T5-CVH-284

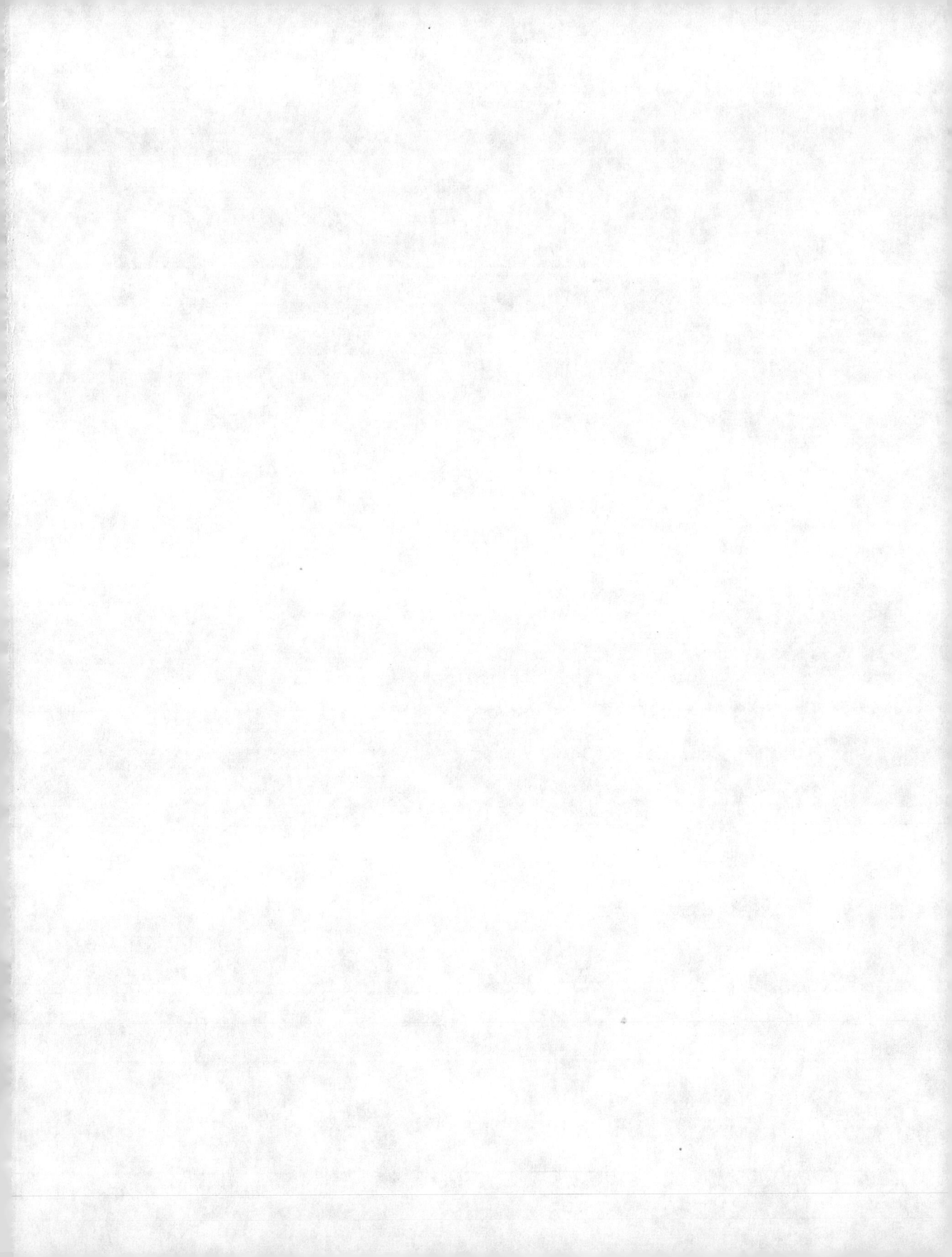

THE HEBREW ENGLISH CONCORDANCE

TO THE OLD TESTAMENT

WITH THE NEW INTERNATIONAL VERSION

JOHN R. KOHLENBERGER III

JAMES A. SWANSON

ZondervanPublishingHouse
Grand Rapids, Michigan

A Division of HarperCollins*Publishers*

Requests for information should be addressed to:
Zondervan Publishing House
Grand Rapids, Michigan 49530

Library of Congress Cataloging-in-Publication Data

Kohlenberger, John R.
The Hebrew-English concordance to the Old Testament / John R. Kohlenberger III and James A. Swanson.
p. cm.
ISBN: 0-310-20839-4 (hardcover)
1. Bible. O.T.—Concordances, Hebrew. 2. Bible. O.T.—Concordances, English—New International. I. Swanson, James A. II. Title.
BS 1121.K65 1998
221.4'4—dc21 98-27107
CIP

This edition printed on acid-free paper and meets the American National Standards Institute Z39.48 standard.

Printed in the United States of America

98 99 00 01 02 03 04 /❖ DC/ 10 9 8 7 6 5 4 3 2 1

Contents

Acknowledgments

THANKS TO Stan Gundry, vice president and editor-in-chief, and Bruce Ryskamp, president of Zondervan Publishing House, for their support and encouragement in permitting us to do this book. Thanks to editors Verlyn Verbrugge and Ed van der Maas for their expert guidance and interaction.

Thanks to Dr. Ronald F. Youngblood of Bethel Seminary West for interacting with text-critical questions relating to the NIV.

Thanks to Roger Green and Tim Hare of Telios Systems for their work in developing the programming to analyze, sort, and set the contexts for this concordance.

Special thanks to our wives and children—Carolyn, Sarah, and Joshua Kohlenberger, and Sandra, Jon, David, and Natanya Lee Swanson—for their loving encouragement and boundless patience.

Introduction

A CONCORDANCE is an index to a book. It is usually arranged in alphabetical order and shows the location of each word in the book. In addition, it often supplies several words of the context in which each word is found.

The Hebrew-English Concordance to the Old Testament (*HECOT*) is prepared for those who are not fluent in Old Testament Hebrew. All headings in this volume are in Hebrew or Aramaic, but are also transliterated into English, and the contexts are in the English of the New International Version (NIV). All headings are also numbered according to the Goodrick/Kohlenberger numbering system so that readers can move from the English-oriented *NIV Exhaustive Concordance* (Zondervan, 1990) into this Hebrew-oriented concordance. Further, the current volume contains a complete listing of NIV OT vocabulary that is indexed to the Hebrew and Aramaic, so that readers can move directly from the English text into the Hebrew or Aramaic concordance. Also unique to this volume are concise Hebrew-English and Aramaic-English dictionaries that both define every word in the Hebrew Bible and index these words to the standard word study resources.

The Hebrew-English Concordance to the Old Testament provides an exhaustive index to the vocabulary of the Hebrew Old Testament according to *The Biblia Hebraica Stuttgartensia*, Fourth Edition (BHS), edited by Karl Elliger and Wilhelm Rudolph (Stuttgart: Deutsche Bibelstiftung, 1990). In addition, the *HECOT* notes all variant readings between BHS and the Masoretic Text it represents and the Hebrew text that underlies the NIV.[1] Most of the vocabulary is indexed with full contexts; 42 highly frequent words are indexed by reference only.

The *HECOT* is the first complete Hebrew-English concordance published in more than 150 years. The first Hebrew-English concordance, based on the King James Version, is still widely used. Samuel Bagster and Sons of London first published George V. Wigram's *The Englishman's Hebrew and Chaldee Concordance of the Old Testament* in 1843. The fifth edition of 1860 has been reprinted by several publishers, including Zondervan. Its most popular editions are indexed to Strong's numbering system, but contain no further enhancements or updates. The editors of the *HECOT* have attempted to update and improve on Wigram's pioneering work by including all his well-designed features, including English contexts, a Hebrew and English index, and an English and Hebrew index.

Two Hebrew-English concordances that followed Wigram provide an index to the Hebrew OT by means of KJV vocabulary; however, neither of them include contexts. These are William Wilson's *The Bible Student's Guide to the More Correct Understanding of the English Translation of the Old Testament* (reprinted as *New Wilson's Old Testament Word Studies* [Grand Rapids: Kregel, 1987]), and Aaron Pick's *The Bible Students Concordance* (reprinted as *Dictionary of Old Testament Words for English Readers* [Grand Rapids: Kregel, 1977]). Three standard all-Hebrew concordances are also available: Solomon Mandelkern's *Veteris Testamenti Concordantiae Hebraicae Atque Chaldaicae* (Tel Aviv: Schocken, 1896; reprint 1978), Gerhard Lisowsky's *Konkordanz zum Hebräischen Alten Testament* (Stuttgart: Württembergische Bibelanstalt, 3rd edition 1993), and Abraham Even-Shoshan's *A New Concordance of the Bible* (Grand Rapids: Baker, 2nd edition 1990).

1. Because there is no available documentation from the International Bible Society or the Committee on Bible Translation, the Hebrew text that underlies the NIV has been reconstructed by the editors with the assistance of Dr. Ronald F. Youngblood of Bethel Seminary West. The variant readings noted in this concordance do not officially represent the International Bible Society or the Committee on Bible Translation, but are the full responsibility of the editors.

Features of *The Hebrew-English Concordance to the Old Testament*

THE *HECOT* expands on the features of these previously published concordances, presenting exhaustive indexes, generous contexts, valuable statistics, and unique features in a manageable volume. It is divided into four major sections: (1) the Main Concordance (Hebrew-English and Aramaic-English), (2) the Select Index of Adverbs, Conjunctions, Particles, and Pronouns, (3) the NIV English–Hebrew & Aramaic Index to the Old Testament, and (4) Concise Hebrew-English and Aramaic-English Dictionaries to the Old Testament.

THE MAIN CONCORDANCE

The following presents elements from a typical entry in the Main Concordance:

43 אֲבִימֶלֶךְ ***ʾabîmelek***, n.pr.m. [67 / 66] [√ 3 + 4889]
Abimelech [60], Abimelech's [2], he[s] [2], him[s] [1], his[s] [1]
2Sa 11:21 who killed **Abimelech** son of Jerub-Besheth? Didn't a woman
1Ch 18:16 and Ahimelech [BHS ***Abimelech***; NIV 316] son of Abiathar were

The heading consists of:

(1) the Goodrick/Kohlenberger (G/K) number: **43**;

(2) the indexed word in Hebrew, אֲבִימֶלֶךְ, and in transliteration, ***ʾabîmelek***;

(3) the part of speech: n.pr.m.;

(4) the frequency count in parentheses, BHS first, NIV second: [67 / 66];

(5) the reference to related words in brackets, listed by G/K number, following the root symbol: √ ;

(6) the list of NIV translations, in descending order of frequency: Abimelech [60], Abimelech's [2], etc.

The context lines consist of:

(1) the book-chapter-verse reference;

(2) the context for the indexed word;

(3) the textual variant information: [BHS ***Abimelech***; NIV 316].

Headings

There are five kinds of headings: (1) Hebrew and Aramaic word headings, (2) Hebrew and Aramaic words not in the BHS and NIV texts, (3) related words lists, (4) NIV translations, and (5) "See" references.

(1) *Hebrew and Aramaic Word Headings*

The Hebrew Bible contains 474,365 words (when each element of a word cluster is counted as one word), with a vocabulary of 8,783 Hebrew words and 714 Aramaic words. The *HECOT* is an exhaustive alphabetical index to every major word of the Hebrew Bible. Note that the standard lexicons and concordances do not always agree on how to analyze Hebrew and Aramaic words. For example, because their definitions are similar and some of their forms are identical, no two sources agree on how many times the verbs דָּחָה, דָּחָה, and נָדָה occur or in which contexts they appear. The word identifications and resulting statistics of the *HECOT* are based as much as is possible on the translation choices of the NIV as compared to the more up-do-date lexicons.

The simplest heading is a word with its G/K number, its part of speech, and its frequency count:

2 אֶבֶה ***'ēbeh***, n.[m.]. [1]

The heading presents the word in its lexical form, both in Hebrew and in English transliteration. Thus the frequency count lists the total number of times the word occurs in the OT, regardless of spelling. If the frequency counts differ between the BHS and NIV texts, the BHS total is given first:

31 אֲבִיָּה ***'ᵃbiyyâ***, n.pr.m. & f. [23 / 29]

In this example, 31 אֲבִיָּה (*'ᵃbiyyâ*) occurs 23 times in BHS and 29 times in the NIV. The variant readings are noted within the contexts of 1 and 2 Kings.

(2) Hebrew and Aramaic Words Not in BHS and NIV

As mentioned above, the Hebrew Bible has a vocabulary of 8,783 Hebrew words and 714 Aramaic words. The G/K numbering system, however, accounts for 9,597 Hebrew words (numbered from 1 through 9597) and 779 Aramaic words (numbered from 10001 through 10779). This vocabulary list was developed by collating the standard Hebrew lexicons—such as those by Brown, Driver, and Briggs; Koehler and Baumgartner; and Holladay—alphabetizing the lists, and then assigning each word a sequential number corresponding to its alphabetical order. The list and its numbering system were developed to replace the useful but dated system developed by James Strong for his *Exhaustive Concordance* of 1890. The G/K numbering system was introduced in *The NIV Exhaustive Concordance*, which also includes two complete indices showing the correspondence of the G/K system to Strong's. The G/K numbering system has also been used in the *Zondervan NIV Nave's Topical Bible* (Zondervan, 1992), the *NIV Compact Nave's Topical Bible* (Zondervan, 1993), the *Zondervan NIV Bible Commentary* (Zondervan, 1994), *The Exhaustive Concordance to the Greek New Testament* (Zondervan, 1995), *The Greek-English Concordance to the New Testament* (Zondervan, 1996), *The New International Dictionary of Old Testament Theology & Exegesis* (Zondervan, 1997), and Zondervan's *NIV Study Bible Library for Windows* software.

Of the 10,376 total words in the G/K numbering system, 879 words are variant readings or alternate spellings that are not indexed in the *HECOT*:

107 אָגַם² ***'ᵃgam²***, n.[m.]. Not used in NIV/BHS

These words are listed without contexts to show that they were not accidentally omitted from the concordance.

(3) *Related Words Lists*

Following most Hebrew word headings in brackets is a list of words that are related by root or share common elements. For convenience of space, the words are listed by G/K number rather than in Hebrew or Aramaic:

121 אֱדוֹם ***'ᵉdôm***, n.pr.m. [100/104] [→ 122, 6273; cf. 131]
122 אֲדוֹמִי ***'ᵃdômî***, a.g. [12] [√ 121; cf. 131]

Rather than listing all related words after each Hebrew or Aramaic word heading, one word was selected to act as the organizing head. Related words point to the organizing head with a root symbol (√), while the organizing word points to the related word list with an arrow (→). On occasion, the list includes more distantly related words for comparison (cf.). Tentative connections are followed by question marks (?).

James A. Swanson collated the related words lists from the standard lexicons, which do not always agree and which sometimes relate words to presumed roots that do not appear in the Hebrew Bible. Please note that although the root symbol is used as the pointer to the organizing head, this does not mean that the editors understand this word to be the etymological "root" of all related forms. The related words lists are included as pointers to cognate studies; however, the editors do not encourage speculative etymology. The reader is encouraged to consult *The New International Dictionary of Old Testament Theology & Exegesis*, in which the entries are organized by carefully defined cognate groups.

(4) *NIV Translations*

The *HECOT* shows the relationship of the Hebrew Bible to the English of the NIV in several ways. In the headings, the list of NIV translations shows every way in which the NIV renders any Hebrew or Aramaic word. This list is organized in descending order of frequency:

8 אֲבֵדָה *'abēdâ*, n.f. [4] [√ 6]

lost property [3], loses [+6+4946]

43 אֲבִימֶלֶךְ *'ᵃbîmelek*, n.pr.m. [67 / 66] [√ 3 + 4889]

Abimelech [60], Abimelech's [2], he[s] [2], him[s] [1], his[s] [1]

Most proper and place names have only one or two translations: absolute and possessive, as in the case of "Abimelech" and "Abimelech's" above, although frequently occurring names are often translated by pronouns (see "Substitute Translation," p. x). Verbs like 170 אָהַב (*'āhab*) may have several forms, such as "love," "loved," "loves," and "lovers." Many words have multiple word translations, such as "lost property" for 8 אֲבֵדָה above. And, if more than one Hebrew word is translated by an NIV word or phrase, the G/K number of the additional word or words is included in brackets with a plus sign (+), as in "loses [+6+4946]" above. If a word is not directly translated in the NIV, the italicized word "*untranslated*" appears in the list, with the total number of times the word was not translated in brackets. NIV-Hebrew relationships are also shown in the contexts by means of bold and italic typefaces, G/K numbers, and abbreviations, as detailed below.

(5) *"See" References*

One hundred fourteen words in the Hebrew Bible occur a total of 231,664 times. Because of space limitations, the most frequent words, such as the conjunction וְ־ and the article הַ־, are not indexed at all. Forty-two independent pronouns and other significant terms are indexed exhaustively, but without contexts, in the Select Index of Adverbs, Conjunctions, Particles, and Pronouns (see p. xv). All of these words are also represented by headings in the Main Concordance, including NIV translations, with a message referring to their indexing:

2256 וְ־ *wᵉ-*, c.pref. [50303 / 50284] [→ Ar 10221] Not indexed

untranslated [20020], and [19276], but [1877], then [1821], ...

4946 מִן *min*, p.p. [7522 / 7521] [→ 4403, ...] See Select Index

from [2541], *untranslated* [1138], of [592], than [182], out of [179], ...

Context Lines

The two-column format of the *HECOT* allows for sizeable contexts, often containing complete sentences or even whole verses. The purpose of context lines in a concordance is simply to help the reader locate a specific verse in the Bible. For word study—or any kind of Bible study—the context offered by a concordance is rarely enough, even when an entire verse fits on one line, as do Job 9:1 and 12:1.

Taken by themselves, context lines can and do misrepresent the teaching of Scripture by taking statements out the larger biblical context. The words "There is no God" are taken directly from Psalms 14:1 and 53:1, but are not statements of fact; they are what "The fool says in his heart." Great care has been taken by the editors and programmer of the *HECOT* to create contexts that are informative and accurate. But the reader should always check these limited contexts against the larger text of the English or Hebrew OT.

(1) *Context Lines: General Format*

The following examples are from the entry for word 185 [1]אֹהֶל (*'ōhel*[1]). The simplest context line presents three items of information: first, the location of the indexed word by book (abbreviated in English and in English canonical order), chapter, and verse; second, the context line; third, within the context line, the NIV translation of the word in bold type. Because the contexts show the relationship of the Hebrew and the NIV, each occurrence of a word has its own context line:

Ge 31:33 So Laban went into Jacob's **tent** and into Leah's tent and into the
31:33 So Laban went into Jacob's tent and into Leah's **tent** and into the

(2) *Context Lines: Multiple Word Translation*

If more than one NIV word is used to define a Hebrew word, all the NIV words are bold:

1Ch 17: 5 I have moved from one **tent site** to another, from one dwelling

If more than one Hebrew word is translated by an NIV word or phrase, the G/K number of the additional word (or words) is included in brackets in the context, as in the following contexts, which occur under words 185 אֹהֶל¹ (*'ōhel*[1]) and 8905 שָׁכַן (*šākan*) respectively:

Jdg 8:11 Gideon went up by the route of the **nomads** [+928+8905] east of
Jdg 8:11 Gideon went up by the route of the **nomads** [+185+928] east of

When NIV words are used to assist in the translation of Hebrew inflections, such as the tense of verbs and the case of nouns and adjectives, these words are italicized.

Ge 9:27 may Japheth live in the **tents** *of* Shem, and may Canaan be his

Because these NIV words show the *form* of the Hebrew word rather than its *definition*, a different typeface is used to show this different relationship. Both defining and assisting words are necessary in translation. In the *HECOT*, as in the *NIV Exhaustive Concordance* and *The Greek-English Concordance to the New Testament*, defining words are in bold and assisting words are in italics.

(3) *Context Lines: Abbreviations for Untranslated and Substituted Words*

Under "NIV Translations" on page viii, it was noted that some Hebrew words are not directly translated in the NIV. This is true of all English Bible translations, because the biblical languages cannot always be translated word for word into understandable English. So for stylistic reasons, the NIV sometimes does not translate repetitive Hebrew words or translates nouns with pronouns and pronouns with nouns. But even words left untranslated in the NIV are indexed with contexts. These stylistic translation choices are indicated by a system of abbreviations within the context.

Untranslated Words: Not In English (NIE). Most words left untranslated in the NIV, as in the KJV and other English versions, are articles, conjunctions, and prepositions, most of which are not indexed with contexts. Word 408 אִישׁ¹ (*'îš*[1]), often "man" or "men," is untranslated in the NIV 241 of its 2189 occurrences. These contexts in the *HECOT* contain the abbreviation [**NIE**] to indicate the word is not in English. Note the following contexts with and without direct translation:

Ge 37:17 "They have moved on from here," the **man** answered. "I heard
37:28 So when the Midianite merchants **[NIE]** came by, his brothers

Untranslated Words: Repeated Hebrew Word (RPH). The NIV sometimes leaves a repeated Hebrew word untranslated for the sake of English style. These words are included in the *HECOT*, but are marked with the abbreviation [**RPH**]. Word 1201 בֵּן¹ (*ben*[1]), often "son(s)" or "descendant(s)," is untranslated in the NIV 227 of its 1430 occurrences, especially in genealogical lists, for example:

Ezr 2: 3 the **descendants** *of* Parosh 2,172
2: 4 **[RPH]** of Shephatiah 372

Because the contexts are in biblical order, the context preceding an RPH context shows the contextual definition of the Hebrew word that is not translated in the RPH context.

Substitute translation (s). Substitute translation occurs when the NIV substitutes pronouns or other "substitute" words to eliminate redundancy when words are repeated in contexts. The most common substitutes are pronouns for proper names. Genesis 1:4 is rendered below first word-for-word and second in the NIV:

And God saw that the light was good, and God separated the light from the darkness.
God saw that the light was good, and he separated the light from the darkness.

The contexts in the *HECOT* are as follows:

Ge 1: 4 **God** saw that the light was good, and he separated the light from
1: 4 the light was good, and **he**s separated the light from the darkness.

The first context shows the one-to-one relationship of word 446 אֱלֹהִים (*'elōhîm*) with the NIV "God." The second context shows the *substitute* translation of "he" for אֱלֹהִים. The substitution is shown by the superscript "s" in both the list of NIV translations (see p. x) and in the context.

(4) *Context Lines: Difference Between BHS and NIV versification*

Whenever versification differs between English and Hebrew, both references are included—English first, and then Hebrew in brackets—as in the following example from 446 אֱלֹהִים (*'elōhîm*):

Ps 4: 1 [4:2] Answer me when I call to you, O my righteous **God**.

(5) *Context Lines: Hebrew and Aramaic Verbal Stem Abbreviations*

The Englishman's Hebrew and Chaldee Concordance (and some all-Hebrew concordances) subdivides verb entries according to their stem. The editors wanted to present all contexts in English canonical order, but also wanted to indicate verb stems. To accomplish both, a system of abbreviations is used to indicate verb stems and the key to the abbreviations runs at the foot of each page spread. This abbreviation appears at the beginning of the context line, as in the following examples from 170 אָהַב (*'āhab*):

Ps 26: 8 [A] *I* **love** the house where you live, O LORD, the place where
31:23 [31:24] [A] **Love** the LORD, all his saints! The LORD

In these examples, [A] indicates the verb is in the Qal stem.

(6) *Context Lines: Textual Variants—NIV and BHS*

The Hebrew text underlying the NIV varies from BHS in three ways: additions, omissions, and differences. Each variant has its own format.

Words Not in BHS but in the NIV [BHS-]. When a word occurs in the NIV but not in BHS, the bolded word is followed by [BHS-], as in the following example from 3 אָב (*āb*):

2Ch 10:14 young men and said, "My **father** [UBS-] made your yoke heavy;

Words Not in the NIV but in BHS [BHS+]. When a word occurs in BHS but not in the NIV, the bracketed code [BHS+] is inserted in the appropriate place in the context. Included in the brackets is a translation of the word or phrase in italics, with the indexed word in bold italics, as in the following example from 285 אֶחָד (*'eḥād*):

Eze 40: 6 it was one rod deep. [BHS+ *the **first** threshold, one rod deep*]
40: 6 it was one rod deep. [BHS+ *the first threshold, **one** rod deep*]

Words That Differ in Identical Contexts. Contexts in which the indexed word differs between BHS and the NIV are flagged with a cross-reference to the variant reading, as in the case of BHS word 285 אֶחָד (*'eḥād*) and NIV word 4395 ¹מֵאָה (*mē'â¹*) in Ezekiel 42:4:

Eze 42: 4 ten cubits wide and a hundred [BHS ***one***; NIV 4395] cubits long.

Eze 42: 4 ten cubits wide and a **hundred** [BHS 285] cubits long.

The first context for the word 285 represents BHS but points to the NIV reading, word 4395. Because the word "hundred" represents the NIV text, it is underlined rather than bold. The translation of the BHS text is once again within the brackets in bold italics. The second context for word 4395 represents the NIV but points to the BHS reading, word 285. Note, too, that Hebrew and Aramaic stem abbreviations are in lower case in every context involving a variant reading, as in the following from 3655 יָצָא (*yāṣā'*):

Jer 48:49 [a] for *she will be* laid waste [+3655]; [BHS ***fly away***; NIV 5898]

(7) *Context Lines: Textual Variants—Masoretic Ketib-Qere*

The ancient, precritical Masoretic texts had a system of variants, offering alternate readings (*Qere*) to what was written (*Ketib*). Although 2,245 words in BHS have such alternate readings, many are simply variant spellings or forms of the same word. These are not represented in the *HECOT*. When the *Qere* (Q) is a different word than the *Ketib* (K), the alternate reading is represented in the *HECOT*. For example, seventeen times in Deuteronomy 22, the K word 5853 ²נַעַר (*na'ar²*) has the Q 5855 ¹נַעֲרָה (*na'ᵃrâ¹*). The NIV translates the Q each time and the contexts for word 5855 point to K 5853. These contexts are duplicated at 5853, but are in brackets with a reference to "see Q 5855" to indicate that these are alternate readings and not the choice of the NIV:

Dt 22:15 the **girl's** [K 5853] father and mother shall bring proof that she

Dt 22:15 [the **girl's** [K; see Q 5855] father and mother shall bring proof that]

Conversely, if the NIV translates the *Ketib* rather than the *Qere*, the presentation of the contexts is the same, and the abbreviations indicate which reading is accepted and which is the variant. In the following examples, the NIV translates the K 76 אֲבָנָה (*'ᵃbānâ*) in preference to the Q 592 ²אֲמָנָה (*'amānâ²*):

2Ki 5:12 Are not **Abana** [Q 592] and Pharpar, the rivers of Damascus,

2Ki 5:12 [not **Abana** [Q; see K 76] and Pharpar, the rivers of Damascus,]

Note that bracketed contexts are not added to the statistics for occurrences of Hebrew word or of NIV translations, because these words are not translated in the NIV.

THE SELECT INDEX OF ADVERBS, CONJUNCTIONS, PARTICLES, AND PRONOUNS

The Main Concordance offers 237,194 contexts, exhaustively indexing 8,705 Hebrew words and 636 Aramaic words and their variants. The Select Index of Adverbs, Conjunctions, Particles, and Pronouns indexes 44,370 references to 38 highly frequent Hebrew words and 4 Aramaic words.

The format of the Index of Adverbs, Etc. is simple. Each of the 42 words has its own heading, followed by its part of speech and frequency count. Words are followed by an exhaustive index of occurrences:

339 אַחַר **'aḥar**, subst. & adv. & pp. [714]

Ge 5:4, 7, 10, 13, 16, 19, 22, 26, 30; 6:4; 9:9, 28; 10:1, 18, 32;

THE NIV ENGLISH–HEBREW & ARAMAIC INDEX

The NIV English–Hebrew & Aramaic Index assists users in moving directly from the NIV OT into the *HECOT*. This index lists every word in the NIV OT in alphabetical order, followed by a complete list of the Hebrew and Aramaic words translated by any NIV phrase that includes the indexed word:

SLAVE [55]

slave, 6269, *'ebed*[1] [15]
slave drivers, 5601, *nāgaś* [5]
slave, *NIH/RPE* [3]
female [slave], 563, *'āmâ* [2]
male slave, 6269, *'ebed*[1] [2]
slave by birth, 3535+1074, *yālîd+bayit*[1] [1]
that slave[s], 2085, *hû'* [1]

The index of NIV–Hebrew & Aramaic equivalents is listed in descending order of frequency. Thus, the first line indicates that the Hebrew word 6269, *'ebed*[1], is the word most frequently rendered "slave" in the NIV. English phrases including the word "slave" are also indexed, as in the case of "slave drivers." Hebrew phrases translated by the word "slave" or by phrases including the word are similarly indexed, as in the case of 3535+1074, *yālîd+bayit*[1].

The use of brackets in "female [slave]" indicates that the word "slave" does double duty in the NIV translation. This example is taken from Exodus 21:20 and 32, in which both verses contain the phrase "male or female slave." This phrase has two Hebrew nouns: 6269, *'ebed*[1], listed as "male slave" in the index, and 563, *'āmâ*, listed as "female slave" in the index. The word "slave" is in bold in both contexts in the main concordance to show each word's contextual meaning. But since the word "slave" is only used once in each of these verses in the NIV, it is in brackets with one of the Hebrew words to indicate that it was not counted twice in the total NIV word statistic of 55.

NIV words that do not directly translate the Hebrew are also listed with statistics and abbreviations. *AIT* is the abbreviation for "assists in translation," referring to NIV words that are used to render Hebrew tenses, number, and cases (see page ix). Because *AIT* words do not define Hebrew words, they are not linked to a specific G/K number. The abbreviations *NIH*, "not in Hebrew," and *RPE*, "repeated English word," both indicate NIV words that are supplied for purposes of style or clarity, but are not direct translations of any Hebrew and Aramaic word. These statistics are included for the sake of completeness, but cannot be further researched in the *HECOT*. However, *The NIV Exhaustive Concordance* can be consulted to find every *AIT*, *NIH*, or *RPE* use of any English word in the entire NIV.

This index also indicates "substitute translation" with a superscript "s," as in "that slave[s], 2085, *hû'* [1]" (see page x).

Every word in the NIV OT is listed in the Index; however, not every occurrence of every word is listed. To save space, entries for 41 highly frequent words were edited—but without any loss of content. Lines were eliminated from words like "and" and "the" where the entry word was part of a phrase that only occurred once or twice. Note that those phrases can still be located by their other words. So "flesh and blood" does not appear under the word "and," but does appear under the words "flesh" and "blood." Index entries that have been edited have an asterisk after the NIV frequency statistic, as in "AND [22881]*."

The NIV English–Hebrew & Aramaic Index does represent the entire vocabulary of the NIV OT. However, it does not indicate the Hebrew word that underlies a specific NIV word in a specific context. Again, *The NIV Exhaustive Concordance* is the best resource for determining NIV English-Hebrew and English-Aramaic relationships within a specific verse.

CONCISE HEBREW-ENGLISH AND ARAMAIC-ENGLISH DICTIONARIES TO THE OLD TESTAMENT

The final section of the *HECOT* offers a concise definition for each word of the Hebrew Bible, including words that do not appear in the NIV and BHS Hebrew texts. In addition, each word is indexed to four standard word study resources for further research.

3 אָב *'āb*, father, grandfather; forefather, ancestor, S: 1, B: 3A, K: 1C, H: 1A

170 אָהַב *'āhab*, [A] to love, like, be a friend; [C] to be loved; [D] be a lover, an ally, S: 157, B: 12C, K: 15C, H: 5B & 76A

10139 גִּזְבַר *gizbar*, treasurer, S: 1490†, B*, K: 1061B, H: 401A

10144 גְּלָה *g^elâ*, [J] to reveal (mysteries); [K] to be revealed (i.e., mysteries); [P] to deport, S: 1541, B: 1086B, K: 1061D, H: 401C

Each entry has eight elements. The first three identify the word and are identical to the headings in the main concordance: G/K number, Hebrew or Aramaic word, and transliteration. The fourth elements is the concise definition, based on NIV translation choices and the standard lexicons. Definitions of Hebrew and Aramaic verbs are subdivided by stems, using the same abbreviation system as appears in the main concordance. The final four elements relate to standard word study resources: the index to Strong's numbering system (following S:); the index to the Brown, Driver, and Briggs *Lexicon* (following B:); the index to the Koehler and Baumgartner *Lexicon* (following K:); and the index to the Holladay *Lexicon* (following H:).

The reference to Strong's numbering system keys the *HECOT* to a number of resources that use this standard, but dated system. Note that sometimes the Strong number has a dagger (†), as in entry 10139, which means that the spelling in the *HECOT* is not exactly the same as Strong's spelling.

A Hebrew and English Lexicon of the Old Testament by Brown, Driver, and Briggs (Oxford University Press, corrected edition 1972) is an indispensable resource to students of the OT. Also of immense value are *Lexicon in Veteris Testamenti Libros* by Koehler and Baumgartner (Brill/Eerdmans, 1958) and its handy edition *A Concise Hebrew and Aramaic Lexicion of the Old Testament* by William L. Holladay (Brill/Eerdmans, 1971). The number in the B, K, or H index refers to the page; the letter of the alphabet refers to the "quadrant" of the page: A is the upper half of the left column, B is the lower left column, C is upper right, and D is lower right. If a word does not appear in these works, the abbreviation letter is followed by an asterisk, as in "B*" in word 10139. Consult these standard resources for more thorough definitions and more specific contextual renderings.

Because it is already keyed to Strong, the editors chose not to include indexing to the useful *Theological Wordbook of the Old Testament* (Moody, 1980). Three additional resources appeared too late to be included in the indexes of the *HECOT*, and a fourth was not included as it is incomplete. Fortunately, the five-volume *New International Dictionary of Old Testament Theology & Exegesis*, edited by Willem A. VanGemeren (Zondervan, 1997) is already keyed to the G/K numbering system and can easily be consulted by those without a reading facility in Hebrew. Similarly the three-volume English translation of the *Theological Lexicon of the Old Testament* by Jenni and Westermann (Hendrickson, 1997) is keyed to Strong, BDB, and *NIDOTTE* as well as the incomplete *Theological Dictionary of the Old Testament* by Botterweck and Ringgren (Eerdmans, 1974–). The three volumes of the revised Koehler and Baumgartner *Hebrew & Aramaic Lexicon of the Old Testament* that have appeared so far are a vast improvement over the 1958 edition (Brill, א-ח 1994, ט-ע 1995, פ-שׂ 1996), but are only accessible to those who can (at least) read the Hebrew alphabet.

ABBREVIATIONS

Books of the Old Testament

1Ch	1 Chronicles
1Ki	1 Kings
1Sa	1 Samuel
2Ch	2 Chronicles
2Ki	2 Kings
2Sa	2 Samuel
Am	Amos
Da	Daniel
Dt	Deuteronomy
Ecc	Ecclesiastes
Est	Esther
Ex	Exodus
Eze	Ezekiel
Ezr	Ezra
Ge	Genesis
Hab	Habakkuk
Hag	Haggai
Hos	Hosea
Isa	Isaiah
Jdg	Judges
Jer	Jeremiah
Jnh	Jonah
Job	Job
Joel	Joel
Jos	Joshua
La	Lamentations
Lev	Leviticus
Mal	Malachi
Mic	Micah
Na	Nahum
Ne	Nehemiah
Nu	Numbers
Ob	Obadiah
Pr	Proverbs
Ps	Psalms
Ru	Ruth
SS	Song of Songs
Zec	Zechariah
Zep	Zephaniah

Parts of Speech, Translation Codes, and Book Titles

&	and
+	plus: in combination with
?	uncertain
1	first person
2	second person
3	third person
a.	adjective
abst.	abstract
adv.	adverb
AIT	assist in translation
art.	article
B:	Brown, Driver & Briggs *Lexicon*
c.	conjunction
col.	collective
com.	common gender
demo.	demonstrative
den.	denominative
du.	dual number
emph.	emphatic
excl.	exclamation
f.	feminine
g.	gentilic
H:	Holladay *Lexicon*
HECOT:	*Hebrew-English Concordance to the Old Testament*
indecl.	indeclinable
indef.	indefinite
inf.	infinitive
intens.	intensive
inter.	interrogative
interj.	interjection
K:	Koehler & Baumgartner *Lexicon*
l.	loanword
loc.	location
m.	masculine
n.	noun
neg.	negative
NIE	not in English
NIH	not in Hebrew
NIV	New International Version
num.	numeral
ord.	ordinal
p.	pronoun
pl.	plural
pp.	preposition
pr.	proper [noun]
pref.	prefix
pt.	particle
ptcp.	participle
rel.	relative
S:	Strong's number
s.	singular
subst.	substantive
suf.	suffix
temp.	temporal
tt.	technical term in Psalm title
v.	verb
var.	variant
vbl.	verbal

Hebrew Verbal Stems

Code	Stem
[A]	Qal
[B]	Qal passive
[C]	Niphal
[D]	Piel
[E]	Pual
[F]	Hitpael
[G]	Hiphil
[H]	Hophal
[I]	Hishtaphel

Aramaic Verbal Stems

Code	Stem
[J]	Peal
[Jp]	Peal passive
[K]	Peil
[L]	Hithpeel
[M]	Pael
[Mp]	Pael passive
[N]	Pual
[O]	Hithpaal
[P]	Haphel
[Pp]	Haphel passive
[Q]	Hophal
[R]	Hishtaphal

HEBREW AND ARAMAIC TRANSLITERATION

Consonants

א	ʾ
ב	*b*
ג	*g*
ד	*d*
ה	*h*
ו	*w*
ז	*z*
ח	*ḥ*
ט	*ṭ*
י	*y*
כ, ך	*k*
ל	*l*
מ, ם	*m*
נ, ן	*n*
ס	*s*
ע	ʿ
פ, ף	*p*
צ, ץ	*ṣ*
ק	*q*
ר	*r*
שׂ	*ś*
שׁ	*š*
ת	*t*

Vowels

ָה	*â*
ָ	*ā*
ַ	*a*
ֲ	^{a}
וּ	*û*
ֻ	*u*
ֵי	*ê*
ֵ	*ē*
ֶ	*e*
ְ if (vocal)	^{e}
ֱ	^{e}
ִי	*î*
ִ	*i*
וֹ	*ô*
ֹ	*ō*
ָ	*o*
ֳ	^{o}

THE

HEBREW-ENGLISH CONCORDANCE

AND

ARAMAIC-ENGLISH CONCORDANCE

TO THE

OLD TESTAMENT

KEY FEATURES OF THE MAIN CONCORDANCE

G/K NUMBER
A code that matches the alphabetic order of Hebrew & Aramaic words. See the intro, pages vi-vii.

ENTRY WORD
First in Hebrew letters, then in English, then its part of speech. See the intro, pages vi-vii.

FREQUENCY
The total number of times this word occurs in the Old Testament. See the introduction, pages vi-ix.

RELATED WORDS
A list of words related by cognate or common elements. See the introduction, page vii.

3655 יָצָא *yāṣāʾ*, v. [1069 / 1067] [→ 3448, 3665, 4604, 4605,

NIV TRANSLATIONS
Every way in which the word is translated in the NIV, with frequency. See the introduction, page viii.

brought out [100], came out [84], went out [82], go out [57],

Ge 1:12 [G] The land **produced** vegetation: plants bearing seed according

BOLD TYPE
Bold type highlights the NIV word or phrase that translates the Hebrew or Aramaic word. See the introduction, pages ix-xi.

Ge 4:16 [A] So Cain **went out** from the LORD's presence and lived in

ITALIC TYPE
Italic type highlights NIV words that assist in translating the Hebrew or Aramaic word inflections. See the introduction, page ix.

ADDITIONAL G/K NUMBERS
When the NIV word or phrase translates more than one word, the additional words are represented by G/K number. See the introduction, page ix.

Ge 27:30 [A] Jacob *had* scarcely **left** [+907+3655+4946] his father's

ABBREVIATIONS
Verb stems, textual variants and untranslated words are indicated by special codes in the context line. See the introduction, pages ix-xi.

Ezr 8:17 [g] [*I* **sent** [K; see Q 7422] them to Iddo, the leader in Casiphia.]

The Hebrew-English Concordance to the Old Testament

א, ’

1 א ’, letter. Not used in NIV/BHS [cf. 66; Ar 10001]

2 אָ- *-ā’*, p.suf.3.f.s. [2 / 1] [cf. 2023]

untranslated [1]

Jer 46:20 a gadfly is coming against <u>her</u> [BHS; NIV 2023] from the north.
Eze 36: 5 against all **[RPR]** Edom, for with glee and with malice in their

3 אָב *’āb*, n.m. [1211] [→ Ar 10003; *also used with compound proper names*]

father [528], fathers [269], father's [121], forefathers [80], families [+1074] [57], families [36], family [+1074] [25], family [14], forefather [11], *untranslated* [10], ancestral [9], them[s] [+2257] [9], father's [+4200] [4], forefathers [+3] [4], parents [+562+2256] [3], ancestor [2], ancestors [2], clans [2], grandfather's [2], he[s] [+3870] [2], him[s] [+2257] [2], parents [2], clan [+1074+5476] [1], clans [+1074] [1], family possessions [1], fatherless [+401] [1], forefather's [1], forefathers [+8037] [1], grandfather [1], group [+1074+2755] [1], he[s] [+2023] [1], he[s] [+3276] [1], him[s] [+2023] [1], him[s] [+3276] [1], his[s] [+2023] [1], his[s] [+2257] [1], them[s] [+3870] [1], them[s] [+4013] [1], they[s] [+4013] [1]

Ge 2:24 For this reason a man will leave his **father** and mother and be
4:20 he was the **father** *of* those who live in tents and raise livestock.
4:21 was Jubal; he was the **father** *of* all who play the harp and flute.
9:18 were Shem, Ham and Japheth. (Ham was the **father** *of* Canaan.)
9:22 Ham, the **father** *of* Canaan, saw his father's nakedness and told his
9:22 saw his **father's** nakedness and told his two brothers outside.
9:23 they walked in backward and covered their **father's** nakedness.
9:23 the other way so that they would not see their **father's** nakedness.
10:21 was Japheth; Shem was the **ancestor** *of* all the sons of Eber.
11:28 While his **father** Terah was still alive, Haran died in Ur of the
11:29 was the daughter of Haran, the **father** *of* both Milcah and Iscah.
11:29 the daughter of Haran, the father of both Milcah and **[RPH]** Iscah.
12: 1 your people and your **father's** household and go to the land I will
15:15 will go to your **fathers** in peace and be buried at a good old age.
17: 4 is my covenant with you: You will be the **father** *of* many nations.
17: 5 will be Abraham, for I have made you a **father** *of* many nations.
19:31 "Our **father** is old, and there is no man around here to lie with us,
19:32 Let's get our **father** to drink wine and then lie with him
19:32 then lie with him and preserve our family line through our **father**."
19:33 That night they got their **father** to drink wine, and the older
19:33 and the older daughter went in and lay with **him**[s] [+2023].
19:34 daughter said to the younger, "Last night I lay with my **father**.
19:34 with him so we can preserve our family line through our **father**."
19:35 So they got their **father** to drink wine that night also,
19:36 So both of Lot's daughters became pregnant by their **father**.
19:37 she named him Moab; he is the **father** *of* the Moabites of today.
19:38 him Ben-Ammi; he is the **father** *of* the Ammonites of today.
20:12 is my sister, the daughter of my **father** though not of my mother;
20:13 And when God had me wander from my **father's** household,
22: 7 Isaac spoke up and said to his **father** Abraham, "Father?"
22: 7 Isaac spoke up and said to his father Abraham, "**Father**?"
22:21 Uz the firstborn, Buz his brother, Kemuel (the **father** *of* Aram),
24: 7 who brought me out of my **father's** household and my native land
24:23 is there room in your **father's** house for us to spend the night?"
24:38 go to my **father's** family and to my own clan, and get a wife for
24:40 a wife for my son from my own clan and from my **father's** family.
26: 3 and will confirm the oath I swore to your **father** Abraham.
26:15 So all the wells that his **father's** servants had dug in the time of his
26:15 his father's servants had dug in the time of his **father** Abraham,
26:18 Isaac reopened the wells that had been dug in the time of his **father**
26:18 and he gave them the same names his **father** had given them.
26:24 appeared to him and said, "I am the God of your **father** Abraham.
27: 6 "Look, I overheard your **father** say to your brother Esau,
27: 9 so I can prepare some tasty food for your **father**, just the way he
27:10 take it to your **father** to eat, so that he may give you his blessing
27:12 What if my **father** touches me? I would appear to be tricking him
27:14 and she prepared some tasty food, just the way his **father** liked it.
27:18 He went to his **father** and said, "My father." "Yes, my son,"
27:18 He went to his father and said, "My **father**." "Yes, my son,"
27:19 Jacob said to his **father**, "I am Esau your firstborn. I have done as
27:22 Jacob went close to his **father** Isaac, who touched him and said,
27:26 his **father** Isaac said to him, "Come here, my son, and kiss me."
27:30 blessing him and Jacob had scarcely left his **father's** presence,
27:31 He too prepared some tasty food and brought it to his **father**.
27:31 he said to **him**[s] [+2257], "My father, sit up and eat some of my
27:31 Then he said to him, "My **father**, sit up and eat some of my game,
27:32 His **father** Isaac asked him, "Who are you?" "I am your son,"
27:34 When Esau heard his **father's** words, he burst out with a loud
27:34 he burst out with a loud and bitter cry and said to his **father**,
27:34 bitter cry and said to his father, "Bless me—me too, my **father**!"
27:38 Esau said to his **father**, "Do you have only one blessing,
27:38 said to his father, "Do you have only one blessing, my **father**?
27:38 you have only one blessing, my father? Bless me too, my **father**!"
27:39 His **father** Isaac answered him, "Your dwelling will be away from
27:41 against Jacob because of the blessing his **father** had given him.
27:41 He said to himself, "The days of mourning for my **father** are near;
28: 2 to Paddan Aram, to the house of your mother's **father** Bethuel.
28: 7 that Jacob had obeyed his **father** and mother and had gone to
28: 8 realized how displeasing the Canaanite women were to his **father**
28:13 the God of your **father** Abraham and the God of Isaac.
28:21 so that I return safely to my **father's** house, then the LORD will
29: 9 Rachel came with her **father's** [+4200] sheep, for she was a
29:12 He had told Rachel that he was a relative of her **father** and a son of
29:12 of her father and a son of Rebekah. So she ran and told her **father**.
31: 1 "Jacob has taken everything our **father** owned and has gained all
31: 1 and has gained all this wealth from what belonged to our **father**."
31: 3 "Go back to the land of your **fathers** and to your relatives,
31: 5 "I see that your **father's** attitude toward me is not what it was
31: 5 what it was before, but the God of my **father** has been with me.
31: 6 You know that I've worked for your **father** with all my strength,
31: 7 yet your **father** has cheated me by changing my wages ten times.
31: 9 So God has taken away your **father's** livestock and has given them
31:14 "Do we still have any share in the inheritance of our **father's**
31:16 Surely all the wealth that God took away from our **father** belongs
31:18 in Paddan Aram, to go to his **father** Isaac in the land of Canaan.

Ge 31:19 shear his sheep, Rachel stole her **father's** [+4200] household gods.
31:29 last night the God of your **father** said to me, 'Be careful not to say
31:30 have gone off because you longed to return to your **father's** house.
31:35 Rachel said to her **father**, "Don't be angry, my lord, that I cannot
31:42 If the God of my **father**, the God of Abraham and the Fear of
31:53 and the God of Nahor, the God of their **father**, judge between us."
31:53 So Jacob took an oath in the name of the Fear of his **father** Isaac.
32: 9 [32:10] Jacob prayed, "O God of my **father** Abraham, God of my
32: 9 [32:10] God of my **father** Isaac, O LORD, who said to me,
33:19 he bought from the sons of Hamor, the **father** *of* Shechem,
34: 4 Shechem said to his **father** Hamor, "Get me this girl as my wife."
34: 6 Then Shechem's **father** Hamor went out to talk with Jacob.
34:11 Shechem said to Dinah's **father** and brothers, "Let me find favor
34:13 deceitfully as they spoke to Shechem and his **father** Hamor.
34:19 who was the most honored of all his **father's** household,
35:18 she named her son Ben-Oni. But his **father** named him Benjamin.
35:22 Reuben went in and slept with his **father's** concubine Bilhah,
35:27 Jacob came home to his **father** Isaac in Mamre, near Kiriath Arba
36: 9 This is the account of Esau the **father** *of* the Edomites in the hill
36:24 the desert while he was grazing the donkeys of his **father** Zibeon.
36:43 the land they occupied. This was Esau the **father** *of* the Edomites.
37: 1 Jacob lived in the land where his **father** had stayed, the land of
37: 2 the sons of Bilhah and the sons of Zilpah, his **father's** wives,
37: 2 and he brought their **father** a bad report about them.
37: 4 When his brothers saw that their **father** loved him more than any
37:10 When he told his **father** as well as his brothers, his father rebuked
37:10 his **father** rebuked him and said, "What is this dream you had?
37:11 were jealous of him, but his **father** kept the matter in mind.
37:12 Now his brothers had gone to graze their **father's** flocks near
37:22 said this to rescue him from them and take him back to his **father**.
37:32 They took the ornamented robe back to their **father** and said,
37:35 will I go down to the grave to my son." So his **father** wept for him.
38:11 "Live as a widow in your **father's** house until my son Shelah
38:11 just like his brothers." So Tamar went to live in her **father's** house.
41:51 has made me forget all my trouble and all my **father's** household."
42:13 The youngest is now with our **father**, and one is no more."
42:29 When they came to their **father** Jacob in the land of Canaan,
42:32 We were twelve brothers, sons of one **father**. One is no more,
42:32 is no more, and the youngest is now with our **father** in Canaan.'
42:35 When they and their **father** saw the money pouches, they were
42:36 Their **father** Jacob said to them, "You have deprived me of my
42:37 Reuben said to his **father**, "You may put both of my sons to death
43: 2 their **father** said to them, "Go back and buy us a little more food."
43: 7 and our family. 'Is your **father** still living?' he asked us.
43: 8 Then Judah said to Israel his **father**, "Send the boy along with me
43:11 Then their **father** Israel said to them, "If it must be, then do this:
43:23 Your God, the God of your **father**, has given you treasure in your
43:27 then he said, "How is your aged **father** you told me about?
43:28 They replied, "Your servant our **father** is still alive and well."
44:17 my slave. The rest of you, go back to your **father** in peace."
44:19 My lord asked his servants, 'Do you have a **father** or a brother?'
44:20 we answered, 'We have an aged **father**, and there is a young son
44:20 is the only one of his mother's sons left, and his **father** loves him.'
44:22 And we said to my lord, 'The boy cannot leave his **father**;
44:22 boy cannot leave his father; if he leaves him, his **father** will die.'
44:24 When we went back to your servant my **father**, we told him what
44:25 "Then our **father** said, 'Go back and buy a little more food.'
44:27 "Your servant my **father** said to us, 'You know that my wife bore
44:30 if the boy is not with us when I go back to your servant my **father**
44:31 Your servants will bring the gray head of our **father** down to the
44:32 Your servant guaranteed the boy's safety to my **father**. I said,
44:32 to you, I will bear the blame before you, my **father**, all my life!'
44:34 How can I go back to my **father** if the boy is not with me?
44:34 Do not let me see the misery that would come upon my **father**."
45: 3 said to his brothers, "I am Joseph! Is my **father** still living?"
45: 8 He made me **father** to Pharaoh, lord of his entire household
45: 9 Now hurry back to my **father** and say to him, 'This is what your
45:13 Tell my **father** about all the honor accorded me in Egypt and about
45:13 you have seen. And bring my **father** down here quickly."
45:18 bring your **father** and your families back to me. I will give you the
45:19 for your children and your wives, and get your **father** and come.
45:23 this is what he sent to his **father**: ten donkeys loaded with the best
45:23 with grain and bread and other provisions for **his**[s] [+2257] journey.
45:25 out of Egypt and came to their **father** Jacob in the land of Canaan.
45:27 had sent to carry him back, the spirit of their **father** Jacob revived.
46: 1 he offered sacrifices to the God of his **father** Isaac.
46: 3 "I am God, the God of your **father**," he said. "Do not be afraid to
46: 5 and Israel's sons took their **father** Jacob and their children
46:29 chariot made ready and went to Goshen to meet his **father** Israel.
46:31 Then Joseph said to his brothers and to his **father's** household,
46:31 and will say to him, 'My brothers and my **father's** household,
46:34 tended livestock from our boyhood on, just as our **fathers** did.'
47: 1 "My **father** and brothers, with their flocks and herds and
47: 3 are shepherds," they replied to Pharaoh, "just as our **fathers** were."
47: 5 said to Joseph, "Your **father** and your brothers have come to you,
47: 6 settle your **father** and your brothers in the best part of the land.
47: 7 Joseph brought his **father** Jacob in and presented him before
47: 9 and they do not equal the years of the pilgrimage of my **fathers**."
47:11 So Joseph settled his **father** and his brothers in Egypt and gave
47:12 Joseph also provided his **father** and his brothers and all his father's
47:12 and his brothers and all his **father's** household with food,
47:30 when I rest with my **fathers**, carry me out of Egypt and bury me
48: 1 Some time later Joseph was told, "Your **father** is ill." So he took
48: 9 are the sons God has given me here," Joseph said to his **father**.
48:15 "May the God before whom my **fathers** Abraham and Isaac
48:16 by my name and the names of my **fathers** Abraham and Isaac,
48:17 When Joseph saw his **father** placing his right hand on Ephraim's
48:17 so he took hold of his **father's** hand to move it from Ephraim's
48:18 Joseph said to **him**[s] [+2257], "No, my father, this one is the
48:18 Joseph said to him, "No, my **father**, this one is the firstborn;
48:19 But his **father** refused and said, "I know, my son, I know.
48:21 will be with you and take you back to the land of your **fathers**.
49: 2 "Assemble and listen, sons of Jacob; listen to your **father** Israel.
49: 4 for you went up onto your **father's** bed, onto my couch and defiled
49: 8 neck of your enemies; your **father's** sons will bow down to you.
49:25 because of your **father's** God, who helps you, because of the
49:26 Your **father's** blessings are greater than the blessings of the
49:28 and this is what their **father** said to them when he blessed them,
49:29 Bury me with my **fathers** in the cave in the field of Ephron the
50: 1 Joseph threw himself upon his **father** and wept over him
50: 2 Joseph directed the physicians in his service to embalm his **father**
50: 5 'My **father** made me swear an oath and said, "I am about to die;
50: 5 Now let me go up and bury my **father**; then I will return.' "
50: 6 Pharaoh said, "Go up and bury your **father**, as he made you swear
50: 7 So Joseph went up to bury his **father**. All Pharaoh's officials
50: 8 and his brothers and those belonging to his **father's** household.
50:10 Joseph observed a seven-day period of mourning for his **father**.
50:14 After burying his **father**, Joseph returned to Egypt, together with
50:14 and all the others who had gone with him to bury his **father**.
50:15 When Joseph's brothers saw that their **father** was dead, they said,
50:16 saying, "Your **father** left these instructions before he died:
50:17 please forgive the sins of the servants of the God of your **father**."
50:22 Joseph stayed in Egypt, along with all his **father's** family.
Ex 2:16 to draw water and fill the troughs to water their **father's** flock.
2:18 When the girls returned to Reuel their **father**, he asked them,
3: 6 Then he said, "I am the God of your **father**, the God of Abraham,
3:13 and say to them, 'The God of your **fathers** has sent me to you,'
3:15 "Say to the Israelites, 'The LORD, the God of your **fathers**—
3:16 of Israel and say to them, 'The LORD, the God of your **fathers**—
4: 5 that they may believe that the LORD, the God of their **fathers**—
6:14 These were the heads of their **families** [+1074]: The sons of
6:25 These were the heads of the Levite **families**, clan by clan.
10: 6 something neither your **fathers** nor your forefathers have ever seen
10: 6 something neither your fathers nor your **forefathers** [+3] have ever
10: 6 something neither your fathers nor your **forefathers** [+3] have ever
12: 3 of this month each man is to take a lamb for his **family** [+1074],
13: 5 the land he swore to your **forefathers** to give you, a land flowing
13:11 it to you, as he promised on oath to you and your **forefathers**,
15: 2 and I will praise him, my **father's** God, and I will exalt him.
18: 4 was named Eliezer, for he said, "My **father's** God was my helper;
20: 5 punishing the children for the sin of the **fathers** to the third
20:12 "Honor your **father** and your mother, so that you may live long in
21:15 "Anyone who attacks his **father** or his mother must be put to
21:17 "Anyone who curses his **father** or mother must be put to death.
22:17 [22:16] If her **father** absolutely refuses to give her to him,
34: 7 their children for the sin of the **fathers** to the third and fourth
40:15 Anoint them just as you anointed their **father**, so they may serve
Lev 16:32 ordained to succeed his **father** as high priest is to make atonement.
18: 7 " 'Do not dishonor your **father** by having sexual relations with
18: 8 " 'Do not have sexual relations with your **father's** wife; that would
18: 8 relations with your father's wife; that would dishonor your **father**.
18: 9 either your **father's** daughter or your mother's daughter,
18:11 " 'Do not have sexual relations with the daughter of your **father's**
18:11 with the daughter of your father's wife, born to your **father**;
18:12 " 'Do not have sexual relations with your **father's** sister; she is
18:12 with your father's sister; she is your **father's** close relative.
18:14 " 'Do not dishonor your **father's** brother by approaching his wife
19: 3 " 'Each of you must respect his mother and **father**, and you must
20: 9 " 'If anyone curses his **father** or mother, he must be put to death.
20: 9 He has cursed his **father** or his mother, and his blood will be on his
20:11 " 'If a man sleeps with his **father's** wife, he has dishonored his
20:11 a man sleeps with his father's wife, he has dishonored his **father**.
20:17 marries his sister, the daughter of either his **father** or his mother,
20:19 relations with the sister of either your mother or your **father**,
21: 2 such as his mother or **father**, his son or daughter, his brother,
21: 9 defiles herself by becoming a prostitute, she disgraces her **father**;
21:11 He must not make himself unclean, even for his **father** or mother,
22:13 and she returns to live in her **father's** house as in her youth,

Lev 22:13 father's house as in her youth, she may eat of her **father's** food.
25:41 will go back to his own clan and to the property of his **forefathers**.
26:39 their sins; also because of their **fathers'** sins they will waste away.
26:40 " 'But if they will confess their sins and the sins of their **fathers**—
Nu 1: 2 the whole Israelite community by their clans and **families** [+1074],
1: 4 each tribe, each the head of his **family** [+1074], is to help you.
1:16 from the community, the leaders of their **ancestral** tribes.
1:18 people indicated their ancestry by their clans and **families** [+1074],
1:20 according to the records of their clans and **families** [+1074].
1:22 according to the records of their clans and **families** [+1074].
1:24 according to the records of their clans and **families** [+1074].
1:26 according to the records of their clans and **families** [+1074].
1:28 according to the records of their clans and **families** [+1074].
1:30 according to the records of their clans and **families** [+1074].
1:32 according to the records of their clans and **families** [+1074].
1:34 according to the records of their clans and **families** [+1074].
1:36 according to the records of their clans and **families** [+1074].
1:38 according to the records of their clans and **families** [+1074].
1:40 according to the records of their clans and **families** [+1074].
1:42 according to the records of their clans and **families** [+1074].
1:44 twelve leaders of Israel, each one representing his **family** [+1074].
1:45 in Israel's army were counted according to their **families** [+1074].
1:47 The **families** of the tribe of Levi, however, were not counted along
2: 2 man under his standard with the banners of his **family** [+1074]."
2:32 are the Israelites, counted according to their **families** [+1074].
2:34 that is the way they set out, each with his clan and **family** [+1074].
3: 4 Ithamar served as priests during the lifetime of their **father** Aaron.
3:15 "Count the Levites by their **families** [+1074] and clans. Count
3:20 These were the Levite clans, according to their **families** [+1074].
3:24 The leader of the **families** [+1074] of the Gershonites was Eliasaph
3:30 The leader of the **families** [+1074] of the Kohathite clans was
3:35 The leader of the **families** [+1074] of the Merarite clans was Zuriel
4: 2 branch of the Levites by their clans and **families** [+1074].
4:22 "Take a census also of the Gershonites by their **families** [+1074]
4:29 "Count the Merarites by their clans and **families** [+1074].
4:34 counted the Kohathites by their clans and **families** [+1074].
4:38 The Gershonites were counted by their clans and **families** [+1074].
4:40 counted by their clans and **families** [+1074], were 2,630.
4:42 The Merarites were counted by their clans and **families** [+1074].
4:46 Israel counted all the Levites by their clans and **families** [+1074].
6: 7 Even if his own **father** or mother or brother or sister dies,
7: 2 the heads of **families** [+1074] who were the tribal leaders in charge
11:12 an infant, to the land you promised on oath to their **forefathers**?
12:14 The LORD replied to Moses, "If her **father** had spit in her face,
13: 2 to the Israelites. From each **ancestral** tribe send one of its leaders."
14:18 he punishes the children for the sin of the **fathers** to the third
14:23 them will ever see the land I promised on oath to their **forefathers**.
17: 2 [17:17] one from the leader of each of their **ancestral** tribes.
17: 2 [17:17] **[RPH]** Write the name of each man on his staff.
17: 3 [17:18] for there must be one staff for the head of each **ancestral**
17: 6 [17:21] one for the leader of each of their **ancestral** tribes, and
18: 1 your **father's** family are to bear the responsibility for offenses
18: 2 Bring your fellow Levites from your **ancestral** tribe to join you
20:15 Our **forefathers** went down into Egypt, and we lived there many
20:15 there many years. The Egyptians mistreated us and our **fathers**,
25:14 was Zimri son of Salu, the leader of a Simeonite **family** [+1074].
25:15 daughter of Zur, a tribal chief of a Midianite **family** [+1074].
26: 2 a census of the whole Israelite community by **families** [+1074]—
26:55 inherits will be according to the names for its **ancestral** tribe.
27: 3 "Our **father** died in the desert. He was not among Korah's
27: 4 Why should our **father's** name disappear from his clan because he
27: 4 he had no son? Give us property among our **father's** relatives."
27: 7 give them property as an inheritance among their **father's** relatives
27: 7 father's relatives and turn their **father's** inheritance over to them.
27:10 If he has no brothers, give his inheritance to his **father's** brothers.
27:11 If his **father** had no brothers, give his inheritance to the nearest
30: 3 [30:4] "When a young woman still living in her **father's** house
30: 4 [30:5] her **father** hears about her vow or pledge but says nothing
30: 4 [30:5] **[RPH]** then all her vows and every pledge by which she
30: 5 [30:6] if her **father** forbids her when he hears about it, none of
30: 5 [30:6] will release her because her **father** has forbidden her.
30:16 [30:17] between a **father** and his young daughter still living in his
30:16 [30:17] and his young daughter still living in **his**[s] [+2023] house.
31:26 and the **family** heads of the community are to count all the people
32: 8 This is what your **fathers** did when I sent them from Kadesh
32:14 standing in the place of your **fathers** and making the LORD even
32:28 Joshua son of Nun and to the **family** heads of the Israelite tribes.
33:54 lot will be theirs. Distribute it according to your **ancestral** tribes.
34:14 because the **families of** [+1074] the tribe of Reuben, the tribe of
34:14 **[RPH]** and the half-tribe of Manasseh have received their
36: 1 The **family** heads of the clan of Gilead son of Makir, the son of
36: 1 before Moses and the leaders, the heads of the Israelite **families**.
36: 3 then their inheritance will be taken from our **ancestral** inheritance
36: 4 will be taken from the tribal inheritance of our **forefathers**."
36: 6 please as long as they marry within the tribal clan of their **father**.
36: 7 Israelite shall keep the tribal land inherited from his **forefathers**.
36: 8 any Israelite tribe must marry someone in her **father's** tribal clan,
36: 8 so that every Israelite will possess the inheritance of his **fathers**.
36:12 and their inheritance remained in their **father's** clan and tribe.
Dt 1: 8 of the land that the LORD swore he would give to your **fathers**—
1:11 May the LORD, the God of your **fathers**, increase you a thousand
1:21 possession of it as the LORD, the God of your **fathers**, told you.
1:35 shall see the good land I swore to give your **forefathers**,
4: 1 the land that the LORD, the God of your **fathers**, is giving you.
4:31 or destroy you or forget the covenant with your **forefathers**,
4:37 Because he loved your **forefathers** and chose their descendants
5: 3 It was not with our **fathers** that the LORD made this covenant,
5: 9 punishing the children for the sin of the **fathers** to the third
5:16 "Honor your **father** and your mother, as the LORD your God has
6: 3 just as the LORD, the God of your **fathers**, promised you.
6:10 your God brings you into the land he swore to your **fathers**,
6:18 good land that the LORD promised on oath to your **forefathers**,
6:23 and give us the land that he promised on oath to our **forefathers**.
7: 8 kept the oath he swore to your **forefathers** that he brought you out
7:12 his covenant of love with you, as he swore to your **forefathers**.
7:13 flocks in the land that he swore to your **forefathers** to give you.
8: 1 the land that the LORD promised on oath to your **forefathers**.
8: 3 you with manna, which neither you nor your **fathers** had known,
8:16 something your **fathers** had never known, to humble and to test
8:18 his covenant, which he swore to your **forefathers**, as it is today.
9: 5 to accomplish what he swore to your **fathers**, to Abraham,
10:11 and possess the land that I swore to their **fathers** to give them."
10:15 Yet the LORD set his affection on your **forefathers** and loved
10:22 Your **forefathers** who went down into Egypt were seventy in all,
11: 9 the land that the LORD swore to your **forefathers** to give to them
11:21 many in the land that the LORD swore to give your **forefathers**,
12: 1 the LORD, the God of your **fathers**, has given you to possess—
13: 6 [13:7] gods" (gods that neither you nor your **fathers** have known,
13:17 [13:18] as he promised on oath to your **forefathers**,
18: 8 though he has received money from the sale of **family possessions**.
19: 8 enlarges your territory, as he promised on oath to your **forefathers**,
19: 8 and gives you the whole land he promised **them**[s] [+3870],
21:13 in your house and mourned her **father** and mother for a full month,
21:18 and rebellious son who does not obey his **father** and mother
21:19 his **father** and mother shall take hold of him and bring him to the
22:15 the girl's **father** and mother shall bring proof that she was a virgin
22:16 The girl's **father** will say to the elders, "I gave my daughter in
22:19 him a hundred shekels of silver and give them to the girl's **father**,
22:21 she shall be brought to the door of her **father's** house and there the
22:21 in Israel by being promiscuous while still in her **father's** house.
22:29 he shall pay the girl's **father** fifty shekels of silver. He must marry
22:30 [23:1] A man is not to marry his **father's** wife; he must not
22:30 [23:1] his father's wife; he must not dishonor his **father's** bed.
24:16 **Fathers** shall not be put to death for their children, nor children put
24:16 death for their children, nor children put to death for their **fathers**;
26: 3 come to the land the LORD swore to our **forefathers** to give us."
26: 5 "My **father** was a wandering Aramean, and he went down into
26: 7 the God of our **fathers**, and the LORD heard our voice and saw
26:15 you have given us as you promised on oath to our **forefathers**,
27: 3 just as the LORD, the God of your **fathers**, promised you.
27:16 "Cursed is the man who dishonors his **father** or his mother."
27:20 "Cursed is the man who sleeps with his **father's** wife, for he
27:20 sleeps with his father's wife, for he dishonors his **father's** bed."
27:22 his sister, the daughter of his **father** or the daughter of his mother."
28:11 in the land he swore to your **forefathers** to give you.
28:36 king you set over you to a nation unknown to you or your **fathers**.
28:64 and stone, which neither you nor your **fathers** have known.
29:13 [29:12] God as he promised you and as he swore to your **fathers**,
29:25 [29:24] the covenant of the LORD, the God of their **fathers**,
30: 5 He will bring you to the land that belonged to your **fathers**,
30: 5 will make you more prosperous and numerous than your **fathers**.
30: 9 and make you prosperous, just as he delighted in your **fathers**,
30:20 give you many years in the land he swore to give to your **fathers**,
31: 7 the land that the LORD swore to their **forefathers** to give them,
31:16 "You are going to rest with your **fathers**, and these people will
31:20 and honey, the land I promised on oath to their **forefathers**,
32: 6 Is he not your **Father**, your Creator, who made you and formed
32: 7 Ask your **father** and he will tell you, your elders, and they will
32:17 gods that recently appeared, gods your **fathers** did not fear.
33: 9 He said of his **father** and mother, 'I have no regard for them.'
Jos 1: 6 people to inherit the land I swore to their **forefathers** to give them.
2:12 by the LORD that you will show kindness to my **family** [+1074],
2:13 that you will spare the lives of my **father** and mother, my brothers
2:18 and unless you have brought your **father** and mother, your brothers
2:18 your brothers and all your **family** [+1074] into your house.
4:21 "In the future when your descendants ask their **fathers**,
5: 6 see the land that he had solemnly promised their **fathers** to give us,
6:23 her **father** and mother and brothers and all who belonged to her.

[F] Hitpael (hitpoel, hitpoal, hitpolel, hitpolal, hitpalel, hitpalal, hitpalpel, hitpalpal, hotpael, hotpaal) [G] Hiphil (hiphtil) [H] Hophal [I] Hishtaphel

Jos 6:25 with her **family** [+1074] and all who belonged to her,
14: 1 and the heads of the tribal **clans** of Israel allotted to them.
15:13 Kiriath Arba, that is, Hebron. (Arba was the **forefather** *of* Anak.)
15:18 she came to Othniel, she urged him to ask her **father** for a field.
17: 1 Makir was the **ancestor** *of* the Gileadites, who had received Gilead
17: 4 gave them an inheritance along with the brothers of their **father**,
18: 3 the land that the LORD, the God of your **fathers**, has given you?
19:47 They settled in Leshem and named it Dan after their **forefather**.)
19:51 the heads of the tribal **clans** of Israel assigned by lot at Shiloh in
21: 1 Now the **family** heads of the Levites approached Eleazar the priest,
21: 1 son of Nun, and the heads of the other tribal **families** of Israel
21:11 in the hill country of Judah. (Arba was the **forefather** *of* Anak.)
21:43 gave Israel all the land he had sworn to give their **forefathers**,
21:44 them rest on every side, just as he had sworn to their **forefathers**.
22:14 ten of the chief men, one **[RPH]** for each of the tribes of Israel,
22:14 each the head of a **family** division among the Israelite clans.
22:28 which our **fathers** built, not for burnt offerings and sacrifices,
24: 2 'Long ago your **forefathers**, including Terah the father of Abraham
24: 2 including Terah the **father** *of* Abraham and Nahor, lived beyond
24: 2 including Terah the father of Abraham and **[RPH]** Nahor,
24: 3 But I took your **father** Abraham from the land beyond the River
24: 6 When I brought your **fathers** out of Egypt, you came to the sea,
24: 6 the Egyptians pursued **them**[s] [+4013] with chariots and horsemen
24:14 Throw away the gods your **forefathers** worshiped beyond the
24:15 whether the gods your **forefathers** served beyond the River,
24:17 our God himself who brought us and our **fathers** up out of Egypt,
24:32 pieces of silver from the sons of Hamor, the **father** *of* Shechem.
Jdg 1:14 she came to Othniel, she urged him to ask her **father** for a field.
2: 1 and led you into the land that I swore to give to your **forefathers**.
2:10 After that whole generation had been gathered to their **fathers**,
2:12 They forsook the LORD, the God of their **fathers**, who had
2:17 they quickly turned from the way in which their **fathers** had
2:19 returned to ways even more corrupt than those of their **fathers**,
2:20 has violated the covenant that I laid down for their **forefathers**
2:22 the way of the LORD and walk in it as their **forefathers** did."
3: 4 which he had given their **forefathers** through Moses.
6:13 Where are all his wonders that our **fathers** told us about when they
6:15 weakest in Manasseh, and I am the least in my **family** [+1074]."
6:25 "Take the second bull from your **father's** herd, the one seven years
6:25 Tear down your **father's** [+4200] altar to Baal and cut down the
6:27 because he was afraid of his **family** [+1074] and the men of the
8:32 was buried in the tomb of his **father** Joash in Ophrah of the
9: 1 and said to them and to all his mother's **clan** [+1074+5476],
9: 5 He went to his **father's** home in Ophrah and on one stone
9:17 to think that my **father** fought for you, risked his life to rescue you
9:18 (but today you have revolted against my **father's** family, murdered
9:28 Zebul his deputy? Serve the men of Hamor, Shechem's **father**!
9:56 had done to his **father** by murdering his seventy brothers.
11: 2 "You are not going to get any inheritance in our **family** [+1074],"
11: 7 "Didn't you hate me and drive me from my **father's** house?
11:36 "My **father**," she replied, "you have given your word to the
11:37 **[RPH]** "Give me two months to roam the hills and weep with my
11:39 she returned to her **father** and he did to her as he had vowed.
14: 2 When he returned, he said to his **father** and mother, "I have seen a
14: 3 His **father** and mother replied, "Isn't there an acceptable woman
14: 3 Samson said to his **father**, "Get her for me. She's the right one for
14: 4 (His **parents** [+562+2256] did not know that this was from the
14: 5 Samson went down to Timnah together with his **father**
14: 6 But he told neither his **father** nor his mother what he had done.
14: 9 When he rejoined his **parents** [+562+2256], he gave them some,
14:10 Now his **father** went down to see the woman. And Samson made a
14:15 or we will burn you and your **father's** household to death.
14:16 "I haven't even explained it to my **father** or mother," he replied,
14:19 the riddle. Burning with anger, he went up to his **father's** house.
15: 1 going to my wife's room." But her **father** would not let him go in.
15: 2 hated her," **he**[s] [+2023] said, "that I gave her to your friend.
15: 6 So the Philistines went up and burned her and her **father** to death.
16:31 his brothers and his **father's** whole family went down to get him.
16:31 him between Zorah and Eshtaol in the tomb of Manoah his **father**.
17:10 Micah said to him, "Live with me and be my **father** and priest,
18:19 Don't say a word. Come with us, and be our **father** and priest.
18:29 They named it Dan after their **forefather** Dan, who was born to
19: 2 She left him and went back to her **father's** house in Bethlehem,
19: 3 She took him into her **father's** house, and when her father saw
19: 3 and when her **father** saw him, he gladly welcomed him.
19: 4 His father-in-law, the girl's **father**, prevailed upon him to stay;
19: 5 he prepared to leave, but the girl's **father** said to his son-in-law,
19: 6 Afterward the girl's **father** said, "Please stay tonight and enjoy
19: 8 when he rose to go, the girl's **father** said, "Refresh yourself.
19: 9 up to leave, his father-in-law, the girl's **father**, said, "Now look,
21:22 When their **fathers** or brothers complain to us, we will say to
Ru 2:11 how you left your **father** and mother and your homeland and came
4:17 named him Obed. He was the **father** *of* Jesse, the father of David.
4:17 named him Obed. He was the father of Jesse, the **father** *of* David.
1Sa 2:25 His sons, however, did not listen to their **father's** rebuke,
2:27 'Did I not clearly reveal myself to your **father's** house when they
2:28 I also gave your **father's** house all the offerings made with fire by
2:30 and your **father's** house would minister before me forever.'
2:31 cut short your strength and the strength of your **father's** house,
9: 3 Now the donkeys belonging to Saul's **father** Kish were lost,
9: 5 or my **father** will stop thinking about the donkeys and start
9:20 desire of Israel turned, if not to you and all your **father's** family?"
10: 2 now your **father** has stopped thinking about them and is worried
10:12 A man who lived there answered, "And who is their **father**?"
12: 6 and Aaron and brought your **forefathers** up out of Egypt.
12: 7 righteous acts performed by the LORD for you and your **fathers**.
12: 8 **they**[s] [+4013] cried to the LORD for help, and the LORD sent
12: 8 who brought your **forefathers** out of Egypt and settled them in this
12:15 his hand will be against you, as it was against your **fathers**.
14: 1 Philistine outpost on the other side." But he did not tell his **father**.
14:27 Jonathan had not heard that his **father** had bound the people with
14:28 told him, "Your **father** bound the army under a strict oath, saying,
14:29 Jonathan said, "My **father** has made trouble for the country.
14:51 Saul's **father** Kish and Abner's father Ner were sons of Abiel.
14:51 Saul's father Kish and Abner's **father** Ner were sons of Abiel.
17:15 and forth from Saul to tend his **father's** sheep at Bethlehem.
17:25 and will exempt his **father's** family from taxes in Israel."
17:34 "Your servant has been keeping his **father's** [+4200] sheep.
18: 2 David with him and did not let him return to his **father's** house.
18:18 "Who am I, and what is my family or my **father's** clan in Israel,
19: 2 warned him, "My **father** Saul is looking for a chance to kill you.
19: 3 I will go out and stand with my **father** in the field where you are.
19: 3 I'll speak to **him**[s] [+3276] about you and will tell you what I find
19: 4 Jonathan spoke well of David to Saul his **father** and said to him,
20: 1 How have I wronged your **father**, that he is trying to take my
20: 2 Look, my **father** doesn't do anything, great or small, without
20: 2 in me. Why would **he**[s] [+3276] hide this from me? It's not so!"
20: 3 "Your **father** knows very well that I have found favor in your eyes,
20: 6 If your **father** misses me at all, tell him, 'David earnestly asked my
20: 8 then kill me yourself! Why hand me over to your **father**?"
20: 9 "If I had the least inkling that my **father** was determined to harm
20:10 "Who will tell me if your **father** answers you harshly?"
20:12 I will surely sound out my **father** by this time the day after
20:13 if my **father** is inclined to harm you, may the LORD deal with
20:13 May the LORD be with you as he has been with my **father**.
20:32 he be put to death? What has he done?" Jonathan asked his **father**.
20:33 Then Jonathan knew that his **father** intended to kill David.
20:34 because he was grieved at his **father's** shameful treatment of
22: 1 When his brothers and his **father's** household heard about it,
22: 3 "Would you let my **father** and mother come and stay with you
22:11 the priest Ahimelech son of Ahitub and his **father's** whole family,
22:15 Let not the king accuse your servant or any of his **father's** family,
22:16 will surely die, Ahimelech, you and your **father's** whole family."
22:22 I am responsible for the death of your **father's** whole family.
23:17 be afraid," he said. "My **father** Saul will not lay a hand on you.
23:17 and I will be second to you. Even my **father** Saul knows this."
24:11 [24:12] See, my **father**, look at this piece of your robe in my
24:21 [24:22] or wipe out my name from my **father's** family."
2Sa 2:32 took Asahel and buried him in his **father's** tomb at Bethlehem.
3: 7 said to Abner, "Why did you sleep with my **father's** concubine?"
3: 8 This very day I am loyal to the house of your **father** Saul and to
3:29 blood fall upon the head of Joab and upon all his **father's** house!
6:21 who chose me rather than your **father** or anyone from his house
7:12 When your days are over and you rest with your **fathers**, I will
7:14 I will be his **father**, and he will be my son. When he does wrong,
9: 7 "for I will surely show you kindness for the sake of your **father**
9: 7 I will restore to you all the land that belonged to your **grandfather**
10: 2 Hanun son of Nahash, just as his **father** showed kindness to me."
10: 2 to express his sympathy to Hanun concerning his **father**.
10: 3 "Do you think David is honoring your **father** by sending men to
13: 5 "When your **father** comes to see you, say to him, 'I would like my
14: 9 let the blame rest on me and on my **father's** family, and let the
15:34 I was your **father's** servant in the past, but now I will be your
16: 3 'Today the house of Israel will give me back my **grandfather's**
16:19 serve the son? Just as I served your **father**, so I will serve you."
16:21 "Lie with your **father's** concubines whom he left to take care of
16:21 hear that you have made yourself a stench in your **father's** nostrils,
16:22 and he lay with his **father's** concubines in the sight of all Israel.
17: 8 You know your **father** and his men; they are fighters, and as fierce
17: 8 Besides, your **father** is an experienced fighter; he will not spend
17:10 for all Israel knows that your **father** is a fighter and that those with
17:23 hanged himself. So he died and was buried in his **father's** tomb.
19:28 [19:29] All my **grandfather's** descendants deserved nothing
19:37 [19:38] I may die in my own town near the tomb of my **father**
21:14 of Saul and his son Jonathan in the tomb of Saul's **father** Kish,
24:17 they done? Let your hand fall upon me and my **family** [+1074]."
1Ki 1: 6 (His **father** had never interfered with him by asking, "Why do you
1:21 as soon as my lord the king is laid to rest with his **fathers**,

1Ki 2:10 David rested with his **fathers** and was buried in the City of David.
2:12 So Solomon sat on the throne of his **father** David, and his rule was
2:24 he who has established me securely on the throne of my **father**
2:26 carried the ark of the Sovereign LORD before my **father** David
2:26 before my father David and shared all my **father's** hardships."
2:31 my **father's** house of the guilt of the innocent blood that Joab shed.
2:32 because without the knowledge of my **father** David he attacked
2:44 "You know in your heart all the wrong you did to my **father**
3: 3 LORD by walking according to the statutes of his **father** David,
3: 6 my **father** David, because he was faithful to you and righteous
3: 7 you have made your servant king in place of my **father** David.
3:14 and obey my statutes and commands as David your **father** did,
5: 1 [5:15] had been anointed king to succeed his **father** David,
5: 3 [5:17] because of the wars waged against my **father** David from
5: 5 [5:19] as the LORD told my **father** David, when he said,
6:12 I will fulfill through you the promise I gave to David your **father**.
7:14 and whose **father** was a man of Tyre and a craftsman in bronze.
7:51 he brought in the things his **father** David had dedicated—
8: 1 all the heads of the tribes and the chiefs of the Israelite **families**,
8:15 what he promised with his own mouth to my **father** David.
8:17 "My **father** David had it in his heart to build a temple for the
8:18 the LORD said to my **father** David, 'Because it was in your heart
8:20 I have succeeded David my **father** and now I sit on the throne of
8:21 he made with our **fathers** when he brought them out of Egypt."
8:24 You have kept your promise to your servant David my **father**;
8:25 keep for your servant David my **father** the promises you made to
8:26 let your word that you promised your servant David my **father**
8:34 and bring them back to the land you gave to their **fathers**.
8:40 will fear you all the time they live in the land you gave our **fathers**.
8:48 pray to you toward the land you gave their **fathers**, toward the city
8:53 O Sovereign LORD, brought our **fathers** out of Egypt."
8:57 May the LORD our God be with us as he was with our **fathers**;
8:58 keep the commands, decrees and regulations he gave our **fathers**.
9: 4 me in integrity of heart and uprightness, as David your **father** did,
9: 5 over Israel forever, as I promised David your **father** when I said,
9: 9 who brought their **fathers** out of Egypt, and have embraced other
11: 4 to the LORD his God, as the heart of David his **father** had been.
11: 6 not follow the LORD completely, as David his **father** had done.
11:12 Nevertheless, for the sake of David your **father**, I will not do it
11:17 to Egypt with some Edomite officials who had served his **father**.
11:21 Hadad heard that David rested with his **fathers** and that Joab the
11:27 and had filled in the gap in the wall of the city of David his **father**.
11:33 nor kept my statutes and laws as David, Solomon's **father**, did.
11:43 he rested with his **fathers** and was buried in the city of David his
11:43 with his fathers and was buried in the city of David his **father**.
12: 4 "Your **father** put a heavy yoke on us, but now lighten the harsh
12: 4 lighten the harsh labor and the heavy yoke **he**[s] [+3870] put on us,
12: 6 King Rehoboam consulted the elders who had served his **father**
12: 9 people who say to me, 'Lighten the yoke your **father** put on us'?"
12:10 'Your **father** put a heavy yoke on us, but make our yoke lighter'—
12:10 tell them, 'My little finger is thicker than my **father's** waist.
12:11 My **father** laid on you a heavy yoke; I will make it even heavier.
12:11 My **father** scourged you with whips; I will scourge you with
12:14 of the young men and said, "My **father** made your yoke heavy;
12:14 My **father** scourged you with whips; I will scourge you with
13:11 that day. They also told their **father** what he had said to the king.
13:12 Their **father** asked them, "Which way did he go?" And his sons
13:22 your body will not be buried in the tomb of your **fathers**.' "
14:15 uproot Israel from this good land that he gave to their **forefathers**
14:20 He reigned for twenty-two years and then rested with his **fathers**.
14:22 they stirred up his jealous anger more than their **fathers** had done.
14:31 Rehoboam rested with his **fathers** and was buried with them in the
14:31 and was buried with **them**[s] [+2257] in the City of David.
15: 3 He committed all the sins his **father** had done before him;
15: 3 the LORD his God, as the heart of David his **forefather** had been.
15: 8 Abijah rested with his **fathers** and was buried in the City of David.
15:11 was right in the eyes of the LORD, as his **father** David had done.
15:12 from the land and got rid of all the idols his **fathers** had made.
15:15 and gold and the articles that he and his **father** had dedicated.
15:19 he said, "as there was between my **father** and your father.
15:19 he said, "as there was between my father and your **father**.
15:24 Asa rested with his **fathers** and was buried with them in the city of
15:24 and was buried with **them**[s] [+2257] in the city of his father David.
15:24 and was buried with them in the city of his **father** David.
15:26 of the LORD, walking in the ways of his **father** and in his sin,
16: 6 Baasha rested with his **fathers** and was buried in Tirzah. And Elah
16:28 Omri rested with his **fathers** and was buried in Samaria. And Ahab
18:18 for Israel," Elijah replied. "But you and your **father's** family have.
19: 4 he said. "Take my life; I am no better than my **ancestors**."
19:20 "Let me kiss my **father** and mother good-by," he said, "and
20:34 "I will return the cities my **father** took from your father,"
20:34 "I will return the cities my father took from your **father**,"
20:34 your own market areas in Damascus, as my **father** did in Samaria."
21: 3 forbid that I should give you the inheritance of my **fathers**."
21: 4 had said, "I will not give you the inheritance of my **fathers**."
22:40 Ahab rested with his **fathers**. And Ahaziah his son succeeded him
22:43 In everything he walked in the ways of his **father** Asa and did not
22:46 [22:47] who remained there even after the reign of his **father** Asa.
22:50 [22:51] Jehoshaphat rested with his **fathers** and was buried with
22:50 [22:51] was buried with **them**[s] [+2257] in the city of David his
22:50 [22:51] and was buried with them in the city of David his **father**.
22:52 [22:53] because he walked in the ways of his **father** and mother
22:53 [22:54] the God of Israel, to anger, just as his **father** had done.
2Ki 2:12 Elisha saw this and cried out, "My **father**! My father! The chariots
2:12 Elisha saw this and cried out, "My father! My **father**! The chariots
3: 2 the eyes of the LORD, but not as his **father** and mother had done.
3: 2 He got rid of the sacred stone of Baal that his **father** had made.
3:13 Go to the prophets of your **father** and the prophets of your
4:18 The child grew, and one day he went out to his **father**, who was
4:19 "My head! My head!" he said to his **father**. His father told a
5:13 Naaman's servants went to him and said, "My **father**,
6:21 of Israel saw them, he asked Elisha, "Shall I kill them, my **father**?
8:24 Jehoram rested with his **fathers** and was buried with them in the
8:24 and was buried with **them**[s] [+2257] in the City of David.
9:25 I were riding together in chariots behind Ahab his **father** when the
9:28 and buried him with his **fathers** in his tomb in the City of David.
10: 3 worthy of your master's sons and set him on his **father's** throne.
10:35 Jehu rested with his **fathers** and was buried in Samaria.
12:18 [12:19] took all the sacred objects dedicated by his **fathers**—
12:21 [12:22] and was buried with his **fathers** in the City of David.
13: 9 Jehoahaz rested with his **fathers** and was buried in Samaria.
13:13 Jehoash rested with his **fathers**, and Jeroboam succeeded him on
13:14 "My **father**! My father!" he cried. "The chariots and horsemen of
13:14 "My father! My **father**!" he cried. "The chariots and horsemen of
13:25 Hazael the towns he had taken in battle from his **father** Jehoahaz.
14: 3 in the eyes of the LORD, but not as his **father** David had done.
14: 3 In everything he followed the example of his **father** Joash.
14: 5 he executed the officials who had murdered his **father** the king.
14: 6 "**Fathers** shall not be put to death for their children, nor children
14: 6 death for their children, nor children put to death for their **fathers**;
14:16 Jehoash rested with his **fathers** and was buried in Samaria with the
14:20 back by horse and was buried in Jerusalem with his **fathers**,
14:21 years old, and made him king in place of his **father** Amaziah.
14:22 and restored it to Judah after Amaziah rested with his **fathers**.
14:29 Jeroboam rested with his **fathers**, the kings of Israel.
15: 3 in the eyes of the LORD, just as his **father** Amaziah had done.
15: 7 Azariah rested with his **fathers** and was buried near them in the
15: 7 and was buried near **them**[s] [+2257] in the City of David.
15: 9 He did evil in the eyes of the LORD, as his **fathers** had done.
15:22 Menahem rested with his **fathers**. And Pekahiah his son succeeded
15:34 right in the eyes of the LORD, just as his **father** Uzziah had done.
15:38 Jotham rested with his **fathers** and was buried with them in the
15:38 and was buried with **them**[s] [+2257] in the City of David,
15:38 was buried with them in the City of David, the city of his **father**.
16: 2 Unlike David his **father**, he did not do what was right in the eyes
16:20 Ahaz rested with his **fathers** and was buried with them in the City
16:20 and was buried with **them**[s] [+2257] in the City of David.
17:13 in accordance with the entire Law that I commanded your **fathers**
17:14 But they would not listen and were as stiff-necked as their **fathers**,
17:15 his decrees and the covenant he had made with their **fathers**
17:41 their children and grandchildren continue to do as their **fathers** did.
18: 3 right in the eyes of the LORD, just as his **father** David had done.
19:12 Did the gods of the nations that were destroyed by my **forefathers**
20: 5 'This is what the LORD, the God of your **father** David, says:
20:17 all that your **fathers** have stored up until this day, will be carried
20:21 Hezekiah rested with his **fathers**. And Manasseh his son succeeded
21: 3 He rebuilt the high places his **father** Hezekiah had destroyed;
21: 8 feet of the Israelites wander from the land I gave their **forefathers**,
21:15 have provoked me to anger from the day their **forefathers** came
21:18 Manasseh rested with his **fathers** and was buried in his palace
21:20 evil in the eyes of the LORD, as his **father** Manasseh had done.
21:21 He walked in all the ways of his **father**; he worshiped the idols his
21:21 he worshiped the idols his **father** had worshiped, and bowed down
21:22 He forsook the LORD, the God of his **fathers**, and did not walk
22: 2 eyes of the LORD and walked in all the ways of his **father** David,
22:13 because our **fathers** have not obeyed the words of this book;
22:20 Therefore I will gather you to your **fathers**, and you will be buried
23:30 and anointed him and made him king in place of his **father**.
23:32 He did evil in the eyes of the LORD, just as his **fathers** had done.
23:34 Neco made Eliakim son of Josiah king in place of his **father** Josiah
23:37 he did evil in the eyes of the LORD, just as his **fathers** had done.
24: 6 Jehoiakim rested with his **fathers**. And Jehoiachin his son
24: 9 He did evil in the eyes of the LORD, just as his **father** had done.
1Ch 2:17 was the mother of Amasa, whose **father** was Jether the Ishmaelite.
2:21 Hezron lay with the daughter of Makir the **father** *of* Gilead (he had
2:23 All these were descendants of Makir the **father** *of* Gilead.
2:24 Abijah the wife of Hezron bore him Ashhur the **father** *of* Tekoa.
2:42 Mesha his firstborn, who was the **father** *of* Ziph, and his son

1Ch 2:42 of Ziph, and his son Mareshah, who was the **father** *of* Hebron.
2:44 was the father of Raham, and Raham the **father** *of* Jorkeam.
2:45 son of Shammai was Maon, and Maon was the **father** *of* Beth Zur.
2:49 She also gave birth to Shaaph the **father** *of* Madmannah and to
2:49 of Madmannah and to Sheva the **father** *of* Macbenah and Gibea.
2:49 and to Sheva the father of Macbenah and **[RPH]** Gibea.
2:50 the firstborn of Ephrathah: Shobal the **father** *of* Kiriath Jearim,
2:51 Salma the **father** *of* Bethlehem, and Hareph the father of Beth
2:51 the father of Bethlehem, and Hareph the **father** *of* Beth Gader.
2:52 The descendants of Shobal the **father** *of* Kiriath Jearim were:
2:55 who came from Hammath, the **father** *of* the house of Recab.
4:3 These were the sons [BHS *father*; NIV 1201] *of* Etam: Jezreel,
4:4 Penuel was the **father** *of* Gedor, and Ezer the father of Hushah.
4:4 Penuel was the father of Gedor, and Ezer the **father** *of* Hushah.
4:4 of Hur, the firstborn of Ephrathah and **father** *of* Bethlehem.
4:5 Ashhur the **father** *of* Tekoa had two wives, Helah and Naarah.
4:11 was the father of Mehir, who was the **father** *of* Eshton.
4:12 of Beth Rapha, Paseah and Tehinnah the **father** *of* Ir Nahash.
4:14 Seraiah was the father of Joab, the **father** *of* Ge Harashim.
4:17 birth to Miriam, Shammai and Ishbah the **father** *of* Eshtemoa.
4:18 (His Judean wife gave birth to Jered the **father** *of* Gedor, Heber the
4:18 Heber the **father** *of* Soco, and Jekuthiel the father of Zanoah.)
4:18 Heber the father of Soco, and Jekuthiel the **father** *of* Zanoah.)
4:19 the **father** *of* Keilah the Garmite, and Eshtemoa the Maacathite.
4:21 Er the **father** *of* Lecah, Laadah the father of Mareshah
4:21 Laadah the **father** *of* Mareshah and the clans of the linen workers
4:38 leaders of their clans. Their **families** [+1074] increased greatly,
5:1 was the firstborn, but when he defiled his **father's** marriage bed,
5:13 Their relatives, by **families** [+1074], were: Michael, Meshullam,
5:15 son of Abdiel, the son of Guni, was head of their **family** [+1074].
5:24 These were the heads of their **families** [+1074]: Epher, Ishi,
5:24 brave warriors, famous men, and heads of their **families** [+1074].
5:25 they were unfaithful to the God of their **fathers** and prostituted
6:19 [6:4] are the clans of the Levites listed according to their **fathers**:
7:2 Jahmai, Ibsam and Samuel—heads of their **families** [+1074].
7:4 According to their **family** [+1074] genealogy, they had 36,000 men
7:7 Uzzi, Uzziel, Jerimoth and Iri, heads of **families** [+1074]—
7:9 Their genealogical record listed the heads of **families** [+1074]
7:11 All these sons of Jediael were heads of **families**. There were
7:14 Aramean concubine. She gave birth to Makir the **father** *of* Gilead.
7:22 Their **father** Ephraim mourned for them many days, and his
7:31 sons of Beriah: Heber and Malkiel, who was the **father** *of* Birzaith.
7:40 heads of **families** [+1074], choice men, brave warriors
8:6 who were heads of **families** of those living in Geba and were
8:10 Sakia and Mirmah. These were his sons, heads of **families**.
8:13 who were heads of **families** of those living in Aijalon and who
8:28 All these were heads of **families**, chiefs as listed in their
8:29 Jeiel the **father** *of* Gibeon lived in Gibeon. His wife's name was
9:9 numbered 956. All these men were heads **[RPH]** of their families.
9:9 numbered 956. All these men were heads of their **families** [+1074].
9:13 The priests, who were heads of **families** [+1074], numbered 1,760.
9:19 and his fellow gatekeepers from his **family** [+1074] (the Korahites)
9:19 **fathers** had been responsible for guarding the entrance to the
9:33 Those who were musicians, heads of Levite **families**, stayed in the
9:34 All these were heads of Levite **families**, chiefs as listed in their
9:35 Jeiel the **father** *of* Gibeon lived in Gibeon. His wife's name was
12:17 [12:18] may the God of our **fathers** see it and judge you."
12:28 [12:29] young warrior, with 22 officers from his **family** [+1074];
12:30 [12:31] brave warriors, famous in their own **clans** [+1074]—
15:12 He said to them, "You are the heads of the Levitical **families**;
17:11 When your days are over and you go to be with your **fathers**,
17:13 I will be his **father**, and he will be my son. I will never take my
19:2 Hanun son of Nahash, because his **father** showed kindness to me."
19:2 to express his sympathy to Hanun concerning his **father**.
19:3 "Do you think David is honoring your **father** by sending men to
21:17 my God, let your hand fall upon me and my **family** [+1074],
22:10 a house for my Name. He will be my son, and I will be his **father**.
23:9 three in all. These were the heads of the **families** of Ladan.
23:11 so they were counted as one **family** [+1074] with one assignment.
23:24 These were the descendants of Levi by their **families** [+1074]—
23:24 the heads of **families** as they were registered under their names
24:2 Nadab and Abihu died before their **father** did, and they had no
24:4 sixteen heads of **families** [+1074] from Eleazar's descendants
24:4 and eight heads of **families** [+1074] from Ithamar's descendants.
24:6 and the heads of **families** of the priests and of the Levites—
24:6 one **family** [+1074] being taken from Eleazar and then one from
24:19 to the regulations prescribed for them by their **forefather** Aaron,
24:30 These were the Levites, according to their **families** [+1074].
24:31 and the heads of **families** of the priests and of the Levites.
24:31 The **families** *of* the oldest brother were treated the same as those of
25:3 six in all, under the supervision of their **father** Jeduthun,
25:6 All these men were under the supervision of their **fathers** for the
26:6 who were leaders in their **father's** family because they were very
26:10 he was not the firstborn, his **father** had appointed him the first),
26:13 each gate, according to their **families** [+1074], young and old alike.
26:21 who were heads of **families** belonging to Ladan the Gershonite,
26:26 by the heads of **families** who were the commanders of thousands
26:31 their chief according to the genealogical records of their **families**.
26:32 hundred relatives, who were able men and heads of **families**,
27:1 heads of **families**, commanders of thousands and commanders of
28:4 chose me from my whole **family** [+1074] to be king over Israel
28:4 and from the house of Judah he chose my **family** [+1074],
28:4 from my **father's** sons he was pleased to make me king over all
28:6 for I have chosen him to be my son, and I will be his **father**.
28:9 "And you, my son Solomon, acknowledge the God of your **father**,
29:6 Then the leaders of **families**, the officers of the tribes of Israel,
29:10 saying, "Praise be to you, O LORD, God of our **father** Israel,
29:15 are aliens and strangers in your sight, as were all our **forefathers**.
29:18 O LORD, God of our **fathers** Abraham, Isaac and Israel,
29:20 So they all praised the LORD, the God of their **fathers**; they
29:23 on the throne of the LORD as king in place of his **father** David.
2Ch 1:2 to the judges and to all the leaders in Israel, the heads of **families**—
1:8 "You have shown great kindness to David my **father** and have
1:9 LORD God, let your promise to my **father** David be confirmed,
2:3 [2:2] "Send me cedar logs as you did for my **father** David when
2:7 [2:6] my skilled craftsmen, whom my **father** David provided.
2:14 [2:13] mother was from Dan and whose **father** was from Tyre.
2:14 [2:13] and with those of my lord, David your **father**.
2:17 [2:16] were in Israel, after the census his **father** David had taken;
3:1 where the LORD had appeared to his **father** David.
5:1 he brought in the things his **father** David had dedicated—
5:2 all the heads of the tribes and the chiefs of the Israelite **families**,
6:4 has fulfilled what he promised with his mouth to my **father** David.
6:7 "My **father** David had it in his heart to build a temple for the
6:8 the LORD said to my **father** David, 'Because it was in your heart
6:10 I have succeeded David my **father** and now I sit on the throne of
6:15 You have kept your promise to your servant David my **father**;
6:16 keep for your servant David my **father** the promises you made to
6:25 bring them back to the land you gave to them and their **fathers**.
6:31 your ways all the time they live in the land you gave our **fathers**.
6:38 pray toward the land you gave their **fathers**, toward the city you
7:17 "As for you, if you walk before me as David your **father** did,
7:18 royal throne, as I covenanted with David your **father** when I said,
7:22 the God of their **fathers**, who brought them out of Egypt, and have
8:14 In keeping with the ordinance of his **father** David, he appointed
9:31 he rested with his **fathers** and was buried in the city of David his
9:31 with his fathers and was buried in the city of David his **father**.
10:4 "Your **father** put a heavy yoke on us, but now lighten the harsh
10:4 lighten the harsh labor and the heavy yoke **he**[s] [+3870] put on us,
10:6 King Rehoboam consulted the elders who had served his **father**
10:9 people who say to me, 'Lighten the yoke your **father** put on us'?"
10:10 'Your **father** put a heavy yoke on us, but make our yoke lighter'—
10:10 tell them, 'My little finger is thicker than my **father's** waist.
10:11 My **father** laid on you a heavy yoke; I will make it even heavier.
10:11 My **father** scourged you with whips; I will scourge you with
10:14 young men and said, "My **father** [BHS-] made your yoke heavy;
10:14 My **father** scourged you with whips; I will scourge you with
11:16 to offer sacrifices to the LORD, the God of their **fathers**.
12:16 Rehoboam rested with his **fathers** and was buried in the City of
13:12 the LORD, the God of your **fathers**, for you will not succeed."
13:18 because they relied on the LORD, the God of their **fathers**.
14:1 [13:23] Abijah rested with his **fathers** and was buried in the City
14:4 [14:3] the God of their **fathers**, and to obey his laws
15:12 the LORD, the God of their **fathers**, with all their heart and soul.
15:18 and gold and the articles that he and his **father** had dedicated.
16:3 he said, "as there was between my **father** and your father.
16:3 he said, "as there was between my father and your **father**.
16:13 forty-first year of his reign Asa died and rested with his **fathers**.
17:2 and in the towns of Ephraim that his **father** Asa had captured.
17:3 because in his early years he walked in the ways his **father** David
17:4 sought the God of his **father** and followed his commands rather
17:14 Their enrollment by **families** [+1074] was as follows: From Judah,
19:4 and turned them back to the LORD, the God of their **fathers**.
19:8 and heads of Israelite **families** to administer the law of the LORD
20:6 "O LORD, God of our **fathers**, are you not the God who is in
20:32 He walked in the ways of his **father** Asa and did not stray from
20:33 the people still had not set their hearts on the God of their **fathers**.
21:1 Jehoshaphat rested with his **fathers** and was buried with them in
21:1 and was buried with **them**[s] [+2257] in the City of David.
21:3 Their **father** had given them many gifts of silver and gold
21:4 When Jehoram established himself firmly over his **father's**
21:10 because Jehoram had forsaken the LORD, the God of his **fathers**.
21:12 "This is what the LORD, the God of your **father** David, says:
21:12 'You have not walked in the ways of your **father** Jehoshaphat
21:13 members of your **father's** house, men who were better than you.
21:19 His people made no fire in his honor, as they had for his **fathers**.
22:4 for after his **father's** death they became his advisers, to his
23:2 the Levites and the heads of Israelite **families** from all the towns.

2Ch 24:18 the God of their **fathers**, and worshiped Asherah poles and idols.
24:22 King Joash did not remember the kindness Zechariah's **father**
24:24 the God of their **fathers**, judgment was executed on Joash.
25: 3 he executed the officials who had murdered his **father** the king.
25: 4 "**Fathers** shall not be put to death for their children, nor children
25: 4 death for their children, nor children put to death for their **fathers**;
25: 5 assigned them according to their **families** [+1074] to commanders
25:28 back by horse and was buried with his **fathers** in the City of Judah.
26: 1 years old, and made him king in place of his **father** Amaziah.
26: 2 and restored it to Judah after Amaziah rested with his **fathers**.
26: 4 in the eyes of the LORD, just as his **father** Amaziah had done.
26:12 The total number of **family** leaders over the fighting men was
26:23 Uzziah rested with his **fathers** and was buried near them in a field
26:23 was buried near **them**[s] [+2257] in a field for burial that belonged
27: 2 right in the eyes of the LORD, just as his **father** Uzziah had done,
27: 9 Jotham rested with his **fathers** and was buried in the City of David.
28: 1 Unlike David his **father**, he did not do what was right in the eyes
28: 6 because Judah had forsaken the LORD, the God of their **fathers**.
28: 9 the LORD, the God of your **fathers**, was angry with Judah,
28:25 and provoked the LORD, the God of his **fathers**, to anger.
28:27 Ahaz rested with his **fathers** and was buried in the city of
29: 2 right in the eyes of the LORD, just as his **father** David had done.
29: 5 and consecrate the temple of the LORD, the God of your **fathers**.
29: 6 Our **fathers** were unfaithful; they did evil in the eyes of the
29: 9 This is why our **fathers** have fallen by the sword and why our sons
30: 7 Do not be like your **fathers** and brothers, who were unfaithful to
30: 7 who were unfaithful to the LORD, the God of their **fathers**,
30: 8 Do not be stiff-necked, as your **fathers** were; submit to the
30:19 his heart on seeking God—the LORD, the God of his **fathers**—
30:22 and praised the LORD, the God of their **fathers**.
31:17 they distributed to the priests enrolled by their **families** [+1074] in
32:13 and my **fathers** have done to all the peoples of the other lands?
32:14 Who of all the gods of these nations that my **fathers** destroyed has
32:15 able to deliver his people from my hand or the hand of my **fathers**.
32:33 Hezekiah rested with his **fathers** and was buried on the hill where
33: 3 He rebuilt the high places his **father** Hezekiah had demolished;
33: 8 feet of the Israelites leave the land I assigned to your **forefathers**,
33:12 and humbled himself greatly before the God of his **fathers**.
33:20 Manasseh rested with his **fathers** and was buried in his palace.
33:22 evil in the eyes of the LORD, as his **father** Manasseh had done.
33:22 and offered sacrifices to all the idols Manasseh had made. **[RPH]**
33:23 unlike his **father** Manasseh, he did not humble himself before the
34: 2 eyes of the LORD and walked in the ways of his **father** David,
34: 3 he was still young, he began to seek the God of his **father** David.
34:21 because our **fathers** have not kept the word of the LORD;
34:28 Now I will gather you to your **fathers**, and you will be buried in
34:32 in accordance with the covenant of God, the God of their **fathers**.
34:33 they did not fail to follow the LORD, the God of their **fathers**.
35: 4 Prepare yourselves by **families** [+1074] in your divisions,
35: 5 "Stand in the holy place with a **group** [+1074+2755] of Levites for
35: 5 subdivision of the **families** [+1074] of your fellow countrymen,
35:12 of the **families** [+1074] of the people to offer to the LORD,
35:24 He was buried in the tombs of his **fathers**, and all Judah
36: 1 of Josiah and made him king in Jerusalem in place of his **father**.
36:15 The LORD, the God of their **fathers**, sent word to them through
Ezr 1: 5 Then the **family** heads of Judah and Benjamin, and the priests
2:59 they could not show that their **families** [+1074] were descended
2:68 some of the heads of the **families** gave freewill offerings toward
3:12 But many of the older priests and Levites and **family** heads,
4: 2 they came to Zerubbabel and to the heads of the **families** and said,
4: 3 and the rest of the heads of the **families** of Israel answered,
7:27 Praise be to the LORD, the God of our **fathers**, who has put it
8: 1 These are the **family** heads and those registered with them who
8:28 are a freewill offering to the LORD, the God of your **fathers**.
8:29 the leading priests and the Levites and the **family** heads of Israel."
9: 7 From the days of our **forefathers** until now, our guilt has been
10:11 confession to the LORD, the God of your **fathers**, and do his will.
10:16 Ezra the priest selected men who were **family** heads, one from
10:16 one from each **family** division, and all of them designated by
Ne 1: 6 including myself and my **father's** house, have committed against
2: 3 Why should my face not look sad when the city where my **fathers**
2: 5 let him send me to the city in Judah where my **fathers** are buried
7:61 they could not show that their **families** [+1074] were descended
7:70 [7:69] Some of the heads of the **families** contributed to the work.
7:71 [7:70] Some of the heads of the **families** gave to the treasury for
8:13 the heads of all the **families**, along with the priests and the Levites,
9: 2 and confessed their sins and the wickedness of their **fathers**.
9: 9 "You saw the suffering of our **forefathers** in Egypt; you heard
9:16 "But they, our **forefathers**, became arrogant and stiff-necked,
9:23 you brought them into the land that you told their **fathers** to enter
9:32 our priests and prophets, upon our **fathers** and all your people,
9:34 our leaders, our priests and our **fathers** did not follow your law;
9:36 slaves in the land you gave our **forefathers** so they could eat its
10:34 [10:35] **families** [+1074] is to bring to the house of our God at set
11:13 and his associates, who were heads of **families**—242 men;
12:12 the days of Joiakim, these were the heads of the priestly **families**:
12:22 The **family** heads of the Levites in the days of Eliashib, Joiada,
12:23 The **family** heads among the descendants of Levi up to the time of
13:18 Didn't your **forefathers** do the same things, so that our God
Est 2: 7 he had brought up because she had neither **father** nor mother.
2: 7 and Mordecai had taken her as his own daughter when her **father**
4:14 from another place, but you and your **father's** family will perish.
Job 8: 8 the former generations and find out what their **fathers** learned,
15:10 and the aged are on our side, men even older than your **father**.
15:18 men have declared, hiding nothing received from their **fathers**
17:14 'You are my **father**,' and to the worm, 'My mother' or 'My sister,'
29:16 I was a **father** to the needy; I took up the case of the stranger.
30: 1 whose **fathers** I would have disdained to put with my sheep dogs.
31:18 from my youth I reared him as would a **father**, and from my birth I
38:28 Does the rain have a **father**? Who fathers the drops of dew?
42:15 their **father** granted them an inheritance along with their brothers.
Ps 22: 4 [22:5] In you our **fathers** put their trust; they trusted and you
27:10 Though my **father** and mother forsake me, the LORD will
39:12 [39:13] with you as an alien, a stranger, as all my **fathers** were.
44: 1 [44:2] our **fathers** have told us what you did in their days, in days
45:10 [45:11] and give ear: Forget your people and your **father's** house.
45:16 [45:17] Your sons will take the place of your **fathers**; you will
49:19 [49:20] he will join the generation of his **fathers**, who will never
68: 5 [68:6] A **father** *to* the fatherless, a defender of widows, is God in
78: 3 what we have heard and known, what our **fathers** have told us.
78: 5 which he commanded our **forefathers** to teach their children,
78: 8 They would not be like their **forefathers**—a stubborn
78:12 He did miracles in the sight of their **fathers** in the land of Egypt,
78:57 Like their **fathers** they were disloyal and faithless, as unreliable as
89:26 [89:27] 'You are my **Father**, my God, the Rock my Savior.'
95: 9 where your **fathers** tested and tried me, though they had seen what
103:13 As a **father** has compassion on his children, so the LORD has
106: 6 We have sinned, even as our **fathers** did; we have done wrong
106: 7 When our **fathers** were in Egypt, they gave no thought to your
109:14 May the iniquity of his **fathers** be remembered before the LORD;
Pr 1: 8 to your **father's** instruction and do not forsake your mother's
3:12 disciplines those he loves, as a **father** the son he delights in.
4: 1 Listen, my sons, to a **father's** instruction; pay attention and gain
4: 3 When I was a boy in my **father's** house, still tender, and an only
6:20 keep your **father's** commands and do not forsake your mother's
10: 1 A wise son brings joy to his **father**, but a foolish son grief to his
13: 1 A wise son heeds his **father's** instruction, but a mocker does not
15: 5 A fool spurns his **father's** discipline, but whoever heeds correction
15:20 A wise son brings joy to his **father**, but a foolish man despises his
17: 6 are a crown to the aged, and **parents** are the pride of their children.
17:21 a fool for a son brings grief; there is no joy for the **father** *of* a fool.
17:25 A foolish son brings grief to his **father** and bitterness to the one
19:13 A foolish son is his **father's** ruin, and a quarrelsome wife is like a
19:14 Houses and wealth are inherited from **parents**, but a prudent wife
19:26 He who robs his **father** and drives out his mother is a son who
20:20 If a man curses his **father** or mother, his lamp will be snuffed out
22:28 not move an ancient boundary stone set up by your **forefathers**.
23:22 Listen to your **father**, who gave you life, and do not despise your
23:24 The **father** *of* a righteous man has great joy; he who has a wise son
23:25 May your **father** and mother be glad; may she who gave you birth
27:10 Do not forsake your friend and the friend of your **father**, and do
28: 7 a discerning son, but a companion of gluttons disgraces his **father**.
28:24 He who robs his **father** or mother and says, "It's not wrong"—
29: 3 A man who loves wisdom brings joy to his **father**, but a
30:11 "There are those who curse their **fathers** and do not bless their
30:17 "The eye that mocks a **father**, that scorns obedience to a mother,
Isa 3: 6 A man will seize one of his brothers at his **father's** home,
7:17 on the house of your **father** a time unlike any since Ephraim broke
8: 4 Before the boy knows how to say 'My **father**' or 'My mother,'
9: 6 [9:5] Mighty God, Everlasting **Father**, Prince of Peace.
14:21 a place to slaughter his sons for the sins of their **forefathers**;
22:21 He will be a **father** to those who live in Jerusalem and to the house
22:23 a firm place; he will be a seat of honor for the house of his **father**.
22:24 All the glory of his **family** [+1074] will hang on him: its offspring
37:12 Did the gods of the nations that were destroyed by my **forefathers**
38: 5 'This is what the LORD, the God of your **father** David, says:
38:19 am doing today; **fathers** tell their children about your faithfulness.
39: 6 all that your **fathers** have stored up until this day, will be carried
43:27 Your first **father** sinned; your spokesmen rebelled against me.
45:10 Woe to him who says to his **father**, 'What have you begotten?'
51: 2 look to Abraham, your **father**, and to Sarah, who gave you birth.
58:14 of the land and to feast on the inheritance of your **father** Jacob."
63:16 But you are our **Father**, though Abraham does not know us
63:16 you, O LORD, are our **Father**, our Redeemer from of old is your
64: 8 [64:7] Yet, O LORD, you are our **Father**. We are the clay, you
64:11 [64:10] and glorious temple, where our **fathers** praised you,
65: 7 both your sins and the sins of your **fathers**," says the LORD.
Jer 2: 5 "What fault did your **fathers** find in me, that they strayed

Jer 2:27 They say to wood, 'You are my **father**,' and to stone, 'You gave me
3: 4 you not just called to me: 'My **Father**, my friend from my youth,
3:18 northern land to the land I gave your **forefathers** as an inheritance.
3:19 I thought you would call me '**Father**' and not turn away from
3:24 shameful gods have consumed the fruits of our **fathers**' labor—
3:25 have sinned against the LORD our God, both we and our **fathers**;
6:21 **Fathers** and sons alike will stumble over them; neighbors
7: 7 in this place, in the land I gave your **forefathers** for ever and ever.
7:14 the temple you trust in, the place I gave to you and your **fathers**.
7:18 The children gather wood, the **fathers** light the fire,
7:22 For when I brought your **forefathers** out of Egypt and spoke to
7:25 From the time your **forefathers** left Egypt until now, day after day,
7:26 They were stiff-necked and did more evil than their **forefathers**.'
9:14 [9:13] have followed the Baals, as their **fathers** taught them."
9:16 [9:15] nations that neither they nor their **fathers** have known,
11: 4 the terms I commanded your **forefathers** when I brought them out
11: 5 I will fulfill the oath I swore to your **forefathers**, to give them a
11: 7 From the time I brought your **forefathers** up from Egypt until
11:10 They have returned to the sins of their **forefathers** [+8037],
11:10 of Judah have broken the covenant I made with their **forefathers**.
12: 6 Your brothers, your own **family** [+1074]—even they have betrayed
13:14 one against the other, **fathers** and sons alike, declares the LORD.
14:20 we acknowledge our wickedness and the guilt of our **fathers**;
16: 3 women who are their mothers and the men who are their **fathers**:
16: 7 not even for a **father** or a mother—nor will anyone give them a
16:11 say to them, 'It is because your **fathers** forsook me,'
16:12 you have behaved more wickedly than your **fathers**. See how each
16:13 of this land into a land neither you nor your **fathers** have known,
16:15 For I will restore them to the land I gave their **forefathers**.
16:19 the earth and say, "Our **fathers** possessed nothing but false gods,
17:22 but keep the Sabbath day holy, as I commanded your **forefathers**.
19: 4 neither they nor their **fathers** nor the kings of Judah ever knew,
20:15 Cursed be the man who brought my **father** the news, who made
22:11 who succeeded his **father** as king of Judah but has gone from this
22:15 and more cedar? Did not your **father** have food and drink?
23:27 just as their **fathers** forgot my name through Baal worship.
23:39 of my presence along with the city I gave to you and your **fathers**.
24:10 are destroyed from the land I gave to them and their **fathers**.' "
25: 5 land the LORD gave to you and your **fathers** for ever and ever.
30: 3 and restore them to the land I gave their **forefathers** to possess,'
31: 9 because I am Israel's **father**, and Ephraim is my firstborn son.
31:29 'The **fathers** have eaten sour grapes, and the children's teeth are set
31:32 It will not be like the covenant I made with their **forefathers** when
32:18 bring the punishment for the **fathers**' sins into the laps of their
32:22 You gave them this land you had sworn to give their **forefathers**,
34: 5 As people made a funeral fire in honor of your **fathers**, the former
34:13 I made a covenant with your **forefathers** when I brought them out
34:14 Your **fathers**, however, did not listen to me or pay attention to me.
35: 6 because our **forefather** Jonadab son of Recab gave us this
35: 8 We have obeyed everything our **forefather** Jonadab son of Recab
35:10 have fully obeyed everything our **forefather** Jonadab commanded
35:14 do not drink wine, because they obey their **forefather's** command.
35:15 you will live in the land I have given to you and your **fathers**."
35:16 Recab have carried out the command their **forefather** gave them,
35:18 'You have obeyed the command of your **forefather** Jonadab
44: 3 other gods that neither they nor you nor your **fathers** ever knew.
44: 9 Have you forgotten the wickedness committed by your **fathers**
44:10 followed my law and the decrees I set before you and your **fathers**.
44:17 and will pour out drink offerings to her just as we and our **fathers**,
44:21 of Judah and the streets of Jerusalem by you and your **fathers**,
47: 3 **Fathers** will not turn to help their children; their hands will hang
50: 7 their true pasture, the LORD, the hope of their **fathers**.'
La 5: 3 We have become orphans and **fatherless** [+401], our mothers like
5: 7 Our **fathers** sinned and are no more, and we bear their punishment.
Eze 2: 3 and their **fathers** have been in revolt against me to this very day.
5:10 Therefore in your midst **fathers** will eat their children,
5:10 fathers will eat their children, and children will eat their **fathers**.
16: 3 your **father** was an Amorite and your mother a Hittite.
16:45 Your mother was a Hittite and your **father** an Amorite.
18: 2 " 'The **fathers** eat sour grapes, and the children's teeth are set on
18: 4 For every living soul belongs to me, the **father** as well as the son—
18:14 "But suppose this son has a son who sees all the sins his **father**
18:17 my decrees. He will not die for his **father's** sin; he will surely live.
18:18 his **father** will die for his own sin, because he practiced extortion,
18:19 "Yet you ask, 'Why does the son not share the guilt of his **father**?'
18:20 The son will not share the guilt of the **father**, nor will the father
18:20 the guilt of the father, nor will the **father** share the guilt of the son.
20: 4 Then confront them with the detestable practices of their **fathers**
20:18 "Do not follow the statutes of your **fathers** or keep their laws
20:24 my Sabbaths, and their eyes ⌊lusted⌋ after their **fathers**' idols.
20:27 In this also your **fathers** blasphemed me by forsaking me:
20:30 Will you defile yourselves the way your **fathers** did and lust after
20:36 As I judged your **fathers** in the desert of the land of Egypt,
20:42 the land I had sworn with uplifted hand to give to your **fathers**.
22: 7 In you they have treated **father** and mother with contempt;
22:10 In you are those who dishonor their **fathers**' bed; in you are those
22:11 and another violates his sister, his own **father's** daughter.
36:28 You will live in the land I gave your **forefathers**; you will be my
37:25 land I gave to my servant Jacob, the land where your **fathers** lived.
44:25 if the dead person was his **father** or mother, son or daughter,
47:14 Because I swore with uplifted hand to give it to your **forefathers**,
Da 9: 6 our princes and our **fathers**, and to all the people of the land.
9: 8 our princes and our **fathers** are covered with shame because we
9:16 Our sins and the iniquities of our **fathers** have made Jerusalem
11:24 and will achieve what neither his **fathers** nor his forefathers did.
11:24 will achieve what neither his fathers nor his **forefathers** [+3] did.
11:24 will achieve what neither his fathers nor his **forefathers** [+3] did.
11:37 He will show no regard for the gods of his **fathers** or for the one
11:38 a god unknown to his **fathers** he will honor with gold and silver,
Hos 9:10 when I saw your **fathers**, it was like seeing the early fruit on the
Joel 1: 2 this ever happened in your days or in the days of your **forefathers**?
Am 2: 4 been led astray by false gods, the gods their **ancestors** followed,
2: 7 **Father** and son use the same girl and so profane my holy name.
Mic 7: 6 For a son dishonors his **father**, a daughter rises up against her
7:20 as you pledged on oath to our **fathers** in days long ago.
Zec 1: 2 "The LORD was very angry with your **forefathers**.
1: 4 Do not be like your **forefathers**, to whom the earlier prophets
1: 5 Where are your **forefathers** now? And the prophets, do they live
1: 6 commanded my servants the prophets, overtake your **forefathers**?
8:14 upon you and showed no pity when your **fathers** angered me,"
13: 3 his **father** and mother, to whom he was born, will say to him,
13: 3 When he prophesies, his own **parents** [+562+2256] will stab him.
Mal 1: 6 "A son honors his **father**, and a servant his master. If I am a father,
1: 6 If I am a **father**, where is the honor due me? If I am a master,
2:10 Have we not all one **Father**? Did not one God create us? Why do
2:10 Why do we profane the covenant of our **fathers** by breaking faith
3: 7 Ever since the time of your **forefathers** you have turned away
4: 6 [3:24] He will turn the hearts of the **fathers** to their children,
4: 6 [3:24] and the hearts of the children to their **fathers**;

4 אֵב 'ēb, n.[m.]. [2] [cf. 817; Ar 10004]

growing [1], new growth [1]

Job 8:12 While still **growing** and uncut, they wither more quickly than
SS 6:11 I went down to the grove of nut trees to look at the **new growth** *in*

5 אֲבַגְתָא 'ăbagtā', n.pr.m. [1]

Abagtha [1]

Est 1:10 Mehuman, Biztha, Harbona, Bigtha, **Abagtha**, Zethar and Carcas—

6 אָבַד 'ābad, v. [184] [→ 7, 8, 9, 10, 11, 12, 13; Ar 10005]

perish [43], destroy [28], destroyed [18], lost [11], perished [9], destruction [5], gone [5], perishes [4], perishing [4], ruined [4], annihilate [3], come to nothing [3], certainly be destroyed [+6] [2], comes to nothing [2], destroy completely [+6+906] [2], destroys [2], lose [2], perish [+6] [2], surely be destroyed [+6] [2], wipe out [2], *untranslated* [1], annihilation [1], banish [1], be destroyed [1], broken [1], brought ruin [1], come to ruin [1], corrupts [1], dead [1], demolish [1], destroying [1], die [1], died [1], dying [1], elude [1], expelled [1], exterminate [1], give up [1], have no [+4946] [1], have nowhere [+4946] [1], kill [1], loses [+8+4946] [1], not escape [+4960] [1], ruin [1], silence [1], squanders [1], swept [1], vanished [1], wandering [1], wiped out [1], without [1]

Ex 10: 7 [A] their God. Do you not yet realize that Egypt *is* **ruined**?"
Lev 23:30 [G] *I will* **destroy** from among his people anyone who does any
26:38 [A] *You will* **perish** among the nations; the land of your enemies
Nu 16:33 [A] and *they* **perished** and were gone from the community.
17:12 [17:27] [A] "We will die! *We are* **lost**, we are all lost!
17:12 [17:27] [A] to Moses, "We will die! We are lost, we *are* all **lost**!
21:29 [A] to you, O Moab! *You are* **destroyed**, O people of Chemosh!
21:30 [A] Heshbon *is* **destroyed** all the way to Dibon.
24:19 [G] will come out of Jacob and **destroy** the survivors of the city."
33:52 [D] **Destroy** all their carved images and their cast idols, and
33:52 [D] their cast idols, **[RPH]** and demolish all their high places.
Dt 4:26 [A] *you will* quickly **perish** [+6] from the land that you are
4:26 [A] *you will* quickly **perish** [+6] from the land that you are
7:10 [G] who hate him he will repay to their face by **destruction**;
7:20 [A] until even the survivors who hide from you *have* **perished**.
7:24 [G] and *you will* **wipe out** their names from under heaven.
8:19 [A] against you today that *you will* **surely be destroyed** [+6].
8:19 [A] against you today that *you will* **surely be destroyed** [+6].
8:20 [G] Like the nations the LORD **destroyed** before you, so you
8:20 [A] so *you will* **be destroyed** for not obeying the LORD your
9: 3 [G] And you will drive them out and **annihilate** them quickly,
11: 4 [D] and how the LORD **brought** lasting **ruin** *on* them.
11:17 [A] *you will* soon **perish** from the good land the LORD is

Dt 12: 2 [D] **Destroy** [+6+906] **completely** all the places on the high
12: 2 [D] **Destroy completely** [+6+906] all the places on the high
12: 3 [D] of their gods and **wipe out** their names from those places.
22: 3 [A] or his cloak or anything he **loses** [+8+4946].
26: 5 [A] "My father *was* a **wandering** Aramean, and he went down
28: 20 [A] until you are destroyed and **come to** sudden **ruin** because of
28: 22 [A] and mildew, which will plague you until you **perish**.
28: 51 [G] of your herds or lambs of your flocks until you *are* **ruined**.
28: 63 [G] in number, so it will please him to **ruin** and destroy you.
30: 18 [A] to you this day that *you will* **certainly be destroyed** [+6].
30: 18 [A] to you this day that *you will* **certainly be destroyed** [+6].
32: 28 [A] They are a nation **without** sense, there is no discernment in
Jos 7: 7 [G] to deliver us into the hands of the Amorites to **destroy** us?
23: 13 [A] and thorns in your eyes, until you **perish** from this good land,
23: 16 [A] *you will* quickly **perish** from the good land he has given
Jdg 5: 31 [A] "So *may* all your enemies **perish**, O LORD! But may they
1Sa 9: 3 [A] Now the donkeys belonging to Saul's father Kish *were* **lost**,
9: 20 [A] As for the donkeys you **lost** three days ago, do not worry
2Sa 1: 27 [A] the mighty have fallen! The weapons of war *have* **perished**!"
2Ki 9: 8 [A] The whole house of Ahab *will* **perish**. I will cut off from
10: 19 [G] Jehu was acting deceptively in order to **destroy** the ministers
11: 1 [D] was dead, she proceeded *to* **destroy** the whole royal family.
13: 7 [D] for the king of Aram *had* **destroyed** the rest and made them
19: 18 [D] have thrown their gods into the fire and **destroyed** them,
21: 3 [D] rebuilt the high places his father Hezekiah *had* **destroyed**;
24: 2 [G] He sent them to **destroy** Judah, in accordance with the word
Est 3: 9 [D] If it pleases the king, let a decree be issued to **destroy** them,
3: 13 [D] with the order to destroy, kill and **annihilate** all the Jews—
4: 7 [D] to pay into the royal treasury for *the* **destruction** of the Jews.
4: 14 [A] another place, but you and your father's family *will* **perish**.
4: 16 [A] even though it is against the law. And if *I* **perish**, I perish."
4: 16 [A] even though it is against the law. And if I perish, *I* **perish**."
7: 4 [D] been sold for destruction and slaughter and **annihilation**.
8: 5 [D] and wrote to **destroy** the Jews in all the king's provinces.
8: 11 [D] kill and **annihilate** any armed force of any nationality
9: 6 [D] of Susa, the Jews killed and **destroyed** five hundred men.
9: 12 [D] "The Jews have killed and **destroyed** five hundred men
9: 24 [D] had plotted against the Jews to **destroy** them and had cast the
9: 24 [D] cast the *pur* (that is, the lot) for their ruin and **destruction**.
Job 3: 3 [A] "*May* the day of my birth **perish**, and the night it was said,
4: 7 [A] "Consider now: Who, being innocent, *has ever* **perished**?
4: 9 [A] At the breath of God *they are* **destroyed**; at the blast of his
4: 11 [A] The lion **perishes** for lack of prey, and the cubs of the lioness
4: 20 [A] they are broken to pieces; unnoticed, *they* **perish** forever.
6: 18 [A] from their routes; they go up into the wasteland and **perish**.
8: 13 [A] of all who forget God; so **perishes** the hope of the godless.
11: 20 [A] the eyes of the wicked will fail, and escape *will* **elude** them;
12: 23 [D] He makes nations great, and **destroys** them; he enlarges
14: 19 [G] and torrents wash away the soil, so *you* **destroy** man's hope.
18: 17 [A] The memory of him **perishes** from the earth; he has no name
20: 7 [A] *he will* **perish** forever, like his own dung; those who have
29: 13 [A] The *man who was* **dying** blessed me; I made the widow's
30: 2 [A] of their hands to me, since their vigor *had* **gone** from them?
31: 19 [A] if I have seen *anyone* **perishing** for lack of clothing, or a
Ps 1: 6 [A] way of the righteous, but the way of the wicked *will* **perish**.
2: 12 [A] the Son, lest he be angry and *you be* **destroyed** in your way,
5: 6 [5:7] [D] *You* **destroy** those who tell lies; bloodthirsty
9: 3 [9:4] [A] turn back; they stumble and **perish** before you.
9: 5 [9:6] [D] You have rebuked the nations and **destroyed** the
9: 6 [9:7] [A] their cities; even the memory of them *has* **perished**.
9: 18 [9:19] [A] nor the hope of the afflicted ever **perish**.
10: 16 [A] King for ever and ever; the nations *will* **perish** from his land.
21: 10 [21:11] [D] *You will* **destroy** their descendants from the earth,
31: 12 [31:13] [A] I were dead; I have become like **broken** pottery.
37: 20 [A] the wicked *will* **perish**: The LORD's enemies will be like
41: 5 [41:6] [A] in malice, "When will he die and his name **perish**?"
49: 10 [49:11] [A] the foolish and the senseless alike **perish** and leave
68: 2 [68:3] [A] before the fire, *may* the wicked **perish** before God.
73: 27 [A] Those who are far from you *will* **perish**; you destroy all who
80: 16 [80:17] [A] burned with fire; at your rebuke your *people* **perish**.
83: 17 [83:18] [A] and dismayed; *may they* **perish** in disgrace.
92: 9 [92:10] [A] O LORD, surely your enemies *will* **perish**;
102: 26 [102:27] [A] They *will* **perish**, but you remain; they will all
112: 10 [A] the longings of the wicked *will* **come to nothing**.
119: 92 [A] not been my delight, *I would have* **perished** in my affliction.
119: 95 [D] The wicked are waiting to **destroy** me, but I will ponder your
119: 176 [A] I have strayed like a **lost** sheep. Seek your servant, for I have
142: 4 [142:5] [A] I **have no** [+4946] refuge; no one cares for my life.
143: 12 [G] my enemies; **destroy** all my foes, for I am your servant.
146: 4 [A] to the ground; on that very day their plans **come to nothing**.
Pr 1: 32 [D] kill them, and the complacency of fools *will* **destroy** them;
10: 28 [A] is joy, but the hopes of the wicked **come to nothing**.
11: 7 [A] When a wicked man dies, his hope **perishes**; all he expected
11: 7 [A] all he expected from his power **comes to nothing**.
11: 10 [A] when the wicked **perish**, there are shouts of joy.
19: 9 [A] not go unpunished, and he who pours out lies *will* **perish**.
21: 28 [A] A false witness *will* **perish**, and whoever listens to him will
28: 28 [A] into hiding; but when the wicked **perish**, the righteous thrive.
29: 3 [D] but a companion of prostitutes **squanders** his wealth.
31: 6 [A] Give beer to *those who are* **perishing**, wine to those who are
Ecc 3: 6 [D] a time to search and a time to **give up**, a time to keep and a
5: 14 [5:13] [A] or wealth **lost** through some misfortune, so that when
7: 7 [D] turns a wise man into a fool, and a bribe **corrupts** the heart.
7: 15 [A] a righteous man **perishing** in his righteousness, and a wicked
9: 6 [A] their hate and their jealousy *have* long since **vanished**;
9: 18 [D] than weapons of war, but one sinner **destroys** much good.
Isa 26: 14 [D] brought them to ruin; *you* **wiped out** all memory of them.
27: 13 [A] Those *who were* **perishing** in Assyria and those who were
29: 14 [A] the wisdom of the wise *will* **perish**, the intelligence of the
37: 19 [D] have thrown their gods into the fire and **destroyed** them,
41: 11 [A] those who oppose you will be as nothing and **perish**.
57: 1 [A] The righteous **perish**, and no one ponders it in his heart;
60: 12 [A] For the nation or kingdom that will not serve you *will* **perish**;
Jer 1: 10 [G] tear down, to **destroy** and overthrow, to build and to plant."
4: 9 [A] the LORD, "the king and the officials *will* **lose** heart,
6: 21 [A] stumble over them; neighbors and friends *will* **perish**."
7: 28 [A] Truth *has* **perished**; it has vanished from their lips.
9: 12 [9:11] [A] Why *has* the land *been* **ruined** and laid waste like a
10: 15 [A] of mockery; when their judgment comes, *they will* **perish**.
12: 17 [D] I will completely uproot and **destroy** it,"
15: 7 [D] I will bring bereavement and **destruction** *on* my people,
18: 7 [G] or kingdom is to be uprooted, torn down and **destroyed**,
18: 18 [A] for the teaching of the law by the priest *will* not *be* **lost**,
23: 1 [D] "Woe to the shepherds *who are* **destroying** and scattering
25: 10 [G] *I will* **banish** from them the sounds of joy and gladness,
25: 35 [A] The shepherds *will* **have nowhere** [+4946] to flee,
27: 10 [A] far from your lands; I will banish you and *you will* **perish**.
27: 15 [A] I will banish you and *you will* **perish**, both you
31: 28 [G] and tear down, and to overthrow, **destroy** and bring disaster,
40: 15 [A] you to be scattered and the remnant of Judah *to* **perish**?"
46: 8 [G] and cover the earth; *I will* **destroy** cities and their people.'
48: 8 [A] The valley *will be* **ruined** and the plateau destroyed,
48: 36 [A] the men of Kir Hareseth. The wealth they acquired *is* **gone**.
48: 46 [A] The people of Chemosh *are* **destroyed**; your sons are taken
49: 7 [A] *Has* counsel **perished** from the prudent? Has their wisdom
49: 38 [G] set my throne in Elam and **destroy** her king and officials,"
50: 6 [A] "My people have been **lost** sheep; their shepherds have led
51: 18 [A] of mockery; when their judgment comes, *they will* **perish**.
51: 55 [D] LORD will destroy Babylon; *he will* **silence** her noisy din.
La 2: 9 [D] sunk into the ground; their bars he has broken and **destroyed**.
3: 18 [A] "My splendor *is* **gone** and all that I had hoped from the
Eze 6: 3 [D] a sword against you, and *I will* **destroy** your high places.
7: 26 [A] the teaching of the law by the priest *will be* **lost**, as will the
12: 22 [A] 'The days go by and every vision **comes to nothing**'?
19: 5 [A] her expectation **gone**, she took another of her cubs and made
22: 27 [D] they shed blood and **kill** people to make unjust gain.
25: 7 [G] off from the nations and **exterminate** you from the countries.
25: 16 [G] the Kerethites and **destroy** those remaining along the coast.
26: 17 [A] " 'How *you are* **destroyed**, O city of renown, peopled by
28: 16 [D] *I* **expelled** you, O guardian cherub, from among the fiery
30: 13 [G] " '*I will* **destroy** the idols and put an end to the images in
32: 13 [G] *I will* **destroy** all her cattle from beside abundant waters no
34: 4 [A] You have not brought back the strays or searched for the **lost**.
34: 16 [A] I will search for the **lost** and bring back the strays. I will bind
37: 11 [A] They say, 'Our bones are dried up and our hope *is* **gone**;
Joel 1: 11 [A] and the barley, because the harvest of the field *is* **destroyed**.
Am 1: 8 [A] till the last of the Philistines *is* **dead**," says the Sovereign
2: 14 [A] The swift *will* **not escape** [+4960], the strong will not muster
3: 15 [A] the houses adorned with ivory *will be* **destroyed**
Ob 1: 8 [G] the LORD, "*will I* not **destroy** the wise men of Edom,
1: 12 [A] over the people of Judah in the day of their **destruction**,
Jnh 1: 6 [A] Maybe he will take notice of us, and *we will* not **perish**."
1: 14 [A] please *do* not *let us* **die** for taking this man's life.
3: 9 [A] turn from his fierce anger so that *we will* not **perish**."
4: 10 [A] or make it grow. It sprang up overnight and **died** overnight.
Mic 4: 9 [A] *Has* your counselor **perished**, that pain seizes you like that
5: 10 [5:9] [G] horses from among you and **demolish** your chariots.
7: 2 [A] The godly *have been* **swept** from the land; not one upright
Zep 2: 5 [G] of the Philistines. "*I will* **destroy** you, and none will be left."
2: 13 [D] stretch out his hand against the north and **destroy** Assyria,
Zec 9: 5 [A] Gaza *will* **lose** her king and Ashkelon will be deserted.

7 אֲבַד *'ōbēd*, n.[m.]. [2] [√ 6]

ruin [2]

Nu 24: 20 was first among the nations, but he will come to **ruin** at last."
24: 24 they will subdue Asshur and Eber, but they too will come to **ruin**."

8 אֲבֵדָה *ᵃbēdâ*, n.f. [4] [√ 6]
lost property [3], loses [+6+4946] [1]

Ex 22: 9 [22:8] or any other **lost property** about which somebody says,
Lev 6: 3 [5:22] or if he finds **lost property** and lies about it, or if he swears
6: 4 [5:23] what was entrusted to him, or the **lost property** he found,
Dt 22: 3 your brother's donkey or his cloak or anything he **loses** [+6+4946].

9 אֲבַדֹּה *ᵃbaddōh*, n.f. [1] [→ 11; cf. 6]
Destruction [1]

Pr 27:20 Death and **Destruction** [Q 10] are never satisfied, and neither are

10 אֲבַדּוֹ *ᵃbaddô*, n.f. [0] [√ 6]

Pr 27:20 [Death and **Destruction** [Q; see K 9] are never satisfied, and neither are the eyes of man.]

11 אֲבַדּוֹן *ᵃbaddôn*, n.f. [5] [√ 9; cf. 6]
Destruction [5]

Job 26: 6 Death is naked before God; **Destruction** lies uncovered.
28:22 **Destruction** and Death say, 'Only a rumor of it has reached our
31:12 It is a fire that burns to **Destruction**; it would have uprooted my
Ps 88:11 [88:12] declared in the grave, your faithfulness in **Destruction**?
Pr 15:11 Death and **Destruction** lie open before the LORD—how much

12 אַבְדָן *'abdān*, n.[m.]. [1] [√ 6]
destroying [1]

Est 9: 5 all their enemies with the sword, killing and **destroying** them,

13 אָבְדָן *'obdān*, n.[m.]. [1] [√ 6]
destruction [1]

Est 8: 6 my people? How can I bear to see the **destruction** *of* my family?"

14 אָבָה *'ābâ*, v. [53] [→ 16, 20?, 22?, 36?, 1066?; cf. 3277, 9289?]
would [13], refused [+4202] [11], willing [11], unwilling [+4202] [7], accept [2], refuse [+4202] [2], will [2], agree to demands [1], consent [1], submit [1], would have [1], yield [1]

Ge 24: 5 [A] "What if the woman *is* **unwilling** [+4202] to come back with
24: 8 [A] If the woman *is* **unwilling** [+4202] to come back with you,
Ex 10:27 [A] Pharaoh's heart, and *he was* not **willing** to let them go.
Lev 26:21 [A] remain hostile toward me and **refuse** [+4202] to listen to me,
Dt 1:26 [A] *you were* **unwilling** [+4202] to go up; you rebelled against
2:30 [A] Sihon king of Heshbon **refused** [+4202] to let us pass
10:10 [A] to me at this time also. *It was* not his **will** to destroy you.
13: 8 [13:9] [A] *do* not **yield** to him or listen to him. Show him no
23: 5 [23:6] [A] the LORD your God **would** not listen to Balaam
25: 7 [A] *He* **will** not fulfill the duty of a brother-in-law to me."
29:20 [29:19] [A] The LORD *will* never *be* **willing** to forgive him;
Jos 24:10 [A] But *I* **would** not listen to Balaam, so he blessed you again
Jdg 11:17 [A] They sent also to the king of Moab, and *he* **refused** [+4202].
19:10 [A] But, **unwilling** [+4202] to stay another night, the man left
19:25 [A] the men **would** not listen to him. So the man took his
20:13 [A] But the Benjamites **would** not listen to their fellow Israelites.
1Sa 15: 9 [A] These *they were* **unwilling** [+4202] to destroy completely,
22:17 [A] the king's officials *were* not **willing** to raise a hand to strike
26:23 [A] but *I* **would** not lay a hand on the LORD's anointed.
31: 4 [A] his armor-bearer was terrified and **would** not do it; so Saul
2Sa 2:21 [A] of his weapons." But Asahel **would** not stop chasing him.
6:10 [A] He *was* not **willing** to take the ark of the LORD to be with
12:17 [A] *he* **refused** [+4202], and he would not eat any food with
13:14 [A] *he* **refused** [+4202] to listen to her, and since he was stronger
13:16 [A] already done to me." But *he* **refused** [+4202] to listen to her.
13:25 [A] *he still* **refused** [+4202] to go, but gave him his blessing.
14:29 [A] him to the king, but Joab **refused** [+4202] to come to him.
14:29 [A] So he sent a second time, but *he* **refused** [+4202] to come.
23:16 [A] *he* **refused** [+4202] to drink it; instead, he poured it out
23:17 [A] David **would** not drink it. Such were the exploits of the three
1Ki 20: 8 [A] all answered, "Don't listen to him or **agree to** his **demands**."
22:49 [22:50] [A] with your men," but Jehoshaphat **refused** [+4202].
2Ki 8:19 [A] servant David, the LORD *was* not **willing** to destroy Judah.
13:23 [A] To this day *he has been* **unwilling** [+4202] to destroy them
24: 4 [A] innocent blood, and the LORD *was* not **willing** to forgive.
1Ch 10: 4 [A] his armor-bearer was terrified and **would** not do it; so Saul
11:18 [A] he **refused** [+4202] to drink it; instead, he poured it out
11:19 [A] risked their lives to bring it back, David **would** not drink it.
19:19 [A] So the Arameans *were* not **willing** to help the Ammonites
2Ch 21: 7 [A] the LORD *was* not **willing** to destroy the house of David.
Job 39: 9 [A] "*Will* the wild ox **consent** to serve you? Will he stay by your
Ps 81:11 [81:12] [A] not listen to me; Israel *would* not **submit** to me.
Pr 1:25 [A] you ignored all my advice and *would* not **accept** my rebuke,
1:30 [A] since *they would* not **accept** my advice and spurned my
6:35 [A] He will not accept any compensation; *he will* **refuse** [+4202]
Isa 1:19 [A] If *you are* **willing** and obedient, you will eat the best from
28:12 [A] "This is the place of repose"—but *they* **would** not listen.
30: 9 [A] children **unwilling** [+4202] to listen to the LORD's
30:15 [A] and trust is your strength, but *you* **would have** none of it.
42:24 [A] For *they* **would** not follow his ways; they did not obey his
Eze 3: 7 [A] the house of Israel *is* not **willing** to listen to you because they
3: 7 [A] to listen to you because they *are* not **willing** to listen to me,
20: 8 [A] " 'But they rebelled against me and **would** not listen to me;

15 אֵבֶה *'ēbeh*, n.[m.]. [1]
papyrus [1]

Job 9:26 They skim past like boats of **papyrus**, like eagles swooping down

16 אֲבוֹי *ᵃbôy*, interj. [1] [√ 14]
sorrow [1]

Pr 23:29 Who has woe? Who has **sorrow**? Who has strife? Who has

17 אֵבוּס *'ēbûs*, n.m. [3] [√ 80]
manger [3]

Job 39: 9 ox consent to serve you? Will he stay by your **manger** at night?
Pr 14: 4 Where there are no oxen, the **manger** is empty, but from the
Isa 1: 3 the donkey his owner's **manger**, but Israel does not know,

18 אִבְחָה *'ibḥâ*, n.f. [1] [cf. 3181]
slaughter [1]

Eze 21:15 [21:20] I have stationed the sword *for* **slaughter** at all their gates.

19 אֲבַטִּיחַ *ᵃbaṭṭîaḥ*, n.[m.]. [1] [√ 1053]
melons [1]

Nu 11: 5 at no cost—also the cucumbers, **melons**, leeks, onions and garlic.

20 אָבִי¹ *'ābî¹*, interj. [1] [√ 14?]
oh that [1]

Job 34:36 **Oh, that** Job might be tested to the utmost for answering like a

21 אָבִי² *'ābî²*, n.pr.m. Not used in NIV/BHS [cf. 2671]

22 אָבִי³ *'ābî³*, v. Not used in NIV/BHS [√ 14?]

23 אֲבִי *ᵃbî*, n.pr.m. [1 / 0] [√ 31]

2Ki 18: 2 His mother's name was Abijah [BHS *Abi*; NIV 31] daughter of

24 אֲבִיאֵל *ᵃbî'ēl*, n.pr.m. [3] [√ 446 + 3]
Abiel [3]

1Sa 9: 1 of standing, whose name was Kish son of **Abiel**, the son of Zeror,
14:51 Saul's father Kish and Abner's father Ner were sons of **Abiel**.
1Ch 11:32 Hurai from the ravines of Gaash, **Abiel** the Arbathite,

25 אֲבִיאָסָף *ᵃbî'āsāp*, n.pr.m. [1] [√ 47; cf. 3 + 3758]
Abiasaph [1]

Ex 6:24 The sons of Korah were Assir, Elkanah and **Abiasaph**. These were

26 אָבִיב *'ābîb*, n.m. [8] [cf. 9425]
Abib [5], headed [1], heads [1], that[s] [1]

Ex 9:31 since the barley had **headed** and the flax was in bloom.
13: 4 Today, in the month of **Abib**, you are leaving.
23:15 Do this at the appointed time in the month of **Abib**, for in that
34:18 Do this at the appointed time in the month of **Abib**, for in that
34:18 in the month of Abib, for in **that**[s] month you came out of Egypt.
Lev 2:14 the LORD, offer crushed **heads** *of* new grain roasted in the fire.
Dt 16: 1 Observe the month of **Abib** and celebrate the Passover of the
16: 1 because in the month of **Abib** he brought you out of Egypt by

27 אֲבִיבַּעַל *ᵃbîba'al*, n.pr.m. Not used in NIV/BHS [√ 3 + 1251]

28 אֲבִיגַיִל *ᵃbîgayil*, n.pr.f. [17] [√ 3 + 1635?]
Abigail [17]

1Sa 25: 3 His name was Nabal and his wife's name was **Abigail**. She was an
25:14 One of the servants told Nabal's wife **Abigail**: "David sent
25:18 **Abigail** lost no time. She took two hundred loaves of bread,
25:23 When **Abigail** saw David, she quickly got off her donkey

1Sa 25:32 David said to **Abigail**, "Praise be to the LORD, the God of Israel,
25:36 When **Abigail** went to Nabal, he was in the house holding a
25:39 Then David sent word to **Abigail**, asking her to become his wife.
25:40 His servants went to Carmel and said to **Abigail**, "David has sent
25:42 **Abigail** quickly got on a donkey and, attended by her five maids,
27: 3 Ahinoam of Jezreel and **Abigail** of Carmel, the widow of Nabal.
30: 5 Ahinoam of Jezreel and **Abigail**, the widow of Nabal of Carmel.
2Sa 2: 2 Ahinoam of Jezreel and **Abigail**, the widow of Nabal of Carmel.
3: 3 Kileab the son of **Abigail** the widow of Nabal of Carmel;
17:25 an Israelite who had married **Abigail**, the daughter of Nahash
1Ch 2:16 Their sisters were Zeruiah and **Abigail**. Zeruiah's three sons were
2:17 **Abigail** was the mother of Amasa, whose father was Jether the
3: 1 of Jezreel; the second, Daniel the son of **Abigail** of Carmel;

29 אֲבִידָן ***a*bîdān**, n.pr.m. [5] [√ 3 + 1906]

Abidan [5]

Nu 1:11 from Benjamin, **Abidan** son of Gideoni;
2:22 The leader of the people of Benjamin is **Abidan** son of Gideoni.
7:60 On the ninth day **Abidan** son of Gideoni, the leader of the people
7:65 This was the offering of **Abidan** son of Gideoni.
10:24 **Abidan** son of Gideoni was over the division of the tribe of

30 אֲבִידָע ***a*bîdā'**, n.pr.m. [2] [√ 3 + 3359]

Abida [2]

Ge 25: 4 sons of Midian were Ephah, Epher, Hanoch, **Abida** and Eldaah.
1Ch 1:33 The sons of Midian: Ephah, Epher, Hanoch, **Abida** and Eldaah.

31 אֲבִיָּה ***a*biyyâ**, n.pr.m. & f. [23 / 29] [→ 23, 32; cf. 3 + 3378]

Abijah [26], Abijah's [3]

1Sa 8: 2 of his firstborn was Joel and the name of his second was **Abijah**,
1Ki 14: 1 At that time **Abijah** son of Jeroboam became ill,
14:31 And **Abijah** [BHS 41] his son succeeded him as king.
15: 1 Jeroboam son of Nebat, **Abijah** [BHS 41] became king of Judah,
15: 7 As for the other events of **Abijah's** [BHS 41] reign, and all he did,
15: 7 There was war between **Abijah** [BHS 41] and Jeroboam.
15: 8 **Abijah** [BHS 41] rested with his fathers and was buried in the
2Ki 18: 2 His mother's name was **Abijah** [BHS 23] daughter of Zechariah.
1Ch 2:24 **Abijah** the wife of Hezron bore him Ashhur the father of Tekoa.
3:10 was Rehoboam, **Abijah** his son, Asa his son, Jehoshaphat his son,
6:28 [6:13] of Samuel: Joel the firstborn and **Abijah** the second son.
7: 8 Elioenai, Omri, Jeremoth, **Abijah**, Anathoth and Alemeth.
24:10 the seventh to Hakkoz, the eighth to **Abijah**,
2Ch 11:20 of Absalom, who bore him **Abijah**, Attai, Ziza and Shelomith.
11:22 Rehoboam appointed **Abijah** son of Maacah to be the chief prince
12:16 in the City of David. And **Abijah** his son succeeded him as king.
13: 1 year of the reign of Jeroboam, **Abijah** became king of Judah,
13: 2 of Uriel of Gibeah. There was war between **Abijah** and Jeroboam.
13: 3 **Abijah** went into battle with a force of four hundred thousand able
13: 4 **Abijah** stood on Mount Zemaraim, in the hill country of Ephraim,
13:15 God routed Jeroboam and all Israel before **Abijah** and Judah.
13:17 **Abijah** and his men inflicted heavy losses on them, so that there
13:19 **Abijah** pursued Jeroboam and took from him the towns of Bethel,
13:22 The other events of **Abijah's** reign, what he did and what he said,
14: 1 [13:23] **Abijah** rested with his fathers and was buried in the City
29: 1 His mother's name was **Abijah** daughter of Zechariah.
Ne 10: 7 [10:8] Meshullam, **Abijah**, Mijamin,
12: 4 Iddo, Ginnethon, **Abijah**,
12:17 of **Abijah's**, Zicri; of Miniamin's and of Moadiah's, Piltai;

32 אֲבִיָּהוּ ***a*biyyāhû**, n.pr.m. [2] [√ 31; cf. 3 + 3378]

Abijah [2]

2Ch 13:20 Jeroboam did not regain power during the time of **Abijah**.
13:21 **Abijah** grew in strength. He married fourteen wives and had

33 אֲבִיהוּא ***a*bîhû'**, n.pr.m. [12] [√ 3 + 2085]

Abihu [12]

Ex 6:23 and she bore him Nadab and **Abihu**, Eleazar and Ithamar.
24: 1 "Come up to the LORD, you and Aaron, Nadab and **Abihu**,
24: 9 Moses and Aaron, Nadab and **Abihu**, and the seventy elders of
28: 1 along with his sons Nadab and **Abihu**, Eleazar and Ithamar,
Lev 10: 1 Aaron's sons Nadab and **Abihu** took their censers, put fire in them
Nu 3: 2 names of the sons of Aaron were Nadab the firstborn and **Abihu**,
3: 4 Nadab and **Abihu**, however, fell dead before the LORD when
26:60 Aaron was the father of Nadab and **Abihu**, Eleazar and Ithamar.
26:61 **Abihu** died when they made an offering before the LORD with
1Ch 6: 3 [5:29] The sons of Aaron: Nadab, **Abihu**, Eleazar and Ithamar.
24: 1 The sons of Aaron were Nadab, **Abihu**, Eleazar and Ithamar.
24: 2 Nadab and **Abihu** died before their father did, and they had no

34 אֲבִיהוּד ***a*bîhûd**, n.pr.m. [1] [√ 3 + 2086]

Abihud [1]

1Ch 8: 3 The sons of Bela were: Addar, Gera, **Abihud**,

35 אֲבִיהַ֫יִל ***a*bîhayil**, n.pr.m. [2] [√ 3 + 2657]

Abihail [2]

1Ch 2:29 Abishur's wife was named **Abihail**, who bore him Ahban
2Ch 11:18 who was the daughter of David's son Jerimoth and of **Abihail**,

36 אֶבְיוֹן **'ebyôn**, a. [61] [√ 14?]

needy [46], poor [14], needy [+132] [1]

Ex 23: 6 "Do not deny justice to your **poor** *people* in their lawsuits.
23:11 the **poor** *among* your people may get food from it, and the wild
Dt 15: 4 However, there should be no **poor** among you, for in the land the
15: 7 If there is a **poor** *man* among your brothers in any of the towns of
15: 7 do not be hardhearted or tightfisted toward your **poor** brother.
15: 9 so that you do not show ill will toward your **needy** brother
15:11 There will always be **poor** *people* in the land. Therefore I
15:11 toward your brothers and toward the poor and **needy** in your land.
24:14 Do not take advantage of a hired man who is poor and **needy**,
1Sa 2: 8 raises the poor from the dust and lifts the **needy** from the ash heap;
Est 9:22 and giving presents of food to one another and gifts to the **poor**.
Job 5:15 He saves the **needy** from the sword in their mouth; he saves them
24: 4 They thrust the **needy** from the path and force all the poor of the
24:14 is gone, the murderer rises up and kills the poor and **needy**;
29:16 I was a father to the **needy**; I took up the case of the stranger.
30:25 wept for those in trouble? Has not my soul grieved for the **poor**?
31:19 perishing for lack of clothing, or a **needy** *man* without a garment,
Ps 9:18 [9:19] the **needy** will not always be forgotten, nor the hope of the
12: 5 [12:6] the oppression of the weak and the groaning of the **needy**,
35:10 too strong for them, the poor and **needy** from those who rob them."
37:14 the sword and bend the bow to bring down the poor and **needy**,
40:17 [40:18] Yet I am poor and **needy**; may the Lord think of me.
49: 2 [49:3] both low and high, rich and **poor** alike:
69:33 [69:34] The LORD hears the **needy** and does not despise his
70: 5 [70:6] Yet I am poor and **needy**; come quickly to me, O God.
72: 4 the afflicted among the people and save the children of the **needy**;
72:12 For he will deliver the **needy** who cry out, the afflicted who have
72:13 He will take pity on the weak and the **needy** and save the needy
72:13 pity on the weak and the needy and save the **needy** from death.
74:21 retreat in disgrace; may the poor and **needy** praise your name.
82: 4 Rescue the weak and **needy**; deliver them from the hand of the
86: 1 Hear, O LORD, and answer me, for I am poor and **needy**.
107:41 he lifted the **needy** out of their affliction and increased their
109:16 hounded to death the poor and the **needy** and the brokenhearted.
109:22 For I am poor and **needy**, and my heart is wounded within me.
109:31 For he stands at the right hand of the **needy** *one*, to save his life
112: 9 He has scattered abroad his gifts to the **poor**, his righteousness
113: 7 raises the poor from the dust and lifts the **needy** from the ash heap;
132:15 her with abundant provisions; her **poor** will I satisfy with food.
140:12 [140:13] justice for the poor and upholds the cause of the **needy**.
Pr 14:31 for their Maker, but whoever is kind to the **needy** honors God.
30:14 to devour the poor from the earth, the **needy** from among mankind.
31: 9 and judge fairly; defend the rights of the poor and **needy**."
31:20 She opens her arms to the poor and extends her hands to the **needy**.
Isa 14:30 of the poor will find pasture, and the **needy** will lie down in safety.
25: 4 a refuge for the **needy** in his distress, a shelter from the storm
29:19 the **needy** [+132] will rejoice in the Holy One of Israel.
32: 7 destroy the poor with lies, even when the plea of the **needy** is just.
41:17 "The poor and **needy** search for water, but there is none;
Jer 2:34 On your clothes men find the lifeblood of the innocent **poor**,
5:28 of the fatherless to win it, they do not defend the rights of the **poor**.
20:13 He rescues the life of the **needy** from the hands of the wicked.
22:16 He defended the cause of the poor and **needy**, and so all went well.
Eze 16:49 overfed and unconcerned; they did not help the poor and **needy**.
18:12 He oppresses the poor and **needy**. He commits robbery. He does
22:29 they oppress the poor and **needy** and mistreat the alien, denying
Am 2: 6 sell the righteous for silver, and the **needy** for a pair of sandals.
4: 1 oppress the poor and crush the **needy** and say to your husbands,
5:12 and take bribes and you deprive the **poor** of justice in the courts.
8: 4 you who trample the **needy** and do away with the poor of the land,
8: 6 buying the poor with silver and the **needy** for a pair of sandals,

37 אֲבִיּוֹנָה ***a*biyyônâ**, n.f. [1]

desire [1]

Ecc 12: 5 the grasshopper drags himself along and **desire** no longer is stirred.

38 אֲבִיחַ֫יִל ***a*bîḥayil**, n.pr.m. [4] [√ 3 + 2657]

Abihail [4]

Nu 3:35 of the families of the Merarite clans was Zuriel son of **Abihail**;

1Ch 5:14 These were the sons of **Abihail** son of Huri, the son of Jaroah,
Est 2:15 (the girl Mordecai had adopted, the daughter of his uncle **Abihail**)
9:29 So Queen Esther, daughter of **Abihail**, along with Mordecai the

39 אֲבִיטוּב ᵃ*bîṭûb*, n.pr.m. [1] [√ 3 + 3202]

Abitub [1]

1Ch 8:11 By Hushim he had **Abitub** and Elpaal.

40 אֲבִיטַל ᵃ*bîṭal*, n.pr.f. [2] [√ 3 + 3228]

Abital [2]

2Sa 3:4 the son of Haggith; the fifth, Shephatiah the son of **Abital**;
1Ch 3:3 the fifth, Shephatiah the son of **Abital**; and the sixth, Ithream,

41 אֲבִיָּם ᵃ*biyyām*, n.pr.m. [5 / 0] [√ 3 + 3542]

1Ki 14:31 And Abijah [BHS *Abijam*; NIV 31] his son succeeded him as king.
15:1 son of Nebat, Abijah [BHS *Abijam*; NIV 31] became king of Judah,
15:7 As for the other events of Abijah's [BHS *Abijam*; NIV 31] reign,
15:7 war between Abijah [BHS *Abijam*; NIV 31] and Jeroboam.
15:8 Abijah [BHS *Abijam*; NIV 31] rested with his fathers and was

42 אֲבִימָאֵל ᵃ*bîmāʾēl*, n.pr.m. [2] [√ 3 + 446]

Abimael [2]

Ge 10:28 Obal, **Abimael**, Sheba,
1Ch 1:22 Obal, **Abimael**, Sheba,

43 אֲבִימֶלֶךְ ᵃ*bîmelek*, n.pr.m. [67 / 66] [√ 3 + 4889]

Abimelech [60], Abimelech's [2], he[s] [2], him[s] [1], his[s] [1]

Ge 20:2 Then **Abimelech** king of Gerar sent for Sarah and took her.
20:3 But God came to **Abimelech** in a dream one night and said to him,
20:4 Now **Abimelech** had not gone near her, so he said, "Lord,
20:8 Early the next morning **Abimelech** summoned all his officials,
20:9 **Abimelech** called Abraham in and said, "What have you done to
20:10 **Abimelech** asked Abraham, "What was your reason for doing
20:14 **Abimelech** brought sheep and cattle and male and female slaves
20:15 **Abimelech** said, "My land is before you; live wherever you like."
20:17 God healed **Abimelech**, his wife and his slave girls so they could
20:18 for the LORD had closed up every womb in **Abimelech's**
21:22 At that time **Abimelech** and Phicol the commander of his forces
21:25 Abraham complained to **Abimelech** about a well of water that
21:25 about a well of water that **Abimelech's** servants had seized.
21:26 **Abimelech** said, "I don't know who has done this. You did not tell
21:27 Abraham brought sheep and cattle and gave them to **Abimelech**,
21:29 **Abimelech** asked Abraham, "What is the meaning of these seven
21:32 **Abimelech** and Phicol the commander of his forces returned to the
26:1 and Isaac went to **Abimelech** king of the Philistines in Gerar.
26:8 **Abimelech** king of the Philistines looked down from a window
26:9 So **Abimelech** summoned Isaac and said, "She is really your wife!
26:10 Then **Abimelech** said, "What is this you have done to us?
26:11 So **Abimelech** gave orders to all the people: "Anyone who molests
26:16 **Abimelech** said to Isaac, "Move away from us; you have become
26:26 Meanwhile, **Abimelech** had come to him from Gerar,
Jdg 8:31 in Shechem, also bore him a son, whom he named **Abimelech**.
9:1 **Abimelech** son of Jerub-Baal went to his mother's brothers in
9:3 they were inclined to follow **Abimelech**, for they said, "He is our
9:4 **Abimelech** used it to hire reckless adventurers, who became his
9:6 the great tree at the pillar in Shechem to crown **Abimelech** king.
9:16 and in good faith when you made **Abimelech** king,
9:18 made **Abimelech**, the son of his slave girl, king over the citizens of
9:19 may **Abimelech** be your joy, and may you be his, too!
9:20 you have not, let fire come out from **Abimelech** and consume you,
9:20 citizens of Shechem and Beth Millo, and consume **Abimelech**!"
9:21 and he lived there because he was afraid of his brother **Abimelech**.
9:22 After **Abimelech** had governed Israel three years,
9:23 God sent an evil spirit between **Abimelech** and the citizens of
9:23 citizens of Shechem, who acted treacherously against **Abimelech**.
9:24 might be avenged on their brother **Abimelech** and on the citizens
9:25 rob everyone who passed by, and this was reported to **Abimelech**.
9:27 While they were eating and drinking, they cursed **Abimelech**.
9:28 Gaal son of Ebed said, "Who is **Abimelech**, and who is Shechem,
9:29 I would get rid of **him**[s]. I would say to Abimelech, 'Call out your
9:29 of him. I would say to **Abimelech**, 'Call out your whole army!' "
9:31 Under cover he sent messengers to **Abimelech**, saying, "Gaal son
9:34 So **Abimelech** and all his troops set out by night and took up
9:35 and was standing at the entrance to the city gate just as **Abimelech**
9:38 who said, 'Who is **Abimelech** that we should be subject to him?'
9:39 So Gaal led out the citizens of Shechem and fought **Abimelech**.
9:40 **Abimelech** chased him, and many fell wounded in the flight—
9:41 **Abimelech** stayed in Arumah, and Zebul drove Gaal and his
9:42 went out to the fields, and this was reported to **Abimelech**.
9:44 **Abimelech** and the companies with him rushed forward to a
9:45 All that day **Abimelech** pressed his attack against the city until he
9:47 When **Abimelech** heard that they had assembled there,
9:48 **he**[s] and all his men went up Mount Zalmon. He took an ax
9:48 **He**[s] took an ax and cut off some branches, which he lifted to his
9:49 So all the men cut branches and followed **Abimelech**. They piled
9:50 Next **Abimelech** went to Thebez and besieged it and captured it.
9:52 **Abimelech** went to the tower and stormed it. But as he approached
9:53 a woman dropped an upper millstone on **his**[s] head and cracked his
9:55 When the Israelites saw that **Abimelech** was dead, they went
9:56 Thus God repaid the wickedness that **Abimelech** had done to his
10:1 After the time of **Abimelech** a man of Issachar, Tola son of Puah,
2Sa 11:21 Who killed **Abimelech** son of Jerub-Besheth? Didn't a woman
1Ch 18:16 Zadok son of Ahitub and Ahimelech [BHS *Abimelech*; NIV 316]
Ps 34:T [34:1] When he pretended to be insane before **Abimelech**, who

44 אֲבִינָדָב ᵃ*bînādāb*, n.pr.m. [12 / 11] [√ 3 + 5605]

Abinadab [9], Abinadab's [2]

1Sa 7:1 They took it to **Abinadab's** house on the hill and consecrated
16:8 Then Jesse called **Abinadab** and had him pass in front of Samuel.
17:13 was Eliab; the second, **Abinadab**; and the third, Shammah.
31:2 and they killed his sons Jonathan, **Abinadab** and Malki-Shua.
2Sa 6:3 of God on a new cart and brought it from the house of **Abinadab**,
6:3 Uzzah and Ahio, sons of **Abinadab**, were guiding the new cart
6:4 [BHS+ ***Abinadab***] with the ark of God on it, and Ahio was walking
1Ch 2:13 his firstborn; the second son was **Abinadab**, the third Shimea,
8:33 Saul the father of Jonathan, Malki-Shua, **Abinadab** and Esh-Baal.
9:39 Saul the father of Jonathan, Malki-Shua, **Abinadab** and Esh-Baal.
10:2 and they killed his sons Jonathan, **Abinadab** and Malki-Shua.
13:7 They moved the ark of God from **Abinadab's** house on a new cart,

45 אֲבִינֹעַם ᵃ*bînōʿam*, n.pr.m. [4] [√ 3 + 5840]

Abinoam [4]

Jdg 4:6 She sent for Barak son of **Abinoam** from Kedesh in Naphtali
4:12 When they told Sisera that Barak son of **Abinoam** had gone up to
5:1 On that day Deborah and Barak son of **Abinoam** sang this song:
5:12 O Barak! Take captive your captives, O son of **Abinoam**.'

46 אֲבִינֵר ᵃ*bînēr*, n.pr.m. [1] [√ 3 + 5944; cf. 79]

Abner [1]

1Sa 14:50 The name of the commander of Saul's army was **Abner** son of

47 אֶבְיָסָף *ʾebyāsāp*, n.pr.m. [3] [→ 25; cf. 3 + 3758]

Ebiasaph [3]

1Ch 6:23 [6:8] Elkanah his son, **Ebiasaph** his son, Assir his son,
6:37 [6:22] the son of Assir, the son of **Ebiasaph**, the son of Korah,
9:19 Shallum son of Kore, the son of **Ebiasaph**, the son of Korah,

48 אֲבִיעֶזֶר ᵃ*bîʿezer*, n.pr.m. [7] [→ 49; cf. 3 + 6469]

Abiezer [6], Abiezrites [1]

Jos 17:2 the clans of **Abiezer**, Helek, Asriel, Shechem, Hepher and
Jdg 6:34 and he blew a trumpet, summoning the **Abiezrites** to follow him.
8:2 of Ephraim's grapes better than the full grape harvest of **Abiezer**?
2Sa 23:27 **Abiezer** from Anathoth, Mebunnai the Hushathite,
1Ch 7:18 His sister Hammoleketh gave birth to Ishhod, **Abiezer** and Mahlah.
11:28 Ira son of Ikkesh from Tekoa, **Abiezer** from Anathoth,
27:12 for the ninth month, was **Abiezer** the Anathothite, a Benjamite.

49 אֲבִי עֶזְרִי ᵃ*bî ʿezrî*, a.g. [3] [√ 48]

Abiezrites [2], Abiezrite [1]

Jdg 6:11 under the oak in Ophrah that belonged to Joash the **Abiezrite**,
6:24 LORD is Peace. To this day it stands in Ophrah of the **Abiezrites**.
8:32 buried in the tomb of his father Joash in Ophrah of the **Abiezrites**.

50 אֲבִי־עַלְבוֹן ᵃ*bî-ʿalbôn*, n.pr.m. [1] [√ 3 + 6588]

Abi-Albon [1]

2Sa 23:31 **Abi-Albon** the Arbathite, Azmaveth the Barhumite,

51 אֲבִיר *ʾābîr*, a. [6] [→ 52, 87, 88, 89]

Mighty One [6]

Ge 49:24 because of the hand of the **Mighty One** *of* Jacob, because of the
Ps 132:2 oath to the LORD and made a vow to the **Mighty One** *of* Jacob:
132:5 a place for the LORD, a dwelling for the **Mighty One** *of* Jacob."
Isa 1:24 the LORD Almighty, the **Mighty One** *of* Israel, declares:
49:26 am your Savior, your Redeemer, the **Mighty One** *of* Jacob."
60:16 am your Savior, your Redeemer, the **Mighty One** *of* Jacob.

52 אביר **אַבִּיר** **'abbîr**, a. [17] [√ 51]

mighty [4], bulls [2], stallions [2], warriors [2], angels [1], great [1], head [1], steeds [1], strong [1], stubborn-hearted [+4213] [1], valiant men [+4213] [1]

Jdg 5:22 the horses' hoofs—galloping, galloping go his **mighty** steeds.
1Sa 21:7 [21:8] he was Doeg the Edomite, Saul's **head** shepherd.
Job 24:22 God drags away the **mighty** by his power; though they become
34:20 and they pass away; the **mighty** are removed without human hand.
Ps 22:12 [22:13] bulls surround me; **strong** bulls *of* Bashan encircle me.
50:13 Do I eat the flesh of **bulls** or drink the blood of goats?
68:30 [68:31] the herd of **bulls** among the calves of the nations.
76:5 [76:6] **Valiant** [+4213] **men** lie plundered, they sleep their last
78:25 Men ate the bread of **angels**; he sent them all the food they could
Isa 10:13 plundered their treasures; like a **mighty** *one* I subdued their kings.
34:7 wild oxen will fall with them, the bull calves and the **great** bulls.
46:12 Listen to me, you **stubborn-hearted** [+4213], you who are far
Jer 8:16 at the neighing of their **stallions** the whole land trembles.
46:15 Why will your **warriors** be laid low? They cannot stand,
47:3 at the sound of the hoofs of galloping **steeds**, at the noise of enemy
50:11 you frolic like a heifer threshing grain and neigh like **stallions**,
La 1:15 "The Lord has rejected all the **warriors** in my midst; he has

53 אבירם **אֲבִירָם** **'abîrām**, n.pr.m. [11] [√ 3 + 8123; cf. 92]

Abiram [11]

Nu 16:1 Dathan and **Abiram**, sons of Eliab, and On son of Peleth—
16:12 Then Moses summoned Dathan and **Abiram**, the sons of Eliab.
16:24 'Move away from the tents of Korah, Dathan and **Abiram**.' "
16:25 Moses got up and went to Dathan and **Abiram**, and the elders of
16:27 So they moved away from the tents of Korah, Dathan and **Abiram**.
16:27 Dathan and **Abiram** had come out and were standing with their
26:9 the sons of Eliab were Nemuel, Dathan and **Abiram**. The same
26:9 **Abiram** were the community officials who rebelled against Moses
Dt 11:6 what he did to Dathan and **Abiram**, sons of Eliab the Reubenite,
1Ki 16:34 He laid its foundations at the cost of his firstborn son **Abiram**,
Ps 106:17 and swallowed Dathan; it buried the company of **Abiram**.

54 אבישג **אֲבִישַׁג** **'abîšag**, n.pr.f. [5] [√ 3 + 8704]

Abishag [5]

1Ki 1:3 searched throughout Israel for a beautiful girl and found **Abishag**,
1:15 in his room, where **Abishag** the Shunammite was attending him.
2:17 not refuse you—to give me **Abishag** the Shunammite as my wife."
2:21 "Let **Abishag** the Shunammite be given in marriage to your
2:22 "Why do you request **Abishag** the Shunammite for Adonijah?

55 אבישוע **אֲבִישׁוּעַ** **'abîšûa'**, n.pr.m. [5] [√ 3 + 8781]

Abishua [5]

1Ch 6:4 [5:30] was the father of Phinehas, Phinehas the father of **Abishua**,
6:5 [5:31] **Abishua** the father of Bukki, Bukki the father of Uzzi,
6:50 [6:35] Eleazar his son, Phinehas his son, **Abishua** his son,
8:4 **Abishua**, Naaman, Ahoah,
Ezr 7:5 the son of **Abishua**, the son of Phinehas, the son of Eleazar,

56 אבישור **אֲבִישׁוּר** **'abîšûr**, n.pr.m. [2] [√ 3 + 8802]

Abishur [1], Abishur's [1]

1Ch 2:28 Shammai and Jada. The sons of Shammai: Nadab and **Abishur**.
2:29 **Abishur's** wife was named Abihail, who bore him Ahban

57 אבישי **אֲבִישַׁי** **'abîšay**, n.pr.m. [19] [cf. 93]

Abishai [19]

1Sa 26:6 then asked Ahimelech the Hittite and **Abishai** son of Zeruiah,
26:6 into the camp with me to Saul?" "I'll go with you," said **Abishai**.
26:7 So David and **Abishai** went to the army by night, and there was
26:8 **Abishai** said to David, "Today God has delivered your enemy into
26:9 David said to **Abishai**, "Don't destroy him! Who can lay a hand on
2Sa 2:18 The three sons of Zeruiah were there: Joab, **Abishai** and Asahel.
2:24 But Joab and **Abishai** pursued Abner, and as the sun was setting,
3:30 (Joab and his brother **Abishai** murdered Abner because he had
10:14 were fleeing, they fled before **Abishai** and went inside the city.
16:9 **Abishai** son of Zeruiah said to the king, "Why should this dead
16:11 David then said to **Abishai** and all his officials, "My son, who is of
18:2 a third under Joab's brother **Abishai** son of Zeruiah, and a third
18:5 The king commanded Joab, **Abishai** and Ittai, "Be gentle with the
18:12 In our hearing the king commanded you and **Abishai** and Ittai,
19:21 [19:22] **Abishai** son of Zeruiah said, "Shouldn't Shimei be put to
20:6 David said to **Abishai**, "Now Sheba son of Bicri will do us more
20:10 Then Joab and his brother **Abishai** pursued Sheba son of Bicri.
21:17 **Abishai** son of Zeruiah came to David's rescue; he struck the
23:18 **Abishai** the brother of Joab son of Zeruiah was chief of the Three.

58 אבישלום **אֲבִישָׁלוֹם** **'abîšālôm**, n.pr.m. [2] [√ 3 + 8934]

Abishalom [2]

1Ki 15:2 His mother's name was Maacah daughter of **Abishalom**.
15:10 His grandmother's name was Maacah daughter of **Abishalom**.

59 אביתר **אֶבְיָתָר** **'ebyātār**, n.pr.m. [30] [√ 3 + 3855]

Abiathar [28], he[s] [1], them [+2256+7401] [1]

1Sa 22:20 But **Abiathar**, a son of Ahimelech son of Ahitub, escaped
22:21 **He**[s] told David that Saul had killed the priests of the LORD.
22:22 David said to **Abiathar**: "That day, when Doeg the Edomite was
23:6 (Now **Abiathar** son of Ahimelech had brought the ephod down
23:9 against him, he said to **Abiathar** the priest, "Bring the ephod."
30:7 Then David said to **Abiathar** the priest, the son of Ahimelech,
30:7 of Ahimelech, "Bring me the ephod." **Abiathar** brought it to him,
2Sa 8:17 Zadok son of Ahitub and Ahimelech son of **Abiathar** were priests;
15:24 **Abiathar** offered sacrifices until all the people had finished
15:27 in peace, with your son Ahimaaz and Jonathan son of **Abiathar**.
15:29 So Zadok and **Abiathar** took the ark of God back to Jerusalem
15:35 Won't the priests Zadok and **Abiathar** be there with you?
15:35 Tell **them**[s] [+2256+7401] anything you hear in the king's palace.
15:36 two sons, Ahimaaz son of Zadok and Jonathan son of **Abiathar**,
17:15 Hushai told Zadok and **Abiathar**, the priests, "Ahithophel has
19:11 [19:12] King David sent this message to Zadok and **Abiathar**,
20:25 Sheva was secretary; Zadok and **Abiathar** were priests;
1Ki 1:7 conferred with Joab son of Zeruiah and with **Abiathar** the priest,
1:19 **Abiathar** the priest and Joab the commander of the army,
1:25 king's sons, the commanders of the army and **Abiathar** the priest.
1:42 as he was speaking, Jonathan son of **Abiathar** the priest arrived.
2:22 for him and for **Abiathar** the priest and Joab son of Zeruiah!"
2:26 To **Abiathar** the priest the king said, "Go back to your fields in
2:27 So Solomon removed **Abiathar** from the priesthood of the
2:35 in Joab's position and replaced **Abiathar** with Zadok the priest.
4:4 of Jehoiada—commander in chief; Zadok and **Abiathar**—priests;
1Ch 15:11 Then David summoned Zadok and **Abiathar** the priests, and Uriel,
18:16 Zadok son of Ahitub and Ahimelech son of **Abiathar** were priests;
24:6 Ahimelech son of **Abiathar** and the heads of families of the priests
27:34 was succeeded by Jehoiada son of Benaiah and by **Abiathar**.

60 אבך **אָבַךְ** **'ābak**, v. [1] [cf. 2200]

rolls upward [1]

Isa 9:18 [9:17] [F] so that *it* **rolls upward** *in* a column of smoke.

61 אבל **אָבַל** **'ābal[1]**, v. [32] [→ 63, 65]

mourn [11], mourned [9], mourns [4], mourning [2], grieve [1], grieving [1], in mourning [1], lament [1], made lament [1], pretend in mourning [1]

Ge 37:34 [F] put on sackcloth and **mourned** for his son many days.
Ex 33:4 [F] *they began to* **mourn** and no one put on any ornaments.
Nu 14:39 [F] reported this to all the Israelites, they **mourned** bitterly.
1Sa 6:19 [F] The people **mourned** because of the heavy blow the LORD
15:35 [F] not go to see Saul again, though Samuel **mourned** for him.
16:1 [F] LORD said to Samuel, "How long *will* you **mourn** for Saul,
2Sa 13:37 [F] of Geshur. But King David **mourned** for his son every day.
14:2 [F] He said to her, "**Pretend** *you are* **in mourning**. Dress in
14:2 [F] Act like a woman *who has spent* many days **grieving** for the
19:1 [19:2] [F] "The king is weeping and **mourning** for Absalom."
1Ch 7:22 [F] Their father Ephraim **mourned** for them many days, and his
2Ch 35:24 [F] of his fathers, and all Judah and Jerusalem **mourned** for him.
Ezr 10:6 [F] because *he continued to* **mourn** over the unfaithfulness of
Ne 1:4 [F] For some days *I* **mourned** and fasted and prayed before the
8:9 [F] is sacred to the LORD your God. *Do* not **mourn** or weep."
Job 14:22 [A] but the pain of his own body and **mourns** only for himself."
Isa 3:26 [A] The gates of Zion will lament and **mourn**; destitute, she will
19:8 [A] The fishermen will groan and **lament**, all who cast hooks
33:9 [A] The land **mourns** and wastes away, Lebanon is ashamed
66:10 [F] rejoice greatly with her, all you who **mourn** over her.
Jer 4:28 [A] Therefore the earth *will* **mourn** and the heavens above grow
14:2 [A] "Judah **mourns**, her cities languish; they wail for the land,
La 2:8 [G] *He* **made** ramparts and walls **lament**; together they wasted
Eze 7:12 [F] Let not the buyer rejoice nor the seller **grieve**, for wrath is
7:27 [F] The king *will* **mourn**, the prince will be clothed with despair,
31:15 [G] to the grave I covered the deep springs *with* **mourning** for it;
Da 10:2 [F] At that time I, Daniel, **mourned** for three weeks.
Hos 4:3 [A] Because of this the land **mourns**, and all who live in it waste
10:5 [A] Its people *will* **mourn** over it, and so will its idolatrous
Joel 1:9 [A] The priests *are* **in mourning**, those who minister before the
Am 8:8 [A] not the land tremble for this, and all who live in it **mourn**?
9:5 [A] touches the earth and it melts, and all who live in it **mourn**—

[F] Hitpael (hitpoel, hitpoal, hitpolel, hitpolal, hitpalel, hitpalal, hitpalpel, hitpalpal, hotpael, hotpaal) [G] Hiphil (hiphtil) [H] Hophal [I] Hishtaphel

62 ²אָבַל 'ābal², v. [7]
parched [3], dries up [2], dried up [1], dry up [1]

Isa 24: 4 [A] The earth **dries up** and withers, the world languishes and
24: 7 [A] The new wine **dries up** and the vine withers; all the
Jer 12: 4 [A] How long *will* the land *lie* **parched** and the grass in every
12: 11 [A] will be made a wasteland, **parched** and desolate before me;
23: 10 [A] because of the curse the land *lies* **parched** and the pastures in
Joel 1: 10 [A] The fields are ruined, the ground *is* **dried up**; the grain is
Am 1: 2 [A] the pastures of the shepherds **dry up**, and the top of Carmel

63 ¹אָבֵל 'ābēl¹, a. [8] [√ 61]
mourn [2], mourners [2], grief [1], grieve [1], mourning [1], weeping [1]

Ge 37: 35 he said, "*in* **mourning** will I go down to the grave to my son."
Est 6: 12 But Haman rushed home, with his head covered in **grief**,
Job 29: 25 a king among his troops; I was like one who comforts **mourners**.
Ps 35: 14 I bowed my head in grief as though **weeping** *for* my mother.
Isa 57: 19 [57:18] creating praise on the lips of the **mourners** *in* Israel.
61: 2 and the day of vengeance of our God, to comfort all *who* **mourn**,
61: 3 provide for *those who* **grieve** *in* Zion—to bestow on them a crown
La 1: 4 The roads to Zion **mourn**, for no one comes to her appointed

64 ²אָבֵל 'ābēl², n.pr.loc. [2 / 1] [→ 67-73; cf. 3297]
Abel [1]

1Sa 6: 18 The large rock, [BHS ***Greater Abel***; NIV 74] on which they set the
2Sa 20: 18 ago they used to say, 'Get your answer at **Abel**,' and that settled it.

65 אֵבֶל 'ēbel, n.m. [24] [√ 61]
mourning [15], mourn [2], ceremony of mourning [1], moan [1], mourn [+4200+6913] [1], period of mourning [1], sorrow [1], time of mourning [1], weep [1]

Ge 27: 41 He said to himself, "The days of **mourning** *for* my father are near;
50: 10 there Joseph observed a seven-day **period of mourning** for his
50: 11 When the Canaanites who lived there saw the **mourning** at the
50: 11 "The Egyptians are holding a solemn **ceremony of mourning**."
Dt 34: 8 thirty days, until the time of weeping and **mourning** was over.
2Sa 11: 27 After the **time of mourning** was over, David had her brought to
14: 2 Dress in **mourning** clothes, and don't use any cosmetic lotions.
19: 2 [19:3] whole army the victory that day was turned into **mourning**,
Est 4: 3 there was great **mourning** among the Jews, with fasting, weeping
9: 22 was turned into joy and their **mourning** into a day of celebration.
Job 30: 31 My harp is tuned to **mourning**, and my flute to the sound of
Ecc 7: 2 It is better to go to a house of **mourning** than to go to a house of
7: 4 The heart of the wise is in the house of **mourning**, but the heart of
Isa 60: 20 will be your everlasting light, and your days of **sorrow** will end.
61: 3 the oil of gladness instead of **mourning**, and a garment of praise
Jer 6: 26 roll in ashes; **mourn** [+4200+6913] with bitter wailing *as for* an
16: 7 No one will offer food to comfort those who **mourn** for the dead—
31: 13 I will turn their **mourning** into gladness; I will give them comfort
La 5: 15 Joy is gone from our hearts; our dancing has turned to **mourning**.
Eze 24: 17 Groan quietly; do not **mourn** for the dead. Keep your turban
Am 5: 16 The farmers will be summoned to **weep** and the mourners to wail.
8: 10 I will turn your religious feasts into **mourning** and all your singing
8: 10 I will make that time like **mourning** *for* an only son and the end of
Mic 1: 8 and naked. I will howl like a jackal and **moan** like an owl.

66 אֲבָל 'ᵃbāl, adv. [11] [√ 1153 + 1]
but [3], however [2], indeed [1], not at all [1], now [1], surely [1], well [1], yes but [1]

Ge 17: 19 Then God said, "**Yes, but** your wife Sarah will bear you a son,
42: 21 "**Surely** we are being punished because of our brother.
2Sa 14: 5 She said, "I am **indeed** a widow; my husband is dead.
1Ki 1: 43 "**Not at all!**" Jonathan answered. "Our lord King David has made
2Ki 4: 14 Gehazi said, "**Well**, she has no son and her husband is old."
2Ch 1: 4 **Now** David had brought up the ark of God from Kiriath Jearim to
19: 3 There is, **however**, some good in you, for you have rid the land of
33: 17 The people, **however**, continued to sacrifice at the high places,
Ezr 10: 13 **But** there are many people here and it is the rainy season;
Da 10: 7 **but** such terror overwhelmed them that they fled and hid
10: 21 **but** first I will tell you what is written in the Book of Truth.

67 אֻבָל 'ubāl, n.[m.]. [3] [√ 64]
canal [3]

Da 8: 2 in the province of Elam; in the vision I was beside the Ulai **Canal**.
8: 3 two horns, standing beside the **canal**, and the horns were long.
8: 6 toward the two-horned ram I had seen standing beside the **canal**

68 אָבֵל בֵּית מַעֲכָה 'ābēl bêt maᵃkâ, n.pr.loc. [4] [√ 64 + 1074 + 5081]
Abel Beth Maacah [4]

2Sa 20: 14 Sheba passed through all the tribes of Israel to **Abel Beth Maacah**
20: 15 troops with Joab came and besieged Sheba in **Abel Beth Maacah**.
1Ki 15: 20 **Abel Beth Maacah** and all Kinnereth in addition to Naphtali.
2Ki 15: 29 and took Ijon, **Abel Beth Maacah**, Janoah, Kedesh and Hazor.

69 אָבֵל הַשִּׁטִּים 'ābēl haššiṭṭîm, n.pr.loc. [1] [√ 64 + 2243]
Abel Shittim [1]

Nu 33: 49 camped along the Jordan from Beth Jeshimoth to **Abel Shittim**.

70 אָבֵל כְּרָמִים 'ābēl kᵉrāmîm, n.pr.loc. [1] [√ 64 + 4148]
Abel Keramim [1]

Jdg 11: 33 from Aroer to the vicinity of Minnith, as far as **Abel Keramim**.

71 אָבֵל מְחוֹלָה 'ābēl mᵉḥôlâ, n.pr.loc. [3] [√ 64 + 4703; cf. 4716?]
Abel Meholah [3]

Jdg 7: 22 Zererah as far as the border of **Abel Meholah** near Tabbath.
1Ki 4: 12 from Beth Shan to **Abel Meholah** across to Jokmeam;
19: 16 anoint Elisha son of Shaphat from **Abel Meholah** to succeed you

72 אָבֵל מַיִם 'ābēl mayim, n.pr.loc. [1] [√ 64 + 4784]
Abel Maim [1]

2Ch 16: 4 Dan, **Abel Maim** and all the store cities of Naphtali.

73 אָבֵל מִצְרַיִם 'ābēl miṣrayim, n.pr.loc. [1] [√ 64 + 5213]
Abel Mizraim [1]

Ge 50: 11 That is why that place near the Jordan is called **Abel Mizraim**.

74 אֶבֶן 'eben, n.f. [273 / 274] [→ 75, 78?; Ar 10006]
stone [93], stones [86], rock [8], rocks [7], weights [5], *untranslated* [4], differing weights [+74+2256] [4], gems [4], hailstones [+453] [3], precious stones [3], slingstones [+7845] [3], stone [+906+928 +2021+8083] [3], blocks [2], onyx [+8732] [2], ore [2], sapphire [+6209] [2], some[s] [2], stone [+928+2021+6232] [2], stone [+928+2021+8083] [2], stoned [+906+8083] [2], stoned [+928+8083] [2], two differing weights [+74+2256] [2], another[s] [1], capstone [+8036] [1], charm [+2834] [1], chrysolite [+9577] [1], cornerstone [+7157] [1], cover [1], fieldstones [+8969] [1], gem [1], hail [+1352] [1], hailstones [+1352] [1], hailstones [1], jewels [1], marble [+8880] [1], masons [+3093] [1], plumb line [+974] [1], plumb line [1], sling stones [+928+2021] [1], sparkling jewels [+734] [1], standard [1], stone [+6584+8083] [1], stonecutters [+2935] [1], stoned [+906+928+2021+6232] [1], stoned [+906+928+2021+8083] [1], stoned [+928+2021+6232] [1], stoned to death [+8083] [1], stonemasons [+3093+7815] [1], stoning [+906+928+2021+8083] [1], them [+928+2021+4392] [1], them[s] [+2021+9109] [1], them[s] [1], these[s] [+2021] [1]

Ge 2: 12 that land is good; aromatic resin and **onyx** [+8732] are also there.)
11: 3 They used brick instead of **stone**, and tar for mortar.
28: 11 Taking one of the **stones** there, he put it under his head and lay
28: 18 Early the next morning Jacob took the **stone** he had placed under
28: 22 and this **stone** that I have set up as a pillar will be God's house,
29: 2 from that well. The **stone** over the mouth of the well was large.
29: 3 the shepherds would roll the **stone** away from the well's mouth
29: 3 they would return the **stone** to its place over the mouth of the well.
29: 8 and the **stone** has been rolled away from the mouth of the well.
29: 10 he went over and rolled the **stone** away from the mouth of the well
31: 45 So Jacob took a **stone** and set it up as a pillar.
31: 46 He said to his relatives, "Gather *some* **stones**." So they took stones
31: 46 So they took **stones** and piled them in a heap, and they ate there by
35: 14 Jacob set up a **stone** pillar at the place where God had talked with
49: 24 Mighty One of Jacob, because of the Shepherd, the **Rock** *of* Israel,
Ex 7: 19 everywhere in Egypt, even in the wooden buckets and **stone** *jars*."
15: 5 waters have covered them; they sank to the depths like a **stone**.
15: 16 By the power of your arm they will be as still as a **stone**—
17: 12 grew tired, they took a **stone** and put it under him and he sat on it.
20: 25 If you make an altar of **stones** for me, do not build it with dressed
21: 18 "If men quarrel and one hits the other with a **stone** or with his fist
24: 12 I will give you the tablets of **stone**, with the law and commands I
25: 7 and onyx **stones** and other gems to be mounted on the ephod
25: 7 and *other* **gems** to be mounted on the ephod and breastpiece.
28: 9 "Take two onyx **stones** and engrave on them the names of the sons
28: 10 six names on one **stone** and the remaining six on the other.
28: 10 names on one stone and the remaining six on the other. **[RPH]**
28: 11 Engrave the names of the sons of Israel on the two **stones** the way

Ex 28:11 of Israel on the two stones the way a **gem** cutter engraves a seal.
28:12 fasten **them**[s] [+2021+9109] on the shoulder pieces of the ephod as
28:12 pieces of the ephod as memorial **stones** for the sons of Israel.
28:17 mount four rows of **precious stones** on it. In the first row there
28:17 In the first row **[RPH]** there shall be a ruby, a topaz and a beryl;
28:21 There are to be twelve **stones**, one for each of the names of the
31: 5 to cut and set **stones**, to work in wood, and to engage in all kinds
31:18 the Testimony, the tablets of **stone** inscribed by the finger of God.
34: 1 said to Moses, "Chisel out two **stone** tablets like the first ones,
34: 4 So Moses chiseled out two **stone** tablets like the first ones
34: 4 commanded him; and he carried the two **stone** tablets in his hands.
35: 9 and onyx **stones** and other gems to be mounted on the ephod
35: 9 and other **gems** to be mounted on the ephod and breastpiece.
35:27 The leaders brought onyx **stones** and other gems to be mounted on
35:27 and other **gems** to be mounted on the ephod and breastpiece.
35:33 to cut and set **stones**, to work in wood and to engage in all kinds of
39: 6 They mounted the onyx **stones** in gold filigree settings
39: 7 pieces of the ephod as memorial **stones** for the sons of Israel,
39:10 they mounted four rows of **precious stones** on it. In the first row
39:14 There were twelve **stones**, one for each of the names of the sons of
Lev 14:40 he is to order that the contaminated **stones** be torn out and thrown
14:42 they are to take other **stones** to replace these and take new clay
14:42 Then they are to take other stones to replace **these**[s] [+2021]
14:43 "If the mildew reappears in the house after the **stones** have been
14:45 It must be torn down—its **stones**, timbers and all the plaster—
19:36 Use honest scales and honest **weights**, an honest ephah and an
20: 2 The people of the community *are to* **stone** [+928+2021+8083] him.
20:27 *You are to* **stone** [+906+928+2021+8083] them; their blood will be
24:23 the blasphemer outside the camp and **stoned** [+906+8083] him.
26: 1 do not place a carved **stone** in your land to bow down before it.
Nu 14:10 assembly talked about **stoning** [+906+928+2021+8083] them.
15:35 The whole assembly *must* **stone** [+906+928+2021+8083] him
15:36 and **stoned** [+906+928+2021+8083] him to death, as the LORD
35:17 Or if anyone has a **stone** *in* his hand that could kill, and he strikes
35:23 seeing him, drops a **stone** on him that could kill him, and he dies,
Dt 4:13 you to follow and then wrote them on two **stone** tablets.
4:28 There you will worship man-made gods of wood and **stone**,
5:22 Then he wrote them on two **stone** tablets and gave them to me.
8: 9 a land where the **rocks** are iron and you can dig copper out of the
9: 9 When I went up on the mountain to receive the tablets of **stone**,
9:10 The LORD gave me two **stone** tablets inscribed by the finger of
9:11 and forty nights, the LORD gave me the two **stone** tablets,
10: 1 "Chisel out two **stone** tablets like the first ones and come up to me
10: 3 acacia wood and chiseled out two **stone** tablets like the first ones,
13:10 [13:11] Stone **[NIE]** him to death, because he tried to turn you
17: 5 to your city gate and **stone** [+928+2021+6232] that person to death.
21:21 the men of his town *shall* **stone** [+928+2021+8083] him to death.
22:21 the men of her town *shall* **stone** [+928+2021+6232] her to death.
22:24 to the gate of that town and stone **them** [+928+2021+4392] to death
25:13 Do not have **two differing weights** [+74+2256] in your bag—
25:13 Do not have **two differing weights** [+74+2256] in your bag—
25:15 You must have accurate and honest **weights** and measures,
27: 2 is giving you, set up *some* large **stones** and coat them with plaster.
27: 4 set up these **stones** on Mount Ebal, as I command you today,
27: 5 Build there an altar to the LORD your God, an altar of **stones**.
27: 6 Build the altar of the LORD your God with **fieldstones** [+8969]
27: 8 clearly all the words of this law on these **stones** you have set up."
28:36 There you will worship other gods, gods of wood and **stone**.
28:64 gods of wood and **stone**, which neither you nor your fathers have
29:17 [29:16] them their detestable images and idols of wood and **stone**,
Jos 4: 3 tell them to take up twelve **stones** from the middle of the Jordan
4: 5 Each of you is to take up a **stone** on his shoulder, according to the
4: 6 when your children ask you, 'What do these **stones** mean?'
4: 7 These **stones** are to be a memorial to the people of Israel forever."
4: 8 They took twelve **stones** from the middle of the Jordan,
4: 9 Joshua set up the twelve **stones** that had been in the middle of the
4:20 Joshua set up at Gilgal the twelve **stones** they had taken out of the
4:21 your descendants ask their fathers, 'What do these **stones** mean?'
7:25 all Israel **stoned** [+906+8083] him, and after they had stoned the
7:25 and after *they had* **stoned** [+906+928+2021+6232] the rest,
7:26 Over Achan they heaped up a large pile of **rocks**, which remains to
8:29 they raised a large pile of **rocks** over it, which remains to this day.
8:31 an altar of uncut **stones**, on which no iron tool had been used.
8:32 Joshua copied on **stones** the law of Moses, which he had written.
10:11 the LORD hurled large **hailstones** down on them from the sky,
10:11 more of them died from the **hailstones** [+1352] than were killed by
10:18 he said, "Roll large **rocks** up to the mouth of the cave, and post
10:27 At the mouth of the cave they placed large **rocks**, which are there
15: 6 continued north of Beth Arabah to the **Stone** *of* Bohan son of
18:17 of Adummim, and ran down to the **Stone** *of* Bohan son of Reuben.
24:26 he took a large **stone** and set it up there under the oak near the holy
24:27 he said to all the people. "This **stone** will be a witness against us.
Jdg 9: 5 home in Ophrah and on one **stone** murdered his seventy brothers,
9:18 murdered his seventy sons on a single **stone**, and made Abimelech,
20:16 each of whom could sling a **stone** at a hair and not miss.
1Sa 6:14 Joshua of Beth Shemesh, and there it stopped beside a large **rock**.
6:15 containing the gold objects, and placed them on the large **rock**.
6:18 The large **rock**, [BHS 64] on which they set the ark of the
7:12 Then Samuel took a **stone** and set it up between Mizpah and Shen.
14:33 have broken faith," he said. "Roll a large **stone** over here at once."
17:40 his staff in his hand, chose five smooth **stones** from the stream,
17:49 Reaching into his bag and taking out a **stone**, he slung it and struck
17:49 The **stone** sank into his forehead, and he fell facedown on the
17:50 So David triumphed over the Philistine with a sling and a **stone**;
20:19 where you hid when this trouble began, and wait by the **stone** Ezel.
25:37 these things, and his heart failed him and he became like a **stone**.
2Sa 5:11 and **stonemasons** [+3093+7815], and they built a palace for David.
12:30 weight was a talent of gold, and it was set with precious **stones**—
14:26 and its weight was two hundred shekels by the royal **standard**.
16: 6 He pelted David and all the king's officials with **stones**, though all
16:13 cursing as he went and throwing **stones** at him and showering him
18:17 a big pit in the forest and piled up a large heap of **rocks** over him.
20: 8 While they were at the great **rock** in Gibeon, Amasa came to meet
1Ki 1: 9 and fattened calves at the **Stone** *of* Zoheleth near En Rogel.
5:17 [5:31] **blocks** of quality stone to provide a foundation of dressed
5:17 [5:31] **stone** to provide a foundation of dressed stone for the
5:17 [5:31] to provide a foundation of dressed **stone** for the temple.
5:18 [5:32] the timber and **stone** for the building of the temple.
6: 7 only **blocks** dressed at the quarry were used, and no hammer,
6:18 and open flowers. Everything was cedar; no **stone** was to be seen.
7: 9 were made of *blocks of* high-grade **stone** cut to size and trimmed
7:10 The foundations were laid with large **stones** of good quality,
7:10 good quality, **[RPH]** some measuring ten cubits and some eight.
7:10 stones of good quality, **some**[s] measuring ten cubits and some eight.
7:10 stones of good quality, some measuring ten cubits and **some**[s] eight.
7:11 Above were high-grade **stones**, cut to size, and cedar beams.
8: 9 There was nothing in the ark except the two **stone** tablets that
10: 2 carrying spices, large quantities of gold, and precious **stones**—
10:10 120 talents of gold, large quantities of spices, and precious **stones**.
10:11 they brought great cargoes of almugwood and precious **stones**.
10:27 The king made silver as common in Jerusalem as **stones**, and cedar
12:18 of forced labor, but all Israel **stoned** [+928+8083] him to death.
15:22 they carried away *from* Ramah the **stones** and timber Baasha had
18:31 Elijah took twelve **stones**, one for each of the tribes descended
18:32 With the **stones** he built an altar in the name of the LORD,
18:38 and burned up the sacrifice, the wood, the **stones** and the soil,
21:13 him outside the city and **stoned** [+928+2021+6232] him to death.
2Ki 3:19 stop up all the springs, and ruin every good field with **stones**."
3:25 each man threw a **stone** on every good field until it was covered.
3:25 Only Kir Hareseth was left with its **stones** in place, but men armed
12:12 [12:13] the masons and **stonecutters** [+2935]. They purchased
12:12 [12:13] dressed **stone** for the repair of the temple of the LORD,
16:17 from the bronze bulls that supported it and set it on a **stone** base.
19:18 destroyed them, for they were not gods but only wood and **stone**,
22: 6 have them purchase timber and dressed **stone** to repair the temple.
1Ch 12: 2 or to **sling stones** [+928+2021] right-handed or left-handed;
20: 2 found to be a talent of gold, and it was set with precious **stones**—
22: 2 to prepare dressed **stone** for building the house of God.
22:14 of bronze and iron too great to be weighed, and wood and **stone**.
22:15 stonecutters, **masons** [+3093] and carpenters, as well as men
29: 2 for the wood, as well as **onyx** [+8732] for the settings, turquoise,
29: 2 turquoise, **stones** *of* various colors, and all kinds of fine stone
29: 2 stones of various colors, and all kinds of fine **stone** and marble—
29: 2 of various colors, and all kinds of fine stone and **marble** [+8880]—
29: 8 Any who had **precious stones** gave them to the treasury of the
2Ch 1:15 The king made silver and gold as common in Jerusalem as **stones**,
2:14 [2:13] work in gold and silver, bronze and iron, **stone** and wood,
3: 6 He adorned the temple with precious **stones**. And the gold he used
9: 1 carrying spices, large quantities of gold, and precious **stones**—
9: 9 120 talents of gold, large quantities of spices, and precious **stones**.
9:10 from Ophir; they also brought algumwood and precious **stones**.
9:27 The king made silver as common in Jerusalem as **stones**, and cedar
10:18 forced labor, but the Israelites **stoned** [+928+8083] him to death.
16: 6 they carried away *from* Ramah the **stones** and timber Baasha had
24:21 by order of the king *they* **stoned** him **to death** [+8083] in the
26:14 coats of armor, bows and **slingstones** [+7845] for the entire army.
26:15 and on the corner defenses to shoot arrows and hurl large **stones**.
32:27 made treasuries for his silver and gold and for his precious **stones**,
34:11 money to the carpenters and builders to purchase dressed **stone**,
Ne 4: 2 [3:34] Can they bring the **stones** back to life from those heaps of
4: 3 [3:35] up on it, he would break down their wall of **stones**!"
9:11 their pursuers into the depths, like a **stone** into mighty waters.
Job 5:23 For you will have a covenant with the **stones** *of* the field,
6:12 Do I have the strength of **stone**? Is my flesh bronze?
8:17 around a pile of rocks and looks for a place among the **stones**.
14:19 as water wears away **stones** and torrents wash away the soil,
28: 2 Iron is taken from the earth, and copper is smelted from **ore**.
28: 3 he searches the farthest recesses for **ore** in the blackest darkness.

Job 28: 6 sapphires come from its **rocks**, and its dust contains nuggets of
38: 6 what were its footings set, or who laid its **cornerstone** [+7157]—
38:30 when the waters become hard as **stone**, when the surface of the
41:24 [41:16] His chest is hard as **rock**, hard as a lower millstone.
41:28 [41:20] make him flee; **slingstones** [+7845] are like chaff to him.
Ps 91:12 in their hands, so that you will not strike your foot against a **stone**.
102:14 [102:15] For her **stones** are dear to your servants; her very dust
118:22 The **stone** the builders rejected has become the capstone;
Pr 11: 1 abhors dishonest scales, but accurate **weights** are his delight.
16:11 are from the LORD; all the **weights** *in* the bag are of his making.
17: 8 A bribe is a **charm** [+2834] to the one who gives it; wherever he
20:10 **Differing weights** [+74+2256] and differing measures—the
20:10 **Differing weights** [+74+2256] and differing measures—the
20:23 The LORD detests **differing weights** [+74+2256], and dishonest
20:23 The LORD detests **differing weights** [+74+2256], and dishonest
24:31 ground was covered with weeds, and the **stone** wall was in ruins.
26: 8 Like tying a **stone** in a sling is the giving of honor to a fool.
26:27 he will fall into it; if a man rolls a **stone**, it will roll back on him.
27: 3 **Stone** is heavy and sand a burden, but provocation by a fool is
Ecc 3: 5 a time to scatter **stones** and a time to gather them, a time to
3: 5 a time to scatter stones and a time to gather **them**[s], a time to
10: 9 Whoever quarries **stones** may be injured by them; whoever splits
Isa 8:14 for both houses of Israel he will be a **stone** *that* causes men to
14:19 pierced by the sword, those who descend to the **stones** *of* the pit.
27: 9 When he makes all the altar **stones** to be like chalk stones crushed
27: 9 When he makes all the altar stones to be like chalk **stones** crushed
28:16 "See, I lay a **stone** in Zion, a tested stone, a precious cornerstone
28:16 "See, I lay a stone in Zion, a tested **stone**, a precious cornerstone
30:30 consuming fire, with cloudburst, thunderstorm and **hail** [+1352].
34:11 the measuring line of chaos and the **plumb line** *of* desolation.
37:19 destroyed them, for they were not gods but only wood and **stone**,
54:11 and not comforted, I will build you with **stones** *of* turquoise,
54:12 your gates of **sparkling jewels** [+734], and all your walls of
54:12 gates of sparkling jewels, and all your walls of precious **stones**.
60:17 of wood I will bring you bronze, and iron in place of **stones**.
62:10 Build up, build up the highway! Remove the **stones**. Raise a
Jer 2:27 They say to wood, 'You are my father,' and to **stone**, 'You gave me
3: 9 she defiled the land and committed adultery with **stone** and wood.
43: 9 take *some* large **stones** with you and bury them in clay in the brick
43:10 and I will set his throne over these **stones** I have buried here;
51:26 No **rock** will be taken from you for a cornerstone, nor any stone
51:26 nor any **stone** for a foundation, for you will be desolate forever,"
51:63 reading this scroll, tie a **stone** to it and throw it into the Euphrates.
La 3:53 They tried to end my life in a pit and threw **stones** at me;
4: 1 The sacred **gems** are scattered at the head of every street.
Eze 1:26 their heads was what looked like a throne of **sapphire** [+6209],
10: 1 I saw the likeness of a throne of **sapphire** [+6209] above the
10: 9 each of the cherubim; the wheels sparkled like **chrysolite** [+9577].
11:19 I will remove from them their heart of **stone** and give them a heart
13:11 come in torrents, and I will send **hailstones** [+453] hurtling down,
13:13 in my anger **hailstones** [+453] and torrents of rain will fall with
16:40 *who will* **stone** [+906+928+2021+8083] you and hack you to pieces
20:32 like the peoples of the world, who serve wood and **stone**."
23:47 The mob *will* **stone** [+6584+8083] them and cut them down with
26:12 your walls and demolish your fine houses and throw your **stones**,
27:22 exchanged the finest of all kinds of spices and precious **stones**,
28:13 in Eden, the garden of God; every precious **stone** adorned you:
28:14 on the holy mount of God; you walked among the fiery **stones**.
28:16 I expelled you, O guardian cherub, from among the fiery **stones**.
36:26 I will remove from you your heart of **stone** and give you a heart of
38:22 **hailstones** [+453] and burning sulfur on him and on his troops
40:42 There were also four tables of dressed **stone** for the burnt
Da 11:38 honor with gold and silver, with precious **stones** and costly gifts.
Mic 1: 6 I will pour her **stones** into the valley and lay bare her foundations.
6:11 I acquit a man with dishonest scales, with a bag of false **weights**?
Hab 2:11 The **stones** of the wall will cry out, and the beams of the
2:19 who says to wood, 'Come to life!' Or to lifeless **stone**, 'Wake up!'
Hag 2:15 consider how things were before one **stone** was laid on another in
2:15 consider how things were before one stone was laid on **another**[s] in
Zec 3: 9 See, the **stone** I have set in front of Joshua! There are seven eyes
3: 9 There are seven eyes on that one **stone**, and I will engrave an
4: 7 he will bring out the **capstone** [+8036] to shouts of 'God bless it!
4:10 Men will rejoice when they see the **plumb** [+974] **line** in the hand
5: 4 in his house and destroy it, both its timbers and its **stones**.' "
5: 8 into the basket and pushed the lead **cover** down over its mouth.
9:15 They will destroy and overcome with **slingstones** [+7845].
9:16 of his people. They will sparkle in his land like **jewels** *in* a crown.
12: 3 I will make Jerusalem an immovable **rock** for all the nations.

75 אֶבֶן הָעֵזֶר *'eben hā'ēzer*, n.pr.loc. [3] [√ 74 + 6469]

Ebenezer [3]

1Sa 4: 1 The Israelites camped at **Ebenezer**, and the Philistines at Aphek.
5: 1 captured the ark of God, they took it from **Ebenezer** to Ashdod.
7:12 He named it **Ebenezer**, saying, "Thus far has the LORD helped

76 אֲבָנָה *ᵃbānâ*, n.pr.loc. [1] [cf. 592]

Abana [1]

2Ki 5:12 Are not **Abana** [Q 592] and Pharpar, the rivers of Damascus,

77 אַבְנֵט *'abnēṭ*, n.[m.]. [9]

sash [6], sashes [3]

Ex 28: 4 a breastpiece, an ephod, a robe, a woven tunic, a turban and a **sash**.
28:39 turban of fine linen. The **sash** is to be the work of an embroiderer.
28:40 Make tunics, **sashes** and headbands for Aaron's sons, to give them
29: 9 put headbands on them. Then tie **sashes** on Aaron and his sons.
39:29 The **sash** was of finely twisted linen and blue, purple and scarlet
Lev 8: 7 tied the **sash** around him, clothed him with the robe and put the
8:13 on them, tied **sashes** around them and put headbands on them,
16: 4 he is to tie the linen **sash** around him and put on the linen turban.
Isa 22:21 I will clothe him with your robe and fasten your **sash** around him

78 אָבְנַיִם *'obnayim*, n.[m.]. [2] [√ 74?]

delivery stool [1], wheel [1]

Ex 1:16 women in childbirth and observe them on the **delivery stool**,
Jer 18: 3 down to the potter's house, and I saw him working at the **wheel**.

79 אַבְנֵר *'abnēr*, n.pr.m. [62] [√ 3 + 5944; cf. 46]

Abner [55], Abner's [3], him[s] [2], *untranslated* [1], he[s] [1]

1Sa 14:51 Saul's father Kish and **Abner's** father Ner were sons of Abiel.
17:55 he said to **Abner**, commander of the army, "Abner, whose son is
17:55 he said to Abner, commander of the army, "**Abner**, whose son is
17:55 **Abner** replied, "As surely as you live, O king, I don't know."
17:57 **Abner** took him and brought him before Saul, with David still
20:25 opposite Jonathan, and **Abner** sat next to Saul, but David's place
26: 5 He saw where Saul and **Abner** son of Ner, the commander of the
26: 7 near his head. **Abner** and the soldiers were lying around him.
26:14 He called out to the army and to **Abner** son of Ner, "Aren't you
26:14 to Abner son of Ner, "Aren't you going to answer me, **Abner**?"
26:14 Abner?" **Abner** replied, "Who are you who calls to the king?"
26:15 David said, **[RPH]** "You're a man, aren't you? And who is like
2Sa 2: 8 Meanwhile, **Abner** son of Ner, the commander of Saul's army,
2:12 **Abner** son of Ner, together with the men of Ish-Bosheth son of
2:14 **Abner** said to Joab, "Let's have some of the young men get up
2:17 and **Abner** and the men of Israel were defeated by David's men.
2:19 He chased **Abner**, turning neither to the right nor to the left as he
2:19 turning neither to the right nor to the left as he pursued **him**[s].
2:20 **Abner** looked behind him and asked, "Is that you, Asahel?"
2:21 Then **Abner** said to him, "Turn aside to the right or to the left;
2:22 Again **Abner** warned Asahel, "Stop chasing me! Why should I
2:23 so **Abner** thrust the butt of his spear into Asahel's stomach,
2:24 But Joab and Abishai pursued **Abner**, and as the sun was setting,
2:25 the men of Benjamin rallied behind **Abner**. They formed
2:26 **Abner** called out to Joab, "Must the sword devour forever?
2:29 All that night **Abner** and his men marched through the Arabah.
2:30 Joab returned from pursuing **Abner** and assembled all his men.
2:31 killed three hundred and sixty Benjamites who were with **Abner**.
3: 6 **Abner** had been strengthening his own position in the house of
3: 7 Ish-Bosheth said to **Abner**, "Why did you sleep with my father's
3: 8 **Abner** was very angry because of what Ish-Bosheth said and he
3: 9 May God deal with **Abner**, be it ever so severely, if I do not do
3:11 Ish-Bosheth did not dare to say another word to **Abner**, because he
3:12 Then **Abner** sent messengers on his behalf to say to David,
3:16 Then **Abner** said to him, "Go back home!" So he went back.
3:17 **Abner** conferred with the elders of Israel and said, "For some time
3:19 **Abner** also spoke to the Benjamites in person. Then he went to
3:19 Then **he**[s] went to Hebron to tell David everything that Israel
3:20 When **Abner**, who had twenty men with him, came to David at
3:20 to David at Hebron, David prepared a feast for **him**[s] and his men.
3:21 **Abner** said to David, "Let me go at once and assemble all Israel
3:21 heart desires." So David sent **Abner** away, and he went in peace.
3:22 **Abner** was no longer with David in Hebron, because David had
3:23 he was told that **Abner** son of Ner had come to the king and that
3:24 and said, "What have you done? Look, **Abner** came to you.
3:25 You know **Abner** son of Ner; he came to deceive you and observe
3:26 Joab then left David and sent messengers after **Abner**, and they
3:27 Now when **Abner** returned to Hebron, Joab took him aside into the
3:28 before the LORD concerning the blood of **Abner** son of Ner.
3:30 (Joab and his brother Abishai murdered **Abner** because he had
3:31 and put on sackcloth and walk in mourning in front of **Abner**."
3:32 They buried **Abner** in Hebron, and the king wept aloud at Abner's
3:32 buried Abner in Hebron, and the king wept aloud at **Abner's** tomb.
3:33 The king sang this lament for **Abner**: "Should Abner have died as
3:33 lament for Abner: "Should **Abner** have died as the lawless die?
3:37 all Israel knew that the king had no part in the murder of **Abner**

2Sa 4: 1 When Ish-Bosheth son of Saul heard that **Abner** had died in
4: 12 the head of Ish-Bosheth and buried it in **Abner's** tomb at Hebron.
1Ki 2: 5 of Israel's armies, **Abner** son of Ner and Amasa son of Jether.
2: 32 **Abner** son of Ner, commander of Israel's army, and Amasa son of
1Ch 26: 28 by Saul son of Kish, **Abner** son of Ner and Joab son of Zeruiah,
27: 21 Iddo son of Zechariah; over Benjamin: Jaasiel son of **Abner**;

80 אָבַס *'ābas*, v. [2] [→ 17, 4393]

choice [1], fattened [1]

1Ki 4: 23 [5:3] [B] as well as deer, gazelles, roebucks and **choice** fowl.
Pr 15: 17 [B] a meal of vegetables where there is love than a **fattened**

81 אֲבַעְבֻּעֹת *ᵃba'bu'ōt*, n.f.pl. [2] [√ 5580]

festering [2]

Ex 9: 9 **festering** boils will break out on men and animals throughout the
9: 10 it into the air, and **festering** boils broke out on men and animals.

82 אֶבֶץ *'ebeṣ*, n.pr.loc. [1] [→ 83]

Ebez [1]

Jos 19: 20 Rabbith, Kishion, **Ebez**,

83 אִבְצָן *'ibṣān*, n.pr.m. [2] [√ 82]

Ibzan [2]

Jdg 12: 8 After him, **Ibzan** of Bethlehem led Israel.
12: 10 Then **Ibzan** died, and was buried in Bethlehem.

84 אָבַק *'ābaq*, v.den. [2] [cf. 3909?]

wrestled [2]

Ge 32: 24 [32:25] [C] and a man **wrestled** with him till daybreak.
32: 25 [32:26] [C] so that his hip was wrenched as he **wrestled** with

85 אָבָק *'ābāq*, n.m. [6] [→ 86]

dust [4], fine dust [1], powder [1]

Ex 9: 9 It will become **fine dust** over the whole land of Egypt,
Dt 28: 24 LORD will turn the rain of your country into dust and **powder**;
Isa 5: 24 so their roots will decay and their flowers blow away like **dust**;
29: 5 your many enemies will become like fine **dust**, the ruthless hordes
Eze 26: 10 His horses will be so many that they will cover you with **dust**.
Na 1: 3 in the whirlwind and the storm, and clouds are the **dust** *of* his feet.

86 אֲבָקָה *ᵃbāqâ*, n.f. [1] [√ 85]

spices [1]

SS 3: 6 with myrrh and incense made from all the **spices** *of* the merchant?

87 אָבַר *'ābar*, v.den. [1] [√ 88; cf. 51]

take flight [1]

Job 39: 26 [G] "*Does* the hawk **take flight** by your wisdom and spread his

88 אֵבֶר *'ēber*, n.[m.]. [3] [→ 87, 89; cf. 51]

wings [2], feathers [1]

Ps 55: 6 [55:7] I said, "Oh, that I had the **wings** of a dove! I would fly
Isa 40: 31 They will soar on **wings** like eagles; they will run and not grow
Eze 17: 3 long **feathers** and full plumage of varied colors came to Lebanon.

89 אֶבְרָה *'ebrâ*, n.f. [4] [√ 88; cf. 51]

feathers [2], pinions [2]

Dt 32: 11 spreads its wings to catch them and carries them on its **pinions**.
Job 39: 13 but they cannot compare with the **pinions** and feathers *of* the stork.
Ps 68: 13 [68:14] are sheathed with silver, its **feathers** with shining gold."
91: 4 He will cover you with his **feathers**, and under his wings you will

90 אַבְרָהָם *'abrāhām*, n.pr.m. [175] [cf. 92]

Abraham [153], Abraham's [11], he[s] [6], him[s] [2], *untranslated* [1], his[s] [+4200] [1], his[s] [1]

Ge 17: 5 your name will be **Abraham**, for I have made you a father of many
17: 9 God said to **Abraham**, "As for you, you must keep my covenant,
17: 15 God also said to **Abraham**, "As for Sarai your wife, you are no
17: 17 **Abraham** fell facedown; he laughed and said to himself, "Will a
17: 18 **Abraham** said to God, "If only Ishmael might live under your
17: 22 When he had finished speaking with **Abraham**, God went up from
17: 23 On that very day **Abraham** took his son Ishmael and all those born
17: 23 every male in **his[s]** household, and circumcised them, as God told
17: 24 **Abraham** was ninety-nine years old when he was circumcised,
17: 26 **Abraham** and his son Ishmael were both circumcised on that same
18: 6 So **Abraham** hurried into the tent to Sarah. "Quick," he said,
18: 7 Then **he[s]** ran to the herd and selected a choice, tender calf
18: 11 **Abraham** and Sarah were already old and well advanced in years,
18: 13 Then the LORD said to **Abraham**, "Why did Sarah laugh
18: 16 and **Abraham** walked along with them to see them on their way.
18: 17 LORD said, "Shall I hide from **Abraham** what I am about to do?
18: 18 **Abraham** will surely become a great and powerful nation,
18: 19 so that the LORD will bring about for **Abraham** what he has
18: 22 but **Abraham** remained standing before the LORD.
18: 23 **Abraham** approached him and said: "Will you sweep away the
18: 27 **Abraham** spoke up again: "Now that I have been so bold as to
18: 33 When the LORD had finished speaking with **Abraham**, he left,
18: 33 speaking with Abraham, he left, and **Abraham** returned home.
19: 27 Early the next morning **Abraham** got up and returned to the place
19: 29 God destroyed the cities of the plain, he remembered **Abraham**,
20: 1 Now **Abraham** moved on from there into the region of the Negev
20: 2 and there **Abraham** said of his wife Sarah, "She is my sister."
20: 9 Abimelech called **Abraham** in and said, "What have you done to
20: 10 Abimelech asked **Abraham**, "What was your reason for doing
20: 11 **Abraham** replied, "I said to myself, 'There is surely no fear of God
20: 14 and cattle and male and female slaves and gave them to **Abraham**,
20: 17 Then **Abraham** prayed to God, and God healed Abimelech,
20: 18 in Abimelech's household because of **Abraham's** wife Sarah.
21: 2 Sarah became pregnant and bore a son to **Abraham** in his old age,
21: 3 **Abraham** gave the name Isaac to the son Sarah bore him.
21: 4 days old, **Abraham** circumcised him, as God commanded him.
21: 5 **Abraham** was a hundred years old when his son Isaac was born to
21: 7 "Who would have said to **Abraham** that Sarah would nurse
21: 8 and on the day Isaac was weaned **Abraham** held a great feast.
21: 9 whom Hagar the Egyptian had borne to **Abraham** was mocking,
21: 10 she said to **Abraham**, "Get rid of that slave woman and her son,
21: 11 The matter distressed **Abraham** greatly because it concerned his
21: 12 But God said to **him[s]**, "Do not be so distressed about the boy
21: 14 Early the next morning **Abraham** took some food and a skin of
21: 22 and Phicol the commander of his forces said to **Abraham**,
21: 24 **Abraham** said, "I swear it."
21: 25 **Abraham** complained to Abimelech about a well of water that
21: 27 So **Abraham** brought sheep and cattle and gave them to
21: 28 **Abraham** set apart seven ewe lambs from the flock,
21: 29 Abimelech asked **Abraham**, "What is the meaning of these seven
21: 34 And **Abraham** stayed in the land of the Philistines for a long time.
22: 1 Some time later God tested **Abraham**. He said to him,
22: 1 He said to him, "**Abraham**!" "Here I am," he replied.
22: 3 Early the next morning **Abraham** got up and saddled his donkey.
22: 4 On the third day **Abraham** looked up and saw the place in the
22: 5 **He[s]** said to his servants, "Stay here with the donkey while I
22: 6 **Abraham** took the wood for the burnt offering and placed it on his
22: 7 Isaac spoke up and said to his father **Abraham**, "Father?"
22: 8 **Abraham** answered, "God himself will provide the lamb for the
22: 9 **Abraham** built an altar there and arranged the wood on it.
22: 10 Then **he[s]** reached out his hand and took the knife to slay his son.
22: 11 angel of the LORD called out to him from heaven, "**Abraham**!
22: 11 LORD called out to him from heaven, "Abraham! **Abraham**!"
22: 13 **Abraham** looked up and there in a thicket he saw a ram caught by
22: 13 **He[s]** went over and took the ram and sacrificed it as a burnt
22: 14 So **Abraham** called that place The LORD Will Provide.
22: 15 The angel of the LORD called to **Abraham** from heaven a
22: 19 **Abraham** returned to his servants, and they set off together for
22: 19 set off together for Beersheba. And **Abraham** stayed in Beersheba.
22: 20 Some time later **Abraham** was told, "Milcah is also a mother;
22: 23 Milcah bore these eight sons to **Abraham's** brother Nahor.
23: 2 and **Abraham** went to mourn for Sarah and to weep over her.
23: 3 **Abraham** rose from beside his dead wife and spoke to the Hittites.
23: 5 The Hittites replied to **Abraham**,
23: 7 **Abraham** rose and bowed down before the people of the land,
23: 10 he replied to **Abraham** in the hearing of all the Hittites who had
23: 12 Again **Abraham** bowed down before the people of the land
23: 14 Ephron answered **Abraham**,
23: 16 **Abraham** agreed to Ephron's terms and weighed out for him the
23: 16 **[RPH]** weighed out for him the price he had named in the hearing
23: 18 to **Abraham** as his property in the presence of all the Hittites who
23: 19 Afterward **Abraham** buried his wife Sarah in the cave in the field
23: 20 the cave in it were deeded to **Abraham** by the Hittites as a burial
24: 1 **Abraham** was now old and well advanced in years,
24: 1 advanced in years, and the LORD had blessed **him[s]** in every way.
24: 2 **He[s]** said to the chief servant in his household, the one in charge of
24: 6 sure that you do not take my son back there," **Abraham** said.
24: 9 So the servant put his hand under the thigh of his master **Abraham**
24: 12 Then he prayed, "O LORD, God of my master **Abraham**,
24: 12 me success today, and show kindness to my master **Abraham**.
24: 15 son of Milcah, who was the wife of **Abraham's** brother Nahor.
24: 27 "Praise be to the LORD, the God of my master **Abraham**,
24: 34 So he said, "I am **Abraham's** servant.
24: 42 I said, 'O LORD, God of my master **Abraham**, if you will,
24: 48 I praised the LORD, the God of my master **Abraham**, who had
24: 52 When **Abraham's** servant heard what they said, he bowed down to

[F] Hitpael (hitpoel, hitpoal, hitpolel, hitpolal, hitpalel, hitpalal, hitpalpel, hitpalpal, hotpael, hotpaal) [G] Hiphil (hiphtil) [H] Hophal [I] Hishtaphel

Ge 24:59 along with her nurse and **Abraham's** servant and his men.
25: 1 **Abraham** took another wife, whose name was Keturah.
25: 5 **Abraham** left everything he owned to Isaac.
25: 6 **he**[s] gave gifts to the sons of his concubines and sent them away
25: 6 he gave gifts to the sons of **his**[s] [+4200] concubines and sent them
25: 7 Altogether, **Abraham** lived a hundred and seventy-five years.
25: 8 Then **Abraham** breathed his last and died at a good old age,
25:10 the field **Abraham** had bought from the Hittites. There Abraham
25:10 from the Hittites. There **Abraham** was buried with his wife Sarah.
25:11 After **Abraham's** death, God blessed his son Isaac, who then lived
25:12 This is the account of **Abraham's** son Ishmael, whom Sarah's
25:12 Sarah's maidservant, Hagar the Egyptian, bore to **Abraham**.
25:19 This is the account of **Abraham's** son Isaac. Abraham became the
25:19 of Abraham's son Isaac. **Abraham** became the father of Isaac,
26: 1 in the land—besides the earlier famine of **Abraham's** time—
26: 3 and will confirm the oath I swore to your father **Abraham**.
26: 5 because **Abraham** obeyed me and kept my requirements,
26:15 his father's servants had dug in the time of his father **Abraham**,
26:18 the wells that had been dug in the time of his father **Abraham**,
26:18 which the Philistines had stopped up after **Abraham** died,
26:24 appeared to him and said, "I am the God of your father **Abraham**.
26:24 number of your descendants for the sake of my servant **Abraham**."
28: 4 he give you and your descendants the blessing given to **Abraham**,
28: 4 where you now live as an alien, the land God gave to **Abraham**."
28: 9 the sister of Nebaioth and daughter of Ishmael son of **Abraham**,
28:13 the God of your father **Abraham** and the God of Isaac.
31:42 the God of **Abraham** and the Fear of Isaac, had not been with me,
31:53 May the God of **Abraham** and the God of Nahor, the God of their
32: 9 [32:10] Jacob prayed, "O God of my father **Abraham**, God of my
35:12 The land I gave to **Abraham** and Isaac I also give to you,
35:27 Arba (that is, Hebron), where **Abraham** and Isaac had stayed.
48:15 "May the God before whom my fathers **Abraham** and Isaac
48:16 by my name and the names of my fathers **Abraham** and Isaac,
49:30 which **Abraham** bought as a burial place from Ephron the Hittite,
49:31 There **Abraham** and his wife Sarah were buried, there Isaac
50:13 which **Abraham** had bought as a burial place from Ephron the
50:24 up out of this land to the land he promised on oath to **Abraham**,
Ex 2:24 their groaning and he remembered his covenant with **Abraham**,
3: 6 the God of **Abraham**, the God of Isaac and the God of Jacob."
3:15 the God of **Abraham**, the God of Isaac and the God of Jacob—
3:16 the God of **Abraham**, Isaac and Jacob—appeared to me and said:
4: 5 the God of **Abraham**, the God of Isaac and the God of Jacob—
6: 3 I appeared to **Abraham**, to Isaac and to Jacob as God Almighty,
6: 8 you to the land I swore with uplifted hand to give to **Abraham**,
32:13 Remember your servants **Abraham**, Isaac and Israel, to whom you
33: 1 and go up to the land I promised on oath to **Abraham**, Isaac
Lev 26:42 and my covenant with Isaac and my covenant with **Abraham**,
Nu 32:11 up out of Egypt will see the land I promised on oath to **Abraham**,
Dt 1: 8 to **Abraham**, Isaac and Jacob—and to their descendants after
6:10 swore to your fathers, to **Abraham**, Isaac and Jacob, to give you—
9: 5 what he swore to your fathers, to **Abraham**, Isaac and Jacob.
9:27 Remember your servants **Abraham**, Isaac and Jacob. Overlook the
29:13 [29:12] as he swore to your fathers, **Abraham**, Isaac and Jacob.
30:20 land he swore to give to your fathers, **Abraham**, Isaac and Jacob.
34: 4 "This is the land I promised on oath to **Abraham**, Isaac and Jacob
Jos 24: 2 including Terah the father of **Abraham** and Nahor, lived beyond
24: 3 But I took your father **Abraham** from the land beyond the River
1Ki 18:36 "O LORD, God of **Abraham**, Isaac and Israel, let it be known
2Ki 13:23 showed concern for them because of his covenant with **Abraham**,
1Ch 1:27 and Abram (that is, **Abraham**).
1:28 The sons of **Abraham**: Isaac and Ishmael.
1:32 The sons born to Keturah, **Abraham's** concubine: Zimran,
1:34 **Abraham** was the father of Isaac. The sons of Isaac: Esau
16:16 the covenant he made with **Abraham**, the oath he swore to Isaac.
29:18 O LORD, God of our fathers **Abraham**, Isaac and Israel,
2Ch 20: 7 and give it forever to the descendants of **Abraham** your friend?
30: 6 return to the LORD, the God of **Abraham**, Isaac and Israel,
Ne 9: 7 brought him out of Ur of the Chaldeans and named him **Abraham**.
Ps 47: 9 [47:10] nations assemble as the people of the God of **Abraham**,
105: 6 O descendants of **Abraham** his servant, O sons of Jacob,
105: 9 the covenant he made with **Abraham**, the oath he swore to Isaac.
105:42 he remembered his holy promise given to his servant **Abraham**.
Isa 29:22 the LORD, who redeemed **Abraham**, says to the house of Jacob:
41: 8 whom I have chosen, you descendants of **Abraham** my friend,
51: 2 look to **Abraham**, your father, and to Sarah, who gave you birth.
63:16 though **Abraham** does not know us or Israel acknowledge us;
Jer 33:26 choose one of his sons to rule over the descendants of **Abraham**,
Eze 33:24 '**Abraham** was only one man, yet he possessed the land.
Mic 7:20 You will be true to Jacob, and show mercy to **Abraham**, as you

91 אַבְרֵךְ *'abrēk*, I.excl. [1]

make way [1]

Ge 41:43 and men shouted before him, "**Make way!**"

92 אַבְרָם *'abrām*, n.pr.m. [61] [√ 3 + 8123; cf. 53, 90]

Abram [50], Abram's [5], him[s] [3], *untranslated* [1], he[s] [1], his[s] [1]

Ge 11:26 lived 70 years, he became the father of **Abram**, Nahor and Haran.
11:27 of Terah. Terah became the father of **Abram**, Nahor and Haran.
11:29 **Abram** and Nahor both married. The name of Abram's wife was
11:29 The name of **Abram's** wife was Sarai, and the name of Nahor's
11:31 Terah took his son **Abram**, his grandson Lot son of Haran,
11:31 and his daughter-in-law Sarai, the wife of his son **Abram**,
12: 1 The LORD had said to **Abram**, "Leave your country, your people
12: 4 So **Abram** left, as the LORD had told him; and Lot went with
12: 4 **Abram** was seventy-five years old when he set out from Haran.
12: 5 **He**[s] took his wife Sarai, his nephew Lot, all the possessions they
12: 6 **Abram** traveled through the land as far as the site of the great tree
12: 7 The LORD appeared to **Abram** and said, "To your offspring I
12: 9 Then **Abram** set out and continued toward the Negev.
12:10 **Abram** went down to Egypt to live there for a while
12:14 When **Abram** came to Egypt, the Egyptians saw that she was a
12:16 He treated **Abram** well for her sake, and Abram acquired sheep
12:17 on Pharaoh and his household because of **Abram's** wife Sarai.
12:18 So Pharaoh summoned **Abram**. "What have you done to me?"
13: 1 So **Abram** went up from Egypt to the Negev, with his wife
13: 2 **Abram** had become very wealthy in livestock and in silver
13: 4 built an altar. There **Abram** called on the name of the LORD.
13: 5 Now Lot, who was moving about with **Abram**, also had flocks
13: 7 quarreling arose between **Abram's** herdsmen and the herdsmen of
13: 8 So **Abram** said to Lot, "Let's not have any quarreling between you
13:12 **Abram** lived in the land of Canaan, while Lot lived among the
13:14 The LORD said to **Abram** after Lot had parted from him,
13:18 So **Abram** moved his tents and went to live near the great trees of
14:12 They also carried off **Abram's** nephew Lot and his possessions,
14:13 who had escaped came and reported this to **Abram** the Hebrew.
14:13 brother of Eshcol and Aner, all of whom were allied with **Abram**.
14:14 When **Abram** heard that his relative had been taken captive,
14:19 saying, "Blessed be **Abram** by God Most High, Creator of heaven
14:21 The king of Sodom said to **Abram**, "Give me the people and keep
14:22 **Abram** said to the king of Sodom, "I have raised my hand to the
14:23 so that you will never be able to say, 'I made **Abram** rich.'
15: 1 After this, the word of the LORD came to **Abram** in a vision:
15: 1 "Do not be afraid, **Abram**. I am your shield, your very great
15: 2 **Abram** said, "O Sovereign LORD, what can you give me since I
15: 3 **Abram** said, "You have given me no children; so a servant in my
15:11 of prey came down on the carcasses, but **Abram** drove them away.
15:12 **Abram** fell into a deep sleep, and a thick and dreadful darkness
15:13 the LORD said to **him**[s], "Know for certain that your descendants
15:18 On that day the LORD made a covenant with **Abram** and said,
16: 1 Now Sarai, **Abram's** wife, had borne him no children. But she had
16: 2 so she said to **Abram**, "The LORD has kept me from having
16: 2 can build a family through her." **Abram** agreed to what Sarai said.
16: 3 So after **Abram** had been living in Canaan ten years, Sarai his wife
16: 3 Sarai **his**[s] wife took her Egyptian maidservant Hagar and gave her
16: 3 and gave her to her husband to be his wife. **[RPH]**
16: 5 Sarai said to **Abram**, "You are responsible for the wrong I am
16: 6 "Your servant is in your hands," **Abram** said. "Do with her
16:15 So Hagar bore **Abram** a son, and Abram gave the name Ishmael to
16:15 and **Abram** gave the name Ishmael to the son she had borne.
16:16 **Abram** was eighty-six years old when Hagar bore him Ishmael.
16:16 Abram was eighty-six years old when Hagar bore **him**[s] Ishmael.
17: 1 When **Abram** was ninety-nine years old, the LORD appeared to
17: 1 the LORD appeared to **him**[s] and said, "I am God Almighty;
17: 3 **Abram** fell facedown, and God said to him,
17: 5 No longer will you be called **Abram**; your name will be Abraham,
1Ch 1:27 and **Abram** (that is, Abraham).
Ne 9: 7 who chose **Abram** and brought him out of Ur of the Chaldeans

93 אַבְשַׁי *'abšay*, n.pr.m. [6] [cf. 57]

Abishai [6]

2Sa 10:10 He put the rest of the men under the command of **Abishai** his
1Ch 2:16 and Abigail. Zeruiah's three sons were **Abishai**, Joab and Asahel.
11:20 **Abishai** the brother of Joab was chief of the Three. He raised his
18:12 **Abishai** son of Zeruiah struck down eighteen thousand Edomites
19:11 He put the rest of the men under the command of **Abishai** his
19:15 they too fled before his brother **Abishai** and went inside the city.

94 אַבְשָׁלוֹם *'abšālôm*, n.pr.m. [109] [√ 3 + 8934]

Absalom [88], Absalom's [10], he[s] [6], *untranslated* [2], him[s] [2], Absalom's [+4200] [1]

2Sa 3: 3 **Absalom** the son of Maacah daughter of Talmai king of Geshur;
13: 1 in love with Tamar, the beautiful sister of **Absalom** son of David.
13: 4 to him, "I'm in love with Tamar, my brother **Absalom's** sister."
13:20 Her brother **Absalom** said to her, "Has that Amnon, your brother,
13:20 Tamar lived in her brother **Absalom's** house, a desolate woman.

2Sa 13:22 **Absalom** never said a word to Amnon, either good or bad;
13:22 **he**[s] hated Amnon because he had disgraced his sister Tamar.
13:23 when **Absalom's** [+4200] sheepshearers were at Baal Hazor near
13:23 border of Ephraim, **he**[s] invited all the king's sons to come there.
13:24 **Absalom** went to the king and said, "Your servant has had shearers
13:25 **[RPH]** "All of us should not go; we would only be a burden to
13:26 **Absalom** said, "If not, please let my brother Amnon come with
13:27 **Absalom** urged him, so he sent with him Amnon and the rest of
13:28 **Absalom** ordered his men, "Listen! When Amnon is in high spirits
13:29 So **Absalom's** men did to Amnon what Absalom had ordered.
13:29 So Absalom's men did to Amnon what **Absalom** had ordered.
13:30 "**Absalom** has struck down all the king's sons; not one of them is
13:32 This has been **Absalom's** expressed intention ever since the day
13:34 Meanwhile, **Absalom** had fled. Now the man standing watch
13:37 **Absalom** fled and went to Talmai son of Ammihud, the king of
13:38 After **Absalom** fled and went to Geshur, he stayed there three
13:39 the spirit of the king longed to go to **Absalom**, for he was consoled
14:1 son of Zeruiah knew that the king's heart longed for **Absalom**.
14:21 "Very well, I will do it. Go, bring back the young man **Absalom**."
14:23 Joab went to Geshur and brought **Absalom** back to Jerusalem.
14:24 So **Absalom** went to his own house and did not see the face of the
14:25 so highly praised for his handsome appearance as **Absalom**.
14:27 Three sons and a daughter were born to **Absalom**. The daughter's
14:28 **Absalom** lived two years in Jerusalem without seeing the king's
14:29 Then **Absalom** sent for Joab in order to send him to the king,
14:30 and set it on fire." So **Absalom's** servants set the field on fire.
14:31 Then Joab did go to **Absalom's** house and he said to him,
14:32 **Absalom** said to Joab, "Look, I sent word to you and said,
14:33 the king summoned **Absalom**, and he came in and bowed down
14:33 face to the ground before the king. And the king kissed **Absalom**.
15:1 **Absalom** provided himself with a chariot and horses and with fifty
15:2 **He**[s] would get up early and stand by the side of the road leading to
15:2 **Absalom** would call out to him, "What town are you from?"
15:3 Then **Absalom** would say to him, "Look, your claims are valid
15:4 **Absalom** would add, "If only I were appointed judge in the land!
15:6 **Absalom** behaved in this way toward all the Israelites who came to
15:6 asking for justice, and so **he**[s] stole the hearts of the men of Israel.
15:7 **Absalom** said to the king, "Let me go to Hebron and fulfill a vow I
15:10 **Absalom** sent secret messengers throughout the tribes of Israel to
15:10 sound of the trumpets, then say, '**Absalom** is king in Hebron.' "
15:11 Two hundred men from Jerusalem had accompanied **Absalom**.
15:12 While **Absalom** was offering sacrifices, he also sent for
15:12 gained strength, and **Absalom's** following kept on increasing.
15:13 told David, "The hearts of the men of Israel are with **Absalom**."
15:14 "Come! We must flee, or none of us will escape from **Absalom**.
15:31 been told, "Ahithophel is among the conspirators with **Absalom**."
15:34 if you return to the city and say to **Absalom**, 'I will be your
15:37 So David's friend Hushai arrived at Jerusalem as **Absalom** was
16:8 The LORD has handed the kingdom over to your son **Absalom**.
16:15 Meanwhile, **Absalom** and all the men of Israel came to Jerusalem,
16:16 David's friend, went to **Absalom** and said to him, "Long live the
16:16 David's friend, went to Absalom and said to **him**[s], "Long live the
16:17 **Absalom** asked Hushai, "Is this the love you show your friend?
16:18 Hushai said to **Absalom**, "No, the one chosen by the LORD,
16:20 **Absalom** said to Ahithophel, "Give us your advice. What should
16:21 **[RPH]** "Lie with your father's concubines whom he left to take
16:22 So they pitched a tent for **Absalom** on the roof, and he lay with his
16:22 and **he**[s] lay with his father's concubines in the sight of all Israel.
16:23 how both David and **Absalom** regarded all of Ahithophel's advice.
17:1 Ahithophel said to **Absalom**, "I would choose twelve thousand
17:4 This plan seemed good to **Absalom** and to all the elders of Israel.
17:5 **Absalom** said, "Summon also Hushai the Arkite, so we can hear
17:6 When Hushai came to **him**[s], Absalom said, "Ahithophel has given
17:6 When Hushai came to him, **Absalom** said, "Ahithophel has given
17:7 Hushai replied to **Absalom**, "The advice Ahithophel has given is
17:9 has been a slaughter among the troops who follow **Absalom**.'
17:14 **Absalom** and all the men of Israel said, "The advice of Hushai the
17:14 good advice of Ahithophel in order to bring disaster on **Absalom**.
17:15 "Ahithophel has advised **Absalom** and the elders of Israel to do
17:18 a young man saw them and told **Absalom**. So the two of them left
17:20 When **Absalom's** men came to the woman at the house, they
17:24 and **Absalom** crossed the Jordan with all the men of Israel.
17:25 **Absalom** had appointed Amasa over the army in place of Joab.
17:26 The Israelites and **Absalom** camped in the land of Gilead.
18:5 and Ittai, "Be gentle with the young man **Absalom** for my sake."
18:5 all the troops heard the king giving orders concerning **Absalom** to
18:9 Now **Absalom** happened to meet David's men. He was riding his
18:9 **He**[s] was riding his mule, and as the mule went under the thick
18:10 he told Joab, "I just saw **Absalom** hanging in an oak tree."
18:12 and Ittai, 'Protect the young man **Absalom** for my sake.'
18:14 plunged them into **Absalom's** heart while Absalom was still alive
18:15 And ten of Joab's armor-bearers surrounded **Absalom**, struck him
18:17 They took **Absalom**, threw him into a big pit in the forest
18:18 During his lifetime **Absalom** had taken a pillar and erected it in the
18:18 after himself, and it is called **Absalom's** Monument to this day.
18:29 The king asked, "Is the young man **Absalom** safe?" Ahimaaz
18:32 The king asked the Cushite, "Is the young man **Absalom** safe?"
18:33 [19:1] As he went, he said: "O my son **Absalom**! My son, my son
18:33 [19:1] he said: "O my son Absalom! My son, my son **Absalom**!
18:33 [19:1] I had died instead of you—O **Absalom**, my son, my son!"
19:1 [19:2] "The king is weeping and mourning for **Absalom**."
19:4 [19:5] covered his face and cried aloud, "O my son **Absalom**!
19:4 [19:5] "O my son Absalom! O **Absalom**, my son, my son!"
19:6 [19:7] I see that you would be pleased if **Absalom** were alive
19:9 [19:10] But now he has fled the country because of **Absalom**;
19:10 [19:11] **Absalom**, whom we anointed to rule over us, has died in
20:6 "Now Sheba son of Bicri will do us more harm than **Absalom** did.
1Ki 1:6 He was also very handsome and was born next after **Absalom**.)
2:7 They stood by me when I fled from your brother **Absalom**.
2:28 who had conspired with Adonijah though not with **Absalom**,
1Ch 3:2 **Absalom** the son of Maacah daughter of Talmai king of Geshur;
2Ch 11:20 he married Maacah daughter of **Absalom**, who bore him Abijah,
11:21 Rehoboam loved Maacah daughter of **Absalom** more than any of
Ps 3:T [3:1] A psalm of David. When he fled from his son **Absalom**.

95 אֹבֹת *'ōbōt*, n.pr.loc. [4] [√ 3277?]

Oboth [4]

Nu 21:10 The Israelites moved on and camped at **Oboth**.
21:11 Then they set out from **Oboth** and camped in Iye Abarim,
33:43 They left Punon and camped at **Oboth**.
33:44 They left **Oboth** and camped at Iye Abarim, on the border of

96 אָגֵא *'āgē'*, n.pr.m. [1]

Agee [1]

2Sa 23:11 Next to him was Shammah son of **Agee** the Hararite.

97 אֲגַג *'agag*, n.pr.m. [8] [→ 98?]

Agag [7], *untranslated* [1]

Nu 24:7 "Their king will be greater than **Agag**; their kingdom will be
1Sa 15:8 He took **Agag** king of the Amalekites alive, and all his people he
15:9 But Saul and the army spared **Agag** and the best of the sheep
15:20 destroyed the Amalekites and brought back **Agag** their king.
15:32 Then Samuel said, "Bring me **Agag** king of the Amalekites."
15:32 **Agag** came to him confidently, thinking, "Surely the bitterness of
15:32 **[RPH]** "Surely the bitterness of death is past."
15:33 And Samuel put **Agag** to death before the LORD at Gilgal.

98 אֲגָגִי *'agāgî*, a.g. [5] [√ 97?]

Agagite [5]

Est 3:1 the **Agagite**, elevating him and giving him a seat of honor higher
3:10 Haman son of Hammedatha, the **Agagite**, the enemy of the Jews.
8:3 begged him to put an end to the evil plan of Haman the **Agagite**,
8:5 the **Agagite**, devised and wrote to destroy the Jews in all the king's
9:24 son of Hammedatha, the **Agagite**, the enemy of all the Jews,

99 אֲגֻדָּה *'aguddâ*, n.f. [4]

bunch [1], cords [1], foundation [1], group [1]

Ex 12:22 Take a **bunch** *of* hyssop, dip it into the blood in the basin and put
2Sa 2:25 They formed themselves into a **group** and took their stand on top
Isa 58:6 to loose the chains of injustice and untie the **cords** *of* the yoke,
Am 9:6 his lofty palace in the heavens and sets its **foundation** on the earth,

100 אֱגוֹז *'egôz*, n.[m.]. [1]

nut trees [1]

SS 6:11 I went down to the grove of **nut trees** to look at the new growth in

101 אָגוּר *'āgûr*, n.pr.m. [1] [√ 112]

Agur [1]

Pr 30:1 The sayings of **Agur** son of Jakeh—an oracle: This man declared

102 אֲגוֹרָה *'agôrâ*, n.f. [1] [→ 115]

piece [1]

1Sa 2:36 and bow down before him for a **piece** *of* silver and a crust of bread

103 אֶגֶל *'ēgel*, n.[m.]. [1] [→ 104]

drops [1]

Job 38:28 Does the rain have a father? Who fathers the **drops** *of* dew?

104 אֶגְלַיִם *'eglayim*, n.pr.loc. [1] [√ 103]

Eglaim [1]

Isa 15:8 their wailing reaches as far as **Eglaim**, their lamentation as far as

105 אָגַם *'āgam*, v. Not used in NIV/BHS

106 אֲגַם¹ *'ᵃgam¹*, n.[m.]. [9] [→ 109]

pools [3], ponds [2], marshes [1], pool [+4784] [1], pool [1], swampland [+4784] [1]

Ex 7: 19 the streams and canals, over the **ponds** and all the reservoirs'—
8: 5 [8:1] hand with your staff over the streams and canals and **ponds**,
Ps 107: 35 He turned the desert into **pools** *of* water and the parched ground
114: 8 who turned the rock into a **pool** [+4784], the hard rock into springs
Isa 14: 23 "I will turn her into a place for owls and into **swampland** [+4784];
35: 7 The burning sand will become a **pool**, the thirsty ground bubbling
41: 18 I will turn the desert into **pools** *of* water, and the parched ground
42: 15 their vegetation; I will turn rivers into islands and dry up the **pools**.
Jer 51: 32 the river crossings seized, the **marshes** set on fire, and the soldiers

107 אֲגַם² *'ᵃgam²*, n.[m.]. Not used in NIV/BHS

108 אָגֵם *'āgēm*, a. [1] [cf. 6327]

sick [1]

Isa 19: 10 will be dejected, and all the wage earners will be **sick** *at* heart.

109 אַגְמוֹן *'agmôn*, n.[m.]. [5] [√ 106]

reed [3], cord [1], reeds [1]

Job 41: 2 [40:26] Can you put a **cord** through his nose or pierce his jaw
41: 20 [41:12] from his nostrils as from a boiling pot over a fire of **reeds**.
Isa 9: 14 [9:13] and tail, both palm branch and **reed** in a single day;
19: 15 There is nothing Egypt can do—head or tail, palm branch or **reed**.
58: 5 Is it only for bowing one's head like a **reed** and for lying on

110 אַגָּן *'aggān*, n.[m.]. [3]

bowls [2], goblet [1]

Ex 24: 6 Moses took half of the blood and put it in **bowls**, and the other half
SS 7: 2 [7:3] Your navel is a rounded **goblet** that never lacks blended
Isa 22: 24 and offshoots—all its lesser vessels, from the **bowls** to all the jars.

111 אֲגַף *'ᵃgap*, n.[m.]. [7] [√ 1727]

troops [7]

Eze 12: 14 his staff and all his **troops**—and I will pursue them with drawn
17: 21 All his fleeing **troops** will fall by the sword, and the survivors will
38: 6 also Gomer with all its **troops**, and Beth Togarmah from the far
38: 6 and Beth Togarmah from the far north with all its **troops**—
38: 9 You and all your **troops** and the many nations with you will go up,
38: 22 hailstones and burning sulfur on him and on his **troops** and on the
39: 4 you will fall, you and all your **troops** and the nations with you.

112 אָגַר *'āgar*, v. [3] [→ 101]

gather grapes [1], gathers crops [1], gathers [1]

Dt 28: 39 [A] but you will not drink the wine or **gather** *the* **grapes**,
Pr 6: 8 [A] its provisions in summer and **gathers** its food at harvest.
10: 5 [A] *He who* **gathers crops** in summer is a wise son, but he who

113 אֲגַרְטָל *'ᵃgarṭāl*, n.m. [2]

dishes [2]

Ezr 1: 9 the inventory: gold **dishes** 30 silver dishes 1,000 silver pans 29
1: 9 the inventory: gold dishes 30 silver **dishes** 1,000 silver pans 29

114 אֶגְרֹף *'egrōp*, n.[m.]. [2] [√ 1759?]

fist [1], fists [1]

Ex 21: 18 or with his **fist** and he does not die but is confined to bed,
Isa 58: 4 and strife, and in striking each other with wicked **fists**.

115 אִגֶּרֶת *'iggeret*, n.f. [10] [√ 102; Ar 10007]

letters [6], letter [4]

2Ch 30: 1 and Judah and also wrote **letters** to Ephraim and Manasseh,
30: 6 and Judah with **letters** from the king and from his officials,
Ne 2: 7 the king, may I have **letters** to the governors of Trans-Euphrates,
2: 8 And may I have a **letter** to Asaph, keeper of the king's forest,
2: 9 the governors of Trans-Euphrates and gave them the king's **letters**.
6: 5 me with the same message, and in his hand was an unsealed **letter**
6: 17 in those days the nobles of Judah were sending many **letters** to
6: 19 telling him what I said. And Tobiah sent **letters** to intimidate me.
Est 9: 26 Because of everything written in this **letter** and because of what
9: 29 wrote with full authority to confirm this second **letter** *concerning*

116 אֵד *'ēd*, n.m. [2]

streams [2]

Ge 2: 6 **streams** came up from the earth and watered the whole surface of
Job 36: 27 draws up the drops of water, which distill as rain to the **streams**;

117 אָדַב *'ādab*, v. [1] [→ 118]

grieve [1]

1Sa 2: 33 [G] only to blind your eyes with tears and to **grieve** your heart,

118 אַדְבְּאֵל *'adbᵉ'ēl*, n.pr.m. [2] [√ 117 + 446]

Adbeel [2]

Ge 25: 13 Nebaioth the firstborn of Ishmael, Kedar, **Adbeel**, Mibsam,
1Ch 1: 29 Nebaioth the firstborn of Ishmael, Kedar, **Adbeel**, Mibsam,

119 אֲדַד *'ᵃdad*, n.pr.m. [1] [√ 2060]

Hadad [1]

1Ki 11: 17 **Hadad**, still only a boy, fled to Egypt with some Edomite officials

120 אִדּוֹ *'iddô*, n.pr.m. [2]

Iddo [2]

Ezr 8: 17 I sent them to **Iddo**, the leader in Casiphia. I told them what to say
8: 17 I told them what to say to **Iddo** and his kinsmen, the temple

121 אֱדוֹם *'ᵉdôm*, n.pr.m. [100 / 104] [→ 122, 6273; cf. 131]

Edom [79], Edom [+824] [11], Edomites [10], Edom's [2], *untranslated* [1], Edomites [+1201] [1]

Ge 25: 30 red stew! I'm famished!" (That is why he was also called **Edom**.)
32: 3 [32:4] his brother Esau in the land of Seir, the country of **Edom**.
36: 1 This is the account of Esau (that is, **Edom**).
36: 8 So Esau (that is, **Edom**) settled in the hill country of Seir.
36: 9 This is the account of Esau the father of the **Edomites** in the hill
36: 16 These were the chiefs descended from Eliphaz in **Edom** [+824];
36: 17 These were the chiefs descended from Reuel in **Edom** [+824];
36: 19 were the sons of Esau (that is, **Edom**), and these were their chiefs.
36: 21 These sons of Seir in **Edom** [+824] were Horite chiefs.
36: 31 These were the kings who reigned in **Edom** [+824] before any
36: 32 Bela son of Beor became king of **Edom**. His city was named
36: 43 These were the chiefs of **Edom**, according to their settlements in
36: 43 the land they occupied. This was Esau the father of the **Edomites**.
Ex 15: 15 The chiefs of **Edom** will be terrified, the leaders of Moab will be
Nu 20: 14 Moses sent messengers from Kadesh to the king of **Edom**,
20: 18 But **Edom** answered: "You may not pass through here; if you try,
20: 20 **Edom** came out against them with a large and powerful army.
20: 21 Since **Edom** refused to let them go through their territory,
20: 23 At Mount Hor, near the border of **Edom** [+824], the LORD said
21: 4 Hor along the route to the Red Sea, to go around **Edom** [+824].
24: 18 **Edom** will be conquered; Seir, his enemy, will be conquered,
33: 37 and camped at Mount Hor, on the border of **Edom** [+824].
34: 3 will include some of the Desert of Zin along the border of **Edom**.
Jos 15: 1 of Judah, clan by clan, extended down to the territory of **Edom**,
15: 21 tribe of Judah in the Negev toward the boundary of **Edom** were:
Jdg 5: 4 when you marched from the land of **Edom**, the earth shook,
11: 17 Then Israel sent messengers to the king of **Edom**, saying,
11: 17 go through your country,' but the king of **Edom** would not listen.
11: 18 traveled through the desert, skirted the lands of **Edom** and Moab,
1Sa 14: 47 Moab, the Ammonites, **Edom**, the kings of Zobah, and the
2Sa 8: 12 **Edom** [BHS 806] and Moab, the Ammonites and the Philistines,
8: 13 eighteen thousand **Edomites** [BHS 806] in the Valley of Salt.
8: 14 He put garrisons throughout **Edom**, and all the Edomites became
8: 14 **[RPH]** and all the Edomites became subject to David.
8: 14 throughout Edom, and all the **Edomites** became subject to David.
1Ki 9: 26 which is near Elath in **Edom** [+824], on the shore of the Red Sea.
11: 14 an adversary, Hadad the Edomite, from the royal line of **Edom**.
11: 15 Earlier when David was fighting with **Edom**, Joab the commander
11: 15 gone up to bury the dead, had struck down all the men in **Edom**.
11: 16 there for six months, until they had destroyed all the men in **Edom**.
22: 47 [22:48] There was then no king in **Edom**; a deputy ruled.
2Ki 3: 8 he asked. "Through the Desert of **Edom**," he answered.
3: 9 king of Israel set out with the king of Judah and the king of **Edom**.
3: 12 and Jehoshaphat and the king of **Edom** went down to him.
3: 20 there it was—water flowing from the direction of **Edom**!
3: 26 seven hundred swordsmen to break through to the king of **Edom**,
8: 20 of Jehoram, **Edom** rebelled against Judah and set up its own king.
8: 21 The **Edomites** surrounded him and his chariot commanders,
8: 22 To this day **Edom** has been in rebellion against Judah. Libnah
14: 7 He was the one who defeated ten thousand **Edomites** in the Valley
14: 10 You have indeed defeated **Edom** and now you are arrogant.
1Ch 1: 43 These were the kings who reigned in **Edom** [+824] before any
1: 51 Hadad also died. The chiefs of **Edom** were: Timna, Alvah, Jetheth,

1Ch 1:54 Magdiel and Iram. These were the chiefs of **Edom**.
18:11 **Edom** and Moab, the Ammonites and the Philistines, and Amalek.
18:12 Abishai son of Zeruiah struck down eighteen thousand **Edomites**
18:13 He put garrisons in **Edom**, and all the Edomites became subject to
18:13 garrisons in Edom, and all the **Edomites** became subject to David.
2Ch 8:17 went to Ezion Geber and Elath on the coast of **Edom** [+824].
20:2 "A vast army is coming against you from **Edom**, [BHS 806]
21:8 of Jehoram, **Edom** rebelled against Judah and set up its own king.
21:9 The **Edomites** surrounded him and his chariot commanders,
21:10 To this day **Edom** has been in rebellion against Judah. Libnah
25:19 You say to yourself that you have defeated **Edom**, and now you
25:20 them over to ⌞Jehoash⌟, because they sought the gods of **Edom**.
Ps 60:T [60:2] struck down twelve thousand **Edomites** in the Valley of
60:8 [60:10] Moab is my washbasin, upon **Edom** I toss my sandal;
60:9 [60:11] me to the fortified city? Who will lead me to **Edom**?
83:6 [83:7] the tents of **Edom** and the Ishmaelites, of Moab
108:9 [108:10] Moab is my washbasin, upon **Edom** I toss my sandal;
108:10 [108:11] me to the fortified city? Who will lead me to **Edom**?
137:7 what the **Edomites** [+1201] did on the day Jerusalem fell.
Isa 11:14 They will lay hands on **Edom** and Moab, and the Ammonites will
34:5 see, it descends in judgment on **Edom**, the people I have totally
34:6 has a sacrifice in Bozrah and a great slaughter in **Edom** [+824].
63:1 Who is this coming from **Edom**, from Bozrah, with his garments
Jer 9:26 [9:25] Egypt, Judah, **Edom**, Ammon, Moab and all who live in
25:21 **Edom**, Moab and Ammon;
27:3 Then send word to the kings of **Edom**, Moab, Ammon, Tyre
40:11 **Edom** and all the other countries heard that the king of Babylon
49:7 Concerning **Edom**: This is what the LORD Almighty says:
49:17 "**Edom** will become an object of horror; all who pass by will be
49:20 Therefore, hear what the LORD has planned against **Edom**,
49:22 In that day the hearts of **Edom's** warriors will be like the heart of a
La 4:21 Rejoice and be glad, O Daughter of **Edom**, you who live in the
4:22 But, O Daughter of **Edom**, he will punish your sin and expose your
Eze 16:57 you are now scorned by the daughters of **Edom** [BHS 806]
25:12 'Because **Edom** took revenge on the house of Judah and became
25:13 I will stretch out my hand against **Edom** and kill its men and their
25:14 I will take vengeance on **Edom** by the hand of my people Israel,
25:14 and they will deal with **Edom** in accordance with my anger
32:29 "**Edom** is there, her kings and all her princes; despite their power,
35:15 You will be desolate, O Mount Seir, you and all of **Edom**.
36:5 against all **Edom**, for with glee and with malice in their hearts they
Da 11:41 **Edom**, Moab and the leaders of Ammon will be delivered from his
Joel 3:19 [4:19] Egypt will be desolate, **Edom** a desert waste, because of
Am 1:6 she took captive whole communities and sold them to **Edom**,
1:9 Because she sold whole communities of captives to **Edom**,
1:11 "For three sins of **Edom**, even for four, I will not turn back ⌞my
2:1 Because he burned, as if to lime, the bones of **Edom's** king,
9:12 so that they may possess the remnant of **Edom** and all the nations
Ob 1:1 This is what the Sovereign LORD says about **Edom**—We have
1:8 declares the LORD, "will I not destroy the wise men of **Edom**,
Mal 1:4 **Edom** may say, "Though we have been crushed, we will rebuild

122 אֲדוֹמִי *'ᵃdômî*, a.g. [12] [√ 121; cf. 131]

Edomite [8], Edomites [4]

Dt 23:7 [23:8] Do not abhor an **Edomite**, for he is your brother. Do not
1Sa 21:7 [21:8] he was Doeg the **Edomite**, Saul's head shepherd.
22:9 But Doeg the **Edomite**, who was standing with Saul's officials,
22:18 the priests." So Doeg the **Edomite** turned and struck them down.
22:22 "That day, when Doeg the **Edomite** was there, I knew he would be
1Ki 11:1 Moabites, Ammonites, **Edomites**, Sidonians and Hittites.
11:14 an adversary, Hadad the **Edomite**, from the royal line of Edom.
11:17 fled to Egypt with some **Edomite** officials who had served his
2Ki 16:6 **Edomites** [K 812] then moved into Elath and have lived there to
2Ch 25:14 When Amaziah returned from slaughtering the **Edomites**,
28:17 The **Edomites** had again come and attacked Judah and carried
Ps 52:T [52:2] When Doeg the **Edomite** had gone to Saul and told him:

123 אָדוֹן *'ādôn*, n.m. [331] [→ 151, 152, 153, 154, 155, 156, 157]

Lord [159], master [105], master's [28], *untranslated* [6], lords [5], Lord's [+4200] [4], masters [4], sir [3], you[s] [+3276] [3], Lord's [2], Sovereign [2], fellow officers [+6269] [1], gods [1], he[s] [+3276] [1], her[s] [+851+2257] [1], him[s] [+3276] [1], husbands [1], owner [1], supervisors [1], the Lord [1], your[s] [+3276] [1]

Ge 18:3 found favor in your eyes, my **lord**, do not pass your servant by.
18:12 "After I am worn out and my **master** is old, will I now have this
19:2 "My **lords**," he said, "please turn aside to your servant's house.
19:18 But Lot said to them, "No, my **lords**, please!
23:6 "**Sir**, listen to us. You are a mighty prince among us. Bury your
23:11 "No, my **lord**," he said. "Listen to me; I give you the field,
23:15 "Listen to me, my **lord**; the land is worth four hundred shekels of
24:9 So the servant put his hand under the thigh of his **master** Abraham
24:10 Then the servant took ten of his **master's** camels and left,
24:10 taking with him all kinds of good things from his **master**.
24:12 Then he prayed, "O LORD, God of my **master** Abraham,
24:12 give me success today, and show kindness to my **master** Abraham.
24:14 By this I will know that you have shown kindness to my **master**."
24:18 "Drink, my **lord**," she said, and quickly lowered the jar to her
24:27 "Praise be to the LORD, the God of my **master** Abraham,
24:27 has not abandoned his kindness and faithfulness to my **master**.
24:27 the LORD has led me on the journey to the house of my **master's**
24:35 The LORD has blessed my **master** abundantly, and he has
24:36 My **master's** wife Sarah has borne him a son in her old age,
24:36 My master's wife Sarah has borne **him**[s] [+3276] a son in her old
24:37 my **master** made me swear an oath, and said, 'You must not get a
24:39 "Then I asked my **master**, 'What if the woman will not come back
24:42 I said, 'O LORD, God of my **master** Abraham, if you will,
24:44 let her be the one the LORD has chosen for my **master's** son.'
24:48 I praised the LORD, the God of my **master** Abraham, who had
24:48 road to get the granddaughter of my **master's** brother for his son.
24:49 Now if you will show kindness and faithfulness to my **master**,
24:51 and go, and let her become the wife of your **master's** son,
24:54 up the next morning, he said, "Send me on my way to my **master**."
24:56 to my journey. Send me on my way so I may go to my **master**."
24:65 "He is my **master**," the servant answered. So she took her veil
31:35 Rachel said to her father, "Don't be angry, my **lord**, that I cannot
32:4 [32:5] "This is what you are to say to my **master** Esau:
32:5 [32:6] Now I am sending this message to my **lord**, that I may
32:18 [32:19] They are a gift sent to my **lord** Esau, and he is coming
33:8 droves I met?" "To find favor in your eyes, my **lord**," he said.
33:13 "My **lord** knows that the children are tender and that I must care
33:14 So let my **lord** go on ahead of his servant, while I move along
33:14 and that of the children, until I come to my **lord** in Seir."
33:15 Jacob asked. "Just let me find favor in the eyes of my **lord**."
39:2 he prospered, and he lived in the house of his Egyptian **master**.
39:3 When his **master** saw that the LORD was with him and that the
39:7 and after a while his **master's** wife took notice of Joseph and said,
39:8 "With me in charge," he told **her**[s] [+851+2257], "my master does
39:8 "my **master** does not concern himself with anything in the house;
39:16 She kept his cloak beside her until his **master** came home.
39:19 When his **master** heard the story his wife told him, saying,
39:20 Joseph's **master** took him and put him in prison, the place where
40:1 and the baker of the king of Egypt offended their **master**,
40:7 officials who were in custody with him in his **master's** house,
42:10 "No, my **lord**," they answered. "Your servants have come to buy
42:30 "The man who is **lord** *over* the land spoke harshly to us
42:33 "Then the man who is **lord** *over* the land said to us, 'This is how I
43:20 "Please, **sir**," they said, "we came down here the first time to buy
44:5 Isn't this the cup my **master** drinks from and also uses for
44:7 But they said to him, "Why does my **lord** say such things?
44:8 So why would we steal silver or gold from your **master's** house?
44:9 and the rest of us will become my **lord's** [+4200] slaves."
44:16 "What can we say to my **lord**?" Judah replied. "What can we say?
44:16 We are now my **lord's** [+4200] slaves—we ourselves and the one
44:18 "Please, my **lord**, let your servant speak a word to my lord.
44:18 "Please, my lord, let your servant speak a word to my **lord**.
44:19 My **lord** asked his servants, 'Do you have a father or a brother?'
44:20 we answered, **[RPH]** 'We have an aged father, and there is a
44:22 And we said to my **lord**, 'The boy cannot leave his father;
44:24 to your servant my father, we told him what my **lord** had said.
44:33 please let your servant remain here as my **lord's** [+4200] slave in
45:8 to Pharaoh, **lord** of his entire household and ruler of all Egypt.
45:9 God has made me **lord** of all Egypt. Come down to me;
47:18 "We cannot hide from our **lord** the fact that since our money is
47:18 our money is gone and our livestock belongs to **you**[s] [+3276],
47:18 there is nothing left for our **lord** except our bodies and our land.
47:25 "May we find favor in the eyes of our **lord**; we will be in bondage
Ex 21:4 If his **master** gives him a wife and she bears him sons
21:4 the woman and her children shall belong to her **master**,
21:5 'I love my **master** and my wife and children and do not want to go
21:6 his **master** must take him before the judges. He shall take him to
21:6 to the door or the doorpost and **[RPH]** pierce his ear with an awl.
21:8 If she does not please the **master** who has selected her for himself,
21:32 the owner must pay thirty shekels of silver to the **master** *of* the
23:17 "Three times a year all the men are to appear before the **Sovereign**
32:22 "Do not be angry, my **lord**," Aaron answered. "You know how
34:23 Three times a year all your men are to appear before the **Sovereign**
Nu 11:28 aide since youth, spoke up and said, "Moses, my **lord**, stop them!"
12:11 he said to Moses, "Please, my **lord**, do not hold against us the sin
32:25 said to Moses, "We your servants will do as our **lord** commands.
32:27 will cross over to fight before the LORD, just as our **lord** says."
36:2 "When the LORD commanded my **lord** to give the land as an
36:2 he ordered **you**[s] [+3276] to give the inheritance of our brother
Dt 10:17 For the LORD your God is God of gods and **Lord** *of* lords,
10:17 For the LORD your God is God of gods and Lord of **lords**,
23:15 [23:16] with you, **[RPH]** do not hand him over to his master.

Dt 23:15 [23:16] refuge with you, do not hand him over to his **master**.
Jos 3:11 the ark of the covenant of the **Lord** *of* all the earth will go into the
3:13 the **Lord** *of* all the earth—set foot in the Jordan, its waters flowing
5:14 asked him, "What message does my **Lord** have for his servant?"
Jdg 3:25 unlocked them. There they saw their **lord** fallen to the floor, dead.
4:18 out to meet Sisera and said to him, "Come, my **lord**, come right in.
6:13 "But **sir**," Gideon replied, "if the LORD is with us, why has all
19:11 the day was almost gone, the servant said to his **master**, "Come,
19:12 His **master** replied, "No. We won't go into an alien city,
19:26 At daybreak the woman went back to the house where her **master**
19:27 When her **master** got up in the morning and opened the door of the
Ru 2:13 "May I continue to find favor in your eyes, my **lord**," she said.
1Sa 1:15 "Not so, my **lord**," Hannah replied, "I am a woman who is deeply
1:26 she said to him, "As surely as you live, my **lord**, I am the woman
1:26 **[RPH]** I am the woman who stood here beside you praying to the
16:16 Let our **lord** command his servants here to search for someone
20:38 The boy picked up the arrow and returned to his **master**.
22:12 "Listen now, son of Ahitub." "Yes, my **lord**," he answered.
24:6 [24:7] LORD forbid that I should do such a thing to my **master**,
24:8 [24:9] out of the cave and called out to Saul, "My **lord** the king!"
24:10 [24:11] I said, 'I will not lift my hand against my **master**,
25:10 Many servants are breaking away from their **masters** these days.
25:14 "David sent messengers from the desert to give our **master** his
25:17 because disaster is hanging over our **master** and his whole
25:24 fell at his feet and said: "My **lord**, let the blame be on me alone.
25:25 May my **lord** pay no attention to that wicked man Nabal. He is just
25:25 But as for me, your servant, I did not see the men my **master** sent.
25:26 my **master**, from bloodshed and from avenging yourself with your
25:26 your enemies and all who intend to harm my **master** be like Nabal.
25:27 And let this gift, which your servant has brought to my **master**,
25:27 to my master, be given to the men who follow **you**[s] [+3276].
25:28 the LORD will certainly make a lasting dynasty for my **master**,
25:28 for my master, because **he**[s] [+3276] fights the LORD's battles.
25:29 the life of my **master** will be bound securely in the bundle of the
25:30 When the LORD has done for my **master** every good thing he
25:31 my **master** will not have on his conscience the staggering burden
25:31 **[RPH]** And when the LORD has brought my master success,
25:31 when the LORD has brought my **master** success, remember your
25:41 ready to serve you and wash the feet of my **master's** servants."
26:15 is like you in Israel? Why didn't you guard your **lord** the king?
26:15 your lord the king? Someone came to destroy your **lord** the king.
26:16 because you did not guard your **master**, the LORD's anointed.
26:17 David my son?" David replied, "Yes it is, my **lord** the king."
26:18 he added, "Why is my **lord** pursuing his servant? What have I
26:19 Now let my **lord** the king listen to his servant's words.
29:4 How better could he regain his **master's** favor than by taking the
29:8 Why can't I go and fight against the enemies of my **lord** the king?"
29:10 along with your **master's** servants who have come with you,
30:13 My **master** abandoned me when I became ill three days ago.
30:15 God that you will not kill me or hand me over to my **master**,
2Sa 1:10 and the band on his arm and have brought them here to my **lord**."
2:5 you for showing this kindness to Saul your **master** by burying him.
2:7 Now then, be strong and brave, for Saul your **master** is dead,
3:21 "Let me go at once and assemble all Israel for my **lord** the king,
4:8 This day the LORD has avenged my **lord** the king against Saul
9:9 "I have given your **master's** grandson everything that belonged to
9:10 in the crops, so that your **master's** grandson may be provided for.
9:10 Mephibosheth, grandson of your **master**, will always eat at my
9:11 "Your servant will do whatever my **lord** the king commands his
10:3 the Ammonite nobles said to Hanun their **lord**, "Do you think
11:9 Uriah slept at the entrance to the palace with all his **master's**
11:11 my **master** Joab and my lord's men are camped in the open fields.
11:11 my master Joab and my **lord's** men are camped in the open fields.
11:13 Uriah went out to sleep on his mat among his **master's** servants;
12:8 I gave your **master's** house to you, and your master's wives into
12:8 master's house to you, and your **master's** wives into your arms.
13:32 "My **lord** should not think that they killed all the princes;
13:33 My **lord** the king should not be concerned about the report that all
14:9 "My **lord** the king, let the blame rest on me and on my father's
14:12 woman said, "Let your servant speak a word to my **lord** the king."
14:15 "And now I have come to say this to my **lord** the king
14:17 servant says, 'May the word of my **lord** the king bring me rest,
14:17 for my **lord** the king is like an angel of God in discerning good
14:18 going to ask you." "Let my **lord** the king speak," the woman said.
14:19 The woman answered, "As surely as you live, my **lord** the king,
14:19 turn to the right or to the left from anything my **lord** the king says.
14:20 My **lord** has wisdom like that of an angel of God—he knows
14:22 my **lord** the king, because the king has granted his servant's
15:15 "Your servants are ready to do whatever our **lord** the king
15:21 "As surely as the LORD lives, and as my **lord** the king lives,
15:21 wherever my **lord** the king may be, whether it means life or death,
16:3 The king then asked, "Where is your **master's** grandson?"
16:4 Ziba said. "May I find favor in your eyes, my **lord** the king."
16:9 to the king, "Why should this dead dog curse my **lord** the king?
18:28 up the men who lifted their hands against my **lord** the king."
18:31 the Cushite arrived and said, "My **lord** the king, hear the good
18:32 "May the enemies of my **lord** the king and all who rise up to harm
19:19 [19:20] said to him, "May my **lord** not hold me guilty. Do not
19:19 [19:20] did wrong on the day my **lord** the king left Jerusalem.
19:20 [19:21] of Joseph to come down and meet my **lord** the king."
19:26 [19:27] He said, "My **lord** the king, since I your servant am lame,
19:27 [19:28] he has slandered your servant to my **lord** the king. My
19:27 [19:28] My **lord** the king is like an angel of God; so do whatever
19:28 [19:29] deserved nothing but death from my **lord** the king,
19:30 [19:31] now that my **lord** the king has arrived home safely."
19:35 [19:36] Why should your servant be an added burden to my **lord**
19:37 [19:38] Let him cross over with my **lord** the king.
20:6 Take your **master's** men and pursue him, or he will find fortified
24:3 a hundred times over, and may the eyes of my **lord** the king see it.
24:3 But why does my **lord** the king want to do such a thing?"
24:21 Araunah said, "Why has my **lord** the king come to his servant?"
24:22 "Let my **lord** the king take whatever pleases him and offer it up.
1Ki 1:2 "Let us look for **[RPH]** a young virgin to attend the king
1:2 She can lie beside him so that our **lord** the king may keep warm."
1:11 of Haggith, has become king without our **lord** David's knowing it?
1:13 Go in to King David and say to him, 'My **lord** the king, did you not
1:17 She said to him, "My **lord**, you yourself swore to me your servant
1:18 has become king, and you, my **lord** the king, do not know about it.
1:20 My **lord** the king, the eyes of all Israel are on you, to learn from
1:20 to learn from you who will sit on the throne of my **lord** the king
1:21 as soon as my **lord** the king is laid to rest with his fathers,
1:24 Nathan said, "Have you, my **lord** the king, declared that Adonijah
1:27 Is this something my **lord** the king has done without letting his
1:27 know who should sit on the throne of my **lord** the king after him?"
1:31 before the king, said, "May my **lord** King David live forever!"
1:33 "Take your **lord's** servants with you and set Solomon my son on
1:36 May the LORD, the God of my **lord** the king, so declare it.
1:37 As the LORD was with my **lord** the king, so may he be with
1:37 his throne even greater than the throne of my **lord** King David!"
1:43 "Our **lord** King David has made Solomon king.
1:47 the royal officials have come to congratulate our **lord** King David,
2:38 say is good. Your servant will do as my **lord** the king has said."
3:17 of them said, "My **lord**, this woman and I live in the same house.
3:26 with compassion for her son and said to the king, "Please, my **lord**,
11:23 Rezon son of Eliada, who had fled from his **master**,
12:27 they will again give their allegiance to their **lord**, Rehoboam king
16:24 it Samaria, after Shemer, the name of the former **owner** *of* the hill.
18:7 down to the ground, and said, "Is it really you, my **lord** Elijah?"
18:8 "Yes," he replied. "Go tell your **master**, 'Elijah is here.' "
18:10 or kingdom where my **master** has not sent someone to look for
18:11 But now you tell me to go to my **master** and say, 'Elijah is here.'
18:13 Haven't you heard, my **lord**, what I did while Jezebel was killing
18:14 And now you tell me to go to my **master** and say, 'Elijah is here.'
20:4 The king of Israel answered, "Just as you say, my **lord** the king.
20:9 So he replied to Ben-Hadad's messengers, "Tell my **lord** the king,
22:17 a shepherd, and the LORD said, 'These people have no **master**.
2Ki 2:3 "Do you know that the LORD is going to take your **master** from
2:5 "Do you know that the LORD is going to take your **master** from
2:16 have fifty able men. Let them go and look for your **master**.
2:19 "Look, our **lord**, this town is well situated, as you can see,
4:16 "No, my **lord**," she objected. "Don't mislead your servant,
4:28 "Did I ask you for a son, my **lord**?" she said. "Didn't I tell you,
5:1 He was a great man in the sight of his **master** and highly regarded,
5:3 "If only my **master** would see the prophet who is in Samaria!
5:4 Naaman went to his **master** and told him what the girl from Israel
5:18 When my **master** enters the temple of Rimmon to bow down
5:20 to himself, "My **master** was too easy on Naaman, this Aramean,
5:22 "My **master** sent me to say, 'Two young men from the company of
5:25 he went in and stood before his **master** Elisha. "Where have you
6:5 fell into the water. "Oh, my **lord**," he cried out, "it was borrowed!"
6:12 "None of us, my **lord** the king," said one of his officers,
6:15 the city. "Oh, my **lord**, what shall we do?" the servant asked.
6:22 so that they may eat and drink and then go back to their **master**."
6:23 he sent them away, and they returned to their **master**.
6:26 on the wall, a woman cried to him, "Help me, my **lord** the king!"
6:32 Is not the sound of his **master's** footsteps behind him?"
8:5 Gehazi said, "This is the woman, my **lord** the king, and this is her
8:12 "Why is my **lord** weeping?" asked Hazael. "Because I know the
8:14 Hazael left Elisha and returned to his **master**. When Ben-Hadad
9:7 You are to destroy the house of Ahab your **master**, and I will
9:11 When Jehu went out to his **fellow officers** [+6269], one of them
9:31 "Have you come in peace, Zimri, you murderer of your **master**?"
10:2 since your **master's** sons are with you and you have chariots
10:3 choose the best and most worthy of your **master's** sons and set
10:3 him on his father's throne. Then fight for your **master's** house."
10:6 take the heads of your **master's** sons and come to me in Jezreel by
10:9 It was I who conspired against my **master** and killed him,
18:23 " 'Come now, make a bargain with my **master**, the king of Assyria:

2Ki 18:24 How can you repulse one officer of the least of my **master's**
18:27 "Was it only to your **master** and you that my master sent me to say
18:27 to your master and you that my **master** sent me to say these things,
19: 4 whom his **master**, the king of Assyria, has sent to ridicule the
19: 6 Isaiah said to them, "Tell your **master**, 'This is what the LORD
1Ch 12:19 [12:20] "It will cost us our heads if he deserts to his **master**
21: 3 My **lord** the king, are they not all my lord's subjects? Why does
21: 3 My lord the king, are they not all my **lord's** [+4200] subjects?
21: 3 they not all my lord's subjects? Why does my **lord** want to do this?
21:23 Let my **lord** the king do whatever pleases him. Look, I will give
2Ch 2:14 [2:13] will work with your craftsmen and with those of my **lord**,
2:15 [2:14] "Now let my **lord** send his servants the wheat and barley
13: 6 an official of Solomon son of David, rebelled against his **master**.
18:16 a shepherd, and the LORD said, 'These people have no **master**.
Ezr 10: 3 in accordance with the counsel of my **lord** and of those who fear
Ne 3: 5 would not put their shoulders to the work under their **supervisors**.
Job 3:19 and the great are there, and the slave is freed from his **master**.
Ps 8: 1 [8:2] O LORD, our **Lord**, how majestic is your name in all the
8: 9 [8:10] O LORD, our **Lord**, how majestic is your name in all the
12: 4 [12:5] with our tongues; we own our lips—who is our **master**?"
45:11 [45:12] enthralled by your beauty; honor him, for he is your **lord**.
97: 5 melt like wax before the LORD, before the **Lord** *of* all the earth.
105:21 He made him **master** of his household, ruler over all he possessed,
110: 1 The LORD says to my **Lord**: "Sit at my right hand until I make
114: 7 Tremble, O earth, at the presence of **the Lord**, at the presence of
123: 2 As the eyes of slaves look to the hand of their **master**, as the eyes
136: 3 Give thanks to the Lord of **lords**: *His love endures*
Pr 25:13 to those who send him; he refreshes the spirit of his **masters**.
27:18 eat its fruit, and he who looks after his **master** will be honored.
30:10 "Do not slander a servant to his **master**, or he will curse you,
Isa 1:24 Therefore the **Lord**, the LORD Almighty, the Mighty One of
3: 1 See now, the **Lord**, the LORD Almighty, is about to take from
10:16 Therefore, the **Lord**, the LORD Almighty, will send a wasting
10:33 See, the **Lord**, the LORD Almighty, will lop off the boughs with
19: 4 I will hand the Egyptians over to the power of a cruel **master**,
19: 4 will rule over them," declares the **Lord**, the LORD Almighty.
21: 8 the lookout shouted, "Day after day, my **lord**, I stand on the
22:18 chariots will remain—you disgrace to your **master's** house!
24: 2 for **master** as for servant, for mistress as for maid, for seller as for
26:13 O LORD, our God, other **lords** besides you have ruled over us,
36: 8 " 'Come now, make a bargain with my **master**, the king of Assyria:
36: 9 can you repulse one officer of the least of my **master's** officials,
36:12 "Was it only to your **master** and you that my master sent me to say
36:12 to your master and you that my **master** sent me to say these things,
37: 4 whom his **master**, the king of Assyria, has sent to ridicule the
37: 6 Isaiah said to them, "Tell your **master**, 'This is what the LORD
Jer 22:18 will not mourn for him: 'Alas, my **master**! Alas, his splendor!'
27: 4 Give them a message for their **masters** and say, 'This is what the
27: 4 the God of Israel, says: "Tell this to your **masters**:
34: 5 they will make a fire in your honor and lament, "Alas, O **master**!"
37:20 now, my **lord** the king, please listen. Let me bring my petition
38: 9 "My **lord** the king, these men have acted wickedly in all they have
Da 1:10 but the official told Daniel, "I am afraid of my **lord** the king,
10:16 with anguish because of the vision, my **lord**, and I am helpless.
10:17 How can I, **your**[s] [+3276] servant, talk with you, my lord?
10:17 How can I, your servant, talk with you, my **lord**? My strength is
10:19 he spoke to me, I was strengthened and said, "Speak, my **lord**,
12: 8 So I asked, "My **lord**, what will the outcome of all this be?"
Am 4: 1 oppress the poor and crush the needy and say to your **husbands**,
Mic 4:13 gains to the LORD, their wealth to the **Lord** *of* all the earth.
Zep 1: 9 who fill the temple of their **gods** with violence and deceit.
Zec 1: 9 I asked, "What are these, my **lord**?" The angel who was talking
4: 4 I asked the angel who talked with me, "What are these, my **lord**?"
4: 5 "Do you not know what these are?" "No, my **lord**," I replied.
4:13 "Do you not know what these are?" "No, my **lord**," I said.
4:14 "These are the two who are anointed to serve the **Lord** *of* all the
6: 4 the angel who was speaking to me, "What are these, my **lord**?"
6: 5 going out from standing in the presence of the **Lord** *of* the whole
Mal 1: 6 "A son honors his father, and a servant his **master**. If I am a father,
1: 6 If I am a **master**, where is the respect due me?" says the LORD
3: 1 Then suddenly the **Lord** you are seeking will come to his temple;

124 אַדּוֹן *'addôn*, n.pr.loc. [1] [cf. 150]

Addon [1]

Ne 7:61 the towns of Tel Melah, Tel Harsha, Kerub, **Addon** and Immer,

125 אֲדֹנִיָּה *'ᵃdôniyyâ*, n.pr.m. Not used in NIV/BHS [→ 3207]

126 אֲדוֹרַיִם *'ᵃdôrayim*, n.pr.m. [1] [√ 1884?]

Adoraim [1]

2Ch 11: 9 **Adoraim**, Lachish, Azekah,

127 אֲדוֹרָם *'ᵃdôrām*, n.pr.m. Not used in NIV/BHS [√ 157]

128 אֹדוֹת *'ōdôt*, n.f. [11]

because of [+6584] [4], about [+6584] [3], *untranslated* [2], concerned [1], for sake [+6584] [1]

Ge 21:11 matter distressed Abraham greatly because it **concerned** his son.
21:25 Abraham complained to Abimelech **about** [+6584] a well of water
26:32 servants came and told him **about** [+6584] the well they had dug.
Ex 18: 8 the Egyptians **for** Israel's **sake** [+6584] and about all the hardships
Nu 12: 1 began to talk against Moses **because of** [+6584] his Cushite wife,
13:24 **because of** [+6584] the cluster of grapes the Israelites cut off there.
Jos 14: 6 to Moses the man of God at Kadesh Barnea **about** [+6584] you
14: 6 the man of God at Kadesh Barnea about you and **[RPH]** me.
Jdg 6: 7 the Israelites cried to the LORD **because of** [+6584] Midian,
2Sa 13:16 **[NIE]** "Sending me away would be a greater wrong than what
Jer 3: 8 of divorce and sent her away **because of** [+6584] all her adulteries.

129 אַדִּיר *'addîr*, a. [27] [√ 158]

nobles [7], mighty [6], leaders [3], majestic [3], Mighty One [2], glorious [1], leader [1], mightier [1], picked troops [1], splendid [1], stately [1]

Ex 15:10 the sea covered them. They sank like lead in the **mighty** waters.
Jdg 5:13 "Then the men who were left came down to the **nobles**; the people
5:25 him milk; in a bowl fit for **nobles** she brought him curdled milk.
1Sa 4: 8 Who will deliver us from the hand of these **mighty** gods?
2Ch 23:20 the **nobles**, the rulers of the people and all the people of the land
Ne 3: 5 their **nobles** would not put their shoulders to the work under their
10:29 [10:30] all these now join their brothers the **nobles**, and bind
Ps 8: 1 [8:2] our Lord, how **majestic** is your name in all the earth!
8: 9 [8:10] our Lord, how **majestic** is your name in all the earth!
16: 3 in the land, they are the **glorious** *ones* in whom is all my delight.
76: 4 [76:5] with light, more **majestic** than mountains rich with game.
93: 4 thunder of the great waters, **mightier** than the breakers of the sea—
93: 4 than the breakers of the sea—the LORD on high is **mighty**.
136:18 and killed **mighty** kings—*His love endures forever.*
Isa 10:34 thickets with an ax; Lebanon will fall before the **Mighty One**.
33:21 There the LORD will be our **Mighty One**. It will be like a place
33:21 No galley with oars will ride them, no **mighty** ship will sail them.
Jer 14: 3 The **nobles** send their servants for water; they go to the cisterns
25:34 and wail, you shepherds; roll in the dust, you **leaders** *of* the flock.
25:35 have nowhere to flee, the **leaders** *of* the flock no place to escape.
25:36 the cry of the shepherds, the wailing of the **leaders** *of* the flock,
30:21 Their **leader** will be one of their own; their ruler will arise from
Eze 17:23 will produce branches and bear fruit and become a **splendid** cedar.
32:18 to the earth below both her and the daughters of **mighty** nations,
Na 2: 5 [2:6] He summons his **picked troops**, yet they stumble on their
3:18 of Assyria, your shepherds slumber; your **nobles** lie down to rest.
Zec 11: 2 O pine tree, for the cedar has fallen; the **stately** trees are ruined!

130 אֲדַלְיָא *'ᵃdalyā'*, n.pr.m. [1]

Adalia [1]

Est 9: 8 Poratha, **Adalia**, Aridatha,

131 אדם *'ādēm*, v. [10] [→ 121, 122, 132, 133?, 134, 135, 136, 137, 138, 139, 140, 141, 143, 145, 147]

dyed red [6], red [3], ruddy [1]

Ex 25: 5 [E] ram skins **dyed red** and hides of sea cows; acacia wood;
26:14 [E] Make for the tent a covering of ram skins **dyed red**, and over
35: 7 [E] ram skins **dyed red** and hides of sea cows; acacia wood;
35:23 [E] ram skins **dyed red** or hides of sea cows brought them.
36:19 [E] they made for the tent a covering of ram skins **dyed red**,
39:34 [E] the covering of ram skins **dyed red**, the covering of hides of
Pr 23:31 [F] Do not gaze at wine when *it is* **red**, when it sparkles in the
Isa 1:18 [G] though *they are* **red** as crimson, they shall be like wool.
La 4: 7 [A] and whiter than milk, their bodies more **ruddy** than rubies,
Na 2: 3 [2:4] [E] The shields of his soldiers *are* **red**; the warriors are

132 אָדָם¹ *'ādām¹*, n.m. [549] [√ 131]

man [278], men [82], men [+1201] [23], people [20], human [13], man's [13], one [13], man [+1201] [10], mankind [10], anyone [9], *untranslated* [8], mankind [+1201] [6], person [5], men's [3], persons [3], someone [3], body [2], everyone [2], man's [+1201] [2], man's [+4200] [2], mortal men [+1201] [2], all mankind [+1201] [1], all men [+1201+2021] [1], another[s] [+2021] [1], any [1], anyone [+3972] [1], charioteers [+8207] [1], deserted [+401+4946] [1], else[s] [1], every [1], everyone [+2021+3972] [1], everyone [+3972] [1], giver[s] [1], he[s] [1], him[s] [+2021] [1], his[s] [+2021] [1], his[s] [1], human [+1201] [1], human being [1], low [+1201] [1], low among men [+1201] [1], lowborn men [+1201] [1], man-made [+3338+5126] [1], men [+1201+2021] [1], mortals [1], natural [+2021+3869+3972] [1], needy

[+36] [1], nobody [+4202] [1], other[s] [1], others[s] [1], people [+1201] [1], people [+5883] [1], rabble [+8044] [1], reflects the man [+2021+4200] [1], scoundrel [+1175] [1], slaves [+5883] [1], son [1], successor [+339+995+8611] [1], they[s] [+2021] [1], those[s] [1], whoever [+2021+3972] [1]

Ge 1:26 Then God said, "Let us make **man** in our image, in our likeness,
1:27 So God created **man** in his own image, in the image of God he
2: 5 sent rain on the earth and there was no **man** to work the ground,
2: 7 the LORD God formed the **man** from the dust of the ground
2: 7 his nostrils the breath of life, and the **man** became a living being.
2: 8 in the east, in Eden; and there he put the **man** he had formed.
2:15 The LORD God took the **man** and put him in the Garden of Eden
2:16 the LORD God commanded the **man**, "You are free to eat from
2:18 The LORD God said, "It is not good for the **man** to be alone.
2:19 He brought them to the **man** to see what he would name them;
2:19 whatever the **man** called each living creature, that was its name.
2:20 So the **man** gave names to all the livestock, the birds of the air
2:21 So the LORD God caused the **man** to fall into a deep sleep;
2:22 God made a woman from the rib he had taken out of the **man**,
2:22 the rib he had taken out of the man, and he brought her to the **man**.
2:23 The **man** said, "This is now bone of my bones and flesh of my
2:25 The **man** and his wife were both naked, and they felt no shame.
3: 8 the **man** and his wife heard the sound of the LORD God as he
3: 9 But the LORD God called to the **man**, "Where are you?"
3:12 The **man** said, "The woman you put here with me—she gave me
3:22 "The **man** has now become like one of us, knowing good and evil.
3:24 After he drove the **man** out, he placed on the east side of the
5: 1 When God created **man**, he made him in the likeness of God.
5: 2 blessed them. And when they were created, he called them "**man**."
6: 1 When **men** began to increase in number on the earth and daughters
6: 2 the sons of God saw that the daughters of **men** were beautiful,
6: 3 "My Spirit will not contend with **man** forever, for he is mortal;
6: 4 when the sons of God went to the daughters of **men** and had
6: 5 The LORD saw how great **man's** wickedness on the earth had
6: 6 The LORD was grieved that he had made **man** on the earth,
6: 7 So the LORD said, "I will wipe **mankind**, whom I have created,
6: 7 **men** and animals, and creatures that move along the ground,
7:21 all the creatures that swarm over the earth, and all **mankind**.
7:23 **men** and animals and the creatures that move along the ground
8:21 "Never again will I curse the ground because of **man**, even though
8:21 even though every inclination of **his**[s] [+2021] heart is evil from
9: 5 from each **man**, too, I will demand an accounting for the life of his
9: 5 I will demand an accounting for the life of his *fellow* **man**.
9: 6 "Whoever sheds the blood of **man**, by man shall his blood be shed;
9: 6 "Whoever sheds the blood of man, by **man** shall his blood be shed;
9: 6 his blood be shed; for in the image of God has God made **man**.
11: 5 to see the city and the tower that the **men** [+1201] were building.
16:12 He will be a wild donkey of a **man**; his hand will be against
Ex 4:11 The LORD said to him, "Who gave **man** his mouth? Who makes
8:17 [8:13] the dust of the ground, gnats came upon **men** and animals.
8:18 [8:14] they could not. And the gnats were on **men** and animals.
9: 9 festering boils will break out on **men** and animals throughout the
9:10 it into the air, and festering boils broke out on **men** and animals.
9:19 because the hail will fall on every **man** and animal that has not
9:22 on **men** and animals and on everything growing in the fields of
9:25 both **men** and animals; it beat down everything growing in the
12:12 and strike down every firstborn—both **men** and animals—
13: 2 among the Israelites belongs to me, whether **man** or animal."
13:13 break its neck. Redeem every firstborn **[NIE]** among your sons.
13:15 the LORD killed every firstborn in Egypt, both **man** and animal.
30:32 Do not pour it on **men's** bodies and do not make any oil with the
33:20 "you cannot see my face, for no **one** may see me and live."
Lev 1: 2 'When **any** of you brings an offering to the LORD, bring as your
5: 3 " 'Or if he touches **human** uncleanness—anything that would
5: 4 or evil—in any matter **one** might carelessly swear about—
6: 3 [5:22] or if he commits any such sin that **people** may do—
7:21 whether **human** uncleanness or an unclean animal or any unclean,
13: 2 "When **anyone** has a swelling or a rash or a bright spot on his skin
13: 9 "When **anyone** has an infectious skin disease, he must be brought
16:17 No **one** is to be in the Tent of Meeting from the time Aaron goes in
18: 5 and laws, for the **man** who obeys them will live by them.
22: 5 or *any* **person** who makes him unclean, whatever the uncleanness
24:17 " 'If anyone takes the life of a **human being**, he must be put to
24:20 tooth for tooth. As he has injured the **other**[s], so he is to be injured.
24:21 make restitution, but whoever kills a **man** must be put to death.
27:28 whether **man** or animal or family land—may be sold or redeemed;
27:29 " 'No **person** devoted to destruction may be ransomed; he must be
Nu 3:13 apart for myself every firstborn in Israel, whether **man** or animal.
5: 6 'When a man or woman wrongs **another**[s] [+2021] in any way and
8:17 Every firstborn male in Israel, whether **man** or animal, is mine.
9: 6 they were ceremonially unclean on account of a dead **body**.
9: 7 said to Moses, "We have become unclean because of a dead **body**,
12: 3 more humble than anyone **else**[s] on the face of the earth.)
16:29 If these men die a **natural** [+2021+3869+3972] death and
16:29 a natural death and experience only what usually happens to **men**,
16:32 with their households and all Korah's **men** and all their
18:15 The first offspring of every womb, both **man** and animal, that is
18:15 you must redeem every firstborn **son** and every firstborn male of
19:11 "Whoever touches the dead body of **anyone** [+3972] will be
19:13 Whoever touches the dead body of **anyone** and fails to purify
19:14 "This is the law that applies when a **person** dies in a tent:
19:16 or anyone who touches a **human** bone or a grave, will be unclean
23:19 God is not a man, that he should lie, nor a son of **man**, that he
31:11 took all the plunder and spoils, including the **people** and animals,
31:26 and the family heads of the community are to count all the **people**
31:28 five hundred, whether **persons**, cattle, donkeys, sheep or goats.
31:30 whether **persons**, cattle, donkeys, sheep, goats or other animals.
31:35 and 32,000 **[RPH]** women who had never slept with a man.
31:40 16,000 **people**, of which the tribute for the LORD was 32.
31:46 and 16,000 **people**.
31:47 Moses selected one out of every fifty **persons** and animals,
Dt 4:28 There you will worship **man-made** [+3338+5126] gods of wood
4:32 long before your time, from the day God created **man** on the earth;
5:24 Today we have seen that a **man** can live even if God speaks with
8: 3 to teach you that **man** does not live on bread alone but on every
8: 3 on every word that comes from the mouth of the LORD. **[RPH]**
20:19 Are the trees of the field **people**, that you should besiege them?
32: 8 nations their inheritance, when he divided all **mankind** [+1201],
Jos 11:14 all the **people** they put to the sword until they completely
14:15 Arba after Arba, who was the greatest **man** among the Anakites.)
Jdg 16: 7 that have not been dried, I'll become as weak as any other **man**."
16:11 that have never been used, I'll become as weak as any other **man**."
16:13 it with the pin, I'll become as weak as any other **man**." [BHS-]
16:17 would leave me, and I would become as weak as any other **man**."
18: 7 way from the Sidonians and had no relationship with **anyone** else.
18:28 a long way from Sidon and had no relationship with **anyone** else.
1Sa 15:29 his mind; for he is not a **man**, that he should change his mind."
16: 7 The LORD does not look at the things **man** looks at.
16: 7 **Man** looks at the outward appearance, but the LORD looks at the
17:32 said to Saul, "Let no **one** lose heart on account of this Philistine;
24: 9 [24:10] He said to Saul, "Why do you listen when **men** say,
25:29 Even though **someone** is pursuing you to take your life, the life of
26:19 If, however, **men** [+1201+2021] have done it, may they be cursed
2Sa 7:14 him with the rod of men, with floggings inflicted by **men** [+1201].
7:19 Is this your usual way of dealing with **man**, O Sovereign LORD?
23: 3 'When one rules over **men** in righteousness, when he rules in the
24:14 his mercy is great; but do not let me fall into the hands of **men**."
1Ki 4:31 [5:11] He was wiser than any other **man**, including Ethan the
8:38 a prayer or plea is made by any **[NIE]** of your people Israel—
8:39 know his heart (for you alone know the hearts of all **men** [+1201]),
8:46 they sin against you—for there is no **one** who does not sin—
13: 2 make offerings here, and **human** bones will be burned on you.' "
2Ki 7:10 not a sound of **anyone**—only tethered horses and donkeys,
19:18 were not gods but only wood and stone, fashioned by **men's** hands.
23:14 down the Asherah poles and covered the sites with **human** bones.
23:20 those high places on the altars and burned **human** bones on them.
1Ch 5:21 They also took one hundred thousand **people** [+5883] captive,
17:17 You have looked on me as though I were the most exalted of **men**,
21:13 mercy is very great; but do not let me fall into the hands of **men**."
29: 1 because this palatial structure is not for **man** but for the LORD
2Ch 6:18 "But will God really dwell on earth with **men**? The heavens,
6:29 a prayer or plea is made by any of **[NIE]** your people Israel—
6:30 know his heart (for you alone know the hearts of **men** [+1201]),
6:36 they sin against you—for there is no **one** who does not sin—
19: 6 you do, because you are not judging for **man** but for the LORD,
32:19 gods of the other peoples of the world—the work of **men's** hands.
Ne 2:10 they were very much disturbed that **someone** had come to promote
2:12 I had not told **anyone** what my God had put in my heart to do for
9:29 your ordinances, by which a **man** will live if he obeys them.
Job 5: 7 Yet **man** is born to trouble as surely as sparks fly upward.
7:20 If I have sinned, what have I done to you, O watcher of **men**?
11:12 more become wise than a wild donkey's colt can be born a **man**.
14: 1 "**Man** born of woman is of few days and full of trouble.
14:10 But man dies and is laid low; **he**[s] breathes his last and is no more.
15: 7 "Are you the first **man** ever born? Were you brought forth before
16:21 on behalf of a man he pleads with God as a **man** [+1201] pleads
20: 4 it has been from of old, ever since **man** was placed on the earth,
20:29 Such is the fate God allots the **[NIE]** wicked, the heritage
21: 4 "Is my complaint directed to **man**? Why should I not be impatient?
21:33 all **men** follow after him, and a countless throng goes before him.
25: 6 who is but a maggot—a son of **man**, who is only a worm!"
27:13 "Here is the fate God allots to the **[NIE]** wicked, the heritage a
28:28 And he said to **man**, 'The fear of the Lord—that is wisdom,
31:33 if I have concealed my sin as **men** do, by hiding my guilt in my
32:21 I will show partiality to no one, nor will I flatter *any* **man**;
33:17 to turn **man** from wrongdoing and keep him from pride,
33:23 one out of a thousand, to tell a **man** what is right for him,

Job 34: 11 He repays a **man** for what he has done; he brings upon him what
34: 15 mankind would perish together and **man** would return to the dust.
34: 29 his face, who can see him? Yet he is over **man** and nation alike,
34: 30 to keep a godless **man** from ruling, from laying snares for the
35: 8 a man like yourself, and your righteousness only the sons of **men**.
36: 25 All **mankind** has seen it; men gaze on it from afar.
36: 28 pour down their moisture and abundant showers fall on **mankind**.
37: 7 has made may know his work, he stops every **man** from his labor.
38: 26 to water a land where no man lives, a desert with no **one** in it,
Ps 8: 4 [8:5] are mindful of him, the son of **man** that you care for him?
11: 4 He observes the sons of **men**; his eyes examine them.
12: 1 [12:2] the faithful have vanished from among **men** [+1201].
12: 8 [12:9] about when what is vile is honored among **men** [+1201].
14: 2 The LORD looks down from heaven on the sons of **men** to see if
17: 4 As for the deeds of **men**—by the word of your lips I have kept
21: 10 [21:11] from the earth, their posterity from **mankind** [+1201].
22: 6 [22:7] and not a man, scorned by **men** and despised by the people.
31: 19 [31:20] which you bestow in the sight of **men** [+1201] on those
32: 2 Blessed is the **man** whose sin the LORD does not count against
33: 13 heaven the LORD looks down and sees all **mankind** [+1201];
36: 6 [36:7] great deep. O LORD, you preserve both **man** and beast.
36: 7 [36:8] **low among men** [+1201] find refuge in the shadow of your
39: 5 [39:6] before you. Each **man's** life is but a breath. *Selah*
39: 11 [39:12] their wealth like a moth—each **man** is but a breath.
45: 2 [45:3] You are the most excellent of **men** [+1201] and your lips
49: 2 [49:3] both **low** [+1201] and high, rich and poor alike:
49: 12 [49:13] **man**, despite his riches, does not endure; he is like the
49: 20 [49:21] A **man** who has riches without understanding is like the
53: 2 [53:3] God looks down from heaven on the sons of **men** to see if
56: 11 [56:12] God I trust; I will not be afraid. What can **man** do to me?
57: 4 [57:5] I lie among ravenous beasts—**men** [+1201] whose teeth are
58: 1 [58:2] speak justly? Do you judge uprightly among **men** [+1201]?
58: 11 [58:12] **men** will say, "Surely the righteous still are rewarded;
60: 11 [60:13] aid against the enemy, for the help of **man** is worthless.
62: 9 [62:10] **Lowborn** [+1201] **men** are but a breath, the highborn are
64: 9 [64:10] All **mankind** will fear; they will proclaim the works of
66: 5 God has done, how awesome his works in **man's** [+1201] behalf!
68: 18 [68:19] you received gifts from **men**, even from the rebellious—
73: 5 the burdens common to man; they are not plagued by **human** ills.
76: 10 [76:11] Surely your wrath against **men** brings you praise,
78: 60 the tabernacle of Shiloh, the tent he had set up among **men**.
80: 17 [80:18] the son of **man** you have raised up for yourself.
82: 7 you will die like mere **men**; you will fall like every other ruler."
84: 5 [84:6] Blessed are **those**[s] whose strength is in you, who have set
84: 12 [84:13] LORD Almighty, blessed is the **man** who trusts in you.
89: 47 [89:48] For what futility you have created all **men** [+1201]!
90: 3 turn men back to dust, saying, "Return to dust, O sons of **men**."
94: 10 nations not punish? Does he who teaches **man** lack knowledge?
94: 11 The LORD knows the thoughts of **man**; he knows that they are
104: 14 makes grass grow for the cattle, and plants for **man** to cultivate—
104: 23 Then **man** goes out to his work, to his labor until evening.
105: 14 He allowed no **one** to oppress them; for their sake he rebuked
107: 8 for his unfailing love and his wonderful deeds for **men** [+1201],
107: 15 for his unfailing love and his wonderful deeds for **men** [+1201],
107: 21 for his unfailing love and his wonderful deeds for **men** [+1201].
107: 31 for his unfailing love and his wonderful deeds for **men** [+1201].
108: 12 [108:13] aid against the enemy, for the help of **man** is worthless.
115: 4 But their idols are silver and gold, made by the hands of **men**.
115: 16 belong to the LORD, but the earth he has given to **man** [+1201].
116: 11 And in my dismay I said, "All **men** are liars."
118: 6 LORD is with me; I will not be afraid. What can **man** do to me?
118: 8 It is better to take refuge in the LORD than to trust in **man**.
119:134 Redeem me from the oppression of **men**, that I may obey your
124: 2 if the LORD had not been on our side when **men** attacked us,
135: 8 down the firstborn of Egypt, the firstborn of **men** and animals.
135: 15 idols of the nations are silver and gold, made by the hands of **men**.
140: 1 [140:2] Rescue me, O LORD, from evil **men**; protect me from
144: 3 O LORD, what is **man** that you care for him, the son of man that
144: 4 **Man** is like a breath; his days are like a fleeting shadow.
145: 12 so that **all men** [+1201+2021] may know of your mighty acts
146: 3 put your trust in princes, in **mortal men** [+1201], who cannot save.
Pr 3: 4 you will win favor and a good name in the sight of God and **man**.
3: 13 Blessed is the **man** who finds wisdom, the man who gains
3: 13 is the man who finds wisdom, the **man** who gains understanding,
3: 30 Do not accuse a **man** for no reason—when he has done you no
6: 12 A **scoundrel** [+1175] and villain, who goes about with a corrupt
8: 4 O men, I call out; I raise my voice to **all mankind** [+1201].
8: 31 rejoicing in his whole world and delighting in **mankind** [+1201].
8: 34 Blessed is the **man** who listens to me, watching daily at my doors,
11: 7 When a wicked **man** dies, his hope perishes; all he expected from
12: 3 A **man** cannot be established through wickedness,
12: 14 with good things as surely as the work of **his**[s] hands rewards him.
12: 23 A prudent **man** keeps his knowledge to himself, but the heart of
12: 27 not roast his game, but the diligent **man** prizes his possessions.
15: 11 before the LORD—how much more the hearts of **men** [+1201]!
15: 20 son brings joy to his father, but a foolish **man** despises his mother.
16: 1 To **man** belong the plans of the heart, but from the LORD comes
16: 9 In his heart a **man** plans his course, but the LORD determines his
17: 18 A **man** lacking in judgment strikes hands in pledge and puts up
18: 16 A gift opens the way for the **giver**[s] and ushers him into the
19: 3 A **man's** *own* folly ruins his life, yet his heart rages against the
19: 11 A **man's** wisdom gives him patience; it is to his glory to overlook
19: 22 What a **man** desires is unfailing love; better to be poor than a liar.
20: 6 Many a **man** claims to have unfailing love, but a faithful man who
20: 24 by the LORD. How then can **anyone** understand his own way?
20: 25 It is a trap for a **man** to dedicate something rashly and only later to
20: 27 The lamp of the LORD searches the spirit of a **man**; it searches
21: 16 A **man** who strays from the path of understanding comes to rest in
21: 20 stores of choice food and oil, but a foolish **man** devours all he has.
23: 28 a bandit she lies in wait, and multiplies the unfaithful among **men**.
24: 9 The schemes of folly are sin, and **men** detest a mocker.
24: 12 Will he not repay *each* **person** according to what he has done?
24: 30 of the sluggard, past the vineyard of the **man** *who* lacks judgment;
27: 19 As water reflects a face, so a **man's** heart reflects the man.
27: 19 reflects a face, so a man's heart **reflects the man** [+2021+4200].
27: 20 Destruction are never satisfied, and neither are the eyes of **man**.
28: 2 but a **man** of understanding and knowledge maintains order.
28: 12 but when the wicked rise to power, **men** go into hiding.
28: 14 Blessed is the **man** who always fears the LORD, but he who
28: 17 A **man** tormented by the guilt of murder will be a fugitive till
28: 23 He who rebukes a **man** will in the end gain more favor than he
28: 28 When the wicked rise to power, **people** go into hiding; but when
29: 23 A **man's** pride brings him low, but a man of lowly spirit gains
29: 25 Fear of **man** will prove to be a snare, but whoever trusts in the
30: 2 am the most ignorant of men; I do not have a **man's** understanding.
30: 14 devour the poor from the earth, the needy from among **mankind**.
Ecc 1: 3 What does **man** gain from all his labor at which he toils under the
1: 13 under heaven. What a heavy burden God has laid on **men** [+1201]!
2: 3 I wanted to see what was worthwhile for **men** [+1201] to do under
2: 8 and a harem as well—the delights of the heart of **man** [+1201].
2: 12 What more can the king's **successor** [+339+995+8611] do than
2: 18 because I must leave them to the **one** who comes after me.
2: 21 For a **man** may do his work with wisdom, knowledge and skill,
2: 21 he must leave all he owns to **someone** who has not worked for it.
2: 22 What does a **man** get for all the toil and anxious striving with
2: 24 A **man** can do nothing better than to eat and drink and find
2: 26 To the **man** who pleases him, God gives wisdom, knowledge
3: 10 I have seen the burden God has laid on **men** [+1201].
3: 11 yet **they**[s] [+2021] cannot fathom what God has done from
3: 13 That **everyone** [+2021+3972] may eat and drink, and find
3: 18 I also thought, "As for **men** [+1201], God tests them so that they
3: 19 **Man's** [+1201] fate is like that of the animals; the same fate awaits
3: 19 All have the same breath; **man** has no advantage over the animal.
3: 21 Who knows if the spirit of **man** [+1201] rises upward and if the
3: 22 So I saw that there is nothing better for a **man** than to enjoy his
5: 19 [5:18] when God gives any **man** wealth and possessions,
6: 1 seen another evil under the sun, and it weighs heavily on **men**:
6: 7 All **man's** efforts are for his mouth, yet his appetite is never
6: 10 exists has already been named, and what **man** is has been known;
6: 11 the words, the less the meaning, and how does that profit **anyone**?
6: 12 For who knows what is good for a **man** in life, during the few
6: 12 Who can tell **him**[s] [+2021] what will happen under the sun after he
7: 2 to go to a house of feasting, for death is the destiny of every **man**;
7: 14 Therefore, a **man** cannot discover anything about his future.
7: 20 There is not a righteous **man** on earth who does what is right
7: 28 I found one ⌞upright⌟ **man** among a thousand, but not one ⌞upright⌟
7: 29 God made **mankind** upright, but men have gone in search of many
8: 1 Wisdom brightens a **man's** face and changes its hard appearance.
8: 6 for every matter, though a **man's** misery weighs heavily upon him.
8: 8 No **man** has power over the wind to contain it; so no one has
8: 9 There is a time when a **man** lords it over others to his own hurt.
8: 9 There is a time when a man lords it over **others**[s] to his own hurt.
8: 11 the hearts of the **people** [+1201] are filled with schemes to do
8: 15 because nothing is better for a **man** under the sun than to eat
8: 17 has done. No **one** can comprehend what goes on under the sun.
8: 17 all his efforts to search it out, **man** cannot discover its meaning.
9: 1 God's hands, but no **man** knows whether love or hate awaits him.
9: 3 The hearts of **men** [+1201], moreover, are full of evil and there is
9: 12 Moreover, no **man** knows when his hour will come: As fish are
9: 12 so **men** [+1201] are trapped by evil times that fall unexpectedly
9: 15 by his wisdom. But **nobody** [+4202] remembered that poor man.
10: 14 No **one** knows what is coming—who can tell him what will happen
11: 8 However many years a **man** may live, let him enjoy them all.
12: 5 **man** goes to his eternal home and mourners go about the streets.
12: 13 and keep his commandments, for this is the whole ⌞duty⌟ of **man**.
Isa 2: 9 So **man** will be brought low and mankind humbled—do not
2: 11 The eyes of the arrogant **man** will be humbled and the pride of
2: 17 The arrogance of **man** will be brought low and the pride of men

Isa 2:20 In that day **men** will throw away to the rodents and bats their idols
2:22 Stop trusting in **man**, who has but a breath in his nostrils. Of what
5:15 So **man** will be brought low and mankind humbled, the eyes of the
6:11 until the houses are left **deserted** [+401+4946] and the fields
6:12 until the LORD has sent **everyone** far away and the land is utterly
13:12 scarcer than pure gold, **[RPH]** more rare than the gold of Ophir.
17:7 In that day **men** will look to their Maker and turn their eyes to the
22:6 Elam takes up the quiver, with her **charioteers** [+8207] and horses;
29:19 the LORD; the **needy** [+36] will rejoice in the Holy One of Israel.
29:21 those who with a word make a **man** out to be guilty, who ensnare
31:3 But the Egyptians are **men** and not God; their horses are flesh
31:8 that is not of man; a sword, not *of* **mortals**, will devour them.
37:19 not gods but only wood and stone, fashioned by **human** hands.
38:11 no longer will I look on **mankind**, or be with those who now dwell
43:4 and because I love you, I will give **men** in exchange for you,
44:11 and his kind will be put to shame; craftsmen are nothing but **men**.
44:13 form of man, of **man** in all his glory, that it may dwell in a shrine.
44:15 It is **man's** [+4200] fuel for burning; some of it he takes
45:12 It is I who made the earth and created **mankind** upon it. My own
47:3 your shame uncovered. I will take vengeance; I will spare no **one**."
51:12 you that you fear mortal men, the sons of **men**, who are but grass,
52:14 of any man and his form marred beyond **human** [+1201] likeness—
56:2 is the man who does this, the **man** [+1201] who holds it fast,
58:5 of fast I have chosen, only a day for a **man** to humble himself?
Jer 2:6 and darkness, a land where no one travels and no **one** lives?'
4:25 I looked, and there were no **people**; every bird in the sky had flown
7:20 on **man** and beast, on the trees of the field and on the fruit of the
9:22 [9:21] " 'The dead bodies of **men** will lie like refuse on the open
10:14 **Everyone** [+3972] is senseless and without knowledge;
10:23 I know, O LORD, that a **man's** [+4200] life is not his own;
16:20 Do **men** make their own gods? Yes, but they are not gods!"
17:5 "Cursed is the one who trusts in **man**, who depends on flesh for his
21:6 both **men** and animals—and they will die of a terrible plague.
27:5 arm I made the earth and its **people** and the animals that are on it,
31:27 and the house of Judah with the offspring of **men** and of animals.
31:30 **whoever** [+2021+3972] eats sour grapes—his own teeth will be set
32:19 Your eyes are open to all the ways of **men** [+1201]; you reward
32:20 continued them to this day, both in Israel and among all **mankind**,
32:43 'It is a desolate waste, without **men** or animals, for it has been
33:5 'They will be filled with the dead bodies of the **men** I will slay in
33:10 about this place, "It is a desolate waste, without **men** or animals."
33:10 inhabited by neither **men** nor animals, there will be heard once
33:12 'In this place, desolate and without **men** or animals—in all its
36:29 and destroy this land and cut off both **men** and animals from it?"
47:2 The **people** will cry out; all who dwell in the land will wail
49:15 I will make you small among the nations, despised among **men**.
49:18 "so no one will live there; no **man** [+1201] will dwell in it.
49:33 No one will live there; no **man** [+1201] will dwell in it."
50:3 No one will live in it; both **men** and animals will flee away.
50:40 "so no one will live there; no **man** [+1201] will dwell in it.
51:14 I will surely fill you with **men**, as with a swarm of locusts,
51:17 "Every **man** is senseless and without knowledge; every goldsmith
51:43 a land where no one lives, through which no **man** [+1201] travels.
51:62 destroy this place, so that neither **man** nor animal will live in it;
La 3:36 to deprive a **man** of justice—would not the Lord see such things?
3:39 Why should any living **man** complain when punished for his sins?
Eze 1:5 four living creatures. In appearance their form was that of a **man**,
1:8 Under their wings on their four sides they had the hands of a **man**.
1:10 Each of the four had the face of a **man**, and on the right side each
1:26 and high above on the throne was a figure like that of a **man**.
2:1 He said to me, "Son of **man**, stand up on your feet and I will speak
2:3 "Son of **man**, I am sending you to the Israelites, to a rebellious
2:6 And you, son of **man**, do not be afraid of them or their words.
2:8 you, son of **man**, listen to what I say to you. Do not rebel like that
3:1 he said to me, "Son of **man**, eat what is before you, eat this scroll;
3:3 Then he said to me, "Son of **man**, eat this scroll I am giving you
3:4 "Son of **man**, go now to the house of Israel and speak my words to
3:10 "Son of **man**, listen carefully and take to heart all the words I
3:17 "Son of **man**, I have made you a watchman for the house of Israel;
3:25 And you, son of **man**, they will tie with ropes; you will be bound
4:1 "Now, son of **man**, take a clay tablet, put it in front of you
4:12 it in the sight of the people, using **human** excrement for fuel."
4:15 "I will let you bake your bread over cow manure instead of **human**
4:16 "Son of **man**, I will cut off the supply of food in Jerusalem.
5:1 "Now, son of **man**, take a sharp sword and use it as a barber's
6:2 "Son of **man**, set your face against the mountains of Israel;
7:2 "Son of **man**, this is what the Sovereign LORD says to the land
8:5 Then he said to me, "Son of **man**, look toward the north."
8:6 And he said to me, "Son of **man**, do you see what they are doing—
8:8 He said to me, "Son of **man**, now dig into the wall." So I dug into
8:12 He said to me, "Son of **man**, have you seen what the elders of the
8:15 He said to me, "Do you see this, son of **man**? You will see things
8:17 He said to me, "Have you seen this, son of **man**? Is it a trivial
10:8 the cherubim could be seen what looked like the hands of a **man**.)
10:14 a cherub, the second the face of a **man**, the third the face of a lion,
10:21 and under their wings was what looked like the hands of a **man**.
11:2 The LORD said to me, "Son of **man**, these are the men who are
11:4 Therefore prophesy against them; prophesy, son of **man**."
11:15 "Son of **man**, your brothers—your brothers who are your blood
12:2 "Son of **man**, you are living among a rebellious people. They have
12:3 "Therefore, son of **man**, pack your belongings for exile and in the
12:9 "Son of **man**, did not that rebellious house of Israel ask you,
12:18 "Son of **man**, tremble as you eat your food, and shudder in fear as
12:22 "Son of **man**, what is this proverb you have in the land of Israel:
12:27 "Son of **man**, the house of Israel is saying, 'The vision he sees is
13:2 "Son of **man**, prophesy against the prophets of Israel who are now
13:17 "Now, son of **man**, set your face against the daughters of your
14:3 "Son of **man**, these men have set up idols in their hearts and put
14:13 "Son of **man**, if a country sins against me by being unfaithful
14:13 and send famine upon it and kill its **men** and their animals,
14:17 pass throughout the land,' and I kill its **men** and their animals,
14:19 wrath upon it through bloodshed, killing its **men** and their animals,
14:21 and wild beasts and plague—to kill its **men** and their animals!
15:2 "Son of **man**, how is the wood of a vine better than that of a
16:2 "Son of **man**, confront Jerusalem with her detestable practices
17:2 "Son of **man**, set forth an allegory and tell the house of Israel a
19:3 a strong lion. He learned to tear the prey and he devoured **men**.
19:6 a strong lion. He learned to tear the prey and he devoured **men**.
20:3 "Son of **man**, speak to the elders of Israel and say to them,
20:4 "Will you judge them? Will you judge them, son of **man**?
20:11 to them my laws, for the **man** who obeys them will live by them.
20:13 my laws—although the **man** who obeys them will live by them—
20:21 although the **man** who obeys them will live by them—and they
20:27 "Therefore, son of **man**, speak to the people of Israel and say to
20:46 [21:2] "Son of **man**, set your face toward the south; preach
21:2 [21:7] "Son of **man**, set your face against Jerusalem and preach
21:6 [21:11] "Therefore groan, son of **man**! Groan before them with
21:9 [21:14] "Son of **man**, prophesy and say, 'This is what the Lord
21:12 [21:17] Cry out and wail, son of **man**, for it is against my people;
21:14 [21:19] son of **man**, prophesy and strike your hands together.
21:19 [21:24] "Son of **man**, mark out two roads for the sword of the
21:28 [21:33] "And you, son of **man**, prophesy and say, 'This is what
22:2 "Son of **man**, will you judge her? Will you judge this city of
22:18 "Son of **man**, the house of Israel has become dross to me;
22:24 "Son of **man**, say to the land, 'You are a land that has had no rain
23:2 "Son of **man**, there were two women, daughters of the same
23:36 said to me: "Son of **man**, will you judge Oholah and Oholibah?
23:42 brought from the desert along with men from the **rabble** [+8044],
24:2 "Son of **man**, record this date, this very date, because the king of
24:16 "Son of **man**, with one blow I am about to take away from you the
24:25 "And you, son of **man**, on the day I take away their stronghold,
25:2 "Son of **man**, set your face against the Ammonites and prophesy
25:13 out my hand against Edom and kill its **men** and their animals.
26:2 "Son of **man**, because Tyre has said of Jerusalem, 'Aha! The gate
27:2 "Son of **man**, take up a lament concerning Tyre.
27:13 they exchanged **slaves** [+5883] and articles of bronze for your
28:2 "Son of **man**, say to the ruler of Tyre, 'This is what the Sovereign
28:2 you are a **man** and not a god, though you think you are as wise as a
28:9 You will be but a **man**, not a god, in the hands of those who slay
28:12 "Son of **man**, take up a lament concerning the king of Tyre
28:21 "Son of **man**, set your face against Sidon; prophesy against her
29:2 "Son of **man**, set your face against Pharaoh king of Egypt
29:8 will bring a sword against you and kill your **men** and their animals.
29:11 No foot of **man** or animal will pass through it; no one will live
29:18 "Son of **man**, Nebuchadnezzar king of Babylon drove his army in
30:2 "Son of **man**, prophesy and say: 'This is what the Sovereign
30:21 "Son of **man**, I have broken the arm of Pharaoh king of Egypt.
31:2 "Son of **man**, say to Pharaoh king of Egypt and to his hordes:
31:14 for death, for the earth below, among **mortal men** [+1201],
32:2 "Son of **man**, take up a lament concerning Pharaoh king of Egypt
32:13 beside abundant waters no longer to be stirred by the foot of **man**
32:18 "Son of **man**, wail for the hordes of Egypt and consign to the earth
33:2 "Son of **man**, speak to your countrymen and say to them: 'When I
33:7 "Son of **man**, I have made you a watchman for the house of Israel;
33:10 "Son of **man**, say to the house of Israel, 'This is what you are
33:12 "Therefore, son of **man**, say to your countrymen,
33:24 "Son of **man**, the people living in those ruins in the land of Israel
33:30 "As for you, son of **man**, your countrymen are talking together
34:2 "Son of **man**, prophesy against the shepherds of Israel; prophesy
34:31 my sheep, the sheep of my pasture, are **people**, and I am your God,
35:2 "Son of **man**, set your face against Mount Seir; prophesy against it
36:1 "Son of **man**, prophesy to the mountains of Israel and say,
36:10 I will multiply the number of **people** upon you, even the whole
36:11 I will increase the number of **men** and animals upon you, and they
36:12 I will cause **people**, my people Israel, to walk upon you. They will
36:13 "You devour **men** and deprive your nation of its children,"
36:14 therefore you will no longer devour **men** or make your nation
36:17 "Son of **man**, when the people of Israel were living in their own

Eze 36: 37 do this for them: I will make their **people** as numerous as sheep,
36: 38 So will the ruined cities be filled with flocks of **people**. Then they
37: 3 He asked me, "Son of **man**, can these bones live?" I said,
37: 9 prophesy, son of **man**, and say to it, 'This is what the Sovereign
37: 11 "Son of **man**, these bones are the whole house of Israel. They say,
37: 16 "Son of **man**, take a stick of wood and write on it, 'Belonging to
38: 2 "Son of **man**, set your face against Gog, of the land of Magog,
38: 14 "Therefore, son of **man**, prophesy and say to Gog: 'This is what the
38: 20 all the **people** on the face of the earth will tremble at my presence.
39: 1 "Son of **man**, prophesy against Gog and say: 'This is what the
39: 15 As they go through the land and one of them sees a **human** bone,
39: 17 "Son of **man**, this is what the Sovereign LORD says: Call out to
40: 4 "Son of **man**, look with your eyes and hear with your ears
41: 19 the face of a **man** toward the palm tree on one side and the face of
43: 7 "Son of **man**, this is the place of my throne and the place for the
43: 10 "Son of **man**, describe the temple to the people of Israel, that they
43: 18 he said to me, "Son of **man**, this is what the Sovereign LORD
44: 5 "Son of **man**, look carefully, listen closely and give attention to
44: 25 " 'A priest must not defile himself by going near a dead **person**;
47: 6 He asked me, "Son of **man**, do you see this?" Then he led me back
Da 8: 16 And I heard a **man's** voice from the Ulai calling, "Gabriel,
8: 17 "Son of **man**," he said to me, "understand that the vision concerns
10: 16 Then one who looked like a **man** [+1201] touched my lips,
10: 18 Again the one who looked like a **man** touched me and gave me
Hos 9: 12 Even if they rear children, I will bereave them of **every** *one*.
11: 4 I led them with cords of **human** kindness, with ties of love;
13: 2 these people, "They offer **human** sacrifice and kiss the calf-idols."
Joel 1: 12 are dried up. Surely the joy of **mankind** [+1201] is withered away.
Am 4: 13 the mountains, creates the wind, and reveals his thoughts to **man**,
Jnh 3: 7 Do not let any **man** or beast, herd or flock, taste anything;
3: 8 let **man** and beast be covered with sackcloth. Let everyone call
4: 11 twenty thousand **people** who cannot tell their right hand from their
Mic 2: 12 like a flock in its pasture; the place will throng with **people**.
5: 5 [5:4] against him seven shepherds, even eight leaders of **men**.
5: 7 [5:6] which do not wait for man or linger for **mankind** [+1201].
6: 8 He has showed you, O **man**, what is good. And what does the
7: 2 have been swept from the land; not one upright **man** remains.
Hab 1: 14 You have made **men** like fish in the sea, like sea creatures that
2: 8 For you have shed **man's** blood; you have destroyed lands
2: 17 For you have shed **man's** blood; you have destroyed lands
Zep 1: 3 "I will sweep away both **men** and animals; I will sweep away the
1: 3 The wicked will have only heaps of rubble when I cut off **man**
1: 17 I will bring distress on the **people** and they will walk like blind
Hag 1: 11 on **men** and cattle, and on the labor of your hands."
Zec 2: 4 [2:8] because of the great number of **men** and livestock in it.
8: 10 Before that time there were no wages for **man** or beast. No one
8: 10 of his enemy, for I had turned every **man** against his neighbor.
9: 1 for the eyes of **men** and all the tribes of Israel are on the LORD—
11: 6 "I will hand **everyone** over to his neighbor and his king.
12: 1 of the earth, and who forms the spirit of **man** within him, declares:
13: 5 the land [BHS ***a man***; NIV 141] has been my livelihood since my youth.'
Mal 3: 8 "Will a **man** rob God? Yet you rob me. "But you ask, 'How do we

133 ²אָדָם *'ādām²*, n.m. Not used in NIV/BHS [√ 131?]

134 ³אָדָם *'ādām³*, n.pr.m. [12] [→ 142; cf. 131]

Adam [11], Adam's [1]

Ge 2: 20 the beasts of the field. But for **Adam** no suitable helper was found.
3: 17 To **Adam** he said, "Because you listened to your wife and ate from
3: 20 **Adam** named his wife Eve, because she would become the mother
3: 21 The LORD God made garments of skin for **Adam** and his wife
4: 1 **Adam** lay with his wife Eve, and she became pregnant and gave
4: 25 **Adam** lay with his wife again, and she gave birth to a son
5: 1 This is the written account of **Adam's** line. When God created
5: 3 When **Adam** had lived 130 years, he had a son in his own likeness,
5: 4 was born, **Adam** lived 800 years and had other sons and daughters.
5: 5 Altogether, **Adam** lived 930 years, and then he died.
1Ch 1: 1 **Adam**, Seth, Enosh,
Hos 6: 7 Like **Adam**, they have broken the covenant—they were unfaithful

135 ⁴אָדָם *'ādām⁴*, n.m. Not used in NIV/BHS [√ 131]

136 ⁵אָדָם *'ādām⁵*, n.pr.loc. [1] [√ 131]

Adam [1]

Jos 3: 16 distance away, at a town called **Adam** in the vicinity of Zarethan,

137 אָדֹם *'ādōm*, a. [9] [→ 147; cf. 131]

red [7], *untranslated* [1], ruddy [1]

Ge 25: 30 He said to Jacob, "Quick, let me have some of that **red** *stew*!
25: 30 let me have some of that red stew! **[RPH]** I'm famished!"
Nu 19: 2 Tell the Israelites to bring you a **red** heifer without defect
2Ki 3: 22 To the Moabites across the way, the water looked **red**—like blood.
SS 5: 10 My lover is radiant and **ruddy**, outstanding among ten thousand.
Isa 63: 2 Why are your garments **red**, like those of one treading the
Zec 1: 8 I had a vision—and there before me was a man riding a **red** horse!
1: 8 trees in a ravine. Behind him were **red**, brown and white horses.
6: 2 The first chariot had **red** horses, the second black,

138 אֹדֶם *'ōdem*, n.[f.]. [3] [√ 131]

ruby [3]

Ex 28: 17 on it. In the first row there shall be a **ruby**, a topaz and a beryl;
39: 10 stones on it. In the first row there was a **ruby**, a topaz and a beryl;
Eze 28: 13 **ruby**, topaz and emerald, chrysolite, onyx and jasper, sapphire,

139 אֱדֹם *'ᵉdōm*, n.[m.]. Not used in NIV/BHS [→ 6273; cf. 131]

140 אֲדַמְדָּם *'ᵃdamdām*, a. [6] [√ 131]

reddish-white [+4237] [4], reddish [2]

Lev 13: 19 boil was, a white swelling or **reddish-white** [+4237] spot appears,
13: 24 someone has a burn on his skin and a **reddish-white** [+4237]
13: 42 But if he has a **reddish-white** [+4237] sore on his bald head
13: 43 or forehead is **reddish-white** [+4237] like an infectious skin
13: 49 or knitted material, or any leather article, is greenish or **reddish**,
14: 37 or **reddish** depressions that appear to be deeper than the surface of

141 ¹אֲדָמָה *'ᵃdāmâ¹*, n.f. [225 / 226] [√ 131]

land [120], ground [42], earth [30], soil [11], dust [4], lands [3], clay [2], country [2], crops [2], fields [2], native land [2], below [+2021+6584] [1], crops [+2021+7262] [1], farmer [+408+6268] [1], her[s] [+3776] [1], home [1], homeland [1]

Ge 1: 25 all the creatures that move along the **ground** according to their
2: 5 sent rain on the earth and there was no man to work the **ground**,
2: 6 up from the earth and watered the whole surface of the **ground**—
2: 7 the LORD God formed the man from the dust of the **ground**
2: 9 the LORD God made all kinds of trees grow out of the **ground**—
2: 19 Now the LORD God had formed out of the **ground** all the beasts
3: 17 'You must not eat of it,' "Cursed is the **ground** because of you;
3: 19 of your brow you will eat your food until you return to the **ground**,
3: 23 of Eden to work the **ground** from which he had been taken.
4: 2 his brother Abel. Now Abel kept flocks, and Cain worked the **soil**.
4: 3 In the course of time Cain brought some of the fruits of the **soil** as
4: 10 Listen! Your brother's blood cries out to me from the **ground**.
4: 11 Now you are under a curse and driven from the **ground**,
4: 12 When you work the **ground**, it will no longer yield its crops for
4: 14 Today you are driving me from the **land**, and I will be hidden from
5: 29 painful toil of our hands caused by the **ground** the LORD has
6: 1 When men began to increase in number on the **earth** and daughters
6: 7 wipe mankind, whom I have created, from the face of the **earth**—
6: 20 of every kind of creature that moves along the **ground** will come
7: 4 I will wipe from the face of the **earth** every living creature I have
7: 8 of birds and of all creatures that move along the **ground**,
7: 23 Every living thing on the face of the **earth** was wiped out;
8: 8 to see if the water had receded from the surface of the **ground**.
8: 13 from the ark and saw that the surface of the **ground** was dry.
8: 21 "Never again will I curse the **ground** because of man, even though
9: 2 birds of the air, upon every creature that moves along the **ground**,
9: 20 Noah, a man of the **soil**, proceeded to plant a vineyard.
12: 3 I will curse; and all peoples on **earth** will be blessed through you."
19: 25 all those living in the cities—and also the vegetation in the **land**.
28: 14 All peoples on **earth** will be blessed through you and your
28: 15 over you wherever you go, and I will bring you back to this **land**.
47: 18 there is nothing left for our lord except our bodies and our **land**.
47: 19 Why should we perish before your eyes—we and our **land** as well?
47: 19 Buy us and our **land** in exchange for food, and we with our land
47: 19 for food, and we with our **land** will be in bondage to Pharaoh.
47: 19 may live and not die, and that the **land** may not become desolate."
47: 20 So Joseph bought all the **land** *in* Egypt for Pharaoh. The
47: 22 However, he did not buy the **land** *of* the priests, because they
47: 22 Pharaoh gave them. That is why they did not sell their **land**.
47: 23 "Now that I have bought you and your **land** today for Pharaoh,
47: 23 for Pharaoh, here is seed for you so you can plant the **ground**.
47: 26 So Joseph established it as a law concerning **land** *in* Egypt—
47: 26 It was only the **land** *of* the priests that did not become Pharaoh's.
Ex 3: 5 for the place where you are standing is holy **ground**."
8: 21 [8:17] will be full of flies, and even the **ground** where they are.
10: 6 the day they settled in this **land** till now.' " Then Moses turned
20: 12 so that you may live long in the **land** the LORD your God is
20: 24 " 'Make an altar of **earth** for me and sacrifice on it your burnt
23: 19 "Bring the best of the firstfruits of your **soil** to the house of the
32: 12 them in the mountains and to wipe them off the face of the **earth**'?
33: 16 your people from all the other people on the face of the **earth**?"

[F] Hitpael (hitpoel, hitpoal, hitpolel, hitpolal, hitpalel, hitpalpel, hitpalpal, hotpael, hotpaal) [G] Hiphil (hiphtil) [H] Hophal [I] Hishtaphel

Ex 34:26 "Bring the best of the firstfruits of your **soil** to the house of the
Lev 20:24 I said to you, "You will possess their **land**; I will give it to you as
20:25 by any animal or bird or anything that moves along the **ground**—
Nu 11:12 an infant, to the **land** you promised on oath to their forefathers?
12:3 more humble than anyone else on the face of the **earth**.)
16:30 the **earth** opens its mouth and swallows them, with everything that
16:31 as he finished saying all this, the **ground** under them split apart
32:11 or more who came up out of Egypt will see the **land** I promised on
Dt 4:10 so that they may learn to revere me as long as they live in the **land**
4:18 or like any creature that moves along the **ground** or any fish in the
4:40 that you may live long in the **land** the LORD your God gives you
5:16 that it may go well with you in the **land** the LORD your God is
6:15 against you, and he will destroy you from the face of the **land**.
7:6 you out of all the peoples on the face of the **earth** to be his people,
7:13 He will bless the fruit of your womb, the crops of your **land**—
7:13 the lambs of your flocks in the **land** that he swore to your
11:9 so that you may live long in the **land** that the LORD swore to
11:17 so that it will not rain and the **ground** will yield no produce,
11:21 the days of your children may be many in the **land** that the LORD
12:1 has given you to possess—as long as you live in the **land**.
12:19 careful not to neglect the Levites as long as you live in your **land**.
14:2 Out of all the peoples on the face of the **earth**, the LORD has
21:1 lying in a field in the **land** the LORD your God is giving you to
21:23 You must not desecrate the **land** the LORD your God is giving
25:15 so that you may live long in the **land** the LORD your God is
26:2 take some of the firstfruits of all that you produce from the **soil** of
26:10 and now I bring the firstfruits of the **soil** that you, O LORD,
26:15 the **land** you have given us as you promised on oath to our
28:4 and the crops of your **land** and the young of your livestock—
28:11 the young of your livestock and the crops of your **ground**—
28:11 your ground—in the **land** he swore to your forefathers to give you.
28:18 the crops of your **land**, and the calves of your herds and the lambs
28:21 he has destroyed you from the **land** you are entering to possess.
28:33 A people that you do not know will eat what your **land** and labor
28:42 of locusts will take over all your trees and the crops of your **land**.
28:51 your livestock and the crops of your **land** until you are destroyed.
28:63 You will be uprooted from the **land** you are entering to possess.
29:28 [29:27] in great wrath the LORD uprooted them from their **land**
30:9 the young of your livestock and the crops of your **land**.
30:18 You will not live long in the **land** you are crossing the Jordan to
30:20 he will give you many years in the **land** he swore to give to your
31:13 learn to fear the LORD your God as long as you live in the **land**
31:20 When I have brought them into the **land** flowing with milk
32:43 on his enemies and make atonement for his **land** and people.
32:47 By them you will live long in the **land** you are crossing the Jordan
Jos 23:13 and thorns in your eyes, until you perish from this good **land**,
23:15 until he has destroyed you from this good **land** he has given you.
1Sa 4:12 and went to Shiloh, his clothes torn and **dust** on his head.
20:15 cut off every one of David's enemies from the face of the **earth**."
20:31 As long as the son of Jesse lives on this **earth**, neither you nor your
2Sa 1:2 from Saul's camp, with his clothes torn and with **dust** on his head.
9:10 and your sons and your servants are to farm the **land** for him
14:7 my husband neither name nor descendant on the face of the **earth**."
15:32 Arkite was there to meet him, his robe torn and **dust** on his head.
17:12 be found, and we will fall on him as dew settles on the **ground**.
1Ki 7:46 The king had them cast in **clay** molds in the plain of the Jordan
8:34 and bring them back to the **land** you gave to their fathers.
8:40 so that they will fear you all the time they live in the **land** you gave
9:7 I will cut off Israel from the **land** I have given them and will reject
13:34 led to its downfall and to its destruction from the face of the **earth**.
14:15 He will uproot Israel from this good **land** that he gave to their
17:14 will not run dry until the day the LORD gives rain on the **land**.' "
18:1 and present yourself to Ahab, and I will send rain on the **land**."
2Ki 5:17 your servant, be given as much **earth** as a pair of mules can carry,
17:23 So the people of Israel were taken from their **homeland** into exile
21:8 will not again make the feet of the Israelites wander from the **land**
25:21 them executed. So Judah went into captivity, away from her **land**.
1Ch 27:26 of Kelub was in charge of the field workers who farmed the **land**.
2Ch 4:17 The king had them cast in **clay** molds in the plain of the Jordan
6:25 and bring them back to the **land** you gave to them and their fathers.
6:31 walk in your ways all the time they live in the **land** you gave our
7:20 then I will uproot Israel from my **land**, which I have given them,
26:10 vineyards in the hills and in the fertile lands, for he loved the **soil**.
33:8 I will not again make the feet of the Israelites leave the **land** I
Ne 9:1 fasting and wearing sackcloth and having **dust** on their heads.
9:25 They captured fortified cities and fertile **land**; they took possession
10:35 [10:36] house of the LORD each year the firstfruits of our **crops**
10:37 [10:38] we will bring a tithe of our **crops** to the Levites, for it is
Job 5:6 not spring from the soil, nor does trouble sprout from the **ground**.
31:38 "if my **land** cries out against me and all its furrows are wet with
Ps 49:11 [49:12] though they had named **lands** after themselves.
83:10 [83:11] perished at Endor and became like refuse on the **ground**.
104:30 your Spirit, they are created, and you renew the face of the **earth**.
105:35 up every green thing in their land, ate up the produce of their **soil**.
137:4 How can we sing the songs of the LORD while in a foreign **land**?
146:4 When their spirit departs, they return to the **ground**; on that very
Pr 12:11 He who works his **land** will have abundant food, but he who
28:19 He who works his **land** will have abundant food, but the one who
Isa 1:7 your **fields** are being stripped by foreigners right before you,
6:11 until the houses are left deserted and the **fields** ruined and ravaged,
7:16 the right, the **land** of the two kings you dread will be laid waste.
14:1 again he will choose Israel and will settle them in their own **land**.
14:2 the nations as menservants and maidservants in the LORD's **land**.
15:9 the fugitives of Moab and upon those who remain in the **land**.
19:17 the **land** *of* Judah will bring terror to the Egyptians; everyone to
23:17 will ply her trade with all the kingdoms on the face of the **earth**.
24:21 the powers in the heavens above and the kings on the **earth** below.
24:21 the heavens above and the kings on the earth **below** [+2021+6584].
28:24 Does he keep on breaking up and harrowing the **soil**?
30:23 He will also send you rain for the seed you sow in the **ground**,
30:23 and the food that comes from the **land** will be rich and plentiful.
30:24 The oxen and donkeys that work the **soil** will eat fodder and mash,
32:13 and for the **land** *of* my people, a land overgrown with thorns
45:9 to him who is but a potsherd among the potsherds on the **ground**.
Jer 7:20 and beast, on the trees of the field and on the fruit of the **ground**,
8:2 gathered up or buried, but will be like refuse lying on the **ground**.
12:14 I will uproot them from their **lands** and I will uproot the house of
14:4 The **ground** is cracked because there is no rain in the land;
16:4 be mourned or buried but will be like refuse lying on the **ground**.
16:15 For I will restore them to the **land** I gave their forefathers.
23:8 he had banished them.' Then they will live in their own **land**."
24:10 plague against them until they are destroyed from the **land** I gave
25:5 you can stay in the **land** the LORD gave to you and your fathers
25:26 one after the other—all the kingdoms on the face of the **earth**.
25:33 gathered up or buried, but will be like refuse lying on the **ground**.
27:10 lies to you that will only serve to remove you far from your **lands**;
27:11 I will let that nation remain in its own **land** to till it and to live
28:16 'I am about to remove you from the face of the **earth**.
35:7 Then you will live a long time in the **land** where you are nomads.'
35:15 you will live in the **land** I have given to you and your fathers."
42:12 that he will have compassion on you and restore you to your **land**.'
52:27 them executed. So Judah went into captivity, away from her **land**.
Eze 7:2 this is what the Sovereign LORD says to the **land** *of* Israel:
11:17 been scattered, and I will give you back the **land** *of* Israel again.'
12:19 says about those living in Jerusalem and in the **land** *of* Israel:
12:22 "Son of man, what is this proverb you have in the **land** *of* Israel:
13:9 records of the house of Israel, nor will they enter the **land** *of* Israel.
18:2 you people mean by quoting this proverb about the **land** *of* Israel:
20:38 where they are living, yet they will not enter the **land** *of* Israel.
20:42 that I am the LORD, when I bring you into the **land** *of* Israel,
21:2 [21:7] against the sanctuary. Prophesy against the **land** *of* Israel
21:3 [21:8] say to **her**s [+3776]: 'This is what the LORD says: I am
25:3 it was desecrated and over the **land** *of* Israel when it was laid waste
25:6 rejoicing with all the malice of your heart against the **land** *of*
28:25 they will live in their own **land**, which I gave to my servant Jacob.
33:24 the people living in those ruins in the **land** *of* Israel are saying,
34:13 them from the countries, and I will bring them into their own **land**.
34:27 ground will yield its crops; the people will be secure in their **land**.
36:6 Therefore prophesy concerning the **land** *of* Israel and say to the
36:17 of man, when the people of Israel were living in their own **land**,
36:24 you from all the countries and bring you back into your own **land**.
37:12 bring you up from them; I will bring you back to the **land** *of* Israel.
37:14 in you and you will live, and I will settle you in your own **land**.
37:21 them from all around and bring them back into their own **land**.
38:18 When Gog attacks the **land** *of* Israel, my hot anger will be aroused,
38:19 at that time there shall be a great earthquake in the **land** *of* Israel.
38:20 the beasts of the field, every creature that moves along the **ground**,
38:20 all the people on the face of the **earth** will tremble at my presence.
39:26 they lived in safety in their **land** with no one to make them afraid.
39:28 I will gather them to their own **land**, not leaving any behind.
Da 11:9 realm of the king of the South but will retreat to his own **country**.
11:39 rulers over many people and will distribute the **land** at a price.
12:2 Multitudes who sleep in the dust of the **earth** will awake:
Hos 2:18 [2:20] of the air and the creatures that move along the **ground**.
Joel 1:10 The fields are ruined, the **ground** is dried up; the grain is
2:21 Be not afraid, O **land**; be glad and rejoice. Surely the LORD has
Am 3:2 "You only have I chosen of all the families of the **earth**; therefore I
3:5 Does a trap spring up from the **earth** when there is nothing to
5:2 is Virgin Israel, never to rise again, deserted in her own **land**,
7:11 and Israel will surely go into exile, away from their **native land**.' "
7:17 Your **land** will be measured and divided up, and you yourself will
7:17 and divided up, and you yourself will die in a pagan **country**.
7:17 Israel will certainly go into exile, away from their **native land**.' "
9:8 I will destroy it from the face of the **earth**—yet I will not totally
9:15 I will plant Israel in their own **land**, never again to be uprooted
9:15 never again to be uprooted from the **land** I have given them,"
Jnh 4:2 "O LORD, is this not what I said when I was still at **home**?
Zep 1:2 "I will sweep away everything from the face of the **earth**,"

Zep 1: 3 heaps of rubble when I cut off man from the face of the **earth**,"
Hag 1: 11 the oil and whatever the **ground** produces, on men and cattle,
Zec 2: 12 [2:16] LORD will inherit Judah as his portion in the holy **land**
9: 16 of his people. They will sparkle in his **land** like jewels in a crown.
13: 5 I am a **farmer** [+408+6268]; the land has been my livelihood since
13: 5 the **land** [BHS 132] has been my livelihood since my youth.'
Mal 3: 11 I will prevent pests from devouring your **crops** [+2021+7262],

142 ²אֲדָמָה ***ᵃdāmâ²***, n.pr.loc. [1] [√ 134; cf. 131]

Adamah [1]

Jos 19: 36 **Adamah**, Ramah, Hazor,

143 ³אֲדָמָה ***ᵃdāmâ³***, n.f. Not used in NIV/BHS [√ 131]

144 אַדְמָה ***'admâ***, n.pr.loc. [5]

Admah [5]

Ge 10: 19 toward Sodom, Gomorrah, **Admah** and Zeboiim, as far as Lasha.
14: 2 Birsha king of Gomorrah, Shinab king of **Admah**, Shemeber king
14: 8 the king of **Admah**, the king of Zeboiim and the king of Bela (that
Dt 29: 23 [29:22] of Sodom and Gomorrah, **Admah** and Zeboiim,
Hos 11: 8 can I hand you over, Israel? How can I treat you like **Admah**?

145 אַדְמוֹנִי ***'admônî***, a. [3] [√ 131]

ruddy [2], red [1]

Ge 25: 25 The first to come out was **red**, and his whole body was like a hairy
1Sa 16: 12 He was **ruddy**, with a fine appearance and handsome features.
17: 42 that he was only a boy, **ruddy** and handsome, and he despised him.

146 אֲדָמִי הַנֶּקֶב ***ᵃdāmî hanneqeb***, n.pr.loc. [1] [√ 131 + 2186]

Adami Nekeb [1]

Jos 19: 33 passing **Adami Nekeb** and Jabneel to Lakkum and ending at the

147 אֲדֻמִּים ***ᵃdummîm***, n.pr.loc. [2] [√ 137; cf. 131]

Adummim [2]

Jos 15: 7 to Gilgal, which faces the Pass of **Adummim** south of the gorge.
18: 17 continued to Geliloth, which faces the Pass of **Adummim**,

148 אַדְמָתָא ***'admātā'***, n.pr.m. [1]

Admatha [1]

Est 1: 14 Shethar, **Admatha**, Tarshish, Meres, Marsena and Memucan,

149 אֶדֶן ***'eden***, n.m. [57 / 58]

bases [41], *untranslated* [13], base [2], footings [1], those[s] [1]

Ex 26: 19 make forty silver **bases** to go under them—two bases for each
26: 19 under them—two **bases** for each frame, one under each projection.
26: 19 two bases for each frame, one under each projection. **[RPH]**
26: 21 and forty silver **bases**—two under each frame.
26: 21 and forty silver bases—two **[RPH]** under each frame.
26: 21 and forty silver bases—two under each frame. **[RPH]**
26: 25 So there will be eight frames and sixteen silver **bases**—two under
26: 25 and sixteen silver bases—**[RPH]** two under each frame.
26: 25 and sixteen silver bases—two **[RPH]** under each frame.
26: 25 and sixteen silver bases—two under each frame. **[RPH]**
26: 32 acacia wood overlaid with gold and standing on four silver **bases**.
26: 37 wood overlaid with gold. And cast five bronze **bases** for them.
27: 10 with twenty posts and twenty bronze **bases** and with silver hooks
27: 11 with twenty posts and twenty bronze **bases** and with silver hooks
27: 12 be fifty cubits wide and have curtains, with ten posts and ten **bases**.
27: 14 to be on one side of the entrance, with three posts and three **bases**,
27: 15 long are to be on the other side, with three posts and three **bases**.
27: 16 the work of an embroiderer—with four posts and four **bases**.
27: 17 the courtyard are to have silver bands and hooks, and bronze **bases**.
27: 18 of finely twisted linen five cubits high, and with bronze **bases**.
35: 11 and its covering, clasps, frames, crossbars, posts and **bases**;
35: 17 the curtains of the courtyard with its posts and **bases**, and the
36: 24 made forty silver **bases** to go under them—two bases for each
36: 24 under them—two **bases** for each frame, one under each projection.
36: 24 two bases for each frame, one under each projection. **[RPH]**
36: 26 and forty silver **bases**—two under each frame.
36: 26 and forty silver bases—two **[RPH]** under each frame.
36: 26 and forty silver bases—two under each frame. **[RPH]**
36: 30 So there were eight frames and sixteen silver **bases**—two under
36: 30 and sixteen silver bases—**[RPH]** two under each frame.
36: 30 and sixteen silver bases—two **[RPH]** under each frame.
36: 30 and sixteen silver bases—two **[RPH]** under each frame.
36: 36 They made gold hooks for them and cast their four silver **bases**.
36: 38 and their bases with gold and made their five **bases** *of* bronze.
38: 10 with twenty posts and twenty bronze **bases**, and with silver hooks
38: 11 hundred cubits long and had twenty posts and twenty bronze **bases**,
38: 12 fifty cubits wide and had curtains, with ten posts and ten **bases**,
38: 14 were on one side of the entrance, with three posts and three **bases**,
38: 15 of the entrance to the courtyard, with three posts and three **bases**.
38: 17 The **bases** for the posts were bronze. The hooks and bands on the
38: 19 with four posts and four bronze **bases**. Their hooks and bands were
38: 27 The 100 talents of silver were used to cast the **bases** *for* the
38: 27 to cast the bases for the sanctuary and **[RPH]** for the curtain—
38: 27 100 **bases** from the 100 talents, one talent for each base.
38: 27 100 bases from the 100 talents, one talent for each **base**.
38: 30 They used it to make the **bases** *for* the entrance to the Tent of
38: 31 the **bases** *for* the surrounding courtyard and those for its entrance
38: 31 and **those**[s] *for* its entrance and all the tent pegs for the tabernacle
39: 33 all its furnishings, its clasps, frames, crossbars, posts and **bases**;
39: 40 the curtains of the courtyard with its posts and **bases**, and the
40: 18 he put the **bases** in place, erected the frames, inserted the crossbars
Nu 3: 36 its crossbars, posts, **bases**, all its equipment, and everything related
3: 37 as well as the posts of the surrounding courtyard with their **bases**,
4: 31 to carry the frames of the tabernacle, its crossbars, posts and **bases**,
4: 32 as well as the posts of the surrounding courtyard with their **bases**,
Job 38: 6 On what were its **footings** set, or who laid its cornerstone—
SS 5: 15 His legs are pillars of marble set on **bases** *of* pure gold.
Eze 41: 22 its corners, its **base** [BHS 802] and its sides were of wood.

150 אַדָּן ***'addān***, n.pr.loc. [1] [cf. 124]

Addon [1]

Ezr 2: 59 the towns of Tel Melah, Tel Harsha, Kerub, **Addon** and Immer,

151 אֲדֹנָי ***ᵃdōnāy***, n.[pr.]m. [442] [√ 123]

Sovereign [291], the Lord [91], Lord [57], the Lord's [3]

Ge 15: 2 Abram said, "O **Sovereign** LORD, what can you give me since I
15: 8 Abram said, "O **Sovereign** LORD, how can I know that I will
18: 27 "Now that I have been so bold as to speak to **the Lord**, though I
18: 30 Then he said, "May **the Lord** not be angry, but let me speak.
18: 31 "Now that I have been so bold as to speak to **the Lord**,
18: 32 he said, "May **the Lord** not be angry, but let me speak just once
20: 4 near her, so he said, "**Lord**, will you destroy an innocent nation?
Ex 4: 10 Moses said to the LORD, "O **Lord**, I have never been eloquent,
4: 13 But Moses said, "O **Lord**, please send someone else to do it."
5: 22 Moses returned to the LORD and said, "O **Lord**, why have you
15: 17 for your dwelling, the sanctuary, O **Lord**, your hands established.
34: 9 "O **Lord**, if I have found favor in your eyes," he said, "then let the
34: 9 found favor in your eyes," he said, "then let **the Lord** go with us.
Nu 14: 17 "Now may **the Lord's** strength be displayed, just as you have
Dt 3: 24 "O **Sovereign** LORD, you have begun to show to your servant
9: 26 I prayed to the LORD and said, "O **Sovereign** LORD, do not
Jos 7: 7 Joshua said, "Ah, **Sovereign** LORD, why did you ever bring this
7: 8 O **Lord**, what can I say, now that Israel has been routed by its
Jdg 6: 15 "But **Lord**," Gideon asked, "how can I save Israel? My clan is the
6: 22 the angel of the LORD, he exclaimed, "Ah, **Sovereign** LORD!
13: 8 "O **Lord**, I beg you, let the man of God you sent to us come again
16: 28 prayed to the LORD, "O **Sovereign** LORD, remember me.
2Sa 7: 18 "Who am I, O **Sovereign** LORD, and what is my family,
7: 19 And as if this were not enough in your sight, O **Sovereign** LORD,
7: 19 Is this your usual way of dealing with man, O **Sovereign** LORD?
7: 20 say to you? For you know your servant, O **Sovereign** LORD.
7: 22 "How great you are, O **Sovereign** LORD! There is no one like
7: 28 O **Sovereign** LORD, you are God! Your words are trustworthy,
7: 29 for you, O **Sovereign** LORD, have spoken, and with your
1Ki 2: 26 because you carried the ark of the **Sovereign** LORD before my
3: 10 **The Lord** was pleased that Solomon had asked for this.
3: 15 stood before the ark of **the Lord's** covenant and sacrificed burnt
8: 53 O **Sovereign** LORD, brought our fathers out of Egypt."
22: 6 they answered, "for **the Lord** will give it into the king's hand."
2Ki 7: 6 for **the Lord** had caused the Arameans to hear the sound of
19: 23 By your messengers you have heaped insults on **the Lord**.
Ne 1: 11 O **Lord**, let your ear be attentive to the prayer of this your servant
4: 14 [4:8] Remember **the Lord**, who is great and awesome, and fight
8: 10 This day is sacred to our **Lord**. Do not grieve, for the joy of the
10: 29 [10:30] and decrees of the LORD our **Lord**.
Job 28: 28 And he said to man, 'The fear of **the Lord**—that is wisdom,
Ps 2: 4 The One enthroned in heaven laughs; **the Lord** scoffs at them.
16: 2 I said to the LORD, "You are my **Lord**; apart from you I have no
22: 30 [22:31] serve him; future generations will be told about **the Lord**.
30: 8 [30:9] To you, O LORD, I called; to **the Lord** I cried for mercy:
35: 17 O **Lord**, how long will you look on? Rescue my life from their
35: 22 you have seen this; be not silent. Do not be far from me, O **Lord**.
35: 23 and rise to my defense! Contend for me, my God and **Lord**.
37: 13 **the Lord** laughs at the wicked, for he knows their day is coming.
38: 9 [38:10] All my longings lie open before you, O **Lord**; my sighing
38: 15 [38:16] for you, O LORD; you will answer, O **Lord** my God.

Ps 38:22 [38:23] Come quickly to help me, O **Lord** my Savior.
39: 7 [39:8] "But now, **Lord**, what do I look for? My hope is in you.
40:17 [40:18] Yet I am poor and needy; may **the Lord** think of me.
44:23 [44:24] Awake, O **Lord**! Why do you sleep? Rouse yourself!
51:15 [51:17] O **Lord**, open my lips, and my mouth will declare your
54: 4 [54:6] God is my help; **the Lord** is the one who sustains me.
55: 9 [55:10] Confuse the wicked, O **Lord**, confound their speech, for I
57: 9 [57:10] I will praise you, O **Lord**, among the nations; I will sing
59:11 [59:12] do not kill them, O **Lord** our shield, or my people will
62:12 [62:13] that you, O **Lord**, are loving. Surely you will reward each
66:18 I had cherished sin in my heart, **the Lord** would not have listened;
68:11 [68:12] **The Lord** announced the word, and great was the
68:17 [68:18] **the Lord** ⌞has come⌟ from Sinai into his sanctuary.
68:19 [68:20] Praise be to **the Lord**, to God our Savior, who daily bears
68:20 [68:21] from the **Sovereign** LORD comes escape from death.
68:22 [68:23] **The Lord** says, "I will bring them from Bashan; I will
68:32 [68:33] kingdoms of the earth, sing praise to **the Lord**, *Selah*
69: 6 [69:7] who hope in you not be disgraced because of me, O **Lord**,
71: 5 For you have been my hope, O **Sovereign** LORD, my confidence
71:16 I will come and proclaim your mighty acts, O **Sovereign** LORD;
73:20 As a dream when one awakes, so when you arise, O **Lord**,
73:28 I have made the **Sovereign** LORD my refuge; I will tell of all
77: 2 [77:3] When I was in distress, I sought **the Lord**; at night I
77: 7 [77:8] "Will **the Lord** reject forever? Will he never show his
78:65 **the Lord** awoke as from sleep, as a man wakes from the stupor of
79:12 seven times the reproach they have hurled at you, O **Lord**.
86: 3 Have mercy on me, O **Lord**, for I call to you all day long.
86: 4 Bring joy to your servant, for to you, O **Lord**, I lift up my soul.
86: 5 You are forgiving and good, O **Lord**, abounding in love to all who
86: 8 Among the gods there is none like you, O **Lord**; no deeds can
86: 9 you have made will come and worship before you, O **Lord**;
86:12 I will praise you, O **Lord** my God, with all my heart; I will glorify
86:15 you, O **Lord**, are a compassionate and gracious God, slow to
89:49 [89:50] O **Lord**, where is your former great love, which in your
89:50 [89:51] Remember, **Lord**, how your servant has been mocked,
90: 1 **Lord**, you have been our dwelling place throughout all
90:17 May the favor of **the Lord** our God rest upon us; establish the
109:21 you, O **Sovereign** LORD, deal well with me for your name's
110: 5 **The Lord** is at your right hand; he will crush kings on the day of
130: 2 O **Lord**, hear my voice. Let your ears be attentive to my cry for
130: 3 O LORD, kept a record of sins, O **Lord**, who could stand?
130: 6 My soul waits for **the Lord** more than watchmen wait for the
135: 5 that the LORD is great, that our **Lord** is greater than all gods.
136: 3 Give thanks to the **Lord** *of* lords: *His love endures*
140: 7 [140:8] O **Sovereign** LORD, my strong deliverer, who shields
141: 8 my eyes are fixed on you, O **Sovereign** LORD; in you I take
147: 5 Great is our **Lord** and mighty in power; his understanding has no
Isa 3:15 the faces of the poor?" declares **the Lord**, the LORD Almighty.
3:17 Therefore **the Lord** will bring sores on the heads of the women of
3:18 In that day **the Lord** will snatch away their finery: the bangles
4: 4 **The Lord** will wash away the filth of the women of Zion;
6: 1 Uzziah died, I saw **the Lord** seated on a throne, high and exalted,
6: 8 Then I heard the voice of **the Lord** saying, "Whom shall I send?
6:11 I said, "For how long, O **Lord**?" And he answered: "Until the
7: 7 Yet this is what the **Sovereign** LORD says: " 'It will not take
7:14 Therefore **the Lord** himself will give you a sign: The virgin will
7:20 In that day **the Lord** will use a razor hired from beyond the
8: 7 therefore **the Lord** is about to bring against them the mighty
9: 8 [9:7] **The Lord** has sent a message against Jacob; it will fall on
9:17 [9:16] Therefore **the Lord** will take no pleasure in the young
10:12 When **the Lord** has finished all his work against Mount Zion
10:23 **The Lord**, the LORD Almighty, will carry out the destruction
10:24 Therefore, this is what **the Lord**, the LORD Almighty, says:
11:11 In that day **the Lord** will reach out his hand a second time to
21: 6 This is what **the Lord** says to me: "Go, post a lookout and have
21:16 This is what **the Lord** says to me: "Within one year, as a servant
22: 5 **The Lord**, the LORD Almighty, has a day of tumult
22:12 **The Lord**, the LORD Almighty, called you on that day to weep
22:14 sin will not be atoned for," says **the Lord**, the LORD Almighty.
22:15 This is what **the Lord**, the LORD Almighty, says: "Go, say to
25: 8 The **Sovereign** LORD will wipe away the tears from all faces;
28: 2 See, **the Lord** has one who is powerful and strong. Like a
28:16 So this is what the **Sovereign** LORD says: "See, I lay a stone in
28:22 **the Lord**, the LORD Almighty, has told me of the destruction
29:13 **The Lord** says: "These people come near to me with their mouth
30:15 This is what the **Sovereign** LORD, the Holy One of Israel,
30:20 Although **the Lord** gives you the bread of adversity and the water
37:24 By your messengers you have heaped insults on **the Lord**.
38:14 I looked to the heavens. I am troubled; O **Lord**, come to my aid!"
38:16 **Lord**, by such things men live; and my spirit finds life in them too.
40:10 See, the **Sovereign** LORD comes with power, and his arm rules
48:16 And now the **Sovereign** LORD has sent me, with his Spirit.
49:14 "The LORD has forsaken me, **the Lord** has forgotten me."
49:22 This is what the **Sovereign** LORD says: "See, I will beckon to the
50: 4 The **Sovereign** LORD has given me an instructed tongue,
50: 5 The **Sovereign** LORD has opened my ears, and I have not been
50: 7 Because the **Sovereign** LORD helps me, I will not be disgraced.
50: 9 It is the **Sovereign** LORD who helps me. Who is he that will
51:22 This is what your **Sovereign** LORD says, your God, who defends
52: 4 For this is what the **Sovereign** LORD says: "At first my people
56: 8 The **Sovereign** LORD declares—he who gathers the exiles of
61: 1 The Spirit of the **Sovereign** LORD is on me, because the LORD
61:11 so the **Sovereign** LORD will make righteousness and praise
65:13 Therefore this is what the **Sovereign** LORD says: "My servants
65:15 the **Sovereign** LORD will put you to death, but to his servants he
Jer 1: 6 "Ah, **Sovereign** LORD," I said, "I do not know how to speak;
2:19 and have no awe of me," declares **the Lord**, the LORD Almighty.
2:22 of your guilt is still before me," declares the **Sovereign** LORD.
4:10 I said, "Ah, **Sovereign** LORD, how completely you have
7:20 " 'Therefore this is what the **Sovereign** LORD says: My anger
14:13 I said, "Ah, **Sovereign** LORD, the prophets keep telling them,
32:17 "Ah, **Sovereign** LORD, you have made the heavens and the earth
32:25 you, O **Sovereign** LORD, say to me, 'Buy the field with silver
44:26 my name or swear, "As surely as the **Sovereign** LORD lives."
46:10 But that day belongs to **the Lord**, the LORD Almighty—
46:10 For **the Lord**, the LORD Almighty, will offer sacrifice in the land
49: 5 all those around you," declares **the Lord**, the LORD Almighty.
50:25 for the **Sovereign** LORD Almighty has work to do in the land of
50:31 "See, I am against you, O arrogant one," declares **the Lord**,
La 1:14 have come upon my neck and **the Lord** has sapped my strength.
1:15 "**The Lord** has rejected all the warriors in my midst; he has
1:15 In his winepress **the Lord** has trampled the Virgin Daughter of
2: 1 How **the Lord** has covered the Daughter of Zion with the cloud of
2: 2 Without pity **the Lord** has swallowed up all the dwellings of
2: 5 **The Lord** is like an enemy; he has swallowed up Israel. He has
2: 7 **The Lord** has rejected his altar and abandoned his sanctuary.
2:18 The hearts of the people cry out to **the Lord**. O wall of the
2:19 pour out your heart like water in the presence of **the Lord**.
2:20 Should priest and prophet be killed in the sanctuary of **the Lord**?
3:31 For men are not cast off by **the Lord** forever.
3:36 to deprive a man of justice—would not **the Lord** see such things?
3:37 Who can speak and have it happen if **the Lord** has not decreed it?
3:58 O **Lord**, you took up my case; you redeemed my life.
Eze 2: 4 Say to them, 'This is what the **Sovereign** LORD says.'
3:11 Say to them, 'This is what the **Sovereign** LORD says,'
3:27 you shall say to them, 'This is what the **Sovereign** LORD says.'
4:14 I said, "Not so, **Sovereign** LORD! I have never defiled myself.
5: 5 "This is what the **Sovereign** LORD says: This is Jerusalem,
5: 7 "Therefore this is what the **Sovereign** LORD says: You have
5: 8 "Therefore this is what the **Sovereign** LORD says: I myself am
5:11 Therefore as surely as I live, declares the **Sovereign** LORD,
6: 3 'O mountains of Israel, hear the word of the **Sovereign** LORD.
6: 3 This is what the **Sovereign** LORD says to the mountains
6:11 " 'This is what the **Sovereign** LORD says: Strike your hands
7: 2 this is what the **Sovereign** LORD says to the land of Israel:
7: 5 "This is what the **Sovereign** LORD says: Disaster! An unheard-of
8: 1 before me, the hand of the **Sovereign** LORD came upon me there.
9: 8 left alone, I fell facedown, crying out, "Ah, **Sovereign** LORD!
11: 7 "Therefore this is what the **Sovereign** LORD says: The bodies
11: 8 is what I will bring against you, declares the **Sovereign** LORD.
11:13 and cried out in a loud voice, "Ah, **Sovereign** LORD!
11:16 "Therefore say: 'This is what the **Sovereign** LORD says:
11:17 "Therefore say: 'This is what the **Sovereign** LORD says:
11:21 own heads what they have done, declares the **Sovereign** LORD."
12:10 "Say to them, 'This is what the **Sovereign** LORD says: This
12:19 'This is what the **Sovereign** LORD says about those living in
12:23 Say to them, 'This is what the **Sovereign** LORD says: I am going
12:25 I will fulfill whatever I say, declares the **Sovereign** LORD.' "
12:28 "Therefore say to them, 'This is what the **Sovereign** LORD says:
12:28 whatever I say will be fulfilled, declares the **Sovereign** LORD.' "
13: 3 This is what the **Sovereign** LORD says: Woe to the foolish
13: 8 " 'Therefore this is what the **Sovereign** LORD says: Because of
13: 8 lying visions, I am against you, declares the **Sovereign** LORD.
13: 9 of Israel. Then you will know that I am the **Sovereign** LORD.
13:13 " 'Therefore this is what the **Sovereign** LORD says: In my wrath I
13:16 her when there was no peace, declares the **Sovereign** LORD." '
13:18 say, 'This is what the **Sovereign** LORD says: Woe to the women
13:20 " 'Therefore this is what the **Sovereign** LORD says: I am against
14: 4 to them and tell them, 'This is what the **Sovereign** LORD says:
14: 6 to the house of Israel, 'This is what the **Sovereign** LORD says:
14:11 and I will be their God, declares the **Sovereign** LORD.' "
14:14 themselves by their righteousness, declares the **Sovereign** LORD.
14:16 as surely as I live, declares the **Sovereign** LORD, even if these
14:18 as surely as I live, declares the **Sovereign** LORD, even if these
14:20 declares the **Sovereign** LORD, even if Noah, Daniel and Job
14:21 "For this is what the **Sovereign** LORD says: How much worse
14:23 done nothing in it without cause, declares the **Sovereign** LORD."
15: 6 "Therefore this is what the **Sovereign** LORD says: As I have

Eze 15: 8 they have been unfaithful, declares the **Sovereign** LORD."
16: 3 and say, 'This is what the **Sovereign** LORD says to Jerusalem:
16: 8 with you, declares the **Sovereign** LORD, and you became mine.
16: 14 you made your beauty perfect, declares the **Sovereign** LORD.
16: 19 That is what happened, declares the **Sovereign** LORD.
16: 23 " 'Woe! Woe to you, declares the **Sovereign** LORD. In addition
16: 30 " 'How weak-willed you are, declares the **Sovereign** LORD,
16: 36 This is what the **Sovereign** LORD says: Because you poured out
16: 43 on your head what you have done, declares the **Sovereign** LORD.
16: 48 declares the **Sovereign** LORD, your sister Sodom and her
16: 59 " 'This is what the **Sovereign** LORD says: I will deal with you as
16: 63 because of your humiliation, declares the **Sovereign** LORD.' "
17: 3 Say to them, 'This is what the **Sovereign** LORD says: A great
17: 9 "Say to them, 'This is what the **Sovereign** LORD says: Will it
17: 16 " 'As surely as I live, declares the **Sovereign** LORD, he shall die
17: 19 " 'Therefore this is what the **Sovereign** LORD says: As surely as I
17: 22 " 'This is what the **Sovereign** LORD says: I myself will take a
18: 3 "As surely as I live, declares the **Sovereign** LORD, you will no
18: 9 is righteous; he will surely live, declares the **Sovereign** LORD.
18: 23 declares the **Sovereign** LORD. Rather, am I not pleased when
18: 25 "Yet you say, 'The way of **the Lord** is not just.' Hear, O house of
18: 29 Yet the house of Israel says, 'The way of **the Lord** is not just.'
18: 30 each one according to his ways, declares the **Sovereign** LORD.
18: 32 pleasure in the death of anyone, declares the **Sovereign** LORD.
20: 3 and say to them, 'This is what the **Sovereign** LORD says:
20: 3 I will not let you inquire of me, declares the **Sovereign** LORD.'
20: 5 and say to them: 'This is what the **Sovereign** LORD says:
20: 27 and say to them, 'This is what the **Sovereign** LORD says:
20: 30 to the house of Israel: 'This is what the **Sovereign** LORD says:
20: 31 As surely as I live, declares the **Sovereign** LORD, I will not let
20: 33 As surely as I live, declares the **Sovereign** LORD, I will rule over
20: 36 land of Egypt, so I will judge you, declares the **Sovereign** LORD.
20: 39 O house of Israel, this is what the **Sovereign** LORD says:
20: 40 the high mountain of Israel, declares the **Sovereign** LORD,
20: 44 O house of Israel, declares the **Sovereign** LORD.' "
20: 47 [21:3] This is what the **Sovereign** LORD says: I am about to set
20: 49 [21:5] I said, "Ah, **Sovereign** LORD! They are saying of me,
21: 7 [21:12] It will surely take place, declares the **Sovereign** LORD."
21: 9 [21:14] of man, prophesy and say, 'This is what **the Lord** says:
21: 13 [21:18] does not continue? declares the **Sovereign** LORD.'
21: 24 [21:29] "Therefore this is what the **Sovereign** LORD says:
21: 26 [21:31] this is what the **Sovereign** LORD says: Take off the
21: 28 [21:33] 'This is what the **Sovereign** LORD says about the
22: 3 say: 'This is what the **Sovereign** LORD says: O city that brings
22: 12 And you have forgotten me, declares the **Sovereign** LORD.
22: 19 Therefore this is what the **Sovereign** LORD says: 'Because you
22: 28 They say, 'This is what the **Sovereign** LORD says'—
22: 31 own heads all they have done, declares the **Sovereign** LORD."
23: 22 "Therefore, Oholibah, this is what the **Sovereign** LORD says:
23: 28 "For this is what the **Sovereign** LORD says: I am about to hand
23: 32 "This is what the **Sovereign** LORD says: "You will drink your
23: 34 tear your breasts. I have spoken, declares the **Sovereign** LORD.
23: 35 "Therefore this is what the **Sovereign** LORD says: Since you
23: 46 "This is what the **Sovereign** LORD says: Bring a mob against
23: 49 of idolatry. Then you will know that I am the **Sovereign** LORD."
24: 3 and say to them: 'This is what the **Sovereign** LORD says:
24: 6 " 'For this is what the **Sovereign** LORD says: " 'Woe to the city
24: 9 " 'Therefore this is what the **Sovereign** LORD says: " 'Woe to the
24: 14 your conduct and your actions, declares the **Sovereign** LORD.' "
24: 21 to the house of Israel, 'This is what the **Sovereign** LORD says:
24: 24 this happens, you will know that I am the **Sovereign** LORD.'
25: 3 Say to them, 'Hear the word of the **Sovereign** LORD. This is
25: 3 This is what the **Sovereign** LORD says: Because you said "Aha!"
25: 6 For this is what the **Sovereign** LORD says: Because you have
25: 8 "This is what the **Sovereign** LORD says: 'Because Moab
25: 12 "This is what the **Sovereign** LORD says: 'Because Edom took
25: 13 therefore this is what the **Sovereign** LORD says: I will stretch out
25: 14 they will know my vengeance, declares the **Sovereign** LORD.' "
25: 15 "This is what the **Sovereign** LORD says: 'Because the Philistines
25: 16 therefore this is what the **Sovereign** LORD says: I am about to
26: 3 therefore this is what the **Sovereign** LORD says: I am against
26: 5 spread fishnets, for I have spoken, declares the **Sovereign** LORD.
26: 7 "For this is what the **Sovereign** LORD says: From the north I am
26: 14 for I the LORD have spoken, declares the **Sovereign** LORD.
26: 15 "This is what the **Sovereign** LORD says to Tyre: Will not the
26: 19 "This is what the **Sovereign** LORD says: When I make you a
26: 21 you will never again be found, declares the **Sovereign** LORD."
27: 3 peoples on many coasts, 'This is what the **Sovereign** LORD says:
28: 2 say to the ruler of Tyre, 'This is what the **Sovereign** LORD says:
28: 6 " 'Therefore this is what the **Sovereign** LORD says:
28: 10 of foreigners. I have spoken, declares the **Sovereign** LORD.' "
28: 12 and say to him: 'This is what the **Sovereign** LORD says:
28: 22 say: 'This is what the **Sovereign** LORD says: " 'I am against you,
28: 24 Then they will know that I am the **Sovereign** LORD.
28: 25 " 'This is what the **Sovereign** LORD says: When I gather the
29: 3 Speak to him and say: 'This is what the **Sovereign** LORD says:
29: 8 " 'Therefore this is what the **Sovereign** LORD says: I will bring a
29: 13 " 'Yet this is what the **Sovereign** LORD says: At the end of forty
29: 16 for help. Then they will know that I am the **Sovereign** LORD.' "
29: 19 Therefore this is what the **Sovereign** LORD says: I am going to
29: 20 and his army did it for me, declares the **Sovereign** LORD.
30: 2 'This is what the **Sovereign** LORD says: " 'Wail and say,
30: 6 will fall by the sword within her, declares the **Sovereign** LORD.
30: 10 " 'This is what the **Sovereign** LORD says: " 'I will put an end to
30: 13 " 'This is what the **Sovereign** LORD says: " 'I will destroy the
30: 22 Therefore this is what the **Sovereign** LORD says: I am against
31: 10 " 'Therefore this is what the **Sovereign** LORD says: Because it
31: 15 " 'This is what the **Sovereign** LORD says: On the day it was
31: 18 is Pharaoh and all his hordes, declares the **Sovereign** LORD.' "
32: 3 " 'This is what the **Sovereign** LORD says: " 'With a great throng
32: 8 bring darkness over your land, declares the **Sovereign** LORD.
32: 11 " 'For this is what the **Sovereign** LORD says: " 'The sword of the
32: 14 make her streams flow like oil, declares the **Sovereign** LORD.
32: 16 all her hordes they will chant it, declares the **Sovereign** LORD."
32: 31 that were killed by the sword, declares the **Sovereign** LORD.
32: 32 with those killed by the sword, declares the **Sovereign** LORD."
33: 11 Say to them, 'As surely as I live, declares the **Sovereign** LORD,
33: 17 "Yet your countrymen say, 'The way of **the Lord** is not just.'
33: 20 O house of Israel, you say, 'The way of **the Lord** is not just.'
33: 25 Therefore say to them, 'This is what the **Sovereign** LORD says:
33: 27 "Say this to them: 'This is what the **Sovereign** LORD says:
34: 2 and say to them: 'This is what the **Sovereign** LORD says:
34: 8 As surely as I live, declares the **Sovereign** LORD, because my
34: 10 This is what the **Sovereign** LORD says: I am against the
34: 11 " 'For this is what the **Sovereign** LORD says: I myself will search
34: 15 and have them lie down, declares the **Sovereign** LORD.
34: 17 " 'As for you, my flock, this is what the **Sovereign** LORD says:
34: 20 " 'Therefore this is what the **Sovereign** LORD says to them:
34: 30 the house of Israel, are my people, declares the **Sovereign** LORD.
34: 31 are people, and I am your God, declares the **Sovereign** LORD.' "
35: 3 say: 'This is what the **Sovereign** LORD says: I am against you,
35: 6 therefore as surely as I live, declares the **Sovereign** LORD,
35: 11 therefore as surely as I live, declares the **Sovereign** LORD,
35: 14 This is what the **Sovereign** LORD says: While the whole earth
36: 2 This is what the **Sovereign** LORD says: The enemy said of you,
36: 3 and say, 'This is what the **Sovereign** LORD says:
36: 4 O mountains of Israel, hear the word of the **Sovereign** LORD:
36: 4 This is what the **Sovereign** LORD says to the mountains
36: 5 this is what the **Sovereign** LORD says: In my burning zeal I have
36: 6 the ravines and valleys: 'This is what the **Sovereign** LORD says:
36: 7 Therefore this is what the **Sovereign** LORD says: I swear with
36: 13 " 'This is what the **Sovereign** LORD says: Because people say to
36: 14 or make your nation childless, declares the **Sovereign** LORD.
36: 15 or cause your nation to fall, declares the **Sovereign** LORD.' "
36: 22 to the house of Israel, 'This is what the **Sovereign** LORD says:
36: 23 will know that I am the LORD, declares the **Sovereign** LORD,
36: 32 I am not doing this for your sake, declares the **Sovereign** LORD.
36: 33 " 'This is what the **Sovereign** LORD says: On the day I cleanse
36: 37 "This is what the **Sovereign** LORD says: Once again I will yield
37: 3 these bones live?" I said, "O **Sovereign** LORD, you alone know."
37: 5 This is what the **Sovereign** LORD says to these bones: I will
37: 9 son of man, and say to it, 'This is what the **Sovereign** LORD says:
37: 12 'This is what the **Sovereign** LORD says: O my people, I am going
37: 19 say to them, 'This is what the **Sovereign** LORD says: I am going
37: 21 and say to them, 'This is what the **Sovereign** LORD says:
38: 3 say: 'This is what the **Sovereign** LORD says: I am against you,
38: 10 " 'This is what the **Sovereign** LORD says: On that day thoughts
38: 14 'This is what the **Sovereign** LORD says: In that day, when my
38: 17 " 'This is what the **Sovereign** LORD says: Are you not the one I
38: 18 my hot anger will be aroused, declares the **Sovereign** LORD.
38: 21 against Gog on all my mountains, declares the **Sovereign** LORD.
39: 1 against Gog and say: 'This is what the **Sovereign** LORD says:
39: 5 the open field, for I have spoken, declares the **Sovereign** LORD.
39: 8 It will surely take place, declares the **Sovereign** LORD.
39: 10 and loot those who looted them, declares the **Sovereign** LORD.
39: 13 will be a memorable day for them, declares the **Sovereign** LORD.
39: 17 "Son of man, this is what the **Sovereign** LORD says: Call out to
39: 20 and soldiers of every kind,' declares the **Sovereign** LORD.
39: 25 "Therefore this is what the **Sovereign** LORD says: I will now
39: 29 my Spirit on the house of Israel, declares the **Sovereign** LORD."
43: 18 said to me, "Son of man, this is what the **Sovereign** LORD says:
43: 19 come near to minister before me, declares the **Sovereign** LORD.
43: 27 the altar. Then I will accept you, declares the **Sovereign** LORD."
44: 6 house of Israel, 'This is what the **Sovereign** LORD says:
44: 9 This is what the **Sovereign** LORD says: No foreigner
44: 12 bear the consequences of their sin, declares the **Sovereign** LORD.
44: 15 offer sacrifices of fat and blood, declares the **Sovereign** LORD.
44: 27 to offer a sin offering for himself, declares the **Sovereign** LORD.

Eze 45: 9 " 'This is what the **Sovereign** LORD says: You have gone far
45: 9 Stop dispossessing my people, declares the **Sovereign** LORD.
45: 15 to make atonement for the people, declares the **Sovereign** LORD.
45: 18 " 'This is what the **Sovereign** LORD says: In the first month on
46: 1 " 'This is what the **Sovereign** LORD says: The gate of the inner
46: 16 " 'This is what the **Sovereign** LORD says: If the prince makes a
47: 13 This is what the **Sovereign** LORD says: "These are the
47: 23 are to give him his inheritance," declares the **Sovereign** LORD.
48: 29 and these will be their portions," declares the **Sovereign** LORD.
Da 1: 2 And **the Lord** delivered Jehoiakim king of Judah into his hand,
9: 3 So I turned to **the Lord** God and pleaded with him in prayer
9: 4 "O **Lord**, the great and awesome God, who keeps his covenant of
9: 7 "**Lord**, you are righteous, but this day we are covered with
9: 9 **The Lord** our God is merciful and forgiving, even though we have
9: 15 "Now, O **Lord** our God, who brought your people out of Egypt
9: 16 O **Lord**, in keeping with all your righteous acts, turn away your
9: 17 For your sake, O **Lord**, look with favor on your desolate sanctuary.
9: 19 O **Lord**, listen! O Lord, forgive! O Lord, hear and act! For your
9: 19 O Lord, listen! O **Lord**, forgive! O Lord, hear and act! For your
9: 19 O Lord, listen! O Lord, forgive! O **Lord**, hear and act! For your
Hos 12: 14 [12:15] his **Lord** will leave upon him the guilt of his bloodshed
Am 1: 8 till the last of the Philistines is dead," says the **Sovereign** LORD.
3: 7 Surely the **Sovereign** LORD does nothing without revealing his
3: 8 The **Sovereign** LORD has spoken—who can but prophesy?
3: 11 Therefore this is what the **Sovereign** LORD says: "An enemy
3: 13 house of Jacob," declares **the Lord**, the LORD God Almighty.
4: 2 The **Sovereign** LORD has sworn by his holiness: "The time will
4: 5 for this is what you love to do," declares the **Sovereign** LORD.
5: 3 This is what the **Sovereign** LORD says: "The city that marches
5: 16 Therefore this is what **the Lord**, the LORD God Almighty,
6: 8 The **Sovereign** LORD has sworn by himself—the LORD God
7: 1 This is what the **Sovereign** LORD showed me: He was preparing
7: 2 stripped the land clean, I cried out, "**Sovereign** LORD, forgive!
7: 4 This is what the **Sovereign** LORD showed me: The Sovereign
7: 4 The **Sovereign** LORD was calling for judgment by fire; it dried
7: 5 I cried out, "**Sovereign** LORD, I beg you, stop! How can Jacob
7: 6 "This will not happen either," the **Sovereign** LORD said.
7: 7 **The Lord** was standing by a wall that had been built true to plumb,
7: 8 **the Lord** said, "Look, I am setting a plumb line among my people
8: 1 This is what the **Sovereign** LORD showed me: a basket of ripe
8: 3 "In that day," declares the **Sovereign** LORD, "the songs in the
8: 9 "In that day," declares the **Sovereign** LORD, "I will make the sun
8: 11 "The days are coming," declares the **Sovereign** LORD, "when I
9: 1 I saw **the Lord** standing by the altar, and he said: "Strike the tops
9: 5 **The Lord**, the LORD Almighty, he who touches the earth
9: 8 "Surely the eyes of the **Sovereign** LORD are on the sinful
Ob 1: 1 This is what the **Sovereign** LORD says about Edom—We have
Mic 1: 2 who are in it, that the **Sovereign** LORD may witness against you,
1: 2 LORD may witness against you, **the Lord** from his holy temple.
Hab 3: 19 The **Sovereign** LORD is my strength; he makes my feet like the
Zep 1: 7 Be silent before the **Sovereign** LORD, for the day of the LORD
Zec 9: 4 **the Lord** will take away her possessions and destroy her power on
9: 14 The **Sovereign** LORD will sound the trumpet; he will march in
Mal 1: 12 "But you profane it by saying of **the Lord's** table, 'It is defiled,'
1: 14 vows to give it, but then sacrifices a blemished animal to **the Lord**.

152 אֲדֹנִי בֶזֶק *ᵃdōnî bezeq*, n.pr.m. [3] [√ 123 + 1028]

Adoni-Bezek [3]

Jdg 1: 5 It was there that they found **Adoni-Bezek** and fought against him,
1: 6 **Adoni-Bezek** fled, but they chased him and caught him, and cut
1: 7 Then **Adoni-Bezek** said, "Seventy kings with their thumbs

153 אֲדֹנִיָּה *ᵃdōniyyâ*, n.pr.m. [7] [→ 154; cf. 123 + 3378]

Adonijah [7]

2Sa 3: 4 the fourth, **Adonijah** the son of Haggith; the fifth,
1Ki 1: 5 Now **Adonijah**, whose mother was Haggith, put himself forward
1: 7 **Adonijah** conferred with Joab son of Zeruiah and with Abiathar
1: 18 But now **Adonijah** has become king, and you, my lord the king,
2: 28 who had conspired with **Adonijah** though not with Absalom,
1Ch 3: 2 Talmai king of Geshur; the fourth, **Adonijah** the son of Haggith;
Ne 10: 16 [10:17] **Adonijah**, Bigvai, Adin,

154 אֲדֹנִיָּהוּ *ᵃdōniyyāhû*, n.pr.m. [19] [√ 153; cf. 123 + 3378]

Adonijah [17], *untranslated* [1], Adonijah's [+4200] [1]

1Ki 1: 8 and Rei and David's special guard did not join **Adonijah**.
1: 9 **Adonijah** then sacrificed sheep, cattle and fattened calves at the
1: 11 "Have you not heard that **Adonijah**, the son of Haggith,
1: 13 he will sit on my throne"? Why then has **Adonijah** become king?"
1: 24 my lord the king, declared that **Adonijah** shall be king after you,
1: 25 and drinking with him and saying, 'Long live King **Adonijah**!'
1: 41 **Adonijah** and all the guests who were with him heard it as they
1: 42 son of Abiathar the priest arrived. **Adonijah** said, "Come in.
1: 43 **[RPH]** "Our lord King David has made Solomon king.
1: 49 all **Adonijah's** [+4200] guests rose in alarm and dispersed.
1: 50 **Adonijah**, in fear of Solomon, went and took hold of the horns of
1: 51 "**Adonijah** is afraid of King Solomon and is clinging to the horns
2: 13 Now **Adonijah**, the son of Haggith, went to Bathsheba, Solomon's
2: 19 Bathsheba went to King Solomon to speak to him for **Adonijah**,
2: 21 the Shunammite be given in marriage to your brother **Adonijah**."
2: 22 "Why do you request Abishag the Shunammite for **Adonijah**?
2: 23 so severely, if **Adonijah** does not pay with his life for this request!
2: 24 for me as he promised—**Adonijah** shall be put to death today!"
2Ch 17: 8 Shemiramoth, Jehonathan, **Adonijah**, Tobijah and Tob-Adonijah—

155 אֲדֹנִי־צֶדֶק *ᵃdōnî-ṣedeq*, n.pr.m. [2] [√ 123 + 7406]

Adoni-Zedek [2]

Jos 10: 1 Now **Adoni-Zedek** king of Jerusalem heard that Joshua had taken
10: 3 So **Adoni-Zedek** king of Jerusalem appealed to Hoham king of

156 אֲדֹנִיקָם *ᵃdōnîqām*, n.pr.m. [3] [√ 123 + 7756]

Adonikam [3]

Ezr 2: 13 of **Adonikam** 666
8: 13 of the descendants of **Adonikam**, the last ones, whose names were
Ne 7: 18 of **Adonikam** 667

157 אֲדֹנִירָם *ᵃdōnîrām*, n.pr.m. [2 / 4] [→ 127, 164; cf. 123 + 8123]

Adoniram [4]

2Sa 20: 24 **Adoniram** [BHS 164] was in charge of forced labor; Jehoshaphat
1Ki 4: 6 Ahishar—in charge of the palace; **Adoniram** son of Abda—
5: 14 [5:28] at home. **Adoniram** was in charge of the forced labor.
12: 18 King Rehoboam sent out **Adoniram**, [BHS 164] who was in

158 אדר *'ādar*, v. [3] [→ 129, 159, 160, 168]

majestic [2], glorious [1]

Ex 15: 6 [C] "Your right hand, O LORD, *was* **majestic** in power.
15: 11 [C] **majestic** in holiness, awesome in glory, working wonders?
Isa 42: 21 [G] sake of his righteousness to make his law great and **glorious**.

159 אֶדֶר *'eder*, n.[m.]. [2] [√ 158]

handsome [1], rich [1]

Mic 2: 8 You strip off the **rich** robe from those who pass by without a care,
Zec 11: 13 it to the potter"—the **handsome** price at which they priced me!

160 אֲדָר *ᵃdār*, n.pr.[m.]. [8] [√ 158; Ar 10009]

Adar [8]

Est 3: 7 And the lot fell on the twelfth month, the month of **Adar**.
3: 13 the twelfth month, the month of **Adar**, and to plunder their goods.
8: 12 was the thirteenth day of the twelfth month, the month of **Adar**.
9: 1 On the thirteenth day of the twelfth month, the month of **Adar**,
9: 15 in Susa came together on the fourteenth day of the month of **Adar**,
9: 17 This happened on the thirteenth day of the month of **Adar**,
9: 19 observe the fourteenth of the month of **Adar** as a day of joy
9: 21 annually the fourteenth and fifteenth days of the month of **Adar**

161 אַדָּרי *'addār¹*, n.pr.m. [1]

Addar [1]

1Ch 8: 3 The sons of Bela were: **Addar**, Gera, Abihud,

162 ²אַדָּר *'addār²*, n.pr.loc. [1] [→ 2960, 6501]

Addar [1]

Jos 15: 3 Then it ran past Hezron up to **Addar** and curved around to Karka.

163 אֲדַרְכֹנִים *ᵃdarkōnîm*, n.[m.pl.?]. [2] [√ 2007]

darics [2]

1Ch 29: 7 of God five thousand talents and ten thousand **darics** of gold,
Ezr 8: 27 20 bowls of gold valued at 1,000 **darics**, and two fine articles of

164 אֲדֹרָם *ᵃdōrām*, n.pr.m. [2 / 0] [√ 157]

2Sa 20: 24 Adoniram [BHS *Adoram*; NIV 157] was in charge of forced labor;
1Ki 12: 18 King Rehoboam sent out Adoniram, [BHS *Adoram*; NIV 157] who

165 אַדְרַמֶּלֶךְי *'adrammelek¹*, n.pr.[m.]. [1] [→ 166]

Adrammelech [1]

2Ki 17: 31 burned their children in the fire as sacrifices to **Adrammelech**

166 [2]אַדְרַמֶּלֶךְ ***'adrammelek***[2], n.pr.m. [2] [√ 165]

Adrammelech [2]

2Ki 19:37 his sons **Adrammelech** and Sharezer cut him down with the
Isa 37:38 his sons **Adrammelech** and Sharezer cut him down with the

167 אֶדְרֶעִי ***'edre'î***, n.pr.loc. [8]

Edrei [8]

Nu 21:33 and his whole army marched out to meet them in battle at **Edrei**.
Dt 1: 4 reigned in Heshbon, and at **Edrei** had defeated Og king of Bashan,
3: 1 with his whole army marched out to meet us in battle at **Edrei**.
3:10 and all Gilead, and all Bashan as far as Salecah and **Edrei**,
Jos 12: 4 of the last of the Rephaites, who reigned in Ashtaroth and **Edrei**.
13:12 who had reigned in Ashtaroth and **Edrei** and had survived as one
13:31 and Ashtaroth and **Edrei** (the royal cities of Og in Bashan).
19:37 Kedesh, **Edrei**, En Hazor,

168 אַדֶּרֶת ***'adderet***, n.f. [12] [√ 158]

cloak [5], robe [2], garment [1], prophet's garment [1], rich pastures [1], royal robes [1], splendid [1]

Ge 25:25 come out was red, and his whole body was like a hairy **garment**;
Jos 7:21 When I saw in the plunder a beautiful **robe** *from* Babylonia,
7:24 the silver, the **robe**, the gold wedge, his sons and daughters,
1Ki 19:13 he pulled his **cloak** over his face and went out and stood at the
19:19 Elijah went up to him and threw his **cloak** around him.
2Ki 2: 8 Elijah took his **cloak**, rolled it up and struck the water with it.
2:13 He picked up the **cloak** that had fallen from Elijah and went back
2:14 he took the **cloak** that had fallen from him and struck the water
Eze 17: 8 it would produce branches, bear fruit and become a **splendid** vine.'
Jnh 3: 6 he rose from his throne, took off his **royal robes**, covered himself
Zec 11: 3 to the wail of the shepherds; their **rich pastures** are destroyed!
13: 4 He will not put on a **prophet's garment** *of* hair in order to

169 אָדַשׁ ***'ādaš***, v. Not used in NIV/BHS [cf. 1889]

170 אָהַב ***'āhab***, v. [215] [→ 171, 172, 173, 174?, 175]

love [93], loves [38], loved [33], lovers [12], friends [8], allies [4], friend [4], in love with [3], fell in love with [2], like [2], liked [2], adore [1], attracted to [1], both[s] [+2021+2021+2256+8533] [1], chosen ally [1], dearly [1], desires [1], likes [1], on friendly terms [1], resents [+4202] [1], show love [1], showed love [1], value [1], was loved [1], were loved [1]

Ge 22: 2 [A] "Take your son, your only son, Isaac, whom *you* **love**,
24:67 [A] So she became his wife, and *he* **loved** her; and Isaac was
25:28 [A] a taste for wild game, **loved** Esau, but Rebekah loved Jacob.
25:28 [A] a taste for wild game, loved Esau, but Rebekah **loved** Jacob.
27: 4 [A] Prepare me the kind of tasty food *I* **like** and bring it to me to
27: 9 [A] some tasty food for your father, just the way *he* **likes** it.
27:14 [A] she prepared some tasty food, just the way his father **liked** it.
29:18 [A] Jacob *was* **in love with** Rachel and said, "I'll work for you
29:30 [A] lay with Rachel also, and *he* **loved** Rachel more than Leah.
29:32 [A] has seen my misery. Surely my husband *will* **love** me now."
34: 3 [A] of Jacob, and *he* **loved** the girl and spoke tenderly to her.
37: 3 [A] Now Israel **loved** Joseph more than any of his other sons,
37: 4 [A] When his brothers saw that their father **loved** him more than
44:20 [A] only one of his mother's sons left, and his father **loves** him.'
Ex 20: 6 [A] showing love to a thousand ⌞generations⌟ of *those who* **love**
21: 5 [A] '*I* **love** my master and my wife and children and do not want
Lev 19:18 [A] one of your people, but **love** your neighbor as yourself.
19:34 [A] **Love** him as yourself, for you were aliens in Egypt. I am the
Dt 4:37 [A] Because *he* **loved** your forefathers and chose their
5:10 [A] showing love to a thousand ⌞generations⌟ of *those who* **love**
6: 5 [A] **Love** the LORD your God with all your heart and with all
7: 8 [A] it was because the LORD **loved** you and kept the oath he
7: 9 [A] of love to a thousand generations of *those who* **love** him
7:13 [A] *He will* **love** you and bless you and increase your numbers.
10:12 [A] the LORD your God, to walk in all his ways, to **love** him,
10:15 [A] LORD set his affection on your forefathers and **loved** them,
10:18 [A] the cause of the fatherless and the widow, and **loves** the alien,
10:19 [A] *you are to* **love** those who are aliens, for you yourselves
11: 1 [A] **Love** the LORD your God and keep his requirements, his
11:13 [A] to **love** the LORD your God and to serve him with all your
11:22 [A] to **love** the LORD your God, to walk in all his ways and to
13: 3 [13:4] [A] to find out whether you **love** him with all your heart
15:16 [A] because *he* **loves** you and your family and is well off with
19: 9 [A] to **love** the LORD your God and to walk always in his
21:15 [B] and he **loves** one but not the other, and both bear him sons
21:15 [B] and **both**[s] [+2021+2021+2256+8533] bear him sons but the
21:16 [B] son of the wife *he* **loves** in preference to his actual firstborn,
23: 5 [23:6] [A] for you, because the LORD your God **loves** you.
30: 6 [A] so that you *may* **love** him with all your heart and with all
30:16 [A] For I command you today to **love** the LORD your God,
30:20 [A] that you *may* **love** the LORD your God, listen to his voice,
Jos 22: 5 [A] to **love** the LORD your God, to walk in all his ways, to obey
23:11 [A] So be very careful to **love** the LORD your God.
Jdg 5:31 [A] *may they who* **love** you be like the sun when it rises in its
14:16 [A] on him, sobbing, "You hate me! *You* don't really **love** me.
16: 4 [A] *he* **fell in love with** a woman in the Valley of Sorek whose
16:15 [A] she said to him, "How can you say, '*I* **love** you,' when you
Ru 4:15 [A] who **loves** you and who is better to you than seven sons,
1Sa 1: 5 [A] to Hannah he gave a double portion because *he* **loved** her,
16:21 [A] Saul **liked** him very much, and David became one of his
18: 1 [A] one in spirit with David, and he **loved** him as himself.
18: 3 [A] a covenant with David because he **loved** him as himself.
18:16 [A] all Israel and Judah **loved** David, because he led them in their
18:20 [A] Now Saul's daughter Michal *was* **in love with** David,
18:22 [A] the king is pleased with you, and his attendants all **like** you;
18:28 [A] was with David and that his daughter Michal **loved** David,
20:17 [A] Jonathan had David reaffirm his oath out of **love** *for* him,
20:17 [A] of love for him, because *he* **loved** him as he loved himself.
2Sa 1:23 [C] in life they **were loved** and gracious, and in death they were
12:24 [A] and they named him Solomon. The LORD **loved** him;
13: 1 [A] course of time, Amnon son of David **fell in love with** Tamar,
13: 4 [A] Amnon said to him, "I'm **in love with** Tamar, my brother
13:15 [A] In fact, he hated her more than *he had* **loved** her. Amnon
19: 6 [19:7] [A] You **love** those who hate you and hate those who
19: 6 [19:7] [A] those who hate you and hate *those who* **love** you.
1Ki 3: 3 [A] Solomon **showed** *his* **love** *for* the LORD by walking
5: 1 [5:15] [A] because he had always been **on friendly terms** with
11: 1 [A] **loved** many foreign women besides Pharaoh's daughter—
2Ch 2:11 [2:10] [A] "Because the LORD **loves** his people, he has made
9: 8 [A] Because of the **love** *of* your God *for* Israel and his desire to
11:21 [A] Rehoboam **loved** Maacah daughter of Absalom more than
19: 2 [A] you help the wicked and **love** those who hate the LORD?
20: 7 [A] give it forever to the descendants of Abraham your **friend**?
26:10 [A] in the hills and in the fertile lands, for *he* **loved** the soil.
Ne 1: 5 [A] who keeps his covenant of love with *those who* **love** him
13:26 [B] *He* **was loved** by his God, and God made him king over all
Est 2:17 [A] Now the king *was* **attracted to** Esther more than to any of
5:10 [A] went home. Calling together his **friends** and Zeresh, his wife,
5:14 [A] His wife Zeresh and all his **friends** said to him, "Have a
6:13 [A] and all his **friends** everything that had happened to him.
Job 19:19 [A] friends detest me; those *I* **love** have turned against me.
Ps 4: 2 [4:3] [A] How long *will you* **love** delusions and seek false
5:11 [5:12] [A] that *those who* **love** your name may rejoice in you.
11: 5 [A] but the wicked and *those who* **love** violence his soul hates.
11: 7 [A] For the LORD is righteous, *he* **loves** justice; upright men
26: 8 [A] *I* **love** the house where you live, O LORD, the place where
31:23 [31:24] [A] **Love** the LORD, all his saints! The LORD
33: 5 [A] The LORD **loves** righteousness and justice; the earth is full
34:12 [34:13] [A] of you loves life and **desires** to see many good days,
37:28 [A] For the LORD **loves** the just and will not forsake his faithful
38:11 [38:12] [A] My **friends** and companions avoid me because of
40:16 [40:17] [A] may *those who* **love** your salvation always say,
45: 7 [45:8] [A] *You* **love** righteousness and hate wickedness;
47: 4 [47:5] [A] for us, the pride of Jacob, whom *he* **loved**.
52: 3 [52:5] [A] *You* **love** evil rather than good, falsehood rather than
52: 4 [52:6] [A] *You* **love** every harmful word, O you deceitful
69:36 [69:37] [A] and *those who* **love** his name will dwell there.
70: 4 [70:5] [A] may *those who* **love** your salvation always say,
78:68 [A] but he chose the tribe of Judah, Mount Zion, which *he* **loved**.
87: 2 [A] the LORD **loves** the gates of Zion more than all the
88:18 [88:19] [A] taken my companions and **loved** *ones* from me;
97:10 [A] *Let those who* **love** the LORD hate evil, for he guards the
99: 4 [A] The King is mighty, *he* **loves** justice—you have established
109:17 [A] *He* **loved** to pronounce a curse—may it come on him; he
116: 1 [A] *I* **love** the LORD, for he heard my voice; he heard my cry
119:47 [A] for I delight in your commands because *I* **love** them.
119:48 [A] which *I* **love**, and I meditate on your decrees.
119:97 [A] Oh, how *I* **love** your law! I meditate on it all day long.
119:113 [A] I hate double-minded men, but *I* **love** your law.
119:119 [A] earth you discard like dross; therefore *I* **love** your statutes.
119:127 [A] Because *I* **love** your commands more than gold, more than
119:132 [A] on me, as you always do to *those who* **love** your name.
119:140 [A] have been thoroughly tested, and your servant **loves** them.
119:159 [A] See how *I* **love** your precepts; preserve my life, O LORD,
119:163 [A] I hate and abhor falsehood but *I* **love** your law.
119:165 [A] Great peace have *they who* **love** your law, and nothing can
119:167 [A] I obey your statutes, for *I* **love** them greatly.
122: 6 [A] the peace of Jerusalem: "May *those who* **love** you be secure.
145:20 [A] The LORD watches over all *who* **love** him, but all the
146: 8 [A] those who are bowed down, the LORD **loves** the righteous.
Pr 1:22 [A] "How long *will you* simple ones **love** your simple ways?
3:12 [A] because the LORD disciplines those *he* **loves**, as a father the
4: 6 [A] she will protect you; **love** her, and she will watch over you.

Pr 8:17 [A] I **love** those who love me, and those who seek me find me.
8:17 [A] I love *those who* **love** me, and those who seek me find me.
8:21 [A] bestowing wealth on *those who* **love** me and making their
8:36 [A] fails to find me harms himself; all who hate me **love** death."
9:8 [A] or he will hate you; rebuke a wise man and *he will* **love** you.
12:1 [A] *Whoever* **loves** discipline loves knowledge, but he who hates
12:1 [A] Whoever loves discipline **loves** knowledge, but he who hates
13:24 [A] his son, but *he who* **loves** him is careful to discipline him.
14:20 [A] even by their neighbors, but the rich have many **friends**.
15:9 [A] of the wicked but *he* **loves** those who pursue righteousness.
15:12 [A] A mocker **resents** [+4202] correction; he will not consult the
16:13 [A] in honest lips; *they* **value** a man who speaks the truth.
17:17 [A] A friend **loves** at all times, and a brother is born for
17:19 [A] *He who* **loves** a quarrel loves sin; he who builds a high gate
17:19 [A] He who loves a quarrel **loves** sin; he who builds a high gate
18:21 [A] of life and death, and *those who* **love** it will eat its fruit.
18:24 [A] to ruin, but there is a **friend** who sticks closer than a brother.
19:8 [A] He who gets wisdom **loves** his own soul; he who cherishes
20:13 [A] *Do* not **love** sleep or you will grow poor; stay awake and you
21:17 [A] He *who* **loves** pleasure will become poor; whoever loves
21:17 [A] become poor; *whoever* **loves** wine and oil will never be rich.
22:11 [A] *He who* **loves** a pure heart and whose speech is gracious will
27:6 [A] Wounds from a **friend** can be trusted, but an enemy
29:3 [A] A man *who* **loves** wisdom brings joy to his father, but a
Ecc 3:8 [A] a time to **love** and a time to hate, a time for war and a time
5:10 [5:9] [A] *Whoever* **loves** money never has money enough;
5:10 [5:9] [A] **loves** wealth is never satisfied with his income.
9:9 [A] Enjoy life with your wife, whom *you* **love**, all the days of
SS 1:3 [A] is like perfume poured out. No wonder the maidens **love** you!
1:4 [A] your love more than wine. How right *they are to* **adore** you!
1:7 [A] Tell me, you whom I **love**, where you graze your flock
3:1 [A] All night long on my bed I looked for the one my heart **loves**;
3:2 [A] and squares; I will search for the one my heart **loves**.
3:3 [A] rounds in the city. "Have you seen the one my heart **loves**?"
3:4 [A] had I passed them when I found the one my heart **loves**.
Isa 1:23 [A] of thieves; they all **love** bribes and chase after gifts.
41:8 [A] I have chosen, you descendants of Abraham my **friend**,
43:4 [A] and honored in my sight, and because I **love** you,
48:14 [A] The LORD's **chosen ally** will carry out his purpose against
56:6 [A] to **love** the name of the LORD, and to worship him, all who
56:10 [A] cannot bark; they lie around and dream, *they* **love** to sleep.
57:8 [A] you made a pact with those whose beds *you* **love**, and you
61:8 [A] "For I, the LORD, **love** justice; I hate robbery and iniquity.
66:10 [A] with Jerusalem and be glad for her, all you *who* **love** her;
Jer 2:25 [A] 'It's no use! *I* **love** foreign gods, and I must go after them.'
5:31 [A] rule by their own authority, and my people **love** it this way.
8:2 [A] which *they have* **loved** and served and which they have
14:10 [A] "*They* greatly **love** to wander; they do not restrain their feet.
20:4 [A] 'I will make you a terror to yourself and to all your **friends**;
20:6 [A] and all your **friends** to whom you have prophesied lies.' "
22:20 [D] cry out from Abarim, for all your **allies** are crushed.
22:22 [D] all your shepherds away, and your **allies** will go into exile.
30:14 [D] All your **allies** have forgotten you; they care nothing for you.
31:3 [A] "*I have* **loved** you *with* an everlasting love; I have drawn
La 1:2 [A] Among all her **lovers** there is none to comfort her.
1:19 [D] "I called to my **allies** but they betrayed me. My priests
Eze 16:33 [D] prostitute receives a fee, but you give gifts to all your **lovers**,
16:36 [D] your nakedness in your promiscuity with your **lovers**,
16:37 [D] therefore I am going to gather all your **lovers**, with whom
16:37 [A] found pleasure, those *you* **loved** as well as those you hated.
23:5 [D] and she lusted after her **lovers**, the Assyrians—warriors
23:9 [D] "Therefore I handed her over to her **lovers**, the Assyrians,
23:22 [D] I will stir up your **lovers** against you, those you turned away
Da 9:4 [A] who keeps his covenant of love with *all who* **love** him
Hos 2:5 [2:7] [D] She said, 'I will go after my **lovers**, who give me my
2:7 [2:9] [D] She will chase after her **lovers** but not catch them; she
2:10 [2:12] [D] expose her lewdness before the eyes of her **lovers**;
2:12 [2:14] [D] which she said were her pay from her **lovers**;
2:13 [2:15] [D] with rings and jewelry, and went after her **lovers**,
3:1 [A] LORD said to me, "Go, **show** *your* **love** *to* your wife again,
3:1 [B] though *she is* **loved** *by* another and is an adulteress.
3:1 [A] Love her as the LORD **loves** the Israelites, though they turn
3:1 [A] they turn to other gods and **love** the sacred raisin cakes."
4:18 [A] their prostitution; their rulers **dearly** love shameful ways.
4:18 [A] their prostitution; their rulers dearly **love** shameful ways.
9:1 [A] *you* **love** the wages of a prostitute at every threshing floor.
9:15 [A] *I will* no longer **love** them; all their leaders are rebellious.
10:11 [A] Ephraim is a trained heifer *that* **loves** to thresh; so I will put
11:1 [A] "When Israel was a child, *I* **loved** him, and out of Egypt I
12:7 [12:8] [A] merchant uses dishonest scales; *he* **loves** to defraud.
14:4 [14:5] [A] "I will heal their waywardness and **love** them freely,
Am 4:5 [A] about them, you Israelites, for this is what *you* **love** to do,"
5:15 [A] Hate evil, **love** good; maintain justice in the courts.
Mic 3:2 [A] you who hate good and **love** evil; who tear the skin from my
6:8 [A] To act justly and *to* **love** mercy and to walk humbly with
Zec 8:17 [A] evil against your neighbor, and *do* not **love** to swear falsely.
8:19 [A] happy festivals for Judah. Therefore **love** truth and peace."
13:6 [D] 'The wounds I was given at the house of my **friends**.'
Mal 1:2 [A] "*I have* **loved** you," says the LORD. "But you ask, 'How
1:2 [A] says the LORD. "But you ask, 'How *have you* **loved** us?'
1:2 [A] Jacob's brother?" the LORD says. "Yet *I have* **loved** Jacob,
2:11 [A] Judah has desecrated the sanctuary the LORD **loves**, by

171 אֹהַב *'ōhab*, n.[m.]. [2] [√ 170]

love [1], thing loved [1]

Pr 7:18 drink deep of love till morning; let's enjoy ourselves with **love**!
Hos 9:10 to that shameful idol and became as vile as the **thing** they **loved**.

172 אַהַב *'ahab*, n.[m.]. [2] [√ 170]

lovers [1], loving [1]

Pr 5:19 A **loving** doe, a graceful deer—may her breasts satisfy you always,
Hos 8:9 wild donkey wandering alone. Ephraim has sold herself to **lovers**.

173 אַהֲבָה¹ *'ahᵃbâ¹*, n.f. [33] [√ 170]

love [26], friendship [2], loved [2], *untranslated* [1], lovingly [1], that[s] [1]

Ge 29:20 seemed like only a few days to him because of his **love** *for* her.
1Sa 20:17 oath out of love for him, because he loved him as he **loved** himself.
2Sa 1:26 Your **love** for me was wonderful, more wonderful than that of
1:26 love for me was wonderful, more wonderful than **that**[s] *of* women.
13:15 had loved her. **[RPH]** Amnon said to her, "Get up and get out!"
1Ki 10:9 Because of the LORD's eternal **love** *for* Israel, he has made you
11:2 after their gods." Nevertheless, Solomon held fast to them in **love**.
Ps 109:4 In return for my **friendship** they accuse me, but I am a man of
109:5 They repay me evil for good, and hatred for my **friendship**.
Pr 5:19 breasts satisfy you always, may you ever be captivated by her **love**.
10:12 Hatred stirs up dissension, but **love** covers over all wrongs.
15:17 Better a meal of vegetables where there is **love** than a fattened calf
17:9 He who covers over an offense promotes **love**, but whoever repeats
27:5 Better is open rebuke than hidden **love**.
Ecc 9:1 God's hands, but no man knows whether **love** or hate awaits him.
9:6 Their **love**, their hate and their jealousy have long since vanished;
SS 2:4 has taken me to the banquet hall, and his banner over me is **love**.
2:5 me with raisins, refresh me with apples, for I am faint with **love**.
2:7 does of the field: Do not arouse or awaken **love** until it so desires.
3:5 does of the field: Do not arouse or awaken **love** until it so desires.
3:10 its interior **lovingly** inlaid by the daughters of Jerusalem.
5:8 my lover, what will you tell him? Tell him I am faint with **love**.
7:6 [7:7] How beautiful you are and how pleasing, O **love**, with your
8:4 I charge you: Do not arouse or awaken **love** until it so desires.
8:6 for **love** is as strong as death, its jealousy unyielding as the grave.
8:7 Many waters cannot quench **love**; rivers cannot wash it away.
8:7 If one were to give all the wealth of his house for **love**, it would be
Isa 63:9 In his **love** and mercy he redeemed them; he lifted them up
Jer 2:2 how as a bride you **loved** me and followed me through the desert,
2:33 How skilled you are at pursuing **love**! Even the worst of women
31:3 "I have loved you with an everlasting **love**; I have drawn you with
Hos 11:4 I led them with cords of human kindness, with ties of **love**;
Zep 3:17 He will take great delight in you, he will quiet you with his **love**,

174 ²אַהֲבָה *'ahᵃbâ²*, n.f. Not used in NIV/BHS [cf. 170?]

175 אֲהַבְהָבַי *'ahabhābay*, n.m. Not used in NIV/BHS [√ 170]

176 אֹהַד *'ōhad*, n.pr.m. [2]

Ohad [2]

Ge 46:10 **Ohad**, Jakin, Zohar and Shaul the son of a Canaanite woman.
Ex 6:15 **Ohad**, Jakin, Zohar and Shaul the son of a Canaanite woman.

177 אֲהָהּ *'ahāh*, interj. [15]

ah [9], oh [3], alas [1], not so [1], what [1]

Jos 7:7 Joshua said, "**Ah**, Sovereign LORD, why did you ever bring this
Jdg 6:22 the angel of the LORD, he exclaimed, "**Ah**, Sovereign LORD!
11:35 When he saw her, he tore his clothes and cried, "**Oh**! My daughter!
2Ki 3:10 "**What**!" exclaimed the king of Israel. "Has the LORD called us
6:5 fell into the water. "**Oh**, my lord," he cried out, "it was borrowed!"
6:15 the city. "**Oh**, my lord, what shall we do?" the servant asked.
Jer 1:6 "**Ah**, Sovereign LORD," I said, "I do not know how to speak;
4:10 I said, "**Ah**, Sovereign LORD, how completely you have
14:13 But I said, "**Ah**, Sovereign LORD, the prophets keep telling them,
32:17 "**Ah**, Sovereign LORD, you have made the heavens and the earth
Eze 4:14 I said, "**Not so**, Sovereign LORD! I have never defiled myself.
9:8 left alone, I fell facedown, crying out, "**Ah**, Sovereign LORD!
11:13 and cried out in a loud voice, "**Ah**, Sovereign LORD!
20:49 [21:5] I said, "**Ah**, Sovereign LORD! They are saying of me,

Joel 1:15 **Alas** for that day! For the day of the LORD is near; it will come

178 אַהֲוָא *'ahawā'*, n.pr.loc. [3]

Ahava [3]

Ezr 8:15 I assembled them at the canal that flows toward **Ahava**, and we
8:21 There, by the **Ahava** Canal, I proclaimed a fast, so that we might
8:31 On the twelfth day of the first month we set out from the **Ahava**

179 אֵהוּד *'ēhûd*, n.pr.m. [9] [cf. 287?]

Ehud [8], *untranslated* [1]

Jdg 3:15 **Ehud**, a left-handed man, the son of Gera the Benjamite.
3:16 Now **Ehud** had made a double-edged sword about a foot and a half
3:20 **Ehud** then approached him while he was sitting alone in the upper
3:20 alone in the upper room of his summer palace and **[RPH]** said,
3:21 **Ehud** reached with his left hand, drew the sword from his right
3:23 **Ehud** went out to the porch; he shut the doors of the upper room
3:26 While they waited, **Ehud** got away. He passed by the idols
4:1 After **Ehud** died, the Israelites once again did evil in the eyes of
1Ch 7:10 Jeush, Benjamin, **Ehud**, Kenaanah, Zethan, Tarshish

180 אֱהִי *'ehî*, adv. [3]

where [2], where [+686] [1]

Hos 13:10 **Where** [+686] is your king, that he may save you? Where are your
13:14 **Where**, O death, are your plagues? Where, O grave, is your
13:14 O death, are your plagues? **Where**, O grave, is your destruction?

181 אֶהְיֶה *'ehyeh*, v. (used as n.pr.). Not used in NIV/BHS [√ 2118]

182 אָהַל¹ *'āhal*[1], v.den. [3] [√ 185]

moved tents [1], pitch tent [1], pitched tents [1]

Ge 13:12 [A] the cities of the plain and **pitched** *his* **tents** near Sodom.
13:18 [A] So Abram **moved** *his* **tents** and went to live near the great
Isa 13:20 [D] no Arab *will* **pitch** *his* **tent** there, no shepherd will rest his

183 ²אָהַל *'āhal*[2], v. [1] [√ 2145]

bright [1]

Job 25:5 [G] If even the moon *is* not **bright** and the stars are not pure in

184 אָהָל *'āhāl*, n.m. Not used in NIV/BHS

185 אֹהֶל¹ *'ōhel*[1], n.m. [345 / 344] [→ 182, 186, 188; *also used with compound proper names*]

tent [260], tents [45], home [10], homes [9], dwellings [3], it[s] [+2021] [3], house [2], tabernacle [2], *untranslated* [1], another[s] [1], broke camp [+4946+5825] [1], camps [1], house [+1074] [1], household [1], nomads [+928+8905] [1], sanctuary [1], tent site [1], tent-dwelling [+928+2021] [1]

Ge 4:20 he was the father of those who live in **tents** and raise livestock.
9:21 of its wine, he became drunk and lay uncovered inside his **tent**.
9:27 may Japheth live in the **tents** *of* Shem, and may Canaan be his
12:8 he went on toward the hills east of Bethel and pitched his **tent**,
13:3 to the place between Bethel and Ai where his **tent** had been earlier
13:5 moving about with Abram, also had flocks and herds and **tents**.
18:1 he was sitting at the entrance to his **tent** in the heat of the day.
18:2 he hurried from the entrance of his **tent** to meet them and bowed
18:6 So Abraham hurried into the **tent** to Sarah. "Quick," he said,
18:9 is your wife Sarah?" they asked him. "There, in the **tent**," he said.
18:10 Now Sarah was listening at the entrance to the **tent**, which was
24:67 Isaac brought her into the **tent** *of* his mother Sarah, and he married
25:27 while Jacob was a quiet man, staying among the **tents**.
26:25 There he pitched his **tent**, and there his servants dug a well.
31:25 Jacob had pitched his **tent** in the hill country of Gilead when
31:33 So Laban went into Jacob's **tent** and into Leah's tent and into the
31:33 So Laban went into Jacob's tent and into Leah's **tent** and into the
31:33 and into Leah's tent and into the **tent** *of* the two maidservants,
31:33 After he came out of Leah's **tent**, he entered Rachel's tent.
31:33 After he came out of Leah's tent, he entered Rachel's **tent**.
31:34 Laban searched through everything in the **tent** but found nothing.
33:19 father of Shechem, the plot of ground where he pitched his **tent**.
35:21 Israel moved on again and pitched his **tent** beyond Migdal Eder.
Ex 16:16 he needs. Take an omer for each person you have in your **tent**.' "
18:7 kissed him. They greeted each other and then went into the **tent**.
26:7 "Make curtains of goat hair for the **tent** over the tabernacle—
26:9 another set. Fold the sixth curtain double at the front of the **tent**.
26:11 and put them in the loops to fasten the **tent** together as a unit.
26:12 As for the additional length of the **tent** curtains, the half curtain
26:13 The **tent** curtains will be a cubit longer on both sides; what is left
26:14 Make for the **tent** a covering of ram skins dyed red, and over that a
26:36 "For the entrance to the **tent** make a curtain of blue, purple
27:21 In the **Tent** *of* Meeting, outside the curtain that is in front of the
28:43 his sons must wear them whenever they enter the **Tent** *of* Meeting
29:4 bring Aaron and his sons to the entrance to the **Tent** *of* Meeting
29:10 "Bring the bull to the front of the **Tent** *of* Meeting, and Aaron
29:11 Slaughter it in the LORD's presence at the entrance to the **Tent** *of*
29:30 comes to the **Tent** *of* Meeting to minister in the Holy Place is to
29:32 At the entrance to the **Tent** *of* Meeting, Aaron and his sons are to
29:42 at the entrance to the **Tent** *of* Meeting before the LORD.
29:44 "So I will consecrate the **Tent** *of* Meeting and the altar and will
30:16 the Israelites and use it for the service of the **Tent** *of* Meeting.
30:18 Place it between the **Tent** *of* Meeting and the altar, and put water
30:20 Whenever they enter the **Tent** *of* Meeting, they shall wash with
30:26 use it to anoint the **Tent** *of* Meeting, the ark of the Testimony,
30:36 and place it in front of the Testimony in the **Tent** *of* Meeting,
31:7 the **Tent** *of* Meeting, the ark of the Testimony with the atonement
31:7 atonement cover on it, and all the other furnishings of the **tent**—
33:7 Now Moses used to take a **tent** and pitch it outside the camp some
33:7 the camp some distance away, calling it the "**tent** *of* meeting."
33:7 Anyone inquiring of the LORD would go to the **tent** *of* meeting
33:8 And whenever Moses went out to the **tent**, all the people rose
33:8 all the people rose and stood at the entrances to their **tents**,
33:8 entrances to their tents, watching Moses until he entered the **tent**.
33:9 As Moses went into the **tent**, the pillar of cloud would come down
33:9 stay at the entrance, **[RPH]** while the LORD spoke with Moses.
33:10 people saw the pillar of cloud standing at the entrance to the **tent**,
33:10 they all stood and worshiped, each at the entrance to his **tent**.
33:11 but his young aide Joshua son of Nun did not leave the **tent**.
35:11 the tabernacle with its **tent** and its covering, clasps, frames,
35:21 brought an offering to the LORD for the work on the **Tent** *of*
36:14 They made curtains of goat hair for the **tent** over the tabernacle—
36:18 They made fifty bronze clasps to fasten the **tent** together as a unit.
36:19 Then they made for the **tent** a covering of ram skins dyed red,
36:37 For the entrance to the **tent** they made a curtain of blue, purple
38:8 of the women who served at the entrance to the **Tent** *of* Meeting.
38:30 They used it to make the bases for the entrance to the **Tent** *of*
39:32 the work on the tabernacle, the **Tent** *of* Meeting, was completed.
39:33 the **tent** and all its furnishings, its clasps, frames, crossbars,
39:38 the fragrant incense, and the curtain for the entrance to the **tent**;
39:40 all the furnishings for the tabernacle, the **Tent** *of* Meeting;
40:2 "Set up the tabernacle, the **Tent** *of* Meeting, on the first day of the
40:6 in front of the entrance to the tabernacle, the **Tent** *of* Meeting;
40:7 place the basin between the **Tent** *of* Meeting and the altar
40:12 "Bring Aaron and his sons to the entrance to the **Tent** *of* Meeting
40:19 he spread the **tent** over the tabernacle and put the covering over the
40:19 the tent over the tabernacle and put the covering over the **tent**,
40:22 Moses placed the table in the **Tent** *of* Meeting on the north side of
40:24 He placed the lampstand in the **Tent** *of* Meeting opposite the table
40:26 Moses placed the gold altar in the **Tent** *of* Meeting in front of the
40:29 the **Tent** *of* Meeting, and offered on it burnt offerings and grain
40:30 He placed the basin between the **Tent** *of* Meeting and the altar
40:32 They washed whenever they entered the **Tent** *of* Meeting
40:34 the cloud covered the **Tent** *of* Meeting, and the glory of the
40:35 Moses could not enter the **Tent** *of* Meeting because the cloud had
Lev 1:1 called to Moses and spoke to him from the **Tent** *of* Meeting.
1:3 He must present it at the entrance to the **Tent** *of* Meeting so that it
1:5 against the altar on all sides at the entrance to the **Tent** *of* Meeting.
3:2 his offering and slaughter it at the entrance to the **Tent** *of* Meeting.
3:8 of his offering and slaughter it in front of the **Tent** *of* Meeting.
3:13 hand on its head and slaughter it in front of the **Tent** *of* Meeting.
4:4 He is to present the bull at the entrance to the **Tent** *of* Meeting
4:5 take some of the bull's blood and carry it into the **Tent** *of* Meeting.
4:7 fragrant incense that is before the LORD in the **Tent** *of* Meeting.
4:7 of the altar of burnt offering at the entrance to the **Tent** *of* Meeting.
4:14 bull as a sin offering and present it before the **Tent** *of* Meeting.
4:16 priest is to take some of the bull's blood into the **Tent** *of* Meeting.
4:18 horns of the altar that is before the LORD in the **Tent** *of* Meeting.
4:18 of the altar of burnt offering at the entrance to the **Tent** *of* Meeting.
6:16 [6:9] they are to eat it in the courtyard of the **Tent** *of* Meeting.
6:26 [6:19] in a holy place, in the courtyard of the **Tent** *of* Meeting.
6:30 [6:23] any sin offering whose blood is brought into the **Tent** *of*
8:3 gather the entire assembly at the entrance to the **Tent** *of* Meeting."
8:4 and the assembly gathered at the entrance to the **Tent** *of* Meeting.
8:31 "Cook the meat at the entrance to the **Tent** *of* Meeting and eat it
8:33 Do not leave the entrance to the **Tent** *of* Meeting for seven days,
8:35 You must stay at the entrance to the **Tent** *of* Meeting day and night
9:5 They took the things Moses commanded to the front of the **Tent** *of*
9:23 Moses and Aaron then went into the **Tent** *of* Meeting. When they
10:7 Do not leave the entrance to the **Tent** *of* Meeting or you will die,
10:9 or other fermented drink whenever you go into the **Tent** *of*
12:6 she is to bring to the priest at the entrance to the **Tent** *of* Meeting a
14:8 into the camp, but he must stay outside his **tent** for seven days.
14:11 his offerings before the LORD at the entrance to the **Tent** *of*

Lev 14:23 his cleansing to the priest at the entrance to the **Tent** *of* Meeting,
15:14 come before the LORD to the entrance to the **Tent** *of* Meeting
15:29 and bring them to the priest at the entrance to the **Tent** *of* Meeting.
16:7 present them before the LORD at the entrance to the **Tent** *of*
16:16 He is to do the same for the **Tent** *of* Meeting, which is among them
16:17 No one is to be in the **Tent** *of* Meeting from the time Aaron goes in
16:20 the **Tent** *of* Meeting and the altar, he shall bring forward the live
16:23 "Then Aaron is to go into the **Tent** *of* Meeting and take off the
16:33 for the **Tent** *of* Meeting and the altar, and for the priests and all the
17:4 instead of bringing it to the entrance to the **Tent** *of* Meeting to
17:5 at the entrance to the **Tent** *of* Meeting and sacrifice them as
17:6 the altar of the LORD at the entrance to the **Tent** *of* Meeting
17:9 does not bring it to the entrance to the **Tent** *of* Meeting to sacrifice
19:21 must bring a ram to the entrance to the **Tent** *of* Meeting for a guilt
24:3 Outside the curtain of the Testimony in the **Tent** *of* Meeting,
Nu 1:1 The LORD spoke to Moses in the **Tent** *of* Meeting in the Desert
2:2 "The Israelites are to camp around the **Tent** *of* Meeting some
2:17 the **Tent** *of* Meeting and the camp of the Levites will set out in the
3:7 for the whole community at the **Tent** *of* Meeting by doing the
3:8 They are to take care of all the furnishings of the **Tent** *of* Meeting,
3:25 At the **Tent** *of* Meeting the Gershonites were responsible for the
3:25 were responsible for the care of the tabernacle and **tent**,
3:25 its coverings, the curtain at the entrance to the **Tent** *of* Meeting,
3:38 the tabernacle, toward the sunrise, in front of the **Tent** *of* Meeting.
4:3 of age who come to serve in the work in the **Tent** *of* Meeting.
4:4 "This is the work of the Kohathites in the **Tent** *of* Meeting:
4:15 The Kohathites are to carry those things that are in the **Tent** *of*
4:23 years of age who come to serve in the work at the **Tent** *of* Meeting.
4:25 the **Tent** *of* Meeting, its covering and the outer covering of hides
4:25 of sea cows, the curtains for the entrance to the **Tent** *of* Meeting,
4:28 This is the service of the Gershonite clans at the **Tent** *of* Meeting.
4:30 years of age who come to serve in the work at the **Tent** *of* Meeting.
4:31 This is their duty as they perform service at the **Tent** *of* Meeting:
4:33 This is the service of the Merarite clans as they work at the **Tent** *of*
4:35 years of age who came to serve in the work in the **Tent** *of* Meeting,
4:37 all those in the Kohathite clans who served in the **Tent** *of* Meeting.
4:39 years of age who came to serve in the work at the **Tent** *of* Meeting,
4:41 those in the Gershonite clans who served in the **Tent** *of* Meeting.
4:43 years of age who came to serve in the work at the **Tent** *of* Meeting,
4:47 came to do the work of serving and carrying the **Tent** *of* Meeting
6:10 or two young pigeons to the priest at the entrance to the **Tent** *of*
6:13 He is to be brought to the entrance to the **Tent** *of* Meeting.
6:18 " 'Then at the entrance to the **Tent** *of* Meeting, the Nazirite must
7:5 that they may be used in the work at the **Tent** *of* Meeting.
7:89 When Moses entered the **Tent** *of* Meeting to speak with the
8:9 Bring the Levites to the front of the **Tent** *of* Meeting and assemble
8:15 they are to come to do their work at the **Tent** *of* Meeting.
8:19 his sons to do the work at the **Tent** *of* Meeting on behalf of the
8:22 the Levites came to do their work at the **Tent** *of* Meeting under the
8:24 or more shall come to take part in the work at the **Tent** *of* Meeting,
8:26 their brothers in performing their duties at the **Tent** *of* Meeting,
9:15 the **Tent** *of* the Testimony, was set up, the cloud covered it.
9:17 Whenever the cloud lifted from above the **Tent**, the Israelites set
10:3 is to assemble before you at the entrance to the **Tent** *of* Meeting.
11:10 the people of every family wailing, each at the entrance to his **tent**.
11:16 Have them come to the **Tent** *of* Meeting, that they may stand there
11:24 seventy of their elders and had them stand around the **Tent**.
11:26 They were listed among the elders, but did not go out to the **Tent**.
12:4 Aaron and Miriam, "Come out to the **Tent** *of* Meeting, all three of
12:5 he stood at the entrance to the **Tent** and summoned Aaron
12:10 When the cloud lifted from above the **Tent**, there stood Miriam—
14:10 the glory of the LORD appeared at the **Tent** *of* Meeting to all the
16:18 with Moses and Aaron at the entrance to the **Tent** *of* Meeting.
16:19 in opposition to them at the entrance to the **Tent** *of* Meeting,
16:26 the assembly, "Move back from the **tents** *of* these wicked men!
16:27 their wives, children and little ones at the entrances to their **tents**.
16:42 [17:7] and Aaron and turned toward the **Tent** *of* Meeting,
16:43 [17:8] and Aaron went to the front of the **Tent** *of* Meeting,
16:50 [17:15] Aaron returned to Moses at the entrance to the **Tent** *of*
17:4 [17:19] Place them in the **Tent** *of* Meeting in front of the
17:7 [17:22] Moses placed the staffs before the LORD in the **Tent** *of*
17:8 [17:23] The next day Moses entered the **Tent** *of* the Testimony
18:2 and your sons minister before the **Tent** *of* the Testimony.
18:3 be responsible to you and are to perform all the duties of the **Tent**,
18:4 join you and be responsible for the care of the **Tent** *of* Meeting—
18:4 all the work at the **Tent**—and no one else may come near where
18:6 dedicated to the LORD to do the work at the **Tent** *of* Meeting.
18:21 return for the work they do while serving at the **Tent** *of* Meeting.
18:22 From now on the Israelites must not go near the **Tent** *of* Meeting,
18:23 It is the Levites who are to do the work at the **Tent** *of* Meeting
18:31 for it is your wages for your work at the **Tent** *of* Meeting.
19:4 sprinkle it seven times toward the front of the **Tent** *of* Meeting.
19:14 "This is the law that applies when a person dies in a **tent**:
19:14 Anyone who enters the **tent** and anyone who is in it will be
19:14 and anyone who is in **it**[s] [+2021] will be unclean for seven days,
19:18 dip it in the water and sprinkle the **tent** and all the furnishings
20:6 Aaron went from the assembly to the entrance to the **Tent** *of*
24:5 "How beautiful are your **tents**, O Jacob, your dwelling places,
25:6 while they were weeping at the entrance to the **Tent** *of* Meeting.
27:2 the entrance to the **Tent** *of* Meeting and stood before Moses,
31:54 brought it into the **Tent** *of* Meeting as a memorial for the Israelites
Dt 1:27 You grumbled in your **tents** and said, "The LORD hates us;
5:30 "Go, tell them to return to their **tents**.
11:6 their **tents** and every living thing that belonged to them.
16:7 your God will choose. Then in the morning return to your **tents**.
31:14 Call Joshua and present yourselves at the **Tent** *of* Meeting,
31:14 and Joshua came and presented themselves at the **Tent** *of* Meeting.
31:15 Then the LORD appeared at the **Tent** in a pillar of cloud,
31:15 a pillar of cloud, and the cloud stood over the entrance to the **Tent**.
33:18 Zebulun, in your going out, and you, Issachar, in your **tents**.
Jos 3:14 So when the people **broke camp** [+4946+5825] to cross the
7:21 They are hidden in the ground inside my **tent**, with the silver
7:22 and they ran to the **tent**, and there it was, hidden in his tent,
7:22 and they ran to the tent, and there it was, hidden in his **tent**,
7:23 They took the things from the **tent**, brought them to Joshua
7:24 his cattle, donkeys and sheep, his **tent** and all that he had,
18:1 Israelites gathered at Shiloh and set up the **Tent** *of* Meeting there.
19:51 the presence of the LORD at the entrance to the **Tent** *of* Meeting.
22:4 return to your **homes** in the land that Moses the servant of the
22:6 blessed them and sent them away, and they went to their **homes**.
22:7 their brothers.) When Joshua sent them **home**, he blessed them,
22:8 saying, "Return to your **homes** with your great wealth—with large
Jdg 4:11 and pitched his **tent** by the great tree in Zaanannim near Kedesh.
4:17 Sisera, however, fled on foot to the **tent** *of* Jael, the wife of Heber
4:18 be afraid." So he entered her **tent**, and she put a covering over him.
4:20 "Stand in the doorway of the **tent**," he told her. "If someone comes
4:21 picked up a **tent** peg and a hammer and went quietly to him while
5:24 most blessed of **tent-dwelling** [+928+2021] women.
6:5 came up with their livestock and their **tents** like swarms of locusts.
7:8 So Gideon sent the rest of the Israelites to their **tents** but kept the
7:13 It struck the **tent** with such force that the tent overturned and
7:13 It struck the tent with such force that the **tent** overturned and
8:11 Gideon went up by the route of the **nomads** [+928+8905] east of
19:9 tomorrow morning you can get up and be on your way **home**."
20:8 All the people rose as one man, saying, "None of us will go **home**.
1Sa 2:22 with the women who served at the entrance to the **Tent** *of* Meeting.
4:10 and the Israelites were defeated and every man fled to his **tent**.
13:2 in Benjamin. The rest of the men he sent back to their **homes**.
17:54 to Jerusalem, and he put the Philistine's weapons in his own **tent**.
2Sa 6:17 and set it in its place inside the **tent** that David had pitched for it,
7:6 I have been moving from place to place with a **tent** as my
16:22 So they pitched a **tent** for Absalom on the roof, and he lay with his
18:17 rocks over him. Meanwhile, all the Israelites fled to their **homes**.
19:8 [19:9] Meanwhile, the Israelites had fled to their **homes**.
20:1 in David, no part in Jesse's son! Every man to his **tent**, O Israel!"
20:22 and his men dispersed from the city, each returning to his **home**.
1Ki 1:39 Zadok the priest took the horn of oil from the sacred **tent**
2:28 he fled to the **tent** *of* the LORD and took hold of the horns of the
2:29 King Solomon was told that Joab had fled to the **tent** *of* the
2:30 So Benaiah entered the **tent** *of* the LORD and said to Joab,
8:4 and the **Tent** *of* Meeting and all the sacred furnishings in it.
8:4 the Tent of Meeting and all the sacred furnishings in **it**[s] [+2021].
8:66 They blessed the king and then went **home**, joyful and glad in heart
12:16 have in David, what part in Jesse's son? To your **tents**, O Israel!
12:16 after your own house, O David!" So the Israelites went **home**.
2Ki 7:7 the dusk and abandoned their **tents** and their horses and donkeys.
7:8 leprosy reached the edge of the camp and entered one of the **tents**.
7:8 They returned and entered another **tent** and took some things from
7:10 tethered horses and donkeys, and the **tents** left just as they were."
8:21 and broke through by night; his army, however, fled back **home**.
13:5 So the Israelites lived in their own **homes** as they had before.
14:12 Judah was routed by Israel, and every man fled to his **home**.
1Ch 4:41 They attacked the Hamites in their **dwellings** and also the
5:10 they occupied the **dwellings** *of* the Hagrites throughout the entire
6:32 [6:17] with music before the tabernacle, the **Tent** *of* Meeting,
9:19 were responsible for guarding the thresholds of the **Tent** just as
9:21 was the gatekeeper at the entrance to the **Tent** *of* Meeting.
9:23 the gates of the house of the LORD—the house called the **Tent**.
15:1 he prepared a place for the ark of God and pitched a **tent** for it.
16:1 ark of God and set it inside the **tent** that David had pitched for it,
17:5 I have moved from one **tent site** to another, from one dwelling
17:5 I have moved from one tent site to **another**[s], from one dwelling
23:32 so the Levites carried out their responsibilities for the **Tent** *of*
2Ch 1:3 to the high place at Gibeon, for God's **Tent** *of* Meeting was there,
1:4 prepared for it, because he had pitched a **tent** for it in Jerusalem.
1:6 up to the bronze altar before the LORD in the **Tent** *of* Meeting
1:13 from the high place at Gibeon, from before the **Tent** *of* Meeting.
5:5 they brought up the ark and the **Tent** *of* Meeting and all the sacred

2Ch 5: 5 the Tent of Meeting and all the sacred furnishings in **it**[s] [+2021].
7: 10 day of the seventh month he sent the people to their **homes**,
10: 16 have in David, what part in Jesse's son? To your **tents**, O Israel!
10: 16 after your own house, O David!" So all the Israelites went **home**.
14: 15 [14:14] They also attacked the **camps** *of* the herdsmen and carried
24: 6 and by the assembly of Israel for the **Tent** *of* the Testimony?"
25: 22 Judah was routed by Israel, and every man fled to his **home**.
Job 5: 24 You will know that your **tent** is secure; you will take stock of your
8: 22 be clothed in shame, and the **tents** *of* the wicked will be no more."
11: 14 the sin that is in your hand and allow no evil to dwell in your **tent**,
12: 6 The **tents** of marauders are undisturbed, and those who provoke
15: 34 and fire will consume the **tents** *of* those who love bribes.
18: 6 The light in his **tent** becomes dark; the lamp beside him goes out.
18: 14 He is torn from the security of his **tent** and marched off to the king
18: 15 Fire resides in his **tent**; burning sulfur is scattered over his
19: 12 they build a siege ramp against me and encamp around my **tent**.
20: 26 fire unfanned will consume him and devour what is left in his **tent**.
21: 28 now is the great man's house, the **tents** where wicked men lived?'
22: 23 you will be restored: If you remove wickedness far from your **tent**
29: 4 in my prime, when God's intimate friendship blessed my **house**,
31: 31 if the men of my **household** have never said, 'Who has not had his
Ps 15: 1 LORD, who may dwell in your **sanctuary**? Who may live on
19: 4 [19:5] the world. In the heavens he has pitched a **tent** for the sun,
27: 5 he will hide me in the shelter of his **tabernacle** and set me high
27: 6 at his **tabernacle** will I sacrifice with shouts of joy; I will sing
52: 5 [52:7] He will snatch you up and tear you from your **tent**; he will
61: 4 [61:5] I long to dwell in your **tent** forever and take refuge in the
69: 25 [69:26] be deserted; let there be no one to dwell in their **tents**.
78: 51 firstborn of Egypt, the firstfruits of manhood in the **tents** *of* Ham.
78: 55 as an inheritance; he settled the tribes of Israel in their **homes**.
78: 60 the tabernacle of Shiloh, the **tent** he had set up among men.
78: 67 he rejected the **tents** *of* Joseph, he did not choose the tribe of
83: 6 [83:7] the **tents** *of* Edom and the Ishmaelites, of Moab
84: 10 [84:11] house of my God than dwell in the **tents** *of* the wicked.
91: 10 then no harm will befall you, no disaster will come near your **tent**.
106: 25 They grumbled in their **tents** and did not obey the LORD.
118: 15 Shouts of joy and victory resound in the **tents** *of* the righteous:
120: 5 me that I dwell in Meshech, that I live among the **tents** *of* Kedar!
132: 3 "I will not enter my **house** [+1074] or go to my bed—
Pr 14: 11 wicked will be destroyed, but the **tent** *of* the upright will flourish.
SS 1: 5 yet lovely, O daughters of Jerusalem, dark like the **tents** *of* Kedar,
Isa 16: 5 one from the **house** *of* David—one who in judging seeks justice
33: 20 will see Jerusalem, a peaceful abode, a **tent** that will not be moved;
38: 12 Like a shepherd's **tent** my house has been pulled down and taken
40: 22 heavens like a canopy, and spreads them out like a **tent** to live in.
54: 2 "Enlarge the place of your **tent**, stretch your tent curtains wide,
Jer 4: 20 In an instant my **tents** are destroyed, my shelter in a moment.
6: 3 they will pitch their **tents** around her, each tending his own
10: 20 My **tent** is destroyed; all its ropes are snapped. My sons are gone
10: 20 no one is left now to pitch my **tent** or to set up my shelter.
30: 18 " 'I will restore the fortunes of Jacob's **tents** and have compassion
35: 7 must never have any of these things, but must always live in **tents**.
35: 10 We have lived in **tents** and have fully obeyed everything our
37: 10 is attacking you and only wounded men were left in their **tents**,
49: 29 Their **tents** and their flocks will be taken; their shelters will be
La 2: 4 he has poured out his wrath like fire on the **tent** *of* the Daughter of
Eze 41: 1 the width of the jambs was six cubits on each side. [BHS+ *the width of the tent*]
Da 11: 45 He will pitch his royal **tents** between the seas at the beautiful holy
Hos 9: 6 will be taken over by briers, and thorns will overrun their **tents**.
12: 9 [12:10] I will make you live in **tents** again, as in the days of your
Hab 3: 7 I saw the **tents** *of* Cushan in distress, the dwellings of Midian in
Zec 12: 7 "The LORD will save the **dwellings** *of* Judah first, so that the
Mal 2: 12 he may be, may the LORD cut him off from the **tents** *of* Jacob—

186 ²אֹהֶל *'ōhel²*, n.pr.m. [1] [√ 185]

Ohel [1]

1Ch 3: 20 Hashubah, **Ohel**, Berekiah, Hasadiah and Jushab-Hesed.

187 אֵהֶל *'ēhel*, pr.pl.m. & f. Not used in NIV/BHS [√ 447]

188 אָהֳלָה *'ohºlâ*, n.pr.f. [5] [→ 191, 192; cf. 185]

Oholah [5]

Eze 23: 4 The older was named **Oholah**, and her sister was Oholibah.
23: 4 and daughters. **Oholah** is Samaria, and Oholibah is Jerusalem.
23: 5 "**Oholah** engaged in prostitution while she was still mine;
23: 36 said to me: "Son of man, will you judge **Oholah** and Oholibah?
23: 44 so they slept with those lewd women, **Oholah** and Oholibah.

189 אֲהָלוֹת *'ahālôt*, n.[m.]. [2] [cf. 193, 194]

aloes [2]

Ps 45: 8 [45:9] your robes are fragrant with myrrh and **aloes** and cassia;
SS 4: 14 kind of incense tree, with myrrh and **aloes** and all the finest spices.

190 אָהֳלִיאָב *'ohºlî'āb*, n.pr.m. [5] [√ 185 + 3]

Oholiab [5]

Ex 31: 6 Moreover, I have appointed **Oholiab** son of Ahisamach,
35: 34 And he has given both him and **Oholiab** son of Ahisamach,
36: 1 **Oholiab** and every skilled person to whom the LORD has given
36: 2 Moses summoned Bezalel and **Oholiab** and every skilled person to
38: 23 with him was **Oholiab** son of Ahisamach, of the tribe of Dan—

191 אָהֳלִיבָה *'ohºlîbâ*, n.pr.f. [6] [√ 188 + 928 + 2023]

Oholibah [6]

Eze 23: 4 The older was named Oholah, and her sister was **Oholibah**.
23: 4 and daughters. Oholah is Samaria, and **Oholibah** is Jerusalem.
23: 11 "Her sister **Oholibah** saw this, yet in her lust and prostitution she
23: 22 "Therefore, **Oholibah**, this is what the Sovereign LORD says:
23: 36 said to me: "Son of man, will you judge Oholah and **Oholibah**?
23: 44 so they slept with those lewd women, Oholah and **Oholibah**.

192 אָהֳלִיבָמָה *'ohºlîbāmâ*, n.pr.m. & f. [8] [√ 185 + 1195?]

Oholibamah [8]

Ge 36: 2 **Oholibamah** daughter of Anah and granddaughter of Zibeon the
36: 5 **Oholibamah** bore Jeush, Jalam and Korah. These were the sons of
36: 14 The sons of Esau's wife **Oholibamah** daughter of Anah
36: 18 The sons of Esau's wife **Oholibamah**: Chiefs Jeush, Jalam
36: 18 These were the chiefs descended from Esau's wife **Oholibamah**
36: 25 The children of Anah: Dishon and **Oholibamah** daughter of Anah.
36: 41 **Oholibamah**, Elah, Pinon,
1Ch 1: 52 **Oholibamah**, Elah, Pinon,

193 ¹אֲהָלִים *'ahālîm¹*, n.[m.]. [2] [cf. 189, 194]

aloes [2]

Nu 24: 6 like gardens beside a river, like **aloes** planted by the LORD,
Pr 7: 17 I have perfumed my bed with myrrh, **aloes** and cinnamon.

194 ²אֲהָלִים *'ahālîm²*, n.[m.]. Not used in NIV/BHS [cf. 189, 193]

195 אַהֲרֹן *'aharôn*, n.pr.m. [347]

Aaron [300], Aaron's [31], he[s] [5], *untranslated* [4], his[s] [3], Aaron's [+4200] [1], Aaronic [+1201] [1], family of Aaron [1], him[s] [1]

Ex 4: 14 and he said, "What about your brother, **Aaron** the Levite?
4: 27 The LORD said to **Aaron**, "Go into the desert to meet Moses."
4: 28 Moses told **Aaron** everything the LORD had sent him to say,
4: 29 and **Aaron** brought together all the elders of the Israelites,
4: 30 and **Aaron** told them everything the LORD had said to Moses.
5: 1 Afterward Moses and **Aaron** went to Pharaoh and said, "This is
5: 4 the king of Egypt said, "Moses and **Aaron**, why are you taking the
5: 20 left Pharaoh, they found Moses and **Aaron** waiting to meet them,
6: 13 and **Aaron** about the Israelites and Pharaoh king of Egypt,
6: 20 his father's sister Jochebed, who bore him **Aaron** and Moses.
6: 23 **Aaron** married Elisheba, daughter of Amminadab and sister of
6: 25 Eleazar son of **Aaron** married one of the daughters of Putiel,
6: 26 It was this same **Aaron** and Moses to whom the LORD said,
6: 27 the Israelites out of Egypt. It was the same Moses and **Aaron**.
7: 1 like God to Pharaoh, and your brother **Aaron** will be your prophet.
7: 2 your brother **Aaron** is to tell Pharaoh to let the Israelites go out of
7: 6 Moses and **Aaron** did just as the LORD commanded them.
7: 7 years old and **Aaron** eighty-three when they spoke to Pharaoh.
7: 8 The LORD said to Moses and **Aaron**,
7: 9 say to **Aaron**, 'Take your staff and throw it down before Pharaoh,'
7: 10 So Moses and **Aaron** went to Pharaoh and did just as the LORD
7: 10 **Aaron** threw his staff down in front of Pharaoh and his officials,
7: 12 and it became a snake. But **Aaron's** staff swallowed up their staffs.
7: 19 "Tell **Aaron**, 'Take your staff and stretch out your hand over the
7: 20 Moses and **Aaron** did just as the LORD had commanded.
8: 5 [8:1] the LORD said to Moses, "Tell **Aaron**, 'Stretch out your
8: 6 [8:2] So **Aaron** stretched out his hand over the waters of Egypt,
8: 8 [8:4] Pharaoh summoned Moses and **Aaron** and said, "Pray to the
8: 12 [8:8] After Moses and **Aaron** left Pharaoh, Moses cried out to the
8: 16 [8:12] "Tell **Aaron**, 'Stretch out your staff and strike the dust of
8: 17 [8:13] when **Aaron** stretched out his hand with the staff
8: 25 [8:21] Then Pharaoh summoned Moses and **Aaron** and said, "Go,
9: 8 the LORD said to Moses and **Aaron**, "Take handfuls of soot from
9: 27 Pharaoh summoned Moses and **Aaron**. "This time I have sinned,"
10: 3 So Moses and **Aaron** went to Pharaoh and said to him, "This is

Ex 10: 8 Then Moses and **Aaron** were brought back to Pharaoh. "Go,
10: 16 Pharaoh quickly summoned Moses and **Aaron** and said, "I have
11: 10 Moses and **Aaron** performed all these wonders before Pharaoh,
12: 1 The LORD said to Moses and **Aaron** in Egypt,
12: 28 Israelites did just what the LORD commanded Moses and **Aaron**.
12: 31 During the night Pharaoh summoned Moses and **Aaron** and said,
12: 43 The LORD said to Moses and **Aaron**, "These are the regulations
12: 50 did just what the LORD had commanded Moses and **Aaron**.
15: 20 Miriam the prophetess, **Aaron's** sister, took a tambourine in her
16: 2 desert the whole community grumbled against Moses and **Aaron**.
16: 6 So Moses and **Aaron** said to all the Israelites, "In the evening you
16: 9 Then Moses told **Aaron**, "Say to the entire Israelite community,
16: 10 While **Aaron** was speaking to the whole Israelite community,
16: 33 So Moses said to **Aaron**, "Take a jar and put an omer of manna in
16: 34 **Aaron** put the manna in front of the Testimony, that it might be
17: 10 had ordered, and Moses, **Aaron** and Hur went to the top of the hill.
17: 12 **Aaron** and Hur held his hands up—one on one side, one on the
18: 12 **Aaron** came with all the elders of Israel to eat bread with Moses'
19: 24 The LORD replied, "Go down and bring **Aaron** up with you.
24: 1 "Come up to the LORD, you and **Aaron**, Nadab and Abihu,
24: 9 Moses and **Aaron**, Nadab and Abihu, and the seventy elders of
24: 14 **Aaron** and Hur are with you, and anyone involved in a dispute can
27: 21 **Aaron** and his sons are to keep the lamps burning before the
28: 1 "Have **Aaron** your brother brought to you from among the
28: 1 along with his sons **[RPH]** Nadab and Abihu, Eleazar
28: 1 Eleazar and Ithamar, so they may serve me as priests. **[RPH]**
28: 2 Make sacred garments for your brother **Aaron**, to give him dignity
28: 3 wisdom in such matters that they are to make garments for **Aaron**,
28: 4 They are to make these sacred garments for your brother **Aaron**
28: 12 **Aaron** is to bear the names on his shoulders as a memorial before
28: 29 "Whenever **Aaron** enters the Holy Place, he will bear the names of
28: 30 so they may be over **Aaron's** heart whenever he enters the
28: 30 Thus **Aaron** will always bear the means of making decisions for
28: 35 **Aaron** must wear it when he ministers. The sound of the bells will
28: 38 It will be on **Aaron's** forehead, and he will bear the guilt involved
28: 38 **he**[s] will bear the guilt involved in the sacred gifts the Israelites
28: 40 Make tunics, sashes and headbands for **Aaron's** sons, to give them
28: 41 After you put these clothes on your brother **Aaron** and his sons,
28: 43 **Aaron** and his sons must wear them whenever they enter the Tent
29: 4 bring **Aaron** and his sons to the entrance to the Tent of Meeting
29: 5 Take the garments and dress **Aaron** with the tunic, the robe of the
29: 9 put headbands on them. Then tie sashes on **Aaron** and his sons.
29: 9 lasting ordinance. In this way you shall ordain **Aaron** and his sons.
29: 10 and **Aaron** and his sons shall lay their hands on its head.
29: 15 the rams, and **Aaron** and his sons shall lay their hands on its head.
29: 19 other ram, and **Aaron** and his sons shall lay their hands on its head.
29: 20 and put it on the lobes of the right ears of **Aaron** and his sons,
29: 21 and sprinkle it on **Aaron** and his garments and on his sons
29: 24 Put all these in the hands of **Aaron** and his sons and wave them
29: 26 After you take the breast of the ram for **Aaron's** ordination,
29: 27 "Consecrate those parts of the ordination ram that belong to **Aaron**
29: 28 This is always to be the regular share from the Israelites for **Aaron**
29: 29 "**Aaron's** [+4200] sacred garments will belong to his descendants
29: 32 **Aaron** and his sons are to eat the meat of the ram and the bread
29: 35 "Do for **Aaron** and his sons everything I have commanded you,
29: 44 the altar and will consecrate **Aaron** and his sons to serve me as
30: 7 "**Aaron** must burn fragrant incense on the altar every morning
30: 8 He must burn incense again when **he**[s] lights the lamps at twilight
30: 10 Once a year **Aaron** shall make atonement on its horns. This annual
30: 19 **Aaron** and his sons are to wash their hands and feet with water
30: 30 "Anoint **Aaron** and his sons and consecrate them so they may
31: 10 both the sacred garments for **Aaron** the priest and the garments for
32: 1 they gathered around **Aaron** and said, "Come, make us gods who
32: 2 **Aaron** answered them, "Take off the gold earrings that your wives,
32: 3 all the people took off their earrings and brought them to **Aaron**.
32: 5 When **Aaron** saw this, he built an altar in front of the calf
32: 5 he built an altar in front of the calf and **[RPH]** announced,
32: 21 He said to **Aaron**, "What did these people do to you, that you led
32: 22 "Do not be angry, my lord," **Aaron** answered. "You know how
32: 25 that **Aaron** had let them get out of control and so become a
32: 35 a plague because of what they did with the calf **Aaron** had made.
34: 30 When **Aaron** and all the Israelites saw Moses, his face was radiant,
34: 31 so **Aaron** and all the leaders of the community came back to him,
35: 19 both the sacred garments for **Aaron** the priest and the garments for
38: 21 by the Levites under the direction of Ithamar son of **Aaron**,
39: 1 They also made sacred garments for **Aaron**, as the LORD
39: 27 For **Aaron** and his sons, they made tunics of fine linen—the work
39: 41 both the sacred garments for **Aaron** the priest and the garments for
40: 12 "Bring **Aaron** and his sons to the entrance to the Tent of Meeting
40: 13 dress **Aaron** in the sacred garments, anoint him and consecrate him
40: 31 and Moses and **Aaron** and his sons used it to wash their hands
Lev 1: 5 then **Aaron's** sons the priests shall bring the blood and sprinkle it
1: 7 The sons of **Aaron** the priest are to put fire on the altar and arrange
1: 8 **Aaron's** sons the priests shall arrange the pieces, including the
1: 11 **Aaron's** sons the priests shall sprinkle its blood against the altar on
2: 2 take it to **Aaron's** sons the priests. The priest shall take a handful
2: 3 The rest of the grain offering belongs to **Aaron** and his sons;
2: 10 The rest of the grain offering belongs to **Aaron** and his sons;
3: 2 **Aaron's** sons the priests shall sprinkle the blood against the altar
3: 5 **Aaron's** sons are to burn it on the altar on top of the burnt offering
3: 8 **Aaron's** sons shall sprinkle its blood against the altar on all sides.
3: 13 **Aaron's** sons shall sprinkle its blood against the altar on all sides.
6: 9 [6:2] "Give **Aaron** and his sons this command: 'These are the
6: 14 [6:7] **Aaron's** sons are to bring it before the LORD, in front of
6: 16 [6:9] **Aaron** and his sons shall eat the rest of it, but it is to be
6: 18 [6:11] Any male descendant of **Aaron** may eat it. It is his regular
6: 20 [6:13] "This is the offering **Aaron** and his sons are to bring to the
6: 25 [6:18] "Say to **Aaron** and his sons: 'These are the regulations for
7: 10 mixed with oil or dry, belongs equally to all the sons of **Aaron**.
7: 31 the fat on the altar, but the breast belongs to **Aaron** and his sons.
7: 33 The son of **Aaron** who offers the blood and the fat of the
7: 34 the thigh that is presented and have given them to **Aaron** the priest
7: 35 offerings made to the LORD by fire that were allotted to **Aaron**
8: 2 "Bring **Aaron** and his sons, their garments, the anointing oil,
8: 6 Moses brought **Aaron** and his sons forward and washed them with
8: 12 He poured some of the anointing oil on **Aaron's** head and anointed
8: 13 Then he brought **Aaron's** sons forward, put tunics on them,
8: 14 sin offering, and **Aaron** and his sons laid their hands on its head.
8: 18 burnt offering, and **Aaron** and his sons laid their hands on its head.
8: 22 the ordination, and **Aaron** and his sons laid their hands on its head.
8: 23 took some of its blood and put it on the lobe of **Aaron's** right ear,
8: 24 Moses also brought **Aaron's** sons forward and put some of the
8: 27 He put all these in the hands of **Aaron** and his sons and waved
8: 30 and sprinkled them on **Aaron** and his garments and on his sons
8: 30 So he consecrated **Aaron** and his garments and his sons and their
8: 31 Moses then said to **Aaron** and his sons, "Cook the meat at the
8: 31 as I commanded, saying, '**Aaron** and his sons are to eat it.'
8: 36 So **Aaron** and his sons did everything the LORD commanded
9: 1 On the eighth day Moses summoned **Aaron** and his sons and the
9: 2 He said to **Aaron**, "Take a bull calf for your sin offering and a ram
9: 7 Moses said to **Aaron**, "Come to the altar and sacrifice your sin
9: 8 So **Aaron** came to the altar and slaughtered the calf as a sin
9: 9 **His**[s] sons brought the blood to him, and he dipped his finger into
9: 12 **His**[s] sons handed him the blood, and he sprinkled it against the
9: 18 **His**[s] sons handed him the blood, and he sprinkled it against the
9: 21 **Aaron** waved the breasts and the right thigh before the LORD as
9: 22 Then **Aaron** lifted his hands toward the people and blessed them.
9: 23 Moses and **Aaron** then went into the Tent of Meeting. When they
10: 1 **Aaron's** sons Nadab and Abihu took their censers, put fire in them
10: 3 Moses then said to **Aaron**, "This is what the LORD spoke of
10: 3 in the sight of all the people I will be honored.' " **Aaron** remained
10: 4 summoned Mishael and Elzaphan, sons of **Aaron's** uncle Uzziel,
10: 6 Then Moses said to **Aaron** and his sons Eleazar and Ithamar,
10: 8 Then the LORD said to **Aaron**,
10: 12 Moses said to **Aaron** and his remaining sons, Eleazar and Ithamar,
10: 16 with Eleazar and Ithamar, **Aaron's** remaining sons, and asked,
10: 19 **Aaron** replied to Moses, "Today they sacrificed their sin offering
11: 1 The LORD said to Moses and **Aaron**,
13: 1 The LORD said to Moses and **Aaron**,
13: 2 he must be brought to **Aaron** the priest or to one of his sons who is
14: 33 The LORD said to Moses and **Aaron**,
15: 1 The LORD said to Moses and **Aaron**,
16: 1 two sons of **Aaron** who died when they approached the LORD.
16: 2 "Tell your brother **Aaron** not to come whenever he chooses into
16: 3 "This is how **Aaron** is to enter the sanctuary area: with a young
16: 6 "**Aaron** is to offer the bull for his own sin offering to make
16: 8 **He**[s] is to cast lots for the two goats—one lot for the LORD
16: 9 **Aaron** shall bring the goat whose lot falls to the LORD
16: 11 "**Aaron** shall bring the bull for his own sin offering to make
16: 21 **He**[s] is to lay both hands on the head of the live goat and confess
16: 23 "Then **Aaron** is to go into the Tent of Meeting and take off the
17: 2 "Speak to **Aaron** and his sons and to all the Israelites and say to
21: 1 "Speak to the priests, the sons of **Aaron**, and say to them:
21: 17 "Say to **Aaron**: 'For the generations to come none of your
21: 21 No descendant of **Aaron** the priest who has any defect is to come
21: 24 So Moses told this to **Aaron** and his sons and to all the Israelites.
22: 2 "Tell **Aaron** and his sons to treat with respect the sacred offerings
22: 4 " 'If a descendant of **Aaron** has an infectious skin disease
22: 18 "Speak to **Aaron** and his sons and to all the Israelites and say to
24: 3 **Aaron** is to tend the lamps before the LORD from evening till
24: 9 It belongs to **Aaron** and his sons, who are to eat it in a holy place,
Nu 1: 3 **Aaron** are to number by their divisions all the men in Israel twenty
1: 17 Moses and **Aaron** took these men whose names had been given,
1: 44 men counted by Moses and **Aaron** and the twelve leaders of Israel,
2: 1 The LORD said to Moses and **Aaron**:
3: 1 This is the account of the family of **Aaron** and Moses at the time
3: 2 The names of the sons of **Aaron** were Nadab the firstborn
3: 3 Those were the names of **Aaron's** sons, the anointed priests,

Nu 3: 4 Ithamar served as priests during the lifetime of their father **Aaron**.
3: 6 the tribe of Levi and present them to **Aaron** the priest to assist him.
3: 9 Give the Levites to **Aaron** and his sons; they are the Israelites who
3: 10 Appoint **Aaron** and his sons to serve as priests; anyone else who
3: 32 The chief leader of the Levites was Eleazar son of **Aaron**,
3: 38 Moses and **Aaron** and his sons were to camp to the east of the
3: 39 LORD's command by Moses and **Aaron** according to their clans,
3: 48 the money for the redemption of the additional Israelites to **Aaron**
3: 51 Moses gave the redemption money to **Aaron** and his sons,
4: 1 The LORD said to Moses and **Aaron**:
4: 5 **Aaron** and his sons are to go in and take down the shielding
4: 15 "After **Aaron** and his sons have finished covering the holy
4: 16 "Eleazar son of **Aaron**, the priest, is to have charge of the oil for
4: 17 The LORD said to Moses and **Aaron**,
4: 19 **Aaron** and his sons are to go into the sanctuary and assign to each
4: 27 is to be done under the direction of **Aaron** and his sons.
4: 28 Their duties are to be under the direction of Ithamar son of **Aaron**,
4: 33 the Tent of Meeting under the direction of Ithamar son of **Aaron**,
4: 34 **Aaron** and the leaders of the community counted the Kohathites
4: 37 **Aaron** counted them according to the LORD's command through
4: 41 and **Aaron** counted them according to the LORD's command.
4: 45 **Aaron** counted them according to the LORD's command through
4: 46 **Aaron** and the leaders of Israel counted all the Levites by their
6: 23 "Tell **Aaron** and his sons, 'This is how you are to bless the
7: 8 They were all under the direction of Ithamar son of **Aaron**,
8: 2 "Speak to **Aaron** and say to him, 'When you set up the seven
8: 3 **Aaron** did so; he set up the lamps so that they faced forward on the
8: 11 **Aaron** is to present the Levites before the LORD as a wave
8: 13 Have the Levites stand in front of **Aaron** and his sons and
8: 19 I have given the Levites as gifts to **Aaron** and his sons to do the
8: 20 **Aaron** and the whole Israelite community did with the Levites just
8: 21 Then **Aaron** presented them as a wave offering before the LORD
8: 21 the LORD and made atonement for them **[RPH]** to purify them.
8: 22 their work at the Tent of Meeting under the supervision of **Aaron**
9: 6 of a dead body. So they came to Moses and **Aaron** that same day
10: 8 "The sons of **Aaron**, the priests, are to blow the trumpets.
12: 1 Miriam and **Aaron** began to talk against Moses because of his
12: 4 **Aaron** and Miriam, "Come out to the Tent of Meeting, all three of
12: 5 at the entrance to the Tent and summoned **Aaron** and Miriam.
12: 10 like snow. **Aaron** turned toward her and saw that she had leprosy;
12: 11 **he**[s] said to Moses, "Please, my lord, do not hold against us the sin
13: 26 They came back to Moses and **Aaron** and the whole Israelite
14: 2 All the Israelites grumbled against Moses and **Aaron**,
14: 5 **Aaron** fell facedown in front of the whole Israelite assembly
14: 26 The LORD said to Moses and **Aaron**:
15: 33 wood brought him to Moses and **Aaron** and the whole assembly,
16: 3 came as a group to oppose Moses and **Aaron** and said to them,
16: 11 Who is **Aaron** that you should grumble against him?"
16: 16 to appear before the LORD tomorrow—you and they and **Aaron**.
16: 17 the LORD. You and **Aaron** are to present your censers also."
16: 18 with Moses and **Aaron** at the entrance to the Tent of Meeting.
16: 20 The LORD said to Moses and **Aaron**,
16: 37 [17:2] "Tell Eleazar son of **Aaron**, the priest, to take the censers
16: 40 [17:5] of **Aaron** should come to burn incense before the LORD,
16: 41 [17:6] Israelite community grumbled against Moses and **Aaron**.
16: 42 [17:7] and **Aaron** and turned toward the Tent of Meeting,
16: 43 [17:8] and **Aaron** went to the front of the Tent of Meeting,
16: 46 [17:11] Moses said to **Aaron**, "Take your censer and put incense
16: 47 [17:12] So **Aaron** did as Moses said, and ran into the midst of the
16: 50 [17:15] **Aaron** returned to Moses at the entrance to the Tent of
17: 3 [17:18] On the staff of Levi write **Aaron's** name, for there must
17: 6 [17:21] their ancestral tribes, and **Aaron's** staff was among them.
17: 8 [17:23] the Tent of the Testimony and saw that **Aaron's** staff,
17: 10 [17:25] "Put back **Aaron's** staff in front of the Testimony,
18: 1 The LORD said to **Aaron**, "You, your sons and your father's
18: 8 the LORD said to **Aaron**, "I myself have put you in charge of the
18: 20 The LORD said to **Aaron**, "You will have no inheritance in their
18: 28 From these tithes you must give the LORD's portion to **Aaron**
19: 1 The LORD said to Moses and **Aaron**:
20: 2 and the people gathered in opposition to Moses and **Aaron**.
20: 6 **Aaron** went from the assembly to the entrance to the Tent of
20: 8 and you and your brother **Aaron** gather the assembly together.
20: 10 and **Aaron** gathered the assembly together in front of the rock
20: 12 the LORD said to Moses and **Aaron**, "Because you did not trust
20: 23 near the border of Edom, the LORD said to Moses and **Aaron**,
20: 24 "**Aaron** will be gathered to his people. He will not enter the land I
20: 25 Get **Aaron** and his son Eleazar and take them up Mount Hor.
20: 26 Remove **Aaron's** garments and put them on his son Eleazar,
20: 26 them on his son Eleazar, for **Aaron** will be gathered to his people;
20: 28 Moses removed **Aaron's** garments and put them on his son
20: 28 And **Aaron** died there on top of the mountain. Then Moses
20: 29 and when the whole community learned that **Aaron** had died,
20: 29 had died, the entire house of Israel mourned for **him**[s] thirty days.
25: 7 the son of **Aaron**, the priest, saw this, he left the assembly,
25: 11 "Phinehas son of Eleazar, the son of **Aaron**, the priest, has turned
26: 1 the plague the LORD said to Moses and Eleazar son of **Aaron**,
26: 9 the community officials who rebelled against Moses and **Aaron**
26: 59 To Amram she bore **Aaron**, Moses and their sister Miriam.
26: 60 **Aaron** was the father of Nadab and Abihu, Eleazar and Ithamar.
26: 64 **Aaron** the priest when they counted the Israelites in the Desert of
27: 13 too will be gathered to your people, as your brother **Aaron** was,
33: 1 of Egypt by divisions under the leadership of Moses and **Aaron**.
33: 38 At the LORD's command **Aaron** the priest went up Mount Hor,
33: 39 **Aaron** was a hundred and twenty-three years old when he died on
Dt 9: 20 And the LORD was angry enough with **Aaron** to destroy him,
9: 20 with Aaron to destroy him, but at that time I prayed for **Aaron** too.
10: 6 There **Aaron** died and was buried, and Eleazar his son succeeded
32: 50 just as your brother **Aaron** died on Mount Hor and was gathered to
Jos 21: 4 The Levites who were descendants of **Aaron** the priest were
21: 10 (these towns were assigned to the descendants of **Aaron** who were
21: 13 So to the descendants of **Aaron** the priest they gave Hebron (a city
21: 19 the towns for the priests, the descendants of **Aaron**, were thirteen,
24: 5 " 'Then I sent Moses and **Aaron**, and I afflicted the Egyptians by
24: 33 And Eleazar son of **Aaron** died and was buried at Gibeah,
Jdg 20: 28 Phinehas son of Eleazar, the son of **Aaron**, ministering before it.)
1Sa 12: 6 "It is the LORD who appointed Moses and **Aaron** and brought
12: 8 to the LORD for help, and the LORD sent Moses and **Aaron**,
1Ch 6: 3 [5:29] **Aaron**, Moses and Miriam. The sons of Aaron: Nadab,
6: 3 [5:29] The sons of **Aaron**: Nadab, Abihu, Eleazar and Ithamar.
6: 49 [6:34] **Aaron** and his descendants were the ones who presented
6: 50 [6:35] These were the descendants of **Aaron**: Eleazar his son,
6: 54 [6:39] descendants of **Aaron** who were from the Kohathite clan,
6: 57 [6:42] So the descendants of **Aaron** were given Hebron (a city of
12: 27 [12:28] leader of the **family of Aaron**, with 3,700 men,
15: 4 He called together the descendants of **Aaron** and the Levites:
23: 13 **Aaron** and Moses. Aaron was set apart, he and his descendants
23: 13 **Aaron** was set apart, he and his descendants forever, to consecrate
23: 28 The duty of the Levites was to help **Aaron's** descendants in the
23: 32 the Holy Place and, under their brothers the descendants of **Aaron**,
24: 1 These were the divisions of the sons of **Aaron**: The sons of Aaron
24: 1 The sons of **Aaron** were Nadab, Abihu, Eleazar and Ithamar.
24: 19 to the regulations prescribed for them by their forefather **Aaron**,
24: 31 also cast lots, just as their brothers the descendants of **Aaron** did,
27: 17 over Levi: Hashabiah son of Kemuel; over **Aaron**: Zadok;
2Ch 13: 9 out the priests of the LORD, the sons of **Aaron**, and the Levites,
13: 10 The priests who serve the LORD are sons of **Aaron**,
26: 18 That is for the priests, the descendants of **Aaron**, who have been
29: 21 The king commanded the priests, the descendants of **Aaron**,
31: 19 As for the priests, the descendants of **Aaron**, who lived on the
35: 14 and for the priests, because the priests, the descendants of **Aaron**,
35: 14 preparations for themselves and for the **Aaronic** [+1201] priests.
Ezr 7: 5 of Phinehas, the son of Eleazar, the son of **Aaron** the chief priest—
Ne 10: 38 [10:39] A priest descended from **Aaron** is to accompany the
12: 47 and the Levites set aside the portion for the descendants of **Aaron**.
Ps 77: 20 [77:21] your people like a flock by the hand of Moses and **Aaron**.
99: 6 Moses and **Aaron** were among his priests, Samuel was among
105: 26 He sent Moses his servant, and **Aaron**, whom he had chosen.
106: 16 In the camp they grew envious of Moses and of **Aaron**, who was
115: 10 O house of **Aaron**, trust in the LORD—he is their help
115: 12 He will bless the house of Israel, he will bless the house of **Aaron**,
118: 3 Let the house of **Aaron** say: "His love endures forever."
133: 2 running down on the beard, running down on **Aaron's** beard,
135: 19 praise the LORD; O house of **Aaron**, praise the LORD;
Mic 6: 4 land of slavery. I sent Moses to lead you, also **Aaron** and Miriam.

196 אוֹ *'ô*, c. [320] [→ 218?] See Select Index

or [247], *untranslated* [35], whether or [13], either or [4], if [3], when [3], whether [3], and [2], also [1], at all [+1524+7785] [1], either [1], if [+4537] [1], nor [1], or else [1], or so [1], over a year [+2296+2296+3427+9102] [1], rather than [1], which way [+3545+6584+6584+8520] [1]

197 אָו *'aw*, n.m. [1] [√ 203]

crave [1]

Pr 31: 4 not for kings to drink wine, not for rulers to **crave** [Q 361] beer,

198 אוּאֵל *'û'ēl*, n.pr.m. [1] [√ 203? + 446]

Uel [1]

Ezr 10: 34 From the descendants of Bani: Maadai, Amram, **Uel**,

199 אוֹב[1] *'ôb*[1], n.m. [1] [cf. 200?]

wineskins [1]

Job 32: 19 I am like bottled-up wine, like new **wineskins** ready to burst.

[F] Hitpael (hitpoel, hitpoal, hitpolel, hitpolal, hitpalel, hitpalal, hitpalpel, hitpalpal, hotpael, hotpaal) [G] Hiphil (hiphtil) [H] Hophal [I] Hishtaphel

200 ²אוֹב *'ôb²*, n.m. [16] [cf. 199?]
mediums [9], medium [2], ghostlike [+3869] [1], medium [+1266] [1], medium [+8626] [1], one[s] [+1266] [1], spirit [1]

Lev 19:31 " 'Do not turn to **mediums** or seek out spiritists, for you will be
20: 6 " 'I will set my face against the person who turns to **mediums**
20:27 " 'A man or woman who is a **medium** or spiritist among you must
Dt 18:11 or *who is a* **medium** [+8626] or spiritist or who consults the dead.
1Sa 28: 3 Saul had expelled the **mediums** and spiritists from the land.
28: 7 "Find me a woman who is a **medium** [+1266], so I may go
28: 7 and inquire of her." "There is **one**[s] [+1266] in Endor," they said.
28: 8 "Consult a **spirit** for me," he said, "and bring up for me the one I
28: 9 has done. He has cut off the **mediums** and spiritists from the land.
2Ki 21: 6 and divination, and consulted **mediums** and spiritists.
23:24 Furthermore, Josiah got rid of the **mediums** and spiritists,
1Ch 10:13 word of the LORD and even consulted a **medium** for guidance,
2Ch 33: 6 divination and witchcraft, and consulted **mediums** and spiritists.
Isa 8:19 When men tell you to consult **mediums** and spiritists, who whisper
19: 3 and the spirits of the dead, the **mediums** and the spiritists.
29: 4 Your voice will come **ghostlike** [+3869] from the earth; out of the

201 אוֹבִיל *'ôbîl*, n.pr.m. [1] [√ 3297]
Obil [1]

1Ch 27:30 **Obil** the Ishmaelite was in charge of the camels. Jehdeiah the

202 אוּד *'ûd*, n.m. [3] [→ 369]
burning stick [2], firewood [1]

Isa 7: 4 not lose heart because of these two smoldering stubs of **firewood**—
Am 4:11 You were like a **burning stick** snatched from the fire, yet you have
Zec 3: 2 Is not this man a **burning stick** snatched from the fire?"

203 ¹אָוָה *'āwâ¹*, v. [26] [→ 197, 205, 2094, 4397, 9294; *also used with compound proper names*]
crave [4], desired [3], desires [3], craves [2], longed for [2], crave other food [+9294] [1], craved other food [1], craves for more [+9294] [1], desire [1], enthralled [1], gave in to craving [+9294] [1], like [1], long for [1], pleases [1], set desire on [1], want [1], yearns for [1]

Nu 11: 4 [F] The rabble with them *began to* **crave** [+9294] **other food**,
11:34 [F] there they buried the people who *had* **craved other food**.
Dt 5:21 [F] *You shall* not **set** *your* **desire on** your neighbor's house
12:20 [D] you **crave** meat and say, "I would like some meat," then you
14:26 [D] Use the silver to buy whatever you **like**: cattle, sheep, wine
1Sa 2:16 [D] then take whatever you **want**," the servant would
2Sa 3:21 [D] and that you may rule over all that your heart **desires**."
23:15 [F] David **longed for** water and said, "Oh, that someone would
1Ki 11:37 [D] take you, and you will rule over all that your heart **desires**;
1Ch 11:17 [F] David **longed for** water and said, "Oh, that someone would
Job 23:13 [D] and who can oppose him? He does whatever he **pleases**.
Ps 45:11 [45:12] [F] The king *is* **enthralled** *by* your beauty; honor him,
106:14 [F] In the desert *they* **gave in to** *their* **craving** [+9294]; in the
132:13 [D] LORD has chosen Zion, *he has* **desired** it for his dwelling:
132:14 [D] and ever; here I will sit enthroned, for *I have* **desired** it—
Pr 13: 4 [F] The sluggard **craves** and gets nothing, but the desires of the
21:10 [D] The wicked man **craves** evil; his neighbor gets no mercy
21:26 [F] All day long *he* **craves** [+9294] **for more**, but the righteous
23: 3 [F] *Do* not **crave** his delicacies, for that food is deceptive.
23: 6 [F] not eat the food of a stingy man, *do* not **crave** his delicacies;
24: 1 [F] Do not envy wicked men, *do* not **desire** their company;
Ecc 6: 2 [F] and honor, so that he lacks nothing his heart **desires**.
Isa 26: 9 [D] My soul **yearns for** you in the night; in the morning my
Jer 17:16 [F] you know *I have* not **desired** the day of despair.
Am 5:18 [F] Woe to *you who* **long for** the day of the LORD! Why do
Mic 7: 1 [D] no cluster of grapes to eat, none of the early figs that I **crave**.

204 ²אָוָה *'āwâ²*, v. [1] [→ 253?; cf. 9292, 9295, 9344]
run a line [1]

Nu 34:10 [F] eastern boundary, **run a line** from Hazar Enan to Shepham.

205 אַוָּה *'awwâ*, n.f. [7] [→ 2094; cf. 203]
want [3], craving [+5883] [1], earnestness [+5883] [1], please [1], pleases [1]

Dt 12:15 in any of your towns and eat as much of the meat as you **want**,
12:20 like some meat," then you may eat as much of it as you **want**.
12:21 and in your own towns you may eat as much of them as you **want**.
18: 6 comes in all **earnestness** [+5883] to the place the LORD will
1Sa 23:20 Now, O king, come down whenever it **pleases** you to do so,
Jer 2:24 to the desert, sniffing the wind in her **craving** [+5883]—
Hos 10:10 When I **please**, I will punish them; nations will be gathered against

206 אוּזַי *'ûzay*, n.pr.m. [1]
Uzai [1]

Ne 3:25 Palal son of **Uzai** worked opposite the angle and the tower

207 אוּזָל *'ûzāl*, n.pr.loc. [& m.]. [3]
Uzal [3]

Ge 10:27 Hadoram, **Uzal**, Diklah,
1Ch 1:21 Hadoram, **Uzal**, Diklah,
Eze 27:19 " 'Danites and Greeks from **Uzal** bought your merchandise;

208 אוֹי *'ôy*, interj. [24] [→ 210]
woe [19], alas [3], ah [1], in trouble [1]

Nu 21:29 **Woe** to you, O Moab! You are destroyed, O people of Chemosh!
24:23 Then he uttered his oracle: "**Ah**, who can live when God does this?
1Sa 4: 7 "A god has come into the camp," they said. "We're **in trouble**!
4: 8 **Woe** to us! Who will deliver us from the hand of these mighty
Pr 23:29 Who has **woe**? Who has sorrow? Who has strife? Who has
Isa 3: 9 they parade their sin like Sodom; they do not hide it. **Woe** to them!
3:11 **Woe** to the wicked! Disaster is upon them! They will be paid back
6: 5 "**Woe** to me!" I cried. "I am ruined! For I am a man of unclean
24:16 I said, "I waste away, I waste away! **Woe** to me! The treacherous
Jer 4:13 his horses are swifter than eagles. **Woe** to us! We are ruined!
4:31 gasping for breath, stretching out her hands and saying, "**Alas**!
6: 4 But, **alas**, the daylight is fading, and the shadows of evening grow
10:19 **Woe** to me because of my injury! My wound is incurable!
13:27 acts on the hills and in the fields. **Woe** to you, O Jerusalem!
15:10 **Alas**, my mother, that you gave me birth, a man with whom the
45: 3 You said, '**Woe** to me! The LORD has added sorrow to my pain;
48:46 **Woe** to you, O Moab! The people of Chemosh are destroyed;
La 5:16 crown has fallen from our head. **Woe** to us, for we have sinned!
Eze 16:23 " '**Woe**! Woe to you, declares the Sovereign LORD. In addition to
16:23 " 'Woe! **Woe** to you, declares the Sovereign LORD. In addition to
24: 6 " '**Woe** *to* the city of bloodshed, to the pot now encrusted,
24: 9 " '**Woe** *to* the city of bloodshed! I, too, will pile the wood high.
Hos 7:13 **Woe** to them, because they have strayed from me! Destruction to
9:12 them of every one. **Woe** to them when I turn away from them!

209 אֱוִי *'ᵉwî*, n.pr.m. [2]
Evi [2]

Nu 31: 8 Among their victims were **Evi**, Rekem, Zur, Hur and Reba—
Jos 13:21 and the Midianite chiefs, **Evi**, Rekem, Zur, Hur and Reba—

210 אוֹיָה *'ôyâ*, interj. [1] [√ 208]
woe [1]

Ps 120: 5 **Woe** to me that I dwell in Meshech, that I live among the tents of

211 ¹אֱוִיל *'ᵉwîl¹*, a. [26 / 25] [→ 216, 222; cf. 3282]
fool [16], fools [7], fool's [1], wicked fools [1]

Job 5: 2 Resentment kills a **fool**, and envy slays the simple.
5: 3 I myself have seen a **fool** taking root, but suddenly his house was
Ps 107:17 *Some* became **fools** through their rebellious ways and suffered
Pr 1: 7 beginning of knowledge, but **fools** despise wisdom and discipline.
7:22 the slaughter, like a deer [BHS *fool*; NIV 385] stepping into a noose
10: 8 wise in heart accept commands, but a chattering **fool** comes to ruin.
10:10 winks maliciously causes grief, and a chattering **fool** comes to ruin.
10:14 Wise men store up knowledge, but the mouth of a **fool** invites ruin.
10:21 of the righteous nourish many, but **fools** die for lack of judgment.
11:29 will inherit only wind, and the **fool** will be servant to the wise.
12:15 The way of a **fool** seems right to him, but a wise man listens to
12:16 A **fool** shows his annoyance at once, but a prudent man overlooks
14: 3 A **fool's** talk brings a rod to his back, but the lips of the wise
14: 9 **Fools** mock at making amends for sin, but goodwill is found
15: 5 A **fool** spurns his father's discipline, but whoever heeds correction
16:22 of life to those who have it, but folly brings punishment to **fools**.
17:28 Even a **fool** is thought wise if he keeps silent, and discerning if he
20: 3 to a man's honor to avoid strife, but every **fool** is quick to quarrel.
24: 7 Wisdom is too high for a **fool**; in the assembly at the gate he has
27: 3 and sand a burden, but provocation by a **fool** is heavier than both.
27:22 Though you grind a **fool** in a mortar, grinding him like grain with a
29: 9 If a wise man goes to court with a **fool**, the fool rages and scoffs,
Isa 19:11 The officials of Zoan are nothing but **fools**; the wise counselors of
35: 8 those who walk in that Way; **wicked fools** will not go about on it.
Jer 4:22 "My people are **fools**; they do not know me. They are senseless
Hos 9: 7 and your hostility so great, the prophet is considered a **fool**,

212 ²אֱוִיל *'ᵉwîl²*, n.m. Not used in NIV/BHS [cf. 380?, 446?]

213 אֱוִיל מְרֹדַךְ ***'ewîl merōdak***, n.pr.m. [2]

Evil-Merodach [2]

2Ki 25:27 of Judah, in the year **Evil-Merodach** became king of Babylon,
Jer 52:31 in the year **Evil-Merodach** became king of Babylon, he released

214 [1]אוּל ***'ûl***[1], n.[m.]. [1] [√ 380?]

bodies [1]

Ps 73:4 They have no struggles; their **bodies** are healthy and strong.

215 [2]אוּל ***'ûl***[2], n.[m.]. [0] [√ 380; cf. 3283]

2Ki 24:15 [his officials and the **leading men** [K; see Q 380] *of* the land.]

216 אֱוִלִי ***'ewilî***, a. [1] [√ 211]

foolish [1]

Zec 11:15 said to me, "Take again the equipment of a **foolish** shepherd.

217 [1]אוּלַי ***'ûlay***[1], n.pr.loc. [2]

Ulai [2]

Da 8:2 in the province of Elam; in the vision I was beside the **Ulai** Canal.
8:16 And I heard a man's voice from the **Ulai** calling, "Gabriel,

218 [2]אוּלַי ***'ûlay***[2], adv. [45] [√ 196? + 4202?]

perhaps [25], what if [9], it may be [3], maybe [3], but perhaps [1], but [1], if not [1], may yet [1], were it to [1]

Ge 16:2 with my maidservant; **perhaps** I can build a family through her."
18:24 **What if** there are fifty righteous people in the city? Will you really
18:28 **what if** the number of the righteous is five less than fifty?
18:29 Once again he spoke to him, "**What if** only forty are found there?"
18:30 **What if** only thirty can be found there?" He answered, "I will not
18:31 as to speak to the Lord, **what if** only twenty can be found there?"
18:32 **What if** only ten can be found there?" He answered, "For the sake
24:5 "**What if** the woman is unwilling to come back with me to this
24:39 my master, '**What if** the woman will not come back with me?'
27:12 **What if** my father touches me? I would appear to be tricking him
32:20 [32:21] later, when I see him, **perhaps** he will receive me."
43:12 put back into the mouths of your sacks. **Perhaps** it was a mistake.
Ex 32:30 go up to the LORD; **perhaps** I can make atonement for your sin."
Nu 22:6 **Perhaps** then I will be able to defeat them and drive them out of
22:11 **Perhaps** then I will be able to fight them and drive them away.' "
22:33 **If** she had **not** turned away, I would certainly have killed you by
23:3 **Perhaps** the LORD will come to meet with me. Whatever he
23:27 **Perhaps** it will please God to let you curse them for me from
Jos 9:7 men of Israel said to the Hivites, "**But perhaps** you live near us.
14:12 Anakites were there and their cities were large and fortified, **but**,
1Sa 6:5 **Perhaps** he will lift his hand from you and your gods and your
9:6 Let's go there now. **Perhaps** he will tell us what way to take."
14:6 **Perhaps** the LORD will act in our behalf. Nothing can hinder the
2Sa 14:15 'I will speak to the king; **perhaps** he will do what his servant asks.
16:12 **It may be** that the LORD will see my distress and repay me with
1Ki 18:5 **Maybe** we can find some grass to keep the horses and mules alive
18:27 or traveling. **Maybe** he is sleeping and must be awakened."
20:31 and ropes around our heads. **Perhaps** he will spare your life."
2Ki 19:4 **It may be** that the LORD your God will hear all the words of the
Job 1:5 "**Perhaps** my children have sinned and cursed God in their hearts."
Isa 37:4 **It may be** that the LORD your God will hear the words of the
47:12 **Perhaps** you will succeed, perhaps you will cause terror.
47:12 Perhaps you will succeed, **perhaps** you will cause terror.
Jer 20:10 are waiting for me to slip, saying, "**Perhaps** he will be deceived;
21:2 **Perhaps** the LORD will perform wonders for us as in times past
26:3 **Perhaps** they will listen and each will turn from his evil way.
36:3 **Perhaps** when the people of Judah hear about every disaster I plan
36:7 **Perhaps** they will bring their petition before the LORD,
51:8 Wail over her! Get balm for her pain; **perhaps** she can be healed.
La 3:29 Let him bury his face in the dust—there **may yet** be hope.
Eze 12:3 **Perhaps** they will understand, though they are a rebellious house.
Hos 8:7 no flour. **Were it to** yield grain, foreigners would swallow it up.
Am 5:15 **Perhaps** the LORD God Almighty will have mercy on the
Jnh 1:6 your god! **Maybe** he will take notice of us, and we will not perish."
Zep 2:3 **perhaps** you will be sheltered on the day of the LORD's anger.

219 [1]אוּלָם ***'ûlām***[1], adv. [19]

but [9], nevertheless [2], though [2], *untranslated* [1], but if [1], however [1], if [1], otherwise [1], yet [1]

Ge 28:19 He called that place Bethel, **though** the city used to be called Luz.
48:19 **Nevertheless**, his younger brother will be greater than he,
Ex 9:16 **But** I have raised you up for this very purpose, that I might show
Nu 14:21 **Nevertheless**, as surely as I live and as surely as the glory of the
Jdg 18:29 who was born to Israel—**though** the city used to be called Laish.
1Sa 20:3 **Yet** as surely as the LORD lives and as you live, there is only a
25:34 **Otherwise**, as surely as the LORD, the God of Israel, lives,
1Ki 20:23 **if** we fight them on the plains, surely we will be stronger than they.
Job 1:11 **But** stretch out your hand and strike everything he has, and he will
2:5 **But** stretch out your hand and strike his flesh and bones, and he
5:8 "**But if** it were I, I would appeal to God; I would lay my cause
11:5 **[NIE]** Oh, how I wish that God would speak, that he would open
12:7 "**But** ask the animals, and they will teach you, or the birds of the
13:3 **But** I desire to speak to the Almighty and to argue my case with
13:4 You, **however**, smear me with lies; you are worthless physicians,
14:18 "**But** as a mountain erodes and crumbles and as a rock is moved
17:10 "**But** come on, all of you, try again! I will not find a wise man
33:1 "**But** now, Job, listen to my words; pay attention to everything I
Mic 3:8 **But** as for me, I am filled with power, with the Spirit of the

220 [2]אוּלָם ***'ûlām***[2], n.pr.m. [4]

Ulam [4]

1Ch 7:16 brother was named Sheresh, and his sons were **Ulam** and Rakem.
7:17 The son of **Ulam**: Bedan. These were the sons of Gilead son of
8:39 **Ulam** his firstborn, Jeush the second son and Eliphelet the third.
8:40 The sons of **Ulam** were brave warriors who could handle the bow.

221 [3]אוּלָם ***'ûlām***[3], n.m. Not used in NIV/BHS [√ 395]

222 אִוֶּלֶת ***'iwwelet***, n.f. [25] [√ 211]

folly [22], foolish [2], sinful folly [1]

Ps 38:5 [38:6] and are loathsome because of my **sinful folly**.
69:5 [69:6] You know my **folly**, O God; my guilt is not hidden from
Pr 5:23 He will die for lack of discipline, led astray by his own great **folly**.
12:23 his knowledge to himself, but the heart of fools blurts out **folly**.
13:16 prudent man acts out of knowledge, but a fool exposes his **folly**.
14:1 her house, but with her own hands the **foolish** *one* tears hers down.
14:8 is to give thought to their ways, but the **folly** *of* fools is deception.
14:17 A quick-tempered man does **foolish** *things*, and a crafty man is
14:18 The simple inherit **folly**, but the prudent are crowned with
14:24 wealth of the wise is their crown, but the **folly** *of* fools yields folly.
14:24 wealth of the wise is their crown, but the folly of fools yields **folly**.
14:29 has great understanding, but a quick-tempered man displays **folly**.
15:2 wise commends knowledge, but the mouth of the fool gushes **folly**.
15:14 heart seeks knowledge, but the mouth of a fool feeds on **folly**.
15:21 **Folly** delights a man who lacks judgment, but a man of
16:22 of life to those who have it, but **folly** brings punishment to fools.
17:12 Better to meet a bear robbed of her cubs than a fool in his **folly**.
18:13 He who answers before listening—that is his **folly** and his shame.
19:3 A man's own **folly** ruins his life, yet his heart rages against the
22:15 **Folly** is bound up in the heart of a child, but the rod of discipline
24:9 The schemes of **folly** are sin, and men detest a mocker.
26:4 Do not answer a fool according to his **folly**, or you will be like him
26:5 Answer a fool according to his **folly**, or he will be wise in his own
26:11 As a dog returns to its vomit, so a fool repeats his **folly**.
27:22 like grain with a pestle, you will not remove his **folly** from him.

223 אוֹמָר ***'ômār***, n.pr.m. [3] [√ 606]

Omar [3]

Ge 36:11 The sons of Eliphaz: Teman, **Omar**, Zepho, Gatam and Kenaz.
36:15 the firstborn of Esau: Chiefs Teman, **Omar**, Zepho, Kenaz,
1Ch 1:36 Teman, **Omar**, Zepho, Gatam and Kenaz; by Timna: Amalek.

224 [1]אָוֶן ***'āwen***[1], n.m. [77 / 76] [→ 1077, 1204, 9303?]

evil [23], evildoers [+7188] [16], wicked [6], sin [3], wrong [3], calamity [1], deceit [1], disaster [1], distress [1], evildoer [+7188] [1], false [1], hardship [1], harm [1], idol [1], iniquity [1], injustice [1], malice [1], malicious [1], misfortune [1], nothing [1], punishment [1], sins [1], slander [1], sorrow [1], suffering [1], trouble [1], unjust [1], villain [+408] [1], wicked men [+7188] [1], wickedness [1]

Nu 23:21 "No **misfortune** is seen in Jacob, no misery observed in Israel.
1Sa 15:23 is like the sin of divination, and arrogance like the **evil** of idolatry.
Job 4:8 those who plow **evil** and those who sow trouble reap it.
5:6 For **hardship** does not spring from the soil, nor does trouble sprout
11:11 deceitful men; and when he sees **evil**, does he not take note?
11:14 if you put away the **sin** that is in your hand and allow no evil to
15:35 They conceive trouble and give birth to **evil**; their womb fashions
18:12 **Calamity** is hungry for him; disaster is ready for him when he
21:19 ⸤It is said,⸥ 'God stores up a man's **punishment** for his sons.'
22:15 Will you keep to the old path that **evil** men have trod?
31:3 Is it not ruin for the wicked, disaster for those who do **wrong**?
34:8 He keeps company with **evildoers** [+7188]; he associates with
34:22 no dark place, no deep shadow, where **evildoers** [+7188] can hide.
34:36 that Job might be tested to the utmost for answering like a **wicked**
36:10 listen to correction and commands them to repent of their **evil**.
36:21 Beware of turning to **evil**, which you seem to prefer to affliction.
Ps 5:5 [5:6] cannot stand in your presence; you hate all who do **wrong**.

[F] Hitpael (hitpoel, hitpoal, hitpolel, hitpolal, hitpalel, hitpalal, hitpalpel, hitpalpal, hotpael, hotpaal) [G] Hiphil (hiphtil) [H] Hophal [I] Hishtaphel

Ps 6: 8 [6:9] Away from me, all you who do **evil**, for the LORD has
7: 14 [7:15] He who is pregnant with **evil** and conceives trouble gives
10: 7 and lies and threats; trouble and **evil** are under his tongue.
14: 4 Will **evildoers** [+7188] never learn—those who devour my people
28: 3 Do not drag me away with the wicked, with those who do **evil**,
36: 3 [36:4] The words of his mouth are **wicked** and deceitful; he has
36: 4 [36:5] Even on his bed he plots **evil**; he commits himself to a
36: 12 [36:13] See how the **evildoers** [+7188] lie fallen—thrown down,
41: 6 [41:7] see me, he speaks falsely, while his heart gathers **slander**;
53: 4 [53:5] Will the **evildoers** [+7188] never learn—those who devour
55: 3 [55:4] for they bring down **suffering** upon me and revile me in
55: 10 [55:11] prowl about on its walls; **malice** and abuse are within it.
56: 7 [56:8] On no [BHS *On account of wickedness*; NIV 401] **account** let them escape;
59: 2 [59:3] Deliver me from **evildoers** [+7188] and save me from
59: 5 [59:6] to punish all the nations; show no mercy to **wicked** traitors.
64: 2 [64:3] of the wicked, from that noisy crowd of **evildoers** [+7188].
66: 18 If I had cherished **sin** in my heart, the Lord would not have
90: 10 yet their span is but trouble and **sorrow**, for they quickly pass,
92: 7 [92:8] spring up like grass and all **evildoers** [+7188] flourish,
92: 9 [92:10] will perish; all **evildoers** [+7188] will be scattered.
94: 4 out arrogant words; all the **evildoers** [+7188] are full of boasting.
94: 16 Who will take a stand for me against **evildoers** [+7188]?
94: 23 He will repay them for their **sins** and destroy them for their
101: 8 I will cut off every **evildoer** [+7188] from the city of the LORD.
119: 133 my footsteps according to your word; let no **sin** rule over me.
125: 5 crooked ways the LORD will banish with the **evildoers** [+7188].
141: 4 to take part in wicked deeds with men *who are* **evildoers** [+7188];
141: 9 they have laid for me, from the traps set by **evildoers** [+7188].
Pr 6: 12 A scoundrel and **villain** [+408], who goes about with a corrupt
6: 18 a heart that devises **wicked** schemes, feet that are quick to rush into
10: 29 is a refuge for the righteous, but it is the ruin of those who do **evil**.
12: 21 No **harm** befalls the righteous, but the wicked have their fill of
17: 4 A wicked man listens to **evil** lips; a liar pays attention to a
19: 28 mocks at justice, and the mouth of the wicked gulps down **evil**.
21: 15 it brings joy to the righteous but terror to **evildoers** [+7188].
22: 8 He who sows wickedness reaps **trouble**, and the rod of his fury
30: 20 and wipes her mouth and says, 'I've done nothing **wrong**.'
Isa 1: 13 Sabbaths and convocations—I cannot bear your **evil** assemblies.
10: 1 Woe to those who make **unjust** laws, to those who issue
29: 20 will disappear, and all who have an eye for **evil** will be cut down—
31: 2 the house of the wicked, against those who help **evildoers** [+7188].
32: 6 For the fool speaks folly, his mind is busy with **evil**: He practices
41: 29 See, they are all **false**! Their deeds amount to nothing; their images
55: 7 Let the wicked forsake his way and the **evil** man his thoughts.
58: 9 yoke of oppression, with the pointing finger and **malicious** talk,
59: 4 and speak lies; they conceive trouble and give birth to **evil**.
59: 6 Their deeds are **evil** deeds, and acts of violence are in their hands.
59: 7 Their thoughts are **evil** thoughts; ruin and destruction mark their
66: 3 whoever burns memorial incense, like one who worships an **idol**.
Jer 4: 14 and be saved. How long will you harbor **wicked** thoughts?
4: 15 from Dan, proclaiming **disaster** from the hills of Ephraim.
Eze 11: 2 these are the men who are plotting **evil** and giving wicked advice
Hos 6: 8 Gilead is a city of **wicked** [+7188] **men**, stained with footprints of
10: 8 The high places of **wickedness** will be destroyed—it is the sin of
12: 11 [12:12] Is Gilead **wicked**? Its people are worthless! Do they
Am 5: 5 will surely go into exile, and Bethel will be reduced to **nothing**."
Mic 2: 1 Woe to those who plan **iniquity**, to those who plot evil on their
Hab 1: 3 Why do you make me look at **injustice**? Why do you tolerate
3: 7 I saw the tents of Cushan in **distress**, the dwellings of Midian in
Zec 10: 2 The idols speak **deceit**, diviners see visions that lie; they tell

225 ²אָוֶן *'āwen²*, n.pr.loc. [2]

Aven [1], Heliopolis [1]

Eze 30: 17 The young men of **Heliopolis** and Bubastis will fall by the sword,
Am 1: 5 I will destroy the king who is in the Valley of **Aven** and the one

226 ¹אוֹן *'ôn¹*, n.m. [12] [→ 227, 229, 231, 232]

power [3], manhood [2], man [1], sign of strength [1], strength [1], vigor [1], weak [+401] [1], wealth [1], wealthy [1]

Ge 49: 3 my might, the first sign of my **strength**, excelling in honor,
Dt 21: 17 That son is the first **sign of** his father's **strength**. The right of the
Job 18: 7 The **vigor** *of* his step is weakened; his own schemes throw him
20: 10 amends to the poor; his own hands must give back his **wealth**.
40: 16 he has in his loins, what **power** in the muscles of his belly!
Ps 78: 51 firstborn of Egypt, the firstfruits of **manhood** in the tents of Ham.
105: 36 all the firstborn in their land, the firstfruits of all their **manhood**.
Pr 11: 7 hope perishes; all he expected from his **power** comes to nothing.
Isa 40: 26 Because of his great **power** and mighty strength, not one of them is
40: 29 strength to the weary and increases the power of the **weak** [+401].
Hos 12: 3 [12:4] his brother's heel; as a **man** he struggled with God.
12: 8 [12:9] Ephraim boasts, "I am very rich; I have become **wealthy**.

227 ²אוֹן *'ôn²*, n.pr.m. [1] [√ 231; cf. 226]

On [1]

Nu 16: 1 Dathan and Abiram, sons of Eliab, and **On** son of Peleth—

228 ³אוֹן *'ôn³*, n.pr.loc. [3]

On [3]

Ge 41: 45 him Asenath daughter of Potiphera, priest of **On**, to be his wife.
41: 50 born to Joseph by Asenath daughter of Potiphera, priest of **On**.
46: 20 born to Joseph by Asenath daughter of Potiphera, priest of **On**.

229 אוֹנוֹ *'ônô*, n.pr.loc. [5] [√ 226]

Ono [5]

1Ch 8: 12 Shemed (who built **Ono** and Lod with its surrounding villages),
Ezr 2: 33 of Lod, Hadid and **Ono** 725
Ne 6: 2 let us meet together in one of the villages on the plain of **Ono**."
7: 37 of Lod, Hadid and **Ono** 721
11: 35 in Lod and **Ono**, and in the Valley of the Craftsmen.

230 אוֹנִי *'ônî*, n.pr.m. [1] [√ 627]

mourners [1]

Hos 9: 4 Such sacrifices will be to them like the bread of **mourners**;

231 אוֹנָם *'ônām*, n.pr.m. [4] [√ 227; cf. 226]

Onam [4]

Ge 36: 23 The sons of Shobal: Alvan, Manahath, Ebal, Shepho and **Onam**.
1Ch 1: 40 The sons of Shobal: Alvan, Manahath, Ebal, Shepho and **Onam**.
2: 26 whose name was Atarah; she was the mother of **Onam**.
2: 28 The sons of **Onam**: Shammai and Jada. The sons of Shammai:

232 אוֹנָן *'ônān*, n.pr.m. [8] [√ 226]

Onan [7], *untranslated* [1]

Ge 38: 4 She conceived again and gave birth to a son and named him **Onan**.
38: 8 Judah said to **Onan**, "Lie with your brother's wife and fulfill your
38: 9 **Onan** knew that the offspring would not be his; so whenever he
46: 12 Er, **Onan**, Shelah, Perez and Zerah (but Er and Onan had died in
46: 12 and Zerah (but Er and **Onan** had died in the land of Canaan).
Nu 26: 19 Er and **Onan** were sons of Judah, but they died in Canaan.
26: 19 and Onan were sons of Judah, but **[RPH]** they died in Canaan.
1Ch 2: 3 The sons of Judah: Er, **Onan** and Shelah. These three were born to

233 אוּפָז *'ûpāz*, n.pr.loc. [2]

finest gold [+4188] [1], Uphaz [1]

Jer 10: 9 Hammered silver is brought from Tarshish and gold from **Uphaz**.
Da 10: 5 in linen, with a belt of the **finest gold** [+4188] around his waist.

234 ¹אוֹפִיר *'ôpîr¹*, n.pr.loc. [11] [→ 235; cf. 709]

Ophir [9], gold of Ophir [1], there[s] [1]

1Ki 9: 28 They sailed to **Ophir** and brought back 420 talents of gold,
10: 11 (Hiram's ships brought gold from **Ophir**; and from there they
10: 11 and from **there**[s] they brought great cargoes of almugwood
22: 48 [22:49] built a fleet of trading ships to go to **Ophir** for gold,
1Ch 29: 4 three thousand talents of gold (gold of **Ophir**) and seven thousand
2Ch 8: 18 sailed to **Ophir** and brought back four hundred and fifty talents of
9: 10 men of Hiram and the men of Solomon brought gold from **Ophir**;
Job 22: 24 nuggets to the dust, your **gold of Ophir** to the rocks in the ravines,
28: 16 It cannot be bought with the gold of **Ophir**, with precious onyx
Ps 45: 9 [45:10] at your right hand is the royal bride in gold of **Ophir**.
Isa 13: 12 man scarcer than pure gold, more rare than the gold of **Ophir**.

235 ²אוֹפִיר *'ôpîr²*, n.pr.m. [2] [√ 234; cf. 709]

Ophir [2]

Ge 10: 29 **Ophir**, Havilah and Jobab. All these were sons of Joktan.
1Ch 1: 23 **Ophir**, Havilah and Jobab. All these were sons of Joktan.

236 אוֹפַן *'ôpan*, n.m. [35] [cf. 698?]

wheels [23], wheel [8], *untranslated* [3], cartwheel [+6322] [1]

Ex 14: 25 He made the **wheels** *of* their chariots come off so that they had
1Ki 7: 30 Each stand had four bronze **wheels** with bronze axles, and each
7: 32 The four **wheels** were under the panels, and the axles of the wheels
7: 32 the panels, and the axles of the **wheels** were attached to the stand.
7: 32 to the stand. The diameter of each **wheel** was a cubit and a half.
7: 33 The **wheels** were made like chariot wheels; the axles, rims,
7: 33 The wheels were made like chariot **wheels**; the axles, rims,
Pr 20: 26 winnows out the wicked; he drives the *threshing* **wheel** over them.
Isa 28: 27 with a sledge, nor is a **cartwheel** [+6322] rolled over cummin;
Eze 1: 15 I saw a **wheel** on the ground beside each creature with its four

Eze 1:16 This was the appearance and structure of the **wheels**:
1:16 Each appeared to be made like a **wheel** intersecting a wheel.
1:16 Each appeared to be made like a wheel intersecting a **wheel**.
1:19 When the living creatures moved, the **wheels** beside them moved;
1:19 the living creatures rose from the ground, the **wheels** also rose.
1:20 they would go, and the **wheels** would rise along with them,
1:20 because the spirit of the living creatures was in the **wheels**.
1:21 creatures rose from the ground, the **wheels** rose along with them,
1:21 because the spirit of the living creatures was in the **wheels**.
3:13 against each other and the sound of the **wheels** beside them,
10:6 among the cherubim," the man went in and stood beside a **wheel**.
10:9 I looked, and I saw beside the cherubim four **wheels**, one beside
10:9 cherubim four wheels, one **[RPH]** beside each of the cherubim;
10:9 each of the cherubim; **[RPH]** the wheels sparkled like chrysolite.
10:9 beside each of the cherubim; the **wheels** sparkled like chrysolite.
10:10 of them looked alike; each was like a **wheel** intersecting a wheel.
10:10 of them looked alike; each was like a wheel intersecting a **wheel**.
10:12 were completely full of eyes, as were their four **wheels**.
10:12 were completely full of eyes, as were their four wheels. **[RPH]**
10:13 I heard the **wheels** being called "the whirling wheels."
10:16 When the cherubim moved, the **wheels** beside them moved;
10:16 wings to rise from the ground, the **wheels** did not leave their side.
10:19 from the ground, and as they went, the **wheels** went with them.
11:22 the cherubim, with the **wheels** beside them, spread their wings,
Na 3:2 the clatter of **wheels**, galloping horses and jolting chariots!

237 אוּץ *'ûṣ*, v. [10]

delayed [+4202] [1], eager [1], haste [1], hasty [+928+8079] [1], in haste [1], pressing [1], run [1], small [1], try [1], urged [1]

Ge 19:15 [G] the coming of dawn, the angels **urged** Lot, saying, "Hurry!
Ex 5:13 [A] The slave drivers *kept* **pressing** them, saying,
Jos 10:13 [A] of the sky and **delayed** [+4202] going down about a full day.
17:15 [A] "and if the hill country of Ephraim *is too* **small** for you,
Pr 19:2 [A] nor *to be* **hasty** [+928+8079] and miss the way.
21:5 [A] The plans of the diligent lead to profit as surely as **haste**
28:20 [A] but *one* **eager** to get rich will not go unpunished.
29:20 [A] Do you see a man *who* speaks **in haste**? There is more hope
Isa 22:4 [G] *Do* not **try** to console me over the destruction of my people."
Jer 17:16 [A] I *have* not **run** away from being your shepherd; you know I

238 אוֹצָר *'ôṣār*, n.m. [79] [√ 732]

treasures [22], treasuries [20], storehouses [9], treasury [7], *untranslated* [2], riches [2], storehouse [2], supplies [2], treasure [2], arsenal [1], fortune [1], put in charge of the storerooms [+732+6584] [1], storehouse [+1074] [1], storerooms [+4200+5969] [1], storerooms [1], stores [1], treasury [+1074] [1], vats [1], vaults [1], wealth [1]

Dt 28:12 the **storehouse** *of* his bounty, to send rain on your land in season
32:34 "Have I not kept this in reserve and sealed it in my **vaults**?
Jos 6:19 and iron are sacred to the LORD and must go into his **treasury**."
6:24 of bronze and iron into the **treasury** *of* the LORD's house.
1Ki 7:51 and he placed them in the **treasuries** *of* the LORD's temple.
14:26 He carried off the **treasures** *of* the temple of the LORD and the
14:26 of the temple of the LORD and the **treasures** *of* the royal palace.
15:18 and gold that was left in the **treasuries** *of* the LORD's temple
15:18 treasuries of the LORD's temple and **[RPH]** of his own palace.
2Ki 12:18 [12:19] all the gold found in the **treasuries** *of* the temple of the
14:14 the temple of the LORD and in the **treasuries** *of* the royal palace.
16:8 in the **treasuries** *of* the royal palace and sent it as a gift to the king
18:15 the temple of the LORD and in the **treasuries** *of* the royal palace.
20:13 fine oil—his armory and everything found among his **treasures**.
20:15 "There is nothing among my **treasures** that I did not show them."
24:13 Nebuchadnezzar removed all the **treasures** *from* the temple of the
24:13 from the temple of the LORD and **[RPH]** from the royal palace,
1Ch 9:26 responsibility for the rooms and **treasuries** *in* the house of God.
26:20 Their fellow Levites were in charge of the **treasuries** *of* the house
26:20 of the house of God and the **treasuries** *for* the dedicated things.
26:22 They were in charge of the **treasuries** *of* the temple of the LORD.
26:24 Gershom son of Moses, was the officer in charge of the **treasuries**.
26:26 his relatives were in charge of all the **treasuries** *for* the things
27:25 Azmaveth son of Adiel was in charge of the royal **storehouses**.
27:25 Jonathan son of Uzziah was in charge of the **storehouses** in the
27:27 was in charge of the produce of the vineyards for the wine **vats**.
27:28 western foothills. Joash was in charge of the **supplies** *of* olive oil.
28:12 for the **treasuries** *of* the temple of God and for the treasuries for
28:12 the temple of God and for the **treasuries** *for* the dedicated things.
29:8 Any who had precious stones gave them to the **treasury** *of* the
2Ch 5:1 and he placed them in the **treasuries** *of* God's temple.
8:15 or to the Levites in any matter, including that of the **treasuries**.
11:11 put commanders in them, with **supplies** *of* food, olive oil and wine.
12:9 he carried off the **treasures** *of* the temple of the LORD and the
12:9 of the temple of the LORD and the **treasures** *of* the royal palace.
16:2 the silver and gold out of the **treasuries** *of* the LORD's temple
25:24 together with the palace **treasures** and the hostages, and returned
32:27 he made **treasuries** for his silver and gold and for his precious
36:18 the **treasures** *of* the LORD's temple and the treasures of the king
36:18 LORD's temple and the **treasures** *of* the king and his officials.
Ezr 2:69 According to their ability they gave to the **treasury** *for* this work
Ne 7:70 [7:69] The governor gave to the **treasury** 1,000 drachmas of gold,
7:71 [7:70] Some of the heads of the families gave to the **treasury** *for*
10:38 [10:39] of our God, to the storerooms of the **treasury** [+1074].
12:44 in charge of the **storerooms** [+4200+5969] for the contributions,
13:12 brought the tithes of grain, new wine and oil into the **storerooms**.
13:13 *I* **put** Shelemiah the priest, Zadok the scribe, and a Levite named Pedaiah **in charge of the storerooms** [+732+6584] and made
Job 38:22 "Have you entered the **storehouses** *of* the snow or seen the
38:22 the storehouses of the snow or seen the **storehouses** *of* the hail,
Ps 33:7 the waters of the sea into jars; he puts the deep into **storehouses**.
135:7 with the rain and brings out the wind from his **storehouses**.
Pr 8:21 wealth on those who love me and making their **treasuries** full.
10:2 Ill-gotten **treasures** are of no value, but righteousness delivers
15:16 Better a little with the fear of the LORD than great **wealth** with
21:6 A **fortune** made by a lying tongue is a fleeting vapor and a deadly
21:20 In the house of the wise are **stores** *of* choice food and oil,
Isa 2:7 land is full of silver and gold; there is no end to their **treasures**.
30:6 their **treasures** on the humps of camels, to that unprofitable nation,
33:6 and knowledge; the fear of the LORD is the key to this **treasure**.
39:2 his entire armory and everything found among his **treasures**.
39:4 "There is nothing among my **treasures** that I did not show them."
45:3 I will give you the **treasures** *of* darkness, riches stored in secret
Jer 10:13 with the rain and brings out the wind from his **storehouses**.
15:13 Your wealth and your **treasures** I will give as plunder, without
17:3 and your wealth and all your **treasures** I will give away as plunder,
20:5 all its valuables and all the **treasures** *of* the kings of Judah.
38:11 men with him and went to a room under the **treasury** in the palace.
48:7 Since you trust in your deeds and **riches**, you too will be taken
49:4 you trust in your **riches** and say, 'Who will attack me?'
50:25 The LORD has opened his **arsenal** and brought out the weapons
50:37 A sword against her **treasures**! They will be plundered.
51:13 You who live by many waters and are rich in **treasures**, your end
51:16 with the rain and brings out the wind from his **storehouses**.
Eze 28:4 wealth for yourself and amassed gold and silver in your **treasuries**.
Da 1:2 of his god in Babylonia and put in the **treasure** house of his god.
Hos 13:15 well dry up. His **storehouse** will be plundered of all its treasures.
Joel 1:17 The **storehouses** are in ruins, the granaries have been broken
Mic 6:10 O wicked house, your ill-gotten **treasures** and the short ephah,
Mal 3:10 Bring the whole tithe into the **storehouse** [+1074], that there may

239 אוֹר[1] *'ôr*[1], v. [43] [→ 240, 241, 244, 245, 246, 247, 251?, 797, 4401, 4402?; *also used with compound proper names*]

give light [6], make shine [6], shine [6], light [4], brightened [2], gives light [2], brightens [1], dawned [1], daybreak [1], give light [+240] [1], gives sight [1], giving light [1], keep burning [1], leaves glistening [1], light fires [1], lights up [1], lit up [1], look with favor [+7156] [1], made light shine [1], make fires [1], radiant [1], resplendent with light [1], shining ever brighter [+2143+2256] [1]

Ge 1:15 [G] let them be lights in the expanse of the sky to **give light** on
1:17 [G] God set them in the expanse of the sky to **give light** on the
44:3 [A] *As* morning **dawned**, the men were sent on their way with
Ex 13:21 [G] their way and by night in a pillar of fire to **give** them **light**,
14:20 [G] brought darkness to the one side and **light** *to* the other side;
25:37 [G] set them up on it so that *they* **light** the space in front of it.
Nu 6:25 [G] the LORD **make** his face **shine** upon you and be gracious to
8:2 [G] *they are to* **light** the area in front of the lampstand.' "
1Sa 14:27 [A] his hand to his mouth, and his eyes **brightened**. [K 8011]
14:29 [A] See how my eyes **brightened** when I tasted a little of this
29:10 [A] with you, and leave in the morning as soon as *it is* **light**."
2Sa 2:32 [A] men marched all night and arrived at Hebron *by* **daybreak**.
Ezr 9:8 [G] so our God **gives light** *to* our eyes and a little relief in our
Ne 9:12 [G] by night with a pillar of fire to **give** them **light** *on* the way
9:19 [G] nor the pillar of fire by night to **shine** on the way they were
Job 33:30 [C] his soul from the pit, that the light of life *may* **shine** *on* him.
41:32 [41:24] [G] Behind him *he* **leaves** a **glistening** wake; one would
Ps 13:3 [13:4] [G] **Give light** *to* my eyes, or I will sleep in death;
18:28 [18:29] [G] You, O LORD, **keep** my lamp **burning**; my God
19:8 [19:9] [G] of the LORD are radiant, **giving light** *to* the eyes.
31:16 [31:17] [G] *Let* your face **shine** on your servant; save me in
67:1 [67:2] [G] to us and bless us and **make** his face **shine** upon us,
76:4 [76:5] [C] You *are* **resplendent with light**, more majestic than
77:18 [77:19] [G] in the whirlwind, your lightning **lit up** the world;
80:3 [80:4] [G] **make** your face **shine** upon us, that we may be saved.
80:7 [80:8] [G] **make** your face **shine** upon us, that we may be saved.
80:19 [80:20] [G] **make** your face **shine** upon us, that we may be
97:4 [G] His lightning **lights up** the world; the earth sees

Ps 105: 39 [G] out a cloud as a covering, and a fire to **give light** at night.
118: 27 [G] LORD is God, and *he has* **made** *his* **light shine** upon us.
119: 130 [G] The unfolding of your words **gives light**; it gives
119: 135 [G] **Make** your face **shine** upon your servant and teach me your
139: 12 [G] the night *will* **shine** like the day, for darkness is as light to
Pr 4: 18 [A] first gleam of dawn, **shining** [+2143+2256] **ever brighter**
29: 13 [G] this in common: The LORD **gives sight** *to* the eyes of both.
Ecc 8: 1 [G] Wisdom **brightens** a man's face and changes its hard
Isa 27: 11 [G] are broken off and women come and **make fires** *with* them.
60: 1 [A] "Arise, **shine**, for your light has come, and the glory of the
60: 19 [G] by day, nor *will* the brightness of the moon **shine** on you,
Eze 32: 7 [G] sun with a cloud, and the moon *will* not **give** its **light** [+240].
43: 2 [G] of rushing waters, and the land *was* **radiant** with his glory.
Da 9: 17 [G] O Lord, **look with favor** [+7156] on your desolate sanctuary.
Mal 1: 10 [G] so that *you would* not **light** useless **fires** *on* my altar!

240 [2]אוֹר *'ôr[2]*, n.m. [121 / 122] [→ 245, 246; cf. 239]

light [84], lightning [7], daybreak [+1332+2021] [3], daylight [3], dawn [+1332+2021] [2], shine [2], shining [2], sun [2], *untranslated* [1], brightens [1], broad daylight [+3427] [1], dawn [1], daybreak [1], daylight [+1332+2021] [1], give light [+239] [1], gleam [1], glint [1], lamp [1], light of day [1], lights [1], new day [1], shine [+2118] [1], sunlight [+2780] [1], sunrise [1], sunshine [1]

Ge 1: 3 And God said, "Let there be **light**," and there was light.
1: 3 And God said, "Let there be light," and there was **light**.
1: 4 God saw that the **light** was good, and he separated the light from
1: 4 the light was good, and he separated the **light** from the darkness.
1: 5 God called the **light** "day," and the darkness he called "night."
1: 18 govern the day and the night, and to separate **light** from darkness.
Ex 10: 23 Yet all the Israelites had **light** in the places where they lived.
Jdg 16: 2 during the night, saying, "At **dawn** [+1332+2021] we'll kill him."
19: 26 was staying, fell down at the door and lay there until **daylight**.
1Sa 14: 36 the Philistines by night and plunder them till **dawn** [+1332+2021],
25: 34 to Nabal would have been left alive by **daybreak** [+1332+2021]."
25: 36 So she told him nothing until **daybreak** [+1332+2021].
2Sa 17: 22 By **daybreak** [+1332+2021], no one was left who had not crossed
23: 4 he is like the **light** *of* morning at sunrise on a cloudless morning,
2Ki 7: 9 If we wait until **daylight** [+1332+2021], punishment will overtake
Ne 8: 3 He read it aloud from **daybreak** till noon as he faced the square
Job 3: 9 may it wait for **daylight** in vain and not see the first rays of dawn,
3: 16 a stillborn child, like an infant who never saw the **light of day**?
3: 20 "Why is **light** given to those in misery, and life to the bitter of soul,
12: 22 the deep things of darkness and brings deep shadows into the **light**.
12: 25 They grope in darkness with no **light**; he makes them stagger like
17: 12 turn night into day; in the face of darkness they say, '**Light** is near.'
18: 5 "The **lamp** *of* the wicked is snuffed out; the flame of his fire stops
18: 6 The **light** in his tent becomes dark; the lamp beside him goes out.
18: 18 He is driven from **light** into darkness and is banished from the
22: 28 you decide on will be done, and **light** will shine on your ways.
24: 13 "There are those who rebel against the **light**, who do not know its
24: 14 When **daylight** is gone, the murderer rises up and kills the poor
24: 16 day they shut themselves in; they want nothing to do with the **light**.
25: 3 Can his forces be numbered? Upon whom does his **light** not rise?
26: 10 the horizon on the face of the waters for a boundary between **light**
28: 11 searches the sources of the rivers and brings hidden things to **light**.
29: 3 shone upon my head and by his **light** I walked through darkness!
29: 24 scarcely believed it; the **light** *of* my face was precious to them.
30: 26 for good, evil came; when I looked for **light**, then came darkness.
31: 26 if I have regarded the **sun** in its radiance or the moon moving in
33: 28 soul from going down to the pit, and I will live to enjoy the **light**.'
33: 30 back his soul from the pit, that the **light** *of* life may shine on him.
36: 30 See how he scatters his **lightning** about him, bathing the depths of
36: 32 He fills his hands with **lightning** and commands it to strike its
37: 3 He unleashes his **lightning** beneath the whole heaven and sends it
37: 11 the clouds with moisture; he scatters his **lightning** through them.
37: 15 know how God controls the clouds and makes his **lightning** flash?
37: 21 Now no one can look at the **sun**, bright as it is in the skies after the
38: 15 The wicked are denied their **light**, and their upraised arm is broken.
38: 19 "What is the way to the abode of **light**? And where does darkness
38: 24 What is the way to the place where the **lightning** is dispersed,
41: 18 [41:10] His snorting throws out flashes of **light**; his eyes are like
Ps 4: 6 [4:7] Let the **light** *of* your face shine upon us, O LORD.
27: 1 The LORD is my **light** and my salvation—whom shall I fear?
36: 9 [36:10] with you is the fountain of life; in your **light** we see light.
36: 9 [36:10] with you is the fountain of life; in your light we see **light**.
37: 6 He will make your righteousness shine like the **dawn**, the justice of
38: 10 [38:11] strength fails me; even the **light** has gone from my eyes.
43: 3 Send forth your **light** and your truth, let them guide me; let them
44: 3 [44:4] your arm, and the **light** *of* your face, for you loved them.
49: 19 [49:20] of his fathers, who will never see the **light** ⌞of life⌟.
56: 13 [56:14] that I may walk before God in the **light** *of* life.
78: 14 them with the cloud by day and with **light** *from* the fire all night.
89: 15 [89:16] who walk in the **light** *of* your presence, O LORD.
97: 11 **Light** is shed upon the righteous and joy on the upright in heart.
104: 2 He wraps himself in **light** as with a garment; he stretches out the
112: 4 Even in darkness **light** dawns for the upright, for the gracious
119: 105 Your word is a lamp to my feet and a **light** for my path.
136: 7 who made the great **lights**—*His love endures forever.*
139: 11 the darkness will hide me and the **light** become night around me,"
148: 3 Praise him, sun and moon, praise him, all you **shining** stars.
Pr 4: 18 The path of the righteous is like the *first* **gleam** *of* dawn, shining
6: 23 For these commands are a lamp, this teaching is a **light**,
13: 9 The **light** *of* the righteous shines brightly, but the lamp of the
16: 15 When a king's face **brightens**, it means life; his favor is like a rain
Ecc 2: 13 wisdom is better than folly, just as **light** is better than darkness.
11: 7 **Light** is sweet, and it pleases the eyes to see the sun.
12: 2 before the sun and the **light** and the moon and the stars grow dark,
Isa 2: 5 Come, O house of Jacob, let us walk in the **light** *of* the LORD.
5: 20 and good evil, who put darkness for **light** and light for darkness,
5: 20 and good evil, who put darkness for light and **light** for darkness,
5: 30 and distress; even the **light** will be darkened by the clouds.
9: 2 [9:1] The people walking in darkness have seen a great **light**;
9: 2 [9:1] on those living in the land of the shadow of death a **light** has
10: 17 The **Light** *of* Israel will become a fire, their Holy One a flame;
13: 10 stars of heaven and their constellations will not show their **light**.
13: 10 rising sun will be darkened and the moon will not give its **light**.
18: 4 on from my dwelling place, like shimmering heat in the **sunshine**,
30: 26 The moon *will* **shine** [+2118] like the sun, and the sunlight will be
30: 26 The moon will shine like **[RPH]** the sun, and the sunlight will be
30: 26 the **sunlight** [+2780] will be seven times brighter, like the light of
30: 26 will be seven times brighter, like the **light** *of* seven full days,
42: 6 you to be a covenant for the people and a **light** *for* the Gentiles,
42: 16 I will turn the darkness into **light** before them and make the rough
45: 7 I form the **light** and create darkness, I bring prosperity and create
49: 6 I will also make you a **light** *for* the Gentiles, that you may bring
51: 4 will go out from me; my justice will become a **light** *to* the nations.
53: 11 of his soul, he will see the **light** [BHS-] ⌞of life⌟ and be satisfied;
58: 8 your **light** will break forth like the dawn, and your healing will
58: 10 needs of the oppressed, then your **light** will rise in the darkness,
59: 9 We look for **light**, but all is darkness; for brightness, but we walk
60: 1 "Arise, shine, for your **light** has come, and the glory of the LORD
60: 3 Nations will come to your **light**, and kings to the brightness of your
60: 19 The sun will no more be your **light** by day, nor will the brightness
60: 19 for the LORD will be your everlasting **light**, and your God will be
60: 20 the LORD will be your everlasting **light**, and your days of sorrow
Jer 4: 23 and empty; and at the heavens, and their **light** was gone.
13: 16 You hope for **light**, but he will turn it to thick darkness and change
25: 10 and bridegroom, the sound of millstones and the **light** *of* the lamp.
31: 35 he who appoints the sun to **shine** by day, who decrees the moon
31: 35 who decrees the moon and stars to **shine** by night, who stirs up the
La 3: 2 driven me away and made me walk in darkness rather than **light**;
Eze 32: 7 the sun with a cloud, and the moon *will* not **give** its **light** [+239].
32: 8 All the **shining** lights in the heavens I will darken over you;
Hos 6: 5 of my mouth; my judgments flashed like **lightning** upon you.
Am 5: 18 for the day of the LORD? That day will be darkness, not **light**.
5: 20 Will not the day of the LORD be darkness, not **light**—pitch-dark,
8: 9 go down at noon and darken the earth in **broad daylight** [+3427].
Mic 2: 1 At morning's **light** they carry it out because it is in their power to
7: 8 I will rise. Though I sit in darkness, the LORD will be my **light**.
7: 9 He will bring me out into the **light**; I will see his righteousness.
Hab 3: 4 His splendor was like the **sunrise**; rays flashed from his hand,
3: 11 moon stood still in the heavens at the **glint** *of* your flying arrows,
Zep 3: 5 every **new day** he does not fail, yet the unrighteous know no
Zec 14: 6 On that day there will be no **light**, no cold or frost.
14: 7 known to the LORD. When evening comes, there will be **light**.

241 [1]אוּר *'ûr[1]*, n.m. [6] [→ 797; cf. 239]

fire [4], east [1], light [1]

Isa 24: 15 Therefore in the **east** give glory to the LORD; exalt the name of
31: 9 declares the LORD, whose **fire** is in Zion, whose furnace is in
44: 16 He also warms himself and says, "Ah! I am warm; I see the **fire**."
47: 14 Here are no coals to warm anyone; here is no **fire** to sit by.
50: 11 walk in the **light** *of* your fires and of the torches you have set
Eze 5: 2 come to an end, burn a third of the hair with **fire** inside the city.

242 [2]אוּר *'ûr[2]*, n.m. [7] [cf. 239?]

Urim [7]

Ex 28: 30 Also put the **Urim** and the Thummim in the breastpiece, so they
Lev 8: 8 He placed the breastpiece on him and put the **Urim** and Thummim
Nu 27: 21 who will obtain decisions for him by inquiring of the **Urim** before
Dt 33: 8 "Your Thummim and **Urim** belong to the man you favored.
1Sa 28: 6 the LORD did not answer him by dreams or **Urim** or prophets.
Ezr 2: 63 most sacred food until there was a priest ministering with the **Urim**
Ne 7: 65 food until there should be a priest ministering with the **Urim**

243 ³אוּר **'ûr[3]**, n.pr.loc. [4]

Ur [4]

Ge 11:28 Haran died in **Ur** *of* the Chaldeans, in the land of his birth.
11:31 together they set out from **Ur** *of* the Chaldeans to go to Canaan.
15: 7 who brought you out of **Ur** *of* the Chaldeans to give you this land
Ne 9: 7 who chose Abram and brought him out of **Ur** *of* the Chaldeans

244 ⁴אוּר **'ûr[4]**, n.pr.m. [1] [√ 239]

Ur [1]

1Ch 11:35 Ahiam son of Sacar the Hararite, Eliphal son of **Ur**,

245 ¹אוֹרָה **'ôrâ[1]**, n.f. [3] [√ 240; cf. 239]

light [1], morning [1], time of happiness [1]

Est 8:16 For the Jews it was a **time of happiness** and joy, gladness
Ps 139:12 the night will shine like the day, for darkness is as **light** to you.
Isa 26:19 Your dew is like the dew of the **morning**; the earth will give birth

246 ²אוֹרָה **'ôrâ[2]**, n.f. [1] [√ 240; cf. 239]

herbs [1]

2Ki 4:39 One of them went out into the fields to gather **herbs** and found a

247 אוּרִי **'ûrî**, n.pr.m. [7] [√ 239]

Uri [7]

Ex 31: 2 "See, I have chosen Bezalel son of **Uri**, the son of Hur, of the tribe
35:30 "See, the LORD has chosen Bezalel son of **Uri**, the son of Hur,
38:22 (Bezalel son of **Uri**, the son of Hur, of the tribe of Judah,
1Ch 2:20 Hur was the father of **Uri**, and Uri the father of Bezalel.
2:20 Hur was the father of Uri, and **Uri** the father of Bezalel.
2Ch 1: 5 But the bronze altar that Bezalel son of **Uri**, the son of Hur,
Ezr 10:24 Eliashib. From the gatekeepers: Shallum, Telem and **Uri**.

248 אוּרִיאֵל **'ûrî'ēl**, n.pr.m. [4] [√ 239 + 446]

Uriel [4]

1Ch 6:24 [6:9] his son, **Uriel** his son, Uzziah his son and Shaul his son.
15: 5 the descendants of Kohath, **Uriel** the leader and 120 relatives;
15:11 **Uriel**, Asaiah, Joel, Shemaiah, Eliel and Amminadab the Levites.
2Ch 13: 2 His mother's name was Maacah, a daughter of **Uriel** of Gibeah.

249 אוּרִיָּה **'ûriyyâ**, n.pr.m. [36] [→ 250; cf. 239 + 3378]

Uriah [29], him[s] [3], *untranslated* [2], Uriah's [2]

2Sa 11: 3 the daughter of Eliam and the wife of **Uriah** the Hittite?"
11: 6 "Send me **Uriah** the Hittite." And Joab sent him to David.
11: 6 "Send me Uriah the Hittite." And Joab sent **him**[s] to David.
11: 7 When **Uriah** came to him, David asked him how Joab was,
11: 8 David said to **Uriah**, "Go down to your house and wash your feet."
11: 8 So **Uriah** left the palace, and a gift from the king was sent after
11: 9 **Uriah** slept at the entrance to the palace with all his master's
11:10 When David was told, "**Uriah** did not go home," he asked him,
11:10 When David was told, "Uriah did not go home," he asked **him**[s],
11:11 **Uriah** said to David, "The ark and Israel and Judah are staying in
11:12 David said to **him**[s], "Stay here one more day, and tomorrow I will
11:12 you back." So **Uriah** remained in Jerusalem that day and the next.
11:14 In the morning David wrote a letter to Joab and sent it with **Uriah**.
11:15 he wrote, "Put **Uriah** in the front line where the fighting is fiercest.
11:16 he put **Uriah** at a place where he knew the strongest defenders
11:17 of the men in David's army fell; moreover, **Uriah** the Hittite died.
11:21 then say to him, 'Also, your servant **Uriah** the Hittite is dead.' "
11:24 men died. Moreover, your servant **Uriah** the Hittite is dead."
11:26 When **Uriah's** wife heard that her husband was dead, she mourned
11:26 When Uriah's wife heard that her husband **[RPH]** was dead,
12: 9 You struck down **Uriah** the Hittite with the sword and took his
12:10 despised me and took the wife of **Uriah** the Hittite to be your own.'
12:15 the LORD struck the child that **Uriah's** wife had borne to David,
23:39 and **Uriah** the Hittite. There were thirty-seven in all.
1Ki 15: 5 all the days of his life—except in the case of **Uriah** the Hittite.
2Ki 16:10 altar in Damascus and sent to **Uriah** the priest a sketch of the altar,
16:11 So **Uriah** the priest built an altar in accordance with all the plans
16:11 from Damascus and finished it **[RPH]** before King Ahaz returned.
16:15 King Ahaz then gave these orders to **Uriah** the priest: "On the
16:16 And **Uriah** the priest did just as King Ahaz had ordered.
1Ch 11:41 **Uriah** the Hittite, Zabad son of Ahlai,
Ezr 8:33 and the sacred articles into the hands of Meremoth son of **Uriah**,
Ne 3: 4 Meremoth son of **Uriah**, the son of Hakkoz, repaired the next
3:21 Next to him, Meremoth son of **Uriah**, the son of Hakkoz,
8: 4 stood Mattithiah, Shema, Anaiah, **Uriah**, Hilkiah and Maaseiah;
Isa 8: 2 I will call in **Uriah** the priest and Zechariah son of Jeberekiah as

250 אוּרִיָּהוּ **'ûriyyāhû**, n.pr.m. [3] [√ 249; cf. 239 + 3378]

Uriah [3]

Jer 26:20 (Now **Uriah** son of Shemaiah from Kiriath Jearim was another
26:21 to put him to death. But **Uriah** heard of it and fled in fear to Egypt.
26:23 They brought **Uriah** out of Egypt and took him to King Jehoiakim,

251 אוּרִים **'ûrîm**, n.m.[pl.]. Not used in NIV/BHS [√ 239? *or* 768? *or* 826?]

252 אוּת **'ût**, v. [4]

give consent [2], agreed [1], consent [1]

Ge 34:15 [C] *We will* **give** *our* **consent** to you on one condition only:
34:22 [C] the men *will* **consent** to live with us as one people only on
34:23 [C] So *let us* **give** *our* **consent** to them, and they will settle
2Ki 12: 8 [12:9] [C] The priests **agreed** that they would not collect any

253 ¹אוֹת **'ôt[1]**, n.m. & f. [79] [√ 204?; Ar 10084]

sign [36], miraculous signs [17], signs [14], miraculous sign [3], symbols [2], *untranslated* [1], accounts [1], banners [1], example [1], mark [1], standards [1], wonders [1]

Ge 1:14 and let them serve as **signs** to mark seasons and days and years,
4:15 the LORD put a **mark** on Cain so that no one who found him
9:12 "This is the **sign** *of* the covenant I am making between me
9:13 and it will be the **sign** *of* the covenant between me and the earth.
9:17 "This is the **sign** *of* the covenant I have established between me
17:11 and it will be the **sign** *of* the covenant between me and you.
Ex 3:12 And this will be the **sign** to you that it is I who have sent you:
4: 8 do not believe you or pay attention to the first **miraculous sign**,
4: 8 to the first miraculous sign, they may believe the second. **[RPH]**
4: 9 But if they do not believe these two **signs** or listen to you,
4:17 staff in your hand so you can perform **miraculous signs** with it."
4:28 also about all the **miraculous signs** he had commanded him to
4:30 had said to Moses. He also performed the **signs** before the people,
7: 3 and though I multiply my **miraculous signs** and wonders in Egypt,
8:23 [8:19] your people. This **miraculous sign** will occur tomorrow.' "
10: 1 so that I may perform these **miraculous signs** *of* mine among
10: 2 with the Egyptians and how I performed my **signs** among them,
12:13 The blood will be a **sign** for you on the houses where you are;
13: 9 This observance will be for you like a **sign** on your hand and a
13:16 it will be like a **sign** on your hand and a symbol on your forehead
31:13 This will be a **sign** between me and you for the generations to
31:17 It will be a **sign** between me and the Israelites forever, for in six
Nu 2: 2 each man under his standard with the **banners** of his family."
14:11 in spite of all the **miraculous signs** I have performed among them?
14:22 and the **miraculous signs** I performed in Egypt and in the desert
16:38 [17:3] have become holy. Let them be a **sign** to the Israelites."
17:10 [17:25] of the Testimony, to be kept as a **sign** to the rebellious.
Dt 4:34 by testings, by **miraculous signs** and wonders, by war, by a
6: 8 Tie them as **symbols** on your hands and bind them on your
6:22 Before our eyes the LORD sent **miraculous signs** and wonders—
7:19 the **miraculous signs** and wonders, the mighty hand
11: 3 the **signs** he performed and the things he did in the heart of Egypt,
11:18 tie them as **symbols** on your hands and bind them on your
13: 1 [13:2] and announces to you a **miraculous sign** or wonder,
13: 2 [13:3] if the **sign** or wonder of which he has spoken takes place,
26: 8 with great terror and with **miraculous signs** and wonders.
28:46 They will be a **sign** and a wonder to you and your descendants
29: 3 [29:2] great trials, those **miraculous signs** and great wonders.
34:11 who did all those **miraculous signs** and wonders the LORD sent
Jos 2:12 because I have shown kindness to you. Give me a sure **sign**
4: 6 to serve as a **sign** among you. In the future, when your children ask
24:17 land of slavery, and performed those great **signs** before our eyes.
Jdg 6:17 in your eyes, give me a **sign** that it is really you talking to me.
1Sa 2:34 to your two sons, Hophni and Phinehas, will be a **sign** to you—
10: 7 Once these **signs** are fulfilled, do whatever your hand finds to do,
10: 9 changed Saul's heart, and all these **signs** were fulfilled that day.
14:10 because that will be our **sign** that the LORD has given them into
2Ki 19:29 "This will be the **sign** for you, O Hezekiah: "This year you will eat
20: 8 "What will be the **sign** that the LORD will heal me and that I will
20: 9 "This is the LORD's **sign** to you that the LORD will do what he
Ne 9:10 You sent **miraculous signs** and wonders against Pharaoh,
Job 21:29 those who travel? Have you paid no regard to their **accounts**—
Ps 65: 8 [65:9] Those living far away fear your **wonders**; where morning
74: 4 place where you met with us; they set up their **standards** as signs.
74: 4 place where you met with us; they set up their standards as **signs**.
74: 9 We are given no **miraculous signs**; no prophets are left, and none
78:43 the day he displayed his **miraculous signs** in Egypt, his wonders in
86:17 Give me a **sign** of your goodness, that my enemies may see it
105:27 They performed his **miraculous signs** among them, his wonders in
135: 9 He sent his **signs** and wonders into your midst, O Egypt,
Isa 7:11 "Ask the LORD your God for a **sign**, whether in the deepest

Isa 7:14 Therefore the Lord himself will give you a **sign**: The virgin will be
8:18 We are **signs** and symbols in Israel from the LORD Almighty,
19:20 It will be a **sign** and witness to the LORD Almighty in the land of
20:3 for three years, as a **sign** and portent against Egypt and Cush,
37:30 "This will be the **sign** for you, O Hezekiah: "This year you will eat
38:7 " 'This is the LORD's **sign** to you that the LORD will do what
38:22 "What will be the **sign** that I will go up to the temple of the
44:25 who foils the **signs** *of* false prophets and makes fools of diviners,
55:13 for an everlasting **sign**, which will not be destroyed."
66:19 "I will set a **sign** among them, and I will send some of those who
Jer 10:2 not learn the ways of the nations or be terrified by **signs** *in* the sky,
32:20 You performed **miraculous signs** and wonders in Egypt and have
32:21 You brought your people Israel out of Egypt with **signs**
44:29 " 'This will be the **sign** to you that I will punish you in this place,'
Eze 4:3 and you shall besiege it. This will be a **sign** to the house of Israel.
14:8 my face against that man and make him an **example** and a byword.
20:12 Also I gave them my Sabbaths as a **sign** between us, so they would
20:20 Keep my Sabbaths holy, that they may be a **sign** between us.

254 אוֹת² *'ôt²*, pt. Not used in NIV/BHS [√ 906]

255 אָז *'āz*, adv. [141] [→ 259, 4403; Ar 10008]

then [65], *untranslated* [29], at that time [11], and [5], long ago [+4946] [5], ever since [+4946] [2], now [2], since [+4946] [2], so [2], time [2], about this time [1], after [1], already [+4946] [1], already [1], and [+2256] [1], distant past [1], from [+4946] [1], meanwhile [1], now [+4946] [1], of old [1], old [1], once [1], past [1], that will mean [1], thus [1], when [+4946] [1]

Ge 4:26 **At that time** men began to call on the name of the LORD.
12:6 Moreh at Shechem. **At that time** the Canaanites were in the land.
13:7 and Perizzites were also living in the land **at that time**.
24:41 **Then**, when you go to my clan, you will be released from my oath
39:5 From *the* **time** he put him in charge of his household and of all that
49:4 you went up onto your father's bed, onto my couch **and** defiled it.
Ex 4:10 neither in the past nor **since** [+4946] you have spoken to your
4:26 (**At that time** she said "bridegroom of blood," referring to
5:23 **Ever since** [+4946] I went to Pharaoh to speak in your name,
9:24 It was the worst storm in all the land of Egypt **since** [+4946] it had
12:44 Any slave you have bought may eat of it **after** you have
12:48 **then** he may take part like one born in the land.
15:1 **Then** Moses and the Israelites sang this song to the LORD:
15:15 **[NIE]** The chiefs of Edom will be terrified, the leaders of Moab
Lev 26:34 **Then** the land will enjoy its sabbath years all the time that it lies
26:34 of your enemies; **then** the land will rest and enjoy its sabbaths.
26:41 **then** when their uncircumcised hearts are humbled and they pay
26:41 when their uncircumcised hearts are humbled **and** [+2256] they
Nu 21:17 **Then** Israel sang this song: "Spring up, O well! Sing about it,
Dt 4:41 **Then** Moses set aside three cities east of the Jordan,
29:20 [29:19] **[NIE]** his wrath and zeal will burn against that man.
Jos 1:8 written in it. **Then** you will be prosperous and successful.
1:8 written in it. Then you will be prosperous and **[RPH]** successful.
8:30 **Then** Joshua built on Mount Ebal an altar to the LORD, the God
10:12 **[NIE]** On the day the LORD gave the Amorites over to Israel,
10:33 **Meanwhile**, Horam king of Gezer had come up to help Lachish,
14:10 he has kept me alive for forty-five years since the **time** he said this
14:11 I'm just as vigorous to go out to battle now as I was **then**.
20:6 **Then** he may go back to his own home in the town from which he
22:1 **Then** Joshua summoned the Reubenites, the Gadites and the
22:31 **Now** you have rescued the Israelites from the LORD's hand."
Jdg 5:8 **[NIE]** war came to the city gates, and not a shield or spear was
5:11 "**Then** the people of the LORD went down to the city gates.
5:13 "**Then** the men who were left came down to the nobles; the people
5:19 **[NIE]** the kings of Canaan fought at Taanach by the waters of
5:22 **Then** thundered the horses' hoofs—galloping, galloping go his
8:3 to you?" **[NIE]** At this, their resentment against him subsided.
13:21 **[NIE]** Manoah realized that it was the angel of the LORD.
Ru 2:7 the field and has worked steadily **from** [+4946] morning till now,
1Sa 6:3 **Then** you will be healed, and you will know why his hand has not
20:12 toward you, **[NIE]** will I not send you word and let you know?
2Sa 2:27 **[NIE]** the men would have continued the pursuit of their brothers
5:24 of marching in the tops of the balsam trees, **[NIE]** move quickly,
5:24 because **that will mean** the LORD has gone out in front of you to
15:34 I was your father's servant in the **past**, but now I will be your
19:6 [19:7] Absalom were alive today and all of us were dead. **[NIE]**
21:17 **Then** David's men swore to him, saying, "Never again will you go
21:18 **At that time** Sibbecai the Hushathite killed Saph, one of the
23:14 **At that time** David was in the stronghold, and the Philistine
23:14 and the Philistine garrison was **[RPH]** at Bethlehem.
1Ki 3:16 **Now** two prostitutes came to the king and stood before him.
8:1 **Then** King Solomon summoned into his presence at Jerusalem the
8:12 **Then** Solomon said, "The LORD has said that he would dwell in
9:11 **[NIE]** King Solomon gave twenty towns in Galilee to Hiram king
9:24 had built for her, **[NIE]** he constructed the supporting terraces.
11:7 **[NIE]** On a hill east of Jerusalem, Solomon built a high place for
16:21 **Then** the people of Israel were split into two factions;
22:49 [22:50] **At that time** Ahaziah son of Ahab said to Jehoshaphat,
2Ki 5:3 who is in Samaria! **[NIE]** He would cure him of his leprosy."
8:22 rebellion against Judah. **[NIE]** Libnah revolted at the same time.
12:17 [12:18] **About this time** Hazael king of Aram went up
13:19 **then** you would have defeated Aram and completely destroyed it.
14:8 **Then** Amaziah sent messengers to Jehoash son of Jehoahaz,
15:16 **At that time** Menahem, starting out from Tirzah, attacked Tiphsah
16:5 **Then** Rezin king of Aram and Pekah son of Remaliah king of
1Ch 11:16 **At that time** David was in the stronghold, and the Philistine
11:16 and the Philistine garrison was **[RPH]** at Bethlehem.
14:15 in the tops of the balsam trees, **[NIE]** move out to battle,
15:2 **Then** David said, "No one but the Levites may carry the ark of
16:7 That day **[NIE]** David first committed to Asaph and his associates
16:33 **Then** the trees of the forest will sing, they will sing for joy before
20:4 **At that time** Sibbecai the Hushathite killed Sippai, one of the
22:13 **Then** you will have success if you are careful to observe the
2Ch 5:2 **Then** Solomon summoned to Jerusalem the elders of Israel,
6:1 **Then** Solomon said, "The LORD has said that he would dwell in
8:12 **[NIE]** On the altar of the LORD that he had built in front of the
8:17 **Then** Solomon went to Ezion Geber and Elath on the coast of
21:10 **[NIE]** Libnah revolted at the same time, because Jehoram had
24:17 Judah came and paid homage to the king, **and** he listened to them.
Job 3:13 now I would be lying down in peace; I would be asleep **and** at rest
9:31 **[NIE]** you would plunge me into a slime pit so that even my
11:15 **then** you will lift up your face without shame; you will stand firm
13:20 me these two things, O God, and **then** I will not hide from you:
22:26 Surely **then** you will find delight in the Almighty and will lift up
28:27 **then** he looked at wisdom and appraised it; he confirmed it
33:16 **[NIE]** he may speak in their ears and terrify them with warnings,
38:21 Surely you know, for you were **already** born! You have lived
Ps 2:5 **Then** he rebukes them in his anger and terrifies them in his wrath,
19:13 [19:14] **Then** will I be blameless, innocent of great transgression.
40:7 [40:8] **Then** I said, "Here I am, I have come—it is written about
51:19 [51:21] **Then** there will be righteous sacrifices, whole burnt
51:19 [51:21] to delight you; **then** bulls will be offered on your altar.
56:9 [56:10] **Then** my enemies will turn back when I call for help.
69:4 [69:5] **[NIE]** I am forced to restore what I did not steal.
76:7 [76:8] Who can stand before you **when** [+4946] you are angry?
89:19 [89:20] **Once** you spoke in a vision, to your faithful people you
93:2 Your throne was established **long** [+4946] **ago**; you are from all
96:12 in them. **Then** all the trees of the forest will sing for joy;
119:6 **Then** I would not be put to shame when I consider all your
119:92 been my delight, **[NIE]** I would have perished in my affliction.
126:2 **[NIE]** Our mouths were filled with laughter, our tongues with
126:2 **Then** it was said among the nations, "The LORD has done great
Pr 1:28 "**Then** they will call to me but I will not answer; they will look for
2:5 **then** you will understand the fear of the LORD and find the
2:9 **Then** you will understand what is right and just and fair—
3:23 **Then** you will go on your way in safety, and your foot will not
8:22 brought me forth as the first of his works, before his deeds of **old**;
20:14 says the buyer; then off he goes **and** boasts about his purchase.
Ecc 2:15 What **then** do I gain by being wise?" I said in my heart, "This too
SS 8:10 **Thus** I have become in his eyes like one bringing contentment.
Isa 14:8 exult over you and say, "**Now** [+4946] that you have been laid low,
16:13 This is the word the LORD has **already** [+4946] spoken
33:23 **Then** an abundance of spoils will be divided and even the lame
35:5 **Then** will the eyes of the blind be opened and the ears of the deaf
35:6 **Then** will the lame leap like a deer, and the mute tongue shout for
41:1 Let them come forward **and** speak; let us meet together at the place
44:8 be afraid. Did I not proclaim this and foretell it **long** [+4946] **ago**?
45:21 Who foretold this long ago, who declared it from the **distant past**?
48:3 I foretold the former things **long** [+4946] **ago**, my mouth
48:5 Therefore I told you these things **long** [+4946] **ago**; before they
48:7 They are created now, and not **long** [+4946] **ago**; you have not
48:8 heard nor understood; from **of old** your ear has not been open.
58:8 **Then** your light will break forth like the dawn, and your healing
58:9 **Then** you will call, and the LORD will answer; you will cry for
58:14 **then** you will find your joy in the LORD, and I will cause you to
60:5 **Then** you will look and be radiant, your heart will throb and swell
Jer 11:15 When you engage in your wickedness, **then** you rejoice."
11:18 I knew it, for **at that time** he showed me what they were doing.
22:15 He did what was right and just, **so** all went well with him.
22:16 He defended the cause of the poor and needy, and **so** all went well.
22:22 **Then** you will be ashamed and disgraced because of all your
31:13 **Then** maidens will dance and be glad, young men and old as well.
32:2 The army of the king of Babylon was **then** besieging Jerusalem,
44:18 **ever since** [+4946] we stopped burning incense to the Queen of
Eze 32:14 **Then** I will let her waters settle and make her streams flow like oil,
Hos 2:7 [2:9] to my husband as at first, for **then** I was better off than now.'
Mic 3:4 **Then** they will cry out to the LORD, but he will not answer them.
Hab 1:11 **Then** they sweep past like the wind and go on—guilty men,
Zep 3:9 "**Then** will I purify the lips of the peoples, that all of them may call

Zep 3:11 because **[NIE]** I will remove from this city those who rejoice in
Mal 3:16 **Then** those who feared the LORD talked with each other,

256 אֶזְבָּי *'ezbāy*, n.pr.m. [1] [√ 257?]

Ezbai [1]

1Ch 11:37 Hezro the Carmelite, Naarai son of **Ezbai**,

257 אֵזוֹב *'ēzôb*, n.m. [10] [→ 256?]

hyssop [10]

Ex 12:22 Take a bunch of **hyssop**, dip it into the blood in the basin and put
Lev 14: 4 scarlet yarn and **hyssop** be brought for the one to be cleansed.
14: 6 together with the cedar wood, the scarlet yarn and the **hyssop**,
14:49 is to take two birds and some cedar wood, scarlet yarn and **hyssop**.
14:51 take the cedar wood, the **hyssop**, the scarlet yarn and the live bird,
14:52 the live bird, the cedar wood, the **hyssop** and the scarlet yarn.
Nu 19: 6 **hyssop** and scarlet wool and throw them onto the burning heifer.
19:18 Then a man who is ceremonially clean is to take *some* **hyssop**,
1Ki 4:33 [5:13] from the cedar of Lebanon to the **hyssop** that grows out of
Ps 51: 7 [51:9] Cleanse me with **hyssop**, and I will be clean; wash me,

258 אֵזוֹר *'ēzôr*, n.m. [14] [→ 273]

belt [9], belt [+5516] [1], belts [+2513] [1], it[s] [+2021] [1], loincloth [1], sash [1]

2Ki 1: 8 with a garment of hair and with a leather **belt** around his waist."
Job 12:18 the shackles put on by kings and ties a **loincloth** around their waist.
Isa 5:27 not a **belt** is loosened at the waist, not a sandal thong is broken.
11: 5 Righteousness will be his **belt** [+5516] and faithfulness the sash
11: 5 will be his belt and faithfulness the **sash** *around* his waist.
Jer 13: 1 "Go and buy a linen **belt** and put it around your waist, but do not
13: 2 So I bought a **belt**, as the LORD directed, and put it around my
13: 4 "Take the **belt** you bought and are wearing around your waist,
13: 6 "Go now to Perath and get the **belt** I told you to hide there."
13: 7 So I went to Perath and dug up the **belt** and took it from the place
13: 7 hidden it, but now **it**[s] [+2021] was ruined and completely useless.
13:10 after other gods to serve and worship them, will be like this **belt**—
13:11 For as a **belt** is bound around a man's waist, so I bound the whole
Eze 23:15 with **belts** [+2513] around their waists and flowing turbans on their

259 אֲזַי *'ᵃzay*, adv. [3] [√ 255]

untranslated [3]

Ps 124: 3 flared against us, **[NIE]** they would have swallowed us alive;
124: 4 **[NIE]** the flood would have engulfed us, the torrent would have
124: 5 **[NIE]** the raging waters would have swept us away.

260 אַזְכָּרָה *'azkārâ*, n.f. [7] [√ 2349]

memorial portion [6], memorial offering [1]

Lev 2: 2 burn this as a **memorial portion** on the altar, an offering made by
2: 9 He shall take out the **memorial portion** from the grain offering
2:16 The priest shall burn the **memorial portion** of the crushed grain
5:12 who shall take a handful of it as a **memorial portion** and burn it
6:15 [6:8] burn the **memorial portion** on the altar as an aroma
24: 7 Along each row put some pure incense as a **memorial portion** to
Nu 5:26 then to take a handful of the grain offering as a **memorial offering**

261 אָזַל *'āzal*, v. [5] [→ Ar 10016]

gone [2], disappears [1], go about [1], off goes [1]

Dt 32:36 [A] on his servants when he sees their strength *is* **gone**
1Sa 9: 7 [A] what can we give the man? The food in our sacks *is* **gone**.
Job 14:11 [A] As water **disappears** from the sea or a riverbed becomes
Pr 20:14 [A] the buyer; then **off** *he* **goes** and boasts about his purchase.
Jer 2:36 [A] Why *do you* **go about** so much, changing your ways?

262 אֶזֶל *'ezel*, n.pr.loc. [1]

Ezel [1]

1Sa 20:19 where you hid when this trouble began, and wait by the stone **Ezel**.

263 אָזַן *'āzan[1]*, v.den. [41] [√ 265]

listen [19], hear [11], pay attention [3], give ear [2], ear perceived [1], give a hearing [+7754] [1], listened [1], paid attention [1], pays attention [1], turned a deaf ear [+4202] [1]

Ge 4:23 [G] and Zillah, listen to me; wives of Lamech, **hear** my words.
Ex 15:26 [G] if *you* **pay attention** to his commands and keep all his
Nu 23:18 [G] his oracle: "Arise, Balak, and listen; **hear** me, son of Zippor.
Dt 1:45 [G] to your weeping and **turned a deaf ear** [+4202] to you.
32: 1 [G] **Listen**, O heavens, and I will speak; hear, O earth, the words
Jdg 5: 3 [G] "Hear this, you kings! **Listen**, *you* rulers! I will sing to the
2Ch 24:19 [G] though they testified against them, *they would* not **listen**.
Ne 9:30 [G] Yet *they* **paid** no **attention**, so you handed them over to the
Job 9:16 [G] I do not believe *he would* **give** me **a hearing** [+7754].
32:11 [G] I waited while you spoke, *I* **listened** to your reasoning;
33: 1 [G] Job, listen to my words; **pay attention** *to* everything I say.
34: 2 [G] my words, you wise men; **listen** to me, you men of learning.
34:16 [G] "If you have understanding, hear this; **listen** to what I say.
37:14 [G] "**Listen** *to* this, Job; stop and consider God's wonders.
Ps 5: 1 [5:2] [G] **Give ear** *to* my words, O LORD, consider my
17: 1 [G] **Give ear** *to* my prayer—it does not rise from deceitful lips.
39:12 [39:13] [G] "Hear my prayer, O LORD, **listen** *to* my cry for
49: 1 [49:2] [G] all you peoples; **listen**, all who live in this world,
54: 2 [54:4] [G] my prayer, O God; **listen** to the words of my mouth.
55: 1 [55:2] [G] **Listen** *to* my prayer, O God, do not ignore my plea;
77: 1 [77:2] [G] out to God for help; I cried out to God *to* **hear** me.
78: 1 [G] O my people, **hear** my teaching; listen to the words of my
80: 1 [80:2] [G] **Hear** us, O Shepherd of Israel, you who lead Joseph
84: 8 [84:9] [G] God Almighty; **listen** to me, O God of Jacob.
86: 6 [G] **Hear** my prayer, O LORD; listen to my cry for mercy.
135:17 [G] they have ears, but cannot **hear**, nor is there breath in their
140: 6 [140:7] [G] are my God." **Hear**, O LORD, my cry for mercy.
141: 1 [G] come quickly to me. **Hear** my voice when I call to you.
143: 1 [G] O LORD, hear my prayer, **listen** to my cry for mercy;
Pr 17: 4 [G] to evil lips; a liar **pays attention** to a malicious tongue.
Isa 1: 2 [G] Hear, O heavens! **Listen**, O earth! For the LORD has
1:10 [G] **listen** *to* the law of our God, you people of Gomorrah!
8: 9 [G] you nations, and be shattered! **Listen**, all *you* distant lands.
28:23 [G] **Listen** and hear my voice; pay attention and hear what I say.
32: 9 [G] you daughters who feel secure, **hear** what I have to say!
42:23 [G] Which of you *will* **listen** *to* this or pay close attention in time
51: 4 [G] "Listen to me, my people; **hear** me, my nation: The law will
64: 4 [64:3] [G] times no one has heard, no **ear** *has* **perceived**,
Jer 13:15 [G] Hear and **pay attention**, do not be arrogant, for the LORD
Hos 5: 1 [G] Pay attention, you Israelites! **Listen**, O royal house!
Joel 1: 2 [G] Hear this, you elders; **listen**, all who live in the land. Has

264 אָזַן *'āzan[2]*, v. [1]

pondered [1]

Ecc 12: 9 [D] *He* **pondered** and searched out and set in order many

265 אֹזֶן *'ōzen*, n.f. [187] [→ 263, 269, 270, 271; cf. 266?]

ears [58], ear [25], hearing [24], to [+928] [19], *untranslated* [6], give ear [+5742] [6], pay attention [+906+5742] [6], heard [+928] [3], revealed [+906+1655] [3], before [+928] [2], let know [+906+1655] [2], listen [+5742] [2], tells [+906+1655] [2], they[s] [2], bring to attention [+1655] [1], confiding in [+906+1655] [1], ear lobe [1], hear [+5742] [1], heard [+606+928] [1], heard [1], in person [+928] [1], listen [+7992] [1], listen carefully [+928+9048] [1], listen closely [+5742] [1], listen closely [+928+9048] [1], listen well [+5742] [1], listened [+928] [1], listened attentively to [+448] [1], listens [+9048] [1], make sure hears [+928+8492] [1], makes listen [+1655] [1], news [+2245] [1], paid any attention [+906+4200+5742+9048] [1], paid attention [+906+5742] [1], pay attention [+5742] [1], speaks [+1655] [1], tell [+906+1655] [1], tell [+928+1819] [1], told [+906+928+1819] [1], wearing [+928] [1], whoever[s] [1]

Ge 20: 8 and when *he* **told** [+906+928+1819] them all that had happened,
23:10 he replied to Abraham in the **hearing** of all the Hittites who had
23:13 and he said to Ephron in their **hearing**, "Listen to me, if you will.
23:16 weighed out for him the price he had named in the **hearing** *of* the
35: 4 gave Jacob all the foreign gods they had and the rings in their **ears**,
44:18 my lord, let your servant speak a word **to** [+928] my lord.
50: 4 I have found favor in your eyes, speak **to** [+928] Pharaoh for me.
Ex 10: 2 that you may tell **[OBJ]** your children and grandchildren how I
11: 2 **Tell** [+928+1819] the people that men and women alike are to ask
17:14 be remembered and **make sure** *that* Joshua **hears** [+928+8492] it,
21: 6 take him to the door or the doorpost and pierce his **ear** with an awl.
24: 7 he took the Book of the Covenant and read it **to** [+928] the people.
29:20 and put it on the lobes of the right **ears** *of* Aaron and his sons,
29:20 put it on the lobes of the right ears of Aaron and **[RPH]** his sons,
32: 2 your sons and your daughters are **wearing** [+928], and bring them
32: 3 people took off their earrings **[RPH]** and brought them to Aaron.
Lev 8:23 took some of its blood and put it on the lobe of Aaron's right **ear**,
8:24 and put some of the blood on the lobes of their right **ears**,
14:14 and put it on the lobe of the right **ear** *of* the one to be cleansed,
14:17 in his palm on the lobe of the right **ear** *of* the one to be cleansed,
14:25 and put it on the lobe of the right **ear** *of* the one to be cleansed,
14:28 on the lobe of the right **ear** *of* the one to be cleansed, on the thumb
Nu 11: 1 Now the people complained about their hardships in the **hearing** *of*
11:18 The LORD **heard** you when you wailed, "If only we had meat to
14:28 I will do to you the very things I **heard** [+928] you say:
Dt 5: 1 O Israel, the decrees and laws I declare in your **hearing** today.
15:17 then take an awl and push it through his **ear lobe** into the door,
29: 4 [29:3] a mind that understands or eyes that see or **ears** that hear.
31:11 will choose, you shall read this law before them in their **hearing**.

Dt 31: 28 so that I can speak these words in their **hearing** and call heaven
31: 30 beginning to end in the **hearing** *of* the whole assembly of Israel:
32: 44 and spoke all the words of this song in the **hearing** *of* the people.
Jos 20: 4 the city gate and state his case **before** [+928] the elders of that city.
Jdg 7: 3 announce now **to** [+928] the people, 'Anyone who trembles with
9: 2 "Ask **[OBJ]** all the citizens of Shechem, 'Which is better for you:
9: 3 When the brothers repeated all this **to** [+928] the citizens of
17: 2 from you and about which I **heard** [+606+928] you utter a curse—
Ru 4: 4 I thought *I should* **bring** the matter **to** your **attention** [+1655]
1Sa 3: 11 I am about to do something in Israel that will make the **ears** *of*
8: 21 all that the people said, he repeated it **before** [+928] the LORD.
9: 15 Saul came, the LORD *had* **revealed** this **to** [+906+1655] Samuel:
11: 4 to Gibeah of Saul and reported these terms **to** [+928] the people,
15: 14 But Samuel said, "What then is this bleating of sheep in my **ears**?
18: 23 They repeated these words **to** [+928] David. But David said,
20: 2 do anything, great or small, without **confiding in** [+906+1655] me.
20: 12 will I not send you word and **let** you **know** [+906+1655]?
20: 13 if *I do* not **let** you **know** [+906+1655] and send you away safely.
22: 8 No *one* **tells** [+906+1655] me when my son makes a covenant with
22: 8 or **tells** [+906+1655] me that my son has incited my servant to lie
22: 17 They knew he was fleeing, yet *they did* not **tell** [+906+1655] me."
25: 24 Please let your servant speak **to** [+928] you; hear what your servant
2Sa 3: 19 Abner also spoke to the Benjamites **in person** [+928]. Then he
3: 19 he went to Hebron to tell **[RPH]** David everything that Israel
7: 22 and there is no God but you, as we have heard with our own **ears**.
7: 27 you *have* **revealed** this **to** [+906+1655] your servant, saying,
18: 12 In our **hearing** the king commanded you and Abishai and Ittai,
22: 7 From his temple he heard my voice; my cry came to his **ears**.
22: 45 come cringing to me; as soon as **they**[s] hear me, they obey me.
2Ki 18: 26 Don't speak to us in Hebrew in the **hearing** *of* the people on the
19: 16 **Give ear** [+5742], O LORD, and hear; open your eyes,
19: 28 you rage against me and your insolence has reached my **ears**,
21: 12 and Judah that the **ears** *of* everyone who hears of it will tingle.
23: 2 He read in their **hearing** all the words of the Book of the
1Ch 17: 20 and there is no God but you, as we have heard with our own **ears**.
17: 25 *have* **revealed to** [+906+1655] your servant that you will build a
28: 8 and of the assembly of the LORD, and in the **hearing** *of* our God:
2Ch 6: 40 and your **ears** attentive to the prayers offered in this place.
7: 15 be open and my **ears** attentive to the prayers offered in this place.
34: 30 He read in their **hearing** all the words of the Book of the
Ne 1: 6 let your **ear** be attentive and your eyes open to hear the prayer your
1: 11 let your **ear** be attentive to the prayer of this your servant and to
8: 3 all the people **listened** [+448] **attentively to** the Book of the Law.
13: 1 On that day the Book of Moses was read aloud in the **hearing** *of*
Job 4: 12 word was secretly brought to me, my **ears** caught a whisper of it.
12: 11 Does not the **ear** test words as the tongue tastes food?
13: 1 "My eyes have seen all this, my **ears** have heard and understood it.
13: 17 Listen carefully to my words; let your **ears** take in what I say.
15: 21 Terrifying sounds fill his **ears**; when all seems well,
28: 22 and Death say, 'Only a rumor of it has reached our **ears**.'
29: 11 **Whoever**[s] heard me spoke well of me, and those who saw me
33: 8 "But you have said in my **hearing**—I heard the very words—
33: 16 he may speak in their **ears** and terrify them with warnings,
34: 3 For the **ear** tests words as the tongue tastes food.
36: 10 *He* **makes** them **listen** [+1655] to correction and commands them
36: 15 in their suffering; *he* **speaks to** [+1655] them in their affliction.
42: 5 My **ears** had heard of you but now my eyes have seen you.
Ps 10: 17 you encourage them, and *you* **listen** [+7992] to their cry,
17: 6 for you will answer me; **give ear** [+5742] to me and hear my
18: 6 [18:7] he heard my voice; my cry came before him, into his **ears**.
18: 44 [18:45] As soon as **they**[s] hear me, they obey me; foreigners
31: 2 [31:3] Turn your **ear** to me, come quickly to my rescue; be my
34: 15 [34:16] are on the righteous and his **ears** are attentive to their cry;
40: 6 [40:7] offering you did not desire, but my **ears** you have pierced;
44: 1 [44:2] We have heard with our **ears**, O God; our fathers have told
45: 10 [45:11] Listen, O daughter, consider and **give ear** [+5742]: Forget
49: 4 [49:5] I will turn my **ear** to a proverb; with the harp I will
58: 4 [58:5] of a snake, like that of a cobra that has stopped its **ears**,
71: 2 deliver me in your righteousness; turn your **ear** to me and save me.
78: 1 hear my teaching; **listen** [+5742] to the words of my mouth.
86: 1 **Hear** [+5742], O LORD, and answer me, for I am poor
88: 2 [88:3] May my prayer come before you; turn your **ear** to my cry.
92: 11 [92:12] my **ears** have heard the rout of my wicked foes.
94: 9 Does he who implanted the **ear** not hear? Does he who formed the
102: 2 [102:3] Turn your **ear** to me; when I call, answer me quickly.
115: 6 they have **ears**, but cannot hear, noses, but they cannot smell;
116: 2 Because he turned his **ear** to me, I will call on him as long as I
130: 2 hear my voice. Let your **ears** be attentive to my cry for mercy.
135: 17 they have **ears**, but cannot hear, nor is there breath in their mouths.
Pr 2: 2 turning your **ear** to wisdom and applying your heart to
4: 20 pay attention to what I say; **listen** [+5742] **closely** to my words.
5: 1 pay attention to my wisdom, **listen** [+5742] **well** to my words of
5: 13 I would not obey my teachers or **listen** [+5742] to my instructors.
15: 31 *He who* **listens to** [+9048] a life-giving rebuke will be at home
18: 15 the discerning acquires knowledge; the **ears** *of* the wise seek it out.
20: 12 **Ears** that hear and eyes that see—the LORD has made them both.
21: 13 If a man shuts his **ears** to the cry of the poor, he too will cry out
22: 17 **Pay attention** [+5742] and listen to the sayings of the wise;
23: 9 Do not speak **to** [+928] a fool, for he will scorn the wisdom of your
23: 12 your heart to instruction and your **ears** to words of knowledge.
25: 12 an ornament of fine gold is a wise man's rebuke to a listening **ear**.
26: 17 Like one who seizes a dog by the **ears** is a passer-by who meddles
28: 9 If anyone turns a deaf **ear** to the law, even his prayers are
Ecc 1: 8 The eye never has enough of seeing, nor the **ear** its fill of hearing.
Isa 5: 9 The LORD Almighty has declared in my **hearing**: "Surely the
6: 10 of this people calloused; make their **ears** dull and close their eyes.
6: 10 hear with their **ears**, understand with their hearts, and turn
11: 3 he sees with his eyes, or decide by what he hears with his **ears**;
22: 14 The LORD Almighty has revealed this in my **hearing**: "Till your
30: 21 or to the left, your **ears** will hear a voice behind you, saying,
32: 3 will no longer be closed, and the **ears** *of* those who hear will listen.
33: 15 who stops his **ears** against plots of murder and shuts his eyes
35: 5 the eyes of the blind be opened and the **ears** *of* the deaf unstopped.
36: 11 Don't speak to us in Hebrew in the **hearing** *of* the people on the
37: 17 **Give ear** [+5742], O LORD, and hear; open your eyes,
37: 29 rage against me and because your insolence has reached my **ears**,
42: 20 have paid no attention; your **ears** are open, but you hear nothing."
43: 8 out those who have eyes but are blind, who have **ears** but are deaf.
48: 8 heard nor understood; from of old your **ear** has not been open.
49: 20 born during your bereavement will yet say in your **hearing**,
50: 4 by morning, wakens my **ear** to listen like one being taught.
50: 5 The Sovereign LORD has opened my **ears**, and I have not been
55: 3 **Give ear** [+5742] and come to me; hear me, that your soul may
59: 1 of the LORD is not too short to save, nor his **ear** too dull to hear.
Jer 2: 2 "Go and proclaim in the **hearing** *of* Jerusalem: " 'I remember the
5: 21 who have eyes but do not see, who have **ears** but do not hear:
6: 10 Who will listen to me? Their **ears** are closed so they cannot hear.
7: 24 But they did not listen or **pay attention** [+906+5742]; instead,
7: 26 But they did not listen to me or **pay attention** [+906+5742].
9: 20 [9:19] of the LORD; open your **ears** to the words of his mouth.
11: 8 But they did not listen or **pay attention** [+906+5742]; instead,
17: 23 Yet they did not listen or **pay attention** [+906+5742]; they were
19: 3 place that will make the **ears** *of* everyone who hears of it tingle.
25: 4 have not listened or **paid any attention** [+906+4200+5742+9048].
26: 11 against this city. You have heard it with your own **ears**!"
26: 15 has sent me to you to speak all these words in your **hearing**."
28: 7 listen to what I have to say in your **hearing** and in the hearing of
28: 7 I have to say in your hearing and in the **hearing** *of* all the people:
29: 29 the priest, however, read the letter **to** [+928] Jeremiah the prophet.
34: 14 did not listen to me or **pay attention** [+906+5742] to me.
35: 15 But *you have* not **paid attention** [+906+5742] or listened to me.
36: 6 read **to** [+928] the people from the scroll the words of the LORD
36: 6 Read them **to** [+928] all the people of Judah who come in from
36: 10 Baruch read **to** [+928] all the people at the LORD's temple the
36: 13 he had heard Baruch read **to** [+928] the people from the scroll,
36: 14 "Bring the scroll from which you have read **to** [+928] the people
36: 15 They said to him, "Sit down, please, and read it **to** [+928] us."
36: 15 please, and read it to us." So Baruch read it **to** [+928] them.
36: 20 to the king in the courtyard and reported everything **to** [+928] him.
36: 21 read it **to** [+928] the king and all the officials standing beside him.
36: 21 read it to the king and **[RPH]** all the officials standing beside him.
44: 5 they did not listen or **pay attention** [+906+5742]; they did not turn
La 3: 56 You heard my plea: "Do not close your **ears** to my cry for relief."
Eze 3: 10 "Son of man, **listen carefully** [+928+9048] and take to heart all the
8: 18 Although they shout in my **ears**, I will not listen to them."
9: 1 I **heard** [+928] him call out in a loud voice, "Bring the guards of
9: 5 As I **listened** [+928], he said to the others, "Follow him through
10: 13 I **heard** [+928] the wheels being called "the whirling wheels."
12: 2 have eyes to see but do not see and **ears** to hear but do not hear,
16: 12 earrings on your **ears** and a beautiful crown on your head.
23: 25 They will cut off your noses and your **ears**, and those of you who
24: 26 on that day a fugitive will come to tell you the **news** [+2245].
40: 4 look with your eyes and hear with your **ears** and pay attention to
44: 5 **listen closely** [+928+9048] and give attention to everything I tell
Da 9: 18 **Give ear** [+5742], O God, and hear; open your eyes and see the
Am 3: 12 from the lion's mouth only two leg bones or a piece of an **ear**,
Mic 7: 16 lay their hands on their mouths and their **ears** will become deaf.
Zec 7: 11 stubbornly they turned their backs and stopped up their **ears**.

266 אֹזֶן ***'āzēn***, n.[m.]. [1] [cf. 265?]

equipment [1]

Dt 23: 13 [23:14] As part of your **equipment** have something to dig with,

267 אֻזֵּן שֶׁאֱרָה ***'uzzēn še'ěrâ***, n.pr.loc. [1] [cf. 8641]

Uzzen Sheerah [1]

1Ch 7: 24 built Lower and Upper Beth Horon as well as **Uzzen Sheerah**.

268 אַזְנוֹת תָּבוֹר ***'aznôt tābôr***, n.pr.loc. [1] [cf. 9314]

Aznoth Tabor [1]

Jos 19:34 The boundary ran west through **Aznoth Tabor** and came out at

269 ¹אָזְנִי ***'oznî***[1], n.pr.m. [1] [→ 270; cf. 265]

Ozni [1]

Nu 26:16 through **Ozni**, the Oznite clan; through Eri, the Erite clan;

270 ²אָזְנִי ***'oznî***[2], a.g. [1] [√ 269; cf. 265]

Oznite [1]

Nu 26:16 through Ozni, the **Oznite** clan; through Eri, the Erite clan;

271 אֲזַנְיָה ***'ᵃzanyâ***, n.pr.m. [1] [√ 265 + 3378]

Azaniah [1]

Ne 10:9 [10:10] Jeshua son of **Azaniah**, Binnui of the sons of Henadad,

272 אֲזִקִּים ***'ᵃziqqîm***, n.[m.] [2] [cf. 2414]

chains [2]

Jer 40:1 He had found Jeremiah bound in **chains** among all the captives
40:4 But today I am freeing you from the **chains** on your wrists.

273 אָזַר ***'āzar***, v. [16 / 17] [√ 258]

armed [4], arms [2], brace [+2743] [2], prepare for battle [2], *untranslated* [1], armed yourself [1], binds [1], clothed [1], get ready [+5516] [1], provide [1], strengthen [1]

1Sa 2:4 [A] but those who stumbled *are* **armed** *with* strength.
2Sa 22:33 [D] It is God *who* **arms** [BHS 5057] me *with* strength
22:40 [D] *You* **armed** me *with* strength for battle; you made my
2Ki 1:8 [B] of hair and with a leather belt **[NIE]** around his waist."
Job 30:18 [A] clothing to me; *he* **binds** me like the neck of my garment.
38:3 [A] **Brace** [+2743] yourself like a man; I will question you,
40:7 [A] "**Brace** [+2743] yourself like a man; I will question you,
Ps 18:32 [18:33] [D] It is God who **arms** me *with* strength and makes my
18:39 [18:40] [D] *You* **armed** me *with* strength for battle; you made
30:11 [30:12] [D] removed my sackcloth and **clothed** me *with* joy,
65:6 [65:7] [C] your power, *having* **armed yourself** with strength,
93:1 [F] the LORD is robed in majesty and *is* **armed** *with* strength.
Isa 8:9 [F] **Prepare for battle**, and be shattered! Prepare for battle,
8:9 [F] and be shattered! **Prepare for battle**, and be shattered!
45:5 [D] *I will* **strengthen** you, though you have not acknowledged
50:11 [D] who light fires and **provide** *yourselves with* flaming torches,
Jer 1:17 [A] "**Get** yourself **ready** [+5516]! Stand up and say to them

274 אֶזְרוֹעַ ***'ezrôa'***, n.f. [2] [cf. 2432; Ar 10013]

arm [1], it[s] [+3276] [1]

Job 31:22 fall from the shoulder, let **it**[s] [+3276] be broken off at the joint.
Jer 32:21 by a mighty hand and an outstretched **arm** and with great terror.

275 אֶזְרָח ***'ezrāḥ***, n.m. [17] [√ 2436]

native-born [12], born [1], citizens [1], native soil [1], native-born [+824] [1], native-born [+824+2021] [1]

Ex 12:19 of Israel, whether he is an alien or **native-born** [+824+2021].
12:48 then he may take part like *one* **born** *in* the land.
12:49 The same law applies to the **native-born** and to the alien living
Lev 16:29 do any work—whether **native-born** or an alien living among you—
17:15 " 'Anyone, whether **native-born** or alien, who eats anything found
18:26 The **native-born** and the aliens living among you must not do any
19:34 alien living with you must be treated as one of your **native-born**.
23:42 for seven days: All **native-born** Israelites are to live in booths
24:16 Whether an alien or **native-born**, when he blasphemes the Name,
24:22 You are to have the same law for the alien and the **native-born**.
Nu 9:14 the same regulations for the alien and the **native-born** [+824].' "
15:13 " 'Everyone who is **native-born** must do these things in this way
15:29 whether he is a **native-born** Israelite or an alien.
15:30 whether **native-born** or alien, blasphemes the LORD,
Jos 8:33 All Israel, aliens and **citizens** alike, with their elders, officials
Ps 37:35 and ruthless man flourishing like a green tree in its **native soil**,
Eze 47:22 You are to consider them as **native-born** Israelites; along with you

276 אֶזְרָחִי ***'ezrāḥî***, a.g. [3] [√ 2438; cf. 2436]

Ezrahite [3]

1Ki 4:31 [5:11] wiser than any other man, including Ethan the **Ezrahite**—
Ps 88:T [88:1] A *maskil* of Heman the **Ezrahite**.
89:T [89:1] A *maskil* of Ethan the **Ezrahite**.

277 ¹אָח ***'āḥ***[1], interj. [2]

alas [1], oh [1]

Eze 6:11 Strike your hands together and stamp your feet and cry out "**Alas**!"
21:15 [21:20] **Oh**! It is made to flash like lightning, it is grasped for

278 ²אָח ***'āḥ***[2], n.m. [630 / 632] [→ 288, 295, 306; Ar 10017; *also used with compound proper names*]

brother [210], brothers [201], relatives [67], fellow [19], associates [17], brother's [17], other[s] [15], *untranslated* [10], countrymen [10], another[s] [7], fellow countrymen [5], kinsmen [5], relative [5], family [3], people [3], brother Israelite [2], countryman [2], cousins [2], friends [2], he[s] [+3870] [2], nephew [+1201] [2], others[s] [2], among yourselves [+408+448] [1], anyone[s] else [1], associate [1], brother Israelites [1], brotherhood [1], brothers [+562] [1], companions [1], each [+408+2257] [1], equally [+408+2257+3869] [1], equally among them [+408+2257+3869] [1], families [1], fellow Jews [1], fellow Levites [1], have brother [1], him[s] [+3870] [1], people from Benjamin [+2157] [1], people from Judah [+2157] [1], priests[s] [+2157] [1], them[s] [+2257] [1], them[s] [1], two men [+408+2256+3481] [1], uncle [1], uncle's [+562] [1], very own brother [+562+1201+3870] [1]

Ge 4:2 Later she gave birth to his **brother** Abel. Now Abel kept flocks,
4:8 Now Cain said to his **brother** Abel, "Let's go out to the field."
4:8 were in the field, Cain attacked his **brother** Abel and killed him.
4:9 Then the LORD said to Cain, "Where is your **brother** Abel?"
4:9 "I don't know," he replied. "Am I my **brother's** keeper?"
4:10 Listen! Your **brother's** blood cries out to me from the ground.
4:11 which opened its mouth to receive your **brother's** blood from your
4:21 His **brother's** name was Jubal; he was the father of all who play
9:5 from **each** [+408+2257] man, too, I will demand an accounting for
9:22 saw his father's nakedness and told his two **brothers** outside.
9:25 be Canaan! The lowest of slaves will he be to his **brothers**."
10:21 Sons were also born to Shem, whose older **brother** was Japheth;
10:25 in his time the earth was divided; his **brother** was named Joktan.
12:5 He took his wife Sarai, his **nephew** [+1201] Lot, all the
13:8 or between your herdsmen and mine, for we are **brothers**.
13:11 and set out toward the east. The two **[RPH]** men parted company:
14:12 They also carried off Abram's **nephew** [+1201] Lot and his
14:13 a **brother** *of* Eshcol and Aner, all of whom were allied with
14:13 a brother of Eshcol and **[RPH]** Aner, all of whom were allied
14:14 When Abram heard that his **relative** had been taken captive,
14:16 the goods and brought back his **relative** Lot and his possessions,
16:12 against him, and he will live in hostility toward all his **brothers**."
19:7 and said, "No, my **friends**. Don't do this wicked thing.
20:5 'She is my sister,' and didn't she also say, 'He is my **brother**'?
20:13 love to me: Everywhere we go, say of me, "He is my **brother**." ' "
20:16 he said, "I am giving your **brother** a thousand shekels of silver.
22:20 is also a mother; she has borne sons to your **brother** Nahor:
22:21 Uz the firstborn, Buz his **brother**, Kemuel (the father of Aram),
22:23 Milcah bore these eight sons to Abraham's **brother** Nahor.
24:15 son of Milcah, who was the wife of Abraham's **brother** Nahor.
24:27 has led me on the journey to the house of my master's **relatives**."
24:29 Now Rebekah had a **brother** named Laban, and he hurried out to
24:48 road to get the granddaughter of my master's **brother** for his son.
24:53 he also gave costly gifts to her **brother** and to her mother.
24:55 her **brother** and her mother replied, "Let the girl remain with us
25:18 And they lived in hostility toward all their **brothers**.
25:26 After this, his **brother** came out, with his hand grasping Esau's
26:31 Early the next morning the men swore an oath to each **other**[s].
27:6 "Look, I overheard your father say to your **brother** Esau,
27:11 "But my **brother** Esau is a hairy man, and I'm a man with smooth
27:23 for his hands were hairy like those of his **brother** Esau;
27:29 Be lord over your **brothers**, and may the sons of your mother bow
27:30 left his father's presence, his **brother** Esau came in from hunting.
27:35 he said, "Your **brother** came deceitfully and took your blessing."
27:37 him lord over you and have made all his **relatives** his servants,
27:40 You will live by the sword and you will serve your **brother**.
27:41 for my father are near; then I will kill my **brother** Jacob."
27:42 "Your **brother** Esau is consoling himself with the thought of
27:43 do what I say: Flee at once to my **brother** Laban in Haran.
27:44 Stay with him for a while until your **brother's** fury subsides.
27:45 When your **brother** is no longer angry with you and forgets what
28:2 from among the daughters of Laban, your mother's **brother**.
28:5 the **brother** *of* Rebekah, who was the mother of Jacob and Esau.
29:4 Jacob asked the shepherds, "My **brothers**, where are you from?"
29:10 his mother's **brother**, and Laban's sheep, he went over and rolled
29:10 Laban's **[RPH]** sheep, he went over and rolled the stone away
29:10 from the mouth of the well and watered his **uncle's** [+562] sheep.
29:12 He had told Rachel that he was a **relative** *of* her father and a son of
29:15 Laban said to him, "Just because you are a **relative** *of* mine,
31:23 Taking his **relatives** with him, he pursued Jacob for seven days
31:25 overtook him, and Laban and his **relatives** camped there too.
31:32 In the presence of our **relatives**, see for yourself whether there is

Ge 31:37 Put it here in front of your **relatives** and mine, and let them judge
31:37 and mine, **[RPH]** and let them judge between the two of us.
31:46 He said to his **relatives**, "Gather some stones." So they took stones
31:54 there in the hill country and invited his **relatives** to a meal.
32: 3 [32:4] Jacob sent messengers ahead of him to his **brother** Esau in
32: 6 [32:7] they said, "We went to your **brother** Esau, and now he is
32:11 [32:12] Save me, I pray, from the hand of my **brother** Esau, for I
32:13 [32:14] he had with him he selected a gift for his **brother** Esau:
32:17 [32:18] "When my **brother** Esau meets you and asks, 'To whom
33: 3 down to the ground seven times as he approached his **brother**.
33: 9 Esau said, "I already have plenty, my **brother**. Keep what you
34:11 Shechem said to Dinah's father and **brothers**, "Let me find favor
34:25 Simeon and Levi, Dinah's **brothers**, took their swords
35: 1 who appeared to you when you were fleeing from your **brother**
35: 7 revealed himself to him when he was fleeing from his **brother**.
36: 6 and moved to a land some distance from his **brother** Jacob.
37: 2 was tending the flocks with his **brothers**, the sons of Bilhah
37: 4 When his **brothers** saw that their father loved him more than any
37: 4 saw that their father loved him more than any of **them**[s] [+2257],
37: 5 Joseph had a dream, and when he told it to his **brothers**, they hated
37: 8 His **brothers** said to him, "Do you intend to reign over us?
37: 9 Then he had another dream, and he told it to his **brothers**.
37:10 When he told his father as well as his **brothers**, his father rebuked
37:10 Will your mother and I and your **brothers** actually come and bow
37:11 His **brothers** were jealous of him, but his father kept the matter in
37:12 Now his **brothers** had gone to graze their father's flocks near
37:13 you know, your **brothers** are grazing the flocks near Shechem.
37:14 "Go and see if all is well with your **brothers** and with the flocks,
37:16 He replied, "I'm looking for my **brothers**. Can you tell me where
37:17 'Let's go to Dothan.' " So Joseph went after his **brothers** and found
37:19 "Here comes that dreamer!" they said to each **other**[s].
37:23 So when Joseph came to his **brothers**, they stripped him of his
37:26 Judah said to his **brothers**, "What will we gain if we kill our
37:26 "What will we gain if we kill our **brother** and cover up his blood?
37:27 on him; after all, he is our **brother**, our own flesh and blood."
37:27 he is our brother, our own flesh and blood." His **brothers** agreed.
37:30 He went back to his **brothers** and said, "The boy isn't there!
38: 1 Judah left his **brothers** and went down to stay with a man of
38: 8 "Lie with your **brother's** wife and fulfill your duty to her as a
38: 8 to her as a brother-in-law to produce offspring for your **brother**."
38: 9 so whenever he lay with his **brother's** wife, he spilled his semen
38: 9 on the ground to keep from producing offspring for his **brother**.
38:11 For he thought, "He may die too, just like his **brothers**." So Tamar
38:29 when he drew back his hand, his **brother** came out, and she said,
38:30 Then his **brother**, who had the scarlet thread on his wrist,
42: 3 ten *of* Joseph's **brothers** went down to buy grain from Egypt.
42: 4 Jacob did not send Benjamin, Joseph's **brother**, with the others,
42: 4 Jacob did not send Benjamin, Joseph's brother, with the **others**[s],
42: 6 So when Joseph's **brothers** arrived, they bowed down to him with
42: 7 As soon as Joseph saw his **brothers**, he recognized them,
42: 8 Although Joseph recognized his **brothers**, they did not recognize
42:13 they replied, "Your servants were twelve **brothers**, the sons of one
42:15 you will not leave this place unless your youngest **brother** comes
42:16 Send one of your number to get your **brother**; the rest of you will
42:19 If you are honest men, let one of your **brothers** stay here in prison,
42:20 you must bring your youngest **brother** to me, so that your words
42:21 They said to one **another**[s], "Surely we are being punished
42:21 "Surely we are being punished because of our **brother**.
42:28 "My silver has been returned," he said to his **brothers**. "Here it is
42:28 hearts sank and they turned to each **other**[s] trembling and said,
42:32 We were twelve **brothers**, sons of one father. One is no more,
42:33 Leave one of your **brothers** here with me, and take food for your
42:34 bring your youngest **brother** to me so I will know that you are not
42:34 I will give your **brother** back to you, and you can trade in the
42:38 there with you; his **brother** is dead and he is the only one left.
43: 3 'You will not see my face again unless your **brother** is with you.'
43: 4 If you will send our **brother** along with us, we will go down
43: 5 'You will not see my face again unless your **brother** is with
43: 6 this trouble on me by telling the man you had another **brother**?"
43: 7 father still living?' he asked us. 'Do you have another **brother**?'
43: 7 were we to know he would say, 'Bring your **brother** down here'?"
43:13 Take your **brother** also and go back to the man at once.
43:14 so that he will let your other **brother** and Benjamin come back
43:29 As he looked about and saw his **brother** Benjamin, his own
43:29 his own mother's son, he asked, "Is this your youngest **brother**,
43:30 Deeply moved at the sight of his **brother**, Joseph hurried out
44:14 Joseph was still in the house when Judah and his **brothers** came in,
44:19 My lord asked his servants, 'Do you have a father or a **brother**?'
44:20 His **brother** is dead, and he is the only one of his mother's sons
44:23 'Unless your youngest **brother** comes down with you,
44:26 go down. Only if our youngest **brother** is with us will we go.
44:26 We cannot see the man's face unless our youngest **brother** is with
44:33 slave in place of the boy, and let the boy return with his **brothers**.
45: 1 no one with Joseph when he made himself known to his **brothers**.
45: 3 Joseph said to his **brothers**, "I am Joseph! Is my father still
45: 3 his **brothers** were not able to answer him, because they were
45: 4 Joseph said to his **brothers**, "Come close to me." When they had
45: 4 When they had done so, he said, "I am your **brother** Joseph,
45:12 "You can see for yourselves, and so can my **brother** Benjamin,
45:14 Then he threw his arms around his **brother** Benjamin and wept,
45:15 he kissed all his **brothers** and wept over them. Afterward his
45:15 and wept over them. Afterward his **brothers** talked with him.
45:16 When the news reached Pharaoh's palace that Joseph's **brothers**
45:17 Pharaoh said to Joseph, "Tell your **brothers**, 'Do this: Load your
45:24 he sent his **brothers** away, and as they were leaving he said to
46:31 Then Joseph said to his **brothers** and to his father's household,
46:31 and will say to him, 'My **brothers** and my father's household,
47: 1 "My father and **brothers**, with their flocks and herds and
47: 2 He chose five of his **brothers** and presented them before Pharaoh.
47: 3 Pharaoh asked the **brothers**, "What is your occupation?" "Your
47: 5 said to Joseph, "Your father and your **brothers** have come to you,
47: 6 settle your father and your **brothers** in the best part of the land.
47:11 So Joseph settled his father and his **brothers** in Egypt and gave
47:12 Joseph also provided his father and his **brothers** and all his
48: 6 inherit they will be reckoned under the names of their **brothers**.
48:19 Nevertheless, his younger **brother** will be greater than he,
48:22 to you, as one who is over your **brothers**, I give the ridge of land I
49: 5 "Simeon and Levi are **brothers**—their swords are weapons of
49: 8 "Judah, your **brothers** will praise you; your hand will be on the
49:26 the head of Joseph, on the brow of the prince among his **brothers**.
50: 8 and his **brothers** and those belonging to his father's household.
50:14 together with his **brothers** and all the others who had gone with
50:15 When Joseph's **brothers** saw that their father was dead, they said,
50:17 I ask you to forgive your **brothers** the sins and the wrongs they
50:18 His **brothers** then came and threw themselves down before him.
50:24 Joseph said to his **brothers**, "I am about to die. But God will
Ex 1: 6 Now Joseph and all his **brothers** and all that generation died,
2:11 he went out to where his own **people** were and watched them at
2:11 He saw an Egyptian beating a Hebrew, one of his own **people**.
4:14 burned against Moses and he said, "What about your **brother**,
4:18 "Let me go back to my own **people** in Egypt to see if any of them
7: 1 like God to Pharaoh, and your **brother** Aaron will be your prophet.
7: 2 your **brother** Aaron is to tell Pharaoh to let the Israelites go out of
10:23 No one could see **anyone**[s] **else** or leave his place for three days.
16:15 When the Israelites saw it, they said to each **other**[s], "What is it?"
25:20 The cherubim are to face each **other**[s], looking toward the cover.
28: 1 "**Have** Aaron your **brother** brought to you from among the
28: 2 Make sacred garments for your **brother** Aaron, to give him dignity
28: 4 They are to make these sacred garments for your **brother** Aaron
28:41 After you put these clothes on your **brother** Aaron and his sons,
32:27 to the other, each killing his **brother** and friend and neighbor.' "
32:29 for you were against your own sons and **brothers**, and he has
37: 9 The cherubim faced each **other**[s], looking toward the cover.
Lev 7:10 belongs **equally** [+408+2257+3869] to all the sons of Aaron.
10: 4 carry your **cousins** outside the camp, away from the front of the
10: 6 your **relatives**, all the house of Israel, may mourn for those the
16: 2 "Tell your **brother** Aaron not to come whenever he chooses into
18:14 " 'Do not dishonor your father's **brother** by approaching his wife
18:16 " 'Do not have sexual relations with your **brother's** wife;
18:16 with your brother's wife; that would dishonor your **brother**.
19:17 " 'Do not hate your **brother** in your heart. Rebuke your neighbor
20:21 " 'If a man marries his **brother's** wife, it is an act of impurity;
20:21 it is an act of impurity; he has dishonored his **brother**.
21: 2 such as his mother or father, his son or daughter, his **brother**,
21:10 the one among his **brothers** who has had the anointing oil poured
25:14 or buy any from him, do not take advantage of each **other**[s].
25:25 " 'If one of your **countrymen** becomes poor and sells some of his
25:25 relative is to come and redeem what his **countryman** has sold.
25:35 " 'If one of your **countrymen** becomes poor and is unable to
25:36 so that your **countryman** may continue to live among you.
25:39 " 'If one of your **countrymen** becomes poor among you and sells
25:46 but you must not rule over your **fellow** Israelites ruthlessly.
25:46 you must not rule over your fellow Israelites **[RPH]** ruthlessly.
25:47 one of your **countrymen** becomes poor and sells himself to the
25:48 after he has sold himself. One of his **relatives** may redeem him:
26:37 They will stumble over one **another**[s] as though fleeing from the
Nu 6: 7 Even if his own father or mother or **brother** or sister dies,
8:26 They may assist their **brothers** in performing their duties at the
14: 4 And they said to each **other**[s], "We should choose a leader
16:10 He has brought you and all your **fellow** Levites near himself,
18: 2 Bring your **fellow** Levites from your ancestral tribe to join you
18: 6 I myself have selected your **fellow** Levites from among the
20: 3 "If only we had died when our **brothers** fell dead before the
20: 8 and you and your **brother** Aaron gather the assembly together.
20:14 the king of Edom, saying: "This is what your **brother** Israel says:
25: 6 an Israelite man brought to his **family** a Midianite woman right
27: 4 he had no son? Give us property among our father's **relatives**."
27: 7 give them property as an inheritance among their father's **relatives**

Nu 27: 9 If he has no daughter, give his inheritance to his **brothers**.
27: 10 If he has no **brothers**, give his inheritance to his father's brothers.
27: 10 If he has no brothers, give his inheritance to his father's **brothers**.
27: 11 If his father had no **brothers**, give his inheritance to the nearest
27: 13 too will be gathered to your people, as your **brother** Aaron was,
32: 6 "Shall your **countrymen** go to war while you sit here?
36: 2 he ordered you to give the inheritance of our **brother** Zelophehad
Dt 1: 16 Hear the disputes between your **brothers** and judge fairly,
1: 16 whether the case is between **brother Israelites** or between one of
1: 28 Our **brothers** have made us lose heart. They say, 'The people are
2: 4 'You are about to pass through the territory of your **brothers** the
2: 8 So we went on past our **brothers** the descendants of Esau,
3: 18 armed for battle, must cross over ahead of your **brother** Israelites.
3: 20 until the LORD gives rest to your **brothers** as he has to you,
10: 9 the Levites have no share or inheritance among their **brothers**;
13: 6 [13:7] If your **very own brother** [+562+1201+3870], or your son
15: 2 He shall not require payment from his fellow Israelite or **brother**,
15: 3 a foreigner, but you must cancel any debt your **brother** owes you.
15: 7 If there is a poor man among your **brothers** in any of the towns of
15: 7 do not be hardhearted or tightfisted toward your poor **brother**.
15: 9 so that you do not show ill will toward your needy **brother**
15: 11 Therefore I command you to be openhanded toward your **brothers**
15: 12 If a **fellow** Hebrew, a man or a woman, sells himself to you
17: 15 He must be from among your own **brothers**. Do not place a
17: 15 not place a foreigner over you, one who is not a **brother** Israelite.
17: 20 not consider himself better than his **brothers** and turn from the law
18: 2 They shall have no inheritance among their **brothers**; the LORD
18: 7 his **fellow** Levites who serve there in the presence of the LORD.
18: 15 raise up for you a prophet like me from among your own **brothers**.
18: 18 raise up for them a prophet like you from among their **brothers**;
19: 18 proves to be a liar, giving false testimony against his **brother**,
19: 19 do to him as he intended to do to his **brother**. You must purge the
20: 8 go home so that his **brothers** will not become disheartened too."
22: 1 If you see your **brother's** ox or sheep straying, do not ignore it
22: 1 do not ignore it but be sure to take it back to **him**[s] [+3870].
22: 2 If the **brother** does not live near you or if you do not know who he
22: 2 home with you and keep it until **he**[s] [+3870] comes looking for it.
22: 3 your brother's donkey or his cloak or anything **he**[s] [+3870] loses.
22: 4 If you see your **brother's** donkey or his ox fallen on the road,
23: 7 [23:8] Do not abhor an Edomite, for he is your **brother**. Do not
23: 19 [23:20] Do not charge your **brother** interest, whether on money
23: 20 [23:21] charge a foreigner interest, but not a **brother Israelite**,
24: 7 If a man is caught kidnapping one of his **brother** Israelites
24: 14 whether he is a **brother Israelite** or an alien living in one of your
25: 3 more than that, your **brother** will be degraded in your eyes.
25: 5 If **brothers** are living together and one of them dies without a son,
25: 6 The first son she bears shall carry on the name of the dead **brother**
25: 7 "My husband's brother refuses to carry on his **brother's** name in
25: 9 done to the man who will not build up his **brother's** family line."
25: 11 If **two men** [+408+2256+3481] are fighting and the wife of one of
28: 54 man among you will have no compassion on his own **brother**
32: 50 just as your **brother** Aaron died on Mount Hor and was gathered
33: 9 He did not recognize his **brothers** or acknowledge his own
33: 16 the head of Joseph, on the brow of the prince among his **brothers**.
33: 24 let him be favored by his **brothers**, and let him bathe his feet in
Jos 1: 14 fighting men, fully armed, must cross over ahead of your **brothers**.
1: 15 until the LORD gives **them**[s] rest, as he has done for you,
2: 13 spare the lives of my father and mother, my **brothers** and sisters,
2: 18 and mother, your **brothers** and all your family into your house.
6: 23 her father and mother and **brothers** and all who belonged to her.
14: 8 my **brothers** who went up with me made the hearts of the people
15: 17 Othniel son of Kenaz, Caleb's **brother**, took it; so Caleb gave his
17: 4 commanded Moses to give us an inheritance among our **brothers**."
17: 4 So Joshua gave them an inheritance along with the **brothers** *of*
22: 3 you have not deserted your **brothers** but have carried out the
22: 4 Now that the LORD your God has given your **brothers** rest as he
22: 7 gave land on the west side of the Jordan with their **brothers**.)
22: 8 and divide with your **brothers** the plunder from your enemies."
Jdg 1: 3 Then the men of Judah said to the Simeonites their **brothers**,
1: 13 Othniel son of Kenaz, Caleb's younger **brother**, took it; so Caleb
1: 17 Then the men of Judah went with the Simeonites their **brothers**
3: 9 Othniel son of Kenaz, Caleb's younger **brother**, who saved them.
8: 19 Gideon replied, "Those were my **brothers**, the sons of my own
9: 1 Abimelech son of Jerub-Baal went to his mother's **brothers** in
9: 3 When the **brothers** [+562] repeated all this to the citizens of
9: 3 inclined to follow Abimelech, for they said, "He is our **brother**."
9: 5 home in Ophrah and on one stone murdered his seventy **brothers**,
9: 18 king over the citizens of Shechem because he is your **brother**)—
9: 21 he lived there because he was afraid of his **brother** Abimelech.
9: 24 might be avenged on their **brother** Abimelech and on the citizens
9: 24 the citizens of Shechem, who had helped him murder his **brothers**.
9: 26 Now Gaal son of Ebed moved with his **brothers** into Shechem,
9: 31 "Gaal son of Ebed and his **brothers** have come to Shechem
9: 41 and Zebul drove Gaal and his **brothers** out of Shechem.
9: 56 had done to his father by murdering his seventy **brothers**.
11: 3 So Jephthah fled from his **brothers** and settled in the land of Tob,
14: 3 "Isn't there an acceptable woman among your **relatives** or among
16: 31 his **brothers** and his father's whole family went down to get him.
18: 8 they returned to Zorah and Eshtaol, their **brothers** asked them,
18: 8 their brothers asked them, **[RPH]** "How did you find things?"
18: 14 men who had spied out the land of Laish said to their **brothers**,
19: 23 went outside and said to them, "No, my **friends**, don't be so vile.
20: 13 But the Benjamites would not listen to their **fellow** Israelites.
20: 23 we go up again to battle against the Benjamites, our **brothers**?"
20: 28 "Shall we go up again to battle with Benjamin our **brother**,
21: 6 Now the Israelites grieved for their **brothers**, the Benjamites.
21: 22 When their fathers or **brothers** complain to us, we will say to
Ru 4: 3 is selling the piece of land that belonged to our **brother** Elimelech.
4: 10 so that his name will not disappear from among his **family**
1Sa 14: 3 He was a son of Ichabod's **brother** Ahitub son of Phinehas,
16: 13 the horn of oil and anointed him in the presence of his **brothers**,
17: 17 these ten loaves of bread for your **brothers** and hurry to their
17: 17 loaves of bread for your brothers and hurry to their camp. **[RPH]**
17: 18 See how your **brothers** are and bring back some assurance from
17: 22 keeper of supplies, ran to the battle lines and greeted his **brothers**.
17: 28 When Eliab, David's oldest **brother**, heard him speaking with the
20: 29 a sacrifice in the town and my **brother** has ordered me to be there.
20: 29 found favor in your eyes, let me get away to see my **brothers**.'
22: 1 When his **brothers** and his father's household heard about it,
26: 6 Ahimelech the Hittite and Abishai son of Zeruiah, Joab's **brother**,
30: 23 David replied, "No, my **brothers**, you must not do that with what
2Sa 1: 26 I grieve for you, Jonathan my **brother**; you were very dear to me.
2: 22 you down? How could I look your **brother** Joab in the face?"
2: 26 long before you order your men to stop pursuing their **brothers**?"
2: 27 the men would have continued the pursuit of their **brothers** until
3: 8 loyal to the house of your father Saul and to his **family** and friends.
3: 27 there, to avenge the blood of his **brother** Asahel, Joab stabbed him
3: 30 (Joab and his **brother** Abishai murdered Abner because he had
3: 30 because he had killed their **brother** Asahel in the battle at Gibeon.)
4: 6 in the stomach. Then Recab and his **brother** Baanah slipped away.
4: 9 David answered Recab and his **brother** Baanah, the sons of
10: 10 put the rest of the men under the command of Abishai his **brother**
13: 3 had a friend named Jonadab son of Shimeah, David's **brother**.
13: 4 to him, "I'm in love with Tamar, my **brother** Absalom's sister."
13: 7 "Go to the house of your **brother** Amnon and prepare some food
13: 8 So Tamar went to the house of her **brother** Amnon, who was lying
13: 10 had prepared and brought it to her **brother** Amnon in his bedroom.
13: 12 "Don't, my **brother**!" she said to him. "Don't force me. Such a
13: 20 Her **brother** Absalom said to her, "Has that Amnon, your brother,
13: 20 said to her, "Has that Amnon, your **brother**, been with you?
13: 20 been with you? Be quiet now, my sister; he is your **brother**.
13: 20 Tamar lived in her **brother** Absalom's house, a desolate woman.
13: 26 "If not, please let my **brother** Amnon come with us."
13: 32 Jonadab son of Shimeah, David's **brother**, said, "My lord should
14: 7 they say, 'Hand over the one who struck his **brother** down,
14: 7 so that we may put him to death for the life of his **brother** whom
15: 20 Go back, and take your **countrymen**. May kindness
18: 2 a third under Joab's **brother** Abishai son of Zeruiah, and a third
19: 12 [19:13] You are my **brothers**, my own flesh and blood. So why
19: 41 [19:42] saying to him, "Why did our **brothers**, the men of Judah,
20: 9 Joab said to Amasa, "How are you, my **brother**?" Then Joab took
20: 10 Then Joab and his **brother** Abishai pursued Sheba son of Bicri.
21: 21 Jonathan son of Shimeah, David's **brother**, killed him.
23: 18 Abishai the **brother** *of* Joab son of Zeruiah was chief of the Three.
23: 24 Asahel the **brother** *of* Joab, Elhanan son of Dodo from Bethlehem,
1Ki 1: 9 He invited all his **brothers**, the king's sons, and all the men of
1: 10 or Benaiah or the special guard or his **brother** Solomon.
2: 7 They stood by me when I fled from your **brother** Absalom.
2: 15 But things changed, and the kingdom has gone to my **brother**;
2: 21 Abishag the Shunammite be given in marriage to your **brother**
2: 22 after all, he is my older **brother**—yes, for him and for Abiathar the
9: 13 "What kind of towns are these you have given me, my **brother**?"
12: 24 Do not go up to fight against your **brothers**, the Israelites.
13: 30 and they mourned over him and said, "Oh, my **brother**!"
20: 32 live.' " The king answered, "Is he still alive? He is my **brother**."
20: 33 "Yes, your **brother** Ben-Hadad!" they said. "Go and get him,"
2Ki 7: 6 and a great army, so that they said to one **another**[s], "Look,
9: 2 get him away from his **companions** and take him into an inner
10: 13 he met *some* **relatives** *of* Ahaziah king of Judah and asked,
10: 13 They said, "We are **relatives** *of* Ahaziah, and we have come down
23: 9 in Jerusalem, they ate unleavened bread with their **fellow** priests.
1Ch 1: 19 in his time the earth was divided; his **brother** was named Joktan.
2: 32 The sons of Jada, Shammai's **brother**: Jether and Jonathan.
2: 42 The sons of Caleb the **brother** *of* Jerahmeel: Mesha his firstborn,
4: 9 Jabez was more honorable than his **brothers**. His mother had
4: 11 Kelub, Shuhah's **brother**, was the father of Mehir, who was the
4: 27 and six daughters, but his **brothers** did not have many children;
5: 2 though Judah was the strongest of his **brothers** and a ruler came

1Ch 5: 7 Their **relatives** by clans, listed according to their genealogical
5: 13 Their **relatives**, by families, were: Michael, Meshullam, Sheba,
6: 39 [6:24] Heman's **associate** Asaph, who served at his right hand:
6: 44 [6:29] from their **associates**, the Merarites, at his left hand:
6: 48 [6:33] Their **fellow** Levites were assigned to all the other duties of
7: 5 The **relatives** who were fighting men belonging to all the clans of
7: 16 His **brother** was named Sheresh, and his sons were Ulam
7: 22 for them many days, and his **relatives** came to comfort him.
7: 35 The sons of his **brother** Helem: Zophah, Imna, Shelesh and Amal.
8: 32 father of Shimeah. They too lived near their **relatives** in Jerusalem.
8: 32 They too lived near their relatives in Jerusalem. **[RPH]**
8: 39 The sons of his **brother** Eshek: Ulam his firstborn,
9: 6 Jeuel. The **people** [+2157] **from Judah** numbered 690.
9: 9 The **people** [+2157] **from Benjamin**, as listed in their genealogy,
9: 13 The **priests**[s] [+2157], who were heads of families, numbered
9: 17 Shallum, Akkub, Talmon, Ahiman and their **brothers**,
9: 19 and his **fellow** gatekeepers from his family (the Korahites)
9: 25 Their **brothers** in their villages had to come from time to time
9: 32 Some of their Kohathite **brothers** were in charge of preparing for
9: 38 of Shimeam. They too lived near their **relatives** in Jerusalem.
9: 38 They too lived near their relatives in Jerusalem. **[RPH]**
11: 20 Abishai the **brother** *of* Joab was chief of the Three. He raised his
11: 26 Asahel the **brother** *of* Joab, Elhanan son of Dodo from Bethlehem,
11: 38 Joel the **brother** *of* Nathan, Mibhar son of Hagri,
11: 45 Jediael son of Shimri, his **brother** Joha the Tizite,
12: 2 they were **kinsmen** *of* Saul from the tribe of Benjamin):
12: 29 [12:30] men of Benjamin, Saul's **kinsmen**—3,000, most of whom
12: 32 [12:33] 200 chiefs, with all their **relatives** under their command;
12: 39 [12:40] for their **families** had supplied provisions for them.
13: 2 wide to the rest of our **brothers** throughout the territories of Israel,
15: 5 the descendants of Kohath, Uriel the leader and 120 **relatives**;
15: 6 the descendants of Merari, Asaiah the leader and 220 **relatives**;
15: 7 the descendants of Gershon, Joel the leader and 130 **relatives**;
15: 8 descendants of Elizaphan, Shemaiah the leader and 200 **relatives**;
15: 9 from the descendants of Hebron, Eliel the leader and 80 **relatives**;
15: 10 descendants of Uzziel, Amminadab the leader and 112 **relatives**.
15: 12 you and your **fellow Levites** are to consecrate yourselves and bring
15: 16 David told the leaders of the Levites to appoint their **brothers** as
15: 17 from his **brothers**, Asaph son of Berekiah; and from their brothers
15: 17 and from their **brothers** the Merarites, Ethan son of Kushaiah;
15: 18 and with them their **brothers** next in rank: Zechariah, Jaaziel,
16: 7 to Asaph and his **associates** this psalm of thanks to the LORD:
16: 37 his **associates** before the ark of the covenant of the LORD to
16: 38 and his sixty-eight **associates** to minister with them.
16: 39 his **fellow** priests before the tabernacle of the LORD at the high
19: 11 put the rest of the men under the command of Abishai his **brother**,
19: 15 they too fled before his **brother** Abishai and went inside the city.
20: 5 Elhanan son of Jair killed Lahmi the **brother** *of* Goliath the Gittite,
20: 7 Jonathan son of Shimea, David's **brother**, killed him.
23: 22 had only daughters. Their **cousins**, the sons of Kish, married them.
23: 32 the Holy Place and, under their **brothers** the descendants of Aaron,
24: 25 The **brother** *of* Micah: Isshiah; from the sons of Isshiah:
24: 31 also cast lots, just as their **brothers** the descendants of Aaron did,
24: 31 The families of the oldest **brother** were treated the same as those
25: 7 Along with their **relatives**—all of them trained and skilled in
25: 9 was for Asaph, fell to Joseph, his sons and **relatives**, [BHS-]
25: 9 12 the second to Gedaliah, he and his **relatives** and sons, 12
25: 10 the third to Zaccur, his sons and **relatives**, 12
25: 11 the fourth to Izri, his sons and **relatives**, 12
25: 12 the fifth to Nethaniah, his sons and **relatives**, 12
25: 13 the sixth to Bukkiah, his sons and **relatives**, 12
25: 14 the seventh to Jesarelah, his sons and **relatives**, 12
25: 15 the eighth to Jeshaiah, his sons and **relatives**, 12
25: 16 the ninth to Mattaniah, his sons and **relatives**, 12
25: 17 the tenth to Shimei, his sons and **relatives**, 12
25: 18 the eleventh to Azarel, his sons and **relatives**, 12
25: 19 the twelfth to Hashabiah, his sons and **relatives**, 12
25: 20 the thirteenth to Shubael, his sons and **relatives**, 12
25: 21 the fourteenth to Mattithiah, his sons and **relatives**, 12
25: 22 the fifteenth to Jerimoth, his sons and **relatives**, 12
25: 23 the sixteenth to Hananiah, his sons and **relatives**, 12
25: 24 the seventeenth to Joshbekashah, his sons and **relatives**, 12
25: 25 the eighteenth to Hanani, his sons and **relatives**, 12
25: 26 the nineteenth to Mallothi, his sons and **relatives**, 12
25: 27 the twentieth to Eliathah, his sons and **relatives**, 12
25: 28 the twenty-first to Hothir, his sons and **relatives**, 12
25: 29 the twenty-second to Giddalti, his sons and **relatives**, 12
25: 30 the twenty-third to Mahazioth, his sons and **relatives**, 12
25: 31 the twenty-fourth to Romamti-Ezer, his sons and **relatives**, 12
26: 7 and Elzabad; his **relatives** Elihu and Semakiah were also able men.
26: 8 their **relatives** were capable men with the strength to do the work—
26: 9 Meshelemiah had sons and **relatives**, who were able men—
26: 11 the fourth. The sons and **relatives** of Hosah were 13 in all.
26: 12 ministering in the temple of the LORD, just as their **relatives** had.
26: 20 Their **fellow** [BHS 308] Levites were in charge of the treasuries of
26: 22 the sons of Jehieli, Zetham and his **brother** Joel. They were in
26: 25 His **relatives** through Eliezer: Rehabiah his son, Jeshaiah his son,
26: 26 his **relatives** were in charge of all the treasuries for the things
26: 28 dedicated things were in the care of Shelomith and his **relatives**.
26: 30 Hashabiah and his **relatives**—seventeen hundred able men—
26: 32 Jeriah had twenty-seven hundred **relatives**, who were able men
27: 7 The fourth, for the fourth month, was Asahel the **brother** *of* Joab;
27: 18 over Judah: Elihu, a **brother** *of* David; over Issachar: Omri son of
28: 2 to his feet and said: "Listen to me, my **brothers** and my people.
2Ch 5: 12 Asaph, Heman, Jeduthun and their sons and **relatives**—stood on
11: 4 Do not go up to fight against your **brothers**. Go home, every one
11: 22 Abijah son of Maacah to be the chief prince among his **brothers**,
19: 10 In every case that comes before you from your **fellow countrymen**
19: 10 otherwise his wrath will come on you and your **brothers**.
21: 2 Jehoram's **brothers**, the sons of Jehoshaphat, were Azariah,
21: 4 he put all his **brothers** to the sword along with some of the princes
21: 13 You have also murdered your own **brothers**, members of your
22: 8 he found the princes of Judah and the sons of Ahaziah's **relatives**,
28: 8 The Israelites took captive from their **kinsmen** two hundred
28: 11 Send back your **fellow countrymen** you have taken as prisoners,
28: 15 So they took them back to their **fellow countrymen** at Jericho,
29: 15 When they had assembled their **brothers** and consecrated
29: 34 so their **kinsmen** the Levites helped them until the task was
30: 7 Do not be like your fathers and **brothers**, who were unfaithful to
30: 9 your **brothers** and your children will be shown compassion by
31: 12 in charge of these things, and his **brother** Shimei was next in rank.
31: 13 Benaiah were supervisors under Conaniah and Shimei his **brother**,
31: 15 distributing to their **fellow** priests according to their divisions,
35: 5 for each subdivision of the families of your **fellow countrymen**,
35: 6 and prepare ⌞the lambs⌟ for your **fellow countrymen**,
35: 9 Also Conaniah along with Shemaiah and Nethanel, his **brothers**,
35: 15 because their **fellow** Levites made the preparations for them.
36: 4 a **brother** *of* Jehoahaz, king over Judah and Jerusalem
36: 4 Neco took Eliakim's **brother** Jehoahaz and carried him off to
36: 10 and he made Jehoiachin's **uncle**, Zedekiah, king over Judah
Ezr 3: 2 Jeshua son of Jozadak and his **fellow** priests and Zerubbabel son of
3: 2 his **associates** began to build the altar of the God of Israel to
3: 8 and the rest of their **brothers** (the priests and the Levites
3: 9 Jeshua and his sons and **brothers** and Kadmiel and his sons
3: 9 the sons of Henadad and their sons and **brothers**—all Levites—
6: 20 for all the exiles, for their **brothers** the priests and for themselves.
8: 17 I told them what to say to Iddo and his **kinsmen**, the temple
8: 18 the son of Israel, and Sherebiah's sons and **brothers**, 18 men;
8: 19 the descendants of Merari, and his **brothers** and nephews, 20 men.
8: 24 together with Sherebiah, Hashabiah and ten of their **brothers**,
10: 18 From the descendants of Jeshua son of Jozadak, and his **brothers**:
Ne 1: 2 Hanani, one of my **brothers**, came from Judah with some other
3: 1 Eliashib the high priest and his **fellow** priests went to work
3: 18 the repairs were made by their **countrymen** under Binnui son of
4: 2 [3:34] in the presence of his **associates** and the army of Samaria,
4: 14 [4:8] and fight for your **brothers**, your sons and your daughters,
4: 19 [4:13] we are widely separated from each **other**[s] along the wall.
4: 23 [4:17] Neither I nor my **brothers** nor my men nor the guards with
5: 1 and their wives raised a great outcry against their Jewish **brothers**.
5: 5 Although we are of the same flesh and blood as our **countrymen**
5: 7 told them, "You are exacting usury from your own **countrymen**!"
5: 8 we have bought back our Jewish **brothers** who were sold to the
5: 8 Now you are selling your **brothers**, only for them to be sold back
5: 10 I and my **brothers** and my men are also lending the people money
5: 14 neither I nor my **brothers** ate the food allotted to the governor.
7: 2 I put in charge of Jerusalem my **brother** Hanani, along with
10: 10 [10:11] their **associates**: Shebaniah, Hodiah, Kelita, Pelaiah,
10: 29 [10:30] all these now join their **brothers** the nobles, and bind
11: 12 and their **associates**, who carried on work for the temple—
11: 13 and his **associates**, who were heads of families—242 men;
11: 14 his **associates**, who were able men—128. Their chief officer was
11: 17 and prayer; Bakbukiah, second among his **associates**;
11: 19 Akkub, Talmon and their **associates**, who kept watch at the gates—
12: 7 the leaders of the priests and their **associates** in the days of Jeshua.
12: 8 Judah, and also Mattaniah, who, together with his **associates**,
12: 9 Bakbukiah and Unni, their **associates**, stood opposite them in the
12: 24 Sherebiah, Jeshua son of Kadmiel, and their **associates**, who stood
12: 36 and his **associates**—Shemaiah, Azarel, Milalai, Gilalai, Maai,
13: 13 made responsible for distributing the supplies to their **brothers**.
Est 10: 3 among the Jews, and held in high esteem by his many **fellow Jews**,
Job 1: 13 were feasting and drinking wine at the oldest **brother's** house,
1: 18 were feasting and drinking wine at the oldest **brother's** house,
6: 15 But my **brothers** are as undependable as intermittent streams,
19: 13 "He has alienated my **brothers** from me; my acquaintances are
22: 6 You demanded security from your **brothers** for no reason;
30: 29 I have become a **brother** of jackals, a companion of owls.
41: 17 [41:9] They are joined fast to one **another**[s]; they cling together
42: 11 All his **brothers** and sisters and everyone who had known him

Job 42:15 their father granted them an inheritance along with their **brothers**.
Ps 22:22 [22:23] I will declare your name to my **brothers**; in the
35:14 I went about mourning as though for my friend or **brother**.
49:7 [49:8] No man can redeem the life of **another**[s] or give to God a
50:20 You speak continually against your **brother** and slander your own
69:8 [69:9] I am a stranger to my **brothers**, an alien to my own
122:8 For the sake of my **brothers** and friends, I will say, "Peace be
133:1 How good and pleasant it is when **brothers** live together in unity!
Pr 6:19 pours out lies and a man who stirs up dissension among **brothers**.
17:2 and will share the inheritance as one of the **brothers**.
17:17 A friend loves at all times, and a **brother** is born for adversity.
18:9 One who is slack in his work is **brother** to one who destroys.
18:19 An offended **brother** is more unyielding than a fortified city,
18:24 come to ruin, but there is a friend who sticks closer than a **brother**.
19:7 A poor man is shunned by all his **relatives**—how much more do
27:10 and do not go to your **brother's** house when disaster strikes you—
27:10 strikes you—better a neighbor nearby than a **brother** far away.
Ecc 4:8 There was a man all alone; he had neither son nor **brother**.
SS 8:1 If only you were to me like a **brother**, who was nursed at my
Isa 3:6 A man will seize *one of* his **brothers** at his father's home,
9:19 [9:18] will be fuel for the fire; no one will spare his **brother**.
19:2 **brother** will fight against **brother**, neighbor against neighbor,
41:6 each helps the other and says to his **brother**, "Be strong!"
66:5 "Your **brothers** who hate you, and exclude you because of my
66:20 And they will bring all your **brothers**, from all the nations,
Jer 7:15 just as I did all your **brothers**, the people of Ephraim.'
9:4 [9:3] "Beware of your friends; do not trust your **brothers**.
9:4 [9:3] For every **brother** is a deceiver, and every friend a
12:6 Your **brothers**, your own family—even they have betrayed you;
13:14 I will smash them one against the **other**[s], fathers and sons alike,
22:18 'Alas, my **brother**! Alas, my sister!' They will not mourn for him:
23:35 This is what each of you keeps on saying to his friend or **relative**:
25:26 and all the kings of the north, near and far, one after the **other**[s]—
29:16 in this city, your **countrymen** who did not go with you into exile—
31:34 or a man his **brother**, saying, 'Know the LORD,' because they
34:9 both male and female; no one was to hold a **fellow** Jew in bondage.
34:14 'Every seventh year each of you must free any **fellow** Hebrew who
34:17 you have not proclaimed freedom for your **fellow** countrymen.
35:3 the son of Habazziniah, and his **brothers** and all his sons—
41:8 So he let them alone and did not kill them with the **others**[s].
49:10 His children, **relatives** and neighbors will perish, and he will be no
Eze 4:17 They will be appalled at the sight of each **other**[s] and will waste
11:15 "Son of man, your **brothers**—your brothers who are your blood
11:15 your **brothers** who are your blood relatives and the whole house of
18:10 a violent son, who sheds blood or does any of these **other**[s] things
18:18 robbed his **brother** and did what was wrong among his people.
24:23 because of your sins and groan **among yourselves** [+408+448].
33:30 **[RPH]** 'Come and hear the message that has come from the
38:21 Every man's sword will be against his **brother**.
44:25 his father or mother, son or daughter, **brother** or unmarried sister,
47:14 You are to divide it **equally among them** [+408+2257+3869].
Hos 2:1 [2:3] "Say of your **brothers**, 'My people,' and of your sisters,
12:3 [12:4] In the womb he grasped his **brother's** heel; as a man he
13:15 even though he thrives among his **brothers**. An east wind from the
Joel 2:8 They do not jostle each **other**[s]; each marches straight ahead.
Am 1:9 of captives to Edom, disregarding a treaty of **brotherhood**,
1:11 Because he pursued his **brother** with a sword, stifling all
Ob 1:10 Because of the violence against your **brother** Jacob, you will be
1:12 You should not look down on your **brother** in the day of his
Mic 5:3 [5:2] and the rest of his **brothers** return to join the Israelites.
7:2 men lie in wait to shed blood; each hunts his **brother** with a net.
Hag 2:22 and their riders will fall, each by the sword of his **brother**.
Zec 7:9 true justice; show mercy and compassion to one **another**[s].
7:10 or the poor. In your hearts do not think evil of each **other**[s].'
Mal 1:2 "Was not Esau Jacob's **brother**?" the LORD says. "Yet I have
2:10 the covenant of our fathers by breaking faith with one **another**[s]?

279 אָח *'aḥ*, n.f. [3]

firepot [2], *untranslated* [1]

Jer 36:22 winter apartment, with a fire burning in the **firepot** in front of him.
36:23 cut them off with a scribe's knife and threw them into the **firepot**,
36:23 the firepot, until the entire scroll was burned in the fire. **[RPH]**

280 אֹחַ *'ōaḥ*, n.[m.] [1]

jackals [1]

Isa 13:21 But desert creatures will lie there, **jackals** will fill her houses;

281 אַחְאָב *'aḥ'āb*, n.pr.m. [92] [√ 278 + 3]

Ahab [79], Ahab's [7], he[s] [3], *untranslated* [2], he[s] [+1201+6687] [1]

1Ki 16:28 was buried in Samaria. And **Ahab** his son succeeded him as king.
16:29 of Asa king of Judah, **Ahab** son of Omri became king of Israel,
16:29 **he**[s] [+1201+6687] reigned in Samaria over Israel twenty-two
16:30 **Ahab** son of Omri did more evil in the eyes of the LORD than
16:33 **Ahab** also made an Asherah pole and did more to provoke the
16:33 an Asherah pole and did more **[RPH]** to provoke the LORD,
17:1 said to **Ahab**, "As the LORD, the God of Israel, lives, whom I
18:1 "Go and present yourself to **Ahab**, and I will send rain on the
18:2 So Elijah went to present himself to **Ahab**. Now the famine was
18:3 **Ahab** had summoned Obadiah, who was in charge of his palace.
18:5 **Ahab** had said to Obadiah, "Go through the land to all the springs
18:6 to cover, **Ahab** going in one direction and Obadiah in another.
18:9 "that you are handing your servant over to **Ahab** to be put to
18:12 If I go and tell **Ahab** and he doesn't find you, he will kill me.
18:16 So Obadiah went to meet **Ahab** and told him, and Ahab went to
18:16 went to meet Ahab and told him, and **Ahab** went to meet Elijah.
18:17 When **he**[s] saw Elijah, he said to him, "Is that you, you troubler of
18:17 When he saw Elijah, **he**[s] said to him, "Is that you, you troubler of
18:20 So **Ahab** sent word throughout all Israel and assembled the
18:41 Elijah said to **Ahab**, "Go, eat and drink, for there is the sound of a
18:42 So **Ahab** went off to eat and drink, but Elijah climbed to the top of
18:44 So Elijah said, "Go and tell **Ahab**, 'Hitch up your chariot and go
18:45 the wind rose, a heavy rain came on and **Ahab** rode off to Jezreel.
18:46 his cloak into his belt, he ran ahead of **Ahab** all the way to Jezreel.
19:1 Now **Ahab** told Jezebel everything Elijah had done and how he
20:2 He sent messengers into the city to **Ahab** king of Israel, saying,
20:13 Meanwhile a prophet came to **Ahab** king of Israel and announced,
20:14 asked **Ahab**. The prophet replied, "This is what the LORD says:
21:1 was in Jezreel, close to the palace of **Ahab** king of Samaria.
21:2 **Ahab** said to Naboth, "Let me have your vineyard to use for a
21:3 **[RPH]** "The LORD forbid that I should give you the inheritance
21:4 So **Ahab** went home, sullen and angry because Naboth the
21:8 So she wrote letters in **Ahab's** name, placed his seal on them,
21:15 she said to **Ahab**, "Get up and take possession of the vineyard of
21:16 When **Ahab** heard that Naboth was dead, he got up and went down
21:16 **he**[s] got up and went down to take possession of Naboth's vineyard.
21:18 "Go down to meet **Ahab** king of Israel, who rules in Samaria.
21:20 **Ahab** said to Elijah, "So you have found me, my enemy!"
21:21 your descendants and cut off from **Ahab** every last male in Israel—
21:24 "Dogs will eat those belonging to **Ahab** who die in the city,
21:25 (There was never a man like **Ahab**, who sold himself to do evil in
21:27 When **Ahab** heard these words, he tore his clothes, put on
21:29 "Have you noticed how **Ahab** has humbled himself before me?
22:20 'Who will entice **Ahab** into attacking Ramoth Gilead and going to
22:39 As for the other events of **Ahab's** reign, including all he did,
22:40 **Ahab** rested with his fathers. And Ahaziah his son succeeded him
22:41 became king of Judah in the fourth year of **Ahab** king of Israel.
22:49 [22:50] At that time Ahaziah son of **Ahab** said to Jehoshaphat,
22:51 [22:52] Ahaziah son of **Ahab** became king of Israel in Samaria in
2Ki 1:1 After **Ahab's** death, Moab rebelled against Israel.
3:1 Joram son of **Ahab** became king of Israel in Samaria in the
3:5 after **Ahab** died, the king of Moab rebelled against the king of
8:16 In the fifth year of Joram son of **Ahab** king of Israel,
8:18 as the house of **Ahab** had done, for he married a daughter of Ahab.
8:18 as the house of Ahab had done, for he married a daughter of **Ahab**.
8:25 In the twelfth year of Joram son of **Ahab** king of Israel,
8:27 He walked in the ways of the house of **Ahab** and did evil in the
8:27 did evil in the eyes of the LORD, as the house of **Ahab** had done,
8:27 Ahab had done, for he was related by marriage to **Ahab's** family.
8:28 Ahaziah went with Joram son of **Ahab** to war against Hazael king
8:29 king of Judah went down to Jezreel to see Joram son of **Ahab**,
9:7 You are to destroy the house of **Ahab** your master, and I will
9:8 The whole house of **Ahab** will perish. I will cut off from Ahab
9:8 I will cut off from **Ahab** every last male in Israel—slave or free.
9:9 I will make the house of **Ahab** like the house of Jeroboam son of
9:25 I were riding together in chariots behind **Ahab** his father when the
9:29 (In the eleventh year of Joram son of **Ahab**, Ahaziah had become
10:1 Now there were in Samaria seventy sons of the house of **Ahab**.
10:1 of Jezreel, to the elders and to the guardians of **Ahab's** children.
10:10 that not a word the LORD has spoken against the house of **Ahab**
10:11 killed everyone in Jezreel who remained of the house of **Ahab**,
10:17 to Samaria, he killed all who were left there of **Ahab's** family;
10:18 all the people together and said to them, "**Ahab** served Baal a little;
10:30 and have done to the house of **Ahab** all I had in mind to do,
21:3 and made an Asherah pole, as **Ahab** king of Israel had done.
21:13 and the plumb line used against the house of **Ahab**.
2Ch 18:1 and honor, and he allied himself with **Ahab** by marriage.
18:2 Some years later he went down to visit **Ahab** in Samaria. Ahab
18:2 **Ahab** slaughtered many sheep and cattle for him and the people
18:3 **Ahab** king of Israel asked Jehoshaphat king of Judah, "Will you go
18:19 'Who will entice **Ahab** king of Israel into attacking Ramoth Gilead
21:6 as the house of **Ahab** had done, for he married a daughter of Ahab.
21:6 as the house of Ahab had done, for he married a daughter of **Ahab**.
21:13 Jerusalem to prostitute themselves, just as the house of **Ahab** did.
22:3 He too walked in the ways of the house of **Ahab**, for his mother
22:4 did evil in the eyes of the LORD, as the house of **Ahab** had done,

2Ch 22: 5 **Ahab** king of Israel to war against Hazael king of Aram at Ramoth
22: 6 king of Judah went down to Jezreel to see Joram son of **Ahab**
22: 7 whom the LORD had anointed to destroy the house of **Ahab**.
22: 8 While Jehu was executing judgment on the house of **Ahab**,
Jer 29: 21 says about **Ahab** son of Kolaiah and Zedekiah son of Maaseiah,
Mic 6: 16 the statutes of Omri and all the practices of **Ahab's** house,

282 אֶחָב *'eḥāb*, n.pr.m. [1] [√ 278 + 3]

Ahab [1]

Jer 29: 22 'The LORD treat you like Zedekiah and **Ahab**, whom the king of

283 אַחְבָּן *'aḥbān*, n.pr.m. [1]

Ahban [1]

1Ch 2: 29 wife was named Abihail, who bore him **Ahban** and Molid.

284 אָחַד *'āḥad*, v. [1] [cf. 2523]

slash [1]

Eze 21: 16 [21:21] [F] O sword, **slash** to the right, then to the left,

285 אֶחָד *'eḥād*, a.num. [970] [→ 287; cf. 2522; Ar 10248]

one [467], a [78], *untranslated* [72], each [58], first [39], same [32], other[s] [27], any [16], single [13], another[s] [12], eleven [+6926] [6], once [6], the [6], together [+285+448] [6], certain [5], an [4], eleventh [+6926] [4], forty-one [+752+2256] [4], man[s] [4], only [4], twenty-first [+2256+6929] [4], twenty-one [+2256+6929] [4], unit [4], any [+3972] [3], common [3], eleven [+6925] [3], next [3], once [+7193] [3], one and the same [3], some [3], thirty-one [+2256+8993] [3], 41,500 [+547+752+2256+2256+2822+4395] [2], 621 [+2256+4395+6929 +9252] [2], agree [+2118+3869] [2], alike [2], all [2], back and forth [+285+2178+2178+2256] [2], did the same[s] [+285+448+2489] [2], identical [2], numbered [+3869] [2], second [2], the other[s] [2], unique [2], yearly [+928+9102] [2], 151,450 [+547+547+752+2256+2256 +2256+2256+2822+2822+4395+4395] [1], 61 [+2256+9252] [1], 61,000 [+547+2256+9252] [1], 721 [+2256+2256+4395+6929+8679] [1], all [+928] [1], all the same [1], all together [+408+3869] [1], alone [+928] [1], annual [+928+2021+9102] [1], another [1], appointed [1], daily [+3427+4200] [1], each one [1], equally [+3869] [1], fellow[s] [1], few [1], for a while [+3427] [1], forty-first [+752+2256] [1], in unison [+3869] [1], joined together [+3869+6641] [1], none [+4202] [1], once for all [1], one time [1], one way [+928] [1], one-tenth [+6928] [1], only a few [1], over here [+4200+6298] [1], over there [+4200+6298] [1], same one [1], shoulder to shoulder [+8900] [1], singleness [1], some[s] other [1], someone [+2021+6639] [1], someone [1], suddenly [+928] [1], third[s] [1], thirty-first [+2256+8993] [1], time and again [+2256+4202+4202+9109] [1], together [+3869] [1], undivided [1], unheard-of [1], unity [1], whatever[s] [1], wherever [+889+928 +2021+5226] [1], whose[s] [+2021+2021+9108] [1]

Ge 1: 5 And there was evening, and there was morning—the **first** day.
1: 9 God said, "Let the water under the sky be gathered to **one** place,
2: 11 The name of the **first** is the Pishon; it winds through the entire land
2: 21 he took **one** of the man's ribs and closed up the place with flesh.
2: 24 and be united to his wife, and they will become **one** flesh.
3: 22 "The man has now become like **one** of us, knowing good and evil.
4: 19 married two women, **one** named Adah and the other Zillah.
8: 5 on the **first** day of the tenth month the tops of the mountains
8: 13 By the **first** day of the first month of Noah's six hundred and first
8: 13 first day of the first month of Noah's six hundred and **first** year,
10: 25 **One** was named Peleg, because in his time the earth was divided;
11: 1 Now the whole world had **one** language and a common speech.
11: 1 Now the whole world had one language and a **common** speech.
11: 6 "If as **one** people speaking the same language they have begun to
11: 6 "If as one people speaking the **same** language they have begun to
19: 9 they said, "This **fellow**[s] came here as an alien, and now he wants to
21: 15 in the skin was gone, she put the boy under **one** *of* the bushes.
22: 2 Sacrifice him there as a burnt offering on **one** *of* the mountains I
22: 13 and there in a thicket he saw **a** [BHS 339] ram caught by its horns.
26: 10 **One** *of* the men might well have slept with your wife, and you
27: 38 Esau said to his father, "Do you have only **one** blessing, my father?
27: 44 Stay with him **for a while** [+3427] until your brother's fury
27: 45 come back from there. Why should I lose both of you in **one** day?"
29: 20 they seemed like **only a few** days to him because of his love for
32: 8 [32:9] He thought, "If Esau comes and attacks **one** group,
32: 22 [32:23] his two maidservants and his **eleven** [+6925] sons
33: 13 If they are driven hard just **one** day, all the animals will die.
34: 16 We'll settle among you and become **one** people with you.
34: 22 the men will consent to live with us as **one** people only on the
37: 9 and moon and **eleven** [+6925] stars were bowing down to me."
37: 20 let's kill him and throw him into **one** *of* these cisterns and say that
40: 5 had a dream the **same** night, and each dream had a meaning of its
41: 5 heads of grain, healthy and good, were growing on a **single** stalk.
41: 11 Each of us had a dream the **same** night, and each dream had a
41: 22 saw seven heads of grain, full and good, growing on a **single** stalk.
41: 25 said to Pharaoh, "The dreams of Pharaoh are **one and the same**.
41: 26 good heads of grain are seven years; it is **one and the same** dream.
42: 11 We are all the sons of **one** man. Your servants are honest men,
42: 13 the sons of **one** man, who lives in the land of Canaan.
42: 13 The youngest is now with our father, and **one** is no more."
42: 16 Send **one** of your number to get your brother; the rest of you will
42: 19 If you are honest men, let **one** *of* your brothers stay here in prison,
42: 27 At the place where they stopped for the night **one** of them opened
42: 32 **One** is no more, and the youngest is now with our father in
42: 33 Leave **one** *of* your brothers here with me, and take food for your
44: 28 **One** *of them* went away from me, and I said, "He has surely been
48: 22 to you, as **one** *who* is over your brothers, I give the ridge of land I
49: 16 "Dan will provide justice for his people as **one** *of* the tribes of
Ex 1: 15 Hebrew midwives, whose names **[NIE]** were Shiphrah and Puah,
8: 31 [8:27] and his officials and his people; not **a** fly remained.
9: 6 Egyptians died, but not **one** animal belonging to the Israelites died.
9: 7 found that not even **one** of the animals of the Israelites had died.
10: 19 them into the Red Sea. Not **a** locust was left anywhere in Egypt.
11: 1 to Moses, "I will bring **one** more plague on Pharaoh and on Egypt.
12: 18 until the evening of the **twenty-first** [+2256+6929] day.
12: 46 "It must be eaten inside **one** house; take none of the meat outside
12: 49 The **same** law applies to the native-born and to the alien living
14: 28 had followed the Israelites into the sea. Not **one** of them survived.
16: 22 they gathered twice as much—two omers for **each** *person*—
16: 33 Moses said to Aaron, "Take **a** jar and put an omer of manna in it.
17: 12 and Hur held his hands up—**one** on one side, one on the other—
17: 12 and Hur held his hands up—one on one side, **one** on the other—
18: 3 **One** son was named Gershom, for Moses said, "I have become an
18: 4 the **other**[s] was named Eliezer, for he said, "My father's God was
23: 29 I will not drive them out in a **single** year, because the land would
24: 3 all the LORD's words and laws, they responded with **one** voice,
25: 12 its four feet, with two rings on **one** side and two rings on the other.
25: 19 Make **one** cherub on one end and the second cherub on the other;
25: 19 Make one cherub on one end and the **second** cherub on the other;
25: 32 sides of the lampstand—three on **one** side and three on the other.
25: 33 almond flowers with buds and blossoms are to be on **one** branch,
25: 33 and blossoms are to be on one branch, three on the **next** branch,
25: 36 and branches shall all be of **one** *piece* with the lampstand,
26: 2 All the curtains are to be the **same** size—twenty-eight cubits long
26: 2 same size—twenty-eight cubits long **[RPH]** and four cubits wide.
26: 2 same size—twenty-eight cubits long and four cubits wide. **[RPH]**
26: 4 loops of blue material along the edge of the end curtain in **one** set,
26: 5 Make fifty loops on **one** curtain and fifty loops on the end curtain
26: 6 them to fasten the curtains together so that the tabernacle is a **unit**.
26: 8 All eleven curtains are to be the **same** size—thirty cubits long
26: 8 be the same size—thirty cubits long **[RPH]** and four cubits wide.
26: 8 be the same size—thirty cubits long and four cubits wide. **[RPH]**
26: 10 Make fifty loops along the edge of the end curtain in **one** set
26: 11 and put them in the loops to fasten the tent together as a **unit**.
26: 16 **Each** frame is to be ten cubits long and a cubit and a half wide,
26: 17 with two projections **[NIE]** set parallel to each other. Make all the
26: 19 under them—two bases for **each** frame, one under each projection.
26: 19 two bases for each frame, one under each projection. **[RPH]**
26: 21 and forty silver bases—two under **each** frame.
26: 21 and forty silver bases—two under each frame. **[RPH]**
26: 24 from the bottom all the way to the top, and fitted into a **single** ring;
26: 25 be eight frames and sixteen silver bases—two under **each** frame.
26: 25 and sixteen silver bases—two under each frame. **[RPH]**
26: 26 of acacia wood: five for the frames on **one** side of the tabernacle,
27: 9 cubits long **[NIE]** and is to have curtains of finely twisted linen,
28: 10 six names on **one** stone and the remaining six on the other.
28: 17 on it. In the **first** row there shall be a ruby, a topaz and a beryl;
29: 1 me as priests: Take **a** young bull and two rams without defect.
29: 3 Put them in **a** basket and present them in it—along with the bull
29: 15 "Take **one** of the rams, and Aaron and his sons shall lay their
29: 23 the LORD, take **a** loaf, and a cake made with oil, and a wafer.
29: 23 the LORD, take a loaf, and **a** cake made with oil, and a wafer.
29: 23 the LORD, take a loaf, and a cake made with oil, and **a** wafer.
29: 39 Offer **one** in the morning and the other at twilight.
29: 40 With the **first** lamb offer a tenth of an ephah of fine flour mixed
30: 10 **Once** a year Aaron shall make atonement on its horns. This annual
30: 10 This **annual** [+928+2021+9102] atonement must be made with the
33: 5 If I were to go with you even for **a** moment, I might destroy you.
36: 9 **All** the curtains were the same size—twenty-eight cubits long
36: 9 All the curtains **[RPH]** were the same size—twenty-eight cubits
36: 9 All the curtains were the **same** size—twenty-eight cubits long
36: 10 They joined five of the curtains **together** [+285+448] and did the
36: 10 They joined five of the curtains **together** [+285+448] and did the
36: 10 and **did**[s] **the same with** [+285+448+2489] the other five.
36: 10 and **did**[s] **the same with** [+285+448+2489] the other five.
36: 11 loops of blue material along the edge of the end curtain in **one** set,
36: 12 They also made fifty loops on **one** curtain and fifty loops on the
36: 12 the end curtain of the other set, with the loops opposite **each** other.

Ex 36:12 end curtain of the other set, with the loops opposite each **other**[s].
36:13 used them to fasten the two sets of curtains **together** [+285+448]
36:13 used them to fasten the two sets of curtains **together** [+285+448]
36:13 the two sets of curtains together so that the tabernacle was a **unit**.
36:15 **All** eleven curtains were the same size—thirty cubits long
36:15 All eleven curtains were the **same** size—thirty cubits long
36:15 the same size—thirty cubits long and four cubits wide. **[RPH]**
36:18 They made fifty bronze clasps to fasten the tent together as a **unit**.
36:21 **Each** frame was ten cubits long and a cubit and a half wide,
36:22 with two projections set parallel to **each** other. They made all the
36:22 with two projections set parallel to each **other**[s]. They made all the
36:22 **[RPH]** They made all the frames of the tabernacle in this way.
36:24 under them—two bases for **each** frame, one under each projection.
36:24 two bases for each frame, one under each projection. **[RPH]**
36:26 and forty silver bases—two under **each** frame.
36:26 and forty silver bases—two under each frame. **[RPH]**
36:29 from the bottom all the way to the top and fitted into a **single** ring;
36:30 were eight frames and sixteen silver bases—two under **each** frame.
36:31 of acacia wood: five for the frames on **one** side of the tabernacle,
37:3 its four feet, with two rings on **one** side and two rings on the other.
37:8 He made **one** cherub on one end and the second cherub on the
37:8 made one cherub on one end and the **second** cherub on the other;
37:18 sides of the lampstand—three on **one** side and three on the other.
37:19 like almond flowers with buds and blossoms were on **one** branch,
37:19 three on the **next** branch and the same for all six branches
37:22 one piece with the lampstand, hammered out of **[NIE]** pure gold.
39:10 stones on it. In the **first** row there was a ruby, a topaz and a beryl;
40:2 the Tent of Meeting, on the **first** day of the first month.
40:17 So the tabernacle was set up on the **first** day of the first month in
Lev 4:2 what is forbidden in any of the LORD's commands—**[RPH]**
4:13 does what is forbidden in **any of** [+3972] the LORD's commands,
4:22 does what is forbidden in **any of** [+3972] the commands of the
4:27 " 'If **a** member of the community sins unintentionally and does
4:27 and does what is forbidden in **any** of the LORD's commands,
5:4 is unaware of it, in **any** case when he learns of it he will be guilty.
5:5 " 'When anyone is guilty in **any** of these ways, he must confess in
5:7 his sin—**one** for a sin offering and the other for a burnt offering.
5:7 his sin—one for a sin offering and the **other**[s] for a burnt offering.
5:13 In this way the priest will make atonement for him for **any** of these
5:17 does what is forbidden in **any of** [+3972] the LORD's commands,
6:3 [5:22] or if he **[NIE]** commits any such sin that people may do—
6:7 [5:26] he will be forgiven for **any** of these things he did that made
7:7 " 'The **same** law applies to both the sin offering and the guilt
7:14 He is to bring **one** of each kind as an offering, a contribution to the
8:26 he took **a** cake of bread, and one made with oil, and a wafer;
8:26 he took a cake of bread, and **one** made with oil, and a wafer;
8:26 he took a cake of bread, and one made with oil, and **a** wafer;
12:8 **one** for a burnt offering and the other for a sin offering.
12:8 one for a burnt offering and the **other**[s] for a sin offering.
13:2 be brought to Aaron the priest or to **one** of his sons who is a priest.
14:5 the priest shall order that **one** of the birds be killed over fresh water
14:10 day he must bring two male lambs and **one** ewe lamb a year old,
14:10 of fine flour mixed with oil for a grain offering, and **one** log of oil.
14:12 "Then the priest is to take **one** of the male lambs and offer it as a
14:21 he must take **one** male lamb as a guilt offering to be waved to
14:21 together with **a** tenth of an ephah of fine flour mixed with oil for a
14:22 can afford, **one** for a sin offering and the other for a burnt offering.
14:22 one for a sin offering and the **other**[s] for a burnt offering.
14:30 Then he shall sacrifice the **[NIE]** doves or the young pigeons,
14:31 **one** as a sin offering and the other as a burnt offering,
14:31 one as a sin offering and the **other**[s] as a burnt offering,
14:50 He shall kill **one** of the birds over fresh water in a clay pot.
15:15 the **one** for a sin offering and the other for a burnt offering.
15:15 the one for a sin offering and the **other**[s] for a burnt offering.
15:30 The priest is to sacrifice **one** for a sin offering and the other for a
15:30 sacrifice one for a sin offering and the **other**[s] for a burnt offering.
16:5 two male goats for a sin offering and **a** ram for a burnt offering.
16:8 two goats—**one** lot for the LORD and the other for the scapegoat.
16:8 one lot for the LORD and the **other**[s] for the scapegoat.
16:34 Atonement is to be made **once** a year for all the sins of the
22:28 Do not slaughter a cow or a sheep and its young on the **same** day.
23:18 each a year old and without defect, **one** young bull and two rams.
23:19 Then sacrifice **one** male goat for a sin offering and two lambs,
23:24 'On the **first** day of the seventh month you are to have a day of
24:5 twelve loaves of bread, using two-tenths of an ephah for **each** loaf.
24:22 You are to have the **same** law for the alien and the native-born.
25:48 after he has sold himself. **One** of his relatives may redeem him:
26:26 of bread, ten women will be able to bake your bread in **one** oven,
Nu 1:1 **first** day of the second month of the second year after the Israelites
1:18 they called the whole community together on the **first** day of the
1:41 tribe of Asher was **41,500** [+547+752+2256+2256+2822+4395].
1:44 and the twelve leaders of Israel, each **one** representing his family.
2:16 of Reuben, according to their divisions, number **151,450** [+547
+547+752+2256+2256+2256+2256+2822+2822+4395+4395].
2:28 His division numbers **41,500** [+547+752+2256+2256+2822+4395].
6:11 The priest is to offer **one** as a sin offering and the other as a burnt
6:11 and the **other**[s] as a burnt offering to make atonement for him
6:14 **a** year-old male lamb without defect for a burnt offering, a year-old
6:14 **a** year-old ewe lamb without defect for a sin offering, a ram
6:14 for a sin offering, **a** ram without defect for a fellowship offering,
6:19 and **a** cake and a wafer from the basket, both made without yeast.
6:19 and a cake and **a** wafer from the basket, both made without yeast.
7:3 twelve oxen—an ox from **each** leader and a cart from every two.
7:11 "Each day **one** leader is to bring his offering for the dedication of
7:11 "Each day one leader **[RPH]** is to bring his offering for the
7:13 His offering was **one** silver plate weighing a hundred and thirty
7:13 and **one** silver sprinkling bowl weighing seventy shekels,
7:14 **one** gold dish weighing ten shekels, filled with incense;
7:15 **one** young bull, one ram and one male lamb a year old, for a burnt
7:15 one young bull, **one** ram and one male lamb a year old, for a burnt
7:15 one young bull, one ram and **one** male lamb a year old, for a burnt
7:16 **one** male goat for a sin offering;
7:19 The offering he brought was **one** silver plate weighing a hundred
7:19 and **one** silver sprinkling bowl weighing seventy shekels,
7:20 **one** gold dish weighing ten shekels, filled with incense;
7:21 **one** young bull, one ram and one male lamb a year old, for a burnt
7:21 one young bull, **one** ram and one male lamb a year old, for a burnt
7:21 one young bull, one ram and **one** male lamb a year old, for a burnt
7:22 **one** male goat for a sin offering;
7:25 His offering was **one** silver plate weighing a hundred and thirty
7:25 and **one** silver sprinkling bowl weighing seventy shekels,
7:26 **one** gold dish weighing ten shekels, filled with incense;
7:27 **one** young bull, one ram and one male lamb a year old, for a burnt
7:27 one young bull, **one** ram and one male lamb a year old, for a burnt
7:27 one young bull, one ram and **one** male lamb a year old, for a burnt
7:28 **one** male goat for a sin offering;
7:31 His offering was **one** silver plate weighing a hundred and thirty
7:31 and **one** silver sprinkling bowl weighing seventy shekels,
7:32 **one** gold dish weighing ten shekels, filled with incense;
7:33 **one** young bull, one ram and one male lamb a year old, for a burnt
7:33 one young bull, **one** ram and one male lamb a year old, for a burnt
7:33 one young bull, one ram and **one** male lamb a year old, for a burnt
7:34 **one** male goat for a sin offering;
7:37 His offering was **one** silver plate weighing a hundred and thirty
7:37 and **one** silver sprinkling bowl weighing seventy shekels,
7:38 **one** gold dish weighing ten shekels, filled with incense;
7:39 **one** young bull, one ram and one male lamb a year old, for a burnt
7:39 one young bull, **one** ram and one male lamb a year old, for a burnt
7:39 one young bull, one ram and **one** male lamb a year old, for a burnt
7:40 **one** male goat for a sin offering;
7:43 His offering was **one** silver plate weighing a hundred and thirty
7:43 and **one** silver sprinkling bowl weighing seventy shekels,
7:44 **one** gold dish weighing ten shekels, filled with incense;
7:45 **one** young bull, one ram and one male lamb a year old, for a burnt
7:45 one young bull, **one** ram and one male lamb a year old, for a burnt
7:45 one young bull, one ram and **one** male lamb a year old, for a burnt
7:46 **one** male goat for a sin offering;
7:49 His offering was **one** silver plate weighing a hundred and thirty
7:49 and **one** silver sprinkling bowl weighing seventy shekels,
7:50 **one** gold dish weighing ten shekels, filled with incense;
7:51 **one** young bull, one ram and one male lamb a year old, for a burnt
7:51 one young bull, **one** ram and one male lamb a year old, for a burnt
7:51 one young bull, one ram and **one** male lamb a year old, for a burnt
7:52 **one** male goat for a sin offering;
7:55 His offering was **one** silver plate weighing a hundred and thirty
7:55 and **one** silver sprinkling bowl weighing seventy shekels,
7:56 **one** gold dish weighing ten shekels, filled with incense;
7:57 **one** young bull, one ram and one male lamb a year old, for a burnt
7:57 one young bull, **one** ram and one male lamb a year old, for a burnt
7:57 one young bull, one ram and **one** male lamb a year old, for a burnt
7:58 **one** male goat for a sin offering;
7:61 His offering was **one** silver plate weighing a hundred and thirty
7:61 and **one** silver sprinkling bowl weighing seventy shekels,
7:62 **one** gold dish weighing ten shekels, filled with incense;
7:63 **one** young bull, one ram and one male lamb a year old, for a burnt
7:63 one young bull, **one** ram and one male lamb a year old, for a burnt
7:63 one young bull, one ram and **one** male lamb a year old, for a burnt
7:64 **one** male goat for a sin offering;
7:67 His offering was **one** silver plate weighing a hundred and thirty
7:67 and **one** silver sprinkling bowl weighing seventy shekels,
7:68 **one** gold dish weighing ten shekels, filled with incense;
7:69 **one** young bull, one ram and one male lamb a year old, for a burnt
7:69 one young bull, **one** ram and one male lamb a year old, for a burnt
7:69 one young bull, one ram and **one** male lamb a year old, for a burnt
7:70 **one** male goat for a sin offering;
7:73 His offering was **one** silver plate weighing a hundred and thirty
7:73 and **one** silver sprinkling bowl weighing seventy shekels,
7:74 **one** gold dish weighing ten shekels, filled with incense;

Nu 7:75 **one** young bull, one ram and one male lamb a year old, for a burnt
7:75 one young bull, **one** ram and one male lamb a year old, for a burnt
7:75 one young bull, one ram and **one** male lamb a year old, for a burnt
7:76 **one** male goat for a sin offering;
7:79 His offering was **one** silver plate weighing a hundred and thirty
7:79 and **one** silver sprinkling bowl weighing seventy shekels,
7:80 **one** gold dish weighing ten shekels, filled with incense;
7:81 **one** young bull, one ram and one male lamb a year old, for a burnt
7:81 one young bull, **one** ram and one male lamb a year old, for a burnt
7:81 one young bull, one ram and **one** male lamb a year old, for a burnt
7:82 **one** male goat for a sin offering;
7:85 **Each** silver plate weighed a hundred and thirty shekels, and each
7:85 and thirty shekels, and **each** sprinkling bowl seventy shekels.
8:12 use the **one** for a sin offering to the LORD and the other for a
8:12 for a sin offering to the LORD and the **other**[s] for a burnt offering,
9:14 You must have the **same** regulations for the alien and the
10:4 If only **one** is sounded, the leaders—the heads of the clans of
11:19 You will not eat it for just **one** day, or two days, or five, ten
11:26 men, **whose**[s] [+2021+2021+9108] names were Eldad and Medad,
13:2 to the Israelites. From each ancestral tribe send **one** of its leaders."
13:2 From each ancestral tribe send one **[RPH]** of its leaders."
13:23 of Eshcol, they cut off a branch bearing a **single** cluster of grapes.
14:15 If you put these people to death all at **one time**, the nations who
15:5 With **each** lamb for the burnt offering or the sacrifice, prepare a
15:11 **Each** bull or ram, each lamb or young goat, is to be prepared in
15:11 Each bull or ram, **[RPH]** each lamb or young goat, is to be
15:12 Do this for **each one**, for as many as you prepare.
15:15 The community is to have the **same** rules for you and for the alien
15:16 The **same** laws and regulations will apply both to you and to the
15:16 The same laws and regulations **[RPH]** will apply both to you
15:24 the whole community is to offer **a** young bull for a burnt offering
15:24 and drink offering, and **a** male goat for a sin offering.
15:27 " 'But if just **one** person sins unintentionally, he must bring a
15:29 **One and the same** law applies to everyone who sins
16:15 I have not taken so much as a donkey from them, nor have I
16:15 so much as a donkey from them, nor have I wronged **any** of them."
16:22 will you be angry with the entire assembly when only **one** man
17:3 [17:18] for there must be **one** staff for the head of each ancestral
17:6 [17:21] **one** for the leader of each of their ancestral tribes, and
17:6 [17:21] **[RPH]** and Aaron's staff was among them.
28:4 Prepare **one** lamb in the morning and the other at twilight,
28:7 is to be a quarter of a hin of fermented drink with **each** lamb.
28:11 **one** ram and seven male lambs a year old, all without defect.
28:12 With **each** bull there is to be a grain offering of three-tenths of an
28:12 of two-tenths of an ephah of fine flour mixed with oil; **[RPH]**
28:13 with **each** lamb, a grain offering of a tenth of an ephah of fine flour
28:15 **one** male goat is to be presented to the LORD as a sin offering.
28:19 **one** ram and seven male lambs a year old, all without defect.
28:21 and with **each** of the seven lambs, one-tenth.
28:22 Include **one** male goat as a sin offering to make atonement for you.
28:27 **one** ram and seven male lambs a year old as an aroma pleasing to
28:28 With **each** bull there is to be a grain offering of three-tenths of an
28:28 of fine flour mixed with oil; with the ram, **[RPH]** two-tenths;
28:29 and with **each** *of* the seven lambs, one-tenth.
28:30 Include **one** male goat to make atonement for you.
29:1 " 'On the **first** day of the seventh month hold a sacred assembly
29:2 prepare a burnt offering of **one** young bull, one ram and seven
29:2 **one** ram and seven male lambs a year old, all without defect.
29:4 and with **each** of the seven lambs, one-tenth.
29:4 and with each of the seven lambs, **one-tenth** [+6928].
29:5 Include **one** male goat as a sin offering to make atonement for you.
29:8 Present as an aroma pleasing to the LORD a burnt offering of **one**
29:8 **one** ram and seven male lambs a year old, all without defect.
29:9 of fine flour mixed with oil; with the ram, **[RPH]** two-tenths;
29:10 and with **each** of the seven lambs, one-tenth.
29:11 Include **one** male goat as a sin offering, in addition to the sin
29:14 With **each** of the thirteen bulls prepare a grain offering of
29:14 of fine flour mixed with oil; with **each** of the two rams, two-tenths;
29:15 and with **each** of the fourteen lambs, one-tenth.
29:16 Include **one** male goat as a sin offering, in addition to the regular
29:19 Include **one** male goat as a sin offering, in addition to the regular
29:22 Include **one** male goat as a sin offering, in addition to the regular
29:25 Include **one** male goat as a sin offering, in addition to the regular
29:28 Include **one** male goat as a sin offering, in addition to the regular
29:31 Include **one** male goat as a sin offering, in addition to the regular
29:34 Include **one** male goat as a sin offering, in addition to the regular
29:36 a burnt offering of **one** bull, one ram and seven male lambs a year
29:36 **one** ram and seven male lambs a year old, all without defect.
29:38 Include **one** male goat as a sin offering, in addition to the regular
31:28 set apart as tribute for the LORD **one** out of every five hundred,
31:30 select **one** out of every fifty, whether persons, cattle, donkeys,
31:34 **61,000** [+547+2256+9252] donkeys
31:39 of which the tribute for the LORD was **61** [+2256+9252];
31:47 Moses selected **one** out of every fifty persons and animals,
33:38 where he died on the **first** day of the fifth month of the fortieth
34:18 And appoint **one** leader from each tribe to help assign the land.
34:18 And appoint one leader from **each** tribe to help assign the land.
35:30 no one is to be put to death on the testimony of only **one** witness.
36:3 Now suppose they marry men from **other**[s] Israelite tribes;
36:8 any Israelite tribe must marry **someone** in her father's tribal clan,
Dt 1:2 (It takes **eleven** [+6925] days to go from Horeb to Kadesh Barnea
1:3 In the fortieth year, on the **first** day of the eleventh month,
1:23 good to me; so I selected twelve of you, **one** man from each tribe.
4:42 He could flee into **one** of these cities and save his life.
6:4 Hear, O Israel: The LORD our God, the LORD is **one**.
12:14 Offer them only at the place the LORD will choose in **one** *of* your
13:12 [13:13] If you hear it said about **one** *of* the towns the LORD
15:7 If there is a poor man among **[RPH]** your brothers in any of the
15:7 If there is a poor man among your brothers in **any** *of* the towns of
16:5 You must not sacrifice the Passover in **any** town the LORD your
17:2 or woman living among you in **one** *of* the towns the LORD gives
17:6 no one shall be put to death on the testimony of only **one** witness.
18:6 If a Levite moves from **one** *of* your towns anywhere in Israel
19:5 That man may flee to **one** *of* these cities and save his life.
19:11 assaults and kills him, and then flees to **one** *of* these cities,
19:15 **One** witness is not enough to convict a man accused of any crime
21:15 and he loves **one** but not the other, and both bear him sons
21:15 and he loves one but not the **other**[s], and both bear him sons
23:16 [23:17] you wherever he likes and in **whatever**[s] town he chooses.
24:5 For **one** year he is to be free to stay at home and bring happiness to
25:5 If brothers are living together and **one** of them dies without a son,
25:11 the wife of **one** of them comes to rescue her husband from his
28:7 They will come at you from **one** direction but flee from you in
28:25 You will come at them from **one** direction but flee from them in
28:55 he will not give to **one** of them any of the flesh of his children that
32:30 How could **one** *man* chase a thousand, or two put ten thousand to
Jos 3:12 choose twelve men from the tribes of Israel, **one** from each tribe.
3:12 twelve men from the tribes of Israel, one **[RPH]** from each tribe.
3:13 waters flowing downstream will be cut off and stand up in **a** heap."
3:16 It piled up in **a** heap a great distance away, at a town called Adam
4:2 "Choose twelve men from among the people, **one** from each tribe,
4:2 twelve men from among the people, one **[RPH]** from each tribe,
4:4 men he had appointed from the Israelites, **one** from each tribe,
4:4 he had appointed from the Israelites, one **[RPH]** from each tribe,
4:5 Each of you is to take up **a** stone on his shoulder, according to the
6:3 March around the city **once** [+7193] with all the armed men.
6:11 ark of the LORD carried around the city, circling it **once** [+7193].
6:14 So on the second day they marched around the city **once** [+7193]
7:21 When I saw in the plunder **a** beautiful robe from Babylonia,
7:21 shekels of silver and **a** wedge of gold weighing fifty shekels,
9:2 they came together to make war against Joshua and Israel. **[NIE]**
10:2 because Gibeon was an important city, like **one** *of* the royal cities;
10:42 All these kings and their lands Joshua conquered in **one** campaign,
12:9 the king of Jericho **one** the king of Ai (near Bethel) one
12:9 the king of Jericho one the king of Ai (near Bethel) **one**
12:10 the king of Jerusalem **one** the king of Hebron one
12:10 the king of Jerusalem one the king of Hebron **one**
12:11 the king of Jarmuth **one** the king of Lachish one
12:11 the king of Jarmuth one the king of Lachish **one**
12:12 the king of Eglon **one** the king of Gezer one
12:12 the king of Eglon one the king of Gezer **one**
12:13 the king of Debir **one** the king of Geder one
12:13 the king of Debir one the king of Geder **one**
12:14 the king of Hormah **one** the king of Arad one
12:14 the king of Hormah one the king of Arad **one**
12:15 the king of Libnah **one** the king of Adullam one
12:15 the king of Libnah one the king of Adullam **one**
12:16 the king of Makkedah **one** the king of Bethel one
12:16 the king of Makkedah one the king of Bethel **one**
12:17 the king of Tappuah **one** the king of Hepher one
12:17 the king of Tappuah one the king of Hepher **one**
12:18 the king of Aphek **one** the king of Lasharon one
12:18 the king of Aphek one the king of Lasharon **one**
12:19 the king of Madon **one** the king of Hazor one
12:19 the king of Madon one the king of Hazor **one**
12:20 the king of Shimron Meron **one** the king of Acshaph one
12:20 the king of Shimron Meron one the king of Acshaph **one**
12:21 the king of Taanach **one** the king of Megiddo one
12:21 the king of Taanach one the king of Megiddo **one**
12:22 the king of Kedesh **one** the king of Jokneam in Carmel one
12:22 the king of Kedesh one the king of Jokneam in Carmel **one**
12:23 king of Dor (in Naphoth Dor) **one** the king of Goyim in Gilgal one
12:23 king of Dor (in Naphoth Dor) one the king of Goyim in Gilgal **one**
12:24 the king of Tirzah **one** thirty-one kings in all.
12:24 the king of Tirzah one **thirty-one** [+2256+8993] kings in all.
15:51 Holon and Giloh—**eleven** [+6926] towns and their villages.
17:14 "Why have you given us only **one** allotment and one portion for an
17:14 given us only one allotment and **one** portion for an inheritance?

Jos 17:17 and very powerful. You will have not only **one** allotment
20: 4 "When he flees to **one** of these cities, he is to stand in the entrance
22:14 they sent ten of the chief men, **one** for each of the tribes of Israel,
22:14 ten of the chief men, one **[RPH]** for each of the tribes of Israel,
22:20 of Israel? He was not the **only** one who died for his sin.' "
23:10 **One** of you routs a thousand, because the LORD your God fights
23:14 soul that not **one** of all the good promises the LORD your God
23:14 has failed. Every promise has been fulfilled; not **one** has failed.
Jdg 4:16 All the troops of Sisera fell by the sword; not a **man**[s] was left.
6:16 you will strike down **all** the Midianites **together** [+408+3869]."
8:18 like you," they answered, "*each* **one** with the bearing of a prince."
9: 2 all seventy of Jerub-Baal's sons rule over you, or just **one** man?'
9: 5 home in Ophrah and on **one** stone murdered his seventy brothers,
9:18 murdered his seventy sons on a **single** stone, and made Abimelech,
9:37 **a** company is coming from the direction of the soothsayers' tree."
9:53 a woman dropped **an** upper millstone on his head and cracked his
13: 2 A **certain** man of Zorah, named Manoah, from the clan of the
15: 4 tail to tail in pairs. He then fastened **a** torch to every pair of tails,
16: 7 that have not been dried, I'll become as weak as **any** other man."
16:11 that have never been used, I'll become as weak as **any** other man."
16:13 it with the pin, I'll become as weak as **any** [BHS-] other man."
16:28 let me with **one** *blow* get revenge on the Philistines for my two
16:29 his right hand on the **one** and his left hand on the other,
16:29 his right hand on the one and his left hand on the **other**[s],
17: 5 an ephod and some idols and installed **one** of his sons as his priest.
17:11 live with him, and the young man was to him like **one** of his sons.
18:19 and clan in Israel as priest rather than just **one** man's household?"
19:13 or Ramah and spend the night in **one** *of* those places."
20: 1 to Beersheba and from the land of Gilead came out as **one** man
20: 8 All the people rose as **one** man, saying, "None of us will go home.
20:11 men of Israel got together and united as **one** man against the city.
20:31 on the roads—the **one** leading to Bethel and the other to Gibeah.
20:31 on the roads—the one leading to Bethel and the **other**[s] to Gibeah.
21: 3 to Israel? Why should **one** tribe be missing from Israel today?"
21: 6 the Benjamites. "Today **one** tribe is cut off from Israel," they said.
21: 8 "Which **one** of the tribes of Israel failed to assemble before the
Ru 1: 4 married Moabite women, **one** named Orpah and the other Ruth.
2:13 though I do not have the standing of **one** *of* your servant girls."
1Sa 1: 1 There was a **certain** man from Ramathaim, a Zuphite from the hill
1: 2 He had two wives; **one** was called Hannah and the other Peninnah.
1: 5 But to Hannah he gave **a** double portion because he loved her,
1:24 with a three-year-old bull, **an** ephah of flour and a skin of wine,
2:34 will be a sign to you—they will both die on the **same** day.
2:36 "Appoint me to **some** priestly office so I can have food to eat." '"
6: 4 because the **same** plague has struck both you and your rulers.
6: 7 "Now then, get **a** new cart ready, with two cows that have calved
6:12 toward Beth Shemesh, keeping on **the** road and lowing all the way;
6:17 **one** *each* for Ashdod, Gaza, Ashkelon, Gath and Ekron.
6:17 one each for Ashdod, Gaza, **[RPH]** Ashkelon, Gath and Ekron.
6:17 one each for Ashdod, Gaza, Ashkelon, **[RPH]** Gath and Ekron.
6:17 one each for Ashdod, Gaza, Ashkelon, Gath **[RPH]** and Ekron.
6:17 one each for Ashdod, Gaza, Ashkelon, Gath and Ekron. **[RPH]**
7: 9 Samuel took **a** suckling lamb and offered it up as a whole burnt
7:12 Then Samuel took **a** stone and set it up between Mizpah and Shen.
9: 3 "Take **one** of the servants with you and go and look for the
9:15 Now **the** day before Saul came, the LORD had revealed this to
10: 3 **One** will be carrying three young goats, another three loaves of
10: 3 **another**[s] three loaves of bread, and another a skin of wine.
10: 3 another three loaves of bread, and **another**[s] a skin of wine.
11: 7 of the LORD fell on the people, and they turned out as **one** man.
13:17 **One** turned toward Ophrah in the vicinity of Shual,
13:18 **another**[s] toward Beth Horon, and the third toward the borderland
13:18 the **third**[s] toward the borderland overlooking the Valley of Zeboim
14: 4 outpost was a cliff; **one** was called Bozez, and the other Seneh.
14: 4 outpost was a cliff; one was called Bozez, and the **other**[s] Seneh.
14: 5 **One** cliff stood to the north toward Micmash, the other to the south
14: 5 to the north toward Micmash, the **other**[s] to the south toward Geba.
14:40 said to all the Israelites, "You stand **over there** [+4200+6298];
14:40 and Jonathan my son will stand **over here** [+4200+6298]."
16:18 **One** of the servants answered, "I have seen a son of Jesse of
16:20 a skin of wine and **a** young goat and sent them with his son David
17:36 this uncircumcised Philistine will be like **one** of them, because he
22:20 **a** son of Ahimelech son of Ahitub, escaped and fled to join David.
24:14 [24:15] come out? Whom are you pursuing? A dead dog? **A** flea?
25:14 **One** of the servants told Nabal's wife Abigail: "David sent
26: 8 Now let me pin him to the ground with **one** thrust of my spear;
26:15 **Someone** [+2021+6639] came to destroy your lord the king.
26:20 The king of Israel has come out to look for **a** flea—as one hunts a
26:22 "Let **one** of your young men come over and get it.
27: 1 "**One** of these days I will be destroyed by the hand of Saul.
27: 5 let a place be assigned to me in **one** *of* the country towns, that I
2Sa 1:15 David called **one** of his men and said, "Go, strike him down!"
2: 1 "Shall I go up to **one** *of* the towns of Judah?" he asked. The
2:18 and Asahel. Now Asahel was as fleet-footed as **a** wild gazelle.
2:21 take on **one** of the young men and strip him of his weapons."
2:25 They formed themselves into **a** group and took their stand on top
2:25 themselves into a group and took their stand on top of **a** hill.
3:13 will make an agreement with you. But I demand **one** thing of you:
4: 2 **One** was named Baanah and the other Recab; they were sons of
6:19 he gave **a** loaf of bread, a cake of dates and a cake of raisins to
6:19 **a** cake of dates and a cake of raisins to each person in the whole
6:19 **a** cake of raisins to each person in the whole crowd of Israelites,
6:20 disrobing in the sight of the slave girls of his servants as **any**
7: 7 did I ever say to **any** *of* their rulers whom I commanded to
7:23 the **one** nation on earth that God went out to redeem as a people for
9:11 So Mephibosheth ate at David's table like **one** of the king's sons.
12: 1 he said, "There were two men in a **certain** town, one rich
12: 1 were two men in a certain town, **one** rich and the other poor.
12: 1 were two men in a certain town, one rich and the **other**[s] poor.
12: 3 the poor man had nothing except **one** little ewe lamb he had
13:13 about you? You would be like **one** *of* the wicked fools in Israel.
13:30 has struck down all the king's sons; not **one** of them is left."
14: 6 was there to separate them. **One** struck the other and killed him.
14: 6 was there to separate them. One struck the **other**[s] and killed him.
14:27 Three sons and **a** daughter were born to Absalom. The daughter's
15: 2 would answer, "Your servant is from **one** *of* the tribes of Israel."
17: 9 Even now, he is hidden in **a** cave or some other place. If he should
17: 9 Even now, he is hidden in a cave or **some**[s] **other** place. If he
17:12 we will attack him **wherever** [+889+928+2021+5226] he may be
17:12 Neither he nor any of his men will be left alive. **[NIE]**
17:22 By daybreak, no **one** was left who had not crossed the Jordan.
18:10 When **one** of the men saw this, he told Joab, "I just saw Absalom
18:11 have had to give you ten shekels of silver and **a** warrior's belt."
19:14 [19:15] of all the men of Judah as though they were **one** man.
23: 8 spear against eight hundred men, whom he killed in **one** encounter.
24:12 Choose **one** of them for me to carry out against you.' "
1Ki 2:16 Now I have **one** request to make of you. Do not refuse me."
2:20 "I have **one** small request to make of you," she said. "Do not refuse
3:17 **One** of them said, "My lord, this woman and I live in the same
3:17 of them said, "My lord, this woman and I live in the **same** house.
3:25 the living child in two and give half to **one** and half to the other."
3:25 the living child in two and give half to one and half to the **other**[s]."
4: 7 Each **one** had to provide supplies for one month in the year.
4:19 of Og king of Bashan). He was the **only** governor over the district.
4:22 [5:2] Solomon's **daily** [+3427+4200] provisions were thirty cors
6:24 One wing of the **first** cherub was five cubits long, and the other
6:25 ten cubits, for the two cherubim were **identical** in size and shape.
6:25 for the two cherubim were identical in size and shape. **[RPH]**
6:26 The height of **each** cherub was ten cubits.
6:27 The wing of **one** cherub touched one wall, while the wing of the
6:34 two pine doors, **each** having two leaves that turned in sockets.
6:38 In the **eleventh** [+6926] year in the month of Bul, the eighth
7:15 **each** eighteen cubits high and twelve cubits around, by line.
7:16 to set on the tops of the pillars; **each** capital was five cubits high.
7:17 festooned the capitals on top of the pillars, seven for **each** capital.
7:18 He made pomegranates in two rows encircling **each** network to
7:27 of bronze; **each** was four cubits long, four wide and three high.
7:30 **Each** stand had four bronze wheels with bronze axles, and each
7:32 to the stand. The diameter of **each** wheel was a cubit and a half.
7:34 **Each** stand had four handles, one on each corner, projecting from
7:37 They were all cast in the **same** molds and were identical in size
7:37 all cast in the same molds and were **identical** in size and shape.
7:37 in the same molds and were identical in size and **[RPH]** shape.
7:38 **each** holding forty baths and measuring four cubits across,
7:38 cubits across, **[RPH]** one basin to go on each of the ten stands.
7:38 four cubits across, **one** basin to go on each of the ten stands.
7:38 four cubits across, one basin to go on **each** of the ten stands.
7:42 two sets of network (two rows of pomegranates for **each** network,
7:44 the Sea **[NIE]** and the twelve bulls under it;
8:56 Not **one** word has failed of all the good promises he gave through
10:14 The weight of the gold that Solomon received **yearly** [+928+9102]
10:16 hammered gold; six hundred bekas of gold went into **each** shield.
10:17 shields of hammered gold, with three minas of gold in **each** shield.
10:22 **Once** every three years it returned, carrying gold, silver and ivory,
11:13 but will give him **one** tribe for the sake of David my servant
11:32 I have chosen out of all the tribes of Israel, he will have **one** tribe.
11:36 I will give **one** tribe to his son so that David my servant may
12:29 **One** he set up in Bethel, and the other in Dan.
12:29 One he set up in Bethel, and the **other**[s] in Dan.
12:30 the people went even as far as Dan to worship the **one** there.
13:11 Now there was a **certain** old prophet living in Bethel, whose sons
14:21 He was **forty-one** [+752+2256] years old when he became king,
15:10 and he reigned in Jerusalem **forty-one** [+752+2256] years.
16:23 In the **thirty-first** [+2256+8993] year of Asa king of Judah, Omri
18: 6 to cover, Ahab going in **one** direction and Obadiah in another.
18: 6 to cover, Ahab going in one direction and Obadiah in **another**[s].
18:23 Let them choose **one** for themselves, and let them cut it into pieces
18:23 I will prepare the **other**[s] bull and put it on the wood but not set fire

1Ki 18:25 "Choose **one** of the bulls and prepare it first, since there are
19: 2 if by this time tomorrow I do not make your life like that of **one** of
19: 4 He came to **a** broom tree, sat down under it and prayed that he
19: 5 he lay down under **the** tree and fell asleep. All at once an angel
20:13 Meanwhile **a** prophet came to Ahab king of Israel and announced,
20:29 thousand casualties on the Aramean foot soldiers in **one** day.
20:35 By the word of the LORD **one** of the sons of the prophets said to
22: 8 "There is still **one** man through whom we can inquire of the
22: 9 So the king of Israel called **one** of his officials and said,
22:13 *as* **one** man the other prophets are predicting success for the king.
22:13 *Let* your word **agree** [+2118+3869] with theirs, and speak
2Ki 2:16 him up and set him down on **some** mountain or in some valley."
2:16 him up and set him down on some mountain or in **some** valley."
3:11 **An** officer of the king of Israel answered, "Elisha son of Shaphat is
4: 1 **The** wife of a man from the company of the prophets cried out to
4:22 "Please send me **one** of the servants and a donkey so I can go to
4:22 "Please send me one of the servants and **a** donkey so I can go to
4:35 and walked **back and forth** [+285+2178+2178+2256] in the room
4:35 and walked **back and forth** [+285+2178+2178+2256] in the room
4:39 **One** of them went out into the fields to gather herbs and found a
6: 2 Let us go to the Jordan, where each of us can get **a** pole; and let us
6: 3 **one** of them said, "Won't you please come with your servants?"
6: 5 As **one** of them was cutting down a tree, the iron axhead fell into
6:10 **Time and again** [+2256+4202+4202+9109] Elisha warned
6:12 of us, my lord the king," said **one** of his officers, "but Elisha,
7: 8 leprosy reached the edge of the camp and entered **one** of the tents.
7:13 **One** of his officers answered, "Have some men take five of the
8: 6 he assigned **an** official to her case and said to him, "Give back
8:26 old when he became king, and he reigned in Jerusalem **one** year.
9: 1 The prophet Elisha summoned a **man**[s] from the company of the
9:29 (In the **eleventh** [+6926] year of Joram son of Ahab, Ahaziah had
12: 9 [12:10] Jehoiada the priest took **a** chest and bored a hole in its lid.
14:23 king in Samaria, and he reigned **forty-one** [+752+2256] years.
15:20 **[NIE]** So the king of Assyria withdrew and stayed in the land no
17:27 "Have **one** of the priests you took captive from Samaria go back to
17:28 So **one** of the priests who had been exiled from Samaria came to
18:24 How can you repulse **one** officer of the least of my master's
22: 1 and he reigned in Jerusalem **thirty-one** [+2256+8993] years.
23:36 he became king, and he reigned in Jerusalem **eleven** [+6926] years.
24:18 Zedekiah was **twenty-one** [+2256+6929] years old when he
24:18 he became king, and he reigned in Jerusalem **eleven** [+6926] years.
25:16 from the two pillars, the Sea **[NIE]** and the movable stands,
25:17 **Each** pillar was twenty-seven feet high. The bronze capital on top
25:19 he took **the** officer in charge of the fighting men and five royal
1Ch 1:19 **One** was named Peleg, because in his time the earth was divided;
11:11 spear against three hundred men, whom he killed in **one** encounter.
12:14 [12:15] **[NIE]** the least was a match for a hundred,
12:38 [12:39] All the rest of the Israelites were also of **one** mind to
17: 6 did I ever say to **any** *of* their leaders whom I commanded to
17:21 the **one** nation on earth whose God went out to redeem a people for
21:10 Choose **one** of them for me to carry out against you.' "
23:11 so they were counted as one family with **one** assignment.
24: 6 **one** family being taken from Eleazar and then one from Ithamar.
24: 6 being taken from Eleazar and then **one** [BHS 296] from Ithamar.
24:17 the **twenty-first** [+2256+6929] to Jakin, the twenty-second to
25:28 the **twenty-first** [+2256+6929] to Hothir, his sons and relatives, 12
27: 1 throughout the year. **Each** division consisted of 24,000 men.
29: 1 the **one** whom God has chosen, is young and inexperienced.
2Ch 3:11 **One** wing of the first cherub was five cubits long and touched the
3:12 also five cubits long, touched the wing of the **first** cherub.
3:17 in the front of the temple, **one** to the south and one to the north.
3:17 in the front of the temple, one to the south and **one** to the north.
4:13 two sets of network (two rows of pomegranates for **each** network,
4:15 the Sea **[NIE]** and the twelve bulls under it;
5:13 The trumpeters and singers joined **in unison** [+3869], as with one
5:13 as with **one** voice, to give praise and thanks to the LORD.
9:13 The weight of the gold that Solomon received **yearly** [+928+9102]
9:15 six hundred bekas of hammered gold went into **each** shield.
9:16 hammered gold, with three hundred bekas of gold in **each** shield.
9:21 **Once** every three years it returned, carrying gold, silver and ivory,
12:13 He was **forty-one** [+752+2256] years old when he became king,
16:13 Then in the **forty-first** [+752+2256] year of his reign Asa died
18: 7 "There is still **one** man through whom we can inquire of the
18: 8 So the king of Israel called **one** of his officials and said,
18:12 *as* **one** man the other prophets are predicting success for the king.
18:12 *Let* your word **agree** [+2118+3869] with theirs, and speak
22: 2 old when he became king, and he reigned in Jerusalem **one** year.
24: 8 At the king's command, **a** chest was made and placed outside,
28: 6 In **one** day Pekah son of Remaliah killed a hundred and twenty
29:17 They began the consecration on the **first** day of the first month,
30:12 the people to give them **unity** of mind to carry out what the king
32:12 'You must worship before **one** altar and burn sacrifices on it'?
34: 1 king, and he reigned in Jerusalem **thirty-one** [+2256+8993] years.
36: 5 he became king, and he reigned in Jerusalem **eleven** [+6926] years.
36:11 Zedekiah was **twenty-one** [+2256+6929] years old when he
36:11 he became king, and he reigned in Jerusalem **eleven** [+6926] years.
36:22 In the **first** year of Cyrus king of Persia, in order to fulfill the word
Ezr 1: 1 In the **first** year of Cyrus king of Persia, in order to fulfill the word
2:26 of Ramah and Geba **621** [+2256+4395+6929+9252]
2:64 The whole company **numbered** [+3869] 42,360,
3: 1 in their towns, the people assembled as **one** man in Jerusalem.
3: 6 On the **first** day of the seventh month they began to offer burnt
3: 9 **joined together** [+3869+6641] in supervising those working on
6:20 had purified themselves and were **[NIE]** all ceremonially clean.
7: 9 He had begun his journey from Babylon on the **first** day of the first
7: 9 and he arrived in Jerusalem on the **first** day of the fifth month,
10:13 Besides, this matter cannot be taken care of in **a** day or two,
10:16 On the **first** day of the tenth month they sat down to investigate the
10:17 by the **first** day of the first month they finished dealing with all the
Ne 1: 2 Hanani, **one** of my brothers, came from Judah with some other
4:17 [4:11] Those who carried materials did their work with **one** hand
4:17 [4:11] their work with one hand and held a weapon in the **other**[s],
5:18 **Each** day one ox, six choice sheep and some poultry were prepared
5:18 Each day **one** ox, six choice sheep and some poultry were prepared
7:30 of Ramah and Geba **621** [+2256+4395+6929+9252]
7:37 of Lod, Hadid and Ono **721** [+2256+2256+4395+6929+8679]
7:66 The whole company **numbered** [+3869] 42,360,
8: 1 all the people assembled as **one** man in the square before the Water
8: 2 So on the **first** day of the seventh month Ezra the priest brought the
11: 1 the rest of the people cast lots to bring **one** out of every ten to live
12:31 **One** [BHS-] was to proceed on top of the wall to the right,
Est 3: 8 "There is a **certain** people dispersed and scattered among the
3:13 on a **single** day, the thirteenth day of the twelfth month, the month
4:11 the inner court without being summoned the king has but **one** law:
7: 9 Then Harbona, **one** of the eunuchs attending the king, said,
8:12 The day **appointed** for the Jews to do this in all the provinces of
Job 2:10 He replied, "You are talking like **a** foolish woman. Shall we accept
9: 3 with him, he could not answer him **one** *time* out of a thousand.
9:22 It is **all the same**; that is why I say, 'He destroys both the blameless
14: 4 Who can bring what is pure from the impure? No **one**!
23:13 "But he stands **alone** [+928], and who can oppose him? He does
31:15 Did not the **same one** form us both within our mothers?
33:14 For God does speak—now **one** [+928] **way**, now another—
33:23 **one** out of a thousand, to tell a man what is right for him,
40: 5 I spoke **once**, but I have no answer—twice, but I will say no
41:16 [41:8] **each** is so close to the next that no air can pass between.
41:16 [41:8] each is so close to the **next** that no air can pass between.
42:11 upon him, and each one gave him **a** piece of silver and a gold ring.
42:11 upon him, and each one gave him a piece of silver and **a** gold ring.
42:14 The **first** daughter he named Jemimah, the second Keziah
Ps 14: 3 become corrupt; there is no one who does good, not even **one**.
27: 4 **One** *thing* I ask of the LORD, this is what I seek: that I may
34:20 [34:21] he protects all his bones, not **one** of them will be broken.
53: 3 [53:4] there is no one who does good, not even **one**.
62:11 [62:12] **One** *thing* God has spoken, two things have I heard:
82: 7 you will die like mere men; you will fall like *every* **other**[s] ruler."
89:35 [89:36] **Once for all**, I have sworn by my holiness—and I will not
106:11 The waters covered their adversaries; not **one** of them survived.
139:16 All the days ordained for me were written in your book before **one**
Pr 1:14 throw in your lot with us, and we will share a **common** purse"—
28:18 but *he* whose ways are perverse will **suddenly** [+928] fall.
Ecc 2:14 but I came to realize that the **same** fate overtakes them both.
3:19 fate is like that of the animals; the **same** fate awaits them both:
3:19 All have the **same** breath; man has no advantage over the animal.
3:20 All go to the **same** place; all come from dust, and to dust all return.
4: 8 There was a **man**[s] all alone; he had neither son nor brother.
4: 9 Two are better than **one**, because they have a good return for their
4:10 If **one** falls down, his friend can help him up. But pity the man who
4:10 But pity the **man**[s] who falls and has no one to help him up!
4:11 they will keep warm. But how can **one** keep warm *alone*?
4:12 Though **one** may be overpowered, two can defend themselves.
6: 6 but fails to enjoy his prosperity. Do not all go to the **same** place?
7:27 "Adding **one** *thing* to another to discover the scheme of things—
7:27 "Adding one thing to **another**[s] to discover the scheme of things—
7:28 I found **one** ⌞upright⌟ man among a thousand, but not one ⌞upright⌟
9: 2 All share a **common** destiny—the righteous and the wicked,
9: 3 The **same** destiny overtakes all. The hearts of men, moreover,
9:18 is better than weapons of war, but **one** sinner destroys much good.
11: 6 whether this or that, or whether both will do **equally** [+3869] well.
12:11 sayings like firmly embedded nails—given by **one** Shepherd.
SS 4: 9 you have stolen my heart with **one** glance of your eyes, with one
4: 9 with one glance of your eyes, with **one** jewel of your necklace.
6: 9 my dove, my perfect one, is **unique**, the only daughter of her
6: 9 my perfect one, is unique, the **only** daughter of her mother,
Isa 4: 1 In that day seven women will take hold of **one** man and say,
5:10 A ten-acre vineyard will produce only **a** bath of wine, a homer of
6: 2 Above him were seraphs, **each** with six wings: With two wings
6: 6 Then **one** of the seraphs flew to me with a live coal in his hand,

Isa 9: 14 [9:13] and tail, both palm branch and reed in a **single** day;
10: 17 in a **single** day it will burn and consume his thorns and his briers.
19: 18 **One** of them will be called the City of Destruction.
23: 15 Tyre will be forgotten for seventy years, the span of **a** king's life.
27: 12 of Egypt, and you, O Israelites, will be gathered up **one** by one.
27: 12 of Egypt, and you, O Israelites, will be gathered up one by **one**.
30: 17 **A** thousand will flee at the threat of one; at the threat of five you
30: 17 A thousand will flee at the threat of **one**; at the threat of five you
34: 16 **None** [+4202] of these will be missing, not one will lack her mate.
36: 9 can you repulse **one** officer of the least of my master's officials,
47: 9 Both of these will overtake you in a moment, on a **single** day:
51: 2 When I called him he was but **one**, and I blessed him and made
65: 25 The wolf and the lamb will feed **together** [+3869], and the lion
66: 8 Can a country be born in **a** day or a nation be brought forth in a
66: 8 country be born in a day or a nation be brought forth in **a** moment?
66: 17 following the **one** in the midst of those who eat the flesh of pigs
Jer 3: 14 I will choose you—**one** from a town and two from a clan—
10: 8 They are **all** [+928] senseless and foolish; they are taught by
24: 2 **One** basket had very good figs, like those that ripen early;
24: 2 the **other**[s] basket had very poor figs, so bad they could not be
32: 39 I will give them **singleness** of heart and action, so that they will
32: 39 I will give them singleness of heart and **[RPH]** action, so that they
35: 2 invite them to come to **one** *of* the side rooms of the house of the
51: 60 Jeremiah had written on **a** scroll about all the disasters that would
52: 1 Zedekiah was **twenty-one** [+2256+6929] years old when he
52: 1 he became king, and he reigned in Jerusalem **eleven** [+6926] years.
52: 20 the Sea **[NIE]** and the twelve bronze bulls under it,
52: 21 **Each** of the pillars was eighteen cubits high and twelve cubits in
52: 22 The bronze capital on top of the one pillar **[RPH]** was five cubits
52: 25 still in the city, he took **the** officer in charge of the fighting men,
Eze 1: 6 but **each** of them had four faces and four wings.
1: 6 but each of them had four faces and four wings. **[RPH]**
1: 15 I saw **a** wheel on the ground beside each creature with its four
1: 16 They sparkled like chrysolite, and all four looked **alike**.
4: 9 put them in **a** storage jar and use them to make bread for yourself.
7: 5 LORD says: Disaster! An **unheard-of** disaster is coming.
8: 7 to the entrance to the court. I looked, and I saw **a** hole in the wall.
8: 8 dig into the wall." So I dug into the wall and saw **a** doorway there.
9: 2 With them was **a** man clothed in linen who had a writing kit at his
10: 9 beside the cherubim four wheels, **one** beside each of the cherubim;
10: 9 beside the cherubim four wheels, one beside **each** of the cherubim;
10: 9 each of the cherubim; **[RPH]** the wheels sparkled like chrysolite.
10: 9 each of the cherubim; **[RPH]** the wheels sparkled like chrysolite.
10: 10 As for their appearance, the four of them looked **alike**; each was
10: 14 **Each** of the cherubim had four faces: One face was that of a
10: 14 **One** face was that of a cherub, the second the face of a man,
10: 21 **Each** had four faces and four wings, and under their wings was
10: 21 **[RPH]** and under their wings was what looked like the hands of a
11: 19 I will give them an **undivided** heart and put a new spirit in them;
16: 5 or had compassion enough to do **any** of these things for you.
17: 7 " 'But there was **another** great eagle with powerful wings
18: 10 a violent son, who sheds blood or does **any** of these other things
19: 3 She brought up **one** of her cubs, and he became a strong lion.
19: 5 she took **another**[s] of her cubs and made him a strong lion.
21: 19 [21:24] of Babylon to take, both starting from the **same** country.
23: 2 of man, there were two women, daughters of the **same** mother.
23: 13 I saw that she too defiled herself; both of them went the **same** way.
26: 1 In the eleventh year, on the **first** day of the month, the word of the
29: 17 In the twenty-seventh year, in the first month on the **first** day,
30: 20 In the **eleventh** [+6926] year, in the first month on the seventh day,
31: 1 In the **eleventh** [+6926] year, in the third month on the first day,
31: 1 In the eleventh year, in the third month on the **first** day, the word
32: 1 In the twelfth year, in the twelfth month on the **first** day, the word
33: 2 the people of the land choose **one** of their men and make him their
33: 24 are saying, 'Abraham was only **one** *man*, yet he possessed the land.
33: 30 saying to each **other**[s], 'Come and hear the message that has come
34: 23 I will place over them **one** shepherd, my servant David, and he will
37: 16 "Son of man, take **a** stick of wood and write on it, 'Belonging to
37: 16 take **another**[s] stick of wood, and write on it, 'Ephraim's stick,
37: 17 Join them **together** [+285+448] into one stick so that they will
37: 17 Join them **together** [+285+448] into one stick so that they will
37: 17 Join them together into **one** stick so that they will become one in
37: 17 together into one stick so that they will become **one** in your hand.
37: 19 and join it to Judah's stick, making them a **single** stick of wood,
37: 19 them a single stick of wood, and they will become **one** in my hand.'
37: 22 I will make them **one** nation in the land, on the mountains of Israel.
37: 22 There will be **one** king over all of them and they will never again
37: 24 David will be king over them, and they will all have **one** shepherd.
40: 5 the wall; it was **one** measuring rod thick and one rod high.
40: 5 the wall; it was one measuring rod thick and **one** rod high.
40: 6 and measured the threshold of the gate; it was **one** rod deep.
40: 6 it was one rod deep. [BHS+ *the* ***first*** *threshold, one rod deep*]
40: 6 it was one rod deep. [BHS+ *the first threshold,* ***one*** *rod deep*]
40: 7 The alcoves for the guards were **one** rod long and one rod wide,
40: 7 The alcoves for the guards were one rod long and **one** rod wide,
40: 7 of the gate next to the portico facing the temple was **one** rod deep.
40: 8 measured the portico of the gateway; [BHS+ *it was* ***one*** *rod deep*]
40: 10 the three had the **same** measurements, and the faces of the
40: 10 the faces of the projecting walls on each side had the **same**
40: 12 In front of each alcove was a wall **one** cubit high, and the alcoves
40: 12 one cubit high, **[RPH]** and the alcoves were six cubits square.
40: 26 on the faces of the projecting walls on each side. **[NIE]**
40: 26 on the faces of the projecting walls on each side. **[NIE]**
40: 42 each **a** cubit and a half long, a cubit and a half wide and a cubit
40: 42 a cubit and a half long, **a** cubit and a half wide and a cubit high.
40: 42 a cubit and a half long, a cubit and a half wide and **a** cubit high.
40: 43 double-pronged hooks, each **a** handbreadth long, were attached to
40: 44 were two rooms, **one** at the side of the north gate and facing south,
40: 49 of stairs, and there were pillars on each side of the jambs. **[NIE]**
40: 49 of stairs, and there were pillars on each side of the jambs. **[NIE]**
41: 11 from the open area, **one** on the north and another on the south;
41: 11 from the open area, one on the north and **another**[s] on the south;
41: 24 Each door had two leaves—two hinged leaves for **each** door.
42: 4 ten cubits wide and a <u>hundred</u> [BHS *one*; NIV 4395] cubits long.
43: 13 and a cubit wide, with a rim of **one** span around the edge.
43: 14 ground up to the lower ledge it is two cubits high and **a** cubit wide,
45: 7 western to the eastern border parallel to **one** *of* the tribal portions.
45: 11 The ephah and the bath are to be the **same** size, the bath containing
45: 15 Also **one** sheep is to be taken from every flock of two hundred
45: 18 In the first month on the **first** day you are to take a young bull
46: 17 he makes a gift from his inheritance to **one** of his servants,
46: 22 each of the courts in the four corners was the **same** size.
48: 1 At the northern frontier, Dan will have **one** *portion*; it will follow
48: 2 "Asher will have **one** *portion*; it will border the territory of Dan
48: 3 "Naphtali will have **one** *portion*; it will border the territory of
48: 4 "Manasseh will have **one** *portion*; it will border the territory of
48: 5 "Ephraim will have **one** *portion*; it will border the territory of
48: 6 "Reuben will have **one** *portion*; it will border the territory of
48: 7 "Judah will have **one** *portion*; it will border the territory of Reuben
48: 8 its length from east to west will equal **one** *of* the tribal portions;
48: 23 Benjamin will have **one** *portion*; it will extend from the east side
48: 24 "Simeon will have **one** *portion*; it will border the territory of
48: 25 "Issachar will have **one** *portion*; it will border the territory of
48: 26 "Zebulun will have **one** *portion*; it will border the territory of
48: 27 "Gad will have **one** *portion*; it will border the territory of Zebulun
48: 31 the gate of Reuben, **[NIE]** the gate of Judah and the gate of Levi.
48: 31 the gate of Reuben, the gate of Judah **[NIE]** and the gate of Levi.
48: 31 the gate of Reuben, the gate of Judah and the gate of Levi. **[NIE]**
48: 32 gate of Joseph, **[NIE]** the gate of Benjamin and the gate of Dan.
48: 32 gate of Joseph, the gate of Benjamin **[NIE]** and the gate of Dan.
48: 32 gate of Joseph, the gate of Benjamin and the gate of Dan. **[NIE]**
48: 33 of Simeon, **[NIE]** the gate of Issachar and the gate of Zebulun.
48: 33 of Simeon, the gate of Issachar **[NIE]** and the gate of Zebulun.
48: 33 of Simeon, the gate of Issachar and the gate of Zebulun. **[NIE]**
48: 34 the gate of Gad, **[NIE]** the gate of Asher and the gate of Naphtali.
48: 34 the gate of Gad, the gate of Asher **[NIE]** and the gate of Naphtali.
48: 34 the gate of Gad, the gate of Asher and the gate of Naphtali. **[NIE]**
Da 1: 21 And Daniel remained there until the **first** year of King Cyrus.
8: 3 I looked up, and there before me was **a** ram with two horns,
8: 3 **One** of the horns was longer than the other but grew up later.
8: 9 Out of **one** of them came another horn, which started small
8: 9 Out of one of them came **another**[s] horn, which started small
8: 13 I heard **a** holy one speaking, and another holy one said to him,
8: 13 I heard a holy one speaking, and **another**[s] holy one said to him,
9: 1 In the **first** year of Darius son of Xerxes (a Mede by descent),
9: 2 in the **first** year of his reign, I, Daniel, understood from the
9: 27 He will confirm a covenant with many for **one** 'seven.' In the
10: 5 I looked up and there before me was **a** man dressed in linen,
10: 13 the Persian kingdom resisted me **twenty-one** [+2256+6929] days.
10: 13 Michael, **one** *of* the chief princes, came to help me, because I was
10: 21 (No **one** supports me against them except Michael, your prince.
11: 1 in the **first** year of Darius the Mede, I took my stand to support
11: 20 In a **few** years, however, he will be destroyed, yet not in anger
11: 27 will sit at the **same** table and lie to each other, but to no avail,
12: 5 **one** on this bank of the river and one on the opposite bank.
12: 5 one on this bank of the river and **one** on the opposite bank.
Hos 1: 11 [2:2] they will appoint **one** leader and will come up out of the
Am 4: 7 I sent rain on **one** town, but withheld it from another. One field had
4: 7 I sent rain on one town, but withheld it from **another**[s]. One field
4: 7 it from another. **One** field had rain; another had none and dried up.
4: 8 People staggered from town to town **[NIE]** for water but did not
6: 9 If ten men are left in **one** house, they too will die.
Ob 1: 11 his gates and cast lots for Jerusalem, you were like **one** of them.
Jnh 3: 4 On the **first** day, Jonah started into the city. He proclaimed:
Zep 3: 9 name of the LORD and serve him **shoulder to shoulder** [+8900].
Hag 1: 1 the second year of King Darius, on the **first** day of the sixth month,
2: 1 On the **twenty-first** [+2256+6929] day of the seventh month,
2: 6 'In a little while I will **once** more shake the heavens and the earth,

Zec 3: 9 There are seven eyes on that **one** stone, and I will engrave an
3: 9 'and I will remove the sin of this land in a **single** day.
4: 3 trees by it, **one** on the right of the bowl and the other on its left."
4: 3 trees by it, one on the right of the bowl and **the other**[s] on its left."
5: 7 the cover of lead was raised, and there in the basket sat **a** woman!
8: 21 and the inhabitants of **one** city will go to another and say,
8: 21 and the inhabitants of one city will go to **another**[s] and say,
11: 7 Then I took two staffs and called **one** Favor and the other Union,
11: 7 Then I took two staffs and called one Favor and **the other**[s] Union,
11: 8 In **one** month I got rid of the three shepherds. The flock detested
14: 7 It will be a **unique** day, without daytime or nighttime—a day
14: 9 On that day there will be **one** LORD, and his name the only
14: 9 that day there will be one LORD, and his name the **only** name.
Mal 2: 10 Have we not all **one** Father? Did not one God create us? Why do
2: 10 Have we not all one Father? Did not **one** God create us? Why do
2: 15 Has not ⌞the LORD⌟ made them **one**? In flesh and spirit they are
2: 15 made them one? In flesh and spirit they are his. And why **one**?

286 אחו אָחוּ *'āḥû*, n.m.col. [3]

reeds [3]

Ge 41: 2 up seven cows, sleek and fat, and they grazed among the **reeds**.
41: 18 up seven cows, fat and sleek, and they grazed among the **reeds**.
Job 8: 11 grow tall where there is no marsh? Can **reeds** thrive without water?

287 אהוד אֵהוּד *'ēhûd*, n.pr.m. [1] [√ 285; cf. 179?]

Ehud [1]

1Ch 8: 6 These were the descendants of **Ehud**, who were heads of families

288 אחוה אַחֲוָה *'aḥ^{a}wâ^1*, n.f. [1] [√ 278]

brotherhood [1]

Zec 11: 14 called Union, breaking the **brotherhood** between Judah and Israel.

289 אחוה אַחֲוָה *'aḥ^{a}wâ^2*, n.f. [1] [√ 2555]

what say [1]

Job 13: 17 Listen carefully to my words; let your ears take in **what I say**.

290 אחוז *'āḥûz*, n.m. *or* v.ptcp. Not used in NIV/BHS [√ 296]

291 אחוח אֲחוֹחַ *'^{a}ḥôaḥ*, n.pr.m. [1] [→ 292]

Ahoah [1]

1Ch 8: 4 Abishua, Naaman, **Ahoah**,

292 אחוחי אֲחוֹחִי *'^{a}ḥôḥî*, a.g. [5] [√ 291]

Ahohite [4], Ahohite [+1201] [1]

2Sa 23: 9 Next to him was Eleazar son of Dodai the **Ahohite** [+1201].
23: 28 Zalmon the **Ahohite**, Maharai the Netophathite,
1Ch 11: 12 Next to him was Eleazar son of Dodai the **Ahohite**, one of the
11: 29 Sibbecai the Hushathite, Ilai the **Ahohite**,
27: 4 of the division for the second month was Dodai the **Ahohite**;

293 אחומי אֲחוּמַי *'^{a}ḥûmay*, n.pr.m. [1]

Ahumai [1]

1Ch 4: 2 the father of Jahath, and Jahath the father of **Ahumai** and Lahad.

294 אחור אָחוֹר *'āḥôr*, subst. [41] [→ 345; cf. 336]

back [14], backs [2], backward [2], behind [2], hindquarters [2], rear [2], west [2], away [1], backsliding [1], backward [+4200] [1], behind [+4946] [1], deserted [+6047] [1], drawn back [+6047] [1], future [1], is driven back [+6047] [1], made retreat [+8740] [1], on both sides [+2256+7156] [1], overthrows [+8740] [1], retreating [+6047] [1], time to come [1], under control [+928] [1], withdrawn [+8740] [1]

Ge 49: 17 that bites the horse's heels so that its rider tumbles **backward**.
Ex 26: 12 the half curtain that is left over is to hang down at the **rear** *of* the
33: 23 I will remove my hand and you will see my **back**; but my face
2Sa 1: 22 the flesh of the mighty, the bow of Jonathan did not turn **back**,
10: 9 there were battle lines in front of him and **behind** [+4946] him;
1Ki 7: 25 on top of them, and their **hindquarters** were toward the center.
1Ch 19: 10 saw that there were battle lines in front of him and **behind** him;
2Ch 4: 4 on top of them, and their **hindquarters** were toward the center.
13: 14 and saw that they were being attacked at both front and **rear**.
Job 23: 8 go to the east, he is not there; if I go to the **west**, I do not find him.
Ps 9: 3 [9:4] My enemies turn **back**; they stumble and perish before you.
35: 4 to shame; may those who plot my ruin be turned **back** in dismay.
40: 14 [40:15] may all who desire my ruin be turned **back** in disgrace.
44: 10 [44:11] *You* **made** us **retreat** [+8740] before the enemy, and our
44: 18 [44:19] Our hearts had not turned **back**; our feet had not strayed
56: 9 [56:10] my enemies will turn **back** when I call for help. By this I
70: 2 [70:3] may all who desire my ruin be turned **back** in disgrace.
78: 66 He beat **back** his enemies; he put them to everlasting shame.
114: 3 The sea looked and fled, the Jordan turned **back**;
114: 5 Why was it, O sea, that you fled, O Jordan, that you turned **back**,
129: 5 May all who hate Zion be turned **back** in shame.
139: 5 You hem me in—**behind** and before; you have laid your hand
Pr 29: 11 to his anger, but a wise man keeps himself **under control** [+928].
Isa 1: 4 spurned the Holy One of Israel and turned their **backs** on him.
9: 12 [9:11] Philistines from the **west** have devoured Israel with open
28: 13 so that they will go and fall **backward**, be injured and snared
41: 23 tell us what the **future** holds, so we may know that you are gods.
42: 17 to images, 'You are our gods,' will be turned **back** in utter shame.
42: 23 of you will listen to this or pay close attention in **time to come**?
44: 25 *who* **overthrows** [+8740] the learning of the wise and turns it into
50: 5 and I have not been rebellious; *I have* not **drawn back** [+6047].
59: 14 So justice **is driven back** [+6047], and righteousness stands at a
Jer 7: 24 of their evil hearts. They went **backward** [+4200] and not forward.
15: 6 rejected me," declares the LORD. "You keep on **backsliding**.
38: 22 feet are sunk in the mud; your friends *have* **deserted** [+6047] you.'
46: 5 They are terrified, *they are* **retreating** [+6047], their warriors are
La 1: 8 they have seen her nakedness; she herself groans and turns **away**.
1: 13 He spread a net for my feet and turned me **back**. He made me
2: 3 *He has* **withdrawn** [+8740] his right hand at the approach of the
Eze 2: 10 **On both sides** [+2256+7156] of it were written words of lament
8: 16 *With* their **backs** toward the temple of the LORD and their faces

295 אחות אָחוֹת *'āḥôt*, n.f. [114] [√ 278]

sister [88], sisters [11], *untranslated* [4], other[s] [4], sister's [4], together [+448+851] [2], another[s] [1]

Ge 4: 22 of tools out of bronze and iron. Tubal-Cain's **sister** was Naamah.
12: 13 Say you are my **sister**, so that I will be treated well for your sake
12: 19 Why did you say, 'She is my **sister**,' so that I took her to be my
20: 2 and there Abraham said of his wife Sarah, "She is my **sister**."
20: 5 Did he not say to me, 'She is my **sister**,' and didn't she also say,
20: 12 Besides, she really is my **sister**, the daughter of my father though
24: 30 as he had seen the nose ring, and the bracelets on his **sister's** arms,
24: 30 and had heard Rebekah **[RPH]** tell what the man said to her,
24: 59 So they sent their **sister** Rebekah on her way, along with her nurse
24: 60 they blessed Rebekah and said to her, "Our **sister**, may you
25: 20 the Aramean from Paddan Aram and **sister** *of* Laban the Aramean.
26: 7 he said, "She is my **sister**," because he was afraid to say, "She is
26: 9 Why did you say, 'She is my **sister**'?" Isaac answered him,
28: 9 the **sister** *of* Nebaioth and daughter of Ishmael son of Abraham,
29: 13 the news about Jacob, his **sister's** son, he hurried to meet him.
30: 1 not bearing Jacob any children, she became jealous of her **sister**.
30: 8 "I have had a great struggle with my **sister**, and I have won."
34: 13 Because their **sister** Dinah had been defiled, Jacob's sons replied
34: 14 a thing; we can't give our **sister** to a man who is not circumcised.
34: 27 dead bodies and looted the city where their **sister** had been defiled.
34: 31 they replied, "Should he have treated our **sister** like a prostitute?"
36: 3 also Basemath daughter of Ishmael and **sister** *of* Nebaioth.
36: 22 The sons of Lotan: Hori and Homam. Timna was Lotan's **sister**.
46: 17 of Asher: Imnah, Ishvah, Ishvi and Beriah. Their **sister** was Serah.
Ex 2: 4 His **sister** stood at a distance to see what would happen to him.
2: 7 his **sister** asked Pharaoh's daughter, "Shall I go and get one of the
6: 23 daughter of Amminadab and **sister** *of* Nahshon, and she bore him
15: 20 Miriam the prophetess, Aaron's **sister**, took a tambourine in her
26: 3 Join five of the curtains **together** [+448+851], and do the same
26: 3 the curtains together, and do the same with the other five. **[RPH]**
26: 5 end curtain of the other set, with the loops opposite each **other**[s].
26: 6 and use them to fasten the curtains **together** [+448+851]
26: 17 with two projections set parallel to each **other**[s]. Make all the
Lev 18: 9 " 'Do not have sexual relations with your **sister**, either your
18: 11 of your father's wife, born to your father; she is your **sister**.
18: 12 " 'Do not have sexual relations with your father's **sister**; she is
18: 13 " 'Do not have sexual relations with your mother's **sister**,
18: 18 " 'Do not take your wife's **sister** as a rival wife and have sexual
20: 17 " 'If a man marries his **sister**, the daughter of either his father
20: 17 He has dishonored his **sister** and will be held responsible.
20: 19 " 'Do not have sexual relations with the **sister** *of* either your
20: 19 with the sister of either your mother or **[RPH]** your father,
21: 3 or an unmarried **sister** who is dependent on him since she has no
Nu 6: 7 Even if his own father or mother or brother or **sister** dies,
25: 18 when they deceived you in the affair of Peor and their **sister** Cozbi,
26: 59 To Amram she bore Aaron, Moses and their **sister** Miriam.
Dt 27: 22 "Cursed is the man who sleeps with his **sister**, the daughter of his
Jos 2: 13 spare the lives of my father and mother, my brothers and **sisters**,
Jdg 15: 2 Isn't her younger **sister** more attractive? Take her instead."
2Sa 13: 1 in love with Tamar, the beautiful **sister** of Absalom son of David.
13: 2 frustrated to the point of illness on account of his **sister** Tamar,
13: 4 to him, "I'm in love with Tamar, my brother Absalom's **sister**."
13: 5 'I would like my **sister** Tamar to come and give me something to
13: 6 "I would like my **sister** Tamar to come and make some special
13: 11 he grabbed her and said, "Come to bed with me, my **sister**."

2Sa 13:20 been with you? Be quiet now, my **sister**; he is your brother.
13:22 he hated Amnon because he had disgraced his **sister** Tamar.
13:32 intention ever since the day Amnon raped his **sister** Tamar.
17:25 the daughter of Nahash and **sister** *of* Zeruiah the mother of Joab.
1Ki 11:19 so pleased with Hadad that he gave him a **sister** *of* his own wife,
11:19 a sister of his own wife, **[RPH]** Queen Tahpenes, in marriage.
11:20 The **sister** *of* Tahpenes bore him a son named Genubath, whom
2Ki 11: 2 the daughter of King Jehoram and **sister** *of* Ahaziah,
1Ch 1:39 The sons of Lotan: Hori and Homam. Timna was Lotan's **sister**.
2:16 Their **sisters** were Zeruiah and Abigail. Zeruiah's three sons were
3: 9 besides his sons by his concubines. And Tamar was their **sister**.
3:19 Meshullam and Hananiah. Shelomith was their **sister**.
4: 3 Jezreel, Ishma and Idbash. Their **sister** was named Hazzelelponi.
4:19 The sons of Hodiah's wife, the **sister** *of* Naham: the father of
7:15 among the Huppites and Shuppites. His **sister's** name was Maacah.
7:18 His **sister** Hammoleketh gave birth to Ishhod, Abiezer and Mahlah.
7:30 of Asher: Imnah, Ishvah, Ishvi and Beriah. Their **sister** was Serah.
7:32 the father of Japhlet, Shomer and Hotham and of their **sister** Shua.
2Ch 22:11 was Ahaziah's **sister**, she hid the child from Athaliah so she could
Job 1: 4 and they would invite their three **sisters** to eat and drink with them.
17:14 'You are my father,' and to the worm, 'My mother' or 'My **sister**,'
42:11 All his brothers and **sisters** and everyone who had known him
Pr 7: 4 Say to wisdom, "You are my **sister**," and call understanding your
SS 4: 9 You have stolen my heart, my **sister**, my bride; you have stolen my
4:10 How delightful is your love, my **sister**, my bride! How much more
4:12 You are a garden locked up, my **sister**, my bride; you are a spring
5: 1 I have come into my garden, my **sister**, my bride; I have gathered
5: 2 "Open to me, my **sister**, my darling, my dove, my flawless one.
8: 8 We have a young **sister**, and her breasts are not yet grown.
8: 8 What shall we do for our **sister** for the day she is spoken for?
Jer 3: 7 return to me but she did not, and her unfaithful **sister** Judah saw it.
3: 8 Yet I saw that her unfaithful **sister** Judah had no fear; she also
3:10 her unfaithful **sister** Judah did not return to me with all her heart,
22:18 'Alas, my brother! Alas, my **sister**!' They will not mourn for him:
Eze 1: 9 their wings touched one **another**[s]. Each one went straight ahead;
1:23 the expanse their wings were stretched out one toward the **other**[s],
3:13 of the wings of the living creatures brushing against each **other**[s]
16:45 you are a true **sister** *of* your sisters, who despised their husbands
16:45 you are a true sister of your **sisters**, who despised their husbands
16:46 Your older **sister** was Samaria, who lived to the north of you with
16:46 your younger **sister**, who lived to the south of you with her
16:48 your **sister** Sodom and her daughters never did what you and your
16:49 " 'Now this was the sin of your **sister** Sodom: She and her
16:51 have made your **sisters** seem righteous by all these things you have
16:52 for you have furnished some justification for your **sisters**.
16:52 your disgrace, for you have made your **sisters** appear righteous.
16:55 your **sisters**, Sodom with her daughters and Samaria with her
16:56 You would not even mention your **sister** Sodom in the day of your
16:61 your ways and be ashamed when you receive your **sisters**,
22:11 and another violates his **sister**, his own father's daughter.
23: 4 The older was named Oholah, and her **sister** was Oholibah.
23:11 "Her **sister** Oholibah saw this, yet in her lust and prostitution she
23:11 in her lust and prostitution she was more depraved than her **sister**.
23:18 away from her in disgust, just as I had turned away from her **sister**.
23:31 You have gone the way of your **sister**; so I will put her cup into
23:32 "You will drink your **sister's** cup, a cup large and deep; it will
23:33 the cup of ruin and desolation, the cup of your **sister** Samaria.
44:25 his father or mother, son or daughter, brother or unmarried **sister**,
Hos 2: 1 [2:3] 'My people,' and of your **sisters**, 'My loved one.'

296 אָחַז **'āḥaz**[1], v. [65 / 64] [→ 290, 297, 298, 299, 303, 304; *also used with compound proper names*]

seized [9], grip [4], *untranslated* [3], seizes [3], caught [2], grips [2], hold [2], seize [2], supports [2], take [2], took hold [2], took [2], accept possession [1], acquire property [1], acquired property [1], acquired [1], are caught [1], are taken [1], bar [1], being taken [1], catch [1], clinging [1], closely followed [1], did[s] so [1], embracing [1], fastened [1], grasp [1], grasping [1], grasps [1], handle [1], held [1], hold fast [1], hold out [1], in [1], inserted [1], kept from closing [+9073] [1], share [1], steady [1], take hold [1], take on [1], wearing [1]

Ge 22:13 [C] and there in a thicket he saw a ram **caught** by its horns.
25:26 [A] his brother came out, with his hand **grasping** Esau's heel;
34:10 [C] to you. Live in it, trade in it, and **acquire property** in it."
47:27 [C] *They* **acquired property** there and were fruitful
Ex 4: 4 [A] said to him, "Reach out your hand and **take** it by the tail."
15:14 [A] and tremble; anguish *will* **grip** the people of Philistia.
15:15 [A] the leaders of Moab *will be* **seized** *with* trembling,
Nu 31:30 [B] select one **[NIE]** out of every fifty, whether persons, cattle,
31:47 [B] Moses selected **[NIE]** one out of every fifty persons
32:30 [C] *they must* **accept** *their* **possession** with you in Canaan."
Dt 32:41 [A] my flashing sword and my hand **grasps** it in judgment,
Jos 22: 9 [C] which *they had* **acquired** in accordance with the command
22:19 [C] the LORD's tabernacle stands, and **share** the land with us.
Jdg 1: 6 [A] Adoni-Bezek fled, but they chased him and **caught** him,
12: 6 [A] *they* **seized** him and killed him at the fords of the Jordan.
16: 3 [A] Then he got up and **took hold** of the doors of the city gate,
16:21 [A] the Philistines **seized** him, gouged out his eyes and took him
20: 6 [A] *I* **took** my concubine, cut her into pieces and sent one piece
Ru 3:15 [A] "Bring me the shawl you are wearing and **hold it out**."
3:15 [A] When *she* **did**[s] **so**, he poured into it six measures of barley
2Sa 1: 9 [A] and kill me! I *am* **in** the throes of death, but I'm still alive.'
2:21 [A] **take on** one of the young men and strip him of his weapons."
4:10 [A] good news, *I* **seized** him and put him to death in Ziklag.
6: 6 [A] Uzzah reached out and **took hold** of the ark of God, because
20: 9 [A] Joab **took** Amasa by the beard *with* his right hand to kiss
1Ki 1:51 [A] of King Solomon and *is* **clinging** to the horns of the altar.
6: 6 [A] so that nothing *would be* **inserted** into the temple walls.
1Ch 13: 9 [A] Uzzah reached out his hand to **steady** the ark,
24: 6 [B] one family **being taken** from Eleazar and then one from
24: 6 [b] and then one [BHS ***being taken***; NIV 285] from Ithamar.
24: 6 [B] being taken from Eleazar and then one **[RPH]** from Ithamar.
2Ch 25: 5 [A] for military service, *able to* **handle** the spear and shield.
Ne 7: 3 [A] are still on duty, have them shut the doors and **bar** them.
Est 1: 6 [B] **fastened** with cords of white linen and purple material to
Job 16:12 [A] he shattered me; *he* **seized** me by the neck and crushed me.
17: 9 [A] Nevertheless, the righteous *will* **hold** *to* their ways, and those
18: 9 [A] A trap **seizes** him by the heel; a snare holds him fast.
18:20 [A] appalled at his fate; men of the east *are* **seized** *with* horror.
21: 6 [A] I think about this, I am terrified; trembling **seizes** my body.
23:11 [A] My feet *have* **closely followed** his steps; I have kept to his
30:16 [A] "And now my life ebbs away; days of suffering **grip** me.
38:13 [A] that *it might* **take** the earth by the edges and shake the
Ps 48: 6 [48:7] [A] Trembling **seized** them there, pain like that of a
56: T [56:1] [A] When the Philistines *had* **seized** him in Gath.
73:23 [A] Yet I am always with you; *you* **hold** me by my right hand.
77: 4 [77:5] [A] *You* **kept** [+9073] my eyes **from closing**; I was too
119:53 [A] Indignation **grips** me because of the wicked, who have
137: 9 [A] *he* who **seizes** your infants and dashes them against the
139:10 [A] your hand will guide me, your right hand *will* **hold** me **fast**.
Ecc 2: 3 [A] I tried cheering myself with wine, and **embracing** folly—my
7:18 [A] It is good *to* **grasp** the one and not let go of the other. The
9:12 [C] As fish **are caught** in a cruel net, or birds are taken in a
9:12 [B] fish are caught in a cruel net, or birds **are taken** in a snare,
SS 2:15 [A] **Catch** for us the foxes, the little foxes that ruin the vineyards,
3: 4 [A] *I* **held** him and would not let him go till I had brought him to
3: 8 [B] all of them **wearing** the sword, all experienced in battle,
7: 8 [7:9] [A] will climb the palm tree; *I will* **take hold** of its fruit."
Isa 5:29 [A] they growl as *they* **seize** their prey and carry it off with no
13: 8 [A] Terror will seize them, pain and anguish *will* **grip** them;
21: 3 [A] with pain, pangs **seize** me, like those of a woman in labor;
33:14 [A] The sinners in Zion are terrified; trembling **grips** the godless:
Jer 13:21 [A] *Will* not pain **grip** you like that of a woman in labor?
49:24 [A] anguish and pain *have* **seized** her, pain like that of a woman
Eze 41: 6 [B] wall of the temple to serve as **supports** for the side rooms,
41: 6 [B] so that the **supports** were not inserted into the wall of the

297 ²אָחַז **'āḥaz**[2], v. [3] [√ 296]

attached to [1], covers [1], was attached [1]

1Ki 6:10 [A] and *they were* **attached to** the temple by beams of cedar.
2Ch 9:18 [H] had six steps, and a footstool of gold **was attached** to it.
Job 26: 9 [D] *He* **covers** the face of the full moon, spreading his clouds

298 אָחָז **'āḥāz**, n.pr.m. [41 / 42] [√ 301; cf. 296]

Ahaz [41], *untranslated* [1]

2Ki 15:38 the city of his father. And **Ahaz** his son succeeded him as king.
16: 1 of Remaliah, **Ahaz** son of Jotham king of Judah began to reign.
16: 2 **Ahaz** was twenty years old when he became king, and he reigned
16: 5 of Israel marched up to fight against Jerusalem and besieged **Ahaz**,
16: 7 **Ahaz** sent messengers to say to Tiglath-Pileser king of Assyria,
16: 8 **Ahaz** took the silver and gold found in the temple of the LORD
16:10 King **Ahaz** went to Damascus to meet Tiglath-Pileser king of
16:10 sketch of the altar, **[RPH]** with detailed plans for its construction.
16:11 with all the plans that King **Ahaz** had sent from Damascus
16:11 sent from Damascus and finished it before King **Ahaz** returned.
16:15 King **Ahaz** then gave these orders to Uriah the priest: "On the
16:16 And Uriah the priest did just as King **Ahaz** had ordered.
16:17 King **Ahaz** took away the side panels and removed the basins from
16:19 As for the other events of the reign of **Ahaz**, and what he did,
16:20 **Ahaz** rested with his fathers and was buried with them in the City
17: 1 In the twelfth year of **Ahaz** king of Judah, Hoshea son of Elah
18: 1 king of Israel, Hezekiah son of **Ahaz** king of Judah began to reign.
20:11 go back the ten steps it had gone down on the stairway of **Ahaz**.
23:12 of Judah had erected on the roof near the upper room of **Ahaz**,
1Ch 3:13 **Ahaz** his son, Hezekiah his son, Manasseh his son,
8:35 The sons of Micah: Pithon, Melech, Tarea and **Ahaz**.

1Ch 8:36 **Ahaz** was the father of Jehoaddah, Jehoaddah was the father of
9:41 The sons of Micah: Pithon, Melech, Tahrea and **Ahaz**. [BHS-]
9:42 **Ahaz** was the father of Jadah, Jadah was the father of Alemeth,
2Ch 27: 9 in the City of David. And **Ahaz** his son succeeded him as king.
28: 1 **Ahaz** was twenty years old when he became king, and he reigned
28:16 At that time King **Ahaz** sent to the king of Assyria for help.
28:19 The LORD had humbled Judah because of **Ahaz** king of Israel,
28:21 **Ahaz** took some of the things from the temple of the LORD
28:22 In his time of trouble King **Ahaz** became even more unfaithful to
28:24 **Ahaz** gathered together the furnishings from the temple of God
28:27 **Ahaz** rested with his fathers and was buried in the city of
29:19 consecrated all the articles that King **Ahaz** removed in his
Isa 1: 1 the reigns of Uzziah, Jotham, **Ahaz** and Hezekiah, kings of Judah.
7: 1 When **Ahaz** son of Jotham, the son of Uzziah, was king of Judah,
7: 3 to meet **Ahaz** at the end of the aqueduct of the Upper Pool,
7:10 Again the LORD spoke to **Ahaz**,
7:12 **Ahaz** said, "I will not ask; I will not put the LORD to the test."
14:28 This oracle came in the year King **Ahaz** died:
38: 8 **Ahaz**.' " So the sunlight went back the ten steps it had gone down.
Hos 1: 1 Jotham, **Ahaz** and Hezekiah, kings of Judah, and during the reign
Mic 1: 1 during the reigns of Jotham, **Ahaz** and Hezekiah, kings of Judah—

299 אֲחֻזָּה *ʾᵃḥuzzâ*, n.f. [66] [√ 296]

property [28], possession [14], land [+824] [4], possess [4], family land [+8441] [3], place [2], site [2], *untranslated* [1], family property [1], hold as a possession [1], hold [1], lands [1], occupied [1], property [+824] [1], territory [1], that[5] [1]

Ge 17: 8 I will give as an everlasting **possession** to you and your
23: 4 Sell me *some* **property** *for* a burial site here so I can bury my
23: 9 Ask him to sell it to me for the full price as a burial **site** among
23:20 cave in it were deeded to Abraham by the Hittites as a burial **site**.
36:43 of Edom, according to their settlements in the land they **occupied**.
47:11 in Egypt and gave them **property** in the best part of the land,
48: 4 I will give this land as an everlasting **possession** to your
49:30 which Abraham bought as a burial **place** from Ephron the Hittite,
50:13 which Abraham had bought as a burial **place** from Ephron the
Lev 14:34 the land of Canaan, which I am giving you as your **possession**,
14:34 and I put a spreading mildew in a house in **that**[5] land,
25:10 each one of you is to return to his **family property** and each to his
25:13 " 'In this Year of Jubilee everyone is to return to his own **property**.
25:24 Throughout the country that you **hold as a possession**, you must
25:25 of your countrymen becomes poor and sells some of his **property**,
25:27 man to whom he sold it; he can then go back to his own **property**.
25:28 be returned in the Jubilee, and he can then go back to his **property**.
25:32 to redeem their houses in the Levitical towns, which they **possess**.
25:33 that is, a house sold in any town they **hold**—and is to be returned
25:33 because the houses in the towns of the Levites are their **property**
25:34 to their towns must not be sold; it is their permanent **possession**.
25:41 will go back to his own clan and to the **property** *of* his forefathers.
25:45 clans born in your country, and they will become your **property**.
25:46 You can will them to your children as inherited **property** and can
27:16 a man dedicates to the LORD part of his **family land** [+8441],
27:21 devoted to the LORD; it will become the **property** of the priests.
27:22 a field he has bought, which is not part of his **family land** [+8441],
27:24 person from whom he bought it, the one whose **land** [+824] it was.
27:28 whether man or animal or **family land** [+8441]—may be sold
Nu 27: 4 he had no son? Give us **property** among our father's relatives."
27: 7 You must certainly give them **property** as an inheritance among
32: 5 "let this land be given to your servants as our **possession**.
32:22 And this land will be your **possession** before the LORD.
32:29 before you, give them the land of Gilead as their **possession**.
32:32 but the **property** we inherit will be on this side of the Jordan."
35: 2 towns to live in from the inheritance the Israelites will **possess**.
35: 8 The towns you give the Levites from the land the Israelites **possess**
35:28 death of the high priest may he return to his own **property** [+824].
Dt 32:49 the land I am giving the Israelites as their own **possession**.
Jos 21:12 city they had given to Caleb son of Jephunneh as his **possession**.
21:41 The towns of the Levites in the **territory** *held by* the Israelites
22: 4 return to your homes in the **land** [+824] that Moses the servant of
22: 9 at Shiloh in Canaan to return to Gilead, their own **land** [+824],
22:19 If the land you **possess** is defiled, come over to the LORD's land,
22:19 you possess is defiled, come over to the LORD's **land** [+824],
1Ch 7:28 Their **lands** and settlements included Bethel and its surrounding
9: 2 Now the first to resettle on their own **property** in their own towns
2Ch 11:14 The Levites even abandoned their pasturelands and **property**,
31: 1 Israelites returned to their own towns and to their own **property**.
Ne 11: 3 towns of Judah, each on his own **property** in the various towns,
Ps 2: 8 the nations your inheritance, the ends of the earth your **possession**.
Eze 44:28 You are to give them no **possession** in Israel; I will be their
44:28 are to give them no possession in Israel; I will be their **possession**.
45: 5 who serve in the temple, as their **possession** for towns to live in.
45: 6 " 'You are to give the city as its **property** an area 5,000 cubits
45: 7 the area formed by the sacred district and the **property** *of* the city.
45: 7 **[RPH]** It will extend westward from the west side and eastward
45: 8 This land will be his **possession** in Israel. And my princes will no
46:16 belong to his descendants; it is to be their **property** by inheritance.
46:18 of the inheritance of the people, driving them off their **property**.
46:18 He is to give his sons their inheritance out of his own **property**,
46:18 so that none of my people will be separated from his **property**.' "
48:20 set aside the sacred portion, along with the **property** *of* the city.
48:21 the sacred portion and the city **property** will belong to the prince.
48:22 So the **property** *of* the Levites and the property of the city will lie
48:22 the **property** *of* the city will lie in the center of the area that

300 אַחְזַי *ʾaḥzay*, n.pr.m. [1] [√ 301; cf. 296 + 3378]

Ahzai [1]

Ne 11:13 Amashsai son of Azarel, the son of **Ahzai**, the son of

301 אֲחַזְיָה *ʾᵃḥazyâ*, n.pr.m. [7] [→ 298, 300, 302, 304; cf. 296 + 3378]

Ahaziah [7]

2Ki 1: 2 Now **Ahaziah** had fallen through the lattice of his upper room in
9:16 and **Ahaziah** king of Judah had gone down to see him.
9:23 and fled, calling out to Ahaziah, "Treachery, **Ahaziah**!"
9:27 When **Ahaziah** king of Judah saw what had happened, he fled up
9:29 year of Joram son of Ahab, **Ahaziah** had become king of Judah.)
11: 2 took Joash son of **Ahaziah** and stole him away from among the
2Ch 20:35 Jehoshaphat king of Judah made an alliance with **Ahaziah** king of

302 אֲחַזְיָהוּ *ʾᵃḥazyāhû*, n.pr.m. [30 / 31] [√ 301; cf. 296 + 3378]

Ahaziah [27], Ahaziah's [4]

1Ki 22:40 with his fathers. And **Ahaziah** his son succeeded him as king.
22:49 [22:50] At that time **Ahaziah** son of Ahab said to Jehoshaphat,
22:51 [22:52] **Ahaziah** son of Ahab became king of Israel in Samaria in
2Ki 1:18 As for all the other events of **Ahaziah's** reign, and what he did,
8:24 in the City of David. And **Ahaziah** his son succeeded him as king.
8:25 of Israel, **Ahaziah** son of Jehoram king of Judah began to reign.
8:26 **Ahaziah** was twenty-two years old when he became king,
8:29 **Ahaziah** son of Jehoram king of Judah went down to Jezreel to see
9:21 Joram king of Israel and **Ahaziah** king of Judah rode out,
9:23 Joram turned about and fled, calling out to **Ahaziah**, "Treachery,
10:13 he met some relatives of **Ahaziah** king of Judah and asked,
10:13 They said, "We are relatives of **Ahaziah**, and we have come down
11: 1 When Athaliah the mother of **Ahaziah** saw that her son was dead,
11: 2 the daughter of King Jehoram and sister of **Ahaziah**,
12:18 [12:19] Jehoshaphat, Jehoram and **Ahaziah**, the kings of Judah—
13: 1 In the twenty-third year of Joash son of **Ahaziah** king of Judah,
14:13 of Judah, the son of Joash, the son of **Ahaziah**, at Beth Shemesh.
1Ch 3:11 Jehoram his son, **Ahaziah** his son, Joash his son,
2Ch 20:37 saying, "Because you have made an alliance with **Ahaziah**,
22: 1 The people of Jerusalem made **Ahaziah**, Jehoram's youngest son,
22: 1 So **Ahaziah** son of Jehoram king of Judah began to reign.
22: 2 **Ahaziah** was twenty-two years old when he became king,
22: 6 **Ahaziah** [BHS 6482] son of Jehoram king of Judah went down to
22: 7 Ahaziah's visit to Joram, God brought about **Ahaziah's** downfall.
22: 8 he found the princes of Judah and the sons of **Ahaziah's** relatives,
22: 8 who had been attending **Ahaziah**, and he killed them.
22: 9 He then went in search of **Ahaziah**, and his men captured him
22: 9 So there was no one in the house of **Ahaziah** powerful enough to
22:10 When Athaliah the mother of **Ahaziah** saw that her son was dead,
22:11 took Joash son of **Ahaziah** and stole him away from among the
22:11 was **Ahaziah's** sister, she hid the child from Athaliah so she could

303 אֲחֻזָּם *ʾᵃḥuzzām*, n.pr.m. [1] [√ 296]

Ahuzzam [1]

1Ch 4: 6 Naarah bore him **Ahuzzam**, Hepher, Temeni and Haahashtari.

304 אֲחֻזַּת *ʾᵃḥuzzat*, n.pr.m. [1] [√ 301; cf. 296]

Ahuzzath [1]

Ge 26:26 with **Ahuzzath** his personal adviser and Phicol the commander of

305 אֵחִי *ʾēḥî*, n.pr.m. [1] [√ 325]

Ehi [1]

Ge 46:21 Bela, Beker, Ashbel, Gera, Naaman, **Ehi**, Rosh, Muppim,

306 אֲחִי *ʾᵃḥî*, n.pr.m. [2] [√ 278]

Ahi [2]

1Ch 5:15 **Ahi** son of Abdiel, the son of Guni, was head of their family.
7:34 The sons of Shomer: **Ahi**, Rohgah, Hubbah and Aram.

307 אֲחִיאָם ʾaḥîʾām, n.pr.m. [2] [√ 278 + 4392?]

Ahiam [2]

2Sa 23:33 son of Shammah the Hararite, **Ahiam** son of Sharar the Hararite,
1Ch 11:35 **Ahiam** son of Sacar the Hararite, Eliphal son of Ur,

308 אֲחִיָּה ʾaḥiyyâ, n.pr.m. [19 / 18] [√ 278 + 3378]

Ahijah [16], Ahiah [1], Ahijah's [1]

1Sa 14: 3 among whom was **Ahijah**, who was wearing an ephod. He was a
14:18 Saul said to **Ahijah**, "Bring the ark of God." (At that time it was
1Ki 4: 3 Elihoreph and **Ahijah**, sons of Shisha—secretaries;
11:29 **Ahijah** the prophet of Shiloh met him on the way, wearing a new
11:30 **Ahijah** took hold of the new cloak he was wearing and tore it into
12:15 spoken to Jeroboam son of Nebat through **Ahijah** the Shilonite.
14: 2 **Ahijah** the prophet is there—the one who told me I would be king
14: 4 wife did what he said and went to **Ahijah's** house in Shiloh.
15:27 Baasha son of **Ahijah** of the house of Issachar plotted against him,
15:29 of the LORD given through his servant **Ahijah** the Shilonite—
15:33 Baasha son of **Ahijah** became king of all Israel in Tirzah,
21:22 that of Jeroboam son of Nebat and that of Baasha son of **Ahijah**,
2Ki 9: 9 son of Nebat and like the house of Baasha son of **Ahijah**.
1Ch 2:25 of Hezron: Ram his firstborn, Bunah, Oren, Ozem and **Ahijah**.
8: 7 Naaman, **Ahijah**, and Gera, who deported them and who was the
11:36 Hepher the Mekerathite, **Ahijah** the Pelonite,
26:20 Their fellow [BHS *Ahijah*; NIV 278] Levites were in charge of the
2Ch 9:29 in the prophecy of **Ahijah** the Shilonite and in the visions of Iddo
Ne 10:26 [10:27] **Ahiah**, Hanan, Anan,

309 אֲחִיָּהוּ ʾaḥiyyāhû, n.pr.m. [5] [√ 278 + 3378]

Ahijah [5]

1Ki 14: 4 Now **Ahijah** could not see; his sight was gone because of his age.
14: 5 the LORD had told **Ahijah**, "Jeroboam's wife is coming to ask
14: 6 So when **Ahijah** heard the sound of her footsteps at the door,
14:18 as the LORD had said through his servant the prophet **Ahijah**.
2Ch 10:15 spoken to Jeroboam son of Nebat through **Ahijah** the Shilonite.

310 אֲחִיהוּד ʾaḥîhûd, n.pr.m. [1] [√ 278 + 2086]

Ahihud [1]

Nu 34:27 **Ahihud** son of Shelomi, the leader from the tribe of Asher;

311 אַחְיוֹ ʾaḥyô, n.pr.m. [6] [√ 278 + 3378]

Ahio [6]

2Sa 6: 3 Uzzah and **Ahio**, sons of Abinadab, were guiding the new cart
6: 4 with the ark of God on it, and **Ahio** was walking in front of it.
1Ch 8:14 **Ahio**, Shashak, Jeremoth,
8:31 Gedor, **Ahio**, Zeker
9:37 Gedor, **Ahio**, Zechariah and Mikloth.
13: 7 Abinadab's house on a new cart, with Uzzah and **Ahio** guiding it.

312 אֲחִיחֻד ʾaḥîḥud, n.pr.m. [1] [√ 278 + 2086]

Ahihud [1]

1Ch 8: 7 who deported them and who was the father of Uzza and **Ahihud**.

313 אֲחִיטוּב ʾaḥîṭûb, n.pr.m. [15] [√ 278 + 3202]

Ahitub [15]

1Sa 14: 3 He was a son of Ichabod's brother **Ahitub** son of Phinehas,
22: 9 "I saw the son of Jesse come to Ahimelech son of **Ahitub** at Nob.
22:11 Then the king sent for the priest Ahimelech son of **Ahitub**
22:12 Saul said, "Listen now, son of **Ahitub**." "Yes, my lord,"
22:20 a son of Ahimelech son of **Ahitub**, escaped and fled to join David.
2Sa 8:17 Zadok son of **Ahitub** and Ahimelech son of Abiathar were priests;
1Ch 6: 7 [5:33] the father of Amariah, Amariah the father of **Ahitub**,
6: 8 [5:34] **Ahitub** the father of Zadok, Zadok the father of Ahimaaz,
6:11 [5:37] the father of Amariah, Amariah the father of **Ahitub**,
6:12 [5:38] **Ahitub** the father of Zadok, Zadok the father of Shallum,
6:52 [6:37] Meraioth his son, Amariah his son, **Ahitub** his son,
9:11 the son of Zadok, the son of Meraioth, the son of **Ahitub**,
18:16 Zadok son of **Ahitub** and Ahimelech son of Abiathar were priests;
Ezr 7: 2 the son of Shallum, the son of Zadok, the son of **Ahitub**,
Ne 11:11 the son of Zadok, the son of Meraioth, the son of **Ahitub**,

314 אֲחִילוּד ʾaḥîlûd, n.pr.m. [5] [√ 278 + 3528?]

Ahilud [5]

2Sa 8:16 was over the army; Jehoshaphat son of **Ahilud** was recorder;
20:24 in charge of forced labor; Jehoshaphat son of **Ahilud** was recorder;
1Ki 4: 3 sons of Shisha—secretaries; Jehoshaphat son of **Ahilud**—recorder;
4:12 Baana son of **Ahilud**—in Taanach and Megiddo, and in all of Beth
1Ch 18:15 was over the army; Jehoshaphat son of **Ahilud** was recorder;

315 אֲחִימוֹת ʾaḥîmôt, n.pr.m. [1] [√ 278 + 4637]

Ahimoth [1]

1Ch 6:25 [6:10] The descendants of Elkanah: Amasai, **Ahimoth**,

316 אֲחִימֶלֶךְ ʾaḥîmelek, n.pr.m. [17 / 18] [√ 278 + 4889]

Ahimelech [18]

1Sa 21: 1 [21:2] David went to Nob, to **Ahimelech** the priest. Ahimelech
21: 1 [21:2] **Ahimelech** trembled when he met him, and asked, "Why
21: 2 [21:3] David answered **Ahimelech** the priest, "The king charged
21: 8 [21:9] David asked **Ahimelech**, "Don't you have a spear or a
22: 9 "I saw the son of Jesse come to **Ahimelech** son of Ahitub at Nob.
22:11 Then the king sent for the priest **Ahimelech** son of Ahitub
22:14 **Ahimelech** answered the king, "Who of all your servants is as
22:16 will surely die, **Ahimelech**, you and your father's whole family."
22:20 a son of **Ahimelech** son of Ahitub, escaped and fled to join David.
23: 6 (Now Abiathar son of **Ahimelech** had brought the ephod down
26: 6 David then asked **Ahimelech** the Hittite and Abishai son of
30: 7 Abiathar the priest, the son of **Ahimelech**, "Bring me the ephod."
2Sa 8:17 Zadok son of Ahitub and **Ahimelech** son of Abiathar were priests;
1Ch 18:16 of Ahitub and **Ahimelech** [BHS 43] son of Abiathar were priests;
24: 3 a descendant of Eleazar and **Ahimelech** a descendant of Ithamar,
24: 6 **Ahimelech** son of Abiathar and the heads of families of the priests
24:31 in the presence of King David and of Zadok, **Ahimelech**,
Ps 52: T [52:2] told him: "David has gone to the house of **Ahimelech**."

317 אֲחִימָן ʾaḥîman, n.pr.m. [4] [√ 278 + ?]

Ahiman [4]

Nu 13:22 and came to Hebron, where **Ahiman**, Sheshai and Talmai,
Jos 15:14 Sheshai, **Ahiman** and Talmai—descendants of Anak.
Jdg 1:10 called Kiriath Arba) and defeated Sheshai, **Ahiman** and Talmai.
1Ch 9:17 Shallum, Akkub, Talmon, **Ahiman** and their brothers,

318 אֲחִימַעַץ ʾaḥîmaʿaṣ, n.pr.m. [15] [√ 278 + 5106]

Ahimaaz [15]

1Sa 14:50 His wife's name was Ahinoam daughter of **Ahimaaz**. The name of
2Sa 15:27 in peace, with your son **Ahimaaz** and Jonathan son of Abiathar.
15:36 two sons, **Ahimaaz** son of Zadok and Jonathan son of Abiathar,
17:17 Jonathan and **Ahimaaz** were staying at En Rogel. A servant girl
17:20 at the house, they asked, "Where are **Ahimaaz** and Jonathan?"
18:19 Now **Ahimaaz** son of Zadok said, "Let me run and take the news
18:22 **Ahimaaz** son of Zadok again said to Joab, "Come what may,
18:23 Then **Ahimaaz** ran by way of the plain and outran the Cushite.
18:27 "It seems to me that the first one runs like **Ahimaaz** son of
18:28 **Ahimaaz** called out to the king, "All is well!" He bowed down
18:29 **Ahimaaz** answered, "I saw great confusion just as Joab was about
1Ki 4:15 **Ahimaaz**—in Naphtali (he had married Basemath daughter of
1Ch 6: 8 [5:34] Ahitub the father of Zadok, Zadok the father of **Ahimaaz**,
6: 9 [5:35] **Ahimaaz** the father of Azariah, Azariah the father of
6:53 [6:38] Zadok his son and **Ahimaaz** his son.

319 אַחְיָן ʾaḥyān, n.pr.m. [1] [√ 278 + 5527?]

Ahian [1]

1Ch 7:19 The sons of Shemida were: **Ahian**, Shechem, Likhi and Aniam.

320 אֲחִינָדָב ʾaḥînādāb, n.pr.m. [1] [√ 278 + 5605]

Ahinadab [1]

1Ki 4:14 **Ahinadab** son of Iddo—in Mahanaim;

321 אֲחִינֹעַם ʾaḥînōʿam, n.pr.f. [7] [√ 278 + 5840]

Ahinoam [7]

1Sa 14:50 His wife's name was **Ahinoam** daughter of Ahimaaz. The name of
25:43 David had also married **Ahinoam** of Jezreel, and they both were
27: 3 **Ahinoam** of Jezreel and Abigail of Carmel, the widow of Nabal.
30: 5 **Ahinoam** of Jezreel and Abigail, the widow of Nabal of Carmel.
2Sa 2: 2 **Ahinoam** of Jezreel and Abigail, the widow of Nabal of Carmel.
3: 2 His firstborn was Amnon the son of **Ahinoam** of Jezreel;
1Ch 3: 1 The firstborn was Amnon the son of **Ahinoam** of Jezreel;

322 אֲחִיסָמָךְ ʾaḥîsāmāk, n.pr.m. [3] [√ 278 + 6164]

Ahisamach [3]

Ex 31: 6 Moreover, I have appointed Oholiab son of **Ahisamach**,
35:34 And he has given both him and Oholiab son of **Ahisamach**,
38:23 with him was Oholiab son of **Ahisamach**, of the tribe of Dan—

323 אֲחִיעֶזֶר ʾaḥîʿezer, n.pr.m. [6] [√ 278 + 6469]

Ahiezer [6]

Nu 1:12 from Dan, **Ahiezer** son of Ammishaddai;

Nu 2:25 The leader of the people of Dan is **Ahiezer** son of Ammishaddai.
7:66 On the tenth day **Ahiezer** son of Ammishaddai, the leader of the
7:71 This was the offering of **Ahiezer** son of Ammishaddai.
10:25 their standard. **Ahiezer** son of Ammishaddai was in command.
1Ch 12:3 **Ahiezer** their chief and Joash the sons of Shemaah the Gibeathite;

324 אֲחִיקָם ʼᵃḥîqām, n.pr.m. [20] [√ 278 + 7756]

Ahikam [20]

2Ki 22:12 **Ahikam** son of Shaphan, Acbor son of Micaiah, Shaphan the
22:14 **Ahikam**, Acbor, Shaphan and Asaiah went to speak to the
25:22 king of Babylon appointed Gedaliah son of **Ahikam**,
2Ch 34:20 **Ahikam** son of Shaphan, Abdon son of Micah, Shaphan the
Jer 26:24 **Ahikam** son of Shaphan supported Jeremiah, and so he was not
39:14 They turned him over to Gedaliah son of **Ahikam**, the son of
40:5 "Go back to Gedaliah son of **Ahikam**, the son of Shaphan,
40:6 So Jeremiah went to Gedaliah son of **Ahikam** at Mizpah
40:7 had appointed Gedaliah son of **Ahikam** as governor over the land
40:9 Gedaliah son of **Ahikam**, the son of Shaphan, took an oath to
40:11 a remnant in Judah and had appointed Gedaliah son of **Ahikam**,
40:14 take your life?" But Gedaliah son of **Ahikam** did not believe them.
40:16 But Gedaliah son of **Ahikam** said to Johanan son of Kareah,
41:1 came with ten men to Gedaliah son of **Ahikam** at Mizpah.
41:2 were with him got up and struck down Gedaliah son of **Ahikam**,
41:6 When he met them, he said, "Come to Gedaliah son of **Ahikam**."
41:10 of the imperial guard had appointed Gedaliah son of **Ahikam**.
41:16 of Nethaniah after he had assassinated Gedaliah son of **Ahikam**:
41:18 Ishmael son of Nethaniah had killed Gedaliah son of **Ahikam**,
43:6 of the imperial guard had left with Gedaliah son of **Ahikam**,

325 אֲחִירָם ʼᵃḥîrām, n.pr.m. [1] [→ 305, 326, 2586, 2587, 2670, 2671; cf. 278 + 8123]

Ahiram [1]

Nu 26:38 the Ashbelite clan; through **Ahiram**, the Ahiramite clan;

326 אֲחִירָמִי ʼᵃḥîrāmî, a.g. [1] [√ 325; cf. 278 + 8123]

Ahiramite [1]

Nu 26:38 the Ashbelite clan; through Ahiram, the **Ahiramite** clan;

327 אֲחִירַע ʼᵃḥîraʻ, n.pr.m. [5] [√ 278 + 8275 *or* 8276 *or* 8277]

Ahira [5]

Nu 1:15 from Naphtali, **Ahira** son of Enan."
2:29 The leader of the people of Naphtali is **Ahira** son of Enan.
7:78 On the twelfth day **Ahira** son of Enan, the leader of the people of
7:83 a fellowship offering. This was the offering of **Ahira** son of Enan.
10:27 **Ahira** son of Enan was over the division of the tribe of Naphtali.

328 אֲחִישָׁחַר ʼᵃḥîšāḥar, n.pr.m. [1] [√ 278 + 8837]

Ahishahar [1]

1Ch 7:10 Benjamin, Ehud, Kenaanah, Zethan, Tarshish and **Ahishahar**.

329 אֲחִישָׁר ʼᵃḥîšār, n.pr.m. [1]

Ahishar [1]

1Ki 4:6 **Ahishar**—in charge of the palace; Adoniram son of Abda—

330 אֲחִיתֹפֶל ʼᵃḥîtōpel, n.pr.m. [20] [√ 278 + 9523?]

Ahithophel [17], Ahithophel's [3]

2Sa 15:12 he also sent for **Ahithophel** the Gilonite, David's counselor,
15:31 been told, "**Ahithophel** is among the conspirators with Absalom."
15:31 "O LORD, turn **Ahithophel's** counsel into foolishness."
15:34 then you can help me by frustrating **Ahithophel's** advice.
16:15 men of Israel came to Jerusalem, and **Ahithophel** was with him.
16:20 Absalom said to **Ahithophel**, "Give us your advice. What should
16:21 **Ahithophel** answered, "Lie with your father's concubines whom
16:23 Now in those days the advice **Ahithophel** gave was like that of one
16:23 how both David and Absalom regarded all of **Ahithophel's** advice.
17:1 **Ahithophel** said to Absalom, "I would choose twelve thousand
17:6 came to him, Absalom said, "**Ahithophel** has given this advice.
17:7 "The advice **Ahithophel** has given is not good this time.
17:14 advice of Hushai the Arkite is better than that of **Ahithophel**."
17:14 good advice of **Ahithophel** in order to bring disaster on Absalom.
17:15 "**Ahithophel** has advised Absalom and the elders of Israel to do
17:21 river at once; **Ahithophel** has advised such and such against you."
17:23 When **Ahithophel** saw that his advice had not been followed,
23:34 of Ahasbai the Maacathite, Eliam son of **Ahithophel** the Gilonite,
1Ch 27:33 **Ahithophel** was the king's counselor. Hushai the Arkite was the
27:34 **Ahithophel** was succeeded by Jehoiada son of Benaiah and by

331 אַחְלָב ʼaḥlāb, n.pr.loc. [1]

Ahlab [1]

Jdg 1:31 or Sidon or **Ahlab** or Aczib or Helbah or Aphek or Rehob,

332 אַחֲלַי ʼaḥᵃlay, subst. [2]

if only [1], oh that [1]

2Ki 5:3 "**If only** my master would see the prophet who is in Samaria!
Ps 119:5 **Oh, that** my ways were steadfast in obeying your decrees!

333 אַחְלַי ʼaḥlay, n.pr. [2] [√ 278 + 446]

Ahlai [2]

1Ch 2:31 who was the father of Sheshan. Sheshan was the father of **Ahlai**.
11:41 Uriah the Hittite, Zabad son of **Ahlai**,

334 אַחְלָמָה ʼaḥlāmâ, n.f. [2]

amethyst [2]

Ex 28:19 in the third row a jacinth, an agate and an **amethyst**;
39:12 in the third row a jacinth, an agate and an **amethyst**;

335 אֲחַסְבַּי ʼᵃḥasbay, n.pr.m. [1] [√ 2879 + 928? + 3378?]

Ahasbai [1]

2Sa 23:34 Eliphelet son of **Ahasbai** the Maacathite, Eliam son of Ahithophel

336 אָחַר ʼāḥar, v. [17] [→ 294, 339, 340, 343, 344, 345, 4737, 4740; cf. 3508]

delay [5], delayed [2], slow [2], detain [1], hold back [1], late [1], linger [1], lost time [1], remained [1], stay up late [1], took longer [1]

Ge 24:56 [D] he said to them, "*Do* not **detain** me, now that the LORD has
32:4 [32:5] [A] with Laban and *have* **remained** there till now.
34:19 [D] **lost** no **time** in doing what they said, because he was
Ex 22:29 [22:28] [D] "*Do* not **hold back** offerings from your granaries
Dt 7:10 [D] *he will* not *be* **slow** to repay to their face those who hate him.
23:21 [23:22] [D] to the LORD your God, *do* not *be* **slow** to pay it,
Jdg 5:28 [D] long in coming? Why *is* the clatter of his chariots **delayed**?'
2Sa 20:5 [G] *he* **took longer** [K 3508] than the time the king had set for
Ps 40:17 [40:18] [D] my help and my deliverer; O my God, *do* not **delay**.
70:5 [70:6] [D] my help and my deliverer; O LORD, *do* not **delay**.
127:2 [D] In vain you rise early and stay up **late**, toiling for food to
Pr 23:30 [D] Those *who* **linger** over wine, who go to sample bowls of
Ecc 5:4 [5:3] [D] you make a vow to God, *do* not **delay** in fulfilling it.
Isa 5:11 [D] *who* **stay up late** at night till they are inflamed with wine.
46:13 [D] it is not far away; and my salvation *will* not *be* **delayed**.
Da 9:19 [D] For your sake, O my God, *do* not **delay**, because your city
Hab 2:3 [D] it linger, wait for it; it will certainly come and *will* not **delay**.

337 אַחֵר¹ ʼaḥēr[1], a. [166] [→ 338]

other [83], another [39], others [12], else [4], next [4], *untranslated* [3], another [+6388] [3], different [2], more [+6388] [2], more [2], additional [1], changed [+2200+4200] [1], new [1], other gods [1], second [1], set farther back [+2021+2958] [1], someone else [1], someone else's [1], strange [1], sword[s] [1], various [1], what[s] [1]

Ge 4:25 saying, "God has granted me **another** child in place of Abel,
8:10 He waited seven **more** [+6388] days and again sent out the dove
8:12 He waited seven **more** [+6388] days and sent the dove out again,
17:21 with Isaac, whom Sarah will bear to you by this time **next** year."
26:21 Then they dug **another** well, but they quarreled over that one also;
26:22 He moved on from there and dug **another** well, and no one
29:19 "It's better that I give her to you than to *some* **other** man.
29:27 one also, in return for **another** [+6388] seven years of work."
29:30 than Leah. And he worked for Laban **another** [+6388] seven years.
30:24 him Joseph, and said, "May the LORD add to me **another** son."
37:9 Then he had **another** [+6388] dream, and he told it to his brothers.
41:3 After them, seven **other** cows, ugly and gaunt, came up out of the
41:19 After them, seven **other** cows came up—scrawny and very ugly
43:14 so that he will let your **other** brother and Benjamin come back
43:22 We have also brought **additional** silver with us to buy food.
Ex 20:3 "You shall have no **other** gods before me.
21:10 If he marries **another** *woman*, he must not deprive the first one of
22:5 [22:4] and lets them stray and they graze in **another** *man's* field,
23:13 Do not invoke the names of **other** gods; do not let them be heard
34:14 Do not worship *any* **other** god, for the LORD, whose name is
Lev 6:11 [6:4] he is to take off these clothes and put on **others**, and carry
14:42 they are to take **other** stones to replace these and take new clay
14:42 stones to replace these and take **new** clay and plaster the house.
27:20 or if he has sold it to someone **else**, it can never be redeemed.
Nu 14:24 because my servant Caleb has a **different** spirit and follows me
23:13 "Come with me to **another** place where you can see them;
23:27 Balak said to Balaam, "Come, let me take you to **another** place.

Nu 36: 9 **[NIE]** for each Israelite tribe is to keep the land it inherits."
Dt 5: 7 "You shall have no **other** gods before me.
6: 14 Do not follow **other** gods, the gods of the peoples around you;
7: 4 for they will turn your sons away from following me to serve **other**
8: 19 and follow **other** gods and worship and bow down to them,
11: 16 to turn away and worship **other** gods and bow down to them.
11: 28 turn from the way that I command you today by following **other**
13: 2 [13:3] "Let us follow **other** gods" (gods you have not known)
13: 6 [13:7] worship **other** gods" (gods that neither you nor your
13: 13 [13:14] and worship **other** gods" (gods you have not known),
17: 3 contrary to my command has worshiped **other** gods, bowing down
18: 20 or a prophet who speaks in the name of **other** gods, must be put to
20: 5 go home, or he may die in battle and someone **else** may dedicate it.
20: 6 him go home, or he may die in battle and someone **else** enjoy it.
20: 7 him go home, or he may die in battle and someone **else** marry her."
24: 2 if after she leaves his house she becomes the wife of **another** man,
28: 14 to the right or to the left, following **other** gods and serving them.
28: 30 to be married to a woman, but **another** will take her and ravish her.
28: 32 Your sons and daughters will be given to **another** nation,
28: 36 There you will worship **other** gods, gods of wood and stone.
28: 64 There you will worship **other** gods—gods of wood and stone,
29: 26 [29:25] They went off and worshiped **other** gods and bowed
29: 28 [29:27] them from their land and thrust them into **another** land,
30: 17 if you are drawn away to bow down to **other** gods and worship
31: 18 that day because of all their wickedness in turning to **other** gods.
31: 20 and thrive, they will turn to **other** gods and worship them,
Jos 23: 16 and go and serve **other** gods and bow down to them,
24: 2 and Nahor, lived beyond the River and worshiped **other** gods.
24: 16 "Far be it from us to forsake the LORD to serve **other** gods!
Jdg 2: 10 had been gathered to their fathers, **another** generation grew up,
2: 12 and worshiped **various** gods of the peoples around them.
2: 17 but prostituted themselves to **other** gods and worshiped them.
2: 19 following **other** gods and serving and worshiping them.
10: 13 you have forsaken me and served **other** gods, so I will no longer
11: 2 they said, "because you are the son of **another** woman."
Ru 2: 8 Don't go and glean in **another** field and don't go away from here.
2: 22 his girls, because in **someone else's** field you might be harmed."
1Sa 8: 8 forsaking me and serving **other** gods, so they are doing to you.
10: 6 with them; and you will be changed into a **different** person.
10: 9 turned to leave Samuel, God **changed** [+2200+4200] Saul's heart,
17: 30 He then turned away to **someone else** and brought up the same
19: 21 Saul was told about it, and he sent **more** men, and they prophesied
21: 9 [21:10] you want it, take it; there is no **sword**[s] here but that one."
26: 19 in the LORD's inheritance and have said, 'Go, serve **other** gods.'
28: 8 putting on **other** clothes, and at night he and two men went to the
2Sa 13: 16 "Sending me away would be a greater wrong than **what**[s] you have
18: 20 "You may take the news **another** time, but you must not do
18: 26 the watchman saw **another** man running, and he called down to
1Ki 3: 22 The **other** woman said, "No! The living one is my son; the dead
7: 8 palace in which he was to live, **set farther back** [+2021+2958],
9: 6 I have given you and go off to serve **other** gods and worship them,
9: 9 and have embraced **other** gods, worshiping and serving them—
11: 4 As Solomon grew old, his wives turned his heart after **other** gods,
11: 10 Although he had forbidden Solomon to follow **other** gods,
13: 10 So he took **another** road and did not return by the way he had
14: 9 You have made for yourself **other** gods, idols made of metal;
20: 37 The prophet found **another** man and said, "Strike me, please."
2Ki 1: 11 At this the king sent to Elijah **another** captain with his fifty men.
5: 17 burnt offerings and sacrifices to *any* **other** god but the LORD.
6: 29 The **next** day I said to her, 'Give up your son so we may eat him,'
7: 8 They returned and entered **another** tent and took some things from
17: 7 the power of Pharaoh king of Egypt. They worshiped **other** gods
17: 35 "Do not worship *any* **other** gods or bow down to them, serve them
17: 37 and commands he wrote for you. Do not worship **other** gods.
17: 38 covenant I have made with you, and do not worship **other** gods.
22: 17 Because they have forsaken me and burned incense to **other** gods
1Ch 2: 26 Jerahmeel had **another** wife, whose name was Atarah; she was the
16: 20 wandered from nation to nation, from one kingdom to **another**.
23: 17 Eliezer had no **other** sons, but the sons of Rehabiah were very
2Ch 3: 11 the temple wall, while its **other** wing, also five cubits long,
3: 11 also five cubits long, touched the wing of the **other** cherub.
3: 12 Similarly one wing of the **second** cherub was five cubits long
3: 12 the other temple wall, and its **other** wing, also five cubits long,
7: 19 I have given you and go off to serve **other** gods and worship them,
7: 22 and have embraced **other** gods, worshiping and serving them—
28: 25 town in Judah he built high places to burn sacrifices to **other** gods
30: 23 then agreed to celebrate the festival seven **more** days;
32: 5 He built **another** wall outside that one and reinforced the
34: 25 Because they have forsaken me and burned incense to **other** gods
Ezr 1: 10 gold bowls 30 matching silver bowls 410 **other** articles 1,000
2: 31 of the **other** Elam 1,254
Ne 5: 5 because our fields and our vineyards belong to **others**."
7: 33 of the **other** Nebo 52
7: 34 of the **other** Elam 1,254
Est 4: 14 and deliverance for the Jews will arise from **another** place,
Job 8: 19 Surely its life withers away, and from the soil **other** plants grow.
31: 8 may **others** eat what I have sown, and may my crops be uprooted.
31: 10 may my wife grind **another** *man's* grain, and may other men sleep
31: 10 wife grind another man's grain, and may **other** *men* sleep with her.
34: 24 inquiry he shatters the mighty and sets up **others** in their place.
Ps 16: 4 The sorrows of those will increase who run after **other gods**.
49: 10 [49:11] the senseless alike perish and leave their wealth to **others**.
105: 13 wandered from nation to nation, from one kingdom to **another**.
109: 8 May his days be few; may **another** take his place of leadership.
109: 13 be cut off, their names blotted out from the **next** generation.
Pr 5: 9 lest you give your best strength to **others** and your years to one
25: 9 case with a neighbor, do not betray **another** *man's* confidence,
Ecc 7: 22 in your heart that many times you yourself have cursed **others**.
Isa 28: 11 foreign lips and **strange** tongues God will speak to this people,
42: 8 I will not give my glory to **another** or my praise to idols.
48: 11 can I let myself be defamed? I will not yield my glory to **another**.
65: 15 put you to death, but to his servants he will give **another** name.
65: 22 No longer will they build houses and **others** live in them, or plant
65: 22 they build houses and others live in them, or plant and **others** eat.
Jer 1: 16 in burning incense to **other** gods and in worshiping what their
3: 1 divorces his wife and she leaves him and marries **another** man,
6: 12 Their houses will be turned over to **others**, together with their
7: 6 this place, and if you do not follow **other** gods to your own harm,
7: 9 burn incense to Baal and follow **other** gods you have not known,
7: 18 They pour out drink offerings to **other** gods to provoke me to
8: 10 Therefore I will give their wives to **other** *men* and their fields to
11: 10 They have followed **other** gods to serve them. Both the house of
13: 10 of their hearts and go after **other** gods to serve and worship them,
16: 11 'and followed **other** gods and served and worshiped them.
16: 13 there you will serve **other** gods day and night, for I will show you
18: 4 so the potter formed it into **another** pot, shaping it as seemed best
19: 4 they have burned sacrifices in it to gods **[NIE]** that neither they
19: 13 all the starry hosts and poured out drink offerings to **other** gods.' "
22: 9 LORD their God and have worshiped and served **other** gods.' "
22: 26 hurl you and the mother who gave you birth into **another** country,
25: 6 Do not follow **other** gods to serve and worship them; do not
32: 29 the roofs to Baal and by pouring out drink offerings to **other** gods.
35: 15 and reform your actions; do not follow **other** gods to serve them.
36: 28 "Take **another** scroll and write on it all the words that were on the
36: 32 So Jeremiah took **another** scroll and gave it to the scribe Baruch
44: 3 by worshiping **other** gods that neither they nor you nor your
44: 5 turn from their wickedness or stop burning incense to **other** gods.
44: 8 burning incense to **other** gods in Egypt, where you have come to
44: 15 who knew that their wives were burning incense to **other** gods,
Eze 12: 3 as they watch, set out and go from where you are to **another** place.
40: 40 were two tables, and on the **other** side of the steps were two tables.
41: 24 door had two leaves—two hinged leaves for each door. **[NIE]**
42: 14 They are to put on **other** clothes before they go near the places that
44: 19 are to leave them in the sacred rooms, and put on **other** clothes,
Da 11: 4 because his empire will be uprooted and given to **others**.
12: 5 Then I, Daniel, looked, and there before me stood two **others**,
Hos 3: 1 though they turn to **other** gods and love the sacred raisin cakes."
Joel 1: 3 tell it to their children, and their children to the **next** generation.
Zec 2: 3 [2:7] speaking to me left, and **another** angel came to meet him

338 ²אַחֵר *'aḥēr²*, n.pr.m. [1] [√ 337]

Aher [1]

1Ch 7: 12 the descendants of Ir, and the Hushites the descendants of **Aher**.

339 אַחַר *'aḥar*, subst. & adv. & pp. [714] [→ 343; cf. 336; Ar 10021] See Select Index

after [205], *untranslated* [80], behind [42], followed [+2143] [27], follow [+2143] [20], next to [17], with [16], afterward [+4027] [15], to [13], follow [12], from [+4946] [12], followed [11], following [11], after that [10], then [10], behind [+4946] [9], in the course of time [+4027] [8], afterward [7], back [6], followed [+995] [6], following [+2143] [6], some time later [+465+1821+2021+2021] [6], pursue [5], pursuing [5], since [5], after [+4027] [4], now [4], of [4], west [4], later [+4027] [3], later [3], some time later [+4027] [3], succeed [3], after this [2], against [2], around [2], away from [+4946] [2], back [+4946] [2], beyond [2], chasing [2], finished [2], flee [2], follow [+2118] [2], followers [2], follows [+995] [2], in addition to [2], join [2], outlived [+799+3427] [2], pursue [+906+8938] [2], pursuing [+4946] [2], rear [2], tending [2], then [+4027] [2], after [+4946] [1], after a while [+465+1821+2021+2021] [1], after the time of [1], again [1], at [1], back [+7155] [1], backs [1], butt [1], calling to arms [+2410] [1], chasing [+1944] [1], departing from [+4946] [1], descendants [1], deserted [+4946+6590] [1], devoted to [+2143] [1], ends up [1], ever [1], far side [1], follow [+1815] [1], follow [+3655] [1], follow [+4946+7756] [1], follow [+6296] [1], follow [+7756] [1], follow [+995] [1], followed [+2118] [1], followed [+3655] [1], followed [+7756] [1], followed in [+995] [1], followers [+2143] [1], followers [+889+2021 +6639] [1], follows [+4027] [1], follows [1], for [1], from then on [+4027+4946] [1], future [1], gave support [+6468] [1], go over the branches a second time [+6994] [1], go over the vines again [+6618] [1], greedy [+2143] [1], how long [+5503+6388] [1], imitated [1], in hot pursuit [1], in the course of time [+4027+4946] [1], in [1], last of all [1], later [+2296] [1], later [+4027+4946] [1], later [+465+1821+2021 +2021] [1], lead on [+3870] [1], lead to do the same[s] [+466+906 +2177+2388] [1], leaves behind [1], led [+2143] [1], left [+4946] [1], loyal to [1], lust after [+2388] [1], lusted after [+2388] [1], next after [1], next in line [1], next [1], over [1], pursue [+2143] [1], pursue [+3655] [1], pursued [+2143] [1], pursuing [+2143] [1], pursuit [1], right behind [1], runs after for favors [+2388] [1], shortly after [1], since [+889] [1], some time after [1], some time later [1], succeeded [1], successive years [+9102+9102] [1], successor [+132+995+8611] [1], successor [1], supported [+2118] [1], supported [1], then [+2256] [1], those[s] [+889+2021+6639] [1], toward [1], under the command of [1], when [1], worshiping [1]

340 אַחֲרוֹן *'aḥarôn*, a.f. [51] [√ 336]

last [11], end [10], next [4], western [4], future [2], later [2], rear [2], second [2], then [+928+2021] [2], to come [2], end [+928+2021 +2118] [1], follow [1], he[s] [+408+2021+2021] [1], later [+928+2021] [1], present [1], then [1], this[s] [1], time [1], west [1], yet to come [1]

Ge 33: 2 Leah and her children **next**, and Rachel and Joseph in the rear.
33: 2 and her children next, and Rachel and Joseph *in* the **rear**.
Ex 4: 8 attention to the first miraculous sign, they may believe the **second**.
Nu 2: 31 Dan number 157,600. They will set out **last**, under their standards.
Dt 11: 24 to Lebanon, and from the Euphrates River to the **western** sea.
13: 9 [13:10] putting him to death, and **then** the hands of all the people.
17: 7 him to death, and **then** [+928+2021] the hands of all the people.
24: 3 her **second** husband dislikes her and writes her a certificate of
24: 3 and sends her from his house, or if **he**[s] [+408+2021+2021] dies,
29: 22 [29:21] Your children who follow you in **later** generations
34: 2 and Manasseh, all the land of Judah as far as the **western** sea,
Ru 3: 10 "**This**[s] kindness is greater than that which you showed earlier:
1Sa 29: 2 David and his men were marching at the **rear** with Achish.
2Sa 2: 26 Don't you realize that *this will* **end** [+928+2021+2118] *in*
19: 11 [19:12] 'Why should you be the **last** to bring the king back to his
19: 12 [19:13] So why should you be the **last** to bring back the king?'
23: 1 These are the **last** words of David: "The oracle of David son of
1Ki 17: 13 and **then** [+928+2021] make something for yourself and your son.
1Ch 23: 27 According to the **last** instructions of David, the Levites were
29: 29 As for the events of King David's reign, from beginning to **end**,
2Ch 9: 29 As for the other events of Solomon's reign, from beginning to **end**,
12: 15 As for the events of Rehoboam's reign, from beginning to **end**,
16: 11 The events of Asa's reign, from beginning to **end**, are written in
20: 34 The other events of Jehoshaphat's reign, from beginning to **end**,
25: 26 As for the other events of Amaziah's reign, from beginning to **end**,
26: 22 The other events of Uzziah's reign, from beginning to **end**,
28: 26 other events of his reign and all his ways, from beginning to **end**,
35: 27 all the events, from beginning to **end**, are written in the book of the
Ezr 8: 13 the **last** *ones*, whose names were Eliphelet, Jeuel and Shemaiah,
Ne 8: 18 Day after day, from the first day to the **last**, Ezra read from the
Job 18: 20 *Men of the* **west** are appalled at his fate; men of the east are seized
19: 25 Redeemer lives, and that *in* the **end** he will stand upon the earth.
Ps 48: 13 [48:14] that you may tell of them to the **next** generation.
78: 4 we will tell the **next** generation the praiseworthy deeds of the
78: 6 so the **next** generation would know them, even the children yet to
102: 18 [102:19] Let this be written for a **future** generation, that a people
Pr 31: 25 with strength and dignity; she can laugh at the days **to come**.
Ecc 1: 11 even those who are **yet to come** will not be remembered by those
1: 11 who are yet to come will not be remembered by those who **follow**.
4: 16 But those *who* came **later** were not pleased with the successor.
Isa 9: 1 [8:23] *in* the **future** he will honor Galilee of the Gentiles,
30: 8 that for the days **to come** it may be an everlasting witness.
41: 4 the LORD—with the first of them and with the **last**—I am he."
44: 6 I am the first and I am the **last**; apart from me there is no God.
48: 12 whom I have called: I am he; I am the first and I am the **last**.
Jer 50: 17 the **last** to crush his bones was Nebuchadnezzar king of Babylon."
Da 8: 3 horns was longer than the other but grew up **later** [+928+2021].
11: 29 but this **time** the outcome will be different from what it was before.
Joel 2: 20 into the eastern sea and those in the rear into the **western** sea.
Hag 2: 9 'The glory of this **present** house will be greater than the glory of
Zec 14: 8 half to the eastern sea and half to the **western** sea, in summer

341 אַחְרַח *'aḥraḥ*, n.pr.m. [1]

Aharah [1]

1Ch 8: 1 of Bela his firstborn, Ashbel the second son, **Aharah** the third,

342 אַחַרְחֵל *'aḥarḥēl*, n.pr.m. [1]

Aharhel [1]

1Ch 4: 8 and Hazzobebah and of the clans of **Aharhel** son of Harum.

343 אַחֲרַי *'aḥaray*, a. [1] [√ 339; cf. 336]

in the end [1]

Pr 28: 23 He who rebukes a man will **in the end** gain more favor than he

344 אַחֲרִית *'aḥarît*, n.f. [61] [√ 336; Ar 10022]

end [20], to come [8], future [7], last [4], future hope [3], left [3], descendants [2], at last [1], end of life [1], far side [1], final destiny [1], final outcome [1], future [+3427] [1], later in time [+928] [1], later [1], latter part of life [1], latter part [1], least [1], outcome [1], what happens [1], what might happen [1]

Ge 49: 1 so I can tell you what will happen to you in days **to come**.
Nu 23: 10 me die the death of the righteous, and may my **end** be like theirs!"
24: 14 you of what this people will do to your people in days **to come**."
24: 20 was first among the nations, but he will come to ruin **at last**."
Dt 4: 30 then in **later** days you will return to the LORD your God
8: 16 and to test you so that in the **end** it might go well with you.
11: 12 God are continually on it from the beginning of the year to its **end**.
31: 29 In days **to come**, disaster will fall upon you because you will do
32: 20 hide my face from them," he said, "and see what their **end** will be;
32: 29 and would understand this and discern what their **end** will be!
Job 8: 7 beginnings will seem humble, so prosperous will your **future** be.
42: 12 The LORD blessed the **latter part of** Job's **life** more than the
Ps 37: 37 observe the upright; there is a **future** for the man of peace.
37: 38 sinners will be destroyed; the **future** *of* the wicked will be cut off.
73: 17 entered the sanctuary of God; then I understood their **final destiny**.
109: 13 May his **descendants** be cut off, their names blotted out from the
139: 9 I rise on the wings of the dawn, if I settle on the **far side** *of* the sea,
Pr 5: 4 but *in* the **end** she is bitter as gall, sharp as a double-edged sword.
5: 11 At the **end of** your **life** you will groan, when your flesh and body
14: 12 is a way that seems right to a man, but *in* the **end** it leads to death.
14: 13 Even in laughter the heart may ache, and joy may **end** in grief.
16: 25 is a way that seems right to a man, but *in* the **end** it leads to death.
19: 20 to advice and accept instruction, and in the **end** you will be wise.
20: 21 quickly gained at the beginning will not be blessed at the **end**.
23: 18 There is surely a **future hope** for you, and your hope will not be
23: 32 *In* the **end** it bites like a snake and poisons like a viper.
24: 14 if you find it, there is a **future hope** for you, and your hope will
24: 20 for the evil man has no **future hope**, and the lamp of the wicked
25: 8 for what will you do in the **end** if your neighbor puts you to
29: 21 man pampers his servant from youth, he will bring grief *in* the **end**.
Ecc 7: 8 The **end** *of* a matter is better than its beginning, and patience is
10: 13 his words are folly; at the **end** they are wicked madness—
Isa 2: 2 In the **last** days the mountain of the LORD's temple will be
41: 22 so that we may consider them and know their **final outcome**.
46: 10 I make known the **end** from the beginning, from ancient times,
47: 7 did not consider these things or reflect on **what might happen**.
Jer 5: 31 and my people love it this way. But what will you do in the **end**?
12: 4 the people are saying, "He will not see **what happens** *to* us."
17: 11 they will desert him, and in the **end** he will prove to be a fool.
23: 20 of his heart. In days **to come** you will understand it clearly.
29: 11 and not to harm you, plans to give you hope and a **future**.
30: 24 the purposes of his heart. In days **to come** you will understand this.
31: 17 So there is hope for your **future**," declares the LORD. "Your
48: 47 "Yet I will restore the fortunes of Moab in days **to come**,"
49: 39 "Yet I will restore the fortunes of Elam in days **to come**,"
50: 12 She will be the **least** *of* the nations—a wilderness, a dry land,
La 1: 9 Her filthiness clung to her skirts; she did not consider her **future**.
Eze 23: 25 and your ears, and *those of* you *who* are **left** will fall by the sword.
23: 25 and *those of* you *who* are **left** will be consumed by fire.
38: 8 In **future** years you will invade a land that has recovered from war,
38: 16 In days **to come**, O Gog, I will bring you against my land,
Da 8: 19 to tell you what will happen **later** [+928] **in** the **time** *of* wrath,
8: 23 "In the **latter part** *of* their reign, when rebels have become
10: 14 to you what will happen to your people in the **future** [+3427],
11: 4 It will not go to his **descendants**, nor will it have the power he
12: 8 So I asked, "My lord, what will the **outcome** *of* all this be?"
Hos 3: 5 come trembling to the LORD and to his blessings in the **last** days.
Am 4: 2 you will be taken away with hooks, the **last** *of* you with fishhooks.
8: 10 like mourning for an only son and the **end** *of* it like a bitter day.
9: 1 of all the people; those who are **left** I will kill with the sword.
Mic 4: 1 In the **last** days the mountain of the LORD's temple will be

345 אֲחֹרַנִּית *'ăḥōrannît*, adv. [7] [→ 294; cf. 336]

back [2], backward [2], go back [+8740] [1], gone down [+3718] [1], turned the other way [1]

Ge 9: 23 they walked in **backward** and covered their father's nakedness.
9: 23 Their faces were **turned the other way** so that they would not see

1Sa 4: 18 ark of God, Eli fell **backward** off his chair by the side of the gate.
1Ki 18: 37 are God, and that you are turning their hearts **back** again."
2Ki 20: 10 said Hezekiah. "Rather, *have* it **go back** [+8740] ten steps."
20: 11 the ten steps *it had* **gone down** [+3718] on the stairway of Ahaz.
Isa 38: 8 I will make the shadow cast by the sun go **back** the ten steps it has

346 אֲחַשְׁדַּרְפָּן ***ʾ^{a}ḥašdarpān***, n.m.pl. [4] [→ Ar 10026]

satraps [4]

Ezr 8: 36 They also delivered the king's orders to the royal **satraps**
Est 3: 12 language of each people all Haman's orders to the king's **satraps**,
8: 9 to the **satraps**, governors and nobles of the 127 provinces
9: 3 the **satraps**, the governors and the king's administrators helped the

347 אֲחַשְׁוֵרוֹשׁ ***ʾ^{a}ḥašwērôš***, n.pr.m. [31] [cf. 348]

Xerxes [31]

Ezr 4: 6 At the beginning of the reign of **Xerxes**, they lodged an accusation
Est 1: 1 This is what happened during the time of **Xerxes**, the Xerxes who
1: 1 the **Xerxes** who ruled over 127 provinces stretching from India to
1: 2 At that time King **Xerxes** reigned from his royal throne in the
1: 9 gave a banquet for the women in the royal palace of King **Xerxes**.
1: 10 the seventh day, when King **Xerxes** was in high spirits from wine,
1: 15 "She has not obeyed the command of King **Xerxes** that the
1: 16 all the nobles and the peoples of all the provinces of King **Xerxes**.
1: 17 'King **Xerxes** commanded Queen Vashti to be brought before him,
1: 19 that Vashti is never again to enter the presence of King **Xerxes**.
2: 1 Later when the anger of King **Xerxes** had subsided,
2: 12 Before a girl's turn came to go in to King **Xerxes**, she had to
2: 16 She was taken to King **Xerxes** in the royal residence in the tenth
2: 21 became angry and conspired to assassinate King **Xerxes**.
3: 1 King **Xerxes** honored Haman son of Hammedatha, the Agagite,
3: 6 the Jews, throughout the whole kingdom of **Xerxes**.
3: 7 In the twelfth year of King **Xerxes**, in the first month, the month of
3: 8 Haman said to King **Xerxes**, "There is a certain people dispersed
3: 12 These were written in the name of King **Xerxes** *himself* and sealed
6: 2 the doorway, who had conspired to assassinate King **Xerxes**.
7: 5 King **Xerxes** asked Queen Esther, "Who is he? Where is the man
8: 1 That same day King **Xerxes** gave Queen Esther the estate of
8: 7 King **Xerxes** replied to Queen Esther and to Mordecai the Jew,
8: 10 Mordecai wrote in the name of King **Xerxes**, sealed the dispatches
8: 12 of King **Xerxes** was the thirteenth day of the twelfth month,
9: 2 provinces of King **Xerxes** to attack those seeking their destruction.
9: 20 letters to all the Jews throughout the provinces of King **Xerxes**,
9: 30 to all the Jews in the 127 provinces of the kingdom of **Xerxes**—
10: 1 King **Xerxes** [K 348] imposed tribute throughout the empire,
10: 3 Mordecai the Jew was second in rank to King **Xerxes**, preeminent
Da 9: 1 In the first year of Darius son of **Xerxes** (a Mede by descent),

348 אֲחַשֵׁרֹשׁ ***ʾ^{a}ḥašērōš***, n.pr.m. [0] [cf. 347]

Est 10: 1 [King **Xerxes** [K; see Q 347] imposed tribute throughout the]

349 אֲחַשְׁתָּרִי ***ʾ^{a}ḥaštārî***, n.pr.m. *or* a.g. Not used in NIV/BHS [→ 2028]

350 אֲחַשְׁתְּרָן ***ʾ^{a}ḥašt^{e}rān***, a. [2]

for king [1], royal [1]

Est 8: 10 who rode fast horses especially bred **for the king**.
8: 14 The couriers, riding the **royal** horses, raced out, spurred on by the

351 אַט ***ʾaṭ***[1], subst. [5]

gently [+4200] [2], gentle [1], meekly [1], slowly [+4200] [1]

Ge 33: 14 while I move along **slowly** [+4200] at the pace of the droves before
2Sa 18: 5 and Ittai, "Be **gentle** with the young man Absalom for my sake."
1Ki 21: 27 and fasted. He lay in sackcloth and went around **meekly**.
Job 15: 11 not enough for you, words spoken **gently** [+4200] to you?
Isa 8: 6 "Because this people has rejected the **gently** [+4200] flowing

352 אַט ***ʾaṭ***[2], v. Not used in NIV/BHS [cf. 5742]

353 אָטָד ***ʾāṭād***[1], n.m. [4] [→ 354]

thornbush [3], thorns [1]

Jdg 9: 14 "Finally all the trees said to the **thornbush**, 'Come and be our
9: 15 "The **thornbush** said to the trees, 'If you really want to anoint me
9: 15 let fire come out of the **thornbush** and consume the cedars of
Ps 58: 9 [58:10] Before your pots can feel ⌞the heat of⌟ the **thorns**—

354 אָטָד ***ʾāṭād***[2], n.pr.loc. [2] [√ 353]

Atad [2]

Ge 50: 10 When they reached the threshing floor of **Atad**, near the Jordan,
50: 11 who lived there saw the mourning at the threshing floor of **Atad**,

355 אֵטוּן ***ʾēṭûn***, n.[m.]. [1]

linens [1]

Pr 7: 16 I have covered my bed with colored **linens** *from* Egypt.

356 אִטִּים ***ʾiṭṭîm***, n.m. [1]

spirits of the dead [1]

Isa 19: 3 they will consult the idols and the **spirits of the dead**, the mediums

357 אָטַם ***ʾāṭam***, v. [8]

narrow [4], holds [1], shuts [1], stopped [1], stops [1]

1Ki 6: 4 [B] He made **narrow** clerestory windows in the temple.
Ps 58: 4 [58:5] [A] a snake, like that of a cobra *that has* **stopped** its ears,
Pr 17: 28 [A] wise if he keeps silent, and discerning if *he* **holds** his tongue.
21: 13 [A] If a *man* **shuts** his ears to the cry of the poor, he too will cry
Isa 33: 15 [A] *who* **stops** his ears against plots of murder and shuts his eyes
Eze 40: 16 [B] were surmounted by **narrow** parapet openings all around,
41: 16 [B] as well as the thresholds and the **narrow** windows
41: 26 [B] On the sidewalls of the portico were **narrow** windows with

358 אָטַר ***ʾāṭar***, v. [1] [→ 359, 360]

close [1]

Ps 69: 15 [69:16] [A] swallow me up or the pit **close** its mouth over me.

359 אָטֵר ***ʾāṭēr***, n.pr.m. [5] [√ 358]

Ater [5]

Ezr 2: 16 of **Ater** (through Hezekiah) 98
2: 42 of Shallum, **Ater**, Talmon, Akkub, Hatita and Shobai 139
Ne 7: 21 of **Ater** (through Hezekiah) 98
7: 45 of Shallum, **Ater**, Talmon, Akkub, Hatita and Shobai 138
10: 17 [10:18] **Ater**, Hezekiah, Azzur,

360 אִטֵּר ***ʾiṭṭēr***, a. [2] [√ 358]

left-handed [+3338+3545] [2]

Jdg 3: 15 cried out to the LORD, and he gave them a deliverer—Ehud, a **left-handed** [+3338+3545] man, the son of Gera the Benjamite.
20: 16 Among all these soldiers there were seven hundred chosen men who were **left-handed** [+3338+3545], each of whom could sling a

361 אֵי ***ʾê***, adv.inter. [38] [→ 372, 377, 378, 379, 402, 407, 686?]

where [16], where [+2296] [9], what [+2296] [3], which [+2296] [2], *untranslated* [1], by what [+2296] [1], no more [1], what [1], where [+5226] [1], which way [+2006+2021+2296] [1], which way [+2296] [1], why [+2296+4200] [1]

Ge 3: 9 But the LORD God called to the man, "**Where** are you?"
4: 9 Then the LORD said to Cain, "**Where** is your brother Abel?"
16: 8 And he said, "Hagar, servant of Sarai, **where** have you come from,
Ex 2: 20 "And **where** is he?" he asked his daughters. "Why did you leave
Dt 32: 37 will say: "Now **where** are their gods, the rock they took refuge in,
Jdg 13: 6 I didn't ask him **where** he came from, and he didn't tell me his
1Sa 9: 18 "Would you please tell me **where** [+2296] the seer's house is?"
25: 11 my shearers, and give it to men coming from who knows **where**?"
26: 16 **Where** are the king's spear and water jug that were near his head?"
30: 13 "To whom do you belong, and **where** do you come from?"
2Sa 1: 3 "**Where** have you come from?" David asked him. He answered,
1: 13 young man who brought him the report, "**Where** are you from?"
15: 2 Absalom would call out to him, "**What** town are you from?"
1Ki 13: 12 Their father asked them, "**Which** [+2296] way did he go?"
22: 24 "**Which** [+2296] **way** did the spirit from the LORD go when he
2Ki 3: 8 "**By what** [+2296] route shall we attack?" he asked. "Through the
19: 13 **Where** is the king of Hamath, the king of Arpad, the king of the
2Ch 18: 23 "**Which** [+2006+2021+2296] **way** did the spirit from the LORD go
Est 7: 5 "**Where** [+2296] is the man who has dared to do such a thing?"
Job 2: 2 And the LORD said to Satan, "**Where** have you come from?"
14: 10 But man dies and is laid low; he breathes his last and is **no more**.
20: 7 his own dung; those who have seen him will say, '**Where** is he?'
28: 12 can wisdom be found? **Where** [+2296] does understanding dwell?
28: 20 wisdom come from? **Where** [+2296] does understanding dwell?
38: 19 "**What** [+2296] is the way to the abode of light? And where does
38: 19 to the abode of light? And **where** [+2296] does darkness reside?
38: 24 **What** [+2296] is the way to the place where the lightning is
Pr 31: 4 [kings to drink wine, not for rulers to **crave** [Q; see K 197] beer,]
Ecc 2: 3 I wanted to see **what** [+2296] was worthwhile for men to do under
11: 6 for you do not know **which** [+2296] will succeed, whether this
Isa 19: 12 **Where** are your wise men now? Let them show you and make
50: 1 "**Where** [+2296] is your mother's certificate of divorce with which

Isa 66: 1 is my footstool. **Where** [+2296] is the house you will build for me?
66: 1 you will build for me? **Where** [+2296] will my resting place be?
Jer 5: 7 "**Why** [+2296+4200] should I forgive you? Your children have
6: 16 ancient paths, ask **where** [+2296] the good way is, and walk in it,
37: 19 [**Where** [K +2257; see Q 372] are your prophets who prophesied]
Jnh 1: 8 What is your country? **[NIE]** From what people are you?"
Mic 7: 10 she who said to me, "**Where** is the LORD your God?"
Na 3: 17 the sun appears they fly away, and no one knows **where** [+5226].

362 [1]אִי 'î[1], n.m. & f. [36] [cf. 363?]

islands [15], coastlands [8], coasts [5], island [2], coast [1], distant shores [+3542] [1], distant shores [1], maritime [1], shore [1], shores [1]

Ge 10: 5 (From these the **maritime** peoples spread out into their territories
Est 10: 1 tribute throughout the empire, to its **distant shores** [+3542].
Ps 72: 10 kings of Tarshish and of **distant shores** will bring tribute to him;
97: 1 LORD reigns, let the earth be glad; let the distant **shores** rejoice.
Isa 11: 11 from Babylonia, from Hamath and from the **islands** *of* the sea.
20: 6 In that day the people who live on this **coast** will say, 'See what has
23: 2 Be silent, you people of the **island** and you merchants of Sidon,
23: 6 Cross over to Tarshish; wail, you people of the **island**.
24: 15 name of the LORD, the God of Israel, in the **islands** *of* the sea.
40: 15 on the scales; he weighs the **islands** as though they were fine dust.
41: 1 "Be silent before me, you **islands**! Let the nations renew their
41: 5 The **islands** have seen it and fear; the ends of the earth tremble.
42: 4 justice on earth. In his law the **islands** will put their hope."
42: 10 the sea, and all that is in it, you **islands**, and all who live in them.
42: 12 give glory to the LORD and proclaim his praise in the **islands**.
42: 15 their vegetation; I will turn rivers into **islands** and dry up the pools.
49: 1 Listen to me, you **islands**; hear this, you distant nations: Before I
51: 5 The **islands** will look to me and wait in hope for my arm.
59: 18 and retribution to his foes; he will repay the **islands** their due.
60: 9 Surely the **islands** look to me; in the lead are the ships of Tarshish,
66: 19 to the distant **islands** that have not heard of my fame or seen my
Jer 2: 10 Cross over to the **coasts** *of* Kittim and look, send to Kedar
25: 22 of Tyre and Sidon; the kings of the **coastlands** across the sea;
31: 10 word of the LORD, O nations; proclaim it in distant **coastlands**:
47: 4 to destroy the Philistines, the remnant from the **coasts** *of* Caphtor.
Eze 26: 15 Will not the **coastlands** tremble at the sound of your fall, when the
26: 18 Now the **coastlands** tremble on the day of your fall; the islands in
26: 18 of your fall; the **islands** in the sea are terrified at your collapse.'
27: 3 at the gateway to the sea, merchant of peoples on many **coasts**,
27: 6 of cypress wood from the **coasts** *of* Cyprus they made your deck,
27: 7 your awnings were of blue and purple from the **coasts** *of* Elishah.
27: 15 traded with you, and many **coastlands** were your customers;
27: 35 All who live in the **coastlands** are appalled at you; their kings
39: 6 fire on Magog and on those who live in safety in the **coastlands**,
Da 11: 18 he will turn his attention to the **coastlands** and will take many of
Zep 2: 11 The nations on every **shore** will worship him, every one in its own

363 [2]אִי 'î[2], n.m. [3] [cf. 362?]

hyenas [3]

Isa 13: 22 **Hyenas** will howl in her strongholds, jackals in her luxurious
34: 14 Desert creatures will meet with **hyenas**, and wild goats will bleat
Jer 50: 39 "So desert creatures and **hyenas** will live there, and there the owl

364 [3]אִי 'î[3], adv. [1] [→ 374?, 376, 388]

not [1]

Job 22: 30 He will deliver even one who is **not** innocent, who will be

365 [4]אִי 'î[4], interj. [2]

pity [1], woe [1]

Ecc 4: 10 But **pity** the man who falls and has no one to help him up!
10: 16 **Woe** to you, O land whose king was a servant and whose princes

366 אָיַב *'āyab*, v. [1] [→ 367, 368, 373]

enemy [1]

Ex 23: 22 [A] *I will be an* **enemy** *to* your enemies and will oppose those

367 אֹיֵב *'ōyēb*, n.m. *or* v.ptcp. [282 / 281] [√ 366]

enemies [191], enemy [70], foes [12], foe [3], *untranslated* [1], enemy's [1], his[s] own [+2021] [1], their[s] [+3870] [1], whom[s] [1]

Ge 22: 17 descendants will take possession of the cities of their **enemies**,
49: 8 will praise you; your hand will be on the neck of your **enemies**;
Ex 15: 6 in power. Your right hand, O LORD, shattered the **enemy**.
15: 9 "The **enemy** boasted, 'I will pursue, I will overtake them. I will
23: 4 "If you come across your **enemy's** ox or donkey wandering off,
23: 22 I will be an enemy to your **enemies** and will oppose those who
23: 27 I will make all your **enemies** turn their backs and run.
Lev 26: 7 You will pursue your **enemies**, and they will fall by the sword
26: 8 ten thousand, and your **enemies** will fall by the sword before you.
26: 16 You will plant seed in vain, because your **enemies** will eat it.
26: 17 my face against you so that you will be defeated by your **enemies**;
26: 25 send a plague among you, and you will be given into **enemy** hands.
26: 32 the land, so that your **enemies** who live there will be appalled.
26: 34 that it lies desolate and you are in the country of your **enemies**;
26: 36 so fearful in the lands of their **enemies** that the sound of a
26: 37 So you will not be able to stand before your **enemies**.
26: 38 among the nations; the land of your **enemies** will devour you.
26: 39 of you who are left will waste away in the lands of their **enemies**
26: 41 toward them so that I sent them into the land of their **enemies**—
26: 44 Yet in spite of this, when they are in the land of their **enemies**,
Nu 10: 9 by the LORD your God and rescued from your **enemies**.
10: 35 May your **enemies** be scattered; may your foes flee before you."
14: 42 the LORD is not with you. You will be defeated by your **enemies**,
23: 11 I brought you to curse my **enemies**, but you have done nothing
24: 10 and said to him, "I summoned you to curse my **enemies**,
24: 18 Seir, his **enemy**, will be conquered, but Israel will grow strong.
32: 21 the LORD until he has driven his **enemies** out before him—
35: 23 since he was not his **enemy** and he did not intend to harm him,
Dt 1: 42 I will not be with you. You will be defeated by your **enemies**.' "
6: 19 thrusting out all your **enemies** before you, as the LORD said.
12: 10 and he will give you rest from all your **enemies** around you
20: 1 When you go to war against your **enemies** and see horses
20: 3 O Israel, today you are going into battle against your **enemies**.
20: 4 you to fight for you against your **enemies** to give you victory."
20: 14 the plunder the LORD your God gives you from your **enemies**.
21: 10 When you go to war against your **enemies** and the LORD your
23: 9 [23:10] When you are encamped against your **enemies**, keep
23: 14 [23:15] camp to protect you and to deliver your **enemies** to you.
25: 19 When the LORD your God gives you rest from all the **enemies**
28: 7 The LORD will grant that the **enemies** who rise up against you
28: 25 The LORD will cause you to be defeated before your **enemies**.
28: 31 Your sheep will be given to your **enemies**, and no one will rescue
28: 48 you will serve the **enemies** the LORD sends against you.
28: 53 Because of the suffering that your **enemy** will inflict on you during
28: 55 because of the suffering your **enemy** will inflict on you during the
28: 57 in the distress that your **enemy** will inflict on you in your cities.
28: 68 There you will offer yourselves for sale to your **enemies** as male
30: 7 The LORD your God will put all these curses on your **enemies**
32: 27 I dreaded the taunt of the **enemy**, lest the adversary misunderstand
32: 31 For their rock is not like our Rock, as even our **enemies** concede.
32: 42 of the slain and the captives, the heads of the **enemy** leaders."
33: 27 He will drive out your **enemy** before you, saying, 'Destroy him!'
33: 29 Your **enemies** will cower before you, and you will trample down
Jos 7: 8 what can I say, now that Israel has been routed by its **enemies**?
7: 12 That is why the Israelites cannot stand against their **enemies**;
7: 12 **[RPH]** because they have been made liable to destruction.
7: 13 You cannot stand against your **enemies** until you remove it.
10: 13 and the moon stopped, till the nation avenged itself on its **enemies**,
10: 19 Pursue your **enemies**, attack them from the rear and don't let them
10: 25 This is what the LORD will do to all the **enemies** you are going
21: 44 Not one of their **enemies** withstood them; the LORD handed all
21: 44 the LORD handed all their **enemies** over to them.
22: 8 and divide with your brothers the plunder from your **enemies**."
23: 1 the LORD had given Israel rest from all their **enemies** around
Jdg 2: 14 He sold them to their **enemies** all around, whom they were no
2: 14 their enemies all around, **whom**[s] they were no longer able to resist.
2: 18 saved them out of the hands of their **enemies** as long as the judge
3: 28 "for the LORD has given Moab, your **enemy**, into your hands."
5: 31 "So may all your **enemies** perish, O LORD! But may they who
8: 34 who had rescued them from the hands of all their **enemies** on every
11: 36 now that the LORD has avenged you of your **enemies**,
16: 23 "Our god has delivered Samson, our **enemy**, into our hands."
16: 24 saying, "Our god has delivered our **enemy** into our hands,
1Sa 2: 1 My mouth boasts over my **enemies**, for I delight in your
4: 3 that it may go with us and save us from the hand of our **enemies**."
12: 10 now deliver us from the hands of our **enemies**, and we will serve
12: 11 he delivered you from the hands of your **enemies** on every side,
14: 24 evening comes, before I have avenged myself on my **enemies**!"
14: 30 had eaten today some of the plunder they took from their **enemies**.
14: 47 rule over Israel, he fought against their **enemies** on every side:
18: 25 to take revenge on his **enemies**.' " Saul's plan was to have David
18: 29 afraid of him, and he remained his **enemy** the rest of his days.
19: 17 me like this and send my **enemy** away so that he escaped?"
20: 15 cut off every one of David's **enemies** from the face of the earth."
20: 16 saying, "May the LORD call David's **enemies** to account."
24: 4 [24:5] 'I will give your **enemy** into your hands for you to deal
24: 19 [24:20] When a man finds his **enemy**, does he let him get away
25: 22 May God deal with [BHS+ ***the enemies of***] David, be it ever so
25: 26 may your **enemies** and all who intend to harm my master be like
25: 29 the lives of your **enemies** he will hurl away as from the pocket of a
26: 8 to David, "Today God has delivered your **enemy** into your hands.
29: 8 Why can't I go and fight against the **enemies** *of* my lord the king?"

1Sa 30:26 is a present for you from the plunder of the LORD's **enemies**."
2Sa 3:18 hand of the Philistines and from the hand of all their **enemies**.' "
4:8 Ish-Bosheth son of Saul, your **enemy**, who tried to take your life.
5:20 the LORD has broken out against my **enemies** before me."
7:1 the LORD had given him rest from all his **enemies** around him,
7:9 have gone, and I have cut off all your **enemies** from before you.
7:11 my people Israel. I will also give you rest from all your **enemies**.
12:14 because by doing this you have made the **enemies** *of* the LORD
18:19 that the LORD has delivered him from the hand of his **enemies**."
18:32 "May the **enemies** *of* my lord the king and all who rise up to harm
19:9 [19:10] "The king delivered us from the hand of our **enemies**;
22:1 when the LORD delivered him from the hand of all his **enemies**
22:4 who is worthy of praise, and I am saved from my **enemies**.
22:18 He rescued me from my powerful **enemy**, from my foes, who were
22:38 "I pursued my **enemies** and crushed them; I did not turn back till
22:41 You made my **enemies** turn their backs in flight, and I destroyed
22:49 who sets me free from my **enemies**. You exalted me above my
1Ki 3:11 nor have asked for the death of your **enemies** but for discernment
8:33 "When your people Israel have been defeated by an **enemy**
8:37 or when an **enemy** besieges them in any of their cities,
8:44 "When your people go to war against their **enemies**, wherever you
8:46 you become angry with them and give them over to the **enemy**,
8:46 who takes them captive to **his**[s] [+2021] **own** land, far away
8:48 and soul in the land of their **enemies** who took them captive,
21:20 Ahab said to Elijah, "So you have found me, my **enemy**!"
2Ki 17:39 it is he who will deliver you from the hand of all your **enemies**."
21:14 remnant of my inheritance and hand them over to their **enemies**.
21:14 their enemies. They will be looted and plundered by all their **foes**,
1Ch 14:11 break out, God has broken out against my **enemies** by my hand."
17:8 have gone, and I have cut off all your **enemies** from before you.
17:10 I will also subdue all your **enemies**. " 'I declare to you that the
21:12 with **their**[s] [+3870] swords overtaking you, or three days of the
22:9 and I will give him rest from all his **enemies** on every side.
2Ch 6:24 "When your people Israel have been defeated by an **enemy**
6:28 or when **enemies** besiege them in any of their cities,
6:34 "When your people go to war against their **enemies**, wherever you
6:36 you become angry with them and give them over to the **enemy**,
20:27 for the LORD had given them cause to rejoice over their **enemies**.
20:29 heard how the LORD had fought against the **enemies** *of* Israel.
25:8 God will overthrow you before the **enemy**, for God has the power
26:13 for war, a powerful force to support the king against his **enemies**.
Ezr 8:22 for soldiers and horsemen to protect us from **enemies** on the road,
8:31 and he protected us from **enemies** and bandits along the way.
Ne 4:15 [4:9] When our **enemies** heard that we were aware of their plot
5:9 the fear of our God to avoid the reproach of our Gentile **enemies**?
6:1 the Arab and the rest of our **enemies** that I had rebuilt the wall
6:16 When all our **enemies** heard about this, all the surrounding nations
9:28 you abandoned them to the hand of their **enemies** so that they ruled
Est 7:6 Esther said, "The adversary and **enemy** is this vile Haman."
8:13 would be ready on that day to avenge themselves on their **enemies**.
9:1 On this day the **enemies** *of* the Jews had hoped to overpower them,
9:5 The Jews struck down all their **enemies** with the sword, killing
9:16 assembled to protect themselves and get relief from their **enemies**.
9:22 as the time when the Jews got relief from their **enemies**, and as the
Job 13:24 Why do you hide your face and consider me your **enemy**?
27:7 "May my **enemies** be like the wicked, my adversaries like the
33:10 Yet God has found fault with me; he considers me his **enemy**.
Ps 3:7 [3:8] Strike all my **enemies** on the jaw; break the teeth of the
6:10 [6:11] All my **enemies** will be ashamed and dismayed; they will
7:5 [7:6] let my **enemy** pursue and overtake me; let him trample my
8:2 [8:3] because of your enemies, to silence the **foe** and the avenger.
9:3 [9:4] My **enemies** turn back; they stumble and perish before you.
9:6 [9:7] Endless ruin has overtaken the **enemy**, you have uprooted
13:2 [13:3] in my heart? How long will my **enemy** triumph over me?
13:4 [13:5] my **enemy** will say, "I have overcome him," and my foes
17:9 wicked who assail me, from my mortal **enemies** who surround me.
18:T [18:1] the LORD delivered him from the hand of all his **enemies**
18:3 [18:4] who is worthy of praise, and I am saved from my **enemies**.
18:17 [18:18] He rescued me from my powerful **enemy**, from my foes,
18:37 [18:38] I pursued my **enemies** and overtook them; I did not turn
18:40 [18:41] You made my **enemies** turn their backs in flight, and I
18:48 [18:49] who saves me from my **enemies**. You exalted me above
21:8 [21:9] Your hand will lay hold on all your **enemies**; your right
25:2 not let me be put to shame, nor let my **enemies** triumph over me.
25:19 See how my **enemies** have increased and how fiercely they hate
27:2 when my enemies and my **foes** attack me, they will stumble
27:6 my head will be exalted above the **enemies** who surround me;
30:1 [30:2] out of the depths and did not let my **enemies** gloat over me.
31:8 [31:9] You have not handed me over to the **enemy** but have set
31:15 [31:16] deliver me from my **enemies** and from those who pursue
35:19 Let not those gloat over me *who* are my **enemies** without cause;
37:20 The LORD's **enemies** will be like the beauty of the fields,
38:19 [38:20] Many are *those who* are my vigorous **enemies**; those who
41:2 [41:3] in the land and not surrender him to the desire of his **foes**.
41:5 [41:6] My **enemies** say of me in malice, "When will he die
41:11 [41:12] with me, for my **enemy** does not triumph over me.
42:9 [42:10] must I go about mourning, oppressed by the **enemy**?"
43:2 Why must I go about mourning, oppressed by the **enemy**?
44:16 [44:17] those who reproach and revile me, because of the **enemy**,
45:5 [45:6] your sharp arrows pierce the hearts of the king's **enemies**;
54:7 [54:9] and my eyes have looked in triumph on my **foes**.
55:3 [55:4] at the voice of the **enemy**, at the stares of the wicked;
55:12 [55:13] If an **enemy** were insulting me, I could endure it; if a foe
56:9 [56:10] my **enemies** will turn back when I call for help. By this I
59:1 [59:2] Deliver me from my **enemies**, O God; protect me from
61:3 [61:4] you have been my refuge, a strong tower against the **foe**.
64:1 [64:2] protect my life from the threat of the **enemy**.
66:3 So great is your power that your **enemies** cringe before you.
68:1 [68:2] May God arise, may his **enemies** be scattered; may his foes
68:21 [68:22] Surely God will crush the heads of his **enemies**, the hairy
68:23 [68:24] that you may plunge your feet in the blood of your **foes**,
69:4 [69:5] many are my **enemies** without cause, those who seek to
69:18 [69:19] and rescue me; redeem me because of my **foes**.
71:10 For my **enemies** speak against me; those who wait to kill me
72:9 tribes will bow before him and his **enemies** will lick the dust.
74:3 all this destruction the **enemy** has brought on the sanctuary.
74:10 enemy mock you, O God? Will the **foe** revile your name forever?
74:18 Remember how the **enemy** has mocked you, O LORD, how
78:53 so they were unafraid; but the sea engulfed their **enemies**.
80:6 [80:7] of contention to our neighbors, and our **enemies** mock us.
81:14 [81:15] how quickly would I subdue their **enemies** and turn my
83:2 [83:3] See how your **enemies** are astir, how your foes rear their
89:10 [89:11] with your strong arm you scattered your **enemies**.
89:22 [89:23] No **enemy** will subject him to tribute; no wicked man will
89:42 [89:43] hand of his foes; you have made all his **enemies** rejoice.
89:51 [89:52] the taunts with which your **enemies** have mocked,
92:9 [92:10] For surely your **enemies**, O LORD, surely your enemies
92:9 [92:10] O LORD, surely your **enemies** will perish;
102:8 [102:9] All day long my **enemies** taunt me; those who rail against
106:10 hand of the foe; from the hand of the **enemy** he redeemed them.
106:42 Their **enemies** oppressed them and subjected them to their power.
110:1 "Sit at my right hand until I make your **enemies** a footstool for
110:2 scepter from Zion; you will rule in the midst of your **enemies**.
119:98 Your commands make me wiser than my **enemies**, for they are
127:5 be put to shame when they contend with their **enemies** in the gate.
132:18 I will clothe his **enemies** with shame, but the crown on his head
138:7 you stretch out your hand against the anger of my **foes**, with your
139:22 I have nothing but hatred for them; I count them my **enemies**.
143:3 The **enemy** pursues me, he crushes me to the ground; he makes me
143:9 Rescue me from my **enemies**, O LORD, for I hide myself in you.
143:12 In your unfailing love, silence my **enemies**; destroy all my foes,
Pr 16:7 to the LORD, he makes even his **enemies** live at peace with him.
24:17 Do not gloat when your **enemy** falls; when he stumbles, do not let
Isa 1:24 I will get relief from my foes and avenge myself on my **enemies**.
9:11 [9:10] foes against them and has spurred their **enemies** on.
42:13 shout he will raise the battle cry and will triumph over his **enemies**.
59:18 so will he repay wrath to his enemies and retribution to his **foes**;
62:8 "Never again will I give your grain as food for your **enemies**,
63:10 So he turned and became their **enemy** and he himself fought
66:6 It is the sound of the LORD repaying his **enemies** all they
66:14 made known to his servants, but his fury will be shown to his **foes**.
Jer 6:25 out to the fields or walk on the roads, for the **enemy** has a sword,
12:7 I will give the one I love into the hands of her **enemies**.
15:9 I will put the survivors to the sword before their **enemies**,"
15:11 surely I will make your **enemies** plead with you in times of disaster
15:14 I will enslave you to your **enemies** in a land you do not know,
17:4 I will enslave you to your **enemies** in a land you do not know,
18:17 Like a wind from the east, I will scatter them before their **enemies**;
19:7 I will make them fall by the sword before their **enemies**, at the
19:9 of the siege imposed on them by the **enemies** who seek their lives.'
20:4 own eyes you will see them fall by the sword of their **enemies**.
20:5 I will hand over to their **enemies** all the wealth of this city—
21:7 king of Babylon and to their **enemies** who seek their lives.
30:14 I have struck you as an **enemy** would and punished you as would
31:16 the LORD. "They will return from the land of the **enemy**.
34:20 I will hand over to their **enemies** who seek their lives. Their dead
34:21 and his officials over to their **enemies** who seek their lives,
44:30 Hophra king of Egypt over to his **enemies** who seek his life,
44:30 king of Babylon, the **enemy** who was seeking his life.' "
49:37 I will shatter Elam before their **foes**, before those who seek their
La 1:2 All her friends have betrayed her; they have become her **enemies**.
1:5 Her foes have become her masters; her **enemies** are at ease.
1:9 O LORD, on my affliction, for the **enemy** has triumphed."
1:16 My children are destitute because the **enemy** has prevailed."
1:21 All my **enemies** have heard of my distress; they rejoice at what
2:3 He has withdrawn his right hand at the approach of the **enemy**.
2:4 Like an **enemy** he has strung his bow; his right hand is ready.
2:5 The Lord is like an **enemy**; he has swallowed up Israel. He has

La 2: 7 He has handed over to the **enemy** the walls of her palaces;
2:16 All your **enemies** open their mouths wide against you; they scoff
2:17 he has let the **enemy** gloat over you, he has exalted the horn of
2:22 those I cared for and reared, my **enemy** has destroyed."
3:46 "All our **enemies** have opened their mouths wide against us.
3:52 *Those who* were my **enemies** without cause hunted me like a bird.
4:12 that **enemies** and foes could enter the gates of Jerusalem.
Eze 36: 2 is what the Sovereign LORD says: The **enemy** said of you, "Aha!
39:27 and have gathered them from the countries of their **enemies**,
Hos 8: 3 But Israel has rejected what is good; an **enemy** will pursue him.
Am 9: 4 Though they are driven into exile by their **enemies**, there I will
Mic 2: 8 Lately my people have risen up like an **enemy**. You strip off the
4:10 the LORD will redeem you out of the hand of your **enemies**.
5: 9 [5:8] over your enemies, and all your **foes** will be destroyed.
7: 6 a man's **enemies** are the members of his own household.
7: 8 Do not gloat over me, my **enemy**! Though I have fallen, I will rise.
7:10 Then my **enemy** will see it and will be covered with shame,
Na 1: 2 vengeance on his foes and maintains his wrath against his **enemies**.
1: 8 make an end of ˻Nineveh˼; he will pursue his **foes** into darkness.
3:11 you will go into hiding and seek refuge from the **enemy**.
3:13 The gates of your land are wide open to your **enemies**; fire has
Zep 3:15 has taken away your punishment, he has turned back your **enemy**.

368 אֵיבָה 'êbâ, n.f. [5] [√ 366]

hostility [4], enmity [1]

Ge 3:15 I will put **enmity** between you and the woman, and between your
Nu 35:21 or if in **hostility** he hits him with his fist so that he dies, that person
35:22 " 'But if without **hostility** someone suddenly shoves another
Eze 25:15 in their hearts, and with ancient **hostility** sought to destroy Judah,
35: 5 " 'Because you harbored an ancient **hostility** and delivered the

369 אֵיד 'êd, n.m. [24] [√ 202]

disaster [16], calamity [3], destruction [2], fall [1], ruin [1], siege ramps [+784] [1]

Dt 32:35 their day of **disaster** is near and their doom rushes upon them."
2Sa 22:19 They confronted me in the day of my **disaster**, but the LORD was
Job 18:12 is hungry for him; **disaster** is ready for him when he falls.
21:17 How often does **calamity** come upon them, the fate God allots in
21:30 that the evil man is spared from the day of **calamity**, that he is
30:12 snares for my feet, they build their **siege ramps** [+784] against me.
31: 3 Is it not **ruin** for the wicked, disaster for those who do wrong?
31:23 For I dreaded **destruction** *from* God, and for fear of his splendor I
Ps 18:18 [18:19] They confronted me in the day of my **disaster**,
Pr 1:26 I in turn will laugh at your **disaster**; I will mock when calamity
1:27 when **disaster** sweeps over you like a whirlwind, when distress
6:15 Therefore **disaster** will overtake him in an instant; he will
17: 5 their Maker; whoever gloats over **disaster** will not go unpunished.
24:22 for those two will send sudden **destruction** upon them, and who
27:10 and do not go to your brother's house when **disaster** strikes you—
Jer 18:17 show them my back and not my face in the day of their **disaster**."
46:21 stand their ground, for the day of **disaster** is coming upon them,
48:16 "The **fall** *of* Moab is at hand; her calamity will come quickly.
49: 8 for I will bring **disaster** on Esau at the time I punish him.
49:32 in distant places and will bring **disaster** on them from every side,"
Eze 35: 5 the Israelites over to the sword at the time of their **calamity**,
Ob 1:13 march through the gates of my people in the day of their **disaster**,
1:13 look down on them in their calamity in the day of their **disaster**,
1:13 of their disaster, nor seize their wealth in the day of their **disaster**.

370 אַיָּה 'ayyâ[1], n.f. [3 / 4] [→ 371]

black kite [2], falcon's [1], vultures [1]

Lev 11:14 the red kite, any kind of **black kite**,
Dt 14:13 the red kite, the **black kite**, any kind of falcon,
Job 15:23 He wanders about—food for **vultures**; [BHS 372] he knows the
28: 7 bird of prey knows that hidden path, no **falcon's** eye has seen it.

371 אַיָּה[2] 'ayyâ[2], n.pr.m. [6] [√ 370]

Aiah [4], Aiah's [2]

Ge 36:24 The sons of Zibeon: **Aiah** and Anah. This is the Anah who
2Sa 3: 7 Now Saul had had a concubine named Rizpah daughter of **Aiah**.
21: 8 and Mephibosheth, the two sons of **Aiah's** daughter Rizpah,
21:10 Rizpah daughter of **Aiah** took sackcloth and spread it out for
21:11 When David was told what **Aiah's** daughter Rizpah,
1Ch 1:40 Ebal, Shepho and Onam. The sons of Zibeon: **Aiah** and Anah.

372 אַיֵּה 'ayyēh, adv.inter. [45 / 44] [√ 361]

where [43], *untranslated* [1]

Ge 18: 9 "**Where** is your wife Sarah?" they asked him. "There, in the tent,"
19: 5 They called to Lot, "**Where** are the men who came to you tonight?
22: 7 Isaac said, "but **where** is the lamb for the burnt offering?"
38:21 "**Where** is the shrine prostitute who was beside the road at
Jdg 6:13 **Where** are all his wonders that our fathers told us about when they
9:38 Zebul said to him, "**Where** is your big talk now, you who said,
2Sa 16: 3 The king then asked, "**Where** is your master's grandson?"
17:20 at the house, they asked, "**Where** are Ahimaaz and Jonathan?"
2Ki 2:14 "**Where** now is the LORD, the God of Elijah?" he asked.
18:34 **Where** are the gods of Hamath and Arpad? Where are the gods of
18:34 and Arpad? **Where** are the gods of Sepharvaim, Hena and Ivvah?
Job 15:23 wanders about—food for vultures; [BHS ***where** is food?*; NIV 370]
17:15 **where** then is my hope? Who can see any hope for me?
21:28 You say, '**Where** now is the great man's house, the tents where
21:28 the great man's house, **[RPH]** the tents where wicked men lived?'
35:10 no one says, '**Where** is God my Maker, who gives songs in the
Ps 42: 3 [42:4] while men say to me all day long, "**Where** is your God?"
42:10 [42:11] saying to me all day long, "**Where** is your God?"
79:10 Why should the nations say, "**Where** is their God?" Before our
89:49 [89:50] O Lord, **where** is your former great love, which in your
115: 2 Why do the nations say, "**Where** is their God?"
Isa 33:18 "**Where** is that chief officer? Where is the one who took the
33:18 is that chief officer? **Where** is the one who took the revenue?
33:18 took the revenue? **Where** is the officer in charge of the towers?"
36:19 **Where** are the gods of Hamath and Arpad? Where are the gods of
36:19 gods of Hamath and Arpad? **Where** are the gods of Sepharvaim?
37:13 **Where** is the king of Hamath, the king of Arpad, the king of the
51:13 is bent on destruction? For **where** is the wrath of the oppressor?
63:11 **where** is he who brought them through the sea, with the shepherd
63:11 of his flock? **Where** is he who set his Holy Spirit among them,
63:15 holy and glorious. **Where** are your zeal and your might?
Jer 2: 6 They did not ask, '**Where** is the LORD, who brought us up out of
2: 8 The priests did not ask, '**Where** is the LORD?' Those who deal
2:28 **Where** then are the gods you made for yourselves? Let them come
13:20 **Where** is the flock that was entrusted to you, the sheep of which
17:15 They keep saying to me, "**Where** is the word of the LORD?
37:19 **Where** [K 361+2257] are your prophets who prophesied to you,
La 2:12 They say to their mothers, "**Where** is bread and wine?" as they
Eze 13:12 not ask you, "**Where** is the whitewash you covered it with?"
Joel 2:17 Why should they say among the peoples, '**Where** is their God?' "
Na 2:11 [2:12] **Where** now is the lions' den, the place where they fed their
Zec 1: 5 **Where** are your forefathers now? And the prophets, do they live
Mal 1: 6 If I am a father, **where** is the honor due me? If I am a master,
1: 6 If I am a master, **where** is the respect due me?" says the LORD
2:17 and he is pleased with them" or "**Where** is the God of justice?"

373 אִיּוֹב 'iyyôb, n.pr.m. [58] [√ 366]

Job [49], Job's [5], he[s] [3], *untranslated* [1]

Job 1: 1 In the land of Uz there lived a man whose name was **Job**.
1: 5 had run its course, **Job** would send and have them purified.
1: 5 **[RPH]** "Perhaps my children have sinned and cursed God in their
1: 5 and cursed God in their hearts." This was **Job's** regular custom.
1: 8 the LORD said to Satan, "Have you considered my servant **Job**?
1: 9 "Does **Job** fear God for nothing?" Satan replied.
1:14 a messenger came to **Job** and said, "The oxen were plowing
1:20 At this, **Job** got up and tore his robe and shaved his head.
1:22 In all this, **Job** did not sin by charging God with wrongdoing.
2: 3 the LORD said to Satan, "Have you considered my servant **Job**?
2: 7 afflicted **Job** with painful sores from the soles of his feet to the top
2:10 and not trouble?" In all this, **Job** did not sin in what he said.
2:11 When **Job's** three friends, Eliphaz the Temanite, Bildad the
3: 1 After this, **Job** opened his mouth and cursed the day of his birth.
3: 2 **He**[s] said:
6: 1 Then **Job** replied:
9: 1 Then **Job** replied:
12: 1 Then **Job** replied:
16: 1 Then **Job** replied:
19: 1 Then **Job** replied:
21: 1 Then **Job** replied:
23: 1 Then **Job** replied:
26: 1 Then **Job** replied:
27: 1 And **Job** continued his discourse:
29: 1 **Job** continued his discourse:
31:40 and weeds instead of barley." The words of **Job** are ended.
32: 1 So these three men stopped answering **Job**, because he was
32: 2 became very angry with **Job** for justifying himself rather than God.
32: 3 because they had found no way to refute **Job**, and yet had
32: 4 Now Elihu had waited before speaking to **Job** because they were
32:12 not one of you has proved **Job** wrong; none of you has answered
33: 1 "But now, **Job**, listen to my words; pay attention to everything I
33:31 "Pay attention, **Job**, and listen to me; be silent, and I will speak.
34: 5 "**Job** says, 'I am innocent, but God denies me justice.
34: 7 What man is like **Job**, who drinks scorn like water?
34:35 '**Job** speaks without knowledge; his words lack insight.'
34:36 that **Job** might be tested to the utmost for answering like a wicked
35:16 So **Job** opens his mouth with empty talk; without knowledge he

Job 37:14 "Listen to this, **Job**; stop and consider God's wonders.
38: 1 Then the LORD answered **Job** out of the storm. He said:
40: 1 The LORD said to **Job**:
40: 3 Then **Job** answered the LORD:
40: 6 Then the LORD spoke to **Job** out of the storm:
42: 1 Then **Job** replied to the LORD:
42: 7 After the LORD had said these things to **Job**, he said to Eliphaz
42: 7 you have not spoken of me what is right, as my servant **Job** has.
42: 8 So now take seven bulls and seven rams and go to my servant **Job**
42: 8 My servant **Job** will pray for you, and I will accept his prayer
42: 8 You have not spoken of me what is right, as my servant **Job** has."
42: 9 the LORD told them; and the LORD accepted **Job's** prayer.
42:10 After **Job** had prayed for his friends, the LORD made him
42:10 prosperous again and gave him twice as much as **he**[s] had before.
42:12 The LORD blessed the latter part of **Job's** life more than the first.
42:15 the land were there found women as beautiful as **Job's** daughters,
42:16 After this, **Job** lived a hundred and forty years; he saw his children
42:17 And so **he**[s] died, old and full of years.
Eze 14:14 Noah, Daniel and **Job**—were in it, they could save only
14:20 the Sovereign LORD, even if Noah, Daniel and **Job** were in it,

374 אִיזֶבֶל *'îzebel*, n.pr.f. [22] [√ 364? + 2292?]

Jezebel [18], Jezebel's [3], she[s] [1]

1Ki 16:31 he also married **Jezebel** daughter of Ethbaal king of the Sidonians,
18: 4 While **Jezebel** was killing off the LORD's prophets, Obadiah had
18:13 what I did while **Jezebel** was killing the prophets of the LORD?
18:19 the four hundred prophets of Asherah, who eat at **Jezebel's** table."
19: 1 Now Ahab told **Jezebel** everything Elijah had done and how he
19: 2 So **Jezebel** sent a messenger to Elijah to say, "May the gods deal
21: 5 His wife **Jezebel** came in and asked him, "Why are you so sullen?
21: 7 **Jezebel** his wife said, "Is this how you act as king over Israel?
21:11 nobles who lived in Naboth's city did as **Jezebel** directed in the
21:14 Then they sent word to **Jezebel**: "Naboth has been stoned
21:15 As soon as **Jezebel** heard that Naboth had been stoned to death,
21:15 **she**[s] said to Ahab, "Get up and take possession of the vineyard of
21:23 "And also concerning **Jezebel** the LORD says: 'Dogs will devour
21:23 the LORD says: 'Dogs will devour **Jezebel** by the wall of Jezreel.'
21:25 to do evil in the eyes of the LORD, urged on by **Jezebel** his wife.
2Ki 9: 7 and the blood of all the LORD's servants shed by **Jezebel**.
9:10 As for **Jezebel**, dogs will devour her on the plot of ground at
9:22 as all the idolatry and witchcraft of your mother **Jezebel** abound?"
9:30 When **Jezebel** heard about it, she painted her eyes, arranged her
9:36 On the plot of ground at Jezreel dogs will devour **Jezebel's** flesh.
9:37 **Jezebel's** body will be like refuse on the ground in the plot at
9:37 at Jezreel, so that no one will be able to say, 'This is **Jezebel**.' "

375 אֵיךְ *'êk*, adv.inter. & excl. [61] [cf. 2120]

how [47], why [6], what [4], *untranslated* [1], how gladly [1], too [1], what else [1]

Ge 26: 9 **Why** did you say, 'She is my sister'?" Isaac answered him,
39: 9 **How** then could I do such a wicked thing and sin against God?"
44: 8 So **why** would we steal silver or gold from your master's house?
44:34 **How** can I go back to my father if the boy is not with me?
Ex 6:12 **why** would Pharaoh listen to me, since I speak with faltering lips?"
6:30 I speak with faltering lips, **why** would Pharaoh listen to me?"
Jos 9: 7 you live near us. **How** then can we make a treaty with you?"
Jdg 16:15 she said to him, "**How** can you say, 'I love you,' when you won't
Ru 3:18 Naomi said, "Wait, my daughter, until you find out **what** happens.
1Sa 16: 2 Samuel said, "**How** can I go? Saul will hear about it and kill me."
2Sa 1: 5 "**How** do you know that Saul and his son Jonathan are dead?"
1:14 "**Why** were you not afraid to lift your hand to destroy the
1:19 O Israel, lies slain on your heights. **How** the mighty have fallen!
1:25 "**How** the mighty have fallen in battle! Jonathan lies slain on your
1:27 "**How** the mighty have fallen! The weapons of war have perished!"
2:22 strike you down? **How** could I look your brother Joab in the face?"
6: 9 and said, "**How** can the ark of the LORD ever come to me?"
12:18 he would not listen to us. **How** can we tell him the child is dead?
1Ki 12: 6 "**How** would you advise me to answer these people?" he asked.
2Ki 10: 4 and said, "If two kings could not resist him, **how** can we?"
17:28 to live in Bethel and taught them **how** to worship the LORD.
18:24 **How** can you repulse one officer of the least of my master's
2Ch 10: 6 "**How** would you advise me to answer these people?" he asked.
Job 21:34 "So **how** can you console me with your nonsense? Nothing is left
Ps 11: 1 In the LORD I take refuge. **How** *then* can you say to me:
73:19 **How** suddenly are they destroyed, completely swept away by
137: 4 **How** can we sing the songs of the LORD while in a foreign land?
Pr 5:12 You will say, "**How** I hated discipline! How my heart spurned
Ecc 2:16 both will be forgotten. Like the fool, the wise man **too** must die!
4:11 they will keep warm. But **how** can one keep warm alone?
Isa 14: 4 **How** the oppressor has come to an end! How his fury has ended!
14:12 **How** you have fallen from heaven, O morning star, son of the
19:11 **How** can you say to Pharaoh, "I am one of the wise men, a disciple
20: 6 deliverance from the king of Assyria! **How** then can we escape?' "
36: 9 **How** then can you repulse one officer of the least of my master's
48:11 for my own sake, I do this. **How** can I let myself be defamed?
Jer 2:21 **How** then did you turn against me into a corrupt, wild vine?
2:23 "**How** can you say, 'I am not defiled; I have not run after the
3:19 " '**How gladly** would I treat you like sons and give you a desirable
9: 7 [9:6] for **what else** can I do because of the sin of my people?
9:19 [9:18] '**How** ruined we are! How great is our shame! We must
12: 5 and they have worn you out, **how** can you compete with horses?
12: 5 safe country, **how** will you manage in the thickets by the Jordan?
36:17 they asked Baruch, "Tell us, **how** did you come to write all this?
47: 7 **how** can it rest when the LORD has commanded it, when he has
48:14 "**How** can you say, 'We are warriors, men valiant in battle'?
48:39 "**How** shattered she is! How they wail! How Moab turns her back
48:39 "How shattered she is! **How** they wail! How Moab turns her back
49:25 **Why** has the city of renown not been abandoned, the town in
50:23 **How** broken and shattered is the hammer of the whole earth!
50:23 of the whole earth! **How** desolate is Babylon among the nations!
51:41 "**How** Sheshach will be captured, the boast of the whole earth
51:41 earth seized! **What** a horror Babylon will be among the nations!
Eze 26:17 " '**How** you are destroyed, O city of renown, peopled by men of the
33:10 we are wasting away because of them. **How** then can we live?" '
Hos 11: 8 "**How** can I give you up, Ephraim? How can I hand you over,
11: 8 How can I hand you over, Israel? **How** can I treat you like Admah?
Ob 1: 5 to you, if robbers in the night—Oh, **what** a disaster awaits you—
1: 6 But **how** Esau will be ransacked, his hidden treasures pillaged!
Mic 2: 4 **[NIE]** He takes it from me! He assigns our fields to traitors.' "
Zep 2:15 **What** a ruin she has become, a lair for wild beasts! All who pass

376 אִי־כָבוֹד, אִיכָבוֹד *'îkābôd, 'î-kābôd*, n.pr.m. [2] [√ 364 + 3883]

Ichabod [1], Ichabod's [1]

1Sa 4:21 She named the boy **Ichabod**, saying, "The glory has departed from
14: 3 He was a son of **Ichabod's** brother Ahitub son of Phinehas,

377 אֵיכָה *'êkâ*, adv.inter. & excl. [17] [√ 361]

how [12], where [2], but how [1], see how [1], what [1]

Dt 1:12 **But how** can I bear your problems and your burdens and your
7:17 nations are stronger than we are. **How** can we drive them out?"
12:30 about their gods, saying, "**How** do these nations serve their gods?
18:21 "**How** can we know when a message has not been spoken by the
32:30 **How** could one man chase a thousand, or two put ten thousand to
Jdg 20: 3 Then the Israelites said, "Tell us **how** this awful thing happened."
2Ki 6:15 the city. "Oh, my lord, **what** shall we do?" the servant asked.
Ps 73:11 They say, "**How** can God know? Does the Most High have
SS 1: 7 **where** you graze your flock and where you rest your sheep at
1: 7 you graze your flock and **where** you rest your sheep at midday.
Isa 1:21 **See how** the faithful city has become a harlot! She once was full of
Jer 8: 8 " '**How** can you say, "We are wise, for we have the law of the
48:17 say, '**How** broken is the mighty scepter, how broken the glorious
La 1: 1 **How** deserted lies the city, once so full of people! How like a
2: 1 **How** the Lord has covered the Daughter of Zion with the cloud of
4: 1 **How** the gold has lost its luster, the fine gold become dull!
4: 2 **How** the precious sons of Zion, once worth their weight in gold,

378 אֵיכֹה *'êkōh*, adv.inter. & excl. [1] [√ 361]

where [1]

2Ki 6:13 "Go, find out **where** he is," the king ordered, "so I can send men

379 אֵיכָכָה *'êkākâ*, adv.inter. [4] [√ 361]

untranslated [2], how [2]

Est 8: 6 For **how** can I bear to see disaster fall on my people? How can I
8: 6 my people? **How** can I bear to see the destruction of my family?"
SS 5: 3 I have taken off my robe—**[NIE]** must I put it on again? I have
5: 3 on again? I have washed my feet—**[NIE]** must I soil them again?

380 אַיִל¹ *'ayil¹*, n.m. [160] [→ 214?, 215, 381, 382?, 383, 385, 442, 463, 464, 471, 473, 475]

ram [88], rams [61], its[s] [+2021] [4], it[s] [+2021] [2], leading men [2], *untranslated* [1], leaders [1], ruler [1]

Ge 15: 9 "Bring me a heifer, a goat and a **ram**, each three years old,
22:13 looked up and there in a thicket he saw a **ram** caught by its horns.
22:13 He went over and took the **ram** and sacrificed it as a burnt offering
31:38 goats have not miscarried, nor have I eaten **rams** *from* your flocks.
32:14 [32:15] twenty male goats, two hundred ewes and twenty **rams**,
Ex 15:15 be terrified, the **leaders** *of* Moab will be seized with trembling,
25: 5 **ram** skins dyed red and hides of sea cows; acacia wood;
26:14 Make for the tent a covering of **ram** skins dyed red, and over that a
29: 1 me as priests: Take a young bull and two **rams** without defect.

Ex 29: 3 and present them in it—along with the bull and the two **rams**.
29:15 "Take one of the **rams**, and Aaron and his sons shall lay their
29:15 and Aaron and his sons shall lay their hands on **its**[s] [+2021] head.
29:16 Slaughter **it**[s] [+2021] and take the blood and sprinkle it against the
29:17 Cut the **ram** into pieces and wash the inner parts and the legs,
29:18 burn the entire **ram** on the altar. It is a burnt offering to the
29:19 "Take the other **ram**, and Aaron and his sons shall lay their hands
29:19 and Aaron and his sons shall lay their hands on **its**[s] [+2021] head.
29:20 Slaughter **it**[s] [+2021], take some of its blood and put it on the lobes
29:22 "Take from this **ram** the fat, the fat tail, the fat around the inner
29:22 on them, and the right thigh. (This is the **ram** *for* the ordination.)
29:26 After you take the breast of the **ram** for Aaron's ordination,
29:27 "Consecrate those parts of the ordination **ram** that belong to Aaron
29:31 "Take the **ram** *for* the ordination and cook the meat in a sacred
29:32 Aaron and his sons are to eat the meat of the **ram** and the bread
35: 7 **ram** skins dyed red and hides of sea cows; acacia wood;
35:23 goat hair, **ram** skins dyed red or hides of sea cows brought them.
36:19 Then they made for the tent a covering of **ram** skins dyed red,
39:34 the covering of **ram** skins dyed red, the covering of hides of sea
Lev 5:15 he is to bring to the LORD as a penalty a **ram** from the flock,
5:16 who will make atonement for him with the **ram** as a guilt offering,
5:18 He is to bring to the priest as a guilt offering a **ram** from the flock,
6: 6 [5:25] to the LORD, his guilt offering, a **ram** from the flock,
8: 2 the two **rams** and the basket containing bread made without yeast,
8:18 He then presented the **ram** *for* the burnt offering, and Aaron
8:18 and Aaron and his sons laid their hands on **its**[s] [+2021] head.
8:20 He cut the **ram** into pieces and burned the head, the pieces
8:21 and burned the whole **ram** on the altar as a burnt offering,
8:22 He then presented the other **ram**, the ram for the ordination,
8:22 the **ram** *for* the ordination, and Aaron and his sons laid their hands
8:22 and Aaron and his sons laid their hands on **its**[s] [+2021] head.
8:29 He also took the breast—Moses' share of the ordination **ram**—
9: 2 a bull calf for your sin offering and a **ram** for your burnt offering,
9: 4 and a **ram** for a fellowship offering to sacrifice before the LORD,
9:18 the ox and the **ram** as the fellowship offering for the people.
9:19 the fat portions of the ox and the **ram**—the fat tail, the layer of fat,
16: 3 with a young bull for a sin offering and a **ram** for a burnt offering.
16: 5 two male goats for a sin offering and a **ram** for a burnt offering.
19:21 must bring a **ram** to the entrance to the Tent of Meeting for a guilt
19:22 With the **ram** *of* the guilt offering the priest is to make atonement
23:18 each a year old and without defect, one young bull and two **rams**.
Nu 5: 8 along with the **ram** with which atonement is made for him.
6:14 for a sin offering, a **ram** without defect for a fellowship offering,
6:17 and is to sacrifice the **ram** as a fellowship offering to the LORD,
6:19 the priest is to place in his hands a boiled shoulder of the **ram**,
7:15 one young bull, one **ram** and one male lamb a year old, for a burnt
7:17 two oxen, five **rams**, five male goats and five male lambs a year
7:21 one young bull, one **ram** and one male lamb a year old, for a burnt
7:23 two oxen, five **rams**, five male goats and five male lambs a year
7:27 one young bull, one **ram** and one male lamb a year old, for a burnt
7:29 two oxen, five **rams**, five male goats and five male lambs a year
7:33 one young bull, one **ram** and one male lamb a year old, for a burnt
7:35 two oxen, five **rams**, five male goats and five male lambs a year
7:39 one young bull, one **ram** and one male lamb a year old, for a burnt
7:41 two oxen, five **rams**, five male goats and five male lambs a year
7:45 one young bull, one **ram** and one male lamb a year old, for a burnt
7:47 two oxen, five **rams**, five male goats and five male lambs a year
7:51 one young bull, one **ram** and one male lamb a year old, for a burnt
7:53 two oxen, five **rams**, five male goats and five male lambs a year
7:57 one young bull, one **ram** and one male lamb a year old, for a burnt
7:59 two oxen, five **rams**, five male goats and five male lambs a year
7:63 one young bull, one **ram** and one male lamb a year old, for a burnt
7:65 two oxen, five **rams**, five male goats and five male lambs a year
7:69 one young bull, one **ram** and one male lamb a year old, for a burnt
7:71 two oxen, five **rams**, five male goats and five male lambs a year
7:75 one young bull, one **ram** and one male lamb a year old, for a burnt
7:77 two oxen, five **rams**, five male goats and five male lambs a year
7:81 one young bull, one **ram** and one male lamb a year old, for a burnt
7:83 two oxen, five **rams**, five male goats and five male lambs a year
7:87 twelve **rams** and twelve male lambs a year old, together with their
7:88 sixty **rams**, sixty male goats and sixty male lambs a year old.
15: 6 " 'With a **ram** prepare a grain offering of two-tenths of an ephah of
15:11 Each bull or **ram**, each lamb or young goat, is to be prepared in
23: 1 seven altars here, and prepare seven bulls and seven **rams** for me."
23: 2 and the two of them offered a bull and a **ram** on each altar.
23: 4 seven altars, and on each altar I have offered a bull and a **ram**."
23:14 he built seven altars and offered a bull and a **ram** on each altar.
23:29 seven altars here, and prepare seven bulls and seven **rams** for me."
23:30 did as Balaam had said, and offered a bull and a **ram** on each altar.
28:11 one **ram** and seven male lambs a year old, all without defect.
28:12 with the **ram**, a grain offering of two-tenths of an ephah of fine
28:14 with the **ram**, a third of a hin; and with each lamb, a quarter of a
28:19 one **ram** and seven male lambs a year old, all without defect.
28:20 of an ephah of fine flour mixed with oil; with the **ram**, two-tenths;
28:27 one **ram** and seven male lambs a year old as an aroma pleasing to
28:28 of an ephah of fine flour mixed with oil; with the **ram**, two-tenths;
29: 2 one **ram** and seven male lambs a year old, all without defect.
29: 3 of an ephah of fine flour mixed with oil; with the **ram**, two-tenths;
29: 8 one **ram** and seven male lambs a year old, all without defect.
29: 9 of an ephah of fine flour mixed with oil; with the **ram**, two-tenths;
29:13 two **rams** and fourteen male lambs a year old, all without defect.
29:14 of fine flour mixed with oil; with each of the two **rams**, two-tenths;
29:14 mixed with oil; with each of the two rams, **[RPH]** two-tenths;
29:17 two **rams** and fourteen male lambs a year old, all without defect.
29:18 With the bulls, **rams** and lambs, prepare their grain offerings
29:20 two **rams** and fourteen male lambs a year old, all without defect.
29:21 With the bulls, **rams** and lambs, prepare their grain offerings
29:23 two **rams** and fourteen male lambs a year old, all without defect.
29:24 With the bulls, **rams** and lambs, prepare their grain offerings
29:26 two **rams** and fourteen male lambs a year old, all without defect.
29:27 With the bulls, **rams** and lambs, prepare their grain offerings
29:29 two **rams** and fourteen male lambs a year old, all without defect.
29:30 With the bulls, **rams** and lambs, prepare their grain offerings
29:32 two **rams** and fourteen male lambs a year old, all without defect.
29:33 With the bulls, **rams** and lambs, prepare their grain offerings
29:36 one **ram** and seven male lambs a year old, all without defect.
29:37 With the bull, the **ram** and the lambs, prepare their grain offerings
Dt 32:14 with choice **rams** of Bashan and the finest kernels of wheat.
1Sa 15:22 is better than sacrifice, and to heed is better than the fat of **rams**.
2Ki 3: 4 thousand lambs and with the wool of a hundred thousand **rams**.
24:15 his wives, his officials and the **leading men** [K 215] *of* the land.
1Ch 15:26 of the LORD, seven bulls and seven **rams** were sacrificed.
29:21 a thousand bulls, a thousand **rams** and a thousand male lambs,
2Ch 13: 9 and seven **rams** may become a priest of what are not gods.
17:11 seven thousand seven hundred **rams** and seven thousand seven
29:21 seven **rams**, seven male lambs and seven male goats as a sin
29:22 next they slaughtered the **rams** and sprinkled their blood on the
29:32 was seventy bulls, a hundred **rams** and two hundred male lambs—
Ezr 8:35 twelve bulls for all Israel, ninety-six **rams**, seventy-seven male
10:19 for their guilt they each presented a **ram** *from* the flock as a guilt
Job 42: 8 So now take seven bulls and seven **rams** and go to my servant Job
Ps 66:15 I will sacrifice fat animals to you and an offering of **rams**;
114: 4 the mountains skipped like **rams**, the hills like lambs.
114: 6 you mountains, that you skipped like **rams**, you hills, like lambs?
Isa 1:11 enough of burnt offerings, of **rams** and the fat of fattened animals;
34: 6 the blood of lambs and goats, fat from the kidneys of **rams**.
60: 7 will be gathered to you, the **rams** *of* Nebaioth will serve you;
Jer 51:40 bring them down like lambs to the slaughter, like **rams** and goats.
Eze 17:13 him under oath. He also carried away the **leading men** *of* the land,
27:21 they did business with you in lambs, **rams** and goats.
31:11 I handed it over to the **ruler** *of* the nations, for him to deal with
34:17 between one sheep and another, and between **rams** and goats.
39:18 and drink the blood of the princes of the earth as if they were **rams**
43:23 you are to offer a young bull and a **ram** from the flock,
43:25 you are also to provide a young bull and a **ram** from the flock,
45:23 and seven **rams** without defect as a burnt offering to the LORD,
45:24 a grain offering an ephah for each bull and an ephah for each **ram**,
46: 4 the LORD on the Sabbath day is to be six male lambs and a **ram**,
46: 5 The grain offering given with the **ram** is to be an ephah,
46: 6 he is to offer a young bull, six lambs and a **ram**, all without defect.
46: 7 one ephah with the **ram**, and with the lambs as much as he wants
46:11 an ephah with a **ram**, and with the lambs as much as one pleases,
Da 8: 3 I looked up, and there before me was a **ram** with two horns,
8: 4 I watched the **ram** as he charged toward the west and the north
8: 6 He came toward the two-horned **ram** I had seen standing beside
8: 7 I saw him attack the **ram** furiously, striking the ram and shattering
8: 7 the ram furiously, striking the **ram** and shattering his two horns.
8: 7 The **ram** was powerless to stand against him; the goat knocked
8: 7 trampled on him, and none could rescue the **ram** from his power.
8:20 The two-horned **ram** that you saw represents the kings of Media
Mic 6: 7 Will the LORD be pleased with thousands of **rams**, with ten

381 [2]אַיִל *'ayil*[2], n.m. [3 / 5] [→ 390, 391, 392, 393?, 396, 397?, 443, 461, 462, 471, 473, 474, 935; cf. 380]

oaks [4], sacred oaks [1]

Ps 29: 9 The voice of the LORD twists the **oaks** [BHS 387] and strips the
56: T [56:1] To ⌞the tune of⌟ "A Dove on Distant **Oaks**." [BHS 521] Of
Isa 1:29 because of the **sacred oaks** in which you have delighted;
57: 5 You burn with lust among the **oaks** and under every spreading tree;
61: 3 They will be called **oaks** *of* righteousness, a planting of the

382 [3]אַיִל *'ayil*[3], n.[m.]. [22 / 20] [→ 444; cf. 380?]

jambs [9], projecting walls [9], jambs [+4647] [1], portico [1]

1Ki 6:31 he made doors of olive wood with five-sided **jambs** [+4647].
Eze 40: 9 it was eight cubits deep and its **jambs** were two cubits thick.
40:10 the faces of the **projecting walls** on each side had the same

Eze 40: 14 He measured along the faces of the **projecting walls** all around the
40: 14 the portico [BHS *projecting wall*; NIV 395] *facing* the courtyard.
40: 16 the **projecting walls** inside the gateway were surmounted by
40: 16 The faces of the **projecting walls** were decorated with palm trees.
40: 21 its **projecting walls** and its portico had the same measurements as
40: 24 He measured its **jambs** and its portico, and they had the same
40: 26 it had palm tree decorations on the faces of the **projecting walls** on
40: 29 its **projecting walls** and its portico had the same measurements as
40: 31 palm trees decorated its **jambs**, and eight steps led up to it.
40: 33 its **projecting walls** and its portico had the same measurements as
40: 34 palm trees decorated the **jambs** on either side, and eight steps led
40: 36 as did its alcoves, its **projecting walls** and its portico, and it had
40: 37 Its **portico** faced the outer court; palm trees decorated the jambs on
40: 37 palm trees decorated the **jambs** on either side, and eight steps led
40: 38 the portico [BHS *jambs*; NIV 395] *in* each of the inner gateways,
40: 48 to the portico of the temple and measured the **jambs** *of* the portico;
40: 49 a flight of stairs, and there were pillars on each side of the **jambs**.
41: 1 man brought me to the outer sanctuary and measured the **jambs**;
41: 3 into the inner sanctuary and measured the **jambs** *of* the entrance;

383 ⁴אַיִל ***'ayil***⁴, n.m. Not used in NIV/BHS [√ 380]

384 אֱיָל ***'ᵉyāl***, n.m. [1] [→ 394; cf. 380]
strength [1]
Ps 88: 4 [88:5] who go down to the pit; I am like a man without **strength**.

385 אַיָּל ***'ayyāl***, n.[m.] & f. [11 / 12] [→ 387, 389; cf. 380]
deer [9], young stag [+6762] [3]
Dt 12: 15 eat as much of the meat as you want, as if it were gazelle or **deer**,
12: 22 Eat them as you would gazelle or **deer**. Both the ceremonially
14: 5 the **deer**, the gazelle, the roe deer, the wild goat, the ibex,
15: 22 and the clean may eat it, as if it were gazelle or **deer**.
1Ki 4: 23 [5:3] as well as **deer**, gazelles, roebucks and choice fowl.
Ps 42: 1 [42:2] As the **deer** pants for streams of water, so my soul pants
Pr 7: 22 to the slaughter, like a **deer** [BHS 211] stepping into a noose
SS 2: 9 My lover is like a gazelle or a **young stag** [+6762]. Look!
2: 17 be like a gazelle or like a **young stag** [+6762] on the rugged hills.
8: 14 or like a **young stag** [+6762] on the spice-laden mountains.
Isa 35: 6 will the lame leap like a **deer**, and the mute tongue shout for joy.
La 1: 6 Her princes are like **deer** that find no pasture; in weakness they

386 אֵיל פָּארָן ***'êl pā'rān***, n.pr.loc. [1] [√ 381 + 7000]
El Paran [1]
Ge 14: 6 in the hill country of Seir, as far as **El Paran** near the desert.

387 אַיָּלָה ***'ayyālâ***, n.f. [11 / 10] [√ 385]
doe [5], deer [3], does [2]
Ge 49: 21 "Naphtali is a **doe** set free that bears beautiful fawns.
2Sa 22: 34 He makes my feet like the feet of a **deer**; he enables me to stand on
Job 39: 1 goats give birth? Do you watch when the **doe** bears her fawn?
Ps 18: 33 [18:34] He makes my feet like the feet of a **deer**; he enables me to
22: T [22:1] To ˻the tune of˼ "The **Doe** *of* the Morning." A psalm of
29: 9 The voice of the LORD twists the oaks [BHS *makes the deer give birth*; NIV 381]
Pr 5: 19 A loving **doe**, a graceful deer—may her breasts satisfy you always,
SS 2: 7 I charge you by the gazelles and by the **does** *of* the field:
3: 5 I charge you by the gazelles and by the **does** *of* the field:
Jer 14: 5 Even the **doe** in the field deserts her newborn fawn because there is
Hab 3: 19 he makes my feet like the feet of a **deer**, he enables me to go on

388 אִילוֹ ***'îlô***, interj. Not used in NIV/BHS [√ 364]

389 אַיָּלוֹן ***'ayyālôn***, n.pr.loc. [10] [√ 385]
Aijalon [10]
Jos 10: 12 stand still over Gibeon, O moon, over the Valley of **Aijalon**."
19: 42 Shaalabbin, **Aijalon**, Ithlah,
21: 24 **Aijalon** and Gath Rimmon, together with their pasturelands—
Jdg 1: 35 **Aijalon** and Shaalbim, but when the power of the house of Joseph
12: 12 Then Elon died, and was buried in **Aijalon** in the land of Zebulun.
1Sa 14: 31 had struck down the Philistines from Micmash to **Aijalon**,
1Ch 6: 69 [6:54] **Aijalon** and Gath Rimmon, together with their
8: 13 who were heads of families of those living in **Aijalon** and who
2Ch 11: 10 Zorah, **Aijalon** and Hebron. These were fortified cities in Judah
28: 18 **Aijalon** and Gederoth, as well as Soco, Timnah and Gimzo,

390 ¹אֵילוֹן ***'êlôn***¹, n.pr.m. [4] [√ 381; cf. 380]
Elon [4]
Ge 26: 34 Beeri the Hittite, and also Basemath daughter of **Elon** the Hittite.
36: 2 Adah daughter of **Elon** the Hittite, and Oholibamah daughter of
Jdg 12: 11 After him, **Elon** the Zebulunite led Israel ten years.
12: 12 Then **Elon** died, and was buried in Aijalon in the land of Zebulun.

391 ²אֵילוֹן ***'êlôn***², n.pr.loc. [1] [→ 381; cf. 380]
Elon [1]
Jos 19: 43 **Elon**, Timnah, Ekron,

392 אֵילוֹן בֵּית חָנָן ***'êlôn bêt ḥānān***, n.pr.loc. [1] [√ 381 + 1074 + 2860]
Elon Bethhanan [1]
1Ki 4: 9 in Makaz, Shaalbim, Beth Shemesh and **Elon Bethhanan**;

393 אֵילוֹת ***'êlôt***, n.pr.loc. [4] [√ 381?]
Elath [3], *untranslated* [1]
1Ki 9: 26 which is near **Elath** in Edom, on the shore of the Red Sea.
2Ki 16: 6 **[RPH]** Edomites then moved into Elath and have lived there to
2Ch 8: 17 Solomon went to Ezion Geber and **Elath** on the coast of Edom.
26: 2 He was the one who rebuilt **Elath** and restored it to Judah after

394 אֱיָלוּת ***'ᵉyālût***, n.m. [1] [√ 384; cf. 380]
Strength [1]
Ps 22: 19 [22:20] be not far off; O my **Strength**, come quickly to help me.

395 אֵילָם ***'êlām***, n.m. [50 / 51] [→ 221]
portico [44], hall [3], *untranslated* [1], colonnade [+6647] [1], porticoes [1], temple porch [1]
1Ki 6: 3 The **portico** at the front of the main hall of the temple extended the
7: 6 He made a **colonnade** [+6647] fifty cubits long and thirty wide.
7: 6 In front of it was a **portico**, and in front of that were pillars
7: 7 He built the throne **hall**, the Hall of Justice, where he was to judge,
7: 7 He built the throne hall, the **Hall** *of* Justice, where he was to judge,
7: 8 he was to live, set farther back, **[RPH]** was similar in design.
7: 8 Solomon also made a palace like this **hall** for Pharaoh's daughter,
7: 12 the inner courtyard of the temple of the LORD with its **portico**.
7: 19 The capitals on top of the pillars in the **portico** were in the shape
7: 21 He erected the pillars at the **portico** *of* the temple. The pillar to the
1Ch 28: 11 David gave his son Solomon the plans for the **portico** of the
2Ch 3: 4 The **portico** at the front of the temple was twenty cubits long
8: 12 On the altar of the LORD that he had built in front of the **portico**,
15: 8 LORD that was in front of the **portico** *of* the LORD's temple.
29: 7 They also shut the doors of the **portico** and put out the lamps.
29: 17 by the eighth day of the month they reached the **portico** *of* the
Eze 8: 16 between the **portico** and the altar, were about twenty-five men.
40: 7 the threshold of the gate next to the **portico** facing the temple was
40: 8 Then he measured the **portico** *of* the gateway;
40: 9 [BHS+ *the portico of the gateway*,] it was eight cubits deep
40: 9 two cubits thick. The **portico** *of* the gateway faced the temple.
40: 14 The measurement was up to the **portico** [BHS 382] *facing* the
40: 15 of the gateway to the far end of its **portico** was fifty cubits.
40: 16 by narrow parapet openings all around, as was the **portico**;
40: 21 its **portico** had the same measurements as those of the first
40: 22 its **portico** and its palm tree decorations had the same
40: 22 facing east. Seven steps led up to it, with its **portico** opposite them.
40: 24 He measured its jambs and its **portico**, and they had the same
40: 25 The gateway and its **portico** had narrow openings all around,
40: 26 Seven steps led up to it, with its **portico** opposite them; it had palm
40: 29 and its **portico** had the same measurements as the others.
40: 29 The gateway and its **portico** had openings all around. It was fifty
40: 30 (The **porticoes** of the gateways around the inner court were
40: 31 Its **portico** faced the outer court; palm trees decorated its jambs,
40: 33 and its **portico** had the same measurements as the others.
40: 33 The gateway and its **portico** had openings all around. It was fifty
40: 34 Its **portico** faced the outer court; palm trees decorated the jambs on
40: 36 as did its alcoves, its projecting walls and its **portico**, and it had
40: 37 Its **portico** faced the outer court; palm trees decorated the jambs on
40: 38 A room with a doorway was by the **portico** [BHS 382] *in* each of
40: 39 In the **portico** *of* the gateway were two tables on each side,
40: 40 By the outside wall of the **portico** *of* the gateway, near the steps at
40: 48 He brought me to the **portico** *of* the temple and measured the
40: 48 to the portico of the temple and measured the jambs of the **portico**;
40: 49 The **portico** was twenty cubits wide, and twelve cubits from front
41: 15 the inner sanctuary and the **portico** *facing* the court,
41: 25 and there was a wooden overhang on the front of the **portico**.
41: 26 On the sidewalls of the **portico** were narrow windows with palm
44: 3 He is to enter by way of the **portico** *of* the gateway and go out the
46: 2 The prince is to enter from the outside through the **portico** *of* the
46: 8 the prince enters, he is to go in through the **portico** *of* the gateway,
Joel 2: 17 before the LORD, weep between the **temple porch** and the altar.

396 אֵילִם *'êlim*, n.pr.loc. [6] [√ 381; cf. 380]

Elim [5], where[s] [+928] [1]

Ex 15: 27 Then they came to **Elim**, where there were twelve springs
16: 1 The whole Israelite community set out from **Elim** and came to the
16: 1 and came to the Desert of Sin, which is between **Elim** and Sinai,
Nu 33: 9 They left Marah and went to **Elim**, where there were twelve
33: 9 and went to Elim, **where**[s] [+928] there were twelve springs
33: 10 They left **Elim** and camped by the Red Sea.

397 אֵילַת *'êlat*, n.pr.loc. [4] [√ 381?]

Elath [4]

Dt 2: 8 the Arabah road, which comes up from **Elath** and Ezion Geber,
2Ki 14: 22 He was the one who rebuilt **Elath** and restored it to Judah after
16: 6 Rezin king of Aram recovered **Elath** for Aram by driving out the
16: 6 Edomites then moved into **Elath** and have lived there to this day.

398 אָיֹם *'āyōm*, a. [3] [√ 399]

majestic [2], feared [1]

SS 6: 4 as Tirzah, lovely as Jerusalem, **majestic** as troops with banners.
6: 10 as the moon, bright as the sun, **majestic** as the stars in procession?
Hab 1: 7 They are a **feared** and dreaded people; they are a law to

399 אֵימָה *'êmâ*, n.f. [17] [→ 398, 400; Ar 10028]

terror [7], terrors [4], fear [2], dreadful [1], fearsome [1], great fear [1], wrath [1]

Ge 15: 12 a deep sleep, and a thick and **dreadful** darkness came over him.
Ex 15: 16 **terror** and dread will fall upon them. By the power of your arm
23: 27 "I will send my **terror** ahead of you and throw into confusion
Dt 32: 25 sword will make them childless; in their homes **terror** will reign.
Jos 2: 9 given this land to you and that a **great fear** *of* you has fallen on us,
Ezr 3: 3 Despite their **fear** of the peoples around them, they built the altar
Job 9: 34 God's rod from me, so that his **terror** would frighten me no more.
13: 21 your hand far from me, and stop frightening me with your **terrors**.
20: 25 the gleaming point out of his liver. **Terrors** will come over him;
33: 7 No **fear** *of* me should alarm you, nor should my hand be heavy
39: 20 him leap like a locust, striking **terror** with his proud snorting?
41: 14 [41:6] doors of his mouth, ringed about with his **fearsome** teeth?
Ps 55: 4 [55:5] is in anguish within me; the **terrors** *of* death assail me.
88: 15 [88:16] to death; I have suffered your **terrors** and am in despair.
Pr 20: 2 A king's **wrath** is like the roar of a lion; he who angers him
Isa 33: 18 In your thoughts you will ponder the former **terror**: "Where is that
Jer 50: 38 For it is a land of idols, idols that will go mad with **terror**.

400 אֵימִים *'êmîm*, n.pr.m.pl. [3] [√ 399]

Emites [3]

Ge 14: 5 the Zuzites in Ham, the **Emites** in Shaveh Kiriathaim
Dt 2: 10 (The **Emites** used to live there—a people strong and numerous,
2: 11 were considered Rephaites, but the Moabites called them **Emites**.

401 אַיִן *'ayin¹*, subst.neg. [788 / 789] [cf. 403] See Select Index

no [209], there is no [98], not [93], nothing [32], there was no [29], without [29], is not [20], *untranslated* [16], none [10], cannot [9], without [+4946] [9], gone [8], there will be no [8], be no more [7], never [7], lack [6], there is none [6], are no more [5], beyond [5], don't [5], is no more [5], neither [5], be no [4], is no [4], is there no [4], no [+4946] [4], nor [+2256] [4], there is not [4], there was none [4], there were no [4], were not [4], it is not [3], nothing [+3972] [3], there is no [+1172] [3], was not [3], is that not [2], is there not [2], isn't [2], it's not [2], lacks [2], none [+408] [2], nothing [+1821] [2], nothing [+4399] [2], senseless [+4213] [2], there are no [2], there is nothing [+4399] [2], there is nothing [2], there was not [2], there was nothing [2], there will be none [2], was no more [2], was there no [2], waterless [+4784] [2], without [+928] [2], won't [2], all alone [+9108] [1], allowed [+646] [1], am no more [1], any[s] [1], are not [1], aren't [1], bare [+928+4399] [1], be nothing [+1194] [1], before [+3954] [1], boundless [+7897] [1], cannot [+3946] [1], countless [+5031] [1], deserted [+132+4946] [1], deserted [+3782+4946] [1], deserted [+928+3782] [1], disappeared [1], endless [+4200+7891] [1], endless [+7897] [1], fatherless [+3] [1], free from [1], gone from [+907] [1], here are no [1], in vain [1], incomprehensible [+1069] [1], incurable [+5340] [1], innumerable [+5031] [1], is never [1], is nothing [1], isn't there [1], it was impossible [1], it was not [1], kept secret [+906+5583] [1], lack [+4200] [1], lack [+928] [1], loses [1], more [+4200] [1], more than [+4200] [1], naught [1], nearly [+3869] [1], neither [+4946] [1], never [+4200+6409] [1], no account [1], none [+4946] [1], none will be [+4946] [1], nor [+1685+2256] [1], nor [+2256+4946] [1], nor [+677] [1], nothing at all [+700+2256] [1], nothing whatever [+1821+3972] [1], or [+561+2256] [1], or [1], otherwise [+561] [1], powerless [+3946] [1], powerless [+445+3338+4200] [1], powerless [+445+4200] [1], regardless [+4200+9068] [1], so[s] [1], surely [+561] [1], than [1], there is neither [1], there is no [+3972] [1], there is no [+4946] [1], there is nothing [+3972] [1], there were no [+1172] [1], there were not [1], there will not be [1], too [1], unclean [+3196] [1], uncovered [+4064] [1], unless [1], unsearchable [+2984] [1], was no [1], weak [+226] [1], will not [1], without [+4200] [1], without [+6330] [1], without any payment [+2855] [1], without equal [+3202+4946] [1], worthless [+2914] [1], wouldn't [1]

402 ²אַיִן *'ayin²*, adv. [17] [→ 4406; cf. 361]

where [12], where [+4946] [5]

Ge 29: 4 Jacob asked the shepherds, "My brothers, **where** are you from?"
42: 7 and spoke harshly to them. "**Where** do you come from?" he asked.
Nu 11: 13 **Where** [+4946] can I get meat for all these people? They keep
Jos 2: 4 men came to me, but I did not know **where** they had come from.
9: 8 But Joshua asked, "Who are you and **where** do you come from?"
Jdg 17: 9 Micah asked him, "**Where** are you from?" "I'm a Levite from
19: 17 man asked, "Where are you going? **Where** did you come from?"
2Ki 5: 25 "**Where** [+4946; K 625] have you been, Gehazi?" Elisha asked.
6: 27 "If the LORD does not help you, **where** [+4946] can I get help
20: 14 "What did those men say, and **where** did they come from?"
Job 1: 7 The LORD said to Satan, "**Where** have you come from?"
28: 12 "But **where** [+4946] can wisdom be found? Where does
28: 20 "**Where** then does wisdom come from? Where does understanding
Ps 121: 1 I lift up my eyes to the hills—**where** does my help come from?
Isa 39: 3 "What did those men say, and **where** did they come from?"
Jnh 1: 8 What do you do? **Where** do you come from? What is your
Na 3: 7 who will mourn for her?' **Where** [+4946] can I find anyone to

403 אִין *'în*, subst.neg. [1] [cf. 401]

don't [1]

1Sa 21: 8 [21:9] "**Don't** you have a spear or a sword here?

404 אִיעֶזֶר *'î'ezer*, n.pr.m. [1] [→ 405; cf. 3 + 3276 + 6469]

Iezer [1]

Nu 26: 30 through **Iezer**, the Iezerite clan; through Helek, the Helekite clan;

405 אִיעֶזְרִי *'î'ezrî*, a.g. [1] [√ 404]

Iezerite [1]

Nu 26: 30 through Iezer, the **Iezerite** clan; through Helek, the Helekite clan;

406 אֵיפָה *'êpâ*, n.f. [40]

ephah [29], basket [4], differing measures [+406+2256] [2], two differing measures [+406+2256] [2], measure [1], measures [1], measuring basket [1]

Ex 16: 36 (An omer is one tenth of an **ephah**.)
Lev 5: 11 he is to bring as an offering for his sin a tenth of an **ephah** *of* fine
6: 20 [6:13] a tenth of an **ephah** *of* fine flour as a regular grain offering,
19: 36 and honest weights, an honest **ephah** and an honest hin.
Nu 5: 15 He must also take an offering of a tenth of an **ephah** *of* barley flour
28: 5 together with a grain offering of a tenth of an **ephah** *of* fine flour
Dt 25: 14 Do not have **two differing measures** [+406+2256] in your house—
25: 14 Do not have **two differing measures** [+406+2256] in your house—
25: 15 You must have accurate and honest weights and **measures**,
Jdg 6: 19 and from an **ephah** *of* flour he made bread without yeast.
Ru 2: 17 the barley she had gathered, and it amounted to about an **ephah**.
1Sa 1: 24 with a three-year-old bull, an **ephah** of flour and a skin of wine,
17: 17 "Take this **ephah** *of* roasted grain and these ten loaves of bread for
Pr 20: 10 and **differing measures** [+406+2256]—the LORD detests them
20: 10 and **differing measures** [+406+2256]—the LORD detests them
Isa 5: 10 only a bath of wine, a homer of seed only an **ephah** of grain."
Eze 45: 10 are to use accurate scales, an accurate **ephah** and an accurate bath.
45: 11 The **ephah** and the bath are to be the same size, the bath containing
45: 11 containing a tenth of a homer and the **ephah** a tenth of a homer;
45: 13 a sixth of an **ephah** from each homer of wheat and a sixth of an
45: 13 of wheat and a sixth of an **ephah** from each homer of barley.
45: 24 He is to provide as a grain offering an **ephah** for each bull
45: 24 a grain offering an ephah for each bull and an **ephah** for each ram,
45: 24 and an ephah for each ram, along with a hin of oil for each **ephah**.
46: 5 The grain offering given with the ram is to be an **ephah**,
46: 5 to be as much as he pleases, along with a hin of oil for each **ephah**.
46: 7 He is to provide as a grain offering *one* **ephah** with the bull,
46: 7 *one* **ephah** with the ram, and with the lambs as much as he wants
46: 7 much as he wants to give, along with a hin of oil with each **ephah**.
46: 11 the grain offering is to be an **ephah** with a bull, an ephah with a
46: 11 an **ephah** with a ram, and with the lambs as much as one pleases,
46: 11 as much as one pleases, along with a hin of oil for each **ephah**.
46: 14 consisting of a sixth of an **ephah** with a third of a hin of oil to
Am 8: 5 skimping the **measure**, boosting the price and cheating with
Mic 6: 10 O wicked house, your ill-gotten treasures and the short **ephah**,
Zec 5: 6 I asked, "What is it?" He replied, "It is a **measuring basket**."

Zec 5: 7 the cover of lead was raised, and there in the **basket** sat a woman!
5: 8 he pushed her back into the **basket** and pushed the lead cover
5: 9 of a stork, and they lifted up the **basket** between heaven and earth.
5: 10 "Where are they taking the **basket**?" I asked the angel who was

407 אֵיפֹה *'êpōh*, adv. [10] [√ 361 + 7024]
where [8], what [1], where from [1]

Ge 37: 16 my brothers. Can you tell me **where** they are grazing their flocks?"
Jdg 8: 18 and Zalmunna, "**What** kind of men did you kill at Tabor?"
Ru 2: 19 Her mother-in-law asked her, "**Where** did you glean today?
1Sa 19: 22 he asked, "**Where** are Samuel and David?" "Over in Naioth at
2Sa 9: 4 "**Where** is he?" the king asked. Ziba answered, "He is at the house
Job 4: 7 has ever perished? **Where** were the upright ever destroyed?
38: 4 "**Where** were you when I laid the earth's foundation? Tell me,
Isa 49: 21 I was left all alone, but these—**where** have they come **from**?' "
Jer 3: 2 and see. Is there *any place* **where** you have not been ravished?
36: 19 and Jeremiah, go and hide. Don't let anyone know **where** you are."

408 אִישׁ *'îš*[1], n.m. [2187 / 2189] [→ 413, 843, 851; *also used with compound proper names*]
man [612], men [523], *untranslated* [241], each [160], one [106], husband [64], man's [32], anyone [29], every [18], everyone [18], people [16], Israelites [+3776] [14], soldiers [+4878] [12], someone [12], any [11], some[s] [10], they[s] [10], they[s] [+2021] [9], person [8], everyone [+3972] [6], he[s] [+2021] [6], Israelite [+1074+3776+4946] [6], them[s] [6], those[s] [6], he[s] [5], Israelite [+3776] [5], none [+4202] [5], swordsmen [+2995+8990] [5], warrior [+4878] [5], all [4], anyone [+408] [4], army [+4878] [4], each [+408] [4], husbands [4], male [4], those[s] [+2021] [4], another[s] [3], anyone [+2021+4769] [3], foot soldiers [+8081] [3], him[s] [+2021] [3], him[s] [3], who [3], any [+408] [2], any man [+408] [2], anyone [+3972] [2], at war with [+4878] [2], champion [+1227+2021] [2], father [2], fellow [2], Israelite [+1201+3776+4946] [2], man [+408+2256] [2], mankind [2], merchants [+9365] [2], mourners[s] [2], neighbor[s] [2], none [+401] [2], servants [2], their[s] [2], them[s] [+2021] [2], valiant fighters [+2657] [2], warriors [+2657] [2], whoever [+2021+4769] [2], whoever [+889] [2], whoever [2], you[s] [2], a[s] [1], accuser [+8190] [1], adulteress [+851] [1], all together [+285+3869] [1], allies [+1382] [1], among yourselves [+278+448] [1], another[s] creature [1], any [+3972] [1], any man [+2021+4769] [1], anyone [+2021] [1], anyone [+2021+3972] [1], anyone's [1], archers [+928+2021+4619+8008] [1], army [1], Benjamin [+1201+3549] [1], Benjamite [+1228] [1], Benjamite [+3549] [1], Benjamites [+1228+4946] [1], blood relatives [+1460] [1], Boaz[s] [+2021] [1], brother [1], captive [1], census [+6296] [1], champions [+2657] [1], child [1], close friend [+8934] [1], counselor [+6783] [1], counselors [+6783] [1], cubs [1], descendant [+2446+4946] [1], deserve to [1], deserved [1], each [+278+2257] [1], eloquent [+1821] [1], enemies [+5194] [1], Ephraimites [+713] [1], equally [+278+2257+3869] [1], equally among them [+278+2257+3869] [1], everyone [+2021+3972] [1], everyone's [+928] [1], experienced fighter [+4878] [1], experienced fighting men [+1475+2657+4878] [1], famous [+9005] [1], farmer [+141+6268] [1], fellow townsmen [+6551] [1], fellowman [1], followers [+889+2143+6640] [1], forces [1], friend[s] [1], friends [+8934] [1], Gibeonites [+1500] [1], Gileadites [+1680] [1], give in marriage [+906+4200+5989] [1], great soldiers [+4878] [1], group [1], guards [+5464] [1], he[s] [+2021+5283] [1], he[s] [+2021+2021+6640+8886] [1], he[s] [+340+2021+2021] [1], high [+1201] [1], highborn [+1201] [1], himself[s] [+2021] [1], his[s] [+2021] [1], hunter [+7473] [1], husband's [1], in the prime of life [1], Israel [+3776] [1], Israelite [+2021+3778] [1], kings[s] [1], leaders [+8031] [1], liar [+3942] [1], madman [+8713] [1], man's body [1], mankind [+1414] [1], marries [+2118+2118+4200] [1], marries [+2118+4200] [1], marry [+2118+4200] [1], members [1], men [+1201] [1], men's [1], Moabites [+4566] [1], mockers [+4371] [1], more[s] [1], neighbor's [1], Ninevites [+5770] [1], none[s] [1], officials [1], one and all [1], one party[s] [1], one[s] [+2424] [1], opponent [1], oppressor [+9412] [1], ready for battle [+2021+4200+4878+7372] [1], remain unmarried [+1194+2118+4200+4200+6328] [1], sailors [+641] [1], scoffers [+4371] [1], scoundrel [+1175] [1], scoundrel [+1175+2021] [1], slanderers [+4383] [1], slept with [+3359+4200+5435] [1], soldier [+7372] [1], soldiers [+1505+4878] [1], soldiers [+7372] [1], soldiers [+8081] [1], some[s] of them [1], son [+2446] [1], son [1], spies [+8078] [1], steward[s] [+889+1074+2021+6584] [1], steward[s] [1], strongest defenders [+2657] [1], talker [+8557] [1], tall [+4500] [1], tend livestock [+2118+5238] [1], tended livestock [+2118+5238] [1], the parties [+2084+2256+8276] [1], their[s] [+2021] [1], their[s] [+3373] [1], they[s] [+3315] [1], they[s] [+7159] [1], this[s] [1], together [+907+2084+8276] [1], townspeople [+6551] [1], tribe of Benjamin [+3549] [1], troublemaker [+1175] [1], trusted friends [+8934] [1], two men [+278+2256+3481] [1], unmarried [+2118+4200+4202] [1], untraveled [+1172+4946+6296] [1], valiant fighter [+1201+2644] [1], valiant fighter [+1201+2657] [1], villain [+224] [1], virgin [+3359+4202] [1], voluntarily [+4213+6584+6590] [1], well-known [+9005] [1], who[s] [+2021+6504] [1], whoever [+889+3972] [1]

Ge 2: 23 she shall be called 'woman,' for she was taken out of **man**."
2: 24 For this reason a **man** will leave his father and mother and be
3: 6 She also gave some to her **husband**, who was with her, and he ate
3: 16 Your desire will be for your **husband**, and he will rule over you."
4: 1 "With the help of the LORD I have brought forth a **man**."
4: 23 I have killed a **man** for wounding me, a young man for injuring
6: 4 children by them. They were the heroes of old, **men** *of* renown.
6: 9 Noah was a righteous **man**, blameless among the people of his
7: 2 a **male** and its mate, and two of every kind of unclean animal,
7: 2 and two of every kind of unclean animal, a **male** and its mate,
9: 5 from **each** [+278+2257] man, too, I will demand an accounting for
9: 20 Noah, a **man** *of* the soil, proceeded to plant a vineyard.
10: 5 by their clans within their nations, **each** with its own language.)
11: 3 They said to **each** other, "Come, let's make bricks and bake them
11: 7 and confuse their language so they will not understand **each** other."
12: 20 Pharaoh gave orders about Abram to his **men**, and they sent him on
13: 8 or between your herdsmen and mine, for we are brothers. **[NIE]**
13: 11 and set out toward the east. The two **men** parted company:
13: 13 Now the **men** *of* Sodom were wicked and were sinning greatly
13: 16 so that if **anyone** could count the dust, then your offspring could be
14: 24 and the share that belongs to the **men** who went with me—
15: 10 cut them in two and arranged the halves opposite **each** other;
16: 3 maidservant Hagar and gave her to her **husband** to be his wife.
17: 23 every male **[NIE]** in his household, and circumcised them,
17: 27 every **male** *in* Abraham's household, including those born in his
18: 2 Abraham looked up and saw three **men** standing nearby. When he
18: 16 When the **men** got up to leave, they looked down toward Sodom,
18: 22 The **men** turned away and went toward Sodom, but Abraham
19: 4 gone to bed, all the **men** from every part of the city of Sodom—
19: 4 all the men from every part of the city of **[RPH]** Sodom—
19: 5 They called to Lot, "Where are the **men** who came to you tonight?
19: 8 Look, I have two daughters who have never slept with a **man**.
19: 8 don't do anything to these **men**, for they have come under the
19: 9 on Lot **[NIE]** and moved forward to break down the door.
19: 10 But the **men** inside reached out and pulled Lot back into the house
19: 11 Then they struck the **men** who were at the door of the house,
19: 12 The two **men** said to Lot, "Do you have anyone else here—
19: 16 the **men** grasped his hand and the hands of his wife and of his two
19: 31 "Our father is old, and there is no **man** around here to lie with us,
20: 7 Now return the **man's** wife, for he is a prophet, and he will pray
20: 8 when he told them all that had happened, **they**[s] [+2021] were very
23: 6 **None** [+4202] of us will refuse you his tomb for burying your
24: 13 the daughters of the **townspeople** [+6551] are coming out to draw
24: 16 girl was very beautiful, a virgin; no **man** had ever lain with her.
24: 21 the **man** watched her closely to learn whether or not the LORD
24: 22 the **man** took out a gold nose ring weighing a beka and two gold
24: 26 Then the **man** bowed down and worshiped the LORD,
24: 29 brother named Laban, and he hurried out to the **man** at the spring.
24: 30 had heard Rebekah tell what the **man** said to her, he went out to
24: 30 he went out to the **man** and found him standing by the camels near
24: 32 So the **man** went to the house, and the camels were unloaded.
24: 32 for the camels, and water for him and his **men** to wash their feet.
24: 54 he and the **men** who were with him ate and drank and spent the
24: 58 they called Rebekah and asked her, "Will you go with this **man**?"
24: 59 along with her nurse and Abraham's servant and his **men**.
24: 61 got ready and mounted their camels and went back with the **man**.
24: 65 the servant, "Who is that **man** in the field coming to meet us?"
25: 27 The boys grew up, and Esau became a skillful **hunter** [+7473],
25: 27 a **man** *of* the open country, while Jacob was a quiet man,
25: 27 while Jacob was a quiet **man**, staying among the tents.
26: 7 When the **men** *of* that place asked him about his wife, he said,
26: 7 "The **men** *of* this place might kill me on account of Rebekah,
26: 11 "Anyone who molests this **man** or his wife shall surely be put to
26: 13 The **man** became rich, and his wealth continued to grow until he
26: 31 Early the next morning the men swore an oath to **each** other.
27: 11 "But my brother Esau is a hairy **man**, and I'm a man with smooth
27: 11 my brother Esau is a hairy man, and I'm a **man** with smooth skin.
29: 19 "It's better that I give her to you than to some other **man**.
29: 22 So Laban brought together all the **people** *of* the place and gave a
29: 32 has seen my misery. Surely my **husband** will love me now."
29: 34 "Now at last my **husband** will become attached to me, because I
30: 15 said to her, "Wasn't it enough that you took away my **husband**?
30: 18 has rewarded me for giving my maidservant to my **husband**."
30: 20 This time my **husband** will treat me with honor, because I have
30: 43 In this way the **man** grew exceedingly prosperous and came to
31: 49 watch between you and me when we are away from **each** other.
31: 50 even though no **one** is with us, remember that God is a witness
32: 6 [32:7] coming to meet you, and four hundred **men** are with him."
32: 24 [32:25] was left alone, and a **man** wrestled with him till daybreak.
32: 28 [32:29] struggled with God and with **men** and have overcome."

Ge 33: 1 looked up and there was Esau, coming with his four hundred **men**;
34: 7 the fields as soon as they heard what had happened. **They**[s] [+2021]
34: 14 a thing; we can't give our sister to a **man** who is not circumcised.
34: 20 to the gate of their city to speak to their **fellow townsmen** [+6551].
34: 21 "These **men** are friendly toward us," they said. "Let them live in
34: 22 the **men** will consent to live with us as one people only on the
34: 25 took **[NIE]** their swords and attacked the unsuspecting city,
37: 15 a **man** found him wandering around in the fields and asked him,
37: 15 in the fields and asked him, **[RPH]** "What are you looking for?"
37: 17 "They have moved on from here," the **man** answered. "I heard
37: 19 "Here comes that dreamer!" they said to **each** other.
37: 28 So when the Midianite merchants **[NIE]** came by, his brothers
38: 1 and went down to stay with a **man** of Adullam named Hirah.
38: 2 There Judah met the daughter of a Canaanite **man** named Shua.
38: 21 He asked the **men** *who lived* there, "Where is the shrine prostitute
38: 22 Besides, the **men** *who lived* there said, 'There hasn't been any
38: 25 "I am pregnant by the **man** who owns these," she said. And she
39: 1 Potiphar, an Egyptian **[NIE]** who was one of Pharaoh's officials,
39: 2 The LORD was with Joseph and **he**[s] prospered, and he lived in
39: 11 his duties, and **none** [+401] of the household servants was inside.
39: 11 to his duties, and none of the household **servants** was inside.
39: 14 she called her household **servants**. "Look," she said to them,
39: 14 "**this**[s] Hebrew has been brought to us to make sport of us!
40: 5 **each** of the two men—the cupbearer and the baker of the king of
40: 5 a dream the same night, and **each** dream had a meaning of its own.
41: 11 a dream the same night, and **each** dream had a meaning of its own.
41: 12 them for us, giving *each* **man** the interpretation of his dream.
41: 33 and wise **man** and put him in charge of the land of Egypt.
41: 38 So Pharaoh asked them, "Can we find anyone like this **man**,
41: 44 but without your word no **one** will lift hand or foot in all Egypt."
42: 11 We are all the sons of one **man**. Your servants are honest men,
42: 13 the sons of one **man**, who lives in the land of Canaan.
42: 21 They said to **one** another, "Surely we are being punished
42: 25 to put **each** man's silver back in his sack, and to give them
42: 28 Their hearts sank and they turned to **each** other trembling and said,
42: 30 "The **man** who is lord over the land spoke harshly to us and treated
42: 33 "Then the **man** who is lord over the land said to us, 'This is how I
42: 35 their sacks, there in **each** man's sack was his pouch of silver!
43: 3 Judah said to him, "The **man** warned us solemnly, 'You will not
43: 5 not send him, we will not go down, because the **man** said to us,
43: 6 "Why did you bring this trouble on me by telling the **man** you had
43: 7 "The **man** questioned us closely about ourselves and our family.
43: 11 of the land in your bags and take them down to the **man** as a gift—
43: 13 Take your brother also and go back to the **man** at once.
43: 14 may God Almighty grant you mercy before the **man** so that he will
43: 15 So the **men** took the gifts and double the amount of silver,
43: 16 "Take these **men** to my house, slaughter an animal and prepare
43: 16 and prepare dinner; **they**[s] [+2021] are to eat with me at noon."
43: 17 The **man** did as Joseph told him and took the men to Joseph's
43: 17 as Joseph told him and **[RPH]** took the men to Joseph's house.
43: 17 man did as Joseph told him and took the **men** to Joseph's house.
43: 18 Now the **men** were frightened when they were taken to his house.
43: 19 So they went up to Joseph's **steward**[s] [+889+1074+2021+6584]
43: 21 for the night we opened our sacks and **each** of us found his silver—
43: 24 The **steward**[s] took the men into Joseph's house, gave them water
43: 24 The steward took the **men** into Joseph's house, gave them water to
43: 33 and **they**[s] [+2021] looked at each other in astonishment.
43: 33 to the youngest; and they looked at **each** other in astonishment.
44: 1 "Fill the **men's** sacks with as much food as they can carry,
44: 1 they can carry, and put *each* **man's** silver in the mouth of his sack.
44: 3 the **men** were sent on their way with their donkeys.
44: 4 "Go after those **men** at once, and when you catch up with them,
44: 11 **Each** of them quickly lowered his sack to the ground and opened
44: 11 quickly lowered his sack to the ground and opened **[RPH]** it.
44: 13 Then they **all** loaded their donkeys and returned to the city.
44: 15 Don't you know that a **man** like me can find things out by
44: 17 Only the **man** who was found to have the cup will become my
44: 26 We cannot see the **man's** face unless our youngest brother is with
45: 1 and he cried out, "Have **everyone** [+3972] leave my presence!"
45: 1 So there was no **one** with Joseph when he made himself known to
45: 22 To each of them he gave **[NIE]** new clothing, but to Benjamin he
46: 32 The **men** are shepherds; they tend livestock, and they have brought
46: 32 The men are shepherds; *they* **tend livestock** [+2118+5238],
46: 34 'Your servants *have* **tended livestock** [+2118+5238] from our
47: 2 He chose five **[NIE]** of his brothers and presented them before
47: 6 And if you know of **any** among them *with* special ability,
47: 20 The Egyptians, **one and all**, sold their fields, because the famine
49: 6 for they have killed **men** in their anger and hamstrung oxen as they
49: 28 when he blessed them, giving **each** the blessing appropriate to him.
Ex 1: 1 sons of Israel who went to Egypt with Jacob, **each** with his family:
2: 1 Now a **man** of the house of Levi married a Levite woman,
2: 11 He saw an Egyptian **[NIE]** beating a Hebrew, one of his own
2: 11 saw an Egyptian beating a Hebrew, **[NIE]** one of his own people.
2: 12 Glancing this way and that and seeing no **one**, he killed the
2: 13 The next day he went out and saw two **[NIE]** Hebrews fighting.
2: 14 The man said, "Who made you **[NIE]** ruler and judge over us?
2: 19 "An **[NIE]** Egyptian rescued us from the shepherds.
2: 20 he asked his daughters. "Why did you leave **him**[s] [+2021]?
2: 21 Moses agreed to stay with the **man**, who gave his daughter
4: 10 said to the LORD, "O Lord, I have never been **eloquent** [+1821],
4: 19 back to Egypt, for all the **men** who wanted to kill you are dead."
5: 9 Make the work harder for the **men** so that they keep working
7: 12 **Each** *one* threw down his staff and it became a snake. But Aaron's
10: 7 Let the **people** go, so that they may worship the LORD their God.
10: 23 No **one** could see anyone else or leave his place for three days.
10: 23 could see anyone else or **[RPH]** leave his place for three days.
11: 2 Tell the people that **men** and women alike are to ask their
11: 3 Moses **himself**[s] [+2021] was highly regarded in Egypt by
11: 7 But among the Israelites not a dog will bark at any **man** or animal.'
12: 3 tenth day of this month *each* **man** is to take a lamb for his family,
12: 4 of lamb needed in accordance with what **each** *person* will eat.
12: 22 Not **one** *of* you shall go out the door of his house until morning.
12: 44 Any slave **[NIE]** you have bought may eat of it after you have
15: 3 The LORD is a **warrior** [+4878]; the LORD is his name.
16: 15 When the Israelites saw it, they said to **each** other, "What is it?"
16: 16 has commanded: '**Each** *one* is to gather as much as he needs.
16: 16 Take an omer for each person you **[RPH]** have in your tent.' "
16: 18 did not have too little. **Each** *one* gathered as much as he needed.
16: 19 Moses said to them, "No **one** is to keep any of it until morning."
16: 20 However, **some**[s] **of them** paid no attention to Moses; they kept
16: 21 Each morning **everyone** gathered as much as he needed, and when
16: 29 **Everyone** is to stay where he is on the seventh day; no one is to go
16: 29 is to stay where he is on the seventh day; no **one** is to go out."
17: 9 "Choose *some of* our **men** and go out to fight the Amalekites.
18: 7 kissed him. They greeted **each** other and then went into the tent.
18: 16 and I decide between **the parties** [+2084+2256+8276] and inform
18: 21 But select capable **men** from all the people—men who fear God,
18: 21 men who fear God, trustworthy **men** who hate dishonest gain—
18: 25 He chose capable **men** from all Israel and made them leaders of the
19: 13 Whether **man** or animal, he shall not be permitted to live.'
21: 7 "If a **man** sells his daughter as a servant, she is not to go free as
21: 12 "Anyone who strikes a **man** and kills him shall surely be put to
21: 14 if a **man** schemes and kills another man deliberately, take him
21: 16 "Anyone who kidnaps **another**[s] and either sells him or still has
21: 18 "If **men** quarrel and one hits the other with a stone or with his fist
21: 18 "If men quarrel and **one** hits the other with a stone or with his fist
21: 20 "If a **man** beats his male or female slave with a rod and the slave
21: 22 "If **men** who are fighting hit a pregnant woman and she gives birth
21: 26 "If a **man** hits a manservant or maidservant in the eye and destroys
21: 28 "If a bull gores a **man** or a woman to death, the bull must be
21: 29 but has not kept it penned up and it kills a **man** or woman,
21: 33 "If a **man** uncovers a pit or digs one and fails to cover it and an ox
21: 33 or digs **[RPH]** one and fails to cover it and an ox or a donkey falls
21: 35 "If a **man's** bull injures the bull of another and it dies, they are to
22: 1 [21:37] "If a **man** steals an ox or a sheep and slaughters it or sells
22: 5 [22:4] "If a **man** grazes his livestock in a field or vineyard
22: 7 [22:6] "If a **man** gives his neighbor silver or goods for
22: 7 [22:6] and they are stolen from the **neighbor's** house,
22: 10 [22:9] "If a **man** gives a donkey, an ox, a sheep or any other
22: 14 [22:13] "If a **man** borrows an animal from his neighbor and it is
22: 16 [22:15] "If a **man** seduces a virgin who is not pledged to be
22: 31 [22:30] "You are to be my holy **people**. So do not eat the meat of
25: 2 You are to receive the offering for me from each **man** whose heart
25: 20 The cherubim are to face **each** other, looking toward the cover.
28: 21 **each** engraved like a seal with the name of one of the twelve tribes.
30: 12 **each** *one* must pay the LORD a ransom for his life at the time he
30: 33 **Whoever** [+889] makes perfume like it and whoever puts it on
30: 38 **Whoever** [+889] makes any like it to enjoy its fragrance must be
32: 1 As for this **fellow** Moses who brought us up out of Egypt,
32: 23 As for this **fellow** Moses who brought us up out of Egypt,
32: 27 the God of Israel, says: '**Each** *man* strap a sword to his side.
32: 27 to the other, **each** killing his brother and friend and neighbor.' "
32: 27 each killing his brother and **[RPH]** friend and neighbor.' "
32: 27 each killing his brother and friend and **[RPH]** neighbor.' "
32: 28 and that day about three thousand **[RPH]** of the people died.
32: 29 for **you**[s] were against your own sons and brothers, and he has
33: 4 they began to mourn and no **one** put on any ornaments.
33: 8 all the people rose and stood **[NIE]** at the entrances to their tents,
33: 10 they all stood and worshiped, **each** at the entrance to his tent.
33: 11 speak to Moses face to face, as a **man** speaks with his friend.
34: 3 No **one** is to come with you or be seen anywhere on the mountain;
34: 3 is to come with you or **[RPH]** be seen anywhere on the mountain;
34: 24 no **one** will covet your land when you go up three times each year
35: 21 **everyone** [+3972] who was willing and whose heart moved him
35: 22 **men** and women alike, came and brought gold jewelry of all kinds:
35: 22 **They**[s] all presented their gold as a wave offering to the LORD.
35: 23 **Everyone** [+3972] who had blue, purple or scarlet yarn or fine
35: 29 All the Israelite **men** and women who were willing brought to the

Ex 36: 1 and every skilled **person** to whom the LORD has given skill
36: 2 and every skilled **person** to whom the LORD had given ability
36: 4 were doing all the work on the sanctuary left **[NIE]** their work
36: 4 were doing all the work on the sanctuary left **[NIE]** their work
36: 6 "No **man** or woman is to make anything else as an offering for the
37: 9 The cherubim faced **each** other, looking toward the cover.
39: 14 **each** engraved like a seal with the name of one of the twelve tribes.
Lev 7: 8 The priest who offers a burnt offering for **anyone** may keep its
7: 10 belongs **equally** [+278+2257+3869] to all the sons of Aaron.
10: 1 took their censers, **[NIE]** put fire in them and added incense;
13: 29 "If a **man** or woman has a sore on the head or on the chin,
13: 38 "When a **man** or woman has white spots on the skin,
13: 40 "When a **man** has lost his hair and is bald, he is clean.
13: 44 the **man** is diseased and is unclean. The priest shall pronounce him
14: 11 The priest who pronounces him clean shall present both the **one** to
15: 2 'When **any man** [+408] has a bodily discharge, the discharge is
15: 2 'When **any man** [+408] has a bodily discharge, the discharge is
15: 5 **Anyone** who touches his bed must wash his clothes and bathe with
15: 16 " 'When a **man** has an emission of semen, he must bathe his whole
15: 18 When a **man** lies with a woman and there is an emission of semen,
15: 24 " 'If a **man** lies with her and her monthly flow touches him,
15: 33 for a **man** who lies with a woman who is ceremonially unclean.
16: 21 He shall send the goat away into the desert in the care of a **man**
17: 3 **Any** Israelite who sacrifices an ox, a lamb or a goat in the camp
17: 3 Any **Israelite** [+1074+3776+4946] who sacrifices an ox, a lamb or
17: 4 that **man** shall be considered guilty of bloodshed; he has shed
17: 4 he has shed blood and must be cut off **[RPH]** from his people.
17: 8 '**Any** Israelite or any alien living among them who offers a burnt
17: 8 "Say to them: 'Any **Israelite** [+1074+3776+4946] or any alien
17: 9 it to the LORD—that **man** must be cut off from his people.
17: 10 " '**Any** Israelite or any alien living among them who eats any
17: 10 " 'Any **Israelite** [+1074+3776+4946] or any alien living among
17: 13 " '**Any** Israelite or any alien living among you who hunts any
17: 13 " 'Any **Israelite** [+1201+3776+4946] or any alien living among
18: 6 " 'No **one** is to approach any close relative to have sexual relations.
18: 6 " 'No one **[RPH]** is to approach any close relative to have sexual
18: 27 for all these things were done by the **people** who lived *in* the land
19: 3 " '**Each** of you must respect his mother and father, and you must
19: 11 " 'Do not steal. " 'Do not lie. " 'Do not deceive **one** another.
19: 20 " 'If a **man** sleeps with a woman who is a slave girl promised to
19: 20 sleeps with a woman who is a slave girl promised to another **man**
20: 2 '**Any** Israelite or any alien living in Israel who gives any of his
20: 2 'Any **Israelite** [+1201+3776+4946] or any alien living in Israel
20: 3 I will set my face against that **man** and I will cut him off from his
20: 4 If the people of the community close their eyes when that **man**
20: 5 I will set my face against that **man** and his family and will cut off
20: 9 " 'If **anyone** [+408] curses his father or mother, he must be put to
20: 9 " 'If **anyone** [+408] curses his father or mother, he must be put to
20: 10 " 'If a **man** commits adultery with another man's wife—with the
20: 10 " 'If a man commits adultery with another **man's** wife—with the
20: 11 " 'If a **man** sleeps with his father's wife, he has dishonored his
20: 12 " 'If a **man** sleeps with his daughter-in-law, both of them must be
20: 13 " 'If a **man** lies with a man as one lies with a woman, both of them
20: 14 " 'If a **man** marries both a woman and her mother, it is wicked.
20: 15 " 'If a **man** has sexual relations with an animal, he must be put to
20: 17 " 'If a **man** marries his sister, the daughter of either his father
20: 18 " 'If a **man** lies with a woman during her monthly period and has
20: 20 " 'If a **man** sleeps with his aunt, he has dishonored his uncle.
20: 21 " 'If a **man** marries his brother's wife, it is an act of impurity;
20: 27 " 'A **man** or woman who is a medium or spiritist among you must
21: 3 sister who is dependent on him since she has no **husband**—
21: 7 women defiled by prostitution or divorced from their **husbands**,
21: 9 " 'If a **[NIE]** priest's daughter defiles herself by becoming a
21: 17 'For the generations to come **none** [+4202] of your descendants
21: 18 No **man** who has any defect may come near: no man who is blind
21: 18 come near: no **man** who is blind or lame, disfigured or deformed;
21: 19 no **man** with a crippled foot or hand,
21: 21 No **[RPH]** descendant of Aaron the priest who has any defect is
22: 3 if **any** [+3972] of your descendants is ceremonially unclean
22: 4 " 'If a **[RPH]** descendant of Aaron has an infectious skin disease
22: 4 " 'If a **descendant of** [+2446+4946] Aaron has an infectious skin
22: 4 defiled by a corpse or by **anyone** who has an emission of semen,
22: 5 or if **he**[s] touches any crawling thing that makes him unclean,
22: 12 If a priest's daughter **marries** [+2118+4200] anyone other than a
22: 14 " 'If **anyone** eats a sacred offering by mistake, he must make
22: 18 'If **any** of you—either an Israelite or an alien living in Israel—
22: 18 'If any of you—either an **Israelite** [+1074+3776+4946] or an alien
22: 21 When **anyone** brings from the herd or flock a fellowship offering
24: 10 and an Egyptian **father** went out among the Israelites,
24: 10 broke out in the camp between him and an **Israelite** [+2021+3778].
24: 15 'If **anyone** [+408] curses his God, he will be held responsible;
24: 15 'If **anyone** [+408] curses his God, he will be held responsible;
24: 17 " 'If **anyone** takes the life of a human being, he must be put to
24: 19 If **anyone** injures his neighbor, whatever he has done must be done
25: 10 **each** *one* of you is to return to his family property and each to his
25: 10 of you is to return to his family property and **each** to his own clan.
25: 13 " 'In this Year of Jubilee **everyone** is to return to his own property.
25: 14 or buy any from him, do not take advantage of **each** other.
25: 17 Do not take advantage of **each** other, but fear your God. I am the
25: 26 a **man** has no one to redeem it for him but he himself prospers
25: 27 he sold it and refund the balance to the **man** to whom he sold it;
25: 29 " 'If a **man** sells a house in a walled city, he retains the right of
25: 46 but you must not rule over your fellow Israelites **[NIE]** ruthlessly.
26: 37 They will stumble over **one** another as though fleeing from the
27: 2 'If **anyone** makes a special vow to dedicate persons to the LORD
27: 14 " 'If a **man** dedicates his house as something holy to the LORD,
27: 16 " 'If a **man** dedicates to the LORD part of his family land,
27: 20 or if he has sold it to **someone** else, it can never be redeemed.
27: 26 " 'No **one**, however, may dedicate the firstborn of an animal,
27: 28 " 'But nothing that a **man** owns and devotes to the LORD—
27: 31 If a **man** redeems any of his tithe, he must add a fifth of the value
Nu 1: 4 **One** man from each tribe, each the head of his family, is to help
1: 4 One **man** from each tribe, each the head of his family, is to help
1: 4 man from each tribe, **each** the head of his family, is to help you.
1: 5 These are the names of the **men** who are to assist you:
1: 17 Moses and Aaron took these **men** whose names had been given,
1: 44 twelve leaders of Israel, **each** [+408] one representing his family.
1: 44 twelve leaders of Israel, **each** [+408] one representing his family.
1: 52 by divisions, *each* **man** in his own camp under his own standard.
1: 52 each man in his own camp **[RPH]** under his own standard.
2: 2 *each* **man** under his standard with the banners of his family."
2: 17 order as they encamp, **each** in his own place under his standard.
2: 34 and that is the way they set out, **each** with his clan and family.
4: 19 and assign to **each** man his work and what he is to carry.
4: 19 and assign to each **man** his work and what he is to carry.
4: 49 **each** [+408] was assigned his work and told what to carry.
4: 49 **each** [+408] was assigned his work and told what to carry.
5: 6 'When a **man** or woman wrongs another in any way and so is
5: 8 if that **person** has no close relative to whom restitution can be
5: 10 *Each* **man's** sacred gifts are his own, but what he gives to the
5: 10 but what **he**[s] gives to the priest will belong to the priest.' "
5: 12 say to them: 'If a **man's** wife goes astray and is unfaithful to him
5: 12 'If a man's **[RPH]** wife goes astray and is unfaithful to him
5: 13 by sleeping with another **man**, and this is hidden from her husband
5: 13 this is hidden from her **husband** and her impurity is undetected
5: 15 **he**[s] [+2021] is to take his wife to the priest. He must also take an
5: 19 "If no other **man** has slept with you and you have not gone astray
5: 19 gone astray and become impure while married to your **husband**,
5: 20 But if you have gone astray while married to your **husband**
5: 20 you have defiled yourself by sleeping with a **man** other than your
5: 20 yourself by sleeping with a man other than your **husband**"—
5: 27 If she has defiled herself and been unfaithful to her **husband**,
5: 29 goes astray and defiles herself while married to her **husband**,
5: 30 or when feelings of jealousy come over a **man** because he suspects
5: 31 The **husband** will be innocent of any wrongdoing, but the woman
6: 2 'If a **man** or woman wants to make a special vow, a vow of
7: 5 Give them to the Levites as *each* **man's** work requires."
9: 6 But **some**[s] *of them* could not celebrate the Passover on that day
9: 7 said **[RPH]** to Moses, "We have become unclean because of a
9: 10 'When **any** [+408] of you or your descendants are unclean
9: 10 'When **any** [+408] of you or your descendants are unclean
9: 13 if a **man** who is ceremonially clean and not on a journey fails to
9: 13 appointed time. That **man** will bear the consequences of his sin.
11: 10 the people of every family wailing, **each** at the entrance to his tent.
11: 16 "Bring me seventy of Israel's elders **[NIE]** who are known to you
11: 24 He brought together seventy **[NIE]** of their elders and had them
11: 25 that was on him and put the Spirit on **[NIE]** the seventy elders.
11: 26 However, two **men**, whose names were Eldad and Medad,
12: 3 (Now Moses was a very humble **man**, more humble than anyone
13: 2 "Send *some* **men** to explore the land of Canaan, which I am giving
13: 2 From each ancestral tribe send one **[RPH]** of its leaders."
13: 2 From each ancestral tribe send one **[RPH]** of its leaders."
13: 3 Desert of Paran. All of them were **leaders of** [+8031] the Israelites.
13: 16 These are the names of the **men** Moses sent to explore the land.
13: 31 the **men** who had gone up with him said, "We can't attack those
13: 32 living in it. All the people we saw there are of **[RPH]** great size.
14: 4 they said to **each** other, "We should choose a leader and go back to
14: 15 If you put these people to death **all** at one time, the nations who
14: 22 not one of the **men** who saw my glory and the miraculous signs I
14: 36 So the **men** Moses had sent to explore the land, who returned
14: 37 these **men** responsible for spreading the bad report about the land
14: 38 Of the **men** who went to explore the land, only Joshua son of Nun
15: 32 in the desert, a **man** was found gathering wood on the Sabbath day.
15: 35 the LORD said to Moses, "The **man** must die. The whole
16: 2 With them were 250 Israelite **men**, well-known community leaders
16: 2 With them were 250 Israelite men, **well-known** [+9005]
16: 7 The **man** the LORD chooses will be the one who is holy.
16: 14 Will you gouge out the eyes of these **men**? No, we will not come!"

Nu 16:17 *Each* **man** is to take his censer and put incense in it—250 censers
16:17 250 censers in all—and present **[RPH]** it before the LORD.
16:17 You and Aaron are to present your censers also." **[RPH]**
16:18 So *each* **man** took his censer, put fire and incense in it, and stood
16:22 will you be angry with the entire assembly when only one **man**
16:26 the assembly, "Move back from the tents of these wicked **men**!
16:30 you will know that these **men** have treated the LORD with
16:35 and consumed the 250 **men** who were offering the incense.
16:40 [17:5] This was to remind the Israelites that no **one**[s] [+2424]
17: 2 [17:17] ancestral tribes. Write the name of *each* **man** on his staff.
17: 5 [17:20] The staff belonging to the **man** I choose will sprout, and I
17: 9 [17:24] They looked at them, and *each* **man** took his own staff.
19: 9 "A **man** who is clean shall gather up the ashes of the heifer
19:18 Then a **man** who is ceremonially clean is to take some hyssop,
19:20 if a **person** who is unclean does not purify himself, he must be cut
21: 9 when **anyone** was bitten by a snake and looked at the bronze
22: 9 God came to Balaam and asked, "Who are these **men** with you?"
22:20 to Balaam and said, "Since these **men** have come to summon you,
22:35 said to Balaam, "Go with the **men**, but speak only what I tell you."
23:19 God is not a **man**, that he should lie, nor a son of man, that he
25: 5 "**Each** of you must put to death those of your men who have joined
25: 5 "Each of you must put to death those of your **men** who have joined
25: 6 an Israelite **man** brought to his family a Midianite woman right
25: 8 followed the **Israelite** [+3776] into the tent. He drove the spear
25: 8 through the **Israelite** [+3776] and into the woman's body.
25:14 The name of the **Israelite** [+3776] who was killed with the
26:10 whose followers died when the fire devoured the 250 **men**.
26:54 **each** is to receive its inheritance according to the number of those
26:64 Not **one** of them was among those counted by Moses and Aaron
26:65 and not **one** of them was left except Caleb son of Jephunneh
27: 8 "Say to the Israelites, 'If a **man** dies and leaves no son, turn his
27:16 of the spirits of all mankind, appoint a **man** over this community
27:18 "Take Joshua son of Nun, a **man** in whom is the spirit, and lay
30: 2 [30:3] When a **man** makes a vow to the LORD or takes an oath
30: 6 [30:7] "If *she* **marries** [+2118+2118+4200] after she makes a vow
30: 7 [30:8] her **husband** hears about it but says nothing to her,
30: 8 [30:9] if her **husband** forbids her when he hears about it, he
30:10 [30:11] "If a woman living with her **husband** makes a vow
30:11 [30:12] her **husband** hears about it but says nothing to her
30:12 [30:13] if her **husband** nullifies them when he hears about them,
30:12 [30:13] Her **husband** has nullified them, and the LORD will
30:13 [30:14] Her **husband** may confirm or nullify any vow she makes
30:13 [30:14] may confirm or **[RPH]** nullify any vow she makes
30:14 [30:15] if her **husband** says nothing to her about it from day to
30:16 [30:17] gave Moses concerning relationships between a **man**
31: 3 "Arm some of your **men** to go to war against the Midianites
31:17 kill every woman *who has* **slept with** [+3359+4200+5435] a man,
31:21 Eleazar the priest said to the **soldiers** [+7372] who had gone into
31:28 From the **soldiers** [+4878] who fought in the battle, set apart as
31:42 which Moses set apart from that of the fighting **men**—
31:49 "Your servants have counted the **soldiers** [+4878] under our
31:49 counted the soldiers under our command, and not **one** is missing.
31:50 as an offering to the LORD the gold articles **each** of us acquired—
31:53 **Each** soldier had taken plunder for himself.
31:53 Each **soldier** [+7372] had taken plunder for himself.
32:11 not one of the **men** twenty years old or more who came up out of
32:14 "And here you are, a brood of **[NIE]** sinners, standing in the place
32:18 We will not return to our homes until **every** Israelite has received
34:17 "These are the names of the **men** who are to assign the land for
34:19 These are **their**[s] [+2021] names: Caleb son of Jephunneh,
35: 8 are to be given in proportion to the inheritance of **each** tribe:
36: 7 for **every** Israelite shall keep the tribal land inherited from his
36: 8 so that **every** Israelite will possess the inheritance of his fathers.
36: 9 tribe to tribe, for **each** Israelite tribe is to keep the land it inherits."
Dt 1:13 understanding and respected **men** from each of your tribes,
1:15 So I took the leading men of your tribes, wise and respected **men**,
1:16 is between brother Israelites or between **one** of them and an alien.
1:17 Do not be afraid of any **man**, for judgment belongs to God.
1:22 "Let us send **men** ahead to spy out the land for us and bring back a
1:23 so I selected twelve **[RPH]** of you, one man from each tribe.
1:23 good to me; so I selected twelve of you, one **man** from each tribe.
1:31 as a **father** carries his son, all the way you went until you reached
1:35 "Not a[s] man of this evil generation shall see the good land I swore
1:35 "Not a **man** of this evil generation shall see the good land I swore
1:41 So **every** *one* of you put on his weapons, thinking it easy to go up
2:14 that entire generation of fighting **men** had perished from the camp,
2:16 Now when the last of these fighting **men** among the people had
3:11 and six feet wide. **[NIE]** It is still in Rabbah of the Ammonites.)
3:20 **each** of you may go back to the possession I have given you."
4: 3 you **everyone** [+2021+3972] who followed the Baal of Peor,
7:24 No **one** will be able to stand up against you; you will destroy them.
8: 5 Know then in your heart that as a **man** disciplines his son,
11:25 No **man** will be able to stand against you. The LORD your God,
12: 8 You are not to do as we do here today, **everyone** as he sees fit,
13:13 [13:14] that wicked **men** have arisen among you and have led the
16:17 **Each** of you must bring a gift in proportion to the way the LORD
17: 2 If a **man** or woman living among you in one of the towns the
17: 5 take the **man** or woman who has done this evil deed to your city
17: 5 evil deed to your city gate **[RPH]** and stone that person to death.
17:12 The **man** who shows contempt for the judge or for the priest who
17:12 must be put to death. **[RPH]** You must purge the evil from Israel.
17:15 not place a foreigner over you, **one** who is not a brother Israelite.
18:19 If **anyone** [+2021] does not listen to my words that the prophet
19:11 But if a **man** hates his neighbor and lies in wait for him, assaults
19:15 One witness is not enough to convict a **man** accused of any crime
19:16 If a malicious witness takes the stand to accuse a **man** of a crime,
19:17 the two **men** involved in the dispute must stand in the presence of
20: 5 "Has **anyone** [+2021+4769] built a new house and not dedicated
20: 5 or he may die in battle and **someone** else may dedicate it.
20: 6 Has **anyone** [+2021+4769] planted a vineyard and not begun to
20: 6 him go home, or he may die in battle and **someone** else enjoy it.
20: 7 Has **anyone** [+2021+4769] become pledged to a woman and not
20: 7 him go home, or he may die in battle and **someone** else marry her."
20: 8 shall add, "Is **any man** [+2021+4769] afraid or fainthearted?
21:15 If a **man** has two wives, and he loves one but not the other,
21:18 If a **man** has a stubborn and rebellious son who does not obey his
21:21 all the **men** *of* his town shall stone him to death. You must purge
21:22 If a **man** guilty of a capital offense is put to death and his body is
22:13 If a **man** takes a wife and, after lying with her, dislikes her
22:16 "I gave my daughter in marriage to this **man**, but he dislikes her.
22:18 and the elders shall take the **man** and punish him.
22:21 and there the **men** *of* her town shall stone her to death.
22:22 If a **man** is found sleeping with another man's wife, both the man
22:22 both the **man** who slept with her and the woman must die.
22:23 If a **man** happens to meet in a town a virgin pledged to be married
22:23 town a virgin pledged to be married **[NIE]** and he sleeps with her,
22:24 for help, and the **man** because he violated another man's wife.
22:25 if out in the country a **man** happens to meet a girl pledged to be
22:25 and rapes her, **[RPH]** only the man who has done this shall die.
22:25 and rapes her, only the **man** who has done this shall die.
22:26 This case is like that of **someone** who attacks and murders his
22:28 If a **man** happens to meet a virgin who is not pledged to be married
22:29 **he**[s] [+2021+2021+6640+8886] shall pay the girl's father fifty
22:30 [23:1] A **man** is not to marry his father's wife; he must not
23:10 [23:11] If one of your **men** is unclean because of a nocturnal
24: 1 If a **man** marries a woman who becomes displeasing to him
24: 2 if after she leaves his house she becomes the wife of another **man**,
24: 3 her second **husband** dislikes her and writes her a certificate of
24: 3 and sends her from his house, or if **he**[s] [+340+2021+2021] dies,
24: 5 If a **man** has recently married, he must not be sent to war or have
24: 7 If a **man** is caught kidnapping one of his brother Israelites
24:11 let the **man** to whom you are making the loan bring the pledge out
24:12 If the **man** is poor, do not go to sleep with his pledge in your
24:16 put to death for their fathers; **each** is to die for his own sin.
25: 1 When **men** have a dispute, they are to take it to court
25: 5 his widow *must* not **marry** [+2118+4200] outside the family.
25: 7 However, if a **man** does not want to marry his brother's wife,
25: 9 "This is what is done to the **man** who will not build up his
25:11 If **two men** [+278+2256+3481] are fighting and the wife of one of
25:11 If two men **[RPH]** are fighting and the wife of one of them comes
25:11 the wife of one of them comes to rescue her **husband** from his
27:14 The Levites shall recite to all the **people** *of* Israel in a loud voice:
27:15 "Cursed is the **man** who carves an image or casts an idol—
28:30 to a woman, but another **[NIE]** will take her and ravish her.
28:54 sensitive **man** among you will have no compassion on his own
28:56 will begrudge the **husband** she loves and her own son or daughter
29:10 [29:9] your elders and officials, and all the other **men** *of* Israel,
29:18 [29:17] Make sure there is no **man** or woman, clan or tribe among
29:20 [29:19] his wrath and zeal will burn against that **man**.
31:12 **men**, women and children, and the aliens living in your towns—
32:25 and young women will perish, infants and gray-haired **men**.
33: 1 This is the blessing that Moses the **man** *of* God pronounced on the
33: 8 "Your Thummim and Urim belong to the **man** you favored.
34: 6 Beth Peor, but to this day no **one** knows where his grave is.
Jos 1: 5 No **one** will be able to stand up against you all the days of your
1:18 **Whoever** [+889+3972] rebels against your word and does not obey
2: 1 Joshua son of Nun secretly sent two **spies** [+8078] from Shittim.
2: 2 **Some**[s] of the Israelites have come here tonight to spy out the
2: 3 "Bring out the **men** who came to you and entered your house,
2: 4 But the woman had taken the two **men** and hidden them. She said,
2: 4 She said, "Yes, the **men** came to me, but I did not know where
2: 5 At dusk, when it was time to close the city gate, the **men** left.
2: 5 the men left. I don't know which way **they**[s] [+2021] went.
2: 7 So the **men** set out in pursuit of the spies on the road that leads to
2: 9 said to **them**[s] [+2021], "I know that the LORD has given this
2:11 and **everyone's** [+928] courage failed because of you,
2:14 "Our lives for your lives!" the **men** assured her. "If you don't tell
2:17 The **men** said to her, "This oath you made us swear will not be

Jos 2:23 Then the two **men** started back. They went down out of the hills,
3:12 Now then, choose twelve **men** from the tribes of Israel, one from
3:12 twelve men from the tribes of Israel, **[RPH]** one from each tribe.
3:12 twelve men from the tribes of Israel, one **[RPH]** from each tribe.
4: 2 "Choose twelve **men** from among the people, one from each tribe,
4: 2 twelve men from among the people, **[RPH]** one from each tribe,
4: 2 twelve men from among the people, one **[RPH]** from each tribe,
4: 4 So Joshua called together the twelve **men** he had appointed from
4: 4 he had appointed from the Israelites, **[RPH]** one from each tribe,
4: 4 he had appointed from the Israelites, one **[RPH]** from each tribe,
4: 5 **Each** of you is to take up a stone on his shoulder, according to the
5: 4 who came out of Egypt—all the men **[NIE]** of military age—
5: 6 the **men** who were *of* military age when they left Egypt had died,
5:13 saw a **man** standing in front of him with a drawn sword in his
6: 3 March around the city once with all the armed **men**. Do this for six
6: 5 will collapse and the people will go up, every **man** straight in."
6:20 so **every** man charged straight in, and they took the city.
6:21 **men** and women, young and old, cattle, sheep and donkeys.
6:22 Joshua said to the two **men** who had spied out the land, "Go into
6:26 "Cursed before the LORD is the **man** who undertakes to rebuild
7: 2 Now Joshua sent **men** from Jericho to Ai, which is near Beth Aven
7: 2 and spy out the region." So the **men** went up and spied out Ai.
7: 3 Send two or three thousand **men** to take it and do not weary all the
7: 3 Send two or three thousand men **[RPH]** to take it and do not
7: 4 So about three thousand **men** went up; but they were routed by the
7: 4 thousand men went up; but they were routed by the **men** *of* Ai,
7: 5 **who**[s] [+2021+6504] killed about thirty-six of them. They chased
7: 5 **[RPH]** They chased the Israelites from the city gate as far as the
8: 3 of his best fighting men **[NIE]** and sent them out at night
8:12 Joshua had taken about five thousand **men** and set them in ambush
8:14 all the **men** *of* the city hurried out early in the morning to meet
8:17 Not a **man** remained in Ai or Bethel who did not go after Israel.
8:20 The **men** *of* Ai looked back and saw the smoke of the city rising
8:21 up from the city, they turned around and attacked the **men** *of* Ai.
8:25 Twelve thousand **men** and women fell that day—all the people of
8:25 thousand men and women fell that day—all the **people** *of* Ai.
9: 6 Joshua in the camp at Gilgal and said to him and the **men** *of* Israel,
9: 7 The **men** *of* Israel said to the Hivites, "But perhaps you live near
9:14 The **men** of Israel sampled their provisions but did not inquire of
10: 2 it was larger than Ai, and all its **men** were good fighters.
10: 6 The **Gibeonites** [+1500] then sent word to Joshua in the camp at
10: 8 into your hand. Not **one** of them will be able to withstand you."
10:14 like it before or since, a day when the LORD listened to a **man**.
10:18 up to the mouth of the cave, and post *some* **men** there to guard it.
10:21 at Makkedah, and no **one** uttered a word against the Israelites.
10:24 he summoned all the **men** *of* Israel and said to the army
10:24 said to the **army** [+4878] commanders who had come with him,
14: 6 "You know what the LORD said to Moses the **man** *of* God at
17: 1 and Bashan because the Makirites were **great soldiers** [+4878].
18: 4 Appoint three **men** from each tribe. I will send them out to make a
18: 8 As the **men** started on their way to map out the land, Joshua
18: 9 So the **men** left and went through the land. They wrote its
21:44 Not **one** of their enemies withstood them; the LORD handed all
22:14 **each** the head of a family division among the Israelite clans.
22:20 of Israel? He was not the only **one** who died for his sin.' "
23: 9 to this day no **one** has been able to withstand you.
23:10 **[RPH]** One of you routs a thousand, because the LORD your
24:28 Then Joshua sent the people away, **each** to his own inheritance.
Jdg 1: 4 into their hands and they struck down ten thousand **men** at Bezek.
1:24 the spies saw a **man** coming out of the city and they said to him,
1:25 put the city to the sword but spared the **man** and his whole family.
1:26 **He**[s] [+2021] then went to the land of the Hittites, where he built a
2: 6 went to take possession of the land, **each** to his own inheritance.
2:21 I will no longer drive out before them **any** of the nations Joshua
3:15 a left-handed **man**, the son of Gera the Benjamite.
3:17 the tribute to Eglon king of Moab, who was a very fat **man**.
3:28 of the Jordan that led to Moab, they allowed no **one** to cross over.
3:29 that time they struck down about ten thousand **Moabites** [+4566],
3:29 all vigorous and strong; **[RPH]** not a man escaped.
3:29 thousand Moabites, all vigorous and strong; not a **man** escaped.
3:31 who struck down six hundred Philistines **[NIE]** with an oxgoad.
4: 6 take with you ten thousand **men** of Naphtali and Zebulun and lead
4:10 Ten thousand **men** followed him, and Deborah also went with him.
4:14 So Barak went down Mount Tabor, followed by ten thousand **men**.
4:20 "If **someone** comes by and asks you, 'Is anyone here?' say 'No.' "
4:20 "If someone comes by and asks you, 'Is **anyone** here?' say 'No.' "
4:22 "Come," she said, "I will show you the **man** you're looking for."
6: 8 he sent them a **[NIE]** prophet, who said, "This is what the
6:16 you will strike down **all** the Midianites **together** [+285+3869]."
6:27 So Gideon took ten **[NIE]** of his servants and did as the LORD
6:27 because he was afraid of his family and the **men** *of* the town,
6:28 In the morning when the **men** *of* the town got up, there was Baal's
6:29 They asked **each** other, "Who did this?" When they carefully
6:30 The **men** *of* the town demanded of Joash, "Bring out your son.
7: 6 Three hundred **men** lapped with their hands to their mouths.
7: 7 "With the three hundred **men** that lapped I will save you and give
7: 7 into your hands. Let all the other men go, **each** to his own place."
7: 8 So Gideon sent the rest of the **Israelites** [+3776] to their tents
7: 8 So Gideon sent the rest of the Israelites **[RPH]** to their tents
7: 8 **[RPH]** who took over the provisions and trumpets of the others.
7:13 Gideon arrived just as a **man** was telling a friend his dream.
7:14 other than the sword of Gideon son of Joash, the **Israelite** [+3776].
7:16 Dividing the three hundred **men** into three companies, he placed
7:19 the hundred **men** with him reached the edge of the camp at the
7:21 While *each* **man** held his position around the camp, all the
7:22 the LORD caused the **men** throughout the camp to turn on each
7:23 **Israelites** [+3776] from Naphtali, Asher and all Manasseh were
7:24 So all the **men** *of* Ephraim were called out and they took the waters
8: 1 Now the **Ephraimites** [+713] asked Gideon, "Why have you
8: 4 Gideon and his three hundred **men**, exhausted yet keeping up the
8: 5 He said to the **men** *of* Succoth, "Give my troops some bread;
8: 8 of them, but **they**[s] [+7159] answered as the men of Succoth had.
8: 8 request of them, but they answered as the **men** *of* Succoth had.
8: 9 So he said to the **men** *of* Peniel, "When I return in triumph,
8:10 a hundred and twenty thousand **swordsmen** [+2995+8990] had
8:14 He caught a young **man** of Succoth and questioned him,
8:14 seventy-seven officials of Succoth, the elders of the town. **[NIE]**
8:15 Gideon came and said to the **men** *of* Succoth, "Here are Zebah
8:15 Why should we give bread to your exhausted **men**?' "
8:16 taught the **men** *of* Succoth a lesson by punishing them with desert
8:17 pulled down the tower of Peniel and killed the **men** *of* the town.
8:18 and Zalmunna, "What kind of **men** did you kill at Tabor?"
8:21 'As is the **man**, so is his strength.' " So Gideon stepped forward
8:22 The **Israelites** [+3776] said to Gideon, "Rule over us—you,
8:24 that **each** of you give me an earring from your share of the
8:25 out a garment, and *each* **man** threw a ring from his plunder onto it.
9: 2 to have all seventy of Jerub-Baal's sons **[NIE]** rule over you,
9: 2 all seventy of Jerub-Baal's sons rule over you, or just one **man**?'
9: 4 and Abimelech used it to hire **[NIE]** reckless adventurers,
9: 5 murdered his seventy brothers, **[NIE]** the sons of Jerub-Baal.
9: 9 'Should I give up my oil, by which both gods and **men** are honored,
9:13 'Should I give up my wine, which cheers both gods and **men**,
9:18 murdered his seventy sons **[NIE]** on a single stone, and made
9:28 Zebul his deputy? Serve the **men** *of* Hamor, Shechem's father!
9:36 "You mistake the shadows of the mountains for **men**."
9:49 So all the men **[NIE]** cut branches and followed Abimelech.
9:49 So all the **people** *in* the tower of Shechem, about a thousand men
9:49 tower of Shechem, about a thousand **men** and women, also died.
9:51 however, was a strong tower, to which all the **men** and women—
9:55 When the **Israelites** [+3776] saw that Abimelech was dead,
9:55 the Israelites saw that Abimelech was dead, **they**[s] went home.
9:57 God also made the **men** *of* Shechem pay for all their wickedness.
10: 1 After the time of Abimelech a **man** *of* Issachar, Tola son of Puah,
10:18 The leaders of the people of Gilead said to **each** other, "Whoever
10:18 to each other, "**Whoever** [+2021+4769] will launch the attack
11: 3 where a **group** of adventurers gathered around him and followed
11:39 did to her as he had vowed. And she *was a* **virgin** [+3359+4202].
12: 1 The **men** *of* Ephraim called out their forces, crossed over to
12: 2 my people were engaged in a great struggle **[NIE]** with the
12: 4 Jephthah then called together the **men** *of* Gilead and fought against
12: 4 The **Gileadites** [+1680] struck them down because the Ephraimites
12: 5 "Let me cross over," the **men** *of* Gilead asked him, "Are you an
13: 2 A certain **man** of Zorah, named Manoah, from the clan of the
13: 6 the woman went to her **husband** and told him, "A man of God
13: 6 went to her husband and told him, "A **man** *of* God came to me.
13: 8 let the **man** *of* God you sent to us come again to teach us how to
13: 9 was out in the field; but her **husband** Manoah was not with her.
13:10 The woman hurried to tell her **husband**, "He's here! The man who
13:10 "He's here! The **man** who appeared to me the other day!"
13:11 When he came to the **man**, he said, "Are you the one who talked to
13:11 to the man, he said, "Are you the **one** who talked to my wife?"
14:15 "Coax your **husband** into explaining the riddle for us, or we will
14:18 Before sunset on the seventh day the **men** *of* the town said to him,
14:19 He went down to Ashkelon, struck down thirty of their **men**,
15:10 The **men** *of* Judah asked, "Why have you come to fight us?"
15:11 three thousand **men** from Judah went down to the cave in the rock
15:15 of a donkey, he grabbed it and struck down a thousand **men**.
15:16 of them. With a donkey's jawbone I have killed a thousand **men**."
16: 5 **Each** *one* of us will give you eleven hundred shekels of silver."
16:19 she called a **man** to shave off the seven braids of his hair,
16:27 Now the temple was crowded with **men** and women; all the rulers
16:27 on the roof were about three thousand **men** and women watching
17: 1 Now a **man** named Micah from the hill country of Ephraim
17: 5 Now this **man** Micah had a shrine, and he made an ephod
17: 6 In those days Israel had no king; **everyone** did as he saw fit.
17: 8 left **[NIE]** that town in search of some other place to stay.
17:11 So the Levite agreed to live with **him**[s] [+2021], and the young man
18: 2 So the Danites sent five **[RPH]** warriors from Zorah and Eshtaol

Jdg 18: 2 out the land and explore it. These **men** represented all their clans.
18: 7 So the five **men** left and came to Laish, where they saw that the
18: 11 six hundred **men** from the clan of the Danites, armed for battle,
18: 14 the five **men** who had spied out the land of Laish said to their
18: 16 The six hundred **[NIE]** Danites, armed for battle, stood at the
18: 17 The five **men** who had spied out the land went inside and took the
18: 17 and the six hundred armed **men** stood at the entrance to the gate.
18: 19 and clan in Israel as priest rather than just one **man's** household?"
18: 22 the **men** who lived near Micah were called together and overtook
18: 25 or *some* hot-tempered **men** will attack you, and you and your
19: 1 Now a **[NIE]** Levite who lived in a remote area in the hill country
19: 3 her **husband** went to her to persuade her to return. He had with
19: 6 girl's father said, **[RPH]** "Please stay tonight and enjoy yourself."
19: 7 And when the **man** got up to go, his father-in-law persuaded him,
19: 9 when the **man**, with his concubine and his servant, got up to leave,
19: 10 the **man** left and went toward Jebus (that is, Jerusalem), with his
19: 15 the city square, but no **one** took them into his home for the night.
19: 16 That evening an old **man** from the hill country of Ephraim,
19: 16 who was living in Gibeah **[RPH]** (the men of the place were
19: 16 who was living in Gibeah (the **men** *of* the place were Benjamites),
19: 17 When he looked and saw **[RPH]** the traveler in the city square,
19: 17 in the city square, the old **man** asked, "Where are you going?
19: 18 to the house of the LORD. No **one** has taken me into his house.
19: 20 "You are welcome at my house," the old **man** said. "Let me supply
19: 22 **some**[s] *of* the wicked men of the city surrounded the house.
19: 22 some of the wicked **men** *of* the city surrounded the house.
19: 22 on the door, they shouted to the old **man** who owned the house,
19: 22 "Bring out the **man** who came to your house so we can have sex
19: 23 **[RPH]** The owner of the house went outside and said to them,
19: 23 Since this **man** is my guest, don't do this disgraceful thing.
19: 24 you wish. But to this **man**, don't do such a disgraceful thing."
19: 25 the **men** would not listen to him. So the man took his concubine
19: 25 So the **man** took his concubine and sent her outside to them,
19: 26 At daybreak the woman went back to the house **[RPH]** where her
19: 28 Then the **man** put her on his donkey and set out for home.
20: 1 to Beersheba and from the land of Gilead came out as one **man**
20: 2 four hundred thousand **soldiers** [+8081] armed with swords.
20: 4 So **[RPH]** the Levite, the husband of the murdered woman,
20: 4 the **husband** *of* the murdered woman, said, "I and my concubine
20: 8 All the people rose as one **man**, saying, "None of us will go home.
20: 8 rose as one man, saying, "**None of** [+4202] us will go home.
20: 8 of us will go home. No, not **one** of us will return to his house.
20: 10 We'll take ten **men** out of every hundred from all the tribes of
20: 11 So all the **men** *of* Israel got together and united as one man against
20: 11 men of Israel got together and united as one **man** against the city.
20: 12 The tribes of Israel sent **men** throughout the tribe of Benjamin,
20: 13 Now surrender those wicked **men** of Gibeah so that we may put
20: 15 mobilized twenty-six thousand **swordsmen** [+2995+8990] from
20: 15 in addition to seven hundred chosen **men** from those living in
20: 16 Among all these soldiers there were seven hundred chosen **men**
20: 17 **Israel** [+3776], apart from Benjamin, mustered four hundred
20: 17 mustered four hundred thousand **swordsmen** [+2995+8990], all of
20: 17 four hundred thousand swordsmen, all of them fighting **men**.
20: 20 The **men** *of* Israel went out to fight the Benjamites and took up
20: 20 and **[RPH]** took up battle positions against them at Gibeah.
20: 21 cut down twenty-two thousand Israelites **[RPH]** on the battlefield
20: 22 the **men** *of* Israel encouraged one another and again took up their
20: 25 thousand Israelites, **[RPH]** all of them armed with swords.
20: 31 so that about thirty **men** fell in the open field and on the roads—
20: 33 All the **men** *of* Israel moved from their places and took up
20: 34 ten thousand of Israel's finest **men** made a frontal attack on
20: 35 struck down 25,100 Benjamites, **[NIE]** all armed with swords.
20: 36 Now the **men** *of* Israel had given way before Benjamin,
20: 38 The **men** *of* Israel had arranged with the ambush that they should
20: 39 then the **men** *of* Israel would turn in the battle. The Benjamites had
20: 39 The Benjamites had begun to inflict casualties on the **men** *of* Israel
20: 39 **[RPH]** and they said, "We are defeating them as in the first
20: 41 the **men** *of* Israel turned on them, and the men of Benjamin were
20: 41 of Israel turned on them, and the **men** *of* Benjamin were terrified,
20: 42 So they fled before the **Israelites** [+3776] in the direction of the
20: 44 thousand Benjamites fell, **[NIE]** all of them valiant fighters.
20: 44 thousand Benjamites fell, all of them **valiant fighters** [+2657].
20: 45 the Israelites cut down five thousand **men** along the roads.
20: 45 Benjamites as far as Gidom and struck down two thousand **more**[s].
20: 46 twenty-five thousand Benjamite **swordsmen** [+2995+8990] fell,
20: 46 Benjamite swordsmen fell, all of them **valiant fighters** [+2657].
20: 47 six hundred **men** turned and fled into the desert to the rock of
20: 48 The **men** *of* Israel went back to Benjamin and put all the towns to
21: 1 The **men** *of* Israel had taken an oath at Mizpah: "Not one of us will
21: 1 "Not **one** of us will give his daughter in marriage to a Benjamite."
21: 8 They discovered that no **one** from Jabesh Gilead had come to the
21: 9 they found that **none** [+401] of the people of Jabesh Gilead were
21: 10 So the assembly sent twelve thousand fighting **men** with
21: 12 four hundred young women who had never slept with a **man**,
21: 21 the vineyards and **each** of you seize a wife from the girls of Shiloh
21: 22 because we did not get wives for them **[NIE]** during the war,
21: 24 left that place and went home **[RPH]** to their tribes and clans,
21: 24 went home to their tribes and clans, **each** to his own inheritance.
21: 25 In those days Israel had no king; **everyone** did as he saw fit.
Ru 1: 1 and a **man** from Bethlehem in Judah, together with his wife
1: 2 The **man's** name was Elimelech, his wife's name Naomi,
1: 3 Now Elimelech, Naomi's **husband**, died, and she was left with her
1: 5 and Naomi was left without her two sons and her **husband**.
1: 9 that each of you will find rest in the home of another **husband**."
1: 11 I going to have any more sons, who could become your **husbands**?
1: 12 my daughters; I am too old to have another **husband**.
1: 12 even if I had a **husband** tonight and then gave birth to sons—
1: 13 *Would you* **remain unmarried** [+1194+2118+4200+4200+6328]
2: 1 Now Naomi had a relative on her **husband's** side, from the clan of
2: 1 the clan of Elimelech, a **man** *of* standing, whose name was Boaz.
2: 11 done for your mother-in-law since the death of your **husband**—
2: 19 "The name of the **man** I worked with today is Boaz," she said.
2: 20 She added, "That **man** is our close relative; he is one of our
3: 3 don't let **him**[s] [+2021] know you are there until he has finished
3: 8 In the middle of the night something startled the **man**, and he
3: 14 feet until morning, but got up before **anyone** could be recognized;
3: 16 Then she told her everything **Boaz**[s] [+2021] had done for her
3: 18 For the **man** will not rest until the matter is settled today."
4: 2 Boaz took ten **[RPH]** of the elders of the town and said,
4: 7 **one party**[s] took off his sandal and gave it to the other.
1Sa 1: 1 There was a certain **man** from Ramathaim, a Zuphite from the hill
1: 3 Year after year this **man** went up from his town to worship
1: 8 Elkanah her **husband** would say to her, "Hannah, why are you
1: 11 and not forget your servant but give her a **son** [+2446],
1: 21 When the **man** Elkanah went up with all his family to offer the
1: 22 She said to her **husband**, "After the boy is weaned, I will take him
1: 23 "Do what seems best to you," Elkanah her **husband** told her.
2: 9 will be silenced in darkness. "It is not by strength that **one** prevails;
2: 13 with the people that whenever **anyone** [+3972] offered a sacrifice
2: 15 of the priest would come and say to the **man** who was sacrificing,
2: 16 If the **man** said to him, "Let the fat be burned up first, and
2: 17 for **they**[s] [+2021] were treating the LORD's offering with
2: 19 took it to him when she went up with her **husband** to offer the
2: 25 If a **man** sins against another man, God may mediate for him;
2: 25 If a man sins against another **man**, God may mediate for him;
2: 25 but if a **man** sins against the LORD, who will intercede for him?"
2: 26 to grow in stature and in favor with the LORD and with **men**.
2: 27 Now a **man** *of* God came to Eli and said to him, "This is what the
2: 33 **Every** *one* of you that I do not cut off from my altar will be spared
2: 33 your heart, and all your descendants will die **in the prime of life**.
4: 2 who killed about four thousand of **them**[s] on the battlefield.
4: 9 Be **men**, or you will be subject to the Hebrews, as they have been
4: 9 to the Hebrews, as they have been to you. Be **men**, and fight!"
4: 10 and the Israelites were defeated and *every* **man** fled to his tent.
4: 12 That same day a **Benjamite** [+1228] ran from the battle line
4: 13 When the **man** entered the town and told what had happened,
4: 14 "What is the meaning of this uproar?" The **man** hurried over to Eli,
4: 16 **He**[s] [+2021] told Eli, "I have just come from the battle line;
4: 18 neck was broken and he died, for he was an old **man** and heavy.
4: 19 and that her father-in-law and her **husband** were dead,
4: 21 ark of God and the deaths of her father-in-law and her **husband**.
5: 7 When the **men** *of* Ashdod saw what was happening, they said,
5: 9 He afflicted the **people** *of* the city, both young and old, with an
5: 12 **Those**[s] [+2021] who did not die were afflicted with tumors,
6: 10 So **they**[s] [+2021] did this. They took two such cows and hitched
6: 15 On that day the **people** *of* Beth Shemesh offered burnt offerings
6: 19 God struck down some of the **men** *of* Beth Shemesh, putting
6: 19 putting seventy **[RPH]** of them to death because they had looked
6: 19 putting seventy [BHS+ *50,070* ***men***] of them to death because they
6: 20 the **men** *of* Beth Shemesh asked, "Who can stand in the presence
7: 1 So the **men** *of* Kiriath Jearim came and took up the ark of the
7: 11 The **men** *of* Israel rushed out of Mizpah and pursued the
8: 22 Samuel said to the **men** *of* Israel, "Everyone go back to his town."
8: 22 Samuel said to the men of Israel, "**Everyone** go back to his town."
9: 1 There was a **[RPH]** Benjamite, a man of standing, whose name
9: 1 the son of Becorath, the son of Aphiah of **Benjamin** [+1201+3549].
9: 2 an impressive young man without equal **[RPH]** among the
9: 6 But the servant replied, "Look, in this town there is a **man** *of* God;
9: 6 in this town there is a man of God; **he**[s] [+2021] is highly respected,
9: 7 Saul said to his servant, "If we go, what can we give the **man**?
9: 7 We have no gift to take to the **man** *of* God. What do we have?"
9: 8 I will give it to the **man** *of* God so that he will tell us what way to
9: 9 in Israel, if a **man** went to inquire of God, he would say, "Come,
9: 10 let's go." So they set out for the town where the **man** *of* God was.
9: 16 "About this time tomorrow I will send you a **man** from the land of
9: 17 the LORD said to him, "This is the **man** I spoke to you about;
9: 22 head of those who were invited—about thirty **[NIE]** in number.
10: 2 you leave me today, you will meet two **men** near Rachel's tomb,

1Sa 10: 3 Three **men** going up to God at Bethel will meet you there.
10: 6 with them; and you will be changed into a different **person**.
10: 11 they asked **each** other, "What is this that has happened to the son
10: 12 A **man** who lived there answered, "And who is their father?"
10: 22 inquired further of the LORD, "Has the **man** come here yet?"
10: 25 Then Samuel dismissed the people, **each** to his own home.
11: 1 And all the **men** *of* Jabesh said to him, "Make a treaty with us,
11: 5 Then they repeated to him what the **men** *of* Jabesh had said.
11: 7 of the LORD fell on the people, and they turned out as one **man**.
11: 8 three hundred thousand and the **men** *of* Judah thirty thousand.
11: 9 "Say to the **men** *of* Jabesh Gilead, 'By the time the sun is hot
11: 9 When the messengers went and reported this to the **men** *of* Jabesh,
11: 10 **They**[s] [+3315] said to the Ammonites, "Tomorrow we will
11: 12 over us?' Bring these **men** to us and we will put them to death."
11: 13 Saul said, "No **one** shall be put to death today, for this day the
11: 15 and Saul and all the **Israelites** [+3776] held a great celebration.
12: 4 they replied. "You have not taken anything from **anyone's** hand."
13: 2 The rest of the men he sent back **[NIE]** to their homes.
13: 6 When the **men** *of* Israel saw that their situation was critical
13: 14 the LORD has sought out a **man** after his own heart
13: 15 the men who were with him. **They**[s] numbered about six hundred.
13: 20 So all Israel went down to the Philistines **[NIE]** to have their
14: 2 tree in Migron. With him were about six hundred **men**,
14: 8 then; we will cross over toward the **men** and let them see us.
14: 12 The **men** *of* the outpost shouted to Jonathan and his armor-bearer,
14: 14 his armor-bearer killed some twenty **men** in an area of about half
14: 20 Philistines in total confusion, striking **each** other with their swords.
14: 22 When all the **Israelites** [+3776] who had hidden in the hill country
14: 24 Now the **men** *of* Israel were in distress that day, because Saul had
14: 24 "Cursed be any **man** who eats food before evening comes,
14: 28 **one** of the soldiers told him, "Your father bound the army under a
14: 28 a strict oath, saying, 'Cursed be any **man** who eats food today!'
14: 34 and tell them, '**Each** of you bring me your cattle and sheep,
14: 34 and tell them, 'Each of you bring me your cattle and **[RPH]** sheep,
14: 34 blood still in it.' " So everyone brought **[RPH]** his ox that night
14: 36 and plunder them till dawn, and let us not leave **one** of them alive."
14: 52 whenever Saul saw a mighty or brave **man**, he took him into his
15: 3 put to death **men** and women, children and infants, cattle
15: 4 hundred thousand foot soldiers and ten thousand **men** *from* Judah.
16: 16 Let our lord command his servants here to search for **someone** who
16: 17 "Find **someone** who plays well and bring him to me."
16: 18 He is a brave man and a **warrior** [+4878]. He speaks well
16: 18 and a warrior. He speaks well and is a fine-looking **man**.
17: 2 Saul and the **Israelites** [+3776] assembled and camped in the
17: 4 A **champion** [+1227+2021] named Goliath, who was from Gath,
17: 8 servants of Saul? Choose a **man** and have him come down to me.
17: 10 the ranks of Israel! Give me a **man** and let us fight each other."
17: 12 Now David was the son of an **[NIE]** Ephrathite named Jesse,
17: 12 and in Saul's time **he**[s] [+2021] was old and well advanced in years.
17: 12 and in Saul's time he was old and well advanced in years. **[NIE]**
17: 19 They are with Saul and all the **men** *of* Israel in the Valley of Elah,
17: 23 Goliath, the Philistine **champion** [+1227+2021] from Gath,
17: 24 When the **Israelites** [+3776] saw the man, they all ran from him in
17: 24 When the Israelites saw the **man**, they all ran from him in great
17: 25 Now the **Israelites** [+3776] had been saying, "Do you see how this
17: 25 had been saying, "Do you see how this **man** keeps coming out?
17: 25 The king will give great wealth to the **man** who kills him.
17: 26 David asked the **men** standing near him, "What will be done for
17: 26 "What will be done for the **man** who kills this Philistine
17: 27 told him, "This is what will be done for the **man** who kills him."
17: 28 David's oldest brother, heard him speaking with the **men**,
17: 33 are only a boy, and he has been a fighting **man** from his youth."
17: 41 the Philistine, with his **[NIE]** shield bearer in front of him,
17: 52 Then the **men** *of* Israel and Judah surged forward with a shout
18: 5 successfully that Saul gave him a high rank in the **army** [+4878].
18: 23 the king's son-in-law? I'm only a poor **man** and little known."
18: 27 David and his **men** went out and killed two hundred Philistines.
18: 27 **[NIE]** He brought their foreskins and presented the full number to
20: 15 not even when the LORD has cut off **every** *one of* David's
20: 41 they kissed **each** other and wept together—but David wept the
20: 41 Then they kissed each other and wept **together** [+907+2084+8276]
21: 1 [21:2] and asked, "Why are you alone? Why is no **one** with you?"
21: 2 [21:3] 'No **one** is to know anything about your mission and your
21: 7 [21:8] Now **one** of Saul's servants was there that day,
21: 14 [21:15] Achish said to his servants, "Look at the **man**! He is
22: 2 All **those**[s] *who* were *in* distress or in debt or discontented gathered
22: 2 All those who were in distress or **[RPH]** in debt or discontented
22: 2 in distress or in debt or **[RPH]** discontented gathered around him,
22: 2 he became their leader. About four hundred **men** were with him.
22: 6 Now Saul heard that David and his **men** had been discovered.
22: 18 That day he killed eighty-five **men** who wore the linen ephod.
22: 19 with its **men** and women, its children and infants, and its cattle,
23: 3 But David's **men** said to him, "Here in Judah we are afraid.
23: 5 So David and his **men** went to Keilah, fought the Philistines
23: 8 for battle, to go down to Keilah to besiege David and his **men**.
23: 12 "Will the citizens of Keilah surrender me and my **men** to Saul?"
23: 13 So David and his **men**, about six hundred in number, left Keilah
23: 13 **[NIE]** left Keilah and kept moving from place to place.
23: 24 Now David and his **men** were in the Desert of Maon, in the Arabah
23: 25 Saul and his **men** began the search, and when David was told about
23: 26 David and his **men** were on the other side, hurrying to get away
23: 26 As Saul and his **forces** were closing in on David and his men to
23: 26 his forces were closing in on David and his **men** to capture them,
24: 2 [24:3] So Saul took three thousand chosen **men** from all Israel
24: 2 [24:3] for David and his **men** near the Crags of the Wild Goats.
24: 3 [24:4] David and his **men** were far back in the cave.
24: 4 [24:5] The **men** said, "This is the day the LORD spoke of when
24: 6 [24:7] He said to his **men**, "The LORD forbid that I should do
24: 7 [24:8] With these words David rebuked his **men** and did not allow
24: 19 [24:20] When a **man** finds his enemy, does he let him get away
24: 22 [24:23] but David and his **men** went up to the stronghold.
25: 2 A certain **man** in Maon, who had property there at Carmel,
25: 2 who had property there at Carmel, **[RPH]** was very wealthy.
25: 3 **His**[s] [+2021] name was Nabal and his wife's name was Abigail.
25: 3 but her **husband**, a Calebite, was surly and mean in his dealings.
25: 10 Many servants **[NIE]** are breaking away from their masters these
25: 11 my shearers, and give it to **men** coming from who knows where?"
25: 13 David said to his **men**, "Put on your swords!" So they put on their
25: 13 **[RPH]** So they put on their swords, and David put on his.
25: 13 your swords!" So **they**[s] put on their swords, and David put on his.
25: 13 About four hundred **men** went up with David, while two hundred
25: 15 Yet these **men** were very good to us. They did not mistreat us,
25: 19 on ahead; I'll follow you." But she did not tell her **husband** Nabal.
25: 20 there were David and his **men** descending toward her, and she met
25: 25 May my lord pay no attention to that wicked **man** Nabal. He is just
26: 2 with his three thousand chosen **men** *of* Israel, to search there for
26: 15 David said, "You're a **man**, aren't you? And who is like you in
26: 23 The LORD rewards every **man** for his righteousness
27: 2 So David and the six hundred **men** with him left and went over to
27: 3 David and his **men** settled in Gath with Achish. Each man had his
27: 3 *Each* **man** had his family with him, and David had his two wives:
27: 8 Now David and his **men** went up and raided the Geshurites,
27: 9 he did not leave a **man** or woman alive, but took sheep and cattle,
27: 11 He did not leave a **man** or woman alive to be brought to Gath,
28: 1 that you and your **men** will accompany me in the army."
28: 8 on other clothes, and at night he and two **men** went to the woman.
28: 14 he asked. "An old **man** wearing a robe is coming up," she said.
29: 2 David and his **men** were marching at the rear with Achish.
29: 4 commanders were angry with him and said, "Send the **man** back,
29: 4 his master's favor than by taking the heads of our own **men**?
29: 11 his **men** got up early in the morning to go back to the land of the
30: 1 David and his **men** reached Ziklag on the third day.
30: 2 They killed none of **them**[s], but carried them off as they went on
30: 3 When David and his **men** came to Ziklag, they found it destroyed
30: 6 each **one** was bitter in spirit because of his sons and daughters.
30: 9 and the six hundred **men** with him came to the Besor Ravine,
30: 10 for two hundred **men** were too exhausted to cross the ravine.
30: 10 the ravine. But David and four hundred **men** continued the pursuit.
30: 11 They found an **[NIE]** Egyptian in a field and brought him to
30: 13 He said, "I am an Egyptian, the slave of an **[NIE]** Amalekite.
30: 17 **none** [+4202] of them got away, except four hundred young men
30: 17 except four hundred young **men** who rode off on camels and fled.
30: 21 David came to the two hundred **men** who had been too exhausted
30: 22 all the evil **men** and troublemakers among David's followers said,
30: 22 troublemakers among David's **followers** [+889+2143+6640] said,
30: 22 However, *each* **man** may take his wife and children and go."
30: 31 those in all the other places where David and his **men** had roamed.
31: 1 the **Israelites** [+3776] fled before them, and many fell slain on
31: 3 and when the **archers** [+928+2021+4619+8008] overtook him,
31: 6 and his armor-bearer and all his **men** died together that same day.
31: 7 When the **Israelites** [+3776] along the valley and those across the
31: 7 and those across the Jordan saw that the Israelite **army** had fled
31: 12 all their valiant **men** journeyed through the night to Beth Shan.
2Sa 1: 2 On the third day a **man** arrived from Saul's camp, with his clothes
1: 11 Then David and all the **men** with him took hold of their clothes
1: 13 "I am the son of an **[NIE]** alien, an Amalekite," he answered.
2: 3 David also took the **men** who were with him, each with his family,
2: 3 **each** with his family, and they settled in Hebron and its towns.
2: 4 the **men** *of* Judah came to Hebron and there they anointed David
2: 4 When David was told that it was the **men** *of* Jabesh Gilead who
2: 5 he sent messengers to the **men** *of* Jabesh Gilead to say to them,
2: 16 *each* **man** grabbed his opponent by the head and thrust his dagger
2: 17 and Abner and the **men** *of* Israel were defeated by David's men.
2: 27 the men would have continued the pursuit of their **[NIE]** brothers
2: 29 All that night Abner and his **men** marched through the Arabah.
2: 30 nineteen **[NIE]** of David's men were found missing.
2: 31 had killed three hundred and sixty **Benjamites** [+1228+4946] who
2: 31 killed three hundred and sixty Benjamites **who** were with Abner.

2Sa 2: 32 Joab and his **men** marched all night and arrived at Hebron by
3: 15 and had her taken away from her **husband** Paltiel son of Laish.
3: 16 Her **husband**, however, went with her, weeping behind her all the
3: 20 When Abner, who had twenty **men** with him, came to David at
3: 20 to David at Hebron, David prepared a feast for him and his **men**.
3: 39 I am weak, and these **[NIE]** sons of Zeruiah are too strong for me.
4: 2 Now Saul's son had two **men** who were leaders of raiding bands.
4: 11 when wicked **men** have killed an innocent man in his own house
4: 11 when wicked men have killed an innocent **man** in his own house
5: 6 and his **men** marched to Jerusalem to attack the Jebusites,
5: 21 their idols there, and David and his **men** carried them off.
6: 19 a cake of raisins **[RPH]** to each person in the whole crowd of
6: 19 person in the whole crowd of Israelites, both **men** and women.
6: 19 and women. And all the people went **[RPH]** to their homes.
7: 14 When he does wrong, I will punish him with the rod of **men**,
8: 4 thousand charioteers and twenty thousand **foot soldiers** [+8081].
8: 5 David struck down twenty-two thousand of them. **[NIE]**
8: 10 in battle over Hadadezer, who had been **at war with** [+4878] Tou.
9: 3 "Is there no **one** still left of the house of Saul to whom I can show
10: 5 David was told about this, he sent messengers to meet the **men**,
10: 6 and Zobah, as well as the king of Maacah with a thousand **men**,
10: 6 a thousand men, and also twelve thousand **[RPH]** men from Tob.
10: 6 with a thousand men, and also twelve thousand **men** *from* Tob.
10: 8 while the Arameans of Zobah and Rehob and the **men** *of* Tob
10: 18 their charioteers and forty thousand of their **[NIE]** foot soldiers.
11: 16 at a place where he knew the **strongest defenders** [+2657] were.
11: 17 When the **men** *of* the city came out and fought against Joab,
11: 23 "The **men** overpowered us and came out against us in the open,
11: 26 When Uriah's wife heard that her **husband** was dead, she mourned
12: 1 he said, "There were two **men** in a certain town, one rich
12: 4 "Now a traveler came to the rich **man**, but the rich man refrained
12: 4 he took the ewe lamb that belonged to the poor **man** and prepared
12: 4 to the poor man and prepared it for the **one** who had come to him."
12: 5 David burned with anger against the **man** and said to Nathan,
12: 5 surely as the LORD lives, the **man** who did this deserves to die!
12: 7 Nathan said to David, "You are the **man**! This is what the LORD,
13: 3 son of Shimeah, David's brother. Jonadab was a very shrewd **man**.
13: 9 refused to eat. "Send **everyone** [+3972] out of here," Amnon said.
13: 9 everyone out of here," Amnon said. So **everyone** [+3972] left him.
13: 29 all the king's sons got up, mounted **[NIE]** their mules and fled.
13: 34 told the king, "I see **men** [BHS-] in the direction of Horonaim,
14: 5 She said, "I am indeed a widow; my **husband** is dead.
14: 7 leaving my **husband** neither name nor descendant on the face of
14: 16 servant from the hand of the **man** who is trying to cut off both me
14: 25 In all Israel there was not a **man** so highly praised for his
15: 1 with a chariot and horses and with fifty **men** to run ahead of him.
15: 2 Whenever **anyone** [+2021+3972] came with a complaint to be
15: 4 **everyone** [+3972] who has a complaint or case could come to me
15: 5 whenever **anyone** approached him to bow down before him,
15: 6 asking for justice, and so he stole the hearts of the **men** *of* Israel.
15: 11 Two hundred **men** from Jerusalem had accompanied Absalom.
15: 13 told David, "The hearts of the **men** *of* Israel are with Absalom."
15: 18 all the six hundred Gittites **[NIE]** who had accompanied him from
15: 22 So Ittai the Gittite marched on with all his **men** and the families
15: 30 All the people with him covered **[NIE]** their heads too and were
16: 5 a **man** from the same clan as Saul's family came out from there.
16: 7 As he cursed, Shimei said, "Get out, get out, you **man** *of* blood,
16: 7 "Get out, get out, you man of blood, you **scoundrel** [+1175+2021]!
16: 8 You have come to ruin because you are a **man** *of* blood!"
16: 13 his **men** continued along the road while Shimei was going along
16: 15 Absalom and all the men of **[RPH]** Israel came to Jerusalem,
16: 18 by the LORD, by these people, and by all the **men** *of* Israel—
16: 23 Ahithophel gave was like that of **one** [no K] who inquires of God.
17: 1 "I would choose twelve thousand **men** and set out tonight in
17: 3 The death of the **man** you seek will mean the return of all;
17: 8 You know your father and his **men**; they are fighters, and as fierce
17: 8 Besides, your father is an **experienced fighter** [+4878]; he will not
17: 12 on the ground. Neither he nor any of his **men** will be left alive.
17: 14 Absalom and all the **men** *of* Israel said, "The advice of Hushai the
17: 18 of them left quickly and went to the house of a **man** in Bahurim.
17: 24 and Absalom crossed the Jordan with all the **men** *of* Israel.
17: 25 Amasa was the son of a **man** named Jether, an Israelite who had
18: 10 When one of the **men** saw this, he told Joab, "I just saw Absalom
18: 11 Joab said to the **man** who had told him this, "What! You saw him?
18: 12 the **man** replied, "Even if a thousand shekels were weighed out
18: 17 over him. Meanwhile, all the Israelites fled **[NIE]** to their homes.
18: 20 "You are not the **one** to take the news today," Joab told him.
18: 24 by the wall. As he looked out, he saw a **man** running alone.
18: 26 the watchman saw another **man** running, and he called down to the
18: 26 down to the gatekeeper, "Look, another **man** running alone!"
18: 27 "He's a good **man**," the king said. "He comes with good news."
18: 28 He has delivered up the **men** who lifted their hands against my lord
19: 7 [19:8] don't go out, not a **man** will be left with you by nightfall.
19: 8 [19:9] Meanwhile, the Israelites had fled **[NIE]** to their homes.
19: 14 [19:15] He won over the hearts of all the **men** *of* Judah as though
19: 14 [19:15] of all the men of Judah as though they were one **man**.
19: 16 [19:17] hurried down with the **men** *of* Judah to meet King David.
19: 17 [19:18] With him were **[NIE]** a thousand Benjamites, along with
19: 22 [19:23] Should **anyone** be put to death in Israel today?
19: 28 [19:29] All my grandfather's descendants **deserved** nothing
19: 32 [19:33] his stay in Mahanaim, for he was a very wealthy **man**.
19: 41 [19:42] Soon all the **men** *of* Israel were coming to the king
19: 41 [19:42] the **men** *of* Judah, steal the king away and bring him
19: 41 [19:42] household across the Jordan, together with all his **men**?"
19: 42 [19:43] All the **men** *of* Judah answered the men of Israel, "We did
19: 42 [19:43] All the men of Judah answered the **men** *of* Israel, "We did
19: 43 [19:44] the **men** *of* Israel answered the men of Judah, "We have
19: 43 [19:44] the men of Israel answered the **men** *of* Judah, "We have
19: 43 [19:44] the **men** *of* Judah responded even more harshly than the
19: 43 [19:44] responded even more harshly than the **men** *of* Israel.
20: 1 Now a **troublemaker** [+1175] named Sheba son of Bicri,
20: 1 Sheba son of Bicri, a **Benjamite** [+3549], happened to be there.
20: 1 in David, no part in Jesse's son! *Every* **man** to his tent, O Israel!"
20: 2 So all the **men** *of* Israel deserted David to follow Sheba son of
20: 2 the **men** *of* Judah stayed by their king all the way from the Jordan
20: 4 "Summon the **men** *of* Judah to come to me within three days,
20: 7 So Joab's **men** and the Kerethites and Pelethites and all the mighty
20: 11 **One** of Joab's men stood beside Amasa and said, "Whoever favors
20: 12 the road, and the **man** saw that all the troops came to a halt there.
20: 13 all the **men** went on with Joab to pursue Sheba son of Bicri.
20: 21 A **man** named Sheba son of Bicri, from the hill country of
20: 22 and his men dispersed from the city, **each** returning to his home.
21: 4 nor do we have the right to put **anyone** in Israel to death."
21: 5 "As for the **man** who destroyed us and plotted against us so that
21: 6 let seven of his **male** descendants be given to us to be killed
21: 17 David's **men** swore to him, saying, "Never again will you go out
21: 20 there was a huge **man** with six fingers on each hand and six toes
22: 49 You exalted me above my foes; from violent **men** you rescued me.
23: 7 **Whoever** touches thorns uses a tool of iron or the shaft of a spear;
23: 9 ⌞at Pas Dammim⌟ for battle. Then the **men** *of* Israel retreated,
23: 17 "Is it not the blood of **men** who went at the risk of their lives?"
23: 20 Benaiah son of Jehoiada was a **valiant fighter** [+1201+2644] from
23: 21 he struck down a **[RPH]** huge Egyptian. Although the Egyptian
23: 21 he struck down a huge **[NIE]** Egyptian. Although the Egyptian
24: 9 In Israel there were eight hundred thousand able-bodied **men** who
24: 9 could handle a sword, and **[RPH]** in Judah five hundred thousand.
24: 9 handle a sword, and in Judah five hundred thousand. **[RPH]**
24: 15 seventy thousand **[NIE]** of the people from Dan to Beersheba
1Ki 1: 5 got chariots and horses ready, with fifty **men** to run ahead of him.
1: 9 the king's sons, and all the **men** *of* Judah who were royal officials,
1: 42 "Come in. A worthy **man** like you must be bringing good news."
1: 49 all Adonijah's guests rose in alarm and dispersed. **[NIE]**
2: 2 way of all the earth," he said. "So be strong, show yourself a **man**,
2: 4 and soul, you will never fail to have a **man** on the throne of Israel.'
2: 9 You are a **man** *of* wisdom; you will know what to do to him.
2: 26 You **deserve to** die, but I will not put you to death now, because
2: 32 without the knowledge of my father David he attacked two **men**
3: 13 so that in your lifetime you will have no equal **[NIE]** among
4: 25 [5:5] lived in safety, *each* **man** under his own vine and fig tree.
4: 27 [5:7] The district officers, **each** *in* his month, supplied provisions
4: 28 [5:8] They also brought to the proper place **[NIE]** their quotas of
5: 6 [5:20] You know that we have no **one** so skilled in felling timber
5: 13 [5:27] conscripted laborers from all Israel—thirty thousand **men**.
7: 14 and whose father was a **man** of Tyre and a craftsman in bronze.
7: 30 a basin resting on four supports, cast with wreaths on **each** side.
7: 36 of the supports and on the panels, in **every** available space,
8: 2 All the **men** *of* Israel came together to King Solomon at the time of
8: 25 'You shall never fail to have a **man** to sit before me on the throne
8: 31 "When a **man** wrongs his neighbor and is required to take an oath
8: 38 **each** *one* aware of the afflictions of his own heart, and spreading
8: 39 deal with each **man** according to all he does, since you know his
9: 5 'You shall never fail to have a **man** on the throne of Israel.'
9: 22 they were his fighting **men**, his government officials, his officers,
9: 27 And Hiram sent his men—**sailors** [+641] who knew the sea—
10: 8 How happy your **men** must be! How happy your officials,
10: 15 not including the revenues from **merchants** [+9365] and traders
10: 25 Year after year, **everyone** who came brought a gift—articles of
11: 17 fled to Egypt with some Edomite **officials** who had served his
11: 18 Then taking **men** from Paran with them, they went to Egypt,
11: 24 He gathered **men** around him and became the leader of a band of
11: 28 Now Jeroboam was a **man** *of* standing, and when Solomon saw
12: 22 But this word of God came to Shemaiah the **man** *of* God:
12: 24 Go home, **every** *one* of you, for this is my doing.' " So they obeyed
13: 1 By the word of the LORD a **man** *of* God came from Judah to
13: 4 When King Jeroboam heard what the **man** *of* God cried out against
13: 5 its ashes poured out according to the sign given by the **man** *of* God
13: 6 the king said to the **man** *of* God, "Intercede with the LORD your
13: 6 So the **man** *of* God interceded with the LORD, and the king's

1Ki 13: 7 The king said to the **man** *of* God, "Come home with me and have
13: 8 the **man** *of* God answered the king, "Even if you were to give me
13: 11 and told him all that the **man** *of* God had done there that day.
13: 12 his sons showed him which road the **man** *of* God from Judah had
13: 14 rode after the **man** *of* God. He found him sitting under an oak tree
13: 14 and asked, "Are you the **man** *of* God who came from Judah?"
13: 21 He cried out to the **man** *of* God who had come from Judah,
13: 25 *Some* **people** who passed by saw the body thrown down there,
13: 26 "It is the **man** *of* God who defied the word of the LORD.
13: 29 So the prophet picked up the body of the **man** *of* God, laid it on the
13: 31 "When I die, bury me in the grave where the **man** *of* God is buried;
17: 18 She said to Elijah, "What do you have against me, **man** *of* God?
17: 24 "Now I know that you are a **man** *of* God and that the word of the
18: 4 and hidden them in two caves, fifty **[NIE]** in each,
18: 13 I hid a hundred **[NIE]** of the LORD's prophets in two caves,
18: 13 fifty **[NIE]** in each, and supplied them with food and water.
18: 22 prophets left, but Baal has four hundred and fifty prophets. **[NIE]**
18: 40 Don't let **anyone** get away!" They seized them, and Elijah had
18: 44 "A cloud as small as a **man's** hand is rising from the sea."
20: 17 who reported, "**Men** are advancing from Samaria."
20: 20 **each** *one* struck down his opponent. At that, the Arameans fled,
20: 20 each one struck down his **opponent**. At that, the Arameans fled,
20: 24 Remove **all** the kings from their commands and replace them with
20: 28 The **man** *of* God came up and told the king of Israel, "This is what
20: 30 where the wall collapsed on twenty-seven thousand of **them**[s].
20: 33 The **men** took this as a good sign and were quick to pick up his
20: 35 By the word of the LORD one **[NIE]** of the sons of the prophets
20: 35 "Strike me with your weapon," but the **man** refused.
20: 37 The prophet found another **man** and said, "Strike me, please."
20: 37 "Strike me, please." So the **man** struck him and wounded him.
20: 39 and **someone** came to me with a captive and said, 'Guard this man.
20: 39 and someone came to me with a **captive** and said, 'Guard this man.
20: 39 and someone came to me with a captive and said, 'Guard this **man**.
20: 42 'You have set free a **man** I had determined should die.
21: 10 seat two **[NIE]** scoundrels opposite him and have them testify that
21: 11 nobles who lived in Naboth's city did **[NIE]** as Jezebel directed in
21: 13 two scoundrels came **[NIE]** and sat opposite him and brought
21: 13 and brought charges against Naboth **[NIE]** before the people,
22: 6 about four hundred **men**—and asked them, "Shall I go to war
22: 8 "There is still one **man** through whom we can inquire of the
22: 10 Jehoshaphat king of Judah were sitting **[NIE]** on their thrones at
22: 17 'These people have no master. Let **each** *one* go home in peace.' "
22: 34 **someone** drew his bow at random and hit the king of Israel
22: 36 through the army: "*Every* **man** to his town; everyone to his land!"
22: 36 through the army: "Every man to his town; **everyone** to his land!"
2Ki 1: 6 "A **man** came to meet us," they replied. "And he said to us,
1: 7 "What kind of **man** was it who came to meet you and told you
1: 8 "He was a **man** with a garment of hair and with a leather belt
1: 9 and said to him, "**Man** *of* God, the king says, 'Come down!' "
1: 10 Elijah answered the captain, "If I am a **man** *of* God, may fire come
1: 11 The captain said to him, "**Man** *of* God, this is what the king says,
1: 12 "If I am a **man** *of* God," Elijah replied, "may fire come down from
1: 13 "**Man** *of* God," he begged, "please have respect for my life
2: 7 Fifty **men** of the company of the prophets went and stood at a
2: 16 "Look," they said, "we your servants have fifty able **men**.
2: 17 they sent fifty **men**, who searched for three days but did not find
2: 19 The **men** *of* the city said to Elisha, "Look, our lord, this town is
3: 23 "Those kings must have fought and slaughtered **each** other.
3: 25 *each* **man** threw a stone on every good field until it was covered.
3: 26 he took with him seven hundred **swordsmen** [+2995+8990] to
4: 1 "Your servant my **husband** is dead, and you know that he revered
4: 7 She went and told the **man** *of* God, and he said, "Go, sell the oil
4: 9 She said to her **husband**, "I know that this man who often comes
4: 9 "I know that this man who often comes our way is a holy **man** *of*
4: 14 Gehazi said, "Well, she has no son and her **husband** is old."
4: 16 she objected. "Don't mislead your servant, O **man** *of* God!"
4: 21 She went up and laid him on the bed of the **man** *of* God, then shut
4: 22 She called her **husband** and said, "Please send me one of the
4: 22 and a donkey so I can go to the **man** *of* God quickly and return."
4: 25 So she set out and came to the **man** *of* God at Mount Carmel.
4: 25 in the distance, the **man** *of* God said to his servant Gehazi, "Look!
4: 26 and ask her, 'Are you all right? Is your **husband** all right?
4: 27 When she reached the **man** *of* God at the mountain, she took hold
4: 27 over to push her away, but the **man** *of* God said, "Leave her alone!
4: 29 If you meet **anyone**, do not greet him, and if anyone greets you,
4: 29 do not greet him, and if **anyone** greets you, do not answer.
4: 40 The stew was poured out for the **men**, but as they began to eat it,
4: 40 they cried out, "O **man** *of* God, there is death in the pot!"
4: 42 A **man** came from Baal Shalishah, bringing the man of God twenty
4: 42 bringing the **man** *of* God twenty loaves of barley bread baked from
4: 43 "How can I set this before a hundred **men**?" his servant asked.
5: 1 He was a great **man** in the sight of his master and highly regarded,
5: 1 through him the LORD had given victory to Aram. **He**[s] [+2021]
5: 7 Why does this fellow send **someone** to me to be cured of his
5: 8 When Elisha the **man** *of* God heard that the king of Israel had torn
5: 14 as the **man** *of* God had told him, and his flesh was restored
5: 15 Then Naaman and all his attendants went back to the **man** *of* God.
5: 20 Gehazi, the servant of Elisha the **man** *of* God, said to himself,
5: 24 put them away in the house. He sent the **men** away and they left.
5: 26 "Was not my spirit with you when the **man** got down from his
6: 2 Let us go to the Jordan, where **each** of us can get a pole; and let us
6: 6 The **man** *of* God asked, "Where did it fall?" When he showed him
6: 9 The **man** *of* God sent word to the king of Israel: "Beware of
6: 10 So the king of Israel checked on the place indicated by the **man** *of*
6: 15 When the servant of the **man** *of* God got up and went out early the
6: 19 Follow me, and I will lead you to the **man** you are looking for."
6: 32 messenger ahead, but before **he**[s] arrived, Elisha said to the elders,
7: 2 The officer on whose arm the king was leaning said to the **man** *of*
7: 3 Now there were four **men** with leprosy at the entrance of the city
7: 3 the city gate. They said to **each** other, "Why stay here until we die?
7: 5 When they reached the edge of the camp, not a **man** was there,
7: 6 and a great army, so that they said to **one** another, "Look,
7: 9 they said to **each** other, "We're not doing right. This is a day of
7: 10 "We went into the Aramean camp and not a **man** was there—
7: 17 just as the **man** *of* God had foretold when the king came down to
7: 18 It happened as the **man** *of* God had said to the king: "About this
7: 19 The officer had said to the **man** *of* God, "Look, even if the LORD
8: 2 The woman proceeded to do as the **man** *of* God said. She
8: 4 talking to Gehazi, the servant of the **man** *of* God, and had said,
8: 7 king was told, "The **man** *of* God has come all the way up here,"
8: 8 to Hazael, "Take a gift with you and go to meet the **man** *of* God.
8: 11 until Hazael felt ashamed. Then the **man** *of* God began to weep.
9: 11 "You know the **man** and the sort of things he says," Jehu replied.
9: 13 They hurried and took **[NIE]** their cloaks and spread them under
9: 21 king of Judah rode out, **each** in his own chariot, to meet Jehu.
10: 5 We will not appoint **anyone** as king; you do whatever you think
10: 6 **[NIE]** and come to me in Jezreel by this time tomorrow."
10: 6 Now the royal princes, seventy of **them**[s], were with the leading
10: 7 these men took the princes and slaughtered all seventy of **them**[s].
10: 14 and slaughtered them by the well of Beth Eked—forty-two **men**.
10: 14 well of Beth Eked—forty-two men. He left no survivor. **[RPH]**
10: 19 See that no **one** is missing, because I am going to hold a great
10: 21 and all the ministers of Baal came; not **one** stayed away.
10: 24 Now Jehu had posted eighty **men** outside with this warning:
10: 24 "If one of you lets **any** of the men I am placing in your hands
10: 24 "If one of you lets any of the **men** I am placing in your hands
10: 25 the guards and officers: "Go in and kill them; let no **one** escape."
11: 8 around the king, *each* **man** with his weapon in his hand.
11: 9 **Each** *one* took his men—those who were going on duty on the
11: 9 Each one took his **men**—those who were going on duty on the
11: 11 The guards, **each** with his weapon in his hand,
12: 4 [12:5] the money collected in the **census** [+6296], the money
12: 4 [12:5] brought **voluntarily** [+4213+6584+6590] to the temple.
12: 5 [12:6] Let **every** priest receive the money from one of the
12: 9 [12:10] on the right side as **one** enters the temple of the LORD.
12: 15 [12:16] They did not require an accounting from **those**[s] [+2021]
13: 19 The **man** *of* God was angry with him and said, "You should have
13: 21 Once while some Israelites were burying a **man**, suddenly they
13: 21 band of raiders; so they threw the **man's body** into Elisha's tomb.
13: 21 Elisha's bones, the **man** came to life and stood up on his feet.
14: 6 put to death for their fathers; **each** is to die for his own sins."
14: 12 Judah was routed by Israel, and *every* **man** fled to his home.
15: 20 **[NIE]** So the king of Assyria withdrew and stayed in the land no
15: 25 Taking fifty **men** of Gilead with him, he assassinated Pekahiah,
17: 30 The **men** *from* Babylon made Succoth Benoth, the men from
17: 30 the **men** *from* Cuthah made Nergal, and the men from Hamath
17: 30 Cuthah made Nergal, and the **men** *from* Hamath made Ashima;
18: 21 which pierces a **man's** hand and wounds him if he leans on it!
18: 27 sent me to say these things, and not to the **men** sitting on the wall—
18: 31 Then **every** *one* of you will eat from his own vine and fig tree
18: 31 and **[RPH]** fig tree and drink water from his own cistern,
18: 31 and fig tree and drink **[RPH]** water from his own cistern,
18: 33 Has the god of any nation ever delivered **[NIE]** his land from the
20: 14 went to King Hezekiah and asked, "What did those **men** say,
22: 15 the God of Israel, says: Tell the **man** who sent you to me,
23: 2 He went up to the temple of the LORD with the **men** *of* Judah,
23: 8 the city governor, which is on the left **[NIE]** of the city gate.
23: 10 so no **one** could use it to sacrifice his son or daughter in the fire to
23: 16 LORD proclaimed by the **man** *of* God who foretold these things.
23: 17 The **men** *of* the city said, "It marks the tomb of the man of God
23: 17 "It marks the tomb of the **man** *of* God who came from Judah
23: 18 "Leave it alone," he said. "Don't let **anyone** disturb his bones."
23: 35 gold from the people of the land **[NIE]** according to their
24: 16 to Babylon the entire force of seven thousand fighting **men**,
25: 4 the whole **army** [+4878] fled at night through the gate between the
25: 19 he took the officer in charge of the fighting **men** and five royal
25: 19 in charge of the fighting men and five **[RPH]** royal advisers.
25: 19 the land and sixty **[RPH]** of his men who were found in the city.

2Ki 25:23 their **men** heard that the king of Babylon had appointed Gedaliah
25:23 Jaazaniah the son of the Maacathite, and their **men**.
25:24 Gedaliah took an oath to reassure them and their **men**. "Do not be
25:25 came with ten **men** and assassinated Gedaliah and also the men of
1Ch 4:12 Tehinnah the father of Ir Nahash. These were the **men** *of* Recah.
4:22 Jokim, the **men** *of* Cozeba, and Joash and Saraph, who ruled in
4:42 And five hundred **[NIE]** of these Simeonites, led by Pelatiah,
5:18 able-bodied **men** who could handle shield and sword, who could
5:24 **They**[s] were brave warriors, famous men, and heads of their
5:24 They were brave warriors, famous **men**, and heads of their
7:21 Ezer and Elead were killed by the native-born **men** *of* Gath,
7:40 The number of **men** ready for battle, as listed in their genealogy,
8:40 The sons of Ulam were **[NIE]** brave warriors who could handle
9: 9 numbered 956. All these **men** were heads of their families.
10: 1 the **Israelites** [+3776] fled before them, and many fell slain on
10: 7 When all the **Israelites** [+3776] in the valley saw that the army had
10:12 all their valiant **men** went and took the bodies of Saul and his sons
11:19 "Should I drink the blood of these **men** who went at the risk of
11:22 Benaiah son of Jehoiada was a **valiant fighter** [+1201+2657] from
11:23 he struck down an Egyptian **[NIE]** who was seven and a half feet
11:23 he struck down an Egyptian **who** was seven and a half feet tall.
12: 8 [12:9] brave warriors, **ready for battle** [+2021+4200+4878+7372]
12:30 [12:31] brave warriors, **famous** [+9005] in their own clans—
12:38 [12:39] All these were fighting **men** who volunteered to serve in
16: 3 and a cake of raisins to each **Israelite** [+3776] man and woman.
16: 3 of dates and a cake of raisins to each Israelite **man** and woman.
16: 3 and a cake of raisins to each Israelite man and woman. **[RPH]**
16:21 He allowed no **man** to oppress them; for their sake he rebuked
16:43 all the people left, **each** for his own home, and David returned
18: 4 thousand charioteers and twenty thousand **foot soldiers** [+8081].
18: 5 David struck down twenty-two thousand of them. **[NIE]**
18:10 in battle over Hadadezer, who had been **at war with** [+4878] Tou.
19: 5 When someone came and told David about the **men**, he sent
19: 5 to meet them, for **they**[s] [+2021] were greatly humiliated.
19:18 their charioteers and forty thousand of their **foot soldiers** [+8081].
20: 6 there was a huge **man** with six fingers on each hand and six toes
21: 5 In all Israel there were one million one hundred thousand **men** who
21: 5 including four hundred and seventy thousand in Judah. **[RPH]**
21:14 a plague on Israel, and seventy thousand **men** of Israel fell dead.
22: 9 But you will have a son who will be a **man** *of* peace and rest,
23:14 The sons of Moses the **man** *of* God were counted as part of the
25: 1 Here is the list of the **men** who performed this service:
26: 8 their relatives were capable **men** with the strength to do the work—
27:32 David's uncle, was a counselor, a **man** *of* insight and a scribe.
28: 3 because you are a **warrior** [+4878] and have shed blood.'
2Ch 2: 2 [2:1] He conscripted seventy thousand **men** as carriers and eighty
2: 2 [2:1] eighty thousand **[RPH]** as stonecutters in the hills
2: 7 [2:6] a **man** skilled to work in gold and silver, bronze and iron,
2:13 [2:12] "I am sending you Huram-Abi, a **man** *of* great skill,
2:14 [2:13] was from Dan and whose father was **[NIE]** from Tyre.
2:17 [2:16] Solomon took a census of all **[NIE]** the aliens who were
5: 3 all the **men** *of* Israel came together to the king at the time of the
6: 5 nor have I chosen **anyone** to be the leader over my people Israel.
6:16 'You shall never fail to have a **man** to sit before me on the throne
6:22 "When a **man** wrongs his neighbor and is required to take an oath
6:29 **each** *one* aware of his afflictions and pains, and spreading out his
6:30 Forgive, and deal with each **man** according to all he does,
7:18 when I said, 'You shall never fail to have a **man** to rule over Israel.'
8: 9 they were his fighting **men**, commanders of his captains,
8:14 because this was what David the **man** *of* God had ordered.
9: 7 How happy your **men** must be! How happy your officials,
9:14 not including the revenues brought in by **merchants** [+9365]
9:24 Year after year, **everyone** who came brought a gift—articles of
10:16 in David, what part in Jesse's son? **[NIE]** To your tents, O Israel!
11: 2 But this word of the LORD came to Shemaiah the **man** *of* God:
11: 4 Go home, **every** *one* of you, for this is my doing.' " So they obeyed
13: 3 with a force of four hundred thousand **[NIE]** able fighting men,
13: 3 line against him with eight hundred thousand **[NIE]** able troops.
13: 7 **Some**[s] worthless scoundrels gathered around him and opposed
13:15 the **men** *of* Judah raised the battle cry. At the sound of their battle
13:15 At the sound of **their**[s] [+3373] battle cry, God routed Jeroboam
13:17 were five hundred thousand casualties among Israel's able **men**.
15:13 were to be put to death, whether small or great, **man** or woman.
17:13 kept **experienced fighting men** [+1475+2657+4878] in Jerusalem.
18: 5 four hundred **men**—and asked them, "Shall we go to war against
18: 7 "There is still one **man** through whom we can inquire of the
18: 9 Jehoshaphat king of Judah were sitting **[NIE]** on their thrones at
18:16 'These people have no master. Let **each** *one* go home in peace.' "
18:33 **someone** drew his bow at random and hit the king of Israel
20:23 the men from Seir, they helped to destroy **one** another.
20:27 all the **men** *of* Judah and Jerusalem returned joyfully to Jerusalem,
23: 7 around the king, *each* **man** with his weapons in his hand.
23: 8 **Each** *one* took his men—those who were going on duty on the
23: 8 Each one took his **men**—those who were going on duty on the
23:10 all the men, **each** with his weapon in his hand, around the king—
24:24 Although the Aramean army had come with only a few **men**,
25: 4 put to death for their fathers; **each** is to die for his own sins."
25: 7 a **man** *of* God came to him and said, "O king, these troops from
25: 9 Amaziah asked the **man** *of* God, "But what about the hundred
25: 9 The **man** *of* God replied, "The LORD can give you much more
25:22 Judah was routed by Israel, and *every* **man** fled to his home.
28:12 Then **some**[s] of the leaders in Ephraim—Azariah son of Jehohanan,
28:15 The **men** designated by name took the prisoners, and from the
30:11 *some* **men** of Asher, Manasseh and Zebulun humbled themselves
30:16 positions as prescribed in the Law of Moses the **man** *of* God.
31: 1 the Israelites returned **[NIE]** to their own towns and to their own
31: 2 **each** of them according to their duties as priests or Levites—
31:19 **men** were designated by name to distribute portions to every male
34:12 The **men** did the work faithfully. Over them to direct them were
34:23 the God of Israel, says: Tell the **man** who sent you to me,
34:30 He went up to the temple of the LORD with the **men** *of* Judah,
Ezr 1: 4 the **people** of any place where survivors may now be living are to
2: 1 (they returned to Jerusalem and Judah, **each** to his own town,
2: 2 Rehum and Baanah): The list of the **men** *of* the people of Israel:
2:22 **[RPH]** of Netophah 56
2:23 **[RPH]** of Anathoth 128
2:27 **[RPH]** of Micmash 122
2:28 **[RPH]** of Bethel and Ai 223
3: 1 in their towns, the people assembled as one **man** in Jerusalem.
3: 2 in accordance with what is written in the Law of Moses the **man** *of*
8:18 they brought us Sherebiah, a capable **man**, from the descendants of
10: 1 of Israelites—**men**, women and children—gathered around him.
10: 9 all the **men** *of* Judah and Benjamin had gathered in Jerusalem.
10:16 Ezra the priest selected **men** who were family heads, one from
10:17 finished dealing with all the **men** who had married foreign women.
Ne 1: 2 one of my brothers, came from Judah with *some other* **men**,
1:11 success today by granting him favor in the presence of this **man**."
2:12 I set out during the night with a few **men**. I had not told anyone
3: 2 The **men** *of* Jericho built the adjoining section, and Zaccur son of
3: 7 to them, repairs were made by **men** *from* Gibeon and Mizpah—
3:22 The repairs next to him were made by the priests from **[RPH]** the
3:28 the priests made repairs, **each** in front of his own house.
4:15 [4:9] we all returned to the wall, **each** to his own work.
4:18 [4:12] **each** of the builders wore his sword at his side as he
4:19 [4:13] we are widely separated from **each** other along the wall.
4:22 [4:16] "Have *every* **man** and his helper stay inside Jerusalem at
4:23 [4:17] men nor the **guards** [+5464] with me took off our clothes;
4:23 [4:17] **each** had his weapon, even when he went for water.
5: 7 "You are exacting usury **[NIE]** from your own countrymen!"
5:13 and possessions every **man** who does not keep this promise.
5:17 **[NIE]** as well as those who came to us from the surrounding
6:11 I said, "Should a **man** like me run away? Or should one like me go
7: 2 because he was a **man** *of* integrity and feared God more than most
7: 3 as guards, **some**[s] at their posts and some near their own houses."
7: 3 as guards, some at their posts and **some**[s] near their own houses."
7: 6 (they returned to Jerusalem and Judah, **each** to his own town,
7: 7 Bigvai, Nehum and Baanah): The list of the **men** *of* Israel:
7:26 the **men** *of* Bethlehem and Netophah 188
7:27 **[RPH]** of Anathoth 128
7:28 **[RPH]** of Beth Azmaveth 42
7:29 **[RPH]** of Kiriath Jearim, Kephirah and Beeroth 743
7:30 **[RPH]** of Ramah and Geba 621
7:31 **[RPH]** of Micmash 122
7:32 **[RPH]** of Bethel and Ai 123
7:33 **[RPH]** of the other Nebo 52
8: 1 all the people assembled as one **man** in the square before the
8: 2 which was made up of **men** and women and all who were able to
8: 3 faced the square before the Water Gate in the presence of the **men**,
8:16 and built themselves booths **[NIE]** on their own roofs,
11: 2 The people commended all the **men** who volunteered to live in
11: 3 the towns of Judah, **each** on his own property in the various towns,
11: 6 descendants of Perez who lived in Jerusalem totaled 468 able **men**.
11:20 were in all the towns of Judah, **each** on his ancestral property.
12:24 responding to the other, as prescribed by David the **man** *of* God.
12:36 with musical instruments ⌊prescribed by⌋ David the **man** *of* God.
12:44 At that time **men** were appointed to be in charge of the storerooms
13:10 that **all** the Levites and singers responsible for the service had gone
13:25 down on them. I beat some of the **men** and pulled out their hair.
13:30 everything foreign, and assigned them duties, **each** to his own task.
Est 1: 8 wine stewards to serve *each* **man** [+408+2256] what he wished.
1: 8 wine stewards to serve *each* **man** [+408+2256] what he wished.
1:22 proclaiming in each people's tongue that every **man** should be
2: 5 Now there was in the citadel of Susa a **[NIE]** Jew of the tribe of
2: 5 was in the citadel of Susa a Jew of the **tribe of Benjamin** [+3549],
4:11 and the people of the royal provinces know that for any **man**
6: 6 "What should be done for the **man** the king delights to honor?"
6: 7 So he answered the king, "For the **man** the king delights to honor,
6: 9 and horse be entrusted to **one** of the king's most noble princes.

Est 6: 9 Let them robe the **man** the king delights to honor, and lead him on
6: 9 'This is what is done for the **man** the king delights to honor!' "
6: 11 "This is what is done for the **man** the king delights to honor!"
7: 6 Esther said, **[NIE]** "The adversary and enemy is this vile Haman."
9: 2 No **one** could stand against them, because the people of all the
9: 4 and **he**[s] [+2021+5283] became more and more powerful.
9: 6 citadel of Susa, the Jews killed and destroyed five hundred **men**.
9: 12 "The Jews have killed and destroyed five hundred **men** and the ten
9: 15 they put to death in Susa three hundred **men**, but they did not lay
9: 19 a day of joy and feasting, a day for giving presents to **each** other.
9: 22 joy and giving presents of food to **one** another and gifts to the
Job 1: 1 In the land of Uz there lived a **man** whose name was Job.
1: 1 This **man** was blameless and upright; he feared God and shunned
1: 3 He was the greatest **man** among all the people of the East.
1: 4 His sons used to take turns holding feasts in **their**[s] homes,
1: 8 he is blameless and upright, a **man** who fears God and shuns evil."
2: 3 he is blameless and upright, a **man** who fears God and shuns evil.
2: 4 Satan replied. "A **man** will give all he has for his own life.
2: 11 **they**[s] set out from their homes and met together by agreement to
2: 12 and they tore **[NIE]** their robes and sprinkled dust on their heads.
4: 13 disquieting dreams in the night, when deep sleep falls on **men**,
9: 32 "He is not a **man** like me that I might answer him, that we might
11: 2 words to go unanswered? Is this **talker** [+8557] to be vindicated?
11: 12 a witless **man** can no more become wise than a wild donkey's colt
12: 10 is the life of every creature and the breath of all **mankind** [+1414].
12: 14 down cannot be rebuilt; the **man** he imprisons cannot be released.
14: 12 so **man** lies down and does not rise; till the heavens are no more,
15: 16 how much less **man**, who is vile and corrupt, who drinks up evil
22: 8 though you were a powerful **man**, owning land—an honored man,
31: 35 let the Almighty answer me; let my **accuser** [+8190] put his
32: 1 So these three **men** stopped answering Job, because he was
32: 5 But when he saw that the three **men** had nothing more to say,
32: 13 Do not say, 'We have found wisdom; let God refute him, not **man**.'
32: 21 I will show partiality to no **one**, nor will I flatter any man;
33: 15 when deep sleep falls on **men** as they slumber in their beds,
33: 16 he may speak in **their**[s] ears and terrify them with warnings,
33: 27 he comes to **men** and says, 'I sinned, and perverted what was right,
34: 8 He keeps company with evildoers; he associates with wicked **men**.
34: 10 "So listen to me, you **men** *of* understanding. Far be it from God to
34: 11 what he has done; he brings upon **him**[s] what his conduct deserves.
34: 21 "His eyes are on the ways of **men**; he sees their every step.
34: 23 God has no need to examine **men** further, that they should come
34: 34 "**Men** *of* understanding declare, wise men who hear me say to me,
34: 36 might be tested to the utmost for answering like a wicked **man**!
35: 8 Your wickedness affects only a **man** like yourself, and your
36: 24 Remember to extol his work, which **men** have praised in song.
37: 7 So that all **men** he has made may know his work, he stops every
37: 20 told that I want to speak? Would any **man** ask to be swallowed up?
37: 24 Therefore, **men** revere him, for does he not have regard for all the
38: 26 to water a land where no **man** lives, a desert with no one in it,
41: 17 [41:9] They are joined fast to **one** another; they cling together
42: 11 upon him, and **each** *one* gave him a piece of silver and a gold ring.
42: 11 and each one gave him a piece of silver and a gold ring. **[RPH]**
Ps 1: 1 Blessed is the **man** who does not walk in the counsel of the wicked
4: 2 [4:3] How long, O **men** [+1201], will you turn my glory into
5: 6 [5:7] tell lies; bloodthirsty and deceitful **men** the LORD abhors.
12: 2 [12:3] **Everyone** lies to his neighbor; their flattering lips speak
18: 48 [18:49] me above my foes; from violent **men** you rescued me.
22: 6 [22:7] I am a worm and not a **man**, scorned by men and despised
25: 12 Who, then, is the **man** that fears the LORD? He will instruct him
26: 9 away my soul along with sinners, my life with bloodthirsty **men**,
31: 20 [31:21] your presence you hide them from the intrigues of **men**;
34: 12 [34:13] **Whoever** [+2021+4769] of you loves life and desires to
37: 7 do not fret when **men** succeed in their ways, when they carry out
37: 37 observe the upright; there is a future for the **man** *of* peace.
38: 14 [38:15] I have become like a **man** who does not hear, whose
39: 6 [39:7] **Man** is a mere phantom as he goes to and fro: He bustles
39: 11 [39:12] You rebuke and discipline **men** for their sin; you consume
41: 9 [41:10] Even my **close friend** [+8934], whom I trusted, he who
43: 1 an ungodly nation; rescue me from deceitful and wicked **men**.
49: 2 [49:3] both low and **high** [+1201], rich and poor alike:
49: 7 [49:8] No **man** can redeem the life of another or give to God a
49: 16 [49:17] Do not be overawed when a **man** grows rich,
55: 23 [55:24] and deceitful **men** will not live out half their days.
59: 2 [59:3] me from evildoers and save me from bloodthirsty **men**.
62: 3 [62:4] How long will you assault a **man**? Would all of you throw
62: 9 [62:10] men are but a breath, the **highborn** [+1201] are but a lie;
62: 12 [62:13] Surely you will reward *each* **person** according to what he
64: 6 [64:7] Surely the mind and heart of **man** are cunning.
76: 5 [76:6] not one of the **warriors** [+2657] can lift his hands.
78: 25 **Men** ate the bread of angels; he sent them all the food they could
80: 17 [80:18] Let your hand rest on the **man** *at* your right hand, the son
87: 5 of Zion it will be said, "*This* **one** and that one were born in her,
87: 5 of Zion it will be said, "This one and *that* **one** were born in her,
90: T [90:1] A prayer of Moses the **man** *of* God.
92: 6 [92:7] The senseless **man** does not know, fools do not understand,
105: 17 and he sent a **man** before them—Joseph, sold as a slave.
109: 16 hounded to death **[NIE]** the poor and the needy
112: 1 Blessed is the **man** who fears the LORD, who finds great delight
112: 5 Good will come to **him**[s] who is generous and lends freely,
119: 24 Your statutes are my delight; they are my **counselors** [+6783].
139: 19 slay the wicked, O God! Away from me, you bloodthirsty **men**!
140: 1 [140:2] from evil men; protect me from **men** *of* violence,
140: 4 [140:5] protect me from **men** *of* violence who plan to trip my feet.
140: 11 [140:12] Let **slanderers** [+4383] not be established in the land;
140: 11 [140:12] in the land; may disaster hunt down **men** *of* violence.
141: 4 is evil, to take part in wicked deeds with **men** who are evildoers;
147: 10 in the strength of the horse, nor his delight in the legs of a **man**;
Pr 2: 12 the ways of wicked men, from **men** whose words are perverse,
3: 31 Do not envy a violent **man** or choose any of his ways,
5: 21 For a **man's** ways are in full view of the LORD, and he examines
6: 11 will come on you like a bandit and scarcity like an armed **man**.
6: 12 A scoundrel and **villain** [+224], who goes about with a corrupt
6: 26 loaf of bread, and the **adulteress** [+851] preys upon your very life.
6: 27 Can a **man** scoop fire into his lap without his clothes being
6: 28 *Can a* **man** walk on hot coals without his feet being scorched?
7: 19 My **husband** is not at home; he has gone on a long journey.
8: 4 "To you, O **men**, I call out; I raise my voice to all mankind.
10: 23 in evil conduct, but a **man** *of* understanding delights in wisdom.
11: 12 derides his neighbor, but a **man** *of* understanding holds his tongue.
11: 17 A kind **man** benefits himself, but a cruel man brings trouble on
12: 2 favor from the LORD, but the LORD condemns a crafty **man**.
12: 8 A **man** is praised according to his wisdom, but men with warped
12: 14 From the fruit of his lips a **man** is filled with good things as surely
12: 25 An anxious heart weighs a **man** down, but a kind word cheers him
13: 2 From the fruit of his lips a **man** enjoys good things,
13: 8 A **man's** riches may ransom his life, but a poor man hears no
14: 7 Stay away from a foolish **man**, for you will not find knowledge on
14: 12 There is a way that seems right to a **man**, but in the end it leads to
14: 14 be fully repaid for their ways, and the good **man** rewarded for his.
14: 17 quick-tempered man does foolish things, and a crafty **man** is hated.
15: 18 A hot-tempered **man** stirs up dissension, but a patient man calms a
15: 21 but a **man** *of* understanding keeps a straight course.
15: 23 A **man** finds joy in giving an apt reply—and how good is a timely
16: 2 All a **man's** ways seem innocent to him, but motives are weighed
16: 7 When a **man's** ways are pleasing to the LORD, he makes even
16: 14 wrath is a messenger of death, but a wise **man** will appease it.
16: 25 There is a way that seems right to a **man**, but in the end it leads to
16: 27 A **scoundrel** [+1175] plots evil, and his speech is like a scorching
16: 28 A perverse **man** stirs up dissension, and a gossip separates close
16: 29 A violent **man** entices his neighbor and leads him down a path that
17: 12 Better to meet a bear robbed of her **cubs** than a fool in his folly.
17: 27 with restraint, and a **man** *of* understanding is even-tempered.
18: 4 The words of a **man's** mouth are deep waters, but the fountain of
18: 12 Before his downfall a **man's** heart is proud, but humility comes
18: 14 A **man's** spirit sustains him in sickness, but a crushed spirit who
18: 20 From the fruit of his mouth a **man's** stomach is filled;
18: 24 A **man** *of* many companions may come to ruin, but there is a
19: 6 with a ruler, and everyone is the friend of a **man** *who gives* gifts.
19: 21 Many are the plans in a **man's** heart, but it is the LORD'S
19: 22 man desires is unfailing love; better to be poor than a **liar** [+3942].
20: 3 It is to a **man's** honor to avoid strife, but every fool is quick to
20: 5 The purposes of a **man's** heart are deep waters, but a man of
20: 5 heart are deep waters, but a **man** *of* understanding draws them out.
20: 6 Many a man claims to have **[RPH]** unfailing love, but a faithful
20: 6 claims to have unfailing love, but a faithful **man** who can find?
20: 17 Food gained by fraud tastes sweet to a **man**, but he ends up with a
21: 2 All a **man's** ways seem right to him, but the LORD weighs the
21: 8 The way of the **[NIE]** guilty is devious, but the conduct of the
21: 17 **He**[s] who loves pleasure will become poor; whoever loves wine
21: 28 will perish, and **whoever** listens to him will be destroyed forever.
21: 29 A wicked **man** puts up a bold front, but an upright man gives
22: 7 over the poor, and the borrower is servant to the **[NIE]** lender.
22: 24 with a hot-tempered man, do not associate with **one** easily angered,
22: 29 Do you see a **man** skilled in his work? He will serve before kings;
24: 1 Do not envy wicked **men**, do not desire their company;
24: 5 man has great power, and a **man** *of* knowledge increases strength;
24: 29 him as he has done to me; I'll pay that **man** back for what he did."
24: 30 I went past the field of the **[NIE]** sluggard, past the vineyard of
24: 34 will come on you like a bandit and scarcity like an armed **man**.
25: 1 of Solomon, copied by the **men** *of* Hezekiah king of Judah:
25: 14 wind without rain is a **man** who boasts of gifts he does not give.
25: 18 or a sharp arrow is the **man** who gives false testimony against his
25: 28 Like a city whose walls are broken down is a **man** who lacks
26: 12 Do you see a **man** wise in his own eyes? There is more hope for a
26: 19 is a **man** who deceives his neighbor and says, "I was only joking!"
26: 21 and as wood to fire, so is a quarrelsome **man** for kindling strife.
27: 8 Like a bird that strays from its nest is a **man** who strays from his

Pr 27:17 As iron sharpens iron, so *one* **man** sharpens another.
27:21 the furnace for gold, but **man** is tested by the praise he receives.
28: 5 Evil **men** do not understand justice, but those who seek the
28:11 A rich **man** may be wise in his own eyes, but a poor man who has
28:20 A faithful **man** will be richly blessed, but one eager to get rich will
28:22 A stingy **man** is eager to get rich and is unaware that poverty
28:24 and says, "It's not wrong"—he is partner to **him**[s] who destroys.
29: 1 A **man** who remains stiff-necked after many rebukes will suddenly
29: 3 A **man** who loves wisdom brings joy to his father, but a
29: 4 a country stability, but **one** *who is greedy for* bribes tears it down.
29: 6 An evil **man** is snared by his own sin, but a righteous one can sing
29: 8 **Mockers** [+4371] stir up a city, but wise men turn away anger.
29: 9 If a wise **man** goes to court with a fool, the fool rages and scoffs,
29: 9 If a wise man goes to court with a **[RPH]** fool, the fool rages
29:10 Bloodthirsty **men** hate a man of integrity and seek to kill the
29:13 The poor man and the **oppressor** [+9412] have this in common:
29:20 Do you see a **man** who speaks in haste? There is more hope for a
29:22 An angry **man** stirs up dissension, and a hot-tempered one
29:26 with a ruler, but it is from the LORD that **man** gets justice.
29:27 The righteous detest the **[NIE]** dishonest; the wicked detest the
30: 2 "I am the most ignorant of **men**; I do not have a man's
Ecc 1: 8 All things are wearisome, more than **one** can say. The eye never
4: 4 and all achievement spring from **man's** envy of his neighbor.
6: 2 God gives a **man** wealth, possessions and honor, so that he lacks
6: 2 him to enjoy them, and a **[NIE]** stranger enjoys them instead.
6: 3 A **man** may have a hundred children and live many years;
7: 5 It is better to heed a wise man's rebuke than **[NIE]** to listen to the
9:14 There was once a small city with only a few **people** in it. And a
9:15 Now there lived in that city a **man** poor but wise, and he saved the
9:15 the city by his wisdom. But nobody remembered that poor **man**.
12: 3 the strong **men** stoop, when the grinders cease because they are
SS 3: 8 all experienced in battle, **each** with his sword at his side,
8: 7 If **one** were to give all the wealth of his house for love, it would be
8:11 **Each** was to bring for its fruit a thousand shekels of silver.
Isa 2: 9 So man will be brought low and **mankind** humbled—do not
2:11 arrogant man will be humbled and the pride of **men** brought low;
2:17 of man will be brought low and the pride of **men** humbled;
3: 2 the hero and **warrior** [+4878], the judge and prophet,
3: 5 oppress each other—**man** against man, neighbor against neighbor.
3: 5 oppress each other—man against **man**, neighbor against neighbor.
3: 5 each other—man against man, **neighbor**[s] against neighbor.
3: 6 A **man** will seize one of his brothers at his father's home,
4: 1 In that day seven women will take hold of one **man** and say,
5: 3 "Now you dwellers in Jerusalem and **men** *of* Judah, judge between
5: 7 house of Israel, and the **men** *of* Judah are the garden of his delight.
5:15 So man will be brought low and **mankind** humbled, the eyes of the
5:22 heroes at drinking wine and **champions** [+2657] at mixing drinks,
6: 5 For I am a **man** *of* unclean lips, and I live among a people of
7:13 you house of David! Is it not enough to try the patience of **men**?
7:21 In that day, a **man** will keep alive a young cow and two goats.
9:19 [9:18] will be fuel for the fire; no **one** will spare his brother.
9:20 [9:19] **Each** will feed on the flesh of his own offspring:
13: 8 in labor. They will look aghast at **each** other, their faces aflame.
13:14 like sheep without a shepherd, **each** will return to his own people,
13:14 each will return to his own people, **each** will flee to his native land.
14:16 "Is this the **man** who shook the earth and made kingdoms tremble,
14:18 All the kings of the nations lie in state, **each** in his own tomb.
19: 2 **brother** will fight against brother, neighbor against neighbor,
19: 2 **neighbor**[s] against neighbor, city against city, kingdom against
21: 9 Look, here comes a **man** in a chariot *with* a team of horses.
28:14 you **scoffers** [+4371] who rule this people in Jerusalem.
29:13 Their worship of me is made up only of rules taught by **men**.
31: 7 For in that day **every** *one* of you will reject the idols of silver
31: 8 "Assyria will fall by a sword that is not *of* **man**; a sword, not of
32: 2 *Each* **man** will be like a shelter from the wind and a refuge from
36: 6 which pierces a **man's** hand and wounds him if he leans on it!
36:12 sent me to say these things, and not to the **men** sitting on the wall—
36:16 Then **every** *one of* you will eat from his own vine and fig tree
36:16 and **[RPH]** fig tree and drink water from his own cistern,
36:16 and fig tree and drink **[RPH]** water from his own cistern,
36:18 Has the god of any nation ever delivered his land **[NIE]** from the
39: 3 went to King Hezekiah and asked, "What did those **men** say,
40:13 mind of the LORD, or instructed him as his **counselor** [+6783]?
40:26 of his great power and mighty strength, not **one** of them is missing.
41: 6 **each** helps the other and says to his brother, "Be strong!"
41:11 **those**[s] *who* oppose you will be as nothing and perish.
41:12 Though you search for your **enemies** [+5194], you will not find
41:12 **Those**[s] *who* wage war against you will be as nothing at all.
41:28 I look but there is no **one**—no one among them to give counsel,
42:13 like a mighty man, like a **warrior** [+4878] he will stir up his zeal;
44:13 He shapes it in the form of **man**, of man in all his glory, that it may
45:14 and the merchandise of Cush, and those **tall** [+4500] Sabeans—
46:11 a bird of prey; from a far-off land, a **man** *to fulfill* my purpose.
47:15 **Each** of them goes on in his error; there is not one that can save
50: 2 When I came, why was there no **one**? When I called, why was
52:14 his appearance was so disfigured beyond that of *any* **man**
53: 3 He was despised and rejected by **men**, a man of sorrows,
53: 3 He was despised and rejected by men, a **man** *of* sorrows,
53: 6 like sheep, have gone astray, **each** of us has turned to his own way;
55: 7 Let the wicked forsake his way and the evil **man** his thoughts.
56:11 they all turn to their own way, **each** seeks his own gain.
57: 1 The righteous perish, and no **one** ponders it in his heart; devout
57: 1 devout **men** are taken away, and no one understands that the
59:16 He saw that there was no **one**, he was appalled that there was no
63: 3 trodden the winepress alone; from the nations no **one** was with me.
66: 3 But whoever sacrifices a bull is like one who kills a **man**,
66:13 As a mother comforts her **child**, so will I comfort you; and you
66:24 and look upon the dead bodies of **those**[s] who rebelled against me;
Jer 1:15 "Their **kings**[s] will come and set up their thrones in the entrance of
2: 6 and darkness, a land where no **one** travels and no one lives?'
3: 1 "If a **man** divorces his wife and she leaves him and marries
3: 1 divorces his wife and she leaves him and marries another **man**,
4: 3 This is what the LORD says to the **men** *of* Judah and to
4: 4 circumcise your hearts, you **men** *of* Judah and people of Jerusalem,
4:29 among the rocks. All the towns are deserted; no **one** lives in them.
5: 1 If you can find but *one* **person** who deals honestly and seeks the
5: 8 are well-fed, lusty stallions, **each** neighing for another man's wife.
5:26 men who snare birds and like those who set traps to catch **men**.
6: 3 will pitch their tents around her, **each** tending his own portion."
6:11 both **husband** and wife will be caught in it, and the old,
6:23 they come like **men** in battle formation to attack you, O Daughter
7: 5 change your ways and your actions and deal with **each** other justly,
8: 6 No **one** repents of his wickedness, saying, "What have I done?"
9: 4 [9:3] "Beware **[RPH]** of your friends; do not trust your brothers.
9: 5 [9:4] **Friend**[s] deceives friend, and no one speaks the truth.
9:10 [9:9] They are desolate and **untraveled** [+1172+4946+6296],
9:12 [9:11] What **man** is wise enough to understand this? Who has
10:23 that a man's life is not his own; it is not for **man** to direct his steps.
11: 2 tell them to the **people** *of* Judah and to those who live in
11: 3 'Cursed is the **man** who does not obey the terms of this covenant—
11: 8 instead, **they**[s] followed the stubbornness of their evil hearts.
11: 9 "There is a conspiracy among the **people** *of* Judah and those who
11:21 "Therefore this is what the LORD says about the **men** *of*
11:23 because I will bring disaster on the **men** *of* Anathoth in the year of
12:11 whole land will be laid waste because there is no **one** who cares.
12:15 will bring **each** of them back to his own inheritance and his own
12:15 of them back to his own inheritance and **[RPH]** his own country.
13:11 For as a belt is bound around a **man's** waist, so I bound the whole
13:14 I will smash them **one** against the other, fathers and sons alike,
14: 9 Why are you like a **man** taken by surprise, like a warrior powerless
15:10 me birth, a **man** with whom the whole land strives and contends!
15:10 a man with whom the whole land strives and **[RPH]** contends!
16:12 See how **each** of you is following the stubbornness of his evil heart
17:10 and examine the mind, to reward a **man** according to his conduct,
17:25 accompanied by the **men** *of* Judah and those living in Jerusalem,
18:11 "Now therefore say to the **people** *of* Judah and those living in
18:11 **each** *one* of you, and reform your ways and your actions.'
18:12 **each** of us will follow the stubbornness of his evil heart.' "
18:21 let their **men** be put to death, their young men slain by the sword in
19: 9 they will eat **one** another's flesh during the stress of the siege
19:10 "Then break the jar while **those**[s] [+2021] who go with you are
20:15 Cursed be the **man** who brought my father the news, who made
20:16 May that **man** be like the towns the LORD overthrew without
22: 7 I will send destroyers against you, *each* **man** with his weapons,
22: 8 from many nations will pass by this city and will ask **one** another,
22:28 Is this **man** Jehoiachin a despised, broken pot, an object no one
22:30 "Record this **man** as if childless, a man who will not prosper in his
22:30 **none**[s] will sit on the throne of David or rule anymore in Judah."
23: 9 I am like a drunken **man**, like a man overcome by wine, because of
23:14 the hands of evildoers, so that no **one** turns from his wickedness.
23:24 Can **anyone** hide in secret places so that I cannot see him?"
23:27 They think the dreams they tell **one** another will make my people
23:30 "I am against the prophets who steal from **one** another words
23:34 oracle of the LORD,' I will punish that **man** and his household.
23:35 This is what **each** of you keeps on saying to his friend or relative:
23:35 what each of you keeps on saying to his friend or **[RPH]** relative:
23:36 because *every* **man's** *own* word becomes his oracle and so you
25: 5 They said, "Turn now, **each** of you, from your evil ways and your
25:26 and all the kings of the north, near and far, **one** after the other—
26: 3 Perhaps they will listen and **each** will turn from his evil way.
26:11 "This **man** should be sentenced to death because he has prophesied
26:16 and the prophets, "This **man** should not be sentenced to death!
26:17 **Some**[s] of the elders of the land stepped forward and said to the
26:20 was another **man** who prophesied in the name of the LORD;
26:22 however, sent Elnathan son of Acbor **[RPH]** to Egypt,
26:22 sent Elnathan son of Acbor to Egypt, along with *some* other **men**.
29: 6 and **give** your daughters **in marriage** [+906+4200+5989], so that
29:26 you should put any **madman** [+8713] who acts like a prophet into

Jer 29:32 He will have no **one** left among this people, nor will he see the
31:30 Instead, **everyone** will die for his own sin; whoever eats sour
31:34 No longer will a **man** teach his neighbor, or a man his brother,
31:34 or a **man** his brother, saying, 'Know the LORD,' because they will
32:19 you reward **everyone** according to his conduct and as his deeds
32:32 and prophets, the **men** *of* Judah and the people of Jerusalem.
33:17 'David will never fail to have a **man** to sit on the throne of the
33:18 ever fail to have a **man** to stand before me continually to offer
34:9 **Everyone** was to free his Hebrew slaves, both male and female;
34:9 was to free his Hebrew slaves, both male and **[RPH]** female;
34:9 both male and female; no **one** was to hold a fellow Jew in bondage.
34:10 people who entered into this covenant agreed that **they**[s] would free
34:10 and female slaves **[RPH]** and no longer hold them in bondage.
34:14 'Every seventh year **each** of you must free any fellow Hebrew who
34:15 in my sight: **Each** of you proclaimed freedom to his countrymen.
34:16 **each** of you has taken back the male and female slaves you had set
34:16 female slaves **[RPH]** you had set free to go where they wished.
34:17 **you**[s] have not proclaimed freedom for your fellow countrymen.
34:17 you have not proclaimed freedom for your fellow **[RPH]**
34:18 The **men** who have violated my covenant and have not fulfilled the
35:4 into the room of the sons of Hanan son of Igdaliah the **man** *of*
35:13 Go and tell the **men** *of* Judah and the people of Jerusalem,
35:15 "**Each** of you must turn from your wicked ways and reform your
35:19 'Jonadab son of Recab will never fail to have a **man** to serve
36:3 to inflict on them, **each** of them will turn from his wicked way;
36:7 **each** will turn from his wicked ways, for the anger and wrath
36:16 these words, they looked at **each** other in fear and said to Baruch,
36:19 and Jeremiah, go and hide. Don't let **anyone** know where you are."
36:31 and the **people** *of* Judah every disaster I pronounced against them,
37:10 is attacking you and only wounded **men** were left in their tents,
37:10 and only wounded men were left **[RPH]** in their tents,
38:4 the officials said to the king, "This **man** should be put to death.
38:4 He is discouraging the **soldiers** [+4878] who are left in this city,
38:4 This **man** is not seeking the good of these people but their ruin."
38:7 But Ebed-Melech, a Cushite, an **[NIE]** official in the royal palace,
38:9 these **men** have acted wickedly in all they have done to Jeremiah
38:10 "Take thirty **men** from here with you and lift Jeremiah the prophet
38:11 So Ebed-Melech took the **men** with him and went to a room under
38:16 I will neither kill you nor hand you over to **[NIE]** those who are
38:22 and overcame you—those **trusted friends of** [+8934] yours.
38:24 "Do not let **anyone** know about this conversation, or you may die.
39:4 Zedekiah king of Judah and all the **soldiers** [+4878] saw them,
39:17 you will not be handed over to **those**[s] [+2021] you fear.
40:7 their **men** who were still in the open country heard that the king of
40:7 as governor over the land and had put him in charge of the **men**,
40:8 and Jaazaniah the son of the Maacathite, and their **men**.
40:9 the son of Shaphan, took an oath to reassure them and their **men**.
40:15 and kill Ishmael son of Nethaniah, and no **one** will know it.
41:1 came with ten **men** to Gedaliah son of Ahikam at Mizpah.
41:2 son of Nethaniah and the ten **men** who were with him got up
41:3 as well as the Babylonian **soldiers** [+4878] who were there.
41:4 day after Gedaliah's assassination, before **anyone** knew about it,
41:5 eighty **men** who had shaved off their beards, torn their clothes
41:5 torn their clothes and cut themselves came **[RPH]** from Shechem,
41:7 of Nethaniah and the **men** who were with him slaughtered them
41:8 ten **[RPH]** of them said to Ishmael, "Don't kill us! We have
41:9 Now the cistern where he threw all the bodies of the **men** he had
41:12 they took all their **men** and went to fight Ishmael son of Nethaniah.
41:15 eight of his **men** escaped from Johanan and fled to the Ammonites.
41:16 the **soldiers** [+1505+4878], women, children and court officials he
42:17 all **[RPH]** who are determined to go to Egypt to settle there will
43:2 Johanan son of Kareah and all the arrogant **men** said to Jeremiah,
43:9 "While the Jews **[NIE]** are watching, take some large stones with
44:7 great disaster on yourselves by cutting off from Judah the **men**
44:15 all the **men** who knew that their wives were burning incense to
44:19 did not our **husbands** know that we were making cakes like her
44:26 'that no **one** *from* Judah living anywhere in Egypt will ever again
44:27 **[RPH]** the Jews in Egypt will perish by sword and famine until
46:16 They will stumble repeatedly; they will fall over **each** other.
48:14 "How can you say, 'We are warriors, **men** valiant in battle'?
48:31 for all Moab I cry out, I moan for the **men** *of* Kir Hareseth.
48:36 like a flute; it laments like a flute for the **men** *of* Kir Hareseth.
49:5 "**Every** *one* of you will be driven away, and no one will gather the
49:18 neighboring towns," says the LORD, "so no **one** will live there;
49:26 all her **soldiers** [+4878] will be silenced in that day,"
49:33 place forever. No **one** will live there; no man will dwell in it."
50:16 Because of the sword of the oppressor let **everyone** return to his
50:16 return to his own people, let **everyone** flee to his own land.
50:30 all her **soldiers** [+4878] will be silenced in that day,"
50:40 declares the LORD, "so no **one** will live there;
50:42 they come like **men** in battle formation to attack you, O Daughter
51:6 Run for **[NIE]** your lives! Do not be destroyed because of her
51:9 let us leave her and **each** go to his own land, for her judgment
51:22 with you I shatter **man** and woman, with you I shatter old man
51:32 the marshes set on fire, and the **soldiers** [+4878] terrified."
51:43 will be desolate, a dry and desert land, a land where no **one** lives,
51:45 for your lives! **[NIE]** Run from the fierce anger of the LORD.
52:7 city wall was broken through, and the whole **army** [+4878] fled.
52:25 still in the city, he took the officer in charge of the fighting **men**,
52:25 in charge of the fighting men, and seven **[RPH]** royal advisers.
52:25 the land and sixty **[RPH]** of his men who were found in the city.
La 3:33 does not willingly bring affliction or grief to the children of **men**.
Eze 1:9 **Each** *one* went straight ahead; they did not turn as they moved.
1:11 **each** had two wings, one touching the wing of another creature on
1:11 one touching the wing of **another**[s] **creature** on either side,
1:12 **Each** *one* went straight ahead. Wherever the spirit would go,
1:23 one toward the other, and **each** had two wings covering its body.
1:23 the other, and each had two wings covering its body. **[RPH]**
3:26 unable to rebuke them, **[NIE]** though they are a rebellious house.
4:17 They will be appalled at the sight of **each** other and will waste
7:13 Because of their sins, not **one** of them will preserve his life.
7:16 moaning like doves of the valleys, **each** because of his sins.
8:2 I looked, and I saw a figure like that of a **man**. [BHS 836]
8:11 In front of them stood seventy **[NIE]** elders of the house of Israel,
8:11 **Each** had a censer in his hand, and a fragrant cloud of incense was
8:12 Israel are doing in the darkness, **each** at the shrine of his own idol?
8:16 between the portico and the altar, were about twenty-five **men**.
9:1 the guards of the city here, **each** with a weapon in his hand."
9:2 And I saw six **men** coming from the direction of the upper gate,
9:2 which faces north, **each** with a deadly weapon in his hand.
9:2 With them was a **man** clothed in linen who had a writing kit at his
9:3 the LORD called to the **man** clothed in linen who had the writing
9:4 of Jerusalem and put a mark on the foreheads of **those**[s] who grieve
9:6 and children, but do not touch **anyone** [+3972] who has the mark.
9:6 So they began with the **[NIE]** elders who were in front of the
9:11 the **man** in linen with the writing kit at his side brought back word,
10:2 The LORD said to the **man** clothed in linen, "Go in among the
10:3 standing on the south side of the temple when the **man** went in,
10:6 When the LORD commanded the **man** in linen, "Take fire from
10:22 those I had seen by the Kebar River. **Each** *one* went straight ahead.
11:1 There at the entrance to the gate were twenty-five **men**, and I saw
11:2 these are the **men** who are plotting evil and giving wicked advice
11:15 your brothers who are your **blood relatives** [+1460] and the whole
12:16 But I will spare a **[NIE]** few of them from the sword, famine
14:1 **Some**[s] of the elders of Israel came to me and sat down in front of
14:3 these **men** have set up idols in their hearts and put wicked
14:4 When **any** Israelite sets up idols in his heart and puts a wicked
14:4 When any **Israelite** [+1074+3776+4946] sets up idols in his heart
14:7 " 'When **any** Israelite or any alien living in Israel separates himself
14:7 " 'When any **Israelite** [+1074+3776+4946] or any alien living in
14:8 I will set my face against that **man** and make him an example
14:14 even if these three **men**—Noah, Daniel and Job—were in it,
14:16 declares the Sovereign LORD, even if these three **men** were in it,
14:18 declares the Sovereign LORD, even if these three **men** were in it,
16:32 adulterous wife! You prefer strangers to your own **husband**!
16:45 of your mother, who despised her **husband** and her children;
16:45 of your sisters, who despised their **husbands** and their children.
18:5 "Suppose there is a righteous **man** who does what is just and right.
18:7 He does not oppress **anyone**, but returns what he took in pledge for
18:8 hand from doing wrong and judges fairly between **man** and man.
18:8 hand from doing wrong and judges fairly between man and **man**.
18:16 He does not oppress **anyone** or require a pledge for a loan.
18:30 house of Israel, I will judge you, **each** *one* according to his ways,
20:1 **some**[s] of the elders of Israel came to inquire of the LORD,
20:7 I said to them, "**Each** of you, get rid of the vile images you have
20:8 **they**[s] did not get rid of the vile images they had set their eyes on,
20:39 LORD says: Go and serve your idols, **every** *one* of you!
21:31 [21:36] I will hand you over to brutal **men**, men skilled in
22:6 " 'See how **each** of the princes of Israel who are in you uses his
22:9 In you are slanderous **men** bent on shedding blood; in you are
22:11 In you *one* **man** commits a detestable offense with his neighbor's
22:11 **another**[s] shamefully defiles his daughter-in-law, and another
22:11 and **another**[s] violates his sister, his own father's daughter.
22:30 "I looked for a **man** among them who would build up the wall
23:14 She saw **men** portrayed on a wall, figures of Chaldeans portrayed
23:40 "They even sent messengers for **men** who came from far away,
23:42 Sabeans were brought from the desert along with **men** from the
23:45 righteous **men** will sentence them to the punishment of women
24:17 lower part of your face or eat the customary food ⌞of **mourners**[s]⌟."
24:22 lower part of your face or eat the customary food ⌞of **mourners**[s]⌟.
24:23 because of your sins and groan **among yourselves** [+278+448].
27:10 of Persia, Lydia and Put served as **soldiers** [+4878] in your army.
27:27 and shipwrights, your merchants and all your **soldiers** [+4878],
32:10 On the day of your downfall **each** of them will tremble every
33:2 the people of the land choose one of their **men** and make him their
33:20 not just.' But I will judge **each** of you according to his own ways."
33:26 do detestable things, and **each** of you defiles his neighbor's wife.
33:30 **[RPH]** 'Come and hear the message that has come from the

Eze 38:21 Sovereign LORD. *Every* **man's** sword will be against his brother.
39:14 " '**Men** will be regularly employed to cleanse the land. Some will
39:20 and riders, mighty men and **soldiers** [+4878] of every kind,'
40: 3 took me there, and I saw a **man** whose appearance was like bronze;
40: 4 The **man** said to me, "Son of man, look with your eyes and hear
40: 5 The length of the measuring rod in the **man's** hand was six long
43: 6 While the **man** was standing beside me, I heard someone speaking
44: 2 It must not be opened; no **one** may enter through it. It is to remain
44:25 son or daughter, brother or **unmarried** [+2118+4200+4202] sister,
45:20 the seventh day of the month for **anyone** who sins unintentionally
46:16 If the prince makes a gift from his inheritance to **one** of his sons,
46:18 so that **none** [+4202] of my people will be separated from his
47: 3 As the **man** went eastward with a measuring line in his hand,
47:14 You are to divide it **equally among them** [+278+2257+3869].
Da 9: 7 the **men** *of* Judah and people of Jerusalem and all Israel, both near
9:21 still in prayer, Gabriel, the **man** I had seen in the earlier vision,
10: 5 I looked up and there before me was a **man** dressed in linen,
10: 7 the **men** with me did not see it, but such terror overwhelmed them
10:11 He said, "Daniel, you **who** are highly esteemed, consider carefully
10:19 "Do not be afraid, O **man** highly esteemed," he said. "Peace!
12: 6 One of them said to the **man** clothed in linen, who was above the
12: 7 The **man** clothed in linen, who was above the waters of the river,
Hos 2: 2 [2:4] for she is not my wife, and I am not her **husband**.
2: 7 [2:9] 'I will go back to my **husband** as at first, for then I was
2:10 [2:12] eyes of her lovers; no **one** will take her out of my hands.
2:16 [2:18] declares the LORD, "you will call me 'my **husband**';
3: 3 you must not be a prostitute or be intimate with any **man**,
4: 4 "But let no **man** bring a charge, let no man accuse another,
4: 4 "But let no man bring a charge, let no **man** accuse another,
6: 9 As marauders lie in ambush for a **man**, so do bands of priests;
9: 7 the prophet is considered a fool, the inspired **man** a maniac.
11: 9 For I am God, and not **man**—the Holy One among you.
Joel 2: 7 They charge like warriors; they scale walls like **soldiers** [+4878].
2: 7 **They**[s] *all* march in line, not swerving from their course.
2: 8 They do not jostle **each** other; each marches straight ahead.
3: 9 [4:9] the warriors! Let all the fighting **men** draw near and attack.
Am 2: 7 Father and **son** use the same girl and so profane my holy name.
5:19 It will be as though a **man** fled from a lion only to meet a bear,
6: 9 If ten **men** are left in one house, they too will die.
Ob 1: 7 All your **allies** [+1382] will force you to the border; your friends
1: 7 the border; your **friends** [+8934] will deceive and overpower you;
1: 9 **everyone** in Esau's mountains will be cut down in the slaughter.
Jnh 1: 5 All the sailors were afraid and **each** cried out to his own god.
1: 7 the sailors said to **each** other, "Come, let us cast lots to find out
1:10 This terrified **them**[s] [+2021] and they asked, "What have you
1:10 "What have you done?" (**They**[s] [+2021] knew he was running
1:13 Instead, the **men** did their best to row back to land. But they could
1:14 "O LORD, please do not let us die for taking this **man's** life.
1:16 At this the **men** greatly feared the LORD, and they offered a
3: 5 The **Ninevites** [+5770] believed God. They declared a fast,
3: 8 on God. Let **them**[s] give up their evil ways and their violence.
Mic 2: 2 They defraud a man of his home, a **fellowman** of his inheritance.
2:11 If a liar and deceiver **[NIE]** comes and says, 'I will prophesy for
4: 4 *Every* **man** will sit under his own vine and under his own fig tree,
4: 5 All the nations may walk **[RPH]** in the name of their gods;
5: 7 [5:6] the grass, which do not wait for **man** or linger for mankind.
7: 2 All men lie in wait to shed blood; **each** hunts his brother with a net.
7: 6 a **man's** enemies are the members of his own household.
7: 6 a man's enemies are the **members** *of* his own household.
Na 2: 3 [2:4] his soldiers are red; the **warriors** [+2657] are clad in scarlet.
Zep 1:12 Jerusalem with lamps and punish **those**[s] who are complacent,
2:11 on every shore will worship him, **every** *one* in its own land.
3: 4 Her prophets are arrogant; they are treacherous **men**. Her priests
3: 6 Their cities are destroyed; no one will be left—no **one** at all.
Hag 1: 9 remains a ruin, while **each** of you is busy with his own house.
2:12 If a **person** carries consecrated meat in the fold of his garment,
2:22 and their riders will fall, **each** by the sword of his brother.
Zec 1: 8 I had a vision—and there before me was a **man** riding a red horse!
1:10 Then the **man** standing among the myrtle trees explained,
1:21 [2:4] that scattered Judah so that no **one** could raise his head,
2: 1 [2:5] there before me was a **man** with a measuring line in his
3: 8 seated before you, who are **men** symbolic of things to come:
3:10 " 'In that day **each** of you will invite his neighbor to sit under his
4: 1 me returned and wakened me, as a **man** is wakened from his sleep.
6:12 'Here is the **man** whose name is the Branch, and he will branch out
7: 2 had sent Sharezer and Regem-Melech, together with their **men**,
7: 9 true justice; show mercy and compassion to **one** another.
7:10 or the poor. In your hearts do not think evil of **each** other.'
8: 4 the streets of Jerusalem, **each** with cane in hand because of his age.
8:10 his enemy, for I had turned every man **[NIE]** against his neighbor.
8:16 Speak the truth to **each** other, and render true and sound judgment
8:17 **[NIE]** do not plot evil against your neighbor, and do not love to
8:23 "In those days ten **men** from all languages and nations will take
8:23 and nations will take firm hold of **one** Jew by the hem of his robe
10: 1 gives showers of rain to men, and plants of the field to **everyone**.
11: 6 "I will hand everyone over **[RPH]** to his neighbor and his king.
13: 3 if **anyone** still prophesies, his father and mother, to whom he was
13: 4 "On that day **every** prophet will be ashamed of his prophetic
13: 5 I am a **farmer** [+141+6268]; the land has been my livelihood since
14:13 *Each* **man** will seize the hand of another, and they will attack each
Mal 2:10 the covenant of our fathers by breaking faith with **one** another?
2:12 As for the **man** who does this, whoever he may be, may the
3:16 Then those who feared the LORD talked with **each** other,
3:17 just as in compassion a **man** spares his son who serves him.

409 אִישׁ² *'îš²*, subst. Not used in NIV/BHS [√ 3780]

410 אִישׁ־בֹּשֶׁת *'îš-bōšet*, n.pr.m. [11] [√ 408 + 1425]

Ish-Bosheth [11]

2Sa 2: 8 had taken **Ish-Bosheth** son of Saul and brought him over to
2:10 **Ish-Bosheth** son of Saul was forty years old when he became king
2:12 together with the men of **Ish-Bosheth** son of Saul, left Mahanaim
2:15 twelve men for Benjamin and **Ish-Bosheth** son of Saul, and twelve
3: 8 very angry because of what **Ish-Bosheth** said and he answered,
3:14 David sent messengers to **Ish-Bosheth** son of Saul, demanding,
3:15 So **Ish-Bosheth** gave orders and had her taken away from her
4: 5 of Rimmon the Beerothite, set out for the house of **Ish-Bosheth**,
4: 8 They brought the head of **Ish-Bosheth** to David at Hebron
4: 8 "Here is the head of **Ish-Bosheth** son of Saul, your enemy,
4:12 they took the head of **Ish-Bosheth** and buried it in Abner's tomb at

411 אִישׁ־טוֹב *'îš-ṭôb*, n.pr.m. Not used in NIV/BHS [√ 408 + 3202]

412 אִישְׁהוֹד *'îšhôd*, n.pr.m. [1] [√ 408 + 2086]

Ishhod [1]

1Ch 7:18 His sister Hammoleketh gave birth to **Ishhod**, Abiezer

413 אִישׁוֹן *'îšôn*, n.[m.]. [4] [√ 408]

apple [2], apple [+1426] [1], dark [+696] [1]

Dt 32:10 and cared for him; he guarded him as the **apple** *of* his eye,
Ps 17: 8 Keep me as the **apple** [+1426] *of* your eye; hide me in the shadow
Pr 7: 2 and you will live; guard my teachings as the **apple** *of* your eye.
7: 9 as the day was fading, as the **dark** [+696] of night set in.
20:20 [his lamp will be snuffed out in **pitch darkness** [K; see Q 854].]

414 אִישַׁי *'îšay*, n.pr.m. [1] [√ 3805]

Jesse [1]

1Ch 2:13 **Jesse** was the father of Eliab his firstborn; the second son was

415 אִיתוֹן *'îtôn*, n.m. [1] [√ 910; cf. 3289]

entrance [1]

Eze 40:15 The distance from the **entrance** *of* the gateway to the far end of its

416 אִיתַי *'îtay*, n.pr.m. [1] [cf. 417, 915]

Ithai [1]

1Ch 11:31 **Ithai** son of Ribai from Gibeah in Benjamin,

417 אִיתִיאֵל *'îtî'ēl*, n.pr.m. [3] [cf. 416]

Ithiel [3]

Ne 11: 7 the son of Maaseiah, the son of **Ithiel**, the son of Jeshaiah,
Pr 30: 1 an oracle: This man declared to **Ithiel**, to Ithiel and to Ucal:
30: 1 an oracle: This man declared to Ithiel, to **Ithiel** and to Ucal:

418 אִיתָמָר *'îtāmār*, n.pr.m. [21]

Ithamar [19], Ithamar's [2]

Ex 6:23 and she bore him Nadab and Abihu, Eleazar and **Ithamar**.
28: 1 along with his sons Nadab and Abihu, Eleazar and **Ithamar**,
38:21 by the Levites under the direction of **Ithamar** son of Aaron,
Lev 10: 6 Then Moses said to Aaron and his sons Eleazar and **Ithamar**,
10:12 Moses said to Aaron and his remaining sons, Eleazar and **Ithamar**,
10:16 he was angry with Eleazar and **Ithamar**, Aaron's remaining sons,
Nu 3: 2 Aaron were Nadab the firstborn and Abihu, Eleazar and **Ithamar**.
3: 4 **Ithamar** served as priests during the lifetime of their father Aaron.
4:28 Their duties are to be under the direction of **Ithamar** son of Aaron,
4:33 the Tent of Meeting under the direction of **Ithamar** son of Aaron,
7: 8 They were all under the direction of **Ithamar** son of Aaron,
26:60 Aaron was the father of Nadab and Abihu, Eleazar and **Ithamar**.
1Ch 6: 3 [5:29] The sons of Aaron: Nadab, Abihu, Eleazar and **Ithamar**.
24: 1 The sons of Aaron were Nadab, Abihu, Eleazar and **Ithamar**.
24: 2 they had no sons; so Eleazar and **Ithamar** served as the priests.

1Ch 24: 3 a descendant of Eleazar and Ahimelech a descendant of **Ithamar**,
24: 4 were found among Eleazar's descendants than among **Ithamar's**,
24: 4 and eight heads of families from **Ithamar's** descendants.
24: 5 of God among the descendants of both Eleazar and **Ithamar**.
24: 6 one family being taken from Eleazar and then one from **Ithamar**.
Ezr 8: 2 of Phinehas, Gershom; of the descendants of **Ithamar**, Daniel;

419 ¹אֵיתָן **'êtān¹**, a. [13] [→ 420; cf. 3851]

rich [2], constant [1], enduring [1], ever flowing [1], everlasting [1], flowing stream [1], hard [1], long established [1], never-failing [1], place [1], secure [1], steady [1]

Ge 49: 24 But his bow remained **steady**, his strong arms stayed limber,
Ex 14: 27 hand over the sea, and at daybreak the sea went back to its **place**.
Nu 24: 21 "Your dwelling place is **secure**, your nest is set in a rock;
Dt 21: 4 not been plowed or planted and where there is a **flowing stream**.
Job 12: 19 leads priests away stripped and overthrows *men* **long established**.
33: 19 Or a man may be chastened on a bed of pain with **constant** distress
Ps 74: 15 up springs and streams; you dried up the **ever flowing** rivers.
Pr 13: 15 understanding wins favor, but the way of the unfaithful is **hard**.
Jer 5: 15 an ancient and **enduring** nation, a people whose language you do
49: 19 "Like a lion coming up from Jordan's thickets to a **rich**
50: 44 Like a lion coming up from Jordan's thickets to a **rich** pastureland,
Am 5: 24 roll on like a river, righteousness like a **never-failing** stream!
Mic 6: 2 listen, you **everlasting** foundations of the earth.

420 ²אֵיתָן **'êtān²**, n.pr.m. [8] [√ 419]

Ethan [8]

1Ki 4: 31 [5:11] wiser than any other man, including **Ethan** the Ezrahite—
1Ch 2: 6 of Zerah: Zimri, **Ethan**, Heman, Calcol and Darda—five in all.
2: 8 The son of **Ethan**: Azariah.
6: 42 [6:27] the son of **Ethan**, the son of Zimmah, the son of Shimei,
6: 44 [6:29] **Ethan** son of Kishi, the son of Abdi, the son of Malluch,
15: 17 and from their brothers the Merarites, **Ethan** son of Kushaiah;
15: 19 Asaph and **Ethan** were to sound the bronze cymbals;
Ps 89: T [89:1] A *maskil* of **Ethan** the Ezrahite.

421 אַךְ **'ak**, adv. [161] [→ 434, 435] See Select Index

but [31], *untranslated* [26], surely [21], only [16], however [8], but only [5], nevertheless [5], yet [5], alone [4], just [4], nothing but [4], also [2], and [2], indeed [2], so [2], after [1], although [1], as long as [1], as surely as [1], be sure [1], both [1], but [+3954] [1], but also [1], but too [1], complete [1], completely [1], except [1], fully [1], furthermore [1], just after [1], mere [1], once more [+2021+7193] [1], only [+8370] [1], provided [+561] [1], really [1], scarcely [1], surely [+6964] [1], though [1], very [1]

422 אַכַּד **'akkad**, n.pr.loc. [1]

Akkad [1]

Ge 10: 10 his kingdom were Babylon, Erech, **Akkad** and Calneh, in Shinar.

423 אַכְזָב **'akzāb**, a. [2] [√ 3941]

deceptive [2]

Jer 15: 18 Will you be to me like a **deceptive** brook, like a spring that fails?
Mic 1: 14 The town of Aczib will prove **deceptive** to the kings of Israel.

424 אַכְזִיב **'akzîb**, n.pr.loc. [4] [√ 3941?]

Aczib [4]

Jos 15: 44 Keilah, **Aczib** and Mareshah—nine towns and their villages.
19: 29 toward Hosah and came out at the sea in the region of **Aczib**,
Jdg 1: 31 or Sidon or Ahlab or **Aczib** or Helbah or Aphek or Rehob,
Mic 1: 14 The town of **Aczib** will prove deceptive to the kings of Israel.

425 אַכְזָר **'akzār**, a. [4] [→ 426, 427]

deadly [1], fierce [1], heartless [1], ruthlessly [+4200] [1]

Dt 32: 33 Their wine is the venom of serpents, the **deadly** poison of cobras.
Job 30: 21 You turn on me **ruthlessly** [+4200]; with the might of your hand
41: 10 [41:2] No *one* is **fierce** *enough* to rouse him. Who then is able to
La 4: 3 but my people have become **heartless** like ostriches in the desert.

426 אַכְזָרִי **'akzārî**, a. [8] [√ 425]

cruel [7], merciless [1]

Pr 5: 9 your best strength to others and your years to *one who* is **cruel**,
11: 17 man benefits himself, but a **cruel** *man* brings trouble on himself.
12: 10 needs of his animal, but the kindest acts of the wicked are **cruel**.
17: 11 only on rebellion; a **merciless** official will be sent against him.
Isa 13: 9 a **cruel** day, with wrath and fierce anger—to make the land
Jer 6: 23 are armed with bow and spear; they are **cruel** and show no mercy.
30: 14 you as an enemy would and punished you as would the **cruel**,
50: 42 are armed with bows and spears; they are **cruel** and without mercy.

427 אַכְזְרִיּוּת **'akzᵉriyyût**, n.f. [1] [√ 425]

cruel [1]

Pr 27: 4 Anger is **cruel** and fury overwhelming, but who can stand before

428 אֲכִילָה **ᵃkîlâ**, n.f. [1] [√ 430]

food [1]

1Ki 19: 8 Strengthened by that **food**, he traveled forty days and forty nights

429 אָכִישׁ **'ākîš**, n.pr.m. [21]

Achish [19], *untranslated* [2]

1Sa 21: 10 [21:11] David fled from Saul and went to **Achish** king of Gath.
21: 11 [21:12] the servants of **Achish** said to him, "Isn't this David,
21: 12 [21:13] and was very much afraid of **Achish** king of Gath.
21: 14 [21:15] **Achish** said to his servants, "Look at the man! He is
27: 2 with him left and went over to **Achish** son of Maoch king of Gath.
27: 3 David and his men settled in Gath with **Achish**. Each man had his
27: 5 Then David said to **Achish**, "If I have found favor in your eyes,
27: 6 So on that day **Achish** gave him Ziklag, and it has belonged to the
27: 9 donkeys and camels, and clothes. Then he returned to **Achish**.
27: 10 When **Achish** asked, "Where did you go raiding today?" David
27: 12 **Achish** trusted David and said to himself, "He has become
28: 1 **Achish** said to David, "You must understand that you and your
28: 2 **[RPH]** "Then you will see for yourself what your servant can do."
28: 2 **Achish** replied, "Very well, I will make you my bodyguard for
29: 2 David and his men were marching at the rear with **Achish**.
29: 3 **Achish** replied, "Is this not David, who was an officer of Saul king
29: 6 So **Achish** called David and said to him, "As surely as the LORD
29: 8 **[RPH]** "What have you found against your servant from the day I
29: 9 **Achish** answered, "I know that you have been as pleasing in my
1Ki 2: 39 two of Shimei's slaves ran off to **Achish** son of Maacah, king of
2: 40 his donkey and went to **Achish** at Gath in search of his slaves.

430 אָכַל **'ākal**, v. [816] [→ 428, 431, 433, 4407, 4408, 4409, 4818; Ar 10030]

eat [359], ate [70], devour [43], consume [30], be eaten [25], eats [25], eaten [23], devoured [22], eating [22], consumed [19], *untranslated* [12], devours [10], consuming [9], food [8], consumes [6], feed on [6], be consumed [5], enjoy [5], ate up [4], burns [4], eaten [+430] [4], gave to eat [4], eater [3], feast [3], fed [3], be devoured [2], been destroyed [2], destroy [2], destroyed [2], devouring [2], eat up [2], eaten [+430+906] [2], eaten provisions [+430] [2], enjoys [2], feasting [2], feed [2], free to eat [+430] [2], give⁸ [2], had to eat [2], have plenty to eat [+430] [2], is eaten [+430] [2], make eat food [2], make eat [2], must eat [+430] [2], needed [2], shared [2], used up [+430+906] [2], burn up [1], burned up [1], burned [1], claimed [1], crushed completely [+2256+4730] [1], dine on [1], dined [1], dried up [1], earn [1], eat away [1], eaten away [1], eats away [1], enjoyed [1], feast on [1], feasting [+2256+9272] [1], feeding [1], feeds on [1], get food [1], give to eat [1], had food enough [1], have food [1], have⁸ [1], is eaten [1], kept [1], lick up [1], like [1], live on [1], meal [+4312] [1], needs [1], pests [1], prepare food to eat [1], prepares [1], provided for [+2118+2256+4200+4312] [1], put an end [1], ruins [1], sap [1], sat [1], scarce [+928+5017] [1], share in [1], sharing [+4946] [1], stay for a meal [+4312] [1], stripped clean [1], stripped [1], supposed to dine [+3782+3782] [1], taste [1], took space [1], use [1], would⁸ [1]

Ge 2: 16 [A] "*You are* **free to eat** [+430] from any tree in the garden;
2: 16 [A] "*You are* **free to eat** [+430] from any tree in the garden;
2: 17 [A] but *you must* not **eat** from the tree of the knowledge of good
2: 17 [A] of good and evil, for when you **eat** of it you will surely die."
3: 1 [A] really say, '*You must* not **eat** from any tree in the garden'?"
3: 2 [A] the serpent, "*We may* **eat** fruit from the trees in the garden,
3: 3 [A] '*You must* not **eat** fruit from the tree that is in the middle of
3: 5 [A] "For God knows that when you **eat** of it your eyes will be
3: 6 [A] also desirable for gaining wisdom, she took some and **ate** it.
3: 6 [A] gave some to her husband, who was with her, and *he* **ate** it.
3: 11 [A] *Have you* **eaten** from the tree that I commanded you not to
3: 11 [A] eaten from the tree that I commanded you not *to* **eat** from?"
3: 12 [A] with me—she gave me some fruit from the tree, and *I* **ate** it."
3: 13 [A] The woman said, "The serpent deceived me, and *I* **ate**."
3: 14 [A] on your belly and *you will* **eat** dust all the days of your life.
3: 17 [A] and **ate** from the tree about which I commanded you,
3: 17 [A] '*You must* not **eat** of it,' "Cursed is the ground because of
3: 17 [A] through painful toil *you will* **eat** *of* it all the days of your life.
3: 18 [A] and thistles for you, and *you will* **eat** the plants of the field.
3: 19 [A] By the sweat of your brow *you will* **eat** your food until you
3: 22 [A] reach out his hand and take also from the tree of life and **eat**,
6: 21 [C] You are to take every kind of food that *is to* **be eaten**

Ge 9: 4 [A] "But *you must* not **eat** meat that has its lifeblood still in it.
14: 24 [A] I will accept nothing but what my men *have* **eaten**
18: 8 [A] before them. While *they* **ate**, he stood near them under a tree.
19: 3 [A] a meal for them, baking bread without yeast, and *they* **ate**.
24: 33 [A] **food** was set before him, but he said, "I will not eat until I
24: 33 [A] "*I will* not **eat** until I have told you what I have to say."
24: 54 [A] he and the men who were with him **ate** and drank and spent
25: 34 [A] some lentil stew. *He* **ate** and drank, and then got up and left.
26: 30 [A] Isaac then made a feast for them, and *they* **ate** and drank.
27: 4 [A] me the kind of tasty food I like and bring it to me *to* **eat**,
27: 7 [A] 'Bring me some game and prepare me some tasty food *to* **eat**,
27: 10 [A] take it to your father *to* **eat**, so that he may give you his
27: 19 [A] Please sit up and **eat** some of my game so that you may give
27: 25 [A] Then he said, "My son, bring me some of your game *to* **eat**,
27: 25 [A] Jacob brought it to him and *he* **ate**; and he brought some
27: 31 [A] he said to him, "My father, sit up and **eat** some of my game,
27: 33 [A] *I* **ate** it just before you came and I blessed him—and indeed
28: 20 [A] I am taking and will give me food to **eat** and clothes to wear
31: 15 [A] but *he has* **used** [+430+906] **up** what was paid for us.
31: 15 [A] but *he has* **used up** [+430+906] what was paid for us.
31: 38 [A] have not miscarried, nor *have I* **eaten** rams from your flocks.
31: 40 [A] The heat **consumed** me in the daytime and the cold at night,
31: 46 [A] and piled them in a heap, and *they* **ate** there by the heap.
31: 54 [A] in the hill country and invited his relatives to a **meal** [+4312].
31: 54 [A] to a meal. After *they had* **eaten**, they spent the night there.
32: 32 [32:33] [A] Therefore to this day the Israelites *do* not **eat** the
37: 20 [A] these cisterns and say that a ferocious animal **devoured** him.
37: 25 [A] As they sat down to **eat** their meal, they looked up and saw a
37: 33 [A] is my son's robe! Some ferocious animal *has* **devoured** him.
39: 6 [A] did not concern himself with anything except the food he **ate**.
40: 17 [A] the birds *were* **eating** them out of the basket on my head."
40: 19 [A] hang you on a tree. And the birds *will* **eat away** your flesh."
41: 4 [A] the cows that were ugly and gaunt **ate up** the seven sleek,
41: 20 [A] ugly cows **ate up** the seven fat cows that came up first.
43: 2 [A] So when *they had* **eaten** all the grain they had brought from
43: 16 [A] and prepare dinner; they *are to* **eat** with me at noon."
43: 25 [A] at noon, because they had heard that *they were to* **eat** there.
43: 32 [A] and the Egyptians who **ate** with him by themselves,
43: 32 [A] because Egyptians could not **eat** with Hebrews, for that is
45: 18 [A] of the land of Egypt and *you can* **enjoy** the fat of the land.'
47: 22 [A] **had food enough** *from* the allotment Pharaoh gave them.
47: 24 [A] and your households and **[NIE]** your children."
49: 27 [A] in the morning *he* **devours** the prey, in the evening he
Ex 2: 20 [A] did you leave him? Invite him *to have* something *to* **eat**."
3: 2 [E] saw that though the bush was on fire it *did* not **burn up**.
10: 5 [A] *They will* **devour** what little you have left after the hail,
10: 5 [A] including **[RPH]** every tree that is growing in your fields.
10: 12 [A] over the land and **devour** everything growing in the fields,
10: 15 [A] *They* **devoured** all that was left after the hail—everything
12: 4 [A] lamb needed in accordance with what each person *will* **eat**.
12: 7 [A] tops of the doorframes of the houses where *they* **eat** the
12: 8 [A] That same night *they are to* **eat** the meat roasted over the
12: 8 [A] with bitter herbs, and bread made without yeast. **[RPH]**
12: 9 [A] *Do* not **eat** the meat raw or cooked in water, but roast it over
12: 11 [A] This is how *you are to* **eat** it: *with* your cloak tucked into
12: 11 [A] in your hand. **Eat** it in haste; it is the LORD's Passover.
12: 15 [A] For seven days *you are to* **eat** bread made without yeast. On
12: 15 [A] for whoever **eats** anything with yeast in it from the first day
12: 16 [C] on these days, except *to* **prepare food** for everyone **to eat**—
12: 18 [A] In the first month *you are to* **eat** bread made without yeast,
12: 19 [A] whoever **eats** anything with yeast in it must be cut off from
12: 20 [A] **Eat** nothing made with yeast. Wherever you live, you must
12: 20 [A] Wherever you live, *you must* **eat** unleavened bread."
12: 43 [A] the regulations for the Passover: "No foreigner *is to* **eat** of it.
12: 44 [A] Any slave you have bought *may* **eat** of it after you have
12: 45 [A] a temporary resident and a hired worker *may* not **eat** of it.
12: 46 [C] "*It must* **be eaten** inside one house; take none of the meat
12: 48 [A] one born in the land. No uncircumcised male *may* **eat** of it.
13: 3 [C] out of it with a mighty hand. **Eat** nothing containing yeast.
13: 6 [A] For seven days **eat** bread made without yeast and on the
13: 7 [C] **Eat** unleavened bread during those seven days; nothing with
15: 7 [A] your burning anger; *it* **consumed** them like stubble.
16: 3 [A] we sat around pots of meat and **ate** all the food we wanted,
16: 8 [A] the LORD when he gives you meat to **eat** in the evening
16: 12 [A] Tell them, 'At twilight *you will* **eat** meat, and in the morning
16: 16 [A] has commanded: 'Each one is to gather as much as he **needs**.
16: 18 [A] not have too little. Each one gathered as much as he **needed**.
16: 21 [A] Each morning everyone gathered as much as he **needed**,
16: 25 [A] "**Eat** it today," Moses said, "because today is a Sabbath to
16: 32 [G] so they can see the bread *I* **gave** you **to eat** in the desert
16: 35 [A] The Israelites **ate** manna forty years, until they came to a
16: 35 [A] *they* **ate** manna until they reached the border of Canaan.
18: 12 [A] Aaron came with all the elders of Israel to **eat** bread with
21: 28 [C] bull must be stoned to death, and its meat *must* not **be eaten**.
22: 6 [22:5] [A] so that *it* **burns** shocks of grain or standing grain
22: 31 [22:30] [A] So *do* not **eat** the meat of an animal torn by wild
23: 11 [A] the poor among your people *may* **get food** from it,
23: 11 [A] food from it, and the wild animals *may* **eat** what they leave.
23: 15 [A] for seven days **eat** bread made without yeast, as I
24: 11 [A] of the Israelites; they saw God, and *they* **ate** and drank.
24: 17 [A] looked like a **consuming** fire on top of the mountain.
29: 32 [A] his sons *are to* **eat** the meat of the ram and the bread that is
29: 33 [A] *They are to* **eat** these offerings by which atonement was
29: 33 [A] But no *one* else *may* **eat** them, because they are sacred.
29: 34 [C] burn it up. *It must* not **be eaten**, because it is sacred.
32: 6 [A] Afterward they sat down to **eat** and drink and got up to
34: 15 [A] to them, they will invite you and *you will* **eat** their sacrifices.
34: 18 [A] For seven days **eat** bread made without yeast, as I
34: 28 [A] and forty nights without **eating** bread or drinking water.
Lev 3: 17 [A] wherever you live: *You must* not **eat** any fat or any blood.' "
6: 10 [6:3] [A] the burnt offering that the fire *has* **consumed** on the
6: 16 [6:9] [A] Aaron and his sons *shall* **eat** the rest of it, but it is to
6: 16 [6:9] [C] of it, but *it is to* **be eaten** without yeast in a holy place;
6: 16 [6:9] [A] *they are to* **eat** it in the courtyard of the Tent of
6: 18 [6:11] [A] Any male descendant of Aaron *may* **eat** it. It is his
6: 23 [6:16] [C] shall be burned completely; *it must* not **be eaten**."
6: 26 [6:19] [A] The priest who offers it *shall* **eat** it; it is to be eaten
6: 26 [6:19] [C] *it is to* **be eaten** in a holy place, in the courtyard of
6: 29 [6:22] [A] Any male in a priest's family *may* **eat** it; it is most
6: 30 [6:23] [C] atonement in the Holy Place *must* not **be eaten**;
7: 6 [A] Any male in a priest's family *may* **eat** it, but it must be eaten
7: 6 [C] family may eat it, but *it must* **be eaten** in a holy place;
7: 15 [C] of thanksgiving *must* **be eaten** on the day it is offered;
7: 16 [C] the sacrifice *shall* **be eaten** on the day he offers it,
7: 16 [C] but anything left over *may* **be eaten** on the next day.
7: 18 [C] If any meat of the fellowship offering *is* **eaten** [+430] on the
7: 18 [C] If any meat of the fellowship offering *is* **eaten** [+430] on the
7: 18 [A] the person who **eats** any of it will be held responsible.
7: 19 [C] touches anything ceremonially unclean *must* not **be eaten**;
7: 19 [A] As for other meat, anyone ceremonially clean *may* **eat** it.
7: 20 [A] if anyone who is unclean **eats** any meat of the fellowship
7: 21 [A] **eats** any of the meat of the fellowship offering belonging to
7: 23 [A] '*Do* not **eat** any of the fat of cattle, sheep or goats.
7: 24 [A] used for any other purpose, but *you* **must** not **eat** [+430] it.
7: 24 [A] used for any other purpose, but *you* **must** not **eat** [+430] it.
7: 25 [A] Anyone *who* **eats** the fat of an animal from which an offering
7: 25 [A] made to the LORD must be cut off **[RPH]** from his people.
7: 26 [A] you live, *you must* not **eat** the blood of any bird or animal.
7: 27 [A] If anyone **eats** blood, that person must be cut off from his
8: 31 [A] **eat** it there with the bread from the basket of ordination
8: 31 [A] as I commanded, saying, 'Aaron and his sons *are to* **eat** it.'
9: 24 [A] **consumed** the burnt offering and the fat portions on the altar.
10: 2 [A] out from the presence of the LORD and **consumed** them,
10: 12 [A] by fire and **eat** it prepared without yeast beside the altar,
10: 13 [A] **Eat** it in a holy place, because it is your share and your sons'
10: 14 [A] your daughters *may* **eat** the breast that was waved and the
10: 17 [A] "Why didn't *you* **eat** the sin offering in the sanctuary area?
10: 18 [A] *you should have* **eaten** [+430+906] the goat in the sanctuary
10: 18 [A] *you should have* **eaten** [+430+906] the goat in the sanctuary
10: 19 [A] Would the LORD have been pleased if *I had* **eaten** the sin
11: 2 [A] the animals that live on land, these are the ones *you may* **eat**:
11: 3 [A] *You may* **eat** any animal that has a split hoof completely
11: 4 [A] the cud or only have a split hoof, but *you must* not **eat** them.
11: 8 [A] *You must* not **eat** their meat or touch their carcasses;
11: 9 [A] and the streams, *you may* **eat** any that have fins and scales.
11: 9 [A] you may eat any that have fins and scales. **[RPH]**
11: 11 [A] *you must* not **eat** their meat and you must detest their
11: 13 [C] you are to detest and not **eat** because they are detestable:
11: 21 [A] winged creatures that walk on all fours that *you may* **eat**:
11: 22 [A] Of these *you may* **eat** any kind of locust, katydid, cricket or
11: 34 [C] Any food that *could* **be eaten** but has water on it from such a
11: 40 [A] Anyone *who* **eats** some of the carcass must wash his clothes,
11: 41 [C] moves about on the ground is detestable; it *is* not *to* **be eaten**.
11: 42 [A] *You are* not *to* **eat** any creature that moves about on the
11: 47 [C] between living creatures that *may* **be eaten** and those that
11: 47 [C] that may be eaten and those that *may* not **be eaten**.' "
14: 47 [A] who sleeps or **eats** in the house must wash his clothes.
17: 10 [A] or any alien living among them who **eats** any blood—
17: 10 [A] I will set my face against that person who **eats** blood and will
17: 12 [A] I say to the Israelites, "None of you *may* **eat** blood,
17: 12 [A] eat blood, nor *may* an alien living among you **eat** blood."
17: 13 [C] or bird that *may* **be eaten** must drain out the blood and cover
17: 14 [A] the Israelites, "*You must* not **eat** the blood of any creature,
17: 14 [A] creature is its blood; anyone *who* **eats** it must be cut off."
17: 15 [A] who **eats** anything found dead or torn by wild animals must
19: 6 [C] *It shall* **be eaten** on the day you sacrifice it or on the next
19: 7 [C] If *any of it* **is eaten** [+430] on the third day, it is impure
19: 7 [C] If *any of it* **is eaten** [+430] on the third day, it is impure

Lev 19: 8 [A] *Whoever* **eats** it will be held responsible because he has
19:23 [C] years you are to consider it forbidden; *it must* not **be eaten**.
19:25 [A] in the fifth year *you may* **eat** its fruit. In this way your
19:26 [A] " '*Do* not **eat** any meat with the blood still in it. " 'Do not
21:22 [A] *He may* **eat** the most holy food of his God, as well as the
22: 4 [A] *he may* not **eat** the sacred offerings until he is cleansed.
22: 6 [A] *He must* not **eat** any of the sacred offerings unless he has
22: 7 [A] will be clean, and after that *he may* **eat** the sacred offerings,
22: 8 [A] *He must* not **eat** anything found dead or torn by wild
22:10 [A] " 'No one outside a priest's family *may* **eat** the sacred
22:10 [A] nor *may* the guest of a priest or his hired worker **eat** it.
22:11 [A] a slave is born in his household, that slave *may* **eat** his food.
22:11 [A] born in his household, that slave may eat his food. **[RPH]**
22:12 [A] than a priest, she *may* not **eat** any of the sacred contributions.
22:13 [A] house as in her youth, *she may* **eat** of her father's food.
22:13 [A] No unauthorized person, however, *may* **eat** any of it.
22:14 [A] " 'If anyone **eats** a sacred offering by mistake, he must make
22:16 [A] by *allowing* them *to* **eat** the sacred offerings and so bring
22:30 [C] *It must* **be eaten** that same day; leave none of it till morning.
23: 6 [A] for seven days *you must* **eat** bread made without yeast.
23:14 [A] *You must* not **eat** any bread, or roasted or new grain,
24: 9 [A] to Aaron and his sons, *who are to* **eat** it in a holy place,
25: 7 [A] in your land. Whatever the land produces may be **eaten.**
25:12 [A] holy for you; **eat** only what is taken directly from the fields.
25:19 [A] its fruit, and *you will* **eat** your fill and live there in safety.
25:20 [A] "What *will we* **eat** in the seventh year if we do not plant
25:22 [A] *you will* **eat** from the old crop and will continue to eat from
25:22 [A] *will continue to* **eat** *from* it until the harvest of the ninth
26: 5 [A] *you will* **eat** all the food you want and live in safety in your
26:10 [A] *You will still be* **eating** last year's harvest when you will
26:16 [A] You will plant seed in vain, because your enemies *will* **eat** it.
26:26 [A] bread by weight. *You will* **eat**, but you will not be satisfied.
26:29 [A] *You will* **eat** the flesh of your sons and the flesh of your
26:29 [A] flesh of your sons and the flesh of your daughters. **[RPH]**
26:38 [A] the nations; the land of your enemies *will* **devour** you.
Nu 6: 3 [A] He must not drink grape juice or **eat** grapes or raisins.
6: 4 [A] *he must* not **eat** anything that comes from the grapevine, not
9:11 [A] *They are to* **eat** the lamb, together with unleavened bread
11: 1 [A] and **consumed** some of the outskirts of the camp.
11: 4 [G] started wailing and said, "If only we **had** meat **to eat**!
11: 5 [A] We remember the fish *we* **ate** in Egypt at no cost—also the
11:13 [A] these people? They keep wailing to me, 'Give us meat *to* **eat**!'
11:18 [A] in preparation for tomorrow, when *you will* **eat** meat.
11:18 [G] heard you when you wailed, "If only we **had** meat **to eat**!
11:18 [A] Now the LORD will give you meat, and *you will* **eat** it.
11:19 [A] *You will* not **eat** it for just one day, or two days, or five, ten
11:21 [A] you say, 'I will give them meat *to* **eat** for a whole month!'
12:12 [C] from its mother's womb with its flesh half **eaten away**."
13:32 [A] They said, "The land we explored **devours** those living in it.
15:19 [A] you **eat** the food of the land, present a portion as an offering
16:35 [A] and **consumed** the 250 men who were offering the incense.
18:10 [A] **Eat** it as something most holy; every male shall eat it.
18:10 [A] Eat it as something most holy; every male *shall* **eat** it.
18:11 [A] in your household who is ceremonially clean *may* **eat** it.
18:13 [A] in your household who is ceremonially clean *may* **eat** it.
18:31 [A] You and your households *may* **eat** the rest of it anywhere,
21:28 [A] *It* **consumed** Ar of Moab, the citizens of Arnon's heights.
23:24 [A] like a lion that does not rest till *he* **devours** his prey
24: 8 [A] *They* **devour** hostile nations and break their bones in pieces;
25: 2 [A] The people **ate** and bowed down before these gods.
26:10 [A] whose followers died when the fire **devoured** the 250 men.
28:17 [C] to be a festival; for seven days **eat** bread made without yeast.
Dt 2: 6 [A] You are to pay them in silver for the food *you* **eat** and the
2:28 [A] Sell us food *to* **eat** and water to drink for their price in silver.
4:24 [A] For the LORD your God is a **consuming** fire, a jealous
4:28 [A] of wood and stone, which cannot see or hear or **eat** or smell.
5:25 [A] This great fire *will* **consume** us, and we will die if we hear
6:11 [A] you did not plant—then when *you* **eat** and are satisfied,
7:16 [A] *You must* **destroy** all the peoples the LORD your God
8: 3 [G] causing you to hunger and then **feeding** you *with* manna,
8: 9 [A] a land where bread *will* not *be* **scarce** [+928+5017] and you
8:10 [A] When *you have* **eaten** and are satisfied, praise the LORD
8:12 [A] Otherwise, when *you* **eat** and are satisfied, when you build
8:16 [G] He **gave** you manna **to eat** in the desert, something your
9: 3 [A] the one who goes across ahead of you like a **devouring** fire.
9: 9 [A] and forty nights; *I* **ate** no bread and drank no water.
9:18 [A] *I* **ate** no bread and drank no water, because of all the sin you
11:15 [A] in the fields for your cattle, and *you will* **eat** and be satisfied.
12: 7 [A] you and your families *shall* **eat** and shall rejoice in
12:15 [A] any of your towns and **eat** as much of the meat as you want,
12:15 [A] Both the ceremonially unclean and the clean *may* **eat** it.
12:16 [A] *you must* not **eat** the blood; pour it out on the ground like
12:17 [A] You must not **eat** in your own towns the tithe of your grain
12:18 [A] *you are to* **eat** them in the presence of the LORD your God
12:20 [A] you crave **[RPH]** meat and say, "I would like some meat,"
12:20 [A] you crave meat and say, "*I would* **like** some meat," then you
12:20 [A] some meat," then *you may* **eat** as much of it as you want.
12:21 [A] in your own towns *you may* **eat** as much of them as you
12:22 [A] **Eat** them as you would gazelle or deer.
12:22 [C] Eat them as you **would**[s] gazelle or deer.
12:22 [A] Both the ceremonially unclean and the clean *may* **eat**.
12:23 [A] be sure you *do* not **eat** the blood, because the blood is the
12:23 [A] blood is the life, and *you must* not **eat** the life with the meat.
12:24 [A] *You must* not **eat** the blood; pour it out on the ground like
12:25 [A] *Do* not **eat** it, so that it may go well with you and your
12:27 [A] the altar of the LORD your God, but *you may* **eat** the meat.
14: 3 [A] *Do* not **eat** any detestable thing.
14: 4 [A] These are the animals *you may* **eat**: the ox, the sheep,
14: 6 [A] *You may* **eat** any animal that has a split hoof divided in two
14: 7 [A] completely divided *you may* not **eat** the camel, the rabbit or
14: 8 [A] *You are* not *to* **eat** their meat or touch their carcasses.
14: 9 [A] living in the water, *you may* **eat** any that has fins and scales.
14: 9 [A] the water, you may eat any that has fins and scales. **[RPH]**
14:10 [A] anything that does not have fins and scales *you may* not **eat**;
14:11 [A] *You may* **eat** any clean bird.
14:12 [A] these *you may* not **eat**: the eagle, the vulture, the black
14:19 [C] insects that swarm are unclean to you; *do* not **eat** *them*.
14:20 [A] But any winged creature that is clean *you may* **eat**.
14:21 [A] *Do* not **eat** anything you find already dead. You may give it
14:21 [A] and *he may* **eat** it, or you may sell it to a foreigner.
14:23 [A] **Eat** the tithe of your grain, new wine and oil, and the
14:26 [A] your household *shall* **eat** there in the presence of the LORD
14:29 [A] who live in your towns may come and **eat** and be satisfied,
15:20 [A] your family *are to* **eat** them in the presence of the LORD
15:22 [A] *You are to* **eat** it in your own towns. Both the ceremonially
15:23 [A] *you must* not **eat** the blood; pour it out on the ground like
16: 3 [A] *Do* not **eat** it with bread made with yeast, but for seven days
16: 3 [A] for seven days **eat** unleavened bread, the bread of affliction,
16: 7 [A] and **eat** it at the place the LORD your God will choose.
16: 8 [A] For six days **eat** unleavened bread and on the seventh day
18: 1 [A] *They shall* **live on** the offerings made to the LORD by fire,
18: 8 [A] *He is to* **share** equally **in** their benefits, even though he has
20:14 [A] *you may* **use** the plunder the LORD your God gives you
20:19 [A] by putting an ax to them, because *you can* **eat** their fruit.
23:24 [23:25] [A] *you may* **eat** all the grapes you want, but do not put
26:12 [A] so that *they may* **eat** in your towns and be satisfied.
26:14 [A] *I have* not **eaten** any of the sacred portion while I was in
27: 7 [A] **eating** them and rejoicing in the presence of the LORD
28:31 [A] be slaughtered before your eyes, but *you will* **eat** none of it.
28:33 [A] A people that you do not know *will* **eat** what your land
28:39 [A] the wine or gather the grapes, because worms *will* **eat** them.
28:51 [A] *They will* **devour** the young of your livestock and the crops
28:53 [A] *you will* **eat** the fruit of the womb, the flesh of the sons
28:55 [A] one of them any of the flesh of his children that *he is* **eating**.
28:57 [A] For *she intends to* **eat** them secretly during the siege and in
29: 6 [29:5] [A] *You* **ate** no bread and drank no wine or other
31:17 [A] I will hide my face from them, and they will be **destroyed**.
31:20 [A] when *they* **eat** their fill and thrive, they will turn to other
32:13 [A] heights of the land and **fed** him *with* the fruit of the fields.
32:22 [A] *It will* **devour** the earth and its harvests and set afire the
32:38 [A] the gods who **ate** the fat of their sacrifices and drank the
32:42 [A] while my sword **devours** flesh: the blood of the slain
Jos 5:11 [A] that very day, *they* **ate** some of the produce of the land:
5:12 [A] The manna stopped the day after they **ate** this food from the
5:12 [A] but that year *they* **ate** of the produce of Canaan.
24:13 [A] you live in them and **eat** *from* vineyards and olive groves
Jdg 6:21 [A] Fire flared from the rock, **consuming** the meat and the bread.
9:15 [A] out of the thornbush and **consume** the cedars of Lebanon!'
9:20 [A] and **consume** you, citizens of Shechem and Beth Millo,
9:20 [A] of Shechem and Beth Millo, and **consume** Abimelech!"
9:27 [A] While *they were* **eating** and drinking, they cursed
13: 4 [A] fermented drink and that *you do* not **eat** anything unclean,
13: 7 [A] or other fermented drink and *do* not **eat** anything unclean,
13:14 [A] *She must* not **eat** anything that comes from the grapevine,
13:14 [A] any wine or other fermented drink nor **eat** anything unclean.
13:16 [A] "Even though you detain me, *I will* not **eat** any of your food.
14: 9 [A] he scooped out with his hands and **ate** as he went along.
14: 9 [A] rejoined his parents, he gave them some, and *they* too **ate** it.
14:14 [A] He replied, "Out of the **eater**, something to eat; out of the
19: 4 [A] with him three days, **eating** and drinking, and sleeping there.
19: 6 [A] So the two of them sat down *to* **eat** and drink together.
19: 8 [A] Wait till afternoon!" So the two of them **ate** together.
19:21 [A] had washed their feet, *they had something to* **eat** and drink.
Ru 2:14 [A] over here. **Have**[s] some bread and dip it in the wine vinegar."
2:14 [A] roasted grain. *She* **ate** all she wanted and had some left over.
3: 3 [A] don't let him know you are there until he has finished **eating**
3: 7 [A] When Boaz *had finished* **eating** and drinking and was in
1Sa 1: 7 [A] her rival provoked her till she wept and *would* not **eat**.

1Sa 1: 8 [A] to her, "Hannah, why are you weeping? Why don't *you* **eat**?
1: 9 [A] Once when *they had* finished **eating** and drinking in Shiloh,
1: 18 [A] she went her way and **ate** something, and her face was no
2: 36 [A] me to some priestly office so I *can have* food *to* **eat**." '"
9: 13 [A] you will find him before he goes up to the high place to **eat**.
9: 13 [A] The people *will* not *begin* **eating** until he comes, because he
9: 13 [A] bless the sacrifice; afterward, those who are invited *will* **eat**.
9: 19 [A] for today *you are to* **eat** with me, and in the morning I will
9: 24 [A] **Eat**, because it was set aside for you for this occasion,
9: 24 [A] 'I have invited guests.' " And Saul **dined** with Samuel that
14: 24 [A] "Cursed be any man who **eats** food before evening comes,
14: 28 [A] strict oath, saying, 'Cursed be any man who **eats** food today!'
14: 30 [A] *had* **eaten** [+430] today some of the plunder they took from
14: 30 [A] *had* **eaten** [+430] today some of the plunder they took from
14: 32 [A] and calves, they butchered them on the ground and **ate** them,
14: 33 [A] the men are sinning against the LORD by **eating** meat that
14: 34 [A] your cattle and sheep, and slaughter them here and **eat** them.
14: 34 [A] Do not sin against the LORD by **eating** meat with blood
20: 5 [A] and I *am* **supposed to dine** [+3782+3782] with the king;
20: 24 [A] when the New Moon festival came, the king sat down to **eat**.
20: 34 [A] on that second day of the month *he did* not **eat**, because he
28: 20 [A] was gone, for *he had* **eaten** nothing all that day and night.
28: 22 [A] your servant and let me give you some food so *you may* **eat**
28: 23 [A] He refused and said, "*I will* not **eat**." But his men joined the
28: 25 [A] she set it before Saul and his men, and *they* **ate**. That same
30: 11 [A] to David. They gave him water to drink and food *to* **eat**—
30: 12 [A] *He* **ate** and was revived, for he had not eaten any food
30: 12 [A] for *he had* not **eaten** any food or drunk any water for three
30: 16 [A] **eating**, drinking and reveling because of the great amount of
2Sa 2: 26 [A] Abner called out to Joab, "*Must* the sword **devour** forever?
9: 7 [A] your grandfather Saul, and you *will* always **eat** at my table."
9: 10 [A] grandson *may be* **provided for** [+2118+2256+4200+4312].
9: 10 [A] grandson of your master, *will* always **eat** at my table."
9: 11 [A] So Mephibosheth **ate** at David's table like one of the king's
9: 13 [A] because he always **ate** at the king's table, and he was
11: 11 [A] How could I go to my house to **eat** and drink and lie with my
11: 13 [A] At David's invitation, *he* **ate** and drank with him, and David
11: 25 [A] let this upset you; the sword **devours** one as well as another.
12: 3 [A] *It* **shared** his food, drank from his cup and even slept in his
12: 20 [A] and at his request they served him food, and *he* **ate**.
12: 21 [A] and wept, but now that the child is dead, you get up and **eat**!"
13: 5 [A] my sight so I may watch her and then **eat** it from her hand.' "
13: 9 [A] took the pan and served him the bread, but he refused to **eat**.
13: 11 [A] But when she took it to him to **eat**, he grabbed her and said,
16: 2 [A] to ride on, the bread and fruit are for the men to **eat**,
17: 29 [A] and cheese from cows' milk for David and his people to **eat**.
18: 8 [A] and the forest **claimed** more lives that day than the sword.
18: 8 [A] the forest claimed more lives that day than **[RPH]** the
19: 28 [19:29] [A] servant a place among *those who* **sat** *at* your table.
19: 35 [19:36] [A] Can your servant taste what *he* **eats** and drinks?
19: 42 [19:43] [A] *Have we* **eaten** [+430] any of the king's **provisions**?
19: 42 [19:43] [A] *Have we* **eaten** any of the king's **provisions** [+430]?
22: 9 [A] **consuming** fire came from his mouth, burning coals blazed
22: 39 [A] *I* **crushed** them **completely** [+2256+4730], and they could not
1Ki 1: 25 [A] Right now they *are* **eating** and drinking with him and saying,
1: 41 [A] who were with him heard it as they were finishing their **feast**.
2: 7 [A] and let them be among *those who* **eat** *at* your table.
4: 20 [A] on the seashore; *they* **ate**, they drank and they were happy.
13: 8 [A] not go with you, nor *would I* **eat** bread or drink water here.
13: 9 [A] '*You must* not **eat** bread or drink water or return by the way
13: 15 [A] So the prophet said to him, "Come home with me and **eat**."
13: 16 [A] nor *can I* **eat** bread or drink water with you in this place.
13: 17 [A] '*You must* not **eat** bread or drink water there or return by the
13: 18 [A] him back with you to your house so that *he may* **eat** bread
13: 19 [A] of God returned with him and **ate** and drank in his house.
13: 22 [A] You came back and **ate** bread and drank water in the place
13: 22 [A] drank water in the place where he told you not *to* **eat** or
13: 23 [A] When the man of God had finished **eating** and drinking, the
13: 28 [A] The lion *had* neither **eaten** the body nor mauled the donkey.
14: 11 [A] Dogs *will* **eat** those belonging to Jeroboam who die in the
14: 11 [A] the birds of the air *will* **feed on** those who die in the country.
16: 4 [A] Dogs *will* **eat** those belonging to Baasha who die in the city,
16: 4 [A] the birds of the air *will* **feed on** those who die in the
17: 12 [A] and make a meal for myself and my son, that *we may* **eat** it—
17: 15 [A] So *there was* **food** every day for Elijah and for the woman
18: 19 [A] hundred prophets of Asherah, *who* **eat** *at* Jezebel's table."
18: 38 [A] **burned up** the sacrifice, the wood, the stones and the soil,
18: 41 [A] Elijah said to Ahab, "Go, **eat** and drink, for there is the sound
18: 42 [A] So Ahab went off to **eat** and drink, but Elijah climbed to the
19: 5 [A] All at once an angel touched him and said, "Get up and **eat**."
19: 6 [A] a jar of water. *He* **ate** and drank and then lay down again.
19: 7 [A] a second time and touched him and said, "Get up and **eat**,
19: 8 [A] So he got up and **ate** and drank. Strengthened by that food,
19: 21 [A] to cook the meat and gave it to the people, and *they* **ate**.
21: 4 [A] of my fathers." He lay on his bed sulking and refused *to* **eat**.
21: 5 [A] asked him, "Why are you so sullen? Why won't you **eat**?"
21: 7 [A] how you act as king over Israel? Get up and **eat**! Cheer up.
21: 23 [A] 'Dogs *will* **devour** Jezebel by the wall of Jezreel.'
21: 24 [A] "Dogs *will* **eat** those belonging to Ahab who die in the city,
21: 24 [A] the birds of the air *will* **feed on** those who die in the
22: 27 [G] Put this fellow in prison and **give**[s] him nothing but bread
2Ki 1: 10 [A] down from heaven and **consume** you and your fifty men!"
1: 10 [A] fire fell from heaven and **consumed** the captain and his men.
1: 12 [A] down from heaven and **consume** you and your fifty men!"
1: 12 [A] God fell from heaven and **consumed** him and his fifty men.
1: 14 [A] and **consumed** the first two captains and all their men.
4: 8 [A] was there, who urged him to **stay for a meal** [+4312].
4: 8 [A] for a meal. So whenever he came by, he stopped there to **eat**.
4: 40 [A] **[RPH]** but as they began to eat it, they cried out, "O man of
4: 40 [A] but as they *began to* **eat** it, they cried out, "O man of God,
4: 40 [A] of God, there is death in the pot!" And they could not **eat** it.
4: 41 [A] He put it into the pot and said, "Serve it to the people *to* **eat**."
4: 42 [A] of new grain. "Give it to the people *to* **eat**," Elisha said.
4: 43 [A] But Elisha answered, "Give it to the people *to* **eat**.
4: 43 [A] the LORD says: 'They *will* **eat** and have some left over.' "
4: 44 [A] he set it before them, and *they* **ate** and had some left over,
6: 22 [A] and water before them so that *they may* **eat** and drink and
6: 23 [A] after *they had finished* **eating** and drinking, he sent them
6: 28 [A] said to me, 'Give up your son so *we may* **eat** him today,
6: 28 [A] so we may eat him today, and tomorrow *we'll* **eat** my son.'
6: 29 [A] So we cooked my son and **ate** him. The next day I said to
6: 29 [A] 'Give up your son so *we may* **eat** him,' but she had hidden
7: 2 [A] own eyes," answered Elisha, "but *you will* not **eat** any of it!"
7: 8 [A] *They* **ate** and drank, and carried away silver, gold
7: 19 [A] see it with your own eyes, but *you will* not **eat** any of it!"
9: 10 [A] dogs *will* **devour** her on the plot of ground at Jezreel,
9: 34 [A] Jehu went in and **ate** and drank. "Take care of that cursed
9: 36 [A] On the plot of ground at Jezreel dogs *will* **devour** Jezebel's
18: 27 [A] *will have to* **eat** their own filth and drink their own urine?"
18: 31 [A] every one of you *will* **eat** *from* his own vine and fig tree
19: 29 [A] "This year you *will* **eat** what grows by itself, and the second
19: 29 [A] third year sow and reap, plant vineyards and **eat** their fruit.
23: 9 [A] *they* **ate** unleavened bread with their fellow priests.
25: 29 [A] and for the rest of his life **ate** regularly at the king's table.
1Ch 12: 39 [12:40] [A] three days there with David, **eating** and drinking,
29: 22 [A] *They* **ate** and drank with great joy in the presence of the
2Ch 7: 1 [A] and **consumed** the burnt offering and the sacrifices,
7: 13 [A] or command locusts to **devour** the land or send a plague
18: 26 [G] Put this fellow in prison and **give**[s] him nothing but bread
28: 15 [G] provided them with clothes and sandals, **food** and drink,
30: 18 [A] yet *they* **ate** the Passover, contrary to what was written.
30: 22 [A] For the seven days *they* **ate** their assigned portion
31: 10 [A] we have had enough *to* **eat** and plenty to spare, because the
Ezr 2: 63 [A] The governor ordered them not *to* **eat** any of the most sacred
6: 21 [A] So the Israelites who had returned from the exile **ate** it,
9: 12 [A] that you may be strong and **eat** the good things of the land
10: 6 [A] While he was there, *he* **ate** no food and drank no water,
Ne 2: 3 [E] lies in ruins, and its gates *have* **been destroyed** by fire?"
2: 13 [E] and its gates, *which had* **been destroyed** by fire.
5: 2 [A] in order for *us to* **eat** and stay alive, we must get grain."
5: 14 [A] neither I nor my brothers **ate** the food allotted to the
7: 65 [A] ordered them not *to* **eat** any of the most sacred food until
8: 10 [A] Nehemiah said, "Go and **enjoy** choice food and sweet drinks,
8: 12 [A] all the people went away to **eat** and drink, to send portions of
9: 25 [A] *They* **ate** to the full and were well-nourished; they reveled in
9: 36 [A] so they *could* **eat** its fruit and the other good things it
Est 4: 16 [A] *Do* not **eat** or drink for three days, night or day. I and my
Job 1: 4 [A] they would invite their three sisters to **eat** and drink with
1: 13 [A] One day when Job's sons and daughters *were* **feasting**
1: 16 [A] **[RPH]** and I am the only one who has escaped to tell you!"
1: 18 [A] "Your sons and daughters *were* **feasting** and drinking wine
5: 5 [A] The hungry **consume** his harvest, taking it even from among
6: 6 [C] **Is** tasteless food **eaten** without salt, or is there flavor in the
13: 28 [A] away like something rotten, like a garment **eaten** *by* moths.
15: 34 [A] and fire *will* **consume** the tents of those who love bribes.
18: 13 [A] *It* **eats away** parts of his skin; death's firstborn devours his
18: 13 [A] away parts of his skin; death's firstborn **devours** his limbs.
20: 21 [A] Nothing is left for him to **devour**; his prosperity will not
20: 26 [A] A fire unfanned *will* **consume** him and devour what is left in
21: 25 [A] in bitterness of soul, never *having* **enjoyed** anything good.
22: 20 [A] 'Surely our foes are destroyed, and fire **devours** their wealth.'
31: 8 [A] *may* others **eat** what I have sown, and may my crops be
31: 12 [A] It is a fire *that* **burns** to Destruction; it would have uprooted
31: 17 [A] if *I have* **kept** my bread to myself, not sharing it with the
31: 17 [A] bread to myself, not **sharing** [+4946] it *with* the fatherless—
31: 39 [A] if *I have* **devoured** its yield without payment or broken the
34: 3 [A] For the ear tests words as the tongue tastes **food**.
40: 15 [A] I made along with you and *which* **feeds on** grass like an ox.

Job 42:11 [A] had known him before came and **ate** with him in his house.
Ps 14: 4 [A] *those who* **devour** my people as men eat bread and who do
14: 4 [A] those who devour my people as *men* **eat** bread and who do
18: 8 [18:9] [A] **consuming** fire came from his mouth, burning coals
21: 9 [21:10] [A] swallow them up, and his fire *will* **consume** them.
22:26 [22:27] [A] The poor *will* **eat** and be satisfied; they who seek
22:29 [22:30] [A] All the rich of the earth *will* **feast** and worship;
27: 2 [A] When evil men advance against me to **devour** my flesh,
41: 9 [41:10] [A] whom I trusted, *he who* **shared** my bread,
50: 3 [A] a fire **devours** before him, and around him a tempest rages.
50:13 [A] *Do I* **eat** the flesh of bulls or drink the blood of goats?
53: 4 [53:5] [A] *those who* **devour** my people as men eat bread
53: 4 [53:5] [A] those who devour my people as *men* **eat** bread
59:15 [59:16] [A] They wander about for **food** and howl if not
69: 9 [69:10] [A] for zeal for your house **consumes** me,
78:24 [A] he rained down manna for the people to **eat**, he gave them
78:25 [A] Men **ate** the bread of angels; he sent them all the food they
78:29 [A] *They* **ate** till they had more than enough, for he had given
78:45 [A] He sent swarms of flies that **devoured** them, and frogs that
78:63 [A] Fire **consumed** their young men, and their maidens had no
79: 7 [A] for *they have* **devoured** Jacob and destroyed his homeland.
80: 5 [80:6] [G] *You have* **fed** them *with* the bread of tears; you have
81:16 [81:17] [G] you *would be* **fed** with the finest of wheat; with
102: 4 [102:5] [A] and withered like grass; I forget *to* **eat** my food.
102: 9 [102:10] [A] For *I* **eat** ashes as my food and mingle my drink
105:35 [A] *they* **ate up** every green thing in their land, ate up the
105:35 [A] green thing in their land, **ate up** the produce of their soil.
106:20 [A] their Glory for an image of a bull, *which* **eats** grass.
106:28 [A] to the Baal of Peor and **ate** sacrifices offered to lifeless gods;
127: 2 [A] vain you rise early and stay up late, toiling for food *to* **eat**—
128: 2 [A] *You will* **eat** the fruit of your labor; blessings and prosperity
Pr 1:31 [A] *they will* **eat** the fruit of their ways and be filled with the
13: 2 [A] From the fruit of his lips a man **enjoys** good things,
13:25 [A] The righteous **eat** to their hearts' content, but the stomach of
18:21 [A] of life and death, and those who love it *will* **eat** its fruit.
23: 7 [A] "**Eat** and drink," he says to you, but his heart is not with you.
23: 8 [A] You will vomit up the little *you have* **eaten** and will have
24:13 [A] **Eat** honey, my son, for it is good; honey from the comb is
25:16 [A] If you find honey, **eat** just enough—too much of it, and you
25:21 [G] If your enemy is hungry, **give** him food **to eat**; if he is thirsty,
25:27 [A] It is not good *to* **eat** too much honey, nor is it honorable to
27:18 [A] He who tends a fig tree *will* **eat** its fruit, and he who looks
30:14 [A] whose jaws are set with knives to **devour** the poor from the
30:17 [A] out by the ravens of the valley, *will be* **eaten** *by* the vultures.
30:20 [A] *She* **eats** and wipes her mouth and says, 'I've done nothing
31:27 [A] of her household and *does* not **eat** the bread of idleness.
Ecc 2:24 [A] A man can do nothing better than *to* **eat** and drink and find
2:25 [A] for without him, who *can* **eat** or find enjoyment?
3:13 [A] That everyone *may* **eat** and drink, and find satisfaction in all
4: 5 [A] The fool folds his hands and **ruins** himself.
5:11 [5:10] [A] As goods increase, so do *those who* **consume** them.
5:12 [5:11] [A] of a laborer is sweet, whether *he* **eats** little or much,
5:17 [5:16] [A] All his days *he* **eats** in darkness, with great
5:18 [5:17] [A] that it is good and proper for a man to **eat** and drink,
5:19 [5:18] [A] enables him to **enjoy** them, to accept his lot and be
6: 2 [A] God does not enable him to **enjoy** them, and a stranger
6: 2 [A] him to enjoy them, and a stranger **enjoys** them instead.
8:15 [A] because nothing is better for a man under the sun than to **eat**
9: 7 [A] Go, **eat** your food with gladness, and drink your wine with a
10:16 [A] king was a servant and whose princes **feast** in the morning.
10:17 [A] is of noble birth and whose princes **eat** at a proper time—
SS 4:16 [A] Let my lover come into his garden and **taste** its choice fruits.
5: 1 [A] *I have* **eaten** my honeycomb and my honey; I have drunk my
5: 1 [A] my milk. **Eat**, O friends, and drink; drink your fill, O lovers.
Isa 1: 7 [A] your fields *are being* **stripped** *by* foreigners right before
1:19 [A] are willing and obedient, *you will* **eat** the best from the land;
1:20 [E] if you resist and rebel, *you will* **be devoured** *by* the sword."
3:10 [A] well with them, for *they will* **enjoy** the fruit of their deeds.
4: 1 [A] "*We will* **eat** our own food and provide our own clothes;
5:17 [A] own pasture; lambs *will* **feed** *among* the ruins of the rich.
5:24 [A] as tongues of fire **lick up** straw and as dry grass sinks down
7:15 [A] *He will* **eat** curds and honey when he knows enough to reject
7:22 [A] abundance of the milk they give, *he will have* curds *to* **eat**.
7:22 [A] to eat. All who remain in the land *will* **eat** curds and honey.
9:12 [9:11] [A] Philistines from the west *have* **devoured** Israel with
9:18 [9:17] [A] *it* **consumes** briers and thorns, it sets the forest
9:20 [9:19] [A] on the left *they will* **eat**, but not be satisfied.
9:20 [9:19] [A] Each *will* **feed on** the flesh of his own offspring:
10:17 [A] single day it will burn and **consume** his thorns and his briers.
11: 7 [A] will lie down together, and the lion *will* **eat** straw like the ox.
21: 5 [A] They set the tables, they spread the rugs, they **eat**, they drink!
22:13 [A] and killing of sheep, **eating** *of* meat and drinking of wine!
22:13 [A] "*Let* us **eat** and drink," you say, "for tomorrow we die!"
23:18 [A] live before the LORD, for abundant **food** and fine clothes.
24: 6 [A] Therefore a curse **consumes** the earth; its people must bear
26:11 [A] *let* the fire reserved for your enemies **consume** them.
29: 6 [A] with windstorm and tempest and flames of a **devouring** fire.
29: 8 [A] as when a hungry man dreams that *he is* **eating**, but he
30:24 [A] The oxen and donkeys that work the soil *will* **eat** fodder
30:27 [A] his lips are full of wrath, and his tongue *is* a **consuming** fire.
30:30 [A] his arm coming down with raging anger and **consuming** fire,
31: 8 [A] that is not of man; a sword, not of mortals, *will* **devour** them.
33:11 [A] give birth to straw; your breath is a fire *that* **consumes** you.
33:14 [A] the godless: "Who of us can dwell with the **consuming** fire?
36:12 [A] *will have to* **eat** their own filth and drink their own urine?"
36:16 [A] every one of you *will* **eat** *from* his own vine and fig tree
37:30 [A] "This year you *will* **eat** what grows by itself, and the second
37:30 [A] third year sow and reap, plant vineyards and **eat** their fruit.
44:16 [A] over it *he* **prepares** his meal, he roasts his meat and eats his
44:19 [A] I even baked bread over its coals, I roasted meat and *I* **ate**.
49:26 [G] *I will* **make** your oppressors **eat** their own flesh; they will be
50: 9 [A] will all wear out like a garment; the moths *will* **eat** them **up**.
51: 8 [A] For the moth *will* **eat** them **up** like a garment; the worm will
51: 8 [A] up like a garment; the worm *will* **devour** them like wool.
55: 1 [A] the waters; and you who have no money, come, buy and **eat**!
55: 2 [A] Listen, listen to me, and **eat** what is good, and your soul will
55:10 [A] so that it yields seed for the sower and bread for the **eater**,
56: 9 [A] Come, all you beasts of the field, come and **devour**, all you
58:14 [G] the land and *to* **feast on** the inheritance of your father Jacob."
59: 5 [A] Whoever **eats** their eggs will die, and when one is broken,
61: 6 [A] *You will* **feed on** the wealth of nations, and in their riches
62: 9 [A] but those who harvest it *will* **eat** it and praise the LORD,
65: 4 [A] who **eat** the flesh of pigs, and whose pots hold broth of
65:13 [A] "My servants *will* **eat**, but you will go hungry; my servants
65:21 [A] dwell in them; they will plant vineyards and **eat** their fruit.
65:22 [A] build houses and others live in them, or plant and others **eat**.
65:25 [A] will feed together, and the lion *will* **eat** straw like the ox,
66:17 [A] following the one in the midst of *those who* **eat** the flesh of
Jer 2: 3 [A] all *who* **devoured** her were held guilty, and disaster overtook
2: 7 [A] I brought you into a fertile land to **eat** its fruit and rich
2:30 [A] Your sword *has* **devoured** your prophets like a ravening
3:24 [A] *have* **consumed** the fruits of our fathers' labor—their flocks
5:14 [A] in your mouth a fire and these people the wood *it* **consumes**.
5:17 [A] *They will* **devour** your harvests and food, devour your sons
5:17 [A] your harvests and food, **devour** your sons and daughters;
5:17 [A] *they will* **devour** your flocks and herds, devour your vines
5:17 [A] your flocks and herds, **devour** your vines and fig trees.
7:21 [A] to your other sacrifices and **eat** the meat *yourselves*!
8:16 [A] They have come *to* **devour** the land and everything in it,
9:15 [9:14] [G] I *will* **make** this people **eat** bitter **food** and drink
10:25 [A] For *they have* **devoured** Jacob; they have devoured him
10:25 [A] *they have* **devoured** him completely and destroyed his
12:12 [A] for the sword of the LORD *will* **devour** from one end of the
15: 3 [A] of the air and the beasts of the earth to **devour** and destroy.
15:16 [A] When your words came, *I* **ate** them; they were my joy
16: 8 [A] a house where there is feasting and sit down to **eat** and drink.
17:27 [A] in the gates of Jerusalem that *will* **consume** her fortresses.' "
19: 9 [G] *I will* **make** them **eat** the flesh of their sons and daughters,
19: 9 [A] *they will* **eat** one another's flesh during the stress of the siege
21:14 [A] I will kindle a fire in your forests *that will* **consume**
22:15 [A] and more cedar? *Did* not your father **have food** and drink?
23:15 [G] "I *will* **make** them **eat** bitter **food** and drink poisoned water,
24: 2 [C] basket had very poor figs, so bad *they could* not **be eaten**.
24: 3 [C] but the poor ones are so bad *they* cannot **be eaten**."
24: 8 [C] which are so bad *they* cannot **be eaten**,' says the LORD,
29: 5 [A] and settle down; plant gardens and **eat** what they produce.
29:17 [C] them like poor figs that are so bad *they* cannot **be eaten**.
29:28 [A] and settle down; plant gardens and **eat** what they produce.' "
30:16 [A] " 'But all *who* **devour** you will be devoured; all your
30:16 [C] " 'But all who devour you *will* **be devoured**; all your
31:29 [A] 'The fathers *have* **eaten** sour grapes, and the children's teeth
31:30 [A] whoever **eats** sour grapes—his own teeth will be set on edge.
41: 1 [A] Ahikam at Mizpah. While *they were* **eating** together there,
46:10 [A] The sword *will* **devour** till it is satisfied, till it has quenched
46:14 [A] and get ready, for the sword **devours** those around you.'
48:45 [A] *it* **burns** the foreheads of Moab, the skulls of the noisy
49:27 [A] of Damascus; *it will* **consume** the fortresses of Ben-Hadad."
50: 7 [A] Whoever found them **devoured** them; their enemies said,
50:17 [A] The first *to* **devour** him was the king of Assyria; the last to
50:32 [A] I will kindle a fire in her towns *that will* **consume** all who
51:34 [A] "Nebuchadnezzar king of Babylon *has* **devoured** us, he has
52:33 [A] and for the rest of his life **ate** regularly at the king's table.
La 2: 3 [A] He has burned in Jacob like a flaming fire *that* **consumes**
2:20 [A] *Should* women **eat** their offspring, the children they have
4: 5 [A] Those *who once* **ate** delicacies are destitute in the streets.
4:11 [A] He kindled a fire in Zion that **consumed** her foundations.
Eze 2: 8 [A] rebellious house; open your mouth and **eat** what I give you."
3: 1 [A] to me, "Son of man, **eat** what is before you, eat this scroll;

Eze 3: 1 [A] to me, "Son of man, eat what is before you, **eat** this scroll;
3: 2 [G] So I opened my mouth, and *he* **gave** me the scroll **to eat**.
3: 3 [G] **eat** this scroll I am giving you and fill your stomach with it."
3: 3 [A] So *I* **ate** it, and it tasted as sweet as honey in my mouth.
4: 9 [A] *You are to* **eat** it during the 390 days you lie on your side.
4: 10 [A] Weigh out twenty shekels of food *to* **eat** each day and eat it
4: 10 [A] twenty shekels of food to eat each day and **eat** it at set times.
4: 12 [A] **Eat** the food as you would a barley cake; bake it in the sight
4: 13 [A] "In this way the people of Israel *will* **eat** defiled food among
4: 14 [A] From my youth until now *I have* never **eaten** anything found
4: 16 [A] *The people will* **eat** rationed food in anxiety and drink
5: 10 [A] Therefore in your midst fathers *will* **eat** their children,
5: 10 [A] will eat their children, and children *will* **eat** their fathers.
7: 15 [A] and those in the city *will be* **devoured** *by* famine and plague.
12: 18 [A] "Son of man, tremble *as you* **eat** your food, and shudder in
12: 19 [A] *They will* **eat** their food in anxiety and drink their water in
15: 4 [A] as fuel and the fire **burns** both ends and chars the middle,
15: 5 [A] it be made into something useful *when* the fire *has* **burned** it
15: 7 [A] have come out of the fire, the fire *will yet* **consume** them.
16: 13 [A] *Your* **food** was fine flour, honey and olive oil.
16: 19 [G] the fine flour, olive oil and honey *I* **gave** you **to eat**—
16: 20 [A] you bore to me and sacrificed them as **food** to the idols.
18: 2 [A] " 'The fathers **eat** sour grapes, and the children's teeth are set
18: 6 [A] *He does* not **eat** at the mountain shrines or look to the idols
18: 11 [A] "*He* **eats** at the mountain shrines. He defiles his neighbor's
18: 15 [A] "*He does* not **eat** at the mountain shrines or look to the idols
19: 3 [A] He learned to tear the prey and *he* **devoured** men.
19: 6 [A] He learned to tear the prey and *he* **devoured** men.
19: 12 [A] its strong branches withered and fire **consumed** them.
19: 14 [A] spread from one of its main branches and **consumed** its fruit.
20: 47 [21:3] [A] *it will* **consume** all your trees, both green and dry.
22: 9 [A] in you are *those who* **eat** at the mountain shrines and commit
22: 25 [A] *they* **devour** people, take treasures and precious things
23: 25 [C] and those of you who are left *will* **be consumed** by fire.
24: 17 [A] part of your face or **eat** the customary food ⌊of mourners⌋."
24: 22 [A] part of your face or **eat** the customary food ⌊of mourners⌋.
25: 4 [A] among you; they *will* **eat** your fruit and drink your milk.
28: 18 [A] So I made a fire come out from you, and it **consumed** you,
33: 25 [A] Since *you* **eat** meat with the blood still in it and look to your
33: 27 [A] in the country I will give to the wild animals to *be* **devoured**,
34: 3 [A] *You* **eat** the curds, clothe yourselves with the wool
34: 28 [A] plundered by the nations, nor *will* wild animals **devour** them.
36: 13 [A] "You **devour** men and deprive your nation of its children,"
36: 14 [A] therefore *you will* no longer **devour** men or make your
39: 17 [A] of Israel. *There you will* **eat** flesh and drink blood.
39: 18 [A] *You will* **eat** the flesh of mighty men and drink the blood of
39: 19 [A] *you will* **eat** fat till you are glutted and drink blood till you
42: 5 [A] for the galleries **took** more **space** from them than from the
42: 13 [A] where the priests who approach the LORD *will* **eat** the most
43: 8 [A] their detestable practices. So *I* **destroyed** them in my anger.
44: 3 [A] sit inside the gateway to **eat** in the presence of the LORD.
44: 29 [A] They *will* **eat** the grain offerings, the sin offerings
44: 31 [A] The priests *must* not **eat** anything, bird or animal,
45: 21 [C] during which you *shall* **eat** bread made without yeast.
Da 1: 12 [A] Give us nothing but vegetables *to* **eat** and water to drink.
1: 13 [A] compare our appearance with that of the young men who **eat**
1: 15 [A] better nourished than any of the young men who **ate** the royal
10: 3 [A] *I* **ate** no choice food; no meat or wine touched my lips; and I
11: 26 [A] *Those who* **eat** *from* the king's provisions will try to destroy
Hos 2: 12 [2:14] [A] them a thicket, and wild animals *will* **devour** them.
4: 8 [A] *They* **feed on** the sins of my people and relish their
4: 10 [A] "*They will* **eat** but not have enough; they will engage in
5: 7 [A] Now their New Moon festivals *will* **devour** them and their
7: 7 [A] All of them are hot as an oven; *they* **devour** their rulers.
7: 9 [A] Foreigners **sap** his strength, but he does not realize it. His
8: 13 [A] They offer sacrifices given to me and *they* **eat** the meat,
8: 14 [A] I will send fire upon their cities *that will* **consume** their
9: 3 [A] will return to Egypt and **eat** unclean food in Assyria.
9: 4 [A] like the bread of mourners; all *who* **eat** them will be unclean.
10: 13 [A] you have reaped evil, *you have* **eaten** the fruit of deception.
11: 4 [G] I lifted the yoke from their neck and bent down *to* **feed** them.
11: 6 [A] destroy the bars of their gates and **put an end** to their plans.
13: 8 [A] Like a lion *I will* **devour** them; a wild animal will tear them
Joel 1: 4 [A] What the locust swarm has left the great locusts *have* **eaten**;
1: 4 [A] the great locusts have left the young locusts *have* **eaten**;
1: 4 [A] what the young locusts have left other locusts *have* **eaten**.
1: 19 [A] for fire *has* **devoured** the open pastures and flames have
1: 20 [A] water have dried up and fire *has* **devoured** the open pastures.
2: 3 [A] Before them fire **devours**, behind them a flame blazes.
2: 5 [A] like a crackling fire **consuming** stubble, like a mighty army
2: 25 [A] "I will repay you for the years the locusts *have* **eaten**—
2: 26 [A] *You will* **have plenty to eat** [+430], until you are full,
2: 26 [A] *You will* **have plenty to eat** [+430], until you are full,
Am 1: 4 [A] I will send fire upon the house of Hazael *that will* **consume**
1: 7 [A] I will send fire upon the walls of Gaza *that will* **consume** her
1: 10 [A] I will send fire upon the walls of Tyre *that will* **consume** her
1: 12 [A] I will send fire upon Teman *that will* **consume** the fortresses
1: 14 [A] I will set fire to the walls of Rabbah *that will* **consume** her
2: 2 [A] I will send fire upon Moab *that will* **consume** the fortresses
2: 5 [A] I will send fire upon Judah *that will* **consume** the fortresses
4: 9 [A] Locusts **devoured** your fig and olive trees, yet you have not
5: 6 [A] *it will* **devour**, and Bethel will have no one to quench it.
6: 4 [A] your couches. *You* **dine on** choice lambs and fattened calves.
7: 2 [A] When *they had* **stripped** the land **clean**, I cried out,
7: 4 [A] by fire; *it* **dried up** the great deep and devoured the land.
7: 4 [A] by fire; it dried up the great deep and **devoured** the land.
7: 12 [A] **Earn** your bread there and do your prophesying there.
9: 14 [A] drink their wine; they will make gardens and **eat** their fruit.
Ob 1: 18 [A] will be stubble, and they will set it on fire and **consume** it.
Mic 3: 3 [A] who **eat** my people's flesh, strip off their skin and break their
6: 14 [A] You *will* **eat** but not be satisfied; your stomach will still be
7: 1 [A] there is no cluster of grapes to **eat**, none of the early figs that
Na 1: 10 [E] from their wine; *they will* **be consumed** like dry stubble.
2: 13 [2:14] [A] and the sword *will* **devour** your young lions.
3: 12 [A] they are shaken, the figs fall into the mouth of the **eater**.
3: 13 [A] are wide open to your enemies; fire *has* **consumed** their bars.
3: 15 [A] There the fire *will* **devour** you; the sword will cut you down
3: 15 [A] will cut you down and, like grasshoppers, **consume** you.
Hab 1: 8 [A] come from afar. They fly like a vulture swooping to **devour**;
3: 14 [A] gloating as though about to **devour** the wretched who were
Zep 1: 18 [C] In the fire of his jealousy the whole world *will* **be consumed**,
3: 8 [C] The whole world *will* **be consumed** by the fire of my jealous
Hag 1: 6 [A] *You* **eat**, but never have enough. You drink, but never have
Zec 7: 6 [A] when *you were* **eating** and drinking, were you not just
7: 6 [A] *were* you not *just* **feasting** [+2256+9272] *for* yourselves?
9: 4 [C] her power on the sea, and she *will* **be consumed** by fire.
9: 15 [A] *They will* **destroy** and overcome with slingstones. They will
11: 1 [A] your doors, O Lebanon, so that fire *may* **devour** your cedars!
11: 9 [A] *Let* those who are left **eat** one another's flesh."
11: 16 [A] or feed the healthy, but *will* **eat** the meat of the choice sheep,
12: 6 [A] *They will* **consume** right and left all the surrounding
Mal 3: 11 [A] I will prevent **pests** from devouring your crops, and the vines

431 אֹכֶל *'ōkel*, n.m. [39] [√ 430]

food [36], it[s] [1], mealtime [+2021+6961] [1], prey [1]

Ge 14: 11 seized all the goods of Sodom and Gomorrah and all their **food**;
41: 35 They should collect all the **food** *of* these good years that are
41: 35 under the authority of Pharaoh, to be kept in the cities for **food**.
41: 36 This **food** should be held in reserve for the country, to be used
41: 48 Joseph collected all the **food** produced *in* those seven years of
41: 48 those seven years of abundance in Egypt and stored **it**[s] in the cities.
41: 48 In each city he put the **food** *grown in* the fields surrounding it.
42: 7 he asked. "From the land of Canaan," they replied, "to buy **food**."
42: 10 my lord," they answered. "Your servants have come to buy **food**.
43: 2 their father said to them, "Go back and buy us a little more **food**."
43: 4 our brother along with us, we will go down and buy **food** for you.
43: 20 they said, "we came down here the first time to buy **food**.
43: 22 We have also brought additional silver with us to buy **food**.
44: 1 "Fill the men's sacks with as much **food** as they can carry,
44: 25 "Then our father said, 'Go back and buy a little more **food**.'
47: 24 as **food** *for* yourselves and your households and your children."
Lev 11: 34 Any **food** that could be eaten but has water on it from such a pot is
25: 37 must not lend him money at interest or sell him **food** at a profit.
Dt 2: 6 You are to pay them in silver for the **food** you eat and the water
2: 28 Sell us **food** to eat and water to drink for their price in silver.
23: 19 [23:20] whether on money or **food** or anything else that may earn
Ru 2: 14 At **mealtime** [+2021+6961] Boaz said to her, "Come over here.
Job 9: 26 like boats of papyrus, like eagles swooping down on their **prey**.
12: 11 Does not the ear test words as the tongue tastes **food**?
36: 31 is the way he governs the nations and provides **food** in abundance.
38: 41 when its young cry out to God and wander about for lack of **food**?
39: 29 From there he seeks out his **food**; his eyes detect it from afar.
Ps 78: 18 They willfully put God to the test by demanding the **food** they
78: 30 before they turned from the **food** they craved, even while it was
104: 21 The lions roar for their prey and seek their **food** from God.
104: 27 These all look to you to give them their **food** at the proper time.
107: 18 They loathed all **food** and drew near the gates of death.
145: 15 of all look to you, and you give them their **food** at the proper time.
Pr 13: 23 A poor man's field may produce abundant **food**, but injustice
La 1: 11 they barter their treasures for **food** to keep themselves alive.
1: 19 my elders perished in the city while they searched for **food** to keep
Joel 1: 16 Has not the **food** been cut off before our very eyes—joy
Hab 3: 17 though the olive crop fails and the fields produce no **food**,
Mal 1: 12 the Lord's table, 'It is defiled,' and of its **food**, 'It is contemptible.'

432 אֻכָל 'ukāl, n.pr.m. [1] [√ 3983]

Ucal [1]

Pr 30: 1 an oracle: This man declared to Ithiel, to Ithiel and to **Ucal**:

433 אָכְלָה 'oklâ, n.f. [18] [√ 430]

food [11], fuel [3], devour [2], eat [2]

Ge 1:29 every tree that has fruit with seed in it. They will be yours for **food**.
1:30 that has the breath of life in it—I give every green plant for **food**."
6:21 that is to be eaten and store it away as **food** for you and for them."
9: 3 Everything that lives and moves will be **food** for you. Just as I
Ex 16:15 said to them, "It is the bread the LORD has given you to **eat**.
Lev 11:39 " 'If an animal that you are allowed to **eat** dies, anyone who
25: 6 Whatever the land yields during the sabbath year will be **food** for
Jer 12: 9 Go and gather all the wild beasts; bring them to **devour**.
Eze 15: 4 after it is thrown on the fire as **fuel** and the fire burns both ends
15: 6 wood of the vine among the trees of the forest as **fuel** for the fire,
21:32 [21:37] You will be **fuel** for the fire, your blood will be shed in
23:37 sacrificed their children, whom they bore to me, as **food** for them.
29: 5 I will give you as **food** to the beasts of the earth and the birds of
34: 5 when they were scattered they became **food** for all the wild
34: 8 has been plundered and has become **food** for all the wild animals,
34:10 my flock from their mouths, and it will no longer be **food** for them.
35:12 have been laid waste and have been given over to us to **devour**."
39: 4 I will give you as **food** to all kinds of carrion birds and to the wild

434 אָכֵן 'ākēn¹, adv. [18] [√ 421 + 2176]

surely [7], but [4], yet [2], *untranslated* [1], actually [1], because surely [1], how [1], truly [1]

Ge 28:16 he thought, "**Surely** the LORD is in this place, and I was not
Ex 2:14 and thought, **[NIE]** "What I did must have become known."
1Sa 15:32 him confidently, thinking, "**Surely** the bitterness of death is past."
1Ki 11: 2 **because** they will **surely** turn your hearts after their gods."
Job 32: 8 **But** it is the spirit in a man, the breath of the Almighty, that gives
Ps 31:22 [31:23] **Yet** you heard my cry for mercy when I called to you for
66:19 but God has **surely** listened and heard my voice in prayer.
82: 7 **But** you will die like mere men; you will fall like every other
Isa 40: 7 breath of the LORD blows on them. **Surely** the people are grass.
45:15 **Truly** you are a God who hides himself, O God and Savior of
49: 4 **Yet** what is due me is in the LORD's hand, and my reward is with
53: 4 **Surely** he took up our infirmities and carried our sorrows,
Jer 3:20 **But** like a woman unfaithful to her husband, so you have been
3:23 **Surely** the ⌊idolatrous⌋ commotion on the hills and mountains is a
3:23 **surely** in the LORD our God is the salvation of Israel.
4:10 **how** completely you have deceived this people and Jerusalem by
8: 8 when **actually** the lying pen of the scribes has handled it falsely?
Zep 3: 7 upon her. **But** they were still eager to act corruptly in all they did.

435 ²אָכֵן 'ākēn², adv. Not used in NIV/BHS [√ 421 + 2176]

436 אָכַף 'ākap, v. [1] [→ 437]

drives on [1]

Pr 16:26 [A] laborer's appetite works for him; his hunger **drives** him **on**.

437 אֶכֶף 'ekep, n.m. [1] [√ 436]

hand [1]

Job 33: 7 of me should alarm you, nor should my **hand** be heavy upon you.

438 אִכָּר 'ikkār, n.m. [7]

farmers [4], farmer [1], people [1], work fields [1]

2Ch 26:10 He had **people** working his fields and vineyards in the hills
Isa 61: 5 your flocks; foreigners will **work** your **fields** and vineyards.
Jer 14: 4 rain in the land; the **farmers** are dismayed and cover their heads.
31:24 its towns—**farmers** and those who move about with their flocks.
51:23 I shatter shepherd and flock, with you I shatter **farmer** and oxen,
Joel 1:11 Despair, you **farmers**, wail, you vine growers; grieve for the wheat
Am 5:16 The **farmers** will be summoned to weep and the mourners to wail.

439 אַכְשָׁף 'akšāp, n.pr.loc. [3] [√ 4175]

Acshaph [3]

Jos 11: 1 to Jobab king of Madon, to the kings of Shimron and **Acshaph**,
12:20 the king of Shimron Meron one the king of **Acshaph** one
19:25 Their territory included: Helkath, Hali, Beten, **Acshaph**,

440 ¹אַל 'al¹, adv.neg. [730] [→ Ar 10031] See Select Index

not [511], don't [64], no [52], *untranslated* [44], nor [+2256] [14], never [11], or [5], nor [3], without [3], cannot [2], from [2], neither [2], never [+4200+6409] [2], nothing [2], stop [2], abstain from sexual relations [+448+851+5602] [1], always [+2893] [1], better than [1], beware [+9068] [1], forget [+2349] [1], immortality [+4638] [1], instead of [1], neither [+2256] [1], never [+6524] [1], or [+2256] [1], overlook [+448+448+448+7155] [1]

441 ²אַל 'al², l.art. Not used in NIV/BHS

442 ¹אֵל 'ēl¹, n.m. Not used in NIV/BHS [√ 380]

443 ²אֵל 'ēl², n.m. Not used in NIV/BHS [√ 381; cf. 380]

444 ³אֵל 'ēl³, n.[m.]. Not used in NIV/BHS [√ 382; cf. 380]

445 ⁴אֵל 'ēl⁴, n.m. [5] [√ 446]

power [+3338] [3], powerless [+401+3338+4200] [1], powerless [+401+4200] [1]

Ge 31:29 I have the **power** [+3338] to harm you; but last night the God of
Dt 28:32 eyes watching for them day after day, **powerless** [+401+4200]
Ne 5: 5 but we are **powerless** [+401+3338+4200], because our fields and
Pr 3:27 from those who deserve it, when it is in your **power** [+3338] to act.
Mic 2: 1 light they carry it out because it is in their **power** [+3338] to do it.

446 ⁵אֵל 'ēl⁵, n.m. [236 / 238] [→ 445, 466, 468; cf. 212?; *also used with compound proper names*]

God [218], God's [5], mighty [4], gods [3], Mighty One [3], great [1], heavenly beings [+1201] [1], his[s] [1], mighty [+1201] [1], rulers [1]

Ge 14:18 brought out bread and wine. He was priest of **God** Most High,
14:19 saying, "Blessed be Abram by **God** Most High, Creator of heaven
14:20 blessed be **God** Most High, who delivered your enemies into your
14:22 **God** Most High, Creator of heaven and earth, and have taken an
16:13 "You are the **God** who sees me," for she said, "I have now seen the
17: 1 the LORD appeared to him and said, "I am **God** Almighty;
21:33 and there he called upon the name of the LORD, the Eternal **God**.
28: 3 May **God** Almighty bless you and make you fruitful and increase
31:13 I am the **God** *of* Bethel, where you anointed a pillar and where you
35: 1 "Go up to Bethel and settle there, and build an altar there to **God**,
35: 3 let us go up to Bethel, where I will build an altar to **God**,
35:11 God said to him, "I am **God** Almighty; be fruitful and increase in
43:14 may **God** Almighty grant you mercy before the man so that he will
46: 3 "I am **God**, the God of your father," he said. "Do not be afraid to
48: 3 "**God** Almighty appeared to me at Luz in the land of Canaan,
49:25 because of your father's **God**, who helps you, because of the
Ex 6: 3 I appeared to Abraham, to Isaac and to Jacob as **God** Almighty,
15: 2 He is my **God**, and I will praise him, my father's God, and I will
15:11 "Who among the **gods** is like you, O LORD? Who is like you—
20: 5 for I, the LORD your God, am a jealous **God**, punishing the
34: 6 the LORD, the compassionate and gracious **God**, slow to anger,
34:14 Do not worship any other **god**, for the LORD, whose name is
34:14 for the LORD, whose name is Jealous, is a jealous **God**.
Nu 12:13 So Moses cried out to the LORD, "O **God**, please heal her!"
16:22 But Moses and Aaron fell facedown and cried out, "O **God**,
23: 8 How can I curse those whom **God** has not cursed? How can I
23:19 **God** is not a man, that he should lie, nor a son of man, that he
23:22 **God** brought them out of Egypt; they have the strength of a wild
23:23 It will now be said of Jacob and of Israel, 'See what **God** has done!'
24: 4 the oracle of one who hears the words of **God**, who sees a vision
24: 8 "**God** brought them out of Egypt; they have the strength of a wild
24:16 the oracle of one who hears the words of **God**, who has knowledge
24:23 Then he uttered his oracle: "Ah, who can live when **God** does this?
Dt 3:24 For what **god** is there in heaven or on earth who can do the deeds
4:24 For the LORD your God is a consuming fire, a jealous **God**.
4:31 For the LORD your God is a merciful **God**; he will not abandon
5: 9 for I, the LORD your God, am a jealous **God**, punishing the
6:15 is among you, is a jealous **God** and his anger will burn against you,
7: 9 he is the faithful **God**, keeping his covenant of love to a thousand
7:21 your God, who is among you, is a great and awesome **God**.
10:17 of gods and Lord of lords, the great **God**, mighty and awesome,
32: 4 A faithful **God** who does no wrong, upright and just is he.
32:12 The LORD alone led him; no foreign **god** was with him.
32:18 who fathered you; you forgot the **God** who gave you birth.
32:21 They made me jealous by what is no **god** and angered me with
33:26 "There is no one like the **God** *of* Jeshurun, who rides on the
Jos 3:10 This is how you will know that the living **God** is among you
22:22 "The **Mighty One**, God, the LORD! The Mighty One, God,
22:22 the LORD! The **Mighty One**, God, the LORD! He knows!
24:19 He is a holy God; he is a jealous **God**. He will not forgive your
1Sa 2: 3 for the LORD is a **God** who knows, and by him deeds are
2Sa 22:31 "As for **God**, his way is perfect; the word of the LORD is
22:32 For who is **God** besides the LORD? And who is the Rock except
22:33 It is **God** who arms me with strength and makes my way perfect.
22:48 He is the **God** who avenges me, who puts the nations under me,
23: 5 "Is not my house right with **God**? Has he not made with me an

Ne 1: 5 "O LORD, God of heaven, the great and awesome **God**,
9: 31 or abandon them, for you are a gracious and merciful **God**.
9: 32 "Now therefore, O our God, the great, mighty and awesome **God**,
Job 5: 8 "But if it were I, I would appeal to **God**; I would lay my cause
8: 3 Does **God** pervert justice? Does the Almighty pervert what is
8: 5 But if you will look to **God** and plead with the Almighty,
8: 13 Such is the destiny of all who forget **God**; so perishes the hope of
8: 20 "Surely **God** does not reject a blameless man or strengthen the
9: 2 that this is true. But how can a mortal be righteous before **God**?
12: 6 are undisturbed, and those who provoke **God** are secure—
13: 3 I desire to speak to the Almighty and to argue my case with **God**.
13: 7 Will you speak wickedly on **God's** behalf? Will you speak
13: 8 Will you show him partiality? Will you argue the case for **God**?
13: 20 two things, O **God**, [BHS 440] and then I will not hide from you:
15: 4 But you even undermine piety and hinder devotion to **God**.
15: 11 Are **God's** consolations not enough for you, words spoken gently
15: 13 so that you vent your rage against **God** and pour out such words
15: 25 because he shakes his fist at **God** and vaunts himself against the
16: 11 **God** has turned me over to evil men and thrown me into the
18: 21 of an evil man; such is the place of one who knows not **God**."
19: 22 Why do you pursue me as **God** does? Will you never get enough of
20: 15 riches he swallowed; **God** will make his stomach vomit them up.
20: 29 God allots the wicked, the heritage appointed for them by **God**."
21: 14 Yet they say to **God**, 'Leave us alone! We have no desire to know
21: 22 "Can anyone teach knowledge to **God**, since he judges even the
22: 2 "Can a man be of benefit to **God**? Can even a wise man benefit
22: 13 Yet you say, 'What does **God** know? Does he judge through such
22: 17 They said to **God**, 'Leave us alone! What can the Almighty do to
23: 16 **God** has made my heart faint; the Almighty has terrified me.
25: 4 How then can a man be righteous before **God**? How can one born
27: 2 "As surely as **God** lives, who has denied me justice, the Almighty,
27: 9 Does **God** listen to his cry when distress comes upon him?
27: 11 "I will teach you about the power of **God**; the ways of the
27: 13 "Here is the fate **God** allots to the wicked, the heritage a ruthless
31: 14 what will I do when **God** confronts me? What will I answer when
31: 23 For I dreaded destruction from **God**, and for fear of his splendor I
31: 28 sins to be judged, for I would have been unfaithful to **God** on high.
32: 13 Do not say, 'We have found wisdom; let **God** refute him, not man.'
33: 4 The Spirit of **God** has made me; the breath of the Almighty gives
33: 6 I am just like you before **God**; I too have been taken from clay.
33: 14 For **God** does speak—now one way, now another—though man
33: 29 "**God** does all these things to a man—twice, even three times—
34: 5 "Job says, 'I am innocent, but **God** denies me justice.
34: 10 Far be it from **God** to do evil, from the Almighty to do wrong.
34: 12 It is unthinkable that **God** would do wrong, that the Almighty
34: 23 **God** has no need to examine men further, that they should come
34: 31 "Suppose a man says to **God**, 'I am guilty but will offend no more.
34: 37 claps his hands among us and multiplies his words against **God**."
35: 2 "Do you think this is just? You say, 'I will be cleared by **God**.'
35: 13 Indeed, **God** does not listen to their empty plea; the Almighty pays
36: 5 "**God** is mighty, but does not despise men; he is mighty, and firm
36: 22 "**God** is exalted in his power. Who is a teacher like him?
36: 26 How great is **God**—beyond our understanding! The number of his
37: 5 **God's** voice thunders in marvelous ways; he does great things
37: 10 The breath of **God** produces ice, and the broad waters become
37: 14 "Listen to this, Job; stop and consider **God's** wonders.
38: 41 Who provides food for the raven when its young cry out to **God**
40: 9 Do you have an arm like **God's**, and can your voice thunder like
40: 19 He ranks first among the works of **God**, yet his Maker can
41: 25 [41:17] When he rises up, the **mighty** are terrified; they retreat
Ps 5: 4 [5:5] You are not a **God** who takes pleasure in evil; with you the
7: 6 [7:7] the rage of my enemies. Awake, my **God**; decree justice.
7: 11 [7:12] righteous judge, a **God** who expresses his wrath every day.
10: 11 He says to himself, "**God** has forgotten; he covers his face
10: 12 Arise, LORD! Lift up your hand, O **God**. Do not forget the
16: 1 Keep me safe, O **God**, for in you I take refuge.
17: 6 I call on you, O **God**, for you will answer me; give ear to me
18: 2 [18:3] my deliverer; my **God** is my rock, in whom I take refuge.
18: 30 [18:31] As for **God**, his way is perfect; the word of the LORD is
18: 32 [18:33] It is **God** who arms me with strength and makes my way
18: 47 [18:48] He is the **God** who avenges me, who subdues nations
19: 1 [19:2] The heavens declare the glory of **God**; the skies proclaim
22: 1 [22:2] My **God**, my God, why have you forsaken me? Why are
22: 1 [22:2] My God, my **God**, why have you forsaken me? Why are
22: 10 [22:11] from my mother's womb you have been my **God**.
29: 1 Ascribe to the LORD, O **mighty** [+1201] *ones*, ascribe to the
29: 3 the **God** *of* glory thunders, the LORD thunders over the mighty
31: 5 [31:6] commit my spirit; redeem me, O LORD, the **God** *of* truth.
36: 6 [36:7] Your righteousness is like the **mighty** mountains,
42: 2 [42:3] My soul thirsts for God, for the living **God**. When can I go
42: 8 [42:9] night his song is with me—a prayer to the **God** *of* my life.
42: 9 [42:10] I say to **God** my Rock, "Why have you forgotten me?
43: 4 Then will I go to the altar of God, to **God**, my joy and my delight.
44: 20 [44:21] name of our God or spread out our hands to a foreign **god**,
50: 1 The **Mighty One**, God, the LORD, speaks and summons the earth
52: 1 [52:3] all day long, you who are a disgrace in the eyes of **God**?
52: 5 [52:7] Surely **God** will bring you down to everlasting ruin: He
55: 19 [55:20] **God**, who is enthroned forever, will hear them and afflict
57: 2 [57:3] I cry out to God Most High, to **God**, who fulfills his
58: 1 [58:2] Do you **rulers** [BHS 521] indeed speak justly? Do you
63: 1 [63:2] O God, you are my **God**, earnestly I seek you; my soul
68: 19 [68:20] Praise be to the Lord, to **God** our Savior, who daily bears
68: 20 [68:21] Our **God** is a God who saves; from the Sovereign LORD
68: 20 [68:21] Our God is a **God** who saves; from the Sovereign LORD
68: 24 [68:25] the procession of my **God** and King into the sanctuary.
68: 35 [68:36] the **God** *of* Israel gives power and strength to his people.
73: 11 They say, "How can **God** know? Does the Most High have
73: 17 till I entered the sanctuary of **God**; then I understood their final
74: 8 They burned every place where **God** was worshiped in the land.
77: 9 [77:10] Has **God** forgotten to be merciful? Has he in anger
77: 13 [77:14] O God, are holy. What **god** is so great as our God?
77: 14 [77:15] You are the **God** who performs miracles; you display
78: 7 and would not forget **his**ˢ deeds but would keep his commands.
78: 8 and rebellious generation, whose hearts were not loyal to **God**,
78: 18 They willfully put **God** to the test by demanding the food they
78: 19 spoke against God, saying, "Can **God** spread a table in the desert?
78: 34 Whenever **God** slew them, they would seek him; they eagerly
78: 35 that God was their Rock, that **God** Most High was their Redeemer.
78: 41 Again and again they put **God** to the test; they vexed the Holy One
80: 10 [80:11] with its shade, the **mighty** cedars with its branches.
81: 9 [81:10] You shall have no foreign **god** among you; you shall not
81: 9 [81:10] god among you; you shall not bow down to an alien **god**.
82: 1 God presides in the **great** assembly; he gives judgment among the
83: 1 [83:2] O God, do not keep silent; be not quiet, O **God**, be not still.
84: 2 [84:3] my heart and my flesh cry out for the living **God**.
85: 8 [85:9] I will listen to what **God** the LORD will say; he promises
86: 15 you, O Lord, are a compassionate and gracious **God**, slow to anger,
89: 6 [89:7] is like the LORD among the **heavenly** [+1201] **beings**?
89: 7 [89:8] In the council of the holy ones **God** is greatly feared; he is
89: 26 [89:27] to me, 'You are my Father, my **God**, the Rock my Savior.'
90: 2 and the world, from everlasting to everlasting you are **God**.
94: 1 O LORD, the **God** *who* avenges, O God who avenges,
94: 1 the God who avenges, O **God** *who* avenges, shine forth.
95: 3 For the LORD is the great **God**, the great King above all gods.
99: 8 you were to Israel a forgiving **God**, though you punished their
102: 24 [102:25] "Do not take me away, O my **God**, in the midst of my
104: 21 The lions roar for their prey and seek their food from **God**.
106: 14 gave in to their craving; in the wasteland they put **God** to the test.
106: 21 They forgot the **God** who saved them, who had done great things
107: 11 for they had rebelled against the words of **God** and despised the
118: 27 The LORD is **God**, and he has made his light shine upon us.
118: 28 You are my **God**, and I will give you thanks; you are my God,
136: 26 Give thanks to the **God** *of* heaven. *His love endures*
139: 17 How precious to me are your thoughts, O **God**! How vast is the
139: 23 Search me, O **God**, and know my heart; test me and know my
140: 6 [140:7] O LORD, I say to you, "You are my **God**." Hear,
146: 5 Blessed is he whose help is the **God** *of* Jacob, whose hope is in the
149: 6 May the praise of **God** be in their mouths and a double-edged
150: 1 Praise **God** in his sanctuary; praise him in his mighty heavens.
Isa 5: 16 and the holy **God** will show himself holy by his righteousness.
8: 10 propose your plan, but it will not stand, for **God** is with us.
9: 6 [9:5] Mighty **God**, Everlasting Father, Prince of Peace.
10: 21 will return, a remnant of Jacob will return to the Mighty **God**.
12: 2 Surely **God** is my salvation; I will trust and not be afraid. The
14: 13 ascend to heaven; I will raise my throne above the stars of **God**;
31: 3 But the Egyptians are men and not **God**; their horses are flesh
40: 18 To whom, then, will you compare **God**? What image will you
42: 5 This is what **God** the LORD says—he who created the heavens
43: 10 Before me no **god** was formed, nor will there be one after me.
43: 12 You are my witnesses," declares the LORD, "that I am **God**.
44: 10 Who shapes a **god** and casts an idol, which can profit him nothing?
44: 15 But he also fashions a **god** and worships it; he makes an idol
44: 17 From the rest he makes a **god**, his idol; he bows down to it
44: 17 and worships. He prays to it and says, "Save me; you are my **god**."
45: 14 before you and plead with you, saying, 'Surely **God** is with you,
45: 15 Truly you are a **God** who hides himself, O God and Savior of
45: 20 who carry about idols of wood, who pray to **gods** that cannot save.
45: 21 And there is no God apart from me, a righteous **God** and a Savior;
45: 22 all you ends of the earth; for I am **God**, and there is no other.
46: 6 they hire a goldsmith to make it into a **god**, and they bow down
46: 9 I am **God**, and there is no other; I am God, and there is none like
Jer 32: 18 O great and powerful **God**, whose name is the LORD Almighty,
51: 56 For the LORD is a **God** *of* retribution; he will repay in full.
La 3: 41 Let us lift up our hearts and our hands to **God** in heaven, and say:
Eze 10: 5 as the outer court, like the voice of **God** Almighty when he speaks.
28: 2 " 'In the pride of your heart you say, "I am a **god**; I sit on the
28: 2 you are a man and not a **god**, though you think you are as wise as a
28: 9 You will be but a man, not a **god**, in the hands of those who slay

Eze 32:21 From within the grave the **mighty** leaders will say of Egypt
Da 9: 4 "O Lord, the great and awesome **God**, who keeps his covenant of
11:36 He will exalt and magnify himself above every **god** and will say
11:36 every god and will say unheard-of things against the **God** *of* gods.
11:36 every god and will say unheard-of things against the God of **gods**.
Hos 1:10 [2:1] not my people,' they will be called 'sons of the living **God**.'
11: 9 For I am **God**, and not man—the Holy One among you.
11:12 [12:1] Judah is unruly against **God**, even against the faithful Holy
Jnh 4: 2 I knew that you are a gracious and compassionate **God**, slow to
Mic 7:18 Who is a **God** like you, who pardons sin and forgives the
Na 1: 2 The LORD is a jealous and avenging **God**; the LORD takes
Mal 1: 9 "Now implore **God** to be gracious to us. With such offerings from
2:10 Have we not all one Father? Did not one **God** create us? Why do
2:11 the LORD loves, by marrying the daughter of a foreign **god**.

447 [6]אֵל ***'ēl***[6], pr.pl.m. & f. [9] [→ 187, 465; Ar 10032]

these [7], those [2]

Ge 19: 8 don't do anything to **these** men, for they have come under the
19:25 Thus he overthrew **those** cities and the entire plain, including all
26: 3 For to you and your descendants I will give all **these** lands
26: 4 numerous as the stars in the sky and will give them all **these** lands,
Lev 18:27 for all **these** things were done by the people who lived in the land
Dt 4:42 He could flee into one of **these** cities and save his life.
7:22 The LORD your God will drive out **those** nations before you,
19:11 assaults and kills him, and then flees to one of **these** cities,
1Ch 20: 8 **These** were descendants of Rapha in Gath, and they fell at the

448 אֶל ***'el***, pp. [5514 / 5513] [→ 492, 493] See Select Index

to [3052], *untranslated* [1166], into [160], against [128], on [114], in [102], at [91], for [74], toward [57], with [51], enter [+995] [36], before [30], over [23], upon [20], of [18], concerning [17], entered [+995] [17], about [16], reached [+995] [13], among [12], by [12], into [+9348] [11], around [10], lay with [+995] [7], near [7], because of [6], sleep with [+995] [6], enters [+995] [5], slept with [+995] [5], along [4], arrived [+995] [4], attack [+6590] [4], attack [4], in front of [+7156] [4], lie with [+995] [4], after [3], as for [3], at [+4578] [3], attack [+995] [3], decorated [3], facedown [+7156] [3], facing [+7156] [3], from [3], in front of [+4578] [3], straight ahead [+6298+7156] [3], together [+285+285] [3], up to [3], wherever [+889+3972] [3], above [+1068] [2], above [2], all the way to [2], along with [2], approaches [+995] [2], be buried [+665+7700] [2], beside [2], down to [2], faced [+7156] [2], facing each other [+4691+4691] [2], fall in [+6015] [2], hands together [+4090+4090] [2], in addition to [2], in front of [2], include [2], inside [+9348] [2], into presence [2], next to [+3338] [2], next to [+6298] [2], on [+4578] [2], onto [2], received [+995] [2], together [+295+851] [2], under [2], abstain from sexual relations [+440+851+5602] [1], abutted [1], according to [1], across [1], adjoining [+7156] [1], among [+9348] [1], among yourselves [+278+408] [1], and [1], approached [+995] [1], arrive [+995] [1], as far as [+4578] [1], as far as [1], as [1], at the sight of [1], ate [+995+7931] [1], attack [+7756] [1], attacked [+7756] [1], attacking [+6590] [1], attentive to [1], away [+2021+2025+2575] [1], because [1], befall [+628] [1], before [+7156] [1], belonged to [+2118] [1], belonged to [1], belongs to [1], beside [+3338] [1], bordering [1], both and [1], buried [+995+7700] [1], call to mind [+4213+8740] [1], care [+4213+8492] [1], care about [+4213+8492] [1], checked on [+8938] [1], committed adultery with [+995] [1], concerned about [+4213+8492] [1], concerned for [1], consult [+2143] [1], consult [1], counting on [+906+5883+5951] [1], covered [1], decorated with [1], definitely [+3922] [1], did the same[s] [+285+285+2489] [1], done so[s] [+995+7931] [1], during [1], entered [+6073] [1], entering [+995] [1], entrusted to [+3338] [1], every kind [+2385+2385+4946] [1], faced forward [+4578+7156] [1], faced [1], filled with gladness [+1637+8524] [1], find [+995] [1], fit for [1], fixed on [1], follow [+3338] [1], for the sake of [1], from [+7156] [1], go sleep with [+995] [1], guest [+995+1074] [1], have on hand [+3338+9393] [1], have [1], here [1], impressed [1], in accordance with [1], in charge of [1], in front of [+4578+7156] [1], in the front line [+4578+7156] [1], in vain [+2855] [1], inherit [+2118] [1], inquire of [+2011] [1], inquire of [+7928] [1], inquired of [+606] [1], inside [+1074+2021] [1], inside [1], into [+7163] [1], invade [+995] [1], invaded [+6590] [1], invaded [+995] [1], invader [+995] [1], join [1], joining [1], keep away [+3870+7928] [1], lie with [+7928] [1], listened attentively to [+265] [1], look in the face [+5951+7156] [1], lusted after [+6311] [1], lying on [1], lying with [+995] [1], make turn [+906+5989] [1], married [+995] [1], meet [+7156] [1], meet [1], occupied [+6641] [1], occupy [+995] [1], on account of [1], on the faces of [1], on the side of [1], onto [+9348] [1], opposite [+7156] [1], opposite [1], out of [1], overboard [+2021+3542] [1], overruled [+2616+6584] [1], overtook [+995] [1], participate in [+2118] [1], reach [+995] [1], reached [+6590] [1], reaches [+995] [1], reflected on [+906+4213+5989] [1], rejoined [+2143] [1], replace [+995+9393] [1], right in [1], see [+6524] [1], showed concern for [+7155] [1], sleeps with [+995] [1], southern [+5582+6991] [1], southward [+2021+3545] [1], square [+752+8062+8063] [1], square [+752+8063] [1], stops to think [+4213+8740] [1], surmounted by [1], that [1], their [+2157] [1], thought [+606+3276] [1], to [+4578] [1], to [+9348] [1], to within [1], took [+995] [1], touched [+995] [1], toward [+2006] [1], toward [+5790] [1], toward [+7156] [1], use [+2143] [1], went in to spend the night with [+995] [1]

449 אֵל אֱלֹהֵי יִשְׂרָאֵל ***'ēl 'ᵉlōhê yiśrā'ēl***, n.pr.loc. [1] [√ 446 + 466 + 3776]

El Elohe Israel [1]

Ge 33:20 There he set up an altar and called it **El Elohe Israel**.

450 אֵל בֵּית־אֵל ***'ēl bêt-'ēl***, n.pr.loc. [1] [√ 446 + 1074 + 446]

El Bethel [1]

Ge 35: 7 There he built an altar, and he called the place **El Bethel**, because

451 אֵל בְּרִית ***'ēl bᵉrît***, n.pr.[loc.?]. [1] [√ 446 + 1382]

El-Berith [1]

Jdg 9:46 of Shechem went into the stronghold of the temple of **El-Berith**.

452 אֵלָא ***'ēlā'***, n.pr.m. [1] [cf. 462]

Ela [1]

1Ki 4:18 Shimei son of **Ela**—in Benjamin;

453 אֶלְגָּבִישׁ ***'elgābîš***, n.[m.]. [3] [cf. 1486]

hailstones [+74] [3]

Eze 13:11 come in torrents, and I will send **hailstones** [+74] hurtling down,
13:13 in my anger **hailstones** [+74] and torrents of rain will fall with
38:22 **hailstones** [+74] and burning sulfur on him and on his troops

454 אַלְגּוּמִּים ***'algûmmîm***, n.[m.]pl. [3] [cf. 523]

algumwood [+6770] [2], algum [1]

2Ch 2: 8 [2:7] "Send me also cedar, pine and **algum** logs from Lebanon,
9:10 they also brought **algumwood** [+6770] and precious stones.
9:11 The king used the **algumwood** [+6770] to make steps for the

455 אֶלְדָּד ***'eldād***, n.pr.m. [2] [√ 446 + 1856]

Eldad [2]

Nu 11:26 However, two men, whose names were **Eldad** and Medad,
11:27 and told Moses, "**Eldad** and Medad are prophesying in the camp."

456 אֶלְדָּעָה ***'eldā'â***, n.pr.m. [2] [√ 446 + 1977?]

Eldaah [2]

Ge 25: 4 sons of Midian were Ephah, Epher, Hanoch, Abida and **Eldaah**.
1Ch 1:33 The sons of Midian: Ephah, Epher, Hanoch, Abida and **Eldaah**.

457 [1]אָלָה ***'ālâ***[1], v. [8] [→ 460, 9297]

swears the oath [2], take an oath [2], bound under an oath [1], cursing [1], take oaths [1], utter a curse [1]

Jdg 17: 2 [A] taken from you and about which I heard you **utter a curse**—
1Sa 14:24 [G] because Saul *had* **bound** the people **under an oath**, saying,
1Ki 8:31 [G] his neighbor and is required to **take an oath** and he comes
8:31 [A] and **swears the oath** before your altar in this temple,
2Ch 6:22 [G] his neighbor and is required to **take an oath** and he comes
6:22 [A] and **swears the oath** before your altar in this temple,
Hos 4: 2 [A] There is only **cursing**, lying and murder, stealing
10: 4 [A] make many promises, **take** false **oaths** and make agreements;

458 [2]אָלָה ***'ālâ***[2], v. [1]

mourn [1]

Joel 1: 8 [A] **Mourn** like a virgin in sackcloth grieving for the husband of

459 [3]אָלָה ***'ālâ***[3], v. Not used in NIV/BHS

460 [4]אָלָה ***'ālâ***[4], n.f. [34] [√ 457]

oath [10], curses [8], curse [7], object of cursing [3], required [+928+5957] [2], accursed [1], public charge [1], put under oath [+9048] [1], sworn agreement [1]

Ge 24:41 you will be released from my **oath** even if they refuse to give her
24:41 they refuse to give her to you—you will be released from my **oath**.'
26:28 so we said, 'There ought to be a **sworn agreement** between us'—
Lev 5: 1 because he does not speak up when he hears a **public charge** to
Nu 5:21 here the priest is to put the woman under this **curse** of the oath—

Nu 5:21 "may the LORD cause your people to **curse** and denounce you
5:23 " 'The priest is to write these **curses** on a scroll and then wash them
5:27 waste away, and she will become **accursed** among her people.
Dt 29:12 [29:11] is making with you this day and sealing with an **oath**,
29:14 [29:13] making this covenant, with its **oath**, not only with you
29:19 [29:18] When such a person hears the words of this **oath**, he
29:20 [29:19] All the **curses** written in this book will fall upon him,
29:21 [29:20] according to all the **curses** *of* the covenant written in this
30: 7 The LORD your God will put all these **curses** on your enemies
1Ki 8:31 and *is* **required** [+928+5957] to take an oath and he comes
2Ch 6:22 and *is* **required** [+928+5957] to take an oath and he comes
34:24 all the **curses** written in the book that has been read in the presence
Ne 10:29 [10:30] bind themselves with a **curse** and an oath to follow the
Job 31:30 I have not allowed my mouth to sin by invoking a **curse** against his
Ps 10: 7 His mouth is full of **curses** and lies and threats; trouble and evil are
59:12 [59:13] be caught in their pride. For the **curses** and lies they utter,
Pr 29:24 his own enemy; *he is* **put under oath** [+9048] and dare not testify.
Isa 24: 6 Therefore a **curse** consumes the earth; its people must bear their
Jer 23:10 because of the **curse** the land lies parched and the pastures in the
29:18 all the kingdoms of the earth and an **object of cursing** and horror,
42:18 You will be an **object of cursing** and horror, of condemnation
44:12 They will become an **object of cursing** and horror, of
Eze 16:59 because you have despised my **oath** by breaking the covenant.
17:13 royal family and made a treaty with him, putting him under **oath**.
17:16 on the throne, whose **oath** he despised and whose treaty he broke.
17:18 He despised the **oath** by breaking the covenant. Because he had
17:19 I will bring down on his head my **oath** that he despised and my
Da 9:11 "Therefore the **curses** and sworn judgments written in the Law of
Zec 5: 3 said to me, "This is the **curse** that is going out over the whole land;

461 [1]אֵלָה 'ēlâ[1], n.f. [13] [→ 462; cf. 381, 380; Ar 10027]

oak [6], oak tree [3], terebinth [2], great tree [1], tree [1]

Ge 35: 4 in their ears, and Jacob buried them under the **oak** at Shechem.
Jdg 6:11 sat down under the **oak** in Ophrah that belonged to Joash the
6:19 he brought them out and offered them to him under the **oak**.
2Sa 18: 9 and as the mule went under the thick branches of a large **oak**,
18: 9 branches of a large oak, Absalom's head got caught in the **tree**.
18:10 he told Joab, "I just saw Absalom hanging in an **oak tree**."
18:14 into Absalom's heart while Absalom was still alive in the **oak tree**.
1Ki 13:14 He found him sitting under an **oak tree** and asked, "Are you the
1Ch 10:12 Then they buried their bones under the **great tree** in Jabesh,
Isa 1:30 You will be like an **oak** with fading leaves, like a garden without
6:13 as the **terebinth** and oak leave stumps when they are cut down,
Eze 6:13 the mountaintops, under every spreading tree and every leafy **oak**—
Hos 4:13 under oak, poplar and **terebinth**, where the shade is pleasant.

462 [2]אֵלָה 'ēlâ[2], n.pr.m. [13] [√ 461; cf. 452]

Elah [12], Elah's [1]

Ge 36:41 Oholibamah, **Elah**, Pinon,
1Ki 16: 6 and was buried in Tirzah. And **Elah** his son succeeded him as king.
16: 8 **Elah** son of Baasha became king of Israel, and he reigned in Tirzah
16:13 because of all the sins Baasha and his son **Elah** had committed
16:14 As for the other events of **Elah's** reign, and all he did, are they not
2Ki 15:30 Hoshea son of **Elah** conspired against Pekah son of Remaliah.
17: 1 Hoshea son of **Elah** became king of Israel in Samaria, and he
18: 1 In the third year of Hoshea son of **Elah** king of Israel,
18: 9 which was the seventh year of Hoshea son of **Elah** king of Israel,
1Ch 1:52 Oholibamah, **Elah**, Pinon,
4:15 son of Jephunneh: Iru, **Elah** and Naam. The son of Elah: Kenaz.
4:15 son of Jephunneh: Iru, Elah and Naam. The son of **Elah**: Kenaz.
9: 8 Ibneiah son of Jeroham; **Elah** son of Uzzi, the son of Micri;

463 [3]אֵלָה 'ēlâ[3], n.pr.loc. [3] [√ 380]

Elah [3]

1Sa 17: 2 and the Israelites assembled and camped in the Valley of **Elah**
17:19 They are with Saul and all the men of Israel in the Valley of **Elah**,
21: 9 [21:10] whom you killed in the Valley of **Elah**, is here;

464 אַלָּה 'allâ, n.f. [1] [√ 380]

oak [1]

Jos 24:26 and set it up there under the **oak** near the holy place of the LORD.

465 אֵלֶּה 'ēlleh, pr.pl.m. & f. [746] [√ 447; Ar 10034] Not indexed

these [481], *untranslated* [68], this [55], those [15], them [12], they [12], this [+1821+2021+2021] [12], such [10], others[s] [7], some time later [+339+1821+2021+2021] [6], some [5], following[s] [4], the [4], here [3], who [3], altogether [+2256] [2], impartially [+465+6640] [2], men[s] [2], now [+928+2021+2021+3427] [2], one group[s] [2], that [2], us[s] [2], what[s] [+1821+2021+2021] [2], after a while [+339+1821 +2021+2021] [1], all this [1], all[s] [1], animals[s] [1], as follows [1], case[s] [1], each other [1], everything [+1821+2021+2021+3972] [1], gave the message [+1819+1821+2021+2021+3972] [1], his[s] [1], later [+339+1821+2021+2021] [1], next[s] [1], share their duties [+6640] [1], she [1], that[s] [+1821+2021+2021] [1], that happened [+1821 +2021+2021] [1], the craftsmen[s] [1], the first[s] [1], the men[s] of the ambush [1], the men[s] [1], the others[s] [1], the total[s] [1], their[s] [+2021] [1], things[s] [1], this is how [+1821+2021+2021+3869] [1], this is how [+928+3972] [1], this is why [+6584] [1], two[s] [1], very [1], what [1], who[s] [1], whose[s] [+1426+2257] [1], your[s] [1]

466 אֱלֹהִים 'ᵉlōhîm, n.pl.m. & f. [2600 / 2602] [√ 468; cf. 446]

God [2302], gods [205], God's [25], *untranslated* [12], he[s] [+3378+3870] [7], he[s] [7], judges [4], him[s] [+3378+3870] [3], angels [+1201+2021] [2], goddess [2], he[s] [+2021] [2], his[s] [+3378+3870] [2], angels [+1201] [1], divine [1], God's [+4200] [1], God's [+4946] [1], God-fearing [+2021+3710] [1], godly [1], great [1], he[s] [+3378] [1], he[s] [+3378+5646] [1], he[s] [+824+2021] [1], heavenly beings [1], high [1], him[s] [+3378+4013] [1], him[s] [+2021] [1], him[s] [1], his[s] [+3276] [1], I[s] [1], idols [1], it[s] [+778+2021] [1], lead to do the same[s] [+339+906+2177+2388] [1], majestic [1], mighty [1], sacred [1], shrine [+1074] [1], spirit [1], them[s] [+1074+2021+3998] [1], them[s] [+2157] [1], there [+928+1074] [1], very [+4200] [1]

Ge 1: 1 In the beginning **God** created the heavens and the earth.
1: 2 of the deep, and the Spirit of **God** was hovering over the waters.
1: 3 And **God** said, "Let there be light," and there was light.
1: 4 **God** saw that the light was good, and he separated the light from
1: 4 the light was good, and **he**[s] separated the light from the darkness.
1: 5 **God** called the light "day," and the darkness he called "night."
1: 6 **God** said, "Let there be an expanse between the waters to separate
1: 7 So **God** made the expanse and separated the water under the
1: 8 **God** called the expanse "sky." And there was evening, and there
1: 9 **God** said, "Let the water under the sky be gathered to one place,
1:10 **God** called the dry ground "land," and the gathered waters he
1:10 gathered waters he called "seas." And **God** saw that it was good.
1:11 **God** said, "Let the land produce vegetation: seed-bearing plants
1:12 seed in it according to their kinds. And **God** saw that it was good.
1:14 **God** said, "Let there be lights in the expanse of the sky to separate
1:16 **God** made two great lights—the greater light to govern the day
1:17 **God** set them in the expanse of the sky to give light on the earth,
1:18 and to separate light from darkness. And **God** saw that it was good.
1:20 **God** said, "Let the water teem with living creatures, and let birds
1:21 So **God** created the great creatures of the sea and every living
1:21 winged bird according to its kind. And **God** saw that it was good.
1:22 **God** blessed them and said, "Be fruitful and increase in number
1:24 **God** said, "Let the land produce living creatures according to their
1:25 **God** made the wild animals according to their kinds, the livestock
1:25 the ground according to their kinds. And **God** saw that it was good.
1:26 Then **God** said, "Let us make man in our image, in our likeness,
1:27 So **God** created man in his own image, in the image of God he
1:27 created man in his own image, in the image of **God** he created him;
1:28 **God** blessed them and said to them, "Be fruitful and increase in
1:28 and said to them, **[RPH]** "Be fruitful and increase in number;
1:29 **God** said, "I give you every seed-bearing plant on the face of the
1:31 **God** saw all that he had made, and it was very good. And there
2: 2 By the seventh day **God** had finished the work he had been doing;
2: 3 **God** blessed the seventh day and made it holy, because on it he
2: 3 because on it he rested from all the work of creating that **he**[s] had
2: 4 When the LORD **God** made the earth and the heavens—
2: 5 for the LORD **God** had not sent rain on the earth and there was
2: 7 the LORD **God** formed the man from the dust of the ground
2: 8 Now the LORD **God** had planted a garden in the east, in Eden;
2: 9 the LORD **God** made all kinds of trees grow out of the ground—
2:15 The LORD **God** took the man and put him in the Garden of Eden
2:16 the LORD **God** commanded the man, "You are free to eat from
2:18 The LORD **God** said, "It is not good for the man to be alone.
2:19 Now the LORD **God** had formed out of the ground all the beasts
2:21 So the LORD **God** caused the man to fall into a deep sleep;
2:22 the LORD **God** made a woman from the rib he had taken out of
3: 1 crafty than any of the wild animals the LORD **God** had made.
3: 1 He said to the woman, "Did **God** really say, 'You must not eat
3: 3 **God** did say, 'You must not eat fruit from the tree that is in the
3: 5 "For **God** knows that when you eat of it your eyes will be opened,
3: 5 will be opened, and you will be like **God**, knowing good and evil."
3: 8 his wife heard the sound of the LORD **God** as he was walking in
3: 8 and they hid from the LORD **God** among the trees of the garden.
3: 9 But the LORD **God** called to the man, "Where are you?"
3:13 the LORD **God** said to the woman, "What is this you have done?"
3:14 So the LORD **God** said to the serpent, "Because you have done
3:21 The LORD **God** made garments of skin for Adam and his wife
3:22 the LORD **God** said, "The man has now become like one of us,
3:23 So the LORD **God** banished him from the Garden of Eden to
4:25 saying, "**God** has granted me another child in place of Abel,

Ge 5: 1 When **God** created man, he made him in the likeness of God.
5: 1 When God created man, he made him in the likeness of **God**.
5: 22 Enoch walked with **God** 300 years and had other sons
5: 24 Enoch walked with **God**; then he was no more, because God took
5: 24 with God; then he was no more, because **God** took him away.
6: 2 the sons of **God** saw that the daughters of men were beautiful,
6: 4 when the sons of **God** went to the daughters of men and had
6: 9 blameless among the people of his time, and he walked with **God**.
6: 11 Now the earth was corrupt in **God's** sight and was full of violence.
6: 12 **God** saw how corrupt the earth had become, for all the people on
6: 13 So **God** said to Noah, "I am going to put an end to all people,
6: 22 Noah did everything just as **God** commanded him.
7: 9 came to Noah and entered the ark, as **God** had commanded Noah.
7: 16 and female of every living thing, as **God** had commanded Noah.
8: 1 **God** remembered Noah and all the wild animals and the livestock
8: 1 and **he**[s] sent a wind over the earth, and the waters receded.
8: 15 Then **God** said to Noah,
9: 1 Then **God** blessed Noah and his sons, saying to them, "Be fruitful
9: 6 his blood be shed; for in the image of **God** has God made man.
9: 8 Then **God** said to Noah and to his sons with him:
9: 12 **God** said, "This is the sign of the covenant I am making between
9: 16 I will see it and remember the everlasting covenant between **God**
9: 17 So **God** said to Noah, "This is the sign of the covenant I have
9: 26 He also said, "Blessed be the LORD, the **God** *of* Shem! May
9: 27 May **God** extend the territory of Japheth; may Japheth live in the
17: 3 Abram fell facedown, and **God** said to him,
17: 7 to be your **God** and the God of your descendants after you.
17: 8 to you and your descendants after you; and I will be their **God**."
17: 9 **God** said to Abraham, "As for you, you must keep my covenant,
17: 15 **God** also said to Abraham, "As for Sarai your wife, you are no
17: 18 Abraham said to **God**, "If only Ishmael might live under your
17: 19 Then **God** said, "Yes, but your wife Sarah will bear you a son,
17: 22 he had finished speaking with Abraham, **God** went up from him.
17: 23 male in his household, and circumcised them, as **God** told him.
19: 29 So when **God** destroyed the cities of the plain, he remembered
19: 29 God destroyed the cities of the plain, **he**[s] remembered Abraham,
20: 3 But **God** came to Abimelech in a dream one night and said to him,
20: 6 **God** said to him in the dream, "Yes, I know you did this with a
20: 11 "I said to myself, 'There is surely no fear of **God** in this place,
20: 13 And when **God** had me wander from my father's household,
20: 17 Then Abraham prayed to **God**, and God healed Abimelech,
20: 17 **God** healed Abimelech, his wife and his slave girls so they could
21: 2 to Abraham in his old age, at the very time **God** had promised him.
21: 4 days old, Abraham circumcised him, as **God** commanded him.
21: 6 Sarah said, "**God** has brought me laughter, and everyone who
21: 12 But **God** said to him, "Do not be so distressed about the boy
21: 17 **God** heard the boy crying, and the angel of God called to Hagar
21: 17 and the angel of **God** called to Hagar from heaven and said to her,
21: 17 Do not be afraid; **God** has heard the boy crying as he lies there.
21: 19 **God** opened her eyes and she saw a well of water. So she went
21: 20 **God** was with the boy as he grew up. He lived in the desert
21: 22 his forces said to Abraham, "**God** is with you in everything you do.
21: 23 Now swear to me here before **God** that you will not deal falsely
22: 1 Some time later **God** tested Abraham. He said to him, "Abraham!"
22: 3 the burnt offering, he set out for the place **God** had told him about.
22: 8 "**God** himself will provide the lamb for the burnt offering,
22: 9 When they reached the place **God** had told him about, Abraham
22: 12 Now I know that you fear **God**, because you have not withheld
23: 6 "Sir, listen to us. You are a **mighty** prince among us. Bury your
24: 3 to swear by the LORD, the **God** *of* heaven and the God of earth,
24: 3 to swear by the LORD, the God of heaven and the **God** *of* earth,
24: 7 "The LORD, the **God** *of* heaven, who brought me out of my
24: 12 Then he prayed, "O LORD, **God** *of* my master Abraham,
24: 27 "Praise be to the LORD, the **God** *of* my master Abraham,
24: 42 I said, 'O LORD, **God** *of* my master Abraham, if you will,
24: 48 I praised the LORD, the **God** *of* my master Abraham, who had
25: 11 **God** blessed his son Isaac, who then lived near Beer Lahai Roi.
26: 24 appeared to him and said, "I am the **God** *of* your father Abraham.
27: 20 my son?" "The LORD your **God** gave me success," he replied.
27: 28 May **God** give you of heaven's dew and of earth's richness—
28: 4 where you now live as an alien, the land **God** gave to Abraham."
28: 12 and the angels of **God** were ascending and descending on it.
28: 13 the LORD, the **God** *of* your father Abraham and the God of Isaac.
28: 13 the LORD, the God of your father Abraham and the **God** *of* Isaac.
28: 17 This is none other than the house of **God**; this is the gate of
28: 20 "If **God** will be with me and will watch over me on this journey I
28: 21 safely to my father's house, then the LORD will be my **God**
28: 22 and this stone that I have set up as a pillar will be **God's** house,
30: 2 Jacob became angry with her and said, "Am I in the place of **God**,
30: 6 Rachel said, "**God** has vindicated me; he has listened to my plea
30: 8 "I have had a **great** struggle with my sister, and I have won."
30: 17 **God** listened to Leah, and she became pregnant and bore Jacob a
30: 18 "**God** has rewarded me for giving my maidservant to my husband."
30: 20 Then Leah said, "**God** has presented me with a precious gift.
30: 22 **God** remembered Rachel; he listened to her and opened her womb.
30: 22 remembered Rachel; **he**[s] listened to her and opened her womb.
30: 23 gave birth to a son and said, "**God** has taken away my disgrace."
31: 5 not what it was before, but the **God** *of* my father has been with me.
31: 7 wages ten times. However, **God** has not allowed him to harm me.
31: 9 So **God** has taken away your father's livestock and has given them
31: 11 The angel of **God** said to me in the dream, 'Jacob.' I answered,
31: 16 Surely all the wealth that **God** took away from our father belongs
31: 16 belongs to us and our children. So do whatever **God** has told you."
31: 24 Then **God** came to Laban the Aramean in a dream at night
31: 29 last night the **God** *of* your father said to me, 'Be careful not to say
31: 30 to return to your father's house. But why did you steal my **gods**?"
31: 32 But if you find anyone who has your **gods**, he shall not live.
31: 42 If the **God** *of* my father, the God of Abraham and the Fear of Isaac,
31: 42 the **God** *of* Abraham and the Fear of Isaac, had not been with me,
31: 42 **God** has seen my hardship and the toil of my hands, and last night
31: 50 is with us, remember that **God** is a witness between you and me."
31: 53 May the **God** *of* Abraham and the God of Nahor, the God of their
31: 53 May the God of Abraham and the **God** *of* Nahor, the God of their
31: 53 and the God of Nahor, the **God** *of* their father, judge between us."
32: 1 [32:2] also went on his way, and the angels of **God** met him.
32: 2 [32:3] When Jacob saw them, he said, "This is the camp of **God**!"
32: 9 [32:10] Jacob prayed, "O **God** *of* my father Abraham, God of my
32: 9 [32:10] **God** *of* my father Isaac, O LORD, who said to me,
32: 28 [32:29] because you have struggled with **God** and with men
32: 30 [32:31] saying, "It is because I saw **God** face to face, and yet my
33: 5 "They are the children **God** has graciously given your servant."
33: 10 For to see your face is like seeing the face of **God**, now that you
33: 11 to you, for **God** has been gracious to me and I have all I need."
35: 1 Then **God** said to Jacob, "Go up to Bethel and settle there,
35: 2 "Get rid of the foreign **gods** you have with you, and purify
35: 4 So they gave Jacob all the foreign **gods** they had and the rings in
35: 5 and the terror of **God** fell upon the towns all around them
35: 7 because it was there that **God** revealed himself to him when he was
35: 9 from Paddan Aram, **God** appeared to him again and blessed him.
35: 10 **God** said to him, "Your name is Jacob, but you will no longer be
35: 11 **God** said to him, "I am God Almighty; be fruitful and increase in
35: 13 **God** went up from him at the place where he had talked with him.
35: 15 Jacob called the place where **God** had talked with him Bethel.
39: 9 then could I do such a wicked thing and sin against **God**?"
40: 8 Then Joseph said to them, "Do not interpretations belong to **God**?
41: 16 to Pharaoh, "but **God** will give Pharaoh the answer he desires."
41: 25 and the same. **God** has revealed to Pharaoh what he is about to do.
41: 28 I said to Pharaoh: **God** has shown Pharaoh what he is about to do.
41: 32 in two forms is that the matter has been firmly decided by **God**,
41: 32 matter has been firmly decided by God, and **God** will do it soon.
41: 38 we find anyone like this man, one in whom is the spirit of **God**?"
41: 39 "Since **God** has made all this known to you, there is no one
41: 51 "It is because **God** has made me forget all my trouble and all my
41: 52 because **God** has made me fruitful in the land of my suffering."
42: 18 Joseph said to them, "Do this and you will live, for I fear **God**:
42: 28 other trembling and said, "What is this that **God** has done to us?"
43: 23 Your **God**, the God of your father, has given you treasure in your
43: 23 Your God, the **God** *of* your father, has given you treasure in your
43: 29 told me about?" And he said, "**God** be gracious to you, my son."
44: 16 **God** has uncovered your servants' guilt. We are now my lord's
45: 5 because it was to save lives that **God** sent me ahead of you.
45: 7 **God** sent me ahead of you to preserve for you a remnant on earth
45: 8 "So then, it was not you who sent me here, but **God**. He made me
45: 9 **God** has made me lord of all Egypt. Come down to me;
46: 1 he offered sacrifices to the **God** *of* his father Isaac.
46: 2 And **God** spoke to Israel in a vision at night and said, "Jacob!
46: 3 "I am God, the **God** *of* your father," he said. "Do not be afraid to
48: 9 "They are the sons **God** has given me here," Joseph said to his
48: 11 face again, and now **God** has allowed me to see your children too."
48: 15 "May the **God** before whom my fathers Abraham and Isaac
48: 15 the **God** who has been my shepherd all my life to this day,
48: 20 'May **God** make you like Ephraim and Manasseh.' " So he put
48: 21 **God** will be with you and take you back to the land of your fathers.
50: 17 Now please forgive the sins of the servants of the **God** *of* your
50: 19 Joseph said to them, "Don't be afraid. Am I in the place of **God**?
50: 20 **God** intended it for good to accomplish what is now being done,
50: 24 **God** will surely come to your aid and take you up out of this land
50: 25 "**God** will surely come to your aid, and then you must carry my
Ex 1: 17 feared **God** and did not do what the king of Egypt had told them to
1: 20 So **God** was kind to the midwives and the people increased
1: 21 because the midwives feared **God**, he gave them families of their
2: 23 and their cry for help because of their slavery went up to **God**.
2: 24 **God** heard their groaning and he remembered his covenant with
2: 24 their groaning and **he**[s] remembered his covenant with Abraham,
2: 25 So **God** looked on the Israelites and was concerned about them.
2: 25 looked on the Israelites and **[RPH]** was concerned about them.
3: 1 the far side of the desert and came to Horeb, the mountain of **God**.
3: 4 over to look, **God** called to him from within the bush, "Moses!

Ex 3: 6 Then he said, "I am the **God** *of* your father, the God of Abraham,
3: 6 the **God** *of* Abraham, the God of Isaac and the God of Jacob."
3: 6 the God of Abraham, the **God** *of* Isaac and the God of Jacob."
3: 6 the God of Abraham, the God of Isaac and the **God** *of* Jacob."
3: 6 Moses hid his face, because he was afraid to look at **God**.
3: 11 But Moses said to **God**, "Who am I, that I should go to Pharaoh
3: 12 the people out of Egypt, you will worship **God** on this mountain."
3: 13 Moses said to **God**, "Suppose I go to the Israelites and say to them,
3: 13 and say to them, 'The **God** *of* your fathers has sent me to you,'
3: 14 **God** said to Moses, "I AM WHO I AM. This is what you are to say
3: 15 **God** also said to Moses, "Say to the Israelites, 'The LORD,
3: 15 "Say to the Israelites, 'The LORD, the **God** *of* your fathers—
3: 15 the **God** *of* Abraham, the God of Isaac and the God of Jacob—
3: 15 the God of Abraham, the **God** *of* Isaac and the God of Jacob—
3: 15 the God of Abraham, the God of Isaac and the **God** *of* Jacob—
3: 16 of Israel and say to them, 'The LORD, the **God** *of* your fathers—
3: 16 the **God** *of* Abraham, Isaac and Jacob—appeared to me and said:
3: 18 of Egypt and say to him, 'The LORD, the **God** *of* the Hebrews,
3: 18 journey into the desert to offer sacrifices to the LORD our **God**.'
4: 5 that they may believe that the LORD, the **God** *of* their fathers—
4: 5 the **God** *of* Abraham, the God of Isaac and the God of Jacob—
4: 5 the God of Abraham, the **God** *of* Isaac and the God of Jacob—
4: 5 the God of Abraham, the God of Isaac and the **God** *of* Jacob—
4: 16 it will be as if he were your mouth and as if you were **God** to him.
4: 20 started back to Egypt. And he took the staff of **God** in his hand.
4: 27 So he met Moses at the mountain of **God** and kissed him.
5: 1 and said, "This is what the LORD, the **God** *of* Israel, says:
5: 3 Then they said, "The **God** *of* the Hebrews has met with us.
5: 3 journey into the desert to offer sacrifices to the LORD our **God**,
5: 8 that is why they are crying out, 'Let us go and sacrifice to our **God**.'
6: 2 **God** also said to Moses, "I am the LORD.
6: 7 I will take you as my own people, and I will be your **God**.
6: 7 you will know that I am the LORD your **God**, who brought you
7: 1 said to Moses, "See, I have made you like **God** to Pharaoh,
7: 16 say to him, 'The LORD, the **God** *of* the Hebrews, has sent me to
8: 10 [8:6] you may know there is no one like the LORD our **God**.
8: 19 [8:15] The magicians said to Pharaoh, "This is the finger of **God**."
8: 25 [8:21] and said, "Go, sacrifice to your **God** here in the land."
8: 26 [8:22] The sacrifices we offer the LORD our **God** would be
8: 27 [8:23] into the desert to offer sacrifices to the LORD our **God**,
8: 28 [8:24] go to offer sacrifices to the LORD your **God** in the desert,
9: 1 to him, 'This is what the LORD, the **God** *of* the Hebrews, says:
9: 13 to him, 'This is what the LORD, the **God** *of* the Hebrews, says:
9: 28 to the LORD, for we have had enough **[RPH]** thunder and hail.
9: 30 that you and your officials still do not fear the LORD **God**."
10: 3 to him, "This is what the LORD, the **God** *of* the Hebrews, says:
10: 7 Let the people go, so that they may worship the LORD their **God**.
10: 8 "Go, worship the LORD your **God**," he said. "But just who will
10: 16 "I have sinned against the LORD your **God** and against you.
10: 17 pray to the LORD your **God** to take this deadly plague away from
10: 25 and burnt offerings to present to the LORD our **God**.
10: 26 We have to use some of them in worshiping the LORD our **God**,
12: 12 and animals—and I will bring judgment on all the **gods** *of* Egypt.
13: 17 **God** did not lead them on the road through the Philistine country,
13: 17 For **God** said, "If they face war, they might change their minds
13: 18 So **God** led the people around by the desert road toward the Red
13: 19 "**God** will surely come to your aid, and then you must carry my
14: 19 the angel of **God**, who had been traveling in front of Israel's army,
15: 2 and I will praise him, my father's **God**, and I will exalt him.
15: 26 "If you listen carefully to the voice of the LORD your **God**
16: 12 Then you will know that I am the LORD your **God**.' "
17: 9 Tomorrow I will stand on top of the hill with the staff of **God** in
18: 1 heard of everything **God** had done for Moses and for his people
18: 4 was named Eliezer, for he said, "My father's **God** was my helper;
18: 5 him in the desert, where he was camped near the mountain of **God**.
18: 11 Now I know that the LORD is greater than all other **gods**,
18: 12 brought a burnt offering and other sacrifices to **God**,
18: 12 to eat bread with Moses' father-in-law in the presence of **God**.
18: 15 "Because the people come to me to seek **God's** will.
18: 16 between the parties and inform them of **God's** decrees and laws."
18: 19 and I will give you some advice, and may **God** be with you.
18: 19 You must be the people's representative before **God** and bring
18: 19 before God and bring their disputes to **him**[s] [+2021].
18: 21 men who fear **God**, trustworthy men who hate dishonest gain—
18: 23 If you do this and **God** so commands, you will be able to stand the
19: 3 Moses went up to **God**, and the LORD called to him from the
19: 17 Then Moses led the people out of the camp to meet with **God**,
19: 19 Then Moses spoke and the voice of **God** answered him.
20: 1 And **God** spoke all these words:
20: 2 "I am the LORD your **God**, who brought you out of Egypt,
20: 3 "You shall have no other **gods** before me.
20: 5 for I, the LORD your **God**, am a jealous God, punishing the
20: 7 "You shall not misuse the name of the LORD your **God**,
20: 10 but the seventh day is a Sabbath to the LORD your **God**.
20: 12 so that you may live long in the land the LORD your **God** is
20: 19 we will listen. But do not have **God** speak to us or we will die."
20: 20 **God** has come to test you, so that the fear of God will be with you
20: 21 while Moses approached the thick darkness where **God** was.
20: 23 do not make for yourselves **gods** *of* silver or gods of gold.
20: 23 do not make for yourselves gods of silver or **gods** *of* gold.
21: 6 his master must take him before the **judges**. He shall take him to
21: 13 However, if he does not do it intentionally, but **God** lets it happen,
22: 8 [22:7] the owner of the house must appear before the **judges** to
22: 9 [22:8] both parties are to bring their cases before the **judges**.
22: 9 [22:8] The one whom the **judges** declare guilty must pay back
22: 20 [22:19] "Whoever sacrifices to any **god** other than the LORD
22: 28 [22:27] "Do not blaspheme **God** or curse the ruler of your people.
23: 13 Do not invoke the names of other **gods**; do not let them be heard
23: 19 of the firstfruits of your soil to the house of the LORD your **God**.
23: 24 Do not bow down before their **gods** or worship them or follow
23: 25 Worship the LORD your **God**, and his blessing will be on your
23: 32 Do not make a covenant with them or with their **gods**.
23: 33 because the worship of their **gods** will certainly be a snare to you."
24: 10 saw the **God** *of* Israel. Under his feet was something like a
24: 11 leaders of the Israelites; they saw **God**, and they ate and drank.
24: 13 with Joshua his aide, and Moses went up on the mountain of **God**.
29: 45 Then I will dwell among the Israelites and be their **God**.
29: 46 They will know that I am the LORD their **God**, who brought
29: 46 so that I might dwell among them. I am the LORD their **God**.
31: 3 and I have filled him with the Spirit of **God**, with skill, ability
31: 18 the Testimony, the tablets of stone inscribed by the finger of **God**.
32: 1 and said, "Come, make us **gods** who will go before us.
32: 4 they said, "These are your **gods**, O Israel, who brought you up out
32: 8 and sacrificed to it and have said, 'These are your **gods**, O Israel,
32: 11 But Moses sought the favor of the LORD his **God**. "O LORD,"
32: 16 The tablets were the work of **God**; the writing was the writing of
32: 16 the writing was the writing of **God**, engraved on the tablets.
32: 23 They said to me, 'Make us **gods** who will go before us. As for this
32: 27 he said to them, "This is what the LORD, the **God** *of* Israel, says:
32: 31 people have committed! They have made themselves **gods** *of* gold.
34: 15 for when they prostitute themselves to their **gods** and sacrifice to
34: 15 prostitute themselves to their gods and sacrifice to **them**[s] [+2157],
34: 16 your sons and those daughters prostitute themselves to their **gods**,
34: 16 *they will* **lead** your sons **to do**[s] **the same** [+339+906+2177+2388].
34: 17 "Do not make cast **idols**.
34: 23 men are to appear before the Sovereign LORD, the **God** *of* Israel.
34: 24 up three times each year to appear before the LORD your **God**.
34: 26 of the firstfruits of your soil to the house of the LORD your **God**.
35: 31 and he has filled him with the Spirit of **God**, with skill, ability
Lev 2: 13 Do not leave the salt of the covenant of your **God** out of your grain
4: 22 what is forbidden in any of the commands of the LORD his **God**,
11: 44 I am the LORD your **God**; consecrate yourselves and be holy,
11: 45 I am the LORD who brought you up out of Egypt to be your **God**;
18: 2 to the Israelites and say to them: 'I am the LORD your **God**.
18: 4 and be careful to follow my decrees. I am the LORD your **God**.
18: 21 to Molech, for you must not profane the name of your **God**.
18: 30 do not defile yourselves with them. I am the LORD your **God**.' "
19: 2 say to them: 'Be holy because I, the LORD your **God**, am holy.
19: 3 and you must observe my Sabbaths. I am the LORD your **God**.
19: 4 " 'Do not turn to idols or make **gods** *of* cast metal for yourselves.
19: 4 gods of cast metal for yourselves. I am the LORD your **God**.
19: 10 Leave them for the poor and the alien. I am the LORD your **God**.
19: 12 swear falsely by my name and so profane the name of your **God**.
19: 14 or put a stumbling block in front of the blind, but fear your **God**.
19: 25 way your harvest will be increased. I am the LORD your **God**.
19: 31 for you will be defiled by them. I am the LORD your **God**.
19: 32 of the aged, show respect for the elderly and revere your **God**.
19: 34 for you were aliens in Egypt. I am the LORD your **God**.
19: 36 I am the LORD your **God**, who brought you out of Egypt.
20: 7 and be holy, because I am the LORD your **God**.
20: 24 I am the LORD your **God**, who has set you apart from the
21: 6 They must be holy to their **God** and must not profane the name of
21: 6 be holy to their God and must not profane the name of their **God**.
21: 6 to the LORD by fire, the food of their **God**, they are to be holy.
21: 7 from their husbands, because priests are holy to their **God**.
21: 8 Regard them as holy, because they offer up the food of your **God**.
21: 12 nor leave the sanctuary of his **God** or desecrate it, because he has
21: 12 because he has been dedicated by the anointing oil of his **God**.
21: 17 who has a defect may come near to offer the food of his **God**.
21: 21 has a defect; he must not come near to offer the food of his **God**.
21: 22 He may eat the most holy food of his **God**, as well as the holy
22: 25 the hand of a foreigner and offer them as the food of your **God**.
22: 33 who brought you out of Egypt to be your **God**. I am the LORD."
23: 14 new grain, until the very day you bring this offering to your **God**.
23: 22 them for the poor and the alien. I am the LORD your **God**.' "
23: 28 when atonement is made for you before the LORD your **God**.
23: 40 and rejoice before the LORD your **God** for seven days.
23: 43 when I brought them out of Egypt. I am the LORD your **God**.' "

Lev 24:15 'If anyone curses his **God**, he will be held responsible;
24:22 for the alien and the native-born. I am the LORD your **God**.' "
25:17 Do not take advantage of each other, but fear your **God**. I am the
25:17 of each other, but fear your God. I am the LORD your **God**.
25:36 Do not take interest of any kind from him, but fear your **God**,
25:38 I am the LORD your **God**, who brought you out of Egypt to give
25:38 out of Egypt to give you the land of Canaan and to be your **God**.
25:43 Do not rule over them ruthlessly, but fear your **God**.
25:55 whom I brought out of Egypt. I am the LORD your **God**.
26: 1 in your land to bow down before it. I am the LORD your **God**.
26:12 I will walk among you and be your **God**, and you will be my
26:13 I am the LORD your **God**, who brought you out of Egypt
26:44 breaking my covenant with them. I am the LORD their **God**.
26:45 I brought out of Egypt in the sight of the nations to be their **God**.
Nu 6: 7 because the symbol of his separation to **God** is on his head.
10: 9 you will be remembered by the LORD your **God** and rescued
10:10 and they will be a memorial for you before your **God**.
10:10 a memorial for you before your God. I am the LORD your **God**."
15:40 to obey all my commands and will be consecrated to your **God**.
15:41 I am the LORD your **God**, who brought you out of Egypt to be
15:41 LORD your God, who brought you out of Egypt to be your **God**.
15:41 you out of Egypt to be your God. I am the LORD your **God**.' "
16: 9 Isn't it enough for you that the **God** *of* Israel has separated you
16:22 and cried out, "O God, **God** *of* the spirits of all mankind,
21: 5 they spoke against **God** and against Moses, and said, "Why have
22: 9 **God** came to Balaam and asked, "Who are these men with you?"
22:10 Balaam said to **God**, "Balak son of Zippor, king of Moab,
22:12 **God** said to Balaam, "Do not go with them. You must not put a
22:18 or small to go beyond the command of the LORD my **God**.
22:20 That night **God** came to Balaam and said, "Since these men have
22:22 **God** was very angry when he went, and the angel of the LORD
22:38 say just anything? I must speak only what **God** puts in my mouth."
23: 4 **God** met with him, and Balaam said, "I have prepared seven altars,
23:21 The LORD their **God** is with them; the shout of the King is
23:27 Perhaps it will please **God** to let you curse them for me from
24: 2 Israel encamped tribe by tribe, the Spirit of **God** came upon him
25: 2 who invited them to the sacrifices to their **gods**. The people ate
25: 2 to their gods. The people ate and bowed down before these **gods**.
25:13 because he was zealous for the honor of his **God** and made
27:16 "May the LORD, the **God** *of* the spirits of all mankind, appoint a
33: 4 among them; for the LORD had brought judgment on their **gods**.
Dt 1: 6 The LORD our **God** said to us at Horeb, "You have stayed long
1:10 The LORD your **God** has increased your numbers so that today
1:11 May the LORD, the **God** *of* your fathers, increase you a thousand
1:17 Do not be afraid of any man, for judgment belongs to **God**.
1:19 Then, as the LORD our **God** commanded us, we set out from
1:20 country of the Amorites, which the LORD our **God** is giving us.
1:21 See, the LORD your **God** has given you the land. Go up
1:21 possession of it as the LORD, the **God** *of* your fathers, told you.
1:25 "It is a good land that the LORD our **God** is giving us."
1:26 you rebelled against the command of the LORD your **God**.
1:30 The LORD your **God**, who is going before you, will fight for you,
1:31 There you saw how the LORD your **God** carried you, as a father
1:32 In spite of this, you did not trust in the LORD your **God**,
1:41 We will go up and fight, as the LORD our **God** commanded us."
2: 7 The LORD your **God** has blessed you in all the work of your
2: 7 These forty years the LORD your **God** has been with you,
2:29 until we cross the Jordan into the land the LORD our **God** is
2:30 For the LORD your **God** had made his spirit stubborn and his
2:33 the LORD our **God** delivered him over to us and we struck him
2:36 was too strong for us. The LORD our **God** gave us all of them.
2:37 But in accordance with the command of the LORD our **God**,
3: 3 So the LORD our **God** also gave into our hands Og king of
3:18 "The LORD your **God** has given you this land to take possession
3:20 they too have taken over the land that the LORD your **God** is
3:21 "You have seen with your own eyes all that the LORD your **God**
3:22 afraid of them; the LORD your **God** himself will fight for you."
4: 1 of the land that the LORD, the **God** *of* your fathers, is giving you.
4: 2 but keep the commands of the LORD your **God** that I give you.
4: 3 The LORD your **God** destroyed from among you everyone who
4: 4 all of you who held fast to the LORD your **God** are still alive
4: 5 you decrees and laws as the LORD my **God** commanded me,
4: 7 so great as to have their **gods** near them the way the LORD our
4: 7 the way the LORD our **God** is near us whenever we pray to him?
4:10 Remember the day you stood before the LORD your **God** at
4:19 worshiping things the LORD your **God** has apportioned to all the
4:21 enter the good land the LORD your **God** is giving you as your
4:23 Be careful not to forget the covenant of the LORD your **God** that
4:23 idol in the form of anything the LORD your **God** has forbidden.
4:24 For the LORD your **God** is a consuming fire, a jealous God.
4:25 doing evil in the eyes of the LORD your **God** and provoking him
4:28 There you will worship man-made **gods** of wood and stone,
4:29 if from there you seek the LORD your **God**, you will find him if
4:30 then in later days you will return to the LORD your **God**
4:31 For the LORD your **God** is a merciful God; he will not abandon
4:32 long before your time, from the day **God** created man on the earth;
4:33 Has any other people heard the voice of **God** speaking out of fire,
4:34 Has any **god** ever tried to take for himself one nation out of another
4:34 like all the things the LORD your **God** did for you in Egypt
4:35 these things so that you might know that the LORD is **God**;
4:39 and take to heart this day that the LORD is **God** in heaven above
4:40 that you may live long in the land the LORD your **God** gives you
5: 2 The LORD our **God** made a covenant with us at Horeb.
5: 6 "I am the LORD your **God**, who brought you out of Egypt,
5: 7 "You shall have no other **gods** before me.
5: 9 for I, the LORD your **God**, am a jealous God, punishing the
5:11 "You shall not misuse the name of the LORD your **God**,
5:12 by keeping it holy, as the LORD your **God** has commanded you.
5:14 but the seventh day is a Sabbath to the LORD your **God**.
5:15 that the LORD your **God** brought you out of there with a mighty
5:15 Therefore the LORD your **God** has commanded you to observe
5:16 and your mother, as the LORD your **God** has commanded you,
5:16 that it may go well with you in the land the LORD your **God** is
5:24 "The LORD our **God** has shown us his glory and his majesty,
5:24 Today we have seen that a man can live even if **God** speaks with
5:25 we will die if we hear the voice of the LORD our **God** any longer.
5:26 For what mortal man has ever heard the voice of the living **God**
5:27 Go near and listen to all that the LORD our **God** says. Then tell
5:27 Then tell us whatever the LORD our **God** tells you. We will listen
5:32 So be careful to do what the LORD your **God** has commanded
5:33 Walk in all the way that the LORD your **God** has commanded
6: 1 laws the LORD your **God** directed me to teach you to observe in
6: 2 their children after them may fear the LORD your **God** as long as
6: 3 just as the LORD, the **God** *of* your fathers, promised you.
6: 4 Hear, O Israel: The LORD our **God**, the LORD is one.
6: 5 Love the LORD your **God** with all your heart and with all your
6:10 When the LORD your **God** brings you into the land he swore to
6:13 Fear the LORD your **God**, serve him only and take your oaths in
6:14 Do not follow other **gods**, the gods of the peoples around you;
6:14 Do not follow other gods, the **gods** *of* the peoples around you;
6:15 for the LORD your **God**, who is among you, is a jealous God
6:15 a jealous God and **his**' [+3378+3870] anger will burn against you,
6:16 Do not test the LORD your **God** as you did at Massah.
6:17 Be sure to keep the commands of the LORD your **God**
6:20 decrees and laws the LORD our **God** has commanded you?"
6:24 us to obey all these decrees and to fear the LORD our **God**,
6:25 if we are careful to obey all this law before the LORD our **God**,
7: 1 When the LORD your **God** brings you into the land you are
7: 2 and when the LORD your **God** has delivered them over to you
7: 4 will turn your sons away from following me to serve other **gods**,
7: 6 For you are a people holy to the LORD your **God**. The LORD
7: 6 The LORD your **God** has chosen you out of all the peoples on the
7: 9 Know therefore that the LORD your **God** is God; he is the
7: 9 Know therefore that the LORD your God is **God**; he is the
7:12 the LORD your **God** will keep his covenant of love with you,
7:16 You must destroy all the peoples the LORD your **God** gives over
7:16 Do not look on them with pity and do not serve their **gods**,
7:18 remember well what the LORD your **God** did to Pharaoh
7:19 with which the LORD your **God** brought you out.
7:19 The LORD your **God** will do the same to all the peoples you now
7:20 the LORD your **God** will send the hornet among them until even
7:21 for the LORD your **God**, who is among you, is a great
7:22 The LORD your **God** will drive out those nations before you,
7:23 the LORD your **God** will deliver them over to you, throwing
7:25 The images of their **gods** you are to burn in the fire. Do not covet
7:25 will be ensnared by it, for it is detestable to the LORD your **God**.
8: 2 Remember how the LORD your **God** led you all the way in the
8: 5 a man disciplines his son, so the LORD your **God** disciplines you.
8: 6 Observe the commands of the LORD your **God**, walking in his
8: 7 For the LORD your **God** is bringing you into a good land—
8:10 praise the LORD your **God** for the good land he has given you.
8:11 Be careful that you do not forget the LORD your **God**, failing to
8:14 heart will become proud and you will forget the LORD your **God**,
8:18 remember the LORD your **God**, for it is he who gives you the
8:19 If you ever forget the LORD your **God** and follow other gods
8:19 and follow other **gods** and worship and bow down to them,
8:20 so you will be destroyed for not obeying the LORD your **God**.
9: 3 be assured today that the LORD your **God** is the one who goes
9: 4 After the LORD your **God** has driven them out before you,
9: 5 the LORD your **God** will drive them out before you, to
9: 6 because of your righteousness that the LORD your **God** is giving
9: 7 never forget how you provoked the LORD your **God** to anger in
9:10 LORD gave me two stone tablets inscribed by the finger of **God**.
9:16 I looked, I saw that you had sinned against the LORD your **God**;
9:23 But you rebelled against the command of the LORD your **God**.
10: 9 LORD is their inheritance, as the LORD your **God** told them.)
10:12 what does the LORD your **God** ask of you but to fear the LORD
10:12 the LORD your God ask of you but to fear the LORD your **God**,

Dt 10:12 to serve the LORD your **God** with all your heart and with all your
10:14 To the LORD your **God** belong the heavens, even the highest
10:17 For the LORD your **God** is God of gods and Lord of lords,
10:17 For the LORD your God is **God** *of* gods and Lord of lords,
10:17 For the LORD your God is God of **gods** and Lord of lords,
10:20 Fear the LORD your **God** and serve him. Hold fast to him
10:21 he is your **God**, who performed for you those great and awesome
10:22 now the LORD your **God** has made you as numerous as the stars
11: 1 Love the LORD your **God** and keep his requirements, his
11: 2 who saw and experienced the discipline of the LORD your **God**:
11:12 It is a land the LORD your **God** cares for; the eyes of the LORD
11:12 the eyes of the LORD your **God** are continually on it from the
11:13 to love the LORD your **God** and to serve him with all your heart
11:16 to turn away and worship other **gods** and bow down to them.
11:22 to love the LORD your **God**, to walk in all his ways and to hold
11:25 The LORD your **God**, as he promised you, will put the terror
11:27 the blessing if you obey the commands of the LORD your **God**
11:28 the curse if you disobey the commands of the LORD your **God**
11:28 from the way that I command you today by following other **gods**,
11:29 When the LORD your **God** has brought you into the land you are
11:31 take possession of the land the LORD your **God** is giving you.
12: 1 the LORD, the **God** *of* your fathers, has given you to possess—
12: 2 tree where the nations you are dispossessing worship their **gods**.
12: 3 cut down the idols of their **gods** and wipe out their names from
12: 4 You must not worship the LORD your **God** in their way.
12: 5 you are to seek the place the LORD your **God** will choose from
12: 7 in the presence of the LORD your **God**, you and your families
12: 7 put your hand to, because the LORD your **God** has blessed you.
12: 9 and the inheritance the LORD your **God** is giving you.
12:10 settle in the land the LORD your **God** is giving you as an
12:11 to the place the LORD your **God** will choose as a dwelling for his
12:12 And there rejoice before the LORD your **God**, you, your sons
12:15 according to the blessing the LORD your **God** gives you.
12:18 you are to eat them in the presence of the LORD your **God** at the
12:18 LORD your God at the place the LORD your **God** will choose—
12:18 you are to rejoice before the LORD your **God** in everything you
12:20 When the LORD your **God** has enlarged your territory as he
12:21 If the place where the LORD your **God** chooses to put his Name
12:27 Present your burnt offerings on the altar of the LORD your **God**,
12:27 sacrifices must be poured beside the altar of the LORD your **God**,
12:28 doing what is good and right in the eyes of the LORD your **God**.
12:29 The LORD your **God** will cut off before you the nations you are
12:30 be careful not to be ensnared by inquiring about their **gods**,
12:30 about their gods, saying, "How do these nations serve their **gods**?
12:31 You must not worship the LORD your **God** in their way,
12:31 because in worshiping their **gods**, they do all kinds of detestable
12:31 burn their sons and daughters in the fire as sacrifices to their **gods**.
13: 2 [13:3] "Let us follow other **gods**" (gods you have not known)
13: 3 [13:4] The LORD your **God** is testing you to find out whether
13: 3 [13:4] whether you love **him**[s] [+3378+4013] with all your heart
13: 4 [13:5] It is the LORD your **God** you must follow, and him you
13: 5 [13:6] he preached rebellion against the LORD your **God**,
13: 5 [13:6] has tried to turn you from the way the LORD your **God**
13: 6 [13:7] worship other **gods**" (gods that neither you nor your fathers
13: 7 [13:8] **gods** *of* the peoples around you, whether near or far, from
13:10 [13:11] he tried to turn you away from the LORD your **God**,
13:12 [13:13] the towns the LORD your **God** is giving you to live in
13:13 [13:14] and worship other **gods**" (gods you have not known),
13:16 [13:17] as a whole burnt offering to the LORD your **God**.
13:18 [13:19] because you obey the LORD your **God**, keeping all his
13:18 [13:19] and doing what is right in **his**[s] [+3378+3870] eyes.
14: 1 You are the children of the LORD your **God**. Do not cut
14: 2 for you are a people holy to the LORD your **God**. Out of all the
14:21 to a foreigner. But you are a people holy to the LORD your **God**.
14:23 flocks in the presence of the LORD your **God** at the place he will
14:23 so that you may learn to revere the LORD your **God** always.
14:24 you have been blessed by the LORD your **God** and cannot carry
14:24 (because the place where the LORD **[RPH]** will choose to put
14:25 with you and go to the place the LORD your **God** will choose.
14:26 household shall eat there in the presence of the LORD your **God**
14:29 so that the LORD your **God** may bless you in all the work of your
15: 4 for in the land the LORD your **God** is giving you to possess as
15: 5 if only you fully obey the LORD your **God** and are careful to
15: 6 For the LORD your **God** will bless you as he has promised,
15: 7 of the towns of the land that the LORD your **God** is giving you,
15:10 because of this the LORD your **God** will bless you in all your
15:14 Give to him as the LORD your **God** has blessed you.
15:15 you were slaves in Egypt and the LORD your **God** redeemed you.
15:18 And the LORD your **God** will bless you in everything you do.
15:19 Set apart for the LORD your **God** every firstborn male of your
15:20 the presence of the LORD your **God** at the place he will choose.
15:21 serious flaw, you must not sacrifice it to the LORD your **God**.
16: 1 of Abib and celebrate the Passover of the LORD your **God**,
16: 1 because in the month of Abib **he**[s] [+3378+3870] brought you out
16: 2 Sacrifice as the Passover to the LORD your **God** an animal from
16: 5 the Passover in any town the LORD your **God** gives you
16: 6 except in the place **he**[s] [+3378+3870] will choose as a dwelling for
16: 7 Roast it and eat it at the place the LORD your **God** will choose.
16: 8 and on the seventh day hold an assembly to the LORD your **God**
16:10 celebrate the Feast of Weeks to the LORD your **God** by giving a
16:10 in proportion to the blessings the LORD your **God** has given you.
16:11 rejoice before the LORD your **God** at the place he will choose as
16:11 rejoice before the LORD your God at the place **he**[s] [+3378+3870]
16:15 For seven days celebrate the Feast to the LORD your **God** at the
16:15 For the LORD your **God** will bless you in all your harvest
16:16 appear before the LORD your **God** at the place he will choose:
16:17 in proportion to the way the LORD your **God** has blessed you.
16:18 for each of your tribes in every town the LORD your **God**
16:20 may live and possess the land the LORD your **God** is giving you.
16:21 Asherah pole beside the altar you build to the LORD your **God**,
16:22 do not erect a sacred stone, for these the LORD your **God** hates.
17: 1 Do not sacrifice to the LORD your **God** an ox or a sheep that has
17: 1 or flaw in it, for that would be detestable to **him**[s] [+3378+3870].
17: 2 woman living among you in one of the towns the LORD **[RPH]**
17: 2 in the eyes of the LORD your **God** in violation of his covenant,
17: 3 contrary to my command has worshiped other **gods**, bowing down
17: 8 take them to the place the LORD your **God** will choose.
17:12 ministering there to the LORD your **God** must be put to death.
17:14 When you enter the land the LORD your **God** is giving you
17:15 be sure to appoint over you the king the LORD your **God**
17:19 days of his life so that he may learn to revere the LORD his **God**
18: 5 for the LORD your **God** has chosen them and their descendants
18: 7 he may minister in the name of the LORD his **God** like all his
18: 9 When you enter the land the LORD your **God** is giving you,
18:12 because of these detestable practices the LORD your **God** will
18:13 You must be blameless before the LORD your **God**.
18:14 as for you, the LORD your **God** has not permitted you to do so.
18:15 The LORD your **God** will raise up for you a prophet like me from
18:16 For this is what you asked of the LORD your **God** at Horeb on
18:16 "Let us not hear the voice of the LORD our **God** nor see this
18:20 or a prophet who speaks in the name of other **gods**, must be put to
19: 1 When the LORD your **God** has destroyed the nations whose land
19: 1 destroyed the nations whose land **he**[s] [+3378+3870] is giving you,
19: 2 located in the land the LORD your **God** is giving you to possess.
19: 3 divide into three parts the land the LORD your **God** is giving you
19: 8 If the LORD your **God** enlarges your territory, as he promised on
19: 9 to love the LORD your **God** and to walk always in his ways—
19:10 which the LORD your **God** is giving you as your inheritance,
19:14 receive in the land the LORD your **God** is giving you to possess.
20: 1 do not be afraid of them, because the LORD your **God**,
20: 4 For the LORD your **God** is the one who goes with you to fight for
20:13 When the LORD your **God** delivers it into your hand, put to the
20:14 you may use the plunder the LORD your **God** gives you from
20:16 in the cities of the nations the LORD your **God** is giving you as
20:17 and Jebusites—as the LORD your **God** has commanded you.
20:18 to follow all the detestable things they do in worshiping their **gods**,
20:18 their gods, and you will sin against the LORD your **God**.
21: 1 lying in a field in the land the LORD your **God** is giving you to
21: 5 for the LORD your **God** has chosen them to minister and to
21:10 the LORD your **God** delivers them into your hands and you take
21:23 because anyone who is hung on a tree is under **God's** curse.
21:23 You must not desecrate the land the LORD your **God** is giving
22: 5 for the LORD your **God** detests anyone who does this.
23: 5 [23:6] the LORD your **God** would not listen to Balaam
23: 5 [23:6] but **[RPH]** turned the curse into a blessing for you,
23: 5 [23:6] blessing for you, because the LORD your **God** loves you.
23:14 [23:15] For the LORD your **God** moves about in your camp to
23:18 [23:19] into the house of the LORD your **God** to pay any vow,
23:18 [23:19] because the LORD your **God** detests them both.
23:20 [23:21] so that the LORD your **God** may bless you in everything
23:21 [23:22] If you make a vow to the LORD your **God**, do not be
23:21 [23:22] for the LORD your **God** will certainly demand it of you
23:23 [23:24] freely to the LORD your **God** with your own mouth.
24: 4 Do not bring sin upon the land the LORD your **God** is giving you
24: 9 Remember what the LORD your **God** did to Miriam along the
24:13 be regarded as a righteous act in the sight of the LORD your **God**.
24:18 in Egypt and the LORD your **God** redeemed you from there.
24:19 so that the LORD your **God** may bless you in all the work of your
25:15 so that you may live long in the land the LORD your **God** is
25:16 For the LORD your **God** detests anyone who does these things,
25:18 and cut off all who were lagging behind; they had no fear of **God**.
25:19 When the LORD your **God** gives you rest from all the enemies
25:19 land **he**[s] [+3378+3870] is giving you to possess as an inheritance,
26: 1 When you have entered the land the LORD your **God** is giving
26: 2 from the soil of the land the LORD your **God** is giving you
26: 2 go to the place the LORD your **God** will choose as a dwelling for
26: 3 "I declare today to the LORD your **God** that I have come to the
26: 4 and set it down in front of the altar of the LORD your **God**.

Dt 26: 5 you shall declare before the LORD your **God**: "My father was a
26: 7 the **God** *of* our fathers, and the LORD heard our voice and saw
26: 10 Place the basket before the LORD your **God** and bow down
26: 10 the LORD your God and bow down before **him**[s] [+3378+3870].
26: 11 in all the good things the LORD your **God** has given to you
26: 13 say to the LORD your **God**: "I have removed from my house the
26: 14 I have obeyed the LORD my **God**; I have done everything you
26: 16 The LORD your **God** commands you this day to follow these
26: 17 You have declared this day that the LORD is your **God** and that
26: 19 and that you will be a people holy to the LORD your **God**,
27: 2 the Jordan into the land the LORD your **God** is giving you,
27: 3 crossed over to enter the land the LORD your **God** is giving you,
27: 3 just as the LORD, the **God** *of* your fathers, promised you.
27: 5 Build there an altar to the LORD your **God**, an altar of stones.
27: 6 Build the altar of the LORD your **God** with fieldstones and offer
27: 6 and offer burnt offerings on it to the LORD your **God**.
27: 7 eating them and rejoicing in the presence of the LORD your **God**.
27: 9 You have now become the people of the LORD your **God**.
27: 10 Obey the LORD your **God** and follow his commands and decrees
28: 1 If you fully obey the LORD your **God** and carefully follow all his
28: 1 the LORD your **God** will set you high above all the nations on
28: 2 upon you and accompany you if you obey the LORD your **God**:
28: 8 The LORD your **God** will bless you in the land he is giving you.
28: 9 if you keep the commands of the LORD your **God** and walk in
28: 13 If you pay attention to the commands of the LORD your **God** that
28: 14 to the right or to the left, following other **gods** and serving them.
28: 15 if you do not obey the LORD your **God** and do not carefully
28: 36 There you will worship other **gods**, gods of wood and stone.
28: 45 because you did not obey the LORD your **God** and observe the
28: 47 Because you did not serve the LORD your **God** joyfully
28: 52 the cities throughout the land the LORD your **God** is giving you.
28: 53 of the sons and daughters the LORD your **God** has given you.
28: 58 revere this glorious and awesome name—the LORD your **God**—
28: 62 few in number, because you did not obey the LORD your **God**.
28: 64 There you will worship other **gods**—gods of wood and stone,
29: 6 [29:5] so that you might know that I am the LORD your **God**.
29: 10 [29:9] standing today in the presence of the LORD your **God**—
29: 12 [29:11] order to enter into a covenant with the LORD your **God**,
29: 12 [29:11] a covenant the LORD **[RPH]** is making with you this
29: 13 [29:12] that he may be your **God** as he promised you and as he
29: 15 [29:14] here with us today in the presence of the LORD our **God**
29: 18 [29:17] whose heart turns away from the LORD our **God** to go
29: 18 [29:17] our God to go and worship the **gods** *of* those nations;
29: 25 [29:24] the covenant of the LORD, the **God** *of* their fathers,
29: 26 [29:25] They went off and worshiped other **gods** and bowed down
29: 26 [29:25] and bowed down to them, **gods** they did not know,
29: 29 [29:28] The secret things belong to the LORD our **God**,
30: 1 you take them to heart wherever the LORD your **God** disperses
30: 2 and when you and your children return to the LORD your **God**
30: 3 the LORD your **God** will restore your fortunes and have
30: 3 gather you again from all the nations where **he**[s] [+3378+3870]
30: 4 from there the LORD your **God** will gather you and bring you
30: 5 **He**[s] [+3378+3870] will bring you to the land that belonged to your
30: 6 The LORD your **God** will circumcise your hearts and the hearts
30: 6 so that you may love **him**[s] [+3378+3870] with all your heart
30: 7 The LORD your **God** will put all these curses on your enemies
30: 9 the LORD your **God** will make you most prosperous in all the
30: 10 if you obey the LORD your **God** and keep his commands
30: 10 turn to the LORD your **God** with all your heart and with all your
30: 16 For I command you today to love the LORD your **God**, to walk in
30: 16 the LORD your **God** will bless you in the land you are entering to
30: 17 if you are drawn away to bow down to other **gods** and worship
30: 20 and that you may love the LORD your **God**, listen to his voice,
31: 3 The LORD your **God** himself will cross over ahead of you.
31: 6 because of them, for the LORD your **God** goes with you;
31: 11 when all Israel comes to appear before the LORD your **God** at the
31: 12 so they can listen and learn to fear the LORD your **God**
31: 13 learn to fear the LORD your **God** as long as you live in the land
31: 16 these people will soon prostitute themselves to the foreign **gods** ***of***
31: 17 not these disasters come upon us because our **God** is not with us?'
31: 18 that day because of all their wickedness in turning to other **gods**.
31: 20 and thrive, they will turn to other **gods** and worship them,
31: 26 place it beside the ark of the covenant of the LORD your **God**.
32: 3 the name of the LORD. Oh, praise the greatness of our **God**!
32: 17 **gods** they had not known, gods that recently appeared, gods your
32: 37 will say: "Now where are their **gods**, the rock they took refuge in,
32: 39 There is no **god** besides me. I put to death and I bring to life,
33: 1 This is the blessing that Moses the man of **God** pronounced on the
33: 27 The eternal **God** is your refuge, and underneath are the everlasting
Jos 1: 9 for the LORD your **God** will be with you wherever you go."
1: 11 take possession of the land the LORD your **God** is giving you for
1: 13 'The LORD your **God** is giving you rest and has granted you this
1: 15 possession of the land that the LORD your **God** is giving them.
1: 17 Only may the LORD your **God** be with you as he was with
2: 11 for the LORD your **God** is God in heaven above and on the earth
2: 11 for the LORD your God is **God** in heaven above and on the earth
3: 3 "When you see the ark of the covenant of the LORD your **God**,
3: 9 "Come here and listen to the words of the LORD your **God**.
4: 5 "Go over before the ark of the LORD your **God** into the middle
4: 23 For the LORD your **God** dried up the Jordan before you until you
4: 23 The LORD your **God** did to the Jordan just what he had done to
4: 24 and so that you might always fear the LORD your **God**."
7: 13 for tomorrow; for this is what the LORD, the **God** *of* Israel, says:
7: 19 glory to the LORD, the **God** *of* Israel, and give him the praise.
7: 20 "It is true! I have sinned against the LORD, the **God** *of* Israel.
8: 7 take the city. The LORD your **God** will give it into your hand.
8: 30 built on Mount Ebal an altar to the LORD, the **God** *of* Israel,
9: 9 very distant country because of the fame of the LORD your **God**.
9: 18 had sworn an oath to them by the LORD, the **God** *of* Israel.
9: 19 by the LORD, the **God** *of* Israel, and we cannot touch them now.
9: 23 serve as woodcutters and water carriers for the house of my **God**."
9: 24 "Your servants were clearly told how the LORD your **God** had
10: 19 for the LORD your **God** has given them into your hand."
10: 40 just as the LORD, the **God** *of* Israel, had commanded.
10: 42 because the LORD, the **God** *of* Israel, fought for Israel.
13: 14 the **God** *of* Israel, are their inheritance, as he promised them.
13: 33 the LORD, the **God** *of* Israel, is their inheritance, as he promised
14: 6 "You know what the LORD said to Moses the man of **God** at
14: 8 I, however, followed the LORD my **God** wholeheartedly.
14: 9 because you have followed the LORD my **God** wholeheartedly.'
14: 14 he followed the LORD, the **God** *of* Israel, wholeheartedly.
18: 3 the land that the LORD, the **God** *of* your fathers, has given you?
18: 6 and I will cast lots for you in the presence of the LORD our **God**.
22: 3 but have carried out the mission the LORD your **God** gave you.
22: 4 Now that the LORD your **God** has given your brothers rest as he
22: 5 to love the LORD your **God**, to walk in all his ways, to obey his
22: 16 'How could you break faith with the **God** *of* Israel like this?
22: 19 an altar for yourselves, other than the altar of the LORD our **God**.
22: 22 "The Mighty One, **God**, the LORD! The Mighty One, God,
22: 22 the LORD! The Mighty One, **God**, the LORD! He knows!
22: 24 'What do you have to do with the LORD, the **God** *of* Israel?
22: 29 other than the altar of the LORD our **God** that stands before his
22: 33 They were glad to hear the report and praised **God**. And they
22: 34 altar this name: A Witness Between Us that the LORD is **God**.
23: 3 You yourselves have seen everything the LORD your **God** has
23: 3 for your sake; it was the LORD your **God** who fought for you.
23: 5 The LORD your **God** himself will drive them out of your way.
23: 5 possession of their land, as the LORD your **God** promised you.
23: 7 do not invoke the names of their **gods** or swear by them.
23: 8 you are to hold fast to the LORD your **God**, as you have until
23: 10 because the LORD your **God** fights for you, just as he promised.
23: 11 So be very careful to love the LORD your **God**.
23: 13 you may be sure that the LORD your **God** will no longer drive
23: 13 from this good land, which the LORD your **God** has given you.
23: 14 soul that not one of all the good promises the LORD your **God**
23: 15 just as every good promise of the LORD your **God** has come true,
23: 15 until he has destroyed you from this good land **he**[s] [+3378] has
23: 16 If you violate the covenant of the LORD your **God**, which he
23: 16 and go and serve other **gods** and bow down to them,
24: 1 and officials of Israel, and they presented themselves before **God**.
24: 2 all the people, "This is what the LORD, the **God** *of* Israel, says:
24: 2 and Nahor, lived beyond the River and worshiped other **gods**.
24: 14 Throw away the **gods** your forefathers worshiped beyond the River
24: 15 whether the **gods** your forefathers served beyond the River,
24: 15 or the **gods** *of* the Amorites, in whose land you are living.
24: 16 "Far be it from us to forsake the LORD to serve other **gods**!
24: 17 It was the LORD our **God** himself who brought us and our fathers
24: 18 in the land. We too will serve the LORD, because he is our **God**."
24: 19 He is a holy **God**; he is a jealous God. He will not forgive your
24: 20 If you forsake the LORD and serve foreign **gods**, he will turn
24: 23 "throw away the foreign **gods** that are among you and yield your
24: 23 and yield your hearts to the LORD, the **God** *of* Israel."
24: 24 to Joshua, "We will serve the LORD our **God** and obey him."
24: 26 And Joshua recorded these things in the Book of the Law of **God**.
24: 27 It will be a witness against you if you are untrue to your **God**."
Jdg 1: 7 Now **God** has paid me back for what I did to them." They brought
2: 3 will be ⌞thorns⌟ in your sides and their **gods** will be a snare to you."
2: 12 They forsook the LORD, the **God** *of* their fathers, who had
2: 12 and worshiped various **gods** of the peoples around them.
2: 12 and worshiped various gods of **[RPH]** the peoples around them.
2: 17 but prostituted themselves to other **gods** and worshiped them.
2: 19 following other **gods** and serving and worshiping them.
3: 6 and gave their own daughters to their sons, and served their **gods**.
3: 7 they forgot the LORD their **God** and served the Baals and the
3: 20 his summer palace and said, "I have a message from **God** for you."
4: 6 and said to him, "The LORD, the **God** *of* Israel, commands you:
4: 23 On that day **God** subdued Jabin, the Canaanite king, before the
5: 3 I will sing; I will make music to the LORD, the **God** *of* Israel.

Jdg 5: 5 the One of Sinai, before the LORD, the **God** *of* Israel.
5: 8 When they chose new **gods**, war came to the city gates, and not a
6: 8 who said, "This is what the LORD, the **God** *of* Israel, says:
6: 10 I said to you, 'I am the LORD your **God**; do not worship the gods
6: 10 do not worship the **gods** *of* the Amorites, in whose land you live.'
6: 20 The angel of **God** said to him, "Take the meat and the unleavened
6: 26 build a proper kind of altar to the LORD your **God** on the top of
6: 31 If Baal really is a **god**, he can defend himself when someone
6: 36 Gideon said to **God**, "If you will save Israel by my hand as you
6: 39 Gideon said to **God**, "Do not be angry with me. Let me make just
6: 40 That night **God** did so. Only the fleece was dry; all the ground was
7: 14 **God** has given the Midianites and the whole camp into his hands."
8: 3 **God** gave Oreb and Zeeb, the Midianite leaders, into your hands.
8: 33 themselves to the Baals. They set up Baal-Berith as their **god**
8: 34 did not remember the LORD their **God**, who had rescued them
9: 7 "Listen to me, citizens of Shechem, so that **God** may listen to you.
9: 9 'Should I give up my oil, by which both **gods** and men are honored,
9: 13 'Should I give up my wine, which cheers both **gods** and men,
9: 23 **God** sent an evil spirit between Abimelech and the citizens of
9: 27 and trodden them, they held a festival in the temple of their **god**.
9: 56 Thus **God** repaid the wickedness that Abimelech had done to his
9: 57 **God** also made the men of Shechem pay for all their wickedness.
10: 6 and the **gods** *of* Aram, the gods of Sidon, the gods of Moab,
10: 6 and the gods of Aram, the **gods** *of* Sidon, the gods of Moab,
10: 6 and the gods of Aram, the gods of Sidon, the **gods** *of* Moab,
10: 6 the **gods** *of* the Ammonites and the gods of the Philistines.
10: 6 the gods of the Ammonites and the **gods** *of* the Philistines.
10: 10 sinned against you, forsaking our **God** and serving the Baals."
10: 13 you have forsaken me and served other **gods**, so I will no longer
10: 14 Go and cry out to the **gods** you have chosen. Let them save you
10: 16 they got rid of the foreign **gods** among them and served the
11: 21 the **God** *of* Israel, gave Sihon and all his men into Israel's hands,
11: 23 "Now since the LORD, the **God** *of* Israel, has driven the
11: 24 Will you not take what your **god** Chemosh gives you? Likewise,
11: 24 Likewise, whatever the LORD our **God** has given us, we will
13: 5 because the boy is to be a Nazirite, set apart to **God** from birth,
13: 6 went to her husband and told him, "A man of **God** came to me.
13: 6 God came to me. He looked like an angel of **God**, very awesome.
13: 7 because the boy will be a Nazirite of **God** from birth until the day
13: 8 let the man of **God** you sent to us come again to teach us how to
13: 9 **God** heard Manoah, and the angel of God came again to the
13: 9 the angel of **God** came again to the woman while she was out in
13: 22 "We are doomed to die!" he said to his wife. "We have seen **God**!"
15: 19 **God** opened up the hollow place in Lehi, and water came out of it.
16: 17 "because I have been a Nazirite set apart to **God** since birth.
16: 23 Philistines assembled to offer a great sacrifice to Dagon their **god**
16: 23 saying, "Our **god** has delivered Samson, our enemy, into our
16: 24 When the people saw him, they praised their **god**, saying,
16: 24 saying, "Our **god** has delivered our enemy into our hands,
16: 28 O **God**, please strengthen me just once more, and let me with one
17: 5 Now this man Micah had a **shrine** [+1074], and he made an ephod
18: 5 "Please inquire of **God** to learn whether our journey will be
18: 10 and a spacious land that **God** has put into your hands,
18: 24 He replied, "You took the **gods** I made, and my priest, and went
18: 31 idols Micah had made, all the time the house of **God** was in Shiloh.
20: 2 of Israel took their places in the assembly of the people of **God**,
20: 18 The Israelites went up to Bethel and inquired of **God**. They said,
20: 27 (In those days the ark of the covenant of **God** was there,
21: 2 where they sat before **God** until evening, raising their voices
21: 3 "O LORD, the **God** *of* Israel," they cried, "why has this happened
Ru 1: 15 "your sister-in-law is going back to her people and her **gods**.
1: 16 I will stay. Your people will be my people and your **God** my God.
1: 16 I will stay. Your people will be my people and your God my **God**.
2: 12 May you be richly rewarded by the LORD, the **God** *of* Israel,
1Sa 1: 17 and may the **God** *of* Israel grant you what you have asked of him."
2: 2 there is no one besides you; there is no Rock like our **God**.
2: 25 If a man sins against another man, **God** may mediate for him;
2: 27 Now a man of **God** came to Eli and said to him, "This is what the
2: 30 "Therefore the LORD, the **God** *of* Israel, declares: 'I promised
3: 3 The lamp of **God** had not yet gone out, and Samuel was lying
3: 3 down in the temple of the LORD, where the ark of **God** was.
3: 17 May **God** deal with you, be it ever so severely, if you hide from
4: 4 and Phinehas, were there with the ark of the covenant of **God**.
4: 7 "A **god** has come into the camp," they said. "We're in trouble!
4: 8 to us! Who will deliver us from the hand of these mighty **gods**?
4: 8 They are the **gods** who struck the Egyptians with all kinds of
4: 11 The ark of **God** was captured, and Eli's two sons, Hophni
4: 13 of the road, watching, because his heart feared for the ark of **God**.
4: 17 and Phinehas, are dead, and the ark of **God** has been captured."
4: 18 When he mentioned the ark of **God**, Eli fell backward off his chair
4: 19 When she heard the news that the ark of **God** had been captured
4: 21 because of the capture of the ark of **God** and the deaths of her
4: 22 has departed from Israel, for the ark of **God** has been captured."
5: 1 After the Philistines had captured the ark of **God**, they took it from
5: 2 they carried the ark **[RPH]** into Dagon's temple and set it beside
5: 7 they said, "The ark of the **god** *of* Israel must not stay here with us,
5: 7 because his hand is heavy upon us and upon Dagon our **god**."
5: 8 asked them, "What shall we do with the ark of the **god** *of* Israel?"
5: 8 They answered, "Have the ark of the **god** *of* Israel moved to Gath."
5: 8 Israel moved to Gath." So they moved the ark of the **God** *of* Israel.
5: 10 So they sent the ark of **God** to Ekron. As the ark of God was
5: 10 As the ark of **God** was entering Ekron, the people of Ekron cried
5: 10 "They have brought the ark of the **god** *of* Israel around to us to kill
5: 11 of the Philistines and said, "Send the ark of the **god** *of* Israel away;
5: 11 had filled the city with panic; **God's** hand was very heavy upon it.
6: 3 They answered, "If you return the ark of the **god** *of* Israel,
6: 5 rats that are destroying the country, and pay honor to Israel's **god**.
6: 5 he will lift his hand from you and your **gods** and your land.
6: 20 "Who can stand in the presence of the LORD, this holy **God**?
7: 3 then rid yourselves of the foreign **gods** and the Ashtoreths
7: 8 to Samuel, "Do not stop crying out to the LORD our **God** for us,
8: 8 forsaking me and serving other **gods**, so they are doing to you.
9: 6 But the servant replied, "Look, in this town there is a man of **God**;
9: 7 We have no gift to take to the man of **God**. What do we have?"
9: 8 I will give it to the man of **God** so that he will tell us what way to
9: 9 in Israel, if a man went to inquire of **God**, he would say, "Come,
9: 10 let's go." So they set out for the town where the man of **God** was.
9: 27 you stay here awhile, so that I may give you a message from **God**."
10: 3 Three men going up to **God** at Bethel will meet you there.
10: 5 "After that you will go to Gibeah of **God**, where there is a
10: 7 do whatever your hand finds to do, for **God** is with you.
10: 9 As Saul turned to leave Samuel, **God** changed Saul's heart,
10: 10 the Spirit of **God** came upon him in power, and he joined in their
10: 18 said to them, "This is what the LORD, the **God** *of* Israel, says:
10: 19 you have now rejected your **God**, who saves you out of all your
10: 26 accompanied by valiant men whose hearts **God** had touched.
11: 6 the Spirit of **God** came upon him in power, and he burned with
12: 9 "But they forgot the LORD their **God**; so he sold them into the
12: 12 rule over us'—even though the LORD your **God** was your king.
12: 14 and the king who reigns over you follow the LORD your **God**—
12: 19 "Pray to the LORD your **God** for your servants so that we will
13: 13 "You have not kept the command the LORD your **God** gave you;
14: 15 raiding parties—and the ground shook. It was a panic sent by **God**.
14: 18 Saul said to Ahijah, "Bring the ark of **God**." (At that time it was
14: 18 ark of God." (At that time **it** [+778+2021] was with the Israelites.)
14: 36 they replied. But the priest said, "Let us inquire of **God** here."
14: 37 So Saul asked **God**, "Shall I go down after the Philistines?
14: 41 to the LORD, the **God** *of* Israel, "Give me the right answer."
14: 44 Saul said, "May **God** deal with me, be it ever so severely,
14: 45 head will fall to the ground, for he did this today with **God's** help."
15: 15 best of the sheep and cattle to sacrifice to the LORD your **God**,
15: 21 in order to sacrifice them to the LORD your **God** at Gilgal."
15: 30 come back with me, so that I may worship the LORD your **God**."
16: 15 said to him, "See, an evil spirit from **God** is tormenting you.
16: 16 He will play when the evil spirit from **God** comes upon you,
16: 23 Whenever the spirit from **God** came upon Saul, David would take
17: 26 Philistine that he should defy the armies of the living **God**?"
17: 36 one of them, because he has defied the armies of the living **God**.
17: 43 at me with sticks?" And the Philistine cursed David by his **gods**.
17: 45 the **God** *of* the armies of Israel, whom you have defied.
17: 46 and the whole world will know that there is a **God** in Israel.
18: 10 The next day an evil spirit from **God** came forcefully upon Saul.
19: 20 the Spirit of **God** came upon Saul's men and they also prophesied.
19: 23 the Spirit of **God** came even upon him, and he walked along
20: 12 "By the LORD, the **God** *of* Israel, I will surely sound out my
22: 3 and stay with you until I learn what **God** will do for me?"
22: 13 giving him bread and a sword and inquiring of **God** for him,
22: 15 Was that day the first time I inquired of **God** for him? Of course
23: 7 had gone to Keilah, and he said, "**God** has handed him over to me,
23: 10 David said, "O LORD, **God** *of* Israel, your servant has heard
23: 11 O LORD, **God** *of* Israel, tell your servant." And the LORD said,
23: 14 Saul searched for him, but **God** did not give David into his hands.
23: 16 went to David at Horesh and helped him find strength in **God**.
25: 22 May **God** deal with David, be it ever so severely, if by morning I
25: 29 securely in the bundle of the living by the LORD your **God**.
25: 32 David said to Abigail, "Praise be to the LORD, the **God** *of* Israel,
25: 34 Otherwise, as surely as the LORD, the **God** *of* Israel, lives,
26: 8 to David, "Today **God** has delivered your enemy into your hands.
26: 19 in the LORD's inheritance and have said, 'Go, serve other **gods**.'
28: 13 The woman said, "I see a **spirit** coming up out of the ground."
28: 15 are fighting against me, and **God** has turned away from me.
29: 9 that you have been as pleasing in my eyes as an angel of **God**;
30: 6 and daughters. But David found strength in the LORD his **God**.
30: 15 "Swear to me before **God** that you will not kill me or hand me over
2Sa 2: 27 Joab answered, "As surely as **God** lives, if you had not spoken,
3: 9 May **God** deal with Abner, be it ever so severely, if I do not do for
3: 35 saying, "May **God** deal with me, be it ever so severely, if I taste
5: 10 more powerful, because the LORD **God** Almighty was with him.

2Sa 6: 2 set out from Baalah of Judah to bring up from there the ark of **God**,
6: 3 They set the ark of **God** on a new cart and brought it from the
6: 4 with the ark of **God** on it, and Ahio was walking in front of it.
6: 6 Uzzah reached out and took hold of the ark of **God**, because the
6: 7 therefore **God** struck him down and he died there beside the ark of
6: 7 God struck him down and he died there beside the ark of **God**.
6:12 of Obed-Edom and everything he has, because of the ark of **God**."
6:12 brought up the ark of **God** from the house of Obed-Edom to the
7: 2 living in a palace of cedar, while the ark of **God** remains in a tent."
7:22 There is no one like you, and there is no **God** but you, as we have
7:23 the one nation on earth that **God** went out to redeem as a people
7:23 by driving out nations and their **gods** from before your people,
7:24 very own forever, and you, O LORD, have become their **God**.
7:25 "And now, LORD **God**, keep forever the promise you have made
7:26 Then men will say, 'The LORD Almighty is **God** over Israel!'
7:27 "O LORD Almighty, **God** *of* Israel, you have revealed this to
7:28 O Sovereign LORD, you are **God**! Your words are trustworthy,
9: 3 left of the house of Saul to whom I can show **God's** kindness?"
10:12 and let us fight bravely for our people and the cities of our **God**.
12: 7 are the man! This is what the LORD, the **God** *of* Israel, says:
12:16 David pleaded with **God** for the child. He fasted and went into his
14:11 "Then let the king invoke the LORD his **God** to prevent the
14:13 then have you devised a thing like this against the people of **God**?
14:14 But **God** does not take away life; instead, he devises ways
14:16 to cut off both me and my son from the inheritance **God** gave us.'
14:17 for my lord the king is like an angel of **God** in discerning good
14:17 and evil. May the LORD your **God** be with you.' "
14:20 My lord has wisdom like that of an angel of **God**—he knows
15:24 who were with him were carrying the ark of the covenant of **God**.
15:24 They set down the ark of **God**, and Abiathar offered sacrifices until
15:25 the king said to Zadok, "Take the ark of **God** back into the city.
15:29 So Zadok and Abiathar took the ark of **God** back to Jerusalem
15:32 David arrived at the summit, where people used to worship **God**,
16:23 advice Ahithophel gave was like that of one who inquires of **God**.
18:28 face to the ground and said, "Praise be to the LORD your **God**!
19:13 [19:14] May **God** deal with me, be it ever so severely, if from
19:27 [19:28] My lord the king is like an angel of **God**; so do whatever
21:14 After that, **God** answered prayer in behalf of the land.
22: 3 my **God** is my rock, in whom I take refuge, my shield and the horn
22: 7 In my distress I called to the LORD; I called out to my **God**.
22:22 ways of the LORD; I have not done evil by turning from my **God**.
22:30 help I can advance against a troop; with my **God** I can scale a wall.
22:32 is God besides the LORD? And who is the Rock except our **God**?
22:47 Praise be to my Rock! Exalted be **God**, the Rock, my Savior!
23: 1 the man anointed by the **God** *of* Jacob, Israel's singer of songs:
23: 3 The **God** *of* Israel spoke, the Rock of Israel said to me: 'When one
23: 3 rules over men in righteousness, when he rules in the fear of **God**,
24: 3 "May the LORD your **God** multiply the troops a hundred times
24:23 also said to him, "May the LORD your **God** accept you."
24:24 I will not sacrifice to the LORD my **God** burnt offerings that cost
1Ki 1:17 you yourself swore to me your servant by the LORD your **God**:
1:30 out today what I swore to you by the LORD, the **God** *of* Israel:
1:36 May the LORD, the **God** *of* my lord the king, so declare it.
1:47 'May your **God** make Solomon's name more famous than yours
1:48 said, 'Praise be to the LORD, the **God** *of* Israel, who has allowed
2: 3 observe what the LORD your **God** requires: Walk in his ways,
2:23 "May **God** deal with me, be it ever so severely, if Adonijah does
3: 5 and **God** said, "Ask for whatever you want me to give you."
3: 7 "Now, O LORD my **God**, you have made your servant king in
3:11 So **God** said to him, "Since you have asked for this and not for
3:28 because they saw that he had wisdom from **God** to administer
4:29 [5:9] **God** gave Solomon wisdom and very great insight, and a
5: 3 [5:17] his **God** until the LORD put his enemies under his feet.
5: 4 [5:18] now the LORD my **God** has given me rest on every side,
5: 5 [5:19] to build a temple for the Name of the LORD my **God**,
8:15 "Praise be to the LORD, the **God** *of* Israel, who with his own
8:17 to build a temple for the Name of the LORD, the **God** *of* Israel.
8:20 built the temple for the Name of the LORD, the **God** *of* Israel.
8:23 "O LORD, **God** *of* Israel, there is no God like you in heaven
8:23 there is no **God** like you in heaven above or on earth below—
8:25 "Now LORD, **God** *of* Israel, keep for your servant David my
8:26 now, O **God** *of* Israel, let your word that you promised your
8:27 "But will **God** really dwell on earth? The heavens, even the highest
8:28 your servant's prayer and his plea for mercy, O LORD my **God**.
8:57 May the LORD our **God** be with us as he was with our fathers;
8:59 before the LORD, be near to the LORD our **God** day and night,
8:60 that all the peoples of the earth may know that the LORD is **God**
8:61 But your hearts must be fully committed to the LORD our **God**,
8:65 They celebrated it before the LORD our **God** for seven days
9: 6 I have given you and go off to serve other **gods** and worship them,
9: 9 will answer, 'Because they have forsaken the LORD their **God**,
9: 9 and have embraced other **gods**, worshiping and serving them—
10: 9 Praise be to the LORD your **God**, who has delighted in you
10:24 with Solomon to hear the wisdom **God** had put in his heart.
11: 2 because they will surely turn your hearts after their **gods**."
11: 4 As Solomon grew old, his wives turned his heart after other **gods**,
11: 4 and his heart was not fully devoted to the LORD his **God**,
11: 5 He followed Ashtoreth the **goddess** *of* the Sidonians, and Molech
11: 8 who burned incense and offered sacrifices to their **gods**.
11: 9 the LORD, the **God** *of* Israel, who had appeared to him twice.
11:10 Although he had forbidden Solomon to follow other **gods**,
11:23 **God** raised up against Solomon another adversary, Rezon son of
11:31 for yourself, for this is what the LORD, the **God** *of* Israel, says:
11:33 and worshiped Ashtoreth the **goddess** *of* the Sidonians,
11:33 Chemosh the **god** *of* the Moabites, and Molech the god of the
11:33 Molech the **god** *of* the Ammonites, and have not walked in my
12:22 But this word of **God** came to Shemaiah the man of God:
12:22 But this word of God came to Shemaiah the man of **God**:
12:28 Here are your **gods**, O Israel, who brought you up out of Egypt."
13: 1 By the word of the LORD a man of **God** came from Judah to
13: 4 When King Jeroboam heard what the man of **God** cried out against
13: 5 its ashes poured out according to the sign given by the man of **God**
13: 6 the king said to the man of **God**, "Intercede with the LORD your
13: 6 "Intercede with the LORD your **God** and pray for me that my
13: 6 So the man of **God** interceded with the LORD, and the king's
13: 7 The king said to the man of **God**, "Come home with me and have
13: 8 the man of **God** answered the king, "Even if you were to give me
13:11 and told him all that the man of **God** had done there that day.
13:12 his sons showed him which road the man of **God** from Judah had
13:14 rode after the man of **God**. He found him sitting under an oak tree
13:14 and asked, "Are you the man of **God** who came from Judah?"
13:21 He cried out to the man of **God** who had come from Judah,
13:21 and have not kept the command the LORD your **God** gave you.
13:26 "It is the man of **God** who defied the word of the LORD.
13:29 So the prophet picked up the body of the man of **God**, laid it on the
13:31 "When I die, bury me in the grave where the man of **God** is buried;
14: 7 tell Jeroboam that this is what the LORD, the **God** *of* Israel, says:
14: 9 You have made for yourself other **gods**, idols made of metal;
14:13 in whom the LORD, the **God** *of* Israel, has found anything good.
15: 3 his heart was not fully devoted to the LORD his **God**, as the heart
15: 4 for David's sake the LORD his **God** gave him a lamp in
15:30 because he provoked the LORD, the **God** *of* Israel, to anger.
16:13 the LORD, the **God** *of* Israel, to anger by their worthless idols.
16:26 the LORD, the **God** *of* Israel, to anger by their worthless idols.
16:33 and did more to provoke the LORD, the **God** *of* Israel,
17: 1 to Ahab, "As the LORD, the **God** *of* Israel, lives, whom I serve,
17:12 "As surely as the LORD your **God** lives," she replied, "I don't
17:14 For this is what the LORD, the **God** *of* Israel, says: 'The jar of
17:18 She said to Elijah, "What do you have against me, man of **God**?
17:20 he cried out to the LORD, "O LORD my **God**, have you brought
17:21 the boy three times and cried to the LORD, "O LORD my **God**,
17:24 "Now I know that you are a man of **God** and that the word of the
18:10 As surely as the LORD your **God** lives, there is not a nation
18:21 If the LORD is **God**, follow him; but if Baal is God, follow him."
18:24 you call on the name of your **god**, and I will call on the name of the
18:24 The **god** who answers by fire—he is God." Then all the people
18:24 The god who answers by fire—he is **God**." Then all the people
18:25 of you. Call on the name of your **god**, but do not light the fire."
18:27 "Shout louder!" he said. "Surely he is a **god**! Perhaps he is deep in
18:36 "O LORD, **God** *of* Abraham, Isaac and Israel, let it be known
18:36 let it be known today that you are **God** in Israel and that I am your
18:37 so these people will know that you, O LORD, are **God**,
18:39 saw this, they fell prostrate and cried, "The LORD—he is **God**!
18:39 and cried, "The LORD—he is God! The LORD—he is **God**!"
19: 2 Elijah to say, "May the **gods** deal with me, be it ever so severely,
19: 8 and forty nights until he reached Horeb, the mountain of **God**.
19:10 "I have been very zealous for the LORD **God** Almighty.
19:14 "I have been very zealous for the LORD **God** Almighty.
20:10 "May the **gods** deal with me, be it ever so severely, if enough dust
20:23 of the king of Aram advised him, "Their **gods** are gods of the hills.
20:23 of the king of Aram advised him, "Their gods are **gods** *of* the hills.
20:28 The man of **God** came up and told the king of Israel, "This is what
20:28 'Because the Arameans think the LORD is a **god** *of* the hills
20:28 think the LORD is a god of the hills and not a **god** *of* the valleys,
21:10 and have them testify that he has cursed both **God** and the king.
21:13 the people, saying, "Naboth has cursed both **God** and the king."
22:53 [22:54] the **God** *of* Israel, to anger, just as his father had done.
2Ki 1: 2 saying to them, "Go and consult Baal-Zebub, the **god** *of* Ekron,
1: 3 because there is no **God** in Israel that you are going off to consult
1: 3 that you are going off to consult Baal-Zebub, the **god** *of* Ekron?'
1: 6 because there is no **God** in Israel that you are sending men to
1: 6 that you are sending men to consult Baal-Zebub, the **god** *of* Ekron?
1: 9 and said to him, "Man of **God**, the king says, 'Come down!' "
1:10 Elijah answered the captain, "If I am a man of **God**, may fire come
1:11 The captain said to him, "Man of **God**, this is what the king says,
1:12 "If I am a man of **God**," Elijah replied, "may fire come down from
1:12 Then the fire of **God** fell from heaven and consumed him
1:13 "Man of **God**," he begged, "please have respect for my life

[F] Hitpael (hitpoel, hitpoal, hitpolel, hitpolal, hitpalel, hitpalal, hitpalpel, hitpalpal, hotpael, hotpaal) [G] Hiphil (hiphtil) [H] Hophal [I] Hishtaphel

2Ki 1:16 because there is no **God** in Israel for you to consult that you have
1:16 have sent messengers to consult Baal-Zebub, the **god** *of* Ekron?
2:14 "Where now is the LORD, the **God** *of* Elijah?" he asked.
4: 7 She went and told the man of **God**, and he said, "Go, sell the oil
4: 9 that this man who often comes our way is a holy man of **God**.
4:16 she objected. "Don't mislead your servant, O man of **God**!"
4:21 She went up and laid him on the bed of the man of **God**, then shut
4:22 and a donkey so I can go to the man of **God** quickly and return."
4:25 So she set out and came to the man of **God** at Mount Carmel.
4:25 in the distance, the man of **God** said to his servant Gehazi, "Look!
4:27 When she reached the man of **God** at the mountain, she took hold
4:27 over to push her away, but the man of **God** said, "Leave her alone!
4:40 to eat it, they cried out, "O man of **God**, there is death in the pot!"
4:42 bringing the man of **God** twenty loaves of barley bread baked from
5: 7 of Israel read the letter, he tore his robes and said, "Am I **God**?
5: 8 When Elisha the man of **God** heard that the king of Israel had torn
5:11 out to me and stand and call on the name of the LORD his **God**,
5:14 as the man of **God** had told him, and his flesh was restored
5:15 Then Naaman and all his attendants went back to the man of **God**.
5:15 "Now I know that there is no **God** in all the world except in Israel.
5:17 burnt offerings and sacrifices to any other **god** but the LORD.
5:20 Gehazi, the servant of Elisha the man of **God**, said to himself,
6: 6 The man of **God** asked, "Where did it fall?" When he showed him
6: 9 The man of **God** sent word to the king of Israel: "Beware of
6:10 king of Israel checked on the place indicated by the man of **God**.
6:15 When the servant of the man of **God** got up and went out early the
6:31 He said, "May **God** deal with me, be it ever so severely, if the head
7: 2 officer on whose arm the king was leaning said to the man of **God**,
7:17 just as the man of **God** had foretold when the king came down to
7:18 It happened as the man of **God** had said to the king: "About this
7:19 The officer had said to the man of **God**, "Look, even if the LORD
8: 2 The woman proceeded to do as the man of **God** said. She and her
8: 4 was talking to Gehazi, the servant of the man of **God**, and had said,
8: 7 king was told, "The man of **God** has come all the way up here,"
8: 8 to Hazael, "Take a gift with you and go to meet the man of **God**.
8:11 until Hazael felt ashamed. Then the man of **God** began to weep.
9: 6 and declared, "This is what the LORD, the **God** *of* Israel, says:
10:31 to keep the law of the LORD, the **God** *of* Israel, with all his heart.
13:19 The man of **God** was angry with him and said, "You should have
14:25 in accordance with the word of the LORD, the **God** *of* Israel,
16: 2 he did not do what was right in the eyes of the LORD his **God**.
17: 7 because the Israelites had sinned against the LORD their **God**,
17: 7 the power of Pharaoh king of Egypt. They worshiped other **gods**
17: 9 The Israelites secretly did things against the LORD their **God** that
17:14 as their fathers, who did not trust in the LORD their **God**.
17:16 They forsook all the commands of the LORD their **God** and made
17:19 even Judah did not keep the commands of the LORD their **God**.
17:26 resettled in the towns of Samaria do not know what the **god** *of* that
17:26 because the people do not know what **he**[s] [+824+2021] requires."
17:27 live there and teach the people what the **god** *of* the land requires."
17:29 each national group made its own **gods** in the several towns where
17:31 and Anammelech, the **gods** [K 468] *of* Sepharvaim.
17:33 they also served their own **gods** in accordance with the customs of
17:35 "Do not worship any other **gods** or bow down to them, serve them
17:37 and commands he wrote for you. Do not worship other **gods**.
17:38 the covenant I have made with you, and do not worship other **gods**.
17:39 Rather, worship the LORD your **God**; it is he who will deliver
18: 5 Hezekiah trusted in the LORD, the **God** *of* Israel. There was no
18:12 This happened because they had not obeyed the LORD their **God**,
18:22 if you say to me, "We are depending on the LORD our **God**"—
18:33 Has the **god** *of* any nation ever delivered his land from the hand of
18:34 Where are the **gods** *of* Hamath and Arpad? Where are the gods of
18:34 and Arpad? Where are the **gods** *of* Sepharvaim, Hena and Ivvah?
18:35 Who of all the **gods** *of* these countries has been able to save his
19: 4 It may be that the LORD your **God** will hear all the words of the
19: 4 his master, the king of Assyria, has sent to ridicule the living **God**,
19: 4 that he will rebuke him for the words the LORD your **God** has
19:10 Do not let the **god** you depend on deceive you when he says,
19:12 Did the **gods** *of* the nations that were destroyed by my forefathers
19:15 "O LORD, **God** *of* Israel, enthroned between the cherubim,
19:15 you alone are **God** over all the kingdoms of the earth.
19:16 listen to the words Sennacherib has sent to insult the living **God**.
19:18 They have thrown their **gods** into the fire and destroyed them,
19:18 destroyed them, for they were not **gods** but only wood and stone,
19:19 Now, O LORD our **God**, deliver us from his hand, so that all
19:19 kingdoms on earth may know that you alone, O LORD, are **God**."
19:20 to Hezekiah: "This is what the LORD, the **God** *of* Israel, says:
19:37 while he was worshiping in the temple of his **god** Nisroch,
20: 5 'This is what the LORD, the **God** *of* your father David, says:
21:12 Therefore this is what the LORD, the **God** *of* Israel, says:
21:22 He forsook the LORD, the **God** *of* his fathers, and did not walk in
22:15 said to them, "This is what the LORD, the **God** *of* Israel, says:
22:17 Because they have forsaken me and burned incense to other **gods**
22:18 'This is what the LORD, the **God** *of* Israel, says concerning the
23:16 LORD proclaimed by the man of **God** who foretold these things.
23:17 "It marks the tomb of the man of **God** who came from Judah
23:21 "Celebrate the Passover to the LORD your **God**, as it is written in
1Ch 4:10 Jabez cried out to the **God** *of* Israel, "Oh, that you would bless me
4:10 so that I will be free from pain." And **God** granted his request.
5:20 and **God** handed the Hagrites and all their allies over to them,
5:22 and many others fell slain, because the battle was **God's** [+4946].
5:25 they were unfaithful to the **God** *of* their fathers and prostituted
5:25 and prostituted themselves to the **gods** *of* the peoples of the land,
5:25 of the peoples of the land, whom **God** had destroyed before them.
5:26 So the **God** *of* Israel stirred up the spirit of Pul king of Assyria
6:48 [6:33] to all the other duties of the tabernacle, the house of **God**.
6:49 [6:34] in accordance with all that Moses the servant of **God** had
9:11 the son of Ahitub, the official in charge of the house of **God**;
9:13 were able men, responsible for ministering in the house of **God**.
9:26 the responsibility for the rooms and treasuries in the house of **God**.
9:27 They would spend the night stationed around the house of **God**,
10:10 They put his armor in the temple of their **gods** and hung up his
11: 2 the LORD your **God** said to you, 'You will shepherd my people
11:19 "**God** forbid that I should do this!" he said. "Should I drink the
12:17 [12:18] may the **God** *of* our fathers see it and judge you."
12:18 [12:19] to those who help you, for your **God** will help you."
12:22 [12:23] until he had a great army, like the army of **God**.
13: 2 it seems good to you and if it is the will of the LORD our **God**,
13: 3 Let us bring the ark of our **God** back to us, for we did not inquire
13: 5 to Lebo Hamath, to bring the ark of **God** from Kiriath Jearim.
13: 6 to bring up from there the ark of **God** the LORD, who is
13: 7 They moved the ark of **God** from Abinadab's house on a new cart,
13: 8 all the Israelites were celebrating with all their might before **God**,
13:10 he had put his hand on the ark. So he died there before **God**.
13:12 David was afraid of **God** that day and asked, "How can I ever
13:12 that day and asked, "How can I ever bring the ark of **God** to me?"
13:14 The ark of **God** remained with the family of Obed-Edom in his
14:10 so David inquired of **God**: "Shall I go and attack the Philistines?
14:11 break out, **God** has broken out against my enemies by my hand."
14:12 The Philistines had abandoned their **gods** there, and David gave
14:14 so David inquired of **God** again, and God answered him, "Do not
14:14 **God** answered him, "Do not go straight up, but circle around them
14:15 because that will mean **God** has gone out in front of you to strike
14:16 So David did as **God** commanded him, and they struck down the
15: 1 he prepared a place for the ark of **God** and pitched a tent for it.
15: 2 David said, "No one but the Levites may carry the ark of **God**,
15:12 the LORD, the **God** *of* Israel, to the place I have prepared for it.
15:13 did not bring it up the first time that the LORD our **God** broke out
15:14 in order to bring up the ark of the LORD, the **God** *of* Israel.
15:15 the Levites carried the ark of **God** with the poles on their
15:24 Eliezer the priests were to blow trumpets before the ark of **God**.
15:26 Because **God** had helped the Levites who were carrying the ark of
16: 1 They brought the ark of **God** and set it inside the tent that David
16: 1 presented burnt offerings and fellowship offerings before **God**.
16: 4 to give thanks, and to praise the LORD, the **God** *of* Israel:
16: 6 blow the trumpets regularly before the ark of the covenant of **God**.
16:14 He is the LORD our **God**; his judgments are in all the earth.
16:25 and most worthy of praise; he is to be feared above all **gods**.
16:26 For all the **gods** *of* the nations are idols, but the LORD made the
16:35 Cry out, "Save us, O **God** our Savior; gather us and deliver us from
16:36 Praise be to the LORD, the **God** *of* Israel, from everlasting to
16:42 and for the playing of the other instruments for **sacred** song.
17: 2 "Whatever you have in mind, do it, for **God** is with you."
17: 3 That night the word of **God** came to Nathan, saying:
17:16 "Who am I, O LORD **God**, and what is my family, that you have
17:17 as if this were not enough in your sight, O **God**, you have spoken
17:17 on me as though I were the most exalted of men, O LORD **God**.
17:20 "There is no one like you, O LORD, and there is no **God** but you,
17:21 the one nation on earth whose **God** went out to redeem a people for
17:22 very own forever, and you, O LORD, have become their **God**.
17:24 'The LORD Almighty, the **God** *over* Israel, is Israel's God!'
17:24 'The LORD Almighty, the God over Israel, is Israel's **God**!'
17:25 "You, my **God**, have revealed to your servant that you will build a
17:26 O LORD, you are **God**! You have promised these good things to
19:13 and let us fight bravely for our people and the cities of our **God**.
21: 7 This command was also evil in the sight of **God**; so he punished
21: 8 Then David said to **God**, "I have sinned greatly by doing this.
21:15 **God** sent an angel to destroy Jerusalem. But as the angel was doing
21:17 David said to **God**, "Was it not I who ordered the fighting men to
21:17 O LORD my **God**, let your hand fall upon me and my family,
21:30 David could not go before it to inquire of **God**, because he was
22: 1 Then David said, "The house of the LORD **God** is to be here,
22: 2 to prepare dressed stone for building the house of **God**.
22: 6 charged him to build a house for the LORD, the **God** *of* Israel.
22: 7 in my heart to build a house for the Name of the LORD my **God**.
22:11 you have success and build the house of the LORD your **God**,
22:12 over Israel, so that you may keep the law of the LORD your **God**.
22:18 He said to them, "Is not the LORD your **God** with you? And has

1Ch 22: 19 Now devote your heart and soul to seeking the LORD your **God**.
22: 19 Begin to build the sanctuary of the LORD **God**, so that you may
22: 19 the sacred articles belonging to **God** into the temple that will be
23: 14 The sons of Moses the man of **God** were counted as part of the
23: 25 For David had said, "Since the LORD, the **God** *of* Israel,
23: 28 and the performance of other duties at the house of **God**.
24: 5 and officials of **God** among the descendants of both Eleazar
24: 19 as the LORD, the **God** *of* Israel, had commanded him.
25: 5 They were given him through the promises of **God** to exalt him.
25: 5 to exalt him. **God** gave Heman fourteen sons and three daughters.
25: 6 lyres and harps, for the ministry at the house of **God**.
26: 5 and Peullethai the eighth. (For **God** had blessed Obed-Edom.)
26: 20 fellow Levites were in charge of the treasuries of the house of **God**
26: 32 and the half-tribe of Manasseh for every matter pertaining to **God**
28: 2 for the footstool of our **God**, and I made plans to build it.
28: 3 But **God** said to me, 'You are not to build a house for my Name,
28: 4 "Yet the LORD, the **God** *of* Israel, chose me from my whole
28: 8 and of the assembly of the LORD, and in the hearing of our **God**:
28: 8 Be careful to follow all the commands of the LORD your **God**,
28: 9 "And you, my son Solomon, acknowledge the **God** *of* your father,
28: 12 for the treasuries of the temple of **God** and for the treasuries for the
28: 20 or discouraged, for the LORD **God**, my God, is with you.
28: 20 or discouraged, for the LORD God, my **God**, is with you.
28: 21 and Levites are ready for all the work on the temple of **God**,
29: 1 the one whom **God** has chosen, is young and inexperienced.
29: 1 this palatial structure is not for man but for the LORD **God**.
29: 2 With all my resources I have provided for the temple of my **God**—
29: 3 in my devotion to the temple of my **God** I now give my personal
29: 3 my personal treasures of gold and silver for the temple of my **God**,
29: 7 They gave toward the work on the temple of **God** five thousand
29: 10 saying, "Praise be to you, O LORD, **God** *of* our father Israel,
29: 13 Now, our **God**, we give you thanks, and praise your glorious name.
29: 16 O LORD our **God**, as for all this abundance that we have
29: 17 I know, my **God**, that you test the heart and are pleased with
29: 18 O LORD, **God** *of* our fathers Abraham, Isaac and Israel,
29: 20 David said to the whole assembly, "Praise the LORD your **God**."
29: 20 So they all praised the LORD, the **God** *of* their fathers; they
2Ch 1: 1 for the LORD his **God** was with him and made him exceedingly
1: 3 to the high place at Gibeon, for **God's** Tent of Meeting was there,
1: 4 Now David had brought up the ark of **God** from Kiriath Jearim to
1: 7 That night **God** appeared to Solomon and said to him, "Ask for
1: 8 Solomon answered **God**, "You have shown great kindness to
1: 9 Now, LORD **God**, let your promise to my father David be
1: 11 **God** said to Solomon, "Since this is your heart's desire and you
2: 4 [2:3] about to build a temple for the Name of the LORD my **God**
2: 4 [2:3] and at the appointed feasts of the LORD our **God**.
2: 5 [2:4] will be great, because our **God** is greater than all other gods.
2: 5 [2:4] will be great, because our God is greater than all other **gods**.
2: 12 [2:11] the **God** *of* Israel, who made heaven and earth!
3: 3 The foundation Solomon laid for building the temple of **God** was
4: 11 work he had undertaken for King Solomon in the temple of **God**:
4: 19 Solomon also made all the furnishings that were in **God's** temple:
5: 1 and he placed them in the treasuries of **God's** temple.
5: 14 of the cloud, for the glory of the LORD filled the temple of **God**.
6: 4 "Praise be to the LORD, the **God** *of* Israel, who with his hands
6: 7 to build a temple for the Name of the LORD, the **God** *of* Israel.
6: 10 built the temple for the Name of the LORD, the **God** *of* Israel.
6: 14 "O LORD, **God** *of* Israel, there is no God like you in heaven
6: 14 God of Israel, there is no **God** like you in heaven or on earth—
6: 16 "Now LORD, **God** *of* Israel, keep for your servant David my
6: 17 now, O LORD, **God** *of* Israel, let your word that you promised
6: 18 "But will **God** really dwell on earth with men? The heavens,
6: 19 your servant's prayer and his plea for mercy, O LORD my **God**.
6: 40 "Now, my **God**, may your eyes be open and your ears attentive to
6: 41 "Now arise, O LORD **God**, and come to your resting place,
6: 41 May your priests, O LORD **God**, be clothed with salvation,
6: 42 O LORD **God**, do not reject your anointed one. Remember the
7: 5 So the king and all the people dedicated the temple of **God**.
7: 19 I have given you and go off to serve other **gods** and worship them,
7: 22 the **God** *of* their fathers, who brought them out of Egypt, and have
7: 22 and have embraced other **gods**, worshiping and serving them—
8: 14 because this was what David the man of **God** had ordered.
9: 8 Praise be to the LORD your **God**, who has delighted in you
9: 8 placed you on his throne as king to rule for the LORD your **God**.
9: 8 Because of the love of your **God** for Israel and his desire to uphold
9: 23 with Solomon to hear the wisdom **God** had put in his heart.
10: 15 did not listen to the people, for this turn of events was from **God**,
11: 2 But this word of the LORD came to Shemaiah the man of **God**:
11: 16 the **God** *of* Israel, followed the Levites to Jerusalem to offer
11: 16 to offer sacrifices to the LORD, the **God** *of* their fathers.
13: 5 Don't you know that the LORD, the **God** *of* Israel, has given the
13: 8 with you the golden calves that Jeroboam made to be your **gods**.
13: 9 and seven rams may become a priest of what are not **gods**.
13: 10 "As for us, the LORD is our **God**, and we have not forsaken him.
13: 11 We are observing the requirements of the LORD our **God**.
13: 12 **God** is with us; he is our leader. His priests with their trumpets will
13: 12 the LORD, the **God** *of* your fathers, for you will not succeed."
13: 15 **God** routed Jeroboam and all Israel before Abijah and Judah.
13: 16 fled before Judah, and **God** delivered them into their hands.
13: 18 because they relied on the LORD, the **God** *of* their fathers.
14: 2 [14:1] was good and right in the eyes of the LORD his **God**.
14: 4 [14:3] the **God** *of* their fathers, and to obey his laws
14: 7 [14:6] is still ours, because we have sought the LORD our **God**;
14: 11 [14:10] Asa called to the LORD his **God** and said, "LORD,
14: 11 [14:10] Help us, O LORD our **God**, for we rely on you, and in
14: 11 [14:10] O LORD, you are our **God**; do not let man prevail
15: 1 The Spirit of **God** came upon Azariah son of Oded.
15: 3 For a long time Israel was without the true **God**, without a priest to
15: 4 the **God** *of* Israel, and sought him, and he was found by them.
15: 6 because **God** was troubling them with every kind of distress.
15: 9 from Israel when they saw that the LORD his **God** was with him.
15: 12 the LORD, the **God** *of* their fathers, with all their heart and soul.
15: 13 the **God** *of* Israel, were to be put to death, whether small or great,
15: 18 He brought into the temple of **God** the silver and gold
16: 7 you relied on the king of Aram and not on the LORD your **God**,
17: 4 sought the **God** *of* his father and followed his commands rather
18: 5 they answered, "for **God** will give it into the king's hand."
18: 13 surely as the LORD lives, I can tell him only what my **God** says."
18: 31 and the LORD helped him. **God** drew them away from him,
19: 3 of the Asherah poles and have set your heart on seeking **God**."
19: 4 and turned them back to the LORD, the **God** *of* their fathers.
19: 7 for with the LORD our **God** there is no injustice or partiality
20: 6 "O LORD, **God** *of* our fathers, are you not the God who is in
20: 6 God of our fathers, are you not the **God** who is in heaven?
20: 7 O our **God**, did you not drive out the inhabitants of this land before
20: 12 O our **God**, will you not judge them? For we have no power to face
20: 15 of this vast army. For the battle is not yours, but **God's** [+4200].
20: 19 and praised the LORD, the **God** *of* Israel, with very loud voice.
20: 20 Have faith in the LORD your **God** and you will be upheld;
20: 29 The fear of **God** came upon all the kingdoms of the countries when
20: 30 was at peace, for his **God** had given him rest on every side.
20: 33 the people still had not set their hearts on the **God** *of* their fathers.
21: 10 because Jehoram had forsaken the LORD, the **God** *of* his fathers.
21: 12 "This is what the LORD, the **God** *of* your father David, says:
22: 7 Ahaziah's visit to Joram, **God** brought about Ahaziah's downfall.
22: 12 He remained hidden with them at the temple of **God** for six years
23: 3 assembly made a covenant with the king at the temple of **God**.
23: 9 had belonged to King David and that were in the temple of **God**.
24: 5 due annually from all Israel, to repair the temple of your **God**.
24: 7 of that wicked woman Athaliah had broken into the temple of **God**
24: 9 that Moses the servant of **God** had required of Israel in the desert.
24: 13 They rebuilt the temple of **God** according to its original design
24: 16 because of the good he had done in Israel for **God** and his temple.
24: 18 the **God** *of* their fathers, and worshiped Asherah poles and idols.
24: 20 the Spirit of **God** came upon Zechariah son of Jehoiada the priest.
24: 20 He stood before the people and said, "This is what **God** says:
24: 24 the **God** *of* their fathers, judgment was executed on Joash.
24: 27 the record of the restoration of the temple of **God** are written in the
25: 7 a man of **God** came to him and said, "O king, these troops from
25: 8 **God** will overthrow you before the enemy, for God has the power
25: 8 before the enemy, for **God** has the power to help or to overthrow."
25: 9 Amaziah asked the man of **God**, "But what about the hundred
25: 9 The man of **God** replied, "The LORD can give you much more
25: 14 the Edomites, he brought back the **gods** *of* the people of Seir.
25: 14 He set them up as his own **gods**, bowed down to them and burned
25: 15 prophet to him, who said, "Why do you consult this people's **gods**,
25: 16 but said, "I know that **God** has determined to destroy you,
25: 20 for **God** so worked that he might hand them over to ⌞Jehoash⌟,
25: 20 them over to ⌞Jehoash⌟, because they sought the **gods** *of* Edom.
25: 24 all the articles found in the temple of **God** that had been in the care
26: 5 He sought **God** during the days of Zechariah, who instructed him
26: 5 the days of Zechariah, who instructed him in the fear of **God**.
26: 5 As long as he sought the LORD, **God** gave him success.
26: 7 **God** helped him against the Philistines and against the Arabs who
26: 16 He was unfaithful to the LORD his **God**, and entered the temple
26: 18 been unfaithful; and you will not be honored by the LORD **God**."
27: 6 because he walked steadfastly before the LORD his **God**.
28: 5 Therefore the LORD his **God** handed him over to the king of
28: 6 because Judah had forsaken the LORD, the **God** *of* their fathers.
28: 9 the LORD, the **God** *of* your fathers, was angry with Judah,
28: 10 But aren't you also guilty of sins against the LORD your **God**?
28: 23 He offered sacrifices to the **gods** *of* Damascus, who had defeated
28: 23 "Since the **gods** *of* the kings of Aram have helped them,
28: 24 Ahaz gathered together the furnishings from the temple of **God**
28: 24 from the temple of God and took **them**[S] [+1074+2021+3998] away.
28: 25 town in Judah he built high places to burn sacrifices to other **gods**
28: 25 and provoked the LORD, the **God** *of* his fathers, to anger.
29: 5 and consecrate the temple of the LORD, the **God** *of* your fathers.

2Ch 29: 6 they did evil in the eyes of the LORD our **God** and forsook him.
29: 7 or present any burnt offerings at the sanctuary to the **God** *of* Israel.
29: 10 the **God** *of* Israel, so that his fierce anger will turn away from us.
29: 36 all the people rejoiced at what **God** had brought about for his
30: 1 and celebrate the Passover to the LORD, the **God** *of* Israel.
30: 5 and celebrate the Passover to the LORD, the **God** *of* Israel.
30: 6 return to the LORD, the **God** *of* Abraham, Isaac and Israel,
30: 7 who were unfaithful to the LORD, the **God** *of* their fathers,
30: 8 Serve the LORD your **God**, so that his fierce anger will turn away
30: 9 this land, for the LORD your **God** is gracious and compassionate.
30: 12 Also in Judah the hand of **God** was on the people to give them
30: 16 positions as prescribed in the Law of Moses the man of **God**.
30: 19 who sets his heart on seeking **God**—the LORD, the God of his
30: 19 his heart on seeking God—the LORD, the **God** *of* his fathers—
30: 22 and praised the LORD, the **God** *of* their fathers.
31: 6 and a tithe of the holy things dedicated to the LORD their **God**,
31: 13 and Azariah the official in charge of the temple of **God**.
31: 14 the East Gate, was in charge of the freewill offerings given to **God**,
31: 20 what was good and right and faithful before the LORD his **God**.
31: 21 In everything that he undertook in the service of **God's** temple
31: 21 and the commands, he sought his **God** and worked wholeheartedly.
32: 8 with us is the LORD our **God** to help us and to fight our battles."
32: 11 'The LORD our **God** will save us from the hand of the king of
32: 13 Were the **gods** *of* those nations ever able to deliver their land from
32: 14 Who of all the **gods** *of* these nations that my fathers destroyed has
32: 14 from me? How then can your **god** deliver you from my hand?
32: 15 How much less will your **god** deliver you from my hand!"
32: 16 Sennacherib's officers spoke further against the LORD **God**
32: 17 the LORD, the **God** *of* Israel, and saying this against him:
32: 17 "Just as the **gods** *of* the peoples of the other lands did not rescue
32: 17 so the **god** *of* Hezekiah will not rescue his people from my hand."
32: 19 They spoke about the **God** *of* Jerusalem as they did about the gods
32: 19 as they did about the **gods** *of* the other peoples of the world—
32: 21 when he went into the temple of his **god**, some of his sons cut him
32: 29 of flocks and herds, for **God** had given him very great riches.
32: 31 **God** left him to test him and to know everything that was in his
33: 7 He took the carved image he had made and put it in **God's** temple,
33: 7 of which **God** had said to David and to his son Solomon, "In this
33: 12 In his distress he sought the favor of the LORD his **God**
33: 12 and humbled himself greatly before the **God** *of* his fathers.
33: 13 and to his kingdom. Then Manasseh knew that the LORD is **God**.
33: 15 He got rid of the foreign **gods** and removed the image from the
33: 16 on it, and told Judah to serve the LORD, the **God** *of* Israel.
33: 17 to sacrifice at the high places, but only to the LORD their **God**.
33: 18 including his prayer to his **God** and the words the seers spoke to
33: 18 the **God** *of* Israel, are written in the annals of the kings of Israel.
34: 3 he was still young, he began to seek the **God** *of* his father David.
34: 8 the recorder, to repair the temple of the LORD his **God**.
34: 9 gave him the money that had been brought into the temple of **God**,
34: 23 said to them, "This is what the LORD, the **God** *of* Israel, says:
34: 25 Because they have forsaken me and burned incense to other **gods**
34: 26 'This is what the LORD, the **God** *of* Israel, says concerning the
34: 27 you humbled yourself before **God** when you heard what he spoke
34: 32 of Jerusalem did this in accordance with the covenant of **God**,
34: 32 in accordance with the covenant of God, the **God** *of* their fathers.
34: 33 he had all who were present in Israel serve the LORD their **God**.
34: 33 they did not fail to follow the LORD, the **God** *of* their fathers.
35: 3 Now serve the LORD your **God** and his people Israel.
35: 8 Zechariah and Jehiel, the administrators of **God's** temple,
35: 21 **God** has told me to hurry; so stop opposing God, who is with me,
35: 21 so stop opposing **God**, who is with me, or he will destroy you."
35: 22 He would not listen to what Neco had said at **God's** command
36: 5 eleven years. He did evil in the eyes of the LORD his **God**.
36: 12 He did evil in the eyes of the LORD his **God** and did not humble
36: 13 who had made him take an oath in **God's** name.
36: 13 his heart and would not turn to the LORD, the **God** *of* Israel.
36: 15 The LORD, the **God** *of* their fathers, sent word to them through
36: 16 they mocked **God's** messengers, despised his words and scoffed at
36: 18 He carried to Babylon all the articles from the temple of **God**,
36: 19 They set fire to **God's** temple and broke down the wall of
36: 23 " 'The LORD, the **God** *of* heaven, has given me all the kingdoms
36: 23 may the LORD his **God** be with him, and let him go up.' "
Ezr 1: 2 " 'The LORD, the **God** *of* heaven, has given me all the kingdoms
1: 3 may his **God** be with him, and let him go up to Jerusalem in Judah
1: 3 of the LORD, the **God** *of* Israel, the God who is in Jerusalem.
1: 3 of the LORD, the God of Israel, the **God** who is in Jerusalem.
1: 4 and with freewill offerings for the temple of **God** in Jerusalem.' "
1: 5 the priests and Levites—everyone whose heart **God** had moved—
1: 7 away from Jerusalem and had placed in the temple of his **god**.
2: 68 offerings toward the rebuilding of the house of **God** on its site.
3: 2 his associates began to build the altar of the **God** *of* Israel to
3: 2 with what is written in the Law of Moses the man of **God**.
3: 8 the second year after their arrival at the house of **God** in Jerusalem,
3: 9 joined together in supervising those working on the house of **God**.
4: 1 exiles were building a temple for the LORD, the **God** *of* Israel,
4: 2 we seek your **God** and have been sacrificing to him since the time
4: 3 "You have no part with us in building a temple to our **God**.
4: 3 the **God** *of* Israel, as King Cyrus, the king of Persia,
6: 21 Gentile neighbors in order to seek the LORD, the **God** *of* Israel.
6: 22 so that he assisted them in the work on the house of **God**, the God
6: 22 assisted them in the work on the house of God, the **God** *of* Israel.
7: 6 Law of Moses, which the LORD, the **God** *of* Israel, had given.
7: 6 he asked, for the hand of the LORD his **God** was on him.
7: 9 of the fifth month, for the gracious hand of his **God** was on him.
7: 27 Praise be to the LORD, the **God** *of* our fathers, who has put it
7: 28 Because the hand of the LORD my **God** was on me, I took
8: 17 so that they might bring attendants to us for the house of our **God**.
8: 18 Because the gracious hand of our **God** was on us, they brought us
8: 21 so that we might humble ourselves before our **God** and ask him for
8: 22 "The gracious hand of our **God** is on everyone who looks to him,
8: 23 So we fasted and petitioned our **God** about this, and he answered
8: 25 and all Israel present there had donated for the house of our **God**.
8: 28 gold are a freewill offering to the LORD, the **God** *of* your fathers.
8: 30 weighed out to be taken to the house of our **God** in Jerusalem.
8: 31 The hand of our **God** was on us, and he protected us from enemies
8: 33 On the fourth day, in the house of our **God**, we weighed out the
8: 35 from captivity sacrificed burnt offerings to the **God** *of* Israel:
8: 36 then gave assistance to the people and to the house of **God**.
9: 4 everyone who trembled at the words of the **God** *of* Israel gathered
9: 5 fell on my knees with my hands spread out to the LORD my **God**
9: 6 "O my **God**, I am too ashamed and disgraced to lift up my face to
9: 6 I am too ashamed and disgraced to lift up my face to you, my **God**,
9: 8 the LORD our **God** has been gracious in leaving us a remnant
9: 8 so our **God** gives light to our eyes and a little relief in our bondage.
9: 9 Though we are slaves, our **God** has not deserted us in our bondage.
9: 9 He has granted us new life to rebuild the house of our **God**
9: 10 "But now, O our **God**, what can we say after this? For we have
9: 13 is a result of our evil deeds and our great guilt, and yet, our **God**,
9: 15 O LORD, **God** *of* Israel, you are righteous! We are left this day as
10: 1 weeping and throwing himself down before the house of **God**,
10: 2 "We have been unfaithful to our **God** by marrying foreign women
10: 3 Now let us make a covenant before our **God** to send away all these
10: 3 of my lord and of those who fear the commands of our **God**.
10: 6 Ezra withdrew from before the house of **God** and went to the room
10: 9 all the people were sitting in the square before the house of **God**,
10: 11 confession to the LORD, the **God** *of* your fathers, and do his will.
10: 14 until the fierce anger of our **God** in this matter is turned away from
Ne 1: 4 days I mourned and fasted and prayed before the **God** *of* heaven.
1: 5 "O LORD, **God** *of* heaven, the great and awesome God,
2: 4 "What is it you want?" Then I prayed to the **God** *of* heaven,
2: 8 because the gracious hand of my **God** was upon me, the king
2: 12 I had not told anyone what my **God** had put in my heart to do for
2: 18 I also told them about the gracious hand of my **God** upon me
2: 20 them by saying, "The **God** *of* heaven will give us success.
4: 4 [3:36] Hear us, O our **God**, for we are despised. Turn their insults
4: 9 [4:3] we prayed to our **God** and posted a guard day and night to
4: 15 [4:9] we were aware of their plot and that **God** had frustrated it,
4: 20 [4:14] of the trumpet, join us there. Our **God** will fight for us!"
5: 9 Shouldn't you walk in the fear of our **God** to avoid the reproach of
5: 13 "In this way may **God** shake out of his house and possessions
5: 15 the people. But out of reverence for **God** I did not act like that.
5: 19 Remember me with favor, O my **God**, for all I have done for these
6: 10 He said, "Let us meet in the house of **God**, inside the temple,
6: 12 I realized that **God** had not sent him, but that he had prophesied
6: 14 Remember Tobiah and Sanballat, O my **God**, because of what they
6: 16 realized that this work had been done with the help of our **God**.
7: 2 he was a man of integrity and feared **God** more than most men do.
7: 5 So my **God** put it into my heart to assemble the nobles, the
8: 6 Ezra praised the LORD, the great **God**; and all the people lifted
8: 8 They read from the Book of the Law of **God**, making it clear
8: 9 said to them all, "This day is sacred to the LORD your **God**.
8: 16 in the courts of the house of **God** and in the square by the Water
8: 18 first day to the last, Ezra read from the Book of the Law of **God**.
9: 3 read from the Book of the Law of the LORD their **God** for a
9: 3 quarter in confession and in worshiping the LORD their **God**.
9: 4 who called with loud voices to the LORD their **God**.
9: 5 "Stand up and praise the LORD your **God**, who is from
9: 7 "You are the LORD **God**, who chose Abram and brought him out
9: 18 cast for themselves an image of a calf and said, 'This is your **god**,
9: 32 "Now therefore, O our **God**, the great, mighty and awesome God,
10: 28 [10:29] the neighboring peoples for the sake of the Law of **God**,
10: 29 [10:30] an oath to follow the Law of **God** given through Moses
10: 29 [10:30] the Law of God given through Moses the servant of **God**
10: 32 [10:33] shekel each year for the service of the house of our **God**:
10: 33 [10:34] for Israel; and for all the duties of the house of our **God**.
10: 34 [10:35] **God** at set times each year a contribution of wood to burn
10: 34 [10:35] of wood to burn on the altar of the LORD our **God**,
10: 36 [10:37] of our herds and of our flocks to the house of our **God**,

Ne 10:36 [10:37] our God, to the priests ministering **there**[s] [+928+1074].
10:37 [10:38] we will bring to the storerooms of the house of our **God**,
10:38 [10:39] to bring a tenth of the tithes up to the house of our **God**,
10:39 [10:40] singers stay. "We will not neglect the house of our **God**."
11:11 son of Meraioth, the son of Ahitub, supervisor in the house of **God**,
11:16 who had charge of the outside work of the house of **God**;
11:22 were the singers responsible for the service of the house of **God**.
12:24 responding to the other, as prescribed by David the man of **God**.
12:36 with musical instruments ⌊prescribed by⌋ David the man of **God**.
12:40 choirs that gave thanks then took their places in the house of **God**;
12:43 great sacrifices, rejoicing because **God** had given them great joy.
12:45 They performed the service of their **God** and the service of
12:46 for the singers and for the songs of praise and thanksgiving to **God**.
13:1 or Moabite should ever be admitted into the assembly of **God**,
13:2 on them. (Our **God**, however, turned the curse into a blessing.)
13:4 had been put in charge of the storerooms of the house of our **God**.
13:7 done in providing Tobiah a room in the courts of the house of **God**.
13:9 then I put back into them the equipment of the house of **God**,
13:11 and asked them, "Why is the house of **God** neglected?"
13:14 Remember me for this, O my **God**, and do not blot out what I have
13:14 so faithfully done for the house of my **God** and its services.
13:18 so that our **God** brought all this calamity upon us and upon this
13:22 Remember me for this also, O my **God**, and show mercy to me
13:25 out their hair. I made them take an oath in **God's** name and said:
13:26 He was loved by his **God**, and God made him king over all Israel,
13:26 He was loved by his God, and **God** made him king over all Israel,
13:27 and are being unfaithful to our **God** by marrying foreign women?"
13:29 Remember them, O my **God**, because they defiled the priestly
13:31 and for the firstfruits. Remember me with favor, O my **God**.
Job 1:1 man was blameless and upright; he feared **God** and shunned evil.
1:5 "Perhaps my children have sinned and cursed **God** in their hearts."
1:6 One day the **angels** [+1201+2021] came to present themselves
1:8 he is blameless and upright, a man who fears **God** and shuns evil."
1:9 "Does Job fear **God** for nothing?" Satan replied.
1:16 "The fire of **God** fell from the sky and burned up the sheep
1:22 In all this, Job did not sin by charging **God** with wrongdoing.
2:1 On another day the **angels** [+1201+2021] came to present
2:3 he is blameless and upright, a man who fears **God** and shuns evil.
2:9 "Are you still holding on to your integrity? Curse **God** and die!"
2:10 Shall we accept good from **God**, and not trouble?" In all this,
5:8 I would appeal to God; I would lay my cause before **him**[s].
20:29 Such is the fate **God** allots the wicked, the heritage appointed for
28:23 **God** understands the way to it and he alone knows where it dwells,
32:2 became very angry with Job for justifying himself rather than **God**.
34:9 For he says, 'It profits a man nothing when he tries to please **God**.'
38:7 stars sang together and all the **angels** [+1201] shouted for joy?
Ps 3:2 [3:3] Many are saying of me, "**God** will not deliver him."
3:7 [3:8] Arise, O LORD! Deliver me, O my **God**! Strike all my
4:1 [4:2] Answer me when I call to you, O my righteous **God**.
5:2 [5:3] to my cry for help, my King and my **God**, for to you I pray.
5:10 [5:11] Declare them guilty, O **God**! Let their intrigues be their
7:1 [7:2] O LORD my **God**, I take refuge in you; save and deliver
7:3 [7:4] O LORD my **God**, if I have done this and there is guilt on
7:9 [7:10] O righteous **God**, who searches minds and hearts, bring to
7:10 [7:11] My shield is **God** Most High, who saves the upright in
7:11 [7:12] **God** is a righteous judge, a God who expresses his wrath
8:5 [8:6] You made him a little lower than the **heavenly beings**
9:17 [9:18] wicked return to the grave, all the nations that forget **God**.
10:4 does not seek him; in all his thoughts there is no room for **God**.
10:13 Why does the wicked man revile **God**? Why does he say to
13:3 [13:4] Look on me and answer, O LORD my **God**. Give light to
14:1 The fool says in his heart, "There is no **God**." They are corrupt,
14:2 of men to see if there are any who understand, any who seek **God**.
14:5 with dread, for **God** is present in the company of the righteous.
18:6 [18:7] distress I called to the LORD; I cried to my **God** for help.
18:21 [18:22] I have not done evil by turning from my **God**.
18:28 [18:29] my lamp burning; my **God** turns my darkness into light.
18:29 [18:30] advance against a troop; with my **God** I can scale a wall.
18:31 [18:32] the LORD? And who is the Rock except our **God**?
18:46 [18:47] Praise be to my Rock! Exalted be **God** my Savior!
20:1 [20:2] in distress; may the name of the **God** *of* Jacob protect you.
20:5 [20:6] and will lift up our banners in the name of our **God**.
20:7 [20:8] in horses, but we trust in the name of the LORD our **God**.
22:2 [22:3] O my **God**, I cry out by day, but you do not answer, by
24:5 blessing from the LORD and vindication from **God** his Savior.
24:6 those who seek him, who seek your face, O **God** [BHS-] *of* Jacob.
25:2 in you I trust, O my **God**. Do not let me be put to shame, nor let
25:5 guide me in your truth and teach me, for you are **God** my Savior,
25:22 Redeem Israel, O **God**, from all their troubles!
27:9 my helper. Do not reject me or forsake me, O **God** my Savior.
30:2 [30:3] O LORD my **God**, I called to you for help and you healed
30:12 [30:13] O LORD my **God**, I will give you thanks forever.
31:14 [31:15] But I trust in you, O LORD; I say, "You are my **God**."
33:12 Blessed is the nation whose **God** is the LORD, the people he
35:23 and rise to my defense! Contend for me, my **God** and Lord.
35:24 Vindicate me in your righteousness, O LORD my **God**; do not let
36:1 [36:2] of the wicked: There is no fear of **God** before his eyes.
36:7 [36:8] Both **high** and low among men find refuge in the shadow
37:31 The law of his **God** is in his heart; his feet do not slip.
38:15 [38:16] for you, O LORD; you will answer, O Lord my **God**.
38:21 [38:22] do not forsake me; be not far from me, O my **God**.
40:3 [40:4] put a new song in my mouth, a hymn of praise to our **God**.
40:5 [40:6] Many, O LORD my **God**, are the wonders you have done.
40:8 [40:9] I desire to do your will, O my **God**; your law is within my
40:17 [40:18] are my help and my deliverer; O my **God**, do not delay.
41:13 [41:14] Praise be to the LORD, the **God** *of* Israel,
42:1 [42:2] for streams of water, so my soul pants for you, O **God**.
42:2 [42:3] My soul thirsts for **God**, for the living God. When can I go
42:2 [42:3] for the living God. When can I go and meet with **God**?
42:3 [42:4] while men say to me all day long, "Where is your **God**?"
42:4 [42:5] leading the procession to the house of **God**, with shouts of
42:5 [42:6] Put your hope in **God**, for I will yet praise him, my Savior
42:6 [42:7] my **God**. My soul is downcast within me; therefore I will
42:10 [42:11] saying to me all day long, "Where is your **God**?"
42:11 [42:12] Put your hope in **God**, for I will yet praise him, my Savior
42:11 [42:12] in God, for I will yet praise him, my Savior and my **God**.
43:1 Vindicate me, O **God**, and plead my cause against an ungodly
43:2 You are **God** my stronghold. Why have you rejected me?
43:4 Then will I go to the altar of **God**, to God, my joy and my delight.
43:4 and my delight. I will praise you with the harp, O **God**, my God.
43:4 and my delight. I will praise you with the harp, O God, my **God**.
43:5 Put your hope in **God**, for I will yet praise him, my Savior
43:5 hope in God, for I will yet praise him, my Savior and my **God**.
44:1 [44:2] We have heard with our ears, O **God**; our fathers have told
44:4 [44:5] You are my King and my **God**, who decrees victories for
44:8 [44:9] In **God** we make our boast all day long, and we will praise
44:20 [44:21] If we had forgotten the name of our **God** or spread out our
44:21 [44:22] would not **God** have discovered it, since he knows the
45:2 [45:3] anointed with grace, since **God** has blessed you forever.
45:6 [45:7] Your throne, O **God**, will last for ever and ever; a scepter
45:7 [45:8] therefore **God**, your God, has set you above your
45:7 [45:8] therefore God, your **God**, has set you above your
46:1 [46:2] **God** is our refuge and strength, an ever-present help in
46:4 [46:5] There is a river whose streams make glad the city of **God**,
46:5 [46:6] **God** is within her, she will not fall; God will help her at
46:5 [46:6] she will not fall; **God** will help her at break of day.
46:7 [46:8] Almighty is with us; the **God** *of* Jacob is our fortress.
46:10 [46:11] "Be still, and know that I am **God**; I will be exalted
46:11 [46:12] Almighty is with us; the **God** *of* Jacob is our fortress.
47:1 [47:2] your hands, all you nations; shout to **God** with cries of joy.
47:5 [47:6] **God** has ascended amid shouts of joy, the LORD amid
47:6 [47:7] Sing praises to **God**, sing praises; sing praises to our King,
47:7 [47:8] For **God** is the King of all the earth; sing to him a psalm of
47:8 [47:9] **God** reigns over the nations; God is seated on his holy
47:8 [47:9] reigns over the nations; **God** is seated on his holy throne.
47:9 [47:10] nations assemble as the people of the **God** *of* Abraham,
47:9 [47:10] of Abraham, for the kings of the earth belong to **God**;
48:1 [48:2] worthy of praise, in the city of our **God**, his holy mountain.
48:3 [48:4] **God** is in her citadels; he has shown himself to be her
48:8 [48:9] in the city of the LORD Almighty, in the city of our **God**:
48:8 [48:9] city of our God: **God** makes her secure forever. *Selah*
48:9 [48:10] Within your temple, O **God**, we meditate on your
48:10 [48:11] Like your name, O **God**, your praise reaches to the ends
48:14 [48:15] For this **God** is our God for ever and ever; he will be our
48:14 [48:15] For this God is our **God** for ever and ever; he will be our
49:7 [49:8] the life of another or give to **God** a ransom for him—
49:15 [49:16] **God** will redeem my life from the grave; he will surely
50:1 **God**, the LORD, speaks and summons the earth from the rising of
50:2 From Zion, perfect in beauty, **God** shines forth.
50:3 Our **God** comes and will not be silent; a fire devours before him,
50:6 the heavens proclaim his righteousness, for **God** himself is judge.
50:7 O Israel, and I will testify against you: I am **God**, your God.
50:7 O Israel, and I will testify against you: I am God, your **God**.
50:14 Sacrifice thank offerings to **God**, fulfill your vows to the Most
50:16 to the wicked, **God** says: "What right have you to recite my laws
50:23 he prepares the way so that I may show him the salvation of **God**."
51:1 [51:3] Have mercy on me, O **God**, according to your unfailing
51:10 [51:12] Create in me a pure heart, O **God**, and renew a steadfast
51:14 [51:16] Save me from bloodguilt, O **God**, the God who saves me,
51:14 [51:16] Save me from bloodguilt, O God, the **God** *who* saves me,
51:17 [51:19] The sacrifices of **God** are a broken spirit; a broken
51:17 [51:19] a broken and contrite heart, O **God**, you will not despise.
52:7 [52:9] "Here now is the man who did not make **God** his
52:8 [52:10] I am like an olive tree flourishing in the house of **God**;
52:8 [52:10] of God; I trust in **God's** unfailing love for ever and ever.
53:1 [53:2] The fool says in his heart, "There is no **God**." They are
53:2 [53:3] **God** looks down from heaven on the sons of men to see if
53:2 [53:3] to see if there are any who understand, any who seek **God**.

Ps 53: 4 [53:5] my people as men eat bread and who do not call on **God**?
53: 5 [53:6] **God** scattered the bones of those who attacked you;
53: 5 [53:6] you put them to shame, for **God** despised them.
53: 6 [53:7] When **God** restores the fortunes of his people, let Jacob
54: 1 [54:3] Save me, O **God**, by your name; vindicate me by your
54: 2 [54:4] Hear my prayer, O **God**; listen to the words of my mouth.
54: 3 [54:5] ruthless men seek my life—men without regard for **God**.
54: 4 [54:6] Surely **God** is my help; the Lord is the one who sustains
55: 1 [55:2] Listen to my prayer, O **God**, do not ignore my plea;
55: 14 [55:15] as we walked with the throng at the house of **God**.
55: 16 [55:17] But I call to **God**, and the LORD saves me.
55: 19 [55:20] who never change their ways and have no fear of **God**.
55: 23 [55:24] you, O **God**, will bring down the wicked into the pit of
56: 1 [56:2] Be merciful to me, O **God**, for men hotly pursue me;
56: 4 [56:5] In **God**, whose word I praise, in God I trust; I will not be
56: 4 [56:5] In God, whose word I praise, in **God** I trust; I will not be
56: 7 [56:8] in your anger, O **God**, bring down the nations.
56: 9 [56:10] I call for help. By this I will know that **God** is for me.
56: 10 [56:11] In **God**, whose word I praise, in the LORD, whose word
56: 11 [56:12] in **God** I trust; I will not be afraid. What can man do to
56: 12 [56:13] I am under vows to you, O **God**; I will present my thank
56: 13 [56:14] that I may walk before **God** in the light of life.
57: 1 [57:2] Have mercy on me, O **God**, have mercy on me, for in you
57: 2 [57:3] I cry out to **God** Most High, to God, who fulfills his
57: 3 [57:4] *Selah* **God** sends his love and his faithfulness.
57: 5 [57:6] Be exalted, O **God**, above the heavens; let your glory be
57: 7 [57:8] My heart is steadfast, O **God**, my heart is steadfast; I will
57: 11 [57:12] Be exalted, O **God**, above the heavens; let your glory be
58: 6 [58:7] Break the teeth in their mouths, O **God**; tear out,
58: 11 [58:12] are rewarded; surely there is a **God** who judges the earth."
59: 1 [59:2] Deliver me from my enemies, O **God**; protect me from
59: 5 [59:6] O LORD **God** Almighty, the God of Israel, rouse yourself
59: 5 [59:6] O LORD God Almighty, the **God** *of* Israel, rouse yourself
59: 9 [59:10] I watch for you; you, O **God**, are my fortress,
59: 10 [59:11] my loving **God**. God will go before me and will let me
59: 10 [59:11] **God** will go before me and will let me gloat over those
59: 13 [59:14] it will be known to the ends of the earth that **God** rules
59: 17 [59:18] to you; you, O **God**, are my fortress, my loving God.
59: 17 [59:18] to you; you, O God, are my fortress, my loving **God**.
60: 1 [60:3] You have rejected us, O **God**, and burst forth upon us;
60: 6 [60:8] **God** has spoken from his sanctuary: "In triumph I will
60: 10 [60:12] Is it not you, O **God**, you who have rejected us and no
60: 10 [60:12] rejected us and no longer go out **[RPH]** with our armies?
60: 12 [60:14] With **God** we will gain the victory, and he will trample
61: 1 [61:2] Hear my cry, O **God**; listen to my prayer.
61: 5 [61:6] For you have heard my vows, O **God**; you have given me
61: 7 [61:8] May he be enthroned in **God's** presence forever;
62: 1 [62:2] My soul finds rest in **God** alone; my salvation comes from
62: 5 [62:6] Find rest, O my soul, in **God** alone; my hope comes from
62: 7 [62:8] My salvation and my honor depend on **God**; he is my
62: 7 [62:8] honor depend on God; **he**[s] is my mighty rock, my refuge.
62: 8 [62:9] pour out your hearts to him, for **God** is our refuge.
62: 11 [62:12] One thing **God** has spoken, two things have I heard:
62: 11 [62:12] two things have I heard: that you, O **God**, are strong,
63: 1 [63:2] O **God**, you are my God, earnestly I seek you; my soul
63: 11 [63:12] the king will rejoice in **God**; all who swear by God's
64: 1 [64:2] Hear me, O **God**, as I voice my complaint; protect my life
64: 7 [64:8] **God** will shoot them with arrows; suddenly they will be
64: 9 [64:10] they will proclaim the works of **God** and ponder what he
65: 1 [65:2] Praise awaits you, O **God**, in Zion; to you our vows will be
65: 5 [65:6] O **God** our Savior, the hope of all the ends of the earth
65: 9 [65:10] The streams of **God** are filled with water to provide the
66: 1 Shout with joy to **God**, all the earth!
66: 3 Say to **God**, "How awesome are your deeds! So great is your
66: 5 Come and see what **God** has done, how awesome his works in
66: 8 Praise our **God**, O peoples, let the sound of his praise be heard;
66: 10 For you, O **God**, tested us; you refined us like silver.
66: 16 Come and listen, all you who fear **God**; let me tell you what he has
66: 19 but **God** has surely listened and heard my voice in prayer.
66: 20 Praise be to **God**, who has not rejected my prayer or withheld his
67: 1 [67:2] May **God** be gracious to us and bless us and make his face
67: 3 [67:4] May the peoples praise you, O **God**; may all the peoples
67: 5 [67:6] May the peoples praise you, O **God**; may all the peoples
67: 6 [67:7] land will yield its harvest, and **God**, our God, will bless us.
67: 6 [67:7] land will yield its harvest, and God, our **God**, will bless us.
67: 7 [67:8] **God** will bless us, and all the ends of the earth will fear
68: 1 [68:2] May **God** arise, may his enemies be scattered; may his foes
68: 2 [68:3] melts before the fire, may the wicked perish before **God**.
68: 3 [68:4] may the righteous be glad and rejoice before **God**; may
68: 4 [68:5] Sing to **God**, sing praise to his name, extol him who rides
68: 5 [68:6] a defender of widows, is **God** in his holy dwelling.
68: 6 [68:7] **God** sets the lonely in families, he leads forth the prisoners
68: 7 [68:8] When you went out before your people, O **God**, when you
68: 8 [68:9] before **God**, the One of Sinai, before God, the God of
68: 8 [68:9] before God, the One of Sinai, before **God**, the God of
68: 8 [68:9] the One of Sinai, before God, the **God** *of* Israel.
68: 9 [68:10] You gave abundant showers, O **God**; you refreshed your
68: 10 [68:11] Your people settled in it, and from your bounty, O **God**,
68: 15 [68:16] The mountains of Bashan are **majestic** mountains;
68: 16 [68:17] at the mountain where **God** chooses to reign,
68: 17 [68:18] The chariots of **God** are tens of thousands and thousands
68: 18 [68:19] that you, O LORD **God**, might dwell there.
68: 21 [68:22] Surely **God** will crush the heads of his enemies, the hairy
68: 24 [68:25] O **God**, the procession of my God and King into the
68: 26 [68:27] Praise **God** in the great congregation; praise the LORD
68: 28 [68:29] Summon your power, O **God**; show us your strength,
68: 28 [68:29] show us your strength, O **God**, as you have done before.
68: 31 [68:32] will come from Egypt; Cush will submit herself to **God**.
68: 32 [68:33] Sing to **God**, O kingdoms of the earth, sing praise to the
68: 34 [68:35] Proclaim the power of **God**, whose majesty is over Israel,
68: 35 [68:36] You are awesome, O **God**, in your sanctuary; the God of
68: 35 [68:36] gives power and strength to his people. Praise be to **God**!
69: 1 [69:2] Save me, O **God**, for the waters have come up to my neck.
69: 3 [69:4] my throat is parched. My eyes fail, looking for my **God**.
69: 5 [69:6] You know my folly, O **God**; my guilt is not hidden from
69: 6 [69:7] you not be put to shame because of me, O **God** *of* Israel.
69: 13 [69:14] in your great love, O **God**, answer me with your sure
69: 29 [69:30] and distress; may your salvation, O **God**, protect me.
69: 30 [69:31] I will praise **God's** name in song and glorify him with
69: 32 [69:33] and be glad—you who seek **God**, may your hearts live!
69: 35 [69:36] for **God** will save Zion and rebuild the cities of Judah.
70: 1 [70:2] Hasten, O **God**, to save me; O LORD, come quickly to
70: 4 [70:5] who love your salvation always say, "Let **God** be exalted!"
70: 5 [70:6] Yet I am poor and needy; come quickly to me, O **God**.
71: 4 Deliver me, O my **God**, from the hand of the wicked,
71: 11 They say, "**God** has forsaken him; pursue him and seize him,
71: 12 Be not far from me, O **God**; come quickly, O my God, to help me.
71: 12 Be not far from me, O God; come quickly, O my **God**, to help me.
71: 17 Since my youth, O **God**, you have taught me, and to this day I
71: 18 Even when I am old and gray, do not forsake me, O **God**,
71: 19 reaches to the skies, O **God**, you who have done great things.
71: 19 you who have done great things. Who, O **God**, is like you?
71: 22 I will praise you with the harp for your faithfulness, O my **God**;
72: 1 Endow the king with your justice, O **God**, the royal son with your
72: 18 Praise be to the LORD **God**, the God of Israel, who alone does
72: 18 Praise be to the LORD God, the **God** *of* Israel, who alone does
73: 1 Surely **God** is good to Israel, to those who are pure in heart.
73: 26 but **God** is the strength of my heart and my portion forever.
73: 28 as for me, it is good to be near **God**. I have made the Sovereign
74: 1 Why have you rejected us forever, O **God**? Why does your anger
74: 10 How long will the enemy mock you, O **God**? Will the foe revile
74: 12 you, O **God**, are my king from of old; you bring salvation upon the
74: 22 Rise up, O **God**, and defend your cause; remember how fools
75: 1 [75:2] to you, O **God**, we give thanks, for your Name is near;
75: 7 [75:8] it is **God** who judges: He brings one down, he exalts
75: 9 [75:10] declare this forever; I will sing praise to the **God** *of* Jacob.
76: 1 [76:2] In Judah **God** is known; his name is great in Israel.
76: 6 [76:7] O **God** *of* Jacob, both horse and chariot lie still.
76: 9 [76:10] when you, O **God**, rose up to judge, to save all the
76: 11 [76:12] Make vows to the LORD your **God** and fulfill them;
77: 1 [77:2] I cried out to **God** for help; I cried out to God to hear me.
77: 1 [77:2] I cried out to God for help; I cried out to **God** to hear me.
77: 3 [77:4] I remembered you, O **God**, and I groaned; I mused, and my
77: 13 [77:14] Your ways, O **God**, are holy. What god is so great as our
77: 13 [77:14] O God, are holy. What god is so great as our **God**?
77: 16 [77:17] waters saw you, O **God**, the waters saw you and writhed;
78: 7 they would put their trust in **God** and would not forget his deeds
78: 10 they did not keep **God's** covenant and refused to live by his law.
78: 19 They spoke against **God**, saying, "Can God spread a table in the
78: 22 for they did not believe in **God** or trust in his deliverance.
78: 31 **God's** anger rose against them; he put to death the sturdiest among
78: 35 They remembered that **God** was their Rock, that God Most High
78: 56 But they put **God** to the test and rebelled against the Most High;
78: 59 When **God** heard them, he was very angry; he rejected Israel
79: 1 O **God**, the nations have invaded your inheritance; they have
79: 9 Help us, O **God** our Savior, for the glory of your name; deliver us
79: 10 Why should the nations say, "Where is their **God**?" Before our
80: 3 [80:4] Restore us, O **God**; make your face shine upon us, that we
80: 4 [80:5] O LORD **God** Almighty, how long will your anger
80: 7 [80:8] Restore us, O **God** Almighty; make your face shine upon
80: 14 [80:15] Return to us, O **God** Almighty! Look down from heaven
80: 19 [80:20] Restore us, O LORD **God** Almighty; make your face
81: 1 [81:2] Sing for joy to **God** our strength; shout aloud to the God of
81: 1 [81:2] joy to God our strength; shout aloud to the **God** *of* Jacob!
81: 4 [81:5] is a decree for Israel, an ordinance of the **God** *of* Jacob.
81: 10 [81:11] I am the LORD your **God**, who brought you up out of
82: 1 **God** presides in the great assembly; he gives judgment among the
82: 1 in the great assembly; he gives judgment among the "**gods**":

Ps 82: 6 "I said, 'You are "**gods**"; you are all sons of the Most High.'
82: 8 Rise up, O **God**, judge the earth, for all the nations are your
83: 1 [83:2] O **God**, do not keep silent; be not quiet, O God, be not still.
83:12 [83:13] "Let us take possession of the pasturelands of **God**."
83:13 [83:14] like tumbleweed, O my **God**, like chaff before the wind.
84: 3 [84:4] your altar, O LORD Almighty, my King and my **God**.
84: 7 [84:8] strength to strength, till each appears before **God** in Zion.
84: 8 [84:9] Hear my prayer, O LORD **God** Almighty; listen to me,
84: 8 [84:9] O LORD God Almighty; listen to me, O **God** *of* Jacob.
84: 9 [84:10] Look upon our shield, O **God**; look with favor on your
84:10 [84:11] I would rather be a doorkeeper in the house of my **God**
84:11 [84:12] For the LORD **God** is a sun and shield; the LORD
85: 4 [85:5] Restore us again, O **God** our Savior, and put away your
86: 2 to you. You are my **God**; save your servant who trusts in you.
86: 8 Among the **gods** there is none like you, O Lord; no deeds can
86:10 For you are great and do marvelous deeds; you alone are **God**.
86:12 I will praise you, O Lord my **God**, with all my heart; I will glorify
86:14 The arrogant are attacking me, O **God**; a band of ruthless men
87: 3 Glorious things are said of you, O city of **God**: *Selah*
88: 1 [88:2] the **God** who saves me, day and night I cry out before you.
89: 8 [89:9] O LORD **God** Almighty, who is like you? You are
90: T [90:1] A prayer of Moses the man of **God**.
90:17 May the favor of the Lord our **God** rest upon us; establish the work
91: 2 "He is my refuge and my fortress, my **God**, in whom I trust."
92:13 [92:14] of the LORD, they will flourish in the courts of our **God**.
94: 7 "The LORD does not see; the **God** *of* Jacob pays no heed."
94:22 become my fortress, and my **God** the rock in whom I take refuge.
94:23 them for their wickedness; the LORD our **God** will destroy them.
95: 3 For the LORD is the great God, the great King above all **gods**.
95: 7 for he is our **God** and we are the people of his pasture, the flock
96: 4 and most worthy of praise; he is to be feared above all **gods**.
96: 5 For all the **gods** *of* the nations are idols, but the LORD made the
97: 7 to shame, those who boast in idols—worship him, all you **gods**!
97: 9 Most High over all the earth; you are exalted far above all **gods**.
98: 3 all the ends of the earth have seen the salvation of our **God**.
99: 5 Exalt the LORD our **God** and worship at his footstool; he is holy.
99: 8 O LORD our **God**, you answered them; you were to Israel a
99: 9 Exalt the LORD our **God** and worship at his holy mountain,
99: 9 and worship at his holy mountain, for the LORD our **God** is holy.
100: 3 Know that the LORD is **God**. It is he who made us, and we are
104: 1 O LORD my **God**, you are very great; you are clothed with
104:33 LORD all my life; I will sing praise to my **God** as long as I live.
105: 7 He is the LORD our **God**; his judgments are in all the earth.
106:47 Save us, O LORD our **God**, and gather us from the nations,
106:48 Praise be to the LORD, the **God** *of* Israel, from everlasting to
108: 1 [108:2] My heart is steadfast, O **God**; I will sing and make music
108: 5 [108:6] Be exalted, O **God**, above the heavens, and let your glory
108: 7 [108:8] **God** has spoken from his sanctuary: "In triumph I will
108:11 [108:12] Is it not you, O **God**, you who have rejected us and no
108:11 [108:12] and no longer go out with our armies? **[RPH]**
108:13 [108:14] With **God** we will gain the victory, and he will trample
109: 1 O **God**, whom I praise, do not remain silent,
109:26 Help me, O LORD my **God**; save me in accordance with your
113: 5 Who is like the LORD our **God**, the One who sits enthroned on
115: 2 Why do the nations say, "Where is their **God**?"
115: 3 Our **God** is in heaven; he does whatever pleases him.
116: 5 LORD is gracious and righteous; our **God** is full of compassion.
118:28 and I will give you thanks; you are my **God**, and I will exalt you.
119:115 you evildoers, that I may keep the commands of my **God**!
122: 9 For the sake of the house of the LORD our **God**, I will seek your
123: 2 so our eyes look to the LORD our **God**, till he shows us his
135: 2 in the house of the LORD, in the courts of the house of our **God**.
135: 5 that the LORD is great, that our Lord is greater than all **gods**.
136: 2 Give thanks to the **God** *of* gods. *His love endures*
136: 2 Give thanks to the God of **gods**. *His love endures*
138: 1 with all my heart; before the "**gods**" I will sing your praise.
143:10 Teach me to do your will, for you are my **God**; may your good
144: 9 I will sing a new song to you, O **God**; on the ten-stringed lyre I
144:15 this is true; blessed are the people whose **God** is the LORD.
145: 1 I will exalt you, my **God** the King; I will praise your name for ever
146: 2 LORD all my life; I will sing praise to my **God** as long as I live.
146: 5 help is the God of Jacob, whose hope is in the LORD his **God**,
146:10 The LORD reigns forever, your **God**, O Zion, for all generations.
147: 1 How good it is to sing praises to our **God**, how pleasant and fitting
147: 7 LORD with thanksgiving; make music to our **God** on the harp.
147:12 Extol the LORD, O Jerusalem; praise your **God**, O Zion,
Pr 2: 5 understand the fear of the LORD and find the knowledge of **God**.
2:17 of her youth and ignored the covenant she made before **God**.
3: 4 you will win favor and a good name in the sight of **God** and man.
25: 2 It is the glory of **God** to conceal a matter; to search out a matter is
30: 9 may become poor and steal, and so dishonor the name of my **God**.
Ecc 1:13 is done under heaven. What a heavy burden **God** has laid on men!
2:24 satisfaction in his work. This too, I see, is from the hand of **God**,
2:26 and storing up wealth to hand it over to the one who pleases **God**.
3:10 I have seen the burden **God** has laid on men.
3:11 yet they cannot fathom what **God** has done from beginning to end.
3:13 and find satisfaction in all his toil—this is the gift of **God**.
3:14 I know that everything **God** does will endure forever; nothing can
3:14 and nothing taken from it. **God** does it so that men will revere him.
3:15 what will be has been before; and **God** will call the past to account.
3:17 "**God** will bring to judgment both the righteous and the wicked,
3:18 **God** tests them so that they may see that they are like the animals.
5: 1 [4:17] Guard your steps when you go to the house of **God**. Go
5: 2 [5:1] do not be hasty in your heart to utter anything before **God**.
5: 2 [5:1] **God** is in heaven and you are on earth, so let your words be
5: 4 [5:3] When you make a vow to **God**, do not delay in fulfilling it.
5: 6 [5:5] Why should **God** be angry at what you say and destroy the
5: 7 [5:6] words are meaningless. Therefore stand in awe of **God**.
5:18 [5:17] the sun during the few days of life **God** has given him—
5:19 [5:18] when **God** gives any man wealth and possessions,
5:19 [5:18] his lot and be happy in his work—this is a gift of **God**.
5:20 [5:19] because **God** keeps him occupied with gladness of heart.
6: 2 **God** gives a man wealth, possessions and honor, so that he lacks
6: 2 **God** does not enable him to enjoy them, and a stranger enjoys
7:13 Consider what **God** has done: Who can straighten what he has
7:14 times are bad, consider: **God** has made the one as well as the other.
7:18 go of the other. The man who fears **God** will avoid all ⌞extremes⌟.
7:26 The man who pleases **God** will escape her, but the sinner she will
7:29 **God** made mankind upright, but men have gone in search of many
8: 2 the king's command, I say, because you took an oath before **God**.
8:12 I know that it will go better with **God-fearing men** [+2021+3710],
8:13 Yet because the wicked do not fear **God**, it will not go well with
8:15 joy will accompany him in his work all the days of the life **God**
8:17 I saw all that **God** has done. No one can comprehend what goes on
9: 1 the righteous and the wise and what they do are in **God's** hands,
9: 7 wine with a joyful heart, for it is now that **God** favors what you do.
11: 5 so you cannot understand the work of **God**, the Maker of all things.
11: 9 but know that for all these things **God** will bring you to judgment.
12: 7 the ground it came from, and the spirit returns to **God** who gave it.
12:13 Fear **God** and keep his commandments, for this is the whole ⌞duty⌟
12:14 For **God** will bring every deed into judgment, including every
Isa 1:10 of Sodom; listen to the law of our **God**, you people of Gomorrah!
2: 3 to the mountain of the LORD, to the house of the **God** *of* Jacob.
7:11 "Ask the LORD your **God** for a sign, whether in the deepest
7:13 try the patience of men? Will you try the patience of my **God** also?
8:19 who whisper and mutter, should not a people inquire of their **God**?
8:21 enraged and, looking upward, will curse their king and their **God**.
13:19 will be overthrown by **God** like Sodom and Gomorrah.
17: 6 on the fruitful boughs," declares the LORD, the **God** *of* Israel.
17:10 You have forgotten **God** your Savior; you have not remembered
21: 9 All the images of its **gods** lie shattered on the ground!' "
21:10 I have heard from the LORD Almighty, from the **God** *of* Israel.
21:17 will be few." The LORD, the **God** *of* Israel, has spoken.
24:15 name of the LORD, the **God** *of* Israel, in the islands of the sea.
25: 1 O LORD, you are my **God**; I will exalt you and praise your name,
25: 9 In that day they will say, "Surely this is our **God**; we trusted in
26:13 O LORD, our **God**, other lords besides you have ruled over us,
28:26 His **God** instructs him and teaches him the right way.
29:23 the Holy One of Jacob, and will stand in awe of the **God** *of* Israel.
30:18 For the LORD is a **God** *of* justice. Blessed are all who wait for
35: 2 they will see the glory of the LORD, the splendor of our **God**.
35: 4 do not fear; your **God** will come, he will come with vengeance;
35: 4 with vengeance; with **divine** retribution he will come to save you."
36: 7 if you say to me, "We are depending on the LORD our **God**"—
36:18 Has the **god** *of* any nation ever delivered his land from the hand of
36:19 Where are the **gods** *of* Hamath and Arpad? Where are the gods of
36:19 gods of Hamath and Arpad? Where are the **gods** *of* Sepharvaim?
36:20 Who of all the **gods** *of* these countries has been able to save his
37: 4 It may be that the LORD your **God** will hear the words of the
37: 4 his master, the king of Assyria, has sent to ridicule the living **God**,
37: 4 that he will rebuke him for the words the LORD your **God** has
37:10 Do not let the **god** you depend on deceive you when he says,
37:12 Did the **gods** *of* the nations that were destroyed by my forefathers
37:16 "O LORD Almighty, **God** *of* Israel, enthroned between the
37:16 you alone are **God** over all the kingdoms of the earth.
37:17 to all the words Sennacherib has sent to insult the living **God**.
37:19 They have thrown their **gods** into the fire and destroyed them,
37:19 destroyed them, for they were not **gods** but only wood and stone,
37:20 Now, O LORD our **God**, deliver us from his hand, so that all
37:20 on earth may know that you alone, O LORD, are **God**." [BHS-]
37:21 to Hezekiah: "This is what the LORD, the **God** *of* Israel, says:
37:38 while he was worshiping in the temple of his **god** Nisroch,
38: 5 'This is what the LORD, the **God** *of* your father David, says:
40: 1 Comfort, comfort my people, says your **God**.
40: 3 make straight in the wilderness a highway for our **God**.
40: 8 and the flowers fall, but the word of our **God** stands forever."
40: 9 do not be afraid; say to the towns of Judah, "Here is your **God**!"
40:27 is hidden from the LORD; my cause is disregarded by my **God**"?

Isa 40:28 The LORD is the everlasting **God**, the Creator of the ends of the
41:10 for I am with you; do not be dismayed, for I am your **God**.
41:13 For I am the LORD, your **God**, who takes hold of your right hand
41:17 will answer them; I, the **God** *of* Israel, will not forsake them.
41:23 tell us what the future holds, so we may know that you are **gods**.
42:17 But those who trust in idols, who say to images, 'You are our **gods**,'
43: 3 For I am the LORD, your **God**, the Holy One of Israel,
44: 6 I am the first and I am the last; apart from me there is no **God**.
45: 3 I am the LORD, the **God** *of* Israel, who summons you by name.
45: 5 the LORD, and there is no other; apart from me there is no **God**.
45:14 God is with you, and there is no other; there is no other **god**.' "
45:15 you are a God who hides himself, O **God** and Savior *of* Israel.
45:18 he who created the heavens, he is **God**; he who fashioned
45:21 And there is no **God** apart from me, a righteous God and a Savior;
46: 9 and there is no other; I am **God**, and there is none like me.
48: 1 oaths in the name of the LORD and invoke the **God** *of* Israel—
48: 2 yourselves citizens of the holy city and rely on the **God** *of* Israel—
48:17 "I am the LORD your **God**, who teaches you what is best for you,
49: 4 due me is in the LORD's hand, and my reward is with my **God**."
49: 5 in the eyes of the LORD and my **God** has been my strength—
50:10 has no light, trust in the name of the LORD and rely on his **God**.
51:15 For I am the LORD your **God**, who churns up the sea so that its
51:20 filled with the wrath of the LORD and the rebuke of your **God**.
51:22 your Sovereign LORD says, your **God**, who defends his people:
52: 7 who proclaim salvation, who say to Zion, "Your **God** reigns!"
52:10 and all the ends of the earth will see the salvation of our **God**.
52:12 will go before you, the **God** *of* Israel will be your rear guard.
53: 4 yet we considered him stricken by **God**, smitten by him,
54: 5 of Israel is your Redeemer; he is called the **God** *of* all the earth.
54: 6 a wife who married young, only to be rejected," says your **God**.
55: 5 because of the LORD your **God**, the Holy One of Israel,
55: 7 will have mercy on him, and to our **God**, for he will freely pardon.
57:21 "There is no peace," says my **God**, "for the wicked."
58: 2 does what is right and has not forsaken the commands of its **God**.
58: 2 me for just decisions and seem eager for **God** to come near them.
59: 2 your iniquities have separated you from your **God**; your sins have
59:13 turning our backs on our **God**, fomenting oppression and revolt,
60: 9 with their silver and gold, to the honor of the LORD your **God**,
60:19 will be your everlasting light, and your **God** will be your glory.
61: 2 year of the LORD's favor and the day of vengeance of our **God**,
61: 6 priests of the LORD, you will be named ministers of our **God**.
61:10 I delight greatly in the LORD; my soul rejoices in my **God**.
62: 3 in the LORD's hand, a royal diadem in the hand of your **God**.
62: 5 rejoices over his bride, so will your **God** rejoice over you.
64: 4 [64:3] ear has perceived, no eye has seen any **God** besides you,
65:16 invokes a blessing in the land will do so by the **God** *of* truth;
65:16 he who takes an oath in the land will swear by the **God** *of* truth.
66: 9 I close up the womb when I bring to delivery?" says your **God**.
Jer 1:16 in burning incense to other **gods** and in worshiping what their
2:11 Has a nation ever changed its **gods**? (Yet they are not gods at all.)
2:11 (Yet they are not **gods** at all.) But my people have exchanged their
2:17 by forsaking the LORD your **God** when he led you in the way?
2:19 and bitter it is for you when you forsake the LORD your **God**
2:28 Where then are the **gods** you made for yourselves? Let them come
2:28 For you have as many **gods** as you have towns, O Judah.
3:13 you have rebelled against the LORD your **God**, you have
3:21 perverted their ways and have forgotten the LORD their **God**.
3:22 "Yes, we will come to you, for you are the LORD our **God**.
3:23 surely in the LORD our **God** is the salvation of Israel.
3:25 We have sinned against the LORD our **God**, both we and our
3:25 our youth till this day we have not obeyed the LORD our **God**."
5: 4 not know the way of the LORD, the requirements of their **God**.
5: 5 they know the way of the LORD, the requirements of their **God**."
5: 7 children have forsaken me and sworn by gods that are not **gods**.
5:14 Therefore this is what the LORD **God** Almighty says:
5:19 the people ask, 'Why has the LORD our **God** done all this to us?'
5:19 you have forsaken me and served foreign **gods** in your own land,
5:24 'Let us fear the LORD our **God**, who gives autumn and spring
7: 3 This is what the LORD Almighty, the **God** *of* Israel, says:
7: 6 this place, and if you do not follow other **gods** to your own harm,
7: 9 burn incense to Baal and follow other **gods** you have not known,
7:18 They pour out drink offerings to other **gods** to provoke me to
7:21 " 'This is what the LORD Almighty, the **God** *of* Israel, says:
7:23 Obey me, and I will be your **God** and you will be my people.
7:28 'This is the nation that has not obeyed the LORD its **God**
8:14 For the LORD our **God** has doomed us to perish and given us
9:15 [9:14] this is what the LORD Almighty, the **God** *of* Israel, says:
10:10 the LORD is the true **God**; he is the living God, the eternal King.
10:10 the LORD is the true God; he is the living **God**, the eternal King.
11: 3 Tell them that this is what the LORD, the **God** *of* Israel, says:
11: 4 command you, and you will be my people, and I will be your **God**.
11:10 They have followed other **gods** to serve them. Both the house of
11:12 will go and cry out to the **gods** to whom they burn incense,
11:13 You have as many **gods** as you have towns, O Judah; and the altars
13:10 of their hearts and go after other **gods** to serve and worship them,
13:12 "Say to them: 'This is what the LORD, the **God** *of* Israel, says:
13:16 Give glory to the LORD your **God** before he brings the darkness,
14:22 No, it is you, O LORD our **God**. Therefore our hope is in you,
15:16 heart's delight, for I bear your name, O LORD **God** Almighty.
16: 9 For this is what the LORD Almighty, the **God** *of* Israel, says:
16:10 What sin have we committed against the LORD our **God**?'
16:11 'and followed other **gods** and served and worshiped them.
16:13 there you will serve other **gods** day and night, for I will show you
16:20 Do men make their own **gods**? Yes, but they are not gods!"
16:20 Do men make their own gods? Yes, but they are not **gods**!"
19: 3 This is what the LORD Almighty, the **God** *of* Israel, says:
19: 4 they have burned sacrifices in it to **gods** that neither they nor their
19:13 all the starry hosts and poured out drink offerings to other **gods**.' "
19:15 "This is what the LORD Almighty, the **God** *of* Israel, says:
21: 4 'This is what the LORD, the **God** *of* Israel, says: I am about to
22: 9 'Because they have forsaken the covenant of the LORD their **God**
22: 9 LORD their God and have worshiped and served other **gods**.' "
23: 2 Therefore this is what the LORD, the **God** *of* Israel, says to the
23:23 "Am I only a **God** nearby," declares the LORD, "and not a God
23:23 a God nearby," declares the LORD, "and not a **God** far away?
23:36 becomes his oracle and so you distort the words of the living **God**,
23:36 the words of the living God, the LORD Almighty, our **God**.
24: 5 "This is what the LORD, the **God** *of* Israel, says: 'Like these good
24: 7 They will be my people, and I will be their **God**, for they will
25: 6 Do not follow other **gods** to serve and worship them; do not
25:15 This is what the LORD, the **God** *of* Israel, said to me: "Take from
25:27 'This is what the LORD Almighty, the **God** *of* Israel, says:
26:13 your ways and your actions and obey the LORD your **God**.
26:16 He has spoken to us in the name of the LORD our **God**."
27: 4 'This is what the LORD Almighty, the **God** *of* Israel, says:
27:21 yes, this is what the LORD Almighty, the **God** *of* Israel,
28: 2 "This is what the LORD Almighty, the **God** *of* Israel, says:
28:14 This is what the LORD Almighty, the **God** *of* Israel, says:
29: 4 This is what the LORD Almighty, the **God** *of* Israel, says to all
29: 8 this is what the LORD Almighty, the **God** *of* Israel, says:
29:21 the **God** *of* Israel, says about Ahab son of Kolaiah and Zedekiah
29:25 "This is what the LORD Almighty, the **God** *of* Israel, says:
30: 2 "This is what the LORD, the **God** *of* Israel, says: 'Write in a book
30: 9 they will serve the LORD their **God** and David their king,
30:22 " 'So you will be my people, and I will be your **God**.' "
31: 1 declares the LORD, "I will be the **God** of all the clans of Israel,
31: 6 'Come, let us go up to Zion, to the LORD our **God**.' "
31:18 and I will return, because you are the LORD my **God**.
31:23 This is what the LORD Almighty, the **God** *of* Israel, says:
31:33 it on their hearts. I will be their **God**, and they will be my people.
32:14 'This is what the LORD Almighty, the **God** *of* Israel, says:
32:15 For this is what the LORD Almighty, the **God** *of* Israel, says:
32:27 "I am the LORD, the **God** *of* all mankind. Is anything too hard for
32:29 the roofs to Baal and by pouring out drink offerings to other **gods**.
32:36 of Babylon'; but this is what the LORD, the **God** *of* Israel, says:
32:38 They will be my people, and I will be their **God**.
33: 4 For this is what the LORD, the **God** *of* Israel, says about the
34: 2 "This is what the LORD, the **God** *of* Israel, says: Go to Zedekiah
34:13 "This is what the LORD, the **God** *of* Israel, says: I made a
35: 4 into the room of the sons of Hanan son of Igdaliah the man of **God**.
35:13 "This is what the LORD Almighty, the **God** *of* Israel, says:
35:15 and reform your actions; do not follow other **gods** to serve them.
35:17 "Therefore, this is what the LORD **God** Almighty, the God of
35:17 this is what the LORD God Almighty, the **God** *of* Israel, says:
35:18 "This is what the LORD Almighty, the **God** *of* Israel, says:
35:19 this is what the LORD Almighty, the **God** *of* Israel, says:
37: 3 with this message: "Please pray to the LORD our **God** for us."
37: 7 "This is what the LORD, the **God** *of* Israel, says: Tell the king of
38:17 "This is what the LORD **God** Almighty, the God of Israel,
38:17 "This is what the LORD God Almighty, the **God** *of* Israel, says:
39:16 'This is what the LORD Almighty, the **God** *of* Israel, says:
40: 2 "The LORD your **God** decreed this disaster for this place.
42: 2 and pray to the LORD your **God** for this entire remnant.
42: 3 Pray that the LORD your **God** will tell us where we should go
42: 4 "I will certainly pray to the LORD your **God** as you have
42: 5 with everything the LORD your **God** sends you to tell us.
42: 6 it is favorable or unfavorable, we will obey the LORD our **God**,
42: 6 that it will go well with us, for we will obey the LORD our **God**."
42: 9 He said to them, "This is what the LORD, the **God** *of* Israel,
42:13 will not stay in this land,' and so disobey the LORD your **God**,
42:15 This is what the LORD Almighty, the **God** *of* Israel, says:
42:18 This is what the LORD Almighty, the **God** *of* Israel, says:
42:20 made a fatal mistake when you sent me to the LORD your **God**
42:20 LORD your God and said, 'Pray to the LORD our **God** for us;
42:20 tell us everything **he**[s] [+3378+5646] says and we will do it.'
42:21 you still have not obeyed the LORD your **God** in all he sent me to
43: 1 finished telling the people all the words of the LORD their **God**—
43: 1 everything the LORD **[RPH]** had sent him to tell them—

Jer 43: 2 The LORD our **God** has not sent you to say, 'You must not go to
43: 10 'This is what the LORD Almighty, the **God** *of* Israel, says:
43: 12 He will set fire to the temples of the **gods** *of* Egypt; he will burn
43: 13 and will burn down the temples of the **gods** *of* Egypt.' "
44: 2 "This is what the LORD Almighty, the **God** *of* Israel, says:
44: 3 by worshiping other **gods** that neither they nor you nor your fathers
44: 5 turn from their wickedness or stop burning incense to other **gods**.
44: 7 "Now this is what the LORD **God** Almighty, the God of Israel,
44: 7 this is what the LORD God Almighty, the **God** *of* Israel, says:
44: 8 burning incense to other **gods** in Egypt, where you have come to
44: 11 this is what the LORD Almighty, the **God** *of* Israel, says:
44: 15 who knew that their wives were burning incense to other **gods**,
44: 25 This is what the LORD Almighty, the **God** *of* Israel, says:
45: 2 "This is what the LORD, the **God** *of* Israel, says to you, Baruch:
46: 25 The LORD Almighty, the **God** *of* Israel, says: "I am about to
46: 25 on Pharaoh, on Egypt and her **gods** and her kings, and on those
48: 1 This is what the LORD Almighty, the **God** *of* Israel, says:
48: 35 make offerings on the high places and burn incense to their **gods**,"
50: 4 of Judah together will go in tears to seek the LORD their **God**.
50: 18 this is what the LORD Almighty, the **God** *of* Israel, says:
50: 28 refugees from Babylon declaring in Zion how the LORD our **God**
50: 40 As **God** overthrew Sodom and Gomorrah along with their
51: 5 For Israel and Judah have not been forsaken by their **God**,
51: 10 come, let us tell in Zion what the LORD our **God** has done.'
51: 33 This is what the LORD Almighty, the **God** *of* Israel, says:
Eze 1: 1 Kebar River, the heavens were opened and I saw visions of **God**.
8: 3 and heaven and in visions of **God** he took me to Jerusalem,
8: 4 there before me was the glory of the **God** *of* Israel, as in the vision
9: 3 Now the glory of the **God** *of* Israel went up from above the
10: 19 and the glory of the **God** *of* Israel was above them.
10: 20 These were the living creatures I had seen beneath the **God** *of*
11: 20 to keep my laws. They will be my people, and I will be their **God**.
11: 22 their wings, and the glory of the **God** *of* Israel was above them.
11: 24 to the exiles in Babylonia in the vision given by the Spirit of **God**.
14: 11 They will be my people, and I will be their **God**,
20: 5 With uplifted hand I said to them, "I am the LORD your **God**."
20: 7 yourselves with the idols of Egypt. I am the LORD your **God**."
20: 19 I am the LORD your **God**; follow my decrees and be careful to
20: 20 between us. Then you will know that I am the LORD your **God**."
28: 2 "I am a god; I sit on the throne of a **god** in the heart of the seas."
28: 2 a man and not a god, though you think you are as wise as a **god**.
28: 6 LORD says: " 'Because you think you are wise, as wise as a **god**,
28: 9 Will you then say, "I am a **god**," in the presence of those who kill
28: 13 You were in Eden, the garden of **God**; every precious stone
28: 14 You were on the holy mount of **God**; you walked among the fiery
28: 16 So I drove you in disgrace from the mount of **God**, and I expelled
28: 26 Then they will know that I am the LORD their **God**.' "
31: 8 The cedars in the garden of **God** could not rival it, nor could the
31: 8 its branches—no tree in the garden of **God** could match its beauty.
31: 9 the envy of all the trees of Eden in the garden of **God**.
34: 24 I the LORD will be their **God**, and my servant David will be
34: 30 the LORD their **God**, am with them and that they, the house of
34: 31 my sheep, the sheep of my pasture, are people, and I am your **God**,
36: 28 your forefathers; you will be my people, and I will be your **God**.
37: 23 will cleanse them. They will be my people, and I will be their **God**.
37: 27 will be with them; I will be their **God**, and they will be my people.
39: 22 the house of Israel will know that I am the LORD their **God**.
39: 28 they will know that I am the LORD their **God**, for though I sent
40: 2 In visions of **God** he took me to the land of Israel and set me on a
43: 2 and I saw the glory of the **God** *of* Israel coming from the east.
44: 2 It is to remain shut because the LORD, the **God** *of* Israel,
Da 1: 2 his hand, along with some of the articles from the temple of **God**.
1: 2 These he carried off to the temple of his **god** in Babylonia
1: 2 of his god in Babylonia and put in the treasure house of his **god**.
1: 9 Now **God** had caused the official to show favor and sympathy to
1: 17 To these four young men **God** gave knowledge and understanding
9: 3 So I turned to the Lord **God** and pleaded with him in prayer
9: 4 I prayed to the LORD my **God** and confessed: "O Lord, the great
9: 9 The Lord our **God** is merciful and forgiving, even though we have
9: 10 we have not obeyed the LORD our **God** or kept the laws he gave
9: 11 the servant of **God**, have been poured out on us, because we have
9: 13 yet we have not sought the favor of the LORD our **God** by
9: 14 for the LORD our **God** is righteous in everything he does;
9: 15 "Now, O Lord our **God**, who brought your people out of Egypt
9: 17 "Now, our **God**, hear the prayers and petitions of your servant.
9: 18 Give ear, O **God**, and hear; open your eyes and see the desolation
9: 19 For your sake, O my **God**, do not delay, because your city
9: 20 and making my request to the LORD my **God** for his holy hill—
9: 20 making my request to the LORD my God for **his**[s] [+3276] holy
10: 12 to gain understanding and to humble yourself before your **God**,
11: 8 He will also seize their **gods**, their metal images and their valuable
11: 32 but the people who know their **God** will firmly resist him.
11: 37 He will show no regard for the **gods** *of* his fathers or for the one
Hos 1: 7 or by horses and horsemen, but by the LORD their **God**."
2: 23 [2:25] are my people'; and they will say, 'You are my **God**.' "
3: 1 though they turn to other **gods** and love the sacred raisin cakes."
3: 5 will return and seek the LORD their **God** and David their king.
4: 1 is no faithfulness, no love, no acknowledgment of **God** in the land.
4: 6 because you have ignored the law of your **God**, I also will ignore
4: 12 of prostitution leads them astray; they are unfaithful to their **God**.
5: 4 "Their deeds do not permit them to return to their **God**. A spirit of
6: 6 and acknowledgment of **God** rather than burnt offerings.
7: 10 but despite all this he does not return to the LORD his **God**
8: 2 Israel cries out to me, 'O our **God**, we acknowledge you!'
8: 6 are from Israel! This calf—a craftsman has made it; it is not **God**.
9: 1 For you have been unfaithful to your **God**; you love the wages of a
9: 8 The prophet, along with my **God**, is the watchman over Ephraim,
9: 8 await him on all his paths, and hostility in the house of his **God**.
9: 17 My **God** will reject them because they have not obeyed him;
12: 3 [12:4] grasped his brother's heel; as a man he struggled with **God**.
12: 5 [12:6] the LORD **God** Almighty, the LORD is his name of
12: 6 [12:7] you must return to your **God**; maintain love and justice,
12: 6 [12:7] maintain love and justice, and wait for your **God** always.
12: 9 [12:10] "I am the LORD your **God**, ⸤who brought you⸥ out of
13: 4 "But I am the LORD your **God**, ⸤who brought you⸥ out of Egypt.
13: 4 You shall acknowledge no **God** but me, no Savior except me.
13: 16 [14:1] their guilt, because they have rebelled against their **God**.
14: 1 [14:2] Return, O Israel, to the LORD your **God**. Your sins have
14: 3 [14:4] We will never again say 'Our **gods**' to what our own hands
Joel 1: 13 spend the night in sackcloth, you who minister before my **God**;
1: 13 and drink offerings are withheld from the house of your **God**.
1: 14 and all who live in the land to the house of the LORD your **God**,
1: 16 our very eyes—joy and gladness from the house of our **God**?
2: 13 Return to the LORD your **God**, for he is gracious
2: 14 grain offerings and drink offerings for the LORD your **God**.
2: 17 Why should they say among the peoples, 'Where is their **God**?' "
2: 23 Be glad, O people of Zion, rejoice in the LORD your **God**,
2: 26 are full, and you will praise the name of the LORD your **God**,
2: 27 that I am the LORD your **God**, and that there is no other;
3: 17 [4:17] that I, the LORD your **God**, dwell in Zion, my holy hill.
Am 2: 8 in pledge. In the house of their **god** they drink wine taken as fines.
3: 13 the house of Jacob," declares the Lord, the LORD **God** Almighty.
4: 11 "I overthrew some of you as **I**[s] overthrew Sodom and Gomorrah.
4: 12 because I will do this to you, prepare to meet your **God**, O Israel."
4: 13 high places of the earth—the LORD **God** Almighty is his name.
5: 14 the LORD **God** Almighty will be with you, just as you say he is.
5: 15 Perhaps the LORD **God** Almighty will have mercy on the
5: 16 Therefore this is what the Lord, the LORD **God** Almighty, says:
5: 26 of your king, the pedestal of your idols, the star of your **god**—
5: 27 says the LORD, whose name is **God** Almighty.
6: 8 has sworn by himself—the LORD **God** Almighty declares:
6: 14 For the LORD **God** Almighty declares, "I will stir up a nation
8: 14 or say, 'As surely as your **god** lives, O Dan,' or, 'As surely as the
9: 15 from the land I have given them," says the LORD your **God**.
Jnh 1: 5 All the sailors were afraid and each cried out to his own **god**.
1: 6 and said, "How can you sleep? Get up and call on your **god**!
1: 6 Maybe **he**[s] [+2021] will take notice of us, and we will not perish."
1: 9 the LORD, the **God** *of* heaven, who made the sea and the land."
2: 1 [2:2] From inside the fish Jonah prayed to the LORD his **God**.
2: 6 [2:7] you brought my life up from the pit, O LORD my **God**.
3: 3 Now Nineveh was a **very** [+4200] important city—a visit required
3: 5 The Ninevites believed **God**. They declared a fast, and all of them,
3: 8 Let everyone call urgently on **God**. Let them give up their evil
3: 9 **God** may yet relent and with compassion turn from his fierce anger
3: 10 When **God** saw what they did and how they turned from their evil
3: 10 how they turned from their evil ways, **he**[s] [+2021] had compassion
4: 6 the LORD **God** provided a vine and made it grow up over Jonah
4: 7 at dawn the next day **God** provided a worm, which chewed the
4: 8 When the sun rose, **God** provided a scorching east wind,
4: 9 **God** said to Jonah, "Do you have a right to be angry about the
Mic 3: 7 will all cover their faces because there is no answer from **God**."
4: 2 to the mountain of the LORD, to the house of the **God** *of* Jacob.
4: 5 All the nations may walk in the name of their **gods**; we will walk
4: 5 we will walk in the name of the LORD our **God** for ever
5: 4 [5:3] in the majesty of the name of the LORD his **God**.
6: 6 I come before the LORD and bow down before the exalted **God**?
6: 8 act justly and to love mercy and to walk humbly with your **God**.
7: 7 I watch in hope for the LORD, I wait for **God** my Savior;
7: 7 for the LORD, I wait for God my Savior; my **God** will hear me.
7: 10 she who said to me, "Where is the LORD your **God**?"
7: 17 they will turn in fear to the LORD our **God** and will be afraid of
Na 1: 14 carved images and cast idols that are in the temple of your **gods**.
Hab 1: 12 My **God**, my Holy One, we will not die. O LORD, you have
3: 18 yet I will rejoice in the LORD, I will be joyful in **God** my Savior.
Zep 2: 7 The LORD their **God** will care for them; he will restore their
2: 9 surely as I live," declares the LORD Almighty, the **God** *of* Israel,
2: 11 will be awesome to them when he destroys all the **gods** *of* the land.
3: 2 does not trust in the LORD, she does not draw near to her **God**.

[F] Hitpael (hitpoel, hitpoal, hitpolel, hitpolal, hitpalel, hitpalal, hitpalpel, hitpalpal, hotpael, hotpaal) [G] Hiphil (hiphtil) [H] Hophal [I] Hishtaphel

Zep 3:17 The LORD your **God** is with you, he is mighty to save. He will
Hag 1:12 remnant of the people obeyed the voice of the LORD their **God**
1:12 the prophet Haggai, because the LORD their **God** had sent him.
1:14 began to work on the house of the LORD Almighty, their **God**,
Zec 6:15 This will happen if you diligently obey the LORD your **God**."
8:8 and I will be faithful and righteous to them as their **God**."
8:23 us go with you, because we have heard that **God** is with you.' "
9:7 Those who are left will belong to our **God** and become leaders in
9:16 The LORD their **God** will save them on that day as the flock of
10:6 for I am the LORD their **God** and I will answer them.
11:4 This is what the LORD my **God** says: "Pasture the flock marked
12:5 Jerusalem are strong, because the LORD Almighty is their **God**.'
12:8 the house of David will be like **God**, like the Angel of the LORD
13:9 are my people,' and they will say, 'The LORD is our **God**.' "
14:5 the LORD my **God** will come, and all the holy ones with him.
Mal 2:15 are his. And why one? Because he was seeking **godly** offspring.
2:16 "I hate divorce," says the LORD **God** *of* Israel, "and I hate a
2:17 and he is pleased with them" or "Where is the **God** *of* justice?"
3:8 "Will a man rob **God**? Yet you rob me. "But you ask, 'How do we
3:14 "You have said, 'It is futile to serve **God**. What did we gain by
3:15 evildoers prosper, and even those who challenge **God** escape.' "
3:18 the wicked, between those who serve **God** and those who do not.

467 אִלּוּ *'illû*, c. [2] [√ 561 + 4273]

if [2]

Est 7:4 **If** we had merely been sold as male and female slaves, I would
Ecc 6:6 even **if** he lives a thousand years twice over but fails to enjoy his

468 אֱלוֹהַּ *'ĕlôah*, n.m. [57] [→ 466; cf. 446; Ar 10033]

God [53], God's [4]

Dt 32:15 He abandoned the **God** who made him and rejected the Rock his
32:17 They sacrificed to demons, which are not **God**—gods they had not
2Ki 17:31 [and Anammelech, the **gods** [K; see Q 466] *of* Sepharvaim.]
2Ch 32:15 for no **god** *of* any nation or kingdom has been able to deliver his
Ne 9:17 But you are a forgiving **God**, gracious and compassionate,
Job 3:4 may it turn to darkness; may **God** above not care about it;
3:23 given to a man whose way is hidden, whom **God** has hedged in?
4:9 At the breath of **God** they are destroyed; at the blast of his anger
4:17 'Can a mortal be more righteous than **God**? Can a man be more
5:17 "Blessed is the man whom **God** corrects; so do not despise the
6:4 drinks in their poison; **God's** terrors are marshaled against me.
6:8 I might have my request, that **God** would grant what I hope for,
6:9 that **God** would be willing to crush me, to let loose his hand
9:13 **God** does not restrain his anger; even the cohorts of Rahab
10:2 I will say to **God**: Do not condemn me, but tell me what charges
11:5 Oh, how I wish that **God** would speak, that he would open his lips
11:6 two sides. Know this: **God** has even forgotten some of your sin.
11:7 "Can you fathom the mysteries of **God**? Can you probe the limits
12:4 to my friends, though I called upon **God** and he answered—
12:6 provoke God are secure—those who carry their **god** in their hands.
15:8 Do you listen in on **God's** council? Do you limit wisdom to
16:20 My intercessor is my friend as my eyes pour out tears to **God**;
16:21 on behalf of a man he pleads with **God** as a man pleads for his
19:6 then know that **God** has wronged me and drawn his net around me.
19:21 my friends, have pity, for the hand of **God** has struck me.
19:26 after my skin has been destroyed, yet in my flesh I will see **God**;
21:9 are safe and free from fear; the rod of **God** is not upon them.
21:19 ⌞It is said,⌟ '**God** stores up a man's punishment for his sons.'
22:12 "Is not **God** in the heights of heaven? And see how lofty are the
22:26 will find delight in the Almighty and will lift up your face to **God**.
24:12 cry out for help. But **God** charges no one with wrongdoing.
27:3 as long as I have life within me, the breath of **God** in my nostrils,
27:8 has the godless when he is cut off, when **God** takes away his life?
27:10 find delight in the Almighty? Will he call upon **God** at all times?
29:2 for the months gone by, for the days when **God** watched over me,
29:4 in my prime, when **God's** intimate friendship blessed my house,
31:2 For what is man's lot from **God** above, his heritage from the
31:6 let **God** weigh me in honest scales and he will know that I am
33:12 I tell you, in this you are not right, for **God** is greater than man.
33:26 He prays to **God** and finds favor with him, he sees God's face
35:10 no one says, 'Where is **God** my Maker, who gives songs in the
36:2 and I will show you that there is more to be said in **God's** behalf.
37:15 Do you know how **God** controls the clouds and makes his
37:22 he comes in golden splendor; **God** comes in awesome majesty.
39:17 for **God** did not endow her with wisdom or give her a share of
40:2 the Almighty correct him? Let him who accuses **God** answer him!"
Ps 18:31 [18:32] For who is **God** besides the LORD? And who is the
50:22 "Consider this, you who forget **God**, or I will tear you to pieces,
114:7 at the presence of the Lord, at the presence of the **God** *of* Jacob,
139:19 If only you would slay the wicked, O **God**! Away from me,
Pr 30:5 "Every word of **God** is flawless; he is a shield to those who take
Isa 44:8 Is there any **God** besides me? No, there is no other Rock; I know
Da 11:37 or for the one desired by women, nor will he regard any **god**,
11:38 Instead of them, he will honor a **god** *of* fortresses; a god unknown
11:38 a **god** unknown to his fathers he will honor with gold and silver,
11:39 will attack the mightiest fortresses with the help of a foreign **god**
Hab 1:11 and go on—guilty men, whose own strength is their **god**."
3:3 **God** came from Teman, the Holy One from Mount Paran.

469 [1]אֱלוּל *'ĕlûl[1]*, n.pr. [1]

Elul [1]

Ne 6:15 So the wall was completed on the twenty-fifth of **Elul**, in fifty-two

470 [2]אֱלוּל *'ĕlûl[2]*, n.m.?. [0] [√ 496]

Jer 14:14 [They are prophesying to you false visions, divinations, **idolatries**
[K; see Q 496] and the delusions of their own minds.]

471 [1]אֵלוֹן *'ēlôn[1]*, n.[f.]. [10] [→ 472; cf. 380; Ar 10027]

great tree [4], great trees [4], large tree [1], tree [1]

Ge 12:6 the land as far as the site of the **great tree** *of* Moreh at Shechem.
13:18 and went to live near the **great trees** *of* Mamre at Hebron,
14:13 Now Abram was living near the **great trees** *of* Mamre the
18:1 The LORD appeared to Abraham near the **great trees** *of* Mamre
Dt 11:30 of the road, toward the setting sun, near the **great trees** *of* Moreh,
Jos 19:33 boundary went from Heleph and the **large tree** in Zaanannim,
Jdg 4:11 and pitched his tent by the **great tree** in Zaanannim near Kedesh.
9:6 Beth Millo gathered beside the **great tree** *at* the pillar in Shechem
9:37 a company is coming from the direction of the soothsayers' **tree**."
1Sa 10:3 "Then you will go on from there until you reach the **great tree** *of*

472 [2]אֵלוֹן *'ēlôn[2]*, n.pr.m. [2] [→ 471, 533; cf. 381]

Elon [2]

Ge 46:14 The sons of Zebulun: Sered, **Elon** and Jahleel.
Nu 26:26 through **Elon**, the Elonite clan; through Jahleel, the Jahleelite clan.

473 [1]אַלּוֹן *'allôn[1]*, n.m. [8] [→ 474; cf. 380]

oak [4], oaks [4]

Ge 35:8 Rebekah's nurse, died and was buried under the **oak** below Bethel.
Isa 2:13 the cedars of Lebanon, tall and lofty, and all the **oaks** *of* Bashan,
6:13 But as the terebinth and **oak** leave stumps when they are cut down,
44:14 He cut down cedars, or perhaps took a cypress or **oak**. He let it
Eze 27:6 Of **oaks** from Bashan they made your oars; of cypress wood from
Hos 4:13 under **oak**, poplar and terebinth, where the shade is pleasant.
Am 2:9 though he was tall as the cedars and strong as the **oaks**.
Zec 11:2 Wail, **oaks** *of* Bashan; the dense forest has been cut down!

474 [2]אַלּוֹן *'allôn[2]*, n.pr.m. [1] [√ 473; cf. 380]

Allon [1]

1Ch 4:37 the son of **Allon**, the son of Jedaiah, the son of Shimri, the son of

475 אַלּוֹן בָּכוּת *'allôn bākût*, n.pr.loc. [1] [√ 380 + 1134]

Allon Bacuth [1]

Ge 35:8 buried under the oak below Bethel. So it was named **Allon Bacuth**.

476 [1]אַלּוּף *'allûp[1]*, a. [9] [√ 544]

close friends [2], friend [2], allies [1], companion [1], gentle [1], oxen [1], partner [1]

Ps 55:13 [55:14] a man like myself, my **companion**, my close friend,
144:14 our **oxen** will draw heavy loads. There will be no breaching of
Pr 2:17 who has left the **partner** *of* her youth and ignored the covenant she
16:28 man stirs up dissension, and a gossip separates **close friends**.
17:9 but whoever repeats the matter separates **close friends**.
Jer 3:4 you not just called to me: 'My Father, my **friend** *from* my youth,
11:19 I had been like a **gentle** lamb led to the slaughter; I did not realize
13:21 LORD⌟ sets over you those you cultivated as your special **allies**?
Mic 7:5 Do not trust a neighbor; put no confidence in a **friend**. Even with

477 [2]אַלּוּף *'allûp[2]*, n.m. [60] [√ 545]

untranslated [40], chiefs [16], leaders [3], divisions [1]

Ge 36:15 These were the **chiefs** *among* Esau's descendants: The sons of
36:15 Eliphaz the firstborn of Esau: **Chiefs** Teman, Omar, Zepho, Kenaz,
36:15 the firstborn of Esau: Chiefs Teman, **[RPH]** Omar, Zepho, Kenaz,
36:15 the firstborn of Esau: Chiefs Teman, Omar, **[RPH]** Zepho, Kenaz,
36:15 the firstborn of Esau: Chiefs Teman, Omar, Zepho, **[RPH]** Kenaz,
36:16 **[RPH]** Korah, Gatam and Amalek. These were the chiefs
36:16 Korah, **[RPH]** Gatam and Amalek. These were the chiefs
36:16 Korah, Gatam and **[RPH]** Amalek. These were the chiefs
36:16 These were the **chiefs** *descended from* Eliphaz in Edom;
36:17 of Esau's son Reuel: **Chiefs** Nahath, Zerah, Shammah and Mizzah.
36:17 son Reuel: Chiefs Nahath, **[RPH]** Zerah, Shammah and Mizzah.

Ge 36: 17 son Reuel: Chiefs Nahath, Zerah, **[RPH]** Shammah and Mizzah.
36: 17 son Reuel: Chiefs Nahath, Zerah, Shammah and **[RPH]** Mizzah.
36: 17 These were the **chiefs** *descended from* Reuel in Edom; they were
36: 18 sons of Esau's wife Oholibamah: **Chiefs** Jeush, Jalam and Korah.
36: 18 Esau's wife Oholibamah: Chiefs Jeush, **[RPH]** Jalam and Korah.
36: 18 Esau's wife Oholibamah: Chiefs Jeush, Jalam and **[RPH]** Korah.
36: 18 These were the **chiefs** *descended from* Esau's wife Oholibamah
36: 19 were the sons of Esau (that is, Edom), and these were their **chiefs**.
36: 21 and Dishan. These sons of Seir in Edom were Horite **chiefs**.
36: 29 These were the Horite **chiefs**: Lotan, Shobal, Zibeon, Anah,
36: 29 were the Horite chiefs: **[RPH]** Lotan, Shobal, Zibeon, Anah,
36: 29 were the Horite chiefs: Lotan, **[RPH]** Shobal, Zibeon, Anah,
36: 29 were the Horite chiefs: Lotan, Shobal, **[RPH]** Zibeon, Anah,
36: 29 were the Horite chiefs: Lotan, Shobal, Zibeon, **[RPH]** Anah,
36: 30 **[RPH]** Dishon, Ezer and Dishan. These were the Horite chiefs,
36: 30 Dishon, **[RPH]** Ezer and Dishan. These were the Horite chiefs,
36: 30 Dishon, Ezer and **[RPH]** Dishan. These were the Horite chiefs,
36: 30 These were the Horite **chiefs**, according to their divisions,
36: 30 the Horite chiefs, according to their **divisions**, in the land of Seir.
36: 40 These were the **chiefs** *descended from* Esau, by name, according
36: 40 to their clans and regions: **[RPH]** Timna, Alvah, Jetheth,
36: 40 to their clans and regions: Timna, **[RPH]** Alvah, Jetheth,
36: 40 to their clans and regions: Timna, Alvah, **[RPH]** Jetheth,
36: 41 **[RPH]** Oholibamah, Elah, Pinon,
36: 41 Oholibamah, **[RPH]** Elah, Pinon,
36: 41 Oholibamah, Elah, **[RPH]** Pinon,
36: 42 **[RPH]** Kenaz, Teman, Mibzar,
36: 42 Kenaz, **[RPH]** Teman, Mibzar,
36: 42 Kenaz, Teman, **[RPH]** Mibzar,
36: 43 **[RPH]** Magdiel and Iram. These were the chiefs of Edom,
36: 43 Magdiel and **[RPH]** Iram. These were the chiefs of Edom,
36: 43 These were the **chiefs** *of* Edom, according to their settlements in
Ex 15: 15 The **chiefs** *of* Edom will be terrified, the leaders of Moab will be
1Ch 1: 51 Hadad also died. The **chiefs** *of* Edom were: Timna, Alvah, Jetheth,
1: 51 The chiefs of Edom were: **[RPH]** Timna, Alvah, Jetheth,
1: 51 The chiefs of Edom were: Timna, **[RPH]** Alvah, Jetheth,
1: 51 The chiefs of Edom were: Timna, Alvah, **[RPH]** Jetheth,
1: 52 **[RPH]** Oholibamah, Elah, Pinon,
1: 52 Oholibamah, **[RPH]** Elah, Pinon,
1: 52 Oholibamah, Elah, **[RPH]** Pinon,
1: 53 **[RPH]** Kenaz, Teman, Mibzar,
1: 53 Kenaz, **[RPH]** Teman, Mibzar,
1: 53 Kenaz, Teman, **[RPH]** Mibzar,
1: 54 **[RPH]** Magdiel and Iram. These were the chiefs of Edom.
1: 54 Magdiel and **[RPH]** Iram. These were the chiefs of Edom.
1: 54 Magdiel and Iram. These were the **chiefs** *of* Edom.
Zec 9: 7 who are left will belong to our God and become **leaders** in Judah,
12: 5 the **leaders** *of* Judah will say in their hearts, 'The people of
12: 6 "On that day I will make the **leaders** *of* Judah like a firepot in a

478 אָלוּשׁ *'ālûš*, n.pr.loc. [2]

Alush [2]

Nu 33: 13 They left Dophkah and camped at **Alush**.
33: 14 They left **Alush** and camped at Rephidim, where there was no

479 אֶלְזָבָד *'elzābād*, n.pr.m. [2] [√ 446 + 2272]

Elzabad [2]

1Ch 12: 12 [12:13] Johanan the eighth, **Elzabad** the ninth,
26: 7 Othni, Rephael, Obed and **Elzabad**; his relatives Elihu

480 אָלַח *'ālaḥ*, v. [3]

corrupt [3]

Job 15: 16 [C] how much less man, who is vile and **corrupt**, who drinks up
Ps 14: 3 [C] All have turned aside, *they have* together *become* **corrupt**;
53: 3 [53:4] [C] turned away, *they have* together *become* **corrupt**;

481 אֶלְחָנָן *'elḥānān*, n.pr.m. [4] [√ 446 + 2860]

Elhanan [4]

2Sa 21: 19 **Elhanan** son of Jaare-Oregim the Bethlehemite killed Goliath the
23: 24 Asahel the brother of Joab, **Elhanan** son of Dodo from Bethlehem,
1Ch 11: 26 Asahel the brother of Joab, **Elhanan** son of Dodo from Bethlehem,
20: 5 **Elhanan** son of Jair killed Lahmi the brother of Goliath the Gittite,

482 אֱלִיאָב *'ᵉlî'āb*, n.pr.m. [21] [√ 446 + 3]

Eliab [20], he[s] [1]

Nu 1: 9 from Zebulun, **Eliab** son of Helon;
2: 7 The leader of the people of Zebulun is **Eliab** son of Helon.
7: 24 On the third day, **Eliab** son of Helon, the leader of the people of
7: 29 a fellowship offering. This was the offering of **Eliab** son of Helon.
10: 16 **Eliab** son of Helon was over the division of the tribe of Zebulun.
16: 1 Dathan and Abiram, sons of **Eliab**, and On son of Peleth—
16: 12 Then Moses summoned Dathan and Abiram, the sons of **Eliab**.
26: 8 The son of Pallu was **Eliab**,
26: 9 the sons of **Eliab** were Nemuel, Dathan and Abiram. The same
Dt 11: 6 what he did to Dathan and Abiram, sons of **Eliab** the Reubenite,
1Sa 16: 6 When they arrived, Samuel saw **Eliab** and thought,
17: 13 The firstborn was **Eliab**; the second, Abinadab; and the third,
17: 28 When **Eliab**, David's oldest brother, heard him speaking with the
17: 28 speaking with the men, **he**[s] burned with anger at him and asked,
1Ch 2: 13 Jesse was the father of **Eliab** his firstborn; the second son was
6: 27 [6:12] **Eliab** his son, Jeroham his son, Elkanah his son
12: 9 [12:10] Obadiah the second in command, **Eliab** the third,
15: 18 Jehiel, Unni, **Eliab**, Benaiah, Maaseiah, Mattithiah, Eliphelehu,
15: 20 Jehiel, Unni, **Eliab**, Maaseiah and Benaiah were to play the lyres
16: 5 Mattithiah, **Eliab**, Benaiah, Obed-Edom and Jeiel.
2Ch 11: 18 son Jerimoth and of Abihail, the daughter of Jesse's son **Eliab**.

483 אֱלִיאֵל *'ᵉlî'ēl*, n.pr.m. [10] [√ 446 + 3276 + 446]

Eliel [10]

1Ch 5: 24 Epher, Ishi, **Eliel**, Azriel, Jeremiah, Hodaviah and Jahdiel.
6: 34 [6:19] the son of Jeroham, the son of **Eliel**, the son of Toah,
8: 20 Elienai, Zillethai, **Eliel**,
8: 22 Ishpan, Eber, **Eliel**,
11: 46 **Eliel** the Mahavite, Jeribai and Joshaviah the sons of Elnaam,
11: 47 **Eliel**, Obed and Jaasiel the Mezobaite.
12: 11 [12:12] Attai the sixth, **Eliel** the seventh,
15: 9 from the descendants of Hebron, **Eliel** the leader and 80 relatives;
15: 11 Asaiah, Joel, Shemaiah, **Eliel** and Amminadab the Levites.
2Ch 31: 13 Jehiel, Azaziah, Nahath, Asahel, Jerimoth, Jozabad, **Eliel**,

484 אֱלִיאָתָה *'ᵉlî'ātâ*, n.pr.m. [1] [√ 446 + 910]

Eliathah [1]

1Ch 25: 4 Hananiah, Hanani, **Eliathah**, Giddalti and Romamti-Ezer;

485 אֱלִידָד *'ᵉlîdād*, n.pr.m. [1] [√ 446 + 1856]

Elidad [1]

Nu 34: 21 **Elidad** son of Kislon, from the tribe of Benjamin;

486 אֶלְיָדָע *'elyādā'*, n.pr.m. [4] [√ 446 + 3359]

Eliada [4]

2Sa 5: 16 Elishama, **Eliada** and Eliphelet.
1Ki 11: 23 Rezon son of **Eliada**, who had fled from his master,
1Ch 3: 8 Elishama, **Eliada** and Eliphelet—nine in all.
2Ch 17: 17 **Eliada**, a valiant soldier, with 200,000 men armed with bows

487 אַלְיָה *'alyâ*, n.f. [5]

fat tail [5]

Ex 29: 22 "Take from this ram the fat, the **fat tail**, the fat around the inner
Lev 3: 9 its fat, the entire **fat tail** cut off close to the backbone, all the fat
7: 3 shall be offered: the **fat tail** and the fat that covers the inner parts,
8: 25 He took the fat, the **fat tail**, all the fat around the inner parts,
9: 19 the **fat tail**, the layer of fat, the kidneys and the covering of the

488 אֵלִיָּה *'ēliyyâ*, n.pr.m. [8] [√ 446 + 3378]

Elijah [8]

2Ki 1: 3 But the angel of the LORD said to **Elijah** the Tishbite, "Go up
1: 4 the bed you are lying on. You will certainly die!' " So **Elijah** went.
1: 8 around his waist." The king said, "That was **Elijah** the Tishbite."
1: 12 "If I am a man of God," **Elijah** replied, "may fire come down from
1Ch 8: 27 Jaareshiah, **Elijah** and Zicri were the sons of Jeroham.
Ezr 10: 21 of Harim: Maaseiah, **Elijah**, Shemaiah, Jehiel and Uzziah.
10: 26 of Elam: Mattaniah, Zechariah, Jehiel, Abdi, Jeremoth and **Elijah**.
Mal 4: 5 [3:23] I will send you the prophet **Elijah** before that great

489 אֵלִיָּהוּ *'ēliyyāhû*, n.pr.m. [63] [√ 446 + 3378]

Elijah [60], *untranslated* [1], Elijah's [1], him[s] [1]

1Ki 17: 1 Now **Elijah** the Tishbite, from Tishbe in Gilead, said to Ahab,
17: 13 **Elijah** said to her, "Don't be afraid. Go home and do as you have
17: 15 She went away and did as **Elijah** had told her. So there was food
17: 16 in keeping with the word of the LORD spoken by **Elijah**.
17: 18 She said to **Elijah**, "What do you have against me, man of God?
17: 22 The LORD heard **Elijah's** cry, and the boy's life returned to him,
17: 23 **Elijah** picked up the child and carried him down from the room
17: 23 He gave him to his mother and said, **[RPH]** "Look, your son is
17: 24 the woman said to **Elijah**, "Now I know that you are a man of God
18: 1 in the third year, the word of the LORD came to **Elijah**:
18: 2 So **Elijah** went to present himself to Ahab. Now the famine was
18: 7 As Obadiah was walking along, **Elijah** met him. Obadiah
18: 7 down to the ground, and said, "Is it really you, my lord **Elijah**?"

1Ki 18: 8 "Yes," he replied. "Go tell your master, '**Elijah** is here.' "
18: 11 But now you tell me to go to my master and say, '**Elijah** is here.'
18: 14 And now you tell me to go to my master and say, '**Elijah** is here.'
18: 15 **Elijah** said, "As the LORD Almighty lives, whom I serve,
18: 16 went to meet Ahab and told him, and Ahab went to meet **Elijah**.
18: 17 When he saw **Elijah**, he said to him, "Is that you, you troubler of
18: 21 **Elijah** went before the people and said, "How long will you waver
18: 22 **Elijah** said to them, "I am the only one of the LORD's prophets
18: 25 **Elijah** said to the prophets of Baal, "Choose one of the bulls
18: 27 At noon **Elijah** began to taunt them. "Shout louder!" he said.
18: 30 **Elijah** said to all the people, "Come here to me." They came to
18: 31 **Elijah** took twelve stones, one for each of the tribes descended
18: 36 time of sacrifice, the prophet **Elijah** stepped forward and prayed:
18: 40 Then **Elijah** commanded them, "Seize the prophets of Baal.
18: 40 **Elijah** had them brought down to the Kishon Valley
18: 41 **Elijah** said to Ahab, "Go, eat and drink, for there is the sound of a
18: 42 went off to eat and drink, but **Elijah** climbed to the top of Carmel,
18: 46 The power of the LORD came upon **Elijah** and, tucking his cloak
19: 1 Now Ahab told Jezebel everything **Elijah** had done and how he
19: 2 So Jezebel sent a messenger to **Elijah** to say, "May the gods deal
19: 9 of the LORD came to him: "What are you doing here, **Elijah**?"
19: 13 When **Elijah** heard it, he pulled his cloak over his face and went
19: 13 Then a voice said to him, "What are you doing here, **Elijah**?"
19: 19 **Elijah** went up to him and threw his cloak around him.
19: 20 Elisha then left his oxen and ran after **Elijah**. "Let me kiss my
19: 21 Then he set out to follow **Elijah** and became his attendant.
21: 17 Then the word of the LORD came to **Elijah** the Tishbite:
21: 20 Ahab said to **Elijah**, "So you have found me, my enemy!"
21: 28 Then the word of the LORD came to **Elijah** the Tishbite:
2Ki 1: 10 **Elijah** answered the captain, "If I am a man of God, may fire come
1: 13 This third captain went up and fell on his knees before **Elijah**.
1: 15 The angel of the LORD said to **Elijah**, "Go down with him;
1: 17 according to the word of the LORD that **Elijah** had spoken.
2: 1 When the LORD was about to take **Elijah** up to heaven in a
2: 1 in a whirlwind, **Elijah** and Elisha were on their way from Gilgal.
2: 2 **Elijah** said to Elisha, "Stay here; the LORD has sent me to
2: 4 **Elijah** said to him, "Stay here, Elisha; the LORD has sent me to
2: 6 **Elijah** said to him, "Stay here; the LORD has sent me to the
2: 8 **Elijah** took his cloak, rolled it up and struck the water with it.
2: 9 When they had crossed, **Elijah** said to Elisha, "Tell me, what can I
2: 11 the two of them, and **Elijah** went up to heaven in a whirlwind.
2: 13 He picked up the cloak that had fallen from **Elijah** and went back
2: 14 he took the cloak that had fallen from **him**[s] and struck the water
2: 14 "Where now is the LORD, the God of **Elijah**?" he asked.
2: 15 were watching, said, "The spirit of **Elijah** is resting on Elisha."
3: 11 of Shaphat is here. He used to pour water on the hands of **Elijah**."
9: 36 the LORD that he spoke through his servant **Elijah** the Tishbite:
10: 10 LORD has done what he promised through his servant **Elijah**."
10: 17 according to the word of the LORD spoken to **Elijah**.
2Ch 21: 12 Jehoram received a letter from **Elijah** the prophet, which said:

490 אֱלִיהוּ ʾelîhû, n.pr.m. [4] [√ 446 + 2085]

Elihu [4]

1Ch 26: 7 and Elzabad; his relatives **Elihu** and Semakiah were also able men.
27: 18 over Judah: **Elihu**, a brother of David; over Issachar: Omri son of
Job 32: 4 Now **Elihu** had waited before speaking to Job because they were
35: 1 Then **Elihu** said:

491 אֱלִיהוּא ʾelîhûʾ, n.pr.m. [7] [√ 446 + 2085]

Elihu [6], he[s] [1]

1Sa 1: the son of **Elihu**, the son of Tohu, the son of Zuph, an Ephraimite.
1Ch 12: 20 [12:21] Jediael, Michael, Jozabad, **Elihu** and Zillethai,
Job 32: 2 But **Elihu** son of Barakel the Buzite, of the family of Ram,
32: 5 But when **he**[s] saw that the three men had nothing more to say,
32: 6 So **Elihu** son of Barakel the Buzite said: "I am young in years,
34: 1 Then **Elihu** said:
36: 1 **Elihu** continued:

492 אֶלְיְהוֹעֵינַי ʾelyehôʿênay, n.pr.m. [2] [√ 448 + 3378 + 6524]

Eliehoenai [2]

1Ch 26: 3 Elam the fifth, Jehohanan the sixth and **Eliehoenai** the seventh.
Ezr 8: 4 **Eliehoenai** son of Zerahiah, and with him 200 men;

493 אֶלְיוֹעֵינַי ʾelyôʿênay, n.pr.m. [7] [√ 448 + 3378 + 6524]

Elioenai [7]

1Ch 3: 23 The sons of Neariah: **Elioenai**, Hizkiah and Azrikam—three in all.
3: 24 The sons of **Elioenai**: Hodaviah, Eliashib, Pelaiah, Akkub,
4: 36 also **Elioenai**, Jaakobah, Jeshohaiah, Asaiah, Adiel, Jesimiel,
7: 8 Zemirah, Joash, Eliezer, **Elioenai**, Omri, Jeremoth, Abijah,
Ezr 10: 22 **Elioenai**, Maaseiah, Ishmael, Nethanel, Jozabad and Elasah.
10: 27 **Elioenai**, Eliashib, Mattaniah, Jeremoth, Zabad and Aziza.
Ne 12: 41 Micaiah, **Elioenai**, Zechariah and Hananiah with their trumpets—

494 אֶלְיַחְבָּא ʾelyaḥbāʾ, n.pr.m. [2] [√ 446 + 2461]

Eliahba [2]

2Sa 23: 32 **Eliahba** the Shaalbonite, the sons of Jashen, Jonathan
1Ch 11: 33 Azmaveth the Baharumite, **Eliahba** the Shaalbonite,

495 אֱלִיחֹרֶף ʾelîḥōrep, n.pr.m. [1]

Elihoreph [1]

1Ki 4: 3 **Elihoreph** and Ahijah, sons of Shisha—secretaries;

496 אֱלִיל ʾelîl, n.m. [20] [→ 470]

idols [15], worthless [2], *untranslated* [1], idolatries [1], images [1]

Lev 19: 4 " 'Do not turn to **idols** or make gods of cast metal for yourselves.
26: 1 " 'Do not make **idols** or set up an image or a sacred stone for
1Ch 16: 26 For all the gods of the nations are **idols**, but the LORD made the
Job 13: 4 smear me with lies; you are **worthless** physicians, all of you!
Ps 96: 5 For all the gods of the nations are **idols**, but the LORD made the
97: 7 who worship images are put to shame, those who boast in **idols**—
Isa 2: 8 Their land is full of **idols**; they bow down to the work of their
2: 18 and the **idols** will totally disappear.
2: 20 away to the rodents and bats their **idols** *of* silver and idols of gold,
2: 20 away to the rodents and bats their idols of silver and **idols** *of* gold,
10: 10 As my hand seized the kingdoms of the **idols**, kingdoms whose
10: 11 and her images as I dealt with Samaria and her **idols**?' "
19: 1 The **idols** *of* Egypt tremble before him, and the hearts of the
19: 3 they will consult the **idols** and the spirits of the dead, the mediums
31: 7 For in that day every one of you will reject the **idols** *of* silver
31: 7 the idols of silver and **[RPH]** gold your sinful hands have made.
Jer 14: 14 **idolatries** [K 470] and the delusions of their own minds.
Eze 30: 13 " 'I will destroy the idols and put an end to the **images** in Memphis.
Hab 2: 18 it trusts in his own creation; he makes **idols** that cannot speak.
Zec 11: 17 "Woe to the **worthless** shepherd, who deserts the flock!

497 אֱלִימֶלֶךְ ʾelîmelek, n.pr.m. [6] [√ 446 + 4889]

Elimelech [6]

Ru 1: 2 The man's name was **Elimelech**, his wife's name Naomi,
1: 3 Now **Elimelech**, Naomi's husband, died, and she was left with her
2: 1 from the clan of **Elimelech**, a man of standing, whose name was
2: 3 in a field belonging to Boaz, who was from the clan of **Elimelech**.
4: 3 is selling the piece of land that belonged to our brother **Elimelech**.
4: 9 that I have bought from Naomi all the property of **Elimelech**,

498 אֶלְיָסָף ʾelyāsāp, n.pr.m. [6] [√ 446 + 3578]

Eliasaph [6]

Nu 1: 14 from Gad, **Eliasaph** son of Deuel;
2: 14 The leader of the people of Gad is **Eliasaph** son of Deuel.
3: 24 The leader of the families of the Gershonites was **Eliasaph** son of
7: 42 On the sixth day **Eliasaph** son of Deuel, the leader of the people of
7: 47 This was the offering of **Eliasaph** son of Deuel.
10: 20 **Eliasaph** son of Deuel was over the division of the tribe of Gad.

499 אֱלִיעֶזֶר ʾelîʿezer, n.pr.m. [14] [√ 446 + 6469]

Eliezer [14]

Ge 15: 2 and the one who will inherit my estate is **Eliezer** of Damascus?"
Ex 18: 4 the other was named **Eliezer**, for he said, "My father's God was
1Ch 7: 8 Zemirah, Joash, **Eliezer**, Elioenai, Omri, Jeremoth, Abijah,
15: 24 **Eliezer** the priests were to blow trumpets before the ark of God.
23: 15 The sons of Moses: Gershom and **Eliezer**.
23: 17 The descendants of **Eliezer**: Rehabiah was the first. Eliezer had no
23: 17 **Eliezer** had no other sons, but the sons of Rehabiah were very
26: 25 His relatives through **Eliezer**: Rehabiah his son, Jeshaiah his son,
27: 16 over the Reubenites: **Eliezer** son of Zicri; over the Simeonites:
2Ch 20: 37 **Eliezer** son of Dodavahu of Mareshah prophesied against
Ezr 8: 16 So I summoned **Eliezer**, Ariel, Shemaiah, Elnathan, Jarib,
10: 18 and his brothers: Maaseiah, **Eliezer**, Jarib and Gedaliah.
10: 23 Shimei, Kelaiah (that is, Kelita), Pethahiah, Judah and **Eliezer**.
10: 31 of Harim: **Eliezer**, Ishijah, Malkijah, Shemaiah, Shimeon,

500 אֱלִיעָם ʾelîʿām, n.pr.m. [2] [√ 446 + 6639]

Eliam [2]

2Sa 11: 3 the daughter of **Eliam** and the wife of Uriah the Hittite?"
23: 34 of Ahasbai the Maacathite, **Eliam** son of Ahithophel the Gilonite,

501 אֱלִיעֵינַי ʾelîʿênay, n.pr.m. [1] [√ 448 + 3378 + 6524]
Elienai [1]
1Ch 8:20 **Elienai**, Zillethai, Eliel,

502 אֱלִיפַז ʾelîpaz, n.pr.m. [15] [√ 446 + 7058]
Eliphaz [14], him[s] [1]
Ge 36: 4 Adah bore **Eliphaz** to Esau, Basemath bore Reuel,
36:10 **Eliphaz**, the son of Esau's wife Adah, and Reuel, the son of Esau's
36:11 The sons of **Eliphaz**: Teman, Omar, Zepho, Gatam and Kenaz.
36:12 Esau's son **Eliphaz** also had a concubine named Timna, who bore
36:12 also had a concubine named Timna, who bore **him**[s] Amalek.
36:15 The sons of **Eliphaz** the firstborn of Esau: Chiefs Teman,
36:16 These were the chiefs descended from **Eliphaz** in Edom; they were
1Ch 1:35 The sons of Esau: **Eliphaz**, Reuel, Jeush, Jalam and Korah.
1:36 The sons of **Eliphaz**: Teman, Omar, Zepho, Gatam and Kenaz;
Job 2:11 **Eliphaz** the Temanite, Bildad the Shuhite and Zophar the
4: 1 Then **Eliphaz** the Temanite replied:
15: 1 Then **Eliphaz** the Temanite replied:
22: 1 Then **Eliphaz** the Temanite replied:
42: 7 he said to **Eliphaz** the Temanite, "I am angry with you and your
42: 9 So **Eliphaz** the Temanite, Bildad the Shuhite and Zophar the

503 אֱלִיפַל ʾelîpal, n.pr.m. [1] [√ 446 + 7136]
Eliphal [1]
1Ch 11:35 Ahiam son of Sacar the Hararite, **Eliphal** son of Ur,

504 אֱלִיפְלֵהוּ ʾelîpelēhû, n.pr.m. [2] [√ 446 + 7098?]
Eliphelehu [2]
1Ch 15:18 Eliab, Benaiah, Maaseiah, Mattithiah, **Eliphelehu**, Mikneiah,
15:21 **Eliphelehu**, Mikneiah, Obed-Edom, Jeiel and Azaziah were to

505 אֱלִיפֶלֶט ʾelîpeleṭ, n.pr.m. [8] [√ 446 + 7118]
Eliphelet [8]
2Sa 5:16 Elishama, Eliada and **Eliphelet**.
23:34 **Eliphelet** son of Ahasbai the Maacathite, Eliam son of Ahithophel
1Ch 3: 6 There were also Ibhar, Elishua, **Eliphelet**,
3: 8 Elishama, Eliada and **Eliphelet**—nine in all.
8:39 Ulam his firstborn, Jeush the second son and **Eliphelet** the third.
14: 7 Elishama, Beeliada and **Eliphelet**.
Ezr 8:13 the last ones, whose names were **Eliphelet**, Jeuel and Shemaiah,
10:33 Mattattah, Zabad, **Eliphelet**, Jeremai, Manasseh and Shimei.

506 אֱלִיצוּר ʾelîṣûr, n.pr.m. [5] [√ 446 + 7446]
Elizur [5]
Nu 1: 5 men who are to assist you: from Reuben, **Elizur** son of Shedeur;
2:10 The leader of the people of Reuben is **Elizur** son of Shedeur.
7:30 On the fourth day **Elizur** son of Shedeur, the leader of the people
7:35 This was the offering of **Elizur** son of Shedeur.
10:18 under their standard. **Elizur** son of Shedeur was in command.

507 אֱלִיצָפָן ʾelîṣāpān, n.pr.m. [4] [√ 446 + 7621]
Elizaphan [4]
Nu 3:30 The leader of the families of the Kohathite clans was **Elizaphan**
34:25 **Elizaphan** son of Parnach, the leader from the tribe of Zebulun;
1Ch 15: 8 from the descendants of **Elizaphan**, Shemaiah the leader and 200
2Ch 29:13 from the descendants of **Elizaphan**, Shimri and Jeiel; from the

508 אֱלִיקָא ʾelîqāʾ, n.pr.m. [1] [√ 446 + 7756?]
Elika [1]
2Sa 23:25 Shammah the Harodite, **Elika** the Harodite,

509 אֶלְיָקִים ʾelyāqîm, n.pr.m. [12] [√ 446 + 7756]
Eliakim [12]
2Ki 18:18 **Eliakim** son of Hilkiah the palace administrator, Shebna the
18:26 **Eliakim** son of Hilkiah, and Shebna and Joah said to the field
18:37 **Eliakim** son of Hilkiah the palace administrator, Shebna the
19: 2 He sent **Eliakim** the palace administrator, Shebna the secretary
23:34 Pharaoh Neco made **Eliakim** son of Josiah king in place of his
2Ch 36: 4 The king of Egypt made **Eliakim**, a brother of Jehoahaz, king over
Ne 12:41 **Eliakim**, Maaseiah, Miniamin, Micaiah, Elioenai, Zechariah
Isa 22:20 "In that day I will summon my servant, **Eliakim** son of Hilkiah.
36: 3 **Eliakim** son of Hilkiah the palace administrator, Shebna the
36:11 Then **Eliakim**, Shebna and Joah said to the field commander,
36:22 **Eliakim** son of Hilkiah the palace administrator, Shebna the
37: 2 He sent **Eliakim** the palace administrator, Shebna the secretary,

510 אֱלִישֶׁבַע ʾelîšebaʿ, n.pr.f. [1] [√ 446 + 8682]
Elisheba [1]
Ex 6:23 Aaron married **Elisheba**, daughter of Amminadab and sister of

511 אֱלִישָׁה ʾelîšâ, n.pr.loc. [3]
Elishah [3]
Ge 10: 4 The sons of Javan: **Elishah**, Tarshish, the Kittim and the Rodanim.
1Ch 1: 7 The sons of Javan: **Elishah**, Tarshish, the Kittim and the Rodanim.
Eze 27: 7 your awnings were of blue and purple from the coasts of **Elishah**.

512 אֱלִישׁוּעַ ʾelîšûaʿ, n.pr.m. [2 / 3] [√ 446 + 8775]
Elishua [3]
2Sa 5:15 Ibhar, **Elishua**, Nepheg, Japhia,
1Ch 3: 6 There were also Ibhar, **Elishua**, [BHS 514] Eliphelet,
14: 5 Ibhar, **Elishua**, Elpelet,

513 אֶלְיָשִׁיב ʾelyāšîb, n.pr.m. [17] [√ 446 + 8740]
Eliashib [15], Eliashib's [1], it[s] [+1074] [1]
1Ch 3:24 **Eliashib**, Pelaiah, Akkub, Johanan, Delaiah and Anani—
24:12 the eleventh to **Eliashib**, the twelfth to Jakim,
Ezr 10: 6 house of God and went to the room of Jehohanan son of **Eliashib**.
10:24 From the singers: **Eliashib**. From the gatekeepers: Shallum,
10:27 Elioenai, **Eliashib**, Mattaniah, Jeremoth, Zabad and Aziza.
10:36 Vaniah, Meremoth, **Eliashib**,
Ne 3: 1 **Eliashib** the high priest and his fellow priests went to work
3:20 from the angle to the entrance of the house of **Eliashib** the high
3:21 from the entrance of **Eliashib's** house to the end of it.
3:21 from the entrance of Eliashib's house to the end of **it**[s] [+1074].
12:10 Joiakim the father of **Eliashib**, Eliashib the father of Joiada,
12:10 Joiakim the father of Eliashib, **Eliashib** the father of Joiada,
12:22 The family heads of the Levites in the days of **Eliashib**, Joiada,
12:23 Johanan son of **Eliashib** were recorded in the book of the annals.
13: 4 **Eliashib** the priest had been put in charge of the storerooms of the
13: 7 Here I learned about the evil thing **Eliashib** had done in providing
13:28 One of the sons of Joiada son of **Eliashib** the high priest was

514 אֱלִישָׁמָע ʾelîšāmāʿ, n.pr.m. [17 / 16] [√ 446 + 9048]
Elishama [16]
Nu 1:10 from Ephraim, **Elishama** son of Ammihud; from Manasseh,
2:18 The leader of the people of Ephraim is **Elishama** son of Ammihud.
7:48 On the seventh day **Elishama** son of Ammihud, the leader of the
7:53 This was the offering of **Elishama** son of Ammihud.
10:22 under their standard. **Elishama** son of Ammihud was in command.
2Sa 5:16 **Elishama**, Eliada and Eliphelet.
2Ki 25:25 the son of **Elishama**, who was of royal blood, came with ten men
1Ch 2:41 the father of Jekamiah, and Jekamiah the father of **Elishama**.
3: 6 also Ibhar, <u>Elishua</u>, [BHS ***Elishama***; NIV 512] Eliphelet,
3: 8 **Elishama**, Eliada and Eliphelet—nine in all.
7:26 Ladan his son, Ammihud his son, **Elishama** his son,
14: 7 **Elishama**, Beeliada and Eliphelet.
2Ch 17: 8 and Tob-Adonijah—and the priests **Elishama** and Jehoram.
Jer 36:12 **Elishama** the secretary, Delaiah son of Shemaiah, Elnathan son of
36:20 After they put the scroll in the room of **Elishama** the secretary,
36:21 and Jehudi brought it from the room of **Elishama** the secretary
41: 1 the son of **Elishama**, who was of royal blood and had been one of

515 אֱלִישָׁע ʾelîšāʿ, n.pr.m. [58] [√ 446 + 3828?]
Elisha [54], Elisha's [3], he[s] [1]
1Ki 19:16 anoint **Elisha** son of Shaphat from Abel Meholah to succeed you
19:17 and **Elisha** will put to death any who escape the sword of Jehu.
19:19 So Elijah went from there and found **Elisha** son of Shaphat.
2Ki 2: 1 in a whirlwind, Elijah and **Elisha** were on their way from Gilgal.
2: 2 Elijah said to **Elisha**, "Stay here; the LORD has sent me to
2: 2 But **Elisha** said, "As surely as the LORD lives and as you live,
2: 3 The company of the prophets at Bethel came out to **Elisha**
2: 4 Elijah said to him, "Stay here, **Elisha**; the LORD has sent me to
2: 5 The company of the prophets at Jericho went up to **Elisha**
2: 9 When they had crossed, Elijah said to **Elisha**, "Tell me, what can I
2: 9 "Let me inherit a double portion of your spirit," **Elisha** replied.
2:12 **Elisha** saw this and cried out, "My father! My father! The chariots
2:14 it divided to the right and to the left, and **he**[s] crossed over.
2:15 were watching, said, "The spirit of Elijah is resting on **Elisha**."
2:19 The men of the city said to **Elisha**, "Look, our lord, this town is
2:22 wholesome to this day, according to the word **Elisha** had spoken.
3:11 of the king of Israel answered, "**Elisha** son of Shaphat is here.
3:13 **Elisha** said to the king of Israel, "What do we have to do with each
3:14 **Elisha** said, "As surely as the LORD Almighty lives, whom I
4: 1 of a man from the company of the prophets cried out to **Elisha**,
4: 2 **Elisha** replied to her, "How can I help you? Tell me, what do you

2Ki 4: 8 One day **Elisha** went to Shunem. And a well-to-do woman was
4: 17 that same time she gave birth to a son, just as **Elisha** had told her.
4: 32 When **Elisha** reached the house, there was the boy lying dead on
4: 38 **Elisha** returned to Gilgal and there was a famine in that region.
5: 8 When **Elisha** the man of God heard that the king of Israel had torn
5: 9 his horses and chariots and stopped at the door of **Elisha's** house.
5: 10 **Elisha** sent a messenger to say to him, "Go, wash yourself seven
5: 20 Gehazi, the servant of **Elisha** the man of God, said to himself,
5: 25 his master Elisha. "Where have you been, Gehazi?" **Elisha** asked.
6: 1 The company of the prophets said to **Elisha**, "Look, the place
6: 12 of us, my lord the king," said one of his officers, "but **Elisha**,
6: 17 And **Elisha** prayed, "O LORD, open his eyes so he may see."
6: 17 saw the hills full of horses and chariots of fire all around **Elisha**.
6: 18 **Elisha** prayed to the LORD, "Strike these people with blindness."
6: 18 So he struck them with blindness, as **Elisha** had asked.
6: 19 **Elisha** told them, "This is not the road and this is not the city.
6: 20 After they entered the city, **Elisha** said, "LORD, open the eyes of
6: 21 of Israel saw them, he asked **Elisha**, "Shall I kill them, my father?
6: 31 if the head of **Elisha** son of Shaphat remains on his shoulders
6: 32 Now **Elisha** was sitting in his house, and the elders were sitting
7: 1 **Elisha** said, "Hear the word of the LORD. This is what the
8: 1 Now **Elisha** had said to the woman whose son he had restored to
8: 4 and had said, "Tell me about all the great things **Elisha** has done."
8: 5 my lord the king, and this is her son whom **Elisha** restored to life."
8: 7 **Elisha** went to Damascus, and Ben-Hadad king of Aram was ill.
8: 10 **Elisha** answered, "Go and say to him, 'You will certainly recover';
8: 13 shown me that you will become king of Aram," answered **Elisha**.
8: 14 Hazael left **Elisha** and returned to his master. When Ben-Hadad
8: 14 When Ben-Hadad asked, "What did **Elisha** say to you?" Hazael
9: 1 The prophet **Elisha** summoned a man from the company of the
13: 14 Now **Elisha** was suffering from the illness from which he died.
13: 15 **Elisha** said, "Get a bow and some arrows," and he did so.
13: 16 When he had taken it, **Elisha** put his hands on the king's hands.
13: 17 he said, and he opened it. "Shoot!" **Elisha** said, and he shot.
13: 20 **Elisha** died and was buried. Now Moabite raiders used to enter the
13: 21 a band of raiders; so they threw the man's body into **Elisha's** tomb.
13: 21 When the body touched **Elisha's** bones, the man came to life

516 אֱלִישָׁפָט ***'elîšāpāṭ***, n.pr.m. [1] [√ 446 + 9149]

Elishaphat [1]

2Ch 23: 1 of Obed, Maaseiah son of Adaiah, and **Elishaphat** son of Zicri.

517 אֱלִיָּתָה ***'eliyyātâ***, n.pr.m. [1] [√ 446 + 910]

Eliathah [1]

1Ch 25: 27 the twentieth to **Eliathah**, his sons and relatives, 12

518 אַלְלַי ***'allay***, interj. [2]

what misery [1], woe [1]

Job 10: 15 If I am guilty—**woe** to me! Even if I am innocent, I cannot lift my
Mic 7: 1 **What misery** is mine! I am like one who gathers summer fruit at

519 ¹אָלַם ***'ālam[1]***, v. [8] [→ 522, 532]

silent [6], be silenced [1], speechless [1]

Ps 31: 18 [31:19] [C] *Let* their lying lips **be silenced**, for with pride
39: 2 [39:3] [C] *when I was* **silent** and still, not even saying anything
39: 9 [39:10] [C] *I was* **silent**; I would not open my mouth, for you
Isa 53: 7 [C] as a sheep before her shearers *is* **silent**, so he did not open his
Eze 3: 26 [C] so that *you will be* **silent** and unable to rebuke them,
24: 27 [C] you will speak with him and *will* no longer *be* **silent**.
33: 22 [C] So my mouth was opened and *I was* no longer **silent**.
Da 10: 15 [C] I bowed with my face toward the ground and *was* **speechless**.

520 ²אָלַם ***'ālam[2]***, v. [1] [→ 524]

binding [1]

Ge 37: 7 [D] We *were* **binding** sheaves of grain out in the field when

521 אֵלֶם ***'ēlem***, n.[m.]. [2 / 0] [cf. 519?, 520?]

Ps 56: T [56:1] "A Dove on Distant Oaks." [BHS *silence*; NIV 381]
58: 1 [58:2] Do you rulers [BHS *silence*; NIV 446] indeed speak justly?

522 אִלֵּם ***'illēm***, a. [6] [√ 519]

mute [4], that cannot speak [1], those who cannot speak [1]

Ex 4: 11 Who makes him deaf or **mute**? Who gives him sight or makes him
Ps 38: 13 [38:14] I am like a deaf man, who cannot hear, like a **mute**,
Pr 31: 8 "Speak up for **those who cannot speak** *for themselves*,
Isa 35: 6 will the lame leap like a deer, and the **mute** tongue shout for joy.
56: 10 they are all **mute** dogs, they cannot bark; they lie around
Hab 2: 18 it trusts in his own creation; he makes idols **that cannot speak**.

523 אַלְמֻגִּים ***'almuggîm***, n.[m.]pl. [3] [cf. 454]

almugwood [+6770] [3]

1Ki 10: 11 and from there they brought great cargoes of **almugwood** [+6770]
10: 12 The king used the **almugwood** [+6770] to make supports for the
10: 12 So much **almugwood** [+6770] has never been imported or seen

524 אֲלֻמָּה ***'ᵃlummâ***, n.f. [5] [√ 520]

sheaves [2], it[s] [1], sheaf [1], sheaves of grain [1]

Ge 37: 7 We were binding **sheaves of grain** out in the field when suddenly
37: 7 sheaves of grain out in the field when suddenly my **sheaf** rose
37: 7 while your **sheaves** gathered around mine and bowed down to it."
37: 7 while your sheaves gathered around mine and bowed down to **it**[s]."
Ps 126: 6 to sow, will return with songs of joy, carrying **sheaves** *with* him.

525 אַלְמוֹדָד ***'almôdād***, n.pr. [2]

Almodad [2]

Ge 10: 26 Joktan was the father of **Almodad**, Sheleph, Hazarmaveth,
1Ch 1: 20 Joktan was the father of **Almodad**, Sheleph, Hazarmaveth,

526 אַלַּמֶּלֶךְ ***'allammelek***, n.pr.loc. [1] [√ 464? + 4889]

Allammelech [1]

Jos 19: 26 **Allammelech**, Amad and Mishal. On the west the boundary

527 ¹אַלְמָן ***'almān[1]***, a. [1] [√ 530]

forsaken [1]

Jer 51: 5 For Israel and Judah have not been **forsaken** by their God,

528 ²אַלְמָן ***'almān[2]***, n.[f.]. [2] [cf. 810]

strongholds [2]

Isa 13: 22 Hyenas will howl in her **strongholds**, jackals in her luxurious
Eze 19: 7 He broke down their **strongholds** and devastated their towns.

529 אַלְמֹן ***'almōn***, n.[m.]. [1] [√ 530]

widowhood [1]

Isa 47: 9 in a moment, on a single day: loss of children and **widowhood**.

530 אַלְמָנָה ***'almānâ***, n.f. [54] [→ 527, 529, 531]

widow [31], widows [18], widow's [4], *untranslated* [1]

Ge 38: 11 "Live *as* a **widow** in your father's house until my son Shelah
Ex 22: 22 [22:21] "Do not take advantage of a **widow** or an orphan.
22: 24 [22:23] your wives will become **widows** and your children
Lev 21: 14 He must not marry a **widow**, a divorced woman, or a woman
22: 13 But if a priest's daughter becomes a **widow** or is divorced,
Nu 30: 9 [30:10] "Any vow or obligation taken by a **widow** or divorced
Dt 10: 18 He defends the cause of the fatherless and the **widow**, and loves
14: 29 and the **widows** who live in your towns may come and eat
16: 11 and the aliens, the fatherless and the **widows** living among you.
16: 14 the aliens, the fatherless and the **widows** who live in your towns.
24: 17 the fatherless of justice, or take the cloak of the **widow** as a pledge.
24: 19 Leave it for the alien, the fatherless and the **widow**, so that the
24: 20 Leave what remains for the alien, the fatherless and the **widow**.
24: 21 Leave what remains for the alien, the fatherless and the **widow**.
26: 12 shall give it to the Levite, the alien, the fatherless and the **widow**,
26: 13 have given it to the Levite, the alien, the fatherless and the **widow**,
27: 19 who withholds justice from the alien, the fatherless or the **widow**."
2Sa 14: 5 She said, "I am indeed a **widow**; my husband is dead.
1Ki 7: 14 whose mother was a **widow** from the tribe of Naphtali and whose
11: 26 from Zeredah, and his mother was a **widow** named Zeruah.
17: 9 I have commanded a **widow** in that place to supply you with food."
17: 10 he came to the town gate, a **widow** was there gathering sticks.
17: 20 have you brought tragedy also upon this **widow** I am staying with,
Job 22: 9 you sent **widows** away empty-handed and broke the strength of the
24: 3 away the orphan's donkey and take the **widow's** ox in pledge.
24: 21 and childless woman, and to the **widow** show no kindness.
27: 15 those who survive him, and their **widows** will not weep for them.
29: 13 man who was dying blessed me; I made the **widow's** heart sing.
31: 16 the desires of the poor or let the eyes of the **widow** grow weary,
Ps 68: 5 [68:6] A father to the fatherless, a defender of **widows**, is God in
78: 64 priests were put to the sword, and their **widows** could not weep.
94: 6 They slay the **widow** and the alien; they murder the fatherless.
109: 9 May his children be fatherless and his wife a **widow**.
146: 9 watches over the alien and sustains the fatherless and the **widow**,
Pr 15: 25 the proud man's house but he keeps the **widow's** boundaries intact.
Isa 1: 17 Defend the cause of the fatherless, plead the case of the **widow**.
1: 23 of the fatherless; the **widow's** case does not come before them.
9: 17 [9:16] nor will he pity the fatherless and **widows**, for everyone is
10: 2 my people, making **widows** their prey and robbing the fatherless.
47: 8 besides me. I will never be a **widow** or suffer the loss of children.'

Jer 7: 6 the fatherless or the **widow** and do not shed innocent blood in this
15: 8 I will make their **widows** more numerous than the sand of the sea.
18: 21 Let their wives be made childless and **widows**; let their men be put
22: 3 Do no wrong or violence to the alien, the fatherless or the **widow**,
49: 11 I will protect their lives. Your **widows** too can trust in me."
La 1: 1 How like a **widow** is she, who once was great among the nations!
5: 3 We have become orphans and fatherless, our mothers like **widows**.
Eze 22: 7 oppressed the alien and mistreated the fatherless and the **widow**.
22: 25 and precious things and make many **widows** within her.
44: 22 They must not marry **widows** or divorced women; they may marry
44: 22 may marry only virgins of Israelite descent or **widows** of priests.
44: 22 only virgins of Israelite descent or widows **[RPH]** of priests.
Zec 7: 10 Do not oppress the **widow** or the fatherless, the alien or the poor.
Mal 3: 5 who oppress the **widows** and the fatherless, and deprive aliens of

531 אַלְמָנוּת *'almānût*, n.f. [4] [√ 530]

widow's [2], widowhood [1], widows [1]

Ge 38: 14 she took off her **widow's** clothes, covered herself with a veil to
38: 19 she took off her veil and put on her **widow's** clothes again.
2Sa 20: 3 kept in confinement till the day of their death, living as **widows**.
Isa 54: 4 and remember no more the reproach of your **widowhood**.

532 אַלְמֹנִי *'almōnî*, a. [3] [√ 519; cf. 7140, 7141]

certain [+7141] [1], friend [+7141] [1], such and such [+7141] [1]

Ru 4: 1 Boaz said, "Come over here, my **friend** [+7141], and sit down."
1Sa 21: 2 [21:3] I have told them to meet me at a **certain** [+7141] place.
2Ki 6: 8 "I will set up my camp in **such and such** [+7141] a place."

533 אֵלֹנִי *'ēlōnî*, a.g. [1] [√ 472; cf. 391]

Elonite [1]

Nu 26: 26 through Elon, the **Elonite** clan; through Jahleel, the Jahleelite clan.

534 אֶלְנָעַם *'elnā'am*, n.pr.m. [1] [√ 446 + 5840]

Elnaam [1]

1Ch 11: 46 Eliel the Mahavite, Jeribai and Joshaviah the sons of **Elnaam**,

535 אֶלְנָתָן *'elnātān*, n.pr.m. [7] [√ 446 + 5989]

Elnathan [7]

2Ki 24: 8 His mother's name was Nehushta daughter of **Elnathan**; she was
Ezr 8: 16 **Elnathan**, Jarib, Elnathan, Nathan, Zechariah and Meshullam,
8: 16 Elnathan, Jarib, **Elnathan**, Nathan, Zechariah and Meshullam,
8: 16 and Meshullam, who were leaders, and Joiarib and **Elnathan**,
Jer 26: 22 King Jehoiakim, however, sent **Elnathan** son of Acbor to Egypt,
36: 12 the secretary, Delaiah son of Shemaiah, **Elnathan** son of Acbor,
36: 25 Even though **Elnathan**, Delaiah and Gemariah urged the king not

536 אֶלָּסָר *'ellāsār*, n.pr.loc. [2]

Ellasar [2]

Ge 14: 1 Arioch king of **Ellasar**, Kedorlaomer king of Elam and Tidal king
14: 9 of Goiim, Amraphel king of Shinar and Arioch king of **Ellasar**—

537 אֶלְעָד *'el'ād*, n.pr.m. [1] [√ 446 + 6386]

Elead [1]

1Ch 7: 21 Ezer and **Elead** were killed by the native-born men of Gath,

538 אֶלְעָדָה *'el'ādâ*, n.pr.m. [1] [√ 446 + 6335]

Eleadah [1]

1Ch 7: 20 Bered his son, Tahath his son, **Eleadah** his son, Tahath his son,

539 אֶלְעוּזַי *'el'ûzay*, n.pr.m. [1] [√ 446 + 6437?]

Eluzai [1]

1Ch 12: 5 [12:6] **Eluzai**, Jerimoth, Bealiah, Shemariah and Shephatiah the

540 אֶלְעָזָר *'el'āzār*, n.pr.m. [72] [√ 446 + 6468]

Eleazar [70], Eleazar's [2]

Ex 6: 23 and she bore him Nadab and Abihu, **Eleazar** and Ithamar.
6: 25 **Eleazar** son of Aaron married one of the daughters of Putiel,
28: 1 along with his sons Nadab and Abihu, **Eleazar** and Ithamar,
Lev 10: 6 Then Moses said to Aaron and his sons **Eleazar** and Ithamar,
10: 12 Moses said to Aaron and his remaining sons, **Eleazar** and Ithamar,
10: 16 he was angry with **Eleazar** and Ithamar, Aaron's remaining sons,
Nu 3: 2 Aaron were Nadab the firstborn and Abihu, **Eleazar** and Ithamar.
3: 4 so only **Eleazar** and Ithamar served as priests during the lifetime
3: 32 The chief leader of the Levites was **Eleazar** son of Aaron,
4: 16 "**Eleazar** son of Aaron, the priest, is to have charge of the oil for
16: 37 [17:2] "Tell **Eleazar** son of Aaron, the priest, to take the censers
16: 39 [17:4] So **Eleazar** the priest collected the bronze censers brought
19: 3 Give it to **Eleazar** the priest; it is to be taken outside the camp
19: 4 Then **Eleazar** the priest is to take some of its blood on his finger
20: 25 Get Aaron and his son **Eleazar** and take them up Mount Hor.
20: 26 Remove Aaron's garments and put them on his son **Eleazar**,
20: 28 removed Aaron's garments and put them on his son **Eleazar**.
20: 28 Then Moses and **Eleazar** came down from the mountain,
25: 7 When Phinehas son of **Eleazar**, the son of Aaron, the priest,
25: 11 "Phinehas son of **Eleazar**, the son of Aaron, the priest, has turned
26: 1 the plague the LORD said to Moses and **Eleazar** son of Aaron,
26: 3 Moses and **Eleazar** the priest spoke with them and said,
26: 60 Aaron was the father of Nadab and Abihu, **Eleazar** and Ithamar.
26: 63 **Eleazar** the priest when they counted the Israelites on the plains of
27: 2 **Eleazar** the priest, the leaders and the whole assembly, and said,
27: 19 Have him stand before **Eleazar** the priest and the entire assembly
27: 21 He is to stand before **Eleazar** the priest, who will obtain decisions
27: 22 He took Joshua and had him stand before **Eleazar** the priest
31: 6 from each tribe, along with Phinehas son of **Eleazar**, the priest,
31: 12 spoils and plunder to Moses and **Eleazar** the priest and the Israelite
31: 13 **Eleazar** the priest and all the leaders of the community went to
31: 21 **Eleazar** the priest said to the soldiers who had gone into battle,
31: 26 "You and **Eleazar** the priest and the family heads of the
31: 29 half share and give it to **Eleazar** the priest as the LORD's part.
31: 31 and **Eleazar** the priest did as the LORD commanded Moses.
31: 41 Moses gave the tribute to **Eleazar** the priest as the LORD's part,
31: 51 Moses and **Eleazar** the priest accepted from them the gold—
31: 54 **Eleazar** the priest accepted the gold from the commanders of
32: 2 So they came to Moses and **Eleazar** the priest and to the leaders of
32: 28 Then Moses gave orders about them to **Eleazar** the priest
34: 17 you as an inheritance: **Eleazar** the priest and Joshua son of Nun.
Dt 10: 6 and was buried, and **Eleazar** his son succeeded him as priest.
Jos 14: 1 which **Eleazar** the priest, Joshua son of Nun and the heads of the
17: 4 They went to **Eleazar** the priest, Joshua son of Nun, and the
19: 51 These are the territories that **Eleazar** the priest, Joshua son of Nun
21: 1 Now the family heads of the Levites approached **Eleazar** the
22: 13 So the Israelites sent Phinehas son of **Eleazar**, the priest,
22: 31 And Phinehas son of **Eleazar**, the priest, said to Reuben, Gad
22: 32 Phinehas son of **Eleazar**, the priest, and the leaders returned to
24: 33 And **Eleazar** son of Aaron died and was buried at Gibeah,
Jdg 20: 28 with Phinehas son of **Eleazar**, the son of Aaron, ministering before
1Sa 7: 1 and consecrated **Eleazar** his son to guard the ark of the LORD.
2Sa 23: 9 Next to him was **Eleazar** son of Dodai the Ahohite. As one of the
1Ch 6: 3 [5:29] The sons of Aaron: Nadab, Abihu, **Eleazar** and Ithamar.
6: 4 [5:30] **Eleazar** was the father of Phinehas, Phinehas the father of
6: 50 [6:35] **Eleazar** his son, Phinehas his son, Abishua his son,
9: 20 In earlier times Phinehas son of **Eleazar** was in charge of the
11: 12 Next to him was **Eleazar** son of Dodai the Ahohite, one of the
23: 21 of Merari: Mahli and Mushi. The sons of Mahli: **Eleazar** and Kish.
23: 22 **Eleazar** died without having sons: he had only daughters.
24: 1 The sons of Aaron were Nadab, Abihu, **Eleazar** and Ithamar.
24: 2 and they had no sons; so **Eleazar** and Ithamar served as the priests.
24: 3 With the help of Zadok a descendant of **Eleazar** and Ahimelech a
24: 4 A larger number of leaders were found among **Eleazar's**
24: 4 sixteen heads of families from **Eleazar's** descendants and eight
24: 5 and officials of God among the descendants of both **Eleazar**
24: 6 one family being taken from **Eleazar** and then one from Ithamar.
24: 28 From Mahli: **Eleazar**, who had no sons.
Ezr 7: 5 the son of Abishua, the son of Phinehas, the son of **Eleazar**,
8: 33 **Eleazar** son of Phinehas was with him, and so were the Levites
10: 25 Izziah, Malkijah, Mijamin, **Eleazar**, Malkijah and Benaiah.
Ne 12: 42 Shemaiah, **Eleazar**, Uzzi, Jehohanan, Malkijah, Elam and Ezer.

541 אֶלְעָלֵא *'el'ālē'*, n.pr.loc. [1] [√ 446 + 6590]

Elealeh [1]

Nu 32: 37 And the Reubenites rebuilt Heshbon, **Elealeh** and Kiriathaim,

542 אֶלְעָלֵה *'el'ālēh*, n.pr.loc. [4] [√ 446? + 6590]

Elealeh [4]

Nu 32: 3 Jazer, Nimrah, Heshbon, **Elealeh**, Sebam, Nebo and Beon—
Isa 15: 4 Heshbon and **Elealeh** cry out, their voices are heard all the way to
16: 9 vines of Sibmah. O Heshbon, O **Elealeh**, I drench you with tears!
Jer 48: 34 "The sound of their cry rises from Heshbon to **Elealeh** and Jahaz,

543 אֶלְעָשָׂה *'el'āśâ*, n.pr.m. [6] [√ 446 + 6913]

Eleasah [4], Elasah [2]

1Ch 2: 39 Azariah the father of Helez, Helez the father of **Eleasah**,
2: 40 **Eleasah** the father of Sismai, Sismai the father of Shallum,
8: 37 of Binea; Raphah was his son, **Eleasah** his son and Azel his son.
9: 43 of Binea; Rephaiah was his son, **Eleasah** his son and Azel his son.
Ezr 10: 22 Elioenai, Maaseiah, Ishmael, Nethanel, Jozabad and **Elasah**.
Jer 29: 3 He entrusted the letter to **Elasah** son of Shaphan and to Gemariah

544 ¹אָלַף *'ālap¹*, v. [4] [→ 476]
learn [1], prompts [1], teach [1], teaches [1]

Job 15: 5 [D] Your sin **prompts** your mouth; you adopt the tongue of the
33: 33 [D] then listen to me; be silent, and *I will* **teach** you wisdom."
35: 11 [D] *who* **teaches** more *to* us than to the beasts of the earth
Pr 22: 25 [A] or *you may* **learn** his ways and get yourself ensnared.

545 ²אָלַף *'ālap²*, v.den. [1] [→ 477, 547, 548; cf. 546]
increase by thousands [1]

Ps 144: 13 [G] Our sheep *will* **increase by thousands**, by tens of thousands

546 ¹אֶלֶף *'elep¹*, n.m. [7] [→ 477, 548; cf. 544]
herds [5], oxen [2]

Dt 7: 13 the calves of your **herds** and the lambs of your flocks in the land
28: 4 the calves of your **herds** and the lambs of your flocks.
28: 18 and the calves of your **herds** and the lambs of your flocks.
28: 51 nor any calves of your **herds** or lambs of your flocks until you are
Ps 8: 7 [8:8] all flocks and **herds**, and the beasts of the field,
Pr 14: 4 Where there are no **oxen**, the manger is empty, but from the
Isa 30: 24 The **oxen** and donkeys that work the soil will eat fodder and mash,

547 ²אֶלֶף *'elep²*, n.m. [494 / 495] [√ 545; Ar 10038]
thousand [223], thousands [31], 24,000 [+752+2256+6929] [14], 25,000 [+2256+2822+6929] [14], 10,000 [+6930] [9], 4,500 [+752+2256+2822+4395] [8], 603,550 [+547+2256+2256+2256 +2822+2822+4395+4395+8993+9252] [6], 1,000 [5], 1,254 [+752+2256+2822+4395] [4], million [+547] [4], 186,400 [+547+547 +752+2256+2256+2256+4395+4395+9046+9252] [3], 337,500 [+547+547+2256+2256+2256+2822+4395+4395+8679+8993+8993] [3], 337,500 [+547+547+2256+2256+2822+4395+4395+8679+8993 +8993] [3], 36,000 [+2256+8993+9252] [3], 40,500 [+752+2256 +2822+4395] [3], 5,000 [+2822] [3], 53,400 [+752+2256+2256 +2822+4395+8993] [3], 675,000 [+547+547+2256+2256+2822+4395 +8679+9252] [3], *untranslated* [3], eleven hundred [+2256+4395] [3], 1,052 [+2256+2822+9109] [2], 1,247 [+752+2256+4395+8679] [2], 1,775 [+2256+2256+2256+2822+4395+8679+8679] [2], 108,100 [+547+2256+2256+4395+4395+9046] [2], 151,450 [+285+547+752 +2256+2256+2256+2256+2822+2822+4395+4395] [2], 153,600 [+547+2256+2256+2256+2822+4395+4395+8993+9252] [2], 157,600 [+547+2256+2256+2256+2822+4395+4395+8679+9252] [2], 16,000 [+6925+9252] [2], 18,000 [+6925+9046] [2], 200,000 [+4395] [2], 30,500 [+2256+2822+4395+8993] [2], 307,500 [+547+2256+2256+2822+4395+4395+8679+8993] [2], 32,200 [+2256+2256+4395+8993+9109] [2], 35,400 [+752+2256+2256 +2822+4395+8993] [2], 4,600 [+752+2256+4395+9252] [2], 41,500 [+285+752+2256+2256+2822+4395] [2], 45,650 [+752+2256+2256 +2256+2822+2822+4395+9252] [2], 46,500 [+752+2256+2256+2822 +4395+9252] [2], 54,400 [+752+752+2256+2256+2822+4395] [2], 57,400 [+752+2256+2256+2822+4395+8679] [2], 59,300 [+2256+2256+2822+4395+8993+9596] [2], 6,720 [+2256+4395 +6929+8679+9252] [2], 601,730 [+547+2256+2256+4395+4395 +8679+8993+9252] [2], 62,700 [+2256+2256+4395+8679+9109 +9252] [2], 7,337 [+2256+4395+8679+8679+8993+8993] [2], 74,600 [+752+2256+2256+4395+8679+9252] [2], fourteen hundred [+752+2256+4395] [2], seventeen hundred [+2256+4395+8679] [2], units of a thousand [2], vast [+547] [2], 1,017 [+2256+6925+8679] [1], 1,017 [+6925+8679] [1], 1,222 [+2256+4395+6929+9109] [1], 1,290 [+2256+4395+9596] [1], 1,335 [+2256+2822+4395+8993 +8993] [1], 1,365 [+2256+2256+2256+2822+4395+8993+9252] [1], 1,760 [+2256+2256+4395+8679+9252] [1], 120,000 [+2256+4395+6929] [1], 14,700 [+752+2256+4395+6925+8679] [1], 16,750 [+2256+2822+4395+6925+8679+9252] [1], 17,200 [+2256+4395+6925+8679] [1], 180,000 [+2256+4395+9046] [1], 2,000 [1], 2,056 [+2256+2822+9252] [1], 2,067 [+2256+8679+9252] [1], 2,172 [+2256+2256+4395+8679+9109] [1], 2,172 [+2256+4395 +8679+9109] [1], 2,200 [+2256+4395] [1], 2,300 [+2256+4395+8993] [1], 2,322 [+2256+4395+6929+8993+9109] [1], 2,400 [+752+2256 +4395] [1], 2,600 [+2256+4395+9252] [1], 2,630 [+2256+2256+4395 +8993+9252] [1], 2,750 [+2256+2822+4395+8679] [1], 2,812 [+2256+4395+6925+9046+9109] [1], 2,818 [+2256+4395+6925 +9046+9046] [1], 20,000 [+6924] [1], 20,200 [+2256+4395+6929] [1], 20,800 [+2256+4395+6929+9046] [1], 22,000 [+2256+6929+9109] [1], 22,034 [+752+2256+2256+2256+6929+8993+9109] [1], 22,200 [+2256+2256+4395+6929+9109] [1], 22,273 [+2256+2256+2256 +4395+6929+8679+8993+9109] [1], 22,600 [+2256+2256+4395 +6929+9109+9252] [1], 23,000 [+2256+6929+8993] [1], 25,100 [+2256+2256+2822+4395+6929] [1], 26,000 [+2256+6929+9252] [1], 28,600 [+2256+2256+4395+6929+9046+9252] [1], 280,000 [+2256+4395+9046] [1], 3,000 [+8993] [1], 3,023 [+2256+2256+6929 +8993+8993] [1], 3,200 [+2256+4395+8993] [1], 3,600 [+2256+4395 +8993+9252] [1], 3,630 [+2256+2256+4395+8993+8993+9252] [1], 3,700 [+2256+4395+8679+8993] [1], 3,930 [+2256+4395+8993 +8993+9596] [1], 300,000 [+4395+8993] [1], 32,000 [+2256+8993 +9109] [1], 32,500 [+2256+2256+2822+4395+8993+9109] [1], 37,000 [+2256+8679+8993] [1], 40,000 [+752] [1], 42,360 [+752+2256+4395+8052+8993+9252] [1], 42,360 [+752+4395+8052 +8993+9252] [1], 43,730 [+752+2256+2256+2256+4395+8679 +8993+8993] [1], 44,760 [+752+752+2256+2256+2256+4395+8679 +9252] [1], 45,400 [+752+752+2256+2256+2822+4395] [1], 45,600 [+752+2256+2256+2822+4395+9252] [1], 5,400 [+752+2256+2822 +4395] [1], 50,000 [+2822] [1], 52,700 [+2256+2256+2822+4395 +8679+9109] [1], 6,200 [+2256+4395+9252] [1], 6,800 [+2256+4395 +9046+9252] [1], 60,500 [+2256+2822+4395+9252] [1], 61,000 [+2256+8052+9252] [1], 61,000 [+285+2256+9252] [1], 64,300 [+752+2256+2256+4395+8993+9252] [1], 64,400 [+752+752+2256 +2256+4395+9252] [1], 7,000 [+8679] [1], 7,100 [+2256+4395+8679] [1], 7,500 [+2256+2822+4395+8679] [1], 70,000 [+8679] [1], 72,000 [+2256+8679+9109] [1], 76,500 [+2256+2256+2822+4395+8679 +9252] [1], 8,580 [+2256+2256+2822+4395+9046+9046] [1], 8,600 [+2256+4395+9046+9252] [1], 80,000 [+9046] [1], 87,000 [+2256+8679+9046] [1], eighteen thousand [+2256+8052+9046] [1], fifteen hundred feet [+564] [1], five hundred yards [+564] [1], thirty-six hundred [+2256+4395+8993+9252] [1], thirty-three hundred [+2256+4395+8993+8993] [1], three thousand feet [+564] [1], twelve hundred [+2256+4395] [1], twenty-seven hundred [+2256+4395+8679] [1], twenty-six hundred [+2256+4395+9252] [1], units of 1,000 [1]

Ge 20: 16 he said, "I am giving your brother a **thousand** shekels *of* silver.
24: 60 "Our sister, may you increase to **thousands** *upon* thousands;
Ex 12: 37 There were about six hundred **thousand** men on foot, besides
18: 21 and appoint them as officials over **thousands**, hundreds, fifties
18: 25 of the people, officials over **thousands**, hundreds, fifties and tens.
20: 6 showing love to a **thousand** ⌞generations⌟ of those who love me
32: 28 and that day about three **thousand** of the people died.
34: 7 maintaining love to **thousands**, and forgiving wickedness,
38: 25 and **1,775** [+2256+2256+2256+2822+4395+8679+8679] shekels,
38: 26 a total of **603,550** [+547+2256+2256+2256+2822+2822 +4395+4395+8993+9252] men.
38: 26 a total of **603,550** [+547+2256+2256+2256+2822+2822 +4395+4395+8993+9252] men.
38: 28 the **1,775** [+2256+2256+2256+2822+4395+8679+8679] shekels to
38: 29 wave offering was 70 talents and **2,400** [+752+2256+4395] shekels.
Nu 1: 21 Reuben was **46,500** [+752+2256+2256+2822+4395+9252].
1: 23 of Simeon was **59,300** [+2256+2256+2822+4395+8993+9596].
1: 25 was **45,650** [+752+2256+2256+2256+2822+2822+4395+9252].
1: 27 tribe of Judah was **74,600** [+752+2256+2256+4395+8679+9252].
1: 29 tribe of Issachar was **54,400** [+752+752+2256+2256+2822+4395].
1: 31 tribe of Zebulun was **57,400** [+752+2256+2256+2822+4395+8679].
1: 33 the tribe of Ephraim was **40,500** [+752+2256+2822+4395].
1: 35 tribe of Manasseh was **32,200** [+2256+2256+4395+8993+9109].
1: 37 of Benjamin was **35,400** [+752+2256+2256+2822+4395+8993].
1: 39 tribe of Dan was **62,700** [+2256+2256+4395+8679+9109+9252].
1: 41 the tribe of Asher was **41,500** [+285+752+2256+2256+2822+4395].
1: 43 of Naphtali was **53,400** [+752+2256+2256+2822+4395+8993].
1: 46 The total number was **603,550** [+547+2256+2256+2256 +2822+2822+4395+4395+8993+9252].
1: 46 The total number was **603,550** [+547+2256+2256+2256 +2822+2822+4395+4395+8993+9252].
2: 4 division numbers **74,600** [+752+2256+2256+4395+8679+9252].
2: 6 His division numbers **54,400** [+752+752+2256+2256+2822+4395].
2: 8 division numbers **57,400** [+752+2256+2256+2822+4395+8679].
2: 9 to the camp of Judah, according to their divisions, number **186,400** [+547+547+752+2256+2256+2256+4395+4395+9046+9252].
2: 9 to the camp of Judah, according to their divisions, number **186,400** [+547+547+752+2256+2256+2256+4395+4395+9046+9252].
2: 9 to the camp of Judah, according to their divisions, number **186,400** [+547+547+752+2256+2256+2256+4395+4395+9046+9252].
2: 11 division numbers **46,500** [+752+2256+2256+2822+4395+9252].
2: 13 division numbers **59,300** [+2256+2256+2822+4395+8993+9596].
2: 15 **45,650** [+752+2256+2256+2256+2822+2822+4395+9252].
2: 16 of Reuben, according to their divisions, number **151,450** [+285 +547+752+2256+2256+2256+2256+2822+2822+4395+4395].
2: 16 of Reuben, according to their divisions, number **151,450** [+285 +547+752+2256+2256+2256+2256+2822+2822+4395+4395].
2: 19 His division numbers **40,500** [+752+2256+2822+4395].
2: 21 His division numbers **32,200** [+2256+2256+4395+8993+9109].
2: 23 division numbers **35,400** [+752+2256+2256+2822+4395+8993].
2: 24 divisions, number **108,100** [+547+2256+2256+4395+4395+9046].
2: 24 divisions, number **108,100** [+547+2256+2256+4395+4395+9046].
2: 26 division numbers **62,700** [+2256+2256+4395+8679+9109+9252].
2: 28 His division numbers **41,500** [+285+752+2256+2256+2822+4395].
2: 30 division numbers **53,400** [+752+2256+2256+2822+4395+8993].
2: 31 All the men assigned to the camp of Dan number **157,600** [+547+2256+2256+2256+2822+4395+4395+8679+9252].

Nu 2:31 All the men assigned to the camp of Dan number **157,600** [+547+2256+2256+2256+2822+4395+4395+8679+9252].
2:32 All those in the camps, by their divisions, number **603,550** [+547+2256+2256+2256+2822+2822+4395+4395+8993+9252].
2:32 All those in the camps, by their divisions, number **603,550** [+547+2256+2256+2256+2822+2822+4395+4395+8993+9252].
3:22 who were counted was **7,500** [+2256+2822+4395+8679].
3:28 males a month old or more was **8,600** [+2256+4395+9046+9252].
3:34 or more who were counted was **6,200** [+2256+4395+9252].
3:39 every male a month old or more, was **22,000** [+2256+6929+9109].
3:43 was **22,273** [+2256+2256+2256+4395+6929+8679+8993+9109].
3:50 **1,365** [+2256+2256+2256+2822+4395+8993+9252] shekels,
4:36 counted by clans, were **2,750** [+2256+2822+4395+8679].
4:40 clans and families, were **2,630** [+2256+2822+4395+8993+9252].
4:44 counted by their clans, were **3,200** [+2256+4395+8993].
4:48 numbered **8,580** [+2256+2256+2822+4395+9046+9046].
7:85 the silver dishes weighed *two* **thousand** four hundred shekels,
10:36 "Return, O LORD, to the countless **thousands** *of* Israel."
11:21 "Here I am among six hundred **thousand** men on foot, and you
16:49 [17:14] **14,700** [+752+2256+4395+6925+8679] people died from
25:9 those who died in the plague numbered **24,000** [+752+2256+6929].
26:7 were **43,730** [+752+2256+2256+2256+4395+8679+8993+8993].
26:14 Simeon; there were **22,200** [+2256+2256+4395+6929+9109] men.
26:18 of Gad; those numbered were **40,500** [+752+2256+2822+4395].
26:22 numbered were **76,500** [+2256+2256+2822+4395+8679+9252].
26:25 numbered were **64,300** [+752+2256+2256+4395+8993+9252].
26:27 Zebulun; those numbered were **60,500** [+2256+2822+4395+9252].
26:34 numbered were **52,700** [+2256+2256+2822+4395+8679+9109].
26:37 numbered were **32,500** [+2256+2256+2822+4395+8993+9109].
26:41 numbered were **45,600** [+752+2256+2256+2822+4395+9252].
26:43 numbered were **64,400** [+752+752+2256+2256+4395+9252].
26:47 numbered were **53,400** [+752+2256+2256+2822+4395+8993].
26:50 numbered were **45,400** [+752+752+2256+2256+2822+4395].
26:51 was **601,730** [+547+2256+2256+4395+4395+8679+8993+9252].
26:51 was **601,730** [+547+2256+2256+4395+4395+8679+8993+9252].
26:62 a month old or more numbered **23,000** [+2256+6929+8993].
31:4 Send into battle a **thousand** *men* from each of the tribes of Israel."
31:4 battle a thousand men from each of the tribes of Israel." **[RPH]**
31:5 So twelve **thousand** men armed for battle, a thousand from each
31:5 a **thousand** from each tribe, were supplied from the clans of Israel.
31:6 Moses sent them into battle, a **thousand** from each tribe,
31:14 the commanders of **thousands** and commanders of hundreds—
31:32 **675,000** [+547+547+2256+2256+2822+4395+8679+9252] sheep,
31:32 **675,000** [+547+547+2256+2256+2822+4395+8679+9252] sheep,
31:32 **675,000** [+547+547+2256+2256+2822+4395+8679+9252] sheep,
31:33 **72,000** [+2256+8679+9109] cattle,
31:34 **61,000** [+285+2256+9252] donkeys
31:35 and **32,000** [+2256+8993+9109] women who had never slept with
31:36 share of those who fought in the battle was: **337,500** [+547+547 +2256+2256+2256+2822+4395+4395+8679+8993+8993] sheep,
31:36 share of those who fought in the battle was: **337,500** [+547+547 +2256+2256+2256+2822+4395+4395+8679+8993+8993] sheep,
31:36 share of those who fought in the battle was: **337,500** [+547+547 +2256+2256+2256+2822+4395+4395+8679+8993+8993] sheep,
31:38 **36,000** [+2256+8993+9252] cattle, of which the tribute for the
31:39 **30,500** [+2256+2822+4395+8993] donkeys, of which the tribute
31:40 **16,000** [+6925+9252] people, of which the tribute for the LORD
31:43 the community's half—was **337,500** [+547+547+2256+2256 +2822+4395+4395+8679+8993+8993] sheep,
31:43 the community's half—was **337,500** [+547+547+2256+2256 +2822+4395+4395+8679+8993+8993] sheep,
31:43 the community's half—was **337,500** [+547+547+2256+2256 +2822+4395+4395+8679+8993+8993] sheep,
31:44 **36,000** [+2256+8993+9252] cattle,
31:45 **30,500** [+2256+2822+4395+8993] donkeys
31:46 and **16,000** [+6925+9252] people.
31:48 the commanders of **thousands** and commanders of hundreds—
31:52 All the gold from the commanders of **thousands** and commanders
31:52 weighed **16,750** [+2256+2822+4395+6925+8679+9252] shekels.
31:54 the priest accepted the gold from the commanders of **thousands**
35:4 will extend out **fifteen hundred feet** [+564] from the town wall.
35:5 the town, measure **three thousand feet** [+564] on the east side,
35:5 *three* **thousand** on the south side, three thousand on the west
35:5 *three* **thousand** on the west and three thousand on the north,
35:5 three thousand on the west and *three* **thousand** on the north,
Dt 1:11 increase you a **thousand** times and bless you as he has promised!
1:15 as commanders of **thousands**, of hundreds, of fifties and of tens
5:10 showing love to a **thousand** ⌞generations⌟ of those who love me
7:9 keeping his covenant of love to a **thousand** generations of those
32:30 How could one man chase a **thousand**, or two put ten thousand to
33:17 ten thousands of Ephraim; such are the **thousands** *of* Manasseh."
Jos 3:4 But keep a distance of about a **thousand** yards between you
4:13 About forty **thousand** armed for battle crossed over before the
7:3 Send *two* or three **thousand** men to take it and do not weary all the
7:3 Send two or three thousand **[RPH]** men to take it and do not
7:4 So about three **thousand** men went up; but they were routed by the
8:3 He chose thirty **thousand** of his best fighting men and sent them
8:12 Joshua had taken about five **thousand** men and set them in ambush
8:25 Twelve **thousand** men and women fell that day—all the people of
23:10 One of you routs a **thousand**, because the LORD your God fights
Jdg 1:4 into their hands and they struck down ten **thousand** men at Bezek.
3:29 At that time they struck down about ten **thousand** Moabites,
4:6 take with you ten **thousand** men of Naphtali and Zebulun
4:10 Ten **thousand** men followed him, and Deborah also went with
4:14 Barak went down Mount Tabor, followed by ten **thousand** men.
5:8 and not a shield or spear was seen among forty **thousand** in Israel.
7:3 and leave Mount Gilead.' " So twenty-two **thousand** men left,
7:3 So twenty-two thousand men left, while ten **thousand** remained.
8:10 Zalmunna were in Karkor with a force of about fifteen **thousand**
8:10 a hundred and twenty **thousand** swordsmen had fallen.
8:26 came to **seventeen hundred** [+2256+4395+8679] shekels,
9:49 tower of Shechem, about a **thousand** men and women, also died.
12:6 Forty-two **thousand** Ephraimites were killed at that time.
15:11 three **thousand** men from Judah went down to the cave in the rock
15:15 of a donkey, he grabbed it and struck down a **thousand** men.
15:16 With a donkey's jawbone I have killed a **thousand** men."
16:5 Each one of us will give you **eleven hundred** [+2256+4395]
16:27 on the roof were about three **thousand** men and women watching
17:2 "The **eleven hundred** [+2256+4395] shekels of silver that were
17:3 When he returned the **eleven hundred** [+2256+4395] shekels of
20:2 of God, four hundred **thousand** soldiers armed with swords.
20:10 and a hundred from a **thousand**, and a thousand from ten thousand,
20:10 and a **thousand** from ten thousand, to get provisions for the army.
20:15 At once the Benjamites mobilized twenty-six **thousand**
20:17 from Benjamin, mustered four hundred **thousand** swordsmen,
20:21 cut down twenty-two **thousand** Israelites on the battlefield that
20:25 they cut down another eighteen **thousand** Israelites, all of them
20:34 ten **thousand** of Israel's finest men made a frontal attack on
20:35 struck down **25,100** [+2256+2256+2822+4395+6929] Benjamites,
20:44 Eighteen **thousand** Benjamites fell, all of them valiant fighters.
20:45 the Israelites cut down five **thousand** men along the roads.
20:45 Benjamites as far as Gidom and struck down *two* **thousand** more.
20:46 On that day twenty-five **thousand** Benjamite swordsmen fell,
21:10 So the assembly sent twelve **thousand** fighting men with
1Sa 4:2 who killed about four **thousand** of them on the battlefield.
4:10 slaughter was very great; Israel lost thirty **thousand** foot soldiers.
6:19 putting seventy [BHS+ *50,070*] of them to death because they had
8:12 Some he will assign to be commanders of **thousands**
11:8 the men of Israel numbered three hundred **thousand** and the men
11:8 three hundred thousand and the men of Judah thirty **thousand**.
13:2 Saul chose three **thousand** *men* from Israel; two thousand were
13:2 *two* **thousand** were with him at Micmash and in the hill country of
13:2 and a **thousand** were with Jonathan at Gibeah in Benjamin.
13:5 fight Israel, with three **thousand** chariots, six thousand charioteers,
13:5 fight Israel, with three thousand chariots, six **thousand** charioteers,
15:4 two hundred **thousand** foot soldiers and ten thousand men from
15:4 hundred thousand foot soldiers and ten **thousand** men from Judah.
17:5 wore a coat of scale armor of bronze weighing five **thousand**
18:7 "Saul has slain his **thousands**, and David his tens of thousands."
18:8 with tens of thousands," he thought, "but me with only **thousands**.
18:13 away from him and gave him command over a **thousand** *men*,
21:11 [21:12] " 'Saul has slain his **thousands**, and David his tens of
22:7 Will he make all of you commanders of **thousands**
24:2 [24:3] So Saul took three **thousand** chosen men from all Israel
25:2 He had a **thousand** goats and three thousand sheep, which he was
25:2 He had a thousand goats and three **thousand** sheep, which he was
26:2 with his three **thousand** chosen men of Israel, to search there for
29:2 rulers marched with their units of hundreds and **thousands**,
29:5 " 'Saul has slain his **thousands**, and David his tens of thousands'?"
2Sa 6:1 brought together out of Israel chosen men, thirty **thousand** in all.
8:4 David captured a **thousand** of his chariots, seven thousand
8:4 seven **thousand** [BHS 4395] charioteers and twenty thousand foot
8:4 seven thousand charioteers and twenty **thousand** foot soldiers.
8:5 king of Zobah, David struck down twenty-two **thousand** of them.
8:13 striking down eighteen **thousand** Edomites in the Valley of Salt.
10:6 they hired twenty **thousand** Aramean foot soldiers from Beth
10:6 and Zobah, as well as the king of Maacah with a **thousand** men,
10:6 with a thousand men, and also twelve **thousand** men from Tob.
10:18 of their charioteers and forty **thousand** *of* their foot soldiers.
17:1 "I would choose twelve **thousand** men and set out tonight in
18:1 appointed over them commanders of **thousands** and commanders
18:3 of us die, they won't care; but you are worth ten **thousand** of us.
18:4 all the men marched out in units of hundreds and of **thousands**.
18:7 and the casualties that day were great—twenty **thousand** men.
18:12 "Even if a **thousand** shekels were weighed out into my hands,
19:17 [19:18] With him were a **thousand** Benjamites, along with Ziba,
24:9 In Israel there were eight hundred **thousand** able-bodied men who
24:9 who could handle a sword, and in Judah five hundred **thousand**.

2Sa 24: 15 and seventy **thousand** of the people from Dan to Beersheba died.
1Ki 3: 4 and Solomon offered a **thousand** burnt offerings on that altar.
4: 26 [5:6] Solomon had four **thousand** stalls for chariot horses,
4: 26 [5:6] stalls for chariot horses, and twelve **thousand** horses.
4: 32 [5:12] He spoke three **thousand** proverbs and his songs numbered
4: 32 [5:12] and his songs numbered a **thousand** and five.
5: 11 [5:25] Solomon gave Hiram twenty **thousand** cors of wheat as
5: 11 [5:25] in addition to twenty **thousand** [BHS-] baths of pressed
5: 13 [5:27] conscripted laborers from all Israel—thirty **thousand** men.
5: 14 [5:28] He sent them off to Lebanon in shifts of ten **thousand** a
5: 15 [5:29] Solomon had seventy **thousand** carriers and eighty
5: 15 [5:29] and eighty **thousand** stonecutters in the hills,
5: 16 [5:30] as well as **thirty-three hundred** [+2256+4395+8993+8993]
7: 26 the rim of a cup, like a lily blossom. It held *two* **thousand** baths.
8: 63 twenty-two **thousand** cattle and a hundred and twenty thousand
8: 63 and a hundred and twenty **thousand** sheep and goats.
10: 26 he had **fourteen hundred** [+752+2256+4395] chariots and twelve
10: 26 he had fourteen hundred chariots and twelve **thousand** horses,
12: 21 tribe of Benjamin—a hundred and eighty **thousand** fighting men—
19: 18 Yet I reserve seven **thousand** in Israel—all whose knees have not
20: 15 Then he assembled the rest of the Israelites, **7,000** [+8679] in all.
20: 29 The Israelites inflicted a hundred **thousand** casualties on the
20: 30 where the wall collapsed on twenty-seven **thousand** of them.
2Ki 3: 4 he had to supply the king of Israel with a hundred **thousand** lambs
3: 4 thousand lambs and with the wool of a hundred **thousand** rams.
5: 5 of silver, six **thousand** shekels of gold and ten sets of clothing.
13: 7 ten chariots and ten **thousand** foot soldiers, for the king of Aram
14: 7 He was the one who defeated ten **thousand** Edomites in the Valley
15: 19 Menahem gave him a **thousand** talents of silver to gain his support
18: 23 I will give you *two* **thousand** horses—if you can put riders on
19: 35 a hundred and eighty-five **thousand** men in the Assyrian camp.
24: 14 and all the craftsmen and artisans—a total of ten **thousand**.
24: 16 to Babylon the entire force of seven **thousand** fighting men,
24: 16 strong and fit for war, and a **thousand** craftsmen and artisans.
1Ch 5: 18 had **44,760** [+752+752+2256+2256+2256+4395+8679+9252] men
5: 21 fifty **thousand** camels, two hundred fifty thousand sheep and two
5: 21 two hundred fifty **thousand** sheep and two thousand donkeys.
5: 21 two hundred fifty thousand sheep and *two* **thousand** donkeys.
5: 21 They also took one hundred **thousand** people captive,
7: 2 numbered **22,600** [+2256+2256+4395+6929+9109+9252].
7: 4 they had **36,000** [+2256+8993+9252] men ready for battle, for they
7: 5 listed in their genealogy, were **87,000** [+2256+8679+9046] in all.
7: 7 **22,034** [+752+2256+2256+2256+6929+8993+9109] fighting men.
7: 9 heads of families and **20,200** [+2256+4395+6929] fighting men.
7: 11 There were **17,200** [+2256+4395+6925+8679] fighting men ready
7: 40 as listed in their genealogy, was **26,000** [+2256+6929+9252].
9: 13 of families, numbered **1,760** [+2256+2256+4395+8679+9252].
12: 14 [12:15] a match for a hundred, and the greatest for a **thousand**.
12: 20 [12:21] leaders of **units of a thousand** in Manasseh.
12: 24 [12:25] spear—**6,800** [+2256+4395+9046+9252] armed for battle;
12: 25 [12:26] warriors ready for battle—**7,100** [+2256+4395+8679];
12: 26 [12:27] men of Levi—**4,600** [+752+2256+4395+9252],
12: 27 [12:28] of Aaron, with **3,700** [+2256+4395+8679+8993] men,
12: 29 [12:30] **3,000** [+8993], most of whom had remained loyal to
12: 30 [12:31] in their own clans—**20,800** [+2256+4395+6929+9046];
12: 31 [12:32] to come and make David king—**18,000** [+6925+9046];
12: 33 [12:34] to help David with undivided loyalty—**50,000** [+2822];
12: 34 [12:35] **1,000** officers, together with 37,000 men carrying shields
12: 34 [12:35] with **37,000** [+2256+8679+8993] men carrying shields and
12: 35 [12:36] for battle—**28,600** [+2256+2256+4395+6929+9046+9252];
12: 36 [12:37] experienced soldiers prepared for battle—**40,000** [+752];
12: 37 [12:38] with every type of weapon—**120,000** [+2256+4395+6929].
13: 1 the commanders of **thousands** and commanders of hundreds.
15: 25 the commanders of **units of a thousand** went to bring up the ark of
16: 15 the word he commanded, for a **thousand** generations,
18: 4 David captured a **thousand** of his chariots, seven thousand
18: 4 seven **thousand** charioteers and twenty thousand foot soldiers.
18: 4 seven thousand charioteers and twenty **thousand** foot soldiers.
18: 5 king of Zobah, David struck down twenty-two **thousand** of them.
18: 12 Abishai son of Zeruiah struck down eighteen **thousand** Edomites
19: 6 the Ammonites sent a **thousand** talents of silver to hire chariots
19: 7 They hired thirty-two **thousand** chariots and charioteers, as well as
19: 18 David killed seven **thousand** of their charioteers and forty
19: 18 of their charioteers and forty **thousand** *of* their foot soldiers.
21: 5 In all Israel there were *one* **million** [+547] one hundred thousand
21: 5 In all Israel there were *one* **million** [+547] one hundred thousand
21: 5 In all Israel there were one million one hundred **thousand** men
21: 5 a sword, including four hundred and seventy **thousand** in Judah.
21: 14 a plague on Israel, and seventy **thousand** men of Israel fell dead.
22: 14 for the temple of the LORD a hundred **thousand** talents of gold,
22: 14 a **million** [+547] talents of silver, quantities of bronze and iron too
22: 14 a **million** [+547] talents of silver, quantities of bronze and iron too
23: 3 and the total number of men was thirty-eight **thousand**.
23: 4 twenty-four **thousand** are to supervise the work of the temple of
23: 4 of the LORD and six **thousand** are to be officials and judges.
23: 5 Four **thousand** are to be gatekeepers and four thousand are to
23: 5 four **thousand** are to praise the LORD with the musical
26: 26 by the heads of families who were the commanders of **thousands**
26: 30 his relatives—**seventeen hundred** [+2256+4395+8679] able men—
26: 32 Jeriah had **twenty-seven** [+2256+4395+8679] **hundred** relatives,
27: 1 commanders of **thousands** and commanders of hundreds,
27: 1 Each division consisted of **24,000** [+752+2256+6929] men.
27: 2 There were **24,000** [+752+2256+6929] men in his division.
27: 4 There were **24,000** [+752+2256+6929] men in his division.
27: 5 chief and there were **24,000** [+752+2256+6929] men in his division.
27: 7 There were **24,000** [+752+2256+6929] men in his division.
27: 8 There were **24,000** [+752+2256+6929] men in his division.
27: 9 There were **24,000** [+752+2256+6929] men in his division.
27: 10 There were **24,000** [+752+2256+6929] men in his division.
27: 11 There were **24,000** [+752+2256+6929] men in his division.
27: 12 There were **24,000** [+752+2256+6929] men in his division.
27: 13 There were **24,000** [+752+2256+6929] men in his division.
27: 14 There were **24,000** [+752+2256+6929] men in his division.
27: 15 There were **24,000** [+752+2256+6929] men in his division.
28: 1 the commanders of **thousands** and commanders of hundreds,
29: 4 three **thousand** talents of gold (gold of Ophir) and seven thousand
29: 4 seven **thousand** talents of refined silver, for the overlaying of the
29: 6 the commanders of **thousands** and commanders of hundreds,
29: 7 They gave toward the work on the temple of God five **thousand**
29: 7 and ten thousand darics of gold, ten **thousand** talents of silver,
29: 7 of silver, **eighteen thousand** [+2256+8052+9046] talents of bronze
29: 7 thousand talents of bronze and a hundred **thousand** talents of iron.
29: 21 a **thousand** bulls, a thousand rams and a thousand male lambs,
29: 21 a thousand bulls, a **thousand** rams and a thousand male lambs,
29: 21 a thousand bulls, a thousand rams and a **thousand** male lambs,
2Ch 1: 2 to the commanders of **thousands** and commanders of hundreds,
1: 6 the Tent of Meeting and offered a **thousand** burnt offerings on it.
1: 14 he had **fourteen hundred** [+752+2256+4395] chariots and twelve
1: 14 he had fourteen hundred chariots and twelve **thousand** horses,
2: 2 [2:1] He conscripted seventy **thousand** men as carriers and eighty
2: 2 [2:1] eighty **thousand** as stonecutters in the hills and thirty-six
2: 2 [2:1] **thirty-six hundred** [+2256+4395+8993+9252] as foremen
2: 10 [2:9] twenty **thousand** cors of ground wheat, twenty thousand
2: 10 [2:9] twenty **thousand** cors of barley, twenty thousand baths of
2: 10 [2:9] twenty **thousand** baths of wine and twenty thousand baths
2: 10 [2:9] baths of wine and twenty **thousand** baths of olive oil."
2: 17 [2:16] his father David had taken; and they were found to be **153,600** [+547+2256+2256+2256+2822+4395+4395+8993+9252].
2: 17 [2:16] his father David had taken; and they were found to be **153,600** [+547+2256+2256+2256+2822+4395+4395+8993+9252].
2: 18 [2:17] He assigned **70,000** [+8679] of them to be carriers
2: 18 [2:17] and **80,000** [+9046] to be stonecutters in the hills,
2: 18 [2:17] with **3,600** [+2256+4395+8993+9252] foremen over them to
4: 5 the rim of a cup, like a lily blossom. It held three **thousand** baths.
7: 5 King Solomon offered a sacrifice of twenty-two **thousand** head of
7: 5 head of cattle and a hundred and twenty **thousand** sheep and goats.
9: 25 Solomon had four **thousand** stalls for horses and chariots,
9: 25 stalls for horses and chariots, and twelve **thousand** horses,
11: 1 and Benjamin—a hundred and eighty **thousand** fighting men—
12: 3 With **twelve hundred** [+2256+4395] chariots and sixty thousand
12: 3 With twelve hundred chariots and sixty **thousand** horsemen
13: 3 Abijah went into battle with a force of four hundred **thousand** able
13: 3 a battle line against him with eight hundred **thousand** able troops.
13: 17 so that there were five hundred **thousand** casualties among Israel's
14: 8 [14:7] Asa had an army of three hundred **thousand** men from
14: 8 [14:7] and two hundred and eighty **thousand** from Benjamin,
14: 9 [14:8] Cushite marched out against them with a **vast** [+547] army
14: 9 [14:8] Cushite marched out against them with a **vast** [+547] army
15: 11 seven **thousand** sheep and goats from the plunder they had
17: 11 seven **thousand** seven hundred rams and seven thousand seven
17: 11 seven hundred rams and seven **thousand** seven hundred goats.
17: 14 From Judah, commanders of **units of 1,000**:
17: 14 Adnah the commander, with **300,000** [+4395+8993] fighting men;
17: 15 Jehohanan the commander, with **280,000** [+2256+4395+9046];
17: 16 himself for the service of the LORD, with **200,000** [+4395].
17: 17 with **200,000** [+4395] men armed with bows and shields;
17: 18 Jehozabad, with **180,000** [+2256+4395+9046] men armed for battle.
25: 5 them according to their families to commanders of **thousands**
25: 5 found that there were three hundred **thousand** men ready for
25: 6 He also hired a hundred **thousand** fighting men from Israel for a
25: 11 to the Valley of Salt, where he killed ten **thousand** men of Seir.
25: 12 The army of Judah also captured ten **thousand** men alive,
25: 13 They killed three **thousand** people and carried off great quantities
26: 12 leaders over the fighting men was **2,600** [+2256+4395+9252].
26: 13 of **307,500** [+547+2256+2256+2822+4395+4395+8679+8993]
26: 13 of **307,500** [+547+2256+2256+2822+4395+4395+8679+8993]
27: 5 ten **thousand** cors of wheat and ten thousand cors of barley.
27: 5 ten thousand cors of wheat and ten **thousand** cors of barley.

2Ch 28: 6 killed a hundred and twenty **thousand** soldiers in Judah—
28: 8 took captive from their kinsmen two hundred **thousand** wives,
29: 33 to six hundred bulls and three **thousand** sheep and goats.
30: 24 Hezekiah king of Judah provided a **thousand** bulls and seven
30: 24 and seven **thousand** sheep and goats for the assembly,
30: 24 the officials provided them with a **thousand** bulls and ten thousand
30: 24 them with a thousand bulls and ten **thousand** sheep and goats.
35: 7 all the lay people who were there a total of thirty **thousand** sheep
35: 7 goats for the Passover offerings, and also three **thousand** cattle—
35: 8 **twenty-six hundred** [+2256+4395+9252] Passover offerings and
35: 9 provided five **thousand** Passover offerings and five hundred head
Ezr 1: 9 the inventory: gold dishes 30 silver dishes **1,000** silver pans 29
1: 10 gold bowls 30 matching silver bowls 410 other articles **1,000**
1: 11 In all, there were **5,400** [+752+2256+2822+4395] articles of gold
2: 3 the descendants of Parosh **2,172** [+2256+4395+8679+9109]
2: 6 line of Jeshua and Joab) **2,812** [+2256+4395+6925+9046+9109]
2: 7 of Elam **1,254** [+752+2256+2822+4395]
2: 12 of Azgad **1,222** [+2256+4395+6929+9109]
2: 14 of Bigvai **2,056** [+2256+2822+9252]
2: 31 of the other Elam **1,254** [+752+2256+2822+4395]
2: 35 of Senaah **3,630** [+2256+2256+4395+8993+8993+9252]
2: 37 of Immer **1,052** [+2256+2822+9109]
2: 38 of Pashhur **1,247** [+752+2256+4395+8679]
2: 39 of Harim **1,017** [+2256+6925+8679]
2: 64 whole company numbered **42,360** [+752+4395+8052+8993+9252],
2: 65 their **7,337** [+2256+4395+8679+8679+8993+8993] menservants
2: 67 435 camels and **6,720** [+2256+4395+6929+8679+9252] donkeys.
2: 69 for this work **61,000** [+2256+8052+9252] drachmas of gold, 5,000
2: 69 of gold, **5,000** [+2822] minas of silver and 100 priestly garments.
8: 27 20 bowls of gold valued at **1,000** darics, and two fine articles of
Ne 3: 13 They also repaired **five hundred yards** [+564] of the wall as far as
7: 8 the descendants of Parosh **2,172** [+2256+2256+4395+8679+9109]
7: 11 line of Jeshua and Joab) **2,818** [+2256+4395+6925+9046+9046]
7: 12 of Elam **1,254** [+752+2256+2822+4395]
7: 17 of Azgad **2,322** [+2256+4395+6929+8993+9109]
7: 19 of Bigvai **2,067** [+2256+8679+9252]
7: 34 of the other Elam **1,254** [+752+2256+2822+4395]
7: 38 of Senaah **3,930** [+2256+4395+8993+8993+9596]
7: 40 of Immer **1,052** [+2256+2822+9109]
7: 41 of Pashhur **1,247** [+752+2256+4395+8679]
7: 42 of Harim **1,017** [+6925+8679]
7: 66 company numbered **42,360** [+752+2256+4395+8052+8993+9252],
7: 67 their **7,337** [+2256+4395+8679+8679+8993+8993] menservants
7: 69 [7:68] camels and **6,720** [+2256+4395+6929+8679+9252] donkeys.
7: 70 [7:69] The governor gave to the treasury **1,000** drachmas of gold,
7: 71 [7:70] drachmas of gold and **2,200** [+2256+4395] minas of silver.
7: 72 [7:71] of gold, **2,000** minas of silver and 67 garments for priests.
Est 3: 9 I will put ten **thousand** talents of silver into the royal treasury for
9: 16 They killed seventy-five **thousand** of them but did not lay their
Job 1: 3 and he owned seven **thousand** sheep, three thousand camels,
1: 3 three **thousand** camels, five hundred yoke of oxen and five
9: 3 with him, he could not answer him one time out of a **thousand**.
33: 23 one out of a **thousand**, to tell a man what is right for him,
42: 12 He had fourteen **thousand** sheep, six thousand camels, a thousand
42: 12 six **thousand** camels, a thousand yoke of oxen and a thousand
42: 12 a **thousand** yoke of oxen and a thousand donkeys.
42: 12 a thousand yoke of oxen and a **thousand** donkeys.
Ps 50: 10 animal of the forest is mine, and the cattle on a **thousand** hills.
60: T [60:2] struck down twelve **thousand** Edomites in the Valley of
68: 17 [68:18] of God are tens of thousands and **thousands** *of* thousands;
84: 10 [84:11] Better is one day in your courts than a **thousand**
90: 4 For a **thousand** years in your sight are like a day that has just gone
91: 7 A **thousand** may fall at your side, ten thousand at your right hand,
105: 8 the word he commanded, for a **thousand** generations,
119: 72 mouth is more precious to me than **thousands** *of pieces of* silver
Ecc 6: 6 even if he lives a **thousand** years twice over but fails to enjoy his
7: 28 I found one ⌞upright⌟ man among a **thousand**, but not one
SS 4: 4 on it hang a **thousand** shields, all of them shields of warriors.
8: 11 Each was to bring for its fruit a **thousand** shekels *of* silver.
8: 12 the **thousand** shekels are for you, O Solomon, and two hundred are
Isa 7: 23 in every place where there were a **thousand** vines worth a
7: 23 there were a thousand vines worth a **thousand** silver shekels,
30: 17 A **thousand** will flee at the threat of one; at the threat of five you
36: 8 I will give you *two* **thousand** horses—if you can put riders on
37: 36 a hundred and eighty-five **thousand** men in the Assyrian camp.
60: 22 The least of you will become a **thousand**, the smallest a mighty
Jer 32: 18 You show love to **thousands** but bring the punishment for the
52: 28 in the seventh year, **3,023** [+2256+2256+6929+8993+8993] Jews;
52: 30 There were **4,600** [+752+2256+4395+9252] people in all.
Eze 45: 1 a sacred district, **25,000** [+2256+2822+6929] cubits long and
45: 1 sacred district, 25,000 cubits long and **20,000** [+6924] cubits wide;
45: 3 measure off a section **25,000** [+2256+2822+6929] cubits long and
45: 3 off a section 25,000 cubits long and **10,000** [+6930] cubits wide.
45: 5 An area **25,000** [+2256+2822+6929] cubits long and 10,000 cubits
45: 5 and **10,000** [+6930] cubits wide will belong to the Levites,
45: 6 " 'You are to give the city as its property an area **5,000** [+2822]
45: 6 5,000 cubits wide and **25,000** [+2256+2822+6929] cubits long,
47: 3 he measured off a **thousand** cubits and then led me through water
47: 4 He measured off another **thousand** cubits and led me through
47: 4 He measured off another **thousand** and led me through water that
47: 5 He measured off another **thousand**, but now it was a river that I
48: 8 It will be **25,000** [+2256+2822+6929] cubits wide, and its length
48: 9 be **25,000** [+2256+2822+6929] cubits long and 10,000 cubits wide.
48: 9 will be 25,000 cubits long and **10,000** [+6930] cubits wide.
48: 10 It will be **25,000** [+2256+2822+6929] cubits long on the north
48: 10 **10,000** [+6930] cubits wide on the west side, 10,000 cubits wide
48: 10 **10,000** [+6930] cubits wide on the east side and 25,000 cubits long
48: 10 and **25,000** [+2256+2822+6929] cubits long on the south side.
48: 13 Levites will have an allotment **25,000** [+2256+2822+6929] cubits
48: 13 an allotment 25,000 cubits long and **10,000** [+6930] cubits wide.
48: 13 Its total length will be **25,000** [+2256+2822+6929] cubits and its
48: 13 length will be 25,000 cubits and its width **10,000** [+6930] cubits.
48: 15 remaining area, **5,000** [+2822] cubits wide and 25,000 cubits long,
48: 15 5,000 cubits wide and **25,000** [+2256+2822+6929] cubits long,
48: 16 the north side **4,500** [+752+2256+2822+4395] cubits, the south
48: 16 the south side **4,500** [+752+2256+2822+4395] cubits, the east side
48: 16 the east side **4,500** [+752+2256+2822+4395] cubits, and the west
48: 16 cubits, and the west side **4,500** [+752+2256+2822+4395] cubits.
48: 18 will be **10,000** [+6930] cubits on the east side and 10,000 cubits on
48: 18 cubits on the east side and **10,000** [+6930] cubits on the west side.
48: 20 will be a square, **25,000** [+2256+2822+6929] cubits on each side.
48: 20 **[RPH]** As a special gift you will set aside the sacred portion,
48: 21 It will extend eastward from the **25,000** [+2256+2822+6929] cubits
48: 21 from the **25,000** [+2256+2822+6929] cubits to the western border.
48: 30 which is **4,500** [+752+2256+2822+4395] cubits long,
48: 32 "On the east side, which is **4,500** [+752+2256+2822+4395] cubits
48: 33 south side, which measures **4,500** [+752+2256+2822+4395] cubits,
48: 34 west side, which is **4,500** [+752+2256+2822+4395] cubits long,
48: 35 "The distance all around will be **18,000** [+6925+9046] cubits.
Da 8: 14 "It will take **2,300** [+2256+4395+8993] evenings and mornings;
12: 11 desolation is set up, there will be **1,290** [+2256+4395+9596] days.
12: 12 reaches the end of the **1,335** [+2256+2822+4395+8993+8993] days.
Am 5: 3 "The city that marches out a **thousand** strong for Israel will have
Mic 6: 7 Will the LORD be pleased with **thousands** *of* rams, with ten

548 ³אֶלֶף *'elep³*, n.m. [12] [√ 545]

clans [9], clan [1], unit [1], units [1]

Nu 1: 16 of their ancestral tribes. They were the heads of the **clans** *of* Israel.
10: 4 only one is sounded, the leaders—the heads of the **clans** *of* Israel—
31: 5 a thousand from each tribe, were supplied from the **clans** *of* Israel.
31: 48 the officers who were over the **units** *of* the army—the commanders
Jos 22: 14 each the head of a family division among the Israelite **clans**.
22: 21 the half-tribe of Manasseh replied to the heads of the **clans** *of*
22: 30 the heads of the **clans** *of* the Israelites—heard what Reuben,
Jdg 6: 15 My **clan** is the weakest in Manasseh, and I am the least in my
1Sa 10: 19 present yourselves before the LORD by your tribes and **clans**."
17: 18 Take along these ten cheeses to the commander of their **unit**.
23: 23 is in the area, I will track him down among all the **clans** *of* Judah."
Mic 5: 2 [5:1] though you are small among the **clans** *of* Judah,

549 ⁴אֶלֶף *'elep⁴*, n.pr.loc. Not used in NIV/BHS

550 אֱלְפֶּלֶט *'elpeleṭ*, n.pr.m. [1] [√ 446 + 7118]

Elpelet [1]

1Ch 14: 5 Ibhar, Elishua, **Elpelet**,

551 אֶלְפַּעַל *'elpa'al*, n.pr.m. [3] [√ 446 + 7188]

Elpaal [3]

1Ch 8: 11 By Hushim he had Abitub and **Elpaal**.
8: 12 The sons of **Elpaal**: Eber, Misham, Shemed (who built Ono
8: 18 Ishmerai, Izliah and Jobab were the sons of **Elpaal**.

552 אָלַץ *'ālaṣ*, v. [1]

prodded [1]

Jdg 16: 16 [D] With such nagging *she* **prodded** him day after day until he

553 אֶלְצָפָן *'elṣāpān*, n.pr.m. [2] [√ 446 + 7621]

Elzaphan [2]

Ex 6: 22 The sons of Uzziel were Mishael, **Elzaphan** and Sithri.
Lev 10: 4 Moses summoned Mishael and **Elzaphan**, sons of Aaron's uncle

554 אַלְקוּם *'alqûm*, n.[m.]?. [1]
army [1]
Pr 30: 31 a strutting rooster, a he-goat, and a king with his **army** around him.

555 אֶלְקָנָה *'elqānâ*, n.pr.m. [21 / 20] [√ 446 + 7865]
Elkanah [20]
Ex 6: 24 The sons of Korah were Assir, **Elkanah** and Abiasaph. These were
1Sa 1: 1 whose name was **Elkanah** son of Jeroham, the son of Elihu,
1: 4 Whenever the day came for **Elkanah** to sacrifice, he would give
1: 8 **Elkanah** her husband would say to her, "Hannah, why are you
1: 19 **Elkanah** lay with Hannah his wife, and the LORD remembered
1: 21 When the man **Elkanah** went up with all his family to offer the
1: 23 "Do what seems best to you," **Elkanah** her husband told her.
2: 11 **Elkanah** went home to Ramah, but the boy ministered before the
2: 20 Eli would bless **Elkanah** and his wife, saying, "May the LORD
1Ch 6: 23 [6:8] **Elkanah** his son, Ebiasaph his son, Assir his son,
6: 25 [6:10] The descendants of **Elkanah**: Amasai, Ahimoth,
6: 26 [6:11] **Elkanah** his son, Zophai his son, Nahath his son,
6: 26 [6:11] Elkanah his son, [BHS+ *the sons of Elkanah*] Zophai his
6: 27 [6:12] Jeroham his son, **Elkanah** his son and Samuel his son.
6: 34 [6:19] the son of **Elkanah**, the son of Jeroham, the son of Eliel,
6: 35 [6:20] the son of Zuph, the son of **Elkanah**, the son of Mahath,
6: 36 [6:21] the son of **Elkanah**, the son of Joel, the son of Azariah,
9: 16 Berekiah son of Asa, the son of **Elkanah**, who lived in the villages
12: 6 [12:7] **Elkanah**, Isshiah, Azarel, Joezer and Jashobeam the
15: 23 Berekiah and **Elkanah** were to be doorkeepers for the ark.
2Ch 28: 7 officer in charge of the palace, and **Elkanah**, second to the king.

556 אֶלְקֹשִׁי *'elqōšî*, a.g. [1]
Elkoshite [1]
Na 1: 1 The book of the vision of Nahum the **Elkoshite**.

557 אֶלְתּוֹלַד *'eltôlad*, n.pr.loc. [2] [cf. 9351]
Eltolad [2]
Jos 15: 30 **Eltolad**, Kesil, Hormah,
19: 4 **Eltolad**, Bethul, Hormah,

558 אֶלְתְּקֵא *'eltᵉqē'*, n.pr.loc. [1] [→ 559]
Elteketh [1]
Jos 21: 23 Also from the tribe of Dan they received **Elteketh**, Gibbethon,

559 אֶלְתְּקֵה *'eltᵉqēh*, n.pr.loc. [1] [√ 558]
Elteketh [1]
Jos 19: 44 **Elteketh**, Gibbethon, Baalath,

560 אֶלְתְּקֹן *'eltᵉqôn*, n.pr.loc. [1]
Eltekon [1]
Jos 15: 59 Maarath, Beth Anoth and **Eltekon**—six towns and their villages.

561 אִם *'im*, c. & pt.inter. [1070] [→ 467, 3955] See Select Index
if [522], *untranslated* [145], but [+3954] [39], or [39], not [34], when [27], except [+3954] [24], though [22], whether [16], surely [+4202] [14], only [+3954] [11], if [+3954] [10], even if [9], that [8], no [7], only [7], but if [6], since [6], unless [+3954] [6], although [5], or [+2256] [5], never [4], unless [+4202] [4], whenever [4], yet if [4], and [3], however [+3954] [3], neither [3], only if [3], until [+6330] [3], but [+4202] [2], but only [+3954] [2], don't [2], if [+3907] [2], instead [+3954] [2], nor [2], other than [+3954] [2], surely [+3954] [2], than [+3954] [2], that [+4202] [2], though [+3954] [2], till [+4202] [2], until [+889+6330] [2], whether [+4202] [2], without [+3954] [2], after [+3983] [1], although [+3954] [1], as if [1], as long as [+6388] [1], as [1], because [+3610+4202] [1], because [1], but [1], cannot [1], certainly [+4202] [1], even [+3954] [1], even though [1], except [+1194] [1], however [1], if even [1], if indeed [1], if only [1], indeed [+3954] [1], never [+2721+4200] [1], never [+4200+5905] [1], never [+6330+6409] [1], nor [+2256] [1], not [+3954] [1], not even [1], not one [1], nothing [+3972+4946] [1], or [+401+2256] [1], other than [1], otherwise [+401] [1], please [1], provided [+421] [1], rather [+3954] [1], rather [1], so [+3610+4202] [1], suppose [1], surely [+401] [1], till [+6330] [1], unless [+1194] [1], unless [+3954+4200+7156] [1], unless [+3954+4202] [1], until [+3954] [1], whether [+2022+4202] [1], while [1], why [+4027+4200+4537] [1], won't until [+3954] [1], yet [+3954] [1], you [+3870] [1]

562 אֵם *'ēm*, n.f. [220] [→ 566]
mother [134], mother's [60], mothers [9], parents [+3+2256] [3], *untranslated* [2], birth [+1061] [2], grandmother [2], she[s] [+2257] [2], birth [+5055] [1], brothers [+278] [1], fork [1], grandmother's [1], uncle's [+278] [1], very own brother [+278+1201+3870] [1]
Ge 2: 24 a man will leave his father and **mother** and be united to his wife,
3: 20 wife Eve, because she would become the **mother** *of* all the living.
20: 12 is my sister, the daughter of my father though not of my **mother**;
21: 21 in the Desert of Paran, his **mother** got a wife for him from Egypt.
24: 28 The girl ran and told her **mother's** household about these things.
24: 53 he also gave costly gifts to her brother and to her **mother**.
24: 55 her brother and her **mother** replied, "Let the girl remain with us
24: 67 Isaac brought her into the tent of his **mother** Sarah, and he married
24: 67 he loved her; and Isaac was comforted after his **mother's** death.
27: 11 Jacob said to Rebekah his **mother**, "But my brother Esau is a hairy
27: 13 His **mother** said to him, "My son, let the curse fall on me.
27: 14 So he went and got them and brought them to his **mother**,
27: 14 **she**[s] [+2257] prepared some tasty food, just the way his father
27: 29 your brothers, and may the sons of your **mother** bow down to you.
28: 2 to Paddan Aram, to the house of your **mother's** father Bethuel.
28: 2 from among the daughters of Laban, your **mother's** brother.
28: 5 the brother of Rebekah, who was the **mother** *of* Jacob and Esau.
28: 7 had obeyed his father and **mother** and had gone to Paddan Aram.
29: 10 his **mother's** brother, and Laban's sheep, he went over and rolled
29: 10 Laban's **[RPH]** sheep, he went over and rolled the stone away
29: 10 from the mouth of the well and watered his **uncle's** [+278] sheep.
30: 14 some mandrake plants, which he brought to his **mother** Leah.
32: 11 [32:12] and attack me, and also the **mothers** with their children.
37: 10 Will your **mother** and I and your brothers actually come and bow
43: 29 his own **mother's** son, he asked, "Is this your youngest brother,
44: 20 brother is dead, and he is the only one of his **mother's** sons left,
Ex 2: 8 she answered. And the girl went and got the baby's **mother**.
20: 12 "Honor your father and your **mother**, so that you may live long in
21: 15 who attacks his father or his **mother** must be put to death.
21: 17 "Anyone who curses his father or **mother** must be put to death.
22: 30 [22:29] Let them stay with their **mothers** for seven days, but give
23: 19 your God. "Do not cook a young goat in its **mother's** milk.
34: 26 your God. "Do not cook a young goat in its **mother's** milk."
Lev 18: 7 dishonor your father by having sexual relations with your **mother**.
18: 7 your mother. She is your **mother**; do not have relations with her.
18: 9 either your father's daughter or your **mother's** daughter,
18: 13 " 'Do not have sexual relations with your **mother's** sister,
18: 13 your mother's sister, because she is your **mother's** close relative.
19: 3 " 'Each of you must respect his **mother** and father, and you must
20: 9 " 'If anyone curses his father or **mother**, he must be put to death.
20: 9 He has cursed his father or his **mother**, and his blood will be on his
20: 14 " 'If a man marries both a woman and her **mother**, it is wicked.
20: 17 marries his sister, the daughter of either his father or his **mother**,
20: 19 not have sexual relations with the sister of either your **mother**
21: 2 such as his **mother** or father, his son or daughter, his brother,
21: 11 He must not make himself unclean, even for his father or **mother**,
22: 27 or a goat is born, it is to remain with its **mother** for seven days.
24: 11 (His **mother's** name was Shelomith, the daughter of Dibri the
Nu 6: 7 Even if his own father or **mother** or brother or sister dies,
12: 12 Do not let her be like a stillborn infant coming from its **mother's**
Dt 5: 16 "Honor your father and your **mother**, as the LORD your God has
13: 6 [13:7] If your **very own brother** [+278+1201+3870], or your son
14: 21 LORD your God. Do not cook a young goat in its **mother's** milk.
21: 13 in your house and mourned her father and **mother** for a full month,
21: 18 and rebellious son who does not obey his father and **mother**
21: 19 his father and **mother** shall take hold of him and bring him to the
22: 6 the ground, and the **mother** is sitting on the young or on the eggs,
22: 6 the young or on the eggs, do not take the **mother** with the young.
22: 7 You may take the young, but be sure to let the **mother** go,
22: 15 **mother** shall bring proof that she was a virgin to the town elders at
27: 16 "Cursed is the man who dishonors his father or his **mother**."
27: 22 his sister, the daughter of his father or the daughter of his **mother**."
33: 9 He said of his father and **mother**, 'I have no regard for them.'
Jos 2: 13 that you will spare the lives of my father and **mother**, my brothers
2: 18 and unless you have brought your father and **mother**, your brothers
6: 23 her father and **mother** and brothers and all who belonged to her.
Jdg 5: 7 ceased until I, Deborah, arose, arose a **mother** in Israel.
5: 28 "Through the window peered Sisera's **mother**; behind the lattice
8: 19 "Those were my brothers, the sons of my own **mother**.
9: 1 Abimelech son of Jerub-Baal went to his **mother's** brothers in
9: 1 brothers in Shechem and said to them and to all his **mother's** clan,
9: 3 When the **brothers** [+278] repeated all this to the citizens of
14: 2 When he returned, he said to his father and **mother**, "I have seen a
14: 3 His father and **mother** replied, "Isn't there an acceptable woman
14: 4 (His **parents** [+3+2256] did not know that this was from the
14: 5 went down to Timnah together with his father and **mother**.
14: 6 But he told neither his father nor his **mother** what he had done.
14: 9 When he rejoined his **parents** [+3+2256], he gave them some,
14: 16 "I haven't even explained it to my father or **mother**," he replied,
16: 17 I have been a Nazirite set apart to God since **birth** [+1061].
17: 2 said to his **mother**, "The eleven hundred shekels of silver that were

Jdg 17: 2 I took it." Then his **mother** said, "The LORD bless you, my son!"
17: 3 he returned the eleven hundred shekels of silver to his **mother**,
17: 3 **[RPH]** "I solemnly consecrate my silver to the LORD for my
17: 4 So he returned the silver to his **mother**, and she took two hundred
17: 4 **she**[s] [+2257] took two hundred shekels of silver and gave them to
Ru 1: 8 "Go back, each of you, to your **mother's** home.
2: 11 how you left your father and **mother** and your homeland and came
1Sa 2: 19 Each year his **mother** made him a little robe and took it to him
15: 33 so will your **mother** be childless among women."
20: 30 to your own shame and to the shame of the **mother** *who bore* you?
22: 3 "Would you let my father and **mother** come and stay with you
2Sa 17: 25 the daughter of Nahash and sister of Zeruiah the **mother** *of* Joab.
19: 37 [19:38] in my own town near the tomb of my father and **mother**.
20: 19 in Israel. You are trying to destroy a city that is a **mother** in Israel.
1Ki 1: 11 Nathan asked Bathsheba, Solomon's **mother**, "Have you not heard
2: 13 the son of Haggith, went to Bathsheba, Solomon's **mother**.
2: 19 He had a throne brought for the king's **mother**, and she sat down
2: 20 The king replied, "Make it, my **mother**; I will not refuse you."
2: 22 King Solomon answered his **mother**, "Why do you request
3: 27 living baby to the first woman. Do not kill him; she is his **mother**."
11: 26 from Zeredah, and his **mother** was a widow named Zeruah.
14: 21 His **mother's** name was Naamah; she was an Ammonite.
14: 31 His **mother's** name was Naamah; she was an Ammonite.
15: 2 His **mother's** name was Maacah daughter of Abishalom.
15: 10 His **grandmother's** name was Maacah daughter of Abishalom.
15: 13 He even deposed his **grandmother** Maacah from her position as
17: 23 He gave him to his **mother** and said, "Look, your son is alive!"
19: 20 "Let me kiss my father and **mother** good-by," he said, "and
22: 42 His **mother's** name was Azubah daughter of Shilhi.
22: 52 [22:53] and **mother** and in the ways of Jeroboam son of Nebat,
2Ki 3: 2 the eyes of the LORD, but not as his father and **mother** had done.
3: 13 to the prophets of your father and the prophets of your **mother**."
4: 19 to his father. His father told a servant, "Carry him to his **mother**."
4: 20 After the servant had lifted him up and carried him to his **mother**,
4: 30 But the child's **mother** said, "As surely as the LORD lives
8: 26 His **mother's** name was Athaliah, a granddaughter of Omri king of
9: 22 as all the idolatry and witchcraft of your **mother** Jezebel abound?"
11: 1 When Athaliah the **mother** *of* Ahaziah saw that her son was dead,
12: 1 [12:2] His **mother's** name was Zibiah; she was from Beersheba.
14: 2 His **mother's** name was Jehoaddin; she was from Jerusalem.
15: 2 His **mother's** name was Jecoliah; she was from Jerusalem.
15: 33 sixteen years. His **mother's** name was Jerusha daughter of Zadok.
18: 2 His **mother's** name was Abijah daughter of Zechariah.
21: 1 in Jerusalem fifty-five years. His **mother's** name was Hephzibah.
21: 19 His **mother's** name was Meshullemeth daughter of Haruz;
22: 1 His **mother's** name was Jedidah daughter of Adaiah; she was from
23: 31 His **mother's** name was Hamutal daughter of Jeremiah; she was
23: 36 His **mother's** name was Zebidah daughter of Pedaiah; she was
24: 8 His **mother's** name was Nehushta daughter of Elnathan; she was
24: 12 his **mother**, his attendants, his nobles and his officials all
24: 15 He also took from Jerusalem to Babylon the king's **mother**,
24: 18 His **mother's** name was Hamutal daughter of Jeremiah; she was
1Ch 2: 26 whose name was Atarah; she was the **mother** *of* Onam.
4: 9 His **mother** had named him Jabez, saying, "I gave birth to him in
2Ch 12: 13 His **mother's** name was Naamah; she was an Ammonite.
13: 2 His **mother's** name was Maacah, a daughter of Uriel of Gibeah.
15: 16 King Asa also deposed his **grandmother** Maacah from her
20: 31 His **mother's** name was Azubah daughter of Shilhi.
22: 2 His **mother's** name was Athaliah, a granddaughter of Omri.
22: 3 the house of Ahab, for his **mother** encouraged him in doing wrong.
22: 10 When Athaliah the **mother** *of* Ahaziah saw that her son was dead,
24: 1 His **mother's** name was Zibiah; she was from Beersheba.
25: 1 His **mother's** name was Jehoaddin; she was from Jerusalem.
26: 3 His **mother's** name was Jecoliah; she was from Jerusalem.
27: 1 sixteen years. His **mother's** name was Jerusha daughter of Zadok.
29: 1 His **mother's** name was Abijah daughter of Zechariah.
Est 2: 7 he had brought up because she had neither father nor **mother**.
2: 7 taken her as his own daughter when her father and **mother** died.
Job 1: 21 "Naked I came from my **mother's** womb, and naked I will depart.
17: 14 'You are my father,' and to the worm, 'My **mother**' or 'My sister,'
31: 18 would a father, and from my **birth** [+1061] I guided the widow—
Ps 22: 9 [22:10] you made me trust in you even at my **mother's** breast.
22: 10 [22:11] from my **mother's** womb you have been my God.
27: 10 Though my father and **mother** forsake me, the LORD will
35: 14 I bowed my head in grief as though weeping for my **mother**.
50: 20 against your brother and slander your own **mother's** son.
51: 5 [51:7] at birth, sinful from the time my **mother** conceived me.
69: 8 [69:9] stranger to my brothers, an alien to my own **mother's** sons;
71: 6 relied on you; you brought me forth from my **mother's** womb.
109: 14 before the LORD; may the sin of his **mother** never be blotted out.
113: 9 He settles the barren woman in her home as a happy **mother** *of*
131: 2 like a weaned child with its **mother**, like a weaned child is my soul
139: 13 my inmost being; you knit me together in my **mother's** womb.
Pr 1: 8 father's instruction and do not forsake your **mother's** teaching.
4: 3 in my father's house, still tender, and an only child of my **mother**,
6: 20 father's commands and do not forsake your **mother's** teaching.
10: 1 son brings joy to his father, but a foolish son grief to his **mother**.
15: 20 son brings joy to his father, but a foolish man despises his **mother**.
19: 26 and drives out his **mother** is a son who brings shame and disgrace.
20: 20 If a man curses his father or **mother**, his lamp will be snuffed out
23: 22 gave you life, and do not despise your **mother** when she is old.
23: 25 May your father and **mother** be glad; may she who gave you birth
28: 24 He who robs his father or **mother** and says, "It's not wrong"—
29: 15 imparts wisdom, but a child left to himself disgraces his **mother**.
30: 11 are those who curse their fathers and do not bless their **mothers**;
30: 17 "The eye that mocks a father, that scorns obedience to a **mother**,
31: 1 The sayings of King Lemuel—an oracle his **mother** taught him:
Ecc 5: 15 [5:14] Naked a man comes from his **mother's** womb, and as he
SS 1: 6 My **mother's** sons were angry with me and made me take care of
3: 4 would not let him go till I had brought him to my **mother's** house,
3: 11 the crown with which his **mother** crowned him on the day of his
6: 9 my perfect one, is unique, the only daughter of her **mother**,
8: 1 were to me like a brother, who was nursed at my **mother's** breasts!
8: 2 I would lead you and bring you to my **mother's** house—she who
8: 5 there your **mother** conceived you, there she who was in labor gave
Isa 8: 4 Before the boy knows how to say 'My father' or 'My **mother**,'
49: 1 from my **birth** [+5055] he has made mention of my name.
50: 1 "Where is your **mother's** certificate of divorce with which I sent
50: 1 because of your transgressions your **mother** was sent away.
66: 13 As a **mother** comforts her child, so will I comfort you; and you
Jer 15: 8 At midday I will bring a destroyer against the **mothers** *of* their
15: 10 Alas, my **mother**, that you gave me birth, a man with whom the
16: 3 born in this land and about the women who are their **mothers**
16: 7 not even for a father or a **mother**—nor will anyone give them a
20: 14 day I was born! May the day my **mother** bore me not be blessed!
20: 17 with my **mother** as my grave, her womb enlarged forever.
22: 26 hurl you and the **mother** who gave you birth into another country,
50: 12 your **mother** will be greatly ashamed; she who gave you birth will
52: 1 His **mother's** name was Hamutal daughter of Jeremiah; she was
La 2: 12 They say to their **mothers**, "Where is bread and wine?" as they
2: 12 streets of the city, as their lives ebb away in their **mothers**' arms.
5: 3 We have become orphans and fatherless, our **mothers** like widows.
Eze 16: 3 your father was an Amorite and your **mother** a Hittite.
16: 44 will quote this proverb about you: "Like **mother**, like daughter."
16: 45 You are a true daughter of your **mother**, who despised her husband
16: 45 Your **mother** was a Hittite and your father an Amorite.
19: 2 and say: " 'What a lioness was your **mother** among the lions!
19: 10 " 'Your **mother** was like a vine in your vineyard planted by the
21: 21 [21:26] For the king of Babylon will stop at the **fork** *in* the road,
22: 7 In you they have treated father and **mother** with contempt;
23: 2 of man, there were two women, daughters of the same **mother**.
44: 25 if the dead person was his father or **mother**, son or daughter,
Hos 2: 2 [2:4] "Rebuke your **mother**, rebuke her, for she is not my wife,
2: 5 [2:7] Their **mother** has been unfaithful and has conceived them in
4: 5 the prophets stumble with you. So I will destroy your **mother**—
10: 14 when **mothers** were dashed to the ground with their children.
Mic 7: 6 a son dishonors his father, a daughter rises up against her **mother**,
Zec 13: 3 his father and **mother**, to whom he was born, will say to him,
13: 3 When he prophesies, his own **parents** [+3+2256] will stab him.

563 אָמָה *'āmâ*, n.f. [56]

maidservant [16], servant [14], maidservants [9], slave girls [4], female slave [2], servant's [2], slave girl [2], female slaves [1], her[s] [+3870] [1], me[s] [+3870] [1], slave born in household [+1201] [1], slave woman [1], slave woman's [1], slaves [+2256+6269] [1]

Ge 20: 17 his wife and his **slave girls** so they could have children again,
21: 10 she said to Abraham, "Get rid of that **slave woman** and her son,
21: 10 for that **slave woman's** son will never share in the inheritance with
21: 12 "Do not be so distressed about the boy and your **maidservant**.
21: 13 I will make the son of the **maidservant** into a nation also,
30: 3 Then she said, "Here is Bilhah, my **maidservant**. Sleep with her
31: 33 and into Leah's tent and into the tent of the two **maidservants**,
Ex 2: 5 saw the basket among the reeds and sent her **slave girl** to get it.
20: 10 nor your son or daughter, nor your manservant or **maidservant**,
20: 17 or his manservant or **maidservant**, his ox or donkey,
21: 7 "If a man sells his daughter as a **servant**, she is not to go free as
21: 20 "If a man beats his male or **female slave** with a rod and the slave
21: 26 a man hits a manservant or **maidservant** in the eye and destroys it,
21: 27 And if he knocks out the tooth of a manservant or **maidservant**,
21: 32 If the bull gores a male or **female slave**, the owner must pay thirty
23: 12 donkey may rest and the **slave born in** your **household** [+1201],
Lev 25: 6 for yourself, your manservant and **maidservant**, and the hired
25: 44 and **female slaves** are to come from the nations around you;
25: 44 nations around you; from them you may buy **slaves** [+2256+6269].
Dt 5: 14 nor your son or daughter, nor your manservant or **maidservant**,
5: 14 so that your manservant and **maidservant** may rest, as you do.
5: 21 or land, his manservant or **maidservant**, his ox or donkey,

[F] Hitpael (hitpoel, hitpoal, hitpolel, hitpolal, hitpalel, hitpalal, hitpalpel, hitpalpal, hotpael, hotpaal) [G] Hiphil (hiphtil) [H] Hophal [I] Hishtaphel

Dt 12:12 your sons and daughters, your menservants and **maidservants**,
12:18 your sons and daughters, your menservants and **maidservants**,
15:17 become your servant for life. Do the same for your **maidservant**.
16:11 your sons and daughters, your menservants and **maidservants**,
16:14 your sons and daughters, your menservants and **maidservants**,
Jdg 9:18 made Abimelech, the son of his **slave girl**, king over the citizens of
19:19 me, your **maidservant**, and the young man with us.
Ru 3:9 "Who are you?" he asked. "I am your **servant** Ruth," she said.
3:9 "Spread the corner of your garment over **me**[s] [+3870], since you
1Sa 1:11 if you will only look upon your **servant's** misery and remember
1:11 and remember me, and not forget your **servant** but give her a son,
1:11 and not forget your servant but give **her**[s] [+3870] a son,
1:16 Do not take your **servant** for a wicked woman; I have been
25:24 Please let your **servant** speak to you; hear what your servant has to
25:24 let your servant speak to you; hear what your **servant** has to say.
25:25 But as for me, your **servant**, I did not see the men my master sent.
25:28 Please forgive your **servant's** offense, for the LORD will
25:31 LORD has brought my master success, remember your **servant**."
25:41 with her face to the ground and said, "Here is your **maidservant**,
2Sa 6:20 disrobing in the sight of the **slave girls** *of* his servants as any
6:22 But by these **slave girls** you spoke of, I will be held in honor."
14:15 'I will speak to the king; perhaps he will do what his **servant** asks.
14:16 Perhaps the king will agree to deliver his **servant** from the hand of
20:17 he answered. She said, "Listen to what your **servant** has to say."
1Ki 1:13 to him, 'My lord the king, did you not swear to me your **servant**:
1:17 you yourself swore to me your **servant** by the LORD your God:
3:20 and took my son from my side while I your **servant** was asleep.
Ezr 2:65 besides their 7,337 menservants and **maidservants**; and they also
Ne 7:67 besides their 7,337 menservants and **maidservants**; and they also
Job 19:15 My guests and my **maidservants** count me a stranger; they look
31:13 and **maidservants** when they had a grievance against me,
Ps 86:16 strength to your servant and save the son of your **maidservant**.
116:16 I am your servant; I am your servant, the son of your **maidservant**;
Na 2:7 [2:8] Its **slave girls** moan like doves and beat upon their breasts.

564 אַמָּה 'ammâ[1], n.f. [247 / 254] [→ Ar 10039]

cubits [164], cubit [37], *untranslated* [27], about six hundred feet [+752+4395] [2], long cubits [2], seventy-five feet [+2822] [2], 18 inches [1], 45 feet [+8993] [1], 450 feet [+4395+8993] [1], 75 feet [+2822] [1], doorposts [1], fifteen feet [+928+2021+6924] [1], fifteen hundred feet [+547] [1], five hundred yards [+547] [1], four and a half feet [+8993] [1], more than thirteen feet [+9596] [1], over nine feet [+2256+2455+9252] [1], seven and a half feet [+928+2021+2822] [1], six feet [+752] [1], thirty feet [+928+2021+6929] [1], three feet [1], three thousand feet [+547] [1], time [1], twenty feet [+2822+6926] [1], twenty-seven feet [+6926+9046] [1], yards [1]

Ge 6:15 The ark is to be **450 feet** [+4395+8993] long, 75 feet wide
6:15 The ark is to be 450 feet long, **75 feet** [+2822] wide and 45 feet
6:15 ark is to be 450 feet long, 75 feet wide and **45 feet** [+8993] high.
6:16 Make a roof for it and finish the ark to within **18 inches** of the top.
7:20 the mountains to a depth of more than **twenty feet** [+2822+6926].
Ex 25:10 *two* and a half **cubits** long, a cubit and a half wide, and a cubit
25:10 cubits long, a **cubit** and a half wide, and a cubit and a half high.
25:10 cubits long, a cubit and a half wide, and a **cubit** and a half high.
25:17 pure gold—*two* and a half **cubits** long and a cubit and a half wide.
25:17 pure gold—two and a half cubits long and a **cubit** and a half wide.
25:23 *two* **cubits** long, a cubit wide and a cubit and a half high.
25:23 two cubits long, a **cubit** wide and a cubit and a half high.
25:23 two cubits long, a cubit wide and a **cubit** and a half high.
26:2 be the same size—twenty-eight **cubits** long and four cubits wide.
26:2 be the same size—twenty-eight cubits long and four **cubits** wide.
26:8 are to be the same size—thirty **cubits** long and four cubits wide.
26:8 are to be the same size—thirty cubits long and four **cubits** wide.
26:13 The tent curtains will be a **cubit** longer on both sides; what is left
26:13 **[RPH]** what is left will hang over the sides of the tabernacle
26:16 Each frame is to be ten **cubits** long and a cubit and a half wide,
26:16 Each frame is to be ten cubits long and a **cubit** and a half wide,
26:16 frame is to be ten cubits long and a cubit and a half **[RPH]** wide,
27:1 "Build an altar of acacia wood, three **cubits** high; it is to be square,
27:1 cubits high; it is to be square, five **cubits** long and five cubits wide.
27:1 cubits high; it is to be square, five cubits long and five **cubits** wide.
27:9 The south side shall be a hundred **cubits** long and is to have
27:12 "The west end of the courtyard shall be fifty **cubits** wide and have
27:13 toward the sunrise, the courtyard shall also be fifty **cubits** wide.
27:14 Curtains fifteen **cubits** long are to be on one side of the entrance,
27:16 provide a curtain twenty **cubits** long, of blue, purple and scarlet
27:18 The courtyard shall be a hundred **cubits** long and fifty cubits wide,
27:18 cubits wide, with curtains of finely twisted linen five **cubits** high,
30:2 It is to be square, a **cubit** long and a cubit wide, and two cubits
30:2 It is to be square, a cubit long and a **cubit** wide, and two cubits
30:2 to be square, a cubit long and a cubit wide, and *two* **cubits** high—
36:9 the same size—twenty-eight **cubits** long and four cubits wide.
36:9 the same size—twenty-eight cubits long and four **cubits** wide.
36:15 were the same size—thirty **cubits** long and four cubits wide.
36:15 were the same size—thirty cubits long and four **cubits** wide.
36:21 Each frame was ten **cubits** long and a cubit and a half wide,
36:21 Each frame was ten cubits long and a **cubit** and a half wide,
36:21 frame was ten cubits long and a cubit and a half **[RPH]** wide,
37:1 *two* and a half **cubits** long, a cubit and a half wide, and a cubit
37:1 cubits long, a **cubit** and a half wide, and a cubit and a half high.
37:1 cubits long, a cubit and a half wide, and a **cubit** and a half high.
37:6 pure gold—*two* and a half **cubits** long and a cubit and a half wide.
37:6 pure gold—two and a half cubits long and a **cubit** and a half wide.
37:10 *two* **cubits** long, a cubit wide, and a cubit and a half high.
37:10 two cubits long, a **cubit** wide, and a cubit and a half high.
37:10 two cubits long, a cubit wide, and a **cubit** and a half high.
37:25 It was square, a **cubit** long and a cubit wide, and two cubits high—
37:25 It was square, a cubit long and a **cubit** wide, and two cubits high—
37:25 It was square, a cubit long and a cubit wide, and *two* **cubits** high—
38:1 built the altar of burnt offering of acacia wood, three **cubits** high;
38:1 cubits high; it was square, five **cubits** long and five cubits wide.
38:1 cubits high; it was square, five cubits long and five **cubits** wide.
38:9 The south side was a hundred **cubits** long and had curtains of
38:11 The north side was also a hundred **cubits** long and had twenty
38:12 The west end was fifty **cubits** wide and had curtains, with ten posts
38:13 The east end, toward the sunrise, was also fifty **cubits** wide.
38:14 Curtains fifteen **cubits** long were on one side of the entrance,
38:15 curtains fifteen **cubits** long were on the other side of the entrance
38:18 It was twenty **cubits** long and, like the curtains of the courtyard,
38:18 cubits long and, like the curtains of the courtyard, five **cubits** high,
Nu 11:31 It brought them down all around the camp to about **three feet**
35:4 will extend out **fifteen hundred feet** [+547] from the town wall.
35:5 the town, measure **three thousand feet** [+547] on the east side,
35:5 three thousand **[RPH]** on the south side, three thousand on the
35:5 three thousand **[RPH]** on the west and three thousand on the
35:5 thousand on the west and three thousand **[RPH]** on the north,
Dt 3:11 and was **more than thirteen feet** [+9596] long and six feet wide.
3:11 and was more than thirteen feet long and **six feet** [+752] wide.
3:11 and six feet wide. **[RPH]** It is still in Rabbah of the Ammonites.)
Jos 3:4 But keep a distance of about a thousand **yards** between you
1Sa 17:4 He was **over nine feet** [+2256+2455+9252] tall.
1Ki 6:2 that King Solomon built for the LORD was sixty **cubits** long,
6:2 was sixty cubits long, twenty wide and thirty **[RPH]** high.
6:3 that is twenty **cubits**, and projected ten cubits from the front of the
6:3 and projected ten **cubits** from the front of the temple.
6:6 The lowest floor was five **cubits** wide, the middle floor six cubits
6:6 cubits wide, the middle floor six **cubits** and the third floor seven.
6:6 **[RPH]** He made offset ledges around the outside of the temple
6:10 The height of each was five **cubits**, and they were attached to the
6:16 He partitioned off twenty **cubits** at the rear of the temple with
6:17 The main hall in front of this room was forty **cubits** long.
6:20 The inner sanctuary was twenty **cubits** long, twenty wide
6:20 was twenty cubits long, twenty **[RPH]** wide and twenty high.
6:20 was twenty cubits long, twenty wide and twenty **[RPH]** high.
6:23 he made a pair of cherubim of olive wood, each ten **cubits** high.
6:24 One wing of the first cherub was five **cubits** long, and the other
6:24 first cherub was five cubits long, and the other wing five **cubits**—
6:24 the other wing five cubits—ten **cubits** from wing tip to wing tip.
6:25 The second cherub also measured ten **cubits**, for the two cherubim
6:26 The height of each cherub was ten **cubits**.
7:2 He built the Palace of the Forest of Lebanon a hundred **cubits** long,
7:2 fifty **[RPH]** wide and thirty high, with four rows of cedar
7:2 fifty wide and thirty **[RPH]** high, with four rows of cedar
7:6 He made a colonnade fifty **cubits** long and thirty wide. In front of
7:6 He made a colonnade fifty cubits long and thirty **[RPH]** wide.
7:10 stones of good quality, some measuring ten **cubits** and some eight.
7:10 good quality, some measuring ten cubits and some eight. **[RPH]**
7:15 each eighteen **cubits** high and twelve cubits around, by line.
7:15 each eighteen cubits high and twelve **cubits** around, by line.
7:16 to set on the tops of the pillars; each capital was five **cubits** high.
7:16 the tops of the pillars; each capital was five cubits high. **[RPH]**
7:19 pillars in the portico were in the shape of lilies, four **cubits** high.
7:23 measuring ten **cubits** from rim to rim and five cubits high.
7:23 measuring ten cubits from rim to rim and five **cubits** high.
7:23 five cubits high. It took a line of thirty **cubits** to measure around it.
7:24 Below the rim, gourds encircled it—ten to a **cubit**. The gourds
7:27 of bronze; each was four **cubits** long, four wide and three high.
7:27 each was four cubits long, four **[RPH]** wide and three high.
7:27 each was four cubits long, four wide and three **[RPH]** high.
7:31 there was an opening that had a circular frame one **cubit** deep.
7:31 was round, and with its basework it measured a **cubit** and a half.
7:31 and a half. **[RPH]** Around its opening there was engraving.
7:32 to the stand. The diameter of each wheel was a **cubit** and a half.
7:32 The diameter of each wheel was a cubit and a half. **[RPH]**
7:35 At the top of the stand there was a circular band half a **cubit** deep.
7:38 each holding forty baths and measuring four **cubits** across,
2Ki 14:13 a section **about six hundred feet** [+752+4395] long.

2Ki 25: 17 Each pillar was **twenty-seven feet** [+6926+9046] high. The bronze
25: 17 capital on top of one pillar was **four and a half feet** [+8993]
1Ch 11: 23 an Egyptian who was **seven and a half feet** [+928+2021+2822]
2Ch 3: 3 Solomon laid for building the temple of God was sixty **cubits** long
3: 3 and twenty **cubits** wide (using the cubit of the old standard).
3: 3 and twenty cubits wide (using the **cubit** of the old standard).
3: 4 The portico at the front of the temple was twenty **cubits** long
3: 4 the width of the building and twenty **cubits** [BHS 4395] high.
3: 8 width of the temple—twenty **cubits** long and twenty cubits wide.
3: 8 width of the temple—twenty cubits long and twenty **cubits** wide.
3: 11 The total wingspan of the cherubim was twenty **cubits**. One wing
3: 11 One wing of the first cherub was five **cubits** long and touched the
3: 11 the temple wall, while its other wing, also five **cubits** long,
3: 12 Similarly one wing of the second cherub was five **cubits** long
3: 12 the other temple wall, and its other wing, also five **cubits** long,
3: 13 The wings of these cherubim extended twenty **cubits**. They stood
3: 15 he made two pillars, which ⌞together⌟ were thirty-five **cubits** long,
3: 15 cubits long, each with a capital on top measuring five **cubits**.
4: 1 He made a bronze altar twenty **cubits** long, twenty cubits wide
4: 1 altar twenty cubits long, twenty **cubits** wide and ten cubits high.
4: 1 altar twenty cubits long, twenty cubits wide and ten **cubits** high.
4: 2 measuring ten **cubits** from rim to rim and five cubits high.
4: 2 measuring ten cubits from rim to rim and five **cubits** high.
4: 2 five cubits high. It took a line of thirty **cubits** to measure around it.
4: 3 Below the rim, figures of bulls encircled it—ten to a **cubit**.
6: 13 five **cubits** long, five cubits wide and three cubits high,
6: 13 five cubits long, five **cubits** wide and three cubits high,
6: 13 five cubits long, five cubits wide and three **cubits** high,
25: 23 a section **about six hundred feet** [+752+4395] long.
Ne 3: 13 They also repaired **five hundred yards** [+547] of the wall as far as
Est 5: 14 said to him, "Have a gallows built, **seventy-five feet** [+2822] high,
7: 9 "A gallows **seventy-five feet** [+2822] high stands by Haman's
Isa 6: 4 At the sound of their voices the **doorposts** and thresholds shook
Jer 51: 13 rich in treasures, your end has come, the **time** *for* you to be cut off.
52: 21 Each of the pillars was eighteen **cubits** high and twelve cubits in
52: 21 was eighteen cubits high and twelve **cubits** in circumference;
52: 22 The bronze capital on top of the one pillar was five **cubits** high
Eze 40: 5 length of the measuring rod in the man's hand was six **long cubits**,
40: 5 was six long cubits, each of which was a **cubit** and a handbreadth.
40: 7 the projecting walls between the alcoves were five **cubits** thick.
40: 9 it was eight **cubits** deep and its jambs were two cubits thick.
40: 9 it was eight cubits deep and its jambs were two **cubits** thick.
40: 11 to the gateway; it was ten **cubits** and its length was thirteen cubits.
40: 11 to the gateway; it was ten cubits and its length was thirteen **cubits**.
40: 12 In front of each alcove was a wall one **cubit** high, and the alcoves
40: 12 one cubit high, **[RPH]** and the alcoves were six cubits square.
40: 12 was a wall one cubit high, and the alcoves were six **cubits** square.
40: 12 one cubit high, and the alcoves were six cubits square. **[RPH]**
40: 13 the distance was twenty-five **cubits** from one parapet opening to
40: 14 projecting walls all around the inside of the gateway—sixty **cubits**.
40: 15 of the gateway to the far end of its portico was fifty **cubits**.
40: 19 it was a hundred **cubits** on the east side as well as on the north.
40: 21 first gateway. It was fifty **cubits** long and twenty-five cubits wide.
40: 21 first gateway. It was fifty cubits long and twenty-five **cubits** wide.
40: 23 from one gate to the opposite one; it was a hundred **cubits**.
40: 25 of the others. It was fifty **cubits** long and twenty-five cubits wide.
40: 25 of the others. It was fifty cubits long and twenty-five **cubits** wide.
40: 27 gate to the outer gate on the south side; it was a hundred **cubits**.
40: 29 all around. It was fifty **cubits** long and twenty-five cubits wide.
40: 29 all around. It was fifty cubits long and twenty-five **cubits** wide.
40: 30 the gateways around the inner court were twenty-five **cubits** wide
40: 30 the inner court were twenty-five cubits wide and five **cubits** deep.)
40: 33 all around. It was fifty **cubits** long and twenty-five cubits wide.
40: 33 all around. It was fifty cubits long and twenty-five **cubits** wide.
40: 36 all around. It was fifty **cubits** long and twenty-five cubits wide.
40: 36 all around. It was fifty cubits long and twenty-five **cubits** wide.
40: 42 each a **cubit** and a half long, a cubit and a half wide and a cubit
40: 42 a cubit and a half long, a **cubit** and a half wide and a cubit high.
40: 42 a cubit and a half long, a cubit and a half wide and a **cubit** high.
40: 47 It was square—a hundred **cubits** long and a hundred cubits wide.
40: 47 It was square—a hundred cubits long and a hundred **cubits** wide.
40: 48 the jambs of the portico; they were five **cubits** wide on either side.
40: 48 **[RPH]** The width of the entrance was fourteen cubits and its
40: 48 The width of the entrance was fourteen **cubits** [BHS-] and its
40: 48 and its projecting walls were three **cubits** wide on either side.
40: 48 its projecting walls were three cubits wide on either side. **[RPH]**
40: 49 The portico was twenty **cubits** wide, and twelve cubits from front
40: 49 was twenty cubits wide, and twelve **cubits** from front to back.
41: 1 the jambs; the width of the jambs was six **cubits** on each side.
41: 1 the width of the jambs was six cubits on each side. **[RPH]**
41: 2 The entrance was ten **cubits** wide, and the projecting walls on each
41: 2 and the projecting walls on each side of it were five **cubits** wide.
41: 2 **[RPH]** He also measured the outer sanctuary; it was forty cubits
41: 2 outer sanctuary; it was forty **cubits** long and twenty cubits wide.
41: 2 outer sanctuary; it was forty cubits long and twenty **cubits** wide.
41: 3 and measured the jambs of the entrance; each was two **cubits** wide.
41: 3 The entrance was six **cubits** wide, and the projecting walls on each
41: 3 and the projecting walls on each side of it were seven **cubits** wide.
41: 4 it was twenty **cubits**, and its width was twenty cubits across the
41: 4 its width was twenty **cubits** across the end of the outer sanctuary.
41: 5 it was six **cubits** thick, and each side room around the temple was
41: 5 and each side room around the temple was four **cubits** wide.
41: 8 of the side rooms. It was the length of the rod, six long **cubits**.
41: 9 The outer wall of the side rooms was five **cubits** thick. The open
41: 10 the ⌞priests'⌟ rooms was twenty **cubits** wide all around the temple.
41: 11 the base adjoining the open area was five **cubits** wide all around.
41: 12 the temple courtyard on the west side was seventy **cubits** wide.
41: 12 The wall of the building was five **cubits** thick all around, and its
41: 12 was five cubits thick all around, and its length was ninety **cubits**.
41: 13 it was a hundred **cubits** long, and the temple courtyard
41: 13 and the building with its walls were also a hundred **cubits** long.
41: 14 the east, including the front of the temple, was a hundred **cubits**.
41: 15 including its galleries on each side; it was a hundred **cubits**.
41: 22 There was a wooden altar three **cubits** high and two cubits square;
41: 22 There was a wooden altar three cubits high and two **cubits** square;
41: 22 **[RPH]** its corners, its base and its sides were of wood.
42: 2 The building whose door faced north was a hundred **cubits** long
42: 2 door faced north was a hundred cubits long and fifty **cubits** wide.
42: 4 In front of the rooms was an inner passageway ten **cubits** wide
42: 4 an inner passageway ten cubits wide and a hundred **cubits** long.
42: 7 the outer court; it extended in front of the rooms for fifty **cubits**.
42: 8 of rooms on the side next to the outer court was fifty **cubits** long,
42: 8 the row on the side nearest the sanctuary was a hundred **cubits**
42: 16 [the measuring rod; it was five **hundred** [K; see Q 4395] cubits.]
42: 16 with the measuring rod; it was five hundred **cubits**. [BHS 7866]
42: 17 it was five hundred **cubits** [BHS 7866] by the measuring rod.
42: 18 it was five hundred **cubits** [BHS 7866] by the measuring rod.
42: 19 it was five hundred **cubits** [BHS 7866] by the measuring rod.
43: 13 "These are the measurements of the altar in **long cubits**, that cubit
43: 13 the altar in long cubits, that **cubit** being a cubit and a handbreadth:
43: 13 the altar in long cubits, that cubit being a **cubit** and a handbreadth:
43: 13 Its gutter is a **cubit** deep and a cubit wide, with a rim of one span
43: 13 Its gutter is a cubit deep and a **cubit** wide, with a rim of one span
43: 14 From the gutter on the ground up to the lower ledge it is two **cubits**
43: 14 ground up to the lower ledge it is two cubits high and a **cubit** wide,
43: 14 from the smaller ledge up to the larger ledge it is four **cubits** high
43: 14 ledge up to the larger ledge it is four cubits high and a **cubit** wide.
43: 15 The altar hearth is four **cubits** high, and four horns project upward
43: 17 with a rim of half a **cubit** and a gutter of a cubit all around.
43: 17 with a rim of half a cubit and a gutter of a **cubit** all around.
45: 2 is to be for the sanctuary, with 50 **cubits** around it for open land.
47: 3 he measured off a thousand **cubits** and then led me through water
Zec 5: 2 "I see a flying scroll, **thirty feet** [+928+2021+6929] long
5: 2 thirty feet long and **fifteen feet** [+928+2021+6924] wide."

565 [2]אַמָּה ***'ammâ[2]***, n.pr.loc. [1]

Ammah [1]

2Sa 2: 24 and as the sun was setting, they came to the hill of **Ammah**,

566 [3]אַמָּה ***'ammâ[3]***, n.f. Not used in NIV/BHS [√ 562]

567 [4]אַמָּה ***'ammâ[4]***, n.f. Not used in NIV/BHS

568 אֵמָה ***'ēmâ***, n.f. Not used in NIV/BHS [cf. 564]

569 אֻמָּה ***'ummâ***, n.f. [7 / 3] [→ Ar 10040]

tribal [2], peoples [1]

Ge 25: 16 these are the names of the twelve **tribal** rulers according to their
Nu 25: 15 was Cozbi daughter of Zur, a **tribal** chief of a Midianite family.
Ps 44: 14 [44:15] the peoples [BHS *no peoples*; NIV 4211] shake their heads
57: 9 [57:10] of you among the peoples. [BHS ***no peoples***; NIV 4211]
108: 3 [108:4] of you among the peoples. [BHS ***no peoples***; NIV 4211]
117: 1 Praise the LORD, all you nations; extol him, all you **peoples**.
149: 7 and punishment on the peoples, [BHS***no peoples***; NIV 4211]

570 [1]אָמוֹן ***'āmôn[1]***, n.m. [2] [→ 588]

craftsman [1], craftsmen [1]

Pr 8: 30 I was the **craftsman** at his side. I was filled with delight day after
Jer 52: 15 along with the rest of the **craftsmen** and those who had gone over

571 [2]אָמוֹן ***'āmôn[2]***, n.pr.m. [17] [→ 577; cf. 572, 586]

Amon [15], Amon's [2]

1Ki 22: 26 "Take Micaiah and send him back to **Amon** the ruler of the city
2Ki 21: 18 the garden of Uzza. And **Amon** his son succeeded him as king.

2Ki 21:19 **Amon** was twenty-two years old when he became king, and he
21:23 **Amon's** officials conspired against him and assassinated the king
21:24 people of the land killed all who had plotted against King **Amon**,
21:25 As for the other events of **Amon's** reign, and what he did,
1Ch 3:14 **Amon** his son, Josiah his son.
2Ch 18:25 "Take Micaiah and send him back to **Amon** the ruler of the city
33:20 buried in his palace. And **Amon** his son succeeded him as king.
33:21 **Amon** was twenty-two years old when he became king, and he
33:22 **Amon** worshiped and offered sacrifices to all the idols Manasseh
33:23 not humble himself before the LORD; **Amon** increased his guilt.
33:25 people of the land killed all who had plotted against King **Amon**,
Ne 7:59 Shephatiah, Hattil, Pokereth-Hazzebaim and **Amon**
Jer 1:2 thirteenth year of the reign of Josiah son of **Amon** king of Judah,
25:3 from the thirteenth year of Josiah son of **Amon** king of Judah until
Zep 1:1 during the reign of Josiah son of **Amon** king of Judah:

572 ³אָמוֹן *'āmôn[3]*, n.pr.[m.]. [1] [→ 5531; cf. 571, 586]

Amon [1]

Jer 46:25 "I am about to bring punishment on **Amon** god of Thebes,

573 ¹אֵמוּן *'ēmûn[1]*, n.[m.]. [2] [√ 586]

faithful [2]

2Sa 20:19 We are the peaceful and **faithful** *in* Israel. You are trying to
Ps 31:23 [31:24] The LORD preserves the **faithful**, but the proud he pays

574 ²אֵמוּן *'ēmûn[2]*, n.[m.]. [6] [√ 586]

faithful [2], faith [1], trustworthy [1], truthful [1], unfaithful [+4202] [1]

Dt 32:20 are a perverse generation, children who are **unfaithful** [+4202].
Ps 12:1 [12:2] are no more; the **faithful** have vanished from among men.
Pr 13:17 falls into trouble, but a **trustworthy** envoy brings healing.
14:5 A **truthful** witness does not deceive, but a false witness pours out
20:6 claims to have unfailing love, but a **faithful** man who can find?
Isa 26:2 that the righteous nation may enter, the nation that keeps **faith**.

575 אֱמוּנָה *'ᵉmûnâ*, n.f. [49] [√ 586]

faithfulness [20], truth [6], faithful [5], faithfully [+928] [5], entrusted with [+928] [2], trustworthy [2], truthful [2], complete honesty [1], faith [1], integrity [1], safe [1], steady [1], sure foundation [1], trust [1]

Ex 17:12 one on the other—so that his hands remained **steady** till sunset.
Dt 32:4 A **faithful** God who does no wrong, upright and just is he.
1Sa 26:23 LORD rewards every man for his righteousness and **faithfulness**.
2Ki 12:15 [12:16] the workers, because they acted with **complete honesty**.
22:7 entrusted to them, because they are acting **faithfully** [+928]."
1Ch 9:22 The gatekeepers had been assigned to their positions of **trust** by
9:26 were **entrusted** [+928] **with** the responsibility for the rooms
9:31 was **entrusted** [+928] **with** the responsibility for baking the
2Ch 19:9 "You must serve **faithfully** [+928] and wholeheartedly in the fear
31:12 Then they **faithfully** [+928] brought in the contributions, tithes
31:15 Shecaniah assisted him **faithfully** [+928] in the towns of the
31:18 For they were **faithful** *in* consecrating themselves.
34:12 The men did the work **faithfully** [+928]. Over them to direct them
Ps 33:4 word of the LORD is right and true; he is **faithful** in all he does.
36:5 [36:6] reaches to the heavens, your **faithfulness** to the skies.
37:3 the LORD and do good; dwell in the land and enjoy **safe** pasture.
40:10 [40:11] in my heart; I speak of your **faithfulness** and salvation.
88:11 [88:12] declared in the grave, your **faithfulness** in Destruction?
89:1 [89:2] with my mouth I will make your **faithfulness** known
89:2 [89:3] that you established your **faithfulness** in heaven itself.
89:5 [89:6] O LORD, your **faithfulness** too, in the assembly of the
89:8 [89:9] O LORD, and your **faithfulness** surrounds you.
89:24 [89:25] My **faithful** love will be with him, and through my name
89:33 [89:34] my love from him, nor will I ever betray my **faithfulness**.
89:49 [89:50] which in your **faithfulness** you swore to David?
92:2 [92:3] your love in the morning and your **faithfulness** at night,
96:13 will judge the world in righteousness and the peoples in his **truth**.
98:3 remembered his love and his **faithfulness** to the house of Israel;
100:5 endures forever; his **faithfulness** continues through all generations.
119:30 I have chosen the way of **truth**; I have set my heart on your laws.
119:75 your laws are righteous, and in **faithfulness** you have afflicted me.
119:86 All your commands are **trustworthy**; help me, for men persecute
119:90 Your **faithfulness** continues through all generations; you
119:138 you have laid down are righteous; they are fully **trustworthy**.
143:1 in your **faithfulness** and righteousness come to my relief.
Pr 12:17 A **truthful** witness gives honest testimony, but a false witness tells
12:22 LORD detests lying lips, but he delights in men who are **truthful**.
28:20 A **faithful** man will be richly blessed, but one eager to get rich will
Isa 11:5 will be his belt and **faithfulness** the sash around his waist.
25:1 for in perfect **faithfulness** you have done marvelous things,
33:6 He will be the **sure foundation** *for* your times, a rich store of
59:4 No one calls for justice; no one pleads his case with **integrity**.
Jer 5:1 can find but one person who deals honestly and seeks the **truth**,
5:3 O LORD, do not your eyes look for **truth**? You struck them,
7:28 to correction. **Truth** has perished; it has vanished from their lips.
9:3 [9:2] to shoot lies; it is not by **truth** that they triumph in the land.
La 3:23 They are new every morning; great is your **faithfulness**.
Hos 2:20 [2:22] I will betroth you in **faithfulness**, and you will
Hab 2:4 desires are not upright—but the righteous will live by his **faith**—

576 אָמוֹץ *'āmôṣ*, n.pr.m. [13] [√ 599]

Amoz [13]

2Ki 19:2 all wearing sackcloth, to the prophet Isaiah son of **Amoz**.
19:20 Isaiah son of **Amoz** sent a message to Hezekiah: "This is what the
20:1 The prophet Isaiah son of **Amoz** went to him and said, "This is
2Ch 26:22 beginning to end, are recorded by the prophet Isaiah son of **Amoz**.
32:20 the prophet Isaiah son of **Amoz** cried out in prayer to heaven about
32:32 the prophet Isaiah son of **Amoz** in the book of the kings of Judah
Isa 1:1 Jerusalem that Isaiah son of **Amoz** saw during the reigns of
2:1 This is what Isaiah son of **Amoz** saw concerning Judah
13:1 An oracle concerning Babylon that Isaiah son of **Amoz** saw:
20:2 at that time the LORD spoke through Isaiah son of **Amoz**.
37:2 all wearing sackcloth, to the prophet Isaiah son of **Amoz**.
37:21 Isaiah son of **Amoz** sent a message to Hezekiah: "This is what the
38:1 The prophet Isaiah son of **Amoz** went to him and said, "This is

577 אָמִי *'āmî*, n.pr.m. [1] [√ 571; cf. 586]

Ami [1]

Ezr 2:57 Shephatiah, Hattil, Pokereth-Hazzebaim and **Ami**

578 אֲמִינוֹן *'ᵃmînôn*, n.pr.m. [1] [√ 596; cf. 586]

Amnon [1]

2Sa 13:20 said to her, "Has that **Amnon**, your brother, been with you?

579 אַמִּיץ *'ammîṣ*, a. [6] [√ 599]

mighty [2], bravest [+4213] [1], strength [1], strong [1], vast [1]

2Sa 15:12 so the conspiracy gained **strength**, and Absalom's following kept
Job 9:4 His wisdom is profound, his power is **vast**. Who has resisted him
9:19 If it is a matter of strength, he is **mighty**! And if it is a matter of
Isa 28:2 See, the Lord has one who is powerful and **strong**. Like a
40:26 Because of his great power and **mighty** strength, not one of them is
Am 2:16 Even the **bravest** [+4213] warriors will flee naked on that day,"

580 אָמִיר *'āmîr*, n.m. [2] [√ 607]

branches [1], undergrowth [1]

Isa 17:6 leaving two or three olives on the topmost **branches**, four
17:9 will be like places abandoned to thickets and **undergrowth**.

581 ¹אָמַל *'āmal[1]*, v. [16] [→ 583, 584; cf. 4908]

languish [2], wither [2], fade [1], fails [1], faint [1], languishes [1], pine away [1], pines away [1], waste away [1], wasted away [1], wastes away [1], weak-willed [+4226] [1], withered [1], withers [1]

1Sa 2:5 [E] seven children, but she who has had many sons **pines away**.
Isa 16:8 [E] The fields of Heshbon **wither**, the vines of Sibmah also.
19:8 [E] the Nile; those who throw nets on the water *will* **pine away**.
24:4 [E] earth dries up and withers, the world **languishes** and withers,
24:4 [E] and withers, the exalted of the earth **languish**.
24:7 [E] The new wine dries up and the vine **withers**; all the
33:9 [E] The land mourns and **wastes away**, Lebanon is ashamed
Jer 14:2 [E] "Judah mourns, her cities **languish**; they wail for the land,
15:9 [E] The mother of seven *will grow* **faint** and breathe her last.
La 2:8 [E] made ramparts and walls lament; together *they* **wasted away**.
Eze 16:30 [B] " 'How **weak-willed** [+4226] you are, declares the Sovereign
Hos 4:3 [E] of this the land mourns, and all who live in it **waste away**;
Joel 1:10 [E] the grain is destroyed, the new wine is dried up, the oil **fails**.
1:12 [E] The vine is dried up and the fig tree *is* **withered**;
Na 1:4 [E] Bashan and Carmel **wither** and the blossoms of Lebanon
1:4 [E] and Carmel wither and the blossoms of Lebanon **fade**.

582 ²אָמַל *'āmal[2]*, v. Not used in NIV/BHS [cf. 4908]

583 אֻמְלַל *'umlal*, a. [1] [√ 581]

faint [1]

Ps 6:2 [6:3] Be merciful to me, LORD, for I am **faint**; O LORD,

584 אֲמֵלָל *'ᵃmēlāl*, a. [1] [√ 581]

feeble [1]

Ne 4:2 [3:34] of Samaria, he said, "What are those **feeble** Jews doing?

[A] Qal [B] Qal passive [C] Niphal [D] Piel (poel, polel, pilel, pilal, pealal, pilpel) [E] Pual (poal, polal, poalal, pulal, pualal)

585 אֲמָם *'ᵃmām*, n.pr.loc. [1] [→ 5497]
Amam [1]

Jos 15:26 **Amam**, Shema, Moladah,

586 ¹אָמַן *'āman¹*, v. [96 / 97] [→ 571, 572, 573, 574, 575, 577, 578, 587, 589, 590, 591, 593, 594, 595, 596, 597, 2124?; Ar 10041, 10327]
believe [20], faithful [15], trust [8], believed [7], trustworthy [4], be established [2], come true [2], firm [2], have faith [2], places trust [2], put trust [2], be confirmed [1], be trusted [1], be upheld [1], be verified [1], believes [1], certain [1], confident [1], despairs [+4202] [1], endure [1], enduring [1], fails [+4202] [1], firmly [1], have assurance [1], lasting [1], lingering [1], loyal [1], never fail [1], not fail [1], prolonged [1], reliable [1], stand firm [+4394] [1], stand firm in faith [1], stand still [1], stand [1], sure [1], trusted advisers [1], trusted [1], trusting [1], trusts [1], trustworthy [+8120] [1], was attested [1]

Ge 15: 6 [G] Abram **believed** the LORD, and he credited it to him as
42:20 [C] so that your words *may* **be verified** and that you may not
45:26 [G] of all Egypt." Jacob was stunned; *he did* not **believe** them.
Ex 4: 1 [G] "What if *they do* not **believe** me or listen to me and say,
4: 5 [G] the LORD, "is so that *they may* **believe** that the LORD,
4: 8 [G] "If *they do* not **believe** you or pay attention to the first
4: 8 [G] to the first miraculous sign, *they may* **believe** the second.
4: 9 [G] But if *they do* not **believe** these two signs or listen to you,
4:31 [G] they **believed**. And when they heard that the LORD was
14:31 [G] and **put** *their* **trust** in him and in Moses his servant.
19: 9 [G] speaking with you and *will* always **put** *their* **trust** in you."
Nu 12: 7 [C] not true of my servant Moses; he *is* **faithful** in all my house.
14:11 [G] How long *will they* refuse *to* **believe** in me, in spite of all the
20:12 [G] "Because *you did* not **trust** in me enough to honor me as
Dt 1:32 [G] In spite of this, you *did* not **trust** in the LORD your God,
7: 9 [C] he is the **faithful** God, keeping his covenant of love to a
9:23 [G] the LORD your God. *You did* not **trust** him or obey him.
28:59 [C] harsh and **prolonged** disasters, and severe and lingering
28:59 [C] and prolonged disasters, and severe and **lingering** illnesses.
28:66 [G] filled with dread both night and day, never **sure** of your life.
Jdg 11:20 [G] however, *did* not **trust** Israel to pass through his territory.
1Sa 2:35 [C] I will raise up for myself a **faithful** priest, who will do
2:35 [C] I will **firmly** establish his house, and he will minister before
3:20 [C] that Samuel **was attested** as a prophet of the LORD.
22:14 [C] "Who of all your servants *is* as **loyal** as David, the king's
25:28 [C] for the LORD will certainly make a **lasting** dynasty for my
27:12 [G] Achish **trusted** David and said to himself, "He has become
2Sa 7:16 [C] and your kingdom *will* **endure** forever before me;
1Ki 8:26 [C] that you promised your servant David my father **come true**.
10: 7 [G] *I did* not **believe** these things until I came and saw with my
11:38 [C] I will build you a dynasty as **enduring** as the one I built for
2Ki 17:14 [G] as their fathers, who *did* not **trust** in the LORD their God.
1Ch 17:23 [C] made concerning your servant and his house **be established**
17:24 [C] so that *it will* **be established** and that your name will be great
2Ch 1: 9 [C] *let* your promise to my father David **be confirmed**,
6:17 [C] *let* your word that you promised your servant David **come true**.
9: 6 [G] *I did* not **believe** what they said until I came and saw with
20:20 [G] **Have faith** in the LORD your God and you will be upheld;
20:20 [C] Have faith in the LORD your God and *you will* **be upheld**;
20:20 [G] **have faith** in his prophets and you will be successful."
32:15 [G] *Do* not **believe** him, for no god of any nation or kingdom has
Ne 9: 8 [C] You found his heart **faithful** to you, and you made a
13:13 [C] because these men were considered **trustworthy**.
Job 4:18 [G] If God **places** no **trust** in his servants, if he charges his
9:16 [G] he responded, *I do* not **believe** he would give me a hearing.
12:20 [C] He silences the lips of **trusted advisers** and takes away the
15:15 [G] If God **places** no **trust** in his holy ones, if even the heavens
15:22 [G] *He* **despairs** [+4202] *of* escaping the darkness; he is marked
15:31 [G] Let him not deceive himself *by* **trusting** what is worthless,
24:22 [G] they become established, *they* **have** no **assurance** of life.
29:24 [G] When I smiled at them, *they* scarcely **believed** it; the light of
39:12 [G] *Can you* **trust** him to bring in your grain and gather it to
39:24 [G] the ground; *he* cannot **stand still** when the trumpet sounds.
Ps 19: 7 [19:8] [C] The statutes of the LORD *are* **trustworthy**,
27:13 [G] *I am* still **confident** of this: I will see the goodness of the
78: 8 [C] not loyal to God, whose spirits *were* not **faithful** to him.
78:22 [G] for *they did* not **believe** in God or trust in his deliverance.
78:32 [G] kept on sinning; in spite of his wonders, *they did* not **believe**.
78:37 [C] were not loyal to him, *they were* not **faithful** to his covenant.
89:28 [89:29] [C] and my covenant with him *will* **never fail**.
89:37 [89:38] [C] like the moon, the **faithful** witness in the sky."
93: 5 [C] Your statutes **stand firm** [+4394]; holiness adorns your
101: 6 [C] My eyes will be on the **faithful** *in* the land, that they may
106:12 [G] Then *they* **believed** his promises and sang his praise.
106:24 [G] despised the pleasant land; *they did* not **believe** his promise.
111: 7 [C] hands are faithful and just; all his precepts *are* **trustworthy**.
116:10 [G] *I* **believed**; therefore I said, "I am greatly afflicted."
119:66 [G] and good judgment, for *I* **believe** in your commands.
145:13 [C] The LORD *is* **faithful** [BHS-] to all his promises
Pr 11:13 [C] a confidence, but a **trustworthy** [+8120] *man* keeps a secret.
14:15 [G] A simple man **believes** anything, but a prudent man gives
25:13 [C] Like the coolness of snow at harvest time is a **trustworthy**
26:25 [G] Though his speech is charming, *do* not **believe** him,
27: 6 [C] Wounds from a friend *can* **be trusted**, but an enemy
Isa 1:21 [C] See how the **faithful** city has become a harlot! She once was
1:26 [C] will be called the City of Righteousness, the **Faithful** City."
7: 9 [G] If *you do* not **stand firm in** *your* **faith**, you will not stand at
7: 9 [C] do not stand firm in your faith, *you will* not **stand** at all.' "
8: 2 [C] Zechariah son of Jeberekiah as **reliable** witnesses for me."
22:23 [C] I will drive him like a peg into a **firm** place; he will be a seat
22:25 [C] "the peg driven into the **firm** place will give way;
28:16 [G] sure foundation; the *one who* **trusts** will never be dismayed.
33:16 [C] His bread will be supplied, and water *will* **not fail** him.
43:10 [G] so that you may know and **believe** me and understand that I
49: 7 [C] who *is* **faithful**, the Holy One of Israel, who has chosen
53: 1 [G] Who *has* **believed** our message and to whom has the arm of
55: 3 [C] covenant with you, my **faithful** love promised to David.
Jer 12: 6 [G] *Do* not **trust** them, though they speak well of you.
15:18 [C] to me like a deceptive brook, like a spring *that* **fails** [+4202]?
40:14 [G] But Gedaliah son of Ahikam *did* not **believe** them.
42: 5 [C] **faithful** witness against us if we do not act in accordance
La 4:12 [G] The kings of the earth *did* not **believe**, nor did any of the
Hos 5: 9 [C] Among the tribes of Israel I proclaim *what is* **certain**.
11:12 [12:1] [C] against God, even against the **faithful** Holy One.
Jnh 3: 5 [G] The Ninevites **believed** God. They declared a fast, and all of
Mic 7: 5 [G] *Do* not **trust** a neighbor; put no confidence in a friend.
Hab 1: 5 [G] to do something in your days that *you would* not **believe**,

587 ²אָמַן *'āman²*, v. [9] [√ 586]
nurse [2], are carried [1], brought up [1], cared [1], foster fathers [1], guardians of children [1], guardians [1], nurtured [1]

Nu 11:12 [A] tell me to carry them in my arms, as a **nurse** carries an infant,
Ru 4:16 [A] Naomi took the child, laid him in her lap and **cared** for him.
2Sa 4: 4 [A] His **nurse** picked him up and fled, but as she hurried to
2Ki 10: 1 [A] to the elders and to the **guardians of** Ahab's **children**.
10: 5 [A] the elders and the **guardians** sent this message to Jehu:
Est 2: 7 [A] whom *he had* **brought up** because she had neither father nor
Isa 49:23 [A] Kings will be your **foster fathers**, and their queens your
60: 4 [C] come from afar, and your daughters **are carried** on the arm.
La 4: 5 [B] the streets. Those **nurtured** in purple now lie on ash heaps.

588 אָמָּן *'ommān*, n.m. [1] [√ 570]
craftsman's [1]

SS 7: 1 [7:2] legs are like jewels, the work of a **craftsman's** hands.

589 אָמֵן *'āmēn*, adv. [30] [√ 586]
amen [26], amen so be it [+589] [2], truth [2]

Nu 5:22 " 'Then the woman is to say, "**Amen** [+589]. **So be it**."
5:22 " 'Then the woman is to say, "**Amen**. **So be it** [+589]."
Dt 27:15 and sets it up in secret." Then all the people shall say, "**Amen**!"
27:16 his father or his mother." Then all the people shall say, "**Amen**!"
27:17 boundary stone." Then all the people shall say, "**Amen**!"
27:18 blind astray on the road." Then all the people shall say, "**Amen**!"
27:19 or the widow." Then all the people shall say, "**Amen**!"
27:20 dishonors his father's bed." Then all the people shall say, "**Amen**!"
27:21 relations with any animal." Then all the people shall say, "**Amen**!"
27:22 daughter of his mother." Then all the people shall say, "**Amen**!"
27:23 with his mother-in-law." Then all the people shall say, "**Amen**!"
27:24 kills his neighbor secretly." Then all the people shall say, "**Amen**!"
27:25 to kill an innocent person." Then all the people shall say, "**Amen**!"
27:26 law by carrying them out." Then all the people shall say, "**Amen**!"
1Ki 1:36 Benaiah son of Jehoiada answered the king, "**Amen**!
1Ch 16:36 Then all the people said "**Amen**" and "Praise the LORD."
Ne 5:13 At this the whole assembly said, "**Amen**," and praised the LORD.
8: 6 and all the people lifted their hands and responded, "**Amen**!
8: 6 all the people lifted their hands and responded, "Amen! **Amen**!"
Ps 41:13 [41:14] from everlasting to everlasting. **Amen** and Amen.
41:13 [41:14] from everlasting to everlasting. Amen and **Amen**.
72:19 may the whole earth be filled with his glory. **Amen** and Amen.
72:19 may the whole earth be filled with his glory. Amen and **Amen**.
89:52 [89:53] Praise be to the LORD forever! **Amen** and Amen.
89:52 [89:53] Praise be to the LORD forever! Amen and **Amen**.
106:48 to everlasting. Let all the people say, "**Amen**!" Praise the LORD.
Isa 65:16 invokes a blessing in the land will do so by the God of **truth**;
65:16 he who takes an oath in the land will swear by the God of **truth**.
Jer 11: 5 the land you possess today." I answered, "**Amen**, LORD."

Jer 28: 6 He said, "**Amen**! May the LORD do so! May the LORD fulfill

590 אֹמֶן *'ōmen*, n.[m.]. [1] [→ 597, 598; cf. 586]

perfect [1]

Isa 25: 1 for in **perfect** faithfulness you have done marvelous things,

591 אֲמָנָה¹ *'ᵃmānâ¹*, n.f. [2] [√ 586]

binding agreement [1], regulated [1]

Ne 9: 38 [10:1] "In view of all this, we are making a **binding agreement**,
11: 23 were under the king's orders, which **regulated** their daily activity.

592 אֲמָנָה² *'ᵃmānâ²*, n.pr.loc. [1] [cf. 76]

Amana [1]

2Ki 5: 12 [Are not **Abana** [Q; see K 76] and Pharpar, the rivers of Damascus,]
SS 4: 8 Descend from the crest of **Amana**, from the top of Senir,

593 אָמְנָה¹ *'omnâ¹*, adv. [2] [√ 586]

really [1], true [1]

Ge 20: 12 Besides, she **really** is my sister, the daughter of my father though
Jos 7: 20 Achan replied, "It is **true**! I have sinned against the LORD,

594 אָמְנָה² *'omnâ²*, n.f. [1] [√ 586]

bringing up [1]

Est 2: 20 instructions as she had done when he was **bringing** her **up**.

595 אֹמְנָה *'ōmᵉnâ*, subst. [1] [√ 586?]

doorposts [1]

2Ki 18: 16 had covered the doors and **doorposts** *of* the temple of the LORD,

596 אַמְנוֹן *'amnôn*, n.pr.m. [27] [→ 578; cf. 586]

Amnon [25], Amnon's [1], him^s [1]

2Sa 3: 2 His firstborn was **Amnon** the son of Ahinoam of Jezreel;
13: 1 the course of time, **Amnon** son of David fell in love with Tamar,
13: 2 **Amnon** became frustrated to the point of illness on account of his
13: 2 a virgin, and it seemed impossible for **him**^s to do anything to her.
13: 3 Now **Amnon** had a friend named Jonadab son of Shimeah,
13: 4 **Amnon** said to him, "I'm in love with Tamar, my brother
13: 6 So **Amnon** lay down and pretended to be ill. When the king came
13: 6 When the king came to see him, **Amnon** said to him, "I would like
13: 7 "Go to the house of your brother **Amnon** and prepare some food
13: 8 So Tamar went to the house of her brother **Amnon**, who was lying
13: 9 but he refused to eat. "Send everyone out of here," **Amnon** said.
13: 10 **Amnon** said to Tamar, "Bring the food here into my bedroom
13: 10 had prepared and brought it to her brother **Amnon** in his bedroom.
13: 15 **Amnon** hated her with intense hatred. In fact, he hated her more
13: 15 than he had loved her. **Amnon** said to her, "Get up and get out!"
13: 22 Absalom never said a word to **Amnon**, either good or bad;
13: 22 he hated **Amnon** because he had disgraced his sister Tamar.
13: 26 "If not, please let my brother **Amnon** come with us."
13: 27 so he sent with him **Amnon** and the rest of the king's sons.
13: 28 When **Amnon** is in high spirits from drinking wine and I say to
13: 28 and I say to you, 'Strike **Amnon** down,' then kill him.
13: 29 So Absalom's men did to **Amnon** what Absalom had ordered.
13: 32 not think that they killed all the princes; only **Amnon** is dead.
13: 33 the report that all the king's sons are dead. Only **Amnon** is dead."
13: 39 to go to Absalom, for he was consoled concerning **Amnon's** death.
1Ch 3: 1 The firstborn was **Amnon** the son of Ahinoam of Jezreel;
4: 20 The sons of Shimon: **Amnon**, Rinnah, Ben-Hanan and Tilon.

597 אָמְנָם *'omnām*, adv. [9] [→ 598; cf. 590, 586]

true [4], indeed [2], be assured [1], doubtless [1], unthinkable [+4202] [1]

Ru 3: 12 Although it is **true** that I am near of kin, there is a
2Ki 19: 17 "It is **true**, O LORD, that the Assyrian kings have laid waste
Job 9: 2 "**Indeed**, I know that this is true. But how can a mortal be
12: 2 "**Doubtless** you are the people, and wisdom will die with you!
19: 4 If it is **true** that I have gone astray, my error remains my concern
19: 5 If **indeed** you would exalt yourselves above me and use my
34: 12 It is **unthinkable** [+4202] that God would do wrong,
36: 4 **Be assured** that my words are not false; one perfect in knowledge
Isa 37: 18 "It is **true**, O LORD, that the Assyrian kings have laid waste all

598 אֻמְנָם *'umnām*, adv. [5] [√ 597; cf. 590, 586]

really [3], indeed [1], really [+677] [1]

Ge 18: 13 "Why did Sarah laugh and say, 'Will I **really** [+677] have a child,
Nu 22: 37 Why didn't you come to me? Am I **really** not able to reward you?"
1Ki 8: 27 "But will God **really** dwell on earth? The heavens,
2Ch 6: 18 "But will God **really** dwell on earth with men? The heavens,
Ps 58: 1 [58:2] Do you rulers **indeed** speak justly? Do you judge uprightly

599 אָמֵץ *'āmēṣ*, v. [41] [→ 576, 579, 600, 601, 602, 4410; *also used with compound proper names*]

courageous [11], strong [4], strengthen [3], managed [2], raised up [2], determined [1], encourage [1], established [1], hardened [1], hardhearted [+906+4222] [1], increases [1], let grow [1], marshal [1], muster [1], obstinate [1], opposed [+6584] [1], reinforced [1], steady [1], strengthened [1], stronger [1], supported [1], take heart [+4213] [1], take heart [+4222] [1], victorious [1]

Ge 25: 23 [A] one people *will be* **stronger** than the other, and the older will
Dt 2: 30 [D] and his heart **obstinate** in order to give him into your hands,
3: 28 [D] But commission Joshua, and encourage and **strengthen** him,
15: 7 [D] *do* not *be* **hardhearted** [+906+4222] or tightfisted toward your
31: 6 [A] Be strong and **courageous**. Do not be afraid or terrified
31: 7 [A] him in the presence of all Israel, "Be strong and **courageous**,
31: 23 [A] "Be strong and **courageous**, for you will bring the Israelites
Jos 1: 6 [A] "Be strong and **courageous**, because you will lead these
1: 7 [A] Be strong and very **courageous**. Be careful to obey all the
1: 9 [A] Be strong and **courageous**. Do not be terrified; do not be
1: 18 [A] will be put to death. Only be strong and **courageous**!"
10: 25 [A] be afraid; do not be discouraged. Be strong and **courageous**.
Ru 1: 18 [F] When Naomi realized that Ruth *was* **determined** to go with
2Sa 22: 18 [A] powerful enemy, from my foes, *who were* too **strong** for me.
1Ki 12: 18 [F] **managed** to get into his chariot and escape to Jerusalem.
1Ch 22: 13 [A] Be strong and **courageous**. Do not be afraid or discouraged.
28: 20 [A] his son, "Be strong and **courageous**, and do the work.
2Ch 10: 18 [F] **managed** to get into his chariot and escape to Jerusalem.
11: 17 [D] and **supported** Rehoboam son of Solomon three years,
13: 7 [F] **opposed** [+6584] Rehoboam son of Solomon when he was
13: 18 [A] the men of Judah *were* **victorious** because they relied on the
24: 13 [D] of God according to its original design and **reinforced** it.
32: 7 [A] "Be strong and **courageous**. Do not be afraid or discouraged
36: 13 [D] He became stiff-necked and **hardened** his heart and would
Job 4: 4 [D] those who stumbled; *you have* **strengthened** faltering knees.
16: 5 [D] my mouth *would* **encourage** you; comfort from my lips
Ps 18: 17 [18:18] [A] from my foes, *who were* too **strong** for me.
27: 14 [G] be strong and **take heart** [+4213] and wait for the LORD.
31: 24 [31:25] [A] Be strong and **take heart** [+4222], all you who hope
80: 15 [80:16] [D] the son *you have* **raised up** for yourself.
80: 17 [80:18] [D] the son of man *you have* **raised up** for yourself.
89: 21 [89:22] [D] sustain him; surely my arm *will* **strengthen** him.
142: 6 [142:7] [A] who pursue me, for *they are* too **strong** for me.
Pr 8: 28 [D] when he **established** the clouds above and fixed securely the
24: 5 [D] has great power, and a man of knowledge **increases** strength;
31: 17 [D] about her work vigorously; her arms *are* **strong** for her tasks.
Isa 35: 3 [D] Strengthen the feeble hands, **steady** the knees that give way;
41: 10 [D] *I will* **strengthen** you and help you; I will uphold you with
44: 14 [D] *He* **let** it **grow** among the trees of the forest, or planted a
Am 2: 14 [D] will not escape, the strong *will* not **muster** their strength,
Na 2: 1 [2:2] [D] the road, brace yourselves, **marshal** all your strength!

600 אָמֹץ *'āmōṣ*, a. [2] [√ 599]

powerful [2]

Zec 6: 3 the third white, and the fourth dappled—*all of them* **powerful**.
6: 7 When the **powerful** horses went out, they were straining to go

601 אֹמֶץ *'ōmeṣ*, n.[m.]. [1] [√ 599]

grow stronger [+3578] [1]

Job 17: 9 and *those with* clean hands *will* **grow stronger** [+3578].

602 אַמְצָה *'amṣâ*, n.f. [1] [√ 599]

strong [1]

Zec 12: 5 'The people of Jerusalem are **strong**, because the LORD

603 אַמְצִי *'amṣî*, n.pr.m. [2] [√ 599; cf. 604?]

Amzi [2]

1Ch 6: 46 [6:31] the son of **Amzi**, the son of Bani, the son of Shemer,
Ne 11: 12 the son of Pelaliah, the son of **Amzi**, the son of Zechariah,

604 אֲמַצְיָה *'ᵃmaṣyâ*, n.pr.m. [9] [→ 603?, 605; cf. 599 + 3378]

Amaziah [9]

2Ki 12: 21 [12:22] of David. And **Amaziah** his son succeeded him as king.
13: 12 including his war against **Amaziah** king of Judah,
14: 8 Then **Amaziah** sent messengers to Jehoash son of Jehoahaz,
15: 1 of Israel, Azariah son of **Amaziah** king of Judah began to reign.
1Ch 4: 34 Meshobab, Jamlech, Joshah son of **Amaziah**,
6: 45 [6:30] son of Hashabiah, the son of **Amaziah**, the son of Hilkiah,

Am 7:10 **Amaziah** the priest of Bethel sent a message to Jeroboam king of
7:12 **Amaziah** said to Amos, "Get out, you seer! Go back to the land of
7:14 Amos answered **Amaziah**, "I was neither a prophet nor a prophet's

605 אֲמַצְיָהוּ *'amaṣyāhû*, n.pr.m. [31] [√ 604; cf. 599 + 3378]

Amaziah [29], Amaziah's [2]

2Ki 14: 1 king of Israel, **Amaziah** son of Joash king of Judah began to reign.
14: 9 But Jehoash king of Israel replied to **Amaziah** king of Judah:
14:11 **Amaziah**, however, would not listen, so Jehoash king of Israel
14:11 **Amaziah** king of Judah faced each other at Beth Shemesh in
14:13 Jehoash king of Israel captured **Amaziah** king of Judah, the son of
14:15 including his war against **Amaziah** king of Judah,
14:17 **Amaziah** son of Joash king of Judah lived for fifteen years after
14:18 As for the other events of **Amaziah's** reign, are they not written in
14:21 years old, and made him king in place of his father **Amaziah**.
14:23 In the fifteenth year of **Amaziah** son of Joash king of Judah,
15: 3 in the eyes of the LORD, just as his father **Amaziah** had done.
1Ch 3:12 **Amaziah** his son, Azariah his son, Jotham his son,
2Ch 24:27 book of the kings. And **Amaziah** his son succeeded him as king.
25: 1 **Amaziah** was twenty-five years old when he became king,
25: 5 **Amaziah** called the people of Judah together and assigned them
25: 9 **Amaziah** asked the man of God, "But what about the hundred
25:10 So **Amaziah** dismissed the troops who had come to him from
25:11 **Amaziah** then marshaled his strength and led his army to the
25:13 Meanwhile the troops that **Amaziah** had sent back and had not
25:14 When **Amaziah** returned from slaughtering the Edomites,
25:15 The anger of the LORD burned against **Amaziah**, and he sent a
25:17 After **Amaziah** king of Judah consulted his advisers, he sent this
25:18 But Jehoash king of Israel replied to **Amaziah** king of Judah:
25:20 **Amaziah**, however, would not listen, for God so worked that he
25:21 **Amaziah** king of Judah faced each other at Beth Shemesh in
25:23 Jehoash king of Israel captured **Amaziah** king of Judah, the son of
25:25 **Amaziah** son of Joash king of Judah lived for fifteen years after
25:26 As for the other events of **Amaziah's** reign, from beginning to end,
25:27 From the time that **Amaziah** turned away from following the
26: 1 years old, and made him king in place of his father **Amaziah**.
26: 4 in the eyes of the LORD, just as his father **Amaziah** had done.

606 אָמַר¹ *'āmar¹*, v. [5308 / 5307] [→ 223, 608, 609, 614, 615, 4411; Ar 10042; *also used with compound proper names*]

said [1958], *untranslated* [867], says [610], say [506], asked [215], replied [185], answered [161], saying [138], tell [93], told [84], thought [47], ask [45], ordered [28], message [18], added [15], spoke [14], commanded [13], answer [12], speak [12], promised [10], declared [9], shouted [9], continued [8], word [8], thinking [7], uttered [+2256+5951] [7], called [6], cried [6], prayed [6], think [6], call [5], exclaimed [5], gave orders [5], asking [4], declare [4], reply [4], reported [4], say [+606] [4], spoken [4], tells [4], asks [3], be called [3], be said [3], called out [3], cried out [3], intend [3], suggested [3], announced [2], be [2], challenge [2], claim [2], claims [2], command [2], commands [2], cry out [2], declares [+606] [2], demanded [2], is said [2], keep saying [+606] [2], name [2], order [2], promised [+606] [2], read [2], replied [+8938] [2], responded [2], set [2], shout [2], shouting [2], so sure [+606] [2], talked [2], telling [2], thinks [2], want [2], add [1], advised [1], afraid[s] [1], agreed [1], assured [1], be named [1], be told [1], been given [1], boast [1], boasted [1], boasts [1], brought up [1], call out [1], called back [1], calling out [1], came [1], claimed [1], commemorate [1], complain [1], confessed [1], cries [1], cry out [+4200+5951] [1], cry [1], demand [1], demanding [1], directed [1], exclaim [1], explain [1], gave an order [1], gave the order [1], gave [1], give [1], goes [1], greeted [1], heard [+265+928] [1], indicate [1], indicated [1], inquired of [+448] [1], insisted [1], instructed [1], intended [1], issued orders [1], makes speech [+609] [1], news [1], objected [1], offered [1], plan [1], plead [1], proclaiming [1], proposed [1], protest [1], provided [1], question [1], realize [+4200+4222] [1], recite [+2256+6699] [1], recite [1], repeated [1], replies [1], report [1], reporting [1], respond [1], say [+2256+6699] [1], saying [+4200] [1], search [+928] [1], sent word [1], shows [1], snorts [1], speaks [1], spoke up [1], suggest [1], swear [1], talking [1], tell [+1821] [1], think [+928+4213] [1], think [+928+4222] [1], thinks [+928+4222] [1], thought [+448+3276] [1], told [+448+4200+8938] [1], urged [1], use [1], used [1], uttered [1], wanted [1], warned [1], warning [1], was said [1], was told [1], words [1]

Ge 1: 3 [A] And God **said**, "Let there be light," and there was light.
1: 6 [A] God **said**, "Let there be an expanse between the waters to
1: 9 [A] God **said**, "Let the water under the sky be gathered to one
1:11 [A] God **said**, "Let the land produce vegetation:
1:14 [A] God **said**, "Let there be lights in the expanse of the sky to
1:20 [A] God **said**, "Let the water teem with living creatures, and let
1:22 [A] God blessed them and **said**, "Be fruitful and increase in
1:24 [A] God **said**, "Let the land produce living creatures according to
1:26 [A] God **said**, "Let us make man in our image, in our likeness,
1:28 [A] God blessed them and **said** to them, "Be fruitful and increase
1:29 [A] God **said**, "I give you every seed-bearing plant on the face of
2:16 [A] **[NIE]** "You are free to eat from any tree in the garden;
2:18 [A] The LORD God **said**, "It is not good for the man to be
2:23 [A] The man **said**, "This is now bone of my bones and flesh of
3: 1 [A] *He* **said** to the woman, "Did God really say, 'You must not
3: 1 [A] He said to the woman, "*Did* God really **say**, 'You must not
3: 2 [A] The woman **said** to the serpent, "We may eat fruit from the
3: 3 [A] God *did* **say**, 'You must not eat fruit from the tree that is in
3: 4 [A] "You will not surely die," the serpent **said** to the woman.
3: 9 [A] the LORD God called to the man, **[NIE]** "Where are you?"
3:10 [A] *He* **answered**, "I heard you in the garden, and I was afraid
3:11 [A] *he* **said**, "Who told you that you were naked? Have you eaten
3:12 [A] The man **said**, "The woman you put here with me—she gave
3:13 [A] the LORD God **said** to the woman, "What is this you have
3:13 [A] The woman **said**, "The serpent deceived me, and I ate."
3:14 [A] So the LORD God **said** to the serpent, "Because you have
3:16 [A] To the woman *he* **said**, "I will greatly increase your pains in
3:17 [A] To Adam *he* **said**, "Because you listened to your wife and ate
3:17 [A] **[NIE]** 'You must not eat of it,' "Cursed is the ground
3:22 [A] the LORD God **said**, "The man has now become like one of
4: 1 [A] *She* **said**, "With the help of the LORD I have brought forth
4: 6 [A] the LORD **said** to Cain, "Why are you angry? Why is your
4: 8 [A] Now Cain **said** to his brother Abel, "Let's go out to the
4: 9 [A] the LORD **said** to Cain, "Where is your brother Abel?"
4: 9 [A] "I don't know," *he* **replied**. "Am I my brother's keeper?"
4:10 [A] The LORD **said**, "What have you done? Listen!
4:13 [A] Cain **said** to the LORD, "My punishment is more than I can
4:15 [A] But the LORD **said** to him, "Not so; if anyone kills Cain,
4:23 [A] Lamech **said** to his wives, "Adah and Zillah, listen to me;
5:29 [A] He named him Noah and **said**, "He will comfort us in the
6: 3 [A] the LORD **said**, "My Spirit will not contend with man
6: 7 [A] So the LORD **said**, "I will wipe mankind, whom I have
6:13 [A] So God **said** to Noah, "I am going to put an end to all people,
7: 1 [A] The LORD then **said** to Noah, "Go into the ark, you
8:15 [A] Then God said to Noah, **[NIE]**
8:21 [A] LORD smelled the pleasing aroma and **said** in his heart:
9: 1 [A] **saying** to them, "Be fruitful and increase in number and fill
9: 8 [A] Then God **said** to Noah and to his sons with him:
9: 8 [A] Then God said to Noah and to his sons with him: **[NIE]**
9:12 [A] God **said**, "This is the sign of the covenant I am making
9:17 [A] So God **said** to Noah, "This is the sign of the covenant I have
9:25 [A] *he* **said**, "Cursed be Canaan! The lowest of slaves will he be
9:26 [A] *He* also **said**, "Blessed be the LORD, the God of Shem!
10: 9 [C] that is why *it* **is said**, "Like Nimrod, a mighty hunter before
11: 3 [A] *They* **said** to each other, "Come, let's make bricks and bake
11: 4 [A] *they* **said**, "Come, let us build ourselves a city, with a tower
11: 6 [A] The LORD **said**, "If as one people speaking the same
12: 1 [A] The LORD *had* **said** to Abram, "Leave your country, your
12: 7 [A] The LORD appeared to Abram and **said**, "To your offspring
12:11 [A] As he was about to enter Egypt, *he* **said** to his wife Sarai,
12:12 [A] When the Egyptians see you, *they will* **say**, 'This is his wife.'
12:13 [A] **Say** you are my sister, so that I will be treated well for your
12:18 [A] summoned Abram. "What have you done to me?" *he* **said**.
12:19 [A] Why *did you* **say**, 'She is my sister,' so that I took her to be
13: 8 [A] So Abram **said** to Lot, "Let's not have any quarreling
13:14 [A] The LORD **said** to Abram after Lot had parted from him,
14:19 [A] he blessed Abram, **saying**, "Blessed be Abram by God Most
14:21 [A] The king of Sodom **said** to Abram, "Give me the people
14:22 [A] Abram **said** to the king of Sodom, "I have raised my hand to
14:23 [A] so that *you will* never *be able to* **say**, 'I made Abram rich.'
15: 1 [A] **[NIE]** "Do not be afraid, Abram. I am your shield,
15: 2 [A] Abram **said**, "O Sovereign LORD, what can you give me
15: 3 [A] Abram **said**, "You have given me no children; so a servant in
15: 4 [A] **[NIE]** "This man will not be your heir, but a son coming
15: 5 [A] He took him outside and **said**, "Look up at the heavens
15: 5 [A] Then *he* **said** to him, "So shall your offspring be."
15: 7 [A] *He* also **said** to him, "I am the LORD, who brought you out
15: 8 [A] Abram **said**, "O Sovereign LORD, how can I know that I
15: 9 [A] So the LORD **said** to him, "Bring me a heifer, a goat and a
15:13 [A] the LORD **said** to him, "Know for certain that your
15:18 [A] that day the LORD made a covenant with Abram and **said**,
16: 2 [A] so she **said** to Abram, "The LORD has kept me from having
16: 5 [A] Sarai **said** to Abram, "You are responsible for the wrong I
16: 6 [A] "Your servant is in your hands," Abram **said**. "Do with her
16: 8 [A] *he* **said**, "Hagar, servant of Sarai, where have you come
16: 8 [A] "I'm running away from my mistress Sarai," *she* **answered**.
16: 9 [A] the angel of the LORD **told** her, "Go back to your mistress
16:10 [A] The angel **added**, "I will so increase your descendants that
16:11 [A] The angel of the LORD also **said** to her: "You are now with
16:13 [A] "You are the God who sees me," for *she* **said**, "I have now
17: 1 [A] the LORD appeared to him and **said**, "I am God Almighty;

Ge 17: 3 [A] Abram fell facedown, and God said to him, **[NIE]**
17: 9 [A] God **said** to Abraham, "As for you, you must keep my
17: 15 [A] God also **said** to Abraham, "As for Sarai your wife, you are
17: 17 [A] he laughed and **said** to himself, "Will a son be born to a man
17: 18 [A] Abraham **said** to God, "If only Ishmael might live under your
17: 19 [A] God **said**, "Yes, but your wife Sarah will bear you a son,
18: 3 [A] *He* **said**, "If I have found favor in your eyes, my lord, do not
18: 5 [A] your servant." "Very well," *they* **answered**, "do as you say."
18: 6 [A] "Quick," *he* **said**, "get three seahs of fine flour and knead it
18: 9 [A] wife Sarah?" *they* **asked** him. "There, in the tent," he said.
18: 9 [A] wife Sarah?" they asked him. "There, in the tent," *he* **said**.
18: 10 [A] the LORD **said**, "I will surely return to you about this time
18: 12 [A] So Sarah laughed to herself *as she* **thought**, "After I am
18: 13 [A] Then the LORD **said** to Abraham, "Why did Sarah laugh
18: 13 [A] "Why did Sarah laugh and **say**, 'Will I really have a child,
18: 15 [A] Sarah was afraid, so she lied and **said**, "I did not laugh."
18: 15 [A] "I did not laugh." But *he* **said**, "Yes, you did laugh."
18: 17 [A] the LORD **said**, "Shall I hide from Abraham what I am
18: 20 [A] the LORD **said**, "The outcry against Sodom and Gomorrah
18: 23 [A] Abraham approached him and **said**: "Will you sweep away
18: 26 [A] The LORD **said**, "If I find fifty righteous people in the city
18: 27 [A] **[NIE]** "Now that I have been so bold as to speak to the
18: 28 [A] "If I find forty-five there," *he* **said**, "I will not destroy it."
18: 29 [A] spoke to him, **[NIE]** "What if only forty are found there?"
18: 29 [A] *He* **said**, "For the sake of forty, I will not do it."
18: 30 [A] Then *he* **said**, "May the Lord not be angry, but let me speak.
18: 30 [A] *He* **answered**, "I will not do it if I find thirty there."
18: 31 [A] Abraham **said**, "Now that I have been so bold as to speak to
18: 31 [A] *He* **said**, "For the sake of twenty, I will not destroy it."
18: 32 [A] *he* **said**, "May the Lord not be angry, but let me speak just
18: 32 [A] *He* **answered**, "For the sake of ten, I will not destroy it."
19: 2 [A] "My lords," *he* **said**, "please turn aside to your servant's
19: 2 [A] "No," *they* **answered**, "we will spend the night in the
19: 5 [A] **[NIE]** "Where are the men who came to you tonight?
19: 7 [A] and **said**, "No, my friends. Don't do this wicked thing.
19: 9 [A] "Get out of our way," *they* **replied**. And they said,
19: 9 [A] *they* **said**, "This fellow came here as an alien, and now he
19: 12 [A] The two men **said** to Lot, "Do you have anyone else here—
19: 14 [A] *He* **said**, "Hurry and get out of this place,
19: 15 [A] the coming of dawn, the angels urged Lot, **saying**, "Hurry!
19: 17 [A] had brought them out, *one of them* **said**, "Flee for your lives!
19: 18 [A] But Lot **said** to them, "No, my lords, please!
19: 21 [A] *He* **said** to him, "Very well, I will grant this request too; I
19: 31 [A] One day the older daughter **said** to the younger, "Our father
19: 34 [A] The next day the older daughter **said** to the younger, "Last
20: 2 [A] and there Abraham **said** of his wife Sarah, "She is my sister."
20: 3 [A] came to Abimelech in a dream one night and **said** to him,
20: 4 [A] so *he* **said**, "Lord, will you destroy an innocent nation?
20: 5 [A] *Did* he not **say** to me, 'She is my sister,' and didn't she also
20: 5 [A] 'She is my sister,' and *didn't* she also **say**, 'He is my brother'?
20: 6 [A] God **said** to him in the dream, "Yes, I know you did this with
20: 9 [A] Abimelech called Abraham in and **said**, "What have you
20: 10 [A] Abimelech **asked** Abraham, "What was your reason for
20: 11 [A] Abraham **replied**, "I said to myself, 'There is surely no fear
20: 11 [A] Abraham replied, "*I* **said** *to myself*, 'There is surely no fear
20: 13 [A] *I* **said** to her, 'This is how you can show your love to me:
20: 13 [A] to me: Everywhere we go, **say** of me, "He is my brother." '"
20: 15 [A] Abimelech **said**, "My land is before you; live wherever you
20: 16 [A] To Sarah *he* **said**, "I am giving your brother a thousand
21: 1 [A] Now the LORD was gracious to Sarah as *he had* **said**,
21: 6 [A] Sarah **said**, "God has brought me laughter, and everyone who
21: 7 [A] *she* **added**, "Who would have said to Abraham that Sarah
21: 10 [A] *she* **said** to Abraham, "Get rid of that slave woman and her
21: 12 [A] But God **said** to him, "Do not be so distressed about the boy
21: 12 [A] Listen to whatever Sarah **tells** you, because it is through
21: 16 [A] sat down nearby, about a bowshot away, for *she* **thought**,
21: 17 [A] angel of God called to Hagar from heaven and **said** to her,
21: 22 [A] and Phicol the commander of his forces **said** to Abraham,
21: 22 [A] to Abraham, **[NIE]** "God is with you in everything you do.
21: 24 [A] Abraham **said**, "I swear it."
21: 26 [A] Abimelech **said**, "I don't know who has done this. You did
21: 29 [A] Abimelech **asked** Abraham, "What is the meaning of these
21: 30 [A] *He* **replied**, "Accept these seven lambs from my hand as a
22: 1 [A] *He* **said** to him, "Abraham!" "Here I am," he replied.
22: 1 [A] He said to him, "Abraham!" "Here I am," *he* **replied**.
22: 2 [A] God **said**, "Take your son, your only son, Isaac, whom you
22: 2 [A] burnt offering on one of the mountains *I will* **tell** you *about*."
22: 3 [A] he set out for the place God *had* **told** him *about*.
22: 5 [A] He **said** to his servants, "Stay here with the donkey while I
22: 7 [A] Isaac **spoke up** and said to his father Abraham, "Father?"
22: 7 [A] Isaac spoke up and **said** to his father Abraham, "Father?"
22: 7 [A] Abraham **replied**. "The fire and wood are here," Isaac said,
22: 7 [A] "The fire and wood are here," Isaac **said**, "but where is the
22: 8 [A] Abraham **answered**, "God himself will provide the lamb for
22: 9 [A] When they reached the place God *had* **told** him *about*,
22: 11 [A] LORD called out to him from heaven, **[NIE]** "Abraham!
22: 11 [A] "Abraham! Abraham!" "Here I am," *he* **replied**.
22: 12 [A] "Do not lay a hand on the boy," *he* **said**. "Do not do anything
22: 14 [C] to this day *it* **is said**, "On the mountain of the LORD it will
22: 16 [A] **said**, "I swear by myself, declares the LORD, that
22: 20 [A] later Abraham was told, **[NIE]** "Milcah is also a mother;
23: 3 [A] from beside his dead wife and spoke to the Hittites. *He* **said**,
23: 5 [A] The Hittites replied to Abraham, **[NIE]**
23: 8 [A] to them, **[NIE]** "If you are willing to let me bury my dead,
23: 11 [23:10] [A] "No, my lord," he **said**. "Listen to me; I give you
23: 13 [A] to Ephron in their hearing, **[NIE]** "Listen to me, if you will.
23: 14 [A] Ephron answered Abraham, **[NIE]**
24: 2 [A] He **said** to the chief servant in his household, the one in
24: 5 [A] The servant **asked** him, "What if the woman is unwilling to
24: 6 [A] sure that you do not take my son back there," Abraham **said**.
24: 7 [A] and who spoke to me and promised me on oath, **saying**,
24: 12 [A] Then *he* **prayed**, "O LORD, God of my master Abraham,
24: 14 [A] May it be that when *I* **say** to a girl, 'Please let down your jar
24: 14 [A] and *she* **says**, 'Drink, and I'll water your camels too'—
24: 17 [A] The servant hurried to meet her and **said**, "Please give me a
24: 18 [A] "Drink, my lord," *she* **said**, and quickly lowered the jar to
24: 19 [A] After she had given him a drink, *she* **said**, "I'll draw water
24: 23 [A] Then *he* **asked**, "Whose daughter are you? Please tell me,
24: 24 [A] *She* **answered** him, "I am the daughter of Bethuel, the son
24: 25 [A] *she* **added**, "We have plenty of straw and fodder, as well as
24: 27 [A] **saying**, "Praise be to the LORD, the God of my master
24: 30 [A] had heard Rebekah **tell** [+1821] what the man said to her,
24: 31 [A] "Come, you who are blessed by the LORD," *he* **said**. "Why
24: 33 [A] food was set before him, but *he* **said**, "I will not eat until I
24: 33 [A] told you what I have to say." "Then tell us," ˻Laban˼ **said**.
24: 34 [A] So *he* **said**, "I am Abraham's servant.
24: 37 [A] my master made me swear an oath, and **said**, 'You must not
24: 39 [A] "Then *I* **asked** my master, 'What if the woman will not come
24: 40 [A] "*He* **replied**, 'The LORD, before whom I have walked,
24: 42 [A] *I* **said**, 'O LORD, God of my master Abraham, if you will,
24: 43 [A] if a maiden comes out to draw water and *I* **say** to her,
24: 44 [A] if *she* **says** to me, "Drink, and I'll draw water for your
24: 45 [A] went down to the spring and drew water, and *I* **said** to her,
24: 46 [A] "She quickly lowered her jar from her shoulder and **said**,
24: 47 [A] "I asked her, **[NIE]** 'Whose daughter are you?' "She said,
24: 47 [A] "*She* **said**, 'The daughter of Bethuel son of Nahor,
24: 50 [A] and Bethuel answered, **[NIE]** "This is from the LORD;
24: 54 [A] When they got up the next morning, *he* **said**, "Send me on
24: 55 [A] her brother and her mother **replied**, "Let the girl remain with
24: 56 [A] *he* **said** to them, "Do not detain me, now that the LORD has
24: 57 [A] Then *they* **said**, "Let's call the girl and ask her about it."
24: 58 [A] So they called Rebekah and **asked** her, "Will you go with
24: 58 [A] "Will you go with this man?" "I will go," *she* **said**.
24: 60 [A] they blessed Rebekah and **said** to her, "Our sister, may you
24: 65 [A] **asked** the servant, "Who is that man in the field coming to
24: 65 [A] "He is my master," the servant **answered**. So she took her
25: 22 [A] within her, and *she* **said**, "Why is this happening to me?"
25: 23 [A] The LORD **said** to her, "Two nations are in your womb,
25: 30 [A] He **said** to Jacob, "Quick, let me have some of that red stew!
25: 31 [A] Jacob **replied**, "First sell me your birthright."
25: 32 [A] "Look, I am about to die," Esau **said**. "What good is the
25: 33 [A] Jacob **said**, "Swear to me first." So he swore an oath to him,
26: 2 [A] The LORD appeared to Isaac and **said**, "Do not go down to
26: 2 [A] go down to Egypt; live in the land where *I* **tell** you to live.
26: 7 [A] *he* **said**, "She is my sister," because he was afraid to say,
26: 7 [A] is my sister," because he was afraid to **say**, "She is my wife."
26: 9 [A] So Abimelech summoned Isaac and **said**, "She is really your
26: 9 [A] Why *did you* **say**, 'She is my sister'?" Isaac answered him,
26: 9 [A] Isaac **answered** him, "Because I thought I might lose my life
26: 9 [A] "Because *I* **thought** I might lose my life on account of her."
26: 10 [A] Then Abimelech **said**, "What is this you have done to us?
26: 11 [A] **[NIE]** "Anyone who molests this man or his wife shall
26: 16 [A] Abimelech **said** to Isaac, "Move away from us; you have
26: 20 [A] herdsmen of Gerar quarreled with Isaac's herdsmen and **said**,
26: 22 [A] He named it Rehoboth, **saying**, "Now the LORD has given
26: 24 [A] That night the LORD appeared to him and **said**, "I am the
26: 27 [A] Isaac **asked** them, "Why have you come to me, since you
26: 28 [A] *They* **answered**, "We saw clearly that the LORD was with
26: 28 [A] so *we* **said**, 'There ought to be a sworn agreement between
26: 32 [A] the well they had dug. *They* **said**, "We've found water!"
27: 1 [A] he called for Esau his older son and **said** to him, "My son."
27: 1 [A] and said to him, "My son." "Here I am," *he* **answered**.
27: 2 [A] Isaac **said**, "I am now an old man and don't know the day of
27: 6 [A] Rebekah **said** to her son Jacob, "Look, I overheard your
27: 6 [A] Rebekah said to her son Jacob, **[RPH]** "Look, I overheard
27: 6 [A] I overheard your father say to your brother Esau, **[NIE]**
27: 11 [A] Jacob **said** to Rebekah his mother, "But my brother Esau is a
27: 13 [A] His mother **said** to him, "My son, let the curse fall on me.

[A] Qal [B] Qal passive [C] Niphal [D] Piel (poel, polel, pilel, pilal, pealal, pilpel) [E] Pual (poal, polal, poalal, pulal, pualal)

Ge 27:18 [A] He went to his father and **said**, "My father." "Yes, my son,"
27:18 [A] "My father." "Yes, my son," *he* **answered**. "Who is it?"
27:19 [A] Jacob **said** to his father, "I am Esau your firstborn. I have
27:20 [A] Isaac **asked** his son, "How did you find it so quickly,
27:20 [A] "The LORD your God gave me success," *he* **replied**.
27:21 [A] Then Isaac **said** to Jacob, "Come near so I can touch you,
27:22 [A] who touched him and **said**, "The voice is the voice of Jacob,
27:24 [A] "Are you really my son Esau?" *he* **asked**. "I am," he replied.
27:24 [A] "Are you really my son Esau?" he asked. "I am," *he* **replied**.
27:25 [A] Then *he* **said**, "My son, bring me some of your game to eat,
27:26 [A] his father Isaac **said** to him, "Come here, my son, and kiss
27:27 [A] caught the smell of his clothes, he blessed him and **said**, "Ah,
27:31 [A] *he* **said** to him, "My father, sit up and eat some of my game,
27:32 [A] His father Isaac **asked** him, "Who are you?" "I am your son,"
27:32 [A] "I am your son," *he* **answered**, "your firstborn, Esau."
27:33 [A] Isaac trembled violently and **said**, "Who was it, then,
27:34 [A] he burst out with a loud and bitter cry and **said** to his father,
27:35 [A] *he* **said**, "Your brother came deceitfully and took your
27:36 [A] Esau **said**, "Isn't he rightly named Jacob? He has deceived
27:36 [A] Then *he* **asked**, "Haven't you reserved any blessing for me?"
27:37 [A] Isaac answered **[NIE]** Esau, "I have made him lord over you
27:38 [A] Esau **said** to his father, "Do you have only one blessing,
27:39 [A] His father Isaac answered **[NIE]** him, "Your dwelling will
27:41 [A] He **said** to himself, "The days of mourning for my father are
27:42 [A] had said, she sent for her younger son Jacob and **said** to him,
27:46 [A] Rebekah **said** to Isaac, "I'm disgusted with living because of
28: 1 [A] commanded him: **[NIE]** "Do not marry a Canaanite woman.
28: 6 [A] **[NIE]** "Do not marry a Canaanite woman,"
28:13 [A] There above it stood the LORD, and *he* **said**: "I am the
28:16 [A] When Jacob awoke from his sleep, *he* **thought**,
28:17 [A] He was afraid and **said**, "How awesome is this place! This is
28:20 [A] **saying**, "If God will be with me and will watch over me on
29: 4 [A] Jacob **asked** the shepherds, "My brothers, where are you
29: 4 [A] where are you from?" "We're from Haran," *they* **replied**.
29: 5 [A] *He* **said** to them, "Do you know Laban, Nahor's grandson?"
29: 5 [A] Nahor's grandson?" "Yes, we know him," *they* **answered**.
29: 6 [A] Then Jacob **asked** them, "Is he well?" "Yes, he is," they said,
29: 6 [A] "Yes, he is," *they* **said**, "and here comes his daughter Rachel
29: 7 [A] "Look," *he* **said**, "the sun is still high; it is not time for the
29: 8 [A] "We can't," *they* **replied**, "until all the flocks are gathered
29:14 [A] Then Laban **said** to him, "You are my own flesh and blood."
29:15 [A] Laban **said** to him, "Just because you are a relative of mine,
29:18 [A] Jacob was in love with Rachel and **said**, "I'll work for you
29:19 [A] Laban **said**, "It's better that I give her to you than to some
29:21 [A] Jacob **said** to Laban, "Give me my wife. My time is
29:25 [A] So Jacob **said** to Laban, "What is this you have done to me?
29:26 [A] Laban **replied**, "It is not our custom here to give the younger
29:32 [A] for *she* **said**, "It is because the LORD has seen my misery.
29:33 [A] conceived again, and when she gave birth to a son *she* **said**,
29:34 [A] she conceived, and when she gave birth to a son *she* **said**,
29:35 [A] conceived again, and when she gave birth to a son *she* **said**,
30: 1 [A] So *she* **said** to Jacob, "Give me children, or I'll die!"
30: 2 [A] Jacob became angry with her and **said**, "Am I in the place of
30: 3 [A] *she* **said**, "Here is Bilhah, my maidservant. Sleep with her
30: 6 [A] Rachel **said**, "God has vindicated me; he has listened to my
30: 8 [A] Rachel **said**, "I have had a great struggle with my sister,
30:11 [A] Leah **said**, "What good fortune!" So she named him Gad.
30:13 [A] Leah **said**, "How happy I am! The women will call me
30:14 [A] Rachel **said** to Leah, "Please give me some of your son's
30:15 [A] *she* **said** to her, "Wasn't it enough that you took away my
30:15 [A] "Very well," Rachel **said**, "he can sleep with you tonight in
30:16 [A] went out to meet him. "You must sleep with me," *she* **said**.
30:18 [A] Leah **said**, "God has rewarded me for giving my maidservant
30:20 [A] Then Leah **said**, "God has presented me with a precious gift.
30:23 [A] She became pregnant and gave birth to a son and **said**,
30:24 [A] She named him Joseph, and **said**, "May the LORD add to
30:25 [A] Jacob **said** to Laban, "Send me on my way so I can go back
30:27 [A] But Laban **said** to him, "If I have found favor in your eyes,
30:28 [A] *He* **added**, "Name your wages, and I will pay them."
30:29 [A] Jacob **said** to him, "You know how I have worked for you
30:31 [A] "What shall I give you?" *he* **asked**. "Don't give me
30:31 [A] he asked. "Don't give me anything," Jacob **replied**.
30:34 [A] "Agreed," **said** Laban. "Let it be as you have said."
31: 1 [A] **[NIE]** "Jacob has taken everything our father owned
31: 3 [A] the LORD **said** to Jacob, "Go back to the land of your
31: 5 [A] *He* **said** to them, "I see that your father's attitude toward me
31: 8 [A] If *he* **said**, 'The speckled ones will be your wages,' then all
31: 8 [A] if *he* **said**, 'The streaked ones will be your wages,' then all the
31:11 [A] The angel of God **said** to me in the dream, 'Jacob.' I
31:11 [A] said to me in the dream, 'Jacob.' *I* **answered**, 'Here I am.'
31:12 [A] *he* **said**, 'Look up and see that all the male goats mating with
31:14 [A] **[NIE]** "Do we still have any share in the inheritance of our
31:16 [A] to us and our children. So do whatever God *has* **told** you."
31:24 [A] to Laban the Aramean in a dream at night and **said** to him,
31:26 [A] Laban **said** to Jacob, "What have you done? You've
31:29 [A] last night the God of your father **said** to me, 'Be careful not
31:29 [A] **[RPH]** 'Be careful not to say anything to Jacob, either good
31:31 [A] Jacob answered **[NIE]** Laban, "I was afraid, because I
31:31 [A] because *I* **thought** you would take your daughters away from
31:35 [A] Rachel **said** to her father, "Don't be angry, my lord, that I
31:36 [A] Laban to task. "What is my crime?" he asked **[NIE]** Laban.
31:43 [A] Laban answered **[NIE]** Jacob, "The women are my
31:46 [A] He **said** to his relatives, "Gather some stones." So they took
31:48 [A] Laban **said**, "This heap is a witness between you and me
31:49 [A] It was also called Mizpah, because *he* **said**,
31:51 [A] Laban also **said** to Jacob, "Here is this heap, and here is this
32: 2 [32:3] [A] When Jacob saw them, *he* **said**, "This is the camp of
32: 4 [32:5] [A] **[NIE]** "This is what you are to say to my master
32: 4 [32:5] [A] "This is what *you are to* **say** to my master Esau:
32: 4 [32:5] [A] 'Your servant Jacob **says**, I have been staying with
32: 6 [32:7] [A] *they* **said**, "We went to your brother Esau, and now
32: 8 [32:9] [A] *He* **thought**, "If Esau comes and attacks one group,
32: 9 [32:10] [A] Jacob **prayed**, "O God of my father Abraham, God
32: 9 [32:10] [A] God of my father Isaac, O LORD, who **said** to me,
32:12 [32:13] [A] you *have* **said**, 'I will surely make you prosper and
32:16 [32:17] [A] by itself, and **said** to his servants, "Go ahead of me,
32:17 [32:18] [A] **[NIE]** "When my brother Esau meets you
32:17 [32:18] [A] and asks, **[NIE]** 'To whom do you belong,
32:18 [32:19] [A] *you are to* **say**, 'They belong to your servant Jacob.
32:19 [32:20] [A] **[NIE]** "You are to say the same thing to Esau
32:20 [32:21] [A] be sure *to* **say**, 'Your servant Jacob is coming
32:20 [32:21] [A] Jacob is coming behind us.' " For *he* **thought**,
32:26 [32:27] [A] the man **said**, "Let me go, for it is daybreak."
32:26 [32:27] [A] Jacob **replied**, "I will not let you go unless you
32:27 [32:28] [A] The man **asked** him, "What is your name?"
32:27 [32:28] [A] "What is your name?" "Jacob," *he* **answered**.
32:28 [32:29] [A] the man **said**, "Your name will no longer be Jacob,
32:28 [32:29] [C] "Your name *will* no longer **be** Jacob, but Israel,
32:29 [32:30] [A] Jacob said, **[NIE]** "Please tell me your name."
32:29 [32:30] [A] *he* **replied**, "Why do you ask my name?" Then he
33: 5 [A] *he* **asked**. Jacob answered, "They are the children God has
33: 5 [A] Jacob **answered**, "They are the children God has graciously
33: 8 [A] Esau **asked**, "What do you mean by all these droves I met?"
33: 8 [A] I met?" "To find favor in your eyes, my lord," *he* **said**.
33: 9 [A] Esau **said**, "I already have plenty, my brother. Keep what
33:10 [A] "No, please!" **said** Jacob. "If I have found favor in your eyes,
33:12 [A] Then Esau **said**, "Let us be on our way; I'll accompany you."
33:13 [A] Jacob **said** to him, "My lord knows that the children are
33:15 [A] Esau **said**, "Then let me leave some of my men with you."
33:15 [A] "But why do that?" Jacob **asked**. "Just let me find favor in
34: 4 [A] Shechem **said** to his father Hamor, "Get me this girl as my
34: 4 [A] to his father Hamor, **[RPH]** "Get me this girl as my wife."
34: 8 [A] **[NIE]** "My son Shechem has his heart set on your daughter.
34:11 [A] Shechem **said** to Dinah's father and brothers, "Let me find
34:11 [A] favor in your eyes, and I will give you whatever *you* **ask**.
34:12 [A] bring as great as you like, and I'll pay whatever *you* **ask** me.
34:14 [A] *They* **said** to them, "We can't do such a thing; we can't give
34:21 [34:20] [A] "These men are friendly toward us," they **said**. "Let
34:30 [A] Jacob **said** to Simeon and Levi, "You have brought trouble
34:31 [A] *they* **replied**, "Should he have treated our sister like a
35: 1 [A] Then God **said** to Jacob, "Go up to Bethel and settle there,
35: 2 [A] So Jacob **said** to his household and to all who were with him,
35:10 [A] God **said** to him, "Your name is Jacob, but you will no
35:11 [A] God **said** to him, "I am God Almighty; be fruitful
35:17 [A] the midwife **said** to her, "Don't be afraid, for you have
37: 6 [A] *He* **said** to them, "Listen to this dream I had:
37: 8 [A] His brothers **said** to him, "Do you intend to reign over us?
37: 9 [A] "Listen," *he* **said**, "I had another dream, and this time the sun
37:10 [A] his father rebuked him and **said**, "What is this dream you
37:13 [A] Israel **said** to Joseph, "As you know, your brothers are
37:13 [A] I am going to send you to them." "Very well," *he* **replied**.
37:14 [A] So *he* **said** to him, "Go and see if all is well with your
37:15 [A] and asked him, **[NIE]** "What are you looking for?"
37:16 [A] *He* **replied**, "I'm looking for my brothers. Can you tell me
37:17 [A] "They have moved on from here," the man **answered**. "I
37:17 [A] "I heard *them* **say**, 'Let's go to Dothan.' " So Joseph went
37:19 [A] "Here comes that dreamer!" *they* **said** to each other.
37:20 [A] these cisterns and **say** *that* a ferocious animal devoured him.
37:21 [A] him from their hands. "Let's not take his life," *he* **said**.
37:22 [A] Reuben **said** this to rescue him from them and take him back
37:26 [A] Judah **said** to his brothers, "What will we gain if we kill our
37:30 [A] He went back to his brothers and **said**, "The boy isn't there!
37:32 [A] They took the ornamented robe back to their father and **said**,
37:33 [A] He recognized it and **said**, "It is my son's robe!
37:35 [A] "No," *he* **said**, "in mourning will I go down to the grave to
38: 8 [A] Judah **said** to Onan, "Lie with your brother's wife and fulfill
38:11 [A] Judah then **said** to his daughter-in-law Tamar, "Live as a
38:11 [A] For *he* **thought**, "He may die too, just like his brothers."

Ge 38:13 [A] **[NIE]** "Your father-in-law is on his way to Timnah to shear
38:16 [A] he went over to her by the roadside and **said**, "Come now,
38:16 [A] "And what will you give me to sleep with you?" *she* **asked**.
38:17 [A] "I'll send you a young goat from my flock," *he* **said**. "Will
38:17 [A] give me something as a pledge until you send it?" *she* **asked**.
38:18 [A] *He* **said**, "What pledge should I give you?" "Your seal
38:18 [A] and its cord, and the staff in your hand," *she* **answered**.
38:21 [A] **[NIE]** "Where is the shrine prostitute who was beside the
38:21 [A] "There hasn't been any shrine prostitute here," *they* **said**.
38:22 [A] So he went back to Judah and **said**, "I didn't find her.
38:22 [A] Besides, the men who lived there **said**, 'There hasn't been
38:23 [A] Judah **said**, "Let her keep what she has, or we will become a
38:24 [A] **[NIE]** "Your daughter-in-law Tamar is guilty of
38:24 [A] Judah **said**, "Bring her out and have her burned to death!"
38:25 [A] "I am pregnant by the man who owns these," *she* **said**.
38:25 [A] And *she* **added**, "See if you recognize whose seal and cord
38:26 [A] Judah recognized them and **said**, "She is more righteous than
38:28 [A] took a scarlet thread and tied it on his wrist and **said**,
38:29 [A] he drew back his hand, his brother came out, and *she* **said**,
39: 7 [A] a while his master's wife took notice of Joseph and **said**,
39: 8 [A] "With me in charge," *he* **told** her, "my master does not
39:12 [A] She caught him by his cloak and **said**, "Come to bed with
39:14 [A] "Look," *she* **said** to them, "this Hebrew has been brought to
39:14 [A] **[RPH]** "this Hebrew has been brought to us to make sport
39:17 [A] **[NIE]** "That Hebrew slave you brought us came to me to
39:19 [A] **saying**, "This is how your slave treated me," he burned with
40: 7 [A] master's house, **[NIE]** "Why are your faces so sad today?"
40: 8 [A] "We both had dreams," *they* **answered**, "but there is no one
40: 8 [A] Joseph **said** to them, "Do not interpretations belong to God?
40: 9 [A] *He* **said** to him, "In my dream I saw a vine in front of me,
40:12 [A] "This is what it means," Joseph **said** to him. "The three
40:16 [A] *he* **said** to Joseph, "I too had a dream:
40:18 [A] Joseph said. **[NIE]** "The three baskets are three days.
41: 9 [A] **[NIE]** "Today I am reminded of my shortcomings.
41:15 [A] Pharaoh **said** to Joseph, "I had a dream, and no one can
41:15 [A] I have heard *it* **said** of you that when you hear a dream you
41:16 [A] **[NIE]** "but God will give Pharaoh the answer he desires."
41:24 [A] *I* **told** this to the magicians, but none could explain it to me."
41:25 [A] Joseph **said** to Pharaoh, "The dreams of Pharaoh are one
41:38 [A] So Pharaoh **asked** them, "Can we find anyone like this man,
41:39 [A] Pharaoh **said** to Joseph, "Since God has made all this known
41:41 [A] So Pharaoh **said** to Joseph, "I hereby put you in charge of the
41:44 [A] Pharaoh **said** to Joseph, "I am Pharaoh, but without your
41:54 [A] and the seven years of famine began, just as Joseph *had* **said**.
41:55 [A] Pharaoh **told** all the Egyptians, "Go to Joseph and do what he
41:55 [A] all the Egyptians, "Go to Joseph and do what *he* **tells** you."
42: 1 [A] he **said** to his sons, "Why do you just keep looking at each
42: 2 [A] *He* **continued**, "I have heard that there is grain in Egypt.
42: 4 [A] because *he was* **afraid**[s] that harm might come to him.
42: 7 [A] *he* **asked**. "From the land of Canaan," they replied, "to buy
42: 7 [A] "From the land of Canaan," *they* **replied**, "to buy food."
42: 9 [A] he remembered his dreams about them and **said** to them,
42:10 [A] "No, my lord," *they* **answered**. "Your servants have come to
42:12 [A] "No!" *he* **said** to them. "You have come to see where our
42:13 [A] *they* **replied**, "Your servants were twelve brothers, the sons
42:14 [A] Joseph **said** to them, "It is just as I told you: You are spies!
42:14 [A] said to them, "It is just as I told you: **[NIE]** You are spies!
42:18 [A] Joseph **said** to them, "Do this and you will live, for I fear
42:21 [A] *They* **said** to one another, "Surely we are being punished
42:22 [A] **[NIE]** "Didn't I tell you not to sin against the boy?
42:22 [A] Reuben replied, "Didn't *I* **tell** you not to sin against the boy?
42:22 [A] "Didn't I tell you **[NIE]** not to sin against the boy?
42:28 [A] "My silver has been returned," *he* **said** to his brothers. "Here
42:28 [A] hearts sank and they turned to each other trembling and **said**,
42:29 [A] they told him all that had happened to them. *They* **said**,
42:31 [A] But *we* **said** to him, 'We are honest men; we are not spies.
42:33 [A] "Then the man who is lord over the land **said** to us, 'This is
42:36 [A] Their father Jacob **said** to them, "You have deprived me of
42:37 [A] Reuben **said** to his father, "You may put both of my sons to
42:37 [A] **[RPH]** "You may put both of my sons to death if I do not
42:38 [A] But Jacob **said**, "My son will not go down there with you;
43: 2 [A] their father **said** to them, "Go back and buy us a little more
43: 3 [A] Judah **said** to him, "The man warned us solemnly, 'You will
43: 3 [A] Judah said to him, **[RPH]** "The man warned us solemnly,
43: 3 [A] **[NIE]** 'You will not see my face again unless your brother is
43: 5 [A] send him, we will not go down, because the man **said** to us,
43: 6 [A] Israel **asked**, "Why did you bring this trouble on me by
43: 7 [A] *They* **replied**, "The man questioned us closely about
43: 7 [A] and our family. 'Is your father still living?' *he* **asked** us.
43: 7 [A] How were we to know *he would* **say**, 'Bring your brother
43: 8 [A] Judah **said** to Israel his father, "Send the boy along with me
43:11 [A] their father Israel **said** to them, "If it must be, then do this:
43:16 [A] *he* **said** to the steward of his house, "Take these men to my
43:17 [A] The man did as Joseph **told** him and took the men to
43:18 [A] *They* **thought**, "We were brought here because of the silver
43:20 [A] "Please, sir," *they* **said**, "we came down here the first time to
43:23 [A] "It's all right," *he* **said**. "Don't be afraid. Your God, the God
43:27 [A] He asked them how they were, and then *he* **said**, "How is
43:27 [A] then he said, "How is your aged father *you* **told** me *about*?
43:28 [A] *They* **replied**, "Your servant our father is still alive
43:29 [A] his own mother's son, *he* **asked**, "Is this your youngest
43:29 [A] "Is this your youngest brother, the one *you* **told** me *about*?"
43:29 [A] me about?" And *he* **said**, "God be gracious to you, my son."
43:31 [A] he came out and, controlling himself, **said**, "Serve the food."
44: 1 [A] **[NIE]** "Fill the men's sacks with as much food as they can
44: 4 [A] They had not gone far from the city when Joseph **said** to his
44: 4 [A] men at once, and when you catch up with them, **say** to them,
44: 7 [A] But *they* **said** to him, "Why does my lord say such things?
44:10 [A] "Very well, then," *he* **said**, "let it be as you say. Whoever is
44:15 [A] Joseph **said** to them, "What is this you have done? Don't you
44:16 [A] "What *can we* **say** to my lord?" Judah replied. "What can we
44:16 [A] can we say to my lord?" Judah **replied**. "What can we say?
44:17 [A] Joseph **said**, "Far be it from me to do such a thing!
44:18 [A] Judah went up to him and **said**: "Please, my lord, let your
44:19 [A] his servants, **[NIE]** 'Do you have a father or a brother?'
44:20 [A] *we* **answered**, 'We have an aged father, and there is a young
44:21 [A] "Then *you* **said** to your servants, 'Bring him down to me so I
44:22 [A] And *we* **said** to my lord, 'The boy cannot leave his father;
44:23 [A] *you* **told** your servants, 'Unless your youngest brother comes
44:25 [A] "Then our father **said**, 'Go back and buy a little more food.'
44:26 [A] *we* **said**, 'We cannot go down. Only if our youngest brother is
44:27 [A] "Your servant my father **said** to us, 'You know that my wife
44:28 [A] One of them went away from me, and *I* **said**, "He has surely
44:32 [A] I **said**, 'If I do not bring him back to you, I will bear the
45: 3 [A] Joseph **said** to his brothers, "I am Joseph! Is my father still
45: 4 [A] Joseph **said** to his brothers, "Come close to me." When they
45: 4 [A] When they had done so, *he* **said**, "I am your brother Joseph,
45: 9 [A] Now hurry back to my father and **say** to him, 'This is what
45: 9 [A] my father and say to him, 'This is what your son Joseph **says**:
45:16 [A] When the news reached Pharaoh's palace that **[NIE]**
45:17 [A] Pharaoh **said** to Joseph, "Tell your brothers, 'Do this:
45:17 [A] Pharaoh said to Joseph, "**Tell** your brothers, 'Do this:
45:24 [A] as they were leaving *he* **said** to them, "Don't quarrel on the
45:26 [A] They told him, **[NIE]** "Joseph is still alive! In fact, he is
45:28 [A] And Israel **said**, "I'm convinced! My son Joseph is still alive.
46: 2 [A] And God **spoke** to Israel in a vision at night and said, "Jacob!
46: 2 [A] And God spoke to Israel in a vision at night and **said**, "Jacob!
46: 2 [A] at night and said, "Jacob! Jacob!" "Here I am," *he* **replied**.
46: 3 [A] "I am God, the God of your father," *he* **said**. "Do not be
46:30 [A] Israel **said** to Joseph, "Now I am ready to die, since I have
46:31 [A] Joseph **said** to his brothers and to his father's household,
46:31 [A] "I will go up and speak to Pharaoh and *will* **say** to him,
46:33 [A] When Pharaoh calls you in and **asks**, 'What is your
46:34 [A] *you should* **answer**, 'Your servants have tended livestock
47: 1 [A] **[NIE]** "My father and brothers, with their flocks and herds
47: 3 [A] Pharaoh **asked** the brothers, "What is your occupation?"
47: 3 [A] *they* **replied** to Pharaoh, "just as our fathers were."
47: 4 [A] *They* also **said** to him, "We have come to live here awhile,
47: 5 [A] Pharaoh **said** to Joseph, "Your father and your brothers have
47: 5 [A] **[RPH]** "Your father and your brothers have come to you,
47: 8 [A] Pharaoh **asked** him, "How old are you?"
47: 9 [A] Jacob **said** to Pharaoh, "The years of my pilgrimage are a
47:15 [A] was gone, all Egypt came to Joseph and **said**, "Give us food.
47:16 [A] "Then bring your livestock," **said** Joseph. "I will sell you
47:18 [A] year was over, they came to him the following year and **said**,
47:23 [A] Joseph **said** to the people, "Now that I have bought you
47:25 [A] "You have saved our lives," *they* **said**. "May we find favor
47:29 [A] he called for his son Joseph and **said** to him, "If I have found
47:30 [A] me where they are buried." "I will do as you say," *he* **said**.
47:31 [A] "Swear to me," *he* **said**. Then Joseph swore to him,
48: 1 [A] Some time later Joseph *was* **told**, "Your father is ill." So he
48: 2 [A] Jacob was told, **[NIE]** "Your son Joseph has come to you,"
48: 3 [A] Jacob **said** to Joseph, "God Almighty appeared to me at Luz
48: 4 [A] **said** to me, 'I am going to make you fruitful and will increase
48: 8 [A] Israel saw the sons of Joseph, *he* **asked**, "Who are these?"
48: 9 [A] the sons God has given me here," Joseph **said** to his father.
48: 9 [A] Then Israel **said**, "Bring them to me so I may bless them."
48:11 [A] Israel **said** to Joseph, "I never expected to see your face
48:15 [A] he blessed Joseph and **said**, "May the God before whom my
48:18 [A] Joseph **said** to him, "No, my father, this one is the firstborn;
48:19 [A] But his father refused and **said**, "I know, my son, I know.
48:20 [A] He blessed them that day and **said**, "In your name will Israel
48:20 [A] **[NIE]** 'May God make you like Ephraim and Manasseh.' "
48:21 [A] Israel **said** to Joseph, "I am about to die, but God will be with
49: 1 [A] Jacob called for his sons and **said**: "Gather around so I can
49:29 [A] **[NIE]** "I am about to be gathered to my people.
50: 4 [A] **[NIE]** "If I have found favor in your eyes, speak to Pharaoh
50: 4 [A] found favor in your eyes, speak to Pharaoh for me. **Tell** him,

Ge 50: 5 [A] 'My father made me swear an oath and **said**, "I am about to
50: 6 [A] Pharaoh **said**, "Go up and bury your father, as he made you
50: 11 [A] *they* **said**, "The Egyptians are holding a solemn ceremony of
50: 15 [A] *they* **said**, "What if Joseph holds a grudge against us
50: 16 [A] So they sent word to Joseph, **saying**, "Your father left these
50: 16 [A] "Your father left these instructions before he died: **[NIE]**
50: 17 [A] 'This is what *you are to* **say** to Joseph: I ask you to forgive
50: 18 [A] down before him. "We are your slaves," *they* **said**.
50: 19 [A] Joseph **said** to them, "Don't be afraid. Am I in the place of
50: 24 [A] Joseph **said** to his brothers, "I am about to die. But God will
50: 25 [A] And Joseph made the sons of Israel swear an oath and **said**,
Ex 1: 9 [A] "Look," *he* **said** to his people, "the Israelites have become
1: 15 [A] The king of Egypt **said** to the Hebrew midwives,
1: 16 [A] **[RPH]** "When you help the Hebrew women in childbirth
1: 18 [A] the king of Egypt summoned the midwives and **asked** them,
1: 19 [A] The midwives **answered** Pharaoh, "Hebrew women are not
1: 22 [A] **[NIE]** "Every boy that is born you must throw into the Nile,
2: 6 [A] sorry for him. "This is one of the Hebrew babies," *she* **said**.
2: 7 [A] his sister **asked** Pharaoh's daughter, "Shall I go and get one
2: 8 [A] "Yes, go," she **answered**. And the girl went and got the
2: 9 [A] Pharaoh's daughter **said** to her, "Take this baby and nurse
2: 10 [A] She named him Moses, **saying**, "I drew him out of the
2: 13 [A] *He* **asked** the one in the wrong, "Why are you hitting your
2: 14 [A] *The man* **said**, "Who made you ruler and judge over us? Are
2: 14 [A] *Are* you **thinking** *of* killing me as you killed the Egyptian?"
2: 14 [A] Moses was afraid and **thought**, "What I did must have
2: 18 [A] *he* **asked** them, "Why have you returned so early today?"
2: 19 [A] *They* **answered**, "An Egyptian rescued us from the
2: 20 [A] "And where is he?" *he* **asked** his daughters. "Why did you
2: 22 [A] gave birth to a son, and Moses named him Gershom, **saying**,
3: 3 [A] So Moses **thought**, "I will go over and see this strange
3: 4 [A] God called to him from within the bush, **[NIE]** "Moses!
3: 4 [A] the bush, "Moses! Moses!" And Moses **said**, "Here I am."
3: 5 [A] "Do not come any closer," God **said**. "Take off your sandals,
3: 6 [A] *he* **said**, "I am the God of your father, the God of Abraham,
3: 7 [A] The LORD **said**, "I have indeed seen the misery of my
3: 11 [A] Moses **said** to God, "Who am I, that I should go to Pharaoh
3: 12 [A] God **said**, "I will be with you. And this will be the sign to
3: 13 [A] Moses **said** to God, "Suppose I go to the Israelites and say to
3: 13 [A] said to God, "Suppose I go to the Israelites and **say** to them,
3: 13 [A] has sent me to you,' and *they* **ask** me, 'What is his name?'
3: 13 [A] ask me, 'What is his name?' Then what *shall I* **tell** them?"
3: 14 [A] God **said** to Moses, "I AM WHO I AM. This is what you are
3: 14 [A] I AM. **[RPH]** This is what you are to say to the Israelites:
3: 14 [A] WHO I AM. This is what *you are to* **say** to the Israelites:
3: 15 [A] God also **said** to Moses, "Say to the Israelites, 'The LORD,
3: 15 [A] God also said to Moses, "**Say** to the Israelites, 'The LORD,
3: 16 [A] "Go, assemble the elders of Israel and **say** to them,
3: 16 [A] God of Abraham, Isaac and Jacob—appeared to me and **said**:
3: 17 [A] *I have* **promised** to bring you up out of your misery in Egypt
3: 18 [A] and the elders are to go to the king of Egypt and **say** to him,
4: 1 [A] **[NIE]** "What if they do not believe me or listen to me
4: 1 [A] "What if they do not believe me or listen to me and **say**,
4: 2 [A] Then the LORD **said** to him, "What is that in your hand?"
4: 2 [A] to him, "What is that in your hand?" "A staff," *he* **replied**.
4: 3 [A] The LORD **said**, "Throw it on the ground." Moses threw it
4: 4 [A] the LORD **said** to him, "Reach out your hand and take it by
4: 6 [A] Then the LORD **said**, "Put your hand inside your cloak."
4: 7 [A] "Now put it back into your cloak," *he* **said**. So Moses put his
4: 10 [A] Moses **said** to the LORD, "O Lord, I have never been
4: 11 [A] The LORD **said** to him, "Who gave man his mouth? Who
4: 13 [A] But Moses **said**, "O Lord, please send someone else to do it."
4: 14 [A] Then the LORD's anger burned against Moses and *he* **said**,
4: 18 [A] Moses went back to Jethro his father-in-law and **said** to him,
4: 18 [A] them are still alive." Jethro **said**, "Go, and I wish you well."
4: 19 [A] Now the LORD *had* **said** to Moses in Midian, "Go back to
4: 21 [A] The LORD **said** to Moses, "When you return to Egypt,
4: 22 [A] **say** to Pharaoh, 'This is what the LORD says: Israel is my
4: 22 [A] say to Pharaoh, 'This is what the LORD **says**: Israel is my
4: 23 [A] *I* **told** you, "Let my son go, so he may worship me." But you
4: 25 [A] "Surely you are a bridegroom of blood to me," *she* **said**.
4: 26 [A] (At that time *she* **said** "bridegroom of blood," referring to
4: 27 [A] The LORD **said** to Aaron, "Go into the desert to meet
5: 1 [A] Afterward Moses and Aaron went to Pharaoh and **said**,
5: 1 [A] and said, "This is what the LORD, the God of Israel, **says**:
5: 2 [A] Pharaoh **said**, "Who is the LORD, that I should obey him
5: 3 [A] Then *they* **said**, "The God of the Hebrews has met with us.
5: 4 [A] the king of Egypt **said**, "Moses and Aaron, why are you
5: 5 [A] Pharaoh **said**, "Look, the people of the land are now
5: 6 [A] slave drivers and foremen in charge of the people: **[NIE]**
5: 8 [A] are crying out, **[NIE]** 'Let us go and sacrifice to our God.'
5: 10 [A] and the foremen went out and **said** to the people,
5: 10 [A] and said to the people, **[RPH]** "This is what Pharaoh says:
5: 10 [A] went out and said to the people, "This is what Pharaoh **says**:
5: 13 [A] The slave drivers kept pressing them, **saying**,
5: 14 [A] by Pharaoh's slave drivers were beaten and *were* **asked**,
5: 15 [A] **[NIE]** "Why have you treated your servants this way?
5: 16 [A] servants are given no straw, yet we *are* **told**, 'Make bricks!'
5: 17 [A] Pharaoh **said**, "Lazy, that's what you are—lazy! That is why
5: 17 [A] That is why you *keep* **saying**, 'Let us go and sacrifice to the
5: 19 [A] foremen realized they were in trouble *when* they *were* **told**,
5: 21 [A] *they* **said**, "May the LORD look upon you and judge you!
5: 22 [A] Moses returned to the LORD and **said**, "O Lord, why have
6: 1 [A] the LORD **said** to Moses, "Now you will see what I will do
6: 2 [A] God also said to Moses, **[NIE]** "I am the LORD.
6: 6 [A] "Therefore, **say** to the Israelites: 'I am the LORD, and I will
6: 10 [A] Then the LORD said to Moses, **[NIE]**
6: 12 [A] to the LORD, **[NIE]** "If the Israelites will not listen to me,
6: 26 [A] It was this same Aaron and Moses to whom the LORD **said**,
6: 29 [A] he said to him, **[NIE]** "I am the LORD. Tell Pharaoh king
6: 30 [A] Moses **said** to the LORD, "Since I speak with faltering lips,
7: 1 [A] the LORD **said** to Moses, "See, I have made you like God
7: 8 [A] The LORD **said** to Moses and Aaron,
7: 8 [A] The LORD said to Moses and Aaron, **[RPH]**
7: 9 [A] **[NIE]** 'Perform a miracle,' then say to Aaron, 'Take your
7: 9 [A] **say** to Aaron, 'Take your staff and throw it down before
7: 14 [A] the LORD **said** to Moses, "Pharaoh's heart is unyielding;
7: 16 [A] **say** to him, 'The LORD, the God of the Hebrews, has sent
7: 16 [A] the God of the Hebrews, has sent me to **say** to you:
7: 17 [A] This is what the LORD **says**: By this you will know that I
7: 19 [A] The LORD **said** to Moses, "Tell Aaron, 'Take your staff
7: 19 [A] "**Tell** Aaron, 'Take your staff and stretch out your hand over
8: 1 [7:26] [A] the LORD **said** to Moses, "Go to Pharaoh and say
8: 1 [7:26] [A] "Go to Pharaoh and **say** to him, 'This is what the
8: 1 [7:26] [A] and say to him, 'This is what the LORD **says**:
8: 5 [8:1] [A] the LORD **said** to Moses, "Tell Aaron, 'Stretch out
8: 5 [8:1] [A] the LORD said to Moses, "**Tell** Aaron, 'Stretch out
8: 8 [8:4] [A] Pharaoh summoned Moses and Aaron and **said**,
8: 9 [8:5] [A] Moses **said** to Pharaoh, "I leave to you the honor of
8: 10 [8:6] [A] "Tomorrow," Pharaoh **said**. Moses replied, "It will be
8: 10 [8:6] [A] Moses **replied**, "It will be as you say, so that you may
8: 16 [8:12] [A] the LORD **said** to Moses, "Tell Aaron, 'Stretch out
8: 16 [8:12] [A] "**Tell** Aaron, 'Stretch out your staff and strike the dust
8: 19 [8:15] [A] The magicians **said** to Pharaoh, "This is the finger of
8: 20 [8:16] [A] the LORD **said** to Moses, "Get up early in the
8: 20 [8:16] [A] Pharaoh as he goes to the water and **say** to him,
8: 20 [8:16] [A] and say to him, 'This is what the LORD **says**:
8: 25 [8:21] [A] Pharaoh summoned Moses and Aaron and **said**, "Go,
8: 26 [8:22] [A] Moses **said**, "That would not be right. The sacrifices
8: 27 [8:23] [A] to the LORD our God, as *he* **commands** us."
8: 28 [8:24] [A] Pharaoh **said**, "I will let you go to offer sacrifices to
8: 29 [8:25] [A] Moses **answered**, "As soon as I leave you, I will pray
9: 1 [A] the LORD **said** to Moses, "Go to Pharaoh and say to him,
9: 1 [A] 'This is what the LORD, the God of the Hebrews, **says**:
9: 5 [A] The LORD set a time and **said**, "Tomorrow the LORD
9: 8 [A] the LORD **said** to Moses and Aaron, "Take handfuls of soot
9: 13 [A] the LORD **said** to Moses, "Get up early in the morning,
9: 13 [A] confront Pharaoh and **say** to him, 'This is what the LORD,
9: 13 [A] 'This is what the LORD, the God of the Hebrews, **says**:
9: 22 [A] the LORD **said** to Moses, "Stretch out your hand toward the
9: 27 [A] and Aaron. "This time I have sinned," *he* **said** to them.
9: 29 [A] Moses **replied**, "When I have gone out of the city, I will
10: 1 [A] the LORD **said** to Moses, "Go to Pharaoh, for I have
10: 3 [A] So Moses and Aaron went to Pharaoh and **said** to him,
10: 3 [A] "This is what the LORD, the God of the Hebrews, **says**:
10: 7 [A] Pharaoh's officials **said** to him, "How long will this man be a
10: 8 [A] "Go, worship the LORD your God," *he* **said**. "But just who
10: 9 [A] Moses **answered**, "We will go with our young and old, with
10: 10 [A] Pharaoh **said**, "The LORD be with you—if I let you go,
10: 12 [A] the LORD **said** to Moses, "Stretch out your hand over
10: 16 [A] Pharaoh quickly summoned Moses and Aaron and **said**,
10: 21 [A] the LORD **said** to Moses, "Stretch out your hand toward the
10: 24 [A] Pharaoh summoned Moses and **said**, "Go, worship the
10: 25 [A] Moses **said**, "You must allow us to have sacrifices and burnt
10: 28 [A] Pharaoh **said** to Moses, "Get out of my sight! Make sure you
10: 29 [A] "Just as you say," Moses **replied**, "I will never appear before
11: 1 [A] Now the LORD *had* **said** to Moses, "I will bring one more
11: 4 [A] So Moses **said**, "This is what the LORD says:
11: 4 [A] So Moses said, "This is what the LORD **says**:
11: 8 [A] bowing down before me and **saying**, 'Go, you and all the
11: 9 [A] The LORD *had* **said** to Moses, "Pharaoh will refuse to
12: 1 [A] The LORD **said** to Moses and Aaron in Egypt,
12: 1 [A] The LORD said to Moses and Aaron in Egypt, **[RPH]**
12: 3 [A] Tell the whole community of Israel that **[NIE]** on the tenth
12: 21 [A] Moses summoned all the elders of Israel and **said** to them,
12: 26 [A] when your children **ask** you, 'What does this ceremony mean
12: 27 [A] **tell** them, 'It is the Passover sacrifice to the LORD,
12: 31 [A] the night Pharaoh summoned Moses and Aaron and **said**,

Ex 12:33 [A] the country. "For otherwise," *they* **said**, "we will all die!"
12:43 [A] The LORD **said** to Moses and Aaron, "These are the
13: 1 [A] The LORD said to Moses, **[NIE]**
13: 3 [A] Moses **said** to the people, "Commemorate this day, the day
13: 8 [A] **[NIE]** 'I do this because of what the LORD did for me
13:14 [A] when your son asks you, **[NIE]** 'What does this mean?'
13:14 [A] **say** to him, 'With a mighty hand the LORD brought us out
13:17 [A] For God **said**, "If they face war, they might change their
13:19 [A] *He had* **said**, "God will surely come to your aid, and
14: 1 [A] Then the LORD said to Moses, **[NIE]**
14: 3 [A] Pharaoh *will* **think**, 'The Israelites are wandering around the
14: 5 [A] and his officials changed their minds about them and **said**,
14:11 [A] *They* **said** to Moses, "Was it because there were no graves in
14:12 [A] Didn't we say to you in Egypt, **[NIE]** 'Leave us alone; let us
14:13 [A] Moses **answered** the people, "Do not be afraid. Stand firm
14:15 [A] the LORD **said** to Moses, "Why are you crying out to me?
14:25 [A] And the Egyptians **said**, "Let's get away from the Israelites!
14:26 [A] the LORD **said** to Moses, "Stretch out your hand over the
15: 1 [A] **[NIE]** "I will sing to the LORD, for he is highly exalted.
15: 1 [A] **[NIE]** "I will sing to the LORD, for he is highly exalted.
15: 9 [A] "The enemy **boasted**, 'I will pursue, I will overtake them.
15:24 [A] grumbled against Moses, **saying**, "What are we to drink?"
15:26 [A] *He* **said**, "If you listen carefully to the voice of the LORD
16: 3 [A] The Israelites **said** to them, "If only we had died by the
16: 4 [A] the LORD **said** to Moses, "I will rain down bread from
16: 6 [A] So Moses and Aaron **said** to all the Israelites, "In the evening
16: 8 [A] Moses also **said**, "You will know that it was the LORD
16: 9 [A] Moses **told** Aaron, "Say to the entire Israelite community,
16: 9 [A] Moses told Aaron, "**Say** to the entire Israelite community,
16:11 [A] The LORD said to Moses, **[NIE]**
16:12 [A] Tell them, **[NIE]** 'At twilight you will eat meat, and in the
16:15 [A] the Israelites saw it, *they* **said** to each other, "What is it?"
16:15 [A] Moses **said** to them, "It is the bread the LORD has given
16:19 [A] Moses **said** to them, "No one is to keep any of it until
16:23 [A] *He* **said** to them, "This is what the LORD commanded:
16:25 [A] "Eat it today," Moses **said**, "because today is a Sabbath to
16:28 [A] the LORD **said** to Moses, "How long will you refuse to
16:32 [A] Moses **said**, "This is what the LORD has commanded:
16:33 [A] So Moses **said** to Aaron, "Take a jar and put an omer of
17: 2 [A] So they quarreled with Moses and **said**, "Give us water to
17: 2 [A] to drink." Moses **replied**, "Why do you quarrel with me?
17: 3 [A] *They* **said**, "Why did you bring us up out of Egypt to make
17: 4 [A] to the LORD, **[NIE]** "What am I to do with these people?
17: 5 [A] The LORD **answered** Moses, "Walk on ahead of the
17: 7 [A] and because they tested the LORD **saying**,
17: 9 [A] Moses **said** to Joshua, "Choose some of our men and go out
17:10 [A] So Joshua fought the Amalekites as Moses *had* **ordered**, and
17:14 [A] the LORD **said** to Moses, "Write this on a scroll as
17:16 [A] *He* **said**, "For hands were lifted up to the throne of the
18: 3 [A] One son was named Gershom, for Moses **said**, "I have
18: 6 [A] Jethro *had* **sent word** to him, "I, your father-in-law Jethro,
18:10 [A] He **said**, "Praise be to the LORD, who rescued you from the
18:14 [A] *he* **said**, "What is this you are doing for the people?
18:15 [A] Moses **answered** him, "Because the people come to me to
18:17 [A] Moses' father-in-law **replied**, "What you are doing is not
18:24 [A] listened to his father-in-law and did everything *he* **said**.
19: 3 [A] and the LORD called to him from the mountain and **said**,
19: 3 [A] "This is what *you are to* **say** to the house of Jacob and what
19: 8 [A] **[NIE]** "We will do everything the LORD has said."
19: 9 [A] The LORD **said** to Moses, "I am going to come to you in a
19:10 [A] the LORD **said** to Moses, "Go to the people and consecrate
19:12 [A] Put limits for the people around the mountain and **tell** them,
19:15 [A] *he* **said** to the people, "Prepare yourselves for the third day.
19:21 [A] and the LORD **said** to him, "Go down and warn the people
19:23 [A] Moses **said** to the LORD, "The people cannot come up
19:23 [A] **[NIE]** 'Put limits around the mountain and set it apart as
19:24 [A] The LORD **replied**, "Go down and bring Aaron up with
19:25 [A] So Moses went down to the people and **told** them.
20: 1 [A] And God spoke all these words: **[NIE]**
20:19 [A] and **said** to Moses, "Speak to us yourself and we will listen.
20:20 [A] Moses **said** to the people, "Do not be afraid. God has come
20:22 [A] the LORD **said** to Moses, "Tell the Israelites this: 'You have
20:22 [A] the LORD said to Moses, "**Tell** the Israelites this: 'You have
21: 5 [A] "But if the servant **declares** [+606], 'I love my master
21: 5 [A] "But if the servant **declares** [+606], 'I love my master
22: 9 [22:8] [A] any other lost property about which *somebody* **says**,
23:13 [A] "Be careful to do everything *I have* **said** to you. Do not
24: 1 [A] *he* **said** to Moses, "Come up to the LORD, you and Aaron,
24: 3 [A] **[NIE]** "Everything the LORD has said we will do."
24: 7 [A] *They* **responded**, "We will do everything the LORD has
24: 8 [A] then took the blood, sprinkled it on the people and **said**,
24:12 [A] The LORD **said** to Moses, "Come up to me on the
24:14 [A] *He* **said** to the elders, "Wait here for us until we come back
25: 1 [A] The LORD said to Moses, **[NIE]**
30:11 [A] Then the LORD said to Moses, **[NIE]**
30:17 [A] Then the LORD said to Moses, **[NIE]**
30:22 [A] Then the LORD said to Moses, **[NIE]**
30:31 [A] **[NIE]** 'This is to be my sacred anointing oil for the
30:34 [A] the LORD **said** to Moses, "Take fragrant spices—
31: 1 [A] Then the LORD said to Moses, **[NIE]**
31:12 [A] Then the LORD **said** to Moses,
31:12 [A] Then the LORD said to Moses, **[NIE]**
31:13 [A] to the Israelites, **[NIE]** 'You must observe my Sabbaths.
32: 1 [A] they gathered around Aaron and **said**, "Come, make us gods
32: 2 [A] Aaron **answered** them, "Take off the gold earrings that your
32: 4 [A] *they* **said**, "These are your gods, O Israel, who brought you
32: 5 [A] **[NIE]** "Tomorrow there will be a festival to the LORD."
32: 8 [A] have bowed down to it and sacrificed to it and *have* **said**,
32: 9 [A] "I have seen these people," the LORD **said** to Moses,
32:11 [A] "O LORD," *he* **said**, "why should your anger burn against
32:12 [A] Why *should* the Egyptians **say**, 'It was with evil intent that
32:12 [A] **[RPH]** 'It was with evil intent that he brought them out,
32:13 [A] I will give your descendants all this land *I* **promised** them,
32:17 [A] *he* **said** to Moses, "There is the sound of war in the camp."
32:18 [A] Moses **replied**: "It is not the sound of victory, it is not the
32:21 [A] He **said** to Aaron, "What did these people do to you, that you
32:22 [A] "Do not be angry, my lord," Aaron **answered**. "You know
32:23 [A] *They* **said** to me, 'Make us gods who will go before us.
32:24 [A] So *I* **told** them, 'Whoever has any gold jewelry, take it off.'
32:26 [A] So he stood at the entrance to the camp and **said**,
32:27 [A] *he* **said** to them, "This is what the LORD, the God of Israel,
32:27 [A] to them, "This is what the LORD, the God of Israel, **says**:
32:29 [A] Moses **said**, "You have been set apart to the LORD today,
32:30 [A] The next day Moses **said** to the people, "You have
32:31 [A] So Moses went back to the LORD and **said**, "Oh, what a
32:33 [A] The LORD **replied** to Moses, "Whoever has sinned against
33: 1 [A] Isaac and Jacob, **saying**, 'I will give it to your descendants.'
33: 5 [A] For the LORD *had* **said** to Moses, "Tell the Israelites,
33: 5 [A] to Moses, "**Tell** the Israelites, 'You are a stiff-necked people.
33:12 [A] Moses **said** to the LORD, "You have been telling me,
33:12 [A] the LORD, "You *have been* **telling** me, 'Lead these people,'
33:12 [A] You *have* **said**, 'I know you by name and you have found
33:14 [A] The LORD **replied**, "My Presence will go with you, and I
33:15 [A] Moses **said** to him, "If your Presence does not go with us,
33:17 [A] the LORD **said** to Moses, "I will do the very thing you have
33:18 [A] Then Moses **said**, "Now show me your glory."
33:19 [A] the LORD **said**, "I will cause all my goodness to pass in
33:20 [A] But," *he* **said**, "you cannot see my face, for no one may see
33:21 [A] the LORD **said**, "There is a place near me where you may
34: 1 [A] The LORD **said** to Moses, "Chisel out two stone tablets like
34: 9 [A] favor in your eyes," *he* **said**, "then let the Lord go with us.
34:10 [A] Then the LORD **said**: "I am making a covenant with you.
34:27 [A] Then the LORD **said** to Moses, "Write down these words,
35: 1 [A] assembled the whole Israelite community and **said** to them,
35: 4 [A] Moses **said** to the whole Israelite community, "This is what
35: 4 [A] **[RPH]** "This is what the LORD has commanded:
35: 4 [A] "This is what the LORD has commanded: **[NIE]**
35:30 [A] Moses **said** to the Israelites, "See, the LORD has chosen
36: 5 [A] **said** to Moses, "The people are bringing more than enough
36: 5 [A] **[RPH]** "The people are bringing more than enough for
36: 6 [A] **[NIE]** "No man or woman is to make anything else as an
40: 1 [A] Then the LORD said to Moses: **[NIE]**
Lev 1: 1 [A] and spoke to him from the Tent of Meeting. *He* **said**,
1: 2 [A] "Speak to the Israelites and **say** to them: 'When any of you
4: 1 [A] The LORD said to Moses, **[NIE]**
4: 2 [A] **[NIE]** 'When anyone sins unintentionally and does what is
5:14 [A] The LORD said to Moses: **[NIE]**
6: 1 [5:20] [A] The LORD said to Moses: **[NIE]**
6: 8 [6:1] [A] The LORD said to Moses: **[NIE]**
6: 9 [6:2] [A] **[NIE]** 'These are the regulations for the burnt
6:19 [6:12] [A] The LORD also said to Moses, **[NIE]**
6:24 [6:17] [A] The LORD said to Moses, **[NIE]**
6:25 [6:18] [A] **[NIE]** 'These are the regulations for the sin offering:
7:22 [A] The LORD said to Moses, **[NIE]**
7:23 [A] **[NIE]** 'Do not eat any of the fat of cattle, sheep or goats.
7:28 [A] The LORD said to Moses, **[NIE]**
7:29 [A] **[NIE]** 'Anyone who brings a fellowship offering to the
8: 1 [A] The LORD said to Moses, **[NIE]**
8: 5 [A] Moses **said** to the assembly, "This is what the LORD has
8:31 [A] Moses then **said** to Aaron and his sons, "Cook the meat at the
8:31 [A] as I commanded, **saying**, 'Aaron and his sons are to eat it.'
9: 2 [A] *He* **said** to Aaron, "Take a bull calf for your sin offering
9: 3 [A] **[NIE]** 'Take a male goat for a sin offering, a calf and a
9: 6 [A] Moses **said**, "This is what the LORD has commanded you
9: 7 [A] Moses **said** to Aaron, "Come to the altar and sacrifice your
10: 3 [A] Moses then **said** to Aaron, "This is what the LORD spoke
10: 3 [A] to Aaron, "This is what the LORD spoke of when *he* **said**:
10: 4 [A] sons of Aaron's uncle Uzziel, and **said** to them, "Come here;

Lev 10: 6 [A] Then Moses **said** to Aaron and his sons Eleazar and Ithamar,
10: 8 [A] Then the LORD said to Aaron, **[NIE]**
10: 16 [A] and Ithamar, Aaron's remaining sons, and **asked**,
11: 1 [A] The LORD said to Moses and Aaron, **[NIE]**
11: 2 [A] **[NIE]** 'Of all the animals that live on land, these are the
12: 1 [A] The LORD said to Moses, **[NIE]**
12: 2 [A] **[NIE]** 'A woman who becomes pregnant and gives birth to a
13: 1 [A] The LORD said to Moses and Aaron, **[NIE]**
14: 1 [A] The LORD said to Moses, **[NIE]**
14: 33 [A] The LORD said to Moses and Aaron, **[NIE]**
14: 35 [A] **[NIE]** 'I have seen something that looks like mildew in my
15: 1 [A] The LORD said to Moses and Aaron, **[NIE]**
15: 2 [A] "Speak to the Israelites and **say** to them: 'When any man has
16: 2 [A] The LORD **said** to Moses: "Tell your brother Aaron not to
17: 1 [A] The LORD said to Moses, **[NIE]**
17: 2 [A] and his sons and to all the Israelites and **say** to them:
17: 2 [A] to them: 'This is what the LORD has commanded: **[RPH]**
17: 8 [A] "**Say** to them: 'Any Israelite or any alien living among them
17: 12 [A] Therefore *I* **say** to the Israelites, "None of you may eat blood,
17: 14 [A] That is why *I have* **said** to the Israelites, "You must not eat
18: 1 [A] The LORD said to Moses, **[NIE]**
18: 2 [A] "Speak to the Israelites and **say** to them: 'I am the LORD
19: 1 [A] The LORD said to Moses, **[NIE]**
19: 2 [A] "Speak to the entire assembly of Israel and **say** to them:
20: 1 [A] The LORD said to Moses, **[NIE]**
20: 2 [A] "**Say** to the Israelites: 'Any Israelite or any alien living in
20: 24 [A] *I* **said** to you, "You will possess their land; I will give it to
21: 1 [A] The LORD **said** to Moses, "Speak to the priests, the sons of
21: 1 [A] "**Speak** to the priests, the sons of Aaron, and say to them:
21: 1 [A] "Speak to the priests, the sons of Aaron, and **say** to them:
21: 16 [A] The LORD said to Moses, **[NIE]**
21: 17 [A] **[NIE]** 'For the generations to come none of your
22: 1 [A] The LORD said to Moses, **[NIE]**
22: 3 [A] "**Say** to them: 'For the generations to come, if any of your
22: 17 [A] The LORD said to Moses, **[NIE]**
22: 18 [A] and his sons and to all the Israelites and **say** to them:
22: 26 [A] The LORD said to Moses, **[NIE]**
23: 1 [A] The LORD said to Moses, **[NIE]**
23: 2 [A] "Speak to the Israelites and **say** to them: 'These are my
23: 9 [A] The LORD said to Moses, **[NIE]**
23: 10 [A] "Speak to the Israelites and **say** to them: 'When you enter the
23: 23 [A] The LORD said to Moses, **[NIE]**
23: 24 [A] **[NIE]** 'On the first day of the seventh month you are to have
23: 26 [A] The LORD said to Moses, **[NIE]**
23: 33 [A] The LORD said to Moses, **[NIE]**
23: 34 [A] **[NIE]** 'On the fifteenth day of the seventh month the
24: 1 [A] The LORD said to Moses, **[NIE]**
24: 13 [A] Then the LORD said to Moses: **[NIE]**
24: 15 [A] **[NIE]** 'If anyone curses his God, he will be held
25: 1 [A] The LORD said to Moses on Mount Sinai, **[NIE]**
25: 2 [A] "Speak to the Israelites and **say** to them: 'When you enter the
25: 20 [A] *You may* **ask**, "What will we eat in the seventh year if we do
27: 1 [A] The LORD said to Moses, **[NIE]**
27: 2 [A] "Speak to the Israelites and **say** to them: 'If anyone makes a
Nu 1: 1 [A] second year after the Israelites came out of Egypt. *He* **said**:
1: 48 [A] The LORD had said to Moses: **[NIE]**
2: 1 [A] The LORD said to Moses and Aaron: **[NIE]**
3: 5 [A] The LORD said to Moses, **[NIE]**
3: 11 [A] The LORD also said to Moses, **[NIE]**
3: 14 [A] The LORD said to Moses in the Desert of Sinai, **[NIE]**
3: 40 [A] The LORD **said** to Moses, "Count all the firstborn Israelite
3: 44 [A] The LORD also said to Moses, **[NIE]**
4: 1 [A] The LORD said to Moses and Aaron: **[NIE]**
4: 17 [A] The LORD said to Moses and Aaron, **[NIE]**
4: 21 [A] The LORD said to Moses, **[NIE]**
5: 1 [A] The LORD said to Moses, **[NIE]**
5: 5 [A] The LORD said to Moses, **[NIE]**
5: 11 [A] Then the LORD said to Moses, **[NIE]**
5: 12 [A] "Speak to the Israelites and **say** to them: 'If a man's wife
5: 19 [A] the priest shall put the woman under oath and **say** to her,
5: 21 [A] **[NIE]** "may the LORD cause your people to curse
5: 22 [A] " 'Then the woman *is to* **say**, "Amen. So be it."
6: 1 [A] The LORD said to Moses, **[NIE]**
6: 2 [A] "Speak to the Israelites and **say** to them: 'If a man or woman
6: 22 [A] The LORD said to Moses, **[NIE]**
6: 23 [A] his sons, **[NIE]** 'This is how you are to bless the Israelites.
6: 23 [A] 'This is how you are to bless the Israelites. **Say** to them:
7: 4 [A] The LORD **said** to Moses,
7: 4 [A] The LORD said to Moses, **[NIE]**
7: 11 [A] For the LORD *had* **said** to Moses, "Each day one leader is
8: 1 [A] The LORD said to Moses, **[NIE]**
8: 2 [A] "Speak to Aaron and **say** to him, 'When you set up the seven
8: 5 [A] The LORD said to Moses: **[NIE]**
8: 23 [A] The LORD said to Moses, **[NIE]**
9: 1 [A] of the second year after they came out of Egypt. *He* **said**,
9: 7 [A] **said** to Moses, "We have become unclean because of a dead
9: 8 [A] Moses **answered** them, "Wait until I find out what the
9: 9 [A] Then the LORD said to Moses, **[NIE]**
9: 10 [A] **[NIE]** 'When any of you or your descendants are unclean
10: 1 [A] The LORD said to Moses: **[NIE]**
10: 29 [A] Now Moses **said** to Hobab son of Reuel the Midianite,
10: 29 [A] are setting out for the place about which the LORD **said**,
10: 30 [A] *He* **answered**, "No, I will not go; I am going back to my own
10: 31 [A] Moses **said**, "Please do not leave us. You know where we
10: 35 [A] Whenever the ark set out, Moses **said**, "Rise up, O LORD!
10: 36 [A] Whenever it came to rest, *he* **said**, "Return, O LORD,
11: 4 [A] again the Israelites started wailing and **said**, "If only we had
11: 11 [A] He **asked** the LORD, "Why have you brought this trouble
11: 12 [A] Why *do you* **tell** me to carry them in my arms, as a nurse
11: 13 [A] They keep wailing to me, **[NIE]** 'Give us meat to eat!'
11: 16 [A] The LORD **said** to Moses: "Bring me seventy of Israel's
11: 18 [A] "**Tell** the people: 'Consecrate yourselves in preparation for
11: 18 [A] you when you wailed, **[NIE]** "If only we had meat to eat!
11: 20 [A] who is among you, and have wailed before him, **saying**,
11: 21 [A] Moses **said**, "Here I am among six hundred thousand men on
11: 21 [A] and you **say**, 'I will give them meat to eat for a whole month!'
11: 23 [A] The LORD **answered** Moses, "Is the LORD's arm too
11: 27 [A] **[NIE]** "Eldad and Medad are prophesying in the camp."
11: 28 [A] spoke up and **said**, "Moses, my lord, stop them!"
11: 29 [A] Moses **replied**, "Are you jealous for my sake? I wish that all
12: 2 [A] *they* **asked**. "Hasn't he also spoken through us?"
12: 4 [A] At once the LORD **said** to Moses, Aaron and Miriam,
12: 6 [A] *he* **said**, "Listen to my words: "When a prophet of the
12: 11 [A] he **said** to Moses, "Please, my lord, do not hold against us the
12: 13 [A] cried out to the LORD, **[NIE]** "O God, please heal her!"
12: 14 [A] The LORD **replied** to Moses, "If her father had spit in her
13: 1 [A] The LORD said to Moses, **[NIE]**
13: 17 [A] *he* **said**, "Go up through the Negev and on into the hill
13: 27 [A] **[NIE]** "We went into the land to which you sent us, and it
13: 30 [A] Caleb silenced the people before Moses and **said**,
13: 31 [A] the men who had gone up with him **said**, "We can't attack
13: 32 [A] They **said**, "The land we explored devours those living in it.
14: 2 [A] and Aaron, and the whole assembly **said** to them,
14: 4 [A] *they* **said** to each other, "We should choose a leader and go
14: 7 [A] **said** to the entire Israelite assembly, "The land we passed
14: 7 [A] **[RPH]** "The land we passed through and explored is
14: 10 [A] the whole assembly **talked** *about* stoning them. Then the
14: 11 [A] The LORD **said** to Moses, "How long will these people
14: 13 [A] Moses **said** to the LORD, "Then the Egyptians will hear
14: 14 [A] *they will* **tell** the inhabitants of this land *about* it. They have
14: 15 [A] the nations who have heard this report about you *will* **say**,
14: 15 [A] who have heard this report about you will say, **[RPH]**
14: 17 [A] strength be displayed, just as you have declared: **[NIE]**
14: 20 [A] The LORD **replied**, "I have forgiven them, as you asked.
14: 26 [A] The LORD said to Moses and Aaron: **[NIE]**
14: 28 [A] So **tell** them, 'As surely as I live, declares the LORD, I will
14: 31 [A] As for your children that *you* **said** would be taken as plunder,
14: 40 [A] "We have sinned," they **said**. "We will go up to the place the
14: 40 [A] "We will go up to the place the LORD **promised**."
14: 41 [A] Moses **said**, "Why are you disobeying the LORD's
15: 1 [A] The LORD said to Moses, **[NIE]**
15: 2 [A] "Speak to the Israelites and **say** to them: 'After you enter the
15: 17 [A] The LORD said to Moses, **[NIE]**
15: 18 [A] "Speak to the Israelites and **say** to them: 'When you enter the
15: 35 [A] the LORD **said** to Moses, "The man must die. The whole
15: 37 [A] The LORD **said** to Moses,
15: 37 [A] The LORD said to Moses, **[RPH]**
15: 38 [A] "Speak to the Israelites and **say** to them: 'Throughout the
16: 3 [A] as a group to oppose Moses and Aaron and **said** to them,
16: 5 [A] **[NIE]** "In the morning the LORD will show who belongs
16: 8 [A] Moses also **said** to Korah, "Now listen, you Levites!
16: 12 [A] the sons of Eliab. But *they* **said**, "We will not come!
16: 15 [A] Moses became very angry and **said** to the LORD, "Do not
16: 16 [A] Moses **said** to Korah, "You and all your followers are to
16: 20 [A] The LORD said to Moses and Aaron, **[NIE]**
16: 22 [A] But Moses and Aaron fell facedown and **cried out**, "O God,
16: 23 [A] Then the LORD said to Moses, **[NIE]**
16: 24 [A] **[NIE]** 'Move away from the tents of Korah, Dathan
16: 26 [A] **[NIE]** "Move back from the tents of these wicked men!
16: 28 [A] Moses **said**, "This is how you will know that the LORD has
16: 34 [A] At their cries, all the Israelites around them fled, **shouting**,
16: 36 [17:1] [A] The LORD said to Moses, **[NIE]**
16: 37 [17:2] [A] "**Tell** Eleazar son of Aaron, the priest, to take the
16: 41 [17:6] [A] "You have killed the LORD's people," *they* **said**.
16: 44 [17:9] [A] and the LORD said to Moses, **[NIE]**
16: 46 [17:11] [A] Moses **said** to Aaron, "Take your censer and put
17: 1 [17:16] [A] The LORD said to Moses, **[NIE]**
17: 10 [17:25] [A] The LORD **said** to Moses, "Put back Aaron's staff

Nu 17:12 [17:27] [A] The Israelites **said** to Moses, "We will die! We are
17:12 [17:27] [A] The Israelites said to Moses, **[RPH]** "We will die!
18: 1 [A] The LORD **said** to Aaron, "You, your sons and your
18:20 [A] The LORD **said** to Aaron, "You will have no inheritance in
18:24 [A] That is why *I* **said** concerning them: 'They will have no
18:25 [A] The LORD said to Moses, **[NIE]**
18:26 [A] "Speak to the Levites and **say** to them: 'When you receive
18:30 [A] "**Say** to the Levites: 'When you present the best part, it will
19: 1 [A] The LORD said to Moses and Aaron: **[NIE]**
19: 2 [A] **[NIE]** Tell the Israelites to bring you a red heifer without
20: 3 [A] They quarreled with Moses and **said**, "If only we had died
20: 3 [A] **[RPH]** "If only we had died when our brothers fell dead
20: 7 [A] The LORD said to Moses, **[NIE]**
20:10 [A] together in front of the rock and Moses **said** to them,
20:12 [A] the LORD **said** to Moses and Aaron, "Because you did not
20:14 [A] king of Edom, saying: "This is what your brother Israel **says**:
20:18 [A] Edom **answered**: "You may not pass through here; if you try,
20:19 [A] The Israelites **replied**: "We will go along the main road,
20:20 [A] Again *they* **answered**: "You may not pass through."
20:23 [A] the border of Edom, the LORD **said** to Moses and Aaron,
20:23 [A] of Edom, the LORD said to Moses and Aaron, **[RPH]**
21: 2 [A] **[NIE]** "If you will deliver these people into our hands, we
21: 7 [A] The people came to Moses and **said**, "We sinned when we
21: 8 [A] The LORD **said** to Moses, "Make a snake and put it up on a
21:14 [C] That is why the Book of the Wars of the LORD **says**:
21:16 [A] the well where the LORD **said** to Moses,
21:21 [A] Israel sent messengers to **say** to Sihon king of the Amorites:
21:27 [A] That is why the poets **say**: "Come to Heshbon and let it be
21:34 [A] The LORD **said** to Moses, "Do not be afraid of him, for I
22: 4 [A] The Moabites **said** to the elders of Midian, "This horde is
22: 5 [A] was at Pethor, near the River, in his native land. Balak **said**:
22: 8 [A] "Spend the night here," Balaam **said** to them, "and I will
22: 9 [A] God came to Balaam and **asked**, "Who are these men with
22:10 [A] Balaam **said** to God, "Balak son of Zippor, king of Moab,
22:12 [A] God **said** to Balaam, "Do not go with them. You must not
22:13 [A] The next morning Balaam got up and **said** to Balak's princes,
22:14 [A] So the Moabite princes returned to Balak and **said**,
22:16 [A] They came to Balaam and **said**: "This is what Balak son of
22:16 [A] to Balaam and said: "This is what Balak son of Zippor **says**:
22:17 [A] I will reward you handsomely and do whatever *you* **say**.
22:18 [A] Balaam answered **[NIE]** them, "Even if Balak gave me his
22:20 [A] That night God came to Balaam and **said**, "Since these men
22:28 [A] LORD opened the donkey's mouth, and *she* **said** to Balaam,
22:29 [A] Balaam **answered** the donkey, "You have made a fool of me!
22:30 [A] The donkey **said** to Balaam, "Am I not your own donkey,
22:30 [A] Have I been in the habit of doing this to you?" "No," *he* **said**.
22:32 [A] The angel of the LORD **asked** him, "Why have you beaten
22:34 [A] Balaam **said** to the angel of the LORD, "I have sinned. I did
22:35 [A] The angel of the LORD **said** to Balaam, "Go with the men,
22:37 [A] Balak **said** to Balaam, "Did I not send you an urgent
22:38 [A] "Well, I have come to you now," Balaam **replied**. "But can I
23: 1 [A] Balaam **said**, "Build me seven altars here, and prepare seven
23: 3 [A] Balaam **said** to Balak, "Stay here beside your offering while
23: 4 [A] God met with him, and Balaam **said**, "I have prepared seven
23: 5 [A] The LORD put a message in Balaam's mouth and **said**,
23: 7 [A] Balaam **uttered** [+2256+5951] his oracle: "Balak brought me
23:11 [A] Balak **said** to Balaam, "What have you done to me?
23:12 [A] **[NIE]** "Must I not speak what the LORD puts in my
23:13 [A] Balak **said** to him, "Come with me to another place where
23:15 [A] Balaam **said** to Balak, "Stay here beside your offering while
23:16 [A] met with Balaam and put a message in his mouth and **said**,
23:17 [A] of Moab. Balak **asked** him, "What did the LORD say?"
23:18 [A] Then *he* **uttered** [+2256+5951] his oracle: "Arise, Balak,
23:19 [A] *Does* he **speak** and then not act? Does he promise and not
23:23 [C] *It will* now **be said** of Jacob and of Israel, 'See what God has
23:25 [A] Balak **said** to Balaam, "Neither curse them at all nor bless
23:26 [A] **[NIE]** "Did I not tell you I must do whatever the LORD
23:26 [A] "Did I not tell you **[NIE]** I must do whatever the LORD
23:27 [A] Balak **said** to Balaam, "Come, let me take you to another
23:29 [A] Balaam **said**, "Build me seven altars here, and prepare seven
23:30 [A] Balak did as Balaam *had* **said**, and offered a bull and a ram
24: 3 [A] *he* **uttered** [+2256+5951] his oracle: "The oracle of Balaam
24:10 [A] He struck his hands together and **said** to him, "I summoned
24:11 [A] *I* **said** I would reward you handsomely, but the LORD has
24:12 [A] Balaam **answered** Balak, "Did I not tell the messengers you
24:12 [A] "Did I not tell the messengers you sent me, **[NIE]**
24:15 [A] *he* **uttered** [+2256+5951] his oracle: "The oracle of Balaam
24:20 [A] Balaam saw Amalek and **uttered** [+2256+5951] his oracle:
24:21 [A] he saw the Kenites and **uttered** [+2256+5951] his oracle:
24:23 [A] *he* **uttered** [+2256+5951] his oracle: "Ah, who can live
25: 4 [A] The LORD **said** to Moses, "Take all the leaders of these
25: 5 [A] So Moses **said** to Israel's judges, "Each of you must put to
25:10 [A] The LORD said to Moses, **[NIE]**
25:12 [A] Therefore **tell** him I am making my covenant of peace with
25:16 [A] The LORD said to Moses, **[NIE]**
26: 1 [A] After the plague the LORD **said** to Moses and Eleazar son
26: 1 [A] said to Moses and Eleazar son of Aaron, the priest, **[NIE]**
26: 3 [A] Moses and Eleazar the priest spoke with them and **said**,
26:52 [A] The LORD said to Moses, **[NIE]**
26:65 [A] For the LORD *had* **told** those Israelites they would surely
27: 2 [A] the priest, the leaders and the whole assembly, and **said**,
27: 6 [A] and the LORD **said** to him,
27: 6 [A] and the LORD said to him, **[RPH]**
27: 8 [A] to the Israelites, **[NIE]** 'If a man dies and leaves no son,
27:12 [A] the LORD **said** to Moses, "Go up this mountain in the
27:15 [A] Moses said to the LORD, **[NIE]**
27:18 [A] So the LORD **said** to Moses, "Take Joshua son of Nun,
28: 1 [A] The LORD said to Moses, **[NIE]**
28: 2 [A] "Give this command to the Israelites and **say** to them:
28: 3 [A] **Say** to them: 'This is the offering made by fire that you are to
29:40 [30:1] [A] Moses **told** the Israelites all that the LORD
30: 1 [30:2] [A] **[NIE]** "This is what the LORD commands:
31: 1 [A] The LORD said to Moses, **[NIE]**
31: 3 [A] **[NIE]** "Arm some of your men to go to war against the
31:15 [A] "Have you allowed all the women to live?" he **asked** them.
31:21 [A] Eleazar the priest **said** to the soldiers who had gone into
31:25 [A] The LORD **said** to Moses,
31:25 [A] The LORD said to Moses, **[RPH]**
31:49 [A] **said** to him, "Your servants have counted the soldiers under
32: 2 [A] the priest and to the leaders of the community, and **said**,
32: 2 [A] and to the leaders of the community, and said, **[RPH]**
32: 5 [A] If we have found favor in your eyes," *they* **said**, "let this land
32: 6 [A] Moses **said** to the Gadites and Reubenites, "Shall your
32:10 [A] anger was aroused that day and he swore this oath: **[NIE]**
32:16 [A] they came up to him and **said**, "We would like to build pens
32:20 [A] Moses **said** to them, "If you will do this—if you will arm
32:25 [A] The Gadites and Reubenites **said** to Moses, "We your
32:25 [A] **[RPH]** "We your servants will do as our lord commands.
32:29 [A] He **said** to them, "If the Gadites and Reubenites, every man
32:31 [A] **[NIE]** "Your servants will do what the LORD has said.
33:50 [A] across from Jericho the LORD said to Moses, **[NIE]**
33:51 [A] "Speak to the Israelites and **say** to them: 'When you cross the
34: 1 [A] The LORD said to Moses, **[NIE]**
34: 2 [A] "Command the Israelites and **say** to them: 'When you enter
34:13 [A] **[NIE]** "Assign this land by lot as an inheritance.
34:16 [A] The LORD said to Moses, **[NIE]**
35: 1 [A] across from Jericho, the LORD said to Moses, **[NIE]**
35: 9 [A] Then the LORD said to Moses: **[NIE]**
35:10 [A] "Speak to the Israelites and **say** to them: 'When you cross the
36: 2 [A] *They* **said**, "When the LORD commanded my lord to give
36: 5 [A] **[NIE]** "What the tribe of the descendants of Joseph is
36: 6 [A] **[NIE]** They may marry anyone they please as long as they
Dt 1: 5 [A] territory of Moab, Moses began to expound this law, **saying**:
1: 6 [A] **[NIE]** "You have stayed long enough at this mountain.
1: 9 [A] At that time *I* **said** to you, "You are too heavy a burden for
1: 9 [A] **[NIE]** "You are too heavy a burden for me to carry alone.
1:14 [A] answered me, **[NIE]** "What you propose to do is good."
1:16 [A] **[NIE]** Hear the disputes between your brothers and judge
1:20 [A] *I* **said** to you, "You have reached the hill country of the
1:22 [A] all of you came to me and **said**, "Let us send men ahead to
1:25 [A] **[NIE]** "It is a good land that the LORD our God is giving
1:27 [A] You grumbled in your tents and **said**, "The LORD hates us;
1:28 [A] *They* **say**, 'The people are stronger and taller than we are;
1:29 [A] *I* **said** to you, "Do not be terrified; do not be afraid of them.
1:34 [A] what you said, he was angry and solemnly swore: **[NIE]**
1:37 [A] of you the LORD became angry with me also and **said**,
1:39 [A] the little ones that *you* **said** would be taken captive, your
1:41 [A] you replied, **[NIE]** "We have sinned against the LORD.
1:42 [A] the LORD **said** to me, "Tell them, 'Do not go up and fight,
1:42 [A] the LORD said to me, "**Tell** them, 'Do not go up and fight,
2: 2 [A] Then the LORD **said** to me,
2: 2 [A] Then the LORD said to me, **[NIE]**
2: 4 [A] **[NIE]** 'You are about to pass through the territory of your
2: 9 [A] Then the LORD **said** to me, "Do not harass the Moabites
2:17 [A] the LORD said to me, **[NIE]**
2:26 [A] to Sihon king of Heshbon offering peace and **saying**,
2:31 [A] The LORD **said** to me, "See, I have begun to deliver Sihon
3: 2 [A] The LORD **said** to me, "Do not be afraid of him, for I have
3:18 [A] **[NIE]** "The LORD your God has given you this land to
3:21 [A] **[NIE]** "You have seen with your own eyes all that the
3:23 [A] At that time I pleaded with the LORD: **[NIE]**
3:26 [A] would not listen to me. "That is enough," the LORD **said**.
4: 6 [A] to the nations, who will hear about all these decrees and **say**,
4:10 [A] when he **said** to me, "Assemble the people before me to hear
5: 1 [A] Moses summoned all Israel and **said**: Hear, O Israel,
5: 5 [A] of the fire and did not go up the mountain.) And *he* **said**:
5:24 [A] And *you* **said**, "The LORD our God has shown us his glory
5:27 [A] Go near and listen to all that the LORD our God **says**.

Dt 5:28 [A] heard you when you spoke to me and the LORD **said** to me,
5:30 [A] "Go, **tell** them to return to their tents.
6:20 [A] **[NIE]** "What is the meaning of the stipulations, decrees
6:21 [A] **tell** him: "We were slaves of Pharaoh in Egypt,
7:17 [A] *You may* **say** to yourselves, "These nations are stronger than
8:17 [A] *You may* **say** to yourself, "My power and the strength of my
9:4 [A] God has driven them out before you, *do* not **say** to yourself,
9:4 [A] **[RPH]** "The LORD has brought me here to take
9:12 [A] the LORD **told** me, "Go down from here at once,
9:13 [A] the LORD **said** to me, "I have seen this people, and they are
9:13 [A] the LORD said to me, **[RPH]** "I have seen this people,
9:23 [A] *he* **said**, "Go up and take possession of the land I have given
9:25 [A] because the LORD *had* **said** he would destroy you.
9:26 [A] I prayed to the LORD and **said**, "O Sovereign LORD,
9:28 [A] Otherwise, the country from which you brought us *will* **say**,
10:1 [A] At that time the LORD **said** to me, "Chisel out two stone
10:11 [A] "Go," the LORD **said** to me, "and lead the people on their
12:20 [A] you crave meat and **say**, "I would like some meat," then you
12:30 [A] their gods, **saying**, "How do these nations serve their gods?
13:2 [13:3] [A] of which he has spoken takes place, and *he* **says**,
13:6 [13:7] [A] **saying**, "Let us go and worship other gods" (gods
13:12 [13:13] [A] If you hear *it* **said** about one of the towns the
13:13 [13:14] [A] **saying**, "Let us go and worship other gods" (gods
15:9 [A] **[NIE]** "The seventh year, the year for canceling debts,
15:11 [A] Therefore I command you **[NIE]** to be openhanded toward
15:16 [A] But if your servant **says** to you, "I do not want to leave you,"
17:11 [A] to the law they teach you and the decisions *they* **give** you.
17:14 [A] and have taken possession of it and settled in it, and *you* **say**,
17:16 [A] for the LORD *has* **told** you, "You are not to go back that
18:16 [A] God at Horeb on the day of the assembly when you **said**,
18:17 [A] The LORD **said** to me: "What they say is good.
18:21 [A] *You may* **say** to yourselves, "How can we know when a
19:7 [A] This is why I command you **[NIE]** to set aside for
20:3 [A] *He shall* **say**: "Hear, O Israel, today you are going into battle
20:5 [A] **[NIE]** "Has anyone built a new house and not dedicated it?
20:8 [A] officers shall add, **[NIE]** "Is any man afraid or fainthearted?
21:7 [A] **[NIE]** "Our hands did not shed this blood, nor did our eyes
21:20 [A] *They shall* **say** to the elders, "This son of ours is stubborn
22:14 [A] and gives her a bad name, **saying**, "I married this woman,
22:16 [A] The girl's father *will* **say** to the elders, "I gave my daughter
22:17 [A] Now he has slandered her and **said**, 'I did not find your
25:7 [A] she shall go to the elders at the town gate and **say**,
25:8 [A] to him. If he persists *in* **saying**, "I do not want to marry her,"
25:9 [A] take off one of his sandals, spit in his face and **say**,
26:3 [A] **say** to the priest in office at the time, "I declare today to the
26:5 [A] Then you shall declare **[NIE]** before the LORD your God:
26:13 [A] **say** to the LORD your God: "I have removed from my
26:17 [G] *You have* **declared** this day that the LORD is your God
26:18 [G] the LORD *has* **declared** this day that you are his people,
27:1 [A] **[NIE]** "Keep all these commands that I give you today.
27:9 [A] said to all Israel, **[NIE]** "Be silent, O Israel, and listen!
27:11 [A] On the same day Moses commanded the people: **[NIE]**
27:14 [A] The Levites *shall* **recite** [+2256+6699] to all the people of
27:15 [A] Then all the people *shall* **say** [+2256+6699], "Amen!"
27:16 [A] or his mother." Then all the people *shall* **say**, "Amen!"
27:17 [A] boundary stone." Then all the people *shall* **say**, "Amen!"
27:18 [A] astray on the road." Then all the people *shall* **say**, "Amen!"
27:19 [A] or the widow." Then all the people *shall* **say**, "Amen!"
27:20 [A] his father's bed." Then all the people *shall* **say**, "Amen!"
27:21 [A] with any animal." Then all the people *shall* **say**, "Amen!"
27:22 [A] of his mother." Then all the people *shall* **say**, "Amen!"
27:23 [A] his mother-in-law." Then all the people *shall* **say**, "Amen!"
27:24 [A] neighbor secretly." Then all the people *shall* **say**, "Amen!"
27:25 [A] an innocent person." Then all the people *shall* **say**, "Amen!"
27:26 [A] carrying them out." Then all the people *shall* **say**, "Amen!"
28:67 [A] In the morning *you will* **say**, "If only it were evening!"
28:67 [A] in the evening, **[RPH]** "If only it were morning!"—
28:68 [A] to Egypt on a journey *I* **said** you should never make again.
29:2 [29:1] [A] Moses summoned all the Israelites and **said** to them:
29:19 [29:18] [A] on himself and therefore **thinks** [+928+4222],
29:22 [29:21] [A] foreigners **[RPH]** who come from distant lands
29:24 [29:23] [A] All the nations *will* **ask**: "Why has the LORD done
29:25 [29:24] [A] *the* **answer** *will be*: "It is because this people
30:12 [A] It is not up in heaven, so that you *have to* **ask**, "Who will
30:13 [A] Nor is it beyond the sea, so that you *have to* **ask**, "Who will
31:2 [A] **[NIE]** "I am now a hundred and twenty years old and I am
31:2 [A] The LORD *has* **said** to me, 'You shall not cross the Jordan.'
31:7 [A] and **said** to him in the presence of all Israel,
31:10 [A] **[NIE]** "At the end of every seven years, in the year for
31:14 [A] The LORD **said** to Moses, "Now the day of your death is
31:16 [A] the LORD **said** to Moses: "You are going to rest with your
31:17 [A] will come upon them, and on that day *they will* **ask**,
31:23 [A] **[NIE]** "Be strong and courageous, for you will bring the
31:25 [A] who carried the ark of the covenant of the LORD: **[NIE]**
32:7 [A] he will tell you, your elders, and *they will* **explain** to you.
32:20 [A] face from them," *he* **said**, "and see what their end will be;
32:26 [A] *I* **said** I would scatter them and blot out their memory from
32:27 [A] lest the adversary misunderstand and **say**, 'Our hand has
32:37 [A] *He will* **say**: "Now where are their gods, the rock they took
32:40 [A] I lift my hand to heaven and **declare**: As surely as I live
32:46 [A] *he* **said** to them, "Take to heart all the words I have solemnly
32:48 [A] On that same day the LORD told Moses, **[NIE]**
33:2 [A] *He* **said**: "The LORD came from Sinai and dawned over
33:7 [A] this *he* **said** about Judah: "Hear, O LORD, the cry of Judah;
33:8 [A] About Levi *he* **said**: "Your Thummim and Urim belong to
33:9 [A] He **said** of his father and mother, 'I have no regard for them.'
33:12 [A] About Benjamin *he* **said**: "Let the beloved of the LORD
33:13 [A] About Joseph *he* **said**: "May the LORD bless his land with
33:18 [A] About Zebulun *he* **said**: "Rejoice, Zebulun, in your going
33:20 [A] About Gad *he* **said**: "Blessed is he who enlarges Gad's
33:22 [A] About Dan *he* **said**: "Dan is a lion's cub, springing out of
33:23 [A] About Naphtali *he* **said**: "Naphtali is abounding with the
33:24 [A] About Asher *he* **said**: "Most blessed of sons is Asher; let him
33:27 [A] will drive out your enemy before you, **saying**, 'Destroy him!'
34:4 [A] the LORD **said** to him, "This is the land I promised on oath
34:4 [A] Isaac and Jacob *when* I **said**, 'I will give it to your
Jos 1:1 [A] the LORD **said** to Joshua son of Nun, Moses' aide:
1:1 [A] the LORD said to Joshua son of Nun, Moses' aide: **[NIE]**
1:10 [A] So Joshua ordered the officers of the people: **[NIE]**
1:11 [A] and tell the people, **[NIE]** 'Get your supplies ready.
1:12 [A] the Gadites and the half-tribe of Manasseh, Joshua **said**,
1:12 [A] and the half-tribe of Manasseh, Joshua said, **[RPH]**
1:13 [A] **[NIE]** 'The LORD your God is giving you rest and has
1:16 [A] **[NIE]** "Whatever you have commanded us we will do,
2:1 [A] "Go, look over the land," he **said**, "especially Jericho."
2:2 [C] The king of Jericho **was told**, "Look! Some of the Israelites
2:2 [A] The king of Jericho was told, **[RPH]** "Look! Some of the
2:3 [A] **[NIE]** "Bring out the men who came to you and entered
2:4 [A] *She* **said**, "Yes, the men came to me, but I did not know
2:9 [A] **said** to them, "I know that the LORD has given this land to
2:14 [A] "Our lives for your lives!" the men **assured** her. "If you
2:16 [A] Now *she had* **said** to them, "Go to the hills so the pursuers
2:17 [A] The men **said** to her, "This oath you made us swear will not
2:21 [A] "Agreed," *she* **replied**. "Let it be as you say." So she sent
2:24 [A] *They* **said** to Joshua, "The LORD has surely given the
3:3 [A] **[NIE]** "When you see the ark of the covenant of the LORD
3:5 [A] Joshua **told** the people, "Consecrate yourselves,
3:6 [A] Joshua **said** to the priests, "Take up the ark of the covenant
3:6 [A] **[RPH]** "Take up the ark of the covenant and pass on ahead
3:7 [A] the LORD **said** to Joshua, "Today I will begin to exalt you
3:8 [A] **[NIE]** 'When you reach the edge of the Jordan's waters, go
3:9 [A] Joshua **said** to the Israelites, "Come here and listen to the
3:10 [A] **[RPH]** This is how you will know that the living God is
4:1 [A] had finished crossing the Jordan, the LORD **said** to Joshua,
4:1 [A] crossing the Jordan, the LORD said to Joshua, **[NIE]**
4:3 [A] tell them **[NIE]** to take up twelve stones from the middle of
4:5 [A] **said** to them, "Go over before the ark of the LORD your
4:6 [A] your children ask you, **[NIE]** 'What do these stones mean?'
4:7 [A] **tell** them that the flow of the Jordan was cut off before the
4:15 [A] Then the LORD **said** to Joshua,
4:15 [A] Then the LORD said to Joshua, **[RPH]**
4:17 [A] commanded the priests, **[NIE]** "Come up out of the Jordan."
4:21 [A] *He* **said** to the Israelites, "In the future when your
4:21 [A] **[RPH]** "In the future when your descendants ask their
4:21 [A] ask their fathers, **[NIE]** 'What do these stones mean?'
4:22 [A] tell them, **[NIE]** 'Israel crossed the Jordan on dry ground.'
5:2 [A] At that time the LORD **said** to Joshua, "Make flint knives
5:9 [A] the LORD **said** to Joshua, "Today I have rolled away the
5:13 [A] Joshua went up to him and **asked**, "Are you for us or for our
5:14 [A] "Neither," *he* **replied**, "but as commander of the army of the
5:14 [A] **asked** him, "What message does my Lord have for his
5:15 [A] The commander of the LORD's army **replied**, "Take off
6:2 [A] the LORD **said** to Joshua, "See, I have delivered Jericho
6:6 [A] So Joshua son of Nun called the priests and **said** to them,
6:7 [A] *he* **ordered** the people, "Advance! March around the city,
6:8 [A] When Joshua *had* **spoken** to the people, the seven priests
6:10 [A] **[NIE]** "Do not give a war cry, do not raise your voices,
6:10 [A] do not say a word until the day I **tell** you to shout.
6:16 [A] the trumpet blast, Joshua **commanded** the people, "Shout!
6:22 [A] Joshua **said** to the two men who had spied out the land,
6:26 [A] **[NIE]** "Cursed before the LORD is the man who
7:2 [A] of Bethel, and **told** them, "Go up and spy out the region."
7:2 [A] and told them, **[RPH]** "Go up and spy out the region."
7:3 [A] When they returned to Joshua, *they* **said**, "Not all the people
7:7 [A] Joshua **said**, "Ah, Sovereign LORD, why did you ever
7:8 [A] O Lord, what *can I* **say**, now that Israel has been routed by
7:10 [A] The LORD **said** to Joshua, "Stand up! What are you doing
7:13 [A] **Tell** them, 'Consecrate yourselves in preparation for

Jos 7: 13 [A] for this is what the LORD, the God of Israel, **says**:
7: 19 [A] Joshua **said** to Achan, "My son, give glory to the LORD,
7: 20 [A] Achan replied, **[NIE]** "It is true! I have sinned against the
7: 25 [A] Joshua **said**, "Why have you brought this trouble on us?
8: 1 [A] the LORD **said** to Joshua, "Do not be afraid; do not be
8: 4 [A] with these orders: **[NIE]** "Listen carefully. You are to set an
8: 6 [A] for *they will* **say**, 'They are running away from us as they did
8: 18 [A] the LORD **said** to Joshua, "Hold out toward Ai the javelin
9: 6 [A] in the camp at Gilgal and **said** to him and the men of Israel,
9: 7 [A] The men of Israel **said** to the Hivites, "But perhaps you live
9: 8 [A] "We are your servants," *they* **said** to Joshua. But Joshua
9: 8 [A] Joshua **asked**, "Who are you and where do you come from?"
9: 9 [A] *They* **answered**: "Your servants have come from a very
9: 11 [A] And our elders and all those living in our country **said** to us,
9: 11 [A] said to us, **[RPH]** 'Take provisions for your journey;
9: 11 [A] go and meet them and **say** to them, "We are your servants;
9: 19 [A] all the leaders **answered**, "We have given them our oath by
9: 21 [A] They **continued**, "Let them live, but let them be woodcutters
9: 22 [A] and said, **[NIE]** "Why did you deceive us by saying,
9: 22 [A] the Gibeonites and said, "Why did you deceive us by **saying**,
9: 24 [A] **[NIE]** "Your servants were clearly told how the LORD
10: 4 [10:3] [A] "Come up and help me attack Gibeon," he **said**,
10: 6 [A] then sent **word** to Joshua in the camp at Gilgal:
10: 8 [A] The LORD **said** to Joshua, "Do not be afraid of them; I
10: 12 [A] Joshua said to the LORD **[NIE]** in the presence of Israel:
10: 17 [A] When Joshua was told **[NIE]** that the five kings had been
10: 18 [A] he **said**, "Roll large rocks up to the mouth of the cave,
10: 22 [A] Joshua **said**, "Open the mouth of the cave and bring those
10: 24 [A] and **said** to the army commanders who had come with him,
10: 25 [A] Joshua **said** to them, "Do not be afraid; do not be
11: 6 [A] The LORD **said** to Joshua, "Do not be afraid of them,
11: 9 [A] Joshua did to them as the LORD *had* **directed**: He
13: 1 [A] in years, the LORD **said** to him, "You are very old,
14: 6 [A] and Caleb son of Jephunneh the Kenizzite **said** to him,
14: 9 [A] **[NIE]** 'The land on which your feet have walked will be
15: 16 [A] Caleb **said**, "I will give my daughter Acsah in marriage to
15: 18 [A] off her donkey, Caleb **asked** her, "What can I do for you?"
15: 19 [A] *She* **replied**, "Do me a special favor. Since you have given
17: 4 [A] the priest, Joshua son of Nun, and the leaders and **said**,
17: 14 [A] **[NIE]** "Why have you given us only one allotment and one
17: 15 [A] "If you are so numerous," Joshua **answered**, "and if the hill
17: 16 [A] The people of Joseph **replied**, "The hill country is not
17: 17 [A] Joshua **said** to the house of Joseph—to Ephraim
17: 17 [A] **[RPH]** "You are numerous and very powerful.
18: 3 [A] So Joshua **said** to the Israelites: "How long will you wait
18: 8 [A] **[NIE]** "Go and make a survey of the land and write a
20: 1 [A] Then the LORD said to Joshua: **[NIE]**
20: 2 [A] "Tell the Israelites **[NIE]** to designate the cities of refuge,
21: 2 [A] **[NIE]** "The LORD commanded through Moses that you
22: 2 [A] **said** to them, "You have done all that Moses the servant of
22: 8 [A] **saying**, "Return to your homes with your great wealth—with
22: 8 [A] **[RPH]** "Return to your homes with your great wealth—
22: 11 [A] when the Israelites heard **[NIE]** that they had built the altar
22: 15 [A] and the half-tribe of Manasseh—they said to them: **[NIE]**
22: 16 [A] "The whole assembly of the LORD **says**: 'How could you
22: 24 [A] We did it for fear **[NIE]** that some day your descendants
22: 24 [A] We did it for fear that some day your descendants *might* **say**
22: 24 [A] **[RPH]** 'What do you have to do with the LORD, the God
22: 26 [A] "That is why *we* **said**, 'Let us get ready and build an altar—
22: 27 [A] in the future your descendants *will* not *be able to* **say** to ours,
22: 28 [A] "And *we* **said**, 'If they ever say this to us, or to our
22: 28 [A] "And we said, 'If *they* ever **say** this to us, or to our
22: 28 [A] ever say this to us, or to our descendants, *we will* **answer**:
22: 31 [A] of Eleazar, the priest, **said** to Reuben, Gad and Manasseh,
22: 33 [A] *they* **talked** no more *about* going to war against them to
23: 2 [A] their elders, leaders, judges and officials—and **said** to them:
24: 2 [A] Joshua **said** to all the people, "This is what the LORD,
24: 2 [A] "This is what the LORD, the God of Israel, **says**:
24: 16 [A] **[NIE]** "Far be it from us to forsake the LORD to serve
24: 19 [A] Joshua **said** to the people, "You are not able to serve the
24: 21 [A] the people **said** to Joshua, "No! We will serve the LORD."
24: 22 [A] Joshua **said**, "You are witnesses against yourselves that you
24: 22 [A] to serve the LORD." "Yes, we are witnesses," *they* **replied**.
24: 24 [A] the people **said** to Joshua, "We will serve the LORD our
24: 27 [A] "See!" he **said** to all the people. "This stone will be a witness
Jdg 1: 1 [A] **[NIE]** "Who will be the first to go up and fight for us
1: 2 [A] The LORD **answered**, "Judah is to go; I have given the
1: 3 [A] Then the men of Judah **said** to the Simeonites their brothers,
1: 7 [A] Then Adoni-Bezek **said**, "Seventy kings with their thumbs
1: 12 [A] Caleb **said**, "I will give my daughter Acsah in marriage to
1: 14 [A] off her donkey, Caleb **asked** her, "What can I do for you?"
1: 15 [A] *She* **replied**, "Do me a special favor. Since you have given
1: 24 [A] spies saw a man coming out of the city and *they* **said** to him,
2: 1 [A] angel of the LORD went up from Gilgal to Bokim and **said**,
2: 1 [A] *I* **said**, 'I will never break my covenant with you,
2: 3 [A] therefore *I* **tell** you that I will not drive them out before you;
2: 20 [A] Therefore the LORD was very angry with Israel and **said**,
3: 19 [A] At the idols near Gilgal he himself turned back and **said**,
3: 19 [A] a secret message for you, O king." The king **said**, "Quiet!"
3: 20 [A] alone in the upper room of his summer palace and **said**,
3: 24 [A] *They* **said**, "He must be relieving himself in the inner room
3: 28 [A] "Follow me," *he* **ordered**, "for the LORD has given Moab,
4: 6 [A] son of Abinoam from Kedesh in Naphtali and **said** to him,
4: 8 [A] Barak **said** to her, "If you go with me, I will go; but if you
4: 9 [A] "Very well," Deborah **said**, "I will go with you. But because
4: 14 [A] Deborah **said** to Barak, "Go! This is the day the LORD has
4: 18 [A] Jael went out to meet Sisera and **said** to him, "Come,
4: 19 [A] "I'm thirsty," *he* **said**. "Please give me some water." She
4: 20 [A] "Stand in the doorway of the tent," *he* **told** her. "If someone
4: 20 [A] "If someone comes by and asks you, **[NIE]** 'Is anyone here?'
4: 20 [A] comes by and asks you, 'Is anyone here?' **say** 'No.' "
4: 22 [A] "Come," *she* **said**, "I will show you the man you're looking
5: 1 [A] and Barak son of Abinoam sang this song: **[NIE]**
5: 23 [A] 'Curse Meroz,' **said** the angel of the LORD. 'Curse its
6: 8 [A] he sent them a prophet, *who* **said**, "This is what the LORD,
6: 8 [A] who said, "This is what the LORD, the God of Israel, **says**:
6: 10 [A] *I* **said** to you, 'I am the LORD your God; do not worship the
6: 12 [A] *he* **said**, "The LORD is with you, mighty warrior."
6: 13 [A] "But sir," Gideon **replied**, "if the LORD is with us, why has
6: 13 [A] all his wonders that our fathers told us about when they **said**,
6: 14 [A] The LORD turned to him and **said**, "Go in the strength you
6: 15 [A] "But Lord," Gideon **asked**, "how can I save Israel? My clan
6: 16 [A] The LORD **answered**, "I will be with you, and you will
6: 17 [A] Gideon **replied**, "If now I have found favor in your eyes,
6: 18 [A] And the LORD **said**, "I will wait until you return."
6: 20 [A] The angel of God **said** to him, "Take the meat and the
6: 22 [A] angel of the LORD, he **exclaimed**, "Ah, Sovereign LORD!
6: 23 [A] the LORD **said** to him, "Peace! Do not be afraid. You are
6: 25 [A] That same night the LORD **said** to him, "Take the second
6: 29 [A] *They* **asked** each other, "Who did this?" When they carefully
6: 29 [A] *they were* **told**, "Gideon son of Joash did it."
6: 30 [A] The men of the town **demanded** of Joash, "Bring out your
6: 31 [A] Joash **replied** to the hostile crowd around him, "Are you
6: 32 [A] **saying**, "Let Baal contend with him," because he broke down
6: 36 [A] Gideon **said** to God, "If you will save Israel by my hand as
6: 39 [A] Gideon **said** to God, "Do not be angry with me. Let me make
7: 2 [A] The LORD **said** to Gideon, "You have too many men for
7: 2 [A] In order that Israel may not boast against me **[NIE]** that her
7: 3 [A] **[NIE]** 'Anyone who trembles with fear may turn back
7: 4 [A] the LORD **said** to Gideon, "There are still too many men.
7: 4 [A] If *I* **say**, 'This one shall go with you,' he shall go; but if I say,
7: 4 [A] but if *I* **say**, 'This one shall not go with you,' he shall not go."
7: 5 [A] There the LORD **told** him, "Separate those who lap the
7: 7 [A] The LORD **said** to Gideon, "With the three hundred men
7: 9 [A] During that night the LORD **said** to Gideon, "Get up,
7: 13 [A] telling a friend his dream. "I had a dream," *he was* **saying**.
7: 14 [A] **[NIE]** "This can be nothing other than the sword of Gideon
7: 15 [A] He returned to the camp of Israel and **called out**, "Get up!
7: 17 [A] "Watch me," *he* **told** them. "Follow my lead. When I get to
7: 18 [A] from all around the camp blow yours and **shout**, 'For the
7: 24 [A] **saying**, "Come down against the Midianites and seize the
8: 1 [A] Now the Ephraimites **asked** Gideon, "Why have you treated
8: 2 [A] *he* **answered** them, "What have I accomplished compared to
8: 5 [A] *He* **said** to the men of Succoth, "Give my troops some bread;
8: 6 [A] the officials of Succoth **said**, "Do you already have the hands
8: 7 [A] Gideon **replied**, "Just for that, when the LORD has given
8: 9 [A] So *he* **said** to the men of Peniel, "When I return in triumph,
8: 9 [A] **[RPH]** "When I return in triumph, I will tear down this
8: 15 [A] Gideon came and **said** to the men of Succoth, "Here are
8: 15 [A] and Zalmunna, about whom you taunted me by **saying**,
8: 18 [A] *he* **asked** Zebah and Zalmunna, "What kind of men did you
8: 18 [A] "Men like you," *they* **answered**, "each one with the bearing
8: 19 [A] Gideon **replied**, "Those were my brothers, the sons of my
8: 20 [A] Turning to Jether, his oldest son, *he* **said**, "Kill them!"
8: 21 [A] Zebah and Zalmunna **said**, "Come, do it yourself. 'As is the
8: 22 [A] The Israelites **said** to Gideon, "Rule over us—you, your son
8: 23 [A] Gideon **told** them, "I will not rule over you, nor will my son
8: 24 [A] he **said**, "I do have one request, that each of you give me an
8: 25 [A] *They* **answered**, "We'll be glad to give them." So they
9: 1 [A] and said to them and to all his mother's clan, **[NIE]**
9: 3 [A] to follow Abimelech, for *they* **said**, "He is our brother."
9: 7 [A] up on the top of Mount Gerizim and shouted **[NIE]** to them,
9: 8 [A] for themselves. *They* **said** to the olive tree, 'Be our king.'
9: 9 [A] "But the olive tree **answered**, 'Should I give up my oil,
9: 10 [A] "Next, the trees **said** to the fig tree, 'Come and be our king.'
9: 11 [A] "But the fig tree **replied**, 'Should I give up my fruit, so good
9: 12 [A] "Then the trees **said** to the vine, 'Come and be our king.'
9: 13 [A] "But the vine **answered**, 'Should I give up my wine,

Jdg 9:14 [A] "Finally all the trees **said** to the thornbush, 'Come and be our
9:15 [A] "The thornbush **said** to the trees, 'If you really want to anoint
9:28 [A] Gaal son of Ebed **said**, "Who is Abimelech, and who is
9:29 [A] *I would* **say** to Abimelech, 'Call out your whole army!' "
9:31 [A] **saying**, "Gaal son of Ebed and his brothers have come to
9:36 [A] When Gaal saw them, *he* **said** to Zebul, "Look, people are
9:36 [A] Zebul **replied**, "You mistake the shadows of the mountains
9:37 [A] **[NIE]** "Look, people are coming down from the center of
9:38 [A] Zebul **said** to him, "Where is your big talk now, you who
9:38 [A] said to him, "Where is your big talk now, *you* who **said**,
9:48 [A] to his shoulders. *He* **ordered** the men with him, "Quick!
9:54 [A] **[NIE]** "Draw your sword and kill me, so that they can't say,
9:54 [A] "Draw your sword and kill me, so that *they* can't **say**,
10:10 [A] **[NIE]** "We have sinned against you, forsaking our God
10:11 [A] The LORD **replied**, "When the Egyptians, the Amorites,
10:15 [A] the Israelites **said** to the LORD, "We have sinned. Do with
10:18 [A] The leaders of the people of Gilead **said** to each other,
11:2 [A] *they* **said**, "because you are the son of another woman."
11:6 [A] "Come," *they* **said**, "be our commander, so we can fight the
11:7 [A] Jephthah **said** to them, "Didn't you hate me and drive me
11:8 [A] The elders of Gilead **said** to him, "Nevertheless, we are
11:9 [A] Jephthah **answered**, "Suppose you take me back to fight the
11:10 [A] The elders of Gilead **replied**, "The LORD is our witness;
11:12 [A] sent messengers to the Ammonite king with the **question**:
11:13 [A] The king of the Ammonites **answered** Jephthah's
11:15 [A] **saying**: "This is what Jephthah says: Israel did not take the
11:15 [A] saying: "This is what Jephthah **says**: Israel did not take the
11:17 [A] **saying**, 'Give us permission to go through your country,'
11:19 [A] who ruled in Heshbon, and **said** to him, 'Let us pass through
11:30 [A] **[NIE]** "If you give the Ammonites into my hands,
11:35 [A] When he saw her, he tore his clothes and **cried**, "Oh!
11:36 [A] "My father," *she* **replied**, "you have given your word to the
11:37 [A] grant me this one request," *she* **said**. "Give me two months to
11:38 [A] "You may go," *he* **said**. And he let her go for two months.
12:1 [A] out their forces, crossed over to Zaphon and **said** to Jephthah,
12:2 [A] Jephthah **answered**, "I and my people were engaged in a
12:4 [A] struck them down because the Ephraimites *had* **said**,
12:5 [A] whenever a survivor of Ephraim **said**, "Let me cross over,"
12:5 [A] "Let me cross over," the men of Gilead **asked** him, "Are you
12:5 [A] asked him, "Are you an Ephraimite?" If *he* **replied**, "No,"
12:6 [A] *they* **said**, "All right, say 'Shibboleth.' " If he said,
12:6 [A] they said, "All right, **say** 'Shibboleth.' " If he said,
12:6 [A] they said, "All right, say 'Shibboleth.' " If *he* **said**,
13:3 [A] The angel of the LORD appeared to her and **said**, "You are
13:6 [A] the woman went to her husband and **told** him, "A man of
13:6 [A] and told him, **[NIE]** "A man of God came to me.
13:7 [A] But *he* **said** to me, 'You will conceive and give birth to a son.
13:8 [A] **[NIE]** "O Lord, I beg you, let the man of God you sent to us
13:10 [A] The woman hurried to tell her husband, **[NIE]** "He's here!
13:11 [A] When he came to the man, *he* **said**, "Are you the one who
13:11 [A] "Are you the one who talked to my wife?" "I am," *he* **said**.
13:12 [A] So Manoah **asked** him, "When your words are fulfilled,
13:13 [A] The angel of the LORD **answered**, "Your wife must do all
13:13 [A] "Your wife must do all that *I have* **told** her.
13:15 [A] Manoah **said** to the angel of the LORD, "We would like
13:16 [A] The angel of the LORD **replied**, "Even though you detain
13:17 [A] Then Manoah **inquired** [+448] **of** the angel of the LORD,
13:18 [A] He **replied**, "Why do you ask my name? It is beyond
13:22 [A] doomed to die!" he **said** to his wife. "We have seen God!"
13:23 [A] But his wife **answered**, "If the LORD had meant to kill us,
14:2 [A] **[NIE]** "I have seen a Philistine woman in Timnah;
14:3 [A] His father and mother **replied**, "Isn't there an acceptable
14:3 [A] Samson **said** to his father, "Get her for me. She's the right
14:12 [A] "Let me tell you a riddle," Samson **said** to them. "If you can
14:13 [A] of clothes." "Tell us your riddle," *they* **said**. "Let's hear it."
14:14 [A] *He* **replied**, "Out of the eater, something to eat; out of the
14:15 [A] On the fourth day, *they* **said** to Samson's wife, "Coax your
14:16 [A] wife threw herself on him, sobbing, **[NIE]** "You hate me!
14:16 [A] even explained it to my father or mother," *he* **replied**,
14:18 [A] Before sunset on the seventh day the men of the town **said** to
14:18 [A] Samson **said** to them, "If you had not plowed with my heifer,
15:1 [A] to visit his wife. *He* **said**, "I'm going to my wife's room."
15:2 [A] "*I was* **so sure** [+606] you thoroughly hated her," he said,
15:2 [A] "*I was* **so sure** [+606] you thoroughly hated her," he said,
15:2 [A] hated her," he **said**, "that I gave her to your friend."
15:3 [A] Samson **said** to them, "This time I have a right to get even
15:6 [A] When the Philistines **asked**, "Who did this?" they were told,
15:6 [A] *they were* **told**, "Samson, the Timnite's son-in-law,
15:7 [A] Samson **said** to them, "Since you've acted like this, I won't
15:10 [A] The men of Judah **asked**, "Why have you come to fight us?"
15:10 [A] *they* **answered**, "to do to him as he did to us."
15:11 [A] down to the cave in the rock of Etam and **said** to Samson,
15:11 [A] *He* **answered**, "I merely did to them what they did to me."
15:12 [A] *They* **said** to him, "We've come to tie you up and hand you
15:12 [A] Samson **said**, "Swear to me that you won't kill me
15:13 [A] "Agreed," *they* **answered**. "We will only tie you up
15:13 [A] **[RPH]** "We will only tie you up and hand you over to them.
15:16 [A] Samson **said**, "With a donkey's jawbone I have made
15:18 [A] **[NIE]** "You have given your servant this great victory.
16:2 [A] The people of Gaza *were* **told**, "Samson is here!" So they
16:2 [A] no move during the night, **saying**, "At dawn we'll kill him."
16:5 [A] The rulers of the Philistines went to her and **said**, "See if you
16:6 [A] So Delilah **said** to Samson, "Tell me the secret of your great
16:7 [A] Samson **answered** her, "If anyone ties me with seven fresh
16:9 [A] *she* **called** to him, "Samson, the Philistines are upon you!"
16:10 [A] Then Delilah **said** to Samson, "You have made a fool of me;
16:11 [A] *He* **said**, "If anyone ties me securely with new ropes that
16:12 [A] with men hidden in the room, *she* **called** to him, "Samson,
16:13 [A] Delilah then **said** to Samson, "Until now, you have been
16:13 [A] *He* **replied**, "If you weave the seven braids of my head into
16:14 [A] Again *she* **called** to him, "Samson, the Philistines are upon
16:15 [A] *she* **said** to him, "How can you say, 'I love you,' when you
16:15 [A] she said to him, "How *can you* **say**, 'I love you,' when you
16:17 [A] "No razor has ever been used on my head," *he* **said**, "because
16:18 [A] the rulers of the Philistines, **[NIE]** "Come back once more;
16:20 [A] *she* **called**, "Samson, the Philistines are upon you!" He
16:20 [A] He awoke from his sleep and **thought**, "I'll go out as before
16:23 [A] a great sacrifice to Dagon their god and to celebrate, **saying**,
16:24 [A] When the people saw him, they praised their god, **saying**,
16:25 [A] While they were in high spirits, *they* **shouted**, "Bring out
16:26 [A] Samson **said** to the servant who held his hand, "Put me
16:28 [A] to the LORD, **[NIE]** "O Sovereign LORD, remember me.
16:30 [A] Samson **said**, "Let me die with the Philistines!" Then he
17:2 [A] **said** to his mother, "The eleven hundred shekels of silver that
17:2 [A] and about which I **heard** [+265+928] you utter a curse—
17:2 [A] Then his mother **said**, "The LORD bless you, my son!"
17:3 [A] the eleven hundred shekels of silver to his mother, *she* **said**,
17:9 [A] Micah **asked** him, "Where are you from?" "I'm a Levite
17:9 [A] in Judah," *he* **said**, "and I'm looking for a place to stay."
17:10 [A] Micah **said** to him, "Live with me and be my father
17:13 [A] Micah **said**, "Now I know that the LORD will be good to
18:2 [A] all their clans. *They* **told** them, "Go, explore the land."
18:3 [A] so they turned in there and **asked** him, "Who brought you
18:4 [A] *He* **told** them what Micah had done for him, and said, "He
18:5 [A] *they* **said** to him, "Please inquire of God to learn whether our
18:6 [A] The priest **answered** them, "Go in peace. Your journey has
18:8 [A] returned to Zorah and Eshtaol, their brothers **asked** them,
18:9 [A] *They* **answered**, "Come on, let's attack them! We have seen
18:14 [A] the five men who had spied out the land of Laish **said** to their
18:18 [A] household gods and the cast idol, the priest **said** to them,
18:19 [A] *They* **answered** him, "Be quiet! Don't say a word. Come
18:23 [A] shouted after them, the Danites turned and **said** to Micah,
18:24 [A] *He* **replied**, "You took the gods I made, and my priest,
18:24 [A] I have? How *can you* **ask**, 'What's the matter with you?' "
18:25 [A] The Danites **answered**, "Don't argue with us, or some
19:5 [A] prepared to leave, but the girl's father **said** to his son-in-law,
19:6 [A] Afterward the girl's father **said**, "Please stay tonight
19:8 [A] when he rose to go, the girl's father **said**, "Refresh yourself.
19:9 [A] to leave, his father-in-law, the girl's father, **said**, "Now look,
19:11 [A] day was almost gone, the servant **said** to his master, "Come,
19:12 [A] His master **replied**, "No. We won't go into an alien city,
19:13 [A] *He* **added**, "Come, let's try to reach Gibeah or Ramah
19:17 [A] in the city square, the old man **asked**, "Where are you going?
19:18 [A] *He* **answered**, "We are on our way from Bethlehem in Judah
19:20 [A] "You are welcome at my house," the old man **said**. "Let me
19:22 [A] the door, *they* **shouted** to the old man who owned the house,
19:22 [A] **[NIE]** "Bring out the man who came to your house so we
19:23 [A] The owner of the house went outside and **said** to them, "No,
19:28 [A] *He* **said** to her, "Get up; let's go." But there was no answer.
19:30 [A] Everyone who saw it **said**, "Such a thing has never been seen
20:3 [A] the Israelites **said**, "Tell us how this awful thing happened."
20:4 [A] **[NIE]** "I and my concubine came to Gibeah in Benjamin to
20:8 [A] people rose as one man, **saying**, "None of us will go home.
20:12 [A] **saying**, "What about this awful crime that was committed
20:18 [A] *They* **said**, "Who of us shall go first to fight against the
20:18 [A] the Benjamites?" The LORD **replied**, "Judah shall go first."
20:23 [A] They **said**, "Shall we go up again to battle against the
20:23 [A] The LORD **answered**, "Go up against them."
20:28 [A] They **asked**, "Shall we go up again to battle with Benjamin
20:28 [A] The LORD **responded**, "Go, for tomorrow I will give them
20:32 [A] While the Benjamites *were* **saying**, "We are defeating them
20:32 [A] the Israelites *were* **saying**, "Let's retreat and draw them
20:39 [A] and *they* **said**, "We are defeating them as in the first battle."
21:1 [A] **[NIE]** "Not one of us will give his daughter in marriage to a
21:3 [A] "O LORD, the God of Israel," *they* **cried**, "why has this
21:5 [A] the Israelites **asked**, "Who from all the tribes of Israel has
21:5 [A] LORD at Mizpah **[NIE]** should certainly be put to death.
21:6 [A] "Today one tribe is cut off from Israel," *they* **said**.

Jdg 21: 8 [A] *they* **asked**, "Which one of the tribes of Israel failed to
21: 11 [21:10] [A] "This is what you are to do," they **said**. "Kill every
21: 16 [A] the elders of the assembly **said**, "With the women of
21: 17 [A] The Benjamite survivors must have heirs," *they* **said**,
21: 18 [A] **[NIE]** 'Cursed be anyone who gives a wife to a Benjamite.'
21: 19 [A] there is **[NIE]** the annual festival of the LORD in Shiloh,
21: 20 [A] the Benjamites, **saying**, "Go and hide in the vineyards
21: 22 [A] their fathers or brothers complain to us, *we will* **say** to them,
Ru 1: 8 [A] Naomi **said** to her two daughters-in-law, "Go back, each of
1: 10 [A] and **said** to her, "We will go back with you to your people."
1: 11 [A] Naomi **said**, "Return home, my daughters. Why would you
1: 12 [A] Even if *I* **thought** there was still hope for me—even if I had
1: 15 [A] "Look," **said** Naomi, "your sister-in-law is going back to her
1: 16 [A] Ruth **replied**, "Don't urge me to leave you or to turn back
1: 19 [A] was stirred because of them, and *the women* **exclaimed**,
1: 20 [A] "Don't call me Naomi," *she* **told** them. "Call me Mara,
2: 2 [A] Ruth the Moabitess **said** to Naomi, "Let me go to the fields
2: 2 [A] I find favor." Naomi **said** to her, "Go ahead, my daughter."
2: 4 [A] Boaz arrived from Bethlehem and **greeted** the harvesters,
2: 4 [A] be with you!" "The LORD bless you!" *they* **called back**.
2: 5 [A] Boaz **asked** the foreman of his harvesters, "Whose young
2: 6 [A] **[NIE]** "She is the Moabitess who came back from Moab
2: 7 [A] *She* **said**, 'Please let me glean and gather among the sheaves
2: 8 [A] So Boaz **said** to Ruth, "My daughter, listen to me. Don't go
2: 10 [A] *She* **exclaimed**, "Why have I found such favor in your eyes
2: 11 [A] **[NIE]** "I've been told all about what you have done for your
2: 13 [A] I continue to find favor in your eyes, my lord," *she* **said**.
2: 14 [A] At mealtime Boaz **said** to her, "Come over here. Have some
2: 15 [A] **[NIE]** "Even if she gathers among the sheaves, don't
2: 19 [A] Her mother-in-law **asked** her, "Where did you glean today?
2: 19 [A] name of the man I worked with today is Boaz," *she* **said**.
2: 20 [A] "The LORD bless him!" Naomi **said** to her daughter-in-law.
2: 20 [A] She **added**, "That man is our close relative; he is one of our
2: 21 [A] Ruth the Moabitess **said**, "He even said to me, 'Stay with my
2: 21 [A] Ruth the Moabitess said, "*He* even **said** to me, 'Stay with my
2: 22 [A] Naomi **said** to Ruth her daughter-in-law, "It will be good for
3: 1 [A] One day Naomi her mother-in-law **said** to her, "My daughter,
3: 5 [A] "I will do whatever *you* **say**," Ruth answered.
3: 5 [A] "I will do whatever you say," Ruth **answered**.
3: 9 [A] "Who are you?" *he* **asked**. "I am your servant Ruth,"
3: 9 [A] are you?" he asked. "I am your servant Ruth," *she* **said**.
3: 10 [A] "The LORD bless you, my daughter," *he* **replied**. "This
3: 11 [A] my daughter, don't be afraid. I will do for you all *you* **ask**.
3: 14 [A] *he* **said**, "Don't let it be known that a woman came to the
3: 15 [A] *He* also **said**, "Bring me the shawl you are wearing and hold
3: 16 [A] Naomi **asked**, "How did it go, my daughter?"
3: 17 [A] **added**, "He gave me these six measures of barley, saying,
3: 17 [A] "He gave me these six measures of barley, **saying**,
3: 18 [A] Naomi **said**, "Wait, my daughter, until you find out what
4: 1 [A] Boaz **said**, "Come over here, my friend, and sit down."
4: 2 [A] Boaz took ten of the elders of the town and **said**, "Sit here,"
4: 3 [A] *he* **said** to the kinsman-redeemer, "Naomi, who has come
4: 4 [A] I **thought** I should bring the matter to your attention and
4: 4 [A] **suggest** that you buy it in the presence of these seated here
4: 4 [A] and I am next in line." "I will redeem it," *he* **said**.
4: 5 [A] Then Boaz **said**, "On the day you buy the land from Naomi
4: 6 [A] At this, the kinsman-redeemer **said**, "Then I cannot redeem it
4: 8 [A] So the kinsman-redeemer **said** to Boaz, "Buy it yourself."
4: 9 [A] Boaz **announced** to the elders and all the people, "Today you
4: 11 [A] the elders and all those at the gate **said**, "We are witnesses.
4: 14 [A] The women **said** to Naomi: "Praise be to the LORD,
4: 17 [A] The women living there **said**, "Naomi has a son." And they
1Sa 1: 8 [A] Elkanah her husband *would* **say** to her, "Hannah, why are
1: 11 [A] she made a vow, **saying**, "O LORD Almighty, if you will
1: 14 [A] and **said** to her, "How long will you keep on getting drunk?
1: 15 [A] **[NIE]** "I am a woman who is deeply troubled.
1: 17 [A] Eli answered, **[NIE]** "Go in peace, and may the God of
1: 18 [A] *She* **said**, "May your servant find favor in your eyes."
1: 22 [A] *She* **said** to her husband, "After the boy is weaned, I will
1: 23 [A] "Do what seems best to you," Elkanah her husband **told** her.
1: 26 [A] *she* **said** to him, "As surely as you live, my lord, I am the
2: 1 [A] Hannah prayed and **said**: "My heart rejoices in the LORD;
2: 15 [A] priest would come and **say** to the man who was sacrificing,
2: 16 [A] If the man **said** to him, "Let the fat be burned up first, and
2: 16 [A] the servant *would* then **answer**, "No, hand it over now;
2: 20 [A] Eli would bless Elkanah and his wife, **saying**,
2: 23 [A] So *he* **said** to them, "Why do you do such things? I hear from
2: 27 [A] Now a man of God came to Eli and **said** to him, "This is
2: 27 [A] came to Eli and said to him, "This is what the LORD **says**:
2: 30 [A] '*I* **promised** [+606] that your house and your father's house
2: 30 [A] '*I* **promised** [+606] that your house and your father's house
2: 36 [A] him for a piece of silver and a crust of bread and **plead**,
3: 4 [A] the LORD called Samuel. Samuel **answered**, "Here I am."
3: 5 [A] he ran to Eli and **said**, "Here I am; you called me." But Eli
3: 5 [A] Eli **said**, "I did not call; go back and lie down." So he went
3: 6 [A] Samuel got up and went to Eli and **said**, "Here I am; you
3: 6 [A] "My son," Eli **said**, "I did not call; go back and lie down."
3: 8 [A] and Samuel got up and went to Eli and **said**, "Here I am;
3: 9 [A] So Eli **told** Samuel, "Go and lie down, and if he calls you,
3: 9 [A] "Go and lie down, and if he calls you, **say**, 'Speak, LORD,
3: 10 [A] Then Samuel **said**, "Speak, for your servant is listening."
3: 11 [A] the LORD **said** to Samuel: "See, I am about to do
3: 16 [A] Eli called him and **said**, "Samuel, my son." Samuel
3: 16 [A] and said, "Samuel, my son." Samuel **answered**, "Here I am."
3: 17 [A] Eli **asked**. "Do not hide it from me. May God deal with you,
3: 18 [A] Eli **said**, "He is the LORD; let him do what is good in his
4: 3 [A] the soldiers returned to camp, the elders of Israel **asked**,
4: 6 [A] Hearing the uproar, the Philistines **asked**, "What's all this
4: 7 [A] "A god has come into the camp," *they* **said**. "We're in
4: 7 [A] come into the camp," they said. **[RPH]** "We're in trouble!
4: 14 [A] Eli heard the outcry and **asked**, "What is the meaning of this
4: 16 [A] He **told** Eli, "I have just come from the battle line; I fled
4: 16 [A] from it this very day." Eli **asked**, "What happened, my son?"
4: 17 [A] **[NIE]** "Israel fled before the Philistines, and the army has
4: 21 [A] She named the boy Ichabod, **saying**, "The glory has departed
4: 22 [A] *She* **said**, "The glory has departed from Israel, for the ark of
5: 7 [A] the men of Ashdod saw what was happening, *they* **said**,
5: 8 [A] together all the rulers of the Philistines and **asked** them,
5: 8 [A] *They* **answered**, "Have the ark of the god of Israel moved to
5: 10 [A] **[NIE]** "They have brought the ark of the god of Israel
5: 11 [A] they called together all the rulers of the Philistines and **said**,
6: 2 [A] the Philistines called for the priests and the diviners and **said**,
6: 3 [A] *They* **answered**, "If you return the ark of the god of Israel,
6: 4 [A] The Philistines **asked**, "What guilt offering should we send
6: 4 [A] *They* **replied**, "Five gold tumors and five gold rats,
6: 20 [A] the men of Beth Shemesh **asked**, "Who can stand in the
6: 21 [A] **saying**, "The Philistines have returned the ark of the LORD.
7: 3 [A] Samuel **said** to the whole house of Israel, "If you are
7: 3 [A] **[RPH]** "If you are returning to the LORD with all your
7: 5 [A] Samuel **said**, "Assemble all Israel at Mizpah and I will
7: 6 [A] On that day they fasted and there *they* **confessed**, "We have
7: 8 [A] They **said** to Samuel, "Do not stop crying out to the LORD
7: 12 [A] He named it Ebenezer, **saying**, "Thus far has the LORD
8: 5 [A] *They* **said** to him, "You are old, and your sons do not walk in
8: 6 [A] when *they* **said**, "Give us a king to lead us," this displeased
8: 7 [A] the LORD **told** him: "Listen to all that the people are saying
8: 7 [A] "Listen to all that the people *are* **saying** to you; it is not you
8: 10 [A] Samuel **told** all the words of the LORD to the people who
8: 11 [A] *He* **said**, "This is what the king who will reign over you will
8: 19 [A] listen to Samuel. "No!" *they* **said**. "We want a king over us.
8: 22 [A] The LORD **answered**, "Listen to them and give them a
8: 22 [A] Samuel **said** to the men of Israel, "Everyone go back to his
9: 3 [A] Kish **said** to his son Saul, "Take one of the servants with you
9: 5 [A] Saul **said** to the servant who was with him, "Come, let's go
9: 6 [A] the servant **replied**, "Look, in this town there is a man of
9: 7 [A] Saul **said** to his servant, "If we go, what can we give the
9: 8 [A] "Look," *he* **said**, "I have a quarter of a shekel of silver. I will
9: 9 [A] inquire of God, *he would* **say**, "Come, let us go to the seer,"
9: 10 [A] "Good," Saul **said** to his servant. "Come, let's go." So they
9: 11 [A] out to draw water, and *they* **asked** them, "Is the seer here?"
9: 12 [A] **[NIE]** "He's ahead of you. Hurry now; he has just come to
9: 15 [A] Saul came, the LORD had revealed this to Samuel: **[NIE]**
9: 17 [A] LORD said to him, "This is the man *I* **spoke** to you *about*;
9: 18 [A] Saul approached Samuel in the gateway and **asked**,
9: 19 [A] **[NIE]** "Go up ahead of me to the high place, for today you
9: 21 [A] Saul answered, **[NIE]** "But am I not a Benjamite, from the
9: 23 [A] Samuel **said** to the cook, "Bring the piece of meat I gave
9: 23 [A] the piece of meat I gave you, the one *I* **told** you to lay aside."
9: 24 [A] Samuel **said**, "Here is what has been kept for you. Eat,
9: 24 [A] was set aside for you for this occasion, from the time I **said**,
9: 26 [A] **[NIE]** "Get ready, and I will send you on your way."
9: 27 [A] Samuel **said** to Saul, "Tell the servant to go on ahead of
9: 27 [A] Samuel said to Saul, "**Tell** the servant to go on ahead of us"—
10: 1 [A] of oil and poured it on Saul's head and kissed him, **saying**,
10: 2 [A] *They will* **say** to you, 'The donkeys you set out to look for
10: 2 [A] about you. He *is* **asking**, "What shall I do about my son?" '
10: 11 [A] they **asked** each other, "What is this that has happened to the
10: 12 [A] who lived there answered, **[NIE]** "And who is their father?"
10: 14 [A] Now Saul's uncle **asked** him and his servant, "Where have
10: 14 [A] have you been?" "Looking for the donkeys," *he* **said**.
10: 15 [A] Saul's uncle **said**, "Tell me what Samuel said to you."
10: 15 [A] Saul's uncle said, "Tell me what Samuel **said** to you."
10: 16 [A] Saul **replied**, "He assured us that the donkeys had been
10: 16 [A] he did not tell his uncle what Samuel *had* **said** *about* the
10: 18 [A] **said** to them, "This is what the LORD, the God of Israel,
10: 18 [A] to them, "This is what the LORD, the God of Israel, **says**:
10: 19 [A] and distresses. And *you have* **said**, 'No, set a king over us.'
10: 22 [A] the LORD **said**, "Yes, he has hidden himself among the

1Sa 10:24 [A] Samuel **said** to all the people, "Do you see the man the
10:24 [A] Then the people shouted, **[NIE]** "Long live the king!"
10:27 [A] some troublemakers **said**, "How can this fellow save us?"
11: 1 [A] all the men of Jabesh **said** to him, "Make a treaty with us,
11: 2 [A] Nahash the Ammonite **replied**, "I will make a treaty with
11: 3 [A] The elders of Jabesh **said** to him, "Give us seven days so we
11: 5 [A] behind his oxen, and he **asked**, "What is wrong with the
11: 7 [A] the pieces by messengers throughout Israel, **proclaiming**,
11: 9 [A] *They* **told** the messengers who had come, "Say to the men of
11: 9 [A] "**Say** to the men of Jabesh Gilead, 'By the time the sun is hot
11:10 [A] They **said** to the Ammonites, "Tomorrow we will surrender
11:12 [A] The people then **said** to Samuel, "Who was it that asked,
11:12 [A] The people then said to Samuel, "Who was it that **asked**,
11:13 [A] Saul **said**, "No one shall be put to death today, for this day
11:14 [A] Then Samuel **said** to the people, "Come, let us go to Gilgal
12: 1 [A] Samuel **said** to all Israel, "I have listened to everything you
12: 1 [A] "I have listened to everything *you* **said** to me and have set a
12: 4 [A] "You have not cheated or oppressed us," *they* **replied**. "You
12: 5 [A] Samuel **said** to them, "The LORD is witness against you,
12: 5 [A] not found anything in my hand." "He is witness," *they* **said**.
12: 6 [A] Samuel **said** to the people, "It is the LORD who appointed
12:10 [A] They cried out to the LORD and **said**, 'We have sinned; we
12:12 [A] *you* **said** to me, 'No, we want a king to rule over us'—
12:19 [A] The people all **said** to Samuel, "Pray to the LORD your
12:20 [A] "Do not be afraid," Samuel **replied**. "You have done all this
13: 3 [A] Saul had the trumpet blown throughout the land and **said**,
13: 4 [A] So all Israel heard the **news**: "Saul has attacked the Philistine
13: 9 [A] So he **said**, "Bring me the burnt offering and the fellowship
13:11 [A] **asked** Samuel. Saul replied, "When I saw that the men were
13:11 [A] Saul **replied**, "When I saw that the men were scattering, and
13:12 [A] *I* **thought**, 'Now the Philistines will come down against me at
13:13 [A] "You acted foolishly," Samuel **said**. "You have not kept the
13:19 [A] because the Philistines *had* **said**, "Otherwise the Hebrews
14: 1 [A] One day Jonathan son of Saul **said** to the young man bearing
14: 6 [A] Jonathan **said** to his young armor-bearer, "Come, let's go
14: 7 [A] "Do all that you have in mind," his armor-bearer **said**. "Go
14: 8 [A] Jonathan **said**, "Come, then; we will cross over toward the
14: 9 [A] If *they* **say** to us, 'Wait there until we come to you,' we will
14:10 [A] if *they* **say**, 'Come up to us,' we will climb up, because that
14:11 [A] to the Philistine outpost. "Look!" **said** the Philistines.
14:12 [A] **[NIE]** "Come up to us and we'll teach you a lesson."
14:12 [A] So Jonathan **said** to his armor-bearer, "Climb up after me;
14:17 [A] Saul **said** to the men who were with him, "Muster the forces
14:18 [A] Saul **said** to Ahijah, "Bring the ark of God." (At that time it
14:19 [A] and more. So Saul **said** to the priest, "Withdraw your hand."
14:24 [A] because Saul had bound the people under an oath, **saying**,
14:28 [A] one of the soldiers told **[NIE]** him, "Your father bound the
14:28 [A] strict oath, **saying**, 'Cursed be any man who eats food today!'
14:29 [A] Jonathan **said**, "My father has made trouble for the country.
14:33 [A] someone said to Saul, **[NIE]** "Look, the men are sinning
14:33 [A] "You have broken faith," *he* **said**. "Roll a large stone over
14:34 [A] he **said**, "Go out among the men and tell them, 'Each of you
14:34 [A] he said, "Go out among the men and **tell** them, 'Each of you
14:36 [A] Saul **said**, "Let us go down after the Philistines by night
14:36 [A] "Do whatever seems best to you," *they* **replied**.
14:36 [A] But the priest **said**, "Let us inquire of God here."
14:38 [A] Saul therefore **said**, "Come here, all you who are leaders of
14:40 [A] Saul then **said** to all the Israelites, "You stand over there; I
14:40 [A] over here." "Do what seems best to you," the men **replied**.
14:41 [A] Saul **prayed** to the LORD, the God of Israel, "Give me the
14:42 [A] Saul **said**, "Cast the lot between me and Jonathan my son."
14:43 [A] Then Saul **said** to Jonathan, "Tell me what you have done."
14:43 [A] with the end of my staff. **[NIE]** And now must I die?"
14:44 [A] Saul **said**, "May God deal with me, be it ever so severely,
14:45 [A] the men **said** to Saul, "Should Jonathan die—he who has
15: 1 [A] Samuel **said** to Saul, "I am the one the LORD sent to anoint
15: 2 [A] This is what the LORD Almighty **says**: 'I will punish the
15: 6 [A] Then he **said** to the Kenites, "Go away, leave the Amalekites
15:10 [A] Then the word of the LORD came to Samuel: **[NIE]**
15:12 [A] meet Saul, but he was told, **[NIE]** "Saul has gone to Carmel.
15:13 [A] Samuel reached him, Saul **said**, "The LORD bless you!
15:14 [A] Samuel **said**, "What then is this bleating of sheep in my ears?
15:15 [A] Saul **answered**, "The soldiers brought them from the
15:16 [A] "Stop!" Samuel **said** to Saul. "Let me tell you what the
15:16 [A] the LORD said to me last night." "Tell me," Saul **replied**.
15:17 [A] Samuel **said**, "Although you were once small in your own
15:18 [A] **saying**, 'Go and completely destroy those wicked people,
15:20 [A] "But I did obey the LORD," Saul **said**. "I went on the
15:22 [A] Samuel **replied**: "Does the LORD delight in burnt offerings
15:24 [A] Saul **said** to Samuel, "I have sinned. I violated the LORD's
15:26 [A] Samuel **said** to him, "I will not go back with you. You have
15:28 [A] Samuel **said** to him, "The LORD has torn the kingdom of
15:30 [A] Saul **replied**, "I have sinned. But please honor me before the
15:32 [A] Then Samuel **said**, "Bring me Agag king of the Amalekites."
15:32 [A] Agag came to him confidently, **thinking**, "Surely the
15:33 [A] But Samuel **said**, "As your sword has made women childless,
16: 1 [A] The LORD **said** to Samuel, "How long will you mourn for
16: 2 [A] Samuel **said**, "How can I go? Saul will hear about it and kill
16: 2 [A] The LORD **said**, "Take a heifer with you and say, 'I have
16: 2 [A] The LORD said, "Take a heifer with you and **say**, 'I have
16: 3 [A] you what to do. You are to anoint for me the one *I* **indicate**."
16: 4 [A] when they met him. *They* **asked**, "Do you come in peace?"
16: 5 [A] Samuel **replied**, "Yes, in peace; I have come to sacrifice to
16: 6 [A] When they arrived, Samuel saw Eliab and **thought**,
16: 7 [A] the LORD **said** to Samuel, "Do not consider his appearance
16: 8 [A] Samuel **said**, "The LORD has not chosen this one either."
16: 9 [A] Jesse then had Shammah pass by, but Samuel **said**, "Nor has
16:10 [A] but Samuel **said** to him, "The LORD has not chosen these."
16:11 [A] So he **asked** Jesse, "Are these all the sons you have?" "There
16:11 [A] "There is still the youngest," Jesse **answered**, "but he is
16:11 [A] Samuel **said**, "Send for him; we will not sit down until he
16:12 [A] Then the LORD **said**, "Rise and anoint him; he is the one."
16:15 [A] Saul's attendants **said** to him, "See, an evil spirit from God is
16:16 [A] *Let* our lord **command** his servants here to search for
16:17 [A] So Saul **said** to his attendants, "Find someone who plays well
16:18 [A] **[NIE]** "I have seen a son of Jesse of Bethlehem who knows
16:19 [A] Saul sent messengers to Jesse and **said**, "Send me your son
16:22 [A] Saul sent word to Jesse, **saying**, "Allow David to remain in
17: 8 [A] **[NIE]** "Why do you come out and line up for battle?
17:10 [A] Then the Philistine **said**, "This day I defy the ranks of Israel!
17:17 [A] Now Jesse **said** to his son David, "Take this ephah of roasted
17:25 [A] Now the Israelites *had been* **saying**, "Do you see how this
17:26 [A] David **asked** the men standing near him, "What will be done
17:26 [A] **[RPH]** "What will be done for the man who kills this
17:27 [A] *They* **repeated** to him what they had been saying and told
17:27 [A] repeated to him what they had been saying and **told** him,
17:28 [A] with the men, he burned with anger at him and **asked**,
17:29 [A] "Now what have I done?" **said** David. "Can't I even speak?"
17:30 [A] away to someone else and **brought up** the same matter,
17:32 [A] David **said** to Saul, "Let no one lose heart on account of this
17:33 [A] Saul **replied**, "You are not able to go out against this
17:34 [A] David **said** to Saul, "Your servant has been keeping his
17:37 [A] **[NIE]** The LORD who delivered me from the paw of the
17:37 [A] Saul **said** to David, "Go, and the LORD be with you."
17:39 [A] "I cannot go in these," he **said** to Saul, "because I am not
17:43 [A] He **said** to David, "Am I a dog, that you come at me with
17:44 [A] "Come here," he **said**, "and I'll give your flesh to the birds of
17:45 [A] David **said** to the Philistine, "You come against me with
17:55 [A] *he* **said** to Abner, commander of the army, "Abner,
17:55 [A] Abner **replied**, "As surely as you live, O king, I don't know."
17:56 [A] The king **said**, "Find out whose son this young man is."
17:58 [A] Saul **asked** him. David said, "I am the son of your servant
17:58 [A] David **said**, "I am the son of your servant Jesse of
18: 7 [A] **[NIE]** "Saul has slain his thousands, and David his tens of
18: 8 [A] of thousands," *he* **thought**, "but me with only thousands.
18:11 [A] he hurled it, **saying** to himself, "I'll pin David to the wall."
18:17 [A] Saul **said** to David, "Here is my older daughter Merab. I will
18:17 [A] For Saul **said** to himself, "I will not raise a hand against him.
18:18 [A] But David **said** to Saul, "Who am I, and what is my family
18:21 [A] "I will give her to him," he **thought**, "so that she may be a
18:21 [A] So Saul **said** to David, "Now you have a second opportunity
18:22 [A] "Speak to David privately and **say**, 'Look, the king is pleased
18:23 [A] David **said**, "Do you think it is a small matter to become the
18:24 [A] When Saul's servants told him **[NIE]** what David had said,
18:25 [A] Saul **replied**, "Say to David, 'The king wants no other price
18:25 [A] Saul replied, "**Say** to David, 'The king wants no other price
19: 2 [A] **[NIE]** "My father Saul is looking for a chance to kill you.
19: 4 [A] spoke well of David to Saul his father and **said** to him,
19:11 [A] warned him, **[NIE]** "If you don't run for your life tonight,
19:14 [A] Saul sent the men to capture David, Michal **said**, "He is ill."
19:15 [A] Saul sent the men back to see David and **told** them,
19:17 [A] Saul **said** to Michal, "Why did you deceive me like this
19:17 [A] Michal **told** him, "He said to me, 'Let me get away.
19:17 [A] Michal told him, "He **said** to me, 'Let me get away.
19:19 [A] Word came to Saul: **[NIE]** "David is in Naioth at Ramah";
19:22 [A] he asked, **[NIE]** "Where are Samuel and David?" "Over in
19:22 [A] and David?" "Over in Naioth at Ramah," *they* **said**.
19:24 [A] This is why *people* **say**, "Is Saul also among the prophets?"
20: 1 [A] fled from Naioth at Ramah and went to Jonathan and **asked**,
20: 2 [A] "Never!" Jonathan **replied**. "You are not going to die! Look,
20: 3 [A] David took an oath and **said**, "Your father knows very well
20: 3 [A] *he has* **said** to himself, 'Jonathan must not know this or he
20: 4 [A] Jonathan **said** to David, "Whatever you want me to do, I'll
20: 4 [A] to David, "Whatever you **want** me to do, I'll do for you."
20: 5 [A] So David **said**, "Look, tomorrow is the New Moon festival,
20: 6 [A] If your father misses me at all, **tell** him, 'David earnestly
20: 7 [A] If *he* **says**, 'Very well,' then your servant is safe. But if he
20: 9 [A] "Never!" Jonathan **said**. "If I had the least inkling that my

1Sa 20:10 [A] David **asked**, "Who will tell me if your father answers you
20:11 [A] "Come," Jonathan **said**, "let's go out into the field." So they
20:12 [A] Jonathan **said** to David: "By the LORD, the God of Israel,
20:18 [A] Jonathan **said** to David: "Tomorrow is the New Moon
20:21 [A] If *I* **say** [+606] to him, 'Look, the arrows are on this side of
20:21 [A] If *I* **say** [+606] to him, 'Look, the arrows are on this side of
20:22 [A] But if *I* **say** to the boy, 'Look, the arrows are beyond you,'
20:26 [A] Saul said nothing that day, for *he* **thought**, "Something must
20:27 [A] Saul **said** to his son Jonathan, "Why hasn't the son of Jesse
20:29 [A] *He* **said**, 'Let me go, because our family is observing a
20:30 [A] Saul's anger flared up at Jonathan and *he* **said** to him,
20:32 [A] What has he done?" Jonathan asked his father. **[NIE]**
20:36 [A] and *he* **said** to the boy, "Run and find the arrows I shoot."
20:37 [A] called out after him, **[NIE]** "Isn't the arrow beyond you?"
20:40 [A] Then Jonathan gave his weapons to the boy and **said**, "Go,
20:42 [A] Jonathan **said** to David, "Go in peace, for we have sworn
20:42 [A] **saying**, 'The LORD is witness between you and me,
21: 1 [21:2] [A] when he met him, and **asked**, "Why are you alone?
21: 2 [21:3] [A] David **answered** Ahimelech the priest, "The king
21: 2 [21:3] [A] charged me with a certain matter and **said** to me,
21: 4 [21:5] [A] **[NIE]** "I don't have any ordinary bread on hand;
21: 5 [21:6] [A] **[NIE]** "Indeed women have been kept from us,
21: 8 [21:9] [A] David **asked** Ahimelech, "Don't you have a spear
21: 9 [21:10] [A] The priest **replied**, "The sword of Goliath the
21: 9 [21:10] [A] David **said**, "There is none like it; give it to me."
21:11 [21:12] [A] the servants of Achish **said** to him, "Isn't this
21:11 [21:12] [A] **[NIE]** " 'Saul has slain his thousands, and David
21:14 [21:15] [A] Achish **said** to his servants, "Look at the man! He is
22: 3 [A] David went to Mizpah in Moab and **said** to the king of Moab,
22: 5 [A] the prophet Gad **said** to David, "Do not stay in the
22: 7 [A] Saul **said** to them, "Listen, men of Benjamin! Will the son of
22: 9 [A] **[NIE]** "I saw the son of Jesse come to Ahimelech son of
22:12 [A] Saul **said**, "Listen now, son of Ahitub." "Yes, my lord,"
22:12 [A] "Listen now, son of Ahitub." "Yes, my lord," *he* **answered**.
22:13 [A] Saul **said** to him, "Why have you conspired against me, you
22:14 [A] **[NIE]** "Who of all your servants is as loyal as David,
22:16 [A] the king **said**, "You will surely die, Ahimelech, you and your
22:17 [A] the king **ordered** the guards at his side: "Turn and kill the
22:18 [A] The king then **ordered** Doeg, "You turn and strike down the
22:22 [A] David **said** to Abiathar: "That day, when Doeg the Edomite
23: 1 [A] When David was told, **[NIE]** "Look, the Philistines are
23: 2 [A] the LORD, **saying**, "Shall I go and attack these Philistines?"
23: 2 [A] The LORD **answered** him, "Go, attack the Philistines
23: 3 [A] But David's men **said** to him, "Here in Judah we are afraid.
23: 4 [A] and the LORD answered him, **[NIE]** "Go down to Keilah,
23: 7 [A] to Keilah, and he **said**, "God has handed him over to me,
23: 9 [A] *he* **said** to Abiathar the priest, "Bring the ephod."
23:10 [A] David **said**, "O LORD, God of Israel, your servant has
23:11 [A] of Israel, tell your servant." And the LORD **said**, "He will."
23:12 [A] Again David **asked**, "Will the citizens of Keilah surrender
23:12 [A] and my men to Saul?" And the LORD **said**, "They will."
23:17 [A] "Don't be afraid," *he* **said**. "My father Saul will not lay a
23:19 [A] The Ziphites went up to Saul at Gibeah and **said**, "Is not
23:21 [A] Saul **replied**, "The LORD bless you for your concern for
23:22 [A] and who has seen him there. *They* **tell** me he is very crafty.
23:27 [A] a messenger came to Saul, **saying**, "Come quickly! The
24: 1 [24:2] [A] was told, **[NIE]** "David is in the Desert of En Gedi."
24: 4 [24:5] [A] The men **said**, "This is the day the LORD spoke of
24: 4 [24:5] [A] "This is the day the LORD spoke of when *he* **said**
24: 6 [24:7] [A] *He* **said** to his men, "The LORD forbid that I should
24: 8 [24:9] [A] and called out to Saul, **[NIE]** "My lord the king!"
24: 9 [24:10] [A] He **said** to Saul, "Why do you listen when men say,
24: 9 [24:10] [A] He said to Saul, "Why do you listen *when* men **say**,
24:10 [24:11] [A] *Some* **urged** me to kill you, but I spared you; I said,
24:10 [24:11] [A] *I* **said**, 'I will not lift my hand against my master,
24:13 [24:14] [A] As the old saying **goes**, 'From evildoers come evil
24:16 [24:17] [A] Saul **asked**, "Is that your voice, David my son?"
24:17 [24:18] [A] "You are more righteous than I," *he* **said**. "You
25: 5 [A] So he sent ten young men and **said** to them, "Go up to Nabal
25: 6 [A] **Say** to him: 'Long life to you! Good health to you and your
25:10 [A] answered David's servants, **[NIE]** "Who is this David?
25:13 [A] David **said** to his men, "Put on your swords!" So they put on
25:14 [A] **[NIE]** "David sent messengers from the desert to give our
25:19 [A] Then *she* **told** her servants, "Go on ahead; I'll follow you."
25:21 [A] David *had just* **said**, "It's been useless—all my watching
25:24 [A] She fell at his feet and **said**: "My lord, let the blame be on me
25:32 [A] David **said** to Abigail, "Praise be to the LORD, the God of
25:35 [A] accepted from her hand what she had brought him and **said**,
25:39 [A] that Nabal was dead, *he* **said**, "Praise be to the LORD,
25:40 [A] **[NIE]** "David has sent us to you to take you to become his
25:41 [A] She bowed down with her face to the ground and **said**,
26: 1 [A] The Ziphites went to Saul at Gibeah and **said**, "Is not David
26: 6 [A] David then asked **[NIE]** Ahimelech the Hittite and Abishai
26: 6 [A] **[NIE]** "Who will go down into the camp with me to Saul?"
26: 6 [A] the camp with me to Saul?" "I'll go with you," **said** Abishai.
26: 8 [A] Abishai **said** to David, "Today God has delivered your
26: 9 [A] David **said** to Abishai, "Don't destroy him! Who can lay a
26:10 [A] As surely as the LORD lives," he **said**, "the LORD
26:14 [A] son of Ner, **[NIE]** "Aren't you going to answer me, Abner?"
26:14 [A] Abner replied, **[NIE]** "Who are you who calls to the king?"
26:15 [A] David **said**, "You're a man, aren't you? And who is like you
26:17 [A] Saul recognized David's voice and **said**, "Is that your voice,
26:17 [A] David my son?" David **replied**, "Yes it is, my lord the king."
26:18 [A] *he* **added**, "Why is my lord pursuing his servant? What have
26:19 [A] from my share in the LORD's inheritance and *have* **said**,
26:21 [A] Then Saul **said**, "I have sinned. Come back, David my son.
26:22 [A] **[NIE]** "Let one of your young men come over and get it.
26:25 [A] Saul **said** to David, "May you be blessed, my son David;
27: 1 [A] David **thought** to himself, "One of these days I will be
27: 5 [A] David **said** to Achish, "If I have found favor in your eyes,
27:10 [A] When Achish **asked**, "Where did you go raiding today?"
27:10 [A] David *would* **say**, "Against the Negev of Judah" or "Against
27:11 [A] to Gath, for *he* **thought**, "They might inform on us and say,
27:11 [A] to Gath, for he thought, "They might inform on us and **say**,
27:12 [A] Achish trusted David and **said** to himself, "He has become
28: 1 [A] Achish **said** to David, "You must understand that you
28: 2 [A] David **said**, "Then you will see for yourself what your
28: 2 [A] Achish **replied**, "Very well, I will make you my bodyguard
28: 7 [A] Saul then **said** to his attendants, "Find me a woman who is a
28: 7 [A] and inquire of her." "There is one in Endor," they **said**.
28: 8 [A] "Consult a spirit for me," *he* **said**, "and bring up for me the
28: 8 [A] spirit for me," he said, "and bring up for me the one *I* **name**."
28: 9 [A] the woman **said** to him, "Surely you know what Saul has
28:10 [A] Saul swore to her by the **[NIE]** LORD, "As surely as the
28:11 [A] Then the woman **asked**, "Whom shall I bring up for you?"
28:11 [A] shall I bring up for you?" "Bring up Samuel," *he* **said**.
28:12 [A] she cried out at the top of her voice and **said** to Saul, "Why
28:12 [A] and said to Saul, **[RPH]** "Why have you deceived me?
28:13 [A] The king **said** to her, "Don't be afraid. What do you see?"
28:13 [A] The woman **said**, "I see a spirit coming up out of the
28:14 [A] "What does he look like?" *he* **asked**. "An old man wearing a
28:14 [A] "An old man wearing a robe is coming up," *she* **said**.
28:15 [A] Samuel **said** to Saul, "Why have you disturbed me by
28:15 [A] "I am in great distress," Saul **said**. "The Philistines are
28:16 [A] Samuel **said**, "Why do you consult me, now that the LORD
28:21 [A] *she* **said**, "Look, your maidservant has obeyed you.
28:23 [A] He refused and **said**, "I will not eat." But his men joined the
29: 3 [A] The commanders of the Philistines **asked**, "What about these
29: 3 [A] Achish **replied**, "Is this not David, who was an officer of
29: 4 [A] the Philistine commanders were angry with him and **said**,
29: 5 [A] **[NIE]** " 'Saul has slain his thousands, and David his tens of
29: 6 [A] So Achish called David and **said** to him, "As surely as the
29: 8 [A] "But what have I done?" **asked** David. "What have you
29: 9 [A] **[NIE]** "I know that you have been as pleasing in my eyes as
29: 9 [A] nevertheless, the Philistine commanders *have* **said**, 'He must
30: 6 [A] because the men *were* **talking** *of* stoning him;
30: 7 [A] David **said** to Abiathar the priest, the son of Ahimelech,
30: 8 [A] of the LORD, **[NIE]** "Shall I pursue this raiding party?
30: 8 [A] Will I overtake them?" "Pursue them," *he* **answered**.
30:13 [A] David **asked** him, "To whom do you belong, and where do
30:13 [A] *He* **said**, "I am an Egyptian, the slave of an Amalekite.
30:15 [A] David **asked** him, "Can you lead me down to this raiding
30:15 [A] *He* **answered**, "Swear to me before God that you will not kill
30:20 [A] of the other livestock, **saying**, "This is David's plunder."
30:22 [A] followers said, **[NIE]** "Because they did not go out with us,
30:23 [A] David **replied**, "No, my brothers, you must not do that with
30:26 [A] to the elders of Judah, who were his friends, **saying** [+4200],
31: 4 [A] Saul **said** to his armor-bearer, "Draw your sword and run me
2Sa 1: 3 [A] David **asked** him. He answered, "I have escaped from the
1: 3 [A] *He* **answered**, "I have escaped from the Israelite camp."
1: 4 [A] David **asked**. "Tell me." He said, "The men fled from the
1: 4 [A] "Tell me." *He* **said**, "The men fled from the battle.
1: 5 [A] David **said** to the young man who brought him the report,
1: 6 [A] the young man **said**, "and there was Saul, leaning on his
1: 7 [A] and saw me, he called out to me, and *I* **said**, 'What can I do?'
1: 8 [A] "*He* **asked** me, 'Who are you?' " 'An Amalekite,' I answered.
1: 8 [A] "He asked me, 'Who are you?' " 'An Amalekite,' *I* **answered**.
1: 9 [A] "Then *he* **said** to me, 'Stand over me and kill me! I am in the
1:13 [A] David **said** to the young man who brought him the report,
1:13 [A] "I am the son of an alien, an Amalekite," *he* **answered**.
1:14 [A] David **asked** him, "Why were you not afraid to lift your hand
1:15 [A] David called one of his men and **said**, "Go, strike him
1:16 [A] For David *had* **said** to him, "Your blood be on your own
1:16 [A] Your own mouth testified against you when you **said**,
1:18 [A] **ordered** that the men of Judah be taught this lament of the
2: 1 [A] he **asked**. The LORD said, "Go up." David asked,
2: 1 [A] he asked. The LORD **said**, "Go up." David asked,
2: 1 [A] LORD said, "Go up." David **asked**, "Where shall I go?"

2Sa 2: 1 [A] "Where shall I go?" "To Hebron," the LORD **answered**.
2: 4 [A] When David was told **[NIE]** that it was the men of Jabesh
2: 5 [A] he sent messengers to the men of Jabesh Gilead *to* **say** to
2: 14 [A] Abner **said** to Joab, "Let's have some of the young men get
2: 14 [A] to hand in front of us." "All right, let them do it," Joab **said**.
2: 20 [A] Abner looked behind him and **asked**, "Is that you, Asahel?"
2: 20 [A] and asked, "Is that you, Asahel?" "It is," *he* **answered**.
2: 21 [A] Abner **said** to him, "Turn aside to the right or to the left;
2: 22 [A] Again Abner **warned** Asahel, "Stop chasing me! Why should
2: 26 [A] called out to Joab, **[NIE]** "Must the sword devour forever?
2: 26 [A] How long before *you* **order** your men to stop pursuing their
2: 27 [A] Joab **answered**, "As surely as God lives, if you had not
3: 7 [A] Ish-Bosheth **said** to Abner, "Why did you sleep with my
3: 8 [A] because of what Ish-Bosheth said and *he* **answered**,
3: 12 [A] Then Abner sent messengers on his behalf to **say** to David,
3: 12 [A] **[RPH]** Make an agreement with me, and I will help you
3: 13 [A] "Good," **said** David. "I will make an agreement with you.
3: 13 [A] **[NIE]** Do not come into my presence unless you bring
3: 14 [A] son of Saul, **demanding**, "Give me my wife Michal,
3: 16 [A] Then Abner **said** to him, "Go back home!" So he went back.
3: 17 [A] Abner conferred with the elders of Israel and **said**, "For some
3: 18 [A] For the LORD **promised** David, 'By my servant David I
3: 18 [A] **[NIE]** 'By my servant David I will rescue my people Israel
3: 21 [A] Abner **said** to David, "Let me go at once and assemble all
3: 23 [A] he was told **[NIE]** that Abner son of Ner had come to the
3: 24 [A] So Joab went to the king and **said**, "What have you done?
3: 28 [A] *he* **said**, "I and my kingdom are forever innocent before the
3: 31 [A] David **said** to Joab and all the people with him, "Tear your
3: 33 [A] **[NIE]** "Should Abner have died as the lawless die?
3: 35 [A] David took an oath, **saying**, "May God deal with me, be it
3: 38 [A] the king **said** to his men, "Do you not realize that a prince
4: 8 [A] head of Ish-Bosheth to David at Hebron and **said** to the king,
4: 9 [A] the Beerothite, **[NIE]** "As surely as the LORD lives,
4: 10 [A] when a man told me, **[NIE]** 'Saul is dead,' and thought he
5: 1 [A] All the tribes of Israel came to David at Hebron and **said**,
5: 1 [A] and said, **[RPH]** "We are your own flesh and blood.
5: 2 [A] the LORD **said** to you, 'You will shepherd my people Israel,
5: 6 [A] The Jebusites **said** to David, "You will not get in here;
5: 6 [A] Jebusites said to David, **[RPH]** "You will not get in here;
5: 6 [A] ward you off." They **thought**, "David cannot get in here."
5: 8 [A] On that day, David **said**, "Anyone who conquers the
5: 8 [A] That is why *they* **say**, "The 'blind and lame' will not enter the
5: 19 [A] of the LORD, **[NIE]** "Shall I go and attack the Philistines?
5: 19 [A] The LORD **answered** him, "Go, for I will surely hand the
5: 20 [A] *He* **said**, "As waters break out, the LORD has broken out
5: 23 [A] *he* **answered**, "Do not go straight up, but circle around
6: 9 [A] David was afraid of the LORD that day and **said**, "How can
6: 12 [A] **[NIE]** "The LORD has blessed the household of
6: 20 [A] Michal daughter of Saul came out to meet him and **said**,
6: 21 [A] David **said** to Michal, "It was before the LORD, who chose
6: 22 [A] by these slave girls *you* **spoke** *of*, I will be held in honor."
7: 2 [A] he **said** to Nathan the prophet, "Here I am, living in a palace
7: 3 [A] Nathan **replied** to the king, "Whatever you have in mind,
7: 4 [A] That night the word of the LORD came to Nathan, **saying**:
7: 5 [A] "Go and **tell** my servant David, 'This is what the LORD
7: 5 [A] and tell my servant David, 'This is what the LORD **says**:
7: 7 [A] **[NIE]** "Why have you not built me a house of cedar?" '
7: 8 [A] "Now then, **tell** my servant David, 'This is what the LORD
7: 8 [A] my servant David, 'This is what the LORD Almighty **says**:
7: 18 [A] King David went in and sat before the LORD, and *he* **said**:
7: 26 [A] men *will* **say**, 'The LORD Almighty is God over Israel!'
7: 27 [A] this to your servant, **saying**, 'I will build a house for you.'
9: 1 [A] David **asked**, "Is there anyone still left of the house of Saul
9: 2 [A] before David, and the king **said** to him, "Are you Ziba?"
9: 2 [A] said to him, "Are you Ziba?" "Your servant," *he* **replied**.
9: 3 [A] The king **asked**, "Is there no one still left of the house of
9: 3 [A] Ziba **answered** the king, "There is still a son of Jonathan;
9: 4 [A] "Where is he?" the king **asked**. Ziba answered, "He is at the
9: 4 [A] Ziba **answered**, "He is at the house of Makir son of Ammiel
9: 6 [A] David **said**, "Mephibosheth!" "Your servant," he replied.
9: 6 [A] David said, "Mephibosheth!" "Your servant," *he* **replied**.
9: 7 [A] "Don't be afraid," David **said** to him, "for I will surely show
9: 8 [A] Mephibosheth bowed down and **said**, "What is your servant,
9: 9 [A] the king summoned Ziba, Saul's servant, and **said** to him,
9: 11 [A] Ziba **said** to the king, "Your servant will do whatever my
10: 2 [A] David **thought**, "I will show kindness to Hanun son of
10: 3 [A] the Ammonite nobles **said** to Hanun their lord, "Do you think
10: 5 [A] The king **said**, "Stay at Jericho till your beards have grown,
10: 11 [A] Joab **said**, "If the Arameans are too strong for me, then you
11: 3 [A] *The man* **said**, "Isn't this Bathsheba, the daughter of Eliam
11: 5 [A] and sent word to David, **saying**, "I am pregnant."
11: 8 [A] David **said** to Uriah, "Go down to your house and wash your
11: 10 [A] was told, **[NIE]** "Uriah did not go home," he asked him,
11: 10 [A] David was told, "Uriah did not go home," he **asked** him,
11: 11 [A] Uriah **said** to David, "The ark and Israel and Judah are
11: 12 [A] David **said** to him, "Stay here one more day, and tomorrow I
11: 15 [A] **[NIE]** "Put Uriah in the front line where the fighting is
11: 19 [A] **[NIE]** "When you have finished giving the king this account
11: 20 [A] *he may* **ask** you, 'Why did you get so close to the city to
11: 21 [A] If he asks you this, then **say** to him, 'Also, your servant
11: 23 [A] The messenger **said** to David, "The men overpowered us
11: 25 [A] David **told** the messenger, "Say this to Joab: 'Don't let this
11: 25 [A] David told the messenger, "**Say** this to Joab: 'Don't let this
12: 1 [A] When he came to him, *he* **said**, "There were two men in a
12: 5 [A] David burned with anger against the man and **said** to Nathan,
12: 7 [A] Nathan **said** to David, "You are the man! This is what the
12: 7 [A] the man! This is what the LORD, the God of Israel, **says**:
12: 11 [A] "This is what the LORD **says**: 'Out of your own household I
12: 13 [A] David **said** to Nathan, "I have sinned against the LORD."
12: 13 [A] Nathan **replied**, "The LORD has taken away your sin.
12: 18 [A] for *they* **thought**, "While the child was still living, we spoke
12: 18 [A] not listen to us. How *can we* **tell** him the child is dead?
12: 19 [A] the child dead?" he **asked**. "Yes," they replied, "he is dead."
12: 19 [A] the child dead?" he asked. "Yes," *they* **replied**, "he is dead."
12: 21 [A] His servants **asked** him, "Why are you acting this way?
12: 22 [A] *He* **answered**, "While the child was still alive, I fasted
12: 22 [A] was still alive, I fasted and wept. *I* **thought**, 'Who knows?
12: 27 [A] **saying**, "I have fought against Rabbah and taken its water
13: 4 [A] *He* **asked** Amnon, "Why do you, the king's son, look
13: 4 [A] Amnon **said** to him, "I'm in love with Tamar, my brother
13: 5 [A] "Go to bed and pretend to be ill," Jonadab **said**. "When your
13: 5 [A] "When your father comes to see you, **say** to him, 'I would
13: 6 [A] When the king came to see him, Amnon **said** to him,
13: 7 [A] David sent **word** to Tamar at the palace: "Go to the house of
13: 9 [A] he refused to eat. "Send everyone out of here," Amnon **said**.
13: 10 [A] Amnon **said** to Tamar, "Bring the food here into my
13: 11 [A] he grabbed her and **said**, "Come to bed with me, my sister."
13: 12 [A] "Don't, my brother!" *she* **said** to him. "Don't force me. Such
13: 15 [A] he had loved her. Amnon **said** to her, "Get up and get out!"
13: 16 [A] "No!" *she* **said** to him. "Sending me away would be a greater
13: 17 [A] He called his personal servant and **said**, "Get this woman out
13: 20 [A] Her brother Absalom **said** to her, "Has that Amnon,
13: 24 [A] Absalom went to the king and **said**, "Your servant has had
13: 25 [A] "No, my son," the king **replied**. "All of us should not go; we
13: 26 [A] Absalom **said**, "If not, please let my brother Amnon come
13: 26 [A] The king **asked** him, "Why should he go with you?"
13: 28 [A] Absalom ordered his men, **[NIE]** "Listen! When Amnon is
13: 28 [A] Amnon is in high spirits from drinking wine and *I* **say** to you,
13: 30 [A] **[NIE]** "Absalom has struck down all the king's sons; not
13: 32 [A] **[NIE]** "My lord should not think that they killed all the
13: 32 [A] "My lord *should* not **think** that they killed all the princes;
13: 33 [A] about the report **[NIE]** that all the king's sons are dead.
13: 34 [A] the king, **[NIE]** "I see men in the direction of Horonaim,
13: 35 [A] Jonadab **said** to the king, "See, the king's sons are here;
14: 2 [A] *He* **said** to her, "Pretend you are in mourning. Dress in
14: 4 [a] When the woman from Tekoa went [BHS *spoke*; NIV 995] to
14: 4 [A] ground to pay him honor, and *she* **said**, "Help me, O king!"
14: 5 [A] The king **asked** her, "What is troubling you?" She said,
14: 5 [A] *She* **said**, "I am indeed a widow; my husband is dead.
14: 7 [A] *they* **say**, 'Hand over the one who struck his brother down,
14: 8 [A] The king **said** to the woman, "Go home, and I will issue an
14: 9 [A] But the woman from Tekoa **said** to him, "My lord the king,
14: 10 [A] The king **replied**, "If anyone says anything to you, bring him
14: 11 [A] *She* **said**, "Then let the king invoke the LORD his God to
14: 11 [A] "As surely as the LORD lives," *he* **said**, "not one hair of
14: 12 [A] the woman **said**, "Let your servant speak a word to my lord
14: 12 [A] speak a word to my lord the king." "Speak," *he* **replied**.
14: 13 [A] The woman **said**, "Why then have you devised a thing like
14: 15 [A] Your servant **thought**, 'I will speak to the king; perhaps he
14: 17 [A] "And now your servant **says**, 'May the word of my lord the
14: 18 [A] the king said **[NIE]** to the woman, "Do not keep from me
14: 18 [A] to ask you." "Let my lord the king speak," the woman **said**.
14: 19 [A] The king **asked**, "Isn't the hand of Joab with you in all this?"
14: 19 [A] **[NIE]** "As surely as you live, my lord the king,
14: 21 [A] The king **said** to Joab, "Very well, I will do it. Go,
14: 22 [A] Joab **said**, "Today your servant knows that he has found
14: 24 [A] the king **said**, "He must go to his own house; he must not see
14: 30 [A] *he* **said** to his servants, "Look, Joab's field is next to mine,
14: 31 [A] Then Joab did go to Absalom's house and *he* **said** to him,
14: 32 [A] Absalom **said** to Joab, "Look, I sent word to you and said,
14: 32 [A] "Look, I sent word to you and **said**, 'Come here so I can send
14: 32 [A] and said, 'Come here so I can send you to the king to **ask**,
15: 2 [A] would call out to him, **[NIE]** "What town are you from?"
15: 2 [A] *He would* **answer**, "Your servant is from one of the tribes of
15: 3 [A] Absalom *would* **say** to him, "Look, your claims are valid
15: 4 [A] Absalom *would* **add**, "If only I were appointed judge in the
15: 7 [A] Absalom **said** to the king, "Let me go to Hebron and fulfill a
15: 8 [A] **[NIE]** 'If the LORD takes me back to Jerusalem, I will

2Sa 15: 9 [A] The king **said** to him, "Go in peace." So he went to Hebron.
15: 10 [A] sent secret messengers throughout the tribes of Israel to **say**,
15: 10 [A] of the trumpets, then **say**, 'Absalom is king in Hebron.' "
15: 13 [A] A messenger came and **told** David, "The hearts of the men of
15: 14 [A] David **said** to all his officials who were with him in
15: 15 [A] The king's officials **answered** him, "Your servants are ready
15: 19 [A] The king **said** to Ittai the Gittite, "Why should you come
15: 21 [A] replied to the king, **[NIE]** "As surely as the LORD lives,
15: 22 [A] David **said** to Ittai, "Go ahead, march on." So Ittai the Gittite
15: 25 [A] the king **said** to Zadok, "Take the ark of God back into the
15: 26 [A] But if *he* **says**, 'I am not pleased with you,' then I am ready;
15: 27 [A] The king also **said** to Zadok the priest, "Aren't you a seer?
15: 31 [A] **[NIE]** "Ahithophel is among the conspirators with
15: 31 [A] So David **prayed**, "O LORD, turn Ahithophel's counsel
15: 33 [A] David **said** to him, "If you go with me, you will be a burden
15: 34 [A] if you return to the city and **say** to Absalom, 'I will be your
16: 2 [A] The king **asked** Ziba, "Why have you brought these?" Ziba
16: 2 [A] Ziba **answered**, "The donkeys are for the king's household
16: 3 [A] The king then **asked**, "Where is your master's grandson?"
16: 3 [A] Ziba **said** to him, "He is staying in Jerusalem, because he
16: 3 [A] said to him, "He is staying in Jerusalem, because *he* **thinks**,
16: 4 [A] the king **said** to Ziba, "All that belonged to Mephibosheth is
16: 4 [A] "I humbly bow," Ziba **said**. "May I find favor in your eyes,
16: 7 [A] As he cursed, Shimei **said**, "Get out, get out, you man of
16: 9 [A] Abishai son of Zeruiah **said** to the king, "Why should this
16: 10 [A] the king **said**, "What do you and I have in common, you sons
16: 10 [A] If he is cursing because the LORD **said** to him,
16: 10 [A] to him, 'Curse David,' who *can* **ask**, 'Why do you do this?' "
16: 11 [A] David then **said** to Abishai and all his officials, "My son,
16: 11 [A] him alone; let him curse, for the LORD *has* **told** him to.
16: 16 [A] David's friend, went to Absalom and **said** to him, "Long live
16: 17 [A] Absalom **asked** Hushai, "Is this the love you show your
16: 18 [A] Hushai **said** to Absalom, "No, the one chosen by the
16: 20 [A] Absalom **said** to Ahithophel, "Give us your advice.
16: 21 [A] Ahithophel **answered**, "Lie with your father's concubines
17: 1 [A] Ahithophel **said** to Absalom, "I would choose twelve
17: 5 [A] Absalom **said**, "Summon also Hushai the Arkite, so we can
17: 6 [A] When Hushai came to him, Absalom **said**, "Ahithophel has
17: 6 [A] Absalom said, **[RPH]** "Ahithophel has given this advice.
17: 7 [A] Hushai **replied** to Absalom, "The advice Ahithophel has
17: 8 [A] **[RPH]** You know your father and his men; they are fighters,
17: 9 [A] attack your troops first, whoever hears about it *will* **say**,
17: 14 [A] Absalom and all the men of Israel **said**, "The advice of
17: 15 [A] Hushai **told** Zadok and Abiathar, the priests, "Ahithophel has
17: 16 [A] **[NIE]** 'Do not spend the night at the fords in the desert;
17: 20 [A] the house, *they* **asked**, "Where are Ahimaaz and Jonathan?"
17: 20 [A] The woman **answered** them, "They crossed over the brook."
17: 21 [A] *They* **said** to him, "Set out and cross the river at once;
17: 29 [A] For *they* **said**, "The people have become hungry and tired
18: 2 [A] The king **told** the troops, "I myself will surely march out
18: 3 [A] the men **said**, "You must not go out; if we are forced to flee,
18: 4 [A] The king **answered**, "I will do whatever seems best to you."
18: 5 [A] **[NIE]** "Be gentle with the young man Absalom for my
18: 10 [A] **[NIE]** "I just saw Absalom hanging in an oak tree."
18: 11 [A] Joab **said** to the man who had told him this, "What! You saw
18: 12 [A] the man **replied**, "Even if a thousand shekels were weighed
18: 12 [A] **[NIE]** 'Protect the young man Absalom for my sake.'
18: 14 [A] Joab **said**, "I'm not going to wait like this for you." So he
18: 18 [A] for *he* **thought**, "I have no son to carry on the memory of my
18: 19 [A] Now Ahimaaz son of Zadok **said**, "Let me run and take the
18: 20 [A] "You are not the one to take the news today," Joab **told** him.
18: 21 [A] Joab **said** to a Cushite, "Go, tell the king what you have
18: 22 [A] Ahimaaz son of Zadok again **said** to Joab, "Come what may,
18: 22 [A] But Joab **replied**, "My son, why do you want to go?
18: 23 [A] "Come what may, I want to run." So Joab **said**, "Run!"
18: 25 [A] The king **said**, "If he is alone, he must have good news."
18: 26 [A] the gatekeeper, **[NIE]** "Look, another man running alone!"
18: 26 [A] The king **said**, "He must be bringing good news, too."
18: 27 [A] The watchman **said**, "It seems to me that the first one runs
18: 27 [A] "He's a good man," the king **said**. "He comes with good
18: 28 [A] Then Ahimaaz called out **[NIE]** to the king, "All is well!"
18: 28 [A] down before the king with his face to the ground and **said**,
18: 29 [A] The king **asked**, "Is the young man Absalom safe?" Ahimaaz
18: 29 [A] Ahimaaz **answered**, "I saw great confusion just as Joab was
18: 30 [A] The king **said**, "Stand aside and wait here." So he stepped
18: 31 [A] the Cushite arrived and **said**, "My lord the king,
18: 32 [A] The king **asked** the Cushite, "Is the young man Absalom
18: 32 [A] The Cushite **replied**, "May the enemies of my lord the king
18: 33 [19:1] [A] over the gateway and wept. As he went, *he* **said**:
19: 2 [19:3] [A] because on that day the troops heard *it* **said**,
19: 5 [19:6] [A] Joab went into the house to the king and **said**,
19: 8 [19:9] [A] **[NIE]** "The king is sitting in the gateway,"
19: 9 [19:10] [A] the people were all arguing with each other, **saying**,
19: 11 [19:12] [A] King David sent this **message** to Zadok
19: 11 [19:12] [A] **[RPH]** 'Why should you be the last to bring the
19: 13 [19:14] [A] **say** to Amasa, 'Are you not my own flesh
19: 19 [19:20] [A] **said** to him, "May my lord not hold me guilty. Do
19: 21 [19:22] [A] **[NIE]** "Shouldn't Shimei be put to death for this?
19: 22 [19:23] [A] David **replied**, "What do you and I have in
19: 23 [19:24] [A] So the king **said** to Shimei, "You shall not die."
19: 25 [19:26] [A] the king **asked** him, "Why didn't you go with me,
19: 26 [19:27] [A] *He* **said**, "My lord the king, since I your servant am
19: 26 [19:27] [A] lord the king, since I your servant am lame, I **said**,
19: 29 [19:30] [A] The king **said** to him, "Why say more? I order you
19: 29 [19:30] [A] *I* **order** you and Ziba to divide the fields."
19: 30 [19:31] [A] Mephibosheth **said** to the king, "Let him take
19: 33 [19:34] [A] The king **said** to Barzillai, "Cross over with me
19: 34 [19:35] [A] Barzillai **answered** the king, "How many more
19: 38 [19:39] [A] The king **said**, "Kimham shall cross over with me,
19: 41 [19:42] [A] of Israel were coming to the king and **saying** to him,
19: 43 [19:44] [A] of Judah, **[NIE]** "We have ten shares in the king;
20: 1 [A] He sounded the trumpet and **shouted**, "We have no share in
20: 4 [A] the king **said** to Amasa, "Summon the men of Judah to come
20: 6 [A] David **said** to Abishai, "Now Sheba son of Bicri will do us
20: 9 [A] Joab **said** to Amasa, "How are you, my brother?" Then Joab
20: 11 [A] One of Joab's men stood beside Amasa and **said**,
20: 16 [A] Listen! **Tell** Joab to come here so I can speak to him."
20: 17 [A] He went toward her, and she **asked**, "Are you Joab?" "I am,"
20: 17 [A] "I am," *he* **answered**. She said, "Listen to what your servant
20: 17 [A] *She* **said**, "Listen to what your servant has to say."
20: 17 [A] to what your servant has to say." "I'm listening," *he* **said**.
20: 18 [A] *She* **continued**, "Long ago they used to say, 'Get your
20: 18 [A] She continued, **[RPH]** "Long ago they used to say, 'Get
20: 18 [A] to say, **[NIE]** 'Get your answer at Abel,' and that settled it.
20: 20 [A] **[NIE]** "Far be it from me to swallow up or destroy!
20: 21 [A] The woman **said** to Joab, "His head will be thrown to you
21: 1 [A] The LORD **said**, "It is on account of Saul and his
21: 2 [A] The king summoned the Gibeonites and **spoke** to them.
21: 3 [A] David **asked** the Gibeonites, "What shall I do for you? How
21: 4 [A] The Gibeonites **answered** him, "We have no right to demand
21: 4 [A] "What *do* you **want** me to do for you?" David asked.
21: 4 [A] "What do you want me to do for you?" David **asked**.
21: 5 [A] *They* **answered** the king, "As for the man who destroyed us
21: 6 [A] chosen one." So the king **said**, "I will give them to you."
21: 16 [A] was armed with a new ⌞sword⌟, **said** he would kill David.
21: 17 [A] David's men swore to him, **saying**, "Never again will you go
22: 2 [A] *He* **said**: "The LORD is my rock, my fortress and my
23: 3 [A] The God of Israel **spoke**, the Rock of Israel said to me:
23: 15 [A] David longed for water and **said**, "Oh, that someone would
23: 17 [A] "Far be it from me, O LORD, to do this!" *he* **said**. "Is it not
24: 1 [A] **saying**, "Go and take a census of Israel and Judah."
24: 2 [A] So the king **said** to Joab and the army commanders with him,
24: 3 [A] Joab **replied** to the king, "May the LORD your God
24: 10 [A] he **said** to the LORD, "I have sinned greatly in what I have
24: 11 [A] LORD had come to Gad the prophet, David's seer: **[NIE]**
24: 12 [A] "Go and tell David, 'This is what the LORD **says**: I am
24: 13 [A] **[NIE]** "Shall there come upon you three years of famine in
24: 14 [A] David **said** to Gad, "I am in deep distress. Let us fall into the
24: 16 [A] and **said** to the angel who was afflicting the people,
24: 17 [A] *he* **said** to the LORD, "I am the one who has sinned
24: 17 [A] **[RPH]** "I am the one who has sinned and done wrong.
24: 18 [A] On that day Gad went to David and **said** to him, "Go up
24: 21 [A] Araunah **said**, "Why has my lord the king come to his
24: 21 [A] "To buy your threshing floor," David **answered**, "so I can
24: 22 [A] Araunah **said** to David, "Let my lord the king take whatever
24: 23 [A] Araunah also **said** to him, "May the LORD your God accept
24: 24 [A] the king **replied** to Araunah, "No, I insist on paying you for
1Ki 1: 2 [A] So his servants **said** to him, "Let us look for a young virgin
1: 5 [A] was Haggith, put himself forward and **said**, "I will be king."
1: 6 [A] (His father had never interfered with him by **asking**,
1: 11 [A] Nathan **asked** Bathsheba, Solomon's mother, "Have you not
1: 11 [A] **[RPH]** "Have you not heard that Adonijah, the son of
1: 13 [A] Go in to King David and **say** to him, 'My lord the king, did
1: 13 [A] **[NIE]** "Surely Solomon your son shall be king after me,
1: 16 [A] knelt before the king. "What is it you want?" the king **asked**.
1: 17 [A] *She* **said** to him, "My lord, you yourself swore to me your
1: 23 [A] And they told the king, **[NIE]** "Nathan the prophet is here."
1: 24 [A] Nathan **said**, "Have you, my lord the king, declared that
1: 24 [A] "*Have* you, my lord the king, **declared** that Adonijah shall
1: 25 [A] Right now they are eating and drinking with him and **saying**,
1: 28 [A] King David said, **[NIE]** "Call in Bathsheba." So she came
1: 29 [A] **[NIE]** "As surely as the LORD lives, who has delivered
1: 30 [A] **[NIE]** Solomon your son shall be king after me, and he will
1: 31 [A] kneeling before the king, **said**, "May my lord King David
1: 32 [A] King David **said**, "Call in Zadok the priest, Nathan the
1: 33 [A] he **said** to them: "Take your lord's servants with you and set
1: 34 [A] Blow the trumpet and **shout**, 'Long live King Solomon!'
1: 36 [A] Benaiah son of Jehoiada answered the king, **[NIE]** "Amen!

1Ki 1:36 [A] *May* the LORD, the God of my lord the king, so **declare** it.
1:39 [A] Then they sounded the trumpet and all the people **shouted**,
1:41 [A] On hearing the sound of the trumpet, Joab **asked**,
1:42 [A] son of Abiathar the priest arrived. Adonijah **said**, "Come in.
1:43 [A] **[NIE]** "Our lord King David has made Solomon king.
1:47 [A] **saying**, 'May your God make Solomon's name more famous
1:48 [A] **said**, 'Praise be to the LORD, the God of Israel, who has
1:51 [A] **[NIE]** "Adonijah is afraid of King Solomon and is clinging
1:51 [A] *He* **says**, 'Let King Solomon swear to me today that he will
1:52 [A] Solomon **replied**, "If he shows himself to be a worthy man,
1:53 [A] to King Solomon, and Solomon **said**, "Go to your home."
2:2 [2:1] [A] "I am about to go the way of all the earth," he **said**.
2:4 [A] **[NIE]** 'If your descendants watch how they live, and if they
2:4 [A] **[NIE]** you will never fail to have a man on the throne of
2:8 [A] **[NIE]** 'I will not put you to death by the sword.'
2:13 [A] Bathsheba **asked** him, "Do you come peacefully?" He
2:13 [A] you come peacefully?" *He* **answered**, "Yes, peacefully."
2:14 [A] *he* **added**, "I have something to say to you." "You may say
2:14 [A] something to say to you." "You may say it," *she* **replied**.
2:15 [A] "As you know," *he* **said**, "the kingdom was mine. All Israel
2:16 [A] of you. Do not refuse me." "You may make it," *she* **said**.
2:17 [A] So *he* **continued**, "Please ask King Solomon—he will not
2:17 [A] So he continued, "Please **ask** King Solomon—he will not
2:18 [A] "Very well," Bathsheba **replied**, "I will speak to the king for
2:20 [A] "I have one small request to make of you," *she* **said**. "Do not
2:20 [A] The king **replied**, "Make it, my mother; I will not refuse
2:21 [A] So *she* **said**, "Let Abishag the Shunammite be given in
2:22 [A] King Solomon answered **[NIE]** his mother, "Why do you
2:23 [A] **[NIE]** "May God deal with me, be it ever so severely, if
2:26 [A] To Abiathar the priest the king **said**, "Go back to your fields
2:29 [A] Benaiah son of Jehoiada, **[NIE]** "Go, strike him down!"
2:30 [A] So Benaiah entered the tent of the LORD and **said** to Joab,
2:30 [A] the tent of the LORD and said to Joab, "The king **says**,
2:30 [A] "The king says, 'Come out!' " But *he* **answered**, "No, I will
2:30 [A] to the king, **[NIE]** "This is how Joab answered me."
2:31 [A] the king **commanded** Benaiah, "Do as he says. Strike him
2:36 [A] the king sent for Shimei and **said** to him, "Build yourself a
2:38 [A] Shimei **answered** the king, "What you say is good.
2:39 [A] and Shimei was told, **[NIE]** "Your slaves are in Gath."
2:42 [A] the king summoned Shimei and **said** to him, "Did I not make
2:42 [A] warn you, **[NIE]** 'On the day you leave to go anywhere else,
2:42 [A] At that time *you* **said** to me, 'What you say is good. I will
2:44 [A] The king also **said** to Shimei, "You know in your heart all
3:5 [A] and God **said**, "Ask for whatever you want me to give you."
3:6 [A] Solomon **answered**, "You have shown great kindness to your
3:11 [A] So God **said** to him, "Since you have asked for this and not
3:17 [A] One of them **said**, "My lord, this woman and I live in the
3:22 [A] The other woman **said**, "No! The living one is my son;
3:22 [A] the first one **insisted**, "No! The dead one is yours; the living
3:23 [A] The king **said**, "This one says, 'My son is alive and your son
3:23 [A] The king said, "This one **says**, 'My son is alive and your son
3:23 [A] son is alive and your son is dead,' while that one **says**, 'No!
3:24 [A] the king **said**, "Bring me a sword." So they brought a sword
3:25 [A] He then **gave an order**: "Cut the living child in two and give
3:26 [A] was filled with compassion for her son and **said** to the king,
3:26 [A] for her son and said to the king, **[RPH]** "Please, my lord,
3:26 [A] But the other **said**, "Neither I nor you shall have him.
3:27 [A] **[NIE]** "Give the living baby to the first woman. Do not kill
5:2 [5:16] [A] Solomon sent back this **message** to Hiram:
5:5 [5:19] [A] I **intend**, therefore, to build a temple for the Name of
5:5 [5:19] [A] as the LORD told my father David, when he **said**,
5:6 [5:20] [A] I will pay you for your men whatever wages *you* **set**.
5:7 [5:21] [A] he was greatly pleased and **said**, "Praise be to the
5:8 [5:22] [A] So Hiram sent **word** to Solomon: "I have received
6:11 [A] The word of the LORD came to Solomon: **[NIE]**
8:12 [A] Solomon **said**, "The LORD has said that he would dwell in
8:12 [A] "The LORD *has* **said** that he would dwell in a dark cloud;
8:15 [A] Then *he* **said**: "Praise be to the LORD, the God of Israel,
8:15 [A] with his own mouth to my father David. For he **said**,
8:18 [A] the LORD **said** to my father David, 'Because it was in your
8:23 [A] **said**: "O LORD, God of Israel, there is no God like you in
8:25 [A] my father the promises you made to him when you **said**,
8:29 [A] this temple night and day, this place of which *you* **said**,
8:47 [A] and plead with you in the land of their conquerors and **say**,
8:55 [A] blessed the whole assembly of Israel in a loud voice, **saying**:
9:3 [A] The LORD **said** to him: "I have heard the prayer and plea
9:5 [A] Israel forever, as I promised David your father when I **said**,
9:8 [A] all who pass by will be appalled and will scoff and **say**,
9:9 [A] *People will* **answer**, 'Because they have forsaken the LORD
9:13 [A] towns are these you have given me, my brother?" *he* **asked**.
10:6 [A] *She* **said** to the king, "The report I heard in my own country
11:2 [A] They were from nations about which the LORD *had* **told**
11:11 [A] So the LORD **said** to Solomon, "Since this is your attitude
11:18 [A] gave Hadad a house and land and **provided** him *with* food.
11:21 [A] Hadad **said** to Pharaoh, "Let me go, that I may return to my
11:22 [A] Pharaoh **asked**. "Nothing," Hadad replied, "but do let me
11:22 [A] "Nothing," Hadad **replied**, "but do let me go!"
11:31 [A] *he* **said** to Jeroboam, "Take ten pieces for yourself, for this is
11:31 [A] for this is what the LORD, the God of Israel, **says**:
12:3 [A] of Israel went to Rehoboam and said to him: **[NIE]**
12:5 [A] Rehoboam **answered**, "Go away for three days and
12:6 [A] would you advise me to answer these people?" he **asked**.
12:7 [A] **[NIE]** "If today you will be a servant to these people
12:9 [A] *He* **asked** them, "What is your advice? How should we
12:9 [A] say to me, **[NIE]** 'Lighten the yoke your father put on us'?"
12:10 [A] **[NIE]** "Tell these people who have said to you, 'Your father
12:10 [A] "**Tell** these people who have said to you, 'Your father put a
12:10 [A] **[NIE]** 'Your father put a heavy yoke on us, but make our
12:12 [A] the king had said, **[NIE]** "Come back to me in three days."
12:14 [A] and said, **[NIE]** "My father made your yoke heavy;
12:16 [A] **[NIE]** "What share do we have in David, what part in
12:22 [A] this word of God came to Shemaiah the man of God: **[NIE]**
12:23 [A] "**Say** to Rehoboam son of Solomon king of Judah, to the
12:23 [A] and Benjamin, and to the rest of the people, **[RPH]**
12:24 [A] 'This is what the LORD **says**: Do not go up to fight against
12:26 [A] Jeroboam **thought** to himself, "The kingdom will now likely
12:28 [A] *He* **said** to the people, "It is too much for you to go up to
13:2 [A] **[NIE]** "O altar, altar! This is what the LORD says: 'A son
13:2 [A] "O altar, altar! This is what the LORD **says**: 'A son named
13:3 [A] **[NIE]** "This is the sign the LORD has declared: The altar
13:4 [A] he stretched out his hand from the altar and **said**,
13:6 [A] the king said **[NIE]** to the man of God, "Intercede with the
13:8 [A] the man of God **answered** the king, "Even if you were to
13:9 [A] **[NIE]** 'You must not eat bread or drink water or return by
13:13 [A] So *he* **said** to his sons, "Saddle the donkey for me."
13:14 [A] He found him sitting under an oak tree and **asked**, "Are you
13:14 [A] the man of God who came from Judah?" "I am," *he* **replied**.
13:15 [A] So the prophet **said** to him, "Come home with me and eat."
13:16 [A] The man of God **said**, "I cannot turn back and go with you,
13:18 [A] The old prophet **answered**, "I too am a prophet, as you are.
13:18 [A] **[NIE]** 'Bring him back with you to your house so that he
13:21 [A] come from Judah, **[NIE]** "This is what the LORD says:
13:21 [A] who had come from Judah, "This is what the LORD **says**:
13:26 [A] *he* **said**, "It is the man of God who defied the word of the
13:27 [A] **[NIE]** "Saddle the donkey for me," and they did so.
13:31 [A] After burying him, *he* **said** to his sons, "When I die, bury me
13:31 [A] After burying him, he said to his sons, **[RPH]** "When I die,
14:2 [A] Jeroboam **said** to his wife, "Go, disguise yourself, so you
14:5 [A] the LORD *had* **told** Ahijah, "Jeroboam's wife is coming to
14:6 [A] footsteps at the door, *he* **said**, "Come in, wife of Jeroboam.
14:7 [A] Go, **tell** Jeroboam that this is what the LORD, the God of
14:7 [A] that this is what the LORD, the God of Israel, **says**:
15:19 [15:18] [A] "Let there be a treaty between me and you," he **said**,
16:1 [A] LORD came to Jehu son of Hanani against Baasha: **[NIE]**
16:16 [A] When the Israelites in the camp heard **[NIE]** that Zimri had
17:1 [A] **said** to Ahab, "As the LORD, the God of Israel, lives,
17:2 [A] Then the word of the LORD came to Elijah: **[NIE]**
17:8 [A] Then the word of the LORD came to him: **[NIE]**
17:10 [A] He called to her and **asked**, "Would you bring me a little
17:11 [A] he called, "And **[NIE]** bring me, please, a piece of bread."
17:12 [A] your God lives," *she* **replied**, "I don't have any bread—
17:13 [A] Elijah **said** to her, "Don't be afraid. Go home and do as you
17:14 [A] For this is what the LORD, the God of Israel, **says**: 'The jar
17:18 [A] *She* **said** to Elijah, "What do you have against me, man of
17:19 [A] "Give me your son," Elijah **replied**. He took him from her
17:20 [A] he cried out to the LORD, **[NIE]** "O LORD my God,
17:21 [A] LORD my God, **[NIE]** let this boy's life return to him!"
17:23 [A] He gave him to his mother and **said**, "Look, your son is
17:24 [A] the woman **said** to Elijah, "Now I know that you are a man
18:1 [A] **[NIE]** "Go and present yourself to Ahab, and I will send
18:5 [A] Ahab *had* **said** to Obadiah, "Go through the land to all the
18:7 [A] to the ground, and **said**, "Is it really you, my lord Elijah?"
18:8 [A] "Yes," *he* **replied**. "Go tell your master, 'Elijah is here.' "
18:8 [A] "Yes," he replied. "Go **tell** your master, 'Elijah is here.' "
18:9 [A] "What have I done wrong," **asked** Obadiah, "that you are
18:10 [A] whenever a nation or kingdom **claimed** you were not there,
18:11 [A] now you **tell** me to go to my master and say, 'Elijah is here.'
18:11 [A] now you tell me to go to my master and **say**, 'Elijah is here.'
18:14 [A] now you **tell** me to go to my master and say, 'Elijah is here.'
18:14 [A] now you tell me to go to my master and **say**, 'Elijah is here.'
18:15 [A] Elijah **said**, "As the LORD Almighty lives, whom I serve,
18:17 [A] When he saw Elijah, he **said** to him, "Is that you,
18:18 [A] "I have not made trouble for Israel," Elijah **replied**. "But you
18:21 [A] Elijah went before the people and **said**, "How long will you
18:22 [A] Elijah **said** to them, "I am the only one of the LORD's
18:24 [A] Then all the people said, **[NIE]** "What you say is good."
18:25 [A] Elijah **said** to the prophets of Baal, "Choose one of the bulls
18:26 [A] "O Baal, answer us!" they **shouted**. But there was no

1Ki 18:27 [A] "Shout louder!" *he* **said**. "Surely he is a god! Perhaps he is
18:30 [A] Elijah **said** to all the people, "Come here to me." They came
18:31 [A] the LORD had come, **saying**, "Your name shall be Israel."
18:33 [18:34] [A] *he* **said** to them, "Fill four large jars with water
18:34 [A] "Do it again," *he* **said**, and they did it again. "Do it a third
18:34 [A] "Do it a third time," *he* **ordered**, and they did it the third
18:36 [A] of sacrifice, the prophet Elijah stepped forward and **prayed**:
18:39 [A] people saw this, they fell prostrate and **cried**, "The LORD—
18:40 [A] Then Elijah **commanded** them, "Seize the prophets of Baal.
18:41 [A] Elijah **said** to Ahab, "Go, eat and drink, for there is the sound
18:43 [A] "Go and look toward the sea," *he* **told** his servant. And he
18:43 [A] he went up and looked. "There is nothing there," *he* **said**.
18:43 [A] nothing there," he said. Seven times Elijah **said**, "Go back."
18:44 [A] The seventh time the servant **reported**, "A cloud as small as
18:44 [A] So Elijah **said**, "Go and tell Ahab, 'Hitch up your chariot
18:44 [A] So Elijah said, "Go and **tell** Ahab, 'Hitch up your chariot
19: 2 [A] So Jezebel sent a messenger to Elijah to **say**, "May the gods
19: 4 [A] "I have had enough, LORD," *he* **said**. "Take my life; I am
19: 5 [A] All at once an angel touched him and **said**, "Get up and eat."
19: 7 [A] LORD came back a second time and touched him and **said**,
19: 9 [A] spent the night. And the word of the LORD **came** to him:
19:10 [A] *He* **replied**, "I have been very zealous for the LORD God
19:11 [A] The LORD **said**, "Go out and stand on the mountain in the
19:13 [A] Then a voice **said** to him, "What are you doing here, Elijah?"
19:14 [A] *He* **replied**, "I have been very zealous for the LORD God
19:15 [A] The LORD **said** to him, "Go back the way you came,
19:20 [A] mother good-by," *he* **said**, "and then I will come with you."
19:20 [A] "and then I will come with you." "Go back," Elijah **replied**.
20: 2 [20:3] [A] king of Israel, **saying**, "This is what Ben-Hadad says:
20: 2 [20:3] [A] king of Israel, saying, "This is what Ben-Hadad **says**:
20: 4 [A] Israel answered, **[NIE]** "Just as you say, my lord the king.
20: 5 [A] The messengers came again and **said**, "This is what
20: 5 [A] came again and said, "This is what Ben-Hadad **says**:
20: 5 [A] **[RPH]** 'I sent to demand your silver and gold, your wives
20: 5 [A] 'I sent to **demand** your silver and gold, your wives and your
20: 7 [A] Israel summoned all the elders of the land and **said** to them,
20: 8 [A] The elders and the people all **answered**, "Don't listen to him
20: 9 [A] So *he* **replied** to Ben-Hadad's messengers, "Tell my lord the
20: 9 [A] replied to Ben-Hadad's messengers, "**Tell** my lord the king,
20:10 [A] Ben-Hadad sent another **message** to Ahab: "May the gods
20:11 [A] The king of Israel answered, **[NIE]** "Tell him: 'One who
20:12 [A] kings were drinking in their tents, and *he* **ordered** his men:
20:13 [A] a prophet came to Ahab king of Israel and **announced**,
20:13 [A] king of Israel and announced, "This is what the LORD **says**:
20:14 [A] **asked** Ahab. The prophet replied, "This is what the LORD
20:14 [A] The prophet **replied**, "This is what the LORD says:
20:14 [A] The prophet replied, "This is what the LORD **says**:
20:14 [A] the battle?" *he* **asked**. The prophet answered, "You will."
20:14 [A] the battle?" he asked. The prophet **answered**, "You will."
20:17 [A] who reported, **[NIE]** "Men are advancing from Samaria."
20:18 [A] *He* **said**, "If they have come out for peace, take them alive;
20:22 [A] Afterward, the prophet came to the king of Israel and **said**,
20:23 [A] Meanwhile, the officials of the king of Aram **advised** him,
20:28 [A] The man of God came up and **told** the king of Israel, "This is
20:28 [A] the king of Israel, **[RPH]** "This is what the LORD says:
20:28 [A] and told the king of Israel, "This is what the LORD **says**:
20:28 [A] 'Because the Arameans **think** the LORD is a god of the hills
20:31 [A] His officials **said** to him, "Look, we have heard that the kings
20:32 [A] around their heads, they went to the king of Israel and **said**,
20:32 [A] to the king of Israel and said, "Your servant Ben-Hadad **says**:
20:32 [A] 'Please let me live.' " The king **answered**, "Is he still alive?
20:33 [A] *they* **said**. "Go and get him," the king said.
20:33 [A] they said. "Go and get him," the king **said**.
20:34 [A] cities my father took from your father," Ben-Hadad **offered**.
20:35 [A] one of the sons of the prophets **said** to his companion,
20:36 [A] So the prophet **said**, "Because you have not obeyed the
20:37 [A] The prophet found another man and **said**, "Strike me,
20:39 [A] **[NIE]** "Your servant went into the thick of the battle,
20:39 [A] someone came to me with a captive and **said**, 'Guard this
20:40 [A] "That is your sentence," the king of Israel **said**.
20:42 [A] *He* **said** to the king, "This is what the LORD says: 'You
20:42 [A] He said to the king, "This is what the LORD **says**: 'You
21: 2 [A] **[NIE]** "Let me have your vineyard to use for a vegetable
21: 3 [A] Naboth **replied**, "The LORD forbid that I should give you
21: 4 [A] **[NIE]** "I will not give you the inheritance of my fathers."
21: 6 [A] said to Naboth the Jezreelite, **[NIE]** 'Sell me your vineyard;
21: 6 [A] in its place.' But *he* **said**, 'I will not give you my vineyard.' "
21: 7 [A] Jezebel his wife **said**, "Is this how you act as king over
21: 9 [A] **[NIE]** "Proclaim a day of fasting and seat Naboth in a
21:10 [A] and have them testify that he **[NIE]** has cursed both God
21:13 [A] **saying**, "Naboth has cursed both God and the king."
21:14 [A] Then they sent **word** to Jezebel: "Naboth has been stoned
21:15 [A] she **said** to Ahab, "Get up and take possession of the
21:17 [A] the word of the LORD came to Elijah the Tishbite: **[NIE]**
21:19 [A] Say to him, **[NIE]** 'This is what the LORD says: Have you
21:19 [A] Say to him, 'This is what the LORD **says**: Have you not
21:19 [A] Then say to him, **[NIE]** 'This is what the LORD says:
21:19 [A] Then say to him, 'This is what the LORD **says**:
21:20 [A] Ahab **said** to Elijah, "So you have found me, my enemy!"
21:20 [A] "I have found you," *he* **answered**, "because you have sold
21:23 [A] **[NIE]** 'Dogs will devour Jezebel by the wall of Jezreel.'
21:28 [A] the word of the LORD came to Elijah the Tishbite: **[NIE]**
22: 3 [A] The king of Israel *had* **said** to his officials, "Don't you know
22: 4 [A] So *he* **asked** Jehoshaphat, "Will you go with me to fight
22: 4 [A] Jehoshaphat **replied** to the king of Israel, "I am as you are,
22: 5 [A] Jehoshaphat also **said** to the king of Israel, "First seek the
22: 6 [A] and **asked** them, "Shall I go to war against Ramoth Gilead,
22: 6 [A] "Go," *they* **answered**, "for the Lord will give it into the
22: 7 [A] Jehoshaphat **asked**, "Is there not a prophet of the LORD
22: 8 [A] The king of Israel **answered** Jehoshaphat, "There is still one
22: 8 [A] "The king *should* not **say** that," Jehoshaphat replied.
22: 8 [A] "The king should not say that," Jehoshaphat **replied**.
22: 9 [A] So the king of Israel called one of his officials and **said**,
22:11 [A] son of Kenaanah had made iron horns and *he* **declared**,
22:11 [A] iron horns and he declared, "This is what the LORD **says**:
22:12 [A] "Attack Ramoth Gilead and be victorious," they **said**,
22:13 [A] had gone to summon Micaiah said to him, **[NIE]** "Look,
22:14 [A] Micaiah **said**, "As surely as the LORD lives, I can tell him
22:14 [A] LORD lives, I can tell him only what the LORD **tells** me."
22:15 [A] When he arrived, the king **asked** him, "Micaiah, shall we go
22:15 [A] "Attack and be victorious," *he* **answered**, "for the LORD
22:16 [A] The king **said** to him, "How many times must I make you
22:17 [A] Micaiah **answered**, "I saw all Israel scattered on the hills like
22:17 [A] and the LORD **said**, 'These people have no master.
22:18 [A] The king of Israel **said** to Jehoshaphat, "Didn't I tell you that
22:18 [A] "Didn't *I* **tell** you that he never prophesies anything good
22:19 [A] Micaiah **continued**, "Therefore hear the word of the LORD:
22:20 [A] the LORD **said**, 'Who will entice Ahab into attacking
22:20 [A] to his death there?' "One **suggested** this, and another that.
22:20 [A] death there?' "One suggested this, and another **[RPH]** that.
22:21 [A] stood before the LORD and **said**, 'I will entice him.'
22:22 [22:21] [A] the LORD **asked**. " 'I will go out and be a lying
22:22 [A] be a lying spirit in the mouths of all his prophets,' *he* **said**.
22:22 [A] " 'You will succeed in enticing him,' **said** the LORD. 'Go
22:24 [A] go when he went from me to speak to you?" *he* **asked**.
22:25 [A] Micaiah **replied**, "You will find out on the day you go to
22:26 [A] The king of Israel then **ordered**, "Take Micaiah and send
22:27 [A] and **say**, 'This is what the king says: Put this fellow in prison
22:27 [A] and say, 'This is what the king **says**: Put this fellow in prison
22:28 [A] Micaiah **declared**, "If you ever return safely, the LORD has
22:28 [A] Then *he* **added**, "Mark my words, all you people!"
22:30 [A] The king of Israel **said** to Jehoshaphat, "I will enter the battle
22:31 [A] **[NIE]** "Do not fight with anyone, small or great, except the
22:32 [A] they **thought**, "Surely this is the king of Israel."
22:34 [A] The king **told** his chariot driver, "Wheel around and get me
22:36 [A] **[NIE]** "Every man to his town; everyone to his land!"
22:49 [22:50] [A] At that time Ahaziah son of Ahab **said** to
2Ki 1: 2 [A] **saying** to them, "Go and consult Baal-Zebub, the god of
1: 4 [A] Therefore this is what the LORD **says**: 'You will not leave
1: 5 [A] to the king, *he* **asked** them, "Why have you come back?"
1: 6 [A] "A man came to meet us," *they* **replied**. "And he said to us,
1: 6 [A] "And *he* **said** to us, 'Go back to the king who sent you
1: 6 [A] who sent you and tell him, "This is what the LORD **says**:
1: 8 [A] *They* **replied**, "He was a man with a garment of hair
1: 8 [A] his waist." The king **said**, "That was Elijah the Tishbite."
1:11 [A] "Man of God, this is what the king **says**, 'Come down at
1:16 [A] He told the king, "This is what the LORD **says**: Is it
2: 2 [A] Elijah **said** to Elisha, "Stay here; the LORD has sent me to
2: 2 [A] Elisha **said**, "As surely as the LORD lives and as you live,
2: 3 [A] of the prophets at Bethel came out to Elisha and **asked**,
2: 3 [A] I know," Elisha **replied**, "but do not speak of it."
2: 4 [A] Elijah **said** to him, "Stay here, Elisha; the LORD has sent
2: 4 [A] *he* **replied**, "As surely as the LORD lives and as you live,
2: 5 [A] of the prophets at Jericho went up to Elisha and **asked** him,
2: 5 [A] "Yes, I know," *he* **replied**, "but do not speak of it."
2: 6 [A] Elijah **said** to him, "Stay here; the LORD has sent me to the
2: 6 [A] *he* **replied**, "As surely as the LORD lives and as you live,
2: 9 [A] When they had crossed, Elijah **said** to Elisha, "Tell me,
2: 9 [A] me inherit a double portion of your spirit," Elisha **replied**.
2:10 [A] "You have asked a difficult thing," Elijah **said**, "yet if you
2:14 [A] "Where now is the LORD, the God of Elijah?" *he* **asked**.
2:15 [A] who were watching, **said**, "The spirit of Elijah is resting on
2:16 [A] "Look," *they* **said**, "we your servants have fifty able men.
2:16 [A] in some valley." "No," Elisha **replied**, "do not send them."
2:17 [A] So *he* **said**, "Send them." And they sent fifty men, who
2:18 [A] who was staying in Jericho, *he* **said** to them, "Didn't I tell
2:18 [A] in Jericho, he said to them, "Didn't *I* **tell** you not to go?"
2:19 [A] The men of the city **said** to Elisha, "Look, our lord, this town

2Ki 2:20 [A] "Bring me a new bowl," *he* **said**, "and put salt in it." So they
2:21 [A] he went out to the spring and threw the salt into it, **saying**,
2:21 [A] threw the salt into it, saying, "This is what the LORD **says**:
2:23 [A] on up, you baldhead!" *they* **said**. "Go on up, you baldhead!"
3: 7 [A] He also sent this **message** to Jehoshaphat king of Judah:
3: 7 [A] "I will go with you," *he* **replied**. "I am as you are, my people
3: 8 [A] *he* **asked**. "Through the Desert of Edom," he answered.
3: 8 [A] he asked. "Through the Desert of Edom," *he* **answered**.
3:10 [A] "What!" **exclaimed** the king of Israel. "Has the LORD
3:11 [A] Jehoshaphat **asked**, "Is there no prophet of the LORD here,
3:11 [A] of Israel answered, **[NIE]** "Elisha son of Shaphat is here.
3:12 [A] Jehoshaphat **said**, "The word of the LORD is with him."
3:13 [A] Elisha **said** to the king of Israel, "What do we have to do
3:13 [A] "No," the king of Israel **answered**, "because it was the
3:14 [A] Elisha **said**, "As surely as the LORD Almighty lives,
3:16 [A] *he* **said**, "This is what the LORD says: Make this valley full
3:16 [A] he said, "This is what the LORD **says**: Make this valley full
3:17 [A] For this is what the LORD **says**: You will see neither wind
3:23 [A] "That's blood!" *they* **said**. "Those kings must have fought
4: 1 [A] **[NIE]** "Your servant my husband is dead, and you know
4: 2 [A] Elisha **replied** to her, "How can I help you? Tell me, what do
4: 2 [A] has nothing there at all," *she* **said**, "except a little oil."
4: 3 [A] Elisha **said**, "Go around and ask all your neighbors for empty
4: 6 [A] jars were full, *she* **said** to her son, "Bring me another one."
4: 6 [A] me another one." But *he* **replied**, "There is not a jar left."
4: 7 [A] of God, and *he* **said**, "Go, sell the oil and pay your debts.
4: 9 [A] *She* **said** to her husband, "I know that this man who often
4:12 [A] *He* **said** to his servant Gehazi, "Call the Shunammite." So he
4:13 [A] Elisha **said** to him, "Tell her, 'You have gone to all this
4:13 [A] Elisha said to him, "**Tell** her, 'You have gone to all this
4:13 [A] to the king or the commander of the army?' " *She* **replied**,
4:14 [A] Elisha **asked**. Gehazi said, "Well, she has no son and her
4:14 [A] Gehazi **said**, "Well, she has no son and her husband is old."
4:15 [A] Elisha **said**, "Call her." So he called her, and she stood in the
4:16 [A] "About this time next year," Elisha **said**, "you will hold a son
4:16 [A] "No, my lord," *she* **objected**. "Don't mislead your servant,
4:19 [A] "My head! My head!" *he* **said** to his father. His father told a
4:19 [A] His father **told** a servant, "Carry him to his mother."
4:22 [A] She called her husband and **said**, "Please send me one of the
4:23 [A] *he* **asked**. "It's not the New Moon or the Sabbath." "It's all
4:23 [A] not the New Moon or the Sabbath." "It's all right," *she* **said**.
4:24 [A] She saddled the donkey and **said** to her servant, "Lead on;
4:24 [A] "Lead on; don't slow down for me unless *I* **tell** you."
4:25 [A] the man of God **said** to his servant Gehazi, "Look!
4:26 [A] Run to meet her and **ask** her, 'Are you all right? Is your
4:26 [A] Is your child all right?' " "Everything is all right," *she* **said**.
4:27 [A] push her away, but the man of God **said**, "Leave her alone!
4:28 [A] "Did I ask you for a son, my lord?" *she* **said**. "Didn't I tell
4:28 [A] she said. "Didn't *I* **tell** you, 'Don't raise my hopes'?"
4:29 [A] Elisha **said** to Gehazi, "Tuck your cloak into your belt, take
4:30 [A] But the child's mother **said**, "As surely as the LORD lives
4:31 [A] and told him, **[NIE]** "The boy has not awakened."
4:36 [A] Elisha summoned Gehazi and **said**, "Call the Shunammite."
4:36 [A] And he did. When she came, *he* **said**, "Take your son."
4:38 [A] *he* **said** to his servant, "Put on the large pot and cook some
4:40 [A] they cried out, **[NIE]** "O man of God, there is death in the
4:41 [A] Elisha **said**, "Get some flour." He put it into the pot and said,
4:41 [A] He put it into the pot and **said**, "Serve it to the people to eat."
4:42 [A] of new grain. "Give it to the people to eat," Elisha **said**.
4:43 [A] his servant **asked**. But Elisha answered, "Give it to the
4:43 [A] But Elisha **answered**, "Give it to the people to eat.
4:43 [A] For this is what the LORD **says**: 'They will eat and have
5: 3 [A] *She* **said** to her mistress, "If only my master would see the
5: 4 [A] and told him **[NIE]** what the girl from Israel had said.
5: 5 [A] "By all means, go," the king of Aram **replied**. "I will send a
5: 6 [A] The letter that he took to the king of Israel **read**: "With this
5: 7 [A] Israel read the letter, he tore his robes and **said**, "Am I God?
5: 8 [A] king of Israel had torn his robes, he sent him *this* **message**:
5:10 [A] Elisha sent a messenger to **say** to him, "Go, wash yourself
5:11 [A] Naaman went away angry and **said**, "I thought that he would
5:11 [A] "*I* **thought** [+448+3276] that he would surely come out to
5:13 [A] Naaman's servants went to him and said, **[NIE]** "My father,
5:13 [A] then, when *he* **tells** you, 'Wash and be cleansed'!"
5:15 [A] He stood before him and **said**, "Now I know that there is no
5:16 [A] The prophet **answered**, "As surely as the LORD lives,
5:17 [A] "If you will not," **said** Naaman, "please let me, your servant,
5:19 [A] "Go in peace," Elisha **said**. After Naaman had traveled some
5:20 [A] the servant of Elisha the man of God, **said** to himself,
5:21 [A] the chariot to meet him. "Is everything all right?" *he* **asked**.
5:22 [A] "Everything is all right," Gehazi **answered**. "My master sent
5:22 [A] "My master sent me to **say**, 'Two young men from the
5:23 [A] "By all means, take two talents," **said** Naaman. He urged
5:25 [A] "Where have you been, Gehazi?" Elisha **asked**.
5:25 [A] "Your servant didn't go anywhere," Gehazi **answered**.
5:26 [A] Elisha **said** to him, "Was not my spirit with you when the
6: 1 [A] The company of the prophets **said** to Elisha, "Look, the place
6: 2 [A] let us build a place there for us to live." And *he* **said**, "Go."
6: 3 [A] one of them **said**, "Won't you please come with your
6: 3 [A] please come with your servants?" "I will," Elisha **replied**.
6: 5 [A] my lord," he cried out, **[NIE]** "it was borrowed!"
6: 6 [A] The man of God **asked**, "Where did it fall?" When he
6: 7 [A] "Lift it out," *he* **said**. Then the man reached out his hand
6: 8 [A] he **said**, "I will set up my camp in such and such a place."
6: 9 [A] The man of God sent **word** to the king of Israel: "Beware of
6:10 [A] So the king of Israel checked on the place **indicated** *by* the
6:11 [A] He summoned his officers and **demanded** of them, "Will
6:12 [A] of us, my lord the king," **said** one of his officers, "but Elisha,
6:13 [A] the king **ordered**, "so I can send men and capture him."
6:13 [A] The report came back: **[NIE]** "He is in Dothan."
6:15 [A] the city. "Oh, my lord, what shall we do?" the servant **asked**.
6:16 [A] "Don't be afraid," the prophet **answered**. "Those who are
6:17 [A] **[NIE]** "O LORD, open his eyes so he may see."
6:18 [A] to the LORD, **[NIE]** "Strike these people with blindness."
6:19 [A] Elisha **told** them, "This is not the road and this is not the city.
6:20 [A] After they entered the city, Elisha **said**, "LORD, open the
6:21 [A] saw them, *he* **asked** Elisha, "Shall I kill them, my father?
6:22 [A] "Do not kill them," *he* **answered**. "Would you kill men you
6:26 [A] a woman cried to him, **[NIE]** "Help me, my lord the king!"
6:27 [A] The king **replied**, "If the LORD does not help you, where
6:28 [A] he **asked** her, "What's the matter?" She answered, "This
6:28 [A] *She* **answered**, "This woman said to me, 'Give up your son
6:28 [A] She answered, "This woman **said** to me, 'Give up your son
6:29 [A] The next day *I* **said** to her, 'Give up your son so we may eat
6:31 [A] *He* **said**, "May God deal with me, be it ever so severely, if
6:32 [A] but before he arrived, Elisha **said** to the elders,
6:33 [A] And ⌊the king⌋ **said**, "This disaster is from the LORD.
7: 1 [A] Elisha **said**, "Hear the word of the LORD. This is what the
7: 1 [A] This is what the LORD **says**: About this time tomorrow,
7: 2 [A] **[NIE]** "Look, even if the LORD should open the
7: 2 [A] own eyes," **answered** Elisha, "but you will not eat any of it!"
7: 3 [A] *They* **said** to each other, "Why stay here until we die?
7: 4 [A] If *we* **say**, 'We'll go into the city'—the famine is there,
7: 6 [A] and a great army, so that *they* **said** to one another, "Look,
7: 9 [A] *they* **said** to each other, "We're not doing right. This is a day
7:10 [A] **[NIE]** "We went into the Aramean camp and not a man was
7:12 [A] The king got up in the night and **said** to his officers, "I will
7:12 [A] **thinking**, 'They will surely come out, and then we will take
7:13 [A] **[NIE]** "Have some men take five of the horses that are left
7:14 [A] *He* **commanded** the drivers, "Go and find out what has
7:18 [A] **[NIE]** "About this time tomorrow, a seah of flour will sell
7:19 [A] The officer had said to the man of God, **[NIE]** "Look,
7:19 [A] The man of God *had* **replied**, "You will see it with your own
8: 1 [A] **[NIE]** "Go away with your family and stay for a while
8: 4 [A] to Gehazi, the servant of the man of God, and *had* **said**,
8: 5 [A] Gehazi **said**, "This is the woman, my lord the king, and this
8: 6 [A] he assigned an official to her case and **said** to him,
8: 7 [A] **[NIE]** "The man of God has come all the way up here,"
8: 8 [A] he **said** to Hazael, "Take a gift with you and go to meet the
8: 8 [A] through him; **ask** him, 'Will I recover from this illness?' "
8: 9 [A] He went in and stood before him, and **said**, "Your son
8: 9 [A] "Your son Ben-Hadad king of Aram has sent me to **ask**,
8:10 [A] Elisha **answered**, "Go and say to him, 'You will certainly
8:10 [A] Elisha answered, "Go and **say** to him, 'You will certainly
8:12 [A] "Why is my lord weeping?" **asked** Hazael. "Because I know
8:12 [A] I know the harm you will do to the Israelites," *he* **answered**.
8:13 [A] Hazael **said**, "How could your servant, a mere dog,
8:13 [A] me that you will become king of Aram," **answered** Elisha.
8:14 [A] When Ben-Hadad **asked**, "What did Elisha say to you?"
8:14 [A] When Ben-Hadad asked, "What *did* Elisha **say** to you?"
8:14 [A] Hazael **replied**, "He told me that you would certainly
8:14 [A] "*He* **told** me that you would certainly recover."
8:19 [A] *He had* **promised** to maintain a lamp for David and his
9: 1 [A] a man from the company of the prophets and **said** to him,
9: 3 [A] Then take the flask and pour the oil on his head and **declare**,
9: 3 [A] oil on his head and declare, 'This is what the LORD **says**:
9: 5 [A] "I have a message for you, commander," *he* **said**. "For which
9: 5 [A] of us?" **asked** Jehu. "For you, commander," he replied.
9: 5 [A] of us?" asked Jehu. "For you, commander," *he* **replied**.
9: 6 [A] Then the prophet poured the oil on Jehu's head and **declared**,
9: 6 [A] "This is what the LORD, the God of Israel, **says**:
9:11 [A] *one* of them **asked** him, "Is everything all right?
9:11 [A] know the man and the sort of things he says," Jehu **replied**.
9:12 [A] *they* **said**. "Tell us." Jehu said, "Here is what he told me:
9:12 [A] they said. "Tell us." Jehu **said**, "Here is what he told me:
9:12 [A] they said. "Tell us." Jehu said, "Here is what *he* **told** me:
9:12 [A] is what he told me: **[NIE]** 'This is what the LORD says:
9:12 [A] "Here is what he told me: 'This is what the LORD **says**:
9:13 [A] Then they blew the trumpet and **shouted**, "Jehu is king!"

2Ki 9:15 [A] Jehu **said**, "If this is the way you feel, don't let anyone slip
9:17 [A] *he* **called out**, "I see some troops coming."
9:17 [A] "Get a horseman," Joram **ordered**. "Send him to meet them
9:17 [A] "Send him to meet them and **ask**, 'Do you come in peace?' "
9:18 [A] The horseman rode off to meet Jehu and **said**, "This is what
9:18 [A] rode off to meet Jehu and said, "This is what the king **says**:
9:18 [A] Jehu **replied**. "Fall in behind me." The lookout reported,
9:18 [A] lookout reported, **[NIE]** "The messenger has reached them,
9:19 [A] When he came to them *he* **said**, "This is what the king says:
9:19 [A] When he came to them he said, "This is what the king **says**:
9:19 [A] 'Do you come in peace?' " Jehu **replied**, "What do you have
9:20 [A] The lookout reported, **[NIE]** "He has reached them, but he
9:21 [A] "Hitch up my chariot," Joram **ordered**. And when it was
9:22 [A] When Joram saw Jehu *he* **asked**, "Have you come in peace,
9:22 [A] Jehu **replied**, "as long as all the idolatry and witchcraft of
9:23 [A] Joram turned about and fled, **calling out** to Ahaziah,
9:25 [A] Jehu **said** to Bidkar, his chariot officer, "Pick him up
9:27 [A] to Beth Haggan. Jehu chased him, **shouting**, "Kill him too!"
9:31 [A] As Jehu entered the gate, *she* **asked**, "Have you come in
9:32 [A] He looked up at the window and **called out**, "Who is on my
9:33 [A] "Throw her down!" Jehu **said**. So they threw her down,
9:34 [A] *he* **said**, "and bury her, for she was a king's daughter."
9:36 [A] They went back and told Jehu, *who* **said**, "This is the word
9:36 [A] **[NIE]** On the plot of ground at Jezreel dogs will devour
9:37 [A] so that no *one will be able to* **say**, 'This is Jezebel.' "
10:1 [A] the elders and to the guardians of Ahab's children. He **said**,
10:4 [A] they were terrified and **said**, "If two kings could not resist
10:5 [A] the elders and the guardians sent this **message** to Jehu:
10:5 [A] "We are your servants and we will do anything *you* **say**. We
10:6 [A] **saying**, "If you are on my side and will obey me, take the
10:8 [A] **[NIE]** "They have brought the heads of the princes."
10:8 [A] Jehu **ordered**, "Put them in two piles at the entrance of the
10:9 [A] He stood before all the people and **said**, "You are innocent.
10:13 [A] he met some relatives of Ahaziah king of Judah and **asked**,
10:13 [A] *They* **said**, "We are relatives of Ahaziah, and we have come
10:14 [A] "Take them alive!" *he* **ordered**. So they took them alive
10:15 [A] Jehu greeted him and **said**, "Are you in accord with me, as I
10:15 [A] "I am," Jehonadab **answered**. "If so," said Jehu, "give me
10:16 [A] Jehu **said**, "Come with me and see my zeal for the LORD."
10:18 [A] Then Jehu brought all the people together and **said** to them,
10:20 [A] Jehu **said**, "Call an assembly in honor of Baal." So they
10:22 [A] Jehu **said** to the keeper of the wardrobe, "Bring robes for all
10:23 [A] Jehu **said** to the ministers of Baal, "Look around and see that
10:24 [A] Now Jehu had posted eighty men outside with *this* **warning**:
10:25 [A] the burnt offering, he **ordered** the guards and officers:
10:30 [A] The LORD **said** to Jehu, "Because you have done well in
11:5 [A] He commanded them, **saying**, "This is what you are to do:
11:12 [A] and the people clapped their hands and **shouted**,
11:15 [A] **[NIE]** "Bring her out between the ranks and put to the
11:15 [A] For the priest *had* **said**, "She must not be put to death in the
12:4 [12:5] [A] Joash **said** to the priests, "Collect all the money that
12:7 [12:8] [A] the priest and the other priests and **asked** them,
13:14 [A] "My father! My father!" *he* **cried**. "The chariots
13:15 [A] Elisha **said**, "Get a bow and some arrows," and he did so.
13:16 [A] "Take the bow in your hands," *he* **said** to the king of Israel.
13:17 [A] "Open the east window," *he* **said**, and he opened it. "Shoot!"
13:17 [A] he said, and he opened it. "Shoot!" Elisha **said**, and he shot.
13:17 [A] of victory, the arrow of victory over Aram!" Elisha **declared**.
13:18 [A] Then *he* **said**, "Take the arrows," and the king took them.
13:18 [A] Elisha **told** him, "Strike the ground." He struck it three times
13:19 [A] The man of God was angry with him and **said**, "You should
14:6 [A] **[NIE]** "Fathers shall not be put to death for their children,
14:8 [A] the son of Jehu, king of Israel, *with the* **challenge**:
14:9 [A] Jehoash king of Israel **replied** [+8938] to Amaziah king of
14:9 [A] "A thistle in Lebanon sent a **message** to a cedar in Lebanon,
15:12 [A] **[NIE]** "Your descendants will sit on the throne of Israel to
16:7 [A] Ahaz sent messengers to **say** to Tiglath-Pileser king of
16:15 [A] **[NIE]** "On the large new altar, offer the morning burnt
17:12 [A] They worshiped idols, though the LORD *had* **said**, "You
17:13 [A] all his prophets and seers: **[NIE]** "Turn from your evil ways.
17:26 [A] *It was* **reported** to the king of Assyria: "The people you
17:26 [A] **[RPH]** "The people you deported and resettled in the towns
17:27 [A] **[NIE]** "Have one of the priests you took captive from
17:35 [A] **[NIE]** "Do not worship any other gods or bow down to
18:14 [A] So Hezekiah king of Judah sent this **message** to the king of
18:19 [A] The field commander **said** to them, "Tell Hezekiah: " 'This is
18:19 [A] The field commander said to them, "**Tell** Hezekiah: " 'This is
18:19 [A] " 'This is what the great king, the king of Assyria, **says**:
18:20 [A] and military strength—but *you* **speak** only empty words.
18:22 [A] if *you* **say** to me, "We are depending on the LORD our
18:22 [A] and altars Hezekiah removed, **saying** to Judah and Jerusalem,
18:25 [A] The LORD *himself* **told** me to march against this country
18:26 [A] and Shebna and Joah **said** to the field commander,
18:27 [A] the commander **replied**, "Was it only to your master and you
18:28 [A] **[NIE]** "Hear the word of the great king, the king of Assyria!
18:29 [A] This is what the king **says**: Do not let Hezekiah deceive you.
18:30 [A] Hezekiah persuade you to trust in the LORD when he **says**,
18:31 [A] This is what the king of Assyria **says**: Make peace with me
18:32 [A] listen to Hezekiah, for he is misleading you when he **says**,
18:36 [A] the king had commanded, **[NIE]** "Do not answer him."
19:3 [A] *They* **told** him, "This is what Hezekiah says: This day is a
19:3 [A] They told him, "This is what Hezekiah **says**: This day is a
19:6 [A] Isaiah **said** to them, "Tell your master, 'This is what the
19:6 [A] Isaiah said to them, "**Tell** your master, 'This is what the
19:6 [A] to them, "Tell your master, 'This is what the LORD **says**:
19:9 [A] Now Sennacherib received a report **[NIE]** that Tirhakah,
19:9 [A] So he again sent messengers to Hezekiah *with this* **word**:
19:10 [A] "**Say** to Hezekiah king of Judah: Do not let the god you
19:10 [A] **[RPH]** Do not let the god you depend on deceive you when
19:10 [A] Do not let the god you depend on deceive you when he **says**,
19:15 [A] **[NIE]** "O LORD, God of Israel, enthroned between the
19:20 [A] Isaiah son of Amoz sent a **message** to Hezekiah: "This is
19:20 [A] "This is what the LORD, the God of Israel, **says**:
19:23 [A] *you have* **said**, "With my many chariots I have ascended the
19:32 [A] "Therefore this is what the LORD **says** concerning the king
20:1 [A] The prophet Isaiah son of Amoz went to him and **said**, "This
20:1 [A] Amoz went to him and said, "This is what the LORD **says**:
20:2 [A] turned his face to the wall and prayed to the LORD, **[NIE]**
20:4 [A] middle court, the word of the LORD came to him: **[NIE]**
20:5 [A] "Go back and **tell** Hezekiah, the leader of my people, 'This is
20:5 [A] 'This is what the LORD, the God of your father David, **says**:
20:7 [A] Then Isaiah **said**, "Prepare a poultice of figs." They did so
20:8 [A] Hezekiah *had* **asked** Isaiah, "What will be the sign that the
20:9 [A] Isaiah **answered**, "This is the LORD's sign to you that the
20:10 [A] for the shadow to go forward ten steps," **said** Hezekiah.
20:14 [A] Then Isaiah the prophet went to King Hezekiah and **asked**,
20:14 [A] went to King Hezekiah and asked, "What *did* those men **say**,
20:14 [A] "From a distant land," Hezekiah **replied**. "They came from
20:15 [A] The prophet **asked**, "What did they see in your palace?"
20:15 [A] "They saw everything in my palace," Hezekiah **said**.
20:16 [A] Then Isaiah **said** to Hezekiah, "Hear the word of the LORD:
20:17 [A] carried off to Babylon. Nothing will be left, **says** the LORD.
20:19 [A] of the LORD you have spoken is good," Hezekiah **replied**.
20:19 [A] For *he* **thought**, "Will there not be peace and security in my
21:4 [A] of which the LORD *had* **said**, "In Jerusalem I will put my
21:7 [A] of which the LORD *had* **said** to David and to his son
21:10 [A] The LORD said through his servants the prophets: **[NIE]**
21:12 [A] Therefore this is what the LORD, the God of Israel, **says**:
22:3 [A] the son of Meshullam, to the temple of the LORD. He **said**:
22:8 [A] Hilkiah the high priest **said** to Shaphan the secretary, "I have
22:9 [A] **[NIE]** "Your officials have paid out the money that was in
22:10 [A] the king, **[NIE]** "Hilkiah the priest has given me a book."
22:12 [A] the secretary and Asaiah the king's attendant: **[NIE]**
22:15 [A] *She* **said** to them, "This is what the LORD, the God of
22:15 [A] to them, "This is what the LORD, the God of Israel, **says**:
22:15 [A] the God of Israel, says: **Tell** the man who sent you to me,
22:16 [A] 'This is what the LORD **says**: I am going to bring disaster
22:18 [A] **Tell** the king of Judah, who sent you to inquire of the
22:18 [A] the God of Israel, **says** concerning the words you heard:
23:17 [A] The king **asked**, "What is that tombstone I see?" The men of
23:17 [A] The men of the city **said**, "It marks the tomb of the man of
23:18 [A] "Leave it alone," *he* **said**. "Don't let anyone disturb his
23:21 [A] **[NIE]** "Celebrate the Passover to the LORD your God,
23:27 [A] So the LORD **said**, "I will remove Judah also from my
23:27 [A] the city I chose, and this temple, about which *I* **said**,
25:24 [A] "Do not be afraid of the Babylonian officials," *he* **said**.
1Ch 4:9 [A] had named him Jabez, **saying**, "I gave birth to him in pain."
4:10 [A] **[NIE]** "Oh, that you would bless me and enlarge my
10:4 [A] Saul **said** to his armor-bearer, "Draw your sword and run me
11:1 [A] All Israel came together to David at Hebron and **said**, "We
11:2 [A] the LORD your God **said** to you, 'You will shepherd my
11:5 [A] **said** to David, "You will not get in here." Nevertheless,
11:6 [A] David *had* **said**, "Whoever leads the attack on the Jebusites
11:17 [A] David longed for water and **said**, "Oh, that someone would
11:19 [A] "God forbid that I should do this!" *he* **said**. "Should I drink
12:17 [12:18] [A] David went out to meet them and **[RPH]** to
12:19 [12:20] [A] They **said**, "It will cost us our heads if he deserts to
13:2 [A] He then **said** to the whole assembly of Israel, "If it seems
13:4 [A] The whole assembly **agreed** to do this, because it seemed
13:12 [A] David was afraid of God that day and **asked**, "How can I
14:10 [A] of God: **[NIE]** "Shall I go and attack the Philistines?
14:10 [A] The LORD **answered** him, "Go, I will hand them over to
14:11 [A] He **said**, "As waters break out, God has broken out against
14:12 [A] gods there, and David **gave orders** to burn them in the fire.
14:14 [A] God **answered** him, "Do not go straight up, but circle around
15:2 [A] David **said**, "No one but the Levites may carry the ark of
15:12 [A] *He* **said** to them, "You are the heads of the Levitical
15:16 [A] David **told** the leaders of the Levites to appoint their brothers

1Ch 16:18 [A] **[NIE]** "To you I will give the land of Canaan as the portion
16:31 [A] *let them* **say** among the nations, "The LORD reigns!"
16:35 [A] **Cry out**, "Save us, O God our Savior; gather us and deliver
16:36 [A] Then all the people **said** "Amen" and "Praise the LORD."
17: 1 [A] he **said** to Nathan the prophet, "Here I am, living in a palace
17: 2 [A] Nathan **replied** to David, "Whatever you have in mind, do it,
17: 3 [A] That night the word of God came to Nathan, **saying**:
17: 4 [A] "Go and **tell** my servant David, 'This is what the LORD
17: 4 [A] and tell my servant David, 'This is what the LORD **says**:
17: 6 [A] **[NIE]** "Why have you not built me a house of cedar?" '
17: 7 [A] "Now then, **tell** my servant David, 'This is what the LORD
17: 7 [A] my servant David, 'This is what the LORD Almighty **says**:
17:16 [A] King David went in and sat before the LORD, and *he* **said**:
17:24 [A] men *will* **say**, 'The LORD Almighty, the God over Israel,
19: 2 [A] David **thought**, "I will show kindness to Hanun son of
19: 3 [A] the Ammonite nobles **said** to Hanun, "Do you think David is
19: 5 [A] The king **said**, "Stay at Jericho till your beards have grown,
19:12 [A] Joab **said**, "If the Arameans are too strong for me, then you
21: 2 [A] So David **said** to Joab and the commanders of the troops,
21: 3 [A] Joab **replied**, "May the LORD multiply his troops a
21: 8 [A] David **said** to God, "I have sinned greatly by doing this.
21: 9 [A] The LORD said to Gad, David's seer, **[NIE]**
21:10 [A] "Go and tell David, **[RPH]** 'This is what the LORD says:
21:10 [A] "Go and tell David, 'This is what the LORD **says**: I am
21:11 [A] So Gad went to David and **said** to him, "This is what the
21:11 [A] to David and said to him, "This is what the LORD **says**:
21:13 [A] David **said** to Gad, "I am in deep distress. Let me fall into the
21:15 [A] and **said** to the angel who was destroying the people,
21:17 [A] David **said** to God, "Was it not I who ordered the fighting
21:17 [A] "Was it not I *who* **ordered** the fighting men to be counted?
21:18 [A] the angel of the LORD **ordered** Gad to tell David to go up
21:18 [A] the angel of the LORD ordered Gad to **tell** David to go up
21:22 [A] David **said** to him, "Let me have the site of your threshing
21:23 [A] Araunah **said** to David, "Take it! Let my lord the king do
21:24 [A] King David **replied** to Araunah, "No, I insist on paying the
21:27 [A] the LORD **spoke** to the angel, and he put his sword back
22: 1 [A] David **said**, "The house of the LORD God is to be here,
22: 2 [A] So David **gave orders** to assemble the aliens living in Israel,
22: 5 [A] David **said**, "My son Solomon is young and inexperienced,
22: 7 [A] David **said** to Solomon: "My son, I had it in my heart to
22: 8 [A] **[NIE]** 'You have shed much blood and have fought many
23:25 [A] For David *had* **said**, "Since the LORD, the God of Israel,
27:23 [A] because the LORD *had* **promised** to make Israel as
28: 2 [A] King David rose to his feet and **said**: "Listen to me,
28: 3 [A] God **said** to me, 'You are not to build a house for my Name,
28: 6 [A] *He* **said** to me: 'Solomon your son is the one who will build
28:20 [A] David also **said** to Solomon his son, "Be strong
29: 1 [A] King David **said** to the whole assembly: "My son Solomon,
29:10 [A] **saying**, "Praise be to you, O LORD, God of our father
29:20 [A] David **said** to the whole assembly, "Praise the LORD your
2Ch 1: 2 [A] Solomon **spoke** to all Israel—to the commanders of
1: 7 [A] That night God appeared to Solomon and **said** to him,
1: 8 [A] Solomon **answered** God, "You have shown great kindness to
1:11 [A] God **said** to Solomon, "Since this is your heart's desire
2: 1 [1:18] [A] Solomon **gave orders** to build a temple for the Name
2: 3 [2:2] [A] Solomon sent this **message** to Hiram king of Tyre:
2:11 [2:10] [A] Hiram king of Tyre **replied** by letter to Solomon:
2:12 [2:11] [A] Hiram **added**: "Praise be to the LORD, the God of
2:15 [2:14] [A] and barley and the olive oil and wine *he* **promised**,
6: 1 [A] Solomon **said**, "The LORD has said that he would dwell in
6: 1 [A] "The LORD *has* **said** that he would dwell in a dark cloud;
6: 4 [A] Then *he* **said**: "Praise be to the LORD, the God of Israel,
6: 4 [A] he promised with his mouth to my father David. For he **said**,
6: 8 [A] the LORD **said** to my father David, 'Because it was in your
6:14 [A] *He* **said**: "O LORD, God of Israel, there is no God like you
6:16 [A] my father the promises you made to him when you **said**,
6:20 [A] this place of which *you* **said** you would put your Name there.
6:37 [A] and plead with you in the land of their captivity and **say**,
7:12 [A] the LORD appeared to him at night and **said**: "I have heard
7:18 [A] as I covenanted with David your father when I **said**,
7:21 [A] is now so imposing, all who pass by will be appalled and **say**,
7:22 [A] *People will* **answer**, 'Because they have forsaken the
8:11 [A] for *he* **said**, "My wife must not live in the palace of David
9: 5 [A] *She* **said** to the king, "The report I heard in my own country
10: 3 [A] and all Israel went to Rehoboam and said to him: **[NIE]**
10: 5 [A] Rehoboam **answered**, "Come back to me in three days."
10: 6 [A] would you advise me to answer these people?" he **asked**.
10: 7 [A] **[NIE]** "If you will be kind to these people and please them
10: 9 [A] *He* **asked** them, "What is your advice? How should we
10: 9 [A] say to me, **[NIE]** 'Lighten the yoke your father put on us'?"
10:10 [A] **[NIE]** "Tell the people who have said to you, 'Your father
10:10 [A] "**Tell** the people who have said to you, 'Your father put a
10:10 [A] **[NIE]** 'Your father put a heavy yoke on us, but make our
10:10 [A] **tell** them, 'My little finger is thicker than my father's waist.
10:12 [A] the king had said, **[NIE]** "Come back to me in three days."
10:14 [A] he followed the advice of the young men and **[NIE]** said,
10:16 [A] **[NIE]** "What share do we have in David, what part in
11: 2 [A] of the LORD came to Shemaiah the man of God: **[NIE]**
11: 3 [A] "**Say** to Rehoboam son of Solomon king of Judah and to all
11: 3 [A] and to all the Israelites in Judah and Benjamin, **[NIE]**
11: 4 [A] 'This is what the LORD **says**: Do not go up to fight against
12: 5 [A] *he* **said** to them, "This is what the LORD says, 'You have
12: 5 [A] he said to them, "This is what the LORD **says**, 'You have
12: 6 [A] leaders of Israel and the king humbled themselves and **said**,
12: 7 [A] **[NIE]** "Since they have humbled themselves, I will not
13: 4 [A] of Ephraim, and **said**, "Jeroboam and all Israel, listen to me!
13: 8 [A] "And now you **plan** to resist the kingdom of the LORD,
14: 4 [14:3] [A] *He* **commanded** Judah to seek the LORD, the God
14: 7 [14:6] [A] *he* **said** to Judah, "and put walls around them,
14:11 [14:10] [A] Asa called to the LORD his God and **said**,
15: 2 [A] He went out to meet Asa and **said** to him, "Listen to me, Asa
16: 3 [16:2] [A] "Let there be a treaty between me and you," he **said**,
16: 7 [A] Hanani the seer came to Asa king of Judah and **said** to him:
18: 3 [A] Ahab king of Israel **asked** Jehoshaphat king of Judah, "Will
18: 3 [A] Jehoshaphat **replied**, "I am as you are, and my people as
18: 4 [A] Jehoshaphat also **said** to the king of Israel, "First seek the
18: 5 [A] and **asked** them, "Shall we go to war against Ramoth Gilead,
18: 5 [A] "Go," *they* **answered**, "for God will give it into the king's
18: 6 [A] Jehoshaphat **asked**, "Is there not a prophet of the LORD
18: 7 [A] The king of Israel **answered** Jehoshaphat, "There is still one
18: 7 [A] "The king *should* not **say** that," Jehoshaphat replied.
18: 7 [A] "The king should not say that," Jehoshaphat **replied**.
18: 8 [A] So the king of Israel called one of his officials and **said**,
18:10 [A] iron horns, and *he* **declared**, "This is what the LORD says:
18:10 [A] iron horns, and he declared, "This is what the LORD **says**:
18:11 [A] "Attack Ramoth Gilead and be victorious," they **said**,
18:12 [A] had gone to summon Micaiah said to him, **[NIE]** "Look,
18:13 [A] Micaiah **said**, "As surely as the LORD lives, I can tell him
18:13 [A] as the LORD lives, I can tell him only what my God **says**."
18:14 [A] When he arrived, the king **asked** him, "Micaiah, shall we go
18:14 [A] "Attack and be victorious," *he* **answered**, "for they will be
18:15 [A] The king **said** to him, "How many times must I make you
18:16 [A] Micaiah **answered**, "I saw all Israel scattered on the hills like
18:16 [A] and the LORD **said**, 'These people have no master.
18:17 [A] The king of Israel **said** to Jehoshaphat, "Didn't I tell you that
18:17 [A] "Didn't *I* **tell** you that he never prophesies anything good
18:18 [A] Micaiah **continued**, "Therefore hear the word of the LORD:
18:19 [A] the LORD **said**, 'Who will entice Ahab king of Israel into
18:19 [A] death there?' **[RPH]** "One suggested this, and another that.
18:19 [A] to his death there?' "One **suggested** this, and another that.
18:19 [A] death there?' "One suggested this, and another **[RPH]** that.
18:20 [A] stood before the LORD and **said**, 'I will entice him.'
18:20 [A] 'I will entice him.' " 'By what means?' the LORD **asked**.
18:21 [A] be a lying spirit in the mouths of all his prophets,' *he* **said**.
18:21 [A] " 'You will succeed in enticing him,' **said** the LORD. 'Go
18:23 [A] go when he went from me to speak to you?" *he* **asked**.
18:24 [A] Micaiah **replied**, "You will find out on the day you go to
18:25 [A] The king of Israel then **ordered**, "Take Micaiah and send
18:26 [A] and **say**, 'This is what the king says: Put this fellow in prison
18:26 [A] and say, 'This is what the king **says**: Put this fellow in prison
18:27 [A] Micaiah **declared**, "If you ever return safely, the LORD has
18:27 [A] Then *he* **added**, "Mark my words, all you people!"
18:29 [A] The king of Israel **said** to Jehoshaphat, "I will enter the battle
18:30 [A] **[NIE]** "Do not fight with anyone, small or great, except the
18:31 [A] saw Jehoshaphat, they **thought**, "This is the king of Israel."
18:33 [A] The king **told** the chariot driver, "Wheel around and get me
19: 2 [A] the son of Hanani, went out to meet him and **said** to the king,
19: 6 [A] *He* **told** them, "Consider carefully what you do, because you
19: 9 [A] **[NIE]** "You must serve faithfully and wholeheartedly in the
20: 2 [A] **[NIE]** "A vast army is coming against you from Edom,
20: 6 [A] **said**: "O LORD, God of our fathers, are you not the God
20: 8 [A] in it and have built in it a sanctuary for your Name, **saying**,
20:15 [A] *He* **said**: "Listen, King Jehoshaphat and all who live in Judah
20:15 [A] and Jerusalem! This is what the LORD **says** to you:
20:20 [A] Jehoshaphat stood and **said**, "Listen to me, Judah and people
20:21 [A] his holiness as they went out at the head of the army, **saying**:
20:37 [A] **saying**, "Because you have made an alliance with Ahaziah,
21: 7 [A] *He had* **promised** to maintain a lamp for him and his
21:12 [A] received a letter from Elijah the prophet, which **said**:
21:12 [A] is what the LORD, the God of your father David, **says**:
22: 9 [A] They buried him, for *they* **said**, "He was a son of
23: 3 [A] Jehoiada **said** to them, "The king's son shall reign, as the
23:11 [A] They anointed him and **shouted**, "Long live the king!"
23:13 [A] Athaliah tore her robes and **shouted**, "Treason! Treason!"
23:14 [A] who were in charge of the troops, and **said** to them:
23:14 [A] For the priest *had* **said**, "Do not put her to death at the
24: 5 [A] He called together the priests and Levites and **said** to them,
24: 6 [A] the king summoned Jehoiada the chief priest and **said** to him,

2Ch 24: 8 [A] *At* the king's **command**, a chest was made and placed
24:20 [A] He stood before the people and **said**, "This is what God says:
24:20 [A] He stood before the people and said, "This is what God **says**:
24:22 [A] had shown him but killed his son, *who* **said** as he lay dying,
25: 4 [A] **[NIE]** "Fathers shall not be put to death for their children,
25: 7 [A] a man of God came to him and **said**, "O king, these troops
25: 9 [A] Amaziah **asked** the man of God, "But what about the
25: 9 [A] The man of God **replied**, "The LORD can give you much
25:15 [A] he sent a prophet to him, *who* **said**, "Why do you consult this
25:16 [A] While he was still speaking, the king **said** to him, "Have we
25:16 [A] So the prophet stopped but **said**, "I know that God has
25:17 [A] he sent this **challenge** to Jehoash son of Jehoahaz, the son of
25:18 [A] Jehoash king of Israel **replied** [+8938] to Amaziah king of
25:18 [A] "A thistle in Lebanon sent a **message** to a cedar in Lebanon,
25:19 [A] *You* **say** *to yourself* that you have defeated Edom, and now
26:18 [A] They confronted him and **said**, "It is not right for you,
26:23 [A] that belonged to the kings, for *people* **said**, "He had leprosy."
28: 9 [A] *He* **said** to them, "Because the LORD, the God of your
28:10 [A] And now you **intend** to make the men and women of Judah
28:13 [A] *they* **said**, "or we will be guilty before the LORD.
28:13 [A] *Do* you **intend** to add to our sin and guilt? For our guilt is
28:23 [A] for *he* **thought**, "Since the gods of the kings of Aram have
29: 5 [A] and **said**: "Listen to me, Levites! Consecrate yourselves now
29:18 [A] they went in to King Hezekiah and **reported**: "We have
29:21 [A] The king **commanded** the priests, the descendants of Aaron,
29:24 [A] because the king *had* **ordered** the burnt offering and the sin
29:27 [A] Hezekiah **gave the order** to sacrifice the burnt offering on
29:30 [A] his officials **ordered** the Levites to praise the LORD with
29:31 [A] **[NIE]** "You have now dedicated yourselves to the LORD.
30: 6 [A] with letters from the king and from his officials, which **read**:
30:18 [A] **saying**, "May the LORD, who is good, pardon everyone
31: 4 [A] *He* **ordered** the people living in Jerusalem to give the
31:10 [A] the chief priest, from the family of Zadok, **answered**,
31:10 [A] **[NIE]** "Since the people began to bring their contributions
31:11 [A] Hezekiah **gave orders** to prepare storerooms in the temple of
32: 1 [A] to the fortified cities, **thinking** to conquer them for himself.
32: 4 [A] kings of Assyria come and find plenty of water?" *they* **said**.
32: 6 [A] at the city gate and encouraged them with *these* **words**:
32: 9 [A] he sent his officers to Jerusalem with *this* **message** for
32:10 [A] "This is what Sennacherib king of Assyria **says**: On what are
32:11 [A] When Hezekiah **says**, 'The LORD our God will save us
32:12 [A] god's high places and altars, **saying** to Judah and Jerusalem,
32:12 [A] **[RPH]** 'You must worship before one altar and burn
32:17 [A] the LORD, the God of Israel, and **saying** this against him:
32:17 [A] **[RPH]** "Just as the gods of the peoples of the other lands
32:24 [A] *who* **answered** him and gave him a miraculous sign.
33: 4 [A] in the temple of the LORD, of which the LORD *had* **said**,
33: 7 [A] of which God *had* **said** to David and to his son Solomon,
33:16 [A] on it, and **told** Judah to serve the LORD, the God of Israel.
34:15 [A] Hilkiah said **[NIE]** to Shaphan the secretary, "I have found
34:16 [A] **[NIE]** "Your officials are doing everything that has been
34:18 [A] the king, **[NIE]** "Hilkiah the priest has given me a book."
34:20 [A] the secretary and Asaiah the king's attendant: **[NIE]**
34:23 [A] *She* **said** to them, "This is what the LORD, the God of
34:23 [A] to them, "This is what the LORD, the God of Israel, **says**:
34:23 [A] the God of Israel, says: **Tell** the man who sent you to me,
34:24 [A] 'This is what the LORD **says**: I am going to bring disaster
34:26 [A] **Tell** the king of Judah, who sent you to inquire of the
34:26 [A] the God of Israel, **says** concerning the words you heard:
35: 3 [A] *He* **said** to the Levites, who instructed all Israel and who had
35:21 [A] Neco sent messengers to him, **saying**, "What quarrel is there
35:21 [A] God *has* **told** me to hurry; so stop opposing God, who is with
35:23 [A] shot King Josiah, and he **told** his officers, "Take me away;
35:25 [A] and women singers **commemorate** Josiah in the laments.
36:22 [A] throughout his realm and to put it in writing: **[NIE]**
36:23 [A] "This is what Cyrus king of Persia **says**: " 'The LORD,
Ezr 1: 1 [A] throughout his realm and to put it in writing: **[NIE]**
1: 2 [A] "This is what Cyrus king of Persia **says**: " 'The LORD,
2:63 [A] The governor **ordered** them not to eat any of the most sacred
4: 2 [A] came to Zerubbabel and to the heads of the families and **said**,
4: 3 [A] and the rest of the heads of the families of Israel **answered**,
8:22 [A] us from enemies on the road, because *we had* **told** the king,
8:22 [A] **[RPH]** "The gracious hand of our God is on everyone who
8:28 [A] *I* **said** to them, "You as well as these articles are consecrated
9: 1 [A] the leaders came to me and **said**, "The people of Israel,
9: 6 [A] **prayed**: "O my God, I am too ashamed and disgraced to lift
9:10 [A] "But now, O our God, what *can we* **say** after this? For we
9:11 [A] you gave through your servants the prophets when you **said**:
10: 2 [A] one of the descendants of Elam, said **[NIE]** to Ezra,
10:10 [A] Ezra the priest stood up and **said** to them, "You have been
10:12 [A] The whole assembly responded **[NIE]** with a loud voice:
Ne 1: 3 [A] *They* **said** to me, "Those who survived the exile and are back
1: 5 [A] *I* **said**: "O LORD, God of heaven, the great and awesome
1: 8 [A] **saying**, 'If you are unfaithful, I will scatter you among the
2: 2 [A] so the king **asked** me, "Why does your face look so sad when
2: 3 [A] *I* **said** to the king, "May the king live forever! Why should
2: 4 [A] The king **said** to me, "What is it you want?" Then I prayed to
2: 5 [A] *I* **answered** the king, "If it pleases the king and if your
2: 6 [A] Then the king, with the queen sitting beside him, **asked** me,
2: 7 [A] *I* also **said** to him, "If it pleases the king, may I have letters
2:17 [A] *I* **said** to them, "You see the trouble we are in: Jerusalem lies
2:18 [A] hand of my God upon me and what the king *had* **said** to me.
2:18 [A] *They* **replied**, "Let us start rebuilding." So they began this
2:19 [A] and ridiculed us. "What is this you are doing?" *they* **asked**.
2:20 [A] I answered them *by* **saying**, "The God of heaven will give us
4: 2 [3:34] [A] of his associates and the army of Samaria, *he* **said**,
4: 2 [3:34] [A] he said, "What **[RPH]** are those feeble Jews doing?
4: 3 [3:35] [A] Tobiah the Ammonite, who was at his side, **said**,
4:10 [4:4] [A] Meanwhile, the people in Judah **said**, "The strength of
4:11 [4:5] [A] Also our enemies **said**, "Before they know it or see us,
4:12 [4:6] [A] who lived near them came and **told** us ten times over,
4:14 [4:8] [A] I stood up and **said** to the nobles, the officials and the
4:19 [4:13] [A] *I* **said** to the nobles, the officials and the rest of the
4:22 [4:16] [A] At that time *I* also **said** to the people, "Have every
5: 2 [A] Some *were* **saying**, "We and our sons and daughters are
5: 3 [A] Others *were* **saying**, "We are mortgaging our fields, our
5: 4 [A] Still others *were* **saying**, "We have had to borrow money to
5: 7 [A] *I* **told** them, "You are exacting usury from your own
5: 8 [A] **said**: "As far as possible, we have bought back our Jewish
5: 9 [A] So *I* **continued**, "What you are doing is not right. Shouldn't
5:12 [A] "We will give it back," *they* **said**. "And we will not demand
5:12 [A] We will do as you **say**." Then I summoned the priests
5:13 [A] I also shook out the folds of my robe and **said**, "In this way
5:13 [A] At this the whole assembly **said**, "Amen," and praised the
6: 2 [A] Sanballat and Geshem sent me *this* **message**: "Come, let us
6: 3 [A] so I sent messengers to them with *this* **reply**: "I am carrying
6: 6 [A] Geshem **says** it is true—that you and the Jews are plotting to
6: 7 [A] **[NIE]** 'There is a king in Judah!' Now this report will get
6: 8 [A] I sent him *this* **reply**: "Nothing like what you are saying is
6: 8 [A] "Nothing like what you *are* **saying** is happening; you are just
6: 9 [A] They were all trying to frighten us, **thinking**, "Their hands
6:10 [A] *He* **said**, "Let us meet in the house of God, inside the temple,
6:11 [A] *I* **said**, "Should a man like me run away? Or should one like
6:19 [A] they kept **reporting** to me his good deeds and then telling
7: 3 [A] *I* **said** to them, "The gates of Jerusalem are not to be opened
7:65 [A] **ordered** them not to eat any of the most sacred food until
8: 1 [A] *They* **told** Ezra the scribe to bring out the Book of the Law
8: 9 [A] the Levites who were instructing the people **said** to them all,
8:10 [A] Nehemiah **said**, "Go and enjoy choice food and sweet drinks,
8:11 [A] all the people, **saying**, "Be still, for this is a sacred day.
8:15 [A] **[NIE]** "Go out into the hill country and bring back branches
9: 5 [A] Sherebiah, Hodiah, Shebaniah and Pethahiah—**said**:
9:15 [A] *you* **told** them to go in and take possession of the land you
9:18 [A] when they cast for themselves an image of a calf and **said**,
9:23 [A] you brought them into the land that *you* **told** their fathers to
13: 9 [A] *I* **gave orders** to purify the rooms, and then I put back into
13:11 [A] So I rebuked the officials and **asked** them, "Why is the house
13:17 [A] I rebuked the nobles of Judah and **said** to them, "What is this
13:19 [A] *I* **ordered** the doors to be shut and not opened until the
13:19 [A] be shut and **[RPH]** not opened until the Sabbath was over.
13:21 [A] I warned them and **said**, "Why do you spend the night by the
13:22 [A] Then *I* **commanded** the Levites to purify themselves and go
Est 1:10 [A] *he* **commanded** the seven eunuchs who served him—
1:13 [A] he **spoke** with the wise men who understood the times
1:16 [A] Memucan **replied** in the presence of the king and the nobles,
1:17 [A] the women, and so they will despise their husbands and **say**,
1:17 [A] 'King Xerxes **commanded** Queen Vashti to be brought
1:18 [A] *will* **respond** to all the king's nobles in the same way.
2: 2 [A] the king's personal attendants **proposed**, "Let a search be
2:13 [A] Anything *she* **wanted** was given her to take with her from
2:15 [A] king's eunuch who was in charge of the harem, **suggested**.
2:22 [A] and told Queen Esther, who in turn **reported** it to the king,
3: 3 [A] Then the royal officials at the king's gate **asked** Mordecai,
3: 4 [A] Day after day they **spoke** to him but he refused to comply.
3: 8 [A] Haman **said** to King Xerxes, "There is a certain people
3:11 [A] "Keep the money," the king **said** to Haman, "and do with the
4: 7 [A] including the exact amount of money Haman *had* **promised**
4:10 [A] Then she **instructed** him to say to Mordecai,
4:13 [A] he sent back *this* **answer**: "Do not think that because you are
4:15 [A] Then Esther sent *this* **reply** to Mordecai:
5: 3 [A] the king **asked**, "What is it, Queen Esther? What is your
5: 4 [A] the king," **replied** Esther, "let the king, together with Haman,
5: 5 [A] "Bring Haman at once," the king **said**, "so that we may do
5: 6 [A] the king again **asked** Esther, "Now what is your petition?
5: 7 [A] Esther replied, **[NIE]** "My petition and my request is this:
5:12 [A] "And that's not all," Haman **added**. "I'm the only person
5:14 [A] His wife Zeresh and all his friends **said** to him, "Have a
5:14 [A] **ask** the king in the morning to have Mordecai hanged on it.

Est 6: 1 [A] so *he* **ordered** the book of the chronicles, the record of his
6: 3 [A] the king **asked**. "Nothing has been done for him," his
6: 3 [A] "Nothing has been done for him," his attendants **answered**.
6: 4 [A] The king **said**, "Who is in the court?" Now Haman had just
6: 4 [A] **speak** to the king *about* hanging Mordecai on the gallows he
6: 5 [A] His attendants **answered**, "Haman is standing in the court."
6: 5 [A] is standing in the court." "Bring him in," the king **ordered**.
6: 6 [A] When Haman entered, the king **asked** him, "What should be
6: 6 [A] Now Haman **thought** to himself, "Who is there that the king
6: 7 [A] So he **answered** the king, "For the man the king delights to
6:10 [A] "Go at once," the king **commanded** Haman. "Get the robe
6:13 [A] His advisers and his wife Zeresh **said** to him,
7: 2 [A] the king again **asked**, "Queen Esther, what is your petition?
7: 3 [A] **[NIE]** "If I have found favor with you, O king, and if it
7: 5 [A] King Xerxes **asked** Queen Esther, "Who is he? Where is the
7: 5 [A] King Xerxes asked **[RPH]** Queen Esther, "Who is he?
7: 6 [A] Esther **said**, "The adversary and enemy is this vile Haman."
7: 8 [A] The king **exclaimed**, "Will he even molest the queen while
7: 9 [A] Then Harbona, one of the eunuchs attending the king, **said**,
7: 9 [A] spoke up to help the king." The king **said**, "Hang him on it!"
8: 5 [A] "If it pleases the king," *she* **said**, "and if he regards me with
8: 7 [A] King Xerxes **replied** to Queen Esther and to Mordecai the
9:12 [A] The king **said** to Queen Esther, "The Jews have killed
9:13 [A] "If it pleases the king," Esther **answered**, "give the Jews in
9:14 [A] So the king **commanded** that this be done. An edict was
9:25 [A] *he* **issued** written **orders** that the evil scheme Haman had
Job 1: 5 [A] **thinking**, "Perhaps my children have sinned and cursed God
1: 7 [A] The LORD **said** to Satan, "Where have you come from?"
1: 7 [A] **[NIE]** "From roaming through the earth and going back
1: 8 [A] the LORD **said** to Satan, "Have you considered my servant
1: 9 [A] "Does Job fear God for nothing?" Satan replied. **[RPH]**
1:12 [A] The LORD **said** to Satan, "Very well, then, everything he
1:14 [A] a messenger came to Job and **said**, "The oxen were plowing
1:16 [A] he was still speaking, another messenger came and **said**,
1:17 [A] he was still speaking, another messenger came and **said**,
1:18 [A] yet another messenger came and **said**, "Your sons
1:21 [A] **said**: "Naked I came from my mother's womb, and naked I
2: 2 [A] the LORD **said** to Satan, "Where have you come from?"
2: 2 [A] **[NIE]** "From roaming through the earth and going back
2: 3 [A] the LORD **said** to Satan, "Have you considered my servant
2: 4 [A] **[NIE]** "A man will give all he has for his own life.
2: 6 [A] The LORD **said** to Satan, "Very well, then, he is in your
2: 9 [A] His wife **said** to him, "Are you still holding on to your
2:10 [A] *He* **replied**, "You are talking like a foolish woman. Shall we
3: 2 [A] He said: **[NIE]**
3: 3 [A] of my birth perish, and the night *it was* **said**, 'A boy is born!'
4: 1 [A] Then Eliphaz the Temanite replied: **[NIE]**
6: 1 [A] Then Job replied: **[NIE]**
6:22 [A] *Have I* ever **said**, 'Give something on my behalf, pay a
7: 4 [A] When I lie down *I* **think**, 'How long before I get up?' The
7:13 [A] When *I* **think** my bed will comfort me and my couch will
8: 1 [A] Then Bildad the Shuhite replied: **[NIE]**
8:10 [A] Will they not instruct you and **tell** you? Will they not bring
9: 1 [A] Then Job replied: **[NIE]**
9: 7 [A] He **speaks** to the sun and it does not shine; he seals off the
9:12 [A] can stop him? Who *can* **say** to him, 'What are you doing?'
9:22 [A] that is why *I* **say**, 'He destroys both the blameless
9:27 [A] If I **say**, 'I will forget my complaint, I will change my
10: 2 [A] *I will* **say** to God: Do not condemn me, but tell me what
11: 1 [A] Then Zophar the Naamathite replied: **[NIE]**
11: 4 [A] *You* **say** to God, 'My beliefs are flawless and I am pure in
12: 1 [A] Then Job replied: **[NIE]**
15: 1 [A] Then Eliphaz the Temanite replied: **[NIE]**
16: 1 [A] Then Job replied: **[NIE]**
18: 1 [A] Then Bildad the Shuhite replied: **[RPH]**
19: 1 [A] Then Job replied: **[NIE]**
19:28 [A] "If *you* **say**, 'How we will hound him, since the root of the
20: 1 [A] Then Zophar the Naamathite replied: **[NIE]**
20: 7 [A] own dung; those who have seen him *will* **say**, 'Where is he?'
21: 1 [A] Then Job replied: **[NIE]**
21:14 [A] Yet *they* **say** to God, 'Leave us alone! We have no desire to
21:28 [A] *You* **say**, 'Where now is the great man's house, the tents
22: 1 [A] Then Eliphaz the Temanite replied: **[NIE]**
22:13 [A] Yet *you* **say**, 'What does God know? Does he judge through
22:17 [A] They **said** to God, 'Leave us alone! What can the Almighty
22:29 [A] When men are brought low and *you* **say**, 'Lift them up!'
23: 1 [A] Then Job replied: **[NIE]**
23: 5 [A] what he would answer me, and consider what *he would* **say**.
24:15 [A] he **thinks**, 'No eye will see me,' and he keeps his face
25: 1 [A] Then Bildad the Shuhite replied: **[NIE]**
26: 1 [A] Then Job replied: **[NIE]**
27: 1 [A] And Job continued his discourse: **[NIE]**
28:14 [A] The deep **says**, 'It is not in me'; the sea says, 'It is not with
28:14 [A] deep says, 'It is not in me'; the sea **says**, 'It is not with me.'
28:22 [A] Destruction and Death **say**, 'Only a rumor of it has reached
28:28 [A] And *he* **said** to man, 'The fear of the Lord—that is wisdom,
29: 1 [A] Job continued his discourse: **[NIE]**
29:18 [A] "*I* **thought**, 'I will die in my own house, my days as
31:24 [A] "If I have put my trust in gold or **said** to pure gold, 'You are
31:31 [A] if the men of my household *have* never **said**, 'Who has not
32: 6 [A] **[NIE]** "I am young in years, and you are old; that is why I
32: 7 [A] *I* **thought**, 'Age should speak; advanced years should teach
32:10 [A] "Therefore *I* **say**: Listen to me; I too will tell you what I
32:13 [A] *Do* not **say**, 'We have found wisdom; let God refute him,
33: 8 [A] "But *you have* **said** in my hearing—I heard the very words—
33:24 [A] to be gracious to him and **say**, 'Spare him from going down
33:27 [A] he comes to men and **says**, 'I sinned, and perverted what was
34: 1 [A] Then Elihu said: **[NIE]**
34: 5 [A] "Job **says**, 'I am innocent, but God denies me justice.
34: 9 [A] For *he* **says**, 'It profits a man nothing when he tries to please
34:18 [A] Is he not the *One who* **says** to kings, 'You are worthless,'
34:31 [A] "Suppose *a man* **says** to God, 'I am guilty but will offend no
34:34 [A] of understanding declare, wise men who hear me **say** to me,
35: 1 [A] Then Elihu said: **[NIE]**
35: 2 [A] you think this is just? *You* **say**, 'I will be cleared by God.'
35: 3 [A] Yet *you* **ask** him, 'What profit is it to me, and what do I gain
35:10 [A] no *one* **says**, 'Where is God my Maker, who gives songs in
35:14 [A] then, will he listen *when you* **say** that you do not see him,
36: 1 [A] Elihu continued: **[NIE]**
36:10 [A] to correction and **commands** them to repent of their evil.
36:23 [A] his ways for him, or **said** to him, 'You have done wrong'?
37: 6 [A] *He* **says** to the snow, 'Fall on the earth,' and to the rain
37:19 [A] "Tell us what *we should* **say** to him; we cannot draw up our
37:20 [A] I want to speak? *Would* any man **ask** to be swallowed up?
38: 1 [A] Then the LORD answered Job out of the storm. *He* **said**:
38:11 [A] when *I* **said**, 'This far you may come and no farther; here is
38:35 [A] bolts on their way? *Do they* **report** to you, 'Here we are'?
39:25 [A] At the blast of the trumpet *he* **snorts**, 'Aha!' He catches the
40: 1 [A] The LORD said to Job: **[NIE]**
40: 3 [A] Then Job answered the LORD: **[NIE]**
40: 6 [A] Then the LORD spoke to Job out of the storm: **[NIE]**
42: 1 [A] Then Job replied to the LORD: **[NIE]**
42: 7 [A] he **said** to Eliphaz the Temanite, "I am angry with you
Ps 2: 7 [A] *He* **said** to me, "You are my Son; today I have become your
3: 2 [3:3] [A] Many *are* **saying** of me, "God will not deliver him."
4: 4 [4:5] [A] on your beds, **search** [+928] your hearts and be silent.
4: 6 [4:7] [A] Many *are* **asking**, "Who can show us any good?"
10: 6 [A] *He* **says** to himself, "Nothing will shake me; I'll always be
10:11 [A] *He* **says** to himself, "God has forgotten; he covers his face
10:13 [A] Why *does he* **say** to himself, "He won't call me to account"?
11: 1 [A] In the LORD I take refuge. How then *can you* **say** to me:
12: 4 [12:5] [A] that **says**, "We will triumph with our tongues;
12: 5 [12:6] [A] of the needy, I will now arise," **says** the LORD.
13: 4 [13:5] [A] my enemy *will* **say**, "I have overcome him," and my
14: 1 [A] The fool **says** in his heart, "There is no God." They are
16: 2 [A] *I* **said** to the LORD, "You are my Lord; apart from you I
18: T [18:2] [A] all his enemies and from the hand of Saul. *He* **said**:
27: 8 [A] My heart **says** of you, "Seek his face!" Your face, LORD,
29: 9 [A] strips the forests bare. And in his temple all **cry**, "Glory!"
30: 6 [30:7] [A] When I felt secure, I **said**, "I will never be shaken."
31:14 [31:15] [A] I trust in you, O LORD; *I* **say**, "You are my God."
31:22 [31:23] [A] In my alarm I **said**, "I am cut off from your sight!"
32: 5 [A] *I* **said**, "I will confess my transgressions to the LORD"—
33: 9 [A] For he **spoke**, and it came to be; he commanded, and it stood
35: 3 [A] those who pursue me. **Say** to my soul, "I am your salvation."
35:10 [A] My whole being *will* **exclaim**, "Who is like you, O LORD?
35:21 [A] They gape at me and **say**, "Aha! Aha! With our own eyes we
35:25 [A] *Do* not *let them* **think** [+928+4213], "Aha, just what we
35:25 [A] just what we wanted!" or **say**, "We have swallowed him up."
35:27 [A] *may they* always **say**, "The LORD be exalted, who delights
38:16 [38:17] [A] For *I* **said**, "Do not let them gloat or exalt
39: 1 [39:2] [A] *I* **said**, "I will watch my ways and keep my tongue
40: 7 [40:8] [A] *I* **said**, "Here I am, I have come—it is written about
40:10 [40:11] [A] my heart; *I* **speak** *of* your faithfulness and salvation.
40:15 [40:16] [A] May those *who* **say** to me, "Aha! Aha!" be appalled
40:16 [40:17] [A] *may* those who love your salvation always **say**,
41: 4 [41:5] [A] I **said**, "O LORD, have mercy on me; heal me, for I
41: 5 [41:6] [A] My enemies **say** of me in malice, "When will he die
42: 3 [42:4] [A] and night, while men **say** to me all day long,
42: 9 [42:10] [A] *I* **say** to God my Rock, "Why have you forgotten
42:10 [42:11] [A] **saying** to me all day long, "Where is your God?"
45: 1 [45:2] [A] My heart is stirred by a noble theme *as* I **recite** my
50:12 [A] If I were hungry *I would* not **tell** you, for the world is mine,
50:16 [A] to the wicked, God **says**: "What right have you to recite my
52: T [52:2] [A] **[NIE]** "David has gone to the house of Ahimelech."
53: 1 [53:2] [A] The fool **says** in his heart, "There is no God."
54: T [54:2] [A] When the Ziphites had gone to Saul and **said**, "Is not
55: 6 [55:7] [A] *I* **said**, "Oh, that I had the wings of a dove! I would

Ps 58:11 [58:12] [A] men *will* **say**, "Surely the righteous still are
64: 5 [64:6] [A] hiding their snares; *they* **say**, "Who will see them?"
66: 3 [A] **Say** to God, "How awesome are your deeds! So great is your
68:22 [68:23] [A] The Lord **says**, "I will bring them from Bashan;
70: 3 [70:4] [A] May those *who* **say** to me, "Aha! Aha!" turn back
70: 4 [70:5] [A] *may* those who love your salvation always **say**,
71:10 [A] For my enemies **speak** against me; those who wait to kill me
71:11 [A] They **say**, "God has forsaken him; pursue him and seize him,
73:11 [A] *They* **say**, "How can God know? Does the Most High have
73:15 [A] If *I had* **said**, "I will speak thus," I would have betrayed your
74: 8 [A] *They* **said** in their hearts, "We will crush them completely!"
75: 4 [75:5] [A] To the arrogant *I* **say**, 'Boast no more,' and to the
77:10 [77:11] [A] *I* **thought**, "To this I will appeal: the years of the
78:19 [A] They spoke against God, **saying**, "Can God spread a table in
79:10 [A] Why *should* the nations **say**, "Where is their God?"
82: 6 [A] "I **said**, 'You are "gods"; you are all sons of the Most High.'
83: 4 [83:5] [A] "Come," *they* **say**, "let us destroy them as a nation,
83:12 [83:13] [A] who **said**, "Let us take possession of the
87: 5 [C] Indeed, of Zion *it will* **be said**, "This one and that one were
89: 2 [89:3] [A] *I will* **declare** that your love stands firm forever,
89:19 [89:20] [A] spoke in a vision, to your faithful people *you* **said**:
90: 3 [A] men back to dust, **saying**, "Return to dust, O sons of men."
91: 2 [A] *I will* **say** of the LORD, "He is my refuge and my fortress,
94: 7 [A] *They* **say**, "The LORD does not see; the God of Jacob pays
94:18 [A] When *I* **said**, "My foot is slipping," your love, O LORD,
95:10 [A] *I* **said**, "They are a people whose hearts go astray, and they
96:10 [A] **Say** among the nations, "The LORD reigns." The world is
102:24 [102:25] [A] So *I* **said**: "Do not take me away, O my God,
105:11 [A] **[NIE]** "To you I will give the land of Canaan as the portion
105:31 [A] *He* **spoke**, and there came swarms of flies, and gnats
105:34 [A] *He* **spoke**, and the locusts came, grasshoppers without
106:23 [A] So *he* **said** he would destroy them—had not Moses,
106:34 [A] destroy the peoples as the LORD *had* **commanded** them,
106:48 [A] *Let* all the people **say**, "Amen!" Praise the LORD.
107: 2 [A] *Let* the redeemed of the LORD **say** this—those he
107:25 [A] For *he* **spoke** and stirred up a tempest that lifted high the
115: 2 [A] Why *do* the nations **say**, "Where is their God?"
116:11 [A] And in my dismay I **said**, "All men are liars."
118: 2 [A] *Let* Israel **say**: "His love endures forever."
118: 3 [A] *Let* the house of Aaron **say**: "His love endures forever."
118: 4 [A] *Let* those who fear the LORD **say**: "His love endures
119:57 [A] O LORD; *I have* **promised** to obey your words.
119:82 [A] for your promise; I **say**, "When will you comfort me?"
122: 1 [A] I rejoiced with *those who* **said** to me, "Let us go to the house
124: 1 [A] If the LORD had not been on our side—*let* Israel **say**—
126: 2 [A] *it was* **said** among the nations, "The LORD has done great
129: 1 [A] have greatly oppressed me from my youth—*let* Israel **say**—
129: 8 [A] *May* those who pass by not **say**, "The blessing of the
137: 7 [A] "Tear it down," they **cried**, "tear it down to its foundations!"
139:11 [A] If *I* **say**, "Surely the darkness will hide me and the light
139:20 [A] *They* **speak** *of* you with evil intent; your adversaries misuse
140: 6 [140:7] [A] O LORD, *I* **say** to you, "You are my God." Hear,
142: 5 [142:6] [A] *I* **say**, "You are my refuge, my portion in the land of
145: 6 [A] *They will* **tell** *of* the power of your awesome works, and I
145:11 [A] *They will* **tell** *of* the glory of your kingdom and speak of
Pr 1:11 [A] If *they* **say**, "Come along with us; let's lie in wait for
1:21 [A] in the gateways of the city *she* **makes** her **speech** [+609]:
3:28 [A] *Do* not **say** to your neighbor, "Come back later; I'll give it
4: 4 [A] he taught me and **said**, "Lay hold of my words with all your
5:12 [A] *You will* **say**, "How I hated discipline! How my heart
7: 4 [A] **Say** to wisdom, "You are my sister," and call understanding
7:13 [A] hold of him and kissed him and with a brazen face *she* **said**:
9: 4 [A] simple come in here!" *she* **says** to those who lack judgment.
9:16 [A] simple come in here!" *she* **says** to those who lack judgment.
20: 9 [A] Who *can* **say**, "I have kept my heart pure; I am clean
20:14 [A] **says** the buyer; then off he goes and boasts about his
20:22 [A] *Do* not **say**, "I'll pay you back for this wrong!" Wait for the
22:13 [A] The sluggard **says**, "There is a lion outside!" or, "I will be
23: 7 [A] "Eat and drink," *he* **says** to you, but his heart is not with you.
24:12 [A] If *you* **say**, "But we knew nothing about this," does not he
24:24 [A] *Whoever* **says** to the guilty, "You are innocent"—
24:29 [A] *Do* not **say**, "I'll do to him as he has done to me; I'll pay that
25: 7 [A] it is better for him *to* **say** to you, "Come up here," than for
26:13 [A] The sluggard **says**, "There is a lion in the road, a fierce lion
26:19 [A] is a man who deceives his neighbor and **says**, "I was only
28:24 [A] He who robs his father or mother and **says**, "It's not
30: 9 [A] Otherwise, I may have too much and disown you and **say**,
30:15 [A] things that are never satisfied, four *that* never **say**, 'Enough!':
30:16 [A] satisfied with water, and fire, *which* never **says**, 'Enough!'
30:20 [A] She eats and wipes her mouth and **says**, 'I've done nothing
Ecc 1: 2 [A] "Meaningless! Meaningless!" **says** the Teacher. "Utterly
1:10 [A] Is there anything of which *one can* **say**, "Look! This is
1:16 [A] **[NIE]** "Look, I have grown and increased in wisdom more
2: 1 [A] I **thought** in my heart, "Come now, I will test you with
2: 2 [A] "Laughter," *I* **said**, "is foolish. And what does pleasure
2:15 [A] I **thought** in my heart, "The fate of the fool will overtake me
3:17 [A] I **thought** in my heart, "God will bring to judgment both the
3:18 [A] I also **thought**, "As for men, God tests them so that they may
5: 6 [5:5] [A] *do* not **protest** to the ⌞temple⌟ messenger, "My vow
6: 3 [A] proper burial, *I* **say** that a stillborn child is better off than he.
7:10 [A] *Do* not **say**, "Why were the old days better than these?" For it
7:23 [A] All this I tested by wisdom and *I* **said**, "I am determined to
7:27 [A] "Look," **says** the Teacher, "this is what I have discovered:
8: 4 [A] is supreme, who *can* **say** to him, "What are you doing?"
8:14 [A] what the righteous deserve. This too, *I* **say**, is meaningless.
8:17 [A] Even if a wise man **claims** he knows, he cannot really
9:16 [A] So I **said**, "Wisdom is better than strength." But the poor
10: 3 [A] the fool lacks sense and **shows** everyone how stupid he is.
12: 1 [A] of trouble come and the years approach when *you will* **say**,
12: 8 [A] "Meaningless! Meaningless!" **says** the Teacher. "Everything
SS 2:10 [A] My lover spoke and **said** to me, "Arise, my darling,
7: 8 [7:9] [A] *I* **said**, "I will climb the palm tree; I will take hold of
Isa 1:11 [A] of your sacrifices—what are they to me?" **says** the LORD.
1:18 [A] "Come now, let us reason together," **says** the LORD.
2: 3 [A] Many peoples will come and **say**, "Come, let us go up to the
3: 7 [A] in that day *he will* **cry** [+4200+5951] **out**, "I have no
3:10 [A] **Tell** the righteous it will be well with them, for they will
3:16 [A] The LORD **says**, "The women of Zion are haughty, walking
4: 1 [A] In that day seven women will take hold of one man and **say**,
4: 3 [C] left in Zion, who remain in Jerusalem, *will* **be called** holy,
5:19 [A] to those *who* **say**, "Let God hurry, let him hasten his work
5:20 [A] Woe to those *who* **call** evil good and good evil, who put
6: 3 [A] **[NIE]** "Holy, holy, holy is the LORD Almighty; the whole
6: 5 [A] "Woe to me!" *I* **cried**. "I am ruined! For I am a man of
6: 7 [A] With it he touched my mouth and **said**, "See, this has
6: 8 [A] I heard the voice of the Lord **saying**, "Whom shall I send?
6: 8 [A] And who will go for us?" And *I* **said**, "Here am I. Send me!"
6: 9 [A] *He* **said**, "Go and tell this people: " 'Be ever hearing, but
6: 9 [A] He said, "Go and **tell** this people: " 'Be ever hearing, but
6:11 [A] *I* **said**, "For how long, O Lord?" And he answered: "Until the
6:11 [A] I said, "For how long, O Lord?" And *he* **answered**:
7: 2 [A] was told, **[NIE]** "Aram has allied itself with Ephraim";
7: 3 [A] the LORD **said** to Isaiah, "Go out, you and your son
7: 4 [A] **Say** to him, 'Be careful, keep calm and don't be afraid. Do
7: 5 [A] Ephraim and Remaliah's son have plotted your ruin, **saying**,
7: 7 [A] Yet this is what the Sovereign LORD **says**: " 'It will not
7:10 [A] Again the LORD spoke to Ahaz, **[NIE]**
7:12 [A] Ahaz **said**, "I will not ask; I will not put the LORD to the
7:13 [A] Isaiah **said**, "Hear now, you house of David! Is it not enough
8: 1 [A] The LORD **said** to me, "Take a large scroll and write on it
8: 3 [A] the LORD **said** to me, "Name him Maher-Shalal-Hash-Baz.
8: 5 [A] The LORD spoke to me again: **[NIE]**
8:11 [A] The LORD **spoke** to me with his strong hand upon me,
8:11 [A] warning me not to follow the way of this people. *He* **said**:
8:12 [A] "*Do* not **call** conspiracy everything that these people call
8:12 [A] "Do not call conspiracy everything that these people **call**
8:19 [A] When *men* **tell** you to consult mediums and spiritists,
8:20 [A] If *they do* not **speak** according to this word, they have no
9: 9 [9:8] [A] *who* **say** with pride and arrogance of heart,
10: 8 [A] 'Are not my commanders all kings?' *he* **says**.
10:13 [A] For *he* **says**: " 'By the strength of my hand I have done this,
10:24 [A] Therefore, this is what the Lord, the LORD Almighty, **says**:
12: 1 [A] In that day *you will* **say**: "I will praise you, O LORD.
12: 4 [A] In that day *you will* **say**: "Give thanks to the LORD, call on
14: 4 [A] **[NIE]** How the oppressor has come to an end! How his fury
14:10 [A] They will all respond, *they will* **say** to you, "You also have
14:13 [A] You **said** in your heart, "I will ascend to heaven; I will raise
14:24 [A] **[NIE]** "Surely, as I have planned, so it will be, and as I have
16:14 [A] **[NIE]** "Within three years, as a servant bound by contract
18: 4 [A] This is what the LORD **says** to me: "I will remain quiet and
19:11 [A] How *can you* **say** to Pharaoh, "I am one of the wise men,
19:18 [C] One of them *will* **be called** the City of Destruction.
19:25 [A] **saying**, "Blessed be Egypt my people, Assyria my
20: 2 [A] *He* **said** to him, "Take off the sackcloth from your body
20: 3 [A] the LORD **said**, "Just as my servant Isaiah has gone
20: 6 [A] In that day the people who live on this coast *will* **say**,
21: 6 [A] This is what the Lord **says** to me: "Go, post a lookout
21: 9 [A] back the answer: **[NIE]** 'Babylon has fallen, has fallen!
21:12 [A] The watchman **replies**, "Morning is coming, but also the
21:16 [A] This is what the Lord **says** to me: "Within one year, as a
22: 4 [A] Therefore *I* **said**, "Turn away from me; let me weep bitterly.
22:14 [A] will not be atoned for," **says** the Lord, the LORD Almighty.
22:15 [A] This is what the Lord, the LORD Almighty, **says**: "Go, say
23: 4 [A] and you, O fortress of the sea, for the sea *has* **spoken**:
23: 4 [A] **[RPH]** "I have neither been in labor nor given birth; I have
23:12 [A] *He* **said**, "No more of your reveling, O Virgin Daughter of
24:16 [A] *I* **said**, "I waste away, I waste away! Woe to me!
25: 9 [A] In that day *they will* **say**, "Surely this is our God; we trusted

Isa 28:12 [A] to whom *he* **said**, "This is the resting place, let the weary
28:15 [A] *You* **boast**, "We have entered into a covenant with death,
28:16 [A] So this is what the Sovereign LORD **says**: "See, I lay a
29:11 [A] and **say** to him, "Read this, please," he will answer, "I can't;
29:11 [A] and say to him, "Read this, please," *he will* **answer**, "I can't;
29:12 [A] **say**, "Read this, please," he will answer, "I don't know how
29:12 [A] say, "Read this, please," *he will* **answer**, "I don't know how
29:13 [A] The Lord **says**: "These people come near to me with their
29:15 [A] who do their work in darkness and **think**, "Who sees us?
29:16 [A] *Shall* what is formed **say** to him who formed it, "He did not
29:16 [A] *Can* the pot **say** of the potter, "He knows nothing"?
29:22 [A] who redeemed Abraham, **says** to the house of Jacob:
30:10 [A] *They* **say** to the seers, "See no more visions!" and to the
30:12 [A] Therefore, this is what the Holy One of Israel **says**:
30:15 [A] is what the Sovereign LORD, the Holy One of Israel, **says**:
30:16 [A] *You* **said**, 'No, we will flee on horses.' Therefore you will
30:21 [A] ears will hear a voice behind you, **saying**, "This is the way;
30:22 [A] will throw them away like a menstrual cloth and **say** to them,
31: 4 [A] This is what the LORD **says** to me: "As a lion growls, a
32: 5 [C] No longer will the fool be called noble nor the scoundrel **be**
33:10 [A] "Now will I arise," **says** the LORD. "Now will I be exalted;
33:24 [A] No one living in Zion *will* **say**, "I am ill"; and the sins of
35: 4 [A] **say** to those with fearful hearts, "Be strong, do not fear; your
36: 4 [A] The field commander **said** to them, "Tell Hezekiah, " 'This is
36: 4 [A] "**Tell** Hezekiah, " 'This is what the great king, the king of
36: 4 [A] " 'This is what the great king, the king of Assyria, **says**:
36: 5 [A] and military strength—but *you* **speak** only empty words.
36: 7 [A] if *you* **say** to me, "We are depending on the LORD our
36: 7 [A] and altars Hezekiah removed, **saying** to Judah and Jerusalem,
36:10 [A] The LORD *himself* **told** me to march against this country
36:11 [A] Then Eliakim, Shebna and Joah **said** to the field commander,
36:12 [A] the commander **replied**, "Was it only to your master and you
36:13 [A] Then the commander stood and called out **[NIE]** in Hebrew,
36:14 [A] This is what the king **says**: Do not let Hezekiah deceive you.
36:15 [A] Hezekiah persuade you to trust in the LORD *when* he **says**,
36:16 [A] This is what the king of Assyria **says**: Make peace with me
36:18 [A] "Do not let Hezekiah mislead you *when* he **says**,
36:21 [A] the king had commanded, **[NIE]** "Do not answer him."
37: 3 [A] *They* **told** him, "This is what Hezekiah says: This day is a
37: 3 [A] They told him, "This is what Hezekiah **says**: This day is a
37: 6 [A] Isaiah **said** to them, "Tell your master, 'This is what the
37: 6 [A] Isaiah said to them, "**Tell** your master, 'This is what the
37: 6 [A] to them, "Tell your master, 'This is what the LORD **says**:
37: 9 [A] Now Sennacherib received a report **[NIE]** that Tirhakah,
37: 9 [A] he heard it, he sent messengers to Hezekiah *with this* **word**:
37:10 [A] "**Say** to Hezekiah king of Judah: Do not let the god you
37:10 [A] **[RPH]** Do not let the god you depend on deceive you when
37:10 [A] Do not let the god you depend on deceive you *when* he **says**,
37:15 [A] And Hezekiah prayed to the LORD: **[NIE]**
37:21 [A] Isaiah son of Amoz sent a **message** to Hezekiah: "This is
37:21 [A] "This is what the LORD, the God of Israel, **says**:
37:24 [A] *you have* **said**, 'With my many chariots I have ascended the
37:33 [A] "Therefore this is what the LORD **says** concerning the king
38: 1 [A] The prophet Isaiah son of Amoz went to him and **said**, "This
38: 1 [A] Amoz went to him and said, "This is what the LORD **says**:
38: 3 [A] **[NIE]** "Remember, O LORD, how I have walked before
38: 4 [A] Then the word of the LORD came to Isaiah: **[NIE]**
38: 5 [A] "Go and **tell** Hezekiah, 'This is what the LORD, the God of
38: 5 [A] 'This is what the LORD, the God of your father David, **says**:
38:10 [A] I **said**, "In the prime of my life must I go through the gates of
38:11 [A] *I* **said**, "I will not again see the LORD, the LORD,
38:15 [A] I say? *He has* **spoken** to me, and he himself has done this.
38:21 [A] Isaiah *had* **said**, "Prepare a poultice of figs and apply it to the
38:22 [A] Hezekiah *had* **asked**, "What will be the sign that I will go up
39: 3 [A] Then Isaiah the prophet went to King Hezekiah and **asked**,
39: 3 [A] went to King Hezekiah and asked, "What *did* those men **say**,
39: 3 [A] they come from?" "From a distant land," Hezekiah **replied**.
39: 4 [A] The prophet **asked**, "What did they see in your palace?"
39: 4 [A] "They saw everything in my palace," Hezekiah **said**.
39: 5 [A] Isaiah **said** to Hezekiah, "Hear the word of the LORD
39: 6 [A] carried off to Babylon. Nothing will be left, **says** the LORD.
39: 8 [A] of the LORD you have spoken is good," Hezekiah **replied**.
39: 8 [A] For *he* **thought**, "There will be peace and security in my
40: 1 [A] Comfort, comfort my people, **says** your God.
40: 6 [A] A voice **says**, "Cry out." And I said, "What shall I cry?"
40: 6 [A] A voice says, "Cry out." And *I* **said**, "What shall I cry?"
40: 9 [A] not be afraid; **say** to the towns of Judah, "Here is your God!"
40:25 [A] you compare me? Or who is my equal?" **says** the Holy One.
40:27 [A] Why *do you* **say**, O Jacob, and complain, O Israel, "My way
41: 6 [A] each helps the other and **says** to his brother, "Be strong!"
41: 7 [A] *He* **says** of the welding, "It is good." He nails down the idol
41: 9 [A] *I* **said**, 'You are my servant'; I have chosen you and have not
41:13 [A] your God, who takes hold of your right hand and **says** to you,
41:21 [A] "Present your case," **says** the LORD. "Set forth your
41:21 [A] the LORD. "Set forth your arguments," **says** Jacob's King.
41:26 [A] could know, or beforehand, so *we could* **say**, 'He was right'?
42: 5 [A] This is what God the LORD **says**—he who created the
42:17 [A] who trust in idols, who **say** to images, 'You are our gods,'
42:22 [A] have been made loot, with no *one to* **say**, "Send them back."
43: 1 [A] But now, this is what the LORD **says**—he who created you,
43: 6 [A] *I will* **say** to the north, 'Give them up!' and to the south,
43: 9 [A] they were right, so that others may hear and **say**, "It is true."
43:14 [A] This is what the LORD **says**—your Redeemer, the Holy
43:16 [A] This is what the LORD **says**—he who made a way through
44: 2 [A] This is what the LORD **says**—he who made you, who
44: 5 [A] One *will* **say**, 'I belong to the LORD'; another will call
44: 6 [A] "This is what the LORD **says**—Israel's King
44:16 [A] He also warms himself and **says**, "Ah! I am warm; I see the
44:17 [A] He prays to it and **says**, "Save me; you are my god."
44:19 [A] to think, no one has the knowledge or understanding to **say**,
44:20 [A] he cannot save himself, or **say**, "Is not this thing in my right
44:24 [A] "This is what the LORD **says**—your Redeemer, who
44:26 [A] who **says** of Jerusalem, 'It shall be inhabited,' of the towns of
44:27 [A] who **says** to the watery deep, 'Be dry, and I will dry up your
44:28 [A] who **says** of Cyrus, 'He is my shepherd and will accomplish
44:28 [A] he *will* **say** of Jerusalem, "Let it be rebuilt," and of the
45: 1 [A] "This is what the LORD **says** to his anointed, to Cyrus,
45: 9 [A] *Does* the clay **say** to the potter, 'What are you making?' Does
45:10 [A] Woe to *him who* **says** to his father, 'What have you
45:11 [A] "This is what the LORD **says**—the Holy One of Israel,
45:13 [A] but not for a price or reward, **says** the LORD Almighty."
45:14 [A] This is what the LORD **says**: "The products of Egypt
45:18 [A] For this is what the LORD **says**—he who created the
45:19 [A] *I have* not **said** to Jacob's descendants, 'Seek me in vain.'
45:24 [A] *They will* **say** of me, 'In the LORD alone are righteousness
46:10 [A] from ancient times, what is still to come. I **say**:
47: 7 [A] *You* **said**, 'I will continue forever—the eternal queen!'
47: 8 [A] lounging in your security and **saying** to yourself, 'I am,
47:10 [A] You have trusted in your wickedness and *have* **said**, 'No one
47:10 [A] and knowledge mislead you when *you* **say** to yourself,
48: 5 [A] I announced them to you so that *you could* not **say**,
48: 7 [A] them before today. So *you* cannot **say**, 'Yes, I knew of them.'
48:17 [A] This is what the LORD **says**—your Redeemer, the Holy
48:20 [A] **say**, "The LORD has redeemed his servant Jacob."
48:22 [A] "There is no peace," **says** the LORD, "for the wicked."
49: 3 [A] *He* **said** to me, "You are my servant, Israel, in whom I will
49: 4 [A] I **said**, "I have labored to no purpose; I have spent my
49: 5 [A] now the LORD **says**—he who formed me in the womb to be
49: 6 [A] *he* **says**: "It is too small a thing for you to be my servant to
49: 7 [A] the LORD **says**—the Redeemer and Holy One of Israel—*to*
49: 8 [A] This is what the LORD **says**: "In the time of my favor I will
49: 9 [A] to **say** to the captives, 'Come out,' and to those in darkness,
49:14 [A] Zion **said**, "The LORD has forsaken me, the Lord has
49:20 [A] The children born during your bereavement *will* yet **say** in
49:21 [A] *you will* **say** in your heart, 'Who bore me these? I was
49:22 [A] This is what the Sovereign LORD **says**: "See, I will beckon
49:25 [A] this is what the LORD **says**: "Yes, captives will be taken
50: 1 [A] This is what the LORD **says**: "Where is your mother's
51:16 [A] of the earth, and *who* **say** to Zion, 'You are my people.' "
51:22 [A] This is what your Sovereign LORD **says**, your God,
51:23 [A] who **said** to you, 'Fall prostrate that we may walk over you.'
52: 3 [A] For this is what the LORD **says**: "You were sold for
52: 4 [A] For this is what the Sovereign LORD **says**: "At first my
52: 7 [A] proclaim salvation, *who* **say** to Zion, "Your God reigns!"
54: 1 [A] woman than of her who has a husband," **says** the LORD.
54: 6 [A] who married young, only to be rejected," **says** your God.
54: 8 [A] have compassion on you," **says** the LORD your Redeemer.
54:10 [A] be removed," **says** the LORD, who has compassion on you.
56: 1 [A] This is what the LORD **says**: "Maintain justice and do what
56: 3 [A] *Let* no foreigner who has bound himself to the LORD **say**,
56: 3 [A] **[RPH]** "The LORD will surely exclude me from his
56: 3 [A] And *let* not any eunuch **complain**, "I am only a dry tree."
56: 4 [A] For this is what the LORD **says**: "To the eunuchs who keep
57:10 [A] by all your ways, but *you would* not **say**, 'It is hopeless.'
57:14 [A] And *it will be* **said**: "Build up, build up, prepare the road!
57:15 [A] For this is what the high and lofty *One* **says**—he who lives
57:19 [A] Peace, peace, to those far and near," **says** the LORD. "And I
57:21 [A] "There is no peace," **says** my God, "for the wicked."
58: 9 [A] LORD will answer; you will cry for help, and *he will* **say**:
59:21 [A] for me, this is my covenant with them," **says** the LORD.
59:21 [A] from this time on and forever," **says** the LORD.
61: 6 [C] of the LORD, you *will* **be named** ministers of our God.
62: 4 [C] No longer *will they* **call** you Deserted, or name your land
62: 4 [C] will they call you Deserted, or **name** your land Desolate.
62:11 [A] "**Say** to the Daughter of Zion, 'See, your Savior comes! See,
63: 8 [A] *He* **said**, "Surely they are my people, sons who will not be
65: 1 [A] that did not call on my name, *I* **said**, 'Here am I, here am I.'
65: 5 [A] who **say**, 'Keep away; don't come near me, for I am too

Isa 65: 7 [A] both your sins and the sins of your fathers," **says** the LORD.
65: 8 [A] This is what the LORD **says**: "As when juice is still found
65: 8 [A] when juice is still found in a cluster of grapes and *men* **say**,
65:13 [A] Therefore this is what the Sovereign LORD **says**: "My
65:25 [A] nor destroy on all my holy mountain," **says** the LORD.
66: 1 [A] This is what the LORD **says**: "Heaven is my throne,
66: 5 [A] exclude you because of my name, *have* **said**,
66: 9 [A] moment of birth and not give delivery?" **says** the LORD.
66: 9 [A] close up the womb when I bring to delivery?" **says** your God.
66:12 [A] For this is what the LORD **says**: "I will extend peace to her
66:20 [A] and wagons, and on mules and camels," **says** the LORD.
66:21 [A] of them also to be priests and Levites," **says** the LORD.
66:23 [A] will come and bow down before me," **says** the LORD.
Jer 1: 4 [A] The word of the LORD came to me, **saying**,
1: 6 [A] "Ah, Sovereign LORD," *I* **said**, "I do not know how to
1: 7 [A] But the LORD **said** to me, "Do not say, 'I am only a child.'
1: 7 [A] But the LORD said to me, "*Do* not **say**, 'I am only a child.'
1: 9 [A] reached out his hand and touched my mouth and **said** to me,
1:11 [A] **[NIE]** "What do you see, Jeremiah?" "I see the branch of an
1:11 [A] Jeremiah?" "I see the branch of an almond tree," *I* **replied**.
1:12 [A] The LORD **said** to me, "You have seen correctly, for I am
1:13 [A] **[NIE]** "What do you see?" "I see a boiling pot, tilting away
1:13 [A] see a boiling pot, tilting away from the north," *I* **answered**.
1:14 [A] The LORD **said** to me, "From the north disaster will be
2: 1 [A] The word of the LORD came to me: **[NIE]**
2: 2 [A] **[RPH]** " 'I remember the devotion of your youth, how as a
2: 2 [A] **[NIE]** " 'I remember the devotion of your youth, how as a
2: 5 [A] This is what the LORD **says**: "What fault did your fathers
2: 6 [A] *They did* not **ask**, 'Where is the LORD, who brought us up
2: 8 [A] The priests *did* not **ask**, 'Where is the LORD?' Those who
2:20 [A] and tore off your bonds; *you* **said**, 'I will not serve you!'
2:23 [A] "How *can you* **say**, 'I am not defiled; I have not run after the
2:25 [A] *you* **said**, 'It's no use! I love foreign gods, and I must go after
2:27 [A] *They* **say** to wood, 'You are my father,' and to stone,
2:27 [A] yet when they are in trouble, *they* **say**, 'Come and save us!'
2:31 [A] Why *do* my people **say**, 'We are free to roam; we will come
2:35 [A] *you* **say**, 'I am innocent; he is not angry with me.' But I will
2:35 [A] I will pass judgment on you because you **say**, 'I have not
3: 1 [A] **[NIE]** "If a man divorces his wife and she leaves him
3: 6 [A] During the reign of King Josiah, the LORD **said** to me,
3: 7 [A] *I* **thought** that after she had done all this she would return to
3:11 [A] The LORD **said** to me, "Faithless Israel is more righteous
3:12 [A] **[NIE]** " 'Return, faithless Israel,' declares the LORD,
3:16 [A] declares the LORD, "*men will* no longer **say**, 'The ark of
3:19 [A] "*I* myself **said**, " 'How gladly would I treat you like sons
3:19 [A] *I* **thought** you would call me 'Father' and not turn away from
4: 3 [A] This is what the LORD **says** to the men of Judah and to
4: 5 [A] "Announce in Judah and proclaim in Jerusalem and **say**:
4: 5 [A] Cry aloud and **say**: 'Gather together! Let us flee to the
4:10 [A] *I* **said**, "Ah, Sovereign LORD, how completely you have
4:10 [A] you have deceived this people and Jerusalem by **saying**,
4:11 [A] At that time this people and Jerusalem *will* **be told**, "A
4:27 [A] This is what the LORD **says**: "The whole land will be
5: 2 [A] Although *they* **say**, 'As surely as the LORD lives,' still they
5: 4 [A] I **thought**, "These are only the poor; they are foolish, for they
5:12 [A] have lied about the LORD; *they* **said**, "He will do nothing!
5:14 [A] Therefore this is what the LORD God Almighty **says**:
5:19 [A] when *the people* **ask**, 'Why has the LORD our God done all
5:19 [A] *you will* **tell** them, 'As you have forsaken me and served
5:20 [A] this to the house of Jacob and proclaim it in Judah: **[NIE]**
5:24 [A] *They do* not **say** to themselves, 'Let us fear the LORD our
6: 6 [A] This is what the LORD Almighty **says**: "Cut down the trees
6: 9 [A] This is what the LORD Almighty **says**: "Let them glean the
6:14 [A] not serious. 'Peace, peace,' they **say**, when there is no peace.
6:15 [A] will be brought down when I punish them," **says** the LORD.
6:16 [A] This is what the LORD **says**: "Stand at the crossroads
6:16 [A] find rest for your souls. But *you* **said**, 'We will not walk in it.'
6:17 [A] the sound of the trumpet!' But *you* **said**, 'We will not listen.'
6:21 [A] Therefore this is what the LORD **says**: "I will put obstacles
6:22 [A] This is what the LORD **says**: "Look, an army is coming
7: 1 [A] is the word that came to Jeremiah from the LORD: **[NIE]**
7: 2 [A] **[NIE]** " 'Hear the word of the LORD, all you people of
7: 3 [A] This is what the LORD Almighty, the God of Israel, **says**:
7: 4 [A] Do not trust in deceptive words and **say**, "This is the temple
7:10 [A] this house, which bears my Name, and **say**, "We are safe"—
7:20 [A] " 'Therefore this is what the Sovereign LORD **says**: My
7:21 [A] " 'This is what the LORD Almighty, the God of Israel, **says**:
7:23 [A] **[NIE]** Obey me, and I will be your God and you will be my
7:28 [A] Therefore **say** to them, 'This is the nation that has not obeyed
7:32 [C] when people *will* no longer **call** *it* Topheth or the Valley of
8: 4 [A] "**Say** to them, 'This is what the LORD says: " 'When men
8: 4 [A] "Say to them, 'This is what the LORD **says**: " 'When men
8: 6 [A] one repents of his wickedness, **saying**, "What have I done?"
8: 8 [A] " 'How *can you* **say**, "We are wise, for we have the law of
8:11 [A] not serious. "Peace, peace," they **say**, when there is no peace.
8:12 [A] be brought down when they are punished, **says** the LORD.
9: 7 [9:6] [A] Therefore this is what the LORD Almighty **says**:
9:13 [9:12] [A] The LORD **said**, "It is because they have forsaken
9:15 [9:14] [A] what the LORD Almighty, the God of Israel, **says**:
9:17 [9:16] [A] This is what the LORD Almighty **says**:
9:23 [9:22] [A] This is what the LORD **says**: "Let not the wise man
10: 2 [A] This is what the LORD **says**: "Do not learn the ways of the
10:18 [A] For this is what the LORD **says**: "At this time I will hurl out
10:19 [A] Yet I **said** to myself, "This is my sickness, and I must endure
11: 1 [A] is the word that came to Jeremiah from the LORD: **[NIE]**
11: 3 [A] **Tell** them that this is what the LORD, the God of Israel,
11: 3 [A] them that this is what the LORD, the God of Israel, **says**:
11: 4 [A] *I* **said**, 'Obey me and do everything I command you, and you
11: 5 [A] you possess today." I answered, **[NIE]** "Amen, LORD."
11: 6 [A] The LORD **said** to me, "Proclaim all these words in the
11: 6 [A] **[NIE]** 'Listen to the terms of this covenant and follow them.
11: 7 [A] I warned them again and again, **saying**, "Obey me."
11: 9 [A] the LORD **said** to me, "There is a conspiracy among the
11:11 [A] Therefore this is what the LORD **says**: 'I will bring on them
11:21 [A] "Therefore this is what the LORD **says** about the men of
11:21 [A] the men of Anathoth who are seeking your life and **saying**,
11:22 [A] therefore this is what the LORD Almighty **says**: 'I will
12: 4 [A] Moreover, *the people are* **saying**, "He will not see what
12:14 [A] This is what the LORD **says**: "As for all my wicked
13: 1 [A] This is what the LORD **said** to me: "Go and buy a linen belt
13: 3 [A] the word of the LORD came to me a second time: **[NIE]**
13: 6 [A] Many days later the LORD **said** to me, "Go now to Perath
13: 8 [A] Then the word of the LORD came to me: **[NIE]**
13: 9 [A] "This is what the LORD **says**: 'In the same way I will ruin
13:12 [A] "**Say** to them: 'This is what the LORD, the God of Israel,
13:12 [A] to them: 'This is what the LORD, the God of Israel, **says**:
13:12 [A] if *they* **say** to you, 'Don't we know that every wineskin
13:13 [A] **tell** them, 'This is what the LORD says: I am going to fill
13:13 [A] tell them, 'This is what the LORD **says**: I am going to fill
13:18 [A] **Say** to the king and to the queen mother, "Come down from
13:21 [A] What *will you* **say** when ⌊the LORD⌋ sets over you those
13:22 [A] And if *you* **ask** yourself, "Why has this happened to me?"—
14:10 [A] This is what the LORD **says** about this people:
14:11 [A] the LORD **said** to me, "Do not pray for the well-being of
14:13 [A] *I* **said**, "Ah, Sovereign LORD, the prophets keep telling
14:13 [A] "Ah, Sovereign LORD, the prophets *keep* **telling** them,
14:14 [A] the LORD **said** to me, "The prophets are prophesying lies in
14:15 [A] this is what the LORD **says** about the prophets who are
14:15 [A] yet they *are* **saying**, 'No sword or famine will touch this
14:17 [A] "**Speak** this word to them: " 'Let my eyes overflow with tears
15: 1 [A] the LORD **said** to me: "Even if Moses and Samuel were to
15: 2 [A] if *they* **ask** you, 'Where shall we go?' tell them, 'This is what
15: 2 [A] shall we go?' **tell** them, 'This is what the LORD says:
15: 2 [A] shall we go?' tell them, 'This is what the LORD **says**:
15:11 [A] The LORD **said**, "Surely I will deliver you for a good
15:19 [A] Therefore this is what the LORD **says**: "If you repent, I will
16: 1 [A] Then the word of the LORD came to me: **[NIE]**
16: 3 [A] For this is what the LORD **says** about the sons
16: 5 [A] For this is what the LORD **says**: "Do not enter a house
16: 9 [A] this is what the LORD Almighty, the God of Israel, **says**:
16:10 [A] "When you tell these people all this and *they* **ask** you, 'Why
16:11 [A] **say** to them, 'It is because your fathers forsook me,'
16:14 [C] declares the LORD, "when *men will* no longer **say**,
16:19 [A] you the nations will come from the ends of the earth and **say**,
17: 5 [A] This is what the LORD **says**: "Cursed is the one who trusts
17:15 [A] They *keep* **saying** to me, "Where is the word of the LORD?
17:19 [A] This is what the LORD **said** to me: "Go and stand at the
17:20 [A] **Say** to them, 'Hear the word of the LORD, O kings of Judah
17:21 [A] This is what the LORD **says**: Be careful not to carry a load
18: 1 [A] is the word that came to Jeremiah from the LORD: **[NIE]**
18: 5 [A] Then the word of the LORD came to me: **[NIE]**
18:10 [A] then I will reconsider the good *I had* **intended** to do for it.
18:11 [A] "Now therefore **say** to the people of Judah and those living in
18:11 [A] living in Jerusalem, **[RPH]** 'This is what the LORD says:
18:11 [A] and those living in Jerusalem, 'This is what the LORD **says**:
18:12 [A] *they will* **reply**, 'It's no use. We will continue with our own
18:13 [A] Therefore this is what the LORD **says**: "Inquire among the
18:18 [A] *They* **said**, "Come, let's make plans against Jeremiah;
19: 1 [A] This is what the LORD **says**: "Go and buy a clay jar from a
19: 3 [A] **say**, 'Hear the word of the LORD, O kings of Judah
19: 3 [A] This is what the LORD Almighty, the God of Israel, **says**:
19:11 [A] and **say** to them, 'This is what the LORD Almighty says:
19:11 [A] and say to them, 'This is what the LORD Almighty **says**:
19:14 [A] the court of the LORD's temple and **said** to all the people,
19:15 [A] "This is what the LORD Almighty, the God of Israel, **says**:
20: 3 [A] Pashhur released him from the stocks, Jeremiah **said** to him,
20: 4 [A] For this is what the LORD **says**: 'I will make you a terror to
20: 9 [A] if *I* **say**, "I will not mention him or speak any more in his

Jer 20:15 [A] who made him very glad, **saying**, "A child is born to you—
21: 1 [A] and the priest Zephaniah son of Maaseiah. They **said**:
21: 3 [A] But Jeremiah **answered** them, "Tell Zedekiah,
21: 3 [A] But Jeremiah answered them, "**Tell** Zedekiah,
21: 4 [A] 'This is what the LORD, the God of Israel, **says**: I am about
21: 8 [A] "Furthermore, **tell** the people, 'This is what the LORD says:
21: 8 [A] "Furthermore, tell the people, 'This is what the LORD **says**:
21:12 [A] O house of David, this is what the LORD **says**:
21:13 [A] the LORD—you who **say**, "Who can come against us?
22: 1 [A] This is what the LORD **says**: "Go down to the palace of the
22: 2 [A] **[NIE]** 'Hear the word of the LORD, O king of Judah,
22: 3 [A] This is what the LORD **says**: Do what is just and right.
22: 6 [A] For this is what the LORD **says** about the palace of the king
22: 8 [A] many nations will pass by this city and *will* **ask** one another,
22: 9 [A] *the* **answer** *will be*: 'Because they have forsaken the
22:11 [A] For this is what the LORD **says** about Shallum son of
22:14 [A] He **says**, 'I will build myself a great palace with spacious
22:18 [A] Therefore this is what the LORD **says** about Jehoiakim son
22:21 [A] you when you felt secure, but *you* **said**, 'I will not listen!'
22:30 [A] This is what the LORD **says**: "Record this man as if
23: 2 [A] the God of Israel, **says** to the shepherds who tend my people:
23: 7 [A] declares the LORD, "when *people will* no longer **say**,
23:15 [A] this is what the LORD Almighty **says** concerning the
23:16 [A] This is what the LORD Almighty **says**: "Do not listen to
23:17 [A] *They* **keep saying** [+606] to those who despise me,
23:17 [A] *They* **keep saying** [+606] to those who despise me,
23:17 [A] to all who follow the stubbornness of their hearts *they* **say**,
23:25 [A] "I have heard what the prophets **say** who prophesy lies in my
23:25 [A] lies in my name. They **say**, 'I had a dream! I had a dream!'
23:33 [A] a priest, ask you, **[NIE]** 'What is the oracle of the LORD?'
23:33 [A] **say** to them, 'What oracle? I will forsake you,
23:34 [A] If a prophet or a priest or anyone else **claims**, 'This is the
23:35 [A] This is what each of *you keeps on* **saying** to his friend
23:37 [A] This is what *you keep* **saying** to a prophet: 'What is the
23:38 [A] Although *you* **claim**, 'This is the oracle of the LORD,' this
23:38 [A] is the oracle of the LORD,' this is what the LORD **says**:
23:38 [A] You **used** the words, 'This is the oracle of the LORD,'
23:38 [A] even though *I* **told** [+448+4200+8938] you that you must not
23:38 [A] even though I told you that *you must* not **claim**, 'This is the
24: 3 [A] Then the LORD **asked** me, "What do you see, Jeremiah?"
24: 3 [A] asked me, "What do you see, Jeremiah?" "Figs," *I* **answered**.
24: 4 [A] Then the word of the LORD came to me: **[NIE]**
24: 5 [A] "This is what the LORD, the God of Israel, **says**: 'Like these
24: 8 [A] which are so bad they cannot be eaten,' **says** the LORD,
25: 2 [A] people of Judah and to all those living in Jerusalem: **[NIE]**
25: 5 [A] They **said**, "Turn now, each of you, from your evil ways
25: 8 [A] Therefore the LORD Almighty **says** this: "Because you
25:15 [A] This is what the LORD, the God of Israel, **said** to me:
25:27 [A] "Then **tell** them, 'This is what the LORD Almighty, the God
25:27 [A] 'This is what the LORD Almighty, the God of Israel, **says**:
25:28 [A] refuse to take the cup from your hand and drink, **tell** them,
25:28 [A] tell them, 'This is what the LORD Almighty **says**:
25:30 [A] prophesy all these words against them and **say** to them:
25:32 [A] This is what the LORD Almighty **says**: "Look! Disaster is
26: 1 [A] king of Judah, this word came from the LORD: **[NIE]**
26: 2 [A] "This is what the LORD **says**: Stand in the courtyard of the
26: 4 [A] **Say** to them, 'This is what the LORD says: If you do not
26: 4 [A] Say to them, 'This is what the LORD **says**: If you do not
26: 8 [A] the prophets and all the people seized him and **said**,
26: 9 [A] Why do you prophesy in the LORD's name **[NIE]** that this
26:11 [A] the priests and the prophets **said** to the officials and all the
26:11 [A] **[RPH]** "This man should be sentenced to death because he
26:12 [A] Jeremiah **said** to all the officials and all the people: "The
26:12 [A] **[NIE]** "The LORD sent me to prophesy against this house
26:16 [A] and all the people **said** to the priests and the prophets,
26:17 [A] stepped forward and **said** to the entire assembly of people,
26:17 [A] and said to the entire assembly of people, **[NIE]**
26:18 [A] *He* **told** all the people of Judah, 'This is what the LORD
26:18 [A] of Judah, **[RPH]** 'This is what the LORD Almighty says:
26:18 [A] the people of Judah, 'This is what the LORD Almighty **says**:
27: 1 [A] this word came to Jeremiah from the LORD: **[NIE]**
27: 2 [A] This is what the LORD **said** to me: "Make a yoke out of
27: 4 [A] Give them a message for their masters and **say**, 'This is what
27: 4 [A] 'This is what the LORD Almighty, the God of Israel, **says**:
27: 4 [A] the God of Israel, says: "**Tell** this to your masters:
27: 9 [A] of dreams, your mediums or your sorcerers who **tell** you,
27: 9 [A] tell you, **[RPH]** 'You will not serve the king of Babylon.'
27:12 [A] I **said**, "Bow your neck under the yoke of the king of
27:14 [A] Do not listen to the words of the prophets who **say** to you,
27:14 [A] **[NIE]** 'You will not serve the king of Babylon,' for they are
27:16 [A] and all these people, **[NIE]** "This is what the LORD says:
27:16 [A] and all these people, "This is what the LORD **says**:
27:16 [A] Do not listen to the prophets *who* **say**, 'Very soon now the
27:19 [A] For this is what the LORD Almighty **says** about the pillars,
27:21 [A] **says** about the things that are left in the house of the LORD
28: 1 [A] **said** to me in the house of the LORD in the presence of the
28: 1 [A] in the presence of the priests and all the people: **[RPH]**
28: 2 [A] "This is what the LORD Almighty, the God of Israel, **says**:
28: 2 [A] says: **[NIE]** 'I will break the yoke of the king of Babylon.
28: 5 [A] the prophet Jeremiah **replied** to the prophet Hananiah before
28: 6 [A] He **said**, "Amen! May the LORD do so! May the LORD
28:11 [A] he **said** before all the people, "This is what the LORD says:
28:11 [A] before all the people, **[RPH]** "This is what the LORD says:
28:11 [A] he said before all the people, "This is what the LORD **says**:
28:12 [A] the word of the LORD came to Jeremiah: **[NIE]**
28:13 [A] "Go and **tell** Hananiah, 'This is what the LORD says:
28:13 [A] and tell Hananiah, **[RPH]** 'This is what the LORD says:
28:13 [A] "Go and tell Hananiah, 'This is what the LORD **says**:
28:14 [A] This is what the LORD Almighty, the God of Israel, **says**:
28:15 [A] the prophet Jeremiah **said** to Hananiah the prophet, "Listen,
28:16 [A] Therefore, this is what the LORD **says**: 'I am about to
29: 3 [A] of Judah sent to King Nebuchadnezzar in Babylon. *It* **said**:
29: 4 [A] **says** to all those I carried into exile from Jerusalem to
29: 8 [A] this is what the LORD Almighty, the God of Israel, **says**:
29:10 [A] This is what the LORD **says**: "When seventy years are
29:15 [A] *You may* **say**, "The LORD has raised up prophets for us in
29:16 [A] this is what the LORD **says** about the king who sits on
29:17 [A] yes, this is what the LORD Almighty **says**: "I will send the
29:21 [A] **says** about Ahab son of Kolaiah and Zedekiah son of
29:22 [A] **[NIE]** 'The LORD treat you like Zedekiah and Ahab,
29:24 [A] **Tell** Shemaiah the Nehelamite,
29:24 [A] Tell Shemaiah the Nehelamite, **[RPH]**
29:25 [A] "This is what the LORD Almighty, the God of Israel, **says**:
29:25 [A] **[NIE]** You sent letters in your own name to all the people in
29:25 [A] the priest, and to all the other priests. You **said** to Zephaniah,
29:28 [A] He has sent this **message** to us in Babylon: It will be a long
29:30 [A] Then the word of the LORD came to Jeremiah: **[NIE]**
29:31 [A] "Send this **message** to all the exiles: 'This is what the
29:31 [A] 'This is what the LORD **says** about Shemaiah the
29:32 [A] this is what the LORD **says**: I will surely punish Shemaiah
30: 1 [A] is the word that came to Jeremiah from the LORD: **[NIE]**
30: 2 [A] "This is what the LORD, the God of Israel, **says**: 'Write in a
30: 2 [A] **[RPH]** 'Write in a book all the words I have spoken to you.
30: 3 [A] land I gave their forefathers to possess,' **says** the LORD."
30: 5 [A] "This is what the LORD **says**: " 'Cries of fear are heard—
30:12 [A] "This is what the LORD **says**: " 'Your wound is incurable,
30:18 [A] "This is what the LORD **says**: " 'I will restore the fortunes
31: 2 [A] This is what the LORD **says**: "The people who survive the
31: 7 [A] This is what the LORD **says**: "Sing with joy for Jacob;
31: 7 [A] and **say**, 'O LORD, save your people, the remnant of Israel.'
31:10 [A] **[NIE]** 'He who scattered Israel will gather them and will
31:15 [A] This is what the LORD **says**: "A voice is heard in Ramah,
31:16 [A] This is what the LORD **says**: "Restrain your voice from
31:23 [A] This is what the LORD Almighty, the God of Israel, **says**:
31:23 [A] *people* in the land of Judah and in its towns *will* once again **use**
31:29 [A] "In those days *people will* no longer **say**, 'The fathers have
31:34 [A] or a man his brother, **saying**, 'Know the LORD,'
31:35 [A] This is what the LORD **says**, he who appoints the sun to
31:37 [A] This is what the LORD **says**: "Only if the heavens above
32: 3 [A] him there, **saying**, "Why do you prophesy as you do?
32: 3 [A] prophesy as you do? You **say**, 'This is what the LORD says:
32: 3 [A] prophesy as you do? You say, 'This is what the LORD **says**:
32: 6 [A] Jeremiah **said**, "The word of the LORD came to me:
32: 6 [A] "The word of the LORD came to me: **[NIE]**
32: 7 [A] son of Shallum your uncle is going to come to you and **say**,
32: 8 [A] Hanamel came to me in the courtyard of the guard and **said**,
32:13 [A] "In their presence I gave Baruch these instructions: **[NIE]**
32:14 [A] 'This is what the LORD Almighty, the God of Israel, **says**:
32:15 [A] this is what the LORD Almighty, the God of Israel, **says**:
32:16 [A] to Baruch son of Neriah, I prayed to the LORD: **[NIE]**
32:25 [A] you, O Sovereign LORD, **say** to me, 'Buy the field with
32:26 [A] Then the word of the LORD came to Jeremiah: **[NIE]**
32:28 [A] Therefore, this is what the LORD **says**: I am about to hand
32:36 [A] "You *are* **saying** about this city, 'By the sword, famine
32:36 [A] but this is what the LORD, the God of Israel, **says**:
32:42 [A] "This is what the LORD **says**: As I have brought all this
32:43 [A] more fields will be bought in this land of which you **say**,
33: 1 [A] the word of the LORD came to him a second time: **[NIE]**
33: 2 [A] "This is what the LORD **says**, he who made the earth,
33: 4 [A] **says** about the houses in this city and the royal palaces of
33:10 [A] "This is what the LORD **says**: 'You say about this place,
33:10 [A] 'You **say** about this place, "It is a desolate waste, without
33:11 [A] **saying**, "Give thanks to the LORD Almighty,
33:11 [A] fortunes of the land as they were before,' **says** the LORD.
33:12 [A] "This is what the LORD Almighty **says**: 'In this place,
33:13 [A] the hand of the one who counts them,' **says** the LORD.
33:17 [A] For this is what the LORD **says**: 'David will never fail to
33:19 [A] The word of the LORD came to Jeremiah: **[NIE]**

Jer 33:20 [A] "This is what the LORD **says**: 'If you can break my
33:23 [A] The word of the LORD came to Jeremiah: **[NIE]**
33:24 [A] **[NIE]** 'The LORD has rejected the two kingdoms he
33:25 [A] This is what the LORD **says**: 'If I have not established my
34: 1 [A] this word came to Jeremiah from the LORD: **[NIE]**
34: 2 [A] "This is what the LORD, the God of Israel, **says**: Go to
34: 2 [A] Go **[RPH]** to Zedekiah king of Judah and tell him, 'This is
34: 2 [A] Go to Zedekiah king of Judah and **tell** him, 'This is what the
34: 2 [A] king of Judah and tell him, 'This is what the LORD **says**:
34: 4 [A] king of Judah. This is what the LORD **says** concerning you:
34:12 [A] Then the word of the LORD came to Jeremiah: **[NIE]**
34:13 [A] "This is what the LORD, the God of Israel, **says**: I made a
34:13 [A] brought them out of Egypt, out of the land of slavery. I **said**,
34:17 [A] "Therefore, this is what the LORD **says**: You have not
35: 1 [A] the reign of Jehoiakim son of Josiah king of Judah: **[NIE]**
35: 5 [A] cups before the men of the Recabite family and **said** to them,
35: 6 [A] *they* **replied**, "We do not drink wine, because our forefather
35: 6 [A] **[NIE]** 'Neither you nor your descendants must ever drink
35:11 [A] *we* **said**, 'Come, we must go to Jerusalem to escape the
35:12 [A] Then the word of the LORD came to Jeremiah, **saying**:
35:13 [A] "This is what the LORD Almighty, the God of Israel, **says**:
35:13 [A] Go and **tell** the men of Judah and the people of Jerusalem,
35:15 [A] They **said**, "Each of you must turn from your wicked ways
35:17 [A] is what the LORD God Almighty, the God of Israel, **says**:
35:18 [A] Jeremiah **said** to the family of the Recabites, "This is what
35:18 [A] "This is what the LORD Almighty, the God of Israel, **says**:
35:19 [A] this is what the LORD Almighty, the God of Israel, **says**:
36: 1 [A] this word came to Jeremiah from the LORD: **[NIE]**
36: 5 [A] Jeremiah told Baruch, **[NIE]** "I am restricted; I cannot go to
36:14 [A] the son of Shelemiah, the son of Cushi, to **say** to Baruch,
36:15 [A] *They* **said** to him, "Sit down, please, and read it to us."
36:16 [A] they looked at each other in fear and **said** to Baruch,
36:17 [A] they asked Baruch, **[NIE]** "Tell us, how did you come to
36:18 [A] "Yes," Baruch **replied**, "he dictated all these words to me,
36:19 [A] the officials **said** to Baruch, "You and Jeremiah, go and hide.
36:27 [A] the word of the LORD came to Jeremiah: **[NIE]**
36:29 [A] Also **tell** Jehoiakim king of Judah, 'This is what the LORD
36:29 [A] tell Jehoiakim king of Judah, 'This is what the LORD **says**:
36:29 [A] You burned that scroll and **said**, "Why did you write on it
36:29 [A] "Why did you write on it that **[NIE]** the king of Babylon
36:30 [A] this is what the LORD **says** about Jehoiakim king of Judah:
37: 3 [A] son of Maaseiah to Jeremiah the prophet with *this* **message**:
37: 6 [A] word of the LORD came to Jeremiah the prophet: **[NIE]**
37: 7 [A] "This is what the LORD, the God of Israel, **says**: Tell the
37: 7 [A] **Tell** the king of Judah, who sent you to inquire of me,
37: 9 [A] "This is what the LORD **says**: Do not deceive yourselves,
37: 9 [A] Do not deceive yourselves, **thinking**, 'The Babylonians will
37:13 [A] the son of Hananiah, arrested him and **said**, "You are
37:14 [A] "That's not true!" Jeremiah **said**. "I am not deserting to the
37:17 [A] him privately, **[NIE]** "Is there any word from the LORD?"
37:17 [A] "Yes," Jeremiah **replied**, "you will be handed over to the
37:17 [A] **[RPH]** "you will be handed over to the king of Babylon."
37:18 [A] Jeremiah **said** to King Zedekiah, "What crime have I
37:19 [A] **[NIE]** 'The king of Babylon will not attack you or this
38: 1 [A] heard what Jeremiah was telling all the people *when* he **said**,
38: 2 [A] "This is what the LORD **says**: 'Whoever stays in this city
38: 3 [A] this is what the LORD **says**: 'This city will certainly be
38: 4 [A] the officials **said** to the king, "This man should be put to
38: 5 [A] "He is in your hands," King Zedekiah **answered**. "The king
38: 8 [A] Ebed-Melech went out of the palace and said to him, **[NIE]**
38:10 [A] **[NIE]** "Take thirty men from here with you and lift
38:12 [A] Ebed-Melech the Cushite **said** to Jeremiah, "Put these old
38:14 [A] am going to ask you something," the king **said** to Jeremiah.
38:15 [A] Jeremiah **said** to Zedekiah, "If I give you an answer, will you
38:16 [A] **[NIE]** "As surely as the LORD lives, who has given us
38:17 [A] Jeremiah **said** to Zedekiah, "This is what the LORD God
38:17 [A] is what the LORD God Almighty, the God of Israel, **says**:
38:19 [A] King Zedekiah **said** to Jeremiah, "I am afraid of the Jews
38:20 [A] "They will not hand you over," Jeremiah **replied**. "Obey the
38:22 [A] Those *women will* **say** to you: " 'They misled you
38:24 [A] Zedekiah **said** to Jeremiah, "Do not let anyone know about
38:25 [A] they come to you and **say**, 'Tell us what you said to the king
38:26 [A] **tell** them, 'I was pleading with the king not to send me back
39:11 [A] Nebuzaradan commander of the imperial guard: **[NIE]**
39:15 [A] of the guard, the word of the LORD came to him: **[NIE]**
39:16 [A] "Go and **tell** Ebed-Melech the Cushite, 'This is what the
39:16 [A] **[RPH]** 'This is what the LORD Almighty, the God of
39:16 [A] 'This is what the LORD Almighty, the God of Israel, **says**:
40: 2 [A] the commander of the guard found Jeremiah, *he* **said** to him,
40: 9 [A] "Do not be afraid to serve the Babylonians," he **said**.
40:14 [A] **said** to him, "Don't you know that Baalis king of the
40:15 [A] Johanan son of Kareah **said** privately to Gedaliah in Mizpah,
40:15 [A] **[RPH]** "Let me go and kill Ishmael son of Nethaniah,
40:16 [A] But Gedaliah son of Ahikam **said** to Johanan son of Kareah,
41: 6 [A] When he met them, *he* **said**, "Come to Gedaliah son of
41: 8 [A] ten of them **said** to Ishmael, "Don't kill us! We have wheat
42: 2 [A] Jeremiah the prophet and **said** to him, "Please hear our
42: 4 [A] "I have heard you," **replied** Jeremiah the prophet. "I will
42: 5 [A] they **said** to Jeremiah, "May the LORD be a true
42: 9 [A] *He* **said** to them, "This is what the LORD, the God of
42: 9 [A] of Israel, to whom you sent me to present your petition, **says**:
42:13 [A] "However, if you **say**, 'We will not stay in this land,' and
42:14 [A] if you **say**, 'No, we will go and live in Egypt, where we will
42:15 [A] This is what the LORD Almighty, the God of Israel, **says**:
42:18 [A] This is what the LORD Almighty, the God of Israel, **says**:
42:20 [A] mistake when you sent me to the LORD your God and **said**,
42:20 [A] our God for us; tell us everything he **says** and we will do it.'
43: 2 [A] son of Kareah and all the arrogant men **said** to Jeremiah,
43: 2 [A] of Kareah and all the arrogant men said **[RPH]** to Jeremiah,
43: 2 [A] The LORD our God has not sent you to **say**, 'You must not
43: 8 [A] the word of the LORD came to Jeremiah: **[NIE]**
43:10 [A] **say** to them, 'This is what the LORD Almighty, the God of
43:10 [A] 'This is what the LORD Almighty, the God of Israel, **says**:
44: 1 [A] and Memphis—and in Upper Egypt: **[NIE]**
44: 2 [A] "This is what the LORD Almighty, the God of Israel, **says**:
44: 4 [A] Again and again I sent my servants the prophets, *who* **said**,
44: 7 [A] is what the LORD God Almighty, the God of Israel, **says**:
44:11 [A] this is what the LORD Almighty, the God of Israel, **says**:
44:15 [A] living in Lower and Upper Egypt, said to Jeremiah, **[NIE]**
44:20 [A] Then Jeremiah **said** to all the people, both men and women,
44:20 [A] both men and women, who were answering him, **[NIE]**
44:24 [A] Then Jeremiah **said** to all the people, including the women,
44:25 [A] This is what the LORD Almighty, the God of Israel, **says**:
44:25 [A] **[RPH]** You and your wives have shown by your actions
44:25 [A] shown by your actions what you promised *when* you **said**,
44:26 [A] 'I swear by my great name,' **says** the LORD, 'that no one
44:26 [A] in Egypt will ever again invoke my name or **swear**,
44:30 [A] This is what the LORD **says**: 'I am going to hand Pharaoh
45: 1 [A] on a scroll the words Jeremiah was then dictating: **[NIE]**
45: 2 [A] is what the LORD, the God of Israel, **says** to you, Baruch:
45: 3 [A] *You* **said**, 'Woe to me! The LORD has added sorrow to my
45: 4 [A] ˻The LORD said,˼ "**Say** this to him: 'This is what the
45: 4 [A] 'This is what the LORD **says**: I will overthrow what I have
46: 8 [A] *She* **says**, 'I will rise and cover the earth; I will destroy cities
46:14 [A] **[RPH]** 'Take your positions and get ready, for the sword
46:16 [A] *They will* **say**, 'Get up, let us go back to our own people
46:25 [A] The LORD Almighty, the God of Israel, **says**: "I am about
47: 2 [A] This is what the LORD **says**: "See how the waters are rising
48: 1 [A] This is what the LORD Almighty, the God of Israel, **says**:
48: 8 [A] and the plateau destroyed, because the LORD *has* **spoken**.
48:14 [A] "How *can you* **say**, 'We are warriors, men valiant in battle'?
48:17 [A] **say**, 'How broken is the mighty scepter, how broken the
48:19 [A] and the woman escaping, **ask** them, 'What has happened?'
48:40 [A] This is what the LORD **says**: "Look! An eagle is swooping
49: 1 [A] This is what the LORD **says**: "Has Israel no sons? Has she
49: 2 [A] will drive out those who drove her out," **says** the LORD.
49: 7 [A] Concerning Edom: This is what the LORD Almighty **says**:
49:12 [A] This is what the LORD **says**: "If those who do not deserve
49:18 [A] **says** the LORD, "so no one will live there;
49:28 [A] This is what the LORD **says**: "Arise, and attack Kedar
49:34 [A] early in the reign of Zedekiah king of Judah: **[NIE]**
49:35 [A] This is what the LORD Almighty **says**: "See, I will break
50: 2 [A] keep nothing back, but **say**, 'Babylon will be captured;
50: 7 [A] their enemies **said**, 'We are not guilty, for they sinned against
50:18 [A] this is what the LORD Almighty, the God of Israel, **says**:
50:33 [A] This is what the LORD Almighty **says**: "The people of
51: 1 [A] This is what the LORD **says**: "See, I will stir up the spirit of
51:33 [A] This is what the LORD Almighty, the God of Israel, **says**:
51:35 [A] to our flesh be upon Babylon," **say** the inhabitants of Zion.
51:35 [A] blood be on those who live in Babylonia," **says** Jerusalem.
51:36 [A] Therefore, this is what the LORD **says**: "See, I will defend
51:58 [A] This is what the LORD Almighty **says**: "Babylon's thick
51:61 [A] He **said** to Seraiah, "When you get to Babylon, see that you
51:62 [A] **say**, 'O LORD, you have said you will destroy this place,
51:64 [A] **say**, 'So will Babylon sink to rise no more because of the
La 2:12 [A] *They* **say** to their mothers, "Where is bread and wine?"
2:15 [A] "Is this the city that *was* **called** the perfection of beauty,
2:16 [A] they scoff and gnash their teeth and **say**, "We have
3:18 [A] So *I* **say**, "My splendor is gone and all that I had hoped from
3:24 [A] I **say** *to* myself, "The LORD is my portion; therefore I will
3:37 [A] Who *can* **speak** and have it happen if the Lord has not
3:54 [A] closed over my head, and *I* **thought** I was about to be cut off.
3:57 [A] came near when I called you, and *you* **said**, "Do not fear."
4:15 [A] they flee and wander about, *people* among the nations **say**,
4:20 [A] *We* **thought** that under his shadow we would live among the
Eze 2: 1 [A] *He* **said** to me, "Son of man, stand up on your feet and I will
2: 3 [A] *He* **said**: "Son of man, I am sending you to the Israelites, to a
2: 4 [A] **Say** to them, 'This is what the Sovereign LORD says.'

Eze 2: 4 [A] Say to them, 'This is what the Sovereign LORD **says**.'
3: 1 [A] *he* **said** to me, "Son of man, eat what is before you, eat this
3: 3 [A] *he* **said** to me, "Son of man, eat this scroll I am giving you
3: 4 [A] *He* then **said** to me: "Son of man, go now to the house of
3: 10 [A] *he* **said** to me, "Son of man, listen carefully and take to heart
3: 11 [A] **Say** to them, 'This is what the Sovereign LORD says,'
3: 11 [A] Say to them, 'This is what the Sovereign LORD **says**,'
3: 16 [A] of seven days the word of the LORD came to me: **[NIE]**
3: 18 [A] When I **say** to a wicked man, 'You will surely die,' and you
3: 22 [A] *he* **said** to me, "Get up and go out to the plain, and there I
3: 24 [A] He spoke to me and **said**: "Go, shut yourself inside your
3: 27 [A] to you, I will open your mouth and *you shall* **say** to them,
3: 27 [A] shall say to them, 'This is what the Sovereign LORD **says**.'
4: 13 [A] The LORD **said**, "In this way the people of Israel will eat
4: 14 [A] *I* **said**, "Not so, Sovereign LORD! I have never defiled
4: 15 [A] "Very well," *he* **said**, "I will let you bake your bread over
4: 16 [A] *He* then **said** to me: "Son of man, I will cut off the supply of
5: 5 [A] "This is what the Sovereign LORD **says**: This is Jerusalem,
5: 7 [A] "Therefore this is what the Sovereign LORD **says**: You
5: 8 [A] "Therefore this is what the Sovereign LORD **says**: I myself
6: 1 [A] The word of the LORD came to me: **[NIE]**
6: 3 [A] **say**: 'O mountains of Israel, hear the word of the Sovereign
6: 3 [A] This is what the Sovereign LORD **says** to the mountains
6: 11 [A] " 'This is what the Sovereign LORD **says**: Strike your hands
6: 11 [A] your hands together and stamp your feet and **cry out** "Alas!"
7: 1 [A] The word of the LORD came to me: **[NIE]**
7: 2 [A] this is what the Sovereign LORD **says** to the land of Israel:
7: 5 [A] "This is what the Sovereign LORD **says**: Disaster!
8: 5 [A] Then *he* **said** to me, "Son of man, look toward the north."
8: 6 [A] *he* **said** to me, "Son of man, do you see what they are
8: 8 [A] *He* **said** to me, "Son of man, now dig into the wall." So I dug
8: 9 [A] *he* **said** to me, "Go in and see the wicked and detestable
8: 12 [A] *He* **said** to me, "Son of man, have you seen what the elders
8: 12 [A] *They* **say**, 'The LORD does not see us; the LORD has
8: 13 [A] Again, *he* **said**, "You will see them doing things that are
8: 15 [A] *He* **said** to me, "Do you see this, son of man? You will see
8: 17 [A] *He* **said** to me, "Have you seen this, son of man? Is it a
9: 1 [A] **[NIE]** "Bring the guards of the city here, each with a
9: 4 [A] **said** to him, "Go throughout the city of Jerusalem and put a
9: 5 [A] As I listened, *he* **said** to the others, "Follow him through the
9: 7 [A] *he* **said** to them, "Defile the temple and fill the courts with
9: 8 [A] I fell facedown, crying out, **[NIE]** "Ah, Sovereign LORD!
9: 9 [A] *He* **answered** me, "The sin of the house of Israel and Judah
9: 9 [A] *They* **say**, 'The LORD has forsaken the land; the LORD
9: 11 [A] back word, **saying**, "I have done as you commanded."
10: 2 [A] The LORD **said** to the man clothed in linen, "Go in among
10: 2 [A] **[NIE]** "Go in among the wheels beneath the cherubim.
10: 6 [A] **[NIE]** "Take fire from among the wheels, from among the
11: 2 [A] The LORD **said** to me, "Son of man, these are the men who
11: 3 [A] They **say**, 'Will it not soon be time to build houses? This city
11: 5 [A] Spirit of the LORD came upon me, and *he* **told** me to say:
11: 5 [A] Spirit of the LORD came upon me, and he told me *to* **say**:
11: 5 [A] and he told me to say: "This is what the LORD **says**:
11: 5 [A] That is what *you are* **saying**, O house of Israel, but I know
11: 7 [A] "Therefore this is what the Sovereign LORD **says**:
11: 13 [A] cried out in a loud voice, **[NIE]** "Ah, Sovereign LORD!
11: 14 [A] The word of the LORD came to me: **[NIE]**
11: 15 [A] are those of whom the people of Jerusalem *have* **said**,
11: 16 [A] "Therefore **say**: 'This is what the Sovereign LORD says:
11: 16 [A] "Therefore say: 'This is what the Sovereign LORD **says**:
11: 17 [A] "Therefore **say**: 'This is what the Sovereign LORD says:
11: 17 [A] "Therefore say: 'This is what the Sovereign LORD **says**:
12: 1 [A] The word of the LORD came to me: **[NIE]**
12: 8 [A] In the morning the word of the LORD came to me: **[NIE]**
12: 9 [A] "Son of man, *did* not that rebellious house of Israel **ask** you,
12: 10 [A] "**Say** to them, 'This is what the Sovereign LORD says: This
12: 10 [A] "Say to them, 'This is what the Sovereign LORD **says**: This
12: 11 [A] **Say** to them, 'I am a sign to you.' "As I have done, so it will
12: 17 [A] The word of the LORD came to me: **[NIE]**
12: 19 [A] **Say** to the people of the land: 'This is what the Sovereign
12: 19 [A] 'This is what the Sovereign LORD **says** about those living
12: 21 [A] The word of the LORD came to me: **[NIE]**
12: 22 [A] **[NIE]** 'The days go by and every vision comes to nothing'?
12: 23 [A] **Say** to them, 'This is what the Sovereign LORD says: I am
12: 23 [A] Say to them, 'This is what the Sovereign LORD **says**: I am
12: 26 [A] The word of the LORD came to me: **[NIE]**
12: 27 [A] "Son of man, the house of Israel *is* **saying**, 'The vision he
12: 28 [A] "Therefore **say** to them, 'This is what the Sovereign LORD
12: 28 [A] say to them, 'This is what the Sovereign LORD **says**:
13: 1 [A] The word of the LORD came to me: **[NIE]**
13: 2 [A] **Say** to those who prophesy out of their own imagination:
13: 3 [A] This is what the Sovereign LORD **says**: Woe to the foolish
13: 6 [A] They **say**, "The LORD declares," when the LORD has not
13: 7 [A] false visions and **uttered** lying divinations when you say,
13: 7 [A] false visions and uttered lying divinations when you **say**,
13: 8 [A] " 'Therefore this is what the Sovereign LORD **says**:
13: 10 [A] **saying**, "Peace," when there is no peace, and because,
13: 11 [A] therefore **tell** those who cover it with whitewash that it is
13: 12 [C] When the wall collapses, *will* people not **ask** you, "Where is
13: 13 [A] " 'Therefore this is what the Sovereign LORD **says**: In my
13: 15 [A] *I will* **say** to you, "The wall is gone and so are those who
13: 18 [A] **say**, 'This is what the Sovereign LORD says: Woe to the
13: 18 [A] say, 'This is what the Sovereign LORD **says**: Woe to the
13: 20 [A] " 'Therefore this is what the Sovereign LORD **says**: I am
14: 2 [A] Then the word of the LORD came to me: **[NIE]**
14: 4 [A] Therefore speak to them and **tell** them, 'This is what the
14: 4 [A] and tell them, 'This is what the Sovereign LORD **says**:
14: 6 [A] "Therefore **say** to the house of Israel, 'This is what the
14: 6 [A] the house of Israel, 'This is what the Sovereign LORD **says**:
14: 12 [A] The word of the LORD came to me: **[NIE]**
14: 17 [A] "Or if I bring a sword against that country and **say**,
14: 21 [A] "For this is what the Sovereign LORD **says**: How much
15: 1 [A] The word of the LORD came to me: **[NIE]**
15: 6 [A] "Therefore this is what the Sovereign LORD **says**: As I
16: 1 [A] The word of the LORD came to me: **[NIE]**
16: 3 [A] **say**, 'This is what the Sovereign LORD says to Jerusalem:
16: 3 [A] 'This is what the Sovereign LORD **says** to Jerusalem:
16: 6 [A] and as you lay there in your blood *I* **said** to you, "Live!"
16: 6 [a] lay there in your blood I said to you, "Live!" [BHS+ *And I* ***said***]
16: 36 [A] This is what the Sovereign LORD **says**: Because you
16: 44 [A] this proverb about you: **[NIE]** "Like mother, like daughter."
16: 59 [A] " 'This is what the Sovereign LORD **says**: I will deal with
17: 1 [A] The word of the LORD came to me: **[NIE]**
17: 3 [A] **Say** to them, 'This is what the Sovereign LORD says:
17: 3 [A] Say to them, 'This is what the Sovereign LORD **says**:
17: 9 [A] "**Say** to them, 'This is what the Sovereign LORD says:
17: 9 [A] "Say to them, 'This is what the Sovereign LORD **says**:
17: 11 [A] Then the word of the LORD came to me: **[NIE]**
17: 12 [A] "**Say** to this rebellious house, 'Do you not know what these
17: 12 [A] **Say** to them: 'The king of Babylon went to Jerusalem
17: 19 [A] " 'Therefore this is what the Sovereign LORD **says**:
17: 22 [A] " 'This is what the Sovereign LORD **says**: I myself will take
18: 1 [A] The word of the LORD came to me: **[NIE]**
18: 2 [A] **[NIE]** " 'The fathers eat sour grapes, and the children's teeth
18: 19 [A] "Yet *you* **ask**, 'Why does the son not share the guilt of his
18: 25 [A] "Yet *you* **say**, 'The way of the Lord is not just.' Hear,
18: 29 [A] Yet the house of Israel **says**, 'The way of the Lord is not just.'
19: 2 [A] and **say**: " 'What a lioness was your mother among the lions!
20: 2 [A] Then the word of the LORD came to me: **[NIE]**
20: 3 [A] "Son of man, speak to the elders of Israel and **say** to them,
20: 3 [A] and say to them, 'This is what the Sovereign LORD **says**:
20: 5 [A] and **say** to them: 'This is what the Sovereign LORD says:
20: 5 [A] and say to them: 'This is what the Sovereign LORD **says**:
20: 5 [A] With uplifted hand I **said** to them, "I am the LORD your
20: 7 [A] *I* **said** to them, "Each of you, get rid of the vile images you
20: 8 [A] So *I* **said** I would pour out my wrath on them and spend my
20: 13 [A] So *I* **said** I would pour out my wrath on them and destroy
20: 18 [A] *I* **said** to their children in the desert, "Do not follow the
20: 21 [A] So *I* **said** I would pour out my wrath on them and spend my
20: 27 [A] son of man, speak to the people of Israel and **say** to them,
20: 27 [A] and say to them, 'This is what the Sovereign LORD **says**:
20: 29 [A] *I* **said** to them: What is this high place you go to?' " (It is
20: 30 [A] "Therefore **say** to the house of Israel: 'This is what the
20: 30 [A] the house of Israel: 'This is what the Sovereign LORD **says**:
20: 32 [A] " 'You **say**, "We want to be like the nations, like the peoples
20: 39 [A] O house of Israel, this is what the Sovereign LORD **says**:
20: 45 [21:1] [A] The word of the LORD came to me: **[NIE]**
20: 47 [21:3] [A] **Say** to the southern forest: 'Hear the word of the
20: 47 [21:3] [A] This is what the Sovereign LORD **says**: I am about
20: 49 [21:5] [A] *I* **said**, "Ah, Sovereign LORD! They are saying of
20: 49 [21:5] [A] *are* **saying** of me, 'Isn't he just telling parables?' "
21: 1 [21:6] [A] The word of the LORD came to me: **[NIE]**
21: 3 [21:8] [A] **say** to her: 'This is what the LORD says: I am
21: 3 [21:8] [A] say to her: 'This is what the LORD **says**: I am
21: 7 [21:12] [A] when *they* **ask** you, 'Why are you groaning?' you
21: 7 [21:12] [A] *you shall* **say**, 'Because of the news that is coming.
21: 8 [21:13] [A] The word of the LORD came to me: **[NIE]**
21: 9 [21:14] [A] "Son of man, prophesy and **say**, 'This is what the
21: 9 [21:14] [A] prophesy and say, 'This is what the Lord **says**:
21: 9 [21:14] [A] **[RPH]** " 'A sword, a sword, sharpened and
21: 18 [21:23] [A] The word of the LORD came to me: **[NIE]**
21: 24 [21:29] [A] "Therefore this is what the Sovereign LORD **says**:
21: 26 [21:31] [A] this is what the Sovereign LORD **says**: Take off
21: 28 [21:33] [A] "And you, son of man, prophesy and **say**, 'This is
21: 28 [21:33] [A] 'This is what the Sovereign LORD **says** about the
21: 28 [21:33] [A] **[NIE]** " 'A sword, a sword, drawn for the
22: 1 [A] The word of the LORD came to me: **[NIE]**
22: 3 [A] **say**: 'This is what the Sovereign LORD says: O city that

Eze 22: 3 [A] say: 'This is what the Sovereign LORD **says**: O city that
22: 17 [A] Then the word of the LORD came to me: **[NIE]**
22: 19 [A] Therefore this is what the Sovereign LORD **says**:
22: 23 [A] Again the word of the LORD came to me: **[NIE]**
22: 24 [A] "Son of man, **say** to the land, 'You are a land that has had no
22: 28 [A] *They* **say**, 'This is what the Sovereign LORD says'—
22: 28 [A] They say, 'This is what the Sovereign LORD **says**'—
23: 1 [A] The word of the LORD came to me: **[NIE]**
23: 22 [A] this is what the Sovereign LORD **says**:
23: 28 [A] "For this is what the Sovereign LORD **says**: I am about to
23: 32 [A] "This is what the Sovereign LORD **says**: "You will drink
23: 35 [A] "Therefore this is what the Sovereign LORD **says**:
23: 36 [A] The LORD **said** to me: "Son of man, will you judge Oholah
23: 43 [A] *I* **said** about the one worn out by adultery, 'Now let them use
23: 46 [A] "This is what the Sovereign LORD **says**: Bring a mob
24: 1 [A] the tenth day, the word of the LORD came to me: **[NIE]**
24: 3 [A] Tell this rebellious house a parable and **say** to them: 'This is
24: 3 [A] and say to them: 'This is what the Sovereign LORD **says**:
24: 6 [A] " 'For this is what the Sovereign LORD **says**: " 'Woe to the
24: 9 [A] " 'Therefore this is what the Sovereign LORD **says**:
24: 15 [A] The word of the LORD came to me: **[NIE]**
24: 19 [A] the people **asked** me, "Won't you tell us what these things
24: 20 [A] So *I* **said** to them, "The word of the LORD came to me:
24: 20 [A] said to them, "The word of the LORD came to me: **[NIE]**
24: 21 [A] **Say** to the house of Israel, 'This is what the Sovereign
24: 21 [A] the house of Israel, 'This is what the Sovereign LORD **says**:
25: 1 [A] The word of the LORD came to me: **[NIE]**
25: 3 [A] **Say** to them, 'Hear the word of the Sovereign LORD.
25: 3 [A] This is what the Sovereign LORD **says**: Because you said
25: 3 [A] what the Sovereign LORD says: Because you **said** "Aha!"
25: 6 [A] For this is what the Sovereign LORD **says**: Because you
25: 8 [A] "This is what the Sovereign LORD **says**: 'Because Moab
25: 8 [A] 'Because Moab and Seir **said**, "Look, the house of Judah has
25: 12 [A] "This is what the Sovereign LORD **says**: 'Because Edom
25: 13 [A] therefore this is what the Sovereign LORD **says**: I will
25: 15 [A] "This is what the Sovereign LORD **says**:
25: 16 [A] therefore this is what the Sovereign LORD **says**: I am about
26: 1 [A] of the month, the word of the LORD came to me: **[NIE]**
26: 2 [A] "Son of man, because Tyre *has* **said** of Jerusalem, 'Aha!
26: 3 [A] therefore this is what the Sovereign LORD **says**: I am
26: 7 [A] "For this is what the Sovereign LORD **says**: From the north
26: 15 [A] "This is what the Sovereign LORD **says** to Tyre: Will not
26: 17 [A] they will take up a lament concerning you and **say** to you:
26: 19 [A] "This is what the Sovereign LORD **says**: When I make you
27: 1 [A] The word of the LORD came to me: **[NIE]**
27: 3 [A] **Say** to Tyre, situated at the gateway to the sea, merchant of
27: 3 [A] on many coasts, 'This is what the Sovereign LORD **says**:
27: 3 [A] LORD says: " 'You **say**, O Tyre, "I am perfect in beauty."
28: 1 [A] The word of the LORD came to me: **[NIE]**
28: 2 [A] "Son of man, **say** to the ruler of Tyre, 'This is what the
28: 2 [A] the ruler of Tyre, 'This is what the Sovereign LORD **says**:
28: 2 [A] " 'In the pride of your heart *you* **say**, "I am a god; I sit on the
28: 6 [A] " 'Therefore this is what the Sovereign LORD **says**:
28: 9 [A] *Will you then* **say** [+606], "I am a god," in the presence of
28: 9 [A] *Will you then* **say** [+606], "I am a god," in the presence of
28: 11 [A] The word of the LORD came to me: **[NIE]**
28: 12 [A] take up a lament concerning the king of Tyre and **say** to him:
28: 12 [A] and say to him: 'This is what the Sovereign LORD **says**:
28: 20 [A] The word of the LORD came to me: **[NIE]**
28: 22 [A] **say**: 'This is what the Sovereign LORD says: " 'I am against
28: 22 [A] say: 'This is what the Sovereign LORD **says**: " 'I am against
28: 25 [A] " 'This is what the Sovereign LORD **says**: When I gather
29: 1 [A] the twelfth day, the word of the LORD came to me: **[NIE]**
29: 3 [A] Speak to him and **say**: 'This is what the Sovereign LORD
29: 3 [A] to him and say: 'This is what the Sovereign LORD **says**:
29: 3 [A] *You* **say**, "The Nile is mine; I made it for myself."
29: 8 [A] " 'Therefore this is what the Sovereign LORD **says**: I will
29: 9 [A] " 'Because *you* **said**, "The Nile is mine; I made it,"
29: 13 [A] " 'Yet this is what the Sovereign LORD **says**: At the end of
29: 17 [A] on the first day, the word of the LORD came to me: **[NIE]**
29: 19 [A] Therefore this is what the Sovereign LORD **says**: I am
30: 1 [A] The word of the LORD came to me: **[NIE]**
30: 2 [A] "Son of man, prophesy and **say**: 'This is what the Sovereign
30: 2 [A] 'This is what the Sovereign LORD **says**: " 'Wail and say,
30: 6 [A] " 'This is what the LORD **says**: " 'The allies of Egypt will
30: 10 [A] " 'This is what the Sovereign LORD **says**: " 'I will put an
30: 13 [A] " 'This is what the Sovereign LORD **says**: " 'I will destroy
30: 20 [A] seventh day, the word of the LORD came to me: **[NIE]**
30: 22 [A] Therefore this is what the Sovereign LORD **says**: I am
31: 1 [A] on the first day, the word of the LORD came to me: **[NIE]**
31: 2 [A] "Son of man, **say** to Pharaoh king of Egypt and to his hordes:
31: 10 [A] " 'Therefore this is what the Sovereign LORD **says**:
31: 15 [A] " 'This is what the Sovereign LORD **says**: On the day it was
32: 1 [A] on the first day, the word of the LORD came to me: **[NIE]**
32: 2 [A] a lament concerning Pharaoh king of Egypt and **say** to him:
32: 3 [A] " 'This is what the Sovereign LORD **says**: " 'With a great
32: 11 [A] " 'For this is what the Sovereign LORD **says**: " 'The sword
32: 17 [A] of the month, the word of the LORD came to me: **[NIE]**
33: 1 [A] The word of the LORD came to me: **[NIE]**
33: 2 [A] "Son of man, speak to your countrymen and **say** to them:
33: 8 [A] When I **say** to the wicked, 'O wicked man, you will surely
33: 10 [A] "Son of man, **say** to the house of Israel, 'This is what you are
33: 10 [A] say to the house of Israel, 'This is what *you are* **saying**:
33: 10 [A] **[NIE]** "Our offenses and sins weigh us down, and we are
33: 11 [A] **Say** to them, 'As surely as I live, declares the Sovereign
33: 12 [A] "Therefore, son of man, **say** to your countrymen,
33: 13 [A] If I **tell** the righteous man that he will surely live, but then he
33: 14 [A] And if I **say** to the wicked man, 'You will surely die,' but he
33: 17 [A] "Yet your countrymen **say**, 'The way of the Lord is not just.'
33: 20 [A] Yet, O house of Israel, *you* **say**, 'The way of the Lord is not
33: 21 [A] man who had escaped from Jerusalem came to me and **said**,
33: 23 [A] Then the word of the LORD came to me: **[NIE]**
33: 24 [A] people living in those ruins in the land of Israel *are* **saying**,
33: 24 [A] **[RPH]** 'Abraham was only one man, yet he possessed the
33: 25 [A] Therefore **say** to them, 'This is what the Sovereign LORD
33: 25 [A] say to them, 'This is what the Sovereign LORD **says**:
33: 27 [A] "**Say** this to them: 'This is what the Sovereign LORD says:
33: 27 [A] "Say this to them: 'This is what the Sovereign LORD **says**:
33: 30 [A] **[RPH]** 'Come and hear the message that has come from the
34: 1 [A] The word of the LORD came to me: **[NIE]**
34: 2 [A] against the shepherds of Israel; prophesy and **say** to them:
34: 2 [A] and say to them: 'This is what the Sovereign LORD **says**:
34: 10 [A] This is what the Sovereign LORD **says**: I am against the
34: 11 [A] " 'For this is what the Sovereign LORD **says**: I myself will
34: 17 [A] for you, my flock, this is what the Sovereign LORD **says**:
34: 20 [A] " 'Therefore this is what the Sovereign LORD **says** to them:
35: 1 [A] The word of the LORD came to me: **[NIE]**
35: 3 [A] **say**: 'This is what the Sovereign LORD says: I am against
35: 3 [A] say: 'This is what the Sovereign LORD **says**: I am against
35: 10 [A] " 'Because you *have* **said**, "These two nations and countries
35: 12 [A] things *you have* **said** against the mountains of Israel.
35: 12 [A] You **said**, "They have been laid waste and have been given
35: 14 [A] This is what the Sovereign LORD **says**: While the whole
36: 1 [A] "Son of man, prophesy to the mountains of Israel and **say**,
36: 2 [A] This is what the Sovereign LORD **says**: The enemy said of
36: 2 [A] the Sovereign LORD says: The enemy **said** of you, "Aha!
36: 3 [A] Therefore prophesy and **say**, 'This is what the Sovereign
36: 3 [A] and say, 'This is what the Sovereign LORD **says**:
36: 4 [A] This is what the Sovereign LORD **says** to the mountains
36: 5 [A] this is what the Sovereign LORD **says**: In my burning zeal I
36: 6 [A] the land of Israel and **say** to the mountains and hills,
36: 6 [A] and valleys: 'This is what the Sovereign LORD **says**:
36: 7 [A] Therefore this is what the Sovereign LORD **says**: I swear
36: 13 [A] " 'This is what the Sovereign LORD **says**: Because people
36: 13 [A] Because *people* **say** to you, "You devour men and deprive
36: 16 [A] Again the word of the LORD came to me: **[NIE]**
36: 20 [A] for *it was* **said** of them, 'These are the LORD's people,
36: 22 [A] "Therefore **say** to the house of Israel, 'This is what the
36: 22 [A] the house of Israel, 'This is what the Sovereign LORD **says**:
36: 33 [A] " 'This is what the Sovereign LORD **says**: On the day I
36: 35 [A] *They will* **say**, "This land that was laid waste has become
36: 37 [A] "This is what the Sovereign LORD **says**: Once again I will
37: 3 [A] *He* **asked** me, "Son of man, can these bones live?" I said,
37: 3 [A] bones live?" *I* **said**, "O Sovereign LORD, you alone know."
37: 4 [A] *he* **said** to me, "Prophesy to these bones and say to them,
37: 4 [A] to me, "Prophesy to these bones and **say** to them, 'Dry bones,
37: 5 [A] This is what the Sovereign LORD **says** to these bones: I
37: 9 [A] *he* **said** to me, "Prophesy to the breath; prophesy, son of
37: 9 [A] prophesy, son of man, and **say** to it, 'This is what the
37: 9 [A] and say to it, 'This is what the Sovereign LORD **says**:
37: 11 [A] *he* **said** to me: "Son of man, these bones are the whole house
37: 11 [A] *They* **say**, 'Our bones are dried up and our hope is gone;
37: 12 [A] Therefore prophesy and **say** to them: 'This is what the
37: 12 [A] 'This is what the Sovereign LORD **says**: O my people, I am
37: 15 [A] The word of the LORD came to me: **[NIE]**
37: 18 [A] "When your countrymen **ask** you, 'Won't you tell us what
37: 18 [A] ask you, **[NIE]** 'Won't you tell us what you mean by this?'
37: 19 [A] say to them, 'This is what the Sovereign LORD **says**: I am
37: 21 [A] and say to them, 'This is what the Sovereign LORD **says**:
38: 1 [A] The word of the LORD came to me: **[NIE]**
38: 3 [A] **say**: 'This is what the Sovereign LORD says: I am against
38: 3 [A] say: 'This is what the Sovereign LORD **says**: I am against
38: 10 [A] " 'This is what the Sovereign LORD **says**: On that day
38: 11 [A] *You will* **say**, "I will invade a land of unwalled villages;
38: 13 [A] the merchants of Tarshish and all her villages *will* **say** to you,
38: 14 [A] "Therefore, son of man, prophesy and **say** to Gog: 'This is
38: 14 [A] 'This is what the Sovereign LORD **says**: In that day,
38: 17 [A] " 'This is what the Sovereign LORD **says**: Are you not the

Eze 39: 1 [A] "Son of man, prophesy against Gog and **say**: 'This is what the
39: 1 [A] and say: 'This is what the Sovereign LORD **says**:
39: 17 [A] "Son of man, this is what the Sovereign LORD **says**:
39: 17 [A] **Call out** to every kind of bird and all the wild animals:
39: 25 [A] "Therefore this is what the Sovereign LORD **says**: I will
41: 4 [A] *He* **said** to me, "This is the Most Holy Place."
42: 13 [A] *he* **said** to me, "The north and south rooms facing the temple
43: 7 [A] *He* **said**: "Son of man, this is the place of my throne and the
43: 18 [A] *he* **said** to me, "Son of man, this is what the Sovereign
43: 18 [A] to me, "Son of man, this is what the Sovereign LORD **says**:
44: 2 [A] The LORD **said** to me, "This gate is to remain shut. It must
44: 5 [A] The LORD **said** to me, "Son of man, look carefully, listen
44: 6 [A] **Say** to the rebellious house of Israel, 'This is what the
44: 6 [A] house of Israel, 'This is what the Sovereign LORD **says**:
44: 9 [A] This is what the Sovereign LORD **says**: No foreigner
45: 9 [A] " 'This is what the Sovereign LORD **says**: You have gone
45: 18 [A] " 'This is what the Sovereign LORD **says**: In the first month
46: 1 [A] " 'This is what the Sovereign LORD **says**: The gate of the
46: 16 [A] " 'This is what the Sovereign LORD **says**: If the prince
46: 20 [A] *He* **said** to me, "This is the place where the priests will cook
46: 24 [A] *He* **said** to me, "These are the kitchens where those who
47: 6 [A] *He* **asked** me, "Son of man, do you see this?" Then he led
47: 8 [A] *He* **said** to me, "This water flows toward the eastern region
47: 13 [A] This is what the Sovereign LORD **says**: "These are the
Da 1: 3 [A] Then the king **ordered** Ashpenaz, chief of his court officials,
1: 10 [A] but the official **told** Daniel, "I am afraid of my lord the king,
1: 11 [A] **said** to the guard whom the chief official had appointed over
1: 18 [A] At the end of the time **set** *by* the king to bring them in,
2: 2 [A] So the king **[NIE]** summoned the magicians, enchanters,
2: 3 [A] he **said** to them, "I have had a dream that troubles me and I
8: 13 [A] heard a holy one speaking, and another holy one **said** to him,
8: 14 [A] *He* **said** to me, "It will take 2,300 evenings and mornings;
8: 16 [A] **[NIE]** "Gabriel, tell this man the meaning of the vision."
8: 17 [A] "Son of man," *he* **said** to me, "understand that the vision
8: 19 [A] *He* **said**: "I am going to tell you what will happen later in the
8: 26 [C] the evenings and mornings that *has* **been given** you is true,
9: 4 [A] **[NIE]** "O Lord, the great and awesome God, who keeps his
9: 22 [A] He instructed me and said to me, **[NIE]** "Daniel, I have now
10: 11 [A] *He* **said**, "Daniel, you who are highly esteemed,
10: 12 [A] *he* **continued**, "Do not be afraid, Daniel. Since the first day
10: 16 [A] *I* **said** to the one standing before me, "I am overcome with
10: 19 [A] "Do not be afraid, O man highly esteemed," *he* **said**. "Peace!
10: 19 [A] spoke to me, I was strengthened and **said**, "Speak, my lord,
10: 20 [A] So *he* **said**, "Do you know why I have come to you? Soon I
12: 6 [A] *One of them* **said** to the man clothed in linen, who was
12: 8 [A] So *I* **asked**, "My lord, what will the outcome of all this be?"
12: 9 [A] *He* **replied**, "Go your way, Daniel, because the words are
Hos 1: 2 [A] the LORD **said** to him, "Go, take to yourself an adulterous
1: 4 [A] the LORD **said** to Hosea, "Call him Jezreel, because I will
1: 6 [A] the LORD **said** to Hosea, "Call her Lo-Ruhamah, for I will
1: 9 [A] the LORD **said**, "Call him Lo-Ammi, for you are not my
1: 10 [2:1] [C] In the place where *it* **was said** to them, 'You are not
1: 10 [2:1] [C] 'You are not my people,' they *will* **be called** 'sons of
2: 1 [2:3] [A] "**Say** of your brothers, 'My people,' and of your sisters,
2: 5 [2:7] [A] *She* **said**, 'I will go after my lovers, who give me my
2: 7 [2:9] [A] *she will* **say**, 'I will go back to my husband as at first,
2: 12 [2:14] [A] which *she* **said** were her pay from her lovers;
2: 23 [2:25] [A] *I will* **say** to those called 'Not my people,' 'You are
2: 23 [2:25] [A] my people'; and they *will* **say**, 'You are my God.' "
3: 1 [A] The LORD **said** to me, "Go, show your love to your wife
3: 3 [A] *I* **told** her, "You are to live with me many days; you must not
7: 2 [A] they *do* not **realize** [+4200+4222] that I remember all their
10: 3 [A] *they will* **say**, "We have no king because we did not revere
10: 8 [A] *they will* **say** to the mountains, "Cover us!" and to the hills,
12: 8 [12:9] [A] Ephraim **boasts**, "I am very rich; I have become
13: 2 [A] *It is* **said** of these people, "They offer human sacrifice
13: 10 [A] your towns, of whom *you* **said**, 'Give me a king and princes'?
14: 2 [14:3] [A] **Say** to him: "Forgive all our sins and receive us
14: 3 [14:4] [A] *We will* never again **say** 'Our gods' to what our own
Joel 2: 17 [A] and the altar. *Let them* **say**, "Spare your people, O LORD.
2: 17 [A] Why *should they* **say** among the peoples, 'Where is their
2: 19 [A] The LORD will reply **[NIE]** to them: "I am sending you
2: 32 [3:5] [A] there will be deliverance, as the LORD *has* **said**,
3: 10 [4:10] [A] into spears. *Let* the weakling **say**, "I am strong!"
Am 1: 2 [A] *He* **said**: "The LORD roars from Zion and thunders from
1: 3 [A] This is what the LORD **says**: "For three sins of Damascus,
1: 5 [A] people of Aram will go into exile to Kir," **says** the LORD.
1: 6 [A] This is what the LORD **says**: "For three sins of Gaza,
1: 8 [A] last of the Philistines is dead," **says** the Sovereign LORD.
1: 9 [A] This is what the LORD **says**: "For three sins of Tyre,
1: 11 [A] This is what the LORD **says**: "For three sins of Edom,
1: 13 [A] This is what the LORD **says**: "For three sins of Ammon,
1: 15 [A] go into exile, he and his officials together," **says** the LORD.
2: 1 [A] This is what the LORD **says**: "For three sins of Moab,
2: 3 [A] and kill all her officials with him," **says** the LORD.
2: 4 [A] This is what the LORD **says**: "For three sins of Judah,
2: 6 [A] This is what the LORD **says**: "For three sins of Israel,
2: 12 [A] and commanded the prophets **[NIE]** not to prophesy.
3: 1 [A] against the whole family I brought up out of Egypt: **[NIE]**
3: 9 [A] **[NIE]** "Assemble yourselves on the mountains of Samaria;
3: 11 [A] Therefore this is what the Sovereign LORD **says**:
3: 12 [A] This is what the LORD **says**: "As a shepherd saves from the
4: 1 [A] the poor and crush the needy and **say** to your husbands,
5: 3 [A] This is what the Sovereign LORD **says**: "The city that
5: 4 [A] This is what the LORD **says** to the house of Israel:
5: 14 [A] God Almighty will be with you, just as *you* **say** he is.
5: 16 [A] this is what the Lord, the LORD God Almighty, **says**:
5: 16 [A] in all the streets and **cries** of anguish in every public square.
5: 17 [A] for I will pass through your midst," **says** the LORD.
5: 27 [A] **says** the LORD, whose name is God Almighty.
6: 10 [A] them out of the house and **asks** anyone still hiding there,
6: 10 [A] with you?" and *he* **says**, "No," then he will say, "Hush!
6: 10 [A] with you?" and he says, "No," then *he will* **say**, "Hush!
6: 13 [A] you who rejoice in the conquest of Lo Debar and **say**, "Did
7: 2 [A] the land clean, *I* **cried out**, "Sovereign LORD, forgive!
7: 3 [A] LORD relented. "This will not happen," the LORD **said**.
7: 5 [A] *I* **cried out**, "Sovereign LORD, I beg you, stop! How can
7: 6 [A] "This will not happen either," the Sovereign LORD **said**.
7: 8 [A] the LORD **asked** me, "What do you see, Amos?" "A plumb
7: 8 [A] "What do you see, Amos?" "A plumb line," *I* **replied**.
7: 8 [A] the Lord **said**, "Look, I am setting a plumb line among my
7: 10 [A] Amaziah the priest of Bethel sent a **message** to Jeroboam
7: 11 [A] For this is what Amos *is* **saying**: " 'Jeroboam will die by the
7: 12 [A] Amaziah **said** to Amos, "Get out, you seer! Go back to the
7: 14 [A] **[NIE]** "I was neither a prophet nor a prophet's son, but I
7: 15 [A] the LORD took me from tending the flock and **said** to me,
7: 16 [A] You **say**, " 'Do not prophesy against Israel, and stop
7: 17 [A] "Therefore this is what the LORD **says**: " 'Your wife will
8: 2 [A] "What do you see, Amos?" *he* **asked**. "A basket of ripe
8: 2 [A] Amos?" he asked. "A basket of ripe fruit," *I* **answered**.
8: 2 [A] the LORD **said** to me, "The time is ripe for my people
8: 5 [A] **saying**, "When will the New Moon be over that we may sell
8: 14 [A] or **say**, 'As surely as your god lives, O Dan,' or, 'As surely as
9: 1 [A] I saw the Lord standing by the altar, and *he* **said**:
9: 10 [A] all those *who* **say**, 'Disaster will not overtake or meet us.'
9: 15 [A] the land I have given them," **says** the LORD your God.
Ob 1: 1 [A] This is what the Sovereign LORD **says** about Edom—
1: 3 [A] make your home on the heights, you *who* **say** to yourself,
Jnh 1: 1 [A] word of the LORD came to Jonah son of Amittai: **[NIE]**
1: 6 [A] The captain went to him and **said**, "How can you sleep?
1: 7 [A] the sailors **said** to each other, "Come, let us cast lots to find
1: 8 [A] So *they* **asked** him, "Tell us, who is responsible for making
1: 9 [A] *He* **answered**, "I am a Hebrew and I worship the LORD,
1: 10 [A] This terrified them and *they* **asked**, "What have you done?"
1: 11 [A] So *they* **asked** him, "What should we do to you to make the
1: 12 [A] throw me into the sea," *he* **replied**, "and it will become calm.
1: 14 [A] they cried to the LORD, **[NIE]** "O LORD, please do not
2: 2 [2:3] [A] *He* **said**: "In my distress I called to the LORD,
2: 4 [2:5] [A] I **said**, 'I have been banished from your sight; yet I will
2: 10 [2:11] [A] the LORD **commanded** the fish, and it vomited
3: 1 [A] word of the LORD came to Jonah a second time: **[NIE]**
3: 4 [A] **[NIE]** "Forty more days and Nineveh will be overturned."
3: 7 [A] he issued a proclamation **[NIE]** in Nineveh: "By the decree
3: 7 [A] **[NIE]** Do not let any man or beast, herd or flock,
4: 2 [A] He prayed to the LORD, **[NIE]** "O LORD, is this not
4: 4 [A] But the LORD **replied**, "Have you any right to be angry?"
4: 8 [A] He wanted to die, and **said**, "It would be better for me to die
4: 9 [A] God **said** to Jonah, "Do you have a right to be angry about
4: 9 [A] about the vine?" "I do," *he* **said**. "I am angry enough to die."
4: 10 [A] the LORD **said**, "You have been concerned about this vine,
Mic 2: 3 [A] Therefore, the LORD **says**: "I am planning disaster against
2: 4 [A] **[NIE]** 'We are utterly ruined; my people's possession is
2: 7 [B] *Should it* **be said**, O house of Jacob: "Is the Spirit of the
3: 1 [A] *I* **said**, "Listen, you leaders of Jacob, you rulers of the house
3: 5 [A] This is what the LORD **says**: "As for the prophets who lead
3: 11 [A] Yet they lean upon the LORD and **say**, "Is not the LORD
4: 2 [A] Many nations will come and **say**, "Come, let us go up to the
4: 11 [A] They **say**, "Let her be defiled, let our eyes gloat over Zion!"
6: 1 [A] Listen to what the LORD **says**: "Stand up, plead your case
7: 10 [A] see it and will be covered with shame, *she who* **said** to me,
Na 1: 12 [A] This is what the LORD **says**: "Although they have allies
3: 7 [A] All who see you will flee from you and **say**, 'Nineveh is in
Hab 2: 2 [A] **[NIE]** "Write down the revelation and make it plain on
2: 6 [A] not all of them taunt him with ridicule and scorn, **saying**,
2: 19 [A] Woe to *him who* **says** to wood, 'Come to life!' Or to lifeless
3: 9 [A] You uncovered your bow, *you* **called** *for* many arrows.
Zep 1: 12 [A] who **think** [+928+4222], 'The LORD will do nothing,
2: 15 [A] She **said** to herself, "I am, and there is none besides me."

Zep 3: 7 [A] *I* **said** to the city, 'Surely you will fear me and accept
3:16 [C] On that day *they will* **say** to Jerusalem, "Do not fear, O Zion;
3:20 [A] your fortunes before your very eyes," **says** the LORD.
Hag 1: 1 [A] and to Joshua son of Jehozadak, the high priest: **[NIE]**
1: 2 [A] This is what the LORD Almighty **says**: "These people say,
1: 2 [A] **[RPH]** "These people say, 'The time has not yet come for
1: 2 [A] "These people **say**, 'The time has not yet come for the
1: 3 [A] of the LORD came through the prophet Haggai: **[NIE]**
1: 5 [A] Now this is what the LORD Almighty **says**: "Give careful
1: 7 [A] This is what the LORD Almighty **says**: "Give careful
1: 8 [A] I may take pleasure in it and be honored," **says** the LORD.
1:13 [A] **gave** this message of the LORD to the people:
1:13 [A] to the people: **[RPH]** "I am with you," declares the LORD.
2: 1 [A] of the LORD came through the prophet Haggai: **[NIE]**
2: 2 [A] "**Speak** to Zerubbabel son of Shealtiel, governor of Judah,
2: 2 [A] the high priest, and to the remnant of the people. **Ask** them,
2: 6 [A] "This is what the LORD Almighty **says**: 'In a little while I
2: 7 [A] I will fill this house with glory,' **says** the LORD Almighty.
2: 9 [A] the glory of the former house,' **says** the LORD Almighty.
2:10 [A] the word of the LORD came to the prophet Haggai: **[NIE]**
2:11 [A] "This is what the LORD Almighty **says**: 'Ask the priests
2:11 [A] LORD Almighty says: 'Ask the priests what the law **says**:
2:12 [A] become consecrated?' " The priests answered, **[NIE]** "No."
2:13 [A] Haggai **said**, "If a person defiled by contact with a dead body
2:13 [A] the priests replied, **[NIE]** "it becomes defiled."
2:14 [A] **[NIE]** " 'So it is with this people and this nation in my
2:20 [A] a second time on the twenty-fourth day of the month: **[NIE]**
2:21 [A] "**Tell** Zerubbabel governor of Judah that I will shake the
2:21 [A] "Tell Zerubbabel governor of Judah **[RPH]** that I will shake
Zec 1: 1 [A] prophet Zechariah son of Berekiah, the son of Iddo: **[NIE]**
1: 3 [A] Therefore **tell** the people: This is what the LORD Almighty
1: 3 [A] This is what the LORD Almighty **says**: 'Return to me,'
1: 3 [A] 'and I will return to you,' **says** the LORD Almighty.
1: 4 [A] **[NIE]** This is what the LORD Almighty says: 'Turn from
1: 4 [A] This is what the LORD Almighty **says**: 'Turn from your evil
1: 6 [A] "Then they repented and **said**, 'The LORD Almighty has
1: 7 [A] prophet Zechariah son of Berekiah, the son of Iddo. **[NIE]**
1: 9 [A] *I* **asked**, "What are these, my lord?" The angel who was
1: 9 [A] The angel who was talking with me **answered**, "I will show
1:10 [A] **[NIE]** "They are the ones the LORD has sent to go
1:11 [A] **[NIE]** "We have gone throughout the earth and found the
1:12 [A] the angel of the LORD said, **[NIE]** "LORD Almighty,
1:14 [A] the angel who was speaking to me **said**, "Proclaim this word:
1:14 [A] the angel who was speaking to me said, "Proclaim this **word**:
1:14 [A] this word: This is what the LORD Almighty **says**:
1:16 [A] "Therefore, this is what the LORD **says**: 'I will return to
1:17 [A] **[NIE]** This is what the LORD Almighty says:
1:17 [A] "Proclaim further: This is what the LORD Almighty **says**:
1:19 [2:2] [A] *I* **asked** the angel who was speaking to me, "What are
1:19 [2:2] [A] *He* **answered** me, "These are the horns that scattered
1:21 [2:4] [A] *I* **asked**, "What are these coming to do?" He
1:21 [2:4] [A] *He* **answered**, "These are the horns that scattered
1:21 [2:4] [A] **[RPH]** "These are the horns that scattered Judah
2: 2 [2:6] [A] *I* **asked**, "Where are you going?" He answered me,
2: 2 [2:6] [A] *He* **answered** me, "To measure Jerusalem, to find out
2: 4 [2:8] [A] **said** to him: "Run, tell that young man, 'Jerusalem will
2: 4 [2:8] [A] **[NIE]** 'Jerusalem will be a city without walls
2: 8 [2:12] [A] For this is what the LORD Almighty **says**: "After he
3: 2 [A] The LORD **said** to Satan, "The LORD rebuke you, Satan!
3: 4 [A] The angel said **[NIE]** to those who were standing before
3: 4 [A] standing before him, **[NIE]** "Take off his filthy clothes."
3: 4 [A] Then *he* **said** to Joshua, "See, I have taken away your sin,
3: 5 [A] *I* **said**, "Put a clean turban on his head." So they put a clean
3: 6 [A] The angel of the LORD gave this charge to Joshua: **[NIE]**
3: 7 [A] "This is what the LORD Almighty **says**: 'If you will walk in
4: 2 [A] *He* **asked** me, "What do you see?" I answered, "I see a solid
4: 2 [A] *I* **answered**, "I see a solid gold lampstand with a bowl at the
4: 4 [A] I asked **[NIE]** the angel who talked with me, "What are
4: 4 [A] who talked with me, **[NIE]** "What are these, my lord?"
4: 5 [A] He answered, **[NIE]** "Do you not know what these are?"
4: 5 [A] "Do you not know what these are?" "No, my lord," *I* **replied**.
4: 6 [A] So he said **[NIE]** to me, "This is the word of the LORD to
4: 6 [A] **[NIE]** "This is the word of the LORD to Zerubbabel:
4: 6 [A] **[NIE]** 'Not by might nor by power, but by my Spirit,'
4: 6 [A] nor by power, but by my Spirit,' **says** the LORD Almighty.
4: 8 [A] Then the word of the LORD came to me: **[NIE]**
4:11 [A] I asked **[NIE]** the angel, "What are these two olive trees on
4:12 [A] Again I asked **[NIE]** him, "What are these two olive
4:13 [A] *He* **replied**, "Do you not know what these are?" "No,
4:13 [A] He replied, **[RPH]** "Do you not know what these are?" "No,
4:13 [A] "Do you not know what these are?" "No, my lord," *I* **said**.
4:14 [A] So *he* **said**, "These are the two who are anointed to serve the
5: 2 [A] *He* **asked** me, "What do you see?" I answered, "I see a flying
5: 2 [A] *I* **answered**, "I see a flying scroll, thirty feet long and fifteen
5: 3 [A] *he* **said** to me, "This is the curse that is going out over the
5: 5 [A] angel who was speaking to me came forward and **said** to me,
5: 6 [A] *I* **asked**, "What is it?" He replied, "It is a measuring basket."
5: 6 [A] I asked, "What is it?" *He* **replied**, "It is a measuring basket."
5: 6 [A] *he* **added**, "This is the iniquity of the people throughout the
5: 8 [A] *He* **said**, "This is wickedness," and he pushed her back into
5:10 [A] the basket?" *I* **asked** the angel who was speaking to me.
5:11 [A] *He* **replied**, "To the country of Babylonia to build a house
6: 4 [A] I asked **[NIE]** the angel who was speaking to me, "What are
6: 5 [A] The angel answered **[NIE]** me, "These are the four spirits of
6: 7 [A] *he* **said**, "Go throughout the earth!" So they went throughout
6: 8 [A] he called to me, **[NIE]** "Look, those going toward the north
6: 9 [A] The word of the LORD came to me: **[NIE]**
6:12 [A] **Tell** him this is what the LORD Almighty says: 'Here is the
6:12 [A] Tell him **[RPH]** this is what the LORD Almighty says:
6:12 [A] Tell him this is what the LORD Almighty **says**: 'Here is the
6:12 [A] **[RPH]** 'Here is the man whose name is the Branch, and he
7: 3 [A] **asking** the priests of the house of the LORD Almighty and
7: 3 [A] **[RPH]** "Should I mourn and fast in the fifth month,
7: 4 [A] Then the word of the LORD Almighty came to me: **[NIE]**
7: 5 [A] "**Ask** all the people of the land and the priests, 'When you
7: 5 [A] **[RPH]** 'When you fasted and mourned in the fifth
7: 8 [A] the word of the LORD came again to Zechariah: **[NIE]**
7: 9 [A] "This is what the LORD Almighty **says**: 'Administer true
7: 9 [A] **[RPH]** 'Administer true justice; show mercy
7:13 [A] they called, I would not listen,' **says** the LORD Almighty.
8: 1 [A] the word of the LORD Almighty came to me. **[NIE]**
8: 2 [A] This is what the LORD Almighty **says**: "I am very jealous
8: 3 [A] This is what the LORD **says**: "I will return to Zion
8: 4 [A] This is what the LORD Almighty **says**: "Once again men
8: 6 [A] This is what the LORD Almighty **says**: "It may seem
8: 7 [A] This is what the LORD Almighty **says**: "I will save my
8: 9 [A] This is what the LORD Almighty **says**: "You who now hear
8:14 [A] This is what the LORD Almighty **says**: "Just as I had
8:14 [A] when your fathers angered me," **says** the LORD Almighty,
8:18 [A] the word of the LORD Almighty came to me. **[NIE]**
8:19 [A] This is what the LORD Almighty **says**: "The fasts of the
8:20 [A] This is what the LORD Almighty **says**: "Many peoples
8:21 [A] and the inhabitants of one city will go to another and **say**,
8:23 [A] This is what the LORD Almighty **says**: "In those days ten
8:23 [A] take firm hold of one Jew by the hem of his robe and **say**,
11: 4 [A] This is what the LORD my God **says**: "Pasture the flock
11: 5 [A] Those who sell them **say**, 'Praise the LORD, I am rich!'
11: 9 [A] **said**, "I will not be your shepherd. Let the dying die,
11:12 [A] *I* **told** them, "If you think it best, give me my pay; but if not,
11:13 [A] the LORD **said** to me, "Throw it to the potter"—
11:15 [A] the LORD **said** to me, "Take again the equipment of a
12: 5 [A] the leaders of Judah *will* **say** in their hearts, 'The people of
13: 3 [A] to whom he was born, *will* **say** to him, 'You must die,
13: 5 [A] *He will* **say**, 'I am not a prophet. I am a famer; the land has
13: 6 [A] If *someone* **asks** him, 'What are these wounds on your body?'
13: 6 [A] *he will* **answer**, 'The wounds I was given at the house of my
13: 9 [A] *I will* **say**, 'They are my people,' and they will say,
13: 9 [A] I will say, 'They are my people,' and they *will* **say**,
Mal 1: 2 [A] "I have loved you," **says** the LORD. "But you ask, 'How
1: 2 [A] says the LORD. "But *you* **ask**, 'How have you loved us?'
1: 4 [A] Edom *may* **say**, "Though we have been crushed, we will
1: 4 [A] this is what the LORD Almighty **says**: "They may build,
1: 5 [A] You will see it with your own eyes and **say**, 'Great is the
1: 6 [A] **says** the LORD Almighty. "It is you, O priests, who show
1: 6 [A] "But *you* **ask**, 'How have we shown contempt for your
1: 7 [A] food on my altar. "But *you* **ask**, 'How have we defiled you?'
1: 7 [A] "By **saying** that the LORD's table is contemptible.
1: 8 [A] Would he accept you?" **says** the LORD Almighty.
1: 9 [A] will he accept you?"—**says** the LORD Almighty.
1:10 [A] I am not pleased with you," **says** the LORD Almighty,
1:11 [A] will be great among the nations," **says** the LORD Almighty.
1:12 [A] "But you profane it by **saying** *of* the Lord's table, 'It is
1:13 [A] *you* **say**, 'What a burden!' and you sniff at it
1:13 [A] you sniff at it contemptuously," **says** the LORD Almighty.
1:13 [A] should I accept them from your hands?" **says** the LORD.
1:14 [A] For I am a great king," **says** the LORD Almighty, "and my
2: 2 [A] **says** the LORD Almighty, "I will send a curse upon you,
2: 4 [A] with Levi may continue," **says** the LORD Almighty.
2: 8 [A] violated the covenant with Levi," **says** the LORD Almighty.
2:14 [A] *You* **ask**, "Why?" It is because the LORD is acting as the
2:16 [A] "I hate divorce," **says** the LORD God of Israel, "and I hate
2:16 [A] as well as with his garment," **says** the LORD Almighty.
2:17 [A] *you* **ask**. By saying, "All who do evil are good in the eyes of
2:17 [A] By **saying**, "All who do evil are good in the eyes of the
3: 1 [A] whom you desire, will come," **says** the LORD Almighty.
3: 5 [A] of justice, but do not fear me," **says** the LORD Almighty.
3: 7 [A] to me, and I will return to you," **says** the LORD Almighty.
3: 7 [A] the LORD Almighty. "But *you* **ask**, 'How are we to return?'

[A] Qal [B] Qal passive [C] Niphal [D] Piel (poel, polel, pilel, pilal, pealal, pilpel) [E] Pual (poal, polal, poalal, pulal, pualal)

Mal 3: 8 [A] "But *you* **ask**, 'How do we rob you?' "In tithes and offerings.
3: 10 [A] Test me in this," **says** the LORD Almighty, "and see if I
3: 11 [A] fields will not cast their fruit," **says** the LORD Almighty.
3: 12 [A] yours will be a delightful land," **says** the LORD Almighty.
3: 13 [A] "You have said harsh things against me," **says** the LORD.
3: 13 [A] the LORD. "Yet *you* **ask**, 'What have we said against you?'
3: 14 [A] "*You have* **said**, 'It is futile to serve God. What did we gain
3: 17 [A] "They will be mine," **says** the LORD Almighty, "in the day
4: 1 [3:19] [A] will set them on fire," **says** the LORD Almighty.
4: 3 [3:21] [A] when I do these things," **says** the LORD Almighty.

607 ²אָמַר *'āmar²*, v. [2] [→ 580, 610, 9473]

boast [1], full of boasting [1]

Ps 94: 4 [F] out arrogant words; all the evildoers *are* **full of boasting**.
Isa 61: 6 [F] on the wealth of nations, and in their riches *you will* **boast**.

608 אֹמֶר *'ōmer*, n.m. [5] [√ 606]

speech [2], promise [1], what[s] [1], word [1]

Job 22: 28 **What**[s] you decide on will be done, and light will shine on your
Ps 19: 2 [19:3] Day after day they pour forth **speech**; night after night they
19: 3 [19:4] There is no **speech** or language where their voice is not
68: 11 [68:12] The Lord announced the **word**, and great was the
77: 8 [77:9] love vanished forever? Has his **promise** failed for all time?

609 ¹אֵמֶר *'ēmer¹*, n.m. [48] [√ 606]

words [33], arguments [2], what say [+7023] [2], words [+7023] [2], answers [1], appointed [1], keeps saying [+8740] [1], lies [+9214] [1], makes speech [+606] [1], pleading [1], those[s] [1], what said [+7023] [1], what say [1]

Nu 24: 4 the oracle of one who hears the **words** *of* God, who sees a vision
24: 16 the oracle of one who hears the **words** *of* God, who has knowledge
Dt 32: 1 O heavens, and I will speak; hear, O earth, the **words** *of* my mouth.
Jos 24: 27 against us. It has heard all the **words** the LORD has said to us.
Jdg 5: 29 her ladies answer her; indeed, she **keeps saying** [+8740] to herself,
Job 6: 10 that I had not denied the **words** *of* the Holy One.
6: 25 How painful are honest **words**! But what do your arguments
6: 26 what I say, and treat the **words** *of* a despairing man as wind?
8: 2 you say such things? Your **words** [+7023] are a blustering wind.
20: 29 God allots the wicked, the heritage **appointed** *for* them by God."
22: 22 instruction from his mouth and lay up his **words** in your heart.
23: 12 I have treasured the **words** *of* his mouth more than my daily bread.
32: 12 has proved Job wrong; none of you has answered his **arguments**.
32: 14 words against me, and I will not answer him with your **arguments**.
33: 3 My **words** come from an upright heart; my lips sincerely speak
34: 37 claps his hands among us and multiplies his **words** against God."
Ps 5: 1 [5:2] Give ear to my **words**, O LORD, consider my sighing.
19: 14 [19:15] May the **words** *of* my mouth and the meditation of my
54: 2 [54:4] Hear my prayer, O God; listen to the **words** *of* my mouth.
78: 1 O my people, hear my teaching; listen to the **words** *of* my mouth.
107: 11 for they had rebelled against the **words** *of* God and despised the
138: 4 praise you, O LORD, when they hear the **words** *of* your mouth.
141: 6 and the wicked will learn that my **words** were well spoken.
Pr 1: 2 and discipline; for understanding **words** *of* insight;
1: 21 in the gateways of the city *she* **makes** her **speech** [+606]:
2: 1 if you accept my **words** and store up my commands within you,
2: 16 the adulteress, from the wayward wife with her seductive **words**,
4: 5 do not forget my **words** [+7023] or swerve from them.
4: 10 Listen, my son, accept **what I say**, and the years of your life will
4: 20 My son, pay attention to what I say; listen closely to my **words**.
5: 7 my sons, listen to me; do not turn aside from **what I say** [+7023].
6: 2 if you have been trapped by **what** you **said** [+7023], ensnared by
6: 2 trapped by what you said, ensnared by the **words** *of* your mouth,
7: 1 My son, keep my **words** and store up my commands within you.
7: 5 the adulteress, from the wayward wife with her seductive **words**.
7: 24 my sons, listen to me; pay attention to **what I say** [+7023].
8: 8 All the **words** *of* my mouth are just; none of them is crooked
15: 26 thoughts of the wicked, but **those**[s] *of* the pure are pleasing to him.
16: 24 Pleasant **words** are a honeycomb, sweet to the soul and healing to
17: 27 A man of knowledge uses **words** with restraint, and a man of
19: 7 Though he pursues them with **pleading**, they are nowhere to be
19: 27 my son, and you will stray from the **words** *of* knowledge.
22: 21 teaching you true and reliable **words**, so that you can give sound
22: 21 so that you can give sound **answers** to him who sent you?
23: 12 your heart to instruction and your ears to **words** *of* knowledge.
Isa 32: 7 he makes up evil schemes to destroy the poor with **lies** [+9214],
41: 26 told of this, no one foretold it, no one heard *any* **words** *from* you.
Hos 6: 5 pieces with my prophets, I killed you with the **words** *of* my mouth;

610 ²אֵמֶר *'ēmer²*, n.m. Not used in NIV/BHS [√ 607]

611 ¹אִמֵּר *'immēr¹*, n.m. [1] [→ 612, 613; Ar 10043]

fawns [1]

Ge 49: 21 "Naphtali is a doe set free that bears beautiful **fawns**.

612 ²אִמֵּר *'immēr²*, n.pr.m. [8] [√ 611]

Immer [8]

1Ch 9: 12 the son of Meshullam, the son of Meshillemith, the son of **Immer**.
24: 14 the fifteenth to Bilgah, the sixteenth to **Immer**,
Ezr 2: 37 of **Immer** 1,052
10: 20 From the descendants of **Immer**: Hanani and Zebadiah.
Ne 3: 29 to them, Zadok son of **Immer** made repairs opposite his house.
7: 40 of **Immer** 1,052
11: 13 the son of Ahzai, the son of Meshillemoth, the son of **Immer**,
Jer 20: 1 When the priest Pashhur son of **Immer**, the chief officer in the

613 ³אִמֵּר *'immēr³*, n.pr.loc. [2] [√ 611]

Immer [2]

Ezr 2: 59 the towns of Tel Melah, Tel Harsha, Kerub, Addon and **Immer**,
Ne 7: 61 the towns of Tel Melah, Tel Harsha, Kerub, Addon and **Immer**,

614 אִמְרָה *'imrâ*, n.f. [37] [√ 606]

word [13], promise [11], words [4], promises [2], speech [2], *untranslated* [1], command [1], prayer [1], what have to say [1], what say [1]

Ge 4: 23 and Zillah, listen to me; wives of Lamech, hear my **words**.
Dt 32: 2 Let my teaching fall like rain and my **words** descend like dew,
33: 9 but he watched over your **word** and guarded your covenant.
2Sa 22: 31 for God, his way is perfect; the **word** *of* the LORD is flawless.
Ps 12: 6 [12:7] the **words** *of* the LORD are flawless, like silver refined in
12: 6 [12:7] the words of the LORD are **[RPH]** flawless, like silver
17: 6 for you will answer me; give ear to me and hear my **prayer**.
18: 30 [18:31] his way is perfect; the **word** *of* the LORD is flawless.
105: 19 foretold came to pass, till the **word** *of* the LORD proved him true.
119: 11 I have hidden your **word** in my heart that I might not sin against
119: 38 Fulfill your **promise** to your servant, so that you may be feared.
119: 41 come to me, O LORD, your salvation according to your **promise**;
119: 50 comfort in my suffering is this: Your **promise** preserves my life.
119: 58 with all my heart; be gracious to me according to your **promise**.
119: 67 Before I was afflicted I went astray, but now I obey your **word**.
119: 76 love be my comfort, according to your **promise** to your servant.
119: 82 My eyes fail, looking for your **promise**; I say, "When will you
119:103 How sweet are your **words** to my taste, sweeter than honey to my
119:116 Sustain me according to your **promise**, and I will live; do not let
119:123 looking for your salvation, looking for your righteous **promise**.
119:133 Direct my footsteps according to your **word**; let no sin rule over
119:140 Your **promises** have been thoroughly tested, and your servant
119:148 the watches of the night, that I may meditate on your **promises**.
119:154 and redeem me; preserve my life according to your **promise**.
119:158 on the faithless with loathing, for they do not obey your **word**.
119:162 I rejoice in your **promise** like one who finds great spoil.
119:170 come before you; deliver me according to your **promise**.
119:172 May my tongue sing of your **word**, for all your commands are
138: 2 for you have exalted above all things your name and your **word**.
147: 15 He sends his **command** to the earth; his word runs swiftly.
Pr 30: 5 "Every **word** *of* God is flawless; he is a shield to those who take
Isa 5: 24 LORD Almighty and spurned the **word** *of* the Holy One of Israel.
28: 23 Listen and hear my voice; pay attention and hear **what I say**.
29: 4 speak from the ground; your **speech** will mumble out of the dust.
29: 4 ghostlike from the earth; out of the dust your **speech** will whisper.
32: 9 to me; you daughters who feel secure, hear **what I have to say**!
La 2: 17 he planned; he has fulfilled his **word**, which he decreed long ago.

615 אֶמְרָה *'emrâ*, n.f. Not used in NIV/BHS [√ 606]

616 אֱמֹרִי *ᵉmōrî*, a.g. [87]

Amorites [76], Amorite [10], it[s] [+1473+2021] [1]

Ge 10: 16 Jebusites, **Amorites**, Girgashites,
14: 7 as well as the **Amorites** who were living in Hazazon Tamar.
14: 13 Now Abram was living near the great trees of Mamre the **Amorite**,
15: 16 for the sin of the **Amorites** has not yet reached its full measure."
15: 21 **Amorites**, Canaanites, Girgashites and Jebusites."
48: 22 I give the ridge of land I took from the **Amorites** with my sword
Ex 3: 8 Hittites, **Amorites**, Perizzites, Hivites and Jebusites.
3: 17 Hittites, **Amorites**, Perizzites, Hivites and Jebusites—
13: 5 land of the Canaanites, Hittites, **Amorites**, Hivites and Jebusites—
23: 23 will go ahead of you and bring you into the land of the **Amorites**,
33: 2 **Amorites**, Hittites, Perizzites, Hivites and Jebusites.
34: 11 I will drive out before you the **Amorites**, Canaanites, Hittites,
Nu 13: 29 the Hittites, Jebusites and **Amorites** live in the hill country;
21: 13 the Arnon, which is in the desert extending into **Amorite** territory.

Nu 21:13 Arnon is the border of Moab, between Moab and the **Amorites**.
21:21 Israel sent messengers to say to Sihon king of the **Amorites**:
21:25 Israel captured all the cities of the **Amorites** and occupied them,
21:26 Heshbon was the city of Sihon king of the **Amorites**, who had
21:29 and his daughters as captives to Sihon king of the **Amorites**.
21:31 So Israel settled in the land of the **Amorites**.
21:32 and drove out the **Amorites** who were there.
21:34 Do to him what you did to Sihon king of the **Amorites**,
22:2 Balak son of Zippor saw all that Israel had done to the **Amorites**,
32:33 son of Joseph the kingdom of Sihon king of the **Amorites**
32:39 to Gilead, captured it and drove out the **Amorites** who were there.
Dt 1:4 This was after he had defeated Sihon king of the **Amorites**,
1:7 Break camp and advance into the hill country of the **Amorites**;
1:19 went toward the hill country of the **Amorites** through all that vast
1:20 I said to you, "You have reached the hill country of the **Amorites**,
1:27 of Egypt to deliver us into the hands of the **Amorites** to destroy us.
1:44 The **Amorites** who lived in those hills came out against you;
2:24 See, I have given into your hand Sihon the **Amorite**, king of
3:2 Do to him what you did to Sihon king of the **Amorites**,
3:8 So at that time we took from these two kings of the **Amorites** the
3:9 is called Sirion by the Sidonians; the **Amorites** call it Senir.)
4:46 in the land of Sihon king of the **Amorites**, who reigned in Heshbon
4:47 of Og king of Bashan, the two **Amorite** kings east of the Jordan.
7:1 **Amorites**, Canaanites, Perizzites, Hivites and Jebusites,
20:17 **Amorites**, Canaanites, Perizzites, Hivites and Jebusites—
31:4 to them what he did to Sihon and Og, the kings of the **Amorites**,
Jos 2:10 and Og, the two kings of the **Amorites** east of the Jordan,
3:10 Hittites, Hivites, Perizzites, Girgashites, **Amorites** and Jebusites.
5:1 Now when all the **Amorite** kings west of the Jordan and all the
7:7 Jordan to deliver us into the hands of the **Amorites** to destroy us?
9:1 **Amorites**, Canaanites, Perizzites, Hivites and Jebusites)—
9:10 all that he did to the two kings of the **Amorites** east of the Jordan—
10:5 Then the five kings of the **Amorites**—the kings of Jerusalem,
10:6 because all the **Amorite** kings from the hill country have joined
10:12 On the day the LORD gave the **Amorites** over to Israel,
11:3 to the **Amorites**, Hittites, Perizzites and Jebusites in the hill
12:2 Sihon king of the **Amorites**, who reigned in Heshbon. He ruled
12:8 **Amorites**, Canaanites, Perizzites, Hivites and Jebusites):
13:4 Arah of the Sidonians as far as Aphek, the region of the **Amorites**,
13:10 all the towns of Sihon king of the **Amorites**, who ruled in
13:21 on the plateau and the entire realm of Sihon king of the **Amorites**,
24:8 " 'I brought you to the land of the **Amorites** who lived east of the
24:11 as did also the **Amorites**, Perizzites, Canaanites, Hittites,
24:12 which drove them out before you—also the two **Amorite** kings.
24:15 or the gods of the **Amorites**, in whose land you are living.
24:18 us all the nations, including the **Amorites**, who lived in the land.
Jdg 1:34 The **Amorites** confined the Danites to the hill country, not
1:35 the **Amorites** were determined also to hold out in Mount Heres,
1:36 The boundary of the **Amorites** was from Scorpion Pass to Sela
3:5 Hittites, **Amorites**, Perizzites, Hivites and Jebusites.
6:10 do not worship the gods of the **Amorites**, in whose land you live.'
10:8 on the east side of the Jordan in Gilead, the land of the **Amorites**.
10:11 the Egyptians, the **Amorites**, the Ammonites, the Philistines,
11:19 "Then Israel sent messengers to Sihon king of the **Amorites**,
11:21 Israel took over all the land of the **Amorites** who lived in that
11:22 capturing all of **it**[s] [+1473+2021] from the Arnon to the Jabbok
11:23 God of Israel, has driven the **Amorites** out before his people Israel,
1Sa 7:14 And there was peace between Israel and the **Amorites**.
2Sa 21:2 were not a part of Israel but were survivors of the **Amorites**;
1Ki 4:19 in Gilead (the country of Sihon king of the **Amorites**
9:20 All the people left from the **Amorites**, Hittites, Perizzites,
21:26 after idols, like the **Amorites** the LORD drove out before Israel.)
2Ki 21:11 He has done more evil than the **Amorites** who preceded him
1Ch 1:14 Jebusites, **Amorites**, Girgashites,
2Ch 8:7 **Amorites**, Perizzites, Hivites and Jebusites (these peoples were not
Ezr 9:1 Jebusites, Ammonites, Moabites, Egyptians and **Amorites**.
Ne 9:8 **Amorites**, Perizzites, Jebusites and Girgashites.
Ps 135:11 Sihon king of the **Amorites**, Og king of Bashan and all the kings
136:19 Sihon king of the **Amorites** *His love endures forever.*
Eze 16:3 your father was an **Amorite** and your mother a Hittite.
16:45 Your mother was a Hittite and your father an **Amorite**.
Am 2:9 "I destroyed the **Amorite** before them, though he was tall as the
2:10 you forty years in the desert to give you the land of the **Amorites**.

617 אִמְרִי *'imrî*, n.pr.m. [2] [√ 606 + 3378]

Imri [2]

1Ch 9:4 of Ammihud, the son of Omri, the son of **Imri**, the son of Bani,
Ne 3:2 the adjoining section, and Zaccur son of **Imri** built next to them.

618 אֲמַרְיָה *'ᵃmaryâ*, n.pr.m. [13] [→ 619; cf. 606 + 3378]

Amariah [12], Amariah's [1]

1Ch 6:7 [5:33] Meraioth the father of **Amariah**, Amariah the father of
6:7 [5:33] the father of Amariah, **Amariah** the father of Ahitub,
6:11 [5:37] Azariah the father of **Amariah**, Amariah the father of
6:11 [5:37] the father of Amariah, **Amariah** the father of Ahitub,
6:52 [6:37] Meraioth his son, **Amariah** his son, Ahitub his son,
23:19 Jeriah the first, **Amariah** the second, Jahaziel the third
Ezr 7:3 the son of **Amariah**, the son of Azariah, the son of Meraioth,
10:42 Shallum, **Amariah** and Joseph.
Ne 10:3 [10:4] Pashhur, **Amariah**, Malkijah,
11:4 the son of Zechariah, the son of **Amariah**, the son of Shephatiah,
12:2 **Amariah**, Malluch, Hattush,
12:13 of Ezra's, Meshullam; of **Amariah's**, Jehohanan;
Zep 1:1 the son of Gedaliah, the son of **Amariah**, the son of Hezekiah,

619 אֲמַרְיָהוּ *'ᵃmaryāhû*, n.pr.m. [3] [√ 618; cf. 606 + 3378]

Amariah [3]

1Ch 24:23 Jeriah the first, **Amariah** the second, Jahaziel the third
2Ch 19:11 "**Amariah** the chief priest will be over you in any matter
31:15 **Amariah** and Shecaniah assisted him faithfully in the towns of the

620 אַמְרָפֶל *'amrāpel*, n.pr.m. [2]

Amraphel [2]

Ge 14:1 At this time **Amraphel** king of Shinar, Arioch king of Ellasar,
14:9 of Goiim, **Amraphel** king of Shinar and Arioch king of Ellasar—

621 אֶמֶשׁ *'emeš*, adv. [5] [cf. 5406?]

last night [3], at night [1], yesterday [1]

Ge 19:34 daughter said to the younger, "**Last night** I lay with my father.
31:29 **last night** the God of your father said to me, 'Be careful not to say
31:42 and the toil of my hands, and **last night** he rebuked you."
2Ki 9:26 '**Yesterday** I saw the blood of Naboth and the blood of his sons,
Job 30:3 they roamed the parched land in desolate wastelands **at night**.

622 אֱמֶת *'ᵉmet*, n.f. [127] [→ 624; cf. 586]

faithfulness [34], truth [29], true [20], faithful [5], sure [5], faithfully [+928] [4], faithfully [4], security [3], truthful [3], honorably [+928] [2], reliable [2], right [2], truly [+928] [2], trustworthy [2], assurance [1], assuredly [+928] [1], fairly [1], fairness [1], faithful [+928+2143] [1], faithfully [+6913] [1], integrity [1], lasting [1], really [+928] [1], sound [1]

Ge 24:27 has not abandoned his kindness and **faithfulness** to my master.
24:48 who had led me on the **right** road to get the granddaughter of my
24:49 Now if you will show kindness and **faithfulness** to my master,
32:10 [32:11] and **faithfulness** you have shown your servant.
42:16 so that your words may be tested to see if you are telling the **truth**.
47:29 and promise that you will show me kindness and **faithfulness**.
Ex 18:21 men who fear God, **trustworthy** men who hate dishonest gain—
34:6 gracious God, slow to anger, abounding in love and **faithfulness**,
Dt 13:14 [13:15] if it is **true** and it has been proved that this detestable
17:4 If it is **true** and it has been proved that this detestable thing has
22:20 the charge is **true** and no proof of the girl's virginity can be found,
Jos 2:12 because I have shown kindness to you. Give me a **sure** sign
2:14 you kindly and **faithfully** when the LORD gives us the land."
24:14 "Now fear the LORD and serve him with all **faithfulness**.
Jdg 9:15 'If you **really** [+928] want to anoint me king over you, come
9:16 "Now if you have acted **honorably** [+928] and in good faith when
9:19 if then you have acted **honorably** [+928] and in good faith toward
1Sa 12:24 the LORD and serve him **faithfully** [+928] with all your heart;
2Sa 2:6 May the LORD now show you kindness and **faithfulness**,
7:28 Your words are **trustworthy**, and you have promised these good
15:20 your countrymen. May kindness and **faithfulness** be with you."
1Ki 2:4 and if they walk **faithfully** [+928] before me with all their heart
3:6 because *he was* **faithful** [+928+2143] to you and righteous
10:6 own country about your achievements and your wisdom is **true**.
17:24 and that the word of the LORD from your mouth is the **truth**."
22:16 swear to tell me nothing but the **truth** in the name of the LORD?"
2Ki 20:3 how I have walked before you **faithfully** [+928] and with
20:19 he thought, "Will there not be peace and **security** in my lifetime?"
2Ch 9:5 own country about your achievements and your wisdom is **true**.
15:3 For a long time Israel was without the **true** God, without a priest to
18:15 swear to tell me nothing but the **truth** in the name of the LORD?"
31:20 what was good and right and **faithful** before the LORD his God.
32:1 After all that Hezekiah had *so* **faithfully** done, Sennacherib king of
Ne 7:2 because he was a man of **integrity** and feared God more than most
9:13 You gave them regulations and laws that are just and **right**,
9:33 you have been just; you have acted **faithfully**, while we did wrong.
Est 9:30 of the kingdom of Xerxes—words of goodwill and **assurance**—
Ps 15:2 who does what is righteous, who speaks the **truth** from his heart
19:9 [19:10] The ordinances of the LORD are **sure** and altogether
25:5 guide me in your **truth** and teach me, for you are God my Savior,
25:10 and **faithful** for those who keep the demands of his covenant.
26:3 your love is ever before me, and I walk continually in your **truth**.
30:9 [30:10] the dust praise you? Will it proclaim your **faithfulness**?

Ps 31: 5 [31:6] my spirit; redeem me, O LORD, the God of **truth**.
40: 10 [40:11] your love and your **truth** from the great assembly.
40: 11 [40:12] may your love and your **truth** always protect me.
43: 3 Send forth your light and your **truth**, let them guide me; let them
45: 4 [45:5] In your majesty ride forth victoriously in behalf of **truth**,
51: 6 [51:8] Surely you desire **truth** in the inner parts; you teach me
54: 5 [54:7] those who slander me; in your **faithfulness** destroy them.
57: 3 [57:4] *Selah* God sends his love and his **faithfulness**.
57: 10 [57:11] to the heavens; your **faithfulness** reaches to the skies.
61: 7 [61:8] appoint your love and **faithfulness** to protect him.
69: 13 [69:14] great love, O God, answer me with your **sure** salvation.
71: 22 I will praise you with the harp for your **faithfulness**, O my God;
85: 10 [85:11] Love and **faithfulness** meet together; righteousness
85: 11 [85:12] **Faithfulness** springs forth from the earth,
86: 11 Teach me your way, O LORD, and I will walk in your **truth**;
86: 15 gracious God, slow to anger, abounding in love and **faithfulness**.
89: 14 [89:15] of your throne; love and **faithfulness** go before you.
91: 4 will find refuge; his **faithfulness** will be your shield and rampart.
108: 4 [108:5] than the heavens; your **faithfulness** reaches to the skies.
111: 7 The works of his hands are **faithful** and just; all his precepts are
111: 8 steadfast for ever and ever, done in **faithfulness** and uprightness.
115: 1 to your name be the glory, because of your love and **faithfulness**.
117: 2 toward us, and the **faithfulness** *of* the LORD endures forever.
119: 43 Do not snatch the word of **truth** from my mouth, for I have put my
119: 142 Your righteousness is everlasting and your law is **true**.
119: 151 Yet you are near, O LORD, and all your commands are **true**.
119: 160 All your words are **true**; all your righteous laws are eternal.
132: 11 swore an oath to David, a **sure** oath that he will not revoke:
138: 2 and will praise your name for your love and your **faithfulness**,
145: 18 is near to all who call on him, to all who call on him in **truth**.
146: 6 everything in them—the LORD, who remains **faithful** forever.
Pr 3: 3 Let love and **faithfulness** never leave you; bind them around your
8: 7 My mouth speaks *what* is **true**, for my lips detest wickedness.
11: 18 but he who sows righteousness reaps a **sure** reward.
12: 19 **Truthful** lips endure forever, but a lying tongue lasts only a
14: 22 But those who plan what is good find love and **faithfulness**.
14: 25 A **truthful** witness saves lives, but a false witness is deceitful.
16: 6 Through love and **faithfulness** sin is atoned for; through the fear of
20: 28 Love and **faithfulness** keep a king safe; through love his throne is
22: 21 teaching you true and **reliable** words, so that you can give sound
22: 21 so that you can give **sound** answers to him who sent you?
23: 23 Buy the **truth** and do not sell it; get wisdom, discipline
29: 14 If a king judges the poor with **fairness**, his throne will always be
Ecc 12: 10 find just the right words, and what he wrote was upright and **true**.
Isa 10: 20 who struck them down but will **truly** [+928] rely on the LORD,
16: 5 in **faithfulness** a man will sit on it—one from the house of David—
38: 3 how I have walked before you **faithfully** [+928] and with
38: 18 those who go down to the pit cannot hope for your **faithfulness**.
38: 19 am doing today; fathers tell their children about your **faithfulness**.
39: 8 For he thought, "There will be peace and **security** in my lifetime."
42: 3 he will not snuff out. In **faithfulness** he will bring forth justice;
43: 9 prove they were right, so that others may hear and say, "It is **true**."
48: 1 and invoke the God of Israel—but not in **truth** or righteousness—
59: 14 a distance; **truth** has stumbled in the streets, honesty cannot enter.
59: 15 **Truth** is nowhere to be found, and whoever shuns evil becomes a
61: 8 In my **faithfulness** I will reward them and make an everlasting
Jer 2: 21 I had planted you like a choice vine of sound and **reliable** stock.
4: 2 if in a **truthful**, just and righteous way you swear, 'As surely as the
9: 5 [9:4] Friend deceives friend, and no one speaks the **truth**.
10: 10 the LORD is the **true** God; he is the living God, the eternal King.
14: 13 suffer famine. Indeed, I will give you **lasting** peace in this place.' "
23: 28 tell his dream, but let the one who has my word speak it **faithfully**.
26: 15 for in **truth** the LORD has sent me to you to speak all these
28: 9 **truly** [+928] sent by the LORD only if his prediction comes
32: 41 and will **assuredly** [+928] plant them in this land with all my heart
33: 6 my people and will let them enjoy abundant peace and **security**.
42: 5 "May the LORD be a **true** and faithful witness against us if we do
Eze 18: 8 hand from doing wrong and judges **fairly** between man and man.
18: 9 He follows my decrees and **faithfully** [+6913] keeps my laws.
Da 8: 12 prospered in everything it did, and **truth** was thrown to the ground.
8: 26 of the evenings and mornings that has been given you is **true**,
9: 13 God by turning from our sins and giving attention to your **truth**.
10: 1 Its message was **true** and it concerned a great war. The
10: 21 but first I will tell you what is written in the Book of **Truth**.
11: 2 "Now then, I tell you the **truth**: Three more kings will appear in
Hos 4: 1 "There is no **faithfulness**, no love, no acknowledgment of God in
Mic 7: 20 You will be **true** to Jacob, and show mercy to Abraham, as you
Zec 7: 9 'Administer **true** justice; show mercy and compassion to one
8: 3 Jerusalem will be called the City of **Truth**, and the mountain of the
8: 8 and I will be **faithful** and righteous to them as their God."
8: 16 Speak the **truth** to each other, and render true and sound judgment
8: 16 to each other, and render **true** and sound judgment in your courts;
8: 19 and happy festivals for Judah. Therefore love **truth** and peace."
Mal 2: 6 **True** instruction was in his mouth and nothing false was found on

623 אַמְתַּחַת *'amtaḥat*, n.f. [15] [√ 5501]

sack [7], sacks [7], it[s] [+2257] [1]

Ge 42: 27 feed for his donkey, and he saw his silver in the mouth of his **sack**.
42: 28 "Here it is in my **sack**." Their hearts sank and they turned to each
43: 12 return the silver that was put back into the mouths of your **sacks**.
43: 18 because of the silver that was put back into our **sacks** the first time.
43: 21 at the place where we stopped for the night we opened our **sacks**
43: 21 of us found his silver—the exact weight—in the mouth of his **sack**.
43: 22 us to buy food. We don't know who put our silver in our **sacks**."
43: 23 the God of your father, has given you treasure in your **sacks**;
44: 1 "Fill the men's **sacks** with as much food as they can carry,
44: 1 they can carry, and put each man's silver in the mouth of his **sack**.
44: 2 my cup, the silver one, in the mouth of the youngest one's **sack**,
44: 8 land of Canaan the silver we found inside the mouths of our **sacks**.
44: 11 Each of them quickly lowered his **sack** to the ground and opened
44: 11 quickly lowered his sack to the ground and opened **it**[s] [+2257].
44: 12 with the youngest. And the cup was found in Benjamin's **sack**.

624 אֲמִתַּי *'amittay*, n.pr.m. [2] [√ 622; cf. 586]

Amittai [2]

2Ki 14: 25 God of Israel, spoken through his servant Jonah son of **Amittai**,
Jnh 1: 1 The word of the LORD came to Jonah son of **Amittai**:

625 אָן *'ān*, adv. [41 / 42]

where [+2025] [17], how long [+2025+6330] [12], anywhere else [+625+2025+2025+2256] [4], anywhere [+625+2025+2025+2256] [2], where [2], which way [+2025] [2], how long [+6330] [1], when [+2025+6330] [1], wherever [+2025] [1]

Ge 16: 8 where have you come from, and **where** [+2025] are you going?"
32: 17 [32:18] whom do you belong, and **where** [+2025] are you going,
37: 30 and said, "The boy isn't there! **Where** [+2025] can I turn now?"
Ex 16: 28 the LORD said to Moses, "**How long** [+2025+6330] will you
Nu 14: 11 The LORD said to Moses, "**How long** [+2025+6330] will these
14: 11 these people treat me with contempt? **How long** [+2025+6330]
Dt 1: 28 **Where** [+2025] can we go? Our brothers have made us lose heart.
Jos 2: 5 the men left. I don't know **which way** [+2025] they went.
18: 3 So Joshua said to the Israelites: "**How long** [+2025+6330] will you
Jdg 19: 17 city square, the old man asked, "**Where** [+2025] are you going?
Ru 2: 19 "Where did you glean today? **Where** [+2025] did you work?
1Sa 10: 14 Saul's uncle asked him and his servant, "**Where** have you been?"
27: 10 Achish asked, "**Where** [BHS 440] did you go raiding today?"
2Sa 2: 1 LORD said, "Go up." David asked, "**Where** [+2025] shall I go?"
13: 13 What about me? **Where** [+2025] could I get rid of my disgrace?
1Ki 2: 36 but do not go **anywhere** [+625+2025+2025+2256] **else**.
2: 36 but do not go **anywhere else** [+625+2025+2025+2256].
2: 42 the day you leave to go **anywhere** [+625+2025+2025+2256] **else**,
2: 42 the day you leave to go **anywhere else** [+625+2025+2025+2256],
2Ki 5: 25 ["**Where** [K; see Q 402] have you been, Gehazi?" Elisha asked.]
5: 25 "Your servant didn't go **anywhere** [+625+2025+2025+2256],"
5: 25 "Your servant didn't go **anywhere** [+625+2025+2025+2256],"
6: 6 The man of God asked, "**Where** [+2025] did it fall?" When he
Ne 2: 16 The officials did not know **where** [+2025] I had gone or what I
Job 8: 2 "**How long** [+6330] will you say such things? Your words are a
18: 2 "**When** [+2025+6330] will you end these speeches? Be sensible,
19: 2 "**How long** [+2025+6330] will you torment me and crush me with
Ps 13: 1 [13:2] **How long** [+2025+6330], O LORD? Will you forget me
13: 1 [13:2] Will you forget me forever? **How long** [+2025+6330] will
13: 2 [13:3] **How long** [+2025+6330] must I wrestle with my thoughts
13: 2 [13:3] day have sorrow in my heart? **How long** [+2025+6330]
62: 3 [62:4] **How long** [+2025+6330] will you assault a man?
139: 7 **Where** [+2025] can I go from your Spirit? Where can I flee from
139: 7 from your Spirit? **Where** [+2025] can I flee from your presence?
SS 6: 1 **Where** [+2025] has your lover gone, most beautiful of women?
6: 1 **Which way** [+2025] did your lover turn, that we may look for him
Isa 10: 3 will you run for help? **Where** [+2025] will you leave your riches?
Jer 15: 2 And if they ask you, '**Where** [+2025] shall we go?' tell them,
47: 6 of the LORD,' ⌞you cry,⌟ '**how long** [+2025+6330] till you rest?
Eze 21: 16 [21:21] then to the left, **wherever** [+2025] your blade is turned.
Hab 1: 2 **How long** [+2025+6330], O LORD, must I call for help,
Zec 2: 2 [2:6] I asked, "**Where** [+2025] are you going?" He answered me,
5: 10 "**Where** [+2025] are they taking the basket?" I asked the angel

626 אָנָּא *'onnā'*, interj. [7] [√ 629; cf. 5528]

O [5], I ask [1], oh [1]

Ge 50: 17 **I ask** you to forgive your brothers the sins and the wrongs they
Ex 32: 31 So Moses went back to the LORD and said, "**Oh**, what a great sin
Ne 1: 5 "**O** LORD, God of heaven, the great and awesome God,
1: 11 **O** Lord, let your ear be attentive to the prayer of this your servant
Ps 118: 25 **O** LORD, save us; O LORD, grant us success.
118: 25 O LORD, save us; **O** LORD, grant us success.
Da 9: 4 "**O** Lord, the great and awesome God, who keeps his covenant of

[F] Hitpael (hitpoel, hitpoal, hitpolel, hitpolal, hitpalel, hitpalal, hitpalpel, hitpalpal, hotpael, hotpaal) [G] Hiphil (hiphtil) [H] Hophal [I] Hishtaphel

627 ¹אָנָה **'ānâ¹**, v. [3] [→ 230, 640, 3433, 9302; cf. 634, 645]
groan [1], lament [1], mourning [1]
Dt 26: 14 [A] not eaten any of the sacred portion while I *was in* **mourning**,
Isa 3: 26 [A] The gates of Zion *will* **lament** and mourn; destitute, she will
19: 8 [A] The fishermen *will* **groan** and lament, all who cast hooks

628 ²אָנָה **'ānâ²**, v. [4] [→ 9299, 9301]
befall [+448] [1], befalls [+4200] [1], lets happen [+3338+4200] [1], trying to pick a quarrel [1]
Ex 21: 13 [D] not do it intentionally, but God **lets** *it* **happen** [+3338+4200],
2Ki 5: 7 [F] See how he *is* **trying to pick a quarrel** with me!"
Ps 91: 10 [E] no harm *will* **befall** [+448] you, no disaster will come near
Pr 12: 21 [E] No harm **befalls** [+4200] the righteous, but the wicked have

629 אָנָּה **'onnâ**, interj. [6] [√ 626; cf. 5528]
O [6]
2Ki 20: 3 "Remember, **O** LORD, how I have walked before you faithfully
Ps 116: 4 Then I called on the name of the LORD: "**O** LORD, save me!"
116: 16 **O** LORD, truly I am your servant; I am your servant, the son of
Isa 38: 3 "Remember, **O** LORD, how I have walked before you faithfully
Jnh 1: 14 they cried to the LORD, "**O** LORD, please do not let us die for
4: 2 He prayed to the LORD, "**O** LORD, is this not what I said when

630 אֲנוּ **'ᵃnû**, p.com.pl. [0] [√ 636]
Jer 42: 6 [to whom **we** [K; see Q 636] are sending you, so that it will go well]

631 אָנוּשׁ **'ānûš**, a.vbl. [8] [√ 653; cf. 5683]
incurable [3], beyond cure [1], despair [1], grievous [1], incurable wound [1], no cure [1]
Job 34: 6 although I am guiltless, his arrow inflicts an **incurable wound**.'
Isa 17: 11 harvest will be as nothing in the day of disease and **incurable** pain.
Jer 15: 18 Why is my pain unending and my wound **grievous** and incurable?
17: 9 The heart is deceitful above all things and **beyond cure**. Who can
17: 16 your shepherd; you know I have not desired the day of **despair**.
30: 12 " 'Your wound is **incurable**, your injury beyond healing.
30: 15 Why do you cry out over your wound, your pain that has **no cure**?
Mic 1: 9 For her wound is **incurable**; it has come to Judah. It has reached

632 ¹אֱנוֹשׁ **'ᵉnôš¹**, n.m. [42] [→ 633; cf. 653; Ar 10046, 10050]
man [20], men [9], mortal [4], man's [2], friends [+8934] [1], he[s] [1], his[s] [1], mankind [1], one [1], ordinary [1], very few [+4663] [1]
Dt 32: 26 I would scatter them and blot out their memory from **mankind**,
2Ch 14: 11 [14:10] you are our God; do not let **man** prevail against you."
Job 4: 17 'Can a **mortal** be more righteous than God? Can a man be more
5: 17 "Blessed is the **man** whom God corrects; so do not despise the
7: 1 "Does not **man** have hard service on earth? Are not his days like
7: 17 "What is **man** that you make so much of him, that you give him
9: 2 that this is true. But how can a **mortal** be righteous before God?
10: 4 Do you have eyes of flesh? Do you see as a **mortal** sees?
10: 5 Are your days like those of a **mortal** or your years like those of a
13: 9 examined you? Could you deceive him as you might deceive **men**?
14: 19 and torrents wash away the soil, so you destroy **man's** hope.
15: 14 "What is **man**, that he could be pure, or one born of woman,
25: 4 How then can a **man** be righteous before God? How can one born
25: 6 how much less **man**, who is but a maggot—a son of man,
28: 4 forgotten by the foot of man; far from **men** he dangles and sways.
28: 13 **Man** does not comprehend its worth; it cannot be found in the land
32: 8 it is the spirit in a **man**, the breath of the Almighty, that gives him
33: 12 I tell you, in this you are not right, for God is greater than **man**.
33: 26 and shouts for joy; **he**[s] is restored by God to his righteous state.
36: 25 All mankind has seen it; **men** gaze on it from afar.
Ps 8: 4 [8:5] what is **man** that you are mindful of him, the son of man
9: 19 [9:20] Arise, O LORD, let not **man** triumph; let the nations be
9: 20 [9:21] O LORD; let the nations know they are but **men**.
10: 18 defending the fatherless and the oppressed, in order that **man**,
55: 13 [55:14] it is you, a **man** like myself, my companion, my close
56: 1 [56:2] Be merciful to me, O God, for **men** hotly pursue me;
66: 12 You let **men** ride over our heads; we went through fire and water,
73: 5 They are free from the burdens common to **man**; they are not
90: 3 You turn **men** back to dust, saying, "Return to dust, O sons of
103: 15 As for **man**, his days are like grass, he flourishes like a flower of
104: 15 wine that gladdens the heart of **man**, oil to make his face shine,
104: 15 oil to make his face shine, and bread that sustains **his**[s] heart.
144: 3 is man that you care for him, the son of **man** that you think of him?
Isa 8: 1 "Take a large scroll and write on it with an **ordinary** pen:
13: 7 of this, all hands will go limp, every **man's** heart will melt.
13: 12 I will make **man** scarcer than pure gold, more rare than the gold of
24: 6 earth's inhabitants are burned up, and **very few** [+4663] are left.
33: 8 treaty is broken, its witnesses are despised, no **one** is respected.
51: 7 Do not fear the reproach of **men** or be terrified by their insults.
51: 12 Who are you that you fear mortal **men**, the sons of men, who are
56: 2 Blessed is the **man** who does this, the man who holds it fast,
Jer 20: 10 All my **friends** [+8934] are waiting for me to slip, saying,

633 ²אֱנוֹשׁ **'ᵉnôš²**, n.pr.m. [7] [√ 632; cf. 653]
Enosh [7]
Ge 4: 26 Seth also had a son, and he named him **Enosh**. At that time men
5: 6 When Seth had lived 105 years, he became the father of **Enosh**.
5: 7 And after he became the father of **Enosh**, Seth lived 807 years
5: 9 When **Enosh** had lived 90 years, he became the father of Kenan.
5: 10 of Kenan, **Enosh** lived 815 years and had other sons and daughters.
5: 11 Altogether, **Enosh** lived 905 years, and then he died.
1Ch 1: 1 Adam, Seth, **Enosh**,

634 אָנַח **'ānaḥ**, v. [12 / 13] [→ 635; cf. 627, 645, 5664]
groan [7], groaning [2], grieve [1], groaned [1], groans [1], moan [1]
Ex 2: 23 [C] The Israelites **groaned** in their slavery and cried out,
Pr 29: 2 [C] the people rejoice; when the wicked rule, the people **groan**.
Isa 24: 7 [C] dries up and the vine withers; all the merrymakers **groan**.
Jer 22: 23 [C] how *you will* **groan** [BHS 2858] when pangs come upon
La 1: 4 [C] her priests **groan**, her maidens grieve, and she is in bitter
1: 8 [C] have seen her nakedness; *she* herself **groans** and turns away.
1: 11 [C] All her people **groan** as they search for bread; they barter
1: 21 [C] "People have heard my **groaning**, but there is no one to
Eze 9: 4 [C] and put a mark on the foreheads of those who **grieve**
21: 6 [21:11] [C] "Therefore **groan**, son of man! Groan before them
21: 6 [21:11] [C] **Groan** before them with broken heart and bitter
21: 7 [21:12] [C] when they ask you, 'Why *are* you **groaning**?' you
Joel 1: 18 [C] How the cattle **moan**! The herds mill about because they

635 אֲנָחָה **'ᵃnāḥâ**, n.f. [11] [√ 634]
groaning [6], sighing [4], groans [1]
Job 3: 24 For **sighing** comes to me instead of food; my groans pour out like
23: 2 my complaint is bitter; his hand is heavy in spite of my **groaning**.
Ps 6: 6 [6:7] I am worn out from **groaning**; all night long I flood my bed
31: 10 [31:11] life is consumed by anguish and my years by **groaning**;
38: 9 [38:10] before you, O Lord; my **sighing** is not hidden from you.
102: 5 [102:6] Because of my loud **groaning** I am reduced to skin and
Isa 21: 2 lay siege! I will bring to an end all the **groaning** she caused.
35: 10 and joy will overtake them, and sorrow and **sighing** will flee away.
51: 11 and joy will overtake them, and sorrow and **sighing** will flee away.
Jer 45: 3 to my pain; I am worn out with **groaning** and find no rest.' "
La 1: 22 because of all my sins. My **groans** are many and my heart is faint."

636 אֲנַחְנוּ **'ᵃnaḥnû**, p.com.pl. [120] [→ 630, 638, 644, 5721; Ar 10047] Not indexed
we [103], *untranslated* [8], us [6], we're [2], our [1]

637 אֲנָחֲרַת **'ᵃnāḥᵃrat**, n.pr.loc. [1]
Anaharath [1]
Jos 19: 19 Hapharaim, Shion, **Anaharath**,

638 אֲנִי **'ᵃnî**, p.com.s. [874] [√ 636; Ar 10044] Not indexed
I [790], me [26], myself [21], *untranslated* [20], we [6], I'll [3], my [2], each of us [+2085+2256] [1], I'm [1], me alone [+3276] [1], mine [1], my life [1], yes[s] [1]

639 אֳנִי **'ᵒnî**, n.m. [7] [→ 641]
ships [3], fleet of trading ships [+9576] [1], fleet [1], galley [1], it[s] [+9576] [1]
1Ki 9: 26 King Solomon also built **ships** at Ezion Geber, which is near Elath
9: 27 who knew the sea—to serve in the **fleet** with Solomon's men.
10: 11 (Hiram's **ships** brought gold from Ophir; and from there they
10: 22 The king had a **fleet of trading ships** [+9576] at sea along with the
10: 22 The king had a fleet of trading ships at sea along with the **ships** *of*
10: 22 Once every three years **it**[s] [+9576] returned, carrying gold,
Isa 33: 21 No **galley** *with* oars will ride them, no mighty ship will sail them.

640 אֲנִיָּה **'ᵃniyyâ**, n.f. [2] [√ 627]
lament [1], lamentation [1]
Isa 29: 2 she will mourn and **lament**, she will be to me like an altar hearth.
La 2: 5 multiplied mourning and **lamentation** for the Daughter of Judah.

641 אֳנִיָּה **'ᵒniyyâ**, n.f. [31] [√ 639]
ships [16], ship [3], boats [1], cargo [+889+928+2021+3998] [1], fleet of ships [1], fleet of trading ships [+2143+4200+9576] [1], fleet of trading ships [+2143+9576] [1], fleet of trading ships [+9576] [1], it[s]

[+9576] [1], sail [+928+2021+2143] [1], sailors [+408] [1], these[s] [1], they[s] [1], trading ship [+9576] [1]
Ge 49:13 "Zebulun will live by the seashore and become a haven for **ships**;
Dt 28:68 The LORD will send you back in **ships** to Egypt on a journey I
Jdg 5:17 Dan, why did he linger by the **ships**? Asher remained on the coast
1Ki 9:27 And Hiram sent his men—**sailors** [+408] who knew the sea—
22:48 [22:49] Now Jehoshaphat built a **fleet of trading ships** [+9576] to
22:48 [22:49] they never set sail—**they**[s] were wrecked at Ezion Geber.
22:49 [22:50] "*Let* my men **sail** [+928+2021+2143] with your men,"
2Ch 8:18 And Hiram sent him **ships** commanded by his own officers,
9:21 The king had a **fleet of trading ships** [+2143+9576] manned by
9:21 Once every three years **it**[s] [+9576] returned, carrying gold,
20:36 to construct a **fleet of trading ships** [+2143+4200+9576].
20:36 a fleet of trading ships. After **these**[s] were built at Ezion Geber,
20:37 The **ships** were wrecked and were not able to set sail to trade.
Job 9:26 They skim past like **boats** *of* papyrus, like eagles swooping down
Ps 48:7 [48:8] You destroyed them like **ships** *of* Tarshish shattered by an
104:26 There the **ships** go to and fro, and the leviathan, which you formed
107:23 Others went out on the sea in **ships**; they were merchants on the
Pr 30:19 the way of a snake on a rock, the way of a **ship** on the high seas,
31:14 She is like the merchant **ships**, bringing her food from afar.
Isa 2:16 for every **trading ship** [+9576] and every stately vessel.
23:1 Wail, O **ships** *of* Tarshish! For Tyre is destroyed and left without
23:14 Wail, you **ships** *of* Tarshish; your fortress is destroyed!
43:14 all the Babylonians, in the **ships** *in which* they took pride.
60:9 in the lead are the **ships** *of* Tarshish, bringing your sons from afar,
Eze 27:9 All the **ships** *of* the sea and their sailors came alongside to trade for
27:25 " 'The **ships** *of* Tarshish serve as carriers for your wares. You are
27:29 All who handle the oars will abandon their **ships**; the mariners
Da 11:40 out against him with chariots and cavalry and a great **fleet of ships**.
Jnh 1:3 He went down to Joppa, where he found a **ship** bound for that port.
1:4 and such a violent storm arose that the **ship** threatened to break up.
1:5 And they threw the **cargo** [+889+928+2021+3998] into the sea to lighten the ship. But Jonah had gone below deck, where he lay down

642 אֲנִיעָם 'anî'ām, n.pr.m. [1]

Aniam [1]
1Ch 7:19 The sons of Shemida were: Ahian, Shechem, Likhi and **Aniam**.

643 אֲנָךְ 'anāk, n.[m.]. [4]

plumb line [3], true to plumb [1]
Am 7:7 Lord was standing by a wall that had been built **true to plumb**,
7:7 that had been built true to plumb, with a **plumb line** in his hand.
7:8 asked me, "What do you see, Amos?" "A **plumb line**," I replied.
7:8 "Look, I am setting a **plumb line** among my people Israel;

644 אָנֹכִי 'ānōkî, p.com.s. [359] [√ 636] Not indexed

I [326], *untranslated* [10], I'm [8], me [5], myself [5], I'll [3], it[s] [1], we [1]

645 אָנַן 'ānan, v. [2] [cf. 627 *or* 634]

complain [1], complained [1]
Nu 11:1 [F] Now the people **complained** *about* their hardships in the
La 3:39 [F] Why *should* any living man **complain** when punished for his

646 אָנַס 'ānas, v. [1] [→ Ar 10048]

allowed [+401] [1]
Est 1:8 [A] By the king's command each guest *was* **allowed** [+401] to

647 אָנַף 'ānap, v. [14] [→ 678, 690, 691, 3018; Ar 10049]

angry [14]
Dt 1:37 [F] Because of you the LORD *became* **angry** with me also and
4:21 [F] The LORD *was* **angry** with me because of you, and he
9:8 [F] LORD's wrath so that he *was* **angry** *enough* to destroy you.
9:20 [F] the LORD *was* **angry** enough with Aaron to destroy him,
1Ki 8:46 [A] *you become* **angry** with them and give them over to the
11:9 [F] The LORD *became* **angry** with Solomon because his heart
2Ki 17:18 [F] So the LORD *was* very **angry** with Israel and removed them
2Ch 6:36 [A] *you become* **angry** with them and give them over to the
Ezr 9:14 [A] *Would you* not *be* **angry** enough with us to destroy us,
Ps 2:12 [A] the Son, lest *he be* **angry** and you be destroyed in your way,
60:1 [60:3] [A] upon us; *you have been* **angry**—now restore us!
79:5 [A] How long, O LORD? *Will you be* **angry** forever? How
85:5 [85:6] [A] *Will you be* **angry** with us forever? Will you prolong
Isa 12:1 [A] Although *you were* **angry** with me, your anger has turned

648 אָנָף 'ānāp, n.m. Not used in NIV/BHS [√ 678; cf. 647]

649 אֲנָפָה 'anāpâ, n.f. [2]

heron [2]
Lev 11:19 the stork, any kind of **heron**, the hoopoe and the bat.
Dt 14:18 the stork, any kind of **heron**, the hoopoe and the bat.

650 אָנַק 'ānaq, v. [4] [→ 651; cf. 5543, 5544]

groan [3], lament [1]
Jer 51:52 [A] her idols, and throughout her land the wounded *will* **groan**.
Eze 9:4 [C] and **lament** over all the detestable things that are done in it."
24:17 [C] **Groan** quietly; do not mourn for the dead. Keep your turban
26:15 [A] when the wounded **groan** and the slaughter takes place in

651 ¹אֲנָקָה 'anāqâ[1], n.f. [4] [√ 650]

groans [2], groaning [1], wail [1]
Ps 12:5 [12:6] the oppression of the weak and the **groaning** *of* the needy,
79:11 May the **groans** *of* the prisoners come before you; by the strength
102:20 [102:21] to hear the **groans** *of* the prisoners and release those
Mal 2:13 You weep and **wail** because he no longer pays attention to your

652 ²אֲנָקָה 'anāqâ[2], n.f. [1]

gecko [1]
Lev 11:30 the **gecko**, the monitor lizard, the wall lizard, the skink

653 אָנַשׁ 'ānaš, v. [1] [→ 631, 632, 633]

ill [1]
2Sa 12:15 [C] that Uriah's wife had borne to David, and *he became* **ill**.

654 אָסָא 'āsā', n.pr.m. [58]

Asa [50], Asa's [7], *untranslated* [1]
1Ki 15:8 in the City of David. And **Asa** his son succeeded him as king.
15:9 year of Jeroboam king of Israel, **Asa** became king of Judah,
15:11 **Asa** did what was right in the eyes of the LORD, as his father
15:13 **Asa** cut the pole down and burned it in the Kidron Valley.
15:14 **Asa's** heart was fully committed to the LORD all his life.
15:16 There was war between **Asa** and Baasha king of Israel throughout
15:17 anyone from leaving or entering the territory of **Asa** king of Judah.
15:18 **Asa** then took all the silver and gold that was left in the treasuries
15:18 and sent them **[RPH]** to Ben-Hadad son of Tabrimmon,
15:20 Ben-Hadad agreed with King **Asa** and sent the commanders of his
15:22 Then King **Asa** issued an order to all Judah—no one was exempt—
15:22 With them King **Asa** built up Geba in Benjamin, and also Mizpah.
15:23 As for all the other events of **Asa's** reign, all his achievements,
15:24 **Asa** rested with his fathers and was buried with them in the city of
15:25 became king of Israel in the second year of **Asa** king of Judah,
15:28 Baasha killed Nadab in the third year of **Asa** king of Judah
15:32 There was war between **Asa** and Baasha king of Israel throughout
15:33 In the third year of **Asa** king of Judah, Baasha son of Ahijah
16:8 In the twenty-sixth year of **Asa** king of Judah, Elah son of Baasha
16:10 and killed him in the twenty-seventh year of **Asa** king of Judah.
16:15 In the twenty-seventh year of **Asa** king of Judah, Zimri reigned in
16:23 In the thirty-first year of **Asa** king of Judah, Omri became king of
16:29 In the thirty-eighth year of **Asa** king of Judah, Ahab son of Omri
22:41 Jehoshaphat son of **Asa** became king of Judah in the fourth year of
22:43 In everything he walked in the ways of his father **Asa** and did not
22:46 [22:47] who remained there even after the reign of his father **Asa**.
1Ch 3:10 was Rehoboam, Abijah his son, **Asa** his son, Jehoshaphat his son,
9:16 Berekiah son of **Asa**, the son of Elkanah, who lived in the villages
2Ch 14:1 [13:23] **Asa** his son succeeded him as king, and in his days the
14:2 [14:1] **Asa** did what was good and right in the eyes of the LORD
14:8 [14:7] **Asa** had an army of three hundred thousand men from
14:10 [14:9] **Asa** went out to meet him, and they took up battle positions
14:11 [14:10] **Asa** called to the LORD his God and said, "LORD,
14:12 [14:11] The LORD struck down the Cushites before **Asa**
14:13 [14:12] **Asa** and his army pursued them as far as Gerar. Such a
15:2 He went out to meet **Asa** and said to him, "Listen to me, Asa
15:2 and said to him, "Listen to me, **Asa** and all Judah and Benjamin.
15:8 When **Asa** heard these words and the prophecy of Azariah son of
15:10 at Jerusalem in the third month of the fifteenth year of **Asa's** reign.
15:16 King **Asa** also deposed his grandmother Maacah from her position
15:16 **Asa** cut the pole down, broke it up and burned it in the Kidron
15:17 **Asa's** heart was fully committed ⌞to the LORD⌟ all his life.
15:19 There was no more war until the thirty-fifth year of **Asa's** reign.
16:1 In the thirty-sixth year of **Asa's** reign Baasha king of Israel went
16:1 anyone from leaving or entering the territory of **Asa** king of Judah.
16:2 **Asa** then took the silver and gold out of the treasuries of the
16:4 Ben-Hadad agreed with King **Asa** and sent the commanders of his
16:6 King **Asa** brought all the men of Judah, and they carried away
16:7 At that time Hanani the seer came to **Asa** king of Judah and said to
16:10 **Asa** was angry with the seer because of this; he was so enraged

2Ch 16:10 At the same time **Asa** brutally oppressed some of the people.
16:11 The events of **Asa's** reign, from beginning to end, are written in
16:12 In the thirty-ninth year of his reign **Asa** was afflicted with a disease
16:13 in the forty-first year of his reign **Asa** died and rested with his
17: 2 and in the towns of Ephraim that his father **Asa** had captured.
20:32 He walked in the ways of his father **Asa** and did not stray from
21:12 in the ways of your father Jehoshaphat or of **Asa** king of Judah.
Jer 41: 9 **Asa** had made as part of his defense against Baasha king of Israel.

655 אָסוּךְ *'āsûk*, n.[m.]. [1] [√ 6057]

little[s] [1]

2Ki 4: 2 servant has nothing there at all," she said, "except a **little**[s] oil."

656 אָסוֹן *'āsôn*, n.m. [5]

harm [3], serious injury [2]

Ge 42: 4 the others, because he was afraid that **harm** might come to him.
42:38 If **harm** comes to him on the journey you are taking, you will
44:29 If you take this one from me too and **harm** comes to him,
Ex 21:22 and she gives birth prematurely but there is no **serious injury**,
21:23 But if there is **serious injury**, you are to take life for life,

657 אֵסוּר *'ēsûr*, n.m. [3] [√ 673; Ar 10054]

bindings [1], chains [1], imprisoned [+906+1074+2021+5989] [1]

Jdg 15:14 like charred flax, and the **bindings** dropped from his hands.
Ecc 7:26 who is a snare, whose heart is a trap and whose hands are **chains**.
Jer 37:15 **imprisoned in** [+906+1074+2021+5989] the house of Jonathan the

658 אָסִיף *'āsîp*, n.[m.]. [2 / 3] [√ 665]

Ingathering [2], harvest [1]

Ex 23:16 "Celebrate the Feast of **Ingathering** at the end of the year,
34:22 wheat harvest, and the Feast of **Ingathering** at the turn of the year.
Jer 8:13 " 'I will take away their **harvest**, [BHS 6066] declares the

659 אָסִיר *'āsîr*, n.m. [12] [√ 673]

prisoners [8], captives [2], captive [1], held [1]

Ge 39:20 the place where the king's **prisoners** [K 673] were confined.
39:22 So the warden put Joseph in charge of all those **held** in the prison,
Jdg 16:21 [they set him to grinding in the **prison** [K; see Q 673].]
16:25 [So they called Samson out of the **prison** [K; see Q 673],]
Job 3:18 **Captives** also enjoy their ease; they no longer hear the slave
Ps 68: 6 [68:7] in families, he leads forth the **prisoners** with singing;
69:33 [69:34] hears the needy and does not despise his **captive** *people*.
79:11 May the groans of the **prisoners** come before you; by the strength
102:20 [102:21] to hear the groans of the **prisoners** and release those
107:10 and the deepest gloom, **prisoners** suffering *in* iron chains,
Isa 14:17 who overthrew its cities and would not let his **captives** go home?"
La 3:34 To crush underfoot all **prisoners** *in* the land,
Zec 9:11 with you, I will free your **prisoners** from the waterless pit.
9:12 Return to your fortress, O **prisoners** *of* hope; even now I announce

660 אַסִּיר¹ *'assîr¹*, n.m.[col.]. [4] [→ 661; cf. 673]

captives [2], captive [1], prisoners [1]

1Ch 3:17 The descendants of Jehoiachin the **captive**: Shealtiel his son,
Isa 10: 4 Nothing will remain but to cringe among the **captives** or fall
24:22 They will be herded together like **prisoners** *bound* in a dungeon;
42: 7 to free **captives** from prison and to release from the dungeon those

661 אַסִּיר² *'assîr²*, n.pr.m. [4] [√ 660; cf. 673]

Assir [4]

Ex 6:24 The sons of Korah were **Assir**, Elkanah and Abiasaph. These were
1Ch 6:22 [6:7] Amminadab his son, Korah his son, **Assir** his son,
6:23 [6:8] Elkanah his son, Ebiasaph his son, **Assir** his son,
6:37 [6:22] the son of Tahath, the son of **Assir**, the son of Ebiasaph,

662 אָסָם *'āsām*, n.m. [2]

barns [2]

Dt 28: 8 The LORD will send a blessing on your **barns** and on everything
Pr 3:10 your **barns** will be filled to overflowing, and your vats will brim

663 אַסְנָה *'asnâ*, n.pr.m. [1]

Asnah [1]

Ezr 2:50 **Asnah**, Meunim, Nephussim,

664 אָסְנַת *'āsᵉnat*, n.pr.f. [3]

Asenath [3]

Ge 41:45 and gave him **Asenath** daughter of Potiphera,
41:50 two sons were born to Joseph by **Asenath** daughter of Potiphera,
46:20 Ephraim were born to Joseph by **Asenath** daughter of Potiphera,

665 אָסַף *'āsap*, v. [200] [→ 658, 666, 667, 668, 669, 670, 671, 4417]

gathered [18], gather [17], assembled [14], be gathered [9], assemble [6], harvest [5], rear guard [5], was gathered [5], brought together [4], gathered together [4], take away [4], are taken away [3], collected [3], cure [3], gather together [3], gathered up [3], mustered [3], accumulated [2], be buried [+448+7700] [2], be gathered [+665] [2], called together [+906+2256+8938] [2], gather in [2], gather up [2], gathers up [2], gathers [2], no longer shine [+5586] [2], put [2], surely gather [+665] [2], withdraw [2], admit [1], are gathered [1], assembling [1], banded together [+2021+2653+4200] [1], be brought back [1], be collected [1], be gathered up [1], be herded together [+669] [1], be recovered [1], been brought [1], been gathered [1], bring back [1], bring [1], brought back [1], brought [1], called together [+448+2256+8938] [1], called together [+448+906+2256+8938] [1], called together [1], came together [1], cured [1], destroy [1], do so more [1], drew up [1], dying [1], gather around [1], gathering [1], get [1], gone [1], got together [1], had brought [1], harvested [1], is gathered in [1], is harvested [1], join forces [1], join [1], joined forces [+3481] [1], joined forces [1], lose [1], massing together [1], muster [1], rallied [1], receive [1], regrouped [+3480] [1], remove [1], return [1], returned [1], set aside [1], steal away [1], store away [1], summon [1], sweep away [+6066] [1], take [1], taken away [1], taken [1], together [1], took into service [1], took [1], victims [1], wane [1], was[s] [1], were brought together [1], were caught [1], were gathered [1], were mustered [1], withdrawn [1], withdraws [1], withdrew [1]

Ge 6:21 [A] to be eaten and **store** it **away** as food for you and for them."
25: 8 [C] old man and full of years; and *he* **was gathered** to his people.
25:17 [C] his last and died, and *he* **was gathered** to his people.
29: 3 [C] When all the flocks **were gathered** there, the shepherds
29: 7 [C] sun is still high; it is not time for the flocks *to* **be gathered**.
29: 8 [C] "until all the flocks **are gathered** and the stone has been
29:22 [A] So Laban **brought together** all the people of the place
30:23 [A] birth to a son and said, "God *has* **taken away** my disgrace."
34:30 [C] *if they* **join forces** against me and attack me, I and my
35:29 [C] he breathed his last and died and **was gathered** to his people,
42:17 [A] And *he* **put** them all in custody for three days.
49: 1 [C] "**Gather around** so I can tell you what will happen to you in
49:29 [C] these instructions: "I *am about to* **be gathered** to my people.
49:33 [A] *he* **drew** his feet **up** into the bed, breathed his last and was
49:33 [C] the bed, breathed his last and **was gathered** to his people.
Ex 3:16 [A] "Go, **assemble** the elders of Israel and say to them,
4:29 [A] and Aaron **brought together** all the elders of the Israelites,
9:19 [C] animal that *has* not **been brought** in and is still out in the
23:10 [A] six years you are to sow your fields and **harvest** the crops,
23:16 [A] of the year, when you **gather in** your crops from the field.
32:26 [C] the LORD, come to me." And all the Levites **rallied** to him.
Lev 23:39 [A] after you *have* **gathered** the crops of the land, celebrate the
25: 3 [A] for six years prune your vineyards and **gather** their crops.
25:20 [A] in the seventh year if we do not plant or **harvest** our crops?"
26:25 [C] When *you* **withdraw** into your cities, I will send a plague
Nu 10:25 [D] Finally, as the **rear guard** for all the units, the divisions of
11:16 [A] "**Bring** me seventy of Israel's elders who are known to you
11:22 [C] have enough if all the fish in the sea **were caught** for them?"
11:24 [A] *He* **brought together** seventy of their elders and had them
11:30 [C] Then Moses and the elders of Israel **returned** to the camp.
11:32 [A] and all the next day the people went out and **gathered** quail.
11:32 [A] and gathered quail. No one **gathered** less than ten homers.
12:14 [C] camp for seven days; after that *she can* **be brought back**."
12:15 [C] and the people did not move on till she *was* **brought back**.
19: 9 [A] "A man who is clean *shall* **gather up** the ashes of the heifer
19:10 [A] The *man who* **gathers up** the ashes of the heifer must also
20:24 [C] "Aaron *will* **be gathered** to his people. He will not enter the
20:26 [C] on his son Eleazar, for Aaron *will* **be gathered** to his people;
21:16 [A] "**Gather** the people **together** and I will give them water."
21:23 [A] He **mustered** his entire army and marched out into the desert
27:13 [C] you have seen it, you too *will* **be gathered** to your people,
27:13 [C] will be gathered to your people, as your brother Aaron **was**[s],
31: 2 [C] After that, *you will* **be gathered** to your people."
Dt 11:14 [A] so that *you may* **gather in** your grain, new wine and oil.
16:13 [A] after you *have* **gathered** the produce of your threshing floor
22: 2 [A] **take** it home with you and keep it until he comes looking for
28:38 [A] will sow much seed in the field but *you will* **harvest** little,
32:50 [C] have climbed you will die and **be gathered** to your people,
32:50 [C] Aaron died on Mount Hor and **was gathered** to his people.
33: 5 [F] over Jeshurun when the leaders of the people **assembled**,
Jos 2:18 [A] *you have* **brought** your father and mother, your brothers and
6: 9 [D] who blew the trumpets, and the **rear guard** followed the ark.
6:13 [D] of them and the **rear guard** followed the ark of the LORD,
10: 5 [C] Jarmuth, Lachish and Eglon—**joined forces**.

Jos 20: 4 [A] *they are to* **admit** him into their city and give him a place to
24: 1 [A] Then Joshua **assembled** all the tribes of Israel at Shechem.
Jdg 2: 10 [C] After that whole generation *had* **been gathered** to their
3: 13 [A] *Getting* the Ammonites and Amalekites *to* **join** him, Eglon
6: 33 [C] Amalekites and other eastern peoples **joined** [+3481] **forces**
9: 6 [C] Beth Millo **gathered** beside the great tree at the pillar in
10: 17 [C] in Gilead, the Israelites **assembled** and camped at Mizpah.
11: 20 [A] He **mustered** all his men and encamped at Jahaz and fought
16: 23 [C] Now the rulers of the Philistines **assembled** to offer a great
18: 25 [A] attack you, and *you* and your family *will* **lose** your lives."
19: 15 [D] city square, but no one **took** them into his home for the night.
19: 18 [D] house of the LORD. No one *has* **taken** me into his house.
20: 11 [C] So all the men of Israel **got together** and united as one man
20: 14 [C] From their towns they **came together** at Gibeah to fight
Ru 2: 7 [A] and **gather** among the sheaves behind the harvesters.'
1Sa 5: 8 [A] So *they* **called together** [+448+906+2256+8938] all the rulers
5: 11 [A] So *they* **called together** [+906+2256+8938] all the rulers of the
13: 5 [C] The Philistines **assembled** to fight Israel, with three thousand
13: 11 [C] and that the Philistines *were* **assembling** at Micmash,
14: 19 [A] and more. So Saul said to the priest, "**Withdraw** your hand."
14: 52 [A] saw a mighty or brave man, *he* **took** him **into** his **service**.
15: 6 [A] the Amalekites so that *I do* not **destroy** you along with them;
17: 1 [A] Now the Philistines **gathered** their forces for war
17: 1 [C] their forces for war and **assembled** *at* Socoh in Judah.
17: 2 [C] Saul and the Israelites **assembled** and camped in the Valley
2Sa 6: 1 [G] David again **brought together** out of Israel chosen men,
10: 15 [C] that they had been routed by Israel, *they* **regrouped** [+3480].
10: 17 [A] *he* **gathered** all Israel, crossed the Jordan and went to
11: 27 [A] David **had** her **brought** to his house, and she became his
12: 28 [A] Now **muster** the rest of the troops and besiege the city
12: 29 [A] So David **mustered** the entire army and went to Rabbah,
14: 14 [C] on the ground, which cannot **be recovered**, so we must die.
17: 11 [C] as numerous as the sand on the seashore—**be gathered** [+665]
17: 11 [C] as numerous as the sand on the seashore—**be gathered** [+665]
17: 13 [C] If *he* **withdraws** into a city, then all Israel will bring ropes to
21: 13 [A] of those who had been killed and exposed *were* **gathered up**.
23: 9 [C] was with David when they taunted the Philistines **gathered**
23: 11 [C] the Philistines **banded** [+2021+2653+4200] **together** at a place
1Ki 10: 26 [A] Solomon **accumulated** chariots and horses; he had fourteen
2Ki 5: 3 [A] who is in Samaria! *He would* **cure** him of his leprosy."
5: 6 [A] Naaman to you so that *you may* **cure** him of his leprosy."
5: 7 [A] Why does this fellow send someone to me to *be* **cured** of his
5: 11 [A] wave his hand over the spot and **cure** me *of* my leprosy.
22: 4 [A] which the doorkeepers *have* **collected** from the people.
22: 20 [A] Therefore I *will* **gather** you to your fathers, and you will be
22: 20 [C] your fathers, and *you will* **be buried** [+448+7700] in peace.
23: 1 [A] Then the king **called together** [+448+2256+8938] all the
1Ch 11: 13 [C] Pas Dammim when the Philistines **gathered** there for battle.
15: 4 [A] He **called together** the descendants of Aaron and the
19: 7 [C] while the Ammonites **were mustered** from their towns
19: 17 [A] told of this, *he* **gathered** all Israel and crossed the Jordan;
23: 2 [A] *He* also **gathered together** all the leaders of Israel, as well as
2Ch 1: 14 [A] Solomon **accumulated** chariots and horses; he had fourteen
12: 5 [C] to the leaders of Judah who *had* **assembled** in Jerusalem for
24: 11 [A] did this regularly and **collected** a great amount of money.
28: 24 [A] Ahaz **gathered together** the furnishings from the temple of
29: 4 [A] the Levites, **assembled** them in the square on the east side
29: 15 [A] When *they had* **assembled** their brothers and consecrated
29: 20 [A] morning King Hezekiah **gathered** the city officials **together**
30: 3 [C] and the people *had* not **assembled** in Jerusalem.
30: 13 [C] A very large crowd of people **assembled** *in* Jerusalem to
34: 9 [A] which the Levites who were the doorkeepers *had* **collected**
34: 28 [A] Now I *will* **gather** you to your fathers, and you will be buried
34: 28 [C] your fathers, and *you will* **be buried** [+448+7700] in peace.
34: 29 [A] Then the king **called together** [+906+2256+8938] all the
Ezr 3: 1 [C] their towns, the people **assembled** as one man in Jerusalem.
9: 4 [C] at the words of the God of Israel **gathered** around me
Ne 8: 1 [C] all the people **assembled** as one man in the square before the
8: 13 [C] **gathered** around Ezra the scribe to give attention to the
9: 1 [C] the Israelites **gathered together**, fasting and wearing
12: 28 [C] The singers also **were brought together** from the region
Job 27: 19 [C] He lies down wealthy, but *will* **do so no more**; when he
34: 14 [A] If it were his intention and *he* **withdrew** his spirit and breath,
39: 12 [A] to bring in your grain and **gather** it *to* your threshing floor?
Ps 26: 9 [A] *Do* not **take away** my soul along with sinners, my life with
27: 10 [A] and mother forsake me, the LORD *will* **receive** me.
35: 15 [C] when I stumbled, *they* **gathered** in glee; attackers gathered
35: 15 [C] in glee; attackers **gathered** against me when I was unaware.
39: 6 [39:7] [A] he heaps up wealth, not knowing who *will* **get** it.
47: 9 [47:10] [C] The nobles of the nations **assemble** as the people of
50: 5 [A] "**Gather** to me my consecrated ones, who made a covenant
85: 3 [85:4] [A] *You* **set aside** all your wrath and turned from your
104: 22 [C] The sun rises, and *they* **steal away**; they return and lie down
104: 29 [A] *when you* **take away** their breath, they die and return to the
Pr 27: 25 [C] growth appears and the grass from the hills **is gathered in**,
30: 4 [A] Who *has* **gathered up** the wind in the hollow of his hands?
Ecc 2: 26 [A] to the sinner he gives the task of **gathering** and storing up
Isa 4: 1 [A] let us be called by your name. **Take away** our disgrace!"
10: 14 [A] as men **gather** abandoned eggs, so I gathered all the
10: 14 [A] men gather abandoned eggs, so I **gathered** all the countries;
11: 12 [A] raise a banner for the nations and **gather** the exiles of Israel;
13: 4 [C] uproar among the kingdoms, like nations **massing together**!
16: 10 [C] Joy and gladness **are taken away** from the orchards; no one
17: 5 [A] It will be as *when* a reaper **gathers** the standing grain
24: 22 [E] *They will* **be herded** [+669] **together** like prisoners bound in
33: 4 [E] Your plunder, O nations, **is harvested** as by young locusts;
43: 9 [C] All the nations gather together and the peoples **assemble**.
49: 5 [C] to bring Jacob back to him and **gather** Israel to himself,
52: 12 [D] go before you, the God of Israel will be your **rear guard**.
57: 1 [C] devout men **are taken away**, and no one understands that the
57: 1 [C] no one understands that the righteous **are taken away** to be
58: 8 [A] and the glory of the LORD *will be* your **rear guard**.
60: 20 [C] sun will never set again, and your moon *will* **wane** no more;
62: 9 [D] but *those who* **harvest** it will eat it and praise the LORD,
Jer 4: 5 [C] Cry aloud and say: '**Gather together**! Let us flee to the
8: 2 [C] *They will* not **be gathered up** or buried, but will be like
8: 13 [A] " '*I will* **take away** their harvest, declares the LORD.
8: 14 [C] "Why are we sitting here? **Gather together**! Let us flee to
9: 22 [9:21] [D] behind the reaper, with no *one to* **gather** them.' "
10: 17 [A] **Gather up** your belongings to leave the land, you who live
12: 9 [A] and **gather** all the wild beasts; bring them to devour.
16: 5 [A] because *I have* **withdrawn** my blessing, my love and my
21: 4 [A] wall besieging you. And *I will* **gather** them inside this city.
25: 33 [C] They will not be mourned or **gathered up** or buried, but will
40: 10 [A] you *are to* **harvest** the wine, summer fruit and oil, and put
40: 12 [A] And *they* **harvested** an abundance of wine and summer fruit.
47: 6 [C] till you rest? **Return** to your scabbard; cease and be still.'
48: 33 [C] Joy and gladness *are* **gone** from the orchards and fields of
Eze 11: 17 [A] **bring** you **back** from the countries where you have been
24: 4 [A] **Put** into it the pieces of meat, all the choice pieces—the leg
29: 5 [C] will fall on the open field and not **be gathered** or picked up.
34: 29 [B] they will no longer be **victims** *of* famine in the land or bear
38: 12 [E] the resettled ruins and the people **gathered** from the nations,
39: 17 [C] come **together** from all around to the sacrifice I am preparing
Da 11: 10 [A] His sons will prepare for war and **assemble** a great army,
Hos 4: 3 [C] and the birds of the air and the fish of the sea *are* **dying**.
10: 10 [E] nations *will* **be gathered** against them to put them in bonds
Joel 1: 14 [A] **Summon** the elders and all who live in the land to the house
2: 10 [A] moon are darkened, and the stars **no longer shine** [+5586].
2: 16 [A] **Gather** the people, consecrate the assembly; bring together
2: 16 [A] bring together the elders, **gather** the children, those nursing
3: 15 [4:15] [A] be darkened, and the stars **no longer shine** [+5586].
Am 3: 9 [C] "**Assemble** *yourselves* on the mountains of Samaria; see the
Mic 2: 12 [A] "*I will* **surely gather** [+665] all of you, O Jacob; I will surely
2: 12 [A] "*I will* **surely gather** [+665] all of you, O Jacob; I will surely
4: 6 [A] "In that day," declares the LORD, "*I will* **gather** the lame;
4: 11 [C] But now many nations *are* **gathered** against you. They say,
Hab 1: 9 [A] advance like a desert wind and **gather** prisoners like sand.
1: 15 [A] catches them in his net, *he* **gathers** them **up** in his dragnet;
2: 5 [A] *he* **gathers** to himself all the nations and takes captive all the
Zep 1: 2 [A] "*I will* **sweep away** [+6066] everything from the face of the
3: 8 [A] I have decided to **assemble** the nations, to gather the
3: 18 [A] "The sorrows for the appointed feasts *I will* **remove** from
Zec 12: 3 [C] when all the nations of the earth *are* **gathered** against her,
14: 2 [A] *I will* **gather** all the nations to Jerusalem to fight against it;
14: 14 [E] The wealth of all the surrounding nations *will* **be collected**—

666 אָסָף *'āsāp*, n.pr.m. [46] [√ 665]

Asaph [45], Asaph's [1]

2Ki 18: 18 and Joah son of **Asaph** the recorder went out to them.
18: 37 and Joah son of **Asaph** the recorder went to Hezekiah,
1Ch 6: 39 [6:24] Heman's associate **Asaph**, who served at his right hand:
6: 39 [6:24] his right hand: **Asaph** son of Berekiah, the son of Shimea,
9: 15 and Mattaniah son of Mica, the son of Zicri, the son of **Asaph**;
15: 17 from his brothers, **Asaph** son of Berekiah; and from their brothers
15: 19 **Asaph** and Ethan were to sound the bronze cymbals;
16: 5 **Asaph** was the chief, Zechariah second, then Jeiel, Shemiramoth,
16: 5 were to play the lyres and harps, **Asaph** was to sound the cymbals,
16: 7 That day David first committed to **Asaph** and his associates this
16: 37 David left **Asaph** and his associates before the ark of the covenant
25: 1 set apart some of the sons of **Asaph**, Heman and Jeduthun for the
25: 2 From the sons of **Asaph**: Zaccur, Joseph, Nethaniah and Asarelah.
25: 2 The sons of **Asaph** were under the supervision of Asaph,
25: 2 The sons of Asaph were under the supervision of **Asaph**,
25: 6 **Asaph**, Jeduthun and Heman were under the supervision of the
25: 9 The first lot, which was for **Asaph**, fell to Joseph, his sons
26: 1 Meshelemiah son of Kore, one of the sons of **Asaph**.

2Ch 5:12 **Asaph**, Heman, Jeduthun and their sons and relatives—stood on
20:14 of Jeiel, the son of Mattaniah, a Levite and descendant of **Asaph**,
29:13 from the descendants of **Asaph**, Zechariah and Mattaniah;
29:30 praise the LORD with the words of David and of **Asaph** the seer.
35:15 The musicians, the descendants of **Asaph**, were in the places
35:15 prescribed by David, **Asaph**, Heman and Jeduthun the king's seer.
Ezr 2:41 The singers: the descendants of **Asaph** 128
3:10 and with trumpets, and the Levites (the sons of **Asaph**)
Ne 2:8 And may I have a letter to **Asaph**, keeper of the king's forest,
7:44 The singers: the descendants of **Asaph** 148
11:17 Mattaniah son of Mica, the son of Zabdi, the son of **Asaph**,
11:22 Uzzi was one of **Asaph's** descendants, who were the singers
12:35 the son of Micaiah, the son of Zaccur, the son of **Asaph**,
12:46 For long ago, in the days of David and **Asaph**, there had been
Ps 50:T [50:1] A psalm of **Asaph**.
73:T [73:1] A psalm of **Asaph**.
74:T [74:1] A *maskil* of **Asaph**.
75:T [75:1] the tune of⌞ "Do Not Destroy." A psalm of **Asaph**. A song.
76:T [76:1] With stringed instruments. A psalm of **Asaph**. A song.
77:T [77:1] the director of music. For Jeduthun. Of **Asaph**. A psalm.
78:T [78:1] A *maskil* of **Asaph**.
79:T [79:1] A psalm of **Asaph**.
80:T [80:1] tune of⌞ "The Lilies of the Covenant." Of **Asaph**. A psalm.
81:T [81:1] the director of music. According to *gittith*. Of **Asaph**.
82:T [82:1] A psalm of **Asaph**.
83:T [83:1] A song. A psalm of **Asaph**.
Isa 36:3 the secretary, and Joah son of **Asaph** the recorder went out to him.
36:22 and Joah son of **Asaph** the recorder went to Hezekiah,

667 אָסֹף *'āsōp*, n.[m.]. [3] [√ 665]

storehouse [+1074] [1], storehouse [1], storerooms [1]

1Ch 26:15 and the lot for the **storehouse** [+1074] fell to his sons.
26:17 four a day on the south and two at a time at the **storehouse**.
Ne 12:25 Akkub were gatekeepers who guarded the **storerooms** *at* the gates.

668 אֹסֶף *'ōsep*, n.m. [3] [√ 665]

untranslated [1], gathers [1], harvest of fruit [1]

Isa 32:10 the grape harvest will fail, and the **harvest of fruit** will not come.
33:4 Your plunder, O nations, is harvested **[RPH]** as by young locusts;
Mic 7:1 I am like *one who* **gathers** summer fruit at the gleaning of the

669 אֲסֵפָה *'ᵃsēpâ*, n.f.vbl. [1] [√ 665]

be herded together [+665] [1]

Isa 24:22 *They will* **be herded together** [+665] like prisoners bound in a

670 אֲסֻפָּה *'ᵃsuppâ*, n.f. [1] [√ 665]

collected sayings [+1251] [1]

Ecc 12:11 their **collected** [+1251] **sayings** like firmly embedded nails—

671 אֲסַפְסֻף *'ᵃsapsup*, n.[m.]. [1] [√ 665]

rabble [1]

Nu 11:4 The **rabble** with them began to crave other food, and again the

672 אַסְפָּתָא *'aspātā'*, n.pr.m. [1]

Aspatha [1]

Est 9:7 They also killed Parshandatha, Dalphon, **Aspatha**,

673 אָסַר *'āsar*, v. [72] [→ 657, 659, 660, 661, 674, 4591, 4593, 4594?, 5035?, 5037?]

bound [9], obligated [4], obligates [4], *untranslated* [2], be tied [2], hitch up [2], prison [+1074] [2], prisoners [2], tie up [+673] [2], tie up [2], tied [2], ties securely [+673] [2], ties [2], are bound [1], be kept in prison [1], be tied up [1], been captured [1], bind [1], binding [1], captives [1], fetters [1], had made ready [1], harness [1], hitch [1], hitched up [1], hitched [1], instruct [1], is held captive [1], join in [1], made ready [1], obligate [1], obligation taken [1], prison [+1074+2021] [1], put in bonds [1], put in chains [1], put [1], start [1], stay [1], take prisoner [1], tether [1], tethered [1], was confined [1], went into [1], were bound [1], were confined [1], were held [1], were taken prisoner [1], wore [1]

Ge 39:20 [b] [where the king's **prisoners** [K; see Q 659] were confined.]
39:20 [B] the place where the king's prisoners **were confined**.
40:3 [B] of the guard, in the same prison where Joseph **was confined**.
40:5 [B] baker of the king of Egypt, who **were** *being* **held** in prison—
42:16 [C] the rest of you *will* **be kept in prison**, so that your words
42:19 [C] are honest men, *let* one of your brothers **stay** here in prison,
42:24 [A] had Simeon taken from them and **bound** before their eyes.
46:29 [A] Joseph *had* his chariot **made ready** and went to Goshen to
49:11 [A] *He will* **tether** his donkey to a vine, his colt to the choicest
Ex 14:6 [A] So *he* **had** his chariot **made ready** and took his army with
Nu 30:2 [30:3] [A] or takes an oath to **obligate** himself by a pledge,
30:3 [30:4] [A] vow to the LORD or **obligates** *herself* by a pledge
30:4 [30:5] [A] her vow or pledge **[RPH]** but says nothing to her,
30:4 [30:5] [A] every pledge by which *she* **obligated** herself will
30:5 [30:6] [A] pledges by which *she* **obligated** herself will stand;
30:6 [30:7] [A] utter a rash promise by which *she* **obligates** herself
30:7 [30:8] [A] pledges by which *she* **obligated** herself will stand.
30:8 [30:9] [A] or the rash promise by which *she* **obligates** herself,
30:9 [30:10] [A] "Any vow or **obligation taken** by a widow
30:10 [30:11] [A] a vow or **obligates** herself by a pledge under oath
30:11 [30:12] [A] pledges by which *she* **obligated** herself will stand.
Jdg 15:10 [A] "We have come to **take** Samson **prisoner**," they answered,
15:12 [A] "We've come to **tie** you **up** and hand you over to the
15:13 [A] "*We will* only **tie** [+673] you **up** and hand you over to them.
15:13 [A] "*We will* only **tie** you **up** [+673] and hand you over to them.
15:13 [A] So *they* **bound** him with two new ropes and led him up from
16:5 [A] can overpower him so *we may* **tie** him **up** and subdue him.
16:6 [C] great strength and how *you can* **be tied up** and subdued."
16:7 [A] "If *anyone* **ties** me with seven fresh thongs that have not
16:8 [A] thongs that had not been dried, and *she* **tied** him with them.
16:10 [C] you lied to me. Come now, tell me how *you can* **be tied**."
16:11 [A] "If *anyone* **ties** [+673] me **securely** with new ropes that have
16:11 [A] "If *anyone* **ties** me **securely** [+673] with new ropes that have
16:12 [A] So Delilah took new ropes and **tied** him with them. Then,
16:13 [C] Tell me how *you can* **be tied**." He replied, "If you weave the
16:21 [A] **Binding** him with bronze shackles, they set him to grinding
16:21 [B] they set him to grinding in the **prison** [+1074; K 659].
16:25 [B] So they called Samson out of the **prison** [+1074; K 659],
1Sa 6:7 [A] **Hitch** the cows to the cart, but take their calves away and pen
6:10 [A] They took two such cows and **hitched** them to the cart
2Sa 3:34 [B] Your hands **were** not **bound**, your feet were not fettered.
1Ki 18:44 [A] '**Hitch up** your chariot and go down before the rain stops
20:14 [A] commanders will do it.' " "And who *will* **start** the battle?"
2Ki 7:10 [B] only **tethered** horses and donkeys, and the tents left just as
7:10 [B] only tethered horses and **[RPH]** donkeys, and the tents left
9:21 [A] "**Hitch up** my chariot," Joram ordered. And when it was
9:21 [A] when *it was* **hitched up**, Joram king of Israel and Ahaziah
17:4 [A] Therefore Shalmaneser seized him and **put** him *in* prison.
23:33 [A] Pharaoh Neco **put** him **in chains** at Riblah in the land of
25:7 [A] **bound** him with bronze shackles and took him to Babylon.
2Ch 13:3 [A] Abijah **went into** battle with a force of four hundred
33:11 [A] **bound** him with bronze shackles and took him to Babylon.
36:6 [A] and **bound** him with bronze shackles to take him to Babylon.
Ne 4:18 [4:12] [B] each of the builders **wore** his sword at his side as he
Job 12:18 [A] put on by kings and **ties** a loincloth around their waist.
36:8 [B] if *men* **are bound** in chains, held fast by cords of affliction,
36:13 [A] even when *he* **fetters** them, they do not cry for help.
Ps 105:22 [A] to **instruct** his princes as he pleased and teach his elders
118:27 [A] **join in** the festal procession up to the horns of the altar.
146:7 [B] gives food to the hungry. The LORD sets **prisoners** free,
149:8 [A] to **bind** their kings with fetters, their nobles with shackles of
Ecc 4:14 [B] The youth may have come from **prison** [+1074+2021] to the
SS 7:5 [7:6] [B] royal tapestry; the king **is held captive** by its tresses.
Isa 22:3 [E] *they have* **been captured** without using the bow.
22:3 [E] All you who were caught **were taken prisoner** together,
49:9 [B] to say to the **captives**, 'Come out,' and to those in darkness,
61:1 [B] for the captives and release from darkness for the **prisoners**,
Jer 39:7 [A] and **bound** him with bronze shackles to take him to Babylon.
40:1 [B] He had found Jeremiah **bound** in chains among all the
46:4 [A] **Harness** the horses, mount the steeds! Take your positions
52:11 [A] **bound** him with bronze shackles and took him to Babylon,
Eze 3:25 [A] you *will be* **bound** so that you cannot go out among the
Hos 10:10 [A] nations will be gathered against them *to* **put** them **in bonds**

674 אִסָּר *'issār*, n.m. [11] [√ 673; Ar 10057]

pledge [6], pledges [5]

Nu 30:2 [30:3] or takes an oath to obligate himself by a **pledge**,
30:3 [30:4] a vow to the LORD or obligates herself by a **pledge**
30:4 [30:5] hears about her vow or **pledge** but says nothing to her,
30:4 [30:5] and every **pledge** by which she obligated herself will stand.
30:5 [30:6] or the **pledges** by which she obligated herself will stand;
30:7 [30:8] or the **pledges** by which she obligated herself will stand.
30:10 [30:11] makes a vow or obligates herself by a **pledge** under oath
30:11 [30:12] or the **pledges** by which she obligated herself will stand.
30:12 [30:13] of the vows or **pledges** that came from her lips will stand.
30:13 [30:14] any vow she makes or any sworn **pledge** to deny herself.
30:14 [30:15] he confirms all her vows or the **pledges** binding on her.

675 אֵסַר־חַדֹּן *'ēsar-ḥaddōn*, n.pr.m. [3]

Esarhaddon [3]

2Ki 19:37 land of Ararat. And **Esarhaddon** his son succeeded him as king.

Ezr 4: 2 have been sacrificing to him since the time of **Esarhaddon** king of
Isa 37:38 land of Ararat. And **Esarhaddon** his son succeeded him as king.

676 אֶסְתֵּר 'estēr, n.pr.f. [55]

Esther [42], Esther's [5], she^s [4], *untranslated* [2], her^s [1], who^s [1]

Est 2: 7 This girl, who was also known as **Esther**, was lovely in form
2: 8 **Esther** also was taken to the king's palace and entrusted to Hegai,
2:10 **Esther** had not revealed her nationality and family background,
2:11 forth near the courtyard of the harem to find out how **Esther** was
2:15 When the turn came for **Esther** (the girl Mordecai had adopted,
2:15 suggested. And **Esther** won the favor of everyone who saw her.
2:16 **She**^s was taken to King Xerxes in the royal residence in the tenth
2:17 Now the king was attracted to **Esther** more than to any of the other
2:18 a great banquet, **Esther's** banquet, for all his nobles and officials.
2:20 **Esther** had kept secret her family background and nationality just
2:20 for **she**^s continued to follow Mordecai's instructions as she had
2:22 But Mordecai found out about the plot and told Queen **Esther**,
2:22 and told Queen Esther, **who**^s in turn reported it to the king,
4: 4 When **Esther's** maids and eunuchs came and told her about
4: 5 **Esther** summoned Hathach, one of the king's eunuchs assigned to
4: 8 been published in Susa, to show to **Esther** and explain it to her,
4: 9 went back and reported to **Esther** what Mordecai had said.
4:10 Then **she**^s instructed him to say to Mordecai,
4:12 When **Esther's** words were reported to Mordecai,
4:13 **[RPH]** "Do not think that because you are in the king's house you
4:15 Then **Esther** sent this reply to Mordecai:
4:17 Mordecai went away and carried out all of **Esther's** instructions.
5: 1 On the third day **Esther** put on her royal robes and stood in the
5: 2 When he saw Queen **Esther** standing in the court, he was pleased
5: 2 and held out to **her**^s the gold scepter that was in his hand.
5: 2 his hand. So **Esther** approached and touched the tip of the scepter.
5: 3 the king asked, "What is it, Queen **Esther**? What is your request?
5: 4 the king," replied **Esther**, "let the king, together with Haman,
5: 5 at once," the king said, "so that we may do what **Esther** asks."
5: 5 So the king and Haman went to the banquet **Esther** had prepared.
5: 6 the king again asked **Esther**, "Now what is your petition?
5: 7 **Esther** replied, "My petition and my request is this:
5:12 "I'm the only person Queen **Esther** invited to accompany the king
6:14 and hurried Haman away to the banquet **Esther** had prepared.
7: 1 So the king and Haman went to dine with Queen **Esther**,
7: 2 the king again asked, **[RPH]** "Queen Esther, what is your
7: 2 the king again asked, "Queen **Esther**, what is your petition?
7: 3 Then Queen **Esther** answered, "If I have found favor with you,
7: 5 King Xerxes asked Queen **Esther**, "Who is he? Where is the man
7: 6 **Esther** said, "The adversary and enemy is this vile Haman."
7: 7 decided his fate, stayed behind to beg Queen **Esther** for his life.
7: 8 Haman was falling on the couch where **Esther** was reclining.
8: 1 That same day King Xerxes gave Queen **Esther** the estate of
8: 1 of the king, for **Esther** had told how he was related to her.
8: 2 it to Mordecai. And **Esther** appointed him over Haman's estate.
8: 3 **Esther** again pleaded with the king, falling at his feet and weeping.
8: 4 Then the king extended the gold scepter to **Esther** and she arose
8: 4 the gold scepter to Esther and **she**^s arose and stood before him.
8: 7 King Xerxes replied to Queen **Esther** and to Mordecai the Jew,
8: 7 Haman attacked the Jews, I have given his estate to **Esther**,
9:12 The king said to Queen **Esther**, "The Jews have killed
9:13 "If it pleases the king," **Esther** answered, "give the Jews in Susa
9:29 So Queen **Esther**, daughter of Abihail, along with Mordecai the
9:31 as Mordecai the Jew and Queen **Esther** had decreed for them,
9:32 **Esther's** decree confirmed these regulations about Purim,

677 ¹אַף 'ap¹, c. [134] [→ Ar 10059] See Select Index

untranslated [37], and [8], too [7], and [+2256] [6], even [6], how much less [+3954] [6], also [4], how much more [+3954] [4], how much more [4], how much worse [+3954] [3], no sooner [+1153] [3], surely [3], all [2], and also [2], how much more so [+3954] [2], now [2], then [2], too [+2256] [2], yes [2], also [+2256] [1], but also [1], but even [1], but now [1], even [+2256] [1], even [+2256+3954] [1], how much better [+3954] [1], how much less [+3954+4202] [1], how much more [+2256+3954] [1], how [1], if [1], in all this [1], indeed [+2256+3954] [1], indeed [1], moreover [1], no [1], nor [+401] [1], or [1], really [+3954] [1], really [+598] [1], really [1], rejoice greatly [+1635+1638] [1], though [1], till [+2256] [1], together with [+2256] [1], true [1], very [1], whether [1], yet [+2256] [1]

678 ²אַף 'ap², n.m. [276 / 277] [→ 648, 690, 691; cf. 647; Ar 10049]

anger [173], wrath [15], face [14], nostrils [12], angry [+3013] [11], nose [10], angry [4], faces [4], very angry [+3013] [4], patient [+800] [3], fury [2], noses [2], *untranslated* [1], anger [+3013] [1], angry [+3019] [1], before [+4200] [1], before [+928] [1], breath [1], brow [1], double [1], fell facedown [+2556+4200] [1], furious [+3013+4394] [1], gives patience [+799] [1], great rage [+3034] [1], hot-tempered [1], life breath [+8120] [1], long-suffering [+800] [1], not angry [+8740] [1], passion [1], patience [+802] [1], pride [+1470] [1], quick-tempered [+7920] [1], resentment [1], snout [1], which^s [+2257] [1]

Ge 2: 7 dust of the ground and breathed into his **nostrils** the breath of life,
3:19 By the sweat of your **brow** you will eat your food until you return
7:22 Everything on dry land that had the breath of life in its **nostrils**
19: 1 got up to meet them and bowed down with his **face** to the ground.
24:47 "Then I put the ring in her **nose** and the bracelets on her arms,
27:45 When your brother is no longer **angry** with you and forgets what
30: 2 Jacob *became* **angry** [+3013] with her and said, "Am I in the place
39:19 "This is how your slave treated me," he burned with **anger**.
42: 6 they bowed down to him with their **faces** to the ground.
44:18 *Do* not *be* **angry** [+3013] with your servant, though you are equal
48:12 from Israel's knees and bowed down with his **face** to the ground.
49: 6 for they have killed men in their **anger** and hamstrung oxen as they
49: 7 Cursed be their **anger**, so fierce, and their fury, so cruel! I will
Ex 4:14 Then the LORD's **anger** burned against Moses and he said,
11: 8 After that I will leave." Then Moses, hot with **anger**, left Pharaoh.
15: 8 By the blast of your **nostrils** the waters piled up. The surging
22:24 [22:23] My **anger** will be aroused, and I will kill you with the
32:10 Now leave me alone so that my **anger** may burn against them
32:11 he said, "why should your **anger** burn against your people,
32:12 Turn from your fierce **anger**; relent and do not bring disaster on
32:19 his **anger** burned and he threw the tablets out of his hands,
32:22 "*Do* not *be* **angry** [+3013], my lord," Aaron answered. "You know
34: 6 gracious God, slow to **anger**, abounding in love and faithfulness,
Nu 11: 1 of the LORD, and when he heard them his **anger** was aroused.
11:10 The LORD *became* exceedingly **angry** [+3013], and Moses was
11:20 until it comes out of your **nostrils** and you loathe it—
11:33 be consumed, the **anger** *of* the LORD burned against the people,
12: 9 The **anger** *of* the LORD burned against them, and he left them.
14:18 'The LORD is slow to **anger**, abounding in love and forgiving sin
22:22 God *was* **very angry** [+3013] when he went, and the angel of the
22:27 and he *was* **angry** [+3013] and beat her with his staff.
22:31 So he bowed low and **fell facedown** [+2556+4200].
24:10 Balak's **anger** burned against Balaam. He struck his hands
25: 3 the Baal of Peor. And the LORD's **anger** burned against them.
25: 4 so that the LORD's fierce **anger** may turn away from Israel."
32:10 The LORD's **anger** was aroused that day and he swore this oath:
32:13 The LORD's **anger** burned against Israel and he made them
32:14 and making the LORD even more **angry** [+3019] with Israel.
Dt 6:15 among you, is a jealous God and his **anger** will burn against you,
7: 4 the LORD's **anger** will burn against you and will quickly destroy
9:19 I feared the **anger** and wrath of the LORD, for he was angry
11:17 the LORD's **anger** will burn against you, and he will shut the
13:17 [13:18] so that the LORD will turn from his fierce **anger**;
29:20 [29:19] his **wrath** and zeal will burn against that man.
29:23 [29:22] which the LORD overthrew in fierce **anger**.
29:24 [29:23] done this to this land? Why this fierce, burning **anger**?"
29:27 [29:26] Therefore the LORD's **anger** burned against this land,
29:28 [29:27] In furious **anger** and in great wrath the LORD uprooted
31:17 On that day I *will become* **angry** [+3013] with them and forsake
32:22 For a fire has been kindled by my **wrath**, one that burns to the
33:10 He offers incense **before** [+928] you and whole burnt offerings on
Jos 7: 1 took some of them. So the LORD's **anger** burned against Israel.
7:26 remains to this day. Then the LORD turned from his fierce **anger**.
23:16 and bow down to them, the LORD's **anger** will burn against you,
Jdg 2:14 *In his* **anger** [+3013] against Israel the LORD handed them over
2:20 Therefore the LORD *was* **very angry** [+3013] with Israel
3: 8 The **anger** *of* the LORD burned against Israel so that he sold
6:39 Then Gideon said to God, "*Do* not *be* **angry** [+3013] with me.
9:30 heard what Gaal son of Ebed said, he *was* **very angry** [+3013].
10: 7 he *became* **angry** [+3013] with them. He sold them into the hands
14:19 the riddle. Burning with **anger**, he went up to his father's house.
1Sa 1: 5 But to Hannah he gave a **double** portion because he loved her,
11: 6 Spirit of God came upon him in power, and he burned with **anger**.
17:28 speaking with the men, he burned with **anger** at him and asked,
20:30 Saul's **anger** flared up at Jonathan and he said to him, "You son of
20:34 Jonathan got up from the table in fierce **anger**; on that second day
20:41 down before Jonathan three times, with his **face** to the ground.
24: 8 [24:9] and prostrated himself with his **face** to the ground.
25:23 bowed down **before** [+4200] David with her face to the ground.
25:41 She bowed down with her **face** to the ground and said, "Here is
28:14 he bowed down and prostrated himself with his **face** to the ground.
28:18 the LORD or carry out his fierce **wrath** against the Amalekites,
2Sa 6: 7 The LORD's **anger** burned against Uzzah because of his
12: 5 David burned with **anger** against the man and said to Nathan,
14: 4 she fell with her **face** to the ground to pay him honor, and she said,
14:33 and bowed down with his **face** to the ground before the king.
18:28 He bowed down before the king with his **face** to the ground
22: 9 Smoke rose from his **nostrils**; consuming fire came from his
22:16 the rebuke of the LORD, at the blast of breath from his **nostrils**.

2Sa 24: 1 Again the **anger** *of* the LORD burned against Israel, and he
24: 20 and bowed down before the king with his **face** to the ground.
1Ki 1: 23 So he went before the king and bowed with his **face** to the ground.
1: 31 Then Bathsheba bowed low with her **face** to the ground and,
2Ki 13: 3 So the LORD's **anger** burned against Israel, and for a long time
19: 28 I will put my hook in your **nose** and my bit in your mouth,
23: 26 the LORD did not turn away from the heat of his fierce **anger**,
23: 26 **which**[s] [+2257] burned against Judah because of all that Manasseh
24: 20 because of the LORD's **anger** that all this happened to Jerusalem
1Ch 13: 10 The LORD's **anger** burned against Uzzah, and he struck him
21: 21 and bowed down before David with his **face** to the ground.
2Ch 7: 3 they knelt on the pavement with their **faces** to the ground,
12: 12 the LORD's **anger** turned from him, and he was not totally
20: 18 Jehoshaphat bowed with his **face** to the ground, and all the people
25: 10 They *were* **furious** [+3013+4394] with Judah and left for home in
25: 10 were furious with Judah and left for home in a **great rage** [+3034].
25: 15 The **anger** *of* the LORD burned against Amaziah, and he sent a
28: 11 taken as prisoners, for the LORD's fierce **anger** rests on you."
28: 13 For our guilt is already great, and his fierce **anger** rests on Israel."
29: 10 the God of Israel, so that his fierce **anger** will turn away from us.
30: 8 your God, so that his fierce **anger** will turn away from you.
Ezr 8: 22 looks to him, but his great **anger** is against all who forsake him."
10: 14 until the fierce **anger** *of* our God in this matter is turned away from
Ne 8: 6 and worshiped the LORD with their **faces** to the ground.
9: 17 and compassionate, slow to **anger** and abounding in love.
Job 4: 9 of God they are destroyed; at the blast of his **anger** they perish.
9: 5 without their knowing it and overturns them in his **anger**.
9: 13 God does not restrain his **anger**; even the cohorts of Rahab
14: 13 hide me in the grave and conceal me till your **anger** has passed!
16: 9 God assails me and tears me in his **anger** and gnashes his teeth at
18: 4 You who tear yourself to pieces in your **anger**, is the earth to be
19: 11 His **anger** burns against me; he counts me among his enemies.
20: 23 God will vent his burning **anger** against him and rain down his
20: 28 will carry off his house, rushing waters on the day of God's **wrath**.
21: 17 does calamity come upon them, the fate God allots in his **anger**?
27: 3 as long as I have life within me, the breath of God in my **nostrils**,
32: 2 *became* **very angry** [+3013] with Job for justifying himself rather
32: 2 became very angry with Job **[RPH]** for justifying himself rather
32: 3 He *was* also **angry** [+3013] with the three friends, because they
32: 5 that the three men had nothing more to say, his **anger** was aroused.
35: 15 that his **anger** never punishes and he does not take the least notice
36: 13 "The godless in heart harbor **resentment**; even when he fetters
40: 11 Unleash the fury of your **wrath**, look at every proud man and bring
40: 24 anyone capture him by the eyes, or trap him and pierce his **nose**?
41: 2 [40:26] Can you put a cord through his **nose** or pierce his jaw
42: 7 the Temanite, "I *am* **angry** [+3013] with you and your two friends,
Ps 2: 5 Then he rebukes them in his **anger** and terrifies them in his wrath,
2: 12 be destroyed in your way, for his **wrath** can flare up in a moment.
6: 1 [6:2] do not rebuke me in your **anger** or discipline me in your
7: 6 [7:7] Arise, O LORD, in your **anger**; rise up against the rage of
10: 4 In his **pride** [+1470] the wicked does not seek him; in all his
18: 8 [18:9] Smoke rose from his **nostrils**; consuming fire came from
18: 15 [18:16] O LORD, at the blast of breath from your **nostrils**.
21: 9 [21:10] In his **wrath** the LORD will swallow them up, and his
27: 9 hide your face from me, do not turn your servant away in **anger**;
30: 5 [30:6] For his **anger** lasts only a moment, but his favor lasts a
37: 8 Refrain from **anger** and turn from wrath; do not fret—it leads only
55: 3 [55:4] down suffering upon me and revile me in their **anger**.
56: 7 [56:8] in your **anger**, O God, bring down the nations.
69: 24 [69:25] your wrath on them; let your fierce **anger** overtake them.
74: 1 Why does your **anger** smolder against the sheep of your pasture?
76: 7 [76:8] be feared. Who can stand before you when you are **angry**?
77: 9 [77:10] Has he in **anger** withheld his compassion?" *Selah*
78: 21 his fire broke out against Jacob, and his **wrath** rose against Israel,
78: 31 God's **anger** rose against them; he put to death the sturdiest among
78: 38 Time after time he restrained his **anger** and did not stir up his full
78: 49 He unleashed against them his hot **anger**, his wrath, indignation
78: 50 He prepared a path for his **anger**; he did not spare them from death
85: 3 [85:4] set aside all your wrath and turned from your fierce **anger**.
85: 5 [85:6] Will you prolong your **anger** through all generations?
86: 15 gracious God, slow to **anger**, abounding in love and faithfulness.
90: 7 We are consumed by your **anger** and terrified by your indignation.
90: 11 Who knows the power of your **anger**? For your wrath is as great as
95: 11 So I declared on oath in my **anger**, "They shall never enter my
103: 8 The LORD is compassionate and gracious, slow to **anger**,
106: 40 Therefore the LORD *was* **angry** [+3013] with his people
110: 5 is at your right hand; he will crush kings on the day of his **wrath**.
115: 6 they have ears, but cannot hear, **noses**, but they cannot smell;
124: 3 when their **anger** flared against us, they would have swallowed us
138: 7 you stretch out your hand against the **anger** *of* my foes, with your
145: 8 is gracious and compassionate, slow to **anger** and rich in love.
Pr 11: 22 Like a gold ring in a pig's **snout** is a beautiful woman who shows
14: 17 A **quick-tempered man** [+7920] does foolish things, and a crafty
14: 29 A **patient man** [+800] has great understanding, but a
15: 1 A gentle answer turns away wrath, but a harsh word stirs up **anger**.
15: 18 man stirs up dissension, but a **patient man** [+800] calms a quarrel.
16: 32 Better a **patient man** [+800] than a warrior, a man who controls
19: 11 A man's wisdom **gives** him **patience** [+799]; it is to his glory to
21: 14 A gift given in secret soothes **anger**, and a bribe concealed in the
22: 24 Do not make friends with a **hot-tempered** man, do not associate
24: 18 will see and disapprove and turn his **wrath** away from him.
25: 15 Through **patience** [+802] a ruler can be persuaded, and a gentle
27: 4 Anger is cruel and **fury** overwhelming, but who can stand before
29: 8 Mockers stir up a city, but wise men turn away **anger**.
29: 22 An **angry** man stirs up dissension, and a hot-tempered one
30: 33 as twisting the **nose** produces blood, so stirring up anger produces
30: 33 the nose produces blood, so stirring up **anger** produces strife."
SS 7: 4 [7:5] Your **nose** is like the tower of Lebanon looking toward
7: 8 [7:9] clusters of the vine, the fragrance of your **breath** like apples,
Isa 2: 22 Stop trusting in man, who has but a breath in his **nostrils**.
3: 21 the signet rings and **nose** rings,
5: 25 Therefore the LORD's **anger** burns against his people; his hand is
5: 25 Yet for all this, his **anger** is not turned away, his hand is still
7: 4 because of the fierce **anger** *of* Rezin and Aram and of the son of
9: 12 [9:11] Yet for all this, his **anger** is not turned away, his hand is
9: 17 [9:16] Yet for all this, his **anger** is not turned away, his hand is
9: 21 [9:20] Yet for all this, his **anger** is not turned away, his hand is
10: 4 Yet for all this, his **anger** is not turned away, his hand is still
10: 5 "Woe to the Assyrian, the rod of my **anger**, in whose hand is the
10: 25 you will end and my **wrath** will be directed to their destruction."
12: 1 with me, your **anger** has turned away and you have comforted me.
13: 3 I have summoned my warriors to carry out my **wrath**—those who
13: 9 a cruel day, with wrath and fierce **anger**—to make the land
13: 13 wrath of the LORD Almighty, in the day of his burning **anger**.
14: 6 and in **fury** subdued nations with relentless aggression.
30: 27 comes from afar, with burning **anger** and dense clouds of smoke;
30: 30 and will make them see his arm coming down with raging **anger**
37: 29 I will put my hook in your **nose** and my bit in your mouth,
42: 25 So he poured out on them his burning **anger**, the violence of war.
48: 9 For my own name's sake I delay my **wrath**; for the sake of my
49: 23 They will bow down before you with their **faces** to the ground;
63: 3 I trampled them in my **anger** and trod them down in my wrath;
63: 6 I trampled the nations in my **anger**; in my wrath I made them
65: 5 Such people are smoke in my **nostrils**, a fire that keeps burning all
66: 15 he will bring down his **anger** with fury, and his rebuke with flames
Jer 2: 35 you say, 'I am innocent; he *is* **not angry** [+8740] with me.'
4: 8 for the fierce **anger** *of* the LORD has not turned away from us.
4: 26 its towns lay in ruins before the LORD, before his fierce **anger**.
7: 20 My **anger** and my wrath will be poured out on this place, on man
10: 24 with justice—not in your **anger**, lest you reduce me to nothing.
12: 13 the shame of your harvest because of the LORD's fierce **anger**."
15: 14 for my **anger** will kindle a fire that will burn against you."
15: 15 You are **long-suffering** [+800]—do not take me away; think of
17: 4 for you have kindled my **anger**, and it will burn forever."
18: 23 overthrown before you; deal with them in the time of your **anger**.
21: 5 and a mighty arm in **anger** and fury and great wrath.
23: 20 The **anger** *of* the LORD will not turn back until he fully
25: 37 will be laid waste because of the fierce **anger** *of* the LORD.
25: 38 sword of the oppressor and because of the LORD's fierce **anger**.
30: 24 The fierce **anger** *of* the LORD will not turn back until he fully
32: 31 this city has so aroused my **anger** and wrath that I must remove it
32: 37 them from all the lands where I banish them in my furious **anger**
33: 5 be filled with the dead bodies of the men I will slay in my **anger**
36: 7 for the **anger** and wrath pronounced against this people by the
42: 18 'As my **anger** and wrath have been poured out on those who lived
44: 6 Therefore, my fierce **anger** was poured out; it raged against the
49: 37 disaster upon them, even my fierce **anger**," declares the LORD.
51: 45 Run for your lives! Run from the fierce **anger** *of* the LORD.
52: 3 because of the LORD's **anger** that all this happened to Jerusalem
La 1: 12 that the LORD brought on me in the day of his fierce **anger**?
2: 1 has covered the Daughter of Zion with the cloud of his **anger**!
2: 1 he has not remembered his footstool in the day of his **anger**.
2: 3 In fierce **anger** he has cut off every horn of Israel. He has
2: 6 in his fierce **anger** he has spurned both king and priest.
2: 21 You have slain them in the day of your **anger**; you have
2: 22 In the day of the LORD's **anger** no one escaped or survived;
3: 43 "You have covered yourself with **anger** and pursued us; you have
3: 66 Pursue them in **anger** and destroy them from under the heavens of
4: 11 has given full vent to his wrath; he has poured out his fierce **anger**.
4: 20 The LORD's anointed, our very **life breath** [+8120], was caught
Eze 5: 13 "Then my **anger** will cease and my wrath against them will
5: 15 the nations around you when I inflict punishment on you in **anger**
7: 3 The end is now upon you and I will unleash my **anger** against you.
7: 8 to pour out my wrath on you and spend my **anger** against you;
8: 17 me to anger? Look at them putting the branch to their **nose**!
13: 13 in my **anger** hailstones and torrents of rain will fall with
16: 12 I put a ring on your **nose**, earrings on your ears and a beautiful
20: 8 out my wrath on them and spend my **anger** against them in Egypt.

Eze 20:21 my wrath on them and spend my **anger** against them in the desert.
22:20 so will I gather you in my **anger** and my wrath and put you inside
23:25 They will cut off your **noses** and your ears, and those of you who
25:14 and they will deal with Edom in accordance with my **anger**
35:11 I will treat you in accordance with the **anger** and jealousy you
38:18 my hot **anger** will be aroused, declares the Sovereign LORD.
43: 8 by their detestable practices. So I destroyed them in my **anger**.
Da 9:16 turn away your **anger** and your wrath from Jerusalem, your city,
11:20 however, he will be destroyed, yet not in **anger** or in battle.
Hos 7: 6 Their **passion** [BHS 685] smolders all night; in the morning it
8: 5 out your calf-idol, O Samaria! My **anger** burns against them.
11: 9 I will not carry out my fierce **anger**, nor will I turn and devastate
13:11 So in my **anger** I gave you a king, and in my wrath I took him
14: 4 [14:5] love them freely, for my **anger** has turned away from them.
Joel 2:13 and compassionate, slow to **anger** and abounding in love,
Am 1:11 because his **anger** raged continually and his fury flamed
4:10 I filled your **nostrils** with the stench of your camps, yet you have
Jnh 3: 9 may yet relent and with compassion turn from his fierce **anger**
4: 2 and compassionate God, slow to **anger** and abounding in love,
Mic 5:15 [5:14] I will take vengeance in **anger** and wrath upon the nations
7:18 You do not stay **angry** forever but delight to show mercy.
Na 1: 3 The LORD is slow to **anger** and great in power; the LORD will
1: 6 Who can endure his fierce **anger**? His wrath is poured out like fire;
Hab 3: 8 with the rivers, O LORD? Was your **wrath** against the streams?
3:12 you strode through the earth and in **anger** you threshed the nations.
Zep 2: 2 like chaff, before the fierce **anger** *of* the LORD comes upon you,
2: 2 upon you, before the day of the LORD's **wrath** comes upon you.
2: 3 perhaps you will be sheltered on the day of the LORD's **anger**.
3: 8 and to pour out my wrath on them—all my fierce **anger**.
Zec 10: 3 "My **anger** burns against the shepherds, and I will punish the

679 אָפַד *'āpad*, v.den. [2] [→ 682]

fasten [1], fastened [1]

Ex 29: 5 [A] **Fasten** the ephod on him by its skillfully woven waistband.
Lev 8: 7 [A] by its skillfully woven waistband; so it *was* **fastened** on him.

680 [1]אֵפֹד *'ēpōd[1]*, n.m. [49] [→ 681?; cf. 679]

ephod [46], *untranslated* [2], it[s] [+2021] [1]

Ex 25: 7 and other gems to be mounted on the **ephod** and breastpiece.
28: 4 a breastpiece, an **ephod**, a robe, a woven tunic, a turban and a sash.
28: 6 "Make the **ephod** of gold, and of blue, purple and scarlet yarn,
28:12 fasten them on the shoulder pieces of the **ephod** as memorial
28:15 Make it like the **ephod**: of gold, and of blue, purple and scarlet
28:25 attaching them to the shoulder pieces of the **ephod** at the front.
28:26 corners of the breastpiece on the inside edge next to the **ephod**.
28:27 to the bottom of the shoulder pieces on the front of the **ephod**,
28:27 close to the seam just above the waistband of the **ephod**.
28:28 The rings of the breastpiece are to be tied to the rings of the **ephod**
28:28 **[RPH]** so that the breastpiece will not swing out from the ephod.
28:28 so that the breastpiece will not swing out from the **ephod**.
28:31 "Make the robe of the **ephod** entirely of blue cloth,
29: 5 the robe of the **ephod**, the ephod itself and the breastpiece.
29: 5 the robe of the ephod, the **ephod** itself and the breastpiece.
29: 5 Fasten the **ephod** on him by its skillfully woven waistband.
35: 9 and other gems to be mounted on the **ephod** and breastpiece.
35:27 and other gems to be mounted on the **ephod** and breastpiece.
39: 2 They made the **ephod** of gold, and of blue, purple and scarlet yarn,
39: 7 they fastened them on the shoulder pieces of the **ephod** as
39: 8 They made it like the **ephod**: of gold, and of blue, purple
39:18 attaching them to the shoulder pieces of the **ephod** at the front.
39:19 corners of the breastpiece on the inside edge next to the **ephod**.
39:20 to the bottom of the shoulder pieces on the front of the **ephod**,
39:20 close to the seam just above the waistband of the **ephod**.
39:21 They tied the rings of the breastpiece to the rings of the **ephod** with
39:21 **[RPH]** so that the breastpiece would not swing out from the
39:21 so that the breastpiece would not swing out from the **ephod**—
39:22 They made the robe of the **ephod** entirely of blue cloth—the work
Lev 8: 7 around him, clothed him with the robe and put the **ephod** on him.
8: 7 He also tied the **ephod** to him by its skillfully woven waistband;
Jdg 8:27 Gideon made the gold into an **ephod**, which he placed in Ophrah,
17: 5 he made an **ephod** and some idols and installed one of his sons as
18:14 "Do you know that one of these houses has an **ephod**, other
18:17 the **ephod**, the other household gods and the cast idol while the
18:18 the **ephod**, the other household gods and the cast idol, the priest
18:20 He took the **ephod**, the other household gods and the carved image
1Sa 2:18 was ministering before the LORD—a boy wearing a linen **ephod**.
2:28 to my altar, to burn incense, and to wear an **ephod** in my presence.
14: 3 among whom was Ahijah, who was wearing an **ephod**. He was a
21: 9 [21:10] of Elah, is here; it is wrapped in a cloth behind the **ephod**.
22:18 That day he killed eighty-five men who wore the linen **ephod**.
23: 6 (Now Abiathar son of Ahimelech had brought the **ephod** down
23: 9 against him, he said to Abiathar the priest, "Bring the **ephod**."
30: 7 Abiathar the priest, the son of Ahimelech, "Bring me the **ephod**."
30: 7 "Bring me the ephod." Abiathar brought **it**[s] [+2021] to him,
2Sa 6:14 David, wearing a linen **ephod**, danced before the LORD with all
1Ch 15:27 charge of the singing of the choirs. David also wore a linen **ephod**.
Hos 3: 4 or prince, without sacrifice or sacred stones, without **ephod** or idol.

681 [2]אֵפֹד *'ēpōd[2]*, n.pr.m. [1] [√ 680?; cf. 679]

Ephod [1]

Nu 34:23 Hanniel son of **Ephod**, the leader from the tribe of Manasseh son

682 אֲפֻדָּה *ᵃpuddâ*, n.f. [3] [√ 679]

skillfully woven [2], covered [1]

Ex 28: 8 Its **skillfully woven** waistband is to be like it—of one piece with
39: 5 Its **skillfully woven** waistband was like it—of one piece with the
Isa 30:22 your idols overlaid with silver and your images **covered** *with* gold;

683 אַפֶּדֶן *'appeden*, n.[m.]. [1]

royal [1]

Da 11:45 He will pitch his **royal** tents between the seas at the beautiful holy

684 אָפָה *'āpâ*, v. [13] [→ 685, 4418; cf. 9519?]

bake [5], baked [5], bakes [1], baking [1], be baked [1]

Ge 19: 3 [A] a meal for them, **baking** bread without yeast, and they ate.
Ex 12:39 [A] brought from Egypt, *they* **baked** cakes of unleavened bread.
16:23 [A] So **bake** what you want to bake and boil what you want to
16:23 [A] So bake what *you want to* **bake** and boil what you want to
Lev 6:17 [6:10] [C] *It must* not **be baked** *with* yeast; I have given it as
7: 9 [C] Every grain offering **baked** in an oven or cooked in a pan
23:17 [C] **baked** *with* yeast, as a wave offering of firstfruits to the
24: 5 [A] "Take fine flour and **bake** twelve loaves of bread,
26:26 [A] ten women *will be able to* **bake** your bread in one oven,
1Sa 28:24 [A] took some flour, kneaded it and **baked** bread without yeast.
Isa 44:15 [A] and warms himself, he kindles a fire and **bakes** bread.
44:19 [A] *I* even **baked** bread over its coals, I roasted meat and I ate.
Eze 46:20 [A] and the sin offering and **bake** the grain offering,

685 אֹפֶה *'ōpeh*, n.m. *or* v.ptcp. [12 / 11] [√ 684]

baker [8], bakers [2], baked goods [+4407+5126] [1]

Ge 40: 1 and the **baker** of the king of Egypt offended their master,
40: 2 with his two officials, the chief cupbearer and the chief **baker**,
40: 5 the cupbearer and the **baker** of the king of Egypt, who were being
40:16 When the chief **baker** saw that Joseph had given a favorable
40:17 In the top basket were all kinds of **baked** [+4407+5126] **goods** *for*
40:20 chief cupbearer and the chief **baker** in the presence of his officials:
40:22 he hanged the chief **baker**, just as Joseph had said to them in his
41:10 and the chief **baker** in the house of the captain of the guard.
1Sa 8:13 He will take your daughters to be perfumers and cooks and **bakers**.
Jer 37:21 given bread from the street of the **bakers** each day until all the
Hos 7: 4 burning like an oven whose fire the **baker** need not stir from the
7: 6 Their passion [BHS *baker*; NIV 678] smolders all night;

686 אֵפוֹא *'ēpô'*, pt. [15] [√ 361? + 7024?]

then [7], now [3], so [2], how [+928+4537] [1], oh [+4769+5989] [1], where [+180] [1]

Ge 27:33 Isaac trembled violently and said, "Who was it, **then**, that hunted
27:37 and new wine. **So** what can I possibly do for you, my son?"
43:11 Then their father Israel said to them, "If it must be, **then** do this:
Ex 33:16 **How** [+928+4537] will anyone know that you are pleased with me
Jdg 9:38 Zebul said to him, "Where is your big talk **now**, you who said,
2Ki 10:10 Know **then**, that not a word the LORD has spoken against the
Job 9:24 the wicked, he blindfolds its judges. If it is not he, **then** who is it?
17:15 where **then** is my hope? Who can see any hope for me?
19: 6 **then** know that God has wronged me and drawn his net around me.
19:23 "**Oh** [+4769+5989], that my words were recorded, that they were
24:25 "If this is not **so**, who can prove me false and reduce my words to
Pr 6: 3 **then** do this, my son, to free yourself, since you have fallen into
Isa 19:12 Where are your wise men **now**? Let them show you and make
22: 1 What troubles you **now**, that you have all gone up on the roofs,
Hos 13:10 **Where** [+180] is your king, that he may save you? Where are your

687 אֲפוּנָה *'āpûnâ*, n.f.?. Not used in NIV/BHS [√ 7041]

688 אֲפִיחַ *ᵃpîaḥ*, n.pr.m. [1]

Aphiah [1]

1Sa 9: 1 son of Zeror, the son of Becorath, the son of **Aphiah** *of* Benjamin.

689 אָפִיל *'āpîl*, a. [1] [√ 694]
ripen later [1]
Ex 9:32 and spelt, however, were not destroyed, because they **ripen later.**)

690 [1]אַפַּיִם *'appayim*[1], n.m. Not used in NIV/BHS [√ 691; cf. 678, 647]

691 [2]אַפַּיִם *'appayim*[2], n.pr.m. [2] [√ 690; cf. 678, 647]
Appaim [2]
1Ch 2:30 The sons of Nadab: Seled and **Appaim**. Seled died without
2:31 The son of **Appaim**: Ishi, who was the father of Sheshan.

692 [1]אָפִיק *'āpîq*[1], n.m. [18] [√ 706]
ravines [8], streams [4], valleys [2], channels [1], rows [1], streams [+5707] [1], tubes [1]
2Sa 22:16 The **valleys** *of* the sea were exposed and the foundations of the
Job 6:15 as intermittent streams, as the **streams** [+5707] that overflow
40:18 His bones are **tubes** *of* bronze, his limbs like rods of iron.
41:15 [41:7] His back has **rows** *of* shields tightly sealed together;
Ps 18:15 [18:16] The **valleys** *of* the sea were exposed and the foundations
42:1 [42:2] As the deer pants for **streams** *of* water, so my soul pants
126:4 Restore our fortunes, O LORD, like **streams** in the Negev.
SS 5:12 His eyes are like doves by the water **streams**, washed in milk,
Isa 8:7 his pomp. It will overflow all its **channels**, run over all its banks
Eze 6:3 LORD says to the mountains and hills, to the **ravines** and valleys:
31:12 the valleys; its branches lay broken in all the **ravines** *of* the land.
32:6 to the mountains, and the **ravines** will be filled with your flesh.
34:13 of Israel, in the **ravines** and in all the settlements in the land.
35:8 will fall on your hills and in your valleys and in all your **ravines**.
36:4 LORD says to the mountains and hills, to the **ravines** and valleys,
36:6 and say to the mountains and hills, to the **ravines** and valleys:
Joel 1:20 the **streams** *of* water have dried up and fire has devoured the open
3:18 [4:18] with milk; all the **ravines** *of* Judah will run with water.

693 [2]אָפִיק *'āpîq*[2], n.m. [1] [√ 706]
mighty [1]
Job 12:21 He pours contempt on nobles and disarms the **mighty**.

694 אֹפֶל *'ōpel*, n.m. [9] [→ 689, 695, 696, 4419?, 4420?]
darkness [4], thick darkness [2], deepest night [+4017+6547] [1], gloom [1], shadows [1]
Job 3:6 That night—may **thick darkness** seize it; may it not be included
10:22 to the land of **deepest night** [+4017+6547], of deep shadow
10:22 deep shadow and disorder, where even the light is like **darkness**."
23:17 by the darkness, by the **thick darkness** that covers my face.
28:3 he searches the farthest recesses for ore in the blackest **darkness**.
30:26 for good, evil came; when I looked for light, then came **darkness**.
Ps 11:2 they set their arrows against the strings to shoot from the **shadows**
91:6 nor the pestilence that stalks in the **darkness**, nor the plague that
Isa 29:18 and out of **gloom** and darkness the eyes of the blind will see.

695 אָפֵל *'āpēl*, a. [1] [√ 694]
pitch-dark [1]
Am 5:20 be darkness, not light—**pitch-dark**, without a ray of brightness?

696 אֲפֵלָה *'ªpēlâ*, n.f. [10] [√ 694]
gloom [2], dark [+413] [1], dark [1], darkness [1], deep darkness [1], deep shadows [1], night [1], total darkness [+3125] [1], utter darkness [1]
Ex 10:22 and **total darkness** [+3125] covered all Egypt for three days.
Dt 28:29 At midday you will grope about like a blind man in the **dark**.
Pr 4:19 the way of the wicked is like **deep darkness**; they do not know
7:9 as the day was fading, as the **dark** [+413] of night set in.
Isa 8:22 and fearful gloom, and they will be thrust into **utter darkness**.
58:10 rise in the darkness, and your **night** will become like the noonday.
59:9 but all is darkness; for brightness, but we walk in **deep shadows**.
Jer 23:12 they will be banished to **darkness** and there they will fall.
Joel 2:2 a day of darkness and **gloom**, a day of clouds and blackness.
Zep 1:15 a day of trouble and ruin, a day of darkness and **gloom**,

697 אֶפְלָל *'eplāl*, n.pr.m. [2] [√ 7136]
Ephlal [2]
1Ch 2:37 Zabad the father of **Ephlal**, Ephlal the father of Obed,
2:37 Zabad the father of Ephlal, **Ephlal** the father of Obed,

698 אֹפֶן *'ōpen*, n.[m.]. [1] [cf. 236?]
aptly [+6584] [1]
Pr 25:11 A word **aptly** [+6584] spoken is like apples of gold in settings of

699 אָפֵס *'āpēs*, v. [5] [→ 700, 702]
come to an end [1], gone [1], used up [1], vanish [1], vanished [1]
Ge 47:15 [A] should we die before your eyes? Our money *is* **used up**."
47:16 [A] in exchange for your livestock, since your money *is* **gone**."
Ps 77:8 [77:9] [A] *Has* his unfailing love **vanished** forever? Has his
Isa 16:4 [A] The oppressor *will* **come to an end**, and destruction will
29:20 [A] The ruthless *will* **vanish**, the mockers will disappear, and all

700 אֶפֶס *'epes*, n.m. [43] [√ 699]
ends [14], no [5], none [5], without [+928] [3], but [+3954] [2], not [2], only [2], amount to nothing [1], but [1], however [+3954] [1], lately [+928] [1], nothing at all [+401+2256] [1], nothing [1], or [+2256] [1], vanish away [1], whether [+2256] [1], yet [+3954] [1]
Nu 13:28 **But** [+3954] the people who live there are powerful, and the cities
22:35 said to Balaam, "Go with the men, but speak **only** what I tell you."
23:13 you can see them; you will see **only** a part but not all of them.
Dt 15:4 **However** [+3954], there should be no poor among you, for in the
32:36 his servants when he sees their strength is gone and **no** one is left,
33:17 them he will gore the nations, even those at the **ends** *of* the earth.
Jdg 4:9 **But** [+3954] because of the way you are going about this,
1Sa 2:10 them from heaven; the LORD will judge the **ends** *of* the earth.
2Sa 9:3 "Is there **no** one still left of the house of Saul to whom I can show
12:14 **But** because by doing this you have made the enemies of the
2Ki 14:26 LORD had seen how bitterly everyone in Israel, **whether** [+2256]
14:26 everyone in Israel, whether slave **or** [+2256] free, was suffering;
Job 7:6 a weaver's shuttle, and they come to an end **without** [+928] hope.
Ps 2:8 the nations your inheritance, the **ends** *of* the earth your possession.
22:27 [22:28] All the **ends** *of* the earth will remember and turn to the
59:13 [59:14] it will be known to the **ends** *of* the earth that God rules
67:7 [67:8] will bless us, and all the **ends** *of* the earth will fear him.
72:8 rule from sea to sea and from the River to the **ends** *of* the earth.
98:3 all the **ends** *of* the earth have seen the salvation of our God.
Pr 14:28 is a king's glory, but **without** [+928] subjects a prince is ruined.
26:20 **Without** [+928] wood a fire goes out; without gossip a quarrel dies
30:4 Who has established all the **ends** *of* the earth? What is his name,
Isa 5:8 join field to field till **no** space is left and you live alone in the land.
34:12 there to be called a kingdom, all her princes will **vanish away**.
40:17 they are regarded by him as worthless and less than **nothing**.
41:12 who wage war against you will be as **nothing at all** [+401+2256].
41:29 Their deeds **amount to nothing**; their images are but wind
45:6 to the place of its setting men may know there is **none** besides me.
45:14 God is with you, and there is no other; there is **no** other god.' "
45:22 "Turn to me and be saved, all you **ends** *of* the earth; for I am God,
46:9 and there is no other; I am God, and there is **none** like me.
47:8 and saying to yourself, 'I am, and there is **none** besides me.
47:10 you when you say to yourself, 'I am, and there is **none** besides me.'
52:4 "At first my people went down to Egypt to live; **lately** [+928],
52:10 and all the **ends** *of* the earth will see the salvation of our God.
54:15 If anyone does attack you, it will **not** be my doing; whoever attacks
Jer 16:19 to you the nations will come from the **ends** *of* the earth and say,
Da 8:25 of princes. Yet he will be destroyed, but **not** by human power.
Am 6:10 "Is anyone with you?" and he says, "**No**," then he will say, "Hush!
9:8 **yet** [+3954] I will not totally destroy the house of Jacob,"
Mic 5:4 [5:3] for then his greatness will reach to the **ends** *of* the earth.
Zep 2:15 She said to herself, "I am, and there is **none** besides me." What a
Zec 9:10 extend from sea to sea and from the River to the **ends** *of* the earth.

701 אֹפֶס *'ōpes*, n.[m.]. [1] [cf. 7168]
ankle-deep [1]
Eze 47:3 and then led me through water that was **ankle-deep**.

702 אֶפֶס דַּמִּים *'epes dammîm*, n.pr.loc. [1] [√ 699 + 1956]
Ephes Dammim [1]
1Sa 17:1 They pitched camp at **Ephes Dammim**, between Socoh

703 אֶפַע *'epa'*, n. *or* a. [1]
worthless [1]
Isa 41:24 you are less than nothing and your works are utterly **worthless**;

704 אֶפְעֶה *'ep'eh*, n.[m.]. [3] [√ 7184?]
adder [2], adders [1]
Job 20:16 suck the poison of serpents; the fangs of an **adder** will kill him.
Isa 30:6 and distress, of lions and lionesses, of **adders** and darting snakes,
59:5 their eggs will die, and when one is broken, an **adder** is hatched.

705 אָפַף *'āpap*, v. [5]

entangled [2], engulfing [1], surround [1], swirled about [1]

2Sa 22: 5 [A] "The waves of death **swirled about** me; the torrents of
Ps 18: 4 [18:5] [A] The cords of death **entangled** me; the torrents of
40: 12 [40:13] [A] For troubles without number **surround** me; my sins
116: 3 [A] The cords of death **entangled** me, the anguish of the grave
Jnh 2: 5 [2:6] [A] The **engulfing** waters threatened me, the deep

706 אָפַק *'āpaq*, v. [7] [→ 692, 693]

are withheld [1], control himself [1], controlling himself [1], felt compelled [1], held myself back [1], hold yourself back [1], restrained himself [1]

Ge 43: 31 [F] he came out and, **controlling himself**, said, "Serve the food."
45: 1 [F] Joseph could no longer **control himself** before all his
1Sa 13: 12 [F] So *I* **felt compelled** to offer the burnt offering."
Est 5: 10 [F] Nevertheless, Haman **restrained himself** and went home.
Isa 42: 14 [F] I have kept silent, I have been quiet and **held myself back**.
63: 15 [F] Your tenderness and compassion **are withheld** from us.
64: 12 [64:11] [F] all this, O LORD, *will you* **hold yourself back**?

707 אֲפֵק *'ᵃpēq*, n.pr.loc. [9] [→ 708]

Aphek [9]

Jos 12: 18 the king of **Aphek** one the king of Lasharon one
13: 4 from Arah of the Sidonians as far as **Aphek**, the region of the
19: 30 Ummah, **Aphek** and Rehob. There were twenty-two towns
Jdg 1: 31 or Sidon or Ahlab or Aczib or Helbah or **Aphek** or Rehob,
1Sa 4: 1 The Israelites camped at Ebenezer, and the Philistines at **Aphek**.
29: 1 The Philistines gathered all their forces at **Aphek**, and Israel
1Ki 20: 26 the Arameans and went up to **Aphek** to fight against Israel.
20: 30 The rest of them escaped to the city of **Aphek**, where the wall
2Ki 13: 17 "You will completely destroy the Arameans at **Aphek**."

708 אֲפֵקָה *'ᵃpēqâ*, n.pr.loc. [1] [√ 707]

Aphekah [1]

Jos 15: 53 Janim, Beth Tappuah, **Aphekah**,

709 אֵפֶר *'ēper*, n.[m.]. [22] [→ 234, 235]

ashes [20], dust [2]

Ge 18: 27 as to speak to the Lord, though I am nothing but dust and **ashes**,
Nu 19: 9 "A man who is clean shall gather up the **ashes** *of* the heifer
19: 10 The man who gathers up the **ashes** *of* the heifer must also wash his
2Sa 13: 19 Tamar put **ashes** on her head and tore the ornamented robe she was
Est 4: 1 he tore his clothes, put on sackcloth and **ashes**, and went out into
4: 3 weeping and wailing. Many lay in sackcloth and **ashes**.
Job 2: 8 and scraped himself with it as he sat among the **ashes**.
13: 12 Your maxims are proverbs of **ashes**; your defenses are defenses of
30: 19 He throws me into the mud, and I am reduced to dust and **ashes**.
42: 6 Therefore I despise myself and repent in dust and **ashes**."
Ps 102: 9 [102:10] For I eat **ashes** as my food and mingle my drink with
147: 16 He spreads the snow like wool and scatters the frost like **ashes**.
Isa 44: 20 He feeds on **ashes**, a deluded heart misleads him; he cannot save
58: 5 one's head like a reed and for lying on sackcloth and **ashes**?
61: 3 to bestow on them a crown of beauty instead of **ashes**, the oil of
Jer 6: 26 O my people, put on sackcloth and roll in **ashes**; mourn with bitter
La 3: 16 has broken my teeth with gravel; he has trampled me in the **dust**.
Eze 27: 30 over you; they will sprinkle dust on their heads and roll in **ashes**.
28: 18 I reduced you to **ashes** on the ground in the sight of all who were
Da 9: 3 him in prayer and petition, in fasting, and in sackcloth and **ashes**.
Jnh 3: 6 covered himself with sackcloth and sat down in the **dust**.
Mal 4: 3 [3:21] they will be **ashes** under the soles of your feet on the day

710 אֲפֵר *'ᵃpēr*, n.[m.]. [2]

headband [2]

1Ki 20: 38 He disguised himself with his **headband** down over his eyes.
20: 41 Then the prophet quickly removed the **headband** from his eyes,

711 אֶפְרֹחַ *'eprōaḥ*, n.m. [4] [√ 7256]

young [2], *untranslated* [1], young ones [1]

Dt 22: 6 **[RPH]** and the mother is sitting on the young or on the eggs,
22: 6 the ground, and the mother is sitting on the **young** or on the eggs,
Job 39: 30 His **young ones** feast on blood, and where the slain are, there is
Ps 84: 3 [84:4] a nest for herself, where she may have her **young**—

712 אַפִּרְיוֹן *'appiryôn*, n.[m.]. [1]

carriage [1]

SS 3: 9 King Solomon made for himself the **carriage**; he made it of wood

713 אֶפְרַיִם *'eprayim*, n.pr.m. [180] [√ 7238?]

Ephraim [148], Ephraim's [12], Ephraim [+1201] [6], Ephraimites [+1201] [4], Ephraim [+824] [2], Ephraimite [+1201] [2], Ephraimites [2], *untranslated* [1], Ephraimite [1], Ephraimites [+408] [1], Ephraimites [+4946] [1]

Ge 41: 52 The second son he named **Ephraim** and said, "It is because God
46: 20 **Ephraim** were born to Joseph by Asenath daughter of Potiphera,
48: 1 So he took his two sons Manasseh and **Ephraim** along with him.
48: 5 **Ephraim** and Manasseh will be mine, just as Reuben and Simeon
48: 13 **Ephraim** on his right toward Israel's left hand and Manasseh on
48: 14 But Israel reached out his right hand and put it on **Ephraim's** head,
48: 17 When Joseph saw his father placing his right hand on **Ephraim's**
48: 17 so he took hold of his father's hand to move it from **Ephraim's**
48: 20 'May God make you like **Ephraim** and Manasseh.' " So he put
48: 20 and Manasseh.' " So he put **Ephraim** ahead of Manasseh.
50: 23 saw the third generation of **Ephraim's** children. Also the children
Nu 1: 10 from **Ephraim**, Elishama son of Ammihud; from Manasseh,
1: 32 From the sons of Joseph: From the descendants of **Ephraim**:
1: 33 The number from the tribe of **Ephraim** was 40,500.
2: 18 On the west will be the divisions of the camp of **Ephraim** under
2: 18 The leader of the people of **Ephraim** is Elishama son of
2: 24 All the men assigned to the camp of **Ephraim**, according to their
7: 48 the leader of the people of **Ephraim**, brought his offering.
10: 22 The divisions of the camp of **Ephraim** [+1201] went next,
13: 8 from the tribe of **Ephraim**, Hoshea son of Nun;
26: 28 of Joseph by their clans through Manasseh and **Ephraim** were:
26: 35 These were the descendants of **Ephraim** by their clans:
26: 37 These were the clans of **Ephraim** [+1201]; those numbered were
34: 24 the leader from the tribe of **Ephraim** [+1201] son of Joseph;
Dt 33: 17 Such are the ten thousands of **Ephraim**; such are the thousands of
34: 2 all of Naphtali, the territory of **Ephraim** and Manasseh, all the
Jos 14: 4 sons of Joseph had become two tribes—Manasseh and **Ephraim**.
16: 4 So Manasseh and **Ephraim**, the descendants of Joseph,
16: 5 This was the territory of **Ephraim** [+1201], clan by clan: The
16: 8 This was the inheritance of the tribe of the **Ephraimites** [+1201],
16: 9 their villages that were set aside for the **Ephraimites** [+1201]
16: 10 to this day the Canaanites live among the people of **Ephraim**
17: 8 the boundary of Manasseh, belonged to the **Ephraimites** [+1201].)
17: 9 There were towns belonging to **Ephraim** lying among the towns of
17: 10 On the south the land belonged to **Ephraim**, on the north to
17: 15 "and if the hill country of **Ephraim** is too small for you,
17: 17 to **Ephraim** and Manasseh—"You are numerous and very
19: 50 town he asked for—Timnath Serah in the hill country of **Ephraim**.
20: 7 Shechem in the hill country of **Ephraim**, and Kiriath Arba (that is,
21: 5 were allotted ten towns from the clans of the tribes of **Ephraim**,
21: 20 of the Levites were allotted towns from the tribe of **Ephraim**:
21: 21 In the hill country of **Ephraim** they were given Shechem (a city of
24: 30 at Timnath Serah in the hill country of **Ephraim**, north of Mount
24: 33 been allotted to his son Phinehas in the hill country of **Ephraim**.
Jdg 1: 29 Nor did **Ephraim** drive out the Canaanites living in Gezer,
2: 9 at Timnath Heres in the hill country of **Ephraim**, north of Mount
3: 27 he arrived there, he blew a trumpet in the hill country of **Ephraim**,
4: 5 between Ramah and Bethel in the hill country of **Ephraim**,
5: 14 Some came from **Ephraim**, whose roots were in Amalek;
7: 24 Gideon sent messengers throughout the hill country of **Ephraim**,
7: 24 So all the men of **Ephraim** were called out and they took the
8: 1 Now the **Ephraimites** [+408] asked Gideon, "Why have you
8: 2 Aren't the gleanings of **Ephraim's** grapes better than the full grape
10: 1 to save Israel. He lived in Shamir, in the hill country of **Ephraim**.
10: 9 to fight against Judah, Benjamin and the house of **Ephraim**;
12: 1 The men of **Ephraim** called out their forces, crossed over to
12: 4 called together the men of Gilead and fought against **Ephraim**.
12: 4 Gileadites struck them down because the **Ephraimites** had said,
12: 4 "You Gileadites are renegades from **Ephraim** and Manasseh."
12: 4 Gileadites are renegades from Ephraim **[RPH]** and Manasseh."
12: 5 Gileadites captured the fords of the Jordan leading to **Ephraim**,
12: 5 and whenever a survivor of **Ephraim** said, "Let me cross over,"
12: 6 Forty-two thousand **Ephraimites** [+4946] were killed at that time.
12: 15 son of Hillel died, and was buried at Pirathon in **Ephraim** [+824],
17: 1 Now a man named Micah from the hill country of **Ephraim**
17: 8 his way he came to Micah's house in the hill country of **Ephraim**.
18: 2 The men entered the hill country of **Ephraim** and came to the
18: 13 From there they went on to the hill country of **Ephraim** and came
19: 1 country of **Ephraim** took a concubine from Bethlehem in Judah.
19: 16 That evening an old man from the hill country of **Ephraim**,
19: 18 Judah to a remote area in the hill country of **Ephraim** where I live.
1Sa 1: 1 a Zuphite from the hill country of **Ephraim**, whose name was
9: 4 So he passed through the hill country of **Ephraim** and through the
14: 22 hill country of **Ephraim** heard that the Philistines were on the run,
2Sa 2: 9 and Jezreel, and also over **Ephraim**, Benjamin and all Israel.
13: 23 sheepshearers were at Baal Hazor near the border of **Ephraim**,
18: 6 to fight Israel, and the battle took place in the forest of **Ephraim**.
20: 21 man named Sheba son of Bicri, from the hill country of **Ephraim**,

1Ki 4: 8 These are their names: Ben-Hur—in the hill country of **Ephraim**;
12: 25 Then Jeroboam fortified Shechem in the hill country of **Ephraim**
2Ki 5: 22 prophets have just come to me from the hill country of **Ephraim**.
14: 13 broke down the wall of Jerusalem from the **Ephraim** Gate to the
1Ch 6: 66 [6:51] given as their territory towns from the tribe of **Ephraim**.
6: 67 [6:52] In the hill country of **Ephraim** they were given Shechem
7: 20 The descendants of **Ephraim**: Shuthelah, Bered his son, Tahath his
7: 22 Their father **Ephraim** mourned for them many days, and his
9: 3 from **Ephraim** [+1201] and Manasseh who lived in Jerusalem
12: 30 [12:31] men of **Ephraim**, brave warriors, famous in their own
27: 10 seventh month, was Helez the Pelonite, an **Ephraimite** [+1201].
27: 14 was Benaiah the Pirathonite, an **Ephraimite** [+1201].
27: 20 over the **Ephraimites** [+1201]: Hoshea son of Azaziah; over half
2Ch 13: 4 in the hill country of **Ephraim**, and said, "Jeroboam and all Israel,
15: 8 and from the towns he had captured in the hills of **Ephraim**.
15: 9 assembled all Judah and Benjamin and the people from **Ephraim**,
17: 2 and in the towns of **Ephraim** that his father Asa had captured.
19: 4 among the people from Beersheba to the hill country of **Ephraim**
25: 7 is not with Israel—not with any of the people of **Ephraim**.
25: 10 dismissed the troops who had come to him from **Ephraim**
25: 23 broke down the wall of Jerusalem from the **Ephraim** Gate to the
28: 7 Zicri, an **Ephraimite** warrior, killed Maaseiah the king's son,
28: 12 some of the leaders in **Ephraim** [+1201]—Azariah son of
30: 1 and Judah and also wrote letters to **Ephraim** and Manasseh,
30: 10 The couriers went from town to town in **Ephraim** [+824]
30: 18 Although most of the many people who came from **Ephraim**,
31: 1 throughout Judah and Benjamin and in **Ephraim** and Manasseh.
34: 6 the towns of Manasseh, **Ephraim** and Simeon, as far as Naphtali,
34: 9 **Ephraim** and the entire remnant of Israel and from all the people
Ne 8: 16 the square by the Water Gate and the one by the Gate of **Ephraim**.
12: 39 over the Gate of **Ephraim**, the Jeshanah Gate, the Fish Gate,
Ps 60: 7 [60:9] is mine; **Ephraim** is my helmet, Judah my scepter.
78: 9 The men of **Ephraim**, though armed with bows, turned back on the
78: 67 the tents of Joseph, he did not choose the tribe of **Ephraim**;
80: 2 [80:3] before **Ephraim**, Benjamin and Manasseh. Awaken your
108: 8 [108:9] is mine; **Ephraim** is my helmet, Judah my scepter.
Isa 7: 2 house of David was told, "Aram has allied itself with **Ephraim**";
7: 5 Aram, **Ephraim** and Remaliah's son have plotted your ruin,
7: 8 Within sixty-five years **Ephraim** will be too shattered to be a
7: 9 The head of **Ephraim** is Samaria, and the head of Samaria is only
7: 17 on the house of your father a time unlike any since **Ephraim** broke
9: 9 [9:8] **Ephraim** and the inhabitants of Samaria—who say with
9: 21 [9:20] Manasseh will feed on **Ephraim**, and Ephraim on
9: 21 [9:20] will feed on Ephraim, and **Ephraim** on Manasseh;
11: 13 **Ephraim's** jealousy will vanish, and Judah's enemies will be cut
11: 13 **Ephraim** will not be jealous of Judah, nor Judah hostile toward
11: 13 will not be jealous of Judah, nor Judah hostile toward **Ephraim**.
17: 3 The fortified city will disappear from **Ephraim**, and royal power
28: 1 Woe to that wreath, the pride of **Ephraim's** drunkards, to the
28: 3 That wreath, the pride of **Ephraim's** drunkards, will be trampled
Jer 4: 15 from Dan, proclaiming disaster from the hills of **Ephraim**.
7: 15 just as I did all your brothers, the people of **Ephraim**.'
31: 6 will be a day when watchmen cry out on the hills of **Ephraim**,
31: 9 because I am Israel's father, and **Ephraim** is my firstborn son.
31: 18 "I have surely heard **Ephraim's** moaning: 'You disciplined me like
31: 20 Is not **Ephraim** my dear son, the child in whom I delight?
50: 19 his appetite will be satisfied on the hills of **Ephraim** and Gilead.
Eze 37: 16 write on it, '**Ephraim's** stick, belonging to Joseph and all the house
37: 19 going to take the stick of Joseph—which is in **Ephraim's** hand—
48: 5 "**Ephraim** will have one portion; it will border the territory of
48: 6 it will border the territory of **Ephraim** from east to west.
Hos 4: 17 **Ephraim** is joined to idols; leave him alone!
5: 3 I know all about **Ephraim**; Israel is not hidden from me. Ephraim,
5: 3 **Ephraim**, you have now turned to prostitution; Israel is corrupt.
5: 5 the Israelites, even **Ephraim**, stumble in their sin; Judah also
5: 9 **Ephraim** will be laid waste on the day of reckoning.
5: 11 **Ephraim** is oppressed, trampled in judgment, intent on pursuing
5: 12 I am like a moth to **Ephraim**, like rot to the people of Judah.
5: 13 "When **Ephraim** saw his sickness, and Judah his sores,
5: 13 his sickness, and Judah his sores, then **Ephraim** turned to Assyria,
5: 14 For I will be like a lion to **Ephraim**, like a great lion to Judah.
6: 4 "What can I do with you, **Ephraim**? What can I do with you,
6: 10 There **Ephraim** is given to prostitution and Israel is defiled.
7: 1 the sins of **Ephraim** are exposed and the crimes of Samaria
7: 8 "**Ephraim** mixes with the nations; Ephraim is a flat cake not
7: 8 mixes with the nations; **Ephraim** is a flat cake not turned over.
7: 11 "**Ephraim** is like a dove, easily deceived and senseless—
8: 9 wild donkey wandering alone. **Ephraim** has sold herself to lovers.
8: 11 "Though **Ephraim** built many altars for sin offerings, these have
9: 3 **Ephraim** will return to Egypt and eat unclean food in Assyria.
9: 8 The prophet, along with my God, is the watchman over **Ephraim**,
9: 11 **Ephraim's** glory will fly away like a bird—no birth, no
9: 13 I have seen **Ephraim**, like Tyre, planted in a pleasant place.
9: 13 But **Ephraim** will bring out their children to the slayer."
9: 16 **Ephraim** is blighted, their root is withered, they yield no fruit.
10: 6 **Ephraim** will be disgraced; Israel will be ashamed of its wooden
10: 11 **Ephraim** is a trained heifer that loves to thresh; so I will put a
10: 11 I will drive **Ephraim**, Judah must plow, and Jacob must break up
11: 3 It was I who taught **Ephraim** to walk, taking them by the arms;
11: 8 "How can I give you up, **Ephraim**? How can I hand you over,
11: 9 carry out my fierce anger, nor will I turn and devastate **Ephraim**.
11: 12 [12:1] **Ephraim** has surrounded me with lies, the house of Israel
12: 1 [12:2] **Ephraim** feeds on the wind; he pursues the east wind all
12: 8 [12:9] **Ephraim** boasts, "I am very rich; I have become wealthy.
12: 14 [12:15] **Ephraim** has bitterly provoked him to anger; his Lord
13: 1 When **Ephraim** spoke, men trembled; he was exalted in Israel.
13: 12 The guilt of **Ephraim** is stored up, his sins are kept on record.
14: 8 [14:9] O **Ephraim**, what more have I to do with idols? I will
Ob 1: 19 They will occupy the fields of **Ephraim** and Samaria,
Zec 9: 10 I will take away the chariots from **Ephraim** and the war-horses
9: 13 I will bend Judah as I bend my bow and fill it with **Ephraim**.
10: 7 The **Ephraimites** will become like mighty men, and their hearts

714 אֶפְרָת[1] *'eprāt[1]*, n.pr.loc. [4] [→ 715, 716, 717, 718]

Ephrath [4]

Ge 35: 16 While they were still some distance from **Ephrath**, Rachel began
35: 19 So Rachel died and was buried on the way to **Ephrath** (that is,
48: 7 while we were still on the way, a little distance from **Ephrath**.
48: 7 So I buried her there beside the road to **Ephrath**" (that is,

715 אֶפְרָת[2] *'eprāt[2]*, n.pr.f. [1] [√ 714]

Ephrath [1]

1Ch 2: 19 When Azubah died, Caleb married **Ephrath**, who bore him Hur.

716 אֶפְרָתָה[1] *'eprātâ[1]*, n.pr.loc. [3] [→ 3980; cf. 714]

Ephrathah [3]

Ru 4: 11 May you have standing in **Ephrathah** and be famous in
Ps 132: 6 We heard it in **Ephrathah**, we came upon it in the fields of Jaar:
Mic 5: 2 [5:1] "But you, Bethlehem **Ephrathah**, though you are small

717 אֶפְרָתָה[2] *'eprātâ[2]*, n.pr.f. [2] [√ 714]

Ephrathah [2]

1Ch 2: 50 The sons of Hur the firstborn of **Ephrathah**: Shobal the father of
4: 4 of Hur, the firstborn of **Ephrathah** and father of Bethlehem.

718 אֶפְרָתִי *'eprātî*, a.g. [5] [√ 714]

Ephraimite [3], Ephrathite [1], Ephrathites [1]

Jdg 12: 5 the men of Gilead asked him, "Are you an **Ephraimite**?"
Ru 1: 2 and Kilion. They were **Ephrathites** from Bethlehem, Judah.
1Sa 1: 1 the son of Elihu, the son of Tohu, the son of Zuph, an **Ephraimite**.
17: 12 Now David was the son of an **Ephrathite** named Jesse, who was
1Ki 11: 26 He was one of Solomon's officials, an **Ephraimite** from Zeredah,

719 אֶצְבֹּן *'eṣbōn*, n.pr.m. [2]

Ezbon [2]

Ge 46: 16 sons of Gad: Zephon, Haggi, Shuni, **Ezbon**, Eri, Arodi and Areli.
1Ch 7: 7 **Ezbon**, Uzzi, Uzziel, Jerimoth and Iri, heads of families—

720 אֶצְבַּע *'eṣba'*, n.f. [31] [→ Ar 10064]

finger [17], fingers [11], forefinger [2], toes [1]

Ex 8: 19 [8:15] magicians said to Pharaoh, "This is the **finger** *of* God."
29: 12 bull's blood and put it on the horns of the altar with your **finger**,
31: 18 the Testimony, the tablets of stone inscribed by the **finger** *of* God.
Lev 4: 6 He is to dip his **finger** into the blood and sprinkle some of it seven
4: 17 He shall dip his **finger** into the blood and sprinkle it before the
4: 25 shall take some of the blood of the sin offering with his **finger**
4: 30 Then the priest is to take some of the blood with his **finger**
4: 34 shall take some of the blood of the sin offering with his **finger**
8: 15 with his **finger** he put it on all the horns of the altar to purify the
9: 9 he dipped his **finger** into the blood and put it on the horns of the
14: 16 dip his right **forefinger** into the oil in his palm, and with his finger
14: 16 with his **finger** sprinkle some of it before the LORD seven times.
14: 27 with his right **forefinger** sprinkle some of the oil from his palm
16: 14 and with his **finger** sprinkle it on the front of the atonement cover;
16: 14 he shall sprinkle some of it with his **finger** seven times before the
16: 19 He shall sprinkle some of the blood on it with his **finger** seven
Nu 19: 4 Then Eleazar the priest is to take some of its blood on his **finger**
Dt 9: 10 The LORD gave me two stone tablets inscribed by the **finger** *of*
2Sa 21: 20 there was a huge man with six **fingers** *on* each hand and six toes
21: 20 huge man with six fingers on each hand and six **toes** *on* each foot—
1Ch 20: 6 there was a huge man with six **fingers** on each hand and six toes
Ps 8: 3 [8:4] the work of your **fingers**, the moon and the stars, which you
144: 1 my Rock, who trains my hands for war, my **fingers** for battle.

Pr 6:13 with his eye, signals with his feet and motions with his **fingers**,
7:3 Bind them on your **fingers**; write them on the tablet of your heart.
SS 5:5 my **fingers** with flowing myrrh, on the handles of the lock.
Isa 2:8 down to the work of their hands, to what their **fingers** have made.
17:8 the Asherah poles and the incense altars their **fingers** have made.
58:9 yoke of oppression, with the pointing **finger** and malicious talk,
59:3 For your hands are stained with blood, your **fingers** with guilt.
Jer 52:21 cubits in circumference; each was four **fingers** thick, and hollow.

721 [1]אָצִיל **'āṣîl[1]**, n.[m.]. [1] [√ 724]

farthest corners [1]

Isa 41:9 from the ends of the earth, from its **farthest corners** I called you.

722 [2]אָצִיל **'āṣîl[2]**, n.[m.]. [1] [→ 727, 728]

leaders [1]

Ex 24:11 God did not raise his hand against these **leaders** *of* the Israelites;

723 אַצִּיל **'aṣṣîl**, n.[f.]. [3] [√ 724]

arms [+3338] [1], long [1], wrists [+3338] [1]

Jer 38:12 and worn-out clothes under your **arms** [+3338] to pad the ropes."
Eze 13:18 to the women who sew magic charms on all their **wrists** [+3338]
41:8 of the side rooms. It was the length of the rod, six **long** cubits.

724 אָצַל **'āṣal**, v.den. [5] [→ 721, 723, 725, 729]

denied [1], reserved [1], smaller [1], take [1], took [1]

Ge 27:36 [A] Then he asked, "Haven't *you* **reserved** any blessing for me?"
Nu 11:17 [A] *I will* **take** of the Spirit that is on you and put the Spirit on
11:25 [A] *he* **took** of the Spirit that was on him and put the Spirit on the
Ecc 2:10 [A] *I* **denied** *myself* nothing my eyes desired; I refused my heart
Eze 42:6 [C] so *they were* **smaller** in floor space than those on the lower

725 [1]אֵצֶל **'ēṣel[1]**, subst.pp. [61] [√ 724] See Select Index

beside [30], near [6], side [4], *untranslated* [3], at side [2], at [2], away [+4946] [2], by [2], next to [2], with [2], close to [+7940] [1], close to [1], go to bed with [+8886] [1], neared [+2143] [1], next to [+4946] [1], to [1]

726 [2]אֵצֶל **'ēṣel[2]**, n.pr.loc. Not used in NIV/BHS [→ 1089]

727 [1]אָצֵל **'āṣēl[1]**, n.pr.m. [6] [√ 722]

Azel [6]

1Ch 8:37 of Binea; Raphah was his son, Eleasah his son and **Azel** his son.
8:38 **Azel** had six sons, and these were their names: Azrikam, Bokeru,
8:38 Sheariah, Obadiah and Hanan. All these were the sons of **Azel**.
9:43 of Binea; Rephaiah was his son, Eleasah his son and **Azel** his son.
9:44 **Azel** had six sons, and these were their names: Azrikam, Bokeru,
9:44 Sheariah, Obadiah and Hanan. These were the sons of **Azel**.

728 [2]אָצֵל **'āṣēl[2]**, n.pr.loc. [1] [√ 722]

Azel [1]

Zec 14:5 You will flee by my mountain valley, for it will extend to **Azel**.

729 אֲצַלְיָהוּ **'aṣalyāhû**, n.pr.m. [2] [√ 724 + 3378]

Azaliah [2]

2Ki 22:3 Shaphan son of **Azaliah**, the son of Meshullam, to the temple of
2Ch 34:8 he sent Shaphan son of **Azaliah** and Maaseiah the ruler of the city,

730 אֹצֶם **'ōṣem**, n.pr.m. [2]

Ozem [2]

1Ch 2:15 the sixth **Ozem** and the seventh David.
2:25 of Hezron: Ram his firstborn, Bunah, Oren, **Ozem** and Ahijah.

731 אֶצְעָדָה **'eṣ'ādâ**, n.f. [2] [√ 7575]

armlets [1], band [1]

Nu 31:50 **armlets**, bracelets, signet rings, earrings and necklaces—to make
2Sa 1:10 and the **band** on his arm and have brought them here to my lord."

732 אָצַר **'āṣar**, v. [5] [→ 238, 733?]

stored up [2], be stored up [1], hoard [1], put in charge of the storerooms [+238+6584] [1]

2Ki 20:17 [A] all that your fathers *have* **stored up** until this day, will be
Ne 13:13 [G] *I* **put** Shelemiah the priest, Zadok the scribe, and a Levite named Pedaiah **in charge of the storerooms** [+238+6584] and
Isa 23:18 [C] apart for the LORD; *they will* not **be stored up** or hoarded.
39:6 [A] all that your fathers *have* **stored up** until this day, will be
Am 3:10 [A] "who **hoard** plunder and loot in their fortresses."

733 אֵצֶר **'ēṣer**, n.pr.m. [5] [√ 732?]

Ezer [5]

Ge 36:21 Dishon, **Ezer** and Dishan. These sons of Seir in Edom were Horite
36:27 The sons of **Ezer**: Bilhan, Zaavan and Akan.
36:30 Dishon, **Ezer** and Dishan. These were the Horite chiefs,
1Ch 1:38 of Seir: Lotan, Shobal, Zibeon, Anah, Dishon, **Ezer** and Dishan.
1:42 The sons of **Ezer**: Bilhan, Zaavan and Akan. The sons of Dishan:

734 אֶקְדָּח **'eqdāḥ**, n.[m.]. [1] [√ 7706]

sparkling jewels [+74] [1]

Isa 54:12 your gates of **sparkling jewels** [+74], and all your walls of

735 אַקּוֹ **'aqqô**, n.m. [1] [√ 3567]

wild goat [1]

Dt 14:5 the **wild goat**, the ibex, the antelope and the mountain sheep.

736 אֲרָא **'arā'**, n.pr.m. [1]

Ara [1]

1Ch 7:38 The sons of Jether: Jephunneh, Pispah and **Ara**.

737 אֶרְאֵל **'er'ēl**, n.[m.]. [1] [√ 738?]

brave men [1]

Isa 33:7 Look, their **brave men** cry aloud in the streets; the envoys of peace

738 אֲרִאֵל **'ari'ēl**, n.pr.m. [2] [√ 737?]

best men [2]

2Sa 23:20 great exploits. He struck down two of Moab's **best men**.
1Ch 11:22 great exploits. He struck down two of Moab's **best men**.

739 [1]אַרְאֵלִי **'ar'ēlî[1]**, n.pr.m. [2] [→ 740; cf. 9550?]

Areli [2]

Ge 46:16 sons of Gad: Zephon, Haggi, Shuni, Ezbon, Eri, Arodi and **Areli**.
Nu 26:17 through Arodi, the Arodite clan; through **Areli**, the Arelite clan.

740 [2]אַרְאֵלִי **'ar'ēlî[2]**, a.g. [1] [√ 739; cf. 9550?]

Arelite [1]

Nu 26:17 through Arodi, the Arodite clan; through Areli, the **Arelite** clan.

741 אָרַב **'ārab**, v. [41] [→ 743, 744, 747?, 4422]

ambush [9], lie in wait [8], lies in wait [5], in ambush [3], set an ambush [3], hidden [2], lay in wait [2], *untranslated* [1], ambush set [1], ambushes [1], bandits [1], hide [1], lurked [1], lurks [1], lying in wait [1], took up concealed positions [1]

Dt 19:11 [A] if a man hates his neighbor and **lies in wait** for him, assaults
Jos 8:2 [A] livestock for yourselves. Set an **ambush** behind the city."
8:4 [A] "Listen carefully. You *are to* **set an ambush** behind the city.
8:7 [A] you are to rise up from **ambush** and take the city. The
8:12 [A] and set them **in ambush** between Bethel and Ai,
8:14 [A] he did not know that an **ambush** *had been* **set** against him
8:19 [A] the *men* **in** *the* **ambush** rose quickly from their position
8:21 [A] and all Israel saw that the **ambush** had taken the city
Jdg 9:25 [D] these citizens of Shechem set men on the hilltops *to* **ambush**
9:32 [A] and your men should come and **lie in wait** in the fields.
9:34 [A] **took up concealed positions** near Shechem in four
9:43 [A] them into three companies and **set an ambush** in the fields.
16:2 [A] the place and **lay in wait** for him all night at the city gate.
16:9 [A] With men **hidden** in the room, she called to him, "Samson,
16:12 [A] Then, with men **hidden** in the room, she called to him,
20:29 [A] Then Israel set an **ambush** around Gibeah.
20:33 [A] the Israelite **ambush** charged out of its place on the west of
20:36 [A] because they relied on the **ambush** they had set near Gibeah.
20:37 [A] The *men who had been* **in ambush** made a sudden dash into
20:37 [A] spread out **[RPH]** and put the whole city to the sword.
20:38 [A] The men of Israel had arranged with the **ambush** that they
21:20 [A] the Benjamites, saying, "Go and **hide** in the vineyards
1Sa 15:5 [G] went to the city of Amalek and **set an ambush** in the ravine.
22:8 [A] or tells me that my son has incited my servant to **lie in wait**
22:13 [A] so that he has rebelled against me and **lies in wait** for me,
2Ch 20:22 [D] the LORD set **ambushes** against the men of Ammon
Ezr 8:31 [A] and he protected us from enemies and **bandits** along the way.
Job 31:9 [A] by a woman, or if *I have* **lurked** at my neighbor's door,
Ps 10:9 [A] *He* **lies in wait** like a lion in cover; he lies in wait to catch
10:9 [A] *he* **lies in wait** to catch the helpless; he catches the helpless
59:3 [59:4] [A] See how *they* **lie in wait** for me! Fierce men conspire
Pr 1:11 [A] *let's* **lie in wait** for someone's blood, let's waylay some
1:18 [A] These men **lie in wait** for their own blood; they waylay only
7:12 [A] in the street, now in the squares, at every corner *she* **lurks**.)

Pr 12: 6 [A] The words of the wicked **lie in wait** *for* blood, but the speech
23: 28 [A] Like a bandit she **lies in wait**, and multiplies the unfaithful
24: 15 [A] *Do* not **lie in wait** like an outlaw against a righteous man's
Jer 51: 12 [A] the guard, station the watchmen, prepare an **ambush**!
La 3: 10 [A] Like a bear **lying in wait**, like a lion in hiding,
4: 19 [A] us over the mountains and **lay in wait** for us in the desert.
Mic 7: 2 [A] All men **lie in wait** to shed blood; each hunts his brother with

742 אֲרָב *ᵃrāb*, n.pr.loc. [1] [cf. 750?]

Arab [1]

Jos 15: 52 **Arab**, Dumah, Eshan,

743 אֶרֶב *'ereb*, n.[m.]. [2] [√ 741]

cover [1], wait [1]

Job 37: 8 The animals take **cover**; they remain in their dens.
38: 40 when they crouch in their dens or lie in **wait** in a thicket?

744 אֹרֶב *'ōreb*, n.[m.]. [2] [√ 741]

intrigue [1], trap [1]

Jer 9: 8 [9:7] to his neighbor, but in his heart he sets a **trap** *for* him.
Hos 7: 6 Their hearts are like an oven; they approach him with **intrigue**.

745 אַרְבֵּאל *'arbē'l*, n.loc. Not used in NIV/BHS [→ 1079]

746 אַרְבֶּה *'arbeh*, n.m. [24] [√ 8049?]

locusts [15], locust [5], great locusts [2], great locust [1], they[s] [+2021] [1]

Ex 10: 4 to let them go, I will bring **locusts** into your country tomorrow.
10: 12 out your hand over Egypt so that **locusts** will swarm over the land
10: 13 and all that night. By morning the wind had brought the **locusts**;
10: 14 **they**[s] [+2021] invaded all Egypt and settled down in every area of
10: 14 Never before had there been such a plague of **locusts**, nor will
10: 19 which caught up the **locusts** and carried them into the Red Sea.
10: 19 them into the Red Sea. Not a **locust** was left anywhere in Egypt.
Lev 11: 22 Of these you may eat any kind of **locust**, katydid, cricket or
Dt 28: 38 the field but you will harvest little, because **locusts** will devour it.
Jdg 6: 5 came up with their livestock and their tents like swarms of **locusts**.
7: 12 the other eastern peoples had settled in the valley, thick as **locusts**.
1Ki 8: 37 comes to the land, or blight or mildew, **locusts** or grasshoppers,
2Ch 6: 28 comes to the land, or blight or mildew, **locusts** or grasshoppers,
Job 39: 20 Do you make him leap like a **locust**, striking terror with his proud
Ps 78: 46 He gave their crops to the grasshopper, their produce to the **locust**.
105: 34 He spoke, and the **locusts** came, grasshoppers without number;
109: 23 I fade away like an evening shadow; I am shaken off like a **locust**.
Pr 30: 27 **locusts** have no king, yet they advance together in ranks;
Jer 46: 23 They are more numerous than **locusts**, they cannot be counted.
Joel 1: 4 What the locust swarm has left the **great locusts** have eaten;
1: 4 what the **great locusts** have left the young locusts have eaten;
2: 25 the **great locust** and the young locust, the other locusts
Na 3: 15 consume you. Multiply like grasshoppers, multiply like **locusts**!
3: 17 Your guards are like **locusts**, your officials like swarms of locusts

747 אָרְבָּה *'orbâ*, n.f. [1] [√ 741?]

cleverness [1]

Isa 25: 11 God will bring down their pride despite the **cleverness** *of* their

748 אֲרֻבָּה *ᵃrubbâ*, n.f. [9]

floodgates [6], nests [1], window [1], windows [1]

Ge 7: 11 deep burst forth, and the **floodgates** *of* the heavens were opened.
8: 2 of the deep and the **floodgates** *of* the heavens had been closed,
2Ki 7: 2 even if the LORD should open the **floodgates** of the heavens,
7: 19 even if the LORD should open the **floodgates** of the heavens,
Ecc 12: 3 they are few, and those looking through the **windows** grow dim;
Isa 24: 18 The **floodgates** of the heavens are opened, the foundations of the
60: 8 "Who are these that fly along like clouds, like doves to their **nests**?
Hos 13: 3 from a threshing floor, like smoke escaping through a **window**.
Mal 3: 10 "and see if I will not throw open the **floodgates** *of* heaven

749 אֲרֻבּוֹת *ᵃrubbôt*, n.pr.loc. [1]

Arubboth [1]

1Ki 4: 10 in **Arubboth** (Socoh and all the land of Hepher were his);

750 אַרְבִּי *'arbî*, a.g. [1] [cf. 742?]

Arbite [1]

2Sa 23: 35 Hezro the Carmelite, Paarai the **Arbite**,

751 ארנבן *'rnbn*, n.pr.loc. Not used in NIV/BHS

752 אַרְבַּע *'arba'*[1], n.m. & f. [454 / 456] [→ 753, 754, 2033, 7957, 7959, 8055, 8062, 8063?, 8065, 8067, 8068; Ar 10065]

four [172], forty [78], fourteenth [+6925] [19], 24,000 [+547+2256 +6929] [14], fourteen [+6925] [12], twenty-fourth [+2256+6929] [9], 4,500 [+547+2256+2822+4395] [8], *untranslated* [6], fourteen [+6926] [6], fourth [5], twenty-four [+2256+6929] [5], 1,254 [+547+2256+2822+4395] [4], 54,400 [+547+752+2256+2256 +2822+4395] [4], all fours [4], forty-one [+285+2256] [4], forty-two [+2256+9109] [4], fourteenth [+6926] [4], 40,500 [+547+2256 +2822 +4395] [3], 430 [+2256+4395+8993] [3], 53,400 [+547+2256+2256 +2822+4395+8993] [3], fortieth [3], forty-five [+2256+2822] [3], 1,247 [+547+2256+4395+8679] [2], 345 [+2256+2822+4395+8993] [2], 35,400 [+547+2256+2256+2822+4395+8993] [2], 4,600 [+547+2256 +4395+9252] [2], 403 [+2256+4395+8993] [2], 41,500 [+285+547 +2256+2256+2822+4395] [2], 42 [+2256+9109] [2], 435 [+2256+2822+4395+8993] [2], 44,760 [+547+752+2256+2256+2256 +4395+8679+9252] [2], 45,400 [+547+752+2256+2256+2822+4395] [2], 45,650 [+547+2256+2256+2256+2822+2822+4395+9252] [2], 454 [+752+2256+2822+4395] [2], 46,500 [+547+2256+2256+2822 +4395+9252] [2], 57,400 [+547+2256+2256+2822+4395+8679] [2], 64,400 [+547+752+2256+2256+4395+9252] [2], 74 [+2256+8679] [2], 74,600 [+547+2256+2256+4395+8679+9252] [2], about six hundred feet [+564+4395] [2], forty-eight [+2256+9046] [2], fourteen hundred [+547+2256+4395] [2], 14,700 [+547+2256+4395 +6925+8679] [1], 148 [+2256+4395+9046] [1], 151,450 [+285+547 +547+2256+2256+2256+2256+2822+2822+4395+4395] [1], 186,400 [+547+547+547+2256+2256+2256+4395+4395+9046+9252] [1], 2,400 [+547+2256+4395] [1], 22,034 [+547+2256+2256+2256+6929 +8993+9109] [1], 242 [+2256+4395+9109] [1], 245 [+2256+2256 +2822+4395] [1], 245 [+2256+2822+4395] [1], 245 [1], 284 [+2256+4395+9046] [1], 324 [+2256+4395+6929+8993] [1], 34 [+2256+8993] [1], 40 [1], 40,000 [+547] [1], 410 [+2256+4395+6927] [1], 42,360 [+547+2256+4395+8052+8993+9252] [1], 42,360 [+547+4395+8052+8993+9252] [1], 420 [+2256+4395+6929] [1], 43,730 [+547+2256+2256+2256+4395+8679+8993+8993] [1], 45,600 [+547+2256+2256+2822+4395+9252] [1], 468 [+2256+4395 +9046+9252] [1], 5,400 [+547+2256+2822+4395] [1], 64,300 [+547+2256+2256+4395+8993+9252] [1], 642 [+2256+2256+4395 +9109+9252] [1], 642 [+2256+4395+9109+9252] [1], 648 [+2256+4395+9046+9252] [1], 743 [+2256+2256+4395+8679+8993] [1], 743 [+2256+4395+8679+8993] [1], 745 [+2256+2822 +4395+8679] [1], 840 [+2256+4395+9046] [1], 845 [+2256+2822 +4395+9046] [1], 945 [+2256+2256+2822+4395+9596] [1], each[s] [1], forty [+2256+9109] [1], forty-first [+285+2256] [1], forty-nine [+2256+9596] [1], forty-seven [+2256+8679] [1], four-fifths [+3338] [1], fourteen [1], six feet [+564] [1], square [+448+8062+8063] [1], square [+448+8063] [1]

Ge 2: 10 from Eden; from there it was separated into **four** headwaters.
5: 13 Kenan lived **840** [+2256+4395+9046] years and had other sons and
7: 4 Seven days from now I will send rain on the earth for **forty** days
7: 4 now I will send rain on the earth for forty days and **forty** nights,
7: 12 And rain fell on the earth **forty** days and forty nights.
7: 12 And rain fell on the earth forty days and **forty** nights.
7: 17 For **forty** days the flood kept coming on the earth, and as the
8: 6 After **forty** days Noah opened the window he had made in the ark
11: 13 Arphaxad lived **403** [+2256+4395+8993] years and had other sons
11: 15 Shelah lived **403** [+2256+4395+8993] years and had other sons
11: 16 When Eber had lived **34** [+2256+8993] years, he became the father
11: 17 Eber lived **430** [+2256+4395+8993] years and had other sons and
14: 5 In the **fourteenth** [+6926] year, Kedorlaomer and the kings allied
14: 9 king of Shinar and Arioch king of Ellasar—**four** kings against five.
15: 13 and they will be enslaved and mistreated **four** hundred years.
18: 28 "If I find **forty-five** [+2256+2822] there," he said, "I will not
18: 29 Once again he spoke to him, "What if only **forty** are found there?"
18: 29 are found there?" He said, "For the sake of **forty**, I will not do it."
23: 15 the land is worth **four** hundred shekels of silver, but what is that
23: 16 **four** hundred shekels of silver, according to the weight current
25: 20 Isaac was **forty** years old when he married Rebekah daughter of
26: 34 When Esau was **forty** years old, he married Judith daughter of
31: 41 I worked for you **fourteen** [+6926] years for your two daughters
32: 6 [32:7] coming to meet you, and **four** hundred men are with him."
32: 15 [32:16] **forty** cows and ten bulls, and twenty female donkeys
33: 1 looked up and there was Esau, coming with his **four** hundred men;
46: 22 sons of Rachel who were born to Jacob—**fourteen** [+6925] in all.
47: 24 The *other* **four-fifths** [+3338] you may keep as seed for the fields
47: 28 the years of his life were a hundred and **forty-seven** [+2256+8679].
50: 3 taking a full **forty** days, for that was the time required for
Ex 12: 6 Take care of them until the **fourteenth** [+6925] day of the month,
12: 18 from the evening of the **fourteenth** [+6925] day until the evening
12: 40 people lived in Egypt was **430** [+2256+4395+8993] years.
12: 41 At the end of the **430** [+2256+4395+8993] years, to the very day,

Ex 16:35 The Israelites ate manna **forty** years, until they came to a land that
22:1 [21:37] five head of cattle for the ox and **four** sheep for the sheep.
24:18 And he stayed on the mountain **forty** days and forty nights.
24:18 And he stayed on the mountain forty days and **forty** nights.
25:12 Cast **four** gold rings for it and fasten them to its four feet,
25:12 Cast four gold rings for it and fasten them to its **four** feet,
25:26 Make **four** gold rings for the table and fasten them to the four
25:26 four gold rings for the table and fasten them to the **four** corners,
25:26 and fasten them to the four corners, where the **four** legs are.
25:34 on the lampstand there are to be **four** cups shaped like almond
26:2 be the same size—twenty-eight cubits long and **four** cubits wide.
26:8 are to be the same size—thirty cubits long and **four** cubits wide.
26:19 make **forty** silver bases to go under them—two bases for each
26:21 and **forty** silver bases—two under each frame.
26:32 Hang it with gold hooks on **four** posts of acacia wood overlaid
26:32 acacia wood overlaid with gold and standing on **four** silver bases.
27:2 Make a horn at each of the **four** corners, so that the horns
27:4 make a **[RPH]** bronze ring at each of the four corners of the
27:4 and make a bronze ring at each of the **four** corners of the network.
27:16 the work of an embroiderer—with **four** posts and four bases.
27:16 the work of an embroiderer—with four posts and **four** bases.
28:17 mount **four** rows of precious stones on it. In the first row there
34:28 Moses was there with the LORD **forty** days and forty nights
34:28 forty days and **forty** nights without eating bread or drinking water.
36:9 the same size—twenty-eight cubits long and **four** cubits wide.
36:15 were the same size—thirty cubits long and **four** cubits wide.
36:24 made **forty** silver bases to go under them—two bases for each
36:26 and **forty** silver bases—two under each frame.
36:36 They made **four** posts of acacia wood for it and overlaid them with
36:36 They made gold hooks for them and cast their **four** silver bases.
37:3 He cast **four** gold rings for it and fastened them to its four feet,
37:3 He cast four gold rings for it and fastened them to its **four** feet,
37:13 They cast **four** gold rings for the table and fastened them to the
37:13 four gold rings for the table and fastened them to the **four** corners,
37:13 and fastened them to the four corners, where the **four** legs were.
37:20 on the lampstand were **four** cups shaped like almond flowers with
38:2 They made a horn at each of the **four** corners, so that the horns
38:5 They cast bronze **[RPH]** rings to hold the poles for the four
38:5 They cast bronze rings to hold the poles for the **four** corners of the
38:19 with **four** posts and four bronze bases. Their hooks and bands were
38:19 with four posts and **four** bronze bases. Their hooks and bands were
38:29 offering was 70 talents and **2,400** [+547+2256+4395] shekels.
39:10 they mounted **four** rows of precious stones on it. In the first row
Lev 11:20 " 'All flying insects that walk on **all fours** are to be detestable to
11:21 some winged creatures that walk on **all fours** that you may eat:
11:23 But all other winged creatures that have **four** legs you are to detest.
11:27 Of all the animals that walk on **all fours**, those that walk on their
11:42 it moves on its belly or walks on **all fours** or on many feet;
23:5 at twilight on the **fourteenth** [+6925] day of the first month.
25:8 years amount to a period of **forty-nine** [+2256+9596] years.
Nu 1:21 of Reuben was **46,500** [+547+2256+2256+2822+4395+9252].
1:25 was **45,650** [+547+2256+2256+2822+2822+4395+9252].
1:27 of Judah was **74,600** [+547+2256+2256+4395+8679+9252].
1:29 of Issachar was **54,400** [+547+752+2256+2256+2822+4395].
1:29 of Issachar was **54,400** [+547+752+2256+2256+2822+4395].
1:31 of Zebulun was **57,400** [+547+2256+2256+2822+4395+8679].
1:33 the tribe of Ephraim was **40,500** [+547+2256+2822+4395].
1:37 of Benjamin was **35,400** [+547+2256+2256+2822+4395+8993].
1:41 tribe of Asher was **41,500** [+285+547+2256+2256+2822+4395].
1:43 of Naphtali was **53,400** [+547+2256+2256+2822+4395+8993].
2:4 division numbers **74,600** [+547+2256+2256+4395+8679+9252].
2:6 His division numbers **54,400** [+547+752+2256+2256+2822+4395].
2:6 His division numbers **54,400** [+547+752+2256+2256+2822+4395].
2:8 division numbers **57,400** [+547+2256+2256+2822+4395+8679].
2:9 to the camp of Judah, according to their divisions, number **186,400** [+547+547+547+2256+2256+2256+4395+4395+9046+9252].
2:11 division numbers **46,500** [+547+2256+2256+2822+4395+9252].
2:15 division numbers **45,650** [+547+2256+2256+2256 +2822+2822+4395+9252].
2:16 of Reuben, according to their divisions, number **151,450** [+285 +547+547+2256+2256+2256+2256+2822+2822+4395+4395].
2:19 His division numbers **40,500** [+547+2256+2822+4395].
2:23 division numbers **35,400** [+547+2256+2256+2822+4395+8993].
2:28 His division numbers **41,500** [+285+547+2256+2256+2822+4395].
2:30 division numbers **53,400** [+547+2256+2256+2822+4395+8993].
7:7 He gave two carts and **four** oxen to the Gershonites, as their work
7:8 he gave **four** carts and eight oxen to the Merarites, as their work
7:85 the silver dishes weighed two thousand **four** hundred shekels,
7:88 the fellowship offering came to **twenty-four** [+2256+6929] oxen,
9:3 at twilight on the **fourteenth** [+6925] day of this month,
9:5 so in the Desert of Sinai at twilight on the **fourteenth** [+6925] day
9:11 They are to celebrate it on the **fourteenth** [+6925] day of the
13:25 At the end of **forty** days they returned from exploring the land.
14:33 Your children will be shepherds here for **forty** years, suffering for
14:34 For **forty** years—one year for each of the forty days you explored
14:34 one year for each of the **forty** days you explored the land—
16:49 [17:14] **14,700** [+547+2256+4395+6925+8679] people died from
25:9 those who died in the plague numbered **24,000** [+547+2256+6929].
26:7 were **43,730** [+547+2256+2256+2256+4395+8679+8993+8993].
26:18 Gad; those numbered were **40,500** [+547+2256+2822+4395].
26:25 numbered were **64,300** [+547+2256+2256+4395+8993+9252].
26:41 numbered were **45,600** [+547+2256+2256+2822+4395+9252].
26:43 numbered were **64,400** [+547+752+2256+2256+4395+9252].
26:43 numbered were **64,400** [+547+752+2256+2256+4395+9252].
26:47 numbered were **53,400** [+547+2256+2256+2822+4395+8993].
26:50 numbered were **45,400** [+547+752+2256+2256+2822+4395].
26:50 numbered were **45,400** [+547+752+2256+2256+2822+4395].
28:16 " 'On the **fourteenth** [+6925] day of the first month the LORD's
29:13 two rams and **fourteen** [+6925] male lambs a year old, all without
29:15 and with each of the **fourteen** [+6925] lambs, one-tenth.
29:17 two rams and **fourteen** [+6925] male lambs a year old, all without
29:20 two rams and **fourteen** [+6925] male lambs a year old, all without
29:23 two rams and **fourteen** [+6925] male lambs a year old, all without
29:26 two rams and **fourteen** [+6925] male lambs a year old, all without
29:29 two rams and **fourteen** [+6925] male lambs a year old, all without
29:32 two rams and **fourteen** [+6925] male lambs a year old, all without
32:13 against Israel and he made them wander in the desert **forty** years,
33:38 where he died on the first day of the fifth month of the **fortieth**
35:6 In addition, give them **forty-two** [+2256+9109] other towns.
35:7 In all you must give the Levites **forty-eight** [+2256+9046] towns,
Dt 1:3 In the **fortieth** year, on the first day of the eleventh month,
2:7 These **forty** years the LORD your God has been with you,
3:11 and was more than thirteen feet long and **six feet** [+564] wide.
8:2 your God led you all the way in the desert these **forty** years,
8:4 not wear out and your feet did not swell during these **forty** years.
9:9 with you, I stayed on the mountain **forty** days and forty nights;
9:9 with you, I stayed on the mountain forty days and **forty** nights;
9:11 At the end of the **forty** days and forty nights, the LORD gave me
9:11 At the end of the forty days and **forty** nights, the LORD gave me
9:18 Then once again I fell prostrate before the LORD for **forty** days
9:18 I fell prostrate before the LORD for forty days and **forty** nights;
9:25 I lay prostrate before the LORD those **forty** days and forty nights
9:25 I lay prostrate before the LORD those forty days and **forty** nights
10:10 Now I had stayed on the mountain **forty** days and nights, as I did
10:10 Now I had stayed on the mountain forty days and **[RPH]** nights,
22:12 Make tassels on the **four** corners of the cloak you wear.
25:3 he must not give him more than **forty** lashes. If he is flogged more
29:5 [29:4] During the **forty** years that I led you through the desert,
Jos 4:13 About **forty** thousand armed for battle crossed over before the
5:6 The Israelites had moved about in the desert **forty** years until all
5:10 On the evening of the **fourteenth** [+6925] day of the month,
14:7 I was **forty** years old when Moses the servant of the LORD sent
14:10 he has kept me alive for **forty-five** [+2256+2822] years since the
15:36 (or Gederothaim)—**fourteen** [+6926] towns and their villages.
18:28 Gibeah and Kiriath—**fourteen** [+6926] towns and their villages.
19:7 Rimmon, Ether and Ashan—**four** towns and their villages—
21:18 and Almon, together with their pasturelands—**four** towns.
21:22 and Beth Horon, together with their pasturelands—**four** towns.
21:24 and Gath Rimmon, together with their pasturelands—**four** towns.
21:29 and En Gannim, together with their pasturelands—**four** towns;
21:31 and Rehob, together with their pasturelands—**four** towns;
21:35 and Nahalal, together with their pasturelands—**four** towns;
21:37 and Mephaath, together with their pasturelands—**four** towns;
21:39 and Jazer, together with their pasturelands—**four** towns in all.
21:41 held by the Israelites were **forty-eight** [+2256+9046] in all,
Jdg 3:11 So the land had peace for **forty** years, until Othniel son of Kenaz
5:8 and not a shield or spear was seen among **forty** thousand in Israel.
5:31 when it rises in its strength." Then the land had peace **forty** years.
8:28 During Gideon's lifetime, the land enjoyed peace **forty** years.
9:34 and took up concealed positions near Shechem in **four** companies.
11:40 that each year the young women of Israel go out for **four** days to
12:6 **Forty-two** [+2256+9109] thousand Ephraimites were killed at that
12:14 He had **forty** sons and thirty grandsons, who rode on seventy
13:1 delivered them into the hands of the Philistines for **forty** years.
19:2 house in Bethlehem, Judah. After she had been there **four** months,
20:2 people of God, **four** hundred thousand soldiers armed with swords.
20:17 apart from Benjamin, mustered **four** hundred thousand swordsmen,
20:47 the desert to the rock of Rimmon, where they stayed **four** months.
21:12 They found among the people living in Jabesh Gilead **four**
1Sa 4:2 who killed about **four** thousand of them on the battlefield.
4:18 for he was an old man and heavy. He had led Israel **forty** years.
13:1 and he reigned over Israel ⌞**forty-** [+2256+9109]⌟two [BHS-] years.
17:16 For **forty** days the Philistine came forward every morning
22:2 he became their leader. About **four** hundred men were with him.
25:13 About **four** hundred men went up with David, while two hundred
27:7 David lived in Philistine territory a year and **four** months.
30:10 the ravine. But David and **four** hundred men continued the pursuit.
30:17 except **four** hundred young men who rode off on camels and fled.

2Sa 2:10 Ish-Bosheth son of Saul was **forty** years old when he became king
5:4 thirty years old when he became king, and he reigned **forty** years.
10:18 of their charioteers and **forty** thousand of their foot soldiers.
12:6 He must pay for that lamb **four** *times over*, because he did such a
15:7 At the end of **four** years, Absalom said to the king, "Let me go to
21:20 and six toes on each foot—**twenty-four** [+2256+6929] in all.
21:22 These **four** were descendants of Rapha in Gath, and they fell at the
1Ki 2:11 He had reigned **forty** years over Israel—seven years in Hebron
4:26 [5:6] Solomon had **four** thousand stalls for chariot horses,
6:1 In the **four** hundred and eightieth year after the Israelites had come
6:17 The main hall in front of this room was **forty** cubits long.
7:2 with **four** rows of cedar columns supporting trimmed cedar beams.
7:3 the columns—**forty-five** [+2256+2822] beams, fifteen to a row.
7:19 pillars in the portico were in the shape of lilies, **four** cubits high.
7:27 of bronze; each was **four** cubits long, four wide and three high.
7:27 of bronze; each was four cubits long, **four** wide and three high.
7:30 Each stand had **four** bronze wheels with bronze axles, and each
7:30 each had a basin resting on **four** supports, cast with wreaths on
7:32 The **four** wheels were under the panels, and the axles of the wheels
7:34 Each stand had **four** handles, one on each corner, projecting from
7:34 had four handles, one on **each**' corner, projecting from the stand.
7:38 each holding **forty** baths and measuring four cubits across,
7:38 each holding forty baths and measuring **four** cubits across,
7:42 the **four** hundred pomegranates for the two sets of network (two
8:65 for seven days and seven days more, **fourteen** [+6925] days in all.
9:28 and brought back **420** [+2256+4395+6929] talents of gold,
10:26 he had **fourteen** [+547+2256+4395] **hundred** chariots and twelve
11:42 Solomon reigned in Jerusalem over all Israel **forty** years.
14:21 He was **forty-one** [+285+2256] years old when he became king,
15:10 and he reigned in Jerusalem **forty-one** [+285+2256] years.
15:33 year of Asa king of Judah, Baasha son of Ahijah became king of all Israel in Tirzah, and he reigned **twenty-four** [+2256+6929] years.
18:19 bring the **four** hundred and fifty prophets of Baal and the four
18:19 fifty prophets of Baal and the **four** hundred prophets of Asherah,
18:22 prophets left, but Baal has **four** hundred and fifty prophets.
18:33 [18:34] "Fill **four** large jars with water and pour it on the offering
19:8 he traveled **forty** days and forty nights until he reached Horeb,
19:8 he traveled forty days and **forty** nights until he reached Horeb,
22:6 about **four** hundred men—and asked them, "Shall I go to war
22:41 Jehoshaphat son of Asa became king of Judah in the **fourth** year of
2Ki 2:24 curse on them in the name of the LORD. Then two bears came out of the woods and mauled **forty-two** [+2256+9109] of the youths.
7:3 Now there were **four** men with leprosy at the entrance of the city
8:9 taking with him as a gift **forty** camel-loads of all the finest wares
10:14 them alive!" he ordered. So they took them alive and slaughtered them by the well of Beth Eked—**forty-two** [+2256+9109] men.
12:1 [12:2] became king, and he reigned in Jerusalem **forty** years.
14:13 a section **about six hundred feet** [+564+4395] long.
14:23 king in Samaria, and he reigned **forty-one** [+285+2256] years.
18:13 In the **fourteenth** [+6926] year of King Hezekiah's reign,
1Ch 3:5 and Solomon. These **four** were by Bathsheba daughter of Ammiel.
5:18 had **44,760** [+547+752+2256+2256+2256+4395+8679+9252] men
5:18 had **44,760** [+547+752+2256+2256+2256+4395+8679+9252] men
7:1 The sons of Issachar: Tola, Puah, Jashub and Shimron—**four** in all.
7:7 **22,034** [+547+2256+2256+2256+6929+8993+9109] fighting men.
9:24 The gatekeepers were on the **four** sides: east, west, north and
9:26 the **four** principal gatekeepers, who were Levites, were entrusted
12:26 [12:27] men of Levi—**4,600** [+547+2256+4395+9252],
12:36 [12:37] experienced soldiers prepared for battle—**40,000** [+547];
19:18 of their charioteers and **forty** thousand of their foot soldiers.
20:6 and six toes on each foot—**twenty-four** [+2256+6929] in all.
21:5 a sword, including **four** hundred and seventy thousand in Judah.
21:20 saw the angel; his **four** sons who were with him hid themselves.
23:4 **twenty-four** [+2256+6929] thousand are to supervise the work of
23:5 **Four** thousand are to be gatekeepers and four thousand are to
23:5 **four** thousand are to praise the LORD with the musical
23:10 Jeush and Beriah. These were the sons of Shimei—**four** in all.
23:12 sons of Kohath: Amram, Izhar, Hebron and Uzziel—**four** in all.
24:13 the thirteenth to Huppah, the **fourteenth** [+6925] to Jeshebeab,
24:18 to Delaiah and the **twenty-fourth** [+2256+6929] to Maaziah.
25:5 God gave Heman **fourteen** [+6925] sons and three daughters.
25:21 the **fourteenth** [+6925] to Mattithiah, his sons and relatives,
25:31 the **twenty-fourth** [+2256+6929] to Romamti-Ezer, his sons and
26:17 **four** a day on the north, four a day on the south and two at a time
26:17 **four** a day on the south and two at a time at the storehouse.
26:18 to the west, there were **four** at the road and two at the court itself.
26:31 In the **fortieth** year of David's reign a search was made in the
27:1 Each division consisted of **24,000** [+547+2256+6929] men.
27:2 There were **24,000** [+547+2256+6929] men in his division.
27:4 There were **24,000** [+547+2256+6929] men in his division.
27:5 and there were **24,000** [+547+2256+6929] men in his division.
27:7 There were **24,000** [+547+2256+6929] men in his division.
27:8 There were **24,000** [+547+2256+6929] men in his division.
27:9 There were **24,000** [+547+2256+6929] men in his division.
27:10 There were **24,000** [+547+2256+6929] men in his division.
27:11 There were **24,000** [+547+2256+6929] men in his division.
27:12 There were **24,000** [+547+2256+6929] men in his division.
27:13 There were **24,000** [+547+2256+6929] men in his division.
27:14 There were **24,000** [+547+2256+6929] men in his division.
27:15 There were **24,000** [+547+2256+6929] men in his division.
29:27 He ruled over Israel **forty** years—seven in Hebron and thirty-three
2Ch 1:14 he had **fourteen** [+547+2256+4395] **hundred** chariots and twelve
3:2 the second day of the second month in the **fourth** year of his reign.
4:13 the **four** hundred pomegranates for the two sets of network (two
8:18 sailed to Ophir and brought back **four** hundred and fifty talents of
9:25 Solomon had **four** thousand stalls for horses and chariots,
9:30 Solomon reigned in Jerusalem over all Israel **forty** years.
12:13 He was **forty-one** [+285+2256] years old when he became king,
13:3 Abijah went into battle with a force of **four** hundred thousand able
13:21 He married **fourteen** [+6926] wives and had twenty-two sons
16:13 Then in the **forty-first** [+285+2256] year of his reign Asa died
18:5 **four** hundred men—and asked them, "Shall we go to war against
22:2 Ahaziah was twenty-two [+2256+9109] [BHS *forty-two*; NIV 6929] years old when he became king,
24:1 old when he became king, and he reigned in Jerusalem **forty** years.
25:23 a section **about six hundred feet** [+564+4395] long.
30:15 They slaughtered the Passover lamb on the **fourteenth** [+6925]
35:1 the Passover lamb was slaughtered on the **fourteenth** [+6925] day
Ezr 1:10 gold bowls 30 matching silver bowls **410** [+2256+4395+6927]
1:11 In all, there were **5,400** [+547+2256+2822+4395] articles of gold
2:7 of Elam **1,254** [+547+2256+2822+4395]
2:8 of Zattu **945** [+2256+2256+2822+4395+9596]
2:10 of Bani **642** [+2256+4395+9109+9252]
2:15 of Adin **454** [+752+2256+2822+4395]
2:15 of Adin **454** [+752+2256+2822+4395]
2:24 of Azmaveth **42** [+2256+9109]
2:25 Kephirah and Beeroth **743** [+2256+2256+4395+8679+8993]
2:31 of the other Elam **1,254** [+547+2256+2822+4395]
2:34 of Jericho **345** [+2256+2822+4395+8993]
2:38 of Pashhur **1,247** [+547+2256+4395+8679]
2:40 and Kadmiel (through the line of Hodaviah) **74** [+2256+8679]
2:64 whole company numbered **42,360** [+547+4395+8052+8993+9252],
2:66 They had 736 horses, **245** [+2256+2822+4395] mules,
2:67 **435** [+2256+2822+4395+8993] camels and 6,720 donkeys.
6:19 On the **fourteenth** [+6925] day of the first month, the exiles
Ne 5:15 and took **forty** shekels of silver from them in addition to food
6:4 **Four** times they sent me the same message, and each time I gave
7:12 of Elam **1,254** [+547+2256+2822+4395]
7:13 of Zattu **845** [+2256+2822+4395+9046]
7:15 of Binnui **648** [+2256+4395+9046+9252]
7:23 of Bezai **324** [+2256+4395+6929+8993]
7:28 of Beth Azmaveth **42** [+2256+9109]
7:29 Kephirah and Beeroth **743** [+2256+4395+8679+8993]
7:34 of the other Elam **1,254** [+547+2256+2822+4395]
7:36 of Jericho **345** [+2256+2822+4395+8993]
7:41 of Pashhur **1,247** [+547+2256+4395+8679]
7:43 (through Kadmiel through the line of Hodaviah) **74** [+2256+8679]
7:44 The singers: the descendants of Asaph **148** [+2256+4395+9046]
7:62 Tobiah and Nekoda **642** [+2256+2256+4395+9109+9252]
7:66 company numbered **42,360** [+547+2256+4395+8052+8993+9252],
7:67 also had **245** [+2256+2256+2822+4395] men and women singers.
7:68 [7:67] There were 736 horses, **245** mules,
7:69 [7:68] **435** [+2256+2822+4395+8993] camels and 6,720 donkeys.
9:1 On the **twenty-fourth** [+2256+6929] day of the same month,
9:21 For **forty** years you sustained them in the desert; they lacked
11:6 in Jerusalem totaled **468** [+2256+4395+9046+9252] able men.
11:13 families—**242** [+2256+4395+9109] men; Amashsai son of Azarel,
11:18 The Levites in the holy city totaled **284** [+2256+4395+9046].
Est 9:15 The Jews in Susa came together on the **fourteenth** [+6925] day of
9:17 on the **fourteenth** [+6925] they rested and made it a day of
9:18 had assembled on the thirteenth and **fourteenth** [+6925], and
9:19 observe the **fourteenth** [+6925] of the month of Adar as a day of
9:21 to have them celebrate annually the **fourteenth** [+6925] and
Job 1:19 swept in from the desert and struck the **four** corners of the house.
42:12 He had **fourteen** [+6925] thousand sheep, six thousand camels,
42:16 After this, Job lived a hundred and **forty** years; he saw his children
42:16 he saw his children and their children to the **fourth** generation.
Ps 95:10 For **forty** years I was angry with that generation; I said, "They are
Pr 30:15 three things that are never satisfied, **four** that never say, 'Enough!':
30:18 things that are too amazing for me, **four** that I do not understand:
30:21 three things the earth trembles, under **four** it cannot bear up:
30:24 "**Four** things on earth are small, yet they are extremely wise:
30:29 that are stately in their stride, **four** that move with stately bearing:
Isa 11:12 he will assemble the scattered people of Judah from the **four**
17:6 **four** or five on the fruitful boughs," declares the LORD,
36:1 In the **fourteenth** [+6926] year of King Hezekiah's reign,
Jer 15:3 "I will send **four** kinds of destroyers against them,"
36:23 Whenever Jehudi had read three or **four** columns of the scroll,

Jer 49:36 I will bring against Elam the **four** winds from the four quarters of
49:36 I will bring against Elam the four winds from the **four** quarters of
52:21 cubits in circumference; each was **four** fingers thick, and hollow.
52:30 **745** [+2256+2822+4395+8679] Jews taken into exile by
52:30 There were **4,600** [+547+2256+4395+9252] people in all.
Eze 1:5 and in the fire was what looked like **four** living creatures.
1:6 but each of them had **four** faces and four wings.
1:6 but each of them had four faces and **four** wings.
1:8 Under their wings on their **four** sides they had the hands of a man.
1:8 they had the hands of a man. *All* **four** *of* them had faces and wings,
1:10 Each of the **four** had the face of a man, and on the right side each
1:10 on the right side each had **[RPH]** the face of a lion, and on the left
1:10 left the face of an ox; each also had **[RPH]** the face of an eagle.
1:15 I saw a wheel on the ground beside each creature with its **four**
1:16 They sparkled like chrysolite, and *all* **four** looked alike.
1:17 they would go in any one of the **four** directions the creatures faced;
1:18 and awesome, and *all* **four** rims were full of eyes all around.
4:6 house of Judah. I have assigned you **40** days, a day for each year.
7:2 The end! The end has come upon the **four** corners of the land.
10:9 I looked, and I saw beside the cherubim **four** wheels, one beside
10:10 As for their appearance, the **four** *of* them looked alike; each was
10:11 they would go in any one of the **four** directions the cherubim
10:12 were completely full of eyes, as were their **four** wheels.
10:14 Each of the cherubim had **four** faces: One face was that of a
10:21 Each had **four** faces and four wings, and under their wings was
10:21 Each had four **[RPH]** faces and four wings, and under their wings
10:21 Each had four faces and **four** wings, and under their wings was
14:21 How much worse will it be when I send against Jerusalem my **four**
29:11 animal will pass through it; no one will live there for **forty** years.
29:12 and her cities will lie desolate **forty** years among ruined cities.
29:13 At the end of **forty** years I will gather the Egyptians from the
37:9 Come from the **four** winds, O breath, and breathe into these slain,
40:1 in the **fourteenth** [+6926] year after the fall of the city—
40:41 So there were **four** tables on one side of the gateway and four on
40:41 were four tables on one side of the gateway and **four** on the other—
40:42 There were also **four** tables of dressed stone for the burnt
40:48 The width of the entrance was **fourteen** [BHS-] cubits and its
41:2 outer sanctuary; it was **forty** cubits long and twenty cubits wide.
41:5 and each side room around the temple was **four** cubits wide.
42:20 So he measured the area on *all* **four** sides. It had a wall around it,
43:14 from the smaller ledge up to the larger ledge it is **four** cubits high
43:15 The altar hearth is **four** cubits high, and four horns project upward
43:15 is four cubits high, and **four** horns project upward from the hearth.
43:16 The altar hearth *is* **square** [+448+8062+8063], twelve cubits long
43:17 The upper ledge also is **square** [+448+8063], fourteen cubits long
43:17 **fourteen** [+6926] cubits long and fourteen cubits wide, with a rim
43:17 fourteen cubits long and **fourteen** [+6926] cubits wide, with a rim
43:20 to take some of its blood and put it on the **four** horns of the altar
43:20 and on the **four** corners of the upper ledge and all around the rim,
45:19 on the **four** corners of the upper ledge of the altar and on the
45:21 " 'In the first month on the **fourteenth** [+6925] day you are to
46:21 me to the outer court and led me around to its **four** corners,
46:22 In the **four** corners of the outer court were enclosed courts,
46:22 were enclosed courts, **forty** cubits long and thirty cubits wide;
46:22 each of the courts in the **four** corners was the same size.
46:23 Around the inside of each of the **four** courts was a ledge of stone,
48:16 the north side **4,500** [+547+2256+2822+4395] cubits, the south
48:16 the south side **4,500** [+547+2256+2822+4395] cubits, the east side
48:16 the east side **4,500** [+547+2256+2822+4395] cubits, and the west
48:16 and the west side **4,500** [+547+2256+2822+4395] cubits.
48:30 north side, which is **4,500** [+547+2256+2822+4395] cubits long,
48:32 the east side, which is **4,500** [+547+2256+2822+4395] cubits long,
48:33 south side, which measures **4,500** [+547+2256+2822+4395] cubits,
48:34 west side, which is **4,500** [+547+2256+2822+4395] cubits long,
Da 1:17 To these **four** young men God gave knowledge and understanding
8:8 in its place **four** prominent horns grew up toward the four winds of
8:8 in its place four prominent horns grew up toward the **four** winds of
8:22 The **four** horns that replaced the one that was broken off represent
8:22 off represent **four** kingdoms that will emerge from his nation
10:4 On the **twenty-fourth** [+2256+6929] day of the first month,
11:4 be broken up and parceled out toward the **four** winds of heaven.
Am 1:3 "For three sins of Damascus, even for **four**, I will not turn back
1:6 "For three sins of Gaza, even for **four**, I will not turn back ⌞my
1:9 "For three sins of Tyre, even for **four**, I will not turn back ⌞my
1:11 "For three sins of Edom, even for **four**, I will not turn back ⌞my
1:13 "For three sins of Ammon, even for **four**, I will not turn back ⌞my
2:1 "For three sins of Moab, even for **four**, I will not turn back ⌞my
2:4 "For three sins of Judah, even for **four**, I will not turn back ⌞my
2:6 "For three sins of Israel, even for **four**, I will not turn back ⌞my
2:10 I led you **forty** years in the desert to give you the land of the
5:25 you bring me sacrifices and offerings **forty** years in the desert,
Jnh 3:4 "**Forty** more days and Nineveh will be overturned."
Hag 1:15 on the **twenty-fourth** [+2256+6929] day of the sixth month in the
2:10 On the **twenty-fourth** [+2256+6929] day of the ninth month, in the
2:18 'From this day on, from this **twenty-fourth** [+2256+6929] day of
2:20 on the **twenty-fourth** [+2256+6929] day of the month:
Zec 1:7 On the **twenty-fourth** [+2256+6929] day of the eleventh month,
1:18 [2:1] Then I looked up—and there before me were **four** horns!
1:20 [2:3] Then the LORD showed me **four** craftsmen.
2:6 [2:10] "for I have scattered you to the **four** winds of heaven,"
6:1 there before me were **four** chariots coming out from between two
6:5 The angel answered me, "These are the **four** spirits of heaven,
7:1 In the **fourth** year of King Darius, the word of the LORD came to
7:1 the word of the LORD came to Zechariah on the **fourth** day of

753 אַרְבַּע[2] *'arba'*[2], n.pr.m. Not used in NIV/BHS [√ 752]

754 אַרְבָּעִים *'arbā'îm*, n.pl.indecl. Not used in NIV/BHS [√ 752]

755 אָרַג *'ārag*, v. [13 / 14] [→ 756]

weaver's [4], weaver [3], weavers [2], did weaving [+1428] [1], spin [1], weave [1], wove [1], woven [+5126] [1]

Ex 28:32 [A] There shall be a **woven** [+5126] edge like a collar around this
35:35 [A] in blue, purple and scarlet yarn and fine linen, and **weavers**—
39:22 [A] of the ephod entirely of blue cloth—the work of a **weaver**—
39:27 [A] they made tunics of fine linen—the work of a **weaver**—
Jdg 16:13 [A] "If *you* **weave** the seven braids of my head into the fabric ⌞on
16:13 [A] seven braids of his head, **wove** [BHS-] them into the fabric
1Sa 17:7 [A] His spear shaft was like a **weaver's** rod, and its iron point
2Sa 21:19 [A] the Gittite, who had a spear with a shaft like a **weaver's** rod.
2Ki 23:7 [A] and where women **did weaving** [+1428] for Asherah.
1Ch 11:23 [A] Although the Egyptian had a spear like a **weaver's** rod in his
20:5 [A] the Gittite, who had a spear with a shaft like a **weaver's** rod.
Isa 19:9 [A] flax will despair, the **weavers** *of* fine linen will lose hope.
38:12 [A] Like a **weaver** I have rolled up my life, and he has cut me off
59:5 [A] They hatch the eggs of vipers and **spin** a spider's web.

756 אֶרֶג *'ereg*, n.[m.]. [2] [√ 755]

loom [1], weaver's shuttle [1]

Jdg 16:14 He awoke from his sleep and pulled up the pin and the **loom**,
Job 7:6 "My days are swifter than a **weaver's shuttle**, and they come to an

757 אַרְגָּב *'argāb*, n.m. Not used in NIV/BHS [→ 758, 759; cf. 8073]

758 אַרְגֹּב[1] *'argōb*[1], n.pr.loc. [4] [√ 757; cf. 8073]

Argob [4]

Dt 3:4 from them—the whole region of **Argob**, Og's kingdom in Bashan.
3:13 (The whole region of **Argob** in Bashan used to be known as a land
3:14 took the whole region of **Argob** as far as the border of the
1Ki 4:13 as well as the district of **Argob** in Bashan and its sixty large walled

759 אַרְגֹּב[2] *'argōb*[2], n.pr.m. [1] [√ 757; cf. 8073]

Argob [1]

2Ki 15:25 with him, he assassinated Pekahiah, along with **Argob** and Arieh,

760 אַרְגְּוָן *'argᵉwān*, n.[m.]. [1] [cf. 763]

purple [1]

2Ch 2:7 [2:6] and iron, and in **purple**, crimson and blue yarn,

761 אַרְגָּז *'argaz*, n.m. [3] [√ 8074]

chest [3]

1Sa 6:8 in a **chest** beside it put the gold objects you are sending back to
6:11 along with it the **chest** containing the gold rats and the models of
6:15 together with the **chest** containing the gold objects, and placed

762 אֹרְגִים *'ōrᵉgîm*, n.pr.m. Not used in NIV/BHS [cf. 3629]

763 אַרְגָּמָן *'argāmān*, n.[m.]. [38] [cf. 760; Ar 10066]

purple [36], purple material [1], tapestry [1]

Ex 25:4 blue, **purple** and scarlet yarn and fine linen; goat hair;
26:1 curtains of finely twisted linen and blue, **purple** and scarlet yarn,
26:31 a curtain of blue, **purple** and scarlet yarn and finely twisted linen,
26:36 a curtain of blue, **purple** and scarlet yarn and finely twisted linen—
27:16 of blue, **purple** and scarlet yarn and finely twisted linen—
28:5 them use gold, and blue, **purple** and scarlet yarn, and fine linen.
28:6 "Make the ephod of gold, and of blue, **purple** and scarlet yarn,
28:8 and made with gold, and with blue, **purple** and scarlet yarn,
28:15 of gold, and of blue, **purple** and scarlet yarn, and of finely twisted
28:33 of blue, **purple** and scarlet yarn around the hem of the robe,

[F] Hitpael (hitpoel, hitpoal, hitpolel, hitpolal, hitpalel, hitpalal, hitpalpel, hitpalpal, hotpael, hotpaal) [G] Hiphil (hiphtil) [H] Hophal [I] Hishtaphel

Ex 35: 6 blue, **purple** and scarlet yarn and fine linen; goat hair;
35:23 **purple** or scarlet yarn or fine linen, or goat hair, ram skins dyed
35:25 what she had spun—blue, **purple** or scarlet yarn or fine linen.
35:35 in blue, **purple** and scarlet yarn and fine linen, and weavers—
36: 8 curtains of finely twisted linen and blue, **purple** and scarlet yarn,
36:35 curtain of blue, **purple** and scarlet yarn and finely twisted linen,
36:37 a curtain of blue, **purple** and scarlet yarn and finely twisted linen—
38:18 was of blue, **purple** and scarlet yarn and finely twisted linen—
38:23 and an embroiderer in blue, **purple** and scarlet yarn and fine linen.)
39: 1 **purple** and scarlet yarn they made woven garments for ministering
39: 2 and of blue, **purple** and scarlet yarn, and of finely twisted linen.
39: 3 to be worked into the blue, **purple** and scarlet yarn and fine linen—
39: 5 and made with gold, and with blue, **purple** and scarlet yarn,
39: 8 of gold, and of blue, **purple** and scarlet yarn, and of finely twisted
39:24 **purple** and scarlet yarn and finely twisted linen around the hem of
39:29 sash was of finely twisted linen and blue, **purple** and scarlet yarn—
Nu 4:13 the ashes from the bronze altar and spread a **purple** cloth over it.
Jdg 8:26 the pendants and the **purple** garments worn by the kings of Midian
2Ch 2:14 [2:13] and with **purple** and blue and crimson yarn and fine linen.
3:14 made the curtain of blue, **purple** and crimson yarn and fine linen,
Est 1: 6 white linen and **purple material** to silver rings on marble pillars.
8:15 and white, a large crown of gold and a **purple** robe of fine linen.
Pr 31:22 coverings for her bed; she is clothed in fine linen and **purple**.
SS 3:10 Its seat was upholstered with **purple**, its interior lovingly inlaid by
7: 5 [7:6] Your hair is like royal **tapestry**; the king is held captive by
Jer 10: 9 and goldsmith have made is then dressed in blue and **purple**—
Eze 27: 7 your awnings were of blue and **purple** from the coasts of Elishah.
27:16 **purple** fabric, embroidered work, fine linen, coral and rubies for

764 אַרְדְּ 'ard, n.pr.m. [2 / 3] [→ 765?, 766, 769?]

Ard [3]

Ge 46:21 Ashbel, Gera, Naaman, Ehi, Rosh, Muppim, Huppim and **Ard**.
Nu 26:40 The descendants of Bela through **Ard** and Naaman were:
26:40 through **Ard**, [BHS-] the Ardite clan; through Naaman,

765 אַרְדּוֹן 'ardôn, n.pr.m. [1] [√ 764?]

Ardon [1]

1Ch 2:18 (and by Jerioth). These were her sons: Jesher, Shobab and **Ardon**.

766 אַרְדִּי 'ardî, a.g. [1] [√ 764]

Ardite [1]

Nu 26:40 through Ard, the **Ardite** clan; through Naaman, the Naamite clan.

767 אֲרַדַּי 'ariday, n.pr.m. [1]

Aridai [1]

Est 9: 9 Parmashta, Arisai, **Aridai** and Vaizatha,

768 אָרָה 'ārâ, v. [2] [√ 251?]

gathered [1], pick [1]

Ps 80:12 [80:13] [A] its walls so that all who pass by **pick** its grapes?
SS 5: 1 [A] my bride; *I have* **gathered** my myrrh with my spice.

769 אֲרוֹד 'arôd, n.pr.m. [1 / 0] [√ 764?]

Nu 26:17 through Arodi, [BHS *Arod*; NIV 771] the Arodite clan;

770 אַרְוָד 'arwād, n.pr.loc. [2] [→ 773]

Arvad [2]

Eze 27: 8 Men of Sidon and **Arvad** were your oarsmen; your skilled men,
27:11 Men of **Arvad** and Helech manned your walls on every side;

771 אֲרוֹדִי 'arôdî[1], n.pr.m. [1 / 2] [→ 772]

Arodi [2]

Ge 46:16 sons of Gad: Zephon, Haggi, Shuni, Ezbon, Eri, **Arodi** and Areli.
Nu 26:17 through **Arodi**, [BHS 769] the Arodite clan; through Areli,

772 אֲרוֹדִי[2] 'arôdî[2], a.g. [1] [√ 771]

Arodite [1]

Nu 26:17 through Arodi, the **Arodite** clan; through Areli, the Arelite clan.

773 אַרְוָדִי 'arwādî, a.g. [2] [√ 770]

Arvadites [2]

Ge 10:18 **Arvadites**, Zemarites and Hamathites. Later the Canaanite clans
1Ch 1:16 **Arvadites**, Zemarites and Hamathites.

774 אֻרְוָה 'urwâ, n.f. [4] [cf. 795]

stalls [3], pens [1]

1Ki 4:26 [5:6] Solomon had four thousand **stalls** for chariot horses,
2Ch 9:25 Solomon had four thousand **stalls** *for* horses and chariots,
32:28 he made **stalls** for various kinds of cattle, and pens for the flocks.
32:28 he made stalls for various kinds of cattle, and **pens** for the flocks.

775 אָרֻז 'ārûz, a. [1] [√ 780?]

tightly knotted [1]

Eze 27:24 and multicolored rugs with cords twisted and **tightly knotted**.

776 אֲרוּכָה 'arûkâ, n.f. [6] [√ 799]

health [2], repairs [2], healing for wound [1], healing [1]

2Ch 24:13 of the work were diligent, and the **repairs** progressed under them.
Ne 4: 7 [4:1] the men of Ashdod heard that the **repairs** to Jerusalem's
Isa 58: 8 break forth like the dawn, and your **healing** will quickly appear;
Jer 8:22 Why then is there no **healing for** the **wound** *of* my people?
30:17 I will restore you to **health** and heal your wounds,' declares the
33: 6 " 'Nevertheless, I will bring **health** and healing to it; I will heal my

777 אֲרוּמָה 'arûmâ, n.pr.loc. [1] [cf. 8126]

Arumah [1]

Jdg 9:41 Abimelech stayed in **Arumah**, and Zebul drove Gaal and his

778 אָרוֹן 'arôn, n.m. & f. [202]

ark [181], chest [10], it[s] [+2021] [4], *untranslated* [2], it[s] [2], coffin [1], it[s] [+1382+2021] [1], it[s] [+466+2021] [1]

Ge 50:26 And after they embalmed him, he was placed in a **coffin** in Egypt.
Ex 25:10 "Have them make a **chest** *of* acacia wood—two and a half cubits
25:14 Insert the poles into the rings on the sides of the **chest** to carry it.
25:14 poles into the rings on the sides of the chest to carry **it**[s] [+2021].
25:15 The poles are to remain in the rings of this **ark**; they are not to be
25:16 Then put in the **ark** the Testimony, which I will give you.
25:21 Place the cover on top of the **ark** and put in the ark the Testimony,
25:21 Place the cover on top of the ark and put in the **ark** the Testimony,
25:22 above the cover between the two cherubim that are over the **ark** *of*
26:33 the clasps and place the **ark** *of* the Testimony behind the curtain.
26:34 Put the atonement cover on the **ark** *of* the Testimony in the Most
30: 6 Put the altar in front of the curtain that is before the **ark** *of* the
30:26 use it to anoint the Tent of Meeting, the **ark** *of* the Testimony,
31: 7 the **ark** of the Testimony with the atonement cover on it,
35:12 the **ark** with its poles and the atonement cover and the curtain that
37: 1 Bezalel made the **ark** of acacia wood—two and a half cubits long,
37: 5 he inserted the poles into the rings on the sides of the **ark** to carry
37: 5 the poles into the rings on the sides of the ark to carry **it**[s] [+2021].
39:35 the **ark** *of* the Testimony with its poles and the atonement cover;
40: 3 Place the **ark** *of* the Testimony in it and shield the ark with the
40: 3 the ark of the Testimony in it and shield the **ark** with the curtain.
40: 5 Place the gold altar of incense in front of the **ark** *of* the Testimony
40:20 He took the Testimony and placed it in the **ark**, attached the poles
40:20 attached the poles to the **ark** and put the atonement cover over it.
40:20 the poles to the ark and put the atonement cover over **it**[s] [+2021].
40:21 he brought the **ark** into the tabernacle and hung the shielding
40:21 hung the shielding curtain and shielded the **ark** *of* the Testimony,
Lev 16: 2 Place behind the curtain in front of the atonement cover on the **ark**,
Nu 3:31 They were responsible for the care of the **ark**, the table,
4: 5 the shielding curtain and cover the **ark** *of* the Testimony with it.
7:89 cherubim above the atonement cover on the **ark** *of* the Testimony.
10:33 The **ark** *of* the covenant of the LORD went before them during
10:35 Whenever the **ark** set out, Moses said, "Rise up, O LORD!
14:44 though neither Moses nor the **ark** *of* the LORD's covenant
Dt 10: 1 and come up to me on the mountain. Also make a wooden **chest**.
10: 2 which you broke. Then you are to put them in the **chest**."
10: 3 So I made the **ark** out of acacia wood and chiseled out two stone
10: 5 back down the mountain and put the tablets in the **ark** I had made,
10: 8 the tribe of Levi to carry the **ark** *of* the covenant of the LORD,
31: 9 sons of Levi, who carried the **ark** *of* the covenant of the LORD,
31:25 he gave this command to the Levites who carried the **ark** *of* the
31:26 place it beside the **ark** *of* the covenant of the LORD your God.
Jos 3: 3 "When you see the **ark** *of* the covenant of the LORD your God,
3: 6 "Take up the **ark** *of* the covenant and pass on ahead of the people."
3: 6 So they took **it**[s] [+1382+2021] up and went ahead of them.
3: 8 Tell the priests who carry the **ark** *of* the covenant: 'When you
3:11 the **ark** *of* the covenant of the Lord of all the earth will go into the
3:13 And as soon as the priests who carry the **ark** *of* the LORD—
3:14 the priests carrying the **ark** *of* the covenant went ahead of them.
3:15 Yet as soon as the priests who carried the **ark** reached the Jordan
3:15 Yet as soon as the priests who carried the ark **[RPH]** reached the
3:17 The priests who carried the **ark** *of* the covenant of the LORD
4: 5 "Go over before the **ark** *of* the LORD your God into the middle

Jos 4: 7 tell them that the flow of the Jordan was cut off before the **ark** *of*
4: 9 where the priests who carried the **ark** *of* the covenant had stood.
4: 10 Now the priests who carried the **ark** remained standing in the
4: 11 the **ark** *of* the LORD and the priests came to the other side while
4: 16 "Command the priests carrying the **ark** *of* the Testimony to come
4: 18 the priests came up out of the river carrying the **ark** *of* the
6: 4 seven priests carry trumpets of rams' horns in front of the **ark**.
6: 6 "Take up the **ark** *of* the covenant of the LORD and have seven
6: 6 the LORD and have seven priests carry trumpets in front of **it**[s]."
6: 7 with the armed guard going ahead of the **ark** *of* the LORD."
6: 8 and the **ark** *of* the LORD's covenant followed them.
6: 9 priests who blew the trumpets, and the rear guard followed the **ark**.
6: 11 So he had the **ark** *of* the LORD carried around the city, circling it
6: 12 the next morning and the priests took up the **ark** *of* the LORD.
6: 13 marching before the **ark** *of* the LORD and blowing the trumpets.
6: 13 ahead of them and the rear guard followed the **ark** *of* the LORD,
7: 6 and fell facedown to the ground before the **ark** *of* the LORD,
8: 33 were standing on both sides of the **ark** *of* the covenant of the
8: 33 ark of the covenant of the LORD, facing those who carried **it**[s]—
Jdg 20: 27 (In those days the **ark** *of* the covenant of God was there,
1Sa 3: 3 down in the temple of the LORD, where the **ark** *of* God was.
4: 3 Let us bring the **ark** *of* the LORD's covenant from Shiloh,
4: 4 they brought back the **ark** *of* the covenant of the LORD
4: 4 and Phinehas, were there with the **ark** *of* the covenant of God.
4: 5 When the **ark** *of* the LORD's covenant came into the camp,
4: 6 When they learned that the **ark** *of* the LORD had come into the
4: 11 The **ark** *of* God was captured, and Eli's two sons, Hophni
4: 13 of the road, watching, because his heart feared for the **ark** *of* God.
4: 17 and Phinehas, are dead, and the **ark** *of* God has been captured."
4: 18 When he mentioned the **ark** *of* God, Eli fell backward off his chair
4: 19 When she heard the news that the **ark** *of* God had been captured
4: 21 because of the capture of the **ark** *of* God and the deaths of her
4: 22 has departed from Israel, for the **ark** *of* God has been captured."
5: 1 After the Philistines had captured the **ark** *of* God, they took it from
5: 2 they carried the **ark** into Dagon's temple and set it beside Dagon.
5: 3 fallen on his face on the ground before the **ark** *of* the LORD!
5: 4 fallen on his face on the ground before the **ark** *of* the LORD!
5: 7 they said, "The **ark** *of* the god of Israel must not stay here with us,
5: 8 asked them, "What shall we do with the **ark** *of* the god of Israel?"
5: 8 "Have the **ark** *of* the god of Israel moved to Gath."
5: 8 Israel moved to Gath." So they moved the **ark** *of* the God of Israel.
5: 10 So they sent the **ark** *of* God to Ekron. As the ark of God was
5: 10 As the **ark** *of* God was entering Ekron, the people of Ekron cried
5: 10 "They have brought the **ark** *of* the god of Israel around to us to kill
5: 11 of the Philistines and said, "Send the **ark** *of* the god of Israel away;
6: 1 When the **ark** *of* the LORD had been in Philistine territory seven
6: 2 and said, "What shall we do with the **ark** *of* the LORD?
6: 3 They answered, "If you return the **ark** *of* the god of Israel,
6: 8 Take the **ark** *of* the LORD and put it on the cart, and in a chest
6: 11 They placed the **ark** *of* the LORD on the cart and along with it
6: 13 when they looked up and saw the **ark**, they rejoiced at the sight.
6: 15 The Levites took down the **ark** *of* the LORD, together with the
6: 18 The large rock, on which they set the **ark** *of* the LORD, is a
6: 19 them to death because they had looked into the **ark** *of* the LORD.
6: 21 saying, "The Philistines have returned the **ark** *of* the LORD.
7: 1 men of Kiriath Jearim came and took up the **ark** *of* the LORD.
7: 1 and consecrated Eleazar his son to guard the **ark** *of* the LORD.
7: 2 twenty years in all, that the **ark** remained at Kiriath Jearim,
14: 18 Saul said to Ahijah, "Bring the **ark** *of* God." (At that time it was
14: 18 ark of God." (At that time **it**[s] [+466+2021] was with the Israelites.)
2Sa 6: 2 out from Baalah of Judah to bring up from there the **ark** *of* God,
6: 3 They set the **ark** *of* God on a new cart and brought it from the
6: 4 with the **ark** *of* God on it, and Ahio was walking in front of it.
6: 4 the ark of God on it, and Ahio was walking in front of **it**[s] [+2021].
6: 6 Uzzah reached out and took hold of the **ark** *of* God, because the
6: 7 God struck him down and he died there beside the **ark** *of* God.
6: 9 and said, "How can the **ark** *of* the LORD ever come to me?"
6: 10 He was not willing to take the **ark** *of* the LORD to be with him in
6: 11 The **ark** *of* the LORD remained in the house of Obed-Edom the
6: 12 of Obed-Edom and everything he has, because of the **ark** *of* God."
6: 12 brought up the **ark** *of* God from the house of Obed-Edom to the
6: 13 When those who were carrying the **ark** *of* the LORD had taken
6: 15 the entire house of Israel brought up the **ark** *of* the LORD with
6: 16 As the **ark** *of* the LORD was entering the City of David,
6: 17 They brought the **ark** *of* the LORD and set it in its place inside
7: 2 living in a palace of cedar, while the **ark** *of* God remains in a tent."
11: 11 "The **ark** and Israel and Judah are staying in tents, and my master
15: 24 all the Levites who were with him were carrying the **ark** *of* the
15: 24 They set down the **ark** *of* God, and Abiathar offered sacrifices
15: 25 the king said to Zadok, "Take the **ark** *of* God back into the city.
15: 29 So Zadok and Abiathar took the **ark** *of* God back to Jerusalem
1Ki 2: 26 because you carried the **ark** *of* the Sovereign LORD before my
3: 15 stood before the **ark** *of* the Lord's covenant and sacrificed burnt
6: 19 He prepared the inner sanctuary within the temple to set the **ark** *of*
8: 1 to bring up the **ark** *of* the LORD's covenant from Zion, the City
8: 3 all the elders of Israel had arrived, the priests took up the **ark**,
8: 4 they brought up the **ark** *of* the LORD and the Tent of Meeting
8: 5 of Israel that had gathered about him were before the **ark**,
8: 6 brought the **ark** *of* the LORD's covenant to its place in the inner
8: 7 The cherubim spread their wings over the place of the **ark**
8: 7 place of the ark and overshadowed the **ark** and its carrying poles.
8: 9 There was nothing in the **ark** except the two stone tablets that
8: 21 I have provided a place there for the **ark**, in which is the covenant
2Ki 12: 9 [12:10] Jehoiada the priest took a **chest** and bored a hole in its lid.
12: 10 [12:11] saw that there was a large amount of money in the **chest**,
1Ch 6: 31 [6:16] in the house of the LORD after the **ark** came to rest there.
13: 3 Let us bring the **ark** *of* our God back to us, for we did not inquire
13: 5 to Lebo Hamath, to bring the **ark** *of* God from Kiriath Jearim.
13: 6 to bring up from there the **ark** *of* God the LORD, who is
13: 7 They moved the **ark** *of* God from Abinadab's house on a new cart,
13: 9 Uzzah reached out his hand to steady the **ark**, because the oxen
13: 10 and he struck him down because he had put his hand on the **ark**.
13: 12 and asked, "How can I ever bring the **ark** *of* God to me?"
13: 13 He did not take the **ark** to be with him in the City of David.
13: 14 The **ark** *of* God remained with the family of Obed-Edom in his
15: 1 he prepared a place for the **ark** *of* God and pitched a tent for it.
15: 2 David said, "No one but the Levites may carry the **ark** *of* God,
15: 2 because the LORD chose them to carry the **ark** *of* the LORD
15: 3 David assembled all Israel in Jerusalem to bring up the **ark** *of* the
15: 12 are to consecrate yourselves and bring up the **ark** *of* the LORD,
15: 14 Levites consecrated themselves in order to bring up the **ark** *of* the
15: 15 the Levites carried the **ark** *of* God with the poles on their
15: 23 Berekiah and Elkanah were to be doorkeepers for the **ark**.
15: 24 Eliezer the priests were to blow trumpets before the **ark** *of* God.
15: 24 Obed-Edom and Jehiah were also to be doorkeepers for the **ark**.
15: 25 the commanders of units of a thousand went to bring up the **ark** *of*
15: 26 Because God had helped the Levites who were carrying the **ark** *of*
15: 27 as were all the Levites who were carrying the **ark**, and as were the
15: 28 So all Israel brought up the **ark** *of* the covenant of the LORD
15: 29 As the **ark** *of* the covenant of the LORD was entering the City of
16: 1 They brought the **ark** *of* God and set it inside the tent that David
16: 4 He appointed some of the Levites to minister before the **ark** *of* the
16: 6 blow the trumpets regularly before the **ark** *of* the covenant of God.
16: 37 his associates before the **ark** *of* the covenant of the LORD to
16: 37 of the covenant of the LORD to minister there **[RPH]** regularly,
17: 1 while the **ark** *of* the covenant of the LORD is under a tent."
22: 19 so that you may bring the **ark** *of* the covenant of the LORD
28: 2 I had it in my heart to build a house as a place of rest for the **ark** *of*
28: 18 their wings and shelter the **ark** *of* the covenant of the LORD.
2Ch 1: 4 Now David had brought up the **ark** *of* God from Kiriath Jearim to
5: 2 to bring up the **ark** *of* the LORD's covenant from Zion, the City
5: 4 all the elders of Israel had arrived, the Levites took up the **ark**,
5: 5 they brought up the **ark** and the Tent of Meeting and all the sacred
5: 6 of Israel that had gathered about him were before the **ark**,
5: 7 brought the **ark** *of* the LORD's covenant to its place in the inner
5: 8 The cherubim spread their wings over the place of the **ark**
5: 8 the place of the ark and covered the **ark** and its carrying poles.
5: 9 These poles were so long that their ends, extending from the **ark**,
5: 10 There was nothing in the **ark** except the two tablets that Moses had
6: 11 There I have placed the **ark**, in which is the covenant of the
6: 41 and come to your resting place, you and the **ark** *of* your might.
8: 11 because the places the **ark** *of* the LORD has entered are holy."
24: 8 At the king's command, a **chest** was made and placed outside,
24: 10 contributions gladly, dropping them into the **chest** until it was full.
24: 11 Whenever the **chest** was brought in by the Levites to the king's
24: 11 would come and empty the **chest** and carry it back to its place.
35: 3 "Put the sacred **ark** in the temple that Solomon son of David king
Ps 132: 8 and come to your resting place, you and the **ark** *of* your might.
Jer 3: 16 "men will no longer say, 'The **ark** *of* the covenant of the LORD.'

779 אֲרַוְנָה ***ᵃrawnâ***, n.pr.m. [9] [cf. 819]

Araunah [8], he[s] [1]

2Sa 24: 16 LORD was then at the threshing floor of **Araunah** the Jebusite.
24: 18 build an altar to the LORD on the threshing floor of **Araunah** the
24: 20 When **Araunah** looked and saw the king and his men coming
24: 20 **he**[s] went out and bowed down before the king with his face to the
24: 21 **Araunah** said, "Why has my lord the king come to his servant?"
24: 22 **Araunah** said to David, "Let my lord the king take whatever
24: 23 O king, **Araunah** gives all this to the king." Araunah also said to
24: 23 **Araunah** also said to him, "May the LORD your God accept
24: 24 But the king replied to **Araunah**, "No, I insist on paying you for it.

780 אֶרֶז ***'erez***, n.m. [73] [→ 775?, 781]

cedar [53], cedars [19], them [+6770] [1]

Lev 14: 4 priest shall order that two live clean birds and some **cedar** wood,
14: 6 then to take the live bird and dip it, together with the **cedar** wood,

Lev 14:49 To purify the house he is to take two birds and some **cedar** wood,
14:51 Then he is to take the **cedar** wood, the hyssop, the scarlet yarn
14:52 the live bird, the **cedar** wood, the hyssop and the scarlet yarn.
Nu 19: 6 The priest is to take some **cedar** wood, hyssop and scarlet wool
24: 6 like aloes planted by the LORD, like **cedars** beside the waters.
Jdg 9:15 come out of the thornbush and consume the **cedars** *of* Lebanon!'
2Sa 5:11 along with **cedar** logs and carpenters and stonemasons, and they
7: 2 said to Nathan the prophet, "Here I am, living in a palace of **cedar**,
7: 7 people Israel, "Why have you not built me a house of **cedar**?" '
1Ki 4:33 [5:13] from the **cedar** of Lebanon to the hyssop that grows out of
5: 6 [5:20] "So give orders that **cedars** of Lebanon be cut for me. My
5: 8 [5:22] will do all you want in providing the **cedar** and pine logs.
5:10 [5:24] this way Hiram kept Solomon supplied with all the **cedar**
6: 9 and completed it, roofing it with beams and **cedar** planks.
6:10 and they were attached to the temple by beams of **cedar**.
6:15 He lined its interior walls with **cedar** boards, paneling them from
6:16 partitioned off twenty cubits at the rear of the temple with **cedar**
6:18 The inside of the temple was **cedar**, carved with gourds and open
6:18 and open flowers. Everything was **cedar**; no stone was to be seen.
6:20 the inside with pure gold, and he also overlaid the altar of **cedar**.
6:36 courses of dressed stone and one course of trimmed **cedar** beams.
7: 2 with four rows of **cedar** columns supporting trimmed cedar beams.
7: 2 with four rows of cedar columns supporting trimmed **cedar** beams.
7: 3 It was roofed with **cedar** above the beams that rested on the
7: 7 he was to judge, and he covered it with **cedar** from floor to ceiling.
7:11 Above were high-grade stones, cut to size, and **cedar** *beams*.
7:12 courses of dressed stone and one course of trimmed **cedar** beams,
9:11 because Hiram had supplied him with all the **cedar** and pine
10:27 and **cedar** as plentiful as sycamore-fig trees in the foothills.
2Ki 14: 9 "A thistle in Lebanon sent a message to a **cedar** in Lebanon,
19:23 I have cut down its tallest **cedars**, the choicest of its pines.
1Ch 14: 1 along with **cedar** logs, stonemasons and carpenters to build a
17: 1 said to Nathan the prophet, "Here I am, living in a palace of **cedar**,
17: 6 my people, "Why have you not built me a house of **cedar**?" '
22: 4 He also provided more **cedar** logs than could be counted,
22: 4 Tyrians had brought large numbers of **them**[s] [+6770] to David.
2Ch 1:15 and **cedar** as plentiful as sycamore-fig trees in the foothills.
2: 3 [2:2] David when you sent him **cedar** to build a palace to live in.
2: 8 [2:7] "Send me also **cedar**, pine and algum logs from Lebanon,
9:27 and **cedar** as plentiful as sycamore-fig trees in the foothills.
25:18 "A thistle in Lebanon sent a message to a **cedar** in Lebanon,
Ezr 3: 7 so that they would bring **cedar** logs by sea from Lebanon to Joppa,
Job 40:17 His tail sways like a **cedar**; the sinews of his thighs are close-knit.
Ps 29: 5 The voice of the LORD breaks the **cedars**; the LORD breaks in
29: 5 the cedars; the LORD breaks in pieces the **cedars** *of* Lebanon.
80:10 [80:11] with its shade, the mighty **cedars** with its branches.
92:12 [92:13] like a palm tree, they will grow like a **cedar** of Lebanon;
104:16 LORD are well watered, the **cedars** *of* Lebanon that he planted.
148: 9 you mountains and all hills, fruit trees and all **cedars**,
SS 1:17 The beams of our house are **cedars**; our rafters are firs.
5:15 of pure gold. His appearance is like Lebanon, choice as its **cedars**.
8: 9 If she is a door, we will enclose her with panels of **cedar**.
Isa 2:13 for all the **cedars** *of* Lebanon, tall and lofty, and all the oaks of
9:10 [9:9] have been felled, but we will replace them with **cedars**."
14: 8 the pine trees and the **cedars** *of* Lebanon exult over you and say,
37:24 I have cut down its tallest **cedars**, the choicest of its pines.
41:19 I will put in the desert the **cedar** and the acacia, the myrtle
44:14 He cut down **cedars**, or perhaps took a cypress or oak. He let it
Jer 22: 7 they will cut up your fine **cedar** *beams* and throw them into the
22:14 large windows in it, panels it with **cedar** and decorates it in red.
22:15 "Does it make you a king to have more and more **cedar**? Did not
22:23 You who live in 'Lebanon,' who are nestled in **cedar** buildings,
Eze 17: 3 varied colors came to Lebanon. Taking hold of the top of a **cedar**,
17:22 I myself will take a shoot from the very top of a **cedar** and plant it;
17:23 will produce branches and bear fruit and become a splendid **cedar**.
27: 5 they took a **cedar** from Lebanon to make a mast for you.
31: 3 Consider Assyria, once a **cedar** in Lebanon, with beautiful
31: 8 The **cedars** in the garden of God could not rival it, nor could the
Am 2: 9 though he was tall as the **cedars** and strong as the oaks.
Zec 11: 1 Open your doors, O Lebanon, so that fire may devour your **cedars**!
11: 2 Wail, O pine tree, for the **cedar** has fallen; the stately trees are

781 אַרְזָה *'arzâ*, n.f.col. [1] [√ 780]

beams of cedar [1]

Zep 2:14 will be in the doorways, the **beams of cedar** will be exposed.

782 ¹אָרַח *'āraḥ¹*, v. [6 / 7] [→ 783?, 784, 785, 786?]

traveler [4], going out [1], keeps company [+2495+4200] [1], travelers [1]

Jdg 19:17 [A] When he looked and saw the **traveler** in the city square,
2Sa 12: 4 [A] or cattle to prepare a meal for the **traveler** who had come to
Job 31:32 [A] for my door was always open to the **traveler**—[BHS 784]
34: 8 [A] *He* **keeps company** [+2495+4200] with evildoers; he
Ps 139: 3 [A] You discern my **going out** and my lying down; you are
Jer 9: 2 [9:1] [A] that I had in the desert a lodging place for **travelers**,
14: 8 [A] a stranger in the land, like a **traveler** who stays only a night?

783 ²אָרַח *'āraḥ²*, n.pr.m. [4] [√ 782?]

Arah [4]

1Ch 7:39 The sons of Ulla: **Arah**, Hanniel and Rizia.
Ezr 2: 5 of **Arah** 775
Ne 6:18 oath to him, since he was son-in-law to Shecaniah son of **Arah**,
7:10 of **Arah** 652

784 אֹרַח *'ōraḥ*, n.m. [56 / 55] [√ 782; Ar 10068]

path [17], paths [11], way [9], ways [5], course [4], roads [2], age of childbearing [+851+2021+3869] [1], conduct [1], destiny [1], end [1], journey [1], path [+2006] [1], siege ramps [+369] [1]

Ge 18:11 and Sarah was past the **age of childbearing** [+851+2021+3869].
49:17 a viper along the **path**, that bites the horse's heels so that its rider
Jdg 5: 6 son of Anath, in the days of Jael, the **roads** were abandoned;
5: 6 the roads were abandoned; travelers took to winding **paths**.
Job 8:13 Such is the **destiny** *of* all who forget God; so perishes the hope of
13:27 you keep close watch on all my **paths** by putting marks on the
16:22 "Only a few years will pass before I go on the **journey** of no
19: 8 He has blocked my **way** so I cannot pass; he has shrouded my
22:15 Will you keep to the old **path** that evil men have trod?
30:12 snares for my feet, they build their **siege ramps** [+369] against me.
31:32 for my door was always open to the traveler—[BHS *path*; NIV 782]
33:11 fastens my feet in shackles; he keeps close watch on all my **paths**.'
34:11 what he has done; he brings upon him what his **conduct** deserves.
Ps 8: 8 [8:9] and the fish of the sea, all that swim the **paths** *of* the seas.
16:11 You have made known to me the **path** *of* life; you will fill me with
17: 4 by the word of your lips I have kept myself from the **ways** *of* the
19: 5 [19:6] his pavilion, like a champion rejoicing to run his **course**.
25: 4 Show me your **ways**, O LORD, teach me your paths;
25:10 All the **ways** *of* the LORD are loving and faithful for those who
27:11 O LORD; lead me in a straight **path** because of my oppressors.
44:18 [44:19] not turned back; our feet had not strayed from your **path**.
119: 9 How can a young man keep his **way** pure? By living according to
119:15 I meditate on your precepts and consider your **ways**.
119:101 I have kept my feet from every evil **path** so that I might obey your
119:104 from your precepts; therefore I hate every wrong **path**.
119:128 because I consider all your precepts right, I hate every wrong **path**.
142: 3 [142:4] In the **path** where I walk men have hidden a snare for me.
Pr 1:19 Such is the **end** *of* all who go after ill-gotten gain; it takes away the
2: 8 for he guards the **course** *of* the just and protects the way of his
2:13 who leave the straight **paths** to walk in dark ways,
2:15 whose **paths** are crooked and who are devious in their ways.
2:19 None who go to her return or attain the **paths** *of* life.
2:20 in the ways of good men and keep to the **paths** *of* the righteous.
3: 6 your ways acknowledge him, and he will make your **paths** straight.
4:14 Do not set foot on the **path** *of* the wicked or walk in the way of
4:18 The **path** *of* the righteous is like the first gleam of dawn, shining
5: 6 She gives no thought to the **way** *of* life; her paths are crooked,
8:20 I walk in the **way** *of* righteousness, along the paths of justice,
9:15 calling out to those who pass by, who go straight on their **way**.
10:17 He who heeds discipline shows the **way** to life, but whoever
12:28 In the **way** *of* righteousness there is life; along that path is
15:10 Stern discipline awaits him who leaves the **path**; he who hates
15:19 is blocked with thorns, but the **path** *of* the upright is a highway.
15:24 The **path** *of* life leads upward for the wise to keep him from going
17:23 A wicked man accepts a bribe in secret to pervert the **course** *of*
22:25 or you may learn his **ways** and get yourself ensnared.
Isa 2: 3 He will teach us his ways, so that we may walk in his **paths**."
3:12 your guides lead you astray; they turn you from the **path** [+2006].
26: 7 The **path** of the righteous is level; O upright One, you make the
26: 8 Yes, LORD, walking in the **way** *of* your laws, we wait for you;
30:11 Leave this way, get off this **path**, and stop confronting us with the
33: 8 The highways are deserted, no travelers are on the **roads**.
40:14 consult to enlighten him, and who taught him the right **way**?
41: 3 moves on unscathed, by a **path** his feet have not traveled before.
Joel 2: 7 They all march in line, not swerving from their **course**.
Mic 4: 2 He will teach us his ways, so that we may walk in his **paths**."

785 אֹרְחָה *'ōrḥâ*, n.f. [4] [√ 782]

caravans [3], caravan [1]

Ge 37:25 looked up and saw a **caravan** *of* Ishmaelites coming from Gilead.
Job 6:18 **Caravans** turn aside from their routes; they go up into the
6:19 The **caravans** *of* Tema look for water, the traveling merchants of
Isa 21:13 You **caravans** *of* Dedanites, who camp in the thickets of Arabia,

786 אֲרֻחָה ***'aruḥâ***, n.f. [6] [√ 782?]

untranslated [2], allowance [2], meal [1], provisions [1]

2Ki 25:30 Day by day the king gave Jehoiachin a regular **allowance** as long
25:30 Day by day the king gave Jehoiachin a regular allowance **[RPH]**
Pr 15:17 Better a **meal** *of* vegetables where there is love than a fattened calf
Jer 40: 5 the commander gave him **provisions** and a present and let him go.
52:34 by day the king of Babylon gave Jehoiachin a regular **allowance**
52:34 gave Jehoiachin a regular allowance **[RPH]** as long as he lived,

787 אֲרִי ***'ărî***, n.m. [35 / 34] [→ 788]

lion [17], lions [14], fierce lion [1], lion's [1], young lion [+4097] [1]

Nu 23:24 they rouse themselves like a **lion** that does not rest till he devours
24: 9 Like a **lion** they crouch and lie down, like a lioness—who dares to
Jdg 14: 5 suddenly a **young lion** [+4097] came roaring toward him.
14:18 What is stronger than a **lion**?" Samson said to them, "If you had
1Sa 17:34 When a **lion** or a bear came and carried off a sheep from the flock,
17:36 Your servant has killed both the **lion** and the bear; this
17:37 The LORD who delivered me from the paw of the **lion** and the
2Sa 1:23 They were swifter than eagles, they were stronger than **lions**.
23:20 went down into a pit on a snowy day and killed a **lion**. [K 793]
1Ki 7:29 On the panels between the uprights were **lions**, bulls
7:29 Above and below the **lions** and bulls were wreaths of hammered
7:36 **lions** and palm trees on the surfaces of the supports and on the
10:19 of the seat were armrests, with a **lion** standing beside each of them.
10:20 Twelve **lions** stood on the six steps, one at either end of each step.
2Ki 17:25 so he sent **lions** among them and they killed some of the people.
17:26 He has sent **lions** among them, which are killing them off,
1Ch 11:22 He also went down into a pit on a snowy day and killed a **lion**.
2Ch 9:18 of the seat were armrests, with a **lion** standing beside each of them.
9:19 Twelve **lions** stood on the six steps, one at either end of each step.
Ps 22:16 [22:17] they have pierced [BHS *like the lion*; NIV 4125] my hands and my feet.
Pr 22:13 The sluggard says, "There is a **lion** outside!" or, "I will be
26:13 "There is a lion in the road, a **fierce lion** roaming the streets!"
28:15 Like a roaring **lion** or a charging bear is a wicked man ruling over
SS 4: 8 from the **lions'** dens and the mountain haunts of the leopards.
Isa 38:13 I waited patiently till dawn, but like a **lion** he broke all my bones;
Jer 50:17 "Israel is a scattered flock that **lions** have chased away. The first to
51:38 Her people all roar like young lions, they growl like **lion** cubs.
La 3:10 Like a bear lying in wait, like a **lion** [K 793] in hiding,
Eze 19: 2 and say: " 'What a lioness was your mother among the **lions**!
19: 6 He prowled among the **lions**, for he was now a strong lion.
22:25 There is a conspiracy of her princes within her like a roaring **lion**
Am 3:12 "As a shepherd saves from the **lion's** mouth only two leg bones
5:19 It will be as though a man fled from a **lion** only to meet a bear,
Na 2:11 [2:12] Where now is the **lions'** den, the place where they fed their
Zep 3: 3 Her officials are roaring **lions**, her rulers are evening wolves,

788 אֻרִי ***'urî***, n.pr.m. [1] [√ 787]

Uri [1]

1Ki 4:19 Geber son of **Uri**—in Gilead (the country of Sihon king of the

789 ¹אֲרִיאֵל ***'ărî'ēl¹***, n.m. [3] [→ 738, 790, 791; cf. 2219]

altar hearth [2], hearth [1]

Isa 29: 2 she will mourn and lament, she will be to me like an **altar hearth**.
Eze 43:15 is four cubits high, and four horns project upward from the **hearth**.
43:16 The **altar hearth** is square, twelve cubits long and twelve cubits

790 ²אֲרִיאֵל ***'ărî'ēl²***, n.pr.f. [4] [√ 789]

Ariel [4]

Isa 29: 1 Woe to you, **Ariel**, Ariel, the city where David settled! Add year to
29: 1 Woe to you, Ariel, **Ariel**, the city where David settled! Add year to
29: 2 Yet I will besiege **Ariel**; she will mourn and lament, she will be to
29: 7 Then the hordes of all the nations that fight against **Ariel**,

791 ³אֲרִיאֵל ***'ărî'ēl³***, n.pr.m. [1] [√ 789]

Ariel [1]

Ezr 8:16 **Ariel**, Shemaiah, Elnathan, Jarib, Elnathan, Nathan, Zechariah

792 אֲרִידָתָא ***'ărîdātā'***, n.pr.m. [1]

Aridatha [1]

Est 9: 8 Poratha, Adalia, **Aridatha**,

793 ¹אַרְיֵה ***'aryēh¹***, n.m. [45 / 44] [→ 794; Ar 10069]

lion [34], lion's [4], lions [4], cubs [+1594] [1], it[s] [+1581+2021] [1]

Ge 49: 9 You are a **lion's** cub, O Judah; you return from the prey, my son.
49: 9 Like a **lion** he crouches and lies down, like a lioness—who dares to
Dt 33:22 About Dan he said: "Dan is a **lion's** cub, springing out of Bashan."
Jdg 14: 8 back to marry her, he turned aside to look at the **lion's** carcass.
14: 8 In **it**[s] [+1581+2021] was a swarm of bees and some honey,
14: 9 he did not tell them that he had taken the honey from the **lion's**
2Sa 17:10 whose heart is like the heart of a **lion**, will melt with fear,
23:20 [down into a pit on a snowy day and killed a **lion**. [K; see Q 787]]
1Ki 13:24 As he went on his way, a **lion** met him on the road and killed him,
13:24 on the road, with both the donkey and the **lion** standing beside it.
13:25 with the **lion** standing beside the body, and they went and reported
13:26 The LORD has given him over to the **lion**, which has mauled him
13:28 down on the road, with the donkey and the **lion** standing beside it.
13:28 The **lion** had neither eaten the body nor mauled the donkey.
20:36 obeyed the LORD, as soon as you leave me a **lion** will kill you."
20:36 And after the man went away, a **lion** found him and killed him.
1Ch 12: 8 [12:9] Their faces were the faces of **lions**, and they were as swift
Job 4:10 The **lions** may roar and growl, yet the teeth of the great lions are
Ps 7: 2 [7:3] or they will tear me like a **lion** and rip me to pieces with no
10: 9 He lies in wait like a **lion** in cover; he lies in wait to catch the
17:12 They are like a **lion** hungry for prey, like a great lion crouching in
22:13 [22:14] Roaring **lions** tearing their prey open their mouths wide
22:21 [22:22] Rescue me from the mouth of the **lions**; save me from the
Ecc 9: 4 the living has hope—even a live dog is better off than a dead **lion**!
Isa 11: 7 will lie down together, and the **lion** will eat straw like the ox.
15: 9 a **lion** upon the fugitives of Moab and upon those who remain in
21: 8 And the lookout [BHS *lion*; NIV 8011] shouted, "Day after day,
31: 4 "As a **lion** growls, a great lion over his prey—and though a whole
35: 9 No **lion** will be there, nor will any ferocious beast get up on it;
65:25 the lamb will feed together, and the **lion** will eat straw like the ox,
Jer 2:30 Your sword has devoured your prophets like a ravening **lion**.
4: 7 A **lion** has come out of his lair; a destroyer of nations has set out.
5: 6 Therefore a **lion** from the forest will attack them, a wolf from the
12: 8 My inheritance has become to me like a **lion** in the forest.
49:19 "Like a **lion** coming up from Jordan's thickets to a rich
50:44 Like a **lion** coming up from Jordan's thickets to a rich pastureland,
La 3:10 [Like a bear lying in wait, like a **lion** [K; see Q 787] in hiding,]
Eze 1:10 on the right side each had the face of a **lion**, and on the left the face
10:14 a cherub, the second the face of a man, the third the face of a **lion**,
Hos 11:10 They will follow the LORD; he will roar like a **lion**. When he
Joel 1: 6 without number; it has the teeth of a **lion**, the fangs of a lioness.
Am 3: 4 Does a **lion** roar in the thicket when he has no prey? Does he growl
3: 8 The **lion** has roared—who will not fear? The Sovereign LORD
Mic 5: 8 [5:7] of many peoples, like a **lion** among the beasts of the forest,
Na 2:11 [2:12] where the **lion** and lioness went, and the cubs, with nothing
2:11 [2:12] where the lion and lioness went, and the **cubs** [+1594],
2:12 [2:13] The **lion** killed enough for his cubs and strangled the prey

794 ²אַרְיֵה ***'aryēh²***, n.pr.m. [1] [√ 793]

Arieh [1]

2Ki 15:25 with him, he assassinated Pekahiah, along with Argob and **Arieh**,

795 אֻרְיָה ***'uryâ***, n.f. Not used in NIV/BHS [cf. 774]

796 אַרְיוֹךְ ***'aryôk***, n.pr.m. [2] [→ Ar 10070]

Arioch [2]

Ge 14: 1 **Arioch** king of Ellasar, Kedorlaomer king of Elam and Tidal king
14: 9 of Goiim, Amraphel king of Shinar and **Arioch** king of Ellasar—

797 אֻרִים ***'urîm***, n.[m.]pl. Not used in NIV/BHS [√ 241]

798 אֲרִיסַי ***'ărîsay***, n.pr.m. [1]

Arisai [1]

Est 9: 9 Parmashta, **Arisai**, Aridai and Vaizatha,

799 אָרַךְ ***'ārak***, v. [34 / 35] [→ 776, 800, 801, 802, 803; Ar 10073]

live long [+3427] [8], lengthen [2], long [2], outlived [+339+3427] [2], prolong [2], so long [2], been long [1], delay [1], endure [1], enjoy a long life [+3427] [1], enjoy long life [+3427] [1], give long [1], gives patience [+678] [1], go by [1], have long [1], lives a long time [1], living long [1], made long [1], maintains [1], patient [1], remained [1], stayed [+8905] [1], stick out [1]

Ge 26: 8 [A] When Isaac *had* **been** there *a* **long** time, Abimelech king of
Ex 20:12 [G] so that you *may* **live long** [+3427] in the land the LORD
Nu 9:19 [G] When the cloud **remained** over the tabernacle a long time,
9:22 [G] Whether the cloud **stayed** [+8905] over the tabernacle for
Dt 4:26 [G] *You will* not **live** there **long** [+3427] but will certainly be
4:40 [G] that *you may* **live long** [+3427] in the land the LORD your
5:16 [G] so that you *may* **live long** [+3427] and that it may go well
5:33 [G] and **prolong** your days in the land that you will possess.
6: 2 [G] that I give you, and so that you *may* **enjoy long** [+3427] **life**.
11: 9 [G] so that *you may* **live long** [+3427] in the land that the

Dt 17:20 [G] his descendants *will* reign a **long** time over his kingdom in
22: 7 [G] that it may go well with you and *you may* **have** *a* **long** life.
25:15 [G] so that you *may* **live long** [+3427] in the land the LORD
30:18 [G] *You will* not **live long** [+3427] in the land you are crossing
32:47 [G] By them *you will* **live long** [+3427] in the land you are
Jos 24:31 [G] of Joshua and of the elders who **outlived** [+339+3427] him
Jdg 2: 7 [G] of Joshua and of the elders who **outlived** [+339+3427] him
1Ki 3:14 [G] as David your father did, *I will* **give** you a **long** life."
8: 8 [G] These poles *were* **so long** that their ends could be seen from
2Ch 5: 9 [G] These poles *were* **so long** that their ends, extending from the
Job 6:11 [G] I should still hope? What prospects, that I *should be* **patient**?
Ps 72: 5 [G] *He will* **endure** [BHS 3707] as long as the sun, as long as
129: 3 [G] have plowed my back and **made** their furrows **long**.
Pr 19:11 [G] A man's wisdom **gives** him **patience** [+678]; it is to his glory
28: 2 [G] but a man of understanding and knowledge **maintains** order.
28:16 [G] he who hates ill-gotten gain *will* **enjoy a long** [+3427] **life**.
Ecc 7:15 [G] and a wicked man **living long** in his wickedness.
8:12 [G] man commits a hundred crimes and still **lives a long time**,
8:13 [G] with them, and their days *will* not **lengthen** like a shadow.
Isa 48: 9 [G] For my own name's sake *I* **delay** my wrath; for the sake of
53:10 [G] he will see his offspring and **prolong** his days, and the will of
54: 2 [G] not hold back; **lengthen** your cords, strengthen your stakes.
57: 4 [G] At whom do you sneer and **stick out** your tongue?
Eze 12:22 [A] 'The days **go by** and every vision comes to nothing'?
31: 5 [A] its boughs increased and its branches *grew* **long**, spreading

800 אָרֵךְ *'ārēk*, a. [15] [√ 799]

slow [9], patient [+678] [3], long [1], long-suffering [+678] [1], patience [+8120] [1]

Ex 34: 6 gracious God, **slow** *to* anger, abounding in love and faithfulness,
Nu 14:18 'The LORD is **slow** *to* anger, abounding in love and forgiving sin
Ne 9:17 gracious and compassionate, **slow** *to* anger and abounding in love.
Ps 86:15 gracious God, **slow** *to* anger, abounding in love and faithfulness.
103: 8 The LORD is compassionate and gracious, **slow** *to* anger,
145: 8 is gracious and compassionate, **slow** *to* anger and rich in love.
Pr 14:29 A **patient** [+678] *man* has great understanding, but a
15:18 man stirs up dissension, but a **patient** [+678] *man* calms a quarrel.
16:32 Better a **patient** [+678] *man* than a warrior, a man who controls
Ecc 7: 8 better than its beginning, and **patience** [+8120] is better than pride.
Jer 15:15 You are **long-suffering** [+678]—do not take me away; think of
Eze 17: 3 **long** feathers and full plumage of varied colors came to Lebanon.
Joel 2:13 and compassionate, **slow** *to* anger and abounding in love,
Jnh 4: 2 and compassionate God, **slow** *to* anger and abounding in love,
Na 1: 3 The LORD is **slow** *to* anger and great in power; the LORD will

801 אָרֹךְ *'ārōk*, a. [3] [√ 799]

long time [2], longer [1]

2Sa 3: 1 the house of Saul and the house of David lasted a **long time**.
Job 11: 9 Their measure is **longer** than the earth and wider than the sea.
Jer 29:28 It will be a **long time**. Therefore build houses and settle down;

802 אֹרֶךְ *'ōrek*, n.[m.]. [95 / 94] [√ 799]

long [65], length [12], *untranslated* [3], wide [2], endless [1], extended [1], forever [+3427+4200] [1], lengthwise [1], longer [1], many years [+3427] [1], patience [+678] [1], prolong [1], so long [+3427] [1], spreading [1], square [1], total wingspan [+4053] [1]

Ge 6:15 The ark is to be 450 feet **long**, 75 feet wide and 45 feet high.
13:17 Go, walk through the **length** and breadth of the land, for I am
Ex 25:10 two and a half cubits **long**, a cubit and a half wide, and a cubit
25:17 pure gold—two and a half cubits **long** and a cubit and a half wide.
25:23 two cubits **long**, a cubit wide and a cubit and a half high.
26: 2 to be the same size—twenty-eight cubits **long** and four cubits wide.
26: 8 are to be the same size—thirty cubits **long** and four cubits wide.
26:13 The tent curtains will be a cubit **longer** on both sides; what is left
26:16 Each frame is to be ten cubits **long** and a cubit and a half wide,
27: 1 cubits high; it is to be square, five cubits **long** and five cubits wide.
27: 9 The south side shall be a hundred cubits **long** and is to have
27:11 The north side shall also be a **[RPH]** hundred cubits long
27:11 The north side shall also be a hundred cubits **long** and is to have
27:18 The courtyard shall be a hundred cubits **long** and fifty cubits wide,
28:16 It is to be square—a span **long** and a span wide—and folded
30: 2 It is to be square, a cubit **long** and a cubit wide, and two cubits
36: 9 were the same size—twenty-eight cubits **long** and four cubits wide.
36:15 were the same size—thirty cubits **long** and four cubits wide.
36:21 Each frame was ten cubits **long** and a cubit and a half wide,
37: 1 two and a half cubits **long**, a cubit and a half wide, and a cubit
37: 6 pure gold—two and a half cubits **long** and a cubit and a half wide.
37:10 two cubits **long**, a cubit wide, and a cubit and a half high.
37:25 It was square, a cubit **long** and a cubit wide, and two cubits high—
38: 1 cubits high; it was square, five cubits **long** and five cubits wide.
38:18 It was twenty cubits **long** and, like the curtains of the courtyard,
39: 9 It was square—a span **long** and a span wide—and folded double.
Dt 3:11 of iron and was more than thirteen feet **long** and six feet wide.
30:20 he will give you **many** [+3427] **years** in the land he swore to give
Jdg 3:16 Ehud had made a double-edged sword about a foot and a half **long**,
1Ki 6: 2 that King Solomon built for the LORD was sixty cubits **long**,
6: 3 **[RPH]** and projected ten cubits from the front of the temple.
6:20 The inner sanctuary was twenty cubits **long**, twenty wide
7: 2 He built the Palace of the Forest of Lebanon a hundred cubits **long**,
7: 6 He made a colonnade fifty cubits **long** and thirty wide. In front of
7:27 of bronze; each was four cubits **long**, four wide and three high.
2Ch 3: 3 Solomon laid for building the temple of God was sixty cubits **long**
3: 4 The portico at the front of the temple was twenty cubits **long**
3: 8 Holy Place, its **length** corresponding to the width of the temple—
3:11 The **total wingspan of** [+4053] the cherubim was twenty cubits.
3:15 he made two pillars, which ⌞together⌟ were thirty-five cubits **long**,
4: 1 He made a bronze altar twenty cubits **long**, twenty cubits wide
6:13 five cubits **long**, five cubits wide and three cubits high,
Job 12:12 found among the aged? Does not **long** life bring understanding?
Ps 21: 4 [21:5] and you gave it to him—**length** *of* days, for ever and ever.
23: 6 I will dwell in the house of the LORD **forever** [+3427+4200].
91:16 With **long** life will I satisfy him and show him my salvation."
93: 5 holiness adorns your house for **endless** days, O LORD.
Pr 3: 2 for they will **prolong** your life many years and bring you
3:16 **Long** life is in her right hand; in her left hand are riches and honor.
25:15 Through **patience** [+678] a ruler can be persuaded, and a gentle
La 5:20 do you always forget us? Why do you forsake us **so long** [+3427]?
Eze 31: 7 It was majestic in beauty, with its **spreading** boughs, for its roots
40: 7 The alcoves for the guards were one rod **long** and one rod wide,
40:11 to the gateway; it was ten cubits and its **length** was thirteen cubits.
40:18 the sides of the gateways and was as wide as they were **long**;
40:20 Then he measured the **length** and width of the gate facing north,
40:21 first gateway. It was fifty cubits **long** and twenty-five cubits wide.
40:25 of the others. It was fifty cubits **long** and twenty-five cubits wide.
40:29 all around. It was fifty cubits **long** and twenty-five cubits wide.
40:30 the gateways around the inner court were twenty-five cubits **wide**
40:33 all around. It was fifty cubits **long** and twenty-five cubits wide.
40:36 all around. It was fifty cubits **long** and twenty-five cubits wide.
40:42 each a cubit and a half **long**, a cubit and a half wide and a cubit
40:47 It was square—a hundred cubits **long** and a hundred cubits wide.
40:49 The portico was twenty cubits **wide**, and twelve cubits from front
41: 2 outer sanctuary; it was forty cubits **long** and twenty cubits wide.
41: 4 he measured the **length** *of* the inner sanctuary; it was twenty
41:12 was five cubits thick all around, and its **length** was ninety cubits.
41:13 it was a hundred cubits **long**, and the temple courtyard
41:13 and the building with its walls were also a hundred cubits **long**.
41:15 he measured the **length** *of* the building facing the courtyard at the
41:22 There was a wooden altar three cubits high and two cubits **square**;
41:22 its base [BHS *length*; NIV 149] and its sides were of wood.
42: 2 The building whose door faced north was a hundred cubits **long**
42: 7 the outer court; it **extended** in front of the rooms for fifty cubits.
42: 8 of rooms on the side next to the outer court was fifty cubits **long**,
42:11 they had the same **length** and width, with similar exits and
42:20 around it, five hundred cubits **long** and five hundred cubits wide,
43:16 altar hearth is square, twelve cubits **long** and twelve cubits wide.
43:17 fourteen cubits **long** and fourteen cubits wide, with a rim of half a
45: 1 as a sacred district, 25,000 cubits **long** and 20,000 cubits wide;
45: 1 sacred district, 25,000 cubits long **[RPH]** and 20,000 cubits wide;
45: 3 measure off a section 25,000 cubits **long** and 10,000 cubits wide.
45: 5 An area 25,000 cubits **long** and 10,000 cubits wide will belong to
45: 6 as its property an area 5,000 cubits wide and 25,000 cubits **long**,
45: 7 running **lengthwise** from the western to the eastern border parallel
46:22 were enclosed courts, forty cubits **long** and thirty cubits wide;
48: 8 its **length** from east to west will equal one of the tribal portions;
48: 9 portion you are to offer to the LORD will be 25,000 cubits **long**
48:10 wide on the east side and 25,000 cubits **long** on the south side.
48:13 the Levites will have an allotment 25,000 cubits **long** and 10,000
48:13 Its total **length** will be 25,000 cubits and its width 10,000 cubits.
48:18 bordering on the sacred portion and running the **length** of it,
Zec 2: 2 [2:6] to find out how wide and how **long** it is."
5: 2 "I see a flying scroll, thirty feet **long** and fifteen feet wide."

803 ¹אֶרֶךְ *'erek¹*, a. Not used in NIV/BHS [√ 799]

804 ²אֶרֶךְ *'erek²*, n.pr.loc. [1] [→ Ar 10074]

Erech [1]

Ge 10:10 his kingdom were Babylon, **Erech**, Akkad and Calneh, in Shinar.

805 אַרְכִּי *'arkî*, a.g. [6]

Arkite [5], Arkites [1]

Jos 16: 2 Luz), crossed over to the territory of the **Arkites** *in* Ataroth,
2Sa 15:32 Hushai the **Arkite** was there to meet him, his robe torn and dust on
16:16 Then Hushai the **Arkite**, David's friend, went to Absalom

2Sa 17: 5 Absalom said, "Summon also Hushai the **Arkite**, so we can hear
17: 14 "The advice of Hushai the **Arkite** is better than that of
1Ch 27: 33 was the king's counselor. Hushai the **Arkite** was the king's friend.

806 אֲרָם *ʾᵃrām*, n.pr.m. [132 / 129] [→ 811, 812, 7020; *also used with compound proper names*]

Aram [69], Arameans [42], Aramean [7], *untranslated* [2], Aramean kingdom [2], their[s] [2], them[s] [2], they[s] [2], it[s] [1]

Ge 10: 22 The sons of Shem: Elam, Asshur, Arphaxad, Lud and **Aram**.
10: 23 The sons of **Aram**: Uz, Hul, Gether and Meshech.
22: 21 Uz the firstborn, Buz his brother, Kemuel (the father of **Aram**),
Nu 23: 7 "Balak brought me from **Aram**, the king of Moab from the eastern
Jdg 3: 10 The LORD gave Cushan-Rishathaim king of **Aram** into the hands
10: 6 and the gods of **Aram**, the gods of Sidon, the gods of Moab,
2Sa 8: 5 When the **Arameans** *of* Damascus came to help Hadadezer king of
8: 5 king of Zobah, David struck down twenty-two thousand of **them**[s].
8: 6 He put garrisons in the **Aramean kingdom** *of* Damascus,
8: 6 and the **Arameans** became subject to him and brought tribute.
8: 12 Edom [BHS *Aram*; NIV 121] and Moab, the Ammonites and the
8: 13 eighteen thousand Edomites [BHS *Arameans*; NIV 121]
10: 6 they hired twenty thousand **Aramean** foot soldiers *from* Beth
10: 6 Aramean foot soldiers from Beth Rehob and **[RPH]** Zobah,
10: 8 while the **Arameans** *of* Zobah and Rehob and the men of Tob
10: 9 the best troops in Israel and deployed them against the **Arameans**.
10: 11 Joab said, "If the **Arameans** are too strong for me, then you are to
10: 13 and the troops with him advanced to fight the **Arameans**,
10: 14 When the Ammonites saw that the **Arameans** were fleeing,
10: 15 After the **Arameans** saw that they had been routed by Israel,
10: 16 Hadadezer had **Arameans** brought from beyond the River;
10: 17 The **Arameans** formed their battle lines to meet David and fought
10: 18 **they**[s] fled before Israel, and David killed seven hundred of their
10: 18 David killed seven hundred of **their**[s] charioteers and forty
10: 19 So the **Arameans** were afraid to help the Ammonites anymore.
15: 8 While your servant was living at Geshur in **Aram**, I made this
1Ki 10: 29 exported them to all the kings of the Hittites and of the **Arameans**.
11: 25 by Hadad. So Rezon ruled in **Aram** and was hostile toward Israel.
15: 18 the son of Hezion, the king of **Aram**, who was ruling in Damascus.
19: 15 of Damascus. When you get there, anoint Hazael king over **Aram**.
20: 1 Now Ben-Hadad king of **Aram** mustered his entire army.
20: 20 At that, the **Arameans** fled, with the Israelites in pursuit.
20: 20 Ben-Hadad king of **Aram** escaped on horseback with some of his
20: 21 and chariots and inflicted heavy losses on the **Arameans**.
20: 22 because next spring the king of **Aram** will attack you again."
20: 23 Meanwhile, the officials of the king of **Aram** advised him,
20: 26 The next spring Ben-Hadad mustered the **Arameans** and went up
20: 27 flocks of goats, while the **Arameans** covered the countryside.
20: 28 'Because the **Arameans** think the LORD is a god of the hills
20: 29 thousand casualties on the **Aramean** foot soldiers in one day.
22: 1 For three years there was no war between **Aram** and Israel.
22: 3 and yet we are doing nothing to retake it from the king of **Aram**?"
22: 11 'With these you will gore the **Arameans** until they are
22: 31 Now the king of **Aram** had ordered his thirty-two chariot
22: 35 and the king was propped up in his chariot facing the **Arameans**.
2Ki 5: 1 Now Naaman was commander of the army of the king of **Aram**.
5: 1 because through him the LORD had given victory to **Aram**.
5: 2 Now bands from **Aram** had gone out and had taken captive a
5: 5 "By all means, go," the king of **Aram** replied. "I will send a letter
6: 8 Now the king of **Aram** was at war with Israel. After conferring
6: 9 passing that place, because the **Arameans** are going down there."
6: 11 This enraged the king of **Aram**. He summoned his officers
6: 23 So the bands from **Aram** stopped raiding Israel's territory.
6: 24 Ben-Hadad king of **Aram** mobilized his entire army and marched
7: 4 So let's go over to the camp of the **Arameans** and surrender.
7: 5 At dusk they got up and went to the camp of the **Arameans**.
7: 5 they reached the edge of the camp, **[RPH]** not a man was there,
7: 6 for the Lord had caused the **Arameans** to hear the sound of
7: 10 "We went into the **Aramean** camp and not a man was there—
7: 12 to his officers, "I will tell you what the **Arameans** have done to us.
7: 14 with their horses, and the king sent them after the **Aramean** army.
7: 15 equipment the **Arameans** had thrown away in their headlong
7: 16 the people went out and plundered the camp of the **Arameans**.
8: 7 Elisha went to Damascus, and Ben-Hadad king of **Aram** was ill.
8: 9 and said, "Your son Ben-Hadad king of **Aram** has sent me to ask,
8: 13 "The LORD has shown me that you will become king of **Aram**,"
8: 28 of Ahab to war against Hazael king of **Aram** at Ramoth Gilead.
8: 29 inflicted on him at Ramoth in his battle with Hazael king of **Aram**.
9: 14 had been defending Ramoth Gilead against Hazael king of **Aram**,
9: 15 had inflicted on him in the battle with Hazael king of **Aram**.)
12: 17 [12:18] About this time Hazael king of **Aram** went up
12: 18 [12:19] he sent them to Hazael king of **Aram**, who then withdrew
13: 3 a long time he kept them under the power of Hazael king of **Aram**
13: 4 for he saw how severely the king of **Aram** was oppressing Israel.
13: 5 a deliverer for Israel, and they escaped from the power of **Aram**.
13: 7 for the king of **Aram** had destroyed the rest and made them like
13: 17 "The LORD's arrow of victory, the arrow of victory over **Aram**!"
13: 17 "You will completely destroy the **Arameans** at Aphek."
13: 19 then you would have defeated **Aram** and completely destroyed it.
13: 19 destroyed it. But now you will defeat **it**[s] only three times."
13: 22 Hazael king of **Aram** oppressed Israel throughout the reign of
13: 24 Hazael king of **Aram** died, and Ben-Hadad his son succeeded him
15: 37 (In those days the LORD began to send Rezin king of **Aram**
16: 5 Rezin king of **Aram** and Pekah son of Remaliah king of Israel
16: 6 Rezin king of **Aram** recovered Elath for Aram by driving out the
16: 6 Rezin king of Aram recovered Elath for **Aram** by driving out the
16: 7 Come up and save me out of the hand of the king of **Aram**
24: 2 **Aramean**, Moabite and Ammonite raiders against him.
1Ch 1: 17 Elam, Asshur, Arphaxad, Lud and **Aram**. The sons of Aram:
1: 17 The sons of **Aram**: [BHS-] Uz, Hul, Gether and Meshech.
2: 23 (But Geshur and **Aram** captured Havvoth Jair, as well as Kenath
7: 34 The sons of Shomer: Ahi, Rohgah, Hubbah and **Aram**.
18: 5 When the **Arameans** *of* Damascus came to help Hadadezer king of
18: 5 king of Zobah, David struck down twenty-two thousand of **them**[s].
18: 6 He put garrisons in the **Aramean kingdom** *of* Damascus,
18: 6 and the **Arameans** became subject to him and brought tribute.
19: 10 the best troops in Israel and deployed them against the **Arameans**.
19: 12 Joab said, "If the **Arameans** are too strong for me, then you are to
19: 14 and the troops with him advanced to fight the **Arameans**,
19: 15 When the Ammonites saw that the **Arameans** were fleeing,
19: 16 After the **Arameans** saw that they had been routed by Israel,
19: 16 and had **Arameans** brought from beyond the River,
19: 17 David formed his lines to meet the **Arameans** in battle, and they
19: 18 **they**[s] fled before Israel, and David killed seven thousand of their
19: 18 David killed seven thousand of **their**[s] charioteers and forty
19: 19 So the **Arameans** were not willing to help the Ammonites
2Ch 1: 17 exported them to all the kings of the Hittites and of the **Arameans**.
16: 2 and of his own palace and sent it to Ben-Hadad king of **Aram**,
16: 7 "Because you relied on the king of **Aram** and not on the LORD
16: 7 the army of the king of **Aram** has escaped from your hand.
18: 10 'With these you will gore the **Arameans** until they are
18: 30 Now the king of **Aram** had ordered his chariot commanders,
18: 34 himself up in his chariot facing the **Arameans** until evening.
20: 2 army is coming against you from Edom, [BHS *Aram*; NIV 121]
22: 5 of Israel to war against Hazael king of **Aram** at Ramoth Gilead.
22: 6 inflicted on him at Ramoth in his battle with Hazael king of **Aram**.
24: 23 At the turn of the year, the army of **Aram** marched against Joash;
24: 24 Although the **Aramean** army had come with only a few men,
28: 5 the LORD his God handed him over to the king of **Aram**.
28: 23 "Since the gods of the kings of **Aram** have helped them,
Isa 7: 1 King Rezin of **Aram** and Pekah son of Remaliah king of Israel
7: 2 house of David was told, "**Aram** has allied itself with Ephraim";
7: 4 of the fierce anger of Rezin and **Aram** and of the son of Remaliah.
7: 5 **Aram**, Ephraim and Remaliah's son have plotted your ruin,
7: 8 for the head of **Aram** is Damascus, and the head of Damascus is
9: 12 [9:11] **Arameans** from the east and Philistines from the west have
17: 3 the remnant of **Aram** will be like the glory of the Israelites,"
Jer 35: 11 go to Jerusalem to escape the Babylonian and **Aramean** armies.'
Eze 16: 57 now scorned by the daughters of Edom [BHS *Aram*; NIV 121]
27: 16 " '**Aram** did business with you because of your many products;
Hos 12: 12 [12:13] Jacob fled to the country of **Aram**; Israel served to get a
Am 1: 5 The people of **Aram** will go into exile to Kir," says the LORD.
9: 7 the Philistines from Caphtor and the **Arameans** from Kir?

807 אֲרַם מַעֲכָה *ʾᵃram maʿᵃkâ*, n.pr.loc. [1] [√ 806 + 5081]

Aram Maacah [1]

1Ch 19: 6 and charioteers from Aram Naharaim, **Aram Maacah** and Zobah.

808 אֲרַם נַהֲרַיִם *ʾᵃram nahᵃrayim*, n.loc. [5] [√ 806 + 5645]

Aram Naharaim [5]

Ge 24: 10 He set out for **Aram Naharaim** and made his way to the town of
Dt 23: 4 [23:5] Pethor in **Aram Naharaim** to pronounce a curse on you.
Jdg 3: 8 into the hands of Cushan-Rishathaim king of **Aram Naharaim**,
1Ch 19: 6 of silver to hire chariots and charioteers from **Aram Naharaim**,
Ps 60: T [60:2] When he fought **Aram Naharaim** and Aram Zobah, and

809 אֲרַם צוֹבָה *ʾᵃram ṣôbâ*, n.pr.loc. [1] [√ 806 + 7420]

Aram Zobah [1]

Ps 60: T [60:2] When he fought Aram Naharaim and **Aram Zobah**, and

810 אַרְמוֹן *'armôn*, n.m. [32] [→ 813; cf. 528, 8227]

fortresses [19], citadels [4], citadel [3], palaces [3], fortress [1], palace [1], stronghold [1]

1Ki 16: 18 he went into the **citadel** *of* the royal palace and set the palace on
2Ki 15: 25 and Arieh, in the **citadel** *of* the royal palace at Samaria.
2Ch 36: 19 they burned all the **palaces** and destroyed everything of value

Ps 48: 3 [48:4] God is in her **citadels**; he has shown himself to be her
48: 13 [48:14] consider well her ramparts, view her **citadels**, that you
122: 7 be peace within your walls and security within your **citadels**."
Pr 18: 19 a fortified city, and disputes are like the barred gates of a **citadel**.
Isa 23: 13 they stripped its **fortresses** bare and turned it into a ruin.
25: 2 the fortified town a ruin, the foreigners' **stronghold** a city no more;
32: 14 The **fortress** will be abandoned, the noisy city deserted; citadel
34: 13 Thorns will overrun her **citadels**, nettles and brambles her
Jer 6: 5 So arise, let us attack at night and destroy her **fortresses**!"
9: 21 [9:20] in through our windows and has entered our **fortresses**;
17: 27 fire in the gates of Jerusalem that will consume her **fortresses**.' "
30: 18 rebuilt on her ruins, and the **palace** will stand in its proper place.
49: 27 walls of Damascus; it will consume the **fortresses** *of* Ben-Hadad."
La 2: 5 He has swallowed up all her **palaces** and destroyed her
2: 7 He has handed over to the enemy the walls of her **palaces**;
Hos 8: 14 will send fire upon their cities that will consume their **fortresses**."
Am 1: 4 house of Hazael that will consume the **fortresses** *of* Ben-Hadad.
1: 7 send fire upon the walls of Gaza that will consume her **fortresses**.
1: 10 send fire upon the walls of Tyre that will consume her **fortresses**."
1: 12 I will send fire upon Teman that will consume the **fortresses** *of*
1: 14 will consume her **fortresses** amid war cries on the day of battle,
2: 2 I will send fire upon Moab that will consume the **fortresses** *of*
2: 5 I will send fire upon Judah that will consume the **fortresses** *of*
3: 9 Proclaim to the **fortresses** of Ashdod and to the fortresses of
3: 9 to the fortresses of Ashdod and to the **fortresses** of Egypt:
3: 10 the LORD, "who hoard plunder and loot in their **fortresses**."
3: 11 he will pull down your strongholds and plunder your **fortresses**."
6: 8 "I abhor the pride of Jacob and detest his **fortresses**; I will deliver
Mic 5: 5 [5:4] invades our land and marches through our **fortresses**,

811 אֲרָמִית ʾᵃrāmîṯ, adv. [5] [√ 806]

in Aramaic [5]

2Ki 18: 26 "Please speak to your servants **in Aramaic**, since we understand it.
Ezr 4: 7 The letter was written **in Aramaic** script and in the Aramaic
4: 7 letter was written in Aramaic script and **in** the **Aramaic** language.
Isa 36: 11 "Please speak to your servants **in Aramaic**, since we understand it.
Da 2: 4 Then the astrologers answered the king **in Aramaic**, "O king,

812 אֲרַמִּי ʾᵃrammî, a.g. [11 / 12] [√ 806]

Aramean [8], Arameans [4]

Ge 25: 20 Rebekah daughter of Bethuel the **Aramean** from Paddan Aram
25: 20 the Aramean from Paddan Aram and sister of Laban the **Aramean**.
28: 5 to Laban son of Bethuel the **Aramean**, the brother of Rebekah,
31: 20 Jacob deceived Laban the **Aramean** by not telling him he was
31: 24 Then God came to Laban the **Aramean** in a dream at night
Dt 26: 5 "My father was a wandering **Aramean**, and he went down into
2Ki 5: 20 to himself, "My master was too easy on Naaman, this **Aramean**,
8: 28 king of Aram at Ramoth Gilead. The **Arameans** wounded Joram;
8: 29 **Arameans** had inflicted on him at Ramoth in his battle with
9: 15 **Arameans** had inflicted on him in the battle with Hazael king of
16: 6 [**Edomites** [K; see Q 122] then moved into Elath and have lived]
1Ch 7: 14 Asriel was his descendant through his **Aramean** concubine.
2Ch 22: 5 at Ramoth Gilead. The **Arameans** [BHS 8246] wounded Joram;

813 אַרְמֹנִי ʾarmōnî, n.pr.m. [1] [√ 810]

Armoni [1]

2Sa 21: 8 the king took **Armoni** and Mephibosheth, the two sons of Aiah's

814 אֲרָן ʾᵃrān, n.pr.m. [2]

Aran [2]

Ge 36: 28 The sons of Dishan: Uz and **Aran**.
1Ch 1: 42 Bilhan, Zaavan and Akan. The sons of Dishan: Uz and **Aran**.

815 ¹אֹרֶן ʾōren[1], n.[m.]. [1] [→ 816, 818?]

pine [1]

Isa 44: 14 the trees of the forest, or planted a **pine**, and the rain made it grow.

816 ²אֹרֶן ʾōren[2], n.pr.m. [1] [√ 815]

Oren [1]

1Ch 2: 25 of Hezron: Ram his firstborn, Bunah, **Oren**, Ozem and Ahijah.

817 אַרְנֶבֶת ʾarnebeṯ, n.f. [2] [cf. 4]

rabbit [2]

Lev 11: 6 The **rabbit**, though it chews the cud, does not have a split hoof;
Dt 14: 7 divided you may not eat the camel, the **rabbit** or the coney.

818 אַרְנוֹן ʾarnôn, n.pr.loc. [25] [√ 815?]

Arnon [24], Arnon's [1]

Nu 21: 13 They set out from there and camped alongside the **Arnon**,
21: 13 The **Arnon** is the border of Moab, between Moab and the
21: 14 the LORD says: "Waheb in Suphah and the ravines, the **Arnon**
21: 24 to the sword and took over his land from the **Arnon** to the Jabbok,
21: 26 of Moab and had taken from him all his land as far as the **Arnon**.
21: 28 It consumed Ar of Moab, the citizens of **Arnon's** heights.
22: 36 he went out to meet him at the Moabite town on the **Arnon** border,
Dt 2: 24 "Set out now and cross the **Arnon** Gorge. See, I have given into
2: 36 From Aroer on the rim of the **Arnon** Gorge, and from the town in
3: 8 east of the Jordan, from the **Arnon** Gorge as far as Mount Hermon.
3: 12 and the Gadites the territory north of Aroer by the **Arnon** Gorge,
3: 16 to the **Arnon** Gorge (the middle of the gorge being the border)
4: 48 This land extended from Aroer on the rim of the **Arnon** Gorge to
Jos 12: 1 from the **Arnon** Gorge to Mount Hermon, including all the eastern
12: 2 He ruled from Aroer on the rim of the **Arnon** Gorge—from the
13: 9 It extended from Aroer on the rim of the **Arnon** Gorge, and from
13: 16 The territory from Aroer on the rim of the **Arnon** Gorge, and from
Jdg 11: 13 they took away my land from the **Arnon** to the Jabbok, all the way
11: 18 the country of Moab, and camped on the other side of the **Arnon**.
11: 18 did not enter the territory of Moab, for the **Arnon** was its border.
11: 22 capturing all of it from the **Arnon** to the Jabbok and from the
11: 26 the surrounding settlements and all the towns along the **Arnon**.
2Ki 10: 33 from Aroer by the **Arnon** Gorge through Gilead to Bashan.
Isa 16: 2 the nest, so are the women of Moab at the fords of the **Arnon**.
Jer 48: 20 and cry out! Announce by the **Arnon** that Moab is destroyed.

819 אֲרַנְיָה ʾᵃranyâ, n.pr.m. Not used in NIV/BHS [cf. 779]

820 אַרְנָן ʾarnān, n.pr.m. [1]

Arnan [1]

1Ch 3: 21 and the sons of Rephaiah, of **Arnan**, of Obadiah and of Shecaniah.

821 אָרְנָן ʾornān, n.pr.m. [12]

Araunah [9], *untranslated* [1], he[s] [1], him[s] [1]

1Ch 21: 15 then standing at the threshing floor of **Araunah** the Jebusite.
21: 18 build an altar to the LORD on the threshing floor of **Araunah** the
21: 20 While **Araunah** was threshing wheat, he turned and saw the angel;
21: 20 While Araunah was threshing wheat, **he**[s] turned and saw the angel;
21: 21 **[RPH]** and when Araunah looked and saw him,
21: 21 Then David approached, and when **Araunah** looked and saw him,
21: 22 David said to **him**[s], "Let me have the site of your threshing floor
21: 23 **Araunah** said to David, "Take it! Let my lord the king do
21: 24 King David replied to **Araunah**, "No, I insist on paying the full
21: 25 So David paid **Araunah** six hundred shekels of gold for the site.
21: 28 had answered him on the threshing floor of **Araunah** the Jebusite,
2Ch 3: 1 It was on the threshing floor of **Araunah** the Jebusite, the place

822 אַרְפָּד ʾarpāḏ, n.pr.loc. [6]

Arpad [6]

2Ki 18: 34 Where are the gods of Hamath and **Arpad**? Where are the gods of
19: 13 Where is the king of Hamath, the king of **Arpad**, the king of the
Isa 10: 9 Is not Hamath like **Arpad**, and Samaria like Damascus?
36: 19 Where are the gods of Hamath and **Arpad**? Where are the gods of
37: 13 Where is the king of Hamath, the king of **Arpad**, the king of the
Jer 49: 23 "Hamath and **Arpad** are dismayed, for they have heard bad news.

823 אַרְפַּכְשַׁד ʾarpakšaḏ, n.pr.m. [9]

Arphaxad [9]

Ge 10: 22 The sons of Shem: Elam, Asshur, **Arphaxad**, Lud and Aram.
10: 24 **Arphaxad** was the father of Shelah, and Shelah the father of Eber.
11: 10 when Shem was 100 years old, he became the father of **Arphaxad**.
11: 11 after he became the father of **Arphaxad**, Shem lived 500 years
11: 12 When **Arphaxad** had lived 35 years, he became the father of
11: 13 **Arphaxad** lived 403 years and had other sons and daughters.
1Ch 1: 17 Elam, Asshur, **Arphaxad**, Lud and Aram. The sons of Aram:
1: 18 **Arphaxad** was the father of Shelah, and Shelah the father of Eber.
1: 24 Shem, **Arphaxad**, Shelah,

824 אֶרֶץ ʾereṣ, n.f. & m. [2504 / 2503] [→ Ar 10075, 10077]

land [1150], earth [524], Egypt [+5213] [184], ground [160], country [92], *untranslated* [40], countries [39], lands [34], Canaan [+4046] [29], world [20], region [18], territory [17], Edom [+121] [11], Gilead [+1680] [8], Israel [+3776] [7], around[s] [6], it[s] [+2021] [6], Judah [+3373] [6], wild [6], area [5], earth's [5], fields [5], Moab [+4566] [5], countryside [4], district [4], Goshen [+1777] [4], land [+299] [4], neighboring [4], soil [4], territories [4], dust [3], floor [3], its[s] [+2021] [3], Assyria [+855] [2], cities [+9133] [2], community [2], empire [2],

Ephraim [+713] [2], Judah[s] [+2021] [2], Lower Egypt [+5213] [2], Midian [+4518] [2], Negev [+5582] [2], Shinar [+9114] [2], the other[s] [+2021+7895] [2], there[s] [+2021] [2], they [+2021+6639] [2], Upper Egypt [+7356] [2], areas of land [1], army [1], Babylon [+4169] [1], Babylon [+951] [1], Babylonia [+9114] [1], Bashan [+1421] [1], battlefield [1], Benjamin [+1228] [1], clay [1], community [+2021+6639] [1], desert [+4497] [1], districts [1], down [+2025] [1], fail [+2025+4946+5877] [1], field [1], floor space [1], foreign [1], Galilee [+1665] [1], he[s] [+466+2021] [1], here[s] [+2021] [1], here[s] [+928+2021] [1], homeland [+4580] [1], homeland [+5226] [1], in midair [+1068+1068+2021+2021+2256+9028] [1], it[s] [+2021+2021+2296] [1], land's [+928] [1], little distance [+3896] [1], Naphtali [+5889] [1], nations [+1580] [1], nations [1], native land [1], native-born [+275] [1], native-born [+275+2021] [1], native-born [+928+2021+3528] [1], neighbors [1], on foot [+2021+6584] [1], other nationalities [+2021+6639] [1], peoples [1], Philistines [+7149] [1], place [1], plain [+6677] [1], plateau [+4793] [1], property [+299] [1], shore [1], soil [+6760] [1], some distance [+2021+3896] [1], some distance [+3896] [1], suitable [1], Tema [+9401] [1], their [+2021+6639] [1], them[s] [+2021+6551] [1], there[s] [+928] [1], there[s] [+2025+4046] [1], there[s] [+928+2021] [1], there[s] [+928+2257] [1], tracts of land [1], Uz [+6420] [1], vicinity [1], where[s] [1], whole earth [+9315] [1], whole world [+9315] [1]

Ge 1: 1 In the beginning God created the heavens and the **earth**.
1: 2 Now the **earth** was formless and empty, darkness was over the
1:10 God called the dry ground "**land**," and the gathered waters he
1:11 God said, "Let the **land** produce vegetation: seed-bearing plants
1:11 and trees on the **land** that bear fruit with seed in it,
1:12 The **land** produced vegetation: plants bearing seed according to
1:15 them be lights in the expanse of the sky to give light on the **earth**."
1:17 God set them in the expanse of the sky to give light on the **earth**,
1:20 and let birds fly above the **earth** across the expanse of the sky."
1:22 fill the water in the seas, and let the birds increase on the **earth**."
1:24 "Let the **land** produce living creatures according to their kinds:
1:24 along the ground, and **wild** animals, each according to its kind."
1:25 God made the **wild** animals according to their kinds, the livestock
1:26 and the birds of the air, over the livestock, over all the **earth**,
1:26 the earth, and over all the creatures that move along the **ground**."
1:28 "Be fruitful and increase in number; fill the **earth** and subdue it.
1:28 and over every living creature that moves on the **ground**."
1:29 "I give you every seed-bearing plant on the face of the whole **earth**
1:30 And to all the beasts of the **earth** and all the birds of the air
1:30 the birds of the air and all the creatures that move on the **ground**—
2: 1 the heavens and the **earth** were completed in all their vast array.
2: 4 the account of the heavens and the **earth** when they were created.
2: 4 When the LORD God made the **earth** and the heavens—
2: 5 no shrub of the field had yet appeared on the **earth** and no plant of
2: 5 for the LORD God had not sent rain on the **earth** and there was
2: 6 streams came up from the **earth** and watered the whole surface of
2:11 it winds through the entire **land** of Havilah, where there is gold.
2:12 (The gold of that **land** is good; aromatic resin and onyx are also
2:13 second river is the Gihon; it winds through the entire **land** *of* Cush.
4:12 its crops for you. You will be a restless wanderer on the **earth**."
4:14 I will be a restless wanderer on the **earth**, and whoever finds me
4:16 went out from the LORD's presence and lived in the **land** *of* Nod,
6: 4 The Nephilim were on the **earth** in those days—and also
6: 5 The LORD saw how great man's wickedness on the **earth** had
6: 6 The LORD was grieved that he had made man on the **earth**,
6:11 Now the **earth** was corrupt in God's sight and was full of violence.
6:11 earth was corrupt in God's sight and was full of violence. **[RPH]**
6:12 God saw how corrupt the **earth** had become, for all the people on
6:12 had become, for all the people on **earth** had corrupted their ways.
6:13 to all people, for the **earth** is filled with violence because of them.
6:13 of them. I am surely going to destroy both them and the **earth**.
6:17 I am going to bring floodwaters on the **earth** to destroy all life
6:17 that has the breath of life in it. Everything on **earth** will perish.
7: 3 and female, to keep their various kinds alive throughout the **earth**.
7: 4 Seven days from now I will send rain on the **earth** for forty days
7: 6 six hundred years old when the floodwaters came on the **earth**.
7:10 And after the seven days the floodwaters came on the **earth**.
7:12 And rain fell on the **earth** forty days and forty nights.
7:14 every creature that moves along the **ground** according to its kind
7:17 For forty days the flood kept coming on the **earth**, and as the
7:17 as the waters increased they lifted the ark high above the **earth**.
7:18 The waters rose and increased greatly on the **earth**, and the ark
7:19 They rose greatly on the **earth**, and all the high mountains under
7:21 Every living thing that moved on the **earth** perished—birds,
7:21 livestock, wild animals, all the creatures that swarm over the **earth**,
7:23 the ground and the birds of the air were wiped from the **earth**.
7:24 The waters flooded the **earth** for a hundred and fifty days.
8: 1 and he sent a wind over the **earth**, and the waters receded.
8: 3 The water receded steadily from the **earth**. At the end of the
8: 7 flying back and forth until the water had dried up from the **earth**.
8: 9 its feet because there was water over all the surface of the **earth**;
8:11 Then Noah knew that the water had receded from the **earth**.
8:13 six hundred and first year, the water had dried up from the **earth**.
8:14 By the twenty-seventh day of the second month the **earth** was
8:17 the animals, and all the creatures that move along the **ground**—
8:17 so they can multiply on the **earth** and be fruitful and increase in
8:17 the earth and be fruitful and increase in number upon **it**[s] [+2021]."
8:19 the ground and all the birds—everything that moves on the **earth**—
8:22 "As long as the **earth** endures, seedtime and harvest, cold
9: 1 to them, "Be fruitful and increase in number and fill the **earth**.
9: 2 The fear and dread of you will fall upon all the beasts of the **earth**
9: 7 increase in number; multiply on the **earth** and increase upon it."
9:10 the birds, the livestock and all the **wild** animals, all those that came
9:10 that came out of the ark with you—every living creature on **earth**.
9:11 of a flood; never again will there be a flood to destroy the **earth**."
9:13 and it will be the sign of the covenant between me and the **earth**.
9:14 Whenever I bring clouds over the **earth** and the rainbow appears in
9:16 between God and all living creatures of every kind on the **earth**."
9:17 covenant I have established between me and all life on the **earth**."
9:19 and from them came the people who were scattered over the **earth**.
10: 5 (From these the maritime peoples spread out into their **territories**
10: 8 father of Nimrod, who grew to be a mighty warrior on the **earth**.
10:10 were Babylon, Erech, Akkad and Calneh, in **Shinar** [+9114].
10:11 From that **land** he went to Assyria, where he built Nineveh,
10:20 Ham by their clans and languages, in their **territories** and nations.
10:25 One was named Peleg, because in his time the **earth** was divided;
10:31 Shem by their clans and languages, in their **territories** and nations.
10:32 From these the nations spread out over the **earth** after the flood.
11: 1 Now the whole **world** had one language and a common speech.
11: 2 they found a plain in **Shinar** [+9114] and settled there.
11: 4 and not be scattered over the face of the whole **earth**."
11: 8 So the LORD scattered them from there over all the **earth**,
11: 9 there the LORD confused the language of the whole **world**.
11: 9 there the LORD scattered them over the face of the whole **earth**.
11:28 Haran died in Ur of the Chaldeans, in the **land** *of* his birth.
11:31 they set out from Ur of the Chaldeans to go to **Canaan** [+4046].
12: 1 "Leave your **country**, your people and your father's household
12: 1 and your father's household and go to the **land** I will show you.
12: 5 and they set out for the **land** *of* Canaan, and they arrived there.
12: 5 out for the land of Canaan, and they arrived **there**[s] [+2025+4046].
12: 6 Abram traveled through the **land** as far as the site of the great tree
12: 6 Moreh at Shechem. At that time the Canaanites were in the **land**.
12: 7 to Abram and said, "To your offspring I will give this **land**."
12:10 Now there was a famine in the **land**, and Abram went down to
12:10 to live there for a while because the famine was severe. **[RPH]**
13: 6 But the **land** could not support them while they stayed together,
13: 7 and Perizzites were also living in the **land** at that time.
13: 9 Is not the whole **land** before you? Let's part company. If you go to
13:10 like the garden of the LORD, like the **land** *of* Egypt, toward Zoar.
13:12 Abram lived in the **land** *of* Canaan, while Lot lived among the
13:15 All the **land** that you see I will give to you and your offspring
13:16 I will make your offspring like the dust of the **earth**, so that if
13:16 count the dust, **[RPH]** then your offspring could be counted.
13:17 Go, walk through the length and breadth of the **land**, for I am
14:19 be Abram by God Most High, Creator of heaven and **earth**.
14:22 God Most High, Creator of heaven and **earth**, and have taken an
15: 7 who brought you out of Ur of the Chaldeans to give you this **land**
15:13 that your descendants will be strangers in a **country** not their own,
15:18 with Abram and said, "To your descendants I give this **land**,
16: 3 So after Abram had been living in **Canaan** [+4046] ten years,
17: 8 The whole **land** *of* Canaan, where you are now an alien, I will give
17: 8 The whole land of Canaan, **where**[s] you are now an alien, I will
18: 2 entrance of his tent to meet them and bowed low to the **ground**.
18:18 and all nations on **earth** will be blessed through him.
18:25 Far be it from you! Will not the Judge of all the **earth** do right?"
19: 1 got up to meet them and bowed down with his face to the **ground**.
19:23 By the time Lot reached Zoar, the sun had risen over the **land**.
19:28 toward Sodom and Gomorrah, toward all the **land** *of* the plain,
19:28 he saw dense smoke rising from the **land**, like smoke from a
19:31 is old, and there is no man around **here**[s] [+2021] to lie with us,
19:31 man around here to lie with us, as is the custom all over the **earth**.
20: 1 Now Abraham moved on from there into the **region** *of* the Negev
20:15 Abimelech said, "My **land** is before you; live wherever you like."
21:21 of Paran, his mother got a wife for him from **Egypt** [+5213].
21:23 the **country** where you are living as an alien the same kindness I
21:32 Phicol the commander of his forces returned to the **land** *of* the
21:34 And Abraham stayed in the **land** *of* the Philistines for a long time.
22: 2 only son, Isaac, whom you love, and go to the **region** *of* Moriah.
22:18 and through your offspring all nations on **earth** will be blessed,
23: 2 in the **land** *of* Canaan, and Abraham went to mourn for Sarah
23: 7 Abraham rose and bowed down before the people of the **land**,
23:12 Again Abraham bowed down before the people of the **land**
23:13 he said to Ephron in **their**[s] [+2021+6639] hearing, "Listen to me,
23:15 the **land** is worth four hundred shekels of silver, but what is that

Ge 23:19 near Mamre (which is at Hebron) in the **land** *of* Canaan.
24: 3 to swear by the LORD, the God of heaven and the God of **earth**,
24: 4 will go to my **country** and my own relatives and get a wife for my
24: 5 if the woman is unwilling to come back with me to this **land**?
24: 5 Shall I then take your son back to the **country** you came from?"
24: 7 my native **land** and who spoke to me and promised me on oath,
24: 7 me on oath, saying, 'To your offspring I will give this **land**'—
24:37 my son from the daughters of the Canaanites, in whose **land** I live,
24:52 what they said, he bowed down to the **ground** before the LORD.
24:62 from Beer Lahai Roi, for he was living in the **Negev** [+5582].
25: 6 and sent them away from his son Isaac to the **land** *of* the east.
26: 1 Now there was a famine in the **land**—besides the earlier famine of
26: 2 "Do not go down to Egypt; live in the **land** where I tell you to live.
26: 3 Stay in this **land** for a while, and I will be with you and will bless
26: 3 For to you and your descendants I will give all these **lands**
26: 4 numerous as the stars in the sky and will give them all these **lands**,
26: 4 and through your offspring all nations on **earth** will be blessed,
26:12 Isaac planted crops in that **land** and the same year reaped a
26:22 the LORD has given us room and we will flourish in the **land**."
27:28 May God give you of heaven's dew and of **earth's** richness—
27:39 "Your dwelling will be away from the **earth's** richness,
27:46 If Jacob takes a wife from among the women of this **land**,
28: 4 so that you may take possession of the **land** *where* you now live as
28:12 He had a dream in which he saw a stairway resting on the **earth**,
28:13 give you and your descendants the **land** on which you are lying.
28:14 Your descendants will be like the dust of the **earth**, and you will
29: 1 on his journey and came to the **land** *of* the eastern peoples.
30:25 me on my way so I can go back to my own **homeland** [+5226].
31: 3 "Go back to the **land** *of* your fathers and to your relatives,
31:13 Now leave this **land** at once and go back to your native land.' "
31:13 Now leave this land at once and go back to your native **land**.' "
31:18 in Paddan Aram, to go to his father Isaac in the **land** *of* Canaan.
32: 3 [32:4] ahead of him to his brother Esau in the **land** *of* Seir,
32: 9 [32:10] said to me, 'Go back to your **country** and your relatives,
33: 3 bowed down to the **ground** seven times as he approached his
33:18 he arrived safely at the city of Shechem in **Canaan** [+4046]
34: 1 Leah had borne to Jacob, went out to visit the women of the **land**.
34: 2 the ruler of that **area**, saw her, he took her and violated her.
34:10 You can settle among us; the **land** is open to you. Live in it,
34:21 "Let them live in our **land** and trade in it; the land has plenty of
34:21 in our land and trade in it; the **land** has plenty of room for them.
34:30 to the Canaanites and Perizzites, the people living in this **land**.
35: 6 with him came to Luz (that is, Bethel) in the **land** *of* Canaan.
35:12 The **land** I gave to Abraham and Isaac I also give to you, and I will
35:12 to you, and I will give this **land** to your descendants after you."
35:16 While they were still **some distance** [+2021+3896] from Ephrath,
35:22 While Israel was living in that **region**, Reuben went in and slept
36: 5 were the sons of Esau, who were born to him in **Canaan** [+4046].
36: 6 and all the goods he had acquired in **Canaan** [+4046],
36: 6 and moved to a **land** some distance from his brother Jacob.
36: 7 the **land** *where* they were staying could not support them both
36:16 These were the chiefs descended from Eliphaz in **Edom** [+121];
36:17 These were the chiefs descended from Reuel in **Edom** [+121];
36:20 were the sons of Seir the Horite, who were living in the **region**:
36:21 These sons of Seir in **Edom** [+121] were Horite chiefs.
36:30 the Horite chiefs, according to their divisions, in the **land** *of* Seir.
36:31 These were the kings who reigned in **Edom** [+121] before any
36:34 Husham from the **land** *of* the Temanites succeeded him as king.
36:43 of Edom, according to their settlements in the **land** they occupied.
37: 1 Jacob lived in the **land** *where* his father had stayed, the land of
37: 1 lived in the land where his father had stayed, the **land** *of* Canaan.
37:10 brothers actually come and bow down to the **ground** before you?"
38: 9 he spilled his semen on the **ground** to keep from producing
40:15 For I was forcibly carried off from the **land** *of* the Hebrews,
41:19 and lean. I had never seen such ugly cows in all the **land** *of* Egypt.
41:29 Seven years of great abundance are coming throughout the **land** *of*
41:30 Then all the abundance in **Egypt** [+5213] will be forgotten,
41:30 in Egypt will be forgotten, and the famine will ravage the **land**.
41:31 The abundance in the **land** will not be remembered, because the
41:33 and wise man and put him in charge of the **land** *of* Egypt.
41:34 Let Pharaoh appoint commissioners over the **land** to take a fifth of
41:34 the harvest of **Egypt** [+5213] during the seven years of abundance.
41:36 This food should be held in reserve for the **country**, to be used
41:36 the seven years of famine that will come upon **Egypt** [+5213],
41:36 upon Egypt, so that the **country** may not be ruined by the famine."
41:41 to Joseph, "I hereby put you in charge of the whole **land** *of* Egypt."
41:43 Thus he put him in charge of the whole **land** *of* Egypt.
41:44 your word no one will lift hand or foot in all **Egypt** [+5213]."
41:45 to be his wife. And Joseph went throughout the **land** *of* Egypt.
41:46 from Pharaoh's presence and traveled throughout **Egypt** [+5213].
41:47 During the seven years of abundance the **land** produced
41:48 food produced in those seven years of abundance in **Egypt** [+5213]
41:52 because God has made me fruitful in the **land** *of* my suffering."
41:53 The seven years of abundance in **Egypt** [+5213] came to an end,
41:54 There was famine in all the other **lands**, but in the whole land of
41:54 all the other lands, but in the whole **land** *of* Egypt there was food.
41:55 When all **Egypt** [+5213] began to feel the famine, the people cried
41:56 When the famine had spread over the whole **country**, Joseph
41:56 for the famine was severe throughout **Egypt** [+5213].
41:57 And all the **countries** came to Egypt to buy grain from Joseph,
41:57 grain from Joseph, because the famine was severe in all the **world**.
42: 5 went to buy grain, for the famine was in the **land** *of* Canaan also.
42: 6 Now Joseph was the governor of the **land**, the one who sold grain
42: 6 of the land, the one who sold grain to all **its**[s] [+2021] people.
42: 6 they bowed down to him with their faces to the **ground**.
42: 7 he asked. "From the **land** *of* Canaan," they replied, "to buy food."
42: 9 are spies! You have come to see where our **land** is unprotected."
42:12 to them. "You have come to see where our **land** is unprotected."
42:13 the sons of one man, who lives in the **land** *of* Canaan.
42:29 When they came to their father Jacob in the **land** *of* Canaan,
42:30 "The man who is lord over the **land** spoke harshly to us and treated
42:30 harshly to us and treated us as though we were spying on the **land**.
42:32 and the youngest is now with our father in **Canaan** [+4046].'
42:33 "Then the man who is lord over the **land** said to us, 'This is how I
42:34 give your brother back to you, and you can trade in the **land**.' "
43: 1 Now the famine was still severe in the **land**.
43:11 Put some of the best products of the **land** in your bags and take
43:26 into the house, and they bowed down before him to the **ground**.
44: 8 We even brought back to you from the **land** *of* Canaan the silver
44:11 Each of them quickly lowered his sack to the **ground** and opened
44:14 came in, and they threw themselves to the **ground** before him.
45: 6 For two years now there has been famine in the **land**, and for the
45: 7 God sent me ahead of you to preserve for you a remnant on **earth**
45: 8 lord of his entire household and ruler of all **Egypt** [+5213].
45:10 You shall live in the **region** *of* Goshen and be near me—you,
45:17 'Do this: Load your animals and return to the **land** *of* Canaan,
45:18 I will give you the best of the **land** *of* Egypt and you can enjoy the
45:18 the best of the land of Egypt and you can enjoy the fat of the **land**.'
45:19 Take some carts from **Egypt** [+5213] for your children and your
45:20 because the best of all **Egypt** [+5213] will be yours.' "
45:25 out of Egypt and came to their father Jacob in the **land** *of* Canaan.
45:26 In fact, he is ruler of all **Egypt** [+5213]." Jacob was stunned;
46: 6 and the possessions they had acquired in **Canaan** [+4046],
46:12 and Zerah (but Er and Onan had died in the **land** *of* Canaan).
46:20 In **Egypt** [+5213], Manasseh and Ephraim were born to Joseph by
46:28 directions to Goshen. When they arrived in the **region** *of* Goshen,
46:31 who were living in the **land** *of* Canaan, have come to me.
46:34 Then you will be allowed to settle in the **region** *of* Goshen,
47: 1 have come from the **land** *of* Canaan and are now in Goshen."
47: 1 come from the land of Canaan and are now in **Goshen** [+1777]."
47: 4 said to him, "We have come to live **here**[s] [+928+2021] awhile,
47: 4 because the famine is severe in **Canaan** [+4046] and your servants'
47: 4 So now, please let your servants settle in **Goshen** [+1777]."
47: 6 the **land** *of* Egypt is before you; settle your father and your
47: 6 settle your father and your brothers in the best part of the **land**.
47: 6 in the best part of the land. Let them live in **Goshen** [+1777].
47:11 So Joseph settled his father and his brothers in **Egypt** [+5213]
47:11 in Egypt and gave them property in the best part of the **land**,
47:11 best part of the land, the **district** *of* Rameses, as Pharaoh directed.
47:13 however, in the whole **region** because the famine was severe;
47:13 both **Egypt** [+5213] and Canaan wasted away because of the
47:13 both Egypt and **Canaan** [+4046] wasted away because of the
47:14 collected all the money that was to be found in **Egypt** [+5213]
47:14 and **Canaan** [+4046] in payment for the grain they were buying,
47:15 When the money of the people of **Egypt** [+5213] and Canaan was
47:15 the money of the people of Egypt and **Canaan** [+4046] was gone,
47:20 the famine was too severe for them. The **land** became Pharaoh's,
47:27 Now the Israelites settled in **Egypt** [+5213] in the region of
47:27 Now the Israelites settled in Egypt in the **region** *of* Goshen.
47:28 Jacob lived in **Egypt** [+5213] seventeen years, and the years of his
48: 3 "God Almighty appeared to me at Luz in the **land** *of* Canaan,
48: 4 I will give this **land** as an everlasting possession to your
48: 5 your two sons born to you in **Egypt** [+5213] before I came to you
48: 7 to my sorrow Rachel died in the **land** *of* Canaan while we were
48: 7 we were still on the way, a **little distance** [+3896] from Ephrath.
48:12 from Israel's knees and bowed down with his face to the **ground**.
48:16 and Isaac, and may they increase greatly upon the **earth**."
48:21 God will be with you and take you back to the **land** *of* your fathers.
49:15 he sees how good is his resting place and how pleasant is his **land**,
49:30 cave in the field of Machpelah, near Mamre in **Canaan** [+4046],
50: 5 bury me in the tomb I dug for myself in the **land** *of* Canaan."
50: 7 dignitaries of his court and all the dignitaries of **Egypt** [+5213]—
50: 8 and their flocks and herds were left in **Goshen** [+1777].
50:11 When the Canaanites who lived **there**[s] [+2021] saw the mourning
50:13 They carried him to the **land** *of* Canaan and buried him in the cave
50:24 take you up out of this **land** to the land he promised on oath to
50:24 take you up out of this land to the **land** he promised on oath to
Ex 1: 7 exceedingly numerous, so that the **land** was filled with them.

Ex 1:10 will join our enemies, fight against us and leave the **country**."
2:15 but Moses fled from Pharaoh and went to live in **Midian** [+4518],
2:22 him Gershom, saying, "I have become an alien in a foreign **land**."
3:8 to bring them up out of that **land** into a good and spacious land,
3:8 to bring them up out of that land into a good and spacious **land**,
3:8 a good and spacious land, a **land** flowing with milk and honey—
3:17 you up out of your misery in Egypt into the **land** *of* the Canaanites,
3:17 Hivites and Jebusites—a **land** flowing with milk and honey.'
4:3 The LORD said, "Throw it on the **ground**." Moses threw it on the
4:3 Moses threw it on the **ground** and it became a snake, and he ran
4:20 and sons, put them on a donkey and started back to **Egypt** [+5213].
5:5 Pharaoh said, "Look, the people of the **land** are now numerous,
5:12 So the people scattered all over **Egypt** [+5213] to gather stubble to
6:1 because of my mighty hand he will drive them out of his **country**."
6:4 I also established my covenant with them to give them the **land** *of*
6:4 give them the land of Canaan, **[RPH]** where they lived as aliens.
6:8 I will bring you to the **land** I swore with uplifted hand to give to
6:11 Pharaoh king of Egypt to let the Israelites go out of his **country**."
6:13 he commanded them to bring the Israelites out of **Egypt** [+5213].
6:26 "Bring the Israelites out of **Egypt** [+5213] by their divisions."
6:28 Now when the LORD spoke to Moses in **Egypt** [+5213],
7:2 Aaron is to tell Pharaoh to let the Israelites go out of his **country**.
7:3 I multiply my miraculous signs and wonders in **Egypt** [+5213],
7:4 I will bring out my divisions, my people the Israelites. **[RPH]**
7:19 Blood will be everywhere in **Egypt** [+5213], even in the wooden
7:21 could not drink its water. Blood was everywhere in **Egypt** [+5213].
8:5 [8:1] and ponds, and make frogs come up on the **land** *of* Egypt.' "
8:6 [8:2] of Egypt, and the frogs came up and covered the **land**.
8:7 [8:3] they also made frogs come up on the **land** *of* Egypt.
8:14 [8:10] They were piled into heaps, and the **land** reeked of them.
8:16 [8:12] 'Stretch out your staff and strike the dust of the **ground**,'
8:16 [8:12] throughout the **land** *of* Egypt the dust will become gnats."
8:17 [8:13] his hand with the staff and struck the dust of the **ground**,
8:17 [8:13] All the dust **[RPH]** throughout the land of Egypt became
8:17 [8:13] All the dust throughout the **land** *of* Egypt became gnats.
8:22 [8:18] " 'But on that day I will deal differently with the **land** *of*
8:22 [8:18] so that you will know that I, the LORD, am in this **land**.
8:24 [8:20] throughout **Egypt** [+5213] the land was ruined by the flies.
8:24 [8:20] and throughout Egypt the **land** was ruined by the flies.
8:25 [8:21] and said, "Go, sacrifice to your God here in the **land**."
9:5 and said, "Tomorrow the LORD will do this in the **land**."
9:9 It will become fine dust over the whole **land** *of* Egypt,
9:9 boils will break out on men and animals throughout the **land**."
9:14 so you may know that there is no one like me in all the **earth**.
9:15 people with a plague that would have wiped you off the **earth**.
9:16 my power and that my name might be proclaimed in all the **earth**.
9:22 hand toward the sky so that hail will fall all over **Egypt** [+5213]—
9:22 and on everything growing in the fields of **Egypt** [+5213]."
9:23 sent thunder and hail, and lightning flashed down to the **ground**.
9:23 to the ground. So the LORD rained hail on the **land** *of* Egypt;
9:24 It was the worst storm in all the **land** *of* Egypt since it had become
9:25 Throughout **Egypt** [+5213] hail struck everything in the fields—
9:26 The only place it did not hail was the **land** *of* Goshen,
9:29 be no more hail, so you may know that the **earth** is the LORD's.
9:33 and hail stopped, and the rain no longer poured down on the **land**.
10:5 They will cover the face of the **ground** so that it cannot be seen.
10:5 cover the face of the ground so that **it**[s] [+2021] cannot be seen.
10:12 "Stretch out your hand over **Egypt** [+5213] so that locusts will
10:12 out your hand over Egypt so that locusts will swarm over the **land**
10:12 swarm over the land and devour everything growing in the **fields**,
10:13 So Moses stretched out his staff over **Egypt** [+5213],
10:13 the LORD made an east wind blow across the **land** all that day
10:14 they invaded all **Egypt** [+5213] and settled down in every area of
10:15 They covered all the **ground** until it was black. They devoured all
10:15 They covered all the ground until **it**[s] [+2021] was black. They
10:15 everything growing in the **fields** and the fruit on the trees.
10:15 Nothing green remained on tree or plant in all the **land** *of* Egypt.
10:21 toward the sky so that darkness will spread over **Egypt** [+5213]—
10:22 and total darkness covered all **Egypt** [+5213] for three days.
11:3 Moses himself was highly regarded in **Egypt** [+5213] by Pharaoh's
11:5 Every firstborn son in **Egypt** [+5213] will die, from the firstborn
11:6 There will be loud wailing throughout **Egypt** [+5213]—worse than
11:9 so that my wonders may be multiplied in **Egypt** [+5213]."
11:10 and he would not let the Israelites go out of his **country**.
12:1 The LORD said to Moses and Aaron in **Egypt** [+5213],
12:12 "On that same night I will pass through **Egypt** [+5213] and strike
12:12 and strike down every firstborn—**[RPH]** both men and animals—
12:13 No destructive plague will touch you when I strike **Egypt** [+5213].
12:17 this very day that I brought your divisions out of **Egypt** [+5213].
12:19 of Israel, whether he is an alien or **native-born** [+275+2021].
12:25 When you enter the **land** that the LORD will give you as he
12:29 the LORD struck down all the firstborn in **Egypt** [+5213],
12:33 The Egyptians urged the people to hurry and leave the **country**.
12:41 to the very day, all the LORD's divisions left **Egypt** [+5213].
12:42 LORD kept vigil that night to bring them out of **Egypt** [+5213],
12:48 then he may take part like one born in the **land**.
12:51 brought the Israelites out of **Egypt** [+5213] by their divisions.
13:5 When the LORD brings you into the **land** *of* the Canaanites,
13:5 your forefathers to give you, a **land** flowing with milk and honey—
13:11 "After the LORD brings you into the **land** *of* the Canaanites
13:15 the LORD killed every firstborn in **Egypt** [+5213], both man
13:17 God did not lead them on the road through the Philistine **country**,
13:18 The Israelites went up out of **Egypt** [+5213] armed for battle.
14:3 'The Israelites are wandering around the **land** in confusion,
15:12 You stretched out your right hand and the **earth** swallowed them.
16:1 of the second month after they had come out of **Egypt** [+5213].
16:3 "If only we had died by the LORD's hand in **Egypt** [+5213]!
16:6 that it was the LORD who brought you out of **Egypt** [+5213],
16:14 thin flakes like frost on the **ground** appeared on the desert floor.
16:32 to eat in the desert when I brought you out of **Egypt** [+5213].' "
16:35 ate manna forty years, until they came to a **land** that was settled;
16:35 they ate manna until they reached the border of **Canaan** [+4046].
18:3 for Moses said, "I have become an alien in a foreign **land**";
18:27 father-in-law on his way, and Jethro returned to his own **country**.
19:1 In the third month after the Israelites left **Egypt** [+5213]—
19:5 be my treasured possession. Although the whole **earth** is mine,
20:2 who brought you out of **Egypt** [+5213], out of the land of slavery.
20:4 in heaven above or on the **earth** beneath or in the waters below.
20:4 or on the earth beneath or in the waters below. **[RPH]**
20:11 For in six days the LORD made the heavens and the **earth**,
22:21 [22:20] or oppress him, for you were aliens in **Egypt** [+5213].
23:9 it feels to be aliens, because you were aliens in **Egypt** [+5213].
23:10 "For six years you are to sow your **fields** and harvest the crops,
23:26 none will miscarry or be barren in your **land**. I will give you a full
23:29 because the **land** would become desolate and the wild animals too
23:30 until you have increased enough to take possession of the **land**.
23:31 I will hand over to you the people who live in the **land** and you
23:33 Do not let them live in your **land**, or they will cause you to sin
29:46 who brought them out of **Egypt** [+5213] so that I might dwell
31:17 for in six days the LORD made the heavens and the **earth**,
32:1 As for this fellow Moses who brought us up out of **Egypt** [+5213],
32:4 your gods, O Israel, who brought you up out of **Egypt** [+5213]."
32:7 because your people, whom you brought up out of **Egypt** [+5213],
32:8 your gods, O Israel, who brought you up out of **Egypt** [+5213].'
32:11 whom you brought out of **Egypt** [+5213] with great power
32:13 and I will give your descendants all this **land** I promised them,
32:23 As for this fellow Moses who brought us up out of **Egypt** [+5213],
33:1 you and the people you brought up out of **Egypt** [+5213],
33:1 and go up to the **land** I promised on oath to Abraham, Isaac
33:3 Go up to the **land** flowing with milk and honey. But I will not go
34:8 Moses bowed to the **ground** at once and worshiped.
34:10 I will do wonders never before done in any nation in all the **world**.
34:12 Be careful not to make a treaty with those who live in the **land**
34:15 "Be careful not to make a treaty with those who live in the **land**;
34:24 no one will covet your **land** when you go up three times each year
Lev 4:27 a member of the **community** [+2021+6639] sins unintentionally
11:2 'Of all the animals that live on **land**, these are the ones you may
11:21 may eat: those that have jointed legs for hopping on the **ground**.
11:29 " 'Of the animals that move about on the **ground**, these are unclean
11:41 " 'Every creature that moves about on the **ground** is detestable;
11:42 You are not to eat any creature that moves about on the **ground**,
11:44 unclean by any creature that moves about on the **ground**.
11:45 I am the LORD who brought you up out of **Egypt** [+5213] to be
11:46 in the water and every creature that moves about on the **ground**.
14:34 "When you enter the **land** *of* Canaan, which I am giving you as
14:34 and I put a spreading mildew in a house in that **land**,
16:22 The goat will carry on itself all their sins to a solitary **place**;
18:3 You must not do as they do in **Egypt** [+5213], where you used to
18:3 used to live, and you must not do as they do in the **land** *of* Canaan,
18:25 Even the **land** was defiled; so I punished it for its sin, and the land
18:25 so I punished it for its sin, and the **land** vomited out its inhabitants.
18:27 for all these things were done by the people who lived in the **land**
18:27 who lived in the land before you, and the **land** became defiled.
18:28 if you defile the **land**, it will vomit you out as it vomited out the
19:9 " 'When you reap the harvest of your **land**, do not reap to the very
19:23 " 'When you enter the **land** and plant any kind of fruit tree,
19:29 or the **land** will turn to prostitution and be filled with wickedness.
19:29 will turn to prostitution and be filled with wickedness. **[RPH]**
19:33 " 'When an alien lives with you in your **land**, do not mistreat him.
19:34 Love him as yourself, for you were aliens in **Egypt** [+5213].
19:36 am the LORD your God, who brought you out of **Egypt** [+5213].
20:2 be put to death. The people of the **community** are to stone him.
20:4 If the people of the **community** close their eyes when that man
20:22 so that the **land** where I am bringing you to live may not vomit you
20:24 it to you as an inheritance, a **land** flowing with milk and honey."
22:24 crushed, torn or cut. You must not do this in your own **land**,
22:33 and who brought you out of **Egypt** [+5213] to be your God.
23:10 'When you enter the **land** I am going to give you and you reap its

Lev 23:22 " 'When you reap the harvest of your **land**, do not reap to the very
23:39 after you have gathered the crops of the **land**, celebrate the festival
23:43 live in booths when I brought them out of **Egypt** [+5213].
25: 2 'When you enter the **land** I am going to give you, the land itself
25: 2 to give you, the **land** itself must observe a sabbath to the LORD.
25: 4 But in the seventh year the **land** is to have a sabbath of rest,
25: 5 grapes of your untended vines. The **land** is to have a year of rest.
25: 6 Whatever the **land** yields during the sabbath year will be food for
25: 7 as well as for your livestock and the wild animals in your **land**.
25: 9 on the Day of Atonement sound the trumpet throughout your **land**.
25:10 and proclaim liberty throughout the **land** to all its inhabitants.
25:18 be careful to obey my laws, and you will live safely in the **land**.
25:19 Then the **land** will yield its fruit, and you will eat your fill
25:23 " 'The **land** must not be sold permanently, because the land is mine
25:23 because the **land** is mine and you are but aliens and my tenants.
25:24 Throughout the **country** *that* you hold as a possession, you must
25:24 as a possession, you must provide for the redemption of the **land**.
25:31 without walls around them are to be considered as open **country**.
25:38 who brought you out of **Egypt** [+5213] to give you the land of
25:38 who brought you out of Egypt to give you the **land** *of* Canaan
25:42 whom I brought out of **Egypt** [+5213], they must not be sold as
25:45 among you and members of their clans born in your **country**,
25:55 They are my servants, whom I brought out of **Egypt** [+5213].
26: 1 do not place a carved stone in your **land** to bow down before it.
26: 4 the **ground** will yield its crops and the trees of the field their fruit.
26: 5 you will eat all the food you want and live in safety in your **land**.
26: 6 " 'I will grant peace in the **land**, and you will lie down and no one
26: 6 I will remove savage beasts from the **land**, and the sword will not
26: 6 from the land, and the sword will not pass through your **country**.
26:13 who brought you out of **Egypt** [+5213] so that you would no
26:19 sky above you like iron and the **ground** *beneath* you like bronze.
26:20 will be spent in vain, because your **soil** will not yield its crops,
26:20 not yield its crops, nor will the trees of the **land** yield their fruit.
26:32 I will lay waste the **land**, so that your enemies who live there will
26:33 Your **land** will be laid waste, and your cities will lie in ruins.
26:34 the **land** will enjoy its sabbath years all the time that it lies desolate
26:34 that it lies desolate and you are in the **country** *of* your enemies;
26:34 of your enemies; then the **land** will rest and enjoy its sabbaths.
26:36 so fearful in the **lands** *of* their enemies that the sound of a
26:38 among the nations; the **land** *of* your enemies will devour you.
26:39 Those of you who are left will waste away in the **lands** *of* their
26:41 toward them so that I sent them into the **land** *of* their enemies—
26:42 and my covenant with Abraham, and I will remember the **land**.
26:43 For the **land** will be deserted by them and will enjoy its sabbaths
26:44 Yet in spite of this, when they are in the **land** *of* their enemies,
26:45 out of **Egypt** [+5213] in the sight of the nations to be their God.
27:24 person from whom he bought it, the one whose **land** [+299] it was.
27:30 " 'A tithe of everything from the **land**, whether grain from the soil
27:30 whether grain from the **soil** or fruit from the trees, belongs to the
Nu 1: 1 of the second year after the Israelites came out of **Egypt** [+5213].
3:13 When I struck down all the firstborn in **Egypt** [+5213], I set apart
8:17 When I struck down all the firstborn in **Egypt** [+5213], I set them
9: 1 month of the second year after they came out of **Egypt** [+5213].
9:14 the same regulations for the alien and the **native-born** [+275].' "
10: 9 When you go into battle in your own **land** against an enemy who is
10:30 will not go; I am going back to my own **land** and my own people."
11:31 down all around the camp to about three feet above the **ground**,
13: 2 "Send some men to explore the **land** *of* Canaan, which I am giving
13:16 These are the names of the men Moses sent to explore the **land**.
13:17 When Moses sent them to explore **Canaan** [+4046], he said,
13:18 See what the **land** is like and whether the people who live there are
13:19 What kind of **land** do they live in? Is it good or bad? What kind of
13:20 How is the **soil**? Is it fertile or poor? Are there trees on it or not?
13:20 or not? Do your best to bring back some of the fruit of the **land**."
13:21 and explored the **land** from the Desert of Zin as far as Rehob,
13:25 At the end of forty days they returned from exploring the **land**.
13:26 and to the whole assembly and showed them the fruit of the **land**.
13:27 "We went into the **land** to which you sent us, and it does flow with
13:28 But the people who live **there**[s] [+928+2021] are powerful,
13:29 The Amalekites live in the **Negev** [+5582]; the Hittites, Jebusites
13:32 they spread among the Israelites a bad report about the **land** they
13:32 They said, "The **land** we explored devours those living in it.
13:32 "The land we explored **[RPH]** devours those living in it.
14: 2 assembly said to them, "If only we had died in **Egypt** [+5213]!
14: 3 Why is the LORD bringing us to this **land** only to let us fall by
14: 6 who were among those who had explored the **land**, tore their
14: 7 "The **land** we passed through and explored is exceedingly good.
14: 7 we passed through and explored is exceedingly good. **[RPH]**
14: 8 he will lead us into that **land**, a land flowing with milk and honey,
14: 8 a **land** flowing with milk and honey, and will give it to us.
14: 9 do not be afraid of the people of the **land**, because we will swallow
14:14 they will tell the inhabitants of this **land** about it. They have
14:16 'The LORD was not able to bring these people into the **land** he
14:21 and as surely as the glory of the LORD fills the whole **earth**,
14:23 not one of them will ever see the **land** I promised on oath to their
14:24 me wholeheartedly, I will bring him into the **land** he went to,
14:30 Not one of you will enter the **land** I swore with uplifted hand to
14:31 I will bring them in to enjoy the **land** you have rejected.
14:34 one year for each of the forty days you explored the **land**—
14:36 So the men Moses had sent to explore the **land**, who returned
14:36 grumble against him by spreading a bad report about **it**[s] [+2021]—
14:37 these men responsible for spreading the bad report about the **land**
14:38 Of the men who went to explore the **land**, only Joshua son of Nun
15: 2 say to them: 'After you enter the **land** I am giving you as a home
15:18 say to them: 'When you enter the **land** to which I am taking you
15:19 you eat the food of the **land**, present a portion as an offering to the
15:41 your God, who brought you out of **Egypt** [+5213] to be your God.
16:13 Isn't it enough that you have brought us up out of a **land** flowing
16:14 you haven't brought us into a **land** flowing with milk and honey
16:32 the **earth** opened its mouth and swallowed them, with their
16:33 the **earth** closed over them, and they perished and were gone from
16:34 them fled, shouting, "The **earth** is going to swallow us too!"
18:13 All the **land's** [+928] firstfruits that they bring to the LORD will
18:20 LORD said to Aaron, "You will have no inheritance in their **land**,
20:12 you will not bring this community into the **land** I give them."
20:17 Please let us pass through your **country**. We will not go through
20:23 At Mount Hor, near the border of **Edom** [+121], the LORD said
20:24 He will not enter the **land** I give the Israelites, because both of you
21: 4 Hor along the route to the Red Sea, to go around **Edom** [+121].
21:22 "Let us pass through your **country**. We will not turn aside into any
21:24 to the sword and took over his **land** from the Arnon to the Jabbok,
21:26 of Moab and had taken from him all his **land** as far as the Arnon.
21:31 So Israel settled in the **land** *of* the Amorites.
21:34 I have handed him over to you, with his whole army and his **land**.
21:35 leaving them no survivors. And they took possession of his **land**.
22: 5 son of Beor, who was at Pethor, near the River, in his native **land**.
22: 5 they cover the face of the **land** and have settled next to me.
22: 6 I will be able to defeat them and drive them out of the **country**.
22:11 'A people that has come out of Egypt covers the face of the **land**.
22:13 and said to Balak's princes, "Go back to your own **country**,
26: 4 These were the Israelites who came out of **Egypt** [+5213]:
26:10 The **earth** opened its mouth and swallowed them along with
26:19 and Onan were sons of Judah, but they died in **Canaan** [+4046].
26:53 "The **land** is to be allotted to them as an inheritance based on the
26:55 Be sure that the **land** is distributed by lot. What each group inherits
27:12 in the Abarim range and see the **land** I have given the Israelites.
32: 1 saw that the **lands** *of* Jazer and Gilead were suitable for livestock.
32: 1 the lands of Jazer and **[RPH]** Gilead were suitable for livestock.
32: 4 the **land** the LORD subdued before the people of Israel—
32: 4 are **suitable** *for* livestock, and your servants have livestock.
32: 5 "let this **land** be given to your servants as our possession.
32: 7 Why do you discourage the Israelites from going over into the **land**
32: 8 did when I sent them from Kadesh Barnea to look over the **land**.
32: 9 After they went up to the Valley of Eshcol and viewed the **land**,
32: 9 they discouraged the Israelites from entering the **land** the LORD
32:17 in fortified cities, for protection from the inhabitants of the **land**.
32:22 then when the **land** is subdued before the LORD, you may return
32:22 And this **land** will be your possession before the LORD.
32:29 when the **land** is subdued before you, give them the land of Gilead
32:29 before you, give them the **land** *of* Gilead as their possession.
32:30 they must accept their possession with you in **Canaan** [+4046]."
32:32 We will cross over before the LORD into **Canaan** [+4046]
32:33 the whole **land** with its cities and the territory around them.
32:33 land with its cities and the territory around **them**[s] [+2021+6551].
33: 1 out of **Egypt** [+5213] by divisions under the leadership of Moses
33:37 and camped at Mount Hor, on the border of **Edom** [+121].
33:38 of the fortieth year after the Israelites came out of **Egypt** [+5213].
33:40 king of Arad, who lived in the Negev of **Canaan** [+4046],
33:51 and say to them: 'When you cross the Jordan into **Canaan** [+4046],
33:52 drive out all the inhabitants of the **land** before you. Destroy all
33:53 Take possession of the **land** and settle in it, for I have given you
33:53 of the land and settle in it, for I have given you the **land** to possess.
33:54 Distribute the **land** by lot, according to your clans. To a larger
33:55 " 'But if you do not drive out the inhabitants of the **land**, those you
33:55 They will give you trouble in the **land** where you will live.
34: 2 'When you enter **Canaan** [+4046], the land that will be allotted to
34: 2 the **land** that will be allotted to you as an inheritance will have
34: 2 to you as an inheritance will have these boundaries: **[RPH]**
34:12 " 'This will be your **land**, with its boundaries on every side.' "
34:13 the Israelites: "Assign this **land** by lot as an inheritance.
34:17 "These are the names of the men who are to assign the **land** for
34:18 And appoint one leader from each tribe to help assign the **land**.
34:29 to assign the inheritance to the Israelites in the **land** *of* Canaan.
35:10 and say to them: 'When you cross the Jordan into **Canaan** [+4046],
35:14 side of the Jordan and three in **Canaan** [+4046] as cities of refuge.
35:28 death of the high priest may he return to his own **property** [+299].
35:32 and live on his own **land** before the death of the high priest.
35:33 " 'Do not pollute the **land** where you are. Bloodshed pollutes the

Nu 35:33 Bloodshed pollutes the **land**, and atonement cannot be made for
35:33 atonement cannot be made for the **land** on which blood has been
35:34 Do not defile the **land** where you live and where I dwell, for I,
36: 2 "When the LORD commanded my lord to give the **land** as an
Dt 1: 5 East of the Jordan in the **territory** *of* Moab, Moses began to
1: 7 and along the coast, to the **land** *of* the Canaanites and to Lebanon,
1: 8 See, I have given you this **land**. Go in and take possession of the
1: 8 take possession of the **land** that the LORD swore he would give
1:21 See, the LORD your God has given you the **land**. Go up
1:22 "Let us send men ahead to spy out the **land** for us and bring back a
1:25 Taking with them some of the fruit of the **land**, they brought it
1:25 "It is a good **land** that the LORD our God is giving us."
1:27 so he brought us out of **Egypt** [+5213] to deliver us into the hands
1:35 "Not a man of this evil generation shall see the good **land** I swore
1:36 and I will give him and his descendants the **land** he set his feet on,
2: 5 not provoke them to war, for I will not give you any of their **land**,
2: 9 provoke them to war, for I will not give you any part of their **land**.
2:12 just as Israel did in the **land** the LORD gave them as their
2:19 for I will not give you possession of any **land** *belonging to* the
2:20 (That too was considered a **land** *of* the Rephaites, who used to live
2:24 your hand Sihon the Amorite, king of Heshbon, and his **country**.
2:27 "Let us pass through your **country**. We will stay on the main road;
2:29 until we cross the Jordan into the **land** the LORD our God is
2:31 I have begun to deliver Sihon and his **country** over to you.
2:31 country over to you. Now begin to conquer and possess his **land**."
2:37 you did not encroach on any of the **land** *of* the Ammonites,
3: 2 I have handed him over to you with his whole army and his **land**.
3: 8 these two kings of the Amorites the **territory** east of the Jordan,
3:12 Of the **land** that we took over at that time, I gave the Reubenites
3:13 of Argob in Bashan used to be known as a **land** *of* the Rephaites.
3:18 "The LORD your God has given you this **land** to take possession
3:20 they too have taken over the **land** that the LORD your God is
3:24 or on **earth** who can do the deeds and mighty works you do?
3:25 Let me go over and see the good **land** beyond the Jordan—
3:28 and will cause them to inherit the **land** that you will see."
4: 1 and may go in and take possession of the **land** that the LORD,
4: 5 so that you may follow them in the **land** you are entering to take
4:14 laws you are to follow in the **land** that you are crossing the Jordan
4:17 or like any animal on **earth** or any bird that flies in the air,
4:18 moves along the ground or any fish in the waters below. **[NIE]**
4:21 enter the good **land** the LORD your God is giving you as your
4:22 I will die in this **land**; I will not cross the Jordan; but you are about
4:22 you are about to cross over and take possession of that good **land**.
4:25 and grandchildren and have lived in the **land** a long time—
4:26 **earth** as witnesses against you this day that you will quickly perish
4:26 perish from the **land** that you are crossing the Jordan to possess.
4:32 long before your time, from the day God created man on the **earth**;
4:36 On **earth** he showed you his great fire, and you heard his words
4:38 to bring you into their **land** to give it to you for your inheritance,
4:39 that the LORD is God in heaven above and on the **earth** below.
4:43 Bezer in the desert **plateau** [+4793], for the Reubenites; Ramoth in
4:46 in the **land** *of* Sihon king of the Amorites, who reigned in Heshbon
4:47 They took possession of his **land** and the land of Og king of
4:47 took possession of his land and the **land** *of* Og king of Bashan,
5: 6 who brought you out of **Egypt** [+5213], out of the land of slavery.
5: 8 in heaven above or on the **earth** beneath or in the waters below.
5: 8 or on the earth beneath or in the waters below. **[RPH]**
5:15 Remember that you were slaves in **Egypt** [+5213] and that the
5:31 laws you are to teach them to follow in the **land** I am giving them
5:33 and prolong your days in the **land** that you will possess.
6: 1 to observe in the **land** that you are crossing the Jordan to possess,
6: 3 and that you may increase greatly in a **land** flowing with milk
6:10 When the LORD your God brings you into the **land** he swore to
6:12 who brought you out of **Egypt** [+5213], out of the land of slavery.
6:18 take over the good **land** that the LORD promised on oath to your
6:23 and give us the **land** that he promised on oath to our forefathers.
7: 1 When the LORD your God brings you into the **land** you are
8: 1 possess the **land** that the LORD promised on oath to your
8: 7 For the LORD your God is bringing you into a good **land**—
8: 7 a **land** *with* streams and pools of water, with springs flowing in the
8: 8 a **land** *with* wheat and barley, vines and fig trees, pomegranates,
8: 8 vines and fig trees, pomegranates, **[RPH]** olive oil and honey;
8: 9 a **land** where bread will not be scarce and you will lack nothing;
8: 9 a **land** where the rocks are iron and you can dig copper out of the
8:10 praise the LORD your God for the good **land** he has given you.
8:14 who brought you out of **Egypt** [+5213], out of the land of slavery.
9: 4 "The LORD has brought me here to take possession of this **land**
9: 5 integrity that you are going in to take possession of their **land**;
9: 6 that the LORD your God is giving you this good **land** to possess,
9: 7 From the day you left **Egypt** [+5213] until you arrived here,
9:23 "Go up and take possession of the **land** I have given you."
9:28 Otherwise, the **country** from which you brought us will say,
9:28 'Because the LORD was not able to take them into the **land** he
10: 7 to Gudgodah and on to Jotbathah, a **land** *with* streams of water.
10:11 and possess the **land** that I swore to their fathers to give them."
10:14 even the highest heavens, the **earth** and everything in it.
10:19 who are aliens, for you yourselves were aliens in **Egypt** [+5213].
11: 3 of Egypt, both to Pharaoh king of Egypt and to his whole **country**;
11: 6 when the **earth** opened its mouth right in the middle of all Israel
11: 8 and take over the **land** that you are crossing the Jordan to possess,
11: 9 and their descendants, a **land** flowing with milk and honey.
11:10 The **land** you are entering to take over is not like the land of Egypt,
11:10 The land you are entering to take over is not like the **land** *of* Egypt,
11:11 the **land** you are crossing the Jordan to take possession of is a land
11:11 are crossing the Jordan to take possession of is a **land** *of* mountains
11:12 It is a **land** the LORD your God cares for; the eyes of the LORD
11:14 then I will send rain on your **land** in its season, both autumn
11:17 you will soon perish from the good **land** the LORD is giving you.
11:21 as many as the days that the heavens are above the **earth**.
11:25 will put the terror and fear of you on the whole **land**, wherever you
11:29 When the LORD your God has brought you into the **land** you are
11:30 in the **territory** *of* those Canaanites living in the Arabah in the
11:31 take possession of the **land** the LORD your God is giving you.
12: 1 laws you must be careful to follow in the **land** that the LORD,
12:10 settle in the **land** the LORD your God is giving you as an
12:16 you must not eat the blood; pour it out on the **ground** like water.
12:24 You must not eat the blood; pour it out on the **ground** like water.
12:29 But when you have driven them out and settled in their **land**,
13: 5 [13:6] who brought you out of **Egypt** [+5213] and redeemed you
13: 7 [13:8] whether near or far, from one end of the **land** to the other),
13: 7 [13:8] from one end of the land to **the other** [+2021+7895]),
13:10 [13:11] who brought you out of **Egypt** [+5213], out of the land of
15: 4 for in the **land** the LORD your God is giving you to possess as
15: 7 of the towns of the **land** that the LORD your God is giving you,
15:11 There will always be poor people in the **land**. Therefore I
15:11 toward your brothers and toward the poor and needy in your **land**.
15:15 Remember that you were slaves in **Egypt** [+5213] and the LORD
15:23 you must not eat the blood; pour it out on the **ground** like water.
16: 3 the bread of affliction, because you left **Egypt** [+5213] in haste—
16: 3 may remember the time of your departure from **Egypt** [+5213].
16:20 and possess the **land** the LORD your God is giving you.
17:14 When you enter the **land** the LORD your God is giving you
18: 9 When you enter the **land** the LORD your God is giving you,
19: 1 When the LORD your God has destroyed the nations whose **land**
19: 2 set aside for yourselves three cities centrally located in the **land** the
19: 3 divide into three parts the **land** the LORD your God is giving you
19: 8 your forefathers, and gives you the whole **land** he promised them,
19:10 Do this so that innocent blood will not be shed in your **land**,
19:14 receive in the **land** the LORD your God is giving you to possess.
20: 1 who brought you up out of **Egypt** [+5213], will be with you.
22: 6 either in a tree or on the **ground**, and the mother is sitting on the
23: 7 [23:8] an Egyptian, because you lived as an alien in his **country**.
23:20 [23:21] put your hand to in the **land** you are entering to possess.
24: 4 Do not bring sin upon the **land** the LORD your God is giving you
24:14 a brother Israelite or an alien living in one of your towns. **[NIE]**
24:22 Remember that you were slaves in **Egypt** [+5213]. That is why I
25:19 you in the **land** he is giving you to possess as an inheritance,
26: 1 When you have entered the **land** the LORD your God is giving
26: 2 from the soil of the **land** the LORD your God is giving you
26: 3 declare today to the LORD your God that I have come to the **land**
26: 9 He brought us to this place and gave us this **land**, a land flowing
26: 9 and gave us this land, a **land** flowing with milk and honey;
26:15 on oath to our forefathers, a **land** flowing with milk and honey."
27: 2 When you have crossed the Jordan into the **land** the LORD your
27: 3 crossed over to enter the **land** the LORD your God is giving you,
27: 3 a **land** flowing with milk and honey, just as the LORD, the God
28: 1 LORD your God will set you high above all the nations on **earth**.
28: 8 The LORD your God will bless you in the **land** he is giving you.
28:10 all the peoples on **earth** will see that you are called by the name of
28:12 to send rain on your **land** in season and to bless all the work of
28:23 sky over your head will be bronze, the **ground** beneath you iron.
28:24 The LORD will turn the rain of your **country** into dust
28:25 you will become a thing of horror to all the kingdoms on **earth**.
28:26 will be food for all the birds of the air and the beasts of the **earth**,
28:49 from the ends of the **earth**, like an eagle swooping down,
28:52 They will lay siege to all the cities throughout your **land** until the
28:52 They will besiege all the cities throughout the **land** the LORD
28:56 gentle that she would not venture to touch the **ground** with the sole
28:64 you among all nations, from one end of the **earth** to the other.
28:64 **[RPH]** There you will worship other gods—gods of wood
29: 1 [28:69] Moses to make with the Israelites in **Moab** [+4566],
29: 2 [29:1] seen all that the LORD did in **Egypt** [+5213] to Pharaoh,
29: 2 [29:1] in Egypt to Pharaoh, to all his officials and to all his **land**.
29: 8 [29:7] We took their **land** and gave it as an inheritance to the
29:16 [29:15] You yourselves know how we lived in **Egypt** [+5213]
29:22 [29:21] foreigners who come from distant **lands** will see the
29:22 [29:21] lands will see the calamities that have fallen on the **land**
29:23 [29:22] The whole **land** will be a burning waste of salt

Dt 29:24 [29:23] "Why has the LORD done this to this **land**? Why this
29:25 [29:24] with them when he brought them out of **Egypt** [+5213].
29:27 [29:26] Therefore the LORD's anger burned against this **land**,
29:28 [29:27] them from their land and thrust them into another **land**,
30: 5 He will bring you to the **land** that belonged to your fathers,
30:16 the LORD your God will bless you in the **land** you are entering to
30:19 and **earth** as witnesses against you that I have set before you life
31: 4 kings of the Amorites, whom he destroyed along with their **land**.
31: 7 for you must go with this people into the **land** that the LORD
31:16 themselves to the foreign gods of the **land** they are entering.
31:21 even before I bring them into the **land** I promised them on oath."
31:23 for you will bring the Israelites into the **land** I promised them on
31:28 in their hearing and call heaven and **earth** to testify against them.
32: 1 and I will speak; hear, O **earth**, the words of my mouth.
32:10 In a desert **land** he found him, in a barren and howling waste.
32:13 He made him ride on the heights of the **land** and fed him with the
32:22 It will devour the **earth** and its harvests and set afire the
32:49 "Go up into the Abarim Range to Mount Nebo in **Moab** [+4566],
32:49 the **land** I am giving the Israelites as their own possession.
32:52 Therefore, you will see the **land** only from a distance; you will not
32:52 you will not enter the **land** I am giving to the people of Israel."
33:13 "May the LORD bless his **land** with the precious dew from
33:16 with the best gifts of the **earth** and its fullness and the favor of him
33:17 them he will gore the nations, even those at the ends of the **earth**.
33:28 Jacob's spring is secure in a **land** *of* grain and new wine, where the
34: 1 There the LORD showed him the whole **land**—from Gilead to
34: 2 all of Naphtali, the **territory** *of* Ephraim and Manasseh, all the
34: 2 and Manasseh, all the **land** *of* Judah as far as the western sea,
34: 4 "This is the **land** I promised on oath to Abraham, Isaac and Jacob
34: 5 And Moses the servant of the LORD died there in **Moab** [+4566],
34: 6 He buried him in **Moab** [+4566], in the valley opposite Beth Peor,
34:11 and wonders the LORD sent him to do in **Egypt** [+5213]—
34:11 in Egypt—to Pharaoh and to all his officials and to his whole **land**.
Jos 1: 2 get ready to cross the Jordan River into the **land** I am about to give
1: 4 and from the great river, the Euphrates—all the Hittite **country**—
1: 6 because you will lead these people to inherit the **land** I swore to
1:11 take possession of the **land** the LORD your God is giving you for
1:13 LORD your God is giving you rest and has granted you this **land**.'
1:14 your livestock may stay in the **land** that Moses gave you east of the
1:15 until they too have taken possession of the **land** that the LORD
1:15 After that, you may go back and occupy your own **land**, which
2: 1 "Go, look over the **land**," he said, "especially Jericho." So they
2: 2 Some of the Israelites have come here tonight to spy out the **land**."
2: 3 your house, because they have come to spy out the whole **land**."
2: 9 "I know that the LORD has given this **land** to you and that a great
2: 9 so that all who live in this **country** are melting in fear because of
2:11 LORD your God is God in heaven above and on the **earth** below.
2:14 you kindly and faithfully when the LORD gives us the **land**."
2:18 unless, when we enter the **land**, you have tied this scarlet cord in
2:24 "The LORD has surely given the whole **land** into our hands;
2:24 all the people **[RPH]** are melting in fear because of us."
3:11 the ark of the covenant of the Lord of all the **earth** will go into the
3:13 the Lord of all the **earth**—set foot in the Jordan, its waters flowing
4:24 so that all the peoples of the **earth** might know that the hand of the
5: 6 the LORD had sworn to them that they would not see the **land**
5: 6 their fathers to give us, a **land** flowing with milk and honey.
5:11 that very day, they ate some of the produce of the **land**:
5:12 The manna stopped the day after they ate this food from the **land**;
5:12 but that year they ate of the produce of **Canaan** [+4046].
5:14 Joshua fell facedown to the **ground** in reverence, and asked him,
6:22 Joshua said to the two men who had spied out the **land**, "Go into
6:27 LORD was with Joshua, and his fame spread throughout the **land**.
7: 2 the east of Bethel, and told them, "Go up and spy out the **region**."
7: 6 and fell facedown to the **ground** before the ark of the LORD,
7: 9 and the other people of the **country** will hear about this
7: 9 and they will surround us and wipe out our name from the **earth**.
7:21 They are hidden in the **ground** inside my tent, with the silver
8: 1 into your hands the king of Ai, his people, his city and his **land**.
9: 6 and the men of Israel, "We have come from a distant **country**;
9: 9 "Your servants have come from a very distant **country** because of
9:11 And our elders and all those living in our **country** said to us,
9:24 God had commanded his servant Moses to give you the whole **land**
9:24 and to wipe out all **its**[s] [+2021] inhabitants from before you.
10:40 So Joshua subdued the whole **region**, including the hill country,
10:41 Barnea to Gaza and from the whole **region** *of* Goshen to Gibeon.
10:42 All these kings and their **lands** Joshua conquered in one campaign,
11: 3 and to the Hivites below Hermon in the **region** *of* Mizpah.
11:16 So Joshua took this entire **land**: the hill country, all the Negev,
11:16 the hill country, all the Negev, the whole **region** *of* Goshen,
11:22 No Anakites were left in Israelite **territory**; only in Gaza,
11:23 So Joshua took the entire **land**, just as the LORD had directed
11:23 according to their tribal divisions. Then the **land** had rest from war.
12: 1 These are the kings of the **land** whom the Israelites had defeated
12: 1 and whose **territory** they took over east of the Jordan,
12: 7 These are the kings of the **land** that Joshua and the Israelites
13: 1 and there are still very large **areas of land** to be taken over.
13: 2 "This is the **land** that remains: all the regions of the Philistines
13: 4 from the south, all the **land** *of* the Canaanites, from Arah of the
13: 5 the **area** *of* the Gebalites; and all Lebanon to the east, from Baal
13: 7 divide **it**[s] [+2021+2021+2296] as an inheritance among the nine
13:21 and Reba—princes allied with Sihon—who lived in that **country**.
13:25 towns of Gilead and half the Ammonite **country** as far as Aroer,
14: 1 the Israelites received as an inheritance in the **land** *of* Canaan,
14: 4 The Levites received no share of the **land** but only towns to live in,
14: 5 So the Israelites divided the **land**, just as the LORD had
14: 7 of the LORD sent me from Kadesh Barnea to explore the **land**.
14: 9 'The **land** on which your feet have walked will be your inheritance
14:15 man among the Anakites.) Then the **land** had rest from war.
15:19 Since you have given me **land** *in* the Negev, give me also springs
17: 5 Manasseh's share consisted of ten **tracts of land** besides Gilead
17: 6 The **land** *of* Gilead belonged to the rest of the descendants of
17: 8 (Manasseh had the **land** *of* Tappuah, but Tappuah itself,
17:12 for the Canaanites were determined to live in that **region**.
17:15 and clear land for yourselves there in the **land** *of* the Perizzites
17:16 all the Canaanites who live in the **plain** [+6677] have iron chariots,
18: 1 of Meeting there. The **country** was brought under their control,
18: 3 before you begin to take possession of the **land** that the LORD,
18: 4 I will send them out to make a survey of the **land** and to write a
18: 6 After you have written descriptions of the seven parts of the **land**,
18: 8 As the men started on their way to map out the **land**, Joshua
18: 8 "Go and make a survey of the **land** and write a description of it.
18: 9 So the men left and went through the **land**. They wrote its
18:10 there he distributed the **land** to the Israelites according to their
19:49 When they had finished dividing the **land** into its allotted portions,
19:51 to the Tent of Meeting. And so they finished dividing the **land**.
21: 2 at Shiloh in **Canaan** [+4046] and said to them, "The LORD
21:43 So the LORD gave Israel all the **land** he had sworn to give their
22: 4 return to your homes in the **land** [+299] that Moses the servant of
22: 9 left the Israelites at Shiloh in **Canaan** [+4046] to return to Gilead,
22: 9 left the Israelites at Shiloh in Canaan to return to **Gilead** [+1680],
22: 9 at Shiloh in Canaan to return to Gilead, their own **land** [+299],
22:10 When they came to Geliloth near the Jordan in the **land** *of* Canaan,
22:11 **Canaan** [+4046] at Geliloth near the Jordan on the Israelite side,
22:13 sent Phinehas son of Eleazar, the priest, to the **land** *of* Gilead—
22:15 When they went to **Gilead** [+1680]—to Reuben, Gad and the
22:19 If the **land** you possess is defiled, come over to the LORD's land,
22:19 you possess is defiled, come over to the LORD's **land** [+299],
22:32 the leaders returned to **Canaan** [+4046] from their meeting with
22:32 and Gadites in **Gilead** [+1680] and reported to the Israelites.
22:33 to war against them to devastate the **country** where the Reubenites
23: 5 them out before you, and you will take possession of their **land**,
23:14 "Now I am about to go the way of all the **earth**. You know with all
23:16 and you will quickly perish from the good **land** he has given you."
24: 3 led him throughout **Canaan** [+4046] and gave him many
24: 8 " 'I brought you to the **land** *of* the Amorites who lived east of the
24: 8 them from before you, and you took possession of their **land**.
24:13 So I gave you a **land** on which you did not toil and cities you did
24:15 or the gods of the Amorites, in whose **land** you are living.
24:17 himself who brought us and our fathers up out of **Egypt** [+5213],
24:18 us all the nations, including the Amorites, who lived in the **land**.
Jdg 1: 2 "Judah is to go; I have given the **land** into their hands."
1:15 Since you have given me **land** in the Negev, give me also springs
1:26 He then went to the **land** *of* the Hittites, where he built a city
1:27 for the Canaanites were determined to live in that **land**.
1:32 people of Asher lived among the Canaanite inhabitants of the **land**.
1:33 Naphtalites too lived among the Canaanite inhabitants of the **land**,
2: 1 and led you into the **land** that I swore to give to your forefathers.
2: 2 and you shall not make a covenant with the people of this **land**,
2: 6 they went to take possession of the **land**, each to his own
2:12 God of their fathers, who had brought them out of **Egypt** [+5213].
3:11 So the **land** had peace for forty years, until Othniel son of Kenaz
3:25 unlocked them. There they saw their lord fallen to the **floor**, dead.
3:30 made subject to Israel, and the **land** had peace for eighty years.
4:21 She drove the peg through his temple into the **ground**, and he died.
5: 4 the **earth** shook, the heavens poured, the clouds poured down
5:31 when it rises in its strength." Then the **land** had peace forty years.
6: 4 They camped on the **land** and ruined the crops all the way to Gaza
6: 5 count the men and their camels; they invaded the **land** to ravage it.
6: 9 I drove them from before you and gave you their **land**.
6:10 do not worship the gods of the Amorites, in whose **land** you live.'
6:37 If there is dew only on the fleece and all the **ground** is dry,
6:39 This time make the fleece dry and the **ground** covered with dew."
6:40 Only the fleece was dry; all the **ground** was covered with dew.
8:28 During Gideon's lifetime, the **land** enjoyed peace forty years.
9:37 "Look, people are coming down from the center of the **land**,
10: 4 They controlled thirty towns in **Gilead** [+1680], which to this day
10: 8 on the east side of the Jordan in Gilead, the **land** *of* the Amorites.
11: 3 So Jephthah fled from his brothers and settled in the **land** *of* Tob,

Jdg 11: 5 the elders of Gilead went to get Jephthah from the **land** *of* Tob.
11: 12 do you have against us that you have attacked our **country**?"
11: 13 they took away my **land** from the Arnon to the Jabbok, all the way
11: 15 Israel did not take the **land** *of* Moab or the land of the Ammonites.
11: 15 Israel did not take the land of Moab or the **land** *of* the Ammonites.
11: 17 saying, 'Give us permission to go through your **country**,'
11: 18 traveled through the desert, skirted the **lands** *of* Edom and Moab,
11: 18 through the desert, skirted the lands of Edom and **[RPH]** Moab,
11: 18 and Moab, passed along the eastern side of the **country** *of* Moab,
11: 19 said to him, 'Let us pass through your **country** to our own place.'
11: 21 Israel took over all the **land** *of* the Amorites who lived in that
11: 21 took over all the land of the Amorites who lived in that **country**,
12: 12 Then Elon died, and was buried in Aijalon in the **land** *of* Zebulun.
12: 15 son of Hillel died, and was buried at Pirathon in **Ephraim** [+713],
13: 20 Manoah and his wife fell with their faces to the **ground**.
16: 24 the one who laid waste our **land** and multiplied our slain."
18: 2 warriors from Zorah and Eshtaol to spy out the **land** and explore it.
18: 2 represented all their clans. They told them, "Go, explore the **land**."
18: 7 And since their **land** lacked nothing, they were prosperous.
18: 9 let's attack them! We have seen that the **land** is very good.
18: 9 do something? Don't hesitate to go there and take **it**' [+2021] over.
18: 10 and a spacious **land** that God has put into your hands,
18: 10 put into your hands, a land that lacks nothing whatever." **[RPH]**
18: 14 the five men who had spied out the **land** *of* Laish said to their
18: 17 The five men who had spied out the **land** went inside and took the
18: 30 for the tribe of Dan until the time of the captivity of the **land**.
19: 30 not since the day the Israelites came up out of **Egypt** [+5213].
20: 1 to Beersheba and from the **land** *of* Gilead came out as one man
20: 21 cut down twenty-two thousand Israelites on the **battlefield** that
20: 25 thousand Israelites, **[RPH]** all of them armed with swords.
21: 12 and they took them to the camp at Shiloh in **Canaan** [+4046].
21: 21 a wife from the girls of Shiloh and go to the **land** *of* Benjamin.
Ru 1: 1 In the days when the judges ruled, there was a famine in the **land**,
1: 7 set out on the road that would take them back to the **land** *of* Judah.
2: 10 At this, she bowed down with her face to the **ground**. She
2: 11 how you left your father and mother and your **homeland** [+4580]
1Sa 2: 8 "For the foundations of the **earth** are the LORD's; upon them he
2: 10 them from heaven; the LORD will judge the ends of the **earth**.
3: 19 as he grew up, and he let none of his words fall to the **ground**.
4: 5 all Israel raised such a great shout that the **ground** shook.
5: 3 fallen on his face on the **ground** before the ark of the LORD!
5: 4 fallen on his face on the **ground** before the ark of the LORD!
6: 5 of the tumors and of the rats that are destroying the **country**,
6: 5 he will lift his hand from you and your gods and your **land**.
9: 4 the hill country of Ephraim and through the **area** *around* Shalisha,
9: 4 They went on into the **district** *of* Shaalim, but the donkeys were
9: 4 he passed through the **territory** *of* Benjamin, but they did not find
9: 5 When they reached the **district** *of* Zuph, Saul said to the servant
9: 16 "About this time tomorrow I will send you a man from the **land** *of*
12: 6 and Aaron and brought your forefathers up out of **Egypt** [+5213].
13: 3 Then Saul had the trumpet blown throughout the **land** and said,
13: 7 Some Hebrews even crossed the Jordan to the **land** *of* Gad
13: 17 One turned toward Ophrah in the **vicinity** *of* Shual,
13: 19 Not a blacksmith could be found in the whole **land** *of* Israel,
14: 15 those in the outposts and raiding parties—and the **ground** shook.
14: 25 The entire **army** entered the woods, and there was honey on the
14: 29 Jonathan said, "My father has made trouble for the **country**.
14: 32 and calves, they butchered them on the **ground** and ate them,
14: 45 as the LORD lives, not a hair of his head will fall to the **ground**,
17: 46 Philistine army to the birds of the air and the beasts of the **earth**,
17: 46 and the whole **world** will know that there is a God in Israel.
17: 49 stone sank into his forehead, and he fell facedown on the **ground**.
20: 41 down before Jonathan three times, with his face to the **ground**.
21: 11 [21:12] said to him, "Isn't this David, the king of the **land**?
22: 5 Go into the **land** *of* Judah." So David left and went to the forest of
23: 23 if he is in the **area**, I will track him down among all the clans of
23: 27 saying, "Come quickly! The Philistines are raiding the **land**."
24: 8 [24:9] and prostrated himself with his face to the **ground**.
25: 23 and bowed down before David with her face to the **ground**.
25: 41 She bowed down with her face to the **ground** and said, "Here is
26: 7 lying asleep inside the camp with his spear stuck in the **ground**
26: 8 Now let me pin him to the **ground** with one thrust of my spear;
26: 20 Now do not let my blood fall to the **ground** far from the presence
27: 1 The best thing I can do is to escape to the **land** *of* the Philistines.
27: 8 (From ancient times these peoples had lived in the **land** extending
27: 8 had lived in the land extending to Shur and **Egypt** [+5213].)
27: 9 Whenever David attacked an **area**, he did not leave a man
28: 3 Saul had expelled the mediums and spiritists from the **land**.
28: 9 has done. He has cut off the mediums and spiritists from the **land**.
28: 13 The woman said, "I see a spirit coming up out of the **ground**."
28: 14 he bowed down and prostrated himself with his face to the **ground**.
28: 20 Immediately Saul fell full length on the **ground**, filled with fear
28: 23 listened to them. He got up from the **ground** and sat on the couch.
29: 11 his men got up early in the morning to go back to the **land** *of* the
30: 16 scattered over the **countryside**, eating, drinking and reveling
30: 16 amount of plunder they had taken from the **land** *of* the Philistines
30: 16 had taken from the land of the Philistines and from **[RPH]** Judah.
31: 9 they sent messengers throughout the **land** *of* the Philistines to
2Sa 1: 2 When he came to David, he fell to the **ground** to pay him honor.
2: 22 "Stop chasing me! Why should I strike you **down** [+2025]?
3: 12 sent messengers on his behalf to say to David, "Whose **land** is it?
4: 11 now demand his blood from your hand and rid the **earth** of you!"
5: 6 to Jerusalem to attack the Jebusites, who lived **there**' [+2021].
7: 9 your name great, like the names of the greatest men of the **earth**.
7: 23 the one nation on **earth** that God went out to redeem as a people
7: 23 wonders by driving out [BHS *wonders for your land*; NIV 1763]
8: 2 He made them lie down on the **ground** and measured them off
10: 2 his father. When David's men came to the **land** *of* the Ammonites,
12: 16 and went into his house and spent the nights lying on the **ground**.
12: 17 of his household stood beside him to get him up from the **ground**,
12: 20 Then David got up from the **ground**. After he had washed,
13: 31 The king stood up, tore his clothes and lay down on the **ground**;
14: 4 she fell with her face to the **ground** to pay him honor, and she said,
14: 11 he said, "not one hair of your son's head will fall to the **ground**."
14: 14 Like water spilled on the **ground**, which cannot be recovered,
14: 20 an angel of God—he knows everything that happens in the **land**."
14: 22 Joab fell with his face to the **ground** to pay him honor, and he
14: 33 and bowed down with his face to the **ground** before the king.
15: 4 Absalom would add, "If only I were appointed judge in the **land**!
15: 23 The whole **countryside** wept aloud as all the people passed by.
17: 26 The Israelites and Absalom camped in the **land** *of* Gilead.
18: 8 The battle spread out over the whole **countryside**, and the forest
18: 9 left hanging **in midair** [+1068+1068+2021+2021+2256+9028],
18: 11 saw him? Why didn't you strike him to the **ground** right there?
18: 28 He bowed down before the king with his face to the **ground**
19: 9 [19:10] But now he has fled the **country** because of Absalom;
20: 10 it into his belly, and his intestines spilled out on the **ground**.
21: 14 at Zela in **Benjamin** [+1228], and did everything the king
21: 14 After that, God answered prayer in behalf of the **land**.
22: 8 "The **earth** trembled and quaked, the foundations of the heavens
22: 43 I beat them as fine as the dust of the **earth**; I pounded and trampled
23: 4 like the brightness after rain that brings the grass from the **earth**.'
24: 6 They went to Gilead and the **region** *of* Tahtim Hodshi, and on to
24: 8 After they had gone through the entire **land**, they came back to
24: 13 "Shall there come upon you three years of famine in your **land**?
24: 13 Or three days of plague in your **land**? Now then, think it over
24: 20 and bowed down before the king with his face to the **ground**.
24: 25 the LORD answered prayer in behalf of the **land**, and the plague
1Ki 1: 23 So he went before the king and bowed with his face to the **ground**.
1: 31 Then Bathsheba bowed low with her face to the **ground** and,
1: 40 and rejoicing greatly, so that the **ground** shook with the sound.
1: 52 to be a worthy man, not a hair of his head will fall to the **ground**;
2: 2 "I am about to go the way of all the **earth**," he said. "So be strong,
4: 10 in Arubboth (Socoh and all the **land** *of* Hepher were his);
4: 19 in **Gilead** [+1680] (the country of Sihon king of the Amorites
4: 19 in Gilead (the **country** *of* Sihon king of the Amorites
4: 19 of Og king of Bashan). He was the only governor over the **district**.
4: 21 [5:1] the kingdoms from the River to the **land** *of* the Philistines,
4: 34 [5:14] sent by all the kings of the **world**, who had heard of his
6: 1 eightieth year after the Israelites had come out of **Egypt** [+5213],
8: 9 covenant with the Israelites after they came out of **Egypt** [+5213].
8: 21 with our fathers when he brought them out of **Egypt** [+5213]."
8: 23 there is no God like you in heaven above or on **earth** below—
8: 27 "But will God really dwell on **earth**? The heavens,
8: 36 and send rain on the **land** you gave your people for an inheritance.
8: 37 "When famine or plague comes to the **land**, or blight or mildew,
8: 37 or when an enemy besieges them in any of their **cities** [+9133],
8: 41 but has come from a distant **land** because of your name—
8: 43 so that all the peoples of the **earth** may know your name and fear
8: 46 who takes them captive to his own **land**, far away or near;
8: 47 if they have a change of heart in the **land** where they are held
8: 47 and plead with you in the **land** *of* their conquerors and say,
8: 48 and soul in the **land** *of* their enemies who took them captive,
8: 48 pray to you toward the **land** you gave their fathers, toward the city
8: 53 For you singled them out from all the nations of the **world** to be
8: 60 so that all the peoples of the **earth** may know that the LORD is
9: 8 'Why has the LORD done such a thing to this **land** and to this
9: 9 who brought their fathers out of **Egypt** [+5213], and have
9: 11 King Solomon gave twenty towns in **Galilee** [+1665] to Hiram
9: 13 he called them the **Land** *of* Cabul, a name they have to this day.
9: 18 Baalath, and Tadmor in the desert, within his **land**,
9: 19 in Jerusalem, in Lebanon and throughout all the **territory** he ruled.
9: 21 that is, their descendants remaining in the **land**,
9: 26 which is near Elath in **Edom** [+121], on the shore of the Red Sea.
10: 6 "The report I heard in my own **country** about your achievements
10: 13 Then she left and returned with her retinue to her own **country**.
10: 15 and from all the Arabian kings and the governors of the **land**.
10: 23 greater in riches and wisdom than all the other kings of the **earth**.

1Ki 10:24 The whole **world** sought audience with Solomon to hear the
11:18 who gave Hadad a house and **land** and provided him with food.
11:21 to Pharaoh, "Let me go, that I may return to my own **country**."
11:22 you lacked here that you want to go back to your own **country**?"
12:28 your gods, O Israel, who brought you up out of **Egypt** [+5213]."
14:24 There were even male shrine prostitutes in the **land**; the people
15:12 He expelled the male shrine prostitutes from the **land** and got rid
15:20 Beth Maacah and all Kinnereth in addition to **Naphtali** [+5889].
17: 7 later the brook dried up because there had been no rain in the **land**.
18: 5 to Obadiah, "Go through the **land** to all the springs and valleys.
18: 6 So they divided the **land** they were to cover, Ahab going in one
18:42 bent down to the **ground** and put his face between his knees.
20: 7 The king of Israel summoned all the elders of the **land** and said to
20:27 flocks of goats, while the Arameans covered the **countryside**.
22:36 through the army: "Every man to his town; everyone to his **land**!"
22:46 [22:47] He rid the **land** of the rest of the male shrine prostitutes
2Ki 2:15 And they went to meet him and bowed to the **ground** before him.
2:19 as you can see, but the water is bad and the **land** is unproductive."
3:20 from the direction of Edom! And the **land** was filled with water.
3:27 Israel was great; they withdrew and returned to their own **land**.
4:37 She came in, fell at his feet and bowed to the **ground**. Then she
4:38 Elisha returned to Gilgal and there was a famine in that **region**.
5: 2 gone out and had taken captive a young girl from **Israel** [+3776],
5: 4 his master and told him what the girl from **Israel** [+3776] had said.
5:15 "Now I know that there is no God in all the **world** except in Israel.
5:19 Elisha said. After Naaman had traveled **some distance** [+3896],
6:23 So the bands from Aram stopped raiding Israel's **territory**.
8: 1 because the LORD has decreed a famine in the **land** that will last
8: 2 went away and stayed in the **land** *of* the Philistines seven years.
8: 3 At the end of the seven years she came back from the **land** *of* the
8: 6 income from her land from the day she left the **country** until now."
10:10 spoken against the house of Ahab *will* **fail** [+2025+4946+5877].
10:33 east of the Jordan in all the **land** *of* Gilead (the region of Gad,
11: 3 temple of the LORD for six years while Athaliah ruled the **land**.
11:14 and all the people of the **land** were rejoicing and blowing trumpets.
11:18 All the people of the **land** went to the temple of Baal and tore it
11:19 of hundreds, the Carites, the guards and all the people of the **land**,
11:20 and all the people of the **land** rejoiced. And the city was quiet,
13:18 Elisha told him, "Strike the **ground**." He struck it three times
13:20 Now Moabite raiders used to enter the **country** every spring.
15: 5 son had charge of the palace and governed the people of the **land**.
15:19 Pul king of Assyria invaded the **land**, and Menahem gave him a
15:20 So the king of Assyria withdrew and stayed in the **land** no longer.
15:29 He took Gilead and Galilee, including all the **land** *of* Naphtali,
16:15 grain offering, and the burnt offering of all the people of the **land**,
17: 5 The king of Assyria invaded the entire **land**, marched against
17: 7 who had brought them up out of **Egypt** [+5213] from under the
17:26 of Samaria do not know what the god of that **country** requires.
17:26 because the people do not know what **he**[s] [+466+2021] requires."
17:27 live there and teach the people what the god of the **land** requires."
17:36 who brought you up out of **Egypt** [+5213] with mighty power
18:25 The LORD himself told me to march against this **country**
18:32 until I come and take you to a **land** like your own, a land of grain
18:32 **[RPH]** a land of grain and new wine, a land of bread
18:32 a **land** *of* grain and new wine, a land of bread and vineyards,
18:32 a land of grain and new wine, a **land** *of* bread and vineyards,
18:32 a land of bread and vineyards, a **land** *of* olive trees and honey.
18:33 Has the god of any nation ever delivered his **land** from the hand of
18:35 Who of all the gods of these **countries** has been able to save his
18:35 the gods of these countries has been able to save his **land** from me?
19: 7 he will return to his own **country**, and there I will have him cut
19: 7 and **there** [+928] I will have him cut down with the sword.' "
19:11 heard what the kings of Assyria have done to all the **countries**,
19:15 you alone are God over all the kingdoms of the **earth**.
19:15 all the kingdoms of the earth. You have made heaven and **earth**.
19:17 the Assyrian kings have laid waste these nations and their **lands**.
19:19 so that all kingdoms on **earth** may know that you alone, O
19:37 him down with the sword, and they escaped to the **land** *of* Ararat.
20:14 "From a distant **land**," Hezekiah replied. "They came from
21:24 the people of the **land** killed all who had plotted against King
21:24 and **they**[s] [+2021+6639] made Josiah his son king in his place.
23:24 the idols and all the other detestable things seen in **Judah** [+3373]
23:30 the people of the **land** took Jehoahaz son of Josiah and anointed
23:33 Pharaoh Neco put him in chains at Riblah in the **land** *of* Hamath
23:33 he imposed on **Judah**[s] [+2021] a levy of a hundred talents of silver
23:35 he taxed the **land** and exacted the silver and gold from the people
23:35 gold from the people of the **land** according to their assessments.
24: 7 The king of Egypt did not march out from his own **country** again,
24:14 total of ten thousand. Only the poorest people of the **land** were left.
24:15 his wives, his officials and the leading men of the **land**.
25: 3 so severe that there was no food for the people **[NIE]** to eat.
25:12 the commander left behind some of the poorest people of the **land**
25:19 was chief officer in charge of conscripting the people of the **land**
25:19 the land and sixty of his men **[RPH]** who were found in the city.
25:21 There at Riblah, in the **land** *of* Hamath, the king had them
25:22 to be over the people he had left behind in **Judah** [+3373].
25:24 "Settle down in the **land** and serve the king of Babylon, and it will
1Ch 1:10 the father of Nimrod, who grew to be a mighty warrior on **earth**.
1:19 One was named Peleg, because in his time the **earth** was divided;
1:43 These were the kings who reigned in **Edom** [+121] before any
1:45 Husham from the **land** *of* the Temanites succeeded him as king.
2:22 of Jair, who controlled twenty-three towns in **Gilead** [+1680].
4:40 good pasture, and the **land** was spacious, peaceful and quiet.
5: 9 because their livestock had increased in **Gilead** [+1680].
5:11 The Gadites lived next to them in **Bashan** [+1421], as far as
5:23 they settled in the **land** from Bashan to Baal Hermon, that is,
5:25 and prostituted themselves to the gods of the peoples of the **land**,
6:55 [6:40] They were given Hebron in **Judah** [+3373] with its
7:21 killed by the **native-born** [+928+2021+3528] men of Gath,
10: 9 sent messengers throughout the **land** *of* the Philistines to proclaim
11: 4 to Jerusalem (that is, Jebus). The Jebusites who lived there **[NIE]**
13: 2 wide to the rest of our brothers throughout the **territories** *of* Israel,
14:17 So David's fame spread throughout every **land**, and the LORD
16:14 He is the LORD our God; his judgments are in all the **earth**.
16:18 "To you I will give the **land** *of* Canaan as the portion you will
16:23 Sing to the LORD, all the **earth**; proclaim his salvation day after
16:30 Tremble before him, all the **earth**! The world is firmly established;
16:31 Let the heavens rejoice, let the **earth** be glad; let them say among
16:33 sing for joy before the LORD, for he comes to judge the **earth**.
17: 8 make your name like the names of the greatest men of the **earth**.
17:21 the one nation on **earth** whose God went out to redeem a people
19: 2 When David's men came to Hanun in the **land** *of* the Ammonites
19: 3 come to you to explore and spy out the **country** and overthrow it?"
20: 1 He laid waste the **land** *of* the Ammonites and went to Rabbah
21:12 days of plague in the **land**, with the angel of the LORD ravaging
21:16 saw the angel of the LORD standing between heaven and **earth**,
21:21 and bowed down before David with his face to the **ground**.
22: 2 David gave orders to assemble the aliens living in **Israel** [+3776],
22: 5 and fame and splendor in the sight of all the **nations**.
22: 8 because you have shed much blood on the **earth** in my sight.
22:18 For he has handed the inhabitants of the **land** over to me,
22:18 to me, and the **land** is subject to the LORD and to his people.
28: 8 that you may possess this good **land** and pass it on as an
29:11 and the splendor, for everything in heaven and **earth** is yours.
29:15 Our days on **earth** are like a shadow, without hope.
29:30 surrounded him and Israel and the kingdoms of all the other **lands**.
2Ch 1: 9 king over a people who are as numerous as the dust of the **earth**.
2:12 [2:11] the God of Israel, who made heaven and **earth**!
2:17 [2:16] took a census of all the aliens who were in **Israel** [+3776],
6: 5 'Since the day I brought my people out of **Egypt** [+5213],
6:14 God of Israel, there is no God like you in heaven or on **earth**—
6:18 "But will God really dwell on **earth** with men? The heavens,
6:27 and send rain on the **land** you gave your people for an inheritance.
6:28 "When famine or plague comes to the **land**, or blight or mildew,
6:28 or when enemies besiege them in any of their **cities** [+9133],
6:32 but has come from a distant **land** because of your great name
6:33 so that all the peoples of the **earth** may know your name and fear
6:36 to the enemy, who takes them captive to a **land** far away or near;
6:37 if they have a change of heart in the **land** where they are held
6:37 and plead with you in the **land** *of* their captivity and say,
6:38 and soul in the **land** *of* their captivity where they were taken,
6:38 pray toward the **land** you gave their fathers, toward the city you
7: 3 they knelt on the pavement with their faces to the **ground**,
7:13 or command locusts to devour the **land** or send a plague among my
7:14 hear from heaven and will forgive their sin and will heal their **land**.
7:21 'Why has the LORD done such a thing to this **land** and to this
7:22 the God of their fathers, who brought them out of **Egypt** [+5213],
8: 6 in Jerusalem, in Lebanon and throughout all the **territory** he ruled.
8: 8 that is, their descendants remaining in the **land**,
8:17 went to Ezion Geber and Elath on the coast of **Edom** [+121].
9: 5 "The report I heard in my own **country** about your achievements
9:11 Nothing like them had ever been seen in **Judah** [+3373].)
9:12 Then she left and returned with her retinue to her own **country**.
9:14 and the governors of the **land** brought gold and silver to Solomon.
9:22 greater in riches and wisdom than all the other kings of the **earth**.
9:23 All the kings of the **earth** sought audience with Solomon to hear
9:26 He ruled over all the kings from the River to the **land** *of* the
9:28 horses were imported from Egypt and from all other **countries**.
11:23 dispersing some of his sons throughout the **districts** *of* Judah
12: 8 between serving me and serving the kings of other **lands**."
13: 9 and make priests of your own as the peoples of other **lands** do?
14: 1 [13:23] and in his days the **country** was at peace for ten years.
14: 6 [14:5] up the fortified cities of Judah, since the **land** was at peace.
14: 7 [14:6] The **land** is still ours, because we have sought the LORD
15: 5 for all the inhabitants of the **lands** were in great turmoil.
15: 8 He removed the detestable idols from the whole **land** *of* Judah
16: 9 For the eyes of the LORD range throughout the **earth** to
17: 2 all the fortified cities of Judah and put garrisons in **Judah** [+3373]

2Ch 17:10 The fear of the LORD fell on all the kingdoms of the **lands**
19: 3 for you have rid the **land** of the Asherah poles and have set your
19: 5 He appointed judges in the **land**, in each of the fortified cities of
20: 7 did you not drive out the inhabitants of this **land** before your
20:10 not allow Israel to invade when they came from **Egypt** [+5213];
20:18 Jehoshaphat bowed with his face to the **ground**, and all the people
20:24 the vast army, they saw only dead bodies lying on the **ground**;
20:29 The fear of God came upon all the kingdoms of the **countries**
22:12 at the temple of God for six years while Athaliah ruled the **land**.
23:13 and all the people of the **land** were rejoicing and blowing trumpets,
23:20 the rulers of the people and all the people of the **land** and brought
23:21 and all the people of the **land** rejoiced. And the city was quiet,
26:21 son had charge of the palace and governed the people of the **land**.
30: 9 compassion by their captors and will come back to this **land**,
30:10 The couriers went from town to town in **Ephraim** [+713]
30:25 including the aliens who had come from **Israel** [+3776] and those
32: 4 all the springs and the stream that flowed through the **land**.
32:13 and my fathers have done to all the peoples of the other **lands**?
32:13 Were the gods of those **nations** [+1580] ever able to deliver their
32:13 Were the gods of those nations ever able to deliver their **land** from
32:17 "Just as the gods of the peoples of the other **lands** did not rescue
32:19 as they did about the gods of the other peoples of the **world**—
32:21 So he withdrew to his own **land** in disgrace. And when he went
32:31 to ask him about the miraculous sign that had occurred in the **land**,
33:25 the people of the **land** killed all who had plotted against King
33:25 and **they**[s] [+2021+6639] made Josiah his son king in his place.
34: 7 and cut to pieces all the incense altars throughout **Israel** [+3776].
34: 8 to purify the **land** and the temple, he sent Shaphan son of Azaliah
34:33 Josiah removed all the detestable idols from all the **territory**
36: 1 the people of the **land** took Jehoahaz son of Josiah and made him
36: 3 imposed on **Judah**[s] [+2021] a levy of a hundred talents of silver
36:21 The **land** enjoyed its sabbath rests; all the time of its desolation it
36:23 has given me all the kingdoms of the **earth** and he has appointed
Ezr 1: 2 has given me all the kingdoms of the **earth** and he has appointed
3: 3 Despite their fear of the peoples **around**[s] them, they built the altar
4: 4 the peoples **around**[s] them set out to discourage the people of
6:21 practices of their Gentile **neighbors** in order to seek the LORD,
9: 1 have not kept themselves separate from the **neighboring** peoples
9: 2 and have mingled the holy race with the peoples **around**[s] them.
9: 7 to pillage and humiliation at the hand of **foreign** kings, as it is
9:11 'The **land** you are entering to possess is a land polluted by the
9:11 'The land you are entering to possess is a **land** polluted by the
9:11 possess is a land polluted by the corruption of **its**[s] [+2021] peoples.
9:12 that you may be strong and eat the good things of the **land**
10: 2 our God by marrying foreign women from the peoples **around**[s] us.
10:11 Separate yourselves from the peoples **around**[s] you and from your
Ne 4: 4 [3:36] Give them over as plunder in a **land** *of* captivity.
5:14 when I was appointed to be their governor in the **land** *of* Judah,
8: 6 and worshiped the LORD with their faces to the **ground**.
9: 6 the **earth** and all that is on it, the seas and all that is in them.
9: 8 with him to give to his descendants the **land** *of* the Canaanites,
9:10 against all his officials and all the people of his **land**,
9:15 take possession of the **land** you had sworn with uplifted hand to
9:22 They took over the **country** *of* Sihon king of Heshbon and the
9:22 the country of Sihon [BHS+ *the **country** of*] king of Heshbon
9:22 of Sihon king of Heshbon and the **country** *of* Og king of Bashan.
9:23 you brought them into the **land** that you told their fathers to enter
9:24 Their sons went in and took possession of the **land**. You subdued
9:24 You subdued before them the Canaanites, who lived in the **land**;
9:24 along with their kings and the peoples of the **land**, to deal with
9:30 no attention, so you handed them over to the **neighboring** peoples.
9:35 goodness to them in the spacious and fertile **land** you gave them,
9:36 slaves in the **land** you gave our forefathers so they could eat its
10:28 [10:29] all who separated themselves from the **neighboring**
10:30 [10:31] give our daughters in marriage to the peoples **around**[s] us
10:31 [10:32] "When the **neighboring** peoples bring merchandise
Est 8:17 many people of **other nationalities** [+2021+6639] became Jews
10: 1 King Xerxes imposed tribute throughout the **empire**, to its distant
Job 1: 1 In the **land** *of* Uz there lived a man whose name was Job.
1: 7 "From roaming through the **earth** and going back and forth in it."
1: 8 There is no one on **earth** like him; he is blameless and upright,
1:10 so that his flocks and herds are spread throughout the **land**.
1:20 and shaved his head. Then he fell to the **ground** in worship
2: 2 "From roaming through the **earth** and going back and forth in it."
2: 3 There is no one on **earth** like him; he is blameless and upright,
2:13 they sat on the **ground** with him for seven days and seven nights.
3:14 with kings and counselors of the **earth**, who built for themselves
5:10 He bestows rain on the **earth**; he sends water upon the countryside.
5:22 and famine, and need not fear the beasts of the **earth**.
5:25 will be many, and your descendants like the grass of the **earth**.
7: 1 "Does not man have hard service on **earth**? Are not his days like
8: 9 and know nothing, and our days on **earth** are but a shadow.
9: 6 He shakes the **earth** from its place and makes its pillars tremble.
9:24 When a **land** falls into the hands of the wicked, he blindfolds its
10:21 go to the place of no return, to the **land** *of* gloom and deep shadow,
10:22 to the **land** *of* deepest night, of deep shadow and disorder,
11: 9 Their measure is longer than the **earth** and wider than the sea.
12: 8 or speak to the **earth**, and it will teach you, or let the fish of the sea
12:15 there is drought; if he lets them loose, they devastate the **land**.
12:24 He deprives the leaders of the **earth** of their reason; he sends them
14: 8 Its roots may grow old in the **ground** and its stump die in the soil,
14:19 water wears away stones and torrents wash away the **soil** [+6760],
15:19 (to whom alone the **land** was given when no alien passed among
15:29 will not endure, nor will his possessions spread over the **land**.
16:13 he pierces my kidneys and spills my gall on the **ground**.
16:18 "O **earth**, do not cover my blood; may my cry never be laid to rest!
18: 4 pieces in your anger, is the **earth** to be abandoned for your sake?
18:10 A noose is hidden for him on the **ground**; a trap lies in his path.
18:17 The memory of him perishes from the **earth**; he has no name in the
20: 4 it has been from of old, ever since man was placed on the **earth**,
20:27 heavens will expose his guilt; the **earth** will rise up against him.
22: 8 though you were a powerful man, owning **land**—an honored man,
24: 4 needy from the path and force all the poor of the **land** into hiding.
24:18 their portion of the **land** is cursed, so that no one goes to the
26: 7 ⌞skies⌟ over empty space; he suspends the **earth** over nothing.
28: 5 The **earth**, from which food comes, is transformed below as by
28:13 comprehend its worth; it cannot be found in the **land** *of* the living.
28:24 for he views the ends of the **earth** and sees everything under the
30: 8 A base and nameless brood, they were driven out of the **land**.
34:13 Who appointed him over the **earth**? Who put him in charge of the
35:11 who teaches more to us than to the beasts of the **earth** and makes
37: 3 beneath the whole heaven and sends it to the ends of the **earth**.
37: 6 He says to the snow, 'Fall on the **earth**,' and to the rain shower,
37:12 of the **whole earth** [+9315] to do whatever he commands them.
37:13 the clouds to punish men, or to water his **earth** and show his love.
37:17 You who swelter in your clothes when the **land** lies hushed under
38: 4 "Where were you when I laid the **earth's** foundation? Tell me,
38:13 that it might take the **earth** by the edges and shake the wicked out
38:18 Have you comprehended the vast expanses of the **earth**? Tell me,
38:24 or the place where the east winds are scattered over the **earth**?
38:26 to water a **land** where no man lives, a desert with no one in it,
38:33 of the heavens? Can you set up ⌞God's⌟ dominion over the **earth**?
39:14 She lays her eggs on the **ground** and lets them warm in the sand,
39:24 In frenzied excitement he eats up the **ground**; he cannot stand still
42:15 Nowhere in all the **land** were there found women as beautiful as
Ps 2: 2 The kings of the **earth** take their stand and the rulers gather
2: 8 the nations your inheritance, the ends of the **earth** your possession.
2:10 Therefore, you kings, be wise; be warned, you rulers of the **earth**.
7: 5 [7:6] let him trample my life to the **ground** and make me sleep in
8: 1 [8:2] our Lord, how majestic is your name in all the **earth**!
8: 9 [8:10] our Lord, how majestic is your name in all the **earth**!
10:16 is King for ever and ever; the nations will perish from his **land**.
10:18 and the oppressed, in order that man, who is of the **earth**,
12: 6 [12:7] like silver refined in a furnace of **clay**, purified seven
16: 3 As for the saints who are in the **land**, they are the glorious ones in
17:11 they now surround me, with eyes alert, to throw me to the **ground**.
18: 7 [18:8] The **earth** trembled and quaked, and the foundations of the
19: 4 [19:5] Their voice goes out into all the **earth**, their words to the
21:10 [21:11] You will destroy their descendants from the **earth**, their
22:27 [22:28] All the ends of the **earth** will remember and turn to the
22:29 [22:30] All the rich of the **earth** will feast and worship; all who
24: 1 The **earth** is the LORD's, and everything in it, the world,
25:13 his days in prosperity, and his descendants will inherit the **land**.
27:13 I will see the goodness of the LORD in the **land** *of* the living.
33: 5 and justice; the **earth** is full of his unfailing love.
33: 8 Let all the **earth** fear the LORD; let all the people of the world
33:14 from his dwelling place he watches all who live on **earth**—
34:16 [34:17] do evil, to cut off the memory of them from the **earth**.
35:20 devise false accusations against those who live quietly in the **land**.
37: 3 the LORD and do good; dwell in the **land** and enjoy safe pasture.
37: 9 be cut off, but those who hope in the LORD will inherit the **land**.
37:11 But the meek will inherit the **land** and enjoy great peace.
37:22 those the LORD blesses will inherit the **land**, but those he curses
37:29 the righteous will inherit the **land** and dwell in it forever.
37:34 He will exalt you to inherit the **land**; when the wicked are cut off,
41: 2 [41:3] he will bless him in the **land** and not surrender him to the
42: 6 [42:7] therefore I will remember you from the **land** *of* the Jordan,
44: 3 [44:4] It was not by their sword that they won the **land**, nor did
44:25 [44:26] brought down to the dust; our bodies cling to the **ground**.
45:16 [45:17] you will make them princes throughout the **land**.
46: 2 [46:3] though the **earth** give way and the mountains fall into the
46: 6 [46:7] in uproar, kingdoms fall; he lifts his voice, the **earth** melts.
46: 8 [46:9] of the LORD, the desolations he has brought on the **earth**.
46: 9 [46:10] He makes wars cease to the ends of the **earth**; he breaks
46:10 [46:11] exalted among the nations, I will be exalted in the **earth**."
47: 2 [47:3] the LORD Most High, the great King over all the **earth**!
47: 7 [47:8] For God is the King of all the **earth**; sing to him a psalm of
47: 9 [47:10] of Abraham, for the kings of the **earth** belong to God;

Ps 48: 2 [48:3] It is beautiful in its loftiness, the joy of the whole **earth**.
48: 10 [48:11] O God, your praise reaches to the ends of the **earth**;
50: 1 summons the **earth** from the rising of the sun to the place where it
50: 4 the heavens above, and the **earth**, that he may judge his people:
52: 5 [52:7] your tent; he will uproot you from the **land** *of* the living.
57: 5 [57:6] above the heavens; let your glory be over all the **earth**.
57: 11 [57:12] above the heavens; let your glory be over all the **earth**.
58: 2 [58:3] and your hands mete out violence on the **earth**.
58: 11 [58:12] surely there is a God who judges the **earth**."
59: 13 [59:14] it will be known to the ends of the **earth** that God rules
60: 2 [60:4] You have shaken the **land** and torn it open; mend its
61: 2 [61:3] From the ends of the **earth** I call to you, I call as my heart
63: 1 [63:2] for you, in a dry and weary **land** where there is no water.
63: 9 [63:10] they will go down to the depths of the **earth**.
65: 5 [65:6] the hope of all the ends of the **earth** and of the farthest
65: 9 [65:10] You care for the **land** and water it; you enrich it
66: 1 Shout with joy to God, all the **earth**!
66: 4 All the **earth** bows down to you; they sing praise to you, they sing
67: 2 [67:3] that your ways may be known on **earth**, your salvation
67: 4 [67:5] rule the peoples justly and guide the nations of the **earth**.
67: 6 [67:7] the **land** will yield its harvest, and God, our God, will bless
67: 7 [67:8] will bless us, and all the ends of the **earth** will fear him.
68: 8 [68:9] the **earth** shook, the heavens poured down rain, before
68: 32 [68:33] Sing to God, O kingdoms of the **earth**, sing praise to the
69: 34 [69:35] Let heaven and **earth** praise him, the seas and all that
71: 20 life again; from the depths of the **earth** you will again bring me up.
72: 6 like rain falling on a mown field, like showers watering the **earth**.
72: 8 rule from sea to sea and from the River to the ends of the **earth**.
72: 16 Let grain abound throughout the **land**; on the tops of the hills may
72: 16 fruit flourish like Lebanon; let it thrive like the grass of the **field**.
72: 19 name forever; may the whole **earth** be filled with his glory.
73: 9 lay claim to heaven, and their tongues take possession of the **earth**.
73: 25 I in heaven but you? And **earth** has nothing I desire besides you.
74: 7 They burned your sanctuary to the **ground**; they defiled the
74: 8 They burned every place where God was worshiped in the **land**.
74: 12 are my king from of old; you bring salvation upon the **earth**.
74: 17 It was you who set all the boundaries of the **earth**; you made both
74: 20 because haunts of violence fill the dark places of the **land**.
75: 3 [75:4] When the **earth** and all its people quake, it is I who hold its
75: 8 [75:9] all the wicked of the **earth** drink it down to its very dregs.
76: 8 [76:9] pronounced judgment, and the **land** feared and was quiet—
76: 9 [76:10] rose up to judge, to save all the afflicted of the **land**.
76: 12 [76:13] the spirit of rulers; he is feared by the kings of the **earth**.
77: 18 [77:19] lightning lit up the world; the **earth** trembled and quaked.
78: 12 He did miracles in the sight of their fathers in the **land** *of* Egypt,
78: 69 like the heights, like the **earth** that he established forever.
79: 2 birds of the air, the flesh of your saints to the beasts of the **earth**.
80: 9 [80:10] the ground for it, and it took root and filled the **land**.
81: 5 [81:6] for Joseph when he went out against **Egypt** [+5213],
81: 10 [81:11] your God, who brought you up out of **Egypt** [+5213].
82: 5 walk about in darkness; all the foundations of the **earth** are shaken.
82: 8 Rise up, O God, judge the **earth**, for all the nations are your
83: 18 [83:19] that you alone are the Most High over all the **earth**.
85: 1 [85:2] You showed favor to your **land**, O LORD; you restored
85: 9 [85:10] those who fear him, that his glory may dwell in our **land**.
85: 11 [85:12] Faithfulness springs forth from the **earth**,
85: 12 [85:13] give what is good, and our **land** will yield its harvest.
88: 12 [88:13] or your righteous deeds in the **land** *of* oblivion?
89: 11 [89:12] The heavens are yours, and yours also the **earth**;
89: 27 [89:28] my firstborn, the most exalted of the kings of the **earth**.
89: 39 [89:40] with your servant and have defiled his crown in the **dust**.
89: 44 [89:45] an end to his splendor and cast his throne to the **ground**.
90: 2 mountains were born or you brought forth the **earth** and the world,
94: 2 Rise up, O Judge of the **earth**; pay back to the proud what they
95: 4 In his hand are the depths of the **earth**, and the mountain peaks
96: 1 Sing to the LORD a new song; sing to the LORD, all the **earth**.
96: 9 in the splendor of his holiness; tremble before him, all the **earth**.
96: 11 Let the heavens rejoice, let the **earth** be glad; let the sea resound,
96: 13 before the LORD, for he comes, he comes to judge the **earth**.
97: 1 The LORD reigns, let the **earth** be glad; let the distant shores
97: 4 His lightning lights up the world; the **earth** sees and trembles.
97: 5 melt like wax before the LORD, before the Lord of all the **earth**.
97: 9 For you, O LORD, are the Most High over all the **earth**;
98: 3 all the ends of the **earth** have seen the salvation of our God.
98: 4 Shout for joy to the LORD, all the **earth**, burst into jubilant song
98: 9 let them sing before the LORD, for he comes to judge the **earth**.
99: 1 he sits enthroned between the cherubim, let the **earth** shake.
100: 1 Shout for joy to the LORD, all the **earth**.
101: 6 My eyes will be on the faithful in the **land**, that they may dwell
101: 8 Every morning I will put to silence all the wicked in the **land**;
102: 15 [102:16] all the kings of the **earth** will revere your glory.
102: 19 [102:20] his sanctuary on high, from heaven he viewed the **earth**,
102: 25 [102:26] In the beginning you laid the foundations of the **earth**,
103: 11 For as high as the heavens are above the **earth**, so great is his love
104: 5 He set the **earth** on its foundations; it can never be moved.
104: 9 boundary they cannot cross; never again will they cover the **earth**.
104: 13 his upper chambers; the **earth** is satisfied by the fruit of his work.
104: 14 plants for man to cultivate—bringing forth food from the **earth**:
104: 24 In wisdom you made them all; the **earth** is full of your creatures.
104: 32 he who looks at the **earth**, and it trembles, who touches the
104: 35 But may sinners vanish from the **earth** and the wicked be no more.
105: 7 He is the LORD our God; his judgments are in all the **earth**.
105: 11 "To you I will give the **land** *of* Canaan as the portion you will
105: 16 He called down famine on the **land** and destroyed all their supplies
105: 23 Israel entered Egypt; Jacob lived as an alien in the **land** *of* Ham.
105: 27 his miraculous signs among them, his wonders in the **land** *of* Ham.
105: 30 Their **land** teemed with frogs, which went up into the bedrooms of
105: 32 He turned their rain into hail, with lightning throughout their **land**;
105: 35 they ate up every green thing in their **land**, ate up the produce of
105: 36 he struck down all the firstborn in their **land**, the firstfruits of all
105: 44 he gave them the **lands** *of* the nations, and they fell heir to what
106: 17 The **earth** opened up and swallowed Dathan; it buried the
106: 22 miracles in the **land** *of* Ham and awesome deeds by the Red Sea.
106: 24 they despised the pleasant **land**; they did not believe his promise.
106: 27 fall among the nations and scatter them throughout the **lands**.
106: 38 to the idols of Canaan, and the **land** was desecrated by their blood.
107: 3 those he gathered from the **lands**, from east and west, from north
107: 34 fruitful **land** into a salt waste, because of the wickedness of those
107: 35 into pools of water and the parched **ground** into flowing springs;
108: 5 [108:6] the heavens, and let your glory be over all the **earth**.
109: 15 that he may cut off the memory of them from the **earth**.
110: 6 heaping up the dead and crushing the rulers of the whole **earth**.
112: 2 His children will be mighty in the **land**; the generation of the
113: 6 who stoops down to look on the heavens and the **earth**?
114: 7 Tremble, O **earth**, at the presence of the Lord, at the presence of
115: 15 you be blessed by the LORD, the Maker of heaven and **earth**.
115: 16 heavens belong to the LORD, but the **earth** he has given to man.
116: 9 that I may walk before the LORD in the **land** *of* the living.
119: 19 I am a stranger on **earth**; do not hide your commands from me.
119: 64 The **earth** is filled with your love, O LORD; teach me your
119: 87 They almost wiped me from the **earth**, but I have not forsaken
119: 90 through all generations; you established the **earth**, and it endures.
119: 119 All the wicked of the **earth** you discard like dross; therefore I love
121: 2 My help comes from the LORD, the Maker of heaven and **earth**.
124: 8 help is in the name of the LORD, the Maker of heaven and **earth**.
134: 3 May the LORD, the Maker of heaven and **earth**, bless you from
135: 6 in the heavens and on the **earth**, in the seas and all their depths.
135: 7 He makes clouds rise from the ends of the **earth**; he sends
135: 12 he gave their **land** as an inheritance, an inheritance to his people
136: 6 who spread out the **earth** upon the waters, *His love endures*
136: 21 gave their **land** as an inheritance, *His love endures*
138: 4 May all the kings of the **earth** praise you, O LORD, when they
139: 15 When I was woven together in the depths of the **earth**,
140: 11 [140:12] Let slanderers not be established in the **land**;
141: 7 ⌞They will say,⌟ "As one plows and breaks up the **earth**, so our
142: 5 [142:6] "You are my refuge, my portion in the **land** *of* the living."
143: 3 The enemy pursues me, he crushes me to the **ground**; he makes me
143: 6 out my hands to you; my soul thirsts for you like a parched **land**.
143: 10 you are my God; may your good Spirit lead me on level **ground**.
146: 6 the Maker of heaven and **earth**, the sea, and everything in them—
147: 6 LORD sustains the humble but casts the wicked to the **ground**.
147: 8 he supplies the **earth** with rain and makes grass grow on the hills.
147: 15 He sends his command to the **earth**; his word runs swiftly.
148: 7 Praise the LORD from the **earth**, you great sea creatures
148: 11 kings of the **earth** and all nations, you princes and all rulers on
148: 11 of the earth and all nations, you princes and all rulers on **earth**,
148: 13 alone is exalted; his splendor is above the **earth** and the heavens.
Pr 2: 21 For the upright will live in the **land**, and the blameless will remain
2: 22 the wicked will be cut off from the **land**, and the unfaithful will be
3: 19 By wisdom the LORD laid the **earth's** foundations,
8: 16 me princes govern, and all nobles who rule on **earth**. [BHS 7406]
8: 23 from eternity, from the beginning, before the **world** began.
8: 26 before he made the **earth** or its fields or any of the dust of the
8: 29 and when he marked out the foundations of the **earth**.
8: 31 rejoicing in his **whole world** [+9315] and delighting in mankind.
10: 30 will never be uprooted, but the wicked will not remain in the **land**.
11: 31 If the righteous receive their due on **earth**, how much more the
17: 24 wisdom in view, but a fool's eyes wander to the ends of the **earth**.
21: 19 Better to live in a **desert** [+4497] than with a quarrelsome
25: 3 As the heavens are high and the **earth** is deep, so the hearts of
25: 25 Like cold water to a weary soul is good news from a distant **land**.
28: 2 When a **country** is rebellious, it has many rulers, but a man of
29: 4 By justice a king gives a **country** stability, but one who is greedy
30: 4 Who has established all the ends of the **earth**? What is his name,
30: 14 whose jaws are set with knives to devour the poor from the **earth**,
30: 16 the grave, the barren womb, **land**, which is never satisfied with
30: 21 "Under three things the **earth** trembles, under four it cannot bear
30: 24 "Four things on **earth** are small, yet they are extremely wise:

Pr 31:23 the city gate, where he takes his seat among the elders of the **land**.
Ecc 1: 4 and generations go, but the **earth** remains forever.
3:21 and if the spirit of the animal goes down into the **earth**?"
5: 2 [5:1] God is in heaven and you are on **earth**, so let your words be
5: 9 [5:8] The increase from the **land** is taken by all; the king himself
7:20 There is not a righteous man on **earth** who does what is right
8:14 There is something else meaningless that occurs on **earth**:
8:16 my mind to know wisdom and to observe man's labor on **earth**—
10: 7 on horseback, while princes go **on foot** [+2021+6584] like slaves.
10:16 O **land** whose king was a servant and whose princes feast in the
10:17 O **land** whose king is of noble birth and whose princes eat at a
11: 2 for you do not know what disaster may come upon the **land**.
11: 3 If clouds are full of water, they pour rain upon the **earth**. Whether
12: 7 the dust returns to the **ground** it came from, and the spirit returns
SS 2:12 Flowers appear on the **earth**; the season of singing has come,
2:12 of singing has come, the cooing of doves is heard in our **land**.
Isa 1: 2 Hear, O heavens! Listen, O **earth**! For the LORD has spoken:
1: 7 Your **country** is desolate, your cities burned with fire; your fields
1:19 If you are willing and obedient, you will eat the best from the **land**;
2: 7 Their **land** is full of silver and gold; there is no end to their
2: 7 Their **land** is full of horses; there is no end to their chariots.
2: 8 Their **land** is full of idols; they bow down to the work of their
2:19 and the splendor of his majesty, when he rises to shake the **earth**.
2:21 and the splendor of his majesty, when he rises to shake the **earth**.
3:26 Zion will lament and mourn; destitute, she will sit on the **ground**.
4: 2 the fruit of the **land** will be the pride and glory of the survivors in
5: 8 join field to field till no space is left and you live alone in the **land**.
5:26 the distant nations, he whistles for those at the ends of the **earth**.
5:30 And if one looks at the **land**, he will see darkness and distress;
6: 3 holy is the LORD Almighty; the whole **earth** is full of his glory."
6:12 has sent everyone far away and the **land** is utterly forsaken.
7:18 the distant streams of Egypt and for bees from the **land** *of* Assyria.
7:22 curds to eat. All who remain in the **land** will eat curds and honey.
7:24 and arrow, for the **land** will be covered with briers and thorns.
8: 8 Its outspread wings will cover the breadth of your **land**,
8: 9 you nations, and be shattered! Listen, all you distant **lands**.
8:22 Then they will look toward the **earth** and see only distress
9: 1 [8:23] In the past he humbled the **land** *of* Zebulun and the land of
9: 1 [8:23] he humbled the land of Zebulun and the **land** *of* Naphtali,
9: 2 [9:1] on those living in the **land** *of* the shadow of death a light has
9:19 [9:18] By the wrath of the LORD Almighty the **land** will be
10:14 as men gather abandoned eggs, so I gathered all the **countries**;
10:23 will carry out the destruction decreed upon the whole **land**.
11: 4 with justice he will give decisions for the poor of the **earth**.
11: 4 He will strike the **earth** with the rod of his mouth; with the breath
11: 9 for the **earth** will be full of the knowledge of the LORD as the
11:12 the scattered people of Judah from the four quarters of the **earth**.
11:16 as there was for Israel when they came up from **Egypt** [+5213].
12: 5 for he has done glorious things; let this be known to all the **world**.
13: 5 They come from faraway **lands**, from the ends of the heavens—
13: 5 and the weapons of his wrath—to destroy the whole **country**.
13: 9 to make the **land** desolate and destroy the sinners within it.
13:13 the **earth** will shake from its place at the wrath of the LORD
13:14 will return to his own people, each will flee to his **native land**.
14: 7 All the **lands** are at rest and at peace; they break into singing.
14: 9 all those who were leaders in the **world**; it makes them rise from
14:12 You have been cast down to the **earth**, you who once laid low the
14:16 "Is this the man who shook the **earth** and made kingdoms tremble,
14:20 in burial, for you have destroyed your **land** and killed your people.
14:21 they are not to rise to inherit the **land** and cover the earth with their
14:25 I will crush the Assyrian in my **land**; on my mountains I will
14:26 This is the plan determined for the whole **world**; this is the hand
16: 1 Send lambs as tribute to the ruler of the **land**, from Sela,
16: 4 and destruction will cease; the aggressor will vanish from the **land**.
18: 1 Woe to the **land** *of* whirring wings along the rivers of Cush,
18: 2 nation of strange speech, whose **land** is divided by rivers.
18: 3 All you people of the world, you who live on the **earth**, when a
18: 6 all be left to the mountain birds of prey and to the **wild** animals;
18: 6 the birds will feed on them all summer, the **wild** animals all winter.
18: 7 nation of strange speech, whose **land** is divided by rivers—
19:18 In that day five cities in **Egypt** [+5213] will speak the language of
19:19 there will be an altar to the LORD in the heart of **Egypt** [+5213],
19:20 and witness to the LORD Almighty in the **land** *of* Egypt.
19:24 be the third, along with Egypt and Assyria, a blessing on the **earth**.
21: 1 an invader comes from the desert, from a **land** *of* terror.
21: 9 All the images of its gods lie shattered on the **ground**!' "
21:14 you who live in **Tema** [+9401], bring food for the fugitives.
22:18 roll you up tightly like a ball and throw you into a large **country**.
23: 1 or harbor. From the **land** *of* Cyprus word has come to them.
23: 8 merchants are princes, whose traders are renowned in the **earth**?
23: 9 of all glory and to humble all who are renowned on the **earth**.
23:10 Till your **land** as along the Nile, O Daughter of Tarshish, for you
23:13 Look at the **land** *of* the Babylonians, this people that is now of no
23:17 will ply her trade with all the kingdoms **[RPH]** on the face of the
24: 1 the LORD is going to lay waste the **earth** and devastate it;
24: 3 The **earth** will be completely laid waste and totally plundered.
24: 4 The **earth** dries up and withers, the world languishes and withers,
24: 4 the world languishes and withers, the exalted of the **earth** languish.
24: 5 The **earth** is defiled by its people; they have disobeyed the laws,
24: 6 Therefore a curse consumes the **earth**; its people must bear their
24: 6 Therefore **earth's** inhabitants are burned up, and very few are left.
24:11 all joy turns to gloom, all gaiety is banished from the **earth**.
24:13 So will it be on the **earth** and among the nations, as when an olive
24:16 From the ends of the **earth** we hear singing: "Glory to the
24:17 Terror and pit and snare await you, O people of the **earth**.
24:18 of the heavens are opened, the foundations of the **earth** shake.
24:19 The **earth** is broken up, the earth is split asunder, the earth is
24:19 The earth is broken up, the **earth** is split asunder, the earth is
24:19 the earth is split asunder, the **earth** is thoroughly shaken.
24:20 The **earth** reels like a drunkard, it sways like a hut in the wind;
25: 8 he will remove the disgrace of his people from all the **earth**.
25:12 them low; he will bring them down to the **ground**, to the very dust.
26: 1 In that day this song will be sung in the **land** *of* Judah: We have a
26: 5 city low; he levels it to the **ground** and casts it down to the dust.
26: 9 When your judgments come upon the **earth**, the people of the
26:10 even in a **land** *of* uprightness they go on doing evil and regard not
26:15 glory for yourself; you have extended all the borders of the **land**.
26:18 We have not brought salvation to the **earth**; we have not given
26:19 like the dew of the morning; the **earth** will give birth to her dead.
26:21 out of his dwelling to punish the people of the **earth** for their sins.
26:21 The **earth** will disclose the blood shed upon her; she will conceal
27:13 Those who were perishing in **Assyria** [+855] and those who were
27:13 in Assyria and those who were exiled in **Egypt** [+5213] will come
28: 2 and a flooding downpour, he will throw it forcefully to the **ground**.
28:22 has told me of the destruction decreed against the whole **land**.
29: 4 Brought low, you will speak from the **ground**; your speech will
29: 4 Your voice will come ghostlike from the **earth**; out of the dust
30: 6 Through a **land** *of* hardship and distress, of lions and lionesses,
32: 2 water in the desert and the shadow of a great rock in a thirsty **land**.
33: 9 The **land** mourns and wastes away, Lebanon is ashamed
33:17 will see the king in his beauty and view a **land** *that* stretches afar.
34: 1 Let the **earth** hear, and all that is in it, the world, and all that
34: 6 has a sacrifice in Bozrah and a great slaughter in **Edom** [+121].
34: 7 Their **land** will be drenched with blood, and the dust will be
34: 9 her dust into burning sulfur; her **land** will become blazing pitch!
36:10 have I come to attack and destroy this **land** without the LORD?
36:10 The LORD himself told me to march against this **country**
36:17 until I come and take you to a **land** like your own—a land of grain
36:17 **[RPH]** a land of grain and new wine, a land of bread
36:17 a **land** *of* grain and new wine, a land of bread and vineyards.
36:17 a land of grain and new wine, a **land** *of* bread and vineyards.
36:18 Has the god of any nation ever delivered his **land** from the hand of
36:20 Who of all the gods of these **countries** has been able to save his
36:20 the gods of these countries has been able to save his **land** from me?
37: 7 when he hears a certain report, he will return to his own **country**,
37: 7 **there**[s] [+928+2257] I will have him cut down with the sword.' "
37:11 heard what the kings of Assyria have done to all the **countries**,
37:16 you alone are God over all the kingdoms of the **earth**.
37:16 all the kingdoms of the earth. You have made heaven and **earth**.
37:18 that the Assyrian kings have laid waste all these **peoples** and their
37:18 Assyrian kings have laid waste all these peoples and their **lands**.
37:20 so that all kingdoms on **earth** may know that you alone, O
37:38 him down with the sword, and they escaped to the **land** *of* Ararat.
38:11 not again see the LORD, the LORD, in the **land** *of* the living;
39: 3 did they come from?" "From a distant **land**," Hezekiah replied.
40:12 Who has held the dust of the **earth** in a basket, or weighed the
40:21 Have you not understood since the **earth** was founded?
40:22 He sits enthroned above the circle of the **earth**, and its people are
40:23 princes to naught and reduces the rulers of this **world** to nothing.
40:24 no sooner do they take root in the **ground**, than he blows on them
40:28 is the everlasting God, the Creator of the ends of the **earth**.
41: 5 The islands have seen it and fear; the ends of the **earth** tremble.
41: 9 I took you from the ends of the **earth**, from its farthest corners I
41:18 the desert into pools of water, and the parched **ground** into springs.
42: 4 will not falter or be discouraged till he establishes justice on **earth**.
42: 5 them out, who spread out the **earth** and all that comes out of it,
42:10 his praise from the ends of the **earth**, you who go down to the sea,
43: 6 my sons from afar and my daughters from the ends of the **earth**—
44:23 for the LORD has done this; shout aloud, O **earth** beneath.
44:24 stretched out the heavens, who spread out the **earth** by myself,
45: 8 Let the **earth** open wide, let salvation spring up, let righteousness
45:12 It is I who made the **earth** and created mankind upon it. My own
45:18 he is God; he who fashioned and made the **earth**, he founded it;
45:19 I have not spoken in secret, from somewhere in a **land** *of* darkness;
45:22 "Turn to me and be saved, all you ends of the **earth**; for I am God,
46:11 a bird of prey; from a far-off **land**, a man to fulfill my purpose.
47: 1 sit on the **ground** without a throne, Daughter of the Babylonians.
48:13 My own hand laid the foundations of the **earth**, and my right hand

Isa 48:20 Send it out to the ends of the **earth**; say, "The LORD has
49: 6 that you may bring my salvation to the ends of the **earth**."
49: 8 to restore the **land** and to reassign its desolate inheritances,
49:12 the north, some from the west, some from the **region** *of* Aswan."
49:13 Shout for joy, O heavens; rejoice, O **earth**; burst into song,
49:19 you were ruined and made desolate and your **land** laid waste,
49:23 They will bow down before you with their faces to the **ground**;
51: 6 Lift up your eyes to the heavens, look at the **earth** beneath;
51: 6 the **earth** will wear out like a garment and its inhabitants die like
51:13 stretched out the heavens and laid the foundations of the **earth**,
51:16 who laid the foundations of the **earth**, and who say to Zion,
51:23 you made your back like the **ground**, like a street to be walked
52:10 and all the ends of the **earth** will see the salvation of our God.
53: 2 before him like a tender shoot, and like a root out of dry **ground**.
53: 8 For he was cut off from the **land** *of* the living; for the transgression
54: 5 of Israel is your Redeemer; he is called the God of all the **earth**.
54: 9 I swore that the waters of Noah would never again cover the **earth**.
55: 9 "As the heavens are higher than the **earth**, so are my ways higher
55:10 do not return to it without watering the **earth** and making it bud
57:13 But the man who makes me his refuge will inherit the **land**
58:14 I will cause you to ride on the heights of the **land** and to feast on
60: 2 darkness covers the **earth** and thick darkness is over the peoples,
60:18 No longer will violence be heard in your **land**, nor ruin
60:21 all your people be righteous and they will possess the **land** forever.
61: 7 so they will inherit a double portion in their **land**, and everlasting
61:11 For as the **soil** makes the sprout come up and a garden causes seeds
62: 4 No longer will they call you Deserted, or name your **land** Desolate.
62: 4 you will be called Hephzibah, and your **land** Beulah;
62: 4 the LORD will take delight in you, and your **land** will be married.
62: 7 till he establishes Jerusalem and makes her the praise of the **earth**.
62:11 The LORD has made proclamation to the ends of the **earth**:
63: 6 wrath I made them drunk and poured their blood on the **ground**."
65:16 Whoever invokes a blessing in the **land** will do so by the God of
65:16 he who takes an oath in the **land** will swear by the God of truth.
65:17 "Behold, I will create new heavens and a new **earth**. The former
66: 1 LORD says: "Heaven is my throne, and the **earth** is my footstool.
66: 8 Can a **country** be born in a day or a nation be brought forth in a
66:22 and the new **earth** that I make will endure before me,"
Jer 1: 1 one of the priests at Anathoth in the **territory** *of* Benjamin.
1:14 the north disaster will be poured out on all who live in the **land**.
1:18 an iron pillar and a bronze wall to stand against the whole **land**—
1:18 kings of Judah, its officials, its priests and the people of the **land**.
2: 2 and followed me through the desert, through a **land** not sown.
2: 6 who brought us up out of **Egypt** [+5213] and led us through the
2: 6 through a **land** *of* deserts and rifts, a land of drought and darkness,
2: 6 through a land of deserts and rifts, a **land** *of* drought and darkness,
2: 6 and darkness, a **land** where no one travels and no one lives?'
2: 7 I brought you into a fertile **land** to eat its fruit and rich produce.
2: 7 you came and defiled my **land** and made my inheritance
2:15 They have laid waste his **land**; his towns are burned and deserted.
2:31 "Have I been a desert to Israel or a **land** *of* great darkness?
3: 1 he return to her again? Would not the **land** be completely defiled?
3: 2 You have defiled the **land** with your prostitution and wickedness.
3: 9 she defiled the **land** and committed adultery with stone and wood.
3:16 when your numbers have increased greatly in the **land**,"
3:18 together they will come from a northern **land** to the land I gave
3:18 together they will come from a northern land to the **land** I gave
3:19 gladly would I treat you like sons and give you a desirable **land**,
4: 5 in Jerusalem and say: 'Sound the trumpet throughout the **land**!'
4: 7 of nations has set out. He has left his place to lay waste your **land**.
4:16 'A besieging army is coming from a distant **land**, raising a war cry
4:20 Disaster follows disaster; the whole **land** lies in ruins. In an instant
4:23 I looked at the **earth**, and it was formless and empty; and at the
4:27 "The whole **land** will be ruined, though I will not destroy it
4:28 Therefore the **earth** will mourn and the heavens above grow dark,
5:19 you have forsaken me and served foreign gods in your own **land**,
5:19 so now you will serve foreigners in a **land** not your own.'
5:30 "A horrible and shocking thing has happened in the **land**:
6: 8 from you and make your **land** desolate so no one can live in it."
6:12 when I stretch out my hand against those who live in the **land**,"
6:19 Hear, O **earth**: I am bringing disaster on this people, the fruit of
6:20 about incense from Sheba or sweet calamus from a distant **land**?
6:22 "Look, an army is coming from the **land** *of* the north; a great
6:22 a great nation is being stirred up from the ends of the **earth**.
7: 7 in this place, in the **land** I gave your forefathers for ever and ever.
7:22 For when I brought your forefathers out of **Egypt** [+5213]
7:25 From the time your forefathers left **Egypt** [+5213] until now,
7:33 become food for the birds of the air and the beasts of the **earth**,
7:34 and the streets of Jerusalem, for the **land** will become desolate.
8:16 at the neighing of their stallions the whole **land** trembles.
8:16 They have come to devour the **land** and everything in it, the city
8:19 Listen to the cry of my people from a **land** far away: "Is the
9: 3 [9:2] to shoot lies; it is not by truth that they triumph in the **land**.
9:12 [9:11] Why has the **land** been ruined and laid waste like a desert
9:19 [9:18] We must leave our **land** because our houses are in ruins.' "
9:24 [9:23] justice and righteousness on **earth**, for in these I delight,"
10:10 When he is angry, the **earth** trembles; the nations cannot endure
10:12 God made the **earth** by his power; he founded the world by his
10:13 the heavens roar; he makes clouds rise from the ends of the **earth**.
10:17 Gather up your belongings to leave the **land**, you who live under
10:18 "At this time I will hurl out those who live in this **land**; I will bring
10:22 report is coming—a great commotion from the **land** *of* the north!
11: 4 your forefathers when I brought them out of **Egypt** [+5213],
11: 5 to give them a **land** flowing with milk and honey'—
11: 7 From the time I brought your forefathers up from **Egypt** [+5213]
11:19 let us cut him off from the **land** *of* the living, that his name be
12: 4 How long will the **land** lie parched and the grass in every field be
12: 5 If you stumble in safe **country**, how will you manage in the
12:11 the whole **land** will be laid waste because there is no one who
12:12 for the sword of the LORD will devour from one end of the **land**
12:12 from one end of the land to the other; **[RPH]** no one will be safe.
12:15 each of them back to his own inheritance and his own **country**.
13:13 I am going to fill with drunkenness all who live in this **land**,
14: 2 they wail for the **land**, and a cry goes up from Jerusalem.
14: 4 The ground is cracked because there is no rain in the **land**;
14: 8 Savior in times of distress, why are you like a stranger in the **land**,
14:15 yet they are saying, 'No sword or famine will touch this **land**.'
14:18 Both prophet and priest have gone to a **land** they know not.' "
15: 3 birds of the air and the beasts of the **earth** to devour and destroy.
15: 4 I will make them abhorrent to all the kingdoms of the **earth**
15: 7 winnow them with a winnowing fork at the city gates of the **land**.
15:10 me birth, a man with whom the whole **land** strives and contends!
15:14 I will enslave you to your enemies in a **land** you do not know,
16: 3 who are their mothers and the men who are their fathers: **[RPH]**
16: 4 become food for the birds of the air and the beasts of the **earth**."
16: 6 "Both high and low will die in this **land**. They will not be buried
16:13 So I will throw you out of this **land** into a land neither you nor
16:13 So I will throw you out of this land into a **land** neither you nor
16:14 LORD lives, who brought the Israelites up out of **Egypt** [+5213],'
16:15 who brought the Israelites up out of the **land** *of* the north and out
16:15 and out of all the **countries** where he had banished them.'
16:18 because they have defiled my **land** with the lifeless forms of their
16:19 to you the nations will come from the ends of the **earth** and say,
17: 4 I will enslave you to your enemies in a **land** you do not know,
17: 6 the parched places of the desert, in a salt **land** where no one lives.
17:13 Those who turn away from you will be written in the **dust**
17:26 from the **territory** *of* Benjamin and the western foothills, from the
18:16 Their **land** will be laid waste, an object of lasting scorn; all who
19: 7 carcasses as food to the birds of the air and the beasts of the **earth**.
22:10 because he will never return nor see his native **land** again.
22:12 where they have led him captive; he will not see this **land** again."
22:26 hurl you and the mother who gave you birth into another **country**,
22:27 You will never come back to the **land** you long to return to."
22:28 and his children be hurled out, cast into a **land** they do not know?
22:29 O **land**, land, land, hear the word of the LORD!
22:29 O land, **land**, land, hear the word of the LORD!
22:29 O land, land, **land**, hear the word of the LORD!
23: 3 of my flock out of all the **countries** where I have driven them
23: 5 who will reign wisely and do what is just and right in the **land**.
23: 7 LORD lives, who brought the Israelites up out of **Egypt** [+5213],'
23: 8 who brought the descendants of Israel up out of the **land** *of* the
23: 8 and out of all the **countries** where he had banished them.'
23:10 The **land** is full of adulterers; because of the curse the land lies
23:10 because of the curse the **land** lies parched and the pastures in the
23:15 of Jerusalem ungodliness has spread throughout the **land**."
23:24 "Do not I fill heaven and **earth**?" declares the LORD.
24: 5 whom I sent away from this place to the **land** *of* the Babylonians.
24: 6 over them for their good, and I will bring them back to this **land**.
24: 8 from Jerusalem, whether they remain in this **land** or live in Egypt.
24: 8 whether they remain in this land or live in **Egypt** [+5213].
24: 9 them abhorrent and an offense to all the kingdoms of the **earth**,
25: 9 "and I will bring them against this **land** and its inhabitants
25:11 This whole **country** will become a desolate wasteland, and these
25:12 the king of Babylon and his nation, the **land** *of* the Babylonians,
25:13 I will bring upon that **land** all the things I have spoken against it,
25:20 and all the foreign people there; all the kings of **Uz** [+6420];
25:20 all the kings of the **Philistines** [+7149] (those of Ashkelon,
25:26 after the other—all the kingdoms **[RPH]** on the face of the earth.
25:29 for I am calling down a sword upon all who live on the **earth**,
25:30 those who tread the grapes, shout against all who live on the **earth**.
25:31 The tumult will resound to the ends of the **earth**, for the LORD
25:32 to nation; a mighty storm is rising from the ends of the **earth**."
25:33 will be everywhere—from one end of the **earth** to the other.
25:33 from one end of the earth to **the other**[s] [+2021+7895].
25:38 their **land** will become desolate because of the sword of the
26: 6 this city an object of cursing among all the nations of the **earth**.' "
26:17 Some of the elders of the **land** stepped forward and said to the
26:20 the same things against this city and this **land** as Jeremiah did.

Jer 27: 5 great power and outstretched arm I made the **earth** and its people
27: 5 the earth and its people and the animals that are on **it**[s] [+2021],
27: 6 Now I will hand all your **countries** over to my servant
27: 7 and his son and his grandson until the time for his **land** comes;
28: 8 disaster and plague against many **countries** and great kingdoms.
29: 18 and will make them abhorrent to all the kingdoms of the **earth**
30: 3 and restore them to the **land** I gave their forefathers to possess,'
30: 10 of a distant place, your descendants from the **land** *of* their exile.
31: 8 I will bring them from the **land** *of* the north and gather them from
31: 8 the land of the north and gather them from the ends of the **earth**.
31: 16 the LORD. "They will return from the **land** *of* the enemy.
31: 22 The LORD will create a new thing on **earth**—a woman will
31: 23 the people in the **land** *of* Judah and in its towns will once again use
31: 32 when I took them by the hand to lead them out of **Egypt** [+5213],
31: 37 the foundations of the **earth** below be searched out will I reject all
32: 8 and said, 'Buy my field at Anathoth in the **territory** *of* Benjamin.
32: 15 Houses, fields and vineyards will again be bought in this **land**.'
32: 17 and the **earth** by your great power and outstretched arm.
32: 20 You performed miraculous signs and wonders in **Egypt** [+5213]
32: 21 You brought your people Israel out of **Egypt** [+5213] with signs
32: 22 You gave them this **land** you had sworn to give their forefathers,
32: 22 to give their forefathers, a **land** flowing with milk and honey.
32: 37 I will surely gather them from all the **lands** where I banish them in
32: 41 and will assuredly plant them in this **land** with all my heart
32: 43 Once more fields will be bought in this **land** of which you say,
32: 44 will be signed, sealed and witnessed in the **territory** *of* Benjamin,
33: 9 honor before all nations on **earth** that hear of all the good things I
33: 11 For I will restore the fortunes of the **land** as they were before,'
33: 13 western foothills and of the Negev, in the **territory** *of* Benjamin,
33: 15 from David's line; he will do what is just and right in the **land**.
33: 25 with day and night and the fixed laws of heaven and **earth**,
34: 1 and peoples in the **empire** he ruled were fighting against Jerusalem
34: 13 with your forefathers when I brought them out of **Egypt** [+5213],
34: 17 I will make you abhorrent to all the kingdoms of the **earth**.
34: 19 all the people of the **land** who walked between the pieces of the
34: 20 become food for the birds of the air and the beasts of the **earth**.
35: 11 But when Nebuchadnezzar king of Babylon invaded this **land**,
36: 29 and destroy this **land** and cut off both men and animals from it?"
37: 1 Zedekiah son of Josiah was made king of **Judah** [+3373] by
37: 2 Neither he nor his attendants nor the people of the **land** paid any
37: 7 marched out to support you, will go back to its own **land**, to Egypt.
37: 12 Jeremiah started to leave the city to go to the **territory** *of*
37: 19 to you, 'The king of Babylon will not attack you or this **land**'?
39: 5 Nebuchadnezzar king of Babylon at Riblah in the **land** *of* Hamath,
39: 10 the commander of the guard left behind in the **land** *of*
40: 4 Look, the whole **country** lies before you; go wherever you please."
40: 6 with him among the people who were left behind in the **land**.
40: 7 had appointed Gedaliah son of Ahikam as governor over the **land**
40: 7 women and children who were the poorest in the **land** and who had
40: 9 "Settle down in the **land** and serve the king of Babylon, and it will
40: 11 all the other **countries** heard that the king of Babylon had left a
40: 12 they all came back to the **land** *of* Judah, to Gedaliah at Mizpah,
41: 2 the king of Babylon had appointed as governor over the **land**.
41: 18 the king of Babylon had appointed as governor over the **land**.
42: 10 'If you stay in this **land**, I will build you up and not tear you down;
42: 13 'We will not stay in this **land**,' and so disobey the LORD your
42: 14 and if you say, 'No, we will go and live in **Egypt** [+5213],
42: 16 **[RPH]** and the famine you dread will follow you into Egypt,
43: 4 disobeyed the LORD's command to stay in the **land** *of* Judah.
43: 5 **land** *of* Judah from all the nations where they had been scattered.
43: 7 So they entered **Egypt** [+5213] in disobedience to the LORD
43: 11 He will come and attack **Egypt** [+5213], bringing death to those
43: 12 so will he wrap **Egypt** [+5213] around himself and depart from
43: 13 There in the temple of the sun in **Egypt** [+5213] he will demolish
44: 1 Jeremiah concerning all the Jews living in **Lower Egypt** [+5213]—
44: 1 Tahpanhes and Memphis—and in **Upper Egypt** [+7356]:
44: 8 burning incense to other gods in **Egypt** [+5213], where you have
44: 8 an object of cursing and reproach among all the nations on **earth**.
44: 9 and your wives in the **land** *of* Judah and the streets of Jerusalem?
44: 12 Judah who were determined to go to **Egypt** [+5213] to settle there.
44: 12 They will all perish in **Egypt** [+5213]; they will fall by the sword
44: 13 I will punish those who live in **Egypt** [+5213] with the sword,
44: 14 of Judah who have gone to live in **Egypt** [+5213] will escape
44: 14 live in Egypt will escape or survive to return to the **land** *of* Judah,
44: 15 and all the people living in **Lower** and Upper **Egypt** [+5213],
44: 21 your kings and your officials and the people of the **land**?
44: 22 your **land** became an object of cursing and a desolate waste
44: 24 the word of the LORD, all you people of Judah in **Egypt** [+5213].
44: 26 hear the word of the LORD, all Jews living in **Egypt** [+5213]:
44: 26 'that no one from Judah living anywhere in **Egypt** [+5213] will
44: 27 the Jews in **Egypt** [+5213] will perish by sword and famine until
44: 28 and return to the **land** *of* Judah from Egypt will be very few.
44: 28 return to the land of Judah from **Egypt** [+5213] will be very few.
44: 28 the whole remnant of Judah who came to live in **Egypt** [+5213]
45: 4 I have built and uproot what I have planted, throughout the **land**.
46: 8 She says, 'I will rise and cover the **earth**; I will destroy cities
46: 10 will offer sacrifice in the **land** *of* the north by the River Euphrates.
46: 12 The nations will hear of your shame; your cries will fill the **earth**.
46: 13 of Nebuchadnezzar king of Babylon to attack **Egypt** [+5213]:
46: 16 'Get up, let us go back to our own people and our native **lands**,
46: 27 of a distant place, your descendants from the **land** *of* their exile.
47: 2 They will overflow the **land** and everything in it, the towns
47: 2 The people will cry out; all who dwell in the **land** will wail
48: 21 Judgment has come to **[NIE]** the plateau—to Holon, Jahzah
48: 24 and Bozrah—to all the towns of **Moab** [+4566], far and near.
48: 33 and gladness are gone from the orchards and **fields** *of* Moab.
49: 21 At the sound of their fall the **earth** will tremble; their cry will
50: 1 the prophet concerning Babylon and the **land** *of* the Babylonians:
50: 3 A nation from the north will attack her and lay waste her **land**.
50: 8 leave the **land** *of* the Babylonians, and be like the goats that lead
50: 9 bring against Babylon an alliance of great nations from the **land** *of*
50: 16 return to his own people, let everyone flee to his own **land**.
50: 18 the king of Babylon and his **land** as I punished the king of Assyria.
50: 21 "Attack the **land** *of* Merathaim and those who live in Pekod.
50: 22 The noise of battle is in the **land**, the noise of great destruction!
50: 23 How broken and shattered is the hammer of the whole **earth**!
50: 25 for the Sovereign LORD Almighty has work to do in the **land** *of*
50: 28 refugees from **Babylon** [+951] declaring in Zion how the LORD
50: 34 defend their cause so that he may bring rest to their **land**,
50: 38 For it is a **land** *of* idols, idols that will go mad with terror.
50: 41 and many kings are being stirred up from the ends of the **earth**.
50: 45 what he has purposed against the **land** *of* the Babylonians:
50: 46 At the sound of Babylon's capture the **earth** will tremble;
51: 2 foreigners to Babylon to winnow her and to devastate her **land**;
51: 4 They will fall down slain in **Babylon** [+4169], fatally wounded in
51: 5 though their **land** is full of guilt before the Holy One of Israel.
51: 7 a gold cup in the LORD's hand; she made the whole **earth** drunk.
51: 9 let us leave her and each go to his own **land**, for her judgment
51: 15 "He made the **earth** by his power; he founded the world by his
51: 16 the heavens roar; he makes clouds rise from the ends of the **earth**.
51: 25 you who destroy the whole **earth**," declares the LORD.
51: 27 "Lift up a banner in the **land**! Blow the trumpet among the nations!
51: 28 and all their officials, and all the **countries** they rule.
51: 29 The **land** trembles and writhes, for the LORD's purposes against
51: 29 to lay waste the **land** *of* Babylon so that no one will live there.
51: 41 Sheshach will be captured, the boast of the whole **earth** seized!
51: 43 a dry **[RPH]** and desert land, a land where no one lives,
51: 43 will be desolate, a dry and desert **land**, a land where no one lives,
51: 46 Do not lose heart or be afraid when rumors are heard in the **land**;
51: 46 the next, rumors of violence in the **land** and of ruler against ruler.
51: 47 her whole **land** will be disgraced and her slain will all lie fallen
51: 48 heaven and **earth** and all that is in them will shout for joy over
51: 49 just as the slain in all the **earth** have fallen because of Babylon.
51: 52 punish her idols, and throughout her **land** the wounded will groan.
51: 54 the sound of great destruction from the **land** *of* the Babylonians.
52: 6 so severe that there was no food for the people **[NIE]** to eat.
52: 9 He was taken to the king of Babylon at Riblah in the **land** *of*
52: 16 Nebuzaradan left behind the rest of the poorest people of the **land**
52: 25 was chief officer in charge of conscripting the people of the **land**
52: 25 the land and sixty of his men **[RPH]** who were found in the city.
52: 27 There at Riblah, in the **land** *of* Hamath, the king had them
La 2: 1 He has hurled down the splendor of Israel from heaven to **earth**;
2: 2 her kingdom and its princes down to the **ground** in dishonor.
2: 9 Her gates have sunk into the **ground**; their bars he has broken
2: 10 The elders of the Daughter of Zion sit on the **ground** in silence;
2: 10 young women of Jerusalem have bowed their heads to the **ground**.
2: 11 my heart is poured out on the **ground** because my people are
2: 15 was called the perfection of beauty, the joy of the whole **earth**?"
2: 21 "Young and old lie together in the **dust** of the streets; my young
3: 34 To crush underfoot all prisoners in the **land**,
4: 12 The kings of the **earth** did not believe, nor did any of the world's
4: 21 and be glad, O Daughter of Edom, you who live in the **land** *of* Uz.
Eze 1: 3 the son of Buzi, by the Kebar River in the **land** *of* the Babylonians.
1: 15 I saw a wheel on the **ground** beside each creature with its four
1: 19 when the living creatures rose from the **ground**, the wheels also
1: 21 when the creatures rose from the **ground**, the wheels rose along
5: 5 have set in the center of the nations, with **countries** all around her.
5: 6 and decrees more than the nations and **countries** around her.
6: 8 you will escape the sword when you are scattered among the **lands**
6: 14 and make the **land** a desolate waste from the desert to Diblah—
7: 2 The end! The end has come upon the four corners of the **land**.
7: 7 Doom has come upon you—you who dwell in the **land**. The time
7: 21 as plunder to foreigners and as loot to the wicked of the **earth**,
7: 23 because the **land** is full of bloodshed and the city is full of
7: 27 with despair, and the hands of the people of the **land** will tremble.
8: 3 The Spirit lifted me up between **earth** and heaven and in visions of
8: 12 'The LORD does not see us; the LORD has forsaken the **land**.' "
8: 17 Must they also fill the **land** with violence and continually provoke

Eze 9: 9 the **land** is full of bloodshed and the city is full of injustice.
9: 9 They say, 'The LORD has forsaken the **land**; the LORD does
10: 16 and when the cherubim spread their wings to rise from the **ground**,
10: 19 the cherubim spread their wings and rose from the **ground**,
11: 15 from the LORD; this **land** was given to us as our possession.'
11: 16 away among the nations and scattered them among the **countries**,
11: 16 been a sanctuary for them in the **countries** where they have gone.'
11: 17 bring you back from the **countries** where you have been scattered,
12: 6 Cover your face so that you cannot see the **land**, for I have made
12: 12 go through. He will cover his face so that he cannot see the **land**.
12: 13 the **land** *of* the Chaldeans, but he will not see it, and there he will
12: 15 them among the nations and scatter them through the **countries**.
12: 19 Say to the people of the **land**: 'This is what the Sovereign LORD
12: 19 for their **land** will be stripped of everything in it because of the
12: 20 inhabited towns will be laid waste and the **land** will be desolate.
13: 14 will level it to the **ground** so that its foundation will be laid bare.
14: 13 if a **country** sins against me by being unfaithful and I stretch out
14: 15 "Or if I send wild beasts through that **country** and they leave it
14: 16 They alone would be saved, but the **land** would be desolate.
14: 17 "Or if I bring a sword against that **country** and say, 'Let the sword
14: 17 that country and say, 'Let the sword pass throughout the **land**,'
14: 19 "Or if I send a plague into that **land** and pour out my wrath upon it
15: 8 I will make the **land** desolate because they have been unfaithful,
16: 3 Your ancestry and birth were in the **land** *of* the Canaanites;
16: 29 a **land** *of* merchants, but even with this you were not satisfied.
17: 4 off its topmost shoot and carried it away to a **land** *of* merchants,
17: 5 " 'He took some of the seed of your **land** and put it in fertile soil.
17: 13 him under oath. He also carried away the leading men of the **land**,
19: 4 trapped in their pit. They led him with hooks to the **land** *of* Egypt.
19: 7 The **land** and all who were in it were terrified by his roaring.
19: 12 it was uprooted in fury and thrown to the **ground**. The east wind
19: 13 Now it is planted in the desert, in a dry and thirsty **land**.
20: 5 the house of Jacob and revealed myself to them in **Egypt** [+5213].
20: 6 them out of **Egypt** [+5213] into a land I had searched out for them,
20: 6 bring them out of Egypt into a **land** I had searched out for them,
20: 6 land flowing with milk and honey, the most beautiful of all **lands**.
20: 8 wrath on them and spend my anger against them in **Egypt** [+5213].
20: 9 myself to the Israelites by bringing them out of **Egypt** [+5213].
20: 10 Therefore I led them out of **Egypt** [+5213] and brought them into
20: 15 desert that I would not bring them into the **land** I had given them—
20: 15 a land flowing with milk and honey, most beautiful of all **lands**—
20: 23 them among the nations and scatter them through the **countries**,
20: 28 When I brought them into the **land** I had sworn to give them
20: 32 like the peoples of the **world**, who serve wood and stone."
20: 34 gather you from the **countries** where you have been scattered—
20: 36 As I judged your fathers in the desert of the **land** *of* Egypt,
20: 38 Although I will bring them out of the **land** *where* they are living,
20: 40 there in the **land** the entire house of Israel will serve me, and there
20: 41 and gather you from the **countries** where you have been scattered,
20: 42 the **land** I had sworn with uplifted hand to give to your fathers.
21: 19 [21:24] of Babylon to take, both starting from the same **country**.
21: 30 [21:35] in the **land** *of* your ancestry, I will judge you.
21: 32 [21:37] be fuel for the fire, your blood will be shed in your **land**,
22: 4 of scorn to the nations and a laughingstock to all the **countries**.
22: 15 you among the nations and scatter you through the **countries**;
22: 24 'You are a **land** that has had no rain or showers in the day of
22: 29 The people of the **land** practice extortion and commit robbery;
22: 30 stand before me in the gap on behalf of the **land** so I would not
23: 15 looked like Babylonian chariot officers, natives of **[NIE]** Chaldea.
23: 19 the days of her youth, when she was a prostitute in **Egypt** [+5213].
23: 27 stop to the lewdness and prostitution you began in **Egypt** [+5213].
23: 48 "So I will put an end to lewdness in the **land**, that all women may
24: 7 she did not pour it on the **ground**, where the dust would cover it.
25: 7 you off from the nations and exterminate you from the **countries**.
25: 9 Baal Meon and Kiriathaim—the glory of that **land**.
26: 11 with the sword, and your strong pillars will fall to the **ground**.
26: 16 Clothed with terror, they will sit on the **ground**, trembling every
26: 20 I will make you dwell in the **earth** below, as in ancient ruins,
26: 20 and you will not return or take your place in the **land** *of* the living.
27: 17 " 'Judah and **Israel** [+3776] traded with you; they exchanged
27: 29 their ships; the mariners and all the seamen will stand on the **shore**.
27: 33 great wealth and your wares you enriched the kings of the **earth**.
28: 17 So I threw you to the **earth**; I made a spectacle of you before
28: 18 I reduced you to ashes on the **ground** in the sight of all who were
29: 5 I will give you as food to the beasts of the **earth** and the birds of
29: 9 **Egypt** [+5213] will become a desolate wasteland. Then they will
29: 10 I will make the **land** *of* Egypt a ruin and a desolate waste from
29: 12 I will make the **land** *of* Egypt desolate among devastated lands,
29: 12 I will make the land of Egypt desolate among devastated **lands**,
29: 12 among the nations and scatter them through the **countries**.
29: 14 back from captivity and return them to **Upper Egypt** [+7356],
29: 14 and return them to Upper Egypt, the **land** *of* their ancestry.
29: 19 I am going to give **Egypt** [+5213] to Nebuchadnezzar king of
29: 20 I have given him **Egypt** [+5213] as a reward for his efforts
30: 5 the people of the covenant **land** will fall by the sword along with
30: 7 " 'They will be desolate among desolate **lands**, and their cities will
30: 11 most ruthless of nations—will be brought in to destroy the **land**.
30: 11 draw their swords against Egypt and fill the **land** with the slain.
30: 12 I will dry up the streams of the Nile and sell the **land** to evil men;
30: 12 by the hand of foreigners I will lay waste the **land** and everything
30: 13 No longer will there be a prince in **Egypt** [+5213], and I will
30: 13 be a prince in Egypt, and I will spread fear throughout the **land**.
30: 23 among the nations and scatter them through the **countries**.
30: 25 of the king of Babylon and he brandishes it against **Egypt** [+5213].
30: 26 among the nations and scatter them through the **countries**.
31: 12 the valleys; its branches lay broken in all the ravines of the **land**.
31: 12 All the nations of the **earth** came out from under its shade
31: 14 are all destined for death, for the **earth** below, among mortal men,
31: 16 the trees that were well-watered, were consoled in the **earth** below.
31: 18 will be brought down with the trees of Eden to the **earth** below;
32: 4 I will throw you on the **land** and hurl you on the open field.
32: 4 on you and all the beasts of the **earth** gorge themselves on you.
32: 6 I will drench the **land** with your flowing blood all the way to the
32: 8 I will bring darkness over your **land**, declares the Sovereign
32: 9 destruction among the nations, among **lands** you have not known.
32: 15 When I make **Egypt** [+5213] desolate and strip the land of
32: 15 When I make Egypt desolate and strip the **land** of everything in it,
32: 18 for the hordes of Egypt and consign to the **earth** below both her
32: 23 All who had spread terror in the **land** *of* the living are slain,
32: 24 All who had spread terror in the **land** *of* the living went down
32: 24 land of the living went down uncircumcised to the **earth** below.
32: 25 Because their terror had spread in the **land** *of* the living, they bear
32: 26 the sword because they spread their terror in the **land** *of* the living.
32: 27 though the terror of these warriors had stalked through the **land** *of*
32: 32 Although I had him spread terror in the **land** *of* the living,
33: 2 'When I bring the sword against a **land**, and the people of the land
33: 2 the people of the **land** choose one of their men and make him their
33: 3 he sees the sword coming against the **land** and blows the trumpet
33: 24 are saying, 'Abraham was only one man, yet he possessed the **land**.
33: 24 are many; surely the **land** has been given to us as our possession.'
33: 25 to your idols and shed blood, should you then possess the **land**?
33: 26 you defiles his neighbor's wife. Should you then possess the **land**?'
33: 28 I will make the **land** a desolate waste, and her proud strength will
33: 29 when I have made the **land** a desolate waste because of all the
34: 6 They were scattered over the whole **earth**, and no one searched
34: 13 them out from the nations and gather them from the **countries**,
34: 13 of Israel, in the ravines and in all the settlements in the **land**.
34: 25 and rid the **land** of wild beasts so that they may live in the desert
34: 27 of the field will yield their fruit and the **ground** will yield its crops;
34: 28 be plundered by the nations, nor will **wild** animals devour them.
34: 29 they will no longer be victims of famine in the **land** or bear the
35: 10 "These two nations and **countries** will be ours and we will take
35: 14 While the whole **earth** rejoices, I will make you desolate.
36: 5 with malice in their hearts they made my **land** their own
36: 18 out my wrath on them because they had shed blood in the **land** and
36: 19 among the nations, and they were scattered through the **countries**;
36: 20 are the LORD's people, and yet they had to leave his **land**.'
36: 24 I will gather you from all the **countries** and bring you back into
36: 28 You will live in the **land** I gave your forefathers; you will be my
36: 34 The desolate **land** will be cultivated instead of lying desolate in the
36: 35 "This **land** that was laid waste has become like the garden of Eden;
37: 22 I will make them one nation in the **land**, on the mountains of
37: 25 They will live in the **land** I gave to my servant Jacob, the land
38: 2 "Son of man, set your face against Gog, of the **land** *of* Magog,
38: 8 In future years you will invade a **land** that has recovered from war,
38: 9 advancing like a storm; you will be like a cloud covering the **land**.
38: 11 You will say, "I will invade a **land** *of* unwalled villages; I will
38: 12 rich in livestock and goods, living at the center of the **land**."
38: 16 advance against my people Israel like a cloud that covers the **land**.
38: 16 In days to come, O Gog, I will bring you against my **land**,
38: 20 the cliffs will crumble and every wall will fall to the **ground**.
39: 12 house of Israel will be burying them in order to cleanse the **land**.
39: 13 All the people of the **land** will bury them, and the day I am
39: 14 Some will go throughout the **land** and, in addition to them,
39: 14 addition to them, others will bury those that remain on the **ground**.
39: 15 As they go through the **land** and one of them sees a human bone,
39: 16 called Hamonah will be there.) And so they will cleanse the **land**.'
39: 18 and drink the blood of the princes of the **earth** as if they were rams
39: 27 and have gathered them from the **countries** *of* their enemies,
40: 2 In visions of God he took me to the **land** *of* Israel and set me on a
41: 16 The **floor**, the wall up to the windows, and the windows were
41: 20 From the **floor** to the area above the entrance, cherubim and palm
42: 6 so they were smaller in **floor space** than those on the lower
43: 2 the roar of rushing waters, and the **land** was radiant with his glory.
43: 14 From the gutter on the **ground** up to the lower ledge it is two
45: 1 " 'When you allot the **land** as an inheritance, you are to present to
45: 1 you are to present to the LORD a portion of the **land** as a sacred
45: 4 It will be the sacred portion of the **land** for the priests,

Eze 45: 8 This **land** will be his possession in Israel. And my princes will no
45: 8 will allow the house of Israel to possess the **land** according to their
45: 16 All the people of the **land** will participate in this special gift for the
45: 22 bull as a sin offering for himself and for all the people of the **land**.
46: 3 New Moons the people of the **land** are to worship in the presence
46: 9 " 'When the people of the **land** come before the LORD at the
47: 13 "These are the boundaries by which you are to divide the **land** for
47: 14 give it to your forefathers, this **land** will become your inheritance.
47: 15 "This is to be the boundary of the **land**: "On the north side it will
47: 18 along the Jordan between Gilead and the **land** *of* Israel,
47: 21 "You are to distribute this **land** among yourselves according to the
48: 12 It will be a special gift to them from the sacred portion of the **land**,
48: 14 This is the best of the **land** and must not pass into other hands,
48: 29 "This is the **land** you are to allot as an inheritance to the tribes of
Da 1: 2 These he carried off to the temple of his god in **Babylonia** [+9114]
8: 5 the west, crossing the whole **earth** without touching the ground.
8: 5 the west, crossing the whole earth without touching the **ground**.
8: 7 the goat knocked him to the **ground** and trampled on him,
8: 10 it threw some of the starry host down to the **earth** and trampled on
8: 12 prospered in everything it did, and truth was thrown to the **ground**.
8: 18 speaking to me, I was in a deep sleep, with my face to the **ground**.
9: 6 our princes and our fathers, and to all the people of the **land**.
9: 7 in all the **countries** where you have scattered us because of our
9: 15 who brought your people out of **Egypt** [+5213] with a mighty hand
10: 9 as I listened to him, I fell into a deep sleep, my face to the **ground**.
10: 15 I bowed with my face toward the **ground** and was speechless.
11: 16 He will establish himself in the Beautiful **Land** and will have the
11: 19 he will turn back toward the fortresses of his own **country**
11: 28 The king of the North will return to his own **country** with great
11: 28 He will take action against it and then return to his own **country**.
11: 40 He will invade *many* **countries** and sweep through them like a
11: 41 He will also invade the Beautiful **Land**. Many countries will fall,
11: 42 He will extend his power over *many* **countries**; Egypt will not
11: 42 He will extend his power over many countries; **Egypt** [+5213] will
Hos 1: 2 because the **land** is guilty of the vilest adultery in departing from
1: 11 [2:2] will appoint one leader and will come up out of the **land**,
2: 3 [2:5] turn her into a parched **land**, and slay her with thirst.
2: 15 [2:17] her youth, as in the day she came up out of **Egypt** [+5213].
2: 18 [2:20] Bow and sword and battle I will abolish from the **land**,
2: 21 [2:23] respond to the skies, and they will respond to the **earth**;
2: 22 [2:24] the **earth** will respond to the grain, the new wine and oil,
2: 23 [2:25] I will plant her for myself in the **land**; I will show my love
4: 1 the LORD has a charge to bring against you who live in the **land**:
4: 1 is no faithfulness, no love, no acknowledgment of God in the **land**.
4: 3 Because of this the **land** mourns, and all who live in it waste away;
6: 3 us like the winter rains, like the spring rains that water the **earth**."
7: 16 insolent words. For this they will be ridiculed in the **land** *of* Egypt.
9: 3 They will not remain in the LORD's **land**; Ephraim will return to
10: 1 more altars; as his **land** prospered, he adorned his sacred stones.
11: 5 "Will they not return to **Egypt** [+5213] and will not Assyria rule
11: 11 trembling like birds from Egypt, like doves from **Assyria** [+855].
12: 9 [12:10] your God, ⌞who brought you⌟ out of **Egypt** [+5213];
13: 4 the LORD your God, ⌞who brought you⌟ out of **Egypt** [+5213].
13: 5 I cared for you in the desert, in the **land** *of* burning heat.
Joel 1: 2 Hear this, you elders; listen, all who live in the **land**. Has anything
1: 6 A nation has invaded my **land**, powerful and without number;
1: 14 and all who live in the **land** to the house of the LORD your God,
2: 1 Let all who live in the **land** tremble, for the day of the LORD is
2: 3 Before them the **land** is like the garden of Eden, behind them,
2: 10 Before them the **earth** shakes, the sky trembles, the sun and moon
2: 18 the LORD will be jealous for his **land** and take pity on his people.
2: 20 army far from you, pushing it into a parched and barren **land**,
2: 30 [3:3] I will show wonders in the heavens and on the **earth**, blood
3: 2 [4:2] my people among the nations and divided up my **land**.
3: 16 [4:16] from Jerusalem; the **earth** and the sky will tremble.
3: 19 [4:19] people of Judah, in whose **land** they shed innocent blood.
Am 2: 7 trample on the heads of the poor as upon the dust of the **ground**
2: 10 "I brought you up out of **Egypt** [+5213], and I led you forty years
2: 10 I led you forty years in the desert to give you the **land** *of* the
3: 1 against the whole family I brought up out of **Egypt** [+5213]:
3: 5 Does a bird fall into a trap on the **ground** where no snare has been
3: 9 to the fortresses of Ashdod and to the fortresses of **Egypt** [+5213]:
3: 11 "An enemy will overrun the **land**; he will pull down your
3: 14 the horns of the altar will be cut off and fall to the **ground**.
4: 13 turns dawn to darkness, and treads the high places of the **earth**—
5: 7 turn justice into bitterness and cast righteousness to the **ground**
5: 8 the waters of the sea and pours them out over the face of the **land**—
7: 2 When they had stripped the **land** clean, I cried out,
7: 10 you in the very heart of Israel. The **land** cannot bear all his words.
7: 12 said to Amos, "Get out, you seer! Go back to the **land** *of* Judah.
8: 4 you who trample the needy and do away with the poor of the **land**,
8: 8 "Will not the **land** tremble for this, and all who live in it mourn?
8: 9 the sun go down at noon and darken the **earth** in broad daylight.
8: 11 Sovereign LORD, "when I will send a famine through the **land**—
9: 5 the LORD Almighty, he who touches the **earth** and it melts,
9: 6 his lofty palace in the heavens and sets its foundation on the **earth**,
9: 6 the waters of the sea and pours them out over the face of the **land**—
9: 7 "Did I not bring Israel up from **Egypt** [+5213], the Philistines from
9: 9 grain is shaken in a sieve, and not a pebble will reach the **ground**.
Ob 1: 3 you who say to yourself, 'Who can bring me down to the **ground**?'
Jnh 1: 8 do you do? Where do you come from? What is your **country**?
2: 6 [2:7] I sank down; the **earth** beneath barred me in forever.
Mic 1: 2 O peoples, all of you, listen, O **earth** and all who are in it,
1: 3 he comes down and treads the high places of the **earth**.
4: 13 gains to the LORD, their wealth to the Lord of all the **earth**.
5: 4 [5:3] for then his greatness will reach to the ends of the **earth**.
5: 5 [5:4] When the Assyrian invades our **land** and marches through
5: 6 [5:5] They will rule the **land** *of* Assyria with the sword, the land
5: 6 [5:5] with the sword, the **land** *of* Nimrod with drawn sword.
5: 6 [5:5] will deliver us from the Assyrian when he invades our **land**
5: 11 [5:10] I will destroy the cities of your **land** and tear down all your
6: 2 listen, you everlasting foundations of the **earth**.
6: 4 I brought you up out of **Egypt** [+5213] and redeemed you from the
7: 2 The godly have been swept from the **land**; not one upright man
7: 13 The **earth** will become desolate because of its inhabitants,
7: 15 "As in the days when you came out of **Egypt** [+5213], I will show
7: 17 will lick dust like a snake, like creatures that crawl on the **ground**.
Na 1: 5 The **earth** trembles at his presence, the world and all who live in it.
2: 13 [2:14] your young lions. I will leave you no prey on the **earth**.
3: 13 The gates of your **land** are wide open to your enemies; fire has
Hab 1: 6 who sweep across the whole **earth** to seize dwelling places not
2: 8 you have destroyed **lands** and cities and everyone in them.
2: 14 For the **earth** will be filled with the knowledge of the glory of the
2: 17 you have destroyed **lands** and cities and everyone in them.
2: 20 is in his holy temple; let all the **earth** be silent before him."
3: 3 His glory covered the heavens and his praise filled the **earth**.
3: 6 He stood, and shook the **earth**; he looked, and made the nations
3: 7 of Cushan in distress, the dwellings of **Midian** [+4518] in anguish.
3: 9 called for many arrows. *Selah* You split the **earth** with rivers;
3: 12 In wrath you strode through the **earth** and in anger you threshed
Zep 1: 18 In the fire of his jealousy the whole **world** will be consumed,
1: 18 for he will make a sudden end of all who live in the **earth**."
2: 3 Seek the LORD, all you humble of the **land**, you who do what he
2: 5 of the LORD is against you, O Canaan, **land** *of* the Philistines.
2: 11 will be awesome to them when he destroys all the gods of the **land**.
3: 8 The whole **world** will be consumed by the fire of my jealous
3: 19 and honor in every **land** *where* they were put to shame.
3: 20 praise among all the peoples of the **earth** when I restore your
Hag 1: 10 of you the heavens have withheld their dew and the **earth** its crops.
1: 11 I called for a drought on the **fields** and the mountains, on the grain,
2: 4 Be strong, all you people of the **land**,' declares the LORD,
2: 6 'In a little while I will once more shake the heavens and the **earth**,
2: 21 governor of Judah that I will shake the heavens and the **earth**.
Zec 1: 10 are the ones the LORD has sent to go throughout the **earth**."
1: 11 "We have gone throughout the **earth** and found the whole world at
1: 11 the earth and found the whole **world** at rest and in peace."
1: 21 [2:4] their horns against the **land** *of* Judah to scatter its people."
2: 6 [2:10] Flee from the **land** *of* the north," declares the LORD,
3: 9 'and I will remove the sin of this **land** in a single day.
4: 10 are the eyes of the LORD, which range throughout the **earth**.)"
4: 14 are the two who are anointed to serve the Lord of all the **earth**."
5: 3 said to me, "This is the curse that is going out over the whole **land**;
5: 6 he added, "This is the iniquity of the people throughout the **land**."
5: 9 of a stork, and they lifted up the basket between heaven and **earth**.
5: 11 He replied, "To the **country** *of* Babylonia to build a house for it.
6: 5 out from standing in the presence of the Lord of the whole **world**.
6: 6 The one with the black horses is going toward the north **country**,
6: 6 and the one with the dappled horses toward **[RPH]** the south."
6: 7 horses went out, they were straining to go throughout the **earth**.
6: 7 he said, "Go throughout the **earth**!" So they went throughout the
6: 7 "Go throughout the earth!" So they went throughout the **earth**.
6: 8 those going toward the north **country** have given my Spirit rest in
6: 8 north country have given my Spirit rest in the **land** *of* the north."
7: 5 "Ask all the people of the **land** and the priests, 'When you fasted
7: 14 The **land** was left so desolate behind them that no one could come
7: 14 or go. This is how they made the pleasant **land** desolate.' "
8: 7 "I will save my people from the **countries** *of* the east and the west.
8: 7 my people from the countries of the east and **[RPH]** the west.
8: 12 the vine will yield its fruit, the **ground** will produce its crops,
9: 1 An Oracle The word of the LORD is against the **land** *of* Hadrach
9: 10 extend from sea to sea and from the River to the ends of the **earth**.
10: 10 I will bring them back from **Egypt** [+5213] and gather them from
10: 10 I will bring them to **Gilead** [+1680] and Lebanon, and there will
11: 6 For I will no longer have pity on the people of the **land**,"
11: 6 They will oppress the **land**, and I will not rescue them from their
11: 16 For I am going to raise up a shepherd over the **land** who will not
12: 1 stretches out the heavens, who lays the foundation of the **earth**,
12: 3 when all the nations of the **earth** are gathered against her,

Zec 12:12 The **land** will mourn, each clan by itself, with their wives by
13: 2 "On that day, I will banish the names of the idols from the **land**,
13: 2 remove both the prophets and the spirit of impurity from the **land**.
13: 8 In the whole **land**," declares the LORD, "two-thirds will be
14: 9 The LORD will be king over the whole **earth**. On that day there
14:10 The whole **land**, from Geba to Rimmon, south of Jerusalem,
14:17 If any of the peoples of the **earth** do not go up to Jerusalem to
Mal 3:12 for yours will be a delightful **land**," says the LORD Almighty.
4: 6 [3:24] or else I will come and strike the **land** with a curse."

825 אַרְצָא *'arṣā'*, n.pr.m. [1]

Arza [1]

1Ki 16: 9 Elah was in Tirzah at the time, getting drunk in the home of **Arza**,

826 אָרַר *'ārar*, v. [63] [→ 251?, 4423]

cursed [32], curse [11], be cursed [7], brings a curse [5], curse bitterly [+826] [2], put a curse on [2], under a curse [2], curse [+4423] [1], this[s] [1]

Ge 3:14 [B] "**Cursed** *are* you above all the livestock and all the wild
3:17 [B] must not eat of it,' "**Cursed** *is* the ground because of you;
4:11 [B] Now you *are* **under a curse** and driven from the ground,
5:29 [D] of our hands caused by the ground the LORD *has* **cursed**."
9:25 [B] he said, "**Cursed** *be* Canaan! The lowest of slaves will he be
12: 3 [A] those who bless you, and whoever curses you *I will* **curse**;
27:29 [A] May *those who* **curse** you be cursed and those who bless you
27:29 [B] *May* those who curse you **be cursed** and those who bless you
49: 7 [B] **Cursed** *be* their anger, so fierce, and their fury, so cruel!
Ex 22:28 [22:27] [A] blaspheme God or **curse** the ruler of your people.
Nu 5:18 [D] while he himself holds the bitter water that **brings a curse**.
5:19 [D] may this bitter water that **brings a curse** not harm you.
5:22 [D] May this water that **brings a curse** enter your body so that
5:24 [D] have the woman drink the bitter water that **brings a curse**,
5:24 [D] and **this**[s] water will enter her and cause bitter suffering.
5:27 [D] then when she is made to drink the water that **brings a curse**,
22: 6 [A] Now come and **put a curse on** these people, because they are
22: 6 [A] those you bless are blessed, and those *you* **curse** are cursed."
22: 6 [H] those you bless are blessed, and those you curse *are* **cursed**."
22:12 [A] *You must* not **put a curse on** those people, because they are
23: 7 [A] 'Come,' he said, '**curse** Jacob for me; come, denounce Israel.'
24: 9 [A] bless you be blessed and *those who* **curse** you be cursed!"
24: 9 [B] bless you be blessed and those who curse you **be cursed**!"
Dt 27:15 [B] "**Cursed** *is* the man who carves an image or casts an idol—
27:16 [B] "**Cursed** *is* the man who dishonors his father or his mother."
27:17 [B] "**Cursed** *is* the man who moves his neighbor's boundary
27:18 [B] "**Cursed** *is* the man who leads the blind astray on the road."
27:19 [B] "**Cursed** *is* the man who withholds justice from the alien,
27:20 [B] "**Cursed** *is* the man who sleeps with his father's wife, for he
27:21 [B] "**Cursed** *is* the man who has sexual relations with any
27:22 [B] "**Cursed** *is* the man who sleeps with his sister, the daughter
27:23 [B] "**Cursed** *is* the man who sleeps with his mother-in-law."
27:24 [B] "**Cursed** *is* the man who kills his neighbor secretly." Then all
27:25 [B] "**Cursed** *is* the man who accepts a bribe to kill an innocent
27:26 [B] "**Cursed** *is* the man who does not uphold the words of this
28:16 [B] You *will* **be cursed** in the city and cursed in the country.
28:16 [B] You will be cursed in the city and **cursed** in the country.
28:17 [B] Your basket and your kneading trough *will* **be cursed**.
28:18 [B] The fruit of your womb *will* **be cursed**, and the crops of your
28:19 [B] You *will* **be cursed** when you come in and cursed when you
28:19 [B] be cursed when you come in and **cursed** when you go out.
Jos 6:26 [B] "**Cursed** before the LORD is the man who undertakes to
9:23 [B] You *are* now **under a curse**: You will never cease to serve
Jdg 5:23 [A] '**Curse** Meroz,' said the angel of the LORD. 'Curse its
5:23 [A] '**Curse** [+826] its people **bitterly**, because they did not come
5:23 [A] '**Curse** its people **bitterly** [+826], because they did not come
21:18 [B] '**Cursed** *be* anyone who gives a wife to a Benjamite.'
1Sa 14:24 [B] "**Cursed** *be* any man who eats food before evening comes,
14:28 [B] strict oath, saying, '**Cursed** *be* any man who eats food today!'
26:19 [B] men have done it, *may* they **be cursed** before the LORD!
2Ki 9:34 [B] "Take care of that **cursed** *woman*," he said, "and bury her,
Job 3: 8 [A] May *those who* **curse** days curse that day, those who are
Ps 119:21 [B] *who are* **cursed** and who stray from your commands.
Jer 11: 3 [B] '**Cursed** *is* the man who does not obey the terms of this
17: 5 [B] "**Cursed** *is* the one who trusts in man, who depends on flesh
20:14 [B] **Cursed** *be* the day I was born! May the day my mother bore
20:15 [B] **Cursed** *be* the man who brought my father the news, who
48:10 [B] "A **curse** *on* him who is lax in doing the LORD's work!
48:10 [B] A **curse** *on* him who keeps his sword from bloodshed!
Mal 1:14 [B] "**Cursed** *is* the cheat who has an acceptable male in his flock
2: 2 [A] will send a curse upon you, and *I will* **curse** your blessings.
2: 2 [A] Yes, *I have already* **cursed** them, because you have not set
3: 9 [C] You *are* under a **curse** [+4423]—the whole nation of you—

827 אֲרָרַט *'ărāraṭ*, n.pr.loc. [4]

Ararat [4]

Ge 8: 4 seventh month the ark came to rest on the mountains of **Ararat**.
2Ki 19:37 him down with the sword, and they escaped to the land of **Ararat**.
Isa 37:38 him down with the sword, and they escaped to the land of **Ararat**.
Jer 51:27 **Ararat**, Minni and Ashkenaz. Appoint a commander against her;

828 אֲרָרִי *'ărārî*, a.g. Not used in NIV/BHS [cf. 2240]

829 אָרַשׂ *'āraś*, v. [11]

pledged to be married [5], betroth [3], betrothed [2], pledged [1]

Ex 22:16 [22:15] [E] seduces a virgin who *is* not **pledged to be married**
Dt 20: 7 [D] *Has* anyone *become* **pledged** *to* a woman and not married
22:23 [E] happens to meet in a town a virgin **pledged to be married**
22:25 [E] country a man happens to meet a girl **pledged to be married**
22:27 [E] though the **betrothed** girl screamed, there was no one to
22:28 [E] happens to meet a virgin who *is* not **pledged to be married**
28:30 [D] *You will be* **pledged to be married** *to* a woman, but another
2Sa 3:14 [D] whom *I* **betrothed** to myself for the price of a hundred
Hos 2:19 [2:21] [D] *I will* **betroth** you to me forever; I will betroth you in
2:19 [2:21] [D] *I will* **betroth** you in righteousness and justice, in
2:20 [2:22] [D] *I will* **betroth** you in faithfulness, and you will

830 אֲרֶשֶׁת *'ărešet*, n.f. [1] [→ 4626]

request [1]

Ps 21: 2 [21:3] of his heart and have not withheld the **request** *of* his lips.

831 אַרְתַּחְשַׁסְתְּא *'artaḥšast'*, אַרְתַּחְשַׁשְׂתְּ *'artaḥšaśt*, אַרְתַּחְשַׁשְׂתָּא *'artaḥšaśtā'*, n.pr.m. [9] [→ Ar 10078]

Artaxerxes [9]

Ezr 4: 7 in the days of **Artaxerxes** king of Persia, Bishlam, Mithredath,
4: 7 and the rest of his associates wrote a letter to **Artaxerxes**.
7: 1 After these things, during the reign of **Artaxerxes** king of Persia,
7: 7 also came up to Jerusalem in the seventh year of King **Artaxerxes**.
7:11 This is a copy of the letter King **Artaxerxes** had given to Ezra the
8: 1 up with me from Babylon during the reign of King **Artaxerxes**:
Ne 2: 1 In the month of Nisan in the twentieth year of King **Artaxerxes**,
5:14 Moreover, from the twentieth year of King **Artaxerxes**, when I
13: 6 for in the thirty-second year of **Artaxerxes** king of Babylon I had

832 אֲשַׂרְאֵל *'ăśar'ēl*, n.pr.m. [1] [→ 833, 834, 835]

Asarel [1]

1Ch 4:16 The sons of Jehallelel: Ziph, Ziphah, Tiria and **Asarel**.

833 אֲשַׂרְאֵלָה *'ăśar'ēlâ*, n.pr.m. [1] [√ 832; cf. 3777]

Asarelah [1]

1Ch 25: 2 From the sons of Asaph: Zaccur, Joseph, Nethaniah and **Asarelah**.

834 אַשְׂרִאֵלִי *'aśri'ēlî*, a.g. [1] [√ 832]

Asrielite [1]

Nu 26:31 through Asriel, the **Asrielite** clan; through Shechem,

835 אַשְׂרִיאֵל *'aśrî'ēl*, n.pr.m. [3] [√ 832]

Asriel [3]

Nu 26:31 through **Asriel**, the Asrielite clan; through Shechem,
Jos 17: 2 clans of Abiezer, Helek, **Asriel**, Shechem, Hepher and Shemida.
1Ch 7:14 **Asriel** was his descendant through his Aramean concubine.

836 אֵשׁ *'ēš*[1], n.f. & m. [377 / 376] [→ 852; Ar 10080]

fire [259], fiery [9], burn down [+928+2021+8596] [7], lightning [7], burning [6], set on fire [+906+928+2021+3675] [6], burned [+906+928+2021+8596] [5], be burned up [+928+2021+8596] [4], burned down [+906+928+2021+8596] [4], set fire [+3675] [4], burning [+2021+6584] [3], flame [3], set on fire [+928+2021+3675] [3], *untranslated* [2], burn down [+906+928+2021+8596] [2], burn up [+906+928+2021+8596] [2], burned [+928+2021+8596] [2], coals [2], fire [+4258] [2], fires [2], flaming [2], it[s] [+2021] [2], set on fire [+906+928+2021+8596] [2], set on fire [+928+2021+8596] [2], use for fuel [+928+1277] [2], are burned up [+928+2021+8596+8596] [1], be burned [+928+2021+8596] [1], be burned down [+928+2021 +8596] [1], blazing [1], burn [+4805] [1], burn [+906+906+906+928 +2021+8596] [1], burn [+906+906+928+2021+8596] [1], burn [+906+928+2021+8596] [1], burn [+928+2021+8596] [1], burn to death [+906+906+928+2021+8596] [1], burn up [+928+2021+8596] [1], burned [+906+906+928+2021+8596] [1], burned [+928+2021 +8938] [1], burned to death [+906+906+928+2021+8596] [1], burned up [+906+906+906+906+928+2021+8596] [1], burned up

[+906+906+906+928+2021+8596] [1], burned up [+906+906+928+2021+8596] [1], burned up [+906+928+2021+8596] [1], charred [+928+1277+2021] [1], firepot [+3963] [1], flashes [+928] [1], fuel for fire [+928+1896] [1], fuel for flames [+928+1896] [1], kindled [+928+7706] [1], lightning [+4259] [1], lit [+928+1277] [1], on fire [+928+1277+2021] [1], set ablaze [+928+2021+3675] [1], set fire to [+906+906+928+2021+8596] [1], set fire to [+928+2021+8938] [1], set on fire [+3675+6584] [1], used for fuel [+1198+8596] [1]

Ge 15:17 a smoking firepot with a **blazing** torch appeared and passed
19:24 the LORD rained down **burning** sulfur on Sodom
22: 6 it on his son Isaac, and he himself carried the **fire** and the knife.
22: 7 "The **fire** and wood are here," Isaac said, "but where is the lamb
Ex 3: 2 There the angel of the LORD appeared to him in flames of **fire**
3: 2 Moses saw that though the bush *was* **on fire** [+928+1277+2021] it
9:23 sent thunder and hail, and **lightning** flashed down to the ground.
9:24 hail fell and **lightning** flashed back and forth. It was the worst
12: 8 That same night they are to eat the meat roasted over the **fire**,
12: 9 not eat the meat raw or cooked in water, but roast it over the **fire**—
12:10 if some is left till morning, *you must* **burn** [+928+2021+8596] it.
13:21 them on their way and by night in a pillar of **fire** to give them light,
13:22 Neither the pillar of cloud by day nor the pillar of **fire** by night left
14:24 watch of the night the LORD looked down from the pillar of **fire**
19:18 covered with smoke, because the LORD descended on it in **fire**.
22: 6 [22:5] "If a **fire** breaks out and spreads into thornbushes so that it
24:17 the LORD looked like a consuming **fire** on top of the mountain.
29:14 But **burn** [+906+906+906+928+2021+8596] the bull's flesh and
29:34 bread is left over till morning, **burn** it **up** [+906+928+2021+8596].
32:20 And he took the calf they had made and burned it in the **fire**;
32:24 me the gold, and I threw it into the **fire**, and out came this calf!"
35: 3 Do not light a **fire** in any of your dwellings on the Sabbath day."
40:38 **fire** was in the cloud by night, in the sight of all the house of Israel
Lev 1: 7 The sons of Aaron the priest are to put **fire** on the altar and arrange
1: 7 the priest are to put fire on the altar and arrange wood on the **fire**.
1: 8 the fat, on the **burning** [+2021+6584] wood that is on the altar.
1:12 the fat, on the **burning** [+2021+6584] wood that is on the altar.
1:17 the priest shall burn it on the wood that is on the **fire** on the altar.
2:14 to the LORD, offer crushed heads of new grain roasted in the **fire**.
3: 5 of the burnt offering that is on the **burning** [+2021+6584] wood,
4:12 the ashes are thrown, and burn it in a wood **fire** on the ash heap.
6: 9 [6:2] till morning, and the **fire** must be kept burning on the altar.
6:10 [6:3] shall remove the ashes of the burnt offering that the **fire** has
6:12 [6:5] The **fire** on the altar must be kept burning; it must not go
6:13 [6:6] The **fire** must be kept burning on the altar continuously;
6:30 [6:23] must not be eaten; *it must* **be burned** [+928+2021+8596].
7:17 left over till the third day *must* **be burned up** [+928+2021+8596].
7:19 must not be eaten; *it must* **be burned up** [+928+2021+8596].
8:17 and its offal *he* **burned up** [+906+906+906+906+928+2021+8596]
8:32 **burn up** [+928+2021+8596] the rest of the meat and the bread.
9:11 the flesh and the hide *he* **burned up** [+906+906+928+2021+8596]
9:24 **Fire** came out from the presence of the LORD and consumed the
10: 1 and Abihu took their censers, put **fire** in them and added incense;
10: 1 they offered unauthorized **fire** before the LORD, contrary to his
10: 2 So **fire** came out from the presence of the LORD and consumed
13:24 "When someone has a **burn** [+4805] on his skin and a
13:52 is destructive; the article *must* **be burned up** [+928+2021+8596].
13:55 Burn it with **fire**, whether the mildew has affected one side
13:57 and whatever has the mildew must be burned with **fire**.
16:12 He is to take a censer full of **burning** coals from the altar before
16:13 He is to put the incense on the **fire** before the LORD,
16:27 and offal *are to be* **burned up** [+906+906+906+928+2021+8596].
19: 6 over until the third day *must* **be burned up** [+928+2021+8596].
20:14 Both he and they must be burned in the **fire**, so that no wickedness
21: 9 she disgraces her father; she must be burned in the **fire**.
Nu 3: 4 offering with unauthorized **fire** before him in the Desert of Sinai.
6:18 put it in the **fire** that is under the sacrifice of the fellowship
9:15 till morning the cloud above the tabernacle looked like **fire**.
9:16 to be; the cloud covered it, and at night it looked like **fire**.
11: 1 **fire** *from* the LORD burned among them and consumed some of
11: 2 out to Moses, he prayed to the LORD and the **fire** died down.
11: 3 because **fire** *from* the LORD had burned among them.
14:14 before them in a pillar of cloud by day and a pillar of **fire** by night.
16: 7 and tomorrow put **fire** and incense in them before the LORD.
16:18 put **fire** and incense in it, and stood with Moses and Aaron at the
16:35 **fire** came out from the LORD and consumed the 250 men who
16:37 [17:2] and scatter the **coals** some distance away,
16:46 [17:11] and put incense in it, along with **fire** from the altar,
18: 9 have the part of the most holy offerings that is kept from the **fire**.
21:28 "**Fire** went out from Heshbon, a blaze from the city of Sihon.
26:10 whose followers died when the **fire** devoured the 250 men.
26:61 they made an offering before the LORD with unauthorized **fire**.)
31:10 *They* **burned** [+906+906+928+2021+8596] all the towns where
31:23 anything else that can withstand **fire** must be put through the fire,
31:23 anything else that can withstand fire must be put through the **fire**,
31:23 whatever cannot withstand **fire** must be put through that water.
Dt 1:33 in **fire** by night and in a cloud by day, to search out places for you
4:11 stood at the foot of the mountain while it blazed with **fire** to the
4:12 the LORD spoke to you out of the **fire**. You heard the sound of
4:15 any kind the day the LORD spoke to you at Horeb out of the **fire**.
4:24 For the LORD your God is a consuming **fire**, a jealous God.
4:33 Has any other people heard the voice of God speaking out of **fire**,
4:36 On earth he showed you his great **fire**, and you heard his words
4:36 you his great fire, and you heard his words from out of the **fire**.
5: 4 The LORD spoke to you face to face out of the **fire** on the
5: 5 because you were afraid of the **fire** and did not go up the
5:22 to your whole assembly there on the mountain from out of the **fire**,
5:23 while the mountain was ablaze with **fire**, all the leading men of
5:24 and his majesty, and we have heard his voice from the **fire**.
5:25 This great **fire** will consume us, and we will die if we hear the
5:26 has ever heard the voice of the living God speaking out of **fire**,
7: 5 cut down their Asherah poles and burn their idols in the **fire**.
7:25 The images of their gods you are to burn in the **fire**. Do not covet
9: 3 God is the one who goes across ahead of you like a devouring **fire**.
9:10 the LORD proclaimed to you on the mountain out of the **fire**,
9:15 and went down from the mountain while it was ablaze with **fire**.
9:21 thing of yours, the calf you had made, and burned it in the **fire**.
10: 4 to you on the mountain, out of the **fire**, on the day of the assembly.
12: 3 smash their sacred stones and burn their Asherah poles in the **fire**;
12:31 burn their sons and daughters in the **fire** as sacrifices to their gods.
13:16 [13:17] completely **burn** [+906+906+928+2021+8596] the town
18:10 be found among you who sacrifices his son or daughter in the **fire**,
18:16 the voice of the LORD our God nor see this great **fire** anymore,
33: 2 [from the south, from his **mountain slopes**. [Q; see K 851]]
32:22 For a **fire** has been kindled by my wrath, one that burns to the
Jos 6:24 Then *they* **burned** [+928+2021+8596] the whole city and
7:15 who is caught with the devoted things shall be destroyed by **fire**,
7:25 had stoned the rest, *they* **burned** [+906+928+2021+8596] them.
8: 8 you have taken the city, **set** it **on fire** [+906+928+2021+3675].
8:19 captured it and quickly **set** it **on fire** [+906+928+2021+3675].
11: 6 their horses and **burn** [+906+928+2021+8596] their chariots."
11: 9 their horses and **burned** [+906+928+2021+8596] their chariots.
11:11 and *he* **burned up** [+906+928+2021+8596] Hazor itself.
Jdg 1: 8 and took it. They put the city to the sword and set it on **fire**.
6:21 **Fire** flared from the rock, consuming the meat and the bread.
9:15 let **fire** come out of the thornbush and consume the cedars of
9:20 you have not, let **fire** come out from Abimelech and consume you,
9:20 of Shechem and Beth Millo, and let **fire** come out from you,
9:49 and **set** it **on fire** [+906+928+2021+3675] over the people inside.
9:52 the entrance to the tower to **set** it **on fire** [+928+2021+8596],
12: 1 *We're going to* **burn down** [+928+2021+8596] your house over
14:15 or *we will* **burn** you … **to death** [+906+906+928+2021+8596].
15: 5 **lit** [+928+1277] the torches and let the foxes loose in the standing
15: 6 **burned** her and her father **to death** [+906+906+928+2021+8596].
15:14 ropes on his arms became like **charred** [+928+1277+2021] flax,
16: 9 as easily as a piece of string snaps when it comes close to a **flame**.
18:27 the sword and **burned down** [+906+928+2021+8596] their city.
20:48 else they found. All the towns they came across they set on **fire**.
1Sa 30: 1 They had attacked Ziklag and **burned** [+906+928+2021+8596] it,
30: 3 they found it destroyed by **fire** and their wives and sons and
30:14 And *we* **burned** [+906+928+2021+8596] Ziklag."
2Sa 14:30 and he has barley there. Go and **set** it **on fire** [+928+2021+3675]."
14:30 Absalom's servants **set** the field **on fire** [+906+928+2021+3675].
14:31 *have* your servants **set** my field **on fire** [+906+928+2021+3675]?"
22: 9 consuming **fire** came from his mouth, burning coals blazed out of
22:13 Out of the brightness of his presence bolts of **lightning** blazed
23: 7 *they* **are burned up** [+928+2021+8596+8596] where they lie."
1Ki 9:16 and captured Gezer. *He had* **set** it **on fire** [+928+2021+8596].
16:18 and **set** the palace **on fire** [+906+928+2021+8596] around him.
18:23 them cut it into pieces and put it on the wood but not set **fire** to it.
18:23 prepare the other bull and put it on the wood but not set **fire** to it.
18:24 The god who answers by **fire**—he is God." Then all the people
18:25 of you. Call on the name of your god, but do not light the **fire**."
18:38 Then the **fire** *of* the LORD fell and burned up the sacrifice,
19:12 After the earthquake came a **fire**, but the LORD was not in the
19:12 the earthquake came a fire, but the LORD was not in the **fire**.
19:12 was not in the fire. And after the **fire** came a gentle whisper.
2Ki 1:10 may **fire** come down from heaven and consume you and your fifty
1:10 Then **fire** fell from heaven and consumed the captain and his men.
1:12 "may **fire** come down from heaven and consume you and your
1:12 Then the **fire** *of* God fell from heaven and consumed him
1:14 **fire** has fallen from heaven and consumed the first two captains
2:11 suddenly a chariot of **fire** and horses of fire appeared and separated
2:11 suddenly a chariot of fire and horses of **fire** appeared and separated
6:17 saw the hills full of horses and chariots of **fire** all around Elisha.
8:12 he answered. "*You will* **set fire** [+928+2021+8938] **to** their
16: 3 ways of the kings of Israel and even sacrificed his son in the **fire**,
17:17 They sacrificed their sons and daughters in the **fire**. They practiced
17:31 the Sepharvites burned their children in the **fire** as sacrifices to

2Ki 19:18 They have thrown their gods into the **fire** and destroyed them,
21: 6 He sacrificed his own son in the **fire**, practiced sorcery and
23:10 could use it to sacrifice his son or daughter in the **fire** to Molech.
23:11 Josiah then **burned** [+906+928+2021+8596] the chariots dedicated
25: 9 important building *he* **burned down** [+906+928+2021+8596].
1Ch 14:12 their gods there, and David gave orders to burn them in the **fire**.
21:26 the LORD answered him with **fire** from heaven on the altar of
2Ch 7: 1 **fire** came down from heaven and consumed the burnt offering
7: 3 When all the Israelites saw the **fire** coming down and the glory of
28: 3 in the Valley of Ben Hinnom and sacrificed his sons in the **fire**,
33: 6 He sacrificed his sons in the **fire** in the Valley of Ben Hinnom,
35:13 They roasted the Passover animals over the **fire** as prescribed,
36:19 *they* **burned** [+928+2021+8596] all the palaces and destroyed
Ne 1: 3 is broken down, and its gates have been burned with **fire**."
2: 3 are buried lies in ruins, and its gates have been destroyed by **fire**?"
2:13 been broken down, and its gates, which had been destroyed by **fire**.
2:17 Jerusalem lies in ruins, and its gates have been burned with **fire**.
9:12 by night with a pillar of **fire** to give them light on the way they
9:19 nor the pillar of **fire** by night to shine on the way they were to take.
Job 1:16 "The **fire** *of* God fell from the sky and burned up the sheep
15:34 be barren, and **fire** will consume the tents of those who love bribes.
18: 5 of the wicked is snuffed out; the flame of his **fire** stops burning.
20:26 A **fire** unfanned will consume him and devour what is left in his
22:20 'Surely our foes are destroyed, and **fire** devours their wealth.'
28: 5 from which food comes, is transformed below as by **fire**;
31:12 It is a **fire** that burns to Destruction; it would have uprooted my
41:19 [41:11] stream from his mouth; sparks of **fire** shoot out.
Ps 11: 6 On the wicked he will rain **fiery** coals and burning sulfur;
18: 8 [18:9] consuming **fire** came from his mouth, burning coals blazed
18:12 [18:13] clouds advanced, with hailstones and bolts of **lightning**.
18:13 [18:14] the voice of the Most High resounded. [BHS+ *amid hailstones and bolts of* ***lightning***]
21: 9 [21:10] your appearing you will make them like a **fiery** furnace.
21: 9 [21:10] will swallow them up, and his **fire** will consume them.
29: 7 The voice of the LORD strikes with flashes of **lightning**.
39: 3 [39:4] grew hot within me, and as I meditated, the **fire** burned;
46: 9 [46:10] and shatters the spear, he burns the shields with **fire**.
50: 3 a **fire** devours before him, and around him a tempest rages.
66:12 we went through **fire** and water, but you brought us to a place of
68: 2 [68:3] as wax melts before the **fire**, may the wicked perish before
74: 7 *They* **burned** [+928+2021+8938] your sanctuary to the ground;
78:14 them with the cloud by day and with light from the **fire** all night.
78:21 his **fire** broke out against Jacob, and his wrath rose against Israel,
78:63 **Fire** consumed their young men, and their maidens had no
79: 5 you be angry forever? How long will your jealousy burn like **fire**?
80:16 [80:17] Your vine is cut down, it is burned with **fire**; at your
83:14 [83:15] As **fire** consumes the forest or a flame sets the mountains
89:46 [89:47] How long will your wrath burn like **fire**?
97: 3 **Fire** goes before him and consumes his foes on every side.
104: 4 He makes winds his messengers, flames of **fire** his servants.
105:32 their rain into hail, with **lightning** [+4259] throughout their land;
105:39 spread out a cloud as a covering, and a **fire** to give light at night.
106:18 **Fire** blazed among their followers; a flame consumed the wicked.
118:12 me like bees, but they died out as quickly as **burning** thorns;
140:10 [140:11] may they be thrown into the **fire**, into miry pits, never to
148: 8 **lightning** and hail, snow and clouds, stormy winds that do his
Pr 6:27 Can a man scoop **fire** into his lap without his clothes being
16:27 A scoundrel plots evil, and his speech is like a scorching **fire**.
26:20 Without wood a **fire** goes out; without gossip a quarrel dies down.
26:21 As charcoal to embers and as wood to **fire**, so is a quarrelsome
30:16 is never satisfied with water, and **fire**, which never says, 'Enough!'
SS 8: 6 as the grave. It burns like blazing **fire**, like a mighty flame.
Isa 1: 7 Your country is desolate, your cities burned with **fire**; your fields
4: 5 there a cloud of smoke by day and a glow of flaming **fire** by night;
5:24 as tongues of **fire** lick up straw and as dry grass sinks down in the
9: 5 [9:4] blood will be destined for burning, will be fuel for the **fire**.
9:18 [9:17] Surely wickedness burns like a **fire**; it consumes briers
9:19 [9:18] will be scorched and the people will be fuel for the **fire**;
10:16 under his pomp a fire will be kindled like a blazing **flame**.
10:17 The Light of Israel will become a **fire**, their Holy One a flame;
26:11 to shame; let the **fire** *reserved for* your enemies consume them.
29: 6 with windstorm and tempest and flames of a devouring **fire**.
30:14 pieces not a fragment will be found for taking **coals** from a hearth
30:27 his lips are full of wrath, and his tongue is a consuming **fire**.
30:30 arm coming down with raging anger and consuming **fire** [+4258],
30:33 been made deep and wide, with an abundance of **fire** and wood;
33:11 you give birth to straw; your breath is a **fire** that consumes you.
33:12 like cut thornbushes *they will be* **set ablaze** [+928+2021+3675]."
33:14 grips the godless: "Who of us can dwell with the consuming **fire**?
37:19 They have thrown their gods into the **fire** and destroyed them,
43: 2 When you walk through the **fire**, you will not be burned;
44:16 Half of the wood he burns in the **fire**; over it he prepares his meal,
44:19 or understanding to say, "Half of it *I* **used for fuel** [+1198+8596];
47:14 Surely they are like stubble; the **fire** will burn them up.
50:11 all you who light **fires** and provide yourselves with flaming
50:11 walk in the light of your **fires** and of the torches you have set
54:16 it is I who created the blacksmith who fans the coals into **flame**
64: 2 [64:1] As when **fire** sets twigs ablaze and causes water to boil,
64: 2 [64:1] **[RPH]** come down to make your name known to your
64:11 [64:10] where our fathers praised you, has been burned with **fire**,
65: 5 people are smoke in my nostrils, a **fire** that keeps burning all day.
66:15 See, the LORD is coming with **fire**, and his chariots are like a
66:15 bring down his anger with fury, and his rebuke with flames of **fire**.
66:16 For with **fire** and with his sword the LORD will execute
66:24 their worm will not die, nor will their **fire** be quenched, and they
Jer 4: 4 or my wrath will break out and burn like **fire** because of the evil
5:14 I will make my words in your mouth a **fire** and these people the
6:29 The bellows blow fiercely to burn away the lead with **fire**,
7:18 The children gather wood, the fathers light the **fire**, and the women
7:31 of Ben Hinnom to burn their sons and daughters in the **fire**—
11:16 the roar of a mighty storm *he will* **set** it **on fire** [+3675+6584],
15:14 for my anger will kindle a **fire** that will burn against you."
17: 4 for *you have* **kindled** [+928+7706] my anger, and it will burn
17:27 I will kindle an unquenchable **fire** in the gates of Jerusalem that
19: 5 have built the high places of Baal to burn their sons in the **fire**
20: 9 his word is in my heart like a **fire**, a fire shut up in my bones.
21:10 the hands of the king of Babylon, and he will destroy it with **fire**.'
21:12 or my wrath will break out and burn like **fire** because of the evil
21:14 I will kindle a **fire** in your forests that will consume everything
22: 7 will cut up your fine cedar beams and throw them into the **fire**.
23:29 "Is not my word like **fire**," declares the LORD, "and like a
29:22 and Ahab, whom the king of Babylon burned in the **fire**.'
32:29 this city will come in and **set** it **on fire** [+906+928+2021+3675];
34: 2 the king of Babylon, and *he will* **burn** it **down** [+928+2021+8596].
34:22 fight against it, take it and **burn** it **down** [+928+2021+8596].
36:22 with a **fire** [BHS 906] burning *in* the firepot in front of him.
36:23 off with a scribe's knife and threw them **[RPH]** into the firepot,
36:23 them into the firepot, until the entire scroll was burned in the **fire**.
36:32 of the scroll that Jehoiakim king of Judah had burned in the **fire**.
37: 8 they will capture it and **burn** it **down** [+928+2021+8596].'
37:10 would come out and **burn** this city **down** [+906+928+2021+8596]."
38:17 spared and this city *will* not **be burned down** [+928+2021+8596];
38:18 the Babylonians and *they will* **burn** it **down** [+928+2021+8596];
38:23 and this city *will be* **burned down** [+906+928+2021+8596]."
39: 8 The Babylonians **set fire to** [+906+906+928+2021+8596] the royal
43:12 *He will* **set fire** [+3675] to the temples of the gods of Egypt;
43:13 and *will* **burn down** [+906+928+2021+8596] the temples of the
48:45 for a **fire** has gone out from Heshbon, a blaze from the midst of
49: 2 and its surrounding villages *will be* **set on fire** [+928+2021+3675].
49:27 "*I will* **set fire** [+3675] to the walls of Damascus; it will consume
50:32 I will kindle a **fire** in her towns that will consume all who are
51:32 the marshes **set on fire** [+906+928+2021+8596], and the soldiers
51:58 will be leveled and her high gates **set on fire** [+928+2021+3675];
51:58 the nations' labor is only **fuel for** the **flames** [+928+1896]."
52:13 important building *he* **burned down** [+906+928+2021+8596].
La 1:13 "From on high he sent **fire**, sent it down into my bones. He spread
2: 3 He has burned in Jacob like a flaming **fire** that consumes
2: 4 he has poured out his wrath like **fire** on the tent of the Daughter of
4:11 He kindled a **fire** in Zion that consumed her foundations.
Eze 1: 4 an immense cloud with flashing **lightning** and surrounded by
1: 4 by brilliant light. The center of the **fire** looked like glowing metal,
1:13 appearance of the living creatures was like burning coals of **fire**
1:13 moved back and forth among the creatures; **it**[s] [+2021] was bright,
1:13 it was bright, and lightning flashed out of **it**[s] [+2021].
1:27 as if full of **fire**, and that from there down he looked like fire;
1:27 as if full of fire, and that from there down he looked like **fire**;
5: 4 take a few of these and throw them into the **fire** and burn them up.
5: 4 into the fire and **burn** them **up** [+906+928+2021+8596].
5: 4 A **fire** will spread from there to the whole house of Israel.
8: 2 I saw a figure like that of a <u>man</u>. [BHS *a* ***fiery*** *figure*; NIV 408]
8: 2 From what appeared to be his waist down he was like **fire**,
10: 2 Fill your hands with **burning** coals from among the cherubim
10: 6 "Take **fire** from among the wheels, from among the cherubim,"
10: 7 one of the cherubim reached out his hand to the **fire** that was
15: 4 after it is thrown on the **fire** as fuel and the fire burns both ends
15: 4 the fire as fuel and the **fire** burns both ends and chars the middle,
15: 5 how much less can it be made into something useful when the **fire**
15: 6 wood of the vine among the trees of the forest as fuel for the **fire**,
15: 7 Although they have come out of the **fire**, the fire will yet consume
15: 7 they have come out of the fire, the **fire** will yet consume them.
16:41 *They will* **burn down** [+928+2021+8596] your houses and inflict
19:12 of its fruit; its strong branches withered and **fire** consumed them.
19:14 **Fire** spread from one of its main branches and consumed its fruit.
20:31 When you offer your gifts—the sacrifice of your sons in the **fire**—
20:47 [21:3] I *am about to* **set fire** [+3675] to you, and it will consume
21:31 [21:36] upon you and breathe out my **fiery** anger against you;
21:32 [21:37] You will be fuel for the **fire**, your blood will be shed in
22:20 iron, lead and tin into a furnace to melt it with a **fiery** blast,

Eze 22:21 I will gather you and I will blow on you with my **fiery** wrath,
22:31 out my wrath on them and consume them with my **fiery** anger,
23:25 and those of you who are left will be consumed by **fire**.
23:47 and daughters and **burn down** [+928+2021+8596] their houses.
24:10 So heap on the wood and kindle the **fire**. Cook the meat well,
24:12 its heavy deposit has not been removed, not even by **fire**.
28:14 on the holy mount of God; you walked among the **fiery** stones.
28:16 I expelled you, O guardian cherub, from among the **fiery** stones.
28:18 So I made a **fire** come out from you, and it consumed you,
30: 8 when I set **fire** to Egypt and all her helpers are crushed.
30:14 Upper Egypt, set **fire** to Zoan and inflict punishment on Thebes.
30:16 I will set **fire** to Egypt; Pelusium will writhe in agony. Thebes will
36: 5 In my **burning** zeal I have spoken against the rest of the nations,
38:19 **fiery** wrath I declare that at that time there shall be a great
38:22 hailstones and **burning** sulfur on him and on his troops and on the
39: 6 I will send **fire** on Magog and on those who live in safety in the
39: 9 For seven years *they will* **use** them **for fuel** [+928+1277].
39:10 because *they will* **use** the weapons **for fuel** [+928+1277].
Da 10: 6 his eyes like **flaming** torches, his arms and legs like the gleam of
Hos 7: 6 smolders all night; in the morning it blazes like a flaming **fire**.
8:14 I will send **fire** upon their cities that will consume their fortresses."
Joel 1:19 for **fire** has devoured the open pastures and flames have burned up
1:20 of water have dried up and **fire** has devoured the open pastures.
2: 3 Before them **fire** devours, behind them a flame blazes. Before
2: 5 like a crackling **fire** [+4258] consuming stubble, like a mighty
2:30 [3:3] and on the earth, blood and **fire** and billows of smoke.
Am 1: 4 I will send **fire** upon the house of Hazael that will consume the
1: 7 I will send **fire** upon the walls of Gaza that will consume her
1:10 I will send **fire** upon the walls of Tyre that will consume her
1:12 I will send **fire** upon Teman that will consume the fortresses of
1:14 *I will* **set fire** [+3675] to the walls of Rabbah that will consume her
2: 2 I will send **fire** upon Moab that will consume the fortresses of
2: 5 I will send **fire** upon Judah that will consume the fortresses of
5: 6 and live, or he will sweep through the house of Joseph like a **fire**;
7: 4 The Sovereign LORD was calling for judgment by **fire**; it dried
Ob 1:18 The house of Jacob will be a **fire** and the house of Joseph a flame;
Mic 1: 4 beneath him and the valleys split apart, like wax before the **fire**,
1: 7 all her temple gifts will be burned with **fire**; I will destroy all her
Na 1: 6 His wrath is poured out like **fire**; the rocks are shattered before
2: 3 [2:4] The metal on the chariots **flashes** [+928] on the day they are
3:13 land are wide open to your enemies; **fire** has consumed their bars.
3:15 There the **fire** will devour you; the sword will cut you down and,
Hab 2:13 that the people's labor is only **fuel for** the **fire** [+928+1896],
Zep 1:18 In the **fire** *of* his jealousy the whole world will be consumed,
3: 8 The whole world will be consumed by the **fire** *of* my jealous anger.
Zec 2: 5 [2:9] I myself will be a wall of **fire** around it,'
3: 2 Is not this man a burning stick snatched from the **fire**?"
9: 4 destroy her power on the sea, and she will be consumed by **fire**.
11: 1 Open your doors, O Lebanon, so that **fire** may devour your cedars!
12: 6 make the leaders of Judah like a **firepot** [+3963] in a woodpile,
12: 6 like a firepot in a woodpile, like a **flaming** torch among sheaves.
13: 9 This third I will bring into the **fire**; I will refine them like silver
Mal 3: 2 For he will be like a refiner's **fire** or a launderer's soap.

837 ²אֵשׁ *'ēš²*, n.f. & m. Not used in NIV/BHS

838 אִשׁ *'iš*, subst. [2 / 1] [√ 3780]

one [1]

2Sa 14:19 no **one** can turn to the right or to the left from anything my lord the
Mic 6:10 *Am I* still *to* forget, [BHS *Are there yet*; NIV 5960] O wicked

839 אַשְׁבֵּל *'ašbēl*, n.pr.m. [3] [→ 840; cf. 8670]

Ashbel [3]

Ge 46:21 Bela, Beker, **Ashbel**, Gera, Naaman, Ehi, Rosh, Muppim,
Nu 26:38 through Bela, the Belaite clan; through **Ashbel**, the Ashbelite clan;
1Ch 8: 1 of Bela his firstborn, **Ashbel** the second son, Aharah the third,

840 אַשְׁבֵּלִי *'ašbēlî*, a.g. [1] [√ 839; cf. 8670]

Ashbelite [1]

Nu 26:38 through Bela, the Belaite clan; through Ashbel, the **Ashbelite** clan;

841 אֶשְׁבָּן *'ešbān*, n.pr.m. [2]

Eshban [2]

Ge 36:26 The sons of Dishon: Hemdan, **Eshban**, Ithran and Keran.
1Ch 1:41 Dishon. The sons of Dishon: Hemdan, **Eshban**, Ithran and Keran.

842 אַשְׁבֵּעַ *'ašbēa'*, n.pr.loc. Not used in NIV/BHS [→ 1080]

843 אֶשְׁבַּעַל *'ešba'al*, n.pr.m. [2] [√ 408 + 1251]

Esh-Baal [2]

1Ch 8:33 Saul the father of Jonathan, Malki-Shua, Abinadab and **Esh-Baal**.
9:39 Saul the father of Jonathan, Malki-Shua, Abinadab and **Esh-Baal**.

844 אֶשֶׁד *'āšēd*, n.f. [7] [→ 845, 850]

slopes [5], mountain slopes [2]

Nu 21:15 the **slopes** *of* the ravines that lead to the site of Ar and lie along the
Dt 3:17 to the Sea of the Arabah (the Salt Sea), below the **slopes** *of* Pisgah.
4:49 as far as the Sea of the Arabah, below the **slopes** *of* Pisgah.
Jos 10:40 the Negev, the western foothills and the **mountain slopes**,
12: 3 to Beth Jeshimoth, and then southward below the **slopes** *of* Pisgah.
12: 8 the Arabah, the **mountain slopes**, the desert and the Negev—
13:20 Beth Peor, the **slopes** *of* Pisgah, and Beth Jeshimoth

845 אֶשֶׁד *'ešed*, n.[m.]. Not used in NIV/BHS [√ 844]

846 אַשְׁדּוֹד *'ašdôd*, n.pr.loc. [17] [→ 847, 848]

Ashdod [15], *untranslated* [2]

Jos 11:22 Israelite territory; only in Gaza, Gath and **Ashdod** did any survive.
15:46 west of Ekron, all that were in the vicinity of **Ashdod**,
15:47 **Ashdod**, its surrounding settlements and villages; and Gaza,
1Sa 5: 1 captured the ark of God, they took it from Ebenezer to **Ashdod**.
5: 5 others who enter Dagon's temple at **Ashdod** step on the threshold.
5: 6 devastation upon them and afflicted them **[RPH]** with tumors.
5: 7 When the men of **Ashdod** saw what was happening, they said,
6:17 one each for **Ashdod**, Gaza, Ashkelon, Gath and Ekron.
2Ch 26: 6 and broke down the walls of Gath, Jabneh and **Ashdod**.
26: 6 He then rebuilt towns near **Ashdod** and elsewhere among the
Isa 20: 1 king of Assyria, came to **Ashdod** and attacked and captured it—
20: 1 of Assyria, came to Ashdod and attacked **[RPH]** and captured it—
Jer 25:20 (those of Ashkelon, Gaza, Ekron, and the people left at **Ashdod**);
Am 1: 8 I will destroy the king of **Ashdod** and the one who holds the
3: 9 Proclaim to the fortresses of **Ashdod** and to the fortresses of
Zep 2: 4 in ruins. At midday **Ashdod** will be emptied and Ekron uprooted.
Zec 9: 6 Foreigners will occupy **Ashdod**, and I will cut off the pride of the

847 אַשְׁדּוֹדִי *'ašdôdî*, a.g. [5] [√ 846]

people of Ashdod [2], Ashdod [1], from Ashdod [1], men of Ashdod [1]

Jos 13: 3 Philistine rulers in Gaza, **Ashdod**, Ashkelon, Gath and Ekron—
1Sa 5: 3 When the **people of Ashdod** rose early the next day, there was
5: 6 The LORD's hand was heavy upon the **people of Ashdod**
Ne 4: 7 [4:1] the **men of Ashdod** heard that the repairs to Jerusalem's
13:23 days I saw men of Judah who had married women **from Ashdod**,

848 אַשְׁדּוֹדִית *'ašdôdît*, adv. [1] [√ 846]

language of Ashdod [1]

Ne 13:24 Half of their children spoke the **language of Ashdod** or the

849 אַשְׁדּוֹת הַפִּסְגָּה *'ašdôt happisgâ*, n.pr.loc. Not used in NIV/BHS [√ 844 + 2021 + 7171]

850 אֶשְׁדָּת *'ēšdāt*, n.f. [1] [√ 844]

mountain slopes [1]

Dt 33: 2 holy ones from the south, from his **mountain slopes**. [Q 836+2017]

851 אִשָּׁה *'iššâ*, n.f. [781] [√ 408; Ar 10493]

wife [253], woman [167], women [103], wives [91], *untranslated* [32], wife's [9], each [7], her[s] [+2021] [6], mother [6], one [6], she[s] [+2021] [6], widow [6], gave in marriage [+906+4200+5989] [5], give in marriage [+906+4200+5989] [5], harem [+1074] [5], woman's [4], married [+906+4200+4200+4374] [3], marry [+2118+4200+4200] [3], marry [+4374] [3], adulteress [+2424] [2], harem [2], her[s] [2], married [+2118+4200] [2], married [+2118+4200+4200] [2], married [+4200+4374] [2], married [+4374] [2], married [+4374+4946] [2], married [+906+4200+4374] [2], marry [+2118+4200] [2], marry [+4200+4200+4374] [2], marry [+4200+4374] [2], mate [2], together [+295+448] [2], abstain from sexual relations [+440+448+5602] [1], adulteress [+408] [1], age of childbearing [+784+2021+3869] [1], be given in marriage [+906+4200+5989] [1], become wife [+4200+4374] [1], gave in marriage [+906+4200+4200+5989] [1], girl [+3251] [1], give [+4200+4200+5989] [1], give in marriage [+2021+4200+5989] [1], give in marriage [+4200+5989] [1], her[s] [+123+2257] [1], her[s] [+2257] [1], married [+4200+4200+4200+4374] [1], married [+4200+5951] [1], married [+906+2257+4200+4200+4374] [1], married [+906+4374] [1], married [+906+906+4374] [1], married to [+2118+4200+4200] [1], marry [+906+4200+4200+4374] [1], Naomi[s] [+2021] [1], others[s] [+2021] [1], period [+2006] [1], queens[s] [1], she[s]

[+2257] [1], stillborn child [+5878] [1], them[s] [1], they[s] [+1201+2021] [1], they[s] [+2021] [1], took in marriage [+906+4200+4200+4374] [1], was given in marriage [+4200+5989] [1], widow [+4637] [1], wife [+1249] [1], women's [1]

Ge 2:22 the LORD God made a **woman** from the rib he had taken out of
2:23 she shall be called '**woman**,' for she was taken out of man."
2:24 a man will leave his father and mother and be united to his **wife**,
2:25 The man and his **wife** were both naked, and they felt no shame.
3: 1 He said to the **woman**, "Did God really say, 'You must not eat
3: 2 The **woman** said to the serpent, "We may eat fruit from the trees in
3: 4 "You will not surely die," the serpent said to the **woman**.
3: 6 When the **woman** saw that the fruit of the tree was good for food
3: 8 his **wife** heard the sound of the LORD God as he was walking in
3:12 The man said, "The **woman** you put here with me—she gave me
3:13 the LORD God said to the **woman**, "What is this you have
3:13 The **woman** said, "The serpent deceived me, and I ate."
3:15 I will put enmity between you and the **woman**, and between your
3:16 To the **woman** he said, "I will greatly increase your pains in
3:17 "Because you listened to your **wife** and ate from the tree about
3:20 Adam named his **wife** Eve, because she would become the mother
3:21 made garments of skin for Adam and his **wife** and clothed them.
4: 1 Adam lay with his **wife** Eve, and she became pregnant and gave
4:17 Cain lay with his **wife**, and she became pregnant and gave birth to
4:19 Lamech married two **women**, one named Adah and the other
4:23 Lamech said to his **wives**, "Adah and Zillah, listen to me;
4:23 and Zillah, listen to me; **wives** *of* Lamech, hear my words.
4:25 Adam lay with his **wife** again, and she gave birth to a son
6: 2 and *they* **married** [+4200+4374] any of them they chose.
6:18 you and your sons and your **wife** and your sons' wives with you.
6:18 and your sons and your wife and your sons' **wives** with you.
7: 2 a male and its **mate**, and two of every kind of unclean animal,
7: 2 and two of every kind of unclean animal, a male and its **mate**,
7: 7 Noah and his sons and his **wife** and his sons' wives entered the ark
7: 7 his sons' **wives** entered the ark to escape the waters of the flood.
7:13 and Japheth, together with his **wife** and the wives of his three sons,
7:13 and Japheth, together with his wife and the **wives** *of* his three sons,
8:16 out of the ark, you and your **wife** and your sons and their wives.
8:16 out of the ark, you and your wife and your sons and their **wives**.
8:18 came out, together with his sons and his **wife** and his sons' wives.
8:18 came out, together with his sons and his wife and his sons' **wives**.
11:29 Abram and Nahor both **married** [+4200+4374]. The name of
11:29 The name of Abram's **wife** was Sarai, and the name of Nahor's
11:29 wife was Sarai, and the name of Nahor's **wife** was Milcah;
11:31 of Haran, and his daughter-in-law Sarai, the **wife** *of* his son Abram,
12: 5 He took his **wife** Sarai, his nephew Lot, all the possessions they
12:11 As he was about to enter Egypt, he said to his **wife** Sarai, "I know
12:11 he said to his wife Sarai, "I know what a beautiful **woman** you are.
12:12 When the Egyptians see you, they will say, 'This is his **wife**.'
12:14 to Egypt, the Egyptians saw that she was a very beautiful **woman**.
12:15 praised her to Pharaoh, and **she**[s] [+2021] was taken into his palace.
12:17 on Pharaoh and his household because of Abram's **wife** Sarai.
12:18 done to me?" he said. "Why didn't you tell me she was your **wife**?
12:19 did you say, 'She is my sister,' so that I took her to be my **wife**?
12:19 her to be my wife? Now then, here is your **wife**. Take her and go!"
12:20 and they sent him on his way, with his **wife** and everything he had.
13: 1 with his **wife** and everything he had, and Lot went with him.
14:16 and his possessions, together with the **women** and the other people.
16: 1 Now Sarai, Abram's **wife**, had borne him no children. But she had
16: 3 Sarai his **wife** took her Egyptian maidservant Hagar and gave her
16: 3 maidservant Hagar and gave her to her husband to be his **wife**.
17:15 God also said to Abraham, "As for Sarai your **wife**, you are no
17:19 Then God said, "Yes, but your **wife** Sarah will bear you a son,
18: 9 "Where is your **wife** Sarah?" they asked him. "There, in the tent,"
18:10 about this time next year, and Sarah your **wife** will have a son."
18:11 and Sarah was past the **age of childbearing** [+784+2021+3869].
19:15 Take your **wife** and your two daughters who are here, or you will
19:16 his hand and the hands of his **wife** and of his two daughters
19:26 But Lot's **wife** looked back, and she became a pillar of salt.
20: 2 and there Abraham said of his **wife** Sarah, "She is my sister."
20: 3 "You are as good as dead because of the **woman** you have taken;
20: 7 Now return the man's **wife**, for he is a prophet, and he will pray for
20:11 fear of God in this place, and they will kill me because of my **wife**.'
20:12 of my father though not of my mother; and she became my **wife**.
20:14 and gave them to Abraham, and he returned Sarah his **wife** to him.
20:17 his **wife** and his slave girls so they could have children again,
20:18 in Abimelech's household because of Abraham's **wife** Sarah.
21:21 in the Desert of Paran, his mother got a **wife** for him from Egypt.
23:19 Afterward Abraham buried his **wife** Sarah in the cave in the field
24: 3 that you will not get a **wife** for my son from the daughters of the
24: 4 my country and my own relatives and get a **wife** for my son Isaac."
24: 5 "What if the **woman** is unwilling to come back with me to this
24: 7 angel before you so that you can get a **wife** for my son from there.
24: 8 If the **woman** is unwilling to come back with you, then you will be
24:15 son of Milcah, who was the **wife** *of* Abraham's brother Nahor.
24:36 My master's **wife** Sarah has borne him a son in her old age,
24:37 'You must not get a **wife** for my son from the daughters of the
24:38 my father's family and to my own clan, and get a **wife** for my son.'
24:39 my master, 'What if the **woman** will not come back with me?'
24:40 so that you can get a **wife** for my son from my own clan and from
24:44 let her be the **one** the LORD has chosen for my master's son.'
24:51 take her and go, and let her become the **wife** of your master's son,
24:67 So she became his **wife**, and he loved her; and Isaac was comforted
25: 1 Abraham took another **wife**, whose name was Keturah.
25:10 from the Hittites. There Abraham was buried with his **wife** Sarah.
25:20 when he **married** [+906+2257+4200+4200+4374] Rebekah
25:21 Isaac prayed to the LORD on behalf of his **wife**, because she was
25:21 answered his prayer, and his **wife** Rebekah became pregnant.
26: 7 When the men of that place asked him about his **wife**, he said,
26: 7 "She is my sister," because he was afraid to say, "She is my **wife**."
26: 8 down from a window and saw Isaac caressing his **wife** Rebekah.
26: 9 So Abimelech summoned Isaac and said, "She is really your **wife**!
26:10 One of the men might well have slept with your **wife**, and you
26:11 who molests this man or his **wife** shall surely be put to death."
26:34 *he* **married** [+906+906+4374] Judith daughter of Beeri the Hittite,
27:46 If Jacob takes a **wife** from among the women of this land,
28: 1 and commanded him: "*Do* not **marry** [+4374] a Canaanite woman.
28: 2 Take a **wife** for yourself there, from among the daughters of Laban,
28: 6 and had sent him to Paddan Aram to take a **wife** from there,
28: 6 he commanded him, "*Do* not **marry** [+4374] a Canaanite woman,"
28: 9 and **married** [+906+4200+4200+4374] Mahalath, the sister of
28: 9 Ishmael son of Abraham, in addition to the **wives** he already had.
29:21 Jacob said to Laban, "Give me my **wife**. My time is completed,
29:28 and then Laban gave him his daughter Rachel to be his **wife**.
30: 4 So she gave him her servant Bilhah as a **wife**. Jacob slept with her,
30: 9 she took her maidservant Zilpah and gave her to Jacob as a **wife**.
30:26 Give me my **wives** and children, for whom I have served you,
31:17 Then Jacob put his children and his **wives** on camels,
31:35 cannot stand up in your presence; I'm having my **period** [+2006]."
31:50 my daughters or if you take any **wives** besides my daughters,
32:22 [32:23] That night Jacob got up and took his two **wives**, his two
33: 5 Esau looked up and saw the **women** and children. "Who are these
34: 4 Shechem said to his father Hamor, "Get me this girl as my **wife**."
34: 8 his heart set on your daughter. Please give her to him as his **wife**.
34:12 I'll pay whatever you ask me. Only give me the girl as my **wife**."
34:21 We *can* **marry** [+906+4200+4200+4374] their daughters and they
34:29 They carried off all their wealth and all their **women** and children,
36: 2 Esau took his **wives** from the women of Canaan: Adah daughter of
36: 6 Esau took his **wives** and sons and daughters and all the members of
36:10 Eliphaz, the son of Esau's **wife** Adah, and Reuel, the son of Esau's
36:10 of Esau's wife Adah, and Reuel, the son of Esau's **wife** Basemath.
36:12 bore him Amalek. These were grandsons of Esau's **wife** Adah.
36:13 and Mizzah. These were grandsons of Esau's **wife** Basemath.
36:14 The sons of Esau's **wife** Oholibamah daughter of Anah
36:17 Reuel in Edom; they were grandsons of Esau's **wife** Basemath.
36:18 The sons of Esau's **wife** Oholibamah: Chiefs Jeush, Jalam
36:18 These were the chiefs descended from Esau's **wife** Oholibamah
36:39 and his **wife's** name was Mehetabel daughter of Matred,
37: 2 the sons of Bilhah and the sons of Zilpah, his father's **wives**,
38: 6 Judah got a **wife** for Er, his firstborn, and her name was Tamar.
38: 8 "Lie with your brother's **wife** and fulfill your duty to her as a
38: 9 so whenever he lay with his brother's **wife**, he spilled his semen on
38:12 After a long time Judah's **wife**, the daughter of Shua, died.
38:14 had now grown up, she had not been given to him as his **wife**.
38:20 the Adullamite in order to get his pledge back from the **woman**,
39: 7 and after a while his master's **wife** took notice of Joseph and said,
39: 8 "With me in charge," he told **her**[s] [+123+2257], "my master does
39: 9 withheld nothing from me except you, because you are his **wife**.
39:19 When his master heard the story his **wife** told him, saying,
41:45 him Asenath daughter of Potiphera, priest of On, to be his **wife**.
44:27 my father said to us, 'You know that my **wife** bore me two sons.
45:19 Take some carts from Egypt for your children and your **wives**,
46: 5 and their **wives** in the carts that Pharaoh had sent to transport him.
46:19 The sons of Jacob's **wife** Rachel: Joseph and Benjamin.
46:26 who were his direct descendants, not counting his sons' **wives**—
49:31 There Abraham and his **wife** Sarah were buried, there Isaac
49:31 there Isaac and his **wife** Rebekah were buried, and there I buried
Ex 1:19 answered Pharaoh, "Hebrew women are not like Egyptian **women**;
2: 2 and **she**[s] [+2021] became pregnant and gave birth to a son.
2: 7 and get one of the Hebrew **women** to nurse the baby for you?"
2: 9 and I will pay you." So the **woman** took the baby and nursed him.
3:22 *Every* **woman** is to ask her neighbor and any woman living in her
4:20 So Moses took his **wife** and sons, put them on a donkey and started
6:20 Amram **married** [+906+4200+4200+4374] his father's sister
6:23 Aaron **married** [+906+4200+4200+4374] Elisheba, daughter of
6:25 Eleazar son of Aaron **married** [+4200+4200+4200+4374] one of
11: 2 and **women** alike are to ask their neighbors for articles of silver
15:20 and all the **women** followed her, with tambourines and dancing.

Ex 18: 2 After Moses had sent away his **wife** Zipporah, his father-in-law
18: 5 Moses' father-in-law, together with Moses' sons and **wife**,
18: 6 am coming to you with your **wife** and her two sons."
19: 15 **Abstain from sexual relations** [+440+448+5602]."
20: 17 You shall not covet your neighbor's **wife**, or his manservant
21: 3 but if he has a **wife** when he comes, she is to go with him.
21: 3 if he has a wife when he comes, **she**[s] [+2257] is to go with him.
21: 4 If his master gives him a **wife** and she bears him sons or daughters,
21: 4 the **woman** and her children shall belong to her master,
21: 5 'I love my master and my **wife** and children and do not want to go
21: 22 "If men who are fighting hit a pregnant **woman** and she gives birth
21: 22 the offender must be fined whatever the **woman's** husband
21: 28 "If a bull gores a man or a **woman** to death, the bull must be
21: 29 but has not kept it penned up and it kills a man or **woman**,
22: 16 [22:15] he must pay the bride-price, and she shall be his **wife**.
22: 24 [22:23] your **wives** will become widows and your children
26: 3 Join five of the curtains **together** [+295+448], and do the same
26: 3 the curtains together, and do the same with the other five. **[RPH]**
26: 5 the end curtain of the other set, with the loops opposite **each** other.
26: 6 and use them to fasten the curtains **together** [+295+448]
26: 17 with two projections set parallel to **each** other. Make all the frames
32: 2 "Take off the gold earrings that your **wives**, your sons and your
35: 22 men and **women** alike, came and brought gold jewelry of all kinds:
35: 25 Every skilled **woman** spun with her hands and brought what she
35: 26 all the **women** who were willing and had the skill spun the goat
35: 29 **women** who were willing brought to the LORD freewill offerings
36: 6 or **woman** is to make anything else as an offering for the
Lev 12: 2 'A **woman** who becomes pregnant and gives birth to a son will be
13: 29 "If a man or **woman** has a sore on the head or on the chin,
13: 38 "When a man or **woman** has white spots on the skin,
15: 18 When a man lies with a **woman** and there is an emission of semen,
15: 19 " 'When a **woman** has her regular flow of blood, the impurity of
15: 25 " 'When a **woman** has a discharge of blood for many days at a time
18: 8 " 'Do not have sexual relations with your father's **wife**; that would
18: 11 not have sexual relations with the daughter of your father's **wife**,
18: 14 " 'Do not dishonor your father's brother by approaching his **wife** to
18: 15 She is your son's **wife**; do not have relations with her.
18: 16 " 'Do not have sexual relations with your brother's **wife**;
18: 17 " 'Do not have sexual relations with both a **woman** and her
18: 18 " 'Do not take your **wife's** sister as a rival wife and have sexual
18: 19 " 'Do not approach a **woman** to have sexual relations during the
18: 20 " 'Do not have sexual relations with your neighbor's **wife**
18: 22 " 'Do not lie with a man as one lies with a **woman**; that is
18: 23 A **woman** must not present herself to an animal to have sexual
19: 20 " 'If a man sleeps with a **woman** who is a slave girl promised to
20: 10 " 'If a man commits adultery with another man's **wife**—with the
20: 10 with the **wife** *of* his neighbor—both the adulterer
20: 11 " 'If a man sleeps with his father's **wife**, he has dishonored his
20: 13 " 'If a man lies with a man as one lies with a **woman**, both of them
20: 14 " 'If a man marries both a **woman** and her mother, it is wicked.
20: 16 " 'If a **woman** approaches an animal to have sexual relations with
20: 16 have sexual relations with it, kill both the **woman** and the animal.
20: 18 " 'If a man lies with a **woman** during her monthly period and has
20: 21 " 'If a man marries his brother's **wife**, it is an act of impurity;
20: 27 " 'A man or **woman** who is a medium or spiritist among you must
21: 7 " 'They must not marry **women** defiled by prostitution or divorced
21: 7 defiled by prostitution or **[RPH]** divorced from their husbands,
21: 13 " 'The **woman** he marries must be a virgin.
21: 14 by prostitution, but only a virgin from his own people, **[RPH]**
24: 10 Now the son of an Israelite **mother** and an Egyptian father went
24: 11 The son of the Israelite **woman** blasphemed the Name with a
26: 26 of bread, ten **women** will be able to bake your bread in one oven,
Nu 5: 6 'When a man or **woman** wrongs another in any way and so is
5: 12 say to them: 'If a man's **wife** goes astray and is unfaithful to him
5: 14 over her husband and he suspects his **wife** and she is impure—
5: 14 and suspects **her**[s] [+2257] even though she is not impure—
5: 15 he is to take his **wife** to the priest. He must also take an offering of
5: 18 After the priest has had the **woman** stand before the LORD,
5: 18 he shall loosen **her**[s] [+2021] hair and place in her hands the
5: 19 Then the priest shall put the **woman** under oath and say to her,
5: 21 here the priest is to put the **woman** under this curse of the oath—
5: 21 **[RPH]** "may the LORD cause your people to curse
5: 22 wastes away." " 'Then the **woman** is to say, "Amen. So be it."
5: 24 He shall have the **woman** drink the bitter water that brings a curse,
5: 25 The priest is to take from **her**[s] [+2021] hands the grain offering for
5: 26 it on the altar; after that, he is to have the **woman** drink the water.
5: 27 and **she**[s] [+2021] will become accursed among her people.
5: 28 the **woman** has not defiled herself and is free from impurity,
5: 29 is the law of jealousy when a **woman** goes astray and defiles
5: 30 feelings of jealousy come over a man because he suspects his **wife**.
5: 30 The priest is to have **her**[s] [+2021] stand before the LORD
5: 31 but the **woman** will bear the consequences of her sin.' "
6: 2 'If a man or **woman** wants to make a special vow, a vow of
12: 1 Aaron began to talk against Moses because of his Cushite **wife**,
12: 1 of his Cushite wife, for *he had* **married** [+4374] a Cushite.
14: 3 Our **wives** and children will be taken as plunder. Wouldn't it be
16: 27 and Abiram had come out and were standing with their **wives**,
25: 8 both of them—through the Israelite and into the **woman's** body.
25: 15 the name of the Midianite **woman** who was put to death was Cozbi
26: 59 the name of Amram's **wife** was Jochebed, a descendant of Levi,
30: 3 [30:4] "When a young **woman** still living in her father's house
30: 16 [30:17] concerning relationships between a man and his **wife**,
31: 9 The Israelites captured the Midianite **women** and children
31: 17 kill all the boys. And kill every **woman** who has slept with a man,
31: 18 save for yourselves every **girl** [+3251] who has never slept with a
31: 35 and 32,000 **women** who had never slept with a man.
32: 26 Our children and **wives**, our flocks and herds will remain here in
36: 3 Now suppose *they* **marry** [+2118+4200+4200] men from other
36: 6 *They may* **marry** [+2118+4200] anyone they please as long as
36: 6 as *they* **marry** [+2118+4200] within the tribal clan of their father.
36: 8 *must* **marry** [+2118+4200+4200] someone in her father's tribal
36: 11 Milcah and Noah—**married** [+2118+4200+4200] their cousins on
36: 12 *They* **married** [+2118+4200] within the clans of the descendants
Dt 2: 34 and completely destroyed them—men, **women** and children.
3: 6 of Heshbon, destroying every city—men, **women** and children.
3: 19 However, your **wives**, your children and your livestock (I know
5: 21 "You shall not covet your neighbor's **wife**. You shall not set your
13: 6 [13:7] own brother, or your son or daughter, or the **wife** you love,
17: 2 or **woman** living among you in one of the towns the LORD gives
17: 5 the man or **woman** who has done this evil deed to your city gate
17: 5 evil deed to your city gate **[RPH]** and stone that person to death.
17: 17 He must not take many **wives**, or his heart will be led astray.
20: 7 Has anyone become pledged to a **woman** and not married her?
20: 14 As for the **women**, the children, the livestock and everything else
21: 11 if you notice among the captives a beautiful **woman** and are
21: 11 and are attracted to her, you may take her as your **wife**.
21: 13 you may go to her and be her husband and she shall be your **wife**.
21: 15 If a man has two **wives**, and he loves one but not the other,
22: 5 A **woman** must not wear men's clothing, nor a man wear women's
22: 5 must not wear men's clothing, nor a man wear **women's** clothing,
22: 13 If a man takes a **wife** and, after lying with her, dislikes her
22: 14 and gives her a bad name, saying, "I married this **woman**,
22: 16 "*I* **gave** my daughter **in marriage** [+906+4200+5989] to this man,
22: 19 She shall continue to be his **wife**; he must not divorce her as long
22: 22 If a man is found sleeping with another man's **wife** [+1249],
22: 22 both the man who slept with **her**[s] [+2021] and the woman must
22: 22 both the man who slept with her and the **woman** must die.
22: 24 for help, and the man because he violated another man's **wife**.
22: 29 He *must* **marry** [+2118+4200+4200] the girl, for he has violated
22: 30 [23:1] A man is not to marry his father's **wife**; he must not
24: 1 If a man marries a **woman** who becomes displeasing to him
24: 3 gives it to her and sends her from his house, or if he dies, **[RPH]**
24: 4 is not allowed to **marry** [+4200+4374] her again after she has been
24: 5 If a man *has* recently **married** [+4374], he must not be sent to war
24: 5 to stay at home and bring happiness to the **wife** he has married.
25: 5 a son, his **widow** [+4637] must not marry outside the family.
25: 5 husband's brother shall take her and **marry** [+4200+4200+4374]
25: 11 the **wife** *of* one of them comes to rescue her husband from his
27: 20 "Cursed is the man who sleeps with his father's **wife**, for he
28: 30 You will be pledged to be married to a **woman**, but another will
28: 54 on his own brother or the **wife** he loves or his surviving children,
29: 11 [29:10] together with your children and your **wives**, and the aliens
29: 18 [29:17] Make sure there is no man or **woman**, clan or tribe among
31: 12 men, **women** and children, and the aliens living in your towns—
Jos 1: 14 Your **wives**, your children and your livestock may stay in the land
2: 1 and entered the house of a **[NIE]** prostitute named Rahab
2: 4 But the **woman** had taken the two men and hidden them. She said,
6: 21 men and **women**, young and old, cattle, sheep and donkeys.
6: 22 "Go into the prostitute's **[NIE]** house and bring her out and all
6: 22 the prostitute's house and bring **her**[s] out and all who belong to her,
8: 25 Twelve thousand men and **women** fell that day—all the people of
8: 35 including the **women** and children, and the aliens who lived among
15: 16 "*I will* **give** my daughter Acsah **in marriage** [+906+4200+5989] to
15: 17 **gave** his daughter Acsah to him **in marriage** [+906+4200+5989].
Jdg 1: 12 "*I will* **give** my daughter Acsah **in marriage** [+906+4200+5989] to
1: 13 **gave** his daughter Acsah to him **in marriage** [+906+4200+5989].
3: 6 *They* **took** their daughters **in marriage** [+906+4200+4200+4374]
4: 4 Deborah, a **[NIE]** prophetess, the wife of Lappidoth, was leading
4: 4 Deborah, a prophetess, the **wife** *of* Lappidoth, was leading Israel at
4: 9 not be yours, for the LORD will hand Sisera over to a **woman**."
4: 17 fled on foot to the tent of Jael, the **wife** *of* Heber the Kenite,
4: 21 But Jael, Heber's **wife**, picked up a tent peg and a hammer
5: 24 "Most blessed of **women** be Jael, the wife of Heber the Kenite,
5: 24 "Most blessed of women be Jael, the **wife** *of* Heber the Kenite,
5: 24 wife of Heber the Kenite, most blessed of tent-dwelling **women**.
8: 30 He had seventy sons of his own, for he had many **wives**.
9: 49 tower of Shechem, about a thousand men and **women**, also died.
9: 51 however, was a strong tower, to which all the men and **women**—

Jdg 9:53 a **woman** dropped an upper millstone on his head and cracked his
9:54 'A **woman** killed him.' " So his servant ran him through, and he
11: 1 His father was Gilead; his **mother** was a prostitute.
11: 2 Gilead's **wife** also bore him sons, and when they were grown up,
11: 2 when **they**[s] [+1201+2021] were grown up, they drove Jephthah
11: 2 they said, "because you are the son of another **woman**."
13: 2 of the Danites, had a **wife** who was sterile and remained childless.
13: 3 The angel of the LORD appeared to **her**[s] [+2021] and said,
13: 6 the **woman** went to her husband and told him, "A man of God
13: 9 the angel of God came again to the **woman** while she was out in
13:10 The **woman** hurried to tell her husband, "He's here! The man who
13:11 Manoah got up and followed his **wife**. When he came to the man,
13:11 to the man, he said, "Are you the one who talked to my **wife**?"
13:13 the LORD answered, "Your **wife** must do all that I have told her.
13:19 LORD did an amazing thing while Manoah and his **wife** watched:
13:20 Manoah and his **wife** fell with their faces to the ground.
13:21 of the LORD did not show himself again to Manoah and his **wife**,
13:22 "We are doomed to die!" he said to his **wife**. "We have seen God!"
13:23 But his **wife** answered, "If the LORD had meant to kill us,
13:24 The **woman** gave birth to a boy and named him Samson. He grew
14: 1 went down to Timnah and saw there a young Philistine **woman**.
14: 2 his father and mother, "I have seen a Philistine **woman** in Timnah;
14: 2 a Philistine woman in Timnah; now get her for me as my **wife**."
14: 3 "Isn't there an acceptable **woman** among your relatives or among
14: 3 Must you go to the uncircumcised Philistines to get a **wife**?"
14: 7 Then he went down and talked with the **woman**, and he liked her.
14:10 Now his father went down to see the **woman**. And Samson made a
14:15 On the fourth day, they said to Samson's **wife**, "Coax your
14:16 Then Samson's **wife** threw herself on him, sobbing, "You hate me!
14:20 Samson's **wife** was given to the friend who had attended him at his
15: 1 Samson took a young goat and went to visit his **wife**.
15: 1 and went to visit his wife. He said, "I'm going to my **wife's** room."
15: 6 Timnite's son-in-law, because his **wife** was given to his friend."
16: 1 One day Samson went to Gaza, where he saw a **[NIE]** prostitute.
16: 4 he fell in love with a **woman** in the Valley of Sorek whose name
16:27 Now the temple was crowded with men and **women**; all the rulers
16:27 about three thousand men and **women** watching Samson perform.
19: 1 of Ephraim took a **[NIE]** concubine from Bethlehem in Judah.
19:26 At daybreak the **woman** went back to the house where her master
19:27 there lay **[NIE]** his concubine, fallen in the doorway of the house,
20: 4 the husband of the murdered **woman**, said, "I and my concubine
21: 1 "Not one of us *will* **give** his daughter **in marriage** [+4200+5989]
21: 7 "How can we provide **wives** for those who are left, since we have
21: 7 who are left, since we have taken an oath by the LORD not *to* **give** [+4200+4200+5989] them any of our daughters in marriage?"
21:10 to the sword those living there, including the **women** and children.
21:11 they said. "Kill every male and every **woman** who is not a virgin."
21:14 and were given the **women** *of* Jabesh Gilead who had been spared.
21:14 been spared. **[RPH]** But there were not enough for all of them.
21:16 of the assembly said, "With the **women** of Benjamin destroyed,
21:16 how shall we provide **wives** for the men who are left?
21:18 We can't give them our daughters as **wives**, since we Israelites
21:18 this oath: 'Cursed be anyone who gives a **wife** to a Benjamite.'
21:21 the vineyards and each of you seize a **wife** from the girls of Shiloh
21:22 because we did not get **wives** *for* them during the war, and you are
21:23 each man caught one and carried her off to be his **wife**.
Ru 1: 1 from Bethlehem in Judah, together with his **wife** and two sons,
1: 2 The man's name was Elimelech, his **wife's** name Naomi,
1: 4 *They* **married** [+4200+5951] Moabite women, one named Orpah
1: 5 **Naomi**[s] [+2021] was left without her two sons and her husband.
1: 8 "Go back, **each** of you, to your mother's home.
1: 9 May the LORD grant that **each** of you will find rest in the home
3: 8 the man, and he turned and discovered a **woman** lying at his feet.
3:11 All my fellow townsmen know that you are a **woman** *of* noble
3:14 "Don't let it be known that a **woman** came to the threshing floor."
4: 5 and from Ruth the Moabitess, you acquire the dead man's **widow**,
4:10 also acquired Ruth the Moabitess, Mahlon's **widow**, as my wife,
4:10 also acquired Ruth the Moabitess, Mahlon's widow, as my **wife**,
4:11 May the LORD make the **woman** who is coming into your home
4:13 So Boaz took Ruth and she became his **wife**. Then he went to her,
4:14 The **women** said to Naomi: "Praise be to the LORD, who this day
1Sa 1: 2 He had two **wives**; one was called Hannah and the other Peninnah.
1: 4 he would give portions of the meat to his **wife** Peninnah and to all
1:15 my lord," Hannah replied, "I am a **woman** who is deeply troubled.
1:18 **she**[s] [+2021] went her way and ate something, and her face was no
1:19 Elkanah lay with Hannah his **wife**, and the LORD remembered
1:23 So the **woman** stayed at home and nursed her son until she had
1:26 I am the **woman** who stood here beside you praying to the
2:20 Eli would bless Elkanah and his **wife**, saying, "May the LORD
2:20 "May the LORD give you children by this **woman** to take the
2:22 how they slept with the **women** who served at the entrance to the
4:19 the **wife** *of* Phinehas, was pregnant and near the time of delivery.
14:50 His **wife's** name was Ahinoam daughter of Ahimaaz. The name of
15: 3 put to death men and **women**, children and infants, cattle
15:33 But Samuel said, "As your sword has made **women** childless,
15:33 women childless, so will your mother be childless among **women**."
18: 6 the **women** came out from all the towns of Israel to meet King Saul
18: 7 As **they**[s] [+2021] danced, they sang: "Saul has slain his thousands,
18:17 *I will* **give** her to you **in marriage** [+906+4200+5989]; only serve
18:19 she **was given in marriage** [+4200+5989] to Adriel of Meholah.
18:27 Then Saul **gave** him his daughter Michal **in marriage** [+906+4200+4200+5989].
19:11 Michal, David's **wife**, warned him, "If you don't run for your life
21: 4 [21:5] provided the men have kept themselves from **women**."
21: 5 [21:6] David replied, "Indeed **women** have been kept from us,
22:19 with its men and **women**, its children and infants, and its cattle,
25: 3 His name was Nabal and his **wife's** name was Abigail. She was an
25: 3 She was an intelligent and beautiful **woman**, but her husband,
25:14 One of the servants told Nabal's **wife** Abigail: "David sent
25:37 when Nabal was sober, his **wife** told him all these things,
25:39 word to Abigail, asking her to **become** his **wife** [+4200+4374].
25:40 "David has sent us to you to take you to become his **wife**."
25:42 five maids, went with David's messengers and became his **wife**.
25:43 also married Ahinoam of Jezreel, and they both were his **wives**.
25:44 David's **wife**, to Paltiel son of Laish, who was from Gallim.
27: 3 Each man had his family with him, and David had his two **wives**:
27: 3 Ahinoam of Jezreel and Abigail of Carmel, the **widow** *of* Nabal.
27: 9 he did not leave a man or **woman** alive, but took sheep and cattle,
27:11 He did not leave a man or **woman** alive to be brought to Gath,
28: 7 "Find me a **woman** who is a medium, so I may go and inquire of
28: 7 and inquire of her." "There is **[RPH]** one in Endor," they said.
28: 8 on other clothes, and at night he and two men went to the **woman**.
28: 9 But the **woman** said to him, "Surely you know what Saul has done.
28:11 Then the **woman** asked, "Whom shall I bring up for you?"
28:12 When the **woman** saw Samuel, she cried out at the top of her voice
28:12 she cried out at the top of her voice and said **[RPH]** to Saul,
28:13 The **woman** said, "I see a spirit coming up out of the ground."
28:21 When the **woman** came to Saul and saw that he was greatly
28:23 his men joined the **woman** in urging him, and he listened to them.
28:24 The **woman** had a fattened calf at the house, which she butchered
30: 2 had taken captive the **women** and all who were in it, both young
30: 3 by fire and their **wives** and sons and daughters taken captive.
30: 5 David's two **wives** had been captured—Ahinoam of Jezreel
30: 5 Ahinoam of Jezreel and Abigail, the **widow** *of* Nabal of Carmel.
30:18 everything the Amalekites had taken, including his two **wives**.
30:22 However, each man may take his **wife** and children and go."
2Sa 1:26 love for me was wonderful, more wonderful than that of **women**.
2: 2 So David went up there with his two **wives**, Ahinoam of Jezreel
2: 2 Ahinoam of Jezreel and Abigail, the **widow** *of* Nabal of Carmel.
3: 3 Kileab the son of Abigail the **widow** *of* Nabal of Carmel;
3: 5 the sixth, Ithream the son of David's **wife** Eglah. These were born
3: 8 Yet now you accuse me of an offense involving this **woman**!
3:14 to Ish-Bosheth son of Saul, demanding, "Give me my **wife** Michal,
5:13 David took more concubines and **wives** in Jerusalem, and more
6:19 person in the whole crowd of Israelites, both men and **women**.
11: 2 From the roof he saw a **woman** bathing. The woman was very
11: 2 the roof he saw a woman bathing. The **woman** was very beautiful,
11: 3 David sent someone to find out about **her**[s] [+2021]. The man said,
11: 3 the daughter of Eliam and the **wife** *of* Uriah the Hittite?"
11: 5 The **woman** conceived and sent word to David, saying, "I am
11:11 How could I go to my house to eat and drink and lie with my **wife**?
11:21 Didn't a **woman** throw an upper millstone on him from the wall,
11:26 When Uriah's **wife** heard that her husband was dead, she mourned
11:27 brought to his house, and she became his **wife** and bore him a son.
12: 8 master's house to you, and your master's **wives** into your arms.
12: 9 Uriah the Hittite with the sword and took his **wife** to be your own.
12: 9 **[RPH]** You killed him with the sword of the Ammonites.
12:10 despised me and took the **wife** *of* Uriah the Hittite to be your own.'
12:10 and took the wife of Uriah the Hittite to be your own.' **[RPH]**
12:11 Before your very eyes I will take your **wives** and give them to one
12:11 is close to you, and he will lie with your **wives** in broad daylight.
12:15 the LORD struck the child that Uriah's **wife** had borne to David,
12:24 Then David comforted his **wife** Bathsheba, and he went to her
14: 2 sent someone to Tekoa and had a wise **woman** brought from there.
14: 2 Act like a **woman** who has spent many days grieving for the dead.
14: 4 When the **woman** from Tekoa went to the king, she fell with her
14: 5 She said, "I am indeed a **[NIE]** widow; my husband is dead.
14: 8 The king said to the **woman**, "Go home, and I will issue an order
14: 9 But the **woman** from Tekoa said to him, "My lord the king,
14:12 the **woman** said, "Let your servant speak a word to my lord the
14:13 The **woman** said, "Why then have you devised a thing like this
14:18 the king said to the **woman**, "Do not keep from me the answer to
14:18 going to ask you." "Let my lord the king speak," the **woman** said.
14:19 The **woman** answered, "As surely as you live, my lord the king,
14:27 daughter's name was Tamar, and she became a beautiful **woman**.
15:16 but he left ten **[NIE]** concubines to take care of the palace.
17:19 His **wife** took a covering and spread it out over the opening of the
17:20 When Absalom's men came to the **woman** at the house, they

2Sa 17:20 The **woman** answered them, "They crossed over the brook."
19: 5 [19:6] and daughters and the lives of your **wives** and concubines.
20: 3 he took the ten **[NIE]** concubines he had left to take care of the
20:16 a wise **woman** called from the city, "Listen! Listen! Tell Joab to
20:17 He went toward her, and **she**ˢ [+2021] asked, "Are you Joab?"
20:21 The **woman** said to Joab, "His head will be thrown to you from the
20:22 Then the **woman** went to all the people with her wise advice,
1Ki 2:17 not refuse you—to give me Abishag the Shunammite as my **wife**."
2:21 So she said, "*Let* Abishag the Shunammite **be given in marriage** [+906+4200+5989] to your brother Adonijah."
3:16 Now two **[NIE]** prostitutes came to the king and stood before
3:17 One of **them**ˢ said, "My lord, this woman and I live in the same
3:17 of them said, "My lord, this **woman** and I live in the same house.
3:18 third day after my child was born, this **woman** also had a baby.
3:19 "During the night this **woman's** son died because she lay on him.
3:22 The other **woman** said, "No! The living one is my son; the dead
3:26 The **woman** whose son was alive was filled with compassion for
4:11 in Naphoth Dor (he *was* **married to** [+2118+4200+4200] Taphath
4:15 (he *had* **married** [+906+4200+4374] Basemath daughter of
7:14 whose **mother** was a widow from the tribe of Naphtali and whose
9:16 then gave it as a wedding gift to his daughter, Solomon's **wife**.
11: 1 loved many foreign **women** besides Pharaoh's daughter—
11: 3 He had seven hundred **wives** of royal birth and three hundred
11: 3 and three hundred concubines, and his **wives** led him astray.
11: 4 As Solomon grew old, his **wives** turned his heart after other gods,
11: 8 He did the same for all his foreign **wives**, who burned incense
11:19 Pharaoh was so pleased with Hadad that *he* **gave** him a sister of his own wife, Queen Tahpenes, **in marriage** [+906+4200+5989].
11:19 so pleased with Hadad that he gave him a sister of his own **wife**,
11:26 from Zeredah, and his mother was a **[NIE]** widow named Zeruah.
14: 2 Jeroboam said to his **wife**, "Go, disguise yourself, so you won't be
14: 2 so you won't be recognized as the **wife** *of* Jeroboam.
14: 4 So Jeroboam's **wife** did what he said and went to Ahijah's house in
14: 5 "Jeroboam's **wife** is coming to ask you about her son, for he is ill,
14: 6 of her footsteps at the door, he said, "Come in, **wife** *of* Jeroboam.
14:17 Then Jeroboam's **wife** got up and left and went to Tirzah.
16:31 *he* also **married** [+906+4374] Jezebel daughter of Ethbaal king of
17: 9 I have commanded a **[NIE]** widow in that place to supply you
17:10 came to the town gate, a **[NIE]** widow was there gathering sticks.
17:17 Some time later the son of the **woman** who owned the house
17:24 the **woman** said to Elijah, "Now I know that you are a man of God
20: 3 gold are mine, and the best of your **wives** and children are mine.' "
20: 5 sent to demand your silver and gold, your **wives** and your children.
20: 7 When he sent for my **wives** and my children, my silver and my
21: 5 His **wife** Jezebel came in and asked him, "Why are you so sullen?
21: 7 Jezebel his **wife** said, "Is this how you act as king over Israel?
21:25 to do evil in the eyes of the LORD, urged on by Jezebel his **wife**.
2Ki 4: 1 The **wife** of a man from the company of the prophets cried out to
4: 1 The wife of a man from **[RPH]** the company of the prophets cried
4: 8 a well-to-do **woman** was there, who urged him to stay for a meal.
4:17 the **woman** became pregnant, and the next year about that same
5: 2 captive a young girl from Israel, and she served Naaman's **wife**.
6:26 on the wall, a **woman** cried to him, "Help me, my lord the king!"
6:28 She answered, "This **woman** said to me, 'Give up your son
6:30 When the king heard the **woman's** words, he tore his robes.
8: 1 Now Elisha had said to the **woman** whose son he had restored to
8: 2 The **woman** proceeded to do as the man of God said. She
8: 3 At the end of the seven years **she**ˢ [+2021] came back from the
8: 5 the **woman** whose son Elisha had brought back to life came to beg
8: 5 Gehazi said, "This is the **woman**, my lord the king, and this is her
8: 6 The king asked the **woman** about it, and she told him. Then he
8:18 for *he* **married** [+2118+4200+4200] a daughter of Ahab.
14: 9 '**Give** your daughter to my son **in marriage** [+906+4200+5989].'
22:14 who was the **wife** *of* Shallum son of Tikvah, the son of Harhas,
23: 7 temple of the LORD and where **women** did weaving for Asherah.
24:15 his **wives**, his officials and the leading men of the land.
1Ch 1:50 and his **wife's** name was Mehetabel daughter of Matred,
2:18 Caleb son of Hezron had children by his **wife** Azubah (and by
2:24 Abijah the **wife** *of* Hezron bore him Ashhur the father of Tekoa.
2:26 Jerahmeel had another **wife**, whose name was Atarah; she was the
2:29 Abishur's **wife** was named Abihail, who bore him Ahban
2:35 Sheshan **gave** his daughter **in marriage** [+906+4200+5989] to his
3: 3 the son of Abital; and the sixth, Ithream, by his **wife** Eglah.
4: 5 Ashhur the father of Tekoa had two **wives**, Helah and Naarah.
4:18 (His Judean **wife** gave birth to Jered the father of Gedor, Heber the
4:19 The sons of Hodiah's **wife**, the sister of Naham: the father of
7: 4 36,000 men ready for battle, for they had many **wives** and children.
7:15 Makir took a **wife** from among the Huppites and Shuppites.
7:16 Makir's **wife** Maacah gave birth to a son and named him Peresh.
7:23 Then he lay with his **wife** again, and she became pregnant
8: 8 to Shaharaim in Moab after he had divorced his **wives** Hushim
8: 9 By his **wife** Hodesh he had Jobab, Zibia, Mesha, Malcam,
8:29 father of Gibeon lived in Gibeon. His **wife's** name was Maacah,
9:35 father of Gibeon lived in Gibeon. His **wife's** name was Maacah,
14: 3 In Jerusalem David took more **wives** and became the father of
16: 3 of dates and a cake of raisins to each Israelite man and **woman**.
2Ch 2:14 [2:13] whose **mother** was from Dan and whose father was from
8:11 "My **wife** must not live in the palace of David king of Israel,
11:18 Rehoboam **married** [+906+4200+4374] Mahalath, who was the
11:21 Maacah daughter of Absalom more than any of his other **wives**
11:21 In all, he had eighteen **wives** and sixty concubines, twenty-eight
11:23 He gave them abundant provisions and took many **wives** for them.
13:21 He married fourteen **wives** and had twenty-two sons and sixteen
15:13 were to be put to death, whether small or great, man or **woman**.
20:13 All the men of Judah, with their **wives** and children and little ones,
21: 6 Ahab had done, for he **married** [+2118+4200] a daughter of Ahab.
21:14 your sons, your **wives** and everything that is yours, with a heavy
21:17 goods found in the king's palace, together with his sons and **wives**.
22:11 the daughter of King Jehoram and **wife** *of* the priest Jehoiada,
24: 3 Jehoiada chose two **wives** for him, and he had sons and daughters.
25:18 '**Give** your daughter to my son **in marriage** [+906+4200+5989].'
28: 8 took captive from their kinsmen two hundred thousand **wives**,
29: 9 and why our sons and daughters and our **wives** are in captivity.
31:18 the **wives**, and the sons and daughters of the whole community
34:22 who was the **wife** *of* Shallum son of Tokhath, the son of Hasrah,
Ezr 2:61 Barzillai (a man who *had* **married** [+4374+4946] a daughter of
10: 1 of Israelites—men, **women** and children—gathered around him.
10: 2 "We have been unfaithful to our God by marrying foreign **women**
10: 3 us make a covenant before our God to send away all these **women**
10:10 you have married foreign **women**, adding to Israel's guilt.
10:11 from the peoples around you and from your foreign **wives**."
10:14 let everyone in our towns who has married a foreign **woman** come
10:17 finished dealing with all the men who had married foreign **women**.
10:18 of the priests, the following had married foreign **women**:
10:19 (They all gave their hands in pledge to put away their **wives**,
10:44 All these had married foreign **women**, and some of them had
10:44 foreign women, and some of them had children by these **wives**.
Ne 4:14 [4:8] your sons and your daughters, your **wives** and your homes."
5: 1 and their **wives** raised a great outcry against their Jewish brothers.
7:63 Barzillai (a man who *had* **married** [+4374+4946] a daughter of
8: 2 which was made up of men and **women** and all who were able to
8: 3 the presence of the men, **women** and others who could understand.
10:28 [10:29] together with their **wives** and all their sons and daughters
12:43 had given them great joy. The **women** and children also rejoiced.
13:23 in those days I saw men of Judah who had married **women** from
13:26 over all Israel, but even he was led into sin by foreign **women**.
13:27 and are being unfaithful to our God by marrying foreign **women**?"
Est 1: 9 Queen Vashti also gave a banquet for the **women** in the royal
1:17 For the queen's conduct will become known to all the **women**,
1:20 all the **women** will respect their husbands, from the least to the
2: 3 these beautiful girls into the **harem** [+1074] at the citadel of Susa.
2: 3 care of Hegai, the king's eunuch, who is in charge of the **women**;
2: 8 and entrusted to Hegai, who had charge of the **harem**.
2: 9 moved her and her maids into the best place in the **harem** [+1074].
2:11 forth near the courtyard of the **harem** [+1074] to find out how
2:12 twelve months of beauty treatments prescribed for the **women**,
2:12 with oil of myrrh and six with perfumes and cosmetics. **[RPH]**
2:13 her to take with her from the **harem** [+1074] to the king's palace.
2:14 in the morning return to another part of the **harem** [+1074] to the
2:15 the king's eunuch who was in charge of the **harem**, suggested.
2:17 king was attracted to Esther more than to any of the other **women**,
3:13 young and old, **women** and little children—on a single day,
4:11 or **woman** who approaches the king in the inner court without
5:10 and went home. Calling together his friends and Zeresh, his **wife**,
5:14 His **wife** Zeresh and all his friends said to him, "Have a gallows
6:13 told Zeresh his **wife** and all his friends everything that had
6:13 His advisers and his **wife** Zeresh said to him, "Since Mordecai,
8:11 or province that might attack them and their **women** and children;
Job 2: 9 His **wife** said to him, "Are you still holding on to your integrity?
14: 1 "Man born of **woman** is of few days and full of trouble.
15:14 "What is man, that he could be pure, or one born of **woman**,
19:17 My breath is offensive to my **wife**; I am loathsome to my own
25: 4 be righteous before God? How can one born of **woman** be pure?
31: 9 "If my heart has been enticed by a **woman**, or if I have lurked at
31:10 may my **wife** grind another man's grain, and may other men sleep
42:15 Nowhere in all the land were there found **women** as beautiful as
Ps 58: 8 [58:9] like a **stillborn child** [+5878], may they not see the sun.
109: 9 May his children be fatherless and his **wife** a widow.
128: 3 Your **wife** will be like a fruitful vine within your house; your sons
Pr 2:16 It will save you also from the **adulteress** [+2424],
5:18 fountain be blessed, and may you rejoice in the **wife** *of* your youth.
6:24 keeping you from the immoral **woman**, from the smooth tongue of
6:26 for the **[NIE]** prostitute reduces you to a loaf of bread,
6:26 loaf of bread, and the **adulteress** [+408] preys upon your very life.
6:29 So is he who sleeps with another man's **wife**; no one who touches
6:32 But a man who commits adultery **[NIE]** lacks judgment;
7: 5 they will keep you from the **adulteress** [+2424], from the wayward
7:10 Then out came a **woman** to meet him, dressed like a prostitute

Pr 9: 13 The **woman** Folly is loud; she is undisciplined and without
11: 16 A kindhearted **woman** gains respect, but ruthless men gain only
11: 22 Like a gold ring in a pig's snout is a beautiful **woman** who shows
12: 4 A **wife** *of* noble character is her husband's crown, but a disgraceful
14: 1 The wise **woman** builds her house, but with her own hands the
18: 22 He who finds a **wife** finds what is good and receives favor from the
19: 13 his father's ruin, and a quarrelsome **wife** is like a constant dripping.
19: 14 are inherited from parents, but a prudent **wife** is from the LORD.
21: 9 on a corner of the roof than share a house with a quarrelsome **wife**.
21: 19 to live in a desert than with a quarrelsome and ill-tempered **wife**.
25: 24 on a corner of the roof than share a house with a quarrelsome **wife**.
27: 15 A quarrelsome **wife** is like a constant dripping on a rainy day;
30: 20 "This is the way of an **[NIE]** adulteress: She eats and wipes her
31: 3 do not spend your strength on **women**, your vigor on those who
31: 10 A **wife** *of* noble character who can find? She is worth far more than
31: 30 is fleeting; but a **woman** who fears the LORD is to be praised.
Ecc 7: 26 I find more bitter than death the **woman** who is a snare, whose
7: 28 among a thousand, but not one ⌊upright⌋ **woman** among them all.
9: 9 Enjoy life with your **wife**, whom you love, all the days of this
SS 1: 8 If you do not know, most beautiful of **women**, follow the tracks of
5: 9 How is your beloved better than others, most beautiful of **women**?
6: 1 Where has your lover gone, most beautiful of **women**? Which way
Isa 3: 12 Youths oppress my people, **women** rule over them. O my people,
4: 1 In that day seven **women** will take hold of one man and say,
13: 16 their eyes; their houses will be looted and their **wives** ravished.
19: 16 In that day the Egyptians will be like **women**. They will shudder
27: 11 they are broken off and **women** come and make fires with them.
32: 9 You **women** who are so complacent, rise up and listen to me;
34: 15 of her wings; there also the falcons will gather, **each** with its mate.
34: 16 None of these will be missing, not **one** will lack her mate.
45: 10 you begotten?' or to his **mother**, 'What have you brought to birth?'
49: 15 "Can a **mother** forget the baby at her breast and have no
54: 6 The LORD will call you back as if you were a **wife** deserted
54: 6 a **wife** *who married* young, only to be rejected," says your God.
Jer 3: 1 "If a man divorces his **wife** and she leaves him and marries another
3: 3 Yet you have the brazen look of a **[NIE]** prostitute; you refuse to
3: 20 like a **woman** unfaithful to her husband, so you have been
5: 8 are well-fed, lusty stallions, each neighing for another man's **wife**.
6: 11 both husband and **wife** will be caught in it, and the old,
6: 12 be turned over to others, together with their fields and their **wives**,
7: 18 the **women** knead the dough and make cakes of bread for the
8: 10 Therefore I will give their **wives** to other men and their fields to
9: 20 [9:19] Now, O **women**, hear the word of the LORD; open your
9: 20 [9:19] your daughters how to wail; teach **one** another a lament.
13: 21 Will not pain grip you like that of a **woman** in labor?
14: 16 There will be no one to bury them or their **wives**, their sons
16: 2 "*You must* not **marry** [+4200+4374] and have sons or daughters
18: 21 Let their **wives** be made childless and widows; let their men be put
29: 6 **Marry** [+4374] and have sons and daughters; find wives for your
29: 6 find **wives** for your sons and give your daughters in marriage,
29: 23 they have committed adultery with their neighbors' **wives** and in
35: 8 Neither we nor our **wives** nor our sons and daughters have ever
38: 22 All the **women** left in the palace of the king of Judah will be
38: 23 "All your **wives** and children will be brought out to the
40: 7 **women** and children who were the poorest in the land and who had
41: 16 **women**, children and court officials he had brought from Gibeon.
43: 6 **women** and children and the king's daughters whom Nebuzaradan
44: 7 on yourselves by cutting off from Judah the men and **women**,
44: 9 by the kings and **queens**[s] of Judah and the wickedness committed
44: 9 and your **wives** in the land of Judah and the streets of Jerusalem?
44: 15 all the men who knew that their **wives** were burning incense to
44: 15 to other gods, along with all the **women** who were present—
44: 20 to all the people, both men and **women**, who were answering him,
44: 24 including the **women**, "Hear the word of the LORD, all you
44: 25 your **wives** have shown by your actions what you promised when
48: 41 of Moab's warriors will be like the heart of a **woman** in labor.
49: 22 of Edom's warriors will be like the heart of a **woman** in labor.
50: 37 They will become **women**. A sword against her treasures!
51: 22 with you I shatter man and **woman**, with you I shatter old man
51: 30 Their strength is exhausted; they have become like **women**.
La 2: 20 Should **women** eat their offspring, the children they have cared
4: 10 With their own hands compassionate **women** have cooked their
5: 11 **Women** have been ravished in Zion, and virgins in the towns of
Eze 1: 9 their wings touched **one** another. Each one went straight ahead;
1: 23 Under the expanse their wings were stretched out **one** toward the
3: 13 of the wings of the living creatures brushing against **each** other
8: 14 and I saw **women** sitting there, mourning for Tammuz.
9: 6 Slaughter old men, young men and maidens, **women** and children,
16: 30 you do all these things, acting like a brazen **[NIE]** prostitute!
16: 32 " 'You adulterous **wife**! You prefer strangers to your own husband!
16: 34 So in your prostitution you are the opposite of **others**[s] [+2021];
16: 41 and inflict punishment on you in the sight of many **women**.
18: 6 He does not defile his neighbor's **wife** or lie with a woman during
18: 6 defile his neighbor's wife or lie with a **woman** during her period.
18: 11 "He eats at the mountain shrines. He defiles his neighbor's **wife**.
18: 15 idols of the house of Israel. He does not defile his neighbor's **wife**.
22: 11 one man commits a detestable offense with his neighbor's **wife**,
23: 2 "Son of man, there were two **women**, daughters of the same
23: 10 She became a byword among **women**, and punishment was
23: 44 As men sleep with a **[NIE]** prostitute, so they slept with those
23: 44 so they slept with those lewd **women**, Oholah and Oholibah.
23: 48 in the land, that all **women** may take warning and not imitate you.
24: 18 to the people in the morning, and in the evening my **wife** died.
33: 26 do detestable things, and each of you defiles his neighbor's **wife**.
44: 22 *They must* not **marry** [+4200+4200+4374] widows or divorced
Da 11: 17 And *he will* **give** him a daughter **in marriage** [+2021+4200+5989]
11: 37 regard for the gods of his fathers or for the one desired by **women**,
Hos 1: 2 take to yourself an adulterous **wife** and children of unfaithfulness,
2: 2 [2:4] "Rebuke your mother, rebuke her, for she is not my **wife**,
3: 1 The LORD said to me, "Go, show your love to your **wife** again,
12: 12 [12:13] Israel served to get a **wife**, and to pay for her he tended
12: 12 [12:13] served to get a wife, and to pay for **her**[s] he tended sheep.
Am 4: 3 You will **each** go straight out through breaks in the wall, and you
7: 17 " 'Your **wife** will become a prostitute in the city, and your sons
Mic 2: 9 You drive the **women** *of* my people from their pleasant homes.
Na 3: 13 Look at your troops—they are all **women**! The gates of your land
Zec 5: 7 the cover of lead was raised, and there in the basket sat a **woman**!
5: 9 there before me were two **women**, with the wind in their wings!
11: 9 perishing perish. Let those who are left eat **one** another's flesh."
12: 12 the clan of the house of David and their **wives**, the clan of the
12: 12 and their wives, the clan of the house of Nathan and their **wives**,
12: 13 the clan of the house of Levi and their **wives**, the clan of Shimei
12: 13 house of Levi and their wives, the clan of Shimei and their **wives**,
12: 14 and all the rest of the clans and their **wives**.
14: 2 city will be captured, the houses ransacked, and the **women** raped.
Mal 2: 14 is acting as the witness between you and the **wife** *of* your youth,
2: 14 though she is your partner, the **wife** *of* your marriage covenant.
2: 15 in your spirit, and do not break faith with the **wife** *of* your youth.

852 אִשֶּׁה *'iššeh*, n.m. [65] [√ 836; Ar 10080]
offering made by fire [38], offerings made by fire [19], made by fire [2], offering by fire [2], sacrifice made by fire [2], offering made by fire [+7933] [1], offerings made with fire [1]

Ex 29: 18 a pleasing aroma, an **offering made** to the LORD **by fire**.
29: 25 aroma to the LORD, an **offering made** to the LORD **by fire**.
29: 41 a pleasing aroma, an **offering made** to the LORD **by fire**.
30: 20 to minister by presenting an **offering made** to the LORD **by fire**,
Lev 1: 9 It is a burnt offering, an **offering made by fire**, an aroma pleasing
1: 13 It is a burnt offering, an **offering made by fire**, an aroma pleasing
1: 17 It is a burnt offering, an **offering made by fire**, an aroma pleasing
2: 2 an **offering made by fire**, an aroma pleasing to the LORD.
2: 3 it is a most holy part of the **offerings made** *to* the LORD **by fire**.
2: 9 grain offering and burn it on the altar as an **offering made by fire**,
2: 10 it is a most holy part of the **offerings made** *to* the LORD **by fire**.
2: 11 any yeast or honey in an **offering made** to the LORD **by fire**.
2: 16 with all the incense, as an **offering made** to the LORD **by fire**.
3: 3 offering he is to bring a **sacrifice made** to the LORD **by fire**:
3: 5 as an **offering made by fire**, an aroma pleasing to the LORD.
3: 9 offering he is to bring a **sacrifice made** to the LORD **by fire**:
3: 11 them on the altar as food, an **offering made** to the LORD **by fire**.
3: 14 what he offers he is to make this **offering** to the LORD **by fire**:
3: 16 on the altar as food, an **offering made by fire**, a pleasing aroma.
4: 35 it on the altar on top of the **offerings made** *to* the LORD **by fire**.
5: 12 it on the altar on top of the **offerings made** *to* the LORD **by fire**.
6: 17 [6:10] given it as their share of the **offerings made** *to* me **by fire**.
6: 18 [6:11] **offerings made** *to* the LORD **by fire** for the generations
7: 5 burn them on the altar as an **offering made** to the LORD **by fire**.
7: 25 who eats the fat of an animal from which an **offering by fire**
7: 30 own hands he is to bring the **offering made** *to* the LORD **by fire**;
7: 35 This is the portion of the **offerings made** *to* the LORD **by fire**
8: 21 a pleasing aroma, an **offering made** to the LORD **by fire**,
8: 28 a pleasing aroma, an **offering made** to the LORD **by fire**.
10: 12 offering left over from the **offerings made** *to* the LORD **by fire**
10: 13 and your sons' share of the **offerings made** *to* the LORD **by fire**;
10: 15 be brought with the fat portions of the **offerings made by fire**,
21: 6 Because they present the **offerings made** *to* the LORD **by fire**,
21: 21 to come near to present the **offerings made** *to* the LORD **by fire**.
22: 22 of these on the altar as an **offering made** to the LORD **by fire**.
22: 27 be acceptable as an **offering made** to the LORD **by fire** [+7933].
23: 8 For seven days present an **offering made** to the LORD **by fire**.
23: 13 an **offering made** to the LORD **by fire**, a pleasing aroma—
23: 18 an **offering made by fire**, an aroma pleasing to the LORD.
23: 25 but present an **offering made** to the LORD **by fire**.' "
23: 27 and present an **offering made** to the LORD **by fire**.
23: 36 For seven days present **offerings made** to the LORD **by fire**,
23: 36 and present an **offering made** to the LORD **by fire**.
23: 37 assemblies for bringing **offerings made** to the LORD **by fire**—

Lev 24: 7 the bread and to be an **offering made** to the LORD **by fire**.
24: 9 their regular share of the **offerings made** *to* the LORD **by fire**."
Nu 15: 3 you present to the LORD **offerings made by fire**, from the herd
15: 10 It will be an **offering made by fire**, an aroma pleasing to the
15: 13 an **offering made by fire** as an aroma pleasing to the LORD.
15: 14 anyone else living among you presents an **offering made by fire**
15: 25 brought to the LORD for their wrong an offering **made by fire**
18: 17 blood on the altar and burn their fat as an **offering made by fire**,
28: 2 me at the appointed time the food for my offerings **made by fire**,
28: 3 'This is the **offering made by fire** that you are to present to the
28: 6 as a pleasing aroma, an **offering made** to the LORD **by fire**.
28: 8 This is an **offering made by fire**, an aroma pleasing to the
28: 13 a pleasing aroma, an **offering made** to the LORD **by fire**.
28: 19 Present to the LORD an **offering made by fire**, a burnt offering
28: 24 In this way prepare the food for the **offering made by fire** every
29: 6 They are **offerings made** to the LORD **by fire**—a pleasing
29: 13 Present an **offering made by fire** as an aroma pleasing to the
29: 36 Present an **offering made by fire** as an aroma pleasing to the
Dt 18: 1 They shall live on the **offerings made** *to* the LORD **by fire**,
Jos 13: 14 since the **offerings made by fire** *to* the LORD, the God of Israel,
1Sa 2: 28 I also gave your father's house all the **offerings made with fire** *by*

853 אֲשׁוּיָה *ʾăšûyâ*, n.f. Not used in NIV/BHS [cf. 859]

854 אֱשׁוּן *ʾᵉšûn*, n.[m.]. [1]

pitch darkness [+3125] [1]

Pr 20: 20 or mother, his lamp will be snuffed out in **pitch darkness** [+3125; K 413].

855 אַשּׁוּר *ʾaššûr*, n.pr.g. & loc. [152 / 151] [√ 894]

Assyria [120], Assyrian [9], Asshur [7], Assyrians [+1201] [5], Assyrians [5], Assyria [+824] [2], *untranslated* [1], Assyria's [1], Shalmaneser[s] [+4889] [1]

Ge 2: 14 of the third river is the Tigris; it runs along the east side of **Asshur**.
10: 11 From that land he went to **Assyria**, where he built Nineveh,
10: 22 The sons of Shem: Elam, **Asshur**, Arphaxad, Lud and Aram.
25: 18 to Shur, near the border of Egypt, as you go toward **Asshur**.
Nu 24: 22 yet you Kenites will be destroyed when **Asshur** takes you captive."
24: 24 they will subdue **Asshur** and Eber, but they too will come to ruin."
2Ki 15: 19 Pul king of **Assyria** invaded the land, and Menahem gave him a
15: 20 contribute fifty shekels of silver to be given to the king of **Assyria**.
15: 20 So the king of **Assyria** withdrew and stayed in the land no longer.
15: 29 Tiglath-Pileser king of **Assyria** came and took Ijon, Abel Beth
15: 29 all the land of Naphtali, and deported the people to **Assyria**.
16: 7 Ahaz sent messengers to say to Tiglath-Pileser king of **Assyria**,
16: 8 of the royal palace and sent it as a gift to the king of **Assyria**.
16: 9 The king of **Assyria** complied by attacking Damascus
16: 9 The king of Assyria complied by attacking **[RPH]** Damascus
16: 10 Ahaz went to Damascus to meet Tiglath-Pileser king of **Assyria**.
16: 18 the temple of the LORD, in deference to the king of **Assyria**.
17: 3 Shalmaneser king of **Assyria** came up to attack Hoshea, who had
17: 4 But the king of **Assyria** discovered that Hoshea was a traitor,
17: 4 he no longer paid tribute to the king of **Assyria**, as he had done
17: 4 Therefore **Shalmaneser**[s] [+4889] seized him and put him in
17: 5 The king of **Assyria** invaded the entire land, marched against
17: 6 the king of **Assyria** captured Samaria and deported the Israelites to
17: 6 of Assyria captured Samaria and deported the Israelites to **Assyria**.
17: 23 of Israel were taken from their homeland into exile in **Assyria**,
17: 24 The king of **Assyria** brought people from Babylon, Cuthah,
17: 26 It was reported to the king of **Assyria**: "The people you deported
17: 27 the king of **Assyria** gave this order: "Have one of the priests you
18: 7 He rebelled against the king of **Assyria** and did not serve him.
18: 9 Shalmaneser king of **Assyria** marched against Samaria and laid
18: 11 The king of **Assyria** deported Israel to Assyria and settled them in
18: 11 The king of Assyria deported Israel to **Assyria** and settled them in
18: 13 Sennacherib king of **Assyria** attacked all the fortified cities of
18: 14 king of Judah sent this message to the king of **Assyria** at Lachish:
18: 14 The king of **Assyria** exacted from Hezekiah king of Judah three
18: 16 of the temple of the LORD, and gave it to the king of **Assyria**.
18: 17 The king of **Assyria** sent his supreme commander, his chief officer
18: 19 " 'This is what the great king, the king of **Assyria**, says:
18: 23 " 'Come now, make a bargain with my master, the king of **Assyria**:
18: 28 in Hebrew: "Hear the word of the great king, the king of **Assyria**!
18: 30 this city will not be given into the hand of the king of **Assyria**.'
18: 31 This is what the king of **Assyria** says: Make peace with me
18: 33 ever delivered his land from the hand of the king of **Assyria**?
19: 4 whom his master, the king of **Assyria**, has sent to ridicule the
19: 6 those words with which the underlings of the king of **Assyria** have
19: 8 When the field commander heard that the king of **Assyria** had left
19: 10 'Jerusalem will not be handed over to the king of **Assyria**.'
19: 11 Surely you have heard what the kings of **Assyria** have done to all
19: 17 that the **Assyrian** kings have laid waste these nations and their
19: 20 I have heard your prayer concerning Sennacherib king of **Assyria**.
19: 32 this is what the LORD says concerning the king of **Assyria**:
19: 35 a hundred and eighty-five thousand men in the **Assyrian** camp.
19: 36 So Sennacherib king of **Assyria** broke camp and withdrew.
20: 6 will deliver you and this city from the hand of the king of **Assyria**.
23: 29 Egypt went up to the Euphrates River to help the king of **Assyria**.
1Ch 1: 17 Elam, **Asshur**, Arphaxad, Lud and Aram. The sons of Aram:
5: 6 his son, whom Tiglath-Pileser king of **Assyria** took into exile.
5: 26 So the God of Israel stirred up the spirit of Pul king of **Assyria**
5: 26 Tiglath-Pileser king of **Assyria**), who took the Reubenites,
2Ch 28: 16 At that time King Ahaz sent to the king of **Assyria** for help.
28: 20 Tiglath-Pileser king of **Assyria** came to him, but he gave him
28: 21 and from the princes and presented them to the king of **Assyria**,
30: 6 are left, who have escaped from the hand of the kings of **Assyria**.
32: 1 Sennacherib king of **Assyria** came and invaded Judah.
32: 4 "Why should the kings of **Assyria** come and find plenty of water?'
32: 7 Do not be afraid or discouraged because of the king of **Assyria**
32: 9 when Sennacherib king of **Assyria** and all his forces were laying
32: 10 "This is what Sennacherib king of **Assyria** says: On what are you
32: 11 our God will save us from the hand of the king of **Assyria**,'
32: 21 and the leaders and officers in the camp of the **Assyrian** king.
32: 22 people of Jerusalem from the hand of Sennacherib king of **Assyria**
33: 11 brought against them the army commanders of the king of **Assyria**,
Ezr 4: 2 sacrificing to him since the time of Esarhaddon king of **Assyria**,
6: 22 them with joy by changing the attitude of the king of **Assyria**,
Ne 9: 32 all your people, from the days of the kings of **Assyria** until today.
Ps 83: 8 [83:9] Even **Assyria** has joined them to lend strength to the
Isa 7: 17 broke away from Judah—he will bring the king of **Assyria**."
7: 18 the distant streams of Egypt and for bees from the land of **Assyria**.
7: 20 the king of **Assyria**—to shave your head and the hair of your legs,
8: 4 the plunder of Samaria will be carried off by the king of **Assyria**."
8: 7 floodwaters of the River—the king of **Assyria** with all his pomp.
10: 5 "Woe to the **Assyrian**, the rod of my anger, in whose hand is the
10: 12 "I will punish the king of **Assyria** for the willful pride of his heart
10: 24 do not be afraid of the **Assyrians**, who beat you with a rod
11: 11 time to reclaim the remnant that is left of his people from **Assyria**,
11: 16 a highway for the remnant of his people that is left from **Assyria**,
14: 25 I will crush the **Assyrian** in my land; on my mountains I will
19: 23 In that day there will be a highway from Egypt to **Assyria**.
19: 23 The **Assyrians** will go to Egypt and the Egyptians to Assyria.
19: 23 The Assyrians will go to Egypt and the Egyptians to **Assyria**.
19: 23 to Assyria. The Egyptians and **Assyrians** will worship together.
19: 24 be the third, along with Egypt and **Assyria**, a blessing on the earth.
19: 25 my people, **Assyria** my handiwork, and Israel my inheritance."
20: 1 sent by Sargon king of **Assyria**, came to Ashdod and attacked
20: 4 so the king of **Assyria** will lead away stripped and barefoot the
20: 6 those we fled to for help and deliverance from the king of **Assyria**!
23: 13 The **Assyrians** have made it a place for desert creatures;
27: 13 Those who were perishing in **Assyria** [+824] and those who were
30: 31 The voice of the LORD will shatter **Assyria**; with his scepter he
31: 8 "**Assyria** will fall by a sword that is not of man; a sword, not of
36: 1 Sennacherib king of **Assyria** attacked all the fortified cities of
36: 2 the king of **Assyria** sent his field commander with a large army
36: 4 " 'This is what the great king, the king of **Assyria**, says:
36: 8 " 'Come now, make a bargain with my master, the king of **Assyria**:
36: 13 in Hebrew, "Hear the words of the great king, the king of **Assyria**!
36: 15 this city will not be given into the hand of the king of **Assyria**.'
36: 16 This is what the king of **Assyria** says: Make peace with me
36: 18 ever delivered his land from the hand of the king of **Assyria**?
37: 4 whom his master, the king of **Assyria**, has sent to ridicule the
37: 6 those words with which the underlings of the king of **Assyria** have
37: 8 When the field commander heard that the king of **Assyria** had left
37: 10 'Jerusalem will not be handed over to the king of **Assyria**.'
37: 11 Surely you have heard what the kings of **Assyria** have done to all
37: 18 that the **Assyrian** kings have laid waste all these peoples and their
37: 21 you have prayed to me concerning Sennacherib king of **Assyria**,
37: 33 this is what the LORD says concerning the king of **Assyria**:
37: 36 a hundred and eighty-five thousand men in the **Assyrian** camp.
37: 37 So Sennacherib king of **Assyria** broke camp and withdrew.
38: 6 will deliver you and this city from the hand of the king of **Assyria**.
52: 4 went down to Egypt to live; lately, **Assyria** has oppressed them.
Jer 2: 18 the Shihor? And why go to **Assyria** to drink water from the River?
2: 36 You will be disappointed by Egypt as you were by **Assyria**.
50: 17 The first to devour him was the king of **Assyria**; the last to crush
50: 18 the king of Babylon and his land as I punished the king of **Assyria**.
La 5: 6 We submitted to Egypt and **Assyria** to get enough bread.
Eze 16: 28 You engaged in prostitution with the **Assyrians** [+1201] too,
23: 5 still mine; and she lusted after her lovers, the **Assyrians**—warriors
23: 7 gave herself as a prostitute to all the elite of the **Assyrians** [+1201]
23: 9 over to her lovers, the **Assyrians** [+1201], for whom she lusted.
23: 12 She too lusted after the **Assyrians** [+1201]—governors
23: 23 and Shoa and Koa, and all the **Assyrians** [+1201] with them,
27: 6 of cypress **wood** [BHS *the daughter of Assyria*; NIV 9309] from
27: 23 and merchants of Sheba, **Asshur** and Kilmad traded with you.

Eze 31: 3 Consider **Assyria**, once a cedar in Lebanon, with beautiful
32: 22 "**Assyria** is there with her whole army; she is surrounded by the
Hos 5: 13 his sickness, and Judah his sores, then Ephraim turned to **Assyria**,
7: 11 and senseless—now calling to Egypt, now turning to **Assyria**.
8: 9 For they have gone up to **Assyria** like a wild donkey wandering
9: 3 Ephraim will return to Egypt and eat unclean food in **Assyria**.
10: 6 It will be carried to **Assyria** as tribute for the great king.
11: 5 "Will they not return to Egypt and will not **Assyria** rule over them
11: 11 trembling like birds from Egypt, like doves from **Assyria** [+824].
12: 1 [12:2] He makes a treaty with **Assyria** and sends olive oil to
14: 3 [14:4] **Assyria** cannot save us; we will not mount war-horses. We
Mic 5: 5 [5:4] When the **Assyrian** invades our land and marches through
5: 6 [5:5] They will rule the land of **Assyria** with the sword, the land
5: 6 [5:5] He will deliver us from the **Assyrian** when he invades our
7: 12 In that day people will come to you from **Assyria** and the cities of
Na 3: 18 O king of **Assyria**, your shepherds slumber; your nobles lie down
Zep 2: 13 He will stretch out his hand against the north and destroy **Assyria**,
Zec 10: 10 I will bring them back from Egypt and gather them from **Assyria**.
10: 11 **Assyria's** pride will be brought down and Egypt's scepter will pass

856 אֲשׁוּרִי *ᵃšûrî*, a.g. [1]

Ashuri [1]

2Sa 2: 9 **Ashuri** and Jezreel, and also over Ephraim, Benjamin and all

857 אַשּׁוּרִם *aššûrim*, n.pr.g.pl. [1]

Asshurites [1]

Ge 25: 3 the descendants of Dedan were the **Asshurites**, the Letushites

858 אַשְׁחוּר *'ašḥûr*, n.pr.m. [2]

Ashhur [2]

1Ch 2: 24 Abijah the wife of Hezron bore him **Ashhur** the father of Tekoa.
4: 5 **Ashhur** the father of Tekoa had two wives, Helah and Naarah.

859 אֹשְׁיָה *'ošyâ*, n.f. [1] [cf. 853]

towers [1]

Jer 50: 15 She surrenders, her **towers** fall, her walls are torn down.

860 אֲשִׁימָא *ᵃšîmā'*, n.pr.[m.]. [1]

Ashima [1]

2Ki 17: 30 Cuthah made Nergal, and the men from Hamath made **Ashima**;

861 אָשִׁישׁ *'āšîš*, n.m. [1]

men [1]

Isa 16: 7 together for Moab. Lament and grieve for the **men** *of* Kir Hareseth.

862 אֲשִׁישָׁה *ᵃšîšâ*, n.f. [4] [√ 899?]

cake of raisins [2], raisins [1], sacred cakes [1]

2Sa 6: 19 a **cake of raisins** to each person in the whole crowd of Israelites,
1Ch 16: 3 of dates and a **cake of raisins** to each Israelite man and woman.
SS 2: 5 Strengthen me with **raisins**, refresh me with apples, for I am faint
Hos 3: 1 though they turn to other gods and love the **sacred** raisin **cakes**."

863 אֶשֶׁךְ *'ešek*, n.[m.]. [1]

testicles [1]

Lev 21: 20 or who has festering or running sores or damaged **testicles**.

864 ¹אֶשְׁכּוֹל *'eškôl¹*, n.m. [9] [→ 865, 866; cf. 8897]

cluster of grapes [3], clusters [3], cluster [2], clusters of fruit [1]

Ge 40: 10 as it budded, it blossomed, and its **clusters** ripened into grapes.
Nu 13: 23 of Eshcol, they cut off a branch bearing a single **cluster** *of* grapes.
13: 24 because of the **cluster of grapes** the Israelites cut off there.
Dt 32: 32 grapes are filled with poison, and their **clusters** *with* bitterness.
SS 1: 14 My lover is to me a **cluster** *of* henna blossoms from the vineyards
7: 7 [7:8] like that of the palm, and your breasts like **clusters of fruit**.
7: 8 [7:9] May your breasts be like the **clusters** *of* the vine,
Isa 65: 8 "As when juice is still found in a **cluster of grapes** and men say,
Mic 7: 1 there is no **cluster of grapes** to eat, none of the early figs that I

865 ²אֶשְׁכּוֹל *'eškôl²*, n.pr.loc. [4] [√ 864]

Eshcol [4]

Nu 13: 23 When they reached the Valley of **Eshcol**, they cut off a branch
13: 24 That place was called the Valley of **Eshcol** because of the cluster
32: 9 After they went up to the Valley of **Eshcol** and viewed the land,
Dt 1: 24 the hill country, and came to the Valley of **Eshcol** and explored it.

866 ³אֶשְׁכֹּל *'eškōl³*, n.pr.m. [2] [√ 864]

Eshcol [2]

Ge 14: 13 a brother of **Eshcol** and Aner, all of whom were allied with Abram.
14: 24 to the men who went with me—to Aner, **Eshcol** and Mamre.

867 אַשְׁכְּנַז *'aškᵉnaz*, n.pr.m. [3]

Ashkenaz [3]

Ge 10: 3 The sons of Gomer: **Ashkenaz**, Riphath and Togarmah.
1Ch 1: 6 The sons of Gomer: **Ashkenaz**, Riphath and Togarmah.
Jer 51: 27 Ararat, Minni and **Ashkenaz**. Appoint a commander against her;

868 אֶשְׁכָּר *'eškār*, n.[m.]. [2]

gifts [1], paid [+8740] [1]

Ps 72: 10 tribute to him; the kings of Sheba and Seba will present him **gifts**.
Eze 27: 15 coastlands were your customers; *they* **paid** [+8740] you *with*

869 אֶשֶׁל *'ešel*, n.m. [3]

tamarisk tree [3]

Ge 21: 33 Abraham planted a **tamarisk tree** in Beersheba, and there he
1Sa 22: 6 in hand, was seated under the **tamarisk tree** on the hill at Gibeah,
31: 13 took their bones and buried them under a **tamarisk tree** at Jabesh,

870 אָשַׁם *'āšam*, v. [35] [→ 871, 872, 873]

guilty [15], bear guilt [3], condemned [2], guilty of wrongdoing [+870] [2], sin [2], very guilty [+870] [2], admit guilt [1], declare guilty [1], devastated [1], held guilty [1], innocent [1], pay for it [1], suffering [1], unpunished [+4202] [1], wronged [1]

Lev 4: 13 [A] the community is unaware of the matter, *they are* **guilty**.
4: 22 [A] in any of the commands of the LORD his God, *he is* **guilty**.
4: 27 [A] is forbidden in any of the LORD's commands, *he is* **guilty**.
5: 2 [A] he is unaware of it, he has become unclean and *is* **guilty**.
5: 3 [A] he is unaware of it, when he learns of it *he will be* **guilty**.
5: 4 [A] of it, in any case when he learns of it *he will be* **guilty**.
5: 5 [A] " 'When *anyone is* **guilty** in any of these ways, he must
5: 17 [A] he does not know it, *he is* **guilty** and will be held responsible.
5: 19 [A] *he has been* **guilty** [+870] **of wrongdoing** against the
5: 19 [A] *he has been* **guilty of wrongdoing** [+870] against the
6: 4 [5:23] [A] when he thus sins and *becomes* **guilty**, he must
Nu 5: 6 [A] and so is unfaithful to the LORD, that person *is* **guilty**
5: 7 [A] one fifth to it and give it all to the person *he has* **wronged**.
Jdg 21: 22 [A] *you are* **innocent**, since you did not give your daughters to
2Ch 19: 10 [A] you are to warn them not *to* **sin** against the LORD;
19: 10 [A] come on you and your brothers. Do this, and *you will* not **sin**.
Ps 5: 10 [5:11] [G] **Declare** them **guilty**, O God! Let their intrigues be
34: 21 [34:22] [A] the foes of the righteous *will be* **condemned**.
34: 22 [34:23] [A] no one *will be* **condemned** who takes refuge in him.
Pr 30: 10 [A] to his master, or he will curse you, and *you will* **pay for it**.
Isa 24: 6 [A] a curse consumes the earth; its people *must* **bear** *their* **guilt**.
Jer 2: 3 [A] all who devoured her *were* **held guilty**, and disaster overtook
50: 7 [A] their enemies said, '*We are* not **guilty**, for they sinned
Eze 6: 6 [A] so that your altars will be laid waste and **devastated**, your
22: 4 [A] *you have become* **guilty** because of the blood you have shed
25: 12 [A] house of Judah and *became* **very guilty** [+870] by doing so,
25: 12 [A] house of Judah and *became* **very guilty** [+870] by doing so,
Hos 4: 15 [A] you commit adultery, O Israel, *let* not Judah *become* **guilty**.
5: 15 [A] Then I will go back to my place until *they* **admit** *their* **guilt**.
10: 2 [A] Their heart is deceitful, and now *they must* **bear** *their* **guilt**.
13: 1 [A] in Israel. But *he became* **guilty** of Baal worship and died.
13: 16 [14:1] [A] The people of Samaria *must* **bear** *their* **guilt**,
Joel 1: 18 [C] they have no pasture; even the flocks of sheep *are* **suffering**.
Hab 1: 11 [A] and go on—**guilty** *men*, whose own strength is their god."
Zec 11: 5 [A] Their buyers slaughter them and *go* **unpunished** [+4202].

871 אָשָׁם *'āšām*, n.m. [46 / 47] [√ 870]

guilt offering [29], guilt offerings [5], penalty [4], guilt [2], wrong [2], *untranslated* [1], its[s] [+2021] [1], making amends for sin [1], restitution [+8740] [1], sins [1]

Ge 26: 10 slept with your wife, and you would have brought **guilt** upon us."
Lev 5: 6 and, as a **penalty** for the sin he has committed, he must bring to the
5: 7 or two young pigeons to the LORD as a **penalty** *for* his sin—
5: 15 he is to bring to the LORD as a **penalty** a ram from the flock,
5: 15 in silver, according to the sanctuary shekel. It is a **guilt offering**.
5: 16 who will make atonement for him with the ram as a **guilt offering**,
5: 18 He is to bring to the priest as a **guilt offering** a ram from the flock,
5: 19 It is a **guilt offering**; he has been guilty of wrongdoing against the
6: 6 [5:25] as a **penalty** he must bring to the priest, that is, to the
6: 6 [5:25] that is, to the LORD, his **guilt offering**, a ram from the
6: 17 [6:10] Like the sin offering and the **guilt offering**, it is most holy.
7: 1 " 'These are the regulations for the **guilt offering**, which is most

Lev 7: 2 The **guilt offering** is to be slaughtered in the place where the burnt
7: 5 as an offering made to the LORD by fire. It is a **guilt offering**.
7: 7 same law applies to both the sin offering and the **guilt offering**:
7: 37 the grain offering, the sin offering, the **guilt offering**, the
14: 12 is to take one of the male lambs and offer it as a **guilt offering**,
14: 13 Like the sin offering, the **guilt offering** belongs to the priest;
14: 14 The priest is to take some of the blood of the **guilt offering**
14: 17 big toe of his right foot, on top of the blood of the **guilt offering**.
14: 21 he must take one male lamb as a **guilt offering** to be waved to
14: 24 The priest is to take the lamb for the **guilt offering**, together with
14: 25 He shall slaughter the lamb for the **guilt offering** and take some of
14: 25 the lamb for the guilt offering and take some of **its**[*] [+2021] blood
14: 28 is to put on the same places he put the blood of the **guilt offering**—
19: 21 must bring a ram **[RPH]** to the entrance to the Tent of Meeting
19: 21 entrance to the Tent of Meeting for a **guilt offering** to the LORD.
19: 22 With the ram of the **guilt offering** the priest is to make atonement
Nu 5: 7 He must make full restitution for his **wrong**, add one fifth to it
5: 8 no close relative to whom restitution can be made for the **wrong**,
5: 8 the **restitution** [+8740] belongs to the LORD and must be given
6: 12 and must bring a year-old male lamb as a **guilt offering**.
18: 9 whether grain or sin or **guilt offerings**, that part belongs to you
1Sa 6: 3 send it away empty, but by all means send a **guilt offering** to him.
6: 4 Philistines asked, "What **guilt offering** should we send to him?"
6: 8 the gold objects you are sending back to him as a **guilt offering**.
6: 17 These are the gold tumors the Philistines sent as a **guilt offering** to
2Ki 12: 16 [12:17] The money from the **guilt offerings** and sin offerings was
Ezr 10: 19 presented a ram from the flock as a **guilt** [BHS 872] **offering**.)
Ps 68: 21 [68:22] the hairy crowns of those who go on in their **sins**.
Pr 14: 9 Fools mock at **making amends for sin**, but goodwill is found
Isa 53: 10 to suffer, and though the LORD makes his life a **guilt offering**,
Jer 51: 5 though their land is full of **guilt** before the Holy One of Israel.
Eze 40: 39 burnt offerings, sin offerings and **guilt offerings** were slaughtered.
42: 13 the grain offerings, the sin offerings and the **guilt offerings**—
44: 29 eat the grain offerings, the sin offerings and the **guilt offerings**;
46: 20 "This is the place where the priests will cook the **guilt offering**

872 אָשֵׁם 'āšēm, a. [3 / 2] [√ 870]

convict [1], punished [1]

Ge 42: 21 "Surely we are being **punished** because of our brother.
2Sa 14: 13 When the king says this, does he not **convict** himself, for the king
Ezr 10: 19 a ram from the flock as a guilt **offering**.) [BHS *guilty*; NIV 871]

873 אַשְׁמָה 'ašmâ, n.f. [19] [√ 870]

guilt [13], guilty [2], guilt offering [1], guilty of sins [1], requiring payment [1], shame [1]

Lev 4: 3 " 'If the anointed priest sins, bringing **guilt** *on* the people,
6: 5 [5:24] it all to the owner on the day he presents his **guilt offering**.
6: 7 [5:26] for any of these things he did that made him **guilty**."
22: 16 sacred offerings and so bring upon them guilt **requiring payment**.
1Ch 21: 3 my lord want to do this? Why should he bring **guilt** on Israel?"
2Ch 24: 18 Because of their **guilt**, God's anger came upon Judah
28: 10 But aren't you also **guilty of sins** against the LORD your God?
28: 13 they said, "or we will be **guilty** *before* the LORD.
28: 13 Do you intend to add to our sin and **guilt**? For our guilt is already
28: 13 For our **guilt** is already great, and his fierce anger rests on Israel."
33: 23 not humble himself before the LORD; Amon increased his **guilt**.
Ezr 9: 6 are higher than our heads and our **guilt** has reached to the heavens.
9: 7 the days of our forefathers until now, our **guilt** has been great.
9: 13 has happened to us is a result of our evil deeds and our great **guilt**,
9: 15 Here we are before you in our **guilt**, though because of it not one
10: 10 you have married foreign women, adding to Israel's **guilt**.
10: 19 for their **guilt** they each presented a ram from the flock as a guilt
Ps 69: 5 [69:6] know my folly, O God; my **guilt** is not hidden from you.
Am 8: 14 They who swear by the **shame** *of* Samaria, or say, 'As surely as

874 אַשְׁמוּרָה 'ašmûrâ, n.f. [7] [√ 9068]

watches of the night [3], watch [2], last watch of the night [+1332] [1], last watch of the night [+1332+2021] [1]

Ex 14: 24 During the **last watch** [+1332] **of the night** the LORD looked
Jdg 7: 19 reached the edge of the camp at the beginning of the middle **watch**,
1Sa 11: 11 during the **last watch** [+1332+2021] **of the night** they broke into
Ps 63: 6 [63:7] I think of you through the **watches of the night**.
90: 4 are like a day that has just gone by, or like a **watch** in the night.
119: 148 My eyes stay open through the **watches of the night**, that I may
La 2: 19 Arise, cry out in the night, as the **watches of the night** begin;

875 אַשְׁמָן 'ašmān, n.[m.]pl. [1] [√ 9043?]

strong [1]

Isa 59: 10 as if it were twilight; among the **strong**, we are like the dead.

876 אֶשְׁנָב 'ešnāb, n.[m.]. [2] [√ 5959]

lattice [2]

Jdg 5: 28 behind the **lattice** she cried out, 'Why is his chariot so long in
Pr 7: 6 At the window of my house I looked out through the **lattice**.

877 אַשְׁנָה 'ašnâ, n.pr.loc. [2]

Ashnah [2]

Jos 15: 33 In the western foothills: Eshtaol, Zorah, **Ashnah**,
15: 43 Iphtah, **Ashnah**, Nezib,

878 אֶשְׁעָן 'eš'ān, n.pr.loc. [1]

Eshan [1]

Jos 15: 52 Arab, Dumah, **Eshan**,

879 אַשָּׁף 'aššāp, n.m. [2] [→ Ar 10081]

enchanters [2]

Da 1: 20 than all the magicians and **enchanters** in his whole kingdom.
2: 2 **enchanters**, sorcerers and astrologers to tell him what he had

880 אַשְׁפָּה 'ašpâ, n.f. [6]

quiver [5], quivers [1]

Job 39: 23 The **quiver** rattles against his side, along with the flashing spear
Ps 127: 5 Blessed is the man whose **quiver** is full of them. They will not be
Isa 22: 6 Elam takes up the **quiver**, with her charioteers and horses;
49: 2 he made me into a polished arrow and concealed me in his **quiver**.
Jer 5: 16 Their **quivers** are like an open grave; all of them are mighty
La 3: 13 He pierced my heart with arrows from his **quiver**.

881 אַשְׁפְּנַז 'ašpᵉnaz, n.pr.m. [1]

Ashpenaz [1]

Da 1: 3 Then the king ordered **Ashpenaz**, chief of his court officials,

882 אֶשְׁפָּר 'ešpār, n.m. [2] [√ 8795]

cake of dates [2]

2Sa 6: 19 a **cake of dates** and a cake of raisins to each person in the whole
1Ch 16: 3 a **cake of dates** and a cake of raisins to each Israelite man

883 אַשְׁפֹּת 'ašpōt, n.[m.]. [7] [√ 9189]

dung [4], ash heap [2], ash heaps [1]

1Sa 2: 8 raises the poor from the dust and lifts the needy from the **ash heap**;
Ne 2: 13 the Valley Gate toward the Jackal Well and the **Dung** Gate,
3: 13 repaired five hundred yards of the wall as far as the **Dung** Gate.
3: 14 The **Dung** Gate was repaired by Malkijah son of Recab, ruler of
12: 31 to proceed on top of the wall to the right, toward the **Dung** Gate.
Ps 113: 7 raises the poor from the dust and lifts the needy from the **ash heap**;
La 4: 5 in the streets. Those nurtured in purple now lie on **ash heaps**.

884 אַשְׁקְלוֹן 'ašqᵉlôn, n.pr.loc. [12] [→ 885]

Ashkelon [12]

Jdg 1: 18 The men of Judah also took Gaza, **Ashkelon** and Ekron—
14: 19 He went down to **Ashkelon**, struck down thirty of their men,
1Sa 6: 17 one each for Ashdod, Gaza, **Ashkelon**, Gath and Ekron.
2Sa 1: 20 "Tell it not in Gath, proclaim it not in the streets of **Ashkelon**,
Jer 25: 20 all the kings of the Philistines (those of **Ashkelon**, Gaza, Ekron,
47: 5 Gaza will shave her head in mourning; **Ashkelon** will be silenced.
47: 7 when he has ordered it to attack **Ashkelon** and the coast?"
Am 1: 8 the king of Ashdod and the one who holds the scepter in **Ashkelon**.
Zep 2: 4 Gaza will be abandoned and **Ashkelon** left in ruins. At midday
2: 7 In the evening they will lie down in the houses of **Ashkelon**.
Zec 9: 5 **Ashkelon** will see it and fear; Gaza will writhe in agony, and
9: 5 will wither. Gaza will lose her king and **Ashkelon** will be deserted.

885 אֶשְׁקְלוֹנִי 'ešqᵉlônî, a.g. [1] [√ 884]

Ashkelon [1]

Jos 13: 3 Philistine rulers in Gaza, Ashdod, **Ashkelon**, Gath and Ekron—

886 אָשַׁר¹ 'āšar¹, v. [6] [→ 892, 893]

walk [2], are guided [1], guide [1], guides [1], keep right [1]

Pr 4: 14 [D] on the path of the wicked or **walk** in the way of evil men.
9: 6 [A] and you will live; **walk** in the way of understanding.
23: 19 [D] my son, and be wise, and **keep** your heart on the **right** path.
Isa 3: 12 [D] O my people, your **guides** lead you astray; they turn you
9: 16 [9:15] [D] *Those who* **guide** this people mislead them,
9: 16 [9:15] [E] and *those who* **are guided** are led astray.

887 ²אָשַׁר ***'āšar²***, v. [10] [→ 888, 890, 891, 896, 897]

call blessed [4], be blessed [1], bless [1], call happy [1], called blessed [1], encourage [1], spoke well of [1]

Ge 30: 13 [D] "How happy I am! The women *will* **call** me **happy**."
Job 29: 11 [D] Whoever heard me **spoke well of** me, and those who saw me
Ps 41: 2 [41:3] [E] he *will* **bless** *him* in the land and not surrender him to
72: 17 [D] will be blessed through him, and *they will* **call** him **blessed**.
Pr 3: 18 [E] who embrace her; those who lay hold of her *will* **be blessed**.
31: 28 [D] Her children arise and **call** her **blessed**; her husband also,
SS 6: 9 [D] The maidens saw her and **called** her **blessed**; the queens
Isa 1: 17 [D] learn to do right! Seek justice, **encourage** the oppressed.
Mal 3: 12 [D] "Then all the nations *will* **call** you **blessed**, for yours will be
3: 15 [D] now we **call** the arrogant **blessed**. Certainly the evildoers

888 אָשֵׁר ***'āšēr***, n.pr.m. [43] [√ 896; cf. 887]

Asher [37], Asher [+1201] [5], Asher's [+4946] [1]

Ge 30: 13 The women will call me happy." So she named him **Asher**.
35: 26 Gad and **Asher**. These were the sons of Jacob, who were born to
46: 17 The sons of **Asher**: Imnah, Ishvah, Ishvi and Beriah. Their sister
49: 20 "**Asher's** [+4946] food will be rich; he will provide delicacies fit
Ex 1: 4 Dan and Naphtali; Gad and **Asher**.
Nu 1: 13 from **Asher**, Pagiel son of Ocran;
1: 40 From the descendants of **Asher**: All the men twenty years old
1: 41 The number from the tribe of **Asher** was 41,500.
2: 27 The tribe of **Asher** will camp next to them. The leader of the
2: 27 to them. The leader of the people of **Asher** is Pagiel son of Ocran.
7: 72 of Ocran, the leader of the people of **Asher**, brought his offering.
10: 26 son of Ocran was over the division of the tribe of **Asher** [+1201],
13: 13 from the tribe of **Asher**, Sethur son of Michael;
26: 44 The descendants of **Asher** by their clans were: through Imnah,
26: 46 (**Asher** had a daughter named Serah.)
26: 47 These were the clans of **Asher** [+1201]; those numbered were
34: 27 son of Shelomi, the leader from the tribe of **Asher** [+1201];
Dt 27: 13 Reuben, Gad, **Asher**, Zebulun, Dan and Naphtali.
33: 24 About **Asher** he said: "Most blessed of sons is Asher; let him be
33: 24 "Most blessed of sons is **Asher**; let him be favored by his brothers,
Jos 17: 7 The territory of Manasseh extended from **Asher** to Micmethath
17: 10 and bordered **Asher** on the north and Issachar on the east.
17: 11 Within Issachar and **Asher**, Manasseh also had Beth Shan,
19: 24 The fifth lot came out for the tribe of **Asher** [+1201], clan by clan.
19: 31 their villages were the inheritance of the tribe of **Asher** [+1201],
19: 34 on the south, **Asher** on the west and the Jordan on the east.
21: 6 **Asher**, Naphtali and the half-tribe of Manasseh in Bashan.
21: 30 from the tribe of **Asher**, Mishal, Abdon,
Jdg 1: 31 Nor did **Asher** drive out those living in Acco or Sidon or Ahlab
5: 17 by the ships? **Asher** remained on the coast and stayed in his coves.
6: 35 calling them to arms, and also into **Asher**, Zebulun and Naphtali,
7: 23 Israelites from Naphtali, **Asher** and all Manasseh were called out,
1Ki 4: 16 Baana son of Hushai—in **Asher** and in Aloth;
1Ch 2: 2 Dan, Joseph, Benjamin, Naphtali, Gad and **Asher**.
6: 62 [6:47] towns from the tribes of Issachar, **Asher** and Naphtali,
6: 74 [6:59] from the tribe of **Asher** they received Mashal, Abdon,
7: 30 The sons of **Asher**: Imnah, Ishvah, Ishvi and Beriah. Their sister
7: 40 All these were descendants of **Asher**—heads of families, choice
12: 36 [12:37] men of **Asher**, experienced soldiers prepared for battle—
2Ch 30: 11 some men of **Asher**, Manasseh and Zebulun humbled themselves
Eze 48: 2 "**Asher** will have one portion; it will border the territory of Dan
48: 3 one portion; it will border the territory of **Asher** from east to west.
48: 34 the gate of Gad, the gate of **Asher** and the gate of Naphtali.

889 אֲשֶׁר ***'ªšer***, pt.rel. [5500 / 5496] [→ 948, 3876, 4424]

untranslated [2614], that [538], who [527], as [+3869] [271], which [222], what [178], whom [120], where [79], just as [+3869] [58], whose [42], those [41], when [41], when [+3869] [38], until [+6330] [30], whatever [+3972] [30], because [28], for [28], how [28], just as [+3869+3972] [24], because [+3610] [21], as [18], what [+3869] [18], whatever [18], just as [+3869+4027] [17], after [+3869] [14], because [+6584] [14], if [13], as [+3869+4027] [12], like [+3869] [12], so that [11], the one[s] [10], wherever [+928+3972] [10], though [8], administrator[s] [+6584] [7], whatever [+3869] [7], anyone [6], because [+9393] [6], he[s] [6], so [6], them[s] [6], because [+3869] [5], since [5], whatever [+3869+3972] [5], as [+3869+3972] [4], him[s] [4], of [4], something [4], the covenant[s] [4], things [4], whoever [4], at [3], because [+6813] [3], before [+4202+6330] [3], for [+3610] [3], for [+9393] [3], if [+3869] [3], just as [3], since [+3610] [3], territory[s] [3], the land[s] [3], these [3], this [3], wherever [+448+3972] [3], wherever [+928+2006+2021] [3], wherever [+928+5226] [3], although [2], as much as [+3869] [2], as soon as [+3869] [2], because [+928] [2], even as [+3869] [2], even though [2], exactly as [+3869+4027] [2], here [2], how much [2], it[s] [2], just the way [+3869] [2], just what [+3869+4027] [2], one[s] [2], others[s] [2], peoples[s] [2], sometimes [+3780] [2], such [2], the creatures[s] [2], the day[s] [2], the man[s] [2], the men[s] [2], the name[s] [2], the ones[s] [2], the property[s] [2], the steward[s] [+6584] [2], the way[s] [2], the ways[s] [2], there [2], they[s] [2], until [+561+6330] [2], what [+3869+4027] [2], whatever [+3869+4027] [2], where [+928] [2], wherever [+928+2021+3972+5226] [2], wherever [2], whoever [+408] [2], whoever [+4769] [2], with [2], abundantly [+3907+6330+6330] [1], according to [+3869] [1], according to [1], although [+928+3972] [1], any [1], anything [+3972] [1], as [+928] [1], as [+928+3972] [1], as easily as [+3869] [1], as long as [+3869] [1], as soon as [1], as though [+3869] [1], because [+3869+7023] [1], because [+4946] [1], because of [+3869] [1], but [1], by [1], cargo [+641+928+2021+3998] [1], closest friend [+3869+3870+5883 +8276] [1], covenant[s] [1], creature[s] [1], creatures[s] [1], crowd [+3972+6641] [1], disaster[s] [1], do not know where am going [+2143+2143+6584] [1], edict[s] [1], else[s] [1], everything else [1], exactly as [+3869+3972] [1], exactly like [+3869+3972+4027] [1], except [+4202] [1], finally [+6330] [1], followers [+339+2021+6639] [1], followers [+408+2143+6640] [1], for [+6584] [1], for [+928] [1], from [+928] [1], gods[s] [1], governor[s] [+6584] [1], have [+4200] [1], houses[s] [1], if only [+3869] [1], in accordance with [+3869] [1], in accordance with [+3972] [1], in proportion to [+3869+5002] [1], in the end [+6330] [1], in [1], including [1], instead of [+9393] [1], it [1], just as [+3869+3972+4027] [1], just as [+3972+4200] [1], just what [+3869] [1], keeper[s] [+6584] [1], kind [+3869] [1], lest [+4202] [1], life [+2118+3427] [1], like [+3869+3972] [1], like [+3869+4027] [1], like [1], living thing[s] [1], make countless [+906+906+4202+6218+8049] [1], man[s] [1], matter[s] [1], men[s] [1], mission [+1821+8938] [1], more [+3869] [1], moving from place to place [+928+2143+2143] [1], my people[s] [1], no sooner than [+3869] [1], nothing [+3972+4202] [1], now that [+3869] [1], one [1], or [+4202] [1], or [1], other[s] [+907] [1], otherwise [+4200+4202+5100] [1], people[s] [+928+3972] [1], place[s] [1], possessions[s] [1], predecessor [+2118+4200+7156] [1], proper place [+2118+5226+9004] [1], property[s] [+2118+4200] [1], property[s] [1], replies[s] [1], responsible for [+928+4200] [1], robe[s] [1], same [+3869] [1], same as [1], share [+3869+4200] [1], shared hardships [+928+6700+6700] [1], she[s] [1], since [+339] [1], since [+4946] [1], since [+928] [1], since [+9393] [1], so [+3869] [1], so that [+3610] [1], so with [+3869] [1], some other place[s] [1], some[s] [1], someone [1], son[s] [1], steward[s] [+408+1074+2021+6584] [1], steward[s] [+1074+6584] [1], such as [1], surviving [+3855+3856] [1], than [+4946] [1], that [+6330] [1], the areas[s] [1], the celebration[s] [1], the cup[s] [1], the girl[s] [1], the gods[s] [1], the person[s] [1], the place[s] [1], the places[s] [1], the plans[s] [1], the storehouses[s] [+928+2157+3972] [1], the temple[s] [1], the terms[s] [1], the territory[s] [1], the total[s] [1], the vineyard[s] [1], then [+3869] [1], then [1], this is how [+3869] [1], those [+339+2021+6639] [1], till [+6330] [1], town[s] [1], under [1], very things [+3869+4027] [1], vows[s] [1], what [+4017] [1], whatever [+3869+3972+4027] [1], whatever [+928+3972] [1], when [+6584] [1], whenever [+3869] [1], whenever [+928+3972] [1], wherever [+2021+3972+5226+6584] [1], wherever [+2025+9004] [1], wherever [+285+928+2021+5226] [1], wherever [+3972+6584] [1], wherever [+3972+9004] [1], wherever [+4946] [1], wherever[s] [+5226] [1], wherever [+928] [1], wherever [+928+2021+5226] [1], while [+3869] [1], while [1], whoever [+408+3972] [1], whose [+4200] [1], yet [+1172+4946] [1], yet [1], you[s] [1]

890 אֶשֶׁר ***'ešer***, n.[m.]. [1 / 2] [√ 887]

blessed [1], happy [1]

Ps 10: 6 I'll always be **happy** [BHS 889] and never have trouble."
Pr 29: 18 the people cast off restraint; but **blessed** is he who keeps the law.

891 אֹשֶׁר ***'ōšer***, n.[m.]. [1] [→ 897; cf. 887]

happy [1]

Ge 30: 13 Leah said, "How **happy** I am! The women will call me happy."

892 אָשֻׁר ***'āšur***, n.f. [9] [√ 886]

steps [4], feet [2], foothold [1], place to stand [1], tracked down [1]

Job 23: 11 My feet have closely followed his **steps**; I have kept to his way
31: 7 if my **steps** have turned from the path, if my heart has been led by
Ps 17: 5 My **steps** have held to your paths; my feet have not slipped.
17: 11 *They have* **tracked** me **down**, they now surround me, with eyes
37: 31 The law of his God is in his heart; his **feet** do not slip.
40: 2 [40:3] set my feet on a rock and gave me a firm **place to stand**.
44: 18 [44:19] not turned back; our **feet** had not strayed from your path.
73: 2 my feet had almost slipped; I had nearly lost my **foothold**.
Pr 14: 15 believes anything, but a prudent man gives thought to his **steps**.

893 ¹אַשֻּׁר ***'aššur¹***, n.f. Not used in NIV/BHS [√ 886]

894 ²אַשֻּׁר ***'aššur²***, n.pr.g. & loc. Not used in NIV/BHS [→ 855]

895 אֲשֵׁרָה ***'ašērâ***, n.pr.f. [40] [cf. 6958?]

Asherah poles [22], Asherah pole [14], Asherah [3], Asherahs [1]

Ex 34:13 smash their sacred stones and cut down their **Asherah poles**.
Dt 7:5 cut down their **Asherah poles** and burn their idols in the fire.
12:3 smash their sacred stones and burn their **Asherah poles** in the fire;
16:21 Do not set up any wooden **Asherah pole** beside the altar you build
Jdg 3:7 the LORD their God and served the Baals and the **Asherahs**.
6:25 father's altar to Baal and cut down the **Asherah pole** beside it.
6:26 Using the wood of the **Asherah pole** that you cut down, offer the
6:28 with the **Asherah pole** beside it cut down and the second bull
6:30 down Baal's altar and cut down the **Asherah pole** beside it."
1Ki 14:15 they provoked the LORD to anger by making **Asherah poles**.
14:23 sacred stones and **Asherah poles** on every high hill and under
15:13 as queen mother, because she had made a repulsive **Asherah pole**.
16:33 Ahab also made an **Asherah pole** and did more to provoke the
18:19 fifty prophets of Baal and the four hundred prophets of **Asherah**,
2Ki 13:6 in them. Also, the **Asherah pole** remained standing in Samaria.
17:10 They set up sacred stones and **Asherah poles** on every high hill
17:16 two idols cast in the shape of calves, and an **Asherah pole**.
18:4 smashed the sacred stones and cut down the **Asherah poles**.
21:3 he also erected altars to Baal and made an **Asherah pole**, as Ahab
21:7 He took the carved **Asherah pole** he had made and put it in the
23:4 all the articles made for Baal and **Asherah** and all the starry hosts.
23:6 He took the **Asherah pole** from the temple of the LORD to the
23:7 temple of the LORD and where women did weaving for **Asherah**.
23:14 Josiah smashed the sacred stones and cut down the **Asherah poles**
23:15 and ground it to powder, and burned the **Asherah pole** also.
2Ch 14:3 [14:2] the sacred stones and cut down the **Asherah poles**.
15:16 as queen mother, because she had made a repulsive **Asherah pole**.
17:6 he removed the high places and the **Asherah poles** from Judah.
19:3 for you have rid the land of the **Asherah poles** and have set your
24:18 the God of their fathers, and worshiped **Asherah poles** and idols.
31:1 smashed the sacred stones and cut down the **Asherah poles**.
33:3 he also erected altars to the Baals and made **Asherah poles**.
33:19 and set up **Asherah poles** and idols before he humbled himself—
34:3 of high places, **Asherah poles**, carved idols and cast images.
34:4 and smashed the **Asherah poles**, the idols and the images.
34:7 he tore down the altars and the **Asherah poles** and crushed the
Isa 17:8 they will have no regard for the **Asherah poles** and the incense
27:9 to pieces, no **Asherah poles** or incense altars will be left standing.
Jer 17:2 and **Asherah poles** beside the spreading trees and on the high hills.
Mic 5:14 [5:13] I will uproot from among you your **Asherah poles**

896 אָשֵׁרִי ***'āšērî***, a.g. [1] [√ 888; cf. 887]

people of Asher [1]

Jdg 1:32 because of this the **people of Asher** lived among the Canaanite

897 אַשְׁרֵי ***'ašrê***, n.[m.]. [44] [√ 891; cf. 887]

blessed [37], how happy [4], *untranslated* [1], blessings [1], happy [1]

Dt 33:29 **Blessed** are you, O Israel! Who is like you, a people saved by the
1Ki 10:8 **How happy** your men must be! How happy your officials,
10:8 **How happy** your officials, who continually stand before you
2Ch 9:7 **How happy** your men must be! How happy your officials,
9:7 **How happy** your officials, who continually stand before you
Job 5:17 "**Blessed** is the man whom God corrects; so do not despise the
Ps 1:1 **Blessed** is the man who does not walk in the counsel of the wicked
2:12 can flare up in a moment. **Blessed** are all who take refuge in him.
32:1 **Blessed** is he whose transgressions are forgiven, whose sins are
32:2 **Blessed** is the man whose sin the LORD does not count against
33:12 **Blessed** is the nation whose God is the LORD, the people he
34:8 [34:9] is good; **blessed** is the man who takes refuge in him.
40:4 [40:5] **Blessed** is the man who makes the LORD his trust, who
41:1 [41:2] **Blessed** is he who has regard for the weak; the LORD
65:4 [65:5] **Blessed** are those you choose and bring near to live in your
84:4 [84:5] **Blessed** are those who dwell in your house; they are ever
84:5 [84:6] **Blessed** are those whose strength is in you, who have set
84:12 [84:13] LORD Almighty, **blessed** is the man who trusts in you.
89:15 [89:16] **Blessed** are those who have learned to acclaim you,
94:12 **Blessed** is the man you discipline, O LORD, the man you teach
106:3 **Blessed** are they who maintain justice, who constantly do what is
112:1 **Blessed** is the man who fears the LORD, who finds great delight
119:1 **Blessed** are they whose ways are blameless, who walk according to
119:2 **Blessed** are they who keep his statutes and seek him with all their
127:5 **Blessed** is the man whose quiver is full of them. They will not be
128:1 **Blessed** are all who fear the LORD, who walk in his ways.
128:2 eat the fruit of your labor; **blessings** and prosperity will be yours.
137:8 **happy** is he who repays you for what you have done to us—
137:9 **[RPH]** he who seizes your infants and dashes them against the
144:15 **Blessed** are the people of whom this is true; blessed are the people
144:15 this is true; **blessed** are the people whose God is the LORD.
146:5 **Blessed** is he whose help is the God of Jacob, whose hope is in the
Pr 3:13 **Blessed** is the man who finds wisdom, the man who gains
8:32 my sons, listen to me; **blessed** are those who keep my ways.
8:34 **Blessed** is the man who listens to me, watching daily at my doors,
14:21 his neighbor sins, but **blessed** is he who is kind to the needy.
16:20 to instruction prospers, and **blessed** is he who trusts in the LORD.
20:7 man leads a blameless life; **blessed** are his children after him.
28:14 **Blessed** is the man who always fears the LORD, but he who
Ecc 10:17 **Blessed** are you, O land whose king is of noble birth and whose
Isa 30:18 the LORD is a God of justice. **Blessed** are all who wait for him!
32:20 *how* **blessed** you will be, sowing your seed by every stream,
56:2 **Blessed** is the man who does this, the man who holds it fast,
Da 12:12 **Blessed** is the one who waits for and reaches the end of the 1,335

898 אֲשֻׁרִים ***'ašurîm***, n.pr.m.?. Not used in NIV/BHS [√ 9309]

899 אָשַׁשׁ ***'āšaš***, v. [1] [→ 862?; Ar 10079]

fix in mind [1]

Isa 46:8 [F] "Remember this, **fix it in mind**, take it to heart, you rebels.

900 אֶשְׁתָּאוֹל ***'eštā'ôl***, n.pr.loc. [7] [→ 901; cf. 8626]

Eshtaol [7]

Jos 15:33 In the western foothills: **Eshtaol**, Zorah, Ashnah,
19:41 territory of their inheritance included: Zorah, **Eshtaol**, Ir Shemesh,
Jdg 13:25 him while he was in Mahaneh Dan, between Zorah and **Eshtaol**.
16:31 him between Zorah and **Eshtaol** in the tomb of Manoah his father.
18:2 warriors from Zorah and **Eshtaol** to spy out the land and explore it.
18:8 When they returned to Zorah and **Eshtaol**, their brothers asked
18:11 of the Danites, armed for battle, set out from Zorah and **Eshtaol**.

901 אֶשְׁתָּאֻלִי ***'eštā'ulî***, a.g. [1] [√ 900]

Eshtaolites [1]

1Ch 2:53 From these descended the Zorathites and **Eshtaolites**.

902 אֶשְׁתּוֹן ***'eštôn***, n.pr.m. [2]

Eshton [2]

1Ch 4:11 was the father of Mehir, who was the father of **Eshton**.
4:12 **Eshton** was the father of Beth Rapha, Paseah and Tehinnah the

903 אֶשְׁתְּמֹה ***'eštemōh***, n.pr.loc. [1] [cf. 904]

Eshtemoh [1]

Jos 15:50 Anab, **Eshtemoh**, Anim,

904 אֶשְׁתְּמֹעַ ***'eštemōa'***, n.pr.loc. & m. [5] [√ 9048; cf. 903]

Eshtemoa [5]

Jos 21:14 Jattir, **Eshtemoa**,
1Sa 30:28 to those in Aroer, Siphmoth, **Eshtemoa**
1Ch 4:17 birth to Miriam, Shammai and Ishbah the father of **Eshtemoa**.
4:19 the father of Keilah the Garmite, and **Eshtemoa** the Maacathite.
6:57 [6:42] Hebron (a city of refuge), and Libnah, Jattir, **Eshtemoa**,

905 אַתְּ ***'att***, p.f.s. [60] [→ 911, 914, 917, 920] Not indexed

you [50], *untranslated* [9], how did it go [+4769] [1]

906 אֵת ***'ēt***[1], pt. [10932 / 10937] [→ 254; Ar 10337] Not indexed

untranslated [10860], aloud [+5951+7754] [5], entreat [+2704+7156] [3], ordained [+3338+4848] [3], sought the favor of [+2704+7156] [3], take a census [+5951+8031] [3], to [3], installed [+3338+4848] [2], let know [+265+1655] [2], ordination [+3338+4848] [2], tells [+265+1655] [2], accepted [+5951+7156] [1], began [+5951+7754] [1], come into presence [+7156+8011] [1], confiding in [+265+1655] [1], consecrated [+3338+4848] [1], count [+928+928+5951+8031] [1], counted [+5951+8031] [1], counting on [+448+5883+5951] [1], did [+3877+4213+4392] [1], did so [+2021+6913+7175] [1], disheartened [+4222+5022] [1], for [1], given word [+7023+7198] [1], hardhearted [+599+4222] [1], has sexual relations with [+1655+6872] [1], have sexual relations [+6872+8011] [1], helped [+2616+3338] [1], helped find strength [+2616+3338] [1], include in the census [+5951+8031] [1], inquire of [+7023+8626] [1], intercede with [+2704+7156] [1], interceded with [+2704+7156] [1], keep themselves alive [+4392+5883+8740] [1], let go [+3338+5663] [1], looked [+6524] [1], offering body [+7316+8079] [1], on [1], openhanded [+3338+4200+7337+7337] [1], openhanded [+3338 +7337+7337] [1], ordain [+3338+4848] [1], out [+5951] [1], relieve himself [+2257+6114+8079] [1], relieving himself [+2257+6114 +8079] [1], revealed [+265+1655] [1], saw [+5951+6524] [1], seek favor [+2704+7156] [1], sent on way [+906+906+8938] [1], sought favor [+2704+7156] [1], stared with a fixed gaze [+2256+6641

[F] Hitpael (hitpoel, hitpoal, hitpolel, hitpolal, hitpalel, hitpalal, hitpalpel, hitpalpal, hotpael, hotpaal) [G] Hiphil (hiphtil) [H] Hophal [I] Hishtaphel

+7156+8492] [1], sulking [+6015+7156] [1], sworn [+3338+5951] [1], tell [+265+1655] [1], tightfisted [+3338+7890] [1], undergo circumcision [+1414+4576+6889] [1], uttered a word [+3076+4383] [1], wanted [+5883+8626] [1], wanted to kill [+1335+5883] [1], wept so loudly [+928+1140+5989+7754] [1], worry [+4213+8492] [1]

907 [2]אֵת **'ēt[2]**, pp. [934] [→ 909, 4425] See Select Index

with [406], *untranslated* [129], from [+4946] [93], against [34], to [28], among [14], along with [13], his [+2257] [13], before [+7156] [9], and [8], have [8], near [7], of [+4946] [7], for [5], in [5], slept with [+8886] [5], by [4], left [+2143+4946] [4], through [+4946] [4], upon [4], doing [+4946] [3], had [+5162] [3], lies with [+8886] [3], pronounced on [+1819] [3], sleeps with [+8886] [3], the LORD's [+3378+4946] [3], allied with [2], away from [+4946] [2], before [2], close to [2], has [2], have [+3780] [2], help [2], in front of [+7156] [2], lay with [+8886] [2], leave [+2143+4946] [2], of [2], within [2], about [1], accompanied [+2143] [1], accompanied [+6590] [1], accompanied by [1], accompany [+3655] [1], according to [1], account for [+3108] [1], adding to [+2256] [1], all around [1], alongside [1], among [+4946] [1], among [+8905] [1], and [+2256] [1], and together [1], any of [+4946] [1], as well as [1], as [1], ask [+4946+8626] [1], assist [+6641] [1], away [+4946] [1], because of [1], both and [1], bring [+995] [1], by [+4946] [1], by myself [+3276+4769] [1], company [+2118] [1], concern [1], confide in [+4213] [1], decreed [1], determined [+4946] [1], fighting with [+2118] [1], following [+6639] [1], for [+4946] [1], forsaking [+4946] [1], gain support [+2118+3338] [1], given to [1], gone from [+401] [1], had [1], help [+2118] [1], helped [1], helping [1], in addition to [1], in hand [1], in possession [1], in sight [+7156] [1], in view [+7156] [1], inquire of [+2011+4946] [1], into [1], know [1], leaves [+2143+4946] [1], left [+4946] [1], lie with [+8886] [1], lies with [+8886+8886] [1], lost [+4946+5877] [1], lying with [+8886] [1], my [+3276] [1], near [+2143] [1], next to [1], on [+4946] [1], on behalf of [+4946] [1], on side [1], oppose [1], other[s] [+889] [1], out of [+4946] [1], over [1], own [1], past [+4946] [1], representative [+4946] [1], send [+995+4946] [1], sent by [+4946] [1], served [+6641+7156] [1], shared with [1], show [1], sleeping with [+2446+8886+8887] [1], sleeps with [+2446+8886+8887] [1], some [+4946] [1], supported [+2118+3338] [1], through [1], to [+7156] [1], together [+408+2084+8276] [1], together with [1], together [1], told [+4946+9048] [1], toward [1], under [+7156] [1], under care [1], under [1], with [+7156] [1], with the help of [+4946] [1], with the help of [1], within sight of [+7156] [1], your [+3870] [1]

908 [3]אֵת **'ēt[3]**, n.[m.] [5]

plowshares [3], mattocks [2]

1Sa 13:20 to have their plowshares, **mattocks**, axes and sickles sharpened.
13:21 two thirds of a shekel for sharpening plowshares and **mattocks**,
Isa 2: 4 They will beat their swords into **plowshares** and their spears into
Joel 3:10 [4:10] Beat your **plowshares** into swords and your pruning hooks
Mic 4: 3 They will beat their swords into **plowshares** and their spears into

909 אֶתְבַּעַל **'etba'al**, n.pr.m. [1] [√ 907 + 1251]

Ethbaal [1]

1Ki 16:31 he also married Jezebel daughter of **Ethbaal** king of the Sidonians,

910 אָתָה **'ātâ**, v. [21] [→ 415, 484, 517; Ar 10085]

come [7], bring [2], comes [2], advance [1], assembled [1], be restored [1], came [1], come forward [1], coming [1], holds [1], pass [1], sweeps over [1], things to come [1]

Dt 33: 2 [A] *He* **came** with myriads of holy ones from the south, from his
33:21 [A] When the heads of the people **assembled**, he carried out the
Job 3:25 [A] What I feared *has* **come** *upon* me; what I dreaded has
16:22 [A] "Only a few years *will* **pass** before I go on the journey of no
30:14 [A] *They* **advance** as *through* a gaping breach; amid the ruins
37:22 [A] Out of the north *he* **comes** in golden splendor; God comes in
Ps 68:31 [68:32] [A] Envoys *will* **come** from Egypt; Cush will submit
Pr 1:27 [A] when disaster **sweeps over** you like a whirlwind,
Isa 21:12 [A] watchman replies, "Morning *is* **coming**, but also the night.
21:12 [A] If you would ask, then ask; and **come** back yet again."
21:14 [G] **bring** water for the thirsty; you who live in Tema, bring food
41: 5 [A] ends of the earth tremble. They approach and **come forward**;
41:23 [A] tell us what the future **holds**, so we may know that you are
41:25 [A] "I have stirred up one from the north, and *he* **comes**—
44: 7 [A] I established my ancient people, and *what is yet to* **come**—
45:11 [A] Concerning **things to come**, do you question me about my
56: 9 [A] **Come**, all *you* beasts of the field, come and devour, all you
56:12 [A] "**Come**," each one cries, "let me get wine! Let us drink our
Jer 3:22 [A] "Yes, we *will* **come** to you, for you are the LORD our God.
12: 9 [G] and gather all the wild beasts; **bring** them to devour.
Mic 4: 8 [A] of Zion, the former dominion *will* **be restored** to you;

911 אַתָּה **'attâ**, p.m.s. [744 / 745] [√ 905; Ar 10051, 10052] Not indexed

you [621], *untranslated* [93], yourself [17], your [4], you alone [+911] [2], you're [2], your own [2], it [1], you yourself [1], you'll [1], yours [1]

912 אָתוֹן **'ātôn**, n.f. [34]

donkey [13], donkeys [12], female donkeys [3], her[s] [+2021] [2], colt [+1201] [1], donkey's [1], she[s] [+2021] [1], them[s] [+2021] [1]

Ge 12:16 and Abram acquired sheep and cattle, male and **female donkeys**,
32:15 [32:16] and twenty **female donkeys** and ten male donkeys.
45:23 ten **female donkeys** loaded with grain and bread and other
49:11 tether his donkey to a vine, his **colt** [+1201] to the choicest branch;
Nu 22:21 saddled his **donkey** and went with the princes of Moab.
22:22 Balaam was riding on his **donkey**, and his two servants were with
22:23 When the **donkey** saw the angel of the LORD standing in the
22:23 standing in the road with a drawn sword in his hand, **she**[s] [+2021]
22:23 into a field. Balaam beat **her**[s] [+2021] to get her back on the road.
22:25 When the **donkey** saw the angel of the LORD, she pressed close
22:27 When the **donkey** saw the angel of the LORD, she lay down
22:27 and he was angry and beat **her**[s] [+2021] with his staff.
22:28 the LORD opened the **donkey's** mouth, and she said to Balaam,
22:29 Balaam answered the **donkey**, "You have made a fool of me!
22:30 The **donkey** said to Balaam, "Am I not your own donkey,
22:30 The donkey said to Balaam, "Am I not your own **donkey**,
22:32 asked him, "Why have you beaten your **donkey** these three times?
22:33 The **donkey** saw me and turned away from me these three times.
Jdg 5:10 "You who ride on white **donkeys**, sitting on your saddle blankets,
1Sa 9: 3 Now the **donkeys** belonging to Saul's father Kish were lost,
9: 3 one of the servants with you and go and look for the **donkeys**."
9: 5 or my father will stop thinking about the **donkeys** and start
9:20 As for the **donkeys** you lost three days ago, do not worry about
10: 2 say to you, 'The **donkeys** you set out to look for have been found.
10: 2 And now your father has stopped thinking about **them**[s] [+2021]
10:14 "Where have you been?" "Looking for the **donkeys**," he said.
10:16 Saul replied, "He assured us that the **donkeys** had been found."
2Ki 4:22 "Please send me one of the servants and a **donkey** so I can go to
4:24 She saddled the **donkey** and said to her servant, "Lead on;
1Ch 27:30 Jehdeiah the Meronothite was in charge of the **donkeys**.
Job 1: 3 five hundred yoke of oxen and five hundred **donkeys**,
1:14 "The oxen were plowing and the **donkeys** were grazing nearby,
42:12 a thousand yoke of oxen and a thousand **donkeys**.
Zec 9: 9 gentle and riding on a donkey, on a colt, the foal of a **donkey**.

913 אַתּוּק **'attûq**, n.m. [0] [cf. 916]

Eze 41:15 [of the temple, including its **galleries** [K; see Q 916] on each side;]

914 אַתִּי **'attî**, p.f.s. [0] [√ 905]

915 אִתַּי **'ittay**, n.pr.m. [8] [cf. 416]

Ittai [7], Ithai [1]

2Sa 15:19 The king said to **Ittai** the Gittite, "Why should you come along
15:21 But **Ittai** replied to the king, "As surely as the LORD lives,
15:22 David said to **Ittai**, "Go ahead, march on." So Ittai the Gittite
15:22 So **Ittai** the Gittite marched on with all his men and the families
18: 2 brother Abishai son of Zeruiah, and a third under **Ittai** the Gittite.
18: 5 The king commanded Joab, Abishai and **Ittai**, "Be gentle with the
18:12 In our hearing the king commanded you and Abishai and **Ittai**,
23:29 the Netophathite, **Ithai** son of Ribai from Gibeah in Benjamin,

916 אַתִּיק **'attîq**, n.m. [5] [cf. 913]

galleries [3], gallery [2]

Eze 41:15 the rear of the temple, including its **galleries** [K 913] on each side;
41:16 and the narrow windows and **galleries** around the three of them—
42: 3 of the outer court, **gallery** faced gallery at the three levels.
42: 3 of the outer court, gallery faced **gallery** at the three levels.
42: 5 for the **galleries** took more space from them than from the rooms

917 אַתֶּם **'attem**, p.m.pl. [283] [√ 905; Ar 10053] Not indexed

you [244], *untranslated* [22], yourselves [10], your [3], yours [2], people[s] [1], you and your men [1]

918 אֵתָם **'ētām**, n.pr.loc. [4]

Etham [4]

Ex 13:20 After leaving Succoth they camped at **Etham** on the edge of the
Nu 33: 6 They left Succoth and camped at **Etham**, on the edge of the desert.
33: 7 They left **Etham**, turned back to Pi Hahiroth, to the east of Baal
33: 8 and when they had traveled for three days in the Desert of **Etham**,

919 אֶתְמוֹל ***'etmôl***, subst.adv. [8] [√ 9453]

before [+8997] [2], day [+3427] [1], formerly [+4946+8997] [1], in the past [+1685+1685+8997] [1], lately [1], long [+4946] [1], previously [+3869+8997] [1]

1Sa 4: 7 "We're in trouble! Nothing like this has happened **before** [+8997].
10: 11 When all those who had **formerly** [+4946+8997] known him saw
14: 21 Those Hebrews who had **previously** [+3869+8997] been with the
19: 7 brought him to Saul, and David was with Saul as **before** [+8997].
2Sa 5: 2 **In the past** [+1685+1685+8997], while Saul was king over us,
Ps 90: 4 For a thousand years in your sight are like a **day** [+3427] that has
Isa 30: 33 Topheth has **long** [+4946] been prepared; it has been made ready
Mic 2: 8 **Lately** my people have risen up like an enemy. You strip off the

920 אַתֵּן ***'attēn***, p.f.pl. [4] [√ 905] Not indexed

you [4]

921 אֶתְנָה ***'etnâ***, n.f. [1] [√ 924]

pay [1]

Hos 2: 12 [2:14] her fig trees, which she said were her **pay** from her lovers;

922 אֶתְנִי ***'etnî***, n.pr.m. [1]

Ethni [1]

1Ch 6: 41 [6:26] the son of **Ethni**, the son of Zerah, the son of Adaiah,

923 אֵתָנִים ***'ētānîm***, n.pr.[m.]. [1] [√ 3851]

Ethanim [1]

1Ki 8: 2 King Solomon at the time of the festival in the month of **Ethanim**,

924 אֶתְנַן ***'etnan***, n.m. [11] [→ 921, 925, 9479; cf. 5989]

earnings [2], payment [2], wages [2], *untranslated* [1], hire as a prostitute [1], pay [+5989] [1], temple gifts [1], wages of a prostitute [1]

Dt 23: 18 [23:19] You must not bring the **earnings** *of* a female prostitute
Isa 23: 17 She will return to her **hire as a prostitute** and will ply her trade
23: 18 Yet her profit and her **earnings** will be set apart for the LORD;
Eze 16: 31 you were unlike a prostitute, because you scorned **payment**.
16: 34 the very opposite, for you give **payment** and none is given to you.
16: 34 for you give payment and none **[RPH]** is given to you.
16: 41 your prostitution, and *you will* no longer **pay** [+5989] your lovers.
Hos 9: 1 you love the **wages of a prostitute** at every threshing floor.
Mic 1: 7 all her **temple gifts** will be burned with fire; I will destroy all her
1: 7 Since she gathered her gifts from the **wages** *of* prostitutes,
1: 7 of prostitutes, as the **wages** *of* prostitutes they will again be used."

925 אֶתְנָן ***'etnān***, n.pr.m. [1] [√ 924]

Ethnan [1]

1Ch 4: 7 The sons of Helah: Zereth, Zohar, **Ethnan**,

926 אֲתָרִים ***'ătārîm***, n.pr.loc. [1]

Atharim [1]

Nu 21: 1 heard that Israel was coming along the road to **Atharim**,

ב, *b*

927 ב ***b***, letter. Not used in NIV/BHS [→ Ar 10088]

928 -בְּ ***b^{e}-***, pp.pref. [15547 / 15552] [→ 948, 972, 1198, 1233, 1236, 1247, 1295, 1417; Ar 10089]

in [4676], *untranslated* [2404], with [1047], on [956], at [580], by [501], when [497], of [303], to [281], into [274], against [260], among [241], through [183], for [160], among [+9348] [111], from [98], over [89], as [80], through [+3338] [62], because of [59], during [59], among [+7931] [52], according to [50], while [48], throughout [+3972] [47], in [+9348] [45], when [+3427] [45], obey [+7754+9048] [36], before [+3270] [35], upon [34], under [33], after [27], there[s] [+2023] [26], throughout [26], along [25], enter [+995] [25], in [+7931] [24], follow [+2143] [21], about [20], whenever [20], with [+3338] [20], within [+7931] [20], within [20], to [+265] [19], by [+3338] [18], hand over [+906+3338+5989] [18], near [18], obeyed [+7754+9048] [17], with [+9348] [17], because [16], how [+4537] [16], if [16], has [15], inquired of [+8626] [15], inside [+9348] [15], to [+3338] [15], to [+7754] [15], within [+9348] [15], hand over [+3338+5989] [14], used [14], handed over [+3338+5989] [13], have [12], here [+2296] [12], for the sake of [+6288] [11], had [11], when [+6961] [11], with [+7931] [11], around [10], followed [+2143] [10], seems [+6524] [10], where [10], wherever [+3972] [10], wherever [+889+3972] [10], because of [+1673] [9], east [+6298] [9], inside [9], into [+9348] [9], safely [+8934] [9], without [+4202] [9], and [8], be handed over [+3338+5989] [8], entered [+995] [8], every morning [+928+1332+1332+2021+2021] [8], in spite of [8], seemed [+6524] [8], think [+6524] [8], through [+9348] [8], before [7], burn down [+836+2021+8596] [7], handed over [+906+3338+5989] [7], outside [+2021+2575] [7], pleased [+3512+6524] [7], that [7], toward [7], along with [+9348] [6], amid [6], any [6], because of [+6288] [6], before [+2021+8037] [6], despite [6], invade [+995] [6], like [6], secretly [+2021+6260] [6], set on fire [+836+906+2021+3675] [6], there[s] [+3731] [6], this is how [+2296] [6], unintentionally [+8705] [6], use [6], within [+6388] [6], against [+7156] [5], always [+3972+6961] [5], at the cost of [5], beyond [+6298] [5], burned [+836+906+2021 +8596] [5], displeased [+6524+8317] [5], faithfully [+575] [5], has [+2118] [5], on account of [5], pleased with [+2834+5162+6524] [5], pleases [+3202+6524] [5], ruthlessly [+7266] [5], so that [+6288] [5], there[s] [+1195+2021] [5], using [5], accidentally [+8705] [4], accompanied by [4], across [+6298] [4], allotted [+1598+2021+4200] [4], be burned up [+836+2021+8596] [4], beside [4], consult [+2011] [4], faithfully [+622] [4], for sake [+6288] [4], have [+3338] [4], in exchange for [4], inner room [+2540+2540] [4], invaded [+995] [4], near [+7931] [4], out of [4], seem [+6524] [4], there[s] [+2023+9348] [4], there[s] [+2257] [4], to [+6288] [4], to [+6524] [4], touch [+2118] [4], unintentionally [+1172+1981] [4], wearing [4], wherever goes [+928+995+2256+3655] [4], whether [4], with [+6524] [4], as [+2006] [3], at the risk of [3], at the time of [3], because [+6288] [3], before [+4202] [3], between [+9348] [3], burned down [+836+906 +2021+8596] [3], called out [+1524+7754+7924] [3], cost [3], daily [+3427+3427] [3], each year [+9102+9102] [3], early [+8040] [3], every last male [+7815+8874] [3], favorably disposed toward [+2834+6524] [3], first [+2021+9378] [3], follows [+2143] [3], has [+3780] [3], heard [+265] [3], including [3], inquire of [+2011] [3], king's [+4889] [3], later [3], like [+3202+6524] [3], made [3], male [+7815+8874] [3], on high [+2021+5294] [3], on the basis of [3], saw [+6524] [3], secret [+4537] [3], set on fire [+836+2021+3675] [3], share [+5951] [3], some [3], stone [+74+906+2021+8083] [3], though [3], through [+7931] [3], throughout [+1473+3972] [3], under [+3338] [3], upon [+7931] [3], whenever [+3972] [3], wherever [+889+2006 +2021] [3], wherever [+889+5226] [3], wild [+2021+8441] [3], without [+700] [3], all day long [+2021+2021+2085+3427] [2], all [2], alone [+1727+2257] [2], along with [2], anywhere [+3972+5226] [2], as [+6961] [2], as before [+3869+7193+7193] [2], as long as live [+6388] [2], as long as [2], as soon as [2], assassinate [+3338+8938] [2], associate with [+995] [2], at [+6961] [2], because [+889] [2], before [+265] [2], before [+3270+4202] [2], bloodshed [+995+1947] [2], boldly [+3338+8123] [2], burn down [+836+906+2021+8596] [2], burn up [+836+906+2021+8596] [2], burned [+836+2021+8596] [2], by [+6524] [2], by means of [2], by what means [+4537] [2], certainly be handed over [+3338+5989+5989] [2], chosen [+7924+9005] [2], deceitfully [+5327] [2], disobeyed [+4202+7754+9048] [2], distressed [+6524+8317] [2], do [2], down [2], each day [+3427+3427] [2], each morning [+928+1332+1332+2021+2021] [2], each [2], earlier [+2021+9378] [2], entrusted with [+575] [2], evening [+928+2021 +2021+6847+6847] [2], every evening [+928+2021+2021+6847 +6847] [2], everywhere [+3972] [2], exceedingly [+4394+4394] [2], fill [2], first [+2021+8037] [2], fleet-footed [+7824+8079] [2], following [+8079] [2], following [2], for [+6288] [2], for each day [+1821+3427+3427] [2], for nothing [+1896+8198] [2], from [+9348] [2], fully obey [+7754+9048+9048] [2], greatly [+4394+4394] [2], guilty [+3338] [2], had [+3338] [2], hand over [+3338+6037] [2], hand over [+906+906+906+906+3338+5989] [2], handed over [+3338+6037] [2], handed over [+906+906+906+3338+5989] [2], have respect for [+3700+6524] [2], honorably [+622] [2], in charge of [2], in each corner [+928+5243+5243] [2], in obedience to [2], in order to [+6288] [2], in return for [2], inside [+1074+2021] [2], intersecting [+9348] [2], invades [+995] [2], its [+2023] [2], joyfully [+8525] [2], just as [2], led by [+8031] [2], make a survey of [+2143] [2], my [+3276+8079] [2], near [+6298] [2], now [+465+2021+2021 +3427] [2], on [+7931] [2], on account of [+6288] [2], on high [+7757] [2], over [+8031] [2], overwhelmed [+2118+4202+6388+8120] [2], play [+3338+5594] [2], playing the harp [+3338+5594] [2], please [+3202+6524] [2], please [+3837+6524] [2], pleased [+3202+6524] [2], pleased [+3837+6524] [2], privately [+2021+6260] [2], purchased [+4374+4697] [2], quietly [+2021+4319] [2], reached [+995] [2], required [+460+5957] [2], Sabbath after Sabbath [+928+2021+2021 +3427+3427+8701+8701] [2], sees [+6524] [2], set on fire [+836+2021+8596] [2], set on fire [+836+906+2021+8596] [2], so [+6288] [2], sold for [+2118] [2], stone [+74+2021+6232] [2], stone [+74+2021+8083] [2], struck [+2118] [2], supervising [2], taking with [+3338] [2], that [+6288] [2], then [+340+2021] [2], there[s] [+1074+2021] [2], there[s] [+2021+2215] [2], there[s] [+9076] [2], there[s] [+2023] [2], thought [+6524] [2], throughout [+6017] [2], throughout

[+9348] [2], truly [+622] [2], up to [2], very [+4394+4394] [2], what [+4537] [2], what [2], when [+2021+3427] [2], where[s] [+2023] [2], where [+889] [2], wherever [+889+2021+3972+5226] [2], wherever [2], while [+3427] [2], wholeheartedly [+3972+4213] [2], wholeheartedly [+3972+4222] [2], wholeheartedly [+4222+8969] [2], with help [2], without [+401] [2], withstand [+6641+7156] [2], withstand [+995] [2], wounds [+995] [2], yearly [+285+9102] [2], ability [+2683+4213] [1], aboard [1], above [+2021+5294] [1], accuse [+1821+8492] [1], across [1], affected [1], after [+1821] [1], after [+1896+4946] [1], after [+3427] [1], after [+8079] [1], after [+9005] [1], again [+1685+2021+2021+2085+7193] [1], against [+6330] [1], alive [+5883] [1], all [+285] [1], all night long [+2021+4326] [1], allotted [+1598+2021+2118+4200] [1], allotted [+906+1598 +2021+5989] [1], allotted [+906+906+1598+2021+5989] [1], alone [+285] [1], along [+6298] [1], along [+9348] [1], along with [+3338] [1], along with [+7931] [1], alongside [1], aloud [+1524+7754] [1], aloud [+7754] [1], already [+2021+9378] [1], although [+889+3972] [1], angry [+3013+6524] [1], annual [+2021+7193+9102] [1], annual [+285+2021+9102] [1], annually [+2256+3972+9102+9102] [1], anywhere in [+1473+3972] [1], appealed to [+3512+6524] [1], appear [+2118+3869+6524] [1], approve of [+3202+6524] [1], archers [+2021+4619+8008] [1], archers [+408+2021+4619+8008] [1], are burned up [+836+2021+8596+8596] [1], arrayed in [1], as [+889] [1], as [+889+3972] [1], as directs [1], as done before [+3869+7193 +7193] [1], as long as [+3427] [1], as long as [+3972+6961] [1], as long as [+6388] [1], as one [+9348] [1], as usually did [+3427+3427 +3869] [1], assaults [+8938] [1], assemble [+2021+6590+7736] [1], assisted [+2616+3338] [1], assuredly [+622] [1], at [+2006+2021] [1], at [+6298] [1], at [+7931] [1], at [+9348] [1], at once [+2021+2021 +2085+3427] [1], at once [+2021+2021+2085+6961] [1], at once [+2021+3427] [1], at other times [+7193+7193] [1], at stake [1], at the blast [+1896] [1], at the time [1], attached to [1], attack [+3338+8938] [1], attack [+3718] [1], attack [+5877] [1], attacked [+3338+8938] [1], attacked [+5877] [1], attacked [+6590] [1], attacks [+3338+8938] [1], bare [+401+4399] [1], based on [1], be a virgin [+1436] [1], be burned [+836+2021+8596] [1], be burned down [+836+2021+8596] [1], be defeated [+3338+5989] [1], be taken captive [+2021+4090 +9530] [1], bears [1], because [+1673] [1], because [+2256+3610 +3610] [1], because [+3610] [1], because [+3610+3610] [1], because of [+3338] [1], been handed over [+3338+5989] [1], before [+2021+9378] [1], before [+3266] [1], before [+678] [1], beginning with [1], behind [1], belong to [+2118] [1], belonged to [+8079] [1], bent on [+6783] [1], beset [+995] [1], beside [+2668] [1], beside [+3338] [1], besiege [+995+2021+4946+5189+7156] [1], besieged [+2837] [1], between [1], bind themselves with [+995] [1], blind [+2021+5782+6427] [1], boasted [+1540+7023] [1], borrowed [+5957] [1], bought [+2021+4084+7864] [1], bring about [+2118] [1], brings [1], brought [+3338] [1], brought with [+2118+3338] [1], brutally [+7266] [1], burn [+836+2021+8596] [1], burn [+836+906+2021+8596] [1], burn [+836+906+906+2021+8596] [1], burn [+836+906+906+906+2021+8596] [1], burn to death [+836+906+906+2021+8596] [1], burn up [+836+2021+8596] [1], burned [+836+2021+8938] [1], burned [+836+906+906+2021+8596] [1], burned to death [+836+906+906+2021+8596] [1], burned up [+836+906+2021+8596] [1], burned up [+836+906+906+2021+8596] [1], burned up [+836+906+906+906+2021+8596] [1], burned up [+836+906+906+906+906+2021+8596] [1], buy [+4084] [1], by [+9348] [1], by day [+3429] [1], by means [1], cargo [+641+889 +2021+3998] [1], carried [+906+906+3338+4374] [1], carry off [+995+2021+8660] [1], carrying [1], cause [+3338] [1], centrally located in [+9348] [1], charred [+836+1277+2021] [1], close to [1], clung to [1], come into [+4200+5877] [1], commit [+2143] [1], committed [+2143] [1], compels [1], concealed in [1], concerning [1], consider [+4222] [1], consider [+6524] [1], considered [+6524] [1], constantly [+3972+6961] [1], consult [+1821+2011] [1], containing [1], contrary to [+3869+4202] [1], counted off [+5031+6296] [1], covered [+2118] [1], covers [+995] [1], cruelly [+2622] [1], customary [+3869+7193+7193] [1], daily [+1821+3427+3427] [1], daily [+2257+3427+3427] [1], day by day [+1821+2257+3427+3427] [1], day by day [+1821+3427+3427] [1], dealing with [1], debtor [+5957] [1], deceived [+4200+5792+5793] [1], deceptively [+6817] [1], defiantly [+7418] [1], delegation [+3338+6269] [1], deliberately [+6893] [1], delivered [+3338] [1], despise [+1022+6524] [1], despise [+6524+7837] [1], despises [+1022+6524] [1], despises [+6524+7837] [1], despite [+4200+8611] [1], diligently obey [+7754+9048+9048] [1], disapprove [+6524+8317] [1], disobedience [+4202+7754+9048] [1], disobey [+1194+7754+9048] [1], displease [+2834+4202+5162+6524] [1], displease [+6524+8273] [1], displeasing [+2834+4202+5162+6524] [1], displeasing [+6524+8273] [1], distributed among [1], do that[s] [+2118+2257+3338] [1], done by [+3338] [1], doubly [+2021+9109] [1], drew [+3338+4848] [1], driving [1], due annually [+1896+4946+9102 +9102] [1], during [+3427] [1], each day's [+2257+3427+3427] [1], each day's [+3427+3427] [1], eagerly [+3972+8356] [1], east [+2025+4667+6298] [1], east [+2025+4667+6298+9087] [1], east [+4667+6298+9087] [1], encounter [+995] [1], end [+340+2021 +2118] [1], entered [+995+9348] [1], entering [+995] [1], entering [+995+7931] [1], entering [+995+9348] [1], enters [+995] [1], entrusted to [+3338] [1], even after [1], even if [1], every day [+3427+3427] [1], every Sabbath [+8701+8701] [1], every [1], everyone's [+408] [1], everywhere [+3972+5226] [1], fairly [+7406] [1], faithful [+622+2143] [1], far back in [+3752] [1], far off [+8158] [1], fault [+4200+8611] [1], favorable toward [+2834+5162+6524] [1], feeds [+5966+9094] [1], few [+5031+5071] [1], fiercely [+2021+6677] [1], fifteen feet [+564+2021+6924] [1], filled [+2118+3972] [1], filled with [+7931] [1], flashed back and forth [+4374+9348] [1], flashes [+836] [1], follow [+2143+8079] [1], follow [+8079] [1], follow [+906+2143] [1], followed [+6590+8079] [1], followed [1], for [+1685+8611] [1], for [+3338] [1], for [+6524] [1], for [+889] [1], for [+9348] [1], for this purpose [+6288] [1], forcefully [+3338] [1], formerly [+2021+8037] [1], fought in [+3655] [1], free from [+4202] [1], from [+3338] [1], from [+6524] [1], from [+889] [1], from now [+6388] [1], from the time [1], fuel for fire [+836+1896] [1], fuel for flames [+836+1896] [1], fully determined [+4222+8969] [1], galled [+6524+8317] [1], gave in [+7754+9048] [1], gave victory [+3338+5989] [1], get [1], give [+3338+5989] [1], given by [1], giving credit to [+9005] [1], glad [+3512+6524] [1], gladly [+3206+4222] [1], go [+2006+2143] [1], gone [+2118+4202] [1], gone [+4202+6641] [1], had [+2118] [1], had [+7023] [1], had [+7931] [1], had chance [+2118+3338] [1], hand over [+906+3338+4835] [1], hand over [+906+3338+5162] [1], hand over [+906+906+3338+5989] [1], hand over to [+906+3338+5989] [1], handed [+906+906+3338+5989] [1], handed over [+3338+5162] [1], handed over [+906+3338+5796] [1], handed over [+906+906+3338+5989] [1], handing over [+3338+6037] [1], handing over [+906+3338+5989] [1], harbor [+4328+7931] [1], harbor in [1], harnessed to [1], harshly [+2622] [1], has [+3338] [1], hasty [+237+8079] [1], have [+2118] [1], have [+3338+5162] [1], have [+3780] [1], have [+5055] [1], have [+7023] [1], have a claim on [1], heard [+265+606] [1], here[s] [+2021+2021+2296+5226] [1], here[s] [+2021+4497] [1], here [+2023] [1], here[s] [+5226] [1], here[s] [+824+2021] [1], his[s] [+2021+4889] [1], his [+2257] [1], hold [+2118+3338] [1], holding [+3338] [1], holds [+2118+3338] [1], how [+686+4537] [1], how [1], hurl insults [+7080+8557] [1], if [+3427] [1], imagine [+3869+5381] [1], imprisoned [+906+906 +5464+5989] [1], in [+1068] [1], in [+4213] [1], in [+4595] [1], in accordance with [1], in charge of [+3338] [1], in equal amounts [+963+963] [1], in keeping with [1], in payment for [1], in person [+265] [1], in possession [1], in regard to [1], in response to [1], in the name of [1], in view of [1], include [+9348] [1], inquire of [+2011 +4200] [1], inquire of [+8626] [1], inquires of [+1821+8626] [1], inquiring of [+8626] [1], inserted into [1], inside [+5055] [1], inside [+7931] [1], insist on paying for [+907+4697+4946+7864+7864] [1], inspire [+906+4222+5989] [1], intentionally [+7402] [1], interwoven [+1808+2021] [1], into [+7931] [1], invade [+6296] [1], invade [+6590] [1], invaded [+6590] [1], invoke [+7023+7924] [1], involved in [1], Israel [1], Israel's [+3776] [1], Israelite [+1201+3776] [1], Israelite [+3776] [1], its[s] [+2021+6551] [1], join [+2118] [1], joined in [+9348] [1], just before [+3270] [1], keep [+2143] [1], keeping watch [+6524+8011] [1], kept [+2143] [1], killing [+3338+8938] [1], lack [+401] [1], lack [+4202] [1], laden with [1], laid siege [+995+2021+5189] [1], lamb [+2021+3897+8445] [1], lamb [+2021+4166+8445] [1], land's [+824] [1], lately [+700] [1], later [+340+2021] [1], later in time [+344] [1], lead life [+2143] [1], leads [+2021+8037] [1], leave [1], led life [+2143] [1], let get away [+2006+8938] [1], let touch [+995] [1], leveled completely [+2021+9164+9168] [1], lie in state [+3883+8886] [1], like [+9348] [1], liked [+3837+6524] [1], likes [+2021+3202+4200] [1], listen carefully [+265+9048] [1], listen carefully [+4200+7754+9048] [1], listen closely [+265+9048] [1], listened [+265] [1], live [+2021+2644] [1], live [+2143] [1], lived [+1074+2021] [1], living in [1], long ago [+2021+8037] [1], look [+6524] [1], look carefully [+6524+8011] [1], looked [+2118+6524] [1], lose heart [+1327+7931+8120] [1], lost self-confidence [+4394+5877+6524] [1], loudly [+1524+7754] [1], made [+906+906+906+4200+4200+4200+4374] [1], made a fatal mistake [+5883+9494] [1], made pay for [+906+8031+8740] [1], made with [1], make enter [+995] [1], make fine speeches [+2488+4863] [1], make full restitution [+906+8031+8740] [1], make sure hears [+265+8492] [1], makes [1], mark [1], measured out [+4500+9419] [1], mention [+7023+9019] [1], monthly [+2544+2544] [1], mortal [+5883] [1], mounted [+2021+6061] [1], moving from place to place [+889+2143+2143] [1], must sell [+2021+4084+4835+4835] [1], my [+3276] [1], nails down [+2616+5021] [1], named [+906+7924+9005] [1], native-born [+824+2021+3528] [1], nomads [+185+8905] [1], not please [+6524+8317] [1], not want [+6524+8273] [1], now [1], obey [+2143] [1], obey fully [+7754+9048+9048] [1], obeyed [+4200+7754+9048] [1], obeying [+7754+9048] [1], obeys [+7754+9048] [1], of [+9348] [1], off [1], offer [1], on [+9348] [1], on board [+9348] [1], on board [1], on each side [1], on fire [+836+1277+2021] [1], on side [1], on the condition that [+2296] [1], on the tip of tongue [+2674+4383] [1], once [1], one by one [+5031] [1], one way [+285] [1], one [1], one[s] of [1], only [+1727+2257] [1], only if [1], oppose [+995] [1], oppressed [+2021+4200+6913+6945] [1], out here [+2021+2575] [1], outdoor [+2021+2575] [1], over [+9348] [1], overrun [1], paid [1], painted [+2021+7037+8531] [1], parallel [+7156] [1], part of [1], pay with [1], peaceably [+8934] [1], peacefully [+8934] [1], penned up [+906+1074+2021+3973] [1], people[s] [+889+3972] [1], pierce [+995] [1], pierce [1], pierced [+5737] [1], pierced [+995] [1], placed seal [+2597+3159] [1], please [+2256+3202+3838+6524] [1], please [+3838+6524] [1], pleased [+3201+6524] [1], pleased [+3838+6524] [1], pleased with [+2834+5951+6524] [1], pleased with [+3202+6524] [1], pleased with [+3512+6524] [1], pleased with [+3837+6524] [1], pleases [+3512+6524] [1], plot against [+906+3108+4222] [1], prefer [+3202+6524] [1], present in [1], preserved [+2021+2645+8492] [1], presumptuously [+2295] [1], prevailed upon [+2616] [1], privately [+2021+4319] [1], privately [+2021+8952] [1], proclaim [+7924] [1], proclaimed [+7924] [1], promised [+1819+7023] [1], prone to [1], protect [+3829+8883] [1], pursues [+8740] [1], put in jeopardy [+1414+5951+9094] [1], put on [+5516+8492] [1], puts up a bold front [+6451+7156] [1], quickly [+4559] [1], raiding [+995] [1], rationed [+5374] [1], rationed [+5486] [1], reached [+2118] [1], reached [+9048] [1], reaches to [1], ready for battle [+2021+4878 +7372] [1], really [+622] [1], regarding [1], regards [+5162+6524] [1], regular flow [+1414+2307] [1], regularly [+3427+3427+4200] [1], repay [+906+8031+8740] [1], responsible for [+4200+8611] [1], responsible for [+6015] [1], responsible for [+889+4200] [1], result of [1], ride [+2143] [1], risked [1], roars [+5989+7754] [1], sacrificed [+906+5989+6296] [1], sail [+641+2021+2143] [1], sandaled [+2021+5837] [1], satisfied [+3512+6524] [1], satisfied [+8934] [1], scarce [+430+5017] [1], scorned the idea [+1022+6524] [1], screamed [+1524+7754+7924] [1], search [+606] [1], seem [+2118+4200+6524] [1], seem [+4017+6524] [1], seemed [+2118+6524] [1], seize [+3338+8492] [1], sell [+4084+4200+5989] [1], sell [+906+4084+4200+5989] [1], sell for [+2118] [1], set ablaze [+836+2021+3675] [1], set fire to [+836+2021+8938] [1], set fire to [+836+906+906+2021+8596] [1], set on [1], set with [1], seven and a half feet [+564+2021+2822] [1], shamefully [+2365] [1], shared hardships [+889+6700+6700] [1], sharply [+2622] [1], shoot [+2021+8008] [1], shout [+7754+7924] [1], shout aloud [+1744+7924] [1], shouted [+7754+7924] [1], shouted [+7754+8123+9558] [1], since [+889] [1], sing [+7023+8492] [1], sing songs [+4200+7754+8123+9048] [1], sins defiantly [+3338+6913+8123] [1], sins unintentionally [+6913+8705] [1], sleeping with [+906+5989+8888] [1], sling stones [+74+2021] [1], smoothly [+4797] [1], so quickly [+7328] [1], some of [1], someone else[s] [+3338] [1], soon [+7940] [1], speak [+7023] [1], spreads feathers to run [+2021+5257+5294] [1], stargazers [+2600+3919] [1], stationed at [1], stoned [+74+2021+6232] [1], stoned [+74+906+2021+6232] [1], stoned [+74+906+2021+8083] [1], stoning [+74+906+2021+8083] [1], strike [+2118] [1], striking [+2118] [1], suddenly [+285] [1], suddenly [+7328+7353] [1], suddenly [+7353] [1], suffer [1], suffered [+2118] [1], surely hand over [+906+3338+5989+5989] [1], surrender [+906+3338+6037] [1], surrounded by [+9348] [1], sweep away [+906+4053+7674] [1], take great delight [+8464+8525] [1], take hold of [+2118] [1], take in [1], taken [+3338] [1], taken great pains [+6715] [1], taken into account [1], takes the stand [+7756] [1], tell [+265+1819] [1], tent-dwelling [+185+2021] [1], that [+3907] [1], the storehouses[s] [+889+2157+3972] [1], their[s] [+2157+4090] [1], them [+74+2021+4392] [1], then[s] [+2021+2021+2085+3427] [1], then [+2296] [1], then [+6288] [1], there[s] [+1014+2021] [1], there[s] [+1028] [1], there[s] [+1074+2021+3752] [1], there[s] [+1078] [1], there[s] [+1618] [1], there[s] [+2006+2021] [1], there[s] [+2021+4722] [1], there[s] [+2021+5207] [1], there[s] [+2021+6551] [1], there[s] [+2023+8148] [1], there[s] [+2025+9463] [1], there[s] [+2157] [1], there[s] [+2257+7931] [1], there[s] [+2257+9348] [1], there[s] [+2972] [1], there [+3720] [1], there[s] [+4392+9348] [1], there[s] [+466+1074] [1], there[s] [+5213] [1], there[s] [+5707+7724] [1], there[s] [+824] [1], there[s] [+824+2021] [1], there[s] [+824+2257] [1], there[s] [+8931] [1], there[s] [+951] [1], there [1], think [+606+4213] [1], think [+606+4222] [1], thinks [+606+4222] [1], thirty feet [+564+2021+6929] [1], this [+3907] [1], this is how [+465+3972] [1], this is the way [+4392] [1], thoughtlessly [+1051+4200+8557] [1], thoughts [+5883+6783] [1], through fault [1], throughout [+7931] [1], thunders [+5989+7754] [1], till [1], timely [+6961] [1], to [+4200+6288] [1], to [+4213] [1], to avenge [1], to each man [+9005] [1], to get [1], together with [1], told [+265+906+1819] [1], told [+7023+8492] [1], took with [+3338] [1], took [1], tried [+4213+9365] [1], troubled [+6524+8273] [1], under control [+294] [1], under cover [+9564] [1], underfoot [+8079] [1], unharmed [+8934] [1], unintentionally [+4202+7402] [1], unnoticed [+2021+4319] [1], unscathed [+8934] [1], upset [+906+6524+8317] [1], urgently [+2622] [1], use name as a curse [+8678] [1], used [+3338] [1], used for [1], uses [+3338] [1], value [+1540+6524] [1], valued [+1540+6524] [1], very old [+995+2021+2416+3427] [1], vigorously [+6437] [1], walk [+2006+2143] [1], walking along [+2006+2021] [1], wanted to do [+3202+6524] [1], watch [+6524] [1], waylaid [+2006+2021+4200+8492] [1], wearing [+265] [1], went aboard [+3718] [1], wept so loudly [+906+1140+5989+7754] [1], were put in chains [+2414+8415] [1], west [+6298] [1], whatever [+889+3972] [1], when [+8040] [1], when began [+3427] [1], whenever [+3427] [1], whenever [+3972+6961] [1], whenever [+6961] [1], whenever [+889+3972] [1], where [+2021+5226] [1], where[s] [+2177] [1], where[s] [+2257] [1], where[s] [+396] [1], where[s] [+5226] [1], where[s] [+6152+8234] [1], wherever [+2021+3972+5226] [1], wherever [+285+889+2021+5226] [1], wherever [+889] [1], wherever [+889+2021+5226] [1], while [+6288] [1], wholeheartedly [+4213+8969] [1], why [+4537] [1], willfully [+4222] [1], wish [+3202+6524] [1], wish [+3512+6524] [1], wished [+3202+6524] [1], with [+2118] [1], with [+8079] [1], with in hand [1], within [+2668] [1], within [+3752] [1], within [+5055+9348] [1], without [+1172] [1], without meaning [+2021+2039] [1], withstood [+6641+7156] [1], won [+5951+6524] [1], workmen [+2021+4856+6913] [1], worn [+5432] [1], worth [1], your [+2257] [1], your [+3870] [1]

929 בִּאָה bi'â, n.f. [1] [√ 995]

entrance [1]

Eze 8: 5 in the **entrance** north of the gate of the altar I saw this idol of

930 בָּאַר bā'ar, v. [3]

clearly [1], expound [1], make plain [1]

Dt 1: 5 [D] territory of Moab, Moses began *to* **expound** this law, saying:
27: 8 [D] you shall write very **clearly** all the words of this law on these
Hab 2: 2 [D] "Write down the revelation and **make** it **plain** on tablets so

931 בְּאֵר[1] b[e]'ēr[1], n.f. [39] [→ 932, 933, 934, 935, 936, 937, 938, 939, 940, 941, 942, 1014, 1015, 1016, 1364, 1365; cf. 1071; *also used with compound proper names*]

well [30], full of pits [+931] [2], pit [2], wells [2], well [+4784] [1], well's [1], wells [+4784] [1]

Ge 14:10 Now the Valley of Siddim was **full of** tar **pits** [+931], and when
14:10 Now the Valley of Siddim was **full of** tar **pits** [+931], and when
16:14 That is why the **well** was called Beer Lahai Roi; it is still there,
21:19 God opened her eyes and she saw a **well** *of* water. So she went
21:25 Abraham complained to Abimelech about a **well** *of* water that
21:30 these seven lambs from my hand as a witness that I dug this **well**."
24:11 He had the camels kneel down near the **well** [+4784] outside the
24:20 ran back to the **well** to draw more water, and drew enough for all
26:15 So all the **wells** that his father's servants had dug in the time of his
26:18 Isaac reopened the **wells** [+4784] that had been dug in the time of
26:19 dug in the valley and discovered a **well** *of* fresh water there.
26:20 So he named the **well** Esek, because they disputed with him.
26:21 Then they dug another **well**, but they quarreled over that one also;
26:22 He moved on from there and dug another **well**, and no one
26:25 There he pitched his tent, and there his servants dug a **well**.
26:32 Isaac's servants came and told him about the **well** they had dug.
29: 2 There he saw a **well** in the field, with three flocks of sheep lying
29: 2 sheep lying near it because the flocks were watered from that **well**.
29: 2 from that well. The stone over the mouth of the **well** was large.
29: 3 the shepherds would roll the stone away from the **well's** mouth
29: 3 they would return the stone to its place over the mouth of the **well**.
29: 8 and the stone has been rolled away from the mouth of the **well**.
29:10 he went over and rolled the stone away from the mouth of the **well**
Ex 2:15 and went to live in Midian, where he sat down by a **well**.
Nu 20:17 not go through any field or vineyard, or drink water from any **well**.
21:16 the **well** where the LORD said to Moses, "Gather the people
21:17 Then Israel sang this song: "Spring up, O **well**! Sing about it,
21:18 about the **well** that the princes dug, that the nobles of the people
21:22 turn aside into any field or vineyard, or drink water from any **well**.
Dt 10: 6 (The Israelites traveled from the **wells** *of* the Jaakanites to
2Sa 17:18 He had a **well** in his courtyard, and they climbed down into it.
17:19 wife took a covering and spread it out over the opening of the **well**
17:21 the two climbed out of the **well** and went to inform King David.
Ps 55:23 [55:24] will bring down the wicked into the **pit** *of* corruption;
69:15 [69:16] depths swallow me up or the **pit** close its mouth over me.
Pr 5:15 water from your own cistern, running water from your own **well**.
23:27 for a prostitute is a deep pit and a wayward wife is a narrow **well**.
SS 4:15 a **well** *of* flowing water streaming down from Lebanon.
Jer 6: 7 As a **well** [K 1014] pours out its water, so she pours out her

932 ²בְּאֵר bᵉʾēr², n.pr.loc. [2] [√ 931]

Beer [2]

Nu 21:16 From there they continued on to **Beer**, the well where the LORD
Jdg 9:21 escaping to **Beer**, and he lived there because he was afraid of his

933 ³בְּאֵר bᵉʾēr³, n.f. Not used in NIV/BHS [√ 931]

934 בֹּאר bōʾr, n.m. Not used in NIV/BHS [√ 1014; cf. 931]

935 בְּאֵר אֵילִים bᵉʾēr ʾêlîm, n.pr.loc. [1] [√ 931 + 381; cf. 380]

Beer Elim [1]

Isa 15: 8 reaches as far as Eglaim, their lamentation as far as **Beer Elim**.

936 בְּאֵר לַחַי רֹאִי bᵉʾēr laḥay rōʾî, n.pr.loc. [3] [√ 931 + 4200 + 2649 + 8022]

Beer Lahai Roi [3]

Ge 16:14 That is why the well was called **Beer Lahai Roi**; it is still there,
24:62 Now Isaac had come from **Beer Lahai Roi**, for he was living in
25:11 God blessed his son Isaac, who then lived near **Beer Lahai Roi**.

937 בְּאֵר שֶׁבַע bᵉʾēr šebaʿ, n.pr.loc. [34] [√ 931 + 8679]

Beersheba [34]

Ge 21:14 She went on her way and wandered in the desert of **Beersheba**.
21:31 So that place was called **Beersheba**, because the two men swore an
21:32 After the treaty had been made at **Beersheba**, Abimelech
21:33 Abraham planted a tamarisk tree in **Beersheba**, and there he called
22:19 returned to his servants, and they set off together for **Beersheba**.
22:19 set off together for Beersheba. And Abraham stayed in **Beersheba**.
26:23 From there he went up to **Beersheba**.
26:33 and to this day the name of the town has been **Beersheba**.
28:10 Jacob left **Beersheba** and set out for Haran.
46: 1 set out with all that was his, and when he reached **Beersheba**,
46: 5 Jacob left **Beersheba**, and Israel's sons took their father Jacob
Jos 15:28 Hazar Shual, **Beersheba**, Biziothiah,
19: 2 It included: **Beersheba** (or Sheba), Moladah,
Jdg 20: 1 all the Israelites from Dan to **Beersheba** and from the land of
1Sa 3:20 all Israel from Dan to **Beersheba** recognized that Samuel was
8: 2 the name of his second was Abijah, and they served at **Beersheba**.
2Sa 3:10 David's throne over Israel and Judah from Dan to **Beersheba**."
17:11 Let all Israel, from Dan to **Beersheba**—as numerous as the sand
24: 2 "Go throughout the tribes of Israel from Dan to **Beersheba**
24: 7 Finally, they went on to **Beersheba** in the Negev of Judah.
24:15 and seventy thousand of the people from Dan to **Beersheba** died.
1Ki 4:25 [5:5] lifetime Judah and Israel, from Dan to **Beersheba**,
19: 3 When he came to **Beersheba** in Judah, he left his servant there,
2Ki 12: 1 [12:2] His mother's name was Zibiah; she was from **Beersheba**.
23: 8 of Judah and desecrated the high places, from Geba to **Beersheba**,
1Ch 4:28 They lived in **Beersheba**, Moladah, Hazar Shual,
21: 2 of the troops, "Go and count the Israelites from **Beersheba** to Dan.
2Ch 19: 4 he went out again among the people from **Beersheba** to the hill
24: 1 His mother's name was Zibiah; she was from **Beersheba**.
30: 5 from **Beersheba** to Dan, calling the people to come to Jerusalem
Ne 11:27 in Hazar Shual, in **Beersheba** and its settlements,
11:30 So they were living all the way from **Beersheba** to the Valley of
Am 5: 5 not seek Bethel, do not go to Gilgal, do not journey to **Beersheba**.
8:14 god lives, O Dan,' or, 'As surely as the god of **Beersheba** lives'—

938 בְּאֵרָא bᵉʾērāʾ, n.pr.m. [1] [√ 931]

Beera [1]

1Ch 7:37 Bezer, Hod, Shamma, Shilshah, Ithran and **Beera**.

939 בְּאֵרָה bᵉʾērâ, n.pr.m. [1] [√ 931]

Beerah [1]

1Ch 5: 6 **Beerah** his son, whom Tiglath-Pileser king of Assyria took into

940 בְּאֵרוֹת bᵉʾērôt, n.pr.loc. [5] [√ 943; cf. 931]

Beeroth [5]

Jos 9:17 to their cities: Gibeon, Kephirah, **Beeroth** and Kiriath Jearim.
18:25 Gibeon, Ramah, **Beeroth**,
2Sa 4: 2 the tribe of Benjamin—**Beeroth** is considered part of Benjamin,
Ezr 2:25 of Kiriath Jearim, Kephirah and **Beeroth** 743
Ne 7:29 of Kiriath Jearim, Kephirah and **Beeroth** 743

941 בְּאֵרִי bᵉʾērî, n.pr.m. [2] [√ 931]

Beeri [2]

Ge 26:34 was forty years old, he married Judith daughter of **Beeri** the Hittite,
Hos 1: 1 The word of the LORD that came to Hosea son of **Beeri** during

942 בְּאֵרֹת בְּנֵי־יַעֲקָן bᵉʾērōt bᵉnê-yaʿᵃqān, n.pr.loc. Not used in NIV/BHS [√ 931 + 1201 + 3622]

943 בְּאֵרֹתִי bᵉʾērōtî, a.g. [5] [√ 940; cf. 1409]

Beerothite [4], people of Beeroth [1]

2Sa 4: 2 they were sons of Rimmon the **Beerothite** from the tribe of
4: 3 because the **people of Beeroth** fled to Gittaim and have lived there
4: 5 Now Recab and Baanah, the sons of Rimmon the **Beerothite**,
4: 9 and his brother Baanah, the sons of Rimmon the **Beerothite**,
23:37 Zelek the Ammonite, Naharai the **Beerothite**, the armor-bearer of

944 בָּאַשׁ bāʾaš, v. [17] [→ 945, 946, 947; Ar 10091]

stench [3], so odious [+944] [2], stink [2], bring shame [1], give a bad smell [+5580] [1], loathsome [1], made stench [+906+8194] [1], made yourself a stench [1], making a stench [1], reeked [1], rot [1], smell [1], smelled bad [1]

Ge 34:30 [G] "You have brought trouble on me by **making** me **a stench** to
Ex 5:21 [G] *You have* **made** us a **stench** [+906+8194] to Pharaoh and his
7:18 [A] The fish in the Nile will die, and the river *will* **stink**;
7:21 [A] the river **smelled** so **bad** that the Egyptians could not drink
8:14 [8:10] [A] were piled into heaps, and the land **reeked** *of* them.
16:20 [A] until morning, but it was full of maggots and *began to* **smell**.
16:24 [G] Moses commanded, and *it did* not **stink** or get maggots in it.
1Sa 13: 4 [C] and now Israel *has become a* **stench** to the Philistines."
27:12 [G] "*He has become* **so odious** [+944] to his people,
27:12 [G] "*He has become* **so odious** [+944] to his people,
2Sa 10: 6 [C] realized that *they had become a* **stench** in David's nostrils,
16:21 [C] all Israel will hear that *you have* **made yourself a stench** in
1Ch 19: 6 [F] realized that *they had become a* **stench** in David's nostrils,
Ps 38: 5 [38:6] [G] My wounds fester and *are* **loathsome** because of my
Pr 13: 5 [G] hate what is false, but the wicked **bring shame** and disgrace.
Ecc 10: 1 [G] As dead flies **give** perfume **a bad smell** [+5580], so a little
Isa 50: 2 [A] into a desert; their fish **rot** for lack of water and die of thirst.

945 בְּאֹשׁ bᵉʾōš, n.m. [3] [√ 944]

stench [3]

Isa 34: 3 slain will be thrown out, their dead bodies will send up a **stench**;
Joel 2:20 its **stench** will go up; its smell will rise." Surely he has done great
Am 4:10 I filled your nostrils with the **stench** *of* your camps, yet you have

946 בְּאֻשִׁים bᵉʾuš, n.[m.]pl. [2] [√ 944]

bad fruit [1], bad [1]

Isa 5: 2 he looked for a crop of good grapes, but it yielded only **bad fruit**.
5: 4 When I looked for good grapes, why did it yield only **bad**?

947 בָּאְשָׁה boʾšâ, n.f. [1] [√ 944]

weeds [1]

Job 31:40 let briers come up instead of wheat and **weeds** instead of barley."

948 בַּאֲשֶׁר baʾᵃšer, adv. & c. Not used in NIV/BHS [√ 928 + 889]

949 בָּבָה bābâ, n.f. [1] [√ 950?]

apple [1]

Zec 2: 8 [2:12] for whoever touches you touches the **apple** *of* his eye—

950 בֵּבַי bēbay, n.pr.m. [6] [√ 949?]

Bebai [6]

Ezr 2:11 of **Bebai** 623
8:11 of the descendants of **Bebai**, Zechariah son of Bebai, and with him
8:11 of Bebai, Zechariah son of **Bebai**, and with him 28 men;
10:28 From the descendants of **Bebai**: Jehohanan, Hananiah, Zabbai
Ne 7:16 of **Bebai** 628
10:15 [10:16] Bunni, Azgad, **Bebai**,

951 בָּבֶל bābel, n.pr.loc. [262] [cf. 4169; Ar 10093]

Babylon [242], *untranslated* [7], Babylon's [3], Babylonians [+1201] [2], Babel [1], Babylon [+824] [1], Babylonia [1], Babylonian [+1201] [1], he[s] [+4889] [1], him[s] [+4889] [1], his[s] [+4889] [1], there[s] [+928] [1]

Ge 10:10 The first centers of his kingdom were **Babylon**, Erech, Akkad
11: 9 That is why it was called **Babel**—because there the LORD
2Ki 17:24 The king of Assyria brought people from **Babylon**, Cuthah,
17:30 The men from **Babylon** made Succoth Benoth, the men from
20:12 At that time Merodach-Baladan son of Baladan king of **Babylon**
20:14 a distant land," Hezekiah replied. "They came from **Babylon**."

2Ki 20: 17 have stored up until this day, will be carried off to **Babylon**.
20: 18 they will become eunuchs in the palace of the king of **Babylon**."
24: 1 Nebuchadnezzar king of **Babylon** invaded the land,
24: 7 because the king of **Babylon** had taken all his territory, from the
24: 10 At that time the officers of Nebuchadnezzar king of **Babylon**
24: 11 Nebuchadnezzar **[RPH]** himself came up to the city while his
24: 12 his nobles and his officials all surrendered to **him**[s] [+4889].
24: 12 In the eighth year of the reign of the king of **Babylon**, he took
24: 15 Nebuchadnezzar took Jehoiachin captive to **Babylon**. He also took
24: 15 He also took from Jerusalem to **Babylon** the king's mother,
24: 16 The king of **Babylon** also deported to Babylon the entire force of
24: 16 The king of Babylon also deported to **Babylon** the entire force of
24: 17 **He**[s] [+4889] made Mattaniah, Jehoiachin's uncle, king in his place
24: 20 his presence. Now Zedekiah rebelled against the king of **Babylon**.
25: 1 Nebuchadnezzar king of **Babylon** marched against Jerusalem with
25: 6 He was taken to the king of **Babylon** at Riblah, where sentence
25: 7 bound him with bronze shackles and took him to **Babylon**.
25: 8 in the nineteenth year of Nebuchadnezzar king of **Babylon**,
25: 8 an official of the king of **Babylon**, came to Jerusalem.
25: 11 the populace and those who had gone over to the king of **Babylon**.
25: 13 the temple of the LORD and they carried the bronze to **Babylon**.
25: 20 took them all and brought them to the king of **Babylon** at Riblah.
25: 21 in the land of Hamath, the king **[RPH]** had them executed.
25: 22 Nebuchadnezzar king of **Babylon** appointed Gedaliah son of
25: 23 their men heard that the king of **Babylon** had appointed Gedaliah
25: 24 "Settle down in the land and serve the king of **Babylon**, and it will
25: 27 king of Judah, in the year Evil-Merodach became king of **Babylon**,
25: 28 than those of the other kings who were with him in **Babylon**.
1Ch 9: 1 The people of Judah were taken captive to **Babylon** because of
2Ch 32: 31 when envoys were sent by the rulers of **Babylon** to ask him about
33: 11 bound him with bronze shackles and took him to **Babylon**.
36: 6 Nebuchadnezzar king of **Babylon** attacked him and bound him
36: 6 and bound him with bronze shackles to take him to **Babylon**.
36: 7 Nebuchadnezzar also took to **Babylon** articles from the temple of
36: 7 temple of the LORD and put them in his temple **there**[s] [+928].
36: 10 King Nebuchadnezzar sent for him and brought him to **Babylon**,
36: 18 He carried to **Babylon** all the articles from the temple of God,
36: 20 He carried into exile to **Babylon** the remnant, who escaped from
Ezr 1: 11 these along when the exiles came up from **Babylon** to Jerusalem.
2: 1 whom Nebuchadnezzar king of **Babylon** had taken captive to
2: 1 Babylon had taken captive to **Babylon** (they returned to Jerusalem
7: 6 this Ezra came up from **Babylon**. He was a teacher well versed in
7: 9 He had begun his journey from **Babylon** on the first day of the first
8: 1 those registered with them who came up with me from **Babylon**
Ne 7: 6 king of **Babylon** had taken captive (they returned to Jerusalem
13: 6 for in the thirty-second year of Artaxerxes king of **Babylon** I had
Est 2: 6 into exile from Jerusalem by Nebuchadnezzar king of **Babylon**,
Ps 87: 4 record Rahab and **Babylon** among those who acknowledge me—
137: 1 By the rivers of **Babylon** we sat and wept when we remembered
137: 8 O Daughter of **Babylon**, doomed to destruction, happy is he who
Isa 13: 1 An oracle concerning **Babylon** that Isaiah son of Amoz saw:
13: 19 **Babylon**, the jewel of kingdoms, the glory of the Babylonians'
14: 4 you will take up this taunt against the king of **Babylon**: How the
14: 22 "I will cut off from **Babylon** her name and survivors, her offspring
21: 9 And he gives back the answer: '**Babylon** has fallen, has fallen!
39: 1 At that time Merodach-Baladan son of Baladan king of **Babylon**
39: 3 distant land," Hezekiah replied. "They came to me from **Babylon**."
39: 6 have stored up until this day, will be carried off to **Babylon**.
39: 7 they will become eunuchs in the palace of the king of **Babylon**."
43: 14 "For your sake I will send to **Babylon** and bring down as fugitives
47: 1 "Go down, sit in the dust, Virgin Daughter of **Babylon**; sit on the
48: 14 LORD's chosen ally will carry out his purpose against **Babylon**;
48: 20 Leave **Babylon**, flee from the Babylonians! Announce this with
Jer 20: 4 I will hand all Judah over to the king of **Babylon**, who will carry
20: 4 who will carry them away to **Babylon** or put them to the sword.
20: 5 They will take it away as plunder and carry it off to **Babylon**.
20: 6 and all who live in your house will go into exile to **Babylon**.
21: 2 because Nebuchadnezzar king of **Babylon** is attacking us.
21: 4 which you are using to fight the king of **Babylon** and the
21: 7 to Nebuchadnezzar king of **Babylon** and to their enemies who seek
21: 10 It will be given into the hands of the king of **Babylon**, and he will
22: 25 to Nebuchadnezzar king of **Babylon** and to the Babylonians.
24: 1 from Jerusalem to **Babylon** by Nebuchadnezzar king of Babylon,
24: 1 from Jerusalem to Babylon by Nebuchadnezzar king of **Babylon**,
25: 1 which was the first year of Nebuchadnezzar king of **Babylon**.
25: 9 of the north and my servant Nebuchadnezzar king of **Babylon**,"
25: 11 and these nations will serve the king of **Babylon** seventy years.
25: 12 I will punish the king of **Babylon** and his nation, the land of the
27: 6 countries over to my servant Nebuchadnezzar king of **Babylon**;
27: 8 or kingdom will not serve Nebuchadnezzar king of **Babylon**
27: 8 king of Babylon or bow its neck under **his**[s] [+4889] yoke,
27: 9 sorcerers who tell you, 'You will not serve the king of **Babylon**.'
27: 11 any nation will bow its neck under the yoke of the king of **Babylon**
27: 12 I said, "Bow your neck under the yoke of the king of **Babylon**;
27: 13 has threatened any nation that will not serve the king of **Babylon**?
27: 14 'You will not serve the king of **Babylon**,' for they are prophesying
27: 16 from the LORD's house will be brought back from **Babylon**.'
27: 17 not listen to them. Serve the king of **Babylon**, and you will live.
27: 18 of the king of Judah and in Jerusalem not be taken to **Babylon**.
27: 20 which Nebuchadnezzar king of **Babylon** did not take away when
27: 20 of Jehoiakim king of Judah into exile from Jerusalem to **Babylon**,
27: 22 'They will be taken to **Babylon** and there they will remain until the
28: 2 God of Israel, says: 'I will break the yoke of the king of **Babylon**.
28: 3 house that Nebuchadnezzar king of **Babylon** removed from here
28: 3 king of Babylon removed from here and took to **Babylon**.
28: 4 and all the other exiles from Judah who went to **Babylon**,'
28: 4 the LORD, 'for I will break the yoke of the king of **Babylon**.' "
28: 6 LORD's house and all the exiles back to this place from **Babylon**.
28: 11 **Babylon** off the neck of all the nations within two years.' " At this,
28: 14 nations to make them serve Nebuchadnezzar king of **Babylon**,
29: 1 Nebuchadnezzar had carried into exile from Jerusalem to **Babylon**.
29: 3 king of Judah sent to King Nebuchadnezzar **[RPH]** in Babylon.
29: 3 Zedekiah king of Judah sent to King Nebuchadnezzar in **Babylon**.
29: 4 says to all those I carried into exile from Jerusalem to **Babylon**:
29: 10 "When seventy years are completed for **Babylon**, I will come to
29: 15 may say, "The LORD has raised up prophets for us in **Babylon**,"
29: 20 all you exiles whom I have sent away from Jerusalem to **Babylon**.
29: 21 "I will hand them over to Nebuchadnezzar king of **Babylon**,
29: 22 all the exiles from Judah who are in **Babylon** will use this curse:
29: 22 and Ahab, whom the king of **Babylon** burned in the fire.'
29: 28 He has sent this message to us in **Babylon**: It will be a long time.
32: 2 The army of the king of **Babylon** was then besieging Jerusalem,
32: 3 I am about to hand this city over to the king of **Babylon**, and he
32: 4 but will certainly be handed over to the king of **Babylon**,
32: 5 He will take Zedekiah to **Babylon**, where he will remain until I
32: 28 over to the Babylonians and to Nebuchadnezzar king of **Babylon**,
32: 36 and plague it will be handed over to the king of **Babylon**';
34: 1 While Nebuchadnezzar king of **Babylon** and all his army and all
34: 2 I am about to hand this city over to the king of **Babylon**, and he
34: 3 You will see the king of **Babylon** with your own eyes, and he will
34: 3 he will speak with you face to face. And you will go to **Babylon**.
34: 7 while the army of the king of **Babylon** was fighting against
34: 21 to the army of the king of **Babylon**, which has withdrawn from
35: 11 But when Nebuchadnezzar king of **Babylon** invaded this land,
36: 29 "Why did you write on it that the king of **Babylon** would certainly
37: 1 was made king of Judah by Nebuchadnezzar king of **Babylon**;
37: 17 "you will be handed over to the king of **Babylon**."
37: 19 to you, 'The king of **Babylon** will not attack you or this land'?
38: 3 will certainly be handed over to the army of the king of **Babylon**,
38: 17 'If you surrender to the officers of the king of **Babylon**, your life
38: 18 But if you will not surrender to the officers of the king of **Babylon**,
38: 22 Judah will be brought out to the officials of the king of **Babylon**.
38: 23 from their hands but will be captured by the king of **Babylon**;
39: 1 Nebuchadnezzar king of **Babylon** marched against Jerusalem with
39: 3 all the officials of the king of **Babylon** came and took seats in the
39: 3 a high official and all the other officials of the king of **Babylon**.
39: 5 took him to Nebuchadnezzar king of **Babylon** at Riblah in the land
39: 6 There at Riblah the king of **Babylon** slaughtered the sons of
39: 6 before his eyes and also killed all the nobles of Judah. **[RPH]**
39: 7 and bound him with bronze shackles to take him to **Babylon**.
39: 9 carried into exile to **Babylon** the people who remained in the city,
39: 11 Now Nebuchadnezzar king of **Babylon** had given these orders
39: 13 a high official and all the other officers of the king of **Babylon**
40: 1 and Judah who were being carried into exile to **Babylon**.
40: 4 Come with me to **Babylon**, if you like, and I will look after you;
40: 4 **[RPH]** Look, the whole country lies before you; go wherever you
40: 5 whom the king of **Babylon** has appointed over the towns of Judah,
40: 7 **Babylon** had appointed Gedaliah son of Ahikam as governor over
40: 7 in the land and who had not been carried into exile to **Babylon**,
40: 9 "Settle down in the land and serve the king of **Babylon**, and it will
40: 11 all the other countries heard that the king of **Babylon** had left a
41: 2 killing the one whom the king of **Babylon** had appointed as
41: 18 whom the king of **Babylon** had appointed as governor over the
42: 11 Do not be afraid of the king of **Babylon**, whom you now fear.
43: 3 so they may kill us or carry us into exile to **Babylon**."
43: 10 I will send for my servant Nebuchadnezzar king of **Babylon**,
44: 30 Zedekiah king of Judah over to Nebuchadnezzar king of **Babylon**,
46: 2 **Babylon** in the fourth year of Jehoiakim son of Josiah king of
46: 13 the coming of Nebuchadnezzar king of **Babylon** to attack Egypt:
46: 26 their lives, to Nebuchadnezzar king of **Babylon** and his officers.
49: 28 of Hazor, which Nebuchadnezzar king of **Babylon** attacked:
49: 30 "Nebuchadnezzar king of **Babylon** has plotted against you;
50: 1 LORD spoke through Jeremiah the prophet concerning **Babylon**
50: 2 proclaim it; keep nothing back, but say, '**Babylon** will be captured;
50: 8 "Flee out of **Babylon**; leave the land of the Babylonians, and be
50: 9 bring against **Babylon** an alliance of great nations from the land of
50: 13 All who pass **Babylon** will be horrified and scoff because of all her
50: 14 "Take up your positions around **Babylon**, all you who draw the

Jer 50:16 Cut off from **Babylon** the sower, and the reaper with his sickle at
50:17 the last to crush his bones was Nebuchadnezzar king of **Babylon**."
50:18 "I will punish the king of **Babylon** and his land as I punished the
50:23 of the whole earth! How desolate is **Babylon** among the nations!
50:24 I set a trap for you, O **Babylon**, and you were caught before you
50:28 refugees from **Babylon** [+824] declaring in Zion how the LORD
50:29 "Summon archers against **Babylon**, all those who draw the bow.
50:34 bring rest to their land, but unrest to those who live in **Babylon**.
50:35 "against those who live in **Babylon** and against her officials
50:42 like men in battle formation to attack you, O Daughter of **Babylon**.
50:43 The king of **Babylon** has heard reports about them, and his hands
50:45 Therefore, hear what the LORD has planned against **Babylon**,
50:46 At the sound of **Babylon's** capture the earth will tremble;
51: 1 I will stir up the spirit of a destroyer against **Babylon** and the
51: 2 I will send foreigners to **Babylon** to winnow her and to devastate
51: 6 "Flee from **Babylon**! Run for your lives! Do not be destroyed
51: 7 **Babylon** was a gold cup in the LORD's hand; she made the
51: 8 **Babylon** will suddenly fall and be broken. Wail over her!
51: 9 " 'We would have healed **Babylon**, but she cannot be healed;
51:11 the kings of the Medes, because his purpose is to destroy **Babylon**.
51:12 Lift up a banner against the walls of **Babylon**! Reinforce the guard,
51:12 carry out his purpose, his decree against the people of **Babylon**.
51:24 "Before your eyes I will repay **Babylon** and all who live in
51:29 and writhes, for the LORD's purposes against **Babylon** stand—
51:29 to lay waste the land of **Babylon** so that no one will live there.
51:30 **Babylon's** warriors have stopped fighting; they remain in their
51:31 messenger follows messenger to announce to the king of **Babylon**
51:33 "The Daughter of **Babylon** is like a threshing floor at the time it is
51:34 "Nebuchadnezzar king of **Babylon** has devoured us, he has thrown
51:35 May the violence done to our flesh be upon **Babylon**,"
51:37 **Babylon** will be a heap of ruins, a haunt of jackals, an object of
51:41 earth seized! What a horror **Babylon** will be among the nations!
51:42 The sea will rise over **Babylon**; its roaring waves will cover her.
51:44 I will punish Bel in **Babylon** and make him spew out what he has
51:44 will no longer stream to him. And the wall of **Babylon** will fall.
51:47 the time will surely come when I will punish the idols of **Babylon**;
51:48 and earth and all that is in them will shout for joy over **Babylon**,
51:49 "**Babylon** must fall because of Israel's slain, just as the slain in all
51:49 just as the slain in all the earth have fallen because of **Babylon**.
51:53 Even if **Babylon** reaches the sky and fortifies her lofty stronghold,
51:54 "The sound of a cry comes from **Babylon**, the sound of great
51:55 The LORD will destroy **Babylon**; he will silence her noisy din.
51:56 A destroyer will come against **Babylon**; her warriors will be
51:58 "**Babylon's** thick wall will be leveled and her high gates set on
51:59 when he went to **Babylon** with Zedekiah king of Judah in the
51:60 on a scroll about all the disasters that would come upon **Babylon**—
51:60 upon Babylon—all that had been recorded concerning **Babylon**.
51:61 He said to Seraiah, "When you get to **Babylon**, see that you read
51:64 'So will **Babylon** sink to rise no more because of the disaster I will
52: 3 his presence. Now Zedekiah rebelled against the king of **Babylon**.
52: 4 Nebuchadnezzar king of **Babylon** marched against Jerusalem with
52: 9 He was taken to the king of **Babylon** at Riblah in the land of
52:10 There at Riblah the king of **Babylon** slaughtered the sons of
52:11 bound him with bronze shackles and took him **[RPH]** to Babylon,
52:11 bound him with bronze shackles and took him to **Babylon**,
52:12 in the nineteenth year of Nebuchadnezzar king of **Babylon**,
52:12 who served the king of **Babylon**, came to Jerusalem.
52:15 the craftsmen and those who had gone over to the king of **Babylon**.
52:17 temple of the LORD and they carried all the bronze to **Babylon**.
52:26 took them all and brought them to the king of **Babylon** at Riblah.
52:27 in the land of Hamath, the king **[RPH]** had them executed.
52:31 in the year Evil-Merodach became king of **Babylon**, he released
52:32 than those of the other kings who were with him in **Babylon**.
52:34 Day by day the king of **Babylon** gave Jehoiachin a regular
Eze 12:13 I will bring him to **Babylonia**, the land of the Chaldeans, but he
17:12 'The king of **Babylon** went to Jerusalem and carried off her king
17:12 and her nobles, bringing them back with him to **Babylon**.
17:16 as I live, declares the Sovereign LORD, he shall die in **Babylon**,
17:20 I will bring him to **Babylon** and execute judgment upon him there
19: 9 pulled him into a cage and brought him to the king of **Babylon**.
21:19 [21:24] mark out two roads for the sword of the king of **Babylon**
21:21 [21:26] For the king of **Babylon** will stop at the fork in the road,
23:15 all of them looked like **Babylonian** [+1201] chariot officers,
23:17 Then the **Babylonians** [+1201] came to her, to the bed of love,
23:23 the **Babylonians** [+1201] and all the Chaldeans, the men of Pekod
24: 2 because the king of **Babylon** has laid siege to Jerusalem this very
26: 7 I am going to bring against Tyre Nebuchadnezzar king of **Babylon**,
29:18 Nebuchadnezzar king of **Babylon** drove his army in a hard
29:19 I am going to give Egypt to Nebuchadnezzar king of **Babylon**,
30:10 hordes of Egypt by the hand of Nebuchadnezzar king of **Babylon**.
30:24 I will strengthen the arms of the king of **Babylon** and put my
30:25 I will strengthen the arms of the king of **Babylon**, but the arms of
30:25 when I put my sword into the hand of the king of **Babylon**
32:11 " 'The sword of the king of **Babylon** will come against you.
Da 1: 1 Nebuchadnezzar king of **Babylon** came to Jerusalem and besieged
Mic 4:10 the open field. You will go to **Babylon**; there you will be rescued.
Zec 2: 7 [2:11] Escape, you who live in the Daughter of **Babylon**!"
6:10 Tobijah and Jedaiah, who have arrived from **Babylon**.

952 בַּג *bag*, var. [0] [cf. 1020, 7329?]

Eze 25: 7 [against you and give you as **plunder** [K; see Q 1020] to the nations.]

953 בָּגַד *bāgad*, v. [49] [→ 954, 955, 956, 957]

unfaithful [16], betrayed [5], broken faith [4], treacherous [4], betray [2], betrays [2], break faith [2], faithless [2], how treacherous [+953] [2], traitor [2], utterly unfaithful [+953] [2], acted treacherously [1], betraying [1], breaking faith [1], faithless [+954] [1], traitors [1], undependable [1]

Ex 21: 8 [A] sell her to foreigners, because he *has* **broken faith** with her.
Jdg 9:23 [A] of Shechem, who **acted treacherously** against Abimelech.
1Sa 14:33 [A] "*You have* **broken faith**," he said. "Roll a large stone over
Job 6:15 [A] my brothers *are* as **undependable** as intermittent streams,
Ps 25: 3 [A] they will be put to shame who *are* **treacherous** without
59: 5 [59:6] [A] all the nations; show no mercy to wicked **traitors**.
73:15 [A] "I will speak thus," *I would have* **betrayed** your children.
78:57 [A] Like their fathers they were disloyal and **faithless**,
119:158 [A] I look on the **faithless** with loathing, for they do not obey
Pr 2:22 [A] cut off from the land, and the **unfaithful** will be torn from it.
11: 3 [A] but the **unfaithful** are destroyed by their duplicity.
11: 6 [A] delivers them, but the **unfaithful** are trapped by evil desires.
13: 2 [A] good things, but the **unfaithful** have a craving for violence.
13:15 [A] wins favor, but the way of the **unfaithful** is hard.
21:18 [A] ransom for the righteous, and the **unfaithful** for the upright.
22:12 [A] but he frustrates the words of the **unfaithful**.
23:28 [A] she lies in wait, and multiplies the **unfaithful** among men.
25:19 [A] or a lame foot is reliance on the **unfaithful** in times of
Isa 21: 2 [A] The **traitor** betrays, the looter takes loot. Elam, attack!
21: 2 [A] The traitor **betrays**, the looter takes loot. Elam, attack!
24:16 [A] I waste away! Woe to me! The **treacherous** betray!
24:16 [A] I waste away! Woe to me! The treacherous **betray**!
24:16 [A] treacherous betray! With treachery the **treacherous** betray!"
24:16 [A] treacherous betray! *With* treachery the treacherous **betray**!"
33: 1 [A] Woe to you, O **traitor**, you who have not been betrayed!
33: 1 [A] Woe to you, O traitor, you who *have* not *been* **betrayed**!
33: 1 [A] when you stop **betraying**, you will be betrayed.
33: 1 [A] when you stop betraying, you *will be* **betrayed**.
48: 8 [A] Well do I know **how treacherous** [+953] *you are*; you were
48: 8 [A] Well do I know **how treacherous** *you* **are** [+953]; you were
Jer 3: 8 [A] Yet I saw that her **unfaithful** sister Judah had no fear; she
3:11 [A] "Faithless Israel is more righteous than **unfaithful** Judah.
3:20 [A] like a woman **unfaithful** to her husband, so you have been
3:20 [A] so *you have been* **unfaithful** to me, O house of Israel,"
5:11 [A] the house of Judah *have been* **utterly unfaithful** [+953] to
5:11 [A] the house of Judah *have been* **utterly unfaithful** [+953] to
9: 2 [9:1] [A] they are all adulterers, a crowd of **unfaithful** *people*.
12: 1 [A] wicked prosper? Why do all the **faithless** [+954] live at ease?
12: 6 [A] your own family—even they *have* **betrayed** you;
La 1: 2 [A] All her friends *have* **betrayed** her; they have become her
Hos 5: 7 [A] *They are* **unfaithful** to the LORD; they give birth to
6: 7 [A] broken the covenant—*they were* **unfaithful** to me there.
Hab 1:13 [A] tolerate wrong. Why then do you tolerate the **treacherous**?
2: 5 [A] indeed, wine **betrays** him; he is arrogant and never at rest.
Mal 2:10 [A] covenant of our fathers *by* **breaking faith** with one another?
2:11 [A] Judah *has* **broken faith**. A detestable thing has been
2:14 [A] because you *have* **broken faith** with her, though she is your
2:15 [A] and *do* not **break faith** with the wife of your youth.
2:16 [A] So guard yourself in your spirit, and *do* not **break faith**.

954 בֶּגֶד¹ *beged¹*, n.[m.]. [2] [√ 953]

faithless [+953] [1], treachery [1]

Isa 24:16 The treacherous betray! With **treachery** the treacherous betray!"
Jer 12: 1 the wicked prosper? Why do all the **faithless** [+953] live at ease?

955 בֶּגֶד² *beged²*, n.m. [215 / 216] [√ 953]

clothes [79], garments [48], clothing [23], robes [17], garment [14], cloak [8], cloth [8], *untranslated* [5], tunic [2], wardrobe [2], articles of clothing [1], blankets [+2927] [1], cloaks [1], clothed [+4252] [1], clothed [1], clothes [+6886] [1], covers [1], fold of cloak [1], rags [1], those[s] [1]

Ge 24:53 silver jewelry and **articles of clothing** and gave them to Rebekah;
27:15 Then Rebekah took the best **clothes** *of* Esau her older son,
27:27 When Isaac caught the smell of his **clothes**, he blessed him
28:20 I am taking and will give me food to eat and **clothes** to wear
37:29 the cistern and saw that Joseph was not there, he tore his **clothes**.

Ge 38:14 she took off her widow's **clothes**, covered herself with a veil to
38:19 she took off her veil and put on her widow's **clothes** again.
39:12 She caught him by his **cloak** and said, "Come to bed with me!"
39:12 But he left his **cloak** in her hand and ran out of the house.
39:13 When she saw that he had left his **cloak** in her hand and had run
39:15 for help, he left his **cloak** beside me and ran out of the house."
39:16 She kept his **cloak** beside her until his master came home.
39:18 for help, he left his **cloak** beside me and ran out of the house."
41:42 He dressed him in **robes** *of* fine linen and put a gold chain around
Ex 28: 2 Make sacred **garments** for your brother Aaron, to give him dignity
28: 3 wisdom in such matters that they are to make **garments** *for* Aaron,
28: 4 These are the **garments** they are to make: a breastpiece, an ephod,
28: 4 They are to make these sacred **garments** for your brother Aaron
29: 5 Take the **garments** and dress Aaron with the tunic, the robe of the
29:21 it on Aaron and his **garments** and on his sons and their garments.
29:21 it on Aaron and his garments and on his sons and their **garments**.
29:21 Then he and his sons and their **garments** will be consecrated.
29:21 and his sons and their garments **[RPH]** will be consecrated.
29:29 "Aaron's sacred **garments** will belong to his descendants
31:10 also the woven **garments**, both the sacred garments for Aaron the
31:10 both the sacred **garments** for Aaron the priest and the garments for
31:10 and the **garments** *for* his sons when they serve as priests,
35:19 the woven **garments** worn for ministering in the sanctuary—
35:19 both the sacred **garments** for Aaron the priest and the garments for
35:19 and the **garments** *for* his sons when they serve as priests."
35:21 Tent of Meeting, for all its service, and for the sacred **garments**.
39: 1 scarlet yarn they made woven **garments** for ministering in the
39: 1 They also made sacred **garments** for Aaron, as the LORD
39:41 and the woven **garments** worn for ministering in the sanctuary,
39:41 both the sacred **garments** for Aaron the priest and the garments for
39:41 the priest and the **garments** *for* his sons when serving as priests.
40:13 dress Aaron in the sacred **garments**, anoint him and consecrate
Lev 6:11 [6:4] he is to take off these **clothes** and put on others, and carry
6:11 [6:4] **[RPH]** and carry the ashes outside the camp to a place that
6:27 [6:20] if any of the blood is spattered on a **garment**, you must
8: 2 "Bring Aaron and his sons, their **garments**, the anointing oil,
8:30 on Aaron and his **garments** and on his sons and their garments.
8:30 on Aaron and his garments and on his sons and their **garments**.
8:30 and his **garments** and his sons and their garments.
8:30 and his garments and his sons and their **garments**.
10: 6 do not tear your **clothes**, or you will die and the LORD will be
11:25 Whoever picks up one of their carcasses must wash his **clothes**,
11:28 Anyone who picks up their carcasses must wash his **clothes**,
11:32 be unclean, whether it is made of wood, **cloth**, hide or sackcloth.
11:40 Anyone who eats some of the carcass must wash his **clothes**,
11:40 Anyone who picks up the carcass must wash his **clothes**, and he
13: 6 only a rash. The man must wash his **clothes**, and he will be clean.
13:34 him clean. He must wash his **clothes**, and he will be clean.
13:45 person with such an infectious disease must wear torn **clothes**,
13:47 "If any **clothing** is contaminated with mildew—any woolen
13:47 contaminated with mildew—any **[RPH]** woolen or linen clothing,
13:47 is contaminated with mildew—any woolen or linen **clothing**,
13:49 and if the contamination in the **clothing**, or leather, or woven
13:51 and if the mildew has spread in the **clothing**, or the woven
13:52 He must burn up the **clothing**, or the woven or knitted material of
13:53 the mildew has not spread in the **clothing**, or the woven or knitted
13:56 he is to tear the contaminated part out of the **clothing**, or the
13:57 if it reappears in the **clothing**, or in the woven or knitted material,
13:58 The **clothing**, or the woven or knitted material, or any leather
13:59 concerning contamination by mildew in woolen or linen **clothing**,
14: 8 "The person to be cleansed must wash his **clothes**, shave off all his
14: 9 He must wash his **clothes** and bathe himself with water, and he
14:47 who sleeps **[RPH]** or eats in the house must wash his clothes.
14:47 Anyone who sleeps or eats in the house must wash his **clothes**.
14:55 for mildew in **clothing** or in a house,
15: 5 Anyone who touches his bed must wash his **clothes** and bathe with
15: 6 that the man with a discharge sat on must wash his **clothes**
15: 7 touches the man who has a discharge must wash his **clothes**
15: 8 that person must wash his **clothes** and bathe with water, and he
15:10 whoever picks up those things must wash his **clothes** and bathe
15:11 touches without rinsing his hands with water must wash his **clothes**
15:13 he must wash his **clothes** and bathe himself with fresh water,
15:17 Any **clothing** or leather that has semen on it must be washed with
15:21 Whoever touches her bed must wash his **clothes** and bathe with
15:22 Whoever touches anything she sits on must wash his **clothes**
15:27 he must wash his **clothes** and bathe with water, and he will be
16: 4 These are sacred **garments**; so he must bathe himself with water
16:23 take off the linen **garments** he put on before he entered the Most
16:24 with water in a holy place and put on his regular **garments**.
16:26 man who releases the goat as a scapegoat must wash his **clothes**
16:28 The man who burns them must wash his **clothes** and bathe himself
16:32 is to make atonement. He is to put on the sacred linen **garments**
16:32 He is to put on the sacred linen garments **[RPH]**
17:15 or torn by wild animals must wash his **clothes** and bathe with
19:19 of seed. " 'Do not wear **clothing** woven of two kinds of material.
21:10 and who has been ordained to wear the priestly **garments**,
21:10 must not let his hair become unkempt or tear his **clothes**.
Nu 4: 6 spread a **cloth** *of* solid blue over that and put the poles in place.
4: 7 "Over the table of the Presence they are to spread a blue **cloth**
4: 8 Over these they are to spread a scarlet **cloth**, cover that with hides
4: 9 "They are to take a blue **cloth** and cover the lampstand that is for
4:11 "Over the gold altar they are to spread a blue **cloth** and cover that
4:12 wrap them in a blue **cloth**, cover that with hides of sea cows
4:13 the ashes from the bronze altar and spread a purple **cloth** over it.
8: 7 then have them shave their whole bodies and wash their **clothes**,
8:21 The Levites purified themselves and washed their **clothes**.
14: 6 were among those who had explored the land, tore their **clothes**
15:38 to come you are to make tassels on the corners of your **garments**,
19: 7 the priest must wash his **clothes** and bathe himself with water.
19: 8 The man who burns it must also wash his **clothes** and bathe with
19:10 who gathers up the ashes of the heifer must also wash his **clothes**,
19:19 The person being cleansed must wash his **clothes** and bathe with
19:21 who sprinkles the water of cleansing must also wash his **clothes**,
20:26 Remove Aaron's **garments** and put them on his son Eleazar,
20:28 Moses removed Aaron's **garments** and put them on his son
31:20 Purify every **garment** as well as everything made of leather,
31:24 On the seventh day wash your **clothes** and you will be clean.
Dt 24:17 the fatherless of justice, or take the **cloak** *of* the widow as a pledge.
Jdg 8:26 the pendants and the purple **garments** worn by the kings of Midian
11:35 When he saw her, he tore his **clothes** and cried, "Oh! My daughter!
14:12 I will give you thirty linen garments and thirty sets of **clothes**.
14:13 you must give me thirty linen garments and thirty sets of **clothes**."
17:10 ten shekels of silver a year, your **clothes** [+6886] and your food."
1Sa 19:13 covering it with a **garment** and putting some goats' hair at the
19:24 He stripped off his **robes** and also prophesied in Samuel's
27: 9 but took sheep and cattle, donkeys and camels, and **clothes**.
28: 8 putting on other **clothes**, and at night he and two men went to the
2Sa 1: 2 from Saul's camp, with his **clothes** torn and with dust on his head.
1:11 Then David and all the men with him took hold of their **clothes**
3:31 "Tear your **clothes** and put on sackcloth and walk in mourning in
13:31 The king stood up, tore his **clothes** and lay down on the ground;
13:31 on the ground; and all his servants stood by with their **clothes** torn.
14: 2 Dress in mourning **clothes**, and don't use any cosmetic lotions.
19:24 [19:25] or washed his **clothes** from the day the king left until the
20:12 him from the road into a field and threw a **garment** over him.
1Ki 1: 1 he could not keep warm even when they put **covers** over him.
21:27 heard these words, he tore his **clothes**, put on sackcloth and fasted.
22:10 Dressed in their royal **robes**, the king of Israel and Jehoshaphat
22:30 "I will enter the battle in disguise, but you wear your royal **robes**."
2Ki 2:12 Then he took hold of his own **clothes** and tore them apart.
4:39 He gathered some of its gourds and filled the **fold of** his **cloak**.
5: 5 of silver, six thousand shekels of gold and ten sets of **clothing**.
5: 7 of Israel read the letter, he tore his **robes** and said, "Am I God?
5: 8 the man of God heard that the king of Israel had torn his **robes**,
5: 8 he sent him this message: "Why have you torn your **robes**?
5:22 Please give them a talent of silver and two sets of **clothing**.' "
5:23 up the two talents of silver in two bags, with two sets of **clothing**.
5:26 or to accept **clothes**, olive groves, vineyards, flocks, herds,
6:30 When the king heard the woman's words, he tore his **robes**.
7: 8 carried away silver, gold and **clothes**, and went off and hid them.
7:15 they found the whole road strewn with the **clothing** and equipment
9:13 They hurried and took their **cloaks** and spread them under him on
11:14 Then Athaliah tore her **robes** and called out, "Treason! Treason!"
18:37 with their **clothes** torn, and told him what the field commander had
19: 1 he tore his **clothes** and put on sackcloth and went into the temple
22:11 the king heard the words of the Book of the Law, he tore his **robes**.
22:14 son of Tikvah, the son of Harhas, keeper of the **wardrobe**.
22:19 and because you tore your **robes** and wept in my presence,
25:29 So Jehoiachin put aside his prison **clothes** and for the rest of his
2Ch 18: 9 Dressed in their royal **robes**, the king of Israel and Jehoshaphat
18:29 "I will enter the battle in disguise, but you wear your royal **robes**."
20:25 of equipment and **clothing** [BHS 7007] and also articles of value—
23:13 Then Athaliah tore her **robes** and shouted, "Treason! Treason!"
34:19 When the king heard the words of the Law, he tore his **robes**.
34:22 son of Tokhath, the son of Hasrah, keeper of the **wardrobe**.
34:27 yourself before me and tore your **robes** and wept in my presence,
Ezr 9: 3 When I heard this, I tore my **tunic** and cloak, pulled hair from my
9: 5 I rose from my self-abasement, with my **tunic** and cloak torn,
Ne 4:23 [4:17] nor my men nor the guards with me took off our **clothes**;
Est 4: 1 he tore his **clothes**, put on sackcloth and ashes, and went out into
4: 4 She sent **clothes** for him to put on instead of his sackcloth,
Job 13:28 wastes away like something rotten, like a **garment** eaten by moths.
22: 6 no reason; you stripped men of their **clothing**, leaving them naked.
37:17 You who swelter in your **clothes** when the land lies hushed under
Ps 22:18 [22:19] They divide my **garments** among them and cast lots for
45: 8 [45:9] All your **robes** are fragrant with myrrh and aloes
102:26 [102:27] but you remain; they will all wear out like a **garment**.
109:19 May it be like a **cloak** wrapped about him, like a belt tied forever

[F] Hitpael (hitpoel, hitpoal, hitpolel, hitpolal, hitpalel, hitpalal, hitpalpel, hitpalpal, hotpael, hotpaal) [G] Hiphil (hiphtil) [H] Hophal [I] Hishtaphel

Pr 6:27 Can a man scoop fire into his lap without his **clothes** being
20:16 Take the **garment** *of* one who puts up security for a stranger;
25:20 Like one who takes away a **garment** on a cold day, or like vinegar
27:13 Take the **garment** *of* one who puts up security for a stranger;
Ecc 9:8 Always be **clothed** *in* white, and always anoint your head with oil.
Isa 36:22 with their **clothes** torn, and told him what the field commander had
37:1 he tore his **clothes** and put on sackcloth and went into the temple
50:9 They will all wear out like a **garment**; the moths will eat them up.
51:6 the earth will wear out like a **garment** and its inhabitants die like
51:8 For the moth will eat them up like a **garment**; the worm will
52:1 Put on your **garments** *of* splendor, O Jerusalem, the holy city.
59:6 Their cobwebs are useless for **clothing**; they cannot cover
59:17 he put on the **garments** *of* vengeance and wrapped himself in zeal
61:10 For he has clothed me with **garments** *of* salvation and arrayed me
63:1 from Edom, from Bozrah, with his **garments** stained crimson?
63:2 are your garments red, like **those**ˢ of one treading the winepress?
63:3 their blood spattered my **garments**, and I stained all my clothing.
64:6 [64:5] is unclean, and all our righteous acts are like filthy **rags**;
Jer 36:24 all these words showed no fear, nor did they tear their **clothes**.
41:5 torn their **clothes** and cut themselves came from Shechem,
43:12 As a shepherd wraps his **garment** around him, so will he wrap
52:33 So Jehoiachin put aside his prison **clothes** and for the rest of his
Eze 16:16 You took some of your **garments** to make gaudy high places,
16:18 you took your embroidered **clothes** to put on them, and you offered
16:39 They will strip you of your **clothes** and take your fine jewelry
18:7 gives his food to the hungry and provides **clothing** for the naked.
18:16 gives his food to the hungry and provides **clothing** for the naked.
23:26 They will also strip you of your **clothes** and take your fine jewelry.
26:16 and lay aside their robes and take off their embroidered **garments**.
27:20 " 'Dedan traded in saddle **blankets** [+2927] with you.
42:14 court until they leave behind the **garments** in which they minister,
42:14 They are to put on other **clothes** before they go near the places that
44:17 enter the gates of the inner court, they are to wear linen **clothes**;
44:19 they are to take off the **clothes** they have been ministering in
44:19 are to leave them in the sacred rooms, and put on other **clothes**,
44:19 that they do not consecrate the people by means of their **garments**.
Joel 2:13 Rend your heart and not your **garments**. Return to the LORD
Am 2:8 They lie down beside every altar on **garments** taken in pledge.
Hag 2:12 If a person carries consecrated meat in the fold of his **garment**,
Zec 3:3 Now Joshua was dressed in filthy **clothes** as he stood before the
3:4 those who were standing before him, "Take off his filthy **clothes**."
3:5 So they put a clean turban on his head and **clothed** [+4252] him,
14:14 will be collected—great quantities of gold and silver and **clothing**.

956 בֹּגְדוֹת *bōgᵉdôt*, n.pl.abst. [1] [√ 953]

treacherous [1]

Zep 3:4 Her prophets are arrogant; they are **treacherous** men. Her priests

957 בָּגוֹד *bāgôd*, a. [2] [√ 953]

unfaithful [2]

Jer 3:7 return to me but she did not, and her **unfaithful** sister Judah saw it.
3:10 her **unfaithful** sister Judah did not return to me with all her heart,

958 בִּגְוַי *bigway*, n.pr.m. [6]

Bigvai [6]

Ezr 2:2 Reelaiah, Mordecai, Bilshan, Mispar, **Bigvai**, Rehum and Baanah):
2:14 of **Bigvai** 2,056
8:14 of the descendants of **Bigvai**, Uthai and Zaccur, and with them 70
Ne 7:7 Mordecai, Bilshan, Mispereth, **Bigvai**, Nehum and Baanah):
7:19 of **Bigvai** 2,067
10:16 [10:17] Adonijah, **Bigvai**, Adin,

959 בִּגְלַל *biglal*, n.m. Not used in NIV/BHS [√ 1673]

960 בִּגְתָא *bigtā'*, n.pr.m. [1] [→ 961, 962]

Bigtha [1]

Est 1:10 Mehuman, Biztha, Harbona, **Bigtha**, Abagtha, Zethar and Carcas—

961 בִּגְתָן *bigtān*, n.pr.m. [1] [√ 960]

Bigthana [1]

Est 2:21 **Bigthana** and Teresh, two of the king's officers who guarded the

962 בִּגְתָנָא *bigtānā'*, n.pr.m. [1] [√ 960]

Bigthana [1]

Est 6:2 It was found recorded there that Mordecai had exposed **Bigthana**

963 בַּד *bad¹*, n.m. [161] [√ 969; cf. 4224]

alone [+4200] [40], *untranslated* [22], in addition to [+4200+4946] [18], only [+4200] [16], besides [+4200+4946] [9], only one [+4200] [8], by themselves [+4200+4392] [4], apart [+4200] [3], as well as [+4200+4946] [2], in addition to [+4200] [2], in equal amounts [+928+963] [2], limbs [2], not counting [+4200+4946] [2], not including [+4200+4946] [2], set [2], all [+4200] [1], all alone [+4200] [1], all by myself [+3276+4200] [1], along with [+4200+4946] [1], also [+4200] [1], anyone [+4200] [1], besides [+4200] [1], by himself [+2257+4200] [1], by itself [+2257+4200] [1], by itself [+4200] [1], by myself [+3276+4200] [1], even though [+4200] [1], in addition [+4200] [1], in addition [+4200+4946] [1], into another set [+4200] [1], into one set [+4200] [1], more than [+4200+4946] [1], myself [+3276] [1], only [+2314+4200] [1], only exception [+4200] [1], only one [+2257+4200] [1], other than [+1194+4200] [1], other than [+4200+4946] [1], parts [1], separate [+4200] [1], separate [+906+3657+4200] [1], this one [+4200] [1]

Ge 2:18 LORD God said, "It is not good for the man to be **alone** [+4200].
21:28 Abraham set **apart** [+4200] seven ewe lambs from the flock,
21:29 seven ewe lambs you have set **apart** [+4200] by themselves?"
26:1 Now there was a famine in the land—**besides** [+4200+4946] the
30:40 Thus he made **separate** [+4200] flocks for himself and did not put
32:16 [32:17] each herd **by itself** [+2257+4200], and said to his
32:24 [32:25] So Jacob was left **alone** [+4200], and a man wrestled with
42:38 his brother is dead and he is the **only** [+2257+4200] **one** left.
43:32 They served him **by himself** [+2257+4200], the brothers by
43:32 served him by himself, the brothers **by themselves** [+4200+4392],
43:32 and the Egyptians who ate with him **by themselves** [+4200+4392],
44:20 is dead, and he is the **only** [+4200] one of his mother's sons left,
46:26 who were his direct descendants, **not** [+4200+4946] **counting**
47:26 It was only the land of the priests **[NIE]** that did not become
Ex 12:16 prepare food for everyone to eat—that is **all** [+4200] you may do.
12:37 about six hundred thousand men on foot, **besides** [+4200+4946]
18:14 Why do you **alone** [+4200] sit as judge, while all these people
18:18 The work is too heavy for you; you cannot handle it **alone** [+4200].
22:20 [22:19] "Whoever sacrifices to any god **other than** [+1194+4200]
22:27 [22:26] because his cloak is the **only** [+4200] covering he has for
24:2 Moses **alone** [+4200] is to approach the LORD; the others must
26:9 Join five of the curtains together **into one set** [+4200] and the other
26:9 together into one set and the other six **into another set** [+4200].
30:34 and pure frankincense, all **in equal amounts** [+928+963],
30:34 and pure frankincense, all **in equal amounts** [+928+963],
36:16 They joined five of the curtains into *one* **set** and the other six into
36:16 five of the curtains into one set and the other six into *another* **set**.
Lev 9:17 burned it on the altar **in addition** [+4200+4946] **to** the morning's
23:38 These offerings are **in addition** [+4200+4946] **to** those for the
23:38 **in addition** [+4200+4946] **to** your gifts and whatever you have
23:38 and in addition to your gifts and **[RPH]** whatever you have vowed
23:38 and **[RPH]** all the freewill offerings you give to the LORD.)
Nu 5:8 must be given to the priest, **along with** [+4200+4946] the ram with
6:21 in accordance with his separation, **in addition** [+4200+4946] **to**
11:14 I cannot carry all these people **by myself** [+3276+4200];
11:17 of the people so that you will not have to carry it **alone** [+4200].
16:49 [17:14] died from the plague, **in addition** [+4200+4946] **to**
28:23 Prepare these **in addition** [+4200+4946] **to** the regular morning
28:31 together with their drink offerings, **in addition** [+4200+4946] **to**
29:6 These are **in addition** [+4200+4946] **to** the monthly and daily
29:11 one male goat as a sin offering, **in addition** [+4200+4946] **to**
29:16 one male goat as a sin offering, **in addition** [+4200+4946] **to**
29:19 one male goat as a sin offering, **in addition** [+4200+4946] **to**
29:22 one male goat as a sin offering, **in addition** [+4200+4946] **to**
29:25 one male goat as a sin offering, **in addition** [+4200+4946] **to**
29:28 one male goat as a sin offering, **in addition** [+4200+4946] **to**
29:31 one male goat as a sin offering, **in addition** [+4200+4946] **to**
29:34 one male goat as a sin offering, **in addition** [+4200+4946] **to**
29:38 one male goat as a sin offering, **in addition** [+4200+4946] **to**
29:39 " '**In addition** [+4200] **to** what you vow and your freewill
Dt 1:9 "You are too heavy a burden *for* me to carry **alone** [+4200].
1:12 and your burdens and your disputes **all by myself** [+3276+4200]?
3:5 and there were **also** [+4200] a great many unwalled villages.
4:35 you might know that the LORD is God; **besides** [+4200+4946]
8:3 to teach you that man does not live on bread **alone** [+4200]
18:8 He is to share equally in their benefits, **even though** [+4200] he
22:25 and rapes her, **only** [+4200] the man who has done this shall die.
29:1 [28:69] with the Israelites in Moab, **in addition** [+4200+4946] **to**
29:14 [29:13] this covenant, with its oath, not **only** [+4200] with you
Jos 11:13 on their mounds—except Hazor, which Joshua burned. **[NIE]**
17:5 Manasseh's share consisted of ten tracts of land **besides** [+4200]
22:29 sacrifices, **other than** [+4200+4946] the altar of the LORD our
Jdg 3:20 approached him while he was sitting **alone** [+4200] in the upper
6:37 If there is dew **only** [+4200] on the fleece and all the ground is dry,
6:39 make the fleece dry **[RPH]** and the ground covered with dew."
6:40 That night God did so. **Only** [+4200] the fleece was dry; all the
7:5 told him, "**Separate** [+906+3657+4200] those who lap the water
8:26 came to seventeen hundred shekels, **not** [+4200+4946] **counting**
8:26 of Midian or **[RPH]** the chains that were on their camels' necks.

Jdg 20:15 thousand swordsmen from their towns, **in addition** [+4200] **to**
20:17 Israel, **apart** [+4200] from Benjamin, mustered four hundred
1Sa 7:3 and commit yourselves to the LORD and serve him **only** [+4200],
7:4 their Baals and Ashtoreths, and served the LORD **only** [+4200].
21:1 [21:2] he met him, and asked, "Why are you **alone** [+4200]?
2Sa 10:8 Maacah were **by themselves** [+4200+4392] in the open country.
13:32 lord should not think that they killed all the princes; **only** [+4200]
13:33 about the report that all the king's sons are dead. **Only** [+4200]
17:2 with him will flee. I would strike down **only** [+4200] the king
18:24 the wall. As he looked out, he saw a man running **alone** [+4200].
18:25 The king said, "If he is **alone** [+4200], he must have good news."
18:26 to the gatekeeper, "Look, another man running **alone** [+4200]!"
20:21 Hand over **this one** [+4200] man, and I'll withdraw from the city."
1Ki 4:23 [5:3] a hundred sheep and goats, **as well** [+4200+4946] **as** deer,
5:16 [5:30] **as well** [+4200+4946] **as** thirty-three hundred foremen who
8:39 since you know his heart (for you **alone** [+4200] know the hearts
10:13 asked for, **besides** [+4200+4946] what he had given her out of his
10:15 **not including** [+4200+4946] the revenues from merchants and
11:29 new cloak. The two of them were **alone** [+4200] out in the country,
12:20 made him king over all Israel. **Only** [+2314+4200] the tribe of
12:33 [the eighth month, a month of **his own** [K; see Q 4213] choosing,]
14:13 He is the **only** [+4200] one belonging to Jeroboam who will be
18:6 Ahab going in one direction **[NIE]** and Obadiah in another.
18:6 Ahab going in one direction and Obadiah in another. **[NIE]**
18:22 "I am the **only** [+4200] **one** of the LORD's prophets left,
19:10 I am the **only** [+4200] **one** left, and now they are trying to kill me
19:14 I am the **only** [+4200] **one** left, and now they are trying to kill me
22:31 "Do not fight with **anyone** [+4200], small or great, except the king
2Ki 10:23 of the LORD are here with you—only ministers of Baal." **[NIE]**
17:18 them from his presence. Only the tribe of Judah was left, **[NIE]**
19:15 you **alone** [+4200] are God over all the kingdoms of the earth.
19:19 so that all kingdoms on earth may know that you **alone** [+4200],
21:16 that he filled Jerusalem from end to end—**besides** [+4200+4946]
1Ch 3:9 All these were the sons of David, **besides** [+4200+4946] his sons
19:9 had come were **by themselves** [+4200+4392] in the open country.
2Ch 6:30 since you know his heart (for you **alone** [+4200] know the hearts
9:12 he gave her **more** [+4200+4946] **than** she had brought to him.
9:14 **not including** [+4200+4946] the revenues brought in by merchants
17:19 These were the men who served the king, **besides** [+4200+4946]
18:30 with anyone, small or great, except the king of Israel." **[NIE]**
31:16 **In addition** [+4200+4946], they distributed to the males three
Ezr 1:6 with valuable gifts, **in addition** [+4200] to all the freewill
2:65 **besides** [+4200+4946] their 7,337 menservants and maidservants;
Ne 7:67 **besides** [+4200+4946] their 7,337 menservants and maidservants;
9:6 You **alone** [+4200] are the LORD. You made the heavens,
Est 1:16 not **only** [+4200] against the king but also against all the nobles
3:6 people were, he scorned the idea of killing **only** [+4200] Mordecai.
4:11 The **only** [+4200] **exception** to this is for the king to extend the
Job 1:15 and I am the **only** [+4200] **one** who has escaped to tell you!"
1:16 and I am the **only** [+4200] **one** who has escaped to tell you!"
1:17 and I am the **only** [+4200] **one** who has escaped to tell you!"
1:19 and I am the **only** [+4200] **one** who has escaped to tell you!"
9:8 He **alone** [+4200] stretches out the heavens and treads on the
15:19 (to whom **alone** [+4200] the land was given when no alien passed
18:13 It eats away **parts** *of* his skin; death's firstborn devours his limbs.
18:13 It eats away parts of his skin; death's firstborn devours his **limbs**.
31:17 if I have kept my bread to **myself** [+3276], not sharing it with the
41:12 [41:4] "I will not fail to speak of his **limbs**, his strength and his
Ps 51:4 [51:6] Against you, you **only** [+4200], have I sinned and done
71:16 I will proclaim your righteousness, yours **alone** [+4200].
72:18 the God of Israel, who **alone** [+4200] does marvelous deeds.
83:18 [83:19] that you **alone** [+4200] are the Most High over all the
86:10 you are great and do marvelous deeds; you **alone** [+4200] are God.
136:4 to him who **alone** [+4200] does great wonders, *His love*
148:13 the name of the LORD, for his name **alone** [+4200] is exalted;
Pr 5:17 Let them be yours **alone** [+4200], never to be shared with
9:12 reward you; if you are a mocker, you **alone** [+4200] will suffer."
Ecc 7:29 This **only** [+4200] have I found: God made mankind upright,
Isa 2:11 brought low; the LORD **alone** [+4200] will be exalted in that day.
2:17 the LORD **alone** [+4200] will be exalted in that day,
5:8 to field till no space is left and you live **alone** [+4200] in the land.
26:13 you have ruled over us, but your name **alone** [+4200] do we honor.
37:16 you **alone** [+4200] are God over all the kingdoms of the earth.
37:20 so that all kingdoms on earth may know that you **alone** [+4200],
44:24 has made all things, who **alone** [+4200] stretched out the heavens,
49:21 I was left **all alone** [+4200], but these—where have they come
63:3 "I have trodden the winepress **alone** [+4200]; from the nations no
Eze 14:16 They **alone** [+4200] would be saved, but the land would be
14:18 their own sons or daughters. They **alone** [+4200] would be saved.
Da 10:7 I, Daniel, was the **only** [+4200] **one** who saw the vision; the men
10:8 So I was left **alone** [+4200], gazing at this great vision; I had no
11:4 because his empire will be uprooted and given to others. **[NIE]**
Zec 12:12 The land will mourn, each clan **by itself** [+4200], with their wives
12:12 the clan of the house of David **[RPH]** and their wives, the clan of
12:12 **[RPH]** the clan of the house of Nathan and their wives,
12:12 the clan of the house of Nathan **[RPH]** and their wives,
12:12 the clan of the house of Nathan and their wives, **[RPH]**
12:13 the clan of the house of Levi **[RPH]** and their wives, the clan of
12:13 and their wives, **[RPH]** the clan of Shimei and their wives,
12:13 and their wives, the clan of Shimei **[RPH]** and their wives,
12:13 and their wives, the clan of Shimei and their wives, **[RPH]**
12:14 and all the rest of the clans **[RPH]** and their wives.
12:14 and all the rest of the clans and their wives. **[RPH]**

964 ²בַּד *bad²*, n.m. [41] [√ 969]

poles [31], carrying poles [2], their[s] [+2021] [2], *untranslated* [1], bars of gates [1], branches [1], gates [1], main branches [+4751] [1], they[s] [+2021] [1]

Ex 25:13 Then make **poles** *of* acacia wood and overlay them with gold.
25:14 Insert the **poles** into the rings on the sides of the chest to carry it.
25:15 The **poles** are to remain in the rings of this ark; they are not to be
25:27 The rings are to be close to the rim to hold the **poles** used in
25:28 Make the **poles** of acacia wood, overlay them with gold and carry
27:6 Make **poles** *of* acacia wood for the altar and overlay them with
27:6 Make poles of **[RPH]** acacia wood for the altar and overlay them
27:7 The **poles** are to be inserted into the rings so they will be on two
27:7 so **they**[s] [+2021] will be on two sides of the altar when it is
30:4 two on opposite sides—to hold the **poles** used to carry it.
30:5 Make the **poles** of acacia wood and overlay them with gold.
35:12 the ark with its **poles** and the atonement cover and the curtain that
35:13 the table with its **poles** and all its articles and the bread of the
35:15 the altar of incense with its **poles**, the anointing oil and the fragrant
35:16 burnt offering with its bronze grating, its **poles** and all its utensils;
37:4 Then he made **poles** *of* acacia wood and overlaid them with gold.
37:5 he inserted the **poles** into the rings on the sides of the ark to carry
37:14 The rings were put close to the rim to hold the **poles** used in
37:15 The **poles** for carrying the table were made of acacia wood
37:27 two on opposite sides—to hold the **poles** used to carry it.
37:28 They made the **poles** *of* acacia wood and overlaid them with gold.
38:5 They cast bronze rings to hold the **poles** for the four corners of the
38:6 They made the **poles** of acacia wood and overlaid them with
38:7 They inserted the **poles** into the rings so they would be on the sides
39:35 the ark of the Testimony with its **poles** and the atonement cover;
39:39 bronze altar with its bronze grating, its **poles** and all its utensils;
40:20 attached the **poles** to the ark and put the atonement cover over it.
Nu 4:6 spread a cloth of solid blue over that and put the **poles** in place.
4:8 cover that with hides of sea cows and put its **poles** in place.
4:11 and cover that with hides of sea cows and put its **poles** in place.
4:14 to spread a covering of hides of sea cows and put its **poles** in place.
1Ki 8:7 place of the ark and overshadowed the ark and its **carrying poles**.
8:8 These **poles** were so long that their ends could be seen from the
8:8 so long that **their**[s] [+2021] ends could be seen from the Holy Place
2Ch 5:8 the place of the ark and covered the ark and its **carrying poles**.
5:9 These **poles** were so long that their ends, extending from the ark,
5:9 These poles were so long that **their**[s] [+2021] ends, extending from
Job 17:16 Will it go down to the **gates** *of* death? Will we descend together
Eze 17:6 So it became a vine and produced **branches** and put out leafy
19:14 Fire spread from one of its **main branches** [+4751] and consumed
Hos 11:6 will destroy the **bars of** their **gates** and put an end to their plans.

965 ³בַּד *bad³*, n.[m.] [23] [√ 969]

linen [22], undergarments [+4829] [1]

Ex 28:42 "Make **linen** undergarments as a covering for the body, reaching
39:28 and the **undergarments** [+4829] of finely twisted linen.
Lev 6:10 [6:3] The priest shall then put on his **linen** clothes, with linen
6:10 [6:3] his linen clothes, with **linen** undergarments next to his body,
16:4 He is to put on the sacred **linen** tunic, with linen undergarments
16:4 the sacred linen tunic, with **linen** undergarments next to his body;
16:4 he is to tie the **linen** sash around him and put on the linen turban.
16:4 he is to tie the linen sash around him and put on the **linen** turban.
16:23 take off the **linen** garments he put on before he entered the Most
16:32 is to make atonement. He is to put on the sacred **linen** garments
1Sa 2:18 was ministering before the LORD—a boy wearing a **linen** ephod.
22:18 That day he killed eighty-five men who wore the **linen** ephod.
2Sa 6:14 David, wearing a **linen** ephod, danced before the LORD with all
1Ch 15:27 charge of the singing of the choirs. David also wore a **linen** ephod.
Eze 9:2 With them was a man clothed in **linen** who had a writing kit at his
9:3 the LORD called to the man clothed in **linen** who had the writing
9:11 the man in **linen** with the writing kit at his side brought back word,
10:2 The LORD said to the man clothed in **linen**, "Go in among the
10:6 When the LORD commanded the man in **linen**, "Take fire from
10:7 He took up some of it and put it into the hands of the man in **linen**,
Da 10:5 I looked up and there before me was a man dressed in **linen**,
12:6 One of them said to the man clothed in **linen**, who was above the
12:7 The man clothed in **linen**, who was above the waters of the river,

966 ⁴בַּד **bad⁴**, n.m. [3] [√ 968]
boasts [2], idle talk [1]

Job 11: 3 Will your **idle talk** reduce men to silence? Will no one rebuke you
Isa 16: 6 her pride and her insolence—but her **boasts** are empty.
Jer 48: 30 declares the LORD, "and her **boasts** accomplish nothing.

967 ⁵בַּד **bad⁵**, n.m. [2] [√ 968]
false prophets [2]

Isa 44: 25 who foils the signs of **false prophets** and makes fools of diviners,
Jer 50: 36 A sword against her **false prophets**! They will become fools.

968 בָּדָא **bādā'**, v. [2] [→ 966, 967]
choosing [1], making up [1]

1Ki 12: 33 [A] day of the eighth month, a month of his own **choosing**,
Ne 6: 8 [A] is happening; you *are* just **making it up** out of your head."

969 בָּדַד **bādad**, v. [3] [→ 963, 964, 965, 970, 4224]
alone [1], straggler [1], wandering alone [1]

Ps 102: 7 [102:8] [A] I have become like a bird **alone** on a roof.
Isa 14: 31 [A] from the north, and there is not a **straggler** in its ranks.
Hos 8: 9 [A] gone up to Assyria like a wild donkey **wandering alone**.

970 בָּדָד **bādād**, n.[m.]. [11] [√ 969]
alone [6], alone [+4200] [1], apart [+4200] [1], by itself [+4200] [1], deserted [1], desolate [1]

Lev 13: 46 He must live **alone**; he must live outside the camp.
Nu 23: 9 I see a people who live **apart** [+4200] and do not consider
Dt 32: 12 The LORD **alone** led him; no foreign god was with him.
33: 28 So Israel will live in safety **alone**; Jacob's spring is secure in a land
Ps 4: 8 [4:9] and sleep in peace, for you **alone** [+4200], O LORD,
Isa 27: 10 The fortified city stands **desolate**, an abandoned settlement,
Jer 15: 17 I sat **alone** because your hand was on me and you had filled me
49: 31 "a nation that has neither gates nor bars; its people live **alone**.
La 1: 1 How **deserted** lies the city, once so full of people! How like a
3: 28 Let him sit **alone** in silence, for the LORD has laid it on him.
Mic 7: 14 which lives **by itself** [+4200] in a forest, in fertile pasturelands.

971 בְּדַד **bᵉdad**, n.pr.m. [2]
Bedad [2]

Ge 36: 35 When Husham died, Hadad son of **Bedad**, who defeated Midian in
1Ch 1: 46 When Husham died, Hadad son of **Bedad**, who defeated Midian in

972 בְּדֵי **bᵉdê**, subst. Not used in NIV/BHS [√ 928 + 1896]

973 בֵּדְיָה **bēdᵉyâ**, n.pr.m. [1]
Bedeiah [1]

Ezr 10: 35 Benaiah, **Bedeiah**, Keluhi,

974 בְּדִיל **bᵉdîl**, n.[m.]. [5] [√ 976?]
tin [4], plumb line [+74] [1]

Nu 31: 22 Gold, silver, bronze, iron, **tin**, lead
Eze 22: 18 all of them are the copper, **tin**, iron and lead left inside a furnace.
22: 20 iron, lead and **tin** into a furnace to melt it with a fiery blast,
27: 12 they exchanged silver, iron, **tin** and lead for your merchandise.
Zec 4: 10 Men will rejoice when they see the **plumb line** [+74] in the hand

975 בָּדִיל **bādîl**, n.[m.]. [1] [√ 976]
impurities [1]

Isa 1: 25 thoroughly purge away your dross and remove all your **impurities**.

976 בָּדַל **bādal**, v. [42] [→ 974?, 975, 977, 4426]
set apart [7], separate [5], separated [4], distinguish [3], separated themselves [3], set aside [3], separate yourselves [2], severing completely [2], surely exclude [+976] [2], be expelled [1], defected [1], dismissed [1], employed [1], excluded [1], kept themselves separate [1], make a distinction [1], selected [1], single out [1], singled out [1], was set apart [1]

Ge 1: 4 [G] light was good, and he **separated** the light from the darkness.
1: 6 [G] "Let there be an expanse between the waters *to* **separate**
1: 7 [G] **separated** the water under the expanse from the water above
1: 14 [G] "Let there be lights in the expanse of the sky to **separate** the
1: 18 [G] the day and the night, and to **separate** light from darkness.
Ex 26: 33 [G] The curtain *will* **separate** the Holy Place from the Most Holy
Lev 1: 17 [G] not **severing** it **completely**, and then the priest shall burn it
5: 8 [G] is to wring its head from its neck, not **severing** it **completely**,
10: 10 [G] You *must* **distinguish** between the holy and the common,
11: 47 [G] You *must* **distinguish** between the unclean and the clean,
20: 24 [G] LORD your God, who *has* **set** you **apart** from the nations.
20: 25 [G] " '*You must* therefore **make a distinction** between clean
20: 25 [G] those which *I have* **set apart** as unclean for you.
20: 26 [G] and *I have* **set** you **apart** from the nations to be my own.
Nu 8: 14 [G] In this way *you are to* **set** the Levites **apart** from the other
16: 9 [G] Isn't it enough for you that the God of Israel *has* **separated**
16: 21 [C] "**Separate yourselves** from this assembly so I can put an end
Dt 4: 41 [G] Then Moses **set aside** three cities east of the Jordan,
10: 8 [G] At that time the LORD **set apart** the tribe of Levi to carry
19: 2 [G] **set aside** for yourselves three cities centrally located in the
19: 7 [G] This is why I command you *to* **set aside** for yourselves three
29: 21 [29:20] [G] The LORD *will* **single** him **out** from all the tribes
1Ki 8: 53 [G] **singled** them **out** from all the nations of the world to be your
1Ch 12: 8 [12:9] [C] Some Gadites **defected** to David at his stronghold in
23: 13 [C] Aaron **was set apart**, he and his descendants forever,
25: 1 [G] **set apart** some of the sons of Asaph, Heman and Jeduthun
2Ch 25: 10 [G] So Amaziah **dismissed** the troops who had come to him from
Ezr 6: 21 [C] together with all who *had* **separated themselves** from the
8: 24 [G] *I* **set apart** twelve of the leading priests, together with
9: 1 [C] *have* not **kept themselves separate** from the neighboring
10: 8 [C] *would* himself **be expelled** from the assembly of the exiles.
10: 11 [C] **Separate yourselves** from the peoples around you and from
10: 16 [C] Ezra the priest **selected** men who were family heads,
Ne 9: 2 [C] *Those of* Israelite descent *had* **separated themselves** from
10: 28 [10:29] [C] all who **separated themselves** from the neighboring
13: 3 [G] *they* **excluded** from Israel all who were of foreign descent.
Isa 56: 3 [G] "The LORD *will* **surely exclude** [+976] me from his
56: 3 [G] "The LORD *will* **surely exclude** [+976] me from his
59: 2 [G] your iniquities *have* **separated** you from your God; your sins
Eze 22: 26 [G] *they do* not **distinguish** between the holy and the common;
39: 14 [G] " 'Men *will be* regularly **employed** to cleanse the land.
42: 20 [G] hundred cubits wide, to **separate** the holy from the common.

977 בָּדָל **bādāl**, n.[m.]. [1] [√ 976]
piece [1]

Am 3: 12 from the lion's mouth only two leg bones or a **piece** *of* an ear,

978 בְּדֹלַח **bᵉdōlaḥ**, n.[m.]. [2]
aromatic resin [1], resin [1]

Ge 2: 12 gold of that land is good; **aromatic resin** and onyx are also there.)
Nu 11: 7 The manna was like coriander seed and looked like **resin**.

979 בְּדָן **bᵉdān**, n.pr.m. [2 / 1]
Bedan [1]

1Sa 12: 11 the LORD sent Jerub-Baal, Barak, [BHS *Bedan*; NIV 1399]
1Ch 7: 17 The son of Ulam: **Bedan**. These were the sons of Gilead son of

980 בָּדַק **bādaq**, v.den. [1] [→ 981; cf. 1438]
repaired [1]

2Ch 34: 10 [A] These men paid the workers *who* **repaired** and restored the

981 בֶּדֶק **bedeq**, n.m. [10] [√ 980]
untranslated [4], damage [2], repair [+2616] [1], repairing [1], seams [1], shipwrights [+2616] [1]

2Ki 12: 5 [12:6] let it be used to repair whatever **damage** is found *in* the
12: 5 [12:6] repair whatever damage is found in the temple." **[RPH]**
12: 6 [12:7] Joash the priests still had not repaired **[RPH]** the temple.
12: 7 [12:8] "Why aren't you repairing the **damage** *done to* the
12: 7 [12:8] your treasurers, but hand it over for **repairing** the temple."
12: 8 [12:9] that they would not repair **[RPH]** the temple themselves.
12: 12 [12:13] dressed stone for the repair of **[RPH]** the temple of the
22: 5 have these men pay the workers who **repair** [+2616] the temple of
Eze 27: 9 of Gebal were on board as shipwrights to caulk your **seams**.
27: 27 and wares, your mariners, seamen and **shipwrights** [+2616],

982 בִּדְקַר **bidqar**, n.pr.m. [1] [√ 1201? + 1992?]
Bidkar [1]

2Ki 9: 25 Jehu said to **Bidkar**, his chariot officer, "Pick him up and throw

983 בֹּהוּ **bōhû**, n.[m.]. [3]
empty [2], desolation [1]

Ge 1: 2 Now the earth was formless and **empty**, darkness was over the
Isa 34: 11 the measuring line of chaos and the plumb line of **desolation**.
Jer 4: 23 I looked at the earth, and it was formless and **empty**; and at the

984 בֹּהֶן behôn, n.[f.]. [2] [√ 991]
thumbs [+3338] [2]

Jdg 1: 6 and caught him, and cut off his **thumbs** [+3338] and big toes.
1: 7 "Seventy kings with their **thumbs** [+3338] and big toes cut off

985 בַּהַט bahaṭ, n.[m.]. [1]
porphyry [1]

Est 1: 6 couches of gold and silver on a mosaic pavement of **porphyry**,

986 בָּהִיר bāhîr, a. [1] [→ 994]
bright [1]

Job 37: 21 **bright** as it is in the skies after the wind has swept them clean.

987 בָּהַל bāhal, v. [39] [→ 988; cf. 1164; Ar 10097, 10218]
terrified [10], dismayed [3], hurried [2], make afraid [2], terrifies [2], alarm [1], alarmed [1], am bewildered [1], dismayed [+4394] [1], eager [1], hurry [1], immediately [1], in a hurry [1], in agony [1], in anguish [+4394] [1], quick [1], quickly gained [1], quickly [1], raced [1], sudden [1], terrify [1], terror seize [1], terror [1], tremble [1], was shaken [1]

Ge 45: 3 [C] to answer him, because *they were* **terrified** at his presence.
Ex 15: 15 [C] The chiefs of Edom *will be* **terrified**, the leaders of Moab
Jdg 20: 41 [C] turned on them, and the men of Benjamin *were* **terrified**,
1Sa 28: 21 [C] the woman came to Saul and saw that *he* **was** greatly **shaken**,
2Sa 4: 1 [C] in Hebron, he lost courage, and all Israel *became* **alarmed**.
2Ch 26: 20 [G] that he had leprosy on his forehead, so *they* **hurried** him out.
32: 18 [D] and **make** them **afraid** in order to capture the city.
35: 21 [D] God has told me to **hurry**; so stop opposing God, who is
Ezr 4: 4 [D] of Judah and **make** them **afraid** [K 1164] to go on building.
Est 2: 9 [D] **Immediately** *he* provided her with her beauty treatments and
6: 14 [G] **hurried** Haman away to the banquet Esther had prepared.
8: 14 [E] The couriers, riding the royal horses, **raced** out, spurred on
Job 4: 5 [C] you are discouraged; it strikes you, and *you are* **dismayed**.
21: 6 [C] When I think about this, *I am* **terrified**; trembling seizes my
22: 10 [D] snares are all around you, why sudden peril **terrifies** you,
23: 15 [C] That is why *I am* **terrified** before him; when I think of all
23: 16 [G] God has made my heart faint; the Almighty *has* **terrified** me.
Ps 2: 5 [D] he rebukes them in his anger and **terrifies** them in his wrath,
6: 2 [6:3] [C] O LORD, heal me, for my bones *are* **in agony**.
6: 3 [6:4] [C] My soul *is* **in anguish** [+4394]. How long, O LORD,
6: 10 [6:11] [C] my enemies will be ashamed and **dismayed** [+4394];
30: 7 [30:8] [C] but when you hid your face, I was **dismayed**.
48: 5 [48:6] [C] saw ⌊her⌋ and were astounded; they fled *in* **terror**.
83: 15 [83:16] [D] your tempest and **terrify** them with your storm.
83: 17 [83:18] [C] May they ever be ashamed and **dismayed**; may they
90: 7 [C] consumed by your anger and **terrified** by your indignation.
104: 29 [C] When you hide your face, *they are* **terrified**; when you take
Pr 20: 21 [E] An inheritance **quickly** [K 1042] **gained** at the beginning
28: 22 [C] A stingy man *is* **eager** to get rich and is unaware that poverty
Ecc 5: 2 [5:1] [D] *Do* not *be* **quick** with your mouth, do not be hasty in
7: 9 [D] Do not be **quickly** provoked in your spirit, for anger resides
8: 3 [C] *Do* not *be* **in a hurry** to leave the king's presence. Do not
Isa 13: 8 [C] **Terror** *will* **seize** *them*, pain and anguish will grip them;
21: 3 [C] am staggered by what I hear, *I* **am bewildered** by what I see.
Jer 51: 32 [C] the marshes set on fire, and the soldiers **terrified**."
Eze 7: 27 [C] and the hands of the people of the land *will* **tremble**.
26: 18 [C] your fall; the islands in the sea *are* **terrified** at your collapse.'
Da 11: 44 [D] reports from the east and the north *will* **alarm** him, and he
Zep 1: 18 [C] for he will make a **sudden** end of all who live in the earth."

988 בֶּהָלָה behālâ, n.f. [4] [√ 987; Ar 10096]
terror [2], misfortune [1], sudden terror [1]

Lev 26: 16 I will bring upon you **sudden terror**, wasting diseases and fever
Ps 78: 33 So he ended their days in futility and their years in **terror**.
Isa 65: 23 They will not toil in vain or bear children doomed to **misfortune**;
Jer 15: 8 suddenly I will bring down on them anguish and **terror**.

989 בְּהֵמָה behēmâ, n.f. [190] [→ 990?]
animals [63], animal [44], livestock [33], cattle [17], beasts [13], beast [5], herds [3], *untranslated* [2], kinds of cattle [+989+2256] [2], another[s] [1], beasts of burden [+2256+2651] [1], brute beast [1], livestock [+5238] [1], mount [1], mounts [1], one[s] [1], wild beasts [1]

Ge 1: 24 **livestock**, creatures that move along the ground, and wild animals,
1: 25 according to their kinds, the **livestock** according to their kinds,
1: 26 and the birds of the air, over the **livestock**, over all the earth,
2: 20 So the man gave names to all the **livestock**, the birds of the air
3: 14 "Cursed are you above all the **livestock** and all the wild animals!
6: 7 men and **animals**, and creatures that move along the ground,
6: 20 of every kind of **animal** and of every kind of creature that moves
7: 2 Take with you seven of every kind of clean **animal**, a male
7: 2 and two of every kind of unclean **animal**, a male and its mate,
7: 8 Pairs of clean and unclean **animals**, of birds and of all creatures
7: 8 **[RPH]** of birds and of all creatures that move along the ground,
7: 14 animal according to its kind, all **livestock** according to their kinds,
7: 21 birds, **livestock**, wild animals, all the creatures that swarm over the
7: 23 men and **animals** and the creatures that move along the ground
8: 1 the wild animals and the **livestock** that were with him in the ark,
8: 17 the birds, the **animals**, and all the creatures that move along the
8: 20 taking some of all the clean **animals** and clean birds, he sacrificed
9: 10 the birds, the **livestock** and all the wild animals, all those that came
34: 23 their property and all their *other* **animals** become ours?
36: 6 as well as his livestock and all his *other* **animals** and all the goods
47: 18 since our money is gone and our **livestock** [+5238] belongs to you,
Ex 8: 17 [8:13] the dust of the ground, gnats came upon men and **animals**.
8: 18 [8:14] they could not. And the gnats were on men and **animals**.
9: 9 boils will break out on men and **animals** throughout the land."
9: 10 it into the air, and festering boils broke out on men and **animals**.
9: 19 and **animal** that has not been brought in and is still out in the field,
9: 22 on men and **animals** and on everything growing in the fields of
9: 25 both men and **animals**; it beat down everything growing in the
11: 5 who is at her hand mill, and all the firstborn of the **cattle** as well.
11: 7 But among the Israelites not a dog will bark at any man or **animal**.'
12: 12 and strike down every firstborn—both men and **animals**—
12: 29 was in the dungeon, and the firstborn of all the **livestock** as well.
13: 2 among the Israelites belongs to me, whether man or **animal**."
13: 12 All the firstborn males of your **livestock** belong to the LORD.
13: 15 the LORD killed every firstborn in Egypt, both man and **animal**.
19: 13 Whether man or **animal**, he shall not be permitted to live.'
20: 10 nor your manservant or maidservant, nor your **animals**,
22: 10 [22:9] or any other **animal** to his neighbor for safekeeping
22: 19 [22:18] "Anyone who has sexual relations with an **animal** must
Lev 1: 2 bring as your offering an **animal** from either the herd or the flock.
5: 2 the carcasses of unclean wild animals or of unclean **livestock**
7: 21 whether human uncleanness or an unclean **animal** or any unclean,
7: 25 Anyone who eats the fat of an **animal** from which an offering by
7: 26 you live, you must not eat the blood of any bird or **animal**.
11: 2 'Of all the **animals** that live on land, these are the ones you may
11: 3 You may eat any **animal** that has a split hoof completely divided
11: 26 " 'Every **animal** that has a split hoof not completely divided
11: 39 " 'If an **animal** that you are allowed to eat dies, anyone who
11: 46 " 'These are the regulations concerning **animals**, birds, every living
18: 23 " 'Do not have sexual relations with an **animal** and defile yourself
18: 23 A woman must not present herself to an **animal** to have sexual
19: 19 " 'Keep my decrees. " 'Do not mate different kinds of **animals**.
20: 15 " 'If a man has sexual relations with an **animal**, he must be put to
20: 15 an animal, he must be put to death, and you must kill the **animal**.
20: 16 " 'If a woman approaches an **animal** to have sexual relations with
20: 16 have sexual relations with it, kill both the woman and the **animal**.
20: 25 and unclean **animals** and between unclean and clean birds.
20: 25 Do not defile yourselves by any **animal** or bird or anything that
24: 18 Anyone who takes the life of someone's **animal** must make
24: 21 Whoever kills an **animal** must make restitution, but whoever kills
25: 7 as well as for your **livestock** and the wild animals in your land.
26: 22 destroy your **cattle** and make you so few in number that your roads
27: 9 " 'If what he vowed is an **animal** that is acceptable as an offering
27: 10 if he should substitute *one* **animal** for another, both it
27: 10 if he should substitute one animal for **another**[s], both it
27: 11 If what he vowed is a ceremonially unclean **animal**—one that is
27: 11 to the LORD—the **animal** must be presented to the priest,
27: 26 " 'No one, however, may dedicate the firstborn of an **animal**,
27: 27 If it is one of the unclean **animals**, he may buy it back at its set
27: 28 whether man or **animal** or family land—may be sold or redeemed;
Nu 3: 13 apart for myself every firstborn in Israel, whether man or **animal**.
3: 41 the **livestock** *of* the Levites in place of all the firstborn of the
3: 41 Levites in place of all the firstborn of the **livestock** *of* the Israelites.
3: 45 and the **livestock** *of* the Levites in place of their livestock.
3: 45 and the livestock of the Levites in place of their **livestock**.
8: 17 Every firstborn male in Israel, whether man or **animal**, is mine.
18: 15 The first offspring of every womb, both man and **animal**,
18: 15 every firstborn son and every firstborn male of unclean **animals**.
31: 9 Midianite women and children and took all the Midianite **herds**,
31: 11 took all the plunder and spoils, including the people and **animals**,
31: 26 are to count all the people and **animals** that were captured.
31: 30 whether persons, cattle, donkeys, sheep, goats or other **animals**.
31: 47 Moses selected one out of every fifty persons and **animals**,
32: 26 our flocks and **herds** will remain here in the cities of Gilead.
35: 3 they will have towns to live in and pasturelands for their **cattle**,
Dt 2: 35 the **livestock** and the plunder from the towns we had captured we
3: 7 all the **livestock** and the plunder from their cities we carried off for
4: 17 or like any **animal** on earth or any bird that flies in the air,
5: 14 or maidservant, nor your ox, your donkey or any of your **animals**,
7: 14 women will be childless, nor any of your **livestock** without young.
11: 15 I will provide grass in the fields for your **cattle**, and you will eat

[F] Hitpael (hitpoel, hitpoal, hitpolel, hitpolal, hitpalel, hitpalal, hitpalpel, hitpalpal, hotpael, hotpaal) [G] Hiphil (hiphtil) [H] Hophal [I] Hishtaphel

Dt 13:15 [13:16] Destroy it completely, both its people and its **livestock**.
14:4 These are the **animals** you may eat: the ox, the sheep, the goat,
14:6 You may eat any **animal** that has a split hoof divided in two
14:6 has a split hoof divided in two and that chews the cud. **[RPH]**
20:14 the children, the **livestock** and everything else in the city,
27:21 "Cursed is the man who has sexual relations with any **animal**."
28:4 and the crops of your land and the young of your **livestock**—
28:11 the young of your **livestock** and the crops of your ground—
28:26 will be food for all the birds of the air and the **beasts** *of* the earth,
28:51 They will devour the young of your **livestock** and the crops of your
30:9 the young of your **livestock** and the crops of your land.
32:24 I will send against them the fangs of **wild beasts**, the venom of
Jos 8:2 that you may carry off their plunder and **livestock** for yourselves.
8:27 Israel did carry off for themselves the **livestock** and plunder of this
11:14 off for themselves all the plunder and **livestock** of these cities,
21:2 you give us towns to live in, with pasturelands for our **livestock**."
Jdg 20:48 the sword, including the **animals** and everything else they found.
1Sa 17:44 give your flesh to the birds of the air and the **beasts** *of* the field!"
1Ki 4:33 [5:13] He also taught about **animals** and birds, reptiles and fish.
18:5 and mules alive so we will not have to kill any of our **animals**."
2Ki 3:9 had no more water for themselves or for the **animals** with them.
3:17 with water, and you, your cattle and your other **animals** will drink.
2Ch 32:28 and he made stalls for various **kinds of cattle** [+989+2256],
32:28 and he made stalls for various **kinds of cattle** [+989+2256],
Ezr 1:4 are to provide him with silver and gold, with goods and **livestock**,
1:6 them with articles of silver and gold, with goods and **livestock**,
Ne 2:12 There were no **mounts** with me except the one I was riding on.
2:12 There were no mounts with me except the **one**[s] I was riding on.
2:14 but there was not enough room for my **mount** to get through;
9:37 They rule over our bodies and our **cattle** as they please. We are in
10:36 [10:37] we will bring the firstborn of our sons and of our **cattle**,
Job 12:7 "But ask the **animals**, and they will teach you, or the birds of the
18:3 Why are we regarded as **cattle** and considered stupid in your sight?
35:11 who teaches more to us than to the **beasts** *of* the earth and makes
Ps 8:7 [8:8] all flocks and herds, and the **beasts** *of* the field,
36:6 [36:7] great deep. O LORD, you preserve both man and **beast**.
49:12 [49:13] does not endure; he is like the **beasts** that perish.
49:20 [49:21] riches without understanding is like the **beasts** that perish.
50:10 animal of the forest is mine, and the **cattle** on a thousand hills.
73:22 I was senseless and ignorant; I was a **brute beast** before you.
104:14 He makes grass grow for the **cattle**, and plants for man to
107:38 numbers greatly increased, and he did not let their **herds** diminish.
135:8 down the firstborn of Egypt, the firstborn of men and **animals**.
147:9 He provides food for the **cattle** and for the young ravens when they
148:10 wild animals and all **cattle**, small creatures and flying birds,
Pr 12:10 A righteous man cares for the needs of his **animal**, but the kindest
30:30 a lion, mighty among **beasts**, who retreats before nothing;
Ecc 3:18 God tests them so that they may see that they are like the **animals**.
3:19 Man's fate is like that of the **animals**; the same fate awaits them
3:19 All have the same breath; man has no advantage over the **animal**.
3:21 and if the spirit of the **animal** goes down into the earth?"
Isa 18:6 all be left to the mountain birds of prey and to the wild **animals**;
18:6 birds will feed on them all summer, the wild **animals** all winter.
30:6 An oracle concerning the **animals** *of* the Negev: Through a land of
46:1 their idols are borne by **beasts of burden** [+2256+2651].
63:14 like **cattle** that go down to the plain, they were given rest by the
Jer 7:20 on man and **beast**, on the trees of the field and on the fruit of the
7:33 become food for the birds of the air and the **beasts** *of* the earth,
9:10 [9:9] The birds of the air have fled and the **animals** are gone.
12:4 who live in it are wicked, the **animals** and birds have perished.
15:3 birds of the air and the **beasts** *of* the earth to devour and destroy.
16:4 become food for the birds of the air and the **beasts** *of* the earth."
19:7 carcasses as food to the birds of the air and the **beasts** *of* the earth.
21:6 both men and **animals**—and they will die of a terrible plague.
27:5 arm I made the earth and its people and the **animals** that are on it,
31:27 and the house of Judah with the offspring of men and of **animals**.
32:43 'It is a desolate waste, without men or **animals**, for it has been
33:10 about this place, "It is a desolate waste, without men or **animals**."
33:10 inhabited by neither men nor **animals**, there will be heard once
33:12 'In this place, desolate and without men or **animals**—in all its
34:20 become food for the birds of the air and the **beasts** *of* the earth.
36:29 and destroy this land and cut off both men and **animals** from it?"
50:3 No one will live in it; both men and **animals** will flee away.
51:62 destroy this place, so that neither man nor **animal** will live in it;
Eze 8:10 and detestable **animals** and all the idols of the house of Israel.
14:13 and send famine upon it and kill its men and their **animals**,
14:17 pass throughout the land,' and I kill its men and their **animals**,
14:19 wrath upon it through bloodshed, killing its men and their **animals**,
14:21 and wild beasts and plague—to kill its men and their **animals**!
25:13 out my hand against Edom and kill its men and their **animals**.
29:8 bring a sword against you and kill your men and their **animals**.
29:11 No foot of man or **animal** will pass through it; no one will live
32:13 I will destroy all her **cattle** from beside abundant waters no longer
32:13 to be stirred by the foot of man or muddied by the hoofs of **cattle**.
36:11 I will increase the number of men and **animals** upon you,
44:31 eat anything, bird or **animal**, found dead or torn by wild animals.
Joel 1:18 How the **cattle** moan! The herds mill about because they have no
1:20 Even the wild **animals** pant for you; the streams of water have
2:22 Be not afraid, O wild **animals**, for the open pastures are becoming
Jnh 3:7 Do not let any man or **beast**, herd or flock, taste anything;
3:8 let man and **beast** be covered with sackcloth. Let everyone call
4:11 cannot tell their right hand from their left, and many **cattle** as well.
Mic 5:8 [5:7] of many peoples, like a lion among the **beasts** *of* the forest,
Hab 2:17 overwhelm you, and your destruction of **animals** will terrify you.
Zep 1:3 "I will sweep away both men and **animals**; I will sweep away the
Hag 1:11 on men and **cattle**, and on the labor of your hands."
Zec 2:4 [2:8] because of the great number of men and **livestock** in it.
8:10 Before that time there were no wages for man or **beast**. No one
14:15 the camels and donkeys, and all the **animals** in those camps.

990 בְּהֵמוֹת *behēmôt*, n.m. [1] [√ 989?]

behemoth [1]

Job 40:15 "Look at the **behemoth**, which I made along with you and which

991 בֹּהֶן *bōhen*, n.[f.]. [14] [→ 984, 992?]

big toe [5], thumb [5], big toes [2], thumbs [2]

Ex 29:20 ears of Aaron and his sons, on the **thumbs** *of* their right hands,
29:20 thumbs of their right hands, and on the **big toes** *of* their right feet.
Lev 8:23 on the **thumb** *of* his right hand and on the big toe of his right foot.
8:23 on the thumb of his right hand and on the **big toe** *of* his right foot.
8:24 on the **thumbs** *of* their right hands and on the big toes of their right
8:24 thumbs of their right hands and on the **big toes** *of* their right feet.
14:14 on the **thumb** *of* his right hand and on the big toe of his right foot.
14:14 on the thumb of his right hand and on the **big toe** *of* his right foot.
14:17 on the **thumb** *of* his right hand and on the big toe of his right foot,
14:17 on the thumb of his right hand and on the **big toe** *of* his right foot,
14:25 on the **thumb** *of* his right hand and on the big toe of his right foot.
14:25 on the thumb of his right hand and on the **big toe** *of* his right foot.
14:28 on the **thumb** *of* his right hand and on the big toe of his right foot.
14:28 on the thumb of his right hand and on the **big toe** *of* his right foot.

992 בֹּהַן *bōhan*, n.pr.m. [2] [√ 991?]

Bohan [2]

Jos 15:6 continued north of Beth Arabah to the Stone of **Bohan** son of
18:17 of Adummim, and ran down to the Stone of **Bohan** son of Reuben.

993 בֹּהַק *bōhaq*, n.m. [1]

harmless rash [1]

Lev 13:39 dull white, it is a **harmless rash** that has broken out on the skin;

994 בַּהֶרֶת *baheret*, n.f. [12] [√ 986]

spot [7], bright spot [2], spots [2], *untranslated* [1]

Lev 13:2 or a **bright spot** on his skin that may become an infectious skin
13:4 If the **spot** on his skin is white but does not appear to be more than
13:19 where the boil was, a white swelling or reddish-white **spot** appears,
13:23 if the **spot** is unchanged and has not spread, it is only a scar from
13:24 a reddish-white or white **spot** appears in the raw flesh of the burn,
13:25 the priest is to examine the **spot**, and if the hair in it has turned
13:26 But if the priest examines it and there is no white hair in the **spot**
13:28 the **spot** is unchanged and has not spread in the skin but has faded,
13:38 "When a man or woman has white **spots** on the skin,
13:38 "When a man or woman has white spots **[RPH]** on the skin,
13:39 the priest is to examine them, and if the **spots** are dull white,
14:56 and for a swelling, a rash or a **bright spot**,

995 בּוֹא *bô'*, v. [2557 / 2559] [→ 929, 4427, 4569, 9311]

come [374], came [285], bring [177], went [174], brought [165], go [105], coming [71], comes [67], *untranslated* [64], arrived [48], enter [+448] [36], enter [31], returned [29], enter [+928] [25], took [22], bringing [19], entered [19], go in [19], went in [18], entered [+448] [17], take [14], bring in [13], gone [13], reached [+448] [13], come in [12], entering [12], brought in [11], came in [11], bring back [10], reached [+6330] [10], went into [10], brings [8], entered [+928] [8], enters [8], brought back [7], fulfilled [7], lay with [+448] [7], put [7], set [7], well advanced [7], followed [+339] [6], get [6], go into [6], invade [+928] [6], reached [6], sleep with [+448] [6], sunset [+2021+9087] [6], went back [6], attack [+6584] [5], enters [+448] [5], goes [5], happened [5], slept with [+448] [5], approached [+6330] [4], arrived [+448] [4], back [4], came back [4], carried off [4], certainly come [+995] [4], entrance [4], flee [4], flows [4], going on duty [4], going [4], included [4], invaded [+928] [4], lie with [+448] [4], overtake [4], reached [+2025] [4], return [4], arriving [3], attack [+4200] [3], attack [+448] [3], bring about [3], bring into [3], brought into [3], comes true [3], entered [+4200] [3], get in [3], give [3], going in [3], is brought [3], marched [3], overtakes [3], returning [3], sailed [3], setting [3], taken [3], toward [+2025+3870] [3], was brought [3], actually come [+995] [2], advance [+995] [2], approach [2], approaches [+448] [2], approaching [2], arrival [2], arrives [2], associate with [+928] [2], at hand [2], attack [2], attacked [+6584] [2], be brought [2], been brought into [2], bloodshed [+928+1947] [2], bow [2], bring down [2], bringing in [2], brought to pass [2], came home [2], came to pass [2], carried [2], carry [2], come into [2], come true [2], comes [+995] [2], comes true [+995] [2], delivered [2], enter [+6584] [2], entering [+4200] [2], follows [+339] [2], get there [2], go back [2], go now [+2143] [2], goes down [2], goes in [2], happens [2], inserted [2], invade [2], invades [+928] [2], kept [2], led in campaigns [+2256+3655+4200+7156] [2], led on military campaigns [+906+2256+3655] [2], led [2], left [+4946] [2], march [2], placed [2], present [2], presented [2], put in [2], reach [+6330] [2], reached [+928] [2], received [+448] [2], return [+995] [2], set out [2], sets [2], sunset [+2021+6961+9087] [2], sweep on [+995] [2], were brought [2], wherever goes [+928+928+2256+3655] [2], withstand [+928] [2], wounds [+928] [2], accompanied [+8079] [1], admitted [1], advance [1], advanced [1], advancing [1], all the way to [+3870+6330] [1], all the way to [+6330] [1], all the way to [1], appear [1], appeared [1], apply [1], approached [+448] [1], approached [1], are brought [1], are [1], arrive [+448] [1], arrive [+6330] [1], arrive [1], arrived [+6330] [1], arrives [+7024] [1], assembled [+7736] [1], associate [1], at hand [+4200+7940] [1], at hand [+7940] [1], ate [+448+7931] [1], attacking [+6584] [1], attacks [+6584] [1], awaits [1], away [1], be brought in [1], be heard[s] [1], be inserted [1], be right there [1], be taken [1], be [1], became [1], been brought [1], been taken into [1], begin [1], beset [+928] [1], besiege [+928+2021+4946+5189+7156] [1], bind themselves with [+928] [1], blessed [+1388+6584] [1], border [1], bound [1], break into [1], bring [+907] [1], bring home [1], bring out [1], bringing into [1], broke [1], brought about [1], brought in as wives [1], built up [1], buried [+448+7700] [1], buried [1], by all means go [+2143] [1], calling together [+906+906+2256+8938] [1], came along [1], came back [+2143+2256] [1], came bringing [1], came up [1], came with [1], carried away [1], carried back [1], carry back [1], carry off [+928+2021+8660] [1], carry off [1], carry out duties [+2256+3655] [1], caused to come [1], check [+4200+7156] [1], collapses [+8691] [1], come back [1], come home [1], come on [1], come to rest [1], comes by [1], comes in [1], committed adultery with [+448] [1], confront [1], consort [1], covers [+928] [1], crept [1], crowded into [1], deported [+906+1583] [1], does[s] [1], done[s] so [+448+7931] [1], edge [1], encounter [+928] [1], encroach [1], enter [+4200] [1], entered [+2025] [1], entered [+6584] [1], entered [+928+9348] [1], entered and went [1], entering [+2025] [1], entering [+448] [1], entering [+6330] [1], entering [+928] [1], entering [+928+7931] [1], entering [+928+9348] [1], enters [+2025] [1], enters [+4200] [1], enters [+928] [1], escort [1], every spring [+9102] [1], extending [1], fallen [1], find [+448] [1], fled [1], float [1], flowing [1], follow [+339] [1], followed in [+339] [1], fulfill [1], future [1], gain [1], gave [1], give in [1], given [1], go [+2143] [1], go about business [+2256+3655] [1], go at once [+2143+2256] [1], go down [1], go home [1], go in [+2143+2256] [1], go sleep with [+448] [1], going down [1], gone into [1], granted [1], guest [+440+1074] [1], had brought in [1], had brought [1], had [1], had[s] [1], hand over [1], happen [1], harvested [1], has [1], have [1], here [1], hid in [1], imported [1], in [1], insert [1], intermarry [1], into [1], invade [+2025+9004] [1], invade [+448] [1], invaded [+448] [1], invaded [+6584] [1], invader [+448] [1], invading [+4200] [1], invited [1], is [1], join [+6330] [1], journeyed [1], laid siege [+928+2021+5189] [1], last [1], lead [+2256+3655] [1], lead [+2256+3655+4200+7156] [1], lead [1], led into [1], ledges [1], let touch [+928] [1], lie with [+6584] [1], listed [1], lying with [+448] [1], made attack [1], make enter [+928] [1], make go down [1], make [1], married [+448] [1], migration [1], moved into [1], moved out [1], moved [1], moves [1], moving [1], myself [1], occupy [+448] [1], offer [1], on duty [+2256+3655] [1], on [1], oppose [+928] [1], out [1], over [1], overtook [+448] [1], overwhelm [+6584] [1], pass [1], passed [1], pierce [+928] [1], pierced [+928] [1], place [1], placing [1], poured [1], produce [1], provide [1], pulled back [1], put [+4200+7156] [1], put [+4200+9202] [1], putting [1], raiding [+928] [1], reach [+448] [1], reach [1], reached [+4200] [1], reached [+448+6330] [1], reaches [+448] [1], received [+4200] [1], received [1], reentered [+2256+8740] [1], replace [+448+9393] [1], report back [1], reported [1], resound [1], rest [1], return [+2143] [1], return [+6388] [1], rose [1], sank in [1], send [+907+4946] [1], send [1], sent [1], serve [+2256+3655] [1], set foot [1], share [1], shave head in mourning [+448+7947] [1], shed [1], sleeps with [+448] [1], stay [+448+4202] [1], stayed away [+4202] [1], stepped [1], stole into [+1704+4200] [1], successor [+132+339 +8611] [1], sunset [+2021+3064] [1], swarm [1], swept in [1], take [+1198] [1], take [+6584] [1], take along [1], take back [1], take home [1], take into [1], take out [1], take part [1], taken place [1], takes place [1], taking [1], time is ripe [+7891] [1], to the vicinity of [+3870 +6330] [1], took [+448] [1], took back [+906+2256+8938] [1], took back [1], took into [1], touch [1], touched [+448] [1], toward [+3870] [1], travel about [+2256+3655] [1], traveled [1], treads [1], turn [1], very old [+928+2021+2416+3427] [1], visit [1], was brought into [1], was taken [1], went in to spend the night with [+448] [1], went inside [1], went on [1], went out [1], went over [1], were taken [1], were [1], what[s] [+2021] [1], wielding [+2025+4200+5087] [1], will[s] [1], work [1]

Ge 2:19 [G] *He* **brought** them to the man to see what he would name
2:22 [G] he had taken out of the man, and *he* **brought** her to the man.
4: 3 [G] In the course of time Cain **brought** some of the fruits of the
4: 4 [G] Abel **brought** fat portions from some of the firstborn of his
6: 4 [A] when the sons of God **went** to the daughters of men and had
6:13 [A] So God said to Noah, "I *am going to* **put** [+4200+7156] an
6:17 [G] I *am going to* **bring** floodwaters on the earth to destroy all
6:18 [A] my covenant with you, and *you will* **enter** [+448] the ark—
6:19 [G] *You are to* **bring** into the ark two of all living creatures,
6:20 [A] moves along the ground *will* **come** to you to be kept alive.
7: 1 [A] said to Noah, "**Go** into the ark, you and your whole family,
7: 7 [A] his sons' wives **entered** [+448] the ark to escape the waters
7: 9 [A] male and female, **came** to Noah and entered the ark, as God
7:13 [A] and the wives of his three sons, **entered** [+448] the ark.
7:15 [A] creatures that have the breath of life in them **came** to Noah
7:16 [A] The *animals* **going in** were male and female of every living
7:16 [A] of every living thing, **[RPH]** as God had commanded Noah.
8: 9 [G] and took the dove and **brought** it **back** to himself in the ark.
8:11 [A] When the dove **returned** to him in the evening, there in its
10:19 [A] from Sidon **toward** [+2025+3870] Gerar as far as Gaza,
10:19 [A] and then **toward** [+2025+3870] Sodom, Gomorrah, Admah
10:30 [A] lived stretched from Mesha **toward** [+2025+3870] Sephar,
11:31 [A] to Canaan. But when *they* **came** to Haran, they settled there.
12: 5 [A] they set out for the land of Canaan, and *they* **arrived** there.
12:11 [A] As he was about to **enter** Egypt, he said to his wife Sarai,
12:14 [A] When Abram **came** to Egypt, the Egyptians saw that she was
13:10 [A] of the LORD, like the land of Egypt, **toward** [+3870] Zoar.
13:18 [A] and **went** to live near the great trees of Mamre at Hebron,
14: 5 [A] Kedorlaomer and the kings allied with him **went out**
14: 7 [A] they turned back and **went** to En Mishpat (that is, Kadesh),
14:13 [A] *One* who had escaped **came** and reported this to Abram the
15:12 [A] As the sun *was* **setting**, Abram fell into a deep sleep, and a
15:15 [A] *will* **go** to your fathers in peace and be buried at a good old
15:17 [A] When the sun *had* **set** and darkness had fallen, a smoking
16: 2 [A] **Go** [+448], **sleep with** my maidservant; perhaps I can build a
16: 4 [A] *He* **slept** [+448] **with** Hagar, and she conceived. When she
16: 8 [A] "Hagar, servant of Sarai, where *have you* **come** from,
18:11 [A] and Sarah were already old and **well advanced** in years,
18:19 [G] so that the LORD *will* **bring about** for Abraham what he
18:21 [A] done is as bad as the outcry that *has* **reached** [+448] me.
19: 1 [A] The two angels **arrived** at Sodom in the evening, and Lot
19: 3 [A] that they did go with him and **entered** [+448] his house.
19: 5 [A] called to Lot, "Where are the men who **came** to you tonight?
19: 8 [A] for *they have* **come** under the protection of my roof."
19: 9 [A] they said, "This fellow **came** here as an alien, and now he
19:10 [G] and **pulled** Lot **back** into the house and shut the door.
19:22 [A] because I cannot do anything until you **reach** it."
19:23 [A] By the time Lot **reached** [+2025] Zoar, the sun had risen
19:31 [A] and there is no man around here to **lie** [+6584] **with** us,
19:33 [A] drink wine, and the older daughter **went in** and lay with him.
19:34 [A] *you* **go in** and lie with him so we can preserve our family line
20: 3 [A] God **came** to Abimelech in a dream one night and said to
20: 9 [G] How have I wronged you that *you have* **brought** such great
20:13 [A] is how you can show your love to me: Everywhere *we* **go**,
22: 9 [A] When *they* **reached** [+448] the place God had told him
23: 2 [A] and Abraham **went** to mourn for Sarah and to weep over her.
23:10 [A] of all the Hittites *who had* **come** *to* the gate of his city.
23:18 [A] of all the Hittites *who had* **come** *to* the gate of the city.
24: 1 [A] Abraham was now old and **well advanced** in years,
24:30 [A] *he* **went** *out* to the man and found him standing by the
24:31 [A] "**Come**, you who are blessed by the LORD," he said. "Why
24:32 [A] So the man **went** to the house, and the camels were unloaded.
24:41 [A] Then, when *you* **go** to my clan, you will be released from my
24:42 [A] "When *I* **came** to the spring today, I said, 'O LORD, God of
24:62 [A] Now Isaac *had* **come** from Beer Lahai Roi, for he was living
24:62 [A] Now Isaac had come from **[RPH]** Beer Lahai Roi, for he
24:63 [A] and as he looked up, he saw camels **approaching**.
24:67 [G] Isaac **brought** her into the tent of his mother Sarah, and he
25:18 [A] to Shur, near the border of Egypt, *as* you **go** toward Asshur.
25:29 [A] some stew, Esau **came in** from the open country, famished.
26:10 [G] with your wife, and *you would have* **brought** guilt upon us."
26:27 [A] Isaac asked them, "Why *have you* **come** to me, since you
26:32 [A] That day Isaac's servants **came** and told him about the well
27: 4 [G] me the kind of tasty food I like and **bring** it to me to eat,
27: 5 [G] left for the open country to hunt game and **bring** it **back**,
27: 7 [G] '**Bring** me some game and prepare me some tasty food to eat,
27:10 [G] **take** it to your father to eat, so that he may give you his

Ge 27:12 [G] *would* **bring down** a curse on myself rather than a blessing."
27:14 [G] So he went and got them and **brought** them to his mother,
27:18 [A] *He* **went** to his father and said, "My father." "Yes, my son,"
27:25 [G] to him and he ate; and *he* **brought** some wine and he drank.
27:30 [A] his father's presence, his brother Esau **came in** from hunting.
27:31 [G] He too prepared some tasty food and **brought** it to his father.
27:33 [G] "Who was it, then, that hunted game and **brought** it to me?
27:33 [A] I ate it just before *you* **came** and I blessed him—and indeed
27:35 [A] "Your brother **came** deceitfully and took your blessing."
28:11 [A] he stopped for the night because the sun *had* **set**.
29: 6 [A] "and here **comes** his daughter Rachel with the sheep."
29: 9 [A] Rachel **came** with her father's sheep, for she was a
29:13 [G] embraced him and kissed him and **brought** him to his home,
29:21 [A] My time is completed, and *I want to* **lie** [+448] **with** her."
29:23 [G] he took his daughter Leah and **gave** her to Jacob, and Jacob
29:23 [A] and gave her to Jacob, and Jacob **lay** [+448] **with** her.
29:30 [A] Jacob **lay** [+448] **with** Rachel also, and he loved Rachel
30: 3 [A] **Sleep** [+448] **with** her so that she can bear children for me
30: 4 [A] her servant Bilhah as a wife. Jacob **slept** [+448] **with** her,
30:11 [a] [Leah said, "**What** [Q; see K 928] good fortune!"]
30:14 [G] mandrake plants, which *he* **brought** to his mother Leah.
30:16 [A] So when Jacob **came in** from the fields that evening, Leah
30:16 [A] to meet him. "*You must* **sleep** [+448] **with** me," she said.
30:33 [A] whenever *you* **check** [+4200+7156] on the wages you have
30:38 [A] be directly in front of the flocks *when they* **came** to drink.
30:38 [A] to drink. When the flocks were in heat and **came** to drink,
31:18 [A] Paddan Aram, to **go** to his father Isaac in the land of Canaan.
31:24 [A] Then God **came** to Laban the Aramean in a dream at night
31:33 [A] So Laban **went** into Jacob's tent and into Leah's tent and into
31:33 [A] he came out of Leah's tent, *he* **entered** [+928] Rachel's tent.
31:39 [G] *I did* not **bring** you animals torn by wild beasts; I bore the
32: 6 [32:7] [A] they said, "*We* **went** to your brother Esau, and now
32: 8 [32:9] [A] He thought, "If Esau **comes** and attacks one group,
32:11 [32:12] [A] for I am afraid he *will* **come** and attack me,
32:13 [32:14] [A] from **what**[s] [+2021] he had with him he selected a
33: 1 [A] and there was Esau, **coming** with his four hundred men;
33:11 [H] Please accept the present that **was brought** to you, for God
33:14 [A] and that of the children, until *I* **come** to my lord in Seir."
33:18 [A] After Jacob **came** from Paddan Aram, he arrived safely at the
33:18 [A] he **arrived** safely *at* the city of Shechem in Canaan
34: 5 [A] his livestock; so he kept quiet about it until they **came home**.
34: 7 [A] Now Jacob's sons *had* **come in** from the fields as soon as
34:20 [A] his son Shechem **went** to the gate of their city to speak to
34:25 [A] their swords and **attacked** [+6584] the unsuspecting city,
34:27 [A] The sons of Jacob **came** upon the dead bodies and looted the
35: 6 [A] Jacob and all the people with him **came** to Luz (that is,
35: 9 [A] After Jacob **returned** from Paddan Aram, God appeared to
35:16 [A] While they were still some distance **[NIE]** from Ephrath,
35:27 [A] Jacob **came home** to his father Isaac in Mamre, near Kiriath
37: 2 [G] and he **brought** their father a bad report about them.
37:10 [A] *Will* your mother and I and your brothers **actually come** [+995]
37:10 [A] *Will* your mother and I and your brothers **actually come** [+995]
37:14 [A] the Valley of Hebron. When Joseph **arrived** at Shechem,
37:19 [A] "Here **comes** that dreamer!" they said to each other.
37:23 [A] So when Joseph **came** to his brothers, they stripped him of
37:25 [A] and saw a caravan of Ishmaelites **coming** from Gilead.
37:28 [G] shekels of silver to the Ishmaelites, *who* **took** him to Egypt.
37:30 [A] and said, "The boy isn't there! Where *can* I **turn** *now*?"
37:32 [G] *They* **took** the ornamented robe **back** [+906+2256+8938] to
38: 2 [A] man named Shua. He married her and **lay** [+448] **with** her;
38: 8 [A] "**Lie** [+448] **with** your brother's wife and fulfill your duty to
38: 9 [A] so whenever *he* **lay** [+448] **with** his brother's wife, he spilled
38:16 [A] and said, "Come now, *let me* **sleep** [+448] **with** you."
38:16 [A] "And what will you give me *to* **sleep** [+448] **with** *you*?" she
38:18 [A] So he gave them to her and **slept** [+448] **with** her, and she
39:11 [A] One day *he* **went** into the house to attend to his duties,
39:14 [G] "this Hebrew *has been* **brought** to us to make sport of us!
39:14 [A] of us! *He* **came** in here to sleep with me, but I screamed.
39:16 [A] She kept his cloak beside her until his master **came** home.
39:17 [G] "That Hebrew slave *you* **brought** us came to me to make
39:17 [A] "That Hebrew slave you brought us **came** to me to make
40: 6 [A] When Joseph **came** to them the next morning, he saw that
41:14 [A] and changed his clothes, *he* **came** before Pharaoh.
41:21 [A] even after they **ate** [+448+7931] *them*, no one could tell that
41:21 [A] no one could tell that they *had* **done**[s] [+448+7931] **so**;
41:29 [A] Seven years of great abundance *are* **coming** throughout the
41:35 [A] collect all the food of these good years that *are* **coming**
41:50 [A] Before the years of famine **came**, two sons were born to
41:54 [A] seven years of famine began, **[NIE]** just as Joseph had said.
41:57 [A] all the countries **came** to Egypt to buy grain from Joseph,
42: 5 [A] So Israel's sons **were** among those who went to buy grain,
42: 5 [A] So Israel's sons were among those *who* **went** to buy grain,
42: 6 [A] So when Joseph's brothers **arrived**, they bowed down to him
42: 7 [A] harshly to them. "Where *do you* **come** from?" he asked.
42: 9 [A] *You have* **come** to see where our land is unprotected."
42:10 [A] they answered. "Your servants *have* **come** to buy food.
42:12 [A] "*You have* **come** to see where our land is unprotected."
42:15 [A] not leave this place unless your youngest brother **comes** here.
42:19 [G] of you go and **take** grain **back** *for* your starving households.
42:20 [G] *you must* **bring** your youngest brother to me, so that your
42:21 [A] would not listen; that's why this distress *has* **come** upon us."
42:29 [A] When *they* **came** to their father Jacob in the land of Canaan,
42:34 [G] **bring** your youngest brother to me so I will know that you
42:37 [G] both of my sons to death if *I do* not **bring** him **back** to you.
43: 2 [G] So when they had eaten all the grain *they had* **brought** from
43: 9 [G] If *I do* not **bring** him **back** to you and set him here before
43:16 [G] "**Take** these men to my house, slaughter an animal
43:17 [G] did as Joseph told him and **took** the men to Joseph's house.
43:18 [H] Now the men were frightened when *they* **were taken** *to* his
43:18 [H] "We **were brought** here because of the silver that was put
43:21 [A] **[NIE]** at the place where we stopped for the night we
43:23 [A] you treasure in your sacks; I **received** [+448] your silver."
43:24 [G] The steward **took** the men into Joseph's house, gave them
43:25 [A] They prepared their gifts for Joseph's **arrival** at noon,
43:26 [A] When Joseph **came** home, they presented to him the gifts
43:26 [G] *they* **presented** to him the gifts they had brought into the
43:30 [A] place to weep. *He* **went** into his private room and wept there.
44:14 [A] was still in the house when Judah and his brothers **came** in,
44:30 [A] if the boy is not with us when I **go back** to your servant my
44:32 [G] I said, 'If *I do* not **bring** him **back** to you, I will bear the
45:16 [A] reached Pharaoh's palace that Joseph's brothers *had* **come**,
45:17 [A] your animals and **return** [+2143] to the land of Canaan,
45:18 [A] bring your father and your families **back** to me. I will give
45:19 [A] your children and your wives, and get your father and **come**.
45:25 [A] and **came** to their father Jacob *in* the land of Canaan.
46: 1 [A] all that was his, and when *he* **reached** [+2025] Beersheba,
46: 6 [A] in Canaan, and Jacob and all his offspring **went** to Egypt.
46: 7 [G] *He* **took** with him to Egypt his sons and grandsons and his
46: 8 [A] of Israel (Jacob and his descendants) who **went** to Egypt:
46:26 [A] All those who **went** to Egypt with Jacob—those who were
46:27 [A] of Jacob's family, which **went** to Egypt, were seventy in all.
46:28 [A] to Goshen. When *they* **arrived** in the region of Goshen,
46:31 [A] who were living in the land of Canaan, *have* **come** to me.
46:32 [G] *they have* **brought** *along* their flocks and herds and
47: 1 [A] Joseph **went** and told Pharaoh, "My father and brothers, with
47: 1 [A] *have* **come** from the land of Canaan and are now in Goshen."
47: 4 [A] They also said to him, "*We have* **come** to live here awhile,
47: 5 [A] to Joseph, "Your father and your brothers *have* **come** to you,
47: 7 [G] Joseph **brought** his father Jacob **in** and presented him before
47:14 [G] they were buying, and he **brought** it to Pharaoh's palace.
47:15 [A] was gone, all Egypt **came** to Joseph and said, "Give us food.
47:17 [G] So *they* **brought** their livestock to Joseph, and he gave them
47:18 [A] year was over, *they* **came** to him the following year and said,
48: 2 [A] When Jacob was told, "Your son Joseph *has* **come** to you,"
48: 5 [A] your two sons born to you in Egypt before I **came** to you
48: 7 [A] As I *was* **returning** from Paddan, to my sorrow Rachel died
48: 7 [A] were still on the way, a little distance **[RPH]** from Ephrath.
49: 6 [A] *Let* me not **enter** [+928] their council, let me not join their
49:10 [A] until *he* **comes** to whom it belongs and the obedience of the
50:10 [A] When *they* **reached** [+6330] the threshing floor of Atad,
Ex 1: 1 [A] These are the names of the sons of Israel who **went** to Egypt
1: 1 [A] went to Egypt with Jacob, each with his family: **[RPH]**
1:19 [A] and give birth before the midwives **arrive** [+448]."
2:10 [G] *she* **took** him to Pharaoh's daughter and he became her son.
2:16 [A] *they* **came** to draw water and fill the troughs to water their
2:17 [A] Some shepherds **came along** and drove them away,
2:18 [A] When *the girls* **returned** to Reuel their father, he asked
2:18 [A] he asked them, "Why *have you* **returned** so early today?"
3: 1 [A] led the flock to the far side of the desert and **came** to Horeb,
3: 9 [A] And now the cry of the Israelites *has* **reached** [+448] me,
3:13 [A] said to God, "Suppose I **go** to the Israelites and say to them,
3:18 [A] you and the elders *are to* **go** to the king of Egypt and say to
4: 6 [G] Then the LORD said, "**Put** your hand inside your cloak."
4: 6 [G] So Moses **put** his hand into his cloak, and when he took it
5: 1 [A] Afterward Moses and Aaron **went** to Pharaoh and said,
5:15 [A] Then the Israelite foremen **went** and appealed to Pharaoh:
5:23 [A] Ever since *I* **went** to Pharaoh to speak in your name, he has
6: 8 [G] *I will* **bring** you to the land I swore with uplifted hand to
6:11 [A] "**Go**, tell Pharaoh king of Egypt to let the Israelites go out of
7:10 [A] So Moses and Aaron **went** to Pharaoh and did just as the
7:23 [A] Instead, he turned and **went** into his palace, and did not take
8: 1 [7:26] [A] "**Go** to Pharaoh and say to him, 'This is what the
8: 3 [7:28] [A] *They will* **come** up into your palace and your
8:24 [8:20] [A] Dense swarms of flies **poured** into Pharaoh's palace
9: 1 [A] "**Go** to Pharaoh and say to him, 'This is what the LORD,
10: 1 [A] "**Go** to Pharaoh, for I have hardened his heart and the hearts
10: 3 [A] So Moses and Aaron **went** to Pharaoh and said to him,
10: 4 [G] let them go, I *will* **bring** locusts into your country tomorrow.

Ex 10:26 [A] until we **get** there we will not know what we are to use to
11: 1 [G] "*I will* **bring** one more plague on Pharaoh and on Egypt.
12:23 [A] he will not permit the destroyer to **enter** [+448] your houses
12:25 [A] When *you* **enter** [+448] the land that the LORD will give
13: 5 [G] When the LORD **brings** you into the land of the
13:11 [G] "After the LORD **brings** you into the land of the Canaanites
14:16 [A] so that the Israelites *can* **go** through the sea on dry ground.
14:17 [A] the hearts of the Egyptians so that *they will* **go in** after them.
14:20 [A] **coming** between the armies of Egypt and Israel. Throughout
14:22 [A] the Israelites **went** through the sea on dry ground, with a wall
14:23 [A] and horsemen **followed** [+339] them into the sea.
14:28 [A] the entire army of Pharaoh that *had* **followed** [+339] the
15:17 [G] *You will* **bring** them *in* and plant them on the mountain of
15:19 [A] Pharaoh's horses, chariots and horsemen **went** into the sea,
15:23 [A] When *they* **came** to Marah, they could not drink its water
15:27 [A] Then *they* **came** to Elim, where there were twelve springs
16: 1 [A] community set out from Elim and **came** to the Desert of Sin,
16: 5 [G] On the sixth day they are to prepare what *they* **bring in**,
16:22 [A] the leaders of the community **came** and reported this to
16:35 [A] manna forty years, until they **came** to a land that was settled;
16:35 [A] they ate manna until they **reached** [+448] the border of
17: 8 [A] The Amalekites **came** and attacked the Israelites at
17:12 [A] so that his hands remained steady till **sunset** [+2021+9087].
18: 5 [A] with Moses' sons and wife, **came** to him in the desert,
18: 6 [A] *am* **coming** to you with your wife and her two sons."
18: 7 [A] They greeted each other and then **went** into the tent.
18:12 [A] Aaron **came** with all the elders of Israel to eat bread with
18:15 [A] "Because the people **come** to me to seek God's will.
18:16 [A] Whenever they have a dispute, *it is* **brought** to me, and I
18:19 [G] representative before God and **bring** their disputes to him.
18:22 [G] at all times, but *have them* **bring** every difficult case to you;
18:23 [A] stand the strain, and all these people *will* **go** home satisfied."
18:26 [G] The difficult cases *they* **brought** to Moses, but the simple
19: 1 [A] on the very day—*they* **came** *to* the Desert of Sinai.
19: 2 [A] set out from Rephidim, *they* **entered** the Desert of Sinai,
19: 4 [G] I carried you on eagles' wings and **brought** you to myself.
19: 7 [A] So Moses **went back** and summoned the elders of the people
19: 9 [A] said to Moses, "I *am going to* **come** to you in a dense cloud,
20:20 [A] God *has* **come** to test you, so that the fear of God will be
20:24 [A] my name to be honored, *I will* **come** to you and bless you.
21: 3 [A] If *he* **comes** alone, he is to go free alone; but if he has a wife
22: 9 [22:8] [A] parties *are to* **bring** their cases before the judges.
22:13 [22:12] [G] *he shall* **bring in** the remains as evidence and he
22:15 [22:14] [A] the money paid for the hire **covers** [+928] the loss.
22:26 [22:25] [A] a pledge, return it to him by **sunset** [+2021+9087],
23:19 [G] "**Bring** the best of the firstfruits of your soil *to* the house of
23:20 [G] along the way and to **bring** you to the place I have prepared.
23:23 [G] go ahead of you and **bring** you into the land of the Amorites,
23:27 [A] throw into confusion every nation *you* **encounter** [+928].
24: 3 [A] When Moses **went** and told the people all the LORD's
24:18 [A] Moses **entered** [+928+9348] the cloud as he went on up the
25:14 [G] **Insert** the poles into the rings on the sides of the chest to
26:11 [G] and **put** them in the loops to fasten the tent together as a unit.
26:33 [G] and **place** the ark of the Testimony behind the curtain.
27: 7 [H] The poles *are to* **be inserted** into the rings so they will be on
28:29 [A] "Whenever Aaron **enters** [+448] the Holy Place, he will bear
28:30 [A] so they may be over Aaron's heart whenever he **enters** the
28:35 [A] The sound of the bells will be heard when he **enters** [+448]
28:43 [A] his sons must wear them whenever they **enter** [+448] the
29:30 [A] **comes** to the Tent of Meeting to minister in the Holy Place is
30:20 [A] Whenever they **enter** [+448] the Tent of Meeting, they shall
32: 2 [G] and your daughters are wearing, and **bring** them to me."
32: 3 [G] people took off their earrings and **brought** them to Aaron.
32:21 [G] people do to you, that *you* **led** them **into** such great sin?"
33: 8 [A] their tents, watching Moses until he **entered** [+2025] the tent.
33: 9 [A] As Moses **went** into the tent, the pillar of cloud would come
34:12 [A] a treaty with those who live in the land where you *are* **going**,
34:26 [G] "**Bring** the best of the firstfruits of your soil to the house of
34:34 [A] whenever he **entered** the LORD's presence to speak with
34:35 [A] Moses would put the veil back over his face until he **went in**
35: 5 [G] Everyone who is willing *is to* **bring** to the LORD an
35:10 [A] "All who are skilled among you *are to* **come** and make
35:21 [A] everyone who was willing and whose heart moved him **came**
35:21 [G] **brought** an offering to the LORD for the work on the Tent
35:22 [A] women alike, **came** and brought gold jewelry of all kinds:
35:22 [G] women alike, came and **brought** gold jewelry of all kinds:
35:23 [G] ram skins dyed red or hides of sea cows **brought** them.
35:24 [G] of silver or bronze **brought** it as an offering to the LORD,
35:24 [G] who had acacia wood for any part of the work **brought** it.
35:25 [G] and **brought** what she had spun—blue, purple or scarlet yarn
35:27 [G] The leaders **brought** onyx stones and other gems to be
35:29 [G] women who were willing **brought** to the LORD freewill
35:29 [G] through Moses had commanded them to do. **[RPH]**
36: 3 [G] *had* **brought** to carry out the work of constructing the
36: 3 [G] the people continued *to* **bring** freewill offerings morning
36: 4 [A] doing all the work on the sanctuary **left** [+4946] their work
36: 5 [G] "The people *are* **bringing** more than enough for doing the
36: 6 [G] And so the people were restrained from **bringing** more,
37: 5 [G] *he* **inserted** the poles into the rings on the sides of the ark to
38: 7 [G] *They* **inserted** the poles into the rings so they would be on
39:33 [G] *they* **brought** the tabernacle to Moses: the tent and all its
40: 4 [G] **Bring in** the table and set out what belongs on it. Then bring
40: 4 [G] on it. Then **bring in** the lampstand and set up its lamps.
40:21 [G] *he* **brought** the ark into the tabernacle and hung the shielding
40:32 [A] They washed whenever they **entered** [+448] the Tent of
40:35 [A] Moses could not **enter** [+448] the Tent of Meeting
Lev 2: 2 [G] **take** it to Aaron's sons the priests. The priest shall take a
2: 8 [G] **Bring** the grain offering made of these things to the LORD;
4: 4 [G] *He is to* **present** the bull at the entrance to the Tent of
4: 5 [G] of the bull's blood and **carry** it into the Tent of Meeting.
4:14 [G] as a sin offering and **present** it before the Tent of Meeting.
4:16 [G] the anointed priest *is to* **take** some of the bull's blood into
4:23 [G] *he must* **bring** as his offering a male goat without defect.
4:28 [G] *he must* **bring** as his offering for the sin he committed a
4:32 [G] " 'If *he* **brings** a lamb as his sin offering, he is to bring a
4:32 [G] as his sin offering, *he is to* **bring** a female without defect.
5: 6 [G] as a penalty for the sin he has committed, *he must* **bring** to
5: 7 [G] *he is to* **bring** two doves or two young pigeons to the LORD as
5: 8 [G] *He is to* **bring** them to the priest, who shall first offer the one
5:11 [G] *he is to* **bring** as an offering for his sin a tenth of an ephah of
5:12 [G] *He is to* **bring** it to the priest, who shall take a handful of it
5:15 [G] *he is to* **bring** to the LORD as a penalty a ram from the
5:18 [G] *He is to* **bring** to the priest as a guilt offering a ram from the
6: 6 [5:25] [G] as a penalty *he must* **bring** to the priest, that is, to the
6:21 [6:14] [G] **bring** it well-mixed and present the grain offering
6:30 [6:23] [H] any sin offering whose blood **is brought** into the
7:29 [G] LORD *is to* **bring** part of it as his sacrifice to the LORD.
7:30 [G] With his own hands *he is to* **bring** the offering made to the
7:30 [G] *he is to* **bring** the fat, together with the breast, and wave the
9:23 [A] Moses and Aaron then **went** into the Tent of Meeting.
10: 9 [A] or other fermented drink whenever you **go** into the Tent of
10:15 [G] the breast that was waved *must be* **brought** with the fat
10:18 [H] Since its blood **was** not **taken** into the Holy Place,
11:32 [H] **Put** *it* in water; it will be unclean till evening, and then it will
11:34 [A] could be eaten but **has** water on it from such a pot is unclean,
12: 4 [A] or **go** to the sanctuary until the days of her purification are
12: 6 [G] *she is to* **bring** to the priest at the entrance to the Tent of
13: 2 [H] *he must* **be brought** to Aaron the priest or to one of his sons
13: 9 [H] an infectious skin disease, *he must* **be brought** to the priest.
13:16 [A] the raw flesh change and turn white, *he must* **go** to the priest.
14: 2 [H] his ceremonial cleansing, when *he is* **brought** to the priest:
14: 8 [A] After this *he may* **come** into the camp, but he must stay
14:23 [G] "On the eighth day *he must* **bring** them for his cleansing to
14:34 [A] "When *you* **enter** [+448] the land of Canaan, which I am
14:35 [A] the owner of the house *must* **go** and tell the priest, 'I have
14:36 [A] to be emptied before he **goes in** to examine the mildew,
14:36 [A] After this the priest *is to* **go in** and inspect the house.
14:42 [G] they are to take other stones *to* **replace** [+448+9393] these
14:44 [A] the priest *is to* **go** and examine it and, if the mildew has
14:46 [A] "Anyone *who* **goes** into the house while it is closed up will
14:48 [A] "But if the priest **comes** [+995] to examine it and the mildew
14:48 [A] "But if the priest **comes** [+995] to examine it and the mildew
15:14 [A] **come** before the LORD to the entrance to the Tent of
15:29 [G] **bring** them to the priest at the entrance to the Tent of
16: 2 [A] "Tell your brother Aaron not *to* **come** whenever he chooses
16: 3 [A] "This is how Aaron *is to* **enter** [+448] the sanctuary area:
16:12 [G] ground fragrant incense and **take** them behind the curtain.
16:15 [G] **take** its blood behind the curtain and do with it as he did with
16:17 [A] **goes in** to make atonement in the Most Holy Place until he
16:23 [A] "Then Aaron *is to* **go** into the Tent of Meeting and take off
16:23 [A] he put on before he **entered** [+448] the Most Holy Place,
16:26 [A] himself with water; afterward *he may* **come** into the camp.
16:27 [H] whose blood **was brought** into the Most Holy Place to make
16:28 [A] himself with water; afterward *he may* **come** into the camp.
17: 4 [G] instead of **bringing** it to the entrance to the Tent of Meeting
17: 5 [G] so the Israelites *will* **bring** to the LORD the sacrifices they
17: 5 [G] *They must* **bring** them to the priest, that is, to the LORD,
17: 9 [G] *does* not **bring** it to the entrance to the Tent of Meeting to
18: 3 [G] as they do in the land of Canaan, where I *am* **bringing** you.
19:21 [G] *must* **bring** a ram to the entrance to the Tent of Meeting for a
19:23 [A] " 'When *you* **enter** [+448] the land and plant any kind of
20:22 [G] so that the land where I *am* **bringing** you to live may not
21:11 [A] *He must* not **enter** [+6584] a place where there is a dead
21:23 [A] *he must* not **go** near the curtain or approach the altar, and
22: 7 [A] When the sun **goes down**, he will be clean, and after that he
23:10 [A] 'When *you* **enter** [+448] the land I am going to give you
23:10 [G] **bring** to the priest a sheaf of the first grain you harvest.
23:14 [G] until the very day you **bring** this offering to your God.

Lev 23:15 [G] the day you **brought** the sheaf of the wave offering,
23:17 [G] **bring** two loaves made of two-tenths of an ephah of fine
24:11 [G] the Name with a curse; so *they* **brought** him to Moses.
25: 2 [A] 'When *you* **enter** [+448] the land I am going to give you,
25:22 [A] to eat from it until the harvest of the ninth year **comes in**.
25:25 [A] his nearest relative *is to* **come** and redeem what his
26:25 [G] *I will* **bring** the sword upon you to avenge the breaking of
26:36 [G] *I will* **make** their hearts so fearful in the lands of their
26:41 [G] so that *I* **sent** them into the land of their enemies—
Nu 4: 3 [A] Count all the men from thirty to fifty years of age *who* **come**
4: 5 [A] Aaron and his sons *are to* **go in** and take down the shielding
4:15 [A] to move, the Kohathites *are to* **come** to do the carrying.
4:19 [A] Aaron and his sons *are to* **go into** the sanctuary and assign to
4:20 [A] But the Kohathites *must* not **go in** to look at the holy things,
4:23 [A] Count all the men from thirty to fifty years of age who **come**
4:30 [A] Count all the men from thirty to fifty years of age who **come**
4:35 [A] All the men from thirty to fifty years of age who **came** to
4:39 [A] All the men from thirty to fifty years of age who **came** to
4:43 [A] All the men from thirty to fifty years of age who **came** to
4:47 [A] All the men from thirty to fifty years of age who **came** to do
5:15 [G] he *is to* **take** his wife to the priest. He must also take an
5:15 [G] *He must* also **take** an offering of a tenth of an ephah of
5:22 [A] *May* this water that brings a curse **enter** [+928] your body
5:24 [A] this water *will* **enter** [+928] her and cause bitter suffering.
5:27 [A] brings a curse, it *will* **go** into her and cause bitter suffering;
6: 6 [A] separation to the LORD *he must* not **go** near a dead body.
6:10 [G] on the eighth day *he must* **bring** two doves or two young
6:12 [G] and *must* **bring** a year-old male lamb as a guilt offering.
6:13 [G] He *is to be* **brought** to the entrance to the Tent of Meeting.
7: 3 [G] *They* **brought** as their gifts before the LORD six covered
7:89 [A] When Moses **entered** [+448] the Tent of Meeting to speak
8:15 [A] they *are to* **come** to do their work at the Tent of Meeting.
8:22 [A] the Levites **came** to do their work at the Tent of Meeting
8:24 [A] or more *shall* **come** to take part in the work at the Tent of
10: 9 [A] When *you* **go into** battle in your own land against an enemy
10:21 [A] The tabernacle was to be set up before they **arrived**.
13:22 [A] They went up through the Negev and **came** to Hebron, where
13:23 [A] When *they* **reached** [+6330] the Valley of Eshcol, they cut
13:26 [A] *They* **came back** [+2143+2256] to Moses and Aaron and the
13:27 [A] "*We* **went** into the land to which you sent us, and it does
14: 3 [G] Why *is* the LORD **bringing** us to this land only to let us fall
14: 8 [G] *he will* **lead** us into that land, a land flowing with milk
14:16 [G] 'The LORD was not able to **bring** these people into the land
14:24 [G] me wholeheartedly, *I will* **bring** him into the land he went to,
14:24 [A] me wholeheartedly, I will bring him into the land *he* **went** to,
14:30 [A] Not one of you *will* **enter** [+448] the land I swore with
14:31 [G] *I will* **bring** them **in** to enjoy the land you have rejected.
15: 2 [A] 'After *you* **enter** [+448] the land I am giving you as a home
15:18 [A] 'When you **enter** [+448] the land to which I am taking you
15:18 [G] to them: 'When you enter the land to which I *am* **taking** you
15:25 [G] they *have* **brought** to the LORD for their wrong an offering
16:14 [G] *you* haven't **brought** us into a land flowing with milk
16:43 [17:8] [A] and Aaron **went** to the front of the Tent of Meeting,
17: 8 [17:23] [A] The next day Moses **entered** [+448] the Tent of the
18:13 [G] All the land's firstfruits that *they* **bring** to the LORD will
19: 7 [A] *He may* then **come** into the camp, but he will be
19:14 [A] Anyone who **enters** [+448] the tent and anyone who is in it
20: 1 [A] In the first month the whole Israelite community **arrived** *at*
20: 4 [G] Why *did you* **bring** the LORD's community into this
20: 5 [G] Why did you bring us up out of Egypt **[NIE]** to this terrible
20: 6 [A] Aaron **went** from the assembly to the entrance to the Tent of
20:12 [G] *you will* not **bring** this community into the land I give
20:22 [A] community set out from Kadesh and **came** *to* Mount Hor.
20:24 [A] *He will* not **enter** [+448] the land I give the Israelites,
21: 1 [A] heard that Israel *was* **coming** *along* the road to Atharim,
21: 7 [A] The people **came** to Moses and said, "We sinned when we
21:23 [A] When *he* **reached** [+2025] Jahaz, he fought with Israel.
21:27 [A] "**Come** *to* Heshbon and let it be rebuilt; let Sihon's city be
22: 7 [A] When *they* **came** to Balaam, they told him what Balak had
22: 9 [A] God **came** to Balaam and asked, "Who are these men with
22:14 [A] So the Moabite princes **returned** to Balak and said,
22:16 [A] *They* **came** to Balaam and said: "This is what Balak son of
22:20 [A] That night God **came** to Balaam and said, "Since these men
22:20 [A] and said, "Since these men *have* **come** to summon you,
22:36 [A] When Balak heard that Balaam *was* **coming**, he went out to
22:38 [A] "Well, *I have* **come** to you now," Balaam replied. "But can I
22:39 [A] Then Balaam went with Balak to **[NIE]** Kiriath Huzoth.
23:17 [A] So *he* **went** to him and found him standing beside his
25: 6 [A] an Israelite man **[NIE]** brought to his family a Midianite
25: 8 [A] **followed** [+339] the Israelite into the tent. He drove the spear
27:17 [A] to go out and **come in** before them, one who will lead them
27:17 [G] before them, one who will lead them out and **bring** them **in**,
27:21 [A] will go out, and at his command *they will* **come in**."
31:12 [G] **brought** the captives, spoils and plunder to Moses
31:14 [A] commanders of hundreds—who **returned** from the battle.
31:21 [A] Eleazar the priest said to the soldiers who *had* **gone** into
31:23 [A] anything else that *can* **withstand** [+928] fire must be put
31:23 [A] whatever cannot **withstand** [+928] fire must be put through
31:24 [A] and you will be clean. Then *you may* **come** into the camp."
31:54 [G] **brought** it into the Tent of Meeting as a memorial for the
32: 2 [A] So they **came** to Moses and Eleazar the priest and to the
32: 6 [A] "*Shall* your countrymen **go** to war while you sit here?
32: 9 [A] they discouraged the Israelites from **entering** [+448] the land
32:17 [G] go ahead of the Israelites until *we have* **brought** them to
32:19 [A] because our inheritance *has* **come** to us on the east side of
33: 9 [A] They left Marah and **went** to Elim, where there were twelve
33:40 [A] the Negev of Canaan, heard that the Israelites *were* **coming**.
34: 2 [A] 'When you **enter** [+448] Canaan, the land that will be
Dt 1: 7 [A] **go** to all the neighboring peoples in the Arabah,
1: 8 [A] **Go in** and take possession of the land that the LORD swore
1:19 [A] you have seen, and so *we* **reached** [+6330] Kadesh Barnea.
1:20 [A] "*You have* **reached** [+6330] the hill country of the
1:22 [A] the route we are to take and the towns *we will* **come** to."
1:24 [A] and **came** to the Valley of Eshcol and explored it.
1:31 [A] all the way you went until you **reached** [+6330] this place."
1:37 [A] angry with me also and said, "You *shall* not **enter** it, either.
1:38 [A] your assistant, Joshua son of Nun, *will* **enter** it.
1:39 [A] do not yet know good from bad—they *will* **enter** the land.
4: 1 [A] Follow them so that you may live and *may* **go in** and take
4: 5 [A] so that you may follow them in the land you *are* **entering** to
4:21 [A] **enter** [+448] the good land the LORD your God is giving
4:34 [A] Has any god ever tried **[NIE]** to take for himself one nation
4:38 [G] to **bring** you **into** their land to give it to you for your
6:10 [G] When the LORD your God **brings** you into the land he
6:18 [A] so that it may go well with you and *you may* **go in** and take
6:23 [G] he brought us out from there to **bring** us **in** and give us the
7: 1 [G] When the LORD your God **brings** you into the land you are
7: 1 [A] God brings you into the land you *are* **entering** to possess
7:26 [G] *Do* not **bring** a detestable thing into your house or you,
8: 1 [A] so that you may live and increase and *may* **enter** and possess
8: 7 [G] For the LORD your God *is* **bringing** you into a good land—
9: 1 [A] You are now about to cross the Jordan to **go in**
9: 4 [G] "The LORD *has* **brought** me here to take possession of this
9: 5 [A] or your integrity that you *are* **going in** to take possession of
9: 7 [A] From the day you left Egypt until you **arrived** [+6330] here,
9:28 [G] 'Because the LORD was not able to **take** them into the land
10:11 [A] so that *they may* **enter** and possess the land that I swore to
11: 5 [A] he did for you in the desert until you **arrived** at this place,
11: 8 [A] so that you may have the strength to **go in** and take over the
11:10 [A] The land you *are* **entering** to take over is not like the land of
11:29 [G] When the LORD your God *has* **brought** you into the land
11:29 [A] has brought you into the land you *are* **entering** to possess,
11:31 [A] You are about to cross the Jordan to **enter** and take
12: 5 [A] his Name there for his dwelling. To that place *you must* **go**;
12: 6 [G] **bring** your burnt offerings and sacrifices, your tithes and
12: 9 [A] since *you have* not yet **reached** [+448] the resting place
12:11 [G] there *you are to* **bring** everything I command you:
12:26 [A] vowed to give, and **go** to the place the LORD will choose.
12:29 [A] you the nations you *are about to* **invade** [+2025+9004]
13: 2 [13:3] [A] or wonder of which he has spoken **takes place**,
14:29 [A] and the widows who live in your towns *may* **come** and eat
16: 6 [A] when the sun **goes down**, on the anniversary of your
17: 9 [A] **Go** to the priests, who are Levites, and to the judge who is in
17:14 [A] When *you* **enter** [+448] the land the LORD your God is
18: 6 [A] If a Levite **moves** from one of your towns anywhere in Israel
18: 6 [A] **comes** in all earnestness to the place the LORD will choose,
18: 9 [A] When you **enter** [+448] the land the LORD your God is
18:22 [A] in the name of the LORD does not take place or **come true**,
19: 5 [A] a man *may* **go** into the forest with his neighbor to cut wood,
20:19 [A] that you *should* **besiege** [+928+2021+4946+5189+7156] them?
21:12 [G] **Bring** her into your home and have her shave her head, trim
21:13 [A] *you may* **go** to her and be her husband and she shall be your
22:13 [A] takes a wife and, after **lying** [+448] **with** her, dislikes her
23: 1 [23:2] [A] or cutting *may* **enter** [+928] the assembly of the
23: 2 [23:3] [A] *may* **enter** [+928] the assembly of the LORD,
23: 2 [23:3] [A] may enter **[RPH]** the assembly of the LORD,
23: 3 [23:4] [A] or any of his descendants *may* **enter** [+928] the
23: 3 [23:4] [A] or any of his descendants may enter **[RPH]** the
23: 8 [23:9] [A] them *may* **enter** [+928] the assembly of the LORD.
23:10 [23:11] [A] to go outside the camp and **stay** [+448+4202] there.
23:11 [23:12] [A] at **sunset** [+2021+9087] he may return to the camp.
23:11 [23:12] [A] and at sunset *he may* **return** to the camp.
23:18 [23:19] [G] *You must* not **bring** the earnings of a female
23:20 [23:21] [A] hand to in the land you *are* **entering** to possess.
23:24 [23:25] [A] If *you* **enter** [+928] your neighbor's vineyard, you
23:25 [23:26] [A] If *you* **enter** [+928] your neighbor's grainfield, you
24:10 [A] *do* not **go** into his house to get what he is offering as a
24:13 [A] Return his cloak to him by **sunset** [+2021+9087] so that he

Dt 24:15 [A] Pay him his wages each day before **sunset** [+2021+9087],
25: 5 [A] Her husband's brother *shall* **take** [+6584] her and marry her
26: 1 [A] When *you have* **entered** [+448] the land the LORD your
26: 2 [G] take some of the firstfruits of all that *you* **produce** *from* the
26: 3 [A] **[RPH]** and say to the priest in office at the time, "I declare
26: 3 [A] "I declare today to the LORD your God that *I have* **come** to
26: 9 [G] *He* **brought** us to this place and gave us this land, a land
26:10 [G] now *I* **bring** the firstfruits of the soil that you, O LORD,
27: 3 [A] to **enter** [+448] the land the LORD your God is giving you,
28: 2 [A] All these blessings *will* **come** upon you and accompany you
28: 6 [A] You will be blessed when you **come in** and blessed when you
28:15 [A] all these curses *will* **come** upon you and overtake you:
28:19 [A] You will be cursed when you **come in** and cursed when you
28:21 [A] has destroyed you from the land you *are* **entering** to possess.
28:45 [A] All these curses *will* **come** upon you. They will pursue you
28:63 [A] You will be uprooted from the land you *are* **entering** to
29: 7 [29:6] [A] When *you* **reached** [+448] this place, Sihon king of
29:22 [29:21] [A] foreigners who **come** from distant lands will see the
29:27 [29:26] [G] so that *he* **brought** on it all the curses written in this
30: 1 [A] and curses I have set before you **come** upon you
30: 5 [G] He *will* **bring** you to the land that belonged to your fathers,
30:16 [A] God will bless you in the land you *are* **entering** to possess.
30:18 [A] not live long in the land you are crossing the Jordan to **enter**
31: 2 [A] years old and I am no longer able to **lead** [+2256+3655] you.
31: 7 [A] for you *must* **go** with this people into the land that the
31:11 [A] when all Israel **comes** to appear before the LORD your God
31:16 [A] the foreign gods of the land they *are* **entering** [+928+7931].
31:20 [G] When *I have* **brought** them into the land flowing with milk
31:21 [G] even before *I* **bring** them into the land I promised them on
31:23 [G] for you *will* **bring** the Israelites into the land I promised them
32:17 [A] gods they had not known, gods that recently **appeared**,
32:44 [A] Moses **came** with Joshua son of Nun and spoke all the words
32:52 [A] *you will* not **enter** [+448] the land I am giving to the people
33: 2 [A] "The LORD **came** from Sinai and dawned over them from
33: 7 [G] "Hear, O LORD, the cry of Judah; **bring** him to his people.
33:16 [A] *Let all these* **rest** on the head of Joseph, on the brow of the
Jos 1:11 [A] Three days from now you will cross the Jordan here to **go in**
2: 1 [A] they went and **entered** the house of a prostitute named Rahab
2: 2 [A] Some of the Israelites *have* **come** here tonight to spy out the
2: 3 [A] "Bring out the men who **came** to you and entered your
2: 3 [A] the men who came to you and **entered** [+4200] your house,
2: 3 [A] because *they have* **come** to spy out the whole land."
2: 4 [A] She said, "Yes, the men **came** to me, but I did not know
2:18 [A] unless, *when* we **enter** [+928] the land, you have tied this
2:22 [A] they left, *they* **went** into the hills and stayed there three days,
2:23 [A] forded the river and **came** to Joshua son of Nun and told him
3: 1 [A] all the Israelites set out from Shittim and **went** to the Jordan,
3: 8 [A] 'When you **reach** [+6330] the edge of the Jordan's waters,
3:15 [A] as the priests who carried the ark **reached** [+6330] the Jordan
5:14 [A] as commander of the army of the LORD I *have* now **come**."
6: 1 [A] of the Israelites. No one went out and no *one* **came in**.
6:11 [A] Then the people **returned** *to* camp and spent the night there.
6:19 [A] iron are sacred to the LORD and *must* **go into** his treasury."
6:22 [A] "**Go into** the prostitute's house and bring her out and all who
6:23 [A] So the young men who had done the spying **went in**
7:23 [G] **brought** them to Joshua and all the Israelites and spread
8:11 [A] and approached the city and **arrived** in front of it.
8:19 [A] *They* **entered** the city and captured it and quickly set it on
8:29 [A] At **sunset** [+2021+9087], Joshua ordered them to take his
9: 6 [A] the men of Israel, "*We have* **come** from a distant country;
9: 8 [A] Joshua asked, "Who are you and where *do you* **come** from?"
9: 9 [A] "Your servants *have* **come** from a very distant country
9:17 [A] the Israelites set out and on the third day **came** to their cities:
10: 9 [A] march from Gilgal, Joshua **took** [+448] them by surprise.
10:13 [A] middle of the sky and delayed **going down** about a full day.
10:19 [A] from the rear and don't let them **reach** [+448] their cities,
10:20 [A] the few who were left **reached** [+448] their fortified cities.
10:27 [A] At **sunset** [+2021+6961+9087] Joshua gave the order and they
11: 5 [A] and **[NIE]** made camp together at the Waters of Merom,
11: 7 [A] his whole army **came** against them suddenly at the Waters of
11:21 [A] At that time Joshua **went** and destroyed the Anakites from
13: 1 [A] When Joshua was old and **well advanced** in years,
13: 1 [A] said to him, "You *are* **very old** [+928+2021+2416+3427], and
14:11 [A] I'm just as vigorous to go out **[NIE]** to battle now as I was
15:18 [A] One day when she **came** to Othniel, she urged him to ask her
18: 3 [A] "How long will you wait before you **begin** to take possession
18: 4 [A] to the inheritance of each. Then *they will* **return** to me.
18: 6 [G] **bring** them here to me and I will cast lots for you in the
18: 9 [A] in seven parts, and **returned** to Joshua in the camp at Shiloh.
20: 6 [A] he may **go** back to his own home in the town from which he
21:45 [A] to the house of Israel failed; every one *was* **fulfilled**.
22:10 [A] When *they* **came** to Geliloth near the Jordan in the land of
22:15 [A] When *they* **went** to Gilead—to Reuben, Gad and the
23: 1 [A] Joshua, by then old and **well advanced** in years,
23: 2 [A] and said to them: "I am old and **well advanced** in years.
23: 7 [A] *Do* not **associate** [+928] **with** these nations that remain
23:12 [A] if you intermarry with them and **associate** [+928] **with** them,
23:14 [A] Every promise *has been* **fulfilled**; not one has failed.
23:15 [A] every good promise of the LORD your God *has* **come true**,
23:15 [G] so the LORD *will* **bring** on you all the evil he has
24: 6 [A] I brought your fathers out of Egypt, *you* **came** to the sea,
24: 7 [G] *he* **brought** the sea over them and covered them.
24: 8 [G] " '*I* **brought** you to the land of the Amorites who lived east
24:11 [A] " 'Then you crossed the Jordan and **came** to Jericho. The
Jdg 1: 7 [G] to them." *They* **brought** him to Jerusalem, and he died there.
1:14 [A] One day when she **came** *to* Othniel, she urged him to ask her
2: 1 [G] **led** you into the land that I swore to give to your forefathers.
3:20 [A] **approached** [+448] him while he was sitting alone in the
3:22 [A] Even the handle **sank in** after the blade, which came out his
3:24 [A] the servants **came** and found the doors of the upper room
3:27 [A] When he **arrived** there, he blew a trumpet in the hill country
4:20 [A] "If someone **comes by** and asks you, 'Is anyone here?' say
4:21 [A] a hammer and **went** quietly to him while he lay fast asleep,
4:22 [A] So *he* **went** in *with* her, and there lay Sisera with the tent peg
5:19 [A] "Kings **came**, they fought; the kings of Canaan fought at
5:23 [A] because *they did* not **come** to help the LORD,
5:28 [A] lattice she cried out, 'Why is his chariot so long in **coming**?
6: 4 [A] on the land and ruined the crops all the way to **[NIE]** Gaza
6: 5 [A] their livestock and their tents **[NIE]** like swarms of locusts.
6: 5 [A] and their camels; *they* **invaded** [+928] the land to ravage it.
6:11 [A] The angel of the LORD **came** and sat down under the oak
6:18 [A] Please do not go away until I **come back** and bring my
6:19 [A] Gideon **went in**, prepared a young goat, and from an ephah
7:13 [A] Gideon **arrived** just as a man was telling a friend his dream.
7:13 [A] **[NIE]** It struck the tent with such force that the tent
7:17 [A] When I **get** to the edge of the camp, do exactly as I do.
7:19 [A] the hundred men with him **reached** [+928] the edge of the
7:25 [G] and **brought** the heads of Oreb and Zeeb to Gideon,
8: 4 [A] yet keeping up the pursuit, **came** to the Jordan and crossed it.
8:15 [A] Gideon **came** and said to the men of Succoth, "Here are
9: 5 [A] *He* **went** *to* his father's home in Ophrah and on one stone
9:15 [A] anoint me king over you, **come** and take refuge in my shade;
9:24 [A] God did this in order that **[NIE]** the crime against
9:26 [A] Now Gaal son of Ebed **moved** with his brothers into
9:27 [A] trodden them, they held a festival **in** the temple of their god.
9:31 [A] "Gaal son of Ebed and his brothers *have* **come** to Shechem
9:37 [A] a company *is* **coming** from the direction of the soothsayers'
9:46 [A] the citizens in the tower of Shechem **went** into the stronghold
9:52 [A] Abimelech **went** to the tower and stormed it. But as he
9:57 [A] The curse of Jotham son of Jerub-Baal **came** on them.
11: 7 [A] Why *do you* **come** to me now, when you're in trouble?"
11:12 [A] "What do you have against us that **[NIE]** you have attacked
11:16 [A] through the desert to the Red Sea and **[NIE]** on to Kadesh.
11:18 [A] **passed** along the eastern side of the country of Moab,
11:18 [A] *They did* not **enter** [+928] the territory of Moab,
11:33 [A] towns from Aroer **to the vicinity of** [+3870+6330] Minnith,
11:34 [A] When Jephthah **returned** to his home in Mizpah, who should
12: 9 [G] for his sons *he* **brought in** thirty young women **as wives**
13: 6 [A] the woman **went** to her husband and told him, "A man of
13: 6 [A] to her husband and told him, "A man of God **came** to me.
13: 8 [A] *let* the man of God you sent to us **come** again to teach us
13: 9 [A] the angel of God **came** again to the woman while she was out
13:10 [A] The man who appeared to me **[NIE]** the other day!"
13:11 [A] When *he* **came** to the man, he said, "Are you the one who
13:12 [A] So Manoah asked him, "When your words *are* **fulfilled**,
13:17 [A] so that we may honor you when your word **comes true**?"
14: 5 [A] As *they* **approached** [+6330] the vineyards of Timnah,
14:18 [A] Before **sunset** [+2021+3064] on the seventh day the men of
15: 1 [A] to visit his wife. He said, "*I'm* **going** to my wife's room."
15: 1 [A] to my wife's room." But her father would not let him **go in**.
15:14 [A] *As* he **approached** [+6330] Lehi, the Philistines came toward
16: 1 [A] a prostitute. *He* **went** [+448] **in to spend the night with** her.
16: 2 [A] The people of Gaza were told, "Samson **is** here!" So they
17: 8 [A] On his way *he* **came** to Micah's house in the hill country of
17: 9 [A] Micah asked him, "Where **are** *you* from?" "I'm a Levite
18: 2 [A] The men **entered** the hill country of Ephraim and came to the
18: 3 [G] they turned in there and asked him, "Who **brought** you here?
18: 7 [A] So the five men left and **came** to Laish, where they saw that
18: 8 [A] When *they* **returned** to Zorah and Eshtaol, their brothers
18: 9 [A] Don't hesitate to go **[RPH]** there and take it over.
18:10 [A] When you **get there**, you will find an unsuspecting people
18:10 [A] *you will* **find** [+448] an unsuspecting people and a spacious
18:13 [A] to the hill country of Ephraim and **came** to Micah's house.
18:15 [A] and **went** to the house of the young Levite at Micah's place
18:17 [A] The five men who had spied out the land **went** inside and
18:18 [A] When these men **went into** Micah's house and took the
18:20 [A] and the carved image and **went** along with the people.
18:27 [A] his priest, and **went on** to Laish, against a peaceful

Jdg 19: 3 [G] *She* **took** him **into** her father's house, and when her father
19: 10 [A] the man left and **went** toward Jebus (that is, Jerusalem), with
19: 14 [A] went on, and the sun **set** as they neared Gibeah in Benjamin.
19: 15 [A] There they stopped **[NIE]** to spend the night. They went
19: 15 [A] *They* **went** and sat in the city square, but no one took them
19: 16 [A] place were Benjamites), **came in** from his work in the fields.
19: 17 [A] "Where are you going? Where *did you* **come** from?"
19: 21 [G] So *he* **took** him into his house and fed his donkeys.
19: 22 [A] "Bring out the man who **came** to your house so we can have
19: 23 [A] Since this man *is* my **guest** [+440+1074], don't do this
19: 26 [A] At daybreak the woman **went back** *to* the house where her
19: 29 [A] When *he* **reached** [+448] home, he took a knife and cut up
20: 4 [A] my concubine **came** to Gibeah in Benjamin to spend the
20: 10 [A] Then, when the army **arrives** at Gibeah in Benjamin, it can
20: 26 [A] Then the Israelites, all the people, went up **[NIE]** to Bethel,
20: 34 [A] ten thousand of Israel's finest men **made** a frontal **attack** on
21: 2 [A] The people **went** *to* Bethel, where they sat before God until
21: 8 [A] They discovered that no one from Jabesh Gilead *had* **come**
21: 12 [G] a man, and *they* **took** them to the camp at Shiloh in Canaan.
21: 22 [A] When their fathers or brothers **[NIE]** complain to us, we
Ru 1: 2 [A] Judah. And *they* **went** *to* Moab and lived there.
1: 19 [A] So the two women went on until they **came** *to* Bethlehem.
1: 19 [A] When they **arrived** *in* Bethlehem, the whole town was
1: 22 [A] **arriving** *in* Bethlehem as the barley harvest was beginning.
2: 3 [A] So she went **out** and began to glean in the fields behind the
2: 4 [A] Just then Boaz **arrived** from Bethlehem and greeted the
2: 7 [A] *She* **went into** the field and has worked steadily from
2: 12 [A] of Israel, under whose wings *you have* **come** to take refuge."
2: 18 [A] She carried it **back** *to* town, and her mother-in-law saw how
3: 4 [A] **go** and uncover his feet and lie down. He will tell you what
3: 7 [A] *he* **went over** to lie down at the far end of the grain pile.
3: 7 [A] Ruth **approached** quietly, uncovered his feet and lay down.
3: 14 [A] "Don't let it be known that a woman **came** *to* the threshing
3: 15 [A] of barley and put it on her. Then *he* **went back** *to* town.
3: 16 [A] When Ruth **came** to her mother-in-law, Naomi asked,
3: 17 [A] 'Don't **go back** to your mother-in-law empty-handed.' "
4: 11 [A] May the LORD make the woman who *is* **coming** into your
4: 13 [A] *he* **went** to her, and the LORD enabled her to conceive,
1Sa 1: 19 [A] the LORD and then **went** back to their home at Ramah.
1: 22 [G] *I will* **take** him and present him before the LORD,
1: 24 [G] and **brought** him *to* the house of the LORD at Shiloh.
1: 25 [G] they had slaughtered the bull, *they* **brought** the boy to Eli,
2: 13 [A] the servant of the priest *would* **come** with a three-pronged
2: 14 [A] This is how they treated all the Israelites who **came** to
2: 15 [A] the servant of the priest *would* **come** and say to the man who
2: 27 [A] Now a man of God **came** to Eli and said to him, "This is
2: 31 [A] The time *is* **coming** when I will cut short your strength
2: 34 [A] " 'And what **happens** to your two sons, Hophni
2: 36 [A] everyone left in your family line *will* **come** and bow down
3: 10 [A] The LORD **came** and stood there, calling as at the other
4: 3 [A] When the soldiers **returned** to camp, the elders of Israel
4: 3 [A] so that *it may* **go** with us and save us from the hand of our
4: 5 [A] When the ark of the LORD's covenant **came** into the camp,
4: 6 [A] When they learned that the ark of the LORD *had* **come** into
4: 7 [A] "A god *has* **come** into the camp," they said. "We're in
4: 12 [A] day a Benjamite ran from the battle line and **went** *to* Shiloh,
4: 13 [A] When *he* **arrived**, there was Eli sitting on his chair by the
4: 13 [A] When the man **entered** [+928] the town and told what had
4: 14 [A] is the meaning of this uproar?" The man hurried **over** to Eli,
4: 16 [A] He told Eli, "I *have just* **come** from the battle line; I fled
5: 1 [G] the ark of God, *they* **took** it from Ebenezer to Ashdod.
5: 2 [G] they carried the ark **[RPH]** into Dagon's temple and set it
5: 5 [A] *others* who **enter** Dagon's temple at Ashdod step on the
5: 10 [A] As the ark of God *was* **entering** Ekron, the people of Ekron
6: 14 [A] The cart **came** to the field of Joshua of Beth Shemesh, and
7: 1 [A] So the men of Kiriath Jearim **came** and took up the ark of the
7: 1 [G] *They* **took** it to Abinadab's house on the hill and consecrated
7: 13 [A] and *did* not **invade** [+928] Israelite territory again.
8: 4 [A] of Israel gathered together and **came** to Samuel at Ramah.
9: 5 [A] When they **reached** [+928] the district of Zuph, Saul said to
9: 6 [A] highly respected, and everything he says **comes true** [+995].
9: 6 [A] highly respected, and everything he says **comes true** [+995].
9: 7 [G] said to his servant, "If we go, what *can we* **give** the man?
9: 7 [G] We have no gift to **take** to the man of God. What do we
9: 12 [A] *he has* just **come** to our town today, for the people have a
9: 13 [A] As soon as you **enter** the town, you will find him before he
9: 13 [A] The people will not begin eating until he **comes**, because he
9: 14 [A] *as* they *were* **entering** [+928+9348] it, there was Samuel,
9: 15 [A] Now the day before Saul **came**, the LORD had revealed this
9: 16 [A] upon my people, for their cry *has* **reached** [+448] me."
9: 22 [G] Samuel **brought** Saul and his servant into the hall and seated
10: 3 [A] "Then you will go on from there until *you* **reach** [+6330] the
10: 5 [A] "After that *you will* **go** *to* Gibeah of God, where there is a
10: 5 [A] As you **approach** the town, you will meet a procession of
10: 7 [A] Once these signs *are* **fulfilled**, do whatever your hand finds
10: 8 [A] you must wait seven days until I **come** to you and tell you
10: 9 [A] Saul's heart, and all these signs *were* **fulfilled** that day.
10: 10 [A] When *they* **arrived** at Gibeah, a procession of prophets met
10: 13 [A] After Saul stopped prophesying, *he* **went** *to* the high place.
10: 14 [A] we saw they were not to be found, *we* **went** to Samuel."
10: 22 [A] further of the LORD, "*Has* the man **come** here yet?"
10: 27 [G] They despised him and **brought** him no gifts. But Saul kept
11: 4 [A] When the messengers **came** *to* Gibeah of Saul and reported
11: 5 [A] Just then Saul *was* **returning** from the fields, behind his
11: 9 [A] They told the messengers who *had* **come**, "Say to the men of
11: 9 [A] you will be delivered.' " When the messengers **went**
11: 11 [A] during the last watch of the night *they* **broke** into the camp
12: 8 [A] "After Jacob **entered** Egypt, they cried to the LORD for
12: 12 [A] that Nahash king of the Ammonites *was* **moving** against you,
13: 8 [A] Samuel *did* not **come** *to* Gilgal, and Saul's men began to
13: 10 [A] the offering, Samuel **arrived**, and Saul went out to greet him.
13: 11 [A] were scattering, and that you *did* not **come** at the set time,
14: 20 [A] Then Saul and all his men assembled and **went** to the battle.
14: 25 [A] The entire army **entered** [+928] the woods, and there was
14: 26 [A] When they **went** into the woods, they saw the honey oozing
15: 5 [A] Saul **went** to the city of Amalek and set an ambush in the
15: 7 [A] Saul attacked the Amalekites **all the way** from Havilah **to**
15: 12 [A] to meet Saul, but he was told, "Saul *has* **gone** to Carmel.
15: 13 [A] When Samuel **reached** [+448] him, Saul said, "The LORD
15: 15 [G] "The soldiers **brought** them from the Amalekites;
15: 20 [G] destroyed the Amalekites and **brought back** Agag their king.
16: 2 [A] with you and say, '*I have* **come** to sacrifice to the LORD.'
16: 4 [A] When *he* **arrived** *at* Bethlehem, the elders of the town
16: 4 [A] when they met him. They asked, "*Do* you **come** in peace?"
16: 5 [A] "Yes, in peace; *I have* **come** to sacrifice to the LORD.
16: 5 [A] Consecrate yourselves and **come** to the sacrifice with me."
16: 6 [A] When they **arrived**, Samuel saw Eliab and thought,
16: 11 [A] for him; we will not sit down until he **arrives** [+7024]."
16: 12 [G] So he sent and **had** him **brought in**. He was ruddy, with a
16: 17 [G] "Find someone who plays well and **bring** him to me."
16: 21 [A] David **came** to Saul and entered his service. Saul liked him
17: 12 [A] and in Saul's time he was old and **well advanced** in years.
17: 18 [G] **Take along** these ten cheeses to the commander of their unit.
17: 20 [A] *He* **reached** the camp as the army was going out to its battle
17: 22 [A] ran to the battle lines **[NIE]** and greeted his brothers.
17: 34 [A] When a lion or a bear **came** and carried off a sheep from the
17: 43 [A] to David, "Am I a dog, that you **come** at me with sticks?"
17: 45 [A] "You **come** against me with sword and spear and javelin,
17: 45 [A] but I **come** against you in the name of the LORD Almighty,
17: 52 [A] pursued the Philistines to the **entrance** *of* Gath and to the
17: 54 [G] David took the Philistine's head and **brought** it *to* Jerusalem,
17: 57 [G] Abner took him and **brought** him before Saul, with David
18: 6 [A] When the men *were* **returning** home after David had killed
18: 13 [A] **led** the troops **in** their **campaigns** [+2256+3655+4200+7156].
18: 16 [A] **led** them **in** their **campaigns** [+2256+3655+4200+7156].
18: 27 [G] He **brought** their foreskins and presented the full number to
19: 7 [G] He **brought** him to Saul, and David was with Saul as before.
19: 16 [A] when the men **entered**, there was the idol in the bed, and at
19: 18 [A] *he* **went** to Samuel at Ramah and told him all that Saul had
19: 22 [A] himself left for Ramah and **went** to the great cistern at Secu.
19: 23 [A] and he walked along prophesying until he **came** to Naioth.
20: 1 [A] fled from Naioth at Ramah and **went** to Jonathan and asked,
20: 8 [G] for *you have* **brought** him into a covenant with you before
20: 8 [G] then kill me yourself! Why **hand** me **over** to your father?"
20: 9 [A] inkling that my father was determined to harm **[NIE]** you,
20: 19 [A] **go** to the place where you hid when this trouble began,
20: 21 [A] bring them here,' then **come**, because, as surely as the
20: 27 [A] "Why hasn't the son of Jesse **come** to the meal,
20: 29 [A] That is why *he has* not **come** to the king's table."
20: 37 [A] When the boy **came** to the place where Jonathan's arrow had
20: 38 [A] The boy picked up the arrow and **returned** to his master.
20: 40 [G] to the boy and said, "Go, **carry** them **back** *to* town."
20: 41 [A] After the boy *had* **gone**, David got up from the south side of
20: 42 [21:1] [A] David left, and Jonathan **went back** *to* the town.
21: 1 [21:2] [A] David **went** to Nob, to Ahimelech the priest.
21: 10 [21:11] [A] fled from Saul and **went** to Achish king of Gath.
21: 14 [21:15] [G] at the man! He is insane! Why **bring** him to me?
21: 15 [21:16] [G] so short of madmen that *you have to* **bring** this
21: 15 [21:16] [A] front of me? *Must* this man **come** into my house?"
22: 5 [A] Go **into** the land of Judah." So David left and went to the
22: 5 [A] of Judah." So David left and **went** *to* the forest of Hereth.
22: 9 [A] "I saw the son of Jesse **come** to Ahimelech son of Ahitub at
22: 11 [A] who were the priests at Nob, and they all **came** to the king.
23: 7 [A] Saul was told that David *had* **gone** *to* Keilah, and he said,
23: 7 [A] for David has imprisoned himself by **entering** [+928] a town
23: 10 [A] your servant has heard definitely that Saul plans to **come** to
23: 27 [A] a messenger **came** to Saul, saying, "Come quickly! The
24: 3 [24:4] [A] *He* **came** to the sheep pens along the way; a cave was

1Sa 24: 3 [24:4] [A] a cave was there, and Saul **went in** to relieve himself.
25: 5 [A] "**Go** up to Nabal at Carmel and greet him in my name.
25: 8 [A] toward my young men, since *we* **come** at a festive time.
25: 9 [A] When David's men **arrived**, they gave Nabal this message in
25: 12 [A] went back. When *they* **arrived**, they reported every word.
25: 19 [A] she told her servants, "Go on ahead; I'll **follow** [+339] you."
25: 26 [A] from **bloodshed** [+928+1947] and from avenging yourself
25: 27 [G] let this gift, which your servant *has* **brought** to my master,
25: 33 [A] and for keeping me from **bloodshed** [+928+1947] this day
25: 34 [A] from harming you, if *you had* not **come** quickly to meet me,
25: 35 [G] David accepted from her hand what *she had* **brought** him
25: 36 [A] When Abigail **went** to Nabal, he was in the house holding a
25: 40 [A] His servants **went** to Carmel and said to Abigail, "David has
26: 1 [A] The Ziphites **went** to Saul at Gibeah and said, "Is not David
26: 3 [A] When he saw that Saul *had* **followed** [+339] him there,
26: 4 [A] sent out scouts and learned that Saul *had* definitely **arrived**.
26: 5 [A] David set out and **went** to the place where Saul had camped.
26: 7 [A] So David and Abishai **went** to the army by night, and there
26: 10 [A] either his time *will* **come** and he will die, or he will go into
26: 15 [A] lord the king? Someone **came** to destroy your lord the king.
27: 8 [A] times these peoples had lived in the land **extending** to Shur
27: 9 [A] and camels, and clothes. Then he returned **[NIE]** to Achish.
27: 11 [G] did not leave a man or woman alive to *be* **brought** *to* Gath,
28: 4 [A] The Philistines assembled and **came** and set up camp at
28: 8 [A] and at night he and two men **went** to the woman.
28: 21 [A] When the woman **came** to Saul and saw that he was greatly
29: 6 [A] I would be pleased *to have* you **serve** [+2256+3655] with me
29: 6 [A] From the day you **came** to me until now, I have found no
29: 8 [A] Why can't *I* **go** and fight against the enemies of my lord the
29: 10 [A] along with your master's servants who *have* **come** with you,
30: 1 [A] David and his men **reached** Ziklag on the third day.
30: 3 [A] When David and his men **came** to Ziklag, they found it
30: 9 [A] and the six hundred men with him **came** to the Besor Ravine,
30: 21 [A] David **came** to the two hundred men who had been too
30: 23 [A] and handed over to us the forces that **came** against us.
30: 26 [A] When David **arrived** in Ziklag, he sent some of the plunder
31: 4 [A] or these uncircumcised fellows *will* **come** and run me
31: 7 [A] and fled. And the Philistines **came** and occupied them.
31: 8 [A] The next day, when the Philistines **came** to strip the dead,
31: 12 [A] and his sons from the wall of Beth Shan and **went** to Jabesh.
2Sa 1: 2 [A] On the third day a man **arrived** from Saul's camp, with his
1: 2 [A] When he **came** to David, he fell to the ground to pay him
1: 3 [A] "Where *have you* **come** from?" David asked him. He
1: 10 [G] band on his arm and *have* **brought** them here to my lord."
2: 4 [A] the men of Judah **came** to Hebron and there they anointed
2: 23 [A] every man stopped when he **came** to the place where Asahel
2: 24 [A] and Abishai pursued Abner, and *as* the sun *was* **setting**,
2: 24 [A] and as the sun was setting, they **came** to the hill of Ammah,
2: 29 [A] through the whole Bithron and **came** *to* Mahanaim.
3: 7 [A] "Why *did you* **sleep** [+448] **with** my father's concubine?"
3: 13 [G] Do not come into my presence unless you **bring** Michal
3: 13 [A] bring Michal daughter of Saul when you **come** to see me."
3: 20 [A] **came** to David at Hebron, David prepared a feast for him
3: 22 [A] Just then David's men and Joab **returned** from a raid
3: 22 [G] from a raid and **brought** with them a great deal of plunder.
3: 23 [A] When Joab and all the soldiers with him **arrived**, he was told
3: 23 [A] he was told that Abner son of Ner *had* **come** to the king
3: 24 [A] So Joab **went** to the king and said, "What have you done?
3: 24 [A] and said, "What have you done? Look, Abner **came** to you.
3: 25 [A] *he* **came** to deceive you and observe your movements
3: 35 [A] they all **came** and urged David to eat something while it was
3: 35 [A] if I taste bread or anything else before the sun **sets**!"
4: 4 [A] when the news about Saul and Jonathan **came** from Jezreel.
4: 5 [A] *they* **arrived** there in the heat of the day while he was taking
4: 6 [A] They **went** into the inner part of the house as if to get some
4: 7 [A] *They had* **gone into** the house while he was lying on the bed
4: 8 [G] *They* **brought** the head of Ish-Bosheth to David at Hebron
5: 1 [A] All the tribes of Israel **came** to David at Hebron and said,
5: 2 [G] **led** Israel **on** their **military campaigns** [+906+2256+3655].
5: 3 [A] When all the elders of Israel *had* **come** to King David at
5: 6 [A] The Jebusites said to David, "*You will* not **get in** here;
5: 6 [A] can ward you off." They thought, "David cannot **get in** here."
5: 8 [A] "The 'blind and lame' *will* not **enter** [+448] the palace."
5: 13 [A] After he **left** [+4946] Hebron, David took more concubines
5: 18 [A] Now the Philistines *had* **come** and spread out in the Valley
5: 20 [A] So David **went** to Baal Perazim, and there he defeated them.
5: 23 [A] and **attack** [+4200] them in front of the balsam trees.
5: 25 [A] the Philistines **all the way** from Gibeon **to** [+6330] Gezer.
6: 6 [A] When *they* **came** to the threshing floor of Nacon, Uzzah
6: 9 [A] "How *can* the ark of the LORD *ever* **come** to me?"
6: 16 [A] As the ark of the LORD *was* **entering** the City of David,
6: 17 [G] *They* **brought** the ark of the LORD and set it in its place
7: 18 [A] King David **went in** and sat before the LORD, and he said:
7: 18 [G] and what is my family, that *you have* **brought** me this far?
8: 5 [A] When the Arameans of Damascus **came** to help Hadadezer
8: 7 [G] to the officers of Hadadezer and **brought** them *to* Jerusalem.
9: 6 [A] the son of Saul, **came** to David, he bowed down to pay him
9: 10 [G] servants are to farm the land for him and **bring in** the crops,
10: 2 [A] When David's men **came** *to* the land of the Ammonites,
10: 14 [A] they fled before Abishai and **went inside** the city.
10: 14 [A] from fighting the Ammonites and **came** *to* Jerusalem.
10: 16 [A] *they* **went** *to* Helam, with Shobach the commander of
10: 17 [A] he gathered all Israel, crossed the Jordan and **went** to Helam.
11: 4 [A] to get her. *She* **came** to him, and he slept with her.
11: 7 [A] When Uriah **came** to him, David asked him how Joab was,
11: 10 [A] he asked him, "Haven't you *just* **come** from a distance?
11: 11 [A] *How could* I **go** to my house to eat and drink and lie with my
11: 22 [A] when *he* **arrived** he told David everything Joab had sent him
12: 1 [A] When *he* **came** to him, he said, "There were two men in a
12: 4 [A] "Now a traveler **came** to the rich man, but the rich man
12: 4 [A] or cattle to prepare a meal for the traveler who *had* **come** to
12: 4 [A] poor man and prepared it for the one who *had* **come** to him."
12: 16 [A] He fasted and **went into** his house and spent the nights lying
12: 20 [A] *he* **went into** the house of the LORD and worshiped.
12: 20 [A] *he* **went** to his own house, and at his request they served him
12: 24 [A] his wife Bathsheba, and *he* **went** to her and lay with her.
13: 5 [A] "When your father **comes** to see you, say to him, 'I would
13: 5 [A] 'I would like my sister Tamar *to* **come** and give me
13: 6 [A] When the king **came** to see him, Amnon said to him,
13: 6 [A] "I would like my sister Tamar *to* **come** and make some
13: 10 [G] "**Bring** the food here **into** my bedroom so I may eat from
13: 10 [G] and **brought** it to her brother Amnon in his bedroom.
13: 11 [A] he grabbed her and said, "**Come** to bed with me, my sister."
13: 24 [A] Absalom **went** to the king and said, "Your servant has had
13: 30 [A] While they were on their way, the report **came** to David:
13: 34 [A] The watchman **went** [BHS-] and told the king, "I see men in
13: 35 [A] Jonadab said to the king, "See, the king's sons *are* **here**;
13: 36 [A] finished speaking, the king's sons **came in**, wailing loudly.
14: 3 [A] **go** to the king and speak these words to him." And Joab put
14: 4 [A] When the woman from Tekoa **went** [BHS 606] to the king,
14: 10 [G] "If anyone says anything to you, **bring** him to me,
14: 15 [A] "And now *I have* **come** to say this to my lord the king
14: 23 [G] went to Geshur and **brought** Absalom **back** *to* Jerusalem.
14: 29 [A] to send him to the king, but Joab refused to **come** to him.
14: 29 [A] to him. So he sent a second time, but he refused to **come**.
14: 31 [A] Then Joab *did* **go** to Absalom's house and he said to him,
14: 32 [A] and said, '**Come** here so I can send you to the king to ask,
14: 32 [A] you to the king to ask, "Why *have I* **come** from Geshur?
14: 33 [A] So Joab **went** to the king and told him this. Then the king
14: 33 [A] *he* **came** in and bowed down with his face to the ground
15: 2 [A] Whenever anyone came with a complaint to *be* **placed** before
15: 4 [A] everyone who has a complaint or case *could* **come** to me
15: 6 [A] all the Israelites who **came** to the king asking for justice,
15: 13 [A] A messenger **came** and told David, "The hearts of the men of
15: 18 [A] all the six hundred Gittites who *had* **accompanied** [+8079]
15: 20 [A] You **came** only yesterday. And today shall I make you
15: 28 [A] I will wait at the fords in the desert until word **comes** from
15: 32 [A] When David **arrived** at the summit, where people used to
15: 37 [A] So David's friend Hushai **arrived** *at* Jerusalem as Absalom
15: 37 [A] arrived at Jerusalem as Absalom *was* **entering** the city.
16: 5 [A] As King David **approached** [+6330] Bahurim, a man from
16: 14 [A] all the people with him **arrived** at their destination
16: 15 [A] Absalom and all the men of Israel **came** *to* Jerusalem,
16: 16 [A] David's friend, **went** to Absalom and said to him, "Long live
16: 21 [A] "**Lie** [+448] **with** your father's concubines whom he left to
16: 22 [A] he **lay** [+448] **with** his father's concubines in the sight of all
17: 2 [A] *I would* **attack** [+6584] him while he is weary and weak.
17: 6 [A] When Hushai **came** to him, Absalom said, "Ahithophel has
17: 12 [A] Then *we will* **attack** [+448] him wherever he may be found,
17: 14 [G] advice of Ahithophel in order to **bring** disaster on Absalom.
17: 17 [A] for they could not risk being seen **entering** [+2025] the city.
17: 18 [A] them left quickly and **went** to the house of a man in Bahurim.
17: 20 [A] When Absalom's men **came** to the woman at the house, they
17: 24 [A] David **went** to Mahanaim, and Absalom crossed the Jordan
17: 25 [A] an Israelite who *had* **married** [+448] Abigail, the daughter
17: 27 [A] When David **came** to Mahanaim, Shobi son of Nahash from
18: 9 [A] and *as* the mule **went** under the thick branches of a large oak,
18: 27 [A] a good man," the king said. "*He* **comes** with good news."
18: 31 [A] the Cushite **arrived** and said, "My lord the king,
19: 3 [19:4] [A] The men **stole into** [+1704+4200] the city that day as
19: 5 [19:6] [A] Joab **went** into the house to the king and said,
19: 7 [19:8] [A] that *have* **come** upon you from your youth till now."
19: 8 [19:9] [A] is sitting in the gateway," they all **came** before him.
19: 11 [19:12] [A] Israel *has* **reached** [+448] the king at his quarters?
19: 15 [19:16] [A] the king returned and **went** as far as the Jordan.
19: 15 [19:16] [A] Now the men of Judah *had* **come** to Gilgal to go out
19: 20 [19:21] [A] today *I have* **come** here as the first of the whole
19: 24 [19:25] [A] day the king left until the day *he* **returned** safely.

2Sa 19:25 [19:26] [A] When *he* **came** *from* Jerusalem to meet the king,
19:30 [19:31] [A] that my lord the king *has* **arrived** home safely."
19:41 [19:42] [A] Soon all the men of Israel *were* **coming** to the king
20: 3 [A] When David **returned** to his palace in Jerusalem, he took the
20: 3 [A] He provided for them, but *did* not **lie** [+448] **with** them.
20: 8 [A] were at the great rock in Gibeon, Amasa **came** to meet them.
20:12 [A] When he realized that everyone who **came** up to Amasa
20:14 [A] the Berites, who gathered together and **followed** [+339] him.
20:15 [A] All the troops with Joab **came** and besieged Sheba in Abel
20:22 [A] Then the woman **went** to all the people with her wise advice,
23:13 [A] three of the thirty chief men **came** down to David at the cave
23:16 [G] well near the gate of Bethlehem and carried it **back** to David.
23:19 [A] even though *he was* not **included** among them.
23:23 [A] any of the Thirty, but *he was* not **included** among the Three.
24: 6 [A] *They* **went** to Gilead and the region of Tahtim Hodshi, and
24: 6 [A] and **on** to Dan Jaan and around toward Sidon.
24: 7 [A] *they* **went** *toward* the fortress of Tyre and all the towns of
24: 8 [A] *they* **came back** *to* Jerusalem at the end of nine months
24:13 [A] So Gad **went** to David and said to him, "Shall there come
24:13 [A] "*Shall there* **come** upon you three years of famine in your
24:18 [A] On that day Gad **went** to David and said to him, "Go up
24:21 [A] "Why *has* my lord the king **come** to his servant?"
1Ki 1: 1 [A] When King David was old and **well advanced** in years, he
1: 3 [G] found Abishag, a Shunammite, and **brought** her to the king.
1:13 [A] **Go in** [+2143+2256] to King David and say to him, 'My lord
1:14 [A] to the king, I *will* **come in** and confirm what you have said."
1:15 [A] So Bathsheba **went** to see the aged king in his room, where
1:22 [A] was still speaking with the king, Nathan the prophet **arrived**.
1:23 [A] So *he* **went** before the king and bowed with his face to the
1:28 [A] So *she* **came** into the king's presence and stood before him.
1:32 [A] Benaiah son of Jehoiada." When *they* **came** before the king,
1:35 [A] he *is to* **come** and sit on my throne and reign in my place.
1:42 [A] he was speaking, Jonathan son of Abiathar the priest **arrived**.
1:42 [A] son of Abiathar the priest arrived. Adonijah said, "**Come in**.
1:47 [A] the royal officials *have* **come** to congratulate our lord King
1:53 [A] Adonijah **came** and bowed down to King Solomon,
2:13 [A] Now Adonijah, the son of Haggith, **went** to Bathsheba,
2:13 [A] Bathsheba asked him, "*Do* you **come** peacefully?" He
2:19 [A] When Bathsheba **went** to King Solomon to speak to him for
2:28 [A] When the news **reached** [+6330] Joab, who had conspired
2:30 [A] So Benaiah **entered** [+448] the tent of the LORD and said
2:40 [G] Shimei went away and **brought** the slaves **back** from Gath.
3: 1 [G] *He* **brought** her to the City of David until he finished
3: 7 [A] and do not know how *to* **carry out** *my* **duties** [+2256+3655].
3:15 [A] *He* **returned** *to* Jerusalem, stood before the ark of the Lord's
3:16 [A] Now two prostitutes **came** to the king and stood before him.
3:24 [G] "Bring me a sword." So *they* **brought** a sword for the king.
4:28 [5:8] [G] *They* also **brought** to the proper place their quotas of
4:34 [5:14] [A] *Men* of all nations **came** to listen to Solomon's
7:14 [A] *He* **came** to King Solomon and did all the work assigned to
7:51 [G] **brought in** the things his father David had dedicated—
8: 3 [A] When all the elders of Israel *had* **arrived**, the priests took up
8: 6 [G] **brought** the ark of the LORD's covenant to its place in the
8:31 [A] his neighbor and is required to take an oath and *he* **comes**
8:41 [A] but *has* **come** from a distant land because of your name—
8:42 [A] when *he* **comes** and prays toward this temple,
9: 9 [G] that is why the LORD **brought** all this disaster on them.' "
9:28 [A] *They* **sailed** to Ophir and brought back 420 talents of gold,
9:28 [G] 420 talents of gold, which *they* **delivered** to King Solomon.
10: 1 [A] of the LORD, *she* **came** to test him with hard questions.
10: 2 [A] **Arriving** at Jerusalem with a very great caravan—
10: 2 [A] *she* **came** to Solomon and talked with him about all that she
10: 7 [A] I did not believe these things until *I* **came** and saw with my
10:10 [A] Never again *were* so many spices **brought in** as those the
10:11 [G] and from there *they* **brought** great cargoes of almugwood
10:12 [A] So much almugwood *has* never *been* **imported** or seen since
10:14 [A] The weight of the gold that Solomon **received** [+4200]
10:22 [A] Once every three years it **returned**, carrying gold, silver
10:25 [G] Year after year, everyone who came **brought** a gift—
11: 2 [A] "*You must* not **intermarry** with them, because they will
11: 2 [A] **[RPH]** because they will surely turn your hearts after their
11:17 [A] fled **[RPH]** to Egypt with some Edomite officials who had
11:18 [A] They set out from Midian and **went** *to* Paran. Then taking
11:18 [A] *they* **went** *to* Egypt, to Pharaoh king of Egypt, who gave
12: 1 [A] for all the Israelites *had* **gone** there to make him king.
12: 3 [A] and he and the whole assembly of Israel **went** *to* Rehoboam
12:12 [A] later Jeroboam and all the people **returned** to Rehoboam,
12:21 [A] When Rehoboam **arrived** *in* Jerusalem, he mustered the
13: 1 [A] By the word of the LORD a man of God **came** from Judah
13: 7 [A] "**Come** home with me and have something to eat, and I will
13: 8 [A] *I would* not **go** with you, nor would I eat bread or drink
13:10 [A] and did not return by the way *he had* **come** to Bethel.
13:11 [A] whose sons **came** and told him all that the man of God had
13:12 [A] his sons showed him which road the man of God **[NIE]**
13:14 [A] "Are you the man of God *who* **came** from Judah?"
13:16 [A] "I cannot turn back and **go** with you, nor can I eat bread
13:21 [A] He cried out to the man of God who *had* **come** from Judah,
13:22 [A] Therefore your body *will* not *be* **buried** in the tomb of your
13:25 [A] *they* **went** and reported it in the city where the old prophet
13:29 [A] and brought it back **[NIE]** to his own city to mourn for him
14: 3 [A] with you, some cakes and a jar of honey, and **go** to him.
14: 4 [A] what he said and went to Ahijah's house **[NIE]** in Shiloh.
14: 5 [A] "Jeroboam's wife *is* **coming** to ask you about her son, for he
14: 5 [A] When she **arrives**, she will pretend to be someone else."
14: 6 [A] So when Ahijah heard the sound of her footsteps **[RPH]** at
14: 6 [A] footsteps at the door, he said, "**Come in**, wife of Jeroboam.
14:10 [G] I *am going to* **bring** disaster on the house of Jeroboam.
14:12 [A] back home. When you **set** foot in your city, the boy will die.
14:13 [A] belonging to Jeroboam *who will be* **buried** [+448+7700],
14:17 [A] Then Jeroboam's wife got up and left and **went** to Tirzah.
14:17 [A] As soon as she **stepped** over the threshold of the house,
14:28 [A] Whenever the king **went** *to* the LORD's temple, the guards
15:15 [G] *He* **brought into** the temple of the LORD the silver and gold
15:17 [A] or **entering** [+4200] the territory of Asa king of Judah.
16:10 [A] Zimri **came in**, struck him down and killed him in the
16:18 [A] *he* **went** into the citadel of the royal palace and set the palace
17: 6 [G] The ravens **brought** him bread and meat in the morning
17:10 [A] When *he* **came** to the town gate, a widow was there
17:12 [A] I am gathering a few sticks *to* **take home** and make a meal
17:13 [A] to her, "Don't be afraid. **Go home** and do as you have said.
17:18 [A] *Did you* **come** to remind me of my sin and kill my son?"
18:12 [A] If *I* **go** and tell Ahab and he doesn't find you, he will kill me.
18:46 [A] he ran ahead of Ahab **all the way to** [+3870+6330] Jezreel.
19: 3 [A] When *he* **came** *to* Beersheba in Judah, he left his servant
19: 4 [A] *He* **came** *to* a broom tree, sat down under it and prayed that
19: 9 [A] There *he* **went** into a cave and spent the night. And the word
19:15 [A] When *you* **get there**, anoint Hazael king over Aram.
20:30 [A] And Ben-Hadad fled to the city and **hid in** an inner room.
20:32 [A] around their heads, *they* **went** to the king of Israel and said,
20:33 [A] they said. "**Go** and get him," the king said.
20:39 [G] someone **came** to me **with** a captive and said, 'Guard this
20:43 [A] the king of Israel went to his palace **[NIE]** in Samaria.
21: 4 [A] So Ahab **went** home, sullen and angry because Naboth the
21: 5 [A] His wife Jezebel **came** in and asked him, "Why are you
21:13 [A] two scoundrels **came** and sat opposite him and brought
21:21 [G] 'I *am going to* **bring** disaster on you. I will consume your
21:29 [G] has humbled himself, *I will* not **bring** this disaster in his day,
21:29 [G] but *I will* **bring** it on his house in the days of his son."
22:15 [A] When *he* **arrived** [+448], the king asked him, "Micaiah,
22:25 [A] "You will find out on the day *you* **go** to hide in an inner
22:27 [A] him nothing but bread and water until I **return** safely.' "
22:30 [A] "*I will* **enter** [+928] the battle in disguise, but you wear your
22:30 [A] So the king of Israel disguised himself and **went** into battle.
22:36 [A] As the sun *was* **setting**, a cry spread through the army:
22:37 [A] So the king died and *was* **brought** *to* Samaria, and they
2Ki 1:13 [A] captain went up **[NIE]** and fell on his knees before Elijah.
2: 4 [A] as you live, I will not leave you." So *they* **went** *to* Jericho.
2:15 [A] *they* **went** to meet him and bowed to the ground before him.
3:20 [A] there it was—water **flowing** from the direction of Edom!
3:24 [A] when the Moabites **came** to the camp of Israel, the Israelites
3:24 [A] And the Israelites **invaded** [+928] [Q 5782] the land and
4: 1 [A] now his creditor *is* **coming** to take my two boys as his
4: 4 [A] Then **go** *inside* and shut the door behind you and your sons.
4: 7 [A] *She* **went** and told the man of God, and he said, "Go, sell the
4:10 [A] for him. Then he can stay there whenever he **comes** to us."
4:11 [A] One day when Elisha **came**, he went up to his room and lay
4:20 [G] the servant had lifted him up and **carried** him to his mother,
4:25 [A] So she set out and **came** to the man of God at Mount Carmel.
4:27 [A] When *she* **reached** [+448] the man of God at the mountain,
4:32 [A] When Elisha **reached** [+2025] the house, there was the boy
4:33 [A] *He* **went in**, shut the door on the two of them and prayed to
4:36 [A] And he did. When *she* **came**, he said, "Take your son."
4:37 [A] *She* **came in**, fell at his feet and bowed to the ground.
4:39 [A] When *he* **returned**, he cut them up into the pot of stew,
4:42 [A] A man **came** from Baal Shalishah, bringing the man of God
4:42 [G] **bringing** the man of God twenty loaves of barley bread
5: 4 [A] Naaman **went** to his master and told him what the girl from
5: 5 [A] "**By all means, go** [+2143]," the king of Aram replied. "I
5: 6 [G] The letter that *he* **took** to the king of Israel read: "With this
5: 6 [A] "With **[NIE]** this letter I am sending my servant Naaman to
5: 8 [A] *Have* the man **come** to me and he will know that there is a
5: 9 [A] So Naaman **went** with his horses and chariots and stopped at
5:15 [A] **[NIE]** He stood before him and said, "Now I know that
5:18 [A] When my master **enters** the temple of Rimmon to bow down
5:20 [G] this Aramean, by not accepting from him what *he* **brought**.
5:22 [A] *have* just **come** to me from the hill country of Ephraim.
5:24 [A] When Gehazi **came** to the hill, he took the things from the
5:25 [A] he **went in** and stood before his master Elisha. "Where have

2Ki 6: 4 [A] *They* **went** to the Jordan and began to cut down trees.
6:14 [A] force there. *They* **went** by night and surrounded the city.
6:20 [A] After they **entered** the city, Elisha said, "LORD, open the
6:23 [A] So the bands from Aram stopped **raiding** [+928] Israel's
6:32 [A] but before he **arrived** [+448], Elisha said to the elders,
6:32 [A] Look, when the messenger **comes**, shut the door and hold it
7: 4 [A] If we say, '*We'll* **go into** the city'—the famine is there,
7: 5 [A] At dusk they got up and **went** to the camp of the Arameans.
7: 5 [A] When *they* **reached** [+6330] the edge of the camp, not a man
7: 6 [A] hired the Hittite and Egyptian kings to **attack** [+6584] us!"
7: 8 [A] The men who had leprosy **reached** [+6330] the edge of the
7: 8 [A] the edge of the camp and **entered** [+448] one of the tents.
7: 8 [A] They returned and **entered** [+448] another tent and took
7: 9 [A] *Let's* **go at once** [+2143+2256] and report this to the royal
7:10 [A] So *they* **went** and called out to the city gatekeepers and told
7:10 [A] "*We* **went** into the Aramean camp and not a man was there—
7:12 [A] and then we will take them alive and **get** into the city.' "
8: 1 [A] has decreed a famine in the land *that will* **last** seven years."
8: 7 [A] Elisha **went** *to* Damascus, and Ben-Hadad king of Aram was
8: 7 [A] was told, "The man of God *has* **come** all the way up here,"
8: 9 [A] *He* **went in** and stood before him, and said, "Your son
8:14 [A] Hazael left Elisha and **returned** to his master.
9: 2 [A] When *you* **get** there, look for Jehu son of Jehoshaphat,
9: 2 [A] **Go** *to* him, get him away from his companions and take him
9: 2 [G] away from his companions and **take** him **into** an inner room.
9: 5 [A] When *he* **arrived**, he found the army officers sitting together.
9: 6 [A] Jehu got up and **went** into the house. Then the prophet
9:11 [A] Why *did* this madman **come** to you?" "You know the man
9:17 [A] on the tower in Jezreel saw Jehu's troops **approaching**,
9:18 [A] "The messenger *has* **reached** [+6330] them,
9:19 [A] When *he* **came** to them he said, "This is what the king says:
9:20 [A] The lookout reported, "*He has* **reached** [+448+6330] them,
9:30 [A] Jehu **went** to Jezreel. When Jezebel heard about it, she
9:31 [A] As Jehu **entered** [+928] the gate, she asked, "Have you come
9:34 [A] Jehu **went in** and ate and drank. "Take care of that cursed
10: 2 [A] "As soon as this letter **reaches** [+448] you, since your
10: 6 [A] and **come** to me in Jezreel by this time tomorrow."
10: 7 [A] When the letter **arrived** [+448], these men took the princes
10: 8 [A] When the messenger **arrived**, he told Jehu, "They have
10: 8 [G] he told Jehu, "*They have* **brought** the heads of the princes."
10:12 [A] Jehu then **set out** and went toward Samaria. At Beth Eked of
10:17 [A] When Jehu **came** *to* Samaria, he killed all who were left
10:21 [A] word throughout Israel, and all the ministers of Baal **came**;
10:21 [A] all the ministers of Baal came; not one **stayed** [+4202] **away**.
10:21 [A] *They* **crowded into** the temple of Baal until it was full from
10:23 [A] and Jehonadab son of Recab **went into** the temple of Baal.
10:24 [A] So *they* **went in** to make sacrifices and burnt offerings.
10:24 [G] "If one of you lets any of the men I *am* **placing** in your
10:25 [A] and officers: "**Go in** and kill them; let no one escape."
11: 4 [G] and **had** them **brought** to him at the temple of the LORD.
11: 5 [A] the three companies *that are* **going on duty** *on* the Sabbath—
11: 8 [A] Anyone *who* **approaches** [+448] your ranks must be put to
11: 8 [A] close to the king **wherever** he **goes** [+928+928+2256+3655]."
11: 9 [A] *those who were* **going on duty** *on* the Sabbath and those
11: 9 [A] who were going off duty—and **came** to Jehoiada the priest.
11:13 [A] *she* **went** to the people at the temple of the LORD.
11:15 [A] and put to the sword anyone *who* **follows** [+339] her."
11:16 [A] So they seized her as *she* **reached** the place where the horses
11:18 [A] All the people of the land **went** *to* the temple of Baal and tore
11:19 [A] from the temple of the LORD and **went into** the palace,
12: 4 [12:5] [H] **is brought** as sacred offerings *to* the temple of the
12: 4 [12:5] [G] and the money **brought** voluntarily *to* the temple.
12: 9 [12:10] [A] right side as one **enters** the temple of the LORD.
12: 9 [12:10] [H] that **was brought** *to* the temple of the LORD.
12:13 [12:14] [H] The money **brought into** the temple was not spent
12:16 [12:17] [H] sin offerings **was** not **brought into** the temple of the
13:20 [A] Now Moabite raiders *used to* **enter** [+928] the country every
13:20 [A] raiders used to enter the country **every spring** [+9102].
14:13 [A] Jehoash **went** *to* Jerusalem and broke down the wall of
15:14 [A] Then Menahem son of Gadi **went** from Tirzah up to Samaria.
15:19 [A] Pul king of Assyria **invaded** [+6584] the land, and Menahem
15:29 [A] Tiglath-Pileser king of Assyria **came** and took Ijon, Abel
16: 6 [A] Edomites then **moved into** Elath and have lived there to this
16:11 [A] from Damascus and finished it before King Ahaz **returned**.
16:12 [A] When the king **came back** from Damascus and saw the altar,
17:24 [G] The king of Assyria **brought** people from Babylon, Cuthah,
17:28 [A] who had been exiled from Samaria **came** to live in Bethel
18:17 [A] *They* **came** up to Jerusalem and stopped at the aqueduct of
18:17 [A] **[RPH]** and stopped at the aqueduct of the Upper Pool,
18:21 [A] a man's hand and **wounds** [+928] him if he leans on it!
18:32 [A] until I **come** and take you to a land like your own, a land of
18:37 [A] and Joah son of Asaph the recorder **went** to Hezekiah,
19: 1 [A] put on sackcloth and **went into** the temple of the LORD.
19: 3 [A] as when children **come** to the point of birth and there is no
19: 5 [A] When King Hezekiah's officials **came** to Isaiah,
19:23 [A] *I have* **reached** its remotest parts, the finest of its forests.
19:25 [G] now *I have* **brought** it **to pass**, that you have turned fortified
19:27 [A] " 'But I know where you stay and *when* you **come** and go
19:28 [A] and I will make you return by the way *you* **came**.'
19:32 [A] "*He will* not **enter** [+448] this city or shoot an arrow here.
19:33 [A] By the way that *he* **came** he will return; he will not enter this
19:33 [A] *he will* not **enter** [+448] this city, declares the LORD.
20: 1 [A] The prophet Isaiah son of Amoz **went** to him and said, "This
20:14 [A] Then Isaiah the prophet **went** to King Hezekiah and asked,
20:14 [A] "What did those men say, and where *did they* **come** from?"
20:14 [A] distant land," Hezekiah replied. "*They* **came** from Babylon."
20:17 [A] The time *will* surely **come** when everything in your palace,
20:20 [G] and the tunnel by which *he* **brought** water into the city,
21:12 [G] I *am going to* **bring** such disaster on Jerusalem and Judah
22: 4 [H] have him get ready the money that *has* **been brought into**
22: 9 [A] Shaphan the secretary **went** to the king and reported to him:
22:16 [G] I *am going to* **bring** disaster on this place and its people,
22:20 [G] Your eyes will not see all the disaster I *am going to* **bring** on
23: 8 [G] Josiah **brought** all the priests from the towns of Judah
23:11 [A] He removed from the **entrance** *to* the temple of the LORD
23:17 [A] "It marks the tomb of the man of God who **came** from Judah
23:18 [A] and those of the prophet who *had* **come** from Samaria.
23:30 [G] Josiah's servants **brought** his body in a chariot from
23:34 [A] he took Jehoahaz and **carried** him **off** *to* Egypt, and there he
24:10 [A] on Jerusalem and **laid siege to** [+928+2021+5189] it,
24:11 [A] Nebuchadnezzar *himself* **came up** to the city while his
24:16 [G] The king of Babylon also **deported** [+906+1583] to Babylon
25: 1 [A] Nebuchadnezzar king of Babylon **marched** against
25: 2 [A] The city *was* **kept** under siege until the eleventh year of King
25: 7 [G] bound him with bronze shackles and **took** him *to* Babylon.
25: 8 [A] an official of the king of Babylon, **came** *to* Jerusalem.
25:23 [A] Gedaliah as governor, *they* **came** to Gedaliah at Mizpah—
25:25 [A] **came** with ten men and assassinated Gedaliah and also the
25:26 [A] the army officers, **fled** *to* Egypt for fear of the Babylonians.
1Ch 2:21 [A] Hezron **lay** [+448] **with** the daughter of Makir the father of
2:55 [A] These are the Kenites who **came** from Hammath, the father
4:10 [G] that I will be free from pain." And God **granted** his request.
4:38 [A] The men **listed** above by name were leaders of their clans.
4:41 [A] The men whose names were listed **came** in the days of
5: 9 [A] To the east they occupied the land up to the **edge** *of* the
5:26 [G] *He* **took** them to Halah, Habor, Hara and the river of Gozan,
7:22 [A] for them many days, and his relatives **came** to comfort him.
7:23 [A] *he* **lay** [+448] **with** his wife again, and she became pregnant
9:25 [A] Their brothers in their villages *had* to **come** from time to
9:28 [G] they counted them *when* they *were* **brought in** and when
10: 4 [A] or these uncircumcised fellows *will* **come** and abuse me."
10: 7 [A] and fled. And the Philistines **came** and occupied them.
10: 8 [A] The next day, when the Philistines **came** to strip the dead,
10:12 [G] the bodies of Saul and his sons and **brought** them to Jabesh.
11: 2 [G] **led** Israel **on** their **military campaigns** [+906+2256+3655].
11: 3 [A] When all the elders of Israel *had* **come** to King David at
11: 5 [A] said to David, "*You will* not **get in** here." Nevertheless,
11:18 [G] well near the gate of Bethlehem and carried it **back** to David.
11:19 [G] Because they risked their lives *to* **bring** it **back**, David would
11:21 [A] even though *he was* not **included** among them.
11:25 [A] any of the Thirty, but *he was* not **included** among the Three.
12: 1 [A] These were the *men who* **came** to David at Ziklag, while he
12:16 [12:17] [A] *some men* from Judah also **came** to David in his
12:17 [12:18] [A] "If *you have* **come** to me in peace, to help me,
12:19 [12:20] [A] he **went** with the Philistines to fight against Saul.
12:22 [12:23] [A] Day after day *men* **came** to help David, until he had
12:23 [12:24] [A] *who* **came** to David at Hebron to turn Saul's
12:31 [12:32] [A] designated by name to **come** and make David king—
12:38 [12:39] [A] *They* **came** to Hebron fully determined to make
12:40 [12:41] [G] Zebulun and Naphtali **came bringing** food on
13: 5 [G] Lebo Hamath, to **bring** the ark of God from Kiriath Jearim.
13: 9 [A] When *they* **came** to the threshing floor of Kidon, Uzzah
13:12 [G] and asked, "How *can I ever* **bring** the ark of God to me?"
14: 9 [A] Now the Philistines *had* **come** and raided the Valley of
14:14 [A] and **attack** [+4200] them in front of the balsam trees.
15:29 [A] of the LORD was **entering** [+6330] the City of David,
16: 1 [G] *They* **brought** the ark of God and set it inside the tent that
16:29 [A] Bring an offering and **come** before him; worship the LORD
16:33 [A] for joy before the LORD, for *he* **comes** to judge the earth.
17:16 [A] King David **went in** and sat before the LORD, and he said:
17:16 [G] and what is my family, that *you have* **brought** me this far?
18: 5 [A] When the Arameans of Damascus **came** to help Hadadezer
18: 7 [G] by the officers of Hadadezer and **brought** them *to* Jerusalem.
19: 2 [A] When David's men **came** to Hanun in the land of the
19: 3 [A] Haven't his men **come** to you to explore and spy out the
19: 7 [A] with his troops, *who* **came** and camped near Medeba,
19: 7 [A] were mustered from their towns and **moved out** for battle.
19: 9 [A] while the kings who *had* **come** were by themselves in the

1Ch 19:15 [A] too fled before his brother Abishai and **went** inside the city.
19:15 [A] and went inside the city. So Joab **went back** *to* Jerusalem.
19:17 [A] *he* **advanced** against them and formed his battle lines
20: 1 [A] land of the Ammonites and **went** *to* Rabbah and besieged it,
21: 2 [G] **report back** to me so that I may know how many there are."
21: 4 [A] went throughout Israel and then **came back** *to* Jerusalem.
21:11 [A] So Gad **went** to David and said to him, "This is what the
21:21 [A] Then David **approached** [+6330], and when Araunah looked
22: 4 [G] and Tyrians *had* **brought** large numbers of them to David.
22:19 [G] so that you *may* **bring** the ark of the covenant of the LORD
24:19 [A] when they **entered** [+4200] the temple of the LORD,
27: 1 [A] *were* **on duty** [+2256+3655] month by month throughout the
2Ch 1:10 [A] that *I may* **lead** [+2256+3655+4200+7156] this people, for who
1:13 [A] Solomon **went** *to* Jerusalem from the high place at Gibeon,
2:16 [2:15] [G] and *will* **float** them *in* rafts by sea *down* to Joppa.
5: 1 [G] **brought in** the things his father David had dedicated—
5: 4 [A] When all the elders of Israel *had* **arrived**, the Levites took
5: 7 [G] **brought** the ark of the LORD's covenant to its place in the
6:22 [A] his neighbor and is required to take an oath and *he* **comes**
6:32 [A] but *has* **come** from a distant land because of your great name
6:32 [A] when *he* **comes** and prays toward this temple,
7: 2 [A] The priests could not **enter** [+448] the temple of the LORD
7:11 [A] had succeeded in carrying out all he **had** in mind to do in the
7:22 [G] that is why *he* **brought** all this disaster on them.' "
8:11 [A] because the places the ark of the LORD *has* **entered** [+448]
8:18 [A] *These*, with Solomon's men, **sailed** to Ophir and brought
8:18 [G] fifty talents of gold, which *they* **delivered** to King Solomon.
9: 1 [A] *she* **came** to Jerusalem to test him with hard questions.
9: 1 [A] *she* **came** to Solomon and talked with him about all she had
9: 6 [A] I did not believe what they said until *I* **came** and saw with
9:10 [G] of Hiram and the men of Solomon **brought** gold from Ophir;
9:10 [G] *they* also **brought** algumwood and precious stones.
9:12 [G] asked for; he gave her more than *she had* **brought** to him.
9:13 [A] The weight of the gold that Solomon **received** yearly was
9:14 [G] not including the revenues **brought in** *by* merchants
9:14 [G] the governors of the land **brought** gold and silver to
9:21 [A] Once every three years it **returned**, carrying gold, silver
9:24 [G] Year after year, everyone who came **brought** a gift—
10: 1 [A] for all the Israelites *had* **gone** there to make him king.
10: 3 [A] and he and all Israel **went** to Rehoboam and said to him:
10:12 [A] later Jeroboam and all the people **returned** to Rehoboam,
11: 1 [A] When Rehoboam **arrived** *in* Jerusalem, he mustered the
11:16 [A] **followed** [+339] the Levites *to* Jerusalem to offer sacrifices
12: 3 [A] Sukkites and Cushites that **came** with him from Egypt,
12: 4 [A] the fortified cities of Judah and **came** as far as Jerusalem.
12: 5 [A] the prophet Shemaiah **came** to Rehoboam and to the leaders
12:11 [A] Whenever the king **went** *to* the LORD's temple, the guards
12:11 [A] the guards **went** with him, bearing the shields,
13: 9 [A] Whoever **comes** to consecrate himself with a young bull
13:13 [A] Now Jeroboam had sent troops around **[NIE]** to the rear,
14: 9 [14:8] [A] three hundred chariots, and **came** as far as Mareshah.
14:11 [14:10] [A] in your name *we have* **come** against this vast army.
15: 5 [A] In those days it was not safe to **travel about** [+2256+3655],
15:11 [G] and goats from the plunder *they had* **brought back**.
15:12 [A] *They* **entered** into a covenant to seek the LORD, the God
15:18 [G] *He* **brought into** the temple of God the silver and gold and
16: 1 [A] or **entering** [+4200] the territory of Asa king of Judah.
16: 7 [A] At that time Hanani the seer **came** to Asa king of Judah
17:11 [G] Some Philistines **brought** Jehoshaphat gifts and silver as
17:11 [G] and silver as tribute, and the Arabs **brought** him flocks:
18:14 [A] When *he* **arrived** [+448], the king asked him, "Micaiah,
18:24 [A] "You will find out on the day *you* **go** to hide in an inner
18:29 [A] "*I will* **enter** [+928] the battle in disguise, but you wear your
18:29 [A] So the king of Israel disguised himself and **went** into battle.
18:34 [A] Then at **sunset** [+2021+6961+9087] he died.
19:10 [A] In every case that **comes** before you from your fellow
20: 1 [A] Ammonites with some of the Meunites **came** to make war on
20: 2 [A] *Some men* **came** and told Jehoshaphat, "A vast army is
20: 2 [A] "A vast army *is* **coming** against you from Edom,
20: 4 [A] indeed, *they* **came** from every town in Judah to seek him.
20: 9 [A] 'If calamity **comes** upon us, whether the sword of judgment,
20:10 [A] whose territory you would not allow Israel to **invade** [+928]
20:10 [A] not allow Israel to invade when they **came** from Egypt;
20:11 [A] See how they are repaying us by **coming** to drive us out of
20:12 [A] no power to face this vast army that *is* **attacking** [+6584] us.
20:22 [A] and Mount Seir who *were* **invading** [+4200] Judah,
20:24 [A] When the men of Judah **came** to the place that overlooks the
20:25 [A] So Jehoshaphat and his men **went** to carry off their plunder,
20:28 [A] *They* **entered** Jerusalem **and went** to the temple of the
21:12 [A] Jehoram **received** [+448] a letter from Elijah the prophet,
22: 1 [A] since the raiders, who **came** with the Arabs into the camp,
22: 7 [A] Through Ahaziah's **visit** to Joram, God brought about
22: 7 [A] When Ahaziah **arrived**, he went out with Joram to meet Jehu
22: 9 [G] He *was* **brought** to Jehu and put to death. They buried him,
23: 2 [A] families from all the towns. When *they* **came** to Jerusalem,
23: 4 [A] Levites *who are* **going on duty** *on* the Sabbath are to keep
23: 6 [A] No *one is to* **enter** the temple of the LORD except the
23: 6 [A] they *may* **enter** because they are consecrated, but all the
23: 7 [A] Anyone *who* **enters** [+448] the temple must be put to death.
23: 7 [A] close to the king **wherever** he **goes** [+928+928+2256+3655]."
23: 8 [A] *those who were* **going on duty** *on* the Sabbath and those
23:12 [A] the king, *she* **went** to them at the temple of the LORD.
23:14 [A] and put to the sword anyone *who* **follows** [+339] her."
23:15 [A] So they seized her as *she* **reached** [+448] the entrance of the
23:17 [A] All the people **went** *to* the temple of Baal and tore it down.
23:19 [A] so that no one who was in any way unclean *might* **enter**.
23:20 [A] *They* **went into** the palace through the Upper Gate
24: 6 [G] required the Levites to **bring in** from Judah and Jerusalem
24: 9 [G] Jerusalem that they *should* **bring** to the LORD the tax that
24:10 [G] and all the people **brought** their contributions gladly,
24:11 [G] Whenever the chest *was* **brought in** by the Levites to the
24:11 [A] royal secretary and the officer of the chief priest *would* **come**
24:14 [G] *they* **brought** the rest of the money to the king and Jehoiada,
24:17 [A] the officials of Judah **came** and paid homage to the king,
24:23 [A] *it* **invaded** [+448] Judah and Jerusalem and killed all the
24:24 [A] Although the Aramean army *had* **come** with only a few men,
25: 7 [A] a man of God **came** to him and said, "O king, these troops
25: 7 [A] "O king, these troops from Israel *must* not **march** with you,
25: 8 [A] Even if you **go** and fight courageously in battle, God will
25:10 [A] So Amaziah dismissed the troops who *had* **come** to him from
25:12 [G] **took** them to the top of a cliff and threw them down so that
25:14 [A] When Amaziah **returned** from slaughtering the Edomites,
25:14 [G] *he* **brought back** the gods of the people of Seir.
25:23 [G] Jehoash **brought** him *to* Jerusalem and broke down the wall
26: 8 [A] his fame spread as far as the **border** *of* Egypt, because he
26:16 [A] **entered** [+448] the temple of the LORD to burn incense on
26:17 [A] courageous priests of the LORD **followed** [+339] him **in**.
27: 2 [A] unlike him *he did* not **enter** [+448] the temple of the
28: 5 [G] of his people as prisoners and **brought** them *to* Damascus.
28: 8 [G] a great deal of plunder, which *they* **carried back** to Samaria.
28: 9 [A] he went out to meet the army when it **returned** to Samaria.
28:12 [A] confronted those *who were* **arriving** from the war.
28:13 [G] "*You must* not **bring** those prisoners here," they said, "or we
28:15 [G] So *they* **took** them **back** to their fellow countrymen at
28:17 [A] The Edomites *had* again **come** and attacked Judah
28:20 [A] Tiglath-Pileser king of Assyria **came** to him, but he gave him
28:27 [G] but he *was* not **placed** in the tombs of the kings of Israel.
29: 4 [G] *He* **brought in** the priests and the Levites, assembled them
29:15 [A] *they* **went in** to purify the temple of the LORD, as the king
29:16 [A] The priests **went** into the sanctuary of the LORD to purify
29:17 [A] by the eighth day of the month *they* **reached** the portico of
29:18 [A] *they* **went** in to King Hezekiah and reported: "We have
29:21 [G] *They* **brought** seven bulls, seven rams, seven male lambs
29:31 [G] Come and **bring** sacrifices and thank offerings to the temple
29:31 [G] So the assembly **brought** sacrifices and thank offerings,
29:32 [G] The number of burnt offerings the assembly **brought** was
30: 1 [A] inviting them to **come** to the temple of the LORD in
30: 5 [A] calling the people to **come** to Jerusalem and celebrate the
30: 8 [A] **Come** to the sanctuary, which he has consecrated forever.
30:11 [A] and Zebulun humbled themselves and **went** to Jerusalem.
30:15 [G] and **brought** burnt offerings *to* the temple of the LORD.
30:25 [A] and Levites and all who *had* **assembled** [+7736] from Israel,
30:25 [A] including the aliens who *had* **come** from Israel and those
30:27 [A] God heard them, for their prayer **reached** [+4200] heaven,
31: 5 [G] *They* **brought** a great amount, a tithe of everything.
31: 6 [G] Judah who lived in the towns of Judah also **brought** a tithe
31: 8 [A] When Hezekiah and his officials **came** and saw the heaps,
31:10 [G] "Since the people began to **bring** their contributions *to* the
31:12 [G] *they* faithfully **brought in** the contributions, tithes
31:16 [A] all who *would* **enter** [+4200] the temple of the LORD to
32: 1 [A] Sennacherib king of Assyria **came** and invaded Judah.
32: 1 [A] king of Assyria came and **invaded** [+928] Judah.
32: 2 [A] When Hezekiah saw that Sennacherib *had* **come** and that he
32: 4 [A] "Why *should* the kings of Assyria **come** and find plenty of
32:21 [A] when *he* **went into** the temple of his god, some of his sons
32:23 [G] Many **brought** offerings to Jerusalem for the LORD
32:26 [A] therefore the LORD's wrath *did* not **come** upon them
33:11 [G] So the LORD **brought** against them the army commanders
33:14 [A] as far as the **entrance** of the Fish Gate and encircling the hill
34: 9 [A] *They* **went** to Hilkiah the high priest and gave him the
34: 9 [H] gave him the money that *had* **been brought into** the temple
34:14 [H] money that *had* **been taken into** the temple of the LORD,
34:16 [G] Then Shaphan **took** the book to the king and reported to him:
34:24 [G] I *am going to* **bring** disaster on this place and its people—
34:28 [G] Your eyes will not see all the disaster I *am going to* **bring** on
35:22 [A] but **went** to fight him on the plain of Megiddo.
36: 4 [G] Eliakim's brother Jehoahaz and **carried** him **off** to Egypt.
36: 7 [G] Nebuchadnezzar also **took** to Babylon articles from the

2Ch 36: 10 [G] Nebuchadnezzar sent for him and **brought** him to Babylon,
36: 18 [G] *He* **carried** *to* Babylon all the articles from the temple of
Ezr 2: 2 [A] **[RPH]** in company with Zerubbabel, Jeshua, Nehemiah,
2: 68 [A] When they **arrived** at the house of the LORD in Jerusalem,
3: 7 [G] so that they *would* **bring** cedar logs by sea from Lebanon to
3: 8 [A] In the second month of the second year after their **arrival** at
3: 8 [A] and all who *had* **returned** from the captivity to Jerusalem)
7: 8 [A] Ezra **arrived** *in* Jerusalem in the fifth month of the seventh
7: 9 [A] *he* **arrived** in Jerusalem on the first day of the fifth month,
8: 15 [A] I assembled them at the canal that **flows** toward Ahava,
8: 17 [G] so that they *might* **bring** attendants to us for the house of our
8: 18 [G] *they* **brought** us Sherebiah, a capable man,
8: 30 [G] sacred articles that had been weighed out to *be* **taken** to the
8: 32 [A] So *we* **arrived** *in* Jerusalem, where we rested three days.
8: 35 [A] the exiles who *had* **returned** from captivity sacrificed burnt
9: 11 [A] 'The land you *are* **entering** to possess is a land polluted by
9: 13 [A] "What *has* **happened** to us is a result of our evil deeds
10: 8 [A] Anyone who failed *to* **appear** within three days would forfeit
10: 14 [A] everyone in our towns who has married a foreign woman **come**
Ne 1: 2 [A] one of my brothers, **came** from Judah with some other men,
1: 9 [G] **bring** them to the place I have chosen as a dwelling for my
2: 7 [A] so that they will provide me safe-conduct until *I* **arrive** in
2: 8 [A] for the city wall and for the residence *I will* **occupy** [+448]?"
2: 9 [A] So *I* **went** to the governors of Trans-Euphrates and gave
2: 10 [A] they were very much disturbed that someone *had* **come** to
2: 11 [A] *I* **went** to Jerusalem, and after staying there three days
2: 15 [A] and **reentered** [+2256+8740] through the Valley Gate.
3: 5 [G] their nobles *would* not **put** their shoulders to the work under
4: 8 [4:2] [A] They all plotted together to **come** and fight against
4: 11 [4:5] [A] *we will* **be right there** among them and will kill them
4: 12 [4:6] [A] the Jews who lived near them **came** and told us ten
5: 17 [A] as well as those *who* **came** to us from the surrounding
6: 10 [A] One day I **went** *to* the house of Shemaiah son of Delaiah,
6: 10 [A] the temple doors, because *men are* **coming** to kill you—
6: 10 [A] coming to kill you—by night *they are* **coming** to kill you."
6: 11 [A] Or *should* one like me **go** into the temple to save his life?
6: 11 [A] one like me go into the temple to save his life? *I will* not **go**!"
6: 17 [A] to Tobiah, and replies from Tobiah *kept* **coming** to them.
7: 7 [A] **[RPH]** in company with Zerubbabel, Jeshua, Nehemiah,
8: 1 [G] They told Ezra the scribe to **bring out** the Book of the Law
8: 2 [G] month Ezra the priest **brought** the Law before the assembly,
8: 15 [G] and **bring back** branches from olive and wild olive trees,
8: 16 [G] So the people went out and **brought back** branches and built
9: 15 [A] you told them to **go in** and take possession of the land you
9: 23 [G] *you* **brought** them into the land that you told their fathers to
9: 23 [A] brought them into the land that you told their fathers to **enter**
9: 24 [A] Their sons **went in** and took possession of the land. You
9: 33 [A] In all that *has* **happened** to us, you have been just; you have
10: 29 [10:30] [A] **bind** [+928] **themselves with** a curse and an oath to
10: 31 [10:32] [G] "When the neighboring peoples **bring** merchandise
10: 34 [10:35] [G] **bring** to the house of our God at set times each year
10: 35 [10:36] [G] **bringing** to the house of the LORD each year the
10: 36 [10:37] [G] *will* **bring** the firstborn of our sons and of our cattle,
10: 37 [10:38] [G] *we will* **bring** to the storerooms of the house of our
10: 39 [10:40] [G] *are to* **bring** their contributions of grain, new wine
11: 1 [G] the rest of the people cast lots to **bring** one out of every ten
12: 27 [G] *were* **brought** to Jerusalem to celebrate joyfully the
13: 1 [A] or Moabite *should* ever *be* **admitted** into the assembly of
13: 6 [A] of Artaxerxes king of Babylon *I had* **returned** to the king.
13: 7 [A] **came back** to Jerusalem. Here I learned about the evil thing
13: 12 [G] All Judah **brought** the tithes of grain, new wine and oil into
13: 15 [G] the Sabbath and **bringing in** grain and loading it on donkeys,
13: 15 [G] *they were* **bringing** all this **into** Jerusalem on the Sabbath.
13: 16 [G] Men from Tyre who lived in Jerusalem *were* **bringing in**
13: 18 [G] so that our God **brought** all this calamity upon us and upon
13: 19 [A] so that no load *could be* **brought in** on the Sabbath day.
13: 21 [A] From that time on *they* no longer **came** on the Sabbath.
13: 22 [A] Then I commanded the Levites to purify themselves and **go**
Est 1: 11 [G] to **bring** before him Queen Vashti, wearing her royal crown,
1: 12 [A] the king's command, Queen Vashti refused to **come**.
1: 17 [G] 'King Xerxes commanded Queen Vashti to *be* **brought**
1: 17 [A] Vashti to be brought before him, but *she would* not **come**.'
1: 19 [A] that Vashti *is* never again *to* **enter** the presence of King
2: 12 [A] Before a girl's turn came to **go in** to King Xerxes, she had to
2: 13 [A] this is how she *would* **go** to the king: Anything she wanted
2: 13 [A] Anything she wanted was given her to **take** with her from the
2: 14 [A] In the evening she *would* **go** there and in the morning return
2: 14 [A] *She would* not **return** [+6388] to the king unless he was
2: 15 [A] to **go** to the king, she asked for nothing other than what
3: 9 [G] *I will* **put** [+4200+9202] ten thousand talents of silver into
4: 2 [A] *he* **went** only as far as the king's gate, because no one
4: 2 [A] no one clothed in sackcloth was allowed to **enter** [+448] it.
4: 4 [A] When Esther's maids and eunuchs **came** and told her about
4: 8 [A] he told him to urge her to **go** into the king's presence to beg
4: 9 [A] Hathach **went back** and reported to Esther what Mordecai
4: 11 [A] or woman who **approaches** [+448] the king in the inner
4: 11 [A] thirty days have passed since I was called to **go** to the king."
4: 16 [A] When this is done, *I will* **go** to the king, even though it is
5: 4 [A] "*let* the king, together with Haman, **come** today to a banquet
5: 5 [A] and Haman **went** to the banquet Esther had prepared.
5: 8 [A] *let* the king and Haman **come** tomorrow to the banquet I will
5: 10 [A] Nevertheless, Haman restrained himself and **went** home.
5: 10 [G] **Calling together** [+906+906+2256+8938] his friends and
5: 12 [G] "I'm the only person Queen Esther **invited** to accompany the
5: 14 [A] **go** with the king to the dinner and be happy." This suggestion
6: 1 [G] the record of his reign, to *be* **brought in** and read to him.
6: 4 [A] Now Haman *had just* **entered** [+4200] the outer court of the
6: 5 [A] is standing in the court." "**Bring** *him* **in**," the king ordered.
6: 6 [A] When Haman **entered**, the king asked him, "What should be
6: 8 [G] *have them* **bring** a royal robe the king has worn and a horse
6: 14 [G] and hurried Haman **away** to the banquet Esther had prepared.
7: 1 [A] So the king and Haman **went** to dine with Queen Esther,
8: 1 [A] Mordecai **came** into the presence of the king, for Esther had
9: 11 [A] the citadel of Susa *was* **reported** to the king that same day.
9: 25 [A] when the plot **came** *to* the king's attention, he issued written
Job 1: 6 [A] One day the angels **came** to present themselves before the
1: 6 [A] before the LORD, and Satan also **came** with them.
1: 7 [A] The LORD said to Satan, "Where *have you* **come** from?"
1: 14 [A] a messenger **came** to Job and said, "The oxen were plowing
1: 16 [A] he was still speaking, another messenger **came** and said,
1: 17 [A] he was still speaking, another messenger **came** and said,
1: 18 [A] yet another messenger **came** and said, "Your sons
1: 19 [A] when suddenly a mighty wind **swept in** from the desert
2: 1 [A] On another day the angels **came** to present themselves before
2: 1 [A] Satan also **came** with them to present himself before him.
2: 2 [A] the LORD said to Satan, "Where *have you* **come** from?"
2: 11 [A] heard about all the troubles that *had* **come** upon him,
2: 11 [A] they **set out** from their homes and met together by agreement
2: 11 [A] met together by agreement to **go** and sympathize with him
3: 6 [A] the days of the year nor *be* **entered** in any of the months.
3: 7 [A] that night be barren; *may* no shout of joy **be heard**[s] in it.
3: 24 [A] For sighing **comes** *to* me instead of food; my groans pour out
3: 25 [A] has come upon me; what I dreaded *has* **happened** to me.
3: 26 [A] no quietness; I have no rest, but only **[NIE]** turmoil."
4: 5 [A] now trouble **comes** to you, and you are discouraged; it strikes
5: 21 [A] of the tongue, and need not fear when destruction **comes**.
5: 26 [A] *You will* **come** to the grave in full vigor, like sheaves
6: 8 [A] "Oh, that I *might* **have** my request, that God would grant
6: 20 [A] *they* **arrive** [+6330] there, only to be disappointed.
9: 32 [A] answer him, that *we might* **confront** each other in court.
12: 6 [G] God are secure—*those* who **carry** their god in their hands.
13: 16 [A] for no godless man *would dare* **come** before him!
14: 3 [G] on such a one? *Will you* **bring** him before you for judgment?
14: 14 [A] days of my hard service I will wait for my renewal *to* **come**.
15: 21 [A] fill his ears; when all seems well, marauders **attack** him.
17: 10 [A] "But **come on**, all of you, try again! I will not find a wise
19: 12 [A] His troops **advance** in force; they build a siege ramp against
20: 22 [A] overtake him; the full force of misery *will* **come** *upon* him.
21: 17 [A] How often *does* calamity **come** upon them, the fate God
22: 4 [A] piety that he rebukes you and **brings** charges against you?
22: 21 [A] at peace with him; in this way prosperity *will* **come** *to* you.
23: 3 [A] I knew where to find him; if only *I could* **go** to his dwelling!
27: 9 [A] Does God listen to his cry when distress **comes** upon him?
28: 20 [A] "Where then *does* wisdom **come** from? Where does
29: 13 [A] The man who was dying **blessed** [+1388+6584] me; I made
30: 26 [A] Yet when I hoped for good, evil **came**; when I looked for
30: 26 [A] evil came; when I looked for light, then **came** darkness.
34: 28 [G] They **caused** the cry of the poor **to come** before him, so that
37: 8 [A] The animals **take** [+1198] cover; they remain in their dens.
37: 9 [A] The tempest **comes** out from its chamber, the cold from the
38: 11 [A] when I said, 'This far *you may* **come** and no farther; here is
38: 16 [A] "*Have you* **journeyed** to the springs of the sea or walked in
38: 22 [A] "*Have you* **entered** [+448] the storehouses of the snow
41: 13 [41:5] [A] outer coat? Who *would* **approach** him with a bridle?
41: 16 [41:8] [A] so close to the next that no air *can* **pass** between.
42: 11 [A] and sisters and everyone who had known him before **came**
42: 11 [G] consoled him over all the trouble the LORD *had* **brought**
Ps 5: 7 [5:8] [A] I, by your great mercy, *will* **come into** your house;
18: 6 [18:7] [A] my voice; my cry **came** before him, into his ears.
22: 30 [22:32] [A] **future** generations will be told about the Lord.
24: 7 [A] you ancient doors, that the King of glory *may* **come in**.
24: 9 [A] you ancient doors, that the King of glory *may* **come in**.
26: 4 [A] not sit with deceitful men, nor *do I* **consort** with hypocrites;
35: 8 [A] *may* ruin **overtake** them by surprise—may the net they hid
36: 11 [36:12] [A] *May* the foot of the proud not **come** *against* me, nor
37: 13 [A] Lord laughs at the wicked, for he knows their day *is* **coming**.
37: 15 [A] their swords *will* **pierce** [+928] their own hearts, and their
40: 7 [40:8] [A] I said, "Here I am, *I have* **come**—it is written about

Ps 41: 6 [41:7] [A] Whenever *one* **comes** to see me, he speaks falsely,
42: 2 [42:3] [A] the living God. When *can I* **go** and meet with God?
43: 3 [G] *let them* **bring** me to your holy mountain, to the place where
43: 4 [A] *will I* **go** to the altar of God, to God, my joy and my delight.
44: 17 [44:18] [A] All this **happened** *to* us, though we had not
45: 14 [45:15] [H] companions follow her and **are brought** to you.
45: 15 [45:16] [A] *they* **enter** [+928] the palace of the king.
49: 19 [49:20] [A] *he will* **join** [+6330] the generation of his fathers,
50: 3 [A] Our God **comes** and will not be silent; a fire devours before
51: T [51:2] [A] When the prophet Nathan **came** to him after David
51: T [51:2] [A] *had* **committed adultery** [+448] **with** Bathsheba.
52: T [52:2] [A] Doeg the Edomite *had* **gone** to Saul and told him:
52: T [52:2] [A] "David *has* **gone** to the house of Ahimelech."
54: T [54:2] [A] When the Ziphites *had* **gone** to Saul and said, "Is not
55: 5 [55:6] [A] Fear and trembling *have* **beset** [+928] me; horror has
63: 9 [63:10] [A] *they will* **go down** to the depths of the earth.
65: 2 [65:3] [A] O you who hear prayer, to you all men *will* **come**.
66: 11 [G] *You* **brought** us into prison and laid burdens on our backs.
66: 12 [A] *we* **went** through fire and water, but you brought us to a
66: 13 [A] *I will* **come** *to* your temple with burnt offerings and fulfill
69: 1 [69:2] [A] O God, for the waters *have* **come** up to my neck.
69: 2 [69:3] [A] *I have* **come** into the deep waters; the floods engulf
69: 27 [69:28] [A] *do* not *let them* **share** in your salvation.
71: 3 [A] Be my rock of refuge, to which I *can* always **go**; give the
71: 16 [A] *I will* **come** and proclaim your mighty acts, O Sovereign
71: 18 [A] to the next generation, your might to all *who are to* **come**.
73: 17 [A] till *I* **entered** [+448] the sanctuary of God; then I understood
74: 5 [G] They behaved like *men* **wielding** [+2025+4200+5087] axes to
78: 29 [G] more than enough, for *he had* **given** them what they craved.
78: 54 [G] Thus *he* **brought** them to the border of his holy land,
78: 71 [G] from tending the sheep *he* **brought** him to be the shepherd of
79: 1 [A] O God, the nations *have* **invaded** [+928] your inheritance;
79: 11 [A] *May* the groans of the prisoners **come** before you;
86: 9 [A] All the nations you have made *will* **come** and worship before
88: 2 [88:3] [A] *May* my prayer **come** before you; turn your ear to my
90: 12 [G] number our days aright, that *we may* **gain** a heart of wisdom.
95: 6 [A] **Come**, let us bow down in worship, let us kneel before the
95: 11 [A] oath in my anger, "*They shall* never **enter** [+448] my rest."
96: 8 [A] due his name; bring an offering and **come** into his courts.
96: 13 [A] the LORD, for *he* **comes**, he comes to judge the earth.
96: 13 [A] the LORD, for he comes, *he* **comes** to judge the earth.
98: 9 [A] sing before the LORD, for *he* **comes** to judge the earth.
100: 2 [A] LORD with gladness; **come** before him with joyful songs.
100: 4 [A] **Enter** his gates with thanksgiving and his courts with praise;
101: 2 [A] careful to lead a blameless life—when *will you* **come** to me?
102: 1 [102:2] [A] O LORD; *let* my cry for help **come** to you.
102: 13 [102:14] [A] to show favor to her; the appointed time *has* **come**.
105: 18 [A] bruised his feet with shackles, his neck *was* **put in** irons,
105: 19 [A] till what he foretold **came to pass**, till the word of the
105: 23 [A] Israel **entered** Egypt; Jacob lived as an alien in the land of
105: 31 [A] He spoke, and *there* **came** swarms of flies, and gnats
105: 34 [A] He spoke, and the locusts **came**, grasshoppers without
105: 40 [G] *he* **brought** them quail and satisfied them with the bread of
109: 17 [A] He loved to pronounce a curse—*may it* **come** *on* him; he
109: 18 [A] *it* **entered** into his body like water, into his bones like oil.
118: 19 [A] *I will* **enter** [+928] and give thanks to the LORD.
118: 20 [A] gate of the LORD through which the righteous *may* **enter**.
118: 26 [A] Blessed is he *who* **comes** in the name of the LORD.
119: 41 [A] *May* your unfailing love **come** *to* me, O LORD,
119: 77 [A] *Let* your compassion **come** *to* me that I may live, for your
119: 170 [A] *May* my supplication **come** before you; deliver me according
121: 1 [A] lift up my eyes to the hills—where *does* my help **come** from?
121: 8 [A] the LORD will watch over your **coming** and going both
126: 6 [A] carrying seed to sow, *will* **return** [+995] with songs of joy,
126: 6 [A] carrying seed to sow, *will* **return** [+995] with songs of joy,
132: 3 [A] "*I will* not **enter** [+928] my house or go to my bed—
132: 7 [A] "*Let us* **go** to his dwelling place; let us worship at his
143: 2 [A] *Do* not **bring** [+907] your servant into judgment, for no one
Pr 1: 10 [A] My son, if sinners entice you, *do* not **give in** *to* them.
1: 26 [A] at your disaster; I will mock when calamity **overtakes** you—
1: 27 [A] when calamity **overtakes** you like a storm, when disaster
1: 27 [A] when distress and trouble **overwhelm** [+6584] you.
2: 10 [A] For wisdom *will* **enter** [+928] your heart, and knowledge
2: 19 [A] None *who* **go** *to* her return or attain the paths of life.
3: 25 [A] of sudden disaster or of the ruin that **overtakes** the wicked,
4: 14 [A] *Do* not **set foot** on the path of the wicked or walk in the way
6: 3 [A] since *you have* **fallen** into your neighbor's hands:
6: 11 [A] poverty *will* **come** *on* you like a bandit and scarcity like an
6: 15 [A] Therefore disaster *will* **overtake** him in an instant; he will
6: 29 [A] So is he *who* **sleeps** [+448] **with** another man's wife; no one
7: 20 [A] purse filled with money and *will* not **be** home till full moon."
7: 22 [A] All at once he followed her like an ox **going** to the slaughter,
10: 24 [A] What the wicked dreads *will* **overtake** him; what the
11: 2 [A] *When* pride **comes**, then comes disgrace, but with humility
11: 2 [A] When pride comes, then **comes** disgrace, but with humility
11: 8 [A] is rescued from trouble, and *it* **comes** *on* the wicked instead.
11: 27 [A] finds goodwill, but evil **comes** *to* him who searches for it.
13: 12 [A] makes the heart sick, but a longing **fulfilled** is a tree of life.
18: 3 [A] When wickedness **comes**, so does contempt, and with shame
18: 3 [A] When wickedness comes, so **does**[s] contempt, and with
18: 6 [A] A fool's lips **bring** him strife, and his mouth invites a
18: 17 [A] seems right, till another **comes** *forward* and questions him.
21: 27 [G] how much more so *when* **brought** with evil intent!
22: 24 [A] hot-tempered man, *do* not **associate** with one easily angered,
23: 10 [A] boundary stone or **encroach** on the fields of the fatherless,
23: 12 [G] **Apply** your heart to instruction and your ears to words of
23: 30 [A] linger over wine, who **go** to sample bowls of mixed wine.
24: 25 [A] convict the guilty, and rich blessing *will* **come** upon them.
24: 34 [A] poverty *will* **come** *on* you like a bandit and scarcity like an
26: 2 [A] darting swallow, an undeserved curse *does* not **come to rest**.
27: 10 [A] *do* not **go** *to* your brother's house when disaster strikes you—
28: 22 [A] is eager to get rich and is unaware that poverty **awaits** him.
31: 14 [G] She is like the merchant ships, **bringing** her food from afar.
Ecc 1: 4 [A] Generations come and generations **go**, but the earth remains
1: 5 [A] The sun rises and the sun **sets**, and hurries back to where it
2: 12 [A] What more can the king's **successor** [+132+339+8611] do than
2: 16 [A] be long remembered; in days *to* **come** both will be forgotten.
3: 22 [G] For who *can* **bring** him to see what will happen after him?
5: 3 [5:2] [A] As a dream **comes** when there are many cares,
5: 15 [5:14] [A] his mother's womb, and as *he* **comes**, so he departs.
5: 16 [5:15] [A] As a *man* **comes**, so he departs, and what does he
6: 4 [A] *It* **comes** without meaning, it departs in darkness, and in
8: 10 [A] *those who used to* **come** and go from the holy place
9: 14 [A] a powerful king **came** against it, surrounded it and built huge
11: 8 [A] for they will be many. Everything *to* **come** is meaningless.
11: 9 [G] know that for all these things God *will* **bring** you to
12: 1 [A] before the days of trouble **come** and the years approach when
12: 14 [G] For God *will* **bring** every deed into judgment,
SS 1: 4 [G] *Let* the king **bring** me **into** his chambers. We rejoice
2: 4 [G] *He has* **taken** me to the banquet hall, and his banner over me
2: 8 [A] Here *he* **comes**, leaping across the mountains, bounding over
3: 4 [G] would not let him go till *I had* **brought** him to my mother's
4: 8 [A] me from Lebanon, my bride, **come** with me from Lebanon.
4: 16 [A] Awake, north wind, and **come**, south wind! Blow on my
4: 16 [A] *Let* my lover **come** into his garden and taste its choice fruits.
5: 1 [A] *I have* **come** into my garden, my sister, my bride; I have
8: 2 [G] I would lead you and **bring** you to my mother's house—
8: 11 [G] Each *was to* **bring** for its fruit a thousand shekels of silver.
Isa 1: 12 [A] When *you* **come** to appear before me, who has asked this of
1: 13 [G] Stop **bringing** meaningless offerings! Your incense is
1: 23 [A] the fatherless; the widow's case *does* not **come** before them.
2: 10 [A] **Go** into the rocks, hide in the ground from dread of the
2: 19 [A] *Men will* **flee** to caves in the rocks and to holes in the ground
2: 21 [A] They *will* **flee** to caverns in the rocks and to the overhanging
3: 14 [A] The LORD **enters** into judgment against the elders
5: 19 [A] Let it approach, *let* the plan of the Holy One of Israel **come**,
5: 26 [A] the ends of the earth. Here *they* **come**, swiftly and speedily!
7: 17 [G] *will* **bring** on you and on your people and on the house of your
7: 17 [A] on the house of your father a time unlike **[RPH]** any since
7: 19 [A] They *will* all **come** and settle in the steep ravines and in the
7: 24 [A] *Men will* **go** there with bow and arrow, for the land will be
7: 25 [A] *you will* no longer **go** there for fear of the briers and thorns;
10: 3 [A] do on the day of reckoning, when disaster **comes** from afar?
10: 28 [A] *They* **enter** [+6584] Aiath; they pass through Migron;
13: 2 [A] to them; beckon to them *to* **enter** the gates of the nobles.
13: 5 [A] *They* **come** from faraway lands, from the ends of the
13: 6 [A] is near; *it will* **come** like destruction from the Almighty.
13: 9 [A] See, the day of the LORD *is* **coming**—a cruel day,
13: 22 [A] Her time *is* **at hand** [+4200+7940], and her days will not be
14: 2 [G] Nations will take them and **bring** them to their own place.
14: 9 [A] The grave below is all astir to meet you *at* your **coming**;
14: 31 [A] A cloud of smoke **comes** from the north, and there is not a
16: 3 [G] "**Give** us counsel, render a decision. Make your shadow like
16: 12 [A] when *she* **goes** to her shrine to pray, it is to no avail.
19: 1 [A] the LORD rides on a swift cloud and *is* **coming** *to* Egypt.
19: 23 [A] The Assyrians *will* **go** to Egypt and the Egyptians to Assyria.
20: 1 [A] of Assyria, **came** to Ashdod and attacked and captured it—
21: 1 [A] *an invader* **comes** from the desert, from a land of terror.
21: 9 [A] Look, here **comes** a man in a chariot with a team of horses.
22: 15 [A] "**Go** [+2143], say to this steward, to Shebna, who is in charge
23: 1 [a] left without house or harbor. [BHS *one entering*; NIV 4427]
24: 10 [A] city lies desolate; the **entrance** *to* every house is barred.
26: 2 [A] Open the gates that the righteous nation *may* **enter**,
26: 20 [A] **enter** [+928] your rooms and shut the doors behind you;
27: 6 [A] *In* days *to* **come** Jacob will take root, Israel will bud
27: 11 [A] they are broken off and women **come** and make fires with
27: 13 [A] in Assyria and those who were exiled in Egypt *will* **come**
28: 15 [A] *it* cannot **touch** us, for we have made a lie our refuge

Isa 30: 8 [A] **Go** now, write it on a tablet for them, inscribe it on a scroll,
30: 13 [A] cracked and bulging, that **collapses** [+8691] suddenly, in an
30: 27 [A] See, the Name of the LORD **comes** from afar, with burning
30: 29 [A] go up with flutes **[RPH]** to the mountain of the LORD,
31: 2 [G] Yet he too is wise and *can* **bring** disaster; he does not take
32: 10 [A] grape harvest will fail, and the harvest of fruit *will* not **come**.
35: 4 [A] not fear; your God will come, *he will* **come** *with* vengeance;
35: 4 [A] with divine retribution he *will* **come** to save you."
35: 10 [A] *They will* **enter** Zion with singing; everlasting joy will
36: 6 [A] a man's hand and **wounds** [+928] him if he leans on it!
36: 17 [A] until I **come** and take you to a land like your own—a land of
36: 22 [A] and Joah son of Asaph the recorder **went** to Hezekiah,
37: 1 [A] put on sackcloth and **went into** the temple of the LORD.
37: 3 [A] as when children **come** to the point of birth and there is no
37: 5 [A] When King Hezekiah's officials **came** to Isaiah,
37: 24 [A] *I have* **reached** its remotest heights, the finest of its forests.
37: 26 [G] now *I have* **brought** it **to pass**, that you have turned fortified
37: 28 [A] "But I know where you stay and *when* you **come** and go and
37: 29 [A] and I will make you return by the way *you* **came**.
37: 33 [A] "*He will* not **enter** [+448] this city or shoot an arrow here.
37: 34 [A] By the way that *he* **came** he will return; he will not enter this
37: 34 [A] *he will* not **enter** [+448] this city," declares the LORD.
38: 1 [A] The prophet Isaiah son of Amoz **went** to him and said, "This
39: 3 [A] Then Isaiah the prophet **went** to King Hezekiah and asked,
39: 3 [A] "What did those men say, and where *did they* **come** from?"
39: 3 [A] Hezekiah replied. "*They* **came** to me from Babylon."
39: 6 [A] The time *will* surely **come** when everything in your palace,
40: 10 [A] See, the Sovereign LORD **comes** with power, and his arm
41: 3 [A] on unscathed, by a path his feet *have* not **traveled** before.
41: 22 [A] their final outcome. Or declare to us the *things to* **come**,
41: 25 [A] *He* **treads** *on* rulers as if they were mortar, as if he were a
42: 9 [A] See, the former things *have* **taken place**, and new things I
43: 5 [G] *I will* **bring** your children from the east and gather you from
43: 6 [G] **Bring** my sons from afar and my daughters from the ends of
43: 23 [G] *You have* not **brought** me sheep for burnt offerings, nor
44: 7 [A] what is yet to come—yes, let him foretell what *will* **come**.
45: 20 [A] "Gather together and **come**; assemble, you fugitives from the
45: 24 [A] strength.' " All who have raged against him *will* **come** to him
46: 11 [G] What I have said, that *will I* **bring about**; what I have
47: 5 [A] "Sit in silence, **go** into darkness, Daughter of the
47: 9 [A] Both of these *will* **overtake** you in a moment, on a single
47: 9 [A] *They will* **come** upon you in full measure, in spite of your
47: 11 [A] Disaster *will* **come** upon you, and you will not know how to
47: 11 [A] a catastrophe you cannot foresee *will* suddenly **come** upon
47: 13 [A] by month, let them save you from what *is* **coming** upon you.
48: 3 [A] them known; then suddenly I acted, and *they* **came to pass**.
48: 5 [A] before *they* **happened** I announced them to you so that you
48: 15 [G] *I will* **bring** him, and he will succeed in his mission.
49: 12 [A] See, they *will* **come** from afar—some from the north, some
49: 18 [A] and look around; all your sons gather and **come** to you.
49: 22 [G] *they will* **bring** your sons in their arms and carry your
50: 2 [A] *When* I **came**, why was there no one? When I called, why
51: 11 [A] *They will* **enter** Zion with singing; everlasting joy will
52: 1 [A] and defiled *will* not **enter** [+928] you again.
56: 1 [A] for my salvation is close **at hand** and my righteousness will
56: 7 [G] these *I will* **bring** to my holy mountain and give them joy in
57: 2 [A] Those who walk uprightly **enter** *into* peace; they find rest as
58: 7 [G] the hungry and *to* **provide** the poor wanderer *with* shelter—
59: 14 [A] truth has stumbled in the streets, honesty cannot **enter**.
59: 19 [A] For *he will* **come** like a pent-up flood that the breath of the
59: 20 [A] "The Redeemer *will* **come** to Zion, to those in Jacob who
60: 1 [A] "Arise, shine, for your light *has* **come**, and the glory of the
60: 4 [A] All assemble and **come** to you; your sons come from afar,
60: 4 [A] your sons **come** from afar, and your daughters are carried on
60: 5 [A] be brought to you, to you the riches of the nations *will* **come**.
60: 6 [A] all from Sheba *will* **come**, bearing gold and incense
60: 9 [G] **bringing** your sons from afar, with their silver and gold,
60: 11 [G] so that men *may* **bring** you the wealth of the nations—
60: 13 [A] "The glory of Lebanon *will* **come** to you, the pine, the fir
60: 17 [G] Instead of bronze *I will* **bring** you gold, and silver in place of
60: 17 [G] Instead of wood *I will* **bring** you bronze, and iron in place of
60: 20 [A] Your sun *will* never **set** again, and your moon will wane no
62: 11 [A] "Say to the Daughter of Zion, 'See, your Savior **comes**! See,
63: 1 [A] Who is this **coming** from Edom, from Bozrah, with his
63: 4 [A] was in my heart, and the year of my redemption *has* **come**.
66: 4 [G] for them and *will* **bring** upon them what they dread.
66: 7 [A] before the pains **come** upon her, she delivers a son.
66: 15 [A] See, the LORD *is* **coming** with fire, and his chariots are like
66: 18 [A] *am about to* **come** and gather all nations and tongues,
66: 18 [A] and tongues, and *they will* **come** and see my glory.
66: 20 [G] And *they will* **bring** all your brothers, from all the nations,
66: 20 [G] will bring them, as the Israelites **bring** their grain offerings,
66: 23 [A] all mankind *will* **come** and bow down before me,"
Jer 1: 15 [A] "Their kings *will* **come** and set up their thrones in the
2: 3 [A] and disaster **overtook** [+448] them,' " declares the LORD.
2: 7 [G] *I* **brought** you into a fertile land to eat its fruit and rich
2: 7 [A] *you* **came** and defiled my land and made my inheritance
2: 31 [A] 'We are free to roam; *we will* **come** to you no more'?
3: 14 [G] from a town and two from a clan—and **bring** you *to* Zion.
3: 18 [A] together *they will* **come** from a northern land to the land I
4: 5 [A] and say: 'Gather together! *Let us* **flee** to the fortified cities!'
4: 6 [G] For I *am* **bringing** disaster from the north, even terrible
4: 12 [A] a wind too strong for that **comes** from me. Now I pronounce
4: 16 [A] 'A besieging army *is* **coming** from a distant land, raising a
4: 29 [A] *Some* **go** into the thickets; some climb up among the rocks.
5: 12 [A] No harm *will* **come** to us; we will never see sword or famine.
5: 15 [G] the LORD, "I *am* **bringing** a distant nation against you—
6: 3 [A] Shepherds with their flocks *will* **come** against her; they will
6: 19 [G] I am **bringing** disaster on this people, the fruit of their
6: 20 [A] from Sheba **[NIE]** or sweet calamus from a distant land?
6: 22 [A] "Look, an army *is* **coming** from the land of the north; a great
6: 26 [A] an only son, for suddenly the destroyer *will* **come** upon us.
7: 2 [A] all you people of Judah who **come** through these gates to
7: 10 [A] then **come** and stand before me in this house, which bears my
7: 32 [A] So beware, the days *are* **coming**, declares the LORD,
8: 7 [A] the swift and the thrush observe the time of their **migration**.
8: 14 [A] *Let us* **flee** to the fortified cities and perish there!
8: 16 [A] *They have* **come** to devour the land and everything in it,
9: 17 [9:16] [A] Call for the wailing women *to* **come**; send for the
9: 17 [9:16] [A] to come; send for the most skillful of them. **[RPH]**
9: 21 [9:20] [A] our windows and *has* **entered** [+928] our fortresses;
9: 25 [9:24] [A] "The days *are* **coming**," declares the LORD,
10: 9 [H] Hammered silver **is brought** from Tarshish and gold from
10: 22 [A] The report *is* **coming**—a great commotion from the land of
11: 8 [G] So *I* **brought** on them all the curses of the covenant I had
11: 11 [G] 'I *will* **bring** on them a disaster they cannot escape. Although
11: 23 [G] because *I will* **bring** disaster on the men of Anathoth in the
12: 12 [A] all the barren heights in the desert destroyers *will* **swarm**,
13: 1 [G] it around your waist, but *do* not **let** it **touch** [+928] water."
13: 20 [A] up your eyes and see those *who are* **coming** from the north.
14: 3 [A] servants for water; *they* **go** to the cisterns but find no water.
14: 18 [A] the sword; if *I* **go into** the city, I see the ravages of famine.
15: 8 [G] At midday *I will* **bring** a destroyer against the mothers of
15: 9 [A] Her sun *will* **set** while it is still day; she will be disgraced
16: 5 [A] "*Do* not **enter** a house where there is a funeral meal; do not
16: 8 [A] "And *do* not **enter** a house where there is feasting and sit
16: 14 [A] "However, the days *are* **coming**," declares the LORD,
16: 19 [A] to you the nations *will* **come** from the ends of the earth
17: 6 [A] in the wastelands; he will not see prosperity when *it* **comes**.
17: 8 [A] It does not fear when heat **comes**; its leaves are always green.
17: 15 [A] "Where is the word of the LORD? *Let it* now *be* **fulfilled**!"
17: 18 [G] **Bring** on them the day of disaster; destroy them with double
17: 19 [A] the people, through which the kings of Judah **go in** and out;
17: 20 [A] everyone living in Jerusalem who **come** through these gates.
17: 21 [G] the Sabbath day or **bring** it through the gates of Jerusalem.
17: 24 [G] **bring** no load through the gates of this city on the Sabbath,
17: 25 [A] kings who sit on David's throne *will* **come** through the gates
17: 26 [A] *People will* **come** from the towns of Judah and the villages
17: 26 [G] and the Negev, **bringing** burnt offerings and sacrifices,
17: 26 [G] and **[RPH]** thank offerings to the house of the LORD.
17: 27 [A] you **come** through the gates of Jerusalem on the Sabbath day,
18: 22 [G] their houses when *you* suddenly **bring** invaders against them,
19: 3 [G] I *am going to* **bring** a disaster on this place that will make
19: 6 [A] So beware, the days *are* **coming**, declares the LORD,
19: 14 [A] Jeremiah then **returned** from Topheth, where the LORD
19: 15 [G] I *am going to* **bring** on this city and the villages around it
20: 5 [G] will take it away as plunder and **carry** it **off** to Babylon.
20: 6 [A] all who live in your house will go into exile **[RPH]** to
21: 13 [A] can come against us? Who *can* **enter** [+928] our refuge?"
22: 2 [A] and your people who **come** through these gates.
22: 4 [A] kings who sit on David's throne *will* **come** through the gates
22: 23 [A] how you will groan when pangs **come** upon you, pain like
23: 5 [A] "The days *are* **coming**," declares the LORD, "when I will
23: 7 [A] "So then, the days are **coming**," declares the LORD,
23: 8 [G] who brought the descendants of Israel up **[NIE]** out of the
23: 12 [G] *I will* **bring** disaster on them in the year they are punished,"
23: 17 [A] of their hearts they say, 'No harm *will* **come** to you.'
24: 1 [G] **[NIE]** to Babylon by Nebuchadnezzar king of Babylon,
25: 9 [G] "and *I will* **bring** them against this land and its inhabitants
25: 13 [G] *I will* **bring** upon that land all the things I have spoken
25: 31 [A] The tumult *will* **resound** to the ends of the earth, for the
26: 2 [A] speak to all the people of the towns of Judah who **come** to
26: 21 [A] But Uriah heard of it and fled in fear to **[NIE]** Egypt.
26: 23 [G] brought Uriah out of Egypt and **took** him to King Jehoiakim,
27: 3 [A] Sidon through the envoys who *have* **come** *to* Jerusalem to
27: 7 [A] his son and his grandson until the time for his land **comes**;
27: 11 [G] if any nation *will* **bow** its neck under the yoke of the king of
27: 12 [G] "**Bow** your neck under the yoke of the king of Babylon;

Jer 27:18 [A] the king of Judah and in Jerusalem not *be* **taken** to Babylon.
27:22 [H] '*They will* **be taken** to Babylon and there they will remain
28: 3 [G] king of Babylon removed from here and **took** *to* Babylon.
28: 4 [A] and all the other exiles from Judah who **went** to Babylon,'
28: 9 [A] truly sent by the LORD only if his prediction **comes true**."
30: 3 [A] The days *are* **coming**,' declares the LORD, 'when I will
31: 8 [G] I *will* **bring** them from the land of the north and gather them
31: 9 [A] *They will* **come** with weeping; they will pray as I bring them
31:12 [A] *They will* **come** and shout for joy on the heights of Zion;
31:27 [A] "The days *are* **coming**," declares the LORD, "when I will
31:31 [A] "The time *is* **coming**," declares the LORD, "when I will
31:38 [A] "The days *are* **coming**," [no K] declares the LORD,
32: 7 [A] Hanamel son of Shallum your uncle *is going to* **come** to you
32: 8 [A] my cousin Hanamel **came** to me in the courtyard of the guard
32:23 [A] *They* **came in** and took possession of it, but they did not
32:24 [A] "See how the siege ramps *are* **built up** to take the city.
32:29 [A] The Babylonians who are attacking this city *will* **come in**
32:42 [G] As *I have* **brought** all this great calamity on this people, so I
32:42 [G] so I *will* **give** them all the prosperity I have promised them.
33: 5 [A] **[NIE]** in the fight with the Babylonians: 'They will be filled
33:11 [G] the voices of *those who* **bring** thank offerings *to* the house
33:14 [A] " 'The days *are* **coming**,' declares the LORD, 'when I will
34: 3 [A] speak with you face to face. And *you will* **go** *to* Babylon.
34:10 [A] people who **entered** into this covenant agreed that they
35: 2 [G] invite them *to* **come** to one of the side rooms of the house of
35: 4 [G] *I* **brought** them into the house of the LORD, into the room
35:11 [A] we said, '**Come**, we must go to Jerusalem to escape the
35:11 [A] *we must* **go** *to* Jerusalem to escape the Babylonian
35:17 [G] *am going to* **bring** on Judah and on everyone living in
36: 5 [A] "I am restricted; I cannot **go** *to* the LORD's temple.
36: 6 [A] So you **go** *to* the house of the LORD on a day of fasting
36: 6 [A] Read them to all the people of Judah who **come in** from their
36: 9 [A] and those *who had* **come** from the towns of Judah.
36:14 [A] So Baruch son of Neriah **went** to them with the scroll in his
36:20 [A] *they* **went** to the king in the courtyard and reported
36:29 [A] on it that the king of Babylon *would* **certainly come** [+995]
36:29 [A] on it that the king of Babylon *would* **certainly come** [+995]
36:31 [G] *I will* **bring** on them and those living in Jerusalem and the
37: 4 [A] Now Jeremiah *was free to* **come** and go among the people,
37:14 [G] he arrested Jeremiah and **brought** him to the officials.
37:16 [A] Jeremiah *was* **put** into a vaulted cell in a dungeon, where he
37:19 [A] 'The king of Babylon *will* not **attack** [+6584] you or this
38:11 [A] with him and **went** to a room under the treasury in the palace.
38:25 [A] *they* **come** to you and say, 'Tell us what you said to the king
38:27 [A] All the officials *did* **come** to Jeremiah and question him,
39: 1 [A] Nebuchadnezzar king of Babylon **marched** against
39: 3 [A] all the officials of the king of Babylon **came** and took seats
39: 7 [G] and bound him with bronze shackles to **take** him to Babylon.
39:16 [G] I *am about to* **fulfill** my words against this city through
40: 3 [G] now the LORD *has* **brought** it **about**; he has done just as
40: 4 [A] **Come** with me to Babylon, if you like, and I will look after
40: 4 [A] me to Babylon, **[RPH]** if you like, and I will look after you;
40: 4 [A] look after you; but if you do not want to, then don't **come**.
40: 6 [A] So Jeremiah **went** to Gedaliah son of Ahikam at Mizpah
40: 8 [A] *they* **came** to Gedaliah at Mizpah—Ishmael son of
40:10 [A] to represent you before the Babylonians who **come** to us,
40:12 [A] they all came back **[NIE]** to the land of Judah, to Gedaliah
40:13 [A] all the army officers still in the open country **came** to
41: 1 [A] **came** with ten men to Gedaliah son of Ahikam at Mizpah.
41: 5 [A] torn their clothes and cut themselves **came** from Shechem,
41: 5 [G] **bringing** grain offerings and incense with them to the house
41: 6 [A] he met them, he said, "**Come** to Gedaliah son of Ahikam."
41: 7 [A] When they **went** into the city, Ishmael son of Nethaniah and
41:17 [A] Kimham near Bethlehem on their way **[NIE]** to Egypt
42:14 [A] if you say, 'No, *we will* **go** and live in Egypt, where we will
42:15 [A] 'If you are determined to **go** *to* Egypt and you do go to settle
42:15 [A] are determined to go to Egypt and *you do* **go** to settle there,
42:17 [A] all who are determined to **go** *to* Egypt to settle there will die
42:17 [G] them will survive or escape the disaster I *will* **bring** on them.'
42:18 [A] so will my wrath be poured out on you when you **go** *to*
42:19 [A] of Judah, the LORD has told you, '*Do* not **go** *to* Egypt.'
42:22 [A] and plague in the place where you want to **go** to settle."
43: 2 [A] sent you to say, '*You must* not **go** *to* Egypt to settle there.'
43: 7 [A] So *they* **entered** Egypt in disobedience to the LORD
43: 7 [A] in disobedience to the LORD and **went** as far as Tahpanhes.
43:11 [A] *He will* **come** and attack Egypt, bringing death to those
44: 2 [G] You saw the great disaster *I* **brought** on Jerusalem and on all
44: 8 [A] to other gods in Egypt, where you *have* **come** to live?
44:12 [A] of Judah who were determined to **go** *to* Egypt to settle there.
44:14 [A] None of the remnant of Judah who *have* **gone** to live in
44:28 [A] the whole remnant of Judah who **came** to live in Egypt will
45: 5 [G] For I *will* **bring** disaster on all people, declares the LORD,
46:13 [A] **coming** *of* Nebuchadnezzar king of Babylon to attack Egypt:
46:18 [A] "*one will* **come** who is like Tabor among the mountains, like
46:20 [A] but a gadfly *is* **coming** against her from the north.
46:21 [A] their ground, for the day of disaster *is* **coming** upon them,
46:22 [A] *they will* **come** against her with axes, like men who cut down
47: 4 [A] For the day *has* **come** to destroy all the Philistines and to cut
47: 5 [A] Gaza *will* **shave** *her* **head in mourning** [+448+7947];
48: 8 [A] The destroyer *will* **come** against every town, and not a town
48:12 [A] days *are* **coming**," declares the LORD, "when I will send
48:16 [A] "The fall of Moab *is* **at hand** [+7940]; her calamity will
48:21 [A] Judgment *has* **come** to the plateau—to Holon, Jahzah
48:44 [G] for *I will* **bring** upon Moab the year of her punishment,"
49: 2 [A] the days *are* **coming**," declares the LORD, "when I will
49: 4 [A] trust in your riches and say, 'Who *will* **attack** [+448] me?'
49: 5 [G] I *will* **bring** terror on you from all those around you,"
49: 8 [G] for *I will* **bring** disaster on Esau at the time I punish him.
49: 9 [A] If grape pickers **came** to you, would they not leave a few
49:14 [A] nations to say, "Assemble yourselves *to* **attack** [+6584] it!
49:32 [G] and *will* **bring** disaster *on* them from every side,"
49:36 [G] *I will* **bring** against Elam the four winds from the four
49:36 [A] and there will not be a nation where Elam's exiles *do* not **go**.
49:37 [G] *I will* **bring** disaster upon them, even my fierce anger,"
50: 4 [A] the people of Judah together *will* **go** in tears to seek the
50: 5 [A] *They will* **come** and bind themselves to the LORD in an
50:26 [A] **Come** against her from afar. Break open her granaries;
50:27 [A] For their day *has* **come**, the time for them to be punished.
50:31 [A] the Lord, the LORD Almighty, "for your day *has* **come**,
50:41 [A] An army *is* **coming** from the north; a great nation and many
51:10 [A] **come**, let us tell in Zion what the LORD our God has done.'
51:13 [A] by many waters and are rich in treasures, your end *has* **come**,
51:33 [A] time it is trampled; the time to harvest her *will* soon **come**."
51:46 [A] one rumor **comes** this year, another the next, rumors of
51:47 [A] For the time *will* surely **come** when I will punish the idols of
51:48 [A] for out of the north destroyers *will* **attack** [+4200] her,"
51:51 [A] because foreigners *have* **entered** [+6584] the holy places of
51:52 [A] "But days *are* **coming**," declares the LORD, "when I will
51:53 [A] I *will* **send** [+907+4946] destroyers against her,"
51:56 [A] A destroyer *will* **come** against Babylon; her warriors will be
51:60 [A] about all the disasters that *would* **come** upon Babylon—
51:61 [A] He said to Seraiah, "When you **get** *to* Babylon, see that you
51:64 [G] to rise no more because of the disaster I *will* **bring** upon her.
52: 4 [A] Nebuchadnezzar king of Babylon **marched** against
52: 5 [A] The city *was* **kept** under siege until the eleventh year of King
52:11 [G] bound him with bronze shackles and **took** him to Babylon,
52:12 [A] who served the king of Babylon, **came** to Jerusalem.
La 1: 4 [A] to Zion mourn, for no *one* **comes** *to* her appointed feasts.
1:10 [A] all her treasures; she saw pagan nations **enter** her sanctuary—
1:10 [A] those you had forbidden *to* **enter** [+928] your assembly.
1:21 [G] *May you* **bring** the day you have announced so they may
1:22 [A] "*Let* all their wickedness **come** before you; deal with them as
3:13 [G] *He* **pierced** [+928] my heart *with* arrows from his quiver.
4:12 [A] and foes *could* **enter** [+928] the gates of Jerusalem.
4:18 [A] was near, our days were numbered, for our end *had* **come**.
5: 4 [A] the water we drink; our wood *can be* **had**[s] only at a price.
5: 9 [G] *We* **get** our bread at the risk of our lives because of the sword
Eze 1: 4 [A] I looked, and I saw a windstorm **coming** out of the north—
2: 2 [A] he spoke, the Spirit **came** into me and raised me to my feet,
3: 4 [A] **go now** [+2143] to the house of Israel and speak my words to
3:11 [A] **Go now** [+2143] to your countrymen in exile and speak to
3:15 [A] *I* **came** to the exiles who lived at Tel Abib near the Kebar
3:24 [A] the Spirit **came** into me and raised me to my feet. He spoke
3:24 [A] spoke to me and said: "**Go**, shut yourself inside your house.
4:14 [A] No unclean meat *has ever* **entered** [+928] my mouth."
5:17 [G] sweep through you, and *I will* **bring** the sword against you.
6: 3 [G] I *am about to* **bring** a sword against you, and I will destroy
7: 2 [A] The end *has* **come** upon the four corners of the land.
7: 5 [A] LORD says: Disaster! An unheard-of disaster *is* **coming**.
7: 6 [A] The end *has* **come**! The end has come! It has roused itself
7: 6 [A] The end has come! The end *has* **come**! It has roused itself
7: 6 [A] end has come! It has roused itself against you. *It has* **come**!
7: 7 [A] Doom *has* **come** upon you—you who dwell in the land.
7: 7 [A] The time *has* **come**, the day is near; there is panic, not joy,
7:10 [A] "The day is here! *It has* **come**! Doom has burst forth, the rod
7:12 [A] The time *has* **come**, the day has arrived. Let not the buyer
7:22 [A] treasured place; robbers *will* **enter** [+928] it and desecrate it.
7:24 [G] *I will* **bring** the most wicked of the nations to take
7:25 [A] *When* terror **comes**, they will seek peace, but there will be
7:26 [A] Calamity upon calamity *will* **come**, and rumor upon rumor.
8: 3 [G] and heaven and in visions of God *he* **took** me to Jerusalem,
8: 7 [G] Then *he* **brought** me to the entrance to the court. I looked,
8: 9 [A] "**Go in** and see the wicked and detestable things they are
8:10 [A] So *I* **went in** and looked, and I saw portrayed all over the
8:14 [G] *he* **brought** me to the entrance to the north gate of the house
8:16 [G] *He* then **brought** me into the inner court of the house of the
9: 2 [A] I saw six men **coming** from the direction of the upper gate,
9: 2 [A] at his side. *They* **came in** and stood beside the bronze altar.

Eze 10: 2 [A] in linen, "**Go** in among the wheels beneath the cherubim.
10: 2 [A] scatter them over the city." And as I watched, *he* **went in**.
10: 3 [A] on the south side of the temple when the man **went in**,
10: 6 [A] the cherubim," the man **went in** and stood beside a wheel.
11: 1 [G] **brought** me to the gate of the house of the LORD that faces
11: 8 [G] the sword, and the sword is what *I will* **bring** against you,
11:16 [A] a sanctuary for them in the countries where *they have* **gone**.'
11:18 [A] "*They will* **return** to it and remove all its vile images
11:24 [G] **brought** me to the exiles in Babylonia in the vision given by
12:13 [G] *I will* **bring** him to Babylonia, the land of the Chaldeans,
12:16 [A] so that in the nations where *they* **go** they may acknowledge
13: 9 [A] house of Israel, nor *will they* **enter** [+448] the land of Israel.
14: 1 [A] Some of the elders of Israel **came** to me and sat down in
14: 4 [A] stumbling block before his face and then **goes** to a prophet,
14: 4 I the LORD will answer him **myself** [BHS 2023] in keeping with
14: 7 [A] before his face and then **goes** to a prophet to inquire of me,
14:17 [G] "Or if *I* **bring** a sword against that country and say,
14:22 [G] you will be consoled regarding the disaster *I have* **brought**
14:22 [G] upon Jerusalem—every disaster *I have* **brought** upon it.
16: 7 [A] and developed and **became** the most beautiful of jewels.
16: 8 [A] you my solemn oath and **entered** into a covenant with you,
16:16 [A] *Such things should* not **happen**, nor should they ever occur.
16:33 [A] bribing them to **come** to you from everywhere for your illicit
17: 3 [A] and full plumage of varied colors **came** to Lebanon.
17: 4 [G] its topmost shoot and **carried** it **away** to a land of merchants,
17:12 [A] 'The king of Babylon **went** *to* Jerusalem and carried off her
17:12 [G] and her nobles, **bringing** them *back* with him to Babylon.
17:13 [G] and made a treaty with him, **putting** him under oath.
17:20 [G] *I will* **bring** him to Babylon and execute judgment upon him
19: 4 [G] in their pit. *They* **led** him with hooks to the land of Egypt.
19: 9 [G] him into a cage and **brought** him to the king of Babylon.
19: 9 [G] *They* **put** him in prison, so his roar was heard no longer on
20: 1 [A] some of the elders of Israel **came** to inquire of the LORD,
20: 3 [A] *Have* you **come** to inquire of me? As surely as I live, I will
20:10 [G] I led them out of Egypt and **brought** them into the desert.
20:15 [G] that I *would* not **bring** them into the land I had given them—
20:28 [G] When *I* **brought** them into the land I had sworn to give them
20:29 [A] What is this high place you **go** *to*?' " (It is called Bamah to
20:35 [G] *I will* **bring** you into the desert of the nations and there,
20:37 [G] my rod, and *I will* **bring** you into the bond of the covenant.
20:38 [A] are living, yet *they will* not **enter** [+448] the land of Israel.
20:42 [G] I am the LORD, when I **bring** you into the land of Israel,
21: 7 [21:12] [A] you shall say, 'Because of the news that *is* **coming**.
21: 7 [21:12] [A] *It is* **coming**! It will surely take place,
21:19 [21:24] [A] roads for the sword of the king of Babylon to **take**,
21:20 [21:25] [A] Mark out one road for the sword to **come** against
21:25 [21:30] [A] and wicked prince of Israel, whose day *has* **come**,
21:27 [21:32] [A] It will not be restored until he **comes** to whom it
21:29 [21:34] [A] whose day *has* **come**, whose time of punishment
22: 3 [A] O city *that* **brings** *on* herself doom by shedding blood in her
22: 4 [A] your days to a close, and the end of your years *has* **come**.
23:17 [A] the Babylonians **came** to her, to the bed of love, and in their
23:22 [G] and *I will* **bring** them against you from every side—
23:24 [A] *They will* **come** against you with weapons, chariots
23:39 [A] *they* **entered** [+448] my sanctuary and desecrated it.
23:40 [A] "They even sent messengers for men *who* **came** from far
23:40 [A] when *they* **arrived** you bathed yourself for them,
23:42 [H] Sabeans **were brought** from the desert along with men from
23:44 [A] *they* **slept** [+448] **with** her. As men sleep with a prostitute,
23:44 [A] As *men* **sleep** [+448] **with** a prostitute, so they slept with
23:44 [A] so *they* **slept** [+448] **with** those lewd women, Oholah
24:14 [A] The time *has* **come** for me to act. I will not hold back; I will
24:16 [A] of your eyes. Yet do not lament or weep or **shed** any tears.
24:24 [A] When this **happens**, you will know that I am the Sovereign
24:26 [A] on that day a fugitive *will* **come** to tell you the news.
26: 7 [G] From the north I *am going to* **bring** against Tyre
26:10 [A] chariots when he **enters** [+928] your gates as men enter a
27:26 [G] Your oarsmen **take** you **out** to the high seas. But the east
28: 7 [G] I *am going to* **bring** foreigners against you, the most ruthless
29: 8 [G] I *will* **bring** a sword against you and kill your men and their
30: 4 [A] A sword *will* **come** against Egypt, and anguish will come
30: 9 [A] of them on the day of Egypt's doom, for it is sure *to* **come**.
30:11 [H] ruthless of nations—*will* **be brought in** to destroy the land.
32: 9 [G] I will trouble the hearts of many peoples when I **bring about**
32:11 [A] " 'The sword of the king of Babylon *will* **come** *against* you.
33: 2 [G] 'When *I* **bring** the sword against a land, and the people of the
33: 3 [A] he sees the sword **coming** against the land and blows the
33: 4 [A] not take warning and the sword **comes** and takes his life,
33: 6 [A] if the watchman sees the sword **coming** and does not blow
33: 6 [A] and the sword **comes** and takes the life of one of them,
33:21 [A] a man who had escaped from Jerusalem **came** to me
33:22 [A] Now the evening before the man **arrived**, the hand of the
33:22 [A] he opened my mouth before the man **came** to me in the
33:30 [A] '**Come** and hear the message that has come from the
33:31 [A] My people **come** to you, as they usually do, and sit before
33:33 [A] "When all this **comes true**—and it surely will—then they
33:33 [A] "When all this comes true—and *it* surely **will**"—then they
34:13 [G] from the countries, and *I will* **bring** them into their own land.
36: 8 [A] fruit for my people Israel, for *they will* soon **come home**.
36:20 [A] wherever *they* **went** among the nations they profaned my
36:20 [A] wherever they went **[RPH]** among the nations they
36:21 [A] of Israel profaned among the nations where *they had* **gone**.
36:22 [A] you have profaned among the nations where *you have* **gone**.
36:24 [G] all the countries and **bring** you **back** into your own land.
37: 5 [G] I *will* **make** breath **enter** [+928] you, and you will come to
37: 9 [A] **Come** from the four winds, O breath, and breathe into these
37:10 [A] as he commanded me, and breath **entered** [+928] them;
37:12 [G] up from them; *I will* **bring** you **back** to the land of Israel.
37:21 [G] from all around and **bring** them **back** into their own land.
38: 8 [A] In future years *you will* **invade** [+448] a land that has
38: 9 [A] many nations with you will go up, **advancing** like a storm;
38:11 [A] *I will* **attack** a peaceful and unsuspecting people—all of
38:13 [A] all her villages will say to you, "*Have* you **come** to plunder?
38:15 [A] *You will* **come** from your place in the far north, you
38:16 [G] In days to come, O Gog, *I will* **bring** you against my land,
38:17 [G] At that time they prophesied for years that I *would* **bring** you
38:18 [A] When Gog **attacks** [+6584] the land of Israel, my hot anger
39: 2 [G] the far north and **send** you against the mountains of Israel.
39: 8 [A] *It is* **coming**! It will surely take place, declares the Sovereign
39:17 [A] **come** together from all around to the sacrifice I am preparing
40: 1 [G] the hand of the LORD was upon me and *he* **took** me there.
40: 2 [G] In visions of God *he* **took** me to the land of Israel and set me
40: 3 [G] *He* **took** me there, and I saw a man whose appearance was
40: 4 [H] to show you, for that is why *you have* **been brought** here.
40: 6 [A] Then *he* **went** to the gate facing east. He climbed its steps
40:17 [G] *he* **brought** me into the outer court. There I saw some rooms
40:28 [G] *he* **brought** me into the inner court through the south gate,
40:32 [G] *he* **brought** me to the inner court on the east side, and he
40:35 [G] *he* **brought** me to the north gate and measured it. It had the
40:48 [G] *He* **brought** me to the portico of the temple and measured
41: 1 [G] the man **brought** me to the outer sanctuary and measured the
41: 3 [A] *he* **went** into the inner sanctuary and measured the jambs of
41: 6 [A] There were **ledges** all around the wall of the temple to serve
42: 1 [G] and **brought** me to the rooms opposite the temple courtyard
42: 9 [g] [The lower rooms had an **entrance** [Q; see K 4427] on the east]
42: 9 [A] east side as one **enters** [+4200] them from the outer court.
42:12 [A] wall extending eastward, by which *one* **enters** the rooms.
42:14 [A] Once the priests **enter** the holy precincts, they are not to go
43: 2 [A] I saw the glory of the God of Israel **coming** from the east.
43: 3 [A] vision I saw was like the vision I had seen when he **came**
43: 4 [A] The glory of the LORD **entered** [+448] the temple through
43: 5 [G] the Spirit lifted me up and **brought** me into the inner court,
44: 2 [A] It must not be opened; no one *may* **enter** through it. It is to
44: 2 [A] the LORD, the God of Israel, *has* **entered** through it.
44: 3 [A] *He is to* **enter** by way of the portico of the gateway and go
44: 4 [G] the man **brought** me by way of the north gate to the front of
44: 7 [G] you **brought** foreigners uncircumcised in heart and flesh into
44: 9 [A] in heart and flesh *is to* **enter** [+448] my sanctuary,
44:16 [A] They alone *are to* **enter** [+448] my sanctuary; they alone are
44:17 [A] " 'When they **enter** [+448] the gates of the inner court,
44:21 [A] No priest is to drink wine when he **enters** [+448] the inner
44:25 [A] " 'A priest must not defile himself by **going** near a dead
44:27 [A] On the day he **goes** into the inner court of the sanctuary to
46: 2 [A] The prince *is to* **enter** from the outside through the portico of
46: 8 [A] When the prince **enters**, he is to go in through the portico of
46: 8 [A] *he is to* **go in** through the portico of the gateway,
46: 9 [A] " 'When the people of the land **come** before the LORD at
46: 9 [A] whoever **enters** by the north gate to worship is to go out the
46: 9 [A] whoever **enters** by the south gate is to go out the north gate.
46: 9 [A] one is to return through the gate by which *he* **entered** [+928],
46:10 [A] **going in** when they go in and going out when they go out.
46:10 [A] going in when they **go in** and going out when they go out.
46:19 [G] the man **brought** me through the entrance at the side of the
47: 8 [A] goes down into the Arabah, where *it* **enters** [+2025] the Sea.
47: 9 [A] Swarms of living creatures will live wherever the river **flows**.
47: 9 [A] because this water **flows** there and makes the salt water fresh;
47: 9 [A] salt water fresh; so where the river **flows** everything will live.
Da 1: 1 [A] Nebuchadnezzar king of Babylon **came** *to* Jerusalem
1: 2 [G] These *he* **carried off** *to* the temple of his god in Babylonia
1: 2 [G] god in Babylonia and **put in** the treasure house of his god.
1: 3 [G] to **bring in** some of the Israelites from the royal family
1:18 [G] At the end of the time set by the king to **bring** them **in**,
1:18 [G] the chief official **presented** them to Nebuchadnezzar.
2: 2 [A] had dreamed. When *they* **came in** and stood before the king,
8: 5 [A] with a prominent horn between his eyes **came** from the west,
8: 6 [A] *He* **came** toward the two-horned ram I had seen standing
8:17 [A] As *he* **came** near the place where I was standing, I was
8:17 [A] I was standing, **[RPH]** I was terrified and fell prostrate.

Da 9:12 [G] and against our rulers by **bringing** upon us great disaster.
9:13 [A] in the Law of Moses, all this disaster *has* **come** upon us,
9:14 [G] The LORD did not hesitate *to* **bring** the disaster upon us,
9:23 [A] an answer was given, which I *have* **come** to tell you, for you
9:24 [G] to **bring in** everlasting righteousness, to seal up vision
9:26 [A] The people of the ruler who *will* **come** will destroy the city
10: 3 [A] ate no choice food; no meat or wine **touched** [+448] my lips;
10:12 [A] words were heard, and I *have* **come** in response to them.
10:13 [A] Michael, one of the chief princes, **came** to help me, because I
10:14 [A] Now *I have* **come** to explain to you what will happen to your
10:20 [A] So he said, "Do you know why *I have* **come** to you? Soon I
10:20 [A] of Persia, and when I go, the prince of Greece *will* **come**;
11: 6 [A] The daughter of the king of the South *will* **go** to the king of
11: 6 [G] together with her royal **escort** and her father and the one who
11: 7 [A] *He will* **attack** [+448] the forces of the king of the North
11: 7 [A] forces of the king of the North and **enter** [+928] his fortress;
11: 8 [G] and **carry** [+928+2021+8660] them **off** *to* Egypt.
11: 9 [A] the king of the North *will* **invade** [+928] the realm of the
11:10 [A] *which will* **sweep** [+995] **on** like an irresistible flood
11:10 [A] *which will* **sweep on** [+995] like an irresistible flood
11:13 [A] *he will* **advance** [+995] with a huge army fully equipped.
11:13 [A] *he will* **advance** [+995] with a huge army fully equipped.
11:15 [A] the king of the North *will* **come** and build up siege ramps
11:16 [A] The **invader** [+448] will do as he pleases; no one will be able
11:17 [A] He will determine to **come** with the might of his entire
11:21 [A] *He will* **invade** the kingdom when its people feel secure,
11:24 [A] *he will* **invade** them and will achieve what neither his fathers
11:29 [A] "At the appointed time *he will* **invade** [+928] the South
11:30 [A] Ships of the western coastlands *will* **oppose** [+928] him,
11:40 [A] *He will* **invade** [+928] many countries and sweep through
11:41 [A] *He will* also **invade** [+928] the Beautiful Land. Many
11:45 [A] Yet *he will* **come** to his end, and no one will help him.
Hos 4:15 [A] "*Do* not **go** *to* Gilgal; do not go up to Beth Aven. And do not
6: 3 [A] *he will* **come** to us like the winter rains, like the spring rains
7: 1 [A] They practice deceit, thieves **break into** houses, bandits rob
9: 4 [A] *it will* not **come into** the temple of the LORD.
9: 7 [A] The days of punishment *are* **coming**, the days of reckoning
9: 7 [A] punishment are coming, the days of reckoning *are* **at hand**.
9:10 [A] when they **came** *to* Baal Peor, they consecrated themselves
10:12 [A] until *he* **comes** and showers righteousness on you.
11: 9 [A] the Holy One among you. *I will* not **come** in wrath.
13:13 [A] Pains as of a woman in childbirth **come** to him, but he is a
13:15 [A] An east wind from the LORD *will* **come**, blowing in from
Joel 1:13 [A] **Come**, spend the night in sackcloth, you who minister before
1:15 [A] is near; *it will* **come** like destruction from the Almighty.
2: 1 [A] live in the land tremble, for the day of the LORD *is* **coming**.
2: 9 [A] into the houses; like thieves *they* **enter** through the windows.
2:31 [3:4] [A] the moon to blood before the **coming** *of* the great
3: 5 [4:5] [G] and **carried off** my finest treasures to your temples.
3:11 [4:11] [A] **Come** quickly, all you nations from every side,
3:13 [4:13] [A] **Come**, trample the grapes, for the winepress is full
Am 4: 1 [G] the needy and say to your husbands, "**Bring** us some drinks!"
4: 2 [A] "The time *will* surely **come** when you will be taken away
4: 4 [A] "**Go** *to* Bethel and sin; go to Gilgal and sin yet more. Bring
4: 4 [G] **Bring** your sacrifices every morning, your tithes every three
5: 5 [A] do not seek Bethel, *do* not **go** *to* Gilgal, do not journey to
5: 9 [A] on the stronghold and **brings** the fortified city to ruin),
5:19 [A] as though *he* **entered** his house and rested his hand on the
6: 1 [A] of the foremost nation, to whom the people of Israel **come**!
8: 2 [A] said to me, "The **time is ripe** [+7891] for my people Israel;
8: 9 [G] "*I will* **make** the sun **go down** at noon and darken the earth
8:11 [A] "The days *are* **coming**," declares the Sovereign LORD,
9:13 [A] "The days *are* **coming**," declares the LORD,
Ob 1: 5 [A] "If thieves **came** to you, if robbers in the night—Oh, what a
1: 5 [A] If grape pickers **came** to you, would they not leave a few
1:11 [A] and foreigners **entered** his gates and cast lots for Jerusalem,
1:13 [A] *You should* not **march** through the gates of my people in the
Jnh 1: 3 [A] down to Joppa, where he found a ship **bound** *for* that port.
1: 3 [A] went aboard and **sailed** for Tarshish to flee from the LORD.
1: 8 [A] What do you do? Where *do you* **come** from? What is your
2: 7 [2:8] [A] I remembered you, LORD, and my prayer **rose** to
3: 4 [A] On the first day, Jonah started **[NIE]** into the city. He
Mic 1: 9 [A] For her wound is incurable; *it has* **come** to Judah. It has
1:15 [G] *I will* **bring** a conqueror against you who live in Mareshah.
1:15 [A] *He* who is the glory of Israel *will* **come** to Adullam.
3: 6 [A] The sun *will* **set** for the prophets, and the day will go dark for
3:11 [A] not the LORD among us? No disaster *will* **come** upon us."
4: 8 [A] to you; kingship *will* **come** to the Daughter of Jerusalem."
4:10 [A] *You will* **go** to Babylon; there you will be rescued.
5: 5 [5:4] [A] When the Assyrian **invades** [+928] our land
5: 6 [5:5] [A] us from the Assyrian when *he* **invades** [+928] our land
7: 4 [A] The day of your watchmen *has* **come**, the day God visits you.
7:12 [A] In that day *people will* **come** to you from Assyria
Na 3:14 [A] **Work** the clay, tread the mortar, repair the brickwork!
Hab 1: 8 [A] cavalry gallops headlong; their horsemen **come** from afar.
1: 9 [A] they all **come** bent on violence. Their hordes advance like a
2: 3 [A] wait for it; *it will* **certainly come** [+995] and will not delay.
2: 3 [A] wait for it; *it will* **certainly come** [+995] and will not delay.
3: 3 [A] God **came** from Teman, the Holy One from Mount Paran.
3:16 [A] the sound; decay **crept** into my bones, and my legs trembled.
Zep 2: 2 [A] before the fierce anger of the LORD **comes** upon you,
2: 2 [A] before the day of the LORD's wrath **comes** upon you.
3:20 [G] time I will gather you; at that time *I will* **bring** you **home**.
Hag 1: 2 [A] 'The time *has* not *yet* **come** for the LORD's house to be
1: 6 [G] You have planted much, but *have* **harvested** little. You eat,
1: 8 [G] the mountains and **bring down** timber and build the house,
1: 9 [G] to be little. What *you* **brought** home, I blew away. Why?"
1:14 [A] *They* **came** and began to work on the house of the LORD
2: 7 [A] shake all nations, and the desired of all nations *will* **come**,
2:16 [A] When anyone **came** to a heap of twenty measures, there were
2:16 [A] *When anyone* **went** to a wine vat to draw fifty measures,
Zec 1:21 [2:4] [A] I asked, "What are these **coming** to do?" He answered,
1:21 [2:4] [A] the craftsmen *have* **come** to terrify them and throw
2:10 [2:14] [A] For I *am* **coming**, and I will live among you,"
3: 8 [G] things to come: I *am going to* **bring** my servant, the Branch.
5: 4 [A] *it will* **enter** [+448] the house of the thief and the house of
6:10 [A] and Jedaiah, who *have* **arrived** from Babylon.
6:10 [A] **Go** the same day *to* the house of Josiah son of Zephaniah.
6:10 [A] Go the same day **[RPH]** to the house of Josiah son of
6:15 [A] Those who are far away *will* **come** and help to build the
8: 8 [G] *I will* **bring** them **back** to live in Jerusalem; they will be my
8:10 [A] No one *could* **go about** *his* **business** [+2256+3655] safely
8:20 [A] and the inhabitants of many cities *will* yet **come**,
8:22 [A] powerful nations *will* **come** to Jerusalem to seek the LORD
9: 9 [A] See, your king **comes** to you, righteous and having salvation,
10:10 [G] *I will* **bring** them to Gilead and Lebanon, and there will not
12: 9 [A] out to destroy all the nations that **attack** [+6584] Jerusalem.
13: 9 [G] This third *I will* **bring** into the fire; I will refine them like
14: 1 [A] A day of the LORD *is* **coming** when your plunder will be
14: 5 [A] the LORD my God *will* **come**, and all the holy ones with
14:16 [A] the survivors from all the nations that *have* **attacked** [+6584]
14:18 [A] If the Egyptian people do not go up and **take part**, they will
14:21 [A] all who **come** to sacrifice will take some of the pots and cook
Mal 1:13 [G] "When *you* **bring** injured, crippled or diseased animals
1:13 [G] or diseased animals and **offer** them as sacrifices,
3: 1 [A] suddenly the Lord you are seeking *will* **come** to his temple;
3: 1 [A] whom you desire, *will* **come**," says the LORD Almighty.
3: 2 [A] who can endure the day of his **coming**? Who can stand when
3:10 [G] **Bring** the whole tithe into the storehouse, that there may be
4: 1 [3:19] [A] "Surely the day *is* **coming**; it will burn like a furnace.
4: 1 [3:19] [A] that day that *is* **coming** will set them on fire," says
4: 5 [3:23] [A] that great and dreadful day of the LORD **comes**.
4: 6 [3:24] [A] or else *I will* **come** and strike the land with a curse."

996 בּוּז bûz[1], v. [14] [→ 997, 998?, 999, 1000, 1001]

despise [4], despises [4], scorns [2], utterly scorned [+996+4200] [2], derides [1], scorn [1]

2Ki 19:21 [A] " 'The Virgin Daughter of Zion **despises** you and mocks you.
Pr 1: 7 [A] of knowledge, but fools **despise** wisdom and discipline.
6:30 [A] *Men do* not **despise** a thief if he steals to satisfy his hunger
11:12 [A] A man who lacks judgment **derides** his neighbor, but a man
13:13 [A] *He who* **scorns** instruction will pay for it, but he who
14:21 [A] *He who* **despises** his neighbor sins, but blessed is he who is
23: 9 [A] speak to a fool, for *he will* **scorn** the wisdom of your words.
23:22 [A] you life, and *do* not **despise** your mother when she is old.
30:17 [A] eye that mocks a father, *that* **scorns** obedience to a mother,
SS 8: 1 [A] you outside, I would kiss you, and no *one would* **despise** me.
8: 7 [A] house for love, it *would be* **utterly scorned** [+996+4200].
8: 7 [A] house for love, it *would be* **utterly scorned** [+996+4200].
Isa 37:22 [A] "The Virgin Daughter of Zion **despises** and mocks you.
Zec 4:10 [A] "Who **despises** the day of small things? Men will rejoice

997 בּוּז[2] bûz[2], n.m. [11] [√ 996]

contempt [9], despised [1], laughingstock [1]

Ge 38:23 "Let her keep what she has, or we will become a **laughingstock**.
Job 12: 5 Men at ease have **contempt** for misfortune as the fate of those
12:21 He pours **contempt** on nobles and disarms the mighty.
31:34 and so dreaded the **contempt** *of* the clans that I kept silent
Ps 31:18 [31:19] and **contempt** they speak arrogantly against the righteous.
107:40 he who pours **contempt** on nobles made them wander in a
119:22 Remove from me scorn and **contempt**, for I keep your statutes.
123: 3 have mercy on us, for we have endured much **contempt**.
123: 4 much ridicule from the proud, much **contempt** from the arrogant.
Pr 12: 8 to his wisdom, but men with warped minds are **despised**.
18: 3 When wickedness comes, so does **contempt**, and with shame

998 ³בּוּז ***bûz³***, n.pr.m. [3] [√ 996?]

Buz [3]

Ge 22: 21 Uz the firstborn, **Buz** his brother, Kemuel (the father of Aram),
1Ch 5: 14 of Michael, the son of Jeshishai, the son of Jahdo, the son of **Buz**.
Jer 25: 23 Dedan, Tema, **Buz** and all who are in distant places;

999 בּוּזָה ***bûzâ***, n.f. [1] [√ 996]

despised [1]

Ne 4: 4 [3:36] Hear us, O our God, for we are **despised**. Turn their insults

1000 בּוּזִי ***bûzî¹***, a.g. [2] [→ 1001; cf. 996]

Buzite [2]

Job 32: 2 But Elihu son of Barakel the **Buzite**, of the family of Ram,
32: 6 So Elihu son of Barakel the **Buzite** said: "I am young in years,

1001 ²בּוּזִי ***bûzî²***, n.pr.m. [1] [√ 1000; cf. 996]

Buzi [1]

Eze 1: 3 the son of **Buzi**, by the Kebar River in the land of the Babylonians.

1002 בַּוַּי ***bawway***, n.pr.m. [1 / 0] [cf. 1218]

Ne 3: 18 made by their countrymen under Binnui [BHS *Bavvai*; NIV 1218]

1003 בּוּךְ ***bûk***, v. [3] [→ 4428]

bewildered [1], mill about [1], wandering around in confusion [1]

Ex 14: 3 [C] 'The Israelites *are* **wandering around** the land **in confusion**,
Est 3: 15 [C] sat down to drink, but the city of Susa *was* **bewildered**.
Joel 1: 18 [C] The herds **mill about** because they have no pasture;

1004 ¹בּוּל ***bûl¹***, n.[m.]. [1]

Bul [1]

1Ki 6: 38 In the eleventh year in the month of **Bul**, the eighth month,

1005 ²בּוּל ***bûl²***, n.[m.]. [1]

block [1]

Isa 44: 19 thing from what is left? Shall I bow down to a **block** *of* wood?"

1006 ³בּוּל ***bûl³***, n.[m.]. [1] [→ 9315?]

produce [1]

Job 40: 20 The hills bring him their **produce**, and all the wild animals play

1007 בּוּנָה ***bûnâ***, n.pr.m. [1]

Bunah [1]

1Ch 2: 25 of Hezron: Ram his firstborn, **Bunah**, Oren, Ozem and Ahijah.

1008 בּוּס ***bûs***, v. [12] [→ 4431, 9313]

trample down [4], kicking about [2], loathes [1], trample [1], trampled down [1], trampled underfoot [1], trampled [1], trampling [1]

Ps 44: 5 [44:6] [A] through your name *we* **trample** our foes.
60: 12 [60:14] [A] the victory, and he *will* **trample down** our enemies.
108: 13 [108:14] [A] and he *will* **trample down** our enemies.
Pr 27: 7 [A] He who is full **loathes** honey, but to the hungry even what is
Isa 14: 19 [H] to the stones of the pit. Like a corpse **trampled underfoot**,
14: 25 [A] in my land; on my mountains *I will* **trample** him **down**.
63: 6 [A] *I* **trampled** the nations in my anger; in my wrath I made
63: 18 [D] but now our enemies *have* **trampled down** your sanctuary.
Jer 12: 10 [D] will ruin my vineyard and **trample down** my field;
Eze 16: 6 [F] I passed by and saw you **kicking about** in your blood,
16: 22 [F] when you were naked and bare, **kicking about** in your blood.
Zec 10: 5 [A] Together they will be like mighty men **trampling** the muddy

1009 בּוּץ ***bûṣ***, n.[m.]. [8] [→ 1010?, 1070]

fine linen [6], linen [1], white linen [1]

1Ch 4: 21 of Mareshah and the clans of the **linen** workers at Beth Ashbea,
15: 27 Now David was clothed in a robe of **fine linen**, as were all the
2Ch 2: 14 [2:13] and with purple and blue and crimson yarn and **fine linen**.
3: 14 made the curtain of blue, purple and crimson yarn and **fine linen**,
5: 12 dressed in **fine linen** and playing cymbals, harps and lyres.
Est 1: 6 fastened with cords of **white linen** and purple material to silver
8: 15 and white, a large crown of gold and a purple robe of **fine linen**.
Eze 27: 16 **fine linen**, coral and rubies for your merchandise.

1010 בּוֹצֵץ ***bôṣēṣ***, n.pr.loc. [1] [√ 1009? *or* 1288?]

Bozez [1]

1Sa 14: 4 outpost was a cliff; one was called **Bozez**, and the other Seneh.

1011 בּוּקָה ***bûqâ***, n.f. [1] [→ 4433, 6443?]

pillaged [1]

Na 2: 10 [2:11] She is **pillaged**, plundered, stripped! Hearts melt, knees

1012 בּוֹקֵר ***bôqēr***, n.m.den. [1] [√ 1330; cf. 1329]

shepherd [1]

Am 7: 14 but I was a **shepherd**, and I also took care of sycamore-fig trees.

1013 בּוּר ***bûr***, v. [1]

concluded [1]

Ecc 9: 1 [A] on all this and **concluded** that the righteous and the wise

1014 בּוֹר ***bôr***, n.m. [70] [→ 934, 1015, 1016, 1071; cf. 931, 3930, 6941]

pit [26], cistern [19], well [7], cisterns [5], dungeon [3], dungeon [+1074] [2], wells [2], death [1], hole [1], one[s] [1], quarry [+5217] [1], slimy pit [+8622] [1], there[s] [+928+2021] [1]

Ge 37: 20 let's kill him and throw him into one of these **cisterns** and say that
37: 22 Throw him into this **cistern** here in the desert, but don't lay a hand
37: 24 they took him and threw him into the **cistern**. Now the cistern was
37: 24 the cistern. Now the **cistern** was empty; there was no water in it.
37: 28 his brothers pulled Joseph up out of the **cistern** and sold him for
37: 29 When Reuben returned to the **cistern** and saw that Joseph was not
37: 29 to the cistern and saw that Joseph was not **there**[s] [+928+2021],
40: 15 even here I have done nothing to deserve being put in a **dungeon**."
41: 14 sent for Joseph, and he was quickly brought from the **dungeon**.
Ex 12: 29 to the firstborn of the prisoner, who was in the **dungeon** [+1074],
21: 33 "If a man uncovers a **pit** or digs one and fails to cover it and an ox
21: 33 or digs **one**[s] and fails to cover it and an ox or a donkey falls into it,
21: 34 the owner of the **pit** must pay for the loss; he must pay its owner,
Lev 11: 36 A spring, however, or a **cistern** *for* collecting water remains clean,
Dt 6: 11 **wells** you did not dig, and vineyards and olive groves you did not
1Sa 13: 6 in caves and thickets, among the rocks, and in pits and **cisterns**.
19: 22 he himself left for Ramah and went to the great **cistern** at Secu.
2Sa 3: 26 after Abner, and they brought him back from the **well** *of* Sirah.
23: 15 get me a drink of water from the **well** near the gate *of* Bethlehem!"
23: 16 drew water from the **well** near the gate *of* Bethlehem and carried it
23: 20 He also went down into a **pit** on a snowy day and killed a lion.
2Ki 10: 14 took them alive and slaughtered them by the **well** *of* Beth Eked—
18: 31 his own vine and fig tree and drink water from his own **cistern**,
1Ch 11: 17 get me a drink of water from the **well** near the gate *of* Bethlehem!"
11: 18 drew water from the **well** near the gate *of* Bethlehem and carried it
11: 22 He also went down into a **pit** on a snowy day and killed a lion.
2Ch 26: 10 He also built towers in the desert and dug many **cisterns**,
Ne 9: 25 **wells** already dug, vineyards, olive groves and fruit trees in
Ps 7: 15 [7:16] He who digs a **hole** and scoops it out falls into the pit he
28: 1 remain silent, I will be like those who have gone down to the **pit**.
30: 3 [30:4] the grave; you spared me from going down into the **pit**.
40: 2 [40:3] He lifted me out of the **slimy pit** [+8622], out of the mud
88: 4 [88:5] I am counted among those who go down to the **pit**; I am
88: 6 [88:7] You have put me in the lowest **pit**, in the darkest depths.
143: 7 your face from me or I will be like those who go down to the **pit**.
Pr 1: 12 like the grave, and whole, like those who go down to the **pit**;
5: 15 Drink water from your own **cistern**, running water from your own
28: 17 man tormented by the guilt of murder will be a fugitive till **death**;
Ecc 12: 6 pitcher is shattered at the spring, or the wheel broken at the **well**,
Isa 14: 15 But you are brought down to the grave, to the depths of the **pit**.
14: 19 pierced by the sword, those who descend to the stones of the **pit**.
24: 22 They will be herded together like prisoners bound in a **dungeon**;
36: 16 his own vine and fig tree and drink water from his own **cistern**,
38: 18 those who go down to the **pit** cannot hope for your faithfulness.
51: 1 were cut and to the **quarry** *from* **which** [+5217] you were hewn;
Jer 2: 13 the spring of living water, and have dug their own **cisterns**,
2: 13 dug their own cisterns, broken **cisterns** that cannot hold water.
6: 7 [As a **well** [K; see Q 931] pours out its water,]
37: 16 Jeremiah was put into a vaulted cell in a **dungeon** [+1074],
38: 6 So they took Jeremiah and put him into the **cistern** *of* Malkijah,
38: 6 They lowered Jeremiah by ropes into the **cistern**; it had no water in
38: 7 the royal palace, heard that they had put Jeremiah into the **cistern**.
38: 9 They have thrown him into a **cistern**, where he will starve to death
38: 10 and lift Jeremiah the prophet out of the **cistern** before he dies."
38: 11 and let them down with ropes to Jeremiah in the **cistern**.
38: 13 they pulled him up with the ropes and lifted him out of the **cistern**.
41: 7 were with him slaughtered them and threw them into a **cistern**.
41: 9 Now the **cistern** where he threw all the bodies of the men he had
La 3: 53 They tried to end my life in a **pit** and threw stones at me;
3: 55 I called on your name, O LORD, from the depths of the **pit**.
Eze 26: 20 then I will bring you down with those who go down to the **pit**,
26: 20 as in ancient ruins, with those who go down to the **pit**, and you will
31: 14 among mortal men, with those who go down to the **pit**.

Eze 31:16 I brought it down to the grave with those who go down to the **pit**.
32:18 daughters of mighty nations, with those who go down to the **pit**.
32:23 Their graves are in the depths of the **pit** and her army lies around
32:24 They bear their shame with those who go down to the **pit**.
32:25 they bear their shame with those who go down to the **pit**;
32:29 lie with the uncircumcised, with those who go down to the **pit**.
32:30 the sword and bear their shame with those who go down to the **pit**.
Zec 9:11 with you, I will free your prisoners from the waterless **pit**.

1015 בּוֹר הַסִּרָה *bôr hassirâ*, n.pr.loc. Not used in NIV/BHS [√ 1014 + 2021 + 6241]

1016 בּוֹר־עָשָׁן *bôr-ʿāšān*, n.pr.loc. [1] [√ 1014 + 6940; cf. 3930, 6941]

Bor Ashan [1]

1Sa 30:30 to those in Hormah, **Bor Ashan**, Athach

1017 בּוֹשׁ *bôš*[1], v. [122 / 121] [→ 1019, 1423, 1425, 4434]

put to shame [41], ashamed [24], disgraced [8], shame [6], have shame at all [+1017] [4], shamed [4], disappointed [3], disgrace [3], disgraceful [3], dismayed [3], be disgraced [2], despair [2], *untranslated* [1], bear shame [1], bring shame [1], brings shame [1], disgraces [1], distressed [1], embarrassment [1], felt ashamed [1], felt shame [1], frustrate [1], humiliated [1], infamy [1], let be dashed [1], let be put to shame [1], shameful [1], shamelessly [+4202] [1], suffer shame [1], utter shame [+1425] [1]

Ge 2:25 [F] and his wife were both naked, and *they* **felt** no **shame**.
Jdg 3:25 [A] They waited to the point of **embarrassment**, but when he did
2Sa 19:5 [19:6] [G] and said, "Today *you have* **humiliated** all your men,
2Ki 2:17 [A] they persisted until *he was* too **ashamed** to refuse. So he
8:11 [A] stared at him with a fixed gaze until Hazael **felt ashamed**.
19:26 [A] drained of power, are dismayed and **put to shame**.
Ezr 8:22 [A] *I was* **ashamed** to ask the king for soldiers and horsemen to
9:6 [A] *I am too* **ashamed** and disgraced to lift up my face to you,
Job 6:20 [A] *They are* **distressed**, because they had been confident;
19:3 [A] times now you have reproached me; **shamelessly** [+4202]
Ps 6:10 [6:11] [A] All my enemies *will be* **ashamed** and dismayed; they
6:10 [6:11] [A] they will turn back *in* sudden **disgrace**.
14:6 [G] *You* evildoers **frustrate** the plans of the poor,
22:5 [22:6] [A] in you they trusted and *were* not **disappointed**.
25:2 [A] *Do* not *let me be* **put to shame**, nor let my enemies triumph
25:3 [A] No one whose hope is in you *will* ever *be* **put to shame**,
25:3 [A] *they will be* **put to shame** who are treacherous without
25:20 [A] *let me* not *be* **put to shame**, for I take refuge in you.
31:1 [31:2] [A] I have taken refuge; *let me* never *be* **put to shame**;
31:17 [31:18] [A] *Let me* not *be* **put to shame**, O LORD, for I have
31:17 [31:18] [A] *let* the wicked *be* **put to shame** and lie silent in the
35:4 [A] *May* those who seek my life *be* **disgraced** and put to shame;
35:26 [A] *May* all who gloat over my distress *be* **put to shame**
40:14 [40:15] [A] May all who seek to take my life *be* **put to shame**
44:7 [44:8] [G] over our enemies, *you* **put** our adversaries **to shame**.
53:5 [53:6] [G] *you* **put** them **to shame**, for God despised them.
69:6 [69:7] [A] *May* those who hope in you not *be* **disgraced**
70:2 [70:3] [A] *May* those who seek my life *be* **put to shame**
71:1 [A] I have taken refuge; *let me* never *be* **put to shame**.
71:13 [A] May my accusers perish *in* **shame**; may those who want to
71:24 [A] for those who wanted to harm me *have been* **put to shame**
83:17 [83:18] [A] *May they* ever *be* **ashamed** and dismayed; may
86:17 [A] that my enemies may see it and *be* **put to shame**, for you,
97:7 [A] All who worship images *are* **put to shame**, those who boast
109:28 [A] when they attack *they will be* **put to shame**, but your servant
119:6 [A] *I would* not *be* **put to shame** when I consider all your
119:31 [G] to your statutes, O LORD; *do* not **let** me **be put to shame**.
119:46 [A] of your statutes before kings and *will* not *be* **put to shame**,
119:78 [A] *May* the arrogant *be* **put to shame** for wronging me without
119:80 [A] toward your decrees, that *I may* not *be* **put to shame**.
119:116 [G] your promise, and I will live; *do* not **let** my hopes **be dashed**.
127:5 [A] *They will* not *be* **put to shame** when they contend with their
129:5 [A] May all who hate Zion be turned back *in* **shame**.
Pr 10:5 [G] but he who sleeps during harvest *is* a **disgraceful** son.
12:4 [G] but a **disgraceful** wife is like decay in his bones.
14:35 [G] in a wise servant, but a **shameful** servant incurs his wrath.
17:2 [G] A wise servant will rule over a **disgraceful** son, and will
19:26 [G] drives out his mother is a son *who* **brings shame**
29:15 [G] but a child left to himself **disgraces** his mother.
Isa 1:29 [A] "*You will be* **ashamed** because of the sacred oaks in which
19:9 [A] Those who work with combed flax *will* **despair**, the weavers
20:5 [A] and boasted in Egypt will be afraid and **put to shame**.
23:4 [A] *Be* **ashamed**, O Sidon, and you, O fortress of the sea,
24:23 [A] The moon will be abashed, the sun **ashamed**; for the LORD
26:11 [A] Let them see your zeal for your people and *be* **put to shame**;
29:22 [A] "No longer *will* Jacob *be* **ashamed**; no longer will their faces
30:5 [G] everyone *will be* **put to shame** because of a people useless to
37:27 [A] drained of power, are dismayed and **put to shame**.
41:11 [A] "All who rage against you *will* surely *be* **ashamed**
42:17 [A] are our gods,' will be turned back *in* **utter shame** [+1425].
44:9 [A] up for them are blind; they are ignorant, to *their own* **shame**.
44:11 [A] *He* and his kind *will be* **put to shame**; craftsmen are nothing
44:11 [A] their stand; they will be brought down to terror and **infamy**.
45:16 [A] All the makers of idols *will be* **put to shame** and disgraced;
45:17 [A] *you will* never *be* **put to shame** or disgraced, to ages
45:24 [A] raged against him will come to him and *be* **put to shame**.
49:23 [A] those who hope in me *will* not *be* **disappointed**."
50:7 [A] set my face like flint, and I know *I will* not *be* **put to shame**.
54:4 [A] "Do not be afraid; *you will* not **suffer shame**. Do not fear
65:13 [A] my servants will rejoice, but you *will be* **put to shame**.
66:5 [A] that we may see your joy!' Yet they *will be* **put to shame**.
Jer 2:26 [G] when he is caught, so the house of Israel *is* **disgraced**—
2:36 [A] *You will be* **disappointed** by Egypt as you were by Assyria.
2:36 [A] You will be disappointed by Egypt as you were **[RPH]** by
6:15 [G] *Are they* **ashamed** *of* their loathsome conduct? No,
6:15 [A] No, *they* **have** no **shame** [+1017] **at all**; they do not even
6:15 [A] No, *they* **have** no **shame at all** [+1017]; they do not even
8:9 [G] The wise *will be* **put to shame**; they will be dismayed
8:12 [G] *Are they* **ashamed** *of* their loathsome conduct? No,
8:12 [A] No, *they* **have** no **shame** [+1017] **at all**; they do not even
8:12 [A] No, *they* **have** no **shame at all** [+1017]; they do not even
9:19 [9:18] [A] 'How ruined we are! How great *is our* **shame**! We
10:14 [G] without knowledge; every goldsmith *is* **shamed** by his idols.
12:13 [A] So **bear** *the* **shame** of your harvest because of the LORD's
14:3 [A] **dismayed** and despairing, they cover their heads.
14:4 [A] in the land; the farmers *are* **dismayed** and cover their heads.
15:9 [A] set while it is still day; *she will be* **disgraced** and humiliated.
17:13 [A] the hope of Israel, all who forsake you *will be* **put to shame**.
17:18 [A] *Let* my persecutors *be* **put to shame**, but keep me from
17:18 [A] my persecutors be put to shame, but *keep* me from **shame**;
20:11 [A] They will fail and *be* thoroughly **disgraced**; their dishonor
22:22 [A] *you will be* **ashamed** and disgraced because of all your
31:19 [A] *I was* **ashamed** and humiliated because I bore the disgrace of
46:24 [G] The Daughter of Egypt *will be* **put to shame**, handed over to
48:1 [G] Kiriathaim *will* **be disgraced** and captured; the stronghold
48:1 [G] and captured; the stronghold *will* **be disgraced** and shattered.
48:13 [A] Moab *will be* **ashamed** of Chemosh, as the house of Israel
48:13 [A] as the house of Israel *was* **ashamed** when they trusted in
48:20 [G] Moab *is* **disgraced**, for she is shattered. Wail and cry out!
48:39 [A] she is! How they wail! How Moab turns her back *in* **shame**!
49:23 [A] "Hamath and Arpad *are* **dismayed**, for they have heard bad
50:2 [G] Bel *will be* **put to shame**, Marduk filled with terror.
50:2 [G] Her images *will be* **put to shame** and her idols filled with
50:12 [A] your mother *will be* greatly **ashamed**; she who gave you
51:17 [G] without knowledge; every goldsmith *is* **shamed** by his idols.
51:47 [A] her whole land *will be* **disgraced** and her slain will all lie
51:51 [A] "*We are* **disgraced**, for we have been insulted and shame
Eze 16:52 [A] So then, *be* **ashamed** and bear your disgrace, for you have
16:63 [A] you will remember and *be* **ashamed** and never again open
32:30 [A] they went down with the slain *in* **disgrace** despite the terror
36:32 [A] *Be* **ashamed** and disgraced for your conduct, O house of
Hos 2:5 [2:7] [G] been unfaithful and has conceived them *in* **disgrace**.
4:19 [A] them away, and their sacrifices *will* **bring** *them* **shame**.
10:6 [A] be disgraced; Israel *will be* **ashamed** of its wooden idols.
13:15 [a] his spring *will* fail [BHS *be ashamed*; NIV 3312] and his well
Joel 1:11 [G] **Despair**, you farmers, wail, you vine growers; grieve for the
2:26 [A] wonders for you; never again *will* my people *be* **shamed**.
2:27 [A] that there is no other; never again *will* my people *be* **shamed**.
Mic 3:7 [A] The seers *will be* **ashamed** and the diviners disgraced. They
7:16 [A] Nations will see and *be* **ashamed**, deprived of all their
Zep 3:11 [A] On that day *you will* not *be* **put to shame** for all the wrongs
Zec 13:4 [A] "On that day every prophet *will be* **ashamed** of his prophetic

1018 בּוֹשׁ *bôš*[2], v. [2]

so long [2]

Ex 32:1 [D] When the people saw that Moses *was* **so long** in coming
Jdg 5:28 [D] lattice she cried out, 'Why *is* his chariot **so long** in coming?

1019 בּוּשָׁה *bûšâ*, n.f. [4] [√ 1017]

shame [4]

Ps 89:45 [89:46] his youth; you have covered him with a mantle of **shame**.
Eze 7:18 Their faces will be covered with **shame** and their heads will be
Ob 1:10 against your brother Jacob, you will be covered with **shame**;
Mic 7:10 Then my enemy will see it and will be covered with **shame**,

1020 בַּז *baz*, n.[m.]. [25] [→ 4561; cf. 1024]

plunder [15], plundered [4], loot [+1024] [2], despoil [+4200+5989] [1], looted [1], plunder [+1024] [1], taken captive [1]

Nu 14: 3 Our wives and children will be taken as **plunder**. Wouldn't it be
14: 31 As for your children that you said would be taken as **plunder**,
31: 32 The **plunder** remaining from the spoils that the soldiers took was
Dt 1: 39 the little ones that you said would be **taken captive**, your children
2Ki 21: 14 their enemies. They will be **looted** and plundered by all their foes,
Isa 10: 6 against a people who anger me, to seize loot and snatch **plunder**,
33: 23 of spoils will be divided and even the lame will carry off **plunder**.
42: 22 They have become **plunder**, with no one to rescue them; they have
Jer 2: 14 a servant, a slave by birth? Why then has he become **plunder**?
15: 13 Your wealth and your treasures I will give as **plunder**, without
17: 3 and your wealth and all your treasures I will give away as **plunder**,
30: 16 all who make spoil of you *I will* **despoil** [+4200+5989].
49: 32 Their camels will become **plunder**, and their large herds will be
Eze 7: 21 I will hand it all over as **plunder** to foreigners and as loot to the
23: 46 a mob against them and give them over to terror and **plunder**.
25: 7 hand against you and give you as **plunder** [K 952] to the nations.
26: 5 the Sovereign LORD. She will become **plunder** for the nations,
29: 19 He will loot and **plunder** [+1024] the land as pay for his army.
34: 8 because my flock lacks a shepherd and so has been **plundered**
34: 22 I will save my flock, and they will no longer be **plundered**.
34: 28 They will no longer be **plundered** by the nations, nor will wild
36: 4 desolate ruins and the deserted towns that have been **plundered**
36: 5 their own possession so that they might **plunder** its pastureland.'
38: 12 I will plunder and **loot** [+1024] and turn my hand against the
38: 13 Have you gathered your hordes to **loot** [+1024], to carry off silver

1021 בָּזָא *bāzā'*, v. [2]

divided [2]

Isa 18: 2 [A] nation of strange speech, whose land *is* **divided** *by* rivers.
18: 7 [A] nation of strange speech, whose land *is* **divided** *by* rivers—

1022 בָּזָה *bāzâ*, v. [43] [→ 1025, 1026, 5802]

despised [20], despise [6], contemptible [3], was despised [3], be despised [2], despises [2], contemptuous [1], despise [+928+6524] [1], despises [+928+6524] [1], ridiculed [1], scorned the idea [+928+6524] [1], show contempt [1], shown contempt [1]

Ge 25: 34 [A] and then got up and left. So Esau **despised** his birthright.
Nu 15: 31 [A] Because *he has* **despised** the LORD's word and broken his
1Sa 2: 30 [A] me I will honor, but *those who* **despise** me will be disdained.
10: 27 [A] *They* **despised** him and brought him no gifts. But Saul kept
15: 9 [C] everything *that* **was despised** and weak they totally
17: 42 [A] was only a boy, ruddy and handsome, and *he* **despised** him.
2Sa 6: 16 [A] dancing before the LORD, *she* **despised** him in her heart.
12: 9 [A] Why *did you* **despise** the word of the LORD by doing what
12: 10 [A] because *you* **despised** me and took the wife of Uriah the
1Ch 15: 29 [A] and celebrating, *she* **despised** him in her heart.
2Ch 36: 16 [A] **despised** his words and scoffed at his prophets until the
Ne 2: 19 [A] the Arab heard about it, they mocked and **ridiculed** us.
Est 1: 17 [G] so they *will* **despise** [+928+6524] their husbands and say,
3: 6 [A] he **scorned** [+928+6524] **the idea** of killing only Mordecai.
Ps 15: 4 [C] *who* **despises** [+928+6524] a vile man but honors those who
22: 6 [22:7] [B] a man, scorned by men and **despised** *by* the people.
22: 24 [22:25] [A] For *he has* not **despised** or disdained the suffering
51: 17 [51:19] [A] and contrite heart, O God, *you will* not **despise**.
69: 33 [69:34] [A] the needy and *does* not **despise** his captive people.
73: 20 [A] when you arise, O Lord, *you will* **despise** them as fantasies.
102: 17 [102:18] [A] of the destitute; *he will* not **despise** their plea.
119: 141 [C] Though I am lowly and **despised**, I do not forget your
Pr 14: 2 [A] the LORD, but he whose ways are devious **despises** him.
15: 20 [A] joy to his father, but a foolish man **despises** his mother.
19: 16 [A] his life, but *he who is* **contemptuous** *of* his ways will die.
Ecc 9: 16 [B] the poor man's wisdom *is* **despised**, and his words are no
Isa 49: 7 [A] to him *who was* **despised** and abhorred by the nation,
53: 3 [C] *He* **was despised** and rejected by men, a man of sorrows,
53: 3 [C] Like one from whom men hide their faces *he* **was despised**,
Jer 22: 28 [C] *Is* this man Jehoiachin *a* **despised**, broken pot, an object no
49: 15 [B] make you small among the nations, **despised** among men.
Eze 16: 59 [A] because *you have* **despised** my oath by breaking the
17: 16 [A] whose oath *he* **despised** and whose treaty he broke.
17: 18 [A] *He* **despised** the oath by breaking the covenant. Because he
17: 19 [A] I will bring down on his head my oath that *he* **despised**
22: 8 [A] *You have* **despised** my holy things and desecrated my
Da 11: 21 [C] "He will be succeeded by a **contemptible** *person* who has
Ob 1: 2 [B] you small among the nations; you *will* **be** utterly **despised**.
Mal 1: 6 [A] "It is you, O priests, *who* **show contempt** *for* my name.
1: 6 [A] you ask, 'How *have we* **shown contempt** *for* your name?'
1: 7 [C] "By saying that the LORD's table *is* **contemptible**.
1: 12 [C] 'It is defiled,' and of its food, 'It *is* **contemptible**.'

2: 9 [C] "So I have caused you *to* **be despised** and humiliated before

1023 בִּזָּה *bizzâ*, n.f. [10] [√ 1024]

plunder [7], booty [1], pillage [1], plundered [1]

2Ch 14: 14 [14:13] all these villages, since there was much **booty** there.
25: 13 three thousand people and carried off great quantities of **plunder**.
28: 14 and **plunder** in the presence of the officials and all the assembly.
Ezr 9: 7 to **pillage** and humiliation at the hand of foreign kings, as it is
Ne 4: 4 [3:36] Give them over as **plunder** in a land of captivity.
Est 9: 10 of the Jews. But they did not lay their hands on the **plunder**.
9: 15 hundred men, but they did not lay their hands on the **plunder**.
9: 16 thousand of them but did not lay their hands on the **plunder**.
Da 11: 24 He will distribute **plunder**, loot and wealth among his followers.
11: 33 they will fall by the sword or be burned or captured or **plundered**.

1024 בָּזַז *bāzaz*, v. [43] [→ 1020, 1023]

plunder [11], carried off [4], carry off [4], plundered [3], loot [+1020] [2], loot [2], looted [2], took [2], totally plundered [+1024] [2], be plundered [1], collect [1], make spoil [1], plunder [+1020] [1], plunderers [1], robbing [1], snatch [1], take [1], taken plunder [1], taking as plunder [1], took as plunder [1]

Ge 34: 27 [A] and **looted** the city where their sister had been defiled.
34: 29 [A] and children, **taking as plunder** everything in the houses.
Nu 31: 9 [A] **took** all the Midianite herds, flocks and goods **as plunder**.
31: 32 [A] The plunder remaining from the spoils that the soldiers **took**
31: 53 [A] Each soldier *had* **taken plunder** for himself.
Dt 2: 35 [A] the plunder from the towns we had captured *we* **carried off**
3: 7 [A] the plunder from their cities *we* **carried off** for ourselves.
20: 14 [A] in the city, *you may* **take** these as plunder for yourselves.
Jos 8: 2 [A] except that *you may* **carry off** their plunder and livestock for
8: 27 [A] Israel *did* **carry off** for themselves the livestock and plunder
11: 14 [A] The Israelites **carried off** for themselves all the plunder
1Sa 14: 36 [A] after the Philistines by night and **plunder** them till dawn,
2Ki 7: 16 [A] people went out and **plundered** the camp of the Arameans.
2Ch 14: 14 [14:13] [A] *They* **plundered** all these villages, since there was
20: 25 [A] So Jehoshaphat and his men went to **carry off** their plunder,
20: 25 [A] so much plunder that it took three days *to* **collect** it.
25: 13 [A] thousand people and **carried off** great quantities of plunder.
28: 8 [A] *They* also **took** a great deal of plunder, which they carried
Est 3: 13 [A] the month of Adar, and to **plunder** their goods.
8: 11 [A] and children; and to **plunder** the property of their enemies.
Ps 109: 11 [A] all he has; *may* strangers **plunder** the fruits of his labor.
Isa 10: 2 [A] making widows their prey and **robbing** the fatherless.
10: 6 [A] a people who anger me, to seize loot and **snatch** plunder,
11: 14 [A] to the west; together *they will* **plunder** the people to the east.
17: 14 [A] of those who loot us, the lot of *those who* **plunder** us.
24: 3 [C] will be completely laid waste and **totally plundered** [+1024].
24: 3 [C] will be completely laid waste and **totally plundered** [+1024].
33: 23 [A] will be divided and even the lame *will* **carry off** plunder.
42: 22 [B] this is a people **plundered** and looted, all of them trapped in
42: 24 [A] Jacob over to become loot, and Israel to the **plunderers**?
Jer 20: 5 [A] They will take it away *as* **plunder** and carry it off to
30: 16 [A] will be plundered; all *who* **make spoil** *of* you I will despoil.
50: 37 [E] A sword against her treasures! *They will* **be plundered**.
Eze 26: 12 [A] They will plunder your wealth and **loot** your merchandise;
29: 19 [A] will loot and **plunder** [+1020] the land as pay for his army.
38: 12 [A] I will plunder and **loot** [+1020] and turn my hand against the
38: 13 [A] Have you gathered your hordes to **loot** [+1020], to carry off
39: 10 [A] those who plundered them and **loot** those who looted them,
39: 10 [A] those who plundered them and loot *those who* **looted** them,
Am 3: 11 [C] pull down your strongholds and **plunder** your fortresses."
Na 2: 9 [2:10] [A] **Plunder** the silver! Plunder the gold! The supply is
2: 9 [2:10] [A] Plunder the silver! **Plunder** the gold! The supply is
Zep 2: 9 [A] The remnant of my people *will* **plunder** them; the survivors

1025 בִּזָּיוֹן *bizzāyôn*, n.[m.]. [1] [→ 1026; cf. 1022]

disrespect [1]

Est 1: 18 in the same way. There will be no end of **disrespect** and discord.

1026 בִּזְיוֹתְיָה *bizyôtᵉyâ*, n.pr.loc. [1] [√ 1025 + 3378]

Biziothiah [1]

Jos 15: 28 Hazar Shual, Beersheba, **Biziothiah**,

1027 בָּזָק *bāzāq*, n.[m.]. [1]

flashes of lightning [1]

Eze 1: 14 The creatures sped back and forth like **flashes of lightning**.

1028 בֶּ֫זֶק *bezeq*, n.pr.loc. [3] [→ 152]
Bezek [2], there[s] [+928] [1]
Jdg 1: 4 into their hands and they struck down ten thousand men at **Bezek**.
1: 5 It was **there**[s] [+928] that they found Adoni-Bezek and fought
1Sa 11: 8 When Saul mustered them at **Bezek**, the men of Israel numbered

1029 בָּזַר *bāzar*, v. [2] [cf. 7061; Ar 10095]
distribute [1], scatter [1]
Ps 68: 30 [68:31] [D] of silver. **Scatter** the nations who delight in war.
Da 11: 24 [A] *He will* **distribute** plunder, loot and wealth among his

1030 בִּזְּתָא *bizz[e]tā'*, n.pr.m. [1]
Biztha [1]
Est 1: 10 Mehuman, **Biztha**, Harbona, Bigtha, Abagtha, Zethar and Carcas—

1031 בָּחוֹן *bāḥôn*, n.[m.]. [1] [√ 1043]
tester of metals [1]
Jer 6: 27 "I have made you a **tester of metals** and my people the ore,

1032 בַּחוּן *baḥûn*, n.[m.]. [1] [→ 1039, 1044]
siege towers [1]
Isa 23: 13 they raised up their **siege towers**, [K 1039] they stripped its

1033 ¹בָּחוּר *bāḥûr[1]*, n.m. [51 / 50] [→ 1035, 1036, 1037]
young men [34], young man [6], able [3], men [3], bridegrooms [1], sons [1], strong young men [1], younger men [1]
Dt 32: 25 **Young men** and young women will perish, infants and gray-haired
Jdg 14: 10 Samson made a feast there, as was customary for **bridegrooms**.
Ru 3: 10 You have not run after the **younger men**, whether rich or poor.
1Sa 8: 16 and the best of your cattle [BHS *young men*; NIV 1330]
9: 2 an impressive **young man** without equal among the Israelites—
1Ki 12: 21 tribe of Benjamin—a hundred and eighty thousand fighting **men**—
2Ki 8: 12 kill their **young men** with the sword, dash their little children to
2Ch 11: 1 and Benjamin—a hundred and eighty thousand fighting **men**—
13: 3 Abijah went into battle with a force of four hundred thousand **able**
13: 3 a battle line against him with eight hundred thousand **able** troops.
13: 17 were five hundred thousand casualties among Israel's **able** men.
25: 5 found that there were three hundred thousand **men** ready for
36: 17 who killed their **young men** with the sword in the sanctuary,
36: 17 and spared neither **young man** nor young woman, old man
Ps 78: 31 the sturdiest among them, cutting down the **young men** *of* Israel.
78: 63 Fire consumed their **young men**, and their maidens had no
89: 19 [89:20] I have exalted a **young man** from among the people.
148: 12 **young men** and maidens, old men and children.
Pr 20: 29 The glory of **young men** is their strength, gray hair the splendor of
Ecc 11: 9 Be happy, **young man**, while you are young, and let your heart
Isa 9: 17 [9:16] Therefore the Lord will take no pleasure in the **young men**,
23: 4 given birth; I have neither reared **sons** nor brought up daughters."
31: 8 before the sword and their **young men** will be put to forced labor.
40: 30 youths grow tired and weary, and **young men** stumble and fall;
62: 5 As a **young man** marries a maiden, so will your sons marry you;
Jer 6: 11 the children in the street and on the **young men** gathered together;
9: 21 [9:20] the streets and the **young men** from the public squares.
11: 22 Their **young men** will die by the sword, their sons and daughters
15: 8 I will bring a destroyer against the mothers of their **young men**;
18: 21 men be put to death, their **young men** slain by the sword in battle.
31: 13 Then maidens will dance and be glad, **young men** and old as well.
48: 15 her finest **young men** will go down in the slaughter,"
49: 26 Surely, her **young men** will fall in the streets; all her soldiers will
50: 30 Therefore, her **young men** will fall in the streets; all her soldiers
51: 3 Do not spare her **young men**; completely destroy her army.
51: 22 old man and youth, with you I shatter **young man** and maiden,
La 1: 15 he has summoned an army against me to crush my **young men**.
1: 18 my suffering. My **young men** and maidens have gone into exile.
2: 21 the streets; my **young men** and maidens have fallen by the sword.
5: 13 **Young men** toil at the millstones; boys stagger under loads of
5: 14 gone from the city gate; the **young men** have stopped their music.
Eze 9: 6 Slaughter old men, **young men** and maidens, women and children,
23: 6 governors and commanders, all of them handsome **young men**,
23: 12 in full dress, mounted horsemen, all handsome **young men**.
23: 23 handsome **young men**, all of them governors and commanders,
30: 17 The **young men** *of* Heliopolis and Bubastis will fall by the sword,
Joel 2: 28 [3:1] men will dream dreams, your **young men** will see visions.
Am 2: 11 from among your sons and Nazirites from among your **young men**.
4: 10 I killed your **young men** with the sword, along with your captured
8: 13 young women and **strong young men** will faint because of thirst.
Zec 9: 17 Grain will make the **young men** thrive, and new wine the young

1034 ²בָּחוּר *bāḥûr[2]*, a. *or* v.ptcp. Not used in NIV/BHS [cf. 1047]

1035 בְּחוּרוֹת *b[e]ḥûrôt*, n.f.pl.abst. [2] [√ 1033]
youth [2]
Ecc 11: 9 and let your heart give you joy in the days of your **youth**.
12: 1 Remember your Creator in the days of your **youth**, before the days

1036 בְּחוּרִים *b[e]ḥûrîm*, n.m.pl.abst. [1] [√ 1033]
youth [1]
Nu 11: 28 who had been Moses' aide since **youth**, spoke up and said,

1037 ¹בַּחוּרִים *baḥûrîm[1]*, n.m. Not used in NIV/BHS [√ 1033]

1038 ²בַּחוּרִים *baḥûrîm[2]*, n.pr.loc. [5] [cf. 1372]
Bahurim [5]
2Sa 3: 16 went with her, weeping behind her all the way to **Bahurim**.
16: 5 As King David approached **Bahurim**, a man from the same clan as
17: 18 of them left quickly and went to the house of a man in **Bahurim**.
19: 16 [19:17] Shimei son of Gera, the Benjamite from **Bahurim**,
1Ki 2: 8 have with you Shimei son of Gera, the Benjamite from **Bahurim**,

1039 בַּחִין *baḥîn*, var. [0] [√ 1032]
Isa 23: 13 [they raised up their **siege towers**, [K; see Q 1032] they stripped its]

1040 בָּחִיר *bāḥîr*, n.m. [13] [√ 1047]
chosen [13]
2Sa 21: 6 before the LORD at Gibeah of Saul—the LORD's **chosen** *one*."
1Ch 16: 13 descendants of Israel his servant, O sons of Jacob, his **chosen** *ones*.
Ps 89: 3 [89:4] You said, "I have made a covenant with my **chosen** *one*,
105: 6 of Abraham his servant, O sons of Jacob, his **chosen** *ones*.
105: 43 out his people with rejoicing, his **chosen** *ones* with shouts of joy;
106: 5 that I may enjoy the prosperity of your **chosen** *ones*, that I may
106: 23 had not Moses, his **chosen** *one*, stood in the breach before him to
Isa 42: 1 is my servant, whom I uphold, my **chosen** *one* in whom I delight;
43: 20 streams in the wasteland, to give drink to my people, my **chosen**,
45: 4 of Israel my **chosen**, I summon you by name and bestow on you a
65: 9 my **chosen** *people* will inherit them, and there will my servants
65: 15 You will leave your name to my **chosen** *ones* as a curse;
65: 22 my **chosen** *ones* will long enjoy the works of their hands.

1041 ¹בָּחַל *bāḥal[1]*, v. [1]
detested [1]
Zec 11: 8 [A] The flock **detested** me, and I grew weary of them

1042 ²בָּחַל *bāḥal[2]*, v. [0]
Pr 20: 21 [e] [An inheritance **quickly** [K; see Q 987] **gained** at the]

1043 בָּחַן *bāḥan*, v. [29] [→ 1031, 1045, 1046]
test [11], be tested [3], examine [3], tested [3], tests [2], *untranslated* [1], challenge [1], examines [1], probe [1], searches [1], testing [1], tried [1]
Ge 42: 15 [C] this is how *you will* **be tested**: As surely as Pharaoh lives,
42: 16 [C] so that your words *may* **be tested** to see if you are telling the
1Ch 29: 17 [A] that you **test** the heart and are pleased with integrity.
Job 7: 18 [A] examine him every morning and **test** him every moment?
12: 11 [A] *Does* not the ear **test** words as the tongue tastes food?
23: 10 [A] that I take; *when he has* **tested** me, I will come forth as gold.
34: 3 [A] For the ear **tests** words as the tongue tastes food.
34: 36 [C] that Job *might* **be tested** to the utmost for answering like a
Ps 7: 9 [7:10] [A] O righteous God, *who* **searches** minds and hearts,
11: 4 [A] He observes the sons of men; his eyes **examine** them.
11: 5 [A] The LORD **examines** the righteous, but the wicked
17: 3 [A] Though *you* **probe** my heart and examine me at night,
26: 2 [A] **Test** me, O LORD, and try me, examine my heart and my
66: 10 [A] For *you*, O God, **tested** us; you refined us like silver.
81: 7 [81:8] [A] *I* **tested** you at the waters of Meribah.
95: 9 [A] where your fathers tested and **tried** me, though they had seen
139: 23 [A] and know my heart; **test** me and know my anxious thoughts.
Pr 17: 3 [A] and the furnace for gold, but the LORD **tests** the heart.
Jer 6: 27 [A] my people the ore, that you may observe and **test** their ways.
9: 7 [9:6] [A] "See, I will refine and **test** them, for what else can I do
11: 20 [A] you who judge righteously and **test** the heart and mind,
12: 3 [A] O LORD; you see me and **test** my thoughts about you.
17: 10 [A] "I the LORD search the heart and **examine** the mind, to
20: 12 [A] you *who* **examine** the righteous and probe the heart
Eze 21: 13 [21:18] [E] " '**Testing** *will* surely *come*. And what if the scepter
Zec 13: 9 [A] the fire; I will refine them like silver and **test** them like gold.

Zec 13: 9 [A] I will refine them like silver and test them like **[RPH]** gold.
Mal 3: 10 [A] **Test** me in this," says the LORD Almighty, "and see if I
3: 15 [A] and even *those who* **challenge** God escape.' "

1044 בַּחַן **bahan**, n.[m.]. [1] [√ 1032]

watchtower [1]

Isa 32: 14 citadel and **watchtower** will become a wasteland forever,

1045 [1]בֹּחַן **bōḥan**[1], n.[m.]. Not used in NIV/BHS [√ 1043]

1046 [2]בֹּחַן **bōḥan**[2], n.[m.]. [1] [√ 1043]

tested [1]

Isa 28: 16 "See, I lay a stone in Zion, a **tested** stone, a precious cornerstone

1047 [1]בָּחַר **bāḥar**[1], v. [164] [→ 1040, 3295, 4435, 4436, 4437; cf. 1034, 1048]

chosen [63], choose [42], chose [27], chooses [7], choice [4], best [3], prefer [3], selected [2], acceptable [1], adopt [1], choose [+7864] [1], decide [1], desirable [1], desire [1], discern [1], find [1], finest [1], selects [1], sided with [+4200] [1], tested [1], would rather be [1]

Ge 6: 2 [A] were beautiful, and they married any of them *they* **chose**.
13: 11 [A] So Lot **chose** for himself the whole plain of the Jordan
Ex 14: 7 [B] He took six hundred of the **best** chariots, along with all the
17: 9 [A] "**Choose** some of our men and go out to fight the
18: 25 [A] He **chose** capable men from all Israel and made them leaders
Nu 16: 5 [A] he will have that person come near him. The man *he* **chooses**
16: 7 [A] The man the LORD **chooses** will be the one who is holy.
17: 5 [17:20] [A] The staff belonging to the man *I* **choose** will sprout,
Dt 4: 37 [A] your forefathers and **chose** their descendants after them,
7: 6 [A] The LORD your God *has* **chosen** you out of all the peoples
7: 7 [A] The LORD did not set his affection on you and **choose** you
10: 15 [A] on your forefathers and loved them, and *he* **chose** you,
12: 5 [A] you are to seek the place the LORD your God *will* **choose**
12: 11 [A] to the place the LORD your God *will* **choose** as a dwelling
12: 14 [A] Offer them only at the place the LORD *will* **choose** in one
12: 18 [A] your God at the place the LORD your God *will* **choose**—
12: 21 [A] If the place where the LORD your God **chooses** to put his
12: 26 [A] vowed to give, and go to the place the LORD *will* **choose**.
14: 2 [A] the LORD *has* **chosen** you to be his treasured possession.
14: 23 [A] God at the place *he will* **choose** as a dwelling for his Name,
14: 24 [A] (because the place where the LORD *will* **choose** to put his
14: 25 [A] and go to the place the LORD your God *will* **choose**.
15: 20 [A] of the LORD your God at the place he *will* **choose**.
16: 2 [A] or herd at the place the LORD *will* **choose** as a dwelling for
16: 6 [A] except in the place he *will* **choose** as a dwelling for his
16: 7 [A] and eat it at the place the LORD your God *will* **choose**.
16: 11 [A] God at the place he *will* **choose** as a dwelling for his Name—
16: 15 [A] to the LORD your God at the place the LORD *will* **choose**.
16: 16 [A] before the LORD your God at the place *he will* **choose**:
17: 8 [A] take them to the place the LORD your God *will* **choose**.
17: 10 [A] decisions they give you at the place the LORD *will* **choose**.
17: 15 [A] to appoint over you the king the LORD your God **chooses**.
18: 5 [A] for the LORD your God *has* **chosen** them and their
18: 6 [A] comes in all earnestness to the place the LORD *will* **choose**,
21: 5 [A] for the LORD your God *has* **chosen** them to minister and to
23: 16 [23:17] [A] wherever he likes and in whatever town *he* **chooses**.
26: 2 [A] go to the place the LORD your God *will* **choose** as a
30: 19 [A] Now **choose** life, so that you and your children may live
31: 11 [A] before the LORD your God at the place *he will* **choose**,
Jos 8: 3 [A] He **chose** thirty thousand of his best fighting men and sent
9: 27 [A] altar of the LORD at the place the LORD *would* **choose**.
24: 15 [A] then **choose** for yourselves this day whom you will serve,
24: 22 [A] "You are witnesses against yourselves that you *have* **chosen**
Jdg 5: 8 [A] *When they* **chose** new gods, war came to the city gates,
10: 14 [A] Go and cry out to the gods *you have* **chosen**. Let them save
20: 15 [B] in addition to seven hundred **chosen** men from those living in
20: 16 [B] Among all these soldiers there were seven hundred **chosen**
20: 34 [B] ten thousand of Israel's **finest** men made a frontal attack on
1Sa 2: 28 [A] I **chose** your father out of all the tribes of Israel to be my
8: 18 [A] you will cry out for relief from the king *you have* **chosen**,
10: 24 [A] all the people, "Do you see the man the LORD *has* **chosen**?
12: 13 [A] Now here is the king *you have* **chosen**, the one you asked
13: 2 [A] Saul **chose** three thousand men from Israel; two thousand
16: 8 [A] Samuel said, "The LORD *has* not **chosen** this one either."
16: 9 [A] but Samuel said, "Nor *has* the LORD **chosen** this one."
16: 10 [A] but Samuel said to him, "The LORD *has* not **chosen** these."
17: 40 [A] staff in his hand, **chose** five smooth stones from the stream,
20: 30 [A] Don't I know that you *have* **sided** [+4200] **with** the son of
24: 2 [24:3] [B] So Saul took three thousand **chosen** men from all
26: 2 [B] with his three thousand **chosen** men of Israel, to search there
2Sa 6: 1 [B] David again brought together out of Israel **chosen** *men*,
6: 21 [A] who **chose** me rather than your father or anyone from his
10: 9 [A] so *he* **selected** some of the best troops in Israel and deployed
10: 9 [B] so he selected some of the **best** *troops in* Israel and deployed
15: 15 [A] servants are ready to do whatever our lord the king **chooses**."
16: 18 [A] "No, the one **chosen** by the LORD, by these people,
17: 1 [A] "*I would* **choose** twelve thousand men and set out tonight in
19: 38 [19:39] [A] anything *you* **desire** from me I will do for you."
24: 12 [A] **Choose** one of them for me to carry out against you.' "
1Ki 3: 8 [A] Your servant is here among the people *you have* **chosen**,
8: 16 [A] *I have* not **chosen** a city in any tribe of Israel to have a
8: 16 [A] be there, but *I have* **chosen** David to rule my people Israel.'
8: 44 [A] they pray to the LORD toward the city *you have* **chosen**
8: 48 [A] toward the city *you have* **chosen** and the temple I have built
11: 13 [A] and for the sake of Jerusalem, which *I have* **chosen**."
11: 32 [A] which *I have* **chosen** out of all the tribes of Israel, he will
11: 34 [A] whom *I* **chose** and who observed my commands and statutes.
11: 36 [A] me in Jerusalem, the city where *I* **chose** to put my Name.
14: 21 [A] the city the LORD *had* **chosen** out of all the tribes of Israel
18: 23 [A] *Let them* **choose** one for themselves, and let them cut it into
18: 25 [A] "**Choose** one of the bulls and prepare it first, since there are
2Ki 21: 7 [A] which *I have* **chosen** out of all the tribes of Israel,
23: 27 [A] the city *I* **chose**, and this temple, about which I said,
1Ch 15: 2 [A] because the LORD **chose** them to carry the ark of the
19: 10 [A] so *he* **selected** some of the best troops in Israel and deployed
19: 10 [B] so he selected some of the **best** *troops* in Israel and deployed
21: 10 [A] **Choose** one of them for me to carry out against you.' "
28: 4 [A] **chose** me from my whole family to be king over Israel
28: 4 [A] *He* **chose** Judah as leader, and from the house of Judah he
28: 5 [A] *he has* **chosen** my son Solomon to sit on the throne of the
28: 6 [A] and my courts, for *I have* **chosen** him to be my son,
28: 10 [A] for the LORD *has* **chosen** you to build a temple as a
29: 1 [A] the one whom God *has* **chosen**, is young and inexperienced.
2Ch 6: 5 [A] *I have* not **chosen** a city in any tribe of Israel to have a
6: 5 [A] nor *have I* **chosen** anyone to be the leader over my people
6: 6 [A] But now *I have* **chosen** Jerusalem for my Name to be there,
6: 6 [A] be there, and *I have* **chosen** David to rule my people Israel.'
6: 34 [A] and when they pray to you toward this city *you have* **chosen**
6: 38 [A] toward the city *you have* **chosen** and toward the temple I
7: 12 [A] *have* **chosen** this place for myself as a temple for sacrifices.
7: 16 [A] *I have* **chosen** and consecrated this temple so that my Name
12: 13 [A] the city the LORD *had* **chosen** out of all the tribes of Israel
29: 11 [A] for the LORD *has* **chosen** you to stand before him
33: 7 [A] which *I have* **chosen** out of all the tribes of Israel,
34: 6 [a] [and **in** [K; see Q 928] the ruins around them,]
Ne 1: 9 [A] bring them to the place *I have* **chosen** as a dwelling for my
9: 7 [A] who **chose** Abram and brought him out of Ur of the
Job 7: 15 [A] so that I **prefer** strangling and death, rather than this body of
9: 14 [A] dispute with him? *How can I* **find** words to argue with him?
15: 5 [A] sin prompts your mouth; *you* **adopt** the tongue of the crafty.
29: 25 [A] *I* **chose** the way for them and sat as their chief; I dwelt as a
34: 4 [A] *Let us* **discern** for ourselves what is right; let us learn
34: 33 [A] You *must* **decide**, not I; so tell me what you know.
36: 21 [A] Beware of turning to evil, which *you seem to* **prefer** to
Ps 25: 12 [A] the LORD? He will instruct him in the way **chosen** for him.
33: 12 [A] God is the LORD, the people *he* **chose** for his inheritance.
47: 4 [47:5] [A] *He* **chose** our inheritance for us, the pride of Jacob,
65: 4 [65:5] [A] Blessed are those *you* **choose** and bring near to live
78: 67 [A] the tents of Joseph, *he did* not **choose** the tribe of Ephraim;
78: 68 [A] but *he* **chose** the tribe of Judah, Mount Zion, which he loved.
78: 70 [A] *He* **chose** David his servant and took him from the sheep
84: 10 [84:11] [A] *I* **would rather be** a doorkeeper in the house of my
105: 26 [A] He sent Moses his servant, and Aaron, whom *he had* **chosen**.
119: 30 [A] *I have* **chosen** the way of truth; I have set my heart on your
119: 173 [A] hand be ready to help me, for *I have* **chosen** your precepts.
132: 13 [A] For the LORD *has* **chosen** Zion, he has desired it for his
135: 4 [A] For the LORD *has* **chosen** Jacob to be his own, Israel to be
Pr 1: 29 [A] hated knowledge and *did* not **choose** to fear the LORD,
3: 31 [A] Do not envy a violent man or **choose** any of his ways,
8: 10 [C] instead of silver, knowledge rather than **choice** gold,
8: 19 [C] is better than fine gold; what I yield surpasses **choice** silver.
10: 20 [C] The tongue of the righteous *is* **choice** silver, but the heart of
16: 16 [C] How much better to get wisdom than gold, *to* **choose** [+7864]
21: 3 [C] and just *is* more **acceptable** to the LORD than sacrifice.
22: 1 [C] A good name *is* more **desirable** than great riches; to be
Ecc 9: 4 [e] [Anyone who *is* **among** [K; see Q 2489] the living has hope—]
SS 5: 15 [B] His appearance is like Lebanon, **choice** as its cedars.
Isa 1: 29 [A] be disgraced because of the gardens that *you have* **chosen**.
7: 15 [A] he knows enough to reject the wrong and **choose** the right.
7: 16 [A] boy knows enough to reject the wrong and **choose** the right,
14: 1 [A] once again *he will* **choose** Israel and will settle them in their
40: 20 [A] A man too poor to present such an offering **selects** wood that
41: 8 [A] "But you, O Israel, my servant, Jacob, whom *I have* **chosen**,
41: 9 [A] my servant'; *I have* **chosen** you and have not rejected you.
41: 24 [A] are utterly worthless; *he who* **chooses** you is detestable.

Isa 43:10 [A] declares the LORD, "and my servant whom *I have* **chosen**,
44: 1 [A] O Jacob, my servant, Israel, whom *I have* **chosen**.
44: 2 [A] O Jacob, my servant, Jeshurun, whom *I have* **chosen**.
48:10 [A] not as silver; *I have* **tested** you in the furnace of affliction.
49: 7 [A] is faithful, the Holy One of Israel, *who has* **chosen** you."
56: 4 [A] *who* **choose** what pleases me and hold fast to my covenant—
58: 5 [A] Is this the kind of fast *I have* **chosen**, only a day for a man to
58: 6 [A] "Is not this the kind of fasting *I have* **chosen**: to loose the
65:12 [A] You did evil in my sight and **chose** what displeases me."
66: 3 [A] They *have* **chosen** their own ways, and their souls delight in
66: 4 [A] so I also *will* **choose** harsh treatment for them and will bring
66: 4 [A] They did evil in my sight and **chose** what displeases me."
Jer 8: 3 [C] all the survivors of this evil nation *will* **prefer** death to life,
33:24 [A] 'The LORD has rejected the two kingdoms *he* **chose**'?
49:19 [B] Who *is the* **chosen** *one* I will appoint for this? Who is like
50:44 [B] Who *is* the **chosen** *one* I will appoint for this? Who is like me
Eze 20: 5 [A] On the day I **chose** Israel, I swore with uplifted hand to the
Hag 2:23 [A] for *I have* **chosen** you,' declares the LORD Almighty."
Zec 1:17 [A] LORD will again comfort Zion and **choose** Jerusalem.' "
2:12 [2:16] [A] in the holy land and *will* again **choose** Jerusalem.
3: 2 [A] Satan! The LORD, who *has* **chosen** Jerusalem, rebuke you!

1048 ²בָּחַר **bāḥar²**, v. Not used in NIV/BHS [cf. 1034, 1047]

1049 בַּחֲרוּמִי **baḥ^a^rûmî**, a.g. [1] [→ 1050]
Baharumite [1]

1Ch 11:33 Azmaveth the **Baharumite**, Eliahba the Shaalbonite,

1050 בַּחֻרְמִי **baḥurimî**, a.g. Not used in NIV/BHS [cf. 1372]

1051 בָּטָא **bāṭā'**, v. [4] [→ 4439]
carelessly [1], rash words came [1], reckless words [1], thoughtlessly [+928+4200+8557] [1]

Lev 5: 4 [D] " 'Or if a person **thoughtlessly** [+928+4200+8557] takes an
5: 4 [D] or evil—in any matter one *might* **carelessly** swear about—
Ps 106:33 [D] the Spirit of God, and **rash words came** from Moses' lips.
Pr 12:18 [A] **Reckless words** pierce like a sword, but the tongue of the

1052 בָּטוּחַ **bāṭûaḥ**, a. Not used in NIV/BHS [√ 1053]

1053 ¹בָּטַח **bāṭaḥ¹**, v. [119] [→ 19, 1052, 1055, 1057, 1058, 1059, 4440; cf. 1054]
trust [45], trusts [15], trusted [10], depending [8], feel secure [4], put trust [4], depend [3], rely [3], secure [3], confident [2], let persuade to trust [2], on basing [2], put confidence [2], relied [2], trusting [2], unsuspecting [2], basing confidence [1], bold [1], depended [1], has full confidence [+4213] [1], led to believe [1], let depend [1], made trust [1], persuaded to trust [1], reckless [1], safe [1]

Dt 28:52 [A] until the high fortified walls in which you **trust** fall down.
Jdg 9:26 [A] into Shechem, and its citizens **put** *their* **confidence** in him.
18: 7 [A] living in safety, like the Sidonians, unsuspecting and **secure**.
18:10 [A] you will find an **unsuspecting** people and a spacious land
18:27 [A] on to Laish, against a peaceful and **unsuspecting** people.
20:36 [A] because *they* **relied** on the ambush they had set near Gibeah.
2Ki 18: 5 [A] Hezekiah **trusted** in the LORD, the God of Israel. There
18:19 [A] says: **On** what *are you* **basing** this confidence of yours?
18:20 [A] On whom *are you* **depending**, that you rebel against me?
18:21 [A] Look now, *you are* **depending** on Egypt, that splintered reed
18:21 [A] Such is Pharaoh king of Egypt to all who **depend** on him.
18:22 [A] say to me, "*We are* **depending** on the LORD our God"—
18:24 [A] even though *you are* **depending** on Egypt for chariots
18:30 [G] *Do* not **let** Hezekiah **persuade** you **to trust** in the LORD
19:10 [A] Do not let the god you **depend** on deceive you when he says,
1Ch 5:20 [A] He answered their prayers, because *they* **trusted** in him.
2Ch 32:10 [A] On what *are* you **basing** your **confidence**, that you remain in
Job 6:20 [A] They are distressed, because *they had been* **confident**;
11:18 [A] *You will be* **secure**, because there is hope; you will look
39:11 [A] *Will you* **rely** on him for his great strength? Will you leave
40:23 [A] *he is* **secure**, though the Jordan should surge against his
Ps 4: 5 [4:6] [A] Offer right sacrifices and **trust** in the LORD.
9:10 [9:11] [A] Those who know your name *will* **trust** in you,
13: 5 [13:6] [A] I **trust** in your unfailing love; my heart rejoices in
21: 7 [21:8] [A] For the king **trusts** in the LORD; through the
22: 4 [22:5] [A] In you our fathers **put** *their* **trust**; they trusted
22: 4 [22:5] [A] put their trust; *they* **trusted** and you delivered them.
22: 5 [22:6] [A] in you *they* **trusted** and were not disappointed.
22: 9 [22:10] [G] **made** me **trust** in you even at my mother's breast.
25: 2 [A] in you *I* **trust**, O my God. Do not let me be put to shame,
26: 1 [A] *I have* **trusted** in the LORD without wavering.
27: 3 [A] war break out against me, even then *will* I *be* **confident**.
28: 7 [A] and my shield; my heart **trusts** in him, and I am helped.
31: 6 [31:7] [A] who cling to worthless idols; I **trust** in the LORD.
31:14 [31:15] [A] I **trust** in you, O LORD; I say, "You are my God."
32:10 [A] the LORD's unfailing love surrounds the *man who* **trusts**
33:21 [A] In him our hearts rejoice, for *we* **trust** in his holy name.
37: 3 [A] **Trust** in the LORD and do good; dwell in the land
37: 5 [A] your way to the LORD; **trust** in him and he will do this:
40: 3 [40:4] [A] will see and fear and **put** *their* **trust** in the LORD.
41: 9 [41:10] [A] Even my close friend, whom *I* **trusted**, he who
44: 6 [44:7] [A] *I do* not **trust** in my bow, my sword does not bring
49: 6 [49:7] [A] those *who* **trust** in their wealth and boast of their
52: 7 [52:9] [A] **trusted** in his great wealth and grew strong by
52: 8 [52:10] [A] *I* **trust** in God's unfailing love for ever and ever.
55:23 [55:24] [A] out half their days. But as for me, *I* **trust** in you.
56: 3 [56:4] [A] When I am afraid, *I will* **trust** in you.
56: 4 [56:5] [A] In God, whose word I praise, in God *I* **trust**; I will
56:11 [56:12] [A] in God *I* **trust**; I will not be afraid. What can man
62: 8 [62:9] [A] **Trust** in him at all times, O people; pour out your
62:10 [62:11] [A] *Do* not **trust** in extortion or take pride in stolen
78:22 [A] for they did not believe in God or **trust** in his deliverance.
84:12 [84:13] [A] blessed is the man *who* **trusts** in you.
86: 2 [A] You are my God; save your servant who **trusts** in you.
91: 2 [A] is my refuge and my fortress, my God, in whom *I* **trust**."
112: 7 [B] of bad news; his heart is steadfast, **trusting** in the LORD.
115: 8 [A] them will be like them, and so will all who **trust** in them.
115: 9 [A] O house of Israel, **trust** in the LORD—he is their help
115:10 [A] O house of Aaron, **trust** in the LORD—he is their help
115:11 [A] *You* who fear him, **trust** in the LORD—he is their help
118: 8 [A] It is better to take refuge in the LORD than *to* **trust** in man.
118: 9 [A] It is better to take refuge in the LORD than *to* **trust** in
119:42 [A] will answer the one who taunts me, for *I* **trust** in your word.
125: 1 [A] Those *who* **trust** in the LORD are like Mount Zion,
135:18 [A] them will be like them, and so will all who **trust** in them.
143: 8 [A] word of your unfailing love, for *I have* **put** *my* **trust** in you.
146: 3 [A] *Do* not **put** *your* **trust** in princes, in mortal men, who cannot
Pr 3: 5 [A] **Trust** in the LORD with all your heart and lean not on your
11:15 [A] but whoever refuses to strike hands in pledge *is* **safe**.
11:28 [A] *Whoever* **trusts** in his riches will fall, but the righteous will
14:16 [A] and shuns evil, but a fool is hotheaded and **reckless**.
16:20 [A] and blessed is he *who* **trusts** in the LORD.
28: 1 [A] no one pursues, but the righteous *are* as **bold** as a lion.
28:25 [A] up dissension, but *he who* **trusts** in the LORD will prosper.
28:26 [A] *He who* **trusts** in himself is a fool, but he who walks in
29:25 [A] to be a snare, but *whoever* **trusts** in the LORD is kept safe.
31:11 [A] Her husband **has full confidence** [+4213] in her and lacks
Isa 12: 2 [A] Surely God is my salvation; *I will* **trust** and not be afraid.
26: 3 [B] peace him whose mind is steadfast, because *he* **trusts** in you.
26: 4 [A] **Trust** in the LORD forever, for the LORD, the LORD,
30:12 [A] this message, **relied** on oppression and depended on deceit,
31: 1 [A] *who* **trust** in the multitude of their chariots and in the great
32: 9 [A] you daughters *who* **feel secure**, hear what I have to say!
32:10 [A] In little more than a year you *who* **feel secure** will tremble;
32:11 [A] shudder, you daughters *who* **feel secure**!
36: 4 [A] says: **On** what *are you* **basing** this confidence of yours?
36: 5 [A] On whom *are you* **depending**, that you rebel against me?
36: 6 [A] Look now, *you are* **depending** on Egypt, that splintered reed
36: 6 [A] Such is Pharaoh king of Egypt to all who **depend** on him.
36: 7 [A] say to me, "*We are* **depending** on the LORD our God"—
36: 9 [A] even though *you are* **depending** on Egypt for chariots
36:15 [G] *Do* not **let** Hezekiah **persuade** you **to trust** in the LORD
37:10 [A] *Do* not **let** the god you **depend** on deceive you when he says,
42:17 [A] those *who* **trust** in idols, who say to images, 'You are our
47:10 [A] *You have* **trusted** in your wickedness and have said, 'No one
50:10 [A] *Let* him who walks in the dark, who has no light, **trust** in the
59: 4 [A] They **rely** on empty arguments and speak lies; they conceive
Jer 5:17 [A] they will destroy the fortified cities in which you **trust**.
7: 4 [A] *Do* not **trust** in deceptive words and say, "This is the temple
7: 8 [A] you *are* **trusting** in deceptive words that are worthless.
7:14 [A] the temple you **trust** in, the place I gave to you and your
9: 4 [9:3] [A] "Beware of your friends; *do* not **trust** your brothers.
13:25 [A] "because you have forgotten me and **trusted** in false gods.
17: 5 [A] "Cursed is the one who **trusts** in man, who depends on flesh
17: 7 [A] "But blessed is the man who **trusts** in the LORD, whose
28:15 [G] sent you, yet you *have* **persuaded** this nation **to trust** in lies.
29:31 [G] though I did not send him, and *has* **led** you **to believe** a lie,
39:18 [A] your life, because *you* **trust** in me, declares the LORD.' "
46:25 [A] her gods and her kings, and on those *who* **rely** on Pharaoh.
48: 7 [A] Since you **trust** in your deeds and riches, you too will be
49: 4 [A] you **trust** in your riches and say, 'Who will attack me?'
49:11 [A] I will protect their lives. Your widows too *can* **trust** in me."
Eze 16:15 [A] " 'But *you* **trusted** in your beauty and used your fame to
33:13 [A] but then he **trusts** in his righteousness and does evil,
Hos 10:13 [A] Because *you have* **depended** on your own strength and on
Am 6: 1 [A] to *you who* **feel secure** on Mount Samaria, you notable men
Mic 7: 5 [A] Do not trust a neighbor; **put** no **confidence** in a friend.

Hab 2:18 [A] For he who makes it **trusts** in his own creation; he makes
Zep 3:2 [A] *She does* not **trust** in the LORD, she does not draw near to

1054 בָּטַח² ***bāṭaḥ²***, v. [1] [cf. 1053]

stumble [1]

Jer 12:5 [A] If you **stumble** in safe country, how will you manage in the

1055 בֶּטַח ***beṭaḥ¹***, n.[m.]. [42] [√ 1053]

safety [24], secure [4], confidence [2], safely [+4200] [2], securely [2], unsuspecting [2], complacency [1], feeling of security [1], security [1], trustfully [+4200] [1], unsuspecting [+4200] [1], without a care [1]

Ge 34:25 took their swords and attacked the **unsuspecting** city,
Lev 25:18 to obey my laws, and you will live **safely** [+4200] in the land.
25:19 yield its fruit, and you will eat your fill and live there in **safety**.
26:5 you will eat all the food you want and live in **safety** in your land.
Dt 12:10 from all your enemies around you so that you will live *in* **safety**.
33:12 "Let the beloved of the LORD rest **secure** in him, for he shields
33:28 So Israel will live *in* **safety** alone; Jacob's spring is secure in a land
Jdg 8:11 east of Nobah and Jogbehah and fell upon the **unsuspecting** army.
18:7 where they saw that the people were living in **safety**, like the
1Sa 12:11 hands of your enemies on every side, so that you lived **securely**.
1Ki 4:25 [5:5] and Israel, from Dan to Beersheba, lived in **safety**,
Job 11:18 there is hope; you will look about you and take your rest in **safety**.
24:23 He may let them rest in a **feeling of security**, but his eyes are on
Ps 4:8 [4:9] for you alone, O LORD, make me dwell in **safety**.
16:9 is glad and my tongue rejoices; my body also will rest **secure**,
78:53 He guided them **safely** [+4200], so they were unafraid; but the sea
Pr 1:33 but whoever listens to me will live *in* **safety** and be at ease,
3:23 you will go on your way in **safety**, and your foot will not stumble;
3:29 against your neighbor, who lives **trustfully** [+4200] near you.
10:9 The man of integrity walks **securely**, but he who takes crooked
Isa 14:30 of the poor will find pasture, and the needy will lie down in **safety**.
32:17 effect of righteousness will be quietness and **confidence** forever.
47:8 lounging in your **security** and saying to yourself, 'I am,
Jer 23:6 In his days Judah will be saved and Israel will live in **safety**.
32:37 I will bring them back to this place and let them live in **safety**.
33:16 In those days Judah will be saved and Jerusalem will live in **safety**.
49:31 a nation at ease, which lives in **confidence**," declares the LORD,
Eze 28:26 They will live there in **safety** and will build houses and plant
28:26 they will live in **safety** when I inflict punishment on all their
30:9 go out from me in ships to frighten Cush out of her **complacency**.
34:25 so that they may live in the desert and sleep in the forests in **safety**.
34:27 ground will yield its crops; the people will be **secure** in their land.
34:28 They will live in **safety**, and no one will make them afraid.
38:8 brought out from the nations, and now all of them live in **safety**.
38:11 I will attack a peaceful and **unsuspecting** [+4200] people—
38:14 In that day, when my people Israel are living in **safety**, will you not
39:6 fire on Magog and on those who live in **safety** in the coastlands,
39:26 they lived in **safety** in their land with no one to make them afraid.
Hos 2:18 [2:20] abolish from the land, so that all may lie down in **safety**.
Mic 2:8 You strip off the rich robe from those who pass by **without a care**,
Zep 2:15 This is the carefree city that lived in **safety**. She said to herself,
Zec 14:11 never again will it be destroyed. Jerusalem will be **secure**.

1056 בֶּטַח² ***beṭaḥ²***, n.pr.loc. [1 / 0] [cf. 3187]

2Sa 8:8 From Tebah [BHS ***Betah***; NIV 3183] and Berothai, towns that

1057 בִּטְחָה ***biṭḥâ***, n.f. [1] [√ 1053]

trust [1]

Isa 30:15 and rest is your salvation, in quietness and **trust** is your strength,

1058 בַּטֻּחָה ***baṭṭuḥâ***, n.f.pl. [1] [√ 1053]

secure [1]

Job 12:6 are undisturbed, and those who provoke God are **secure**—

1059 בִּטָּחוֹן ***biṭṭāḥôn***, n.m. [3] [√ 1053]

confidence [2], hope [1]

2Ki 18:19 of Assyria, says: On what are you basing this **confidence** of yours?
Ecc 9:4 Anyone who is among the living has **hope**—even a live dog is
Isa 36:4 of Assyria, says: On what are you basing this **confidence** of yours?

1060 בָּטַל ***bāṭal***, v. [1] [→ Ar 10098]

cease [1]

Ecc 12:3 [A] men stoop, when the grinders **cease** because they are few,

1061 בֶּטֶן ***beṭen¹***, n.f. [72]

womb [28], belly [4], birth [4], abdomen [3], stomach [3], *untranslated* [2], birth [+562] [2], body [2], heart [2], inmost being [+2540] [2], inmost parts [+2540] [2], bodies [1], born [1], borne [1], bowl-shaped part [1], brothers [+1201] [1], children [+2021+7262] [1], children [+7262] [1], conceived [1], craving [1], depths [1], descendants [+7262] [1], infants [+7262] [1], inside [1], offspring [1], pregnancy [1], still hunger [+4848] [1], waist [1], within [1]

Ge 25:23 The LORD said to her, "Two nations are in your **womb**,
25:24 time came for her to give birth, there were twin boys in her **womb**.
30:2 place of God, who has kept you from *having* **children** [+7262]?"
38:27 time came for her to give birth, there were twin boys in her **womb**.
Nu 5:21 he causes your thigh to waste away and your **abdomen** to swell.
5:22 so that your **abdomen** swells and your thigh wastes away."
5:27 her **abdomen** will swell and her thigh waste away, and she will
Dt 7:13 He will bless the fruit of your **womb**, the crops of your land—
28:4 The fruit of your **womb** will be blessed, and the crops of your land
28:11 in the fruit of your **womb**, the young of your livestock and the
28:18 The fruit of your **womb** will be cursed, and the crops of your land,
28:53 you will eat the fruit of the **womb**, the flesh of the sons
30:9 in all the work of your hands and in the fruit of your **womb**,
Jdg 3:21 the sword from his right thigh and plunged it into the king's **belly**.
3:22 did not pull the sword out, **[RPH]** and the fat closed in over it.
13:5 because the boy is to be a Nazirite, set apart to God from **birth**,
13:7 because the boy will be a Nazirite of God from **birth** until the day
16:17 I have been a Nazirite set apart to God since **birth** [+562].
1Ki 7:20 of both pillars, above the **bowl-shaped part** next to the network,
Job 1:21 "Naked I came from my mother's **womb**, and naked I will depart.
3:10 for it did not shut the doors of the **womb** on me to hide trouble
3:11 "Why did I not perish at birth, and die as I came from the **womb**?
10:19 or had been carried straight from the **womb** to the grave!
15:2 answer with empty notions or fill his **belly** with the hot east wind?
15:35 and give birth to evil; their **womb** fashions deceit."
19:17 to my wife; I am loathsome to my own **brothers** [+1201].
20:15 riches he swallowed; God will make his **stomach** vomit them up.
20:20 "Surely he will have no respite from his **craving**; he cannot save
20:23 When he has filled his **belly**, God will vent his burning anger
31:15 Did not he who made me in the **womb** make them? Did not the
31:18 as would a father, and from my **birth** [+562] I guided the widow—
32:18 For I am full of words, and the spirit **within** me compels me;
32:19 **inside** I am like bottled-up wine, like new wineskins ready to burst.
38:29 From whose **womb** comes the ice? Who gives birth to the frost
40:16 strength he has in his loins, what power in the muscles of his **belly**!
Ps 17:14 *You* **still** *the* **hunger of** [+4848] those you cherish; their sons have
22:9 [22:10] Yet you brought me out of the **womb**; you made me trust
22:10 [22:11] from my mother's **womb** you have been my God.
31:9 [31:10] grow weak with sorrow, my soul and my **body** with grief.
44:25 [44:26] brought down to the dust; our **bodies** cling to the ground.
58:3 [58:4] from the **womb** they are wayward and speak lies.
71:6 From **birth** I have relied on you; you brought me forth from my
127:3 from the LORD, **children** [+2021+7262] a reward from him.
132:11 "One of your own **descendants** [+7262] I will place on your
139:13 my inmost being; you knit me together in my mother's **womb**.
Pr 13:25 to their hearts' content, but the **stomach** *of* the wicked goes hungry.
18:8 choice morsels; they go down to a man's **inmost** [+2540] **parts**.
18:20 From the fruit of his mouth a man's **stomach** is filled;
20:27 the spirit of a man; it searches out his **inmost** [+2540] **being**.
20:30 cleanse away evil, and beatings purge the **inmost** [+2540] **being**.
22:18 for it is pleasing when you keep them in your **heart** and have all of
26:22 choice morsels; they go down to a man's **inmost** [+2540] **parts**.
31:2 "O my son, O son of my **womb**, O son of my vows,
Ecc 5:15 [5:14] Naked a man comes from his mother's **womb**, and as he
11:5 path of the wind, or how the body is formed in a mother's **womb**,
SS 7:2 [7:3] Your **waist** is a mound of wheat encircled by lilies.
Isa 13:18 they will have no mercy on **infants** [+7262] nor will they look with
44:2 he who made you, who formed you in the **womb**, and who will
44:24 the LORD says—your Redeemer, who formed you in the **womb**:
46:3 you whom I have upheld since you were **conceived**, and have
48:8 know how treacherous you are; you were called a rebel from **birth**.
49:1 Before I was **born** the LORD called me; from my birth he has
49:5 he who formed me in the **womb** to be his servant to bring Jacob
49:15 at her breast and have no compassion on the child she has **borne**?
Jer 1:5 "Before I formed you in the **womb** I knew you, before you were
Eze 3:3 **[RPH]** eat this scroll I am giving you and fill your stomach with
Hos 9:11 will fly away like a bird—no birth, no **pregnancy**, no conception.
9:16 Even if they bear children, I will slay their cherished **offspring**."
12:3 [12:4] In the **womb** he grasped his brother's heel; as a man he
Jnh 2:2 [2:3] From the **depths** *of* the grave I called for help, and you
Mic 6:7 for my transgression, the fruit of my **body** for the sin of my soul?
Hab 3:16 I heard and my **heart** pounded, my lips quivered at the sound;

1062 בֶּטֶן² ***beṭen²***, n.pr.loc. [1] [cf. 1063?]

Beten [1]

Jos 19:25 Their territory included: Helkath, Hali, **Beten**, Acshaph,

[F] Hitpael (hitpoel, hitpoal, hitpolel, hitpolal, hitpalel, hitpalal, hitpalpel, hitpalpal, hotpael, hotpaal) [G] Hiphil (hiphtil) [H] Hophal [I] Hishtaphel

1063 בָּטְנָה boṭnâ, n.[m.]pl. [1] [cf. 1062?, 1064?]
pistachio nuts [1]
Ge 43:11 some spices and myrrh, *some* **pistachio nuts** and almonds.

1064 בְּטֹנִים bᵉṭōnîm, n.pr.loc. [1] [cf. 1063?]
Betonim [1]
Jos 13:26 from Heshbon to Ramath Mizpah and **Betonim**, and from

1065 בִּי bî, pt.entreaty. [12]
O [4], please [3], *untranslated* [2], but [2], please [+5528] [1]
Ge 43:20 "**Please**, sir," they said, "we came down here the first time to buy
44:18 "**Please**, my lord, let your servant speak a word to my lord.
Ex 4:10 Moses said to the LORD, "**O** Lord, I have never been eloquent,
4:13 But Moses said, "**O** Lord, please send someone else to do it."
Nu 12:11 he said to Moses, "**Please** [+5528], my lord, do not hold against us
Jos 7:8 **O** Lord, what can I say, now that Israel has been routed by its
Jdg 6:13 "**But** sir," Gideon replied, "if the LORD is with us, why has all
6:15 "**But** Lord," Gideon asked, "how can I save Israel? My clan is the
13:8 "**O** Lord, I beg you, let the man of God you sent to us come again
1Sa 1:26 and she said to him, **[NIE]** "As surely as you live, my lord,
1Ki 3:17 **[NIE]** "My lord, this woman and I live in the same house.
3:26 with compassion for her son and said to the king, "**Please**, my lord,

1066 בָּיַי bāyay, v. Not used in NIV/BHS [√ 14?]

1067 בִּין bîn, v. [170] [→ 1068, 1069, 3296?, 9312]
understand [29], discerning [16], understanding [11], consider [8], understood [5], give understanding [4], have understanding [4], instructed [4], understands [4], discern [3], discernment [3], gain [3], perceive [3], clever [2], gain understanding [2], gives thought [2], gives understanding [2], look [2], note well [+906+1067] [2], ponder [2], realized [2], show regard [2], skilled [2], *untranslated* [1], able [1], acted wisely [1], brilliant [1], cared for [1], checked [1], comprehended [1], consider carefully [1], considers [1], distinguish [1], dwell on [1], enlighten [1], explain [1], explaining [1], feel [1], find [1], gave full attention [1], give discernment [1], give thought [1], have concern [+1981] [1], insight [1], insights have [1], instruct [1], instructing [1], intelligent [1], know [1], knows [1], learned [1], learning [1], let understand [1], look lustfully [1], looked closely [1], master [1], noticed [1], observe [1], pays heed [1], prudent [1], quick to understand [+4529] [1], realize [1], regard [1], see [1], sensible [1], show favor [1], show [1], skillful [1], take heed [1], take note [1], teacher [1], tell the meaning [1], think [1], thinking [1], understand clearly [+928+1069] [1], well [1]
Ge 41:33 [C] "And now let Pharaoh look for a **discerning** and wise man
41:39 [C] known to you, there is no *one so* **discerning** and wise as you.
Dt 1:13 [C] **understanding** and respected men from each of your tribes,
4:6 [C] this great nation is a wise and **understanding** people."
32:7 [A] the days of old; **consider** the generations long past.
32:10 [D] He shielded him and **cared for** him; he guarded him as the
32:29 [A] would understand this and **discern** what their end will be!
1Sa 3:8 [A] Then Eli **realized** that the LORD was calling the boy.
16:18 [C] and a warrior. He speaks **well** and is a fine-looking man.
2Sa 12:19 [A] among themselves and he **realized** the child was dead.
1Ki 3:9 [G] your people and to **distinguish** between right and wrong.
3:11 [G] your enemies but for **discernment** in administering justice,
3:12 [C] I will give you a wise and **discerning** heart, so that there will
3:21 [F] when *I* **looked** at him **closely** in the morning light, I saw that
1Ch 15:22 [G] that was his responsibility because he *was* **skillful** at it.
25:7 [G] all of them trained and **skilled** in music for the LORD—
25:8 [G] Young and old alike, **teacher** as well as student, cast lots for
27:32 [G] was a counselor, a man of **insight** and a scribe.
28:9 [G] and **understands** every motive behind the thoughts.
2Ch 11:23 [A] *He* **acted wisely**, dispersing some of his sons throughout the
26:5 [G] days of Zechariah, who **instructed** him in the fear of God.
34:12 [G] all *who were* **skilled** in playing musical instruments—
35:3 [G] who **instructed** all Israel and who had been consecrated to
Ezr 8:15 [A] When *I* **checked** among the people and the priests, I found
8:16 [G] and Joiarib and Elnathan, *who were men of* **learning**,
Ne 8:2 [G] up of men and women and all *who were* **able** to understand.
8:3 [G] of the men, women and others *who could* **understand**.
8:7 [G] **instructed** the people in the Law while the people were
8:8 [A] so that the people *could* **understand** what was being read.
8:9 [G] the Levites who *were* **instructing** the people said to them all,
8:12 [G] because *they* now **understood** the words that had been made
10:28 [10:29] [G] and daughters who are able *to* **understand**—
13:7 [A] Here *I* **learned** about the evil thing Eliashib had done in
Job 6:24 [G] and I will be quiet; **show** me where I have been wrong.
6:30 [A] wickedness on my lips? *Can* my mouth not **discern** malice?
9:11 [A] I cannot see him; when he goes by, *I* cannot **perceive** him.
11:11 [F] deceitful men; and when he sees evil, *does he* not **take note**?
13:1 [A] have seen all this, my ears have heard and **understood** it.
14:21 [A] does not know it; if they are brought low, *he does* not **see** it.
15:9 [A] not know? What **insights** *do you* **have** that we do not have?
18:2 [A] you end these speeches? *Be* **sensible**, and then we can talk.
23:5 [A] what he would answer me, and **consider** what he would say.
23:8 [A] the east, he is not there; if I go to the west, *I do* not **find** him.
23:15 [F] I am terrified before him; *when I* **think** of all this, I fear him.
26:14 [F] Who then *can* **understand** the thunder of his power?"
28:23 [G] God **understands** the way to it and he alone knows where it
30:20 [F] you do not answer; I stand up, but *you merely* **look** at me.
31:1 [F] "I made a covenant with my eyes not *to* **look lustfully** at a
32:8 [G] the breath of the Almighty, *that* **gives** him **understanding**.
32:9 [A] are wise, not only the aged *who* **understand** what is right.
32:12 [F] *I* **gave** you *my* **full attention**. But not one of you has proved
36:29 [A] *Who can* **understand** how he spreads out the clouds, how he
37:14 [F] "Listen to this, Job; stop and **consider** God's wonders.
38:18 [F] *Have you* **comprehended** the vast expanses of the earth?
38:20 [A] to their places? *Do you* **know** the paths to their dwellings?
42:3 [A] Surely I spoke of things *I did* not **understand**, things too
Ps 5:1 [5:2] [A] ear to my words, O LORD, **consider** my sighing.
19:12 [19:13] [A] Who *can* **discern** his errors? Forgive my hidden
28:5 [A] Since *they* **show** no **regard** for the works of the LORD
32:9 [G] *which* **have** no **understanding** but must be controlled by bit
33:15 [G] forms the hearts of all, who **considers** everything they do.
37:10 [F] no more; though *you* **look** for them, they will not be found.
49:20 [49:21] [A] A man who has riches without **understanding** is
50:22 [A] "**Consider** this, *you* who forget God, or I will tear you to
58:9 [58:10] [A] Before your pots *can* **feel** ⌞the heat of⌟ the thorns—
73:17 [A] the sanctuary of God; then *I* **understood** their final destiny.
82:5 [A] "They know nothing, *they* **understand** nothing. They walk
92:6 [92:7] [A] man does not know, fools *do* not **understand**,
94:7 [A] "The LORD does not see; the God of Jacob **pays** no **heed**."
94:8 [A] **Take heed**, *you* senseless ones among the people; you fools,
107:43 [F] heed these things and **consider** the great love of the LORD.
119:27 [G] **Let** me **understand** the teaching of your precepts; then I will
119:34 [G] **Give** me **understanding**, and I will keep your law and obey
119:73 [G] **give** me **understanding** to learn your commands.
119:95 [F] are waiting to destroy me, but *I will* **ponder** your statutes.
119:100 [F] *I* **have** more **understanding** than the elders, for I obey your
119:104 [F] *I* **gain understanding** from your precepts; therefore I hate
119:125 [G] **give** me **discernment** that I may understand your statutes.
119:130 [G] your words gives light; *it* **gives understanding** *to* the simple.
119:144 [G] are forever right; **give** me **understanding** that I may live.
119:169 [G] O LORD; **give** me **understanding** according to your word.
139:2 [A] I sit and when I rise; *you* **perceive** my thoughts from afar.
Pr 1:2 [G] and discipline; for **understanding** words of insight;
1:5 [C] add to their learning, and let the **discerning** get guidance—
1:6 [G] for **understanding** proverbs and parables, the sayings
2:5 [A] *you will* **understand** the fear of the LORD and find the
2:9 [A] Then *you will* **understand** what is right and just and fair—
7:7 [A] I saw among the simple, *I* **noticed** among the young men,
8:5 [G] You who are simple, **gain** prudence; you who are foolish,
8:5 [G] gain prudence; you who are foolish, **gain** understanding.
8:9 [G] To the **discerning** all of them are right; they are faultless to
10:13 [C] Wisdom is found on the lips of the **discerning**, but a rod is
14:6 [C] finds none, but knowledge comes easily to the **discerning**.
14:8 [G] The wisdom of the prudent is *to* **give thought** *to* their ways,
14:15 [G] but a prudent man **gives thought** to his steps.
14:33 [C] Wisdom reposes in the heart of the **discerning** and even
15:14 [C] The **discerning** heart seeks knowledge, but the mouth of a
16:21 [C] The wise in heart are called **discerning**, and pleasant words
17:10 [G] A rebuke impresses a *man of* **discernment** more than a
17:24 [G] A **discerning** *man* keeps wisdom in view, but a fool's eyes
17:28 [C] wise if he keeps silent, and **discerning** if he holds his tongue.
18:15 [C] The heart of the **discerning** acquires knowledge; the ears of
19:25 [C] rebuke a **discerning** *man*, and he will gain knowledge.
19:25 [A] rebuke a discerning man, and *he will* **gain** knowledge.
20:24 [A] How then *can* anyone **understand** his own way?
21:29 [A] but an upright man **gives thought** [K 3922] *to* his ways.
23:1 [A] dine with a ruler, **note** [+906+1067] **well** what is before you,
23:1 [A] dine with a ruler, **note well** [+906+1067] what is before you,
24:12 [A] about this," *does* not he who weighs the heart **perceive** it?
28:2 [G] but a man of **understanding** and knowledge maintains order.
28:5 [A] Evil men *do* not **understand** justice, but those who seek the
28:5 [A] but those who seek the LORD **understand** it fully.
28:7 [G] He who keeps the law *is* a **discerning** son, but a companion
28:11 [G] but a poor man *who has* **discernment** sees through him.
29:7 [A] for the poor, but the wicked **have** no *such* **concern** [+1981].
29:19 [A] by mere words; though *he* **understands**, he will not respond.
Ecc 9:11 [C] to the wise or wealth to the **brilliant** or favor to the learned;
Isa 1:3 [F] but Israel does not know, my people *do* not **understand**."
3:3 [C] the counselor, skilled craftsman and **clever** enchanter.
5:21 [C] who are wise in their own eyes and **clever** in their own sight.

Isa 6: 9 [A] " 'Be ever hearing, but never **understanding**; be ever seeing,
6: 10 [A] **understand** with their hearts, and turn and be healed."
10: 13 [C] and by my wisdom, because *I* **have understanding**.
14: 16 [F] Those who see you stare at you, *they* **ponder** your fate: "Is
28: 9 [G] "Who is it he is trying to teach? *To* whom *is he* **explaining**
28: 19 [G] The **understanding** *of* this message will bring sheer terror.
29: 14 [C] will perish, the intelligence of the **intelligent** will vanish."
29: 16 [G] Can the pot say of the potter, "*He* **knows** nothing"?
32: 4 [A] The mind of the rash will know and **understand**,
40: 14 [G] Whom did the LORD consult *to* **enlighten** him, and who
40: 21 [G] *Have you* not **understood** since the earth was founded?
43: 10 [A] you may know and believe me and **understand** that I am he.
43: 18 [F] "Forget the former things; *do* not **dwell on** the past.
44: 18 [A] They know nothing, *they* **understand** nothing; their eyes are
52: 15 [F] will see, and what they have not heard, *they will* **understand**.
56: 11 [G] **[RPH]** they all turn to their own way, each seeks his own
57: 1 [G] no *one* **understands** that the righteous are taken away to be
Jer 2: 10 [F] coasts of Kittim and look, send to Kedar and **observe** closely;
4: 22 [C] They are senseless children; they **have** no **understanding**.
9: 12 [9:11] [A] What man is wise enough *to* **understand** this? Who
9: 17 [9:16] [F] "**Consider** now! Call for the wailing women to come;
23: 20 [F] In days to come *you will* **understand** [+928+1069] it **clearly**.
30: 24 [F] of his heart. In days to come *you will* **understand** this.
49: 7 [A] Has counsel perished from the **prudent**? Has their wisdom
Da 1: 4 [G] well informed, **quick to understand** [+4529], and qualified
1: 17 [G] Daniel *could* **understand** visions and dreams of all kinds.
8: 5 [G] As I was **thinking** about this, suddenly a goat with a
8: 16 [G] "Gabriel, **tell** this man **the meaning** *of* the vision."
8: 17 [G] "**understand** that the vision concerns the time of the end."
8: 23 [G] a stern-faced king, a **master** *of* intrigue, will arise.
8: 27 [G] I was appalled by the vision; it was beyond **understanding**.
9: 2 [A] year of his reign, I, Daniel, **understood** from the Scriptures,
9: 22 [G] *He* **instructed** me and said to me, "Daniel, I have now come
9: 23 [A] Therefore, **consider** the message and understand the vision:
9: 23 [G] Therefore, consider the message and **understand** the vision:
10: 1 [A] The **understanding** *of* the message came to him in a vision.
10: 11 [G] *you* who are highly esteemed, **consider carefully** the words I
10: 12 [G] the first day that you set your mind to **gain understanding**
10: 14 [G] Now I have come to **explain** *to* you what will happen to your
11: 30 [A] and **show favor** to those who forsake the holy covenant.
11: 33 [G] "Those who are wise *will* **instruct** many, though for a time
11: 37 [A] *He will* **show** no **regard** for the gods of his fathers or for the
11: 37 [A] for the one desired by women, nor *will he* **regard** any god,
12: 8 [A] I heard, but *I did* not **understand**. So I asked, "My lord,
12: 10 [A] None of the wicked *will* **understand**, but those who are wise
12: 10 [A] will understand, but those who are wise *will* **understand**.
Hos 4: 14 [A] a people without **understanding** will come to ruin!
14: 9 [14:10] [A] Who is wise? *He will* **realize** these things. Who is
14: 9 [14:10] [C] Who *is* **discerning**? He will understand them.
Mic 4: 12 [G] *they do* not **understand** his plan, he who gathers them like

1068 בַּיִן ***bayin***, subst. & pp. [408] [→ 1227; cf. 1067; Ar 10099] See Select Index

between [164], *untranslated* [145], among [31], at twilight [+2021+6847] [11], from [6], at [3], between [+4946] [3], above [+448] [2], as [2], in midair [+824+1068+2021+2021+2256+9028] [2], on forehead [+6524] [2], on foreheads [+6524] [2], or [2], whether [2], with [2], above [+6584] [1], above [1], against [1], alternated with [1], among [+4946] [1], attached to [1], difference between [1], distinction between [1], every [1], from [+4200] [1], front of heads [+6524] [1], have [+2118] [1], in [+928] [1], in the midst of [1], midst [1], of [+4946] [1], on [1], out [+4946] [1], out of [+4946] [1], relationships between [1], separate [+5911] [1], separated [+7233] [1], slung on back [+4190] [1], the difference between [1], to [1], together [1], using [1], witness [+9048] [1], womb [+8079] [1]

1069 בִּינָה ***bînâ***, n.f. [38] [√ 1067; Ar 10100]

understanding [24], insight [2], wisdom [2], *untranslated* [1], discernment [1], good sense [1], great skill [+2682+3359] [1], incomprehensible [+401] [1], intelligence [1], understand [+3359] [1], understand clearly [+928+1067] [1], understand [1], understood [+3359+4200] [1]

Dt 4: 6 for this will show your wisdom and **understanding** to the nations,
1Ch 12: 32 [12:33] men of Issachar, *who* **understood** [+3359+4200] the times
22: 12 and **understanding** when he puts you in command over Israel,
2Ch 2: 12 [2:11] a wise son, endowed with intelligence and **discernment**,
2: 13 [2:12] you Huram-Abi, a man of **great skill** [+2682+3359],
Job 20: 3 that dishonors me, and my **understanding** inspires me to reply.
28: 12 where can wisdom be found? Where does **understanding** dwell?
28: 20 then does wisdom come from? Where does **understanding** dwell?
28: 28 of the Lord—that is wisdom, and to shun evil is **understanding**.' "
34: 16 "If you have **understanding**, hear this; listen to what I say.
38: 4 I laid the earth's foundation? Tell me, if *you* **understand** [+3359].
38: 36 the heart with wisdom or gave **understanding** to the mind?
39: 17 did not endow her with wisdom or give her a share of **good sense**.
39: 26 "Does the hawk take flight by your **wisdom** and spread his wings
Pr 1: 2 and discipline; for understanding words of **insight**;
2: 3 and if you call out for **insight** and cry aloud for understanding,
3: 5 with all your heart and lean not on your own **understanding**;
4: 1 to a father's instruction; pay attention and gain **understanding**.
4: 5 Get wisdom, get **understanding**; do not forget my words or
4: 7 get wisdom. Though it cost all you have, get **understanding**.
7: 4 "You are my sister," and call **understanding** your kinsman;
8: 14 and sound judgment are mine; I have **understanding** and power.
9: 6 simple ways and you will live; walk in the way of **understanding**.
9: 10 of wisdom, and knowledge of the Holy One is **understanding**.
16: 16 get wisdom than gold, to choose **understanding** rather than silver!
23: 4 wear yourself out to get rich; have the **wisdom** to show restraint.
23: 23 and do not sell it; get wisdom, discipline and **understanding**.
30: 2 the most ignorant of men; I do not have a man's **understanding**.
Isa 11: 2 the Spirit of wisdom and of **understanding**, the Spirit of counsel
27: 11 For this is a people without **understanding**; so their Maker has no
29: 14 the wise will perish, the **intelligence** *of* the intelligent will vanish."
29: 24 Those who are wayward in spirit will gain **understanding**;
33: 19 with their strange, **incomprehensible** [+401] tongue.
Jer 23: 20 In days to come *you will* **understand** it **clearly** [+928+1067].
Da 1: 20 and **understanding** about which the king questioned them,
8: 15 Daniel, was watching the vision and trying to **understand** it,
9: 22 I have now come to give you insight and **understanding**.
10: 1 The understanding of the message came **[RPH]** to him in a vision.

1070 בֵּיצָה ***bêṣâ***, n.f. [6] [√ 1009]

eggs [5], *untranslated* [1]

Dt 22: 6 **[RPH]** and the mother is sitting on the young or on the eggs,
22: 6 the ground, and the mother is sitting on the young or on the **eggs**,
Job 39: 14 She lays her **eggs** on the ground and lets them warm in the sand,
Isa 10: 14 as men gather abandoned **eggs**, so I gathered all the countries;
59: 5 They hatch the **eggs** *of* vipers and spin a spider's web.
59: 5 Whoever eats their **eggs** will die, and when one is broken,

1071 בַּיִר ***bayir***, n.[f.]. Not used in NIV/BHS [√ 1014; cf. 931]

1072 בִּירָה ***bîrâ***, n.f. [18] [cf. 1073; Ar 10101]

citadel [14], forts [2], palatial structure [2]

1Ch 29: 1 because this **palatial structure** is not for man but for the LORD
29: 19 to do everything to build the **palatial structure** for which I have
2Ch 17: 12 and more powerful; he built **forts** and store cities in Judah
27: 4 towns in the Judean hills and **forts** and towers in the wooded areas.
Ne 1: 1 of Kislev in the twentieth year, while I was in the **citadel** of Susa,
2: 8 he will give me timber to make beams for the gates of the **citadel**
7: 2 along with Hananiah the commander of the **citadel**, because he
Est 1: 2 King Xerxes reigned from his royal throne in the **citadel** *of* Susa,
1: 5 from the least to the greatest, who were in the **citadel** of Susa.
2: 3 bring all these beautiful girls into the harem at the **citadel** of Susa.
2: 5 Now there was in the **citadel** of Susa a Jew of the tribe of
2: 8 many girls were brought to the **citadel** of Susa and put under the
3: 15 couriers went out, and the edict was issued in the **citadel** of Susa.
8: 14 And the edict was also issued in the **citadel** *of* Susa.
9: 6 In the **citadel** of Susa, the Jews killed and destroyed five hundred
9: 11 The number of those slain in the **citadel** of Susa was reported to
9: 12 five hundred men and the ten sons of Haman in the **citadel** of Susa.
Da 8: 2 In my vision I saw myself in the **citadel** of Susa in the province of

1073 בִּירָנִיָּה ***bîrāniyyâ***, n.f. Not used in NIV/BHS [cf. 1072]

1074 בַּיִת ***bayit[1]***, n.m. [2041 / 2039] [→ 1131; Ar 10103]

house [770], temple [436], palace [120], household [81], houses [81], home [71], family [67], families [+3] [57], *untranslated* [36], family [+3] [25], people [21], land [15], palace [+4889] [15], homes [10], hold [8], buildings [6], households [6], Israelite [+408+3776+4946] [6], place [6], prison [+2021+6045] [6], estate [5], harem [+851] [5], inside [+4946] [5], Israel [+3776] [5], shrines [5], behind [+4946] [4], building [4], families [4], family line [4], hall [4], its[s] [+2021] [4], Judah [+3373] [4], prison [+2021+3975] [4], room [4], that[s] [4], dynasty [3], armory [+3998] [2], center [2], court [2], division [2], dungeon [+1014] [2], inside [+2025] [2], inside [+928+2021] [2], its[s] [+2021] [2], its[s] [+3378] [2], palace grounds [+4889] [2], prison [+2021+3989] [2], prison [+3975] [2], prison [+659] [2], quarters [2], residence [2], sanctuary [2], shelter [2], storehouses [+5800] [2], temple area [2], temples [2], there[s] [+928+2021] [2], those[s] [2], tribe [2], tribes [2], web [2], apartment [1], banquet hall [+3516] [1], born in the same home [+4580] [1], bottles [1], camps [+5661] [1], clan [+3+5476] [1], clan [1], clans [+3] [1], descendants [+5270] [1], descendants [1], dungeon [+3975] [1], dwellings [1], full [+6017] [1], group [+3+2755] [1], guest [+440+995] [1], guests [+1591] [1], house [+185] [1], house [+4632] [1], imprisoned [+657+906+2021+5989] [1], in [+2021+2025] [1], inner [1], inside [+4200+4946] [1], inside [+448+2021] [1], inside [1], interior [+2025+4946] [1], interior [1], inward [+2025] [1], Israelite [+3776] [1], Israelites [+3776] [1], it[s] [+1251] [1], it[s] [+3378] [1], it[s] [+513] [1], kitchens [+1418] [1], lived [+928+2021] [1], living with [1], lodge [+4472] [1], main hall [1], mansions [+8041] [1], mansions [1], palace [+4895] [1], palaces [1], pen up [+2025] [1], penned up [+906+928+2021+3973] [1], possessions [1], prison [+2021+4551] [1], prison [+2021+7213] [1], prison [+5464] [1], prison [+673+2021] [1], prison [1], prisons [+3975] [1], realm [1], sanctuary [+5219] [1], shrine [+466] [1], shrine [1], slave by birth [+3535] [1], stall [1], steward[s] [+408+889+2021 +6584] [1], steward[s] [+889+6584] [1], storehouse [+238] [1], storehouse [+667] [1], strong fortress [+5181] [1], that[s] [+2021+2021 +2296] [1], them[s] [+466+2021+3998] [1], them[s] [+2023] [1], there[s] [+466+928] [1], there[s] [+7281] [1], there[s] [+8235] [1], there[s] [+928+2021+3752] [1], they[s] [+3441] [1], tomb [1], town [1], treasury [+238] [1], under [+4200] [1], underneath [+4946] [1], wall [1], where[s] [1], wine stewards [+8042] [1], workers [+6275] [1]

Ge 6:14 make rooms in it and coat it with pitch **inside** [+4946] and out.
7: 1 then said to Noah, "Go into the ark, you and your whole **family**,
12: 1 your people and your father's **household** and go to the land I will
12:15 they praised her to Pharaoh, and she was taken into his **palace**.
12:17 on Pharaoh and his **household** because of Abram's wife Sarai.
14:14 he called out the 318 trained men born in his **household** and went
15: 2 and the one who will inherit my **estate** is Eliezer of Damascus?"
15: 3 me no children; so a servant in my **household** will be my heir."
17:12 including those born in your **household** or bought with money
17:13 Whether born in your **household** or bought with your money,
17:23 and all those born in his **household** or bought with his money,
17:23 every male in his **household**, and circumcised them, as God told
17:27 every male in Abraham's **household**, including those born in his
17:27 including those born in his **household** or bought from a foreigner,
18:19 his **household** after him to keep the way of the LORD by doing
19: 2 "My lords," he said, "please turn aside to your servant's **house**.
19: 3 so strongly that they did go with him and entered his **house**.
19: 4 of the city of Sodom—both young and old—surrounded the **house**.
19:10 reached out and pulled Lot back into the **house** and shut the door.
19:11 Then they struck the men who were at the door of the **house**,
20:13 And when God had me wander from my father's **household**,
20:18 the LORD had closed up every womb in Abimelech's **household**
24: 2 He said to the chief servant in his **household**, the one in charge of
24: 7 who brought me out of my father's **household** and my native land
24:23 is there room in your father's **house** for us to spend the night?"
24:27 the LORD has led me on the journey to the **house** *of* my master's
24:28 The girl ran and told her mother's **household** about these things.
24:31 out here? I have prepared the **house** and a place for the camels."
24:32 So the man went to the **house**, and the camels were unloaded.
24:38 go to my father's **family** and to my own clan, and get a wife for
24:40 a wife for my son from my own clan and from my father's **family**.
27:15 which she had in the **house**, and put them on her younger son
28: 2 to Paddan Aram, to the **house** *of* your mother's father Bethuel.
28:17 This is none other than the **house** *of* God; this is the gate of
28:21 so that I return safely to my father's **house**, then the LORD will
28:22 and this stone that I have set up as a pillar will be God's **house**,
29:13 He embraced him and kissed him and brought him to his **home**,
30:30 But now, when may I do something for my own **household**?"
31:14 we still have any share in the inheritance of our father's **estate**?
31:30 have gone off because you longed to return to your father's **house**.
31:37 my goods, what have you found that belongs to your **household**?
31:41 It was like this for the twenty years I was in your **household**.
33:17 where he built a **place** for himself and made shelters for his
34:19 who was the most honored of all his father's **household**,
34:26 to the sword and took Dinah from Shechem's **house** and left.
34:29 and children, taking as plunder everything in the **houses**.
34:30 against me and attack me, I and my **household** will be destroyed."
35: 2 So Jacob said to his **household** and to all who were with him,
36: 6 and sons and daughters and all the members of his **household**,
38:11 "Live as a widow in your father's **house** until my son Shelah
38:11 just like his brothers." So Tamar went to live in her father's **house**.
39: 2 and he prospered, and he lived in the **house** *of* his Egyptian master.
39: 4 Potiphar put him in charge of his **household**, and he entrusted to
39: 5 From the time he put him in charge of his **household** and of all that
39: 5 the LORD blessed the **household** *of* the Egyptian because of
39: 5 was on everything Potiphar had, both in the **house** and in the field.
39: 8 "my master does not concern himself with anything in the **house**;
39: 9 No one is greater in this **house** than I am. My master has withheld
39:11 One day he went into the **house** to attend to his duties, and none of
39:11 attend to his duties, and none of the **household** servants was inside.
39:11 and none of the household servants was **inside** [+928+2021].
39:14 she called her **household** servants. "Look," she said to them,
39:16 She kept his cloak beside her until his master came **home**.
39:20 Joseph's master took him and put him in **prison** [+2021+6045],
39:20 But while Joseph was there in *the* **prison** [+2021+6045],
39:21 granted him favor in the eyes of the **prison** [+2021+6045] warden.
39:22 So the warden **[RPH]** put Joseph in charge of all those held in the
39:22 put Joseph in charge of all those held in the **prison** [+2021+6045],
39:23 The warden **[RPH]** paid no attention to anything under Joseph's
40: 3 and put them in custody in the **house** *of* the captain of the guard,
40: 3 in the same **prison** [+2021+6045] where Joseph was confined.
40: 5 the king of Egypt, who were being held in **prison** [+2021+6045]—
40: 7 officials who were in custody with him in his master's **house**,
40:14 me kindness; mention me to Pharaoh and get me out of this **prison**.
41:10 and the chief baker in the **house** *of* the captain of the guard.
41:40 You shall be in charge of my **palace**, and all my people are to
41:51 has made me forget all my trouble and all my father's **household**."
42:19 honest men, let one of your brothers stay here in **prison** [+5464],
42:19 rest of you go and take grain back for your starving **households**.
42:33 here with me, and take food for your starving **households** and go.
43:16 he said to the steward of his **house**, "Take these men to my house,
43:16 "Take these men to my **house**, slaughter an animal and prepare
43:17 man did as Joseph told him and took the men to Joseph's **house**.
43:18 Now the men were frightened when they were taken to his **house**.
43:19 So they went up to Joseph's **steward**[s] [+408+889+2021+6584] and
43:19 to Joseph's steward and spoke to him at the entrance to the **house**.
43:24 The steward took the men into Joseph's **house**, gave them water to
43:26 When Joseph came **home**, they presented to him the gifts they had
43:26 they presented to him the gifts they had brought into the **house**,
44: 1 Now Joseph gave these instructions to the steward of his **house**:
44: 4 far from the city when Joseph said to his **steward**[s] [+889+6584],
44: 8 So why would we steal silver or gold from your master's **house**?
44:14 Joseph was still in the **house** when Judah and his brothers came in,
45: 2 the Egyptians heard him, and Pharaoh's **household** heard about it.
45: 8 to Pharaoh, lord of his entire **household** and ruler of all Egypt.
45:11 Otherwise you and your **household** and all who belong to you will
45:16 When the news reached Pharaoh's **palace** that Joseph's brothers
45:18 bring your father and your **families** back to me. I will give you the
46:27 the members of Jacob's **family**, which went to Egypt, were seventy
46:31 Then Joseph said to his brothers and to his father's **household**,
46:31 and will say to him, 'My brothers and my father's **household**,
47:12 and his brothers and all his father's **household** with food,
47:14 the grain they were buying, and he brought it to Pharaoh's **palace**.
47:24 as food for yourselves and your **households** and your children."
50: 4 Joseph said to Pharaoh's **court**, "If I have found favor in your
50: 7 the dignitaries of his **court** and all the dignitaries of Egypt—
50: 8 besides all the members of Joseph's **household** and his brothers
50: 8 and his brothers and *those belonging to* his father's **household**.
50:22 Joseph stayed in Egypt, along with all his father's **family**.

Ex 1: 1 sons of Israel who went to Egypt with Jacob, each with his **family**:
1:21 the midwives feared God, he gave them **families** of their own.
2: 1 Now a man of the **house** *of* Levi married a Levite woman,
3:22 and any woman living in her **house** for articles of silver and gold
6:14 These were the heads of their **families** [+3]: The sons of Reuben
7:23 Instead, he turned and went into his **palace**, and did not take even
8: 3 [7:28] They will come up into your **palace** and your bedroom and
8: 3 [7:28] into the **houses** *of* your officials and on your people,
8: 9 [8:5] people that you and your **houses** may be rid of the frogs,
8:11 [8:7] The frogs will leave you and your **houses**, your officials
8:13 [8:9] The frogs died in the **houses**, in the courtyards and in the
8:21 [8:17] and your officials, on your people and into your **houses**.
8:21 [8:17] The **houses** *of* the Egyptians will be full of flies, and even
8:24 [8:20] Dense swarms of flies poured into Pharaoh's **palace**
8:24 [8:20] into Pharaoh's palace and into the **houses** *of* his officials,
9:19 animal that has not been brought **in** [+2021+2025] and is still out
9:20 to bring their slaves and their livestock **inside** [+448+2021].
10: 6 They will fill your **houses** and those of all your officials and all the
10: 6 your houses and **those**[s] *of* all your officials and all the Egyptians—
10: 6 and those of all your officials and **[RPH]** all the Egyptians—
12: 3 day of this month each man is to take a lamb for his **family** [+3],
12: 3 each man is to take a lamb for his family, one for each **household**.
12: 4 If any **household** is too small for a whole lamb, they must share
12: 4 **[NIE]** having taken into account the number of people there are.
12: 7 and tops of the doorframes of the **houses** where they eat the lambs.
12:13 The blood will be a sign for you on the **houses** where you are;
12:15 On the first day remove the yeast from your **houses**, for whoever
12:19 For seven days no yeast is to be found in your **houses**. And
12:22 Not one of you shall go out the door of his **house** until morning.
12:23 he will not permit the destroyer to enter your **houses** and strike you
12:27 who passed over the **houses** *of* the Israelites in Egypt and spared
12:27 spared our **homes** when he struck down the Egyptians.' " Then the
12:29 to the firstborn of the prisoner, who was in the **dungeon** [+1014],
12:30 wailing in Egypt, for there was not a **house** without someone dead.
12:46 "It must be eaten inside one **house**; take none of the meat outside
12:46 be eaten inside one house; take none of the meat outside the **house**.
13: 3 the day you came out of Egypt, out of the **land** *of* slavery,

Ex 13:14 the LORD brought us out of Egypt, out of the **land** *of* slavery.
16:31 The **people** *of* Israel called the bread manna. It was white like
19: 3 "This is what you are to say to the **house** *of* Jacob and what you
20: 2 who brought you out of Egypt, out of the **land** *of* slavery.
20:17 "You shall not covet your neighbor's **house**. You shall not covet
22: 7 [22:6] and they are stolen from the neighbor's **house**,
22: 8 [22:7] the owner of the **house** must appear before the judges to
23:19 "Bring the best of the firstfruits of your soil to the **house** *of* the
25:11 Overlay it with pure gold, both **inside** [+4946] and out, and make a
25:27 The rings are to be close to the rim to **hold** the poles used in
26:29 the frames with gold and make gold rings to **hold** the crossbars.
26:33 and place the ark of the Testimony **behind** [+4946] the curtain.
28:26 of the breastpiece on the **inside** [+2025] edge next to the ephod.
30: 4 two on opposite sides—to **hold** the poles used to carry it.
34:26 "Bring the best of the firstfruits of your soil to the **house** *of* the
36:34 the frames with gold and made gold rings to **hold** the crossbars.
37: 2 He overlaid it with pure gold, both **inside** [+4946] and out,
37:14 The rings were put close to the rim to **hold** the poles used in
37:27 two on opposite sides—to **hold** the poles used to carry it.
38: 5 They cast bronze rings to **hold** the poles for the four corners of the
39:19 of the breastpiece on the **inside** [+2025] edge next to the ephod.
40:38 in the sight of all the **house** *of* Israel during all their travels.
Lev 10: 6 your relatives, all the **house** *of* Israel, may mourn for those the
14:34 and I put a spreading mildew in a **house** *in* that land,
14:35 the owner of the **house** must go and tell the priest, 'I have seen
14:35 'I have seen something that looks like mildew in my **house**.'
14:36 The priest is to order the **house** to be emptied before he goes in to
14:36 so that nothing in the **house** will be pronounced unclean.
14:36 After this the priest is to go in and inspect the **house**.
14:37 **[RPH]** and if it has greenish or reddish depressions that appear to
14:38 the priest shall go out **[RPH]** the doorway of the house and close
14:38 the priest shall go out the doorway of the **house** and close it up for
14:38 the doorway of the house and close **it**[s] [+2021] up for seven days.
14:39 inspect the house. If the mildew has spread on the walls, **[RPH]**
14:41 He must have all the **inside** [+4946] walls of the house scraped
14:41 He must have all the inside walls of the **house** scraped and the
14:42 stones to replace these and take new clay and plaster the **house**.
14:43 "If the mildew reappears in the **house** after the stones have been
14:43 the stones have been torn out and the **house** scraped and plastered,
14:44 and examine it and, if the mildew has spread in the **house**,
14:44 in the house, it is a destructive mildew; the **house** is unclean.
14:45 **It**[s] [+2021] must be torn down—its stones, timbers and all the
14:45 the plaster—**[RPH]** and taken out of the town to an unclean place.
14:46 "Anyone who goes into the **house** while it is closed up will be
14:47 who sleeps **[RPH]** or eats in the house must wash his clothes.
14:47 Anyone who sleeps or eats in the **house** must wash his clothes.
14:48 the mildew has not spread **[RPH]** after the house has been
14:48 and the mildew has not spread after the **house** has been plastered,
14:48 he shall pronounce the **house** clean, because the mildew is gone.
14:49 To purify the **house** he is to take two birds and some cedar wood,
14:51 dead bird and the fresh water, and sprinkle the **house** seven times.
14:52 He shall purify the **house** with the bird's blood, the fresh water,
14:53 In this way he will make atonement for the **house**, and it will be
14:55 for mildew in clothing or in a **house**,
16: 2 **behind** [+4946] the curtain in front of the atonement cover on the
16: 6 sin offering to make atonement for himself and his **household**.
16:11 sin offering to make atonement for himself and his **household**,
16:12 ground fragrant incense and take them **behind** [+4946] the curtain.
16:15 take its blood **behind** [+4946] the curtain and do with it as he did
16:17 for himself, his **household** and the whole community of Israel.
17: 3 Any **Israelite** [+408+3776+4946] who sacrifices an ox, a lamb or a
17: 8 "Say to them: 'Any **Israelite** [+408+3776+4946] or any alien
17:10 " 'Any **Israelite** [+408+3776+4946] or any alien living among
18: 9 whether she was **born in the same home** [+4580] or elsewhere.
22:11 or if a slave is born in his **household**, that slave may eat his food.
22:13 and she returns to live in her father's **house** as in her youth,
22:18 'If any of you—either an **Israelite** [+408+3776+4946] or an alien
25:29 " 'If a man sells a **house** [+4632] *in* a walled city, he retains the
25:30 the **house** in the walled city shall belong permanently to the buyer
25:31 **houses** *in* villages without walls around them are to be considered
25:32 " 'The Levites always have the right to redeem their **houses** *in* the
25:33 that is, a **house** sold in any town they hold—and is to be returned
25:33 because the **houses** *in* the towns of the Levites are their property
27:14 " 'If a man dedicates his **house** as something holy to the LORD,
27:15 If the man who dedicates his **house** redeems it, he must add a fifth
Nu 1: 2 of the whole Israelite community by their clans and **families** [+3],
1: 4 from each tribe, each the head of his **family** [+3], is to help you.
1:18 people indicated their ancestry by their clans and **families** [+3],
1:20 by one, according to the records of their clans and **families** [+3].
1:22 by one, according to the records of their clans and **families** [+3].
1:24 by name, according to the records of their clans and **families** [+3].
1:26 by name, according to the records of their clans and **families** [+3].
1:28 by name, according to the records of their clans and **families** [+3].
1:30 by name, according to the records of their clans and **families** [+3].
1:32 by name, according to the records of their clans and **families** [+3].
1:34 by name, according to the records of their clans and **families** [+3].
1:36 by name, according to the records of their clans and **families** [+3].
1:38 by name, according to the records of their clans and **families** [+3].
1:40 by name, according to the records of their clans and **families** [+3].
1:42 by name, according to the records of their clans and **families** [+3].
1:44 the twelve leaders of Israel, each one representing his **family** [+3].
1:45 in Israel's army were counted according to their **families** [+3].
2: 2 each man under his standard with the banners of his **family** [+3]."
2:32 These are the Israelites, counted according to their **families** [+3].
2:34 and that is the way they set out, each with his clan and **family** [+3].
3:15 "Count the Levites by their **families** [+3] and clans. Count every
3:20 These were the Levite clans, according to their **families** [+3].
3:24 The leader of the **families** [+3] of the Gershonites was Eliasaph
3:30 The leader of the **families** [+3] of the Kohathite clans was
3:35 The leader of the **families** [+3] of the Merarite clans was Zuriel
4: 2 Kohathite branch of the Levites by their clans and **families** [+3].
4:22 "Take a census also of the Gershonites by their **families** [+3]
4:29 "Count the Merarites by their clans and **families** [+3].
4:34 counted the Kohathites by their clans and **families** [+3].
4:38 The Gershonites were counted by their clans and **families** [+3].
4:40 counted by their clans and **families** [+3], were 2,630.
4:42 The Merarites were counted by their clans and **families** [+3].
4:46 of Israel counted all the Levites by their clans and **families** [+3].
7: 2 the heads of **families** [+3] who were the tribal leaders in charge of
12: 7 this is not true of my servant Moses; he is faithful in all my **house**.
16:32 with their **households** and all Korah's men and all their
17: 2 [17:17] one from the leader of each of their ancestral **tribes**.
17: 2 [17:17] **[RPH]** Write the name of each man on his staff.
17: 3 [17:18] must be one staff for the head of each ancestral **tribe**.
17: 6 [17:21] one for the leader of each of their ancestral **tribes**, and
17: 8 [17:23] which represented the **house** *of* Levi, had not only
18: 1 your father's **family** are to bear the responsibility for offenses
18: 7 with everything at the altar and **inside** [+4200+4946] the curtain.
18:11 Everyone in your **household** who is ceremonially clean may eat it.
18:13 Everyone in your **household** who is ceremonially clean may eat it.
18:31 You and your **households** may eat the rest of it anywhere,
20:29 had died, the entire **house** *of* Israel mourned for him thirty days.
22:18 "Even if Balak gave me his **palace** filled with silver and gold,
24:13 'Even if Balak gave me his **palace** filled with silver and gold,
25:14 was Zimri son of Salu, the leader of a Simeonite **family** [+3].
25:15 Cozbi daughter of Zur, a tribal chief of a Midianite **family** [+3].
26: 2 a census of the whole Israelite community by **families** [+3]—
30: 3 [30:4] "When a young woman still living in her father's **house**
30:10 [30:11] "If a woman **living with** her husband makes a vow
30:16 [30:17] a father and his young daughter still living in his **house**.
32:18 We will not return to our **homes** until every Israelite has received
34:14 because the **families** [+3] *of* the tribe of Reuben, the tribe of Gad
34:14 **[RPH]** and the half-tribe of Manasseh have received their
Dt 5: 6 who brought you out of Egypt, out of the **land** *of* slavery.
5:21 You shall not set your desire on your neighbor's **house** or land,
6: 7 Talk about them when you sit at **home** and when you walk along
6: 9 Write them on the doorframes of your **houses** and on your gates.
6:11 **houses** filled with all kinds of good things you did not provide,
6:12 who brought you out of Egypt, out of the **land** *of* slavery.
6:22 and terrible—upon Egypt and Pharaoh and his whole **household**.
7: 8 with a mighty hand and redeemed you from the **land** *of* slavery,
7:26 Do not bring a detestable thing into your **house** or you, like it,
8:12 and are satisfied, when you build fine **houses** and settle down,
8:14 who brought you out of Egypt, out of the **land** *of* slavery.
11: 6 middle of all Israel and swallowed them up with their **households**,
11:19 talking about them when you sit at **home** and when you walk along
11:20 Write them on the doorframes of your **houses** and on your gates,
12: 7 you and your **families** shall eat and shall rejoice in everything you
13: 5 [13:6] out of Egypt and redeemed you from the **land** *of* slavery;
13:10 [13:11] who brought you out of Egypt, out of the **land** *of* slavery.
14:26 your **household** shall eat there in the presence of the LORD your
15:16 because he loves you and your **family** and is well off with you,
15:20 your **family** are to eat them in the presence of the LORD your
19: 1 you have driven them out and settled in their towns and **houses**,
20: 5 "Has anyone built a new **house** and not dedicated it? Let him go
20: 5 Let him go **home**, or he may die in battle and someone else may
20: 6 Let him go **home**, or he may die in battle and someone else enjoy
20: 7 Let him go **home**, or he may die in battle and someone else marry
20: 8 Let him go **home** so that his brothers will not become disheartened
21:12 Bring her into your **home** and have her shave her head, trim her
21:13 After she has lived in your **house** and mourned her father
22: 2 take it **home** with you and keep it until he comes looking for it.
22: 8 When you build a new **house**, make a parapet around your roof
22: 8 so that you may not bring the guilt of bloodshed on your **house** if
22:21 she shall be brought to the door of her father's **house** and there the
22:21 in Israel by being promiscuous while still in her father's **house**.
23:18 [23:19] or of a male prostitute into the **house** *of* the LORD your
24: 1 certificate of divorce, gives it to her and sends her from his **house**,

Dt 24: 2 if after she leaves his **house** she becomes the wife of another man,
24: 3 gives it to her and sends her from his **house**, or if he dies,
24: 5 For one year he is to be free to stay at **home** and bring happiness to
24: 10 do not go into his **house** to get what he is offering as a pledge.
25: 9 is done to the man who will not build up his brother's **family line**."
25: 10 That man's line shall be known in Israel as The **Family** *of* the
25: 14 Do not have two differing measures in your **house**—one large,
26: 11 things the LORD your God has given to you and your **household**.
26: 13 "I have removed from my **house** the sacred portion and have given
28: 30 and ravish her. You will build a **house**, but you will not live in it.
Jos 2: 1 So they went and entered the **house** *of* a prostitute named Rahab
2: 3 "Bring out the men who came to you and entered your **house**,
2: 12 me by the LORD that you will show kindness to my **family** [+3],
2: 15 the window, for the **house** she lived in was part of the city wall.
2: 18 your brothers and all your **family** [+3] into your house.
2: 18 and mother, your brothers and all your family into your **house**.
2: 19 If anyone goes outside your **house** into the street, his blood will be
2: 19 As for anyone who is in the **house** with you, his blood will be on
6: 17 the prostitute and all who are with her in her **house** shall be spared,
6: 22 "Go into the prostitute's **house** and bring her out and all who
6: 24 articles of bronze and iron into the treasury of the LORD's **house**.
6: 25 the prostitute, with her **family** [+3] and all who belonged to her,
7: 14 clan that the LORD takes shall come forward family by **family**;
7: 14 the **family** that the LORD takes shall come forward man by man.
7: 18 Joshua had his **family** come forward man by man, and Achan son
9: 12 This bread of ours was warm when we packed it at **home** on the
9: 23 serve as woodcutters and water carriers for the **house** *of* my God."
17: 17 Joshua said to the **house** *of* Joseph—to Ephraim and Manasseh—
18: 5 on the south and the **house** *of* Joseph in its territory on the north.
20: 6 he may go back to his own **home** in the town from which he fled."
21: 45 Not one of all the LORD's good promises to the **house** *of* Israel
22: 14 ten of the chief men, one **[RPH]** for each of the tribes of Israel,
22: 14 each the head of a family **division** among the Israelite clans.
24: 15 But as for me and my **household**, we will serve the LORD."
24: 17 and our fathers up out of Egypt, from that **land** *of* slavery,
Jdg 1: 22 Now the **house** *of* Joseph attacked Bethel, and the LORD was
1: 23 When **they**[s] [+3441] sent men to spy out Bethel (formerly called
1: 35 but when the power of the **house** *of* Joseph increased,
4: 17 between Jabin king of Hazor and the **clan** *of* Heber the Kenite.
6: 8 says: I brought you up out of Egypt, out of the **land** *of* slavery.
6: 15 is the weakest in Manasseh, and I am the least in my **family** [+3]."
6: 27 because he was afraid of his **family** [+3] and the men of the town,
8: 27 it there, and it became a snare to Gideon and his **family**.
8: 29 Jerub-Baal son of Joash went back **home** to live.
8: 35 They also failed to show kindness to the **family** *of* Jerub-Baal (that
9: 1 and said to them and to all his mother's **clan** [+3+5476],
9: 4 They gave him seventy shekels of silver from the **temple** *of*
9: 5 He went to his father's **home** in Ophrah and on one stone
9: 16 if you have been fair to Jerub-Baal and his **family**, and if you have
9: 18 (but today you have revolted against my father's **family**, murdered
9: 19 and in good faith toward Jerub-Baal and his **family** today,
9: 27 and trodden them, they held a festival in the **temple** *of* their god.
9: 46 of Shechem went into the stronghold of the **temple** *of* El-Berith.
10: 9 Jordan to fight against Judah, Benjamin and the **house** *of* Ephraim;
11: 2 "You are not going to get any inheritance in our **family** [+3],"
11: 7 "Didn't you hate me and drive me from my father's **house**?
11: 31 whatever comes out of the door of my **house** to meet me when I
11: 34 When Jephthah returned to his **home** in Mizpah, who should come
12: 1 with you? We're going to burn down your **house** over your head."
14: 15 or we will burn you and your father's **household** to death.
14: 19 the riddle. Burning with anger, he went up to his father's **house**.
16: 21 bronze shackles, they set him to grinding in the **prison** [+659].
16: 25 So they called Samson out of the **prison** [+659], and he performed
16: 26 "Put me where I can feel the pillars that support the **temple**,
16: 27 Now the **temple** was crowded with men and women; all the rulers
16: 29 reached toward the two central pillars on which the **temple** stood.
16: 30 and down came the **temple** on the rulers and all the people in it.
16: 31 his brothers and his father's whole **family** went down to get him.
17: 4 into the image and the idol. And they were put in Micah's **house**.
17: 5 Now this man Micah had a **shrine** [+466], and he made an ephod
17: 8 On his way he came to Micah's **house** in the hill country of
17: 12 and the young man became his priest and lived in his **house**.
18: 2 the hill country of Ephraim and came to the **house** *of* Micah,
18: 3 When they were near Micah's **house**, they recognized the voice of
18: 13 went on to the hill country of Ephraim and came to Micah's **house**.
18: 14 "Do you know that one of these **houses** has an ephod, other
18: 15 and went to the **house** *of* the young Levite at Micah's place
18: 15 and went to the house of the young Levite at Micah's **place**
18: 18 When these men went into Micah's **house** and took the carved
18: 19 and clan in Israel as priest rather than just one man's **household**?"
18: 22 When they had gone some distance from Micah's **house**, the men
18: 22 the men who **lived** [+928+2021] near Micah were called together
18: 22 the men who lived near **[RPH]** Micah were called together
18: 25 men will attack you, and you and your **family** will lose your lives."
18: 26 they were too strong for him, turned around and went back **home**.
18: 31 idols Micah had made, all the time the **house** *of* God was in Shiloh.
19: 2 She left him and went back to her father's **house** in Bethlehem,
19: 3 She took him into her father's **house**, and when her father saw him,
19: 15 the city square, but no one took them into his **home** for the night.
19: 18 in Judah and now I am going to the **house** *of* the LORD.
19: 18 to the house of the LORD. No one has taken me into his **house**.
19: 21 So he took him into his **house** and fed his donkeys. After they had
19: 22 some of the wicked men of the city surrounded the **house**.
19: 22 on the door, they shouted to the old man who owned the **house**,
19: 22 "Bring out the man who came to your **house** so we can have sex
19: 23 The owner of the **house** went outside and said to them, "No,
19: 23 Since this man *is* my **guest** [+440+995], don't do this disgraceful
19: 26 At daybreak the woman went back to the **house** where her master
19: 27 her master got up in the morning and opened the door of the **house**
19: 27 there lay his concubine, fallen in the doorway of the **house**,
19: 29 When he reached **home**, he took a knife and cut up his concubine,
20: 5 night the men of Gibeah came after me and surrounded the **house**,
20: 8 of us will go home. No, not one of us will return to his **house**.
Ru 1: 8 "Go back, each of you, to your mother's **home**.
1: 9 that each of you will find rest in the **home** *of* another husband."
2: 7 from morning till now, except for a short rest in the **shelter**."
4: 11 May the LORD make the woman who is coming into your **home**
4: 11 like Rachel and Leah, who together built up the **house** *of* Israel.
4: 12 may your **family** be like that of Perez, whom Tamar bore to
4: 12 may your family be like **that**[s] *of* Perez, whom Tamar bore to
1Sa 1: 7 Whenever Hannah went up to the **house** *of* the LORD, her rival
1: 19 before the LORD and then went back to their **home** at Ramah.
1: 21 When the man Elkanah went up with all his **family** to offer the
1: 24 of wine, and brought him to the **house** *of* the LORD at Shiloh.
2: 11 Elkanah went **home** to Ramah, but the boy ministered before the
2: 27 'Did I not clearly reveal myself to your father's **house** when they
2: 27 father's house when they were in Egypt **under** [+4200] Pharaoh?
2: 28 I also gave your father's **house** all the offerings made with fire by
2: 30 'I promised that your **house** and your father's house would minister
2: 30 and your father's **house** would minister before me forever.'
2: 31 will cut short your strength and the strength of your father's **house**,
2: 31 so that there will not be an old man in your **family line**
2: 32 done to Israel, in your **family line** there will never be an old man.
2: 33 and all your **descendants** [+5270] will die in the prime of life.
2: 35 I will firmly establish his **house**, and he will minister before my
2: 36 everyone left in your **family line** will come and bow down before
3: 12 I will carry out against Eli everything I spoke against his **family**—
3: 13 For I told him that I would judge his **family** forever because of the
3: 14 Therefore, I swore to the **house** *of* Eli, 'The guilt of Eli's house will
3: 14 'The guilt of Eli's **house** will never be atoned for by sacrifice
3: 15 and then opened the doors of the **house** *of* the LORD.
5: 2 they carried the ark into Dagon's **temple** and set it beside Dagon.
5: 5 others who enter Dagon's **temple** at Ashdod step on the threshold.
6: 7 to the cart, but take their calves away and **pen** [+2025] them **up**.
6: 10 and **penned** [+906+928+2021+3973] **up** their calves.
7: 1 They took it to Abinadab's **house** on the hill and consecrated
7: 2 and all the **people** *of* Israel mourned and sought after the LORD.
7: 3 Samuel said to the whole **house** *of* Israel, "If you are returning to
7: 17 to Ramah, where his **home** was, and there he also judged Israel.
9: 18 and asked, "Would you please tell me where the seer's **house** is?"
9: 20 desire of Israel turned, if not to you and all your father's **family**?"
10: 25 Then Samuel dismissed the people, each to his own **home**.
10: 26 Saul also went to his **home** in Gibeah, accompanied by valiant men
15: 34 left for Ramah, but Saul went up to his **home** *in* Gibeah of Saul.
17: 25 and will exempt his father's **family** from taxes in Israel."
18: 2 David with him and did not let him return to his father's **house**.
18: 10 He was prophesying in his **house**, while David was playing the
19: 9 upon Saul as he was sitting in his **house** with his spear in his hand.
19: 11 Saul sent men to David's **house** to watch it and to kill him in the
20: 15 do not ever cut off your kindness from my **family**—not even when
20: 16 So Jonathan made a covenant with the **house** *of* David, saying,
21: 15 [21:16] this in front of me? Must this man come into my **house**?"
22: 1 When his brothers and his father's **household** heard about it,
22: 11 the priest Ahimelech son of Ahitub and his father's whole **family**,
22: 14 of your bodyguard and highly respected in your **household**?
22: 15 Let not the king accuse your servant or any of his father's **family**,
22: 16 will surely die, Ahimelech, you and your father's whole **family**."
22: 22 I am responsible for the death of your father's whole **family**.
23: 18 Then Jonathan went **home**, but David remained at Horesh.
24: 21 [24:22] or wipe out my name from my father's **family**."
24: 22 [24:23] Saul returned **home**, but David and his men went up to
25: 1 and mourned for him; and they buried him at his **home** in Ramah.
25: 6 'Long life to you! Good health to you and your **household**!
25: 17 disaster is hanging over our master and his whole **household**.
25: 28 for the LORD will certainly make a lasting **dynasty** for my
25: 35 her hand what she had brought him and said, "Go **home** in peace.
25: 36 to Nabal, he was in the **house** holding a banquet like that of a king.
27: 3 Each man had his **family** with him, and David had his two wives:

1Sa 28:24 The woman had a fattened calf at the **house**, which she butchered
31: 9 of the Philistines to proclaim the news in the **temple** *of* their idols
31:10 They put his armor in the **temple** *of* the Ashtoreths and fastened
2Sa 1:12 and for the army of the LORD and the **house** *of* Israel,
2: 3 each with his **family**, and they settled in Hebron and its towns.
2: 4 and there they anointed David king over the **house** *of* Judah.
2: 7 and the **house** *of* Judah has anointed me king over them."
2:10 reigned two years. The **house** *of* Judah, however, followed David.
2:11 The length of time David was king in Hebron over the **house** *of*
3: 1 The war between the **house** *of* Saul and the house of David lasted a
3: 1 the house of Saul and the **house** *of* David lasted a long time.
3: 1 and stronger, while the **house** *of* Saul grew weaker and weaker.
3: 6 During the war between the **house** *of* Saul and the house of David,
3: 6 During the war between the house of Saul and the **house** *of* David,
3: 6 Abner had been strengthening his own position in the **house** *of*
3: 8 This very day I am loyal to the **house** *of* your father Saul and to his
3:10 transfer the kingdom from the **house** *of* Saul and establish David's
3:19 that Israel and the whole **house** *of* Benjamin wanted to do.
3:29 blood fall upon the head of Joab and upon all his father's **house**!
3:29 May Joab's **house** never be without someone who has a running
4: 5 of Rimmon the Beerothite, set out for the **house** *of* Ish-Bosheth,
4: 6 They went into the inner part of the **house** as if to get some wheat,
4: 7 They had gone into the **house** while he was lying on the bed in his
4:11 when wicked men have killed an innocent man in his own **house**
5: 8 is why they say, "The 'blind and lame' will not enter the **palace**."
5: 9 the area around it, from the supporting terraces **inward** [+2025].
5:11 and carpenters and stonemasons, and they built a **palace** for David.
6: 3 of God on a new cart and brought it from the **house** *of* Abinadab,
6: 4 [BHS+ *from the house of Abinadab,*] with the ark of God on it,
6: 5 the whole **house** *of* Israel were celebrating with all their might
6:10 Instead, he took it aside to the **house** *of* Obed-Edom the Gittite.
6:11 The ark of the LORD remained in the **house** *of* Obed-Edom the
6:11 and the LORD blessed him and his entire **household**.
6:12 "The LORD has blessed the **household** *of* Obed-Edom and
6:12 brought up the ark of God from the **house** *of* Obed-Edom to the
6:15 the entire **house** *of* Israel brought up the ark of the LORD with
6:19 both men and women. And all the people went to their **homes**.
6:20 When David returned home to bless his **household**, Michal
6:21 or anyone from his **house** when he appointed me ruler over the
7: 1 After the king was settled in his **palace** and the LORD had given
7: 2 said to Nathan the prophet, "Here I am, living in a **palace** *of* cedar,
7: 5 the LORD says: Are you the one to build me a **house** to dwell in?
7: 6 I have not dwelt in a **house** from the day I brought the Israelites up
7: 7 my people Israel, "Why have you not built me a **house** *of* cedar?"'
7:11 to you that the LORD himself will establish a **house** for you:
7:13 He is the one who will build a **house** for my Name, and I will
7:16 Your **house** and your kingdom will endure forever before me;
7:18 "Who am I, O Sovereign LORD, and what is my **family**,
7:19 you have also spoken about the future of the **house** *of* your servant.
7:25 the promise you have made concerning your servant and his **house**.
7:26 the **house** *of* your servant David will be established before you.
7:27 revealed this to your servant, saying, 'I will build a **house** for you.'
7:29 Now be pleased to bless the **house** *of* your servant, that it may
7:29 with your blessing the **house** *of* your servant will be blessed
9: 1 "Is there anyone still left of the **house** *of* Saul to whom I can show
9: 2 Now there was a servant of Saul's **household** named Ziba.
9: 3 "Is there no one still left of the **house** *of* Saul to whom I can show
9: 4 "He is at the **house** *of* Makir son of Ammiel in Lo Debar."
9: 5 brought from Lo Debar, from the **house** *of* Makir son of Ammiel.
9: 9 master's grandson everything that belonged to Saul and his **family**.
9:12 all the members of Ziba's **household** were servants of
11: 2 from his bed and walked around on the roof of the **palace** [+4889].
11: 4 purified herself from her uncleanness.) Then she went back **home**.
11: 8 David said to Uriah, "Go down to your **house** and wash your feet."
11: 8 So Uriah left the **palace** [+4889], and a gift from the king was sent
11: 9 Uriah slept at the entrance to the **palace** [+4889] with all his
11: 9 with all his master's servants and did not go down to his **house**.
11:10 When David was told, "Uriah did not go **home**," he asked him,
11:10 you just come from a distance? Why didn't you go **home**?"
11:11 How could I go to my **house** to eat and drink and lie with my wife?
11:13 sleep on his mat among his master's servants; he did not go **home**.
11:27 David had her brought to his **house**, and she became his wife
12: 8 I gave your master's **house** to you, and your master's wives into
12: 8 I gave you the **house** *of* Israel and Judah. And if all this had been
12:10 Now, therefore, the sword will never depart from your **house**,
12:11 'Out of your own **household** I am going to bring calamity upon
12:15 After Nathan had gone **home**, the LORD struck the child that
12:17 The elders of his **household** stood beside him to get him up from
12:20 his clothes, he went into the **house** *of* the LORD and worshiped.
12:20 he went to his own **house**, and at his request they served him food,
13: 7 David sent word to Tamar at the **palace**: "Go to the house of your
13: 7 "Go to the **house** *of* your brother Amnon and prepare some food
13: 8 So Tamar went to the **house** *of* her brother Amnon, who was lying
13:20 Tamar lived in her brother Absalom's **house**, a desolate woman.
14: 8 The king said to the woman, "Go **home**, and I will issue an order
14: 9 let the blame rest on me and on my father's **family**, and let the king
14:24 the king said, "He must go to his own **house**; he must not see my
14:24 So Absalom went to his own **house** and did not see the face of the
14:31 Then Joab did go to Absalom's **house** and he said to him,
15:16 The king set out, with his entire **household** following him;
15:16 but he left ten concubines to take care of the **palace**.
15:17 following him, and they halted at a **place** some distance away.
15:35 there with you? Tell them anything you hear in the king's **palace**.
16: 2 "The donkeys are for the king's **household** to ride on, the bread
16: 3 'Today the **house** *of* Israel will give me back my grandfather's
16: 5 a man from the same clan as Saul's **family** came out from there.
16: 8 has repaid you for all the blood you shed in the **household** *of* Saul,
16:21 your father's concubines whom he left to take care of the **palace**.
17:18 of them left quickly and went to the **house** *of* a man in Bahurim.
17:20 When Absalom's men came to the woman at the **house**, they
17:23 he saddled his donkey and set out for his **house** in his hometown.
17:23 He put his **house** in order and then hanged himself. So he died
19: 5 [19:6] Joab went into the **house** to the king and said, "Today you
19:11 [19:12] you be the last to bring the king back to his **palace**,
19:11 [19:12] throughout Israel has reached the king at his **quarters**?
19:17 [19:18] along with Ziba, the steward of Saul's **household**, and his
19:18 [19:19] They crossed at the ford to take the king's **household**
19:20 [19:21] today I have come here as the first of the whole **house** *of*
19:28 [19:29] All my grandfather's **descendants** deserved nothing
19:30 [19:31] now that my lord the king has arrived **home** safely."
19:41 [19:42] and bring him and his **household** across the Jordan,
20: 3 When David returned to his **palace** in Jerusalem, he took the ten
20: 3 he took the ten concubines he had left to take care of the **palace**
20: 3 left to take care of the palace and put them in a **house** under guard.
21: 1 "It is on account of Saul and his blood-stained **house**;
21: 4 have no right to demand silver or gold from Saul or his **family**,
23: 5 "Is not my **house** right with God? Has he not made with me an
24:17 have they done? Let your hand fall upon me and my **family** [+3]."
1Ki 1:53 down to King Solomon, and Solomon said, "Go to your **home**."
2:24 father David and has founded a **dynasty** for me as he promised—
2:27 the word the LORD had spoken at Shiloh about the **house** *of* Eli.
2:31 my father's **house** of the guilt of the innocent blood that Joab shed.
2:33 But on David and his descendants, his **house** and his throne,
2:34 and killed him, and he was buried on his own **land** in the desert.
2:36 said to him, "Build yourself a **house** in Jerusalem and live there,
3: 1 her to the City of David until he finished building his **palace**
3: 1 until he finished building his palace and the **temple** *of* the LORD,
3: 2 because a **temple** had not yet been built for the Name of the
3:17 of them said, "My lord, this woman and I live in the same **house**.
3:17 I had a baby while she was **there**[s] [+928+2021] with me.
3:18 We were alone; there was no one in the **house** but the two of us.
3:18 there was no one in the house but the two of us. **[RPH]**
4: 6 Ahishar—in charge of the **palace**; Adoniram son of Abda—
4: 7 who supplied provisions for the king and the royal **household**.
5: 3 [5:17] he could not build a **temple** for the Name of the LORD
5: 5 [5:19] to build a **temple** for the Name of the LORD my God,
5: 5 [5:19] throne in your place will build the **temple** for my Name.'
5: 9 [5:23] grant my wish by providing food for my royal **household**."
5:11 [5:25] twenty thousand cors of wheat as food for his **household**,
5:14 [5:28] they spent one month in Lebanon and two months at **home**.
5:17 [5:31] to provide a foundation of dressed stone for the **temple**.
5:18 [5:32] the timber and stone for the building of the **temple**.
6: 1 the second month, he began to build the **temple** of the LORD.
6: 2 The **temple** that King Solomon built for the LORD was sixty
6: 3 The portico at the front of the main hall of the **temple** extended the
6: 3 of the main hall of the temple extended the width of the **temple**,
6: 3 and projected ten cubits from the front of the **temple**.
6: 4 He made narrow clerestory windows in the **temple**.
6: 5 Against the walls **[RPH]** of the main hall and inner sanctuary he
6: 5 and inner sanctuary he built a structure around the **building**,
6: 6 He made offset ledges around the outside of the **temple** so that
6: 6 the temple so that nothing would be inserted into the **temple** walls.
6: 7 In building the **temple**, only blocks dressed at the quarry were
6: 7 or any other iron tool was heard at the **temple** site while it was
6: 8 entrance to the lowest floor was on the south side of the **temple**;
6: 9 So he built the **temple** and completed it, roofing it with beams
6: 9 and completed it, roofing **it**[s] [+2021] with beams and cedar planks.
6:10 he built the side rooms all along the **temple**. The height of each
6:10 and they were attached to the **temple** by beams of cedar.
6:12 "As for this **temple** you are building, if you follow my decrees,
6:14 So Solomon built the **temple** and completed it.
6:15 He lined **its**[s] [+2021] interior walls with cedar boards,
6:15 He lined its **interior** [+2025+4946] walls with cedar boards,
6:15 paneling **[RPH]** them from the floor of the temple to the ceiling,
6:15 paneling them from the floor of the **temple** to the ceiling,
6:15 and covered the floor of the **temple** with planks of pine.
6:16 He partitioned off twenty cubits at the rear of the **temple** with
6:16 from floor to ceiling to form within the **temple** an inner sanctuary,

1Ki 6:17 The main hall in front of this **room** was forty cubits long.
6:18 The inside of the **temple** was cedar, carved with gourds and open
6:19 He prepared the inner sanctuary within the **temple** to set the ark of
6:21 Solomon covered the inside of the **temple** with pure gold,
6:22 So he overlaid the whole **interior** with gold. He also overlaid with
6:22 **[RPH]** He also overlaid with gold the altar that belonged to the
6:27 He placed the cherubim inside the innermost room of the **temple**,
6:27 and their wings touched each other in the middle of the **room**.
6:29 On the walls all around the **temple**, in both the inner and outer
6:30 floors of both the inner and outer rooms of the **temple** with gold.
6:37 The foundation of the **temple** *of* the LORD was laid in the fourth
6:38 the **temple** was finished in all its details according to its
7:1 however, to complete **[RPH]** the construction of his palace.
7:1 thirteen years, however, to complete the construction of his **palace**.
7:2 He built the **Palace** *of* the Forest of Lebanon a hundred cubits long,
7:8 the **palace** in which he was to live, set farther back, was similar in
7:8 he was to live, set farther back, **[RPH]** was similar in design.
7:8 Solomon also made a **palace** like this hall for Pharaoh's daughter,
7:9 cut to size and trimmed with a saw on their **inner** and outer faces.
7:12 as was the inner courtyard of the **temple** *of* the LORD with its
7:12 courtyard of the temple of the LORD with **its**[s] [+2021] portico.
7:25 on top of them, and their hindquarters were toward the **center**.
7:31 On the **inside** of the stand there was an opening that had a circular
7:39 He placed five of the stands on the south side of the **temple**
7:39 on the south side of the temple and five on **[RPH]** the north.
7:39 the Sea on the south side, at the southeast corner of the **temple**.
7:40 he had undertaken for King Solomon in the **temple** *of* the LORD:
7:45 Solomon for the **temple** *of* the LORD were of burnished bronze.
7:48 also made all the furnishings that were in the LORD's **temple**:
7:50 and the gold sockets for the doors of the innermost **room**,
7:50 Holy Place, and also for the doors of the main hall of the **temple**.
7:51 When all the work King Solomon had done for the **temple** *of* the
7:51 and he placed them in the treasuries of the LORD's **temple**.
8:6 covenant to its place in the inner sanctuary of the **temple**,
8:10 from the Holy Place, the cloud filled the **temple** *of* the LORD.
8:11 because of the cloud, for the glory of the LORD filled his **temple**.
8:13 I have indeed built a magnificent **temple** for you, a place for you to
8:16 I have not chosen a city in any tribe of Israel to have a **temple** built
8:17 "My father David had it in his heart to build a **temple** for the Name
8:18 'Because it was in your heart to build a **temple** for my Name,
8:19 Nevertheless, you are not the one to build the **temple**, but your son,
8:19 and blood—he is the one who will build the **temple** for my Name.'
8:20 I have built the **temple** for the Name of the LORD, the God of
8:27 cannot contain you. How much less this **temple** I have built!
8:29 May your eyes be open toward this **temple** night and day,
8:31 and he comes and swears the oath before your altar in this **temple**,
8:33 your name, praying and making supplication to you in this **temple**,
8:38 of his own heart, and spreading out his hands toward this **temple**—
8:42 outstretched arm—when he comes and prays toward this **temple**,
8:43 and may know that this **house** I have built bears your Name.
8:44 city you have chosen and the **temple** I have built for your Name,
8:48 city you have chosen and the **temple** I have built for your Name;
8:63 and all the Israelites dedicated the **temple** *of* the LORD.
8:64 middle part of the courtyard in front of the **temple** *of* the LORD,
9:1 When Solomon had finished building the **temple** *of* the LORD
9:1 finished building the temple of the LORD and the royal **palace**,
9:3 I have consecrated this **temple**, which you have built, by putting
9:7 and will reject this **temple** I have consecrated for my Name.
9:8 though this **temple** is now imposing, all who pass by will be
9:8 has the LORD done such a thing to this land and to this **temple**?'
9:10 of twenty years, during which Solomon built these two **buildings**—
9:10 two buildings—the **temple** *of* the LORD and the royal palace—
9:10 two buildings—the temple of the LORD and the royal **palace**—
9:15 labor King Solomon conscripted to build the LORD's **temple**,
9:15 his own **palace**, the supporting terraces, the wall of Jerusalem,
9:24 up from the City of David to the **palace** Solomon had built for her,
9:25 LORD along with them, and so fulfilled the **temple** obligations.
10:4 Sheba saw all the wisdom of Solomon and the **palace** he had built,
10:5 and the burnt offerings he made at the **temple** *of* the LORD,
10:12 The king used the almugwood to make supports for the **temple** *of*
10:12 supports for the temple of the LORD and for the royal **palace**,
10:17 The king put them in the **Palace** *of* the Forest of Lebanon.
10:21 all the household articles in the **Palace** *of* the Forest of Lebanon
11:18 who gave Hadad a **house** and land and provided him with food.
11:20 named Genubath, whom Tahpenes brought up in the royal **palace**.
11:20 **There**[s] [+7281] Genubath lived with Pharaoh's own children.
11:28 he put him in charge of the whole labor force of the **house** *of*
11:38 I will build you a **dynasty** as enduring as the one I built for David
12:16 To your tents, O Israel! Look after your own **house**, O David!"
12:19 So Israel has been in rebellion against the **house** *of* David to this
12:20 Only the tribe of Judah remained loyal to the **house** *of* David.
12:21 he mustered the whole **house** *of* Judah and the tribe of Benjamin—
12:21 to make war against the **house** *of* Israel and to regain the kingdom
12:23 to the whole **house** *of* Judah and Benjamin, and to the rest of the
12:24 Go **home**, every one of you, for this is my doing.' " So they obeyed
12:26 "The kingdom will now likely revert to the **house** *of* David.
12:27 If these people go up to offer sacrifices at the **temple** *of* the
12:31 Jeroboam built **shrines** *on* high places and appointed priests from
13:2 'A son named Josiah will be born to the **house** *of* David.
13:7 "Come **home** with me and have something to eat, and I will give
13:8 "Even if you were to give me half your **possessions**, I would not
13:15 So the prophet said to him, "Come **home** with me and eat."
13:18 'Bring him back with you to your **house** so that he may eat bread
13:19 the man of God returned with him and ate and drank in his **house**.
13:32 against all the **shrines** *on* the high places in the towns of Samaria
13:34 This was the sin of the **house** *of* Jeroboam that led to its downfall
14:4 wife did what he said and went to Ahijah's **house** in Shiloh.
14:8 I tore the kingdom away from the **house** *of* David and gave it to
14:10 of this, I am going to bring disaster on the **house** *of* Jeroboam.
14:10 I will burn up the **house** *of* Jeroboam as one burns dung, until it is
14:12 "As for you, go back **home**. When you set foot in your city,
14:13 because he is the only one in the **house** *of* Jeroboam in whom the
14:14 himself a king over Israel who will cut off the **family** *of* Jeroboam.
14:17 As soon as she stepped over the threshold of the **house**, the boy
14:26 He carried off the treasures of the **temple** *of* the LORD and the
14:26 of the temple of the LORD and the treasures of the royal **palace**.
14:27 of the guard on duty at the entrance to the royal **palace**.
14:28 Whenever the king went to the LORD's **temple**, the guards bore
15:15 He brought into the **temple** *of* the LORD the silver and gold
15:18 and gold that was left in the treasuries of the LORD's **temple**
15:18 left in the treasuries of the LORD's temple and of his own **palace**.
15:27 Baasha son of Ahijah of the **house** *of* Issachar plotted against him,
15:29 As soon as he began to reign, he killed Jeroboam's whole **family**.
16:3 So I am about to consume Baasha and his **house**, and I will make
16:3 and I will make your **house** like that of Jeroboam son of Nebat.
16:3 and I will make your house like **that**[s] *of* Jeroboam son of Nebat.
16:7 through the prophet Jehu son of Hanani to Baasha and his **house**,
16:7 by the things he did, and becoming like the **house** *of* Jeroboam—
16:9 Elah was in Tirzah at the time, getting drunk in the **home** *of* Arza,
16:9 in the home of Arza, the man in charge of the **palace** at Tirzah.
16:11 and was seated on the throne, he killed off Baasha's whole **family**.
16:12 So Zimri destroyed the whole **family** *of* Baasha, in accordance
16:18 he went into the citadel of the royal **palace** and set the palace on
16:18 citadel of the royal palace and set the **palace** on fire around him.
16:32 He set up an altar for Baal in the **temple** *of* Baal that he built in
17:15 was food every day for Elijah and for the woman and her **family**.
17:17 Some time later the son of the woman who owned the **house**
17:23 up the child and carried him down from the room into the **house**.
18:3 Ahab had summoned Obadiah, who was in charge of his **palace**.
18:18 for Israel," Elijah replied. "But you and your father's **family** have.
18:32 he dug a trench around it large enough to **hold** two seahs of seed.
20:6 tomorrow I am going to send my officials to search your **palace**
20:6 my officials to search your palace and the **houses** *of* your officials.
20:31 we have heard that the kings of the **house** *of* Israel are merciful.
20:43 and angry, the king of Israel went to his **palace** in Samaria.
21:2 to use for a vegetable garden, since it is close to my **palace**.
21:4 So Ahab went **home**, sullen and angry because Naboth the
21:22 I will make your **house** like that of Jeroboam son of Nebat
21:22 I will make your house like **that**[s] *of* Jeroboam son of Nebat
21:22 that of Jeroboam son of Nebat and **that**[s] *of* Baasha son of Ahijah,
21:29 in his day, but I will bring it on his **house** in the days of his son."
22:17 'These people have no master. Let each one go **home** in peace.' "
22:27 Put this fellow in **prison** [+2021+3975] and give him nothing
22:39 including all he did, the **palace** he built and inlaid with ivory,
2Ki 4:2 "How can I help you? Tell me, what do you have in your **house**?"
4:2 "Your servant has nothing **there**[s] [+928+2021] at all," she said,
4:32 When Elisha reached the **house**, there was the boy lying dead on
4:35 Elisha turned away and walked back and forth in the **room** and
5:9 his horses and chariots and stopped at the door of Elisha's **house**.
5:18 When my master enters the **temple** *of* Rimmon to bow down
5:18 and he is leaning on my arm and I bow **there**[s] [+8235] also—
5:18 when I bow down in the **temple** *of* Rimmon, may the LORD
5:24 took the things from the servants and put them away in the **house**.
6:30 along the wall, the people looked, and there, **underneath** [+4946],
6:32 Now Elisha was sitting in his **house**, and the elders were sitting
7:9 overtake us. Let's go at once and report this to the royal **palace**."
7:11 shouted the news, and it was reported within the **palace** [+4889].
8:1 "Go away with your **family** and stay for a while wherever you can,
8:2 She and her **family** went away and stayed in the land of the
8:3 the Philistines and went to the king to beg for her **house** and land.
8:5 Elisha had brought back to life came to beg the king for her **house**
8:18 as the **house** *of* Ahab had done, for he married a daughter of Ahab.
8:27 He walked in the ways of the **house** *of* Ahab and did evil in the
8:27 did evil in the eyes of the LORD, as the **house** *of* Ahab had done,
8:27 Ahab had done, for he was related by marriage to Ahab's **family**.
9:6 Jehu got up and went into the **house**. Then the prophet poured the
9:7 You are to destroy the **house** *of* Ahab your master, and I will
9:8 The whole **house** *of* Ahab will perish. I will cut off from Ahab

2Ki 9: 9 I will make the **house** *of* Ahab like the house of Jeroboam son of
9: 9 I will make the house of Ahab like the **house** *of* Jeroboam son of
9: 9 Jeroboam son of Nebat and like the **house** *of* Baasha son of Ahijah.
10: 3 set him on his father's throne. Then fight for your master's **house**."
10: 5 So the **palace** administrator, the city governor, the elders
10: 10 that not a word the LORD has spoken against the **house** *of* Ahab
10: 11 So Jehu killed everyone in Jezreel who remained of the **house** *of*
10: 21 They crowded into the **temple** *of* Baal until it was full from one
10: 21 They crowded into the temple of Baal until **it**[s] [+1251] was full
10: 23 and Jehonadab son of Recab went into the **temple** *of* Baal.
10: 25 bodies out and then entered the inner shrine of the **temple** *of* Baal.
10: 26 They brought the sacred stone out of the **temple** *of* Baal
10: 27 the sacred stone of Baal and tore down the **temple** *of* Baal,
10: 30 and have done to the **house** *of* Ahab all I had in mind to do,
11: 3 He remained hidden with his nurse at the **temple** *of* the LORD for
11: 4 and had them brought to him at the **temple** *of* the LORD.
11: 4 with them and put them under oath at the **temple** *of* the LORD.
11: 5 on duty on the Sabbath—a third of you guarding the royal **palace**,
11: 6 at the gate behind the guard, who take turns guarding the **temple**—
11: 7 go off Sabbath duty are all to guard the **temple** for the king.
11: 10 to King David and that were in the **temple** *of* the LORD.
11: 11 near the altar and the **temple**, from the south side to the north side
11: 11 from the south side **[RPH]** to the north side of the temple.
11: 11 and the temple, from the south side to the north side of the **temple**.
11: 13 the people, she went to the people at the **temple** *of* the LORD.
11: 15 "Bring her out **[RPH]** between the ranks and put to the sword
11: 15 "She must not be put to death in the **temple** *of* the LORD."
11: 16 the place where the horses enter the **palace** [+4889] **grounds**,
11: 18 All the people of the land went to the **temple** *of* Baal and tore it
11: 18 Jehoiada the priest posted guards at the **temple** *of* the LORD.
11: 19 together they brought the king down from the **temple** *of* the
11: 19 from the temple of the LORD and went into the **palace** [+4889],
11: 20 Athaliah had been slain with the sword at the **palace** [+4889].
12: 4 [12:5] brought as sacred offerings to the **temple** *of* the LORD—
12: 4 [12:5] and the money brought voluntarily to the **temple**.
12: 5 [12:6] be used to repair whatever damage is found in the **temple**."
12: 6 [12:7] of King Joash the priests still had not repaired the **temple**.
12: 7 [12:8] "Why aren't you repairing the damage done to the **temple**?
12: 7 [12:8] your treasurers, but hand it over for repairing the **temple**."
12: 8 [12:9] and that they would not repair the **temple** themselves.
12: 9 [12:10] on the right side as one enters the **temple** *of* the LORD.
12: 9 [12:10] the money that was brought to the **temple** *of* the LORD.
12: 10 [12:11] that had been brought into the **temple** *of* the LORD
12: 11 [12:12] to the men appointed to supervise the work on the **temple**.
12: 11 [12:12] With it they paid those who worked on the **temple** *of* the
12: 12 [12:13] dressed stone for the repair of the **temple** *of* the LORD,
12: 12 [12:13] and met all the other expenses of restoring the **temple**.
12: 13 [12:14] The money brought into the **temple** was not spent for
12: 13 [12:14] articles of gold or silver for the **temple** *of* the LORD;
12: 14 [12:15] paid to the workmen, who used it to repair the **temple**.
12: 16 [12:17] sin offerings was not brought into the **temple** *of* the
12: 18 [12:19] all the gold found in the treasuries of the **temple** *of* the
12: 18 [12:19] of the temple of the LORD and of the royal **palace**,
13: 6 But they did not turn away from the sins of the **house** *of* Jeroboam,
14: 10 Glory in your victory, but stay at **home**! Why ask for trouble
14: 14 and silver and all the articles found in the **temple** *of* the LORD
14: 14 the temple of the LORD and in the treasuries of the royal **palace**.
15: 5 with leprosy until the day he died, and he lived in a separate **house**.
15: 5 Jotham the king's son had charge of the **palace** and governed the
15: 25 and Arieh, in the citadel of the royal **palace** at Samaria.
15: 35 Jotham rebuilt the Upper Gate of the **temple** *of* the LORD.
16: 8 Ahaz took the silver and gold found in the **temple** *of* the LORD
16: 8 in the treasuries of the royal **palace** and sent it as a gift to the king
16: 14 stood before the LORD he brought from the front of the **temple**—
16: 14 from between the new altar and the **temple** *of* the LORD—
16: 18 He took away the Sabbath canopy that had been built at the **temple**
16: 18 and removed the royal entryway outside the **temple** *of* the LORD,
17: 4 Therefore Shalmaneser seized him and put him in **prison** [+3975].
17: 21 When he tore Israel away from the **house** *of* David, they made
17: 29 set them up in the **shrines** the people of Samaria had made *at* the
17: 32 to officiate for them as priests in the **shrines** *at* the high places.
18: 15 gave him all the silver that was found in the **temple** *of* the LORD
18: 15 the temple of the LORD and in the treasuries of the royal **palace**.
18: 18 Eliakim son of Hilkiah the **palace** administrator, Shebna the
18: 37 Eliakim son of Hilkiah the **palace** administrator, Shebna the
19: 1 and put on sackcloth and went into the **temple** *of* the LORD.
19: 2 He sent Eliakim the **palace** administrator, Shebna the secretary
19: 14 he went up to the **temple** *of* the LORD and spread it out before
19: 30 Once more a remnant of the **house** *of* Judah will take root below
19: 37 while he was worshiping in the **temple** *of* his god Nisroch,
20: 1 Put your **house** in order, because you are going to die; you will not
20: 5 On the third day from now you will go up to the **temple** *of* the
20: 8 that I will go up to the **temple** *of* the LORD on the third day from
20: 13 and showed them all that was in his **storehouses** [+5800]—
20: 13 his **armory** [+3998] and everything found among his treasures.
20: 13 There was nothing in his **palace** or in all his kingdom that
20: 15 The prophet asked, "What did they see in your **palace**?" "They
20: 15 your palace?" "They saw everything in my **palace**," Hezekiah said.
20: 17 The time will surely come when everything in your **palace**,
21: 4 He built altars in the **temple** *of* the LORD, of which the LORD
21: 5 In both courts of the **temple** *of* the LORD, he built altars to all the
21: 7 took the carved Asherah pole he had made and put it in the **temple**,
21: 7 and to his son Solomon, "In this **temple** and in Jerusalem,
21: 13 and the plumb line used against the **house** *of* Ahab.
21: 18 rested with his fathers and was buried in his **palace** garden,
21: 23 conspired against him and assassinated the king in his **palace**.
22: 3 of Azaliah, the son of Meshullam, to the **temple** *of* the LORD.
22: 4 the money that has been brought into the **temple** *of* the LORD,
22: 5 it to the men appointed to supervise the work on the **temple**.
22: 5 have these men pay the workers who repair the **temple** *of* the
22: 5 pay the workers who repair the temple of the LORD—**[RPH]**
22: 6 have them purchase timber and dressed stone to repair the **temple**.
22: 8 "I have found the Book of the Law in the **temple** *of* the LORD."
22: 9 "Your officials have paid out the money that was in the **temple** *of*
22: 9 have entrusted it to the workers and supervisors at the **temple**."
23: 2 He went up to the **temple** *of* the LORD with the men of Judah,
23: 2 the Covenant, which had been found in the **temple** *of* the LORD.
23: 6 He took the Asherah pole from the **temple** *of* the LORD to the
23: 7 He also tore down the **quarters** *of* the male shrine prostitutes,
23: 7 which were in the **temple** *of* the LORD and where women did
23: 11 He removed from the entrance to the **temple** *of* the LORD the
23: 12 the altars Manasseh had built in the two courts of the **temple** *of* the
23: 19 defiled all the **shrines** *at* the high places that the kings of Israel had
23: 24 that Hilkiah the priest had discovered in the **temple** *of* the LORD.
23: 27 the city I chose, and this **temple**, about which I said,
24: 13 Nebuchadnezzar removed all the treasures from the **temple** *of* the
24: 13 from the temple of the LORD and from the royal **palace**,
25: 9 He set fire to the **temple** *of* the LORD, the royal palace and all
25: 9 of the LORD, the royal **palace** and all the houses of Jerusalem.
25: 9 of the LORD, the royal palace and all the **houses** *of* Jerusalem.
25: 9 houses of Jerusalem. Every important **building** he burned down.
25: 13 **[RPH]** the movable stands and the bronze Sea that were at the
25: 13 and the bronze Sea that were at the **temple** *of* the LORD
25: 16 which Solomon had made for the **temple** *of* the LORD,
25: 27 he released Jehoiachin from **prison** [+3975] on the twenty-seventh
1Ch 2: 55 who came from Hammath, the father of the **house** *of* Recab.
4: 21 and the clans of the linen **workers** [+6275] at Beth Ashbea,
4: 38 were leaders of their clans. Their **families** [+3] increased greatly,
5: 13 Their relatives, by **families** [+3], were: Michael, Meshullam,
5: 15 Ahi son of Abdiel, the son of Guni, was head of their **family** [+3].
5: 24 These were the heads of their **families** [+3]: Epher, Ishi, Eliel,
5: 24 were brave warriors, famous men, and heads of their **families** [+3].
6: 10 [5:36] served as priest in the **temple** Solomon built in Jerusalem),
6: 31 [6:16] in the **house** *of* the LORD after the ark came to rest there.
6: 32 [6:17] until Solomon built the **temple** *of* the LORD in
6: 48 [6:33] to all the other duties of the tabernacle, the **house** *of* God.
7: 2 Jeriel, Jahmai, Ibsam and Samuel—heads of their **families** [+3].
7: 4 According to their **family** [+3] genealogy, they had 36,000 men
7: 7 Ezbon, Uzzi, Uzziel, Jerimoth and Iri, heads of **families** [+3]—
7: 9 Their genealogical record listed the heads of **families** [+3]
7: 23 him Beriah, because there had been misfortune in his **family**.
7: 40 heads of **families** [+3], choice men, brave warriors and outstanding
9: 9 numbered 956. All these men were heads of their **families** [+3].
9: 11 the son of Ahitub, the official in charge of the **house** *of* God;
9: 13 The priests, who were heads of **families** [+3], numbered 1,760.
9: 13 were able men, responsible for ministering in the **house** *of* God.
9: 19 and his fellow gatekeepers from his **family** [+3] (the Korahites)
9: 23 were in charge of guarding the gates of the **house** *of* the LORD—
9: 23 the gates of the house of the LORD—the **house** called the Tent.
9: 26 the responsibility for the rooms and treasuries in the **house** *of* God.
9: 27 They would spend the night stationed around the **house** *of* God,
10: 6 So Saul and his three sons died, and all his **house** died together.
10: 10 They put his armor in the **temple** *of* their gods and hung up his
10: 10 temple of their gods and hung up his head in the **temple** *of* Dagon.
12: 28 [12:29] young warrior, with 22 officers from his **family** [+3];
12: 29 [12:30] most of whom had remained loyal to Saul's **house** until
12: 30 [12:31] brave warriors, famous in their own **clans** [+3]—
13: 7 They moved the ark of God from Abinadab's **house** on a new cart,
13: 13 Instead, he took it aside to the **house** *of* Obed-Edom the Gittite.
13: 14 The ark of God remained with the **family** *of* Obed-Edom in his
13: 14 with the family of Obed-Edom in his **house** for three months,
13: 14 and the LORD blessed his **household** and everything he had.
14: 1 cedar logs, stonemasons and carpenters to build a **palace** for him.
15: 1 After David had constructed **buildings** for himself in the City of
15: 25 ark of the covenant of the LORD from the **house** *of* Obed-Edom,
16: 43 all the people left, each for his own **home**, and David returned
16: 43 for his own home, and David returned home to bless his **family**.
17: 1 After David was settled in his **palace**, he said to Nathan the

1Ch 17: 1 said to Nathan the prophet, "Here I am, living in a **palace** *of* cedar,
17: 4 LORD says: You are not the one to build me a **house** to dwell in.
17: 5 I have not dwelt in a **house** from the day I brought Israel up out of
17: 6 my people, "Why have you not built me a **house** *of* cedar?" '
17: 10 " 'I declare to you that the LORD will build a **house** for you:
17: 12 He is the one who will build a **house** for me, and I will establish
17: 14 I will set him over my **house** and my kingdom forever; his throne
17: 16 "Who am I, O LORD God, and what is my **family**, that you have
17: 17 you have spoken about the future of the **house** *of* your servant.
17: 23 concerning your servant and his **house** be established forever.
17: 24 the **house** *of* your servant David will be established before you.
17: 25 have revealed to your servant that you will build a **house** for him.
17: 27 Now you have been pleased to bless the **house** *of* your servant,
21: 17 LORD my God, let your hand fall upon me and my **family** [+3],
22: 1 Then David said, "The **house** *of* the LORD God is to be here,
22: 2 to prepare dressed stone for building the **house** *of* God.
22: 5 the **house** to be built for the LORD should be of great
22: 6 his son Solomon and charged him to build a **house** for the LORD,
22: 7 I had it in my heart to build a **house** for the Name of the LORD
22: 8 You are not to build a **house** for my Name, because you have shed
22: 10 He is the one who will build a **house** for my Name. He will be my
22: 11 you have success and build the **house** *of* the LORD your God,
22: 14 "I have taken great pains to provide for the **temple** *of* the LORD a
22: 19 the sacred articles belonging to God into the **temple** that will be
23: 4 twenty-four thousand are to supervise the work of the **temple** *of*
23: 11 so they were counted as one **family** [+3] with one assignment.
23: 24 These were the descendants of Levi by their **families** [+3]—
23: 24 twenty years old or more who served in the **temple** *of* the LORD.
23: 28 Aaron's descendants in the service of the **temple** *of* the LORD:
23: 28 and the performance of other duties at the **house** *of* God.
23: 32 descendants of Aaron, for the service of the **temple** *of* the LORD.
24: 4 sixteen heads of **families** [+3] from Eleazar's descendants
24: 4 and eight heads of **families** [+3] from Ithamar's descendants.
24: 6 one **family** [+3] being taken from Eleazar and then one from
24: 19 order of ministering when they entered the **temple** *of* the LORD,
24: 30 These were the Levites, according to their **families** [+3].
25: 6 of their fathers for the music of the **temple** *of* the LORD,
25: 6 lyres and harps, for the ministry at the **house** *of* God.
26: 6 who were leaders in their father's **family** because they were very
26: 12 chief men, had duties for ministering in the **temple** *of* the LORD,
26: 13 for each gate, according to their **families** [+3], young and old alike.
26: 15 and the lot for the **storehouse** [+667] fell to his sons.
26: 20 fellow Levites were in charge of the treasuries of the **house** *of*
26: 22 They were in charge of the treasuries of the **temple** *of* the LORD.
26: 27 in battle they dedicated for the repair of the **temple** *of* the LORD.
28: 2 I had it in my heart to build a **house** as a place of rest for the ark of
28: 3 But God said to me, 'You are not to build a **house** for my Name,
28: 4 chose me from my whole **family** [+3] to be king over Israel
28: 4 Judah as leader, and from the **house** *of* Judah he chose my family,
28: 4 as leader, and from the house of Judah he chose my **family** [+3],
28: 6 'Solomon your son is the one who will build my **house** and my
28: 10 for the LORD has chosen you to build a **temple** as a sanctuary.
28: 11 its **buildings**, its storerooms, its upper parts, its inner rooms
28: 11 its upper parts, its inner rooms and the **place** *of* atonement.
28: 12 had put in his mind for the courts of the **temple** *of* the LORD
28: 12 for the treasuries of the **temple** *of* God and for the treasuries for the
28: 13 and for all the work of serving in the **temple** *of* the LORD,
28: 13 as well as for all the articles to be used in **its**[s] [+3378] service.
28: 20 or forsake you until all the work for the service of the **temple** *of*
28: 21 and Levites are ready for all the work on the **temple** *of* God,
29: 2 With all my resources I have provided for the **temple** *of* my God—
29: 3 in my devotion to the **temple** *of* my God I now give my personal
29: 3 my personal treasures of gold and silver for the **temple** *of* my God,
29: 3 and above everything I have provided for this holy **temple**:
29: 4 of refined silver, for the overlaying of the walls of the **buildings**,
29: 7 They gave toward the work on the **temple** *of* God five thousand
29: 8 the **temple** *of* the LORD in the custody of Jehiel the Gershonite.
29: 16 we have provided for building you a **temple** for your Holy Name,
2Ch 2: 1 [1:18] Solomon gave orders to build a **temple** for the Name of the
2: 1 [1:18] for the Name of the LORD and a royal **palace** for himself.
2: 3 [2:2] David when you sent him cedar to build a **palace** to live in.
2: 4 [2:3] Now I am about to build a **temple** for the Name of the
2: 5 [2:4] "The **temple** I am going to build will be great, because our
2: 6 [2:5] But who is able to build a **temple** for him, since the heavens,
2: 6 [2:5] Who then am I to build a **temple** for him, except as a place
2: 9 [2:8] because the **temple** I build must be large and magnificent.
2: 12 [2:11] who will build a **temple** for the LORD and a palace for
2: 12 [2:11] a temple for the LORD and a **palace** [+4895] for himself.
3: 1 Solomon began to build the **temple** *of* the LORD in Jerusalem on
3: 3 The foundation Solomon laid for building the **temple** *of* God was
3: 4 the temple was twenty cubits long across the width of the **building**
3: 5 He paneled the main **hall** with pine and covered it with fine gold
3: 6 He adorned the **temple** with precious stones. And the gold he used
3: 7 doorframes, walls and doors of the **temple** with gold,
3: 8 He built **[RPH]** the Most Holy Place, its length corresponding to
3: 8 Holy Place, its length corresponding to the width of the **temple**—
3: 10 In the Most Holy **Place** he made a pair of sculptured cherubim
3: 11 the first cherub was five cubits long and touched the **temple** wall,
3: 12 cherub was five cubits long and touched the other **temple** wall,
3: 13 twenty cubits. They stood on their feet, facing the **main hall**.
3: 15 In the front of the **temple** he made two pillars, which ⌊together⌋
4: 4 on top of them, and their hindquarters were toward the **center**.
4: 11 work he had undertaken for King Solomon in the **temple** *of* God:
4: 16 Solomon for the **temple** *of* the LORD were of polished bronze.
4: 19 Solomon also made all the furnishings that were in God's **temple**:
4: 22 dishes and censers; and the gold doors of the **temple**:
4: 22 to the Most Holy Place and the doors of the main hall. **[RPH]**
5: 1 When all the work Solomon had done for the **temple** *of* the
5: 1 and he placed them in the treasuries of God's **temple**.
5: 7 covenant to its place in the inner sanctuary of the **temple**,
5: 13 Then the **temple** *of* the LORD was filled with a cloud,
5: 13 Then the temple of **[RPH]** the LORD was filled with a cloud,
5: 14 of the cloud, for the glory of the LORD filled the **temple** *of* God.
6: 2 I have built a magnificent **temple** for you, a place for you to dwell
6: 5 I have not chosen a city in any tribe of Israel to have a **temple** built
6: 7 "My father David had it in his heart to build a **temple** for the Name
6: 8 'Because it was in your heart to build a **temple** for my Name,
6: 9 Nevertheless, you are not the one to build the **temple**, but your son,
6: 9 and blood—he is the one who will build the **temple** for my Name.'
6: 10 I have built the **temple** for the Name of the LORD, the God of
6: 18 cannot contain you. How much less this **temple** I have built!
6: 20 May your eyes be open toward this **temple** day and night,
6: 22 and he comes and swears the oath before your altar in this **temple**,
6: 24 praying and making supplication before you in this **temple**,
6: 29 and pains, and spreading out his hands toward this **temple**—
6: 32 outstretched arm—when he comes and prays toward this **temple**,
6: 33 and may know that this **house** I have built bears your Name.
6: 34 city you have chosen and the **temple** I have built for your Name,
6: 38 have chosen and toward the **temple** I have built for your Name;
7: 1 and the sacrifices, and the glory of the LORD filled the **temple**.
7: 2 The priests could not enter the **temple** *of* the LORD
7: 2 of the LORD because the glory of the LORD filled **it**[s] [+3378].
7: 3 fire coming down and the glory of the LORD above the **temple**,
7: 5 So the king and all the people dedicated the **temple** *of* God.
7: 7 middle part of the courtyard in front of the **temple** *of* the LORD,
7: 11 When Solomon had finished the **temple** *of* the LORD and the
7: 11 had finished the temple of the LORD and the royal **palace**,
7: 11 carrying out all he had in mind to do in the **temple** *of* the LORD
7: 11 in mind to do in the temple of the LORD and in his own **palace**,
7: 12 and have chosen this place for myself as a **temple** *for* sacrifices.
7: 16 I have chosen and consecrated this **temple** so that my Name may
7: 20 and will reject this **temple** I have consecrated for my Name.
7: 21 though this **temple** is now so imposing, all who pass by will be
7: 21 has the LORD done such a thing to this land and to this **temple**?'
8: 1 during which Solomon built the **temple** *of* the LORD and his own
8: 1 Solomon built the temple of the LORD and his own **palace**,
8: 11 up from the City of David to the **palace** he had built for her,
8: 11 "My wife must not live in the **palace** *of* David king of Israel,
8: 16 from the day the foundation of the **temple** *of* the LORD was laid
8: 16 until its completion. So the **temple** *of* the LORD was finished.
9: 3 saw the wisdom of Solomon, as well as the **palace** he had built,
9: 4 and the burnt offerings he made at the **temple** *of* the LORD,
9: 11 The king used the algumwood to make steps for the **temple** *of* the
9: 11 make steps for the temple of the LORD and for the royal **palace**,
9: 16 The king put them in the **Palace** *of* the Forest of Lebanon.
9: 20 all the household articles in the **Palace** *of* the Forest of Lebanon
10: 16 To your tents, O Israel! Look after your own **house**, O David!"
10: 19 So Israel has been in rebellion against the **house** *of* David to this
11: 1 in Jerusalem, he mustered the **house** *of* Judah and Benjamin—
11: 4 Go **home**, every one of you, for this is my doing.' " So they obeyed
12: 9 he carried off the treasures of the **temple** *of* the LORD and the
12: 9 of the temple of the LORD and the treasures of the royal **palace**.
12: 10 of the guard on duty at the entrance to the royal **palace**.
12: 11 Whenever the king went to the LORD's **temple**, the guards went
15: 18 He brought into the **temple** *of* God the silver and gold
16: 2 the silver and gold out of the treasuries of the LORD's **temple**
16: 2 and of his own **palace** and sent it to Ben-Hadad king of Aram,
16: 10 he was so enraged that he put him in **prison** [+2021+4551].
17: 14 Their enrollment by **families** [+3] was as follows: From Judah,
18: 16 'These people have no master. Let each one go **home** in peace.' "
18: 26 Put this fellow in **prison** [+2021+3975] and give him nothing
19: 1 When Jehoshaphat king of Judah returned safely to his **palace** in
19: 11 and Zebadiah son of Ishmael, the leader of the **tribe** *of* Judah,
20: 5 Jerusalem at the **temple** *of* the LORD in the front of the new
20: 9 we will stand in your presence before this **temple** that bears your
20: 9 before this temple **that**[s] [+2021+2021+2296] bears your Name
20: 28 and went to the **temple** *of* the LORD with harps and lutes
21: 6 as the **house** *of* Ahab had done, for he married a daughter of Ahab.

2Ch 21: 7 the LORD was not willing to destroy the **house** *of* David.
21: 13 Jerusalem to prostitute themselves, just as the **house** *of* Ahab did.
21: 13 *members of* your father's **house**, men who were better than you.
21: 17 invaded it and carried off all the goods found in the king's **palace**,
22: 3 He too walked in the ways of the **house** *of* Ahab, for his mother
22: 4 did evil in the eyes of the LORD, as the **house** *of* Ahab had done,
22: 7 whom the LORD had anointed to destroy the **house** *of* Ahab.
22: 8 While Jehu was executing judgment on the **house** *of* Ahab,
22: 9 So there was no one in the **house** *of* Ahaziah powerful enough to
22: 10 she proceeded to destroy the whole royal family of the **house** *of*
22: 12 He remained hidden with them at the **temple** *of* God for six years
23: 3 whole assembly made a covenant with the king at the **temple** *of*
23: 5 a third of you at the royal **palace** and a third at the Foundation
23: 5 all the other men are to be in the courtyards of the **temple** *of* the
23: 6 No one is to enter the **temple** *of* the LORD except the priests
23: 7 in his hand. Anyone who enters the **temple** must be put to death.
23: 9 had belonged to King David and that were in the **temple** *of* God.
23: 10 near the altar and the **temple**, from the south side to the north side
23: 10 from the south side **[RPH]** to the north side of the temple.
23: 10 and the temple, from the south side to the north side of the **temple**.
23: 12 cheering the king, she went to them at the **temple** *of* the LORD.
23: 14 "Bring her out **[RPH]** between the ranks and put to the sword
23: 14 had said, "Do not put her to death at the **temple** *of* the LORD."
23: 15 the entrance of the Horse Gate on the **palace** [+4889] **grounds**,
23: 17 All the people went to the **temple** *of* Baal and tore it down.
23: 18 Jehoiada placed the oversight of the **temple** *of* the LORD in the
23: 18 were Levites, to whom David had made assignments in the **temple**,
23: 19 He also stationed doorkeepers at the gates of the LORD's **temple**
23: 20 and brought the king down from the **temple** *of* the LORD.
23: 20 They went into the **palace** [+4889] through the Upper Gate
24: 4 Some time later Joash decided to restore the **temple** *of* the
24: 5 due annually from all Israel, to repair the **temple** *of* your God.
24: 7 of that wicked woman Athaliah had broken into the **temple** *of* God
24: 7 and had used even **its**[s] [+3378] sacred objects for the Baals.
24: 8 and placed outside, at the gate of the **temple** *of* the LORD.
24: 12 who carried out the work required for the **temple** *of* the LORD.
24: 12 They hired masons and carpenters to restore the LORD's **temple**,
24: 12 and also workers in iron and bronze to repair the **temple**.
24: 13 They rebuilt the **temple** *of* God according to its original design
24: 14 and with it were made articles for the LORD's **temple**:
24: 14 burnt offerings were presented continually in the **temple** *of* the
24: 16 because of the good he had done in Israel for God and his **temple**.
24: 18 They abandoned the **temple** *of* the LORD, the God of their
24: 21 they stoned him to death in the courtyard of the LORD's **temple**.
24: 27 the record of the restoration of the **temple** *of* God are written in the
25: 5 assigned them according to their **families** [+3] to commanders of
25: 19 and now you are arrogant and proud. But stay at **home**!
25: 24 all the articles found in the **temple** *of* God that had been in the care
25: 24 together with the **palace** [+4889] treasures and the hostages,
26: 19 in their presence before the incense altar in the LORD's **temple**,
26: 21 He lived in a separate **house**—leprous, and excluded from the
26: 21 leprous, and excluded from the **temple** *of* the LORD.
26: 21 Jotham his son had charge of the **palace** [+4889] and governed the
27: 3 Jotham rebuilt the Upper Gate of the **temple** *of* the LORD
28: 7 Azrikam the officer in charge of the **palace**, and Elkanah,
28: 21 Ahaz took some of the things from the **temple** *of* the LORD
28: 21 from the royal **palace** and from the princes and presented them to
28: 24 Ahaz gathered together the furnishings from the **temple** *of* God
28: 24 from the temple of God and took **them**[s] [+466+2021+3998] away.
28: 24 He shut the doors of the LORD's **temple** and set up altars at
29: 3 he opened the doors of the **temple** *of* the LORD and repaired
29: 5 yourselves now and consecrate the **temple** *of* the LORD,
29: 15 they went in to purify the **temple** *of* the LORD, as the king had
29: 16 The priests went into the **sanctuary** *of* the LORD to purify it.
29: 16 They brought out to the courtyard of the LORD's **temple**
29: 17 eight more days they consecrated the **temple** *of* the LORD *itself*,
29: 18 "We have purified the entire **temple** *of* the LORD, the altar of
29: 20 city officials together and went up to the **temple** *of* the LORD.
29: 25 He stationed the Levites in the **temple** *of* the LORD with
29: 31 bring sacrifices and thank offerings to the **temple** *of* the LORD."
29: 35 So the service of the **temple** *of* the LORD was reestablished.
30: 1 inviting them to come to the **temple** *of* the LORD in Jerusalem
30: 15 and brought burnt offerings to the **temple** *of* the LORD.
31: 10 and Azariah the chief priest, from the **family** *of* Zadok, answered,
31: 10 began to bring their contributions to the **temple** *of* the LORD,
31: 11 Hezekiah gave orders to prepare storerooms in the **temple** *of* the
31: 13 and Azariah the official in charge of the **temple** *of* God.
31: 16 all who would enter the **temple** *of* the LORD to perform the daily
31: 17 they distributed to the priests enrolled by their **families** [+3] in the
31: 21 In everything that he undertook in the service of God's **temple**
32: 21 when he went into the **temple** *of* his god, some of his sons cut him
33: 4 He built altars in the **temple** *of* the LORD, of which the LORD
33: 5 In both courts of the **temple** *of* the LORD, he built altars to all the
33: 7 He took the carved image he had made and put it in God's **temple**,
33: 7 and to his son Solomon, "In this **temple** and in Jerusalem,
33: 15 and removed the image from the **temple** *of* the LORD,
33: 15 as well as all the altars he had built on the **temple** hill and in
33: 20 Manasseh rested with his fathers and was buried in his **palace**.
33: 24 officials conspired against him and assassinated him in his **palace**.
34: 6 [as far as Naphtali, and in the **ruins** [K; see Q 2999] around them,]
34: 8 to purify the land and the **temple**, he sent Shaphan son of Azaliah
34: 8 the recorder, to repair the **temple** *of* the LORD his God.
34: 9 gave him the money that had been brought into the **temple** *of* God,
34: 10 the men appointed to supervise the work on the LORD's **temple**.
34: 10 These men paid the workers **[RPH]** who repaired and restored the
34: 10 These men paid the workers who repaired and restored the **temple**.
34: 11 beams for the **buildings** that the kings of Judah had allowed to fall
34: 14 out the money that had been taken into the **temple** *of* the LORD,
34: 15 "I have found the Book of the Law in the **temple** *of* the LORD."
34: 17 They have paid out the money that was in the **temple** *of* the
34: 30 He went up to the **temple** *of* the LORD with the men of Judah,
34: 30 the Covenant, which had been found in the **temple** *of* the LORD.
35: 2 and encouraged them in the service of the LORD's **temple**.
35: 3 "Put the sacred ark in the **temple** that Solomon son of David king
35: 4 Prepare yourselves by **families** [+3] in your divisions, according to
35: 5 "Stand in the holy place with a **group** [+3+2755] of Levites for
35: 5 each subdivision of the **families** [+3] of your fellow countrymen,
35: 8 Zechariah and Jehiel, the administrators of God's **temple**,
35: 12 of the **families** [+3] of the people to offer to the LORD,
35: 20 After all this, when Josiah had set the **temple** in order, Neco king
35: 21 I am attacking at this time, but the **house** *with which* I am at war.
36: 7 Nebuchadnezzar also took to Babylon articles from the **temple** *of*
36: 10 together with articles of value from the **temple** *of* the LORD,
36: 14 practices of the nations and defiling the **temple** *of* the LORD,
36: 17 killed their young men with the sword in the **sanctuary** [+5219],
36: 18 He carried to Babylon all the articles from the **temple** *of* God,
36: 18 the treasures of the LORD's **temple** and the treasures of the king
36: 19 They set fire to God's **temple** and broke down the wall of
36: 23 he has appointed me to build a **temple** for him at Jerusalem in
Ezr 1: 2 he has appointed me to build a **temple** for him at Jerusalem in
1: 3 go up to Jerusalem in Judah and build the **temple** *of* the LORD,
1: 4 and with freewill offerings for the **temple** *of* God in Jerusalem.' "
1: 5 prepared to go up and build the **house** *of* the LORD in Jerusalem.
1: 7 King Cyrus brought out the articles belonging to the **temple** *of* the
1: 7 away from Jerusalem and had placed in the **temple** *of* his god.
2: 36 the descendants of Jedaiah (through the **family** *of* Jeshua)
2: 59 they could not show that their **families** [+3] were descended from
2: 68 When they arrived at the **house** *of* the LORD in Jerusalem,
2: 68 offerings toward the rebuilding of the **house** *of* God on its site.
3: 8 the second year after their arrival at the **house** *of* God in Jerusalem,
3: 8 and older to supervise the building of the **house** *of* the LORD.
3: 9 joined together in supervising those working on the **house** *of* God.
3: 11 because the foundation of the **house** *of* the LORD was laid.
3: 12 and Levites and family heads, who had seen the former **temple**,
3: 12 wept aloud when they saw the foundation of this **temple** being
4: 3 "You have no part with us in building a **temple** to our God.
6: 22 so that he assisted them in the work on the **house** *of* God, the God
7: 27 who has put it into the king's heart to bring honor to the **house** *of*
8: 17 so that they might bring attendants to us for the **house** *of* our God.
8: 25 and all Israel present there had donated for the **house** *of* our God.
8: 29 of the **house** *of* the LORD in Jerusalem before the leading priests
8: 30 weighed out to be taken to the **house** *of* our God in Jerusalem.
8: 33 On the fourth day, in the **house** *of* our God, we weighed out the
8: 36 then gave assistance to the people and to the **house** *of* God.
9: 9 He has granted us new life to rebuild the **house** *of* our God
10: 1 weeping and throwing himself down before the **house** *of* God,
10: 6 Ezra withdrew from before the **house** *of* God and went to the room
10: 9 all the people were sitting in the square before the **house** *of* God,
10: 16 one from each family **division**, and all of them designated by
Ne 1: 6 including myself and my father's **house**, have committed against
2: 3 Why should my face not look sad when the city **where**[s] my fathers
2: 8 me timber to make beams for the gates of the citadel by the **temple**
2: 8 and for the city wall and for the **residence** I will occupy?"
3: 10 Jedaiah son of Harumaph made repairs opposite his **house**,
3: 16 of David, as far as the artificial pool and the **House** *of* the Heroes.
3: 20 from the angle to the entrance of the **house** *of* Eliashib the high
3: 21 from the entrance of Eliashib's **house** to the end of it.
3: 21 from the entrance of Eliashib's house to the end of **it**[s] [+513].
3: 23 Benjamin and Hasshub made repairs in front of their **house**;
3: 23 of Maaseiah, the son of Ananiah, made repairs beside his **house**.
3: 24 another section, from Azariah's **house** to the angle and the corner,
3: 25 the tower projecting from the upper **palace** [+4889] near the court
3: 28 the priests made repairs, each in front of his own **house**.
3: 29 to them, Zadok son of Immer made repairs opposite his **house**.
3: 31 made repairs as far as the **house** *of* the temple servants
4: 14 [4:8] your sons and your daughters, your wives and your **homes**."
4: 16 [4:10] The officers posted themselves behind all the **people** *of*
5: 3 our vineyards and our **homes** to get grain during the famine."

Ne 5:11 vineyards, olive groves and **houses**, and also the usury you are
5:13 "In this way may God shake out of his **house** and possessions
6:10 One day I went to the **house** *of* Shemaiah son of Delaiah, the son
6:10 He said, "Let us meet in the **house** *of* God, inside the temple,
7:3 as guards, some at their posts and some near their own **houses**."
7:4 were few people in it, and the **houses** had not yet been rebuilt.
7:39 the descendants of Jedaiah (through the **family** *of* Jeshua)
7:61 they could not show that their **families** [+3] were descended from
8:16 in the courts of the **house** *of* God and in the square by the Water
9:25 they took possession of **houses** filled with all kinds of good things,
10:32 [10:33] shekel each year for the service of the **house** *of* our God:
10:33 [10:34] for Israel; and for all the duties of the **house** *of* our God.
10:34 [10:35] have cast lots to determine when each of our **families** [+3]
10:34 [10:35] **house** *of* our God at set times each year a contribution of
10:35 [10:36] also assume responsibility for bringing to the **house** *of*
10:36 [10:37] of our herds and of our flocks to the **house** *of* our God,
10:36 [10:37] of our God, to the priests ministering **there**[s] [+466+928].
10:37 [10:38] we will bring to the storerooms of the **house** *of* our God,
10:38 [10:39] to bring a tenth of the tithes up to the **house** *of* our God,
10:38 [10:39] of our God, to the storerooms of the **treasury** [+238].
10:39 [10:40] singers stay. "We will not neglect the **house** *of* our God."
11:11 son of Meraioth, the son of Ahitub, supervisor in the **house** *of* God,
11:12 and their associates, who carried on work for the **temple**—
11:16 who had charge of the outside work of the **house** *of* God;
11:22 who were the singers responsible for the service of the **house** *of*
12:37 passed above the **house** *of* David to the Water Gate on the east.
12:40 choirs that gave thanks then took their places in the **house** *of* God;
13:4 had been put in charge of the storerooms of the **house** *of* our God.
13:7 done in providing Tobiah a room in the courts of the **house** *of* God.
13:8 and threw all Tobiah's **household** goods out of the room.
13:9 then I put back into them the equipment of the **house** *of* God,
13:11 and asked them, "Why is the **house** *of* God neglected?"
13:14 so faithfully done for the **house** *of* my God and its services.
Est 1:8 for the king instructed all the **wine stewards** [+8042] to serve each
1:9 Vashti also gave a banquet for the women in the royal **palace**
1:22 tongue that every man should be ruler over his own **household**.
2:3 these beautiful girls into the **harem** [+851] at the citadel of Susa.
2:8 Esther also was taken to the king's **palace** and entrusted to Hegai,
2:9 He assigned to her seven maids selected from the king's **palace**
2:9 moved her and her maids into the best place in the **harem** [+851].
2:11 forth near the courtyard of the **harem** [+851] to find out how
2:13 her to take with her from the **harem** [+851] to the king's palace.
2:13 was given her to take with her from the harem to the king's **palace**.
2:14 in the morning return to another part of the **harem** [+851] to the
2:16 She was taken to King Xerxes in the royal **residence** in the tenth
4:13 because you are in the king's **house** you alone of all the Jews will
4:14 from another place, but you and your father's **family** will perish.
5:1 her royal robes and stood in the inner court of the **palace** [+4889],
5:1 stood in the inner court of the palace, in front of the king's **hall**.
5:1 The king was sitting on his royal throne in the **hall**, facing the
5:1 sitting on his royal throne in the hall, facing the entrance. **[RPH]**
5:10 Nevertheless, Haman restrained himself and went **home**. Calling
6:4 Now Haman had just entered the outer court of the **palace** [+4889]
6:12 But Haman rushed **home**, with his head covered in grief,
7:8 as the king returned from the palace garden to the banquet **hall**,
7:8 he even molest the queen while she is with me in the **house**?"
7:9 "A gallows seventy-five feet high stands by Haman's **house**.
8:1 That same day King Xerxes gave Queen Esther the **estate** *of*
8:2 it to Mordecai. And Esther appointed him over Haman's **estate**.
8:7 Haman attacked the Jews, I have given his **estate** to Esther,
9:4 Mordecai was prominent in the **palace** [+4889]; his reputation
Job 1:4 His sons used to take turns holding feasts in their **homes**, and they
1:10 put a hedge around him and his **household** and everything he has?
1:13 were feasting and drinking wine at the oldest brother's **house**,
1:18 were feasting and drinking wine at the oldest brother's **house**,
1:19 swept in from the desert and struck the four corners of the **house**.
3:15 with rulers who had gold, who filled their **houses** with silver.
4:19 how much more those who live in **houses** *of* clay,
7:10 He will never come to his **house** again; his place will know him no
8:14 What he trusts in is fragile; what he relies on is a spider's **web**.
8:15 He leans on his **web**, but it gives way; he clings to it, but it does
15:28 he will inhabit ruined towns and **houses** where no one lives,
17:13 If the only **home** I hope for is the grave, if I spread out my bed in
19:15 My **guests** [+1591] and my maidservants count me a stranger;
20:19 and left them destitute; he has seized **houses** he did not build.
20:28 A flood will carry off his **house**, rushing waters on the day of
21:9 Their **homes** are safe and free from fear; the rod of God is not
21:21 For what does he care about the **family** he leaves behind when his
21:28 You say, 'Where now is the great man's **house**, the tents where
22:18 Yet it was he who filled their **houses** with good things, so I stand
24:16 In the dark, men break into **houses**, but by day they shut
27:18 The **house** he builds is like a moth's cocoon, like a hut made by a
30:23 bring me down to death, to the **place** appointed for all the living.
38:20 them to their places? Do you know the paths to their **dwellings**?
39:6 I gave him the wasteland as his **home**, the salt flats as his habitat.
42:11 who had known him before came and ate with him in his **house**.
Ps 5:7 [5:8] I, by your great mercy, will come into your **house**;
23:6 of my life, and I will dwell in the **house** *of* the LORD forever.
26:8 I love the **house** where you live, O LORD, the place where your
27:4 that I may dwell in the **house** *of* the LORD all the days of my life,
30:T [30:1] A psalm. A song. For the dedication of the **temple**.
31:2 [31:3] my rock of refuge, a **strong fortress** [+5181] to save me.
36:8 [36:9] They feast on the abundance of your **house**; you give them
42:4 [42:5] leading the procession to the **house** *of* God, with shouts of
45:10 [45:11] and give ear: Forget your people and your father's **house**.
49:11 [49:12] Their tombs will remain their **houses** forever,
49:16 [49:17] grows rich, when the splendor of his **house** increases;
50:9 I have no need of a bull from your **stall** or of goats from your pens,
52:T [52:2] and told him: "David has gone to the **house** *of* Ahimelech."
52:8 [52:10] I am like an olive tree flourishing in the **house** *of* God;
55:14 [55:15] as we walked with the throng at the **house** *of* God.
59:T [59:1] When Saul had sent men to watch David's **house** in order
65:4 [65:5] We are filled with the good things of your **house**, of your
66:13 I will come to your **temple** with burnt offerings and fulfill my
68:6 [68:7] God sets the lonely in **families**, he leads forth the prisoners
68:12 [68:13] in haste; in the **camps** [+5661] men divide the plunder.
69:9 [69:10] for zeal for your **house** consumes me, and the insults of
84:3 [84:4] Even the sparrow has found a **home**, and the swallow a
84:4 [84:5] Blessed are those who dwell in your **house**; they are ever
84:10 [84:11] I would rather be a doorkeeper in the **house** *of* my God
92:13 [92:14] planted in the **house** *of* the LORD, they will flourish in
93:5 holiness adorns your **house** for endless days, O LORD.
98:3 has remembered his love and his faithfulness to the **house** *of* Israel;
101:2 you come to me? I will walk in my **house** with blameless heart.
101:7 No one who practices deceit will dwell in my **house**; no one who
104:17 the birds make their nests; the stork has its **home** in the pine trees.
105:21 He made him master of his **household**, ruler over all he possessed,
112:3 Wealth and riches are in his **house**, and his righteousness endures
113:9 He settles the barren woman in her **home** as a happy mother of
114:1 out of Egypt, the **house** *of* Jacob from a people of foreign tongue,
115:10 O **house** *of* Aaron, trust in the LORD—he is their help and shield.
115:12 He will bless the **house** *of* Israel, he will bless the house of Aaron,
115:12 He will bless the house of Israel, he will bless the **house** *of* Aaron,
116:19 in the courts of the **house** *of* the LORD—in your midst,
118:3 Let the **house** *of* Aaron say: "His love endures forever."
118:26 name of the LORD. From the **house** *of* the LORD we bless you.
119:54 Your decrees are the theme of my song wherever I **lodge** [+4472].
122:1 those who said to me, "Let us go to the **house** *of* the LORD."
122:5 the thrones for judgment stand, the thrones of the **house** *of* David.
122:9 For the sake of the **house** *of* the LORD our God, I will seek your
127:1 Unless the LORD builds the **house**, its builders labor in vain.
128:3 Your wife will be like a fruitful vine within your **house**; your sons
132:3 "I will not enter my **house** [+185] or go to my bed—
134:1 of the LORD who minister by night in the **house** *of* the LORD.
135:2 you who minister in the **house** *of* the LORD, in the courts of the
135:2 in the house of the LORD, in the courts of the **house** *of* our God.
135:19 O **house** *of* Israel, praise the LORD; O house of Aaron, praise the
135:19 praise the LORD; O **house** *of* Aaron, praise the LORD;
135:20 O **house** *of* Levi, praise the LORD; you who fear him, praise the
Pr 1:13 get all sorts of valuable things and fill our **houses** with plunder;
2:18 For her **house** leads down to death and her paths to the spirits of
3:33 The LORD's curse is on the **house** *of* the wicked, but he blesses
5:8 Keep to a path far from her, do not go near the door of her **house**,
5:10 feast on your wealth and your toil enrich another man's **house**.
6:31 must pay sevenfold, though it costs him all the wealth of his **house**.
7:6 At the window of my **house** I looked out through the lattice.
7:8 street near her corner, walking along in the direction of her **house**
7:11 (She is loud and defiant, her feet never stay at **home**;
7:19 My husband is not at **home**; he has gone on a long journey.
7:20 his purse filled with money and will not be **home** till full moon."
7:27 Her **house** is a highway to the grave, leading down to the chambers
9:1 Wisdom has built her **house**; she has hewn out its seven pillars.
9:14 She sits at the door of her **house**, on a seat at the highest point of
11:29 He who brings trouble on his **family** will inherit only wind,
12:7 and are no more, but the **house** *of* the righteous stands firm.
14:1 The wise woman builds her **house**, but with her own hands the
14:11 The **house** *of* the wicked will be destroyed, but the tent of the
15:6 The **house** *of* the righteous contains great treasure, but the income
15:25 The LORD tears down the proud man's **house** but he keeps the
15:27 A greedy man brings trouble to his **family**, but he who hates bribes
17:1 a dry crust with peace and quiet than a **house** full of feasting,
17:13 If a man pays back evil for good, evil will never leave his **house**.
19:14 **Houses** and wealth are inherited from parents, but a prudent wife is
21:9 Better to live on a corner of the roof than share a **house** with a
21:12 The Righteous One takes note of the **house** *of* the wicked
24:3 By wisdom a **house** is built, and through understanding it is
24:27 and get your fields ready; after that, build your **house**.
25:17 Seldom set foot in your neighbor's **house**—too much of you,

Pr 25:24 Better to live on a corner of the roof than share a **house** with a
27:10 and do not go to your brother's **house** when disaster strikes you—
27:27 milk to feed you and your **family** and to nourish your servant girls.
30:26 are creatures of little power, yet they make their **home** in the crags;
31:15 she provides food for her **family** and portions for her servant girls.
31:21 When it snows, she has no fear for her **household**; for all of them
31:21 for her household; for all of **them**[s] [+2023] are clothed in scarlet.
31:27 She watches over the affairs of her **household** and does not eat the
Ecc 2:4 great projects: I built **houses** for myself and planted vineyards.
2:7 female slaves and had other slaves who were born in my **house**.
4:14 The youth may have come from **prison** [+673+2021] to the
5:1 [4:17] Guard your steps when you go to the **house** *of* God. Go
7:2 It is better to go to a **house** *of* mourning than to go to a house of
7:2 It is better to go to a house of mourning than to go to a **house** *of*
7:4 The heart of the wise is in the **house** *of* mourning, but the heart of
7:4 of mourning, but the heart of fools is in the **house** *of* pleasure.
10:18 a man is lazy, the rafters sag; if his hands are idle, the **house** leaks.
12:3 when the keepers of the **house** tremble, and the strong men stoop,
12:5 man goes to his eternal **home** and mourners go about the streets.
SS 1:17 The beams of our **house** are cedars; our rafters are firs.
2:4 He has taken me to the **banquet hall** [+3516], and his banner over
3:4 would not let him go till I had brought him to my mother's **house**,
8:2 I would lead you and bring you to my mother's **house**—she who
8:7 If one were to give all the wealth of his **house** for love, it would be
Isa 2:2 In the last days the mountain of the LORD's **temple** will be
2:3 to the mountain of the LORD, to the **house** *of* the God of Jacob.
2:5 Come, O **house** *of* Jacob, let us walk in the light of the LORD.
2:6 You have abandoned your people, the **house** *of* Jacob. They are
3:6 A man will seize one of his brothers at his father's **home**,
3:7 I have no food or clothing in my **house**; do not make me the leader
3:14 ruined my vineyard; the plunder from the poor is in your **houses**.
3:20 and ankle chains and sashes, the perfume **bottles** and charms,
5:7 The vineyard of the LORD Almighty is the **house** *of* Israel,
5:8 Woe to you who add **house** to house and join field to field till no
5:8 Woe to you who add house to **house** and join field to field till no
5:9 "Surely the great **houses** will become desolate, the fine mansions
6:4 and thresholds shook and the **temple** was filled with smoke.
6:11 until the **houses** are left deserted and the fields ruined and ravaged,
7:2 Now the **house** *of* David was told, "Aram has allied itself with
7:13 Isaiah said, "Hear now, you **house** *of* David! Is it not enough to try
7:17 on the **house** *of* your father a time unlike any since Ephraim broke
8:14 for both **houses** *of* Israel he will be a stone that causes men to
8:17 for the LORD, who is hiding his face from the **house** *of* Jacob.
10:20 that day the remnant of Israel, the survivors of the **house** *of* Jacob,
10:32 [their fist at the mount of the **Daughter** [K; see Q 1426] *of* Zion,]
13:16 their eyes; their **houses** will be looted and their wives ravished.
13:21 But desert creatures will lie there, jackals will fill her **houses**;
14:1 own land. Aliens will join them and unite with the **house** *of* Jacob.
14:2 And the **house** *of* Israel will possess the nations as menservants
14:17 who overthrew its cities and would not let his captives go **home**?"
14:18 All the kings of the nations lie in state, each in his own **tomb**.
15:2 Dibon goes up to its **temple**, to its high places to weep;
22:8 you looked in that day to the weapons in the **Palace** *of* the Forest;
22:10 You counted the **buildings** *in* Jerusalem and tore down houses to
22:10 in Jerusalem and tore down **houses** to strengthen the wall.
22:15 say to this steward, to Shebna, who is in charge of the **palace**:
22:18 chariots will remain—you disgrace to your master's **house**!
22:21 a father to those who live in Jerusalem and to the **house** *of* Judah.
22:22 I will place on his shoulder the key to the **house** *of* David;
22:23 a firm place; he will be a seat of honor for the **house** *of* his father.
22:24 All the glory of his **family** [+3] will hang on him: its offspring
23:1 For Tyre is destroyed and left without **house** or harbor.
24:10 The ruined city lies desolate; the entrance to every **house** is barred.
29:22 the LORD, who redeemed Abraham, says to the **house** *of* Jacob:
31:2 He will rise up against the **house** *of* the wicked, against those who
32:13 mourn for all **houses** *of* merriment and for this city of revelry.
36:3 Eliakim son of Hilkiah the **palace** administrator, Shebna the
36:22 Eliakim son of Hilkiah the **palace** administrator, Shebna the
37:1 and put on sackcloth and went into the **temple** *of* the LORD.
37:2 He sent Eliakim the **palace** administrator, Shebna the secretary,
37:14 he went up to the **temple** *of* the LORD and spread it out before
37:31 Once more a remnant of the **house** *of* Judah will take root below
37:38 while he was worshiping in the **temple** *of* his god Nisroch,
38:1 Put your **house** in order, because you are going to die; you will not
38:20 instruments all the days of our lives in the **temple** *of* the LORD.
38:22 "What will be the sign that I will go up to the **temple** *of* the
39:2 and showed them what was in his **storehouses** [+5800]—
39:2 his entire **armory** [+3998] and everything found among his
39:2 There was nothing in his **palace** or in all his kingdom that
39:4 The prophet asked, "What did they see in your **palace**?" "They
39:4 your palace?" "They saw everything in my **palace**," Hezekiah said.
39:6 The time will surely come when everything in your **palace**,
42:7 to release from the **dungeon** [+3975] those who sit in darkness.
42:22 all of them trapped in pits or hidden away in **prisons** [+3975].
44:13 form of man, of man in all his glory, that it may dwell in a **shrine**.
46:3 "Listen to me, O **house** *of* Jacob, all you who remain of the house
46:3 O house of Jacob, all you who remain of the **house** *of* Israel,
48:1 "Listen to this, O **house** *of* Jacob, you who are called by the name
56:5 to them I will give within my **temple** and its walls a memorial
56:7 to my holy mountain and give them joy in my **house** *of* prayer.
56:7 for my **house** will be called a house of prayer for all nations."
56:7 for my house will be called a **house** *of* prayer for all nations."
58:1 to my people their rebellion and to the **house** *of* Jacob their sins.
58:7 with the hungry and to provide the poor wanderer with **shelter**—
60:7 as offerings on my altar, and I will adorn my glorious **temple**.
63:7 the many good things he has done for the **house** *of* Israel,
64:11 [64:10] Our holy and glorious **temple**, where our fathers praised
65:21 They will build **houses** and dwell in them; they will plant
66:1 earth is my footstool. Where is the **house** you will build for me?
66:20 to the **temple** *of* the LORD in ceremonially clean vessels.
Jer 2:4 Hear the word of the LORD, O **house** *of* Jacob, all you clans of
2:4 the LORD, O house of Jacob, all you clans of the **house** *of* Israel.
2:14 Is Israel a servant, a **slave by birth** [+3535]? Why then has he
2:26 disgraced when he is caught, so the **house** *of* Israel is disgraced—
3:18 In those days the **house** *of* Judah will join the house of Israel,
3:18 In those days the house of Judah will join the **house** *of* Israel,
3:20 been unfaithful to me, O **house** *of* Israel," declares the LORD.
5:7 they committed adultery and thronged to the **houses** *of* prostitutes.
5:11 The **house** *of* Israel and the house of Judah have been utterly
5:11 and the **house** *of* Judah have been utterly unfaithful to me,"
5:15 O **house** *of* Israel," declares the LORD, "I am bringing a distant
5:20 "Announce this to the **house** *of* Jacob and proclaim it in Judah:
5:27 Like cages full of birds, their **houses** are full of deceit; they have
6:12 Their **houses** will be turned over to others, together with their
7:2 "Stand at the gate of the LORD's **house** and there proclaim this
7:10 then come and stand before me in this **house**, which bears my
7:11 Has this **house**, which bears my Name, become a den of robbers to
7:14 what I did to Shiloh I will now do to the **house** that bears my
7:30 They have set up their detestable idols in the **house** that bears my
9:26 [9:25] even the whole **house** *of* Israel is uncircumcised in heart."
10:1 Hear what the LORD says to you, O **house** *of* Israel.
11:10 Both the **house** *of* Israel and the house of Judah have broken the
11:10 the **house** *of* Judah have broken the covenant I made with their
11:15 "What is my beloved doing in my **temple** as she works out her evil
11:17 because the **house** *of* Israel and the house of Judah have done evil
11:17 because the house of Israel and the **house** *of* Judah have done evil
12:6 Your brothers, your own **family** [+3]—even they have betrayed
12:7 "I will forsake my **house**, abandon my inheritance; I will give the
12:14 their lands and I will uproot the **house** *of* Judah from among them.
13:11 so I bound the whole **house** *of* Israel and the whole house of Judah
13:11 the whole house of Israel and the whole **house** *of* Judah to me,'
16:5 "Do not enter a **house** *where there* is a funeral meal; do not go to
16:8 "And do not enter a **house** *where there* is feasting and sit down to
17:22 Do not bring a load out of your **houses** or do any work on the
17:26 incense and thank offerings to the **house** *of* the LORD.
18:2 "Go down to the potter's **house**, and there I will give you my
18:3 So I went down to the potter's **house**, and I saw him working at the
18:6 "O **house** *of* Israel, can I not do with you as this potter does?"
18:6 in the hand of the potter, so are you in my hand, O **house** *of* Israel.
18:22 Let a cry be heard from their **houses** when you suddenly bring
19:13 The **houses** *in* Jerusalem and those of the kings of Judah will be
19:13 and **those**[s] *of* the kings of Judah will be defiled like this place,
19:13 all the **houses** where they burned incense on the roofs to all the
19:14 stood in the court of the LORD's **temple** and said to all the
20:1 son of Immer, the chief officer in the **temple** *of* the LORD,
20:2 the stocks at the Upper Gate of Benjamin at the LORD's **temple**.
20:6 and all who live in your **house** will go into exile to Babylon.
21:11 "Moreover, say to the royal **house** *of* Judah, 'Hear the word of the
21:12 O **house** *of* David, this is what the LORD says:
22:1 "Go down to the **palace** *of* the king of Judah and proclaim this
22:4 sit on David's throne will come through the gates of this **palace**,
22:5 I swear by myself that this **palace** will become a ruin.' "
22:6 For this is what the LORD says about the **palace** *of* the king of
22:13 "Woe to him who builds his **palace** by unrighteousness, his upper
22:14 'I will build myself a great **palace** with spacious upper rooms.'
23:8 who brought the descendants of **Israel** [+3776] up out of the land
23:11 even in my **temple** I find their wickedness," declares the LORD.
23:34 oracle of the LORD,' I will punish that man and his **household**.
26:2 Stand in the courtyard of the LORD's **house** and speak to all the
26:2 towns of Judah who come to worship in the **house** *of* the LORD.
26:6 I will make this **house** like Shiloh and this city an object of
26:7 all the people heard Jeremiah speak these words in the **house** *of* the
26:9 Why do you prophesy in the LORD's name that this **house** will
26:9 all the people crowded around Jeremiah in the **house** *of* the
26:10 they went up from the royal **palace** to the house of the LORD
26:10 they went up from the royal palace to the **house** *of* the LORD
26:12 "The LORD sent me to prophesy against this **house** and this city
26:18 a heap of rubble, the **temple** hill a mound overgrown with thickets.'

Jer 27:16 'Very soon now the articles from the LORD's **house** will be
27:18 that the furnishings remaining in the **house** *of* the LORD
27:18 in the **palace** *of* the king of Judah and in Jerusalem not be taken to
27:21 says about the things that are left in the **house** *of* the LORD
27:21 and in the **palace** *of* the king of Judah and in Jerusalem:
28: 1 said to me in the **house** *of* the LORD in the presence of the priests
28: 3 **house** that Nebuchadnezzar king of Babylon removed from here
28: 5 and all the people who were standing in the **house** *of* the LORD.
28: 6 have prophesied by bringing the articles of the LORD's **house**
29: 5 "Build **houses** and settle down; plant gardens and eat what they
29:26 in place of Jehoiada to be in charge of the **house** *of* the LORD;
29:28 Therefore build **houses** and settle down; plant gardens and eat
31:27 "when I will plant the **house** *of* Israel and the house of Judah with
31:27 and the **house** *of* Judah with the offspring of men and of animals.
31:31 "when I will make a new covenant with the **house** *of* Israel
31:31 new covenant with the house of Israel and with the **house** *of* Judah.
31:33 "This is the covenant I will make with the **house** *of* Israel after that
32: 2 confined in the courtyard of the guard in the royal **palace** *of* Judah.
32:15 **Houses**, fields and vineyards will again be bought in this land.'
32:29 along with the **houses** where the people provoked me to anger by
32:34 They set up their abominable idols in the **house** that bears my
33: 4 says about the **houses** *in* this city and the royal palaces of Judah
33: 4 the royal **palaces** *of* Judah that have been torn down to be used
33:11 the voices of those who bring thank offerings to the **house** *of* the
33:14 'when I will fulfill the gracious promise I made to the **house** *of*
33:14 promise I made to the house of Israel and to the **house** *of* Judah.
33:17 never fail to have a man to sit on the throne of the **house** *of* Israel,
34:13 when I brought them out of Egypt, out of the **land** *of* slavery.
34:15 You even made a covenant before me in the **house** that bears my
35: 2 "Go to the Recabite **family** and invite them to come to one of the
35: 2 invite them to come to one of the side rooms of the **house** *of* the
35: 3 his brothers and all his sons—the whole **family** *of* the Recabites.
35: 4 I brought them into the **house** *of* the LORD, into the room of the
35: 5 some cups before the men of the Recabite **family** and said to them,
35: 7 Also you must never build **houses**, sow seed or plant vineyards;
35: 9 or built **houses** to live in or had vineyards, fields or crops.
35:18 Jeremiah said to the **family** *of* the Recabites, "This is what the
36: 3 Perhaps when the **people** *of* Judah hear about every disaster I plan
36: 5 told Baruch, "I am restricted; I cannot go to the LORD's **temple**.
36: 6 So you go to the **house** *of* the LORD on a day of fasting and read
36: 8 at the LORD's **temple** he read the words of the LORD from the
36:10 the upper courtyard at the entrance of the New Gate of the **temple**,
36:10 Baruch read to all the people at the LORD's **temple** the words of
36:12 he went down to the secretary's room in the royal **palace**,
36:22 the ninth month and the king was sitting in the winter **apartment**,
37: 4 the people, for he had not yet been put in **prison** [+2021+3989].
37:15 beaten and **imprisoned in** [+657+906+2021+5989] the house of
37:15 him beaten and imprisoned in the **house** *of* Jonathan the secretary,
37:15 the secretary, which they had made into a **prison** [+2021+3975].
37:16 Jeremiah was put into a vaulted cell in a **dungeon** [+1014],
37:17 King Zedekiah sent for him and had him brought to the **palace**,
37:18 or this people, that you have put me in **prison** [+2021+3975]?
37:20 Do not send me back to the **house** *of* Jonathan the secretary,
38: 7 But Ebed-Melech, a Cushite, an official in the royal **palace**,
38: 8 Ebed-Melech went out of the **palace** [+4889] and said to him,
38:11 and went to a room under the treasury in the **palace** [+4889].
38:14 had him brought to the third entrance to the **temple** *of* the LORD.
38:17 this city will not be burned down; you and your **family** will live.
38:22 All the women left in the **palace** *of* the king of Judah will be
38:26 the king not to send me back to Jonathan's **house** to die there.' "
39: 8 The Babylonians set fire to the royal **palace** and the houses of the
39: 8 the **houses** *of* the people and broke down the walls of Jerusalem.
39:14 son of Ahikam, the son of Shaphan, to take him back to his **home**.
41: 5 grain offerings and incense with them to the **house** *of* the LORD.
43: 9 brick pavement at the entrance to Pharaoh's **palace** in Tahpanhes.
43:12 He will set fire to the **temples** *of* the gods of Egypt; he will burn
43:13 There in the **temple** *of* the sun in Egypt he will demolish the sacred
43:13 and will burn down the **temples** *of* the gods of Egypt.' "
48:13 as the **house** *of* Israel was ashamed when they trusted in Bethel.
51:51 foreigners have entered the holy places of the LORD's **house**."
52:11 where he put him in **prison** [+2021+7213] till the day of his death.
52:13 He set fire to the **temple** *of* the LORD, the royal palace and all
52:13 of the LORD, the royal **palace** and all the houses of Jerusalem.
52:13 of the LORD, the royal palace and all the **houses** *of* Jerusalem.
52:13 houses of Jerusalem. Every important **building** he burned down.
52:17 and the bronze Sea that were at the **temple** *of* the LORD
52:17 of the LORD **[RPH]** and they carried all the bronze to Babylon.
52:20 which King Solomon had made for the **temple** *of* the LORD,
52:31 freed him from **prison** [+2021+3989] on the twenty-fifth day of
La 1:20 Outside, the sword bereaves; **inside** [+928+2021], there is only
2: 7 they have raised a shout in the **house** *of* the LORD as on the day
5: 2 inheritance has been turned over to aliens, our **homes** to foreigners.
Eze 1:27 as if **full** [+6017] *of* fire, and that from there down he looked like
2: 5 they listen or fail to listen—for they are a rebellious **house**—
2: 6 they say or terrified by them, though they are a rebellious **house**.
2: 8 Do not rebel like that rebellious **house**; open your mouth and eat
3: 1 eat this scroll; then go and speak to the **house** *of* Israel."
3: 4 go now to the **house** *of* Israel and speak my words to them.
3: 5 obscure speech and difficult language, but to the **house** *of* Israel—
3: 7 the **house** *of* Israel is not willing to listen to you because they are
3: 7 to me, for the whole **house** *of* Israel is hardened and obstinate.
3: 9 of them or terrified by them, though they are a rebellious **house**."
3:17 "Son of man, I have made you a watchman for the **house** *of* Israel;
3:24 He spoke to me and said: "Go, shut yourself inside your **house**.
3:26 and unable to rebuke them, though they are a rebellious **house**.
3:27 whoever will refuse let him refuse; for they are a rebellious **house**.
4: 3 and you shall besiege it. This will be a sign to the **house** *of* Israel.
4: 4 your left side and put the sin of the **house** *of* Israel upon yourself.
4: 5 So for 390 days you will bear the sin of the **house** *of* Israel.
4: 6 this time on your right side, and bear the sin of the **house** *of* Judah.
5: 4 A fire will spread from there to the whole **house** *of* Israel.
6:11 of all the wicked and detestable practices of the **house** *of* Israel,
7:15 "Outside is the sword, **inside** [+4946] are plague and famine;
7:24 the most wicked of the nations to take possession of their **houses**;
8: 1 while I was sitting in my **house** and the elders of Judah were sitting
8: 6 the utterly detestable things the **house** *of* Israel is doing here,
8:10 and detestable animals and all the idols of the **house** *of* Israel.
8:11 In front of them stood seventy elders of the **house** *of* Israel,
8:12 have you seen what the elders of the **house** *of* Israel are doing in
8:14 he brought me to the entrance to the north gate of the **house** *of* the
8:16 then brought me into the inner court of the **house** *of* the LORD,
8:17 Is it a trivial matter for the **house** *of* Judah to do the detestable
9: 3 where it had been, and moved to the threshold of the **temple**.
9: 6 So they began with the elders who were in front of the **temple**.
9: 7 said to them, "Defile the **temple** and fill the courts with the slain.
9: 9 "The sin of the **house** *of* Israel and Judah is exceedingly great;
10: 3 Now the cherubim were standing on the south side of the **temple**
10: 4 above the cherubim and moved to the threshold of the **temple**.
10: 4 The cloud filled the **temple**, and the court was full of the radiance
10:18 of the LORD departed from over the threshold of the **temple**
10:19 stopped at the entrance to the east gate of the LORD's **house**,
11: 1 brought me to the gate of the **house** *of* the LORD that faces east.
11: 3 They say, 'Will it not soon be time to build **houses**? This city is a
11: 5 That is what you are saying, O **house** *of* Israel, but I know what is
11:15 who are your blood relatives and the whole **house** *of* Israel—
12: 2 "Son of man, you are living among a rebellious **people**. They have
12: 2 and ears to hear but do not hear, for they are a rebellious **people**.
12: 3 Perhaps they will understand, though they are a rebellious **house**.
12: 6 see the land, for I have made you a sign to the **house** *of* Israel."
12: 9 "Son of man, did not that rebellious **house** *of* Israel ask you,
12: 9 rebellious house of Israel ask you, **[RPH]** 'What are you doing?'
12:10 prince in Jerusalem and the whole **house** *of* Israel who are there.'
12:24 false visions or flattering divinations among the **people** *of* Israel.
12:25 For in your days, you rebellious **house**, I will fulfill whatever I say,
12:27 "Son of man, the **house** *of* Israel is saying, 'The vision he sees is
13: 5 gone up to the breaks in the wall to repair it for the **house** *of* Israel
13: 9 of my people or be listed in the records of the **house** *of* Israel,
14: 4 When any **Israelite** [+408+3776+4946] sets up idols in his heart
14: 5 I will do this to recapture the hearts of the **people** *of* Israel,
14: 6 "Therefore say to the **house** *of* Israel, 'This is what the Sovereign
14: 7 " 'When any **Israelite** [+408+3776+4946] or any alien living in
14:11 the **people** *of* Israel will no longer stray from me, nor will they
16:41 They will burn down your **houses** and inflict punishment on you in
17: 2 set forth an allegory and tell the **house** *of* Israel a parable.
17:12 "Say to this rebellious **house**, 'Do you not know what these things
18: 6 at the mountain shrines or look to the idols of the **house** *of* Israel.
18:15 at the mountain shrines or look to the idols of the **house** *of* Israel.
18:25 of the Lord is not just.' Hear, O **house** *of* Israel: Is my way unjust?
18:29 Yet the **house** *of* Israel says, 'The way of the Lord is not just.'
18:29 of the Lord is not just.' Are my ways unjust, O **house** *of* Israel?
18:30 "Therefore, O **house** *of* Israel, I will judge you, each one according
18:31 a new heart and a new spirit. Why will you die, O **house** *of* Israel?
20: 5 I swore with uplifted hand to the descendants of the **house** *of* Jacob
20:13 " 'Yet the **people** *of* Israel rebelled against me in the desert.
20:27 son of man, speak to the **people** *of* Israel and say to them,
20:30 "Therefore say to the **house** *of* Israel: 'This is what the Sovereign
20:31 Am I to let you inquire of me, O **house** *of* Israel? As surely as I
20:39 " 'As for you, O **house** *of* Israel, this is what the Sovereign LORD
20:40 there in the land the entire **house** *of* Israel will serve me, and there
20:44 to your evil ways and your corrupt practices, O **house** *of* Israel,
22:18 "Son of man, the **house** *of* Israel has become dross to me;
23:39 my sanctuary and desecrated it. That is what they did in my **house**.
23:47 they will kill their sons and daughters and burn down their **houses**.
24: 3 Tell this rebellious **house** a parable and say to them: 'This is what
24:21 Say to the **house** *of* Israel, 'This is what the Sovereign LORD
25: 3 laid waste and over the **people** *of* Judah when they went into exile,
25: 8 the **house** *of* Judah has become like all the other nations,"
25:12 'Because Edom took revenge on the **house** *of* Judah and became

Eze 26: 12 your walls and demolish your fine **houses** and throw your stones,
28: 24 " 'No longer will the **people** *of* Israel have malicious neighbors
28: 25 When I gather the **people** *of* Israel from the nations where they
28: 26 will live there in safety and will build **houses** and plant vineyards;
29: 6 " 'You have been a staff of reed for the **house** *of* Israel.
29: 16 Egypt will no longer be a source of confidence for the **people** *of*
29: 21 "On that day I will make a horn grow for the **house** *of* Israel,
33: 7 "Son of man, I have made you a watchman for the **house** *of* Israel;
33: 10 "Son of man, say to the **house** *of* Israel, 'This is what you are
33: 11 Turn from your evil ways! Why will you die, O **house** *of* Israel?'
33: 20 Yet, O **house** *of* Israel, you say, 'The way of the Lord is not just.'
33: 30 together about you by the walls and at the doors of the **houses**,
34: 30 am with them and that they, the **house** *of* Israel, are my people,
35: 15 Because you rejoiced when the inheritance of the **house** *of* Israel
36: 10 the number of people upon you, even the whole **house** *of* Israel.
36: 17 of man, when the **people** *of* Israel were living in their own land,
36: 21 which the **house** *of* Israel profaned among the nations where they
36: 22 "Therefore say to the **house** *of* Israel, 'This is what the Sovereign
36: 22 It is not for your sake, O **house** *of* Israel, that I am going to do
36: 32 Be ashamed and disgraced for your conduct, O **house** *of* Israel!
36: 37 Once again I will yield to the plea of the **house** *of* Israel and do this
37: 11 "Son of man, these bones are the whole **house** *of* Israel. They say,
37: 16 to Joseph and all the **house** *of* Israel associated with him.'
39: 12 " 'For seven months the **house** *of* Israel will be burying them in
39: 22 From that day forward the **house** *of* Israel will know that I am the
39: 23 the nations will know that the **people** *of* Israel went into exile for
39: 25 and will have compassion on all the **people** *of* Israel,
39: 29 for I will pour out my Spirit on the **house** *of* Israel,
40: 4 been brought here. Tell the **house** *of* Israel everything you see."
40: 5 I saw a wall completely surrounding the **temple** area. The length of
40: 7 the threshold of the gate next to the portico facing the **temple** was
40: 8 he measured the portico of the gateway; [BHS+ *facing the* ***temple***]
40: 9 two cubits thick. The portico of the gateway faced the **temple**.
40: 43 each a handbreadth long, were attached to the **wall** all around.
40: 45 room facing south is for the priests who have charge of the **temple**,
40: 47 a hundred cubits wide. And the altar was in front of the **temple**.
40: 48 He brought me to the portico of the **temple** and measured the
41: 5 Then he measured the wall of the **temple**; it was six cubits thick,
41: 5 and each side room around the **temple** was four cubits wide.
41: 6 There were ledges all around the wall of the **temple** to serve as
41: 6 so that the supports were not inserted into the wall of the **temple**.
41: 7 The structure surrounding the **temple** was built in ascending
41: 7 **[RPH]** so that the rooms widened as one went upward.
41: 7 so that the rooms widened **[RPH]** as one went upward.
41: 8 I saw that the **temple** had a raised base all around it,
41: 9 cubits thick. The open area between the side rooms of the **temple**
41: 10 the ⌞priests'⌟ rooms was twenty cubits wide all around the **temple**.
41: 13 Then he measured the **temple**; it was a hundred cubits long,
41: 14 the east, including the front of the **temple**, was a hundred cubits.
41: 17 the space above the outside of the entrance to the inner **sanctuary**
41: 19 tree on the other. They were carved all around the whole **temple**.
41: 26 on each side. The side rooms of the **temple** also had overhangs.
42: 15 When he had finished measuring what was inside the **temple area**,
43: 4 The glory of the LORD entered the **temple** through the gate
43: 5 into the inner court, and the glory of the LORD filled the **temple**.
43: 6 I heard someone speaking to me from inside the **temple**.
43: 7 The **house** *of* Israel will never again defile my holy name—
43: 10 "Son of man, describe the **temple** to the people of Israel, that they
43: 10 "Son of man, describe the temple to the **people** *of* Israel, that they
43: 11 all they have done, make known to them the design of the **temple**—
43: 12 "This is the law of the **temple**: All the surrounding area on top of
43: 12 of the mountain will be most holy. Such is the law of the **temple**.
43: 21 burn it in the designated part of the **temple area** outside the
44: 4 brought me by way of the north gate to the front of the **temple**.
44: 4 and saw the glory of the LORD filling the **temple** *of* the LORD,
44: 5 concerning all the regulations regarding the **temple** *of* the LORD.
44: 5 Give attention to the entrance of the **temple** and all the exits of the
44: 6 Say to the rebellious **house** *of* Israel, 'This is what the Sovereign
44: 6 Enough of your detestable practices, O **house** *of* Israel!
44: 7 desecrating my **temple** while you offered me food, fat and blood,
44: 11 having charge of the gates of the **temple** and serving in it;
44: 11 having charge of the gates of the temple and serving in **it**[s] [+2021];
44: 12 presence of their idols and made the **house** *of* Israel fall into sin,
44: 14 Yet I will put them in charge of the duties of the **temple** and all the
44: 17 ministering at the gates of the inner court or inside the **temple**.
44: 22 they may marry only virgins of **Israelite** [+3776] descent
44: 30 your ground meal so that a blessing may rest on your **household**.
45: 4 It will be a place for their **houses** as well as a holy place for the
45: 5 who serve in the **temple**, as their possession for towns to live in.
45: 6 the sacred portion; it will belong to the whole **house** *of* Israel.
45: 8 will allow the **house** *of* Israel to possess the land according to their
45: 17 and the Sabbaths—at all the appointed feasts of the **house** *of* Israel.
45: 17 and fellowship offerings to make atonement for the **house** *of* Israel.
45: 19 blood of the sin offering and put it on the doorposts of the **temple**,
45: 20 through ignorance; so you are to make atonement for the **temple**.
46: 24 "These are the **kitchens** [+1418] where those who minister at the
46: 24 "These are the kitchens where those who minister at the **temple**
47: 1 The man brought me back to the entrance of the **temple**, and I saw
47: 1 I saw water coming out from under the threshold of the **temple**
47: 1 threshold of the temple toward the east (for the **temple** faced east).
47: 1 water was coming down from under the south side of the **temple**,
48: 21 the sacred portion with the **temple** sanctuary will be in the center
Da 1: 2 his hand, along with some of the articles from the **temple** *of* God.
1: 2 These he carried off to the **temple** *of* his god in Babylonia
1: 2 of his god in Babylonia and put in the treasure **house** *of* his god.
Hos 1: 4 because I will soon punish the **house** *of* Jehu for the massacre at
1: 4 at Jezreel, and I will put an end to the kingdom of **Israel** [+3776].
1: 6 for I will no longer show love to the **house** *of* Israel,
1: 7 Yet I will show love to the **house** *of* Judah; and I will save them—
5: 1 Pay attention, you **Israelites** [+3776]! Listen, O royal house!
5: 1 you priests! Pay attention, you Israelites! Listen, O royal **house**!
5: 12 I am like a moth to Ephraim, like rot to the **people** *of* Judah.
5: 14 I will be like a lion to Ephraim, like a great lion to **Judah** [+3373].
6: 10 I have seen a horrible thing in the **house** *of* Israel. There Ephraim
8: 1 An eagle is over the **house** *of* the LORD because the people have
9: 4 be for themselves; it will not come into the **temple** *of* the LORD.
9: 8 await him on all his paths, and hostility in the **house** *of* his God.
9: 15 Because of their sinful deeds, I will drive them out of my **house**.
11: 11 I will settle them in their **homes**," declares the LORD.
11: 12 [12:1] surrounded me with lies, the **house** *of* Israel with deceit.
Joel 1: 9 and drink offerings are cut off from the **house** *of* the LORD.
1: 13 and drink offerings are withheld from the **house** *of* your God.
1: 14 and all who live in the land to the **house** *of* the LORD your God,
1: 16 our very eyes—joy and gladness from the **house** *of* our God?
2: 9 They climb into the **houses**; like thieves they enter through the
3: 18 [4:18] A fountain will flow out of the LORD's **house** and will
Am 1: 4 I will send fire upon the **house** *of* Hazael that will consume the
2: 8 in pledge. In the **house** *of* their god they drink wine taken as fines.
3: 13 "Hear this and testify against the **house** *of* Jacob,"
3: 15 I will tear down the winter **house** along with the summer house;
3: 15 I will tear down the winter house along with the summer **house**;
3: 15 the **houses** *adorned with* ivory will be destroyed and the mansions
3: 15 will be destroyed and the **mansions** [+8041] will be demolished,"
5: 1 Hear this word, O **house** *of* Israel, this lament I take up concerning
5: 3 "The city that marches out a thousand strong for **Israel** [+3776]
5: 4 This is what the LORD says to the **house** *of* Israel: "Seek me
5: 6 and live, or he will sweep through the **house** *of* Joseph like a fire;
5: 11 Therefore, though you have built stone **mansions**, you will not live
5: 19 as though he entered his **house** and rested his hand on the wall only
5: 25 and offerings forty years in the desert, O **house** *of* Israel?
6: 1 men of the foremost nation, to whom the **people** *of* Israel come!
6: 9 If ten men are left in one **house**, they too will die.
6: 10 who is to burn the bodies comes to carry them out of the **house**
6: 10 the house and asks anyone still hiding **there**[s] [+928+2021+3752],
6: 11 he will smash the great **house** into pieces and the small house into
6: 11 smash the great house into pieces and the small **house** into bits.
6: 14 "I will stir up a nation against you, O **house** *of* Israel,
7: 9 with my sword I will rise against the **house** *of* Jeroboam."
7: 10 a conspiracy against you in the very heart of **Israel** [+3776].
7: 13 this is the king's sanctuary and the **temple** *of* the kingdom."
7: 16 against Israel, and stop preaching against the **house** *of* Isaac.'
9: 8 yet I will not totally destroy the **house** *of* Jacob,"
9: 9 I will shake the **house** *of* Israel among all the nations as grain is
Ob 1: 17 it will be holy, and the **house** *of* Jacob will possess its inheritance.
1: 18 The **house** *of* Jacob will be a fire and the house of Joseph a flame;
1: 18 The house of Jacob will be a fire and the **house** *of* Joseph a flame;
1: 18 the **house** *of* Esau will be stubble, and they will set it on fire
1: 18 consume it. There will be no survivors from the **house** *of* Esau."
Mic 1: 5 of Jacob's transgression, because of the sins of the **house** *of* Israel.
1: 14 The **town** *of* Aczib will prove deceptive to the kings of Israel.
2: 2 They covet fields and seize them, and **houses**, and take them.
2: 2 They defraud a man of his **home**, a fellowman of his inheritance.
2: 7 Should it be said, O **house** *of* Jacob: "Is the Spirit of the LORD
2: 9 You drive the women of my people from their pleasant **homes**.
3: 1 "Listen, you leaders of Jacob, you rulers of the **house** *of* Israel.
3: 9 Hear this, you leaders of the **house** *of* Jacob, you rulers of the
3: 9 you rulers of the **house** *of* Israel, who despise justice and distort all
3: 12 a heap of rubble, the **temple** hill a mound overgrown with thickets.
4: 1 In the last days the mountain of the LORD's **temple** will be
4: 2 to the mountain of the LORD, to the **house** *of* the God of Jacob.
6: 4 you up out of Egypt and redeemed you from the **land** *of* slavery.
6: 10 Am I still to forget, O wicked **house**, your ill-gotten treasures
6: 16 the statutes of Omri and all the practices of Ahab's **house**,
7: 6 a man's enemies are the members of his own **household**.
Na 1: 14 carved images and cast idols that are in the **temple** *of* your gods.
Hab 2: 9 "Woe to him who builds his **realm** by unjust gain to set his nest on
2: 10 of many peoples, shaming your own **house** and forfeiting your life.
3: 13 You crushed the leader of the **land** *of* wickedness, you stripped

Zep 1: 9 who fill the **temple** *of* their gods with violence and deceit.
1:13 Their wealth will be plundered, their **houses** demolished. They will
1:13 They will build **houses** but not live in them; they will plant
2: 7 It will belong to the remnant of the **house** *of* Judah; there they will
2: 7 In the evening they will lie down in the **houses** *of* Ashkelon.
Hag 1: 2 'The time has not yet come for the LORD's **house** to be built.' "
1: 4 "Is it a time for you yourselves to be living in your paneled **houses**,
1: 4 be living in your paneled houses, while this **house** remains a ruin?"
1: 8 up into the mountains and bring down timber and build the **house**,
1: 9 out to be little. What you brought **home**, I blew away. Why?"
1: 9 "Because of my **house**, which remains a ruin, while each of you is
1: 9 remains a ruin, while each of you is busy with his own **house**.
1:14 and began to work on the **house** *of* the LORD Almighty,
2: 3 'Who of you is left who saw this **house** in its former glory?
2: 7 and I will fill this **house** with glory,' says the LORD Almighty.
2: 9 'The glory of this present **house** will be greater than the glory of
Zec 1:16 return to Jerusalem with mercy, and there my **house** will be rebuilt.
3: 7 then you will govern my **house** and have charge of my courts,
4: 9 "The hands of Zerubbabel have laid the foundation of this **temple**;
5: 4 it will enter the **house** *of* the thief and the house of him who swears
5: 4 of the thief and the **house** *of* him who swears falsely by my name.
5: 4 It will remain in his **house** and destroy it, both its timbers
5:11 He replied, "To the country of Babylonia to build a **house** for it.
6:10 Go the same day to the **house** *of* Josiah son of Zephaniah.
7: 3 by asking the priests of the **house** *of* the LORD Almighty
8: 9 the foundation was laid for the **house** *of* the LORD Almighty,
8:13 O **Judah** [+3373] and Israel, so will I save you, and you will be a
8:13 O Judah and **Israel** [+3776], so will I save you, and you will be a
8:15 determined to do good again to Jerusalem and **Judah** [+3373].
8:19 and glad occasions and happy festivals for **Judah** [+3373].
9: 8 I will defend my **house** against marauding forces. Never again will
10: 3 the **house** *of* Judah, and make them like a proud horse in battle.
10: 6 "I will strengthen the **house** *of* Judah and save the house of Joseph.
10: 6 "I will strengthen the house of Judah and save the **house** *of* Joseph.
11:13 and threw them into the **house** *of* the LORD to the potter.
12: 4 "I will keep a watchful eye over the **house** *of* Judah, but I will
12: 7 so that the honor of the **house** *of* David and of Jerusalem's
12: 8 the **house** *of* David will be like God, like the Angel of the LORD
12:10 "And I will pour out on the **house** *of* David and the inhabitants of
12:12 the clan of the **house** *of* David and their wives, the clan of the
12:12 and their wives, the clan of the **house** *of* Nathan and their wives,
12:13 the clan of the **house** *of* Levi and their wives, the clan of Shimei
13: 1 "On that day a fountain will be opened to the **house** *of* David
13: 6 will answer, 'The wounds I was given at the **house** *of* my friends.'
14: 2 city will be captured, the **houses** ransacked, and the women raped.
14:20 the cooking pots in the LORD's **house** will be like the sacred
14:21 on that day there will no longer be a Canaanite in the **house** *of* the
Mal 3:10 Bring the whole tithe into the **storehouse** [+238], that there may be
3:10 tithe into the storehouse, that there may be food in my **house**.

1075 ²בַּיִת *bayit*[2], pp. [3]

among [1], between [1], meet [1]

Job 8:17 around a pile of rocks and looks for a *place* **among** the stones.
Pr 8: 2 heights along the way, where the paths **meet**, she takes her stand;
Eze 41: 9 cubits thick. The open area **between** the side rooms of the temple

1076 ³בַּיִת *bayit*[3], n.pr.loc. Not used in NIV/BHS

1077 בֵּית אָוֶן *bêt 'āwen*, n.pr.loc. [7] [√ 1074 + 224]

Beth Aven [7]

Jos 7: 2 which is near **Beth Aven** to the east of Bethel, and told them,
18:12 west into the hill country, coming out at the desert of **Beth Aven**.
1Sa 13: 5 They went up and camped at Micmash, east of **Beth Aven**.
14:23 Israel that day, and the battle moved on beyond **Beth Aven**.
Hos 4:15 "Do not go to Gilgal; do not go up to **Beth Aven**. And do not
5: 8 in Ramah. Raise the battle cry in **Beth Aven**; lead on, O Benjamin.
10: 5 people who live in Samaria fear for the calf-idol of **Beth Aven**.

1078 בֵּית־אֵל *bêt-'ēl*, n.pr.loc. [71] [√ 1074 + 446; cf. 2029]

Bethel [70], there[s] [+928] [1]

Ge 12: 8 From there he went on toward the hills east of **Bethel** and pitched
12: 8 and pitched his tent, with **Bethel** on the west and Ai on the east.
13: 3 the Negev he went from place to place until he came to **Bethel**,
13: 3 to the place between **Bethel** and Ai where his tent had been earlier
28:19 He called that place **Bethel**, though the city used to be called Luz.
31:13 I am the God of **Bethel**, where you anointed a pillar and where you
35: 1 Then God said to Jacob, "Go up to **Bethel** and settle there,
35: 3 come, let us go up to **Bethel**, where I will build an altar to God,
35: 6 Jacob and all the people with him came to Luz (that is, **Bethel**)
35: 8 Rebekah's nurse, died and was buried under the oak below **Bethel**.
35:15 Jacob called the place where God had talked with him **Bethel**.
35:16 they moved on from **Bethel**. While they were still some distance
Jos 7: 2 which is near Beth Aven to the east of **Bethel**, and told them,
8: 9 to the place of ambush and lay in wait between **Bethel** and Ai,
8:12 five thousand men and set them in ambush between **Bethel** and Ai,
8:17 Not a man remained in Ai or **Bethel** who did not go after Israel.
12: 9 the king of Jericho one the king of Ai (near **Bethel**) one
12:16 the king of Makkedah one the king of **Bethel** one
16: 1 up from there through the desert into the hill country of **Bethel**.
16: 2 It went on from **Bethel** (that is, Luz), crossed over to the territory
18:13 From there it crossed to the south slope of Luz (that is, **Bethel**)
18:22 Beth Arabah, Zemaraim, **Bethel**,
Jdg 1:22 Now the house of Joseph attacked **Bethel**, and the LORD was
1:23 When they sent men to spy out **Bethel** (formerly called Luz),
4: 5 between Ramah and **Bethel** in the hill country of Ephraim,
20:18 The Israelites went up to **Bethel** and inquired of God. They said,
20:26 the Israelites, all the people, went up to **Bethel**, and there they sat
20:31 on the roads—the one leading to **Bethel** and the other to Gibeah.
21: 2 The people went to **Bethel**, where they sat before God until
21:19 the annual festival of the LORD in Shiloh, to the north of **Bethel**,
21:19 of Bethel, and east of the road that goes from **Bethel** to Shechem,
1Sa 7:16 From year to year he went on a circuit from **Bethel** to Gilgal to
10: 3 Three men going up to God at **Bethel** will meet you there.
13: 2 were with him at Micmash and in the hill country of **Bethel**,
30:27 He sent it to those who were in **Bethel**, Ramoth Negev and Jattir;
1Ki 12:29 One he set up in **Bethel**, and the other in Dan.
12:32 This he did in **Bethel**, sacrificing to the calves he had made.
12:32 at **Bethel** he also installed priests at the high places he had made.
12:33 he offered sacrifices on the altar he had built at **Bethel**.
13: 1 the word of the LORD a man of God came from Judah to **Bethel**,
13: 4 heard what the man of God cried out against the altar at **Bethel**,
13:10 another road and did not return by the way he had come to **Bethel**.
13:11 Now there was a certain old prophet living in **Bethel**, whose sons
13:11 told him all that the man of God had done **there**[s] [+928] that day.
13:32 he declared by the word of the LORD against the altar in **Bethel**
2Ki 2: 2 said to Elisha, "Stay here; the LORD has sent me to **Bethel**."
2: 2 as you live, I will not leave you." So they went down to **Bethel**.
2: 3 The company of the prophets at **Bethel** came out to Elisha
2:23 From there Elisha went up to **Bethel**. As he was walking along the
10:29 to commit—the worship of the golden calves at **Bethel** and Dan.
17:28 priests who had been exiled from Samaria came to live in **Bethel**
23: 4 in the fields of the Kidron Valley and took the ashes to **Bethel**.
23:15 Even the altar at **Bethel**, the high place made by Jeroboam son of
23:17 pronounced against the altar of **Bethel** the very things you have
23:19 Just as he had done at **Bethel**, Josiah removed and defiled all the
1Ch 7:28 Their lands and settlements included **Bethel** and its surrounding
2Ch 13:19 Abijah pursued Jeroboam and took from him the towns of **Bethel**,
Ezr 2:28 of **Bethel** and Ai 223
Ne 7:32 of **Bethel** and Ai 123
11:31 from Geba lived in Micmash, Aija, **Bethel** and its settlements,
Jer 48:13 as the house of Israel was ashamed when they trusted in **Bethel**.
Hos 10:15 Thus will it happen to you, O **Bethel**, because your wickedness is
12: 4 [12:5] He found him at **Bethel** and talked with him there—
Am 3:14 day I punish Israel for her sins, I will destroy the altars of **Bethel**;
4: 4 "Go to **Bethel** and sin; go to Gilgal and sin yet more. Bring your
5: 5 do not seek **Bethel**, do not go to Gilgal, do not journey to
5: 5 will surely go into exile, and **Bethel** will be reduced to nothing."
5: 6 like a fire; it will devour, and **Bethel** will have no one to quench it.
7:10 Amaziah the priest of **Bethel** sent a message to Jeroboam king of
7:13 Don't prophesy anymore at **Bethel**, because this is the king's
Zec 7: 2 The people of **Bethel** had sent Sharezer and Regem-Melech,

1079 בֵּית אַרְבֵאל *bêt 'arbē'l*, n.pr.loc. [1] [√ 1074 + 745]

Beth Arbel [1]

Hos 10:14 as Shalman devastated **Beth Arbel** on the day of battle,

1080 בֵּית אַשְׁבֵּעַ *bêt 'ašbēa'*, n.pr.loc. [1] [√ 1074 + 842]

Beth Ashbea [1]

1Ch 4:21 of Mareshah and the clans of the linen workers at **Beth Ashbea**,

1081 בֵּית בַּעַל מְעוֹן *bêt ba'al me'ôn*, n.pr.loc. [1] [√ 1074 + 1260]

Beth Baal Meon [1]

Jos 13:17 on the plateau, including Dibon, Bamoth Baal, **Beth Baal Meon**,

1082 בֵּית בִּרְאִי *bêt bir'î*, n.pr.loc. [1] [√ 1074 + 1348]

Beth Biri [1]

1Ch 4:31 Beth Marcaboth, Hazar Susim, **Beth Biri** and Shaaraim.

1083 בֵּית בָּרָה **bêt bārâ**, n.pr.loc. [2] [√ 1074 + [?]]

Beth Barah [2]

Jdg 7: 24 the waters of the Jordan ahead of them as far as **Beth Barah.**"
7: 24 and they took the waters of the Jordan as far as **Beth Barah.**

1084 בֵּית־גָּדֵר **bêt-gādēr**, n.pr.loc. [1] [√ 1074 + 1554; cf. 1559]

Beth Gader [1]

1Ch 2: 51 the father of Bethlehem, and Hareph the father of **Beth Gader.**

1085 בֵּית גָּמוּל **bêt gāmûl**, n.pr.loc. [1] [√ 1074 + 1694]

Beth Gamul [1]

Jer 48: 23 to Kiriathaim, **Beth Gamul** and Beth Meon,

1086 בֵּית דִּבְלָתַיִם **bêt diblātayim**, n.pr.loc. [1] [√ 1074 + 1814]

Beth Diblathaim [1]

Jer 48: 22 to Dibon, Nebo and **Beth Diblathaim,**

1087 בֵּית־דָּגוֹן **bêt-dāgôn**, n.pr.loc. [2] [√ 1074 + 1837]

Beth Dagon [2]

Jos 15: 41 Gederoth, **Beth Dagon,** Naamah and Makkedah—sixteen towns
19: 27 It then turned east toward **Beth Dagon,** touched Zebulun and the

1088 בֵּית הָאֱלִי **bêt hā'ᵉlî**, a.g. [1] [√ 1074 + 466; cf. 468]

of Bethel [1]

1Ki 16: 34 In Ahab's time, Hiel **of Bethel** rebuilt Jericho. He laid its

1089 בֵּית הָאֵצֶל **bêt hā'ēṣel**, n.pr.loc. [1] [√ 1074 + 2021 + 726]

Beth Ezel [1]

Mic 1: 11 **Beth Ezel** is in mourning; its protection is taken from you.

1090 בֵּית הַגִּלְגָּל **bêt haggilgāl**, n.pr.loc. [1] [√ 1074 + 2021 + 1652]

Beth Gilgal [1]

Ne 12: 29 from **Beth Gilgal,** and from the area of Geba and Azmaveth,

1091 בֵּית הַגָּן **bêt haggān**, n.pr.loc.?. [1] [√ 1074 + 2056]

Beth Haggan [1]

2Ki 9: 27 saw what had happened, he fled up the road to **Beth Haggan.**

1092 בֵּית הַמֶּרְחָק **bêt hammerḥāq**, n.pr.loc. Not used in NIV/BHS [√ 1074 + 2021 + 8178]

1093 בֵּית הַיְשִׁימוֹת **bêt hayᵉšîmôt**, n.pr.loc. [4] [√ 1074 + 2127]

Beth Jeshimoth [4]

Nu 33: 49 camped along the Jordan from **Beth Jeshimoth** to Abel Shittim.
Jos 12: 3 to **Beth Jeshimoth,** and then southward below the slopes of
13: 20 Beth Peor, the slopes of Pisgah, and **Beth Jeshimoth**
Eze 25: 9 **Beth Jeshimoth,** Baal Meon and Kiriathaim—the glory of that

1094 בֵּית־הַכֶּרֶם **bêt-hakkerem**, n.pr.loc. [2] [√ 1074 + 2130]

Beth Hakkerem [2]

Ne 3: 14 by Malkijah son of Recab, ruler of the district of **Beth Hakkerem.**
Jer 6: 1 the trumpet in Tekoa! Raise the signal over **Beth Hakkerem!**

1095 בֵּית־הַלַּחְמִי **bêt-hallaḥmî**, a.g. [4] [√ 1074 + 2140]

of Bethlehem [3], the Bethlehemite [1]

1Sa 16: 1 and be on your way; I am sending you to Jesse **of Bethlehem.**
16: 18 "I have seen a son of Jesse **of Bethlehem** who knows how to play
17: 58 David said, "I am the son of your servant Jesse **of Bethlehem.**"
2Sa 21: 19 Elhanan son of Jaare-Oregim **the Bethlehemite** killed Goliath the

1096 בֵּית־הַמַּרְכָּבוֹת **bêt-hammarkābôt**, n.pr.loc. [1] [√ 1074 + 2175]

Beth Marcaboth [1]

Jos 19: 5 Ziklag, **Beth Marcaboth,** Hazar Susah,

1097 בֵּית הָעֵמֶק **bêt hā'ēmeq**, n.pr.loc. [1] [√ 1074 + 2021 + 6677]

Beth Emek [1]

Jos 19: 27 and went north to **Beth Emek** and Neiel, passing Cabul on the left.

1098 בֵּית הָעֲרָבָה **bêt hā'ᵃrābâ**, n.pr.loc. [3 / 4] [√ 1074 + 2196]

Beth Arabah [4]

Jos 15: 6 continued north of **Beth Arabah** to the Stone of Bohan son of
15: 61 In the desert: **Beth Arabah,** Middin, Secacah,
18: 18 It continued to the northern slope of **Beth** [BHS 4578] **Arabah**
18: 22 **Beth Arabah,** Zemaraim, Bethel,

1099 בֵּית הָרָם **bêt hārām**, n.pr.loc. [1] [√ 1074 + 2234]

Beth Haram [1]

Jos 13: 27 **Beth Haram,** Beth Nimrah, Succoth and Zaphon with the rest of

1100 בֵּית הָרָן **bêt hārān**, n.pr.loc. [1] [√ 1074 + 2237]

Beth Haran [1]

Nu 32: 36 Beth Nimrah and **Beth Haran** as fortified cities, and built pens for

1101 בֵּית הַשִּׁטָּה **bêt haššiṭṭâ**, n.pr.loc. [1] [√ 1074 + 2242]

Beth Shittah [1]

Jdg 7: 22 The army fled to **Beth Shittah** toward Zererah as far as the border

1102 בֵּית־חָגְלָה **bêt-ḥoglâ**, n.pr.loc. [3] [√ 1074 + 2519]

Beth Hoglah [3]

Jos 15: 6 went up to **Beth Hoglah** and continued north of Beth Arabah to the
18: 19 It then went to the northern slope of **Beth Hoglah** and came out at
18: 21 had the following cities: Jericho, **Beth Hoglah,** Emek Keziz,

1103 בֵּית־חוֹרוֹן **bêt-ḥôrôn**, n.pr.loc. [14] [√ 1074 + 2582]

Beth Horon [14]

Jos 10: 10 Israel pursued them along the road going up to **Beth Horon**
10: 11 As they fled before Israel on the road down from **Beth Horon** to
16: 3 of the Japhletites as far as the region of Lower **Beth Horon**
16: 5 went from Ataroth Addar in the east to Upper **Beth Horon**
18: 13 down to Ataroth Addar on the hill south of Lower **Beth Horon.**
18: 14 From the hill facing **Beth Horon** on the south the boundary turned
21: 22 Kibzaim and **Beth Horon,** together with their pasturelands—
1Sa 13: 18 another toward **Beth Horon,** and the third toward the borderland
1Ki 9: 17 And Solomon rebuilt Gezer.) He built up Lower **Beth Horon,**
1Ch 6: 68 [6:53] Jokmeam, **Beth Horon,**
7: 24 built Lower and Upper **Beth Horon** as well as Uzzen Sheerah.
2Ch 8: 5 He rebuilt Upper **Beth Horon** and Lower Beth Horon as fortified
8: 5 Upper Beth Horon and Lower **Beth Horon** as fortified cities,
25: 13 part in the war raided Judean towns from Samaria to **Beth Horon.**

1104 בֵּית חָנָן **bêt ḥānān**, n.pr.loc. Not used in NIV/BHS [√ 1074 + 2860]

1105 בֵּית כַּר **bêt kār**, n.pr.loc. [1] [√ 1074 + 4122]

Beth Car [1]

1Sa 7: 11 slaughtering them along the way to a point below **Beth Car.**

1106 בֵּית לְבָאוֹת **bêt lᵉbā'ôt**, n.pr.loc. [1] [√ 1074 + 4219]

Beth Lebaoth [1]

Jos 19: 6 **Beth Lebaoth** and Sharuhen—thirteen towns and their villages;

1107 בֵּית לֶחֶם **bêt leḥem**, n.pr.loc. [41] [√ 1074 + 4312]

Bethlehem [40], *untranslated* [1]

Ge 35: 19 and was buried on the way to Ephrath (that is, **Bethlehem**).
48: 7 I buried her there beside the road to Ephrath" (that is, **Bethlehem**).
Jos 19: 15 Included were Kattath, Nahalal, Shimron, Idalah and **Bethlehem.**
Jdg 12: 8 After him, Ibzan of **Bethlehem** led Israel.
12: 10 Then Ibzan died, and was buried in **Bethlehem.**
17: 7 A young Levite from **Bethlehem** *in* Judah, who had been living
17: 8 left that town **[RPH]** in search of some other place to stay.
17: 9 "I'm a Levite from **Bethlehem** *in* Judah," he said, "and I'm
19: 1 country of Ephraim took a concubine from **Bethlehem** *in* Judah.
19: 2 She left him and went back to her father's house in **Bethlehem,**
19: 18 "We are on our way from **Bethlehem** *in* Judah to a remote area in
19: 18 I have been to **Bethlehem** *in* Judah and now I am going to the
Ru 1: 1 and a man from **Bethlehem** *in* Judah, together with his wife
1: 2 and Kilion. They were Ephrathites from **Bethlehem,** Judah.

Ru 1:19 So the two women went on until they came to **Bethlehem**.
1:19 When they arrived in **Bethlehem**, the whole town was stirred
1:22 arriving in **Bethlehem** as the barley harvest was beginning.
2:4 Just then Boaz arrived from **Bethlehem** and greeted the harvesters,
4:11 May you have standing in Ephrathah and be famous in **Bethlehem**.
1Sa 16:4 When he arrived at **Bethlehem**, the elders of the town trembled
17:12 of an Ephrathite named Jesse, who was from **Bethlehem** *in* Judah.
17:15 and forth from Saul to tend his father's sheep at **Bethlehem**.
20:6 'David earnestly asked my permission to hurry to **Bethlehem**,
20:28 "David earnestly asked me for permission to go to **Bethlehem**.
2Sa 2:32 took Asahel and buried him in his father's tomb at **Bethlehem**.
23:14 in the stronghold, and the Philistine garrison was at **Bethlehem**.
23:15 get me a drink of water from the well near the gate of **Bethlehem**!"
23:16 drew water from the well near the gate of **Bethlehem** and carried it
23:24 Asahel the brother of Joab, Elhanan son of Dodo from **Bethlehem**,
1Ch 2:51 Salma the father of **Bethlehem**, and Hareph the father of Beth
2:54 **Bethlehem**, the Netophathites, Atroth Beth Joab, half the
4:4 of Hur, the firstborn of Ephrathah and father of **Bethlehem**.
11:16 in the stronghold, and the Philistine garrison was at **Bethlehem**.
11:17 get me a drink of water from the well near the gate of **Bethlehem**!"
11:18 drew water from the well near the gate of **Bethlehem** and carried it
11:26 Asahel the brother of Joab, Elhanan son of Dodo from **Bethlehem**,
2Ch 11:6 **Bethlehem**, Etam, Tekoa,
Ezr 2:21 the men of **Bethlehem** 123
Ne 7:26 the men of **Bethlehem** and Netophah 188
Jer 41:17 stopping at Geruth Kimham near **Bethlehem** on their way to
Mic 5:2 [5:1] "But you, **Bethlehem** Ephrathah, though you are small

1108 בֵּית לְעַפְרָה **bêt l^e'aprâ**, n.pr.loc. [1] [√ 1074 + 4364]

Beth Ophrah [1]

Mic 1:10 it not in Gath; weep not at all. In **Beth Ophrah** roll in the dust.

1109 בֵּית מִלּוֹא **bêt millô'**, n.pr.loc. [4] [√ 1074 + 4848]

Beth Millo [4]

Jdg 9:6 **Beth Millo** gathered beside the great tree at the pillar in Shechem
9:20 and consume you, citizens of Shechem and **Beth Millo**,
9:20 citizens of Shechem and **Beth Millo**, and consume Abimelech!"
2Ki 12:20 [12:21] against him and assassinated him at **Beth Millo**,

1110 בֵּית מְעוֹן **bêt m^e'ôn**, n.pr.loc. [1] [√ 1074 + 1260]

Beth Meon [1]

Jer 48:23 to Kiriathaim, Beth Gamul and **Beth Meon**,

1111 בֵּית מַעֲכָה **bêt ma'^akâ**, n.pr.loc. Not used in NIV/BHS [√ 1074 + 5081]

1112 בֵּית מַרְכָּבוֹת **bêt markābôt**, n.pr.loc. [1] [√ 1074 + 5325]

Beth Marcaboth [1]

1Ch 4:31 **Beth Marcaboth**, Hazar Susim, Beth Biri and Shaaraim.

1113 בֵּית נִמְרָה **bêt nimrâ**, n.pr.loc. [2] [√ 1074 + 5809]

Beth Nimrah [2]

Nu 32:36 **Beth Nimrah** and Beth Haran as fortified cities, and built pens for
Jos 13:27 **Beth Nimrah**, Succoth and Zaphon with the rest of the realm of

1114 בֵּית עֶדֶן **bêt 'eden**, n.pr.loc. [1] [√ 1074 + 6361]

Beth Eden [1]

Am 1:5 Valley of Aven and the one who holds the scepter in **Beth Eden**.

1115 בֵּית־עַזְמָוֶת **bêt-'azmāwet**, n.pr.loc. [1] [√ 1074 + 6462]

Beth Azmaveth [1]

Ne 7:28 of **Beth Azmaveth** 42

1116 בֵּית־עֲנוֹת **bêt-'^anôt**, n.pr.loc. [1] [√ 1074 + 6742]

Beth Anoth [1]

Jos 15:59 Maarath, **Beth Anoth** and Eltekon—six towns and their villages.

1117 בֵּית־עֲנָת **bêt-'^anāt**, n.pr.loc. [3] [√ 1074 + 6742]

Beth Anath [3]

Jos 19:38 Iron, Migdal El, Horem, **Beth Anath** and Beth Shemesh. There
Jdg 1:33 Naphtali drive out those living in Beth Shemesh or **Beth Anath**;
1:33 Beth Shemesh and **Beth Anath** became forced laborers for them.

1118 בֵּית־עֵקֶד **bêt-'ēqed**, n.pr.loc. [2] [√ 1074 + 6820]

Beth Eked [2]

2Ki 10:12 and went toward Samaria. At **Beth Eked** *of* the Shepherds,
10:14 took them alive and slaughtered them by the well of **Beth Eked**—

1119 בֵּית עַשְׁתָּרוֹת **bêt 'aštārôt**, n.pr.loc.?. Not used in NIV/BHS [√ 1074 + 6958]

1120 בֵּית פֶּלֶט **bêt peleṭ**, n.pr.loc. [2] [√ 1074 + 7118]

Beth Pelet [2]

Jos 15:27 Hazar Gaddah, Heshmon, **Beth Pelet**,
Ne 11:26 in Jeshua, in Moladah, in **Beth Pelet**,

1121 בֵּית פְּעוֹר **bêt p^e'ôr**, n.pr.loc. [4] [√ 1074 + 7186]

Beth Peor [4]

Dt 3:29 So we stayed in the valley near **Beth Peor**.
4:46 were in the valley near **Beth Peor** east of the Jordan, in the land of
34:6 He buried him in Moab, in the valley opposite **Beth Peor**,
Jos 13:20 **Beth Peor**, the slopes of Pisgah, and Beth Jeshimoth

1122 בֵּית פַּצֵּץ **bêt paṣṣēṣ**, n.pr.loc. [1] [√ 1074 + 7208]

Beth Pazzez [1]

Jos 19:21 Remeth, En Gannim, En Haddah and **Beth Pazzez**.

1123 בֵּית־צוּר **bêt-ṣûr**, n.pr.loc. [4] [√ 1074 + 7446]

Beth Zur [4]

Jos 15:58 Halhul, **Beth Zur**, Gedor,
1Ch 2:45 son of Shammai was Maon, and Maon was the father of **Beth Zur**.
2Ch 11:7 **Beth Zur**, Soco, Adullam,
Ne 3:16 Nehemiah son of Azbuk, ruler of a half-district of **Beth Zur**,

1124 בֵּית־רְחוֹב **bêt-r^eḥôb**, n.pr.loc. [2] [√ 1074 + 8148]

Beth Rehob [2]

Jdg 18:28 The city was in a valley near **Beth Rehob**. The Danites rebuilt the
2Sa 10:6 hired twenty thousand Aramean foot soldiers from **Beth Rehob**

1125 בֵּית רָפָא **bêt rāpā'**, n.pr.[loc.?]. [1] [√ 1074 + 8324]

Beth Rapha [1]

1Ch 4:12 Eshton was the father of **Beth Rapha**, Paseah and Tehinnah the

1126 בֵּית־שְׁאָן **bêt-š^e'ān**, n.pr.loc. [9] [√ 1074 + 8632]

Beth Shan [9]

Jos 17:11 Manasseh also had **Beth Shan**, Ibleam and the people of Dor,
17:16 both those in **Beth Shan** and its settlements and those in the Valley
Jdg 1:27 Manasseh did not drive out the people of **Beth Shan** or Taanach
1Sa 31:10 of the Ashtoreths and fastened his body to the wall of **Beth Shan**.
31:12 and his sons from the wall of **Beth Shan** and went to Jabesh,
2Sa 21:12 had taken them secretly from the public square at **Beth Shan**,
1Ki 4:12 and in all of **Beth Shan** next to Zarethan below Jezreel,
4:12 from **Beth Shan** to Abel Meholah across to Jokmeam;
1Ch 7:29 Along the borders of Manasseh were **Beth Shan**, Taanach,

1127 בֵּית שֶׁמֶשׁ **bêt šemeš**, n.pr.loc. [20] [√ 1074 + 9087]

Beth Shemesh [20]

Jos 15:10 continued down to **Beth Shemesh** and crossed to Timnah.
19:22 Shahazumah and **Beth Shemesh**, and ended at the Jordan.
19:38 Iron, Migdal El, Horem, Beth Anath and **Beth Shemesh**. There
21:16 Ain, Juttah and **Beth Shemesh**, together with their pasturelands—
Jdg 1:33 Neither did Naphtali drive out those living in **Beth Shemesh**
1:33 those living in **Beth Shemesh** and Beth Anath became forced
1Sa 6:9 If it goes up to its own territory, toward **Beth Shemesh**, then the
6:12 the cows went straight up toward **Beth Shemesh**, keeping on the
6:12 Philistines followed them as far as the border of **Beth Shemesh**.
6:13 Now the people of **Beth Shemesh** were harvesting their wheat in
6:15 On that day the people of **Beth Shemesh** offered burnt offerings
6:19 But God struck down some of the men of **Beth Shemesh**,
6:20 the men of **Beth Shemesh** asked, "Who can stand in the presence
1Ki 4:9 in Makaz, Shaalbim, **Beth Shemesh** and Elon Bethhanan;
2Ki 14:11 Amaziah king of Judah faced each other at **Beth Shemesh** in
14:13 of Judah, the son of Joash, the son of Ahaziah, at **Beth Shemesh**.
1Ch 6:59 [6:44] Ashan, Juttah and **Beth Shemesh**, together with their
2Ch 25:21 Amaziah king of Judah faced each other at **Beth Shemesh** in
25:23 of Judah, the son of Joash, the son of Ahaziah, at **Beth Shemesh**.
28:18 They captured and occupied **Beth Shemesh**, Aijalon and Gederoth,

1128 בֵּית־שִׁמְשִׁי *bêt-šimšî*, a.g. [2] [√ 1074 + 9090]

of Beth Shemesh [2]

1Sa 6: 14 The cart came to the field of Joshua **of Beth Shemesh**, and there it
6: 18 is a witness to this day in the field of Joshua **of Beth Shemesh**.

1129 בֵּית תּוֹגַרְמָה *bêt tôgarmâ*, n.pr.loc. [2] [√ 1074 + [?]]

Beth Togarmah [2]

Eze 27: 14 " 'Men of **Beth Togarmah** exchanged work horses, war horses
38: 6 and **Beth Togarmah** from the far north with all its troops—

1130 בֵּית־תַּפּוּחַ *bêt-tappûaḥ*, n.pr.loc. [1] [√ 1074 + 9515]

Beth Tappuah [1]

Jos 15: 53 Janim, **Beth Tappuah**, Aphekah,

1131 בִּיתָן *bîtān*, n.[m.]. [3] [√ 1074]

palace [3]

Est 1: 5 lasting seven days, in the enclosed garden of the king's **palace**,
7: 7 got up in a rage, left his wine and went out into the **palace** garden.
7: 8 Just as the king returned from the **palace** garden to the banquet

1132 בָּכָא¹ *bākā'¹*, n.[m.]. [4] [√ 1134]

balsam trees [4]

2Sa 5: 23 around behind them and attack them in front of the **balsam trees**.
5: 24 as you hear the sound of marching in the tops of the **balsam trees**,
1Ch 14: 14 circle around them and attack them in front of the **balsam trees**.
14: 15 as you hear the sound of marching in the tops of the **balsam trees**,

1133 בָּכָא² *bākā'²*, n.pr.loc. [1] [√ 1134]

Baca [1]

Ps 84: 6 [84:7] As they pass through the Valley of **Baca**, they make it a

1134 בָּכָה *bākâ*, v. [114] [→ 1132, 1133, 1135, 1139, 1140, 1143, 4441; cf. 1141]

wept [36], weep [26], weeping [16], wailing [5], mourned [3], wept [+1140] [3], bitterly weeps [+1134] [2], mourn [2], wailed [2], weep [+1134] [2], weep at all [+1134] [2], weep bitterly [+1134] [2], wept much [+1134] [2], cried [1], crying [1], grieved [1], mourning [1], sob [1], sobbing [1], tears [1], weeping [+1140] [1], wept aloud [1], wept bitterly [+1135+2221] [1], wet with tears [1]

Ge 21: 16 [A] the boy die." And as she sat there nearby, she began *to* **sob**.
23: 2 [A] and Abraham went to mourn for Sarah and to **weep** *over* her.
27: 38 [A] my father? Bless me too, my father!" Then Esau **wept** aloud.
29: 11 [A] Then Jacob kissed Rachel and *began to* **weep** aloud.
33: 4 [A] his arms around his neck and kissed him. And *they* **wept**.
37: 35 [A] go down to the grave to my son." So his father **wept** *for* him.
42: 24 [A] He turned away from them and *began to* **weep**, but
43: 30 [A] Joseph hurried out and looked for a place to **weep**.
43: 30 [A] place to weep. He went into his private room and **wept** there.
45: 14 [A] he threw his arms around his brother Benjamin and **wept**,
45: 14 [A] and wept, and Benjamin embraced him, **weeping**.
45: 15 [A] he kissed all his brothers and **wept** over them. Afterward his
46: 29 [A] he threw his arms around his father and **wept** for a long time.
50: 1 [A] himself upon his father and **wept** over him and kissed him.
50: 3 [A] And the Egyptians **mourned** *for* him seventy days.
50: 17 [A] your father." When their message came to him, Joseph **wept**.
Ex 2: 6 [A] and saw the baby. He *was* **crying**, and she felt sorry for him.
Lev 10: 6 [A] *may* **mourn** *for* those the LORD has destroyed by fire.
Nu 11: 4 [A] again the Israelites *started* **wailing** and said, "If only we had
11: 10 [A] Moses heard the people of every family **wailing**, each at the
11: 13 [A] *They keep* **wailing** to me, 'Give us meat to eat!'
11: 18 [A] The LORD heard you when *you* **wailed**, "If only we had
11: 20 [A] who is among you, and *have* **wailed** before him, saying,
14: 1 [A] people of the community raised their voices and **wept aloud**.
20: 29 [A] the entire house of Israel **mourned** *for* him thirty days.
25: 6 [A] the whole assembly of Israel while they *were* **weeping** at the
Dt 1: 45 [A] You came back and **wept** before the LORD, but he paid no
21: 13 [A] and **mourned** her father and mother for a full month,
34: 8 [A] The Israelites **grieved** *for* Moses in the plains of Moab thirty
Jdg 2: 4 [A] these things to all the Israelites, the people **wept** aloud,
11: 37 [A] me two months to roam the hills and **weep** with my friends,
11: 38 [A] She and the girls went into the hills and **wept** because she
14: 16 [A] Samson's wife threw herself on him, **sobbing**, "You hate me!
14: 17 [A] *She* **cried** the whole seven days of the feast. So on the
20: 23 [A] Israelites went up and **wept** before the LORD until evening,
20: 26 [A] up to Bethel, and there they sat **weeping** before the LORD.
21: 2 [A] raising their voices and **weeping** [+1140] bitterly.
Ru 1: 9 [A] Then she kissed them and *they* **wept** aloud
1: 14 [A] At this *they* **wept** again. Then Orpah kissed her
1Sa 1: 7 [A] her rival provoked her till *she* **wept** and would not eat.
1: 8 [A] husband would say to her, "Hannah, why *are you* **weeping**?
1: 10 [A] In bitterness of soul Hannah **wept** [+1134] **much** and prayed
1: 10 [A] In bitterness of soul Hannah **wept much** [+1134] and prayed
11: 4 [A] and reported these terms to the people, they all **wept** aloud.
11: 5 [A] "What is wrong with the people? Why *are they* **weeping**?"
20: 41 [A] they kissed each other and **wept** together—but David wept
24: 16 [24:17] [A] your voice, David my son?" And he **wept** aloud.
30: 4 [A] his men **wept** aloud until they had no strength left to weep.
30: 4 [A] his men wept aloud until they had no strength left to **weep**.
2Sa 1: 12 [A] They mourned and **wept** and fasted till evening for Saul
1: 24 [A] "O daughters of Israel, **weep** for Saul, who clothed you in
3: 16 [A] went with her, **weeping** behind her all the way to Bahurim.
3: 32 [A] Abner in Hebron, and the king **wept** aloud at Abner's tomb.
3: 32 [A] king wept aloud at Abner's tomb. All the people **wept** also.
3: 34 [A] wicked men." And all the people **wept** over him again.
12: 21 [A] While the child was alive, you fasted and **wept**, but now that
12: 22 [A] "While the child was still alive, I fasted and **wept**.
13: 36 [A] finished speaking, the king's sons came in, **wailing** loudly.
13: 36 [A] The king, too, and all his servants **wept** [+1140] very bitterly.
15: 23 [A] The whole countryside **wept** aloud as all the people passed
15: 30 [A] continued up the Mount of Olives, **weeping** as he went;
15: 30 [A] covered their heads too and *were* **weeping** as they went up.
18: 33 [19:1] [A] He went up to the room over the gateway and **wept**.
19: 1 [19:2] [A] "The king *is* **weeping** and mourning for Absalom."
2Ki 8: 11 [A] Hazael felt ashamed. Then the man of God *began to* **weep**.
8: 12 [A] "Why *is* my lord **weeping**?" asked Hazael. "Because I know
13: 14 [A] king of Israel went down to see him and **wept** over him.
20: 3 [A] is good in your eyes." And Hezekiah **wept** [+1140] bitterly.
22: 19 [A] and because you tore your robes and **wept** in my presence,
2Ch 34: 27 [A] before me and tore your robes and **wept** in my presence,
Ezr 3: 12 [A] **wept** aloud when they saw the foundation of this temple
10: 1 [A] **weeping** and throwing himself down before the house of
10: 1 [A] gathered around him. They too **wept** [+1135+2221] **bitterly**.
Ne 1: 4 [A] When I heard these things, I sat down and **wept**. For some
8: 9 [A] is sacred to the LORD your God. Do not mourn or **weep**."
8: 9 [A] For all the people *had been* **weeping** as they listened to the
Est 8: 3 [A] again pleaded with the king, falling at his feet and **weeping**.
Job 2: 12 [A] *they began to* **weep** aloud, and they tore their robes
27: 15 [A] who survive him, and their widows *will* not **weep** *for* them.
30: 25 [A] *Have I* not **wept** for those in trouble? Has not my soul
30: 31 [A] is tuned to mourning, and my flute to the sound of **wailing**.
31: 38 [A] cries out against me and all its furrows *are* **wet with tears**,
Ps 69: 10 [69:11] [A] When *I* **weep** and fast, I must endure scorn;
78: 64 [A] were put to the sword, and their widows *could* not **weep**.
126: 6 [A] He who goes out **weeping**, carrying seed to sow, will return
137: 1 [A] of Babylon we sat and **wept** when we remembered Zion.
Ecc 3: 4 [A] a time to **weep** and a time to laugh, a time to mourn and a
Isa 16: 9 [A] So *I* **weep**, as Jazer weeps, *for* the vines of Sibmah.
30: 19 [A] who live in Jerusalem, *you will* **weep** [+1134] no *more*.
30: 19 [A] who live in Jerusalem, *you will* **weep** no **more** [+1134].
33: 7 [A] cry aloud in the streets; the envoys of peace **weep** bitterly.
38: 3 [A] is good in your eyes." And Hezekiah **wept** [+1140] bitterly.
Jer 9: 1 [8:23] [A] *I would* **weep** day and night *for* the slain of my
13: 17 [A] you do not listen, I *will* **weep** in secret because of your pride;
22: 10 [A] *Do* not **weep** for the dead king or mourn his loss; rather,
22: 10 [A] rather, **weep** [+1134] **bitterly** for him who is exiled,
22: 10 [A] rather, **weep bitterly** [+1134] for him who is exiled,
31: 15 [D] Rachel **weeping** for her children and refusing to be
41: 6 [A] went out from Mizpah to meet them, **weeping** as he went.
48: 32 [A] *I* **weep** for you, as Jazer weeps, O vines of Sibmah.
50: 4 [A] the people of Judah together will go *in* **tears** to seek the
La 1: 2 [A] **Bitterly** *she* **weeps** [+1134] at night, tears are upon her
1: 2 [A] **Bitterly** *she* **weeps** [+1134] at night, tears are upon her
1: 16 [A] "This is why I **weep** and my eyes overflow with tears. No
Eze 8: 14 [D] and I saw women sitting there, **mourning** *for* Tammuz.
24: 16 [A] of your eyes. Yet do not lament or **weep** or shed any tears.
24: 23 [A] You will not mourn or **weep** but will waste away because of
27: 31 [A] *They will* **weep** over you with anguish of soul and with bitter
Hos 12: 4 [12:5] [A] and overcame him; *he* **wept** and begged for his favor.
Joel 1: 5 [A] Wake up, you drunkards, and **weep**! Wail, all you drinkers of
2: 17 [A] *Let* the priests, who minister before the LORD, **weep**
Mic 1: 10 [A] Tell it not in Gath; **weep** [+1134] not **at all**. In Beth Ophrah
1: 10 [A] Tell it not in Gath; **weep** not **at all** [+1134]. In Beth Ophrah
Zec 7: 3 [A] the prophets, "*Should I* **mourn** and fast in the fifth month,

1135 בֶּכֶה *bekeh*, n.[m.]. [1] [√ 1134]

wept bitterly [+1134+2221] [1]

Ezr 10: 1 gathered around him. They too **wept bitterly** [+1134+2221].

1136 בִּכּוּרָה bikkûrâ, n.f. [4] [√ 1144]
early figs [1], early fruit [1], fig ripe [1], ripen early [1]

Isa 28: 4 the head of a fertile valley, will be like a **fig ripe** before harvest—
Jer 24: 2 One basket had very good figs, like those that **ripen early**;
Hos 9: 10 I saw your fathers, it was like seeing the **early fruit** on the fig tree.
Mic 7: 1 is no cluster of grapes to eat, none of the **early figs** that I crave.

1137 בִּכּוּרִים bikkûrîm, n.m. [17] [√ 1144]
firstfruits [12], *untranslated* [2], first ripe fruit [1], first ripe grain [1], first ripe [1]

Ex 23: 16 "Celebrate the Feast of Harvest with the **firstfruits** *of* the crops
23: 19 "Bring the best of the **firstfruits** *of* your soil to the house of the
34: 22 "Celebrate the Feast of Weeks with the **firstfruits** *of* the wheat
34: 26 "Bring the best of the **firstfruits** *of* your soil to the house of the
Lev 2: 14 " 'If you bring a grain offering of **firstfruits** to the LORD,
2: 14 offer crushed heads of new grain roasted in the fire. **[RPH]**
23: 17 baked with yeast, as a wave offering of **firstfruits** to the LORD.
23: 20 as a wave offering, together with the bread of the **firstfruits**.
Nu 13: 20 the fruit of the land." (It was the season for the **first ripe** grapes.)
18: 13 All the land's **firstfruits** that they bring to the LORD will be
28: 26 " 'On the day of **firstfruits**, when you present to the LORD an
2Ki 4: 42 God twenty loaves of barley bread baked from the **first ripe grain**,
Ne 10: 35 [10:36] house of the LORD each year the **firstfruits** *of* our crops
10: 35 [10:36] the firstfruits of our crops and **[RPH]** of every fruit tree.
13: 31 contributions of wood at designated times, and for the **firstfruits**.
Eze 44: 30 The best of all the **firstfruits** and of all your special gifts will
Na 3: 12 All your fortresses are like fig trees with their **first ripe fruit**;

1138 בְּכוֹרַת b[e]kôrat, n.pr.m. [1] [√ 1144]
Becorath [1]

1Sa 9: 1 the son of Zeror, the son of **Becorath**, the son of Aphiah of

1139 בָּכוּת bākût, n.f. Not used in NIV/BHS [√ 1134]

1140 בְּכִי b[e]kî, n.m. [30 / 29] [√ 1134]
weeping [14], weep [4], wept [+1134] [3], weeping bitterly [+1140] [2], weeps [2], tears [1], weep [+5951] [1], weeping [+1134] [1], wept so loudly [+906+928+5989+7754] [1]

Ge 45: 2 And he **wept** [+906+928+5989+7754] **so loudly** that the Egyptians
Dt 34: 8 thirty days, until the time of **weeping** and mourning was over.
Jdg 21: 2 until evening, raising their voices and **weeping** [+1134] bitterly.
2Sa 13: 36 The king, too, and all his servants **wept** [+1134] very bitterly.
2Ki 20: 3 what is good in your eyes." And Hezekiah **wept** [+1134] bitterly.
Ezr 3: 13 the sound of the shouts of joy from the sound of **weeping**,
Est 4: 3 mourning among the Jews, with fasting, **weeping** and wailing.
Job 16: 16 My face is red with **weeping**, deep shadows ring my eyes;
28: 11 He searches the sources of [BHS *flowing of*; NIV 4441] the rivers
Ps 6: 8 [6:9] all you who do evil, for the LORD has heard my **weeping**.
30: 5 [30:6] **weeping** may remain for a night, but rejoicing comes in the
102: 9 [102:10] I eat ashes as my food and mingle my drink with **tears**
Isa 15: 2 Dibon goes up to its temple, to its high places to **weep**; Moab wails
15: 3 and in the public squares they all wail, prostrate with **weeping**.
15: 5 They go up the way to Luhith, **weeping** as they go; on the road to
16: 9 So I weep, as Jazer **weeps**, for the vines of Sibmah. O Heshbon,
22: 4 Therefore I said, "Turn away from me; let me **weep** bitterly.
22: 12 called you on that day to **weep** and to wail, to tear out your hair
38: 3 what is good in your eyes." And Hezekiah **wept** [+1134] bitterly.
65: 19 the sound of **weeping** and of crying will be heard in it no more.
Jer 3: 21 barren heights, the **weeping** and pleading of the people of Israel,
9: 10 [9:9] *I will* **weep** [+5951] and wail for the mountains and take up
31: 9 They will come with **weeping**; they will pray as I bring them back.
31: 15 "A voice is heard in Ramah, mourning and great **weeping**,
31: 16 "Restrain your voice from **weeping** and your eyes from tears,
48: 5 go up the way to Luhith, **weeping** [+1140] **bitterly** as they go;
48: 5 go up the way to Luhith, **weeping bitterly** [+1140] as they go;
48: 32 I weep for you, as Jazer **weeps**, O vines of Sibmah. Your branches
Joel 2: 12 me with all your heart, with fasting and **weeping** and mourning."
Mal 2: 13 *You* **weep** and wail because he no longer pays attention to your

1141 בֹּכִים bōkîm, n.pr.loc. [2] [cf. 1134]
Bokim [2]

Jdg 2: 1 The angel of the LORD went up from Gilgal to **Bokim** and said,
2: 5 they called that place **Bokim**. There they offered sacrifices to the

1142 בְּכִירָה b[e]kîrâ, n.f. [6] [√ 1144]
older [6]

Ge 19: 31 One day the **older** *daughter* said to the younger, "Our father is
19: 33 to drink wine, and the **older** *daughter* went in and lay with him.
19: 34 The next day the **older** *daughter* said to the younger, "Last night I
19: 37 The **older** *daughter* had a son, and she named him Moab;
29: 26 to give the younger daughter in marriage before the **older** *one*.
1Sa 14: 49 The name of his **older** daughter was Merab, and that of the

1143 בְּכִית b[e]kît, n.f. [1] [√ 1134]
mourning [1]

Ge 50: 4 When the days of **mourning** had passed, Joseph said to Pharaoh's

1144 בָּכַר bākar, v. [4] [→ 1136, 1137, 1138, 1142, 1145, 1146, 1147, 1148, 1149, 1150, 1151, 1152]
bear [1], bearing first child [1], firstborn belongs to [+4200] [1], give the rights of the firstborn [1]

Lev 27: 26 [E] since the **firstborn** [+4200] already **belongs to** the LORD;
Dt 21: 16 [D] he must not **give the rights of the firstborn** *to* the son of the
Jer 4: 31 [G] woman in labor, a groan as of *one* **bearing** *her* **first child**—
Eze 47: 12 [D] Every month *they will* **bear**, because the water from the

1145 בֵּכֶר bēker, n.f. [1] [→ 1146; cf. 1144]
young camels [1]

Isa 60: 6 camels will cover your land, **young camels** *of* Midian and Ephah.

1146 בֶּכֶר beker, n.pr.m. [5] [→ 1145, 1151, 1152; cf. 1144]
Beker [5]

Ge 46: 21 Bela, **Beker**, Ashbel, Gera, Naaman, Ehi, Rosh, Muppim,
Nu 26: 35 through **Beker**, the Bekerite clan; through Tahan, the Tahanite
1Ch 7: 6 Three sons of Benjamin: Bela, **Beker** and Jediael.
7: 8 The sons of **Beker**: Zemirah, Joash, Eliezer, Elioenai, Omri,
7: 8 Anathoth and Alemeth. All these were the sons of **Beker**.

1147 בְּכֹר b[e]kōr, n.m. [122] [√ 1144]
firstborn [108], *untranslated* [5], oldest [3], firstborn male [2], first male offspring [+7081+8167] [1], first male offspring [1], first [1], poorest of the poor [+1924] [1]

Ge 4: 4 Abel brought fat portions from some of the **firstborn** *of* his flock.
10: 15 Canaan was the father of Sidon his **firstborn**, and of the Hittites,
22: 21 Uz the **firstborn**, Buz his brother, Kemuel (the father of Aram),
25: 13 Nebaioth the **firstborn** *of* Ishmael, Kedar, Adbeel, Mibsam,
27: 19 Jacob said to his father, "I am Esau your **firstborn**. I have done as
27: 32 are you?" "I am your son," he answered, "your **firstborn**, Esau."
35: 23 Reuben the **firstborn** *of* Jacob, Simeon, Levi, Judah, Issachar
36: 15 The sons of Eliphaz the **firstborn** *of* Esau: Chiefs Teman,
38: 6 Judah got a wife for Er, his **firstborn**, and her name was Tamar.
38: 7 But Er, Judah's **firstborn**, was wicked in the LORD's sight;
41: 51 Joseph named his **firstborn** Manasseh and said, "It is because God
43: 33 him in the order of their ages, from the **firstborn** to the youngest;
46: 8 who went to Egypt: Reuben the **firstborn** *of* Jacob.
48: 14 on Manasseh's head, even though Manasseh was the **firstborn**.
48: 18 Joseph said to him, "No, my father, this one is the **firstborn**;
49: 3 "Reuben, you are my **firstborn**, my might, the first sign of my
Ex 4: 22 'This is what the LORD says: Israel is my **firstborn** son,
4: 23 But you refused to let him go; so I will kill your **firstborn** son.' "
6: 14 The sons of Reuben the **firstborn** *son of* Israel were Hanoch
11: 5 Every **firstborn** *son* in Egypt will die, from the firstborn son of
11: 5 from the **firstborn** *son of* Pharaoh, who sits on the throne,
11: 5 who sits on the throne, to the **firstborn** *son of* the slave girl,
11: 5 who is at her hand mill, and all the **firstborn** *of* the cattle as well.
12: 12 night I will pass through Egypt and strike down every **firstborn**—
12: 29 At midnight the LORD struck down all the **firstborn** in Egypt,
12: 29 from the **firstborn** *of* Pharaoh, who sat on the throne,
12: 29 who sat on the throne, to the **firstborn** *of* the prisoner, who was in
12: 29 was in the dungeon, and the **firstborn** *of* all the livestock as well.
13: 2 "Consecrate to me every **firstborn** *male*. The first offspring of
13: 13 break its neck. Redeem every **firstborn** among your sons.
13: 15 the LORD killed every **firstborn** in Egypt, both man and animal.
13: 15 killed every firstborn in Egypt, both **[RPH]** man and animal.
13: 15 killed every firstborn in Egypt, both man and **[RPH]** animal.
13: 15 offspring of every womb and redeem each of my **firstborn** sons.'
22: 29 [22:28] your vats. "You must give me the **firstborn** *of* your sons.
34: 20 do not redeem it, break its neck. Redeem all your **firstborn** sons.
Lev 27: 26 " 'No one, however, may dedicate the **firstborn** of an animal,
Nu 1: 20 From the descendants of Reuben the **firstborn** *son of* Israel:
3: 2 The names of the sons of Aaron were Nadab the **firstborn**
3: 12 the **first** [+7081+8167] **male offspring** of every Israelite woman.
3: 13 for all the **firstborn** are mine. When I struck down all the firstborn
3: 13 When I struck down all the **firstborn** in Egypt, I set apart for
3: 13 I set apart for myself every **firstborn** in Israel, whether man
3: 40 "Count all the **firstborn** Israelite males who are a month old
3: 41 Take the Levites for me in place of all the **firstborn** of the
3: 41 the livestock of the Levites in place of all the **firstborn** of the
3: 42 So Moses counted all the **firstborn** of the Israelites, as the LORD

[A] Qal [B] Qal passive [C] Niphal [D] Piel (poel, polel, pilel, pilal, pealal, pilpel) [E] Pual (poal, polal, poalal, pulal, pualal)

Nu 3:43 The total number of **firstborn** males a month old or more,
3:45 "Take the Levites in place of all the **firstborn** of Israel, and the
3:46 To redeem the 273 **firstborn** Israelites who exceed the number of
3:50 From the **firstborn** *of* the Israelites he collected silver weighing
8:16 the firstborn, the **first male offspring** from every Israelite woman.
8:17 Every **firstborn male** in Israel, whether man or animal, is mine.
8:17 When I struck down all the **firstborn** in Egypt, I set them apart for
8:18 I have taken the Levites in place of all the **firstborn** *sons* in Israel.
18:15 you must redeem every **firstborn** son and every firstborn male of
18:15 every firstborn son and every **firstborn male** *of* unclean animals.
18:17 "But you must not redeem the **firstborn** *of* an ox, a sheep
18:17 must not redeem the firstborn of an ox, a **[RPH]** sheep or a goat;
18:17 must not redeem the firstborn of an ox, a sheep or a **[RPH]** goat;
26:5 The descendants of Reuben, the **firstborn** *son of* Israel, were:
33:4 who were burying all their **firstborn**, whom the LORD had struck
Dt 12:6 your freewill offerings, and the **firstborn** *of* your herds and flocks.
12:17 and new wine and oil, or the **firstborn** *of* your herds and flocks,
14:23 the **firstborn** *of* your herds and flocks in the presence of the
15:19 Set apart for the LORD your God every **firstborn** male of your
15:19 Do not put the **firstborn** *of* your oxen to work, and do not shear
15:19 of your oxen to work, and do not shear the **firstborn** *of* your sheep.
21:15 him sons but the **firstborn** is the son of the wife he does not love,
21:16 to the son of the wife he loves in preference to his actual **firstborn**,
21:17 He must acknowledge the son of his unloved wife as the **firstborn**
25:6 The **first** *son* she bears shall carry on the name of the dead brother
33:17 In majesty he is like a **firstborn** bull; his horns are the horns of a
Jos 6:26 "At the cost of his **firstborn** *son* will he lay its foundations;
17:1 was the allotment for the tribe of Manasseh as Joseph's **firstborn**,
17:1 as Joseph's firstborn, that is, for Makir, Manasseh's **firstborn**.
Jdg 8:20 Turning to Jether, his **oldest** *son*, he said, "Kill them!" But Jether
1Sa 8:2 The name of his **firstborn** was Joel and the name of his second
17:13 The **firstborn** was Eliab; the second, Abinadab; and the third,
2Sa 3:2 His **firstborn** was Amnon the son of Ahinoam of Jezreel;
1Ki 16:34 He laid its foundations at the cost of his **firstborn** *son* Abiram,
2Ki 3:27 Then he took his **firstborn** son, who was to succeed him as king,
1Ch 1:13 Canaan was the father of Sidon his **firstborn**, and of the Hittites,
1:29 Nebaioth the **firstborn** *of* Ishmael, Kedar, Adbeel, Mibsam,
2:3 Er, Judah's **firstborn**, was wicked in the LORD's sight;
2:13 Jesse was the father of Eliab his **firstborn**; the second son was
2:25 The sons of Jerahmeel the **firstborn** *of* Hezron: Ram his firstborn,
2:25 of Hezron: Ram his **firstborn**, Bunah, Oren, Ozem and Ahijah.
2:27 The sons of Ram the **firstborn** *of* Jerahmeel: Maaz, Jamin
2:42 Mesha his **firstborn**, who was the father of Ziph, and his son
2:50 The sons of Hur the **firstborn** *of* Ephrathah: Shobal the father of
3:1 The **firstborn** was Amnon the son of Ahinoam of Jezreel;
3:15 Johanan the **firstborn**, Jehoiakim the second son,
4:4 of Hur, the **firstborn** *of* Ephrathah and father of Bethlehem.
5:1 The sons of Reuben the **firstborn** *of* Israel (he was the firstborn,
5:1 The sons of Reuben the firstborn of Israel (he was the **firstborn**,
5:3 the sons of Reuben the **firstborn** *of* Israel: Hanoch, Pallu,
6:28 [6:13] of Samuel: Joel the **firstborn** and Abijah the second son.
8:1 Benjamin was the father of Bela his **firstborn**, Ashbel the second
8:30 and his **firstborn** son was Abdon, followed by Zur, Kish,
8:39 Ulam his **firstborn**, Jeush the second son and Eliphelet the third.
9:5 Of the Shilonites: Asaiah the **firstborn** and his sons.
9:31 named Mattithiah, the **firstborn** son of Shallum the Korahite,
9:36 and his **firstborn** son was Abdon, followed by Zur, Kish,
26:2 Zechariah the **firstborn**, Jediael the second, Zebadiah the third,
26:4 Shemaiah the **firstborn**, Jehozabad the second, Joah the third,
26:10 Shimri the first (although he was not the **firstborn**, his father had
2Ch 21:3 given the kingdom to Jehoram because he was his **firstborn** *son*.
Ne 10:36 [10:37] we will bring the **firstborn** *of* our sons and of our cattle,
10:36 [10:37] **[RPH]** of our herds and of our flocks to the house of our
Job 1:13 were feasting and drinking wine at the **oldest** brother's house,
1:18 were feasting and drinking wine at the **oldest** brother's house,
18:13 It eats away parts of his skin; death's **firstborn** devours his limbs.
Ps 78:51 He struck down all the **firstborn** of Egypt, the firstfruits of
89:27 [89:28] I will also appoint him my **firstborn**, the most exalted of
105:36 he struck down all the **firstborn** in their land, the firstfruits of all
135:8 He struck down the **firstborn** *of* Egypt, the firstborn of men
136:10 to him who struck down the **firstborn** *of* Egypt *His love*
Isa 14:30 The **poorest of the poor** [+1924] will find pasture, and the needy
Jer 31:9 because I am Israel's father, and Ephraim is my **firstborn** *son*.
Mic 6:7 Shall I offer my **firstborn** for my transgression, the fruit of my
Zec 12:10 and grieve bitterly for him as one grieves for a **firstborn** *son*.

1148 בְּכֹרָה *bᵉkōrâ*, n.f. [10] [√ 1144]

birthright [6], ages [+7584] [1], firstborn [1], rights as firstborn [1], rights of the firstborn [1]

Ge 25:31 Jacob replied, "First sell me your **birthright**."
25:32 am about to die," Esau said. "What good is the **birthright** to me?"
25:33 So he swore an oath to him, selling his **birthright** to Jacob.
25:34 and then got up and left. So Esau despised his **birthright**.
27:36 He took my **birthright**, and now he's taken my blessing!"
43:33 men had been seated before him in the order of their **ages** [+7584],
Dt 21:17 of his father's strength. The right of the **firstborn** belongs to him.
1Ch 5:1 his **rights as firstborn** were given to the sons of Joseph son of
5:1 listed in the genealogical record in accordance with his **birthright**,
5:2 came from him, the **rights of the firstborn** belonged to Joseph)—

1149 בִּכְרָה *bikrâ*, n.f. [1] [√ 1144]

she-camel [1]

Jer 2:23 you have done. You are a swift **she-camel** running here and there,

1150 בֹּכְרוּ *bōkᵉrû*, n.pr.m. [2] [√ 1144]

Bokeru [2]

1Ch 8:38 Azrikam, **Bokeru**, Ishmael, Sheariah, Obadiah and Hanan.
9:44 Azrikam, **Bokeru**, Ishmael, Sheariah, Obadiah and Hanan.

1151 בַּכְרִי *bakrî*, a.g. [1] [√ 1146; cf. 1144]

Bekerite [1]

Nu 26:35 through Beker, the **Bekerite** clan; through Tahan, the Tahanite

1152 בִּכְרִי *bikrî*, n.pr.m. *or* a.g. [8] [√ 1146; cf. 1144]

Bicri [8]

2Sa 20:1 Now a troublemaker named Sheba son of **Bicri**, a Benjamite,
20:2 all the men of Israel deserted David to follow Sheba son of **Bicri**.
20:6 "Now Sheba son of **Bicri** will do us more harm than Absalom did.
20:7 They marched out from Jerusalem to pursue Sheba son of **Bicri**.
20:10 Then Joab and his brother Abishai pursued Sheba son of **Bicri**.
20:13 all the men went on with Joab to pursue Sheba son of **Bicri**.
20:21 A man named Sheba son of **Bicri**, from the hill country of
20:22 they cut off the head of Sheba son of **Bicri** and threw it to Joab.

1153 בַּל *bal*^{1}, adv. [73 / 69] [→ 66, 1187; cf. 1162]

not [34], cannot [6], no [5], never [3], no sooner [+677] [3], never [+4200+5905] [2], never [+4200+6409] [2], nor [+2256] [2], nothing [2], *untranslated* [1], blind [+8011] [1], don't [1], ignorant [+3359] [1], immovable [+4572] [1], in order that no [1], never [+2256+6329 +6409] [1], untouched [+7212] [1], without [1], worthless [+3603] [1]

1Ch 16:30 all the earth! The world is firmly established; it **cannot** be moved.
Job 41:23 [41:15] are tightly joined; they are firm and **immovable** [+4572].
Ps 10:4 In his pride the wicked does **not** seek him; in all his thoughts there
10:6 He says to himself, "**Nothing** will shake me; I'll always be happy
10:11 has forgotten; he covers his face and **never** [+4200+5905] sees."
10:15 call him to account for his wickedness that would **not** be found out.
10:18 **in order that** man, who is of the earth, may terrify **no** more.
16:2 "You are my Lord; apart from you I have **no** good thing."
16:4 I will **not** pour out their libations of blood or take up their names
16:4 their libations of blood or **[RPH]** take up their names on my lips.
16:8 before me. Because he is at my right hand, I will **not** be shaken.
17:3 examine me at night, though you test me, you will find **nothing**;
17:3 you will find nothing; I have resolved that my mouth will **not** sin.
17:5 My steps have held to your paths; my feet have **not** slipped.
21:2 [21:3] of his heart and have **not** withheld the request of his lips.
21:7 [21:8] through the unfailing love of the Most High he will **not** be
21:11 [21:12] and devise wicked schemes, they **cannot** succeed;
30:6 [30:7] felt secure, I said, "I will **never** [+4200+6409] be shaken."
32:9 must be controlled by bit and bridle or they will **not** come to you.
44:14 [44:15] the peoples [BHS ***no*** *peoples*; NIV 928] shake their heads
46:5 [46:6] God is within her, she will **not** fall; God will help her at
49:12 [49:13] man, despite his riches, does **not** endure; he is like the
57:9 [57:10] sing of you among [BHS ***no*** *peoples*; NIV 928] the peoples.
58:8 [58:9] like a stillborn child, may they **not** see the sun.
78:44 their rivers to blood; they could **not** drink from their streams.
93:1 with strength. The world is firmly established; it **cannot** be moved.
96:10 The world is firmly established, it **cannot** be moved; he will judge
104:5 on its foundations; it can **never** [+2256+6329+6409] be moved.
104:9 You set a boundary they **cannot** cross; never again will they cover
104:9 boundary they cannot cross; **never** again will they cover the earth.
108:3 [108:4] sing of you among [BHS ***no*** *peoples*; NIV 928] the peoples.
119:121 done what is righteous and just; do **not** leave me to my oppressors.
140:10 [140:11] they be thrown into the fire, into miry pits, **never** to rise.
140:11 [140:12] Let slanderers **not** be established in the land;
141:4 with men who are evildoers; let me **not** eat of their delicacies.
147:20 He has done this for no other nation; they do **not** know his laws.
149:7 and punishment on [BHS ***no*** *peoples*; NIV 928] the peoples,
Pr 9:13 woman Folly is loud; she is undisciplined and **without** knowledge.
10:30 The righteous will **never** [+4200+6409] be uprooted,
12:3 through wickedness, but the righteous **cannot** be uprooted.
14:7 from a foolish man, for you will **not** find knowledge on his lips.
19:23 to life: Then one rests content, **untouched by** [+7212] trouble.
22:29 He will serve before kings; he will **not** serve before obscure men.

Pr 23: 7 "Eat and drink," he says to you, but his heart is **not** with you.
23: 35 "They hit me," you will say, "but I'm **not** hurt! They beat me,
23: 35 you will say, "but I'm not hurt! They beat me, but I **don't** feel it!
24: 23 are sayings of the wise: To show partiality in judging is **not** good:
Isa 14: 21 they are **not** to rise to inherit the land and cover the earth with their
26: 10 grace is shown to the wicked, they do **not** learn righteousness;
26: 10 they go on doing evil and regard **not** the majesty of the LORD.
26: 11 O LORD, your hand is lifted high, but they do **not** see it.
26: 14 They are now dead, they live **no** *more*; those departed spirits do
26: 14 are now dead, they live no more; those departed spirits do **not** rise.
26: 18 We have **not** brought salvation to the earth; we have not given
26: 18 to the earth; we have **not** given birth to people of the world.
33: 20 will see Jerusalem, a peaceful abode, a tent that will **not** be moved;
33: 20 its stakes will **never** [+4200+5905] be pulled up, nor any of its
33: 20 its stakes will never be pulled up, **nor** [+2256] any of its ropes
33: 21 **No** galley with oars will ride them, no mighty ship will sail them.
33: 23 hangs loose: The mast is **not** held secure, the sail is not spread.
33: 23 hangs loose: The mast is not held secure, the sail is **not** spread.
33: 24 **No** one living in Zion will say, "I am ill"; and the sins of those who
35: 9 No lion will be there, **nor** [+2256] will any ferocious beast get up
40: 24 **No** [+677] **sooner** are they planted, no sooner are they sown,
40: 24 No sooner are they planted, **no** [+677] **sooner** are they sown,
40: 24 no sooner are they sown, **no** [+677] **sooner** do they take root in the
43: 17 they lay there, **never** to rise again, extinguished, snuffed out like a
44: 8 any God besides me? No, there is no other Rock; I know **not** one."
44: 9 are nothing, and the things they treasure *are* **worthless** [+3603].
44: 9 Those who would speak up for them *are* **blind** [+8011]; they are
44: 9 would speak up for them are blind; *they are* **ignorant** [+3359],
Hos 7: 2 but they do **not** realize that I remember all their evil deeds.
9: 16 is blighted, their root is withered, they yield **no** [K 1172] fruit.

1154 ²בַּל *bal²*, adv. Not used in NIV/BHS [√ 1162]

1155 בֵּל *bēl*, n.pr.m. [3] [→ 1157, 1161, 1171, 1193]

Bel [3]

Isa 46: 1 **Bel** bows down, Nebo stoops low; their idols are borne by beasts of
Jer 50: 2 be captured; **Bel** will be put to shame, Marduk filled with terror.
51: 44 I will punish **Bel** in Babylon and make him spew out what he has

1156 בַּלְאֲדָן *bal'ᵃdān*, n.pr.m. [2] [→ 5282]

Baladan [2]

2Ki 20: 12 At that time Merodach-Baladan son of **Baladan** king of Babylon
Isa 39: 1 At that time Merodach-Baladan son of **Baladan** king of Babylon

1157 בֵּלְשַׁאצַּר *bēlšaṣṣar*, n.pr.m. [1] [√ 1155; Ar 10105, 10109]

Belshazzar's [1]

Da 8: 1 In the third year of King **Belshazzar's** reign, I, Daniel, had a

1158 בָּלַג *bālag*, v. [4] [→ 1159, 1160]

flashes [1], have joy [1], rejoice [1], smile [1]

Job 9: 27 [G] my complaint, I will change my expression, and **smile**,'
10: 20 [G] Turn away from me so *I can* **have** a moment's **joy**
Ps 39: 13 [39:14] [G] that *I may* **rejoice** *again* before I depart and am no
Am 5: 9 [G] he **flashes** destruction on the stronghold and brings the

1159 בִּלְגָּה *bilgâ*, n.pr.m. [3] [√ 1158]

Bilgah [2], Bilgah's [1]

1Ch 24: 14 the fifteenth to **Bilgah**, the sixteenth to Immer,
Ne 12: 5 Mijamin, Moadiah, **Bilgah**,
12: 18 of **Bilgah's**, Shammua; of Shemaiah's, Jehonathan;

1160 בִּלְגַּי *bilgay*, n.pr.m. [1] [√ 1158]

Bilgai [1]

Ne 10: 8 [10:9] Maaziah, **Bilgai** and Shemaiah. These were the priests.

1161 בִּלְדַּד *bildad*, n.pr.m. [5] [√ 1155? + 1856]

Bildad [5]

Job 2: 11 the Temanite, **Bildad** the Shuhite and Zophar the Naamathite,
8: 1 Then **Bildad** the Shuhite replied:
18: 1 Then **Bildad** the Shuhite replied:
25: 1 Then **Bildad** the Shuhite replied:
42: 9 **Bildad** the Shuhite and Zophar the Naamathite did what the

1162 ¹בָּלָה *bālâ¹*, v. [15] [→ 66, 1153, 1154, 1165, 1170, 1172, 1187, 1194, 4442, 9318; Ar 10106]

wear out [6], worn out [2], decay [1], did[s] [1], long enjoy [1], made grow old [1], oppress [1], wasted away [1], wastes away [1]

Ge 18: 12 [A] "After I *am* **worn out** and my master is old, will I now have
Dt 8: 4 [A] Your clothes *did* not **wear out** and your feet did not swell
29: 5 [29:4] [A] your clothes *did* not **wear out**, nor did the sandals on
29: 5 [29:4] [A] did not wear out, nor **did**[s] the sandals on your feet.
Jos 9: 13 [A] and sandals *are* **worn out** by the very long journey."
1Ch 17: 9 [D] Wicked people *will* not **oppress** them anymore, as they did
Ne 9: 21 [A] their clothes *did* not **wear out** nor did their feet become
Job 13: 28 [A] "So man **wastes away** like something rotten, like a garment
21: 13 [d] [*They* **spend** [K; see Q 3983] their years in prosperity]
Ps 32: 3 [A] my bones **wasted away** through my groaning all day long.
49: 14 [49:15] [D] their forms *will* **decay** in the grave, far from their
102: 26 [102:27] [A] you remain; they *will* all **wear out** like a garment.
Isa 50: 9 [A] They *will* all **wear out** like a garment; the moths will eat
51: 6 [A] the earth *will* **wear out** like a garment and its inhabitants die
65: 22 [D] my chosen ones *will* **long enjoy** the works of their hands.
La 3: 4 [D] *He has* **made** my skin and my flesh **grow old** and has broken

1163 ²בָּלָה *bālâ²*, n.pr.loc. [1] [cf. 1168]

Balah [1]

Jos 19: 3 Hazar Shual, **Balah**, Ezem,

1164 ³בָּלַהּ *bālah³*, v. [0] [→ 1166, 1167?; cf. 987]

Ezr 4: 4 [d] [and **make** them **afraid** [K; see Q 987] to go on building.]

1165 בָּלֶה *bāleh*, a. [5] [√ 1162]

old [2], worn out [1], worn [1], worn-out [1]

Jos 9: 4 as a delegation whose donkeys were loaded with **worn-out** sacks
9: 4 donkeys were loaded with worn-out sacks and **old** wineskins,
9: 5 The men put **worn** and patched sandals on their feet and wore old
9: 5 put worn and patched sandals on their feet and wore **old** clothes.
Eze 23: 43 I said about the *one* **worn out** *by* adultery, 'Now let them use her

1166 בַּלָּהָה *ballāhâ*, n.f. [10] [√ 1164]

terrors [6], horrible end [3], sudden terror [1]

Job 18: 11 **Terrors** startle him on every side and dog his every step.
18: 14 from the security of his tent and marched off to the king of **terrors**.
24: 17 is their morning; they make friends with the **terrors** *of* darkness.
27: 20 **Terrors** overtake him like a flood; a tempest snatches him away in
30: 15 **Terrors** overwhelm me; my dignity is driven away as by the wind,
Ps 73: 19 suddenly are they destroyed, completely swept away by **terrors**!
Isa 17: 14 In the evening, **sudden terror**! Before the morning, they are gone!
Eze 26: 21 I will bring you to a **horrible end** and you will be no more.
27: 36 at you; you have come to a **horrible end** and will be no more.' "
28: 19 at you; you have come to a **horrible end** and will be no more.' "

1167 ¹בִּלְהָה *bilhâ¹*, n.pr.f. [10] [√ 1164?]

Bilhah [9], she[s] [1]

Ge 29: 29 Laban gave his servant girl **Bilhah** to his daughter Rachel as her
30: 3 Then she said, "Here is **Bilhah**, my maidservant. Sleep with her
30: 4 So she gave him her servant **Bilhah** as a wife. Jacob slept with her,
30: 5 and **she**[s] became pregnant and bore him a son.
30: 7 Rachel's servant **Bilhah** conceived again and bore Jacob a second
35: 22 Reuben went in and slept with his father's concubine **Bilhah**.
35: 25 The sons of Rachel's maidservant **Bilhah**: Dan and Naphtali.
37: 2 the sons of **Bilhah** and the sons of Zilpah, his father's wives,
46: 25 These were the sons born to Jacob by **Bilhah**, whom Laban had
1Ch 7: 13 Jahziel, Guni, Jezer and Shillem—the descendants of **Bilhah**.

1168 ²בִּלְהָה *bilhâ²*, n.pr.loc. [1] [√ 1266; cf. 1163]

Bilhah [1]

1Ch 4: 29 **Bilhah**, Ezem, Tolad,

1169 בִּלְהָן *bilhān*, n.pr.m. [4]

Bilhan [4]

Ge 36: 27 The sons of Ezer: **Bilhan**, Zaavan and Akan.
1Ch 1: 42 The sons of Ezer: **Bilhan**, Zaavan and Akan. The sons of Dishan:
7: 10 The son of Jediael: **Bilhan**. The sons of Bilhan: Jeush, Benjamin,
7: 10 The sons of **Bilhan**: Jeush, Benjamin, Ehud, Kenaanah, Zethan,

1170 בְּלוֹי *bᵉlôy*, n.[m.]. [3] [√ 1162]

old [2], worn-out [1]

Jer 38: 11 He took some **old** rags and worn-out clothes from there and let
38: 11 He took some old rags and **worn-out** clothes from there and let

Jer 38:12 "Put these **old** rags and worn-out clothes under your arms to pad

1171 בֵּלְטְשַׁאצַּר bēlṭešaʾṣṣar, n.pr.m. [2] [√ 1155; Ar 10108]

Belteshazzar [2]

Da 1: 7 to Daniel, the name **Belteshazzar**; to Hananiah, Shadrach;
10: 1 a revelation was given to Daniel (who was called **Belteshazzar**).

1172 בְּלִי belî, subst. [58 / 57] [→ 1174, 1175; cf. 1162] See Select Index

no [9], not [7], lack [6], without [6], unintentionally [+928+1981] [4], there is no [+401] [3], no [+4946] [2], without [+4200] [2], *untranslated* [1], deserted [+3782+4946] [1], destruction [1], guiltless [+7322] [1], lacking [+4946] [1], lacking [1], nameless [+9005] [1], no longer [1], no more [1], nothing [+4537] [1], relentless [+3104] [1], there were no [+401] [1], unnoticed [+4946+8492] [1], untraveled [+408+4946+6296] [1], without [+3869] [1], without [+4946] [1], without [+928] [1], yet [+889+4946] [1]

1173 בְּלִיל belîl, n.m. [3] [√ 1177]

fodder [3]

Job 6: 5 bray when it has grass, or an ox bellow when it has **fodder**?
24: 6 They gather **fodder** in the fields and glean in the vineyards of the
Isa 30:24 The oxen and donkeys that work the soil will eat **fodder** and mash,

1174 בְּלִימָה belîmâ, n.[m.]. Not used in NIV/BHS [√ 1172 + 4537]

1175 בְּלִיַּעַל beliyyaʿal, n.[m.]. [27] [√ 1172 + 3603]

wicked [6], scoundrels [+1201] [3], wicked [+1201] [3], destruction [2], vile [2], *untranslated* [1], corrupt [1], evil men [1], scoundrel [+132] [1], scoundrel [+408] [1], scoundrel [+408+2021] [1], troublemaker [+408] [1], troublemakers [+1201] [1], troublemakers [1], wickedness [1], worthless [1]

Dt 13:13 [13:14] that **wicked** [+1201] men have arisen among you
15: 9 Be careful not to harbor this **wicked** thought: "The seventh year,
Jdg 19:22 some of the **wicked** [+1201] men of the city surrounded the house.
20:13 Now surrender those **wicked** [+1201] men of Gibeah so that we
1Sa 1:16 Do not take your servant for a **wicked** woman; I have been praying
2:12 Eli's sons were **wicked** men; they had no regard for the LORD.
10:27 *some* **troublemakers** [+1201] said, "How can this fellow save
25:17 He is such a **wicked** man that no one can talk to him."
25:25 May my lord pay no attention to that **wicked** man Nabal. He is just
30:22 all the evil men and **troublemakers** among David's followers said,
2Sa 16: 7 "Get out, get out, you man of blood, you **scoundrel** [+408+2021]!
20: 1 Now a **troublemaker** [+408] named Sheba son of Bicri,
22: 5 swirled about me; the torrents of **destruction** overwhelmed me.
23: 6 **evil men** are all to be cast aside like thorns, which are not gathered
1Ki 21:10 seat two **scoundrels** [+1201] opposite him and have them testify
21:13 two **scoundrels** [+1201] came and sat opposite him and brought
21:13 and brought charges against Naboth **[RPH]** before the people,
2Ch 13: 7 Some worthless **scoundrels** [+1201] gathered around him
Job 34:18 to kings, 'You are **worthless**,' and to nobles, 'You are wicked,'
Ps 18: 4 [18:5] the torrents of **destruction** overwhelmed me.
41: 8 [41:9] "A **vile** disease has beset him; he will never get up from the
101: 3 I will set before my eyes no **vile** thing. The deeds of faithless men I
Pr 6:12 A **scoundrel** [+132] and villain, who goes about with a corrupt
16:27 A **scoundrel** [+408] plots evil, and his speech is like a scorching
19:28 A **corrupt** witness mocks at justice, and the mouth of the wicked
Na 1:11 forth who plots evil against the LORD and counsels **wickedness**.
1:15 [2:1] No more will the **wicked** invade you; they will be

1176 בָּלַל bālal¹, v. [43] [→ 8671?, 9316, 9319; cf. 1182?]

mixed [38], confuse [1], confused [1], fed [1], mixes [1], poured [1]

Ge 11: 7 [A] let us go down and **confuse** their language so they will not
11: 9 [A] because there the LORD **confused** the language of the
Ex 29: 2 [B] without yeast, make bread, and cakes **mixed** with oil,
29:40 [B] flour **mixed** with a quarter of a hin of oil from pressed olives,
Lev 2: 4 [B] cakes made without yeast and **mixed** with oil, or wafers
2: 5 [B] it is to be made of fine flour **mixed** with oil, and without
7:10 [B] every grain offering, whether **mixed** with oil or dry,
7:12 [B] offer cakes of bread made without yeast and **mixed** with oil,
7:12 [B] and cakes of fine flour well-kneaded and **mixed** with oil.
9: 4 [B] the LORD, together with a grain offering **mixed** with oil.
14:10 [B] along with three-tenths of an ephah of fine flour **mixed** with
14:21 [B] together with a tenth of an ephah of fine flour **mixed** with oil
23:13 [B] of two-tenths of an ephah of fine flour **mixed** with oil—
Nu 6:15 [B] cakes made of fine flour **mixed** with oil, and wafers spread
7:13 [B] each filled with fine flour **mixed** with oil as a grain offering;
7:19 [B] each filled with fine flour **mixed** with oil as a grain offering;
7:25 [B] each filled with fine flour **mixed** with oil as a grain offering;
7:31 [B] each filled with fine flour **mixed** with oil as a grain offering;
7:37 [B] each filled with fine flour **mixed** with oil as a grain offering;
7:43 [B] each filled with fine flour **mixed** with oil as a grain offering;
7:49 [B] each filled with fine flour **mixed** with oil as a grain offering;
7:55 [B] each filled with fine flour **mixed** with oil as a grain offering;
7:61 [B] each filled with fine flour **mixed** with oil as a grain offering;
7:67 [B] each filled with fine flour **mixed** with oil as a grain offering;
7:73 [B] each filled with fine flour **mixed** with oil as a grain offering;
7:79 [B] each filled with fine flour **mixed** with oil as a grain offering;
8: 8 [B] bull with its grain offering of fine flour **mixed** with oil;
15: 4 [B] of an ephah of fine flour **mixed** with a quarter of a hin of oil.
15: 6 [B] of an ephah of fine flour **mixed** with a third of a hin of oil,
15: 9 [B] of an ephah of fine flour **mixed** with half a hin of oil.
28: 5 [B] flour **mixed** with a quarter of a hin of oil from pressed olives.
28: 9 [B] a grain offering of two-tenths of an ephah of fine flour **mixed**
28:12 [B] of three-tenths of an ephah of fine flour **mixed** with oil;
28:12 [B] a grain offering of two-tenths of an ephah of fine flour **mixed**
28:13 [B] a grain offering of a tenth of an ephah of fine flour **mixed**
28:20 [B] of three-tenths of an ephah of fine flour **mixed** with oil;
28:28 [B] of three-tenths of an ephah of fine flour **mixed** with oil;
29: 3 [B] of three-tenths of an ephah of fine flour **mixed** with oil;
29: 9 [B] of three-tenths of an ephah of fine flour **mixed** with oil;
29:14 [B] of three-tenths of an ephah of fine flour **mixed** with oil;
Jdg 19:21 [A] So he took him into his house and **fed** his donkeys.
Ps 92:10 [92:11] [A] of a wild ox; fine oils *have been* **poured** *upon me*.
Hos 7: 8 [F] "Ephraim **mixes** with the nations; Ephraim is a flat cake not

1177 בָּלַל bālal², v.den. Not used in NIV/BHS [→ 1173]

1178 בָּלַם bālam, v. [1]

controlled [1]

Ps 32: 9 [A] *must be* **controlled** by bit and bridle or they will not come to

1179 בָּלַס bālas, v.den. [1]

took care of [1]

Am 7:14 [A] I was a shepherd, and I also **took care of** sycamore-fig trees.

1180 בָּלַע bālaʿ¹, v. [43] [→ 1183, 1185, 1186, 1188, 1189, 1190?, 3300?]

swallowed up [9], swallow up [7], swallowed [7], swallow [3], be swallowed up [2], destroy [2], swallows [2], consumed [1], destroying [1], devoured [1], devours [1], for an instant [+6330+8371] [1], gulps down [1], is swallowed up [1], moment [1], ruin [1], torn [1], uneaten [+4202] [1]

Ge 41: 7 [A] The thin heads of grain **swallowed up** the seven healthy, full
41:24 [A] The thin heads of grain **swallowed up** the seven good heads.
Ex 7:12 [A] became a snake. But Aaron's staff **swallowed up** their staffs.
15:12 [A] stretched out your right hand and the earth **swallowed** them.
Nu 4:20 [D] look at the holy things, even for a **moment**, or they will die."
16:30 [A] and **swallows** them, with everything that belongs to them,
16:32 [A] **swallowed** them, with their households and all Korah's men
16:34 [A] them fled, shouting, "The earth *is going to* **swallow** us too!"
26:10 [A] opened its mouth and **swallowed** them along with Korah,
Dt 11: 6 [A] **swallowed** them **up** with their households, their tents and
2Sa 17:16 [E] and all the people with him *will* **be swallowed up**.' "
20:19 [D] Why *do you want to* **swallow up** the LORD's
20:20 [D] Joab replied, "Far be it from me *to* **swallow up** or destroy!
Job 2: 3 [D] though you incited me against him to **ruin** him without any
7:19 [A] from me, or let me alone even **for an instant** [+6330+8371]?
8:18 [D] when it *is* **torn** from its spot, that place disowns it and says,
10: 8 [D] and made me. Will *you* now turn and **destroy** me?
20:15 [A] He will spit out the riches *he* **swallowed**; God will make his
20:18 [A] What he toiled for he must give back **uneaten** [+4202]; he
37:20 [E] I want to speak? Would any man ask *to* **be swallowed up**?
Ps 21: 9 [21:10] [D] In his wrath the LORD *will* **swallow** them **up**,
35:25 [D] what we wanted!" or say, "*We have* **swallowed** him **up**."
69:15 [69:16] [A] or the depths **swallow** me **up** or the pit close its
106:17 [A] The earth opened up and **swallowed** Dathan; it buried the
124: 3 [A] flared against us, *they would have* **swallowed** us alive;
Pr 1:12 [A] *let's* **swallow** them alive, like the grave, and whole,
19:28 [D] at justice, and the mouth of the wicked **gulps down** evil.
21:20 [D] of choice food and oil, but a foolish man **devours** all he has.
Ecc 10:12 [D] mouth are gracious, but a fool *is* **consumed** *by* his own lips.
Isa 25: 7 [D] On this mountain *he will* **destroy** the shroud that enfolds all
25: 8 [D] *he will* **swallow up** death forever. The Sovereign LORD
28: 4 [A] as someone sees it and takes it in his hand, *he* **swallows** it.
49:19 [D] your people, and *those who* **devoured** you will be far away.
Jer 51:34 [A] Like a serpent *he has* **swallowed** us and filled his stomach
La 2: 2 [D] Without pity the Lord *has* **swallowed up** all the dwellings of
2: 5 [D] The Lord is like an enemy; *he has* **swallowed up** Israel.
2: 5 [D] *He has* **swallowed up** all her palaces and destroyed her

La 2: 8 [D] and did not withhold his hand from **destroying**.
2: 16 [D] and gnash their teeth and say, "*We have* **swallowed** her **up**.
Hos 8: 7 [A] Were it to yield grain, foreigners *would* **swallow** it **up**.
8: 8 [C] Israel **is swallowed up**; now she is among the nations like a
Jnh 1: 17 [2:1] [A] the LORD provided a great fish to **swallow** Jonah,
Hab 1: 13 [D] Why are you silent while the wicked **swallow up** those more

1181 ²בָּלַע **bāla'²**, v. Not used in NIV/BHS [→ 3300?]

1182 ³בָּלַע **bāla'³**, v. [6] [→ 1184, 3300?; cf. 1176?]

are led astray [1], at wits end [+2683+3972] [1], befuddled [1], bring to nothing [1], confuse [1], turn [1]

Ps 55: 9 [55:10] [D] **Confuse** the wicked, O Lord, confound their
107: 27 [F] drunken men; they *were* **at** their **wits' end** [+2683+3972].
Isa 3: 12 [D] your guides lead you astray; *they* **turn** you *from* the path.
9: 16 [9:15] [E] and those who are guided **are led astray**.
19: 3 [D] will lose heart, and *I will* **bring** their plans **to nothing**;
28: 7 [C] prophets stagger from beer and *are* **befuddled** with wine;

1183 ¹בֶּלַע **bela'¹**, n.[m.]. [1] [√ 1180]

what swallowed [1]

Jer 51: 44 Bel in Babylon and make him spew out **what** he has **swallowed**.

1184 ²בֶּלַע **bela'²**, n.[m.]. [1] [√ 1182]

harmful [1]

Ps 52: 4 [52:6] You love every **harmful** word, O you deceitful tongue!

1185 ³בֶּלַע **bela'³**, n.pr.m. [12] [√ 1180]

Bela [12]

Ge 36: 32 **Bela** son of Beor became king of Edom. His city was named
36: 33 When **Bela** died, Jobab son of Zerah from Bozrah succeeded him
46: 21 **Bela**, Beker, Ashbel, Gera, Naaman, Ehi, Rosh, Muppim,
Nu 26: 38 through **Bela**, the Belaite clan; through Ashbel, the Ashbelite clan;
26: 40 The descendants of **Bela** through Ard and Naaman were:
1Ch 1: 43 king reigned: **Bela** son of Beor, whose city was named Dinhabah.
1: 44 When **Bela** died, Jobab son of Zerah from Bozrah succeeded him
5: 8 **Bela** son of Azaz, the son of Shema, the son of Joel. They settled
7: 6 Three sons of Benjamin: **Bela**, Beker and Jediael.
7: 7 The sons of **Bela**: Ezbon, Uzzi, Uzziel, Jerimoth and Iri, heads of
8: 1 Benjamin was the father of **Bela** his firstborn, Ashbel the second
8: 3 The sons of **Bela** were: Addar, Gera, Abihud,

1186 ⁴בֶּלַע **bela'⁴**, n.pr.loc. [2] [√ 1180]

Bela [2]

Ge 14: 2 Shemeber king of Zeboiim, and the king of **Bela** (that is, Zoar).
14: 8 of Admah, the king of Zeboiim and the king of **Bela** (that is, Zoar)

1187 בַּלְעֲדֵי **bal'ădê**, adv. [17] [√ 1153 + 6330]

apart from [+4946] [3], besides [+4946] [3], cannot [2], other than [+4946] [2], without [+4946] [2], besides [1], except [+4946] [1], not [+4946] [1], nothing [1], without [1]

Ge 14: 24 I will accept **nothing** but what my men have eaten and the share
41: 16 "**I cannot** do it," Joseph replied to Pharaoh, "but God will give
41: 44 but **without** your word no one will lift hand or foot in all Egypt."
Nu 5: 20 by sleeping with a man **other** [+4946] **than** your husband"—
Jos 22: 19 against us by building an altar for yourselves, **other than** [+4946]
2Sa 22: 32 For who is God **besides** [+4946] the LORD? And who is the
22: 32 the LORD? And who is the Rock **except** [+4946] our God?
2Ki 18: 25 and destroy this place **without** [+4946] word from the LORD?
Job 34: 32 Teach me what I **cannot** see; if I have done wrong, I will not do
Ps 18: 31 [18:32] For who is God **besides** [+4946] the LORD? And who is
Isa 36: 10 come to attack and destroy this land **without** [+4946] the LORD?
43: 11 am the LORD, and **apart** [+4946] **from** me there is no savior.
44: 6 and I am the last; **apart** [+4946] **from** me there is no God.
44: 8 Is there any God **besides** [+4946] me? No, there is no other Rock;
45: 6 to the place of its setting men may know there is none **besides** me.
45: 21 And there is no God **apart** [+4946] **from** me, a righteous God
Jer 44: 19 did **not** [+4946] our husbands know that we were making cakes

1188 בַּלְעִי **bal'î**, a.g. [1] [√ 1180]

Belaite [1]

Nu 26: 38 through Bela, the **Belaite** clan; through Ashbel, the Ashbelite clan;

1189 ¹בִּלְעָם **bil'ām¹**, n.pr.m. [60] [√ 1180]

Balaam [53], Balaam's [4], he[s] [1], him[s] [1], the two of them[s] [+1192+2256] [1]

Nu 22: 5 sent messengers to summon **Balaam** son of Beor, who was at
22: 7 When they came to **Balaam**, they told him what Balak had said.
22: 8 "Spend the night here," **Balaam** said to them, "and I will bring you
22: 9 God came to **Balaam** and asked, "Who are these men with you?"
22: 10 **Balaam** said to God, "Balak son of Zippor, king of Moab,
22: 12 God said to **Balaam**, "Do not go with them. You must not put a
22: 13 The next morning **Balaam** got up and said to Balak's princes,
22: 14 returned to Balak and said, "**Balaam** refused to come with us."
22: 16 They came to **Balaam** and said: "This is what Balak son of Zippor
22: 18 **Balaam** answered them, "Even if Balak gave me his palace filled
22: 20 That night God came to **Balaam** and said, "Since these men have
22: 21 **Balaam** got up in the morning, saddled his donkey and went with
22: 23 the road into a field. **Balaam** beat her to get her back on the road.
22: 25 she pressed close to the wall, crushing **Balaam's** foot against it.
22: 27 she lay down under **Balaam**, and he was angry and beat her with
22: 27 down under Balaam, and **he**[s] was angry and beat her with his staff.
22: 28 the LORD opened the donkey's mouth, and she said to **Balaam**,
22: 29 **Balaam** answered the donkey, "You have made a fool of me!
22: 30 The donkey said to **Balaam**, "Am I not your own donkey,
22: 31 the LORD opened **Balaam's** eyes, and he saw the angel of the
22: 34 **Balaam** said to the angel of the LORD, "I have sinned. I did not
22: 35 The angel of the LORD said to **Balaam**, "Go with the men,
22: 35 only what I tell you." So **Balaam** went with the princes of Balak.
22: 36 When Balak heard that **Balaam** was coming, he went out to meet
22: 37 Balak said to **Balaam**, "Did I not send you an urgent summons?
22: 38 "Well, I have come to you now," **Balaam** replied. "But can I say
22: 39 Then **Balaam** went with Balak to Kiriath Huzoth.
22: 40 and gave some to **Balaam** and the princes who were with him.
22: 41 The next morning Balak took **Balaam** up to Bamoth Baal,
23: 1 **Balaam** said, "Build me seven altars here, and prepare seven bulls
23: 2 Balak did as **Balaam** said, and the two of them offered a bull
23: 2 **the two of them**[s] [+1192+2256] offered a bull and a ram on each
23: 3 **Balaam** said to Balak, "Stay here beside your offering while I go
23: 4 God met with him, and **Balaam** said, "I have prepared seven altars,
23: 5 The LORD put a message in **Balaam's** mouth and said, "Go back
23: 11 Balak said to **Balaam**, "What have you done to me? I brought you
23: 16 The LORD met with **Balaam** and put a message in his mouth
23: 25 Balak said to **Balaam**, "Neither curse them at all nor bless them at
23: 26 **Balaam** answered, "Did I not tell you I must do whatever the
23: 27 Balak said to **Balaam**, "Come, let me take you to another place.
23: 28 Balak took **Balaam** to the top of Peor, overlooking the wasteland.
23: 29 **Balaam** said, "Build me seven altars here, and prepare seven bulls
23: 30 Balak did as **Balaam** had said, and offered a bull and a ram on
24: 1 Now when **Balaam** saw that it pleased the LORD to bless Israel,
24: 2 When **Balaam** looked out and saw Israel encamped tribe by tribe,
24: 3 "The oracle of **Balaam** son of Beor, the oracle of one whose eye
24: 10 Balak's anger burned against **Balaam**. He struck his hands
24: 10 He struck his hands together and said to **him**[s], "I summoned you to
24: 12 **Balaam** answered Balak, "Did I not tell the messengers you sent
24: 15 "The oracle of **Balaam** son of Beor, the oracle of one whose eye
24: 25 **Balaam** got up and returned home and Balak went his own way.
31: 8 of Midian. They also killed **Balaam** son of Beor with the sword.
31: 16 "They were the ones who followed **Balaam's** advice and were the
Dt 23: 4 [23:5] they hired **Balaam** son of Beor from Pethor in Aram
23: 5 [23:6] the LORD your God would not listen to **Balaam**
Jos 13: 22 the Israelites had put to the sword **Balaam** son of Beor,
24: 9 he sent for **Balaam** son of Beor to put a curse on you.
24: 10 But I would not listen to **Balaam**, so he blessed you again
Ne 13: 2 and water but had hired **Balaam** to call a curse down on them.
Mic 6: 5 king of Moab counseled and what **Balaam** son of Beor answered.

1190 ²בִּלְעָם **bil'ām²**, n.pr.loc. [1] [√ 1180?]

Bileam [1]

1Ch 6: 70 [6:55] the tribe of Manasseh the Israelites gave Aner and **Bileam**,

1191 בָּלַק **bālaq**, v. [2] [→ 1192, 4444]

devastate [1], stripped [1]

Isa 24: 1 [A] the LORD is going to lay waste the earth and **devastate** it;
Na 2: 10 [2:11] [E] She is pillaged, plundered, **stripped**! Hearts melt,

1192 בָּלָק **bālāq**, n.pr.m. [43] [√ 1191]

Balak [34], *untranslated* [5], Balak's [2], the two of them[s] [+1189+2256] [1], them[s] [+6269] [1]

Nu 22: 2 Now **Balak** son of Zippor saw all that Israel had done to the
22: 4 So **Balak** son of Zippor, who was king of Moab at that time,
22: 7 When they came to Balaam, they told him what **Balak** had said.
22: 10 Balaam said to God, "**Balak** son of Zippor, king of Moab,
22: 13 The next morning Balaam got up and said to **Balak's** princes,
22: 14 So the Moabite princes returned to **Balak** and said,
22: 15 **Balak** sent other princes, more numerous and more distinguished
22: 16 came to Balaam and said: "This is what **Balak** son of Zippor says:
22: 18 Balaam answered **them**[s] [+6269], "Even if Balak gave me his
22: 18 "Even if **Balak** gave me his palace filled with silver and gold,

Nu 22:35 only what I tell you." So Balaam went with the princes of **Balak**.
22:36 When **Balak** heard that Balaam was coming, he went out to meet
22:37 **Balak** said to Balaam, "Did I not send you an urgent summons?
22:38 you now," Balaam replied. **[RPH]** "But can I say just anything?
22:39 Then Balaam went with **Balak** to Kiriath Huzoth.
22:40 **Balak** sacrificed cattle and sheep, and gave some to Balaam
22:41 The next morning **Balak** took Balaam up to Bamoth Baal,
23: 1 Balaam said, **[RPH]** "Build me seven altars here, and prepare
23: 2 **Balak** did as Balaam said, and the two of them offered a bull
23: 2 **the two of them**[s] [+1189+2256] offered a bull and a ram on each
23: 3 Balaam said to **Balak**, "Stay here beside your offering while I go
23: 5 and said, "Go back to **Balak** and give him this message."
23: 7 "**Balak** brought me from Aram, the king of Moab from the eastern
23:11 **Balak** said to Balaam, "What have you done to me? I brought you
23:13 **Balak** said to him, "Come with me to another place where you can
23:15 Balaam said to **Balak**, "Stay here beside your offering while I meet
23:16 and said, "Go back to **Balak** and give him this message."
23:17 princes of Moab. **Balak** asked him, "What did the LORD say?"
23:18 his oracle: "Arise, **Balak**, and listen; hear me, son of Zippor.
23:25 **Balak** said to Balaam, "Neither curse them at all nor bless them at
23:26 **[RPH]** "Did I not tell you I must do whatever the LORD says?"
23:27 **Balak** said to Balaam, "Come, let me take you to another place.
23:28 **Balak** took Balaam to the top of Peor, overlooking the wasteland.
23:29 Balaam said, **[RPH]** "Build me seven altars here, and prepare
23:30 **Balak** did as Balaam had said, and offered a bull and a ram on
24:10 **Balak's** anger burned against Balaam. He struck his hands together
24:10 He struck his hands together and said **[RPH]** to him,
24:12 Balaam answered **Balak**, "Did I not tell the messengers you sent
24:13 'Even if **Balak** gave me his palace filled with silver and gold,
24:25 Balaam got up and returned home and **Balak** went his own way.
Jos 24: 9 When **Balak** son of Zippor, the king of Moab, prepared to fight
Jdg 11:25 Are you better than **Balak** son of Zippor, king of Moab? Did he
Mic 6: 5 remember what **Balak** king of Moab counseled and what Balaam

1193 בִּלְשָׁן *bilšān*, n.pr.m. [2] [√ 1155]

Bilshan [2]

Ezr 2: 2 Mordecai, **Bilshan**, Mispar, Bigvai, Rehum and Baanah):
Ne 7: 7 Mordecai, **Bilshan**, Mispereth, Bigvai, Nehum and Baanah):

1194 בִּלְתִּי *biltî*, subst. & adv. & pp. [112] [√ 1162]

not [37], no [14], *untranslated* [7], keep from [5], nothing [5], neither [4], without [3], except [2], fail [2], never [2], prevent [+5989] [2], unless [2], avoid [1], be kept from [+1757+4200] [1], be nothing [+401] [1], besides [1], but [1], ceremonially unclean [+3196] [1], didn't [1], disobey [+928+7754+9048] [1], except [+561] [1], except for [1], failing [1], forbidden [+448+6584+7422] [1], free from [1], from [1], insatiable [+8429] [1], instead of [+4200] [1], no more [1], not [+4946] [1], only [+4202] [1], other than [+963+4200] [1], refusing [1], remain unmarried [+408+2118+4200+4200+6328] [1], stop [1], unable [1], unceasing [+6239] [1], unless [+561] [1], worthless [+3603] [1]

Ge 3:11 Have you eaten from the tree that I commanded you **not** to eat
4:15 put a mark on Cain so that **no** one who found him would kill him.
19:21 grant this request too; I will **not** overthrow the town you speak of.
21:26 You did not tell me, and I heard about it **only** [+4202] today."
38: 9 he spilled his semen on the ground to **keep from** producing
43: 3 'You will not see my face again **unless** your brother is with you.'
43: 5 'You will not see my face again **unless** your brother is with you.' "
47:18 there is nothing left for our lord **except** [+561] our bodies
Ex 8:22 [8:18] **no** swarms of flies will be there, so that you will know that
8:29 [8:25] **not** letting the people go to offer sacrifices to the LORD."
9:17 You still set yourself against my people and will **not** let them go.
20:20 so that the fear of God will be with you to **keep** you **from** sinning."
22:20 [22:19] "Whoever sacrifices to any god **other** [+963+4200] **than**
Lev 18:30 do **not** follow any of the detestable customs that were practiced
20: 4 one of his children to Molech and they **fail** to put him to death,
26:15 and abhor my laws and **fail** to carry out all my commands and
Nu 9: 7 why *should we* **be kept from** [+1757+4200] presenting the
11: 6 we have lost our appetite; we never see anything **but** this manna!"
14:16 'The LORD was **not** [+4946] able to bring these people into the
21:35 with his sons and his whole army, leaving them **no** survivors.
32: 9 they discouraged the Israelites **from** entering the land the LORD
32:12 not one **except** Caleb son of Jephunneh the Kenizzite and Joshua
Dt 3: 3 and all his army. We struck them down, leaving **no** survivors.
4:21 he solemnly swore that I would **not** cross the Jordan and enter the
4:21 **[RPH]** enter the good land the LORD your God is giving you as
8:11 **failing** to observe his commands, his laws and his decrees that I am
12:23 But be sure you do **not** eat the blood, because the blood is the life,
17:12 or **[NIE]** for the priest who stands ministering there to the
17:20 **not** consider himself better than his brothers and turn from the law
17:20 and **[RPH]** turn from the law to the right or to the left.
Jos 5: 6 For the LORD had sworn to them that they would **not** see the
8:22 Israel cut them down, leaving them **neither** survivors nor fugitives.
10:33 Joshua defeated him and his army—until **no** survivors were left.
11: 8 to the Valley of Mizpah on the east, until **no** survivors were left.
11:19 **Except for** the Hivites living in Gibeon, not one city made a treaty
11:20 he might destroy them totally, exterminating them **without** mercy,
22:25 So your descendants might cause ours to stop **[NIE]** fearing the
23: 6 the Law of Moses, **without** turning aside to the right or to the left.
23: 7 Do **not** associate with these nations that remain among you;
Jdg 2:23 he did **not** drive them out at once by giving them into the hands of
7:14 "This can **be nothing** [+401] other than the sword of Gideon son
8: 1 Why **didn't** you call us when you went to fight Midian?" And they
21: 7 since we have taken an oath by the LORD **not** to give them any
Ru 1:13 *Would you* **remain unmarried** [+408+2118+4200+4200+6328]
2: 9 I have told the men **not** to touch you. And whenever you are
3:10 You have **not** run after the younger men, whether rich or poor.
1Sa 2: 2 there is no one **besides** you; there is no Rock like our God.
20:26 happened to David to make him **ceremonially unclean** [+3196]—
2Sa 14: 7 leaving my husband **neither** name nor descendant on the face of
14:13 for the king has **not** brought back his banished son?
14:14 so that a banished person may **not** remain estranged from him.
1Ki 6: 6 the temple so that **nothing** would be inserted into the temple walls.
11:10 Although *he had* **forbidden** [+448+6584+7422] Solomon to
15:17 and fortified Ramah to **prevent** anyone **from** [+5989] leaving
2Ki 10:11 his close friends and his priests, leaving him **no** survivor.
12: 8 [12:9] The priests agreed that they would **not** collect any more
12: 8 [12:9] and that they would **not** repair the temple themselves.
17:15 "Do **not** do as they do," and they did the things the LORD had
23:10 so **no** one could use it to sacrifice his son or daughter in the fire to
1Ch 4:10 with me, and keep me from harm so that I will be **free from** pain."
2Ch 16: 1 and fortified Ramah to **prevent** anyone **from** [+5989] leaving
Job 14:12 till the heavens are **no more**, men will not awake or be roused
42: 8 accept his prayer and **not** deal with you according to your folly.
Isa 10: 4 **Nothing** will remain but to cringe among the captives or fall
14: 6 which in anger struck down peoples with **unceasing** [+6239]
44:10 Who shapes a god and casts an idol, which can profit him **nothing**?
48: 9 sake of my praise I hold it back from you, so as **not** to cut you off.
65: 8 so will I do in behalf of my servants; I will **not** destroy them all.
Jer 7: 8 you are trusting in deceptive words *that are* **worthless** [+3603].
16:12 the stubbornness of his evil heart **instead** [+4200] **of** obeying me.
17:23 they were stiff-necked and would **not** listen or respond to
17:23 and would not listen or **[RPH]** respond to discipline.
17:24 and bring **no** load through the gates of this city on the Sabbath,
17:24 but keep the Sabbath day holy by **not** doing any work on it,
17:27 if you do not obey me to keep the Sabbath day holy by **not**
18:10 if it does evil in my sight and does **not** obey me, then I will
19:15 they were stiff-necked and would **not** listen to my words.' "
23:14 the hands of evildoers, so that **no** one turns from his wickedness.
26:24 so he was **not** handed over to the people to be put to death.
27:18 of the king of Judah and in Jerusalem **not** be taken to Babylon.
32:40 inspire them to fear me, so that they will **never** turn away from me.
33:20 so that day and night **no** longer come at their appointed time,
34: 9 both male and female; **no** one was to hold a fellow Jew in bondage.
34:10 their male and female slaves and **no** longer hold them in bondage.
35: 8 **Neither** we nor our wives nor our sons and daughters have ever
35: 9 or **[RPH]** built houses to live in or had vineyards, fields or crops.
35:14 'Jonadab son of Recab ordered his sons **not** to drink wine and this
36:25 Delaiah and Gemariah urged the king **not** to burn the scroll,
38:26 'I was pleading with the king **not** to send me back to Jonathan's
42:13 and so **disobey** [+928+7754+9048] the LORD your God,
44: 5 turn from their wickedness or **stop** burning incense to other gods.
44: 7 and infants, and so leave yourselves **without** a remnant?
51:62 destroy this place, so that **neither** man nor animal will live in it;
Eze 3:21 if you do warn the righteous man **not** to sin and he does not sin,
13: 3 prophets who follow their own spirit and have seen **nothing!**
13:22 because you encouraged the wicked **not** to turn from their evil
16:28 with the Assyrians too, because you *were* **insatiable** [+8429];
17:14 **unable** to rise again, surviving only by keeping his treaty.
20: 9 for the sake of my name I did what would **keep** it **from** being
20:14 for the sake of my name I did what would **keep** it **from** being
20:15 desert that I would **not** bring them into the land I had given them—
20:22 for the sake of my name I did what would **keep** it **from** being
22:30 in the gap on behalf of the land so I would **not** have to destroy it,
24: 8 I put her blood on the bare rock, so that it would **not** be covered.
29:15 will make it so weak that it will **never** *again* rule over the nations.
33:15 the decrees that give life, and does **no** evil, he will surely live;
46:20 to **avoid** bringing them into the outer court and consecrating the
Da 9:11 has transgressed your law and turned away, **refusing** to obey you.
11:18 to his insolence and **[NIE]** will turn his insolence back upon him.
Hos 13: 4 You shall acknowledge no God but me, no Savior **except** me.
Am 3: 3 Do two walk together **unless** [+561] they have agreed to do so?
3: 4 no prey? Does he growl in his den when he has caught **nothing**?

[F] Hitpael (hitpoel, hitpoal, hitpolel, hitpolal, hitpalel, hitpalal, hitpalpel, hitpalpal, hotpael, hotpaal) [G] Hiphil (hiphtil) [H] Hophal [I] Hishtaphel

1195 ¹בָּמָה bāmâ[1], n.f. [102] [→ 192?, 1196, 1199, 1200]

high places [62], high place [20], heights [9], there[s] [+928+2021] [4], mound [2], *untranslated* [1], shrines [1], there[s] [+928+2021] [1], tops [1], waves [1]

Lev 26:30 I will destroy your **high places**, cut down your incense altars
Nu 21:28 It consumed Ar of Moab, the citizens of Arnon's **heights**.
33:52 and their cast idols, and demolish all their **high places**.
Dt 32:13 He made him ride on the **heights** *of* the land and fed him with the
33:29 cower before you, and you will trample down their **high places**."
1Sa 9:12 to our town today, for the people have a sacrifice at the **high place**.
9:13 you will find him before he goes up to the **high place** to eat.
9:14 was Samuel, coming toward them on his way up to the **high place**.
9:19 "Go up ahead of me to the **high place**, for today you are to eat with
9:25 After they came down from the **high place** to the town, Samuel
10:5 of prophets coming down from the **high place** with lyres,
10:13 After Saul stopped prophesying, he went to the **high place**.
2Sa 1:19 "Your glory, O Israel, lies slain on your **heights**. How the mighty
1:25 mighty have fallen in battle! Jonathan lies slain on your **heights**.
22:34 feet like the feet of a deer; he enables me to stand on the **heights**.
1Ki 3:2 The people, however, were still sacrificing at the **high places**,
3:3 that he offered sacrifices and burned incense on the **high places**.
3:4 to offer sacrifices, for that was the most important **high place**,
11:7 Solomon built a **high place** for Chemosh the detestable god of
12:31 Jeroboam built shrines on **high places** and appointed priests from
12:32 at Bethel he also installed priests at the **high places** he had made.
13:2 On you he will sacrifice the priests of the **high places** who now
13:32 against all the shrines on the **high places** in the towns of Samaria
13:33 once more appointed priests for the **high places** from all sorts of
13:33 who wanted to become a priest he consecrated for the **high places**.
14:23 They also set up for themselves **high places**, sacred stones
15:14 Although he did not remove the **high places**, Asa's heart was fully
22:43 [22:44] The **high places**, however, were not removed,
22:43 [22:44] to offer sacrifices and burn incense **there**[s] [+928+2021].
2Ki 12:3 [12:4] The **high places**, however, were not removed; the people
12:3 [12:4] to offer sacrifices and burn incense **there** [+928+2021].
14:4 The **high places**, however, were not removed; the people
14:4 continued to offer sacrifices and burn incense **there**[s] [+928+2021].
15:4 The **high places**, however, were not removed; the people
15:4 continued to offer sacrifices and burn incense **there**[s] [+928+2021].
15:35 The **high places**, however, were not removed; the people
15:35 continued to offer sacrifices and burn incense **there**[s] [+928+2021].
16:4 He offered sacrifices and burned incense at the **high places**,
17:9 fortified city they built themselves **high places** in all their towns.
17:11 At every **high place** they burned incense, as the nations whom the
17:29 in the shrines the people of Samaria had made at the **high places**.
17:32 for them as priests **[RPH]** in the shrines at the high places.
17:32 to officiate for them as priests in the shrines at the **high places**.
18:4 He removed the **high places**, smashed the sacred stones and cut
18:22 isn't he the one whose **high places** and altars Hezekiah removed,
21:3 He rebuilt the **high places** his father Hezekiah had destroyed;
23:5 of Judah to burn incense on the **high places** of the towns of Judah
23:8 the priests from the towns of Judah and desecrated the **high places**,
23:8 He broke down the **shrines** *at* the gates—at the entrance to the
23:9 Although the priests of the **high places** did not serve at the altar of
23:13 The king also desecrated the **high places** that were east of
23:15 the altar at Bethel, the **high place** made by Jeroboam son of Nebat,
23:15 caused Israel to sin—even that altar and **high place** he demolished.
23:15 He burned the **high place** and ground it to powder, and burned the
23:19 defiled all the shrines at the **high places** that the kings of Israel had
23:20 Josiah slaughtered all the priests of those **high places** on the altars
1Ch 16:39 before the tabernacle of the LORD at the **high place** in Gibeon
21:29 the altar of burnt offering were at that time on the **high place** at
2Ch 1:3 and the whole assembly went to the **high place** at Gibeon,
1:13 Then Solomon went to Jerusalem from the **high place** at Gibeon,
11:15 he appointed his own priests for the **high places** and for the goat
14:3 [14:2] He removed the foreign altars and the **high places**,
14:5 [14:4] He removed the **high places** and incense altars in every
15:17 Although he did not remove the **high places** from Israel,
17:6 he removed the **high places** and the Asherah poles from Judah.
20:33 The **high places**, however, were not removed, and the people still
21:11 He had also built **high places** on the hills of Judah and had caused
28:4 He offered sacrifices and burned incense at the **high places**,
28:25 In every town in Judah he built **high places** to burn sacrifices to
31:1 They destroyed the **high places** and the altars throughout Judah
32:12 Did not Hezekiah himself remove this god's **high places**
33:3 He rebuilt the **high places** his father Hezekiah had demolished;
33:17 The people, however, continued to sacrifice at the **high places**,
33:19 and the sites where he built **high places** and set up Asherah poles
34:3 year he began to purge Judah and Jerusalem of **high places**,
Job 9:8 alone stretches out the heavens and treads on the **waves** *of* the sea.
Ps 18:33 [18:34] the feet of a deer; he enables me to stand on the **heights**.
78:58 They angered him with their **high places**; they aroused his jealousy
Isa 14:14 I will ascend above the **tops** *of* the clouds; I will make myself like
15:2 Dibon goes up to its temple, to its **high places** to weep;
16:12 When Moab appears at her **high place**, she only wears herself out;
36:7 isn't he the one whose **high places** and altars Hezekiah removed,
58:14 I will cause you to ride on the **heights** *of* the land and to feast on
Jer 7:31 They have built the **high places** *of* Topheth in the Valley of Ben
17:3 together with your **high places**, because of sin throughout your
19:5 They have built the **high places** *of* Baal to burn their sons in the
26:18 heap of rubble, the temple hill a **mound** *overgrown with* thickets.'
32:35 They built **high places** *for* Baal in the Valley of Ben Hinnom to
48:35 I will put an end to those who make offerings on the **high places**
Eze 6:3 to bring a sword against you, and I will destroy your **high places**.
6:6 the towns will be laid waste and the **high places** demolished,
16:16 You took some of your garments to make gaudy **high places**,
20:29 What is this **high place** you go to?' " (It is called Bamah to this
36:2 "Aha! The ancient **heights** have become our possession." '
43:7 and the lifeless idols of their kings at their **high places**.
Hos 10:8 The **high places** *of* wickedness will be destroyed—it is the sin of
Am 4:13 turns dawn to darkness, and treads the **high places** *of* the earth—
7:9 "The **high places** *of* Isaac will be destroyed and the sanctuaries of
Mic 1:3 he comes down and treads the **high places** *of* the earth.
1:5 Is it not Samaria? What is Judah's **high place**? Is it not Jerusalem?
3:12 a heap of rubble, the temple hill a **mound** overgrown with thickets.
Hab 3:19 my feet like the feet of a deer, he enables me to go on the **heights**.

1196 ²בָּמָה bāmâ[2], n.pr.loc. [1] [√ 1195]

Bamah [1]

Eze 20:29 What is this high place you go to?' " (It is called **Bamah** to this

1197 בִּמְהָל bimhāl, n.pr.m. [1] [√ 1201 + 4543]

Bimhal [1]

1Ch 7:33 The sons of Japhlet: Pasach, **Bimhal** and Ashvath. These were

1198 בְּמוֹ b[e]mô, pp. [10] [√ 928]

untranslated [2], in [2], with [2], from [1], take [+995] [1], through [1], used for fuel [+836+8596] [1]

Job 9:30 Even if I washed myself **with** [Q 928+4784] soap and my hands
16:4 make fine speeches against you and shake **[OBJ]** my head at you.
16:5 **[OBJ]** comfort from my lips would bring you relief.
19:16 but he does not answer, though I beg him **with** my own mouth.
37:8 The animals **take** [+995] cover; they remain in their dens.
Ps 11:2 they set their arrows against the strings to shoot **from** the shadows
Isa 25:10 Moab will be trampled under him as straw is trampled down **in** the
43:2 When you walk **through** the fire, you will not be burned;
44:16 Half of the wood he burns **in** the fire; over it he prepares his meal,
44:19 or understanding to say, "Half of it *I* **used for fuel** [+836+8596];

1199 בָּמוֹת bāmôt, n.pr.loc. [2] [√ 1195]

Bamoth [2]

Nu 21:19 from Mattanah to Nahaliel, from Nahaliel to **Bamoth**,
21:20 from **Bamoth** to the valley in Moab where the top of Pisgah

1200 בָּמוֹת בַּעַל bāmôt ba'al, n.pr.loc. [2] [√ 1195 + 1251]

Bamoth Baal [2]

Nu 22:41 The next morning Balak took Balaam up to **Bamoth Baal**,
Jos 13:17 on the plateau, including Dibon, **Bamoth Baal**, Beth Baal Meon,

1201 ¹בֵּן bēn[1], n.m. [4921 / 4930] [→ 1202, 1217, 1232; cf. 1215, 1337; Ar 10120; *also used with compound proper names*]

son [1846], sons [820], Israelites [+3776] [485], descendants [229], *untranslated* [227], children [175], old [153], people [85], Ammonites [+6648] [79], young [54], Israelite [+3776] [50], men [35], men [+132] [23], Israel [+3776] [21], Benjamites [+1228] [17], Reubenites [+8017] [17], Gadites [+1514] [16], Levites [+4290] [15], Benjamin [+1228] [13], descendant [12], son's [12], them[s] [+3776] [12], Judah [+3373] [11], age [10], foreigners [+5797] [10], man [+132] [10], Ammon [+6648] [9], children's [9], company [9], Danites [+1968] [9], Hittites [+3147] [9], Merarites [+5356] [9], they[s] [+3776] [9], Ammonite [+6648] [8], grandchildren [+1201] [8], people [+6639] [8], Gad [+1514] [7], Kohathite [+7740] [7], Merarite [+5356] [7], countrymen [+6639] [6], Ephraim [+713] [6], exiles [+1583] [6], Gershonites [+1767] [6], grandson [+1201] [6], grandson [6], grandsons [+1201] [6], mankind [+132] [6], Reuben [+8017] [6], Asher [+888] [5], Assyrians [+855] [5], boy [5], foreigner [+5797] [5], line [5], Manasseh [+4985] [5], Naphtali [+5889] [5], peoples [5], Simeon [+9058] [5], their[s] [+2257] [5], year-old [+9102] [5], Zebulun [+2282] [5], able men [+2657] [4], age [+9102] [4], Anakites [+6737] [4], brave [+2657] [4], cousin [+1856] [4], Dan [+1968] [4], descended [4], Ephraimites [+713] [4], grandsons [4], Issachar [+3779] [4], Kohathites [+7740]

[4], man [4], Simeonites [+9058] [4], child [3], Kohathites [+7741] [3], Levites [+4291] [3], one[s] [3], princes [+4889] [3], princes [3], scoundrels [+1175] [3], their[s] [+3870] [3], whose[s] [3], wicked [+1175] [3], ages [+9102] [2], angels [+466+2021] [2], Babylonians [+951] [2], born [2], calf [+1330] [2], calves [2], common people [+6639] [2], condemned to [2], cubs [2], Ephraimite [+713] [2], father[s] [2], fruitful vine [+7238] [2], Gershonite [+1767] [2], grandchildren [2], him[s] [+3870] [2], hostages [+9510] [2], Israelite [+408+3776+4946] [2], Israelites [+3776+4946] [2], Joseph [+3441] [2], lambs [+7366] [2], lay people [+6639] [2], man's [+132] [2], Manassites [+4985] [2], mortal men [+132] [2], nephew [+278] [2], overnight [+4326] [2], they[s] [+1201+1514+2256+8017] [2], they[s] [+5797] [2], young men [2], Aaronic [+195] [1], able [+2657] [1], able-bodied [+2657] [1], Ahohite [+292] [1], all mankind [+132] [1], all men [+132+2021] [1], angels [+466] [1], anointed [+2021+3658] [1], army [1], arrows [+8008] [1], arrows[s] [1], babies [1], Babylonian [+951] [1], Benjamin [+408+3549] [1], birth [1], bravely [+2657+4200] [1], bravest soldier [+2657] [1], brood [1], brothers [+1061] [1], bull [+1330] [1], calves [+1330] [1], children [+1887] [1], children's [+4200] [1], choice [1], clans [1], colt [+912] [1], courageous [+2657] [1], cousins on their father's side [+1856] [1], Cushites [+3934] [1], deserve to [1], deserves to [1], deserves [1], destitute [+2710] [1], disciple [1], Edomites [+121] [1], Egyptians [+5213] [1], especially bred [+2021+8247] [1], evildoers [+6594] [1], families [1], fertile [+9043] [1], fighting [+2657] [1], foal [1], foreigner [+2021+5797] [1], foreigners [+2021+5797] [1], Gad [+1532] [1], Gershonite [+1769] [1], Gershonites [+1768] [1], Gershonites [+1769] [1], Gilead [+1680] [1], goats [+6436] [1], granddaughters [+1426] [1], Greeks [+3436] [1], Hacmonite [+2685] [1], he[s] [+281+6687] [1], heavenly beings [+446] [1], high [+408] [1], highborn [+408] [1], him[s] [+2021+3778] [1], him[s] [+2023] [1], his people[s] [+3147] [1], human [+132] [1], Israelite [+3776+4200] [1], Israelite [+3776+4946] [1], Israelite [+928+3776] [1], Israelites [+3776+6639] [1], Israelites [+906+3776] [1], Jaakanites [+3622] [1], Judah's [+3373] [1], Kedar [+7723] [1], Kohathite [+7741] [1], Korahites [+7948] [1], low [+132] [1], low among men [+132] [1], lowborn men [+132] [1], Maacathite [+5084] [1], members [1], men [+132+2021] [1], men [+408] [1], mighty [+446] [1], Moabites [+4566] [1], murderer [+8357] [1], must die [+4638] [1], my[s] [+2257] [1], native [+6639] [1], nephews [+2157] [1], noisy boasters [+8623] [1], of Gilead [+1682] [1], of Judah [+3373] [1], one who will inherit [+5479] [1], one [1], opening of the womb [+5402] [1], oppressed [+6715] [1], people [+132] [1], prince [+4889] [1], proud [+8832] [1], proud beasts [+8832] [1], rebellious [+5308] [1], Reuben [+8018] [1], Reubenite [+8017] [1], servant [1], singers [+8876] [1], slave born in household [+563] [1], soldiers [+2657] [1], some[s] [1], sparks [+8404] [1], successors [1], their[s] [+6648] [1], their[s] [+1769+2021] [1], their[s] [1], them[s] [+3620] [1], them[s] [+6648] [1], them[s] [+4013] [1], these men[s] [+2021+5566] [1], they[s] [+1228] [1], they[s] [+1968] [1], they[s] [+6648] [1], they[s] [+2257] [1], they[s] [+851+2021] [1], tribe [1], tribes [1], troops [+1522] [1], troublemakers [+1175] [1], valiant fighter [+408+2644] [1], valiant fighter [+408+2657] [1], vassal [1], very own brother [+278+562+3870] [1], vultures [+5979] [1], warriors [+2657] [1], who[s] [+3776] [1], Zadokites [+7401] [1], Zerahites [+2438] [1]

Ge 3:16 pains in childbearing; with pain you will give birth to **children**.
4:17 Cain was then building a city, and he named it after his **son** Enoch.
4:25 and she gave birth to a **son** and named him Seth, saying,
4:26 Seth also had a **son**, and he named him Enosh. At that time men
5: 4 was born, Adam lived 800 years and had other **sons** and daughters.
5: 7 of Enosh, Seth lived 807 years and had other **sons** and daughters.
5:10 of Kenan, Enosh lived 815 years and had other **sons** and daughters.
5:13 Kenan lived 840 years and had other **sons** and daughters.
5:16 Mahalalel lived 830 years and had other **sons** and daughters.
5:19 of Enoch, Jared lived 800 years and had other **sons** and daughters.
5:22 walked with God 300 years and had other **sons** and daughters.
5:26 Methuselah lived 782 years and had other **sons** and daughters.
5:28 When Lamech had lived 182 years, he had a **son**.
5:30 Lamech lived 595 years and had other **sons** and daughters.
5:32 After Noah was 500 years **old**, he became the father of Shem,
6: 2 the **sons** *of* God saw that the daughters of men were beautiful,
6: 4 when the **sons** *of* God went to the daughters of men and had
6:10 Noah had three **sons**: Shem, Ham and Japheth.
6:18 you and your **sons** and your wife and your sons' wives with you.
6:18 and your sons and your wife and your **sons'** wives with you.
7: 6 Noah was six hundred years **old** when the floodwaters came on the
7: 7 Noah and his **sons** and his wife and his sons' wives entered the ark
7: 7 his **sons'** wives entered the ark to escape the waters of the flood.
7:13 On that very day Noah and his **sons**, Shem, Ham and Japheth,
7:13 and Japheth, together with his wife and the wives of his three **sons**,
8:16 out of the ark, you and your wife and your **sons** and their wives.
8:16 you and your wife and your sons and **their**[s] [+3870] wives.
8:18 came out, together with his **sons** and his wife and his sons' wives.
8:18 came out, together with his sons and his wife and his **sons'** wives.
9: 1 Then God blessed Noah and his **sons**, saying to them, "Be fruitful
9: 8 Then God said to Noah and to his **sons** with him:
9:18 The **sons** *of* Noah who came out of the ark were Shem, Ham
9:19 These were the three **sons** *of* Noah, and from them came the people
9:24 his wine and found out what his youngest **son** had done to him,
10: 1 This is the account of Shem, Ham and Japheth, Noah's **sons**,
10: 1 and Japheth, Noah's sons, who themselves had **sons** after the flood.
10: 2 The **sons** *of* Japheth: Gomer, Magog, Madai, Javan, Tubal,
10: 3 The **sons** *of* Gomer: Ashkenaz, Riphath and Togarmah.
10: 4 The **sons** *of* Javan: Elishah, Tarshish, the Kittim and the Rodanim.
10: 6 The **sons** *of* Ham: Cush, Mizraim, Put and Canaan.
10: 7 The **sons** *of* Cush: Seba, Havilah, Sabtah, Raamah and Sabteca.
10: 7 Raamah and Sabteca. The **sons** *of* Raamah: Sheba and Dedan.
10:20 These are the **sons** *of* Ham by their clans and languages, in their
10:21 brother was Japheth; Shem was the ancestor of all the **sons** *of* Eber.
10:22 The **sons** *of* Shem: Elam, Asshur, Arphaxad, Lud and Aram.
10:23 The **sons** *of* Aram: Uz, Hul, Gether and Meshech.
10:25 Two **sons** were born to Eber: One was named Peleg, because in his
10:29 Ophir, Havilah and Jobab. All these were **sons** *of* Joktan.
10:31 These are the **sons** *of* Shem by their clans and languages, in their
10:32 These are the clans of Noah's **sons**, according to their lines of
11: 5 to see the city and the tower that the **men** [+132] were building.
11:10 Two years after the flood, when Shem was 100 years **old**,
11:11 Shem lived 500 years and had other **sons** and daughters.
11:13 Arphaxad lived 403 years and had other **sons** and daughters.
11:15 of Eber, Shelah lived 403 years and had other **sons** and daughters.
11:17 of Peleg, Eber lived 430 years and had other **sons** and daughters.
11:19 of Reu, Peleg lived 209 years and had other **sons** and daughters.
11:21 of Serug, Reu lived 207 years and had other **sons** and daughters.
11:23 of Nahor, Serug lived 200 years and had other **sons** and daughters.
11:25 of Terah, Nahor lived 119 years and had other **sons** and daughters.
11:31 Terah took his **son** Abram, his grandson Lot son of Haran,
11:31 took his son Abram, his **grandson** [+1201] Lot son of Haran,
11:31 took his son Abram, his **grandson** [+1201] Lot son of Haran,
11:31 Terah took his son Abram, his grandson Lot **son** *of* Haran,
11:31 and his daughter-in-law Sarai, the wife of his **son** Abram,
12: 4 Abram was seventy-five years **old** when he set out from Haran.
12: 5 He took his wife Sarai, his **nephew** [+278] Lot, all the possessions
14:12 They also carried off Abram's **nephew** [+278] Lot and his
15: 2 the **one who will inherit** [+5479] my estate is Eliezer of
15: 3 me no children; so a **servant** *in* my household will be my heir."
16:11 "You are now with child and you will have a **son**. You shall name
16:15 So Hagar bore Abram a **son**, and Abram gave the name Ishmael to
16:15 and Abram gave the name Ishmael to the **son** she had borne.
16:16 Abram was eighty-six years **old** when Hagar bore him Ishmael.
17: 1 When Abram was ninety-nine years **old**, the LORD appeared to
17:12 every male among you who is eight days **old** must be circumcised,
17:12 your household or bought with money from a **foreigner** [+5797]—
17:16 I will bless her and will surely give you a **son** by her. I will bless
17:17 said to himself, "Will a son be born to a *man* a hundred years **old**?
17:19 Then God said, "Yes, but your wife Sarah will bear you a **son**,
17:23 On that very day Abraham took his **son** Ishmael and all those born
17:24 Abraham was ninety-nine years **old** when he was circumcised,
17:25 and his **son** Ishmael was thirteen;
17:25 and his son Ishmael was thirteen; **[RPH]**
17:26 and his **son** Ishmael were both circumcised on that same day.
17:27 those born in his household or bought from a **foreigner** [+5797],
18: 7 and selected a choice, tender **calf** [+1330] and gave it to a servant,
18: 8 some curds and milk and the **calf** [+1330] that had been prepared,
18:10 about this time next year, and Sarah your wife will have a **son**."
18:14 to you at the appointed time next year and Sarah will have a **son**."
18:19 so that he will direct his **children** and his household after him to
19:12 sons-in-law, **sons** or daughters, or anyone else in the city who
19:37 The older daughter had a **son**, and she named him Moab; he is the
19:38 The younger daughter also had a **son**, and she named him
19:38 he is the father of the **Ammonites** [+6648] of today.
21: 2 Sarah became pregnant and bore a **son** to Abraham in his old age,
21: 3 Abraham gave the name Isaac to the **son** Sarah bore him.
21: 4 When his **son** Isaac was eight days old, Abraham circumcised him,
21: 4 When his son Isaac was eight days **old**, Abraham circumcised him,
21: 5 Abraham was a hundred years **old** when his son Isaac was born to
21: 5 Abraham was a hundred years old when his **son** Isaac was born to
21: 7 would have said to Abraham that Sarah would nurse **children**?
21: 7 would nurse children? Yet I have borne him a **son** in his old age."
21: 9 Sarah saw that the **son** whom Hagar the Egyptian had borne to
21:10 she said to Abraham, "Get rid of that slave woman and her **son**,
21:10 for that slave woman's **son** will never share in the inheritance with
21:10 son will never share in the inheritance with my **son** Isaac."
21:11 matter distressed Abraham greatly because it concerned his **son**.
21:13 I will make the **son** *of* the maidservant into a nation also,
22: 2 God said, "Take your **son**, your only son, Isaac, whom you love,
22: 3 his donkey. He took with him two of his servants and his **son** Isaac.
22: 6 took the wood for the burnt offering and placed it on his **son** Isaac,
22: 7 and said to his father Abraham, "Father?" "Yes, my **son**?"
22: 8 himself will provide the lamb for the burnt offering, my **son**."

Ge 22: 9 He bound his **son** Isaac and laid him on the altar, on top of the
22: 10 Then he reached out his hand and took the knife to slay his **son**.
22: 12 because you have not withheld from me your **son**, your only son."
22: 13 took the ram and sacrificed it as a burnt offering instead of his **son**.
22: 16 because you have done this and have not withheld your **son**,
22: 20 is also a mother; she has borne **sons** to your brother Nahor:
23: 3 rose from beside his dead wife and spoke to the **Hittites** [+3147].
23: 5 The **Hittites** [+3147] replied to Abraham,
23: 7 bowed down before the people of the land, the **Hittites** [+3147].
23: 8 listen to me and intercede with Ephron **son** *of* Zohar on my behalf
23: 10 Ephron the Hittite was sitting among **his people**[s] [+3147]
23: 10 he replied to Abraham in the hearing of all the **Hittites** [+3147]
23: 11 I give it to you in the presence of my **people** [+6639]. Bury your
23: 16 him the price he had named in the hearing of the **Hittites** [+3147]:
23: 18 of all the **Hittites** [+3147] who had come to the gate of the city.
23: 20 the cave in it were deeded to Abraham by the **Hittites** [+3147] as a
24: 3 that you will not get a wife for my **son** from the daughters of the
24: 4 my country and my own relatives and get a wife for my **son** Isaac."
24: 5 Shall I then take your **son** back to the country you came from?"
24: 6 "Make sure that you do not take my **son** back there," Abraham
24: 7 angel before you so that you can get a wife for my **son** from there.
24: 8 from this oath of mine. Only do not take my **son** back there."
24: 15 She was the daughter of Bethuel **son** *of* Milcah, who was the wife
24: 24 "I am the daughter of Bethuel, the **son** that Milcah bore to Nahor."
24: 36 My master's wife Sarah has borne him a **son** in her old age,
24: 37 'You must not get a wife for my **son** from the daughters of the
24: 38 my father's family and to my own clan, and get a wife for my **son**.'
24: 40 so that you can get a wife for my **son** from my own clan and from
24: 44 let her be the one the LORD has chosen for my master's **son**.'
24: 47 "She said, 'The daughter of Bethuel **son** *of* Nahor, whom Milcah
24: 48 road to get the granddaughter of my master's brother for his **son**.
24: 51 and go, and let her become the wife of your master's **son**,
25: 3 the **descendants** *of* Dedan were the Asshurites, the Letushites
25: 4 The **sons** *of* Midian were Ephah, Epher, Hanoch, Abida
25: 4 Abida and Eldaah. All these were **descendants** *of* Keturah.
25: 6 he gave gifts to the **sons** *of* his concubines and sent them away
25: 6 and sent them away from his **son** Isaac to the land of the east.
25: 9 His **sons** Isaac and Ishmael buried him in the cave of Machpelah
25: 9 near Mamre, in the field of Ephron **son** *of* Zohar the Hittite,
25: 10 the field Abraham had bought from the **Hittites** [+3147].
25: 11 God blessed his **son** Isaac, who then lived near Beer Lahai Roi.
25: 12 This is the account of Abraham's **son** Ishmael, whom Sarah's
25: 13 These are the names of the **sons** *of* Ishmael, listed in the order of
25: 16 These were the **sons** *of* Ishmael, and these are the names of the
25: 19 This is the account of Abraham's **son** Isaac. Abraham became the
25: 20 Isaac was forty years **old** when he married Rebekah daughter of
25: 22 The **babies** jostled each other within her, and she said, "Why is
25: 26 Isaac was sixty years **old** when Rebekah gave birth to them.
26: 34 When Esau was forty years **old**, he married Judith daughter of
27: 1 he called for Esau his older **son** and said to him, "My son."
27: 1 he called for Esau his older son and said to him, "My **son**."
27: 5 Now Rebekah was listening as Isaac spoke to his **son** Esau.
27: 6 Rebekah said to her **son** Jacob, "Look, I overheard your father say
27: 8 Now, my **son**, listen carefully and do what I tell you:
27: 13 His mother said to him, "My **son**, let the curse fall on me.
27: 15 Then Rebekah took the best clothes of Esau her older **son**,
27: 15 she had in the house, and put them on her younger **son** Jacob.
27: 17 she handed to her **son** Jacob the tasty food and the bread she had
27: 18 and said, "My father." "Yes, my **son**," he answered. "Who is it?"
27: 20 Isaac asked his **son**, "How did you find it so quickly, my son?"
27: 20 Isaac asked his son, "How did you find it so quickly, my **son**?"
27: 21 Then Isaac said to Jacob, "Come near so I can touch you, my **son**,
27: 21 my son, to know whether you really are my **son** Esau or not."
27: 24 "Are you really my **son** Esau?" he asked. "I am," he replied.
27: 25 Then he said, "My **son**, bring me some of your game to eat,
27: 26 his father Isaac said to him, "Come here, my **son**, and kiss me."
27: 27 the smell of my **son** is like the smell of a field that the LORD has
27: 29 your brothers, and may the **sons** *of* your mother bow down to you.
27: 31 said to him, "My father, sit up and eat some of **my**[s] [+2257] game,
27: 32 are you?" "I am your **son**," he answered, "your firstborn, Esau."
27: 37 and new wine. So what can I possibly do for you, my **son**?"
27: 42 When Rebekah was told what her older **son** Esau had said,
27: 42 Esau had said, she sent for her younger **son** Jacob and said to him,
27: 43 Now then, my **son**, do what I say: Flee at once to my brother
28: 5 to Laban **son** *of* Bethuel the Aramean, the brother of Rebekah,
28: 9 the sister of Nebaioth and daughter of Ishmael **son** *of* Abraham,
29: 1 on his journey and came to the land of the eastern **peoples**.
29: 5 He said to them, "Do you know Laban, Nahor's **grandson**?"
29: 12 Rachel that he was a relative of her father and a **son** *of* Rebekah.
29: 13 the news about Jacob, his sister's **son**, he hurried to meet him.
29: 32 Leah became pregnant and gave birth to a **son**. She named him
29: 33 She conceived again, and when she gave birth to a **son** she said,
29: 34 Again she conceived, and when she gave birth to a **son** she said,
29: 34 will become attached to me, because I have borne him three **sons**."
29: 35 She conceived again, and when she gave birth to a **son** she said,
30: 1 of her sister. So she said to Jacob, "Give me **children**, or I'll die!"
30: 5 and she became pregnant and bore him a **son**.
30: 6 has vindicated me; he has listened to my plea and given me a **son**."
30: 7 servant Bilhah conceived again and bore Jacob a second **son**.
30: 10 Leah's servant Zilpah bore Jacob a **son**.
30: 12 Leah's servant Zilpah bore Jacob a second **son**.
30: 14 said to Leah, "Please give me some of your **son's** mandrakes."
30: 15 Will you take my **son's** mandrakes too?" "Very well," Rachel said,
30: 15 "he can sleep with you tonight in return for your **son's**
30: 16 with me," she said. "I have hired you with my **son's** mandrakes."
30: 17 to Leah, and she became pregnant and bore Jacob a fifth **son**.
30: 19 Leah conceived again and bore Jacob a sixth **son**.
30: 20 will treat me with honor, because I have borne him six **sons**."
30: 23 She became pregnant and gave birth to a **son** and said, "God has
30: 24 him Joseph, and said, "May the LORD add to me another **son**."
30: 35 the dark-colored lambs, and he placed them in the care of his **sons**.
31: 1 Jacob heard that Laban's **sons** were saying, "Jacob has taken
31: 16 God took away from our father belongs to us and our **children**.
31: 17 Then Jacob put his **children** and his wives on camels,
31: 28 You didn't even let me kiss my **grandchildren** and my daughters
31: 43 the **children** are my children, and the flocks are my flocks.
31: 43 the children are my **children**, and the flocks are my flocks.
31: 43 these daughters of mine, or about the **children** they have borne?
31: 55 [32:1] Early the next morning Laban kissed his **grandchildren**
32: 11 [32:12] and attack me, and also the mothers with their **children**.
32: 15 [32:16] thirty female camels with their **young**, forty cows and ten
32: 32 [32:33] Therefore to this day the **Israelites** [+3776] do not eat the
33: 19 he bought from the **sons** *of* Hamor, the father of Shechem,
34: 2 When Shechem **son** *of* Hamor the Hivite, the ruler of that area,
34: 5 had been defiled, his **sons** were in the fields with his livestock;
34: 7 Now Jacob's **sons** had come in from the fields as soon as they
34: 8 said to them, "My **son** Shechem has his heart set on your daughter.
34: 13 Jacob's **sons** replied deceitfully as they spoke to Shechem
34: 18 Their proposal seemed good to Hamor and his **son** Shechem.
34: 20 his **son** Shechem went to the gate of their city to speak to their
34: 24 went out of the city gate agreed with Hamor and his **son** Shechem,
34: 25 two of Jacob's **sons**, Simeon and Levi, Dinah's brothers, took their
34: 26 They put Hamor and his **son** Shechem to the sword and took Dinah
34: 27 The **sons** *of* Jacob came upon the dead bodies and looted the city
35: 5 the towns all around them so that no one pursued **them**[s] [+3620].
35: 17 midwife said to her, "Don't be afraid, for you have another **son**."
35: 22 concubine Bilhah, and Israel heard of it. Jacob had twelve **sons**:
35: 23 The **sons** *of* Leah: Reuben the firstborn of Jacob, Simeon,
35: 24 The **sons** *of* Rachel: Joseph and Benjamin.
35: 25 The **sons** *of* Rachel's maidservant Bilhah: Dan and Naphtali.
35: 26 The **sons** *of* Leah's maidservant Zilpah: Gad and Asher.
35: 26 These were the **sons** *of* Jacob, who were born to him in Paddan
35: 29 and full of years. And his **sons** Esau and Jacob buried him.
36: 5 These were the **sons** *of* Esau, who were born to him in Canaan.
36: 6 Esau took his wives and **sons** and daughters and all the members of
36: 10 These are the names of Esau's **sons**: Eliphaz, the son of Esau's
36: 10 Eliphaz, the **son** *of* Esau's wife Adah, and Reuel, the son of Esau's
36: 10 of Esau's wife Adah, and Reuel, the **son** *of* Esau's wife Basemath.
36: 11 The **sons** *of* Eliphaz: Teman, Omar, Zepho, Gatam and Kenaz.
36: 12 Esau's **son** Eliphaz also had a concubine named Timna, who bore
36: 12 bore him Amalek. These were **grandsons** *of* Esau's wife Adah.
36: 13 The **sons** *of* Reuel: Nahath, Zerah, Shammah and Mizzah.
36: 13 and Mizzah. These were **grandsons** *of* Esau's wife Basemath.
36: 14 The **sons** *of* Esau's wife Oholibamah daughter of Anah
36: 15 These were the chiefs among Esau's **descendants**: The sons of
36: 15 The **sons** *of* Eliphaz the firstborn of Esau: Chiefs Teman, Omar,
36: 16 descended from Eliphaz in Edom; they were **grandsons** *of* Adah.
36: 17 The **sons** *of* Esau's son Reuel: Chiefs Nahath, Zerah, Shammah
36: 17 The sons of Esau's **son** Reuel: Chiefs Nahath, Zerah, Shammah
36: 17 Reuel in Edom; they were **grandsons** *of* Esau's wife Basemath.
36: 18 The **sons** *of* Esau's wife Oholibamah: Chiefs Jeush, Jalam
36: 19 These were the **sons** *of* Esau (that is, Edom), and these were their
36: 20 These were the **sons** *of* Seir the Horite, who were living in the
36: 21 and Dishan. These **sons** *of* Seir in Edom were Horite chiefs.
36: 22 The **sons** *of* Lotan: Hori and Homam. Timna was Lotan's sister.
36: 23 The **sons** *of* Shobal: Alvan, Manahath, Ebal, Shepho and Onam.
36: 24 The **sons** *of* Zibeon: Aiah and Anah. This is the Anah who
36: 25 The **children** *of* Anah: Dishon and Oholibamah daughter of Anah.
36: 26 The **sons** *of* Dishon: Hemdan, Eshban, Ithran and Keran.
36: 27 The **sons** *of* Ezer: Bilhan, Zaavan and Akan.
36: 28 The **sons** *of* Dishan: Uz and Aran.
36: 31 who reigned in Edom before any **Israelite** [+3776] king reigned:
36: 32 Bela **son** *of* Beor became king of Edom. His city was named
36: 33 Bela died, Jobab **son** *of* Zerah from Bozrah succeeded him as king.
36: 35 When Husham died, Hadad **son** *of* Bedad, who defeated Midian in
36: 38 Shaul died, Baal-Hanan **son** *of* Acbor succeeded him as king.
36: 39 When Baal-Hanan **son** *of* Acbor died, Hadad succeeded him as
37: 2 **[NIE]** was tending the flocks with his brothers, the sons of Bilhah

Ge 37: 2 the **sons** *of* Bilhah and the sons of Zilpah, his father's wives,
37: 2 the sons of Bilhah and the **sons** *of* Zilpah, his father's wives,
37: 3 Now Israel loved Joseph more than any of his *other* **sons**,
37: 3 of his other sons, because he had been **born** to him *in* his old age;
37:32 "We found this. Examine it to see whether it is your **son's** robe."
37:33 He recognized it and said, "It is my **son's** robe! Some ferocious
37:34 his clothes, put on sackcloth and mourned for his **son** many days.
37:35 All his **sons** and daughters came to comfort him, but he refused to
37:35 he said, "in mourning will I go down to the grave to my **son**."
38: 3 she became pregnant and gave birth to a **son**, who was named Er.
38: 4 She conceived again and gave birth to a **son** and named him Onan.
38: 5 She gave birth to still another **son** and named him Shelah.
38:11 "Live as a widow in your father's house until my **son** Shelah grows
38:26 more righteous than I, since I wouldn't give her to my **son** Shelah."
41:46 Joseph was thirty years **old** when he entered the service of Pharaoh
41:50 two **sons** were born to Joseph by Asenath daughter of Potiphera,
42: 1 he said to his **sons**, "Why do you just keep looking at each other?"
42: 5 So Israel's **sons** were among those who went to buy grain,
42:11 We are all the **sons** *of* one man. Your servants are honest men,
42:13 the **sons** *of* one man, who lives in the land of Canaan.
42:32 We were twelve brothers, **sons** *of* one father. One is no more,
42:37 "You may put both of my **sons** to death if I do not bring him back
42:38 But Jacob said, "My **son** will not go down there with you;
43:29 his own mother's **son**, he asked, "Is this your youngest brother,
43:29 told me about?" And he said, "God be gracious to you, my **son**."
45: 9 to my father and say to him, 'This is what your **son** Joseph says:
45:10 you, your **children** and grandchildren, your flocks and herds,
45:10 you, your children and **grandchildren** [+1201], your flocks
45:10 you, your children and **grandchildren** [+1201], your flocks
45:21 So the **sons** *of* Israel did this. Joseph gave them carts, as Pharaoh
45:28 My **son** Joseph is still alive. I will go and see him before I die."
46: 5 and Israel's **sons** took their father Jacob and their children
46: 7 He took with him to Egypt his **sons** and grandsons and his
46: 7 and **grandsons** [+1201] and his daughters and granddaughters—
46: 7 and **grandsons** [+1201] and his daughters and granddaughters—
46: 7 and his daughters and **granddaughters** [+1426]—all his offspring.
46: 8 These are the names of the **sons** *of* Israel (Jacob and his
46: 8 are the names of the sons of Israel (Jacob and his **descendants**)
46: 9 The **sons** *of* Reuben: Hanoch, Pallu, Hezron and Carmi.
46:10 The **sons** *of* Simeon: Jemuel, Jamin, Ohad, Jakin, Zohar and Shaul
46:10 Ohad, Jakin, Zohar and Shaul the **son** *of* a Canaanite woman.
46:11 The **sons** *of* Levi: Gershon, Kohath and Merari.
46:12 The **sons** *of* Judah: Er, Onan, Shelah, Perez and Zerah (but Er
46:12 died in the land of Canaan). The **sons** *of* Perez: Hezron and Hamul.
46:13 The **sons** *of* Issachar: Tola, Puah, Jashub and Shimron.
46:14 The **sons** *of* Zebulun: Sered, Elon and Jahleel.
46:15 These were the **sons** Leah bore to Jacob in Paddan Aram, besides
46:15 These **sons** and daughters of his were thirty-three in all.
46:16 The **sons** *of* Gad: Zephon, Haggi, Shuni, Ezbon, Eri, Arodi
46:17 The **sons** *of* Asher: Imnah, Ishvah, Ishvi and Beriah. Their sister
46:17 Their sister was Serah. The **sons** *of* Beriah: Heber and Malkiel.
46:18 These were the **children** born to Jacob *by* Zilpah, whom Laban
46:19 The **sons** *of* Jacob's wife Rachel: Joseph and Benjamin.
46:21 The **sons** *of* Benjamin: Bela, Beker, Ashbel, Gera, Naaman,
46:22 These were the **sons** *of* Rachel who were born to Jacob—fourteen
46:23 The **son** *of* Dan: Hushim.
46:24 The **sons** *of* Naphtali: Jahziel, Guni, Jezer and Shillem.
46:25 These were the **sons** born to Jacob *by* Bilhah, whom Laban had
46:26 who were his direct descendants, not counting his **sons'** wives—
46:27 With the two **sons** who had been born to Joseph in Egypt,
47:29 he called for his **son** Joseph and said to him, "If I have found favor
48: 1 So he took his two **sons** Manasseh and Ephraim along with him.
48: 2 When Jacob was told, "Your **son** Joseph has come to you,"
48: 5 your two **sons** born to you in Egypt before I came to you here will
48: 8 When Israel saw the **sons** *of* Joseph, he asked, "Who are these?"
48: 9 "They are the **sons** God has given me here," Joseph said to his
48:19 his father refused and said, "I know, my **son**, I know. He too will
49: 1 Jacob called for his **sons** and said: "Gather around so I can tell you
49: 2 "Assemble and listen, **sons** *of* Jacob; listen to your father Israel.
49: 8 neck of your enemies; your father's **sons** will bow down to you.
49: 9 You are a lion's cub, O Judah; you return from the prey, my **son**.
49:11 tether his donkey to a vine, his **colt** [+912] to the choicest branch;
49:22 "Joseph is a **fruitful vine** [+7238], a fruitful vine near a spring,
49:22 "Joseph is a fruitful vine, a **fruitful vine** [+7238] near a spring,
49:32 and the cave in it were bought from the **Hittites** [+3147]."
49:33 When Jacob had finished giving instructions to his **sons**, he drew
50:12 So Jacob's **sons** did as he had commanded them:
50:13 **They**[s] [+2257] carried him to the land of Canaan and buried him in
50:23 saw the third generation of Ephraim's **children**. Also the children
50:23 Also the **children** *of* Makir son of Manasseh were placed at birth
50:23 Also the children of Makir **son** *of* Manasseh were placed at birth
50:25 And Joseph made the **sons** *of* Israel swear an oath and said,
50:26 So Joseph died at the **age** [+9102] *of* a hundred and ten. And after
Ex 1: 1 These are the names of the **sons** *of* Israel who went to Egypt with
1: 7 but the **Israelites** [+3776] were fruitful and multiplied greatly
1: 9 "the **Israelites** [+3776+6639] have become much too numerous for
1:12 and spread; so the Egyptians came to dread the **Israelites** [+3776]
1:13 and worked **them**[s] [+3776] ruthlessly.
1:16 and observe them on the delivery stool, if it is a **boy**, kill him;
1:22 "Every **boy** that is born you must throw into the Nile, but let every
2: 2 she became pregnant and gave birth to a **son**. When she saw that he
2:10 she took him to Pharaoh's daughter and he became her **son**.
2:22 Zipporah gave birth to a **son**, and Moses named him Gershom,
2:23 The **Israelites** [+3776] groaned in their slavery and cried out,
2:25 So God looked on the **Israelites** [+3776] and was concerned about
3: 9 And now the cry of the **Israelites** [+3776] has reached me,
3:10 Pharaoh to bring my people the **Israelites** [+3776] out of Egypt."
3:11 go to Pharaoh and bring the **Israelites** [+3776] out of Egypt?"
3:13 to God, "Suppose I go to the **Israelites** [+3776] and say to them,
3:14 WHO I AM. This is what you are to say to the **Israelites** [+3776]:
3:15 also said to Moses, "Say to the **Israelites** [+3776], 'The LORD,
3:22 and for clothing, which you will put on your **sons** and daughters.
4:20 So Moses took his wife and **sons**, put them on a donkey and started
4:22 'This is what the LORD says: Israel is my firstborn **son**,
4:23 I told you, "Let my **son** go, so he may worship me." But you
4:23 But you refused to let him go; so I will kill your firstborn **son**.' "
4:25 cut off her **son's** foreskin and touched ⌊Moses'⌋ feet with it.
4:29 and Aaron brought together all the elders of the **Israelites** [+3776],
4:31 they heard that the LORD was concerned about **them**[s] [+3776]
5:14 The **Israelite** [+3776] foremen appointed by Pharaoh's slave
5:15 Then the **Israelite** [+3776] foremen went and appealed to Pharaoh:
5:19 The **Israelite** [+3776] foremen realized they were in trouble when
6: 5 Moreover, I have heard the groaning of the **Israelites** [+3776],
6: 6 "Therefore, say to the **Israelites** [+3776]: 'I am the LORD,
6: 9 Moses reported this to the **Israelites** [+3776], but they did not
6:11 tell Pharaoh king of Egypt to let the **Israelites** [+3776] go out of
6:12 said to the LORD, "If the **Israelites** [+3776] will not listen to me,
6:13 and Aaron about the **Israelites** [+3776] and Pharaoh king of Egypt,
6:13 he commanded them to bring the **Israelites** [+3776] out of Egypt.
6:14 The **sons** *of* Reuben the firstborn son of Israel were Hanoch
6:15 The **sons** *of* Simeon were Jemuel, Jamin, Ohad, Jakin, Zohar
6:15 Ohad, Jakin, Zohar and Shaul the **son** *of* a Canaanite woman.
6:16 These were the names of the **sons** *of* Levi according to their
6:17 The **sons** *of* Gershon, by clans, were Libni and Shimei.
6:18 The **sons** *of* Kohath were Amram, Izhar, Hebron and Uzziel.
6:19 The **sons** *of* Merari were Mahli and Mushi. These were the clans of
6:21 The **sons** *of* Izhar were Korah, Nepheg and Zicri.
6:22 The **sons** *of* Uzziel were Mishael, Elzaphan and Sithri.
6:24 The **sons** *of* Korah were Assir, Elkanah and Abiasaph. These were
6:25 Eleazar **son** *of* Aaron married one of the daughters of Putiel,
6:26 "Bring the **Israelites** [+3776] out of Egypt by their divisions."
6:27 king of Egypt about bringing the **Israelites** [+3776] out of Egypt.
7: 2 your brother Aaron is to tell Pharaoh to let the **Israelites** [+3776]
7: 4 I will bring out my divisions, my people the **Israelites** [+3776].
7: 5 my hand against Egypt and bring the **Israelites** [+3776] out of it."
7: 7 Moses was eighty years **old** and Aaron eighty-three when they
7: 7 and Aaron eighty-three **[RPH]** when they spoke to Pharaoh.
9: 4 so that no animal belonging to the **Israelites** [+3776] will die.' "
9: 6 but not one animal belonging to the **Israelites** [+3776] died.
9:26 hail was the land of Goshen, where the **Israelites** [+3776] were.
9:35 heart was hard and he would not let the **Israelites** [+3776] go,
10: 2 that you may tell your **children** and grandchildren how I dealt
10: 2 and **grandchildren** [+1201] how I dealt harshly with the Egyptians
10: 2 and **grandchildren** [+1201] how I dealt harshly with the Egyptians
10: 9 "We will go with our young and old, with our **sons** and daughters,
10:20 Pharaoh's heart, and he would not let the **Israelites** [+3776] go.
10:23 Yet all the **Israelites** [+3776] had light in the places where they
11: 7 But among the **Israelites** [+3776] not a dog will bark at any man
11:10 and he would not let the **Israelites** [+3776] go out of his country.
12: 5 The animals you choose must be **year-old** [+9102] males without
12:24 instructions as a lasting ordinance for you and your **descendants**.
12:26 when your **children** ask you, 'What does this ceremony mean to
12:27 who passed over the houses of the **Israelites** [+3776] in Egypt
12:28 The **Israelites** [+3776] did just what the LORD commanded
12:31 Leave my people, you and the **Israelites** [+3776]! Go, worship the
12:35 The **Israelites** [+3776] did as Moses instructed and asked the
12:37 The **Israelites** [+3776] journeyed from Rameses to Succoth.
12:40 Now the length of time the **Israelite people** [+3776] lived in Egypt
12:42 on this night all the **Israelites** [+3776] are to keep vigil to honor
12:43 regulations for the Passover: "No **foreigner** [+5797] is to eat of it.
12:50 All the **Israelites** [+3776] did just what the LORD had
12:51 on that very day the LORD brought the **Israelites** [+3776] out of
13: 2 The first offspring of every womb among the **Israelites** [+3776]
13: 8 On that day tell your **son**, 'I do this because of what the LORD
13:13 break its neck. Redeem every firstborn among your **sons**.
13:14 "In days to come, when your **son** asks you, 'What does this mean?'
13:15 offspring of every womb and redeem each of my firstborn **sons**.'
13:18 The **Israelites** [+3776] went up out of Egypt armed for battle.

Ex 13:19 because Joseph had made the **sons** *of* Israel swear an oath.
14: 2 "Tell the **Israelites** [+3776] to turn back and encamp near Pi
14: 3 'The **Israelites** [+3776] are wandering around the land in
14: 8 so that he pursued the **Israelites** [+3776], who were marching out
14: 8 so that he pursued the Israelites, **who**[s] [+3776] were marching out
14:10 As Pharaoh approached, the **Israelites** [+3776] looked up,
14:10 They were terrified and cried out **[RPH]** to the LORD.
14:15 are you crying out to me? Tell the **Israelites** [+3776] to move on.
14:16 so that the **Israelites** [+3776] can go through the sea on dry
14:22 and the **Israelites** [+3776] went through the sea on dry ground,
14:29 But the **Israelites** [+3776] went through the sea on dry ground,
15: 1 and the **Israelites** [+3776] sang this song to the LORD:
15:19 but the **Israelites** [+3776] walked through the sea on dry ground.
16: 1 The whole **Israelite** [+3776] community set out from Elim
16: 2 In the desert the whole community **[RPH]** grumbled against
16: 3 The **Israelites** [+3776] said to them, "If only we had died by the
16: 6 So Moses and Aaron said to all the **Israelites** [+3776],
16: 9 Moses told Aaron, "Say to the entire **Israelite** [+3776] community,
16:10 While Aaron was speaking to the whole **Israelite** [+3776]
16:12 "I have heard the grumbling of the **Israelites** [+3776]. Tell them,
16:15 When the **Israelites** [+3776] saw it, they said to each other,
16:17 The **Israelites** [+3776] did as they were told; some gathered much,
16:35 The **Israelites** [+3776] ate manna forty years, until they came to a
17: 1 The whole **Israelite** [+3776] community set out from the Desert of
17: 3 of Egypt to make us and our **children** and livestock die of thirst?"
17: 7 and Meribah because the **Israelites** [+3776] quarreled and
18: 3 and her two **sons**. One son was named Gershom, for Moses said,
18: 5 Moses' father-in-law, together with Moses' **sons** and wife,
18: 6 am coming to you with your wife and her two **sons**."
19: 1 In the third month after the **Israelites** [+3776] left Egypt—
19: 3 to the house of Jacob and what you are to tell the **people** *of* Israel:
19: 6 These are the words you are to speak to the **Israelites** [+3776]."
20: 5 punishing the **children** for the sin of the fathers to the third
20:10 neither you, nor your **son** or daughter, nor your manservant
20:22 Then the LORD said to Moses, "Tell the **Israelites** [+3776] this:
21: 4 If his master gives him a wife and she bears him **sons** or daughters,
21: 5 'I love my master and my wife and **children** and do not want to go
21: 9 If he selects her for his **son**, he must grant her the rights of a
21:31 This law also applies if the bull gores a **son** or daughter.
22:24 [22:23] wives will become widows and your **children** fatherless.
22:29 [22:28] your vats. "You must give me the firstborn of your **sons**.
23:12 donkey may rest and the **slave** [+563] **born in** your **household**,
24: 5 he sent young **Israelite** [+3776] men, and they offered burnt
24:11 not raise his hand against these leaders of the **Israelites** [+3776];
24:17 To the **Israelites** [+3776] the glory of the LORD looked like a
25: 2 "Tell the **Israelites** [+3776] to bring me an offering. You are to
25:22 and give you all my commands for the **Israelites** [+3776].
27:20 "Command the **Israelites** [+3776] to bring you clear oil of pressed
27:21 his **sons** are to keep the lamps burning before the LORD from
27:21 This is to be a lasting ordinance among the **Israelites** [+3776] for
28: 1 your brother brought to you from among the **Israelites** [+3776],
28: 1 along with his **sons** Nadab and Abihu, Eleazar and Ithamar,
28: 1 Eleazar and Ithamar, so they may serve me as priests. **[RPH]**
28: 4 make these sacred garments for your brother Aaron and his **sons**,
28: 9 onyx stones and engrave on them the names of the **sons** *of* Israel
28:11 Engrave the names of the **sons** *of* Israel on the two stones the way
28:12 pieces of the ephod as memorial stones for the **sons** *of* Israel.
28:21 to be twelve stones, one for each of the names of the **sons** *of* Israel,
28:29 he will bear the names of the **sons** *of* Israel over his heart on the
28:30 for the **Israelites** [+3776] over his heart before the LORD.
28:38 guilt involved in the sacred gifts the **Israelites** [+3776] consecrate,
28:40 Make tunics, sashes and headbands for Aaron's **sons**, to give them
28:41 After you put these clothes on your brother Aaron and his **sons**,
28:43 his **sons** must wear them whenever they enter the Tent of Meeting
29: 1 me as priests: Take a **young** bull and two rams without defect.
29: 4 bring Aaron and his **sons** to the entrance to the Tent of Meeting
29: 8 Bring his **sons** and dress them in tunics
29: 9 and put headbands on them. Then tie sashes on Aaron and his **sons**.
29: 9 lasting ordinance. In this way you shall ordain Aaron and his **sons**.
29:10 and Aaron and his **sons** shall lay their hands on its head.
29:15 the rams, and Aaron and his **sons** shall lay their hands on its head.
29:19 other ram, and Aaron and his **sons** shall lay their hands on its head.
29:20 and put it on the lobes of the right ears of Aaron and his **sons**,
29:21 it on Aaron and his garments and on his **sons** and their garments.
29:21 and his garments and on his sons and **their**[s] [+2257] garments.
29:21 Then he and his **sons** and their garments will be consecrated.
29:21 and his sons and **their**[s] [+2257] garments will be consecrated.
29:24 Put all these in the hands of Aaron and his **sons** and wave them
29:27 those parts of the ordination ram that belong to Aaron and his **sons**:
29:28 This is always to be the regular share from the **Israelites** [+3776]
29:28 to be the regular share from the Israelites for Aaron and his **sons**.
29:28 It is the contribution the **Israelites** [+3776] are to make to the
29:29 "Aaron's sacred garments will belong to his **descendants**
29:30 The **son** who succeeds him as priest and comes to the Tent of
29:32 Aaron and his **sons** are to eat the meat of the ram and the bread that
29:35 "Do for Aaron and his **sons** everything I have commanded you,
29:38 are to offer on the altar regularly each day: two lambs a year **old**.
29:43 there also I will meet with the **Israelites** [+3776], and the place
29:44 and will consecrate Aaron and his **sons** to serve me as priests.
29:45 Then I will dwell among the **Israelites** [+3776] and be their God.
30:12 "When you take a census of the **Israelites** [+3776] to count them,
30:14 All who cross over, those twenty years **old** or more, are to give an
30:16 Receive the atonement money from the **Israelites** [+3776]
30:16 It will be a memorial for the **Israelites** [+3776] before the LORD,
30:19 Aaron and his **sons** are to wash their hands and feet with water
30:30 "Anoint Aaron and his **sons** and consecrate them so they may serve
30:31 Say to the **Israelites** [+3776], 'This is to be my sacred anointing oil
31: 2 "See, I have chosen Bezalel **son** *of* Uri, the son of Hur, of the tribe
31: 2 chosen Bezalel son of Uri, the **son** *of* Hur, of the tribe of Judah,
31: 6 Moreover, I have appointed Oholiab **son** *of* Ahisamach, of the tribe
31:10 the priest and the garments for his **sons** when they serve as priests,
31:13 "Say to the **Israelites** [+3776], 'You must observe my Sabbaths.
31:16 The **Israelites** [+3776] are to observe the Sabbath, celebrating it
31:17 It will be a sign between me and the **Israelites** [+3776] forever,
32: 2 your **sons** and your daughters are wearing, and bring them to me."
32:20 scattered it on the water and made the **Israelites** [+3776] drink it.
32:26 come to me." And all the **Levites** [+4290] rallied to him.
32:28 The **Levites** [+4290] did as Moses commanded, and that day about
32:29 for you were against your own **sons** and brothers, and he has
33: 5 "Tell the **Israelites** [+3776], 'You are a stiff-necked people.
33: 6 So the **Israelites** [+3776] stripped off their ornaments at Mount
33:11 but his young aide Joshua **son** *of* Nun did not leave the tent.
34: 7 he punishes the **children** and their children for the sin of the
34: 7 **their**[s] children for the sin of the fathers to the third and fourth
34: 7 their **children** for the sin of the fathers to the third and fourth
34:16 when you choose some of their daughters as wives for your **sons**
34:16 themselves to their gods, they will lead your **sons** to do the same.
34:20 do not redeem it, break its neck. Redeem all your firstborn **sons**.
34:30 When Aaron and all the **Israelites** [+3776] saw Moses, his face
34:32 Afterward all the **Israelites** [+3776] came near him, and he gave
34:34 and told the **Israelites** [+3776] what he had been commanded,
34:35 **they**[s] [+3776] saw that his face was radiant. Then Moses would
35: 1 Moses assembled the whole **Israelite** [+3776] community
35: 4 Moses said to the whole **Israelite** [+3776] community, "This is
35:19 and the garments for his **sons** when they serve as priests."
35:20 the whole **Israelite** [+3776] community withdrew from Moses'
35:29 All the **Israelite** [+3776] men and women who were willing
35:30 Moses said to the **Israelites** [+3776], "See, the LORD has chosen
35:30 "See, the LORD has chosen Bezalel **son** *of* Uri, the son of Hur,
35:30 has chosen Bezalel son of Uri, the **son** *of* Hur, of the tribe of Judah,
35:34 And he has given both him and Oholiab **son** *of* Ahisamach,
36: 3 They received from Moses all the offerings the **Israelites** [+3776]
38:21 by the Levites under the direction of Ithamar **son** *of* Aaron,
38:22 (Bezalel **son** *of* Uri, the son of Hur, of the tribe of Judah,
38:22 (Bezalel son of Uri, the **son** *of* Hur, of the tribe of Judah,
38:23 with him was Oholiab **son** *of* Ahisamach, of the tribe of Dan—
38:26 to those counted, twenty years **old** or more, a total of 603,550 men.
39: 6 and engraved them like a seal with the names of the **sons** *of* Israel.
39: 7 pieces of the ephod as memorial stones for the **sons** *of* Israel,
39:14 were twelve stones, one for each of the names of the **sons** *of* Israel,
39:27 For Aaron and his **sons**, they made tunics of fine linen—the work
39:32 The **Israelites** [+3776] did everything just as the LORD
39:41 the priest and the garments for his **sons** when serving as priests.
39:42 The **Israelites** [+3776] had done all the work just as the LORD
40:12 "Bring Aaron and his **sons** to the entrance to the Tent of Meeting
40:14 Bring his **sons** and dress them in tunics.
40:31 and Aaron and his **sons** used it to wash their hands and feet.
40:36 In all the travels of the **Israelites** [+3776], whenever the cloud
Lev 1: 2 "Speak to the **Israelites** [+3776] and say to them: 'When any of
1: 5 He is to slaughter the **young** bull before the LORD, and
1: 5 then Aaron's **sons** the priests shall bring the blood and sprinkle it
1: 7 The **sons** *of* Aaron the priest are to put fire on the altar and arrange
1: 8 Aaron's **sons** the priests shall arrange the pieces, including the
1:11 Aaron's **sons** the priests shall sprinkle its blood against the altar on
1:14 is a burnt offering of birds, he is to offer a dove or a **young** pigeon.
2: 2 take it to Aaron's **sons** the priests. The priest shall take a handful
2: 3 The rest of the grain offering belongs to Aaron and his **sons**;
2:10 The rest of the grain offering belongs to Aaron and his **sons**;
3: 2 Aaron's **sons** the priests shall sprinkle the blood against the altar
3: 5 Aaron's **sons** are to burn it on the altar on top of the burnt offering
3: 8 Aaron's **sons** shall sprinkle its blood against the altar on all sides.
3:13 Aaron's **sons** shall sprinkle its blood against the altar on all sides.
4: 2 "Say to the **Israelites** [+3776]: 'When anyone sins unintentionally
4: 3 he must bring to the LORD a **young** bull without defect as a sin
4:14 the assembly must bring a **young** bull as a sin offering and present
5: 7 or two **young** pigeons to the LORD as a penalty for his sin—
5:11 however, he cannot afford two doves or two **young** pigeons,
6: 9 [6:2] "Give Aaron and his **sons** this command: 'These are the

Lev 6:14 [6:7] Aaron's **sons** are to bring it before the LORD, in front of
6:16 [6:9] Aaron and his **sons** shall eat the rest of it, but it is to be eaten
6:18 [6:11] Any male **descendant** of Aaron may eat it. It is his regular
6:20 [6:13] his **sons** are to bring to the LORD on the day he is
6:22 [6:15] The **son** who is to succeed him as anointed priest shall
6:25 [6:18] "Say to Aaron and his **sons**: 'These are the regulations for
7:10 mixed with oil or dry, belongs equally to all the **sons** *of* Aaron.
7:23 "Say to the **Israelites** [+3776]: 'Do not eat any of the fat of cattle,
7:29 "Say to the **Israelites** [+3776]: 'Anyone who brings a fellowship
7:31 the fat on the altar, but the breast belongs to Aaron and his **sons**.
7:33 The **son** *of* Aaron who offers the blood and the fat of the
7:34 From the fellowship offerings of the **Israelites** [+3776], I have
7:34 the priest and his **sons** as their regular share from the Israelites.' "
7:34 and his sons as their regular share from the **Israelites** [+3776].' "
7:35 his **sons** on the day they were presented to serve the LORD as
7:36 the LORD commanded that the **Israelites** [+3776] give this to
7:38 the **Israelites** [+3776] to bring their offerings to the LORD,
8:2 "Bring Aaron and his **sons**, their garments, the anointing oil,
8:6 Moses brought Aaron and his **sons** forward and washed them with
8:13 Then he brought Aaron's **sons** forward, put tunics on them,
8:14 sin offering, and Aaron and his **sons** laid their hands on its head.
8:18 burnt offering, and Aaron and his **sons** laid their hands on its head.
8:22 the ordination, and Aaron and his **sons** laid their hands on its head.
8:24 Moses also brought Aaron's **sons** forward and put some of the
8:27 He put all these in the hands of Aaron and his **sons** and waved
8:30 on Aaron and his garments and on his **sons** and their garments.
8:30 and his garments and on his sons and **their**[s] [+2257] garments.
8:30 and his garments and his **sons** and their garments.
8:30 and his garments and his sons and **their**[s] [+2257] garments.
8:31 Moses then said to Aaron and his **sons**, "Cook the meat at the
8:31 as I commanded, saying, 'Aaron and his **sons** are to eat it.'
8:36 his **sons** did everything the LORD commanded through Moses.
9:1 day Moses summoned Aaron and his **sons** and the elders of Israel.
9:2 "Take a **bull** [+1330] calf for your sin offering and a ram for your
9:3 say to the **Israelites** [+3776]: 'Take a male goat for a sin offering,
9:3 a calf and a lamb—*both* a year **old** and without defect—
9:9 His **sons** brought the blood to him, and he dipped his finger into
9:12 His **sons** handed him the blood, and he sprinkled it against the altar
9:18 His **sons** handed him the blood, and he sprinkled it against the altar
10:1 Aaron's **sons** Nadab and Abihu took their censers, put fire in them
10:4 summoned Mishael and Elzaphan, **sons** *of* Aaron's uncle Uzziel,
10:6 Then Moses said to Aaron and his **sons** Eleazar and Ithamar,
10:9 "You and your **sons** are not to drink wine or other fermented drink
10:11 you must teach the **Israelites** [+3776] all the decrees the LORD
10:12 Moses said to Aaron and his remaining **sons**, Eleazar and Ithamar,
10:13 and your **sons**' share of the offerings made to the LORD by fire;
10:14 you and your **sons** and your daughters may eat the breast that was
10:14 your **children** as your share of the Israelites' fellowship offerings.
10:14 your children as your share of the **Israelites** [+3776]' fellowship
10:15 This will be the regular share for you and your **children**, as the
10:16 with Eleazar and Ithamar, Aaron's remaining **sons**, and asked,
11:2 "Say to the **Israelites** [+3776]: 'Of all the animals that live on land,
12:2 "Say to the **Israelites** [+3776]: 'A woman who becomes pregnant
12:6 " 'When the days of her purification for a **son** or daughter are over,
12:6 the Tent of Meeting a **year-old** [+9102] lamb for a burnt offering
12:6 a burnt offering and a **young** pigeon or a dove for a sin offering.
12:8 she is to bring two doves or two **young** pigeons, one for a burnt
13:2 be brought to Aaron the priest or to one of his **sons** who is a priest.
14:22 and two doves or two **young** pigeons, which he can afford,
14:30 he shall sacrifice the doves or the **young** pigeons, which the person
15:2 "Speak to the **Israelites** [+3776] and say to them: 'When any man
15:14 On the eighth day he must take two doves or two **young** pigeons
15:29 On the eighth day she must take two doves or two **young** pigeons
15:31 " 'You must keep the **Israelites** [+3776] separate from things that
16:1 The LORD spoke to Moses after the death of the two **sons** *of*
16:3 with a **young** bull for a sin offering and a ram for a burnt offering.
16:5 From the **Israelite** [+3776] community he is to take two male goats
16:16 because of the uncleanness and rebellion of the **Israelites** [+3776],
16:19 and to consecrate it from the uncleanness of the **Israelites** [+3776].
16:21 over it all the wickedness and rebellion of the **Israelites** [+3776]—
16:34 is to be made once a year for all the sins of the **Israelites** [+3776]."
17:2 "Speak to Aaron and his **sons** and to all the Israelites and say to
17:2 and his sons and to all the **Israelites** [+3776] and say to them:
17:5 so the **Israelites** [+3776] will bring to the LORD the sacrifices
17:12 Therefore I say to the **Israelites** [+3776], "None of you may eat
17:13 " 'Any **Israelite** [+408+3776+4946] or any alien living among you
17:14 That is why I have said to the **Israelites** [+3776], "You must not
18:2 "Speak to the **Israelites** [+3776] and say to them: 'I am the LORD
18:10 " 'Do not have sexual relations with your **son's** daughter or your
18:15 She is your **son's** wife; do not have relations with her.
18:17 Do not have sexual relations with either her **son's** daughter
19:2 "Speak to the entire assembly of **Israel** [+3776] and say to them:
19:18 not seek revenge or bear a grudge against **one**[s] *of* your people,
20:2 "Say to the **Israelites** [+3776]: 'Any Israelite or any alien living in
20:2 'Any **Israelite** [+408+3776+4946] or any alien living in Israel who
20:17 They must be cut off before the eyes of their **people** [+6639].
21:1 "Speak to the priests, the **sons** *of* Aaron, and say to them:
21:2 such as his mother or father, his **son** or daughter, his brother,
21:24 So Moses told this to Aaron and his **sons** and to all the Israelites.
21:24 told this to Aaron and his sons and to all the **Israelites** [+3776].
22:2 his **sons** to treat with respect the sacred offerings the Israelites
22:2 the sacred offerings the **Israelites** [+3776] consecrate to me,
22:3 yet comes near the sacred offerings that the **Israelites** [+3776]
22:15 the sacred offerings the **Israelites** [+3776] present to the LORD
22:18 "Speak to Aaron and his **sons** and to all the Israelites and say to
22:18 and his sons and to all the **Israelites** [+3776] and say to them:
22:25 must not accept such animals from the hand of a **foreigner** [+5797]
22:28 Do not slaughter a cow or a sheep and its **young** on the same day.
22:32 I must be acknowledged as holy by the **Israelites** [+3776].
23:2 "Speak to the **Israelites** [+3776] and say to them: 'These are my
23:10 "Speak to the **Israelites** [+3776] and say to them: 'When you enter
23:12 as a burnt offering to the LORD a lamb a year **old** without defect,
23:18 each a year **old** and without defect, one young bull and two rams.
23:18 each a year old and without defect, one **young** bull and two rams.
23:19 one male goat for a sin offering and two lambs, each a year **old**,
23:24 "Say to the **Israelites** [+3776]: 'On the first day of the seventh
23:34 "Say to the **Israelites** [+3776]: 'On the fifteenth day of the seventh
23:43 so your descendants will know that I had the **Israelites** [+3776]
23:44 So Moses announced to the **Israelites** [+3776] the appointed feasts
24:2 "Command the **Israelites** [+3776] to bring you clear oil of pressed
24:8 on behalf of the **Israelites** [+3776], as a lasting covenant.
24:9 It belongs to Aaron and his **sons**, who are to eat it in a holy place,
24:10 Now the **son** *of* an Israelite mother and an Egyptian father went out
24:10 and an **[RPH]** Egyptian father went out among the Israelites,
24:10 and an Egyptian father went out among the **Israelites** [+3776],
24:10 and a fight broke out in the camp between **him**[s] [+2021+3778]
24:11 The **son** *of* the Israelite woman blasphemed the Name with a curse;
24:15 Say to the **Israelites** [+3776]: 'If anyone curses his God, he will be
24:23 Moses spoke to the **Israelites** [+3776], and they took the
24:23 The **Israelites** [+3776] did as the LORD commanded Moses.
25:2 "Speak to the **Israelites** [+3776] and say to them: 'When you enter
25:33 of the Levites are their property among the **Israelites** [+3776].
25:41 he and his **children** are to be released, and he will go back to his
25:45 among you and **members** *of* their clans born in your country,
25:46 You can will them to your **children** as inherited property and can
25:46 you must not rule over your fellow **Israelites** [+3776] ruthlessly.
25:49 An uncle or a **cousin** [+1856] or any blood relative in his clan may
25:54 and his **children** are to be released in the Year of Jubilee,
25:55 for the **Israelites** [+3776] belong to me as servants. They are my
26:29 You will eat the flesh of your **sons** and the flesh of your daughters.
26:46 Sinai between himself and the **Israelites** [+3776] through Moses.
27:2 "Speak to the **Israelites** [+3776] and say to them: 'If anyone makes
27:3 set the value of a male between the **ages of** [+9102] twenty
27:3 the ages of twenty and **[RPH]** sixty at fifty shekels of silver,
27:5 If it is a person between the **ages of** [+9102] five and twenty,
27:5 If it is a person between the ages of five and **[RPH]** twenty,
27:6 If it is a person between **[RPH]** one month and five years,
27:6 If it is a person between one month and **[RPH]** five years,
27:7 If it is a person sixty years **old** or more, set the value of a male at
27:34 the LORD gave Moses on Mount Sinai for the **Israelites** [+3776].
Nu 1:2 "Take a census of the whole **Israelite** [+3776] community by their
1:3 to number by their divisions all the men in Israel twenty years **old**
1:5 men who are to assist you: from Reuben, Elizur **son** *of* Shedeur;
1:6 from Simeon, Shelumiel **son** *of* Zurishaddai;
1:7 from Judah, Nahshon **son** *of* Amminadab;
1:8 from Issachar, Nethanel **son** *of* Zuar;
1:9 from Zebulun, Eliab **son** *of* Helon;
1:10 from the **sons** *of* Joseph: from Ephraim, Elishama son of
1:10 from Ephraim, Elishama **son** *of* Ammihud; from Manasseh,
1:10 son of Ammihud; from Manasseh, Gamaliel **son** *of* Pedahzur;
1:11 from Benjamin, Abidan **son** *of* Gideoni;
1:12 from Dan, Ahiezer **son** *of* Ammishaddai;
1:13 from Asher, Pagiel **son** *of* Ocran;
1:14 from Gad, Eliasaph **son** *of* Deuel;
1:15 from Naphtali, Ahira **son** *of* Enan."
1:18 and the men twenty years **old** or more were listed by name,
1:20 From the **descendants** *of* Reuben the firstborn son of Israel:
1:20 All the men twenty years **old** or more who were able to serve in the
1:22 From the **descendants** *of* Simeon: All the men twenty years old
1:22 All the men twenty years **old** or more who were able to serve in the
1:24 From the **descendants** *of* Gad: All the men twenty years old
1:24 All the men twenty years **old** or more who were able to serve in the
1:26 From the **descendants** *of* Judah: All the men twenty years old
1:26 All the men twenty years **old** or more who were able to serve in the
1:28 From the **descendants** *of* Issachar: All the men twenty years old
1:28 All the men twenty years **old** or more who were able to serve in the
1:30 From the **descendants** *of* Zebulun: All the men twenty years old
1:30 All the men twenty years **old** or more who were able to serve in the

Nu 1:32 From the **sons** *of* Joseph: From the descendants of Ephraim:
1:32 From the sons of Joseph: From the **descendants** *of* Ephraim:
1:32 All the men twenty years **old** or more who were able to serve in the
1:34 From the **descendants** *of* Manasseh: All the men twenty years old
1:34 All the men twenty years **old** or more who were able to serve in the
1:36 From the **descendants** *of* Benjamin: All the men twenty years old
1:36 All the men twenty years **old** or more who were able to serve in the
1:38 From the **descendants** *of* Dan: All the men twenty years old
1:38 All the men twenty years **old** or more who were able to serve in the
1:40 From the **descendants** *of* Asher: All the men twenty years old
1:40 All the men twenty years **old** or more who were able to serve in the
1:42 From the **descendants** *of* Naphtali: All the men twenty years old
1:42 All the men twenty years **old** or more who were able to serve in the
1:45 All the **Israelites** [+3776] twenty years old or more who were able
1:45 All the Israelites twenty years **old** or more who were able to serve
1:49 or include them in the census of the other **Israelites** [+3776].
1:52 The **Israelites** [+3776] are to set up their tents by divisions,
1:53 so that wrath will not fall on the **Israelite** [+3776] community.
1:54 The **Israelites** [+3776] did all this just as the LORD commanded
2:2 "The **Israelites** [+3776] are to camp around the Tent of Meeting
2:3 The leader of the **people** *of* Judah is Nahshon son of Amminadab.
2:3 The leader of the people of Judah is Nahshon **son** *of* Amminadab.
2:5 The leader of the **people** *of* Issachar is Nethanel son of Zuar.
2:5 The leader of the people of Issachar is Nethanel **son** *of* Zuar.
2:7 The leader of the **people** *of* Zebulun is Eliab son of Helon.
2:7 The leader of the people of Zebulun is Eliab **son** *of* Helon.
2:10 The leader of the **people** *of* Reuben is Elizur son of Shedeur.
2:10 The leader of the people of Reuben is Elizur **son** *of* Shedeur.
2:12 The leader of the **people** *of* Simeon is Shelumiel son of
2:12 The leader of the people of Simeon is Shelumiel **son** *of*
2:14 The leader of the **people** *of* Gad is Eliasaph son of Deuel.
2:14 The leader of the people of Gad is Eliasaph **son** *of* Deuel.
2:18 The leader of the **people** *of* Ephraim is Elishama son of Ammihud.
2:18 The leader of the people of Ephraim is Elishama **son** *of* Ammihud.
2:20 The leader of the **people** *of* Manasseh is Gamaliel son of Pedahzur.
2:20 The leader of the people of Manasseh is Gamaliel **son** *of* Pedahzur.
2:22 The leader of the **people** *of* Benjamin is Abidan son of Gideoni.
2:22 The leader of the people of Benjamin is Abidan **son** *of* Gideoni.
2:25 The leader of the **people** *of* Dan is Ahiezer son of Ammishaddai.
2:25 The leader of the people of Dan is Ahiezer **son** *of* Ammishaddai.
2:27 to them. The leader of the **people** *of* Asher is Pagiel son of Ocran.
2:27 to them. The leader of the people of Asher is Pagiel **son** *of* Ocran.
2:29 The leader of the **people** *of* Naphtali is Ahira son of Enan.
2:29 The leader of the people of Naphtali is Ahira **son** *of* Enan.
2:32 These are the **Israelites** [+3776], counted according to their
2:33 were not counted along with the other **Israelites** [+3776],
2:34 So the **Israelites** [+3776] did everything the LORD commanded
3:2 The names of the **sons** *of* Aaron were Nadab the firstborn
3:3 Those were the names of Aaron's **sons**, the anointed priests,
3:4 They had no **sons**; so only Eleazar and Ithamar served as priests
3:8 fulfilling the obligations of the **Israelites** [+3776] by doing the
3:9 Give the Levites to Aaron and his **sons**; they are the Israelites who
3:9 they are the **Israelites** [+3776] who are to be given wholly to him.
3:10 Appoint Aaron and his **sons** to serve as priests; anyone else who
3:12 "I have taken the Levites from among the **Israelites** [+3776] in
3:12 place of the first male offspring of every **Israelite** [+3776] woman.
3:15 "Count the **Levites** [+4290] by their families and clans. Count
3:15 their families and clans. Count every male a month **old** or more."
3:17 These were the names of the **sons** *of* Levi: Gershon, Kohath
3:18 These were the names of the **Gershonite** [+1767] clans: Libni
3:19 The **Kohathite** [+7740] clans: Amram, Izhar, Hebron and Uzziel.
3:20 The **Merarite** [+5356] clans: Mahli and Mushi. These were the
3:22 The number of all the males a month **old** or more who were
3:24 The leader of the families of the Gershonites was Eliasaph **son** *of*
3:25 At the Tent of Meeting the **Gershonites** [+1767] were responsible
3:28 The number of all the males a month **old** or more was 8,600.
3:29 The **Kohathite** [+7740] clans were to camp on the south side of
3:30 of the families of the Kohathite clans was Elizaphan **son** *of* Uzziel.
3:32 The chief leader of the Levites was Eleazar **son** *of* Aaron,
3:34 The number of all the males a month **old** or more who were
3:35 The leader of the families of the Merarite clans was Zuriel **son** *of*
3:36 The **Merarites** [+5356] were appointed to take care of the frames
3:38 and Aaron and his **sons** were to camp to the east of the tabernacle,
3:38 for the care of the sanctuary on behalf of the **Israelites** [+3776].
3:39 their clans, including every male a month **old** or more, was 22,000.
3:40 "Count all the firstborn **Israelite** [+3776] males who are a month
3:40 "Count all the firstborn Israelite males who are a month **old**
3:41 for me in place of all the firstborn of the **Israelites** [+3776],
3:41 place of all the firstborn of the livestock of the **Israelites** [+3776].
3:42 So Moses counted all the firstborn of the **Israelites** [+3776],
3:43 The total number of firstborn males a month **old** or more, listed by
3:45 "Take the Levites in place of all the firstborn of **Israel** [+3776],
3:46 To redeem the 273 firstborn **Israelites** [+3776] who exceed the
3:48 the redemption of the additional Israelites to Aaron and his **sons**."
3:50 From the firstborn of the **Israelites** [+3776] he collected silver
3:51 Moses gave the redemption money to Aaron and his **sons**,
4:2 "Take a census of the **Kohathite** [+7740] branch of the Levites by
4:2 "Take a census of the Kohathite branch of the **Levites** [+4290] by
4:3 Count all the men from thirty to fifty years *of* **age** who come to
4:3 Count all the men from thirty to fifty years of age **[RPH]** who
4:4 "This is the work of the **Kohathites** [+7740] in the Tent of
4:5 Aaron and his **sons** are to go in and take down the shielding curtain
4:15 and his **sons** have finished covering the holy furnishings
4:15 to move, the **Kohathites** [+7740] are to come to do the carrying.
4:15 The **Kohathites** [+7740] are to carry those things that are in the
4:16 "Eleazar **son** *of* Aaron, the priest, is to have charge of the oil for
4:19 Aaron and his **sons** are to go into the sanctuary and assign to each
4:22 "Take a census also of the **Gershonites** [+1767] by their families
4:23 Count all the men from thirty to fifty years *of* **age** who come to
4:23 Count all the men from thirty to fifty years of age **[RPH]** who
4:27 All **their**[s] [+1769+2021] service, whether carrying or doing other
4:27 other work, is to be done under the direction of Aaron and his **sons**.
4:28 This is the service of the **Gershonite** [+1769] clans at the Tent of
4:28 Their duties are to be under the direction of Ithamar **son** *of* Aaron,
4:29 "Count the **Merarites** [+5356] by their clans and families.
4:30 Count all the men from thirty to fifty years *of* **age** who come to
4:30 Count all the men from thirty to fifty years of age **[RPH]** who
4:33 This is the service of the **Merarite** [+5356] clans as they work at
4:33 at the Tent of Meeting under the direction of Ithamar **son** *of* Aaron,
4:34 the leaders of the community counted the **Kohathites** [+7741] by
4:35 All the men from thirty to fifty years *of* **age** who came to serve in
4:35 All the men from thirty to fifty years of age **[RPH]** who came to
4:38 The **Gershonites** [+1767] were counted by their clans
4:39 All the men from thirty to fifty years *of* **age** who came to serve in
4:39 All the men from thirty to fifty years of age **[RPH]** who came to
4:41 This was the total of those in the **Gershonite** [+1767] clans who
4:42 The **Merarites** [+5356] were counted by their clans and families.
4:43 All the men from thirty to fifty years *of* **age** who came to serve in
4:43 All the men from thirty to fifty years of age **[RPH]** who came to
4:45 This was the total of those in the **Merarite** [+5356] clans.
4:47 All the men from thirty to fifty years *of* **age** who came to do the
4:47 All the men from thirty to fifty years of age **[RPH]** who came to
5:2 "Command the **Israelites** [+3776] to send away from the camp
5:4 The **Israelites** [+3776] did this; they sent them outside the camp.
5:4 they sent them outside the camp. **They**[s] [+3776] did just as the
5:6 "Say to the **Israelites** [+3776]: 'When a man or woman wrongs
5:9 All the sacred contributions the **Israelites** [+3776] bring to a priest
5:12 "Speak to the **Israelites** [+3776] and say to them: 'If a man's wife
6:2 "Speak to the **Israelites** [+3776] and say to them: 'If a man
6:10 or two **young** pigeons to the priest at the entrance to the Tent of
6:12 and must bring a **year-old** [+9102] male lamb as a guilt offering.
6:14 a **year-old** [+9102] male lamb without defect for a burnt offering,
6:23 "Tell Aaron and his **sons**, 'This is how you are to bless the
6:23 and his sons, 'This is how you are to bless the **Israelites** [+3776].
6:27 "So they will put my name on the **Israelites** [+3776], and I will
7:7 He gave two carts and four oxen to the **Gershonites** [+1767],
7:8 and he gave four carts and eight oxen to the **Merarites** [+5356],
7:8 They were all under the direction of Ithamar **son** *of* Aaron,
7:9 Moses did not give any to the **Kohathites** [+7740], because they
7:12 the first day was Nahshon **son** *of* Amminadab of the tribe of Judah.
7:15 one **young** bull, one ram and one male lamb a year old, for a burnt
7:15 one young bull, one ram and one male lamb a year **old**, for a burnt
7:17 five rams, five male goats and five male lambs a year **old**,
7:17 This was the offering of Nahshon **son** *of* Amminadab.
7:18 On the second day Nethanel **son** *of* Zuar, the leader of Issachar,
7:21 one **young** bull, one ram and one male lamb a year old, for a burnt
7:21 one young bull, one ram and one male lamb a year **old**, for a burnt
7:23 five rams, five male goats and five male lambs a year **old**,
7:23 fellowship offering. This was the offering of Nethanel **son** *of* Zuar.
7:24 On the third day, Eliab **son** *of* Helon, the leader of the people of
7:24 third day, Eliab son of Helon, the leader of the **people** *of* Zebulun,
7:27 one **young** bull, one ram and one male lamb a year old, for a burnt
7:27 one young bull, one ram and one male lamb a year **old**, for a burnt
7:29 five rams, five male goats and five male lambs a year **old**,
7:29 a fellowship offering. This was the offering of Eliab **son** *of* Helon.
7:30 On the fourth day Elizur **son** *of* Shedeur, the leader of the people
7:30 the leader of the **people** *of* Reuben, brought his offering.
7:33 one **young** bull, one ram and one male lamb a year old, for a burnt
7:33 one young bull, one ram and one male lamb a year **old**, for a burnt
7:35 five rams, five male goats and five male lambs a year **old**,
7:35 This was the offering of Elizur **son** *of* Shedeur.
7:36 On the fifth day Shelumiel **son** *of* Zurishaddai, the leader of the
7:36 the leader of the **people** *of* Simeon, brought his offering.
7:39 one **young** bull, one ram and one male lamb a year old, for a burnt
7:39 one young bull, one ram and one male lamb a year **old**, for a burnt
7:41 five rams, five male goats and five male lambs a year **old**,
7:41 This was the offering of Shelumiel **son** *of* Zurishaddai.
7:42 On the sixth day Eliasaph **son** *of* Deuel, the leader of the people of

Nu 7:42 son of Deuel, the leader of the **people** *of* Gad, brought his offering.
7:45 one **young** bull, one ram and one male lamb a year old, for a burnt
7:45 one young bull, one ram and one male lamb a year **old**, for a burnt
7:47 five rams, five male goats and five male lambs a year **old**,
7:47 This was the offering of Eliasaph **son** *of* Deuel.
7:48 On the seventh day Elishama **son** *of* Ammihud, the leader of the
7:48 the leader of the **people** *of* Ephraim, brought his offering.
7:51 one **young** bull, one ram and one male lamb a year old, for a burnt
7:51 one young bull, one ram and one male lamb a year **old**, for a burnt
7:53 five rams, five male goats and five male lambs a year **old**,
7:53 This was the offering of Elishama **son** *of* Ammihud.
7:54 On the eighth day Gamaliel **son** *of* Pedahzur, the leader of the
7:54 the leader of the **people** *of* Manasseh, brought his offering.
7:57 one **young** bull, one ram and one male lamb a year old, for a burnt
7:57 one young bull, one ram and one male lamb a year **old**, for a burnt
7:59 five rams, five male goats and five male lambs a year **old**,
7:59 This was the offering of Gamaliel **son** *of* Pedahzur.
7:60 On the ninth day Abidan **son** *of* Gideoni, the leader of the people
7:60 the leader of the **people** *of* Benjamin, brought his offering.
7:63 one **young** bull, one ram and one male lamb a year old, for a burnt
7:63 one young bull, one ram and one male lamb a year **old**, for a burnt
7:65 five rams, five male goats and five male lambs a year **old**,
7:65 This was the offering of Abidan **son** *of* Gideoni.
7:66 On the tenth day Ahiezer **son** *of* Ammishaddai, the leader of the
7:66 the leader of the **people** *of* Dan, brought his offering.
7:69 one **young** bull, one ram and one male lamb a year old, for a burnt
7:69 one young bull, one ram and one male lamb a year **old**, for a burnt
7:71 five rams, five male goats and five male lambs a year **old**,
7:71 This was the offering of Ahiezer **son** *of* Ammishaddai.
7:72 On the eleventh day Pagiel **son** *of* Ocran, the leader of the people
7:72 of Ocran, the leader of the **people** *of* Asher, brought his offering.
7:75 one **young** bull, one ram and one male lamb a year old, for a burnt
7:75 one young bull, one ram and one male lamb a year **old**, for a burnt
7:77 five rams, five male goats and five male lambs a year **old**,
7:77 a fellowship offering. This was the offering of Pagiel **son** *of* Ocran.
7:78 On the twelfth day Ahira **son** *of* Enan, the leader of the people of
7:78 the leader of the **people** *of* Naphtali, brought his offering.
7:81 one **young** bull, one ram and one male lamb a year old, for a burnt
7:81 one young bull, one ram and one male lamb a year **old**, for a burnt
7:83 five rams, five male goats and five male lambs a year **old**,
7:83 a fellowship offering. This was the offering of Ahira **son** *of* Enan.
7:87 twelve rams and twelve male lambs a year **old**, together with their
7:88 sixty rams, sixty male goats and sixty male lambs a year **old**.
8:6 "Take the Levites from among the other **Israelites** [+3776]
8:8 Have them take a **young** bull with its grain offering of fine flour
8:8 then you are to take a second **young** bull for a sin offering.
8:9 of Meeting and assemble the whole **Israelite** [+3776] community.
8:10 and the **Israelites** [+906+3776] are to lay their hands on them.
8:11 before the LORD as a wave offering from the **Israelites** [+3776],
8:13 Have the Levites stand in front of Aaron and his **sons** and
8:14 you are to set the Levites apart from the other **Israelites** [+3776],
8:16 They are the **Israelites** [+3776] who are to be given wholly to me.
8:16 the first male offspring from every **Israelite** [+3776] woman.
8:17 Every firstborn male in **Israel** [+3776], whether man or animal,
8:18 the Levites in place of all the firstborn sons in **Israel** [+3776].
8:19 Of all the **Israelites** [+3776], I have given the Levites as gifts to
8:19 his **sons** to do the work at the Tent of Meeting on behalf of the
8:19 the work at the Tent of Meeting on behalf of the **Israelites** [+3776]
8:19 to make atonement for **them**[s] [+3776] so that no plague will strike
8:19 so that no plague will strike the **Israelites** [+3776] when they go
8:19 so that no plague will strike the Israelites when **they**[s] [+3776] go
8:20 the whole **Israelite** [+3776] community did with the Levites just as
8:20 with the Levites just as the LORD commanded Moses. **[RPH]**
8:22 the Tent of Meeting under the supervision of Aaron and his **sons**.
8:24 Men twenty-five years **old** or more shall come to take part in the
8:25 but at the **age** *of* fifty, they must retire from their regular service
9:2 "Have the **Israelites** [+3776] celebrate the Passover at the
9:4 So Moses told the **Israelites** [+3776] to celebrate the Passover,
9:5 The **Israelites** [+3776] did everything just as the LORD
9:7 offering with the other **Israelites** [+3776] at the appointed time?"
9:10 "Tell the **Israelites** [+3776]: 'When any of you or your descendants
9:17 the cloud lifted from above the Tent, the **Israelites** [+3776] set out;
9:17 wherever the cloud settled, the **Israelites** [+3776] encamped.
9:18 At the LORD's command the **Israelites** [+3776] set out,
9:19 the **Israelites** [+3776] obeyed the LORD's order and did not set
9:22 the **Israelites** [+3776] would remain in camp and not set out;
10:8 "The **sons** *of* Aaron, the priests, are to blow the trumpets. This is to
10:12 Then the **Israelites** [+3776] set out from the Desert of Sinai
10:14 The divisions of the camp of **Judah** [+3373] went first, under their
10:14 their standard. Nahshon **son** *of* Amminadab was in command.
10:15 Nethanel **son** *of* Zuar was over the division of the tribe of Issachar,
10:15 son of Zuar was over the division of the tribe of **Issachar** [+3779],
10:16 Eliab **son** *of* Helon was over the division of the tribe of Zebulun.
10:16 of Helon was over the division of the tribe of **Zebulun** [+2282].
10:17 and the **Gershonites** [+1767] and Merarites, who carried it,
10:17 and the Gershonites and **Merarites** [+5356], who carried it,
10:18 under their standard. Elizur **son** *of* Shedeur was in command.
10:19 Shelumiel **son** *of* Zurishaddai was over the division of the tribe of
10:19 Zurishaddai was over the division of the tribe of **Simeon** [+9058],
10:20 Eliasaph **son** *of* Deuel was over the division of the tribe of Gad.
10:20 son of Deuel was over the division of the tribe of **Gad** [+1514].
10:22 The divisions of the camp of **Ephraim** [+713] went next,
10:22 under their standard. Elishama **son** *of* Ammihud was in command.
10:23 Gamaliel **son** *of* Pedahzur was over the division of the tribe of
10:23 Pedahzur was over the division of the tribe of **Manasseh** [+4985],
10:24 Abidan **son** *of* Gideoni was over the division of the tribe of
10:24 of Gideoni was over the division of the tribe of **Benjamin** [+1228].
10:25 the divisions of the camp of **Dan** [+1968] set out, under their
10:25 their standard. Ahiezer **son** *of* Ammishaddai was in command.
10:26 Pagiel **son** *of* Ocran was over the division of the tribe of Asher,
10:26 son of Ocran was over the division of the tribe of **Asher** [+888],
10:27 Ahira **son** *of* Enan was over the division of the tribe of Naphtali.
10:27 son of Enan was over the division of the tribe of **Naphtali** [+5889].
10:28 This was the order of march for the **Israelite** [+3776] divisions as
10:29 Now Moses said to Hobab **son** *of* Reuel the Midianite,
11:4 again the **Israelites** [+3776] started wailing and said, "If only we
11:28 Joshua **son** *of* Nun, who had been Moses' aide since youth,
13:2 the land of Canaan, which I am giving to the **Israelites** [+3776].
13:3 Desert of Paran. All of them were leaders of the **Israelites** [+3776].
13:4 their names: from the tribe of Reuben, Shammua **son** *of* Zaccur;
13:5 from the tribe of Simeon, Shaphat **son** *of* Hori;
13:6 from the tribe of Judah, Caleb **son** *of* Jephunneh;
13:7 from the tribe of Issachar, Igal **son** *of* Joseph;
13:8 from the tribe of Ephraim, Hoshea **son** *of* Nun;
13:9 from the tribe of Benjamin, Palti **son** *of* Raphu;
13:10 from the tribe of Zebulun, Gaddiel **son** *of* Sodi;
13:11 from the tribe of Manasseh (a tribe of Joseph), Gaddi **son** *of* Susi;
13:12 from the tribe of Dan, Ammiel **son** *of* Gemalli;
13:13 from the tribe of Asher, Sethur **son** *of* Michael;
13:14 from the tribe of Naphtali, Nahbi **son** *of* Vophsi;
13:15 from the tribe of Gad, Geuel **son** *of* Maki.
13:16 the land. (Moses gave Hoshea **son** *of* Nun the name Joshua.)
13:24 because of the cluster of grapes the **Israelites** [+3776] cut off
13:26 the whole **Israelite** [+3776] community at Kadesh in the Desert of
13:32 they spread among the **Israelites** [+3776] a bad report about the
13:33 We saw the Nephilim there (the **descendants** *of* Anak come from
14:2 All the **Israelites** [+3776] grumbled against Moses and Aaron,
14:5 Aaron fell facedown in front of the whole **Israelite** [+3776]
14:6 Joshua **son** *of* Nun and Caleb son of Jephunneh, who were among
14:6 Joshua son of Nun and Caleb **son** *of* Jephunneh, who were among
14:7 said to the entire **Israelite** [+3776] assembly, "The land we passed
14:10 appeared at the Tent of Meeting to all the **Israelites** [+3776].
14:18 he punishes the **children** for the sin of the fathers to the third
14:27 I have heard the complaints of these grumbling **Israelites** [+3776].
14:29 every one of you twenty years **old** or more who was counted in the
14:30 your home, except Caleb **son** *of* Jephunneh and Joshua son of Nun.
14:30 your home, except Caleb son of Jephunneh and Joshua **son** *of* Nun.
14:33 Your **children** will be shepherds here for forty years, suffering for
14:38 only Joshua **son** *of* Nun and Caleb son of Jephunneh survived.
14:38 only Joshua son of Nun and Caleb **son** *of* Jephunneh survived.
14:39 When Moses reported this to all the **Israelites** [+3776], they
15:2 "Speak to the **Israelites** [+3776] and say to them: 'After you enter
15:8 " 'When you prepare a **young** bull as a burnt offering or sacrifice,
15:9 bring with the **[RPH]** bull a grain offering of three-tenths of an
15:18 "Speak to the **Israelites** [+3776] and say to them: 'When you enter
15:24 the whole community is to offer a **young** bull for a burnt offering
15:25 The priest is to make atonement for the whole **Israelite** [+3776]
15:26 The whole **Israelite** [+3776] community and the aliens living
15:29 whether he is a native-born **Israelite** [+928+3776] or an alien.
15:32 While the **Israelites** [+3776] were in the desert, a man was found
15:38 "Speak to the **Israelites** [+3776] and say to them: 'Throughout the
16:1 Korah **son** *of* Izhar, the son of Kohath, the son of Levi, and certain
16:1 Korah son of Izhar, the **son** *of* Kohath, the son of Levi, and certain
16:1 Korah son of Izhar, the son of Kohath, the **son** *of* Levi, and certain
16:1 son of Kohath, the son of Levi, and certain **Reubenites** [+8017]—
16:1 Dathan and Abiram, **sons** *of* Eliab, and On son of Peleth—
16:1 Dathan and Abiram, sons of Eliab, and On **son** *of* Peleth—
16:2 With them were 250 **Israelite** [+3776] men, well-known
16:7 be the one who is holy. You **Levites** [+4290] have gone too far!"
16:8 Moses also said to Korah, "Now listen, you **Levites** [+4290]!
16:10 has brought you and all your fellow **Levites** [+4290] near himself,
16:12 Then Moses summoned Dathan and Abiram, the **sons** *of* Eliab.
16:27 their wives, **children** and little ones at the entrances to their tents.
16:37 [17:2] "Tell Eleazar **son** *of* Aaron, the priest, to take the censers
16:38 [17:3] become holy. Let them be a sign to the **Israelites** [+3776]."
16:40 [17:5] This was to remind the **Israelites** [+3776] that no one
16:41 [17:6] The next day the whole **Israelite** [+3776] community
17:2 [17:17] "Speak to the **Israelites** [+3776] and get twelve staffs

Nu 17: 5 [17:20] grumbling against you by the **Israelites** [+3776]."
17: 6 [17:21] So Moses spoke to the **Israelites** [+3776], and their
17: 9 [17:24] from the LORD's presence to all the **Israelites** [+3776].
17: 10 [17:25] to be kept as a sign to the **rebellious** [+5308].
17: 12 [17:27] The **Israelites** [+3776] said to Moses, "We will die!
18: 1 your **sons** and your father's family are to bear the responsibility for
18: 1 your **sons** alone are to bear the responsibility for offenses against
18: 2 when you and your **sons** minister before the Tent of the Testimony.
18: 5 so that wrath will not fall on the **Israelites** [+3776] again.
18: 6 fellow Levites from among the **Israelites** [+3776] as a gift to you,
18: 7 your **sons** may serve as priests in connection with everything at the
18: 8 all the holy offerings the **Israelites** [+3776] give me I give to you
18: 8 me I give to you and your **sons** as your portion and regular share.
18: 9 or sin or guilt offerings, that part belongs to you and your **sons**.
18: 11 from the gifts of all the wave offerings of the **Israelites** [+3776].
18: 11 I give this to you and your **sons** and daughters as your regular
18: 16 When they are a month **old**, you must redeem them at the
18: 19 is set aside from the holy offerings the **Israelites** [+3776]
18: 19 I give to you and your **sons** and daughters as your regular share.
18: 20 I am your share and your inheritance among the **Israelites** [+3776].
18: 21 "I give to the **Levites** [+4290] all the tithes in Israel as their
18: 22 From now on the **Israelites** [+3776] must not go near the Tent of
18: 23 They will receive no inheritance among the **Israelites** [+3776].
18: 24 that the **Israelites** [+3776] present as an offering to the LORD.
18: 24 'They will have no inheritance among the **Israelites** [+3776].' "
18: 26 'When you receive from the **Israelites** [+3776] the tithe I give you
18: 28 LORD from all the tithes you receive from the **Israelites** [+3776].
18: 32 you will not defile the holy offerings of the **Israelites** [+3776],
19: 2 Tell the **Israelites** [+3776] to bring you a red heifer without defect
19: 9 They shall be kept by the **Israelite** [+3776] community for use in
19: 10 This will be a lasting ordinance both for the **Israelites** [+3776]
20: 1 In the first month the whole **Israelite** [+3776] community arrived
20: 12 enough to honor me as holy in the sight of the **Israelites** [+3776],
20: 13 where the **Israelites** [+3776] quarreled with the LORD and where
20: 19 The **Israelites** [+3776] replied: "We will go along the main road,
20: 22 The whole **Israelite** [+3776] community set out from Kadesh
20: 24 He will not enter the land I give the **Israelites** [+3776],
20: 25 Get Aaron and his **son** Eleazar and take them up Mount Hor.
20: 26 Remove Aaron's garments and put them on his **son** Eleazar,
20: 28 removed Aaron's garments and put them on his **son** Eleazar.
21: 10 The **Israelites** [+3776] moved on and camped at Oboth.
21: 24 only as far as the **Ammonites** [+6648], because their border was
21: 24 far as the Ammonites, because **their**[s] [+6648] border was fortified.
21: 29 He has given up his **sons** as fugitives and his daughters as captives
21: 35 they struck him down, together with his **sons** and his whole army,
22: 1 Then the **Israelites** [+3776] traveled to the plains of Moab
22: 2 Now Balak **son** *of* Zippor saw all that Israel had done to the
22: 3 Moab was filled with dread because of the **Israelites** [+3776].
22: 4 So Balak **son** *of* Zippor, who was king of Moab at that time,
22: 5 sent messengers to summon Balaam **son** *of* Beor, who was at
22: 5 who was at Pethor, near the River, in his **native** [+6639] land.
22: 10 Balaam said to God, "Balak **son** *of* Zippor, king of Moab,
22: 16 came to Balaam and said: "This is what Balak **son** *of* Zippor says:
23: 18 his oracle: "Arise, Balak, and listen; hear me, **son** *of* Zippor.
23: 19 God is not a man, that he should lie, nor a **son** *of* man, that he
24: 3 "The oracle of Balaam **son** *of* Beor, the oracle of one whose eye
24: 15 "The oracle of Balaam **son** *of* Beor, the oracle of one whose eye
24: 17 crush the foreheads of Moab, the skulls of all the **sons** *of* Sheth.
25: 6 an **Israelite** [+3776+4946] man brought to his family a Midianite
25: 6 the whole assembly of **Israel** [+3776] while they were weeping at
25: 7 When Phinehas **son** *of* Eleazar, the son of Aaron, the priest,
25: 7 the **son** *of* Aaron, the priest, saw this, he left the assembly,
25: 8 Then the plague against the **Israelites** [+3776] was stopped;
25: 11 "Phinehas **son** *of* Eleazar, the son of Aaron, the priest, has turned
25: 11 "Phinehas son of Eleazar, the **son** *of* Aaron, the priest, has turned
25: 11 the priest, has turned my anger away from the **Israelites** [+3776];
25: 11 so that in my zeal I did not put an end to **them**[s] [+3776].
25: 13 honor of his God and made atonement for the **Israelites** [+3776]."
25: 14 who was killed with the Midianite woman was Zimri **son** *of* Salu,
26: 1 the plague the LORD said to Moses and Eleazar **son** *of* Aaron,
26: 2 "Take a census of the whole **Israelite** [+3776] community by
26: 2 all those twenty years **old** or more who are able to serve in the
26: 4 "Take a census of the *men* twenty years **old** or more, as the
26: 4 These were the **Israelites** [+3776] who came out of Egypt:
26: 5 The **descendants** *of* Reuben, the firstborn son of Israel, were:
26: 8 The **son** *of* Pallu was Eliab,
26: 9 the **sons** *of* Eliab were Nemuel, Dathan and Abiram. The same
26: 11 The **line** *of* Korah, however, did not die out.
26: 12 The **descendants** *of* Simeon by their clans were: through Nemuel,
26: 15 The **descendants** *of* Gad by their clans were: through Zephon,
26: 18 These were the clans of **Gad** [+1514]; those numbered were
26: 19 Er and Onan were **sons** *of* Judah, but they died in Canaan.
26: 20 The **descendants** *of* Judah by their clans were: through Shelah,
26: 21 The **descendants** *of* Perez were: through Hezron, the Hezronite
26: 23 The **descendants** *of* Issachar by their clans were: through Tola,
26: 26 The **descendants** *of* Zebulun by their clans were: through Sered,
26: 28 The **descendants** *of* Joseph by their clans through Manasseh
26: 29 The **descendants** *of* Manasseh: through Makir, the Makirite clan
26: 30 These were the **descendants** *of* Gilead: through Iezer, the Iezerite
26: 33 (Zelophehad **son** *of* Hepher had no sons; he had only daughters,
26: 33 (Zelophehad son of Hepher had no **sons**; he had only daughters,
26: 35 These were the **descendants** *of* Ephraim by their clans:
26: 36 These were the **descendants** *of* Shuthelah: through Eran,
26: 37 These were the clans of **Ephraim** [+713]; those numbered were
26: 37 were 32,500. These were the **descendants** *of* Joseph by their clans.
26: 38 The **descendants** *of* Benjamin by their clans were: through Bela,
26: 40 The **descendants** *of* Bela through Ard and Naaman were:
26: 41 These were the clans of **Benjamin** [+1228]; those numbered were
26: 42 These were the **descendants** *of* Dan by their clans:
26: 44 The **descendants** *of* Asher by their clans were: through Imnah,
26: 45 through the **descendants** *of* Beriah: through Heber, the Heberite
26: 47 These were the clans of **Asher** [+888]; those numbered were
26: 48 The **descendants** *of* Naphtali by their clans were: through Jahzeel,
26: 51 The total number of the **men** *of* Israel was 601,730.
26: 62 All the male Levites a month **old** or more numbered 23,000.
26: 62 They were not counted along with the other **Israelites** [+3776]
26: 62 because they received no inheritance among **them**[s] [+3776].
26: 63 Eleazar the priest when they counted the **Israelites** [+3776] on the
26: 64 Aaron the priest when they counted the **Israelites** [+3776] in the
26: 65 and not one of them was left except Caleb **son** *of* Jephunneh
26: 65 was left except Caleb son of Jephunneh and Joshua **son** *of* Nun.
27: 1 The daughters of Zelophehad **son** *of* Hepher, the son of Gilead,
27: 1 the **son** *of* Gilead, the son of Makir, the son of Manasseh,
27: 1 the son of Gilead, the **son** *of* Makir, the son of Manasseh,
27: 1 the son of Gilead, the son of Makir, the **son** *of* Manasseh,
27: 1 son of Manasseh, belonged to the clans of Manasseh **son** *of* Joseph.
27: 3 against the LORD, but he died for his own sin and left no **sons**.
27: 4 our father's name disappear from his clan because he had no **son**?
27: 8 "Say to the **Israelites** [+3776], 'If a man dies and leaves no son,
27: 8 "Say to the Israelites, 'If a man dies and leaves no **son**, turn his
27: 11 This is to be a legal requirement for the **Israelites** [+3776],
27: 12 Abarim range and see the land I have given the **Israelites** [+3776].
27: 18 "Take Joshua **son** *of* Nun, a man in whom is the spirit, and lay
27: 20 so the whole **Israelite** [+3776] community will obey him.
27: 21 and the entire community of the **Israelites** [+3776] will go out,
28: 2 "Give this command to the **Israelites** [+3776] and say to them:
28: 3 two lambs a year **old** without defect, as a regular burnt offering
28: 9 make an offering of two lambs a year **old** without defect,
28: 11 present to the LORD a burnt offering of two **young** bulls,
28: 11 one ram and seven male lambs a year **old**, all without defect.
28: 19 a burnt offering of two **young** bulls, one ram and seven male lambs
28: 19 one ram and seven male lambs a year **old**, all without defect.
28: 27 Present a burnt offering of two **young** bulls, one ram and seven
28: 27 seven male lambs a year **old** as an aroma pleasing to the LORD.
29: 2 prepare a burnt offering of one **young** bull, one ram and seven
29: 2 one ram and seven male lambs a year **old**, all without defect.
29: 8 aroma pleasing to the LORD a burnt offering of one **young** bull,
29: 8 one ram and seven male lambs a year **old**, all without defect.
29: 13 a burnt offering of thirteen **young** bulls, two rams and fourteen
29: 13 two rams and fourteen male lambs a year **old**, all without defect.
29: 17 " 'On the second day prepare twelve **young** bulls, two rams
29: 17 two rams and fourteen male lambs a year **old**, all without defect.
29: 20 two rams and fourteen male lambs a year **old**, all without defect.
29: 23 two rams and fourteen male lambs a year **old**, all without defect.
29: 26 two rams and fourteen male lambs a year **old**, all without defect.
29: 29 two rams and fourteen male lambs a year **old**, all without defect.
29: 32 two rams and fourteen male lambs a year **old**, all without defect.
29: 36 one ram and seven male lambs a year **old**, all without defect.
29: 40 [30:1] Moses told the **Israelites** [+3776] all that the LORD
30: 1 [30:2] Moses said to the heads of the tribes of **Israel** [+3776]:
31: 2 "Take vengeance on the Midianites for the **Israelites** [+3776].
31: 6 from each tribe, along with Phinehas **son** *of* Eleazar, the priest,
31: 8 of Midian. They also killed Balaam **son** *of* Beor with the sword.
31: 9 The **Israelites** [+3776] captured the Midianite women and children
31: 12 the **Israelite** [+3776] assembly at their camp on the plains of
31: 16 were the means of turning the **Israelites** [+3776] away from the
31: 30 From the **Israelites** [+3776]' half, select one out of every fifty,
31: 42 The half belonging to the **Israelites** [+3776], which Moses set
31: 47 From the **Israelites** [+3776]' half, Moses selected one out of every
31: 54 as a memorial for the **Israelites** [+3776] before the LORD.
32: 1 The **Reubenites** [+8017] and Gadites, who had very large herds
32: 1 The Reubenites and **Gadites** [+1514], who had very large herds
32: 2 So **they**[s] [+1201+1514+2256+8017] came to Moses and Eleazar
32: 2 So **they**[s] [+1201+1514+2256+8017] came to Moses and Eleazar
32: 6 Moses said to the **Gadites** [+1514] and Reubenites, "Shall your
32: 6 Moses said to the Gadites and **Reubenites** [+8017], "Shall your
32: 7 Why do you discourage the **Israelites** [+3776] from going over
32: 9 they discouraged the **Israelites** [+3776] from entering the land the

Nu 32:11 not one of the men twenty years **old** or more who came up out of
32:12 not one except Caleb **son** *of* Jephunneh the Kenizzite and Joshua
32:12 Caleb son of Jephunneh the Kenizzite and Joshua **son** *of* Nun,
32:17 go ahead of the **Israelites** [+3776] until we have brought them to
32:18 We will not return to our homes until every **Israelite** [+3776] has
32:25 The **Gadites** [+1514] and Reubenites said to Moses, "We your
32:25 The Gadites and **Reubenites** [+8017] said to Moses, "We your
32:28 Joshua **son** *of* Nun and to the family heads of the Israelite tribes.
32:28 son of Nun and to the family heads of the **Israelite** [+3776] tribes.
32:29 He said to them, "If the **Gadites** [+1514] and Reubenites,
32:29 He said to them, "If the Gadites and **Reubenites** [+8017],
32:31 The **Gadites** [+1514] and Reubenites answered, "Your servants
32:31 The Gadites and **Reubenites** [+8017] answered, "Your servants
32:33 Moses gave to the **Gadites** [+1514], the Reubenites and the
32:33 the **Reubenites** [+8017] and the half-tribe of Manasseh son of
32:33 the half-tribe of Manasseh **son** *of* Joseph the kingdom of Sihon
32:34 The **Gadites** [+1514] built up Dibon, Ataroth, Aroer,
32:37 the **Reubenites** [+8017] rebuilt Heshbon, Elealeh and Kiriathaim,
32:39 The **descendants** *of* Makir son of Manasseh went to Gilead,
32:39 The descendants of Makir **son** *of* Manasseh went to Gilead,
32:40 the **descendants** *of* Manasseh, and they settled there.
32:41 Jair, a **descendant** *of* Manasseh, captured their settlements
33:1 Here are the stages in the journey of the **Israelites** [+3776] when
33:3 The **Israelites** [+3776] set out from Rameses on the fifteenth day
33:5 The **Israelites** [+3776] left Rameses and camped at Succoth.
33:38 of the fortieth year after the **Israelites** [+3776] came out of Egypt.
33:39 a hundred and twenty-three years **old** when he died on Mount Hor.
33:40 Negev of Canaan, heard that the **Israelites** [+3776] were coming.
33:51 "Speak to the **Israelites** [+3776] and say to them: 'When you cross
34:2 "Command the **Israelites** [+3776] and say to them: 'When you
34:13 Moses commanded the **Israelites** [+3776]: "Assign this land by lot
34:14 because the families of the tribe of **Reuben** [+8018], the tribe of
34:14 the tribe of **Gad** [+1532] and the half-tribe of Manasseh have
34:17 for you as an inheritance: Eleazar the priest and Joshua **son** *of* Nun.
34:19 are their names: Caleb **son** *of* Jephunneh, from the tribe of Judah;
34:20 Shemuel **son** *of* Ammihud, from the tribe of Simeon;
34:20 Shemuel son of Ammihud, from the tribe of **Simeon** [+9058];
34:21 Elidad **son** *of* Kislon, from the tribe of Benjamin;
34:22 Bukki **son** *of* Jogli, the leader from the tribe of Dan;
34:22 Bukki son of Jogli, the leader from the tribe of **Dan** [+1968];
34:23 Hanniel **son** *of* Ephod, the leader from the tribe of Manasseh son of
34:23 the leader from the tribe of **Manasseh** [+4985] son of Joseph;
34:23 son of Ephod, the leader from the tribe of Manasseh **son** *of* Joseph;
34:24 Kemuel **son** *of* Shiphtan, the leader from the tribe of Ephraim son
34:24 the leader from the tribe of **Ephraim** [+713] son of Joseph;
34:25 Elizaphan **son** *of* Parnach, the leader from the tribe of Zebulun;
34:25 son of Parnach, the leader from the tribe of **Zebulun** [+2282];
34:26 Paltiel **son** *of* Azzan, the leader from the tribe of Issachar;
34:26 Paltiel son of Azzan, the leader from the tribe of **Issachar** [+3779];
34:27 Ahihud **son** *of* Shelomi, the leader from the tribe of Asher;
34:27 Ahihud son of Shelomi, the leader from the tribe of **Asher** [+888];
34:28 Pedahel **son** *of* Ammihud, the leader from the tribe of Naphtali."
34:28 son of Ammihud, the leader from the tribe of **Naphtali** [+5889]."
34:29 the inheritance to the **Israelites** [+3776] in the land of Canaan.
35:2 "Command the **Israelites** [+3776] to give the Levites towns to live
35:8 towns you give the Levites from the land the **Israelites** [+3776]
35:10 "Speak to the **Israelites** [+3776] and say to them: 'When you cross
35:15 These six towns will be a place of refuge for **Israelites** [+3776],
35:34 for I, the LORD, dwell among the **Israelites** [+3776].' "
36:1 The family heads of the clan of **Gilead** [+1680] son of Makir,
36:1 The family heads of the clan of Gilead **son** *of* Makir, the son of
36:1 heads of the clan of Gilead son of Makir, the **son** *of* Manasseh,
36:1 who were from the clans of the **descendants** *of* Joseph, came
36:1 and the leaders, the heads of the **Israelite** [+3776] families.
36:2 to give the land as an inheritance to the **Israelites** [+3776] by lot,
36:3 Now suppose they marry **men** from other Israelite tribes; then their
36:3 Now suppose they marry men from other **Israelite** [+3776] tribes;
36:4 When the Year of Jubilee for the **Israelites** [+3776] comes,
36:5 command Moses gave this order to the **Israelites** [+3776]:
36:5 "What the tribe of the **descendants** *of* Joseph is saying is right.
36:7 No inheritance in **Israel** [+3776] is to pass from tribe to tribe,
36:7 for every **Israelite** [+3776] shall keep the tribal land inherited from
36:8 Every daughter who inherits land in any **Israelite** [+3776] tribe
36:8 so that every **Israelite** [+3776] will possess the inheritance of his
36:9 for each **Israelite** [+3776] tribe is to keep the land it inherits."
36:11 and Noah—married their **cousins** [+1856] **on their father's side**.
36:12 They married within the clans of the **descendants** *of* Manasseh son
36:12 within the clans of the descendants of Manasseh **son** *of* Joseph,
36:13 **Israelites** [+3776] on the plains of Moab by the Jordan across from
Dt 1:3 Moses proclaimed to the **Israelites** [+3776] all that the LORD
1:28 walls up to the sky. We even saw the **Anakites** [+6737] there.' "
1:31 as a father carries his **son**, all the way you went until you reached
1:36 except Caleb **son** *of* Jephunneh. He will see it, and I will give him
1:36 and I will give him and his **descendants** the land he set his feet on,
1:38 your assistant, Joshua **son** *of* Nun, will enter it. Encourage him,
1:39 taken captive, your **children** who do not yet know good from bad—
2:4 through the territory of your brothers the **descendants** *of* Esau,
2:8 So we went on past our brothers the **descendants** *of* Esau,
2:9 I have given Ar to the **descendants** *of* Lot as a possession."
2:12 used to live in Seir, but the **descendants** *of* Esau drove them out.
2:19 When you come to the **Ammonites** [+6648], do not harass them
2:19 you possession of any land belonging to the **Ammonites** [+6648].
2:19 I have given it as a possession to the **descendants** *of* Lot."
2:22 The LORD had done the same for the **descendants** *of* Esau,
2:29 as the **descendants** *of* Esau, who live in Seir, and the Moabites,
2:33 we struck him down, together with his **sons** and his whole army.
2:37 did not encroach on any of the land of the **Ammonites** [+6648],
3:11 and six feet wide. It is still in Rabbah of the **Ammonites** [+6648].)
3:14 Jair, a **descendant** *of* Manasseh, took the whole region of Argob as
3:16 the Jabbok River, which is the border of the **Ammonites** [+6648].
3:18 all your able-bodied **men**, armed for battle, must cross over ahead
3:18 must cross over ahead of your brother **Israelites** [+3776].
4:9 Teach them to your **children** and to their children after them.
4:9 them to your children and to **their**[s] [+3870] children after them.
4:9 Teach them to your children and to their **children** after them.
4:10 long as they live in the land and may teach them to their **children**."
4:25 After you have had **children** and grandchildren and have lived in
4:25 After you have had children and **grandchildren** [+1201] and have
4:25 After you have had children and **grandchildren** [+1201] and have
4:40 so that it may go well with you and your **children** after you
4:44 This is the law Moses set before the **Israelites** [+3776].
4:45 laws Moses gave **them**[s] [+3776] when they came out of Egypt
4:46 by Moses and the **Israelites** [+3776] as they came out of Egypt.
5:9 punishing the **children** for the sin of the fathers to the third
5:14 neither you, nor your **son** or daughter, nor your manservant
5:29 so that it might go well with them and their **children** forever!
6:2 your **children** and their children after them may fear the LORD
6:2 **their**[s] [+3870] children after them may fear the LORD your God
6:2 their **children** after them may fear the LORD your God as long as
6:7 Impress them on your **children**. Talk about them when you sit at
6:20 In the future, when your **son** asks you, "What is the meaning of the
6:21 tell **him**[s] [+3870]: "We were slaves of Pharaoh in Egypt,
7:3 Do not give your daughters to their **sons** or take their daughters for
7:3 your daughters to their sons or take their daughters for your **sons**,
7:4 for they will turn your **sons** away from following me to serve other
8:5 Know then in your heart that as a man disciplines his **son**,
9:2 The people are strong and tall—**Anakites** [+6737]! You know
9:2 heard it said: "Who can stand up against the **Anakites** [+6737]?"
10:6 (The **Israelites** [+3776] traveled from the wells of the Jaakanites to
10:6 (The Israelites traveled from the wells of the **Jaakanites** [+3622]
10:6 and was buried, and Eleazar his **son** succeeded him as priest.
11:2 Remember today that your **children** were not the ones who saw
11:6 what he did to Dathan and Abiram, **sons** *of* Eliab the Reubenite,
11:6 did to Dathan and Abiram, sons of Eliab the **Reubenite** [+8017],
11:19 Teach them to your **children**, talking about them when you sit at
11:21 the days of your **children** may be many in the land that the
12:12 you, your **sons** and daughters, your menservants and maidservants,
12:18 you, your **sons** and daughters, your menservants and maidservants,
12:25 so that it may go well with you and your **children** after you,
12:28 that it may always go well with you and your **children** after you,
12:31 They even burn their **sons** and daughters in the fire as sacrifices to
13:6 [13:7] If your **very own brother** [+278+562+3870], or your son or
13:6 [13:7] own brother, or your **son** or daughter, or the wife you love,
13:13 [13:14] that **wicked** [+1175] men have arisen among you
14:1 You are the **children** of the LORD your God. Do not cut
16:11 you, your **sons** and daughters, your menservants and maidservants,
16:14 you, your **sons** and daughters, your menservants and maidservants,
17:20 his **descendants** will reign a long time over his kingdom in Israel.
18:5 chosen them and their **descendants** out of all your tribes to stand
18:10 Let no one be found among you who sacrifices his **son** or daughter
21:5 The priests, the **sons** *of* Levi, shall step forward, for the LORD
21:15 both bear him **sons** but the firstborn is the son of the wife he does
21:15 him sons but the firstborn is the **son** of the wife he does not love,
21:16 when he wills his property to his **sons**, he must not give the rights
21:16 he must not give the rights of the firstborn to the **son** *of* the wife he
21:16 to his actual firstborn, the **son** *of* the wife he does not love.
21:17 He must acknowledge the **son** *of* his unloved wife as the firstborn
21:18 and rebellious **son** who does not obey his father and mother
21:20 shall say to the elders, "This **son** *of* ours is stubborn and rebellious.
22:6 the young or on the eggs, do not take the mother with the **young**.
22:7 You may take the **young**, but be sure to let the mother go,
23:4 [23:5] they hired Balaam **son** *of* Beor from Pethor in Aram
23:8 [23:9] The third generation of **children** born to them may enter
23:17 [23:18] No Israelite **man** or woman is to become a shrine
24:7 is caught kidnapping one of his brother **Israelites** [+3776+4946]
24:16 Fathers shall not be put to death for their **children**, nor children put
24:16 death for their children, nor **children** put to death for their fathers;
25:2 If the guilty man **deserves** to be beaten, the judge shall make him

Dt 25: 5 If brothers are living together and one of them dies without a **son**,
28: 32 Your **sons** and daughters will be given to another nation, and you
28: 41 You will have **sons** and daughters but you will not keep them,
28: 53 the flesh of the **sons** and daughters the LORD your God has given
28: 54 on his own brother or the wife he loves or his surviving **children**,
28: 55 he will not give to one of them any of the flesh of his **children** that
28: 56 will begrudge the husband she loves and her own **son** or daughter
28: 57 the afterbirth from her womb and the **children** she bears. For she
29: 1 [28:69] Moses to make with the **Israelites** [+3776] in Moab,
29: 22 [29:21] Your **children** who follow you in later generations
29: 29 [29:28] things revealed belong to us and to our **children** forever,
30: 2 and when you and your **children** return to the LORD your God
31: 2 "I am now a hundred and twenty years **old** and I am no longer able
31: 9 wrote down this law and gave it to the priests, the **sons** *of* Levi,
31: 13 Their **children**, who do not know this law, must hear it and learn to
31: 19 and teach it to the **Israelites** [+3776] and have them sing it,
31: 19 so that it may be a witness for me against **them**[s] [+3776].
31: 22 down this song that day and taught it to the **Israelites** [+3776].
31: 23 The LORD gave this command to Joshua **son** *of* Nun: "Be strong
31: 23 for you will bring the **Israelites** [+3776] into the land I promised
32: 5 to their shame they are no longer his **children**, but a warped
32: 8 the nations their inheritance, when he divided all **mankind** [+132],
32: 8 for the peoples according to the number of the **sons** *of* Israel.
32: 14 with **choice** rams *of* Bashan and the finest kernels of wheat.
32: 19 rejected them because he was angered by his **sons** and daughters.
32: 20 for they are a perverse generation, **children** who are unfaithful.
32: 44 Moses came with Joshua **son** *of* Nun and spoke all the words of
32: 46 so that you may command your **children** to obey carefully all the
32: 49 the land I am giving the **Israelites** [+3776] as their own
32: 51 **Israelites** [+3776] at the waters of Meribah Kadesh in the Desert
32: 51 you did not uphold my holiness among the **Israelites** [+3776].
32: 52 you will not enter the land I am giving to the **people** *of* Israel."
33: 1 man of God pronounced on the **Israelites** [+3776] before his death.
33: 9 did not recognize his brothers or acknowledge his own **children**,
33: 24 "Most blessed of **sons** is Asher; let him be favored by his brothers,
34: 7 Moses was a hundred and twenty years **old** when he died,
34: 8 The **Israelites** [+3776] grieved for Moses in the plains of Moab
34: 9 Now Joshua **son** *of* Nun was filled with the spirit of wisdom
34: 9 So the **Israelites** [+3776] listened to him and did what the LORD
Jos 1: 1 the LORD, the LORD said to Joshua **son** *of* Nun, Moses' aide:
1: 2 into the land I am about to give to them—to the **Israelites** [+3776].
2: 1 Then Joshua **son** *of* Nun secretly sent two spies from Shittim.
2: 2 Some of the **Israelites** [+3776] have come here tonight to spy out
2: 23 forded the river and came to Joshua **son** *of* Nun and told him
3: 1 all the **Israelites** [+3776] set out from Shittim and went to the
3: 9 Joshua said to the **Israelites** [+3776], "Come here and listen to the
4: 4 the twelve men he had appointed from the **Israelites** [+3776],
4: 5 according to the number of the tribes of the **Israelites** [+3776],
4: 6 In the future, when your **children** ask you, 'What do these stones
4: 7 These stones are to be a memorial to the **people** *of* Israel forever."
4: 8 So the **Israelites** [+3776] did as Joshua commanded them.
4: 8 according to the number of the tribes of the **Israelites** [+3776],
4: 12 The **men** *of* Reuben, Gad and the half-tribe of Manasseh crossed
4: 12 **[RPH]** Gad and the half-tribe of Manasseh crossed over,
4: 12 armed, in front of the **Israelites** [+3776], as Moses had directed
4: 21 He said to the **Israelites** [+3776], "In the future when your
4: 21 "In the future when your **descendants** ask their fathers,
4: 22 tell **them**[s] [+4013], 'Israel crossed the Jordan on dry ground.'
5: 1 the Jordan before the **Israelites** [+3776] until we had crossed over,
5: 1 and they no longer had the courage to face the **Israelites** [+3776].
5: 2 "Make flint knives and circumcise the **Israelites** [+3776] again."
5: 3 and circumcised the **Israelites** [+3776] at Gibeath Haaraloth.
5: 6 The **Israelites** [+3776] had moved about in the desert forty years
5: 7 So he raised up their **sons** in their place, and these were the ones
5: 10 camped at Gilgal on the plains of Jericho, the **Israelites** [+3776]
5: 12 there was no longer any manna for the **Israelites** [+3776],
6: 1 Now Jericho was tightly shut up because of the **Israelites** [+3776].
6: 6 So Joshua **son** *of* Nun called the priests and said to them, "Take up
7: 1 the **Israelites** [+3776] acted unfaithfully in regard to the devoted
7: 1 Achan **son** *of* Carmi, the son of Zimri, the son of Zerah, of the tribe
7: 1 the **son** *of* Zimri, the son of Zerah, of the tribe of Judah, took some
7: 1 the son of Zimri, the **son** *of* Zerah, of the tribe of Judah, took some
7: 1 of them. So the LORD's anger burned against **Israel** [+3776].
7: 12 That is why the **Israelites** [+3776] cannot stand against their
7: 18 and Achan **son** *of* Carmi, the son of Zimri, the son of Zerah,
7: 18 the **son** *of* Zimri, the son of Zerah, of the tribe of Judah, was taken.
7: 18 the son of Zimri, the **son** *of* Zerah, of the tribe of Judah, was taken.
7: 19 "My **son**, give glory to the LORD, the God of Israel, and give
7: 23 brought them to Joshua and all the **Israelites** [+3776] and spread
7: 24 took Achan **son** *of* Zerah, the silver, the robe, the gold wedge,
7: 24 his **sons** and daughters, his cattle, donkeys and sheep, his tent
8: 31 the servant of the LORD had commanded the **Israelites** [+3776].
8: 32 There, in the presence of the **Israelites** [+3776], Joshua copied on
9: 17 So the **Israelites** [+3776] set out and on the third day came to their
9: 18 the **Israelites** [+3776] did not attack them, because the leaders of
9: 26 So Joshua saved them from the **Israelites** [+3776], and they did
10: 4 it has made peace with Joshua and the **Israelites** [+3776]."
10: 11 hailstones than were killed by the swords of the **Israelites** [+3776].
10: 12 On the day the LORD gave the Amorites over to **Israel** [+3776],
10: 20 So Joshua and the **Israelites** [+3776] destroyed them completely—
10: 21 and no one uttered a word against the **Israelites** [+3776].
11: 14 The **Israelites** [+3776] carried off for themselves all the plunder
11: 19 not one city made a treaty of peace with the **Israelites** [+3776],
11: 22 No Anakites were left in **Israelite** [+3776] territory; only in Gaza,
12: 1 These are the kings of the land whom the **Israelites** [+3776] had
12: 2 the Jabbok River, which is the border of the **Ammonites** [+6648].
12: 6 servant of the LORD, and the **Israelites** [+3776] conquered them.
12: 7 the **Israelites** [+3776] conquered on the west side of the Jordan,
13: 6 I myself will drive them out before the **Israelites** [+3776].
13: 10 ruled in Heshbon, out to the border of the **Ammonites** [+6648].
13: 13 But the **Israelites** [+3776] did not drive out the people of Geshur
13: 15 This is what Moses had given to the tribe of **Reuben** [+8017],
13: 22 the **Israelites** [+3776] had put to the sword Balaam son of Beor,
13: 22 the Israelites had put to the sword Balaam **son** *of* Beor,
13: 23 The boundary of the **Reubenites** [+8017] was the bank of the
13: 23 and their villages were the inheritance of the **Reubenites** [+8017],
13: 24 is what Moses had given to the tribe of Gad, **[RPH]** clan by clan:
13: 25 of Gilead and half the **Ammonite** [+6648] country as far as Aroer,
13: 28 and their villages were the inheritance of the **Gadites** [+1514],
13: 29 that is, to half the family of the **descendants** *of* Manasseh,
13: 31 This was for the **descendants** *of* Makir son of Manasseh—
13: 31 This was for the descendants of Makir **son** *of* Manasseh—
13: 31 son of Manasseh—for half of the **sons** *of* Makir, clan by clan.
14: 1 Now these are the areas the **Israelites** [+3776] received as an
14: 1 Joshua **son** *of* Nun and the heads of the tribal clans of Israel
14: 1 and the heads of the tribal clans of **Israel** [+3776] allotted to them.
14: 4 for the **sons** *of* Joseph had become two tribes—Manasseh
14: 5 So the **Israelites** [+3776] divided the land, just as the LORD had
14: 6 Now the **men** *of* Judah approached Joshua at Gilgal, and Caleb son
14: 6 at Gilgal, and Caleb **son** *of* Jephunneh the Kenizzite said to him,
14: 7 I was forty years **old** when Moses the servant of the LORD sent
14: 9 walked will be your inheritance and that of your **children** forever,
14: 10 about in the desert. So here I am today, eighty-five years **old**!
14: 13 Joshua blessed Caleb **son** *of* Jephunneh and gave him Hebron as
14: 14 So Hebron has belonged to Caleb **son** *of* Jephunneh the Kenizzite
15: 1 The allotment for the tribe of **Judah** [+3373], clan by clan,
15: 6 continued north of Beth Arabah to the Stone of Bohan **son** *of*
15: 12 These are the boundaries around the **people** *of* Judah by their
15: 13 Joshua gave to Caleb **son** *of* Jephunneh a portion in Judah—
15: 13 gave to Caleb son of Jephunneh a portion in **Judah** [+3373]—
15: 14 From Hebron Caleb drove out the three **Anakites** [+6737]—
15: 17 Othniel **son** *of* Kenaz, Caleb's brother, took it; so Caleb gave his
15: 20 This is the inheritance of the tribe of **Judah** [+3373], clan by clan:
15: 21 The southernmost towns of the tribe of **Judah** [+3373] in the
15: 63 **Judah** [+3373] could not dislodge the Jebusites, who were living
15: 63 to this day the Jebusites live there with the **people** *of* Judah.
16: 1 The allotment for **Joseph** [+3441] began at the Jordan of Jericho,
16: 4 So Manasseh and Ephraim, the **descendants** *of* Joseph,
16: 5 This was the territory of **Ephraim** [+713], clan by clan: The
16: 8 This was the inheritance of the tribe of the **Ephraimites** [+713],
16: 9 their villages that were set aside for the **Ephraimites** [+713] within
16: 9 the Ephraimites within the inheritance of the **Manassites** [+4985].
17: 2 So this allotment was for the rest of the **people** *of* Manasseh—
17: 2 the **clans** *of* Abiezer, Helek, Asriel, Shechem, Hepher and
17: 2 of Abiezer, **[RPH]** Helek, Asriel, Shechem, Hepher and Shemida.
17: 2 of Abiezer, Helek, **[RPH]** Asriel, Shechem, Hepher and Shemida.
17: 2 of Abiezer, Helek, Asriel, **[RPH]** Shechem, Hepher and Shemida.
17: 2 of Abiezer, Helek, Asriel, Shechem, **[RPH]** Hepher and Shemida.
17: 2 of Abiezer, Helek, Asriel, Shechem, Hepher **[RPH]** and Shemida.
17: 2 These are the other male **descendants** *of* Manasseh son of Joseph
17: 2 These are the other male descendants of Manasseh **son** *of* Joseph
17: 3 Now Zelophehad **son** *of* Hepher, the son of Gilead, the son of
17: 3 the **son** *of* Gilead, the son of Makir, the son of Manasseh,
17: 3 the son of Gilead, the **son** *of* Makir, the son of Manasseh,
17: 3 of Makir, the **son** *of* Manasseh, had no sons but only daughters,
17: 3 of Makir, the son of Manasseh, had no **sons** but only daughters,
17: 4 to Eleazar the priest, Joshua **son** *of* Nun, and the leaders and said,
17: 6 of the tribe of Manasseh received an inheritance among the **sons**.
17: 6 The land of Gilead belonged to the rest of the **descendants** *of*
17: 8 the boundary of Manasseh, belonged to the **Ephraimites** [+713].)
17: 12 Yet the **Manassites** [+4985] were not able to occupy these towns,
17: 13 However, when the **Israelites** [+3776] grew stronger, they
17: 14 The **people** *of* Joseph said to Joshua, "Why have you given us only
17: 16 The **people** *of* Joseph replied, "The hill country is not enough for
18: 1 The whole assembly of the **Israelites** [+3776] gathered at Shiloh
18: 2 there were still seven **Israelite** [+3776] tribes who had not yet
18: 3 So Joshua said to the **Israelites** [+3776]: "How long will you wait
18: 10 there he distributed the land to the **Israelites** [+3776] according to

Jos 18:11 The lot came up for the tribe of **Benjamin** [+1228], clan by clan.
18:11 Their allotted territory lay between the **tribes** *of* Judah and Joseph:
18:11 territory lay between the tribes of Judah and **Joseph** [+3441]:
18:14 Baal (that is, Kiriath Jearim), a town of the **people** *of* Judah.
18:17 of Adummim, and ran down to the Stone of Bohan **son** *of* Reuben.
18:20 out the inheritance of the clans of **Benjamin** [+1228] on all sides.
18:21 The tribe of **Benjamin** [+1228], clan by clan, had the following
18:28 This was the inheritance of **Benjamin** [+1228] for its clans.
19: 1 The second lot came out for the tribe of **Simeon** [+9058], clan by
19: 1 Their inheritance lay within the territory of **Judah** [+3373].
19: 8 This was the inheritance of the tribe of the **Simeonites** [+9058],
19: 9 The inheritance of the **Simeonites** [+9058] was taken from the
19: 9 of the Simeonites was taken from the share of **Judah** [+3373],
19: 9 because **Judah's** [+3373] portion was more than they needed.
19: 9 So the **Simeonites** [+9058] received their inheritance within the
19:10 The third lot came up for **Zebulun** [+2282], clan by clan: The
19:16 and their villages were the inheritance of **Zebulun** [+2282],
19:17 The fourth lot came out for **Issachar** [+3779], clan by clan.
19:23 their villages were the inheritance of the tribe of **Issachar** [+3779],
19:24 The fifth lot came out for the tribe of **Asher** [+888], clan by clan.
19:31 and their villages were the inheritance of the tribe of **Asher** [+888],
19:32 The sixth lot came out for **Naphtali** [+5889], clan by clan:
19:32 The sixth lot came out for Naphtali, clan by clan: **[RPH]**
19:39 their villages were the inheritance of the tribe of **Naphtali** [+5889],
19:40 The seventh lot came out for the tribe of **Dan** [+1968], clan by
19:47 (But the **Danites** [+1968] had difficulty taking possession of their
19:47 so **they**[s] [+1968] went up and attacked Leshem, took it, put it to
19:48 and their villages were the inheritance of the tribe of **Dan** [+1968],
19:49 the **Israelites** [+3776] gave Joshua son of Nun an inheritance
19:49 the Israelites gave Joshua **son** *of* Nun an inheritance among them,
19:51 Joshua **son** *of* Nun and the heads of the tribal clans of Israel
19:51 the heads of the tribal clans of **Israel** [+3776] assigned by lot at
20: 2 "Tell the **Israelites** [+3776] to designate the cities of refuge,
20: 9 Any of the **Israelites** [+3776] or any alien living among them who
21: 1 Joshua **son** *of* Nun, and the heads of the other tribal families of
21: 1 and the heads of the other tribal families of **Israel** [+3776]
21: 3 the **Israelites** [+3776] gave the Levites the following towns
21: 4 The Levites who were **descendants** *of* Aaron the priest were
21: 5 The rest of Kohath's **descendants** were allotted ten towns from the
21: 6 The **descendants** *of* Gershon were allotted thirteen towns from the
21: 7 The **descendants** *of* Merari, clan by clan, received twelve towns
21: 8 So the **Israelites** [+3776] allotted to the Levites these towns
21: 9 From the tribes of **Judah** [+3373] and Simeon they allotted the
21: 9 and **Simeon** [+9058] they allotted the following towns by name
21:10 (these towns were assigned to the **descendants** *of* Aaron who were
21:10 Aaron who were from the Kohathite clans of the **Levites** [+4290],
21:12 villages around the city they had given to Caleb **son** *of* Jephunneh
21:13 So to the **descendants** *of* Aaron the priest they gave Hebron (a city
21:19 the towns for the priests, the **descendants** *of* Aaron, were thirteen,
21:20 The rest of the **Kohathite** [+7740] clans of the Levites were
21:20 The rest of the Kohathite clans **[RPH]** of the Levites were allotted
21:26 their pasturelands were given to the rest of the **Kohathite** [+7740]
21:27 The Levite clans of the **Gershonites** [+1767] were given:
21:34 The **Merarite** [+5356] clans (the rest of the Levites) were given:
21:40 All the towns allotted to the **Merarite** [+5356] clans, who were the
21:41 the territory held by the **Israelites** [+3776] were forty-eight in all,
22: 9 So the **Reubenites** [+8017], the Gadites and the half-tribe of
22: 9 the **Gadites** [+1514] and the half-tribe of Manasseh left the
22: 9 the half-tribe of Manasseh left the **Israelites** [+3776] at Shiloh in
22:10 the **Reubenites** [+8017], the Gadites and the half-tribe of
22:10 the **Gadites** [+1514] and the half-tribe of Manasseh built an
22:11 when the **Israelites** [+3776] heard that they had built the altar on
22:11 of Canaan at Geliloth **[RPH]** near the Jordan on the Israelite side,
22:11 of Canaan at Geliloth **[RPH]** near the Jordan on the Israelite side,
22:11 of Canaan at Geliloth near the Jordan on the **Israelite** [+3776] side,
22:12 the whole assembly of **Israel** [+3776] gathered at Shiloh to go to
22:12 the whole assembly of Israel gathered **[RPH]** at Shiloh to go to
22:13 So the **Israelites** [+3776] sent Phinehas son of Eleazar, the priest,
22:13 So the Israelites sent Phinehas **son** *of* Eleazar, the priest,
22:13 to **Reuben** [+8017], Gad and the half-tribe of Manasseh.
22:13 to Reuben, **Gad** [+1514] and the half-tribe of Manasseh.
22:15 to **Reuben** [+8017], Gad and the half-tribe of Manasseh—
22:15 to Reuben, **Gad** [+1514] and the half-tribe of Manasseh—
22:20 When Achan **son** *of* Zerah acted unfaithfully regarding the devoted
22:21 **Reuben** [+8017], Gad and the half-tribe of Manasseh replied to the
22:21 Reuben, **Gad** [+1514] and the half-tribe of Manasseh replied to the
22:24 We did it for fear that some day your **descendants** might say to
22:24 **[RPH]** 'What do you have to do with the LORD, the God of
22:25 between us and you—you **Reubenites** [+8017] and Gadites!
22:25 between us and you—you Reubenites and **Gadites** [+1514]!
22:25 So your **descendants** might cause ours to stop fearing the LORD.
22:25 So your descendants might cause ours to stop **[RPH]** fearing the
22:27 Then in the future your **descendants** will not be able to say to ours,
22:27 be able to say to ours, **[RPH]** 'You have no share in the LORD.'
22:30 heard what **Reuben** [+8017], Gad and Manasseh had to say,
22:30 heard what Reuben, **Gad** [+1514] and Manasseh had to say,
22:30 Gad and **Manasseh** [+4985] had to say, they were pleased.
22:31 And Phinehas **son** *of* Eleazar, the priest, said to Reuben, Gad
22:31 of Eleazar, the priest, said to **Reuben** [+8017], Gad and Manasseh,
22:31 of Eleazar, the priest, said to Reuben, **Gad** [+1514] and Manasseh,
22:31 of Eleazar, the priest, said to Reuben, Gad and **Manasseh** [+4985],
22:31 Now you have rescued the **Israelites** [+3776] from the LORD's
22:32 Phinehas **son** *of* Eleazar, the priest, and the leaders returned to
22:32 to Canaan from their meeting with the **Reubenites** [+8017]
22:32 and **Gadites** [+1514] in Gilead and reported to the Israelites.
22:32 and Gadites in Gilead and reported to the **Israelites** [+3776].
22:33 **They**[s] [+3776] were glad to hear the report and praised God.
22:33 **[RPH]** And they talked no more about going to war against them
22:33 them to devastate the country where the **Reubenites** [+8017]
22:33 the country where the Reubenites and the **Gadites** [+1514] lived.
22:34 the **Reubenites** [+8017] and the Gadites gave the altar this name:
22:34 the Reubenites and the **Gadites** [+1514] gave the altar this name:
24: 4 of Seir to Esau, but Jacob and his **sons** went down to Egypt.
24: 9 When Balak **son** *of* Zippor, the king of Moab, prepared to fight
24: 9 he sent for Balaam **son** *of* Beor to put a curse on you.
24:29 After these things, Joshua **son** *of* Nun, the servant of the LORD,
24:29 of the LORD, died at the **age** [+9102] *of* a hundred and ten.
24:32 which the **Israelites** [+3776] had brought up from Egypt,
24:32 bought for a hundred pieces of silver from the **sons** *of* Hamor,
24:32 of Shechem. This became the inheritance of Joseph's **descendants**.
24:33 And Eleazar **son** *of* Aaron died and was buried at Gibeah,
24:33 which had been allotted to his **son** Phinehas in the hill country of
Jdg 1: 1 the death of Joshua, the **Israelites** [+3776] asked the LORD,
1: 8 The **men** *of* Judah attacked Jerusalem also and took it. They put
1: 9 the **men** *of* Judah went down to fight against the Canaanites living
1:13 Othniel **son** *of* Kenaz, Caleb's younger brother, took it; so Caleb
1:16 The **descendants** *of* Moses' father-in-law, the Kenite, went up
1:16 went up from the City of Palms with the **men** *of* Judah to live
1:20 was given to Caleb, who drove from it the three **sons** *of* Anak.
1:21 The **Benjamites** [+1228], however, failed to dislodge the Jebusites,
1:21 to this day the Jebusites live there with the **Benjamites** [+1228].
1:34 The Amorites confined the **Danites** [+1968] to the hill country,
2: 4 the LORD had spoken these things to all the **Israelites** [+3776],
2: 6 After Joshua had dismissed the **Israelites** [+3776], they went to
2: 8 Joshua **son** *of* Nun, the servant of the LORD, died at the age of a
2: 8 of the LORD, died at the **age** [+9102] *of* a hundred and ten.
2:11 Then the **Israelites** [+3776] did evil in the eyes of the LORD
3: 2 **Israelites** [+3776] who had not had previous battle experience):
3: 5 The **Israelites** [+3776] lived among the Canaanites, Hittites,
3: 6 daughters in marriage and gave their own daughters to their **sons**,
3: 7 The **Israelites** [+3776] did evil in the eyes of the LORD;
3: 8 to whom the **Israelites** [+3776] were subject for eight years.
3: 9 when **they**[s] [+3776] cried out to the LORD, he raised up for them
3: 9 he raised up for **them**[s] [+3776] a deliverer, Othniel son of Kenaz,
3: 9 Othniel **son** *of* Kenaz, Caleb's younger brother, who saved them.
3:11 the land had peace for forty years, until Othniel **son** *of* Kenaz died.
3:12 Once again the **Israelites** [+3776] did evil in the eyes of the
3:13 Getting the **Ammonites** [+6648] and Amalekites to join him,
3:14 The **Israelites** [+3776] were subject to Eglon king of Moab for
3:15 Again the **Israelites** [+3776] cried out to the LORD, and he gave
3:15 a left-handed man, the **son** *of* Gera the Benjamite.
3:15 The **Israelites** [+3776] sent him with tribute to Eglon king of
3:27 and the **Israelites** [+3776] went down with him from the hills,
3:31 After Ehud came Shamgar **son** *of* Anath, who struck down six
4: 1 the **Israelites** [+3776] once again did evil in the eyes of the
4: 3 and had cruelly oppressed the **Israelites** [+3776] for twenty years,
4: 3 had cruelly oppressed the Israelites for twenty years, **they**[s] [+3776]
4: 5 the **Israelites** [+3776] came to her to have their disputes decided.
4: 6 She sent for Barak **son** *of* Abinoam from Kedesh in Naphtali
4: 6 take with you ten thousand men of **Naphtali** [+5889] and Zebulun
4: 6 and **Zebulun** [+2282] and lead the way to Mount Tabor.
4:11 other Kenites, the **descendants** *of* Hobab, Moses' brother-in-law,
4:12 When they told Sisera that Barak **son** *of* Abinoam had gone up to
4:23 subdued Jabin, the Canaanite king, before the **Israelites** [+3776].
4:24 the hand of the **Israelites** [+3776] grew stronger and stronger
5: 1 On that day Deborah and Barak **son** *of* Abinoam sang this song:
5: 6 "In the days of Shamgar **son** *of* Anath, in the days of Jael,
5:12 O Barak! Take captive your captives, O **son** *of* Abinoam.'
6: 1 Again the **Israelites** [+3776] did evil in the eyes of the LORD,
6: 2 the **Israelites** [+3776] prepared shelters for themselves in
6: 3 Amalekites and other eastern **peoples** invaded the country.
6: 6 so impoverished the Israelites that **they**[s] [+3776] cried out to the
6: 7 When the **Israelites** [+3776] cried to the LORD because of
6: 8 he sent **them**[s] [+3776] a prophet, who said, "This is what the
6:11 where his **son** Gideon was threshing wheat in a winepress to keep
6:29 carefully investigated, they were told, "Gideon **son** *of* Joash did it."
6:30 The men of the town demanded of Joash, "Bring out your **son**.
6:33 Amalekites and other eastern **peoples** joined forces and crossed

Jdg 7:12 and all the other eastern **peoples** had settled in the valley,
7:14 "This can be nothing other than the sword of Gideon **son** *of* Joash,
8:10 all that were left of the armies of the eastern **peoples**;
8:13 Gideon **son** *of* Joash then returned from the battle by the Pass of
8:18 they answered, "each one with the bearing of a **prince** [+4889]."
8:19 "Those were my brothers, the **sons** *of* my own mother.
8:22 said to Gideon, "Rule over us—you, your **son** and your grandson—
8:22 "Rule over us—you, your son and your **grandson** [+1201]—
8:22 "Rule over us—you, your son and your **grandson** [+1201]—
8:23 told them, "I will not rule over you, nor will my **son** rule over you.
8:28 Thus Midian was subdued before the **Israelites** [+3776] and did
8:29 Jerub-Baal **son** *of* Joash went back home to live.
8:30 He had seventy **sons** of his own, for he had many wives.
8:31 His concubine, who lived in Shechem, also bore him a **son**,
8:32 Gideon **son** *of* Joash died at a good old age and was buried in the
8:33 No sooner had Gideon died than the **Israelites** [+3776] again
8:34 did not remember **[RPH]** the LORD their God, who had rescued
9:1 Abimelech **son** *of* Jerub-Baal went to his mother's brothers in
9:2 to have all seventy *of* Jerub-Baal's **sons** rule over you, or just one
9:5 one stone murdered his seventy brothers, the **sons** *of* Jerub-Baal.
9:5 But Jotham, the youngest **son** *of* Jerub-Baal, escaped by hiding.
9:18 murdered his seventy **sons** on a single stone, and made Abimelech,
9:18 made Abimelech, the **son** *of* his slave girl, king over the citizens of
9:24 did this in order that the crime against Jerub-Baal's seventy **sons**,
9:26 Now Gaal **son** *of* Ebed moved with his brothers into Shechem,
9:28 Gaal **son** *of* Ebed said, "Who is Abimelech, and who is Shechem,
9:28 Isn't he Jerub-Baal's **son**, and isn't Zebul his deputy? Serve the
9:30 When Zebul the governor of the city heard what Gaal **son** *of* Ebed
9:31 "Gaal **son** *of* Ebed and his brothers have come to Shechem
9:35 Now Gaal **son** *of* Ebed had gone out and was standing at the
9:57 The curse of Jotham **son** *of* Jerub-Baal came on them.
10:1 of Issachar, Tola **son** *of* Puah, the son of Dodo, rose to save Israel.
10:1 of Issachar, Tola son of Puah, the **son** *of* Dodo, rose to save Israel.
10:4 He had thirty **sons**, who rode thirty donkeys. They controlled thirty
10:6 Again the **Israelites** [+3776] did evil in the eyes of the LORD.
10:6 the gods of the **Ammonites** [+6648] and the gods of the
10:7 them into the hands of the Philistines and the **Ammonites** [+6648],
10:8 who that year shattered and crushed **them**[s] [+3776]. For eighteen
10:8 For eighteen years they oppressed all the **Israelites** [+3776] on the
10:9 The **Ammonites** [+6648] also crossed the Jordan to fight against
10:10 the **Israelites** [+3776] cried out to the LORD, "We have sinned
10:11 **[RPH]** "When the Egyptians, the Amorites, the Ammonites,
10:11 the Amorites, the **Ammonites** [+6648], the Philistines,
10:15 But the **Israelites** [+3776] said to the LORD, "We have sinned.
10:17 When the **Ammonites** [+6648] were called to arms and camped in
10:17 in Gilead, the **Israelites** [+3776] assembled and camped at Mizpah.
10:18 "Whoever will launch the attack against the **Ammonites** [+6648]
11:1 His father was Gilead; his **[RPH]** mother was a prostitute.
11:2 Gilead's wife also bore him **sons**, and when they were grown up,
11:2 when **they**[s] [+851+2021] were grown up, they drove Jephthah
11:2 they said, "because you are the **son** *of* another woman."
11:4 time later, when the **Ammonites** [+6648] made war on Israel,
11:5 the **[RPH]** elders of Gilead went to get Jephthah from the land of
11:6 "be our commander, so we can fight the **Ammonites** [+6648]."
11:8 come with us to fight the **Ammonites** [+6648], and you will be our
11:9 "Suppose you take me back to fight the **Ammonites** [+6648]
11:12 Jephthah sent messengers to the **Ammonite** [+6648] king with the
11:13 The king of the **Ammonites** [+6648] answered Jephthah's
11:14 Jephthah sent back messengers to the **Ammonite** [+6648] king,
11:15 not take the land of Moab or the land of the **Ammonites** [+6648].
11:25 Are you better than Balak **son** *of* Zippor, king of Moab? Did he
11:27 decide the dispute this day between the **Israelites** [+3776]
11:27 this day between the Israelites and the **Ammonites** [+6648]."
11:28 The king of **Ammon** [+6648], however, paid no attention to the
11:29 and from there he advanced against the **Ammonites** [+6648].
11:30 the LORD: "If you give the **Ammonites** [+6648] into my hands,
11:31 in triumph from the **Ammonites** [+6648] will be the LORD's,
11:32 Then Jephthah went over to fight the **Ammonites** [+6648],
11:33 as far as Abel Keramim. Thus **Israel** [+3776] subdued Ammon.
11:33 as far as Abel Keramim. Thus Israel subdued **Ammon** [+6648].
11:34 was an only child. Except for her he had neither **son** nor daughter.
11:36 has avenged you of your enemies, the **Ammonites** [+6648].
12:1 "Why did you go to fight the **Ammonites** [+6648] without calling
12:2 were engaged in a great struggle with the **Ammonites** [+6648],
12:3 life in my hands and crossed over to fight the **Ammonites** [+6648],
12:9 He had thirty **sons** and thirty daughters. He gave his daughters
12:9 for his **sons** he brought in thirty young women as wives from
12:13 After him, Abdon **son** *of* Hillel, from Pirathon, led Israel.
12:14 He had forty **sons** and thirty grandsons, who rode on seventy
12:14 He had forty sons and thirty **grandsons** [+1201], who rode on
12:14 He had forty sons and thirty **grandsons** [+1201], who rode on
12:15 Abdon **son** *of* Hillel died, and was buried at Pirathon in Ephraim,
13:1 Again the **Israelites** [+3776] did evil in the eyes of the LORD,
13:3 and childless, but you are going to conceive and have a **son**.
13:5 because you will conceive and give birth to a **son**. No razor may be
13:7 But he said to me, 'You will conceive and give birth to a **son**.
13:24 The woman gave birth to a **boy** and named him Samson. He grew
14:16 You've given my **people** [+6639] a riddle, but you haven't told me
14:17 press him. She in turn explained the riddle to her **people** [+6639].
17:2 I took it." Then his mother said, "The LORD bless you, my **son**!"
17:3 "I solemnly consecrate my silver to the LORD for my **son** to
17:5 an ephod and some idols and installed one of his **sons** as his priest.
17:11 live with him, and the young man was to him like one of his **sons**.
18:2 So the **Danites** [+1968] sent five warriors from Zorah and Eshtaol
18:2 So the Danites sent five **warriors** [+2657] from Zorah and Eshtaol
18:16 The six hundred **Danites** [+1968], armed for battle, stood at the
18:22 Micah were called together and overtook the **Danites** [+1968].
18:23 shouted after them, the **Danites** [+1968] turned and said to Micah,
18:25 The **Danites** [+1968] answered, "Don't argue with us, or some
18:26 So the **Danites** [+1968] went their way, and Micah, seeing that
18:30 There the **Danites** [+1968] set up for themselves the idols,
18:30 the idols, and Jonathan **son** *of* Gershom, the son of Moses,
18:30 the idols, and Jonathan son of Gershom, the **son** *of* Moses,
18:30 his **sons** were priests for the tribe of Dan until the time of the
19:12 into an alien city, whose people are not **Israelites** [+3776+4946].
19:22 some of the **wicked** [+1175] men of the city surrounded the house.
19:30 not since the day the **Israelites** [+3776] came up out of Egypt.
20:1 all the **Israelites** [+3776] from Dan to Beersheba and from the land
20:3 (The **Benjamites** [+1228] heard that the Israelites had gone up to
20:3 (The Benjamites heard that the **Israelites** [+3776] had gone up to
20:3 the **Israelites** [+3776] said, "Tell us how this awful thing
20:7 Now, all you **Israelites** [+3776], speak up and give your verdict."
20:13 Now surrender those **wicked** [+1175] men of Gibeah so that we
20:13 the **Benjamites** [+1228] would not listen to their fellow Israelites.
20:13 the Benjamites would not listen to their fellow **Israelites** [+3776].
20:14 From their towns **they**[s] [+1228] came together at Gibeah to fight
20:14 came together at Gibeah to fight against the **Israelites** [+3776].
20:15 At once the **Benjamites** [+1228] mobilized twenty-six thousand
20:18 The **Israelites** [+3776] went up to Bethel and inquired of God.
20:18 "Who of us shall go first to fight against the **Benjamites** [+1228]?"
20:19 The next morning the **Israelites** [+3776] got up and pitched camp
20:21 The **Benjamites** [+1228] came out of Gibeah and cut down
20:23 The **Israelites** [+3776] went up and wept before the LORD until
20:23 "Shall we go up again to battle against the **Benjamites** [+1228],
20:24 Then the **Israelites** [+3776] drew near to Benjamin the second day.
20:24 Then the Israelites drew near to **Benjamin** [+1228] the second day.
20:25 they cut down another eighteen thousand **Israelites** [+3776],
20:26 Then the **Israelites** [+3776], all the people, went up to Bethel,
20:27 the **Israelites** [+3776] inquired of the LORD. (In those days the
20:28 with Phinehas **son** *of* Eleazar, the son of Aaron, ministering before
20:28 Phinehas son of Eleazar, the **son** *of* Aaron, ministering before it.)
20:28 "Shall we go up again to battle with **Benjamin** [+1228] our
20:30 **They**[s] [+3776] went up against the Benjamites on the third day
20:30 They went up against the **Benjamites** [+1228] on the third day
20:31 The **Benjamites** [+1228] came out to meet them and were drawn
20:32 While the **Benjamites** [+1228] were saying, "We are defeating
20:32 the **Israelites** [+3776] were saying, "Let's retreat and draw them
20:35 on that day the **Israelites** [+3776] struck down 25,100 Benjamites,
20:36 the **Benjamites** [+1228] saw that they were beaten. Now the men
20:48 The men of Israel went back to **Benjamin** [+1228] and put all the
21:5 the **Israelites** [+3776] asked, "Who from all the tribes of Israel has
21:6 Now the **Israelites** [+3776] grieved for their brothers,
21:10 So the assembly sent twelve thousand **fighting** [+2657] men with
21:13 offer of peace to the **Benjamites** [+1228] at the rock of Rimmon.
21:18 as wives, since we **Israelites** [+3776] have taken this oath:
21:20 So they instructed the **Benjamites** [+1228], saying, "Go and hide
21:23 So that is what the **Benjamites** [+1228] did. While the girls were
21:24 At that time the **Israelites** [+3776] left that place and went home to
Ru 1:1 from Bethlehem in Judah, together with his wife and two **sons**,
1:2 and the names of his two **sons** were Mahlon and Kilion.
1:3 Naomi's husband, died, and she was left with her two **sons**.
1:11 Am I going to have any more **sons**, who could become your
1:12 even if I had a husband tonight and then gave birth to **sons**—
4:13 the LORD enabled her to conceive, and she gave birth to a **son**.
4:15 who loves you and who is better to you than seven **sons**, has given
4:17 The women living there said, "Naomi has a **son**." And they named
1Sa 1:1 whose name was Elkanah **son** *of* Jeroham, the son of Elihu,
1:1 the **son** *of* Elihu, the son of Tohu, the son of Zuph, an Ephraimite.
1:1 the son of Elihu, the **son** *of* Tohu, the son of Zuph, an Ephraimite.
1:1 the son of Elihu, the son of Tohu, the **son** *of* Zuph, an Ephraimite.
1:3 where Hophni and Phinehas, the two **sons** *of* Eli, were priests of
1:4 of the meat to his wife Peninnah and to all her **sons** and daughters.
1:8 are you downhearted? Don't I mean more to you than ten **sons**?"
1:20 So in the course of time Hannah conceived and gave birth to a **son**.
1:23 stayed at home and nursed her **son** until she had weaned him.
2:5 borne seven children, but she who has had many **sons** pines away.
2:12 Eli's **sons** were wicked men; they had no regard for the LORD.
2:12 Eli's sons were wicked **men**; they had no regard for the LORD.

1Sa 2:21 she conceived and gave birth to three **sons** and two daughters.
2:22 heard about everything his **sons** were doing to all Israel and how
2:24 No, my **sons**; it is not a good report that I hear spreading among
2:28 house all the offerings made with fire by the **Israelites** [+3776].
2:29 Why do you honor your **sons** more than me by fattening yourselves
2:34 " 'And what happens to your two **sons**, Hophni and Phinehas,
3: 6 "My **son**," Eli said, "I did not call; go back and lie down."
3:13 his **sons** made themselves contemptible, and he failed to restrain
3:16 but Eli called him and said, "Samuel, my **son**." Samuel answered,
4: 4 Eli's two **sons**, Hophni and Phinehas, were there with the ark of
4:11 God was captured, and Eli's two **sons**, Hophni and Phinehas, died.
4:15 who was ninety-eight years **old** and whose eyes were set so that he
4:16 I fled from it this very day." Eli asked, "What happened, my **son**?"
4:17 Also your two **sons**, Hophni and Phinehas, are dead, and the ark of
4:20 attending her said, "Don't despair; you have given birth to a **son**."
6: 7 the cows to the cart, but take their **calves** away and pen them up.
6:10 such cows and hitched them to the cart and penned up their **calves**.
7: 1 and consecrated Eleazar his **son** to guard the ark of the LORD.
7: 4 So the **Israelites** [+3776] put away their Baals and Ashtoreths,
7: 6 the LORD." And Samuel was leader of **Israel** [+3776] at Mizpah.
7: 7 When the Philistines heard that **Israel** [+3776] had assembled at
7: 7 And when the **Israelites** [+3776] heard of it, they were afraid
7: 8 **They**[s] [+3776] said to Samuel, "Do not stop crying out to the
8: 1 When Samuel grew old, he appointed his **sons** as judges for Israel.
8: 2 The name of his **[RPH]** firstborn was Joel and the name of his
8: 3 his **sons** did not walk in his ways. They turned aside after dishonest
8: 5 said to him, "You are old, and your **sons** do not walk in your ways;
8:11 He will take your **sons** and make them serve with his chariots
9: 1 of standing, whose name was Kish **son** *of* Abiel, the son of Zeror,
9: 1 the **son** *of* Zeror, the son of Becorath, the son of Aphiah of
9: 1 the son of Zeror, the **son** *of* Becorath, the son of Aphiah of
9: 1 son of Zeror, the son of Becorath, the **son** *of* Aphiah of Benjamin.
9: 1 the son of Becorath, the son of Aphiah of **Benjamin** [+408+3549].
9: 2 He had a **son** named Saul, an impressive young man without equal
9: 2 young man without equal among the **Israelites** [+3776]—
9: 3 and Kish said to his **son** Saul, "Take one of the servants with you
10: 2 about you. He is asking, "What shall I do about my **son**?" '
10:11 each other, "What is this that has happened to the **son** *of* Kish?
10:18 said to **them**[s] [+3776], "This is what the LORD, the God of
10:21 and Matri's clan was chosen. Finally Saul **son** *of* Kish was chosen.
10:27 *some* **troublemakers** [+1175] said, "How can this fellow save
11: 8 the **men** *of* Israel numbered three hundred thousand and the men of
12: 2 As for me, I am old and gray, and my **sons** are here with you.
12:12 "But when you saw that Nahash king of the **Ammonites** [+6648]
13: 1 Saul was ⌞thirty⌟ years **old** when he became king, and he reigned
13:16 Saul and his **son** Jonathan and the men with them were staying in
13:22 or spear in his hand; only Saul and his **son** Jonathan had them.
14: 1 One day Jonathan **son** *of* Saul said to the young man bearing his
14: 3 He was a **son** *of* Ichabod's brother Ahitub son of Phinehas,
14: 3 He was a son of Ichabod's brother Ahitub **son** *of* Phinehas,
14: 3 son of Phinehas, the **son** *of* Eli, the LORD's priest in Shiloh.
14:18 the ark of God." (At that time it was with the **Israelites** [+3776].)
14:32 on the plunder and, taking sheep, cattle and **calves** [+1330],
14:39 Israel lives, even if it lies with my **son** Jonathan, he must die."
14:40 stand over there; I and Jonathan my **son** will stand over here."
14:42 Saul said, "Cast the lot between me and Jonathan my **son**."
14:47 Moab, the **Ammonites** [+6648], Edom, the kings of Zobah,
14:49 Saul's **sons** were Jonathan, Ishvi and Malki-Shua. The name of his
14:50 The name of the commander of Saul's army was Abner **son** *of* Ner,
14:51 Saul's father Kish and Abner's father Ner were **sons** *of* Abiel.
14:52 whenever Saul saw a mighty or **brave** [+2657] man, he took him
15: 6 for you showed kindness to all the **Israelites** [+3776] when they
16: 1 to Jesse of Bethlehem. I have chosen one of his **sons** to be king."
16: 5 he consecrated Jesse and his **sons** and invited them to the sacrifice.
16:10 Jesse had seven of his **sons** pass before Samuel, but Samuel said to
16:18 "I have seen a **son** of Jesse of Bethlehem who knows how to play
16:19 Saul sent messengers to Jesse and said, "Send me your **son** David,
16:20 and a young goat and sent them with his **son** David to Saul.
17:12 Now David was the **son** *of* an Ephrathite named Jesse, who was
17:12 Jesse had eight **sons**, and in Saul's time he was old and well
17:13 Jesse's three oldest **sons** had followed Saul to the war: The
17:13 **[RPH]** The firstborn was Eliab; the second, Abinadab;
17:17 Now Jesse said to his **son** David, "Take this ephah of roasted grain
17:53 When the **Israelites** [+3776] returned from chasing the Philistines,
17:55 commander of the army, "Abner, whose **son** is that young man?"
17:56 The king said, "Find out whose **son** this young man is."
17:58 "Whose **son** are you, young man?" Saul asked him. David said,
17:58 David said, "I am the **son** *of* your servant Jesse of Bethlehem."
18:17 only serve me **bravely** [+2657+4200] and fight the battles of the
19: 1 Saul told his **son** Jonathan and all the attendants to kill David.
19: 1 to kill David. But Jonathan **[NIE]** was very fond of David
20:27 Saul said to his **son** Jonathan, "Why hasn't the son of Jesse come
20:27 "Why hasn't the **son** *of* Jesse come to the meal, either yesterday
20:30 and he said to him, "You **son** *of* a perverse and rebellious woman!
20:30 Don't I know that you have sided with the **son** *of* Jesse to your
20:31 As long as the **son** *of* Jesse lives on this earth, neither you nor your
20:31 Now send and bring him to me, for he **must die** [+4638]!"
22: 7 Will the **son** *of* Jesse give all of you fields and vineyards?
22: 8 No one tells me when my **son** makes a covenant with the son of
22: 8 No one tells me when my son makes a covenant with the **son** *of*
22: 8 or tells me that my **son** has incited my servant to lie in wait for me,
22: 9 "I saw the **son** *of* Jesse come to Ahimelech son of Ahitub at Nob.
22: 9 "I saw the son of Jesse come to Ahimelech **son** *of* Ahitub at Nob.
22:11 Then the king sent for the priest Ahimelech **son** *of* Ahitub
22:12 Saul said, "Listen now, **son** *of* Ahitub." "Yes, my lord,"
22:13 you and the **son** *of* Jesse, giving him bread and a sword
22:20 a **son** of Ahimelech son of Ahitub, escaped and fled to join David.
22:20 a son of Ahimelech **son** *of* Ahitub, escaped and fled to join David.
23: 6 (Now Abiathar **son** *of* Ahimelech had brought the ephod down
23:16 Saul's **son** Jonathan went to David at Horesh and helped him find
24:16 [24:17] Saul asked, "Is that your voice, David my **son**?"
25: 8 and your **son** David whatever you can find for them.' "
25:10 David's servants, "Who is this David? Who is this **son** *of* Jesse?
25:17 He is such a wicked **man** that no one can talk to him."
25:44 David's wife, to Paltiel **son** *of* Laish, who was from Gallim.
26: 5 He saw where Saul and Abner **son** *of* Ner, the commander of the
26: 6 then asked Ahimelech the Hittite and Abishai **son** *of* Zeruiah,
26:14 He called out to the army and to Abner **son** *of* Ner, "Aren't you
26:16 As surely as the LORD lives, you and your men **deserve to** die,
26:17 David's voice and said, "Is that your voice, David my **son**?"
26:19 If, however, **men** [+132+2021] have done it, may they be cursed
26:21 Then Saul said, "I have sinned. Come back, David my **son**.
26:25 Then Saul said to David, "May you be blessed, my **son** David;
27: 2 with him left and went over to Achish **son** *of* Maoch king of Gath.
28:19 the Philistines, and tomorrow you and your **sons** will be with me.
30: 3 by fire and their wives and **sons** and daughters taken captive.
30: 6 each one was bitter in spirit because of his **sons** and daughters.
30: 7 Abiathar the priest, the **son** *of* Ahimelech, "Bring me the ephod."
30:19 young or old, **boy** or girl, plunder or anything else they had taken.
30:22 However, each man may take his wife and **children** and go."
31: 2 The Philistines pressed hard after Saul and his **sons**, and they killed
31: 2 and they killed his **sons** Jonathan, Abinadab and Malki-Shua.
31: 6 So Saul and his three **sons** and his armor-bearer and all his men
31: 7 that the Israelite army had fled and that Saul and his **sons** had died,
31: 8 they found Saul and his three **sons** fallen on Mount Gilboa.
31:12 and his **sons** from the wall of Beth Shan and went to Jabesh,
2Sa 1: 4 of them fell and died. And Saul and his **son** Jonathan are dead."
1: 5 "How do you know that Saul and his **son** Jonathan are dead?"
1:12 and wept and fasted till evening for Saul and his **son** Jonathan,
1:13 you from?" "I am the **son** *of* an alien, an Amalekite," he answered.
1:17 David took up this lament concerning Saul and his **son** Jonathan,
1:18 ordered that the **men** *of* Judah be taught this lament of the bow (it
2: 7 Now then, be strong and **brave** [+2657], for Saul your master is
2: 8 Meanwhile, Abner **son** *of* Ner, the commander of Saul's army,
2: 8 had taken Ish-Bosheth **son** *of* Saul and brought him over to
2:10 Ish-Bosheth **son** *of* Saul was forty years old when he became king
2:10 Ish-Bosheth son of Saul was forty years **old** when he became king
2:12 Abner **son** *of* Ner, together with the men of Ish-Bosheth son of
2:12 together with the men of Ish-Bosheth **son** *of* Saul, left Mahanaim
2:13 Joab **son** *of* Zeruiah and David's men went out and met them at the
2:15 twelve men for Benjamin and Ish-Bosheth **son** *of* Saul, and twelve
2:18 The three **sons** *of* Zeruiah were there: Joab, Abishai and Asahel.
2:25 the **men** *of* Benjamin rallied behind Abner. They formed
3: 2 **Sons** were born to David in Hebron: His firstborn was Amnon the
3: 3 Absalom the **son** *of* Maacah daughter of Talmai king of Geshur;
3: 4 the fourth, Adonijah the **son** *of* Haggith; the fifth,
3: 4 the son of Haggith; the fifth, Shephatiah the **son** *of* Abital;
3:14 David sent messengers to Ish-Bosheth **son** *of* Saul, demanding,
3:15 and had her taken away from her husband Paltiel **son** *of* Laish.
3:23 he was told that Abner **son** *of* Ner had come to the king and that
3:25 You know Abner **son** *of* Ner; he came to deceive you and observe
3:28 before the LORD concerning the blood of Abner **son** *of* Ner.
3:34 feet were not fettered. You fell as one falls before wicked **men**."
3:37 knew that the king had no part in the murder of Abner **son** *of* Ner.
3:39 I am weak, and these **sons** *of* Zeruiah are too strong for me.
4: 1 When Ish-Bosheth **son** *of* Saul heard that Abner had died in
4: 2 Now Saul's **son** had two men who were leaders of raiding bands.
4: 2 they were **sons** *of* Rimmon the Beerothite from the tribe of
4: 2 they were sons of Rimmon the Beerothite from the **tribe** *of*
4: 4 (Jonathan **son** *of* Saul had a son who was lame in both feet.
4: 4 (Jonathan son of Saul had a **son** who was lame in both feet.
4: 4 He was five years **old** when the news about Saul and Jonathan
4: 5 Now Recab and Baanah, the **sons** *of* Rimmon the Beerothite,
4: 8 "Here is the head of Ish-Bosheth **son** *of* Saul, your enemy,
4: 9 and his brother Baanah, the **sons** *of* Rimmon the Beerothite,
5: 4 David was thirty years **old** when he became king, and he reigned
5:13 in Jerusalem, and more **sons** and daughters were born to him.
6: 3 Uzzah and Ahio, **sons** *of* Abinadab, were guiding the new cart

2Sa 7: 6 day I brought the **Israelites** [+3776] up out of Egypt to this day.
7: 7 Wherever I have moved with all the **Israelites** [+3776], did I ever
7: 10 Wicked **people** will not oppress them anymore, as they did at the
7: 14 I will be his father, and he will be my **son**. When he does wrong,
7: 14 him with the rod of men, with floggings inflicted by **men** [+132].
8: 3 Moreover, David fought Hadadezer **son** *of* Rehob, king of Zobah,
8: 10 he sent his **son** Joram to King David to greet him and congratulate
8: 12 Edom and Moab, the **Ammonites** [+6648] and the Philistines,
8: 12 He also dedicated the plunder taken from Hadadezer **son** *of* Rehob,
8: 16 Joab **son** *of* Zeruiah was over the army; Jehoshaphat son of Ahilud
8: 16 was over the army; Jehoshaphat **son** *of* Ahilud was recorder;
8: 17 Zadok **son** *of* Ahitub and Ahimelech son of Abiathar were priests;
8: 17 Zadok son of Ahitub and Ahimelech **son** *of* Abiathar were priests;
8: 18 Benaiah **son** *of* Jehoiada was over the Kerethites and Pelethites;
8: 18 and Pelethites; and David's **sons** were royal advisers.
9: 3 Ziba answered the king, "There is still a **son** of Jonathan; he is
9: 4 "He is at the house of Makir **son** *of* Ammiel in Lo Debar."
9: 5 brought from Lo Debar, from the house of Makir **son** *of* Ammiel.
9: 6 When Mephibosheth **son** *of* Jonathan, the son of Saul, came to
9: 6 the **son** *of* Saul, came to David, he bowed down to pay him honor.
9: 9 "I have given your master's **grandson** everything that belonged to
9: 10 You and your **sons** and your servants are to farm the land for him
9: 10 in the crops, so that your master's **grandson** may be provided for.
9: 10 Mephibosheth, **grandson** *of* your master, will always eat at my
9: 10 eat at my table." (Now Ziba had fifteen **sons** and twenty servants.)
9: 11 So Mephibosheth ate at David's table like one of the king's **sons**.
9: 12 Mephibosheth had a young **son** named Mica, and all the members
10: 1 In the course of time, the king of the **Ammonites** [+6648] died,
10: 1 of the Ammonites died, and his **son** Hanun succeeded him as king.
10: 2 David thought, "I will show kindness to Hanun **son** *of* Nahash,
10: 2 When David's men came to the land of the **Ammonites** [+6648],
10: 3 the **Ammonite** [+6648] nobles said to Hanun their lord, "Do you
10: 6 When the **Ammonites** [+6648] realized that they had become a
10: 6 that they had become a stench in David's nostrils, **they**[s] [+6648]
10: 8 The **Ammonites** [+6648] came out and drew up in battle formation
10: 10 his brother and deployed them against the **Ammonites** [+6648].
10: 11 if the **Ammonites** [+6648] are too strong for you, then I will come
10: 14 When the **Ammonites** [+6648] saw that the Arameans were
10: 14 So Joab returned from fighting the **Ammonites** [+6648] and came
10: 19 So the Arameans were afraid to help the **Ammonites** [+6648]
11: 1 They destroyed the **Ammonites** [+6648] and besieged Rabbah.
11: 21 Who killed Abimelech **son** *of* Jerub-Besheth? Didn't a woman
11: 27 brought to his house, and she became his wife and bore him a **son**.
12: 3 He raised it, and it grew up with him and his **children**. It shared his
12: 5 surely as the LORD lives, the man who did this **deserves to** die!
12: 9 You killed him with the sword of the **Ammonites** [+6648].
12: 14 of the LORD show utter contempt, the **son** born to you will die."
12: 24 with her. She gave birth to a **son**, and they named him Solomon.
12: 26 Meanwhile Joab fought against Rabbah of the **Ammonites** [+6648]
12: 31 He did this to all the **Ammonite** [+6648] towns. Then David
13: 1 In the course of time, Amnon **son** *of* David fell in love with Tamar,
13: 1 in love with Tamar, the beautiful sister of Absalom **son** *of* David.
13: 3 Now Amnon had a friend named Jonadab **son** *of* Shimeah,
13: 4 do you, the king's **son**, look so haggard morning after morning?
13: 23 the border of Ephraim, he invited all the king's **sons** to come there.
13: 25 "No, my **son**," the king replied. "All of us should not go; we would
13: 27 so he sent with him Amnon and the rest of the king's **sons**.
13: 28 Have not I given you this order? Be strong and **brave** [+2657]."
13: 29 Then all the king's **sons** got up, mounted their mules and fled.
13: 30 "Absalom has struck down all the king's **sons**; not one of them is
13: 32 Jonadab **son** *of* Shimeah, David's brother, said, "My lord should
13: 32 "My lord should not think that they killed all the **princes** [+4889];
13: 33 not be concerned about the report that all the king's **sons** are dead.
13: 35 Jonadab said to the king, "See, the king's **sons** are here; it has
13: 36 As he finished speaking, the king's **sons** came in, wailing loudly.
13: 37 Absalom fled and went to Talmai **son** *of* Ammihud, the king of
13: 37 king of Geshur. But King David mourned for his **son** every day.
14: 1 Joab **son** *of* Zeruiah knew that the king's heart longed for
14: 6 I your servant had two **sons**. They got into a fight with each other
14: 11 adding to the destruction, so that my **son** will not be destroyed."
14: 11 he said, "not one hair of your **son's** head will fall to the ground."
14: 16 to cut off both me and my **son** from the inheritance God gave us.'
14: 27 Three **sons** and a daughter were born to Absalom. The daughter's
15: 27 in peace, with your **son** Ahimaaz and Jonathan son of Abiathar.
15: 27 in peace, with your son Ahimaaz and Jonathan **son** *of* Abiathar.
15: 27 son of Abiathar. You and Abiathar take your two **sons** with you.
15: 36 Their two **sons**, Ahimaaz son of Zadok and Jonathan son of
16: 3 The king then asked, "Where is your master's **grandson**?"
16: 5 His name was Shimei **son** *of* Gera, and he cursed as he came out.
16: 8 The LORD has handed the kingdom over to your **son** Absalom.
16: 9 Abishai **son** *of* Zeruiah said to the king, "Why should this dead dog
16: 10 "What do you and I have in common, you **sons** *of* Zeruiah?
16: 11 David then said to Abishai and all his officials, "My **son**, who is of
16: 19 Furthermore, whom should I serve? Should I not serve the **son**?
17: 10 even the **bravest soldier** [+2657], whose heart is like the heart of a
17: 10 your father is a fighter and that those with him are **brave** [+2657].
17: 25 Amasa was the **son** *of* a man named Jether, an Israelite who had
17: 27 Shobi **son** *of* Nahash from Rabbah of the Ammonites,
17: 27 Shobi son of Nahash from Rabbah of the **Ammonites** [+6648],
17: 27 Makir **son** *of* Ammiel from Lo Debar, and Barzillai the Gileadite
18: 2 a third under Joab's brother Abishai **son** *of* Zeruiah, and a third
18: 12 out into my hands, I would not lift my hand against the king's **son**.
18: 18 he thought, "I have no **son** to carry on the memory of my name."
18: 19 Now Ahimaaz **son** *of* Zadok said, "Let me run and take the news to
18: 20 but you must not do so today, because the king's **son** is dead."
18: 22 Ahimaaz **son** *of* Zadok again said to Joab, "Come what may,
18: 22 the Cushite." But Joab replied, "My **son**, why do you want to go?
18: 27 "It seems to me that the first one runs like Ahimaaz **son** *of* Zadok."
18: 33 [19:1] As he went, he said: "O my **son** Absalom! My son, my son
18: 33 [19:1] he said: "O my son Absalom! My **son**, my son Absalom!
18: 33 [19:1] he said: "O my son Absalom! My son, my **son** Absalom!
18: 33 [19:1] I had died instead of you—O Absalom, my **son**, my son!"
18: 33 [19:1] I had died instead of you—O Absalom, my son, my **son**!"
19: 2 [19:3] the troops heard it said, "The king is grieving for his **son**."
19: 4 [19:5] covered his face and cried aloud, "O my **son** Absalom!
19: 4 [19:5] "O my son Absalom! O Absalom, my **son**, my son!"
19: 4 [19:5] "O my son Absalom! O Absalom, my son, my **son**!"
19: 5 [19:6] the lives of your **sons** and daughters and the lives of your
19: 16 [19:17] Shimei **son** *of* Gera, the Benjamite from Bahurim,
19: 17 [19:18] and his fifteen **sons** and twenty servants.
19: 18 [19:19] When Shimei **son** *of* Gera crossed the Jordan, he fell
19: 21 [19:22] Abishai **son** *of* Zeruiah said, "Shouldn't Shimei be put to
19: 22 [19:23] do you and I have in common, you **sons** *of* Zeruiah?
19: 24 [19:25] Mephibosheth, Saul's **grandson**, also went down to meet
19: 32 [19:33] Now Barzillai was a very old man, eighty years *of* **age**.
19: 35 [19:36] I am now eighty years **old**. Can I tell the difference
20: 1 Now a troublemaker named Sheba **son** *of* Bicri, a Benjamite,
20: 1 and shouted, "We have no share in David, no part in Jesse's **son**!
20: 2 So all the men of Israel deserted David to follow Sheba **son** *of*
20: 6 "Now Sheba **son** *of* Bicri will do us more harm than Absalom did.
20: 7 They marched out from Jerusalem to pursue Sheba **son** *of* Bicri.
20: 10 Then Joab and his brother Abishai pursued Sheba **son** *of* Bicri.
20: 13 all the men went on with Joab to pursue Sheba **son** *of* Bicri.
20: 21 A man named Sheba **son** *of* Bicri, from the hill country of
20: 22 they cut off the head of Sheba **son** *of* Bicri and threw it to Joab.
20: 23 Benaiah **son** *of* Jehoiada was over the Kerethites and Pelethites;
20: 24 in charge of forced labor; Jehoshaphat **son** *of* Ahilud was recorder;
21: 2 (Now the Gibeonites were not a part of **Israel** [+3776] but were
21: 2 the **Israelites** [+3776] had sworn to ⌞spare⌟ them, but Saul in his
21: 2 Saul in his zeal for **Israel** [+3776] and Judah had tried to annihilate
21: 6 let seven of his male **descendants** be given to us to be killed
21: 7 The king spared Mephibosheth **son** *of* Jonathan, the son of Saul,
21: 7 The king spared Mephibosheth son of Jonathan, the **son** *of* Saul,
21: 7 oath before the LORD between David and Jonathan **son** *of* Saul.
21: 8 and Mephibosheth, the two **sons** *of* Aiah's daughter Rizpah,
21: 8 to Saul, together with the five **sons** *of* Saul's daughter Merab,
21: 8 whom she had borne to Adriel **son** *of* Barzillai the Meholathite.
21: 12 of Saul and his **son** Jonathan from the citizens of Jabesh Gilead.
21: 13 David brought the bones of Saul and his **son** Jonathan from there,
21: 14 of Saul and his **son** Jonathan in the tomb of Saul's father Kish,
21: 17 Abishai **son** *of* Zeruiah came to David's rescue; he struck the
21: 19 Elhanan **son** *of* Jaare-Oregim the Bethlehemite killed Goliath the
21: 21 Jonathan **son** *of* Shimeah, David's brother, killed him.
22: 45 **foreigners** [+5797] come cringing to me; as soon as they hear me,
22: 46 **They**[s] **all** [+5797] lose heart; they come trembling from their
23: 1 "The oracle of David **son** *of* Jesse, the oracle of the man exalted by
23: 9 Next to him was Eleazar **son** *of* Dodai the Ahohite. As one of the
23: 9 Next to him was Eleazar son of Dodai the **Ahohite** [+292].
23: 11 Next to him was Shammah **son** *of* Agee the Hararite.
23: 18 Abishai the brother of Joab **son** *of* Zeruiah was chief of the Three.
23: 20 Benaiah **son** *of* Jehoiada was a valiant fighter from Kabzeel,
23: 20 Benaiah son of Jehoiada was a **valiant fighter** [+408+2644] from
23: 22 Such were the exploits of Benaiah **son** *of* Jehoiada; he too was as
23: 24 Asahel the brother of Joab, Elhanan **son** *of* Dodo from Bethlehem,
23: 26 Helez the Paltite, Ira **son** *of* Ikkesh from Tekoa,
23: 29 Heled **son** *of* Baanah the Netophathite, Ithai son of Ribai from
23: 29 the Netophathite, Ithai **son** *of* Ribai from Gibeah in Benjamin,
23: 29 Ithai son of Ribai from Gibeah in **Benjamin** [+1228],
23: 32 Eliahba the Shaalbonite, the **sons** *of* Jashen, Jonathan
23: 33 **son** [BHS-] *of* Shammah the Hararite, Ahiam son of Sharar the
23: 33 son of Shammah the Hararite, Ahiam **son** *of* Sharar the Hararite,
23: 34 Eliphelet **son** *of* Ahasbai the Maacathite, Eliam son of Ahithophel
23: 34 Eliphelet son of Ahasbai the **Maacathite** [+5084], Eliam son of
23: 34 of Ahasbai the Maacathite, Eliam **son** *of* Ahithophel the Gilonite,
23: 36 Igal **son** *of* Nathan from Zobah, the son of Hagri,
23: 36 Igal son of Nathan from Zobah, the **son** [BHS 1220] *of* Hagri,
23: 37 Naharai the Beerothite, the armor-bearer of Joab **son** *of* Zeruiah,
1Ki 1: 5 Now Adonijah, **whose**[s] mother was Haggith, put himself forward

1Ki 1: 7 Adonijah conferred with Joab **son** *of* Zeruiah and with Abiathar the
1: 8 Benaiah **son** *of* Jehoiada, Nathan the prophet, Shimei and Rei
1: 9 He invited all his brothers, the king's **sons**, and all the men of
1: 11 "Have you not heard that Adonijah, the **son** *of* Haggith,
1: 12 how you can save your own life and the life of your **son** Solomon.
1: 13 "Surely Solomon your **son** shall be king after me, and he will sit on
1: 17 'Solomon your **son** shall be king after me, and he will sit on my
1: 19 fattened calves, and sheep, and has invited all the king's **sons**,
1: 21 his fathers, I and my **son** Solomon will be treated as criminals."
1: 25 He has invited all the king's **sons**, the commanders of the army
1: 26 your servant, and Zadok the priest, and Benaiah **son** *of* Jehoiada,
1: 30 Solomon your **son** shall be king after me, and he will sit on my
1: 32 the priest, Nathan the prophet and Benaiah **son** *of* Jehoiada."
1: 33 set Solomon my **son** on my own mule and take him down to
1: 36 Benaiah **son** *of* Jehoiada answered the king, "Amen!
1: 38 Benaiah **son** *of* Jehoiada, the Kerethites and the Pelethites went
1: 42 as he was speaking, Jonathan **son** *of* Abiathar the priest arrived.
1: 44 Benaiah **son** *of* Jehoiada, the Kerethites and the Pelethites,
1: 52 Solomon replied, "If he shows himself to be a worthy **man**,
2: 1 drew near for David to die, he gave a charge to Solomon his **son**.
2: 4 'If your **descendants** watch how they live, and if they walk
2: 5 "Now you yourself know what Joab **son** *of* Zeruiah did to me—
2: 5 of Israel's armies, Abner **son** *of* Ner and Amasa son of Jether.
2: 5 of Israel's armies, Abner son of Ner and Amasa **son** *of* Jether.
2: 7 "But show kindness to the **sons** *of* Barzillai of Gilead and let them
2: 8 "And remember, you have with you Shimei **son** *of* Gera,
2: 13 Now Adonijah, the **son** *of* Haggith, went to Bathsheba, Solomon's
2: 22 for him and for Abiathar the priest and Joab **son** *of* Zeruiah!"
2: 25 So King Solomon gave orders to Benaiah **son** *of* Jehoiada,
2: 29 Solomon ordered Benaiah **son** *of* Jehoiada, "Go, strike him down!"
2: 32 Abner **son** *of* Ner, commander of Israel's army, and Amasa son of
2: 32 son of Ner, commander of Israel's army, and Amasa **son** *of* Jether,
2: 34 So Benaiah **son** *of* Jehoiada went up and struck down Joab
2: 35 The king put Benaiah **son** *of* Jehoiada over the army in Joab's
2: 39 two of Shimei's slaves ran off to Achish **son** *of* Maacah, king of
2: 46 the king gave the order to Benaiah **son** *of* Jehoiada, and he went
3: 6 and have given him a **son** to sit on his throne this very day.
3: 19 "During the night this woman's **son** died because she lay on him.
3: 20 and took my **son** from my side while I your servant was asleep.
3: 20 She put him by her breast and put her dead **son** by my breast.
3: 21 The next morning, I got up to nurse my **son**—and he was dead!
3: 21 in the morning light, I saw that it wasn't the **son** I had borne."
3: 22 "No! The living one is my **son**; the dead one is yours."
3: 22 **[RPH]** But the first one insisted, "No! The dead one is yours;
3: 22 The dead one is yours; **[RPH]** the living one is mine." And
3: 22 living one is mine." **[RPH]** And so they argued before the king.
3: 23 king said, "This one says, 'My **son** is alive and your son is dead,'
3: 23 king said, "This one says, 'My son is alive and your **son** is dead,'
3: 23 while that one says, 'No! Your **son** is dead and mine is alive.' "
3: 23 that one says, 'No! Your son is dead and mine **[RPH]** is alive.' "
3: 26 The woman whose **son** was alive was filled with compassion for
3: 26 whose son was alive was filled with compassion for her **son**
4: 2 these were his chief officials: Azariah **son** *of* Zadok—the priest;
4: 3 Elihoreph and Ahijah, **sons** *of* Shisha—secretaries;
4: 3 sons of Shisha—secretaries; Jehoshaphat **son** *of* Ahilud—recorder;
4: 4 Benaiah **son** *of* Jehoiada—commander in chief; Zadok
4: 5 Azariah **son** *of* Nathan—in charge of the district officers; Zabud
4: 5 Zabud **son** *of* Nathan—a priest and personal adviser to the king;
4: 6 Ahishar—in charge of the palace; Adoniram **son** *of* Abda—
4: 12 Baana **son** *of* Ahilud—in Taanach and Megiddo, and in all of Beth
4: 13 in Ramoth Gilead (the settlements of Jair **son** *of* Manasseh in
4: 14 Ahinadab **son** *of* Iddo—in Mahanaim;
4: 16 Baana **son** *of* Hushai—in Asher and in Aloth;
4: 17 Jehoshaphat **son** *of* Paruah—in Issachar;
4: 18 Shimei **son** *of* Ela—in Benjamin;
4: 19 Geber **son** *of* Uri—in Gilead (the country of Sihon king of the
4: 30 [5:10] was greater than the wisdom of all the **men** *of* the East,
4: 31 [5:11] wiser than Heman, Calcol and Darda, the **sons** *of* Mahol.
5: 5 [5:19] 'Your **son** whom I will put on the throne in your place will
5: 7 [5:21] for he has given David a wise **son** to rule over this great
6: 1 eightieth year after the **Israelites** [+3776] had come out of Egypt,
6: 13 I will live among the **Israelites** [+3776] and will not abandon my
7: 14 **whose**[s] mother was a widow from the tribe of Naphtali and whose
8: 1 heads of the tribes and the chiefs of the **Israelite** [+3776] families,
8: 9 where the LORD made a covenant with the **Israelites** [+3776]
8: 19 build the temple, but your **son**, who is your own flesh and blood—
8: 25 if only your **sons** are careful in all they do to walk before me as
8: 39 know his heart (for you alone know the hearts of all **men** [+132]),
8: 63 and all the **Israelites** [+3776] dedicated the temple of the LORD.
9: 6 "But if you or your **sons** turn away from me and do not observe the
9: 20 and Jebusites (these peoples were not **Israelites** [+3776]),
9: 21 that is, their **descendants** remaining in the land,
9: 21 in the land, whom the **Israelites** [+3776] could not exterminate—
9: 22 But Solomon did not make slaves of any of the **Israelites** [+3776];
11: 2 nations about which the LORD had told the **Israelites** [+3776],
11: 7 and for Molech the detestable god of the **Ammonites** [+6648].
11: 12 do it during your lifetime. I will tear it out of the hand of your **son**.
11: 13 will give **him**[s] [+3870] one tribe for the sake of David my servant
11: 20 The sister of Tahpenes bore him a **son** named Genubath, whom
11: 20 royal palace. There Genubath lived with Pharaoh's own **children**.
11: 23 Rezon **son** *of* Eliada, who had fled from his master,
11: 26 Also, Jeroboam **son** *of* Nebat rebelled against the king. He was one
11: 33 Molech the god of the **Ammonites** [+6648], and have not walked
11: 35 I will take the kingdom from his **son's** hands and give you ten
11: 36 I will give one tribe to his **son** so that David my servant may
11: 43 of David his father. And Rehoboam his **son** succeeded him as king.
12: 2 When Jeroboam **son** *of* Nebat heard this (he was still in Egypt,
12: 15 to fulfill the word the LORD had spoken to Jeroboam **son** *of*
12: 16 "What share do we have in David, what part in Jesse's **son**?
12: 17 as for the **Israelites** [+3776] who were living in the towns of
12: 21 and to regain the kingdom for Rehoboam **son** *of* Solomon.
12: 23 "Say to Rehoboam **son** *of* Solomon king of Judah, to the whole
12: 24 Do not go up to fight against your brothers, the **Israelites** [+3776].
12: 31 all sorts of people, even though they were not **Levites** [+4290].
12: 33 So he instituted the festival for the **Israelites** [+3776] and went up
13: 2 'A **son** named Josiah will be born to the house of David.
13: 11 whose **sons** came and told him all that the man of God had done
13: 12 his **sons** showed him which road the man of God from Judah had
13: 13 So he said to his **sons**, "Saddle the donkey for me." And when they
13: 27 The prophet said to his **sons**, "Saddle the donkey for me,"
13: 31 After burying him, he said to his **sons**, "When I die, bury me in the
14: 1 At that time Abijah **son** *of* Jeroboam became ill,
14: 5 "Jeroboam's wife is coming to ask you about her **son**, for he is ill,
14: 20 rested with his fathers. And Nadab his **son** succeeded him as king.
14: 21 Rehoboam **son** *of* Solomon was king in Judah. He was forty-one
14: 21 He was forty-one years **old** when he became king, and he reigned
14: 24 nations the LORD had driven out before the **Israelites** [+3776].
14: 31 she was an Ammonite. And Abijah his **son** succeeded him as king.
15: 1 In the eighteenth year of the reign of Jeroboam **son** *of* Nebat,
15: 4 gave him a lamp in Jerusalem by raising up a **son** to succeed him
15: 8 in the City of David. And Asa his **son** succeeded him as king.
15: 18 it to his officials and sent them to Ben-Hadad **son** *of* Tabrimmon,
15: 18 the **son** *of* Hezion, the king of Aram, who was ruling in Damascus.
15: 24 his father David. And Jehoshaphat his **son** succeeded him as king.
15: 25 Nadab **son** *of* Jeroboam became king of Israel in the second year of
15: 27 Baasha **son** *of* Ahijah of the house of Issachar plotted against him,
15: 33 Baasha **son** *of* Ahijah became king of all Israel in Tirzah, and he
16: 1 the word of the LORD came to Jehu **son** *of* Hanani against
16: 3 and I will make your house like that of Jeroboam **son** *of* Nebat.
16: 6 and was buried in Tirzah. And Elah his **son** succeeded him as king.
16: 7 the word of the LORD came through the prophet Jehu **son** *of*
16: 8 Elah **son** *of* Baasha became king of Israel, and he reigned in Tirzah
16: 13 because of all the sins Baasha and his **son** Elah had committed
16: 21 half supported Tibni **son** *of* Ginath for king, and the other half
16: 22 Omri's followers proved stronger than those of Tibni **son** *of*
16: 26 He walked in all the ways of Jeroboam **son** *of* Nebat and in his sin,
16: 28 was buried in Samaria. And Ahab his **son** succeeded him as king.
16: 29 of Asa king of Judah, Ahab **son** *of* Omri became king of Israel,
16: 29 **he**[s] [+281+6687] reigned in Samaria over Israel twenty-two years.
16: 30 Ahab **son** *of* Omri did more evil in the eyes of the LORD than
16: 31 considered it trivial to commit the sins of Jeroboam **son** *of* Nebat,
16: 34 with the word of the LORD spoken by Joshua **son** *of* Nun.
17: 12 a few sticks to take home and make a meal for myself and my **son**,
17: 13 bring it to me, and then make something for yourself and your **son**.
17: 17 Some time later the **son** *of* the woman who owned the house
17: 18 of God? Did you come to remind me of my sin and kill my **son**?"
17: 19 "Give me your **son**," Elijah replied. He took him from her arms,
17: 20 upon this widow I am staying with, by causing her **son** to die?"
17: 23 He gave him to his mother and said, "Look, your **son** is alive!"
18: 20 So Ahab sent word throughout all **Israel** [+3776] and assembled
18: 31 twelve stones, one for each of the tribes **descended** *from* Jacob,
19: 10 The **Israelites** [+3776] have rejected your covenant, broken down
19: 14 The **Israelites** [+3776] have rejected your covenant, broken down
19: 16 Also, anoint Jehu **son** *of* Nimshi king over Israel, and anoint Elisha
19: 16 anoint Elisha **son** *of* Shaphat from Abel Meholah to succeed you as
19: 19 So Elijah went from there and found Elisha **son** *of* Shaphat.
20: 3 are mine, and the best of your wives and **children** are mine.' "
20: 5 to demand your silver and gold, your wives and your **children**.
20: 7 When he sent for my wives and my **children**, my silver and my
20: 15 Then he assembled the rest of the **Israelites** [+3776], 7,000 in all.
20: 27 When the **Israelites** [+3776] were also mustered and given
20: 27 The **Israelites** [+3776] camped opposite them like two small flocks
20: 29 The **Israelites** [+3776] inflicted a hundred thousand casualties on
20: 35 By the word of the LORD one of the **sons** *of* the prophets said to
21: 10 seat two **scoundrels** [+1175] opposite him and have them testify
21: 13 two **scoundrels** [+1175] came and sat opposite him and brought
21: 22 I will make your house like that of Jeroboam **son** *of* Nebat
21: 22 that of Jeroboam son of Nebat and that of Baasha **son** *of* Ahijah,

1Ki 21:26 like the Amorites the LORD drove out before **Israel** [+3776].)
21:29 in his day, but I will bring it on his house in the days of his **son**."
22: 8 good about me, but always bad. He is Micaiah **son** *of* Imlah."
22: 9 one of his officials and said, "Bring Micaiah **son** *of* Imlah at once."
22:11 Now Zedekiah **son** *of* Kenaanah had made iron horns and he
22:24 Zedekiah **son** *of* Kenaanah went up and slapped Micaiah in the
22:26 him back to Amon the ruler of the city and to Joash the king's **son**
22:40 with his fathers. And Ahaziah his **son** succeeded him as king.
22:41 Jehoshaphat **son** *of* Asa became king of Judah in the fourth year of
22:42 Jehoshaphat was thirty-five years **old** when he became king,
22:49 [22:50] At that time Ahaziah **son** *of* Ahab said to Jehoshaphat,
22:50 [22:51] of David his father. And Jehoram his **son** succeeded him.
22:51 [22:52] Ahaziah **son** *of* Ahab became king of Israel in Samaria in
22:52 [22:53] and mother and in the ways of Jeroboam **son** *of* Nebat,
2Ki 1:17 Because Ahaziah had no **son**, Joram succeeded him as king in the
1:17 Joram succeeded him as king in the second year of Jehoram **son** *of*
2: 3 The **company** *of* the prophets at Bethel came out to Elisha
2: 5 The **company** *of* the prophets at Jericho went up to Elisha
2: 7 Fifty men of the **company** *of* the prophets went and stood at a
2:15 The **company** *of* the prophets from Jericho, who were watching,
2:16 they said, "we your servants have fifty **able** [+2657] men.
3: 1 Joram **son** *of* Ahab became king of Israel in Samaria in the
3: 3 Nevertheless he clung to the sins of Jeroboam **son** *of* Nebat,
3:11 of the king of Israel answered, "Elisha **son** *of* Shaphat is here.
3:27 Then he took his firstborn **son**, who was to succeed him as king,
4: 1 The wife of a man from the **company** *of* the prophets cried out to
4: 4 Then go inside and shut the door behind you and your **sons**.
4: 5 She left him and afterward shut the door behind her and her **sons**.
4: 6 all the jars were full, she said to her **son**, "Bring me another one."
4: 7 and pay your debts. You and your **sons** can live on what is left."
4:14 Gehazi said, "Well, she has no **son** and her husband is old."
4:16 time next year," Elisha said, "you will hold a **son** in your arms."
4:17 and the next year about that same time she gave birth to a **son**,
4:28 "Did I ask you for a **son**, my lord?" she said. "Didn't I tell you,
4:36 And he did. When she came, he said, "Take your **son**."
4:37 and bowed to the ground. Then she took her **son** and went out.
4:38 While the **company** *of* the prophets was meeting with him,
4:38 the large pot and cook some stew for **these men**[s] [+2021+5566]."
5:22 'Two young men from the **company** *of* the prophets have just come
6: 1 The **company** *of* the prophets said to Elisha, "Look, the place
6:28 woman said to me, 'Give up your **son** so we may eat him today,
6:28 so we may eat him today, and tomorrow we'll eat my **son**.'
6:29 So we cooked my **son** and ate him. The next day I said to her,
6:29 'Give up your **son** so we may eat him,' but she had hidden him."
6:29 your son so we may eat him,' but she had hidden **him**[s] [+2023]."
6:31 if the head of Elisha **son** *of* Shaphat remains on his shoulders
6:32 "Don't you see how this **murderer** [+8357] is sending someone to
8: 1 Now Elisha had said to the woman whose **son** he had restored to
8: 5 the woman whose **son** Elisha had brought back to life came to beg
8: 5 my lord the king, and this is her **son** whom Elisha restored to life."
8: 9 and said, "Your **son** Ben-Hadad king of Aram has sent me to ask,
8:12 "Because I know the harm you will do to the **Israelites** [+3776],"
8:16 In the fifth year of Joram **son** *of* Ahab king of Israel,
8:16 Jehoram **son** *of* Jehoshaphat began his reign as king of Judah.
8:17 He was thirty-two years **old** when he became king, and he reigned
8:19 to maintain a lamp for David and his **descendants** forever.
8:24 in the City of David. And Ahaziah his **son** succeeded him as king.
8:25 In the twelfth year of Joram **son** *of* Ahab king of Israel,
8:25 of Israel, Ahaziah **son** *of* Jehoram king of Judah began to reign.
8:26 Ahaziah was twenty-two years **old** when he became king,
8:28 Ahaziah went with Joram **son** *of* Ahab to war against Hazael king
8:29 Ahaziah **son** *of* Jehoram king of Judah went down to Jezreel to see
8:29 king of Judah went down to Jezreel to see Joram **son** *of* Ahab,
9: 1 The prophet Elisha summoned a man from the **company** *of* the
9: 2 you get there, look for Jehu **son** *of* Jehoshaphat, the son of Nimshi.
9: 2 you get there, look for Jehu son of Jehoshaphat, the **son** *of* Nimshi.
9: 9 I will make the house of Ahab like the house of Jeroboam **son** *of*
9: 9 Jeroboam son of Nebat and like the house of Baasha **son** *of* Ahijah.
9:14 So Jehu **son** *of* Jehoshaphat, the son of Nimshi, conspired against
9:14 son of Jehoshaphat, the **son** *of* Nimshi, conspired against Joram.
9:20 The driving is like that of Jehu **son** *of* Nimshi—he drives like a
9:26 'Yesterday I saw the blood of Naboth and the blood of his **sons**,
9:29 (In the eleventh year of Joram **son** *of* Ahab, Ahaziah had become
10: 1 Now there were in Samaria seventy **sons** of the house of Ahab.
10: 2 since your master's **sons** are with you and you have chariots
10: 3 choose the best and most worthy of your master's **sons** and set him
10: 6 take the heads of your master's **sons** and come to me in Jezreel by
10: 6 Now the royal **princes**, seventy of them, were with the leading
10: 7 these men took the **princes** [+4889] and slaughtered all seventy of
10: 8 told Jehu, "They have brought the heads of the **princes** [+4889]."
10:13 we have come down to greet the **families** *of* the king and of the
10:13 to greet the families of the king and of the queen mother." **[RPH]**
10:15 After he left there, he came upon Jehonadab **son** *of* Recab,
10:23 and Jehonadab **son** *of* Recab went into the temple of Baal.
10:29 he did not turn away from the sins of Jeroboam **son** *of* Nebat,
10:30 your **descendants** will sit on the throne of Israel to the fourth
10:35 buried in Samaria. And Jehoahaz his **son** succeeded him as king.
11: 1 When Athaliah the mother of Ahaziah saw that her **son** was dead,
11: 2 took Joash **son** *of* Ahaziah and stole him away from among the
11: 2 son of Ahaziah and stole him away from among the royal **princes**,
11: 4 at the temple of the LORD. Then he showed them the king's **son**.
11:12 Jehoiada brought out the king's **son** and put the crown on him;
11:21 [12:1] Joash was seven years **old** when he began to reign.
12:21 [12:22] The officials who murdered him were Jozabad **son** *of*
12:21 [12:22] Jozabad son of Shimeath and Jehozabad **son** *of* Shomer.
12:21 [12:22] of David. And Amaziah his **son** succeeded him as king.
13: 1 In the twenty-third year of Joash **son** *of* Ahaziah king of Judah,
13: 1 Jehoahaz **son** *of* Jehu became king of Israel in Samaria, and he
13: 2 of the LORD by following the sins of Jeroboam **son** *of* Nebat,
13: 3 under the power of Hazael king of Aram and Ben-Hadad his **son**.
13: 5 So the **Israelites** [+3776] lived in their own homes as they had
13: 9 buried in Samaria. And Jehoash his **son** succeeded him as king.
13:10 Jehoash **son** *of* Jehoahaz became king of Israel in Samaria,
13:11 did not turn away from any of the sins of Jeroboam **son** *of* Nebat,
13:24 king of Aram died, and Ben-Hadad his **son** succeeded him as king.
13:25 Jehoash **son** *of* Jehoahaz recaptured from Ben-Hadad son of
13:25 Jehoash son of Jehoahaz recaptured from Ben-Hadad **son** *of*
14: 1 In the second year of Jehoash **son** *of* Jehoahaz king of Israel,
14: 1 king of Israel, Amaziah **son** *of* Joash king of Judah began to reign.
14: 2 He was twenty-five years **old** when he became king, and he
14: 6 Yet he did not put the **sons** *of* the assassins to death, in accordance
14: 6 "Fathers shall not be put to death for their **children**, nor children
14: 6 death for their children, nor **children** put to death for their fathers;
14: 8 Then Amaziah sent messengers to Jehoash **son** *of* Jehoahaz,
14: 8 son of Jehoahaz, the **son** *of* Jehu, king of Israel, with the challenge:
14: 9 to a cedar in Lebanon, 'Give your daughter to my **son** in marriage.'
14:13 of Judah, the **son** *of* Joash, the son of Ahaziah, at Beth Shemesh.
14:13 of Judah, the son of Joash, the **son** *of* Ahaziah, at Beth Shemesh.
14:14 He also took **hostages** [+9510] and returned to Samaria.
14:16 the kings of Israel. And Jeroboam his **son** succeeded him as king.
14:17 Amaziah **son** *of* Joash king of Judah lived for fifteen years after the
14:17 years after the death of Jehoash **son** *of* Jehoahaz king of Israel.
14:21 all the people of Judah took Azariah, who was sixteen years **old**,
14:23 In the fifteenth year of Amaziah **son** *of* Joash king of Judah,
14:23 Jeroboam **son** *of* Jehoash king of Israel became king in Samaria,
14:24 did not turn away from any of the sins of Jeroboam **son** *of* Nebat,
14:25 the God of Israel, spoken through his servant Jonah **son** *of* Amittai,
14:27 he saved them by the hand of Jeroboam **son** *of* Jehoash.
14:29 the kings of Israel. And Zechariah his **son** succeeded him as king.
15: 1 of Israel, Azariah **son** *of* Amaziah king of Judah began to reign.
15: 2 He was sixteen years **old** when he became king, and he reigned in
15: 5 Jotham the king's **son** had charge of the palace and governed the
15: 7 in the City of David. And Jotham his **son** succeeded him as king.
15: 8 Zechariah **son** *of* Jeroboam became king of Israel in Samaria,
15: 9 He did not turn away from the sins of Jeroboam **son** *of* Nebat,
15:10 Shallum **son** *of* Jabesh conspired against Zechariah. He attacked
15:12 "Your **descendants** will sit on the throne of Israel to the fourth
15:13 Shallum **son** *of* Jabesh became king in the thirty-ninth year of
15:14 Then Menahem **son** *of* Gadi went from Tirzah up to Samaria.
15:14 He attacked Shallum **son** *of* Jabesh in Samaria, assassinated him
15:17 Menahem **son** *of* Gadi became king of Israel, and he reigned in
15:18 reign he did not turn away from the sins of Jeroboam **son** *of* Nebat,
15:22 with his fathers. And Pekahiah his **son** succeeded him as king.
15:23 Pekahiah **son** *of* Menahem became king of Israel in Samaria,
15:24 He did not turn away from the sins of Jeroboam **son** *of* Nebat,
15:25 his chief officers, Pekah **son** *of* Remaliah, conspired against him.
15:25 Taking fifty men **of Gilead** [+1682] with him, he assassinated
15:27 Pekah **son** *of* Remaliah became king of Israel in Samaria,
15:28 He did not turn away from the sins of Jeroboam **son** *of* Nebat,
15:30 Hoshea **son** *of* Elah conspired against Pekah son of Remaliah.
15:30 Hoshea son of Elah conspired against Pekah **son** *of* Remaliah.
15:30 succeeded him as king in the twentieth year of Jotham **son** *of*
15:32 In the second year of Pekah **son** *of* Remaliah king of Israel,
15:32 king of Israel, Jotham **son** *of* Uzziah king of Judah began to reign.
15:33 He was twenty-five years **old** when he became king, and he
15:37 Rezin king of Aram and Pekah **son** *of* Remaliah against Judah.)
15:38 the city of his father. And Ahaz his **son** succeeded him as king.
16: 1 In the seventeenth year of Pekah **son** *of* Remaliah, Ahaz son of
16: 1 son of Remaliah, Ahaz **son** *of* Jotham king of Judah began to reign.
16: 2 Ahaz was twenty years **old** when he became king, and he reigned
16: 3 ways of the kings of Israel and even sacrificed his **son** in the fire,
16: 3 nations the LORD had driven out before the **Israelites** [+3776].
16: 5 Pekah **son** *of* Remaliah king of Israel marched up to fight against
16: 7 to Tiglath-Pileser king of Assyria, "I am your servant and **vassal**.
16:20 in the City of David. And Hezekiah his **son** succeeded him as king.
17: 1 Hoshea **son** *of* Elah became king of Israel in Samaria, and he
17: 7 because the **Israelites** [+3776] had sinned against the LORD their
17: 8 of the nations the LORD had driven out before **them**[s] [+3776],

2Ki 17: 9 The **Israelites** [+3776] secretly did things against the LORD their
17:17 They sacrificed their **sons** and daughters in the fire. They practiced
17:21 the house of David, they made Jeroboam **son** *of* Nebat their king.
17:22 The **Israelites** [+3776] persisted in all the sins of Jeroboam
17:24 them in the towns of Samaria to replace the **Israelites** [+3776].
17:31 the Sepharvites burned their **children** in the fire as sacrifices to
17:34 and commands that the LORD gave the **descendants** *of* Jacob,
17:41 To this day their **children** and grandchildren continue to do as their
17:41 and **grandchildren** [+1201] continue to do as their fathers did.
17:41 and **grandchildren** [+1201] continue to do as their fathers did.
18: 1 In the third year of Hoshea **son** *of* Elah king of Israel,
18: 1 king of Israel, Hezekiah **son** *of* Ahaz king of Judah began to reign.
18: 2 He was twenty-five years **old** when he became king, and he
18: 4 for up to that time the **Israelites** [+3776] had been burning incense
18: 9 which was the seventh year of Hoshea **son** *of* Elah king of Israel,
18:18 Eliakim **son** *of* Hilkiah the palace administrator, Shebna the
18:18 the secretary, and Joah **son** *of* Asaph the recorder went out to them.
18:26 Eliakim **son** *of* Hilkiah, and Shebna and Joah said to the field
18:37 Eliakim **son** *of* Hilkiah the palace administrator, Shebna the
18:37 the secretary and Joah **son** *of* Asaph the recorder went to Hezekiah,
19: 2 all wearing sackcloth, to the prophet Isaiah **son** *of* Amoz.
19: 3 as when **children** come to the point of birth and there is no
19:12 Haran, Rezeph and the **people** *of* Eden who were in Tel Assar?
19:20 Isaiah **son** *of* Amoz sent a message to Hezekiah: "This is what the
19:37 his **sons** [Q; no K] Adrammelech and Sharezer cut him down with
19:37 the land of Ararat. And Esarhaddon his **son** succeeded him as king.
20: 1 The prophet Isaiah **son** *of* Amoz went to him and said, "This is
20:12 At that time Merodach-Baladan **son** *of* Baladan king of Babylon
20:18 And some of your **descendants**, your own flesh and blood,
20:21 with his fathers. And Manasseh his **son** succeeded him as king.
21: 1 Manasseh was twelve years **old** when he became king, and he
21: 2 nations the LORD had driven out before the **Israelites** [+3776].
21: 6 He sacrificed his own **son** in the fire, practiced sorcery and
21: 7 of which the LORD had said to David and to his **son** Solomon,
21: 9 nations the LORD had destroyed before the **Israelites** [+3776].
21:18 the garden of Uzza. And Amon his **son** succeeded him as king.
21:19 Amon was twenty-two years **old** when he became king, and he
21:24 King Amon, and they made Josiah his **son** king in his place.
21:26 in the garden of Uzza. And Josiah his **son** succeeded him as king.
22: 1 Josiah was eight years **old** when he became king, and he reigned in
22: 3 Shaphan **son** *of* Azaliah, the son of Meshullam, to the temple of
22: 3 Shaphan son of Azaliah, the **son** *of* Meshullam, to the temple of
22:12 Ahikam **son** *of* Shaphan, Acbor son of Micaiah, Shaphan the
22:12 Acbor **son** *of* Micaiah, Shaphan the secretary and Asaiah the king's
22:14 who was the wife of Shallum **son** *of* Tikvah, the son of Harhas,
22:14 Shallum son of Tikvah, the **son** *of* Harhas, keeper of the wardrobe.
23: 6 scattered the dust over the graves of the **common people** [+6639].
23:10 [which was in the Valley of **Ben** [K; see Q 1208] **Hinnom**,]
23:10 so no one could use it to sacrifice his **son** or daughter in the fire to
23:13 and for Molech the detestable god of the **people** *of* Ammon.
23:15 the altar at Bethel, the high place made by Jeroboam **son** *of* Nebat,
23:30 the people of the land took Jehoahaz **son** *of* Josiah and anointed
23:31 Jehoahaz was twenty-three years **old** when he became king,
23:34 Pharaoh Neco made Eliakim **son** *of* Josiah king in place of his
23:36 Jehoiakim was twenty-five years **old** when he became king,
24: 2 Aramean, Moabite and **Ammonite** [+6648] raiders against him.
24: 6 with his fathers. And Jehoiachin his **son** succeeded him as king.
24: 8 Jehoiachin was eighteen years **old** when he became king, and he
24:18 Zedekiah was twenty-one years **old** when he became king,
25: 7 They killed the **sons** *of* Zedekiah before his eyes. Then they put out
25:22 Nebuchadnezzar king of Babylon appointed Gedaliah **son** *of*
25:22 the **son** *of* Shaphan, to be over the people he had left behind in
25:23 Ishmael **son** *of* Nethaniah, Johanan son of Kareah, Seraiah son of
25:23 Ishmael son of Nethaniah, Johanan **son** *of* Kareah, Seraiah son of
25:23 son of Kareah, Seraiah **son** *of* Tanhumeth the Netophathite,
25:23 Jaazaniah the **son** *of* the Maacathite, and their men.
25:25 however, Ishmael **son** *of* Nethaniah, the son of Elishama,
25:25 the **son** *of* Elishama, who was of royal blood, came with ten men
1Ch 1: 4 The **sons** [BHS-] *of* Noah: Shem, Ham and Japheth.
1: 5 The **sons** *of* Japheth: Gomer, Magog, Madai, Javan, Tubal,
1: 6 The **sons** *of* Gomer: Ashkenaz, Riphath and Togarmah.
1: 7 The **sons** *of* Javan: Elishah, Tarshish, the Kittim and the Rodanim.
1: 8 The **sons** *of* Ham: Cush, Mizraim, Put and Canaan.
1: 9 The **sons** *of* Cush: Seba, Havilah, Sabta, Raamah and Sabteca.
1: 9 Raamah and Sabteca. The **sons** *of* Raamah: Sheba and Dedan.
1:17 The **sons** *of* Shem: Elam, Asshur, Arphaxad, Lud and Aram.
1:17 The **sons** [BHS-] *of* Aram: Uz, Hul, Gether and Meshech.
1:19 Two **sons** were born to Eber: One was named Peleg, because in his
1:23 Ophir, Havilah and Jobab. All these were **sons** *of* Joktan.
1:28 The **sons** *of* Abraham: Isaac and Ishmael.
1:31 Jetur, Naphish and Kedemah. These were the **sons** *of* Ishmael.
1:32 The **sons** born to Keturah, Abraham's concubine: Zimran,
1:32 Ishbak and Shuah. The **sons** *of* Jokshan: Sheba and Dedan.
1:33 The **sons** *of* Midian: Ephah, Epher, Hanoch, Abida and Eldaah.
1:33 Abida and Eldaah. All these were **descendants** *of* Keturah.
1:34 was the father of Isaac. The **sons** *of* Isaac: Esau and Israel.
1:35 The **sons** *of* Esau: Eliphaz, Reuel, Jeush, Jalam and Korah.
1:36 The **sons** *of* Eliphaz: Teman, Omar, Zepho, Gatam and Kenaz;
1:37 The **sons** *of* Reuel: Nahath, Zerah, Shammah and Mizzah.
1:38 The **sons** *of* Seir: Lotan, Shobal, Zibeon, Anah, Dishon, Ezer
1:39 The **sons** *of* Lotan: Hori and Homam. Timna was Lotan's sister.
1:40 The **sons** *of* Shobal: Alvan, Manahath, Ebal, Shepho and Onam.
1:40 Ebal, Shepho and Onam. The **sons** *of* Zibeon: Aiah and Anah.
1:41 The **son** *of* Anah: Dishon. The sons of Dishon: Hemdan, Eshban,
1:41 Dishon. The **sons** *of* Dishon: Hemdan, Eshban, Ithran and Keran.
1:42 The **sons** *of* Ezer: Bilhan, Zaavan and Akan. The sons of Dishan:
1:42 Bilhan, Zaavan and Akan. The **sons** *of* Dishan: Uz and Aran.
1:43 reigned in Edom before any **Israelite** [+3776+4200] king reigned:
1:43 king reigned: Bela **son** *of* Beor, whose city was named Dinhabah.
1:44 Bela died, Jobab **son** *of* Zerah from Bozrah succeeded him as king.
1:46 When Husham died, Hadad **son** *of* Bedad, who defeated Midian in
1:49 Shaul died, Baal-Hanan **son** *of* Acbor succeeded him as king.
2: 1 These were the **sons** *of* Israel: Reuben, Simeon, Levi, Judah,
2: 3 The **sons** *of* Judah: Er, Onan and Shelah. These three were born to
2: 4 bore him Perez and Zerah. Judah had five **sons** in all.
2: 5 The **sons** *of* Perez: Hezron and Hamul.
2: 6 The **sons** *of* Zerah: Zimri, Ethan, Heman, Calcol and Darda—
2: 7 The **son** *of* Carmi: Achar, who brought trouble on Israel by
2: 8 The **son** *of* Ethan: Azariah.
2: 9 The **sons** born to Hezron were: Jerahmeel, Ram and Caleb.
2:10 the father of Nahshon, the leader of the **people** *of* Judah.
2:16 and Abigail. Zeruiah's three **sons** were Abishai, Joab and Asahel.
2:18 Caleb **son** *of* Hezron had children by his wife Azubah (and by
2:18 (and by Jerioth). These were her **sons**: Jesher, Shobab and Ardon.
2:21 father of Gilead (he had married her when he was sixty years **old**),
2:23 All these were **descendants** *of* Makir the father of Gilead.
2:25 The **sons** *of* Jerahmeel the firstborn of Hezron: Ram his firstborn,
2:27 The **sons** *of* Ram the firstborn of Jerahmeel: Maaz, Jamin
2:28 The **sons** *of* Onam: Shammai and Jada. The sons of Shammai:
2:28 Shammai and Jada. The **sons** *of* Shammai: Nadab and Abishur.
2:30 The **sons** *of* Nadab: Seled and Appaim. Seled died without
2:30 sons of Nadab: Seled and Appaim. Seled died without **children**.
2:31 The **son** *of* Appaim: Ishi, who was the father of Sheshan. Sheshan
2:31 The son of Appaim: Ishi, who was the **father**[s] *of* Sheshan.
2:31 who was the father of Sheshan. Sheshan was the **father**[s] *of* Ahlai.
2:32 The **sons** *of* Jada, Shammai's brother: Jether and Jonathan.
2:32 Jether and Jonathan. Jether died without **children**.
2:33 The **sons** *of* Jonathan: Peleth and Zaza. These were the
2:33 Peleth and Zaza. These were the **descendants** *of* Jerahmeel.
2:34 Sheshan had no **sons**—only daughters. He had an Egyptian servant
2:42 The **sons** *of* Caleb the brother of Jerahmeel: Mesha his firstborn,
2:42 his firstborn, who was the father of Ziph, and his **son** Mareshah,
2:43 The **sons** *of* Hebron: Korah, Tappuah, Rekem and Shema.
2:45 The **son** *of* Shammai was Maon, and Maon was the father of Beth
2:47 The **sons** *of* Jahdai: Regem, Jotham, Geshan, Pelet, Ephah
2:50 These were the **descendants** *of* Caleb. The sons of Hur the
2:50 The **sons** *of* Hur the firstborn of Ephrathah: Shobal the father of
2:52 The **descendants** of Shobal the father of Kiriath Jearim were:
2:54 The **descendants** *of* Salma: Bethlehem, the Netophathites,
3: 1 These were the **sons** *of* David born to him in Hebron: The firstborn
3: 2 Absalom the **son** *of* Maacah daughter of Talmai king of Geshur;
3: 2 of Talmai king of Geshur; the fourth, Adonijah the **son** *of* Haggith;
3: 9 All these were the **sons** *of* David, besides his sons by his
3: 9 these were the sons of David, besides his **sons** *by* his concubines.
3:10 Solomon's **son** was Rehoboam, Abijah his son, Asa his son,
3:10 was Rehoboam, Abijah his **son**, Asa his son, Jehoshaphat his son,
3:10 was Rehoboam, Abijah his son, Asa his **son**, Jehoshaphat his son,
3:10 was Rehoboam, Abijah his son, Asa his son, Jehoshaphat his **son**,
3:11 Jehoram his **son**, Ahaziah his son, Joash his son,
3:11 Jehoram his son, Ahaziah his **son**, Joash his son,
3:11 Jehoram his son, Ahaziah his son, Joash his **son**,
3:12 Amaziah his **son**, Azariah his son, Jotham his son,
3:12 Amaziah his son, Azariah his **son**, Jotham his son,
3:12 Amaziah his son, Azariah his son, Jotham his **son**,
3:13 Ahaz his **son**, Hezekiah his son, Manasseh his son,
3:13 Ahaz his son, Hezekiah his **son**, Manasseh his son,
3:13 Ahaz his son, Hezekiah his son, Manasseh his **son**,
3:14 Amon his **son**, Josiah his son.
3:14 Amon his son, Josiah his **son**.
3:15 The **sons** *of* Josiah: Johanan the firstborn, Jehoiakim the second
3:16 The **successors** *of* Jehoiakim: Jehoiachin his son, and Zedekiah.
3:16 The successors of Jehoiakim: Jehoiachin his **son**, and Zedekiah.
3:16 of Jehoiakim: Jehoiachin his son, and Zedekiah. **[RPH]**
3:17 The **descendants** *of* Jehoiachin the captive: Shealtiel his son,
3:17 The descendants of Jehoiachin the captive: Shealtiel his **son**,
3:19 The **sons** *of* Pedaiah: Zerubbabel and Shimei. The sons of
3:19 and Shimei. The **sons** *of* Zerubbabel: Meshullam and Hananiah.
3:21 The **descendants** *of* Hananiah: Pelatiah and Jeshaiah, and the sons

1Ch 3:21 and the **sons** *of* Rephaiah, of Arnan, of Obadiah and of Shecaniah.
3:21 sons of Rephaiah, **[RPH]** of Arnan, of Obadiah and of Shecaniah.
3:21 sons of Rephaiah, of Arnan, **[RPH]** of Obadiah and of Shecaniah.
3:21 sons of Rephaiah, of Arnan, of Obadiah and **[RPH]** of Shecaniah.
3:22 The **descendants** *of* Shecaniah: Shemaiah and his sons: Hattush,
3:22 Shemaiah and his **sons**: Hattush, Igal, Bariah, Neariah
3:23 The **sons** *of* Neariah: Elioenai, Hizkiah and Azrikam—three in all.
3:24 The **sons** *of* Elioenai: Hodaviah, Eliashib, Pelaiah, Akkub,
4:1 The **descendants** *of* Judah: Perez, Hezron, Carmi, Hur and Shobal.
4:2 Reaiah **son** *of* Shobal was the father of Jahath, and Jahath the
4:3 These were the **sons** [BHS 3] *of* Etam: Jezreel, Ishma and Idbash.
4:4 These were the **descendants** *of* Hur, the firstborn of Ephrathah
4:6 Temeni and Haahashtari. These were the **descendants** *of* Naarah.
4:7 The **sons** *of* Helah: Zereth, Zohar, Ethnan,
4:8 and Hazzobebah and of the clans of Aharhel **son** *of* Harum.
4:13 The **sons** *of* Kenaz: Othniel and Seraiah. The sons of Othniel:
4:13 and Seraiah. The **sons** *of* Othniel: Hathath and Meonothai.
4:15 The **sons** *of* Caleb son of Jephunneh: Iru, Elah and Naam.
4:15 The sons of Caleb **son** *of* Jephunneh: Iru, Elah and Naam.
4:15 son of Jephunneh: Iru, Elah and Naam. The **son** *of* Elah: Kenaz.
4:16 The **sons** *of* Jehallelel: Ziph, Ziphah, Tiria and Asarel.
4:17 The **sons** *of* Ezrah: Jether, Mered, Epher and Jalon. One of
4:18 These were the **children** *of* Pharaoh's daughter Bithiah,
4:19 The **sons** *of* Hodiah's wife, the sister of Naham: the father of
4:20 The **sons** *of* Shimon: Amnon, Rinnah, Ben-Hanan and Tilon.
4:20 and Tilon. The **descendants** *of* Ishi: Zoheth and Ben-Zoheth.
4:21 The **sons** *of* Shelah son of Judah: Er the father of Lecah, Laadah
4:21 The sons of Shelah **son** *of* Judah: Er the father of Lecah, Laadah
4:24 The **descendants** *of* Simeon: Nemuel, Jamin, Jarib, Zerah
4:25 Shallum was Shaul's **son**, Mibsam his son and Mishma his son.
4:25 Shallum was Shaul's son, Mibsam his **son** and Mishma his son.
4:25 Shallum was Shaul's son, Mibsam his son and Mishma his **son**.
4:26 The **descendants** *of* Mishma: Hammuel his son, Zaccur his son
4:26 of Mishma: Hammuel his **son**, Zaccur his son and Shimei his son.
4:26 of Mishma: Hammuel his son, Zaccur his **son** and Shimei his son.
4:26 of Mishma: Hammuel his son, Zaccur his son and Shimei his **son**.
4:27 Shimei had sixteen **sons** and six daughters, but his brothers did not
4:27 and six daughters, but his brothers did not have many **children**;
4:27 so their entire clan did not become as numerous as the **people** *of*
4:34 Meshobab, Jamlech, Joshah **son** *of* Amaziah,
4:35 Joel, Jehu **son** *of* Joshibiah, the son of Seraiah, the son of Asiel,
4:35 Jehu son of Joshibiah, the **son** *of* Seraiah, the son of Asiel,
4:35 Jehu son of Joshibiah, the son of Seraiah, the **son** *of* Asiel,
4:37 and Ziza **son** *of* Shiphi, the son of Allon, the son of Jedaiah,
4:37 the **son** *of* Allon, the son of Jedaiah, the son of Shimri, the son of
4:37 the son of Allon, the **son** *of* Jedaiah, the son of Shimri, the son of
4:37 the son of Allon, the son of Jedaiah, the **son** *of* Shimri, the son of
4:37 the son of Jedaiah, the son of Shimri, the **son** *of* Shemaiah.
4:42 And five hundred of these **Simeonites** [+9058], led by Pelatiah,
4:42 led by Pelatiah, Neariah, Rephaiah and Uzziel, the **sons** *of* Ishi,
5:1 The **sons** *of* Reuben the firstborn of Israel (he was the firstborn,
5:1 his rights as firstborn were given to the **sons** *of* Joseph son of
5:1 his rights as firstborn were given to the sons of Joseph **son** *of*
5:3 the **sons** *of* Reuben the firstborn of Israel: Hanoch, Pallu, Hezron
5:4 The **descendants** *of* Joel: Shemaiah his son, Gog his son,
5:4 of Joel: Shemaiah his **son**, Gog his son, Shimei his son,
5:4 of Joel: Shemaiah his son, Gog his **son**, Shimei his son,
5:4 of Joel: Shemaiah his son, Gog his son, Shimei his **son**,
5:5 Micah his **son**, Reaiah his son, Baal his son,
5:5 Micah his son, Reaiah his **son**, Baal his son,
5:5 Micah his son, Reaiah his son, Baal his **son**,
5:6 Beerah his **son**, whom Tiglath-Pileser king of Assyria took into
5:8 Bela **son** *of* Azaz, the son of Shema, the son of Joel. They settled
5:8 Bela son of Azaz, the **son** *of* Shema, the son of Joel. They settled
5:8 Bela son of Azaz, the son of Shema, the **son** *of* Joel. They settled
5:11 The **Gadites** [+1514] lived next to them in Bashan, as far as
5:14 These were the **sons** *of* Abihail son of Huri, the son of Jaroah,
5:14 These were the sons of Abihail **son** *of* Huri, the son of Jaroah,
5:14 the **son** *of* Jaroah, the son of Gilead, the son of Michael, the son of
5:14 the son of Jaroah, the **son** *of* Gilead, the son of Michael, the son of
5:14 the son of Jaroah, the son of Gilead, the **son** *of* Michael, the son of
5:14 of Michael, the **son** *of* Jeshishai, the son of Jahdo, the son of Buz.
5:14 of Michael, the son of Jeshishai, the **son** *of* Jahdo, the son of Buz.
5:14 of Michael, the son of Jeshishai, the son of Jahdo, the **son** *of* Buz.
5:15 Ahi **son** *of* Abdiel, the son of Guni, was head of their family.
5:15 Ahi son of Abdiel, the **son** *of* Guni, was head of their family.
5:18 The **Reubenites** [+8017], the Gadites and the half-tribe of
5:18 had 44,760 men ready for military service—**able-bodied** [+2657]
5:23 The **people** *of* the half-tribe of Manasseh were numerous;
6:1 [5:27] The **sons** *of* Levi: Gershon, Kohath and Merari.
6:2 [5:28] The **sons** *of* Kohath: Amram, Izhar, Hebron and Uzziel.
6:3 [5:29] The **children** *of* Amram: Aaron, Moses and Miriam. The
6:3 [5:29] The **sons** *of* Aaron: Nadab, Abihu, Eleazar and Ithamar.
6:16 [6:1] The **sons** *of* Levi: Gershon, Kohath and Merari.
6:17 [6:2] These are the names of the **sons** *of* Gershon: Libni
6:18 [6:3] The **sons** *of* Kohath: Amram, Izhar, Hebron and Uzziel.
6:19 [6:4] The **sons** *of* Merari: Mahli and Mushi. These are the clans of
6:20 [6:5] Of Gershon: Libni his **son**, Jehath his son, Zimmah his son,
6:20 [6:5] Of Gershon: Libni his son, Jehath his **son**, Zimmah his son,
6:20 [6:5] Of Gershon: Libni his son, Jehath his son, Zimmah his **son**,
6:21 [6:6] Joah his **son**, Iddo his son, Zerah his son and Jeatherai his
6:21 [6:6] Joah his son, Iddo his **son**, Zerah his son and Jeatherai his
6:21 [6:6] his son, Iddo his son, Zerah his **son** and Jeatherai his son.
6:21 [6:6] his son, Iddo his son, Zerah his son and Jeatherai his **son**.
6:22 [6:7] The **descendants** *of* Kohath: Amminadab his son, Korah his
6:22 [6:7] Amminadab his **son**, Korah his son, Assir his son,
6:22 [6:7] Amminadab his son, Korah his **son**, Assir his son,
6:22 [6:7] Amminadab his son, Korah his son, Assir his **son**,
6:23 [6:8] Elkanah his **son**, Ebiasaph his son, Assir his son,
6:23 [6:8] Elkanah his son, Ebiasaph his **son**, Assir his son,
6:23 [6:8] Elkanah his son, Ebiasaph his son, Assir his **son**,
6:24 [6:9] Tahath his **son**, Uriel his son, Uzziah his son and Shaul his
6:24 [6:9] his son, Uriel his **son**, Uzziah his son and Shaul his son.
6:24 [6:9] his son, Uriel his son, Uzziah his **son** and Shaul his son.
6:24 [6:9] his son, Uriel his son, Uzziah his son and Shaul his **son**.
6:25 [6:10] The **descendants** *of* Elkanah: Amasai, Ahimoth,
6:26 [6:11] Elkanah his **son**, Zophai his son, Nahath his son,
6:26 [6:11] Elkanah his son, Zophai his **son**, Nahath his son,
6:26 [6:11] Elkanah his son, Zophai his son, Nahath his **son**,
6:27 [6:12] Eliab his **son**, Jeroham his son, Elkanah his son
6:27 [6:12] Eliab his son, Jeroham his **son**, Elkanah his son
6:27 [6:12] Jeroham his son, Elkanah his **son** and Samuel his son.
6:27 [6:12] his son, Elkanah his son and Samuel his **son**. [BHS-]
6:28 [6:13] The **sons** *of* Samuel: Joel the firstborn and Abijah the
6:29 [6:14] The **descendants** *of* Merari: Mahli, Libni his son,
6:29 [6:14] Mahli, Libni his **son**, Shimei his son, Uzzah his son,
6:29 [6:14] Mahli, Libni his son, Shimei his **son**, Uzzah his son,
6:29 [6:14] Mahli, Libni his son, Shimei his son, Uzzah his **son**,
6:30 [6:15] Shimea his **son**, Haggiah his son and Asaiah his son.
6:30 [6:15] Shimea his son, Haggiah his **son** and Asaiah his son.
6:30 [6:15] Shimea his son, Haggiah his son and Asaiah his **son**.
6:33 [6:18] Here are the men who served, together with their **sons**:
6:33 [6:18] From **[RPH]** the Kohathites: Heman, the musician,
6:33 [6:18] Heman, the musician, the **son** *of* Joel, the son of Samuel,
6:33 [6:18] Heman, the musician, the son of Joel, the **son** *of* Samuel,
6:34 [6:19] the **son** *of* Elkanah, the son of Jeroham, the son of Eliel,
6:34 [6:19] the **son** *of* Jeroham, the son of Eliel, the son of Toah,
6:34 [6:19] the son of Jeroham, the **son** *of* Eliel, the son of Toah,
6:34 [6:19] the son of Jeroham, the son of Eliel, the **son** *of* Toah,
6:35 [6:20] the **son** *of* Zuph, the son of Elkanah, the son of Mahath,
6:35 [6:20] the son of Zuph, the **son** *of* Elkanah, the son of Mahath,
6:35 [6:20] the son of Elkanah, the **son** *of* Mahath, the son of Amasai,
6:35 [6:20] the son of Elkanah, the son of Mahath, the **son** *of* Amasai,
6:36 [6:21] the **son** *of* Elkanah, the son of Joel, the son of Azariah,
6:36 [6:21] the son of Elkanah, the **son** *of* Joel, the son of Azariah,
6:36 [6:21] the son of Elkanah, the son of Joel, the **son** *of* Azariah,
6:36 [6:21] the son of Joel, the son of Azariah, the **son** *of* Zephaniah,
6:37 [6:22] the **son** *of* Tahath, the son of Assir, the son of Ebiasaph,
6:37 [6:22] the son of Tahath, the **son** *of* Assir, the son of Ebiasaph,
6:37 [6:22] the son of Assir, the **son** *of* Ebiasaph, the son of Korah,
6:37 [6:22] the son of Assir, the son of Ebiasaph, the **son** *of* Korah,
6:38 [6:23] the **son** *of* Izhar, the son of Kohath, the son of Levi, the son
6:38 [6:23] the son of Izhar, the **son** *of* Kohath, the son of Levi, the son
6:38 [6:23] the son of Kohath, the **son** *of* Levi, the son of Israel;
6:38 [6:23] the son of Kohath, the son of Levi, the **son** *of* Israel;
6:39 [6:24] his right hand: Asaph **son** *of* Berekiah, the son of Shimea,
6:39 [6:24] his right hand: Asaph son of Berekiah, the **son** *of* Shimea,
6:40 [6:25] the **son** *of* Michael, the son of Baaseiah, the son of
6:40 [6:25] the son of Michael, the **son** *of* Baaseiah, the son of
6:40 [6:25] son of Michael, the son of Baaseiah, the **son** *of* Malkijah,
6:41 [6:26] the **son** *of* Ethni, the son of Zerah, the son of Adaiah,
6:41 [6:26] the son of Ethni, the **son** *of* Zerah, the son of Adaiah,
6:41 [6:26] the son of Ethni, the son of Zerah, the **son** *of* Adaiah,
6:42 [6:27] the **son** *of* Ethan, the son of Zimmah, the son of Shimei,
6:42 [6:27] the son of Ethan, the **son** *of* Zimmah, the son of Shimei,
6:42 [6:27] the son of Ethan, the son of Zimmah, the **son** *of* Shimei,
6:43 [6:28] the **son** *of* Jahath, the son of Gershon, the son of Levi;
6:43 [6:28] the son of Jahath, the **son** *of* Gershon, the son of Levi;
6:43 [6:28] the son of Jahath, the son of Gershon, the **son** *of* Levi;
6:44 [6:29] their associates, the **Merarites** [+5356], at his left hand:
6:44 [6:29] Ethan **son** *of* Kishi, the son of Abdi, the son of Malluch,
6:44 [6:29] Ethan son of Kishi, the **son** *of* Abdi, the son of Malluch,
6:44 [6:29] Ethan son of Kishi, the son of Abdi, the **son** *of* Malluch,
6:45 [6:30] the **son** *of* Hashabiah, the son of Amaziah, the son of
6:45 [6:30] son of Hashabiah, the **son** *of* Amaziah, the son of Hilkiah,
6:45 [6:30] son of Hashabiah, the son of Amaziah, the **son** *of* Hilkiah,
6:46 [6:31] the **son** *of* Amzi, the son of Bani, the son of Shemer,
6:46 [6:31] the son of Amzi, the **son** *of* Bani, the son of Shemer,

1Ch 6:46 [6:31] the son of Amzi, the son of Bani, the **son** *of* Shemer,
6:47 [6:32] the **son** *of* Mahli, the son of Mushi, the son of Merari,
6:47 [6:32] the son of Mahli, the **son** *of* Mushi, the son of Merari,
6:47 [6:32] the son of Mushi, the **son** *of* Merari, the son of Levi.
6:47 [6:32] the son of Mushi, the son of Merari, the **son** *of* Levi.
6:49 [6:34] his **descendants** were the ones who presented offerings on
6:50 [6:35] These were the **descendants** *of* Aaron: Eleazar his son,
6:50 [6:35] Eleazar his **son**, Phinehas his son, Abishua his son,
6:50 [6:35] Eleazar his son, Phinehas his **son**, Abishua his son,
6:50 [6:35] Eleazar his son, Phinehas his son, Abishua his **son**,
6:51 [6:36] Bukki his **son**, Uzzi his son, Zerahiah his son,
6:51 [6:36] Bukki his son, Uzzi his **son**, Zerahiah his son,
6:51 [6:36] Bukki his son, Uzzi his son, Zerahiah his **son**,
6:52 [6:37] Meraioth his **son**, Amariah his son, Ahitub his son,
6:52 [6:37] Meraioth his son, Amariah his **son**, Ahitub his son,
6:52 [6:37] Meraioth his son, Amariah his son, Ahitub his **son**,
6:53 [6:38] Zadok his **son** and Ahimaaz his son.
6:53 [6:38] Zadok his son and Ahimaaz his **son**.
6:54 [6:39] **descendants** *of* Aaron who were from the Kohathite clan,
6:56 [6:41] villages around the city were given to Caleb **son** *of*
6:57 [6:42] So the **descendants** *of* Aaron were given Hebron (a city of
6:61 [6:46] The rest of Kohath's **descendants** were allotted ten towns
6:62 [6:47] The **descendants** *of* Gershon, clan by clan, were allotted
6:63 [6:48] The **descendants** *of* Merari, clan by clan, were allotted
6:64 [6:49] So the **Israelites** [+3776] gave the Levites these towns
6:65 [6:50] From the tribes of **Judah** [+3373], Simeon and Benjamin
6:65 [6:50] From the tribes of Judah, **Simeon** [+9058] and Benjamin
6:65 [6:50] **Benjamin** [+1228] they allotted the previously named
6:66 [6:51] Some of the **Kohathite** [+7740] clans were given as their
6:70 [6:55] to the rest of the **Kohathite** [+7740] clans.
6:71 [6:56] The **Gershonites** [+1768] received the following:
6:77 [6:62] The **Merarites** [+5356] (the rest of the Levites)
7:1 The **sons** *of* Issachar: Tola, Puah, Jashub and Shimron—four in all.
7:2 The **sons** *of* Tola: Uzzi, Rephaiah, Jeriel, Jahmai, Ibsam
7:3 The **son** *of* Uzzi: Izrahiah. The sons of Izrahiah: Michael,
7:3 Izrahiah. The **sons** *of* Izrahiah: Michael, Obadiah, Joel and Isshiah.
7:4 men ready for battle, for they had many wives and **children**.
7:7 The **sons** *of* Bela: Ezbon, Uzzi, Uzziel, Jerimoth and Iri, heads of
7:8 The **sons** *of* Beker: Zemirah, Joash, Eliezer, Elioenai, Omri,
7:8 Abijah, Anathoth and Alemeth. All these were the **sons** *of* Beker.
7:10 The **son** *of* Jediael: Bilhan. The sons of Bilhan: Jeush, Benjamin,
7:10 The **sons** *of* Bilhan: Jeush, Benjamin, Ehud, Kenaanah, Zethan,
7:11 All these **sons** *of* Jediael were heads of families. There were
7:12 The Shuppites and Huppites were the **descendants** *of* Ir,
7:12 the descendants of Ir, and the Hushites the **descendants** *of* Aher.
7:13 The **sons** *of* Naphtali: Jahziel, Guni, Jezer and Shillem—
7:13 Jahziel, Guni, Jezer and Shillem—the **descendants** *of* Bilhah.
7:14 The **descendants** *of* Manasseh: Asriel was his descendant through
7:16 Makir's wife Maacah gave birth to a **son** and named him Peresh.
7:16 brother was named Sheresh, and his **sons** were Ulam and Rakem.
7:17 The **son** *of* Ulam: Bedan. These were the sons of Gilead son of
7:17 These were the **sons** *of* Gilead son of Makir, the son of Manasseh.
7:17 These were the sons of Gilead **son** *of* Makir, the son of Manasseh.
7:17 These were the sons of Gilead son of Makir, the **son** *of* Manasseh.
7:19 The **sons** *of* Shemida were: Ahian, Shechem, Likhi and Aniam.
7:20 The **descendants** *of* Ephraim: Shuthelah, Bered his son, Tahath his
7:20 Shuthelah, Bered his **son**, Tahath his son, Eleadah his son,
7:20 Shuthelah, Bered his son, Tahath his **son**, Eleadah his son,
7:20 Bered his son, Tahath his son, Eleadah his **son**, Tahath his son,
7:20 Bered his son, Tahath his son, Eleadah his son, Tahath his **son**,
7:21 Zabad his **son** and Shuthelah his son. Ezer and Elead were killed
7:21 Zabad his son and Shuthelah his **son**. Ezer and Elead were killed
7:23 his wife again, and she became pregnant and gave birth to a **son**.
7:25 Rephah was his **son**, Resheph his son, Telah his son, Tahan his
7:25 was his son, Resheph his son, Telah his **son**, Tahan his son,
7:25 was his son, Resheph his son, Telah his son, Tahan his **son**,
7:26 Ladan his **son**, Ammihud his son, Elishama his son,
7:26 Ladan his son, Ammihud his **son**, Elishama his son,
7:26 Ladan his son, Ammihud his son, Elishama his **son**,
7:27 Nun his **son** and Joshua his son.
7:27 Nun his son and Joshua his **son**.
7:29 Along the borders of **Manasseh** [+4985] were Beth Shan,
7:29 The **descendants** *of* Joseph son of Israel lived in these towns.
7:29 The descendants of Joseph **son** *of* Israel lived in these towns.
7:30 The **sons** *of* Asher: Imnah, Ishvah, Ishvi and Beriah. Their sister
7:31 The **sons** *of* Beriah: Heber and Malkiel, who was the father of
7:33 The **sons** *of* Japhlet: Pasach, Bimhal and Ashvath. These were
7:33 Pasach, Bimhal and Ashvath. These were Japhlet's **sons**.
7:34 The **sons** *of* Shomer: Ahi, Rohgah, Hubbah and Aram.
7:35 The **sons** *of* his brother Helem: Zophah, Imna, Shelesh and Amal.
7:36 The **sons** *of* Zophah: Suah, Harnepher, Shual, Beri, Imrah,
7:38 The **sons** *of* Jether: Jephunneh, Pispah and Ara.
7:39 The **sons** *of* Ulla: Arah, Hanniel and Rizia.
7:40 All these were **descendants** *of* Asher—heads of families,
8:3 The **sons** of Bela were: Addar, Gera, Abihud,
8:6 These were the **descendants** *of* Ehud, who were heads of families
8:10 Sakia and Mirmah. These were his **sons**, heads of families.
8:12 The **sons** *of* Elpaal: Eber, Misham, Shemed (who built Ono
8:16 Michael, Ishpah and Joha were the **sons** *of* Beriah.
8:18 Ishmerai, Izliah and Jobab were the **sons** *of* Elpaal.
8:21 Adaiah, Beraiah and Shimrath were the **sons** *of* Shimei.
8:25 Iphdeiah and Penuel were the **sons** *of* Shashak.
8:27 Jaareshiah, Elijah and Zicri were the **sons** *of* Jeroham.
8:30 and his firstborn **son** was Abdon, followed by Zur, Kish, Baal,
8:34 The **son** *of* Jonathan: Merib-Baal, who was the father of Micah.
8:35 The **sons** *of* Micah: Pithon, Melech, Tarea and Ahaz.
8:37 of Binea; Raphah was his **son**, Eleasah his son and Azel his son.
8:37 of Binea; Raphah was his son, Eleasah his **son** and Azel his son.
8:37 of Binea; Raphah was his son, Eleasah his son and Azel his **son**.
8:38 Azel had six **sons**, and these were their names: Azrikam, Bokeru,
8:38 Sheariah, Obadiah and Hanan. All these were the **sons** *of* Azel.
8:39 The **sons** *of* his brother Eshek: Ulam his firstborn,
8:40 The **sons** *of* Ulam were brave warriors who could handle the bow.
8:40 They had many **sons** and grandsons—150 in all. All these were the
8:40 They had many sons and **grandsons** [+1201]—150 in all.
8:40 They had many sons and **grandsons** [+1201]—150 in all.
8:40 150 in all. All these were the **descendants** *of* Benjamin.
9:3 Those from **Judah** [+3373], from Benjamin, and from Ephraim
9:3 from **Benjamin** [+1228], and from Ephraim and Manasseh who
9:3 from **Ephraim** [+713] and Manasseh who lived in Jerusalem were:
9:4 Uthai **son** *of* Ammihud, the son of Omri, the son of Imri, the son of
9:4 son of Ammihud, the **son** *of* Omri, the son of Imri, the son of Bani,
9:4 son of Ammihud, the son of Omri, the **son** *of* Imri, the son of Bani,
9:4 son of Ammihud, the son of Omri, the son of Imri, the **son** *of* Bani,
9:4 son of Imri, the son of Bani, a **descendant** *of* Perez son of Judah.
9:4 son of Imri, the son of Bani, a descendant of Perez **son** *of* Judah.
9:5 Of the Shilonites: Asaiah the firstborn and his **sons**.
9:6 Of the **Zerahites** [+2438]: Jeuel. The people from Judah numbered
9:7 Of the **Benjamites** [+1228]: Sallu son of Meshullam, the son of
9:7 Sallu **son** *of* Meshullam, the son of Hodaviah, the son of
9:7 son of Meshullam, the **son** *of* Hodaviah, the son of Hassenuah;
9:7 son of Meshullam, the son of Hodaviah, the **son** *of* Hassenuah;
9:8 Ibneiah **son** *of* Jeroham; Elah son of Uzzi, the son of Micri;
9:8 Ibneiah son of Jeroham; Elah **son** *of* Uzzi, the son of Micri;
9:8 Ibneiah son of Jeroham; Elah son of Uzzi, the **son** *of* Micri;
9:8 Meshullam **son** *of* Shephatiah, the son of Reuel, the son of Ibnijah.
9:8 Meshullam son of Shephatiah, the **son** *of* Reuel, the son of Ibnijah.
9:8 Meshullam son of Shephatiah, the son of Reuel, the **son** *of* Ibnijah.
9:11 Azariah **son** *of* Hilkiah, the son of Meshullam, the son of Zadok,
9:11 the **son** *of* Meshullam, the son of Zadok, the son of Meraioth,
9:11 the **son** *of* Zadok, the son of Meraioth, the son of Ahitub,
9:11 the son of Zadok, the **son** *of* Meraioth, the son of Ahitub,
9:11 the son of Zadok, the son of Meraioth, the **son** *of* Ahitub,
9:12 Adaiah **son** *of* Jeroham, the son of Pashhur, the son of Malkijah;
9:12 Adaiah son of Jeroham, the **son** *of* Pashhur, the son of Malkijah;
9:12 Adaiah son of Jeroham, the son of Pashhur, the **son** *of* Malkijah;
9:12 Maasai **son** *of* Adiel, the son of Jahzerah, the son of Meshullam,
9:12 the **son** *of* Jahzerah, the son of Meshullam, the son of
9:12 the son of Jahzerah, the **son** *of* Meshullam, the son of
9:12 the son of Meshullam, the **son** *of* Meshillemith, the son of Immer.
9:12 the son of Meshullam, the son of Meshillemith, the **son** *of* Immer.
9:14 Shemaiah **son** *of* Hasshub, the son of Azrikam, the son of
9:14 of Hasshub, the **son** *of* Azrikam, the son of Hashabiah, a Merarite;
9:14 of Hasshub, the son of Azrikam, the **son** *of* Hashabiah, a Merarite;
9:14 the son of Azrikam, the son of Hashabiah, a **Merarite** [+5356];
9:15 Bakbakkar, Heresh, Galal and Mattaniah **son** *of* Mica, the son of
9:15 and Mattaniah son of Mica, the **son** *of* Zicri, the son of Asaph;
9:15 and Mattaniah son of Mica, the son of Zicri, the **son** *of* Asaph;
9:16 Obadiah **son** *of* Shemaiah, the son of Galal, the son of Jeduthun;
9:16 Obadiah son of Shemaiah, the **son** *of* Galal, the son of Jeduthun;
9:16 Obadiah son of Shemaiah, the son of Galal, the **son** *of* Jeduthun;
9:16 Berekiah **son** *of* Asa, the son of Elkanah, who lived in the villages
9:16 Berekiah son of Asa, the **son** *of* Elkanah, who lived in the villages
9:18 the gatekeepers belonging to the camp of the **Levites** [+4290].
9:19 Shallum **son** *of* Kore, the son of Ebiasaph, the son of Korah,
9:19 Shallum son of Kore, the **son** *of* Ebiasaph, the son of Korah,
9:19 Shallum son of Kore, the son of Ebiasaph, the **son** *of* Korah,
9:20 In earlier times Phinehas **son** *of* Eleazar was in charge of the
9:21 Zechariah **son** *of* Meshelemiah was the gatekeeper at the entrance
9:23 their **descendants** were in charge of guarding the gates of the
9:30 But some of **[NIE]** the priests took care of mixing the spices.
9:32 Some of their **Kohathite** [+7741] brothers were in charge of
9:36 and his firstborn **son** was Abdon, followed by Zur, Kish, Baal,
9:40 The **son** *of* Jonathan: Merib-Baal, who was the father of Micah.
9:41 The **sons** *of* Micah: Pithon, Melech, Tahrea and Ahaz.
9:43 of Binea; Rephaiah was his **son**, Eleasah his son and Azel his son.
9:43 of Binea; Rephaiah was his son, Eleasah his **son** and Azel his son.
9:43 of Binea; Rephaiah was his son, Eleasah his son and Azel his **son**.

1Ch 9:44 Azel had six **sons**, and these were their names: Azrikam, Bokeru,
9:44 Sheariah, Obadiah and Hanan. These were the **sons** *of* Azel.
10: 2 The Philistines pressed hard after Saul and his **sons**, and they killed
10: 2 and they killed his **sons** Jonathan, Abinadab and Malki-Shua.
10: 6 So Saul and his three **sons** died, and all his house died together.
10: 7 saw that the army had fled and that Saul and his **sons** had died,
10: 8 the dead, they found Saul and his **sons** fallen on Mount Gilboa.
10:12 all their valiant men went and took the bodies of Saul and his **sons**
10:14 him to death and turned the kingdom over to David **son** *of* Jesse.
11: 6 Joab **son** *of* Zeruiah went up first, and so he received the
11:11 Jashobeam, a **Hacmonite** [+2685], was chief of the officers;
11:12 Next to him was Eleazar **son** *of* Dodai the Ahohite, one of the three
11:22 Benaiah **son** *of* Jehoiada was a valiant fighter from Kabzeel,
11:22 Benaiah son of Jehoiada was a **valiant fighter** [+408+2657] from
11:24 Such were the exploits of Benaiah **son** *of* Jehoiada; he too was as
11:26 Asahel the brother of Joab, Elhanan **son** *of* Dodo from Bethlehem,
11:28 Ira **son** *of* Ikkesh from Tekoa, Abiezer from Anathoth,
11:30 Maharai the Netophathite, Heled **son** *of* Baanah the Netophathite,
11:31 Ithai **son** *of* Ribai from Gibeah in Benjamin,
11:31 Ithai son of Ribai from Gibeah in **Benjamin** [+1228],
11:34 the **sons** *of* Hashem the Gizonite, Jonathan son of Shagee the
11:34 sons of Hashem the Gizonite, Jonathan **son** *of* Shagee the Hararite,
11:35 Ahiam **son** *of* Sacar the Hararite, Eliphal son of Ur,
11:35 Ahiam son of Sacar the Hararite, Eliphal **son** *of* Ur,
11:37 Hezro the Carmelite, Naarai **son** *of* Ezbai,
11:38 Joel the brother of Nathan, Mibhar **son** *of* Hagri,
11:39 Naharai the Berothite, the armor-bearer of Joab **son** *of* Zeruiah,
11:41 Uriah the Hittite, Zabad **son** *of* Ahlai,
11:42 Adina **son** *of* Shiza the Reubenite, who was chief of the
11:43 Hanan **son** *of* Maacah, Joshaphat the Mithnite,
11:44 the Ashterathite, Shama and Jeiel the **sons** *of* Hotham the Aroerite,
11:45 Jediael **son** *of* Shimri, his brother Joha the Tizite,
11:46 Eliel the Mahavite, Jeribai and Joshaviah the **sons** *of* Elnaam,
12: 1 while he was banished from the presence of Saul **son** *of* Kish (they
12: 3 Ahiezer their chief and Joash the **sons** *of* Shemaah the Gibeathite;
12: 3 Jeziel and Pelet the **sons** *of* Azmaveth; Beracah, Jehu the
12: 7 [12:8] and Joelah and Zebadiah the **sons** *of* Jeroham from Gedor.
12:14 [12:15] These **Gadites** [+1514] were army commanders; the least
12:16 [12:17] Other **Benjamites** [+1228] and some men from Judah
12:18 [12:19] We are with you, O **son** *of* Jesse! Success, success to you,
12:24 [12:25] **men** *of* Judah, carrying shield and spear—6,800 armed
12:25 [12:26] **men** of Simeon, warriors ready for battle—7,100;
12:26 [12:27] **men** of Levi—4,600,
12:29 [12:30] **men** of Benjamin, Saul's kinsmen—3,000, most of whom
12:30 [12:31] **men** of Ephraim, brave warriors, famous in their own
12:32 [12:33] **men** of Issachar, who understood the times and knew
14: 3 more wives and became the father of more **sons** and daughters.
15: 4 He called together the **descendants** *of* Aaron and the Levites:
15: 5 From the **descendants** *of* Kohath, Uriel the leader and 120
15: 6 from the **descendants** *of* Merari, Asaiah the leader and 220
15: 7 from the **descendants** *of* Gershon, Joel the leader and 130
15: 8 from the **descendants** *of* Elizaphan, Shemaiah the leader and 200
15: 9 from the **descendants** *of* Hebron, Eliel the leader and 80 relatives;
15:10 from the **descendants** *of* Uzziel, Amminadab the leader and 112
15:15 the **Levites** [+4291] carried the ark of God with the poles on their
15:17 So the Levites appointed Heman **son** *of* Joel; from his brothers,
15:17 from his brothers, Asaph **son** *of* Berekiah; and from their brothers
15:17 from their brothers the **Merarites** [+5356], Ethan son of Kushaiah;
15:17 and from their brothers the Merarites, Ethan **son** *of* Kushaiah;
15:18 Zechariah, [BHS+ ***Ben*** or ***son***] Jaaziel, Shemiramoth,
16:13 descendants of Israel his servant, O **sons** *of* Jacob, his chosen ones.
16:38 Obed-Edom **son** *of* Jeduthun, and also Hosah, were gatekeepers.
16:42 for sacred song. The **sons** *of* Jeduthun were stationed at the gate.
17: 9 Wicked **people** will not oppress them anymore, as they did at the
17:11 one of your own **sons**, and I will establish his kingdom.
17:13 I will be his father, and he will be my **son**. I will never take my
18:10 he sent his **son** Hadoram to King David to greet him
18:11 Edom and Moab, the **Ammonites** [+6648] and the Philistines,
18:12 Abishai **son** *of* Zeruiah struck down eighteen thousand Edomites in
18:15 Joab **son** *of* Zeruiah was over the army; Jehoshaphat son of Ahilud
18:15 was over the army; Jehoshaphat **son** *of* Ahilud was recorder;
18:16 Zadok **son** *of* Ahitub and Ahimelech son of Abiathar were priests;
18:16 Zadok son of Ahitub and Ahimelech **son** *of* Abiathar were priests;
18:17 Benaiah **son** *of* Jehoiada was over the Kerethites and Pelethites;
18:17 and David's **sons** were chief officials at the king's side.
19: 1 the course of time, Nahash king of the **Ammonites** [+6648] died,
19: 1 king of the Ammonites died, and his **son** succeeded him as king.
19: 2 David thought, "I will show kindness to Hanun **son** *of* Nahash,
19: 2 in the land of the **Ammonites** [+6648] to express sympathy to him,
19: 3 the **Ammonite** [+6648] nobles said to Hanun, "Do you think David
19: 6 When the **Ammonites** [+6648] realized that they had become a
19: 6 the **Ammonites** [+6648] sent a thousand talents of silver to hire
19: 7 while the **Ammonites** [+6648] were mustered from their towns
19: 9 The **Ammonites** [+6648] came out and drew up in battle formation
19:11 and they were deployed against the **Ammonites** [+6648].
19:12 if the **Ammonites** [+6648] are too strong for you, then I will rescue
19:15 When the **Ammonites** [+6648] saw that the Arameans were
19:19 So the Arameans were not willing to help the **Ammonites** [+6648]
20: 1 He laid waste the land of the **Ammonites** [+6648] and went to
20: 3 and axes. David did this to all the **Ammonite** [+6648] towns.
20: 5 Elhanan **son** *of* Jair killed Lahmi the brother of Goliath the Gittite,
20: 7 Jonathan **son** *of* Shimea, David's brother, killed him.
21:20 saw the angel; his four **sons** who were with him hid themselves.
22: 5 David said, "My **son** Solomon is young and inexperienced,
22: 6 he called for his **son** Solomon and charged him to build a house for
22: 7 "My **son**, I had it in my heart to build a house for the Name of the
22: 9 But you will have a **son** who will be a man of peace and rest,
22:10 a house for my Name. He will be my **son**, and I will be his father.
22:11 "Now, my **son**, the LORD be with you, and may you have
22:17 David ordered all the leaders of Israel to help his **son** Solomon.
23: 1 and full of years, he made his **son** Solomon king over Israel.
23: 3 The Levites thirty years **old** or more were counted, and the total
23: 6 David divided the Levites into groups corresponding to the **sons** *of*
23: 8 The **sons** *of* Ladan: Jehiel the first, Zetham and Joel—three in all.
23: 9 The **sons** *of* Shimei: Shelomoth, Haziel and Haran—three in all.
23:10 the **sons** *of* Shimei: Jahath, Ziza, Jeush and Beriah. These were the
23:10 Jeush and Beriah. These were the **sons** *of* Shimei—four in all.
23:11 and Ziza the second, but Jeush and Beriah did not have many **sons**;
23:12 The **sons** *of* Kohath: Amram, Izhar, Hebron and Uzziel—four in
23:13 The **sons** *of* Amram: Aaron and Moses. Aaron was set apart,
23:13 Aaron was set apart, he and his **descendants** forever, to consecrate
23:14 The **sons** *of* Moses the man of God were counted as part of the
23:15 The **sons** *of* Moses: Gershom and Eliezer.
23:16 The **descendants** *of* Gershom: Shubael was the first.
23:17 The **descendants** *of* Eliezer: Rehabiah was the first. Eliezer had no
23:17 Eliezer had no other **sons**, but the sons of Rehabiah were very
23:17 had no other sons, but the **sons** *of* Rehabiah were very numerous.
23:18 The **sons** *of* Izhar: Shelomith was the first.
23:19 The **sons** *of* Hebron: Jeriah the first, Amariah the second,
23:20 The **sons** *of* Uzziel: Micah the first and Isshiah the second.
23:21 The **sons** *of* Merari: Mahli and Mushi. The sons of Mahli:
23:21 of Merari: Mahli and Mushi. The **sons** *of* Mahli: Eleazar and Kish.
23:22 Eleazar died without having **sons**: he had only daughters. Their
23:22 had only daughters. Their cousins, the **sons** *of* Kish, married them.
23:23 The **sons** *of* Mushi: Mahli, Eder and Jerimoth—three in all.
23:24 These were the **descendants** *of* Levi by their families—the heads
23:24 the workers twenty years **old** or more who served in the temple of
23:27 the **Levites** [+4290] were counted from those twenty years old
23:27 the Levites were counted from *those* twenty years **old** or more.
23:28 The duty of the Levites was to help Aaron's **descendants** in the
23:32 the Holy Place and, under their brothers the **descendants** *of* Aaron,
24: 1 These were the divisions of the **sons** *of* Aaron: The sons of Aaron
24: 1 The **sons** *of* Aaron were Nadab, Abihu, Eleazar and Ithamar.
24: 2 and Abihu died before their father did, and they had no **sons**;
24: 3 With the help of Zadok a **descendant** *of* Eleazar and Ahimelech a
24: 3 a descendant of Eleazar and Ahimelech a **descendant** *of* Ithamar,
24: 4 were found among Eleazar's **descendants** than among Ithamar's,
24: 4 than among Ithamar's, **[RPH]** and they were divided accordingly:
24: 4 sixteen heads of families from Eleazar's **descendants** and eight
24: 4 and eight heads of families from Ithamar's **descendants**.
24: 5 and officials of God among the **descendants** *of* both Eleazar
24: 5 God among the descendants of both Eleazar and **[RPH]** Ithamar.
24: 6 The scribe Shemaiah **son** *of* Nethanel, a Levite, recorded their
24: 6 Ahimelech **son** *of* Abiathar and the heads of families of the priests
24:20 As for the rest of the **descendants** *of* Levi: from the sons of
24:20 from the **sons** *of* Amram: Shubael; from the sons of Shubael:
24:20 the sons of Amram: Shubael; from the **sons** *of* Shubael: Jehdeiah.
24:21 As for Rehabiah, from his **sons**: Isshiah was the first.
24:22 the Izharites: Shelomoth; from the **sons** *of* Shelomoth: Jahath.
24:23 The **sons** *of* Hebron: Jeriah the first, Amariah the second,
24:24 The **son** *of* Uzziel: Micah; from the sons of Micah: Shamir.
24:24 The son of Uzziel: Micah; from the **sons** *of* Micah: Shamir.
24:25 The brother of Micah: Isshiah; from the **sons** *of* Isshiah: Zechariah.
24:26 The **sons** *of* Merari: Mahli and Mushi. The son of Jaaziah:
24:26 The sons of Merari: Mahli and Mushi. The **son** *of* Jaaziah: Beno.
24:27 The **sons** *of* Merari: from Jaaziah: Beno, Shoham, Zaccur
24:28 From Mahli: Eleazar, who had no **sons**.
24:29 From Kish: the **son** *of* Kish: Jerahmeel.
24:30 the **sons** *of* Mushi: Mahli, Eder and Jerimoth. These were the
24:30 These were the **Levites** [+4290], according to their families.
24:31 also cast lots, just as their brothers the **descendants** *of* Aaron did,
25: 1 set apart some of the **sons** *of* Asaph, Heman and Jeduthun for the
25: 2 From the **sons** *of* Asaph: Zaccur, Joseph, Nethaniah and Asarelah.
25: 2 The **sons** *of* Asaph were under the supervision of Asaph,
25: 3 As for Jeduthun, from his **sons**: Gedaliah, Zeri, Jeshaiah, Shimei,
25: 4 As for Heman, from his **sons**: Bukkiah, Mattaniah, Uzziel,
25: 5 All these were **sons** of Heman the king's seer. They were given
25: 5 to exalt him. God gave Heman fourteen **sons** and three daughters.

1Ch 25: 9 was for Asaph, fell to Joseph, his **sons** [BHS-] and relatives,
25: 9 12 the second to Gedaliah, he and his relatives and **sons**, 12
25: 10 the third to Zaccur, his **sons** and relatives, 12
25: 11 the fourth to Izri, his **sons** and relatives, 12
25: 12 the fifth to Nethaniah, his **sons** and relatives, 12
25: 13 the sixth to Bukkiah, his **sons** and relatives, 12
25: 14 the seventh to Jesarelah, his **sons** and relatives, 12
25: 15 the eighth to Jeshaiah, his **sons** and relatives, 12
25: 16 the ninth to Mattaniah, his **sons** and relatives, 12
25: 17 the tenth to Shimei, his **sons** and relatives, 12
25: 18 the eleventh to Azarel, his **sons** and relatives, 12
25: 19 the twelfth to Hashabiah, his **sons** and relatives, 12
25: 20 the thirteenth to Shubael, his **sons** and relatives, 12
25: 21 the fourteenth to Mattithiah, his **sons** and relatives, 12
25: 22 the fifteenth to Jerimoth, his **sons** and relatives, 12
25: 23 the sixteenth to Hananiah, his **sons** and relatives, 12
25: 24 the seventeenth to Joshbekashah, his **sons** and relatives, 12
25: 25 the eighteenth to Hanani, his **sons** and relatives, 12
25: 26 the nineteenth to Mallothi, his **sons** and relatives, 12
25: 27 the twentieth to Eliathah, his **sons** and relatives, 12
25: 28 the twenty-first to Hothir, his **sons** and relatives, 12
25: 29 the twenty-second to Giddalti, his **sons** and relatives, 12
25: 30 the twenty-third to Mahazioth, his **sons** and relatives, 12
25: 31 the twenty-fourth to Romamti-Ezer, his **sons** and relatives, 12
26: 1 the Korahites: Meshelemiah **son** *of* Kore, one of the sons of Asaph.
26: 1 the Korahites: Meshelemiah son of Kore, one of the **sons** *of* Asaph.
26: 2 Meshelemiah had **sons**: Zechariah the firstborn, Jediael the second,
26: 4 Obed-Edom also had **sons**: Shemaiah the firstborn,
26: 6 His **son** Shemaiah also had sons, who were leaders in their father's
26: 6 His son Shemaiah also had **sons**, who were leaders in their father's
26: 7 The **sons** *of* Shemaiah: Othni, Rephael, Obed and Elzabad;
26: 7 his relatives Elihu and Semakiah were also **able men** [+2657].
26: 8 All these were **descendants** *of* Obed-Edom; they and their sons
26: 8 they and their **sons** and their relatives were capable men with the
26: 9 Meshelemiah had **sons** and relatives, who were able men—
26: 9 had sons and relatives, who were **able men** [+2657]—
26: 10 Hosah the **Merarite** [+5356] had sons: Shimri the first (although
26: 10 Hosah the Merarite had **sons**: Shimri the first (although he was not
26: 11 the fourth. The **sons** and relatives of Hosah were 13 in all.
26: 14 Then lots were cast for his **son** Zechariah, a wise counselor,
26: 15 fell to Obed-Edom, and the lot for the storehouse fell to his **sons**.
26: 19 the divisions of the gatekeepers who were **descendants** *of* Korah
26: 19 gatekeepers who were descendants of Korah and **[NIE]** Merari.
26: 21 The **descendants** *of* Ladan, who were Gershonites through Ladan
26: 21 who were **Gershonites** [+1769] through Ladan and who were
26: 22 the **sons** *of* Jehieli, Zetham and his brother Joel. They were in
26: 24 Shubael, a **descendant** *of* Gershom son of Moses, was the officer
26: 24 Shubael, a descendant of Gershom **son** *of* Moses, was the officer in
26: 25 Rehabiah his **son**, Jeshaiah his son, Joram his son, Zicri his son
26: 25 Jeshaiah his **son**, Joram his son, Zicri his son and Shelomith his
26: 25 his son, Joram his **son**, Zicri his son and Shelomith his son.
26: 25 his son, Joram his son, Zicri his **son** and Shelomith his son.
26: 25 his son, Joram his son, Zicri his son and Shelomith his **son**.
26: 28 everything dedicated by Samuel the seer and by Saul **son** *of* Kish,
26: 28 by Saul son of Kish, Abner **son** *of* Ner and Joab son of Zeruiah,
26: 28 by Saul son of Kish, Abner son of Ner and Joab **son** *of* Zeruiah,
26: 29 Kenaniah and his **sons** were assigned duties away from the temple,
26: 30 and his relatives—seventeen hundred **able men** [+2657]—
26: 32 who were **able men** [+2657] and heads of families,
27: 1 This is the list of the **Israelites** [+3776]—heads of families,
27: 2 first division, for the first month, was Jashobeam **son** *of* Zabdiel.
27: 3 He was a **descendant** *of* Perez and chief of all the army officers for
27: 5 for the third month, was Benaiah **son** *of* Jehoiada the priest.
27: 6 over the Thirty. His **son** Ammizabad was in charge of his division.
27: 7 Asahel the brother of Joab; his **son** Zebadiah was his successor.
27: 9 for the sixth month, was Ira the **son** *of* Ikkesh the Tekoite.
27: 10 the seventh month, was Helez the Pelonite, an **Ephraimite** [+713].
27: 14 was Benaiah the Pirathonite, an **Ephraimite** [+713].
27: 16 over the Reubenites: Eliezer **son** *of* Zicri; over the Simeonites:
27: 16 son of Zicri; over the Simeonites: Shephatiah **son** *of* Maacah;
27: 17 over Levi: Hashabiah **son** *of* Kemuel; over Aaron: Zadok;
27: 18 Elihu, a brother of David; over Issachar: Omri **son** *of* Michael;
27: 19 over Zebulun: Ishmaiah **son** *of* Obadiah; over Naphtali:
27: 19 Ishmaiah son of Obadiah; over Naphtali: Jerimoth **son** *of* Azriel;
27: 20 over the **Ephraimites** [+713]: Hoshea son of Azaziah; over half
27: 20 Hoshea **son** *of* Azaziah; over half the tribe of Manasseh: Joel son
27: 20 of Azaziah; over half the tribe of Manasseh: Joel **son** *of* Pedaiah;
27: 21 Iddo **son** *of* Zechariah; over Benjamin: Jaasiel son of Abner;
27: 21 Iddo son of Zechariah; over Benjamin: Jaasiel **son** *of* Abner;
27: 22 over Dan: Azarel **son** *of* Jeroham. These were the officers over the
27: 23 David did not take the number of the men twenty years **old**
27: 24 Joab **son** *of* Zeruiah began to count the men but did not finish.
27: 25 Azmaveth **son** *of* Adiel was in charge of the royal storehouses.
27: 25 Jonathan **son** *of* Uzziah was in charge of the storehouses in the
27: 26 Ezri **son** *of* Kelub was in charge of the field workers who farmed
27: 29 Shaphat **son** *of* Adlai was in charge of the herds in the valleys.
27: 32 and a scribe. Jehiel **son** *of* Hacmoni took care of the king's sons.
27: 32 and a scribe. Jehiel son of Hacmoni took care of the king's **sons**.
27: 34 Ahithophel was succeeded by Jehoiada **son** *of* Benaiah and by
28: 1 of all the property and livestock belonging to the king and his **sons**,
28: 4 from my father's **sons** he was pleased to make me king over all
28: 5 Of all my **sons**—and the LORD has given me many—he has
28: 5 **[RPH]** he has chosen my son Solomon to sit on the throne of the
28: 5 he has chosen my **son** Solomon to sit on the throne of the kingdom
28: 6 'Solomon your **son** is the one who will build my house and my
28: 6 build my house and my courts, for I have chosen him to be my **son**,
28: 8 and pass it on as an inheritance to your **descendants** forever.
28: 9 "And you, my **son** Solomon, acknowledge the God of your father,
28: 11 David gave his **son** Solomon the plans for the portico of the
28: 20 David also said to Solomon his **son**, "Be strong and courageous,
29: 1 "My **son** Solomon, the one whom God has chosen, is young
29: 19 give my **son** Solomon the wholehearted devotion to keep your
29: 22 they acknowledged Solomon **son** *of* David as king a second time,
29: 24 the officers and mighty men, as well as all of King David's **sons**,
29: 26 David **son** *of* Jesse was king over all Israel.
29: 28 wealth and honor. His **son** Solomon succeeded him as king.
2Ch 1: 1 Solomon **son** *of* David established himself firmly over his
1: 5 But the bronze altar that Bezalel **son** *of* Uri, the son of Hur,
1: 5 But the bronze altar that Bezalel son of Uri, the **son** *of* Hur,
2: 12 [2:11] He has given King David a wise **son**, endowed with
2: 14 [2:13] **whose**[s] mother was from Dan and whose father was from
5: 2 heads of the tribes and the chiefs of the **Israelite** [+3776] families,
5: 10 where the LORD made a covenant with the **Israelites** [+3776]
5: 12 Asaph, Heman, Jeduthun and their **sons** and relatives—stood on
6: 9 build the temple, but your **son**, who is your own flesh and blood—
6: 11 covenant of the LORD that he made with the **people** *of* Israel."
6: 16 if only your **sons** are careful in all they do to walk before me
6: 30 you know his heart (for you alone know the hearts of **men** [+132]),
7: 3 When all the **Israelites** [+3776] saw the fire coming down
8: 2 that Hiram had given him, and settled **Israelites** [+3776] in them.
8: 8 that is, their **descendants** remaining in the land,
8: 8 in the land, whom the **Israelites** [+3776] had not destroyed—
8: 9 Solomon did not make slaves of the **Israelites** [+3776] for his
9: 29 in the visions of Iddo the seer concerning Jeroboam **son** *of* Nebat?
9: 31 of David his father. And Rehoboam his **son** succeeded him as king.
10: 2 When Jeroboam **son** *of* Nebat heard this (he was in Egypt,
10: 15 to fulfill the word the LORD had spoken to Jeroboam **son** *of*
10: 16 "What share do we have in David, what part in Jesse's **son**?
10: 17 as for the **Israelites** [+3776] who were living in the towns of
10: 18 of forced labor, but the **Israelites** [+3776] stoned him to death.
11: 3 "Say to Rehoboam **son** *of* Solomon king of Judah and to all the
11: 14 and his **sons** had rejected them as priests of the LORD.
11: 17 of Judah and supported Rehoboam **son** *of* Solomon three years,
11: 18 [Mahalath, who was the **daughter** [K; see Q 1426] *of* David's son]
11: 18 who was the daughter of David's **son** Jerimoth and of Abihail,
11: 18 son Jerimoth and of Abihail, the daughter of Jesse's **son** Eliab.
11: 19 She bore him **sons**: Jeush, Shemariah and Zaham.
11: 21 and sixty concubines, twenty-eight **sons** and sixty daughters.
11: 22 Rehoboam appointed Abijah **son** *of* Maacah to be the chief prince
11: 23 dispersing some of his **sons** throughout the districts of Judah
12: 13 He was forty-one years **old** when he became king, and he reigned
12: 16 in the City of David. And Abijah his **son** succeeded him as king.
13: 5 Israel to David and his **descendants** forever by a covenant of salt?
13: 6 Yet Jeroboam **son** *of* Nebat, an official of Solomon son of David,
13: 6 an official of Solomon **son** *of* David, rebelled against his master.
13: 7 Some worthless **scoundrels** [+1175] gathered around him
13: 7 and opposed Rehoboam **son** *of* Solomon when he was young
13: 8 of the LORD, which is in the hands of David's **descendants**.
13: 9 out the priests of the LORD, the **sons** *of* Aaron, and the Levites,
13: 9 Whoever comes to consecrate himself with a **young** bull and seven
13: 10 The priests who serve the LORD are **sons** *of* Aaron,
13: 12 **Men** *of* Israel, do not fight against the LORD, the God of your
13: 16 The **Israelites** [+3776] fled before Judah, and God delivered them
13: 18 The **men** *of* Israel were subdued on that occasion, and the men of
13: 18 the **men** *of* Judah were victorious because they relied on the
13: 21 fourteen wives and had twenty-two **sons** and sixteen daughters.
14: 1 [13:23] Asa his **son** succeeded him as king, and in his days the
15: 1 The Spirit of God came upon Azariah **son** *of* Oded.
15: 8 and the prophecy of Azariah **son** [BHS-] *of* Oded the prophet,
17: 1 Jehoshaphat his **son** succeeded him as king and strengthened
17: 16 next, Amasiah **son** *of* Zicri, who volunteered himself for the
18: 7 good about me, but always bad. He is Micaiah **son** *of* Imlah."
18: 8 one of his officials and said, "Bring Micaiah **son** *of* Imlah at once."
18: 10 Now Zedekiah **son** *of* Kenaanah had made iron horns, and he
18: 23 Zedekiah **son** *of* Kenaanah went up and slapped Micaiah in the
18: 25 him back to Amon the ruler of the city and to Joash the king's **son**,
19: 2 Jehu the seer, the **son** *of* Hanani, went out to meet him and said to
19: 11 and Zebadiah **son** *of* Ishmael, the leader of the tribe of Judah,

2Ch 20: 1 the **Moabites** [+4566] and Ammonites with some of the Meunites
20: 1 **Ammonites** [+6648] with some of the Meunites came to make war
20: 10 "But now here are **men** *from* Ammon, Moab and Mount Seir,
20: 13 All the men of Judah, with their wives and **children** and little ones,
20: 14 the Spirit of the LORD came upon Jahaziel **son** *of* Zechariah,
20: 14 the **son** *of* Benaiah, the son of Jeiel, the son of Mattaniah,
20: 14 the son of Benaiah, the **son** *of* Jeiel, the son of Mattaniah,
20: 14 of Jeiel, the **son** *of* Mattaniah, a Levite and descendant of Asaph,
20: 14 of Jeiel, the son of Mattaniah, a Levite and **descendant** *of* Asaph,
20: 19 some Levites from the **Kohathites** [+7741] and Korahites stood up
20: 19 and **Korahites** [+7948] stood up and praised the LORD,
20: 22 the LORD set ambushes against the **men** *of* Ammon and Moab
20: 23 The **men** *of* Ammon and Moab rose up against the men from
20: 31 He was thirty-five years **old** when he became king of Judah,
20: 34 beginning to end, are written in the annals of Jehu **son** *of* Hanani,
20: 37 Eliezer **son** *of* Dodavahu of Mareshah prophesied against
21: 1 in the City of David. And Jehoram his **son** succeeded him as king.
21: 2 the **sons** *of* Jehoshaphat, were Azariah, Jehiel, Zechariah,
21: 2 and Shephatiah. All these were **sons** *of* Jehoshaphat king of Israel.
21: 5 Jehoram was thirty-two years **old** when he became king, and he
21: 7 promised to maintain a lamp for him and his **descendants** forever.
21: 14 your **sons**, your wives and everything that is yours, with a heavy
21: 17 goods found in the king's palace, together with his **sons** and wives.
21: 17 and wives. Not a **son** was left to him except Ahaziah, the youngest.
21: 17 Not a son was left to him except Ahaziah, the youngest. **[RPH]**
21: 20 Jehoram was thirty-two years **old** when he became king, and he
22: 1 Jehoram's youngest **son**, king in his place, since the raiders,
22: 1 So Ahaziah **son** *of* Jehoram king of Judah began to reign.
22: 2 Ahaziah was twenty-two years **old** when he became king,
22: 5 He also followed their counsel when he went with Joram **son** *of*
22: 6 Ahaziah **son** *of* Jehoram king of Judah went down to Jezreel to see
22: 6 king of Judah went down to Jezreel to see Joram **son** *of* Ahab
22: 7 he went out with Joram to meet Jehu **son** *of* Nimshi,
22: 8 he found the princes of Judah and the **sons** *of* Ahaziah's relatives,
22: 9 They buried him, for they said, "He was a **son** *of* Jehoshaphat,
22: 10 When Athaliah the mother of Ahaziah saw that her **son** was dead,
22: 11 took Joash **son** *of* Ahaziah and stole him away from among the
22: 11 stole him away from among the royal **princes** who were about to
23: 1 Azariah **son** *of* Jeroham, Ishmael son of Jehohanan, Azariah son of
23: 1 son of Jeroham, Ishmael **son** *of* Jehohanan, Azariah son of Obed,
23: 1 son of Jehohanan, Azariah **son** *of* Obed, Maaseiah son of Adaiah,
23: 1 son of Jehohanan, Azariah son of Obed, Maaseiah **son** *of* Adaiah,
23: 1 son of Obed, Maaseiah son of Adaiah, and Elishaphat **son** *of* Zicri.
23: 3 Jehoiada said to them, "The king's **son** shall reign, as the LORD
23: 3 as the LORD promised concerning the **descendants** *of* David.
23: 11 Jehoiada and his **sons** brought out the king's son and put the crown
23: 11 Jehoiada and his sons brought out the king's **son** and put the crown
24: 1 Joash was seven years **old** when he became king, and he reigned in
24: 3 Jehoiada chose two wives for him, and he had **sons** and daughters.
24: 7 Now the **sons** *of* that wicked woman Athaliah had broken into the
24: 15 of years, and he died at the **age** [+9102] *of* a hundred and thirty.
24: 20 the Spirit of God came upon Zechariah **son** *of* Jehoiada the priest.
24: 22 Zechariah's father Jehoiada had shown him but killed his **son**,
24: 25 His officials conspired against him for murdering the **son** *of*
24: 26 **son** *of* Shimeath an Ammonite woman, and Jehozabad, son of
24: 26 and Jehozabad, **son** *of* Shimrith a Moabite woman.
24: 27 The account of his **sons**, the many prophecies about him,
24: 27 book of the kings. And Amaziah his **son** succeeded him as king.
25: 1 Amaziah was twenty-five years **old** when he became king,
25: 4 Yet he did not put their **sons** to death, but acted in accordance with
25: 4 "Fathers shall not be put to death for their **children**, nor children
25: 4 death for their children, nor **children** put to death for their fathers;
25: 5 He then mustered those twenty years **old** or more and found that
25: 7 LORD is not with Israel—not with any of the **people** *of* Ephraim.
25: 11 to the Valley of Salt, where he killed ten thousand **men** *of* Seir.
25: 12 The **army** *of* Judah also captured ten thousand men alive,
25: 13 Meanwhile the **troops** [+1522] that Amaziah had sent back
25: 14 the Edomites, he brought back the gods of the **people** *of* Seir.
25: 17 he sent this challenge to Jehoash **son** *of* Jehoahaz, the son of Jehu,
25: 17 to Jehoash son of Jehoahaz, the **son** *of* Jehu, king of Israel:
25: 18 to a cedar in Lebanon, 'Give your daughter to my **son** in marriage.'
25: 23 of Judah, the **son** *of* Joash, the son of Ahaziah, at Beth Shemesh.
25: 23 of Judah, the son of Joash, the **son** *of* Ahaziah, at Beth Shemesh.
25: 24 together with the palace treasures and the **hostages** [+9510],
25: 25 Amaziah **son** *of* Joash king of Judah lived for fifteen years after the
25: 25 years after the death of Jehoash **son** *of* Jehoahaz king of Israel.
26: 1 all the people of Judah took Uzziah, who was sixteen years **old**,
26: 3 Uzziah was sixteen years **old** when he became king, and he reigned
26: 17 Azariah the priest with eighty other **courageous** [+2657] priests of
26: 18 That is for the priests, the **descendants** *of* Aaron, who have been
26: 21 Jotham his **son** had charge of the palace and governed the people
26: 22 beginning to end, are recorded by the prophet Isaiah **son** *of* Amoz.
26: 23 "He had leprosy." And Jotham his **son** succeeded him as king.
27: 1 Jotham was twenty-five years **old** when he became king, and he
27: 5 Jotham made war on the king of the **Ammonites** [+6648]
27: 5 That year the **Ammonites** [+6648] paid him a hundred talents of
27: 5 The **Ammonites** [+6648] brought him the same amount also in the
27: 8 He was twenty-five years **old** when he became king, and he
27: 9 in the City of David. And Ahaz his **son** succeeded him as king.
28: 1 Ahaz was twenty years **old** when he became king, and he reigned
28: 3 in the Valley of Ben Hinnom and sacrificed his **sons** in the fire,
28: 3 nations the LORD had driven out before the **Israelites** [+3776].
28: 6 In one day Pekah **son** *of* Remaliah killed a hundred and twenty
28: 6 killed a hundred and twenty thousand **soldiers** [+2657] in Judah—
28: 7 Zicri, an Ephraimite warrior, killed Maaseiah the king's **son**,
28: 8 The **Israelites** [+3776] took captive from their kinsmen two
28: 8 their kinsmen two hundred thousand wives, **sons** and daughters.
28: 10 and women **of Judah** [+3373] and Jerusalem your slaves.
28: 12 some of the leaders in **Ephraim** [+713]—Azariah son of
28: 12 Azariah **son** *of* Jehohanan, Berekiah son of Meshillemoth,
28: 12 Berekiah **son** *of* Meshillemoth, Jehizkiah son of Shallum,
28: 12 Jehizkiah **son** *of* Shallum, and Amasa son of Hadlai—
28: 12 Jehizkiah son of Shallum, and Amasa **son** *of* Hadlai—
28: 27 the kings of Israel. And Hezekiah his **son** succeeded him as king.
29: 1 Hezekiah was twenty-five years **old** when he became king,
29: 9 and why our **sons** and daughters and our wives are in captivity.
29: 11 My **sons**, do not be negligent now, for the LORD has chosen you
29: 12 from the **Kohathites** [+7741], Mahath son of Amasai and Joel son
29: 12 the Kohathites, Mahath **son** *of* Amasai and Joel son of Azariah;
29: 12 the Kohathites, Mahath son of Amasai and Joel **son** *of* Azariah;
29: 12 from the **Merarites** [+5356], Kish son of Abdi and Azariah son of
29: 12 the Merarites, Kish **son** *of* Abdi and Azariah son of Jehallelel;
29: 12 the Merarites, Kish son of Abdi and Azariah **son** *of* Jehallelel;
29: 12 from the Gershonites, Joah **son** *of* Zimmah and Eden son of Joah;
29: 12 from the Gershonites, Joah son of Zimmah and Eden **son** *of* Joah;
29: 13 from the **descendants** *of* Elizaphan, Shimri and Jeiel; from the
29: 13 from the **descendants** *of* Asaph, Zechariah and Mattaniah;
29: 14 from the **descendants** *of* Heman, Jehiel and Shimei; from the
29: 14 from the **descendants** *of* Jeduthun, Shemaiah and Uzziel.
29: 21 The king commanded the priests, the **descendants** *of* Aaron,
30: 6 "**People** *of* Israel, return to the LORD, the God of Abraham,
30: 9 and your **children** will be shown compassion by their captors
30: 21 The **Israelites** [+3776] who were present in Jerusalem celebrated
30: 26 for since the days of Solomon **son** *of* David king of Israel there had
31: 1 the **Israelites** [+3776] returned to their own towns and to their own
31: 5 the **Israelites** [+3776] generously gave the firstfruits of their grain,
31: 6 The **men** *of* Israel and Judah who lived in the towns of Judah also
31: 14 Kore **son** *of* Imnah the Levite, keeper of the East Gate, was in
31: 16 they distributed to the males three years **old** or more whose names
31: 17 and likewise to the Levites twenty years **old** or more,
31: 18 the **sons** and daughters of the whole community listed in these
31: 19 As for the priests, the **descendants** *of* Aaron, who lived on the
32: 20 the prophet Isaiah **son** *of* Amoz cried out in prayer to heaven about
32: 32 the prophet Isaiah **son** *of* Amoz in the book of the kings of Judah
32: 33 was buried on the hill where the tombs of David's **descendants**
32: 33 him when he died. And Manasseh his **son** succeeded him as king.
33: 1 Manasseh was twelve years **old** when he became king, and he
33: 2 nations the LORD had driven out before the **Israelites** [+3776].
33: 6 He sacrificed his **sons** in the fire in the Valley of Ben Hinnom,
33: 7 of which God had said to David and to his **son** Solomon, "In this
33: 9 nations the LORD had destroyed before the **Israelites** [+3776].
33: 20 buried in his palace. And Amon his **son** succeeded him as king.
33: 21 Amon was twenty-two years **old** when he became king, and he
33: 25 King Amon, and they made Josiah his **son** king in his place.
34: 1 Josiah was eight years **old** when he became king, and he reigned in
34: 8 he sent Shaphan **son** *of* Azaliah and Maaseiah the ruler of the city,
34: 8 the ruler of the city, with Joah **son** *of* Joahaz, the recorder,
34: 12 them were Jahath and Obadiah, Levites **descended** from Merari,
34: 12 and Zechariah and Meshullam, **descended** from Kohath.
34: 20 Ahikam **son** *of* Shaphan, Abdon son of Micah, Shaphan the
34: 20 Abdon **son** *of* Micah, Shaphan the secretary and Asaiah the king's
34: 22 who was the wife of Shallum **son** *of* Tokhath, the son of Hasrah,
34: 22 son of Tokhath, the **son** *of* Hasrah, keeper of the wardrobe.
34: 33 idols from all the territory belonging to the **Israelites** [+3776],
35: 3 "Put the sacred ark in the temple that Solomon **son** *of* David king
35: 4 directions written by David king of Israel and by his **son** Solomon.
35: 5 of the families of your fellow countrymen, the **lay people** [+6639].
35: 7 Josiah provided for all the **lay people** [+6639] who were there a
35: 7 thirty thousand sheep and **goats** [+6436] for the Passover offerings,
35: 12 of the families of the **people** [+6639] to offer to the LORD,
35: 13 and pans and served them quickly to all the **people** [+6639].
35: 14 and for the priests, because the priests, the **descendants** *of* Aaron,
35: 14 preparations for themselves and for the **Aaronic** [+195] priests.
35: 15 The musicians, the **descendants** *of* Asaph, were in the places
35: 17 The **Israelites** [+3776] who were present celebrated the Passover
36: 1 the people of the land took Jehoahaz **son** *of* Josiah and made him
36: 2 Jehoahaz was twenty-three years **old** when he became king,
36: 5 Jehoiakim was twenty-five years **old** when he became king,

2Ch 36: 8 and Judah. And Jehoiachin his **son** succeeded him as king.
36: 9 Jehoiachin was eighteen years **old** when he became king, and he
36: 11 Zedekiah was twenty-one years **old** when he became king,
36: 20 to him and his **sons** until the kingdom of Persia came to power.
Ezr 2: 1 Now these are the **people** *of* the province who came up from the
2: 3 the **descendants** *of* Parosh 2,172
2: 4 **[RPH]** of Shephatiah 372
2: 5 **[RPH]** of Arah 775
2: 6 **[RPH]** of Pahath-Moab (through the line of Jeshua and Joab)
2: 6 of Pahath-Moab (through the **line** *of* Jeshua and Joab) 2,812
2: 7 **[RPH]** of Elam 1,254
2: 8 **[RPH]** of Zattu 945
2: 9 **[RPH]** of Zaccai 760
2: 10 **[RPH]** of Bani 642
2: 11 **[RPH]** of Bebai 623
2: 12 **[RPH]** of Azgad 1,222
2: 13 **[RPH]** of Adonikam 666
2: 14 **[RPH]** of Bigvai 2,056
2: 15 **[RPH]** of Adin 454
2: 16 **[RPH]** of Ater (through Hezekiah) 98
2: 17 **[RPH]** of Bezai 323
2: 18 **[RPH]** of Jorah 112
2: 19 **[RPH]** of Hashum 223
2: 20 **[RPH]** of Gibbar 95
2: 21 the **men** *of* Bethlehem 123
2: 24 **[RPH]** of Azmaveth 42
2: 25 **[RPH]** of Kiriath Jearim, Kephirah and Beeroth 743
2: 26 **[RPH]** of Ramah and Geba 621
2: 29 **[RPH]** of Nebo 52
2: 30 **[RPH]** of Magbish 156
2: 31 **[RPH]** of the other Elam 1,254
2: 32 **[RPH]** of Harim 320
2: 33 **[RPH]** of Lod, Hadid and Ono 725
2: 34 **[RPH]** of Jericho 345
2: 35 **[RPH]** of Senaah 3,630
2: 36 the **descendants** *of* Jedaiah (through the family of Jeshua)
2: 37 **[RPH]** of Immer 1,052
2: 38 **[RPH]** of Pashhur 1,247
2: 39 **[RPH]** of Harim 1,017
2: 40 the **descendants** *of* Jeshua and Kadmiel (through the line of
2: 40 descendants of Jeshua and Kadmiel (through the **line** *of* Hodaviah)
2: 41 The singers: the **descendants** *of* Asaph 128
2: 42 **[RPH]** The gatekeepers of the temple: the descendants of
2: 42 the **descendants** *of* Shallum, Ater, Talmon, Akkub, Hatita
2: 42 of Shallum, **[RPH]** Ater, Talmon, Akkub, Hatita and Shobai 139
2: 42 of Shallum, Ater, **[RPH]** Talmon, Akkub, Hatita and Shobai 139
2: 42 of Shallum, Ater, Talmon, **[RPH]** Akkub, Hatita and Shobai 139
2: 42 of Shallum, Ater, Talmon, Akkub, **[RPH]** Hatita and Shobai 139
2: 42 of Shallum, Ater, Talmon, Akkub, Hatita and **[RPH]** Shobai 139
2: 43 The temple servants: the **descendants** *of* Ziha, Hasupha, Tabbaoth,
2: 43 the descendants of Ziha, **[RPH]** Hasupha, Tabbaoth,
2: 43 the descendants of Ziha, Hasupha, **[RPH]** Tabbaoth,
2: 44 **[RPH]** Keros, Siaha, Padon,
2: 44 Keros, **[RPH]** Siaha, Padon,
2: 44 Keros, Siaha, **[RPH]** Padon,
2: 45 **[RPH]** Lebanah, Hagabah, Akkub,
2: 45 Lebanah, **[RPH]** Hagabah, Akkub,
2: 45 Lebanah, Hagabah, **[RPH]** Akkub,
2: 46 **[RPH]** Hagab, Shalmai, Hanan,
2: 46 Hagab, **[RPH]** Shalmai, Hanan,
2: 46 Hagab, Shalmai, **[RPH]** Hanan,
2: 47 **[RPH]** Giddel, Gahar, Reaiah,
2: 47 Giddel, **[RPH]** Gahar, Reaiah,
2: 47 Giddel, Gahar, **[RPH]** Reaiah,
2: 48 **[RPH]** Rezin, Nekoda, Gazzam,
2: 48 Rezin, **[RPH]** Nekoda, Gazzam,
2: 48 Rezin, Nekoda, **[RPH]** Gazzam,
2: 49 **[RPH]** Uzza, Paseah, Besai,
2: 49 Uzza, **[RPH]** Paseah, Besai,
2: 49 Uzza, Paseah, **[RPH]** Besai,
2: 50 **[RPH]** Asnah, Meunim, Nephussim,
2: 50 Asnah, **[RPH]** Meunim, Nephussim,
2: 50 Asnah, Meunim, **[RPH]** Nephussim,
2: 51 **[RPH]** Bakbuk, Hakupha, Harhur,
2: 51 Bakbuk, **[RPH]** Hakupha, Harhur,
2: 51 Bakbuk, Hakupha, **[RPH]** Harhur,
2: 52 **[RPH]** Bazluth, Mehida, Harsha,
2: 52 Bazluth, **[RPH]** Mehida, Harsha,
2: 52 Bazluth, Mehida, **[RPH]** Harsha,
2: 53 **[RPH]** Barkos, Sisera, Temah,
2: 53 Barkos, **[RPH]** Sisera, Temah,
2: 53 Barkos, Sisera, **[RPH]** Temah,
2: 54 **[RPH]** Neziah and Hatipha
2: 54 Neziah and **[RPH]** Hatipha
2: 55 The **descendants** *of* the servants of Solomon: the descendants of
2: 55 of Solomon: the **descendants** *of* Sotai, Hassophereth, Peruda,
2: 55 the descendants of Sotai, **[RPH]** Hassophereth, Peruda,
2: 55 the descendants of Sotai, Hassophereth, **[RPH]** Peruda,
2: 56 **[RPH]** Jaala, Darkon, Giddel,
2: 56 Jaala, **[RPH]** Darkon, Giddel,
2: 56 Jaala, Darkon, **[RPH]** Giddel,
2: 57 **[RPH]** Shephatiah, Hattil, Pokereth-Hazzebaim and Ami
2: 57 Shephatiah, **[RPH]** Hattil, Pokereth-Hazzebaim and Ami
2: 57 Shephatiah, Hattil, **[RPH]** Pokereth-Hazzebaim and Ami
2: 57 Shephatiah, Hattil, Pokereth-Hazzebaim and **[RPH]** Ami
2: 58 and the **descendants** *of* the servants of Solomon 392
2: 60 The **descendants** *of* Delaiah, Tobiah and Nekoda 652
2: 60 The descendants of Delaiah, **[RPH]** Tobiah and Nekoda 652
2: 60 The descendants of Delaiah, Tobiah and **[RPH]** Nekoda 652
2: 61 And from among **[RPH]** the priests: The descendants of Hobaiah,
2: 61 The **descendants** *of* Hobaiah, Hakkoz and Barzillai (a man who
2: 61 **[RPH]** Hakkoz and Barzillai (a man who had married a daughter
2: 61 **[RPH]** Barzillai (a man who had married a daughter of Barzillai
3: 1 month came and the **Israelites** [+3776] had settled in their towns,
3: 2 Jeshua **son** *of* Jozadak and his fellow priests and Zerubbabel son of
3: 2 of Jozadak and his fellow priests and Zerubbabel **son** *of* Shealtiel
3: 8 Zerubbabel **son** *of* Shealtiel, Jeshua son of Jozadak and the rest of
3: 8 Jeshua **son** *of* Jozadak and the rest of their brothers (the priests
3: 8 appointing Levites twenty years *of* **age** and older to supervise the
3: 9 Jeshua and his **sons** and brothers and Kadmiel and his sons
3: 9 and brothers and Kadmiel and his **sons** (descendants of Hodaviah)
3: 9 and brothers and Kadmiel and his sons (**descendants** *of* Hodaviah)
3: 9 and the **sons** *of* Henadad and their sons and brothers—all Levites—
3: 9 and the sons of Henadad and their **sons** and brothers—all Levites—
3: 10 and with trumpets, and the Levites (the **sons** *of* Asaph)
4: 1 Benjamin heard that the **exiles** [+1583] were building a temple for
6: 19 day of the first month, the **exiles** [+1583] celebrated the Passover.
6: 20 Levites slaughtered the Passover lamb for all the **exiles** [+1583],
6: 21 So the **Israelites** [+3776] who had returned from the exile ate it,
7: 1 Ezra **son** *of* Seraiah, the son of Azariah, the son of Hilkiah,
7: 1 Ezra son of Seraiah, the **son** *of* Azariah, the son of Hilkiah,
7: 1 Ezra son of Seraiah, the son of Azariah, the **son** *of* Hilkiah,
7: 2 the **son** *of* Shallum, the son of Zadok, the son of Ahitub,
7: 2 the son of Shallum, the **son** *of* Zadok, the son of Ahitub,
7: 2 the son of Shallum, the son of Zadok, the **son** *of* Ahitub,
7: 3 the **son** *of* Amariah, the son of Azariah, the son of Meraioth,
7: 3 the son of Amariah, the **son** *of* Azariah, the son of Meraioth,
7: 3 the son of Amariah, the son of Azariah, the **son** *of* Meraioth,
7: 4 the **son** *of* Zerahiah, the son of Uzzi, the son of Bukki,
7: 4 the son of Zerahiah, the **son** *of* Uzzi, the son of Bukki,
7: 4 the son of Zerahiah, the son of Uzzi, the **son** *of* Bukki,
7: 5 the **son** *of* Abishua, the son of Phinehas, the son of Eleazar,
7: 5 the son of Abishua, the **son** *of* Phinehas, the son of Eleazar,
7: 5 the son of Abishua, the son of Phinehas, the **son** *of* Eleazar,
7: 5 of Phinehas, the son of Eleazar, the **son** *of* Aaron the chief priest—
7: 7 Some of the **Israelites** [+3776], including priests, Levites,
8: 2 of the **descendants** *of* Phinehas, Gershom; of the descendants of
8: 2 of Phinehas, Gershom; of the **descendants** *of* Ithamar, Daniel;
8: 2 of Ithamar, Daniel; of the **descendants** *of* David, Hattush
8: 3 of the **descendants** *of* Shecaniah; of the descendants of Parosh,
8: 3 of the **descendants** *of* Parosh, Zechariah, and with him were
8: 4 of the **descendants** *of* Pahath-Moab, Eliehoenai son of Zerahiah,
8: 4 Eliehoenai **son** *of* Zerahiah, and with him 200 men;
8: 5 of the **descendants** *of* Zattu, Shecaniah son of Jahaziel, and with
8: 5 of Zattu, Shecaniah **son** *of* Jahaziel, and with him 300 men;
8: 6 of the **descendants** *of* Adin, Ebed son of Jonathan, and with him
8: 6 descendants of Adin, Ebed **son** *of* Jonathan, and with him 50 men;
8: 7 of the **descendants** *of* Elam, Jeshaiah son of Athaliah, and with
8: 7 of Elam, Jeshaiah **son** *of* Athaliah, and with him 70 men;
8: 8 of the **descendants** *of* Shephatiah, Zebadiah son of Michael,
8: 8 of Shephatiah, Zebadiah **son** *of* Michael, and with him 80 men;
8: 9 of the **descendants** *of* Joab, Obadiah son of Jehiel, and with him
8: 9 descendants of Joab, Obadiah **son** *of* Jehiel, and with him 218 men;
8: 10 of the **descendants** *of* Bani, Shelomith son of Josiphiah, and with
8: 10 of Bani, Shelomith **son** *of* Josiphiah, and with him 160 men;
8: 11 of the **descendants** *of* Bebai, Zechariah son of Bebai, and with him
8: 11 of Bebai, Zechariah **son** *of* Bebai, and with him 28 men;
8: 12 of the **descendants** *of* Azgad, Johanan son of Hakkatan, and with
8: 12 of Azgad, Johanan **son** *of* Hakkatan, and with him 110 men;
8: 13 of the **descendants** *of* Adonikam, the last ones, whose names were
8: 14 of the **descendants** *of* Bigvai, Uthai and Zaccur, and with them 70
8: 15 the people and the priests, I found no **Levites** [+4291] there.
8: 18 a capable man, from the **descendants** *of* Mahli son of Levi,
8: 18 a capable man, from the descendants of Mahli **son** *of* Levi,
8: 18 the **son** *of* Israel, and Sherebiah's sons and brothers, 18 men;
8: 18 the son of Israel, and Sherebiah's **sons** and brothers, 18 men;
8: 19 together with Jeshaiah from the **descendants** *of* Merari,
8: 19 of Merari, and his brothers and **nephews** [+2157], 20 men.

Ezr 8:33 and the sacred articles into the hands of Meremoth **son** *of* Uriah,
8:33 Eleazar **son** *of* Phinehas was with him, and so were the Levites
8:33 so were the Levites Jozabad **son** *of* Jeshua and Noadiah son of
8:33 the Levites Jozabad son of Jeshua and Noadiah **son** *of* Binnui.
8:35 the **exiles** [+1583] who had returned from captivity sacrificed burnt
9:2 some of their daughters as wives for themselves and their **sons**,
9:12 do not give your daughters in marriage to their **sons** or take their
9:12 in marriage to their sons or take their daughters for your **sons**.
9:12 and leave it to your **children** as an everlasting inheritance.'
10:2 Then Shecaniah **son** *of* Jehiel, one of the descendants of Elam,
10:2 son of Jehiel, one of the **descendants** *of* Elam, said to Ezra,
10:6 house of God and went to the room of Jehohanan **son** *of* Eliashib.
10:7 and Jerusalem for all the **exiles** [+1583] to assemble in Jerusalem.
10:15 Only Jonathan **son** *of* Asahel and Jahzeiah son of Tikvah,
10:15 Only Jonathan son of Asahel and Jahzeiah **son** *of* Tikvah,
10:16 So the **exiles** [+1583] did as was proposed. Ezra the priest selected
10:18 Among the **descendants** *of* the priests, the following had married
10:18 From the **descendants** *of* Jeshua son of Jozadak, and his brothers:
10:18 From the descendants of Jeshua **son** *of* Jozadak, and his brothers:
10:20 From the **descendants** *of* Immer: Hanani and Zebadiah.
10:21 From the **descendants** *of* Harim: Maaseiah, Elijah, Shemaiah,
10:22 From the **descendants** *of* Pashhur: Elioenai, Maaseiah, Ishmael,
10:25 From the **descendants** *of* Parosh: Ramiah, Izziah, Malkijah,
10:26 From the **descendants** *of* Elam: Mattaniah, Zechariah, Jehiel,
10:27 From the **descendants** *of* Zattu: Elioenai, Eliashib, Mattaniah,
10:28 From the **descendants** *of* Bebai: Jehohanan, Hananiah, Zabbai
10:29 From the **descendants** *of* Bani: Meshullam, Malluch, Adaiah,
10:30 From the **descendants** *of* Pahath-Moab: Adna, Kelal, Benaiah,
10:31 From the **descendants** *of* Harim: Eliezer, Ishijah, Malkijah,
10:33 From the **descendants** *of* Hashum: Mattenai, Mattattah, Zabad,
10:34 From the **descendants** *of* Bani: Maadai, Amram, Uel,
10:38 From the **descendants** [BHS 1220] *of* Binnui: Shimei,
10:43 From the **descendants** *of* Nebo: Jeiel, Mattithiah, Zabad, Zebina,
10:44 foreign women, and some of them had **children** by these wives.
Ne 1:1 The words of Nehemiah **son** *of* Hacaliah: In the month of Kislev in
1:6 before you day and night for your servants, the **people** *of* Israel.
1:6 I confess the sins we **Israelites** [+3776], including myself
2:10 had come to promote the welfare of the **Israelites** [+3776].
3:2 the adjoining section, and Zaccur **son** *of* Imri built next to them.
3:3 The Fish Gate was rebuilt by the **sons** *of* Hassenaah. They laid its
3:4 Meremoth **son** *of* Uriah, the son of Hakkoz, repaired the next
3:4 Meremoth son of Uriah, the **son** *of* Hakkoz, repaired the next
3:4 Next to him Meshullam **son** *of* Berekiah, the son of Meshezabel,
3:4 Meshullam son of Berekiah, the **son** *of* Meshezabel, made repairs,
3:4 and next to him Zadok **son** *of* Baana also made repairs.
3:6 The Jeshanah Gate was repaired by Joiada **son** *of* Paseah
3:6 repaired by Joiada son of Paseah and Meshullam **son** *of* Besodeiah.
3:8 Uzziel **son** *of* Harhaiah, one of the goldsmiths, repaired the next
3:8 Hananiah, **one**[s] *of* the perfume-makers, made repairs next to that.
3:9 Rephaiah **son** *of* Hur, ruler of a half-district of Jerusalem,
3:10 Jedaiah **son** *of* Harumaph made repairs opposite his house,
3:10 and Hattush **son** *of* Hashabneiah made repairs next to him.
3:11 Malkijah **son** *of* Harim and Hasshub son of Pahath-Moab repaired
3:11 and Hasshub **son** *of* Pahath-Moab repaired another section
3:12 Shallum **son** *of* Hallohesh, ruler of a half-district of Jerusalem,
3:14 The Dung Gate was repaired by Malkijah **son** *of* Recab, ruler of
3:15 The Fountain Gate was repaired by Shallun **son** *of* Col-Hozeh,
3:16 Beyond him, Nehemiah **son** *of* Azbuk, ruler of a half-district of
3:17 the repairs were made by the Levites under Rehum **son** *of* Bani.
3:18 the repairs were made by their countrymen under Binnui **son** *of*
3:19 Next to him, Ezer **son** *of* Jeshua, ruler of Mizpah, repaired another
3:20 to him, Baruch **son** *of* Zabbai zealously repaired another section,
3:21 Next to him, Meremoth **son** *of* Uriah, the son of Hakkoz,
3:21 Next to him, Meremoth son of Uriah, the **son** *of* Hakkoz,
3:23 and next to them, Azariah **son** *of* Maaseiah, the son of Ananiah,
3:23 and next to them, Azariah son of Maaseiah, the **son** *of* Ananiah,
3:24 Next to him, Binnui **son** *of* Henadad repaired another section,
3:25 Palal **son** *of* Uzai worked opposite the angle and the tower
3:25 near the court of the guard. Next to him, Pedaiah **son** *of* Parosh
3:29 to them, Zadok **son** *of* Immer made repairs opposite his house.
3:29 Next to him, Shemaiah **son** *of* Shecaniah, the guard at the East
3:30 Next to him, Hananiah **son** *of* Shelemiah, and Hanun, the sixth son
3:30 and Hanun, the sixth **son** *of* Zalaph, repaired another section.
3:30 Meshullam **son** *of* Berekiah made repairs opposite his living
3:31 Next to him, Malkijah, **one**[s] *of* the goldsmiths, made repairs as far
4:14 [4:8] your **sons** and your daughters, your wives and your homes."
5:2 Some were saying, "We and our **sons** and daughters are numerous;
5:5 blood as our countrymen and though our **sons** are as good as theirs,
5:5 **[RPH]** yet we have to subject our sons and daughters to slavery.
5:5 as theirs, yet we have to subject our **sons** and daughters to slavery.
6:10 One day I went to the house of Shemaiah **son** *of* Delaiah, the son
6:10 son of Delaiah, the **son** *of* Mehetabel, who was shut in at his home.
6:18 oath to him, since he was son-in-law to Shecaniah **son** *of* Arah,
6:18 his **son** Jehohanan had married the daughter of Meshullam son of
6:18 his son Jehohanan had married the daughter of Meshullam **son** *of*
7:6 These are the **people** *of* the province who came up from the
7:8 the **descendants** *of* Parosh 2,172
7:9 **[RPH]** of Shephatiah 372
7:10 **[RPH]** of Arah 652
7:11 **[RPH]** of Pahath-Moab (through the line of Jeshua and Joab)
7:11 of Pahath-Moab (through the **line** *of* Jeshua and Joab) 2,818
7:12 **[RPH]** of Elam 1,254
7:13 **[RPH]** of Zattu 845
7:14 **[RPH]** of Zaccai 760
7:15 **[RPH]** of Binnui 648
7:16 **[RPH]** of Bebai 628
7:17 **[RPH]** of Azgad 2,322
7:18 **[RPH]** of Adonikam 667
7:19 **[RPH]** of Bigvai 2,067
7:20 **[RPH]** of Adin 655
7:21 **[RPH]** of Ater (through Hezekiah) 98
7:22 **[RPH]** of Hashum 328
7:23 **[RPH]** of Bezai 324
7:24 **[RPH]** of Hariph 112
7:25 **[RPH]** of Gibeon 95
7:34 **[RPH]** of the other Elam 1,254
7:35 **[RPH]** of Harim 320
7:36 **[RPH]** of Jericho 345
7:37 **[RPH]** of Lod, Hadid and Ono 721
7:38 **[RPH]** of Senaah 3,930
7:39 the **descendants** *of* Jedaiah (through the family of Jeshua)
7:40 **[RPH]** of Immer 1,052
7:41 **[RPH]** of Pashhur 1,247
7:42 **[RPH]** of Harim 1,017
7:43 the **descendants** *of* Jeshua (through Kadmiel through the line of
7:43 the descendants of Jeshua (through Kadmiel through the **line** of
7:44 The singers: the **descendants** *of* Asaph 148
7:45 the **descendants** *of* Shallum, Ater, Talmon, Akkub, Hatita
7:45 of Shallum, **[RPH]** Ater, Talmon, Akkub, Hatita and Shobai 138
7:45 of Shallum, Ater, **[RPH]** Talmon, Akkub, Hatita and Shobai 138
7:45 of Shallum, Ater, Talmon, **[RPH]** Akkub, Hatita and Shobai 138
7:45 of Shallum, Ater, Talmon, Akkub, **[RPH]** Hatita and Shobai 138
7:45 of Shallum, Ater, Talmon, Akkub, Hatita and **[RPH]** Shobai 138
7:46 The temple servants: the **descendants** *of* Ziha, Hasupha, Tabbaoth,
7:46 the descendants of Ziha, **[RPH]** Hasupha, Tabbaoth,
7:46 the descendants of Ziha, Hasupha, **[RPH]** Tabbaoth,
7:47 **[RPH]** Keros, Sia, Padon,
7:47 Keros, **[RPH]** Sia, Padon,
7:47 Keros, Sia, **[RPH]** Padon,
7:48 **[RPH]** Lebana, Hagaba, Shalmai,
7:48 Lebana, **[RPH]** Hagaba, Shalmai,
7:48 Lebana, Hagaba, **[RPH]** Shalmai,
7:49 **[RPH]** Hanan, Giddel, Gahar,
7:49 Hanan, **[RPH]** Giddel, Gahar,
7:49 Hanan, Giddel, **[RPH]** Gahar,
7:50 **[RPH]** Reaiah, Rezin, Nekoda,
7:50 Reaiah, **[RPH]** Rezin, Nekoda,
7:50 Reaiah, Rezin, **[RPH]** Nekoda,
7:51 **[RPH]** Gazzam, Uzza, Paseah,
7:51 Gazzam, **[RPH]** Uzza, Paseah,
7:51 Gazzam, Uzza, **[RPH]** Paseah,
7:52 **[RPH]** Besai, Meunim, Nephussim,
7:52 Besai, **[RPH]** Meunim, Nephussim,
7:52 Besai, Meunim, **[RPH]** Nephussim,
7:53 **[RPH]** Bakbuk, Hakupha, Harhur,
7:53 Bakbuk, **[RPH]** Hakupha, Harhur,
7:53 Bakbuk, Hakupha, **[RPH]** Harhur,
7:54 **[RPH]** Bazluth, Mehida, Harsha,
7:54 Bazluth, **[RPH]** Mehida, Harsha,
7:54 Bazluth, Mehida, **[RPH]** Harsha,
7:55 **[RPH]** Barkos, Sisera, Temah,
7:55 Barkos, **[RPH]** Sisera, Temah,
7:55 Barkos, Sisera, **[RPH]** Temah,
7:56 **[RPH]** Neziah and Hatipha
7:56 Neziah and **[RPH]** Hatipha
7:57 The **descendants** *of* the servants of Solomon: the descendants of
7:57 servants of Solomon: the **descendants** *of* Sotai, Sophereth, Perida,
7:57 of Solomon: the descendants of Sotai, **[RPH]** Sophereth, Perida,
7:57 of Solomon: the descendants of Sotai, Sophereth, **[RPH]** Perida,
7:58 **[RPH]** Jaala, Darkon, Giddel,
7:58 Jaala, **[RPH]** Darkon, Giddel,
7:58 Jaala, Darkon, **[RPH]** Giddel,
7:59 **[RPH]** Shephatiah, Hattil, Pokereth-Hazzebaim and Amon
7:59 Shephatiah, **[RPH]** Hattil, Pokereth-Hazzebaim and Amon
7:59 Shephatiah, Hattil, **[RPH]** Pokereth-Hazzebaim and Amon
7:59 Shephatiah, Hattil, Pokereth-Hazzebaim and **[RPH]** Amon
7:60 and the **descendants** *of* the servants of Solomon 392
7:62 the **descendants** *of* Delaiah, Tobiah and Nekoda 642

Ne 7:62 the descendants of Delaiah, **[RPH]** Tobiah and Nekoda 642
7:62 the descendants of Delaiah, Tobiah and **[RPH]** Nekoda 642
7:63 the **descendants** *of* Hobaiah, Hakkoz and Barzillai (a man who had
7:63 **[RPH]** Hakkoz and Barzillai (a man who had married a daughter
7:63 **[RPH]** Barzillai (a man who had married a daughter of Barzillai
7:73 [7:72] and the **Israelites** [+3776] had settled in their towns,
8:14 that the **Israelites** [+3776] were to live in booths during the feast
8:17 From the days of Joshua **son** *of* Nun until that day, the Israelites
8:17 until that day, the **Israelites** [+3776] had not celebrated it like this.
9: 1 the **Israelites** [+3776] gathered together, fasting and wearing
9: 2 descent had separated themselves from all **foreigners** [+5797].
9:23 You made their **sons** as numerous as the stars in the sky, and you
9:24 Their **sons** went in and took possession of the land. You subdued
10: 1 [10:2] Nehemiah the governor, the **son** *of* Hacaliah. Zedekiah,
10: 9 [10:10] Jeshua **son** *of* Azaniah, Binnui of the sons of Henadad,
10: 9 [10:10] son of Azaniah, Binnui of the **sons** *of* Henadad, Kadmiel,
10:28 [10:29] together with their wives and all their **sons** and daughters
10:30 [10:31] the peoples around us or take their daughters for our **sons**.
10:36 [10:37] we will bring the firstborn of our **sons** and of our cattle, of
10:38 [10:39] A priest **descended** *from* Aaron is to accompany the
10:39 [10:40] The **people** *of* Israel, including the Levites, are to bring
10:39 [10:40] The people of Israel, including the **Levites** [+4291], are to
11: 3 **descendants** *of* Solomon's servants lived in the towns of Judah,
11: 4 while other **people** from both Judah and Benjamin lived in
11: 4 people from both Judah and **[RPH]** Benjamin lived in Jerusalem):
11: 4 From the **descendants** *of* Judah: Athaiah son of Uzziah, the son of
11: 4 Athaiah **son** *of* Uzziah, the son of Zechariah, the son of Amariah,
11: 4 the **son** *of* Zechariah, the son of Amariah, the son of Shephatiah,
11: 4 the son of Zechariah, the **son** *of* Amariah, the son of Shephatiah,
11: 4 the son of Zechariah, the son of Amariah, the **son** *of* Shephatiah,
11: 4 the son of Amariah, the son of Shephatiah, the **son** *of* Mahalalel,
11: 4 son of Shephatiah, the son of Mahalalel, a **descendant** *of* Perez;
11: 5 Maaseiah **son** *of* Baruch, the son of Col-Hozeh, the son of
11: 5 the **son** *of* Col-Hozeh, the son of Hazaiah, the son of Adaiah,
11: 5 the **son** *of* Hazaiah, the son of Adaiah, the son of Joiarib, the son of
11: 5 the son of Hazaiah, the **son** *of* Adaiah, the son of Joiarib, the son of
11: 5 the son of Hazaiah, the son of Adaiah, the **son** *of* Joiarib, the son of
11: 5 the son of Adaiah, the son of Joiarib, the **son** *of* Zechariah,
11: 5 the son of Joiarib, the son of Zechariah, a **descendant** *of* Shelah.
11: 6 The **descendants** *of* Perez who lived in Jerusalem totaled 468 able
11: 7 From the **descendants** *of* Benjamin: Sallu son of Meshullam,
11: 7 Sallu **son** *of* Meshullam, the son of Joed, the son of Pedaiah,
11: 7 the **son** *of* Joed, the son of Pedaiah, the son of Kolaiah, the son of
11: 7 the son of Joed, the **son** *of* Pedaiah, the son of Kolaiah, the son of
11: 7 the son of Joed, the son of Pedaiah, the **son** *of* Kolaiah, the son of
11: 7 the son of Kolaiah, the **son** *of* Maaseiah, the son of Ithiel,
11: 7 the son of Maaseiah, the **son** *of* Ithiel, the son of Jeshaiah,
11: 7 the son of Maaseiah, the son of Ithiel, the **son** *of* Jeshaiah,
11: 9 Joel **son** *of* Zicri was their chief officer, and Judah son of
11: 9 Judah **son** *of* Hassenuah was over the Second District of the city.
11:10 From the priests: Jedaiah; the **son** *of* Joiarib; Jakin;
11:11 Seraiah **son** *of* Hilkiah, the son of Meshullam, the son of Zadok,
11:11 the **son** *of* Meshullam, the son of Zadok, the son of Meraioth,
11:11 the **son** *of* Zadok, the son of Meraioth, the son of Ahitub,
11:11 the son of Zadok, the **son** *of* Meraioth, the son of Ahitub,
11:11 the son of Zadok, the son of Meraioth, the **son** *of* Ahitub,
11:12 Adaiah **son** *of* Jeroham, the son of Pelaliah, the son of Amzi,
11:12 the **son** *of* Pelaliah, the son of Amzi, the son of Zechariah,
11:12 the son of Pelaliah, the **son** *of* Amzi, the son of Zechariah,
11:12 the son of Amzi, the **son** *of* Zechariah, the son of Pashhur,
11:12 the son of Zechariah, the **son** *of* Pashhur, the son of Malkijah,
11:12 the son of Zechariah, the son of Pashhur, the **son** *of* Malkijah,
11:13 Amashsai **son** *of* Azarel, the son of Ahzai, the son of
11:13 Amashsai son of Azarel, the **son** *of* Ahzai, the son of
11:13 the son of Ahzai, the **son** *of* Meshillemoth, the son of Immer,
11:13 the son of Ahzai, the son of Meshillemoth, the **son** *of* Immer,
11:14 128. Their chief officer was Zabdiel **son** *of* Haggedolim.
11:15 Shemaiah **son** *of* Hasshub, the son of Azrikam, the son of
11:15 the **son** *of* Azrikam, the son of Hashabiah, the son of Bunni;
11:15 the son of Azrikam, the **son** *of* Hashabiah, the son of Bunni;
11:15 the son of Azrikam, the son of Hashabiah, the **son** *of* Bunni;
11:17 Mattaniah **son** *of* Mica, the son of Zabdi, the son of Asaph,
11:17 Mattaniah son of Mica, the **son** *of* Zabdi, the son of Asaph,
11:17 Mattaniah son of Mica, the son of Zabdi, the **son** *of* Asaph,
11:17 and Abda **son** *of* Shammua, the son of Galal, the son of Jeduthun.
11:17 and Abda son of Shammua, the **son** *of* Galal, the son of Jeduthun.
11:17 and Abda son of Shammua, the son of Galal, the **son** *of* Jeduthun.
11:22 The chief officer of the Levites in Jerusalem was Uzzi **son** *of* Bani,
11:22 the **son** *of* Hashabiah, the son of Mattaniah, the son of Mica.
11:22 the son of Hashabiah, the **son** *of* Mattaniah, the son of Mica.
11:22 the son of Hashabiah, the son of Mattaniah, the **son** *of* Mica.
11:22 Uzzi was one of Asaph's **descendants**, who were the singers
11:24 Pethahiah **son** *of* Meshezabel, one of the descendants of Zerah son
11:24 son of Meshezabel, one of the **descendants** *of* Zerah son of Judah,
11:24 son of Meshezabel, one of the descendants of Zerah **son** *of* Judah,
11:25 some of the **people** *of* Judah lived in Kiriath Arba and its
11:31 The **descendants** *of* the Benjamites from Geba lived in Micmash,
12: 1 and Levites who returned with Zerubbabel **son** *of* Shealtiel
12:23 The family heads among the **descendants** *of* Levi up to the time of
12:23 of Johanan **son** *of* Eliashib were recorded in the book of the annals.
12:24 Sherebiah, Jeshua **son** *of* Kadmiel, and their associates, who stood
12:26 They served in the days of Joiakim **son** *of* Jeshua, the son of
12:26 the **son** *of* Jozadak, and in the days of Nehemiah the governor
12:28 The **singers** [+8876] also were brought together from the region
12:35 as well as some **[RPH]** priests with trumpets, and also Zechariah
12:35 and also Zechariah **son** *of* Jonathan, the son of Shemaiah,
12:35 the **son** *of* Shemaiah, the son of Mattaniah, the son of Micaiah,
12:35 the **son** *of* Mattaniah, the son of Micaiah, the son of Zaccur,
12:35 the **son** *of* Micaiah, the son of Zaccur, the son of Asaph,
12:35 the son of Micaiah, the **son** *of* Zaccur, the son of Asaph,
12:35 the son of Micaiah, the son of Zaccur, the **son** *of* Asaph,
12:45 according to the commands of David and his **son** Solomon.
12:47 and the Levites set aside the portion for the **descendants** *of* Aaron.
13: 2 because they had not met the **Israelites** [+3776] with food
13:13 in charge of the storerooms and made Hanan **son** *of* Zaccur,
13:13 made Hanan son of Zaccur, the **son** *of* Mattaniah, their assistant,
13:16 selling them in Jerusalem on the Sabbath to the **people** *of* Judah.
13:24 Half of their **children** spoke the language of Ashdod or the
13:25 "You are not to give your daughters in marriage to their **sons**,
13:25 nor are you to take their daughters in marriage for your **sons**
13:28 One of the **sons** *of* Joiada son of Eliashib the high priest was
13:28 One of the sons of Joiada **son** *of* Eliashib the high priest was
Est 2: 5 named Mordecai **son** *of* Jair, the son of Shimei, the son of Kish,
2: 5 named Mordecai son of Jair, the **son** *of* Shimei, the son of Kish,
2: 5 named Mordecai son of Jair, the son of Shimei, the **son** *of* Kish,
3: 1 King Xerxes honored Haman **son** *of* Hammedatha, the Agagite,
3:10 ring from his finger and gave it to Haman **son** *of* Hammedatha,
5:11 his many **sons**, and all the ways the king had honored him
8: 5 let an order be written overruling the dispatches that Haman **son** *of*
8:10 who rode fast horses **especially bred** [+2021+8247] for the king.
9:10 the ten **sons** *of* Haman son of Hammedatha, the enemy of the Jews.
9:10 the ten sons of Haman **son** *of* Hammedatha, the enemy of the Jews.
9:12 five hundred men and the ten **sons** *of* Haman in the citadel of Susa.
9:13 tomorrow also, and let Haman's ten **sons** be hanged on gallows."
9:14 edict was issued in Susa, and they hanged the ten **sons** *of* Haman.
9:24 For Haman **son** *of* Hammedatha, the Agagite, the enemy of all the
9:25 and that he and his **sons** should be hanged on the gallows.
Job 1: 2 He had seven **sons** and three daughters,
1: 3 He was the greatest man among all the **people** *of* the East.
1: 4 His **sons** used to take turns holding feasts in their homes, and they
1: 5 "Perhaps my **children** have sinned and cursed God in their hearts."
1: 6 One day the **angels** [+466+2021] came to present themselves
1:13 One day when Job's **sons** and daughters were feasting and drinking
1:18 "Your **sons** and daughters were feasting and drinking wine at the
2: 1 On another day the **angels** [+466+2021] came to present
4:11 perishes for lack of prey, and the **cubs** *of* the lioness are scattered.
5: 4 His **children** are far from safety, crushed in court without a
5: 7 Yet man is born to trouble as surely as **sparks** [+8404] fly upward.
8: 4 When your **children** sinned against him, he gave them over to the
14:21 If his **sons** are honored, he does not know it; if they are brought
16:21 on behalf of a man he pleads with God as a **man** [+132] pleads for
17: 5 denounces his friends for reward, the eyes of his **children** will fail.
19:17 to my wife; I am loathsome to my own **brothers** [+1061].
20:10 His **children** must make amends to the poor; his own hands must
21:19 ⌊It is said,⌋ 'God stores up a man's punishment for his **sons**.'
25: 6 who is but a maggot—a **son** *of* man, who is only a worm!"
27:14 However many his **children**, their fate is the sword; his offspring
28: 8 **Proud beasts** [+8832] do not set foot on it, and no lion prowls
30: 8 **[RPH]** A base and nameless brood, they were driven out of the
30: 8 A base and nameless **brood**, they were driven out of the land.
32: 2 But Elihu **son** *of* Barakel the Buzite, of the family of Ram,
32: 6 So Elihu **son** *of* Barakel the Buzite said: "I am young in years,
35: 8 a man like yourself, and your righteousness only the **sons** *of* men.
38: 7 stars sang together and all the **angels** [+466] shouted for joy?
38:32 constellations in their seasons or lead out the Bear with its **cubs**?
39: 4 Their **young** thrive and grow strong in the wilds; they leave
39:16 She treats her **young** harshly, as if they were not hers; she cares not
41:28 [41:20] **Arrows** [+8008] do not make him flee; slingstones are
41:34 [41:26] are haughty; he is king over all that are **proud** [+8832]."
42:13 And he also had seven **sons** and three daughters.
42:16 he saw his **children** and their children to the fourth generation.
42:16 his children and **their**[s] [+2257] children to the fourth generation.
42:16 he saw his children and their **children** to the fourth generation.
Ps 2: 7 He said to me, "You are my **Son**; today I have become your Father.
3: T [3:1] A psalm of David. When he fled from his **son** Absalom.
4: 2 [4:3] How long, O **men** [+408], will you turn my glory into
8: 4 [8:5] are mindful of him, the **son** *of* man that you care for him?
9: T [9:1] To ⌊the tune of,⌋ "The Death of the **Son**." A psalm of David.

[F] Hitpael (hitpoel, hitpoal, hitpolel, hitpolal, hitpalel, hitpalal, hitpalpel, hitpalpal, hotpael, hotpaal) [G] Hiphil (hiphtil) [H] Hophal [I] Hishtaphel

Ps 11: 4 He observes the **sons** *of* men; his eyes examine them.
12: 1 [12:2] the faithful have vanished from among **men** [+132].
12: 8 [12:9] about when what is vile is honored among **men** [+132].
14: 2 The LORD looks down from heaven on the **sons** *of* men to see if
17: 14 their **sons** have plenty, and they store up wealth for their children.
18: 44 [18:45] they obey me; **foreigners** [+5797] cringe before me.
18: 45 [18:46] **They**[s] **all** [+5797] lose heart; they come trembling from
21: 10 [21:11] from the earth, their posterity from **mankind** [+132].
29: 1 Ascribe to the LORD, O **mighty ones** [+446], ascribe to the
29: 6 He makes Lebanon skip like a calf, Sirion like a **young** wild ox.
31: 19 [31:20] which you bestow in the sight of **men** [+132] on those
33: 13 heaven the LORD looks down and sees all **mankind** [+132];
34: 11 [34:12] Come, my **children**, listen to me; I will teach you the fear
36: 7 [36:8] **low among men** [+132] find refuge in the shadow of your
42: T [42:1] the director of music. A *maskil* of the **Sons** *of* Korah.
44: T [44:1] the director of music. Of the **Sons** *of* Korah. A *maskil*.
45: T [45:1] Of the **Sons** *of* Korah. A *maskil*. A wedding song.
45: 2 [45:3] You are the most excellent of **men** [+132] and your lips
45: 16 [45:17] Your **sons** will take the place of your fathers; you will
46: T [46:1] Of the **Sons** *of* Korah. According to *alamoth*. A song.
47: T [47:1] For the director of music. Of the **Sons** *of* Korah. A psalm.
48: T [48:1] A song. A psalm of the **Sons** *of* Korah.
49: T [49:1] For the director of music. Of the **Sons** *of* Korah. A psalm.
49: 2 [49:3] both **low** [+132] and high, rich and poor alike:
49: 2 [49:3] both low and **high** [+408], rich and poor alike:
50: 20 against your brother and slander your own mother's **son**.
53: 2 [53:3] God looks down from heaven on the **sons** *of* men to see if
57: 4 [57:5] I lie among ravenous beasts—**men** [+132] whose teeth are
58: 1 [58:2] speak justly? Do you judge uprightly among **men** [+132]?
62: 9 [62:10] **Lowborn men** [+132] are but a breath, the highborn are
62: 9 [62:10] men are but a breath, the **highborn** [+408] are but a lie;
66: 5 God has done, how awesome his works in **man's** [+132] behalf!
69: 8 [69:9] stranger to my brothers, an alien to my own mother's **sons**;
72: 1 with your justice, O God, the royal **son** with your righteousness.
72: 4 the afflicted among the people and save the **children** *of* the needy;
72: 20 This concludes the prayers of David **son** *of* Jesse.
73: 15 "I will speak thus," I would have betrayed your **children** [+1887].
77: 15 [77:16] your people, the **descendants** *of* Jacob and Joseph.
78: 4 We will not hide them from their **children**; we will tell the next
78: 5 which he commanded our forefathers to teach their **children**,
78: 6 even the **children** yet to be born, and they in turn would tell their
78: 6 children yet to be born, and they in turn would tell their **children**.
78: 9 The **men** *of* Ephraim, though armed with bows, turned back on the
79: 11 by the strength of your arm preserve *those* **condemned to** die.
80: 15 [80:16] hand has planted, the **son** you have raised up for yourself.
80: 17 [80:18] the **son** *of* man you have raised up for yourself.
82: 6 "I said, 'You are "gods"; you are all **sons** *of* the Most High.'
83: 8 [83:9] has joined them to lend strength to the **descendants** *of* Lot.
84: T [84:1] According to *gittith*. Of the **Sons** *of* Korah. A psalm.
85: T [85:1] For the director of music. Of the **Sons** *of* Korah. A psalm.
86: 16 your strength to your servant and save the **son** *of* your maidservant.
87: T [87:1] Of the **Sons** *of* Korah. A psalm. A song.
88: T [88:1] A song. A psalm of the **Sons** *of* Korah. For the director of
89: 6 [89:7] is like the LORD among the **heavenly beings** [+446]?
89: 22 [89:23] subject him to tribute; no wicked **man** will oppress him.
89: 30 [89:31] "If his **sons** forsake my law and do not follow my statutes,
89: 47 [89:48] For what futility you have created all **men** [+132]!
90: 3 turn men back to dust, saying, "Return to dust, O **sons** *of* men."
90: 16 deeds be shown to your servants, your splendor to their **children**.
102: 20 [102:21] of the prisoners and release *those* **condemned to** death."
102: 28 [102:29] The **children** *of* your servants will live in your presence;
103: 7 made known his ways to Moses, his deeds to the **people** *of* Israel:
103: 13 As a father has compassion on his **children**, so the LORD has
103: 17 fear him, and his righteousness with their **children's** children—
103: 17 fear him, and his righteousness with their children's **children**—
105: 6 of Abraham his servant, O **sons** *of* Jacob, his chosen ones.
106: 37 They sacrificed their **sons** and their daughters to demons.
106: 38 They shed innocent blood, the blood of their **sons** and daughters,
107: 8 for his unfailing love and his wonderful deeds for **men** [+132],
107: 15 for his unfailing love and his wonderful deeds for **men** [+132],
107: 21 for his unfailing love and his wonderful deeds for **men** [+132].
107: 31 for his unfailing love and his wonderful deeds for **men** [+132].
109: 9 May his **children** be fatherless and his wife a widow.
109: 10 May his **children** be wandering beggars; may they be driven from
113: 9 the barren woman in her home as a happy mother of **children**.
114: 4 the mountains skipped like rams, the hills like **lambs** [+7366].
114: 6 that you skipped like rams, you hills, like **lambs** [+7366]?
115: 14 May the LORD make you increase, both you and your **children**.
115: 16 belong to the LORD, but the earth he has given to **man** [+132].
116: 16 I am your servant; I am your servant, the **son** *of* your maidservant;
127: 3 **Sons** are a heritage from the LORD, children a reward from him.
127: 4 Like arrows in the hands of a warrior are **sons** *born in* one's youth.
128: 3 your house; your **sons** will be like olive shoots around your table.
128: 6 and may you live to see your **children's** [+4200] children.
128: 6 may you live to see your children's **children**. Peace be upon Israel.
132: 12 if your **sons** keep my covenant and the statutes I teach them,
132: 12 then their **sons** will sit on your throne for ever and ever."
137: 7 what the **Edomites** [+121] did on the day Jerusalem fell.
144: 3 is man that you care for him, the **son** *of* man that you think of him?
144: 7 me from the mighty waters, from the hands of **foreigners** [+5797]
144: 11 rescue me from the hands of **foreigners** [+5797] whose mouths are
144: 12 Then our **sons** in their youth will be like well-nurtured plants,
145: 12 so that **all men** [+132+2021] may know of your mighty acts
146: 3 put your trust in princes, in **mortal men** [+132], who cannot save.
147: 9 food for the cattle and for the **young** ravens when they call.
147: 13 the bars of your gates and blesses your **people** within you.
148: 14 the praise of all his saints, of **Israel** [+3776], the people close to his
149: 2 rejoice in their Maker; let the **people** *of* Zion be glad in their King.
Pr 1: 1 The proverbs of Solomon **son** *of* David, king of Israel:
1: 8 Listen, my **son**, to your father's instruction and do not forsake your
1: 10 My **son**, if sinners entice you, do not give in to them.
1: 15 my **son**, do not go along with them, do not set foot on their paths;
2: 1 My **son**, if you accept my words and store up my commands within
3: 1 My **son**, do not forget my teaching, but keep my commands in
3: 11 My **son**, do not despise the LORD's discipline and do not resent
3: 12 disciplines those he loves, as a father the **son** he delights in.
3: 21 My **son**, preserve sound judgment and discernment, do not let them
4: 1 Listen, my **sons**, to a father's instruction; pay attention and gain
4: 3 When I was a **boy** in my father's house, still tender, and an only
4: 10 Listen, my **son**, accept what I say, and the years of your life will be
4: 20 My **son**, pay attention to what I say; listen closely to my words.
5: 1 My **son**, pay attention to my wisdom, listen well to my words of
5: 7 Now then, my **sons**, listen to me; do not turn aside from what I say.
5: 20 Why be captivated, my **son**, by an adulteress? Why embrace the
6: 1 My **son**, if you have put up security for your neighbor, if you have
6: 3 do this, my **son**, to free yourself, since you have fallen into your
6: 20 My **son**, keep your father's commands and do not forsake your
7: 1 My **son**, keep my words and store up my commands within you.
7: 7 I saw among the simple, I noticed among the **young men**,
7: 24 Now then, my **sons**, listen to me; pay attention to what I say.
8: 4 O men, I call out; I raise my voice to **all mankind** [+132].
8: 31 rejoicing in his whole world and delighting in **mankind** [+132].
8: 32 "Now then, my **sons**, listen to me; blessed are those who keep my
10: 1 A wise **son** brings joy to his father, but a foolish son grief to his
10: 1 son brings joy to his father, but a foolish **son** grief to his mother.
10: 5 He who gathers crops in summer is a wise **son**, but he who sleeps
10: 5 is a wise son, but he who sleeps during harvest is a disgraceful **son**.
13: 1 A wise **son** heeds his father's instruction, but a mocker does not
13: 22 A good man leaves an inheritance for his **children's** children,
13: 22 A good man leaves an inheritance for his children's **children**,
13: 24 He who spares the rod hates his **son**, but he who loves him is
14: 26 has a secure fortress, and for his **children** it will be a refuge.
15: 11 before the LORD—how much more the hearts of **men** [+132]!
15: 20 A wise **son** brings joy to his father, but a foolish man despises his
17: 2 A wise servant will rule over a disgraceful **son**, and will share the
17: 6 **Children's** children are a crown to the aged, and parents are the
17: 6 Children's **children** are a crown to the aged, and parents are the
17: 6 are a crown to the aged, and parents are the pride of their **children**.
17: 25 A foolish **son** brings grief to his father and bitterness to the one
19: 13 A foolish **son** is his father's ruin, and a quarrelsome wife is like a
19: 18 Discipline your **son**, for in that there is hope; do not be a willing
19: 26 and drives out his mother is a **son** who brings shame and disgrace.
19: 27 Stop listening to instruction, my **son**, and you will stray from the
20: 7 man leads a blameless life; blessed are his **children** after him.
23: 15 My **son**, if your heart is wise, then my heart will be glad;
23: 19 Listen, my **son**, and be wise, and keep your heart on the right path.
23: 26 My **son**, give me your heart and let your eyes keep to my ways,
24: 13 Eat honey, my **son**, for it is good; honey from the comb is sweet to
24: 21 Fear the LORD and the king, my **son**, and do not join with the
27: 11 Be wise, my **son**, and bring joy to my heart; then I can answer
28: 7 He who keeps the law is a discerning **son**, but a companion of
29: 17 Discipline your **son**, and he will give you peace; he will bring
30: 1 The sayings of Agur **son** *of* Jakeh—an oracle: This man declared
30: 4 What is his name, and the name of his **son**? Tell me if you know!
30: 17 by the ravens of the valley, will be eaten by the **vultures** [+5979].
31: 5 law decrees, and deprive all the **oppressed** [+6715] of their rights.
31: 8 for themselves, for the rights of all *who* are **destitute** [+2710].
31: 28 Her **children** arise and call her blessed; her husband also,
Ecc 1: 1 The words of the Teacher, **son** *of* David, king in Jerusalem:
1: 13 under heaven. What a heavy burden God has laid on **men** [+132]!
2: 3 I wanted to see what was worthwhile for **men** [+132] to do under
2: 7 female slaves and had other slaves *who* were **born** *in* my house.
2: 8 and a harem as well—the delights of the heart of **man** [+132].
3: 10 I have seen the burden God has laid on **men** [+132].
3: 18 I also thought, "As for **men** [+132], God tests them so that they
3: 19 **Man's** [+132] fate is like that of the animals; the same fate awaits
3: 21 Who knows if the spirit of **man** [+132] rises upward and if the
4: 8 There was a man all alone; he had neither **son** nor brother.

Ecc 5:14 [5:13] so that when he has a **son** there is nothing left for him.
8:11 the hearts of the **people** [+132] are filled with schemes to do
9:3 The hearts of **men** [+132], moreover, are full of evil and there is
9:12 so **men** [+132] are trapped by evil times that fall unexpectedly
10:17 O land whose king is of noble **birth** and whose princes eat at a
12:12 Be warned, my **son**, of anything in addition to them. Of making
SS 1:6 My mother's **sons** were angry with me and made me take care of
2:3 among the trees of the forest is my lover among the **young men**.
Isa 1:1 Jerusalem that Isaiah **son** *of* Amoz saw during the reigns of
1:2 "I reared **children** and brought them up, but they have rebelled
1:4 with guilt, a brood of evildoers, **children** given to corruption!
2:1 This is what Isaiah **son** *of* Amoz saw concerning Judah
5:1 My loved one had a vineyard on a **fertile** [+9043] hillside.
7:1 When Ahaz **son** *of* Jotham, the son of Uzziah, was king of Judah,
7:1 the **son** *of* Uzziah, was king of Judah, King Rezin of Aram
7:1 Pekah **son** *of* Remaliah king of Israel marched up to fight against
7:3 LORD said to Isaiah, "Go out, you and your **son** Shear-Jashub,
7:4 of the fierce anger of Rezin and Aram and of the **son** *of* Remaliah.
7:5 Aram, Ephraim and Remaliah's **son** have plotted your ruin,
7:6 it among ourselves, and make the **son** *of* Tabeel king over it."
7:9 is Samaria, and the head of Samaria is only Remaliah's **son**.
7:14 The virgin will be with child and will give birth to a **son**, and will
8:2 and Zechariah **son** *of* Jeberekiah as reliable witnesses for me."
8:3 I went to the prophetess, and she conceived and gave birth to a **son**.
8:6 waters of Shiloah and rejoices over Rezin and the **son** *of* Remaliah,
9:6 [9:5] For to us a child is born, to us a **son** is given,
11:14 to the west; together they will plunder the **people** *to* the east.
11:14 and Moab, and the **Ammonites** [+6648] will be subject to them.
13:1 An oracle concerning Babylon that Isaiah **son** *of* Amoz saw:
13:18 mercy on infants nor will they look with compassion on **children**.
14:12 you have fallen from heaven, O morning star, **son** *of* the dawn!
14:21 Prepare a place to slaughter his **sons** for the sins of their
17:3 remnant of Aram will be like the glory of the **Israelites** [+3776],"
17:9 strong cities, which they left because of the **Israelites** [+3776],
19:11 How can you say to Pharaoh, "I am **one** *of* the wise men, a disciple
19:11 "I am one of the wise men, a **disciple** *of* the ancient kings"?
20:2 at that time the LORD spoke through Isaiah **son** *of* Amoz.
21:10 O my **people**, crushed on the threshing floor, I tell you what I have
21:17 of the bowmen, the warriors of **Kedar** [+7723], will be few."
22:20 "In that day I will summon my servant, Eliakim **son** *of* Hilkiah.
27:12 and you, O **Israelites** [+3776], will be gathered up one by one.
30:1 "Woe to the obstinate **children**," declares the LORD, "to those
30:9 These are rebellious people, deceitful **children**, children unwilling
30:9 **children** unwilling to listen to the LORD's instruction.
31:6 to him you have so greatly revolted against, O **Israelites** [+3776].
36:3 Eliakim **son** *of* Hilkiah the palace administrator, Shebna the
36:3 the secretary, and Joah **son** *of* Asaph the recorder went out to him.
36:22 Eliakim **son** *of* Hilkiah the palace administrator, Shebna the
36:22 and Joah **son** *of* Asaph the recorder went to Hezekiah,
37:2 all wearing sackcloth, to the prophet Isaiah **son** *of* Amoz.
37:3 as when **children** come to the point of birth and there is no
37:12 Haran, Rezeph and the **people** *of* Eden who were in Tel Assar?
37:21 Isaiah **son** *of* Amoz sent a message to Hezekiah: "This is what the
37:38 his **sons** Adrammelech and Sharezer cut him down with the sword,
37:38 the land of Ararat. And Esarhaddon his **son** succeeded him as king.
38:1 The prophet Isaiah **son** *of* Amoz went to him and said, "This is
38:19 am doing today; fathers tell their **children** about your faithfulness.
39:1 At that time Merodach-Baladan **son** *of* Baladan king of Babylon
39:7 some of your **descendants**, your own flesh and blood who will be
43:6 Bring my **sons** from afar and my daughters from the ends of the
45:11 things to come, do you question me about my **children**,
49:15 at her breast and have no compassion on the **child** she has borne?
49:17 Your **sons** hasten back, and those who laid you waste depart from
49:20 The **children** *born during* your bereavement will yet say in your
49:22 they will bring your **sons** in their arms and carry your daughters on
49:25 with those who contend with you, and your **children** I will save.
51:12 you that you fear mortal men, the **sons** *of* men, who are but grass,
51:18 Of all the **sons** she bore there was none to guide her; of all the sons
51:18 of all the **sons** she reared there was none to take her by the hand.
51:20 Your **sons** have fainted; they lie at the head of every street,
52:14 of any man and his form marred beyond **human** [+132] likeness—
54:1 because more are the **children** *of* the desolate woman than of her
54:1 because more are the children of the desolate woman than **[RPH]**
54:13 All your **sons** will be taught by the LORD, and great will be your
54:13 be taught by the LORD, and great will be your **children's** peace.
56:2 is the man who does this, the **man** [+132] who holds it fast,
56:3 Let no **foreigner** [+2021+5797] who has bound himself to the
56:5 its walls a memorial and a name better than **sons** and daughters;
56:6 And **foreigners** [+2021+5797] who bind themselves to the LORD
57:3 come here, you **sons** *of* a sorceress, you offspring of adulterers
60:4 your **sons** come from afar, and your daughters are carried on the
60:9 bringing your **sons** from afar, with their silver and gold,
60:10 "**Foreigners** [+5797] will rebuild your walls, and their kings will
60:14 The **sons** *of* your oppressors will come bowing before you;
61:5 Aliens will shepherd your flocks; **foreigners** [+5797] will work
62:5 As a young man marries a maiden, so will your **sons** marry you;
62:8 never again will **foreigners** [+5797] drink the new wine for which
63:8 "Surely they are my people, **sons** who will not be false to me";
65:20 he who dies at a hundred **[NIE]** will be thought a mere youth;
65:20 he who fails to reach **[NIE]** a hundred will be considered
66:8 Yet no sooner is Zion in labor than she gives birth to her **children**.
66:20 bring them, as the **Israelites** [+3776] bring their grain offerings,
Jer 1:1 The words of Jeremiah **son** *of* Hilkiah, one of the priests at
1:2 thirteenth year of the reign of Josiah **son** *of* Amon king of Judah,
1:3 and through the reign of Jehoiakim **son** *of* Josiah king of Judah,
1:3 down to the fifth month of the eleventh year of Zedekiah **son** *of*
2:9 "And I will bring charges against your **children's** children.
2:9 "And I will bring charges against your children's **children**.
2:16 the **men** *of* Memphis and Tahpanhes have shaved the crown of
2:30 "In vain I punished your **people**; they did not respond to
3:14 "Return, faithless **people**," declares the LORD, "for I am your
3:19 " 'How gladly would I treat you like **sons** and give you a desirable
3:21 barren heights, the weeping and pleading of the **people** *of* Israel,
3:22 "Return, faithless **people**; I will cure you of backsliding."
3:24 our fathers' labor—their flocks and herds, their **sons** and daughters.
4:22 They are senseless **children**; they have no understanding.
5:7 Your **children** have forsaken me and sworn by gods that are not
5:17 devour your harvests and food, devour your **sons** and daughters;
6:1 "Flee for safety, **people** *of* Benjamin! Flee from Jerusalem!
6:21 Fathers and **sons** alike will stumble over them; neighbors
7:18 The **children** gather wood, the fathers light the fire,
7:30 " 'The **people** *of* Judah have done evil in my eyes,
7:31 places of Topheth in the Valley of Ben Hinnom to burn their **sons**
9:26 [9:25] Edom, **Ammon** [+6648], Moab and all who live in the
10:20 My **sons** are gone from me and are no more; no one is left now to
11:22 men will die by the sword, their **sons** and daughters by famine.
13:14 one against the other, fathers and **sons** alike, declares the LORD.
14:16 be no one to bury them or their wives, their **sons** or their daughters.
15:4 because of what Manasseh **son** *of* Hezekiah king of Judah did in
16:2 "You must not marry and have **sons** or daughters in this place."
16:3 For this is what the LORD says about the **sons** and daughters
16:14 LORD lives, who brought the **Israelites** [+3776] up out of Egypt,'
16:15 who brought the **Israelites** [+3776] up out of the land of the north
17:2 Even their **children** remember their altars and Asherah poles
17:19 "Go and stand at the gate of the **people** [+6639], through which the
18:21 So give their **children** over to famine; hand them over to the power
19:5 They have built the high places of Baal to burn their **sons** in the
19:9 I will make them eat the flesh of their **sons** and daughters,
20:1 When the priest Pashhur **son** *of* Immer, the chief officer in the
20:15 who made him very glad, saying, "A **child** is born to you—
21:1 LORD when King Zedekiah sent to him Pashhur **son** *of* Malkijah
21:1 Pashhur son of Malkijah and the priest Zephaniah **son** *of* Maaseiah.
22:11 For this is what the LORD says about Shallum **son** *of* Josiah,
22:18 Therefore this is what the LORD says about Jehoiakim **son** *of*
22:24 "even if you, Jehoiachin **son** *of* Jehoiakim king of Judah,
23:7 LORD lives, who brought the **Israelites** [+3776] up out of Egypt,'
24:1 After Jehoiachin **son** *of* Jehoiakim king of Judah and the officials,
25:1 Judah in the fourth year of Jehoiakim **son** *of* Josiah king of Judah,
25:3 from the thirteenth year of Josiah **son** *of* Amon king of Judah until
25:21 Edom, Moab and **Ammon** [+6648];
26:1 Early in the reign of Jehoiakim **son** *of* Josiah king of Judah,
26:20 (Now Uriah **son** *of* Shemaiah from Kiriath Jearim was another man
26:22 King Jehoiakim, however, sent Elnathan **son** *of* Acbor to Egypt,
26:23 body thrown into the burial place of the **common people** [+6639].)
26:24 Ahikam **son** *of* Shaphan supported Jeremiah, and so he was not
27:1 Early in the reign of Zedekiah **son** *of* Josiah king of Judah,
27:3 Moab, **Ammon** [+6648], Tyre and Sidon through the envoys who
27:7 All nations will serve him and his **son** and his grandson until the
27:7 and his **grandson** [+1201] until the time for his land comes;
27:7 and his **grandson** [+1201] until the time for his land comes;
27:20 **son** *of* Jehoiakim king of Judah into exile from Jerusalem to
28:1 the prophet Hananiah **son** *of* Azzur, who was from Gibeon,
28:4 I will also bring back to this place Jehoiachin **son** *of* Jehoiakim
29:3 He entrusted the letter to Elasah **son** *of* Shaphan and to Gemariah
29:3 letter to Elasah son of Shaphan and to Gemariah **son** *of* Hilkiah,
29:6 Marry and have **sons** and daughters; find wives for your sons
29:6 find wives for your **sons** and give your daughters in marriage,
29:6 in marriage, so that they too may have **sons** and daughters.
29:21 says about Ahab **son** *of* Kolaiah and Zedekiah son of Maaseiah,
29:21 says about Ahab son of Kolaiah and Zedekiah **son** *of* Maaseiah,
29:25 to Zephaniah **son** *of* Maaseiah the priest, and to all the other
30:20 Their **children** will be as in days of old, and their community will
31:12 the new wine and the oil, the **young** *of* the flocks and herds.
31:15 Rachel weeping for her **children** and refusing to be comforted,
31:15 and refusing to be comforted, because her **children** are no more."
31:17 declares the LORD. "Your **children** will return to their own land.
31:20 Is not Ephraim my dear **son**, the child in whom I delight? Though I
31:29 have eaten sour grapes, and the **children's** teeth are set on edge.'

Jer 32: 7 Hanamel **son** *of* Shallum your uncle is going to come to you
32: 8 my **cousin** [+1856] Hanamel came to me in the courtyard of the
32: 9 so I bought the field at Anathoth from my **cousin** [+1856] Hanamel
32: 12 and I gave this deed to Baruch **son** *of* Neriah, the son of Mahseiah,
32: 12 the **son** *of* Mahseiah, in the presence of my cousin Hanamel
32: 12 in the presence of my **cousin** [+1856] [BHS-] Hanamel and of the
32: 16 "After I had given the deed of purchase to Baruch **son** *of* Neriah,
32: 18 for the fathers' sins into the laps of their **children** after them.
32: 19 Your eyes are open to all the ways of **men** [+132]; you reward
32: 30 "The **people** *of* Israel and Judah have done nothing but evil in my
32: 30 "The people of Israel and **[RPH]** Judah have done nothing
32: 30 the **people** *of* Israel have done nothing but provoke me with what
32: 32 The **people** *of* Israel and Judah have provoked me by all the evil
32: 32 **[RPH]** Judah have provoked me by all the evil they have done—
32: 35 places for Baal in the Valley of Ben Hinnom to sacrifice their **sons**
32: 39 me for their own good and the good of their **children** after them.
33: 21 and David will no longer have a **descendant** to reign on his throne.
35: 1 LORD during the reign of Jehoiakim **son** *of* Josiah king of Judah:
35: 3 So I went to get Jaazaniah **son** *of* Jeremiah, the son of
35: 3 the **son** *of* Habazziniah, and his brothers and all his sons—
35: 3 the son of Habazziniah, and his brothers and all his **sons**—
35: 4 into the room of the **sons** *of* Hanan son of Igdaliah the man of God.
35: 4 into the room of the sons of Hanan **son** *of* Igdaliah the man of God.
35: 4 which was over that of Maaseiah **son** *of* Shallum the doorkeeper.
35: 5 some cups before the **men** *of* the Recabite family and said to them,
35: 6 because our forefather Jonadab **son** *of* Recab gave us this
35: 6 'Neither you nor your **descendants** must ever drink wine.
35: 8 We have obeyed everything our forefather Jonadab **son** *of* Recab
35: 8 Neither we nor our wives nor our **sons** and daughters have ever
35: 14 'Jonadab **son** *of* Recab ordered his sons not to drink wine and this
35: 14 'Jonadab son of Recab ordered his **sons** not to drink wine and this
35: 16 The **descendants** *of* Jonadab son of Recab have carried out the
35: 16 The descendants of Jonadab **son** *of* Recab have carried out the
35: 19 'Jonadab **son** *of* Recab will never fail to have a man to serve me.' "
36: 1 In the fourth year of Jehoiakim **son** *of* Josiah king of Judah,
36: 4 So Jeremiah called Baruch **son** *of* Neriah, and while Jeremiah
36: 8 Baruch **son** *of* Neriah did everything Jeremiah the prophet told him
36: 9 In the ninth month of the fifth year of Jehoiakim **son** *of* Josiah king
36: 10 From the room of Gemariah **son** *of* Shaphan the secretary,
36: 11 When Micaiah **son** *of* Gemariah, the son of Shaphan, heard all the
36: 11 When Micaiah son of Gemariah, the **son** *of* Shaphan, heard all the
36: 12 the secretary, Delaiah **son** *of* Shemaiah, Elnathan son of Acbor,
36: 12 the secretary, Delaiah son of Shemaiah, Elnathan **son** *of* Acbor,
36: 12 of Shemaiah, Elnathan son of Acbor, Gemariah **son** *of* Shaphan,
36: 12 of Shaphan, Zedekiah **son** *of* Hananiah, and all the other officials.
36: 14 all the officials sent Jehudi **son** *of* Nethaniah, the son of Shelemiah,
36: 14 the **son** *of* Shelemiah, the son of Cushi, to say to Baruch,
36: 14 the son of Shelemiah, the **son** *of* Cushi, to say to Baruch,
36: 14 So Baruch **son** *of* Neriah went to them with the scroll in his hand.
36: 26 a **son** *of* the king, Seraiah son of Azriel and Shelemiah son of
36: 26 Seraiah **son** *of* Azriel and Shelemiah son of Abdeel to arrest
36: 26 of Azriel and Shelemiah **son** *of* Abdeel to arrest Baruch the scribe
36: 32 took another scroll and gave it to the scribe Baruch **son** *of* Neriah,
37: 1 Zedekiah **son** *of* Josiah was made king of Judah by
37: 1 of Babylon; he reigned in place of Jehoiachin **son** *of* Jehoiakim.
37: 3 sent Jehucal **son** *of* Shelemiah with the priest Zephaniah son of
37: 3 sent Jehucal son of Shelemiah with the priest Zephaniah **son** *of*
37: 13 whose name was Irijah **son** *of* Shelemiah, the son of Hananiah,
37: 13 the **son** *of* Hananiah, arrested him and said, "You are deserting to
38: 1 Shephatiah **son** *of* Mattan, Gedaliah son of Pashhur, Jehucal son of
38: 1 son of Mattan, Gedaliah **son** *of* Pashhur, Jehucal son of Shelemiah,
38: 1 son of Mattan, Gedaliah son of Pashhur, Jehucal **son** *of* Shelemiah,
38: 1 Pashhur **son** *of* Malkijah heard what Jeremiah was telling all the
38: 6 the king's **son**, which was in the courtyard of the guard.
38: 23 your wives and **children** will be brought out to the Babylonians.
39: 6 There at Riblah the king of Babylon slaughtered the **sons** *of*
39: 14 They turned him over to Gedaliah **son** *of* Ahikam, the son of
39: 14 son of Ahikam, the **son** *of* Shaphan, to take him back to his home.
40: 5 "Go back to Gedaliah **son** *of* Ahikam, the son of Shaphan,
40: 5 "Go back to Gedaliah son of Ahikam, the **son** *of* Shaphan,
40: 6 So Jeremiah went to Gedaliah **son** *of* Ahikam at Mizpah and stayed
40: 7 had appointed Gedaliah **son** *of* Ahikam as governor over the land
40: 8 Ishmael **son** *of* Nethaniah, Johanan and Jonathan the sons of
40: 8 son of Nethaniah, Johanan and Jonathan the **sons** *of* Kareah,
40: 8 and Jonathan the sons of Kareah, Seraiah **son** *of* Tanhumeth,
40: 8 Seraiah son of Tanhumeth, the **sons** *of* Ephai the Netophathite,
40: 8 and Jaazaniah the **son** *of* the Maacathite, and their men.
40: 9 Gedaliah **son** *of* Ahikam, the son of Shaphan, took an oath to
40: 9 Gedaliah son of Ahikam, the **son** *of* Shaphan, took an oath to
40: 11 When all the Jews in Moab, **Ammon** [+6648], Edom and all the
40: 11 a remnant in Judah and had appointed Gedaliah **son** *of* Ahikam,
40: 11 son of Ahikam, the **son** *of* Shaphan, as governor over them,
40: 13 Johanan **son** *of* Kareah and all the army officers still in the open
40: 14 "Don't you know that Baalis king of the **Ammonites** [+6648] has
40: 14 Ammonites has sent Ishmael **son** *of* Nethaniah to take your life?"
40: 14 take your life?" But Gedaliah **son** *of* Ahikam did not believe them.
40: 15 Then Johanan **son** *of* Kareah said privately to Gedaliah in Mizpah,
40: 15 "Let me go and kill Ishmael **son** *of* Nethaniah, and no one will
40: 16 But Gedaliah **son** *of* Ahikam said to Johanan son of Kareah,
40: 16 But Gedaliah son of Ahikam said to Johanan **son** *of* Kareah,
41: 1 In the seventh month Ishmael **son** *of* Nethaniah, the son of
41: 1 the **son** *of* Elishama, who was of royal blood and had been one of
41: 1 came with ten men to Gedaliah **son** *of* Ahikam at Mizpah.
41: 2 Ishmael **son** *of* Nethaniah and the ten men who were with him got
41: 2 were with him got up and struck down Gedaliah **son** *of* Ahikam,
41: 2 Gedaliah son of Ahikam, the **son** *of* Shaphan, with the sword,
41: 6 Ishmael **son** *of* Nethaniah went out from Mizpah to meet them,
41: 6 When he met them, he said, "Come to Gedaliah **son** *of* Ahikam."
41: 7 Ishmael **son** *of* Nethaniah and the men who were with him
41: 9 king of Israel. Ishmael **son** *of* Nethaniah filled it with the dead.
41: 10 of the imperial guard had appointed Gedaliah **son** *of* Ahikam.
41: 10 Ishmael **son** *of* Nethaniah took them captive and set out to cross
41: 10 them captive and set out to cross over to the **Ammonites** [+6648].
41: 11 When Johanan **son** *of* Kareah and all the army officers who were
41: 11 about all the crimes Ishmael **son** *of* Nethaniah had committed,
41: 12 they took all their men and went to fight Ishmael **son** *of* Nethaniah.
41: 13 When all the people Ishmael had with him saw Johanan **son** *of*
41: 14 captive at Mizpah turned and went over to Johanan **son** *of* Kareah.
41: 15 Ishmael **son** *of* Nethaniah and eight of his men escaped from
41: 15 men escaped from Johanan and fled to the **Ammonites** [+6648].
41: 16 Johanan **son** *of* Kareah and all the army officers who were with
41: 16 **son** *of* Nethaniah after he had assassinated Gedaliah son of
41: 16 of Nethaniah after he had assassinated Gedaliah **son** *of* Ahikam:
41: 18 because Ishmael **son** *of* Nethaniah had killed Gedaliah son of
41: 18 because Ishmael son of Nethaniah had killed Gedaliah **son** *of*
42: 1 including Johanan **son** *of* Kareah and Jezaniah son of Hoshaiah,
42: 1 including Johanan son of Kareah and Jezaniah **son** *of* Hoshaiah,
42: 8 So he called together Johanan **son** *of* Kareah and all the army
43: 2 Azariah **son** *of* Hoshaiah and Johanan son of Kareah and all the
43: 2 Azariah son of Hoshaiah and Johanan **son** *of* Kareah and all the
43: 3 Baruch **son** *of* Neriah is inciting you against us to hand us over to
43: 4 So Johanan **son** *of* Kareah and all the army officers and all the
43: 5 Johanan **son** *of* Kareah and all the army officers led away all the
43: 6 of the imperial guard had left with Gedaliah **son** *of* Ahikam,
43: 6 the **son** *of* Shaphan, and Jeremiah the prophet and Baruch son of
43: 6 of Shaphan, and Jeremiah the prophet and Baruch **son** *of* Neriah.
45: 1 This is what Jeremiah the prophet told Baruch **son** *of* Neriah in the
45: 1 Neriah in the fourth year of Jehoiakim **son** *of* Josiah king of Judah,
46: 2 in the fourth year of Jehoiakim **son** *of* Josiah king of Judah:
47: 3 Fathers will not turn to help their **children**; their hands will hang
48: 45 the foreheads of Moab, the skulls of the **noisy boasters** [+8623].
48: 46 your **sons** are taken into exile and your daughters into captivity.
49: 1 Concerning the **Ammonites** [+6648]: This is what the LORD
49: 1 "Has Israel no **sons**? Has she no heirs? Why then has Molech taken
49: 2 sound the battle cry against Rabbah of the **Ammonites** [+6648];
49: 6 I will restore the fortunes of the **Ammonites** [+6648],"
49: 18 "so no one will live there; no **man** [+132] will dwell in it.
49: 28 "Arise, and attack Kedar and destroy the **people** *of* the East.
49: 33 No one will live there; no **man** [+132] will dwell in it."
50: 4 "the **people** *of* Israel and the people of Judah together will go in
50: 4 the **people** *of* Judah together will go in tears to seek the LORD
50: 33 "The **people** *of* Israel are oppressed, and the people of Judah as
50: 33 people of Israel are oppressed, and the **people** *of* Judah as well.
50: 40 "so no one will live there; no **man** [+132] will dwell in it.
51: 43 a land where no one lives, through which no **man** [+132] travels.
51: 59 message Jeremiah gave to the staff officer Seraiah **son** *of* Neriah,
51: 59 to the staff officer Seraiah son of Neriah, the **son** *of* Mahseiah,
52: 1 Zedekiah was twenty-one years **old** when he became king,
52: 10 There at Riblah the king of Babylon slaughtered the **sons** *of*
La 1: 16 My **children** are destitute because the enemy has prevailed."
3: 13 He pierced my heart with **arrows**[s] *from* his quiver.
3: 33 does not willingly bring affliction or grief to the **children** *of* men.
4: 2 How the precious **sons** *of* Zion, once worth their weight in gold,
Eze 1: 3 the **son** *of* Buzi, by the Kebar River in the land of the Babylonians.
2: 1 He said to me, "**Son** *of* man, stand up on your feet and I will speak
2: 3 "**Son** *of* man, I am sending you to the Israelites, to a rebellious
2: 3 "Son of man, I am sending you to the **Israelites** [+3776], to a
2: 4 The **people** to whom I am sending you are obstinate and stubborn.
2: 6 And you, **son** *of* man, do not be afraid of them or their words.
2: 8 you, **son** *of* man, listen to what I say to you. Do not rebel like that
3: 1 he said to me, "**Son** *of* man, eat what is before you, eat this scroll;
3: 3 Then he said to me, "**Son** *of* man, eat this scroll I am giving you
3: 4 "**Son** *of* man, go now to the house of Israel and speak my words to
3: 10 "**Son** *of* man, listen carefully and take to heart all the words I speak
3: 11 Go now to your **countrymen** [+6639] in exile and speak to them.
3: 17 "**Son** *of* man, I have made you a watchman for the house of Israel;
3: 25 And you, **son** *of* man, they will tie with ropes; you will be bound
4: 1 "Now, **son** *of* man, take a clay tablet, put it in front of you

Eze 4:13 "In this way the **people** *of* Israel will eat defiled food among the
4:16 "**Son** *of* man, I will cut off the supply of food in Jerusalem.
5:1 "Now, **son** *of* man, take a sharp sword and use it as a barber's
5:10 Therefore in your midst fathers will eat their **children**,
5:10 fathers will eat their children, and **children** will eat their fathers.
6:2 "**Son** *of* man, set your face against the mountains of Israel;
6:5 I will lay the dead bodies of the **Israelites** [+3776] in front of their
7:2 "**Son** *of* man, this is what the Sovereign LORD says to the land of
8:5 Then he said to me, "**Son** *of* man, look toward the north."
8:6 And he said to me, "**Son** *of* man, do you see what they are doing—
8:8 He said to me, "**Son** *of* man, now dig into the wall." So I dug into
8:11 of Israel, and Jaazaniah **son** *of* Shaphan was standing among them.
8:12 He said to me, "**Son** *of* man, have you seen what the elders of the
8:15 He said to me, "Do you see this, **son** *of* man? You will see things
8:17 He said to me, "Have you seen this, **son** *of* man? Is it a trivial
11:1 I saw among them Jaazaniah **son** *of* Azzur and Pelatiah son of
11:1 among them Jaazaniah son of Azzur and Pelatiah **son** *of* Benaiah,
11:2 The LORD said to me, "**Son** *of* man, these are the men who are
11:4 Therefore prophesy against them; prophesy, **son** *of* man."
11:13 Now as I was prophesying, Pelatiah **son** *of* Benaiah died. Then I
11:15 "**Son** *of* man, your brothers—your brothers who are your blood
12:2 "**Son** *of* man, you are living among a rebellious people. They have
12:3 "Therefore, **son** *of* man, pack your belongings for exile and in the
12:9 "**Son** *of* man, did not that rebellious house of Israel ask you,
12:18 "**Son** *of* man, tremble as you eat your food, and shudder in fear as
12:22 "**Son** *of* man, what is this proverb you have in the land of Israel:
12:27 "**Son** *of* man, the house of Israel is saying, 'The vision he sees is
13:2 "**Son** *of* man, prophesy against the prophets of Israel who are now
13:17 "Now, **son** *of* man, set your face against the daughters of your
14:3 "**Son** *of* man, these men have set up idols in their hearts and put
14:13 "**Son** *of* man, if a country sins against me by being unfaithful
14:16 men were in it, they could not save their own **sons** or daughters.
14:18 men were in it, they could not save their own **sons** or daughters.
14:20 and Job were in it, they could save neither **son** nor daughter.
14:22 some survivors—**sons** and daughters who will be brought out of it.
15:2 "**Son** *of* man, how is the wood of a vine better than that of a branch
16:2 "**Son** *of* man, confront Jerusalem with her detestable practices
16:20 " 'And you took your **sons** and daughters whom you bore to me
16:21 You slaughtered my **children** and sacrificed them to the idols.
16:26 You engaged in prostitution with the **Egyptians** [+5213],
16:28 You engaged in prostitution with the **Assyrians** [+855] too,
16:36 and because you gave them your **children's** blood,
16:45 of your mother, who despised her husband and her **children**;
16:45 of your sisters, who despised their husbands and their **children**.
17:2 "**Son** *of* man, set forth an allegory and tell the house of Israel a
18:2 fathers eat sour grapes, and the **children's** teeth are set on edge'?
18:4 For every living soul belongs to me, the father as well as the **son**—
18:10 "Suppose he has a violent **son**, who sheds blood or does any of
18:14 "But suppose this son has a **son** who sees all the sins his father
18:19 "Yet you ask, 'Why does the **son** not share the guilt of his father?'
18:19 Since the **son** has done what is just and right and has been careful
18:20 The **son** will not share the guilt of the father, nor will the father
18:20 the guilt of the father, nor will the father share the guilt of the **son**.
20:3 "**Son** *of* man, speak to the elders of Israel and say to them,
20:4 "Will you judge them? Will you judge them, **son** *of* man?
20:18 I said to their **children** in the desert, "Do not follow the statutes of
20:21 " 'But the **children** rebelled against me: They did not follow my
20:27 "Therefore, **son** *of* man, speak to the people of Israel and say to
20:31 When you offer your gifts—the sacrifice of your **sons** in the fire—
20:46 [21:2] "**Son** *of* man, set your face toward the south; preach
21:2 [21:7] "**Son** *of* man, set your face against Jerusalem and preach
21:6 [21:11] "Therefore groan, **son** *of* man! Groan before them with
21:9 [21:14] "**Son** *of* man, prophesy and say, 'This is what the Lord
21:10 [21:15] " 'Shall we rejoice in the scepter of my **son** ⌞Judah⌟?
21:12 [21:17] Cry out and wail, **son** *of* man, for it is against my people;
21:14 [21:19] **son** *of* man, prophesy and strike your hands together.
21:19 [21:24] "**Son** *of* man, mark out two roads for the sword of the
21:20 [21:25] to come against Rabbah of the **Ammonites** [+6648]
21:28 [21:33] "And you, **son** *of* man, prophesy and say, 'This is what the
21:28 [21:33] Sovereign LORD says about the **Ammonites** [+6648]
22:2 "**Son** *of* man, will you judge her? Will you judge this city of
22:18 "**Son** *of* man, the house of Israel has become dross to me;
22:24 "**Son** *of* man, say to the land, 'You are a land that has had no rain
23:2 "**Son** *of* man, there were two women, daughters of the same
23:4 They were mine and gave birth to **sons** and daughters. Oholah is
23:7 gave herself as a prostitute to all the elite of the **Assyrians** [+855]
23:9 her over to her lovers, the **Assyrians** [+855], for whom she lusted.
23:10 took away her **sons** and daughters and killed her with the sword.
23:12 She too lusted after the **Assyrians** [+855]—governors
23:15 all of them looked like **Babylonian** [+951] chariot officers,
23:17 Then the **Babylonians** [+951] came to her, to the bed of love,
23:23 the **Babylonians** [+951] and all the Chaldeans, the men of Pekod
23:23 and Shoa and Koa, and all the **Assyrians** [+855] with them,
23:25 They will take away your **sons** and daughters, and those of you
23:36 said to me: "**Son** *of* man, will you judge Oholah and Oholibah?
23:37 they even sacrificed their **children**, whom they bore to me,
23:39 On the very day they sacrificed their **children** to their idols,
23:47 they will kill their **sons** and daughters and burn down their houses.
24:2 "**Son** *of* man, record this date, this very date, because the king of
24:16 "**Son** *of* man, with one blow I am about to take away from you the
24:21 The **sons** and daughters you left behind will fall by the sword.
24:25 "And you, **son** *of* man, on the day I take away their stronghold,
24:25 their heart's desire, and their **sons** and daughters as well—
25:2 "**Son** *of* man, set your face against the Ammonites and prophesy
25:2 set your face against the **Ammonites** [+6648] and prophesy against
25:3 Say to **them**[s] [+6648], 'Hear the word of the Sovereign LORD.
25:4 therefore I am going to give you to the **people** *of* the East as a
25:5 for camels and **Ammon** [+6648] into a resting place for sheep.
25:10 I will give Moab along with the **Ammonites** [+6648] to the people
25:10 I will give Moab along with the Ammonites to the **people** *of* the
25:10 so that the **Ammonites** [+6648] will not be remembered among the
26:2 "**Son** *of* man, because Tyre has said of Jerusalem, 'Aha! The gate
27:2 "**Son** *of* man, take up a lament concerning Tyre.
27:11 **Men** *of* Arvad and Helech manned your walls on every side;
27:15 " 'The **men** *of* Rhodes traded with you, and many coastlands were
28:2 "**Son** *of* man, say to the ruler of Tyre, 'This is what the Sovereign
28:12 "**Son** *of* man, take up a lament concerning the king of Tyre
28:21 "**Son** *of* man, set your face against Sidon; prophesy against her
29:2 "**Son** *of* man, set your face against Pharaoh king of Egypt
29:18 "**Son** *of* man, Nebuchadnezzar king of Babylon drove his army in a
30:2 "**Son** *of* man, prophesy and say: 'This is what the Sovereign
30:5 the **people** *of* the covenant land will fall by the sword along with
30:21 "**Son** *of* man, I have broken the arm of Pharaoh king of Egypt.
31:2 "**Son** *of* man, say to Pharaoh king of Egypt and to his hordes:
31:14 destined for death, for the earth below, among **mortal men** [+132],
32:2 "**Son** *of* man, take up a lament concerning Pharaoh king of Egypt
32:18 "**Son** *of* man, wail for the hordes of Egypt and consign to the earth
33:2 "**Son** *of* man, speak to your countrymen and say to them: 'When I
33:2 "Son of man, speak to your **countrymen** [+6639] and say to them:
33:7 "**Son** *of* man, I have made you a watchman for the house of Israel;
33:10 "**Son** *of* man, say to the house of Israel, 'This is what you are
33:12 "Therefore, **son** *of* man, say to your countrymen,
33:12 "Therefore, son of man, say to your **countrymen** [+6639],
33:17 "Yet your **countrymen** [+6639] say, 'The way of the Lord is not
33:24 "**Son** *of* man, the people living in those ruins in the land of Israel
33:30 "As for you, **son** *of* man, your countrymen are talking together
33:30 your **countrymen** [+6639] are talking together about you by the
34:2 "**Son** *of* man, prophesy against the shepherds of Israel; prophesy
35:2 "**Son** *of* man, set your face against Mount Seir; prophesy against it
35:5 delivered the **Israelites** [+3776] over to the sword at the time of
36:1 "**Son** *of* man, prophesy to the mountains of Israel and say,
36:17 "**Son** *of* man, when the people of Israel were living in their own
37:3 He asked me, "**Son** *of* man, can these bones live?" I said,
37:9 prophesy, **son** *of* man, and say to it, 'This is what the Sovereign
37:11 "**Son** *of* man, these bones are the whole house of Israel. They say,
37:16 "**Son** *of* man, take a stick of wood and write on it, 'Belonging to
37:16 to Judah and the **Israelites** [+3776] associated with him.'
37:18 "When your **countrymen** [+6639] ask you, 'Won't you tell us what
37:21 I will take the **Israelites** [+3776] out of the nations where they
37:25 They and their **children** and their children's children will live there
37:25 their children and their **children's** children will live there forever,
37:25 their children and their children's **children** will live there forever,
38:2 "**Son** *of* man, set your face against Gog, of the land of Magog,
38:14 "Therefore, **son** *of* man, prophesy and say to Gog: 'This is what the
39:1 "**Son** *of* man, prophesy against Gog and say: 'This is what the
39:17 "**Son** *of* man, this is what the Sovereign LORD says: Call out to
40:4 "**Son** *of* man, look with your eyes and hear with your ears
40:46 These are the **sons** *of* Zadok, who are the only Levites who may
40:46 who are the only **Levites** [+4290] who may draw near to the
43:7 "**Son** *of* man, this is the place of my throne and the place for the
43:7 This is where I will live among the **Israelites** [+3776] forever.
43:10 "**Son** *of* man, describe the temple to the people of Israel, that they
43:18 he said to me, "**Son** *of* man, this is what the Sovereign LORD
43:19 You are to give a **young** bull as a sin offering to the priests,
43:23 you are to offer a **young** bull and a ram from the flock,
43:25 you are also to provide a **young** bull and a ram from the flock,
44:5 "**Son** *of* man, look carefully, listen closely and give attention to
44:7 you brought **foreigners** [+5797] uncircumcised in heart and flesh
44:9 No **foreigner** [+5797] uncircumcised in heart and flesh is to enter
44:9 not even the **foreigners** [+5797] who live among the Israelites.
44:9 not even the foreigners who live among the **Israelites** [+3776].
44:15 who are Levites and **descendants** *of* Zadok and who faithfully
44:15 of my sanctuary when the **Israelites** [+3776] went astray from me,
44:25 his father or mother, **son** or daughter, brother or unmarried sister,
45:18 In the first month on the first day you are to take a **young** bull
46:6 On the day of the New Moon he is to offer a **young** bull, six lambs
46:13 " 'Every day you are to provide a **year-old** [+9102] lamb without
46:16 If the prince makes a gift from his inheritance to one of his **sons**,

Eze 46:16 to one of his sons, it will also belong to his **descendants**;
46:17 to the prince. His inheritance belongs to his **sons** only; it is theirs.
46:18 He is to give his **sons** their inheritance out of his own property,
47: 6 He asked me, "**Son** *of* man, do you see this?" Then he led me back
47:22 for the aliens who have settled among you and who have **children**.
47:22 You are to consider them as native-born **Israelites** [+3776];
48:11 the **Zadokites** [+7401], who were faithful in serving me and did
48:11 did not go astray as the Levites did when the **Israelites** [+3776]
Da 1: 3 to bring in some of the **Israelites** [+3776] from the royal family
1: 6 Among these were **some**[s] from Judah: Daniel, Hananiah, Mishael
8:17 "**Son** *of* man," he said to me, "understand that the vision concerns
9: 1 In the first year of Darius **son** *of* Xerxes (a Mede by descent),
10:16 Then one who looked like a **man** [+132] touched my lips,
11:10 His **sons** will prepare for war and assemble a great army, which
11:14 The violent **men** among your own people will rebel in fulfillment
11:41 the leaders of **Ammon** [+6648] will be delivered from his hand.
12: 1 the great prince who protects your **people** [+6639], will arise.
Hos 1: 1 The word of the LORD that came to Hosea **son** *of* Beeri during
1: 1 and during the reign of Jeroboam **son** *of* Jehoash king of Israel:
1: 3 daughter of Diblaim, and she conceived and bore him a **son**.
1: 8 After she had weaned Lo-Ruhamah, Gomer had another **son**.
1:10 [2:1] "Yet the **Israelites** [+3776] will be like the sand on the
1:10 [2:1] not my people,' they will be called '**sons** *of* the living God.'
1:11 [2:2] The **people** *of* Judah and the people of Israel will be
1:11 [2:2] people of Judah and the **people** *of* Israel will be reunited,
2: 4 [2:6] I will not show my love to her **children**, because they are
2: 4 [2:6] to her children, because they are the **children** *of* adultery.
3: 1 Love her as the LORD loves the **Israelites** [+3776], though they
3: 4 For the **Israelites** [+3776] will live many days without king
3: 5 Afterward the **Israelites** [+3776] will return and seek the LORD
4: 1 Hear the word of the LORD, you **Israelites** [+3776],
4: 6 have ignored the law of your God, I also will ignore your **children**.
5: 7 unfaithful to the LORD; they give birth to illegitimate **children**.
9:12 Even if they rear **children**, I will bereave them of every one.
9:13 But Ephraim will bring out their **children** to the slayer."
10: 9 Did not war overtake the **evildoers** [+6594] in Gibeah?
10:14 when mothers were dashed to the ground with their **children**.
11: 1 Israel was a child, I loved him, and out of Egypt I called my **son**.
11:10 When he roars, his **children** will come trembling from the west.
13:13 in childbirth come to him, but he is a **child** without wisdom;
13:13 he does not come to the **opening of the womb** [+5402].
Joel 1: 1 The word of the LORD that came to Joel **son** *of* Pethuel.
1: 3 Tell it to your **children**, and let your children tell it to their
1: 3 it to your children, and let your **children** tell it to their children,
1: 3 it to your children, and let your children tell it to their **children**,
1: 3 tell it to their children, and their **children** to the next generation.
1:12 are dried up. Surely the joy of **mankind** [+132] is withered away.
2:23 Be glad, O **people** *of* Zion, rejoice in the LORD your God,
2:28 [3:1] Your **sons** and daughters will prophesy, your old men will
3: 6 [4:6] You sold the **people** *of* Judah and Jerusalem to the Greeks,
3: 6 [4:6] the people of Judah and **[RPH]** Jerusalem to the Greeks,
3: 6 [4:6] the people of Judah and Jerusalem to the **Greeks** [+3436],
3: 8 [4:8] I will sell your **sons** and daughters to the people of Judah,
3: 8 [4:8] I will sell your sons and daughters to the **people** *of* Judah,
3:16 [4:16] refuge for his people, a stronghold for the **people** *of* Israel.
3:19 [4:19] because of violence done to the **people** *of* Judah,
Am 1: 1 was king of Judah and Jeroboam **son** *of* Jehoash was king of Israel.
1:13 "For three sins of **Ammon** [+6648], even for four, I will not turn
2:11 I also raised up prophets from among your **sons** and Nazirites from
2:11 Is this not true, **people** *of* Israel?" declares the LORD.
3: 1 this word the LORD has spoken against you, O **people** *of* Israel—
3:12 or a piece of an ear, so will the **Israelites** [+3776] be saved,
4: 5 boast about them, you **Israelites** [+3776], for this is what you love
7:14 "I was neither a prophet nor a prophet's **son**, but I was a shepherd,
7:17 in the city, and your **sons** and daughters will fall by the sword.
9: 7 "Are not you **Israelites** [+3776] the same to me as the Cushites?"
9: 7 "Are not you Israelites the same to me as the **Cushites** [+3934]?"
Ob 1:12 nor rejoice over the **people** *of* Judah in the day of their destruction,
1:20 This company of **Israelite** [+3776] exiles who are in Canaan will
Jnh 1: 1 The word of the LORD came to Jonah **son** *of* Amittai:
4:10 make it grow. It sprang up **overnight** [+4326] and died overnight.
4:10 make it grow. It sprang up overnight and died **overnight** [+4326].
Mic 1:16 Shave your heads in mourning for the **children** *in whom* you
5: 3 [5:2] the rest of his brothers return to join the **Israelites** [+3776].
5: 7 [5:6] which do not wait for man or linger for **mankind** [+132].
6: 5 king of Moab counseled and what Balaam **son** *of* Beor answered.
6: 6 I come before him with burnt offerings, with calves a year **old**?
7: 6 For a **son** dishonors his father, a daughter rises up against her
Zep 1: 1 The word of the LORD that came to Zephaniah **son** *of* Cushi,
1: 1 the **son** *of* Gedaliah, the son of Amariah, the son of Hezekiah,
1: 1 the son of Gedaliah, the **son** *of* Amariah, the son of Hezekiah,
1: 1 the son of Gedaliah, the son of Amariah, the **son** *of* Hezekiah,
1: 1 during the reign of Josiah **son** *of* Amon king of Judah:
1: 8 and the king's **sons** and all those clad in foreign clothes.
2: 8 the insults of Moab and the taunts of the **Ammonites** [+6648],
2: 9 will become like Sodom, the **Ammonites** [+6648] like Gomorrah—
Hag 1: 1 came through the prophet Haggai to Zerubbabel **son** *of* Shealtiel,
1: 1 governor of Judah, and to Joshua **son** *of* Jehozadak, the high priest:
1:12 Then Zerubbabel **son** *of* Shealtiel, Joshua son of Jehozadak,
1:12 son of Shealtiel, Joshua **son** *of* Jehozadak, the high priest,
1:14 So the LORD stirred up the spirit of Zerubbabel **son** *of* Shealtiel,
1:14 of Judah, and the spirit of Joshua **son** *of* Jehozadak, the high priest,
2: 2 "Speak to Zerubbabel **son** *of* Shealtiel, governor of Judah,
2: 2 governor of Judah, to Joshua **son** *of* Jehozadak, the high priest,
2: 4 'Be strong, O Joshua **son** *of* Jehozadak, the high priest. Be strong,
2:23 'I will take you, my servant Zerubbabel **son** *of* Shealtiel,'
Zec 1: 1 the word of the LORD came to the prophet Zechariah **son** *of*
1: 1 came to the prophet Zechariah son of Berekiah, the **son** *of* Iddo:
1: 7 the word of the LORD came to the prophet Zechariah **son** *of*
1: 7 came to the prophet Zechariah son of Berekiah, the **son** *of* Iddo.
4:14 "These are the two *who are* **anointed** [+2021+3658] to serve the
6:10 Go the same day to the house of Josiah **son** *of* Zephaniah.
6:11 and set it on the head of the high priest, Joshua **son** *of* Jehozadak.
6:14 Hen **son** *of* Zephaniah as a memorial in the temple of the LORD.
9: 9 gentle and riding on a donkey, on a colt, the **foal** *of* a donkey.
9:13 I will rouse your **sons**, O Zion, against your sons, O Greece,
9:13 I will rouse your sons, O Zion, against your **sons**, O Greece,
10: 7 Their **children** will see it and be joyful; their hearts will rejoice in
10: 9 They and their **children** will survive, and they will return.
Mal 1: 6 "A **son** honors his father, and a servant his master. If I am a father,
3: 3 he will purify the **Levites** [+4290] and refine them like gold
3: 6 do not change. So you, O **descendants** *of* Jacob, are not destroyed.
3:17 just as in compassion a man spares his **son** who serves him.
4: 6 [3:24] He will turn the hearts of the fathers to their **children**,
4: 6 [3:24] and the hearts of the **children** to their fathers;

1202 בֵּן[2] ***bēn***[2], n.pr.m. Not used in NIV/BHS [√ 1201]

1203 בֶּן־אֲבִינָדָב ***ben-'abînādāb***, n.pr.m. [1] [√ 1201 + 3 + 5605]

Ben-Abinadab [1]

1Ki 4:11 **Ben-Abinadab**—in Naphoth Dor (he was married to Taphath

1204 בֶּן־אוֹנִי ***ben-'ônî***, n.pr.m. [1] [√ 1201 + 224]

Ben-Oni [1]

Ge 35:18 her last—for she was dying—she named her son **Ben-Oni**.

1205 בֶּן־גֶּבֶר ***ben-geber***, n.pr.m. [1] [√ 1201 + 1505]

Ben-Geber [1]

1Ki 4:13 **Ben-Geber**—in Ramoth Gilead (the settlements of Jair son of

1206 בֶּן־דֶּקֶר ***ben-deqer***, n.pr.[loc.?]. [1] [√ 1201 + 1991]

Ben-Deker [1]

1Ki 4: 9 **Ben-Deker**—in Makaz, Shaalbim, Beth Shemesh and Elon

1207 בֶּן־הֲדַד ***ben-hadad***, n.pr.m. [25] [√ 1201 + 2060]

Ben-Hadad [24], Ben-Hadad's [1]

1Ki 15:18 it to his officials and sent them to **Ben-Hadad** son of Tabrimmon,
15:20 **Ben-Hadad** agreed with King Asa and sent the commanders of his
20: 1 Now **Ben-Hadad** king of Aram mustered his entire army.
20: 2 [20:3] king of Israel, saying, "This is what **Ben-Hadad** says:
20: 5 messengers came again and said, "This is what **Ben-Hadad** says:
20: 9 So he replied to **Ben-Hadad's** messengers, "Tell my lord the king,
20:10 **Ben-Hadad** sent another message to Ahab: "May the gods deal
20:16 They set out at noon while **Ben-Hadad** and the 32 kings allied
20:17 Now **Ben-Hadad** had dispatched scouts, who reported, "Men are
20:20 **Ben-Hadad** king of Aram escaped on horseback with some of his
20:26 The next spring **Ben-Hadad** mustered the Arameans and went up
20:30 And **Ben-Hadad** fled to the city and hid in an inner room.
20:32 to the king of Israel and said, "Your servant **Ben-Hadad** says:
20:33 "Yes, your brother **Ben-Hadad**!" they said. "Go and get him,"
20:33 When **Ben-Hadad** came out, Ahab had him come up into his
2Ki 6:24 **Ben-Hadad** king of Aram mobilized his entire army and marched
8: 7 Elisha went to Damascus, and **Ben-Hadad** king of Aram was ill.
8: 9 and said, "Your son **Ben-Hadad** king of Aram has sent me to ask,
13: 3 under the power of Hazael king of Aram and **Ben-Hadad** his son.
13:24 king of Aram died, and **Ben-Hadad** his son succeeded him as king.
13:25 Jehoash son of Jehoahaz recaptured from **Ben-Hadad** son of
2Ch 16: 2 and of his own palace and sent it to **Ben-Hadad** king of Aram,
16: 4 **Ben-Hadad** agreed with King Asa and sent the commanders of his
Jer 49:27 walls of Damascus; it will consume the fortresses of **Ben-Hadad**."
Am 1: 4 house of Hazael that will consume the fortresses of **Ben-Hadad**.

1208 בֶּן־הִנֹּם *ben-hinnōm*, n.pr.loc. [10] [√ 1201 + 2183]

Ben Hinnom [10]

Jos 15: 8 it ran up the Valley of **Ben Hinnom** along the southern slope of the
18: 16 down to the foot of the hill facing the Valley of **Ben Hinnom**,
2Ki 23: 10 which was in the Valley of **Ben** [K 1201] **Hinnom**,
2Ch 28: 3 He burned sacrifices in the Valley of **Ben Hinnom** and sacrificed
33: 6 He sacrificed his sons in the fire in the Valley of **Ben Hinnom**,
Jer 7: 31 places of Topheth in the Valley of **Ben Hinnom** to burn their sons
7: 32 will no longer call it Topheth or the Valley of **Ben Hinnom**,
19: 2 go out to the Valley of **Ben Hinnom**, near the entrance of the
19: 6 no longer call this place Topheth or the Valley of **Ben Hinnom**,
32: 35 They built high places for Baal in the Valley of **Ben Hinnom** to

1209 בֶּן־זוֹחֵת *ben-zôḥēt*, n.pr.m. [1] [√ 1201 + 2311]

Ben-Zoheth [1]

1Ch 4: 20 and Tilon. The descendants of Ishi: Zoheth and **Ben-Zoheth**.

1210 בֶּן־חוּר *ben-ḥûr*, n.pr.m. [1] [√ 1201 + 2581]

Ben-Hur [1]

1Ki 4: 8 These are their names: **Ben-Hur**—in the hill country of Ephraim;

1211 בֶּן־חַיִל *ben-ḥayil*, n.pr.m. [1] [√ 1201 + 2657]

Ben-Hail [1]

2Ch 17: 7 In the third year of his reign he sent his officials **Ben-Hail**,

1212 בֶּן־חָנָן *ben-ḥānān*, n.pr.m. [1] [√ 1201 + 2860]

Ben-Hanan [1]

1Ch 4: 20 The sons of Shimon: Amnon, Rinnah, **Ben-Hanan** and Tilon.

1213 בֶּן־חֶסֶד *ben-ḥesed*, n.pr.m. [1] [√ 1201 + 2876]

Ben-Hesed [1]

1Ki 4: 10 **Ben-Hesed**—in Arubboth (Socoh and all the land of Hepher were

1214 בֶּן־עַמִּי *ben-'ammî*, n.pr.m. [1] [√ 1201 + 6639 + 3276]

Ben-Ammi [1]

Ge 19: 38 younger daughter also had a son, and she named him **Ben-Ammi**;

1215 בָּנָה *bānâ*, v. [376] [→ 1218, 1220, 1221, 1224, 1230, 4445, 4447, 9322; cf. 1201, 1426; Ar 10111; *also used with compound proper names*]

built [114], build [96], building [24], rebuilt [23], rebuild [14], be rebuilt [12], built up [12], builders [9], build up [7], builds [6], *untranslated* [4], be built [4], fortified [4], rebuilding [3], been built [2], been rebuilt [2], build a family [2], erect [2], indeed built [+1215] [2], is built [2], made [2], rebuilt [+906+2256+8740] [2], set up [2], using[s] [2], be established [1], be restored [1], besieged [+6584] [1], builds up [1], constructed [1], construction [1], craftsmen [1], did work [1], done[s] this [+3378+4200+4640] [1], erected [1], establish [1], form [1], lined [1], make firm [1], newly built [1], partitioned off [1], prosper [1], rebuild [+2256+8740] [1], repairing [1], restored [1], stands firm [1], was built [1], were used [1], worked [1]

Ge 2: 22 [A] the LORD God **made** a woman *from* the rib he had taken
4: 17 [A] Cain was then **building** a city, and he named it after his son
8: 20 [A] Noah **built** an altar to the LORD and, taking some of all the
10: 11 [A] to Assyria, where *he* **built** Nineveh, Rehoboth Ir, Calah
11: 4 [A] they said, "Come, *let us* **build** ourselves a city, with a tower
11: 5 [A] to see the city and the tower that the men *were* **building**.
11: 8 [A] there over all the earth, and they stopped **building** the city.
12: 7 [A] So *he* **built** an altar there to the LORD, who had appeared
12: 8 [A] There *he* **built** an altar to the LORD and called on the name
13: 18 [A] of Mamre at Hebron, where *he* **built** an altar to the LORD.
16: 2 [C] my maidservant; perhaps *I can* **build a family** through her."
22: 9 [A] Abraham **built** an altar there and arranged the wood on it.
26: 25 [A] Isaac **built** an altar there and called on the name of the
30: 3 [C] for me and that through her I too *can* **build a family**."
33: 17 [A] where *he* **built** a place for himself and made shelters for his
35: 7 [A] There *he* **built** an altar, and he called the place El Bethel,
Ex 1: 11 [A] *they* **built** Pithom and Rameses as store cities for Pharaoh.
17: 15 [A] Moses **built** an altar and called it The LORD is my Banner.
20: 25 [A] an altar of stones for me, *do* not **build** it *with* dressed stones,
24: 4 [A] next morning and **built** an altar at the foot of the mountain
32: 5 [A] saw this, *he* **built** an altar in front of the calf and announced,
Nu 13: 22 [C] (Hebron *had* **been built** seven years before Zoan in Egypt.)
21: 27 [C] "Come to Heshbon and *let it* **be rebuilt**; let Sihon's city be
23: 1 [A] Balaam said, "**Build** me seven altars here, and prepare seven
23: 14 [A] there *he* **built** seven altars and offered a bull and a ram on
23: 29 [A] Balaam said, "**Build** me seven altars here, and prepare seven
32: 16 [A] "*We would like to* **build** pens here for our livestock
32: 24 [A] **Build** cities for your women and children, and pens for your
32: 34 [A] The Gadites **built up** Dibon, Ataroth, Aroer,
32: 37 [A] the Reubenites **rebuilt** Heshbon, Elealeh and Kiriathaim,
32: 38 [A] and Sibmah. They gave names to the cities *they* **rebuilt**.
Dt 6: 10 [A] a land with large, flourishing cities *you did* not **build**,
8: 12 [A] are satisfied, when *you* **build** fine houses and settle down,
13: 16 [13:17] [C] It is to remain a ruin forever, never *to* **be rebuilt**.
20: 5 [A] "*Has* anyone **built** a new house and not dedicated it? Let him
20: 20 [A] *use* them *to* **build** siege works until the city at war with you
22: 8 [A] When *you* **build** a new house, make a parapet around your
25: 9 [A] "This is what is done to the man who *will* not **build up** his
27: 5 [A] **Build** there an altar to the LORD your God, an altar of
27: 6 [A] **Build** the altar of the LORD your God *with* fieldstones and
28: 30 [A] ravish her. *You will* **build** a house, but you will not live in it.
Jos 6: 26 [A] the LORD is the man who undertakes *to* **rebuild** this city,
8: 30 [A] Joshua **built** on Mount Ebal an altar to the LORD, the God
19: 50 [A] of Ephraim. And *he* **built up** the town and settled there.
22: 10 [A] the half-tribe of Manasseh **built** an imposing altar there by
22: 11 [A] when the Israelites heard that *they had* **built** the altar on the
22: 16 [A] and **build** yourselves an altar in rebellion against him now?
22: 19 [A] the LORD or against us by **building** an altar for yourselves,
22: 23 [A] If we *have* **built** our own altar to turn away from the LORD
22: 26 [A] "That is why we said, 'Let us get ready and **build** an altar—
22: 29 [A] turn away from him today by **building** an altar for burnt
24: 13 [A] a land on which you did not toil and cities *you did* not **build**;
Jdg 1: 26 [A] where *he* **built** a city and called it Luz, which is its name to
6: 24 [A] So Gideon **built** an altar to the LORD there and called it
6: 26 [A] **build** a proper kind of altar to the LORD your God on the
6: 28 [B] and the second bull sacrificed on the **newly built** altar!
18: 28 [A] Beth Rehob. The Danites **rebuilt** the city and settled there.
21: 4 [A] Early the next day the people **built** an altar and presented
21: 23 [A] to their inheritance and **rebuilt** the towns and settled in them.
Ru 4: 11 [A] and Leah, who together **built up** the house of Israel.
1Sa 2: 35 [A] *I will* firmly **establish** his house, and he will minister before
7: 17 [A] also judged Israel. And *he* **built** an altar there to the LORD.
14: 35 [A] Saul **built** an altar to the LORD; it was the first time he had
14: 35 [A] Then Saul built an altar to the LORD; it was the first time *he had* **done**[s] [+3378+4200+4640] **this**.
2Sa 5: 9 [A] He **built up** the area around it, from the supporting terraces
5: 11 [A] and stonemasons, and *they* **built** a palace for David.
7: 5 [A] Are you the one *to* **build** me a house to dwell in?
7: 7 [A] "Why *have you* not **built** me a house of cedar?"'
7: 13 [A] He is the one *who will* **build** a house for my Name, and I
7: 27 [A] this to your servant, saying, '*I will* **build** a house for you.'
24: 21 [A] David answered, "so I *can* **build** an altar to the LORD,
24: 25 [A] David **built** an altar to the LORD there and sacrificed burnt
1Ki 2: 36 [A] to him, "**Build** yourself a house in Jerusalem and live there,
3: 1 [A] **building** his palace and the temple of the LORD, and
3: 2 [C] because a temple *had* not yet **been built** for the Name of the
5: 3 [5:17] [A] he could not **build** a temple for the Name of the
5: 5 [5:19] [A] **build** a temple for the Name of the LORD my God,
5: 5 [5:19] [A] in your place *will* **build** the temple for my Name.'
5: 18 [5:32] [A] The **craftsmen** *of* Solomon and Hiram and the men
5: 18 [5:32] [A] **[RPH]** Hiram and the men of Gebal cut
5: 18 [5:32] [A] the timber and stone for the **building** *of* the temple.
6: 1 [A] second month, *he began to* **build** the temple of the LORD.
6: 2 [A] The temple that King Solomon **built** for the LORD was
6: 5 [A] and inner sanctuary *he* **built** a structure around the building,
6: 7 [C] In **building** the temple, only blocks dressed at the quarry
6: 7 [C] only blocks dressed at the quarry **were used**, and no hammer,
6: 7 [C] tool was heard at the temple site while it **was** *being* **built**.
6: 9 [A] So *he* **built** the temple and completed it, roofing it with
6: 10 [A] *he* **built** the side rooms all along the temple. The height of
6: 12 [A] "As for this temple you *are* **building**, if you follow my
6: 14 [A] So Solomon **built** the temple and completed it.
6: 15 [A] *He* **lined** its interior walls with cedar boards, paneling them
6: 16 [A] *He* **partitioned off** twenty cubits at the rear of the temple
6: 16 [A] floor to ceiling *to* **form** within the temple an inner sanctuary,
6: 36 [A] *he* **built** the inner courtyard of three courses of dressed stone
6: 38 [A] to its specifications. *He had spent* seven years **building** it.
7: 1 [A] however, to complete the **construction** *of* his palace.
7: 2 [A] *He* **built** the Palace of the Forest of Lebanon a hundred
8: 13 [A] *I have* **indeed built** [+1215] a magnificent temple for you,
8: 13 [A] *I have* **indeed built** [+1215] a magnificent temple for you,
8: 16 [A] of Israel to *have* a temple **built** for my Name to be there,
8: 17 [A] "My father David had it in his heart to **build** a temple for the
8: 18 [A] 'Because it was in your heart to **build** a temple for my Name,
8: 19 [A] you *are* not *the one to* **build** the temple, but your son,
8: 19 [A] he *is the one who will* **build** the temple for my Name.'
8: 20 [A] *I have* **built** the temple for the Name of the LORD, the God
8: 27 [A] cannot contain you. How much less this temple *I have* **built**!
8: 43 [A] and may know that this house *I have* **built** bears your Name.
8: 44 [A] you have chosen and the temple *I have* **built** for your Name,

1Ki 8:48 [A] you have chosen and the temple *I have* **built** for your Name;
9: 1 [A] **building** the temple of the LORD and the royal palace, and
9: 3 [A] I have consecrated this temple, which *you have* **built**,
9:10 [A] **built** these two buildings—the temple of the LORD and
9:15 [A] King Solomon conscripted to **build** the LORD's temple,
9:17 [A] Solomon **rebuilt** Gezer.) He built up Lower Beth Horon,
9:19 [A] whatever he desired to **build** in Jerusalem, in Lebanon
9:24 [A] the City of David to the palace Solomon *had* **built** for her,
9:24 [A] had built for her, *he* **constructed** the supporting terraces.
9:25 [A] fellowship offerings on the altar *he had* **built** for the
10: 4 [A] saw all the wisdom of Solomon and the palace *he had* **built**,
11: 7 [A] Solomon **built** a high place for Chemosh the detestable god
11:27 [A] Solomon *had* **built** the supporting terraces and had filled in
11:38 [A] *I will* **build** you a dynasty as enduring as the one I built for
11:38 [A] I will build you a dynasty as enduring as the one *I* **built** for
12:25 [A] Jeroboam **fortified** Shechem in the hill country of Ephraim
12:25 [A] and lived there. From there he went out and **built up** Peniel.
14:23 [A] They also **set up** for themselves high places, sacred stones
15:17 [A] and **fortified** Ramah to prevent anyone from leaving
15:21 [A] he stopped **building** Ramah and withdrew to Tirzah.
15:22 [A] Ramah the stones and timber Baasha *had been* **using**[s] there.
15:22 [A] With them King Asa **built up** Geba in Benjamin, and also
15:23 [A] all his achievements, all he did and the cities *he* **built**,
16:24 [A] Shemer for two talents of silver and **built** a city *on* the hill,
16:24 [A] a city on the hill, calling **[RPH]** it Samaria, after Shemer,
16:32 [A] He set up an altar for Baal in the temple of Baal that *he* **built**
16:34 [A] In Ahab's time, Hiel of Bethel **rebuilt** Jericho. He laid its
18:32 [A] *With* the stones *he* **built** an altar in the name of the LORD,
22:39 [A] including all he did, the palace *he* **built** and inlaid with ivory,
22:39 [A] he built and inlaid with ivory, and the cities *he* **fortified**,
2Ki 12:11 [12:12] [A] temple of the LORD—the carpenters and **builders**,
14:22 [A] He was the *one who* **rebuilt** Elath and restored it to Judah
15:35 [A] Jotham **rebuilt** the Upper Gate of the temple of the LORD.
16:11 [A] So Uriah the priest **built** an altar in accordance with all the
16:18 [A] He took away the Sabbath canopy that *had been* **built** at the
17: 9 [A] From watchtower to fortified city *they* **built** themselves high
21: 3 [A] *He* **rebuilt** [+906+2256+8740] the high places his father Hezekiah had destroyed; he also erected altars to Baal and made an
21: 4 [A] *He* **built** altars in the temple of the LORD, of which the
21: 5 [A] temple of the LORD, *he* **built** altars to all the starry hosts.
22: 6 [A] the carpenters, the **builders** and the masons. Also have them
23:13 [A] the ones Solomon king of Israel *had* **built** for Ashtoreth the
25: 1 [A] encamped outside the city and **built** siege works all around it.
1Ch 6:10 [5:36] [A] as priest in the temple Solomon **built** in Jerusalem),
6:32 [6:17] [A] until Solomon **built** the temple of the LORD in
7:24 [A] *who* **built** Lower and Upper Beth Horon as well as Uzzen
8:12 [A] Shemed (who **built** Ono and Lod with its surrounding
11: 8 [A] *He* **built up** the city around it, from the supporting terraces
14: 1 [A] stonemasons and carpenters to **build** a palace for him.
17: 4 [A] You are not the one *to* **build** me a house to dwell in.
17: 6 [A] "Why *have you* not **built** me a house of cedar?" '
17:10 [A] " 'I declare to you that the LORD *will* **build** a house for
17:12 [A] He *is the one who will* **build** a house for me, and I will
17:25 [A] have revealed to your servant that you *will* **build** a house for
21:22 [A] of your threshing floor so *I can* **build** an altar to the LORD,
21:26 [A] David **built** an altar to the LORD there and sacrificed burnt
22: 2 [A] to prepare dressed stone for **building** the house of God.
22: 5 [A] the house to *be* **built** for the LORD should be of great
22: 6 [A] and charged him to **build** a house for the LORD,
22: 7 [A] I had it in my heart to **build** a house for the Name of the
22: 8 [A] *You are* not *to* **build** a house for my Name, because you
22:10 [A] He *is the one who will* **build** a house for my Name. He will
22:11 [A] have success and **build** the house of the LORD your God,
22:19 [A] Begin *to* **build** the sanctuary of the LORD God, so that you
22:19 [C] the temple that *will* **be built** for the Name of the LORD."
28: 2 [A] I had it in my heart to **build** a house as a place of rest for the
28: 2 [A] for the footstool of our God, and I made plans to **build** it.
28: 3 [A] God said to me, '*You are* not *to* **build** a house for my Name,
28: 6 [A] 'Solomon your son is the one *who will* **build** my house
28:10 [A] for the LORD has chosen you to **build** a temple as a
29:16 [A] provided for **building** you a temple for your Holy Name,
29:19 [A] to do everything to **build** the palatial structure for which I
2Ch 2: 1 [1:18] [A] Solomon gave orders to **build** a temple for the Name
2: 3 [2:2] [A] when you sent him cedar to **build** a palace to live in.
2: 4 [2:3] [A] Now I *am about to* **build** a temple for the Name of
2: 5 [2:4] [A] "The temple I *am going to* **build** will be great,
2: 6 [2:5] [A] who is able to **build** a temple for him,
2: 6 [2:5] [A] Who then am I *to* **build** a temple for him, except as a
2: 9 [2:8] [A] because the temple I **build** must be large
2:12 [2:11] [A] who *will* **build** a temple for the LORD and a palace
3: 1 [A] Solomon began to **build** the temple of the LORD in
3: 2 [A] He began **building** on the second day of the second month in
3: 3 [A] The foundation Solomon laid for **building** the temple of God
6: 2 [A] I *have* **built** a magnificent temple for you, a place for you to
6: 5 [A] of Israel to *have* a temple **built** for my Name to be there,
6: 7 [A] "My father David had it in his heart to **build** a temple for the
6: 8 [A] 'Because it was in your heart to **build** a temple for my Name,
6: 9 [A] you are not *the one to* **build** the temple, but your son,
6: 9 [A] he is *the one who will* **build** the temple for my Name.'
6:10 [A] *I have* **built** the temple for the Name of the LORD, the God
6:18 [A] cannot contain you. How much less this temple *I have* **built**!
6:33 [A] and may know that this house *I have* **built** bears your Name.
6:34 [A] you have chosen and the temple *I have* **built** for your Name,
6:38 [A] and toward the temple *I have* **built** for your Name;
8: 1 [A] during which Solomon **built** the temple of the LORD and
8: 2 [A] Solomon **rebuilt** the villages that Hiram had given him,
8: 4 [A] *He* also **built up** Tadmor in the desert and all the store cities
8: 4 [A] in the desert and all the store cities *he had* **built** in Hamath.
8: 5 [A] *He* **rebuilt** Upper Beth Horon and Lower Beth Horon as
8: 6 [A] whatever he desired to **build** in Jerusalem, in Lebanon
8:11 [A] up from the City of David to the palace *he had* **built** for her,
8:12 [A] On the altar of the LORD that *he had* **built** in front of the
9: 3 [A] the wisdom of Solomon, as well as the palace *he had* **built**,
11: 5 [A] lived in Jerusalem and **built up** towns for defense in Judah:
11: 6 [A] **[RPH]** Bethlehem, Etam, Tekoa,
14: 6 [14:5] [A] *He* **built up** the fortified cities of Judah,
14: 7 [14:6] [A] "*Let us* **build up** these towns," he said to Judah,
14: 7 [14:6] [A] us rest on every side." So *they* **built** and prospered.
16: 1 [A] **fortified** Ramah to prevent anyone from leaving or entering
16: 5 [A] he stopped **building** Ramah and abandoned his work.
16: 6 [A] from Ramah the stones and timber Baasha *had been* **using**[s].
16: 6 [A] had been using. With them *he* **built up** Geba and Mizpah.
17:12 [A] and more powerful; *he* **built** forts and store cities in Judah
20: 8 [A] lived in it and *have* **built** in it a sanctuary for your Name,
26: 2 [A] He was the one *who* **rebuilt** Elath and restored it to Judah
26: 6 [A] *He* then **rebuilt** towns near Ashdod and elsewhere among the
26: 9 [A] Uzziah **built** towers in Jerusalem at the Corner Gate, at the
26:10 [A] *He* also **built** towers in the desert and dug many cisterns,
27: 3 [A] Jotham **rebuilt** the Upper Gate of the temple of the LORD
27: 3 [A] and **did** extensive **work** on the wall at the hill of Ophel.
27: 4 [A] *He* **built** towns in the Judean hills and forts and towers in the
27: 4 [A] and forts and towers in the wooded areas. **[RPH]**
32: 5 [A] he worked hard **repairing** all the broken sections of the wall
33: 3 [A] *He* **rebuilt** [+906+2256+8740] the high places his father
33: 4 [A] *He* **built** altars in the temple of the LORD, of which the
33: 5 [A] temple of the LORD, *he* **built** altars to all the starry hosts.
33:14 [A] Afterward *he* **rebuilt** the outer wall of the City of David,
33:15 [A] as well as all the altars *he had* **built** on the temple hill and in
33:16 [A] *he* **restored** [K 3922] the altar of the LORD and sacrificed
33:19 [A] the sites where *he* **built** high places and set up Asherah poles
34:11 [A] to the carpenters and **builders** to purchase dressed stone,
35: 3 [A] in the temple that Solomon son of David king of Israel **built**.
36:23 [A] he has appointed me to **build** a temple for him at Jerusalem
Ezr 1: 2 [A] he has appointed me to **build** a temple for him at Jerusalem
1: 3 [A] to Jerusalem in Judah and **build** the temple of the LORD,
1: 5 [A] to go up and **build** the house of the LORD in Jerusalem.
3: 2 [A] his associates began *to* **build** the altar of the God of Israel to
3:10 [A] When the **builders** laid the foundation of the temple of the
4: 1 [A] Benjamin heard that the exiles *were* **building** a temple for
4: 2 [A] and said, "*Let us* help you **build** because, like you,
4: 3 [A] "You have no part with us in **building** a temple to our God.
4: 3 [A] We alone *will* **build** it for the LORD, the God of Israel,
4: 4 [A] the people of Judah and make them afraid to *go on* **building**.
Ne 2: 5 [A] Judah where my fathers are buried so that *I can* **rebuild** it."
2:17 [A] Come, *let us* **rebuild** the wall of Jerusalem, and we will no
2:18 [A] They replied, "Let us start **rebuilding**." So they began this
2:20 [A] We his servants will start **rebuilding**, but as for you,
3: 1 [A] his fellow priests went to work and **rebuilt** the Sheep Gate.
3: 2 [A] The men of Jericho **built** the adjoining section, and Zaccur
3: 2 [A] adjoining section, and Zaccur son of Imri **built** next to them.
3: 3 [A] The Fish Gate *was* **rebuilt** *by* the sons of Hassenaah.
3:13 [A] They **rebuilt** it and put its doors and bolts and bars in place.
3:14 [A] He **rebuilt** it and put its doors and bolts and bars in place.
3:15 [A] He **rebuilt** it, roofing it over and putting its doors and bolts
4: 1 [3:33] [A] When Sanballat heard that we *were* **rebuilding** the
4: 3 [3:35] [A] who was at his side, said, "What they *are* **building**—
4: 5 [3:37] [A] they have thrown insults in the face of the **builders**.
4: 6 [3:38] [A] So *we* **rebuilt** the wall till all of it reached half its
4:10 [4:4] [A] so much rubble that we cannot **rebuild** the wall."
4:17 [4:11] [A] who *were* **building** the wall. Those who carried
4:18 [4:12] [A] each of the **builders** wore his sword at his side as he
4:18 [4:12] [A] the builders wore his sword at his side as *he* **worked**.
6: 1 [A] and the rest of our enemies that *I had* **rebuilt** the wall
6: 6 [A] plotting to revolt, and therefore you *are* **building** the wall.
7: 1 [C] After the wall *had* **been rebuilt** and I had set the doors in
7: 4 [B] few people in it, and the houses *had* not yet **been rebuilt**.
12:29 [A] for the singers *had* **built** villages for themselves around
Job 3:14 [A] the earth, who **built** for themselves places now lying in ruins,

Job 12:14 [C] What he tears down cannot **be rebuilt**; the man he imprisons
20:19 [A] left them destitute; he has seized houses *he did* not **build**.
22:23 [C] If you return to the Almighty, *you will* **be restored**: If you
27:18 [A] The house *he* **builds** is like a moth's cocoon, like a hut made
Ps 28:5 [A] he will tear them down and never **build** them **up** *again*.
51:18 [51:20] [A] Zion prosper; **build up** the walls of Jerusalem.
69:35 [69:36] [A] for God will save Zion and **rebuild** the cities of
78:69 [A] *He* **built** his sanctuary like the heights, like the earth that he
89:2 [89:3] [C] I will declare that your love **stands firm** forever,
89:4 [89:5] [A] **make** your throne **firm** through all generations.' "
102:16 [102:17] [A] For the LORD *will* **rebuild** Zion and appear in
118:22 [A] The stone the **builders** rejected has become the capstone;
122:3 [B] Jerusalem **is built** like a city that is closely compacted
127:1 [A] Unless the LORD **builds** the house, its builders labor in
127:1 [A] the LORD builds the house, its **builders** labor in vain.
147:2 [A] The LORD **builds up** Jerusalem; he gathers the exiles of
Pr 9:1 [A] Wisdom *has* **built** her house; she has hewn out its seven
14:1 [A] The wise woman **builds** her house, but with her own hands
24:3 [C] By wisdom a house **is built**, and through understanding it is
24:27 [A] and get your fields ready; after that, **build** your house.
Ecc 2:4 [A] *I* **built** houses for myself and planted vineyards.
3:3 [A] and a time to heal, a time to tear down and a time to **build**,
9:14 [A] against it, surrounded it and **built** huge siegeworks against it.
SS 4:4 [B] Your neck is like the tower of David, **built** with elegance;
8:9 [C] If she is a wall, *we will* **build** towers of silver on her. If she is
Isa 5:2 [A] *He* **built** a watchtower in it and cut out a winepress as well.
9:10 [9:9] [A] fallen down, but *we will* **rebuild** *with* dressed stone;
25:2 [C] stronghold a city no more; *it will* never **be rebuilt**.
44:26 [C] '*They shall* **be built**,' and of their ruins, 'I will restore them,'
44:28 [C] will say of Jerusalem, "*Let it* **be rebuilt**," and of the temple,
45:13 [A] He *will* **rebuild** my city and set my exiles free, but not for a
58:12 [A] *Your people will* **rebuild** the ancient ruins and will raise up
60:10 [A] "Foreigners *will* **rebuild** your walls, and their kings will
61:4 [A] *They will* **rebuild** the ancient ruins and restore the places
65:21 [A] *They will* **build** houses and dwell in them; they will plant
65:22 [A] No longer *will they* **build** houses and others live in them,
66:1 [A] is my footstool. Where is the house *you will* **build** for me?
Jer 1:10 [A] tear down, to destroy and overthrow, to **build** and to plant."
7:31 [A] *They have* **built** the high places of Topheth in the Valley of
12:16 [C] by Baal—then *they will* **be established** among my people.
18:9 [A] that a nation or kingdom *is to be* **built up** and planted,
19:5 [A] *They have* **built** the high places of Baal to burn their sons in
22:13 [A] "Woe to *him who* **builds** his palace by unrighteousness, his
22:14 [A] '*I will* **build** myself a great palace with spacious upper
24:6 [A] *I will* **build** them **up** and not tear them down; I will plant
29:5 [A] "**Build** houses and settle down; plant gardens and eat what
29:28 [A] Therefore **build** houses and settle down; plant gardens
30:18 [C] the city *will* **be rebuilt** on her ruins, and the palace will stand
31:4 [A] *I will* **build** you **up** again and you will be rebuilt, O Virgin
31:4 [C] I will build you up again and *you will* **be rebuilt**, O Virgin
31:28 [A] so I will watch over them to **build** and to plant,"
31:38 [C] "when this city *will* **be rebuilt** for me from the Tower of
32:31 [A] From the day it *was* **built** until now, this city has so aroused
32:35 [A] *They* **built** high places for Baal in the Valley of Ben Hinnom
33:7 [A] from captivity and *will* **rebuild** them as they were before.
35:7 [A] Also *you must* never **build** houses, sow seed or plant
35:9 [A] or **built** houses to live in or had vineyards, fields or crops.
42:10 [A] stay in this land, *I will* **build** you **up** and not tear you down;
45:4 [A] I will overthrow what *I have* **built** and uproot what I have
52:4 [A] camped outside the city and **built** siege works all around it.
La 3:5 [A] *He has* **besieged** [+6584] me and surrounded me with
Eze 4:2 [A] **Erect** siege works against it, build a ramp up to it, set up
11:3 [A] They say, 'Will it not soon be time *to* **build** houses? This city
13:10 [A] there is no peace, and because, when a flimsy wall *is* **built**,
16:24 [A] *you* **built** a mound for yourself and made a lofty shrine in
16:25 [A] At the head of every street *you* **built** your lofty shrines
16:31 [A] When you **built** your mounds at the head of every street
17:17 [A] are built and siege works **erected** to destroy many lives.
21:22 [21:27] [A] the gates, to build a ramp and to **erect** siege works.
26:14 [C] *You will* never **be rebuilt**, for I the LORD have spoken,
27:4 [A] high seas; your **builders** brought your beauty to perfection.
27:5 [A] *They* **made** all your timbers *of* pine trees from Senir;
28:26 [A] there in safety and *will* **build** houses and plant vineyards;
36:10 [C] of Israel. The towns will be inhabited and the ruins **rebuilt**.
36:33 [C] I will resettle your towns, and the ruins *will* **be rebuilt**.
36:36 [A] know that I the LORD *have* **rebuilt** what was destroyed
39:15 [A] *he will* **set up** a marker beside it until the gravediggers have
Da 9:25 [A] to restore and **rebuild** Jerusalem until the Anointed One,
9:25 [C] *It will* **be rebuilt** with streets and a trench, but in times of
Hos 8:14 [A] Israel has forgotten his Maker and **built** palaces; Judah has
Am 5:11 [A] Therefore, though *you have* **built** stone mansions, you will
9:6 [A] he *who* **builds** his lofty palace in the heavens and sets its
9:11 [A] broken places, restore its ruins, and **build** it as it used to be,
9:14 [A] *they will* **rebuild** the ruined cities and live in them.
Mic 3:10 [A] *who* **build** Zion with bloodshed, and Jerusalem with
7:11 [A] The day for **building** your walls will come, the day for
Hab 2:12 [A] "Woe to *him who* **builds** a city with bloodshed
Zep 1:13 [A] *They will* **build** houses but not live in them; they will plant
Hag 1:2 [C] time has not yet come for the LORD's house to **be built**.' "
1:8 [A] the mountains and bring down timber and **build** the house,
Zec 1:16 [C] to Jerusalem with mercy, and there my house *will* **be rebuilt**.
5:11 [A] "To the country of Babylonia to **build** a house for it.
6:12 [A] out from his place and **build** the temple of the LORD.
6:13 [A] It is he *who will* **build** the temple of the LORD, and he will
6:15 [A] away will come and *help to* **build** the temple of the LORD,
8:9 [C] let your hands be strong so that the temple *may* **be built**.
9:3 [A] Tyre *has* **built** herself a stronghold; she has heaped up silver
Mal 1:4 [A] have been crushed, *we will* **rebuild** [+2256+8740] the ruins."
1:4 [A] "They *may* **build**, but I will demolish. They will be called
3:15 [C] Certainly the evildoers **prosper**, and even those who

1216 בְּנֹב ***bᵉnōb***, n.pr.m. Not used in NIV/BHS [→ 3785, 3787]

1217 בְּנוֹ ***bᵉnô***, n.pr.m. *or* n.m.+p.m.s.suf. [2] [√ 1201]

Beno [2]

1Ch 24:26 The sons of Merari: Mahli and Mushi. The son of Jaaziah: **Beno**.
24:27 The sons of Merari: from Jaaziah: **Beno**, Shoham, Zaccur and Ibri.

1218 בִּנּוּי ***binnûy***, n.pr.m. [7 / 8] [√ 1215; cf. 1002]

Binnui [8]

Ezr 8:33 the Levites Jozabad son of Jeshua and Noadiah son of **Binnui**.
10:30 Benaiah, Maaseiah, Mattaniah, Bezalel, **Binnui** and Manasseh.
10:38 From the descendants of **Binnui**: Shimei,
Ne 3:18 by their countrymen under **Binnui** [BHS 1002] son of Henadad,
3:24 Next to him, **Binnui** son of Henadad repaired another section,
7:15 of **Binnui** 648
10:9 [10:10] son of Azaniah, **Binnui** of the sons of Henadad, Kadmiel,
12:8 **Binnui**, Kadmiel, Sherebiah, Judah, and also Mattaniah, who,

1219 בְּנוֹת ***bᵉnôt***, n.pr. Not used in NIV/BHS [→ 6112]

1220 בָּנִי ***bānî***, n.pr.m. [15 / 14] [√ 1215]

Bani [14]

2Sa 23:36 the <u>son</u> *of* [BHS *Bani*; NIV 1201] Hagri,
1Ch 6:46 [6:31] the son of Amzi, the son of **Bani**, the son of Shemer,
9:4 the son of Omri, the son of Imri, the son of **Bani**, [K 1228]
Ezr 2:10 of **Bani** 642
8:10 of the descendants of **Bani**, [BHS-] Shelomith son of Josiphiah,
10:29 From the descendants of **Bani**: Meshullam, Malluch, Adaiah,
10:34 From the descendants of **Bani**: Maadai, Amram, Uel,
10:38 From the <u>descendants</u> [BHS *Bani*; NIV 1201] *of* Binnui:
Ne 3:17 the repairs were made by the Levites under Rehum son of **Bani**.
8:7 Jeshua, **Bani**, Sherebiah, Jamin, Akkub, Shabbethai, Hodiah,
9:4 Jeshua, **Bani**, Kadmiel, Shebaniah, Bunni, Sherebiah, Bani
9:4 Kadmiel, Shebaniah, Bunni, Sherebiah, **Bani** and Kenani—
9:5 Jeshua, Kadmiel, **Bani**, Hashabneiah, Sherebiah, Hodiah,
10:13 [10:14] Hodiah, **Bani** and Beninu.
10:14 [10:15] of the people: Parosh, Pahath-Moab, Elam, Zattu, **Bani**,
11:22 The chief officer of the Levites in Jerusalem was Uzzi son of **Bani**,

1221 בֻּנִּי ***bunnî***, n.pr.m. [3] [√ 1215]

Bunni [3]

Ne 9:4 Kadmiel, Shebaniah, **Bunni**, Sherebiah, Bani and Kenani—
10:15 [10:16] **Bunni**, Azgad, Bebai,
11:15 the son of Azrikam, the son of Hashabiah, the son of **Bunni**;

1222 בְּנֵי־בְרַק ***bᵉnê-bᵉraq***, n.pr.loc. [1] [√ 1201 + 1400]

Bene Berak [1]

Jos 19:45 Jehud, **Bene Berak**, Gath Rimmon,

1223 בְּנֵי יַעֲקָן ***bᵉnê yaʿᵃqān***, n.pr.loc. [2]

Bene Jaakan [2]

Nu 33:31 They left Moseroth and camped at **Bene Jaakan**.
33:32 They left **Bene Jaakan** and camped at Hor Haggidgad.

1224 בִּנְיָה ***binyâ***, n.f. [1] [√ 1215]

building [1]

Eze 41:13 and the **building** with its walls were also a hundred cubits long.

1225 בְּנָיָה ***bᵉnāyâ***, n.pr.m. [11] [√ 1215 + 3378]

Benaiah [11]

2Sa 20:23 **Benaiah** son of Jehoiada was over the Kerethites and Pelethites;

1Ch 4:36 Jaakobah, Jeshohaiah, Asaiah, Adiel, Jesimiel, **Benaiah**,
11:22 **Benaiah** son of Jehoiada was a valiant fighter from Kabzeel,
11:31 son of Ribai from Gibeah in Benjamin, **Benaiah** the Pirathonite,
27:14 the eleventh month, was **Benaiah** the Pirathonite, an Ephraimite.
2Ch 20:14 the son of **Benaiah**, the son of Jeiel, the son of Mattaniah,
Ezr 10:25 Izziah, Malkijah, Mijamin, Eleazar, Malkijah and **Benaiah**.
10:30 Adna, Kelal, **Benaiah**, Maaseiah, Mattaniah, Bezalel, Binnui
10:35 **Benaiah**, Bedeiah, Keluhi,
10:43 Jeiel, Mattithiah, Zabad, Zebina, Jaddai, Joel and **Benaiah**.
Eze 11:13 Now as I was prophesying, Pelatiah son of **Benaiah** died.

1226 בְּנָיָהוּ *benāyāhû*, n.pr.m. [31] [√ 1215 + 3378]

Benaiah [31]

2Sa 8:18 **Benaiah** son of Jehoiada was over the Kerethites and Pelethites;
23:20 **Benaiah** son of Jehoiada was a valiant fighter from Kabzeel,
23:22 Such were the exploits of **Benaiah** son of Jehoiada; he too was as
23:30 **Benaiah** the Pirathonite, Hiddai from the ravines of Gaash,
1Ki 1:8 **Benaiah** son of Jehoiada, Nathan the prophet, Shimei and Rei
1:10 or **Benaiah** or the special guard or his brother Solomon.
1:26 your servant, and Zadok the priest, and **Benaiah** son of Jehoiada,
1:32 the priest, Nathan the prophet and **Benaiah** son of Jehoiada."
1:36 **Benaiah** son of Jehoiada answered the king, "Amen!
1:38 **Benaiah** son of Jehoiada, the Kerethites and the Pelethites went
1:44 **Benaiah** son of Jehoiada, the Kerethites and the Pelethites,
2:25 So King Solomon gave orders to **Benaiah** son of Jehoiada,
2:29 Solomon ordered **Benaiah** son of Jehoiada, "Go, strike him
2:30 So **Benaiah** entered the tent of the LORD and said to Joab,
2:30 **Benaiah** reported to the king, "This is how Joab answered me."
2:34 So **Benaiah** son of Jehoiada went up and struck down Joab
2:35 The king put **Benaiah** son of Jehoiada over the army in Joab's
2:46 Then the king gave the order to **Benaiah** son of Jehoiada,
4:4 **Benaiah** son of Jehoiada—commander in chief; Zadok
1Ch 11:24 Such were the exploits of **Benaiah** son of Jehoiada; he too was as
15:18 Jehiel, Unni, Eliab, **Benaiah**, Maaseiah, Mattithiah, Eliphelehu,
15:20 and **Benaiah** were to play the lyres according to *alamoth,*
15:24 **Benaiah** and Eliezer the priests were to blow trumpets before the
16:5 Jehiel, Mattithiah, Eliab, **Benaiah**, Obed-Edom and Jeiel.
16:6 **Benaiah** and Jahaziel the priests were to blow the trumpets
18:17 **Benaiah** son of Jehoiada was over the Kerethites and Pelethites;
27:5 for the third month, was **Benaiah** son of Jehoiada the priest.
27:6 This was the **Benaiah** who was a mighty man among the Thirty
27:34 Ahithophel was succeeded by Jehoiada son of **Benaiah** and by
2Ch 31:13 Mahath and **Benaiah** were supervisors under Conaniah and Shimei
Eze 11:1 among them Jaazaniah son of Azzur and Pelatiah son of **Benaiah**,

1227 בֵּנַיִם *bēnayim*, subst.[du.]. [2] [√ 1068]

champion [+408+2021] [2]

1Sa 17:4 A **champion** [+408+2021] named Goliath, who was from Gath,
17:23 Goliath, the Philistine **champion** [+408+2021] from Gath,

1228 בִּנְיָמִין *binyāmîn*, בֶּן־יָמִין *ben-yāmîn*, n.pr.m. [166] [→ 1229, 3549; cf. 1201 + 3545]

Benjamin [111], Benjamites [+1201] [16], Benjamin [+1201] [13], Benjamites [12], Benjamite [4], Benjamin's [2], tribe of Benjamin [2], Benjamin [+824] [1], Benjamite [+408] [1], Benjamite [+4946] [1], Benjamites [+408+4946] [1], Benjamites [+4946] [1], they[s] [+1201] [1]

Ge 35:18 she named her son Ben-Oni. But his father named him **Benjamin**.
35:24 The sons of Rachel: Joseph and **Benjamin**.
42:4 Jacob did not send **Benjamin**, Joseph's brother, with the others,
42:36 and Simeon is no more, and now you want to take **Benjamin**.
43:14 he will let your other brother and **Benjamin** come back with you.
43:15 took the gifts and double the amount of silver, and **Benjamin** also.
43:16 When Joseph saw **Benjamin** with them, he said to the steward of
43:29 As he looked about and saw his brother **Benjamin**, his own
43:34 **Benjamin's** portion was five times as much as anyone else's.
44:12 with the youngest. And the cup was found in **Benjamin's** sack.
45:12 "You can see for yourselves, and so can my brother **Benjamin**,
45:14 Then he threw his arms around his brother **Benjamin** and wept,
45:14 and wept, and **Benjamin** embraced him, weeping.
45:22 to **Benjamin** he gave three hundred shekels of silver and five sets
46:19 The sons of Jacob's wife Rachel: Joseph and **Benjamin**.
46:21 The sons of **Benjamin**: Bela, Beker, Ashbel, Gera, Naaman,
49:27 "**Benjamin** is a ravenous wolf; in the morning he devours the prey,
Ex 1:3 Issachar, Zebulun and **Benjamin**;
Nu 1:11 from **Benjamin**, Abidan son of Gideoni;
1:36 From the descendants of **Benjamin**: All the men twenty years old
1:37 The number from the tribe of **Benjamin** was 35,400.
2:22 The tribe of **Benjamin** will be next. The leader of the people of
2:22 The leader of the people of **Benjamin** is Abidan son of Gideoni.
7:60 the leader of the people of **Benjamin**, brought his offering.
10:24 of Gideoni was over the division of the tribe of **Benjamin** [+1201].
13:9 from the tribe of **Benjamin**, Palti son of Raphu;
26:38 The descendants of **Benjamin** by their clans were: through Bela,
26:41 These were the clans of **Benjamin** [+1201]; those numbered were
34:21 Elidad son of Kislon, from the tribe of **Benjamin**;
Dt 27:12 the people: Simeon, Levi, Judah, Issachar, Joseph and **Benjamin**.
33:12 About **Benjamin** he said: "Let the beloved of the LORD rest
Jos 18:11 The lot came up for the tribe of **Benjamin** [+1201], clan by clan.
18:20 out the inheritance of the clans of **Benjamin** [+1201] on all sides.
18:21 The tribe of **Benjamin** [+1201], clan by clan, had the following
18:28 This was the inheritance of **Benjamin** [+1201] for its clans.
21:4 thirteen towns from the tribes of Judah, Simeon and **Benjamin**.
21:17 And from the tribe of **Benjamin** they gave them Gibeon, Geba,
Jdg 1:21 The **Benjamites** [+1201], however, failed to dislodge the Jebusites,
1:21 to this day the Jebusites live there with the **Benjamites** [+1201].
5:14 in Amalek; **Benjamin** was with the people who followed you.
10:9 Jordan to fight against Judah, **Benjamin** and the house of Ephraim;
19:14 they went on, and the sun set as they neared Gibeah in **Benjamin**.
20:3 (The **Benjamites** [+1201] heard that the Israelites had gone up to
20:4 and my concubine came to Gibeah in **Benjamin** to spend the night.
20:10 Then, when the army arrives at Gibeah in **Benjamin**, it can give
20:12 The tribes of Israel sent men throughout the tribe of **Benjamin**,
20:13 the **Benjamites** [no K] would not listen to their fellow Israelites.
20:14 From their towns **they**[s] [+1201] came together at Gibeah to fight
20:15 At once the **Benjamites** [+1201] mobilized twenty-six thousand
20:17 Israel, apart from **Benjamin**, mustered four hundred thousand
20:18 "Who of us shall go first to fight against the **Benjamites** [+1201]?"
20:20 The men of Israel went out to fight the **Benjamites** and took up
20:21 The **Benjamites** [+1201] came out of Gibeah and cut down
20:23 "Shall we go up again to battle against the **Benjamites** [+1201],
20:24 Then the Israelites drew near to **Benjamin** [+1201] the second day.
20:25 when the **Benjamites** came out from Gibeah to oppose them,
20:28 "Shall we go up again to battle with **Benjamin** [+1201] our
20:30 They went up against the **Benjamites** [+1201] on the third day
20:31 The **Benjamites** [+1201] came out to meet them and were drawn
20:32 While the **Benjamites** [+1201] were saying, "We are defeating
20:35 The LORD defeated **Benjamin** before Israel, and on that day the
20:35 and on that day the Israelites struck down 25,100 **Benjamites**,
20:36 the **Benjamites** [+1201] saw that they were beaten. Now the men
20:36 Now the men of Israel had given way before **Benjamin**,
20:39 The **Benjamites** had begun to inflict casualties on the men of Israel
20:40 the **Benjamites** turned and saw the smoke of the whole city going
20:41 of Israel turned on them, and the men of **Benjamin** were terrified,
20:43 They surrounded the **Benjamites**, chased them and easily overran
20:44 Eighteen thousand **Benjamites** fell, all of them valiant fighters.
20:46 On that day twenty-five thousand **Benjamite** swordsmen fell,
20:48 The men of Israel went back to **Benjamin** [+1201] and put all the
21:1 "Not one of us will give his daughter in marriage to a **Benjamite**."
21:6 Now the Israelites grieved for their brothers, the **Benjamites**.
21:13 offer of peace to the **Benjamites** [+1201] at the rock of Rimmon.
21:14 So the **Benjamites** returned at that time and were given the women
21:15 The people grieved for **Benjamin**, because the LORD had made a
21:16 of the assembly said, "With the women of **Benjamin** destroyed,
21:17 The **Benjamite** survivors must have heirs," they said, "so that a
21:18 this oath: 'Cursed be anyone who gives a wife to a **Benjamite**.'
21:20 So they instructed the **Benjamites** [+1201], saying, "Go and hide
21:21 a wife from the girls of Shiloh and go to the land of **Benjamin**.
21:23 So that is what the **Benjamites** [+1201] did. While the girls were
1Sa 4:12 That same day a **Benjamite** [+408] ran from the battle line
9:1 There was a **Benjamite** [+4946], a man of standing, whose name
9:16 time tomorrow I will send you a man from the land of **Benjamin**.
9:21 is not my clan the least of all the clans of the tribe of **Benjamin**?
10:2 two men near Rachel's tomb, at Zelzah on the border of **Benjamin**.
10:20 all the tribes of Israel near, the tribe of **Benjamin** was chosen.
10:21 Then he brought forward the tribe of **Benjamin**, clan by clan,
13:2 and a thousand were with Jonathan at Gibeah in **Benjamin**.
13:15 Then Samuel left Gilgal and went up to Gibeah in **Benjamin**,
13:16 and the men with them were staying in Gibeah in **Benjamin**,
14:16 Saul's lookouts at Gibeah in **Benjamin** saw the army melting away
2Sa 2:9 and Jezreel, and also over Ephraim, **Benjamin** and all Israel.
2:15 twelve men for **Benjamin** and Ish-Bosheth son of Saul, and twelve
2:25 the men of **Benjamin** rallied behind Abner. They formed
2:31 had killed three hundred and sixty **Benjamites** [+408+4946] who
3:19 Abner also spoke to the **Benjamites** in person. Then he went to
3:19 that Israel and the whole house of **Benjamin** wanted to do.
4:2 were sons of Rimmon the Beerothite from the tribe of **Benjamin**—
4:2 the tribe of Benjamin—Beeroth is considered part of **Benjamin**,
19:17 [19:18] With him were a thousand **Benjamites** [+4946],
21:14 at Zela in **Benjamin** [+824], and did everything the king
23:29 Ithai son of Ribai from Gibeah in **Benjamin** [+1201],
1Ki 4:18 Shimei son of Ela—in **Benjamin**;
12:21 he mustered the whole house of Judah and the tribe of **Benjamin**—
12:23 to the whole house of Judah and **Benjamin**, and to the rest of the
15:22 With them King Asa built up Geba in **Benjamin**, and also Mizpah.
1Ch 2:2 Dan, Joseph, **Benjamin**, Naphtali, Gad and Asher.

1Ch 6:60 [6:45] And from the tribe of **Benjamin** they were given Gibeon,
6:65 [6:50] **Benjamin** [+1201] they allotted the previously named
7: 6 Three sons of **Benjamin**: Bela, Beker and Jediael.
7:10 Jeush, **Benjamin**, Ehud, Kenaanah, Zethan, Tarshish
8: 1 **Benjamin** was the father of Bela his firstborn, Ashbel the second
8:40 150 in all. All these were the descendants of **Benjamin**.
9: 3 from **Benjamin** [+1201], and from Ephraim and Manasseh who
9: 4 [the son of Omri, the son of Imri, the son of **Bani**, [K; see Q 1220]]
9: 7 Of the **Benjamites** [+1201]: Sallu son of Meshullam, the son of
11:31 Ithai son of Ribai from Gibeah in **Benjamin** [+1201],
12: 2 they were kinsmen of Saul from the **tribe of Benjamin**):
12:16 [12:17] Other **Benjamites** [+1201] and some men from Judah
12:29 [12:30] men of **Benjamin**, Saul's kinsmen—3,000, most of whom
21: 6 But Joab did not include Levi and **Benjamin** in the numbering,
27:21 Iddo son of Zechariah; over **Benjamin**: Jaasiel son of Abner;
2Ch 11: 1 in Jerusalem, he mustered the house of Judah and **Benjamin**—
11: 3 king of Judah and to all the Israelites in Judah and **Benjamin**,
11:10 and Hebron. These were fortified cities in Judah and **Benjamin**.
11:12 and made them very strong. So Judah and **Benjamin** were his.
11:23 some of his sons throughout the districts of Judah and **Benjamin**,
14: 8 [14:7] and two hundred and eighty thousand from **Benjamin**,
15: 2 and said to him, "Listen to me, Asa and all Judah and **Benjamin**.
15: 8 **Benjamin** and from the towns he had captured in the hills of
15: 9 he assembled all Judah and **Benjamin** and the people from
17:17 From **Benjamin**: Eliada, a valiant soldier, with 200,000 men
25: 5 and commanders of hundreds for all Judah and **Benjamin**.
31: 1 throughout Judah and **Benjamin** and in Ephraim and Manasseh.
34: 9 remnant of Israel and from all the people of Judah and **Benjamin**
34:32 had everyone in Jerusalem and **Benjamin** pledge themselves to it;
Ezr 1: 5 Then the family heads of Judah and **Benjamin**, and the priests
4: 1 **Benjamin** heard that the exiles were building a temple for the
10: 9 all the men of Judah and **Benjamin** had gathered in Jerusalem.
10:32 **Benjamin**, Malluch and Shemariah.
Ne 3:23 **Benjamin** and Hasshub made repairs in front of their house;
11: 4 other people from both Judah and **Benjamin** lived in Jerusalem):
11: 7 From the descendants of **Benjamin**: Sallu son of Meshullam,
11:31 The descendants of the **Benjamites** from Geba lived in Micmash,
11:36 Some of the divisions of the Levites of Judah settled in **Benjamin**.
12:34 Judah, **Benjamin**, Shemaiah, Jeremiah,
Ps 68:27 [68:28] There is the little **tribe of Benjamin**, leading them,
80: 2 [80:3] before Ephraim, **Benjamin** and Manasseh. Awaken your
Jer 1: 1 one of the priests at Anathoth in the territory of **Benjamin**.
6: 1 "Flee for safety, people of **Benjamin**! Flee from Jerusalem!
17:26 from the territory of **Benjamin** and the western foothills, from the
20: 2 put in the stocks at the Upper Gate of **Benjamin** at the LORD's
32: 8 and said, 'Buy my field at Anathoth in the territory of **Benjamin**.
32:44 will be signed, sealed and witnessed in the territory of **Benjamin**,
33:13 western foothills and of the Negev, in the territory of **Benjamin**,
37:12 Jeremiah started to leave the city to go to the territory of **Benjamin**
37:13 But when he reached the **Benjamin** Gate, the captain of the guard,
38: 7 into the cistern. While the king was sitting in the **Benjamin** Gate,
Eze 48:22 will lie between the border of Judah and the border of **Benjamin**.
48:23 **Benjamin** will have one portion; it will extend from the east side
48:24 it will border the territory of **Benjamin** from east to west.
48:32 the gate of Joseph, the gate of **Benjamin** and the gate of Dan.
Hos 5: 8 in Ramah. Raise the battle cry in Beth Aven; lead on, O **Benjamin**.
Ob 1:19 fields of Ephraim and Samaria, and **Benjamin** will possess Gilead.
Zec 14:10 from the **Benjamin** Gate to the site of the First Gate, to the Corner

1229 בֶּן־יְמִינִי ***ben-y^{e}mînî***, בֶּנְיְמִינִי ***beny^{e}mînî***, a.g. [9] [√ 1128; cf. 1201 + 3545]

Benjamite [7], Benjamites [1], men of Benjamin [1]

Jdg 3:15 a left-handed man, the son of Gera the **Benjamite**.
19:16 who was living in Gibeah (the men of the place were **Benjamites**),
1Sa 9:21 Saul answered, "But am I not a **Benjamite**, from the smallest tribe
22: 7 Saul said to them, "Listen, **men of Benjamin**! Will the son of
2Sa 16:11 How much more, then, this **Benjamite**! Leave him alone;
19:16 [19:17] Shimei son of Gera, the **Benjamite** from Bahurim,
1Ki 2: 8 have with you Shimei son of Gera, the **Benjamite** from Bahurim,
1Ch 27:12 for the ninth month, was Abiezer the Anathothite, a **Benjamite**.
Ps 7: T [7:1] he sang to the LORD concerning Cush, a **Benjamite**.

1230 בִּנְיָן ***binyān***, n.m. [7] [√ 1215; Ar 10112]

building [4], outer wall [2], wall [1]

Eze 40: 5 He measured the **wall**; it was one measuring rod thick and one rod
41:12 The **building** facing the temple courtyard on the west side was
41:12 The wall of the **building** was five cubits thick all around, and its
41:15 he measured the length of the **building** facing the courtyard at the
42: 1 the temple courtyard and opposite the **outer wall** on the north side.
42: 5 from the rooms on the lower and middle floors of the **building**.
42:10 adjoining the temple courtyard and opposite the **outer wall**,

1231 בְּנִינוּ ***b^{e}nînû***, n.pr.m. [1] [√ 1201]

Beninu [1]

Ne 10:13 [10:14] Hodiah, Bani and **Beninu**.

1232 בִּנְעָא ***bin'ā'***, n.pr.m. [2] [√ 1201 + *]

Binea [2]

1Ch 8:37 Moza was the father of **Binea**; Raphah was his son, Eleasah his son
9:43 Moza was the father of **Binea**; Rephaiah was his son, Eleasah his

1233 בְּסוֹדְיָה ***b^{e}sôd^{e}yâ***, n.pr.m. [1] [√ 928 + 6051 + 3378; cf. 1234?]

Besodeiah [1]

Ne 3: 6 by Joiada son of Paseah and Meshullam son of **Besodeiah**.

1234 בֵּסַי ***bēsay***, n.pr.m. [2] [cf. 1233?]

Besai [2]

Ezr 2:49 Uzza, Paseah, **Besai**,
Ne 7:52 **Besai**, Meunim, Nephussim,

1235 בֹּסֶר ***bōser***, n.m. [5]

sour grapes [3], grape [1], unripe grapes [1]

Job 15:33 He will be like a vine stripped of its **unripe grapes**, like an olive
Isa 18: 5 the blossom is gone and the flower becomes a ripening **grape**,
Jer 31:29 'The fathers have eaten **sour grapes**, and the children's teeth are
31:30 whoever eats **sour grapes**—his own teeth will be set on edge.
Eze 18: 2 " 'The fathers eat **sour grapes**, and the children's teeth are set on

1236 בַּעֲבוּר ***ba'^{a}bûr***, pp.+c. Not used in NIV/BHS [√ 928 + 6288]

1237 בַּעַד[1] ***ba'ad[1]***, subst.pp. [105 / 104] [→ 1238] See Select Index

for [48], *untranslated* [20], through [8], behind [5], from [4], behind [+4946] [3], in [3], around [2], on behalf of [2], around [+4946+6017] [1], barred in [+1378] [1], by [1], for [+3954] [1], of [1], on behalf [1], on [1], over [1], seals off [+3159] [1]

1238 בַּעַד[2] ***ba'ad[2]***, subst. Not used in NIV/BHS [√ 1237]

1239 בָּעָה[1] ***bā'â[1]***, v. [3] [→ Ar 10114]

ask [2], pillaged [1]

Isa 21:12 [A] If *you would* **ask**, then ask; and come back yet again."
21:12 [A] If you would ask, then **ask**; and come back yet again."
Ob 1: 6 [C] how Esau will be ransacked, his hidden treasures **pillaged**!

1240 בָּעָה[2] ***bā'â[2]***, v. [2]

bulging [1], causes to boil [1]

Isa 30:13 [C] cracked and **bulging**, that collapses suddenly, in an instant.
64: 2 [64:1] [A] when fire sets twigs ablaze and **causes** water **to boil**,

1241 בְּעוּלָה ***b^e'ûlâ***, n.pr.f. [1] [√ 1249]

Beulah [1]

Isa 62: 4 you will be called Hephzibah, and your land **Beulah**;

1242 בְּעוֹר ***b^e'ôr***, n.pr.m. [10]

Beor [10]

Ge 36:32 Bela son of **Beor** became king of Edom. His city was named
Nu 22: 5 sent messengers to summon Balaam son of **Beor**, who was at
24: 3 "The oracle of Balaam son of **Beor**, the oracle of one whose eye
24:15 "The oracle of Balaam son of **Beor**, the oracle of one whose eye
31: 8 of Midian. They also killed Balaam son of **Beor** with the sword.
Dt 23: 4 [23:5] they hired Balaam son of **Beor** from Pethor in Aram
Jos 13:22 the Israelites had put to the sword Balaam son of **Beor**,
24: 9 he sent for Balaam son of **Beor** to put a curse on you.
1Ch 1:43 king reigned: Bela son of **Beor**, whose city was named Dinhabah.
Mic 6: 5 king of Moab counseled and what Balaam son of **Beor** answered.

1243 בִּעוּת ***bi'ût***, n.m.pl. [2] [√ 1286]

terrors [2]

Job 6: 4 drinks in their poison; God's **terrors** are marshaled against me.
Ps 88:16 [88:17] has swept over me; your **terrors** have destroyed me.

1244 בֹּ֫עַז bōʿaz[1], n.pr.m. [22]

Boaz [22]

Ru 2: 1 the clan of Elimelech, a man of standing, whose name was **Boaz**.
2: 3 turned out, she found herself working in a field belonging to **Boaz**,
2: 4 Just then **Boaz** arrived from Bethlehem and greeted the harvesters,
2: 5 **Boaz** asked the foreman of his harvesters, "Whose young woman
2: 8 So **Boaz** said to Ruth, "My daughter, listen to me. Don't go
2: 11 **Boaz** replied, "I've been told all about what you have done for
2: 14 At mealtime **Boaz** said to her, "Come over here. Have some bread
2: 15 As she got up to glean, **Boaz** gave orders to his men, "Even if she
2: 19 "The name of the man I worked with today is **Boaz**," she said.
2: 23 So Ruth stayed close to the servant girls of **Boaz** to glean until the
3: 2 Is not **Boaz**, with whose servant girls you have been, a kinsman of
3: 7 When **Boaz** had finished eating and drinking and was in good
4: 1 Meanwhile **Boaz** went up to the town gate and sat there. When the
4: 1 **Boaz** said, "Come over here, my friend, and sit down."
4: 5 Then **Boaz** said, "On the day you buy the land from Naomi
4: 8 So the kinsman-redeemer said to **Boaz**, "Buy it yourself."
4: 9 **Boaz** announced to the elders and all the people, "Today you are
4: 13 So **Boaz** took Ruth and she became his wife. Then he went to her,
4: 21 Salmon the father of **Boaz**, Boaz the father of Obed,
4: 21 Salmon the father of Boaz, **Boaz** the father of Obed,
1Ch 2: 11 Nahshon was the father of Salmon, Salmon the father of **Boaz**,
2: 12 **Boaz** the father of Obed and Obed the father of Jesse.

1245 בֹּ֫עַז[2] bōʿaz[2], n.pr.m. [2]

Boaz [2]

1Ki 7: 21 pillar to the south he named Jakin and the one to the north **Boaz**.
2Ch 3: 17 The one to the south he named Jakin and the one to the north **Boaz**.

1246 בָּעַט bāʿaṭ, v. [2]

kicked [1], scorn [1]

Dt 32: 15 [A] Jeshurun grew fat and **kicked**; filled with food, he became
1Sa 2: 29 [A] Why *do you* **scorn** my sacrifice and offering that I

1247 בְּעִי beʿî, n.[m.]. Not used in NIV/BHS [√ 928 + 6505]

1248 בְּעִיר beʿîr, n.m. [6] [→ 1279, 1280]

livestock [4], animals [1], cattle [1]

Ge 45: 17 'Do this: Load your **animals** and return to the land of Canaan,
Ex 22: 5 [22:4] "If a man grazes his **livestock** in a field or vineyard
Nu 20: 4 into this desert, that we and our **livestock** should die here?
20: 8 the rock for the community so they and their **livestock** can drink."
20: 11 Water gushed out, and the community and their **livestock** drank.
Ps 78: 48 He gave over their **cattle** to the hail, their livestock to bolts of

1249 בָּעַל[1] bāʿal[1], v. [15] [→ 1241]

husband [4], be married [1], has a husband [1], married [+1251] [1], married [1], marries [+2256+4374] [1], marries [1], marry [1], marrying [1], ruled over [1], ruled [1], wife [+851] [1]

Ge 20: 3 [B] woman you have taken; she *is a* **married** [+1251] *woman*."
Dt 21: 13 [A] you may go to her and *be* her **husband** and she shall be your
22: 22 [B] If a man is found sleeping with another man's **wife** [+851],
24: 1 [A] If a man **marries** [+2256+4374] a woman who becomes
1Ch 4: 22 [A] and Saraph, who **ruled** in Moab and Jashubi Lehem.
Pr 30: 23 [C] an unloved woman *who is* **married**, and a maidservant who
Isa 26: 13 [A] our God, other lords besides you *have* **ruled over** us,
54: 1 [B] of the desolate woman than of *her who* **has a husband**,"
54: 5 [A] For your Maker *is* your **husband**—the LORD Almighty is
62: 4 [C] will take delight in you, and your land *will* **be married**.
62: 5 [A] As a young man **marries** a maiden, so will your sons marry
62: 5 [A] a young man marries a maiden, so *will* your sons **marry** you;
Jer 3: 14 [A] declares the LORD, "for I *am* your **husband**.
31: 32 [A] though I *was a* **husband** to them," declares the LORD.
Mal 2: 11 [A] LORD loves, *by* **marrying** the daughter of a foreign god.

1250 בָּעַל[2] bāʿal[2], v. Not used in NIV/BHS

1251 בַּ֫עַל baʿal[1], n.m. [165 / 164] [→ 1252, 1266, 1272; cf. 1249; Ar 10116; *also used with compound proper names*]

Baal [55], Baals [18], citizens [18], owner [14], husband [6], Baal worship [3], Baal's [3], husbands [2], two-horned [+2021+7967] [2], with [2], accuser [+5477] [1], allied [+1382] [1], archers [+2932] [1], bird on the wing [+4053] [1], birds [+4053] [1], captain [1], charmer [+4383] [1], collected sayings [+670] [1], creditor [+2257+3338+5408] [1], dreamer [+2021+2706] [1], filled with [1], given to gluttony [+5883] [1], has [1], him[s] [+2023] [1], hot-tempered [+2779] [1], husband's [1], involved in [1], it[s] [+1074] [1], man [1], man's [1], married [+1249] [1], master [1], men [1], one who destroys [+5422] [1], one who gives [1], owned [1], owner's [1], people [1], possessor [1], practice [1], related by marriage [1], riders [+7304] [1], rulers [1], schemer [+4659] [1], tenants [1], they[s] [+3972+4463+8901] [1], those who deserve [1], those who get [1], those who have [1], under oath [+8652] [1], who[s] [+8901] [1]

Ge 14: 13 of Eshcol and Aner, all of whom were **allied with** [+1382] Abram.
20: 3 of the woman you have taken; she *is a* **married woman** [+1249]."
37: 19 "Here comes that **dreamer** [+2021+2706]!" they said to each other.
49: 23 With bitterness **archers** [+2932] attacked him; they shot at him
Ex 21: 3 but if he **has** a wife when he comes, she is to go with him.
21: 22 the offender must be fined whatever the woman's **husband**
21: 28 be eaten. But the **owner** *of* the bull will not be held responsible.
21: 29 and the **owner** has been warned but has not kept it penned up
21: 29 the bull must be stoned and the **owner** also must be put to death.
21: 34 the **owner** *of* the pit must pay for the loss; he must pay its owner,
21: 34 the loss; he must pay its **owner**, and the dead animal will be his.
21: 36 yet the **owner** did not keep it penned up, the owner must pay,
22: 8 [22:7] the **owner** *of* the house must appear before the judges to
22: 11 [22:10] The **owner** is to accept this, and no restitution is required.
22: 12 [22:11] from the neighbor, he must make restitution to the **owner**.
22: 14 [22:13] and it is injured or dies while the **owner** is not present,
22: 15 [22:14] if the **owner** is with the animal, the borrower will not
24: 14 are with you, and anyone **involved in** a dispute can go to them."
Lev 21: 4 not make himself unclean for people **related** *to* him **by marriage**,
Nu 21: 28 It consumed Ar of Moab, the **citizens** *of* Arnon's heights.
25: 3 So Israel joined in worshiping the **Baal** *of* Peor. And the LORD's
25: 5 of your men who have joined in worshiping the **Baal** *of* Peor."
Dt 4: 3 from among you everyone who followed the **Baal** *of* Peor,
15: 2 Every **creditor** [+2257+3338+5408] shall cancel the loan he has
22: 22 If a man is found sleeping with another **man's** wife, both the man
24: 4 her first **husband**, who divorced her, is not allowed to marry her
Jos 24: 11 The **citizens** of Jericho fought against you, as did also the
Jdg 2: 11 Israelites did evil in the eyes of the LORD and served the **Baals**.
2: 13 because they forsook him and served **Baal** and the Ashtoreths.
3: 7 the LORD their God and served the **Baals** and the Asherahs.
6: 25 Tear down your father's altar to **Baal** and cut down the Asherah
6: 28 there was **Baal's** altar, demolished, with the Asherah pole beside it
6: 30 because he has broken down **Baal's** altar and cut down the
6: 31 hostile crowd around him, "Are you going to plead **Baal's** cause?
6: 32 saying, "Let **Baal** contend with him," because he broke down
8: 33 died than the Israelites again prostituted themselves to the **Baals**.
9: 2 "Ask all the **citizens** *of* Shechem, 'Which is better for you:
9: 3 When the brothers repeated all this to the **citizens** *of* Shechem,
9: 6 all the **citizens** *of* Shechem and Beth Millo gathered beside the
9: 7 and shouted to them, "Listen to me, **citizens** *of* Shechem,
9: 18 king over the **citizens** *of* Shechem because he is your brother)—
9: 20 and consume you, **citizens** *of* Shechem and Beth Millo,
9: 20 **citizens** *of* Shechem and Beth Millo, and consume Abimelech!"
9: 23 sent an evil spirit between Abimelech and the **citizens** *of* Shechem,
9: 23 the citizens of Shechem, **who**[s] [+8901] acted treacherously against
9: 24 on their brother Abimelech and on the **citizens** *of* Shechem,
9: 25 In opposition to him these **citizens** *of* Shechem set men on the
9: 26 brothers into Shechem, and its **citizens** put their confidence in him.
9: 39 So Gaal led out the **citizens** *of* Shechem and fought Abimelech.
9: 46 the **citizens** *in* the tower of Shechem went into the stronghold of
9: 47 Abimelech heard that **they**[s] [+3972+4463+8901] had assembled
9: 51 to which all the men and women—all the **people** *of* the city—fled.
10: 6 They served the **Baals** and the Ashtoreths, and the gods of Aram,
10: 10 sinned against you, forsaking our God and serving the **Baals**."
19: 22 on the door, they shouted to the old man who **owned** the house,
19: 23 The **owner** *of* the house went outside and said to them, "No,
20: 5 During the night the **men** *of* Gibeah came after me and surrounded
1Sa 7: 4 So the Israelites put away their **Baals** and Ashtoreths, and served
12: 10 forsaken the LORD and served the **Baals** and the Ashtoreths.
23: 11 Will the **citizens** *of* Keilah surrender me to him? Will Saul come
23: 12 "Will the **citizens** *of* Keilah surrender me and my men to Saul?"
2Sa 1: 6 his spear, with the chariots and **riders** [+7304] almost upon him.
6: 2 all his men set out from Baalah [BHS *Baale*; NIV 1267] *of* Judah
11: 26 heard that her husband was dead, she mourned for **him**[s] [+2023].
21: 12 of Saul and his son Jonathan from the **citizens** *of* Jabesh Gilead.
1Ki 16: 31 king of the Sidonians, and began to serve **Baal** and worship him.
16: 32 He set up an altar for **Baal** *in* the temple of Baal that he built in
16: 32 He set up an altar for Baal in the temple of **Baal** that he built in
18: 18 abandoned the LORD's commands and have followed the **Baals**.
18: 19 bring the four hundred and fifty prophets of **Baal** and the four
18: 21 If the LORD is God, follow him; but if **Baal** is God, follow him."
18: 22 prophets left, but **Baal** has four hundred and fifty prophets.
18: 25 Elijah said to the prophets of **Baal**, "Choose one of the bulls
18: 26 Then they called on the name of **Baal** from morning till noon.
18: 26 "O **Baal**, answer us!" they shouted. But there was no response;
18: 40 Then Elijah commanded them, "Seize the prophets of **Baal**.
19: 18 all whose knees have not bowed down to **Baal** and all whose
22: 53 [22:54] He served and worshiped **Baal** and provoked the LORD,

2Ki 1: 8 "He was a man **with** a garment of hair and with a leather belt
3: 2 He got rid of the sacred stone of **Baal** that his father had made.
10: 18 all the people together and said to them, "Ahab served **Baal** a little;
10: 19 Now summon all the prophets of **Baal**, all his ministers and all his
10: 19 is missing, because I am going to hold a great sacrifice for **Baal**.
10: 19 was acting deceptively in order to destroy the ministers of **Baal**.
10: 20 Jehu said, "Call an assembly in honor of **Baal**." So they
10: 21 he sent word throughout Israel, and all the ministers of **Baal** came;
10: 21 They crowded into the temple of **Baal** until it was full from one
10: 21 They crowded into the temple of Baal until **it**[s] [+1074] was full
10: 22 keeper of the wardrobe, "Bring robes for all the ministers of **Baal**."
10: 23 and Jehonadab son of Recab went into the temple of **Baal**.
10: 23 Jehu said to the ministers of **Baal**, "Look around and see that no
10: 23 of the LORD are here with you—only ministers of **Baal**."
10: 25 bodies out and then entered the inner shrine of the temple of **Baal**.
10: 26 They brought the sacred stone out of the temple of **Baal**
10: 27 They demolished the sacred stone of **Baal** and tore down the
10: 27 the sacred stone of Baal and tore down the temple of **Baal**,
10: 28 So Jehu destroyed **Baal worship** in Israel.
11: 18 All the people of the land went to the temple of **Baal** and tore it
11: 18 to pieces and killed Mattan the priest of **Baal** in front of the altars.
17: 16 They bowed down to all the starry hosts, and they worshiped **Baal**.
21: 3 he also erected altars to **Baal** and made an Asherah pole, as Ahab
23: 4 from the temple of the LORD all the articles made for **Baal**
23: 5 those who burned incense to **Baal**, to the sun and moon, to the
2Ch 17: 3 ways his father David had followed. He did not consult the **Baals**
23: 17 All the people went to the temple of **Baal** and tore it down.
23: 17 and idols and killed Mattan the priest of **Baal** in front of the altars.
24: 7 temple of God and had used even its sacred objects for the **Baals**.
28: 2 kings of Israel and also made cast idols for worshiping the **Baals**.
33: 3 he also erected altars to the **Baals** and made Asherah poles.
34: 4 Under his direction the altars of the **Baals** were torn down;
Ne 6: 18 For many in Judah were **under oath** [+8652] to him, since he was
Est 1: 17 to all the women, and so they will despise their **husbands** and say,
1: 20 all the women will respect their **husbands**, from the least to the
Job 31: 39 its yield without payment or broken the spirit of its **tenants**,
Ps 106: 28 They yoked themselves to the **Baal** *of* Peor and ate sacrifices
Pr 1: 17 How useless to spread a net in full view of all the **birds** [+4053]!
1: 19 go after ill-gotten gain; it takes away the lives of **those who get** it.
3: 27 Do not withhold good from **those who deserve** it, when it is in
12: 4 A wife of noble character is her **husband's** crown, but a
16: 22 Understanding is a fountain of life to **those who have** it, but folly
17: 8 A bribe is a charm to the **one who gives** it; wherever he turns,
18: 9 who is slack in his work is brother to **one who destroys** [+5422].
22: 24 Do not make friends with a hot-tempered **man**, do not associate
23: 2 and put a knife to your throat if you are **given to gluttony** [+5883].
24: 8 He who plots evil will be known as a **schemer** [+4659].
29: 22 and a **hot-tempered one** [+2779] commits many sins.
31: 11 Her **husband** has full confidence in her and lacks nothing of value.
31: 23 Her **husband** is respected at the city gate, where he takes his seat
31: 28 and call her blessed; her **husband** also, and he praises her:
Ecc 5: 11 [5:10] what benefit are they to the **owner** except to feast his eyes
5: 13 [5:12] under the sun: wealth hoarded to the harm of its **owner**,
7: 12 knowledge is this: that wisdom preserves the life of its **possessor**.
8: 8 time of war, so wickedness will not release *those who* **practice** it.
10: 11 before it is charmed, there is no profit for the **charmer** [+4383].
10: 20 and a **bird on the wing** [+4053] may report what you say.
12: 11 their **collected sayings** [+670] like firmly embedded nails—
Isa 1: 3 the donkey his **owner's** manger, but Israel does not know,
16: 8 The **rulers** *of* the nations have trampled down the choicest vines,
41: 15 make you into a threshing sledge, new and sharp, **with** many teeth.
50: 8 each other! Who is my **accuser** [+5477]? Let him confront me!
Jer 2: 8 The prophets prophesied by **Baal**, following worthless idols.
2: 23 can you say, 'I am not defiled; I have not run after the **Baals**'?
7: 9 burn incense to **Baal** and follow other gods you have not known,
9: 14 [9:13] they have followed the **Baals**, as their fathers taught them."
11: 13 to that shameful god **Baal** are as many as the streets of Jerusalem.'
11: 17 done evil and provoked me to anger by burning incense to **Baal**.
12: 16 even as they once taught my people to swear by **Baal**—
19: 5 They have built the high places of **Baal** to burn their sons in the
19: 5 places of Baal to burn their sons in the fire as offerings to **Baal**—
23: 13 They prophesied by **Baal** and led my people Israel astray.
23: 27 just as their fathers forgot my name through **Baal worship**.
32: 29 provoked me to anger by burning incense on the roofs to **Baal**
32: 35 They built high places for **Baal** in the Valley of Ben Hinnom to
37: 13 But when he reached the Benjamin Gate, the **captain** *of* the guard,
Da 8: 6 He came toward the **two-horned** [+2021+7967] ram I had seen
8: 20 The **two-horned** [+2021+7967] ram that you saw represents the
Hos 2: 8 [2:10] on her the silver and gold—which they used for **Baal**.
2: 13 [2:15] punish her for the days she burned incense to the **Baals**;
2: 16 [2:18] me 'my husband'; you will no longer call me 'my **master**.'
2: 17 [2:19] I will remove the names of the **Baals** from her lips; no
11: 2 They sacrificed to the **Baals** and they burned incense to images.
13: 1 exalted in Israel. But he became guilty of **Baal worship** and died.
Joel 1: 8 Mourn like a virgin in sackcloth grieving for the **husband** *of* her
Na 1: 2 the LORD takes vengeance and is **filled with** wrath.
Zep 1: 4 I will cut off from this place every remnant of **Baal**, the names of

1252 ²בַּעַל ba'al², n.pr.m. [4 / 3] [√ 1251]

Baal [3]

1Ch 4: 33 around these towns as far as Baalath. [BHS *Baal*; NIV 1272]
5: 5 Micah his son, Reaiah his son, **Baal** his son,
8: 30 son was Abdon, followed by Zur, Kish, **Baal**, Ner, Nadab,
9: 36 son was Abdon, followed by Zur, Kish, **Baal**, Ner, Nadab,

1253 בַּעַל בְּרִית ba'al bᵉrît, n.pr. [2] [√ 1251 + 1382]

Baal-Berith [2]

Jdg 8: 33 themselves to the Baals. They set up **Baal-Berith** as their god
9: 4 gave him seventy shekels of silver from the temple of **Baal-Berith**,

1254 בַּעַל גָּד ba'al gād, n.pr.loc. [3] [√ 1251 + 1514]

Baal Gad [3]

Jos 11: 17 to **Baal Gad** in the Valley of Lebanon below Mount Hermon.
12: 7 from **Baal Gad** in the Valley of Lebanon to Mount Halak,
13: 5 to the east, from **Baal Gad** below Mount Hermon to Lebo Hamath.

1255 בַּעַל הָמוֹן ba'al hāmôn, n.pr.loc. [1] [√ 1251 + 2162]

Baal Hamon [1]

SS 8: 11 Solomon had a vineyard in **Baal Hamon**; he let out his vineyard to

1256 בַּעַל זְבוּב ba'al zᵉbûb, n.pr. [4] [√ 1251 + 2279]

Baal-Zebub [4]

2Ki 1: 2 saying to them, "Go and consult **Baal-Zebub**, the god of Ekron,
1: 3 is no God in Israel that you are going off to consult **Baal-Zebub**,
1: 6 no God in Israel that you are sending men to consult **Baal-Zebub**,
1: 16 to consult that you have sent messengers to consult **Baal-Zebub**,

1257 בַּעַל חָנָן ba'al ḥānān, n.pr.m. [5] [√ 1251 + 2860]

Baal-Hanan [5]

Ge 36: 38 Shaul died, **Baal-Hanan** son of Acbor succeeded him as king.
36: 39 When **Baal-Hanan** son of Acbor died, Hadad succeeded him as
1Ch 1: 49 Shaul died, **Baal-Hanan** son of Acbor succeeded him as king.
1: 50 When **Baal-Hanan** died, Hadad succeeded him as king. His city
27: 28 **Baal-Hanan** the Gederite was in charge of the olive

1258 בַּעַל חָצוֹר ba'al ḥāṣôr, n.pr.loc. [1] [√ 1251 + 2959]

Baal Hazor [1]

2Sa 13: 23 when Absalom's sheepshearers were at **Baal Hazor** near the

1259 בַּעַל חֶרְמוֹן ba'al ḥermôn, n.pr.loc. [2] [√ 1251 + 3056]

Baal Hermon [2]

Jdg 3: 3 Lebanon mountains from Mount **Baal Hermon** to Lebo Hamath.
1Ch 5: 23 they settled in the land from Bashan to **Baal Hermon**, that is,

1260 בַּעַל מְעוֹן ba'al mᵉ'ôn, n.pr.loc. [3] [√ 1251 + 5061?]

Baal Meon [3]

Nu 32: 38 as well as Nebo and **Baal Meon** (these names were changed)
1Ch 5: 8 They settled in the area from Aroer to Nebo and **Baal Meon**.
Eze 25: 9 Beth Jeshimoth, **Baal Meon** and Kiriathaim—the glory of that

1261 בַּעַל פְּעוֹר ba'al pᵉ'ôr, n.pr.m. [2] [√ 1251 + 7186]

Baal Peor [2]

Dt 4: 3 You saw with your own eyes what the LORD did at **Baal Peor**.
Hos 9: 10 when they came to **Baal Peor**, they consecrated themselves to that

1262 בַּעַל־פְּרָצִים ba'al-pᵉrāṣîm, n.pr.loc. [4] [√ 1251 + 7288]

Baal Perazim [4]

2Sa 5: 20 So David went to **Baal Perazim**, and there he defeated them.
5: 20 my enemies before me." So that place was called **Baal Perazim**.
1Ch 14: 11 So David and his men went up to **Baal Perazim**, and there he
14: 11 my enemies by my hand." So that place was called **Baal Perazim**.

1263 בַּעַל צְפֹן ba'al ṣᵉpōn, n.pr.loc. [3] [√ 1251 + 7600]

Baal Zephon [3]

Ex 14: 2 They are to encamp by the sea, directly opposite **Baal Zephon**.
14: 9 they camped by the sea near Pi Hahiroth, opposite **Baal Zephon**.

Nu 33: 7 Pi Hahiroth, to the east of **Baal Zephon**, and camped near Migdol.

1264 בַּעַל שָׁלִשָׁה ba'al šālišâ, n.pr.loc. [1] [√ 1251 + 8995]

Baal Shalishah [1]

2Ki 4:42 A man came from **Baal Shalishah**, bringing the man of God

1265 בַּעַל תָּמָר ba'al tāmār, n.pr.loc. [1] [√ 1251 + 9469]

Baal Tamar [1]

Jdg 20:33 moved from their places and took up positions at **Baal Tamar**,

1266 בַּעֲלָה¹ ba'ᵃlâ¹, n.f. [4] [→ 1168, 1267?, 1268; cf. 1251]

medium [+200] [1], mistress [1], one[s] [+200] [1], owned [1]

1Sa 28: 7 "Find me a woman who is a **medium** [+200], so I may go
28: 7 and inquire of her." "There is **one**[s] [+200] in Endor," they said.
1Ki 17:17 Some time later the son of the woman who **owned** the house
Na 3: 4 of the wanton lust of a harlot, alluring, the **mistress** *of* sorceries,

1267 בַּעֲלָה² ba'ᵃlâ², n.pr.loc. [5 / 6] [√ 1266?]

Baalah [6]

Jos 15: 9 the towns of Mount Ephron and went down toward **Baalah** (that is,
15:10 it curved westward from **Baalah** to Mount Seir, ran along the
15:11 passed along to Mount **Baalah** and reached Jabneel.
15:29 **Baalah**, Iim, Ezem,
2Sa 6: 2 all his men set out from **Baalah** [BHS 1251] *of* Judah to bring up
1Ch 13: 6 all the Israelites with him went to **Baalah** of Judah (Kiriath Jearim)

1268 בְּעָלוֹת bᵉ'ālôt, n.pr.loc. [1] [√ 1266]

Bealoth [1]

Jos 15:24 Ziph, Telem, **Bealoth**,

1269 בְּעֶלְיָדָע bᵉ'elyādā', n.pr.m. [1] [√ 1251 + 3359]

Beeliada [1]

1Ch 14: 7 Elishama, **Beeliada** and Eliphelet.

1270 בְּעַלְיָה bᵉ'alyâ, n.pr.m. [1] [√ 1251 + 3359 + 3378]

Bealiah [1]

1Ch 12: 5 [12:6] Eluzai, Jerimoth, **Bealiah**, Shemariah and Shephatiah the

1271 בַּעֲלִיס ba'ᵃlîs, n.pr.m. [1]

Baalis [1]

Jer 40:14 "Don't you know that **Baalis** king of the Ammonites has sent

1272 בַּעֲלָת ba'ᵃlāt, n.pr.loc. [3 / 4] [→ 1251]

Baalath [4]

Jos 19:44 Eltekeh, Gibbethon, **Baalath**,
1Ki 9:18 **Baalath**, and Tadmor in the desert, within his land,
1Ch 4:33 all the villages around these towns as far as **Baalath**. [BHS 1252]
2Ch 8: 6 as well as **Baalath** and all his store cities, and all the cities for his

1273 בַּעֲלַת בְּאֵר ba'ᵃlat bᵉ'ēr, n.pr.loc. [1] [√ 1251 + 931]

Baalath Beer [1]

Jos 19: 8 all the villages around these towns as far as **Baalath Beer** (Ramah

1274 בְּעֹן bᵉ'ōn, n.pr.loc. [1]

Beon [1]

Nu 32: 3 Jazer, Nimrah, Heshbon, Elealeh, Sebam, Nebo and **Beon**—

1275 בַּעֲנָא ba'ᵃnā', n.pr.m. [3] [→ 1276]

Baana [3]

1Ki 4:12 **Baana** son of Ahilud—in Taanach and Megiddo, and in all of Beth
4:16 **Baana** son of Hushai—in Asher and in Aloth;
Ne 3: 4 and next to him Zadok son of **Baana** also made repairs.

1276 בַּעֲנָה ba'ᵃnâ, n.pr.m. [9] [√ 1275]

Baanah [9]

2Sa 4: 2 One was named **Baanah** and the other Recab; they were sons of
4: 5 Now Recab and **Baanah**, the sons of Rimmon the Beerothite,
4: 6 in the stomach. Then Recab and his brother **Baanah** slipped away.
4: 9 David answered Recab and his brother **Baanah**, the sons of
23:29 Heled son of **Baanah** the Netophathite, Ithai son of Ribai from
1Ch 11:30 Maharai the Netophathite, Heled son of **Baanah** the Netophathite,
Ezr 2: 2 Mordecai, Bilshan, Mispar, Bigvai, Rehum and **Baanah**):
Ne 7: 7 Mordecai, Bilshan, Mispereth, Bigvai, Nehum and **Baanah**):
10:27 [10:28] Malluch, Harim and **Baanah**.

1277 בָּעַר¹ bā'ar¹, v. [63] [→ 1281, 1282, 9323; cf. 1278]

burn [11], burned [5], burning [5], blazed [4], burn up [3], fire [3], light [3], ablaze [2], blazing [2], burned up [2], burns [2], consume [2], set ablaze [2], use for fuel [+836+928] [2], blazed forth [1], blazes [1], charred [+836+928+2021] [1], consumed [1], consumes [1], fires [1], flare up [1], kindled [1], lit [+836+928] [1], on fire [+836+928+2021] [1], raged [1], sacrificed [1], sets ablaze [1], started [1], use for fuel [1]

Ex 3: 2 [A] the bush *was* **on fire** [+836+928+2021] it did not burn up.
3: 3 [A] and see this strange sight—why the bush *does* not **burn up**."
22: 6 [22:5] [G] the *one who* **started** the fire must make restitution.
35: 3 [D] *Do* not **light** a fire in any of your dwellings on the Sabbath
Lev 6:12 [6:5] [D] and arrange the burnt offering on *the* **fire**
Nu 11: 1 [A] fire from the LORD **burned** among them and consumed
11: 3 [A] because fire from the LORD *had* **burned** among them.
Dt 4:11 [A] stood at the foot of the mountain while it **blazed** with fire to
5:23 [A] while the mountain *was* **ablaze** with fire, all the leading men
9:15 [A] went down from the mountain while it *was* **ablaze** with fire.
Jdg 15: 5 [G] **lit** [+836+928] the torches and let the foxes loose in the
15: 5 [G] *He* **burned up** the shocks and standing grain, together with
15:14 [A] ropes on his arms became like **charred** [+836+928+2021] flax,
2Sa 22: 9 [A] fire came from his mouth, burning coals **blazed** out of it.
22:13 [A] the brightness of his presence bolts of lightning **blazed forth**.
1Ki 14:10 [D] *I will* **burn up** the house of Jeroboam as one burns dung,
14:10 [D] I will burn up the house of Jeroboam as *one* **burns** dung,
16: 3 [G] So I *am about to* **consume** Baasha and his house, and I will
21:21 [D] *I will* **consume** your descendants and cut off from Ahab
2Ch 4:20 [D] to **burn** in front of the inner sanctuary as prescribed;
13:11 [D] and **light** the lamps on the gold lampstand every evening.
28: 3 [G] the Valley of Ben Hinnom and **sacrificed** his sons in the fire,
Ne 10:34 [10:35] [D] wood to **burn** on the altar of the LORD our God,
Est 1:12 [A] Then the king became furious and **burned** *with* anger.
Job 1:16 [A] fell from the sky and **burned up** the sheep and the servants,
Ps 2:12 [A] in your way, for his wrath *can* **flare up** in a moment.
18: 8 [18:9] [A] came from his mouth, burning coals **blazed** out of it.
39: 3 [39:4] [A] hot within me, and as I meditated, the fire **burned**;
79: 5 [A] angry forever? How long *will* your jealousy **burn** like fire?
83:14 [83:15] [A] As fire **consumes** the forest or a flame sets the
89:46 [89:47] [A] How long *will* your wrath **burn** like fire?
106:18 [A] Fire **blazed** among their followers; a flame consumed the
Isa 1:31 [A] both *will* **burn** together, with no one to quench the fire."
4: 4 [D] from Jerusalem by a spirit of judgment and a spirit of **fire**.
9:18 [9:17] [A] Surely wickedness **burns** like a fire; it consumes
10:17 [A] in a single day *it will* **burn** and consume his thorns and his
30:27 [A] from afar, with **burning** anger and dense clouds of smoke;
30:33 [A] of the LORD, like a stream of burning sulfur, **sets** it **ablaze**.
34: 9 [A] dust into burning sulfur; her land will become **blazing** pitch!
40:16 [D] Lebanon is not sufficient for *altar* **fires**, nor its animals
42:25 [A] *it* **consumed** them, but they did not take it to heart.
43: 2 [A] you will not be burned; the flames *will* not **set** you **ablaze**.
44:15 [D] It is man's fuel for **burning**; some of it he takes and warms
50:11 [D] the light of your fires and of the torches *you have* **set ablaze**.
62: 1 [A] shines out like the dawn, her salvation like a **blazing** torch.
Jer 4: 4 [A] or my wrath will break out and **burn** like fire because of the
7:18 [D] The children gather wood, the fathers **light** the fire,
7:20 [A] the fruit of the ground, and *it will* **burn** and not be quenched.
20: 9 [A] his word is in my heart like a fire, a **fire** shut up in my bones.
21:12 [A] or my wrath will break out and **burn** like fire because of the
36:22 [E] with a fire **burning** in the firepot in front of him.
44: 6 [A] *it* **raged** against the towns of Judah and the streets of
La 2: 3 [A] *He has* **burned** in Jacob like a flaming fire that consumes
Eze 1:13 [A] The appearance of the living creatures was like **burning**
5: 2 [G] to an end, **burn** a third of the hair with fire inside the city.
20:48 [21:4] [D] Everyone will see that I the LORD *have* **kindled** it;
39: 9 [D] will go out and use the weapons **for fuel** and burn them up—
39: 9 [D] For seven years *they will* **use** them **for fuel** [+836+928].
39:10 [D] because *they will* **use** the weapons **for fuel** [+836+928].
Hos 7: 4 [A] **burning** like an oven whose fire the baker need not stir from
7: 6 [A] all night; in the morning it **blazes** like a flaming fire.
Na 2:13 [2:14] [G] "*I will* **burn up** your chariots in smoke,
Mal 4: 1 [3:19] [A] "Surely the day is coming; *it will* **burn** like a

1278 בָּעַר² bā'ar², v. [24] [cf. 1277]

purge [12], rid [3], destroyed [2], removed [2], got rid of [1], graze [1], grazes [1], laid waste [1], ruined [1]

Ex 22: 5 [22:4] [G] "If a man **grazes** his livestock *in* a field or vineyard
22: 5 [22:4] [D] lets them stray and *they* **graze** in another man's field,
Nu 24:22 [D] yet you Kenites will be **destroyed** when Asshur takes you
Dt 13: 5 [13:6] [D] to follow. *You must* **purge** the evil from among you.
17: 7 [D] of all the people. *You must* **purge** the evil from among you.
17:12 [D] must be put to death. *You must* **purge** the evil from Israel.
19:13 [D] *You must* **purge** from Israel the guilt of shedding innocent
19:19 [D] do to his brother. *You must* **purge** the evil from among you.

Dt 21: 9 [D] So you *will* **purge** from yourselves the guilt of shedding
21:21 [D] *You must* **purge** the evil from among you. All Israel will
22:21 [D] father's house. *You must* **purge** the evil from among you.
22:22 [D] the woman must die. *You must* **purge** the evil from Israel.
22:24 [D] man's wife. *You must* **purge** the evil from among you.
24: 7 [D] must die. *You must* **purge** the evil from among you.
26:13 [D] "*I have* **removed** from my house the sacred portion and have
26:14 [D] nor *have I* **removed** any of it while I was unclean, nor have I
Jdg 20:13 [D] we may put them to death and **purge** the evil from Israel."
2Sa 4:11 [D] demand his blood from your hand and **rid** the earth *of* you!"
1Ki 22:46 [22:47] [D] *He* **rid** the land *of* the rest of the male shrine
2Ki 23:24 [D] **got rid of** the mediums and spiritists, the household gods,
2Ch 19: 3 [D] for *you have* **rid** the land *of* the Asherah poles and have set
Isa 3:14 [D] "It is you *who have* **ruined** my vineyard; the plunder from
5: 5 [D] I will take away its hedge, and it will be **destroyed**; I will
6:13 [D] a tenth remains in the land, it will again be **laid waste**.

1279 ³בָּעַר bā'ar³, v.den. [7] [√ 1248]

senseless [5], brutal [1], give senseless [1]

Ps 94: 8 [A] Take heed, you **senseless** *ones* among the people; you fools,
Isa 19:11 [C] the wise counselors of Pharaoh **give senseless** advice.
Jer 10: 8 [A] *They are* all **senseless** and foolish; they are taught by
10:14 [C] Everyone *is* **senseless** and without knowledge;
10:21 [C] The shepherds *are* **senseless** and do not inquire of the
51:17 [C] "Every man *is* **senseless** and without knowledge;
Eze 21:31 [21:36] [A] I will hand you over to **brutal** men, men skilled in

1280 בַּעַר ba'ar, n.m. [5] [√ 1248]

senseless [3], ignorant [1], stupid [1]

Ps 49:10 [49:11] the foolish and the **senseless** alike perish and leave their
73:22 I was **senseless** and ignorant; I was a brute beast before you.
92: 6 [92:7] The **senseless** man does not know, fools do not understand,
Pr 12: 1 discipline loves knowledge, but he who hates correction is **stupid**.
30: 2 "I *am the* most **ignorant** of men; I do not have a man's

1281 בַּעֲרָא ba'ărā', n.pr.f. [1] [√ 1282; cf. 1277]

Baara [1]

1Ch 8: 8 in Moab after he had divorced his wives Hushim and **Baara**.

1282 בְּעֵרָה be'ērâ, n.f. [1] [→ 1281; cf. 1277]

fire [1]

Ex 22: 6 [22:5] the one who started the **fire** must make restitution.

1283 בַּעֲשֵׂיָה ba'ăśēyâ, n.pr.m. [1]

Baaseiah [1]

1Ch 6:40 [6:25] the son of Michael, the son of **Baaseiah**, the son of

1284 בַּעְשָׁא ba'šā', n.pr.m. [28]

Baasha [25], Baasha's [2], he[s] [1]

1Ki 15:16 between Asa and **Baasha** king of Israel throughout their reigns.
15:17 **Baasha** king of Israel went up against Judah and fortified Ramah
15:19 Now break your treaty with **Baasha** king of Israel so he will
15:21 When **Baasha** heard this, he stopped building Ramah
15:22 from Ramah the stones and timber **Baasha** had been using there.
15:27 **Baasha** son of Ahijah of the house of Issachar plotted against him,
15:27 **he**[s] struck him down at Gibbethon, a Philistine town, while Nadab
15:28 **Baasha** killed Nadab in the third year of Asa king of Judah
15:32 between Asa and **Baasha** king of Israel throughout their reigns.
15:33 **Baasha** son of Ahijah became king of all Israel in Tirzah,
16: 1 word of the LORD came to Jehu son of Hanani against **Baasha**:
16: 3 So I am about to consume **Baasha** and his house, and I will make
16: 4 Dogs will eat those belonging to **Baasha** who die in the city,
16: 5 As for the other events of **Baasha's** reign, what he did and his
16: 6 **Baasha** rested with his fathers and was buried in Tirzah. And Elah
16: 7 LORD came through the prophet Jehu son of Hanani to **Baasha**
16: 8 Elah son of **Baasha** became king of Israel, and he reigned in
16:11 and was seated on the throne, he killed off **Baasha's** whole family.
16:12 So Zimri destroyed the whole family of **Baasha**, in accordance
16:12 in accordance with the word of the LORD spoken against **Baasha**
16:13 because of all the sins **Baasha** and his son Elah had committed
21:22 that of Jeroboam son of Nebat and that of **Baasha** son of Ahijah,
2Ki 9: 9 son of Nebat and like the house of **Baasha** son of Ahijah.
2Ch 16: 1 In the thirty-sixth year of Asa's reign **Baasha** king of Israel went
16: 3 Now break your treaty with **Baasha** king of Israel so he will
16: 5 When **Baasha** heard this, he stopped building Ramah
16: 6 away from Ramah the stones and timber **Baasha** had been using.
Jer 41: 9 Asa had made as part of his defense against **Baasha** king of Israel.

1285 בְּעֶשְׁתְּרָה be'ešterâ, n.pr.loc. [1] [cf. 6958?]

Be Eshtarah [1]

Jos 21:27 and **Be Eshtarah**, together with their pasturelands—two towns;

1286 בָּעַת bā'at, v. [16] [→ 1287, 1243]

overwhelmed [2], terrified [2], terrify [2], afraid [1], alarm [1], fill with terror [1], frighten [1], frightening [1], makes tremble [1], overwhelm [1], startle [1], tormented [1], tormenting [1]

1Sa 16:14 [D] and an evil spirit from the LORD **tormented** him.
16:15 [D] said to him, "See, an evil spirit from God *is* **tormenting** you.
2Sa 22: 5 [D] about me; the torrents of destruction **overwhelmed** me.
1Ch 21:30 [C] because *he was* **afraid** of the sword of the angel of the
Est 7: 6 [C] Then Haman *was* **terrified** before the king and queen.
Job 3: 5 [D] a cloud settle over it; *may* blackness **overwhelm** its light.
7:14 [D] you frighten me with dreams and **terrify** me with visions,
9:34 [D] rod from me, so that his terror *would* **frighten** me no more.
13:11 [D] *Would* not his splendor **terrify** you? Would not the dread of
13:21 [D] hand far from me, and stop **frightening** me *with* your terrors.
15:24 [D] Distress and anguish **fill** him **with terror**; they overwhelm
18:11 [D] Terrors **startle** him on every side and dog his every step.
33: 7 [D] No fear of me *should* **alarm** you, nor should my hand be
Ps 18: 4 [18:5] [D] the torrents of destruction **overwhelmed** me.
Isa 21: 4 [D] My heart falters, fear **makes** me **tremble**; the twilight I
Da 8:17 [C] place where I was standing, *I was* **terrified** and fell prostrate.

1287 בְּעָתָה be'ātâ, n.f. [2] [√ 1286]

terror [2]

Jer 8:15 no good has come, for a time of healing but there was only **terror**.
14:19 no good has come, for a time of healing but there is only **terror**.

1288 בֹּץ bōṣ, n.[m.]. [1] [→ 1010?, 1289, 9324?]

mud [1]

Jer 38:22 Your feet are sunk in the **mud**; your friends have deserted you.'

1289 בִּצָּה biṣṣâ, n.f. [3] [√ 1288]

marsh [2], swamps [1]

Job 8:11 Can papyrus grow tall where there is no **marsh**? Can reeds thrive
40:21 the lotus plants he lies, hidden among the reeds in the **marsh**.
Eze 47:11 the **swamps** and marshes will not become fresh; they will be left

1290 בָּצוּר bāṣûr, a. [25] [√ 1307]

fortified [22], walls [2], unsearchable [1]

Nu 13:28 live there are powerful, and the cities are **fortified** and very large.
Dt 1:28 and taller than we are; the cities are large, with **walls** up to the sky.
3: 5 All these cities were **fortified** with high walls and with gates
9: 1 stronger than you, with large cities that have **walls** up to the sky.
28:52 land until the high **fortified** walls in which you trust fall down.
Jos 14:12 the Anakites were there and their cities were large and **fortified**,
2Sa 20: 6 pursue him, or he will find **fortified** cities and escape from us."
2Ki 18:13 Sennacherib king of Assyria attacked all the **fortified** cities of
19:25 it to pass, that you have turned **fortified** cities into piles of stone.
2Ch 17: 2 He stationed troops in all the **fortified** cities of Judah and put
19: 5 judges in the land, in each of the **fortified** cities of Judah.
32: 1 He laid siege to the **fortified** cities, thinking to conquer them for
33:14 He stationed military commanders in all the **fortified** cities in
Ne 9:25 They captured **fortified** cities and fertile land; they took possession
Isa 2:15 for every lofty tower and every **fortified** wall,
25: 2 You have made the city a heap of rubble, the **fortified** town a ruin,
27:10 The **fortified** city stands desolate, an abandoned settlement,
36: 1 Sennacherib king of Assyria attacked all the **fortified** cities of
37:26 it to pass, that you have turned **fortified** cities into piles of stone.
Jer 15:20 I will make you a wall to this people, a **fortified** wall of bronze;
33: 3 and tell you great and **unsearchable** *things* you do not know.'
Eze 21:20 [21:25] and another against Judah and **fortified** Jerusalem.
36:35 in ruins, desolate and destroyed, are now **fortified** and inhabited."
Hos 8:14 his Maker and built palaces; Judah has **fortified** many towns.
Zep 1:16 a day of trumpet and battle cry against the **fortified** cities
Zec 11: 2 [the **dense** [K; see Q 1293] forest has been cut down!]

1291 בֵּצַי bēṣay, n.pr.m. [3]

Bezai [3]

Ezr 2:17 of **Bezai** 323
Ne 7:23 of **Bezai** 324
10:18 [10:19] Hodiah, Hashum, **Bezai**,

1292 ¹בָּצִיר bāṣîr¹, n.m. [7] [√ 1305]

grape harvest [4], full grape harvest [1], grapes [1], vineyard [1]

Lev 26: 5 Your threshing will continue until **grape harvest** and the grape

Lev 26: 5 grape harvest and the **grape harvest** will continue until planting,
Jdg 8: 2 of Ephraim's grapes better than the **full grape harvest** *of* Abiezer?
Isa 24: 13 is beaten, or as when gleanings are left after the **grape harvest**.
32: 10 the **grape harvest** will fail, and the harvest of fruit will not come.
Jer 48: 32 The destroyer has fallen on your ripened fruit and **grapes**.
Mic 7: 1 like one who gathers summer fruit at the gleaning of the **vineyard**;

1293 ²בָּצִיר *bāṣîr*[2], n.m. [1] [√ 1307]

dense [1]

Zec 11: 2 oaks of Bashan; the **dense** [K 1290] forest has been cut down!

1294 בָּצָל *bāṣāl*, n.m. [1] [→ 1296?, 1297?]

onions [1]

Nu 11: 5 at no cost—also the cucumbers, melons, leeks, **onions** and garlic.

1295 בְּצַלְאֵל *beṣal'ēl*, n.pr.m. [9] [√ 928 + 7498 + 446]

Bezalel [9]

Ex 31: 2 "See, I have chosen **Bezalel** son of Uri, the son of Hur, of the tribe
35: 30 "See, the LORD has chosen **Bezalel** son of Uri, the son of Hur,
36: 1 So **Bezalel**, Oholiab and every skilled person to whom the LORD
36: 2 Moses summoned **Bezalel** and Oholiab and every skilled person to
37: 1 **Bezalel** made the ark of acacia wood—two and a half cubits long,
38: 22 (**Bezalel** son of Uri, the son of Hur, of the tribe of Judah,
1Ch 2: 20 Hur was the father of Uri, and Uri the father of **Bezalel**.
2Ch 1: 5 But the bronze altar that **Bezalel** son of Uri, the son of Hur,
Ezr 10: 30 Benaiah, Maaseiah, Mattaniah, **Bezalel**, Binnui and Manasseh.

1296 בַּצְלוּת *baṣlût*, n.pr.m. [1 / 2] [√ 1294?]

Bazluth [2]

Ezr 2: 52 **Bazluth**, Mehida, Harsha,
Ne 7: 54 **Bazluth**, [BHS 1297] Mehida, Harsha,

1297 בַּצְלִית *baṣlît*, n.pr.m. [1 / 0] [√ 1294?]

Ne 7: 54 Bazluth, [BHS *Bazlith*; NIV 1296] Mehida, Harsha,

1298 בָּצַע *bāṣa'*, v. [16] [→ 1299]

cut off [3], greedy [3], breaking ranks [1], bring down [1], builds [1], complete [1], finished [1], fulfilled [1], go after ill-gotten gain [+1299] [1], greedy [+1299] [1], make unjust gain [+1299] [1], make unjust gain [1]

Job 6: 9 [D] be willing to crush me, to let loose his hand and **cut** me **off**!
27: 8 [A] For what hope has the godless when *he is* **cut off**, when God
Ps 10: 3 [A] of his heart; he blesses the **greedy** and reviles the LORD.
Pr 1: 19 [A] Such is the end of all *who* **go after ill-gotten gain** [+1299];
15: 27 [A] A **greedy** [+1299] *man* brings trouble to his family, but he
Isa 10: 12 [D] When the Lord *has* **finished** all his work against Mount Zion
38: 12 [D] have rolled up my life, and *he has* **cut** me **off** from the loom;
Jer 6: 13 [A] "From the least to the greatest, all *are* **greedy** *for* gain;
8: 10 [A] From the least to the greatest, all *are* **greedy** *for* gain;
La 2: 17 [D] *he has* **fulfilled** his word, which he decreed long ago.
Eze 22: 12 [D] and **make unjust gain** *from* your neighbors by extortion.
22: 27 [A] shed blood and kill people to **make unjust gain** [+1299].
Joel 2: 8 [A] They plunge through defenses without **breaking ranks**.
Am 9: 1 [A] **Bring** them **down** on the heads of all the people; those who
Hab 2: 9 [A] "Woe to *him who* **builds** his realm by unjust gain to set his
Zec 4: 9 [D] the foundation of this temple; his hands *will* also **complete** it.

1299 בֶּצַע *beṣa'*, n.m. [23] [√ 1298]

gain [9], dishonest gain [3], unjust gain [2], cut off [1], go after ill-gotten gain [+1298] [1], greed [1], greedy [+1298] [1], ill-gotten gain [1], ill-gotten gains [1], make unjust gain [+1298] [1], plunder [1], selfish gain [1]

Ge 37: 26 "What will we **gain** if we kill our brother and cover up his blood?
Ex 18: 21 men who fear God, trustworthy men who hate **dishonest gain**—
Jdg 5: 19 the waters of Megiddo, but they carried off no silver, no **plunder**.
1Sa 8: 3 They turned aside after **dishonest gain** and accepted bribes
Job 22: 3 were righteous? What would he **gain** if your ways were blameless?
Ps 30: 9 [30:10] "What **gain** is there in my destruction, in my going down
119: 36 Turn my heart toward your statutes and not toward **selfish gain**.
Pr 1: 19 Such is the end of all *who* **go after ill-gotten gain** [+1298];
15: 27 A **greedy man** [+1298] brings trouble to his family, but he who
28: 16 but he who hates **ill-gotten gain** will enjoy a long life.
Isa 33: 15 who rejects **gain** *from* extortion and keeps his hand from accepting
56: 11 they all turn to their own way, each seeks his own **gain**.
57: 17 I was enraged by his sinful **greed**; I punished him, and hid my face
Jer 6: 13 "From the least to the greatest, all are greedy for **gain**; prophets
8: 10 From the least to the greatest, all are greedy for **gain**; prophets
22: 17 "But your eyes and your heart are set only on **dishonest gain**,
51: 13 rich in treasures, your end has come, the time for you to be **cut off**.
Eze 22: 13 " 'I will surely strike my hands together at the **unjust gain** you
22: 27 they shed blood and kill people to **make unjust gain** [+1298].
33: 31 they express devotion, but their hearts are greedy for **unjust gain**.
Mic 4: 13 You will devote their **ill-gotten gains** to the LORD, their wealth
Hab 2: 9 "Woe to him who builds his realm by unjust **gain** to set his nest on
Mal 3: 14 What did we **gain** by carrying out his requirements and going

1300 בְּצַעֲנַנִּים *beṣa'anannîm*, n.pr.loc. Not used in NIV/BHS [cf. 7588]

1301 ¹בָּצֵק *bāṣēq*[1], v. [2] [→ 1302, 1304]

swell [1], swollen [1]

Dt 8: 4 [A] wear out and your feet *did* not **swell** during these forty years.
Ne 9: 21 [A] clothes did not wear out nor *did* their feet *become* **swollen**.

1302 ²בָּצֵק *bāṣēq*[2], n.[m.]. [5] [√ 1301]

dough [5]

Ex 12: 34 So the people took their **dough** before the yeast was added,
12: 39 *With* the **dough** they had brought from Egypt, they baked cakes of
2Sa 13: 8 She took some **dough**, kneaded it, made the bread in his sight
Jer 7: 18 the women knead the **dough** and make cakes of bread for the
Hos 7: 4 the baker need not stir from the kneading of the **dough** till it rises.

1303 בִּצְקָלוֹן *biṣqālôn*, n.[m.]. Not used in NIV/BHS

1304 בָּצְקַת *boṣqat*, n.pr.loc. [2] [√ 1301]

Bozkath [2]

Jos 15: 39 Lachish, **Bozkath**, Eglon,
2Ki 22: 1 name was Jedidah daughter of Adaiah; she was from **Bozkath**.

1305 ¹בָּצַר *bāṣar*[1], v. [7] [→ 1292]

grape pickers [2], harvest [2], gathered [1], gathering grapes [1], harvest grapes [1]

Lev 25: 5 [A] grows of itself or **harvest** the grapes of your untended vines.
25: 11 [A] not reap what grows of itself or **harvest** the untended vines.
Dt 24: 21 [A] When *you* **harvest** *the* **grapes** *in* your vineyard, do not go
Jdg 9: 27 [A] out into the fields and **gathered** the grapes and trodden them,
Jer 6: 9 [A] hand over the branches again, like *one* **gathering grapes**."
49: 9 [A] If **grape pickers** came to you, would they not leave a few
Ob 1: 5 [A] If **grape pickers** came to you, would they not leave a few

1306 ²בָּצַר *bāṣar*[2], v. [1] [→ 1314, 1316]

breaks [1]

Ps 76: 12 [76:13] [A] *He* **breaks** the spirit of rulers; he is feared by the

1307 ³בָּצַר *bāṣar*[3], v. [4] [→ 1290, 1293, 1310?, 1311, 1312, 1313, 1315, 4448, 4449, 4450?]

be thwarted [1], fortifies [1], impossible [1], strengthen [1]

Ge 11: 6 [C] then nothing they plan to do *will be* **impossible** for them.
Job 42: 2 [C] that you can do all things; no plan of yours *can* **be thwarted**.
Isa 22: 10 [D] in Jerusalem and tore down houses to **strengthen** the wall.
Jer 51: 53 [D] if Babylon reaches the sky and **fortifies** her lofty stronghold,

1308 ⁴בָּצַר *bāṣar*[4], n.m. Not used in NIV/BHS [→ 1309, 1310?, 4450]

1309 ¹בֶּצֶר *beṣer*[1], n.[m.]. [2] [√ 1308]

gold [1], nuggets [1]

Job 22: 24 assign your **nuggets** to the dust, your gold of Ophir to the rocks in
22: 25 then the Almighty will be your **gold**, the choicest silver for you.

1310 ²בֶּצֶר *beṣer*[2], n.pr.m. [1] [√ 1308 *or* 1307]

Bezer [1]

1Ch 7: 37 **Bezer**, Hod, Shamma, Shilshah, Ithran and Beera.

1311 ³בֶּצֶר *beṣer*[3], n.pr.loc. [4] [√ 1307 *or possibly* 1308]

Bezer [4]

Dt 4: 43 **Bezer** in the desert plateau, for the Reubenites; Ramoth in Gilead,
Jos 20: 8 On the east side of the Jordan of Jericho they designated **Bezer** in
21: 36 from the tribe of Reuben, **Bezer**, Jahaz,
1Ch 6: 78 [6:63] the Jordan east of Jericho they received **Bezer** in the desert,

1312 ¹בָּצְרָה *boṣrâ*[1], n.f. [1] [√ 1307]

pen [1]

Mic 2: 12 I will bring them together like sheep in a **pen**, like a flock in its

1313 ²בָּצְרָה ***boṣrâ²***, n.pr.loc. [8] [√ 1307]

Bozrah [8]

Ge 36:33 Bela died, Jobab son of Zerah from **Bozrah** succeeded him as king.
1Ch 1:44 Bela died, Jobab son of Zerah from **Bozrah** succeeded him as king.
Isa 34: 6 For the LORD has a sacrifice in **Bozrah** and a great slaughter in
63: 1 Who is this coming from Edom, from **Bozrah**, with his garments
Jer 48:24 to Kerioth and **Bozrah**—to all the towns of Moab, far and near.
49:13 "that **Bozrah** will become a ruin and an object of horror, of
49:22 eagle will soar and swoop down, spreading its wings over **Bozrah**.
Am 1:12 send fire upon Teman that will consume the fortresses of **Bozrah**."

1314 בַּצָּרָה ***baṣṣārâ***, n.f. [3] [√ 1306]

trouble [2], drought [1]

Ps 9: 9 [9:10] refuge for the oppressed, a stronghold in times of **trouble**.
10: 1 you stand far off? Why do you hide yourself in times of **trouble**?
Jer 14: 1 is the word of the LORD to Jeremiah concerning the **drought**:

1315 בִּצָּרוֹן ***biṣṣārôn***, n.[m.]. [1] [√ 1307]

fortress [1]

Zec 9:12 Return to your **fortress**, O prisoners of hope; even now I announce

1316 בַּצֹּרֶת ***baṣṣōret***, n.f. [1] [√ 1306]

drought [1]

Jer 17: 8 It has no worries in a year of **drought** and never fails to bear fruit."

1317 בַּקְבּוּק ***baqbûq***, n.pr.m. [2] [√ 1318]

Bakbuk [2]

Ezr 2:51 **Bakbuk**, Hakupha, Harhur,
Ne 7:53 **Bakbuk**, Hakupha, Harhur,

1318 בַּקְבֻּק ***baqbuq***, n.[m.]. [3] [→ 1317, 1319, 1321, 1322]

jar [3]

1Ki 14: 3 of bread with you, some cakes and a **jar** *of* honey, and go to him.
Jer 19: 1 is what the LORD says: "Go and buy a clay **jar** *from* a potter.
19:10 "Then break the **jar** while those who go with you are watching,

1319 בַּקְבֻּקְיָה ***baqbuqyâ***, n.pr.m. [3] [√ 1318 + 3378]

Bakbukiah [3]

Ne 11:17 and prayer; **Bakbukiah**, second among his associates;
12: 9 **Bakbukiah** and Unni, their associates, stood opposite them in the
12:25 Mattaniah, **Bakbukiah**, Obadiah, Meshullam, Talmon and Akkub

1320 בַּקְבַּקַּר ***baqbaqqar***, n.pr.m. [1]

Bakbakkar [1]

1Ch 9:15 **Bakbakkar**, Heresh, Galal and Mattaniah son of Mica, the son of

1321 בֻּקִּי ***buqqî***, n.pr.m. [5] [√ 1318; cf. 1322]

Bukki [5]

Nu 34:22 **Bukki** son of Jogli, the leader from the tribe of Dan;
1Ch 6: 5 [5:31] Abishua the father of **Bukki**, Bukki the father of Uzzi,
6: 5 [5:31] Abishua the father of Bukki, **Bukki** the father of Uzzi,
6:51 [6:36] **Bukki** his son, Uzzi his son, Zerahiah his son,
Ezr 7: 4 the son of Zerahiah, the son of Uzzi, the son of **Bukki**,

1322 בֻּקִּיָּהוּ ***buqqiyyāhû***, n.pr.m. [2] [√ 1318 + 3378?; cf. 1321]

Bukkiah [2]

1Ch 25: 4 **Bukkiah**, Mattaniah, Uzziel, Shubael and Jerimoth; Hananiah,
25:13 the sixth to **Bukkiah**, his sons and relatives, 12

1323 בָּקִיעַ ***bāqîa'***, n.[m.]. [2] [√ 1324]

bits [1], breaches in defenses [1]

Isa 22: 9 you saw that the City of David had many **breaches in** its **defenses**;
Am 6:11 smash the great house into pieces and the small house into **bits**.

1324 בָּקַע ***bāqa'***, v. [51] [→ 1323, 1325, 1326]

divided [3], ripped open [3], split [3], was broken through [3], broke [2], burst forth [2], cracked [2], divide [2], hatch [2], opened up [2], split apart [2], were divided [2], be split [1], been broken through [1], break forth [1], break through [1], breaks up [1], burst [1], chopped up [1], conquer [1], cut [1], gush forth [1], invaded [1], is hatched [1], mauled [1], ready to burst [1], rip open [1], shook [1], splits [1], taken by storm [1], tear apart [1], tore open [1], tunnels [+3284] [1], unleash [1], were dashed to pieces [1]

Ge 7:11 [C] on that day all the springs of the great deep **burst forth**,
22: 3 [D] When *he had* **cut** enough wood for the burnt offering, he set
Ex 14:16 [A] and stretch out your hand over the sea *to* **divide** the water
14:21 [C] and turned it into dry land. The waters **were divided**,
Nu 16:31 [C] he finished saying all this, the ground under them **split apart**
Jos 9: 4 [E] worn-out sacks and old wineskins, **cracked** and mended.
9:13 [F] that we filled were new, but see how **cracked** *they are*.
Jdg 15:19 [A] God **opened up** the hollow place in Lehi, and water came out
1Sa 6:14 [D] The people **chopped up** the wood of the cart and sacrificed
2Sa 23:16 [A] So the three mighty men **broke** through the Philistine lines,
1Ki 1:40 [C] rejoicing greatly, so that the ground **shook** with the sound.
2Ki 2:24 [D] came out of the woods and **mauled** forty-two of the youths.
3:26 [G] hundred swordsmen to **break through** to the king of Edom,
8:12 [D] children to the ground, and **rip open** their pregnant women."
15:16 [D] He sacked Tiphsah and **ripped open** all the pregnant women.
25: 4 [C] the city wall **was broken through**, and the whole army fled
1Ch 11:18 [A] So the Three **broke** through the Philistine lines, drew water
2Ch 21:17 [A] **invaded** it and carried off all the goods found in the king's
25:12 [C] and threw them down so that all **were dashed to pieces**.
32: 1 [A] to the fortified cities, thinking to **conquer** them for himself.
Ne 9:11 [A] *You* **divided** the sea before them, so that they passed through
Job 26: 8 [C] in his clouds, yet the clouds *do* not **burst** under their weight.
28:10 [D] *He* **tunnels** [+3284] through the rock; his eyes see all its
32:19 [C] am like bottled-up wine, like new wineskins **ready to burst**.
Ps 74:15 [A] It was you *who* **opened up** springs and streams; you dried up
78:13 [A] *He* **divided** the sea and led them through; he made the water
78:15 [D] *He* **split** the rocks in the desert and gave them water as
141: 7 [A] ⌞They will say,⌟ "As one plows and **breaks up** the earth,
Pr 3:20 [C] by his knowledge the deeps **were divided**, and the clouds let
Ecc 10: 9 [A] by them; *whoever* **splits** logs may be endangered by them.
Isa 7: 6 [G] let us tear it apart and **divide** it among ourselves, and make
34:15 [A] The owl will nest there and lay eggs, *she will* **hatch** them,
35: 6 [C] Water *will* **gush forth** in the wilderness and streams in the
48:21 [A] them from the rock; *he* **split** the rock and water gushed out.
58: 8 [C] your light *will* **break forth** like the dawn, and your healing
59: 5 [D] *They* **hatch** the eggs of vipers and spin a spider's web.
59: 5 [C] eggs will die, and when one is broken, an adder **is hatched**.
63:12 [A] *who* **divided** the waters before them, to gain for himself
Jer 39: 2 [H] Zedekiah's eleventh year, the city wall **was broken through**.
52: 7 [C] the city wall **was broken through**, and the whole army fled.
Eze 13:11 [D] hailstones hurtling down, and violent winds *will* **burst forth**.
13:13 [D] In my wrath *I will* **unleash** a violent wind, and in my anger
26:10 [E] as men enter a city whose walls *have* **been broken through**.
29: 7 [A] you splintered and *you* **tore open** their shoulders;
30:16 [C] Thebes will be **taken by storm**; Memphis will be in constant
Hos 13: 8 [D] lion I will devour them; a wild animal *will* **tear** them **apart**.
13:16 [14:1] [E] to the ground, their pregnant women **ripped open**."
Am 1:13 [A] Because he **ripped open** the pregnant women of Gilead in
Mic 1: 4 [F] The mountains melt beneath him and the valleys **split apart**,
Hab 3: 9 [D] for many arrows. *Selah You* **split** the earth with rivers;
Zec 14: 4 [C] the Mount of Olives *will* **be split** in two from east to west,

1325 בֶּקַע ***beqa'***, n.[m.]. [2] [√ 1324]

beka [2]

Ge 24:22 the man took out a gold nose ring weighing a **beka** and two gold
Ex 38:26 *one* **beka** per person, that is, half a shekel, according to the

1326 בִּקְעָה ***biq'â***, n.f. [20] [√ 1324; Ar 10117]

plain [9], valley [7], valleys [4]

Ge 11: 2 moved eastward, they found a **plain** in Shinar and settled there.
Dt 8: 7 and pools of water, with springs flowing in the **valleys** and hills;
11:11 of is a land of mountains and **valleys** that drinks rain from heaven.
34: 3 the Negev and the whole region from the **Valley** *of* Jericho,
Jos 11: 8 to Misrephoth Maim, and to the **Valley** *of* Mizpah on the east,
11:17 to Baal Gad in the **Valley** *of* Lebanon below Mount Hermon.
12: 7 from Baal Gad in the **Valley** *of* Lebanon to Mount Halak,
2Ch 35:22 at God's command but went to fight him on the **plain** *of* Megiddo.
Ne 6: 2 let us meet together in one of the villages on the **plain** *of* Ono."
Ps 104: 8 they flowed over the mountains, they went down into the **valleys**,
Isa 40: 4 the rough ground shall become level, the rugged places a **plain**.
41:18 make rivers flow on barren heights, and springs within the **valleys**.
63:14 like cattle that go down to the **plain**, they were given rest by the
Eze 3:22 he said to me, "Get up and go out to the **plain**, and there I will
3:23 So I got up and went out to the **plain**. And the glory of the LORD
8: 4 glory of the God of Israel, as in the vision I had seen in the **plain**.
37: 1 by the Spirit of the LORD and set me in the middle of a **valley**;
37: 2 and I saw a great many bones on the floor of the **valley**,
Am 1: 5 I will destroy the king who is in the **Valley** *of* Aven and the one
Zec 12:11 like the weeping of Hadad Rimmon in the **plain** *of* Megiddo.

1327 ¹בָּקַק **bāqaq¹**, v. [8] [cf. 3309?]

be completely laid waste [+1327] [2], destroyers [1], devastate [1], laid waste [1], lay waste [1], lose heart [+928+7931+8120] [1], ruin [1]

Isa 19: 3 [C] The Egyptians *will* **lose heart** [+928+7931+8120], and I will bring their plans to nothing; they will consult the idols and the
24: 1 [A] the LORD *is going to* **lay waste** the earth and devastate it;
24: 3 [C] The earth *will* **be completely laid waste** [+1327] and totally
24: 3 [C] The earth *will* **be completely laid waste** [+1327] and totally
Jer 19: 7 [A] " 'In this place *I will* **ruin** the plans of Judah and Jerusalem.
51: 2 [D] to Babylon to winnow her and *to* **devastate** her land;
Na 2: 2 [2:3] [A] though **destroyers** have laid them waste and have
2: 2 [2:3] [A] though destroyers *have* **laid** them **waste** and have

1328 ²בָּקַק **bāqaq²**, v. [1]

spreading [1]

Hos 10: 1 [A] Israel *was* a **spreading** vine; he brought forth fruit for

1329 בָּקַר **bāqar**, v. [7] [→ 1330, 1331, 1332, 1333, 1334; Ar 10118]

look after [2], consider [1], look [1], pick out [1], seek [1], seeking guidance [1]

Lev 13:36 [D] in the skin, the priest *does* not *need to* **look** for yellow hair;
27:33 [D] *He must* not **pick out** the good from the bad or make any
2Ki 16:15 [D] But I will use the bronze altar for **seeking guidance**."
Ps 27: 4 [D] upon the beauty of the LORD and to **seek** him in his temple.
Pr 20:25 [D] something rashly and only later to **consider** his vows.
Eze 34:11 [D] I myself will search for my sheep and **look after** them.
34:12 [D] flock when he is with them, so *will I* **look after** my sheep.

1330 בָּקָר **bāqār**, n.m. [183 / 184] [→ 1012; cf. 1329]

cattle [40], herds [32], oxen [31], bull [+7228] [27], bulls [14], herd [10], bulls [+7228] [5], bull [4], ox [4], animals [2], calf [+1201] [2], cows [2], heifer [+6320] [2], bull [+1201] [1], calves [+1201] [1], cattle [+5238] [1], cow [1], herds [+5238] [1], herds [+6373] [1], oxgoad [+4913] [1], plowing [1], young cow [+6320] [1]

Ge 12:16 and Abram acquired sheep and **cattle**, male and female donkeys,
13: 5 moving about with Abram, also had flocks and **herds** and tents.
18: 7 Then he ran to the **herd** and selected a choice, tender calf
18: 7 and selected a choice, tender **calf** [+1201] and gave it to a servant,
18: 8 some curds and milk and the **calf** [+1201] that had been prepared,
20:14 and **cattle** and male and female slaves and gave them to Abraham,
21:27 So Abraham brought sheep and **cattle** and gave them to
24:35 He has given him sheep and **cattle**, silver and gold, menservants
26:14 He had so many flocks and **herds** [+5238] and servants that the
32: 7 [32:8] two groups, and the flocks and **herds** and camels as well.
33:13 that I must care for the ewes and **cows** that are nursing their young.
34:28 They seized their flocks and **herds** and donkeys and everything
45:10 and grandchildren, your flocks and **herds**, and all you have.
46:32 brought along their flocks and **herds** and everything they own.'
47: 1 and brothers, with their flocks and **herds** and everything they own,
47:17 their sheep and goats, their **cattle** [+5238] and donkeys.
50: 8 Only their children and their flocks and **herds** were left in Goshen.
Ex 9: 3 and donkeys and camels and on your **cattle** and sheep and goats.
10: 9 with our sons and daughters, and with our flocks and **herds**,
10:24 may go with you; only leave your flocks and **herds** behind."
12:32 Take your flocks and **herds**, as you have said, and go. And also
12:38 as well as large droves of livestock, both flocks and **herds**.
20:24 and fellowship offerings, your sheep and goats and your **cattle**.
22: 1 [21:37] he must pay back five *head of* **cattle** for the ox and four
29: 1 as priests: Take a young **bull** [+7228] and two rams without defect.
34: 3 not even the flocks and **herds** may graze in front of the mountain."
Lev 1: 2 bring as your offering an animal from either the **herd** or the flock.
1: 3 " 'If the offering is a burnt offering from the **herd**, he is to offer a
1: 5 He is to slaughter the young **bull** before the LORD, and
3: 1 and he offers an animal from the **herd**, whether male or female,
4: 3 he must bring to the LORD a young **bull** [+7228] without defect
4:14 the assembly must bring a young **bull** [+7228] as a sin offering
9: 2 "Take a **bull** [+1201] calf for your sin offering and a ram for your
16: 3 with a young **bull** [+7228] for a sin offering and a ram for a burnt
22:19 you must present a male without defect from the **cattle**, sheep
22:21 When anyone brings from the **herd** or flock a fellowship offering
23:18 and without defect, one young **bull** [+7228] and two rams.
27:32 The entire tithe of the **herd** and flock—every tenth animal that
Nu 7: 3 their gifts before the LORD six covered carts and twelve **oxen**—
7: 6 So Moses took the carts and **oxen** and gave them to the Levites.
7: 7 He gave two carts and four **oxen** to the Gershonites, as their work
7: 8 he gave four carts and eight **oxen** to the Merarites, as their work
7:15 one young **bull** [+7228], one ram and one male lamb a year old,
7:17 two **oxen**, five rams, five male goats and five male lambs a year
7:21 one young **bull** [+7228], one ram and one male lamb a year old,
7:23 two **oxen**, five rams, five male goats and five male lambs a year
7:27 one young **bull** [+7228], one ram and one male lamb a year old,
7:29 two **oxen**, five rams, five male goats and five male lambs a year
7:33 one young **bull** [+7228], one ram and one male lamb a year old,
7:35 two **oxen**, five rams, five male goats and five male lambs a year
7:39 one young **bull** [+7228], one ram and one male lamb a year old,
7:41 two **oxen**, five rams, five male goats and five male lambs a year
7:45 one young **bull** [+7228], one ram and one male lamb a year old,
7:47 two **oxen**, five rams, five male goats and five male lambs a year
7:51 one young **bull** [+7228], one ram and one male lamb a year old,
7:53 two **oxen**, five rams, five male goats and five male lambs a year
7:57 one young **bull** [+7228], one ram and one male lamb a year old,
7:59 two **oxen**, five rams, five male goats and five male lambs a year
7:63 one young **bull** [+7228], one ram and one male lamb a year old,
7:65 two **oxen**, five rams, five male goats and five male lambs a year
7:69 one young **bull** [+7228], one ram and one male lamb a year old,
7:71 two **oxen**, five rams, five male goats and five male lambs a year
7:75 one young **bull** [+7228], one ram and one male lamb a year old,
7:77 two **oxen**, five rams, five male goats and five male lambs a year
7:81 one young **bull** [+7228], one ram and one male lamb a year old,
7:83 two **oxen**, five rams, five male goats and five male lambs a year
7:87 The total number of **animals** for the burnt offering came to twelve
7:88 The total number of **animals** *for* the sacrifice of the fellowship
8: 8 Have them take a young **bull** [+7228] with its grain offering of fine
8: 8 then you are to take a second young **bull** [+7228] for a sin offering.
11:22 they have enough if flocks and **herds** were slaughtered for them?
15: 3 from the **herd** or the flock, as an aroma pleasing to the LORD—
15: 8 " 'When you prepare a young **bull** as a burnt offering or sacrifice,
15: 9 bring with the **bull** a grain offering of three-tenths of an ephah of
15:24 the whole community is to offer a young **bull** [+7228] for a burnt
22:40 Balak sacrificed **cattle** and sheep, and gave some to Balaam
28:11 present to the LORD a burnt offering of two young **bulls** [+7228],
28:19 a burnt offering of two young **bulls** [+7228], one ram and seven
28:27 Present a burnt offering of two young **bulls** [+7228], one ram
29: 2 prepare a burnt offering of one young **bull** [+7228], one ram
29: 8 pleasing to the LORD a burnt offering of one young **bull** [+7228],
29:13 a burnt offering of thirteen young **bulls** [+7228], two rams
29:17 " 'On the second day prepare twelve young **bulls** [+7228],
31:28 five hundred, whether persons, **cattle**, donkeys, sheep or goats.
31:30 whether persons, **cattle**, donkeys, sheep, goats or other animals.
31:33 72,000 **cattle**,
31:38 36,000 **cattle**, of which the tribute for the LORD was 72;
31:44 36,000 **cattle**,
Dt 8:13 and when your **herds** and flocks grow large and your silver
12: 6 your freewill offerings, and the firstborn of your **herds** and flocks.
12:17 and new wine and oil, or the firstborn of your **herds** and flocks,
12:21 you may slaughter animals from the **herds** and flocks the LORD
14:23 the firstborn of your **herds** and flocks in the presence of the
14:26 **cattle**, sheep, wine or other fermented drink, or anything you wish.
15:19 apart for the LORD your God every firstborn male of your **herds**
16: 2 or **herd** at the place the LORD will choose as a dwelling for his
21: 3 the elders of the town nearest the body shall take a **heifer** [+6320]
32:14 with curds and milk from **herd** and flock and with fattened lambs
Jdg 3:31 who struck down six hundred Philistines with an **oxgoad** [+4913].
1Sa 8:16 and maidservants and the best of your **cattle** [BHS 1033]
11: 5 behind his **oxen**, and he asked, "What is wrong with the people?
11: 7 He took a pair of **oxen**, cut them into pieces, and sent the pieces by
11: 7 "This is what will be done to the **oxen** *of* anyone who does not
14:32 They pounced on the plunder and, taking sheep, **cattle** and calves,
14:32 on the plunder and, taking sheep, cattle and **calves** [+1201],
15: 9 and the army spared Agag and the best of the sheep and **cattle**,
15:14 of sheep in my ears? What is this lowing of **cattle** that I hear?"
15:15 best of the sheep and **cattle** to sacrifice to the LORD your God,
15:21 The soldiers took sheep and **cattle** from the plunder, the best of
16: 2 The LORD said, "Take a **heifer** [+6320] with you and say,
27: 9 but took sheep and **cattle**, donkeys and camels, and clothes.
30:20 He took all the flocks and **herds**, and his men drove them ahead of
2Sa 6: 6 and took hold of the ark of God, because the **oxen** stumbled.
12: 2 The rich man had a very large number of sheep and **cattle**,
12: 4 or **cattle** to prepare a meal for the traveler who had come to him.
17:29 and cheese from **cows**' milk for David and his people to eat.
24:22 Here are **oxen** for the burnt offering, and here are threshing sledges
24:22 and here are threshing sledges and **ox** yokes for the wood.
24:24 So David bought the threshing floor and the **oxen** and paid fifty
1Ki 1: 9 **cattle** and fattened calves at the Stone of Zoheleth near En Rogel.
4:23 [5:3] ten *head of* stall-fed **cattle**, twenty of pasture-fed cattle
4:23 [5:3] twenty of pasture-fed **cattle** and a hundred sheep and goats,
7:25 The Sea stood on twelve **bulls**, three facing north, three facing
7:29 the panels between the uprights were lions, **bulls** and cherubim—
7:29 and below the lions and **bulls** were wreaths of hammered work.
7:44 the Sea and the twelve **bulls** under it;
8: 5 many sheep and **cattle** that they could not be recorded or counted.
8:63 twenty-two thousand **cattle** and a hundred and twenty thousand
19:20 Elisha then left his **oxen** and ran after Elijah. "Let me kiss my

1Ki 19:21 and went back. He took his yoke of **oxen** and slaughtered them.
19:21 He burned the **plowing** equipment to cook the meat and gave it to
2Ki 5:26 olive groves, vineyards, flocks, **herds**, or menservants
16:17 He removed the Sea from the bronze **bulls** that supported it
1Ch 12:40 [12:41] came bringing food on donkeys, camels, mules and **oxen**.
12:40 [12:41] fig cakes, raisin cakes, wine, oil, **cattle** and sheep,
13:9 reached out his hand to steady the ark, because the **oxen** stumbled.
21:23 Look, I will give the **oxen** for the burnt offerings, the threshing
27:29 Shitrai the Sharonite was in charge of the **herds** grazing in Sharon.
27:29 Shaphat son of Adlai was in charge of the **herds** in the valleys.
2Ch 4:3 Below the rim, figures of **bulls** encircled it—ten to a cubit.
4:3 The **bulls** were cast in two rows in one piece with the Sea.
4:4 The Sea stood on twelve **bulls**, three facing north, three facing
4:15 the Sea and the twelve **bulls** under it;
5:6 many sheep and **cattle** that they could not be recorded or counted.
7:5 Solomon offered a sacrifice of twenty-two thousand *head of* **cattle**
13:9 Whoever comes to consecrate himself with a young **bull** and seven
15:11 time they sacrificed to the LORD seven hundred *head of* **cattle**
18:2 slaughtered many sheep and **cattle** for him and the people with him
29:22 So they slaughtered the **bulls**, and the priests took the blood
29:32 number of burnt offerings the assembly brought was seventy **bulls**,
29:33 animals consecrated as sacrifices amounted to six hundred **bulls**
31:6 who lived in the towns of Judah also brought a tithe of their **herds**
32:29 He built villages and acquired great numbers of flocks and **herds**,
35:7 goats for the Passover offerings, and also three thousand **cattle**—
35:8 twenty-six hundred Passover offerings and three hundred **cattle**.
35:9 Passover offerings and five hundred *head of* **cattle** for the Levites.
35:12 is written in the Book of Moses. They did the same with the **cattle**.
Ne 10:36 [10:37] of our **herds** and of our flocks to the house of our God,
Job 1:3 five hundred yoke of **oxen** and five hundred donkeys,
1:14 "The **oxen** were plowing and the donkeys were grazing nearby,
40:15 which I made along with you and which feeds on grass like an **ox**.
42:12 a thousand yoke of **oxen** and a thousand donkeys.
Ps 66:15 animals to you and an offering of rams; I will offer **bulls** and goats.
Ecc 2:7 I also owned more **herds** and flocks than anyone in Jerusalem
Isa 7:21 a man will keep alive a **young cow** [+6320] and two goats.
11:7 will lie down together, and the lion will eat straw like the **ox**.
22:13 there is joy and revelry, slaughtering of **cattle** and killing of sheep,
65:10 the Valley of Achor a resting place for **herds**, for my people who
65:25 the lamb will feed together, and the lion will eat straw like the **ox**,
Jer 3:24 fathers' labor—their flocks and **herds**, their sons and daughters.
5:17 they will devour your flocks and **herds**, devour your vines
31:12 the new wine and the oil, the young of the flocks and **herds**.
52:20 the Sea and the twelve bronze **bulls** under it, and the movable
Eze 4:15 "I will let you bake your bread over **cow** manure instead of human
43:19 You are to give a young **bull** [+7228] as a sin offering to the
43:23 you are to offer a young **bull** [+7228] and a ram from the flock,
43:25 you are also to provide a young **bull** [+7228] and a ram from the
45:18 on the first day you are to take a young **bull** [+7228] without defect
46:6 On the day of the New Moon he is to offer a young **bull** [+7228],
Hos 5:6 When they go with their flocks and **herds** to seek the LORD,
Joel 1:18 The **herds** [+6373] mill about because they have no pasture;
Am 6:12 Do horses run on the rocky crags? Does one plow there with **oxen**?
Jnh 3:7 Do not let any man or beast, **herd** or flock, taste anything;
Hab 3:17 though there are no sheep in the pen and no **cattle** in the stalls,

1331 ¹בֹּקֶר *bōqer¹*, n.m. Not used in NIV/BHS [√ 1329]

1332 ²בֹּקֶר *bōqer²*, n.m. [214 / 215] [√ 1329]

morning [179], every morning [+928+928+1332+2021+2021] [8], *untranslated* [4], dawn [3], daybreak [+240+2021] [3], dawn [+240+2021] [2], each morning [+1332+2021+2021+4200+4200] [2], each morning [+928+928+1332+2021+2021] [2], morning's [2], mornings [2], break of day [+7155] [1], daybreak [+2021+7155] [1], daybreak [+7155] [1], daylight [+240+2021] [1], hold back overnight [+907+4328+6330] [1], last watch of the night [+874] [1], last watch of the night [+874+2021] [1], morning light [1]

Ge 1:5 And there was evening, and there was **morning**—the first day.
1:8 And there was evening, and there was **morning**—the second day.
1:13 And there was evening, and there was **morning**—the third day.
1:19 And there was evening, and there was **morning**—the fourth day.
1:23 And there was evening, and there was **morning**—the fifth day.
1:31 And there was evening, and there was **morning**—the sixth day.
19:27 Early the next **morning** Abraham got up and returned to the place
20:8 Early the next **morning** Abimelech summoned all his officials,
21:14 Early the next **morning** Abraham took some food and a skin of
22:3 Early the next **morning** Abraham got up and saddled his donkey.
24:54 When they got up the next **morning**, he said, "Send me on my way
26:31 Early the next **morning** the men swore an oath to each other.
28:18 Early the next **morning** Jacob took the stone he had placed under
29:25 When **morning** came, there was Leah! So Jacob said to Laban,
31:55 [32:1] Early the next **morning** Laban kissed his grandchildren
40:6 When Joseph came to them the next **morning**, he saw that they
41:8 In the **morning** his mind was troubled, so he sent for all the
44:3 As **morning** dawned, the men were sent on their way with their
49:27 in the **morning** he devours the prey, in the evening he divides the
Ex 7:15 Go to Pharaoh in the **morning** as he goes out to the water.
8:20 [8:16] "Get up early in the **morning** and confront Pharaoh as he
9:13 "Get up early in the **morning**, confront Pharaoh and say to him,
10:13 and all that night. *By* **morning** the wind had brought the locusts;
12:10 Do not leave any of it till **morning**; if some is left till morning,
12:10 any of it till morning; if some is left till **morning**, you must burn it.
12:22 Not one of you shall go out the door of his house until **morning**.
14:24 During the **last watch of the night** [+874] the LORD looked
14:27 the sea, and at **daybreak** [+7155] the sea went back to its place.
16:7 and *in* the **morning** you will see the glory of the LORD,
16:8 to eat in the evening and all the bread you want in the **morning**,
16:12 will eat meat, and in the **morning** you will be filled with bread.
16:13 and in the **morning** there was a layer of dew around the camp.
16:19 Moses said to them, "No one is to keep any of it until **morning**."
16:20 they kept part of it until **morning**, but it was full of maggots
16:21 **Each morning** [+928+928+1332+2021+2021] everyone gathered
16:21 **Each morning** [+928+928+1332+2021+2021] everyone gathered
16:23 want to boil. Save whatever is left and keep it until **morning**.' "
16:24 So they saved it until **morning**, as Moses commanded, and it did
18:13 the people, and they stood around him from **morning** till evening.
18:14 while all these people stand around you from **morning** till
19:16 On the **morning** of the third day there was thunder and lightning,
23:18 "The fat of my festival offerings must not be kept until **morning**.
24:4 He got up early the next **morning** and built an altar at the foot of
27:21 the lamps burning before the LORD from evening till **morning**.
29:34 meat of the ordination ram or any bread is left over till **morning**,
29:39 Offer one in the **morning** and the other at twilight.
29:41 the same grain offering and its drink offering as in the **morning**—
30:7 incense on the altar **every morning** [+928+928+1332+2021+2021]
30:7 incense on the altar **every morning** [+928+928+1332+2021+2021]
34:2 Be ready in the **morning**, and then come up on Mount Sinai.
34:2 ready in the morning, and then come up **[RPH]** on Mount Sinai.
34:4 like the first ones and went up Mount Sinai early in the **morning**,
34:25 any of the sacrifice from the Passover Feast remain until **morning**.
36:3 the people continued to bring freewill offerings **morning** after
36:3 continued to bring freewill offerings morning after **morning**.
Lev 6:9 [6:2] till **morning**, and the fire must be kept burning on the altar.
6:12 [6:5] **Every morning** [+928+928+1332+2021+2021] the priest is
6:12 [6:5] **Every morning** [+928+928+1332+2021+2021] the priest is
6:20 [6:13] half of it in the **morning** and half in the evening.
7:15 eaten on the day it is offered; he must leave none of it till **morning**.
9:17 burned it on the altar in addition to the **morning's** burnt offering.
19:13 " '*Do* not **hold back** the wages of a hired man **overnight** [+907+4328+6330].
22:30 It must be eaten that same day; leave none of it till **morning**.
24:3 is to tend the lamps before the LORD from evening till **morning**,
Nu 9:12 They must not leave any of it till **morning** or break any of its
9:15 From evening till **morning** the cloud above the tabernacle looked
9:21 Sometimes the cloud stayed only from evening till **morning**,
9:21 till morning, and when it lifted in the **morning**, they set out.
14:40 Early the next **morning** they went up toward the high hill country.
16:5 "In the **morning** the LORD will show who belongs to him
22:13 The next **morning** Balaam got up and said to Balak's princes,
22:21 Balaam got up in the **morning**, saddled his donkey and went with
22:41 The next **morning** Balak took Balaam up to Bamoth Baal,
28:4 Prepare one lamb in the **morning** and the other at twilight,
28:8 grain offering and drink offering that you prepare in the **morning**.
28:23 Prepare these in addition to the regular **morning** burnt offering.
Dt 16:4 you sacrifice on the evening of the first day remain until **morning**.
16:7 your God will choose. Then in the **morning** return to your tents.
28:67 In the **morning** you will say, "If only it were evening!" and in the
28:67 in the evening, "If only it were **morning**!"—because of the terror
Jos 3:1 Early in the **morning** Joshua and all the Israelites set out from
6:12 Joshua got up early the next **morning** and the priests took up the
7:14 " 'In the **morning**, present yourselves tribe by tribe. The tribe that
7:16 Early the next **morning** Joshua had Israel come forward by tribes,
8:10 Early the next **morning** Joshua mustered his men, and he
Jdg 6:28 In the **morning** when the men of the town got up, there was Baal's
6:31 Whoever fights for him shall be put to death by **morning**!
9:33 In the **morning** at sunrise, advance against the city. When Gaal
16:2 during the night, saying, "At **dawn** [+240+2021] we'll kill him."
19:5 the fourth day they got up early **[NIE]** and he prepared to leave,
19:8 On the **morning** of the fifth day, when he rose to go, the girl's
19:25 her throughout the night, **[NIE]** and at dawn they let her go.
19:26 At **daybreak** [+2021+7155] the woman went back to the house
19:27 When her master got up in the **morning** and opened the door of the
20:19 The next **morning** the Israelites got up and pitched camp near
Ru 2:7 went into the field and has worked steadily from **morning** till now,
3:13 here for the night, and in the **morning** if he wants to redeem, good;
3:13 as surely as the LORD lives I will do it. Lie here until **morning**."
3:14 So she lay at his feet until **morning**, but got up before anyone

1Sa 1:19 Early the next **morning** they arose and worshiped before the
3:15 Samuel lay down until **morning** and then opened the doors of the
5:4 But the following **morning** when they rose, there was Dagon,
9:19 in the **morning** I will let you go and will tell you all that is in your
11:11 during the **last watch of the night** [+874+2021] they broke into
14:36 the Philistines by night and plunder them till **dawn** [+240+2021],
15:12 Early in the **morning** Samuel got up and went to meet Saul,
17:20 Early in the **morning** David left the flock with a shepherd,
19:2 Be on your guard tomorrow **morning**; go into hiding and stay
19:11 men to David's house to watch it and to kill him in the **morning**.
20:35 In the **morning** Jonathan went out to the field for his meeting with
25:22 if by **morning** I leave alive one male of all who belong to him!"
25:34 to Nabal would have been left alive by **daybreak** [+240+2021]."
25:36 very drunk. So she told him nothing until **daybreak** [+240+2021].
25:37 in the **morning**, when Nabal was sober, his wife told him all these
29:10 **[RPH]** along with your master's servants who have come with
29:10 come with you, and leave in the **morning** as soon as it is light."
29:11 his men got up early in the **morning** to go back to the land of the
2Sa 2:27 would have continued the pursuit of their brothers until **morning**."
11:14 In the **morning** David wrote a letter to Joab and sent it with Uriah.
13:4 do you, the king's son, look so haggard **morning** after morning?
13:4 do you, the king's son, look so haggard morning after **morning**?
17:22 By **daybreak** [+240+2021], no one was left who had not crossed
23:4 he is like the light of **morning** at sunrise on a cloudless morning,
23:4 he is like the light of morning at sunrise on a cloudless **morning**,
24:11 Before David got up the next **morning**, the word of the LORD
24:15 So the LORD sent a plague on Israel from that **morning** until the
1Ki 3:21 The next **morning**, I got up to nurse my son—and he was dead!
3:21 when I looked at him closely in the **morning light**, I saw that it
17:6 and meat in the **morning** and bread and meat in the evening,
18:26 Then they called on the name of Baal from **morning** till noon.
2Ki 3:20 The next **morning**, about the time for offering the sacrifice,
3:22 When they got up early in the **morning**, the sun was shining on the
7:9 If we wait until **daylight** [+240+2021], punishment will overtake
10:8 them in two piles at the entrance of the city gate until **morning**."
10:9 The next **morning** Jehu went out. He stood before all the people
16:15 offer the **morning** burnt offering and the evening grain offering,
19:35 When the people got up the next **morning**—there were all the dead
1Ch 9:27 key for opening it **each morning** [+1332+2021+2021+4200+4200].
9:27 key for opening it **each morning** [+1332+2021+2021+4200+4200].
16:40 **morning** and evening, in accordance with everything written in the
23:30 to stand **every morning** [+928+928+1332+2021+2021] to thank
23:30 to stand **every morning** [+928+928+1332+2021+2021] to thank
2Ch 2:4 [2:3] and for making burnt offerings every **morning** and evening
13:11 **Every morning** [+928+928+1332+2021+2021] and evening they
13:11 **Every morning** [+928+928+1332+2021+2021] and evening they
20:20 Early in the **morning** they left for the Desert of Tekoa. As they set
31:3 The king contributed from his own possessions for the **morning**
Ezr 3:3 on it to the LORD, both the **morning** and evening sacrifices.
Est 2:14 in the **morning** return to another part of the harem to the care of
5:14 and ask the king in the **morning** to have Mordecai hanged on it.
Job 1:5 Early in the **morning** he would sacrifice a burnt offering for each
4:20 Between **dawn** and dusk they are broken to pieces; unnoticed,
7:18 that you examine him every **morning** and test him every moment?
11:17 be brighter than noonday, and darkness will become like **morning**.
24:17 For all of them, deep darkness is their **morning**; they make friends
38:7 while the **morning** stars sang together and all the angels shouted
38:12 "Have you ever given orders to the **morning**, or shown the dawn
Ps 5:3 [5:4] *In* the **morning**, O LORD, you hear my voice;
5:3 [5:4] *in* the **morning** I lay my requests before you and wait in
30:5 [30:6] remain for a night, but rejoicing comes in the **morning**.
46:5 [46:6] will not fall; God will help her at **break of day** [+7155].
49:14 [49:15] The upright will rule over them in the **morning**; their
55:17 [55:18] Evening, **morning** and noon I cry out in distress, and he
59:16 [59:17] of your strength, in the **morning** I will sing of your love;
65:8 [65:9] where **morning** dawns and evening fades you call forth
73:14 long I have been plagued; I have been punished every **morning**.
88:13 [88:14] O LORD; in the **morning** my prayer comes before you.
90:5 in the sleep of death; they are like the new grass of the **morning**—
90:6 though in the **morning** it springs up new, by evening it is dry
90:14 Satisfy us in the **morning** with your unfailing love, that we may
92:2 [92:3] to proclaim your love in the **morning** and your faithfulness
101:8 Every **morning** I will put to silence all the wicked in the land;
130:6 soul waits for the Lord more than watchmen wait for the **morning**,
130:6 wait for the morning, more than watchmen wait for the **morning**.
143:8 Let the **morning** bring me word of your unfailing love, for I have
Pr 7:18 Come, let's drink deep of love till **morning**; let's enjoy ourselves
27:14 If a man loudly blesses his neighbor early in the **morning**,
Ecc 10:16 whose king was a servant and whose princes feast in the **morning**.
11:6 Sow your seed in the **morning**, and at evening let not your hands
Isa 5:11 Woe to those who rise early in the **morning** to run after their
17:11 you make them grow, and on the **morning** when you plant them,
17:14 In the evening, sudden terror! Before the **morning**, they are gone!
21:12 The watchman replies, "**Morning** is coming, but also the night.
26:9 in the night; in the **morning** [BHS 7931] my spirit longs for you.
28:19 **morning** after morning, by day and by night, it will sweep
28:19 morning after **morning**, by day and by night, it will sweep
33:2 Be our strength every **morning**, our salvation in time of distress.
37:36 When the people got up the next **morning**—there were all the dead
38:13 I waited patiently till **dawn**, but like a lion he broke all my bones;
50:4 He wakens me **morning** by morning, wakens my ear to listen like
50:4 He wakens me morning by **morning**, wakens my ear to listen like
Jer 20:16 May he hear wailing in the **morning**, a battle cry at noon.
21:12 " 'Administer justice every **morning**; rescue from the hand of his
La 3:23 They are new every **morning**; great is your faithfulness.
Eze 12:8 In the **morning** the word of the LORD came to me:
24:18 So I spoke to the people in the **morning**, and in the evening my
24:18 my wife died. The next **morning** I did as I had been commanded.
33:22 he opened my mouth before the man came to me in the **morning**.
46:13 offering to the LORD; **morning** by morning you shall provide it.
46:13 offering to the LORD; morning by **morning** you shall provide it.
46:14 You are also to provide with it **morning** by morning a grain
46:14 You are also to provide with it morning by **morning** a grain
46:15 the oil shall be provided **morning** by morning for a regular burnt
46:15 the oil shall be provided morning by **morning** for a regular burnt
Da 8:14 He said to me, "It will take 2,300 evenings and **mornings**;
8:26 of the evenings and **mornings** that has been given you is true,
Hos 6:4 Your love is like the **morning** mist, like the early dew that
7:6 smolders all night; in the **morning** it blazes like a flaming fire.
13:3 Therefore they will be like the **morning** mist, like the early dew
Am 4:4 Bring your sacrifices every **morning**, your tithes every three years.
5:8 who turns blackness into **dawn** and darkens day into night,
Mic 2:1 At **morning's** light they carry it out because it is in their power to
Zep 3:3 her rulers are evening wolves, who leave nothing for the **morning**.
3:5 **Morning** by morning he dispenses his justice, and every new day
3:5 Morning by **morning** he dispenses his justice, and every new day

1333 בַּקָּרָה *baqqārâ*, n.f.vbl. [1] [√ 1329]

looks after [1]

Eze 34:12 As a shepherd **looks after** his scattered flock when he is with them,

1334 בִּקֹּרֶת *biqqōret*, n.f. [1] [√ 1329]

due punishment [1]

Lev 19:20 or given her freedom, there must be **due punishment**.

1335 בָּקַשׁ *bāqaš*, v. [225] [→ 1336]

seek [58], seeking [12], look for [10], looked for [10], search for [10], searched for [7], looking for [6], sought [5], tried [5], searched [4], seeks [4], find [3], hold accountable [+3338+4946] [3], search out [3], search [3], trying [3], bent on [2], call to account [2], conspired [2], demand [2], in search of [2], intend [2], searching for [2], seek out [2], sought out [2], take [2], trying to take [2], want [2], about to [1], ask for [1], asked for permission [1], asked for [1], asked [1], asking for [1], be sought [1], beg [1], begging [1], call to account [+3338+4946] [1], carefully investigated [+2011+2256] [1], demanded payment [1], demanded [1], finds [1], gone in search of [1], hold responsible [+3338+4946] [1], inquiring of [1], intended [1], invites [1], looking for a chance [1], looks for [1], looks to [1], petitioned [1], plans [1], plead with [1], pleaded with [1], pleaded [1], promote [1], promotes [1], pursue [1], pursues [1], pursuing [1], questioned [1], search be made for [1], search made for [1], searching [1], seek an audience with [+7156] [1], seek help [1], seek to [1], set out [1], snare [1], sought to [1], straining [1], tried to take [1], try to find [1], try to get [1], trying to get [1], trying to [1], want to do [1], want to [1], wanted to kill [+906+5883] [1], wanted to make [+906+4200] [1], wanted to [1], was investigated [1], went in search of [1]

Ge 31:39 [D] *you* **demanded payment** from me *for* whatever was stolen
37:15 [D] in the fields and asked him, "What *are you* **looking for**?"
37:16 [D] He replied, "I'm **looking for** my brothers. Can you tell me
43:9 [D] *you can* **hold** me personally **responsible** [+3338+4946] *for* him.
43:30 [D] Joseph hurried out and **looked for** a place to weep.
Ex 2:15 [D] When Pharaoh heard of this, *he* **tried** to kill Moses,
4:19 [D] for all the men who **wanted** [+906+5883] **to kill** you are
4:24 [D] the way, the LORD met ⸤Moses⸥ and *was* **about to** kill him.
10:11 [D] the LORD, since that's what you *have been* **asking for**."
33:7 [D] Anyone **inquiring of** the LORD would go to the tent of
Lev 19:31 [D] " 'Do not turn to mediums or **seek out** spiritists, for you will
Nu 16:10 [D] but now *you are* **trying to get** the priesthood too.
35:23 [D] he was not his enemy and *he did* not **intend** *to* harm him,
Dt 4:29 [D] if from there *you* **seek** the LORD your God, you will find
13:10 [13:11] [D] because *he* **tried** to turn you away from the LORD
Jos 2:22 [D] until the pursuers *had* **searched** all along the road
22:23 [D] offerings on it, *may* the LORD himself **call** us **to account**.
Jdg 4:22 [D] she said, "I will show you the man you're **looking for**."
6:29 [D] When *they* **carefully investigated** [+2011+2256], they were

Jdg 14: 4 [D] who *was* **seeking** an occasion to confront the Philistines;
18: 1 [D] in those days the tribe of the Danites *was* **seeking** a place of
Ru 3: 1 [D] "My daughter, *should I* not **try to find** a home for you,
1Sa 9: 3 [D] of the servants with you and go and **look for** the donkeys."
10: 2 [D] 'The donkeys you set out to **look for** have been found.
10: 14 [D] have you been?" "**Looking for** the donkeys," he said.
10: 21 [D] But when *they* **looked for** him, he was not to be found.
13: 14 [D] the LORD *has* **sought out** a man after his own heart
14: 4 [D] On each side of the pass that Jonathan **intended** to cross to
16: 16 [D] Let our lord command his servants here *to* **search for**
19: 2 [D] "My father Saul *is* **looking for a chance** to kill you.
19: 10 [D] Saul **tried** to pin him to the wall with his spear, but David
20: 1 [D] I wronged your father, that *he is* **trying to take** my life?"
20: 16 [D] the LORD **call** David's enemies **to account** [+3338+4946].
22: 23 [D] *the man* who *is* **seeking** your life is seeking mine also.
22: 23 [D] the man who is seeking your life *is* **seeking** mine also.
23: 10 [D] your servant has heard definitely that Saul **plans** to come to
23: 14 [D] Day after day Saul **searched for** him, but God did not give
23: 15 [D] of Ziph, he learned that Saul had come out to **take** his life.
23: 25 [D] Saul and his men began the **search**, and when David was told
24: 2 [24:3] [D] set out to **look for** David and his men near the Crags
24: 9 [24:10] [D] when men say, 'David *is* **bent on** harming you'?
25: 26 [D] and all who **intend** *to* harm my master be like Nabal.
25: 29 [D] Even though someone is pursuing you to **take** your life,
26: 2 [D] thousand chosen men of Israel, to **search** there **for** David.
26: 20 [D] The king of Israel has come out to **look for** a flea—as one
27: 1 [D] Then Saul will give up **searching for** me anywhere in Israel,
27: 4 [D] that David had fled to Gath, he no longer **searched for** him.
28: 7 [D] "**Find** me a woman who is a medium, so I may go and
2Sa 3: 17 [D] "For some time *you have* **wanted** [+906+4200] **to make**
4: 8 [D] son of Saul, your enemy, who **tried to take** your life.
4: 11 [D] *should I* not now **demand** his blood from your hand and rid
5: 17 [D] they went up in full force to **search for** him, but David heard
12: 16 [D] David **pleaded** *with* God for the child. He fasted and went
16: 11 [D] "My son, who is of my own flesh, *is* **trying to take** my life.
17: 3 [D] The death of the man you **seek** will mean the return of all;
17: 20 [D] The men **searched** but found no one, so they returned to
20: 19 [D] You *are* **trying** to destroy a city that is a mother in Israel.
21: 1 [D] successive years; so David **sought** the face of the LORD.
21: 2 [D] in his zeal for Israel and Judah *had* **tried** to annihilate them.)
1Ki 1: 2 [D] "*Let us* **look for** a young virgin to attend the king and take
1: 3 [D] *they* **searched** throughout Israel **for** a beautiful girl
2: 40 [D] and went to Achish at Gath **in search of** his slaves.
10: 24 [D] The whole world **sought** audience with Solomon to hear the
11: 22 [D] "What have you lacked here that you **want** to go back to
11: 40 [D] Solomon **tried** to kill Jeroboam, but Jeroboam fled to Egypt,
18: 10 [D] where my master has not sent someone to **look for** you.
19: 10 [D] the only one left, and now *they are* **trying** to kill me too."
19: 14 [D] the only one left, and now *they are* **trying** to kill me too."
20: 7 [D] and said to them, "See how this man *is* **looking for** trouble!
2Ki 2: 16 [D] have fifty able men. Let them go and **look for** your master.
2: 17 [D] fifty men, *who* **searched** for three days but did not find him.
6: 19 [D] and I will lead you to the man *you are* **looking for**."
1Ch 4: 39 [D] to the east of the valley **in search of** pasture for their flocks.
14: 8 [D] they went up in full force to **search for** him, but David heard
16: 10 [D] let the hearts of *those who* **seek** the LORD rejoice.
16: 11 [D] Look to the LORD and his strength; **seek** his face always.
21: 3 [D] all my lord's subjects? Why *does* my lord **want to do** this?
2Ch 7: 14 [D] will humble themselves and pray and **seek** my face and turn
9: 23 [D] All the kings of the earth **sought** audience with Solomon to
11: 16 [D] tribe of Israel who set their hearts on **seeking** the LORD,
15: 4 [D] the God of Israel, and **sought** him, and he was found by
15: 15 [D] *They* **sought** God eagerly, and he was found by them.
20: 4 [D] The people of Judah came together to **seek help** from the
20: 4 [D] indeed, they came from every town in Judah to **seek** him.
22: 9 [D] *He* then **went in search of** Ahaziah, and his men captured
Ezr 2: 62 [D] These **searched for** their family records, but they could not
8: 21 [D] and **ask** him **for** a safe journey for us and our children,
8: 22 [D] "The gracious hand of our God is on everyone *who* **looks to**
8: 23 [D] So we fasted and **petitioned** our God about this, and he
Ne 2: 4 [D] The king said to me, "What is it you **want**?" Then I prayed to
2: 10 [D] someone had come to **promote** the welfare of the Israelites.
5: 12 [D] "And *we will* not **demand** anything more from them.
5: 18 [D] all this, *I* never **demanded** the food allotted to the governor,
7: 64 [D] These **searched for** their family records, but they could not
12: 27 [D] the Levites *were* **sought out** from where they lived and were
Est 2: 2 [D] "*Let a* **search** *be* **made for** beautiful young virgins for the
2: 15 [D] go to the king, *she* **asked for** nothing other than what Hegai,
2: 21 [D] became angry and **conspired** to assassinate King Xerxes.
2: 23 [E] And when the report **was investigated** and found to be true,
3: 6 [D] Instead Haman **looked for** a way to destroy all Mordecai's
4: 8 [D] to beg for mercy and **plead with** him for her people.
6: 2 [D] who *had* **conspired** to assassinate King Xerxes.
7: 7 [D] his fate, stayed behind to **beg** Queen Esther for his life.
9: 2 [D] of King Xerxes to attack *those* **seeking** their destruction.
Job 10: 6 [D] that *you must* **search out** my faults and probe after my sin—
Ps 4: 2 [4:3] [D] How long will you love delusions and **seek** false
24: 6 [D] of those who seek him, *who* **seek** your face, O God of Jacob.
27: 4 [D] One thing I ask of the LORD, this is what *I* **seek**: that I may
27: 8 [D] My heart says of you, "**Seek** his face!" Your face, LORD,
27: 8 [D] says of you, "Seek his face!" Your face, LORD, *I will* **seek**.
34: 14 [34:15] [D] from evil and do good; **seek** peace and pursue it.
35: 4 [D] May *those who* **seek** my life be disgraced and put to shame;
37: 25 [D] seen the righteous forsaken or their children **begging** bread.
37: 32 [D] wicked lie in wait for the righteous, **seeking** their very lives;
37: 36 [D] no more; though *I* **looked for** him, he could not be found.
38: 12 [38:13] [D] *Those who* **seek** my life set their traps, those who
40: 14 [40:15] [D] *May* all *who* **seek** to take my life be put to shame
40: 16 [40:17] [D] may all *who* **seek** you rejoice and be glad in you;
54: 3 [54:5] [D] Strangers are attacking me; ruthless men **seek** my
63: 9 [63:10] [D] They *who* **seek** my life will be destroyed; they will
69: 6 [69:7] [D] may *those who* **seek** you not be put to shame
70: 2 [70:3] [D] May *those who* **seek** my life be put to shame
70: 4 [70:5] [D] may all *who* **seek** you rejoice and be glad in you;
71: 13 [D] may *those who* **want to** harm me be covered with scorn
71: 24 [D] for *those who* **wanted to** harm me have been put to shame
83: 16 [83:17] [D] faces with shame so that *men will* **seek** your name,
86: 14 [D] attacking me, O God; a band of ruthless men **seeks** my life—
104: 21 [D] The lions roar for their prey and **seek** their food from God.
105: 3 [D] let the hearts of *those who* **seek** the LORD rejoice.
105: 4 [D] Look to the LORD and his strength; **seek** his face always.
119: 176 [D] **Seek** your servant, for I have not forgotten your commands.
122: 9 [D] house of the LORD our God, *I will* **seek** your prosperity.
Pr 2: 4 [D] if *you* **look for** it as for silver and search for it as for hidden
11: 27 [D] He who seeks good **finds** goodwill, but evil comes to him
14: 6 [D] The mocker **seeks** wisdom and finds none, but knowledge
15: 14 [D] The discerning heart **seeks** knowledge, but the mouth of a
17: 9 [D] He who covers over an offense **promotes** love, but whoever
17: 11 [D] An evil man *is* **bent** only **on** rebellion; a merciless official
17: 19 [D] loves sin; he who builds a high gate **invites** destruction.
18: 1 [D] An unfriendly man **pursues** selfish ends; he defies all sound
18: 15 [D] acquires knowledge; the ears of the wise **seek** it **out**.
21: 6 [D] by a lying tongue is a fleeting vapor and a deadly **snare**.
23: 35 [D] feel it! When will I wake up so *I can* **find** another drink?"
28: 5 [D] but *those who* **seek** the LORD understand it fully.
29: 10 [D] men hate a man of integrity and **seek to** kill the upright.
29: 26 [D] Many **seek** [+7156] **an audience with** a ruler, but it is from
Ecc 3: 6 [D] a time to **search** and a time to give up, a time to keep and a
3: 15 [D] be has been before; and God *will* **call** the past **to account**.
7: 25 [D] to investigate and *to* **search out** wisdom and the scheme of
7: 28 [D] while I *was* still **searching** but not finding—I found one
7: 29 [D] but men *have* **gone in search of** many schemes."
8: 17 [D] Despite all his efforts to **search** *it* **out**, man cannot discover
12: 10 [D] The Teacher **searched** to find just the right words, and what
SS 3: 1 [D] All night long on my bed *I* **looked for** the one my heart
3: 1 [D] one my heart loves; *I* **looked for** him but did not find him.
3: 2 [D] and squares; *I will* **search for** the one my heart loves.
3: 2 [D] one my heart loves. So *I* **looked for** him but did not find him.
5: 6 [D] *I* **looked for** him but did not find him. I called him but he did
6: 1 [D] way did your lover turn, that *we may* **look for** him with you?
Isa 1: 12 [D] who *has* **asked** this of you, this trampling of my courts?
40: 20 [D] *He* **looks for** a skilled craftsman to set up an idol that will
41: 12 [D] Though *you* **search for** your enemies, you will not find
41: 17 [D] "The poor and needy **search for** water, but there is none;
45: 19 [D] I have not said to Jacob's descendants, '**Seek** me in vain.'
51: 1 [D] you who pursue righteousness and *who* **seek** the LORD:
65: 1 [D] not ask for me; I was found by *those who did* not **seek** me.
Jer 2: 24 [D] Any *males that* **pursue** her need not tire themselves;
2: 33 [D] How skilled you are at **pursuing** love! Even the worst of
4: 30 [D] in vain. Your lovers despise you; *they* **seek** your life.
5: 1 [D] look around and consider, **search** through her squares.
5: 1 [D] but one person who deals honestly and **seeks** the truth,
11: 21 [D] says about the men of Anathoth who *are* **seeking** your life
19: 7 [D] their enemies, at the hands of *those who* **seek** their lives,
19: 9 [D] siege imposed on them by the enemies *who* **seek** their lives.'
21: 7 [D] king of Babylon and to their enemies *who* **seek** their lives.
22: 25 [D] I will hand you over to *those who* **seek** your life, those you
26: 21 [D] heard his words, the king **sought to** put him to death.
29: 13 [D] *You will* **seek** me and find me when you seek me with all
34: 20 [D] I will hand over to their enemies *who* **seek** their lives. Their
34: 21 [D] and his officials over to their enemies *who* **seek** their lives,
38: 16 [D] you nor hand you over to those who *are* **seeking** your life."
44: 30 [D] Hophra king of Egypt over to his enemies *who* **seek** his life,
44: 30 [D] king of Babylon, the enemy *who was* **seeking** his life.' "
45: 5 [D] *Should* you then **seek** great things for yourself? Seek them
45: 5 [D] then seek great things for yourself? **Seek** them not.
46: 26 [D] I will hand them over to *those who* **seek** their lives, to
49: 37 [D] Elam before their foes, before *those who* **seek** their lives;

Jer 50: 4 [D] the people of Judah together will go in tears *to* **seek** the
50: 20 [E] "**search** *will* **be made for** Israel's guilt, but there will be none,
La 1: 11 [D] All her people groan *as they* **search for** bread; they barter
1: 19 [D] my elders perished in the city while *they* **searched for** food
Eze 3: 18 [D] and *I will* **hold** you **accountable** [+3338+4946] *for* his blood.
3: 20 [D] and *I will* **hold** you **accountable** [+3338+4946] *for* his blood.
7: 25 [D] When terror comes, *they will* **seek** peace, but there will be
7: 26 [D] *They will* **try to get** a vision from the prophet; the teaching
22: 30 [D] "*I* **looked for** a man among them who would build up the
26: 21 [E] *You will* **be sought**, but you will never again be found,
33: 8 [D] and *I will* **hold** you **accountable** [+3338+4946] *for* his blood.
34: 4 [D] have not brought back the strays or **searched for** the lost.
34: 6 [D] the whole earth, and no one searched or **looked for** them.
34: 16 [D] *I will* **search for** the lost and bring back the strays. I will
Da 1: 8 [D] *he* **asked** the chief official **for permission** not to defile
1: 20 [D] and understanding about which the king **questioned** them,
8: 15 [D] Daniel, was watching the vision and **trying to** understand it,
9: 3 [D] the Lord God and **pleaded with** him in prayer and petition,
Hos 2: 7 [2:9] [D] catch them; *she will* **look for** them but not find them.
3: 5 [D] and **seek** the LORD their God and David their king.
5: 6 [D] they go with their flocks and herds to **seek** the LORD,
5: 15 [D] *they will* **seek** my face; in their misery they will earnestly
7: 10 [D] he does not return to the LORD his God or **search for** him.
Am 8: 12 [D] **searching for** the word of the LORD, but they will not find
Na 3: 7 [D] mourn for her?' Where *can I* **find** anyone to comfort you?"
3: 11 [D] you will go into hiding and **seek** refuge from the enemy.
Zep 1: 6 [D] the LORD and neither **seek** the LORD nor inquire of him.
2: 3 [D] **Seek** the LORD, all you humble of the land, you who do
2: 3 [D] **Seek** righteousness, seek humility; perhaps you will be
2: 3 [D] Seek righteousness, **seek** humility; perhaps you will be
Zec 6: 7 [D] went out, *they were* **straining** to go throughout the earth.
8: 21 [D] once to entreat the LORD and **seek** the LORD Almighty.
8: 22 [D] powerful nations will come to Jerusalem to **seek** the LORD
11: 16 [D] or **seek** the young, or heal the injured, or feed the healthy,
12: 9 [D] On that day *I will* **set out** to destroy all the nations that attack
Mal 2: 7 [D] and from his mouth *men should* **seek** instruction—
2: 15 [D] And why one? Because *he was* **seeking** godly offspring.
3: 1 [D] suddenly the Lord you *are* **seeking** will come to his temple;

1336 בַּקָּשָׁה **baqqāšâ**, n.m. [8] [√ 1335]

request [7], asked [1]

Ezr 7: 6 The king had granted him everything he **asked**, for the hand of the
Est 5: 3 the king asked, "What is it, Queen Esther? What *is* your **request**?
5: 6 is your petition? It will be given you. And what is your **request**?
5: 7 Esther replied, "My petition and my **request** is this:
5: 8 if it pleases the king to grant my petition and fulfill my **request**,
7: 2 what is your petition? It will be given you. What is your **request**?
7: 3 this is my petition. And spare my people—this is my **request**.
9: 12 It will be given you. What is your **request**? It will also be granted."

1337 [1]בַּר **bar[1]**, n.m. [4] [→ 1401; cf. 1201; Ar 10120]

son [4]

Ps 2: 12 Kiss the **Son**, lest he be angry and you be destroyed in your way,
Pr 31: 2 "O my **son**, O son of my womb, O son of my vows,
31: 2 "O my son, O **son** *of* my womb, O son of my vows,
31: 2 "O my son, O son of my womb, O **son** *of* my vows,

1338 [2]בַּר **bar[2]**, a. [7] [√ 1405]

pure [3], bright [1], empty [1], favorite [1], radiant [1]

Job 11: 4 say to God, 'My beliefs are flawless and I am **pure** in your sight.'
Ps 19: 8 [19:9] The commands of the LORD are **radiant**, giving light to
24: 4 He who has clean hands and a **pure** heart, who does not lift up his
73: 1 Surely God is good to Israel, to *those who* are **pure** *in* heart.
Pr 14: 4 Where there are no oxen, the manger is **empty**, but from the
SS 6: 9 only daughter of her mother, the **favorite** of the one who bore her.
6: 10 fair as the moon, **bright** as the sun, majestic as the stars in

1339 [3]בַּר **bar[3]**, n.m. [13] [√ 1405; cf. 1350?]

grain [11], wheat [2]

Ge 41: 35 are coming and store up the **grain** under the authority of Pharaoh,
41: 49 Joseph stored up huge quantities of **grain**, like the sand of the sea;
42: 3 Then ten of Joseph's brothers went down to buy **grain** from Egypt.
42: 25 Joseph gave orders to fill their bags with **grain**, to put each man's
45: 23 ten female donkeys loaded with **grain** and bread and other
Ps 65: 13 [65:14] with flocks and the valleys are mantled with **grain**;
72: 16 Let **grain** abound throughout the land; on the tops of the hills may
Pr 11: 26 People curse the man who hoards **grain**, but blessing crowns him
Jer 23: 28 For what has straw to do with **grain**?" declares the LORD.
Joel 2: 24 The threshing floors will be filled with **grain**; the vats will
Am 5: 11 You trample on the poor and force him to give you **grain**.
8: 5 sell grain, and the Sabbath be ended that we may market **wheat**?"—
8: 6 for a pair of sandals, selling even the sweepings with the **wheat**.

1340 [4]בַּר **bar[4]**, n.m. [1] [→ Ar 10119]

wilds [1]

Job 39: 4 Their young thrive and grow strong in the **wilds**; they leave

1341 [1]בֹּר **bōr[1]**, n.m. [5] [√ 1405]

cleanness [5]

2Sa 22: 21 according to the **cleanness** *of* my hands he has rewarded me.
22: 25 to my righteousness, according to my **cleanness** in his sight.
Job 22: 30 who will be delivered through the **cleanness** *of* your hands."
Ps 18: 20 [18:21] according to the **cleanness** *of* my hands he has rewarded
18: 24 [18:25] according to the **cleanness** *of* my hands in his sight.

1342 [2]בֹּר **bōr[2]**, n.m. [2] [√ 1405]

thoroughly purge away [+2021+3869+7671] [1], washing soda [1]

Job 9: 30 if I washed myself with soap and my hands with **washing soda**,
Isa 1: 25 *I will* **thoroughly purge away** [+2021+3869+7671] your dross and

1343 [1]בָּרָא **bārā'[1]**, v. [48] [→ 1349, 1375]

created [21], create [10], were created [6], Creator [3], are created [2], creating [2], brings about [1], creates [1], done [1], not yet created [1]

Ge 1: 1 [A] In the beginning God **created** the heavens and the earth.
1: 21 [A] So God **created** the great creatures of the sea and every
1: 27 [A] So God **created** man in his own image, in the image of God
1: 27 [A] man in his own image, in the image of God *he* **created** him;
1: 27 [A] of God he created him; male and female *he* **created** them.
2: 3 [A] because on it he rested from all the work *of* **creating** that he
2: 4 [C] of the heavens and the earth when they **were created**.
5: 1 [A] When God **created** man, he made him in the likeness of God.
5: 2 [A] *He* **created** them male and female and blessed them.
5: 2 [C] And when they **were created**, he called them "man."
6: 7 [A] LORD said, "I will wipe mankind, whom *I have* **created**,
Ex 34: 10 [C] Before all your people I will do wonders never before **done**
Nu 16: 30 [A] if the LORD **brings about** something totally new,
Dt 4: 32 [A] your time, from the day God **created** man on the earth;
Ps 51: 10 [51:12] [A] **Create** in me a pure heart, O God, and renew a
89: 12 [89:13] [A] You **created** the north and the south; Tabor
89: 47 [89:48] [A] my life. For what futility *you have* **created** all men!
102: 18 [102:19] [C] a people **not yet created** may praise the LORD:
104: 30 [C] When you send your Spirit, *they* **are created**, and you renew
148: 5 [C] of the LORD, for he commanded and *they* **were created**.
Ecc 12: 1 [A] Remember your **Creator** in the days of your youth,
Isa 4: 5 [A] the LORD *will* **create** over all of Mount Zion and over
40: 26 [A] your eyes and look to the heavens: Who **created** all these?
40: 28 [A] is the everlasting God, the **Creator** *of* the ends of the earth.
41: 20 [A] has done this, that the Holy One of Israel *has* **created** it.
42: 5 [A] *he who* **created** the heavens and stretched them out,
43: 1 [A] *he who* **created** you, O Jacob, he who formed you, O Israel:
43: 7 [A] whom *I* **created** for my glory, whom I formed and made."
43: 15 [A] the LORD, your Holy One, Israel's **Creator**, your King."
45: 7 [A] I form the light and **create** darkness, I bring prosperity
45: 7 [A] and create darkness, I bring prosperity and **create** disaster;
45: 8 [A] righteousness grow with it; I, the LORD, *have* **created** it.
45: 12 [A] It is I who made the earth and **created** mankind upon it. My
45: 18 [A] *he who* **created** the heavens, he is God; he who fashioned
45: 18 [A] *he did* not **create** it to be empty, but formed it to be
48: 7 [C] *They* **are created** now, and not long ago; you have not heard
54: 16 [A] it is I *who* **created** the blacksmith who fans the coals into
54: 16 [A] And it is I *who have* **created** the destroyer to work havoc;
57: 19 [A] **creating** praise on the lips of the mourners in Israel. Peace,
65: 17 [A] "Behold, I *will* **create** new heavens and a new earth. The
65: 18 [A] be glad and rejoice forever in what I *will* **create**, for I will
65: 18 [A] for I *will* **create** Jerusalem to be a delight and its people a
Jer 31: 22 [A] The LORD *will* **create** a new thing on earth—a woman will
Eze 21: 30 [21:35] [C] In the place where *you* **were created**, in the land of
28: 13 [C] of gold; on the day you **were created** they were prepared.
28: 15 [C] the day you **were created** till wickedness was found in you.
Am 4: 13 [A] He who forms the mountains, **creates** the wind, and reveals
Mal 2: 10 [A] Have we not all one Father? *Did* not one God **create** us?

1344 [2]בָּרָא **bārā'[2]**, v. [1] [→ 1374; cf. 5258]

fattening [1]

1Sa 2: 29 [G] Why do you honor your sons more than me by **fattening**

1345 [3]בָּרָא **bārā'[3]**, v. [5]

untranslated [1], clear land [1], clear [1], cut down [1], make [1]

Jos 17: 15 [D] **clear land** for yourselves there in the land of the Perizzites

Jos 17:18 [D] **Clear** it, and its farthest limits will be yours;
Eze 21:19 [21:24] [D] **Make** a signpost where the road branches off to the
21:19 [21:24] [D] where the road branches off to the city. **[RPH]**
23:47 [D] mob will stone them and **cut** them **down** with their swords;

1346 ⁴בָּרָא bārā'⁴, v. Not used in NIV/BHS [√ 1356]

1347 בְּרֹאדַךְ־בַּלְאֲדָן bᵉrō'dak-bal'ᵃdān, n.pr.m. [1 / 0] [√ 5282]

2Ki 20:12 At that time Merodach-Baladan [BHS ***Berodach-Baladan***; NIV 5282] son of Baladan

1348 בִּרְאִי bir'î, n.pr.loc. Not used in NIV/BHS [→ 1082]

1349 בְּרָאיָה bᵉrā'yâ, n.pr.m. [1] [√ 1343 + 3378]

Beraiah [1]

1Ch 8:21 Adaiah, **Beraiah** and Shimrath were the sons of Shimei.

1350 בַּרְבֻּר barbur, n.m.pl. [1] [cf. 1339?]

fowl [1]

1Ki 4:23 [5:3] as well as deer, gazelles, roebucks and choice **fowl**.

1351 בָּרַד bārad, v.den. [1] [→ 1352]

hail [1]

Isa 32:19 [A] Though **hail** flattens the forest and the city is leveled

1352 בָּרָד bārād, n.m. [29 / 28] [√ 1351]

hail [21], hail [+74] [1], hailstones [+74] [1], hailstones [1], hailstorm [+2443] [1], hailstorm [1], it^s [+2021] [1], storm [1]

Ex 9:18 at this time tomorrow I will send the worst **hailstorm** that has ever
9:19 because the **hail** will fall on every man and animal that has not
9:22 out your hand toward the sky so that **hail** will fall all over Egypt—
9:23 the LORD sent thunder and **hail**, and lightning flashed down to
9:23 to the ground. So the LORD rained **hail** on the land of Egypt;
9:24 **hail** fell and lightning flashed back and forth. It was the worst
9:24 It was the worst **storm** in all the land of Egypt since it had become
9:25 Throughout Egypt **hail** struck everything in the fields—both men
9:25 animals; **it**^s [+2021] beat down everything growing in the fields
9:26 The only place it did not **hail** was the land of Goshen,
9:28 Pray to the LORD, for we have had enough thunder and **hail**.
9:29 The thunder will stop and there will be no more **hail**, so you may
9:33 the thunder and **hail** stopped, and the rain no longer poured down
9:34 When Pharaoh saw that the rain and **hail** and thunder had stopped,
10:5 They will devour what little you have left after the **hail**,
10:12 everything growing in the fields, everything left by the **hail**."
10:15 They devoured all that was left after the **hail**—everything growing
Jos 10:11 more of them died from the **hailstones** [+74] than were killed by
Job 38:22 the storehouses of the snow or seen the storehouses of the **hail**,
Ps 18:12 [18:13] clouds advanced, with **hailstones** and bolts of lightning.
18:13 [18:14] the voice of the Most High resounded. [BHS+ *amid hailstones and bolts of lightning*]
78:47 He destroyed their vines with **hail** and their sycamore-figs with
78:48 He gave over their cattle to the **hail**, their livestock to bolts of
105:32 He turned their rain into **hail**, with lightning throughout their land;
148:8 lightning and **hail**, snow and clouds, stormy winds that do his
Isa 28:2 Like a **hailstorm** [+2443] and a destructive wind, like a driving
28:17 **hail** will sweep away your refuge, the lie, and water will overflow
30:30 and consuming fire, with cloudburst, thunderstorm and **hail** [+74].
Hag 2:17 mildew and **hail**, yet you did not turn to me,' declares the LORD.

1353 בָּרֹד bārōd, a. [4]

dappled [2], spotted [2]

Ge 31:10 goats mating with the flock were streaked, speckled or **spotted**.
31:12 speckled or **spotted**, for I have seen all that Laban has been doing
Zec 6:3 the third white, and the fourth **dappled**—all of them powerful.
6:6 the west, and the one with the **dappled** horses toward the south."

1354 ¹בֶּרֶד bered¹, n.pr.loc. [1]

Bered [1]

Ge 16:14 called Beer Lahai Roi; it is still there, between Kadesh and **Bered**.

1355 ²בֶּרֶד bered², n.pr.m. [1]

Bered [1]

1Ch 7:20 Shuthelah, **Bered** his son, Tahath his son, Eleadah his son,

1356 ¹בָּרָה bārâ¹, v. [6] [→ 1346, 1362, 1376]

eat [3], food [1], give to eat [1], urged to eat [1]

2Sa 3:35 [G] and **urged** David **to eat** something while it was still day;
12:17 [A] but he refused, and *he would* not **eat** any food with them.
13:5 [G] like my sister Tamar to come and **give** me something **to eat**.
13:6 [A] some special bread in my sight, so *I may* **eat** from her hand."
13:10 [A] food here into my bedroom so *I may* **eat** from your hand."
La 4:10 [D] who became their **food** when my people were destroyed.

1357 ²בָּרָה bārâ², v. Not used in NIV/BHS [√ 1382]

1358 בָּרוּךְ bārûk, n.pr.m. [26] [√ 1385]

Baruch [26]

Ne 3:20 **Baruch** son of Zabbai zealously repaired another section,
10:6 [10:7] Daniel, Ginnethon, **Baruch**,
11:5 Maaseiah son of **Baruch**, the son of Col-Hozeh, the son of
Jer 32:12 and I gave this deed to **Baruch** son of Neriah, the son of Mahseiah,
32:13 "In their presence I gave **Baruch** these instructions:
32:16 "After I had given the deed of purchase to **Baruch** son of Neriah,
36:4 So Jeremiah called **Baruch** son of Neriah, and while Jeremiah
36:4 the LORD had spoken to him, **Baruch** wrote them on the scroll.
36:5 Jeremiah told **Baruch**, "I am restricted; I cannot go to the
36:8 **Baruch** son of Neriah did everything Jeremiah the prophet told
36:10 **Baruch** read to all the people at the LORD's temple the words of
36:13 After Micaiah told them everything he had heard **Baruch** read to
36:14 the son of Shelemiah, the son of Cushi, to say to **Baruch**,
36:14 So **Baruch** son of Neriah went to them with the scroll in his hand.
36:15 "Sit down, please, and read it to us." So **Baruch** read it to them.
36:16 these words, they looked at each other in fear and said to **Baruch**,
36:17 they asked **Baruch**, "Tell us, how did you come to write all this?
36:18 "Yes," **Baruch** replied, "he dictated all these words to me,
36:19 Then the officials said to **Baruch**, "You and Jeremiah, go
36:26 of Azriel and Shelemiah son of Abdeel to arrest **Baruch** the scribe
36:27 After the king burned the scroll containing the words that **Baruch**
36:32 took another scroll and gave it to the scribe **Baruch** son of Neriah,
43:3 **Baruch** son of Neriah is inciting you against us to hand us over to
43:6 of Shaphan, and Jeremiah the prophet and **Baruch** son of Neriah.
45:1 This is what Jeremiah the prophet told **Baruch** son of Neriah in the
45:2 "This is what the LORD, the God of Israel, says to you, **Baruch**:

1359 בָּרוּר bārûr, a. *or* v.ptcp. [2] [√ 1405]

purify [+448+2200] [1], sincerely [1]

Job 33:3 come from an upright heart; my lips **sincerely** speak what I know.
Zep 3:9 "Then *will I* **purify** [+448+2200] the lips of the peoples, that all of

1360 בְּרוֹשׁ bᵉrôš, n.m. [20 / 19] [cf. 1361]

pine [7], pine trees [4], pine tree [3], pines [3], pine [+6770] [1], spears of pine [1]

2Sa 6:5 with songs [BHS ***instruments made of pine***; NIV 8877] and with
1Ki 5:8 [5:22] will do all you want in providing the cedar and **pine** logs.
5:10 [5:24] supplied with all the cedar and **pine** logs he wanted,
6:15 and covered the floor of the temple with planks of **pine**.
6:34 He also made two **pine** doors, each having two leaves that turned
9:11 had supplied him with all the cedar and **pine** and gold he wanted.
2Ki 19:23 I have cut down its tallest cedars, the choicest of its **pines**.
2Ch 2:8 [2:7] "Send me also cedar, **pine** and algum logs from Lebanon,
3:5 He paneled the main hall with **pine** [+6770] and covered it with
Ps 104:17 the birds make their nests; the stork has its home in the **pine trees**.
Isa 14:8 Even the **pine trees** and the cedars of Lebanon exult over you
37:24 I have cut down its tallest cedars, the choicest of its **pines**.
41:19 I will set **pines** in the wasteland, the fir and the cypress together,
55:13 Instead of the thornbush will grow the **pine tree**, and instead of
60:13 the **pine**, the fir and the cypress together, to adorn the place of my
Eze 27:5 They made all your timbers of **pine trees** from Senir; they took a
31:8 of God could not rival it, nor could the **pine trees** equal its boughs,
Hos 14:8 [14:9] I am like a green **pine tree**; your fruitfulness comes from
Na 2:3 [2:4] day they are made ready; the **spears of pine** are brandished.
Zec 11:2 Wail, O **pine tree**, for the cedar has fallen; the stately trees are

1361 בְּרוֹת bᵉrôt, n.m. [1] [cf. 1360]

firs [1]

SS 1:17 The beams of our house are cedars; our rafters are **firs**.

1362 בָּרוּת bārût, n.f. [1] [√ 1356]

food [1]

Ps 69:21 [69:22] They put gall in my **food** and gave me vinegar for my

1363 בֵּרוֹתָה bērôtâ, n.pr.loc. [1]

Berothah [1]

Eze 47:16 **Berothah** and Sibraim (which lies on the border between

1364 בִּרְזָוִת birzāwit, n.pr.f. [0] [√ 1365]

1Ch 7:31 [The sons of Beriah: Heber and Malkiel, who was the father of **Birzaith**. [K; see Q 1365]]

1365 בִּרְזָיִת birzāyit, n.pr.f. [1] [√ 931 + 2339]

Birzaith [1]

1Ch 7:31 Heber and Malkiel, who was the father of **Birzaith**. [K 1364]

1366 בַּרְזֶל barzel, n.m. [76] [→ 1367; Ar 10591]

iron [62], iron-smelting [3], ax [2], iron tool [2], *untranslated* [1], blacksmith [+3093] [1], head [1], iron axhead [1], iron chains [1], irons [1], tool of iron [1]

Ge 4:22 Tubal-Cain, who forged all kinds of tools out of bronze and **iron**.
Lev 26:19 down your stubborn pride and make the sky above you like **iron**
Nu 31:22 Gold, silver, bronze, **iron**, tin, lead
35:16 " 'If a man strikes someone with an **iron** object so that he dies,
Dt 3:11 His bed was made of **iron** and was more than thirteen feet long
4:20 took you and brought you out of the **iron-smelting** furnace,
8:9 a land where the rocks are **iron** and you can dig copper out of the
19:5 fell a tree, the **head** may fly off and hit his neighbor and kill him.
27:5 your God, an altar of stones. Do not use any **iron tool** upon them.
28:23 sky over your head will be bronze, the ground beneath you **iron**.
28:48 He will put an **iron** yoke on your neck until he has destroyed you.
33:25 The bolts of your gates will be **iron** and bronze, and your strength
Jos 6:19 and the articles of bronze and **iron** are sacred to the LORD
6:24 articles of bronze and **iron** into the treasury of the LORD's house.
8:31 an altar of uncut stones, on which no **iron tool** had been used.
17:16 and all the Canaanites who live in the plain have **iron** chariots,
17:18 though the Canaanites have **iron** chariots and though they are
22:8 with large herds of livestock, with silver, gold, bronze and **iron**,
Jdg 1:19 to drive the people from the plains, because they had **iron** chariots.
4:3 Because he had nine hundred **iron** chariots and had cruelly
4:13 Sisera gathered together his nine hundred **iron** chariots and all the
1Sa 17:7 a weaver's rod, and its **iron** point weighed six hundred shekels.
2Sa 12:31 consigning them to labor with saws and with **iron** picks and axes,
12:31 and axes, **[RPH]** and he made them work at brickmaking.
23:7 Whoever touches thorns uses a **tool of iron** or the shaft of a spear;
1Ki 6:7 or any other **iron** tool was heard at the temple site while it was
8:51 whom you brought out of Egypt, out of that **iron-smelting** furnace.
22:11 Now Zedekiah son of Kenaanah had made **iron** horns and he
2Ki 6:5 them was cutting down a tree, the **iron axhead** fell into the water.
6:6 Elisha cut a stick and threw it there, and made the **iron** float.
1Ch 20:3 consigning them to labor with saws and with **iron** picks and axes.
22:3 He provided a large amount of **iron** to make nails for the doors of
22:14 quantities of bronze and **iron** too great to be weighed, and wood
22:16 in gold and silver, bronze and **iron**—craftsmen beyond number.
29:2 bronze for the bronze, **iron** for the iron and wood for the wood,
29:2 bronze for the bronze, iron for the **iron** and wood for the wood,
29:7 thousand talents of bronze and a hundred thousand talents of **iron**.
2Ch 2:7 [2:6] a man skilled to work in gold and silver, bronze and **iron**,
2:14 [2:13] work in gold and silver, bronze and **iron**, stone and wood,
18:10 Now Zedekiah son of Kenaanah had made **iron** horns, and he
24:12 and also workers in **iron** and bronze to repair the temple.
Job 19:24 that they were inscribed with an **iron** tool on lead, or engraved in
20:24 Though he flees from an **iron** weapon, a bronze-tipped arrow
28:2 **Iron** is taken from the earth, and copper is smelted from ore.
40:18 His bones are tubes of bronze, his limbs like rods of **iron**.
41:27 [41:19] **Iron** he treats like straw and bronze like rotten wood.
Ps 2:9 You will rule them with an **iron** scepter; you will dash them to
105:18 They bruised his feet with shackles, his neck was put in **irons**,
107:10 and the deepest gloom, prisoners suffering in **iron chains**,
107:16 for he breaks down gates of bronze and cuts through bars of **iron**.
149:8 to bind their kings with fetters, their nobles with shackles of **iron**,
Pr 27:17 As **iron** sharpens iron, so one man sharpens another.
27:17 As iron sharpens **iron**, so one man sharpens another.
Ecc 10:10 If the **ax** is dull and its edge unsharpened, more strength is needed
Isa 10:34 He will cut down the forest thickets with an **ax**; Lebanon will fall
44:12 The **blacksmith** [+3093] takes a tool and works with it in the
45:2 I will break down gates of bronze and cut through bars of **iron**.
48:4 the sinews of your neck were **iron**, your forehead was bronze.
60:17 Instead of bronze I will bring you gold, and silver in place of **iron**.
60:17 of wood I will bring you bronze, and **iron** in place of stones.
Jer 1:18 an **iron** pillar and a bronze wall to stand against the whole land—
6:28 about to slander. They are bronze and **iron**; they all act corruptly.
11:4 I brought them out of Egypt, out of the **iron-smelting** furnace.'
15:12 "Can a man break **iron**—iron from the north—or bronze?
15:12 "Can a man break iron—**iron** from the north—or bronze?
17:1 "Judah's sin is engraved with an **iron** tool, inscribed with a flint
28:13 broken a wooden yoke, but in its place you will get a yoke of **iron**.
28:14 I will put an **iron** yoke on the necks of all these nations to make
Eze 4:3 Then take an **iron** pan, place it as an iron wall between you
4:3 place it as an **iron** wall between you and the city and turn your face
22:18 all of them are the copper, tin, **iron** and lead left inside a furnace.
22:20 **iron**, lead and tin into a furnace to melt it with a fiery blast,
27:12 they exchanged silver, **iron**, tin and lead for your merchandise.
27:19 they exchanged wrought **iron**, cassia and calamus for your wares.
Am 1:3 Because she threshed Gilead with sledges having **iron** teeth,
Mic 4:13 and thresh, O Daughter of Zion, for I will give you horns of **iron**;

1367 בַּרְזִלַּי barzillay, n.pr.m. [12] [√ 1366]

Barzillai [12]

2Sa 17:27 Ammiel from Lo Debar, and **Barzillai** the Gileadite from Rogelim
19:31 [19:32] **Barzillai** the Gileadite also came down from Rogelim to
19:32 [19:33] Now **Barzillai** was a very old man, eighty years of age.
19:33 [19:34] The king said to **Barzillai**, "Cross over with me and stay
19:34 [19:35] **Barzillai** answered the king, "How many more years will
19:39 [19:40] The king kissed **Barzillai** and gave him his blessing,
21:8 whom she had borne to Adriel son of **Barzillai** the Meholathite.
1Ki 2:7 "But show kindness to the sons of **Barzillai** of Gilead and let them
Ezr 2:61 **Barzillai** (a man who had married a daughter of Barzillai the
2:61 Barzillai (a man who had married a daughter of **Barzillai** the
Ne 7:63 **Barzillai** (a man who had married a daughter of Barzillai the
7:63 Barzillai (a man who had married a daughter of **Barzillai** the

1368 בָּרַח bāraḥ[1], v. [65] [→ 1371, 4451; cf. 1369, 1370]

fled [32], flee [5], fleeing [3], running away [3], flees headlong [+1368] [2], come away [1], drives out [1], drove away [1], drove out [1], escaping [1], extend [1], extended [1], flees [1], fleeting [1], fly away [1], go back [1], gone back [1], leave at once [1], make flee [1], put to flight [1], ran away [1], ran off [1], run away [1], run off [1], takes to flight [1]

Ge 16:6 [A] Then Sarai mistreated Hagar; so *she* **fled** from her.
16:8 [A] "I'm **running away** from my mistress Sarai," she answered.
27:43 [A] do what I say: **Flee** at once to my brother Laban in Haran.
31:20 [A] the Aramean by not telling him he *was* **running away**.
31:21 [A] So he **fled** with all he had, and crossing the River, he headed
31:22 [A] On the third day Laban was told that Jacob *had* **fled**.
31:27 [A] Why *did you* **run off** secretly and deceive me? Why didn't
35:1 [A] who appeared to you when you *were* **fleeing** from your
35:7 [A] himself to him when he *was* **fleeing** from his brother.
Ex 2:15 [A] but Moses **fled** from Pharaoh and went to live in Midian,
14:5 [A] When the king of Egypt was told that the people *had* **fled**,
26:28 [G] The center crossbar *is to* **extend** from end to end at the
36:33 [A] so that *it* **extended** from end to end at the middle of the
Nu 24:11 [A] Now **leave at once** and go home! I said I would reward you
Jdg 9:21 [A] **escaping** to Beer, and he lived there because he was afraid of
11:3 [A] So Jephthah **fled** from his brothers and settled in the land of
1Sa 19:12 [A] let David down through a window, and *he* **fled** and escaped.
19:18 [A] When David *had* **fled** and made his escape, he went to
20:1 [A] Then David **fled** from Naioth at Ramah and went to Jonathan
21:10 [21:11] [A] That day David **fled** from Saul and went to Achish
22:17 [A] They knew he *was* **fleeing**, yet they did not tell me."
22:20 [A] of Ahimelech son of Ahitub, escaped and **fled** to join David.
23:6 [A] the ephod down with him when he **fled** to David *at* Keilah.)
27:4 [A] When Saul was told that David *had* **fled** *to* Gath, he no
2Sa 4:3 [A] because the people of Beeroth **fled** to Gittaim and have lived
13:34 [A] Meanwhile, Absalom *had* **fled**. Now the man standing watch
13:37 [A] Absalom **fled** and went to Talmai son of Ammihud, the king
13:38 [A] After Absalom **fled** and went to Geshur, he stayed there three
15:14 [A] *We must* **flee**, or none of us will escape from Absalom.
19:9 [19:10] [A] now *he has* **fled** the country because of Absalom;
1Ki 2:7 [A] They stood by me when I **fled** from your brother Absalom.
2:39 [A] two of Shimei's slaves **ran off** to Achish son of Maacah,
11:17 [A] **fled** to Egypt with some Edomite officials who had served
11:23 [A] Rezon son of Eliada, who *had* **fled** from his master,
11:40 [A] but Jeroboam **fled** to Egypt, to Shishak the king,
12:2 [A] where *he had* **fled** from King Solomon), he returned from
1Ch 8:13 [G] living in Aijalon and who **drove out** the inhabitants of Gath.
12:15 [12:16] [G] *they* **put to flight** everyone living in the valleys,
2Ch 10:2 [A] where *he had* **fled** from King Solomon), he returned from
Ne 6:11 [A] I said, "*Should* a man like me **run away**? Or should one like
13:10 [A] singers responsible for the service *had* **gone back** to their
13:28 [G] to Sanballat the Horonite. And *I* **drove** him **away** from me.
Job 9:25 [A] than a runner; *they* **fly away** without a glimpse of joy.
14:2 [A] withers away; like a **fleeting** shadow, he does not endure.
20:24 [A] Though *he* **flees** from an iron weapon, a bronze-tipped arrow
27:22 [A] without mercy *as he* **flees** [+1368] **headlong** from its power.
27:22 [A] without mercy *as he* **flees headlong** [+1368] from its power.
41:28 [41:20] [G] Arrows *do* not **make** him **flee**; slingstones are like

Ps 3: T [3:1] [A] psalm of David. When he **fled** from his son Absalom.
57: T [57:1] [A] When he *had* **fled** from Saul into the cave.
139: 7 [A] I go from your Spirit? Where *can I* **flee** from your presence?
Pr 19:26 [G] **drives out** his mother is a son who brings shame
SS 8:14 [A] **Come away**, my lover, and be like a gazelle or like a young
Isa 22: 3 [A] *having* **fled** while the enemy was still far away.
48:20 [A] Leave Babylon, **flee** from the Babylonians! Announce this
Jer 4:29 [A] sound of horsemen and archers every town **takes to flight**.
26:21 [A] him to death. But Uriah heard of it and **fled** in fear *to* Egypt.
39: 4 [A] king of Judah and all the soldiers saw them, *they* **fled**;
52: 7 [A] the city wall was broken through, and the whole army **fled**.
Da 10: 7 [A] such terror overwhelmed them that *they* **fled** and hid
Hos 12:12 [12:13] [A] Jacob **fled** *to* the country of Aram; Israel served to
Am 7:12 [A] to Amos, "Get out, you seer! **Go back** to the land of Judah.
Jnh 1: 3 [A] Jonah **ran away** from the LORD and headed for Tarshish.
1:10 [A] (They knew he *was* **running away** from the LORD,
4: 2 [A] That is why I was so quick to **flee** to Tarshish. I knew that

1369 ²בָּרַח bāraḥ², v. Not used in NIV/BHS [cf. 1368, 1370]

1370 ³בָּרַח bāraḥ³, v. Not used in NIV/BHS [→ 1378; cf. 1368, 1369]

1371 בָּרִחַ bāriaḥ, a. [4] [√ 1368]

fugitives [2], gliding [2]

Job 26:13 breath the skies became fair; his hand pierced the **gliding** serpent.
Isa 15: 5 her **fugitives** flee as far as Zoar, as far as Eglath Shelishiyah.
27: 1 his fierce, great and powerful sword, Leviathan the **gliding** serpent,
43:14 send to Babylon and bring down as **fugitives** all the Babylonians,

1372 בַּרְחֻמִי barḥumî, a.g. [1] [cf. 1038, 1050]

Barhumite [1]

2Sa 23:31 Abi-Albon the Arbathite, Azmaveth the **Barhumite**,

1373 בֵּרִי bērî, n.pr.m. [1]

Beri [1]

1Ch 7:36 The sons of Zophah: Suah, Harnepher, Shual, **Beri**, Imrah,

1374 בָּרִיא bārî', a. [14] [√ 1344; cf. 5258]

fat [4], fat [+1414] [2], healthy [2], choice sheep [1], choice [1], choicest [1], nourished [+1414] [1], stall-fed [1], strong [1]

Ge 41: 2 sleek and **fat** [+1414], and they grazed among the reeds.
41: 4 the cows that were ugly and gaunt ate up the seven sleek, **fat** cows.
41: 5 Seven heads of grain, **healthy** and good, were growing on a single
41: 7 The thin heads of grain swallowed up the seven **healthy**, full
41:18 **fat** [+1414] and sleek, and they grazed among the reeds.
41:20 The lean, ugly cows ate up the seven **fat** cows that came up first.
Jdg 3:17 the tribute to Eglon king of Moab, who was a very **fat** man.
1Ki 4:23 [5:3] ten head of **stall-fed** cattle, twenty of pasture-fed cattle
Ps 73: 4 They have no struggles; their bodies are healthy and **strong**.
Eze 34: 3 clothe yourselves with the wool and slaughter the **choice** *animals*,
34:20 I myself will judge between the **fat** sheep and the lean sheep.
Da 1:15 better **nourished** [+1414] than any of the young men who ate the
Hab 1:16 for by his net he lives in luxury and enjoys the **choicest** food.
Zec 11:16 or feed the healthy, but will eat the meat of the **choice sheep**,

1375 בְּרִיאָה b^erî'â, n.f. [1] [√ 1343]

something totally new [1]

Nu 16:30 if the LORD brings about **something totally new**, and the earth

1376 בִּרְיָה biryâ, n.f. [3] [√ 1356]

food [3]

2Sa 13: 5 Let her prepare the **food** in my sight so I may watch her and
13: 7 the house of your brother Amnon and prepare some **food** for him."
13:10 "Bring the **food** here into my bedroom so I may eat from your

1377 בָּרִיחַ bārîaḥ, n.pr.m. [1]

Bariah [1]

1Ch 3:22 his sons: Hattush, Igal, **Bariah**, Neariah and Shaphat—six in all.

1378 בְּרִיחַ b^erîaḥ, n.m. [40] [√ 1370]

bars [17], crossbars [11], *untranslated* [4], crossbar [2], bar [1], barred gates [1], barred in [+1237] [1], bars of gates [1], gate bars [1], gate [1]

Ex 26:26 "Also make **crossbars** *of* acacia wood: five for the frames on one
26:27 five **[RPH]** for those on the other side, and five for the frames on
26:27 five **[RPH]** for the frames on the west, at the far end of the
26:28 The center **crossbar** is to extend from end to end at the middle of
26:29 the frames with gold and make gold rings to hold the **crossbars**.
26:29 rings to hold the crossbars. Also overlay the **crossbars** with gold.
35:11 and its covering, clasps, frames, **crossbars**, posts and bases;
36:31 They also made **crossbars** *of* acacia wood: five for the frames on
36:32 five **[RPH]** for those on the other side, and five for the frames on
36:32 five **[RPH]** for the frames on the west, at the far end of the
36:33 They made the center **crossbar** so that it extended from end to end
36:34 the frames with gold and made gold rings to hold the **crossbars**.
36:34 to hold the crossbars. They also overlaid the **crossbars** with gold.
39:33 all its furnishings, its clasps, frames, **crossbars**, posts and bases;
40:18 erected the frames, inserted the **crossbars** and set up the posts.
Nu 3:36 its **crossbars**, posts, bases, all its equipment, and everything
4:31 carry the frames of the tabernacle, its **crossbars**, posts and bases,
Dt 3: 5 these cities were fortified with high walls and with gates and **bars**,
Jdg 16: 3 together with the two posts, and tore them loose, **bar** and all.
1Sa 23: 7 has imprisoned himself by entering a town with gates and **bars**."
1Ki 4:13 in Bashan and its sixty large walled cities with bronze **gate bars**);
2Ch 8: 5 Beth Horon as fortified cities, with walls and with gates and **bars**,
14: 7 [14:6] "and put walls around them, with towers, gates and **bars**.
Ne 3: 3 They laid its beams and put its doors and bolts and **bars** in place.
3: 6 They laid its beams and put its doors and bolts and **bars** in place.
3:13 They rebuilt it and put its doors and bolts and **bars** in place.
3:14 He rebuilt it and put its doors and bolts and **bars** in place.
3:15 roofing it over and putting its doors and bolts and **bars** in place.
Job 38:10 when I fixed limits for it and set its doors and **bars** in place,
Ps 107:16 for he breaks down gates of bronze and cuts through **bars** *of* iron.
147:13 for he strengthens the **bars** *of* your gates and blesses your people
Pr 18:19 a fortified city, and disputes are like the **barred gates** *of* a citadel.
Isa 45: 2 I will break down gates of bronze and cut through **bars** *of* iron.
Jer 49:31 declares the LORD, "a nation that has neither gates nor **bars**;
51:30 Her dwellings are set on fire; the **bars of** her **gates** are broken.
La 2: 9 have sunk into the ground; their **bars** he has broken and destroyed.
Eze 38:11 all of them living without walls and without gates and **bars**.
Am 1: 5 I will break down the **gate** *of* Damascus; I will destroy the king
Jnh 2: 6 [2:7] sank down; the earth beneath **barred** [+1237] me **in** forever.
Na 3:13 land are wide open to your enemies; fire has consumed their **bars**.

1379 בֵּרִים bērîm, a.g. [1]

Berites [1]

2Sa 20:14 to Abel Beth Maacah and through the entire region of the **Berites**,

1380 בְּרִיעָה b^erî'â, n.pr.m. [11] [→ 1381]

Beriah [11]

Ge 46:17 The sons of Asher: Imnah, Ishvah, Ishvi and **Beriah**. Their sister
46:17 Their sister was Serah. The sons of **Beriah**: Heber and Malkiel.
Nu 26:44 through Ishvi, the Ishvite clan; through **Beriah**, the Beriite clan;
26:45 through the descendants of **Beriah**: through Heber, the Heberite
1Ch 7:23 He named him **Beriah**, because there had been misfortune in his
7:30 The sons of Asher: Imnah, Ishvah, Ishvi and **Beriah**. Their sister
7:31 The sons of **Beriah**: Heber and Malkiel, who was the father of
8:13 **Beriah** and Shema, who were heads of families of those living in
8:16 Michael, Ishpah and Joha were the sons of **Beriah**.
23:10 the sons of Shimei: Jahath, Ziza, Jeush and **Beriah**. These were the
23:11 and Ziza the second, but Jeush and **Beriah** did not have many sons;

1381 בְּרִיעִי b^erî'î, a.g. [1] [√ 1380]

Beriite [1]

Nu 26:44 through Ishvi, the Ishvite clan; through Beriah, the **Beriite** clan;

1382 בְּרִית b^erît, n.f. [284] [→ 451, 1253, 1357]

covenant [246], treaty [26], agreement [3], compact [3], agreements [1], alliance [1], allied [+1251] [1], allies [+408] [1], it[s] [+778+2021] [1], marriage covenant [1]

Ge 6:18 I will establish my **covenant** with you, and you will enter the ark—
9: 9 "I now establish my **covenant** with you and with your descendants
9:11 I establish my **covenant** with you: Never again will all life be cut
9:12 "This is the sign of the **covenant** I am making between me
9:13 and it will be the sign of the **covenant** between me and the earth.
9:15 I will remember my **covenant** between me and you and all living
9:16 I will see it and remember the everlasting **covenant** between God
9:17 "This is the sign of the **covenant** I have established between me
14:13 of Eshcol and Aner, all of whom were **allied** [+1251] *with* Abram.
15:18 On that day the LORD made a **covenant** with Abram and said,
17: 2 I will confirm my **covenant** between me and you and will greatly
17: 4 "As for me, this is my **covenant** with you: You will be the father
17: 7 I will establish my **covenant** as an everlasting covenant between
17: 7 I will establish my covenant as an everlasting **covenant** between
17: 9 you must keep my **covenant**, you and your descendants after you
17:10 This is my **covenant** with you and your descendants after you,
17:11 and it will be the sign of the **covenant** between me and you.

Ge 17:13 My **covenant** in your flesh is to be an everlasting covenant.
17:13 My covenant in your flesh is to be an everlasting **covenant**.
17:14 will be cut off from his people; he has broken my **covenant**."
17:19 I will establish my **covenant** with him as an everlasting covenant
17:19 I will establish my covenant with him as an everlasting **covenant**
17:21 my **covenant** I will establish with Isaac, whom Sarah will bear to
21:27 and gave them to Abimelech, and the two men made a **treaty**.
21:32 After the **treaty** had been made at Beersheba, Abimelech
26:28 between us'—between us and you. Let us make a **treaty** with you
31:44 Come now, let's make a **covenant**, you and I, and let it serve as a
Ex 2:24 their groaning and he remembered his **covenant** with Abraham,
6:4 I also established my **covenant** with them to give them the land of
6:5 the Egyptians are enslaving, and I have remembered my **covenant**.
19:5 Now if you obey me fully and keep my **covenant**, then out of all
23:32 Do not make a **covenant** with them or with their gods.
24:7 Then he took the Book of the **Covenant** and read it to the people.
24:8 "This is the blood of the **covenant** that the LORD has made with
31:16 celebrating it for the generations to come as a lasting **covenant**.
34:10 Then the LORD said: "I am making a **covenant** with you.
34:12 Be careful not to make a **treaty** with those who live in the land
34:15 "Be careful not to make a **treaty** with those who live in the land;
34:27 for in accordance with these words I have made a **covenant** with
34:28 he wrote on the tablets the words of the **covenant**—the Ten
Lev 2:13 Do not leave the salt of the **covenant** *of* your God out of your grain
24:8 after Sabbath, on behalf of the Israelites, as a lasting **covenant**.
26:9 and increase your numbers, and I will keep my **covenant** with you.
26:15 and fail to carry out all my commands and so violate my **covenant**,
26:25 bring the sword upon you to avenge the breaking of the **covenant**.
26:42 I will remember my **covenant** *with* Jacob and my covenant with
26:42 and my **covenant** *with* Isaac and my covenant with Abraham,
26:42 and my covenant with Isaac and my **covenant** *with* Abraham,
26:44 as to destroy them completely, breaking my **covenant** with them.
26:45 for their sake I will remember the **covenant** *with* their ancestors
Nu 10:33 The ark of the **covenant** *of* the LORD went before them during
14:44 though neither Moses nor the ark of the LORD's **covenant**
18:19 It is an everlasting **covenant** *of* salt before the LORD for both
25:12 Therefore tell him I am making my **covenant** *of* peace with him.
25:13 and his descendants will have a **covenant** *of* a lasting priesthood,
Dt 4:13 He declared to you his **covenant**, the Ten Commandments,
4:23 Be careful not to forget the **covenant** *of* the LORD your God that
4:31 or destroy you or forget the **covenant** *with* your forefathers,
5:2 The LORD our God made a **covenant** with us at Horeb.
5:3 It was not with our fathers that the LORD made this **covenant**,
7:2 them totally. Make no **treaty** with them, and show them no mercy.
7:9 keeping his **covenant** *of* love to a thousand generations of those
7:12 the LORD your God will keep his **covenant** *of* love with you,
8:18 and so confirms his **covenant**, which he swore to your forefathers,
9:9 the tablets of the **covenant** that the LORD had made with you,
9:11 LORD gave me the two stone tablets, the tablets of the **covenant**.
9:15 with fire. And the two tablets of the **covenant** were in my hands.
10:8 the tribe of Levi to carry the ark of the **covenant** *of* the LORD,
17:2 in the eyes of the LORD your God in violation of his **covenant**,
29:1 [28:69] These are the terms of the **covenant** the LORD
29:1 [28:69] in addition to the **covenant** he had made with them at
29:9 [29:8] Carefully follow the terms of this **covenant**, so that you
29:12 [29:11] order to enter into a **covenant** *with* the LORD your God,
29:14 [29:13] I am making this **covenant**, with its oath, not only with
29:21 [29:20] according to all the curses of the **covenant** written in this
29:25 [29:24] because this people abandoned the **covenant** *of* the
31:9 sons of Levi, who carried the ark of the **covenant** *of* the LORD,
31:16 They will forsake me and break the **covenant** I made with them.
31:20 and worship them, rejecting me and breaking my **covenant**.
31:25 to the Levites who carried the ark of the **covenant** *of* the LORD:
31:26 place it beside the ark of the **covenant** *of* the LORD your God.
33:9 but he watched over your word and guarded your **covenant**.
Jos 3:3 "When you see the ark of the **covenant** *of* the LORD your God,
3:6 "Take up the ark of the **covenant** and pass on ahead of the people."
3:6 So they took **it**[s] [+778+2021] up and went ahead of them.
3:8 Tell the priests who carry the ark of the **covenant**: 'When you
3:11 the ark of the **covenant** *of* the Lord of all the earth will go into the
3:14 the priests carrying the ark of the **covenant** went ahead of them.
3:17 The priests who carried the ark of the **covenant** *of* the LORD
4:7 Jordan was cut off before the ark of the **covenant** *of* the LORD.
4:9 where the priests who carried the ark of the **covenant** had stood.
4:18 up out of the river carrying the ark of the **covenant** *of* the LORD.
6:6 "Take up the ark of the **covenant** *of* the LORD and have seven
6:8 and the ark of the LORD's **covenant** followed them.
7:11 they have violated my **covenant**, which I commanded them to
7:15 He has violated the **covenant** *of* the LORD and has done a
8:33 were standing on both sides of the ark of the **covenant** *of* the
9:6 "We have come from a distant country; make a **treaty** with us."
9:7 you live near us. How then can we make a **treaty** with you?"
9:11 and say to them, "We are your servants; make a **treaty** with us." '
9:15 Then Joshua made a **treaty** of peace with them to let them live,
9:16 Three days after they made the **treaty** with the Gibeonites,
23:16 If you violate the **covenant** *of* the LORD your God, which he
24:25 On that day Joshua made a **covenant** for the people, and there at
Jdg 2:1 your forefathers. I said, 'I will never break my **covenant** with you,
2:2 and you shall not make a **covenant** with the people of this land,
2:20 "Because this nation has violated the **covenant** that I laid down for
20:27 (In those days the ark of the **covenant** *of* God was there,
1Sa 4:3 Let us bring the ark of the LORD's **covenant** from Shiloh,
4:4 they brought back the ark of the **covenant** *of* the LORD
4:4 and Phinehas, were there with the ark of the **covenant** *of* God.
4:5 When the ark of the LORD's **covenant** came into the camp,
11:1 to him, "Make a **treaty** with us, and we will be subject to you."
18:3 Jonathan made a **covenant** with David because he loved him as
20:8 for you have brought him into a **covenant** with you *before* the
23:18 The two of them made a **covenant** before the LORD.
2Sa 3:12 Make an **agreement** with me, and I will help you bring all Israel
3:13 "Good," said David. "I will make an **agreement** with you.
3:21 for my lord the king, so that they may make a **compact** with you,
5:3 the king made a **compact** with them at Hebron before the LORD,
15:24 who were with him were carrying the ark of the **covenant** *of* God.
23:5 Has he not made with me an everlasting **covenant**, arranged
1Ki 3:15 stood before the ark of the Lord's **covenant** and sacrificed burnt
5:12 [5:26] and Solomon, and the two of them made a **treaty**.
6:19 the temple to set the ark of the **covenant** *of* the LORD there.
8:1 to bring up the ark of the LORD's **covenant** from Zion, the City
8:6 brought the ark of the LORD's **covenant** to its place in the inner
8:21 in which is the **covenant** *of* the LORD that he made with our
8:23 you who keep your **covenant** of love with your servants who
11:11 your attitude and you have not kept my **covenant** and my decrees,
15:19 "Let there be a **treaty** between me and you," he said, "as there was
15:19 Now break your **treaty** with Baasha king of Israel so he will
19:10 The Israelites have rejected your **covenant**, broken down your
19:14 The Israelites have rejected your **covenant**, broken down your
20:34 ⌞Ahab said,⌟ "On the basis of a **treaty** I will set you free."
20:34 I will set you free." So he made a **treaty** with him, and let him go.
2Ki 11:4 He made a **covenant** with them and put them under oath at the
11:17 Jehoiada then made a **covenant** between the LORD and the king
13:23 showed concern for them because of his **covenant** with Abraham,
17:15 his decrees and the **covenant** he had made with their fathers
17:35 When the LORD made a **covenant** with the Israelites, he
17:38 Do not forget the **covenant** I have made with you, and do not
18:12 not obeyed the LORD their God, but had violated his **covenant**—
23:2 read in their hearing all the words of the Book of the **Covenant**,
23:3 and renewed the **covenant** in the presence of the LORD—
23:3 thus confirming the words of the **covenant** written in this book.
23:3 this book. Then all the people pledged themselves to the **covenant**.
23:21 LORD your God, as it is written in this Book of the **Covenant**."
1Ch 11:3 he made a **compact** with them at Hebron before the LORD,
15:25 ark of the **covenant** *of* the LORD from the house of Obed-Edom,
15:26 Levites who were carrying the ark of the **covenant** *of* the LORD,
15:28 So all Israel brought up the ark of the **covenant** *of* the LORD
15:29 As the ark of the **covenant** *of* the LORD was entering the City of
16:6 blow the trumpets regularly before the ark of the **covenant** *of* God.
16:15 He remembers his **covenant** forever, the word he commanded,
16:17 it to Jacob as a decree, to Israel as an everlasting **covenant**:
16:37 his associates before the ark of the **covenant** *of* the LORD to
17:1 while the ark of the **covenant** *of* the LORD is under a tent."
22:19 so that you may bring the ark of the **covenant** *of* the LORD
28:2 house as a place of rest for the ark of the **covenant** *of* the LORD,
28:18 their wings and shelter the ark of the **covenant** *of* the LORD.
2Ch 5:2 to bring up the ark of the LORD's **covenant** from Zion, the City
5:7 brought the ark of the LORD's **covenant** to its place in the inner
6:11 in which is the **covenant** *of* the LORD that he made with the
6:14 you who keep your **covenant** of love with your servants who
13:5 Israel to David and his descendants forever by a **covenant** *of* salt?
15:12 They entered into a **covenant** to seek the LORD, the God of their
16:3 "Let there be a **treaty** between me and you," he said, "as there was
16:3 Now break your **treaty** with Baasha king of Israel so he will
21:7 because of the **covenant** the LORD had made with David,
23:1 He made a **covenant** with the commanders of units of a hundred:
23:3 the whole assembly made a **covenant** with the king at the temple
23:16 Jehoiada then made a **covenant** that he and the people and the king
29:10 Now I intend to make a **covenant** with the LORD, the God of
34:30 read in their hearing all the words of the Book of the **Covenant**,
34:31 and renewed the **covenant** in the presence of the LORD—
34:31 and to obey the words of the **covenant** written in this book.
34:32 of Jerusalem did this in accordance with the **covenant** *of* God,
Ezr 10:3 Now let us make a **covenant** before our God to send away all these
Ne 1:5 who keeps his **covenant** of love with those who love him and obey
9:8 you made a **covenant** with him to give to his descendants the land
9:32 mighty and awesome God, who keeps his **covenant** of love,
13:29 and the **covenant** *of* the priesthood and of the Levites.
Job 5:23 For you will have a **covenant** with the stones of the field,
31:1 "I made a **covenant** with my eyes not to look lustfully at a girl.

Job 41: 4 [40:28] Will he make an **agreement** with you for you to take him
Ps 25: 10 and faithful for those who keep the demands of his **covenant**.
25: 14 in those who fear him; he makes his **covenant** known to them.
44: 17 [44:18] we had not forgotten you or been false to your **covenant**.
50: 5 my consecrated ones, who made a **covenant** *with* me by sacrifice."
50: 16 right have you to recite my laws or take my **covenant** on your lips?
55: 20 [55:21] companion attacks his friends; he violates his **covenant**.
74: 20 Have regard for your **covenant**, because haunts of violence fill the
78: 10 they did not keep God's **covenant** and refused to live by his law.
78: 37 were not loyal to him, they were not faithful to his **covenant**.
83: 5 [83:6] they plot together; they form an **alliance** against you—
89: 3 [89:4] You said, "I have made a **covenant** with my chosen one,
89: 28 [89:29] to him forever, and my **covenant** with him will never fail.
89: 34 [89:35] I will not violate my **covenant** or alter what my lips have
89: 39 [89:40] You have renounced the **covenant** *with* your servant
103: 18 with those who keep his **covenant** and remember to obey his
105: 8 He remembers his **covenant** forever, the word he commanded,
105: 10 it to Jacob as a decree, to Israel as an everlasting **covenant**:
106: 45 for their sake he remembered his **covenant** and out of his great
111: 5 food for those who fear him; he remembers his **covenant** forever.
111: 9 he ordained his **covenant** forever—holy and awesome is his name.
132: 12 if your sons keep my **covenant** and the statutes I teach them,
Pr 2: 17 of her youth and ignored the **covenant** she *made before* God.
Isa 24: 5 violated the statutes and broken the everlasting **covenant**.
28: 15 You boast, "We have entered into a **covenant** with death,
28: 18 Your **covenant** with death will be annulled; your agreement with
33: 8 The **treaty** is broken, its witnesses are despised, no one is
42: 6 I will keep you and will make you to be a **covenant** *for* the people
49: 8 I will keep you and will make you to be a **covenant** *for* the people,
54: 10 for you will not be shaken nor my **covenant** *of* peace be removed,"
55: 3 I will make an everlasting **covenant** with you, my faithful love
56: 4 who choose what pleases me and hold fast to my **covenant**—
56: 6 Sabbath without desecrating it and who hold fast to my **covenant**—
59: 21 "As for me, this is my **covenant** with them," says the LORD.
61: 8 I will reward them and make an everlasting **covenant** with them.
Jer 3: 16 "men will no longer say, 'The ark of the **covenant** *of* the LORD.'
11: 2 "Listen to the terms of this **covenant** and tell them to the people of
11: 3 'Cursed is the man who does not obey the terms of this **covenant**—
11: 6 'Listen to the terms of this **covenant** and follow them.
11: 8 So I brought on them all the curses of the **covenant** I had
11: 10 the house of Judah have broken the **covenant** I made with their
14: 21 Remember your **covenant** with us and do not break it.
22: 9 'Because they have forsaken the **covenant** *of* the LORD their God
31: 31 "when I will make a new **covenant** with the house of Israel
31: 32 It will not be like the **covenant** I made with their forefathers when
31: 32 because they broke my **covenant**, though I was a husband to
31: 33 "This is the **covenant** I will make with the house of Israel after that
32: 40 I will make an everlasting **covenant** with them: I will never stop
33: 20 'If you can break my **covenant** *with* the day and my covenant with
33: 20 break my covenant with the day and my **covenant** *with* the night,
33: 21 my **covenant** with David my servant—and my covenant with the
33: 25 'If I have not established my **covenant** with day and night
34: 8 **covenant** with all the people in Jerusalem to proclaim freedom for
34: 10 people who entered into this **covenant** agreed that they would free
34: 13 I made a **covenant** with your forefathers when I brought them out
34: 15 You even made a **covenant** before me in the house that bears my
34: 18 The men who have violated my **covenant** and have not fulfilled the
34: 18 have not fulfilled the terms of the **covenant** they made before me,
50: 5 bind themselves to the LORD in an everlasting **covenant** that will
Eze 16: 8 I gave you my solemn oath and entered into a **covenant** with you,
16: 59 because you have despised my oath by breaking the **covenant**.
16: 60 Yet I will remember the **covenant** I made with you in the days of
16: 60 your youth, and I will establish an everlasting **covenant** with you.
16: 61 to you as daughters, but not on the basis of my **covenant** *with* you.
16: 62 So I will establish my **covenant** with you, and you will know that I
17: 13 he took a member of the royal family and made a **treaty** with him,
17: 14 unable to rise again, surviving only by keeping his **treaty**.
17: 15 does such things escape? Will he break the **treaty** and yet escape?
17: 16 on the throne, whose oath he despised and whose **treaty** he broke.
17: 18 He despised the oath by breaking the **covenant**. Because he had
17: 19 his head my oath that he despised and my **covenant** that he broke.
20: 37 under my rod, and I will bring you into the bond of the **covenant**.
30: 5 the people of the **covenant** land will fall by the sword along with
34: 25 " 'I will make a **covenant** *of* peace with them and rid the land of
37: 26 I will make a **covenant** *of* peace with them; it will be an
37: 26 a covenant of peace with them; it will be an everlasting **covenant**.
44: 7 you offered me food, fat and blood, and you broke my **covenant**.
Da 9: 4 who keeps his **covenant** of love with all who love him and obey
9: 27 He will confirm a **covenant** with many for one 'seven.' In the
11: 22 before him; both it and a prince of the **covenant** will be destroyed.
11: 28 great wealth, but his heart will be set against the holy **covenant**.
11: 30 Then he will turn back and vent his fury against the holy **covenant**.
11: 30 will return and show favor to those who forsake the holy **covenant**.
11: 32 With flattery he will corrupt those who have violated the **covenant**,
Hos 2: 18 [2:20] In that day I will make a **covenant** for them with the beasts
6: 7 Like Adam, they have broken the **covenant**—they were unfaithful
8: 1 because the people have broken my **covenant** and rebelled against
10: 4 They make many promises, take false oaths and make **agreements**;
12: 1 [12:2] He makes a **treaty** with Assyria and sends olive oil to
Am 1: 9 of captives to Edom, disregarding a **treaty** *of* brotherhood,
Ob 1: 7 All your **allies** [+408] will force you to the border; your friends
Zec 9: 11 As for you, because of the blood of my **covenant** *with* you,
11: 10 broke it, revoking the **covenant** I had made with all the nations.
Mal 2: 4 you this admonition so that my **covenant** with Levi may continue,"
2: 5 "My **covenant** was with him, a covenant of life and peace,
2: 8 you have violated the **covenant** *with* Levi," says the LORD
2: 10 Why do we profane the **covenant** *of* our fathers by breaking faith
2: 14 though she is your partner, the wife of your **marriage covenant**.
3: 1 the messenger of the **covenant**, whom you desire, will come,"

1383 בֹּרִית bōrît, n.f. [2] [√ 1405]

soap [2]

Jer 2: 22 you wash yourself with soda and use an abundance of **soap**,
Mal 3: 2 For he will be like a refiner's fire or a launderer's **soap**.

1384 ¹בָּרַךְ bārak¹, v. [3] [√ 1386; Ar 10121]

had kneel down [1], kneel [1], knelt down [+1386+6584] [1]

Ge 24: 11 [G] *He* **had** the camels **kneel down** near the well outside the
2Ch 6: 13 [A] **knelt** [+1386+6584] **down** before the whole assembly of
Ps 95: 6 [A] down in worship, *let us* **kneel** before the LORD our Maker;

1385 ²בָּרַךְ bārak², v. [327] [→ 1358, 1387, 1388, 3310; cf. 1386?, Ar 10122]

blessed [86], bless [79], praise [63], be blessed [23], praised [8], blesses [7], give blessing [6], congratulate [3], curse [3], cursed [3], extol [3], pronounce blessings [3], bless [+1385] [2], bless abundant [+1385] [2], bless at all [+1385] [2], blessed [+1385] [2], blessed again and again [+906+1385] [2], blessing [2], done nothing but bless [+1385] [2], gave blessing [2], richly bless [+1385] [2], surely bless [+1385] [2], *untranslated* [1], be praised [1], blessings given [1], commended [1], counted blessed [1], do[s] so [1], give greetings [1], given [1], giving blessing [+906+1388] [1], greet [+7925] [1], greet [1], greeted [1], greets [1], invokes a blessing on himself [1], invokes a blessing [1], is blessed [1], pronounce blessing [1], pronounced [1], thank [1], worships [1]

Ge 1: 22 [D] God **blessed** them and said, "Be fruitful and increase in
1: 28 [D] God **blessed** them and said to them, "Be fruitful and increase
2: 3 [D] God **blessed** the seventh day and made it holy, because on it
5: 2 [D] He created them male and female and **blessed** them.
9: 1 [D] God **blessed** Noah and his sons, saying to them, "Be fruitful
9: 26 [B] He also said, "**Blessed** *be* the LORD, the God of Shem!
12: 2 [D] "I will make you into a great nation and *I will* **bless** you; I
12: 3 [D] *I will* **bless** those who bless you, and whoever curses you I
12: 3 [D] I will bless *those who* **bless** you, and whoever curses you I
12: 3 [C] and all peoples on earth *will* **be blessed** through you."
14: 19 [D] *he* **blessed** Abram, saying, "Blessed be Abram by God Most
14: 19 [B] saying, "**Blessed** *be* Abram by God Most High, Creator of
14: 20 [B] **blessed** *be* God Most High, who delivered your enemies into
17: 16 [D] *I will* **bless** her and will surely give you a son by her. I will
17: 16 [D] *I will* **bless** her so that she will be the mother of nations;
17: 20 [D] *I will* surely **bless** him; I will make him fruitful and will
18: 18 [C] and all nations on earth *will* **be blessed** through him.
22: 17 [D] *I will* **surely bless** [+1385] you and make your descendants
22: 17 [D] *I will* **surely bless** [+1385] you and make your descendants
22: 18 [F] through your offspring all nations on earth *will* **be blessed**,
24: 1 [D] in years, and the LORD *had* **blessed** him in every way.
24: 27 [B] saying, "**Praise** *be to* the LORD, the God of my master
24: 31 [B] "Come, *you who are* **blessed** *by* the LORD," he said. "Why
24: 35 [D] The LORD *has* **blessed** my master abundantly, and he has
24: 48 [D] *I* **praised** the LORD, the God of my master Abraham,
24: 60 [D] *they* **blessed** Rebekah and said to her, "Our sister, may you
25: 11 [D] God **blessed** his son Isaac, who then lived near Beer Lahai
26: 3 [D] land for a while, and I will be with you and *will* **bless** you.
26: 4 [F] through your offspring all nations on earth *will* **be blessed**,
26: 12 [D] year reaped a hundredfold, because the LORD **blessed** him.
26: 24 [D] *I will* **bless** you and will increase the number of your
26: 29 [B] away in peace. And now you are **blessed** *by* the LORD."
27: 4 [D] me to eat, so that I *may* **give** you my **blessing** before I die."
27: 7 [D] so that *I may* **give** you *my* **blessing** in the presence of the
27: 10 [D] to eat, so that *he may* **give** you *his* **blessing** before he dies."
27: 19 [D] some of my game so that you *may* **give** me your **blessing**."
27: 23 [D] were hairy like those of his brother Esau; so *he* **blessed** him.
27: 25 [D] of your game to eat, so that I *may* **give** you my **blessing**."
27: 27 [D] the smell of his clothes, *he* **blessed** him and said, "Ah,
27: 27 [D] son is like the smell of a field that the LORD *has* **blessed**.

Ge 27:29 [D] curse you be cursed and *those who* **bless** you be blessed."
27:29 [B] curse you be cursed and those who bless you **be blessed**."
27:30 [D] After Isaac finished **blessing** him and Jacob had scarcely left
27:31 [D] some of my game, so that you *may* **give** me your **blessing**."
27:33 [D] I ate it just before you came and *I* **blessed** him—and indeed
27:33 [B] and I blessed him—and indeed he will **be blessed**!"
27:34 [D] with a loud and bitter cry and said to his father, "**Bless** me—
27:38 [D] have only one blessing, my father? **Bless** me too, my father!"
27:41 [D] because of the blessing his father *had* **given** him.
28: 1 [D] Isaac called for Jacob and **blessed** him and commanded him:
28: 3 [D] *May* God Almighty **bless** you and make you fruitful
28: 6 [D] Now Esau learned that Isaac *had* **blessed** Jacob and had sent
28: 6 [D] that when he **blessed** him he commanded him, "Do not marry
28:14 [C] All peoples on earth *will* **be blessed** through you and your
30:27 [D] I have learned by divination that the LORD *has* **blessed** me
30:30 [D] and the LORD *has* **blessed** you wherever I have been.
31:55 [32:1] [D] and his daughters and **blessed** them.
32:26 [32:27] [D] "I will not let you go unless *you* **bless** me."
32:29 [32:30] [D] do you ask my name?" Then *he* **blessed** him there.
35: 9 [D] Paddan Aram, God appeared to him again and **blessed** him.
39: 5 [D] the LORD **blessed** the household of the Egyptian because
47: 7 [D] presented him before Pharaoh. After Jacob **blessed** Pharaoh,
47:10 [D] Then Jacob **blessed** Pharaoh and went out from his presence.
48: 3 [D] to me at Luz in the land of Canaan, and there *he* **blessed** me
48: 9 [D] Then Israel said, "Bring them to me so *I may* **bless** them."
48:15 [D] *he* **blessed** Joseph and said, "May the God before whom my
48:16 [D] has delivered me from all harm—*may he* **bless** these boys.
48:20 [D] *He* **blessed** them that day and said, "In your name will Israel
48:20 [D] and said, "In your name *will* Israel **pronounce** *this* **blessing**:
49:25 [D] *who* **blesses** you *with* blessings of the heavens above,
49:28 [D] this is what their father said to them when *he* **blessed** them,
49:28 [D] **giving** each the **blessing** [+906+1388] appropriate to him.
Ex 12:32 [D] and herds, as you have said, and go. And also **bless** me."
18:10 [B] He said, "**Praise** *be to* the LORD, who rescued you from
20:11 [D] Therefore the LORD **blessed** the Sabbath day and made it
20:24 [D] my name to be honored, I will come to you and **bless** you.
23:25 [D] your God, and *his* **blessing** *will be on* your food and water.
39:43 [D] just as the LORD had commanded. So Moses **blessed** them.
Lev 9:22 [D] Aaron lifted his hands toward the people and **blessed** them.
9:23 [D] When they came out, *they* **blessed** the people; and the glory
Nu 6:23 [D] and his sons, 'This is how *you are to* **bless** the Israelites.
6:24 [D] " ' "The LORD **bless** you and keep you;
6:27 [D] will put my name on the Israelites, and I *will* **bless** them."
22: 6 [D] For I know that those *you* **bless** are blessed, and those you
22: 6 [E] For I know that those you bless *are* **blessed**, and those you
22:12 [B] not put a curse on those people, because they *are* **blessed**."
23:11 [D] but *you have* **done nothing but bless** [+1385] them!"
23:11 [D] but *you have* **done nothing but bless** [+1385] them!"
23:20 [D] I have received a command *to* **bless**; he has blessed, and I
23:20 [D] a command to bless; *he has* **blessed**, and I cannot change it.
23:25 [D] "Neither curse them at all nor **bless** [+1385] them **at all**!"
23:25 [D] "Neither curse them at all nor **bless** them **at all** [+1385]!"
24: 1 [D] Now when Balaam saw that it pleased the LORD to **bless**
24: 9 [D] "*May those who* **bless** you be blessed and those who curse
24: 9 [B] "May those who bless you **be blessed** and those who curse
24:10 [D] but *you have* **blessed** [+1385] them these three times.
24:10 [D] but *you have* **blessed** [+1385] them these three times.
Dt 1:11 [D] you a thousand times and **bless** you as he has promised!
2: 7 [D] The LORD your God *has* **blessed** you in all the work of
7:13 [D] He will love you and **bless** you and increase your numbers.
7:13 [D] *He will* **bless** the fruit of your womb, the crops of your
7:14 [B] You will **be blessed** more than any other people; none of
8:10 [D] **praise** the LORD your God for the good land he has given
10: 8 [D] LORD to minister and to **pronounce blessings** in his name,
12: 7 [D] hand to, because the LORD your God *has* **blessed** you.
14:24 [D] you *have been* **blessed** *by* the LORD your God and cannot
14:29 [D] so that the LORD your God *may* **bless** you in all the work
15: 4 [D] possess as your inheritance, he *will* **richly bless** [+1385] you,
15: 4 [D] possess as your inheritance, he *will* **richly bless** [+1385] you,
15: 6 [D] For the LORD your God *will* **bless** you as he has promised,
15:10 [D] because of this the LORD your God *will* **bless** you in all
15:14 [D] Give to him as the LORD your God *has* **blessed** you.
15:18 [D] the LORD your God *will* **bless** you in everything you do.
16:10 [D] to the **blessings** the LORD your God *has* **given** you.
16:15 [D] For the LORD your God *will* **bless** you in all your harvest
21: 5 [D] to **pronounce blessings** in the name of the LORD and to
23:20 [23:21] [D] so that the LORD your God *may* **bless** you in
24:13 [D] *he will* **thank** you, and it will be regarded as a righteous act
24:19 [D] so that the LORD your God *may* **bless** you in all the work
26:15 [D] **bless** your people Israel and the land you have given us as
27:12 [D] these tribes shall stand on Mount Gerizim to **bless** the
28: 3 [B] You *will* **be blessed** in the city and blessed in the country.
28: 3 [B] You will be blessed in the city and **blessed** in the country.
28: 4 [B] The fruit of your womb *will* **be blessed**, and the crops of
28: 5 [B] Your basket and your kneading trough *will* **be blessed**.
28: 6 [B] You *will* **be blessed** when you come in and blessed when you
28: 6 [B] be blessed when you come in and **blessed** when you go out.
28: 8 [D] The LORD your God *will* **bless** you in the land he is giving
28:12 [D] your land in season and to **bless** all the work of your hands.
29:19 [29:18] [F] *he* **invokes a blessing on himself** and
30:16 [D] the LORD your God *will* **bless** you in the land you are
33: 1 [D] man of God **pronounced** *on* the Israelites before his death.
33:11 [D] **Bless** all his skills, O LORD, and be pleased with the work
33:13 [E] "*May* the LORD **bless** his land with the precious dew from
33:20 [B] Gad he said: "**Blessed** *is* he who enlarges Gad's domain!
33:24 [B] "*Most* **blessed** of sons *is* Asher; let him be favored by his
Jos 8:33 [D] when he gave instructions to **bless** the people of Israel.
14:13 [D] Joshua **blessed** Caleb son of Jephunneh and gave him
17:14 [D] and the LORD *has* **blessed** us abundantly."
22: 6 [D] Joshua **blessed** them and sent them away, and they went to
22: 7 [D] When Joshua sent them home, *he* **blessed** them,
22:33 [D] They were glad to hear the report and **praised** God. And they
24:10 [D] to Balaam, so *he* **blessed** [+906+1385] you **again and again**,
24:10 [D] to Balaam, so *he* **blessed** you **again and again** [+906+1385],
Jdg 5: 2 [D] the people willingly offer themselves—**praise** the LORD!
5: 9 [D] the willing volunteers among the people. **Praise** the LORD!
5:24 [E] "Most **blessed** of women *be* Jael, the wife of Heber the
5:24 [E] of Heber the Kenite, most **blessed** of tent-dwelling women.
13:24 [D] named him Samson. He grew and the LORD **blessed** him,
17: 2 [B] Then his mother said, "The LORD **bless** you, my son!"
Ru 2: 4 [D] be with you!" "The LORD **bless** you!" they called back.
2:19 [B] did you work? **Blessed** be the man who took notice of you!"
2:20 [B] "The LORD **bless** him!" Naomi said to her daughter-in-law.
3:10 [B] "The LORD **bless** you, my daughter," he replied. "This
4:14 [B] "**Praise** *be to* the LORD, who this day has not left you
1Sa 2:20 [D] Eli *would* **bless** Elkanah and his wife, saying,
9:13 [D] eating until he comes, because he *must* **bless** the sacrifice;
13:10 [D] Samuel arrived, and Saul went out to **greet** [+7925] him.
15:13 [B] Samuel reached him, Saul said, "The LORD **bless** you!
23:21 [B] "The LORD **bless** you for your concern for me.
25:14 [D] messengers from the desert to **give** our master his **greetings**,
25:32 [B] said to Abigail, "**Praise** *be to* the LORD, the God of Israel,
25:33 [B] *May* you **be blessed** *for* your good judgment and for keeping
25:33 [B] and **[RPH]** for keeping me from bloodshed this day
25:39 [B] that Nabal was dead, he said, "**Praise** *be to* the LORD,
26:25 [B] Saul said to David, "*May* you **be blessed**, my son David;
2Sa 2: 5 [B] "The LORD **bless** you for showing this kindness to Saul
6:11 [D] and the LORD **blessed** him and his entire household.
6:12 [D] "The LORD *has* **blessed** the household of Obed-Edom and
6:18 [D] *he* **blessed** the people in the name of the LORD Almighty.
6:20 [D] When David returned home to **bless** his household, Michal
7:29 [D] Now be pleased *to* **bless** the house of your servant, that it
7:29 [E] with your blessing the house of your servant *will* **be blessed**
8:10 [D] **congratulate** him on his victory in battle over Hadadezer,
13:25 [D] urged him, he still refused to go, but **gave** him *his* **blessing**.
14:22 [D] face to the ground to pay him honor, and *he* **blessed** the king.
18:28 [B] to the ground and said, "**Praise** *be to* the LORD your God!
19:39 [19:40] [D] king kissed Barzillai and **gave** him *his* **blessing**,
21: 3 [D] so that *you will* **bless** the LORD's inheritance?"
22:47 [B] **Praise** *be to* my Rock! Exalted be God, the Rock, my Savior!
1Ki 1:47 [D] the royal officials have come to **congratulate** our lord King
1:48 [B] said, '**Praise** *be to* the LORD, the God of Israel, who has
2:45 [B] King Solomon *will* **be blessed**, and David's throne will
5: 7 [5:21] [B] and said, "**Praise** *be to* the LORD today,
8:14 [D] was standing there, the king turned around and **blessed** them.
8:15 [B] "**Praise** *be to* the LORD, the God of Israel, who with his
8:55 [D] and **blessed** the whole assembly of Israel in a loud voice,
8:56 [B] "**Praise** *be to* the LORD, who has given rest to his people
8:66 [D] *They* **blessed** the king and then went home, joyful and glad
10: 9 [B] **Praise** be *to* the LORD your God, who has delighted in you
21:10 [D] have them testify that he *has* **cursed** both God and the king.
21:13 [D] saying, "Naboth *has* **cursed** both God and the king."
2Ki 4:29 [D] If you meet anyone, *do* not **greet** him, and if anyone greets
4:29 [D] do not greet him, and if anyone **greets** you, do not answer.
10:15 [D] Jehu **greeted** him and said, "Are you in accord with me, as I
1Ch 4:10 [D] that *you would* **bless** [+1385] me and enlarge my territory!
4:10 [D] that *you would* **bless** [+1385] me and enlarge my territory!
13:14 [D] the LORD **blessed** his household and everything he had.
16: 2 [D] *he* **blessed** the people in the name of the LORD.
16:36 [B] **Praise** *be to* the LORD, the God of Israel, from everlasting
16:43 [D] his own home, and David returned home to **bless** his family.
17:27 [D] Now you have been pleased to **bless** the house of your
17:27 [D] for you, O LORD, *have* **blessed** it, and it will be blessed
17:27 [E] O LORD, have blessed it, and *it will* **be blessed** forever."
18:10 [D] **congratulate** him on his victory in battle over Hadadezer,
23:13 [D] before him and to **pronounce blessings** in his name forever.
26: 5 [D] Peullethai the eighth. (For God *had* **blessed** Obed-Edom.)
29:10 [D] David **praised** the LORD in the presence of the whole

1Ch 29: 10 [B] saying, "**Praise** *be to* you, O LORD, God of our father
29: 20 [D] said to the whole assembly, "**Praise** the LORD your God."
29: 20 [D] So they all **praised** the LORD, the God of their fathers;
2Ch 2: 12 [2:11] [B] "**Praise** *be to* the LORD, the God of Israel,
6: 3 [D] was standing there, the king turned around and **blessed** them.
6: 4 [B] "**Praise** *be to* the LORD, the God of Israel, who with his
9: 8 [B] **Praise** be *to* the LORD your God, who has delighted in you
20: 26 [D] in the Valley of Beracah, where *they* **praised** the LORD.
30: 27 [D] The priests and the Levites stood *to* **bless** the people,
31: 8 [D] *they* praised the LORD and **blessed** his people Israel.
31: 10 [D] plenty to spare, because the LORD *has* **blessed** his people,
Ezr 7: 27 [B] **Praise** *be to* the LORD, the God of our fathers, who has
Ne 8: 6 [D] Ezra **praised** the LORD, the great God; and all the people
9: 5 [D] "Stand up and **praise** the LORD your God, who is from
9: 5 [D] "**Blessed** *be* your glorious name, and may it be exalted above
11: 2 [D] The people **commended** all the men who volunteered to live
Job 1: 5 [D] my children have sinned and **cursed** God in their hearts."
1: 10 [D] *You have* **blessed** the work of his hands, so that his flocks
1: 11 [D] he has, and *he will* surely **curse** you to your face."
1: 21 [E] has taken away; may the name of the LORD be **praised**."
2: 5 [D] and bones, and *he will* surely **curse** you to your face."
2: 9 [D] you still holding on to your integrity? **Curse** God and die!"
31: 20 [D] his heart *did* not **bless** me for warming him with the fleece
42: 12 [D] The LORD **blessed** the latter part of Job's life more than the
Ps 5: 12 [5:13] [D] For surely, O LORD, you **bless** the righteous;
10: 3 [D] of his heart; *he* **blesses** the greedy and reviles the LORD.
16: 7 [D] *I will* **praise** the LORD, who counsels me; even at night my
18: 46 [18:47] [B] The LORD lives! **Praise** *be to* my Rock! Exalted
26: 12 [D] level ground; in the great assembly *I will* **praise** the LORD.
28: 6 [B] **Praise** *be to* the LORD, for he has heard my cry for mercy.
28: 9 [D] Save your people and **bless** your inheritance; be their
29: 11 [D] to his people; the LORD **blesses** his people with peace.
31: 21 [31:22] [B] **Praise** *be to* the LORD, for he showed his
34: 1 [34:2] [D] *I will* **extol** the LORD at all times; his praise will
37: 22 [E] *those* the LORD **blesses** will inherit the land, but those he
41: 13 [41:14] [B] **Praise** *be to* the LORD, the God of Israel,
45: 2 [45:3] [D] with grace, since God *has* **blessed** you forever.
49: 18 [49:19] [D] while he lived *he* **counted** himself **blessed**—
62: 4 [62:5] [D] With their mouths *they* **bless**, but in their hearts they
63: 4 [63:5] [D] *I will* **praise** you as long as I live, and in your name I
65: 10 [65:11] [D] you soften it with showers and **bless** its crops.
66: 8 [D] **Praise** our God, O peoples, let the sound of his praise be
66: 20 [B] **Praise** *be to* God, who has not rejected my prayer
67: 1 [67:2] [D] May God be gracious to us and **bless** us and make his
67: 6 [67:7] [D] yield its harvest, and God, our God, *will* **bless** us.
67: 7 [67:8] [D] God *will* **bless** us, and all the ends of the earth will
68: 19 [68:20] [B] **Praise** *be to* the Lord, to God our Savior, who daily
68: 26 [68:27] [D] **Praise** God in the great congregation;
68: 35 [68:36] [B] and strength to his people. **Praise** *be to* God!
72: 15 [D] May people ever pray for him and **bless** him all day long.
72: 17 [F] All nations *will* **be blessed** through him, and they will call
72: 18 [B] **Praise** *be to* the LORD God, the God of Israel, who alone
72: 19 [B] **Praise** *be to* his glorious name forever; may the whole earth
89: 52 [89:53] [B] **Praise** *be to* the LORD forever! Amen and Amen.
96: 2 [D] Sing to the LORD, **praise** his name; proclaim his salvation
100: 4 [D] courts with praise; give thanks to him and **praise** his name.
103: 1 [D] **Praise** the LORD, O my soul; all my inmost being, praise
103: 2 [D] **Praise** the LORD, O my soul, and forget not all his
103: 20 [D] **Praise** the LORD, you his angels, you mighty ones who do
103: 21 [D] **Praise** the LORD, all his heavenly hosts, you his servants
103: 22 [D] **Praise** the LORD, all his works everywhere in his
103: 22 [D] everywhere in his dominion. **Praise** the LORD, O my soul.
104: 1 [D] **Praise** the LORD, O my soul. O LORD my God, you are
104: 35 [D] no more. **Praise** the LORD, O my soul. Praise the LORD.
106: 48 [B] **Praise** *be to* the LORD, the God of Israel, from everlasting
107: 38 [D] *he* **blessed** them, and their numbers greatly increased, and he
109: 28 [D] They may curse, but you *will* **bless**; when they attack they
112: 2 [E] in the land; the generation of the upright *will* **be blessed**.
113: 2 [E] Let the name of the LORD be **praised**, both now
115: 12 [D] The LORD remembers us and *will* **bless** us: He will bless
115: 12 [D] *He will* **bless** the house of Israel, he will bless the house of
115: 12 [D] bless the house of Israel, *he will* **bless** the house of Aaron,
115: 13 [D] *he will* **bless** those who fear the LORD—small and great
115: 15 [B] *May* you **be blessed** by the LORD, the Maker of heaven
115: 18 [D] it is we *who* **extol** the LORD, both now and forevermore.
118: 26 [B] **Blessed** *is* he who comes in the name of the LORD.
118: 26 [D] of the LORD. From the house of the LORD *we* **bless** you.
119: 12 [B] **Praise** *be to* you, O LORD; teach me your decrees.
124: 6 [B] **Praise** *be to* the LORD, who has not let us be torn by their
128: 4 [E] Thus **is** the man **blessed** who fears the LORD.
128: 5 [D] *May* the LORD **bless** you from Zion all the days of your
129: 8 [D] be upon you; *we* **bless** you in the name of the LORD."
132: 15 [D] *I will* **bless** [+1385] her *with* **abundant** provisions; her poor
132: 15 [D] *I will* **bless** her *with* **abundant** [+1385] provisions; her poor
134: 1 [D] **Praise** the LORD, all *you* servants of the LORD who
134: 2 [D] Lift up your hands in the sanctuary and **praise** the LORD.
134: 3 [D] *May* the LORD, the Maker of heaven and earth, **bless** you
135: 19 [D] O house of Israel, **praise** the LORD; O house of Aaron,
135: 19 [D] praise the LORD; O house of Aaron, **praise** the LORD;
135: 20 [D] O house of Levi, **praise** the LORD; you who fear him,
135: 20 [D] praise the LORD; *you* who fear him, **praise** the LORD.
135: 21 [B] **Praise** *be to* the LORD from Zion, *to* him who dwells in
144: 1 [B] **Praise** *be to* the LORD my Rock, who trains my hands for
145: 1 [D] my God the King; *I will* **praise** your name for ever and ever.
145: 2 [D] Every day *I will* **praise** you and extol your name for ever
145: 10 [D] made will praise you, O LORD; your saints *will* **extol** you.
145: 21 [D] *Let* every creature **praise** his holy name for ever and ever.
147: 13 [D] the bars of your gates and **blesses** your people within you.
Pr 3: 33 [D] of the wicked, but *he* **blesses** the home of the righteous.
5: 18 [B] May your fountain be **blessed**, and may you rejoice in the
20: 21 [E] gained at the beginning *will* not **be blessed** at the end.
22: 9 [E] A generous man *will* himself **be blessed**, for he shares his
27: 14 [D] If a *man* loudly **blesses** his neighbor early in the morning,
30: 11 [D] those who curse their fathers and *do* not **bless** their mothers;
Isa 19: 25 [D] The LORD Almighty *will* **bless** them, saying, "Blessed be
19: 25 [B] saying, "**Blessed** *be* Egypt my people, Assyria my
51: 2 [D] him he was but one, and *I* **blessed** him and made him many.
61: 9 [D] that they are a people the LORD *has* **blessed**."
65: 16 [F] Whoever **invokes a blessing** in the land will do so by the
65: 16 [F] Whoever invokes a blessing in the land *will* **do**[s] **so** by the
65: 23 [B] for they will be a people **blessed** *by* the LORD, they
66: 3 [D] burns memorial incense, like *one who* **worships** an idol.
Jer 4: 2 [F] the nations *will* **be blessed** by him and in him they will
17: 7 [B] "But **blessed** *is* the man who trusts in the LORD, whose
20: 14 [B] I was born! May the day my mother bore me not be **blessed**!
31: 23 [D] 'The LORD **bless** you, O righteous dwelling, O sacred
Eze 3: 12 [B] *May* the glory of the LORD **be praised** in his dwelling
Hag 2: 19 [D] have not borne fruit. " 'From this day on *I will* **bless** you.' "
Zec 11: 5 [B] Those who sell them say, '**Praise** the LORD, I am rich!'

1386 בֶּרֶךְ **berek**, n.f. [25] [→ 1384, 1392, 1393; cf. 1385?; Ar 10072, 10123]

knees [15], knee [3], lap [2], for [+6584] [1], knee-deep [1], kneel [1], kneeling [+4156+6584] [1], knelt down [+1384+6584] [1]

Ge 30: 3 Sleep with her so that she can bear children **for** [+6584] me
48: 12 Joseph removed them from Israel's **knees** and bowed down with
50: 23 of Makir son of Manasseh were placed at birth on Joseph's **knees**.
Dt 28: 35 The LORD will afflict your **knees** and legs with painful boils that
Jdg 7: 5 with their tongues like a dog from those who **kneel** down to drink."
7: 6 to their mouths. All the rest got down on their **knees** to drink.
16: 19 Having put him to sleep on her **lap**, she called a man to shave off
1Ki 8: 54 where *he had been* **kneeling** [+4156+6584] with his hands spread
18: 42 bent down to the ground and put his face between his **knees**.
19: 18 all whose **knees** have not bowed down to Baal and all whose
2Ki 1: 13 This third captain went up and fell on his **knees** before Elijah.
4: 20 to his mother, the boy sat on her **lap** until noon, and then he died.
2Ch 6: 13 **knelt down** [+1384+6584] before the whole assembly of Israel
Ezr 9: 5 fell on my **knees** with my hands spread out to the LORD my God
Job 3: 12 Why were there **knees** to receive me and breasts that I might be
4: 4 those who stumbled; you have strengthened faltering **knees**.
Ps 109: 24 My **knees** give way from fasting; my body is thin and gaunt.
Isa 35: 3 Strengthen the feeble hands, steady the **knees** that give way;
45: 23 Before me every **knee** will bow; by me every tongue will swear.
66: 12 you will nurse and be carried on her arm and dandled on her **knees**.
Eze 7: 17 hand will go limp, and every **knee** will become as weak as water.
21: 7 [21:12] become faint and every **knee** become as weak as water.'
47: 4 thousand cubits and led me through water that was **knee-deep**.
Da 10: 10 A hand touched me and set me trembling on my hands and **knees**.
Na 2: 10 [2:11] Hearts melt, **knees** give way, bodies tremble, every face

1387 בַּרַכְאֵל **barak'ēl**, n.pr.m. [2] [√ 1385 + 446]

Barakel [2]

Job 32: 2 But Elihu son of **Barakel** the Buzite, of the family of Ram,
32: 6 So Elihu son of **Barakel** the Buzite said: "I am young in years,

1388 בְּרָכָה¹ **berākâ¹**, n.f. [69 / 68] [→ 1389, 1390; cf. 1385]

blessing [37], blessings [14], blessed [2], gift [2], peace [2], present [2], special favor [2], bless [+906+5989] [1], blessed [+4200+5989] [1], blessed [+5989+6584] [1], blessed [+995+6584] [1], generous [1], giving blessing [+906+1385] [1], good [1]

Ge 12: 2 bless you; I will make your name great, and you will be a **blessing**.
27: 12 and would bring down a curse on myself rather than a **blessing**."
27: 35 he said, "Your brother came deceitfully and took your **blessing**."
27: 36 He took my birthright, and now he's taken my **blessing**!" Then he
27: 36 Then he asked, "Haven't you reserved any **blessing** for me?"

Ge 27:38 said to his father, "Do you have only one **blessing**, my father?
27:41 against Jacob because of the **blessing** his father had given him.
28: 4 he give you and your descendants the **blessing** *given to* Abraham,
33:11 Please accept the **present** that was brought to you, for God has
39: 5 The **blessing** *of* the LORD was on everything Potiphar had,
49:25 who blesses you with **blessings** *of* the heavens above,
49:25 **blessings** *of* the deep that lies below, blessings of the breast
49:25 of the deep that lies below, **blessings** *of* the breast and womb.
49:26 Your father's **blessings** are greater than the blessings of the ancient
49:26 Your father's blessings are greater than the **blessings** *of* the ancient
49:28 **giving** each the **blessing** [+906+1385] appropriate to him.
Ex 32:29 and brothers, and he *has* **blessed** [+5989+6584] you this day."
Lev 25:21 I will send you such a **blessing** in the sixth year that the land will
Dt 11:26 See, I am setting before you today a **blessing** and a curse—
11:27 the **blessing** if you obey the commands of the LORD your God
11:29 you are to proclaim on Mount Gerizim the **blessings**, and on
12:15 according to the **blessing** the LORD your God gives you.
16:17 to the way the LORD your God *has* **blessed** [+4200+5989] you.
23: 5 [23:6] to Balaam but turned the curse into a **blessing** for you,
28: 2 All these **blessings** will come upon you and accompany you if you
28: 8 The LORD will send a **blessing** on your barns and on everything
30: 1 When all these **blessings** and curses I have set before you come
30:19 you that I have set before you life and death, **blessings** and curses.
33: 1 This is the **blessing** that Moses the man of God pronounced on the
33:23 abounding with the favor of the LORD and is full of his **blessing**;
Jos 8:34 read all the words of the law—the **blessings** and the curses—
15:19 She replied, "Do me a **special favor**. Since you have given me
Jdg 1:15 She replied, "Do me a **special favor**. Since you have given me
1Sa 25:27 And let this **gift**, which your servant has brought to my master,
30:26 "Here is a **present** for you from the plunder of the LORD's
2Sa 7:29 with your **blessing** the house of your servant will be blessed
2Ki 5:15 world except in Israel. Please accept now a **gift** from your servant."
18:31 the king of Assyria says: Make **peace** with me and come out to me.
Ne 9: 5 glorious name, and may it be exalted above all **blessing** and praise.
13: 2 on them. (Our God, however, turned the curse into a **blessing**.)
Job 29:13 The man who was dying **blessed** [+995+6584] me; I made the
Ps 3: 8 [3:9] May your **blessing** be on your people. *Selah*
21: 3 [21:4] You welcomed him with rich **blessings** and placed a crown
21: 6 [21:7] Surely you have granted him eternal **blessings** and made
24: 5 He will receive **blessing** from the LORD and vindication from
37:26 are always generous and lend freely; their children will be **blessed**.
84: 6 [84:7] rains also cover it with pools. [BHS *blessings*; NIV 1391]
109:17 may it come on him; he found no pleasure in **blessing**—may it be
129: 8 who pass by not say, "The **blessing** *of* the LORD be upon you;
133: 3 For there the LORD bestows his **blessing**, even life forevermore.
Pr 10: 6 **Blessings** crown the head of the righteous, but violence
10: 7 The memory of the righteous will be a **blessing**, but the name of
10:22 The **blessing** *of* the LORD brings wealth, and he adds no trouble
11:11 Through the **blessing** *of* the upright a city is exalted, but by the
11:25 A **generous** man will prosper; he who refreshes others will himself
11:26 who hoards grain, but **blessing** crowns him who is willing to sell.
24:25 who convict the guilty, and rich **blessing** will come upon them.
28:20 A faithful man will be richly **blessed**, but one eager to get rich will
Isa 19:24 be the third, along with Egypt and Assyria, a **blessing** on the earth.
36:16 the king of Assyria says: Make **peace** with me and come out to me.
44: 3 my Spirit on your offspring, and my **blessing** on your descendants.
65: 8 and men say, 'Don't destroy it, there is yet *some* **good** in it,'
Eze 34:26 *I will* **bless** [+906+5989] them and the places surrounding my hill.
34:26 send down showers in season; there will be showers of **blessing**.
44:30 of your ground meal so that a **blessing** may rest on your household.
Joel 2:14 He may turn and have pity and leave behind a **blessing**—
Zec 8:13 O Judah and Israel, so will I save you, and you will be a **blessing**.
Mal 2: 2 "I will send a curse upon you, and I will curse your **blessings**.
3:10 so much **blessing** that you will not have room enough for it.

1389 ²בְּרָכָה bᵉrākâ², n.pr.m. [1] [√ 1388; cf. 1385]

Beracah [1]

1Ch 12: 3 and Pelet the sons of Azmaveth; **Beracah**, Jehu the Anathothite,

1390 ³בְּרָכָה bᵉrākâ³, n.pr.loc. [2] [√ 1388; cf. 1385]

Beracah [2]

2Ch 20:26 On the fourth day they assembled in the Valley of **Beracah**,
20:26 This is why it is called the Valley of **Beracah** to this day.

1391 בְּרֵכָה bᵉrēkâ, n.f. [17 / 18]

pool [13], pools [2], *untranslated* [1], pool [+4784] [1], reservoirs [+4784] [1]

2Sa 2:13 and David's men went out and met them at the **pool** *of* Gibeon.
2:13 One group sat down on one side of the **pool** and one group on the
2:13 on one side of the pool and one group on the other side. **[RPH]**
4:12 off their hands and feet and hung the bodies by the **pool** in Hebron.
1Ki 22:38 They washed the chariot at a **pool** *in* Samaria (where the
2Ki 18:17 up to Jerusalem and stopped at the aqueduct of the Upper **Pool**,
20:20 all his achievements and how he made the **pool** and the tunnel by
Ne 2:14 Then I moved on toward the Fountain Gate and the King's **Pool**,
3:15 He also repaired the wall of the **Pool** *of* Siloam, by the King's
3:16 of David, as far as the artificial **pool** and the House of the Heroes.
Ps 84: 6 [84:7] the autumn rains also cover it with **pools**. [BHS 1388]
Ecc 2: 6 I made **reservoirs** [+4784] to water groves of flourishing trees.
SS 7: 4 [7:5] Your eyes are the **pools** of Heshbon by the gate of Bath
Isa 7: 3 to meet Ahaz at the end of the aqueduct of the Upper **Pool**,
22: 9 breaches in its defenses; you stored up water in the Lower **Pool**.
22:11 a reservoir between the two walls for the water of the Old **Pool**,
36: 2 When the commander stopped at the aqueduct of the Upper **Pool**,
Na 2: 8 [2:9] Nineveh is like a **pool** [+4784], and its water is draining

1392 בֶּרֶכְיָה berekyâ, n.pr.m. [7] [√ 1386 + 3378]

Berekiah [7]

1Ch 3:20 Hashubah, Ohel, **Berekiah**, Hasadiah and Jushab-Hesed.
9:16 **Berekiah** son of Asa, the son of Elkanah, who lived in the villages
15:23 **Berekiah** and Elkanah were to be doorkeepers for the ark.
Ne 3: 4 Next to him Meshullam son of **Berekiah**, the son of Meshezabel,
3:30 Meshullam son of **Berekiah** made repairs opposite his living
6:18 had married the daughter of Meshullam son of **Berekiah**.
Zec 1: 1 of the LORD came to the prophet Zechariah son of **Berekiah**,

1393 בֶּרֶכְיָהוּ berekyāhû, n.pr.m. [4] [√ 1386 + 3378]

Berekiah [4]

1Ch 6:39 [6:24] his right hand: Asaph son of **Berekiah**, the son of Shimea,
15:17 from his brothers, Asaph son of **Berekiah**; and from their brothers
2Ch 28:12 **Berekiah** son of Meshillemoth, Jehizkiah son of Shallum,
Zec 1: 7 of the LORD came to the prophet Zechariah son of **Berekiah**,

1394 בְּרֹמִים bᵉrōmîm, n.[m.]. [1]

multicolored [1]

Eze 27:24 embroidered work and **multicolored** rugs with cords twisted

1395 בַּרְנֵעַ barnēaʿ, n.pr.loc. Not used in NIV/BHS [→ 7732]

1396 בֶּרַע beraʿ, n.pr.m. [1]

Bera [1]

Ge 14: 2 went to war against **Bera** king of Sodom, Birsha king of

1397 בָּרַק bāraq, v. [1] [→ 1398, 1399, 1402]

send forth lightning [+1398] [1]

Ps 144: 6 [A] **Send forth lightning** [+1398] and scatter ⌊the enemies⌋;

1398 ¹בָּרָק bārāq¹, n.m. [21] [→ 1399, 1402; cf. 1397]

lightning [11], flash like lightning [3], bolts of lightning [2], flashing [1], gleaming point [1], glittering [1], lightning bolts [1], send forth lightning [+1397] [1]

Ex 19:16 On the morning of the third day there was thunder and **lightning**,
Dt 32:41 when I sharpen my **flashing** sword and my hand grasps it in
2Sa 22:15 and scattered ⌊the enemies⌋, **bolts of lightning** and routed them.
Job 20:25 He pulls it out of his back, the **gleaming point** out of his liver.
38:35 Do you send the **lightning bolts** on their way? Do they report to
Ps 18:14 [18:15] ⌊the enemies⌋, great **bolts of lightning** and routed them.
77:18 [77:19] heard in the whirlwind, your **lightning** lit up the world;
97: 4 His **lightning** lights up the world; the earth sees and trembles.
135: 7 he sends **lightning** with the rain and brings out the wind from his
144: 6 **Send forth lightning** [+1397] and scatter ⌊the enemies⌋;
Jer 10:13 He sends **lightning** with the rain and brings out the wind from his
51:16 He sends **lightning** with the rain and brings out the wind from his
Eze 1:13 among the creatures; it was bright, and **lightning** flashed out of it.
21:10 [21:15] for the slaughter, polished to **flash like lightning**!
21:15 [21:20] It is made to **flash like lightning**, it is grasped for
21:28 [21:33] polished to consume and to **flash like lightning**!
Da 10: 6 His body was like chrysolite, his face like **lightning**, his eyes like
Na 2: 4 [2:5] look like flaming torches; they dart about like **lightning**.
3: 3 Charging cavalry, flashing swords and **glittering** spears! Many
Hab 3:11 glint of your flying arrows, at the **lightning** *of* your flashing spear.
Zec 9:14 LORD will appear over them; his arrow will flash like **lightning**.

1399 ²בָּרָק bārāq², n.pr.m. [13 / 14] [√ 1398; cf. 1397]

Barak [12], Barak's [1], he[s] [1]

Jdg 4: 6 She sent for **Barak** son of Abinoam from Kedesh in Naphtali
4: 8 **Barak** said to her, "If you go with me, I will go; but if you don't
4: 9 Sisera over to a woman." So Deborah went with **Barak** to Kedesh,
4:10 where **he**[s] summoned Zebulun and Naphtali. Ten thousand men
4:12 When they told Sisera that **Barak** son of Abinoam had gone up to

Jdg 4:14 Deborah said to **Barak**, "Go! This is the day the LORD has given
4:14 So **Barak** went down Mount Tabor, followed by ten thousand
4:15 At **Barak's** advance, the LORD routed Sisera and all his chariots
4:16 **Barak** pursued the chariots and army as far as Harosheth
4:22 **Barak** came by in pursuit of Sisera, and Jael went out to meet him.
5:1 On that day Deborah and **Barak** son of Abinoam sang this song:
5:12 Deborah! Wake up, wake up, break out in song! Arise, O **Barak**!
5:15 yes, Issachar was with **Barak**, rushing after him into the valley.
1Sa 12:11 LORD sent Jerub-Baal, **Barak**, [BHS 979] Jephthah and Samuel,

1400 בְּרַק ***b^{e}raq***, n.pr.loc. Not used in NIV/BHS [→ 1222]

1401 בַּרְקוֹס ***barqôs***, n.pr.m. [2] [√ 1337 + *]

Barkos [2]

Ezr 2:53 **Barkos**, Sisera, Temah,
Ne 7:55 **Barkos**, Sisera, Temah,

1402 בַּרְקָן ***barqōn***, n.m.pl. [2] [√ 1398; cf. 1397]

briers [2]

Jdg 8:7 into my hand, I will tear your flesh with desert thorns and **briers**."
8:16 Succoth a lesson by punishing them with desert thorns and **briers**.

1403 בָּרֶקֶת ***bāreqet***, n.f. [2] [→ 1404]

beryl [2]

Ex 28:17 on it. In the first row there shall be a ruby, a topaz and a **beryl**;
39:10 stones on it. In the first row there was a ruby, a topaz and a **beryl**;

1404 בָּרְקַת ***bār^{e}qat***, n.f. [1] [√ 1403]

beryl [1]

Eze 28:13 chrysolite, onyx and jasper, sapphire, turquoise and **beryl**.

1405 בָּרַר[1] ***bārar[1]***, v. [14 / 15] [→ 1338, 1339, 1341, 1342, 1359, 1383; cf. 1406]

pure [3], choice [2], chosen [2], show yourself pure [2], be purified [1], choose [1], cleanse [1], purge [1], purified [1], tests [1]

1Sa 17:8 [A] **Choose** [BHS-] a man and have him come down to me.
2Sa 22:27 [C] to the **pure** you show yourself pure, but to the crooked you
22:27 [F] to the pure *you* **show yourself pure**, but to the crooked you
1Ch 7:40 [B] **choice** *men*, brave warriors and outstanding leaders.
9:22 [B] those **chosen** to be gatekeepers at the thresholds numbered
16:41 [B] them were Heman and Jeduthun and the rest of those **chosen**
Ne 5:18 [B] six **choice** sheep and some poultry were prepared for me,
Ps 18:26 [18:27] [C] to the **pure** you show yourself pure, but to the
18:26 [18:27] [F] to the pure *you* **show yourself pure**, but to the
Ecc 3:18 [A] God **tests** them so that they may see that they are like the
Isa 52:11 [C] and *be* **pure**, *you* who carry the vessels of the LORD.
Jer 4:11 [G] blows toward my people, but not to winnow or **cleanse**;
Eze 20:38 [A] *I will* **purge** you of those who revolt and rebel against me.
Da 11:35 [D] **purified** and made spotless until the time of the end,
12:10 [F] Many *will* **be purified**, made spotless and refined,

1406 בָּרַר[2] ***bārar[2]***, v. [2] [cf. 1405]

polished [1], sharpen [1]

Isa 49:2 [B] he made me into a **polished** arrow and concealed me in his
Jer 51:11 [G] "**Sharpen** the arrows, take up the shields! The LORD has

1407 בִּרְשַׁע ***birša'***, n.pr.m. [1]

Birsha [1]

Ge 14:2 **Birsha** king of Gomorrah, Shinab king of Admah, Shemeber king

1408 בֵּרֹתַי ***bērōtay***, n.pr.loc. [1]

Berothai [1]

2Sa 8:8 From Tebah and **Berothai**, towns that belonged to Hadadezer,

1409 בֵּרֹתִי ***bērōtî***, a.g. [1] [cf. 943]

Berothite [1]

1Ch 11:39 Zelek the Ammonite, Naharai the **Berothite**, the armor-bearer of

1410 בְּשׂוֹר ***b^{e}śôr***, n.pr.loc. [3]

Besor [2], *untranslated* [1]

1Sa 30:9 and the six hundred men with him came to the **Besor** Ravine,
30:10 **[RPH]** But David and four hundred men continued the pursuit.
30:21 to follow him and who were left behind at the **Besor** Ravine.

1411 בֹּשֶׂם ***bōśem***, n.m. [30] [→ 1412, 3311]

spices [21], spice [3], fragrance [2], fragrant [2], perfumes [1], spice-laden [1]

Ex 25:6 the light; **spices** for the anointing oil and for the fragrant incense;
30:23 "Take the following fine **spices**: 500 shekels of liquid myrrh,
30:23 250 shekels) of **fragrant** cinnamon, 250 shekels of fragrant cane,
30:23 250 shekels) of fragrant cinnamon, 250 shekels of **fragrant** cane,
35:8 the light; **spices** for the anointing oil and for the fragrant incense;
35:28 They also brought **spices** and olive oil for the light and for the
1Ki 10:2 with camels carrying **spices**, large quantities of gold, and precious
10:10 120 talents of gold, large quantities of **spices**, and precious stones.
10:10 so many **spices** brought in as those the queen of Sheba gave to
10:25 articles of silver and gold, robes, weapons and **spices**, and horses
2Ki 20:13 the silver, the gold, the **spices** and the fine oil—his armory
1Ch 9:29 as well as the flour and wine, and the oil, incense and **spices**.
9:30 But some of the priests took care of mixing the **spices**.
2Ch 9:1 with camels carrying **spices**, large quantities of gold, and precious
9:9 120 talents of gold, large quantities of **spices**, and precious stones.
9:9 There had never been such **spices** as those the queen of Sheba gave
9:24 articles of silver and gold, and robes, weapons and **spices**,
16:14 They laid him on a bier covered with **spices** and various blended
32:27 for his precious stones, **spices**, shields and all kinds of valuables.
Est 2:12 six months with oil of myrrh and six with **perfumes** and cosmetics.
SS 4:10 love than wine, and the fragrance of your perfume than any **spice**!
4:14 kind of incense tree, with myrrh and aloes and all the finest **spices**.
4:16 Blow on my garden, that its **fragrance** may spread abroad.
5:1 my sister, my bride; I have gathered my myrrh with my **spice**.
5:13 His cheeks are like beds of **spice** yielding perfume. His lips are like
6:2 to the beds of **spices**, to browse in the gardens and to gather lilies.
8:14 be like a gazelle or like a young stag on the **spice-laden** mountains.
Isa 3:24 Instead of **fragrance** there will be a stench; instead of a sash,
39:2 the silver, the gold, the **spices**, the fine oil, his entire armory
Eze 27:22 your merchandise they exchanged the finest of all kinds of **spices**

1412 בָּשְׂמַת ***bāś^{e}mat***, n.pr.f. [7] [√ 1411]

Basemath [7]

Ge 26:34 Beeri the Hittite, and also **Basemath** daughter of Elon the Hittite.
36:3 also **Basemath** daughter of Ishmael and sister of Nebaioth.
36:4 Adah bore Eliphaz to Esau, **Basemath** bore Reuel,
36:10 of Esau's wife Adah, and Reuel, the son of Esau's wife **Basemath**.
36:13 and Mizzah. These were grandsons of Esau's wife **Basemath**.
36:17 Reuel in Edom; they were grandsons of Esau's wife **Basemath**.
1Ki 4:15 in Naphtali (he had married **Basemath** daughter of Solomon);

1413 בָּשַׂר ***bāśar***, v. [24] [→ 1415]

proclaim [4], bring good tidings [2], bringing good news [2], brought the news [2], proclaim the news [2], take the news [2], bring good news [1], bring tidings [1], bringing news [1], brings good news [1], do[s] so [1], hear good news [1], messenger of good tidings [1], preach good news [1], proclaimed [1], proclaiming [1]

1Sa 4:17 [D] The *man who* **brought the news** replied, "Israel fled before
31:9 [D] Philistines to **proclaim the news** *in* the temple of their idols
2Sa 1:20 [D] it not in Gath, **proclaim** it not in the streets of Ashkelon,
4:10 [D] thought he was **bringing good news**, I seized him and put
18:19 [D] **take the news** *to* the king that the LORD has delivered him
18:20 [D] "*You may* **take the news** another time, but you must not do
18:20 [D] *you must* not **do[s] so** today, because the king's son is dead."
18:26 [D] The king said, "He *must be* **bringing good news**, too."
18:31 [F] and said, "My lord the king, **hear** *the* **good news**!
1Ki 1:42 [D] A worthy man like you *must be* **bringing** good **news**."
1Ch 10:9 [D] the Philistines to **proclaim the news** *among* their idols and
16:23 [D] all the earth; **proclaim** his salvation day after day.
Ps 40:9 [40:10] [D] *I* **proclaim** righteousness in the great assembly; I do
68:11 [68:12] [D] great was the company of those *who* **proclaimed** it:
96:2 [D] praise his name; **proclaim** his salvation day after day.
Isa 40:9 [D] You *who* **bring good tidings** *to* Zion, go up on a high
40:9 [D] You *who* **bring good tidings** *to* Jerusalem, lift up your voice
41:27 [D] they are!' I gave to Jerusalem a **messenger of good tidings**.
52:7 [D] on the mountains are the feet of *those who* **bring good news**,
52:7 [D] who proclaim peace, *who* **bring** good **tidings**, who proclaim
60:6 [D] and incense and **proclaiming** the praise of the LORD.
61:1 [D] LORD has anointed me to **preach good news** *to* the poor.
Jer 20:15 [D] Cursed be the man who **brought** my father **the news**, who
Na 1:15 [2:1] [D] the feet of *one who* **brings good news**, who proclaims

1414 בָּשָׂר ***bāśār***, n.m. [270] [→ Ar 10125]

flesh [75], meat [64], body [21], *untranslated* [12], himself [+2257] [10], mankind [10], skin [+6425] [8], creature [7], bodies [5], people [5], life [4], flesh and blood [3], men [3], creatures [2], everyone [+3972] [2], fat [+1374] [2], gaunt [+1987] [2], it[s] [2], kind [2], living thing [2], mortal man [2], skin [2], be circumcised [+4576+6889] [1],

[F] Hitpael (hitpoel, hitpoal, hitpolel, hitpolal, hitpalel, hitpalal, hitpalpel, hitpalpal, hotpael, hotpaal) [G] Hiphil (hiphtil) [H] Hophal [I] Hishtaphel

blood relative [+8638] [1], bodily [+4946] [1], body [+6872] [1], circumcised [+906+4576+6889] [1], close relative [+8638] [1], completely [+2256+4946+5883+6330] [1], genitals [1], lean [+8369] [1], lustful [+1541] [1], mankind [+408] [1], meal [1], mortal [1], myself [+3276] [1], nothing but skin [+2256+6425] [1], nourished [+1374] [1], one[s] [+3972] [1], put in jeopardy [+928+5951+9094] [1], regular flow [+928+2307] [1], that[s] [1], them [+4392] [1], those[s] [1], undergo circumcision [+906+4576+6889] [1], was circumcised [+4576+6889] [1], you [+3870] [1]

Ge 2:21 he took one of the man's ribs and closed up the place with **flesh**.
2:23 man said, "This is now bone of my bones and **flesh** of my flesh;
2:23 man said, "This is now bone of my bones and flesh of my **flesh**;
2:24 and be united to his wife, and they will become one **flesh**.
6: 3 "My Spirit will not contend with man forever, for he is **mortal**;
6:12 had become, for all the **people** on earth had corrupted their ways.
6:13 So God said to Noah, "I am going to put an end to all **people**,
6:17 I am going to bring floodwaters on the earth to destroy all **life**
6:19 You are to bring into the ark two of all living **creatures**, male
7:15 Pairs of all **creatures** that have the breath of life in them came to
7:16 The animals going in were male and female of every **living thing**,
7:21 Every **living thing** that moved on the earth perished—birds,
8:17 Bring out every kind of living **creature** that is with you—
9: 4 "But you must not eat **meat** that has its lifeblood still in it.
9:11 Never again will all **life** be cut off by the waters of a flood;
9:15 between me and you and all living creatures of every **kind**.
9:15 Never again will the waters become a flood to destroy all **life**.
9:16 between God and all living creatures of every **kind** on the earth."
9:17 covenant I have established between me and all **life** on the earth."
17:11 You *are to* **undergo circumcision** [+906+4576+6889], and it will
17:13 My covenant in your **flesh** is to be an everlasting covenant.
17:14 uncircumcised male, who has not been circumcised in the **flesh**,
17:23 and **circumcised** [+906+4576+6889] them, as God told him.
17:24 ninety-nine years old when he **was circumcised** [+4576+6889],
17:25 and his son Ishmael was thirteen; **[RPH]**
29:14 Then Laban said to him, "You are my own **flesh** and blood."
37:27 on him; after all, he is our brother, our own **flesh and blood**."
40:19 and hang you on a tree. And the birds will eat away your **flesh**."
41: 2 sleek and **fat** [+1374], and they grazed among the reeds.
41: 3 After them, seven other cows, ugly and **gaunt** [+1987], came up
41: 4 the cows that were ugly and **gaunt** [+1987] ate up the seven sleek,
41:18 **fat** [+1374] and sleek, and they grazed among the reeds.
41:19 other cows came up—scrawny and very ugly and **lean** [+8369].
Ex 4: 7 and when he took it out, it was restored, like the rest of his **flesh**.
12: 8 That same night they are to eat the **meat** roasted over the fire,
12:46 be eaten inside one house; take none of the **meat** outside the house.
16: 3 There we sat around pots of **meat** and ate all the food we wanted,
16: 8 "You will know that it was the LORD when he gives you **meat** to
16:12 Tell them, 'At twilight you will eat **meat**, and in the morning you
21:28 the bull must be stoned to death, and its **meat** must not be eaten.
22:31 [22:30] So do not eat the **meat** of an animal torn by wild beasts;
28:42 "Make linen undergarments as a covering for the **body** [+6872],
29:14 But burn the bull's **flesh** and its hide and its offal outside the camp.
29:31 the ram for the ordination and cook the **meat** in a sacred place.
29:32 Aaron and his sons are to eat the **meat** *of* the ram and the bread
29:34 if any of the **meat** *of* the ordination ram or any bread is left over
30:32 Do not pour it on men's **bodies** and do not make any oil with the
Lev 4:11 But the hide of the bull and all its **flesh**, as well as the head
6:10 [6:3] his linen clothes, with linen undergarments next to his **body**,
6:27 [6:20] Whatever touches any of the **flesh** will become holy, and if
7:15 The **meat** *of* his fellowship offering of thanksgiving must be eaten
7:17 Any **meat** *of* the sacrifice left over till the third day must be burned
7:18 If any **meat** *of* the fellowship offering is eaten on the third day,
7:19 " '**Meat** that touches anything ceremonially unclean must not be
7:19 As for other **meat**, anyone ceremonially clean may eat it.
7:19 As for other meat, anyone ceremonially clean may eat **it**[s].
7:20 if anyone who is unclean eats any **meat** of the fellowship offering
7:21 eats any of the **meat** *of* the fellowship offering belonging to the
8:17 the bull with its hide and its **flesh** and its offal he burned up outside
8:31 "Cook the **meat** at the entrance to the Tent of Meeting and eat it
8:32 Then burn up the rest of the **meat** and the bread.
9:11 the **flesh** and the hide he burned up outside the camp.
11: 8 You must not eat their **meat** or touch their carcasses; they are
11:11 you must not eat their **meat** and you must detest their carcasses.
12: 3 On the eighth day the boy *is to* **be circumcised** [+4576+6889].
13: 2 or a bright spot on his **skin** [+6425] that may become an infectious
13: 2 or a bright spot on his skin that may become **[RPH]** an infectious
13: 3 The priest is to examine the sore on his **skin** [+6425], and if the
13: 3 and the sore appears to be more than **skin** [+6425] deep,
13: 4 If the spot on his **skin** [+6425] is white but does not appear to be
13:10 has turned the hair white and if there is raw **flesh** in the swelling,
13:11 skin disease **[RPH]** and the priest shall pronounce him unclean.
13:13 is to examine him, and if the disease has covered his whole **body**,
13:14 But whenever raw **flesh** appears on him, he will be unclean.
13:15 When the priest sees the raw **flesh**, he shall pronounce him
13:15 The raw **flesh** is unclean; he has an infectious disease.
13:16 Should the raw **flesh** change and turn white, he must go to the
13:18 "When someone has a boil on his **skin** [+6425] and it heals,
13:24 "When someone has a burn on his **skin** [+6425] and a
13:38 "When a man or woman has white spots on the **skin** [+6425],
13:39 **[RPH]** it is a harmless rash that has broken out on the skin;
13:43 or forehead is reddish-white like an infectious **skin** [+6425]
14: 9 He must wash his clothes and bathe **himself** [+2257] with water,
15: 2 'When any man has a **bodily** [+4946] discharge, the discharge is
15: 3 Whether it continues flowing from his **body** or is blocked,
15: 3 from his body or is blocked, **[RPH]** it will make him unclean.
15: 7 " 'Whoever touches **[NIE]** the man who has a discharge must
15:13 must wash his clothes and bathe **himself** [+2257] with fresh water,
15:16 he must bathe his whole **body** with water, and he will be unclean
15:19 " 'When a woman has her **regular flow of** [+928+2307] blood,
16: 4 the sacred linen tunic, with linen undergarments next to his **body**;
16: 4 so he must bathe **himself** [+2257] with water before he puts them
16:24 He shall bathe **himself** [+2257] with water in a holy place
16:26 must wash his clothes and bathe **himself** [+2257] with water;
16:27 outside the camp; their hides, **flesh** and offal are to be burned up.
16:28 them must wash his clothes and bathe **himself** [+2257] with water;
17:11 For the life of a **creature** is in the blood, and I have given it to you
17:14 because the life of every **creature** is its blood. That is why I have
17:14 said to the Israelites, "You must not eat the blood of any **creature**,
17:14 of any creature, because the life of every **creature** is its blood;
17:16 But if he does not wash his clothes and bathe **himself** [+2257],
18: 6 " 'No one is to approach any **close relative** [+8638] to have sexual
19:28 " 'Do not cut your **bodies** for the dead or put tattoo marks on
21: 5 or shave off the edges of their beards or cut their **bodies**.
22: 6 sacred offerings unless he has bathed **himself** [+2257] with water.
25:49 or any **blood relative** [+8638] in his clan may redeem him.
26:29 You will eat the **flesh** *of* your sons and the flesh of your daughters.
26:29 You will eat the flesh of your sons and the **flesh** *of* your daughters.
Nu 8: 7 then have them shave their whole **bodies** and wash their clothes,
11: 4 the Israelites started wailing and said, "If only we had **meat** to eat!
11:13 Where can I get **meat** for all these people? They keep wailing to
11:13 all these people? They keep wailing to me, 'Give us **meat** to eat!'
11:18 yourselves in preparation for tomorrow, when you will eat **meat**.
11:18 LORD heard you when you wailed, "If only we had **meat** to eat!
11:18 Now the LORD will give you **meat**, and you will eat it.
11:21 and you say, 'I will give them **meat** to eat for a whole month!'
11:33 while the **meat** was still between their teeth and before it could be
12:12 coming from its mother's womb with its **flesh** half eaten away."
16:22 and cried out, "O God, God of the spirits of all **mankind**,
18:15 The first offspring of every womb, **[NIE]** both man and animal,
18:18 Their **meat** is to be yours, just as the breast of the wave offering
19: 5 the heifer is to be burned—its hide, **flesh**, blood and offal.
19: 7 priest must wash his clothes and bathe **himself** [+2257] with water.
19: 8 burns it must also wash his clothes and bathe **[RPH]** with water,
27:16 "May the LORD, the God of the spirits of all **mankind**, appoint a
Dt 5:26 For what **mortal man** has ever heard the voice of the living God
12:15 in any of your towns and eat as much of the **meat** as you want,
12:20 you crave **meat** and say, "I would like some meat," then you may
12:20 you crave meat and say, "I would like *some* **meat**," then you may
12:20 like some meat," then you may eat as much of **it**[s] as you want.
12:23 the blood is the life, and you must not eat the life with the **meat**.
12:27 on the altar of the LORD your God, both the **meat** and the blood.
12:27 the altar of the LORD your God, but you may eat the **meat**.
14: 8 the cud. You are not to eat their **meat** or touch their carcasses.
16: 4 Do not let any of the **meat** you sacrifice on the evening of the first
28:53 the **flesh** *of* the sons and daughters the LORD your God has given
28:55 he will not give to one of them any of the **flesh** *of* his children that
32:42 make my arrows drunk with blood, while my sword devours **flesh**:
Jdg 6:19 Putting the **meat** in a basket and its broth in a pot, he brought them
6:20 "Take the **meat** and the unleavened bread, place them on this rock,
6:21 the angel of the LORD touched the **meat** and the unleavened
6:21 Fire flared from the rock, consuming the **meat** and the bread.
8: 7 into my hand, I will tear your **flesh** with desert thorns and briers."
9: 2 or just one man?' Remember, I am your **flesh** and blood."
1Sa 2:13 anyone offered a sacrifice and while the **meat** was being boiled,
2:15 the man who was sacrificing, "Give the priest *some* **meat** to roast;
2:15 to roast; he won't accept boiled **meat** from you, but only raw."
17:44 "and I'll give your **flesh** to the birds of the air and the beasts of the
2Sa 5: 1 to David at Hebron and said, "We are your own **flesh** and blood.
19:12 [19:13] You are my brothers, my own **flesh** and blood. So why
19:13 [19:14] And say to Amasa, 'Are you not my own **flesh** and blood?
1Ki 17: 6 and **meat** in the morning and bread and meat in the evening,
17: 6 and meat in the morning and bread and **meat** in the evening,
19:21 He burned the plowing equipment to cook the **meat** and gave it to
21:27 he tore his clothes, put on sackcloth **[NIE]** and fasted.
2Ki 4:34 As he stretched himself out upon him, the boy's **body** grew warm.
5:10 and your **flesh** will be restored and you will be cleansed."
5:14 his **flesh** was restored and became clean like that of a young boy.

2Ki 5:14 his flesh was restored and became clean like **that**ˢ *of* a young boy.
6:30 and there, underneath, he had sackcloth on his **body**.
9:36 On the plot of ground at Jezreel dogs will devour Jezebel's **flesh**.
1Ch 11:1 to David at Hebron and said, "We are your own **flesh** and blood.
2Ch 32:8 With him is only the arm of **flesh**, but with us is the LORD our
Ne 5:5 Although **[RPH]** we are of the same flesh and blood as our
5:5 Although we are of the same **flesh and blood** as our countrymen
Job 2:5 stretch out your hand and strike his **flesh** and bones, and he will
4:15 spirit glided past my face, and the hair on my **body** stood on end.
6:12 Do I have the strength of stone? Is my **flesh** bronze?
7:5 My **body** is clothed with worms and scabs, my skin is broken
10:4 Do you have eyes of **flesh**? Do you see as a mortal sees?
10:11 clothe me with skin and **flesh** and knit me together with bones
12:10 is the life of every creature and the breath of all **mankind** [+408].
13:14 Why *do I* **put** myself **in jeopardy** [+928+5951+9094] and take my
14:22 He feels but the pain of his own **body** and mourns only for
19:20 I am **nothing but skin** [+2256+6425] and bones; I have escaped
19:22 pursue me as God does? Will you never get enough of my **flesh**?
19:26 after my skin has been destroyed, yet in my **flesh** I will see God;
21:6 When I think about this, I am terrified; trembling seizes my **body**.
31:31 have never said, 'Who has not had his fill of Job's **meat**?'—
33:21 His **flesh** wastes away to nothing, and his bones, once hidden,
33:25 his **flesh** is renewed like a child's; it is restored as in the days of his
34:15 all **mankind** would perish together and man would return to the
41:23 [41:15] The folds of his **flesh** are tightly joined; they are firm and
Ps 16:9 heart is glad and my tongue rejoices; my **body** also will rest secure,
27:2 When evil men advance against me to devour my **flesh**, when my
38:3 [38:4] Because of your wrath there is no health in my **body**;
38:7 [38:8] is filled with searing pain; there is no health in my **body**.
50:13 Do I eat the **flesh** *of* bulls or drink the blood of goats?
56:4 [56:5] I will not be afraid. What can **mortal man** do to me?
63:1 [63:2] my **body** longs for you, in a dry and weary land where
65:2 [65:3] O you who hear prayer, to you all **men** will come.
78:39 He remembered that they were but **flesh**, a passing breeze that does
79:2 birds of the air, the **flesh** *of* your saints to the beasts of the earth.
84:2 [84:3] my heart and my **flesh** cry out for the living God.
102:5 [102:6] Because of my loud groaning I am reduced to **skin** and
109:24 My knees give way from fasting; my **body** is thin and gaunt.
119:120 My **flesh** trembles in fear of you; I stand in awe of your laws.
136:25 who gives food to every **creature**. *His love endures*
145:21 Let every **creature** praise his holy name for ever and ever.
Pr 4:22 are life to those who find them and health to a man's whole **body**.
5:11 of your life you will groan, when your **flesh** and body are spent.
14:30 A heart at peace gives life to the **body**, but envy rots the bones.
23:20 join those who drink too much wine or gorge themselves on **meat**,
Ecc 2:3 I tried cheering **myself** [+3276] with wine, and embracing folly—
4:5 The fool folds his hands and ruins **himself** [+2257].
5:6 [5:5] Do not let your mouth lead **you** [+3870] into sin. And do not
11:10 anxiety from your heart and cast off the troubles of your **body**,
12:12 many books there is no end, and much study wearies the **body**.
Isa 9:20 [9:19] Each will feed on the **flesh** *of* his own offspring:
10:18 fertile fields it will **completely** [+2256+4946+5883+6330] destroy,
17:4 the glory of Jacob will fade; the fat of his **body** will waste away.
22:13 and killing of sheep, eating of **meat** and drinking of wine!
31:3 are men and not God; their horses are **flesh** and not spirit.
40:5 the LORD will be revealed, and all **mankind** together will see it.
40:6 "All **men** are like grass, and all their glory is like the flowers of the
44:16 over it he prepares his **meal**, he roasts his meat and eats his fill.
44:19 I even baked bread over its coals, I roasted **meat** and I ate.
49:26 I will make your oppressors eat their own **flesh**; they will be drunk
49:26 Then all **mankind** will know that I, the LORD, am your Savior,
58:7 clothe him, and not to turn away from your own **flesh and blood**?
65:4 who eat the **flesh** *of* pigs, and whose pots hold broth of unclean
66:16 with his sword the LORD will execute judgment upon all **men**,
66:17 following the one in the midst of those who eat the **flesh** *of* pigs
66:23 all **mankind** will come and bow down before me,"
66:24 fire be quenched, and they will be loathsome to all **mankind**."
Jer 7:21 offerings to your other sacrifices and eat the **meat** yourselves!
11:15 Can consecrated **meat** avert ⌞your punishment⌟? When you engage
12:12 from one end of the land to the other; no **one**ˢ [+3972] will be safe.
17:5 who depends on **flesh** for his strength and whose heart turns away
19:9 I will make them eat the **flesh** *of* their sons and daughters,
19:9 I will make them eat the flesh of their sons and **[RPH]** daughters,
19:9 they will eat one another's **flesh** during the stress of the siege
25:31 he will bring judgment on all **mankind** and put the wicked to the
32:27 "I am the LORD, the God of all **mankind**. Is anything too hard
45:5 For I will bring disaster on all **people**, declares the LORD,
La 3:4 He has made my **skin** and my flesh grow old and has broken my
Eze 4:14 by wild animals. No unclean **meat** has ever entered my mouth."
10:12 Their entire **bodies**, including their backs, their hands and their
11:3 to build houses? This city is a cooking pot, and we are the **meat**.'
11:7 The bodies you have thrown there are the **meat** and this city is the
11:11 This city will not be a pot for you, nor will you be the **meat** in it;
11:19 I will remove from **them** [+4392] their heart of stone and give
11:19 from them their heart of stone and give them a heart of **flesh**.
16:26 in prostitution with the Egyptians, your **lustful** [+1541] neighbors,
20:48 [21:4] **Everyone** [+3972] will see that I the LORD have kindled
21:4 [21:9] my sword will be unsheathed against **everyone** [+3972]
21:5 [21:10] all **people** will know that I the LORD have drawn my
23:20 whose **genitals** were like those of donkeys and whose emission
23:20 whose genitals were like **those**ˢ *of* donkeys and whose emission
24:10 Cook the **meat** well, mixing in the spices; and let the bones be
32:5 I will spread your **flesh** on the mountains and fill the valleys with
36:26 I will remove from **[RPH]** you your heart of stone and give you a
36:26 remove from you your heart of stone and give you a heart of **flesh**.
37:6 to you and make **flesh** come upon you and cover you with skin;
37:8 and tendons and **flesh** appeared on them and skin covered them,
39:17 the mountains of Israel. There you will eat **flesh** and drink blood.
39:18 You will eat the **flesh** *of* mighty men and drink the blood of the
40:43 the wall all around. The tables were for the **flesh** *of* the offerings.
44:7 foreigners uncircumcised in heart and **flesh** into my sanctuary,
44:9 foreigner uncircumcised in heart and **flesh** is to enter my sanctuary,
Da 1:15 better **nourished** [+1374] than any of the young men who ate the
10:3 I ate no choice food; no **meat** or wine touched my lips; and I used
Hos 8:13 They offer sacrifices given to me and they eat the **meat**,
Joel 2:28 [3:1] "And afterward, I will pour out my Spirit on all **people**.
Mic 3:3 who chop them up like meat for the pan, like **flesh** for the pot?"
Hag 2:12 If a person carries consecrated **meat** in the fold of his garment,
Zec 2:13 [2:17] Be still before the LORD, all **mankind**, because he has
11:9 perishing perish. Let those who are left eat one another's **flesh**."
11:16 or feed the healthy, but will eat the **meat** *of* the choice sheep,
14:12 Their **flesh** will rot while they are still standing on their feet,

1415 בְּשׂרָה **bᵉśōrâ**, n.f. [6] [√ 1413]

news [3], good news [2], reward for news [1]

2Sa 4:10 to death in Ziklag. That was the **reward** I gave him **for** his **news**!
18:20 "You are not the one to take the **news** today," Joab told him.
18:22 to go? You don't have any **news** that will bring you a reward."
18:25 The king said, "If he is alone, he must have **good news**."
18:27 "He's a good man," the king said. "He comes with good **news**."
2Ki 7:9 This is a day of **good news** and we are keeping it to ourselves.

1416 בַּשֶּׁבֶת **baššebet**, n.pr.m. Not used in NIV/BHS [→ 3783]

1417 בְּשַׁגַּם **bᵉšaggam**, pp. & rel. & adv. Not used in NIV/BHS [√ 928 + 8611 + 1685]

1418 בָּשַׁל **bāšal**, v. [28] [→ 1419, 4453]

cook [10], cooked [5], boiled [3], boil [2], baked [1], burned to cook [1], cooked [+1419] [1], kitchens [+1074] [1], ripe [1], ripened [1], roast [1], roasted [1]

Ge 40:10 [G] it budded, it blossomed, and its clusters **ripened** *into* grapes.
Ex 12:9 [E] Do not eat the meat raw or **cooked** [+1419] in water,
16:23 [D] bake what you want to bake and **boil** what you want to boil.
16:23 [D] bake what you want to bake and boil what *you want to* **boil**.
23:19 [D] your God. "*Do* not **cook** a young goat in its mother's milk.
29:31 [D] ram for the ordination and **cook** the meat in a sacred place.
34:26 [D] your God. "*Do* not **cook** a young goat in its mother's milk."
Lev 6:28 [6:21] [E] The clay pot the meat *is* **cooked** in must be broken;
6:28 [6:21] [E] if *it is* **cooked** in a bronze pot, the pot is to be scoured
8:31 [D] "**Cook** the meat at the entrance to the Tent of Meeting
Nu 11:8 [D] it in a mortar. *They* **cooked** it in a pot or made it into cakes.
Dt 14:21 [D] your God. *Do* not **cook** a young goat in its mother's milk.
16:7 [D] **Roast** it and eat it at the place the LORD your God will
1Sa 2:13 [D] offered a sacrifice and while the meat *was being* **boiled**,
2:15 [E] he won't accept **boiled** meat from you, but only raw."
2Sa 13:8 [D] kneaded it, made the bread in his sight and **baked** it.
1Ki 19:21 [D] *He* **burned** the plowing equipment **to cook** the meat
2Ki 4:38 [D] "Put on the large pot and **cook** some stew for these men."
6:29 [D] So *we* **cooked** my son and ate him. The next day I said to
2Ch 35:13 [D] *They* **roasted** the Passover animals over the fire as
35:13 [D] **boiled** the holy offerings in pots, caldrons and pans
La 4:10 [D] *With* their own hands compassionate women *have* **cooked**
Eze 24:5 [A] it for the bones; bring it to a boil and **cook** the bones in it.
46:20 [D] is the place where the priests *will* **cook** the guilt offering and
46:24 [D] "These are the **kitchens** [+1074] where those who minister at
46:24 [D] minister at the temple *will* **cook** the sacrifices of the people."
Joel 3:13 [4:13] [A] Swing the sickle, for the harvest *is* **ripe**. Come,
Zec 14:21 [D] to sacrifice will take some of the pots and **cook** in them.

1419 בָּשֵׁל **bāšēl**, a. [2] [√ 1418]

boiled [1], cooked [+1418] [1]

Ex 12:9 Do not eat the meat raw or **cooked** [+1418] in water, but roast it
Nu 6:19 the priest is to place in his hands a **boiled** shoulder of the ram,

1420 בִּשְׁלָם bišlām, n.pr.m. [1] [cf. 8967]
Bishlam [1]

Ezr 4: 7 **Bishlam**, Mithredath, Tabeel and the rest of his associates wrote a

1421 בָּשָׁן bāšān[1], n.pr.loc. [60]
Bashan [59], Bashan [+824] [1]

Nu 21: 33 Then they turned and went up along the road toward **Bashan**,
21: 33 Og king of **Bashan** and his whole army marched out to meet them
32: 33 king of the Amorites and the kingdom of Og king of **Bashan**—
Dt 1: 4 reigned in Heshbon, and at Edrei had defeated Og king of **Bashan**,
3: 1 Next we turned and went up along the road toward **Bashan**,
3: 1 Og king of **Bashan** with his whole army marched out to meet us in
3: 3 the LORD our God also gave into our hands Og king of **Bashan**
3: 4 from them—the whole region of Argob, Og's kingdom in **Bashan**.
3: 10 and all Gilead, and all **Bashan** as far as Salecah and Edrei,
3: 10 as far as Salecah and Edrei, towns of Og's kingdom in **Bashan**.
3: 11 (Only Og king of **Bashan** was left of the remnant of the Rephaites.
3: 13 The rest of Gilead and also all of **Bashan**, the kingdom of Og,
3: 13 (The whole region of Argob in **Bashan** used to be known as a land
3: 14 after him, so that to this day **Bashan** is called Havvoth Jair.)
4: 43 for the Gadites; and Golan in **Bashan**, for the Manassites.
4: 47 took possession of his land and the land of Og king of **Bashan**,
29: 7 [29:6] and Og king of **Bashan** came out to fight against us,
32: 14 with choice rams of **Bashan** and the finest kernels of wheat.
33: 22 About Dan he said: "Dan is a lion's cub, springing out of **Bashan**."
Jos 9: 10 Sihon king of Heshbon, and Og king of **Bashan**, who reigned in
12: 4 the territory of Og king of **Bashan**, one of the last of the Rephaites,
12: 5 all of **Bashan** to the border of the people of Geshur and Maacah,
13: 11 all of Mount Hermon and all **Bashan** as far as Salecah—
13: 12 that is, the whole kingdom of Og in **Bashan**, who had reigned in
13: 30 territory extending from Mahanaim and including all of **Bashan**,
13: 30 including all of Bashan, the entire realm of Og king of **Bashan**—
13: 30 king of Bashan—all the settlements of Jair in **Bashan**, sixty towns,
13: 31 and Ashtaroth and Edrei (the royal cities of Og in **Bashan**).
17: 1 who had received Gilead and **Bashan** because the Makirites were
17: 5 of ten tracts of land besides Gilead and **Bashan** east of the Jordan,
20: 8 in the tribe of Gad, and Golan in **Bashan** in the tribe of Manasseh.
21: 6 Asher, Naphtali and the half-tribe of Manasseh in **Bashan**.
21: 27 Golan in **Bashan** (a city of refuge for one accused of murder)
22: 7 (To the half-tribe of Manasseh Moses had given land in **Bashan**,
1Ki 4: 13 as well as the district of Argob in **Bashan** and its sixty large walled
4: 19 Sihon king of the Amorites and the country of Og king of **Bashan**).
2Ki 10: 33 from Aroer by the Arnon Gorge through Gilead to **Bashan**.
1Ch 5: 11 The Gadites lived next to them in **Bashan** [+824], as far as
5: 12 the chief, Shapham the second, then Janai and Shaphat, in **Bashan**.
5: 16 The Gadites lived in Gilead, in **Bashan** and its outlying villages,
5: 23 they settled in the land from **Bashan** to Baal Hermon, that is,
6: 62 [6:47] from the part of the tribe of Manasseh that is in **Bashan**.
6: 71 [6:56] the half-tribe of Manasseh they received Golan in **Bashan**
Ne 9: 22 of Sihon king of Heshbon and the country of Og king of **Bashan**.
Ps 22: 12 [22:13] bulls surround me; strong bulls of **Bashan** encircle me.
68: 15 [68:16] The mountains of **Bashan** are majestic mountains;
68: 15 [68:16] majestic mountains; rugged are the mountains of **Bashan**.
68: 22 [68:23] The Lord says, "I will bring them from **Bashan**; I will
135: 11 of the Amorites, Og king of **Bashan** and all the kings of Canaan—
136: 20 and Og king of **Bashan**—*His love endures forever.*
Isa 2: 13 the cedars of Lebanon, tall and lofty, and all the oaks of **Bashan**,
33: 9 is like the Arabah, and **Bashan** and Carmel drop their leaves.
Jer 22: 20 "Go up to Lebanon and cry out, let your voice be heard in **Bashan**,
50: 19 back to his own pasture and he will graze on Carmel and **Bashan**;
Eze 27: 6 Of oaks from **Bashan** they made your oars; of cypress wood from
39: 18 goats and bulls—all of them fattened animals from **Bashan**.
Am 4: 1 Hear this word, you cows of **Bashan** on Mount Samaria,
Mic 7: 14 Let them feed in **Bashan** and Gilead as in days long ago.
Na 1: 4 **Bashan** and Carmel wither and the blossoms of Lebanon fade.
Zec 11: 2 Wail, oaks of **Bashan**; the dense forest has been cut down!

1422 בָּשָׁן² bāšān[2], n.m. Not used in NIV/BHS

1423 בָּשְׁנָה bošnâ, n.f. [1] [√ 1017]
disgraced [+4374] [1]

Hos 10: 6 Ephraim *will be* **disgraced** [+4374]; Israel will be ashamed of its

1424 בָּשַׁס bāšas, v. [1]
trample [1]

Am 5: 11 [D] You **trample** on the poor and force him to give you grain.

1425 בֹּשֶׁת bōšet, n.f. [30] [→ 410; cf. 1017]
shame [20], disgraced [2], disgrace [+7156] [1], humiliation [+7156] [1], shame [+6872] [1], shameful god [1], shameful gods [1], shameful idol [1], shaming [1], utter shame [+1017] [1]

1Sa 20: 30 know that you have sided with the son of Jesse to your own **shame**
20: 30 own shame and to the **shame** [+6872] *of* the mother who bore you?
2Ch 32: 21 So he withdrew to his own land in **disgrace** [+7156]. And when he
Ezr 9: 7 to pillage and **humiliation** [+7156] at the hand of foreign kings,
Job 8: 22 Your enemies will be clothed in **shame**, and the tents of the wicked
Ps 35: 26 may all who exalt themselves over me be clothed with **shame**
40: 15 [40:16] say to me, "Aha! Aha!" be appalled at their own **shame**.
44: 15 [44:16] me all day long, and my face is covered with **shame**
69: 19 [69:20] You know how I am scorned, **disgraced** and shamed; all
70: 3 [70:4] say to me, "Aha! Aha!" turn back because of their **shame**.
109: 29 will be clothed with disgrace and wrapped in **shame** as in a cloak.
132: 18 I will clothe his enemies with **shame**, but the crown on his head
Isa 30: 3 Pharaoh's protection will be to your **shame**, Egypt's shade will
30: 5 bring neither help nor advantage, but only **shame** and disgrace."
42: 17 'You are our gods,' will be turned back *in* **utter shame** [+1017].
54: 4 You will forget the **shame** *of* your youth and remember no more
61: 7 Instead of their **shame** my people will receive a double portion,
Jer 2: 26 "As a thief is **disgraced** when he is caught, so the house of Israel is
3: 24 From our youth **shameful gods** have consumed the fruits of our
3: 25 Let us lie down in our **shame**, and let our disgrace cover us.
7: 19 Are they not rather harming themselves, to their own **shame**?
11: 13 the altars you have set up to burn incense to that **shameful god**
20: 18 the womb to see trouble and sorrow and to end my days in **shame**?
Da 9: 7 you are righteous, but this day we are covered with **shame**—
9: 8 our princes and our fathers are covered with **shame** because we
Hos 9: 10 they consecrated themselves to that **shameful idol** and became as
Mic 1: 11 Pass on in nakedness and **shame**, you who live in Shaphir.
Hab 2: 10 of many peoples, **shaming** your own house and forfeiting your life.
Zep 3: 5 new day he does not fail, yet the unrighteous know no **shame**.
3: 19 them praise and honor in every land where they were put to **shame**.

1426 בַּת¹ bat[1], n.f. [588 / 587] [→ 1442, 1444, 1445; cf. 1215]
daughter [245], daughters [204], *untranslated* [23], women [15], people [+6639] [14], surrounding settlements [10], settlements [9], villages [7], surrounding villages [6], granddaughter [5], woman [5], owls [+3613] [4], daughter's [3], girl [3], girls [2], horned owl [+3613] [2], maidens [2], owl [+3613] [2], year-old [+9102] [2], young women [2], adopted [+4200+4200+4374] [1], age [+9102] [1], apple [+413] [1], branches [1], city [1], cousin [+1856] [1], daughters in marriage [1], descendant [1], Egypt [+5213] [1], eyes [+6524] [1], granddaughters [+1201] [1], inhabitants [1], old [1], outlying villages [1], people [1], princess [+4889] [1], she[s] [+7281] [1], sister [1], songs [+8877] [1], whose[s] [+465+2257] [1], whose[s] [+7524] [1], young [1]

Ge 5: 4 Adam lived 800 years and had other sons and **daughters**.
5: 7 of Enosh, Seth lived 807 years and had other sons and **daughters**.
5: 10 Enosh lived 815 years and had other sons and **daughters**.
5: 13 Kenan lived 840 years and had other sons and **daughters**.
5: 16 Mahalalel lived 830 years and had other sons and **daughters**.
5: 19 of Enoch, Jared lived 800 years and had other sons and **daughters**.
5: 22 walked with God 300 years and had other sons and **daughters**.
5: 26 Methuselah lived 782 years and had other sons and **daughters**.
5: 30 Lamech lived 595 years and had other sons and **daughters**.
6: 1 increase in number on the earth and **daughters** were born to them,
6: 2 the sons of God saw that the **daughters** *of* men were beautiful,
6: 4 when the sons of God went to the **daughters** *of* men and had
11: 11 Shem lived 500 years and had other sons and **daughters**.
11: 13 Arphaxad lived 403 years and had other sons and **daughters**.
11: 15 Shelah lived 403 years and had other sons and **daughters**.
11: 17 of Peleg, Eber lived 430 years and had other sons and **daughters**.
11: 19 of Reu, Peleg lived 209 years and had other sons and **daughters**.
11: 21 of Serug, Reu lived 207 years and had other sons and **daughters**.
11: 23 of Nahor, Serug lived 200 years and had other sons and **daughters**.
11: 25 Nahor lived 119 years and had other sons and **daughters**.
11: 29 she was the **daughter** *of* Haran, the father of both Milcah
17: 17 years old? Will Sarah bear a child *at* the **age** [+9102] *of* ninety?"
19: 8 Look, I have two **daughters** who have never slept with a man.
19: 12 sons-in-law, sons or **daughters**, or anyone else in the city who
19: 14 to his sons-in-law, who were pledged to marry his **daughters**.
19: 15 Take your wife and your two **daughters** who are here, or you will
19: 16 his hand and the hands of his wife and of his two **daughters**
19: 30 Lot and his two **daughters** left Zoar and settled in the mountains,
19: 30 afraid to stay in Zoar. He and his two **daughters** lived in a cave.
19: 36 So both of Lot's **daughters** became pregnant by their father.
20: 12 is my sister, the **daughter** *of* my father though not *of* my mother;
20: 12 the daughter of my father though not of **[RPH]** my mother;
24: 3 that you will not get a wife for my son from the **daughters** *of* the
24: 13 the **daughters** *of* the townspeople are coming out to draw water.

[A] Qal [B] Qal passive [C] Niphal [D] Piel (poel, polel, pilel, pilal, pealal, pilpel) [E] Pual (poal, polal, poalal, pulal, pualal)

Ge 24:23 Then he asked, "Whose **daughter** are you? Please tell me,
24:24 She answered him, "I am the **daughter** *of* Bethuel, the son that
24:37 'You must not get a wife for my son from the **daughters** *of* the
24:47 "I asked her, 'Whose **daughter** are you?' "She said, 'The daughter
24:47 "She said, 'The **daughter** *of* Bethuel son of Nahor, whom Milcah
24:48 who had led me on the right road to get the **granddaughter** *of* my
25:20 Isaac was forty years old when he married Rebekah **daughter** *of*
26:34 forty years old, he married Judith **daughter** *of* Beeri the Hittite,
26:34 Beeri the Hittite, and also Basemath **daughter** *of* Elon the Hittite.
27:46 "I'm disgusted with living because of these Hittite **women**.
27:46 If Jacob takes a wife from among the **women** *of* this land,
27:46 from Hittite **women** like these, my life will not be worth living."
28: 1 and commanded him: "Do not marry a Canaanite **woman**.
28: 2 from among the **daughters** *of* Laban, your mother's brother.
28: 6 him he commanded him, "Do not marry a Canaanite **woman**,"
28: 8 realized how displeasing the Canaanite **women** were to his father
28: 9 the sister of Nebaioth and **daughter** *of* Ishmael son of Abraham,
29: 6 they said, "and here comes his **daughter** Rachel with the sheep."
29:10 When Jacob saw Rachel **daughter** *of* Laban, his mother's brother,
29:16 Now Laban had two **daughters**; the name of the older was Leah,
29:18 "I'll work for you seven years in return for your younger **daughter**
29:23 he took his **daughter** Leah and gave her to Jacob, and Jacob lay
29:24 Laban gave his servant girl Zilpah to his **daughter** as her
29:28 and then Laban gave him his **daughter** Rachel to be his wife.
29:29 Laban gave his servant girl Bilhah to his **daughter** Rachel as her
30:13 Leah said, "How happy I am! The **women** will call me happy."
30:21 Some time later she gave birth to a **daughter** and named her
31:26 and you've carried off my **daughters** like captives in war.
31:28 even let me kiss my grandchildren and my **daughters** good-by.
31:31 because I thought you would take your **daughters** away from me
31:41 I worked for you fourteen years for your two **daughters** and six
31:43 Laban answered Jacob, "The **women** are my daughters,
31:43 Laban answered Jacob, "The women are my **daughters**,
31:43 Yet what can I do today about these **daughters** *of* mine, or about
31:50 If you mistreat my **daughters** or if you take any wives besides my
31:50 my daughters or if you take any wives besides my **daughters**,
31:55 [32:1] his grandchildren and his **daughters** and blessed them.
34: 1 Now Dinah, the **daughter** Leah had borne to Jacob, went out to
34: 1 Leah had borne to Jacob, went out to visit the **women** *of* the land.
34: 3 His heart was drawn to Dinah **daughter** *of* Jacob, and he loved the
34: 5 When Jacob heard that his **daughter** Dinah had been defiled,
34: 7 done a disgraceful thing in Israel by lying with Jacob's **daughter**—
34: 8 to them, "My son Shechem has his heart set on your **daughter**.
34: 9 give us your **daughters** and take our daughters for yourselves.
34: 9 give us your daughters and take our **daughters** for yourselves.
34:16 we will give you our **daughters** and take your daughters for
34:16 will give you our daughters and take your **daughters** for ourselves.
34:17 you will not agree to be circumcised, we'll take our **sister** and go."
34:19 what they said, because he was delighted with Jacob's **daughter**.
34:21 for them. We can marry their **daughters** and they can marry ours.
34:21 We can marry their daughters and they can marry ours. **[RPH]**
36: 2 Esau took his wives from the **women** *of* Canaan: Adah daughter of
36: 2 Adah **daughter** *of* Elon the Hittite, and Oholibamah daughter of
36: 2 Oholibamah **daughter** *of* Anah and granddaughter of Zibeon the
36: 2 daughter of Anah and **granddaughter** *of* Zibeon the Hivite—
36: 3 also Basemath **daughter** *of* Ishmael and sister of Nebaioth.
36: 6 Esau took his wives and sons and **daughters** and all the members
36:14 The sons of Esau's wife Oholibamah **daughter** *of* Anah
36:14 wife Oholibamah daughter of Anah and **granddaughter** *of* Zibeon,
36:18 chiefs descended from Esau's wife Oholibamah **daughter** *of* Anah.
36:25 The children of Anah: Dishon and Oholibamah **daughter** *of* Anah.
36:39 and his wife's name was Mehetabel **daughter** *of* Matred,
36:39 was Mehetabel daughter of Matred, the **daughter** *of* Me-Zahab.
37:35 All his sons and **daughters** came to comfort him, but he refused to
38: 2 There Judah met the **daughter** *of* a Canaanite man named Shua.
38:12 After a long time Judah's wife, the **daughter** *of* Shua, died.
41:45 and gave him Asenath **daughter** *of* Potiphera,
41:50 two sons were born to Joseph by Asenath **daughter** *of* Potiphera,
46: 7 his sons and grandsons and his **daughters** and granddaughters—
46: 7 his daughters and **granddaughters** [+1201]—all his offspring.
46:15 Leah bore to Jacob in Paddan Aram, besides his **daughter** Dinah.
46:15 These sons and **daughters** *of* his were thirty-three in all.
46:18 to Jacob by Zilpah, whom Laban had given to his **daughter** Leah—
46:20 Ephraim were born to Joseph by Asenath **daughter** *of* Potiphera,
46:25 Jacob by Bilhah, whom Laban had given to his **daughter** Rachel—
49:22 a fruitful vine near a spring, whose **branches** climb over a wall.
Ex 1:16 delivery stool, if it is a boy, kill him; but if it is a **girl**, let her live."
1:22 that is born you must throw into the Nile, but let every **girl** live."
2: 1 Now a man of the house of Levi married a Levite **woman**,
2: 5 Then Pharaoh's **daughter** went down to the Nile to bathe,
2: 7 his sister asked Pharaoh's **daughter**, "Shall I go and get one of the
2: 8 "Yes, go," **she**[s] [+7281] answered. And the girl went and got the
2: 9 Pharaoh's **daughter** said to her, "Take this baby and nurse him for
2:10 she took him to Pharaoh's **daughter** and he became her son.
2:16 Now a priest of Midian had seven **daughters**, and they came to
2:20 "And where is he?" he asked his **daughters**. "Why did you leave
2:21 the man, who gave his **daughter** Zipporah to Moses in marriage.
3:22 and for clothing, which you will put on your sons and **daughters**.
6:23 **daughter** *of* Amminadab and sister of Nahshon, and she bore him
6:25 Eleazar son of Aaron married one of the **daughters** *of* Putiel,
10: 9 "We will go with our young and old, with our sons and **daughters**,
20:10 neither you, nor your son or **daughter**, nor your manservant
21: 4 his master gives him a wife and she bears him sons or **daughters**,
21: 7 "If a man sells his **daughter** as a servant, she is not to go free as
21: 9 selects her for his son, he must grant her the rights of a **daughter**.
21:31 This law also applies if the bull gores a son or **daughter**.
32: 2 your sons and your **daughters** are wearing, and bring them to me."
34:16 when you choose some of their **daughters** as wives for your sons
34:16 your sons and those **daughters** prostitute themselves to their gods,
Lev 10:14 your sons and your **daughters** may eat the breast that was waved
11:16 the **horned owl** [+3613], the screech owl, the gull, any kind of
12: 6 the days of her purification for a son or **daughter** are over,
14:10 day he must bring two male lambs and one ewe lamb a year **old**,
18: 9 either your father's **daughter** or your mother's daughter,
18: 9 either your father's daughter or your mother's **daughter**,
18:10 " 'Do not have sexual relations with your son's **daughter** or your
18:10 relations with your son's daughter or your **daughter's** daughter;
18:10 relations with your son's daughter or your daughter's **daughter**;
18:11 " 'Do not have sexual relations with the **daughter** *of* your father's
18:17 not have sexual relations with both a woman and her **daughter**.
18:17 Do not have sexual relations with either her son's **daughter**
18:17 with either her son's daughter or her **daughter's** daughter;
18:17 with either her son's daughter or her daughter's **daughter**;
19:29 " 'Do not degrade your **daughter** by making her a prostitute,
20:17 marries his sister, the **daughter** *of* either his father or his mother,
20:17 his sister, the daughter of either his father or **[RPH]** his mother,
21: 2 such as his mother or father, his son or **daughter**, his brother,
21: 9 " 'If a priest's **daughter** defiles herself by becoming a prostitute,
22:12 If a priest's **daughter** marries anyone other than a priest, she may
22:13 But if a priest's **daughter** becomes a widow or is divorced,
24:11 mother's name was Shelomith, the **daughter** *of* Dibri the Danite.)
26:29 will eat the flesh of your sons and the flesh of your **daughters**.
Nu 6:14 a **year-old** [+9102] ewe lamb without defect for a sin offering,
15:27 he must bring a **year-old female** [+9102] goat for a sin offering.
18:11 this to you and your sons and **daughters** as your regular share.
18:19 I give to you and your sons and **daughters** as your regular share.
21:25 including Heshbon and all its **surrounding settlements**.
21:29 and his **daughters** as captives to Sihon king of the Amorites.
21:32 the Israelites captured its **surrounding settlements** and drove out
25: 1 men began to indulge in sexual immorality with Moabite **women**,
25:15 woman who was put to death was Cozbi **daughter** *of* Zur,
25:18 and their sister Cozbi, the **daughter** *of* a Midianite leader,
26:33 he had only **daughters**, whose names were Mahlah, Noah,
26:33 **whose**[s] [+7524] names were Mahlah, Noah, Hoglah, Milcah
26:46 (Asher had a **daughter** named Serah.)
26:59 a **descendant** *of* Levi, who was born to the Levites in Egypt.
27: 1 The **daughters** *of* Zelophehad son of Hepher, the son of Gilead,
27: 1 The names of the **daughters** were Mahlah, Noah, Hoglah,
27: 7 "What Zelophehad's **daughters** are saying is right. You must
27: 8 and leaves no son, turn his inheritance over to his **daughter**.
27: 9 If he has no **daughter**, give his inheritance to his brothers.
30:16 [30:17] a father and his young **daughter** still living in his house.
32:42 And Nobah captured Kenath and its **surrounding settlements**
36: 2 to give the inheritance of our brother Zelophehad to his **daughters**.
36: 6 This is what the LORD commands for Zelophehad's **daughters**:
36: 8 Every **daughter** who inherits land in any Israelite tribe must marry
36:10 So Zelophehad's **daughters** did as the LORD commanded
36:11 Zelophehad's **daughters**—Mahlah, Tirzah, Hoglah, Milcah
Dt 5:14 neither you, nor your son or **daughter**, nor your manservant
7: 3 Do not give your **daughters** to their sons or take their daughters
7: 3 your daughters to their sons or take their **daughters** for your sons,
12:12 you, your sons and **daughters**, your menservants
12:18 you, your sons and **daughters**, your menservants
12:31 burn their sons and **daughters** in the fire as sacrifices to their gods.
13: 6 [13:7] or your son or **daughter**, or the wife you love,
14:15 the **horned owl** [+3613], the screech owl, the gull, any kind of
16:11 you, your sons and **daughters**, your menservants
16:14 you, your sons and **daughters**, your menservants
18:10 be found among you who sacrifices his son or **daughter** in the fire,
22:16 "I gave my **daughter** in marriage to this man, but he dislikes her.
22:17 and said, 'I did not find your **daughter** to be a virgin.'
22:17 to be a virgin.' But here is the proof of my **daughter's** virginity."
23:17 [23:18] Israelite man or **woman** is to become a shrine prostitute.
27:22 the **daughter** *of* his father or the daughter of his mother."
27:22 the daughter of his father or the **daughter** *of* his mother."
28:32 Your sons and **daughters** will be given to another nation,
28:41 You will have sons and **daughters** but you will not keep them,
28:53 of the sons and **daughters** the LORD your God has given you.

Dt 28:56 will begrudge the husband she loves and her own son or **daughter**
32:19 rejected them because he was angered by his sons and **daughters**.
Jos 7:24 his sons and **daughters**, his cattle, donkeys and sheep, his tent
15:16 "I will give my **daughter** Acsah in marriage to the man who
15:17 took it; so Caleb gave his **daughter** Acsah to him in marriage.
15:45 Ekron, with its **surrounding settlements** and villages;
15:47 Ashdod, its **surrounding settlements** and villages; and Gaza,
15:47 and Gaza, its **settlements** and villages, as far as the Wadi of Egypt
17: 3 of Makir, the son of Manasseh, had no sons but only **daughters**,
17: 3 but only daughters, **whose**˚ [+465+2257] names were Mahlah,
17: 6 because the **daughters** *of* the tribe of Manasseh received an
17:11 **[RPH]** Ibleam and the people of Dor, Endor, Taanach and
17:11 Ibleam **[RPH]** and the people of Dor, Endor, Taanach and
17:11 and the people of Dor, **[RPH]** Endor, Taanach and Megiddo,
17:11 and the people of Dor, Endor, **[RPH]** Taanach and Megiddo,
17:11 and the people of Dor, Endor, Taanach **[RPH]** and Megiddo,
17:11 together with their **surrounding settlements** (the third in the list is
17:16 both those in Beth Shan and its **settlements** and those in the Valley
Jdg 1:12 "I will give my **daughter** Acsah in marriage to the man who
1:13 took it; so Caleb gave his **daughter** Acsah to him in marriage.
1:27 or **[RPH]** Taanach or Dor or Ibleam or Megiddo and their
1:27 or Taanach **[RPH]** or Dor or Ibleam or Megiddo and their
1:27 or Taanach or Dor **[RPH]** or Ibleam or Megiddo and their
1:27 or Taanach or Dor or Ibleam **[RPH]** or Megiddo and their
1:27 or Ibleam or Megiddo and their **surrounding settlements**,
3: 6 They took their **daughters** in marriage and gave their own
3: 6 daughters in marriage and gave their own **daughters** to their sons,
11:26 **[RPH]** Aroer, the surrounding settlements and all the towns along
11:26 the **surrounding settlements** and all the towns along the Arnon.
11:34 who should come out to meet him but his **daughter**, dancing to the
11:34 was an only child. Except for her he had neither son nor **daughter**.
11:35 he saw her, he tore his clothes and cried, "Oh! My **daughter**!
11:40 that each year the **young women** *of* Israel go out for four days to
11:40 four days to commemorate the **daughter** *of* Jephthah the Gileadite.
12: 9 He had thirty sons and thirty **daughters**. He gave his daughters
12: 9 for his sons he brought in thirty **young women** as wives from
14: 1 went down to Timnah and saw there a **young** Philistine woman.
14: 2 and mother, "I have seen a Philistine **[RPH]** woman in Timnah;
14: 3 "Isn't there an acceptable woman among **[RPH]** your relatives
19:24 Look, here is my virgin **daughter**, and his concubine. I will bring
21: 1 "Not one of us will give his **daughter** in marriage to a Benjamite."
21: 7 the LORD not to give them any of our **daughters in marriage**?"
21:18 We can't give them our **daughters** as wives, since we Israelites
21:21 When the **girls** *of* Shiloh come out to join in the dancing, then rush
21:21 the vineyards and each of you seize a wife from the **girls** *of* Shiloh
Ru 1:11 Naomi said, "Return home, my **daughters**. Why would you come
1:12 Return home, my **daughters**; I am too old to have another
1:13 No, my **daughters**. It is more bitter for me than for you,
2: 2 eyes I find favor." Naomi said to her, "Go ahead, my **daughter**."
2: 8 So Boaz said to Ruth, "My **daughter**, listen to me. Don't go
2:22 "It will be good for you, my **daughter**, to go with his girls,
3: 1 "My **daughter**, should I not try to find a home for you, where you
3:10 "The LORD bless you, my **daughter**," he replied. "This kindness
3:11 now, my **daughter**, don't be afraid. I will do for you all you ask.
3:16 her mother-in-law, Naomi asked, "How did it go, my **daughter**?"
3:18 Naomi said, "Wait, my **daughter**, until you find out what happens.
1Sa 1: 4 of the meat to his wife Peninnah and to all her sons and **daughters**.
1:16 Do not take your servant for a wicked **woman**; I have been praying
2:21 she conceived and gave birth to three sons and two **daughters**.
8:13 He will take your **daughters** to be perfumers and cooks
14:49 The name of his older **daughter** was Merab, and that of the
14:50 His wife's name was Ahinoam **daughter** *of* Ahimaaz. The name of
17:25 He will also give him his **daughter** in marriage and will exempt
18:17 Saul said to David, "Here is my older **daughter** Merab. I will give
18:19 the time came for Merab, Saul's **daughter**, to be given to David,
18:20 Now Saul's **daughter** Michal was in love with David, and when
18:27 Then Saul gave him his **daughter** Michal in marriage.
18:28 was with David and that his **daughter** Michal loved David,
25:44 Saul had given his **daughter** Michal, David's wife, to Paltiel son
30: 3 by fire and their wives and sons and **daughters** taken captive.
30: 6 each one was bitter in spirit because of his sons and **daughters**.
30:19 young or old, boy or **girl**, plunder or anything else they had taken.
2Sa 1:20 streets of Ashkelon, lest the **daughters** *of* the Philistines be glad,
1:20 be glad, lest the **daughters** *of* the uncircumcised rejoice.
1:24 "O **daughters** *of* Israel, weep for Saul, who clothed you in scarlet
3: 3 Absalom the son of Maacah **daughter** *of* Talmai king of Geshur;
3: 7 Now Saul had had a concubine named Rizpah **daughter** *of* Aiah.
3:13 not come into my presence unless you bring Michal **daughter** *of*
5:13 in Jerusalem, and more sons and **daughters** were born to him.
6:16 City of David, Michal **daughter** *of* Saul watched from a window.
6:20 Michal **daughter** *of* Saul came out to meet him and said,
6:23 Michal **daughter** *of* Saul had no children to the day of her death.
11: 3 the **daughter** *of* Eliam and the wife of Uriah the Hittite?"
12: 3 his cup and even slept in his arms. It was like a **daughter** to him.
13:18 for this was the kind of garment the virgin **daughters** *of* the king
14:27 Three sons and a **daughter** were born to Absalom. The daughter's
17:25 the **daughter** *of* Nahash and sister of Zeruiah the mother of Joab.
19: 5 [19:6] the lives of your sons and **daughters** and the lives of your
21: 8 and Mephibosheth, the two sons of Aiah's **daughter** Rizpah,
21: 8 to Saul, together with the five sons of Saul's **daughter** Merab,
21:10 Rizpah **daughter** *of* Aiah took sackcloth and spread it out for
21:11 When David was told what Aiah's **daughter** Rizpah,
1Ki 3: 1 an alliance with Pharaoh king of Egypt and married his **daughter**.
4:11 in Naphoth Dor (he was married to Taphath **daughter** *of*
4:15 in Naphtali (he had married Basemath **daughter** *of* Solomon);
7: 8 Solomon also made a palace like this hall for Pharaoh's **daughter**,
9:16 and then gave it as a wedding gift to his **daughter**,
9:24 After Pharaoh's **daughter** had come up from the City of David to
11: 1 loved many foreign women besides Pharaoh's **daughter**—
15: 2 His mother's name was Maacah **daughter** *of* Abishalom.
15:10 His grandmother's name was Maacah **daughter** *of* Abishalom.
16:31 he also married Jezebel **daughter** *of* Ethbaal king of the Sidonians,
22:42 His mother's name was Azubah **daughter** *of* Shilhi.
2Ki 8:18 the house of Ahab had done, for he married a **daughter** *of* Ahab.
8:26 name was Athaliah, a **granddaughter** *of* Omri king of Israel.
9:34 he said, "and bury her, for she was a king's **daughter**."
11: 2 the **daughter** *of* King Jehoram and sister of Ahaziah,
14: 9 to a cedar in Lebanon, 'Give your **daughter** to my son in marriage.'
15:33 sixteen years. His mother's name was Jerusha **daughter** *of* Zadok.
17:17 They sacrificed their sons and **daughters** in the fire. They
18: 2 His mother's name was Abijah **daughter** *of* Zechariah.
19:21 " 'The Virgin **Daughter** *of* Zion despises you and mocks you.
19:21 The **Daughter** *of* Jerusalem tosses her head as you flee.
21:19 His mother's name was Meshullemeth **daughter** *of* Haruz;
22: 1 His mother's name was Jedidah **daughter** *of* Adaiah; she was from
23:10 could use it to sacrifice his son or **daughter** in the fire to Molech.
23:31 His mother's name was Hamutal **daughter** *of* Jeremiah; she was
23:36 His mother's name was Zebidah **daughter** *of* Pedaiah; she was
24: 8 His mother's name was Nehushta **daughter** *of* Elnathan; she was
24:18 His mother's name was Hamutal **daughter** *of* Jeremiah; she was
1Ch 1:50 and his wife's name was Mehetabel **daughter** *of* Matred,
1:50 was Mehetabel daughter of Matred, the **daughter** *of* Me-Zahab.
2: 3 were born to him by a Canaanite woman, the **daughter** *of* Shua.
2:21 Hezron lay with the **daughter** *of* Makir the father of Gilead (he
2:23 as well as Kenath with its **surrounding settlements**—
2:34 Sheshan had no sons—only **daughters**. He had an Egyptian
2:35 Sheshan gave his **daughter** in marriage to his servant Jarha,
2:49 the father of Macbenah and Gibea. Caleb's **daughter** was Acsah.
3: 2 Absalom the son of Maacah **daughter** *of* Talmai king of Geshur;
3: 5 and Solomon. These four were by Bathsheba **daughter** *of* Ammiel.
4:18 These were the children of Pharaoh's **daughter** Bithiah,
4:27 Shimei had sixteen sons and six **daughters**, but his brothers did
5:16 The Gadites lived in Gilead, in Bashan and its **outlying villages**,
7:15 descendant was named Zelophehad, who had only **daughters**.
7:24 His **daughter** was Sheerah, who built Lower and Upper Beth
7:28 and settlements included Bethel and its **surrounding villages**,
7:28 Gezer and its **villages** to the west, and Shechem and its villages all
7:28 and Shechem and its **villages** all the way to Ayyah and its villages.
7:28 and Shechem and its villages all the way to Ayyah and its **villages**.
7:29 **[RPH]** Taanach, Megiddo and Dor, together with their villages.
7:29 Taanach, **[RPH]** Megiddo and Dor, together with their villages.
7:29 Taanach, Megiddo and **[RPH]** Dor, together with their villages.
7:29 Taanach, Megiddo and Dor, together with their **villages**.
8:12 Shemed (who built Ono and Lod with its **surrounding villages**),
14: 3 more wives and became the father of more sons and **daughters**.
15:29 City of David, Michal **daughter** *of* Saul watched from a window.
18: 1 and its **surrounding villages** from the control of the Philistines.
23:22 he had only **daughters**. Their cousins, the sons of Kish,
25: 5 to exalt him. God gave Heman fourteen sons and three **daughters**.
2Ch 2:14 [2:13] whose mother was from **[NIE]** Dan and whose father was
8:11 Solomon brought Pharaoh's **daughter** up from the City of David
11:18 who was the **daughter** [K 1201] *of* David's son Jerimoth
11:18 son Jerimoth and of Abihail, the **daughter** *of* Jesse's son Eliab.
11:20 he married Maacah **daughter** *of* Absalom, who bore him Abijah,
11:21 Rehoboam loved Maacah **daughter** *of* Absalom more than any of
11:21 and sixty concubines, twenty-eight sons and sixty **daughters**.
13: 2 His mother's name was Maacah, a **daughter** *of* Uriel of Gibeah.
13:19 **[RPH]** Jeshanah and Ephron, with their surrounding villages.
13:19 Jeshanah **[RPH]** and Ephron, with their surrounding villages.
13:19 of Bethel, Jeshanah and Ephron, with their **surrounding villages**.
13:21 fourteen wives and had twenty-two sons and sixteen **daughters**.
20:31 His mother's name was Azubah **daughter** *of* Shilhi.
21: 6 the house of Ahab had done, for he married a **daughter** *of* Ahab.
22: 2 His mother's name was Athaliah, a **granddaughter** *of* Omri.
22:11 Jehosheba, the **daughter** *of* King Jehoram, took Joash son of
22:11 the **daughter** *of* King Jehoram and wife of the priest Jehoiada,
24: 3 Jehoiada chose two wives for him, and he had sons and **daughters**.
25:18 to a cedar in Lebanon, 'Give your **daughter** to my son in marriage.'

2Ch 27: 1 sixteen years. His mother's name was Jerusha **daughter** *of* Zadok.
28: 8 their kinsmen two hundred thousand wives, sons and **daughters**.
28: 18 and Gederoth, as well as Soco, **[RPH]** Timnah and Gimzo,
28: 18 and Gederoth, as well as Soco, Timnah **[RPH]** and Gimzo,
28: 18 well as Soco, Timnah and Gimzo, with their **surrounding villages**.
29: 1 His mother's name was Abijah **daughter** *of* Zechariah.
29: 9 and why our sons and **daughters** and our wives are in captivity.
31: 18 **daughters** of the whole community listed in these genealogical
Ezr 2: 61 Barzillai (a man who had married a **daughter** *of* Barzillai the
9: 2 They have taken some of their **daughters** as wives for themselves
9: 12 do not give your **daughters** in marriage to their sons or take their
9: 12 in marriage to their sons or take their **daughters** for your sons.
Ne 3: 12 repaired the next section with the help of his **daughters**.
4: 14 [4:8] your sons and your **daughters**, your wives and your
5: 2 were saying, "We and our sons and **daughters** are numerous;
5: 5 yet we have to subject our sons and **daughters** to slavery.
5: 5 Some of our **daughters** have already been enslaved, but we are
6: 18 his son Jehohanan had married the **daughter** *of* Meshullam son of
7: 63 Barzillai (a man who had married a **daughter** *of* Barzillai the
10: 28 [10:29] all their sons and **daughters** who are able to understand—
10: 30 [10:31] "We promise not to give our **daughters** in marriage to the
10: 30 [10:31] peoples around us or take their **daughters** for our sons.
11: 25 of Judah lived in Kiriath Arba and its **surrounding settlements**,
11: 25 in Dibon and its **settlements**, in Jekabzeel and its villages,
11: 27 in Hazar Shual, in Beersheba and its **settlements**,
11: 28 in Ziklag, in Meconah and its **settlements**,
11: 30 in Lachish and its fields, and in Azekah and its **settlements**.
11: 31 from Geba lived in Micmash, Aija, Bethel and its **settlements**,
13: 25 "You are not to give your **daughters** in marriage to their sons,
13: 25 nor are you to take their **daughters** in marriage for your sons
Est 2: 7 Mordecai had a **cousin** [+1856] named Hadassah, whom he had
2: 7 and Mordecai had taken her as his own **daughter** when her father
2: 15 When the turn came for Esther (the girl Mordecai *had* **adopted** [+4200+4200+4374], the daughter of his uncle Abihail) to go to the
2: 15 (the girl Mordecai had adopted, the **daughter** *of* his uncle Abihail)
9: 29 So Queen Esther, **daughter** *of* Abihail, along with Mordecai the
Job 1: 2 He had seven sons and three **daughters**,
1: 13 One day when Job's sons and **daughters** were feasting
1: 18 "Your sons and **daughters** were feasting and drinking wine at the
30: 29 I have become a brother of jackals, a companion of **owls** [+3613].
42: 13 And he also had seven sons and three **daughters**.
42: 15 the land were there found women as beautiful as Job's **daughters**,
Ps 9: 14 [9:15] declare your praises in the gates of the **Daughter** *of* Zion
17: 8 Keep me as the **apple of** [+413] your eye; hide me in the shadow
45: 9 [45:10] **Daughters** *of* kings are among your honored women;
45: 10 [45:11] Listen, O **daughter**, consider and give ear: Forget your
45: 12 [45:13] The **Daughter** *of* Tyre will come with a gift, men of
45: 13 [45:14] All glorious is the **princess** [+4889] within ˻her chamber˼;
48: 11 [48:12] the **villages** *of* Judah are glad because of your judgments.
97: 8 Zion hears and rejoices and the **villages** *of* Judah are glad
106: 37 They sacrificed their sons and their **daughters** to demons.
106: 38 They shed innocent blood, the blood of their sons and **daughters**,
137: 8 O **Daughter** *of* Babylon, doomed to destruction, happy is he who
144: 12 and our **daughters** will be like pillars carved to adorn a palace.
Pr 30: 15 "The leech has two **daughters**. 'Give! Give!' they cry. "There are
31: 29 "Many **women** do noble things, but you surpass them all."
Ecc 12: 4 rise up at the sound of birds, but all their **songs** [+8877] grow faint;
SS 1: 5 Dark am I, yet lovely, O **daughters** *of* Jerusalem, dark like the
2: 2 Like a lily among thorns is my darling among the **maidens**.
2: 7 **Daughters** *of* Jerusalem, I charge you by the gazelles and by the
3: 5 **Daughters** *of* Jerusalem, I charge you by the gazelles and by the
3: 10 its interior lovingly inlaid by the **daughters** *of* Jerusalem.
3: 11 Come out, you **daughters** *of* Zion, and look at King Solomon
5: 8 O **daughters** *of* Jerusalem, I charge you—if you find my lover,
5: 16 This is my lover, this my friend, O **daughters** *of* Jerusalem.
6: 9 The **maidens** saw her and called her blessed; the queens
7: 1 [7:2] How beautiful your sandaled feet, O prince's **daughter**!
8: 4 **Daughters** *of* Jerusalem, I charge you: Do not arouse or awaken
Isa 1: 8 The **Daughter** *of* Zion is left like a shelter in a vineyard, like a hut
3: 16 The LORD says, "The **women** *of* Zion are haughty, walking
3: 17 Therefore the Lord will bring sores on the heads of the **women** *of*
4: 4 The Lord will wash away the filth of the **women** *of* Zion; he will
10: 30 Cry out, O **Daughter** *of* Gallim! Listen, O Laishah!
10: 32 they will shake their fist at the mount of the **Daughter** [K 1074] *of*
13: 21 there the **owls** [+3613] will dwell, and there the wild goats will
16: 1 from Sela, across the desert, to the mount of the **Daughter** *of* Zion.
16: 2 from the nest, so are the **women** *of* Moab at the fords of the Arnon.
22: 4 not try to console me over the destruction of my **people** [+6639]."
23: 10 Till your land as along the Nile, O **Daughter** *of* Tarshish,
23: 12 more of your reveling, O Virgin **Daughter** *of* Sidon, now crushed!
32: 9 to me; you **daughters** who feel secure, hear what I have to say!
34: 13 She will become a haunt for jackals, a home for **owls** [+3613].
37: 22 "The Virgin **Daughter** *of* Zion despises and mocks you.
37: 22 The **Daughter** *of* Jerusalem tosses her head as you flee.
43: 6 my sons from afar and my **daughters** from the ends of the earth—
43: 20 The wild animals honor me, the jackals and the **owls** [+3613],
47: 1 "Go down, sit in the dust, Virgin **Daughter** *of* Babylon; sit on the
47: 1 sit on the ground without a throne, **Daughter** *of* the Babylonians.
47: 5 "Sit in silence, go into darkness, **Daughter** *of* the Babylonians;
49: 22 sons in their arms and carry your **daughters** on their shoulders.
52: 2 from the chains on your neck, O captive **Daughter** *of* Zion.
56: 5 its walls a memorial and a name better than sons and **daughters**;
60: 4 sons come from afar, and your **daughters** are carried on the arm.
62: 11 "Say to the **Daughter** *of* Zion, 'See, your Savior comes! See,
Jer 3: 24 fathers' labor—their flocks and herds, their sons and **daughters**.
4: 11 the barren heights in the desert blows toward my **people** [+6639],
4: 31 the cry of the **Daughter** *of* Zion gasping for breath, stretching out
5: 17 devour your harvests and food, devour your sons and **daughters**;
6: 2 I will destroy the **Daughter** *of* Zion, so beautiful and delicate.
6: 23 like men in battle formation to attack you, O **Daughter** *of* Zion."
6: 26 O my **people** [+6639], put on sackcloth and roll in ashes; mourn
7: 31 of Ben Hinnom to burn their sons and **daughters** in the fire—
8: 11 They dress the wound of my **people** [+6639] as though it were not
8: 19 Listen to the cry of my **people** [+6639] from a land far away:
8: 21 Since my **people** [+6639] are crushed, I am crushed; I mourn,
8: 22 then is there no healing for the wound of my **people** [+6639]?
9: 1 [8:23] weep day and night for the slain of my **people** [+6639].
9: 7 [9:6] what else can I do because of the sin of my **people** [+6639]?
9: 20 [9:19] Teach your **daughters** how to wail; teach one another a
11: 22 men will die by the sword, their sons and **daughters** by famine.
14: 16 no one to bury them or their wives, their sons or their **daughters**.
14: 17 and day without ceasing; for my virgin **daughter**—my people—
16: 2 "You must not marry and have sons or **daughters** in this place."
16: 3 **daughters** born in this land and about the women who are their
19: 9 I will make them eat the flesh of their sons and **daughters**,
29: 6 Marry and have sons and **daughters**; find wives for your sons
29: 6 find wives for your sons and give your **daughters** in marriage,
29: 6 in marriage, so that they too may have sons and **daughters**.
31: 22 How long will you wander, O unfaithful **daughter**? The LORD
32: 35 of Ben Hinnom to sacrifice their sons and **daughters** to Molech,
35: 8 nor our wives nor our sons and **daughters** have ever drunk wine
41: 10 the king's **daughters** along with all the others who were left there,
43: 6 the king's **daughters** whom Nebuzaradan commander of the
46: 11 "Go up to Gilead and get balm, O Virgin **Daughter** *of* Egypt.
46: 19 you who live in **Egypt** [+5213], for Memphis will be laid waste
46: 24 The **Daughter** *of* Egypt will be put to shame, handed over to the
48: 18 sit on the parched ground, O inhabitants of the **Daughter** *of* Dibon,
48: 46 your sons are taken into exile and your **daughters** into captivity.
49: 2 a mound of ruins, and its **surrounding villages** will be set on fire.
49: 3 Cry out, O **inhabitants** *of* Rabbah! Put on sackcloth and mourn;
49: 4 O unfaithful **daughter**, you trust in your riches and say, 'Who will
50: 39 and hyenas will live there, and there the **owl** [+3613] will dwell.
50: 42 men in battle formation to attack you, O **Daughter** *of* Babylon.
51: 33 "The **Daughter** *of* Babylon is like a threshing floor at the time it is
52: 1 His mother's name was Hamutal **daughter** *of* Jeremiah; she was
La 1: 6 All the splendor has departed from the **Daughter** *of* Zion.
1: 15 In his winepress the Lord has trampled the Virgin **Daughter** *of*
2: 1 How the Lord has covered the **Daughter** *of* Zion with the cloud of
2: 2 in his wrath he has torn down the strongholds of the **Daughter** *of*
2: 4 he has poured out his wrath like fire on the tent of the **Daughter** *of*
2: 5 multiplied mourning and lamentation for the **Daughter** *of* Judah.
2: 8 determined to tear down the wall around the **Daughter** *of* Zion.
2: 10 The elders of the **Daughter** *of* Zion sit on the ground in silence;
2: 11 out on the ground because my **people** [+6639] are destroyed,
2: 13 With what can I compare you, O **Daughter** *of* Jerusalem?
2: 13 I liken you, that I may comfort you, O Virgin **Daughter** *of* Zion?
2: 15 they scoff and shake their heads at the **Daughter** *of* Jerusalem:
2: 18 O wall of the **Daughter** *of* Zion, let your tears flow like a river day
2: 18 and night; give yourself no relief, your **eyes** [+6524] no rest.
3: 48 tears flow from my eyes because my **people** [+6639] are destroyed.
3: 51 I see brings grief to my soul because of all the **women** *of* my city.
4: 3 my **people** [+6639] have become heartless like ostriches in the
4: 6 The punishment of my **people** [+6639] is greater than that of
4: 10 who became their food when my **people** [+6639] were destroyed.
4: 21 Rejoice and be glad, O **Daughter** *of* Edom, you who live in the
4: 22 O **Daughter** *of* Zion, your punishment will end; he will not
4: 22 But, O **Daughter** *of* Edom, he will punish your sin and expose
Eze 13: 17 set your face against the **daughters** *of* your people who prophesy
14: 16 men were in it, they could not save their own sons or **daughters**.
14: 18 men were in it, they could not save their own sons or **daughters**.
14: 20 and Job were in it, they could save neither son nor **daughter**.
14: 22 sons and **daughters** who will be brought out of it.
16: 20 " 'And you took your sons and **daughters** whom you bore to me
16: 27 the **daughters** *of* the Philistines, who were shocked by your lewd
16: 44 will quote this proverb about you: "Like mother, like **daughter**."
16: 45 You are a true **daughter** *of* your mother, who despised her
16: 46 was Samaria, who lived to the north of you with her **daughters**;
16: 46 who lived to the south of you with her **daughters**, was Sodom.

Eze 16:48 your sister Sodom and her **daughters** never did what you and your
16:48 her daughters never did what you and your **daughters** have done.
16:49 She and her **daughters** were arrogant, overfed and unconcerned;
16:53 of Sodom and her **daughters** and of Samaria and her daughters,
16:53 of Sodom and her daughters and of Samaria and her **daughters**,
16:55 Sodom with her **daughters** and Samaria with her daughters,
16:55 Sodom with her daughters and Samaria with her **daughters**,
16:55 and you and your **daughters** will return to what you were before.
16:57 you are now scorned by the **daughters** *of* Edom and all her
16:57 and all her neighbors and the **daughters** *of* the Philistines—
16:61 I will give them to you as **daughters**, but not on the basis of my
22:11 and another violates his sister, his own father's **daughter**.
23:2 of man, there were two women, **daughters** *of* the same mother.
23:4 They were mine and gave birth to sons and **daughters**. Oholah is
23:10 took away her sons and **daughters** and killed her with the sword.
23:25 They will take away your sons and **daughters**, and those of you
23:47 they will kill their sons and **daughters** and burn down their houses.
24:21 The sons and **daughters** you left behind will fall by the sword.
24:25 their heart's desire, and their sons and **daughters** as well—
26:6 and her **settlements** on the mainland will be ravaged by the sword.
26:8 He will ravage your **settlements** on the mainland with the sword;
27:6 of [BHS *daughter of Assyria*; NIV 928] cypress wood from the
30:18 will be covered with clouds, and her **villages** will go into captivity.
32:16 The **daughters** *of* the nations will chant it; for Egypt and all her
32:18 to the earth below both her and the **daughters** *of* mighty nations,
44:25 his father or mother, son or **daughter**, brother or unmarried sister,
Da 11:6 The **daughter** *of* the king of the South will go to the king of the
11:17 he will give him a **daughter** in marriage in order to overthrow the
Hos 1:3 So he married Gomer **daughter** *of* Diblaim, and she conceived
1:6 Gomer conceived again and gave birth to a **daughter**.
4:13 Therefore your **daughters** turn to prostitution and your
4:14 "I will not punish your **daughters** when they turn to prostitution,
Joel 2:28 [3:1] Your sons and **daughters** will prophesy, your old men will
3:8 [4:8] I will sell your sons and **daughters** to the people of Judah,
Am 7:17 in the city, and your sons and **daughters** will fall by the sword.
Mic 1:8 and naked. I will howl like a jackal and moan like an **owl** [+3613].
1:13 You were the beginning of sin to the **Daughter** *of* Zion,
4:8 O watchtower of the flock, O stronghold of the **Daughter** *of* Zion,
4:8 restored to you; kingship will come to the **Daughter** *of* Jerusalem."
4:10 Writhe in agony, O **Daughter** *of* Zion, like a woman in labor,
4:13 "Rise and thresh, O **Daughter** *of* Zion, for I will give you horns of
5:1 [4:14] Marshal your troops, O **city** *of* troops, for a siege is laid
7:6 a son dishonors his father, a **daughter** rises up against her mother,
Zep 3:10 Cush my worshipers, my scattered **people**, will bring me offerings.
3:14 Sing, O **Daughter** *of* Zion; shout aloud, O Israel! Be glad
3:14 and rejoice with all your heart, O **Daughter** *of* Jerusalem!
Zec 2:7 [2:11] Escape, you who live in the **Daughter** *of* Babylon!"
2:10 [2:14] "Shout and be glad, O **Daughter** *of* Zion. For I am coming,
9:9 Rejoice greatly, O **Daughter** *of* Zion! Shout, Daughter of
9:9 Shout, **Daughter** *of* Jerusalem! See, your king comes to you,
Mal 2:11 the LORD loves, by marrying the **daughter** *of* a foreign god.

1427 ²בַּת *bat²*, n.m. & f. [13 / 14] [→ Ar 10126]

baths [8], bath [6]

1Ki 5:11 [5:25] in addition to twenty thousand **baths** [BHS 4123] *of*
7:26 the rim of a cup, like a lily blossom. It held two thousand **baths**.
7:38 each holding forty **baths** and measuring four cubits across,
2Ch 2:10 [2:9] twenty thousand **baths** of wine and twenty thousand baths
2:10 [2:9] baths of wine and twenty thousand **baths** of olive oil."
4:5 the rim of a cup, like a lily blossom. It held three thousand **baths**.
Isa 5:10 A ten-acre vineyard will produce only a **bath** of wine, a homer of
Eze 45:10 are to use accurate scales, an accurate ephah and an accurate **bath**.
45:11 The ephah and the **bath** are to be the same size, the bath containing
45:11 the **bath** containing a tenth of a homer and the ephah a tenth of a
45:14 The prescribed portion of oil, measured by the **bath**, is a tenth of a
45:14 is a tenth of a **bath** from each cor (which consists of ten baths
45:14 is a tenth of a bath from each cor (which consists of ten **baths**
45:14 of ten baths or one homer, for ten **baths** are equivalent to a homer).

1428 ³בַּת *bat³*, n.f. [1]

did weaving [+755] [1]

2Ki 23:7 of the LORD and where women **did weaving** [+755] for Asherah.

1429 בָּתָה *bātâ*, n.f. [1] [→ 1431?]

wasteland [1]

Isa 5:6 I will make it a **wasteland**, neither pruned nor cultivated,

1430 בֹּתָה *bōtâ*, var. Not used in NIV/BHS

1431 בַּתָּה *battâ*, n.f. [1] [√ 1429?]

steep [1]

Isa 7:19 They will all come and settle in the **steep** ravines and in the

1432 ¹בְּתוּאֵל *beṯû'ēl¹*, n.pr.m. [9] [√ 5493 + 446]

Bethuel [9]

Ge 22:22 Kesed, Hazo, Pildash, Jidlaph and **Bethuel**."
22:23 **Bethuel** became the father of Rebekah. Milcah bore these eight
24:15 She was the daughter of **Bethuel** son of Milcah, who was the wife
24:24 She answered him, "I am the daughter of **Bethuel**, the son that
24:47 "She said, 'The daughter of **Bethuel** son of Nahor, whom Milcah
24:50 Laban and **Bethuel** answered, "This is from the LORD; we can
25:20 Rebekah daughter of **Bethuel** the Aramean from Paddan Aram
28:2 to Paddan Aram, to the house of your mother's father **Bethuel**.
28:5 to Laban son of **Bethuel** the Aramean, the brother of Rebekah,

1433 ²בְּתוּאֵל *beṯû'ēl²*, n.pr.loc. [1] [cf. 1434?]

Bethuel [1]

1Ch 4:30 **Bethuel**, Hormah, Ziklag,

1434 בְּתוּל *beṯûl*, n.pr.loc. [1] [cf. 1433?]

Bethul [1]

Jos 19:4 Eltolad, **Bethul**, Hormah,

1435 בְּתוּלָה *beṯûlâ*, n.f. [51] [→ 1436]

virgin [25], maidens [7], virgins [6], young women [4], maiden [3], daughters [1], girl [1], girls [+5855] [1], unmarried [1], women [1], young woman [1]

Ge 24:16 The girl was very beautiful, a **virgin**; no man had ever lain with
Ex 22:16 [22:15] "If a man seduces a **virgin** who is not pledged to be
22:17 [22:16] her to him, he must still pay the bride-price for **virgins**.
Lev 21:3 or an **unmarried** sister who is dependent on him since she has no
21:14 defiled by prostitution, but only a **virgin** from his own people,
Dt 22:19 because this man has given an Israelite **virgin** a bad name.
22:23 If a man happens to meet in a town a **virgin** pledged to be married
22:28 If a man happens to meet a **virgin** who is not pledged to be married
32:25 Young men and **young women** will perish, infants and gray-haired
Jdg 19:24 Look, here is my **virgin** daughter, and his concubine. I will bring
21:12 four hundred young **women** who had never slept with a man,
2Sa 13:2 for she was a **virgin**, and it seemed impossible for him to do
13:18 for this was the kind of garment the **virgin** daughters of the king
1Ki 1:2 "Let us look for a young **virgin** to attend the king and take care of
2Ki 19:21 " 'The **Virgin** Daughter of Zion despises you and mocks you.
2Ch 36:17 and spared neither young man nor **young woman**, old man
Est 2:2 "Let a search be made for beautiful young **virgins** for the king.
2:3 these beautiful **girls** [+5855] into the harem at the citadel of Susa.
2:17 she won his favor and approval more than any of the other **virgins**.
2:19 When the **virgins** were assembled a second time, Mordecai was
Job 31:1 "I made a covenant with my eyes not to look lustfully at a **girl**.
Ps 45:14 [45:15] her **virgin** companions follow her and are brought to you.
78:63 their young men, and their **maidens** had no wedding songs;
148:12 young men and **maidens**, old men and children.
Isa 23:4 given birth; I have neither reared sons nor brought up **daughters**."
23:12 more of your reveling, O **Virgin** Daughter of Sidon, now crushed!
37:22 "The **Virgin** Daughter of Zion despises and mocks you.
47:1 "Go down, sit in the dust, **Virgin** Daughter of Babylon; sit on the
62:5 As a young man marries a **maiden**, so will your sons marry you;
Jer 2:32 Does a **maiden** forget her jewelry, a bride her wedding ornaments?
14:17 and day without ceasing; for my **virgin** daughter—my people—
18:13 like this? A most horrible thing has been done by **Virgin** Israel.
31:4 I will build you up again and you will be rebuilt, O **Virgin** Israel.
31:13 Then **maidens** will dance and be glad, young men and old as well.
31:21 road that you take. Return, O **Virgin** Israel, return to your towns.
46:11 "Go up to Gilead and get balm, O **Virgin** Daughter of Egypt.
51:22 old man and youth, with you I shatter young man and **maiden**,
La 1:4 her priests groan, her **maidens** grieve, and she is in bitter anguish.
1:15 In his winepress the Lord has trampled the **Virgin** Daughter of
1:18 my suffering. My young men and **maidens** have gone into exile.
2:10 The **young women** *of* Jerusalem have bowed their heads to the
2:13 I liken you, that I may comfort you, O **Virgin** Daughter of Zion?
2:21 the streets; my young men and **maidens** have fallen by the sword.
5:11 have been ravished in Zion, and **virgins** in the towns of Judah.
Eze 9:6 Slaughter old men, young men and **maidens**, women and children,
23:8 caressed her **virgin** bosom and poured out their lust upon her.
44:22 they may marry only **virgins** of Israelite descent or widows of
Joel 1:8 Mourn like a **virgin** in sackcloth grieving for the husband of her
Am 5:2 "Fallen is **Virgin** Israel, never to rise again, deserted in her own
8:13 "In that day "the lovely **young women** and strong young men will
Zec 9:17 will make the young men thrive, and new wine the **young women**.

1436 בְּתוּלִים b^etûlîm, n.f. [9] [√ 1435]
proof of virginity [3], never marry [2], be a virgin [+928] [1], proof that a virgin [1], to be a virgin [1], virgin [1]

Lev 21:13 " 'The woman he marries must **be a virgin** [+928].
Dt 22:14 but when I approached her, I did not find **proof of** her **virginity**,"
22:15 mother shall bring **proof that** she was **a virgin** to the town elders
22:17 slandered her and said, 'I did not find your daughter **to be a virgin**.'
22:17 to be a virgin.' But here is the **proof of** my daughter's **virginity**."
22:20 the charge is true and no **proof of** the girl's **virginity** can be found,
Jdg 11:37 the hills and weep with my friends, because I will **never marry**."
11:38 girls went into the hills and wept because she would **never marry**.
Eze 23:3 land their breasts were fondled and their **virgin** bosoms caressed.

1437 בִּתְיָה bityâ, n.pr.f. [1]
Bithiah [1]

1Ch 4:18 These were the children of Pharaoh's daughter **Bithiah**,

1438 בָּתַק bātaq, v. [1] [cf. 980]
hack to pieces [1]

Eze 16:40 [D] will stone you and **hack** you **to pieces** with their swords.

1439 בָּתַר bātar, v. [2] [→ 1440, 1441, 1443]
cut in half [1], cut [1]

Ge 15:10 [D] **cut** them in two and arranged the halves opposite each other;
15:10 [A] each other; the birds, however, *he did* not **cut in half**.

1440 בֶּתֶר¹ beter¹, n.m. [3] [√ 1439]
pieces [2], halves [1]

Ge 15:10 cut them in two and arranged the **halves** opposite each other;
Jer 34:18 like the calf they cut in two and then walked between its **pieces**.
34:19 all the people of the land who walked between the **pieces** *of* the

1441 בֶּתֶר² beter², n.m. [1] [√ 1439]
rugged [1]

SS 2:17 and be like a gazelle or like a young stag on the **rugged** hills.

1442 בַּת־רַבִּים bat-rabbîm, n.pr.loc. [1] [√ 1426 + 8049]
Bath Rabbim [1]

SS 7:4 [7:5] eyes are the pools of Heshbon by the gate of **Bath Rabbim**.

1443 בִּתְרוֹן bitrôn, n.[pr.loc.?]. [1] [√ 1439]
Bithron [1]

2Sa 2:29 continued through the whole **Bithron** and came to Mahanaim.

1444 בַּת־שֶׁבַע bat-šeba', n.pr.f. [11 / 12] [√ 1426 + 8682]
Bathsheba [12]

2Sa 11:3 The man said, "Isn't this **Bathsheba**, the daughter of Eliam
12:24 Then David comforted his wife **Bathsheba**, and he went to her
1Ki 1:11 Nathan asked **Bathsheba**, Solomon's mother, "Have you not heard
1:15 So **Bathsheba** went to see the aged king in his room, where
1:16 **Bathsheba** bowed low and knelt before the king. "What is it you
1:28 King David said, "Call in **Bathsheba**." So she came into the king's
1:31 Then **Bathsheba** bowed low with her face to the ground and,
2:13 Now Adonijah, the son of Haggith, went to **Bathsheba**, Solomon's
2:18 "Very well," **Bathsheba** replied, "I will speak to the king for you."
2:19 When **Bathsheba** went to King Solomon to speak to him for
1Ch 3:5 These four were by **Bathsheba** [BHS 1445] daughter of Ammiel.
Ps 51:T [51:2] him after David had committed adultery with **Bathsheba**.

1445 בַּת־שׁוּעַ bat-šûa', n.pr.f. [1 / 0] [√ 1426 + 8679?]

1Ch 3:5 These four were by Bathsheba [BHS *Bathshua*; NIV 1444]

ג, g

1446 ג g, letter. Not used in NIV/BHS [→ Ar 10127]

1447 גֵּא gē', a. [1] [√ 1448]
pride [1]

Isa 16:6 her overweening **pride** and conceit, her pride and her insolence—

1448 גָּאָה gā'â, v. [7] [→ 1447, 1449, 1450, 1452, 1454, 1455, 1456, 1575]
highly exalted [+1448] [4], grow tall [1], hold head high [1], risen [1]

Ex 15:1 [A] "I will sing to the LORD, for *he is* **highly exalted** [+1448].
15:1 [A] "I will sing to the LORD, for *he is* **highly exalted** [+1448].
15:21 [A] "Sing to the LORD, for *he is* **highly exalted** [+1448]. The
15:21 [A] "Sing to the LORD, for *he is* **highly exalted** [+1448]. The
Job 8:11 [A] *Can* papyrus **grow tall** where there is no marsh? Can reeds
10:16 [A] If I **hold** my **head high**, you stalk me like a lion and again
Eze 47:5 [A] because the water *had* **risen** and was deep enough to swim

1449 גֵּאָה gē'â, n.f. [1] [√ 1448]
pride [1]

Pr 8:13 I hate **pride** and arrogance, evil behavior and perverse speech.

1450 גֵּאֶה gē'eh, a. [8] [√ 1448]
proud [7], pride [1]

Job 40:11 fury of your wrath, look at every **proud** *man* and bring him low,
40:12 look at every **proud** *man* and humble him, crush the wicked where
Ps 94:2 O Judge of the earth; pay back to the **proud** what they deserve.
123:4 [much contempt from the **arrogant**. [Q +3561; see K 1456]]
140:5 [140:6] **Proud** *men* have hidden a snare for me; they have spread
Pr 15:25 The LORD tears down the **proud** *man's* house but he keeps the
16:19 and among the oppressed than to share plunder with the **proud**.
Isa 2:12 The LORD Almighty has a day in store for all the **proud**
Jer 48:29 her overweening **pride** and conceit, her pride and arrogance

1451 גְּאוּאֵל g^e'û'ēl, n.pr.m. [1] [√ 1447 + 446]
Geuel [1]

Nu 13:15 from the tribe of Gad, **Geuel** son of Maki.

1452 גַּאֲוָה ga'ᵃwâ, n.f. [19 / 18] [√ 1448]
pride [7], arrogance [2], majesty [2], back [1], conceit [1], glorious [1], proud [+6913] [1], proud [1], surging [1], triumph [1]

Dt 33:26 rides on the heavens to help you and on the clouds in his **majesty**.
33:29 He is your shield and helper and your **glorious** sword.
Job 41:15 [41:7] His back [BHS *His pride is*; NIV 1568] has rows of shields
Ps 10:2 In his **arrogance** the wicked man hunts down the weak, who are
31:18 [31:19] for with **pride** and contempt they speak arrogantly against
31:23 [31:24] the faithful, but the **proud** [+6913] he pays back in full.
36:11 [36:12] May the foot of the **proud** not come against me, nor the
46:3 [46:4] and foam and the mountains quake with their **surging**.
68:34 [68:35] Proclaim the power of God, whose **majesty** is over Israel,
73:6 Therefore **pride** is their necklace; they clothe themselves with
Pr 14:3 A fool's talk brings a rod to his **back**, but the lips of the wise
29:23 A man's **pride** brings him low, but a man of lowly spirit gains
Isa 9:9 [9:8] of Samaria—who say with **pride** and arrogance of heart,
13:3 warriors to carry out my wrath—those who rejoice in my **triumph**.
13:11 arrogance of the haughty and will humble the **pride** *of* the ruthless.
16:6 her overweening pride and **conceit**, her pride and her insolence—
25:11 God will bring down their **pride** despite the cleverness of their
Jer 48:29 her pride and **arrogance** and the haughtiness of her heart.
Zep 3:11 I will remove from this city those who rejoice in their **pride**.

1453 גְּאוּלִים g^e'ûlîm, n.m.pl.abst. [1] [√ 1457]
redemption [1]

Isa 63:4 was in my heart, and the year of my **redemption** has come.

1454 גָּאוֹן gā'ôn, n.m. [49] [√ 1448]
pride [23], majesty [6], arrogance [5], proud [5], thickets [3], splendor [2], arrogant [1], glory [1], lush thicket [1], majestic [1], pomp [1]

Ex 15:7 In the greatness of your **majesty** you threw down those who
Lev 26:19 I will break down your stubborn **pride** and make the sky above
Job 35:12 answer when men cry out because of the **arrogance** *of* the wicked.
37:4 comes the sound of his roar; he thunders with his **majestic** voice.
38:11 may come and no farther; here is where your **proud** waves halt'?
40:10 adorn yourself with **glory** and splendor, and clothe yourself in
Ps 47:4 [47:5] our inheritance for us, the **pride** *of* Jacob, whom he loved.
59:12 [59:13] the words of their lips, let them be caught in their **pride**.
Pr 8:13 I hate pride and **arrogance**, evil behavior and perverse speech.
16:18 **Pride** goes before destruction, a haughty spirit before a fall.
Isa 2:10 ground from dread of the LORD and the splendor of his **majesty**!
2:19 ground from dread of the LORD and the splendor of his **majesty**,
2:21 crags from dread of the LORD and the splendor of his **majesty**,
4:2 the fruit of the land will be the **pride** and glory of the survivors in
13:11 I will put an end to the **arrogance** *of* the haughty and will humble
13:19 the jewel of kingdoms, the glory of the Babylonians' **pride**,
14:11 All your **pomp** has been brought down to the grave, along with the

Isa 16: 6 We have heard of Moab's **pride**—her overweening pride
16: 6 her overweening pride and conceit, her **pride** and her insolence—
23: 9 to bring low the **pride** *of* all glory and to humble all who are
24: 14 shout for joy; from the west they acclaim the LORD's **majesty**.
60: 15 I will make you the everlasting **pride** and the joy of all
Jer 12: 5 safe country, how will you manage in the **thickets** *by* the Jordan?
13: 9 'In the same way I will ruin the **pride** *of* Judah and the great pride
13: 9 way I will ruin the pride of Judah and the great **pride** *of* Jerusalem.
48: 29 "We have heard of Moab's **pride**—her overweening pride
48: 29 her **pride** and arrogance and the haughtiness of her heart.
49: 19 "Like a lion coming up from Jordan's **thickets** to a rich
50: 44 Like a lion coming up from Jordan's **thickets** to a rich pastureland,
Eze 7: 20 They were **proud** of their beautiful jewelry and used it to make
7: 24 I will put an end to the **pride** *of* the mighty, and their sanctuaries
16: 49 She and her daughters were **arrogant**, overfed and unconcerned;
16: 56 not even mention your sister Sodom in the day of your **pride**,
24: 21 the stronghold in which you take **pride**, the delight of your eyes,
30: 6 " 'The allies of Egypt will fall and her **proud** strength will fail.
30: 18 the yoke of Egypt; there her **proud** strength will come to an end.
32: 12 They will shatter the **pride** *of* Egypt, and all her hordes will be
33: 28 land a desolate waste, and her **proud** strength will come to an end,
Hos 5: 5 Israel's **arrogance** testifies against them; the Israelites,
7: 10 Israel's **arrogance** testifies against him, but despite all this he does
Am 6: 8 "I abhor the **pride** *of* Jacob and detest his fortresses; I will deliver
8: 7 The LORD has sworn by the **Pride** *of* Jacob: "I will never forget
Mic 5: 4 [5:3] in the **majesty** *of* the name of the LORD his God.
Na 2: 2 [2:3] The LORD will restore the **splendor** *of* Jacob like the
2: 2 [2:3] will restore the splendor of Jacob like the **splendor** *of* Israel,
Zep 2: 10 This is what they will get in return for their **pride**, for insulting
Zec 9: 6 will occupy Ashdod, and I will cut off the **pride** *of* the Philistines.
10: 11 Assyria's **pride** will be brought down and Egypt's scepter will
11: 3 to the roar of the lions; the **lush thicket** *of* the Jordan is ruined!

1455 גֵּאוּת gē'ût, n.f. [8] [√ 1448]

majesty [2], pride [2], arrogance [1], column [1], glorious things [1], surging [1]

Ps 17: 10 up their callous hearts, and their mouths speak with **arrogance**.
89: 9 [89:10] You rule over the **surging** sea; when its waves mount up,
93: 1 The LORD reigns, he is robed in **majesty**; the LORD is robed in
Isa 9: 18 [9:17] so that it rolls upward in a **column** *of* smoke.
12: 5 Sing to the LORD, for he has done **glorious things**; let this be
26: 10 they go on doing evil and regard not the **majesty** *of* the LORD.
28: 1 Woe to that wreath, the **pride** *of* Ephraim's drunkards, to the
28: 3 That wreath, the **pride** *of* Ephraim's drunkards, will be trampled

1456 גַּאֲיוֹן ga'ᵃyôn, a. [1] [√ 1448]

arrogant [1]

Ps 123: 4 from the proud, much contempt from the **arrogant**. [Q 1450+3561]

1457 גָּאַל¹ gā'al¹, v. [103] [→ 1453, 1460, 3319]

redeemed [18], redeem [17], Redeemer [17], avenger [13], kinsman-redeemer [7], *untranslated* [3], be redeemed [3], do[s] it [2], redeem [+1457] [2], redeem [+906+1457] [2], redeems [+1457] [2], redeems [2], relative [2], rescue [2], claim [1], close relative [1], defender [1], delivered [1], do[s] so [1], has the right to do[s] it [1], is redeemed [1], kinsman-redeemers [1], near of kin [1], redeem himself [1], redeemable [1]

Ge 48: 16 [A] the Angel who *has* **delivered** me from all harm—may he
Ex 6: 6 [A] *I will* **redeem** you with an outstretched arm and with mighty
15: 13 [A] unfailing love you will lead the people *you have* **redeemed**.
Lev 25: 25 [A] his nearest **relative** is to come and redeem what his
25: 25 [A] is to come and **redeem** what his countryman has sold.
25: 26 [A] a man has no *one to* **redeem** it *for* him but he himself
25: 30 [C] If *it is* not **redeemed** before a full year has passed, the house
25: 33 [A] So the property of the Levites *is* **redeemable**—that is,
25: 48 [A] he has sold himself. One of his relatives *may* **redeem** him:
25: 49 [A] a cousin or any blood relative in his clan *may* **redeem** him.
25: 49 [A] **[RPH]** Or if he prospers, he may redeem himself.
25: 49 [C] may redeem him. Or if he prospers, *he may* **redeem himself**.
25: 54 [C] " 'Even if *he* **is** not **redeemed** in any of these ways, he
27: 13 [A] If the owner *wishes to* **redeem** [+1457] the animal, he must
27: 13 [A] If the owner *wishes to* **redeem** [+1457] the animal, he must
27: 15 [A] If the man who dedicates his house **redeems** it, he must add a
27: 19 [A] who dedicates the field *wishes to* **redeem** [+906+1457] it,
27: 19 [A] who dedicates the field *wishes to* **redeem** [+906+1457] it,
27: 20 [A] If, however, *he does* not **redeem** the field, or if he has sold it
27: 20 [C] if he has sold it to someone else, *it can* never **be redeemed**.
27: 27 [C] to it. If he *does* not **redeem** *it*, it is to be sold at its set value.
27: 28 [C] may be sold or **redeemed**; everything so devoted is most
27: 31 [A] If a man **redeems** [+1457] any of his tithe, he must add a
27: 31 [A] If a man **redeems** [+1457] any of his tithe, he must add a
27: 33 [C] and its substitute become holy and cannot **be redeemed**.' "
Nu 5: 8 [A] if that person has no **close relative** to whom restitution can
35: 12 [A] They will be places of refuge from the **avenger**, so that a
35: 19 [A] The **avenger** *of* blood shall put the murderer to death; when
35: 21 [A] The **avenger** *of* blood shall put the murderer to death when
35: 24 [A] and the **avenger** *of* blood according to these regulations.
35: 25 [A] protect the one accused of murder from the **avenger** *of* blood
35: 27 [A] the **avenger** *of* blood finds him outside the city, the avenger
35: 27 [A] the **avenger** *of* blood may kill the accused without being
Dt 19: 6 [A] Otherwise, the **avenger** *of* blood might pursue him in a rage,
19: 12 [A] the city, and hand him over to the **avenger** *of* blood to die.
Jos 20: 3 [A] flee there and find protection from the **avenger** *of* blood.
20: 5 [A] If the **avenger** *of* blood pursues him, they must not surrender
20: 9 [A] not be killed by the **avenger** *of* blood prior to standing trial
Ru 2: 20 [A] is our close relative; he is one of our **kinsman-redeemers**."
3: 9 [A] your garment over me, since you *are a* **kinsman-redeemer**."
3: 12 [A] Although it is true that I *am* **near of kin**, there is a
3: 12 [A] I am near of kin, there is a **kinsman-redeemer** nearer than I.
3: 13 [A] the night, and in the morning if *he wants to* **redeem**, good;
3: 13 [A] in the morning if he wants to redeem, good; *let him* **redeem**.
3: 13 [A] **[RPH]** as surely as the LORD lives I will do it.
3: 13 [A] he is not willing, as surely as the LORD lives I *will* **do[s] it**.
4: 1 [A] When the **kinsman-redeemer** he had mentioned came along,
4: 3 [A] he said to the **kinsman-redeemer**, "Naomi, who has come
4: 4 [A] If *you will* **redeem** it, do so. But if you will not, tell me, so I
4: 4 [A] If you will redeem it, **do[s] so**. But if you will not, tell me, so I
4: 4 [A] do so. But if you will not, **[RPH]** tell me, so I will know.
4: 4 [A] For no *one* **has the right to do[s] it** except you, and I am next
4: 4 [A] and I am next in line." "I *will* **redeem** it," he said.
4: 6 [A] At this, the **kinsman-redeemer** said, "Then I cannot redeem
4: 6 [A] "Then I cannot **redeem** it because I might endanger my own
4: 6 [A] my own estate. You **redeem** it yourself. I cannot do it."
4: 6 [A] my own estate. You redeem it yourself. I cannot **do[s] it**."
4: 8 [A] So the **kinsman-redeemer** said to Boaz, "Buy it yourself."
4: 14 [A] who this day has not left you without a **kinsman-redeemer**.
2Sa 14: 11 [A] prevent the **avenger** *of* blood from adding to the destruction,
1Ki 16: 11 [A] He did not spare a single male, whether **relative** or friend.
Job 3: 5 [A] *May* darkness and deep shadow **claim** it once more; may a
19: 25 [A] I know that my **Redeemer** lives, and that in the end he will
Ps 19: 14 [19:15] [A] your sight, O LORD, my Rock and my **Redeemer**.
69: 18 [69:19] [A] Come near and **rescue** me; redeem me because of
72: 14 [A] *He will* **rescue** them from oppression and violence,
74: 2 [A] of old, the tribe of your inheritance, whom *you* **redeemed**—
77: 15 [77:16] [A] With your mighty arm *you* **redeemed** your people,
78: 35 [A] was their Rock, that God Most High was their **Redeemer**.
103: 4 [A] who **redeems** your life from the pit and crowns you with
106: 10 [A] of the foe; from the hand of the enemy *he* **redeemed** them.
107: 2 [B] Let the **redeemed** *of* the LORD say this—those he
107: 2 [A] say this—those *he* **redeemed** from the hand of the foe,
119: 154 [A] Defend my cause and **redeem** me; preserve my life
Pr 23: 11 [A] for their **Defender** is strong; he will take up their case against
Isa 35: 9 [B] not be found there. But only the **redeemed** will walk there,
41: 14 [A] declares the LORD, your **Redeemer**, the Holy One of
43: 1 [A] "Fear not, for *I have* **redeemed** you; I have summoned you
43: 14 [A] the LORD says—your **Redeemer**, the Holy One of Israel:
44: 6 [A] Israel's King and **Redeemer**, the LORD Almighty:
44: 22 [A] the morning mist. Return to me, for *I have* **redeemed** you."
44: 23 [A] and all your trees, for the LORD *has* **redeemed** Jacob,
44: 24 [A] your **Redeemer**, who formed you in the womb:
47: 4 [A] Our **Redeemer**—the LORD Almighty is his name—
48: 17 [A] the LORD says—your **Redeemer**, the Holy One of Israel:
48: 20 [A] say, "The LORD *has* **redeemed** his servant Jacob."
49: 7 [A] the **Redeemer** and Holy One of Israel—to him who was
49: 26 [A] the LORD, am your Savior, your **Redeemer**, the Mighty
51: 10 [B] the depths of the sea so that the **redeemed** might cross over?
52: 3 [C] sold for nothing, and without money *you will* **be redeemed**."
52: 9 [A] has comforted his people, *he has* **redeemed** Jerusalem.
54: 5 [A] the Holy One of Israel *is* your **Redeemer**; he is called the
54: 8 [A] have compassion on you," says the LORD your **Redeemer**.
59: 20 [A] "The **Redeemer** will come to Zion, to those in Jacob who
60: 16 [A] the LORD, am your Savior, your **Redeemer**, the Mighty
62: 12 [B] be called the Holy People, the **Redeemed** *of* the LORD;
63: 9 [A] In his love and mercy he **redeemed** them; he lifted them up
63: 16 [A] are our Father, our **Redeemer** from of old is your name.
Jer 31: 11 [A] and **redeem** them from the hand of those stronger than they.
50: 34 [A] Yet their **Redeemer** is strong; the LORD Almighty is his
La 3: 58 [A] O Lord, you took up my case; *you* **redeemed** my life.
Hos 13: 14 [A] from the power of the grave; *I will* **redeem** them from death.
Mic 4: 10 [A] There the LORD *will* **redeem** you out of the hand of your

1458 גָּאַל² gā'al², v. [11] [→ 1459; cf. 1718]

defiled [4], defile himself [2], unclean [2], are defiled [1], are stained [1], stained [1]

Ezr 2: 62 [E] and so were excluded from the priesthood *as* **unclean**.

Ne 7:64 [E] and so *were* excluded from the priesthood *as* **unclean**.
Isa 59: 3 [C] For your hands **are stained** with blood, your fingers with
63: 3 [G] blood spattered my garments, and *I* **stained** all my clothing.
La 4:14 [C] *They* **are** *so* **defiled** with blood that no one dares to touch
Da 1: 8 [F] But Daniel resolved not *to* **defile himself** with the royal food
1: 8 [F] chief official for permission not *to* **defile himself** this way.
Zep 3: 1 [C] Woe to the city of oppressors, rebellious and **defiled**!
Mal 1: 7 [E] "You place **defiled** food on my altar. "But you ask, 'How
1: 7 [D] food on my altar. "But you ask, 'How *have we* **defiled** you?'
1:12 [E] Lord's table, 'It *is* **defiled**,' and of its food, 'It is contemptible.'

1459 גֹּאַל *gō'al*, n.[m.]. [1] [√ 1458]

defiled [1]

Ne 13:29 because they **defiled** the priestly office and the covenant of the

1460 גְּאֻלָּה *geullâ*, n.f. [14] [√ 1457]

redemption [4], redeem [3], right of redemption [2], as nearest relative duty [1], blood relatives [+408] [1], it[s] [+3276] [1], redeemed [1], right to redeem [1]

Lev 25:24 as a possession, you must provide for the **redemption** of the land.
25:26 but he himself prospers and acquires sufficient means to **redeem** it,
25:29 he retains the **right of redemption** a full year after its sale.
25:29 a full year after its sale. During that time he may **redeem** it.
25:31 They can be **redeemed**, and they are to be returned in the Jubilee.
25:32 " 'The Levites always have the **right to redeem** their houses in the
25:48 he retains the **right of redemption** after he has sold himself.
25:51 he must pay for his **redemption** a larger share of the price paid for
25:52 he is to compute that and pay for his **redemption** accordingly.
Ru 4: 6 my own estate. You redeem **it**[s] [+3276] yourself. I cannot do it."
4: 7 for the **redemption** and transfer of property to become final,
Jer 32: 7 because **as nearest relative** it is your right and **duty** to buy it.'
32: 8 Since it is your right to **redeem** it and possess it, buy it for
Eze 11:15 your brothers who are your **blood relatives** [+408] and the whole

1461 גַּב *gab*[1], n.m. & f. [11 / 10] [→ 1462; Ar 10128]

rims [3], mounds [2], back [1], backs [1], eyebrows [+6524] [1], mound [1], strong [1]

Lev 14: 9 his head, his beard, his **eyebrows** [+6524] and the rest of his hair.
1Ki 7:33 the axles, **rims**, spokes and hubs were all of cast metal.
Job 15:26 defiantly charging against him with a thick, **strong** shield.
Ps 129: 3 Plowmen have plowed my **back** and made their furrows long.
Eze 1:18 Their **rims** were high and awesome, and all four rims were full of
1:18 and awesome, and all four **rims** were full of eyes all around.
10:12 entire bodies, including their **backs**, their hands and their wings,
16:24 you built a **mound** for yourself and made a lofty shrine in every
16:31 When you built your **mounds** at the head of every street and made
16:39 they will tear down your **mounds** and destroy your lofty shrines.
43:13 And this is the height [BHS *rim*; NIV 1470] *of* the altar:

1462 גַּב *gab*[2], n.m. [2] [√ 1461]

defenses [2]

Job 13:12 maxims are proverbs of ashes; your **defenses** are defenses of clay.
13:12 maxims are proverbs of ashes; your defenses are **defenses** *of* clay.

1463 גֵּב *gēb*[1], n.[m.]. [3] [→ 1481; Ar 10129]

full of ditches [+1463] [2], cisterns [1]

2Ki 3:16 is what the LORD says: Make this valley **full of ditches** [+1463].
3:16 is what the LORD says: Make this valley **full of ditches** [+1463].
Jer 14: 3 their servants for water; they go to the **cisterns** but find no water.

1464 גֵּב *gēb*[2], n.[m.]. [1]

beams [1]

1Ki 6: 9 and completed it, roofing it with **beams** and cedar planks.

1465 גֶּבֶא *gebe'*, n.m. [2]

cistern [1], marshes [1]

Isa 30:14 for taking coals from a hearth or scooping water out of a **cistern**."
Eze 47:11 the swamps and **marshes** will not become fresh; they will be left

1466 גֵּבָה *gēbâ*, n.[m.]. [1] [→ 1479]

locusts [1]

Isa 33: 4 as by young locusts; like a swarm of **locusts** men pounce on it.

1467 גָּבַהּ *gābah*, v. [33] [→ 1468, 1469, 1470, 1471, 1510, 3322]

proud [5], exalted [3], haughty [3], towered [3], high [2], higher [2], soar [2], arrogant [1], build high [1], builds high [1], devoted [1], exalts [1], highest [1], made higher [1], make grow tall [1], pride [+4213] [1], pride [1], taller [1], tower proudly [1], upward [1]

1Sa 10:23 [A] as he stood among the people *he was* a head **taller** than any
2Ch 17: 6 [A] His heart *was* **devoted** to the ways of the LORD;
26:16 [A] became powerful, his **pride** [+4213] led to his downfall.
32:25 [A] Hezekiah's heart *was* **proud** and he did not respond to the
33:14 [G] encircling the hill of Ophel; *he* also **made** it much **higher**.
Job 5: 7 [G] Yet man is born to trouble as surely as sparks fly **upward**.
35: 5 [A] at the heavens and see; gaze at the clouds *so* **high** above you.
36: 7 [A] he enthrones them with kings and **exalts** *them* forever.
39:27 [G] *Does* the eagle **soar** at your command and build his nest on
Ps 113: 5 [G] the LORD our God, the *One who* sits enthroned *on* **high**,
131: 1 [A] My heart *is* not **proud**, O LORD, my eyes are not haughty;
Pr 17:19 [G] loves sin; *he who* **builds** a **high** gate invites destruction.
18:12 [A] Before his downfall a man's heart *is* **proud**, but humility
Isa 3:16 [A] The LORD says, "The women of Zion *are* **haughty**,
5:16 [A] the LORD Almighty *will be* **exalted** by his justice,
7:11 [G] whether in the deepest depths or in the **highest** heights."
52:13 [A] act wisely; he will be raised and lifted up and highly **exalted**.
55: 9 [A] "As the heavens *are* **higher** than the earth, so are my ways
55: 9 [A] so *are* my ways **higher** than your ways and my thoughts than
Jer 13:15 [A] Hear and pay attention, *do* not *be* **arrogant**, for the LORD
49:16 [G] Though *you* **build** your nest as **high** as the eagle's,
Eze 16:50 [A] *They were* **haughty** and did detestable things before me.
17:24 [G] bring down the tall tree and **make** the low tree **grow tall**.
19:11 [A] *It* **towered** high above the thick foliage, conspicuous for its
21:26 [21:31] [G] The lowly *will be* **exalted** and the exalted will be
28: 2 [A] " 'In *the* **pride** *of* your heart you say, "I am a god; I sit on the
28: 5 [A] and because of your wealth your heart *has grown* **proud**.
28:17 [A] Your heart *became* **proud** on account of your beauty,
31: 5 [A] So *it* **towered** higher than all the trees of the field; its boughs
31:10 [A] Because *it* **towered** on high, lifting its top above the thick
31:14 [A] other trees by the waters *are ever to* **tower proudly** on high,
Ob 1: 4 [G] Though *you* **soar** like the eagle and make your nest among
Zep 3:11 [A] Never again *will you be* **haughty** on my holy hill.

1468 גָּבֵהַּ *gābēah*, a. [4] [√ 1467]

haughty [1], pride [+8120] [1], proud [1], towered [1]

Ps 101: 5 whoever has **haughty** eyes and a proud heart, him will I not
Pr 16: 5 The LORD detests all the **proud** *of* heart. Be sure of this:
Ecc 7: 8 better than its beginning, and patience is better than **pride** [+8120].
Eze 31: 3 the forest; it **towered** on high, its top above the thick foliage.

1469 גָּבֹהַּ *gābōah*, a. [38] [√ 1467]

high [19], so proudly [+1469] [2], tall [2], *untranslated* [1], arrogant [1], exalted [1], haughty [1], height [+7757] [1], heights [1], lofty [1], long [1], longer [1], official [1], one[s] [1], others[s] [1], proud [1], taller [1], towers [1]

Ge 7:19 and all the **high** mountains under the entire heavens were covered.
Dt 3: 5 All these cities were fortified with **high** walls and with gates
28:52 land until the **high** fortified walls in which you trust fall down.
1Sa 2: 3 "Do not keep talking **so proudly** [+1469] or let your mouth speak
2: 3 "Do not keep talking **so proudly** [+1469] or let your mouth speak
9: 2 equal among the Israelites—a head **taller** than any of the others.
16: 7 "Do not consider his appearance or his **height** [+7757], for I have
1Ki 14:23 sacred stones and Asherah poles on every **high** hill and under
2Ki 17:10 They set up sacred stones and Asherah poles on every **high** hill
Est 5:14 friends said to him, "Have a gallows built, seventy-five feet **high**,
7: 9 "A gallows seventy-five feet **high** stands by Haman's house.
Job 41:34 [41:26] He looks down on all *that* are **haughty**; he is king over
Ps 103:11 For as **high** as the heavens are above the earth, so great is his love
104:18 The **high** mountains belong to the wild goats; the crags are a
138: 6 he looks upon the lowly, but the **proud** he knows from afar.
Ecc 5: 8 [5:7] for *one* **official** is eyed by a higher one, and over them both
5: 8 [5:7] for one official is eyed by a higher **one**[s], and over them both
5: 8 [5:7] by a higher one, and over them both are **others**[s] higher still.
12: 5 when men are afraid of **heights** and of dangers in the streets;
Isa 2:15 for every **lofty** tower and every fortified wall,
5:15 and mankind humbled, the eyes of the **arrogant** humbled.
10:33 The lofty trees will be felled, the **tall** *ones* will be brought low.
30:25 streams of water will flow on every **high** mountain and every lofty
40: 9 You who bring good tidings to Zion, go up on a **high** mountain.
57: 7 You have made your bed on a **high** and lofty hill; there you went
Jer 2:20 on every **high** hill and under every spreading tree you lay down as
3: 6 She has gone up on every **high** hill and under every spreading tree
17: 2 and Asherah poles beside the spreading trees and on the **high** hills.
51:58 thick wall will be leveled and her **high** gates set on fire;
Eze 17:22 from its topmost shoots and plant it on a **high** and lofty mountain.
17:24 of the field will know that I the LORD bring down the **tall** tree
21:26 [21:31] lowly will be exalted and the **exalted** will be brought low.
40: 2 took me to the land of Israel and set me on a very **high** mountain,
41:22 There was a wooden altar three cubits **high** and two cubits square;

Da 8: 3 with two horns, standing beside the canal, and the horns were **long**.
8: 3 One of the horns was **longer** than the other but grew up later.
8: 3 of the horns was longer than the other but **[RPH]** grew up later.
Zep 1: 16 battle cry against the fortified cities and against the corner **towers**.

1470 גֹּבַהּ gōbah, n.m. [17 / 18] [√ 1467]

height [4], high [3], tall [2], *untranslated* [1], conceit [1], haughty [1], heights [1], higher [1], pride [+678] [1], pride [1], raised [1], splendor [1]

1Sa 17: 4 came out of the Philistine camp. He was over nine feet **tall**.
2Ch 3: 4 cubits long across the width of the building and twenty cubits **high**.
32: 26 Hezekiah repented of the **pride** *of* his heart, as did the people of
Job 11: 8 They are **higher** *than* the heavens—what can you do? They are
22: 12 "Is not God in the **heights** *of* heaven? And see how lofty are the
40: 10 adorn yourself with glory and **splendor**, and clothe yourself in
Ps 10: 4 In his **pride** [+678] the wicked does not seek him; in all his
Pr 16: 18 Pride goes before destruction, a **haughty** spirit before a fall.
Jer 48: 29 her overweening pride and **conceit**, her pride and arrogance
Eze 1: 18 Their rims were **high** and awesome, and all four rims were full of
19: 11 thick foliage, conspicuous for its **height** and for its many branches.
31: 10 top above the thick foliage, and because it was proud of its **height**,
31: 14 No other trees so well-watered are ever to reach *such* a **height**;
40: 42 a cubit and a half long, a cubit and a half wide and a cubit **high**.
41: 8 I saw that the temple had a **raised** *base* all around it,
43: 13 And this is the **height** [BHS 1461] *of* the altar:
Am 2: 9 though he **[RPH]** was tall as the cedars and strong as the oaks.
2: 9 though he was **tall** as the cedars and strong as the oaks.

1471 גַּבְהוּת gabhût, n.f. [2] [√ 1467]

arrogance [1], arrogant [1]

Isa 2: 11 The eyes of the **arrogant** man will be humbled and the pride of
2: 17 The **arrogance** *of* man will be brought low and the pride of men

1472 גָּבוֹל gābôl, var. Not used in NIV/BHS [cf. 1473]

1473 גְּבוּל g^ebûl, n.m. [240] [→ 1474, 1487; cf. 1472]

territory [57], boundary [44], border [36], *untranslated* [22], borders [10], it^s [+2021] [9], country [7], land [7], area [4], boundaries [4], boundary stone [4], region [3], rim [3], throughout [+928+3972] [3], coastline [2], vicinity [2], allotted territory [1], anywhere [+3972] [1], anywhere in [+928+3972] [1], areas [1], bank [1], borderland [1], boundary stones [1], coast [1], districts [1], domain [1], Egypt [+5213] [1], end [+7895] [1], homeland [1], it^s [+616+2021] [1], it^s [1], limits [1], neighboring territory [1], part [1], parts [1], places [1], the borders [1], wall [1], walls [1]

Ge 10: 19 the **borders** *of* Canaan reached from Sidon toward Gerar as far as
23: 17 and the cave in it, and all the trees within the **borders** of the field—
47: 21 people to servitude, from *one* **end** *of* [+7895] Egypt to the other.
Ex 8: 2 [7:27] let them go, I will plague your whole **country** with frogs.
10: 4 to let them go, I will bring locusts into your **country** tomorrow.
10: 14 and settled down in every **area** *of* the country in great numbers.
10: 19 into the Red Sea. Not a locust was left anywhere in **Egypt** [+5213].
13: 7 nor shall any yeast be seen anywhere within your **borders**.
23: 31 "I will establish your **borders** from the Red Sea to the Sea of the
34: 24 I will drive out nations before you and enlarge your **territory**,
Nu 20: 16 "Now we are here at Kadesh, a town on the edge of your **territory**.
20: 17 or to the left until we have passed through your **territory**."
20: 21 Since Edom refused to let them go through their **territory**,
20: 23 At Mount Hor, near the **border** *of* Edom, the LORD said to
21: 13 the Arnon, which is in the desert extending into Amorite **territory**.
21: 13 The Arnon is the **border** *of* Moab, between Moab and the
21: 15 that lead to the site of Ar and lie along the **border** *of* Moab."
21: 22 the king's highway until we have passed through your **territory**."
21: 23 But Sihon would not let Israel pass through his **territory**.
21: 24 only as far as the Ammonites, because their **border** was fortified.
22: 36 he went out to meet him at the Moabite town on the Arnon **border**,
22: 36 the Moabite town on the Arnon border, at the edge of his **territory**.
33: 44 left Oboth and camped at Iye Abarim, on the **border** *of* Moab.
34: 3 your southern **boundary** will start from the end of the Salt Sea,
34: 4 cross **[RPH]** south of Scorpion Pass, continue on to Zin and go
34: 5 where **it**^s [+2021] will turn, join the Wadi of Egypt and end at the
34: 6 " 'Your western **boundary** will be the coast of the Great Sea.
34: 6 " 'Your western boundary will be the **coast** of the Great Sea.
34: 6 coast of the Great Sea. This will be your **boundary** *on* the west.
34: 7 " 'For your northern **boundary**, run a line from the Great Sea to
34: 8 Mount Hor to Lebo Hamath. Then the **boundary** will go to Zedad,
34: 9 continue **[RPH]** to Ziphron and end at Hazar Enan. This will be
34: 9 and end at Hazar Enan. This will be your **boundary** *on* the north.
34: 10 " 'For your eastern **boundary**, run a line from Hazar Enan to
34: 11 The **boundary** will go down from Shepham to Riblah on the east
34: 11 and **[RPH]** continue along the slopes east of the Sea of Kinnereth.
34: 12 the **boundary** will go down along the Jordan and end at the Salt
35: 26 " 'But if the accused ever goes outside the **limits** *of* the city of
35: 27 and the avenger of blood finds him outside **[RPH]** the city,
Dt 2: 4 'You are about to pass through the **territory** *of* your brothers the
2: 18 "Today you are to pass by the **region** *of* Moab at Ar.
3: 14 took the whole region of Argob as far as the **border** *of* the
3: 16 to the Arnon Gorge (the middle of the gorge being the **border**)
3: 16 out to the Jabbok River, which is the **border** *of* the Ammonites.
3: 17 Its western **border** was the Jordan in the Arabah, from Kinnereth
11: 24 Your **territory** will extend from the desert to Lebanon, and from
12: 20 When the LORD your God has enlarged your **territory** as he
16: 4 Let no yeast be found in your possession in all your **land** for seven
19: 3 divide into three **parts** the land the LORD your God is giving you
19: 8 If the LORD your God enlarges your **territory**, as he promised
19: 14 Do not move your neighbor's **boundary stone** set up by your
27: 17 "Cursed is the man who moves his neighbor's **boundary stone**."
28: 40 You will have olive trees throughout your **country** but you will not
Jos 1: 4 Your **territory** will extend from the desert to Lebanon, and from
12: 2 to the Jabbok River, which is the **border** *of* the Ammonites.
12: 4 the **territory** *of* Og king of Bashan, one of the last of the
12: 5 all of Bashan to the **border** *of* the people of Geshur and Maacah,
12: 5 and half of Gilead to the **border** *of* Sihon king of Heshbon.
13: 3 from the Shihor River on the east of Egypt to the **territory** *of*
13: 4 Arah of the Sidonians as far as Aphek, the **region** *of* the Amorites,
13: 10 who ruled in Heshbon, out to the **border** *of* the Ammonites.
13: 11 the **territory** *of* the people of Geshur and Maacah, all of Mount
13: 16 The **territory** from Aroer on the rim of the Arnon Gorge,
13: 23 The **boundary** *of* the Reubenites was the bank of the Jordan.
13: 23 The boundary of the Reubenites was the **bank** *of* the Jordan.
13: 25 The **territory** *of* Jazer, all the towns of Gilead and half the
13: 26 and Betonim, and from Mahanaim to the **territory** of Debir;
13: 27 of the Jordan, the **territory** up to the end of the Sea of Kinnereth).
13: 30 The **territory** extending from Mahanaim and including all of
15: 1 of Judah, clan by clan, extended down to the **territory** *of* Edom,
15: 2 Their southern **boundary** started from the bay at the southern end
15: 4 ending at the sea. **[RPH]** This is their southern boundary.
15: 4 Wadi of Egypt, ending at the sea. This is their southern **boundary**.
15: 5 The eastern **boundary** is the Salt Sea as far as the mouth of the
15: 5 The northern **boundary** started from the bay of the sea at the
15: 6 went up **[RPH]** to Beth Hoglah and continued north of Beth
15: 6 continued north of Beth Arabah **[RPH]** to the Stone of Bohan son
15: 7 The **boundary** then went up to Debir from the Valley of Achor
15: 7 which faces the Pass of Adummim south of the gorge. **It**^s [+2021]
15: 8 **it**^s [+2021] ran up the Valley of Ben Hinnom along the southern
15: 8 From there **it**^s [+2021] climbed to the top of the hill west of the
15: 9 From the hilltop the **boundary** headed toward the spring of the
15: 9 of Mount Ephron and **[RPH]** went down toward Baalah (that is,
15: 10 Then **it**^s [+2021] curved westward from Baalah to Mount Seir,
15: 11 **It**^s [+2021] went to the northern slope of Ekron, turned toward
15: 11 **[RPH]** turned toward Shikkeron, passed along to Mount Baalah
15: 11 and reached Jabneel. The **boundary** ended at the sea.
15: 12 The western **boundary** is the coastline of the Great Sea. These are
15: 12 The western boundary is the **coastline** of the Great Sea. These are
15: 12 These are the **boundaries** around the people of Judah by their
15: 21 tribe of Judah in the Negev toward the **boundary** *of* Edom were:
15: 47 as far as the Wadi of Egypt and the **coastline** of the Great Sea.
15: 47 [of Egypt and the coastline of the **Great** [K; see Q 1524] Sea.]
16: 2 Luz), crossed over to the **territory** *of* the Arkites in Ataroth,
16: 3 descended westward to the **territory** *of* the Japhletites as far as the
16: 3 of the Japhletites as far as the **region** *of* Lower Beth Horon
16: 5 This was the **territory** *of* Ephraim, clan by clan: The boundary of
16: 5 The **boundary** *of* their inheritance went from Ataroth Addar in the
16: 6 continued **[RPH]** to the sea. From Micmethath on the north it
16: 6 From Micmethath on the north **it**^s [+2021] curved eastward to
16: 8 From Tappuah the **border** went west to the Kanah Ravine
17: 7 The **territory** *of* Manasseh extended from Asher to Micmethath
17: 7 The **boundary** ran southward from there to include the people
17: 8 Tappuah itself, on the **boundary** *of* Manasseh, belonged to the
17: 9 Then the **boundary** continued south to the Kanah Ravine.
17: 9 but the **boundary** *of* Manasseh was the northern side of the ravine
17: 10 The **territory** *of* Manasseh reached the sea and bordered Asher on
18: 5 Judah is to remain in its **territory** on the south and the house of
18: 5 on the south and the house of Joseph in its **territory** on the north.
18: 11 Their allotted **territory** lay between the tribes of Judah and Joseph:
18: 12 On the north side their **boundary** began at the Jordan, passed the
18: 12 **[RPH]** passed the northern slope of Jericho and headed west into
18: 13 From there **it**^s [+2021] crossed to the south slope of Luz (that is,
18: 13 **[RPH]** went down to Ataroth Addar on the hill south of Lower
18: 14 From the hill facing Beth Horon on the south the **boundary** turned
18: 15 the **boundary** came out at the spring of the waters of Nephtoah.
18: 16 The **boundary** went down to the foot of the hill facing the Valley
18: 19 **It**^s [+2021] then went to the northern slope of Beth Hoglah
18: 19 and came out **[RPH]** at the northern bay of the Salt Sea,
18: 19 mouth of the Jordan in the south. This was the southern **boundary**.

Jos 19:10 by clan: The **boundary** *of* their inheritance went as far as Sarid.
19:11 Going west it[s] ran to Maralah, touched Dabbesheth, and extended
19:12 It turned east from Sarid toward the sunrise to the **territory** *of*
19:14 There the **boundary** went around on the north to Hannathon
19:18 Their **territory** included: Jezreel, Kesulloth, Shunem,
19:22 The **boundary** touched Tabor, Shahazumah and Beth Shemesh,
19:22 Shahazumah and Beth Shemesh, and ended **[RPH]** at the Jordan.
19:25 Their **territory** included: Helkath, Hali, Beten, Acshaph,
19:29 The **boundary** then turned back toward Ramah and went to the
19:29 turned toward **[RPH]** Hosah and came out at the sea in the region
19:33 Their **boundary** went from Heleph and the large tree in
19:34 The **boundary** ran west through Aznoth Tabor and came out at
19:41 The **territory** *of* their inheritance included: Zorah, Eshtaol,
19:46 Me Jarkon and Rakkon, with the **area** facing Joppa.
19:47 (But the Danites had difficulty taking possession of their **territory**,
22:25 The LORD has made the Jordan a **boundary** between us
24:30 they buried him in the **land** *of* his inheritance, at Timnath Serah in
Jdg 1:18 The men of Judah also took Gaza, **[RPH]** Ashkelon and Ekron—
1:18 The men of Judah also took Gaza, Ashkelon **[RPH]** and Ekron—
1:18 also took Gaza, Ashkelon and Ekron—each city with its **territory**.
1:36 The **boundary** *of* the Amorites was from Scorpion Pass to Sela
2:9 they buried him in the **land** *of* his inheritance, at Timnath Heres in
11:18 They did not enter the **territory** *of* Moab, for the Arnon was its
11:18 did not enter the territory of Moab, for the Arnon was its **border**.
11:20 however, did not trust Israel to pass through his **territory**.
11:22 capturing all of it[s] [+616+2021] from the Arnon to the Jabbok
19:29 into twelve parts and sent them into all the **areas** *of* Israel.
1Sa 5:6 hand was heavy upon the people of Ashdod and its **vicinity**;
6:9 If it goes up to its own **territory**, toward Beth Shemesh, then the
6:12 The rulers of the Philistines followed them as far as the **border** *of*
7:13 were subdued and did not invade Israelite **territory** again.
7:14 Israel delivered the **neighboring territory** from the power of the
10:2 men near Rachel's tomb, at Zelzah on the **border** *of* Benjamin.
11:3 so we can send messengers **throughout** [+928+3972] Israel;
11:7 sent the pieces by messengers **throughout** [+928+3972] Israel,
13:18 the third toward the **borderland** overlooking the Valley of Zeboim
27:1 Saul will give up searching for me **anywhere** [+3972] in Israel,
2Sa 21:5 and have no place **anywhere in** [+928+3972] Israel,
1Ki 1:3 they searched **throughout** [+928+3972] Israel for a beautiful girl
4:21 [5:1] to the land of the Philistines, as far as the **border** *of* Egypt.
2Ki 3:21 who could bear arms was called up and stationed on the **border**.
10:32 Hazael overpowered the Israelites throughout their **territory**
14:25 He was the one who restored the **boundaries** *of* Israel from Lebo
15:16 attacked Tiphsah and everyone in the city and its **vicinity**,
18:8 he defeated the Philistines, as far as Gaza and its **territory**.
1Ch 4:10 of Israel, "Oh, that you would bless me and enlarge my **territory**!
6:54 [6:39] **allotted** as their **territory** (they were assigned to the
6:66 [6:51] Some of the Kohathite clans were given as their **territory**
21:12 with the angel of the LORD ravaging every **part** *of* Israel.'
2Ch 9:26 River to the land of the Philistines, as far as the **border** *of* Egypt.
11:13 Levites from all their **districts** throughout Israel sided with him.
Job 38:20 Can you take them to their **places**? Do you know the paths to their
Ps 78:54 Thus he brought them to the **border** *of* his holy land, to the hill
104:9 You set a **boundary** they cannot cross; never again will they cover
105:31 there came swarms of flies, and gnats throughout their **country**.
105:33 their vines and fig trees and shattered the trees of their **country**.
147:14 He grants peace to your **borders** and satisfies you with the finest
Pr 15:25 proud man's house but he keeps the widow's **boundaries** intact.
22:28 Do not move an ancient **boundary stone** set up by your
23:10 Do not move an ancient **boundary stone** or encroach on the fields
Isa 15:8 Their outcry echoes along the **border** *of* Moab; their wailing
19:19 in the heart of Egypt, and a monument to the LORD at its **border**.
54:12 gates of sparkling jewels, and all your **walls** of precious stones.
60:18 nor ruin or destruction within your **borders**, but you will call your
Jer 5:22 I made the sand a **boundary** for the sea, an everlasting barrier it
15:13 without charge, because of all your sins throughout your **country**.
17:3 with your high places, because of sin throughout your **country**.
31:17 declares the LORD. "Your children will return to their own **land**.
Eze 11:10 and I will execute judgment on you at the **borders** *of* Israel.
11:11 meat in it; I will execute judgment on you at the **borders** *of* Israel.
27:4 Your **domain** was on the high seas; your builders brought your
29:10 waste from Migdol to Aswan, as far as the **border** *of* Cush.
40:12 In front of each alcove was a **wall** one cubit high, and the alcoves
40:12 one cubit high, **[RPH]** and the alcoves were six cubits square.
43:12 All the surrounding **area** on top of the mountain will be most holy.
43:13 and a cubit wide, with a **rim** of one span around the edge.
43:17 with a **rim** of half a cubit and a gutter of a cubit all around.
43:20 and on the four corners of the upper ledge and all around the **rim**,
45:1 cubits long and 20,000 cubits wide; the entire **area** will be holy.
45:7 running lengthwise from the **[RPH]** western to the eastern border
45:7 running lengthwise from the western to the eastern **border** parallel
47:13 "These are the **boundaries** by which you are to divide the land for
47:15 "This is to be the **boundary** *of* the land: "On the north side it will
47:16 and Sibraim (which lies on the **border** between Damascus
47:16 lies on the border between Damascus and **[RPH]** Hamath),
47:16 as far as Hazer Hatticon, which is on the **border** *of* Hauran.
47:17 The **boundary** will extend from the sea to Hazar Enan, along the
47:17 along the northern **border** *of* Damascus, with the border of
47:17 border of Damascus, with the **border** *of* Hamath to the north.
47:18 "On the east side the **boundary** will run between Hauran
47:20 the Great Sea will be the **boundary** to a point opposite Lebo
48:1 the northern **border** *of* Damascus next to Hamath will be part of its
48:2 one portion; it will border the **territory** *of* Dan from east to west.
48:3 one portion; it will border the **territory** *of* Asher from east to west.
48:4 it will border the **territory** *of* Naphtali from east to west.
48:5 it will border the **territory** *of* Manasseh from east to west.
48:6 it will border the **territory** *of* Ephraim from east to west.
48:7 it will border the **territory** *of* Reuben from east to west.
48:8 "Bordering the **territory** *of* Judah from east to west will be the
48:12 a most holy portion, bordering the **territory** *of* the Levites.
48:13 "Alongside the **territory** *of* the priests, the Levites will have an
48:21 from the 25,000 cubits of the sacred portion to the eastern **border**,
48:21 and westward from the 25,000 cubits to the western **border**.
48:22 The area belonging to the prince will lie between the **border** *of*
48:22 will lie between the border of Judah and the **border** *of* Benjamin.
48:24 it will border the **territory** *of* Benjamin from east to west.
48:25 it will border the **territory** *of* Simeon from east to west.
48:26 it will border the **territory** *of* Issachar from east to west.
48:27 it will border the **territory** *of* Zebulun from east to west.
48:28 "The southern **boundary** *of* Gad will run south from Tamar to the
48:28 "The southern boundary of Gad will run **[RPH]** south from
Hos 5:10 Judah's leaders are like those who move **boundary stones**.
Joel 3:6 [4:6] that you might send them far from their **homeland**.
Am 1:13 open the pregnant women of Gilead in order to extend his **borders**,
6:2 better off than your two kingdoms? Is their **land** larger than yours?
6:2 than your two kingdoms? Is their land larger than yours? **[RPH]**
Ob 1:7 All your allies will force you to the **border**; your friends will
Mic 5:6 [5:5] when he invades our land and marches into our **borders**.
Zep 2:8 who insulted my people and made threats against their **land**.
Mal 1:4 They will be called the Wicked **Land**, a people always under the
1:5 'Great is the LORD—even beyond **the borders** *of* Israel!'

1474 גְּבוּלָה *gᵉbûlâ*, n.f. [10] [√ 1473]

boundaries [6], allotted portions [1], boundary stones [1], field [1], territory [1]

Nu 32:33 the whole land with its cities and the **territory** around them.
34:2 be allotted to you as an inheritance will have these **boundaries**:
34:12 " 'This will be your land, with its **boundaries** on every side.' "
Dt 32:8 he set up **boundaries** *for* the peoples according to the number of
Jos 18:20 These were the **boundaries** that marked out the inheritance of the
19:49 they had finished dividing the land into its **allotted portions**,
Job 24:2 Men move **boundary stones**; they pasture flocks they have stolen.
Ps 74:17 It was you who set all the **boundaries** *of* the earth; you made both
Isa 10:13 I removed the **boundaries** *of* nations, I plundered their treasures;
28:25 not plant wheat in its place, barley in its plot, and spelt *in* its **field**?

1475 גִּבּוֹר *gibbôr*, a. [159] [√ 1504; Ar 10132]

warriors [27], mighty [22], mighty men [17], fighting men [+2657] [12], warrior [12], brave warriors [+2657] [6], mighty man [4], strong [4], heroes [3], man [3], special guard [3], able men [+2657] [2], best fighting men [+2657] [2], fighting men [2], hero [2], mighty warrior [2], mighty warriors [2], powerful [2], standing [+2657] [2], valiant soldier [+2657] [2], warrior's [2], *untranslated* [1], another[s] [1], blameless [+9459] [1], brave fighting men [+2657] [1], brave man [+2657] [1], brave warrior [+2657] [1], capable men [+2657] [1], champion [1], experienced fighting men [+408+2657+4878] [1], fighter [1], fighters [1], good fighters [1], leaders [1], men [1], mighty [+3946] [1], mighty men [+2657] [1], mighty warrior [+2657] [1], military staff [1], noblest [+4946] [1], officers [1], principal [1], soldiers [1], strong man [1], troops [+2657] [1], very capable men [+2657] [1], warriors [+2657] [1]

Ge 6:4 children by them. They were the **heroes** of old, men of renown.
10:8 father of Nimrod, who grew to be a **mighty warrior** on the earth.
10:9 He was a **mighty** hunter before the LORD; that is why it is said,
10:9 why it is said, "Like Nimrod, a **mighty** hunter before the LORD."
Dt 10:17 of gods and Lord of lords, the great God, **mighty** and awesome,
Jos 1:14 all your **fighting men** [+2657], fully armed, must cross over ahead
6:2 into your hands, along with its king and its **fighting men** [+2657].
8:3 He chose thirty thousand of his **best fighting men** [+2657]
10:2 it was larger than Ai, and all its men were **good fighters**.
10:7 with his entire army, including all the **best fighting men** [+2657].
Jdg 5:13 the nobles; the people of the LORD came to me with the **mighty**.
5:23 come to help the LORD, to help the LORD against the **mighty**.'
6:12 to Gideon, he said, "The LORD is with you, mighty **warrior**."
11:1 Jephthah the Gileadite was a **mighty warrior** [+2657]. His father
Ru 2:1 of Elimelech, a man of **standing** [+2657], whose name was Boaz.
1Sa 2:4 "The bows of the **warriors** are broken, but those who stumbled are

1Sa 9: 1 There was a Benjamite, a **man** *of* standing, whose name was Kish
14:52 whenever Saul saw a **mighty** or brave man, he took him into his
16:18 He is a **brave man** [+2657] and a warrior. He speaks well
17:51 When the Philistines saw that their **hero** was dead, they turned
2Sa 1:19 O Israel, lies slain on your heights. How the **mighty** have fallen!
1:21 For there the shield of the **mighty** was defiled, the shield of Saul—
1:22 From the blood of the slain, from the flesh of the **mighty**,
1:25 "How the **mighty** have fallen in battle! Jonathan lies slain on your
1:27 "How the **mighty** have fallen! The weapons of war have
10: 7 David sent Joab out with the entire army of **fighting men**.
16: 6 all the troops and the **special guard** were on David's right and left.
17: 8 they are **fighters**, and as fierce as a wild bear robbed of her cubs.
17:10 for all Israel knows that your father is a **fighter** and that those with
20: 7 all the **mighty warriors** went out under the command of Abishai.
22:26 to the **blameless** [+9459] you show yourself blameless,
23: 8 These are the names of David's **mighty men**: Josheb-Basshebeth,
23: 9 As one of the three **mighty men**, he was with David when they
23:16 So the three **mighty men** broke through the Philistine lines,
23:17 not drink it. Such were the exploits of the three **mighty men**.
23:22 son of Jehoiada; he too was as famous as the three **mighty men**.
1Ki 1: 8 and Rei and David's **special guard** did not join Adonijah.
1:10 or Benaiah or the **special guard** or his brother Solomon.
11:28 Now Jeroboam was a man of **standing** [+2657], and when
2Ki 5: 1 to Aram. He was a **valiant soldier** [+2657], but he had leprosy.
15:20 Every wealthy **man** had to contribute fifty shekels of silver to be
24:14 all the officers and **fighting men** [+2657], and all the craftsmen
24:16 **strong** and fit for war, and a thousand craftsmen and artisans.
1Ch 1:10 the father of Nimrod, who grew to be a **mighty warrior** on earth.
5:24 They were brave **warriors**, famous men, and heads of their
7: 2 the descendants of Tola listed as **fighting men** [+2657] in their
7: 5 The relatives who were **fighting men** [+2657] belonging to all the
7: 7 Their genealogical record listed 22,034 **fighting men** [+2657].
7: 9 listed the heads of families and 20,200 **fighting men** [+2657].
7:11 There were 17,200 **fighting men** [+2657] ready to go out to war.
7:40 choice men, **brave warriors** [+2657] and outstanding leaders.
8:40 The sons of Ulam were **brave warriors** [+2657] who could handle
9:13 They were **able men** [+2657], responsible for ministering in the
9:26 the four **principal** gatekeepers, who were Levites, were entrusted
11:10 These were the chiefs of David's **mighty men**—they,
11:11 this is the list of David's **mighty men**: Jashobeam, a Hacmonite,
11:12 Eleazar son of Dodai the Ahohite, one of the three **mighty men**.
11:19 not drink it. Such were the exploits of the three **mighty men**.
11:24 son of Jehoiada; he too was as famous as the three **mighty men**.
11:26 The **mighty** [+2657] **men** were: Asahel the brother of Joab,
12: 1 of Kish (they were among the **warriors** who helped him in battle;
12: 4 and Ishmaiah the Gibeonite, a **mighty man** among the Thirty,
12: 8 [12:9] They were **brave warriors** [+2657], ready for battle
12:21 [12:22] for all of them were **brave warriors** [+2657], and they
12:25 [12:26] men of Simeon, **warriors** [+2657] ready for battle—
12:28 [12:29] Zadok, a **brave** young **warrior** [+2657], with 22 officers
12:30 [12:31] men of Ephraim, **brave warriors** [+2657], famous in
19: 8 David sent Joab out with the entire army of **fighting men**.
26: 6 father's family because they were **very capable men** [+2657].
26:31 **capable men** [+2657] among the Hebronites were found at Jazer in
27: 6 This was the Benaiah who was a **mighty man** *among* the Thirty
28: 1 the palace officials, the **mighty men** and all the brave warriors.
28: 1 the mighty men and all the **brave warriors** [+2657].
29:24 All the officers and **mighty men**, as well as all of King David's
2Ch 13: 3 battle with a force of four hundred thousand able fighting **men**,
13: 3 line against him with eight hundred thousand able **troops** [+2657].
14: 8 [14:7] with bows. All these were **brave fighting men** [+2657].
17:13 He also kept **experienced fighting men** [+408+2657+4878] in
17:14 Adnah the commander, with 300,000 **fighting men** [+2657];
17:16 himself for the service of the LORD, with 200,000. **[RPH]**
17:17 Eliada, a **valiant soldier** [+2657], with 200,000 men armed with
25: 6 He also hired a hundred thousand **fighting men** [+2657] from
26:12 The total number of family leaders over the **fighting men** [+2657]
28: 7 Zicri, an Ephraimite **warrior**, killed Maaseiah the king's son,
32: 3 **military staff** about blocking off the water from the springs
32:21 who annihilated all the **fighting men** [+2657] and the leaders
Ezr 7:28 the king and his advisers and all the king's **powerful** officials.
Ne 3:16 of David, as far as the artificial pool and the House of the **Heroes**.
9:32 "Now therefore, O our God, the great, **mighty** and awesome God,
11:14 his associates, who were **able men** [+2657]—128. Their chief
Job 16:14 and again he bursts upon me; he rushes at me like a **warrior**.
Ps 19: 5 [19:6] his pavilion, like a **champion** rejoicing to run his course.
24: 8 The LORD strong and **mighty**, the LORD mighty in battle.
24: 8 The LORD strong and mighty, the LORD **mighty** *in* battle.
33:16 by the size of his army; no **warrior** escapes by his great strength.
45: 3 [45:4] Gird your sword upon your side, O **mighty** *one*;
52: 1 [52:3] Why do you boast of evil, you **mighty man**? Why do you
78:65 awoke as from sleep, as a **man** wakes from the stupor of wine.
89:19 [89:20] "I have bestowed strength on a **warrior**; I have exalted a
103:20 you his angels, you **mighty** [+3946] *ones* who do his bidding,
112: 2 His children will be **mighty** in the land; the generation of the
120: 4 He will punish you with a **warrior's** sharp arrows, with burning
127: 4 Like arrows in the hands of a **warrior** are sons born in one's
Pr 16:32 Better a patient man than a **warrior**, a man who controls his
21:22 A wise man attacks the city of the **mighty** and pulls down the
30:30 a lion, **mighty** among beasts, who retreats before nothing;
Ecc 9:11 The race is not to the swift or the battle to the **strong**, nor does
SS 3: 7 escorted by sixty **warriors**, the noblest of Israel,
3: 7 escorted by sixty warriors, the **noblest** [+4946] *of* Israel,
4: 4 on it hang a thousand shields, all of them shields of **warriors**.
Isa 3: 2 the **hero** and warrior, the judge and prophet, the soothsayer
5:22 Woe to *those who* are **heroes** at drinking wine and champions at
9: 6 [9:5] **Mighty** God, Everlasting Father, Prince of Peace.
10:21 will return, a remnant of Jacob will return to the **Mighty** God.
13: 3 I have summoned my **warriors** to carry out my wrath—those who
21:17 The survivors of the bowmen, the **warriors** *of* Kedar, will be few."
42:13 The LORD will march out like a **mighty man**, like a warrior he
49:24 Can plunder be taken from **warriors**, or captives rescued from the
49:25 "Yes, captives will be taken from **warriors**, and plunder retrieved
Jer 5:16 quivers are like an open grave; all of them are **mighty warriors**.
9:23 [9:22] or the **strong man** boast of his strength or the rich man
14: 9 you like a man taken by surprise, like a **warrior** powerless to save?
20:11 the LORD is with me like a mighty **warrior**; so my persecutors
26:21 When King Jehoiakim and all his **officers** and officials heard his
32:18 O great and **powerful** God, whose name is the LORD Almighty,
46: 5 They are terrified, they are retreating, their **warriors** are defeated.
46: 6 "The swift cannot flee nor the **strong** escape. In the north by the
46: 9 March on, O **warriors**—men of Cush and Put who carry shields,
46:12 *One* **warrior** will stumble over another; both will fall down
46:12 One warrior will stumble over **another**[s]; both will fall down
48:14 "How can you say, 'We are **warriors**, men valiant in battle'?
48:41 In that day the hearts of Moab's **warriors** will be like the heart of a
49:22 In that day the hearts of Edom's **warriors** will be like the heart of
50: 9 Their arrows will be like skilled **warriors** who do not return
50:36 They will become fools. A sword against her **warriors**! They will
51:30 Babylon's **warriors** have stopped fighting; they remain in their
51:56 her **warriors** will be captured, and their bows will be broken.
51:57 and wise men drunk, her governors, officers and **warriors** as well;
Eze 32:12 I will cause your hordes to fall by the swords of **mighty men**—
32:21 From within the grave the mighty **leaders** will say of Egypt
32:27 Do they not lie with the other uncircumcised **warriors** who have
32:27 though the terror of these **warriors** had stalked through the land of
39:18 You will eat the flesh of **mighty men** and drink the blood of the
39:20 fill of horses and riders, **mighty men** and soldiers of every kind,'
Da 11: 3 Then a **mighty** king will appear, who will rule with great power
Hos 10:13 have depended on your own strength and on your many **warriors**,
Joel 2: 7 They charge like **warriors**; they scale walls like soldiers. They all
3: 9 [4:9] among the nations: Prepare for war! Rouse the **warriors**!
3:10 [4:10] hooks into spears. Let the weakling say, "I am **strong**!"
3:11 [4:11] assemble there. Bring down your **warriors**, O LORD!
Am 2:14 not muster their strength, and the **warrior** will not save his life.
2:16 Even the bravest **warriors** will flee naked on that day,"
Ob 1: 9 Your **warriors**, O Teman, will be terrified, and everyone in Esau's
Na 2: 3 [2:4] The shields of his **soldiers** are red; the warriors are clad in
Zep 1:14 day of the LORD will be bitter, the shouting of the **warrior** there.
3:17 The LORD your God is with you, he is **mighty** to save. He will
Zec 9:13 your sons, O Greece, and make you like a **warrior's** sword.
10: 5 Together they will be like **mighty men** trampling the muddy
10: 7 The Ephraimites will become like **mighty men**, and their hearts

1476 גְּבוּרָה gᵉbûrâ, n.f. [61] [√ 1504; Ar 10130]

power [16], strength [14], might [11], achievements [8], mighty acts [4], things[s] [2], acts of power [1], mighty power [1], mighty works [1], source of strength [1], victory [1], warriors [1]

Ex 32:18 "It is not the sound of **victory**, it is not the sound of defeat;
Dt 3:24 or on earth who can do the deeds and **mighty works** you do?
Jdg 5:31 they who love you be like the sun when it rises in its **strength**."
8:21 so is his **strength**.' " So Gideon stepped forward and killed them,
1Ki 15:23 Asa's reign, all his **achievements**, all he did and the cities he built,
16: 5 other events of Baasha's reign, what he did and his **achievements**,
16:27 events of Omri's reign, what he did and the **things**[s] he achieved,
22:45 [22:46] the **things**[s] he achieved and his military exploits,
2Ki 10:34 other events of Jehu's reign, all he did, and all his **achievements**,
13: 8 events of the reign of Jehoahaz, all he did and his **achievements**,
13:12 events of the reign of Jehoash, all he did and his **achievements**,
14:15 events of the reign of Jehoash, what he did and his **achievements**,
14:28 of Jeroboam's reign, all he did, and his military **achievements**,
18:20 You say you have strategy and military **strength**—but you speak
20:20 all his **achievements** and how he made the pool and the tunnel by
1Ch 29:11 is the greatness and the **power** and the glory and the majesty
29:12 your hands are strength and **power** to exalt and give strength to all.
29:30 together with the details of his reign and **power**, and the
2Ch 20: 6 Power and **might** are in your hand, and no one can withstand you.

Est 10: 2 all his acts of power and **might**, together with a full account of the
Job 12:13 "To God belong wisdom and **power**; counsel and understanding
26:14 hear of him! Who then can understand the thunder of his **power**?"
39:19 "Do you give the horse his **strength** or clothe his neck with a
41:12 [41:4] to speak of his limbs, his **strength** and his graceful form.
Ps 20: 6 [20:7] his holy heaven with the saving **power** *of* his right hand.
21:13 [21:14] in your strength; we will sing and praise your **might**.
54: 1 [54:3] O God, by your name; vindicate me by your **might**.
65: 6 [65:7] by your power, having armed yourself with **strength**,
66: 7 He rules forever by his **power**, his eyes watch the nations—
71:16 I will come and proclaim your **mighty acts**, O Sovereign LORD;
71:18 power to the next generation, your **might** to all who are to come.
80: 2 [80:3] and Manasseh. Awaken your **might**; come and save us.
89:13 [89:14] Your arm is endued with **power**; your hand is strong,
90:10 or eighty, if we have the **strength**; yet their span is but trouble
106: 2 Who can proclaim the **mighty acts** *of* the LORD or fully declare
106: 8 saved them for his name's sake, to make his **mighty power** known.
145: 4 your works to another; they will tell of your **mighty acts**.
145:11 will tell of the glory of your kingdom and speak of your **might**,
145:12 so that all men may know of your **mighty acts** and the glorious
147:10 His pleasure is not in the **strength** *of* the horse, nor his delight in
150: 2 Praise him for his **acts of power**; praise him for his surpassing
Pr 8:14 and sound judgment are mine; I have understanding and **power**.
Ecc 9:16 So I said, "Wisdom is better than **strength**." But the poor man's
10:17 princes eat at a proper time—for **strength** and not for drunkenness.
Isa 3:25 Your men will fall by the sword, your **warriors** in battle.
11: 2 and of understanding, the Spirit of counsel and of **power**,
28: 6 a **source of strength** to those who turn back the battle at the gate.
30:15 and rest is your salvation, in quietness and trust is your **strength**,
33:13 hear what I have done; you who are near, acknowledge my **power**!
36: 5 You say you have strategy and military **strength**—but you speak
63:15 holy and glorious. Where are your zeal and your **might**?
Jer 9:23 [9:22] or the strong man boast of his **strength** or the rich man
10: 6 O LORD; you are great, and your name is mighty in **power**.
16:21 will teach them—this time I will teach them my power and **might**.
23:10 The ⌊prophets⌋ follow an evil course and use their **power** unjustly.
49:35 I will break the bow of Elam, the mainstay of their **might**.
51:30 Their **strength** is exhausted; they have become like women.
Eze 32:29 despite their **power**, they are laid with those killed by the sword.
32:30 with the slain in disgrace despite the terror caused by their **power**.
Mic 3: 8 with the Spirit of the LORD, and with justice and **might**,
7:16 Nations will see and be ashamed, deprived of all their **power**.

1477 גִּבֵּחַ *gibbēaḥ*, a. [1] [→ 1478]

bald forehead [1]

Lev 13:41 lost his hair from the front of his scalp and has a **bald forehead**,

1478 גַּבַּחַת *gabbaḥat*, n.f. [4] [√ 1477]

forehead [3], other[s] [1]

Lev 13:42 But if he has a reddish-white sore on his bald head or **forehead**,
13:42 it is an infectious disease breaking out on his head or **forehead**.
13:43 or **forehead** is reddish-white like an infectious skin disease,
13:55 it with fire, whether the mildew has affected one side or the **other**[s].

1479 גֹּבַי *gōbay*, n.m.col. [2] [√ 1466]

locusts [1], swarms of locusts [1]

Am 7: 1 He was preparing **swarms of locusts** after the king's share had
Na 3:17 your officials like swarms of **locusts** that settle in the walls on a

1480 גַּבַּי *gabbay*, n.pr.m. [1]

Gabbai [1]

Ne 11: 8 and his followers, **Gabbai** and Sallai—928 men.

1481 גֵּבִים *gēbîm*, n.pr.loc. [1] [√ 1463]

Gebim [1]

Isa 10:31 Madmenah is in flight; the people of **Gebim** take cover.

1482 גְּבִינָה *gᵉbînâ*, n.f. [1] [cf. 1492]

cheese [1]

Job 10:10 Did you not pour me out like milk and curdle me like **cheese**,

1483 גָּבִיעַ *gābîa'*, n.m. [14] [→ 1499, 4457?]

cups [6], cup [4], *untranslated* [2], bowls [1], one[s] [1]

Ge 44: 2 put my **cup**, the silver one, in the mouth of the youngest one's
44: 2 put my cup, the silver **one**[s], in the mouth of the youngest one's
44:12 with the youngest. And the **cup** was found in Benjamin's sack.
44:16 we ourselves and the one who was found to have the **cup**."
44:17 Only the man who was found to have the **cup** will become my
Ex 25:31 its flowerlike **cups**, buds and blossoms shall be of one piece with
25:33 Three **cups** shaped like almond flowers with buds and blossoms
25:33 are to be on one branch, three **[RPH]** on the next branch,
25:34 on the lampstand there are to be four **cups** shaped like almond
37:17 its flowerlike **cups**, buds and blossoms were of one piece with it.
37:19 Three **cups** shaped like almond flowers with buds and blossoms
37:19 three **[RPH]** on the next branch and the same for all six branches
37:20 on the lampstand were four **cups** shaped like almond flowers with
Jer 35: 5 I set **bowls** full of wine and some cups before the men of the

1484 גְּבִיר *gᵉbîr*, n.m. [2] [→ 1484; cf. 1504]

lord [2]

Ge 27:29 Be **lord** over your brothers, and may the sons of your mother bow
27:37 "I have made him **lord** over you and have made all his relatives his

1485 גְּבִירָה *gᵉbîrâ*, n.f. [13] [√ 1484; cf. 1504]

mistress [7], queen mother [3], position as queen mother [2], queen [1]

Ge 16: 4 she knew she was pregnant, she began to despise her **mistress**.
16: 8 "I'm running away from my **mistress** Sarai," she answered.
16: 9 LORD told her, "Go back to your **mistress** and submit to her."
1Ki 11:19 gave him a sister of his own wife, **Queen** Tahpenes, in marriage.
15:13 his grandmother Maacah from her **position as queen mother**,
2Ki 5: 3 She said to her **mistress**, "If only my master would see the prophet
10:13 down to greet the families of the king and of the **queen mother**."
2Ch 15:16 his grandmother Maacah from her **position as queen mother**,
Ps 123: 2 as the eyes of a maid look to the hand of her **mistress**, so our eyes
Pr 30:23 who is married, and a maidservant who displaces her **mistress**.
Isa 24: 2 as for servant, for **mistress** as for maid, for seller as for buyer,
Jer 13:18 Say to the king and to the **queen mother**, "Come down from your
29: 2 (This was after King Jehoiachin and the **queen mother**, the court

1486 גָּבִישׁ *gābîš*, n.m. [1] [cf. 453]

jasper [1]

Job 28:18 Coral and **jasper** are not worthy of mention; the price of wisdom is

1487 גָּבַל *gābal*, v.den. [5] [√ 1473]

borders [1], formed the boundary [1], put limits around [1], put limits [1], set up [1]

Ex 19:12 [G] **Put limits** *for* the people around the mountain and tell them,
19:23 [G] **'Put limits around** the mountain and set it apart as holy.' "
Dt 19:14 [A] Do not move your neighbor's boundary stone **set up** by your
Jos 18:20 [A] The Jordan **formed the boundary** on the eastern side.
Zec 9: 2 [A] Hamath too, *which* **borders** on it, and upon Tyre and Sidon,

1488 גְּבַל *gᵉbal*, n.pr.loc. [1] [→ 1490]

Gebal [1]

Eze 27: 9 Veteran craftsmen of **Gebal** were on board as shipwrights to caulk

1489 גְּבָל *gᵉbāl*, n.pr.loc. [1]

Gebal [1]

Ps 83: 7 [83:8] **Gebal**, Ammon and Amalek, Philistia, with the people of

1490 גִּבְלִי *giblî*, a.g. [2] [√ 1488]

Gebalites [1], men of Gebal [1]

Jos 13: 5 the area of the **Gebalites**; and all Lebanon to the east, from Baal
1Ki 5:18 [5:32] Hiram and the **men of Gebal** cut and prepared the timber

1491 גַּבְלֻת *gablut*, n.f. [2] [→ 4456]

braided [2]

Ex 28:22 "For the breastpiece make **braided** chains of pure gold, like a rope.
39:15 For the breastpiece they made **braided** chains of pure gold,

1492 גִּבֵּן *gibbēn*, a. [1] [→ 1493; cf. 1482]

hunchbacked [1]

Lev 21:20 or who is **hunchbacked** or dwarfed, or who has any eye defect,

1493 גַּבְנֹן *gabnôn*, n.[m.]. [2] [√ 1492]

rugged [2]

Ps 68:15 [68:16] majestic mountains; **rugged** are the mountains of Bashan.
68:16 [68:17] Why gaze in envy, O **rugged** mountains, at the mountain

1494 גֶּבַע *geba'*, n.pr.loc. [19 / 15] [√ 1496]

Geba [15]

Jos 18:24 Kephar Ammoni, Ophni and **Geba**—twelve towns and their
21:17 And from the tribe of Benjamin they gave them Gibeon, **Geba**,
Jdg 20:10 the army arrives at Gibeah [BHS ***Geba***; NIV 1497] *in* Benjamin,
20:33 out of its place on the west of Gibeah. [BHS ***Geba***; NIV 1497]

1Sa 13: 3 Jonathan attacked the Philistine outpost at **Geba**,
13: 16 were staying in Gibeah [BHS *Geba*; NIV 1497] *in* Benjamin,
14: 5 to the north toward Micmash, the other to the south toward **Geba**.
2Sa 5: 25 all the way from Gibeon [BHS *Geba*; NIV 1500] to Gezer.
1Ki 15: 22 With them King Asa built up **Geba** *in* Benjamin, and also Mizpah.
2Ki 23: 8 of Judah and desecrated the high places, from **Geba** to Beersheba,
1Ch 6: 60 [6:45] **Geba**, Alemeth and Anathoth, together with their
8: 6 who were heads of families of those living in **Geba** and were
2Ch 16: 6 Baasha had been using. With them he built up **Geba** and Mizpah.
Ezr 2: 26 of Ramah and **Geba** 621
Ne 7: 30 of Ramah and **Geba** 621
11: 31 The descendants of the Benjamites from **Geba** lived in Micmash,
12: 29 from Beth Gilgal, and from the area of **Geba** and Azmaveth,
Isa 10: 29 go over the pass, and say, "We will camp overnight at **Geba**."
Zec 14: 10 The whole land, from **Geba** to Rimmon, south of Jerusalem,

1495 גִּבְעָא *gib'ā'*, n.pr.m. [1] [√ 1496?]

Gibea [1]

1Ch 2: 49 of Madmannah and to Sheva the father of Macbenah and **Gibea**.

1496 גִּבְעָה *gib'â*[1], n.f. [67 / 66] [→ 1494, 1495?, 1497, 1500, 1501, 1502, 1648]

hills [36], hill [26], heights [2], hilltops [2]

Ge 49: 26 of the ancient mountains, than the bounty of the age-old **hills**.
Ex 17: 9 Tomorrow I will stand on top of the **hill** with the staff of God in
17: 10 had ordered, and Moses, Aaron and Hur went to the top of the **hill**.
Nu 23: 9 From the rocky peaks I see them, from the **heights** I view them.
Dt 12: 2 completely all the places on the high mountains and on the **hills**
33: 15 the ancient mountains and the fruitfulness of the everlasting **hills**;
Jdg 7: 1 of Midian was north of them in the valley near the **hill** *of* Moreh.
1Sa 7: 1 They took it to Abinadab's house on the **hill** and consecrated
23: 19 strongholds at Horesh, on the **hill** *of* Hakilah, south of Jeshimon?
26: 1 at Gibeah and said, "Is not David hiding on the **hill** *of* Hakilah,
26: 3 Saul made his camp beside the road on the **hill** *of* Hakilah facing
2Sa 2: 24 and as the sun was setting, they came to the **hill** *of* Ammah,
2: 25 themselves into a group and took their stand on top of a **hill**.
6: 3 and brought it from the house of Abinadab, which was on the **hill**.
6: 4 [BHS+ *which was on the hill*] with the ark of God on it,
1Ki 14: 23 sacred stones and Asherah poles on every high **hill** and under every
2Ki 16: 4 at the high places, on the **hilltops** and under every spreading tree.
17: 10 They set up sacred stones and Asherah poles on every high **hill**
2Ch 28: 4 at the high places, on the **hilltops** and under every spreading tree.
Job 15: 7 the first man ever born? Were you brought forth before the **hills**?
Ps 65: 12 [65:13] of the desert overflow; the **hills** are clothed with gladness.
72: 3 bring prosperity to the people, the **hills** the fruit of righteousness.
114: 4 the mountains skipped like rams, the **hills** like lambs.
114: 6 you mountains, that you skipped like rams, you **hills**, like lambs?
148: 9 you mountains and all **hills**, fruit trees and all cedars,
Pr 8: 25 mountains were settled in place, before the **hills**, I was given birth,
SS 2: 8 he comes, leaping across the mountains, bounding over the **hills**.
4: 6 I will go to the mountain of myrrh and to the **hill** *of* incense.
Isa 2: 2 it will be raised above the **hills**, and all nations will stream to it.
2: 14 for all the towering mountains and all the high **hills**,
10: 32 fist at the mount of the Daughter of Zion, at the **hill** *of* Jerusalem.
30: 17 are left like a flagstaff on a mountaintop, like a banner on a **hill**."
30: 25 of water will flow on every high mountain and every lofty **hill**.
31: 4 will come down to do battle on Mount Zion and on its **heights**.
40: 4 Every valley shall be raised up, every mountain and **hill** made low;
40: 12 or weighed the mountains on the scales and the **hills** in a balance?
41: 15 thresh the mountains and crush them, and reduce the **hills** to chaff.
42: 15 I will lay waste the mountains and **hills** and dry up all their
54: 10 Though the mountains be shaken and the **hills** be removed,
55: 12 the mountains and **hills** will burst into song before you, and all the
65: 7 they burned sacrifices on the mountains and defied me on the **hills**,
Jer 2: 20 on every high **hill** and under every spreading tree you lay down as
3: 23 Surely the ⌞idolatrous⌟ commotion on the **hills** and mountains is a
4: 24 the mountains, and they were quaking; all the **hills** were swaying.
13: 27 I have seen your detestable acts on the **hills** and in the fields.
16: 16 on every mountain and **hill** and from the crevices of the rocks.
17: 2 and Asherah poles beside the spreading trees and on the high **hills**.
31: 39 The measuring line will stretch from there straight to the **hill** *of*
49: 16 live in the clefts of the rocks, who occupy the heights of the **hill**.
50: 6 They wandered over mountain and **hill** and forgot their own resting
Eze 6: 3 This is what the Sovereign LORD says to the mountains and **hills**,
6: 13 on every high **hill** and on all the mountaintops, under every
20: 28 sworn to give them and they saw any high **hill** or any leafy tree,
34: 6 My sheep wandered over all the mountains and on every high **hill**.
34: 26 I will bless them and the places surrounding my **hill**. I will send
35: 8 those killed by the sword will fall on your **hills** and in your valleys
36: 4 This is what the Sovereign LORD says to the mountains and **hills**,
36: 6 concerning the land of Israel and say to the mountains and **hills**,
Hos 4: 13 They sacrifice on the mountaintops and burn offerings on the **hills**,
10: 8 say to the mountains, "Cover us!" and to the **hills**, "Fall on us!"
Joel 3: 18 [4:18] will drip new wine, and the **hills** will flow with milk;
Am 9: 13 New wine will drip from the mountains and flow from all the **hills**.
Mic 4: 1 it will be raised above the **hills**, and peoples will stream to it.
6: 1 case before the mountains; let the **hills** hear what you have to say.
Na 1: 5 The mountains quake before him and the **hills** melt away.
Hab 3: 6 The ancient mountains crumbled and the age-old **hills** collapsed.
Zep 1: 10 wailing from the New Quarter, and a loud crash from the **hills**.

1497 גִּבְעָה *gib'â*[2], n.pr.loc. [46 / 49] [→ 1503; cf. 1496]

Gibeah [48], *untranslated* [1]

Jos 15: 57 Kain, **Gibeah** and Timnah—ten towns and their villages.
18: 28 the Jebusite city (that is, Jerusalem), **Gibeah** and Kiriath—
24: 33 And Eleazar son of Aaron died and was buried at **Gibeah**,
Jdg 19: 12 whose people are not Israelites. We will go on to **Gibeah**."
19: 13 let's try to reach **Gibeah** or Ramah and spend the night in one of
19: 14 they went on, and the sun set as they neared **Gibeah** in Benjamin.
19: 15 **[RPH]** They went and sat in the city square, but no one took them
19: 16 who was living in **Gibeah** (the men of the place were Benjamites),
20: 4 and my concubine came to **Gibeah** in Benjamin to spend the night.
20: 5 During the night the men of **Gibeah** came after me and surrounded
20: 9 now this is what we'll do to **Gibeah**: We'll go up against it as the
20: 10 when the army arrives at **Gibeah** [BHS 1494] *in* Benjamin,
20: 13 Now surrender those wicked men of **Gibeah** so that we may put
20: 14 From their towns they came together at **Gibeah** to fight against the
20: 15 to seven hundred chosen men from those living in **Gibeah**.
20: 19 next morning the Israelites got up and pitched camp near **Gibeah**.
20: 20 and took up battle positions against them at **Gibeah**.
20: 21 The Benjamites came out of **Gibeah** and cut down twenty-two
20: 25 when the Benjamites came out from **Gibeah** to oppose them,
20: 29 Then Israel set an ambush around **Gibeah**.
20: 30 and took up positions against **Gibeah** as they had done before.
20: 31 on the roads—the one leading to Bethel and the other to **Gibeah**.
20: 33 charged out of its place on the west of **Gibeah**. [BHS 1494]
20: 34 thousand of Israel's finest men made a frontal attack on **Gibeah**.
20: 36 because they relied on the ambush they had set near **Gibeah**.
20: 37 men who had been in ambush made a sudden dash into **Gibeah**,
20: 43 and easily overran them in the vicinity of **Gibeah** on the east.
1Sa 10: 5 "After that you will go to **Gibeah** *of* God, where there is a
10: 10 When they arrived at **Gibeah**, a procession of prophets met him;
10: 26 Saul also went to his home in **Gibeah**, accompanied by valiant
11: 4 When the messengers came to **Gibeah** *of* Saul and reported these
13: 2 and a thousand were with Jonathan at **Gibeah** *in* Benjamin.
13: 15 Then Samuel left Gilgal and went up to **Gibeah** *in* Benjamin,
13: 16 the men with them were staying in **Gibeah** [BHS 1494] *in*
14: 2 Saul was staying on the outskirts of **Gibeah** under a pomegranate
14: 16 Saul's lookouts at **Gibeah** *in* Benjamin saw the army melting away
15: 34 left for Ramah, but Saul went up to his home in **Gibeah** *of* Saul.
22: 6 in hand, was seated under the tamarisk tree on the hill at **Gibeah**,
23: 19 The Ziphites went up to Saul at **Gibeah** and said, "Is not David
26: 1 The Ziphites went to Saul at **Gibeah** and said, "Is not David hiding
2Sa 21: 6 us to be killed and exposed before the LORD at **Gibeah** *of* Saul—
23: 29 the Netophathite, Ithai son of Ribai from **Gibeah** *in* Benjamin,
1Ch 11: 31 Ithai son of Ribai from **Gibeah** *in* Benjamin,
2Ch 13: 2 His mother's name was Maacah, a daughter of Uriel of **Gibeah**.
Isa 10: 29 camp overnight at Geba." Ramah trembles; **Gibeah** *of* Saul flees.
Hos 5: 8 "Sound the trumpet in **Gibeah**, the horn in Ramah. Raise the battle
9: 9 They have sunk deep into corruption, as in the days of **Gibeah**.
10: 9 "Since the days of **Gibeah**, you have sinned, O Israel, and there
10: 9 you have remained. Did not war overtake the evildoers in **Gibeah**?

1498 גִּבְעֹנִי *gib'ônî*, a.g. [8] [√ 1500; cf. 1496]

Gibeonites [6], Gibeonite [1], of Gibeon [1]

2Sa 21: 1 blood-stained house; it is because he put the **Gibeonites** to death."
21: 2 The king summoned the **Gibeonites** and spoke to them.
21: 2 (Now the **Gibeonites** were not a part of Israel but were survivors
21: 3 David asked the **Gibeonites**, "What shall I do for you? How shall I
21: 4 The **Gibeonites** answered him, "We have no right to demand silver
21: 9 He handed them over to the **Gibeonites**, who killed and exposed
1Ch 12: 4 and Ishmaiah the **Gibeonite**, a mighty man among the Thirty,
Ne 3: 7 and Mizpah—Melatiah **of Gibeon** and Jadon of Meronoth—

1499 גִּבְעֹל *gib'ōl*, n.[m.] [1] [√ 1483]

in bloom [1]

Ex 9: 31 since the barley had headed and the flax was **in bloom**.

1500 גִּבְעוֹן gibʿōn, n.pr.loc. [37 / 39] [→ 1498; cf. 1496]
Gibeon [38], Gibeonites [+408] [1]

Jos 9: 3 when the people of **Gibeon** heard what Joshua had done to Jericho
9: 17 to their cities: **Gibeon**, Kephirah, Beeroth and Kiriath Jearim.
10: 1 that the people of **Gibeon** had made a treaty of peace with Israel
10: 2 because **Gibeon** was an important city, like one of the royal cities;
10: 4 "Come up and help me attack **Gibeon**," he said, "because it has
10: 5 their troops and took up positions against **Gibeon** and attacked it.
10: 6 The **Gibeonites** [+408] then sent word to Joshua in the camp at
10: 10 before Israel, who defeated them in a great victory at **Gibeon**.
10: 12 "O sun, stand still over **Gibeon**, O moon, over the Valley of
10: 41 Barnea to Gaza and from the whole region of Goshen to **Gibeon**.
11: 19 Except for the Hivites living in **Gibeon**, not one city made a treaty
18: 25 **Gibeon**, Ramah, Beeroth,
21: 17 And from the tribe of Benjamin they gave them **Gibeon**, Geba,
2Sa 2: 12 of Ish-Bosheth son of Saul, left Mahanaim and went to **Gibeon**.
2: 13 and David's men went out and met them at the pool of **Gibeon**.
2: 16 So that place in **Gibeon** was called Helkath Hazzurim.
2: 24 hill of Ammah, near Giah on the way to the wasteland of **Gibeon**.
3: 30 because he had killed their brother Asahel in the battle at **Gibeon**.)
5: 25 struck down the Philistines all the way from **Gibeon** [BHS 1494]
20: 8 While they were at the great rock in **Gibeon**, Amasa came to meet
1Ki 3: 4 The king went to **Gibeon** to offer sacrifices, for that was the most
3: 5 At **Gibeon** the LORD appeared to Solomon during the night in a
9: 2 to him a second time, as he had appeared to him at **Gibeon**.
1Ch 6: 60 [6:45] the tribe of Benjamin they were given **Gibeon**, [BHS-]
8: 29 Jeiel the father of **Gibeon** lived in Gibeon. His wife's name was
8: 29 Jeiel the father of Gibeon lived in **Gibeon**. His wife's name was
9: 35 Jeiel the father of **Gibeon** lived in Gibeon. His wife's name was
9: 35 Jeiel the father of Gibeon lived in **Gibeon**. His wife's name was
14: 16 down the Philistine army, all the way from **Gibeon** to Gezer.
16: 39 before the tabernacle of the LORD at the high place in **Gibeon**
21: 29 of burnt offering were at that time on the high place at **Gibeon**.
2Ch 1: 3 and the whole assembly went to the high place at **Gibeon**,
1: 13 Then Solomon went to Jerusalem from the high place at **Gibeon**,
Ne 3: 7 to them, repairs were made by men from **Gibeon** and Mizpah—
7: 25 of **Gibeon** 95
Isa 28: 21 Mount Perazim, he will rouse himself as in the Valley of **Gibeon**—
Jer 28: 1 the prophet Hananiah son of Azzur, who was from **Gibeon**,
41: 12 They caught up with him near the great pool in **Gibeon**.
41: 16 women, children and court officials he had brought from **Gibeon**.

1501 גִּבְעַת gibʿat, n.pr.loc. Not used in NIV/BHS [√ 1496]

1502 גִּבְעַת הָעֲרָלוֹת gibʿat hāʿărālôt, n.pr.loc. [1] [√ 1496 + 2197]
Gibeath Haaraloth [1]

Jos 5: 3 flint knives and circumcised the Israelites at **Gibeath Haaraloth**.

1503 גִּבְעָתִי gibʿātî, a.g. [1] [√ 1497]
Gibeathite [1]

1Ch 12: 3 Ahiezer their chief and Joash the sons of Shemaah the **Gibeathite**;

1504 גָּבַר gābar, v. [25] [→ 1475, 1476, 1484, 1485, 1505, 1506, 1507, 1508, 1509]
rose [3], triumph [3], great [2], strengthen [2], winning [2], arrogantly [1], confirm [1], flooded [1], greater [1], increasing [1], needed [1], overpowered [1], overwhelmed [1], prevailed [1], prevails [1], stronger [1], strongest [1], vaunts himself [1]

Ge 7: 18 [A] The waters **rose** and increased greatly on the earth,
7: 19 [A] They **rose** greatly on the earth, and all the high mountains
7: 20 [A] The waters **rose** and covered the mountains to a depth of
7: 24 [A] The waters **flooded** the earth for a hundred and fifty days.
49: 26 [A] Your father's blessings *are* **greater** than the blessings of the
Ex 17: 11 [A] the Israelites *were* **winning**, but whenever he lowered his
17: 11 [A] he lowered his hands, the Amalekites *were* **winning**.
1Sa 2: 9 [A] silenced in darkness. "It is not by strength that one **prevails**;
2Sa 1: 23 [A] were swifter than eagles, *they were* **stronger** than lions.
11: 23 [A] "The men **overpowered** us and came out against us in the
1Ch 5: 2 [A] though Judah *was the* **strongest** of his brothers and a ruler
Job 15: 25 [F] his fist at God and **vaunts himself** against the Almighty,
21: 7 [A] do the wicked live on, growing old and **increasing** *in* power?
36: 9 [F] what they have done—that they have sinned **arrogantly**.
Ps 12: 4 [12:5] [G] that says, "*We will* **triumph** with our tongues;
65: 3 [65:4] [A] *When* we *were* **overwhelmed** *by* sins, you forgave
103: 11 [A] above the earth, *so* **great** *is* his love for those who fear him;
117: 2 [A] For **great** *is* his love toward us, and the faithfulness of the
Ecc 10: 10 [D] more strength *is* **needed** but skill will bring success.
Isa 42: 13 [F] will raise the battle cry and *will* **triumph** over his enemies.
Jer 9: 3 [9:2] [A] it is not by truth that *they* **triumph** in the land.
La 1: 16 [A] My children are destitute because the enemy *has* **prevailed**."
Da 9: 27 [G] *He will* **confirm** a covenant with many for one 'seven.' In the
Zec 10: 6 [D] "*I will* **strengthen** the house of Judah and save the house of
10: 12 [D] *I will* **strengthen** them in the LORD and in his name they

1505 ¹גֶּבֶר geber¹, n.m. [66] [→ 1205, 1506, 1508; cf. 1504; Ar 10131]
man [39], men [7], one [3], man's [2], *untranslated* [1], any[s] [1], blameless [+9459] [1], boy [1], each[s] [1], families [1], he[s] [1], him[s] [1], husband's [1], men's [1], mighty man [1], ruler [+8133] [1], soldiers [+408+4878] [1], strong man [1], whoever[s] [1]

Ex 10: 11 Have only the **men** go; and worship the LORD, since that's what
12: 37 There were about six hundred thousand **men** on foot, besides
Nu 24: 3 of Balaam son of Beor, the oracle of **one** whose eye sees clearly,
24: 15 of Balaam son of Beor, the oracle of **one** whose eye sees clearly,
Dt 22: 5 A woman must not wear **men's** clothing, nor a man wear women's
22: 5 must not wear men's clothing, nor a **man** wear women's clothing,
Jos 7: 14 the family that the LORD takes shall come forward man by **man**.
7: 17 He had the clan of the Zerahites come forward by **families**,
7: 18 Joshua had his family come forward man by **man**, and Achan son
Jdg 5: 30 a girl or two for each **man**, colorful garments as plunder for Sisera,
2Sa 23: 1 son of Jesse, the oracle of the **man** exalted by the Most High,
1Ch 23: 3 and the total number of **men** was thirty-eight thousand.
24: 4 A larger number of leaders **[NIE]** were found among Eleazar's
26: 12 These divisions of the gatekeepers, through their chief **men**,
Job 3: 3 day of my birth perish, and the night it was said, 'A **boy** is born!'
3: 23 Why is life given to a **man** whose way is hidden, whom God has
4: 17 righteous than God? Can a **man** be more pure than his Maker?
10: 5 your days like those of a mortal or your years like those of a **man**,
14: 10 But **man** dies and is laid low; he breathes his last and is no more.
14: 14 If a **man** dies, will he live again? All the days of my hard service I
16: 21 on behalf of a **man** he pleads with God as a man pleads for his
22: 2 "Can a **man** be of benefit to God? Can even a wise man benefit
33: 17 to turn man from wrongdoing and keep **him**[s] from pride,
33: 29 "God does all these things to a **man**—twice, even three times—
34: 7 What **man** is like Job, who drinks scorn like water?
34: 9 For he says, 'It profits a **man** nothing when he tries to please God.'
34: 34 "Men of understanding declare, wise **men** who hear me say to me,
38: 3 Brace yourself like a **man**; I will question you, and you shall
40: 7 "Brace yourself like a **man**; I will question you, and you shall
Ps 18: 25 [18:26] to the **blameless** [+9459] you show yourself blameless,
34: 8 [34:9] is good; blessed is the **man** who takes refuge in him.
37: 23 If the LORD delights in a **man's** way, he makes his steps firm;
40: 4 [40:5] Blessed is the **man** who makes the LORD his trust, who
52: 7 [52:9] "Here now is the **man** who did not make God his
88: 4 [88:5] who go down to the pit; I am like a **man** without strength.
89: 48 [89:49] What **man** can live and not see death, or save himself
94: 12 Blessed is the **man** you discipline, O LORD, the man you teach
127: 5 Blessed is the **man** whose quiver is full of them. They will not be
128: 4 Thus is the **man** blessed who fears the LORD.
Pr 6: 34 for jealousy arouses a **husband's** fury, and he will show no mercy
20: 24 A **man's** steps are directed by the LORD. How then can anyone
24: 5 A wise **man** has great power, and a man of knowledge increases
28: 3 A **ruler** [+8133] who oppresses the poor is like a driving rain that
28: 21 is not good—yet a **man** will do wrong for a piece of bread.
29: 5 **Whoever**[s] flatters his neighbor is spreading a net for his feet.
30: 1 an oracle: This **man** declared to Ithiel, to Ithiel and to Ucal:
30: 19 of a ship on the high seas, and the way of a **man** with a maiden.
Isa 22: 17 to take firm hold of you and hurl you away, O you **mighty man**.
Jer 17: 5 "Cursed is the **one** who trusts in man, who depends on flesh for his
17: 7 "But blessed is the **man** who trusts in the LORD, whose
22: 30 this man as if childless, a **man** who will not prosper in his lifetime,
23: 9 like a **man** overcome by wine, because of the LORD and his holy
30: 6 why do I see every **strong man** with his hands on his stomach like
31: 22 will create a new thing on earth—a woman will surround a **man**."
41: 16 the **soldiers** [+408+4878], women, children and court officials he
43: 6 They also led away all the **men**, women and children
44: 20 to all the people, both **men** and women, who were answering him,
La 3: 1 I am the **man** who has seen affliction by the rod of his wrath.
3: 27 It is good for a **man** to bear the yoke while he is young.
3: 35 to deny a **man** his rights before the Most High,
3: 39 Why should **any**[s] living man complain when punished for his sins?
Da 8: 15 to understand it, there before me stood one who looked like a **man**.
Joel 2: 8 They do not jostle each other; **each**[s] marches straight ahead.
Mic 2: 2 They defraud a **man** of his home, a fellowman of his inheritance.
Hab 2: 5 indeed, wine betrays him; **he**[s] is arrogant and never at rest.
Zec 13: 7 against my shepherd, against the **man** who is close to me!"

1506 ²גֶּבֶר geber², n.pr.m. [1] [√ 1505; cf. 1504]
Geber [1]

1Ki 4: 19 **Geber** son of Uri—in Gilead (the country of Sihon king of the

1507 גִּבָּר gibbār, n.pr.m. [1] [√ 1504]

Gibbar [1]

Ezr 2:20 of **Gibbar** 95

1508 גַּבְרִיאֵל gabrî'ēl, n.pr.m. [2] [√ 1505 + 446]

Gabriel [2]

Da 8:16 the Ulai calling, "**Gabriel**, tell this man the meaning of the vision."
9:21 while I was still in prayer, **Gabriel**, the man I had seen in the

1509 גְּבֶרֶת g[e]beret, n.f. [2] [√ 1504]

queen [2]

Isa 47: 5 the Babylonians; no more will you be called **queen** *of* kingdoms.
47: 7 You said, 'I will continue forever—the eternal **queen**!' But you did

1510 גִּבְּתוֹן gibb[e]tôn, n.pr.loc. [6] [√ 1467]

Gibbethon [5], it[s] [1]

Jos 19:44 Eltekeh, **Gibbethon**, Baalath,
21:23 Also from the tribe of Dan they received Eltekeh, **Gibbethon**,
1Ki 15:27 he struck him down at **Gibbethon**, a Philistine town, while Nadab
15:27 a Philistine town, while Nadab and all Israel were besieging **it**[s].
16:15 The army was encamped near **Gibbethon**, a Philistine town.
16:17 and all the Israelites with him withdrew from **Gibbethon**

1511 גָּג gāg, n.m. [30]

roof [18], roofs [7], top [3], roof of house [1], top of the wall [1]

Ex 30: 3 Overlay the **top** and all the sides and the horns with pure gold,
37:26 They overlaid the **top** and all the sides and the horns with pure
Dt 22: 8 make a parapet around your **roof** so that you may not bring the
Jos 2: 6 (But she had taken them up to the **roof** and hidden them under the
2: 6 hidden them under the stalks of flax she had laid out on the **roof**.)
2: 8 Before the spies lay down for the night, she went up on the **roof**
Jdg 9:51 They locked themselves in and climbed up on the tower **roof**.
16:27 on the **roof** were about three thousand men and women watching
1Sa 9:25 to the town, Samuel talked with Saul on the **roof of** his **house**.
9:26 rose about daybreak and Samuel called to Saul on the **roof**,
2Sa 11: 2 got up from his bed and walked around on the **roof** *of* the palace.
11: 2 From the **roof** he saw a woman bathing. The woman was very
16:22 So they pitched a tent for Absalom on the **roof**, and he lay with his
18:24 the watchman went up to the **roof** *of* the gateway by the wall.
2Ki 19:26 like tender green shoots, like grass sprouting on the **roof**, scorched
23:12 of Judah had erected on the **roof** *near* the upper room of Ahaz,
Ne 8:16 back branches and built themselves booths on their own **roofs**,
Ps 102: 7 [102:8] I lie awake; I have become like a bird alone on a **roof**.
129: 6 May they be like grass on the **roof**, which withers before it can
Pr 21: 9 Better to live on a corner of the **roof** than share a house with a
25:24 Better to live on a corner of the **roof** than share a house with a
Isa 15: 3 on the **roofs** and in the public squares they all wail, prostrate with
22: 1 What troubles you now, that you have all gone up on the **roofs**,
37:27 like tender green shoots, like grass sprouting on the **roof**, scorched
Jer 19:13 all the houses where they burned incense on the **roofs** to all the
32:29 provoked me to anger by burning incense on the **roofs** to Baal
48:38 On all the **roofs** *in* Moab and in the public squares there is nothing
Eze 40:13 he measured the gateway from the **top of the** *rear* **wall** *of* one
40:13 the top of the rear wall of one alcove to the **top** *of* the opposite one;
Zep 1: 5 those who bow down on the **roofs** to worship the starry host,

1512 גַּד gad[1], n.m. [2]

coriander [2]

Ex 16:31 It was white like **coriander** seed and tasted like wafers made with
Nu 11: 7 The manna was like **coriander** seed and looked like resin.

1513 גַּד gad[2], n.[m.]. [2] [→ 1514, 1534, 1535]

Fortune [1], good fortune [1]

Ge 30:11 Then Leah said, "What **good fortune**!" So she named him Gad.
Isa 65:11 who spread a table for **Fortune** and fill bowls of mixed wine for

1514 גָּד gād, n.pr.m. [70] [→ 1254, 1532, 1533; cf. 1513]

Gad [43], Gadites [+1201] [16], Gad [+1201] [7], *untranslated* [2], Gad's [1], they[s] [+1201+1201+2256+8017] [1]

Ge 30:11 Then Leah said, "What good fortune!" So she named him **Gad**.
35:26 **Gad** and Asher. These were the sons of Jacob, who were born to
46:16 The sons of **Gad**: Zephon, Haggi, Shuni, Ezbon, Eri, Arodi
49:19 "**Gad** will be attacked by a band of raiders, but he will attack them
Ex 1: 4 Dan and Naphtali; **Gad** and Asher.
Nu 1:14 from **Gad**, Eliasaph son of Deuel;
1:24 From the descendants of **Gad**: All the men twenty years old
1:25 The number from the tribe of **Gad** was 45,650.
2:14 The tribe of **Gad** will be next. The leader of the people of Gad is
2:14 The leader of the people of **Gad** is Eliasaph son of Deuel.
7:42 son of Deuel, the leader of the people of **Gad**, brought his offering.
10:20 son of Deuel was over the division of the tribe of **Gad** [+1201].
13:15 from the tribe of **Gad**, Geuel son of Maki.
26:15 The descendants of **Gad** by their clans were: through Zephon,
26:18 These were the clans of **Gad** [+1201]; those numbered were
32: 1 The Reubenites and **Gadites** [+1201], who had very large herds
32: 2 So **they**[s] [+1201+1201+2256+8017] came to Moses and Eleazar
32: 6 Moses said to the **Gadites** [+1201] and Reubenites, "Shall your
32:25 The **Gadites** [+1201] and Reubenites said to Moses, "We your
32:29 He said to them, "If the **Gadites** [+1201] and Reubenites,
32:31 The **Gadites** [+1201] and Reubenites answered, "Your servants
32:33 Moses gave to the **Gadites** [+1201], the Reubenites and the
32:34 The **Gadites** [+1201] built up Dibon, Ataroth, Aroer,
Dt 27:13 Reuben, **Gad**, Asher, Zebulun, Dan and Naphtali.
33:20 About **Gad** he said: "Blessed is he who enlarges Gad's domain!
33:20 About Gad he said: "Blessed is he who enlarges **Gad's** domain!
Jos 4:12 **Gad** and the half-tribe of Manasseh crossed over, armed,
13:24 This is what Moses had given to the tribe of **Gad**, clan by clan:
13:24 is what Moses had given to the tribe of Gad, **[RPH]** clan by clan:
13:28 and their villages were the inheritance of the **Gadites** [+1201],
18: 7 **Gad**, Reuben and the half-tribe of Manasseh have already received
20: 8 Ramoth in Gilead in the tribe of **Gad**, and Golan in Bashan in the
21: 7 twelve towns from the tribes of Reuben, **Gad** and Zebulun.
21:38 from the tribe of **Gad**, Ramoth in Gilead (a city of refuge for one
22: 9 the **Gadites** [+1201] and the half-tribe of Manasseh left the
22:10 the **Gadites** [+1201] and the half-tribe of Manasseh built an
22:11 of Canaan at Geliloth **[RPH]** near the Jordan on the Israelite side,
22:13 to Reuben, **Gad** [+1201] and the half-tribe of Manasseh.
22:15 to Reuben, **Gad** [+1201] and the half-tribe of Manasseh—
22:21 Reuben, **Gad** [+1201] and the half-tribe of Manasseh replied to the
22:25 between us and you—you Reubenites and **Gadites** [+1201]!
22:30 heard what Reuben, **Gad** [+1201] and Manasseh had to say,
22:31 of Eleazar, the priest, said to Reuben, **Gad** [+1201] and Manasseh,
22:32 and **Gadites** [+1201] in Gilead and reported to the Israelites.
22:33 the country where the Reubenites and the **Gadites** [+1201] lived.
22:34 the Reubenites and the **Gadites** [+1201] gave the altar this name:
1Sa 13: 7 Some Hebrews even crossed the Jordan to the land of **Gad**
22: 5 But the prophet **Gad** said to David, "Do not stay in the stronghold.
2Sa 24: 5 the town in the gorge, and then went through **Gad** and on to Jazer.
24:11 the word of the LORD had come to **Gad** the prophet,
24:13 So **Gad** went to David and said to him, "Shall there come upon
24:14 David said to **Gad**, "I am in deep distress. Let us fall into the hands
24:18 On that day **Gad** went to David and said to him, "Go up and build
24:19 So David went up, as the LORD had commanded through **Gad**.
1Ch 2: 2 Dan, Joseph, Benjamin, Naphtali, **Gad** and Asher.
5:11 The **Gadites** [+1201] lived next to them in Bashan, as far as
6:63 [6:48] twelve towns from the tribes of Reuben, **Gad** and Zebulun.
6:80 [6:65] and from the tribe of **Gad** they received Ramoth in Gilead,
12:14 [12:15] These **Gadites** [+1201] were army commanders; the least
21: 9 The LORD said to **Gad**, David's seer,
21:11 So **Gad** went to David and said to him, "This is what the LORD
21:13 David said to **Gad**, "I am in deep distress. Let me fall into the
21:18 Then the angel of the LORD ordered **Gad** to tell David to go up
21:19 So David went up in obedience to the word that **Gad** had spoken in
29:29 the records of Nathan the prophet and the records of **Gad** the seer,
2Ch 29:25 by David and **Gad** the king's seer and Nathan the prophet;
Jer 49: 1 Has she no heirs? Why then has Molech taken possession of **Gad**?
Eze 48:27 "**Gad** will have one portion; it will border the territory of Zebulun
48:28 "The southern boundary of **Gad** will run south from Tamar to the
48:34 the gate of **Gad**, the gate of Asher and the gate of Naphtali.

1515 גִּדְגָּד gidgād, n.pr.loc. Not used in NIV/BHS [cf. 2044]

1516 גֻּדְגֹּדָה gudgōdâ, n.pr.loc. [2]

untranslated [1], Gudgodah [1]

Dt 10: 7 From there they traveled to **Gudgodah** and on to Jotbathah,
10: 7 there they traveled to Gudgodah and **[RPH]** on to Jotbathah,

1517 גָּדַד gādad[1], v. [5] [→ 1518, 1521, 1522, 1523, 1574?; Ar 10134]

cut yourselves [2], cut himself [1], cut themselves [1], slashed themselves [1]

Dt 14: 1 [F] *Do* not **cut yourselves** or shave the front of your heads for
1Ki 18:28 [F] and **slashed themselves** with swords and spears,
Jer 16: 6 [F] and no *one will* **cut himself** or shave his head for them.
41: 5 [F] torn their clothes and **cut themselves** came from Shechem,
47: 5 [F] O remnant on the plain, how long *will you* **cut yourselves**?

1518 ²גָּדַד **gādad^2**, v. [3] [√ 1517]

band together [1], marshal troops [1], thronged [1]

Ps 94: 21 [A] *They* **band together** against the righteous and condemn the
Jer 5: 7 [F] and **thronged** *to* the houses of prostitutes.
Mic 5: 1 [4:14] [F] **Marshal** *your* **troops**, O city of troops, for a siege is

1519 גָּדָה **gādâ**, n.f. Not used in NIV/BHS [→ 1536]

1520 גַּדָּה **gaddâ**, n.pr.loc. Not used in NIV/BHS [→ 2961]

1521 ¹גְּדוּדִי **g^{e}dûd^1**, n.m. & f. [1] [√ 1517]

ridges [1]

Ps 65: 10 [65:11] You drench its furrows and level its **ridges**; you soften it

1522 ²גְּדוּד **g^{e}dûd^2**, n.m. [33] [√ 1517]

troops [5], *untranslated* [3], raiders [3], raiding bands [3], band of raiders [2], bands [2], forces [2], raiding party [2], troop [2], band of rebels [1], bandits [1], divisions [1], invaders [1], marauders [1], men ready for battle [+4878+7372] [1], raid [1], them[s] [+2021] [1], troops [+1201] [1]

Ge 49: 19 "Gad will be attacked by a **band of raiders**, but he will attack
1Sa 30: 8 David inquired of the LORD, "Shall I pursue this **raiding party**?
30: 15 David asked him, "Can you lead me down to this **raiding party**?"
30: 15 over to my master, and I will take you down to **them**[s] [+2021]."
30: 23 protected us and handed over to us the **forces** that came against us.
2Sa 3: 22 Just then David's men and Joab returned from a **raid** and brought
4: 2 Now Saul's son had two men who were leaders of **raiding bands**.
22: 30 With your help I can advance against a **troop**; with my God I can
1Ki 11: 24 became the leader of a **band of rebels** when David destroyed the
2Ki 5: 2 Now **bands** from Aram had gone out and had taken captive a
6: 23 So the **bands** *from* Aram stopped raiding Israel's territory.
13: 20 Now Moabite **raiders** used to enter the country every spring.
13: 21 were burying a man, suddenly they saw a **band of raiders**;
24: 2 The LORD sent **[RPH]** Babylonian, Aramean, Moabite
24: 2 **[RPH]** Aramean, Moabite and Ammonite raiders against him.
24: 2 Aramean, **[RPH]** Moabite and Ammonite raiders against him.
24: 2 Moabite and Ammonite **raiders** against him.
1Ch 7: 4 they had 36,000 **men ready for battle** [+4878+7372], for they had
12: 18 [12:19] and made them leaders of his **raiding bands**.
12: 21 [12:22] They helped David against **raiding bands**, for all of them
2Ch 22: 1 Jehoram's youngest son, king in his place, since the **raiders**,
25: 9 what about the hundred talents I paid for these Israelite **troops**?"
25: 10 So Amaziah dismissed the **troops** who had come to him from
25: 13 Meanwhile the **troops** [+1201] that Amaziah had sent back
26: 11 ready to go out by **divisions** according to their numbers as
Job 19: 12 His **troops** advance in force; they build a siege ramp against me
25: 3 Can his **forces** be numbered? Upon whom does his light not rise?
29: 25 and sat as their chief; I dwelt as a king among his **troops**;
Ps 18: 29 [18:30] With your help I can advance against a **troop**; with my
Jer 18: 22 from their houses when you suddenly bring **invaders** against them,
Hos 6: 9 As **marauders** lie in ambush for a man, so do bands of priests;
7: 1 thieves break into houses, **bandits** rob in the streets;
Mic 5: 1 [4:14] Marshal your troops, O city of **troops**, for a siege is laid

1523 גְּדוּדָה **g^{e}dûdâ**, n.m. & f. [1] [√ 1517]

slashed [1]

Jer 48: 37 every hand is **slashed** and every waist is covered with sackcloth.

1524 גָּדוֹל **gādôl**, a. [528] [→ 2045; cf. 1540]

great [244], large [41], high [23], greatest [17], loud [16], greater [9], mighty [9], older [9], heavy [8], old [7], vast [7], very [6], greatly [5], terrible [5], bitterly [4], important [4], much [4], oldest [4], powerful [4], strong [4], called out [+928+7754+7924] [3], even more [3], larger [3], many [3], aloud [+7754] [2], awful [2], became more and more powerful [+2143+2143+2256] [2], deep [2], fierce [2], great [+4394] [2], huge [2], louder [2], loudly [2], more [2], such [2], wealthy [2], wonders [2], *untranslated* [1], all [1], aloud [+928+7754] [1], at all [+196+7785] [1], awful [+2098] [1], became more and more powerful [+2143+2256] [1], better [1], big [1], boastful [+1819] [1], chief [1], deeds [1], destroyed [+4394+4804+5782] [1], devastated [+4394+4804+5782] [1], difficult [1], far [1], feat [+1821] [1], fine [+2256+3202] [1], great amount [1], grievous [1], hard [1], harsh [1], highly regarded [+4394] [1], hot-tempered [+2779] [1], huge [+4200+4394+6330] [1], immense [1], imposing [+4200+5260] [1], intense [+4394] [1], large [+4394] [1], leaders [1], leading [1], loud [+4394+6330] [1], loudly [+928+7754] [1], main [1], most important [1], nobles [1], noisy din [+7754] [1], nothing [+1821+2256+4202+7785] [1], older [+4946] [1], power [1], preeminent [1], prominent [1], rich [1], screamed [+928+7754+7924] [1], serious [1], shout [+7754+7924] [1], so much [1], solemn [1], strange [1], stronger [1], such [+2296] [1], terrified [+3707+3711] [1], thick [1], top [1], total [+4394] [1], trembled violently [+3006+3010+4394+6330] [1], utterly [1], vast [+4394] [1], vast [+4394+4394] [1], violent [1], well-to-do [1]

Ge 1: 16 God made two **great** lights—the greater light to govern the day
1: 16 the **greater** light to govern the day and the lesser light to govern
1: 21 So God created the **great** creatures of the sea and every living
4: 13 Cain said to the LORD, "My punishment is **more** than I can bear.
10: 12 which is between Nineveh and Calah; that is the **great** city.
10: 21 Sons were also born to Shem, whose **older** brother was Japheth;
12: 2 "I will make you into a **great** nation and I will bless you; I will
12: 17 the LORD inflicted **serious** diseases on Pharaoh and his
15: 12 a deep sleep, and a **thick** and dreadful darkness came over him.
15: 14 as slaves, and afterward they will come out with **great** possessions.
15: 18 from the river of Egypt to the **great** river, the Euphrates—
17: 20 the father of twelve rulers, and I will make him into a **great** nation.
18: 18 Abraham will surely become a **great** and powerful nation,
19: 11 young and **old**, with blindness so that they could not find the door.
20: 9 How have I wronged you that you have brought *such* **great** guilt
21: 8 and on the day Isaac was weaned Abraham held a **great** feast.
21: 18 and take him by the hand, for I will make him into a **great** nation."
27: 1 he called for Esau his **older** son and said to him, "My son."
27: 15 Then Rebekah took the best clothes of Esau her **older** son,
27: 33 Isaac **trembled violently** [+3006+3010+4394+6330] and said,
27: 34 he burst out with a **loud** [+4394+6330] and bitter cry and said to
27: 42 When Rebekah was told what her **older** son Esau had said,
29: 2 from that well. The stone over the mouth of the well was **large**.
29: 7 "Look," he said, "the sun is still **high**; it is not time for the flocks
29: 16 the name of the **older** was Leah, and the name of the younger was
39: 9 No one is **greater** in this house than I am. My master has withheld
39: 9 How then could I do **such** [+2296] a wicked thing and sin against
39: 14 came in here to sleep with me, but *I* **screamed** [+928+7754+7924].
41: 29 Seven years of **great** abundance are coming throughout the land of
44: 12 to search, beginning with the **oldest** and ending with the youngest.
45: 7 a remnant on earth and to save your lives by a **great** deliverance.
46: 3 to go down to Egypt, for I will make you into a **great** nation there.
50: 10 floor of Atad, near the Jordan, they lamented **loudly** and bitterly;
Ex 3: 3 So Moses thought, "I will go over and see this **strange** sight—
6: 6 you with an outstretched arm and with **mighty** acts of judgment.
7: 4 and with **mighty** acts of judgment I will bring out my divisions,
11: 3 Moses himself was **highly** [+4394] **regarded** in Egypt by
11: 6 There will be **loud** wailing throughout Egypt—worse than there
12: 30 got up during the night, and there was **loud** wailing in Egypt,
14: 31 when the Israelites saw the **great** power the LORD displayed
15: 16 By the **power** *of* your arm they will be as still as a stone—
18: 11 Now I know that the LORD is **greater** than all other gods,
18: 22 people at all times, but have them bring every **difficult** case to you;
32: 10 that I may destroy them. Then I will make you into a **great** nation."
32: 11 whom you brought out of Egypt with **great** power and a mighty
32: 21 did these people do to you, that you led them into *such* **great** sin?"
32: 30 day Moses said to the people, "You have committed a **great** sin.
32: 31 and said, "Oh, what a **great** sin these people have committed!
Lev 19: 15 do not show partiality to the poor or favoritism to the **great**,
21: 10 " 'The **high** priest, the one among his brothers who has had the
Nu 13: 28 live there are powerful, and the cities are fortified and very **large**.
14: 12 but I will make you into a nation **greater** and stronger than they."
22: 18 I could not do *anything* **great** or small to go beyond the command
34: 6 " 'Your western boundary will be the coast of the **Great** Sea.
34: 7 northern boundary, run a line from the **Great** Sea to Mount Hor
35: 25 He must stay there until the death of the **high** priest, who was
35: 28 must stay in his city of refuge until the death of the **high** priest;
35: 28 only after the death of the **high** priest may he return to his own
Dt 1: 7 and to Lebanon, as far as the **great** river, the Euphrates.
1: 17 Do not show partiality in judging; hear both small and **great** alike.
1: 19 went toward the hill country of the Amorites through all that **vast**
1: 28 They say, 'The people are **stronger** and taller than we are;
1: 28 and taller than we are; the cities are **large**, with walls up to the sky.
2: 7 He has watched over your journey through this **vast** desert.
2: 10 a people **strong** and numerous, and as tall as the Anakites.
2: 21 They were a people **strong** and numerous, and as tall as the
4: 6 "Surely this **great** nation is a wise and understanding people."
4: 7 so **great** as to have their gods near them the way the LORD our
4: 8 what other nation is so **great** as to have such righteous decrees
4: 32 Has anything so **great** as this ever happened, or has anything like it
4: 34 and an outstretched arm, or by **great** and awesome deeds,
4: 36 On earth he showed you his **great** fire, and you heard his words
4: 37 brought you out of Egypt by his Presence and his **great** strength,
4: 38 to drive out before you nations **greater** and stronger than you
5: 22 These are the commandments the LORD proclaimed in a **loud**
5: 25 This **great** fire will consume us, and we will die if we hear the
6: 10 to give you—a land with **large**, flourishing cities you did not build,
6: 22 **great** and terrible—upon Egypt and Pharaoh and his whole
7: 19 You saw with your own eyes the **great** trials, the miraculous signs
7: 21 your God, who is among you, is a **great** and awesome God.

Dt 7:23 throwing them into **great** confusion until they are destroyed.
8:15 He led you through the **vast** and dreadful desert, that thirsty
9: 1 to go in and dispossess nations **greater** and stronger than you,
9: 1 stronger than you, with **large** cities that have walls up to the sky.
9: 2 The people are **strong** and tall—Anakites! You know about them
9:29 your inheritance that you brought out by your **great** power
10:17 of gods and Lord of lords, the **great** God, mighty and awesome,
10:21 who performed for you those **great** and awesome wonders you saw
11: 7 it was your own eyes that saw all these **great** things the LORD
11:23 and you will dispossess nations **larger** and stronger than you.
18:16 us not hear the voice of the LORD our God nor see this **great**
25:13 not have two differing weights in your bag—one **heavy**, one light.
25:14 have two differing measures in your house—one **large**, one small.
26: 5 with a few people and lived there and became a **great** nation,
26: 8 with **great** terror and with miraculous signs and wonders.
27: 2 is giving you, set up some **large** stones and coat them with plaster.
28:59 **harsh** and prolonged disasters, and severe and lingering illnesses.
29: 3 [29:2] With your own eyes you saw those **great** trials, those
29: 3 [29:2] great trials, those miraculous signs and **great** wonders.
29:24 [29:23] done this to this land? Why this **fierce**, burning anger?"
29:28 [29:27] in **great** wrath the LORD uprooted them from their land
34:12 or performed the awesome **deeds** that Moses did in the sight of all
Jos 1: 4 the desert to Lebanon, and from the **great** river, the Euphrates—
1: 4 all the Hittite country—to the **Great** Sea on the west.
6: 5 a long blast on the trumpets, have all the people give a **loud** shout;
6:20 the trumpet, when the people gave a **loud** shout, the wall collapsed;
7: 9 from the earth. What then will you do for your own **great** name?"
7:26 Over Achan they heaped up a **large** pile of rocks, which remains to
8:29 they raised a **large** pile of rocks over it, which remains to this day.
9: 1 along the entire coast of the **Great** Sea as far as Lebanon (the kings
10: 2 because Gibeon was an **important** city, like one of the royal cities;
10: 2 it was **larger** than Ai, and all its men were good fighters.
10:10 before Israel, who defeated them in a **great** victory at Gibeon.
10:11 the LORD hurled **large** hailstones down on them from the sky,
10:18 he said, "Roll **large** rocks up to the mouth of the cave, and post
10:20 So Joshua and the Israelites **destroyed** [+4394+4804+5782] them
10:27 At the mouth of the cave they placed **large** rocks, which are there
14:12 the Anakites were there and their cities were **large** and fortified,
14:15 Arba after Arba, who was the **greatest** man among the Anakites.)
15:12 The western boundary is the coastline of the **Great** Sea. These are
15:47 as the Wadi of Egypt and the coastline of the **Great** [K 1473] Sea.
17:17 and Manasseh—"You are numerous and **very** powerful.
20: 6 and until the death of the **high** priest who is serving at that time.
22:10 the half-tribe of Manasseh built an **imposing** [+4200+5260] altar
23: 4 I conquered—between the Jordan and the **Great** Sea in the west.
23: 9 "The LORD has driven out before you **great** and powerful
24:17 land of slavery, and performed those **great** signs before our eyes.
24:26 he took a **large** stone and set it up there under the oak near the holy
Jdg 2: 7 who had seen all the **great** things the LORD had done for Israel.
5:15 In the districts of Reuben there was **much** searching of heart.
5:16 In the districts of Reuben there was **much** searching of heart.
11:33 *He* **devastated** [+4394+4804+5782] twenty towns from Aroer to
15: 8 He attacked them viciously and slaughtered **many** of them.
15:18 to the LORD, "You have given your servant this **great** victory.
16: 5 "See if you can lure him into showing you the secret of his **great**
16: 6 "Tell me the secret of your **great** strength and how you can be tied
16:15 a fool of me and haven't told me the secret of your **great** strength."
16:23 Now the rulers of the Philistines assembled to offer a **great**
21: 2 God until evening, raising their voices and weeping **bitterly**.
21: 5 For they had taken a **solemn** oath that anyone who failed to
1Sa 2:17 This sin of the young men was very **great** in the LORD's sight,
4: 5 all Israel raised such a **great** shout that the ground shook.
4: 6 Philistines asked, "What's **all** this shouting in the Hebrew camp?"
4:10 The slaughter was very **great**; Israel lost thirty thousand foot
4:17 fled before the Philistines, and the army has suffered **heavy** losses.
5: 9 hand was against that city, throwing it into a **great** [+4394] panic.
5: 9 people of the city, both young and **old**, with an outbreak of tumors.
6: 9 then the LORD has brought this **great** disaster on us.
6:14 Joshua of Beth Shemesh, and there it stopped beside a **large** rock.
6:15 containing the gold objects, and placed them on the **large** rock.
6:18 The **large** rock, on which they set the ark of the LORD, is a
6:19 because of the **heavy** blow the LORD had dealt them,
7:10 that day the LORD thundered with **loud** thunder against the
12:16 see this **great** thing the LORD is about to do before your eyes!
12:22 For the sake of his **great** name the LORD will not reject his
14:20 They found the Philistines in **total** [+4394] confusion,
14:33 have broken faith," he said. "Roll a **large** stone over here at once."
14:45 he who has brought about this **great** deliverance in Israel?
17:13 Jesse's three **oldest** sons had followed Saul to the war: The
17:14 David was the youngest. The three **oldest** followed Saul,
17:25 The king will give **great** wealth to the man who kills him.
17:28 When Eliab, David's **oldest** brother, heard him speaking with the
18:17 Saul said to David, "Here is my **older** daughter Merab. I will give
19: 5 The LORD won a **great** victory for all Israel, and you saw it
19: 8 He struck them with **such** force that they fled before him.
19:22 he himself left for Ramah and went to the **great** cistern at Secu.
20: 2 doesn't do anything, **great** or small, without confiding in me.
22:15 for your servant knows nothing **at all** [+196+7785] about this
23: 5 He inflicted **heavy** losses on the Philistines and saved the people of
25: 2 in Maon, who had property there at Carmel, was very **wealthy**.
25:36 So she told him **nothing** [+1821+2256+4202+7785] until daybreak.
28:12 she cried out at the **top** of her voice and said to Saul, "Why have
30: 2 captive the women and all who were in it, both young and **old**.
30:16 because of the **great amount** of plunder they had taken from the
30:19 young or **old**, boy or girl, plunder or anything else they had taken.
2Sa 3:38 realize that a prince and a **great** *man* has fallen in Israel this day?
5:10 And he **became more and more powerful** [+2143+2143+2256],
7: 9 Now I will make your name **great**, like the names of the greatest
7: 9 your name great, like the names of the **greatest** *men* of the earth.
13:15 Then Amnon hated her with **intense** [+4394] hatred. In fact,
13:15 In fact, he hated her **more** than he had loved her. Amnon said to
13:16 "Sending me away would be a **greater** wrong than what you have
13:36 The king, too, and all his servants wept very **bitterly**.
15:23 The whole countryside wept **aloud** [+7754] as all the people
18: 7 defeated by David's men, and the casualties that day were **great**—
18: 9 and as the mule went under the thick branches of a **large** oak,
18:17 threw him into a **big** pit in the forest and piled up a large heap of
18:17 in the forest and piled up a **large** [+4394] heap of rocks over him.
18:29 "I saw **great** confusion just as Joab was about to send the king's
19: 4 [19:5] The king covered his face and cried **aloud** [+7754], "O my
19:32 [19:33] his stay in Mahanaim, for he was a very **wealthy** man.
20: 8 While they were at the **great** rock in Gibeon, Amasa came to meet
23:10 to the sword. The LORD brought about a **great** victory that day.
23:12 Philistines down, and the LORD brought about a **great** victory.
1Ki 1:40 the people went up after him, playing flutes and rejoicing **greatly**,
2:22 after all, he is my **older** [+4946] brother—yes, for him and for
3: 4 to offer sacrifices, for that was the **most important** high place,
3: 6 "You have shown **great** kindness to your servant, my father David,
3: 6 You have continued this **great** kindness to him and have given him
4:13 in Bashan and its sixty **large** walled cities with bronze gate bars);
5:17 [5:31] **large** blocks of quality stone to provide a foundation of
7: 9 from the outside to the **great** courtyard and from foundation to
7:10 The foundations were laid with **large** stones of good quality,
7:12 The **great** courtyard was surrounded by a wall of three courses of
8:42 for men will hear of your **great** name and your mighty hand
8:55 He stood and blessed the whole assembly of Israel in a **loud** voice,
8:65 a **vast** assembly, people from Lebo Hamath to the Wadi of Egypt.
10:18 the king made a **great** throne inlaid with ivory and overlaid with
18:27 "Shout **louder**!" he said. "Surely he is a god! Perhaps he is deep in
18:28 So they shouted **louder** and slashed themselves with swords
18:45 the wind rose, a **heavy** rain came on and Ahab rode off to Jezreel.
19:11 a **great** and powerful wind tore the mountains apart and shattered
20:13 "This is what the LORD says: 'Do you see this **vast** army?
20:21 and chariots and inflicted **heavy** losses on the Arameans.
20:28 a god of the valleys, I will deliver this **vast** army into your hands,
22:31 not fight with anyone, small or **great**, except the king of Israel."
2Ki 3:27 The fury against Israel was **great**; they withdrew and returned to
4: 8 a **well-to-do** woman was there, who urged him to stay for a meal.
4:38 "Put on the **large** pot and cook some stew for these men."
5: 1 He was a **great** man in the sight of his master and highly regarded,
5:13 "My father, if the prophet had told you to do some **great** thing,
6:23 So he prepared a **great** feast for them, and after they had finished
6:25 There was a **great** famine in the city; the siege lasted so long that a
7: 6 to hear the sound of chariots and horses and a **great** army,
8: 4 and had said, "Tell me about all the **great** *things* Elisha has done."
8:13 could your servant, a mere dog, accomplish such a **feat** [+1821]?"
10: 6 seventy of them, were with the **leading** *men of* the city,
10:11 as well as all his **chief** *men*, his close friends and his priests,
10:19 is missing, because I am going to hold a **great** sacrifice for Baal.
12:10 [12:11] the royal secretary and the **high** priest came, counted the
16:15 "On the **large** new altar, offer the morning burnt offering and the
17:21 following the LORD and caused them to commit a **great** sin.
17:36 who brought you up out of Egypt with **mighty** power
18:19 " 'This is what the **great** king, the king of Assyria, says:
18:28 commander stood and **called out** [+928+7754+7924] in Hebrew:
18:28 in Hebrew: "Hear the word of the **great** king, the king of Assyria!
20: 3 done what is good in your eyes." And Hezekiah wept **bitterly**.
22: 4 "Go up to Hilkiah the **high** priest and have him get ready the
22: 8 Hilkiah the **high** priest said to Shaphan the secretary, "I have found
22:13 **Great** is the LORD's anger that burns against us because our
23: 2 and the prophets—all the people from the least to the **greatest**.
23: 4 The king ordered Hilkiah the **high** priest, the priests next in rank
23:26 the LORD did not turn away from the heat of his **fierce** anger,
25: 9 houses of Jerusalem. Every **important** building he burned down.
25:26 At this, all the people from the least to the **greatest**, together with
1Ch 11: 9 David **became more and more powerful** [+2143+2143+2256],
11:14 Philistines down, and the LORD brought about a **great** victory.
12:14 [12:15] a match for a hundred, and the **greatest** for a thousand.

1Ch 12:22 [12:23] until he had a **great** army, like the army of God.
16:25 For **great** is the LORD and most worthy of praise; he is to be
17: 8 Now I will make your name like the names of the **greatest** *men* of
22: 8 to me: 'You have shed much blood and have fought **many** wars.
25: 8 Young and **old** alike, teacher as well as student, cast lots for their
26:13 cast for each gate, according to their families, young and **old** alike.
29: 1 The task is **great**, because this palatial structure is not for man
29: 9 to the LORD. David the king also rejoiced **greatly**.
29:22 and drank with **great** joy in the presence of the LORD that day.
2Ch 1: 8 "You have shown **great** kindness to David my father and have
1:10 this people, for who is able to govern this **great** people of yours?"
2: 5 [2:4] "The temple I am going to build will be **great**, because our
2: 5 [2:4] be great, because our God is **greater** than all other gods.
2: 9 [2:8] because the temple I build must be **large** and magnificent.
3: 5 He paneled the **main** hall with pine and covered it with fine gold
4: 9 the **large** court and the doors for the court, and overlaid the doors
6:32 because of your **great** name and your mighty hand and your
7: 8 a **vast** [+4394] assembly, people from Lebo Hamath to the Wadi of
9:17 the king made a **great** throne inlaid with ivory and overlaid with
15:13 were to be put to death, whether small or **great**, man or woman.
15:14 They took an oath to the LORD with **loud** acclamation, with
16:14 and they made a **huge** [+4200+4394+6330] fire in his honor.
18:30 not fight with anyone, small or **great**, except the king of Israel."
20:19 and praised the LORD, the God of Israel, with very **loud** voice.
21:14 your wives and everything that is yours, with a **heavy** blow.
26:15 and on the corner defenses to shoot arrows and hurl **large** stones.
28: 5 Arameans defeated him and took **many** of his *people* as prisoners
28: 5 hands of the king of Israel, who inflicted **heavy** casualties on him.
30:21 the Feast of Unleavened Bread for seven days with **great** rejoicing,
30:26 There was **great** joy in Jerusalem, for since the days of Solomon
31:15 fellow priests according to their divisions, **old** and young alike.
32:18 *they* **called out** [+928+7754+7924] in Hebrew to the people of
34: 9 They went to Hilkiah the **high** priest and gave him the money that
34:21 **Great** is the LORD's anger that is poured out on us because our
34:30 and the Levites—all the people from the least to the **greatest**.
36:18 both **large** and small, and the treasures of the LORD's temple
Ezr 3:11 And all the people gave a **great** shout of praise to the LORD,
3:12 wept **aloud** [+928+7754] when they saw the foundation of this
3:13 the sound of weeping, because the people made **so much** noise.
9: 7 the days of our forefathers until now, our guilt has been **great**.
9:13 has happened to us is a result of our evil deeds and our **great** guilt,
10:12 The whole assembly responded with a **loud** voice: "You are right!
Ne 1: 3 and are back in the province are in **great** trouble and disgrace.
1: 5 "O LORD, God of heaven, the **great** and awesome God,
1:10 whom you redeemed by your **great** strength and your mighty hand.
2:10 they were very **much** disturbed that someone had come to promote
3: 1 Eliashib the **high** priest and his fellow priests went to work
3:20 from the angle to the entrance of the house of Eliashib the **high**
3:27 from the **great** projecting tower to the wall of Ophel.
4:14 [4:8] Remember the Lord, who is **great** and awesome, and fight
5: 1 and their wives raised a **great** outcry against their Jewish brothers.
5: 7 So I called together a **large** meeting to deal with them
6: 3 "I am carrying on a **great** project and cannot go down. Why should
7: 4 Now the city was **large** and spacious, but there were few people in
8: 6 Ezra praised the LORD, the **great** God; and all the people lifted
8:12 and drink, to send portions of food and to celebrate with **great** joy,
8:17 had not celebrated it like this. And their joy was very **great**.
9: 4 who called with **loud** voices to the LORD their God.
9:18 you up out of Egypt,' or when they committed **awful** blasphemies.
9:25 and were well-nourished; they reveled in your **great** goodness.
9:26 order to turn them back to you; they committed **awful** blasphemies.
9:32 "Now therefore, O our God, the **great**, mighty and awesome God,
9:37 our bodies and our cattle as they please. We are in **great** distress.
12:31 I also assigned two **large** choirs to give thanks. One was to proceed
12:43 on that day they offered **great** sacrifices, rejoicing because God
12:43 great sacrifices, rejoicing because God had given them **great** joy.
13: 5 he had provided him with a **large** room formerly used to store the
13:27 Must we hear now that you too are doing all this **terrible**
13:28 One of the sons of Joiada son of Eliashib the **high** priest was
Est 1: 5 for all the people from the least to the **greatest**, who were in the
1:20 women will respect their husbands, from the least to the **greatest**."
2:18 the king gave a **great** banquet, Esther's banquet, for all his nobles
4: 1 and ashes, and went out into the city, wailing **loudly** and bitterly.
4: 3 there was **great** mourning among the Jews, with fasting, weeping
8:15 and white, a **large** crown of gold and a purple robe of fine linen.
9: 4 Mordecai was **prominent** in the palace; his reputation spread
9: 4 and he **became more and more powerful** [+2143+2256].
10: 3 **preeminent** among the Jews, and held in high esteem by his many
Job 1: 3 He was the **greatest** man among all the people of the East.
1:19 when suddenly a **mighty** wind swept in from the desert and struck
3:19 The small and the **great** are there, and the slave is freed from his
5: 9 He performs **wonders** that cannot be fathomed, miracles that
9:10 He performs **wonders** that cannot be fathomed, miracles that
37: 5 marvelous ways; he does **great** *things* beyond our understanding.
Ps 12: 3 [12:4] off all flattering lips and every **boastful** [+1819] tongue
21: 5 [21:6] Through the victories you gave, his glory is **great**;
47: 2 [47:3] the LORD Most High, the **great** King over all the earth!
48: 1 [48:2] **Great** is the LORD, and most worthy of praise, in the city
57:10 [57:11] For **great** is your love, reaching to the heavens; your
71:19 reaches to the skies, O God, you who have done **great** *things*.
76: 1 [76:2] In Judah God is known; his name is **great** in Israel.
77:13 [77:14] O God, are holy. What god is *so* **great** as our God?
86:10 For you are **great** and do marvelous deeds; you alone are God.
86:13 For **great** is your love toward me; you have delivered me from the
95: 3 For the LORD is the **great** God, the great King above all gods.
95: 3 For the LORD is the great God, the **great** King above all gods.
96: 4 For **great** is the LORD and most worthy of praise; he is to be
99: 2 **Great** is the LORD in Zion; he is exalted over all the nations.
99: 3 Let them praise your **great** and awesome name—he is holy.
104:25 There is the sea, **vast** and spacious, teeming with creatures beyond
104:25 with creatures beyond number—living things both **large** and small.
106:21 the God who saved them, who had done **great** *things* in Egypt,
108: 4 [108:5] For **great** is your love, higher than the heavens; your
111: 2 **Great** are the works of the LORD; they are pondered by all who
115:13 he will bless those who fear the LORD—small and **great** alike.
131: 1 I do not concern myself with **great** *matters* or things too
135: 5 I know that the LORD is **great**, that our Lord is greater than all
136: 4 to him who alone does **great** wonders, *His love endures*
136: 7 who made the **great** lights—*His love endures forever.*
136:17 who struck down **great** kings, *His love endures forever.*
138: 5 of the ways of the LORD, for the glory of the LORD is **great**.
145: 3 **Great** is the LORD and most worthy of praise; his greatness no
145: 8 is gracious and compassionate, slow to anger and **rich** *in* love.
147: 5 **Great** is our Lord and mighty in power; his understanding has no
Pr 18:16 the way for the giver and ushers him into the presence of the **great**.
19:19 A **hot-tempered man** [+2779] must pay the penalty; if you rescue
25: 6 in the king's presence, and do not claim a place among **great** *men*;
27:14 If a man **loudly** [+928+7754] blesses his neighbor early in the
Ecc 9:13 I also saw under the sun this example of wisdom that **greatly**
9:14 a **powerful** king came against it, surrounded it and built huge
9:14 came against it, surrounded it and built **huge** siegeworks against it.
10: 4 do not leave your post; calmness can lay **great** errors to rest.
Isa 5: 9 the **fine** [+2256+3202] mansions left without occupants.
8: 1 to me, "Take a **large** scroll and write on it with an ordinary pen:
9: 2 [9:1] The people walking in darkness have seen a **great** light;
12: 6 people of Zion, for **great** is the Holy One of Israel among you."
27: 1 his fierce, **great** and powerful sword, Leviathan the gliding
27:13 in that day a **great** trumpet will sound. Those who were perishing
29: 6 Almighty will come with thunder and earthquake and **great** noise,
34: 6 LORD has a sacrifice in Bozrah and a **great** slaughter in Edom.
36: 4 "Tell Hezekiah, " 'This is what the **great** king, the king of Assyria,
36:13 commander stood and **called out** [+928+7754+7924] in Hebrew,
36:13 in Hebrew, "Hear the words of the **great** king, the king of Assyria!
38: 3 done what is good in your eyes." And Hezekiah wept **bitterly**.
54: 7 I abandoned you, but with **deep** compassion I will bring you back.
56:12 fill of beer! And tomorrow will be like today, or even far **better**."
Jer 4: 6 I am bringing disaster from the north, even **terrible** destruction."
5: 5 So I will go to the **leaders** and speak to them; surely they know the
6: 1 For disaster looms out of the north, even **terrible** destruction.
6:13 "From the least to the **greatest**, all are greedy for gain; prophets
6:22 a **great** nation is being stirred up from the ends of the earth.
8:10 From the least to the **greatest**, all are greedy for gain; prophets
10: 6 O LORD; you are **great**, and your name is mighty in power.
10: 6 O LORD; you are great, and your name is **mighty** in power.
10:22 report is coming—a **great** commotion from the land of the north!
11:16 with the roar of a **mighty** storm he will set it on fire, and its
14:17 my people—has suffered a **grievous** wound, a crushing blow.
16: 6 "Both **high** and low will die in this land. They will not be buried
16:10 'Why has the LORD decreed such a **great** disaster against us?
21: 5 and a mighty arm in anger and fury and **great** wrath.
21: 6 both men and animals—and they will die of a **terrible** plague.
22: 8 'Why has the LORD done such a thing to this **great** city?'
25:14 themselves will be enslaved by many nations and **great** kings;
25:32 to nation; a **mighty** storm is rising from the ends of the earth."
26:19 We are about to bring a **terrible** disaster on ourselves!"
27: 5 With my **great** power and outstretched arm I made the earth
27: 7 land comes; then many nations and **great** kings will subjugate him.
28: 8 disaster and plague against many countries and **great** kingdoms.
30: 7 How **awful** [+2098] that day will be! None will be like it.
31: 8 expectant mothers and women in labor; a **great** throng will return.
31:34 from the least of them to the **greatest**," declares the LORD.
32:17 and the earth by your **great** power and outstretched arm.
32:18 O **great** and powerful God, whose name is the LORD Almighty,
32:19 **great** are your purposes and mighty are your deeds. Your eyes are
32:21 by a mighty hand and an outstretched arm and with **great** terror.
32:37 lands where I banish them in my furious anger and **great** wrath;
32:42 As I have brought all this **great** calamity on this people, so I will
33: 3 'Call to me and I will answer you and tell you **great**

Jer 36: 7 wrath pronounced against this people by the LORD are **great.**"
42: 1 and all the people from the least to the **greatest** approached
42: 8 were with him and all the people from the least to the **greatest.**
43: 9 take some **large** stones with you and bury them in clay in the brick
44: 7 Why bring *such* **great** disaster on yourselves by cutting off from
44: 12 From the least to the **greatest**, they will die by sword or famine.
44: 15 a **large** assembly—and all the people living in Lower and Upper
44: 26 'I swear by my **great** name,' says the LORD, 'that no one from
45: 5 Should you then seek **great** *things* for yourself? Seek them not.
48: 3 to the cries from Horonaim, cries of **great** havoc and destruction.
50: 9 bring against Babylon an alliance of **great** nations from the land of
50: 22 The noise of battle is in the land, the noise of **great** destruction!
50: 41 a **great** nation and many kings are being stirred up from the ends
51: 54 the sound of **great** destruction from the land of the Babylonians.
51: 55 will destroy Babylon; he will silence her **noisy din** [+7754].
52: 13 houses of Jerusalem. Every **important** building he burned down.
La 2: 13 of Zion? Your wound is as **deep** as the sea. Who can heal you?
Eze 1: 4 an **immense** cloud with flashing lightning and surrounded by
3: 12 Spirit lifted me up, and I heard behind me a **loud** rumbling sound—
3: 13 and the sound of the wheels beside them, a **loud** rumbling sound.
8: 6 the **utterly** detestable things the house of Israel is doing here,
8: 6 But you will see things that are **even more** detestable."
8: 13 "You will see them doing things that are **even more** detestable."
8: 15 You will see things that are **even more** detestable than this."
8: 18 Although *they* **shout** [+7754+7924] in my ears, I will not listen to
9: 1 I heard him call out in a **loud** voice, "Bring the guards of the city
9: 9 "The sin of the house of Israel and Judah is exceedingly **great**;
11: 13 I fell facedown and cried out in a **loud** voice, "Ah,
16: 46 Your **older** sister was Samaria, who lived to the north of you with
16: 61 both those *who* are **older** than you and those who are younger.
17: 3 A **great** eagle with powerful wings, long feathers and full plumage
17: 3 A great eagle with **powerful** wings, long feathers and full plumage
17: 7 " 'But there was another **great** eagle with powerful wings
17: 7 " 'But there was another great eagle with **powerful** wings
17: 9 It will not take a **strong** arm or many people to pull it up by the
17: 17 Pharaoh with his **mighty** army and great horde will be of no help
21: 14 [21:19] a sword for **great** slaughter, closing in on them from
23: 4 The **older** was named Oholah, and her sister was Oholibah.
25: 17 I will carry out **great** vengeance on them and punish them in my
29: 3 king of Egypt, you **great** monster lying among your streams.
29: 18 Nebuchadnezzar king of Babylon drove his army in a **hard**
36: 23 I will show the holiness of my **great** name, which has been
37: 10 to life and stood up on their feet—a **vast** [+4394+4394] army.
38: 13 to take away livestock and goods and to seize **much** plunder?" '
38: 15 all of them riding on horses, a **great** horde, a mighty army.
38: 19 fiery wrath I declare that at that time there shall be a **great**
39: 17 preparing for you, the **great** sacrifice on the mountains of Israel.
43: 14 from the smaller ledge up to the **larger** ledge it is four cubits high
47: 10 The fish will be of many kinds—like the fish of the **Great** Sea.
47: 15 "On the north side it will run from the **Great** Sea by the Hethlon
47: 19 Meribah Kadesh, then along the Wadi ˪of Egypt˩ to the **Great** Sea.
47: 20 the **Great** Sea will be the boundary to a point opposite Lebo
48: 28 Meribah Kadesh, then along the Wadi ˪of Egypt˩ to the **Great** Sea.
Da 8: 8 but at the height of his power his **large** horn was broken off,
8: 21 of Greece, and the **large** horn between his eyes is the first king.
9: 4 "O Lord, the **great** and awesome God, who keeps his covenant of
9: 12 and against our rulers by bringing upon us **great** disaster.
10: 1 Its message was true and it concerned a **great** war. The
10: 4 as I was standing on the bank of the **great** river, the Tigris,
10: 7 **such** terror overwhelmed them that they fled and hid themselves.
10: 8 So I was left alone, gazing at this **great** vision; I had no strength
11: 2 and then a fourth, who will be **far** richer than all the others.
11: 13 several years, he will advance with a **huge** army fully equipped.
11: 25 "With a **large** army he will stir up his strength and courage against
11: 25 The king of the South will wage war with a **large** and very
11: 28 The king of the North will return to his own country with **great**
11: 44 and he will set out in a **great** rage to destroy and annihilate many.
12: 1 the **great** prince who protects your people, will arise.
Hos 1: 11 [2:2] come up out of the land, for **great** will be the day of Jezreel.
Joel 2: 11 The day of the LORD is **great**; it is dreadful. Who can endure it?
2: 25 and the locust swarm—my **great** army that I sent among you.
2: 31 [3:4] the moon to blood before the coming of the **great**
Am 6: 11 he will smash the **great** house into pieces and the small house into
Jnh 1: 2 "Go to the **great** city of Nineveh and preach against it, because its
1: 4 the LORD sent a **great** wind on the sea, and such a violent storm
1: 4 and such a **violent** storm arose that the ship threatened to break up.
1: 10 This **terrified** [+3707+3711] them and they asked, "What have
1: 12 I know that it is my fault that this **great** storm has come upon you."
1: 16 At this the men **greatly** feared the LORD, and they offered a
1: 17 [2:1] the LORD provided a **great** fish to swallow Jonah,
3: 2 "Go to the **great** city of Nineveh and proclaim to it the message I
3: 3 Now Nineveh was a very **important** city—a visit required three
3: 5 and all of them, from the **greatest** to the least, put on sackcloth.
3: 7 "By the decree of the king and his **nobles**: Do not let any man
4: 1 But Jonah was **greatly** displeased and became angry.
4: 6 to ease his discomfort, and Jonah was **very** happy about the vine.
4: 11 cattle as well. Should I not be concerned about that **great** city?"
Mic 7: 3 the judge accepts bribes, the **powerful** dictate what they desire—
Na 1: 3 The LORD is slow to anger and **great** *in* power; the LORD will
3: 10 were cast for her nobles, and all her **great** *men* were put in chains.
Zep 1: 10 wailing from the New Quarter, and a **loud** crash from the hills.
1: 14 "The **great** day of the LORD is near—near and coming quickly.
Hag 1: 1 governor of Judah, and to Joshua son of Jehozadak, the **high** priest:
1: 12 son of Shealtiel, Joshua son of Jehozadak, the **high** priest,
1: 14 and the spirit of Joshua son of Jehozadak, the **high** priest,
2: 2 governor of Judah, to Joshua son of Jehozadak, the **high** priest,
2: 4 'Be strong, O Joshua son of Jehozadak, the **high** priest. Be strong,
2: 9 'The glory of this present house will be **greater** than the glory of
Zec 1: 14 LORD Almighty says: 'I am **very** jealous for Jerusalem and Zion,
1: 15 I am **very** angry with the nations that feel secure. I was only a little
3: 1 he showed me Joshua the **high** priest standing before the angel of
3: 8 O **high** priest Joshua and your associates seated before you,
4: 7 "What are you, O **mighty** mountain? Before Zerubbabel you will
6: 11 and make a crown, and set it on the head of the **high** priest,
7: 12 the earlier prophets. So the LORD Almighty was **very** angry.
8: 2 "I am **very** jealous for Zion; I am burning with jealousy for her."
8: 2 very jealous for Zion; I am burning with jealousy **[RPH]** for her."
14: 4 forming a **great** [+4394] valley, with half of the mountain moving
Mal 1: 11 My name will be **great** among the nations, from the rising to the
1: 11 because my name will be **great** among the nations,"
1: 14 For I am a **great** king," says the LORD Almighty, "and my name
4: 5 [3:23] I will send you the prophet Elijah before that **great**

1525 גְּדוּלָּה *gᵉdûllâ*, n.f. [12] [√ 1540]

great [3], greatness [3], great thing [2], great deeds [1], honor [1], majesty [1], recognition [1]

2Sa 7: 21 you have done this **great thing** and made it known to your servant.
7: 23 and to perform **great** and awesome wonders by driving out nations
1Ch 17: 19 you have done this **great thing** and made known all these great
17: 19 done this great thing and made known all these **great** *promises.*
17: 21 to perform **great** and awesome wonders by driving out nations
29: 11 is the **greatness** and the power and the glory and the majesty
Est 1: 4 wealth of his kingdom and the splendor and glory of his **majesty.**
6: 3 "What honor and **recognition** has Mordecai received for this?"
10: 2 together with a full account of the **greatness** *of* Mordecai to which
Ps 71: 21 You will increase my **honor** and comfort me once again.
145: 3 and most worthy of praise; his **greatness** no one can fathom.
145: 6 of your awesome works, and I will proclaim your **great deeds.**

1526 גִּדּוּף *giddûp*, n.m.pl. [2] [√ 1552]

scorn [1], taunts [1]

Isa 43: 28 and I will consign Jacob to destruction and Israel to **scorn.**
Zep 2: 8 have heard the insults of Moab and the **taunts** *of* the Ammonites,

1527 גְּדוּפָה *gᵉdûpâ*, n.f. [1] [√ 1552]

taunt [1]

Eze 5: 15 You will be a reproach and a **taunt**, a warning and an object of

1528 גִּדּוּפָה *giddûpâ*, n.m.pl. [1] [√ 1552]

insults [1]

Isa 51: 7 Do not fear the reproach of men or be terrified by their **insults.**

1529 גְּדוֹר¹ *gᵉdôr¹*, n.pr.m. [4] [√ 1553]

Gedor [4]

1Ch 4: 4 Penuel was the father of **Gedor**, and Ezer the father of Hushah.
4: 18 (His Judean wife gave birth to Jered the father of **Gedor**, Heber the
8: 31 **Gedor**, Ahio, Zeker
9: 37 **Gedor**, Ahio, Zechariah and Mikloth.

1530 גְּדוֹר² *gᵉdôr²*, n.pr.loc. [3]

Gedor [3]

Jos 15: 58 Halhul, Beth Zur, **Gedor**,
1Ch 4: 39 they went to the outskirts of **Gedor** to the east of the valley in
12: 7 [12:8] and Joelah and Zebadiah the sons of Jeroham from **Gedor.**

1531 גְּדִי *gᵉdî*, n.m. [16 / 17] [→ 1537, 6527]

young goat [+6436] [7], young goat [5], goat [1], goatskins [+6425+6436] [1], lambs [1], young goats [+6436] [1], young goats [1]

Ge 27: 9 Go out to the flock and bring me two choice **young goats** [+6436],
27: 16 and the smooth part of his neck with the **goatskins** [+6425+6436].
38: 17 "I'll send you a **young goat** [+6436] from my flock," he said.
38: 20 Meanwhile Judah sent the **young goat** [+6436] by his friend the
38: 23 After all, I did send her this **young goat**, but you didn't find her."

Ex 23: 19 your God. "Do not cook a **young goat** in its mother's milk.
34: 26 your God. "Do not cook a **young goat** in its mother's milk."
Dt 14: 21 LORD your God. Do not cook a **young goat** in its mother's milk.
Jdg 6: 19 Gideon went in, prepared a **young goat** [+6436], and from an
13: 15 "We would like you to stay until we prepare a **young goat** [+6436]
13: 19 Manoah took a **young goat** [+6436], together with the grain
14: 6 lion apart with his bare hands as he might have torn a **young goat**.
15: 1 Samson took a **young goat** [+6436] and went to visit his wife.
1Sa 10: 3 One will be carrying three **young goats**, another three loaves of
16: 20 a skin of wine and a **young goat** [+6436] and sent them with his
Isa 5: 17 **lambs** [BHS 1731] will feed among the ruins of the rich.
11: 6 the leopard will lie down with the **goat**, the calf and the lion

1532 גָּדִי¹ *gādî¹*, a.g. [16 / 15] [√ 1514]

Gadites [12], Gad [+1201] [1], Gad [1], of Gad [1]

Nu 34: 14 the tribe of **Gad** [+1201] and the half-tribe of Manasseh have
Dt 3: 12 and the **Gadites** the territory north of Aroer by the Arnon Gorge,
3: 16 the **Gadites** I gave the territory extending from Gilead down to the
4: 43 for the Reubenites; Ramoth in Gilead, for the **Gadites**;
29: 8 [29:7] the Reubenites, the **Gadites** and the half-tribe of Manasseh.
Jos 1: 12 the **Gadites** and the half-tribe of Manasseh, Joshua said,
12: 6 the **Gadites** and the half-tribe of Manasseh to be their possession.
13: 8 the **Gadites** had received the inheritance that Moses had given
22: 1 the Reubenites, the **Gadites** and the half-tribe of Manasseh
2Sa 23: 36 the son of Hagri, [BHS *the Gadite* or *Haggadi*; NIV 2058]
2Ki 10: 33 east of the Jordan in all the land of Gilead (the region **of Gad**,
1Ch 5: 18 the **Gadites** and the half-tribe of Manasseh had 44,760 men ready
5: 26 the **Gadites** and the half-tribe of Manasseh into exile.
12: 8 [12:9] Some **Gadites** defected to David at his stronghold in the
12: 37 [12:38] men of Reuben, **Gad** and the half-tribe of Manasseh,
26: 32 the **Gadites** and the half-tribe of Manasseh for every matter

1533 גָּדִי² *gādî²*, n.pr.m. [2] [√ 1514]

Gadi [2]

2Ki 15: 14 Then Menahem son of **Gadi** went from Tirzah up to Samaria.
15: 17 Menahem son of **Gadi** became king of Israel, and he reigned in

1534 גַּדִּי *gaddî*, n.pr.m. [1] [√ 1513]

Gaddi [1]

Nu 13: 11 from the tribe of Manasseh (a tribe of Joseph), **Gaddi** son of Susi;

1535 גַּדִּיאֵל *gaddî'ēl*, n.pr.m. [1] [√ 1513 + 446]

Gaddiel [1]

Nu 13: 10 from the tribe of Zebulun, **Gaddiel** son of Sodi;

1536 גִּדְיָה *gidyâ*, n.f. [4] [√ 1519]

banks [2], at flood stage [+3972+4848+6584] [1], at flood stage [+3972+6584] [1]

Jos 3: 15 Now the Jordan *is* **at flood stage** [+3972+4848+6584] all during
harvest. Yet as soon as the priests who carried the ark reached the
4: 18 to their place and ran **at flood stage** [+3972+6584] as before.
1Ch 12: 15 [12:16] in the first month when it was overflowing all its **banks**,
Isa 8: 7 his pomp. It will overflow all its channels, run over all its **banks**

1537 גְּדִיָּה *gᵉdiyyâ*, n.f. [1] [√ 1531]

young goats [1]

SS 1: 8 and graze your **young goats** by the tents of the shepherds.

1538 גָּדִישׁ¹ *gādîš¹*, n.m. [3] [→ 1539]

sheaves [1], shocks of grain [1], shocks [1]

Ex 22: 6 [22:5] so that it burns **shocks of grain** or standing grain
Jdg 15: 5 He burned up the **shocks** and standing grain, together with the
Job 5: 26 come to the grave in full vigor, like **sheaves** gathered in season.

1539 גָּדִישׁ² *gādîš²*, n.[m.]. [1] [√ 1538]

tomb [1]

Job 21: 32 He is carried to the grave, and watch is kept over his **tomb**.

1540 גָּדַל *gādal*, v. [115 / 116] [→ 1524, 1525, 1541, 1542, 1543, 1544?, 1547, 4460, 4463, 4464, 4465; *also used with compound proper names*]

great [17], greater [8], grown up [7], exalted [6], grew up [6], exalt [5], grew [5], reared [4], defied [+6584] [2], glorify [2], honored [2], gives great [2], make great [2], wealthy [2], boast so much [+3870+7023] [1], boast [1], boasted [+928+7023] [1], boosting [1], brought up [1], developed [1], displayed [1], exalt himself [1], great [+4394] [1], great things done [1], greatness [1], grew older [1], grow long [1], grown [1], grows up [1], increased [1], lifted up [1], made great [1], made grow [1], made threats [1], magnificent [1], magnify [1], make greater [1], make grow [1], make so much of [1], mocking [1], most [1], nourished [1], pile high [1], powerful [1], raised [1], raising [1], reached [+6330] [1], rear [1], rearing [1], rich [1], set up to be great [1], show greatness [1], superior [1], trained [1], triumphed [1], undertook great [1], value [+928+6524] [1], valued [+928+6524] [1], well-nurtured [1], yielding [1]

Ge 12: 2 [D] *I will* **make** your name **great**, and you will be a blessing.
19: 13 [A] The outcry to the LORD against its people *is* so **great** that
19: 19 [G] and you *have* shown **great** kindness to me in sparing my life.
21: 8 [A] The child **grew** and was weaned, and on the day Isaac was
21: 20 [A] God was with the boy as *he* **grew up**. He lived in the desert
24: 35 [A] blessed my master abundantly, and *he has become* **wealthy**.
25: 27 [A] The boys **grew up**, and Esau became a skillful hunter, a man
26: 13 [A] The man *became* **rich**, and his wealth continued to grow
26: 13 [A] his wealth continued to grow until *he became* very **wealthy**.
38: 11 [A] in your father's house until my son Shelah **grows up**."
38: 14 [A] For she saw that, *though* Shelah *had* now **grown up**, she had
41: 40 [A] Only with respect to the throne *will I be* **greater** than you."
48: 19 [A] He too will become a people, and he too *will become* **great**.
48: 19 [A] Nevertheless, his younger brother *will be* **greater** than he,
Ex 2: 10 [A] When the child **grew older**, she took him to Pharaoh's
2: 11 [A] One day, after Moses *had* **grown up**, he went out to where
Nu 6: 5 [D] LORD is over; *he must let* the hair of his head **grow long**.
14: 17 [A] "Now *may* the Lord's strength *be* **displayed**, just as you
Jos 3: 7 [D] "Today I will begin *to* **exalt** you in the eyes of all Israel,
4: 14 [D] That day the LORD **exalted** Joshua in the sight of all Israel;
Jdg 11: 2 [A] and when they *were* **grown up**, they drove Jephthah away.
13: 24 [A] named him Samson. He **grew** and the LORD blessed him,
Ru 1: 13 [A] would you wait until *they* **grew up**? Would you remain
1Sa 2: 21 [A] the boy Samuel **grew up** in the presence of the LORD.
3: 19 [A] The LORD was with Samuel as he **grew up**, and he let none
12: 24 [G] your heart; consider what **great things** *he has* **done** for you.
20: 41 [G] each other and wept together—but David wept *the* **most**.
26: 24 [A] As surely as I **valued** [+928+6524] your life today, so may
26: 24 [A] so *may* the LORD **value** [+928+6524] my life and deliver
2Sa 7: 22 [A] "How **great** *you are*, O Sovereign LORD! There is no one
7: 26 [A] so that your name *will be* **great** forever. Then men will say,
12: 3 [A] He raised it, and *it* **grew up** with him and his children.
22: 51 [G] *He* **gives** his king **great** [Q 4460] victories; he shows
1Ki 1: 37 [D] so may he be with Solomon *to* **make** his throne *even* **greater**
1: 47 [D] more famous than yours and his throne **greater** than yours!'
10: 23 [A] King Solomon *was* **greater** in riches and wisdom than all the
12: 8 [A] and consulted the young men who *had* **grown up** with him
12: 10 [A] The young men who *had* **grown up** with him replied, "Tell
2Ki 4: 18 [A] The child **grew**, and one day he went out to his father,
10: 6 [D] with the leading men of the city, *who were* **rearing** them.
1Ch 17: 24 [A] will be established and that your name *will be* **great** forever.
22: 5 [G] the house to be built for the LORD *should be* of **great**
29: 12 [D] are strength and power to **exalt** and give strength to all.
29: 25 [D] The LORD highly **exalted** Solomon in the sight of all Israel
2Ch 1: 1 [D] his God was with him and **made** him exceedingly **great**.
9: 22 [A] King Solomon *was* **greater** in riches and wisdom than all the
10: 8 [A] and consulted the young men who *had* **grown up** with him
10: 10 [A] The young men who *had* **grown up** with him replied, "Tell
Ezr 9: 6 [A] our heads and our guilt *has* **reached** [+6330] to the heavens.
Est 3: 1 [D] King Xerxes **honored** Haman son of Hammedatha,
5: 11 [D] all the ways the king *had* **honored** him and how he had
10: 2 [D] the greatness of Mordecai to which the king *had* **raised** him,
Job 2: 13 [A] because they saw how **great** [+4394] his suffering *was*.
7: 17 [D] "What is man that *you* **make so much of** him, that you give
19: 5 [G] If indeed *you would* **exalt** *yourselves* above me and use my
31: 18 [A] from my youth I **reared** *him* as would a father, and from my
Ps 18: 50 [18:51] [G] *He* **gives** his king **great** victories; he shows
34: 3 [34:4] [D] **Glorify** the LORD with me; let us exalt his name
35: 26 [G] may *all* who **exalt** *themselves* over me be clothed with
35: 27 [A] may they always say, "The LORD *be* **exalted**, who delights
38: 16 [38:17] [G] or **exalt** *themselves* over me when my foot slips."
40: 16 [40:17] [A] salvation always say, "The LORD *be* **exalted**!"
41: 9 [41:10] [G] shared my bread, *has* **lifted up** his heel against me.
55: 12 [55:13] [G] if a foe *were* **raising** *himself* against me, I could
69: 30 [69:31] [D] name in song and **glorify** him with thanksgiving.
70: 4 [70:5] [A] your salvation always say, "*Let* God *be* **exalted**!"
92: 5 [92:6] [A] How **great** *are* your works, O LORD,
104: 1 [A] O LORD my God, *you are* very **great**; you are clothed with
126: 2 [G] the nations, "The LORD has done **great** *things* for them."
126: 3 [G] The LORD has done **great** *things* for us, and we are filled
138: 2 [G] for *you have* **exalted** above all things your name and your
144: 12 [E] our sons in their youth will be like **well-nurtured** plants,
Ecc 1: 16 [G] I *have* **grown** and increased in wisdom more than anyone
2: 4 [G] *I* **undertook great** projects: I built houses for myself
2: 9 [A] *I became* **greater** by far than anyone in Jerusalem before

SS 5:13 [D] His cheeks are like beds of spice **yielding** [BHS 4463]
Isa 1:2 [D] "*I* **reared** children and brought them up, but they have
9:3 [9:2] [G] You have enlarged the nation and **increased** their joy;
10:15 [F] him who swings it, or the saw **boast** against him who uses it?
23:4 [D] *I have* neither **reared** sons nor brought up daughters."
28:29 [G] wonderful in counsel and **magnificent** *in* wisdom.
42:21 [G] for the sake of his righteousness *to* **make** *his* law **great**
44:14 [D] of the forest, or planted a pine, and the rain **made** it **grow**.
49:21 [D] I was exiled and rejected. Who **brought** these **up**?
51:18 [D] of all the sons *she* **reared** there was none to take her by the
Jer 5:27 [A] are full of deceit; they have become rich and **powerful**
48:26 [G] "Make her drunk, for *she has* **defied** [+6584] the LORD.
48:42 [G] as a nation because *she* **defied** [+6584] the LORD.
La 1:9 [G] O LORD, on my affliction, for the enemy *has* **triumphed**."
4:6 [A] The punishment of my people *is* **greater** than that of Sodom,
Eze 16:7 [A] You grew up and **developed** and became the most beautiful
24:9 [G] to the city of bloodshed! I, too, *will* **pile** the wood **high**.
31:4 [D] The waters **nourished** it, deep springs made it grow tall; their
35:13 [G] You **boasted** [+928+7023] against me and spoke against me
38:23 [F] so *I will* **show** *my* **greatness** and my holiness, and I will
Da 1:5 [D] They *were* to *be* **trained** for three years, and after that they
8:4 [G] from his power. He did as he pleased and *became* **great**.
8:8 [G] The goat *became* very **great**, but at the height of his power
8:9 [A] started small but **grew** *in* power to the south and to the east
8:10 [A] *It* **grew** until it reached the host of the heavens, and it threw
8:11 [G] *It* **set** *itself* **up to be** as **great** as the Prince of the host; it took
8:25 [G] deceit to prosper, and *he will* consider himself **superior**.
11:36 [F] He will exalt and **magnify** himself above every god and will
11:37 [F] will he regard any god, but *will* **exalt himself** above them all.
Hos 9:12 [D] Even if *they* **rear** children, I will bereave them of every one.
Joel 2:20 [G] go up; its smell will rise." Surely he has done **great** *things*.
2:21 [G] and rejoice. Surely the LORD has done **great** *things*.
Am 8:5 [G] **boosting** the price and cheating with dishonest scales,
Ob 1:12 [D] nor **boast** [+3870+7023] **so much** in the day of their trouble.
Jnh 4:10 [D] about this vine, though you did not tend it or **make** it **grow**.
Mic 5:4 [5:3] [A] then *his* **greatness** will reach to the ends of the earth.
Zep 2:8 [G] who insulted my people and **made threats** against their land.
2:10 [G] and **mocking** the people of the LORD Almighty.
Zec 12:7 [A] of Jerusalem's inhabitants *may* not *be* **greater** than that of
12:11 [A] On that day the weeping in Jerusalem *will be* **great**,
Mal 1:5 [A] see it with your own eyes and say, '**Great** *is* the LORD—

1541 גָּדֵל *gādēl*, a.vbl. *or* v.ptcp. [4] [√ 1540]

lustful [+1414] [1], more and more powerful [+2025+2143+2256+4200+5087+6330] [1], stature [1], wealth [1]

Ge 26:13 and his **wealth** continued to grow until he became very wealthy.
1Sa 2:26 the boy Samuel continued to grow *in* **stature** and in favor with the
2Ch 17:12 Jehoshaphat became **more and more powerful** [+2025+2143 +2256+4200+5087+6330]; he built forts and store cities in Judah
Eze 16:26 in prostitution with the Egyptians, your **lustful** [+1414] neighbors,

1542 גֹּדֶל *gōdel*, n.m. [13] [√ 1540]

majesty [4], greatness [3], arrogance [1], beauty [1], great power [1], great [1], strength [1], willful pride [+7262] [1]

Nu 14:19 In accordance with your **great** love, forgive the sin of these people,
Dt 3:24 you have begun to show to your servant your **greatness** and your
5:24 "The LORD our God has shown us his glory and his **majesty**,
9:26 your own inheritance that you redeemed by your **great power**
11:2 your God: his **majesty**, his mighty hand, his outstretched arm;
32:3 the name of the LORD. Oh, praise the **greatness** of our God!
Ps 79:11 by the **strength** *of* your arm preserve those condemned to die.
150:2 him for his acts of power; praise him for his surpassing **greatness**.
Isa 9:9 [9:8] of Samaria—who say with pride and **arrogance** *of* heart,
10:12 "I will punish the king of Assyria for the **willful pride** [+7262] *of*
Eze 31:2 and to his hordes: " 'Who can be compared with you in **majesty**?
31:7 It was majestic in **beauty**, with its spreading boughs, for its roots
31:18 trees of Eden can be compared with you in splendor and **majesty**?

1543 גִּדֵּל *giddēl*, n.pr.m. [4] [√ 1540]

Giddel [4]

Ezr 2:47 **Giddel**, Gahar, Reaiah,
2:56 Jaala, Darkon, **Giddel**,
Ne 7:49 Hanan, **Giddel**, Gahar,
7:58 Jaala, Darkon, **Giddel**,

1544 גָּדִיל *gādil*, n.[m.]pl. [2] [√ 1540?]

festooned [1], tassels [1]

Dt 22:12 Make **tassels** on the four corners of the cloak you wear.
1Ki 7:17 A network of interwoven chains **festooned** the capitals on top of

1545 גְּדַלְיָה *g^e^dalyâ*, n.pr.m. [6] [√ 1540 + 3378]

Gedaliah [6]

Ezr 10:18 and his brothers: Maaseiah, Eliezer, Jarib and **Gedaliah**.
Jer 40:5 "Go back to **Gedaliah** son of Ahikam, the son of Shaphan,
40:6 So Jeremiah went to **Gedaliah** son of Ahikam at Mizpah
40:8 they came to **Gedaliah** at Mizpah—Ishmael son of Nethaniah,
41:16 of Nethaniah after he had assassinated **Gedaliah** son of Ahikam:
Zep 1:1 the son of **Gedaliah**, the son of Amariah, the son of Hezekiah,

1546 גְּדַלְיָהוּ *g^e^dalyāhû*, n.pr.m. [26] [√ 1540 + 3378]

Gedaliah [25], Gedaliah's [1]

2Ki 25:22 Nebuchadnezzar king of Babylon appointed **Gedaliah** son of
25:23 their men heard that the king of Babylon had appointed **Gedaliah**
25:23 Gedaliah as governor, they came to **Gedaliah** at Mizpah—
25:24 **Gedaliah** took an oath to reassure them and their men. "Do not be
25:25 came with ten men and assassinated **Gedaliah** and also the men of
1Ch 25:3 **Gedaliah**, Zeri, Jeshaiah, Shimei, Hashabiah and Mattithiah,
25:9 12 the second to **Gedaliah**, he and his relatives and sons, 12
Jer 38:1 of Mattan, **Gedaliah** son of Pashhur, Jehucal son of Shelemiah,
39:14 They turned him over to **Gedaliah** son of Ahikam, the son of
40:7 had appointed **Gedaliah** son of Ahikam as governor over the land
40:9 **Gedaliah** son of Ahikam, the son of Shaphan, took an oath to
40:11 a remnant in Judah and had appointed **Gedaliah** son of Ahikam,
40:12 they all came back to the land of Judah, to **Gedaliah** at Mizpah,
40:13 all the army officers still in the open country came to **Gedaliah** at
40:14 take your life?" But **Gedaliah** son of Ahikam did not believe them.
40:15 Then Johanan son of Kareah said privately to **Gedaliah** in Mizpah,
40:16 But **Gedaliah** son of Ahikam said to Johanan son of Kareah,
41:1 came with ten men to **Gedaliah** son of Ahikam at Mizpah.
41:2 were with him got up and struck down **Gedaliah** son of Ahikam,
41:3 Ishmael also killed all the Jews who were with **Gedaliah** at
41:4 The day after **Gedaliah's** assassination, before anyone knew about
41:6 When he met them, he said, "Come to **Gedaliah** son of Ahikam."
41:9 **Gedaliah** was the one King Asa had made as part of his defense
41:10 of the imperial guard had appointed **Gedaliah** son of Ahikam.
41:18 because Ishmael son of Nethaniah had killed **Gedaliah** son of
43:6 of the imperial guard had left with **Gedaliah** son of Ahikam,

1547 גִּדַּלְתִּי *giddaltî*, n.pr.m. [2] [√ 1540]

Giddalti [2]

1Ch 25:4 Hananiah, Hanani, Eliathah, **Giddalti** and Romamti-Ezer;
25:29 the twenty-second to **Giddalti**, his sons and relatives, 12

1548 גָּדַע *gāda'*, v. [22 / 23] [→ 1549, 1550, 1551]

cut down [4], cut off [3], broke [2], cut to pieces [2], be cut off [1], be felled [1], be sheared off [1], been cast down [1], been felled [1], broke down [1], broken down [1], broken [1], cut short [1], cut through [1], cuts through [1], is cut off [1]

Dt 7:5 [D] **cut down** their Asherah poles and burn their idols in the fire.
12:3 [D] **cut down** the idols of their gods and wipe out their names
Jdg 21:6 [C] "Today one tribe *is* **cut off** from Israel," they said.
1Sa 2:31 [A] The time is coming when *I will* **cut short** your strength and
2Ch 14:3 [14:2] [D] the sacred stones and **cut down** the Asherah poles.
31:1 [D] smashed the sacred stones and **cut down** the Asherah poles.
34:4 [D] *he* **cut to pieces** the incense altars that were above them,
34:7 [D] and **cut to pieces** all the incense altars throughout Israel.
Ps 75:10 [75:11] [D] *I will* **cut off** the horns of all the wicked,
107:16 [D] breaks down gates of bronze and **cuts through** bars of iron.
Isa 9:10 [9:9] [E] the fig trees *have* **been felled**, but we will replace
10:33 [B] The lofty trees *will* **be felled**, the tall ones will be brought
14:12 [C] *You have* **been cast down** to the earth, you who once laid
22:25 [C] *it will* **be sheared off** and will fall, and the load hanging on it
45:2 [D] break down gates of bronze and **cut through** bars of iron.
Jer 48:25 [C] Moab's horn **is cut off**; her arm is broken,"
50:23 [C] How **broken** and shattered is the hammer of the whole earth!
La 2:3 [A] In fierce anger *he has* **cut off** every horn of Israel. He has
Eze 6:6 [C] idols smashed and ruined, your incense altars **broken down**,
19:7 [A] *He* **broke** [BHS 3359] **down** their strongholds
Am 3:14 [C] the horns of the altar *will* **be cut off** and fall to the ground.
Zec 11:10 [A] I took my staff called Favor and **broke** it, revoking the
11:14 [A] *I* **broke** my second staff called Union, breaking the

1549 גִּדְעוֹן *gid'ôn*, n.pr.m. [39] [→ 1551; cf. 1548]

Gideon [35], he[s] [3], Gideon's [1]

Jdg 6:11 where his son **Gideon** was threshing wheat in a winepress to keep
6:13 "But sir," **Gideon** replied, "if the LORD is with us, why has all
6:19 **Gideon** went in, prepared a young goat, and from an ephah of flour
6:22 When **Gideon** realized that it was the angel of the LORD,
6:22 the angel of the LORD, **he**[s] exclaimed, "Ah, Sovereign LORD!
6:24 So **Gideon** built an altar to the LORD there and called it The

Jdg 6:27 So **Gideon** took ten of his servants and did as the LORD told
6:29 they were told, "**Gideon** son of Joash did it."
6:34 the Spirit of the LORD came upon **Gideon**, and he blew a
6:36 **Gideon** said to God, "If you will save Israel by my hand as you
6:39 **Gideon** said to God, "Do not be angry with me. Let me make just
7:1 Early in the morning, Jerub-Baal (that is, **Gideon**) and all his men
7:2 The LORD said to **Gideon**, "You have too many men for me to
7:4 But the LORD said to **Gideon**, "There are still too many men.
7:5 So **Gideon** took the men down to the water. There the LORD told
7:7 The LORD said to **Gideon**, "With the three hundred men that
7:13 **Gideon** arrived just as a man was telling a friend his dream.
7:14 "This can be nothing other than the sword of **Gideon** son of Joash,
7:15 When **Gideon** heard the dream and its interpretation, he worshiped
7:18 camp blow yours and shout, 'For the LORD and for **Gideon**.' "
7:19 **Gideon** and the hundred men with him reached the edge of the
7:20 they shouted, "A sword for the LORD and for **Gideon**!"
7:24 **Gideon** sent messengers throughout the hill country of Ephraim,
7:25 the Midianites and brought the heads of Oreb and Zeeb to **Gideon**,
8:4 **Gideon** and his three hundred men, exhausted yet keeping up the
8:7 **Gideon** replied, "Just for that, when the LORD has given Zebah
8:11 **Gideon** went up by the route of the nomads east of Nobah
8:13 **Gideon** son of Joash then returned from the battle by the Pass of
8:21 so is his strength.' " So **Gideon** stepped forward and killed them,
8:22 The Israelites said to **Gideon**, "Rule over us—you, your son
8:23 **Gideon** told them, "I will not rule over you, nor will my son rule
8:24 **he**[s] said, "I do have one request, that each of you give me an
8:27 **Gideon** made the gold into an ephod, which he placed in Ophrah,
8:27 it there, and it became a snare to **Gideon** and his family.
8:28 During **Gideon's** lifetime, the land enjoyed peace forty years.
8:30 **He**[s] had seventy sons of his own, for he had many wives.
8:32 **Gideon** son of Joash died at a good old age and was buried in the
8:33 No sooner had **Gideon** died than the Israelites again prostituted
8:35 to show kindness to the family of Jerub-Baal (that is, **Gideon**)

1550 גִּדְעֹם *gid'ōm*, n.pr.loc. [1] [√ 1548]

Gidom [1]

Jdg 20:45 They kept pressing after the Benjamites as far as **Gidom** and struck

1551 גִּדְעֹנִי *gid'ōnî*, n.pr.m. [5] [√ 1549; cf. 1548]

Gideoni [5]

Nu 1:11 from Benjamin, Abidan son of **Gideoni**;
2:22 The leader of the people of Benjamin is Abidan son of **Gideoni**.
7:60 On the ninth day Abidan son of **Gideoni**, the leader of the people
7:65 This was the offering of Abidan son of **Gideoni**.
10:24 Abidan son of **Gideoni** was over the division of the tribe of

1552 גָּדַף *gādap*, v. [7] [→ 1526, 1527, 1528]

blasphemed [5], blasphemes [1], revile [1]

Nu 15:30 [D] whether native-born or alien, **blasphemes** the LORD,
2Ki 19:6 [D] the underlings of the king of Assyria *have* **blasphemed** me.
19:22 [D] Who is it you have insulted and **blasphemed**? Against whom
Ps 44:16 [44:17] [D] at the taunts of those who reproach and **revile** me,
Isa 37:6 [D] the underlings of the king of Assyria *have* **blasphemed** me.
37:23 [D] Who is it you have insulted and **blasphemed**? Against whom
Eze 20:27 [D] In this also your fathers **blasphemed** me by forsaking me:

1553 גָּדַר *gādar*, v. [10] [→ 1529, 1554, 1555, 1556, 1557, 1558, 1560, 1561, 1562]

masons [2], repair [2], barred [1], blocked [1], build up [1], Repairer of Walls [1], wall in [+906+1555] [1], walled [1]

2Ki 12:12 [12:13] [A] the **masons** and stonecutters. They purchased
22:6 [A] the carpenters, the builders and the **masons**. Also have them
Job 19:8 [A] *He has* **blocked** my way so I cannot pass; he has shrouded
Isa 58:12 [A] you will be called **Repairer of** Broken **Walls**, Restorer of
La 3:7 [A] *He has* **walled** me in so I cannot escape; he has weighed me
3:9 [A] *He has* **barred** my way with blocks of stone; he has made
Eze 13:5 [A] You have not gone up to the breaks in the wall *to* **repair** it
22:30 [A] "I looked for a man among them *who would* **build up** the
Hos 2:6 [2:8] [A] *I will* **wall** [+906+1555] her **in** so that she cannot find
Am 9:11 [A] *I will* **repair** its broken places, restore its ruins, and build it

1554 גֶּדֶר *geder*, n.pr.loc. [1] [→ 1084; cf. 1084, 1553]

Geder [1]

Jos 12:13 the king of Debir one the king of **Geder** one

1555 גָּדֵר *gādēr*, n.m. [14] [√ 1553]

wall [7], walls [3], *untranslated* [1], fence [1], wall in [+906+1553] [1], wall of protection [1]

Nu 22:24 in a narrow path between two vineyards, with **walls** on both sides.
22:24 path between two vineyards, with walls **[RPH]** on both sides.
Ezr 9:9 and he has given us a **wall of protection** in Judah and Jerusalem.
Ps 62:3 [62:4] throw him down—this leaning wall, this tottering **fence**?
80:12 [80:13] Why have you broken down its **walls** so that all who pass
Pr 24:31 ground was covered with weeds, and the stone **wall** was in ruins.
Ecc 10:8 into it; whoever breaks through a **wall** may be bitten by a snake.
Isa 5:5 be destroyed; I will break down its **wall**, and it will be trampled.
Eze 13:5 You have not gone up to the breaks in the **wall** to repair it for the
22:30 "I looked for a man among them who would build up the **wall**
42:7 There was an outer **wall** parallel to the rooms and the outer court;
42:10 On the south side along the length of the **wall** *of* the outer court,
Hos 2:6 [2:8] *I will* **wall** her **in** [+906+1553] so that she cannot find her
Mic 7:11 The day for building your **walls** will come, the day for extending

1556 גְּדֵרָה¹ *gᵉdērâ¹*, n.f. [9] [→ 1557, 1558, 1561, 1562; cf. 1553]

pens [4], walls [3], pens [+7366] [1], wall [1]

Nu 32:16 "We would like to build **pens** [+7366] here for our livestock
32:24 cities for your women and children, and **pens** for your flocks,
32:36 and Beth Haran as fortified cities, and built **pens** *for* their flocks.
1Sa 24:3 [24:4] He came to the sheep **pens** along the way; a cave was
Ps 89:40 [89:41] You have broken through all his **walls** and reduced his
Jer 49:3 rush here and there inside the **walls**, for Molech will go into exile,
Eze 42:12 that was parallel to the corresponding **wall** extending eastward,
Na 3:17 your officials like swarms of locusts that settle in the **walls** on a
Zep 2:6 the Kerethites dwell, will be a place for shepherds and sheep **pens**.

1557 גְּדֵרָה² *gᵉdērâ²*, n.pr.loc. [2] [√ 1556; cf. 1553]

Gederah [2]

Jos 15:36 Shaaraim, Adithaim and **Gederah** (or Gederothaim)—
1Ch 4:23 They were the potters who lived at Netaim and **Gederah**;

1558 גְּדֵרוֹת *gᵉdērôt*, n.pr.loc. [2] [√ 1556; cf. 1553]

Gederoth [2]

Jos 15:41 **Gederoth**, Beth Dagon, Naamah and Makkedah—sixteen towns
2Ch 28:18 Aijalon and **Gederoth**, as well as Soco, Timnah and Gimzo,

1559 גְּדֵרִי *gᵉdērî*, a.g. [1] [cf. 1084]

Gederite [1]

1Ch 27:28 Baal-Hanan the **Gederite** was in charge of the olive

1560 גְּדֶרֶת *gᵉderet*, n.f. Not used in NIV/BHS [√ 1553]

1561 גְּדֵרָתִי *gᵉdērātî*, a.g. [1] [√ 1556; cf. 1553]

Gederathite [1]

1Ch 12:4 [12:5] Jahaziel, Johanan, Jozabad the **Gederathite**,

1562 גְּדֵרֹתַיִם *gᵉdērōtayim*, n.pr.loc. [1] [√ 1556; cf. 1553]

Gederothaim [1]

Jos 15:36 Shaaraim, Adithaim and Gederah (or **Gederothaim**)—

1563 גֵּה *gēh*, var. [1 / 0]

Eze 47:13 "These [BHS *these*?; NIV 2296] are the boundaries by which you

1564 גָּהָה *gāhâ*, v. [1] [→ 1565, 4443]

heal [1]

Hos 5:13 [A] But he is not able to cure you, not able *to* **heal** your sores.

1565 גֵּהָה *gēhâ*, n.f. [1] [√ 1564]

medicine [1]

Pr 17:22 A cheerful heart is good **medicine**, but a crushed spirit dries up the

1566 גָּהַר *gāhar*, v. [3]

stretched out [2], bent down [1]

1Ki 18:42 [A] **bent down** to the ground and put his face between his knees.
2Ki 4:34 [A] As *he* **stretched** *himself* **out** upon him, the boy's body grew
4:35 [A] then got on the bed and **stretched out** upon him once more.

1567 גַּו *gaw*, n.[m.]. [3] [√ 1568]

back [2], backs [1]

1Ki 14:9 you have provoked me to anger and thrust me behind your **back**.
Ne 9:26 and rebelled against you; they put your law behind their **backs**.
Eze 23:35 Since you have forgotten me and thrust me behind your **back**,

1568 גֵּוִ¹ **gēw¹**, n.[m.]. [6 / 7] [→ 1567, 1576, 1581]

back [5], backs [2]

Job 41: 15 [41:7] His **back** [BHS 1452] has rows of shields tightly sealed
Pr 10: 13 but a rod is for the **back** *of* him who lacks judgment.
19: 29 are prepared for mockers, and beatings for the **backs** *of* fools.
26: 3 the horse, a halter for the donkey, and a rod for the **backs** *of* fools!
Isa 38: 17 the pit of destruction; you have put all my sins behind your **back**.
50: 6 I offered my **back** to those who beat me, my cheeks to those who
51: 23 you made your **back** like the ground, like a street to be walked

1569 גֵּוִ² **gēw²**, n.[m.]. [1] [√ 1580?; Ar 10135]

fellow men [1]

Job 30: 5 They were banished from their **fellow men**, shouted at as if they

1570 גּוֹב¹ **gôb¹**, n.pr.loc. [2] [√ 1572?]

Gob [2]

2Sa 21: 18 of time, there was another battle with the Philistines, at **Gob**.
21: 19 In another battle with the Philistines at **Gob**, Elhanan son of

1571 גּוֹב² **gôb²**, n.[m.]. [1]

swarms [1]

Na 3: 17 your officials like **swarms** *of* locusts that settle in the walls on a

1572 גּוּב **gûb**, v. Not used in NIV/BHS [√ 1570?]

1573 גּוֹג **gôg**, n.pr.m. [10] [→ 2163, 4470]

Gog [10]

1Ch 5: 4 of Joel: Shemaiah his son, **Gog** his son, Shimei his son,
Eze 38: 2 "Son of man, set your face against **Gog**, *of* the land of Magog,
38: 3 I am against you, O **Gog**, chief prince of Meshech and Tubal.
38: 14 "Therefore, son of man, prophesy and say to **Gog**: 'This is what the
38: 16 In days to come, O **Gog**, I will bring you against my land,
38: 18 When **Gog** attacks the land of Israel, my hot anger will be aroused,
39: 1 "Son of man, prophesy against **Gog** and say: 'This is what the
39: 1 I am against you, O **Gog**, chief prince of Meshech and Tubal.
39: 11 " 'On that day I will give **Gog** a burial place in Israel, in the valley
39: 11 of travelers, because **Gog** and all his hordes will be buried there.

1574 גּוּד **gûd**, v. [3] [√ 1517?]

attack [1], attacked [1], invading [1]

Ge 49: 19 [A] "Gad *will be* **attacked** *by* a band of raiders, but he will
49: 19 [A] by a band of raiders, but he *will* **attack** them *at* their heels.
Hab 3: 16 [A] for the day of calamity to come on the nation **invading** us.

1575 גֵּוָה¹ **gēwâ¹**, n.f. [3] [√ 1448; Ar 10136]

pride [2], lift up [1]

Job 22: 29 When men are brought low and you say, '**Lift** them **up**!' then he
33: 17 to turn man from wrongdoing and keep him from **pride**,
Jer 13: 17 if you do not listen, I will weep in secret because of your **pride**;

1576 גֵּוָה² **gēwâ²**, n.f. [1] [√ 1568]

back [1]

Job 20: 25 He pulls it out of his **back**, the gleaming point out of his liver.

1577 גּוּז **gûz**, v. [2]

drove in [1], pass [1]

Nu 11: 31 [A] went out from the LORD and **drove** quail **in** from the sea.
Ps 90: 10 [A] their span is but trouble and sorrow, for *they* quickly **pass**,

1578 גּוֹזָל **gôzāl**, n.m. [2]

young pigeon [1], young [1]

Ge 15: 9 each three years old, along with a dove and a **young pigeon**."
Dt 32: 11 like an eagle that stirs up its nest and hovers over its **young**,

1579 גּוֹזָן **gôzān**, n.pr.loc. [5]

Gozan [5]

2Ki 17: 6 in **Gozan** on the Habor River and in the towns of the Medes.
18: 11 in Halah, in **Gozan** on the Habor River and in towns of the Medes.
19: 12 the gods of **Gozan**, Haran, Rezeph and the people of Eden who
1Ch 5: 26 He took them to Halah, Habor, Hara and the river of **Gozan**,
Isa 37: 12 the gods of **Gozan**, Haran, Rezeph and the people of Eden who

1580 גּוֹי **gôy**, n.m. [555] [→ 1582]

nations [410], nation [114], people [8], Gentiles [5], *untranslated* [4], each national group [+1580] [2], Gentile [2], peoples [2], another[s] [1], countries [1], foreign [1], it[s] [+2021] [1], kind [1], nations [+824] [1], pagan nations [1], they[s] [1]

Ge 10: 5 (From these the maritime **peoples** spread out into their territories
10: 5 spread out into their territories by their clans within their **nations**,
10: 20 Ham by their clans and languages, in their territories and **nations**.
10: 31 Shem by their clans and languages, in their territories and **nations**.
10: 32 according to their lines of descent, within their **nations**.
10: 32 From these the **nations** spread out over the earth after the flood.
12: 2 "I will make you into a great **nation** and I will bless you; I will
15: 14 I will punish the **nation** they serve as slaves, and afterward they
17: 4 is my covenant with you: You will be the father of many **nations**.
17: 5 will be Abraham, for I have made you a father of many **nations**.
17: 6 I will make **nations** of you, and kings will come from you.
17: 16 I will bless her so that she will be the mother of **nations**; kings of
17: 20 the father of twelve rulers, and I will make him into a great **nation**.
18: 18 Abraham will surely become a great and powerful **nation**,
18: 18 and all **nations** *on* earth will be blessed through him.
20: 4 near her, so he said, "Lord, will you destroy an innocent **nation**?
21: 13 I will make the son of the maidservant into a **nation** also,
21: 18 and take him by the hand, for I will make him into a great **nation**."
22: 18 and through your offspring all **nations** *on* earth will be blessed,
25: 23 The LORD said to her, "Two **nations** are in your womb,
26: 4 and through your offspring all **nations** *on* earth will be blessed,
35: 11 A **nation** and a community of nations will come from you,
35: 11 A nation and a community of **nations** will come from you,
46: 3 to go down to Egypt, for I will make you into a great **nation** there.
48: 19 than he, and his descendants will become a group of **nations**."
Ex 9: 24 worst storm in all the land of Egypt since it had become a **nation**.
19: 6 you will be for me a kingdom of priests and a holy **nation**.'
32: 10 that I may destroy them. Then I will make you into a great **nation**."
33: 13 to find favor with you. Remember that this **nation** is your people."
34: 10 I will do wonders never before done in any **nation** in all the world.
34: 24 I will drive out **nations** before you and enlarge your territory,
Lev 18: 24 because this is how the **nations** that I am going to drive out before
18: 28 it will vomit you out as it vomited out the **nations** that were before
20: 23 You must not live according to the customs of the **nations** I am
25: 44 and female slaves are to come from the **nations** around you;
26: 33 I will scatter you among the **nations** and will draw out my sword
26: 38 You will perish among the **nations**; the land of your enemies will
26: 45 I brought out of Egypt in the sight of the **nations** to be their God.
Nu 14: 12 but I will make you into a **nation** greater and stronger than they."
14: 15 the **nations** who have heard this report about you will say,
23: 9 who live apart and do not consider themselves one of the **nations**.
24: 8 They devour hostile **nations** and break their bones in pieces;
24: 20 "Amalek was first among the **nations**, but he will come to ruin at
Dt 4: 6 "Surely this great **nation** is a wise and understanding people."
4: 7 What other **nation** is so great as to have their gods near them the
4: 8 what other **nation** is so great as to have such righteous decrees
4: 27 only a few of you will survive among the **nations** to which the
4: 34 Has any god ever tried to take for himself one **nation** out of
4: 34 god ever tried to take for himself one nation out of another **nation**,
4: 38 to drive out before you **nations** greater and stronger than you
7: 1 are entering to possess and drives out before you many **nations**—
7: 1 and Jebusites, seven **nations** larger and stronger than you—
7: 17 may say to yourselves, "These **nations** are stronger than we are.
7: 22 The LORD your God will drive out those **nations** before you,
8: 20 Like the **nations** the LORD destroyed before you, so you will be
9: 1 to go in and dispossess **nations** greater and stronger than you,
9: 4 it is on account of the wickedness of these **nations** that the LORD
9: 5 on account of the wickedness of these **nations**, the LORD your
9: 14 I will make you into a **nation** stronger and more numerous than
11: 23 then the LORD will drive out all these **nations** before you,
11: 23 and you will dispossess **nations** larger and stronger than you.
12: 2 under every spreading tree where the **nations** you are
12: 29 The LORD your God will cut off before you the **nations** you are
12: 30 about their gods, saying, "How do these **nations** serve their gods?
15: 6 and you will lend to many **nations** but will borrow from none.
15: 6 You will rule over many **nations** but none will rule over you.
17: 14 you say, "Let us set a king over us like all the **nations** around us,"
18: 9 do not learn to imitate the detestable ways of the **nations** there.
18: 14 The **nations** you will dispossess listen to those who practice
19: 1 When the LORD your God has destroyed the **nations** whose land
20: 15 are at a distance from you and do not belong to the **nations** nearby.
26: 5 with a few people and lived there and became a great **nation**,
26: 19 fame and honor high above all the **nations** he has made and that
28: 1 the LORD your God will set you high above all the **nations** *on*
28: 12 You will lend to many **nations** but will borrow from none.
28: 36 and the king you set over you to a **nation** unknown to you
28: 49 The LORD will bring a **nation** against you from far away,
28: 49 swooping down, a **nation** whose language you will not understand,
28: 50 a fierce-looking **nation** without respect for the old or pity for the
28: 65 Among those **nations** you will find no repose, no resting place for
29: 16 [29:15] how we passed through the **countries** on the way here.

Dt 29:18 [29:17] our God to go and worship the gods of those **nations**;
29:24 [29:23] All the **nations** will ask: "Why has the LORD done this
30: 1 wherever the LORD your God disperses you among the **nations**,
31: 3 He will destroy these **nations** before you, and you will take
32: 8 When the Most High gave the **nations** their inheritance, when he
32:21 I will make them angry by a **nation** that has no understanding.
32:28 They are a **nation** without sense, there is no discernment in them.
32:43 Rejoice, O **nations**, with his people, for he will avenge the blood
Jos 3:17 while all Israel passed by until the whole **nation** had completed the
4: 1 When the whole **nation** had finished crossing the Jordan,
5: 6 **[NIE]** men who were of military age when they left Egypt had
5: 8 after the whole **nation** had been circumcised, they remained where
10:13 and the moon stopped, till the **nation** avenged itself on its enemies,
23: 3 the LORD your God has done to all these **nations** for your sake;
23: 4 inheritance for your tribes all the land of the **nations** that remain—
23: 4 the **nations** I conquered—between the Jordan and the Great Sea in
23: 7 Do not associate with these **nations** that remain among you;
23: 9 LORD has driven out before you great and powerful **nations**;
23:12 ally yourselves with the survivors of these **nations** that remain
23:13 your God will no longer drive out these **nations** before you.
Jdg 2:20 "Because this **nation** has violated the covenant that I laid down for
2:21 I will no longer drive out before them any of the **nations** Joshua
2:23 The LORD had allowed those **nations** to remain; he did not drive
3: 1 These are the **nations** the LORD left to test all those Israelites
1Sa 8: 5 now appoint a king to lead us, such as all the other **nations** have."
8:20 Then we will be like all the other **nations**, with a king to lead us
2Sa 7:23 the one **nation** on earth that God went out to redeem as a people
7:23 and to perform great and awesome wonders by driving out **nations**
8:11 done with the silver and gold from all the **nations** he had subdued:
22:44 of my people; you have preserved me as the head of **nations**.
22:50 Therefore I will praise you, O LORD, among the **nations**;
1Ki 4:31 [5:11] And his fame spread to all the surrounding **nations**.
11: 2 They were from **nations** about which the LORD had told the
14:24 the people engaged in all the detestable practices of the **nations** the
18:10 there is not a **nation** or kingdom where my master has not sent
18:10 And whenever a **nation** or kingdom claimed you were not there,
2Ki 6:18 Elisha prayed to the LORD, "Strike these **people** with blindness."
16: 3 following the detestable ways of the **nations** the LORD had
17: 8 followed the practices of the **nations** the LORD had driven out
17:11 as the **nations** whom the LORD had driven out before them had
17:15 They imitated the **nations** around them although the LORD had
17:26 "The **people** you deported and resettled in the towns of Samaria do
17:29 **each national** [+1580] **group** made its own gods in the several
17:29 **each national group** [+1580] made its own gods in the several
17:29 set them up in the shrines the people of Samaria **[RPH]** had made
17:29 set them up in the shrines the people of Samaria **[RPH]** had made
17:33 with the customs of the **nations** from which they had been brought.
17:41 Even while these **people** were worshiping the LORD, they were
18:33 Has the god of any **nation** ever delivered his land from the hand of
19:12 Did the gods of the **nations** that were destroyed by my forefathers
19:17 that the Assyrian kings have laid waste these **nations** and their
21: 2 following the detestable practices of the **nations** the LORD had
21: 9 so that they did more evil than the **nations** the LORD had
1Ch 14:17 every land, and the LORD made all the **nations** fear him.
16:20 they wandered from **nation** to nation, from one kingdom to
16:20 they wandered from nation to **nation**, from one kingdom to
16:24 Declare his glory among the **nations**, his marvelous deeds among
16:31 be glad; let them say among the **nations**, "The LORD reigns!"
16:35 gather us and deliver us from the **nations**, that we may give thanks
17:21 the one **nation** on earth whose God went out to redeem a people
17:21 awesome wonders by driving out **nations** from before your people,
18:11 done with the silver and gold he had taken from all these **nations**:
2Ch 15: 6 *One* **nation** was being crushed by another and one city by another,
15: 6 One nation was being crushed by **another**[s] and one city by
20: 6 You rule over all the kingdoms of the **nations**. Power and might
28: 3 following the detestable ways of the **nations** the LORD had
32:13 Were the gods of those **nations** [+824] ever able to deliver their
32:14 Who of all the gods of these **nations** that my fathers destroyed has
32:15 for no god of any **nation** or kingdom has been able to deliver his
32:17 "Just as the gods of the **peoples** *of* the other lands did not rescue
32:23 of Judah. From then on he was highly regarded by all the **nations**.
33: 2 following the detestable practices of the **nations** the LORD had
33: 9 so that they did more evil than the **nations** the LORD had
36:14 following all the detestable practices of the **nations** and defiling
Ezr 6:21 practices of their **Gentile** neighbors in order to seek the LORD,
Ne 5: 8 bought back our Jewish brothers who were sold to the **Gentiles**.
5: 9 the fear of our God to avoid the reproach of our **Gentile** enemies?
5:17 as well as those who came to us from the surrounding **nations**.
6: 6 "It is reported among the **nations**—and Geshem says it is true—
6:16 all the surrounding **nations** were afraid and lost their
13:26 Among the many **nations** there was no king like him. He was
Job 12:23 He makes **nations** great, and destroys them; he enlarges nations,
12:23 and destroys them; he enlarges **nations**, and disperses them.
34:29 his face, who can see him? Yet he is over man and **nation** alike,
Ps 2: 1 Why do the **nations** conspire and the peoples plot in vain?
2: 8 Ask of me, and I will make the **nations** your inheritance, the ends
9: 5 [9:6] You have rebuked the **nations** and destroyed the wicked;
9:15 [9:16] The **nations** have fallen into the pit they have dug;
9:17 [9:18] wicked return to the grave, all the **nations** that forget God.
9:19 [9:20] man triumph; let the **nations** be judged in your presence.
9:20 [9:21] O LORD; let the **nations** know they are but men.
10:16 is King for ever and ever; the **nations** will perish from his land.
18:43 [18:44] you have made me the head of **nations**; people I did not
18:49 [18:50] Therefore I will praise you among the **nations**,
22:27 [22:28] all the families of the **nations** will bow down before him,
22:28 [22:29] belongs to the LORD and he rules over the **nations**.
33:10 The LORD foils the plans of the **nations**; he thwarts the purposes
33:12 Blessed is the **nation** whose God is the LORD, the people he
43: 1 O God, and plead my cause against an ungodly **nation**;
44: 2 [44:3] With your hand you drove out the **nations** and planted our
44:11 [44:12] like sheep and have scattered us among the **nations**.
44:14 [44:15] You have made us a byword among the **nations**;
46: 6 [46:7] **Nations** are in uproar, kingdoms fall; he lifts his voice,
46:10 [46:11] I will be exalted among the **nations**, I will be exalted in
47: 8 [47:9] God reigns over the **nations**; God is seated on his holy
59: 5 [59:6] the God of Israel, rouse yourself to punish all the **nations**;
59: 8 [59:9] O LORD, laugh at them; you scoff at all those **nations**.
66: 7 He rules forever by his power, his eyes watch the **nations**—
67: 2 [67:3] may be known on earth, your salvation among all **nations**.
72:11 All kings will bow down to him and all **nations** will serve him.
72:17 All **nations** will be blessed through him, and they will call him
78:55 He drove out **nations** before them and allotted their lands to them
79: 1 O God, the **nations** have invaded your inheritance; they have
79: 6 Pour out your wrath on the **nations** that do not acknowledge you,
79:10 Why should the **nations** say, "Where is their God?" Before our
79:10 make known among the **nations** that you avenge the outpoured
80: 8 [80:9] vine out of Egypt; you drove out the **nations** and planted it.
82: 8 O God, judge the earth, for all the **nations** are your inheritance.
83: 4 [83:5] "Come," they say, "let us destroy them as a **nation**,
86: 9 All the **nations** you have made will come and worship before you,
94:10 Does he who disciplines **nations** not punish? Does he who teaches
96: 3 Declare his glory among the **nations**, his marvelous deeds among
96:10 Say among the **nations**, "The LORD reigns." The world is firmly
98: 2 his salvation known and revealed his righteousness to the **nations**.
102:15 [102:16] The **nations** will fear the name of the LORD, all the
105:13 they wandered from **nation** to nation, from one kingdom to
105:13 they wandered from nation to **nation**, from one kingdom to
105:44 he gave them the lands of the **nations**, and they fell heir to what
106: 5 that I may share in the joy of your **nation** and join your inheritance
106:27 make their descendants fall among the **nations** and scatter them
106:35 but they mingled with the **nations** and adopted their customs.
106:41 He handed them over to the **nations**, and their foes ruled over
106:47 Save us, O LORD our God, and gather us from the **nations**,
110: 6 He will judge the **nations**, heaping up the dead and crushing the
111: 6 the power of his works, giving them the lands of other **nations**.
113: 4 The LORD is exalted over all the **nations**, his glory above the
115: 2 Why do the **nations** say, "Where is their God?"
117: 1 Praise the LORD, all you **nations**; extol him, all you peoples.
118:10 All the **nations** surrounded me, but in the name of the LORD I
126: 2 it was said among the **nations**, "The LORD has done great things
135:10 He struck down many **nations** and killed mighty kings—
135:15 The idols of the **nations** are silver and gold, made by the hands of
147:20 He has done this for no other **nation**; they do not know his laws.
149: 7 to inflict vengeance on the **nations** and punishment on the peoples,
Pr 14:34 Righteousness exalts a **nation**, but sin is a disgrace to any people.
Isa 1: 4 Ah, sinful **nation**, a people loaded with guilt, a brood of evildoers,
2: 2 it will be raised above the hills, and all **nations** will stream to it.
2: 4 He will judge between the **nations** and will settle disputes for
2: 4 **Nation** will not take up sword against nation, nor will they train for
2: 4 Nation will not take up sword against **nation**, nor will they train
5:26 He lifts up a banner for the distant **nations**, he whistles for those at
9: 1 [8:23] in the future he will honor Galilee of the **Gentiles**,
9: 3 [9:2] You have enlarged the **nation** and increased their joy;
10: 6 I send him against a godless **nation**, I dispatch him against a
10: 7 in mind; his purpose is to destroy, to put an end to many **nations**.
11:10 the **nations** will rally to him, and his place of rest will be glorious.
11:12 He will raise a banner for the **nations** and gather the exiles of
13: 4 an uproar among the kingdoms, like **nations** massing together!
14: 6 and in fury subdued **nations** with relentless aggression.
14: 9 rise from their thrones—all those who were kings over the **nations**.
14:12 been cast down to the earth, you who once laid low the **nations**!
14:18 All the kings of the **nations** lie in state, each in his own tomb.
14:26 for the whole world; this is the hand stretched out over all **nations**.
14:32 What answer shall be given to the envoys of that **nation**? "The
16: 8 The rulers of the **nations** have trampled down the choicest vines,
18: 2 Go, swift messengers, to a **people** tall and smooth-skinned,
18: 2 people feared far and wide, an aggressive **nation** *of* strange speech,
18: 7 people feared far and wide, an aggressive **nation** *of* strange speech,

[F] Hitpael (hitpoel, hitpoal, hitpolel, hitpolal, hitpalel, hitpalal, hitpalpel, hitpalpal, hotpael, hotpaal) [G] Hiphil (hiphtil) [H] Hophal [I] Hishtaphel

Isa 23: 3 revenue of Tyre, and she became the marketplace of the **nations**.
25: 3 peoples will honor you; cities of ruthless **nations** will revere you.
25: 7 shroud that enfolds all peoples, the sheet that covers all **nations**;
26: 2 Open the gates that the righteous **nation** may enter, the nation that
26: 15 You have enlarged the **nation**, O LORD; you have enlarged the
26: 15 enlarged the nation, O LORD; you have enlarged the **nation**.
29: 7 Then the hordes of all the **nations** that fight against Ariel,
29: 8 So will it be with the hordes of all the **nations** that fight against
30: 28 He shakes the **nations** in the sieve of destruction; he places in the
33: 3 your voice, the peoples flee; when you rise up, the **nations** scatter.
34: 1 Come near, you **nations**, and listen; pay attention, you peoples!
34: 2 The LORD is angry with all **nations**; his wrath is upon all their
36: 18 Has the god of any **nation** ever delivered his land from the hand of
37: 12 Did the gods of the **nations** that were destroyed by my forefathers
40: 15 Surely the **nations** are like a drop in a bucket; they are regarded as
40: 17 Before him all the **nations** are as nothing; they are regarded by him
41: 2 He hands **nations** over to him and subdues kings before him.
42: 1 I will put my Spirit on him and he will bring justice to the **nations**.
42: 6 you to be a covenant for the people and a light for the **Gentiles**,
43: 9 All the **nations** gather together and the peoples assemble.
45: 1 whose right hand I take hold of to subdue **nations** before him
45: 20 and come; assemble, you fugitives from the **nations**.
49: 6 I will also make you a light for the **Gentiles**, that you may bring
49: 7 to him who was despised and abhorred by the **nation**,
49: 22 "See, I will beckon to the **Gentiles**, I will lift up my banner to the
52: 10 LORD will lay bare his holy arm in the sight of all the **nations**,
52: 15 so will he sprinkle many **nations**, and kings will shut their mouths
54: 3 your descendants will dispossess **nations** and settle in their
55: 5 Surely you will summon **nations** you know not, and nations that
55: 5 **nations** that do not know you will hasten to you, because of the
58: 2 as if they were a **nation** that does what is right and has not
60: 3 **Nations** will come to your light, and kings to the brightness of
60: 5 will be brought to you, to you the riches of the **nations** will come.
60: 11 or night, so that men may bring you the wealth of the **nations**—
60: 12 For the **nation** or kingdom that will not serve you will perish;
60: 12 or kingdom that will not serve you will perish; **it**[s] [+2021] will be
60: 16 You will drink the milk of **nations** and be nursed at royal breasts.
60: 22 least of you will become a thousand, the smallest a mighty **nation**.
61: 6 You will feed on the wealth of **nations**, and in their riches you will
61: 9 Their descendants will be known among the **nations** and their
61: 11 will make righteousness and praise spring up before all **nations**.
62: 2 The **nations** will see your righteousness, and all kings your glory;
64: 2 [64:1] your enemies and cause the **nations** to quake before you!
65: 1 To a **nation** that did not call on my name, I said, 'Here am I,
66: 8 country be born in a day or a **nation** be brought forth in a moment?
66: 12 to her like a river, and the wealth of **nations** like a flooding stream;
66: 18 am about to come and gather all **nations** and tongues, and they will
66: 19 and I will send some of those who survive to the **nations**—
66: 19 or seen my glory. They will proclaim my glory among the **nations**.
66: 20 And they will bring all your brothers, from all the **nations**,
Jer 1: 5 born I set you apart; I appointed you as a prophet to the **nations**."
1: 10 today I appoint you over **nations** and kingdoms to uproot and tear
2: 11 Has a **nation** ever changed its gods? (Yet they are not gods at all.)
3: 17 all **nations** will gather in Jerusalem to honor the name of the
3: 19 you a desirable land, the most beautiful inheritance of *any* **nation**.'
4: 2 the **nations** will be blessed by him and in him they will glory."
4: 7 A lion has come out of his lair; a destroyer of **nations** has set out.
4: 16 "Tell this to the **nations**, proclaim it to Jerusalem: 'A besieging
5: 9 the LORD. "Should I not avenge myself on such a **nation** as this?
5: 15 declares the LORD, "I am bringing a distant **nation** against you—
5: 15 an **[RPH]** ancient and enduring nation, a people whose language
5: 15 an ancient and enduring **nation**, a people whose language you do
5: 15 and enduring nation, a **people** whose language you do not know,
5: 29 the LORD. "Should I not avenge myself on such a **nation** as this?
6: 18 Therefore hear, O **nations**; observe, O witnesses, what will happen
6: 22 a great **nation** is being stirred up from the ends of the earth.
7: 28 'This is the **nation** that has not obeyed the LORD its God
9: 9 [9:8] "Should I not avenge myself on such a **nation** as this?"
9: 16 [9:15] I will scatter them among **nations** that neither they nor
9: 26 [9:25] For all these **nations** are really uncircumcised, and even
10: 2 "Do not learn the ways of the **nations** or be terrified by signs in the
10: 2 by signs in the sky, though the **nations** are terrified by them.
10: 7 Who should not revere you, O King of the **nations**? This is your
10: 7 Among all the wise men of the **nations** and in all their kingdoms,
10: 10 is angry, the earth trembles; the **nations** cannot endure his wrath.
10: 25 Pour out your wrath on the **nations** that do not acknowledge you,
12: 17 But if any **nation** does not listen, I will completely uproot
14: 22 Do any of the worthless idols of the **nations** bring rain? Do the
16: 19 to you the **nations** will come from the ends of the earth and say,
18: 7 If at any time I announce that a **nation** or kingdom is to be
18: 8 and if that **nation** I warned repents of its evil, then I will relent
18: 9 if at another time I announce that a **nation** or kingdom is to be
18: 13 "Inquire among the **nations**: Who has ever heard anything like
22: 8 "People from many **nations** will pass by this city and will ask one
25: 9 and its inhabitants and against all the surrounding **nations**.
25: 11 and these **nations** will serve the king of Babylon seventy years.
25: 12 I will punish the king of Babylon and his **nation**, the land of the
25: 13 in this book and prophesied by Jeremiah against all the **nations**.
25: 14 They themselves will be enslaved by many **nations** and great
25: 15 of my wrath and make all the **nations** to whom I send you drink it.
25: 17 and made all the **nations** to whom he sent me drink it:
25: 31 of the earth, for the LORD will bring charges against the **nations**;
25: 32 Disaster is spreading from **nation** to nation; a mighty storm is
25: 32 Disaster is spreading from nation to **nation**; a mighty storm is
26: 6 this city an object of cursing among all the **nations** *of* the earth.' "
27: 7 All **nations** will serve him and his son and his grandson until the
27: 7 land comes; then many **nations** and great kings will subjugate him.
27: 8 any **nation** or kingdom will not serve Nebuchadnezzar king of
27: 8 I will punish that **nation** with the sword, famine and plague,
27: 11 if any **nation** will bow its neck under the yoke of the king of
27: 13 plague with which the LORD has threatened any **nation** that will
28: 11 Babylon off the neck of all the **nations** within two years.' " At this,
28: 14 I will put an iron yoke on the necks of all these **nations** to make
29: 14 I will gather you from all the **nations** and places where I have
29: 18 of scorn and reproach, among all the **nations** where I drive them.
30: 11 'Though I completely destroy all the **nations** among which I scatter
31: 7 "Sing with joy for Jacob; shout for the foremost of the **nations**.
31: 10 "Hear the word of the LORD, O **nations**; proclaim it in distant
31: 36 "will the descendants of Israel ever cease to be a **nation** before
33: 9 honor before all **nations** *on* earth that hear of all the good things I
33: 24 So they despise my people and no longer regard them as a **nation**.
36: 2 all the other **nations** from the time I began speaking to you in the
43: 5 land of Judah from all the **nations** where they had been scattered.
44: 8 an object of cursing and reproach among all the **nations** *on* earth.
46: 1 LORD that came to Jeremiah the prophet concerning the **nations**:
46: 12 The **nations** will hear of your shame; your cries will fill the earth.
46: 28 "Though I completely destroy all the **nations** among which I
48: 2 'Come, let us put an end to that **nation**.' You too, O Madmen,
49: 14 An envoy was sent to the **nations** to say, "Assemble yourselves to
49: 15 "Now I will make you small among the **nations**, despised among
49: 31 "Arise and attack a **nation** at ease, which lives in confidence,"
49: 36 and there will not be a **nation** where Elam's exiles do not go.
50: 2 "Announce and proclaim among the **nations**, lift up a banner
50: 3 A **nation** from the north will attack her and lay waste her land.
50: 9 bring against Babylon an alliance of great **nations** from the land of
50: 12 She will be the least of the **nations**—a wilderness, a dry land,
50: 23 of the whole earth! How desolate is Babylon among the **nations**!
50: 41 a great **nation** and many kings are being stirred up from the ends
50: 46 the earth will tremble; its cry will resound among the **nations**.
51: 7 The **nations** drank her wine; therefore they have now gone mad.
51: 7 The nations drank her wine; therefore **they**[s] have now gone mad.
51: 20 with you I shatter **nations**, with you I destroy kingdoms,
51: 27 up a banner in the land! Blow the trumpet among the **nations**!
51: 27 Prepare the **nations** for battle against her; summon against her
51: 28 Prepare the **nations** for battle against her—the kings of the Medes,
51: 41 earth seized! What a horror Babylon will be among the **nations**!
51: 44 The **nations** will no longer stream to him. And the wall of Babylon
La 1: 1 How like a widow is she, who once was great among the **nations**!
1: 3 She dwells among the **nations**; she finds no resting place.
1: 10 on all her treasures; she saw **pagan nations** enter her sanctuary—
2: 9 Her king and her princes are exiled among the **nations**, the law is
4: 15 When they flee and wander about, people among the **nations** say,
4: 17 from our towers we watched for a **nation** that could not save us.
4: 20 thought that under his shadow we would live among the **nations**.
Eze 2: 3 to the Israelites, to a rebellious **nation** that has rebelled against me;
4: 13 will eat defiled food among the **nations** where I will drive them."
5: 5 This is Jerusalem, which I have set in the center of the **nations**,
5: 6 and decrees more than the **nations** and countries around her.
5: 7 You have been more unruly than the **nations** around you and have
5: 7 You have not even conformed to the standards of the **nations**
5: 8 and I will inflict punishment on you in the sight of the **nations**.
5: 14 make you a ruin and a reproach among the **nations** around you,
5: 15 an object of horror to the **nations** around you when I inflict
6: 8 the sword when you are scattered among the lands and **nations**.
6: 9 Then in the **nations** where they have been carried captive,
7: 24 I will bring the most wicked of the **nations** to take possession of
11: 12 but have conformed to the standards of the **nations** around you."
11: 16 Although I sent them far away among the **nations** and scattered
12: 15 when I disperse them among the **nations** and scatter them through
12: 16 so that in the **nations** where they go they may acknowledge all
16: 14 your fame spread among the **nations** on account of your beauty,
19: 4 The **nations** heard about him, and he was trapped in their pit.
19: 8 the **nations** came against him, those from regions round about.
20: 9 it from being profaned in the eyes of the **nations** they lived among
20: 14 in the eyes of the **nations** in whose sight I had brought them out.
20: 22 in the eyes of the **nations** in whose sight I had brought them out.
20: 23 to them in the desert that I would disperse them among the **nations**
20: 32 " 'You say, "We want to be like the **nations**, like the peoples of the

Eze 20:41 and I will show myself holy among you in the sight of the **nations**.
22: 4 Therefore I will make you an object of scorn to the **nations**
22:15 I will disperse you among the **nations** and scatter you through the
22:16 When you have been defiled in the eyes of the **nations**, you will
23:30 because you lusted after the **nations** and defiled yourself with their
25: 7 out my hand against you and give you as plunder to the **nations**.
25: 8 the house of Judah has become like all the other **nations**,"
25:10 so that the Ammonites will not be remembered among the **nations**;
26: 3 am against you, O Tyre, and I will bring many **nations** against you,
26: 5 the Sovereign LORD. She will become plunder for the **nations**,
28: 7 going to bring foreigners against you, the most ruthless of **nations**;
28:25 I will show myself holy among them in the sight of the **nations**.
29:12 I will disperse the Egyptians among the **nations** and scatter them
29:15 and will never again exalt itself above the other **nations**.
29:15 I will make it so weak that it will never again rule over the **nations**.
30: 3 LORD is near—a day of clouds, a time of doom for the **nations**.
30:11 He and his army—the most ruthless of **nations**—will be brought in
30:23 I will disperse the Egyptians among the **nations** and scatter them
30:26 I will disperse the Egyptians among the **nations** and scatter them
31: 6 birth under its branches; all the great **nations** lived in its shade.
31:11 I handed it over to the ruler of the **nations**, for him to deal with
31:12 and the most ruthless of foreign **nations** cut it down and left it.
31:16 I made the **nations** tremble at the sound of its fall when I brought it
31:17 Those who lived in its shade, its allies among the **nations**,
32: 2 " 'You are like a lion among the **nations**; you are like a monster in
32: 9 peoples when I bring about your destruction among the **nations**,
32:12 fall by the swords of mighty men—the most ruthless of all **nations**.
32:16 The daughters of the **nations** will chant it; for Egypt and all her
32:18 to the earth below both her and the daughters of mighty **nations**,
34:28 They will no longer be plundered by the **nations**, nor will wild
34:29 be victims of famine in the land or bear the scorn of the **nations**.
35:10 "These two **nations** and countries will be ours and we will take
36: 3 so that you became the possession of the rest of the **nations**
36: 4 and ridiculed by the rest of the **nations** around you—
36: 5 In my burning zeal I have spoken against the rest of the **nations**,
36: 6 jealous wrath because you have suffered the scorn of the **nations**.
36: 7 I swear with uplifted hand that the **nations** around you will also
36:13 "You devour men and deprive your **nation** of its children,"
36:14 you will no longer devour men or make your **nation** childless,
36:15 No longer will I make you hear the taunts of the **nations**, and no
36:15 you suffer the scorn of the peoples or cause your **nation** to fall,
36:19 I dispersed them among the **nations**, and they were scattered
36:20 wherever they went among the **nations** they profaned my holy
36:21 which the house of Israel profaned among the **nations** where they
36:22 which you have profaned among the **nations** where you have gone.
36:23 which has been profaned among the **nations**, the name you have
36:23 the **nations** will know that I am the LORD,
36:24 " 'For I will take you out of the **nations**; I will gather you from all
36:30 so that you will no longer suffer disgrace among the **nations**
36:36 the **nations** around you that remain will know that I the LORD
37:21 I will take the Israelites out of the **nations** where they have gone.
37:22 I will make them one **nation** in the land, on the mountains of
37:22 they will never again be two **nations** or be divided into two
37:28 Then the **nations** will know that I the LORD make Israel holy,
38:12 the resettled ruins and the people gathered from the **nations**,
38:16 so that the **nations** may know me when I show myself holy
38:23 and I will make myself known in the sight of many **nations**.
39: 7 the **nations** will know that I the LORD am the Holy One in Israel.
39:21 "I will display my glory among the **nations**, and all the nations will
39:21 all the **nations** will see the punishment I inflict and the hand I lay
39:23 the **nations** will know that the people of Israel went into exile for
39:27 I will show myself holy through them in the sight of many **nations**.
39:28 for though I sent them into exile among the **nations**, I will gather
Da 8:22 off represent four kingdoms that will emerge from his **nation**
11:23 act deceitfully, and with only a few **people** he will rise to power.
12: 1 such as has not happened from the beginning of **nations** until then.
Hos 8: 8 now she is among the **nations** like a worthless thing.
8:10 Although they have sold themselves among the **nations**, I will now
9:17 have not obeyed him; they will be wanderers among the **nations**.
Joel 1: 6 A **nation** has invaded my land, powerful and without number;
2:17 your inheritance an object of scorn, a byword among the **nations**.
2:19 never again will I make you an object of scorn to the **nations**.
3: 2 [4:2] I will gather all **nations** and bring them down to the Valley
3: 2 [4:2] for they scattered my people among the **nations** and divided
3: 8 [4:8] and they will sell them to the Sabeans, a **nation** far away."
3: 9 [4:9] Proclaim this among the **nations**: Prepare for war!
3:11 [4:11] Come quickly, all you **nations** from every side,
3:12 [4:12] "Let the **nations** be roused; let them advance into the
3:12 [4:12] for there I will sit to judge all the **nations** on every side.
Am 6: 1 you notable men of the foremost **nation**, to whom the people of
6:14 "I will stir up a **nation** against you, O house of Israel,
9: 9 I will shake the house of Israel among all the **nations** as grain is
9:12 the remnant of Edom and all the **nations** that bear my name,"
Ob 1: 1 An envoy was sent to the **nations** to say, "Rise, and let us go
1: 2 "See, I will make you small among the **nations**; you will be utterly
1:15 "The day of the LORD is near for all **nations**. As you have done,
1:16 drank on my holy hill, so all the **nations** will drink continually;
Mic 4: 2 Many **nations** will come and say, "Come, let us go up to the
4: 3 and will settle disputes for strong **nations** far and wide.
4: 3 **Nation** will not take up sword against nation, nor will they train for
4: 3 Nation will not take up sword against **nation**, nor will they train
4: 7 I will make the lame a remnant, those driven away a strong **nation**.
4:11 But now many **nations** are gathered against you. They say,
5: 8 [5:7] The remnant of Jacob will be among the **nations**,
5:15 [5:14] and wrath upon the **nations** that have not obeyed me."
7:16 **Nations** will see and be ashamed, deprived of all their power.
Na 3: 4 who enslaved **nations** by her prostitution and peoples by her
3: 5 I will show the **nations** your nakedness and the kingdoms your
Hab 1: 5 "Look at the **nations** and watch—and be utterly amazed. For I am
1: 6 am raising up the Babylonians, that ruthless and impetuous **people**,
1:17 he to keep on emptying his net, destroying **nations** without mercy?
2: 5 he gathers to himself all the **nations** and takes captive all the
2: 8 Because you have plundered many **nations**, the peoples who are
3: 6 and shook the earth; he looked, and made the **nations** tremble.
3:12 you strode through the earth and in anger you threshed the **nations**.
Zep 2: 1 Gather together, gather together, O shameful **nation**,
2: 5 Woe to you who live by the sea, O Kerethite **people**; the word of
2: 9 plunder them; the survivors of my **nation** will inherit their land."
2:11 The **nations** on every shore will worship him, every one in its own
2:14 Flocks and herds will lie down there, creatures of every **kind**.
3: 6 "I have cut off **nations**; their strongholds are demolished.
3: 8 I have decided to assemble the **nations**, to gather the kingdoms
Hag 2: 7 I will shake all **nations**, and the desired of all nations will come,
2: 7 I will shake all nations, and the desired of all **nations** will come,
2:14 " 'So it is with this people and this **nation** in my sight,'
2:22 royal thrones and shatter the power of the **foreign** kingdoms.
Zec 1:15 I am very angry with the **nations** that feel secure. I was only a little
1:21 [2:4] throw down these horns of the **nations** who lifted up their
2: 8 [2:12] has sent me against the **nations** that have plundered you—
2:11 [2:15] "Many **nations** will be joined with the LORD in that day
7:14 'I scattered them with a whirlwind among all the **nations**,
8:13 As you have been an object of cursing among the **nations**,
8:22 powerful **nations** will come to Jerusalem to seek the LORD
8:23 and **nations** will take firm hold of one Jew by the hem of his robe
9:10 battle bow will be broken. He will proclaim peace to the **nations**.
12: 3 when all the **nations** *of* the earth are gathered against her,
12: 9 On that day I will set out to destroy all the **nations** that attack
14: 2 I will gather all the **nations** to Jerusalem to fight against it;
14: 3 Then the LORD will go out and fight against those **nations**,
14:14 The wealth of all the surrounding **nations** will be collected—
14:16 the survivors from all the **nations** that have attacked Jerusalem will
14:18 LORD will bring on them the plague he inflicts on the **nations**
14:19 the punishment of all the **nations** that do not go up to celebrate the
Mal 1:11 My name will be great among the **nations**, from the rising to the
1:11 because my name will be great among the **nations**,"
1:14 "and my name is to be feared among the **nations**.
3: 9 You are under a curse—the whole **nation** of you—because you are
3:12 "Then all the **nations** will call you blessed, for yours will be a

1581 גְּוִיָּה *g^ewiyyâ*, n.f. [13] [√ 1568]

bodies [4], body [4], *untranslated* [1], carcass [1], corpses [1], dead [1], it[s] [+793+2021] [1]

Ge 47:18 there is nothing left for our lord except our **bodies** and our land.
Jdg 14: 8 In **it**[s] [+793+2021] was a swarm of bees and some honey,
14: 9 not tell them that he had taken the honey from the lion's **carcass**.
1Sa 31:10 of the Ashtoreths and fastened his **body** to the wall of Beth Shan.
31:12 They took down the **bodies** *of* Saul and his sons from the wall of
31:12 **[RPH]** his sons from the wall of Beth Shan and went to Jabesh,
Ne 9:37 They rule over our **bodies** and our cattle as they please. We are in
Ps 110: 6 heaping up the **dead** and crushing the rulers of the whole earth.
Eze 1:11 another creature on either side, and two wings covering its **body**.
1:23 one toward the other, and each had two wings covering its **body**.
Da 10: 6 His **body** was like chrysolite, his face like lightning, his eyes like
Na 3: 3 Many casualties, piles of dead, **bodies** without number, people
3: 3 bodies without number, people stumbling over the **corpses**—

1582 גּוֹיִם *gôyim*, n.pr.g. [3] [√ 1580]

Goiim [2], Goyim [1]

Ge 14: 1 of Ellasar, Kedorlaomer king of Elam and Tidal king of **Goiim**
14: 9 Tidal king of **Goiim**, Amraphel king of Shinar and Arioch king of
Jos 12:23 king of Dor (in Naphoth Dor) one the king of **Goyim** in Gilgal one

[F] Hitpael (hitpoel, hitpoal, hitpolel, hitpolal, hitpalel, hitpalal, hitpalpel, hitpalpal, hotpael, hotpaal) [G] Hiphil (hiphtil) [H] Hophal [I] Hishtaphel

1583 גּוֹלָה gôlâ, n.f. [41] [√ 1655; Ar 10145]
exile [16], exiles [15], exiles [+1201] [6], captive [1], deported [+906 +995] [1], those[s] [+2021] [1], took [+906+906+906+906+2143] [1]

2Ki 24:15 *He* also **took** [+906+906+906+906+2143] from Jerusalem to
24:16 The king of Babylon also **deported** [+906+995] to Babylon the
1Ch 5:22 the battle was God's. And they occupied the land until the **exile**.
Ezr 1:11 Sheshbazzar brought all these along when the **exiles** came up from
2: 1 of the province who came up from the captivity of the **exiles**,
4: 1 Benjamin heard that the **exiles** [+1201] were building a temple for
6:19 day of the first month, the **exiles** [+1201] celebrated the Passover.
6:20 Levites slaughtered the Passover lamb for all the **exiles** [+1201],
6:21 So the Israelites who had returned from the **exile** ate it,
8:35 the **exiles** [+1201] who had returned from captivity sacrificed burnt
9: 4 gathered around me because of this unfaithfulness of the **exiles**.
10: 6 he continued to mourn over the unfaithfulness of the **exiles**.
10: 7 and Jerusalem for all the **exiles** [+1201] to assemble in Jerusalem.
10: 8 and would himself be expelled from the assembly of the **exiles**.
10:16 So the **exiles** [+1201] did as was proposed. Ezra the priest selected
Ne 7: 6 **exiles** whom Nebuchadnezzar king of Babylon had taken captive
Jer 28: 6 LORD's house and all the **exiles** back to this place from Babylon.
29: 1 sent from Jerusalem to the surviving elders among the **exiles**
29: 4 says to all **those**[s] [+2021] I carried into exile from Jerusalem to
29:16 in this city, your countrymen who did not go with you into **exile**—
29:20 all you **exiles** whom I have sent away from Jerusalem to Babylon.
29:31 "Send this message to all the **exiles**: 'This is what the LORD says
46:19 Pack your belongings for **exile**, you who live in Egypt,
48: 7 Chemosh will go into **exile**, together with his priests and officials.
48:11 not poured from one jar to another—she has not gone into **exile**.
49: 3 for Molech will go into **exile**, together with his priests
Eze 1: 1 while I was among the **exiles** by the Kebar River, the heavens were
3:11 Go now to your countrymen in **exile** and speak to them. Say to
3:15 I came to the **exiles** who lived at Tel Abib near the Kebar River.
11:24 brought me to the **exiles** in Babylonia in the vision given by the
11:25 and I told the **exiles** everything the LORD had shown me.
12: 3 son of man, pack your belongings for **exile** and in the daytime,
12: 4 while they watch, bring out your belongings packed for **exile**.
12: 4 while they are watching, go out like those who go into **exile**.
12: 7 During the day I brought out my things packed for **exile**.
12:11 so it will be done to them. They will go into **exile** as captives.
25: 3 laid waste and over the people of Judah when they went into **exile**,
Am 1:15 Her king will go into **exile**, he and his officials together,"
Na 3:10 Yet she was taken **captive** and went into exile. Her infants were
Zec 6:10 "Take ⸤silver and gold⸥ from the **exiles** Heldai, Tobijah
14: 2 Half of the city will go into **exile**, but the rest of the people will not

1584 גּוֹלָן gôlān, n.pr.loc. [4] [→ 1660]
Golan [4]

Dt 4:43 for the Gadites; and **Golan** in Bashan, for the Manassites.
Jos 20: 8 in the tribe of Gad, and **Golan** in Bashan in the tribe of Manasseh.
21:27 **Golan** in Bashan (a city of refuge for one accused of murder)
1Ch 6:71 [6:56] the half-tribe of Manasseh they received **Golan** in Bashan

1585 גּוּמָּץ gûmmāṣ, n.m. [1]
pit [1]

Ecc 10: 8 Whoever digs a **pit** may fall into it; whoever breaks through a wall

1586 גּוּנִי gûnî[1], n.pr.m. [4] [→ 1587]
Guni [4]

Ge 46:24 The sons of Naphtali: Jahziel, **Guni**, Jezer and Shillem.
Nu 26:48 the Jahzeelite clan; through **Guni**, the Gunite clan;
1Ch 5:15 Ahi son of Abdiel, the son of **Guni**, was head of their family.
7:13 Jahziel, **Guni**, Jezer and Shillem—the descendants of Bilhah.

1587 גּוּנִי gûnî[2], a.g. [1] [√ 1586]
Gunite [1]

Nu 26:48 the Jahzeelite clan; through Guni, the **Gunite** clan;

1588 גָּוַע gāwa', v. [24]
die [8], breathed his last [4], died [4], perish [3], perished [2], breathes his last [1], close to death [1], fell dead [1]

Ge 6:17 [A] has the breath of life in it. Everything on earth *will* **perish**.
7:21 [A] Every living thing that moved on the earth **perished**—birds,
25: 8 [A] Then Abraham **breathed his last** and died at a good old age,
25:17 [A] *He* **breathed his last** and died, and he was gathered to his
35:29 [A] he **breathed his last** and died and was gathered to his
49:33 [A] the bed, **breathed his last** and was gathered to his people.
Nu 17:12 [17:27] [A] The Israelites said to Moses, "*We will* **die**! We are
17:13 [17:28] [A] of the LORD will die. Are we all *going to* **die**?"
20: 3 [A] "If only *we had* **died** when our brothers fell dead before the
20: 3 [A] "If only we had died when our brothers **fell dead** before the
20:29 [A] when the whole community learned that Aaron *had* **died**,
Jos 22:20 [A] of Israel? He was not the only one *who* **died** for his sin.' "
Job 3:11 [A] did I not perish at birth, and **die** as I came from the womb?
10:18 [A] out of the womb? *I wish I had* **died** before any eye saw me.
13:19 [A] bring charges against me? If so, I will be silent and **die**.
14:10 [A] and is laid low; he **breathes his last** and is no more.
27: 5 [A] you are in the right; till *I* **die**, I will not deny my integrity.
29:18 [A] "I thought, '*I will* **die** in my own house, my days as
34:15 [A] all mankind *would* **perish** together and man would return to
36:12 [A] they will perish by the sword and **die** without knowledge.
Ps 88:15 [88:16] [A] my youth I have been afflicted and **close to death**;
104:29 [A] you take away their breath, *they* **die** and return to the dust.
La 1:19 [A] my elders **perished** in the city while they searched for food
Zec 13: 8 [A] the LORD, "two-thirds will be struck down and **perish**;

1589 גּוּף gûp, v. [1]
shut [1]

Ne 7: 3 [G] are still on duty, *have them* **shut** the doors and bar them.

1590 גּוּפָה gûpâ, n.f. [2] [√ 1727]
untranslated [1], bodies [1]

1Ch 10:12 all their valiant men went and took the **bodies** *of* Saul and his sons
10:12 valiant men went and took the bodies of Saul and **[RPH]** his sons

1591 גּוּר gûr[1], v. [81] [→ 1595?, 1731, 1745, 4472]
living [24], dwell [10], live [7], settle [6], stay [4], stayed [3], aliens [2], live for a while [2], lived [2], settled [2], stay for a while [2], staying [2], strangers [2], *untranslated* [1], alien [1], can[s] [1], for a while stayed [1], gather together [1], guests [+1074] [1], linger [1], live awhile [1], lived as an alien [1], lives [1], living as an alien [1], nomads [1], settles [1]

Ge 12:10 [A] Abram went down to Egypt to **live** there **for a while**
19: 9 [A] they said, "This fellow came here *as an* **alien**, and now he
20: 1 [A] between Kadesh and Shur. **For a while** *he* **stayed** in Gerar,
21:23 [A] the country where *you are* **living as an alien** the same
21:34 [A] Abraham **stayed** in the land of the Philistines for a long time.
26: 3 [A] **Stay** in this land **for a while**, and I will be with you and will
32: 4 [32:5] [A] *I have been* **staying** with Laban and have remained
35:27 [A] (that is, Hebron), where Abraham and Isaac *had* **stayed**.
47: 4 [A] They also said to him, "We have come to **live** here **awhile**,
Ex 3:22 [A] *any woman* **living** *in* her house for articles of silver and gold
6: 4 [A] to give them the land of Canaan, where they lived *as* **aliens**.
12:48 [A] "An alien **living** among you who wants to celebrate the
12:49 [A] applies to the native-born and to the alien **living** among you."
Lev 16:29 [A] whether native-born or an alien **living** among you—
17: 8 [A] or any alien **living** among them who offers a burnt offering
17:10 [A] or any alien **living** among them who eats any blood—
17:12 [A] eat blood, nor may an alien **living** among you eat blood."
17:13 [A] or any alien **living** among you who hunts any animal
18:26 [A] the aliens **living** among you must not do any of these
19:33 [A] " 'When an alien **lives** with you in your land, do not mistreat
19:34 [A] The alien **living** with you must be treated as one of your
20: 2 [A] or any alien **living** in Israel who gives any of his children to
25: 6 [A] hired worker and temporary resident who **live** among you,
25:45 [A] You may also buy some of the temporary residents **living**
Nu 9:14 [A] " 'An alien **living** among you who wants to celebrate the
15:14 [A] or anyone else **living** among you presents an offering made
15:15 [A] the same rules for you and for the alien **living** among you;
15:16 [A] will apply both to you and to the alien **living** among you.' "
15:26 [A] and the aliens **living** among them will be forgiven,
15:29 [A] whether he is a native-born Israelite or an alien. **[RPH]**
19:10 [A] both for the Israelites and for the aliens **living** among them.
Dt 18: 6 [A] one of your towns anywhere in Israel where he *is* **living**,
26: 5 [A] with a few people and **lived** there and became a great nation,
Jos 20: 9 [A] or any alien **living** among them who killed someone
Jdg 5:17 [A] Dan, why *did he* **linger** *by* the ships? Asher remained on the
17: 7 [A] in Judah, who *had been* **living** within the clan of Judah,
17: 8 [A] left that town in search of some other place to **stay**. On his
17: 9 [A] in Judah," he said, "and I'm looking for a place to **stay**."
19: 1 [A] Now a Levite *who* **lived** in a remote area in the hill country
19:16 [A] who *was* **living** in Gibeah (the men of the place were
Ru 1: 1 [A] two sons, went to **live for a while** in the country of Moab.
2Sa 4: 3 [A] fled to Gittaim and have lived there *as* **aliens** to this day.
1Ki 17:20 [F] have you brought tragedy also upon this widow I *am* **staying**
2Ki 8: 1 [A] with your family and **stay for a while** wherever you can,
8: 1 [A] with your family and stay for a while wherever *you* **can**[s],
8: 2 [A] and **stayed** in the land of the Philistines seven years.
1Ch 16:19 [A] but few in number, few indeed, and **strangers** in it,
2Ch 15: 9 [A] *people* from Ephraim, Manasseh and Simeon *who had* **settled**
Ezr 1: 4 [A] the people of any place where survivors *may now be* **living**

Job 19:15 [A] My **guests** [+1074] and my maidservants count me a
28: 4 [A] Far from where *people* **dwell** he cuts a shaft, in places
Ps 5: 4 [5:5] [A] pleasure in evil; *with* you the wicked cannot **dwell**.
15: 1 [A] LORD, who *may* **dwell** in your sanctuary? Who may live
61: 4 [61:5] [A] *I long to* **dwell** in your tent forever and take refuge in
105:12 [A] but few in number, few indeed, and **strangers** in it,
105:23 [A] entered Egypt; Jacob **lived as an alien** in the land of Ham.
120: 5 [A] Woe to me that *I* **dwell** *in* Meshech, that I live among the
Isa 11: 6 [A] The wolf *will* **live** with the lamb, the leopard will lie down
16: 4 [A] *Let* the Moabite fugitives **stay** with you; be their shelter from
23: 7 [A] old city, whose feet have taken her to **settle** in far-off lands?
33:14 [A] the godless: "Who of us *can* **dwell** *with* the consuming fire?
33:14 [A] Who of us *can* **dwell** *with* everlasting burning?"
52: 4 [A] "At first my people went down to Egypt to **live**; lately,
Jer 35: 7 [A] you will live a long time in the land where you *are* **nomads**.'
42:15 [A] are determined to go to Egypt and you do go to **settle** there,
42:17 [A] all who are determined to go to Egypt to **settle** there will die
42:22 [A] and plague in the place where you want to go to **settle**."
43: 2 [A] sent you to say, 'You must not go to Egypt to **settle** there.'
43: 5 [A] **live** in the land of Judah from all the nations where they had
44: 8 [A] incense to other gods in Egypt, where you have come to **live**?
44:12 [A] of Judah who were determined to go to Egypt to **settle** there.
44:14 [A] None of the remnant of Judah who have gone to **live** in Egypt
44:28 [A] the whole remnant of Judah who came to **live** in Egypt will
49:18 [A] "so no one will live there; no man *will* **dwell** in it.
49:33 [A] No one will live there; no man *will* **dwell** in it."
50:40 [A] "so no one will live there; no man *will* **dwell** in it.
La 4:15 [A] among the nations say, "*They can* **stay** here no longer."
Eze 14: 7 [A] or any alien **living** in Israel separates himself from me
47:22 [A] for the aliens who *have* **settled** among you and who have
47:23 [A] In whatever tribe the alien **settles**, there you are to give him
Hos 7:14 [F] *They* **gather together** for grain and new wine but turn away

1592 ²גּוּר gûr², v. [6] [cf. 1741, 1594?]

attack [+1592] [2], conspire [2], attacks [1], stir up [1]

Ps 56: 6 [56:7] [A] *They* **conspire**, they lurk, they watch my steps, eager
59: 3 [59:4] [A] Fierce men **conspire** against me for no offense or sin
140: 2 [140:3] [A] evil plans in their hearts and **stir up** war every day.
Isa 54:15 [A] If *anyone does* **attack** [+1592] you, it will not be my doing;
54:15 [A] If *anyone does* **attack** [+1592] you, it will not be my doing;
54:15 [A] not be my doing; whoever **attacks** you will surrender to you.

1593 ³גּוּר gûr³, v. [10] [→ 4471, 4474, 4475; cf. 3336]

afraid [3], fear [2], revere [2], terrified [2], dreaded [1]

Nu 22: 3 [A] and Moab *was* **terrified** because there were so many people.
Dt 1:17 [A] *Do* not *be* **afraid** of any man, for judgment belongs to God.
18:22 [A] has spoken presumptuously. *Do* not *be* **afraid** of him.
32:27 [A] *I* **dreaded** the taunt of the enemy, lest the adversary
1Sa 18:15 [A] Saul saw how successful he was, *he was* **afraid** of him.
Job 19:29 [A] *you should* **fear** the sword yourselves; for wrath will bring
41:25 [41:17] [A] When he rises up, the mighty *are* **terrified**;
Ps 22:23 [22:24] [A] **Revere** him, all *you* descendants of Israel!
33: 8 [A] fear the LORD; *let* all the people of the world **revere** him.
Hos 10: 5 [A] The people who live in Samaria **fear** for the calf-idol of Beth

1594 ⁴גּוּר gûr⁴, n.m. [7] [→ 1596; cf. 1592?]

cubs [3], cub [2], cubs [+793] [1], young [1]

Ge 49: 9 You are a lion's **cub**, O Judah; you return from the prey, my son.
Dt 33:22 About Dan he said: "Dan is a lion's **cub**, springing out of Bashan."
La 4: 3 Even jackals offer their breasts to nurse their **young**, but my people
Eze 19: 2 She lay down among the young lions and reared her **cubs**.
19: 3 She brought up one of her **cubs**, and he became a strong lion.
19: 5 she took another of her **cubs** and made him a strong lion.
Na 2:11 [2:12] where the lion and lioness went, and the **cubs** [+793], with

1595 ⁵גּוּר gûr⁵, n.pr.loc. [1] [√ 1591?]

Gur [1]

2Ki 9:27 They wounded him in his chariot on the way up to **Gur** near

1596 גֹּר gôr, n.[m.]. [2] [√ 1594]

cubs [2]

Jer 51:38 Her people all roar like young lions, they growl like lion **cubs**.
Na 2:12 [2:13] The lion killed enough for his **cubs** and strangled the prey

1597 גּוּר־בָּעַל gûr-bāʿal, n.pr.loc. [1] [cf. 3327]

Gur Baal [1]

2Ch 26: 7 against the Arabs who lived in **Gur Baal** and against the Meunites.

1598 גּוֹרָל gôrāl, n.m. [77]

lot [37], lots [17], allotment [5], allotted [+928+2021+4200] [4], allotted [3], *untranslated* [2], allotted [+2118] [1], allotted [+2118 +4200] [1], allotted [+906+906+928+2021+5989] [1], allotted [+906 +928+2021+5989] [1], allotted [+928+2021+2118+4200] [1], allotted inheritance [1], drawing lots [1], portions [1], territory allotted [1]

Lev 16: 8 He is to cast **lots** for the two goats—one lot for the LORD
16: 8 two goats—one **lot** for the LORD and the other for the scapegoat.
16: 8 one lot for the LORD and the other **[RPH]** for the scapegoat.
16: 9 Aaron shall bring the goat whose **lot** falls to the LORD
16:10 the goat chosen by **lot** as the scapegoat shall be presented alive
Nu 26:55 Be sure that the land is distributed by **lot**. What each group inherits
26:56 Each inheritance is to be distributed by **lot** among the larger
33:54 Distribute the land by **lot**, according to your clans. To a larger
33:54 group a smaller one. Whatever falls to them by **lot** will be theirs.
34:13 the Israelites: "Assign this land by **lot** as an inheritance.
36: 2 my lord to give the land as an inheritance to the Israelites by **lot**,
36: 3 so part of the inheritance **allotted** to us will be taken away.
Jos 14: 2 Their inheritances were assigned by **lot** to the nine-and-a-half
15: 1 The **allotment** for the tribe of Judah, clan by clan, extended down
16: 1 The **allotment** for Joseph began at the Jordan of Jericho, east of
17: 1 This was the **allotment** for the tribe of Manasseh as Joseph's
17:14 "Why have you given us only one **allotment** and one portion for
17:17 and very powerful. You will have not only one **allotment**
18: 6 and I will cast **lots** for you in the presence of the LORD our God.
18: 8 I will cast **lots** for you here at Shiloh in the presence of the
18:10 then cast **lots** for them in Shiloh in the presence of the LORD,
18:11 The **lot** came up *for* the tribe of Benjamin, clan by clan. Their
18:11 Their **allotted** territory lay between the tribes of Judah and Joseph:
19: 1 The second **lot** came out for the tribe of Simeon, clan by clan.
19:10 The third **lot** came up for Zebulun, clan by clan: The boundary of
19:17 The fourth **lot** came out for Issachar, clan by clan.
19:24 The fifth **lot** came out for the tribe of Asher, clan by clan.
19:32 The sixth **lot** came out for Naphtali, clan by clan:
19:40 The seventh **lot** came out for the tribe of Dan, clan by clan.
19:51 the heads of the tribal clans of Israel assigned by **lot** at Shiloh in
21: 4 The first **lot** came out for the Kohathites, clan by clan. The Levites
21: 4 the priest *were* **allotted** [+928+2021+2118+4200] thirteen towns
21: 5 of Kohath's descendants were **allotted** [+928+2021+4200] ten
21: 6 The descendants of Gershon were **allotted** [+928+2021+4200]
21: 8 the Israelites **allotted** [+906+906+928+2021+5989] to the Levites
21:10 Kohathite clans of the Levites, because the first **lot** fell to them):
21:20 *were* **allotted** [+2118+4200] towns from the tribe of Ephraim:
21:40 All the towns **allotted** [+2118] to the Merarite clans, who were the
Jdg 1: 3 "Come up with us into the **territory allotted** *to* us, to fight against
1: 3 with you into yours." **[RPH]** So the Simeonites went with them.
20: 9 is what we'll do to Gibeah: We'll go up against it as the **lot** directs.
1Ch 6:54 [6:39] the Kohathite clan, because the first **lot** was for them):
6:61 [6:46] of Kohath's descendants were **allotted** [+928+2021+4200]
6:63 [6:48] of Merari, clan by clan, were **allotted** [+928+2021+4200]
6:65 [6:50] and Benjamin *they* **allotted** [+906+928+2021+5989] the
24: 5 They divided them impartially by **drawing lots**, for there were
24: 7 The first **lot** fell to Jehoiarib, the second to Jedaiah,
24:31 They also cast **lots**, just as their brothers the descendants of Aaron
25: 8 and old alike, teacher as well as student, cast **lots** for their duties.
25: 9 The first **lot**, which was for Asaph, fell to Joseph, his sons
26:13 **Lots** were cast for each gate, according to their families, young
26:14 The **lot** for the East Gate fell to Shelemiah. Then lots were cast for
26:14 Then **lots** were cast for his son Zechariah, a wise counselor,
26:14 a wise counselor, and the **lot** for the North Gate fell to him.
Ne 10:34 [10:35] have cast **lots** to determine when each of our families is to
11: 1 the rest of the people cast **lots** to bring one out of every ten to live
Est 3: 7 the month of Nisan, they cast the *pur* (that is, the **lot**)
9:24 the Jews to destroy them and had cast the *pur* (that is, the **lot**)
Ps 16: 5 assigned me my portion and my cup; you have made my **lot** secure.
22:18 [22:19] my garments among them and cast **lots** for my clothing.
125: 3 The scepter of the wicked will not remain over the *land* **allotted** *to*
Pr 1:14 throw in your **lot** with us, and we will share a common purse"—
16:33 The **lot** is cast into the lap, but its every decision is from the
18:18 Casting the **lot** settles disputes and keeps strong opponents apart.
Isa 17:14 is the portion of those who loot us, the **lot** of those who plunder us.
34:17 He allots their **portions**; his hand distributes them by measure.
57: 6 stones of the ravines are your portion; they, they are your **lot**.
Jer 13:25 This is your **lot**, the portion I have decreed for you," declares the
Eze 24: 6 not go away! Empty it piece by piece without casting **lots** for them.
Da 12:13 end of the days you will rise to receive your **allotted inheritance**."
Joel 3: 3 [4:3] They cast **lots** for my people and traded boys for prostitutes;
Ob 1:11 and foreigners entered his gates and cast **lots** for Jerusalem,
Jnh 1: 7 let us cast **lots** to find out who is responsible for this calamity."
1: 7 for this calamity." They cast **lots** and the lot fell on Jonah.
1: 7 for this calamity." They cast lots and the **lot** fell on Jonah.
Mic 2: 5 no one in the assembly of the LORD to divide the land by **lot**.
Na 3:10 **Lots** were cast for her nobles, and all her great men were put in

1599 גּוּשׁ gûš, n.[m.]. [1] [→ 1641]

scabs [+6760] [1]

Job 7: 5 My body is clothed with worms and **scabs** [+6760], [K 1641] my skin is broken and festering.

1600 גֵּז gēz, n.[m.]. [4] [√ 1605]

fleece [1], harvested [1], mown field [1], wool from shearing [1]

Dt 18: 4 and oil, and the first **wool from** *the* **shearing** *of* your sheep,
Job 31: 20 his heart did not bless me for warming him with the **fleece** *from*
Ps 72: 6 He will be like rain falling on a **mown field**, like showers watering
Am 7: 1 swarms of locusts after the king's share *had been* **harvested**

1601 גִּזְבָּר gizbār, n.m. [1] [→ Ar 10133, 10139]

treasurer [1]

Ezr 1: 8 king of Persia had them brought by Mithredath the **treasurer**,

1602 גָּזָה gāzâ, v. [1] [→ 1607]

brought forth [1]

Ps 71: 6 [A] on you; you **brought** me **forth** from my mother's womb.

1603 גִּזָּה gizzâ, n.f. [7] [√ 1605]

fleece [6], *untranslated* [1]

Jdg 6: 37 look, I will place a wool **fleece** on the threshing floor. If there is
6: 37 If there is dew only on the **fleece** and all the ground is dry,
6: 38 he squeezed the **fleece** and wrung out the dew—a bowlful of water.
6: 38 the fleece and wrung out the dew—**[RPH]** a bowlful of water.
6: 39 Allow me one more test with the **fleece**. This time make the fleece
6: 39 This time make the **fleece** dry and the ground covered with dew."
6: 40 Only the **fleece** was dry; all the ground was covered with dew.

1604 גִּזוֹנִי gizônî, a.g. [1]

Gizonite [1]

1Ch 11: 34 the sons of Hashem the **Gizonite**, Jonathan son of Shagee the

1605 גָּזַז gāzaz, v. [15] [→ 1600, 1603, 1606]

shear [3], shearers [3], shearing [3], be cut off [1], cut off [1], shave heads [+7942] [1], shaved [1], sheep-shearing time [1], sheepshearers [1]

Ge 31: 19 [A] When Laban had gone to **shear** his sheep, Rachel stole her
38: 12 [A] up to Timnah, to the *men who were* **shearing** his sheep,
38: 13 [A] "Your father-in-law is on his way to Timnah to **shear** his
Dt 15: 19 [A] oxen to work, and *do* not **shear** the firstborn of your sheep.
1Sa 25: 2 [A] and three thousand sheep, which he was **shearing** in Carmel.
25: 4 [A] was in the desert, he heard that Nabal *was* **shearing** sheep.
25: 7 [A] " 'Now I hear that *it is* **sheep-shearing time**. When your
25: 11 [A] and water, and the meat I have slaughtered for my **shearers**,
2Sa 13: 23 [A] when Absalom's **sheepshearers** were at Baal Hazor near the
13: 24 [A] to the king and said, "Your servant has had **shearers** come.
Job 1: 20 [A] At this, Job got up and tore his robe and **shaved** his head.
Isa 53: 7 [A] as a sheep before her **shearers** is silent, so he did not open
Jer 7: 29 [A] **Cut off** your hair and throw it away; take up a lament on the
Mic 1: 16 [A] **Shave** *your* **heads** [+7942] in mourning for the children in
Na 1: 12 [C] and are numerous, *they will* **be cut off** and pass away.

1606 גָּזֵז gāzēz, n.pr.m. [2] [√ 1605]

Gazez [2]

1Ch 2: 46 concubine Ephah was the mother of Haran, Moza and **Gazez**.
2: 46 mother of Haran, Moza and Gazez. Haran was the father of **Gazez**.

1607 גָּזִית gāzît, n.f. [11] [√ 1602]

dressed stone [3], dressed [3], cut [2], blocks of stone [1], dressed stones [1], stone [1]

Ex 20: 25 make an altar of stones for me, do not build it with **dressed stones**,
1Ki 5: 17 [5:31] to provide a foundation of **dressed** stone for the temple.
6: 36 And he built the inner courtyard of three courses of **dressed stone**
7: 9 were made of blocks of high-grade stone **cut** to size and trimmed
7: 11 Above were high-grade stones, **cut** to size, and cedar beams.
7: 12 was surrounded by a wall of three courses of **dressed stone**
1Ch 22: 2 from among them he appointed stonecutters to prepare **dressed**
Isa 9: 10 [9:9] have fallen down, but we will rebuild with **dressed stone**;
La 3: 9 He has barred my way with **blocks of stone**; he has made my paths
Eze 40: 42 There were also four tables of **dressed** stone for the burnt
Am 5: 11 Therefore, though you have built **stone** mansions, you will not live

1608 גָּזַל gāzal, v. [30] [→ 1609, 1610, 1611]

rob [3], snatched [3], been robbed [2], commit robbery [+1611] [2], seized [2], are robbed [1], be forcibly taken [1], caught [1], commit robbery [+1610] [1], commits robbery [+1611] [1], exploit [1], injured [1], robbed [+1609] [1], robbed [1], robs [1], seize [1], snatch away [1], steal [1], stolen [+1611] [1], stolen [1], take by force [1], tear [1], withhold [1]

Ge 21: 25 [A] about a well of water that Abimelech's servants *had* **seized**.
31: 31 [A] *you* would **take** your daughters away from me **by force**.
Lev 6: 4 [5:23] [A] he must return what *he has* **stolen** [+1611] or taken
19: 13 [A] " 'Do not defraud your neighbor or **rob** him. " 'Do not hold
Dt 28: 29 [B] day after day you will be oppressed and **robbed**, with no one
28: 31 [B] Your donkey *will* **be forcibly taken** from you and will not be
Jdg 9: 25 [A] on the hilltops to ambush and **rob** everyone who passed by,
21: 23 [A] each man **caught** one and carried her off to be his wife.
2Sa 23: 21 [A] *He* **snatched** the spear from the Egyptian's hand and killed
1Ch 11: 23 [A] *He* **snatched** the spear from the Egyptian's hand and killed
Job 20: 19 [A] left them destitute; *he has* **seized** houses he did not build.
24: 2 [A] move boundary stones; they pasture flocks *they have* **stolen**.
24: 9 [A] The fatherless child *is* **snatched** from the breast; the infant of
24: 19 [A] As heat and drought **snatch away** the melted snow,
Ps 35: 10 [A] for them, the poor and needy from *those who* **rob** them."
69: 4 [69:5] [A] I am forced to restore what *I did* not **steal**.
Pr 4: 16 [C] they **are robbed** *of* slumber till they make someone fall.
22: 22 [A] *Do* not **exploit** the poor because they are poor and do not
28: 24 [A] *He who* **robs** his father or mother and says, "It's not
Isa 10: 2 [A] and **withhold** justice *from* the oppressed of my people,
Jer 21: 12 [B] the hand of his oppressor the *one who has* **been robbed**,
22: 3 [B] the hand of his oppressor the *one who has* **been robbed**.
Eze 18: 7 [A] *He does* not **commit robbery** [+1611] but gives his food to
18: 12 [A] the poor and needy. *He* **commits robbery** [+1611].
18: 16 [A] *He does* not **commit robbery** [+1611] but gives his food to
18: 18 [A] **robbed** [+1609] his brother and did what was wrong among
22: 29 [A] of the land practice extortion and **commit robbery** [+1610];
Mic 2: 2 [A] They covet fields and **seize** them, and houses, and take them.
3: 2 [A] *who* **tear** the skin from my people and the flesh from their
Mal 1: 13 [B] "When you bring **injured**, crippled or diseased animals

1609 גֵּזֶל gēzel, n.[m.]. [2] [√ 1608]

denied [1], robbed [+1608] [1]

Ecc 5: 8 [5:7] justice and rights **denied**, do not be surprised at such things;
Eze 18: 18 **robbed** [+1608] his brother and did what was wrong among his

1610 גָּזֵל gāzēl, n.[m.]. [4] [→ 1611; cf. 1608]

commit robbery [+1608] [1], robbery [1], stolen goods [1], stolen [1]

Lev 6: 2 [5:21] something entrusted to him or left in his care or **stolen**,
Ps 62: 10 [62:11] Do not trust in extortion or take pride in **stolen goods**;
Isa 61: 8 "For I, the LORD, love justice; I hate **robbery** and iniquity.
Eze 22: 29 of the land practice extortion and **commit robbery** [+1608];

1611 גְּזֵלָה gezēlâ, n.f. [6] [√ 1610; cf. 1608]

commit robbery [+1608] [2], commits robbery [+1608] [1], plunder [1], stolen [+1608] [1], what stolen [1]

Lev 6: 4 [5:23] he must return what *he has* **stolen** [+1608] or taken by
Isa 3: 14 ruined my vineyard; the **plunder** *from* the poor is in your houses.
Eze 18: 7 *He does* not **commit robbery** [+1608] but gives his food to the
18: 12 He oppresses the poor and needy. *He* **commits robbery** [+1608].
18: 16 *He does* not **commit robbery** [+1608] but gives his food to the
33: 15 returns **what** he has **stolen**, follows the decrees that give life,

1612 גָּזָם gāzām, n.m. [3] [→ 1613; cf. 4080]

locust swarm [2], locusts [1]

Joel 1: 4 What the **locust swarm** has left the great locusts have eaten;
2: 25 and the young locust, the other locusts and the **locust swarm**—
Am 4: 9 **Locusts** devoured your fig and olive trees, yet you have not

1613 גַּזָּם gazzām, n.pr.m. [2] [√ 1612]

Gazzam [2]

Ezr 2: 48 Rezin, Nekoda, **Gazzam**,
Ne 7: 51 **Gazzam**, Uzza, Paseah,

1614 גֶּזַע geza', n.m. [3]

stump [2], take root [+9245] [1]

Job 14: 8 Its roots may grow old in the ground and its **stump** die in the soil,
Isa 11: 1 A shoot will come up from the **stump** *of* Jesse; from his roots a
40: 24 no sooner *do they* **take root** [+9245] in the ground, than he blows

1615 [1]גָּזַר ***gāzar***[1], v. [12] [→ 1617, 1618?, 1619, 1620, 1621, 4477; cf. 1616, 1746; Ar 10140, 10141]

are cut off [2], be cut off [1], cut down [1], cut in two [1], cut [1], decide [1], decreed [1], divided [1], excluded [1], there are no [1], was cut off [1]

1Ki 3:25 [A] "**Cut** the living child in two and give half to one and half to
3:26 [A] "Neither I nor you shall have him. **Cut** him **in two**!"
2Ki 6:4 [A] They went to the Jordan and *began to* **cut down** trees.
2Ch 26:21 [C] leprous, and **excluded** from the temple of the LORD.
Est 2:1 [C] and what she had done and what *he had* **decreed** about her.
Job 22:28 [A] What *you* **decide** *on* will be done, and light will shine on
Ps 88:5 [88:6] [C] remember no more, who **are cut off** from your care.
136:13 [A] to *him who* **divided** the Red Sea asunder *His love*
Isa 53:8 [C] For *he* **was cut off** from the land of the living;
La 3:54 [C] over my head, and I thought *I was about to* **be cut off**.
Eze 37:11 [C] 'Our bones are dried up and our hope is gone; we **are cut off**.'
Hab 3:17 [A] though **there are no** sheep in the pen and no cattle in the

1616 [2]גָּזַר ***gāzar***[2], v. [1] [cf. 1615]

devour [1]

Isa 9:20 [9:19] [A] On the right *they will* **devour**, but still be hungry; on

1617 [1]גֶּזֶר ***gezer***[1], n.[m.]. [2] [√ 1615]

asunder [1], pieces [1]

Ge 15:17 with a blazing torch appeared and passed between the **pieces**.
Ps 136:13 to him who divided the Red Sea **asunder** *His love endures*

1618 [2]גֶּזֶר ***gezer***[2], n.pr.loc. [15] [→ 1621; cf. 1615?]

Gezer [14], there[s] [+928] [1]

Jos 10:33 Meanwhile, Horam king of **Gezer** had come up to help Lachish,
12:12 the king of Eglon one the king of **Gezer** one
16:3 as far as the region of Lower Beth Horon and on to **Gezer**,
16:10 They did not dislodge the Canaanites living in **Gezer**; to this day
21:21 Shechem (a city of refuge for one accused of murder) and **Gezer**,
Jdg 1:29 Nor did Ephraim drive out the Canaanites living in **Gezer**,
1:29 but the Canaanites continued to live **there**[s] [+928] among them.
2Sa 5:25 he struck down the Philistines all the way from Gibeon to **Gezer**.
1Ki 9:15 the wall of Jerusalem, and Hazor, Megiddo and **Gezer**.
9:16 (Pharaoh king of Egypt had attacked and captured **Gezer**.
9:17 And Solomon rebuilt **Gezer**.) He built up Lower Beth Horon,
1Ch 6:67 [6:52] they were given Shechem (a city of refuge), and **Gezer**,
7:28 **Gezer** and its villages to the west, and Shechem and its villages all
14:16 down the Philistine army, all the way from Gibeon to **Gezer**.
20:4 In the course of time, war broke out with the Philistines, at **Gezer**.

1619 גִּזְרָה ***gizrâ***, n.f. [8] [√ 1615]

courtyard [7], appearance [1]

La 4:7 bodies more ruddy than rubies, their **appearance** like sapphires.
Eze 41:12 The building facing the temple **courtyard** on the west side was
41:13 the temple **courtyard** and the building with its walls were also a
41:14 The width of the temple **courtyard** on the east, including the front
41:15 he measured the length of the building facing the **courtyard** at the
42:1 and brought me to the rooms opposite the temple **courtyard**
42:10 adjoining the temple **courtyard** and opposite the outer wall,
42:13 south rooms facing the temple **courtyard** are the priests' rooms,

1620 גְּזֵרָה ***g***[e]***zērâ***, n.f. [3] [√ 1615; Ar 10141]

announced [1], decree [1], solitary [1]

Lev 16:22 The goat will carry on itself all their sins to a **solitary** place;
Da 4:17 [4:14] " 'The decision is **announced** *by* messengers, the holy ones
4:24 [4:21] this is the **decree** the Most High has issued against my lord

1621 גִּזְרִי ***gizrî***, a.g. [0] [√ 1618; cf. 1615, 1747]

Girzites [0]

1Sa 27:8 [Now David and his men went up and raided the Geshurites, the **Girzites** [Q; see K 1747] and the Amalekites. (From ancient times]

1622 גָּהָה ***gāhâ***, v. Not used in NIV/BHS [√ 1631]

1623 גָּחוֹן ***gāḥôn***, n.m. [2]

belly [2]

Ge 3:14 You will crawl on your **belly** and you will eat dust all the days of
Lev 11:42 whether it moves on its **belly** or walks on all fours or on many feet;

1624 גַּחַל ***gaḥal***, n.f. [16 / 15] [→ 1625]

coals [6], burning coals [5], bolts [2], embers [1], hot coals [1]

Lev 16:12 He is to take a censer full of burning **coals** from the altar before the
2Sa 22:9 fire came from his mouth, **burning coals** blazed out of it.
22:13 Out of the brightness of his presence **bolts** *of* lightning blazed
Job 41:21 [41:13] His breath sets **coals** ablaze, and flames dart from his
Ps 18:8 [18:9] fire came from his mouth, **burning coals** blazed out of it.
18:12 [18:13] clouds advanced, with hailstones and **bolts** *of* lightning.
18:13 [18:14] the voice of the Most High resounded. [BHS+ *amid hailstones and* **bolts** *of lightning*]
120:4 a warrior's sharp arrows, with **burning coals** *of* the broom tree.
140:10 [140:11] Let **burning coals** fall upon them; may they be thrown
Pr 6:28 Can a man walk on **hot coals** without his feet being scorched?
25:22 In doing this, you will heap **burning coals** on his head,
26:21 As charcoal to **embers** and as wood to fire, so is a quarrelsome
Isa 44:19 I even baked bread over its **coals**, I roasted meat and I ate.
Eze 1:13 The appearance of the living creatures was like burning **coals** *of*
10:2 Fill your hands with burning **coals** from among the cherubim
24:11 set the empty pot on the **coals** till it becomes hot and its copper

1625 גַּחֶלֶת ***gaḥelet***, n.f. [2] [√ 1624]

burning coal [1], coals [1]

2Sa 14:7 They would put out the only **burning coal** I have left, leaving my
Isa 47:14 Here are no **coals** to warm anyone; here is no fire to sit by.

1626 גַּחַם ***gaḥam***, n.pr.m. [1]

Gaham [1]

Ge 22:24 was Reumah, also had sons: Tebah, **Gaham**, Tahash and Maacah.

1627 גַּחַר ***gaḥar***, n.pr.m. [2]

Gahar [2]

Ezr 2:47 Giddel, **Gahar**, Reaiah,
Ne 7:49 Hanan, Giddel, **Gahar**,

1628 גַּיְא ***gay'***, n.m. & f. [59 / 58] [→ 1629]

valley [50], valleys [7], it[s] [+2215] [1]

Nu 21:20 from Bamoth to the **valley** in Moab where the top of Pisgah
Dt 3:29 So we stayed in the **valley** near Beth Peor.
4:46 were in the **valley** near Beth Peor east of the Jordan, in the land of
34:6 He buried him in Moab, in the **valley** opposite Beth Peor,
Jos 8:11 set up camp north of Ai, with the **valley** between them and the city.
15:8 it ran up the **Valley** *of* Ben Hinnom along the southern slope of the
15:8 the Hinnom **Valley** at the northern end of the Valley of Rephaim.
18:16 The boundary went down to the foot of the hill facing the **Valley** *of*
18:16 It continued down the Hinnom **Valley** along the southern slope of
19:14 on the north to Hannathon and ended at the **Valley** *of* Iphtah El.
19:27 touched Zebulun and the **Valley** *of* Iphtah El, and went north to
1Sa 13:18 the third toward the borderland overlooking the **Valley** *of* Zeboim
17:3 one hill and the Israelites another, with the **valley** between them.
17:52 the Philistines to the entrance of Gath [BHS *a valley*; NIV 1781]
2Sa 8:13 striking down eighteen thousand Edomites in the **Valley** *of* Salt.
2Ki 2:16 him up and set him down on some mountain or in some **valley**."
14:7 the one who defeated ten thousand Edomites in the **Valley** *of* Salt
23:10 He desecrated Topheth, which was in the **Valley** *of* Ben Hinnom,
1Ch 4:39 they went to the outskirts of Gedor to the east of the **valley** in
18:12 struck down eighteen thousand Edomites in the **Valley** *of* Salt.
2Ch 14:10 [14:9] they took up battle positions in the **Valley** *of* Zephathah
25:11 then marshaled his strength and led his army to the **Valley** *of* Salt,
26:9 at the **Valley** Gate and at the angle of the wall, and he fortified
28:3 He burned sacrifices in the **Valley** *of* Ben Hinnom and sacrificed
33:6 He sacrificed his sons in the fire in the **Valley** *of* Ben Hinnom,
Ne 2:13 By night I went out through the **Valley** Gate toward the Jackal
2:15 Finally, I turned back and reentered through the **Valley** Gate.
3:13 The **Valley** Gate was repaired by Hanun and the residents of
11:30 So they were living all the way from Beersheba to the **Valley** *of*
11:35 in Lod and Ono, and in the **Valley** *of* the Craftsmen.
Ps 23:4 Even though I walk through the **valley** *of* the shadow of death,
60:T [60:2] struck down twelve thousand Edomites in the **Valley** *of*
Isa 22:1 An oracle concerning the **Valley** *of* Vision: What troubles you
22:5 a day of tumult and trampling and terror in the **Valley** *of* Vision,
28:1 his glorious beauty, set on the head of a fertile **valley**—
28:4 his glorious beauty, set on the head of a fertile **valley**,
40:4 Every **valley** shall be raised up, every mountain and hill made low;
Jer 2:23 See how you behaved in the **valley**; consider what you have done.
7:31 They have built the high places of Topheth in the **Valley** *of* Ben
7:32 people will no longer call it Topheth or the **Valley** *of* Ben Hinnom,
7:32 or the Valley of Ben Hinnom, but the **Valley** *of* Slaughter,
19:2 go out to the **Valley** *of* Ben Hinnom, near the entrance of the
19:6 no longer call this place Topheth or the **Valley** *of* Ben Hinnom,
19:6 or the Valley of Ben Hinnom, but the **Valley** *of* Slaughter.
32:35 They built high places for Baal in the **Valley** *of* Ben Hinnom to
Eze 6:3 LORD says to the mountains and hills, to the ravines and **valleys**:
7:16 moaning like doves of the **valleys**, each because of his sins.
31:12 Its boughs fell on the mountains and in all the **valleys**; its branches

Eze 32: 5 your flesh on the mountains and fill the **valleys** with your remains.
35: 8 will fall on your hills and in your **valleys** and in all your ravines.
36: 4 LORD says to the mountains and hills, to the ravines and **valleys**,
36: 6 and say to the mountains and hills, to the ravines and **valleys**:
39: 11 in Israel, in the **valley** *of* those who travel east toward the Sea.
39: 11 will be buried there. So it will be called the **Valley** *of* Hamon Gog.
39: 15 until the gravediggers have buried it in the **Valley** *of* Hamon Gog.
Mic 1: 6 I will pour her stones into the **valley** and lay bare her foundations.
Zec 14: 4 forming a great **valley**, with half of the mountain moving north
14: 5 You will flee by my mountain **valley**, for it will extend to Azel.
14: 5 flee by my mountain valley, for **it**[s] [+2215] will extend to Azel.

1629 גֵּיא חֲרָשִׁים gê' ḥ^arāšîm, n.pr.loc. [1] [√ 1628 + 3096]

Ge Harashim [1]

1Ch 4: 14 Seraiah was the father of Joab, the father of **Ge Harashim**.

1630 גִּיד gîd, n.m. [7]

sinews [3], tendon [+5962] [2], tendons [2]

Ge 32: 32 [32:33] eat the **tendon** [+5962] attached to the socket of the hip,
32: 32 [32:33] of Jacob's hip was touched near the **tendon** [+5962].
Job 10: 11 with skin and flesh and knit me together with bones and **sinews**?
40: 17 His tail sways like a cedar; the **sinews** *of* his thighs are close-knit.
Isa 48: 4 the **sinews** *of* your neck were iron, your forehead was bronze.
Eze 37: 6 I will attach **tendons** to you and make flesh come upon you
37: 8 and **tendons** and flesh appeared on them and skin covered them,

1631 גִּיחַ gîaḥ[1], v. [6] [→ 1622, 1632, 1633; Ar 10137]

brought [1], burst [1], charged out [1], in agony [1], surge [1], thrashing about [1]

Jdg 20: 33 [G] the Israelite ambush **charged out** of its place on the west of
Job 38: 8 [A] "Who shut up the sea behind doors when it **burst** forth from
40: 23 [A] is secure, though the Jordan *should* **surge** against his mouth.
Ps 22: 9 [22:10] [A] Yet you **brought** me out of the womb; you made
Eze 32: 2 [G] you are like a monster in the seas **thrashing about** in your
Mic 4: 10 [A] Writhe **in agony**, O Daughter of Zion, like a woman in labor,

1632 גִּיחַ gîaḥ[2], n.pr.loc. [1] [√ 1631]

Giah [1]

2Sa 2: 24 hill of Ammah, near **Giah** on the way to the wasteland of Gibeon.

1633 גִּיחוֹן giḥôn, n.pr.loc. [6] [√ 1631]

Gihon [6]

Ge 2: 13 The name of the second river is the **Gihon**; it winds through the
1Ki 1: 33 Solomon my son on my own mule and take him down to **Gihon**.
1: 38 put Solomon on King David's mule and escorted him to **Gihon**.
1: 45 and Nathan the prophet have anointed him king at **Gihon**.
2Ch 32: 30 It was Hezekiah who blocked the upper outlet of the **Gihon** spring
33: 14 west of the **Gihon** spring in the valley, as far as the entrance of the

1634 גֵּיחֲזִי gêḥ^azî, n.pr.m. [12]

Gehazi [12]

2Ki 4: 12 He said to his servant **Gehazi**, "Call the Shunammite." So he
4: 14 **Gehazi** said, "Well, she has no son and her husband is old."
4: 25 in the distance, the man of God said to his servant **Gehazi**, "Look!
4: 27 **Gehazi** came over to push her away, but the man of God said,
4: 29 Elisha said to **Gehazi**, "Tuck your cloak into your belt, take my
4: 31 **Gehazi** went on ahead and laid the staff on the boy's face,
4: 36 Elisha summoned **Gehazi** and said, "Call the Shunammite."
5: 20 **Gehazi**, the servant of Elisha the man of God, said to himself,
5: 21 So **Gehazi** hurried after Naaman. When Naaman saw him running
5: 25 his master Elisha. "Where have you been, **Gehazi**?" Elisha asked.
8: 4 The king was talking to **Gehazi**, the servant of the man of God,
8: 5 **Gehazi** said, "This is the woman, my lord the king, and this is her

1635 גִּיל gîl[1], v. [45] [→ 28?, 1636, 1637, 1638]

rejoice [25], glad [11], rejoices [3], great joy [+1635] [2], joy [1], joyful [1], rejoice greatly [+677+1638] [1], rejoiced [1]

1Ch 16: 31 [A] Let the heavens rejoice, *let* the earth *be* **glad**; let them say
Ps 2: 11 [A] Serve the LORD with fear and **rejoice** with trembling.
9: 14 [9:15] [A] Daughter of Zion and there **rejoice** in your salvation.
13: 4 [13:5] [A] overcome him," and my foes *will* **rejoice** when I fall.
13: 5 [13:6] [A] unfailing love; my heart **rejoices** in your salvation.
14: 7 [A] fortunes of his people, *let* Jacob **rejoice** and Israel be glad!
16: 9 [A] Therefore my heart is glad and my tongue **rejoices**; my body
21: 1 [21:2] [A] How great *is his* **joy** in the victories you give!
31: 7 [31:8] [A] *I will be* **glad** and rejoice in your love, for you saw
32: 11 [A] Rejoice in the LORD and *be* **glad**, *you* righteous; sing,
35: 9 [A] my soul *will* **rejoice** in the LORD and delight in his
48: 11 [48:12] [A] the villages of Judah *are* **glad** because of your
51: 8 [51:10] [A] *let* the bones you have crushed **rejoice**.
53: 6 [53:7] [A] of his people, *let* Jacob **rejoice** and Israel be glad!
89: 16 [89:17] [A] *They* **rejoice** in your name all day long; they exult
96: 11 [A] Let the heavens rejoice, *let* the earth *be* **glad**; let the sea
97: 1 [A] let the earth be glad; *let* the distant shores **rejoice**.
97: 8 [A] Zion hears and rejoices and the villages of Judah *are* **glad**
118: 24 [A] day the LORD has made; *let us* **rejoice** and be glad in it.
149: 2 [A] in their Maker; *let* the people of Zion *be* **glad** in their King.
Pr 2: 14 [A] in doing wrong and **rejoice** in the perverseness of evil,
23: 24 [A] The father of a righteous man *has* **great joy** [+1635]; he who
23: 24 [A] The father of a righteous man *has* **great joy** [+1635]; he who
23: 25 [A] and mother be glad; *may* she who gave you birth **rejoice**!
24: 17 [A] enemy falls; when he stumbles, *do* not *let* your heart **rejoice**,
SS 1: 4 [A] *We* **rejoice** and delight in you; we will praise your love more
Isa 9: 3 [9:2] [A] the harvest, as *men* **rejoice** when dividing the plunder.
25: 9 [A] trusted in him; *let us* **rejoice** and be glad in his salvation."
29: 19 [A] the LORD; the needy *will* **rejoice** in the Holy One of Israel.
35: 1 [A] land will be glad; the wilderness *will* **rejoice** and blossom.
35: 2 [A] *it will* **rejoice** [+677+1638] **greatly** and shout for joy.
41: 16 [A] you *will* **rejoice** in the LORD and glory in the Holy One of
49: 13 [A] Shout for joy, O heavens; **rejoice**, O earth; burst into song,
61: 10 [A] I delight greatly in the LORD; my soul **rejoices** in my God.
65: 18 [A] be glad and **rejoice** forever *in* what I will create, for I will
65: 19 [A] *I will* **rejoice** over Jerusalem and take delight in my people;
66: 10 [A] with Jerusalem and *be* **glad** for her, all *you* who love her;
Hos 10: 5 [A] idolatrous priests, *those who had* **rejoiced** over its splendor,
Joel 2: 21 [A] Be not afraid, O land; *be* **glad** and rejoice.
2: 23 [A] *Be* **glad**, O people of Zion, rejoice in the LORD your God,
Hab 1: 15 [A] gathers them up in his dragnet; and so he rejoices and *is* **glad**.
3: 18 [A] rejoice in the LORD, *I will be* **joyful** in God my Savior.
Zep 3: 17 [A] you with his love, *he will* **rejoice** over you with singing."
Zec 9: 9 [A] **Rejoice** greatly, O Daughter of Zion! Shout, Daughter of
10: 7 [A] see it and be joyful; their hearts *will* **rejoice** in the LORD.

1636 גִּיל gîl[2], n.[m.]. [1] [√ 1635]

age [1]

Da 1: 10 he see you looking worse than the other young men your **age**?

1637 גִּיל gîl[3], n.[m.]. [8] [√ 1635]

gladness [5], delight [1], filled with gladness [+448+8524] [1], jubilant [1]

Job 3: 22 who are **filled with gladness** [+448+8524] and rejoice when they
Ps 43: 4 Then will I go to the altar of God, to God, my joy and my **delight**.
45: 15 [45:16] They are led in with joy and **gladness**; they enter the
65: 12 [65:13] of the desert overflow; the hills are clothed with **gladness**.
Isa 16: 10 Joy and **gladness** are taken away from the orchards; no one sings
Jer 48: 33 Joy and **gladness** are gone from the orchards and fields of Moab.
Hos 9: 1 Do not rejoice, O Israel; *do* not *be* **jubilant** like the other nations.
Joel 1: 16 our very eyes—joy and **gladness** from the house of our God?

1638 גִּילָה gîlâ, n.f. [2] [√ 1635]

delight [1], rejoice greatly [+677+1635] [1]

Isa 35: 2 into bloom; *it will* **rejoice greatly** [+677+1635] and shout for joy.
65: 18 for I will create Jerusalem to be a **delight** and its people a joy.

1639 גִּילֹנִי gîlōnî, a.g. [2] [√ 1656; cf. 1655]

Gilonite [2]

2Sa 15: 12 he also sent for Ahithophel the **Gilonite**, David's counselor,
23: 34 of Ahasbai the Maacathite, Eliam son of Ahithophel the **Gilonite**,

1640 גִּינַת gînat, n.pr.m. [2]

Ginath [2]

1Ki 16: 21 half supported Tibni son of **Ginath** for king, and the other half
16: 22 followers proved stronger than those of Tibni son of **Ginath**.

1641 גִּישׁ gîš, var. [0] [√ 1599]

Job 7: 5 [My body is clothed with worms and **scabs**, [K; see Q 1599]]

1642 גֵּישָׁן gêšān, n.pr.m. [1]

Geshan [1]

1Ch 2: 47 sons of Jahdai: Regem, Jotham, **Geshan**, Pelet, Ephah and Shaaph.

1643 גַּל gal[1], n.m. [18] [→ 1668; cf. 1670]

heap [8], heap of ruins [2], pile [2], piles of stone [+5898] [2], heap of rubble [1], pile of rocks [1], piles of stones [1], rubble [1]

Ge 31: 46 So they took stones and piled them in a **heap**, and they ate there by
31: 46 and piled them in a heap, and they ate there by the **heap**.
31: 48 Laban said, "This **heap** is a witness between you and me today."

Ge 31:51 Laban also said to Jacob, "Here is this **heap**, and here is this pillar
31:52 This **heap** is a witness, and this pillar is a witness, that I will not go
31:52 that I will not go past this **heap** to your side to harm you and that
31:52 that you will not go past this **heap** and pillar to my side to harm
Jos 7:26 Over Achan they heaped up a large **pile** *of* rocks, which remains to
8:29 they raised a large **pile** *of* rocks over it, which remains to this day.
2Sa 18:17 a big pit in the forest and piled up a large **heap** *of* rocks over him.
2Ki 19:25 that you have turned fortified cities into **piles** [+5898] **of stone**.
Job 8:17 it entwines its roots around a **pile of rocks** and looks for a place
15:28 and houses where no one lives, houses crumbling to **rubble**.
Isa 25:2 You have made the city a **heap of rubble**, the fortified town a ruin,
37:26 that you have turned fortified cities into **piles** [+5898] **of stone**.
Jer 9:11 [9:10] "I will make Jerusalem a **heap of ruins**, a haunt of jackals;
51:37 Babylon will be a **heap of ruins**, a haunt of jackals, an object of
Hos 12:11 [12:12] Their altars will be like **piles of stones** on a plowed field.

1644 ²גַּל ***gal²***, n.m. [16] [√ 1670]

waves [13], breakers [1], fountain [1], surging [1]

Job 38:11 may come and no farther; here is where your proud **waves** halt'?
Ps 42:7 [42:8] all your waves and **breakers** have swept over me.
65:7 [65:8] the roaring of their **waves**, and the turmoil of the nations.
89:9 [89:10] the surging sea; when its **waves** mount up, you still them.
107:25 For he spoke and stirred up a tempest that lifted high the **waves**.
107:29 stilled the storm to a whisper; the **waves** *of* the sea were hushed.
SS 4:12 my sister, my bride; you are a spring enclosed, a sealed **fountain**.
Isa 48:18 have been like a river, your righteousness like the **waves** *of* the sea.
51:15 LORD your God, who churns up the sea so that its **waves** roar—
Jer 5:22 The **waves** may roll, but they cannot prevail; they may roar,
31:35 stars to shine by night, who stirs up the sea so that its **waves** roar—
51:42 The sea will rise over Babylon; its roaring **waves** will cover her.
51:55 **Waves** ⌞*of* enemies⌟ will rage like great waters; the roar of their
Eze 26:3 bring many nations against you, like the sea casting up its **waves**.
Jnh 2:3 [2:4] about me; all your **waves** and breakers swept over me.
Zec 10:11 the **surging** sea will be subdued and all the depths of the Nile will

1645 גֵּל ***gēl***, n.m. [3] [√ 1670]

dung [1], excrement [+7362] [1], excrement [1]

Job 20:7 he will perish forever, like his own **dung**; those who have seen him
Eze 4:12 the sight of the people, using human **excrement** [+7362] for fuel."
4:15 bake your bread over cow manure instead of human **excrement**."

1646 גֹּל ***gōl***, n.f.?. Not used in NIV/BHS [√ 1657]

1647 גַּלָּב ***gallāb***, n.[m.]. [1]

barber's [1]

Eze 5:1 and use it as a **barber's** razor to shave your head and your beard.

1648 גִּלְבֹּעַ ***gilbōa'***, n.pr.loc. [8] [√ 1496]

Gilboa [8]

1Sa 28:4 while Saul gathered all the Israelites and set up camp at **Gilboa**.
31:1 Israelites fled before them, and many fell slain on Mount **Gilboa**.
31:8 they found Saul and his three sons fallen on Mount **Gilboa**.
2Sa 1:6 "I happened to be on Mount **Gilboa**," the young man said,
1:21 "O mountains of **Gilboa**, may you have neither dew nor rain,
21:12 Philistines had hung them after they struck Saul down on **Gilboa**.)
1Ch 10:1 Israelites fled before them, and many fell slain on Mount **Gilboa**.
10:8 the dead, they found Saul and his sons fallen on Mount **Gilboa**.

1649 ¹גַּלְגַּל ***galgal¹***, n.m. [9] [→ 1650; cf. 1670; Ar 10143]

wheels [3], wagons [2], chariot wheels [1], wheel [1], whirling wheels [1], whirlwind [1]

Ps 77:18 [77:19] Your thunder was heard in the **whirlwind**, your lightning
Ecc 12:6 pitcher is shattered at the spring, or the **wheel** broken at the well,
Isa 5:28 horses' hoofs seem like flint, their **chariot wheels** like a whirlwind.
Jer 47:3 at the noise of enemy chariots and the rumble of their **wheels**.
Eze 10:2 clothed in linen, "Go in among the **wheels** beneath the cherubim.
10:6 "Take fire from among the **wheels**, from among the cherubim,"
10:13 I heard the wheels being called "the **whirling wheels**."
23:24 with weapons, chariots and **wagons** and with a throng of people;
26:10 **wagons** and chariots when he enters your gates as men enter a city

1650 ²גַּלְגַּל ***galgal²***, n.m. [2] [√ 1649; cf. 1670]

tumbleweed [2]

Ps 83:13 [83:14] Make them like **tumbleweed**, O my God, like chaff
Isa 17:13 the wind like chaff on the hills, like **tumbleweed** before a gale.

1651 ¹גִּלְגָּל ***gilgāl¹***, n.[m.]. [1] [√ 1670; Ar 10143]

wheels [1]

Isa 28:28 Though he drives the **wheels** *of* his threshing cart over it, his

1652 ²גִּלְגָּל ***gilgāl²***, n.pr.loc. [40] [→ 1090; cf. 1670]

Gilgal [39], *untranslated* [1]

Dt 11:30 of those Canaanites living in the Arabah in the vicinity of **Gilgal**.
Jos 4:19 the Jordan and camped at **Gilgal** on the eastern border of Jericho.
4:20 Joshua set up at **Gilgal** the twelve stones they had taken out of the
5:9 Egypt from you." So the place has been called **Gilgal** to this day.
5:10 while camped at **Gilgal** on the plains of Jericho, the Israelites
9:6 Then they went to Joshua in the camp at **Gilgal** and said to him
10:6 The Gibeonites then sent word to Joshua in the camp at **Gilgal**:
10:7 So Joshua marched up from **Gilgal** with his entire army, including
10:9 After an all-night march from **Gilgal**, Joshua took them by
10:15 Then Joshua returned with all Israel to the camp at **Gilgal**.
10:43 Then Joshua returned with all Israel to the camp at **Gilgal**.
12:23 king of Dor (in Naphoth Dor) one the king of Goyim in **Gilgal** one
14:6 Now the men of Judah approached Joshua at **Gilgal**, and Caleb son
15:7 up to Debir from the Valley of Achor and turned north to **Gilgal**,
Jdg 2:1 The angel of the LORD went up from **Gilgal** to Bokim and said,
3:19 At the idols near **Gilgal** he himself turned back and said, "I have a
1Sa 7:16 From year to year he went on a circuit from Bethel to **Gilgal** to
10:8 "Go down ahead of me to **Gilgal**. I will surely come down to you
11:14 "Come, let us go to **Gilgal** and there reaffirm the kingship."
11:15 So all the people went to **Gilgal** and confirmed Saul as king in the
11:15 **[RPH]** There they sacrificed fellowship offerings before the
13:4 And the people were summoned to join Saul at **Gilgal**.
13:7 Saul remained at **Gilgal**, and all the troops with him were quaking
13:8 Samuel did not come to **Gilgal**, and Saul's men began to scatter.
13:12 'Now the Philistines will come down against me at **Gilgal**,
13:15 Then Samuel left **Gilgal** and went up to Gibeah in Benjamin,
15:12 in his own honor and has turned and gone on down to **Gilgal**."
15:21 in order to sacrifice them to the LORD your God at **Gilgal**."
15:33 And Samuel put Agag to death before the LORD at **Gilgal**.
2Sa 19:15 [19:16] Now the men of Judah had come to **Gilgal** to go out
19:40 [19:41] When the king crossed over to **Gilgal**, Kimham crossed
2Ki 2:1 in a whirlwind, Elijah and Elisha were on their way from **Gilgal**.
4:38 Elisha returned to **Gilgal** and there was a famine in that region.
Hos 4:15 "Do not go to **Gilgal**; do not go up to Beth Aven. And do not
9:15 "Because of all their wickedness in **Gilgal**, I hated them there.
12:11 [12:12] people are worthless! Do they sacrifice bulls in **Gilgal**?
Am 4:4 "Go to Bethel and sin; go to **Gilgal** and sin yet more. Bring your
5:5 do not seek Bethel, do not go to **Gilgal**, do not journey to
5:5 For **Gilgal** will surely go into exile, and Bethel will be reduced to
Mic 6:5 Remember ⌞your journey⌟ from Shittim to **Gilgal**, that you may

1653 גֻּלְגֹּלֶת ***gulgōlet***, n.f. [12] [√ 1670]

one by one [+4200+4392] [4], skull [2], each [+5031] [1], each one [1], head [1], individually [+4200] [1], person [1], total [1]

Ex 16:16 Take an omer for **each** [+5031] person you have in your tent.' "
38:26 one beka per **person**, that is, half a shekel, according to the
Nu 1:2 listing every man by name, **one** [+4200+4392] **by one**.
1:18 years old or more were listed by name, **one** [+4200+4392] **by one**,
1:20 serve in the army were listed by name, **one** [+4200+4392] **by one**,
1:22 army were counted and listed by name, **one** [+4200+4392] **by one**,
3:47 collect five shekels for **each one**, according to the sanctuary
Jdg 9:53 dropped an upper millstone on his head and cracked his **skull**.
2Ki 9:35 they found nothing except her **skull**, her feet and her hands.
1Ch 10:10 temple of their gods and hung up his **head** in the temple of Dagon.
23:3 and the **total** number of men was thirty-eight thousand.
23:24 registered under their names and counted **individually** [+4200],

1654 גֶּלֶד ***gēled***, n.m. [1]

skin [1]

Job 16:15 "I have sewed sackcloth over my **skin** and buried my brow in the

1655 גָּלָה ***gālâ***, v. [189] [→ 1583, 1639, 1661, 1663, 1656; Ar 10144]

carried into exile [11], have sexual relations with [+6872] [10], deported [7], be exposed [4], dishonored [+6872] [4], expose [4], surely go into exile [+1655] [4], uncovered [4], exposed [3], go into exile [3], have sexual relations [+6872] [3], open [3], opened [3], revealed [+265+906] [3], revealed [3], taken captive [3], taken into exile [3], *untranslated* [2], be revealed [2], been carried into exile [2], been revealed [2], betray [2], betrays [2], carried into exile [+906+906+906+1655] [2], certainly go into exile [+1655] [2], clearly reveal myself [+1655] [2], committed [2], departed [2], exile [2], exiled [2], go into exile [+1655] [2], have relations with [+6872] [2], laid bare [2], let know [+265+906] [2], made known [2], revealed himself [2], sent into exile [2], tells [+265+906] [2], took captive [2], took into exile [2], uncover [2], unsealed [2], went into captivity [2], went into exile [2], would[s] [+1655] [2], airing [1], banished [1], bare [1], be carried into exile [1], be exiled [1], be laid bare [1], been shown [1], been torn off [1], being carried into exile [1], bring to attention [+265] [1], brought [1], captive [1], captivity [1], carried away [1], carried on openly [1], carry away [1], carry into exile [1], carry off [1], confiding in [+265+906] [1], disclose [1], dishonor bed [+4053] [1], dishonor bed [+6872] [1], dishonor by having sexual relations with [+6872] [1], dishonor by to have sexual relations [+6872] [1], dishonors bed [+4053] [1], disrobing [1], driven out [1], free [1], go [1], gone into exile [1], has sexual relations with [+906+6872] [1], have sexual relations with [+906+6872] [1], lay bare [1], led captive [1], let enjoy [1], let see [1], lift [1], makes listen [+265] [1], remove [1], removed [1], revealing [1], reveals [1], send into exile [1], set out [1], showed themselves [1], speak [1], speaks [+265] [1], strip [+6872] [1], strip off [1], stripped away [1], stripped [1], take off [1], taken [1], tell [+265+906] [1], was given [1], was uncovered [1], were taken captive [1], word come [1]

Ge 9:21 [F] its wine, he became drunk and *lay* **uncovered** inside his tent.
35: 7 [C] because it was there that God **revealed himself** to him when
Ex 20:26 [C] to my altar on steps, lest your nakedness **be exposed** on it.'
Lev 18: 6 [D] any close relative to **have sexual** [+6872] **relations**.
18: 7 [D] " '*Do* not **dishonor** your father **by having sexual** [+6872] **relations with** your mother.
18: 7 [D] She is your mother; *do* not **have relations** [+6872] **with** her.
18: 8 [D] " '*Do* not **have sexual** [+6872] **relations with** your father's
18: 9 [D] " '*Do* not **have sexual** [+6872] **relations with** your sister,
18:10 [D] " '*Do* not **have sexual** [+6872] **relations with** your son's
18:11 [D] " '*Do* not **have sexual** [+6872] **relations with** the daughter
18:12 [D] " '*Do* not **have sexual** [+6872] **relations with** your father's
18:13 [D] " '*Do* not **have sexual** [+6872] **relations with** your mother's
18:14 [D] " '*Do* not **dishonor** your father's brother **by** approaching his wife **to have sexual** [+6872] **relations;**
18:15 [D] " '*Do* not **have sexual** [+6872] **relations with** your
18:15 [D] is your son's wife; *do* not **have relations** [+6872] **with** her.
18:16 [D] " '*Do* not **have sexual** [+6872] **relations with** your brother's
18:17 [D] " '*Do* not **have sexual** [+6872] **relations with** both a woman
18:17 [D] *Do* not **have sexual** [+906+6872] **relations with** either her
18:18 [D] **have sexual** [+6872] **relations** with her while your wife is
18:19 [D] not approach a woman to **have sexual** [+6872] **relations**
20:11 [D] with his father's wife, *he has* **dishonored** [+6872] his father.
20:17 [D] *He has* **dishonored** [+6872] his sister and will be held
20:18 [D] and **has sexual** [+906+6872] **relations with** her,
20:18 [D] the source of her flow, and she *has* also **uncovered** it.
20:19 [D] " '*Do* not **have sexual** [+6872] **relations with** the sister of
20:20 [D] sleeps with his aunt, *he has* **dishonored** [+6872] his uncle.
20:21 [D] is an act of impurity; *he has* **dishonored** [+6872] his brother.
Nu 22:31 [D] the LORD **opened** Balaam's eyes, and he saw the angel of
24: 4 [B] who falls prostrate, and whose eyes *are* **opened**:
24:16 [B] who falls prostrate, and whose eyes *are* **opened**:
Dt 22:30 [23:1] [D] *he must* not **dishonor** [+4053] his father's **bed**.
27:20 [D] his father's wife, for *he* **dishonors** [+4053] his father's **bed**."
29:29 [29:28] [C] the *things* **revealed** belong to us and to our children
Jdg 18:30 [A] for the tribe of Dan until the time of the **captivity** *of* the land.
Ru 3: 4 [D] go and **uncover** his feet and lie down. He will tell you what
3: 7 [D] Ruth approached quietly, **uncovered** his feet and lay down.
4: 4 [A] I thought *I should* **bring** the matter **to** your **attention** [+265]
1Sa 2:27 [C] '*Did I* not **clearly reveal** [+1655] **myself** to your father's
2:27 [C] '*Did I* not **clearly reveal myself** [+1655] to your father's
3: 7 [C] The word of the LORD *had* not yet **been revealed** to him.
3:21 [C] and there he **revealed himself** to Samuel through his word.
4:21 [A] boy Ichabod, saying, "The glory *has* **departed** from Israel"—
4:22 [A] She said, "The glory *has* **departed** from Israel, for the ark of
9:15 [A] the LORD *had* **revealed** [+265+906] this *to* Samuel:
14: 8 [C] then; we will cross over toward the men and **let** them **see** *us*.
14:11 [C] So both of them **showed themselves** to the Philistine outpost.
20: 2 [A] great or small, without **confiding** [+265+906] **in** me.
20:12 [A] will I not send you word and **let** you **know** [+265+906]?
20:13 [A] if *I do* not **let** you **know** [+265+906] and send you away
22: 8 [A] No *one* **tells** [+265+906] me when my son makes a covenant
22: 8 [A] or **tells** [+265+906] me that my son has incited my servant to
22:17 [A] knew he was fleeing, yet *they did* not **tell** [+265+906] me."
2Sa 6:20 [C] **disrobing** in the sight of the slave girls of his servants as any
6:20 [C] girls of his servants as any vulgar fellow **would**[s] [+1655]!"
6:20 [C] girls of his servants as any vulgar fellow **would**[s] [+1655]!"
7:27 [A] you *have* **revealed** [+265+906] this *to* your servant, saying,
15:19 [A] You are a foreigner, an **exile** from your homeland.
22:16 [C] the foundations of the earth **laid bare** at the rebuke of the
2Ki 15:29 [G] all the land of Naphtali, and **deported** the people to Assyria.
16: 9 [G] *He* **deported** its inhabitants to Kir and put Rezin to death.
17: 6 [G] captured Samaria and **deported** the Israelites to Assyria.
17:11 [G] as the nations whom the LORD *had* **driven out** before
17:23 [A] Israel *were* **taken** from their homeland **into exile** in Assyria,
17:26 [G] "The people *you* **deported** and resettled in the towns of
17:27 [G] "Have one of the priests *you took* **captive** from Samaria go
17:28 [G] So one of the priests who *had been* **exiled** from Samaria
17:33 [G] customs of the nations from which they *had been* **brought**.
18:11 [G] The king of Assyria **deported** Israel to Assyria and settled
24:14 [G] *He* **carried into exile** [+906+906+906+1655] all Jerusalem:
24:14 [A] *He* **carried into exile** [+906+906+906+1655] all Jerusalem:
24:15 [G] Nebuchadnezzar **took** Jehoiachin **captive** to Babylon.
25:11 [G] **carried into exile** the people who remained in the city,
25:21 [A] So Judah **went into captivity**, away from her land.
1Ch 5: 6 [G] whom Tiglath-Pileser king of Assyria **took into exile**.
5:26 [G] *who* **took** the Reubenites, the Gadites and the half-tribe of Manasseh **into exile**.
6:15 [5:41] [G] the LORD **sent** Judah and Jerusalem **into exile**
8: 6 [G] of those living in Geba and *were* **deported** to Manahath:
8: 7 [G] who **deported** them and who was the father of Uzza
9: 1 [H] The people of Judah **were taken captive** to Babylon
17:25 [A] *have* **revealed** [+265+906] *to* your servant that you will
2Ch 36:20 [G] *He* **carried into exile** to Babylon the remnant, who escaped
Ezr 2: 1 [G] whom Nebuchadnezzar king of Babylon *had* **taken captive**
Ne 7: 6 [G] of Babylon *had* **taken captive** (they returned to Jerusalem
Est 2: 6 [H] who *had* **been carried into exile** from Jerusalem by
2: 6 [G] who had been carried into exile from Jerusalem by **[RPH]**
2: 6 [A] among those **[RPH]** taken captive with Jehoiachin king of
2: 6 [H] among those **taken captive** with Jehoiachin king of Judah.
3:14 [B] **made known** to the people of every nationality so they
8:13 [B] and **made known** to the people of every nationality
Job 12:22 [D] *He* **reveals** the deep things of darkness and brings deep
20:27 [D] The heavens *will* **expose** his guilt; the earth will rise up
20:28 [A] A flood *will* **carry off** his house, rushing waters on the day
33:16 [A] *he may* **speak** *in* their ears and terrify them with warnings,
36:10 [A] *He* **makes** them **listen** [+265] to correction and commands
36:15 [A] their suffering; *he* **speaks** [+265] *to* them in their affliction.
38:17 [C] *Have* the gates of death **been shown** to you? Have you seen
41:13 [41:5] [D] Who *can* **strip off** his outer coat? Who would
Ps 18:15 [18:16] [C] the foundations of the earth **laid bare** at your
98: 2 [D] and **revealed** his righteousness to the nations.
119:18 [D] **Open** my eyes that I may see wonderful things in your law.
119:22 [D] **Remove** from me scorn and contempt, for I keep your
Pr 11:13 [D] A gossip **betrays** a confidence, but a trustworthy man keeps
18: 2 [F] in understanding but delights in **airing** his own opinions.
20:19 [A] A gossip **betrays** a confidence; so avoid a man who talks too
25: 9 [D] with a neighbor, *do* not **betray** another man's confidence,
26:26 [C] but his wickedness *will* **be exposed** in the assembly.
27: 5 [E] Better is **open** rebuke than hidden love.
27:25 [A] *When* the hay *is* **removed** and new growth appears
Isa 5:13 [A] Therefore my people *will* **go into exile** for lack of
16: 3 [D] at high noon. Hide the fugitives, *do* not **betray** the refugees.
22: 8 [D] the defenses of Judah *are* **stripped away**. And you looked in
22:14 [C] The LORD Almighty *has* **revealed** this in my hearing:
23: 1 [C] or harbor. From the land of Cyprus **word** *has* **come** to them.
24:11 [A] all joy turns to gloom, all gaiety *is* **banished** *from* the earth.
26:21 [D] The earth *will* **disclose** the blood shed upon her; she will
38:12 [C] tent my house has been pulled down and **taken** from me.
40: 5 [C] the glory of the LORD *will* **be revealed**, and all mankind
47: 2 [D] Take millstones and grind flour; **take off** your veil. Lift up
47: 2 [D] Lift up your skirts, **bare** *your* legs, and wade through the
47: 3 [C] Your nakedness *will* **be exposed** and your shame uncovered.
49: 9 [C] the captives, 'Come out,' and to those in darkness, '*Be* **free**!'
49:21 [A] I was bereaved and barren; I *was* **exiled** and rejected.
53: 1 [C] and to whom *has* the arm of the LORD **been revealed**?
56: 1 [C] is close at hand and my righteousness *will* soon **be revealed**.
57: 8 [D] Forsaking me, *you* **uncovered** your bed, you climbed into it
Jer 1: 3 [A] king of Judah, when the people of Jerusalem **went into exile**.
11:20 [D] upon them, for to you *I have* **committed** my cause.
13:19 [H] All Judah *will* **be carried into exile**, carried completely
13:19 [H] Judah will be carried into exile, **carried** completely **away**.
13:22 [C] of your many sins that your skirts *have* **been torn off**
20: 4 [G] *who will* **carry** them **away** to Babylon or put them to the
20:12 [D] upon them, for to you *I have* **committed** my cause.
22:12 [G] He will die in the place where *they have* **led** him **captive**;
24: 1 [G] the craftsmen and the artisans of Judah *were* **carried into exile**
27:20 [A] **carried** Jehoiachin son of Jehoiakim king of Judah **into exile**
29: 1 [G] all the other people Nebuchadnezzar *had* **carried into exile**
29: 4 [G] says to all those *I* **carried into exile** from Jerusalem to
29: 7 [G] prosperity of the city to which *I have* **carried** you **into exile**.
29:14 [G] you back to the place from which *I* **carried** you **into exile**."
32:11 [B] the terms and conditions, as well as the **unsealed** *copy*—
32:14 [B] both the sealed and **unsealed** *copies* of the deed of purchase,
33: 6 [D] and *will* **let** them **enjoy** abundant peace and security.
39: 9 [G] **carried into exile** *to* Babylon the people who remained in
40: 1 [H] and Judah who *were* **being carried into exile** to Babylon.
40: 7 [H] and who *had* not **been carried into exile** to Babylon,
43: 3 [G] so they may kill us or **carry** us **into exile** *to* Babylon."
49:10 [D] *I will* **uncover** his hiding places, so that he cannot conceal
52:15 [G] Nebuzaradan the commander of the guard **carried into exile**
52:27 [A] So Judah **went into captivity**, away from her land.
52:28 [G] the number of the people Nebuchadnezzar **carried into exile**:

Jer 52:30 [G] 745 Jews **taken into exile** *by* Nebuzaradan the commander
La 1: 3 [A] After affliction and harsh labor, Judah *has* **gone into exile**.
2:14 [D] *they did* not **expose** your sin to ward off your captivity.
4:22 [G] your punishment will end; he will not prolong your **exile**.
4:22 [D] he will punish your sin and **expose** your wickedness.
Eze 12: 3 [A] **set out** and go from where you are to another place.
12: 3 [A] set out and **go** from where you are to another place.
13:14 [C] level it to the ground so that its foundation *will* **be laid bare**.
16:36 [C] **exposed** your nakedness in your promiscuity with your
16:37 [D] from all around and *will* **strip** [+6872] you in front of them,
16:57 [C] before your wickedness **was uncovered**. Even so, you are
21:24 [21:29] [C] brought to mind your guilt by your **open** rebellion,
22:10 [D] In you are *those who* **dishonor** [+6872] their fathers' **bed**;
23:10 [D] They **stripped** her naked, took away her sons and daughters
23:18 [D] When *she* **carried on** her prostitution **openly** and exposed
23:18 [D] on her prostitution openly and **exposed** her nakedness,
23:29 [C] and bare, and the shame of your prostitution *will* **be exposed**.
39:23 [A] nations will know that the people of Israel **went into exile**
39:28 [G] for though I **sent** them **into exile** among the nations, I will
Da 10: 1 [C] a revelation **was given** to Daniel (who was called
Hos 2:10 [2:12] [D] So now *I will* **expose** her lewdness before the eyes of
7: 1 [C] the sins of Ephraim *are* **exposed** and the crimes of Samaria
10: 5 [A] over its splendor, because *it is* **taken** from them **into exile**.
Am 1: 5 [A] The people of Aram *will* **go into exile** to Kir,"
1: 6 [G] Because she **took captive** whole communities and sold them
3: 7 [A] without **revealing** his plan to his servants the prophets.
5: 5 [A] For Gilgal *will* **surely go into exile** [+1655], and Bethel will
5: 5 [A] For Gilgal *will* **surely go into exile** [+1655], and Bethel will
5:27 [G] Therefore *I will* **send** you **into exile** beyond Damascus,"
6: 7 [A] *you will* be among the first to **go into exile** [+1655];
6: 7 [A] *you will* be among the first to **go into exile** [+1655];
7:11 [A] Israel *will* **surely go into exile** [+1655], away from their
7:11 [A] Israel *will* **surely go into exile** [+1655], away from their
7:17 [A] Israel *will* **certainly go into exile** [+1655], away from their
7:17 [A] Israel *will* **certainly go into exile** [+1655], away from their
Mic 1: 6 [D] pour her stones into the valley and **lay bare** her foundations.
1:16 [A] as bald as the vulture, for *they will* **go** from you **into exile**.
Na 2: 7 [2:8] [E] It is decreed that ⌞the city⌟ **be exiled** and carried away.
3: 5 [D] the LORD Almighty. "*I will* **lift** your skirts over your face.

1656 גִּלֹה gilōh, n.pr.loc. [2] [→ 1639; cf. 1655]

Giloh [2]

Jos 15:51 Goshen, Holon and **Giloh**—eleven towns and their villages.
2Sa 15:12 David's counselor, to come from **Giloh**, his hometown.

1657 גֻּלָּה gullâ, n.f. [15] [→ 1646, 1684]

bowl-shaped [6], springs [4], bowl [3], *untranslated* [2]

Jos 15:19 have given me land in the Negev, give me also **springs** *of* water."
15:19 of water." So Caleb gave her the upper **[RPH]** and lower springs.
15:19 springs of water." So Caleb gave her the upper and lower **springs**.
Jdg 1:15 have given me land in the Negev, give me also **springs** *of* water."
1:15 Then Caleb gave her the upper **[RPH]** and lower springs.
1:15 of water." Then Caleb gave her the upper and lower **springs**.
1Ki 7:41 the two pillars; the two **bowl-shaped** capitals on top of the pillars;
7:41 the two sets of network decorating the two **bowl-shaped** capitals
7:42 decorating the **bowl-shaped** capitals on top of the pillars);
2Ch 4:12 the two pillars; the two **bowl-shaped** capitals on top of the pillars;
4:12 the two sets of network decorating the two **bowl-shaped** capitals
4:13 decorating the **bowl-shaped** capitals on top of the pillars);
Ecc 12: 6 before the silver cord is severed, or the golden **bowl** is broken;
Zec 4: 2 "I see a solid gold lampstand with a **bowl** at the top and seven
4: 3 trees by it, one on the right of the **bowl** and the other on its left."

1658 גִּלּוּלִים gillûlîm, n.m. [48] [√ 1670]

idols [46], idolatry [2]

Lev 26:30 and pile your dead bodies on the lifeless forms of your **idols**,
Dt 29:17 [29:16] them their detestable images and **idols** of wood and stone,
1Ki 15:12 from the land and got rid of all the **idols** his fathers had made.
21:26 He behaved in the vilest manner by going after **idols**, like the
2Ki 17:12 They worshiped **idols**, though the LORD had said, "You shall not
21:11 who preceded him and has led Judah into sin with his **idols**.
21:21 he worshiped the **idols** his father had worshiped, and bowed down
23:24 the **idols** and all the other detestable things seen in Judah
Jer 50: 2 Her images will be put to shame and her **idols** filled with terror.'
Eze 6: 4 will be smashed; and I will slay your people in front of your **idols**.
6: 5 I will lay the dead bodies of the Israelites in front of their **idols**,
6: 6 will be laid waste and devastated, your **idols** smashed and ruined,
6: 9 from me, and by their eyes, which have lusted after their **idols**.
6:13 when their people lie slain among their **idols** around their altars,
6:13 places where they offered fragrant incense to all their **idols**.
8:10 and detestable animals and all the **idols** *of* the house of Israel.
14: 3 these men have set up **idols** in their hearts and put wicked
14: 4 When any Israelite sets up **idols** in his heart and puts a wicked
14: 4 LORD will answer him myself in keeping with his great **idolatry**.
14: 5 of the people of Israel, who have all deserted me for their **idols**.'
14: 6 Turn from your **idols** and renounce all your detestable practices!
14: 7 sets up **idols** in his heart and puts a wicked stumbling block before
16:36 because of all your detestable **idols**, and because you gave them
18: 6 at the mountain shrines or look to the **idols** *of* the house of Israel.
18:12 he took in pledge. He looks to the **idols**. He does detestable things.
18:15 at the mountain shrines or look to the **idols** *of* the house of Israel.
20: 7 your eyes on, and do not defile yourselves with the **idols** *of* Egypt.
20: 8 they had set their eyes on, nor did they forsake the **idols** *of* Egypt.
20:16 my Sabbaths. For their hearts were devoted to their **idols**.
20:18 your fathers or keep their laws or defile yourselves with their **idols**.
20:24 my Sabbaths, and their eyes ⌞lusted⌟ after their fathers' **idols**.
20:31 you continue to defile yourselves with all your **idols** to this day.
20:39 LORD says: Go and serve your **idols**, every one of you!
20:39 and no longer profane my holy name with your gifts and **idols**.
22: 3 by shedding blood in her midst and defiles herself by making **idols**,
22: 4 have shed and have become defiled by the **idols** you have made.
23: 7 and defiled herself with all the **idols** *of* everyone she lusted after.
23:30 you lusted after the nations and defiled yourself with their **idols**.
23:37 They committed adultery with their **idols**; they even sacrificed
23:39 On the very day they sacrificed their children to their **idols**,
23:49 your lewdness and bear the consequences of your sins of **idolatry**.
30:13 " 'I will destroy the **idols** and put an end to the images in Memphis.
33:25 with the blood still in it and look to your **idols** and shed blood,
36:18 blood in the land and because they had defiled it with their **idols**.
36:25 I will cleanse you from all your impurities and from all your **idols**.
37:23 They will no longer defile themselves with their **idols** and vile
44:10 who wandered from me after their **idols** must bear the
44:12 But because they served them in the presence of their **idols**

1659 גְּלוֹם gᵉlôm, n.[m.]. [1] [√ 1676?]

fabric [1]

Eze 27:24 blue **fabric**, embroidered work and multicolored rugs with cords

1660 גָּלוֹן gālôn, n.pr.loc. Not used in NIV/BHS [√ 1584]

1661 גָּלוּת gālût, n.f. [15] [√ 1655; Ar 10145]

exiles [7], exile [5], captives [1], communities of captives [1], communities [1]

2Ki 25:27 In the thirty-seventh year of the **exile** *of* Jehoiachin king of Judah,
Isa 20: 4 and barefoot the Egyptian captives and Cushite **exiles**,
45:13 He will rebuild my city and set my **exiles** free, but not for a price
Jer 24: 5 'Like these good figs, I regard as good the **exiles** *from* Judah,
28: 4 and all the other **exiles** *from* Judah who went to Babylon,'
29:22 all the **exiles** *from* Judah who are in Babylon will use this curse:
40: 1 Jeremiah bound in chains among all the **captives** *from* Jerusalem
52:31 In the thirty-seventh year of the **exile** *of* Jehoiachin king of Judah,
Eze 1: 2 the month—it was the fifth year of the **exile** *of* King Jehoiachin—
33:21 In the twelfth year of our **exile**, in the tenth month on the fifth day,
40: 1 In the twenty-fifth year of our **exile**, at the beginning of the year,
Am 1: 6 Because she took captive whole **communities** and sold them to
1: 9 Because she sold whole **communities of captives** to Edom,
Ob 1:20 This company of Israelite **exiles** who are in Canaan will possess
1:20 the **exiles** *from* Jerusalem who are in Sepharad will possess the

1662 גָּלַח gālaḥ, v. [23]

shave off [5], shave [5], *untranslated* [3], shaved off [3], cut hair [2], shaved [2], be shaved [1], been shaved [1], were shaved [1]

Ge 41:14 [D] When *he had* **shaved** and changed his clothes, he came
Lev 13:33 [F] *he must* **be shaved** except for the diseased area,
13:33 [D] he must be shaved except for **[RPH]** the diseased area,
14: 8 [D] wash his clothes, **shave off** all his hair and bathe with water;
14: 9 [D] On the seventh day *he must* **shave off** all his hair; he must
14: 9 [D] *he must* **shave** his head, his beard, his eyebrows and the rest
21: 5 [D] or **shave off** the edges of their beards or cut their bodies.
Nu 6: 9 [D] *he must* **shave** his head on the day of his cleansing—
6: 9 [D] head on the day of his cleansing—the seventh day. **[RPH]**
6:18 [D] the Nazirite *must* **shave off** the hair that he dedicated.
6:19 [F] " 'After the Nazirite *has* **shaved off** the hair of his dedication,
Dt 21:12 [D] Bring her into your home and *have her* **shave** her head, trim
Jdg 16:17 [E] If my head **were shaved**, my strength would leave me, and I
16:19 [D] she called a man *to* **shave off** the seven braids of his hair,
16:22 [E] on his head began to grow again after *it had* **been shaved**.
2Sa 10: 4 [D] seized David's men, **shaved off** half of each man's beard,
14:26 [D] Whenever he **cut** *the* **hair** *of* his head—he used to cut his
14:26 [D] he used to **cut** *his* **hair** from time to time when it became too
14:26 [D] **[RPH]** he would weigh it, and its weight was two hundred
1Ch 19: 4 [D] So Hanun seized David's men, **shaved** them, cut off their

Isa 7:20 [D] king of Assyria—*to* **shave** your head and the hair of your legs,
Jer 41:5 [E] eighty men *who had* **shaved off** their beards, torn their
Eze 44:20 [D] " '*They must* not **shave** their heads or let their hair grow

1663 גִּלָּיוֹן gillāyôn, n.m. [2] [√ 1655]

mirrors [1], scroll [1]

Isa 3:23 and **mirrors**, and the linen garments and tiaras and shawls.
8:1 to me, "Take a large **scroll** and write on it with an ordinary pen:

1664 ¹גָּלִיל gālîl¹, a. [4] [√ 1670]

untranslated [1], rings [1], rods [1], turned in sockets [1]

1Ki 6:34 two pine doors, each having two leaves *that* **turned in sockets**.
6:34 pine doors, each having two leaves that turned in sockets. **[RPH]**
Est 1:6 of white linen and purple material to silver **rings** on marble pillars.
SS 5:14 His arms are **rods** *of* gold set with chrysolite. His body is like

1665 ²גָּלִיל gālîl², n.pr.loc. [6] [→ 1666, 1667; cf. 1670]

Galilee [5], Galilee [+824] [1]

Jos 20:7 So they set apart Kedesh in **Galilee** in the hill country of Naphtali,
21:32 Kedesh in **Galilee** (a city of refuge for one accused of murder),
1Ki 9:11 King Solomon gave twenty towns in **Galilee** [+824] to Hiram king
2Ki 15:29 He took Gilead and **Galilee**, including all the land of Naphtali,
1Ch 6:76 [6:61] from the tribe of Naphtali they received Kedesh in **Galilee**,
Isa 9:1 [8:23] in the future he will honor **Galilee** *of* the Gentiles,

1666 גְּלִילָה gᵉlîlâ, n.f. [3] [→ 1667; cf. 1665]

regions [2], region [1]

Jos 13:2 land that remains: all the **regions** *of* the Philistines and Geshurites:
Eze 47:8 "This water flows toward the eastern **region** and goes down into
Joel 3:4 [4:4] O Tyre and Sidon and all you **regions** *of* Philistia?

1667 גְּלִילוֹת gᵉlîlôt, n.pr.loc. [3] [√ 1666]

Geliloth [3]

Jos 18:17 then curved north, went to En Shemesh, continued to **Geliloth**,
22:10 When they came to **Geliloth** *near* the Jordan in the land of
22:11 border of Canaan at **Geliloth** *near* the Jordan on the Israelite side,

1668 גַּלִּים gallîm, n.pr.loc. [2] [√ 1643; cf. 1670]

Gallim [2]

1Sa 25:44 David's wife, to Paltiel son of Laish, who was from **Gallim**.
Isa 10:30 Cry out, O Daughter of **Gallim**! Listen, O Laishah! Poor Anathoth!

1669 גָּלְיָת golyāt, n.pr.m. [6]

Goliath [6]

1Sa 17:4 A champion named **Goliath**, who was from Gath, came out of the
17:23 As he was talking with them, **Goliath**, the Philistine champion
21:9 [21:10] The priest replied, "The sword of **Goliath** the Philistine,
22:10 also gave him provisions and the sword of **Goliath** the Philistine."
2Sa 21:19 Elhanan son of Jaare-Oregim the Bethlehemite killed **Goliath** the
1Ch 20:5 Elhanan son of Jair killed Lahmi the brother of **Goliath** the Gittite,

1670 ¹גָּלַל gālal¹, v. [17] [→ 1643, 1644, 1645, 1649, 1650, 1651, 1652, 1653, 1658, 1664, 1665, 1666, 1667, 1668, 1672, 1674, 2055, 4479; cf. 1671, 4478?; Ar 10146]

roll [4], rolled [3], commit [2], attack [1], come rolling in [1], lay wallowing [1], roll on [1], rolled away [1], rolled up [1], rolls [1], trusts [1]

Ge 29:3 [A] the shepherds *would* **roll** the stone away from the well's
29:8 [A] the stone *has been* **rolled** away from the mouth of the well.
29:10 [A] and **rolled** the stone away from the mouth of the well
43:18 [F] He wants to **attack** us and overpower us and seize us as
Jos 5:9 [A] "Today *I have* **rolled away** the reproach of Egypt from you."
10:18 [A] he said, "**Roll** large rocks up to the mouth of the cave,
1Sa 14:33 [A] broken faith," he said. "**Roll** a large stone over here at once."
2Sa 20:12 [F] Amasa **lay wallowing** in his blood in the middle of the road,
Job 30:14 [F] a gaping breach; amid the ruins *they* **come rolling in**.
Ps 22:8 [22:9] [A] "*He* **trusts** in the LORD; let the LORD rescue
37:5 [A] **Commit** your way to the LORD; trust in him and he will do
Pr 16:3 [A] **Commit** to the LORD whatever you do, and your plans will
26:27 [A] fall into it; if a *man* **rolls** a stone, it will roll back on him.
Isa 9:5 [9:4] [E] every garment **rolled** in blood will be destined for
34:4 [C] heavens will be dissolved and the sky **rolled up** like a scroll;
Jer 51:25 [D] **roll** you off the cliffs, and make you a burned-out mountain.
Am 5:24 [C] *let* justice **roll on** like a river, righteousness like a

1671 ²גָּלַל gālal², v. Not used in NIV/BHS [cf. 1670]

1672 ¹גָּלָל gālāl¹, n.[m.]. [2] [√ 1670]

dung [1], filth [1]

1Ki 14:10 I will burn up the house of Jeroboam as one burns **dung**, until it is
Zep 1:17 Their blood will be poured out like dust and their entrails like **filth**.

1673 ²גָּלָל gālāl², n.[m.]. [10] [√ 959]

because of [+928] [9], because [+928] [1]

Ge 12:13 for your sake and my life will be spared **because** [+928] **of** you."
30:27 by divination that the LORD has blessed me **because** [+928] **of**
39:5 LORD blessed the household of the Egyptian **because** [+928] **of**
Dt 1:37 **Because** [+928] **of** you the LORD became angry with me also
15:10 **because** [+928] **of** this the LORD your God will bless you in all
18:12 **because** [+928] **of** these detestable practices the LORD your God
1Ki 14:16 he will give Israel up **because** [+928] **of** the sins Jeroboam has
Jer 11:17 has decreed disaster for you, **because** [+928] the house of Israel
15:4 them abhorrent to all the kingdoms of the earth **because** [+928] **of**
Mic 3:12 Therefore **because** [+928] **of** you, Zion will be plowed like a field,

1674 ³גָּלָל gālāl³, n.pr.m. [3] [→ 1675; cf. 1670]

Galal [3]

1Ch 9:15 Bakbakkar, Heresh, **Galal** and Mattaniah son of Mica, the son of
9:16 Obadiah son of Shemaiah, the son of **Galal**, the son of Jeduthun;
Ne 11:17 and Abda son of Shammua, the son of **Galal**, the son of Jeduthun.

1675 גִּלֲלַי gilᵃlay, n.pr.m. [1] [√ 1674]

Gilalai [1]

Ne 12:36 Azarel, Milalai, **Gilalai**, Maai, Nethanel, Judah and Hanani—

1676 גָּלַם gālam, v. [1] [→ 1659?, 1677]

rolled up [1]

2Ki 2:8 [A] took his cloak, **rolled it up** and struck the water with it.

1677 גֹּלֶם gōlem, n.[m.]. [1] [√ 1676]

unformed body [1]

Ps 139:16 your eyes saw my **unformed body**. All the days ordained for me

1678 גַּלְמוּד galmûd, a. [4]

barren [3], haggard [1]

Job 3:7 May that night be **barren**; may no shout of joy be heard in it.
15:34 For the company of the godless will be **barren**, and fire will
30:3 **Haggard** from want and hunger, they roamed the parched land in
Isa 49:21 me these? I was bereaved and **barren**; I was exiled and rejected.

1679 גָּלַע gāla', v. [3]

breaks out [1], defies [1], quick to quarrel [1]

Pr 17:14 [F] a dam; so drop the matter before a dispute **breaks out**.
18:1 [F] man pursues selfish ends; *he* **defies** all sound judgment.
20:3 [F] honor to avoid strife, but every fool *is* **quick to quarrel**.

1680 גִּלְעָד gil'ād, n.pr.loc. [& m.?]. [102] [→ 1682, 3316, 8240]

Gilead [85], Gilead [+824] [8], Gileadites [3], *untranslated* [1], Gilead [+1201] [1], Gilead's [1], Gileadites [+408] [1], them^s [+2418] [1], there^s [+5206] [1]

Ge 31:21 and crossing the River, he headed for the hill country of **Gilead**.
31:23 seven days and caught up with him in the hill country of **Gilead**.
31:25 Jacob had pitched his tent in the hill country of **Gilead** when
37:25 looked up and saw a caravan of Ishmaelites coming from **Gilead**.
Nu 26:29 through Makir, the Makirite clan (Makir was the father of **Gilead**);
26:29 was the father of Gilead); through **Gilead**, the Gileadite clan.
26:30 These were the descendants of **Gilead**: through Iezer, the Iezerite
27:1 the son of **Gilead**, the son of Makir, the son of Manasseh,
32:1 saw that the lands of Jazer and **Gilead** were suitable for livestock.
32:26 our flocks and herds will remain here in the cities of **Gilead**.
32:29 before you, give them the land of **Gilead** as their possession.
32:39 The descendants of Makir son of Manasseh went to **Gilead**,
32:40 So Moses gave **Gilead** to the Makirites, the descendants of
36:1 The family heads of the clan of **Gilead** [+1201] son of Makir,
Dt 2:36 from the town in the gorge, even as far as **Gilead**, not one town
3:10 and all **Gilead**, and all Bashan as far as Salecah and Edrei,
3:12 including half the hill country of **Gilead**, together with its towns.
3:13 The rest of **Gilead** and also all of Bashan, the kingdom of Og,
3:15 And I gave **Gilead** to Makir.
3:16 the Gadites I gave the territory extending from **Gilead** down to the
4:43 for the Reubenites; Ramoth in **Gilead**, for the Gadites;
34:1 the LORD showed him the whole land—from **Gilead** to Dan,
Jos 12:2 is the border of the Ammonites. This included half of **Gilead**.

Jos 12: 5 and half of **Gilead** to the border of Sihon king of Heshbon.
13: 11 It also included **Gilead**, the territory of the people of Geshur
13: 25 all the towns of **Gilead** and half the Ammonite country as far as
13: 31 half of **Gilead**, and Ashtaroth and Edrei (the royal cities of Og in
17: 1 Makir was the ancestor of the **Gileadites**, who had received Gilead
17: 1 who had received **Gilead** and Bashan because the Makirites were
17: 3 the son of **Gilead**, the son of Makir, the son of Manasseh,
17: 5 Manasseh's share consisted of ten tracts of land besides **Gilead**
17: 6 The land of **Gilead** belonged to the rest of the descendants of
20: 8 Ramoth in **Gilead** in the tribe of Gad, and Golan in Bashan in the
21: 38 Ramoth in **Gilead** (a city of refuge for one accused of murder),
22: 9 left the Israelites at Shiloh in Canaan to return to **Gilead** [+824],
22: 13 sent Phinehas son of Eleazar, the priest, to the land of **Gilead**—
22: 15 When they went to **Gilead** [+824]—to Reuben, Gad and the
22: 32 and Gadites in **Gilead** [+824] and reported to the Israelites.
Jdg 5: 17 **Gilead** stayed beyond the Jordan. And Dan, why did he linger by
7: 3 and leave Mount **Gilead**.' " So twenty-two thousand men left,
10: 4 They controlled thirty towns in **Gilead** [+824], which to this day
10: 8 oppressed all the Israelites on the east side of the Jordan in **Gilead**,
10: 17 When the Ammonites were called to arms and camped in **Gilead**,
10: 18 The leaders of the people of **Gilead** said to each other, "Whoever
10: 18 the Ammonites will be the head of all those living in **Gilead**."
11: 1 mighty warrior. His father was **Gilead**; his mother was a prostitute.
11: 2 **Gilead's** wife also bore him sons, and when they were grown up,
11: 5 the elders of **Gilead** went to get Jephthah from the land of Tob.
11: 7 Jephthah said to **them**[s] [+2418], "Didn't you hate me and drive me
11: 8 The elders of **Gilead** said to him, "Nevertheless, we are turning to
11: 8 and you will be our head over all who live in **Gilead**."
11: 9 **[RPH]** "Suppose you take me back to fight the Ammonites
11: 10 The elders of **Gilead** replied, "The LORD is our witness;
11: 11 So Jephthah went with the elders of **Gilead**, and the people made
11: 29 He crossed **Gilead** and Manasseh, passed through Mizpah of
11: 29 crossed Gilead and Manasseh, passed through Mizpah of **Gilead**,
11: 29 and from **there**[s] [+5206] he advanced against the Ammonites.
12: 4 Jephthah then called together the men of **Gilead** and fought against
12: 4 The **Gileadites** [+408] struck them down because the Ephraimites
12: 4 "You **Gileadites** are renegades from Ephraim and Manasseh."
12: 5 The **Gileadites** captured the fords of the Jordan leading to
12: 5 "Let me cross over," the men of **Gilead** asked him, "Are you an
12: 7 Jephthah the Gileadite died, and was buried in a town in **Gilead**.
20: 1 to Beersheba and from the land of **Gilead** came out as one man
1Sa 13: 7 Hebrews even crossed the Jordan to the land of Gad and **Gilead**.
2Sa 2: 9 He made him king over **Gilead**, Ashuri and Jezreel, and also over
17: 26 The Israelites and Absalom camped in the land of **Gilead**.
24: 6 They went to **Gilead** and the region of Tahtim Hodshi, and on to
1Ki 4: 13 Gilead (the settlements of Jair son of Manasseh in **Gilead** were his,
4: 19 in **Gilead** [+824] (the country of Sihon king of the Amorites
17: 1 from Tishbe in **Gilead**, said to Ahab, "As the LORD, the God of
2Ki 10: 33 east of the Jordan in all the land of **Gilead** (the region of Gad,
10: 33 from Aroer by the Arnon Gorge through **Gilead** to Bashan.
15: 29 He took **Gilead** and Galilee, including all the land of Naphtali,
1Ch 2: 21 Hezron lay with the daughter of Makir the father of **Gilead** (he had
2: 22 father of Jair, who controlled twenty-three towns in **Gilead** [+824].
2: 23 All these were descendants of Makir the father of **Gilead**.
5: 9 because their livestock had increased in **Gilead** [+824].
5: 10 of the Hagrites throughout the entire region east of **Gilead**.
5: 14 the son of Jaroah, the son of **Gilead**, the son of Michael, the son of
5: 16 The Gadites lived in **Gilead**, in Bashan and its outlying villages,
6: 80 [6:65] and from the tribe of Gad they received Ramoth in **Gilead**,
7: 14 Aramean concubine. She gave birth to Makir the father of **Gilead**.
7: 17 These were the sons of **Gilead** son of Makir, the son of Manasseh.
26: 31 capable men among the Hebronites were found at Jazer in **Gilead**.
27: 21 over the half-tribe of Manasseh in **Gilead**: Iddo son of Zechariah;
Ps 60: 7 [60:9] **Gilead** is mine, and Manasseh is mine; Ephraim is my
108: 8 [108:9] **Gilead** is mine, Manasseh is mine; Ephraim is my helmet,
SS 4: 1 Your hair is like a flock of goats descending from Mount **Gilead**.
6: 5 Your hair is like a flock of goats descending from **Gilead**.
Jer 8: 22 Is there no balm in **Gilead**? Is there no physician there? Why
22: 6 "Though you are like **Gilead** to me, like the summit of Lebanon,
46: 11 "Go up to **Gilead** and get balm, O Virgin Daughter of Egypt.
50: 19 his appetite will be satisfied on the hills of Ephraim and **Gilead**.
Eze 47: 18 along the Jordan between **Gilead** and the land of Israel,
Hos 6: 8 **Gilead** is a city of wicked men, stained with footprints of blood.
12: 11 [12:12] Is **Gilead** wicked? Its people are worthless! Do they
Am 1: 3 Because she threshed **Gilead** with sledges having iron teeth,
1: 13 Because he ripped open the pregnant women of **Gilead** in order to
Ob 1: 19 fields of Ephraim and Samaria, and Benjamin will possess **Gilead**.
Mic 7: 14 Let them feed in Bashan and **Gilead** as in days long ago.
Zec 10: 10 I will bring them to **Gilead** [+824] and Lebanon, and there will not

1681 גַּלְעֵד *gal'ēd*, n.pr.loc. [2] [→ Ar 10310]

Galeed [2]

Ge 31: 47 Laban called it Jegar Sahadutha, and Jacob called it **Galeed**.
31: 48 between you and me today." That is why it was called **Galeed**.

1682 גִּלְעָדִי *gil'ādî*, a.g. [11] [√ 1680]

Gileadite [8], of Gilead [2], of Gilead [+1201] [1]

Nu 26: 29 was the father of Gilead); through Gilead, the **Gileadite** clan.
Jdg 10: 3 He was followed by Jair **of Gilead**, who led Israel twenty-two
11: 1 Jephthah the **Gileadite** was a mighty warrior. His father was
11: 40 four days to commemorate the daughter of Jephthah the **Gileadite**.
12: 7 Jephthah the **Gileadite** died, and was buried in a town in Gilead.
2Sa 17: 27 Ammiel from Lo Debar, and Barzillai the **Gileadite** from Rogelim
19: 31 [19:32] Barzillai the **Gileadite** also came down from Rogelim to
1Ki 2: 7 "But show kindness to the sons of Barzillai **of Gilead** and let them
2Ki 15: 25 Taking fifty men **of Gilead** [+1201] with him, he assassinated
Ezr 2: 61 (a man who had married a daughter of Barzillai the **Gileadite**
Ne 7: 63 (a man who had married a daughter of Barzillai the **Gileadite**

1683 גָּלַשׁ *gālaš*, v. [2]

descending [2]

SS 4: 1 [A] Your hair is like a flock of goats **descending** from Mount
6: 5 [A] Your hair is like a flock of goats **descending** from Gilead.

1684 גֻּלֹּת *gullōt*, n.pr.loc. Not used in NIV/BHS [√ 1657]

1685 גַּם *gam*, adv. [769] [→ 1417; cf. 4480] See Select Index

untranslated [200], also [106], even [64], too [62], and [+2256] [53], and [49], also [+2256] [26], even [+2256] [15], both [13], then [9], moreover [+2256] [8], but [6], or [6], yes [6], either [5], moreover [5], now [5], though [5], as well [4], neither [+4202] [4], or [+2256] [4], too [+2256] [4], again [3], as well as [+2256] [3], indeed [3], just as [3], nor [+4202] [3], nor [3], now [+2256] [3], then [+2256] [3], and also [2], another [2], as for [2], besides [+2256] [2], but [+2256] [2], but also [2], even [+3954] [2], for some time [+1685+8997+9453] [2], in the past [+919+1685+8997] [2], in turn [2], indeed [+2256] [2], more [2], neither [2], no [2], so [+2256] [2], surely [2], therefore [+2256] [2], together with [+2256] [2], yes [+2256] [2], yet [+2256] [2], yet [2], after [+2256] [1], again [+928+2021+2021+2085+7193] [1], along with [+2256] [1], although [+3954] [1], and even [1], and indeed [1], and now [1], as well as [1], besides [1], both and [1], but even [+2256] [1], but even [1], certainly [1], even if [1], ever [1], finally [+2256] [1], for [+928+8611] [1], furthermore [+2256] [1], furthermore [1], in spite of [1], including [+2256] [1], instead [+2256] [1], joined [+2256] [1], kept provoking [+4087+4088] [1], mere [1], moreover [+3954] [1], next [1], no sooner than [1], nor [+2256] [1], nor [+2256+4202] [1], nor [+401+2256] [1], or [+3954] [1], rather [+2256] [1], since [1], so [1], still [+2256] [1], than [+2256] [1], that [+2256] [1], therefore [1], very well [1], when [1], whether [1], with [+2256] [1], with [1]

1686 גָּמָא *gāmā'*, v. [2] [→ 1687?]

eats up [1], give [1]

Ge 24: 17 [G] and said, "Please **give** me a little water from your jar."
Job 39: 24 [D] In frenzied excitement *he* **eats up** the ground; he cannot

1687 גֹּמֶא *gōme'*, n.m. [4] [√ 1686?]

papyrus [4]

Ex 2: 3 she got a **papyrus** basket for him and coated it with tar and pitch.
Job 8: 11 Can **papyrus** grow tall where there is no marsh? Can reeds thrive
Isa 18: 2 which sends envoys by sea in **papyrus** boats over the water.
35: 7 where jackals once lay, grass and reeds and **papyrus** will grow.

1688 גֹּמֶד *gōmed*, n.m. [1] [→ 1689?]

about a foot and a half [1]

Jdg 3: 16 Ehud had made a double-edged sword **about a foot and a half**

1689 גַּמָּדִים *gammādîm*, n.pr.g. [1] [√ 1688?]

men of Gammad [1]

Eze 27: 11 your walls on every side; **men of Gammad** were in your towers.

1690 גָּמוּל *gāmûl*, n.pr.m. [1] [√ 1694]

Gamul [1]

1Ch 24: 17 the twenty-first to Jakin, the twenty-second to **Gamul**,

1691 גְּמוּל *g^e mûl*, n.m. [19] [√ 1694]

what done [4], what deserve [3], retribution [2], benefits [1], deeds [1], deserve [1], deserves [+3338] [1], due [1], kindness [1], something done [1], what deserves [1], what[s] [1], work [1]

Jdg 9: 16 his family, and if you have treated him as he **deserves** [+3338]—

2Ch 32: 25 was proud and he did not respond to the **kindness** *shown* him;
Ps 28: 4 hands have done and bring back upon them **what** they **deserve**.
94: 2 O Judge of the earth; pay back to the proud **what** they **deserve**.
103: 2 Praise the LORD, O my soul, and forget not all his **benefits**—
137: 8 happy is he who repays you for **what**[s] you have done to us—
Pr 12: 14 with good things as surely as the **work** *of* his hands rewards him.
19: 17 lends to the LORD, and he will reward him for **what** he has **done**.
Isa 3: 11 They will be paid back for **what** their hands have **done**.
35: 4 with divine **retribution** he will come to save you."
59: 18 so will he repay wrath to his enemies and **retribution** to his foes;
59: 18 and retribution to his foes; he will repay the islands their **due**.
66: 6 is the sound of the LORD repaying his enemies *all* they **deserve**.
Jer 51: 6 for the LORD's vengeance; he will pay her **what** she **deserves**.
La 3: 64 Pay them back **what** they **deserve**, O LORD, for what their hands
Joel 3: 4 [4:4] Are you repaying me for **something** I have **done**? If you are
3: 4 [4:4] and speedily return on your own heads **what** you have **done**.
3: 7 [4:7] and I will return on your own heads **what** you have **done**.
Ob 1: 15 it will be done to you; your **deeds** will return upon your own head.

1692 גְּמוּלָה g^emûlâ, n.f. [3] [√ 1694]

retribution [1], way[s] [1], what done [1]

2Sa 19: 36 [19:37] but why should the king reward me in this **way**[s]?
Isa 59: 18 According to **what** they have **done**, so will he repay wrath to his
Jer 51: 56 For the LORD is a God of **retribution**; he will repay in full.

1693 גִּמְזוֹ gimzô, n.pr.loc. [1]

Gimzo [1]

2Ch 28: 18 Aijalon and Gederoth, as well as Soco, Timnah and **Gimzo**,

1694 גָּמַל gāmal, v. [37] [→ 1085, 1690, 1691, 1692, 1695?, 1696, 1697, 9326]

weaned [7], done [5], dealt with [2], repay [2], treated [2], was weaned [2], been good [1], benefits [1], brings [1], brought up [1], brought [1], committed [1], did [1], do good [1], good [1], goodness [1], is weaned [1], paying back [1], produced [1], repaying [1], reward [1], ripening [1], young child [1]

Ge 21: 8 [C] The child grew and **was weaned**, and on the day Isaac was
21: 8 [C] on the day Isaac **was weaned** Abraham held a great feast.
50: 15 [A] and pays us back for all the wrongs *we* **did** *to* him?"
50: 17 [A] and the wrongs *they* **committed** *in treating* you so badly.'
Nu 17: 8 [17:23] [A] but had budded, blossomed and **produced** almonds.
Dt 32: 6 [A] Is this the way *you* **repay** the LORD, O foolish and unwise
1Sa 1: 22 [C] "After the boy **is weaned**, I will take him and present him
1: 23 [A] "Stay here until you *have* **weaned** him; only may the
1: 23 [A] at home and nursed her son until she *had* **weaned** him.
1: 24 [A] After he *was* **weaned**, she took the boy with her, young as he
24: 17 [24:18] [A] "You *have* **treated** me well, but I have treated you
24: 17 [24:18] [A] have treated me well, but I *have* **treated** you badly.
2Sa 19: 36 [19:37] [A] but why *should* the king **reward** me *in* this way?
22: 21 [A] "The LORD *has* **dealt with** me according to my
1Ki 11: 20 [A] whom Tahpenes **brought up** in the royal palace.
2Ch 20: 11 [A] See *how* they *are* **repaying** us by coming to drive us out of
Ps 7: 4 [7:5] [A] if *I have* **done** evil *to* him who is at peace with me
13: 6 [A] I will sing to the LORD, for *he has* **been good** to me.
18: 20 [18:21] [A] The LORD *has* **dealt with** me according to my
103: 10 [A] us as our sins deserve or **repay** us according to our iniquities.
116: 7 [A] O my soul, for the LORD *has been* **good** to you.
119: 17 [A] **Do good** to your servant, and I will live; I will obey your
131: 2 [B] like a **weaned** *child* with its mother, like a weaned child is
131: 2 [B] with its mother, like a **weaned** *child* is my soul within me.
137: 8 [A] happy is he who repays you for what *you have* **done** to us—
142: 7 [142:8] [A] gather about me because of *your* **goodness** to me.
Pr 3: 30 [A] a man for no reason—when *he has* **done** you no harm.
11: 17 [A] A kind man **benefits** himself, but a cruel man brings trouble
31: 12 [A] *She* **brings** him good, not harm, all the days of her life.
Isa 3: 9 [A] Woe to them! *They have* **brought** disaster upon themselves.
11: 8 [B] and the **young child** put his hand into the viper's nest.
18: 5 [A] blossom is gone and the flower becomes a **ripening** grape,
28: 9 [B] To *children* **weaned** from their milk, to those just taken from
63: 7 [A] to be praised, according to all the LORD *has* **done** *for* us—
63: 7 [A] the many good things *he has* **done** for the house of Israel,
Hos 1: 8 [A] After *she had* **weaned** Lo-Ruhamah, Gomer had another
Joel 3: 4 [4:4] [A] If you *are* **paying** me **back**, I will swiftly and speedily

1695 גָּמָל gāmāl, n.m. [54] [√ 1694?]

camels [48], camel [3], *untranslated* [1], camel's [1], camel-loads [+5362] [1]

Ge 12: 16 and female donkeys, menservants and maidservants, and **camels**.
24: 10 the servant took ten of his master's **camels** and left, taking with
24: 10 Then the servant took ten of his master's camels **[RPH]** and left,
24: 11 He had the **camels** kneel down near the well outside the town;
24: 14 a drink,' and she says, 'Drink, and I'll water your **camels** too'—
24: 19 given him a drink, she said, "I'll draw water for your **camels** too,
24: 20 the well to draw more water, and drew enough for all his **camels**.
24: 22 When the **camels** had finished drinking, the man took out a gold
24: 30 to the man and found him standing by the **camels** near the spring.
24: 31 out here? I have prepared the house and a place for the **camels**."
24: 32 So the man went to the house, and the **camels** were unloaded.
24: 32 Straw and fodder were brought for the **camels**, and water for him
24: 35 and gold, menservants and maidservants, and **camels** and donkeys.
24: 44 if she says to me, "Drink, and I'll draw water for your **camels** too,"
24: 46 from her shoulder and said, 'Drink, and I'll water your **camels** too.'
24: 46 your camels too.' So I drank, and she watered the **camels** also.
24: 61 Then Rebekah and her maids got ready and mounted their **camels**
24: 63 to meditate, and as he looked up, he saw **camels** approaching.
24: 64 also looked up and saw Isaac. She got down from her **camel**
30: 43 and maidservants and menservants, and **camels** and donkeys.
31: 17 Then Jacob put his children and his wives on **camels**,
31: 34 and put them inside her **camel's** saddle and was sitting on them.
32: 7 [32:8] two groups, and the flocks and herds and **camels** as well.
32: 15 [32:16] thirty female **camels** with their young, forty cows and ten
37: 25 Their **camels** were loaded with spices, balm and myrrh, and they
Ex 9: 3 on your horses and donkeys and **camels** and on your cattle
Lev 11: 4 The **camel**, though it chews the cud, does not have a split hoof;
Dt 14: 7 have a split hoof completely divided you may not eat the **camel**,
Jdg 6: 5 It was impossible to count the men and their **camels**; they invaded
7: 12 Their **camels** could no more be counted than the sand on the
8: 21 and killed them, and took the ornaments off their **camels**' necks.
8: 26 the kings of Midian or the chains that were on their **camels**' necks.
1Sa 15: 3 children and infants, cattle and sheep, **camels** and donkeys.' "
27: 9 but took sheep and cattle, donkeys and **camels**, and clothes.
30: 17 except four hundred young men who rode off on **camels** and fled.
1Ki 10: 2 with **camels** carrying spices, large quantities of gold, and precious
2Ki 8: 9 taking with him as a gift forty **camel-loads** [+5362] of all the finest
1Ch 5: 21 fifty thousand **camels**, two hundred fifty thousand sheep and two
12: 40 [12:41] came bringing food on donkeys, **camels**, mules and oxen.
27: 30 Obil the Ishmaelite was in charge of the **camels**. Jehdeiah the
2Ch 9: 1 with **camels** carrying spices, large quantities of gold, and precious
14: 15 [14:14] and carried off droves of sheep and goats and **camels**.
Ezr 2: 67 435 **camels** and 6,720 donkeys.
Ne 7: 69 [7:68] 435 **camels** and 6,720 donkeys.
Job 1: 3 three thousand **camels**, five hundred yoke of oxen and five
1: 17 and swept down on your **camels** and carried them off.
42: 12 six thousand **camels**, a thousand yoke of oxen and a thousand
Isa 21: 7 riders on donkeys or riders on **camels**, let him be alert, fully alert."
30: 6 their treasures on the humps of **camels**, to that unprofitable nation,
60: 6 Herds of **camels** will cover your land, young camels of Midian
Jer 49: 29 their shelters will be carried off with all their goods and **camels**.
49: 32 Their **camels** will become plunder, and their large herds will be
Eze 25: 5 I will turn Rabbah into a pasture for **camels** and Ammon into a
Zec 14: 15 plague will strike the horses and mules, the **camels** and donkeys,

1696 גְּמַלִּי g^emallî, n.pr.m. [1] [√ 1694]

Gemalli [1]

Nu 13: 12 from the tribe of Dan, Ammiel son of **Gemalli**;

1697 גַּמְלִיאֵל gamlî'ēl, n.pr.m. [5] [√ 1694 + 446]

Gamaliel [5]

Nu 1: 10 son of Ammihud; from Manasseh, **Gamaliel** son of Pedahzur;
2: 20 The leader of the people of Manasseh is **Gamaliel** son of
7: 54 On the eighth day **Gamaliel** son of Pedahzur, the leader of the
7: 59 This was the offering of **Gamaliel** son of Pedahzur.
10: 23 **Gamaliel** son of Pedahzur was over the division of the tribe of

1698 גָּמַר gāmar, v. [5] [→ 1700, 1701, 1702; Ar 10147]

bring to an end [1], failed [1], fulfill [1], fulfills [1], no more [1]

Ps 7: 9 [7:10] [A] **bring to an end** the violence of the wicked and make
12: 1 [12:2] [A] Help, LORD, for the godly *are* **no more**;
57: 2 [57:3] [A] Most High, to God, *who* **fulfills** ˻his purpose˼ for me.
77: 8 [77:9] [A] *Has* his promise **failed** for all time?
138: 8 [A] The LORD *will* **fulfill** ˻his purpose˼ for me; your love,

1699 גֹּמֶר gōmer[1], n.pr.m. [5]

Gomer [5]

Ge 10: 2 **Gomer**, Magog, Madai, Javan, Tubal, Meshech and Tiras.
10: 3 The sons of **Gomer**: Ashkenaz, Riphath and Togarmah.
1Ch 1: 5 **Gomer**, Magog, Madai, Javan, Tubal, Meshech and Tiras.
1: 6 The sons of **Gomer**: Ashkenaz, Riphath and Togarmah.
Eze 38: 6 also **Gomer** with all its troops, and Beth Togarmah from the far

1700 [2]גֹּמֶר **gōmer**[2], n.pr.f. [1] [√ 1698]

Gomer [1]

Hos 1: 3 So he married **Gomer** daughter of Diblaim, and she conceived

1701 גְּמַרְיָה **g^{e}maryâ**, n.pr.m. [1] [√ 1698 + 3378]

Gemariah [1]

Jer 29: 3 letter to Elasah son of Shaphan and to **Gemariah** son of Hilkiah,

1702 גְּמַרְיָהוּ **g^{e}maryāhû**, n.pr.m. [4] [√ 1698 + 3378]

Gemariah [4]

Jer 36: 10 From the room of **Gemariah** son of Shaphan the secretary,
36: 11 When Micaiah son of **Gemariah**, the son of Shaphan, heard all the
36: 12 of Shemaiah, Elnathan son of Acbor, **Gemariah** son of Shaphan,
36: 25 Delaiah and **Gemariah** urged the king not to burn the scroll,

1703 גַּן **gan**, n.m. [41] [→ 1708; cf. 1713]

garden [39], gardens [2]

Ge 2: 8 Now the LORD God had planted a **garden** in the east, in Eden;
2: 9 In the middle of the **garden** were the tree of life and the tree of the
2: 10 A river watering the **garden** flowed from Eden; from there it was
2: 15 and put him in the **Garden** *of* Eden to work it and take care of it.
2: 16 the man, "You are free to eat from any tree in the **garden**;
3: 1 God really say, 'You must not eat from any tree in the **garden**'?"
3: 2 said to the serpent, "We may eat fruit from the trees in the **garden**,
3: 3 must not eat fruit from the tree that is in the middle of the **garden**,
3: 8 God as he was walking in the **garden** in the cool of the day,
3: 8 and they hid from the LORD God among the trees of the **garden**.
3: 10 He answered, "I heard you in the **garden**, and I was afraid
3: 23 So the LORD God banished him from the **Garden** *of* Eden to
3: 24 he placed on the east side of the **Garden** *of* Eden cherubim
13: 10 like the **garden** *of* the LORD, like the land of Egypt,
Dt 11: 10 planted your seed and irrigated it by foot as in a vegetable **garden**.
1Ki 21: 2 "Let me have your vineyard to use for a vegetable **garden**,
2Ki 21: 18 rested with his fathers and was buried in his palace **garden**,
21: 18 and was buried in his palace garden, the **garden** *of* Uzza.
21: 26 He was buried in his grave in the **garden** *of* Uzza. And Josiah his
25: 4 through the gate between the two walls near the king's **garden**,
Ne 3: 15 repaired the wall of the Pool of Siloam, by the King's **Garden**,
SS 4: 12 You are a **garden** locked up, my sister, my bride; you are a spring
4: 15 You are a **garden** fountain, a well of flowing water streaming
4: 16 Blow on my **garden**, that its fragrance may spread abroad.
4: 16 Let my lover come into his **garden** and taste its choice fruits.
5: 1 I have come into my **garden**, my sister, my bride; I have gathered
6: 2 My lover has gone down to his **garden**, to the beds of spices,
6: 2 to the beds of spices, to browse in the **gardens** and to gather lilies.
8: 13 You who dwell in the **gardens** with friends in attendance,
Isa 51: 3 deserts like Eden, her wastelands like the **garden** *of* the LORD.
58: 11 You will be like a well-watered **garden**, like a spring whose waters
Jer 31: 12 They will be like a well-watered **garden**, and they will sorrow no
39: 4 they left the city at night by way of the king's **garden**,
52: 7 through the gate between the two walls near the king's **garden**,
La 2: 6 He has laid waste his dwelling like a **garden**; he has destroyed his
Eze 28: 13 You were in Eden, the **garden** *of* God; every precious stone
31: 8 The cedars in the **garden** *of* God could not rival it, nor could the
31: 8 its branches—no tree in the **garden** *of* God could match its beauty.
31: 9 the envy of all the trees of Eden in the **garden** *of* God.
36: 35 "This land that was laid waste has become like the **garden** *of*
Joel 2: 3 Before them the land is like the **garden** *of* Eden, behind them,

1704 גָּנַב **gānab**, v. [40] [→ 1705, 1706, 1707?]

steal [9], stolen [3], steals [2], stole away [2], stole [2], was forcibly carried off [+1704] [2], was stolen [+1704] [2], *untranslated* [1], are stolen [1], be considered stolen [1], deceive [1], deceived [+906+4213] [1], deceived [+906+4222] [1], kidnapping [+5883] [1], kidnaps [1], snatches away [1], steal away [1], steal in [1], stealing [1], stole into [+995+4200] [1], swept away [1], taken secretly [1], thief [1], was secretly brought [1], was stolen [1]

Ge 30: 33 [B] lamb that is not dark-colored, *will* **be considered stolen**."
31: 19 [A] to shear his sheep, Rachel **stole** her father's household gods.
31: 20 [A] Jacob **deceived** [+906+4213] Laban the Aramean by not
31: 26 [A] *You've* **deceived** [+906+4222] me, and you've carried off
31: 27 [A] Why did you run off secretly and **deceive** me? Why didn't
31: 30 [A] to your father's house. But why *did you* **steal** my gods?"
31: 32 [A] Now Jacob did not know that Rachel *had* **stolen** the gods.
31: 39 [B] you demanded payment from me for *whatever* **was stolen** *by*
31: 39 [B] from me for whatever was stolen by day or **[RPH]** night.
40: 15 [E] For *I* **was forcibly carried** [+1704] **off** from the land of the
40: 15 [E] For *I* **was forcibly carried off** [+1704] from the land of the
44: 8 [A] So why *would we* **steal** silver or gold from your master's
Ex 20: 15 [A] "*You shall* not **steal**.
21: 16 [A] "*Anyone who* **kidnaps** another and either sells him or still
22: 1 [21:37] [A] "If a man **steals** an ox or a sheep and slaughters it
22: 7 [22:6] [E] and *they* **are stolen** from the neighbor's house,
22: 12 [22:11] [C] if the animal **was stolen** [+1704] from the neighbor,
22: 12 [22:11] [A] if the animal **was stolen** [+1704] from the neighbor,
Lev 19: 11 [A] " '*Do* not **steal**. " 'Do not lie. " 'Do not deceive one another.
Dt 5: 19 [A] "*You shall* not **steal**.
24: 7 [A] If a man is caught **kidnapping** [+5883] one of his brother
Jos 7: 11 [A] *they have* **stolen**, they have lied, they have put them with
2Sa 15: 6 [D] for justice, and so he **stole** the hearts of the men of Israel.
19: 3 [19:4] [F] The men **stole** [+995+4200] **into** the city that day as
19: 3 [19:4] [F] The men stole into the city that day as men **steal in**
19: 41 [19:42] [A] *did* our brothers, the men of Judah, **steal** the king **away**
21: 12 [A] (*They had* **taken** them **secretly** from the public square at
2Ki 11: 2 [A] **stole** him **away** from among the royal princes, who were about
2Ch 22: 11 [A] **stole** him **away** from among the royal princes who were
Job 4: 12 [E] "A word **was secretly brought** to me, my ears caught a
21: 18 [A] like straw before the wind, like chaff **swept away** *by* a gale?
27: 20 [A] him like a flood; a tempest **snatches** him **away** in the night.
Pr 6: 30 [A] Men do not despise a thief if *he* **steals** to satisfy his hunger
9: 17 [B] "**Stolen** water is sweet; food eaten in secret is delicious!"
30: 9 [A] Or I may become poor and **steal**, and so dishonor the name
Jer 7: 9 [A] " '*Will you* **steal** and murder, commit adultery and perjury,
23: 30 [D] "I am against the prophets *who* **steal** from one another words
Hos 4: 2 [A] is only cursing, lying and murder, **stealing** and adultery;
Ob 1: 5 [A] *would they* not **steal** only as much as they wanted?
Zec 5: 3 [A] to what it says on one side, every **thief** will be banished,

1705 גַּנָּב **gannāb**, n.m. [17] [√ 1704]

thief [9], thieves [7], kidnapper [1]

Ex 22: 2 [22:1] "If a **thief** is caught breaking in and is struck so that he
22: 7 [22:6] the **thief**, if he is caught, must pay back double.
22: 8 [22:7] if the **thief** is not found, the owner of the house must
Dt 24: 7 and treats him as a slave or sells him, the **kidnapper** must die.
Job 24: 14 kills the poor and needy; in the night he steals forth like a **thief**.
30: 5 banished from their fellow men, shouted at as if they were **thieves**.
Ps 50: 18 When you see a **thief**, you join with him; you throw in your lot
Pr 6: 30 Men do not despise a **thief** if he steals to satisfy his hunger when
29: 24 The accomplice of a **thief** is his own enemy; he is put under oath
Isa 1: 23 Your rulers are rebels, companions of **thieves**; they all love bribes
Jer 2: 26 "As a **thief** is disgraced when he is caught, so the house of Israel is
48: 27 Was she caught among **thieves**, that you shake your head in scorn
49: 9 If **thieves** came during the night, would they not steal only as much
Hos 7: 1 They practice deceit, **thieves** break into houses, bandits rob in the
Joel 2: 9 climb into the houses; like **thieves** they enter through the windows.
Ob 1: 5 "If **thieves** came to you, if robbers in the night—Oh, what a
Zec 5: 4 it will enter the house of the **thief** and the house of him who swears

1706 גְּנֵבָה **g^{e}nēbâ**, n.f. [2] [√ 1704]

stolen [1], theft [1]

Ex 22: 3 [22:2] but if he has nothing, he must be sold to pay for his **theft**.
22: 4 [22:3] "If the **stolen** *animal* is found alive in his possession—

1707 גְּנֻבַת **g^{e}nubat**, n.pr.m. [2] [√ 1704?]

Genubath [2]

1Ki 11: 20 The sister of Tahpenes bore him a son named **Genubath**, whom
11: 20 royal palace. There **Genubath** lived with Pharaoh's own children.

1708 גַּנָּה **gannâ**, n.f. [16] [√ 1703; cf. 1713]

gardens [9], garden [6], grove [1]

Nu 24: 6 "Like valleys they spread out, like **gardens** beside a river,
Est 1: 5 lasting seven days, in the enclosed **garden** *of* the king's palace,
7: 7 got up in a rage, left his wine and went out into the palace **garden**.
7: 8 Just as the king returned from the palace **garden** to the banquet
Job 8: 16 plant in the sunshine, spreading its shoots over the **garden**;
Ecc 2: 5 I made **gardens** and parks and planted all kinds of fruit trees in
SS 6: 11 I went down to the **grove** *of* nut trees to look at the new growth in
Isa 1: 29 will be disgraced because of the **gardens** that you have chosen.
1: 30 will be like an oak with fading leaves, like a **garden** without water.
61: 11 soil makes the sprout come up and a **garden** causes seeds to grow,
65: 3 offering sacrifices in **gardens** and burning incense on altars of
66: 17 who consecrate and purify themselves to go into the **gardens**,
Jer 29: 5 and settle down; plant **gardens** and eat what they produce.
29: 28 and settle down; plant **gardens** and eat what they produce.' "
Am 4: 9 "Many times I struck your **gardens** and vineyards, I struck them
9: 14 and drink their wine; they will make **gardens** and eat their fruit.

1709 גֶּנֶז **genez**[1], n.[m.]. [2] [→ 1711; Ar 10148]

treasury [2]

Est 3: 9 I will put ten thousand talents of silver into the royal **treasury** for

[F] Hitpael (hitpoel, hitpoal, hitpolel, hitpolal, hitpalel, hitpalal, hitpalpel, hitpalpal, hotpael, hotpaal) [G] Hiphil (hiphtil) [H] Hophal [I] Hishtaphel

Est 4: 7 to pay into the royal **treasury** for the destruction of the Jews.

1710 ²גֶּנֶז genez², n.[m.]. [1]
rugs [1]
Eze 27:24 embroidered work and multicolored **rugs** with cords twisted

1711 גַּנְזַךְ ganzak, n.[m.]. [1] [√ 1709]
storerooms [1]
1Ch 28:11 its buildings, its **storerooms**, its upper parts, its inner rooms

1712 גַּנִּים gannîm, n.pr.loc. Not used in NIV/BHS [→ 6528]

1713 גָּנַן gānan, v. [8] [→ 1703, 1708, 4482]
defend [4], shield [4]
2Ki 19:34 [A] *I will* **defend** this city and save it, for my sake and for the
20: 6 [A] *I will* **defend** this city for my sake and for the sake of my
Isa 31: 5 [A] the LORD Almighty *will* **shield** Jerusalem;
31: 5 [A] he *will* **shield** it and deliver it, he will 'pass over' it and will
37:35 [A] "*I will* **defend** this city and save it, for my sake and for the
38: 6 [A] from the hand of the king of Assyria. *I will* **defend** this city.
Zec 9:15 [A] the LORD Almighty *will* **shield** them. They will destroy
12: 8 [A] On that day the LORD *will* **shield** those who live in

1714 גִּנְּתוֹי ginnᵉtôy, n.pr.m. [1 / 0] [cf. 1715]
Ne 12: 4 Iddo, Ginnethon, [BHS *Ginnethoi*; NIV 1715] Abijah,

1715 גִּנְּתוֹן ginnᵉtôn, n.pr.m. [2 / 3] [cf. 1714]
Ginnethon [2], Ginnethon's [1]
Ne 10: 6 [10:7] Daniel, **Ginnethon**, Baruch,
12: 4 Iddo, **Ginnethon**, [BHS 1714] Abijah,
12:16 of Iddo's, Zechariah; of **Ginnethon's**, Meshullam;

1716 גָּעָה gā'â, v. [2] [cf. 7880]
bellow [1], lowing [1]
1Sa 6:12 [A] Beth Shemesh, keeping on the road and **lowing** all the way;
Job 6: 5 [A] bray when it has grass, or an ox **bellow** when it has fodder?

1717 גֹּעָה gō'â, n.pr.loc. [1]
Goah [1]
Jer 31:39 from there straight to the hill of Gareb and then turn to **Goah**.

1718 גָּעַל gā'al, v. [10] [→ 1719, 1720; cf. 1458]
abhor [4], despised [2], abhorred [1], despise [1], fail [1], was defiled [1]
Lev 26:11 [A] put my dwelling place among you, and I *will* not **abhor** you.
26:15 [A] if you reject my decrees and **abhor** my laws and fail to carry
26:30 [A] on the lifeless forms of your idols, and I *will* **abhor** you.
26:43 [A] because they rejected my laws and **abhorred** my decrees.
26:44 [A] I will not reject them or **abhor** them so as to destroy them
2Sa 1:21 [C] For there the shield of the mighty **was defiled**, the shield of
Job 21:10 [G] Their bulls never **fail** to breed; their cows calve and do not
Jer 14:19 [A] *Do* you **despise** Zion? Why have you afflicted us so that we
Eze 16:45 [A] of your mother, *who* **despised** her husband and her children;
16:45 [A] your sisters, who **despised** their husbands and their children.

1719 גֹּעַל gō'al, n.m. [1] [√ 1718]
despised [1]
Eze 16: 5 the open field, for on the day you were born you were **despised**.

1720 גַּעַל ga'al, n.pr.m. [9] [√ 1718]
Gaal [9]
Jdg 9:26 Now **Gaal** son of Ebed moved with his brothers into Shechem,
9:28 **Gaal** son of Ebed said, "Who is Abimelech, and who is Shechem,
9:30 When Zebul the governor of the city heard what **Gaal** son of Ebed
9:31 "**Gaal** son of Ebed and his brothers have come to Shechem
9:35 Now **Gaal** son of Ebed had gone out and was standing at the
9:36 When **Gaal** saw them, he said to Zebul, "Look, people are coming
9:37 **Gaal** spoke up again: "Look, people are coming down from the
9:39 So **Gaal** led out the citizens of Shechem and fought Abimelech.
9:41 and Zebul drove **Gaal** and his brothers out of Shechem.

1721 גָּעַר gā'ar, v. [14] [→ 1722, 4486]
rebuke [7], rebuked [3], rebukes [2], prevent [1], reprimanded [1]
Ge 37:10 [A] his father **rebuked** him and said, "What is this dream you
Ru 2:16 [A] and leave them for her to pick up, and don't **rebuke** her."
Ps 9: 5 [9:6] [A] *You have* **rebuked** the nations and destroyed the
68:30 [68:31] [A] **Rebuke** the beast among the reeds, the herd of bulls
106: 9 [A] *He* **rebuked** the Red Sea, and it dried up; he led them
119:21 [A] *You* **rebuke** the arrogant, who are cursed and who stray from
Isa 17:13 [A] when *he* **rebukes** them they flee far away, driven before the
54: 9 [A] sworn not to be angry with you, never *to* **rebuke** you again.
Jer 29:27 [A] So why *have you* not **reprimanded** Jeremiah from
Na 1: 4 [A] *He* **rebukes** the sea and dries it up; he makes all the rivers
Zec 3: 2 [A] The LORD said to Satan, "The LORD **rebuke** you, Satan!
3: 2 [A] Satan! The LORD, who has chosen Jerusalem, **rebuke** you!
Mal 2: 3 [A] "Because of you I *will* **rebuke** your descendants; I will
3:11 [A] *I will* **prevent** pests from devouring your crops, and the

1722 גְּעָרָה gᵉ'ārâ, n.f. [15] [√ 1721]
rebuke [12], threat [3]
2Sa 22:16 the foundations of the earth laid bare at the **rebuke** *of* the LORD,
Job 26:11 The pillars of the heavens quake, aghast at his **rebuke**.
Ps 18:15 [18:16] and the foundations of the earth laid bare at your **rebuke**,
76: 6 [76:7] At your **rebuke**, O God of Jacob, both horse and chariot lie
80:16 [80:17] it is burned with fire; at your **rebuke** your people perish.
104: 7 at your **rebuke** the waters fled, at the sound of your thunder they
Pr 13: 1 his father's instruction, but a mocker does not listen to **rebuke**.
13: 8 man's riches may ransom his life, but a poor man hears no **threat**.
17:10 A **rebuke** impresses a man of discernment more than a hundred
Ecc 7: 5 It is better to heed a wise man's **rebuke** than to listen to the song
Isa 30:17 A thousand will flee at the **threat** *of* one; at the threat of five you
30:17 at the **threat** *of* five you will all flee away, till you are left like a
50: 2 By a mere **rebuke** I dry up the sea, I turn rivers into a desert;
51:20 filled with the wrath of the LORD and the **rebuke** *of* your God.
66:15 bring down his anger with fury, and his **rebuke** with flames of fire.

1723 גָּעַשׁ gā'aš, v. [9]
trembled [4], surging [2], are shaken [1], roll [1], stagger [1]
2Sa 22: 8 [F] "The earth **trembled** and quaked, the foundations of the
22: 8 [F] of the heavens shook; *they* **trembled** because he was angry.
Job 34:20 [E] of the night; the people **are shaken** and they pass away;
Ps 18: 7 [18:8] [A] The earth **trembled** and quaked, and the foundations
18: 7 [18:8] [F] *they* **trembled** because he was angry.
Jer 5:22 [F] The waves *may* **roll**, but they cannot prevail; they may roar,
25:16 [F] *they will* **stagger** and go mad because of the sword I will
46: 7 [F] is this that rises like the Nile, like rivers of **surging** waters?
46: 8 [F] Egypt rises like the Nile, like rivers of **surging** waters. She

1724 גַּעַשׁ ga'aš, n.pr.loc. [4]
Gaash [4]
Jos 24:30 Serah in the hill country of Ephraim, north of Mount **Gaash**.
Jdg 2: 9 Heres in the hill country of Ephraim, north of Mount **Gaash**.
2Sa 23:30 Benaiah the Pirathonite, Hiddai from the ravines of **Gaash**,
1Ch 11:32 Hurai from the ravines of **Gaash**, Abiel the Arbathite,

1725 גַּעְתָּם ga'tām, n.pr.m. [3]
Gatam [3]
Ge 36:11 The sons of Eliphaz: Teman, Omar, Zepho, **Gatam** and Kenaz.
36:16 Korah, **Gatam** and Amalek. These were the chiefs descended from
1Ch 1:36 Teman, Omar, Zepho, **Gatam** and Kenaz; by Timna: Amalek.

1726 ¹גַּף gap¹, n.m. [1]
highest point [+5294] [1]
Pr 9: 3 her maids, and she calls from the **highest point of** [+5294] the city.

1727 ²גַּף gap², n.m. [3] [→ 111, 1590]
alone [+928+2257] [2], only [+928+2257] [1]
Ex 21: 3 If he comes **alone** [+928+2257], he is to go free alone; but if he has
21: 3 If he comes alone, he is to go free **alone** [+928+2257]; but if he has
21: 4 belong to her master, and **only** [+928+2257] the man shall go free.

1728 גֶּפֶן gepen, n.f. & m. [55]
vine [36], vines [16], grapevine [+3516] [2], grapevines [1]
Ge 40: 9 He said to him, "In my dream I saw a **vine** in front of me,
40:10 and on the **vine** were three branches. As soon as it budded,
49:11 He will tether his donkey to a **vine**, his colt to the choicest branch;
Nu 6: 4 he must not eat anything that comes from the **grapevine** [+3516],
20: 5 It has no grain or figs, **grapevines** or pomegranates. And there is
Dt 8: 8 a land with wheat and barley, **vines** and fig trees, pomegranates,
32:32 Their **vine** comes from the vine of Sodom and from the fields of
32:32 Their vine comes from the **vine** *of* Sodom and from the fields of
Jdg 9:12 "Then the trees said to the **vine**, 'Come and be our king.'
9:13 "But the **vine** answered, 'Should I give up my wine, which cheers
13:14 She must not eat anything that comes from the **grapevine** [+3516],
1Ki 4:25 [5:5] lived in safety, each man under his own **vine** and fig tree.

2Ki 4:39 them went out into the fields to gather herbs and found a wild **vine**.
18:31 Then every one of you will eat from his own **vine** and fig tree
Job 15:33 He will be like a **vine** stripped of its unripe grapes, like an olive
Ps 78:47 He destroyed their **vines** with hail and their sycamore-figs with
80: 8 [80:9] You brought a **vine** out of Egypt; you drove out the nations
80:14 [80:15] Look down from heaven and see! Watch over this **vine**,
105:33 he struck down their **vines** and fig trees and shattered the trees of
128: 3 Your wife will be like a fruitful **vine** within your house; your sons
SS 2:13 forms its early fruit; the blossoming **vines** spread their fragrance.
6:11 to see if the **vines** had budded or the pomegranates were in bloom.
7: 8 [7:9] May your breasts be like the clusters of the **vine**,
7:12 [7:13] Let us go early to the vineyards to see if the **vines** have
Isa 7:23 in every place where there were a thousand **vines** worth a thousand
16: 8 The fields of Heshbon wither, the **vines** *of* Sibmah also. The rulers
16: 9 So I weep, as Jazer weeps, for the **vines** *of* Sibmah. O Heshbon,
24: 7 The new wine dries up and the **vine** withers; all the merrymakers
32:12 Beat your breasts for the pleasant fields, for the fruitful **vines**
34: 4 all the starry host will fall like withered leaves from the **vine**,
36:16 Then every one of you will eat from his own **vine** and fig tree
Jer 2:21 How then did you turn against me into a corrupt, wild **vine**?
5:17 will devour your flocks and herds, devour your **vines** and fig trees.
6: 9 "Let them glean the remnant of Israel as thoroughly as a **vine**;
8:13 declares the LORD. There will be no grapes on the **vine**.
48:32 I weep for you, as Jazer weeps, O **vines** *of* Sibmah. Your branches
Eze 15: 2 how is the wood of a **vine** better than that of a branch on any of the
15: 6 As I have given the wood of the **vine** among the trees of the forest
17: 6 it sprouted and became a low, spreading **vine**. Its branches turned
17: 6 So it became a **vine** and produced branches and put out leafy
17: 7 The **vine** now sent out its roots toward him from the plot where it
17: 8 it would produce branches, bear fruit and become a splendid **vine**.'
19:10 " 'Your mother was like a **vine** in your vineyard planted by the
Hos 2:12 [2:14] I will ruin her **vines** and her fig trees, which she said were
10: 1 Israel was a spreading **vine**; he brought forth fruit for himself.
14: 7 [14:8] He will blossom like a **vine**, and his fame will be like the
Joel 1: 7 It has laid waste my **vines** and ruined my fig trees. It has stripped
1:12 The **vine** is dried up and the fig tree is withered; the pomegranate,
2:22 are bearing their fruit; the fig tree and the **vine** yield their riches.
Mic 4: 4 Every man will sit under his own **vine** and under his own fig tree,
Hab 3:17 the fig tree does not bud and there are no grapes on the **vines**,
Hag 2:19 Until now, the **vine** and the fig tree, the pomegranate and the olive
Zec 3:10 that day each of you will invite his neighbor to sit under his **vine**
8:12 "The seed will grow well, the **vine** will yield its fruit, the ground
Mal 3:11 the **vines** in your fields will not cast their fruit," says the LORD

1729 גֹּפֶר gōper, n.[m.]. [1]

cypress [1]

Ge 6:14 So make yourself an ark of **cypress** wood; make rooms in it

1730 גָּפְרִית goprît, n.f. [7]

burning sulfur [4], sulfur [3]

Ge 19:24 the LORD rained down burning **sulfur** on Sodom
Dt 29:23 [29:22] whole land will be a burning waste of salt and **sulfur**—
Job 18:15 resides in his tent; **burning sulfur** is scattered over his dwelling.
Ps 11: 6 On the wicked he will rain fiery coals and **burning sulfur**;
Isa 30:33 of the LORD, like a stream of **burning sulfur**, sets it ablaze.
34: 9 streams will be turned into pitch, her dust into **burning sulfur**;
Eze 38:22 hailstones and burning **sulfur** on him and on his troops and on the

1731 גֵּר gēr, n.m. [93 / 92] [→ 1745; cf. 1591]

alien [61], aliens [26], stranger [3], alien's [1], strangers [1]

Ge 15:13 "Know for certain that your descendants will be **strangers** in a
23: 4 "I am an **alien** and a stranger among you. Sell me some property
Ex 2:22 him Gershom, saying, "I have become an **alien** in a foreign land."
12:19 the community of Israel, whether he is an **alien** or native-born.
12:48 "An **alien** living among you who wants to celebrate the LORD's
12:49 law applies to the native-born and to the **alien** living among you."
18: 3 for Moses said, "I have become an **alien** in a foreign land";
20:10 or maidservant, nor your animals, nor the **alien** within your gates.
22:21 [22:20] "Do not mistreat an **alien** or oppress him, for you were
22:21 [22:20] an alien or oppress him, for you were **aliens** in Egypt.
23: 9 "Do not oppress an **alien**; you yourselves know how it feels to be
23: 9 you yourselves know how it feels to be **aliens**, because you were
23: 9 know how it feels to be aliens, because you were **aliens** in Egypt.
23:12 born in your household, and the **alien** as well, may be refreshed.
Lev 16:29 do any work—whether native-born or an **alien** living among you—
17: 8 or any **alien** living among them who offers a burnt offering
17:10 or any **alien** living among them who eats any blood—
17:12 you may eat blood, nor may an **alien** living among you eat blood."
17:13 or any **alien** living among you who hunts any animal
17:15 " 'Anyone, whether native-born or **alien**, who eats anything found
18:26 the **aliens** living among you must not do any of these detestable
19:10 Leave them for the poor and the **alien**. I am the LORD your God.
19:33 " 'When an **alien** lives with you in your land, do not mistreat him.
19:34 The **alien** living with you must be treated as one of your
19:34 Love him as yourself, for you were **aliens** in Egypt. I am the
20: 2 or any **alien** living in Israel who gives any of his children to
22:18 'If any of you—either an Israelite or an **alien** living in Israel—
23:22 Leave them for the poor and the **alien**. I am the LORD your
24:16 Whether an **alien** or native-born, when he blasphemes the Name,
24:22 You are to have the same law for the **alien** and the native-born.
25:23 because the land is mine and you are but **aliens** and my tenants.
25:35 help him as you would an **alien** or a temporary resident, so he can
25:47 " 'If an **alien** or a temporary resident among you becomes rich
25:47 sells himself to the **alien** living among you or to a member of the
25:47 to the alien living among you or to a member of the **alien's** clan,
Nu 9:14 " 'An **alien** living among you who wants to celebrate the LORD's
9:14 You must have the same regulations for the **alien** and the
15:14 whenever an **alien** or anyone else living among you presents an
15:15 to have the same rules for you and for the **alien** living among you;
15:15 to come. You and the **alien** shall be the same before the LORD:
15:16 will apply both to you and to the **alien** living among you.' "
15:26 and the **aliens** living among them will be forgiven,
15:29 whether he is a native-born Israelite or an **alien**.
15:30 whether native-born or **alien**, blasphemes the LORD,
19:10 both for the Israelites and for the **aliens** living among them.
35:15 for Israelites, **aliens** and any other people living among them,
Dt 1:16 is between brother Israelites or between one of them and an **alien**.
5:14 or any of your animals, nor the **alien** within your gates,
10:18 the cause of the fatherless and the widow, and loves the **alien**,
10:19 you are to love those who are **aliens**, for you yourselves were
10:19 love those who are aliens, for you yourselves were **aliens** in Egypt.
14:21 You may give it to an **alien** living in any of your towns, and he
14:29 the **aliens**, the fatherless and the widows who live in your towns
16:11 and the **aliens**, the fatherless and the widows living among you.
16:14 the **aliens**, the fatherless and the widows who live in your towns.
23: 7 [23:8] an Egyptian, because you lived as an **alien** in his country.
24:14 he is a brother Israelite or an **alien** living in one of your towns.
24:17 Do not deprive the **alien** or the fatherless of justice, or take the
24:19 Leave it for the **alien**, the fatherless and the widow, so that the
24:20 Leave what remains for the **alien**, the fatherless and the widow.
24:21 Leave what remains for the **alien**, the fatherless and the widow.
26:11 the **aliens** among you shall rejoice in all the good things the
26:12 shall give it to the Levite, the **alien**, the fatherless and the widow,
26:13 have given it to the Levite, the **alien**, the fatherless and the widow,
27:19 "Cursed is the man who withholds justice from the **alien**,
28:43 The **alien** who lives among you will rise above you higher
29:11 [29:10] the **aliens** living in your camps who chop your wood
31:12 women and children, and the **aliens** living in your towns—
Jos 8:33 All Israel, **aliens** and citizens alike, with their elders, officials
8:35 the women and children, and the **aliens** who lived among them.
20: 9 or any **alien** living among them who killed someone accidentally
2Sa 1:13 you from?" "I am the son of an **alien**, an Amalekite," he answered.
1Ch 22: 2 So David gave orders to assemble the **aliens** living in Israel,
29:15 We are **aliens** and strangers in your sight, as were all our
2Ch 2:17 [2:16] Solomon took a census of all the **aliens** who were in Israel,
30:25 including the **aliens** who had come from Israel and those who lived
Job 31:32 no **stranger** had to spend the night in the street, for my door was
Ps 39:12 [39:13] For I dwell with you as an **alien**, a stranger, as all my
94: 6 They slay the widow and the **alien**; they murder the fatherless.
119:19 I am a **stranger** on earth; do not hide your commands from me.
146: 9 The LORD watches over the **alien** and sustains the fatherless
Isa 5:17 <u>lambs</u> [BHS ***strangers***; NIV 1531] will feed among the ruins of the
14: 1 own land. **Aliens** will join them and unite with the house of Jacob.
Jer 7: 6 if you do not oppress the **alien**, the fatherless or the widow
14: 8 Savior in times of distress, why are you like a **stranger** in the land,
22: 3 Do no wrong or violence to the **alien**, the fatherless or the widow,
Eze 14: 7 any Israelite or any **alien** living in Israel separates himself from me
22: 7 in you they have oppressed the **alien** and mistreated the fatherless
22:29 they oppress the poor and needy and mistreat the **alien**, denying
47:22 for the **aliens** who have settled among you and who have children.
47:23 In whatever tribe the **alien** settles, there you are to give him his
Zec 7:10 Do not oppress the widow or the fatherless, the **alien** or the poor.
Mal 3: 5 the widows and the fatherless, and deprive **aliens** of justice,

1732 גִּיר gir, n.[m.]. [1] [→ Ar 10142]

chalk [1]

Isa 27: 9 When he makes all the altar stones to be like **chalk** stones crushed

1733 גֵּרָא gērā', n.pr.m. [9]

Gera [9]

Ge 46:21 Bela, Beker, Ashbel, **Gera**, Naaman, Ehi, Rosh, Muppim,
Jdg 3:15 a left-handed man, the son of **Gera** the Benjamite.
2Sa 16: 5 His name was Shimei son of **Gera**, and he cursed as he came out.

2Sa 19: 16 [19:17] Shimei son of **Gera**, the Benjamite from Bahurim,
19: 18 [19:19] When Shimei son of **Gera** crossed the Jordan, he fell
1Ki 2: 8 "And remember, you have with you Shimei son of **Gera**,
1Ch 8: 3 The sons of Bela were: Addar, **Gera**, Abihud,
8: 5 **Gera**, Shephuphan and Huram.
8: 7 Naaman, Ahijah, and **Gera**, who deported them and who was the

1734 גָּרָב *gārāb*, n.[m.]. [3] [→ 1735, 1736]

festering [2], festering sores [1]

Lev 21: 20 or who has **festering** or running sores or damaged testicles.
22: 22 the maimed, or anything with warts or **festering** or running sores.
Dt 28: 27 the boils of Egypt and with tumors, **festering sores** and the itch,

1735 גָּרֵב¹ *gārēb¹*, n.pr.m. [2] [√ 1734]

Gareb [2]

2Sa 23: 38 Ira the Ithrite, **Gareb** the Ithrite,
1Ch 11: 40 Ira the Ithrite, **Gareb** the Ithrite,

1736 גָּרֵב² *gārēb²*, n.pr.loc. [1] [√ 1734]

Gareb [1]

Jer 31: 39 measuring line will stretch from there straight to the hill of **Gareb**

1737 גַּרְגַּר *gargar*, n.m. [1]

olives [1]

Isa 17: 6 leaving two or three **olives** on the topmost branches, four or five on

1738 גַּרְגְּרוֹת *gargᵉrôt*, n.f.pl. [4]

neck [4]

Pr 1: 9 be a garland to grace your head and a chain to adorn your **neck**.
3: 3 bind them around your **neck**, write them on the tablet of your
3: 22 they will be life for you, an ornament to grace your **neck**.
6: 21 Bind them upon your heart forever; fasten them around your **neck**.

1739 גִּרְגָּשִׁי *girgāšî*, a.g. [7]

Girgashites [7]

Ge 10: 16 Jebusites, Amorites, **Girgashites**,
15: 21 Amorites, Canaanites, **Girgashites** and Jebusites."
Dt 7: 1 **Girgashites**, Amorites, Canaanites, Perizzites, Hivites
Jos 3: 10 Hittites, Hivites, Perizzites, **Girgashites**, Amorites and Jebusites.
24: 11 Perizzites, Canaanites, Hittites, **Girgashites**, Hivites and Jebusites,
1Ch 1: 14 Jebusites, Amorites, **Girgashites**,
Ne 9: 8 Amorites, Perizzites, Jebusites and **Girgashites**.

1740 גָּרַד *gārad*, v. [1]

scraped himself [1]

Job 2: 8 [F] and **scraped himself** with it as he sat among the ashes.

1741 גָּרָה *gārâ*, v. [14] [→ 9327; cf. 1592]

stirs up [3], ask [2], provoke to war [2], carry the battle [+2256+8740] [1], engage [1], opposed [1], prepare for war [1], provoke [1], resist [1], wage war [+2021+4200+4878] [1]

Dt 2: 5 [F] *Do* not **provoke** them **to war**, for I will not give you any of
2: 9 [F] to me, "Do not harass the Moabites or **provoke** them *to* war,
2: 19 [F] the Ammonites, do not harass them or **provoke** them **to war**,
2: 24 [F] Begin to take possession of it and **engage** him *in* battle.
2Ki 14: 10 [F] Why **ask** for trouble and cause your own downfall and that of
2Ch 25: 19 [F] Why **ask** for trouble and cause your own downfall and that of
Pr 15: 18 [D] A hot-tempered man **stirs up** dissension, but a patient man
28: 4 [F] praise the wicked, but those who keep the law **resist** them.
28: 25 [D] A greedy man **stirs up** dissension, but he who trusts in the
29: 22 [D] An angry man **stirs up** dissension, and a hot-tempered one
Jer 50: 24 [F] were found and captured because *you* **opposed** the LORD.
Da 11: 10 [F] His sons *will* **prepare for war** and assemble a great army,
11: 10 [F] and **carry the battle** [+2256+8740] as far as his fortress.
11: 25 [F] The king of the South *will* **wage war** [+2021+4200+4878] with

1742 גֵּרָה¹ *gērâ¹*, n.f. [11] [√ 1760]

cud [11]

Lev 11: 3 that has a split hoof completely divided and that chews the **cud**.
11: 4 " 'There are some that only chew the **cud** or only have a split hoof,
11: 4 The camel, though it chews the **cud**, does not have a split hoof;
11: 5 The coney, though it chews the **cud**, does not have a split hoof;
11: 6 The rabbit, though it chews the **cud**, does not have a split hoof;
11: 7 it has a split hoof completely divided, does not chew the **cud**;
11: 26 or that does not chew the **cud** is unclean for you;
Dt 14: 6 animal that has a split hoof divided in two and that chews the **cud**.
14: 7 of those that chew the **cud** or that have a split hoof completely
14: 7 Although they chew the **cud**, they do not have a split hoof;
14: 8 also unclean; although it has a split hoof, it does not chew the **cud**.

1743 גֵּרָה² *gērâ²*, n.f. [5]

gerahs [5]

Ex 30: 13 according to the sanctuary shekel, which weighs twenty **gerahs**.
Lev 27: 25 set according to the sanctuary shekel, twenty **gerahs** to the shekel.
Nu 3: 47 according to the sanctuary shekel, which weighs twenty **gerahs**.
18: 16 according to the sanctuary shekel, which weighs twenty **gerahs**.
Eze 45: 12 The shekel is to consist of twenty **gerahs**. Twenty shekels plus

1744 גָּרוֹן *gārôn*, n.m. [8] [√ 1760]

throat [3], mouths [1], neck [1], necks [1], shout aloud [+928+7924] [1], throats [1]

Ps 5: 9 [5:10] Their **throat** is an open grave; with their tongue they speak
69: 3 [69:4] I am worn out calling for help; my **throat** is parched.
115: 7 but they cannot walk; nor can they utter a sound with their **throats**.
149: 6 May the praise of God be in their **mouths** and a double-edged
Isa 3: 16 walking along with outstretched **necks**, flirting with their eyes,
58: 1 "**Shout** it **aloud** [+928+7924], do not hold back. Raise your voice
Jer 2: 25 Do not run until your feet are bare and your **throat** is dry.
Eze 16: 11 I put bracelets on your arms and a necklace around your **neck**,

1745 גֵּרוּת כִּמְהָם *gērût kimhām*, n.f. [1] [√ 1731 + 4016]

Geruth Kimham [1]

Jer 41: 17 stopping at **Geruth Kimham** near Bethlehem on their way to

1746 גָּרַז *gāraz*, v. [1] [→ 1749; cf. 1615]

am cut off [1]

Ps 31: 22 [31:23] [C] In my alarm I said, "*I* **am cut off** from your sight!"

1747 גִּרְזִי *girzî*, a.g. [1] [cf. 1621]

Girzites [1]

1Sa 27: 8 raided the Geshurites, the **Girzites** [Q 1621] and the Amalekites.

1748 גְּרִזִים *gᵉrizîm*, n.pr.loc. [4]

Gerizim [4]

Dt 11: 29 you are to proclaim on Mount **Gerizim** the blessings, and on
27: 12 these tribes shall stand on Mount **Gerizim** to bless the people:
Jos 8: 33 Half of the people stood in front of Mount **Gerizim** and half of
Jdg 9: 7 he climbed up on the top of Mount **Gerizim** and shouted to them,

1749 גַּרְזֶן *garzen*, n.m. [4] [√ 1746]

ax [3], chisel [1]

Dt 19: 5 and as he swings his **ax** to fell a tree, the head may fly off
20: 19 do not destroy its trees by putting an **ax** to them, because you can
1Ki 6: 7 **chisel** or any other iron tool was heard at the temple site while it
Isa 10: 15 Does the **ax** raise itself above him who swings it, or the saw boast

1750 גָּרַם¹ *gāram¹*, v. [1]

leave [1]

Zep 3: 3 [A] are evening wolves, *who* **leave** nothing for the morning.

1751 גָּרַם² *gāram²*, v.den. [2] [√ 1752]

break in pieces [1], dash [1]

Nu 24: 8 [D] They devour hostile nations and **break** their bones **in pieces**;
Eze 23: 34 [D] drain it dry; *you will* **dash** it *to* pieces and tear your breasts.

1752 גֶּרֶם *gerem*, n.[m.]. [5] [→ 1751, 1753?; Ar 10150]

bare [1], bone [1], bones [1], limbs [1], rawboned [1]

Ge 49: 14 "Issachar is a **rawboned** donkey lying down between two
2Ki 9: 13 and took their cloaks and spread them under him on the **bare** steps.
Job 40: 18 His bones are tubes of bronze, his **limbs** like rods of iron.
Pr 17: 22 heart is good medicine, but a crushed spirit dries up the **bones**.
25: 15 a ruler can be persuaded, and a gentle tongue can break a **bone**.

1753 גַּרְמִי *garmî*, a.g. [1] [√ 1752?]

Garmite [1]

1Ch 4: 19 the father of Keilah the **Garmite**, and Eshtemoa the Maacathite.

1754 גָּרֹל *gārōl*, a. [0]

Pr 19: 19 [A **hot-tempered man** [K; see Q 1524] must pay the penalty;]

1755 גֹּרֶן gōren, n.m. [36]
threshing floor [32], threshing floors [3], threshing floor [+1841] [1]

Ge 50:10 When they reached the **threshing floor** *of* Atad, near the Jordan,
50:11 who lived there saw the mourning at the **threshing floor** *of* Atad,
Nu 15:20 ground meal and present it as an offering from the **threshing floor**.
18:27 offering will be reckoned to you as grain from the **threshing floor**
18:30 it will be reckoned to you as the product of the **threshing floor**
Dt 15:14 from your flock, your **threshing floor** and your winepress.
16:13 days after you have gathered the produce of your **threshing floor**
Jdg 6:37 look, I will place a wool fleece on the **threshing floor**. If there is
Ru 3:2 Tonight he will be winnowing barley on the **threshing floor**.
3:3 go down to the **threshing floor**, but don't let him know you are
3:6 So she went down to the **threshing floor** and did everything her
3:14 "Don't let it be known that a woman came to the **threshing floor**."
1Sa 23:1 are fighting against Keilah and are looting the **threshing floors**,"
2Sa 6:6 When they came to the **threshing floor** *of* Nacon, Uzzah reached
24:16 LORD was then at the **threshing floor** *of* Araunah the Jebusite.
24:18 build an altar to the LORD on the **threshing floor** *of* Araunah the
24:21 "To buy your **threshing floor**," David answered, "so I can build an
24:24 So David bought the **threshing floor** and the oxen and paid fifty
1Ki 22:10 at the **threshing floor** *by* the entrance of the gate of Samaria,
2Ki 6:27 get help for you? From the **threshing floor**? From the winepress?"
1Ch 13:9 When they came to the **threshing floor** *of* Kidon, Uzzah reached
21:15 then standing at the **threshing floor** *of* Araunah the Jebusite.
21:18 build an altar to the LORD on the **threshing floor** *of* Araunah the
21:21 he left the **threshing floor** and bowed down before David with his
21:22 "Let me have the site of your **threshing floor** so I can build an
21:28 had answered him on the **threshing floor** *of* Araunah the Jebusite,
2Ch 3:1 It was on the **threshing floor** *of* Araunah the Jebusite, the place
18:9 at the **threshing floor** *by* the entrance to the gate of Samaria,
Job 39:12 him to bring in your grain and gather it to your **threshing floor**?
Isa 21:10 O my people, crushed on the **threshing floor**, I tell you what I
Jer 51:33 "The Daughter of Babylon is like a **threshing floor** at the time it is
Hos 9:1 love the wages of a prostitute at every **threshing** [+1841] **floor**.
9:2 **Threshing floors** and winepresses will not feed the people;
13:3 dew that disappears, like chaff swirling from a **threshing floor**,
Joel 2:24 The **threshing floors** will be filled with grain; the vats will
Mic 4:12 his plan, he who gathers them like sheaves to the **threshing floor**.

1756 גָּרַס gāras, v. [2]
broken [1], consumed [1]

Ps 119:20 [A] My soul *is* **consumed** with longing for your laws at all times.
La 3:16 [G] *He has* **broken** my teeth with gravel; he has trampled me in

1757 גָּרַע gāraʿ[1], v. [21] [→ 1758, 4492]
be reduced [2], be taken [2], cut off [2], be kept from [+1194+4200] [1], be taken away [1], deprive [1], disappear [1], hinder [1], limit [1], omit [1], reduce the number [1], reduce [1], reduced [1], subtract [1], take away [1], take [1], taken [1], withdraw favor [1]

Ex 5:8 [A] the same number of bricks as before; don't **reduce** the quota.
5:11 [C] you can find it, but your work *will* not **be reduced** at all.' "
5:19 [A] "*You are* not *to* **reduce the number** *of* bricks required of
21:10 [A] *he must* not **deprive** the first one *of* her food, clothing
Lev 27:18 [C] the next Year of Jubilee, and its set value *will* **be reduced**.
Nu 9:7 [C] why *should we* **be kept** [+1194+4200] **from** presenting the
27:4 [C] Why *should* our father's name **disappear** from his clan
36:3 [C] their inheritance *will* **be taken** from our ancestral inheritance
36:3 [C] so part of the inheritance allotted to us *will* **be taken away**.
36:4 [C] their property *will* **be taken** from the tribal inheritance of our
Dt 4:2 [A] not add to what I command you and *do* not **subtract** from it,
12:32 [13:1] [A] command you; do not add to it or **take away** from it.
Job 15:4 [A] But you even undermine piety and **hinder** devotion to God.
15:8 [A] in on God's council? *Do you* **limit** wisdom to yourself?
36:7 [A] *He does* not **take** his eyes off the righteous; he enthrones
Ecc 3:14 [A] nothing can be added to it and nothing **taken** from it.
Isa 15:2 [B] and Medeba. Every head is shaved and every beard **cut off**.
Jer 26:2 [A] Tell them everything I command you; *do* not **omit** a word.
48:37 [B] Every head is shaved and every beard **cut off**; every hand is
Eze 5:11 [A] and detestable practices, *I* myself *will* **withdraw** *my* **favor**;
16:27 [A] out my hand against you and **reduced** your territory;

1758 גָּרַע gāraʿ[2], v. [1] [√ 1757]
draws up [1]

Job 36:27 [D] "*He* **draws up** the drops of water, which distill as rain to the

1759 גָּרַף gārap, v. [1] [→ 114, 4493]
swept away [1]

Jdg 5:21 [A] The river Kishon **swept** them **away**, the age-old river,

1760 גָּרַר gārar, v. [5] [→ 1742, 1744, 4490; cf. 5599]
catches [1], chew [1], drag away [1], driving [1], trimmed [1]

Lev 11:7 [A] it has a split hoof completely divided, *does* not **chew** the cud;
1Ki 7:9 [E] and **trimmed** with a saw on their inner and outer faces.
Pr 21:7 [A] The violence of the wicked *will* **drag** them **away**, for they
Jer 30:23 [F] a **driving** wind swirling down on the heads of the wicked.
Hab 1:15 [A] *he* **catches** them in his net, he gathers them up in his dragnet;

1761 גְּרָר gᵉrār, n.pr.loc. [10]
Gerar [10]

Ge 10:19 the borders of Canaan reached from Sidon toward **Gerar** as far as
20:1 lived between Kadesh and Shur. For a while he stayed in **Gerar**,
20:2 Then Abimelech king of **Gerar** sent for Sarah and took her.
26:1 and Isaac went to Abimelech king of the Philistines in **Gerar**.
26:6 So Isaac stayed in **Gerar**.
26:17 from there and encamped in the Valley of **Gerar** and settled there.
26:20 But the herdsmen of **Gerar** quarreled with Isaac's herdsmen
26:26 Meanwhile, Abimelech had come to him from **Gerar**,
2Ch 14:13 [14:12] Asa and his army pursued them as far as **Gerar**. Such a
14:14 [14:13] They destroyed all the villages around **Gerar**,

1762 גֶּרֶשׂ gereś, n.[m.] [2]
crushed grain [1], crushed [1]

Lev 2:14 the LORD, offer **crushed** heads of new grain roasted in the fire.
2:16 The priest shall burn the memorial portion of the **crushed grain**

1763 גָּרַשׁ gāraš[1], v. [44 / 46] [→ 1766, 4494, 4495; cf. 1764]
drive out [8], drive [7], divorced [5], drove out [5], drove away [3], drive out [+906+1763+4946] [2], driven [2], driving out [2], drove [2], be driven [1], been banished [1], been driven out [1], cast aside [1], drive away [1], driving [1], emptied [1], get rid of [1], removed [1], were banished [1]

Ge 3:24 [D] After *he* **drove** the man **out**, he placed on the east side of the
4:14 [D] Today *you are* **driving** me from the land, and I will be
21:10 [D] said to Abraham, "**Get rid of** that slave woman and her son,
Ex 2:17 [D] Some shepherds came along and **drove** them **away**,
6:1 [D] because of my mighty hand *he will* **drive** them **out** of his
10:11 [D] and Aaron *were* **driven** out of Pharaoh's presence.
11:1 [D] *he will* **drive** [+906+1763+4946] you **out** completely.
11:1 [D] *he will* **drive** you **out** [+906+1763+4946] completely.
12:39 [E] without yeast because *they had* **been driven out** of Egypt
23:28 [D] the hornet ahead of you *to* **drive** the Hivites, Canaanites and
23:29 [D] *I will* not **drive** them out in a single year, because the land
23:30 [D] Little by little *I will* **drive** them out before you, until you
23:31 [D] who live in the land and *you will* **drive** them out before you.
33:2 [D] I will send an angel before you and **drive out** the Canaanites,
34:11 [A] I *will* **drive out** before you the Amorites, Canaanites,
Lev 21:7 [B] defiled by prostitution or **divorced** from their husbands,
21:14 [B] He must not marry a widow, a **divorced** *woman*, or a woman
22:13 [B] But if a priest's daughter becomes a widow or *is* **divorced**,
Nu 22:6 [D] be able to defeat them and **drive** them **out** of the country.
22:11 [D] then I will be able to fight them and **drive** them **away**.' "
30:9 [30:10] [B] or **divorced** *woman* will be binding on her.
Dt 33:27 [D] *He will* **drive out** your enemy before you, saying,
Jos 24:12 [D] the hornet ahead of you, *which* **drove** them **out** before you—
24:18 [D] the LORD **drove out** before us all the nations, including the
Jdg 2:3 [D] therefore I tell you that *I will* not **drive** them **out** before you;
6:9 [D] *I* **drove** them from before you and gave you their land.
9:41 [D] and Zebul **drove** Gaal and his brothers out of Shechem.
11:2 [D] and when they were grown up, *they* **drove** Jephthah **away**.
11:7 [D] "Didn't you hate me and **drive** me from my father's house?
1Sa 26:19 [D] *They have* now **driven** me from my share in the LORD's
2Sa 7:23 [D] and awesome wonders by **driving** [BHS 824] **out** nations
1Ki 2:27 [D] So Solomon **removed** Abiathar from the priesthood of the
1Ch 17:21 [D] awesome wonders by **driving out** nations from before your
2Ch 20:11 [D] See how they are repaying us by coming to **drive** us **out** of
Job 30:5 [E] *They* **were banished** from their fellow men, shouted at as if
Ps 34:T [34:1] [D] before Abimelech, *who* **drove** him **away**, and he left.
78:55 [D] *He* **drove out** nations before them and allotted their lands to
80:8 [80:9] [D] of Egypt; *you* **drove out** the nations and planted it.
109:10 [E] *may they* **be driven** [BHS 2011] from their ruined homes.
Pr 22:10 [D] **Drive out** the mocker, and out goes strife; quarrels
Eze 31:11 [D] him to deal with according to its wickedness. *I* **cast it aside**,
44:22 [B] They must not marry widows or **divorced** *women*; they may
Hos 9:15 [D] of their sinful deeds, *I will* **drive** them out of my house.
Jnh 2:4 [2:5] [C] I said, '*I have* **been banished** from your sight; yet I
Mic 2:9 [D] *You* **drive** the women of my people from their pleasant
Zep 2:4 [D] At midday Ashdod *will be* **emptied** and Ekron uprooted.

1764 ²גָּרַשׁ **gāraš²**, v. [3] [√ 1765; cf. 1763]
be stirred up [1], cast up [1], tossing [1]
Isa 57:20 [C] But the wicked are like the **tossing** sea, which cannot rest,
57:20 [A] which cannot rest, whose waves **cast up** mire and mud.
Am 8: 8 [C] *it will* **be stirred up** and then sink like the river of Egypt.

1765 גֶּרֶשׁ **gereš**, n.[m.]. [1] [√ 1764]
yield [1]
Dt 33:14 with the best the sun brings forth and the finest the moon can **yield**;

1766 גְּרֻשָׁה **g^eruša**, n.f. [1] [√ 1763]
dispossessing [1]
Eze 45: 9 Stop **dispossessing** my people, declares the Sovereign LORD.

1767 גֵּרְשׁוֹן **gēršôn**, n.pr.m. [17] [→ 1768, 1769]
Gershon [9], Gershonites [+1201] [6], Gershonite [+1201] [2]
Ge 46:11 The sons of Levi: **Gershon**, Kohath and Merari.
Ex 6:16 their records: **Gershon**, Kohath and Merari. Levi lived 137 years.
6:17 The sons of **Gershon**, by clans, were Libni and Shimei.
Nu 3:17 were the names of the sons of Levi: **Gershon**, Kohath and Merari.
3:18 These were the names of the **Gershonite** [+1201] clans: Libni
3:21 To **Gershon** belonged the clans of the Libnites and Shimeites;
3:25 At the Tent of Meeting the **Gershonites** [+1201] were responsible
4:22 "Take a census also of the **Gershonites** [+1201] by their families
4:38 The **Gershonites** [+1201] were counted by their clans
4:41 This was the total of those in the **Gershonite** [+1201] clans who
7: 7 He gave two carts and four oxen to the **Gershonites** [+1201],
10:17 and the **Gershonites** [+1201] and Merarites, who carried it,
26:57 through **Gershon**, the Gershonite clan; through Kohath,
Jos 21: 6 The descendants of **Gershon** were allotted thirteen towns from the
21:27 The Levite clans of the **Gershonites** [+1201] were given:
1Ch 6: 1 [5:27] The sons of Levi: **Gershon**, Kohath and Merari.
23: 6 corresponding to the sons of Levi: **Gershon**, Kohath and Merari.

1768 גֵּרְשֹׁם **gēršōm**, n.pr.m. [14] [√ 1767]
Gershom [7], Gershon [6], Gershonites [+1201] [1]
Ex 2:22 gave birth to a son, and Moses named him **Gershom**, saying,
18: 3 One son was named **Gershom**, for Moses said, "I have become an
Jdg 18:30 the idols, and Jonathan son of **Gershom**, the son of Moses,
1Ch 6:16 [6:1] The sons of Levi: **Gershon**, Kohath and Merari.
6:17 [6:2] These are the names of the sons of **Gershon**: Libni
6:20 [6:5] Of **Gershon**: Libni his son, Jehath his son, Zimmah his son,
6:43 [6:28] the son of Jahath, the son of **Gershon**, the son of Levi;
6:62 [6:47] The descendants of **Gershon**, clan by clan, were allotted
6:71 [6:56] The **Gershonites** [+1201] received the following:
15: 7 from the descendants of **Gershon**, Joel the leader and 130
23:15 The sons of Moses: **Gershom** and Eliezer.
23:16 The descendants of **Gershom**: Shubael was the first.
26:24 Shubael, a descendant of **Gershom** son of Moses, was the officer
Ezr 8: 2 of the descendants of Phinehas, **Gershom**; of the descendants of

1769 גֵּרְשֻׁנִּי **gēršunnî**, a.g. [13] [√ 1767]
Gershonite [7], Gershonites [3], Gershonite [+1201] [1], Gershonites [+1201] [1], their^s [+1201+2021] [1]
Nu 3:21 of the Libnites and Shimeites; these were the **Gershonite** clans.
3:23 The **Gershonite** clans were to camp on the west,
3:24 The leader of the families of the **Gershonites** was Eliasaph son of
4:24 "This is the service of the **Gershonite** clans as they work and carry
4:27 All **their**^s [+1201+2021] service, whether carrying or doing other
4:28 This is the service of the **Gershonite** [+1201] clans at the Tent of
26:57 through Gershon, the **Gershonite** clan; through Kohath,
Jos 21:33 All the towns of the **Gershonite** clans were thirteen, together with
1Ch 23: 7 Belonging to the **Gershonites**: Ladan and Shimei.
26:21 who were **Gershonites** [+1201] through Ladan and who were
26:21 who were heads of families belonging to Ladan the **Gershonite**,
29: 8 the temple of the LORD in the custody of Jehiel the **Gershonite**.
2Ch 29:12 from the **Gershonites**, Joah son of Zimmah and Eden son of Joah;

1770 גְּשׁוּר **g^ešûr**, n.pr.m. [9] [→ 1771]
Geshur [8], they^s [+2256+5083] [1]
Jos 13:13 so **they**^s [+2256+5083] continue to live among the Israelites to this
2Sa 3: 3 Absalom the son of Maacah daughter of Talmai king of **Geshur**;
13:37 and went to Talmai son of Ammihud, the king of **Geshur**.
13:38 After Absalom fled and went to **Geshur**, he stayed there three
14:23 Joab went to **Geshur** and brought Absalom back to Jerusalem.
14:32 I can send you to the king to ask, "Why have I come from **Geshur**?
15: 8 While your servant was living at **Geshur** in Aram, I made this
1Ch 2:23 (But **Geshur** and Aram captured Havvoth Jair, as well as Kenath
3: 2 Absalom the son of Maacah daughter of Talmai king of **Geshur**;

1771 גְּשׁוּרִי **g^ešûrî**, a.g. [6] [√ 1770]
Geshurites [3], people of Geshur [3]
Dt 3:14 the whole region of Argob as far as the border of the **Geshurites**
Jos 12: 5 all of Bashan to the border of the **people of Geshur** and Maacah,
13: 2 land that remains: all the regions of the Philistines and **Geshurites**:
13:11 the territory of the **people of Geshur** and Maacah, all of Mount
13:13 the Israelites did not drive out the **people of Geshur** and Maacah,
1Sa 27: 8 Now David and his men went up and raided the **Geshurites**,

1772 גָּשַׁם **gāšam**, v.den. [2] [→ 1773, 1774, 1775, 1776]
bring rain [1], showers [1]
Jer 14:22 [G] *Do* any of the worthless idols of the nations **bring rain**? Do
Eze 22:24 [E] a land that has had no rain or **showers** in the day of wrath.'

1773 ¹גֶּשֶׁם **gešem¹**, n.m. [35] [→ 1774, 1775; cf. 1772]
rain [24], showers [3], rains [2], rainy [2], abundant showers [1], downpour [+4764] [1], shower [1], winter rains [1]
Ge 7:12 And **rain** fell on the earth forty days and forty nights.
8: 2 had been closed, and the **rain** had stopped falling from the sky.
Lev 26: 4 I will send you **rain** in its season, and the ground will yield its
1Ki 17: 7 later the brook dried up because there had been no **rain** in the land.
17:14 the jug of oil will not run dry until the day the LORD gives **rain**
18:41 "Go, eat and drink, for there is the sound of a heavy **rain**."
18:44 'Hitch up your chariot and go down before the **rain** stops you.' "
18:45 the wind rose, a heavy **rain** came on and Ahab rode off to Jezreel.
2Ki 3:17 You will see neither wind nor **rain**, yet this valley will be filled
Ezr 10: 9 greatly distressed by the occasion and because of the **rain**.
10:13 But there are many people here and it is the **rainy** season;
Job 37: 6 He says to the snow, 'Fall on the earth,' and to the rain **shower**,
37: 6 and to the rain shower, 'Be a mighty **downpour** [+4764].'
Ps 68: 9 [68:10] You gave abundant **showers**, O God; you refreshed your
105:32 He turned their **rain** into hail, with lightning throughout their land;
Pr 25:14 wind without **rain** is a man who boasts of gifts he does not give.
25:23 As a north wind brings **rain**, so a sly tongue brings angry looks.
Ecc 11: 3 If clouds are full of water, they pour **rain** upon the earth. Whether
12: 2 and the stars grow dark, and the clouds return after the **rain**;
SS 2:11 See! The winter is past; the **rains** are over and gone.
Isa 44:14 the trees of the forest, or planted a pine, and the **rain** made it grow.
55:10 As the **rain** and the snow come down from heaven, and do not
Jer 5:24 LORD our God, who gives autumn and spring **rains** in season,
14: 4 The ground is cracked because there is no **rain** in the land;
Eze 1:28 Like the appearance of a rainbow in the clouds on a **rainy** day,
13:11 **Rain** will come in torrents, and I will send hailstones hurtling
13:13 anger hailstones and torrents of **rain** will fall with destructive fury.
34:26 I will send down **showers** in season; there will be showers of
34:26 send down showers in season; there will be **showers** *of* blessing.
38:22 I will pour down torrents of **rain**, hailstones and burning sulfur on
Hos 6: 3 he will come to us like the **winter rains**, like the spring rains that
Joel 2:23 He sends you **abundant showers**, both autumn and spring rains,
Am 4: 7 "I also withheld **rain** from you when the harvest was still three
Zec 10: 1 He gives showers of **rain** to men, and plants of the field to
14:17 to worship the King, the LORD Almighty, they will have no **rain**.

1774 ²גֶּשֶׁם **gešem²**, n.pr.m. [3] [→ 1776; cf. 1772, 1773]
Geshem [3]
Ne 2:19 the Ammonite official and **Geshem** the Arab heard about it,
6: 1 **Geshem** the Arab and the rest of our enemies that I had rebuilt the
6: 2 Sanballat and **Geshem** sent me this message: "Come, let us meet

1775 גֹּשֶׁם **gōšem**, n.[m.]. Not used in NIV/BHS [√ 1773; cf. 1772]

1776 גַּשְׁמוּ **gašmû**, n.pr.m. [1] [√ 1774; cf. 1772]
Geshem [1]
Ne 6: 6 **Geshem** says it is true—that you and the Jews are plotting to

1777 גֹּשֶׁן **gōšen**, n.pr.loc. [15]
Goshen [11], Goshen [+824] [4]
Ge 45:10 You shall live in the region of **Goshen** and be near me—you,
46:28 sent Judah ahead of him to Joseph to get directions to **Goshen**.
46:28 directions to Goshen. When they arrived in the region of **Goshen**,
46:29 chariot made ready and went to **Goshen** to meet his father Israel.
46:34 Then you will be allowed to settle in the region of **Goshen**,
47: 1 come from the land of Canaan and are now in **Goshen** [+824]."
47: 4 So now, please let your servants settle in **Goshen** [+824]."
47: 6 in the best part of the land. Let them live in **Goshen** [+824].
47:27 Now the Israelites settled in Egypt in the region of **Goshen**.
50: 8 and their flocks and herds were left in **Goshen** [+824].
Ex 8:22 [8:18] on that day I will deal differently with the land of **Goshen**,

Ex 9:26 The only place it did not hail was the land of **Goshen**,
Jos 10:41 Barnea to Gaza and from the whole region of **Goshen** to Gibeon.
11:16 the hill country, all the Negev, the whole region of **Goshen**,
15:51 **Goshen**, Holon and Giloh—eleven towns and their villages.

1778 גִּשְׁפָּא *gišpā'*, n.pr.m. [1]

Gishpa [1]

Ne 11:21 on the hill of Ophel, and Ziha and **Gishpa** were in charge of them.

1779 גָּשַׁשׁ *gāšaš*, v. [2]

feeling way [1], grope along [1]

Isa 59:10 [D] Like the blind *we* **grope along** the wall, feeling our way like
59:10 [D] grope along the wall, **feeling** *our* **way** like men without eyes.

1780 ¹גַּת *gat¹*, n.f. [5] [→ 1781, 1782, 1783, 1784, 1785, 1786, 1787]

winepress [4], winepresses [1]

Jdg 6:11 where his son Gideon was threshing wheat in a **winepress** to keep
Ne 13:15 In those days I saw men in Judah treading **winepresses** on the
Isa 63:2 are your garments red, like those of one treading the **winepress**?
La 1:15 In his **winepress** the Lord has trampled the Virgin Daughter of
Joel 3:13 [4:13] the grapes, for the **winepress** is full and the vats overflow—

1781 ²גַּת *gat²*, n.pr.loc. [33 / 34] [→ 1785, 1787; cf. 1780]

Gath [34]

Jos 11:22 Israelite territory; only in Gaza, **Gath** and Ashdod did any survive.
1Sa 5:8 "Have the ark of the god of Israel moved to **Gath**."
6:17 one each for Ashdod, Gaza, Ashkelon, **Gath** and Ekron.
7:14 The towns from Ekron to **Gath** that the Philistines had captured
17:4 A champion named Goliath, who was from **Gath**, came out of the
17:23 Goliath, the Philistine champion from **Gath**, stepped out from his
17:52 and pursued the Philistines to the entrance of **Gath** [BHS 1628]
17:52 Their dead were strewn along the Shaaraim road to **Gath**
21:10 [21:11] David fled from Saul and went to Achish king of **Gath**.
21:12 [21:13] and was very much afraid of Achish king of **Gath**.
27:2 with him left and went over to Achish son of Maoch king of **Gath**.
27:3 David and his men settled in **Gath** with Achish. Each man had his
27:4 When Saul was told that David had fled to **Gath**, he no longer
27:11 He did not leave a man or woman alive to be brought to **Gath**,
2Sa 1:20 "Tell it not in **Gath**, proclaim it not in the streets of Ashkelon,
15:18 all the six hundred Gittites who had accompanied him from **Gath**
21:20 In still another battle, which took place at **Gath**, there was a huge
21:22 These four were descendants of Rapha in **Gath**, and they fell at the
1Ki 2:39 king of **Gath**, and Shimei was told, "Your slaves are in Gath."
2:39 king of Gath, and Shimei was told, "Your slaves are in **Gath**."
2:40 his donkey and went to Achish at **Gath** in search of his slaves.
2:40 So Shimei went away and brought the slaves back from **Gath**.
2:41 Solomon was told that Shimei had gone from Jerusalem to **Gath**
2Ki 12:17 [12:18] king of Aram went up and attacked **Gath** and captured it.
1Ch 7:21 Ezer and Elead were killed by the native-born men of **Gath**,
8:13 those living in Aijalon and who drove out the inhabitants of **Gath**.
18:1 he took **Gath** and its surrounding villages from the control of the
20:6 In still another battle, which took place at **Gath**, there was a huge
20:8 These were descendants of Rapha in **Gath**, and they fell at the
2Ch 11:8 **Gath**, Mareshah, Ziph,
26:6 to war against the Philistines and broke down the walls of **Gath**,
Ps 56:T [56:1] A *miktam*. When the Philistines had seized him in **Gath**.
Am 6:2 from there to great Hamath, and then go down to **Gath** *in* Philistia.
Mic 1:10 Tell it not in **Gath**; weep not at all. In Beth Ophrah roll in the dust.

1782 ³גַּת *gat³*, n.pr.loc. Not used in NIV/BHS [√ 1780]

1783 גַּת הַחֵפֶר *gat haḥēper*, גַּת חֵפֶר *gat ḥēper*, n.pr.loc. [2] [√ 1780 + 2021 + 2919]

Gath Hepher [2]

Jos 19:13 Then it continued eastward to **Gath Hepher** and Eth Kazin;
2Ki 14:25 his servant Jonah son of Amittai, the prophet from **Gath Hepher**.

1784 גַּת־רִמּוֹן *gat-rimmôn*, n.pr.loc. [4] [√ 1780 + 8232]

Gath Rimmon [4]

Jos 19:45 Jehud, Bene Berak, **Gath Rimmon**,
21:24 Aijalon and **Gath Rimmon**, together with their pasturelands—
21:25 the tribe of Manasseh they received Taanach and **Gath Rimmon**,
1Ch 6:69 [6:54] Aijalon and **Gath Rimmon**, together with their

1785 גִּתִּי *gittî*, a.g. [10] [√ 1781; cf. 1780]

Gittite [8], Gath [1], Gittites [1]

Jos 13:3 Philistine rulers in Gaza, Ashdod, Ashkelon, **Gath** and Ekron—
2Sa 6:10 Instead, he took it aside to the house of Obed-Edom the **Gittite**.
6:11 remained in the house of Obed-Edom the **Gittite** for three months,
15:18 all the six hundred **Gittites** who had accompanied him from Gath
15:19 The king said to Ittai the **Gittite**, "Why should you come along
15:22 So Ittai the **Gittite** marched on with all his men and the families
18:2 brother Abishai son of Zeruiah, and a third under Ittai the **Gittite**.
21:19 son of Jaare-Oregim the Bethlehemite killed Goliath the **Gittite**,
1Ch 13:13 Instead, he took it aside to the house of Obed-Edom the **Gittite**.
20:5 Elhanan son of Jair killed Lahmi the brother of Goliath the **Gittite**,

1786 גִּתַּיִם *gittayim*, n.pr.loc. [2] [√ 1780]

Gittaim [2]

2Sa 4:3 because the people of Beeroth fled to **Gittaim** and have lived there
Ne 11:33 in Hazor, Ramah and **Gittaim**,

1787 גִּתִּית *gittît*, tt. [3] [√ 1781; cf. 1780]

gittith [3]

Ps 8:T [8:1] director of music. According to ***gittith***. A psalm of David.
81:T [81:1] the director of music. According to ***gittith***. Of Asaph.
84:T [84:1] According to ***gittith***. Of the Sons of Korah. A psalm.

1788 גֶּתֶר *geter*, n.pr.m. [2]

Gether [2]

Ge 10:23 The sons of Aram: Uz, Hul, **Gether** and Meshech.
1Ch 1:17 and Aram. The sons of Aram: Uz, Hul, **Gether** and Meshech.

ד, d

1789 ד *d*, letter. Not used in NIV/BHS [→ Ar 10152]

1790 דָּאַב *dā'ab*, v. [3] [→ 1791, 1792]

dim [1], faint [+5883] [1], sorrow [1]

Ps 88:9 [88:10] [A] my eyes *are* **dim** with grief. I call to you,
Jer 31:12 [A] be like a well-watered garden, and they will **sorrow** no more.
31:25 [A] I will refresh the weary and satisfy the **faint** [+5883]."

1791 דְּאָבָה *de'ābâ*, n.f. [1] [√ 1790]

dismay [1]

Job 41:22 [41:14] Strength resides in his neck; **dismay** goes before him.

1792 דְּאָבוֹן *de'ābôn*, n.[m.]. [1] [√ 1790]

despairing [1]

Dt 28:65 an anxious mind, eyes weary with longing, and a **despairing** heart.

1793 דָּאַג *dā'ag*, v. [7] [→ 1795, 1796, 1869]

afraid [1], dread [1], dreaded [1], has worries [1], troubled [1], worried [1], worrying [1]

1Sa 9:5 [A] thinking about the donkeys and *start* **worrying** about us."
10:2 [A] has stopped thinking about them and *is* **worried** about you.
Ps 38:18 [38:19] [A] I confess my iniquity; *I am* **troubled** by my sin.
Isa 57:11 [A] "Whom *have you so* **dreaded** and feared that you have been
Jer 17:8 [A] *It* **has** no **worries** in a year of drought and never fails to bear
38:19 [A] "*I am* **afraid** *of* the Jews who have gone over to the
42:16 [A] the famine you **dread** will follow you into Egypt, and there

1794 דָּאג *dāg*, n.m. [1] [√ 1834]

fish [1]

Ne 13:16 Men from Tyre who lived in Jerusalem were bringing in **fish**

1795 דֹּאֵג *dō'ēg*, n.pr.m. [6] [√ 1793]

Doeg [6]

1Sa 21:7 [21:8] he was **Doeg** the Edomite, Saul's head shepherd.
22:9 But **Doeg** the Edomite, who was standing with Saul's officials,
22:18 The king then ordered **Doeg**, [K 1869] "You turn and strike down
22:18 the priests." So **Doeg** the Edomite turned and struck them down.
22:22 "That day, when **Doeg** the Edomite was there, I knew he would be
Ps 52:T [52:2] When **Doeg** the Edomite had gone to Saul and told him:

1796 דְּאָגָה *de'āgâ*, n.f. [6] [√ 1793]

anxiety [2], fear [2], anxious [1], restless [1]

Jos 22:24 We did it for **fear** that some day your descendants might say to
Pr 12:25 An **anxious** heart weighs a man down, but a kind word cheers him
Jer 49:23 bad news. They are disheartened, troubled like the **restless** sea.
Eze 4:16 The people will eat rationed food in **anxiety** and drink rationed

Eze 12:18 as you eat your food, and shudder in **fear** as you drink your water.
12:19 They will eat their food in **anxiety** and drink their water in despair,

1797 ¹דָּאָה **dā'â¹**, v. [4 / 5] [→ 1798; cf. 1901]

soared [2], swooping down [2], swoop down [1]

Dt 28:49 [A] from the ends of the earth, like an eagle **swooping down**,
2Sa 22:11 [A] and flew; *he* **soared** [BHS 8011] on the wings of the wind.
Ps 18:10 [18:11] [A] and flew; *he* **soared** on the wings of the wind.
Jer 48:40 [A] An eagle *is* **swooping down**, spreading its wings over Moab.
49:22 [A] An eagle will soar and **swoop down**, spreading its wings

1798 ²דָּאָה **dā'â²**, n.f. [1] [√ 1797]

red kite [1]

Lev 11:14 the **red kite**, any kind of black kite,

1799 דֹּאר **dō'r**, n.pr.loc. [1] [→ 1888, 2831, 5869, 6529; cf. 1883, 1884]

Dor [1]

Jos 17:11 Ibleam and the people of **Dor**, Endor, Taanach and Megiddo,

1800 דֹּב **dōb**, n.m. [12] [√ 1803; Ar 10155]

bear [10], bears [2]

1Sa 17:34 When a lion or a **bear** came and carried off a sheep from the flock,
17:36 Your servant has killed both the lion and the **bear**; this
17:37 the paw of the **bear** will deliver me from the hand of this
2Sa 17: 8 they are fighters, and as fierce as a wild **bear** robbed of her cubs.
2Ki 2:24 two **bears** came out of the woods and mauled forty-two of the
Pr 17:12 Better to meet a **bear** robbed of her cubs than a fool in his folly.
28:15 or a charging **bear** is a wicked man ruling over a helpless people.
Isa 11: 7 The cow will feed with the **bear**, their young will lie down
59:11 We all growl like **bears**; we moan mournfully like doves.
La 3:10 Like a **bear** lying in wait, like a lion in hiding,
Hos 13: 8 Like a **bear** robbed of her cubs, I will attack them and rip them
Am 5:19 It will be as though a man fled from a lion only to meet a **bear**,

1801 דֹּבֶא **dōbe'**, n.[m.]. [1]

strength [1]

Dt 33:25 will be iron and bronze, and your **strength** will equal your days.

1802 דְּבָאָה **d^ebā'â**, n.f. Not used in NIV/BHS

1803 דָּבַב **dābab**, v. [1] [→ 1800, 1804?, 1807?]

flowing gently [1]

SS 7: 9 [7:10] [A] to my lover, **flowing gently** *over* lips and teeth.

1804 דִּבָּה **dibbâ**, n.f. [9] [√ 1803?]

slander [3], bad report [2], report [2], bad reputation [1], whispering [1]

Ge 37: 2 and he brought their father a bad **report** *about* them.
Nu 13:32 they spread among the Israelites a **bad report** *about* the land they
14:36 grumble against him by spreading a **bad report** about it—
14:37 these men responsible for spreading the bad **report** *about* the land
Ps 31:13 [31:14] For I hear the **slander** *of* many; there is terror on every
Pr 10:18 his hatred has lying lips, and whoever spreads **slander** is a fool.
25:10 it may shame you and you will never lose your **bad reputation**.
Jer 20:10 I hear many **whispering**, "Terror on every side! Report him!
Eze 36: 3 the nations and the object of people's malicious talk and **slander**,

1805 ¹דְּבוֹרָה **d^ebôrâ¹**, n.f. [4] [→ 1806; cf. 1819]

bees [3], swarm of bees [1]

Dt 1:44 they chased you like a **swarm of bees** and beat you down from
Jdg 14: 8 at the lion's carcass. In it was a swarm of **bees** and some honey,
Ps 118:12 They swarmed around me like **bees**, but they died out as quickly as
Isa 7:18 the distant streams of Egypt and for **bees** from the land of Assyria.

1806 ²דְּבוֹרָה **d^ebôrâ²**, n.pr.f. [10] [√ 1805; cf. 1819]

Deborah [10]

Ge 35: 8 Now **Deborah**, Rebekah's nurse, died and was buried under the
Jdg 4: 4 **Deborah**, a prophetess, the wife of Lappidoth, was leading Israel
4: 5 She held court under the Palm of **Deborah** between Ramah
4: 9 Sisera over to a woman." So **Deborah** went with Barak to Kedesh,
4:10 thousand men followed him, and **Deborah** also went with him.
4:14 **Deborah** said to Barak, "Go! This is the day the LORD has given
5: 1 On that day **Deborah** and Barak son of Abinoam sang this song:
5: 7 ceased until I, **Deborah**, arose, arose a mother in Israel.
5:12 'Wake up, wake up, **Deborah**! Wake up, wake up, break out in
5:15 The princes of Issachar were with **Deborah**; yes, Issachar was with

1807 דִּבְיֹנִים **dibyōnîm**, n.[m.]. [1] [√ 1803? + 3433]

seed pods [1]

2Ki 6:25 a quarter of a cab of **seed pods** [K 2989] for five shekels.

1808 ¹דְּבִיר **d^ebîr¹**, n.m. [16 / 15] [→ 1809, 1810; cf. 1818?, 1819?]

inner sanctuary [14], Most Holy Place [+7731] [1]

1Ki 6: 5 and **inner sanctuary** he built a structure around the building,
6:16 floor to ceiling to form within the temple an **inner sanctuary**,
6:19 He prepared the **inner sanctuary** within the temple to set the ark
6:20 The **inner sanctuary** was twenty cubits long, twenty wide
6:21 he extended gold chains across the front of the **inner sanctuary**,
6:22 overlaid with gold the altar that belonged to the **inner sanctuary**.
6:23 In the **inner sanctuary** he made a pair of cherubim of olive wood,
6:31 For the entrance of the **inner sanctuary** he made doors of olive
7:49 on the right and five on the left, in front of the **inner sanctuary**);
8: 6 covenant to its place in the **inner sanctuary** *of* the temple,
8: 8 could be seen from the Holy Place in front of the **inner sanctuary**,
2Ch 3:16 made interwoven [BHS *in the inner sanctuary*; NIV 8054] chains
4:20 their lamps, to burn in front of the **inner sanctuary** as prescribed;
5: 7 covenant to its place in the **inner sanctuary** *of* the temple,
5: 9 from the ark, could be seen from in front of the **inner sanctuary**,
Ps 28: 2 as I lift up my hands toward your **Most Holy Place** [+7731].

1809 ²דְּבִיר **d^ebîr²**, n.pr.m. [1] [√ 1808; cf. 1818]

Debir [1]

Jos 10: 3 king of Jarmuth, Japhia king of Lachish and **Debir** king of Eglon.

1810 ³דְּבִיר **d^ebîr³**, n.pr.loc. [13] [√ 1808; cf. 1818]

Debir [11], *untranslated* [2]

Jos 10:38 and all Israel with him turned around and attacked **Debir**.
10:39 They did to **Debir** and its king as they had done to Libnah
11:21 from Hebron, **Debir** and Anab, from all the hill country of Judah,
12:13 the king of **Debir** one the king of Geder one
13:26 and Betonim, and from Mahanaim to the territory of **Debir**;
15: 7 The boundary then went up to **Debir** from the Valley of Achor
15:15 From there he marched against the people living in **Debir**
15:15 From there he marched against the people living in Debir **[RPH]**
15:49 Dannah, Kiriath Sannah (that is, **Debir**),
21:15 Holon, **Debir**,
Jdg 1:11 From there they advanced against the people living in **Debir**
1:11 people living in Debir (formerly **[RPH]** called Kiriath Sepher).
1Ch 6:58 [6:43] Hilen, **Debir**,

1811 דְּבֵלָה **d^ebēlâ**, n.f. [5] [→ 1813?]

poultice [2], cake of pressed figs [1], cakes of pressed figs [1], fig cakes [1]

1Sa 25:18 a hundred cakes of raisins and two hundred **cakes of pressed figs**,
30:12 part of a **cake of pressed figs** and two cakes of raisins. He ate
2Ki 20: 7 Then Isaiah said, "Prepare a **poultice** of figs." They did so
1Ch 12:40 [12:41] **fig cakes**, raisin cakes, wine, oil, cattle and sheep,
Isa 38:21 Isaiah had said, "Prepare a **poultice** *of* figs and apply it to the boil,

1812 דִּבְלָה **diblâ**, n.pr.loc. [1]

Diblah [1]

Eze 6:14 and make the land a desolate waste from the desert to **Diblah**—

1813 דִּבְלַיִם **diblayim**, n.pr.m. [1] [√ 1811?]

Diblaim [1]

Hos 1: 3 So he married Gomer daughter of **Diblaim**, and she conceived

1814 דִּבְלָתַיִם **diblātayim**, n.pr.loc. Not used in NIV/BHS [→ 1086, 6627]

1815 דָּבַק **dābaq**, v. [54] [→ 1816, 1817; Ar 10158]

hold fast [7], cling [5], bound [2], clung [2], held fast [2], keep [2], make stick [2], stay [2], sticks [2], *untranslated* [1], ally [1], almost upon [1], are joined fast [1], caught up [1], clings [1], defiled [+928+4583] [1], drawn [1], follow [+339] [1], found [1], froze [1], joined [1], laid low [1], not escape [1], overtake [1], overtook [1], plague [1], pressed hard after [1], pressed hard [1], pressing [1], reduced to [1], stayed close [1], stayed [1], stick together [1], sticking [1], stuck [1], tightly joined [1], united [1]

Ge 2:24 [A] will leave his father and mother and *be* **united** to his wife,
19:19 [A] to the mountains; this disaster *will* **overtake** me, and I'll die.
31:23 [G] and **caught up** *with* him in the hill country of Gilead.
34: 3 [A] His heart *was* **drawn** to Dinah daughter of Jacob, and he

Nu 36: 7 [A] for every Israelite *shall* **keep** the tribal land inherited from
36: 9 [A] to tribe, for each Israelite tribe *is to* **keep** the land it inherits."
Dt 10: 20 [A] serve him. **Hold fast** to him and take your oaths in his name.
11: 22 [A] your God, to walk in all his ways and to **hold fast** to him—
13: 4 [13:5] [A] and obey him; serve him and **hold fast** to him.
13: 17 [13:18] [A] None of those condemned things *shall be* **found** in
28: 21 [G] The LORD *will* **plague** you *with* diseases until he has
28: 60 [A] of Egypt that you dreaded, and *they will* **cling** to you.
30: 20 [A] LORD your God, listen to his voice, and **hold fast** to him.
Jos 22: 5 [A] to **hold fast** to him and to serve him with all your heart
23: 8 [A] *you are to* **hold fast** to the LORD your God, as you have
23: 12 [A] **ally** *yourselves* with the survivors of these nations that
Jdg 18: 22 [G] near Micah were called together and **overtook** the Danites.
20: 42 [G] direction of the desert, but they *could* **not escape** the battle.
20: 45 [G] *They kept* **pressing** after the Benjamites as far as Gidom
Ru 1: 14 [A] kissed her mother-in-law good-by, but Ruth **clung** to her.
2: 8 [A] don't go away from here. **Stay** here with my servant girls.
2: 21 [A] '**Stay** with my workers until they finish harvesting all my
2: 23 [A] So Ruth **stayed close** to the servant girls of Boaz to glean
1Sa 14: 22 [G] were on the run, they **joined** the battle in hot pursuit.
31: 2 [G] The Philistines **pressed hard after** Saul and his sons,
2Sa 1: 6 [G] on his spear, with the chariots and riders **almost upon** him.
20: 2 [A] the men of Judah **stayed** by their king all the way from the
23: 10 [A] the Philistines till his hand grew tired and **froze** to the sword.
1Ki 11: 2 [A] their gods." Nevertheless, Solomon **held fast** to them in love.
2Ki 3: 3 [A] Nevertheless *he* **clung** to the sins of Jeroboam son of Nebat,
5: 27 [A] Naaman's leprosy *will* **cling** to you and to your descendants
18: 6 [A] *He* **held fast** to the LORD and did not cease to follow him;
1Ch 10: 2 [G] The Philistines **pressed hard** after Saul and his sons,
Job 19: 20 [A] **[NIE]** I am nothing but skin and bones; I have escaped with
29: 10 [A] and their tongues **stuck** to the roof of their mouths.
31: 7 [A] by my eyes, or if my hands *have been* **defiled** [+928+4583],
38: 38 [E] the dust becomes hard and the clods of earth **stick together**?
41: 17 [41:9] [E] *They* **are joined fast** to one another; they cling
41: 23 [41:15] [A] The folds of his flesh *are* **tightly joined**; they are
Ps 22: 15 [22:16] [H] and my tongue **sticks** *to* the roof of my mouth;
44: 25 [44:26] [A] down to the dust; our bodies **cling** to the ground.
63: 8 [63:9] [A] My soul **clings** to you; your right hand upholds me.
101: 3 [A] The deeds of faithless men I hate; *they will* not **cling** to me.
102: 5 [102:6] [A] Because of my loud groaning I *am* **reduced to** skin
119: 25 [A] I *am* **laid low** in the dust; preserve my life according to your
119: 31 [A] *I* **hold fast** to your statutes, O LORD; do not let me be put
137: 6 [A] *May* my tongue **cling** to the roof of my mouth if I do not
Jer 13: 11 [A] For as a belt *is* **bound** around a man's waist, so I bound the
13: 11 [G] so *I* **bound** the whole house of Israel and the whole house of
42: 16 [A] and the famine you dread *will* **follow** [+339] you *into* Egypt,
La 4: 4 [A] Because of thirst the infant's tongue **sticks** to the roof of its
Eze 3: 26 [G] *I will* **make** your tongue **stick** to the roof of your mouth
29: 4 [G] and **make** the fish of your streams **stick** to your scales.
29: 4 [A] among your streams, with all the fish **sticking** to your scales.

1816 דָּבֵק dābēq, a. [3] [√ 1815]

held fast [1], sticks closer [1], touched [1]

Dt 4: 4 all of you who **held fast** to the LORD your God are still alive
2Ch 3: 12 also five cubits long, **touched** the wing of the first cherub.
Pr 18: 24 come to ruin, but there is a friend *who* **sticks closer** than a brother.

1817 דֶּבֶק debeq, n.m. [3] [√ 1815]

sections [2], welding [1]

1Ki 22: 34 and hit the king of Israel between the **sections** of his armor.
2Ch 18: 33 and hit the king of Israel between the **sections** of his armor.
Isa 41: 7 He says of the **welding**, "It is good." He nails down the idol

1818 ¹דָּבַר dābar¹, v. [5] [→ 1808?, 1809, 1810, 1822, 1823, 1824, 1827, 1829, 4497]

departure [1], destroy [1], destroyed [1], subdued [1], subdues [1]

2Ch 22: 10 [D] she proceeded *to* **destroy** the whole royal family of the house
Ps 18: 47 [18:48] [G] who avenges me, *who* **subdues** nations under me,
47: 3 [47:4] [G] *He* **subdued** nations under us, peoples under our feet.
Pr 21: 28 [D] and whoever listens to him *will be* **destroyed** forever.
SS 5: 6 [D] lover had left; he was gone. My heart sank at his **departure**.

1819 ²דָּבַר dābar², v. [1137 / 1138] [→ 1805, 1806, 1808?, 1821, 1825, 1826, 1830, 4498]

said [197], speak [170], spoken [99], spoke [85], say [67], promised [51], tell [49], speaking [38], told [37], *untranslated* [24], speaks [18], talked [17], says [14], talking [14], talk [11], saying [10], gave [6], pronounced [6], reported [6], declared [5], decreed [5], directed [5], made [5], proclaimed [5], repeated [5], replied [5], warned [5], asked [4], given [4], praying [4], promise [4], say [+1821] [4], speak out [4], words [4], ask [3], give [3], instructed [3], preached [3], pronounce [3], pronounced on [+907] [3], spoke up [3], telling [3], threatened [3], announce [2], answered [2], declare [2], foretold [2], full of [2], give answer [+448+1821] [2], give message [2], liars [+9214] [2], proclaim [2], promises made [2], propose [2], sang [2], speak up [2], speak well [+1819] [2], spreads [2], tells [2], threaten [2], used to say [+1819] [2], address [1], announced [1], are said [1], argued [1], asking [1], asks [1], boastful [+1524] [1], break out [1], commanded [1], complain [1], contend [1], decree [1], described [1], dictate [1], discussed [1], encourage [+4213+6584] [1], encouraged [+4222+6584] [1], ever say [+906+1821] [1], explained [1], fluent [+4200+4554] [1], fomenting [1], gave the message [+465+1821 +2021+2021+3972] [1], give an answer [1], give opinion [1], gives [1], giving [1], imagine [1], instructed [+448+7023] [1], invite [1], is spoken [1], lie [+3942] [1], lie [+9214] [1], lied [+3942] [1], lies [+8736] [1], lying [+3942] [1], lying [+9214] [1], made request [1], make many promises [+1821] [1], make promise [+1821] [1], make request [1], make [1], mention [1], mentioned [1], message came [1], message [1], named [1], ordered [1], persuade [+4213+6584] [1], plea [1], pleaded [1], pleads [1], predicted [1], proclaiming [1], proclaims [1], promise [+1821] [1], promised [+928+7023] [1], promises [+1821] [1], promises [1], prophesied [+5553] [1], rebukes [1], recited [1], reciting [1], recommended [1], request [+906+1821] [1], requested [1], ridicule [1], said [+1821] [1], said [+448+1821 +2021] [1], said a word [1], say [+906+1821] [1], shouted [1], silent [+4202] [1], slander [1], speak with words [1], speech [+4537] [1], spoken [+1821] [1], spoken [+7023] [1], spoken kindly [+4213+6584] [1], state [1], suggested [1], talking together [1], taught [1], tell [+265+928] [1], thought [1], told [+265+906+928] [1], urging [1], utter [1], will° [+1821] [1]

Ge 8: 15 [D] Then God **said** to Noah,
12: 4 [D] So Abram left, as the LORD *had* **told** him; and Lot went
16: 13 [A] She gave this name to the LORD who **spoke** to her:
17: 3 [D] Abram fell facedown, and God **said** to him,
17: 22 [D] When he had finished **speaking** with Abraham, God went up
17: 23 [D] in his household, and circumcised them, as God **told** him.
18: 5 [D] your servant." "Very well," they answered, "do as *you* **say**."
18: 19 [D] will bring about for Abraham what *he has* **promised** him."
18: 27 [D] "Now that I have been so bold as to **speak** to the Lord,
18: 29 [D] Once again *he* **spoke** to him, "What if only forty are found
18: 30 [D] Then he said, "May the Lord not be angry, but *let me* **speak**.
18: 31 [D] "Now that I have been so bold as to **speak** to the Lord,
18: 32 [D] the Lord not be angry, but *let me* **speak** just once more.
18: 33 [D] When the LORD had finished **speaking** with Abraham, he
19: 14 [D] So Lot went out and **spoke** to his sons-in-law, who were
19: 21 [D] this request too; I will not overthrow the town *you* **speak** *of*.
20: 8 [D] when *he* **told** [+265+906+928] them all that had happened,
21: 1 [D] and the LORD did for Sarah what *he had* **promised**.
21: 2 [D] in his old age, at the very time God *had* **promised** him.
23: 3 [D] rose from beside his dead wife and **spoke** to the Hittites.
23: 8 [D] *He* **said** to them, "If you are willing to let me bury my dead,
23: 13 [D] *he* **said** to Ephron in their hearing, "Listen to me, if you will.
23: 16 [A] weighed out for him the price *he had* **named** in the hearing
24: 7 [D] my native land and who **spoke** to me and promised me on
24: 15 [D] Before he had finished **praying**, Rebekah came out with her
24: 30 [D] had heard Rebekah tell what the man **said** to her, he went out
24: 33 [D] "I will not eat until *I have* **told** you what I have to say."
24: 33 [D] told you what I have to say." "Then **tell** us," ⌞Laban⌟ said.
24: 45 [D] "Before I finished **praying** in my heart, Rebekah came out,
24: 50 [D] the LORD; we can **say** nothing to you one way or the other.
24: 51 [D] the wife of your master's son, as the LORD *has* **directed**."
27: 5 [D] Now Rebekah was listening as Isaac **spoke** to his son Esau.
27: 6 [D] I overheard your father **say** to your brother Esau,
27: 19 [D] I have done as *you* **told** me. Please sit up and eat some of my
28: 15 [D] I will not leave you until I have done what *I have* **promised**
29: 9 [D] While he *was* still **talking** with them, Rachel came with her
31: 24 [D] "Be careful not *to* **say** *anything* to Jacob, either good
31: 29 [D] 'Be careful not *to* **say** anything to Jacob, either good or bad.'
32: 19 [32:20] [A] "*You are to* **say** the same thing to Esau when you
34: 3 [D] of Jacob, and he loved the girl and **spoke** tenderly to her.
34: 6 [D] Then Shechem's father Hamor went out to **talk** with Jacob.
34: 8 [D] Hamor **said** to them, "My son Shechem has his heart set on
34: 13 [D] Jacob's sons replied deceitfully as *they* **spoke** *to* Shechem
34: 20 [D] his son Shechem went to the gate of their city *to* **speak** to
35: 13 [D] God went up from him at the place where *he had* **talked**
35: 14 [D] Jacob set up a stone pillar at the place where God *had* **talked**
35: 15 [D] Jacob called the place where God *had* **talked** with him
37: 4 [D] they hated him and could not **speak** a kind *word to* him.
39: 10 [D] though she **spoke** to Joseph day after day, he refused to go to
39: 17 [D] *she* **told** him this story: "That Hebrew slave you brought us
39: 19 [D] When his master heard the story his wife **told** him, saying,
41: 9 [D] the chief cupbearer **said** to Pharaoh, "Today I am reminded
41: 17 [D] Pharaoh **said** to Joseph, "In my dream I was standing on the

Ge 41:28 [D] "It is just as *I* **said** to Pharaoh: God has shown Pharaoh what
42: 7 [D] but he pretended to be a stranger and **spoke** harshly to them.
42:14 [D] Joseph said to them, "It is just as *I* **told** you: You are spies!
42:24 [D] to weep, but then turned back and **spoke** to them again.
42:30 [D] "The man who is lord over the land **spoke** harshly to us
43:19 [D] and **spoke** to him at the entrance to the house.
44: 2 [D] with the silver for his grain." And he did as Joseph **said**.
44: 6 [D] he caught up with them, *he* **repeated** these words to them.
44: 7 [D] But they said to him, "Why *does* my lord **say** such things?
44:16 [D] can we say to my lord?" Judah replied. "What *can we* **say**?
44:18 [D] "Please, my lord, *let* your servant **speak** a word to my lord.
45:12 [D] brother Benjamin, that it is really I who *am* **speaking** to you.
45:15 [D] and wept over them. Afterward his brothers **talked** with him.
45:27 [D] But when *they* **told** him everything Joseph had said to them,
45:27 [D] But when they told him everything Joseph *had* **said** to them,
49:28 [D] this is what their father **said** to them when he blessed them,
50: 4 [D] Joseph **said** to Pharaoh's court, "If I have found favor in your
50: 4 [D] "If I have found favor in your eyes, **speak** to Pharaoh for me.
50:17 [D] your father." When their **message came** to him, Joseph wept.
50:21 [D] And he reassured them and **spoke** kindly to them.
Ex 1:17 [D] and did not do what the king of Egypt *had* **told** them to do;
4:10 [D] neither in the past nor since you *have* **spoken** to your
4:12 [D] I will help you speak and will teach you what *to* **say**."
4:14 [D] Aaron the Levite? I know he *can* **speak** [+1819] **well**.
4:14 [D] Aaron the Levite? I know he *can* **speak well** [+1819].
4:15 [D] *You shall* **speak** to him and put words in his mouth; I will
4:16 [D] He *will* **speak** to the people for you, and it will be as if he
4:30 [D] Aaron **told** them everything the LORD had said to Moses.
4:30 [D] Aaron told them everything the LORD *had* **said** to Moses.
5:23 [D] Ever since I went to Pharaoh to **speak** in your name, he has
6: 2 [D] God also **said** to Moses, "I am the LORD.
6: 9 [D] Moses **reported** this to the Israelites, but they did not listen
6:10 [D] Then the LORD **said** to Moses,
6:11 [D] **tell** Pharaoh king of Egypt to let the Israelites go out of his
6:12 [D] Moses **said** to the LORD, "If the Israelites will not listen to
6:13 [D] Now the LORD **spoke** to Moses and Aaron about the
6:27 [D] *were the ones who* **spoke** to Pharaoh king of Egypt *about*
6:28 [D] Now when the LORD **spoke** to Moses in Egypt,
6:29 [D] he **said** to him, "I am the LORD. Tell Pharaoh king of
6:29 [D] **Tell** Pharaoh king of Egypt everything I tell you."
6:29 [A] Tell Pharaoh king of Egypt everything I **tell** you."
7: 2 [D] You *are to* **say** everything I command you, and your brother
7: 2 [D] your brother Aaron *is to* **tell** Pharaoh to let the Israelites go
7: 7 [D] and Aaron eighty-three when they **spoke** to Pharaoh.
7: 9 [D] "When Pharaoh **says** to you, 'Perform a miracle,' then say to
7:13 [D] and he would not listen to them, just as the LORD *had* **said**.
7:22 [D] not listen to Moses and Aaron, just as the LORD *had* **said**.
8:15 [8:11] [D] to Moses and Aaron, just as the LORD *had* **said**.
8:19 [8:15] [D] and he would not listen, just as the LORD *had* **said**.
9: 1 [D] "Go to Pharaoh and **say** to him, 'This is what the LORD,
9:12 [D] to Moses and Aaron, just as the LORD *had* **said** to Moses.
9:35 [D] the Israelites go, just as the LORD *had* **said** through Moses.
10:29 [D] "Just as *you* **say**," Moses replied, "I will never appear before
11: 2 [D] **Tell** [+265+928] the people that men and women alike are to
12: 3 [D] **Tell** the whole community of Israel that on the tenth day of
12:25 [D] enter the land that the LORD will give you as *he* **promised**,
12:31 [D] Go, worship the LORD as you *have* **requested**.
12:32 [D] Take your flocks and herds, as *you have* **said**, and go.
13: 1 [D] The LORD **said** to Moses,
14: 1 [D] Then the LORD **said** to Moses,
14: 2 [D] "**Tell** the Israelites to turn back and encamp near Pi Hahiroth,
14:12 [D] Didn't *we* **say** [+1821] to you in Egypt, 'Leave us alone; let
14:15 [D] are you crying out to me? **Tell** the Israelites to move on.
16:10 [D] While Aaron *was* **speaking** to the whole Israelite
16:11 [D] The LORD **said** to Moses,
16:12 [D] **Tell** them, 'At twilight you will eat meat, and in the morning
16:23 [D] He said to them, "This is what the LORD **commanded**:
19: 6 [D] These are the words *you are to* **speak** to the Israelites."
19: 8 [D] "We will do everything the LORD *has* **said**."
19: 9 [D] so that the people will hear me **speaking** with you and will
19:19 [D] Then Moses **spoke** and the voice of God answered him.
20: 1 [D] And God **spoke** all these words:
20:19 [D] and said to Moses, "**Speak** to us yourself and we will listen.
20:19 [D] will listen. But *do* not *have* God **speak** to us or we will die."
20:22 [D] 'You have seen for yourselves that *I have* **spoken** to you
23:22 [D] If you listen carefully to what he says and do all that *I* **say**,
24: 3 [D] one voice, "Everything the LORD *has* **said** we will do."
24: 7 [D] "We will do everything the LORD *has* **said**;
25: 1 [D] The LORD **said** to Moses,
25: 2 [D] "**Tell** the Israelites to bring me an offering. You are to
25:22 [D] with you and **give** you all my commands for the Israelites.
28: 3 [D] **Tell** all the skilled men to whom I have given wisdom in
29:42 [D] before the LORD. There I will meet you and **speak** to you;
30:11 [D] Then the LORD **said** to Moses,
30:17 [D] Then the LORD **said** to Moses,
30:22 [D] Then the LORD **said** to Moses,
30:31 [D] **Say** to the Israelites, 'This is to be my sacred anointing oil for
31: 1 [D] Then the LORD **said** to Moses,
31:13 [D] "**Say** to the Israelites, 'You must observe my Sabbaths. This
31:18 [D] When the LORD finished **speaking** to Moses on Mount
32: 7 [D] the LORD **said** to Moses, "Go down, because your people,
32:13 [D] **[NIE]** 'I will make your descendants as numerous as the
32:14 [D] did not bring on his people the disaster *he had* **threatened**.
32:34 [D] Now go, lead the people to the place *I* **spoke** *of*, and my
33: 1 [D] the LORD **said** to Moses, "Leave this place, you
33: 9 [D] stay at the entrance, while the LORD **spoke** with Moses.
33:11 [D] The LORD *would* **speak** to Moses face to face, as a man
33:11 [D] speak to Moses face to face, as a man **speaks** with his friend.
33:17 [D] "I will do the very thing *you have* **asked**, because I am
34:29 [D] face was radiant because he *had* **spoken** with the LORD.
34:31 [D] of the community came back to him, and he **spoke** to them.
34:32 [D] he gave them all the commands the LORD *had* **given** him
34:33 [D] When Moses finished **speaking** to them, he put a veil over
34:34 [D] whenever he entered the LORD's presence to **speak** with
34:34 [D] and **told** the Israelites what he had been commanded,
34:35 [D] back over his face until he went in to **speak** with the LORD.
40: 1 [D] Then the LORD **said** to Moses:
Lev 1: 1 [D] called to Moses and **spoke** to him from the Tent of Meeting.
1: 2 [D] "**Speak** to the Israelites and say to them: 'When any of you
4: 1 [D] The LORD **said** to Moses,
4: 2 [D] "**Say** to the Israelites: 'When anyone sins unintentionally
5:14 [D] The LORD **said** to Moses:
6: 1 [5:20] [D] The LORD **said** to Moses:
6: 8 [6:1] [D] The LORD **said** to Moses:
6:19 [6:12] [D] The LORD also **said** to Moses,
6:24 [6:17] [D] The LORD **said** to Moses,
6:25 [6:18] [D] "**Say** to Aaron and his sons: 'These are the
7:22 [D] The LORD **said** to Moses,
7:23 [D] "**Say** to the Israelites: 'Do not eat any of the fat of cattle,
7:28 [D] The LORD **said** to Moses,
7:29 [D] "**Say** to the Israelites: 'Anyone who brings a fellowship
8: 1 [D] The LORD **said** to Moses,
9: 3 [D] **say** to the Israelites: 'Take a male goat for a sin offering,
10: 3 [D] to Aaron, "This is what the LORD **spoke** *of* when he said:
10: 5 [D] still in their tunics, outside the camp, as Moses **ordered**.
10: 8 [D] Then the LORD **said** to Aaron,
10:11 [D] all the decrees the LORD *has* **given** them through Moses."
10:12 [D] Moses **said** to Aaron and his remaining sons, Eleazar
10:19 [D] Aaron **replied** to Moses, "Today they sacrificed their sin
11: 1 [D] The LORD **said** to Moses and Aaron,
11: 2 [D] "**Say** to the Israelites: 'Of all the animals that live on land,
12: 1 [D] The LORD **said** to Moses,
12: 2 [D] "**Say** to the Israelites: 'A woman who becomes pregnant
13: 1 [D] The LORD **said** to Moses and Aaron,
14: 1 [D] The LORD **said** to Moses,
14:33 [D] The LORD **said** to Moses and Aaron,
15: 1 [D] The LORD **said** to Moses and Aaron,
15: 2 [D] "**Speak** to the Israelites and say to them: 'When any man has
16: 1 [D] The LORD **spoke** to Moses after the death of the two sons
16: 2 [D] "**Tell** your brother Aaron not to come whenever he chooses
17: 1 [D] The LORD **said** to Moses,
17: 2 [D] "**Speak** to Aaron and his sons and to all the Israelites and say
18: 1 [D] The LORD **said** to Moses,
18: 2 [D] "**Speak** to the Israelites and say to them: 'I am the LORD
19: 1 [D] The LORD **said** to Moses,
19: 2 [D] "**Speak** to the entire assembly of Israel and say to them:
20: 1 [D] The LORD **said** to Moses,
21:16 [D] The LORD **said** to Moses,
21:17 [D] "**Say** to Aaron: 'For the generations to come none of your
21:24 [D] So Moses **told** this to Aaron and his sons and to all the
22: 1 [D] The LORD **said** to Moses,
22: 2 [D] "**Tell** Aaron and his sons to treat with respect the sacred
22:17 [D] The LORD **said** to Moses,
22:18 [D] "**Speak** to Aaron and his sons and to all the Israelites and say
22:26 [D] The LORD **said** to Moses,
23: 1 [D] The LORD **said** to Moses,
23: 2 [D] "**Speak** to the Israelites and say to them: 'These are my
23: 9 [D] The LORD **said** to Moses,
23:10 [D] "**Speak** to the Israelites and say to them: 'When you enter the
23:23 [D] The LORD **said** to Moses,
23:24 [D] "**Say** to the Israelites: 'On the first day of the seventh month
23:26 [D] The LORD **said** to Moses,
23:33 [D] The LORD **said** to Moses,
23:34 [D] "**Say** to the Israelites: 'On the fifteenth day of the seventh
23:44 [D] So Moses **announced** to the Israelites the appointed feasts of
24: 1 [D] The LORD **said** to Moses,
24:13 [D] Then the LORD **said** to Moses:
24:15 [D] **Say** to the Israelites: 'If anyone curses his God, he will be

Lev 24:23 [D] Moses **spoke** to the Israelites, and they took the blasphemer
25: 1 [D] The LORD **said** to Moses on Mount Sinai,
25: 2 [D] "**Speak** to the Israelites and say to them: 'When you enter the
27: 1 [D] The LORD **said** to Moses,
27: 2 [D] "**Speak** to the Israelites and say to them: 'If anyone makes a
Nu 1: 1 [D] The LORD **spoke** to Moses in the Tent of Meeting in the
1:48 [D] The LORD *had* **said** to Moses:
2: 1 [D] The LORD **said** to Moses and Aaron:
3: 1 [D] Moses at the time the LORD **talked** with Moses on Mount
3: 5 [D] The LORD **said** to Moses,
3:11 [D] The LORD also **said** to Moses,
3:14 [D] The LORD **said** to Moses in the Desert of Sinai,
3:44 [D] The LORD also **said** to Moses,
4: 1 [D] The LORD **said** to Moses and Aaron:
4:17 [D] The LORD **said** to Moses and Aaron,
4:21 [D] The LORD **said** to Moses,
5: 1 [D] The LORD **said** to Moses,
5: 4 [D] They did just as the LORD *had* **instructed** Moses.
5: 5 [D] The LORD **said** to Moses,
5: 6 [D] "**Say** to the Israelites: 'When a man or woman wrongs
5:11 [D] Then the LORD **said** to Moses,
5:12 [D] "**Speak** to the Israelites and say to them: 'If a man's wife
6: 1 [D] The LORD **said** to Moses,
6: 2 [D] "**Speak** to the Israelites and say to them: 'If a man or woman
6:22 [D] The LORD **said** to Moses,
6:23 [D] "**Tell** Aaron and his sons, 'This is how you are to bless the
7:89 [D] When Moses entered the Tent of Meeting to **speak** with the
7:89 [F] he heard the voice **speaking** to him from between the two
7:89 [D] cover on the ark of the Testimony. And *he* **spoke** with him.
8: 1 [D] The LORD **said** to Moses,
8: 2 [D] "**Speak** to Aaron and say to him, 'When you set up the seven
8: 5 [D] The LORD **said** to Moses:
8:23 [D] The LORD **said** to Moses,
9: 1 [D] The LORD **spoke** to Moses in the Desert of Sinai in the
9: 4 [D] So Moses **told** the Israelites to celebrate the Passover,
9: 9 [D] Then the LORD **said** to Moses,
9:10 [D] "**Tell** the Israelites: 'When any of you or your descendants
10: 1 [D] The LORD **said** to Moses:
10:29 [D] for the LORD *has* **promised** good things to Israel."
11:17 [D] I will come down and **speak** with you there, and I will take
11:24 [D] went out and **told** the people what the LORD had said.
11:25 [D] the LORD came down in the cloud and **spoke** with him,
12: 1 [D] Miriam and Aaron *began to* **talk** against Moses because of
12: 2 [D] "*Has* the LORD **spoken** only through Moses?" they asked.
12: 2 [D] they asked. "Hasn't *he* also **spoken** through us?"
12: 6 [D] I reveal myself to him in visions, *I* **speak** to him in dreams.
12: 8 [D] With him *I* **speak** face to face, clearly and not in riddles; he
12: 8 [D] were you not afraid to **speak** against my servant Moses?"
13: 1 [D] The LORD **said** to Moses,
14:17 [D] the Lord's strength be displayed, just as *you have* **declared**:
14:26 [D] The LORD **said** to Moses and Aaron:
14:28 [D] the LORD, I will do to you the very things I heard *you* **say**:
14:35 [D] I, the LORD, *have* **spoken**, and I will surely do these things
14:39 [D] When Moses **reported** this to all the Israelites, they mourned
15: 1 [D] The LORD **said** to Moses,
15: 2 [D] "**Speak** to the Israelites and say to them: 'After you enter the
15:17 [D] The LORD **said** to Moses,
15:18 [D] "**Speak** to the Israelites and say to them: 'When you enter
15:22 [D] to keep any of these commands the LORD **gave** Moses—
15:38 [D] "**Speak** to the Israelites and say to them: 'Throughout the
16: 5 [D] *he* **said** to Korah and all his followers: "In the morning the
16:20 [D] The LORD **said** to Moses and Aaron,
16:23 [D] Then the LORD **said** to Moses,
16:24 [D] "**Say** to the assembly, 'Move away from the tents of Korah,
16:26 [D] *He* **warned** the assembly, "Move back from the tents of
16:31 [D] As soon as he finished **saying** all this, the ground under
16:36 [17:1] [D] The LORD **said** to Moses,
16:40 [17:5] [D] as the LORD **directed** him through Moses.
16:44 [17:9] [D] and the LORD **said** to Moses,
16:47 [17:12] [D] So Aaron did as Moses **said**, and ran into the midst
17: 1 [17:16] [D] The LORD **said** to Moses,
17: 2 [17:17] [D] "**Speak** to the Israelites and get twelve staffs from
17: 6 [17:21] [D] So Moses **spoke** to the Israelites, and their leaders
18: 8 [D] the LORD **said** to Aaron, "I myself have put you in charge
18:25 [D] The LORD **said** to Moses,
18:26 [D] "**Speak** to the Levites and say to them: 'When you receive
19: 1 [D] The LORD **said** to Moses and Aaron:
19: 2 [D] **Tell** the Israelites to bring you a red heifer without defect or
20: 7 [D] The LORD **said** to Moses,
20: 8 [D] **Speak** to that rock before their eyes and it will pour out its
21: 5 [D] they **spoke** against God and against Moses, and said, "Why
21: 7 [D] "We sinned when *we* **spoke** against the LORD and against
22: 7 [D] they came to Balaam, *they* **told** him what Balak had said.
22: 8 [D] "and I will bring you back the answer the LORD **gives** me."
22:19 [D] and I will find out what else the LORD *will* **tell** me."
22:20 [D] to summon you, go with them, but do only what *I* **tell** you."
22:35 [D] "Go with the men, but **speak** only what I tell you."
22:35 [D] "Go with the men, but speak only what *I* **tell** you."
22:38 [D] to you now," Balaam replied. "But can I **say** just anything?
22:38 [D] *I must* **speak** only what God puts in my mouth."
23: 2 [D] Balak did as Balaam **said**, and the two of them offered a bull
23: 5 [D] and said, "Go back to Balak and **give** him this **message**."
23:12 [D] "Must I not **speak** what the LORD puts in my mouth?"
23:16 [D] and said, "Go back to Balak and **give** him this **message**."
23:17 [D] of Moab. Balak asked him, "What *did* the LORD **say**?"
23:19 [D] he speak and then not act? *Does he* **promise** and not fulfill?
23:26 [D] "*Did I* not **tell** you I must do whatever the LORD says?"
23:26 [D] "Did I not tell you I must do whatever the LORD **says**?"
24:12 [D] answered Balak, "*Did I* not **tell** the messengers you sent me,
24:13 [D] of the LORD—and *I must* **say** only what the LORD says'?
24:13 [D] of the LORD—and I must say only what the LORD **says**'?
25:10 [D] The LORD **said** to Moses,
25:16 [D] The LORD **said** to Moses,
26: 3 [D] Moses and Eleazar the priest **spoke** with them and said,
26:52 [D] The LORD **said** to Moses,
27: 7 [A] "*What* Zelophehad's daughters *are* **saying** is right.
27: 8 [D] "**Say** to the Israelites, 'If a man dies and leaves no son, turn
27:15 [D] Moses **said** to the LORD,
27:23 [D] as the LORD **instructed** through Moses.
28: 1 [D] The LORD **said** to Moses,
30: 1 [30:2] [D] Moses **said** to the heads of the tribes of Israel: "This
31: 1 [D] The LORD **said** to Moses,
31: 3 [D] So Moses **said** to the people, "Arm some of your men to go
32:27 [A] cross over to fight before the LORD, just as our lord **says**."
32:31 [D] "Your servants will do what the LORD *has* **said**.
33:50 [D] by the Jordan across from Jericho the LORD **said** to Moses,
33:51 [D] "**Speak** to the Israelites and say to them: 'When you cross the
34: 1 [D] The LORD **said** to Moses,
34:16 [D] The LORD **said** to Moses,
35: 1 [D] the Jordan across from Jericho, the LORD **said** to Moses,
35: 9 [D] Then the LORD **said** to Moses:
35:10 [D] "**Speak** to the Israelites and say to them: 'When you cross the
36: 1 [D] came and **spoke** before Moses and the leaders, the heads of
36: 5 [A] "What the tribe of the descendants of Joseph *is* **saying** is
Dt 1: 1 [D] These are the words Moses **spoke** to all Israel in the desert
1: 3 [D] Moses **proclaimed** to the Israelites all that the LORD had
1: 6 [D] The LORD our God **said** to us at Horeb, "You have stayed
1:11 [D] you a thousand times and bless you as *he has* **promised**!
1:14 [D] You answered me, "What *you* **propose** to do is good."
1:21 [D] of it as the LORD, the God of your fathers, **told** you.
1:43 [D] So *I* **told** you, but you would not listen. You rebelled against
2: 1 [D] the route to the Red Sea, as the LORD *had* **directed** me.
2:17 [D] the LORD **said** to me,
3:26 [D] "*Do* not **speak** to me anymore about this matter.
4:12 [D] the LORD **spoke** to you out of the fire. You heard the sound
4:15 [D] You saw no form of any kind the day the LORD **spoke** to
4:33 [D] Has any other people heard the voice of God **speaking** out of
4:45 [D] and laws Moses **gave** them when they came out of Egypt
5: 1 [A] the decrees and laws I **declare** in your hearing today.
5: 4 [D] The LORD **spoke** to you face to face out of the fire on the
5:22 [D] These are the commandments the LORD **proclaimed** in a
5:24 [D] Today we have seen that a man can live even if God **speaks**
5:26 [D] ever heard the voice of the living God **speaking** out of fire,
5:27 [D] **tell** us whatever the LORD our God tells you. We will listen
5:27 [D] tell us whatever the LORD our God **tells** you. We will listen
5:28 [D] The LORD heard you when you **spoke** to me
5:28 [D] said to me, "I have heard what this people **said** to you.
5:28 [D] what this people said to you. Everything *they* **said** was good.
5:31 [D] stay here with me so that *I may* **give** you all the commands,
6: 3 [D] just as the LORD, the God of your fathers, **promised** you.
6: 7 [D] **Talk** about them when you sit at home and when you walk
6:19 [D] out all your enemies before you, as the LORD **said**.
9: 3 [D] annihilate them quickly, as the LORD *has* **promised** you.
9:10 [D] LORD **proclaimed** to you on the mountain out of the fire,
9:28 [D] not able to take them into the land *he had* **promised** them,
10: 4 [D] the Ten Commandments *he had* **proclaimed** to you on the
10: 9 [D] is their inheritance, as the LORD your God **told** them.)
11:19 [D] **talking** about them when you sit at home and when you walk
11:25 [D] as *he* **promised** you, will put the terror and fear of you on the
12:20 [D] your God has enlarged your territory as *he* **promised** you,
13: 2 [13:3] [D] or wonder of which *he has* **spoken** takes place,
13: 5 [13:6] [D] because *he* **preached** rebellion against the LORD
15: 6 [D] the LORD your God will bless you as *he has* **promised**,
18: 2 [D] the LORD is their inheritance, as *he* **promised** them.
18:17 [D] The LORD said to me: "What *they* **say** is good.
18:18 [D] his mouth, and *he will* **tell** them everything I command him.
18:19 [D] If anyone does not listen to my words that the prophet **speaks**
18:20 [D] a prophet who presumes to **speak** in my name anything I

Dt 18:20 [D] in my name anything I have not commanded him to **say**,
18:20 [D] or a prophet who **speaks** in the name of other gods, must be
18:21 [D] "How can we know when a message *has* not *been* **spoken** by
18:22 [D] If what a prophet **proclaims** in the name of the LORD does
18:22 [D] or come true, that is a message the LORD *has* not **spoken**.
18:22 [D] That prophet *has* **spoken** presumptuously. Do not be afraid
19: 8 [D] and gives you the whole land *he* **promised** them,
20: 2 [D] the priest shall come forward and **address** the army.
20: 5 [D] The officers *shall* **say** to the army: "Has anyone built a new
20: 8 [D] shall add, **[RPH]** "Is any man afraid or fainthearted?
20: 9 [D] When the officers have finished **speaking** to the army, they
23:23 [23:24] [D] LORD your God with your own mouth. **[RPH]**
25: 8 [D] the elders of his town shall summon him and **talk** to him.
26:18 [D] his treasured possession as *he* **promised**, and that you are to
26:19 [D] be a people holy to the LORD your God, as *he* **promised**.
27: 3 [D] just as the LORD, the God of your fathers, **promised** you.
27: 9 [D] are Levites, **said** to all Israel, "Be silent, O Israel, and listen!
29:13 [29:12] [D] that he may be your God as *he* **promised** you and as
31: 1 [D] Then Moses went out and **spoke** these words to all Israel:
31: 3 [D] Joshua also will cross over ahead of you, as the LORD **said**.
31:28 [D] so that *I can* **speak** these words in their hearing and call
31:30 [D] Moses **recited** the words of this song from beginning to end
32: 1 [D] Listen, O heavens, and *I will* **speak**; hear, O earth, the words
32:44 [D] **spoke** all the words of this song in the hearing of the people.
32:45 [D] When Moses finished **reciting** all these words to all Israel,
32:48 [D] On that same day the LORD **told** Moses,
Jos 1: 3 [D] every place where you set your foot, as *I* **promised** Moses.
4: 8 [D] of the tribes of the Israelites, as the LORD *had* **told** Joshua;
4:10 [D] had commanded Joshua **[NIE]** was done by the people,
4:12 [D] armed, in front of the Israelites, as Moses *had* **directed** them.
5:14 [D] "What **message** *does* my Lord *have* for his servant?"
9:21 [D] So the leaders' **promise** to them *was kept*.
9:22 [D] Joshua summoned the Gibeonites and **said**, "Why did you
10:12 [D] to Israel, Joshua **said** to the LORD in the presence of Israel:
11:23 [D] took the entire land, just as the LORD *had* **directed** Moses,
13:14 [D] the God of Israel, are their inheritance, as *he* **promised** them.
13:33 [D] the God of Israel, is their inheritance, as *he* **promised** them.
14: 6 [D] "You know what the LORD **said** to Moses the man of God
14:10 [D] "Now then, just as the LORD **promised**, he has kept me
14:10 [D] has kept me alive for forty-five years since the time he **said**
14:12 [D] Now give me this hill country that the LORD **promised** me
14:12 [D] LORD helping me, I will drive them out just as he **said**."
17:14 [D] The people of Joseph **said** to Joshua, "Why have you given
20: 1 [D] Then the LORD **said** to Joshua:
20: 2 [D] "**Tell** the Israelites to designate the cities of refuge, as I
20: 2 [D] the cities of refuge, as *I* **instructed** you through Moses,
20: 4 [D] the city gate and **state** his case before the elders of that city.
21: 2 [D] at Shiloh in Canaan and **said** to them, "The LORD
21:45 [D] Not one of all the LORD's good **promises** [+1821] to the
22: 4 [D] your God has given your brothers rest as *he* **promised**,
22:15 [D] and the half-tribe of Manasseh—*they* **said** to them:
22:21 [D] the half-tribe of Manasseh replied **[NIE]** to the heads of the
22:30 [D] Gad and Manasseh *had to* **say**, they were pleased.
23: 5 [D] of their land, as the LORD your God **promised** you.
23:10 [D] the LORD your God fights for you, just as *he* **promised**.
23:14 [D] the good promises the LORD your God **gave** you has failed.
23:15 [D] **[NIE]** so the LORD will bring on you all the evil he has
24:27 [D] It has heard all the words the LORD *has* **said** to us.
Jdg 1:20 [D] As Moses *had* **promised**, Hebron was given to Caleb, who
2: 4 [D] When the angel of the LORD *had* **spoken** these things to all
2:15 [D] as he had sworn to them. **[RPH]** They were in great distress.
5:12 [D] Wake up, wake up, **break out** *in* song! Arise, O Barak!
6:17 [D] your eyes, give me a sign that it is really you **talking** to me.
6:27 [D] took ten of his servants and did as the LORD **told** him.
6:36 [D] "If you will save Israel by my hand as *you have* **promised**—
6:37 [D] will know that you will save Israel by my hand, as *you* **said**."
6:39 [D] not be angry with me. *Let me* **make** just one more **request**.
7:11 [D] listen to what *they are* **saying**. Afterward, you will be
8: 3 [D] At **[RPH]** this, their resentment against him subsided.
8: 8 [D] he went up to Peniel and **made** *the* same **request** of them,
9: 1 [D] in Shechem and **said** to them and to all his mother's clan,
9: 2 [D] "**Ask** all the citizens of Shechem, 'Which is better for you:
9: 3 [D] When the brothers **repeated** all this to the citizens of
9:37 [D] Gaal **spoke up** again: "Look, people are coming down from
11:11 [D] And he **repeated** all his words before the LORD in Mizpah.
12: 6 [D] because *he* could not **pronounce** the word correctly,
13:11 [D] the man, he said, "Are you the one who **talked** to my wife?"
14: 7 [D] he went down and **talked** with the woman, and he liked her.
15:17 [D] When he finished **speaking**, he threw away the jawbone; and
16:10 [D] "You have made a fool of me; *you* **lied** [+3942] to me.
16:13 [D] you have been making a fool of me and **lying** [+3942] to me.
19: 3 [D] her husband went to her to **persuade** [+4213+6584] her to
19:30 [D] of Egypt. Think about it! Consider it! **Tell** us what to do!"
20: 3 [D] the Israelites said, "**Tell** us how this awful thing happened."
21:13 [D] the whole assembly sent **[NIE]** an offer of peace to the
Ru 1:18 [D] Ruth was determined to go with her, she stopped **urging** her.
2:13 [D] and *have* **spoken** [+4213+6584] **kindly** *to* your servant—
4: 1 [D] When the kinsman-redeemer *he had* **mentioned** came along,
1Sa 1:13 [D] Hannah *was* **praying** in her heart, and her lips were moving
1:16 [D] *I have been* **praying** here out of my great anguish
2: 3 [D] "Do not keep **talking** so proudly or let your mouth speak
3: 9 [D] "Go and lie down, and if he calls you, say, '**Speak**, LORD,
3:10 [D] Then Samuel said, "**Speak**, for your servant is listening."
3:12 [D] At that time I will carry out against Eli everything *I* **spoke**
3:17 [D] "What was it *he* **said** to you?" Eli asked. "Do not hide it
3:17 [D] so severely, if you hide from me anything *he* **told** you."
4:20 [D] was dying, the women attending her **said**, "Don't despair;
8:21 [D] all that the people said, *he* **repeated** it before the LORD.
9: 6 [D] he is highly respected, and everything *he* **says** comes true.
9:21 [D] the tribe of Benjamin? Why *do you* **say** such a thing to me?"
9:25 [D] the town, Samuel **talked** with Saul on the roof of his house.
10:25 [D] Samuel **explained** to the people the regulations of the
11: 4 [D] to Gibeah of Saul and **reported** these terms to the people,
14:19 [D] While Saul *was* **talking** to the priest, the tumult in the
15:16 [D] "Let me tell you what the LORD **said** to me last night."
15:16 [D] the LORD said to me last night." "**Tell** me," Saul replied.
16: 4 [D] Samuel did what the LORD **said**. When he arrived at
17:23 [D] As he *was* **talking** with them, Goliath, the Philistine
17:23 [D] stepped out from his lines and **shouted** his usual defiance,
17:28 [D] David's oldest brother, heard him **speaking** with the men,
17:31 [D] What David **said** was overheard and reported to Saul,
18: 1 [D] After David had finished **talking** with Saul, Jonathan became
18:22 [D] "**Speak** to David privately and say, 'Look, the king is pleased
18:23 [D] They **repeated** these words to David. But David said, "Do
18:24 [D] When Saul's servants told him what David *had* **said**,
19: 1 [D] Saul **told** his son Jonathan and all the attendants to kill
19: 3 [D] I'll **speak** to him about you and will tell you what I find out."
19: 4 [D] Jonathan **spoke** well of David to Saul his father and said to
20:23 [D] about the matter you and I **discussed**—remember,
20:26 [D] Saul **said** nothing that day, for he thought, "Something must
24:16 [24:17] [D] When David finished **saying** this, Saul asked, "Is
25: 9 [D] men arrived, *they* **gave** Nabal this message in David's name.
25:17 [D] He is such a wicked man that no *one can* **talk** to him."
25:24 [D] Please *let* your servant **speak** to you; hear what your servant
25:30 [D] for my master every good thing *he* **promised** concerning him
25:39 [D] David sent word to Abigail, **asking** her to become his wife.
25:40 [D] His servants went to Carmel and **said** to Abigail, "David has
28:17 [D] The LORD has done what *he* **predicted** through me. The
28:21 [D] I took my life in my hands and did what *you* **told** me to do.
2Sa 2:27 [D] "As surely as God lives, if *you had* not **spoken**,
3:19 [D] Abner also **spoke** *to* the Benjamites in person. Then he went
3:19 [D] Then he went to Hebron to **tell** David everything that Israel
3:27 [D] into the gateway, as though to **speak** with him privately.
7: 7 [D] *did I* **ever say** [+906+1821] *to* any of their rulers whom I
7:17 [D] Nathan **reported** to David all the words of this entire
7:19 [D] *you have* also **spoken** about the future of the house of your
7:20 [D] "What more *can* David **say** to you? For you know your
7:25 [D] keep forever the promise *you have* **made** concerning your
7:25 [D] concerning your servant and his house. Do as *you* **promised**,
7:28 [D] and *you have* **promised** these good things to your servant.
7:29 [D] for you, O Sovereign LORD, *have* **spoken**, and with your
11:19 [D] "When you have finished **giving** the king this account of the
12:18 [D] still living, *we* **spoke** to David but he would not listen to us.
13:13 [D] Please **speak** to the king; he will not keep me from being
13:22 [D] Absalom never **said a word** to Amnon, either good or bad;
13:36 [D] As he finished **speaking**, the king's sons came in, wailing
14: 3 [D] go to the king and **speak** these words to him." And Joab put
14:10 [D] "If anyone **says** anything to you, bring him to me,
14:12 [D] "*Let* your servant **speak** a word to my lord the king."
14:12 [D] speak a word to my lord the king." "**Speak**," he replied.
14:13 [D] When the king **says** this, does he not convict himself,
14:15 [D] "And now I have come to **say** this to my lord the king
14:15 [D] Your servant thought, '*I will* **speak** to the king; perhaps he
14:18 [D] to ask you." "*Let* my lord the king **speak**," the woman said.
14:19 [D] to the right or to the left from anything my lord the king **says**.
17: 6 [D] to him, Absalom said, "Ahithophel *has* **given** this advice.
17: 6 [D] Should we do what he says? If not, **give** us your **opinion**."
19: 7 [19:8] [D] Now go out and **encourage** [+4213+6584] your men.
19:11 [19:12] [D] "**Ask** the elders of Judah, 'Why should you be the
19:29 [19:30] [D] The king said to him, "Why **say** [+1821] more?
20:16 [D] Listen! Tell Joab to come here so *I can* **speak** to him."
20:18 [D] She continued, "Long ago *they* **used to say** [+1819], 'Get
20:18 [D] She continued, "Long ago *they* **used to say** [+1819], 'Get
22: 1 [D] David **sang** to the LORD the words of this song when the
23: 2 [D] "The Spirit of the LORD **spoke** through me; his word was
23: 3 [D] The God of Israel spoke, the Rock of Israel **said** to me:
24:12 [D] "Go and **tell** David, 'This is what the LORD says: I am
1Ki 1:14 [D] While you *are* still there **talking** to the king, I will come in

1Ki 1:22 [D] While she *was* still **speaking** with the king, Nathan the
1:42 [D] Even as he *was* **speaking**, Jonathan son of Abiathar the priest
2:4 [D] and that the LORD may keep his **promise** [+1821] to me:
2:14 [D] something to say to you." "*You may* **say** it," she replied.
2:16 [D] of you. Do not refuse me." "*You may* **make** it," she said.
2:18 [D] Bathsheba replied, "I *will* **speak** to the king for you."
2:19 [D] When Bathsheba went to King Solomon to **speak** to him for
2:23 [D] does not pay with his life for this **request** [+906+1821]!
2:24 [D] and has founded a dynasty for me as *he* **promised**—
2:27 [D] fulfilling the word the LORD *had* **spoken** at Shiloh about
2:30 [D] to the king, "This is how Joab **[NIE]** answered me."
2:31 [D] the king commanded Benaiah, "Do as *he* **says**. Strike him
2:38 [D] is good. Your servant will do as my lord the king *has* **said**."
3:22 [D] the living one is mine." And so *they* **argued** before the king.
4:32 [5:12] [D] *He* **spoke** three thousand proverbs and his songs
4:33 [5:13] [D] *He* **described** plant life, from the cedar of Lebanon
4:33 [5:13] [D] *He* also **taught** about animals and birds, reptiles
5:5 [5:19] [D] as the LORD **told** my father David, when he said,
5:12 [5:26] [D] Solomon wisdom, just as *he had* **promised** him.
6:12 [D] I will fulfill through you the promise *I* **gave** to David your
8:15 [D] what *he* **promised** with his own mouth *to* my father David.
8:20 [D] "The LORD has kept the promise *he* **made**: I have
8:20 [D] I sit on the throne of Israel, just as the LORD **promised**,
8:24 [D] You have kept *your* **promise** to your servant David my
8:24 [D] with your mouth *you have* **promised** and with your hand
8:25 [D] my father *the* **promises** *you* **made** to him when you said,
8:26 [D] let your word that *you* **promised** your servant David my
8:53 [D] just as *you* **declared** through your servant Moses when you,
8:56 [D] who has given rest to his people Israel just as *he* **promised**.
8:56 [D] Not one word has failed of all the good promises *he* **gave**
9:5 [D] Israel forever, as *I* **promised** David your father when I said,
10:2 [D] and **talked** with him *about* all that she had on her mind.
12:3 [D] whole assembly of Israel went to Rehoboam and **said** to him:
12:7 [D] *They* **replied**, "If today you will be a servant to these people
12:7 [D] serve them and **give** them a favorable **answer** [+448+1821],
12:9 [D] How should we answer these people who **say** to me, 'Lighten
12:10 [D] The young men who had grown up with him **replied**, "Tell
12:10 [D] "Tell these people who *have* **said** to you, 'Your father put a
12:10 [D] **tell** them, 'My little finger is thicker than my father's waist.
12:12 [D] as the king *had* **said**, "Come back to me in three days."
12:14 [D] he followed the advice of the young men and **said**, "My
12:15 [D] to fulfill the word the LORD *had* **spoken** to Jeroboam son
13:3 [D] "This is the sign the LORD *has* **declared**: The altar will be
13:7 [D] The king **said** to the man of God, "Come home with me
13:11 [D] They also told their father what *he had* **said** to the king.
13:12 [D] Their father **asked** them, "Which way did he go?" And his
13:18 [D] you are. And an angel **said** to me by the word of the LORD:
13:22 [D] drank water in the place where *he* **told** you not to eat or
13:25 [D] and **reported** it in the city where the old prophet lived.
13:26 [D] killed him, as the word of the LORD *had* **warned** him."
13:27 [D] The prophet **said** to his sons, "Saddle the donkey for me,"
14:2 [D] the one *who* **told** me I would be king over this people.
14:5 [D] he is ill, and *you are to* **give** her such and such **an answer**.
14:11 [D] on those who die in the country. The LORD *has* **spoken**!'
14:18 [D] as the LORD *had* **said** [+1821] through his servant the
15:29 [D] according to the word of the LORD **given** through his
16:12 [D] in accordance with the word of the LORD **spoken** against
16:34 [D] in accordance with the word of the LORD **spoken** by
17:16 [D] in keeping with the word of the LORD **spoken** by Elijah.
20:11 [D] The king of Israel answered, "**Tell** him: 'One who puts on
21:2 [D] Ahab **said** to Naboth, "Let me have your vineyard to use for
21:4 [D] Naboth the Jezreelite *had* **said** [+448+1821+2021], "I will not
21:5 [D] His wife Jezebel came in and **asked** him, "Why are you
21:6 [D] *He* **answered** her, "Because I said to Naboth the Jezreelite,
21:6 [D] He answered her, "Because *I* **said** to Naboth the Jezreelite,
21:19 [D] **Say** to him, 'This is what the LORD says: Have you not
21:19 [D] Then **say** to him, 'This is what the LORD says:
21:23 [D] "And also concerning Jezebel the LORD **says**: 'Dogs will
22:13 [D] The messenger who had gone to summon Micaiah **said** to
22:13 [D] Let your word agree with theirs, and **speak** favorably."
22:14 [D] LORD lives, *I can* **tell** him only what the LORD tells me."
22:16 [D] "How many times must I make you swear *to* **tell** me nothing
22:23 [D] of yours. The LORD *has* **decreed** disaster for you."
22:24 [D] the LORD go when he went from me to **speak** *to* you?"
22:28 [D] ever return safely, the LORD *has* not **spoken** through me."
22:38 [D] up his blood, as the word of the LORD *had* **declared**.
2Ki 1:3 [D] the angel of the LORD **said** to Elijah the Tishbite, "Go up
1:3 [D] meet the messengers of the king of Samaria and **ask** them,
1:6 [D] he said to us, 'Go back to the king who sent you and **tell** him,
1:7 [D] The king **asked** them, "What kind of man was it who came to
1:7 [D] kind of man was it who came to meet you and **told** you this?"
1:9 [D] **said** to him, "Man of God, the king says, 'Come down!'"
1:9 [D] said to him, "Man of God, the king **says**, 'Come down!'"
1:10 [D] Elijah answered **[NIE]** the captain, "If I am a man of God,
1:11 [D] The captain said **[NIE]** to him, "Man of God, this is what
1:12 [D] **[NIE]** "may fire come down from heaven and consume you
1:13 [D] **[NIE]** "please have respect for my life and the lives of these
1:15 [D] The angel of the LORD **said** to Elijah, "Go down with him;
1:16 [D] *He* **told** the king, "This is what the LORD says: Is it
1:17 [D] according to the word of the LORD that Elijah *had* **spoken**.
2:11 [D] As they were walking along and **talking** together, suddenly a
2:22 [D] to this day, according to the word Elisha *had* **spoken**.
4:13 [D] *Can* we **speak** on your behalf to the king or the commander
4:17 [D] same time she gave birth to a son, just as Elisha *had* **told** her.
5:4 [D] to his master and told him what the girl from Israel *had* **said**.
5:13 [D] Naaman's servants went to him and **said**, "My father,
5:13 [D] if the prophet *had* **told** you to do some great thing,
6:12 [D] tells the king of Israel the very words *you* **speak** in your
6:33 [D] While he *was* still **talking** to them, the messenger came
7:17 [D] just as the man of God *had* **foretold** when the king came
7:17 [D] just as the man of God had foretold **[RPH]** when the king
7:18 [D] It happened as the man of God *had* **said** to the king: "About
8:1 [D] Now Elisha *had* **said** to the woman whose son he had
8:4 [D] The king *was* **talking** to Gehazi, the servant of the man of
9:36 [D] "This is the word of the LORD that *he* **spoke** through his
10:10 [D] that not a word the LORD *has* **spoken** against the house of
10:10 [D] The LORD has done what *he* **promised** through his servant
10:17 [D] according to the word of the LORD **spoken** to Elijah.
14:25 [D] of Israel, **spoken** through his servant Jonah son of Amittai,
14:27 [D] since the LORD *had* not **said** he would blot out the name of
15:12 [D] So the word of the LORD **spoken** to Jehu was fulfilled:
17:23 [D] as *he had* **warned** through all his servants the prophets.
18:26 [D] "Please **speak** to your servants in Aramaic, since we
18:26 [D] Don't **speak** to us in Hebrew in the hearing of the people on
18:27 [D] and you that my master sent me to **say** these things,
18:28 [D] **[NIE]** "Hear the word of the great king, the king of Assyria!
19:21 [D] This is the word that the LORD *has* **spoken** against him:
20:9 [D] sign to you that the LORD will do what *he has* **promised**:
20:19 [D] "The word of the LORD *you have* **spoken** is good,"
21:10 [D] The LORD **said** through his servants the prophets:
22:14 [D] Shaphan and Asaiah went *to* **speak** to the prophetess Huldah,
22:19 [D] when you heard what *I have* **spoken** against this place
24:2 [D] in accordance with the word of the LORD **proclaimed** by
24:13 [D] As the LORD *had* **declared**, Nebuchadnezzar removed all
25:6 [D] at Riblah, where sentence *was* **pronounced** [+907] **on** him.
25:28 [D] *He* **spoke** kindly to him and gave him a seat of honor higher
1Ch 17:6 [D] *did I ever* **say** [+906+1821] *to* any of their leaders whom I
17:15 [D] Nathan **reported** to David all the words of this entire
17:17 [D] *you have* **spoken** about the future of the house of your
17:23 [D] let the promise *you have* **made** concerning your servant
17:23 [D] and his house be established forever. Do as *you* **promised**,
17:26 [D] *You have* **promised** these good things to your servant.
21:9 [D] The LORD **said** to Gad, David's seer,
21:10 [D] "Go and **tell** David, 'This is what the LORD says: I am
21:19 [D] to the word that Gad *had* **spoken** in the name of the LORD.
22:11 [D] the house of the LORD your God, as *he* **said** you would.
2Ch 6:4 [D] what *he* **promised** with his mouth *to* my father David.
6:10 [D] "The LORD has kept the promise *he* **made**. I have
6:10 [D] I sit on the throne of Israel, just as the LORD **promised**,
6:15 [D] You have kept *your* **promise** to your servant David my
6:15 [D] with your mouth *you have* **promised** and with your hand
6:16 [D] my father *the* **promises** *you* **made** to him when you said,
6:17 [D] let your word that *you* **promised** your servant David come
9:1 [D] and **talked** with him *about* all she had on her mind.
10:3 [D] and he and all Israel went to Rehoboam and **said** to him:
10:7 [D] *They* **replied**, "If you will be kind to these people and please
10:7 [D] please them and **give** them a favorable **answer** [+448+1821],
10:9 [A] How should we answer these people who **say** to me, 'Lighten
10:10 [D] The young men who had grown up with him **replied**, "Tell
10:10 [D] "Tell the people who *have* **said** to you, 'Your father put a
10:12 [D] as the king *had* **said**, "Come back to me in three days."
10:14 [D] he followed the advice of the young men and **said**, "My
10:15 [D] to fulfill the word the LORD *had* **spoken** to Jeroboam son
18:12 [D] The messenger who had gone to summon Micaiah **said** to
18:12 [D] Let your word agree with theirs, and **speak** favorably."
18:13 [D] as the LORD lives, *I can* **tell** him only what my God says."
18:15 [D] "How many times must I make you swear *to* **tell** me nothing
18:22 [D] of yours. The LORD *has* **decreed** disaster for you."
18:23 [D] the LORD go when he went from me to **speak** *to* you?"
18:27 [D] ever return safely, the LORD *has* not **spoken** through me."
23:3 [D] as the LORD **promised** concerning the descendants of
25:16 [D] While he was still **speaking**, the king said to him, "Have we
30:22 [D] Hezekiah **spoke** encouragingly *to* all the Levites,
32:6 [D] and **encouraged** [+4222+6584] them with these words:
32:16 [D] Sennacherib's officers **spoke** further against the LORD God
32:19 [D] *They* **spoke** about the God of Jerusalem as they did about the
33:10 [D] The LORD **spoke** to Manasseh and his people, but they
33:18 [D] the words the seers **spoke** to him in the name of the LORD,

2Ch 34:22 [D] those the king had sent with him went *to* **speak** to the
Ezr 8:17 [D] I told them what to **say** to Iddo and his kinsmen, the temple
Ne 6:12 [D] that *he had* **prophesied** [+5553] against me because Tobiah
9:13 [D] came down on Mount Sinai; *you* **spoke** to them from heaven.
13:24 [D] Half of their children **spoke** the language of Ashdod or the
13:24 [D] and did not know how to **speak** the language of Judah.
Est 1:22 [D] **proclaiming** in each people's tongue that every man should
6:10 [D] and do just as *you have* **suggested** for Mordecai the Jew,
6:10 [D] Do not neglect anything *you have* **recommended**."
6:14 [D] While they *were* still **talking** with him, the king's eunuchs
7:9 [D] had it made for Mordecai, who **spoke up** to help the king."
8:3 [D] Esther again **pleaded** with the king, falling at his feet
10:3 [A] of his people and **spoke up** *for* the welfare of all the Jews.
Job 1:16 [D] While he *was* still **speaking**, another messenger came
1:17 [D] While he *was* still **speaking**, another messenger came
1:18 [D] While he *was* still **speaking**, yet another messenger came
2:10 [D] He replied, "*You are* **talking** like a foolish woman. Shall we
2:10 [D] He replied, "You are talking like **[RPH]** a foolish woman.
2:13 [A] No *one* **said** a word to him, because they saw how great his
7:11 [D] *I will* **speak out** in the anguish of my spirit, I will complain
9:35 [D] *I would* **speak up** without fear of him, but as it now stands
10:1 [D] to my complaint and **speak out** in the bitterness of my soul.
11:5 [D] Oh, how I wish that God *would* **speak**, that he would open
13:3 [D] I desire *to* **speak** to the Almighty and to argue my case with
13:7 [D] *Will you* **speak** wickedly on God's behalf? Will you speak
13:7 [D] on God's behalf? *Will you* **speak** deceitfully for him?
13:13 [D] "Keep silent and *let* me **speak**; then let come to me what
13:22 [D] and I will answer, or *let me* **speak**, and you reply.
16:4 [D] I also *could* **speak** like you, if you were in my place; I could
16:6 [D] "Yet if *I* **speak**, my pain is not relieved; and if I refrain,
18:2 [D] you end these speeches? Be sensible, and then *we can* **talk**.
19:18 [D] the little boys scorn me; when I appear, *they* **ridicule** me.
21:3 [D] Bear with me while I **speak**, and after I have spoken,
21:3 [D] with me while I speak, and after I *have* **spoken**, mock on.
27:4 [D] my lips *will* not **speak** wickedness, and my tongue will utter
32:7 [D] I thought, 'Age *should* **speak**; advanced years should teach
32:16 [D] Must I wait, now that *they are* **silent** [+4202], now that they
32:20 [D] *I must* **speak** and find relief; I must open my lips and reply.
33:2 [D] to open my mouth; my **words** *are* on the tip of my tongue.
33:14 [D] For God *does* **speak**—now one way, now another—
33:31 [D] Job, and listen to me; be silent, and I *will* **speak**.
33:32 [D] to say, answer me; **speak up**, for I want you to be cleared.
34:33 [D] to repent? You must decide, not I; so **tell** me what you know.
34:35 [D] 'Job **speaks** without knowledge; his words lack insight.'
37:20 [D] Should he be told that *I want to* **speak**? Would any man ask
40:5 [D] *I* **spoke** once, but I have no answer—twice, but I will say no
41:3 [40:27] [D] *Will he* **speak** to you **with** gentle **words**?
42:4 [D] ⌞"You said,⌟ 'Listen now, and I *will* **speak**; I will question
42:7 [D] After the LORD *had* **said** these things to Job, he said to
42:7 [D] because *you have* not **spoken** of me what is right,
42:8 [D] *You have* not **spoken** of me what is right, as my servant Job
42:9 [D] and Zophar the Naamathite did what the LORD **told** them;
Ps 2:5 [D] *he* **rebukes** them in his anger and terrifies them in his wrath,
5:6 [5:7] [A] You destroy *those who* **tell** lies; bloodthirsty
12:2 [12:3] [D] Everyone **lies** [+8736] to his neighbor; their flattering
12:2 [12:3] [D] their flattering lips **speak** with deception.
12:3 [12:4] [D] all flattering lips and every **boastful** [+1524] tongue
15:2 [A] does what is righteous, *who* **speaks** the truth from his heart
17:10 [D] their callous hearts, and their mouths **speak** with arrogance.
18:T [18:1] [D] *He* **sang** to the LORD the words of this song when
28:3 [A] *who* **speak** cordially with their neighbors but harbor malice
31:18 [31:19] [A] contempt they **speak** arrogantly against the
34:13 [34:14] [D] tongue from evil and your lips from **speaking** lies.
35:20 [D] *They do* not **speak** peaceably, but devise false accusations
37:30 [D] man utters wisdom, and his tongue **speaks** what is just.
38:12 [38:13] [D] those who would harm me **talk** *of* my ruin;
39:3 [39:4] [D] the fire burned; then *I* **spoke** with my tongue:
40:5 [40:6] [D] were I to speak and **tell** of them, they would be too
41:6 [41:7] [D] *he* **speaks** falsely, while his heart gathers slander;
41:6 [41:7] [D] then he goes out and **spreads** it abroad.
49:3 [49:4] [D] My mouth *will* **speak** words of wisdom; the utterance
50:1 [D] **speaks** and summons the earth from the rising of the sun to
50:7 [D] "Hear, O my people, and *I will* **speak**, O Israel, and I will
50:20 [D] *You* **speak** continually against your brother and slander your
51:4 [51:6] [A] so that you are proved right when you **speak**
52:3 [52:5] [D] than good, falsehood rather than **speaking** the truth.
58:1 [58:2] [D] *Do you* rulers indeed **speak** justly? Do you judge
58:3 [58:4] [A] from the womb they are wayward and **speak** lies.
60:6 [60:8] [D] God *has* **spoken** from his sanctuary: "In triumph I
62:11 [62:12] [D] One thing God *has* **spoken**, two things have I heard:
63:11 [63:12] [A] while the mouths of **liars** [+9214] will be silenced.
66:14 [A] lips promised and my mouth **spoke** when I was in trouble.
73:8 [D] They scoff, and **speak** with malice; in their arrogance they
73:8 [D] with malice; in their arrogance *they* **threaten** oppression.
75:5 [75:6] [D] *do* not **speak** with outstretched neck.' "
77:4 [77:5] [D] my eyes from closing; I was too troubled *to* **speak**.
78:19 [D] *They* **spoke** against God, saying, "Can God spread a table in
85:8 [85:9] [D] I will listen to what God the LORD *will* **say**; he
85:8 [85:9] [D] *he* **promises** peace to his people, his saints—but let
87:3 [E] Glorious things **are said** of you, O city of God: *Selah*
89:19 [89:20] [D] Once *you* **spoke** in a vision, to your faithful people
94:4 [D] They pour out arrogant **words**; all the evildoers are full of
99:7 [D] *He* **spoke** to them from the pillar of cloud; they kept his
101:7 [A] no *one who* **speaks** falsely will stand in my presence.
108:7 [108:8] [D] God *has* **spoken** from his sanctuary: "In triumph I
109:2 [D] *they have* **spoken** against me *with* lying tongues.
109:20 [A] payment to my accusers, to those *who* **speak** evil of me.
115:5 [D] They have mouths, but cannot **speak**, eyes, but they cannot
116:10 [D] I believed; therefore *I* **said**, "I am greatly afflicted."
119:23 [C] Though rulers sit together and **slander** me, your servant will
119:46 [D] *I will* **speak** of your statutes before kings and will not be put
120:7 [D] I am a man of peace; but when *I* **speak**, they are for war.
122:8 [D] For the sake of my brothers and friends, *I will* **say**, "Peace be
127:5 [D] They will not be put to shame when *they* **contend** with their
135:16 [D] They have mouths, but cannot **speak**, eyes, but they cannot
144:8 [D] whose mouths *are* **full of** lies, whose right hands are
144:11 [D] from the hands of foreigners whose mouths *are* **full of** lies,
145:5 [D] *They will* **speak** [BHS 1821] *of* the glorious splendor of
145:11 [D] tell of the glory of your kingdom and **speak** *of* your might,
145:21 [D] My mouth *will* **speak** in praise of the LORD. Let every
Pr 2:12 [D] ways of wicked men, from men *whose* **words** are perverse,
8:6 [D] Listen, for *I have* worthy things *to* **say**; I open my lips to
16:13 [A] in honest lips; they value a *man who* **speaks** the truth.
18:23 [D] A poor man **pleads** *for* mercy, but a rich man answers
23:9 [D] *Do* not **speak** to a fool, for he will scorn the wisdom of your
23:16 [D] my inmost being will rejoice when your lips **speak** what is
23:33 [D] see strange sights and your mind **imagine** confusing things.
24:2 [D] plot violence, and their lips **talk** *about* making trouble.
25:11 [B] A word aptly **spoken** is like apples of gold in settings of
Ecc 1:8 [D] All things are wearisome, more than one can **say**. The eye
1:16 [D] I **thought** to myself, "Look, I have grown and increased in
2:15 [D] being wise?" *I* **said** in my heart, "This too is meaningless."
3:7 [D] and a time to mend, a time to be silent and a time to **speak**,
7:21 [D] Do not pay attention to every word *people* **say**, or you may
SS 8:8 [E] What shall we do for our sister for the day she **is spoken** for?
Isa 1:2 [D] O heavens! Listen, O earth! For the LORD *has* **spoken**:
1:20 [D] by the sword." For the mouth of the LORD *has* **spoken**.
7:10 [D] Again the LORD **spoke** to Ahaz,
8:5 [D] The LORD **spoke** to me again:
8:10 [D] **propose** your plan, but it will not stand, for God is with us.
9:17 [9:16] [A] is ungodly and wicked, every mouth **speaks** vileness.
16:13 [D] This is the word the LORD *has* already **spoken** concerning
16:14 [D] now the LORD **says**: "Within three years, as a servant
19:18 [D] In that day five cities in Egypt *will* **speak** the language of
20:2 [D] at that time the LORD **spoke** through Isaiah son of Amoz.
21:17 [D] will be few." The LORD, the God of Israel, *has* **spoken**.
22:25 [D] hanging on it will be cut down." The LORD *has* **spoken**.
24:3 [D] and totally plundered. The LORD *has* **spoken** this word.
25:8 [D] of his people from all the earth. The LORD *has* **spoken**.
28:11 [D] and strange tongues God *will* **speak** to this people,
29:4 [D] Brought low, *you will* **speak** from the ground; your speech
30:10 [D] of what is right! **Tell** us pleasant things, prophesy illusions.
32:4 [D] the stammering tongue *will be* **fluent** [+4200+4554] and
32:6 [D] For the fool **speaks** folly, his mind is busy with evil: He
32:6 [D] and **spreads** error concerning the LORD;
32:7 [D] the poor with lies, even when the **plea** *of* the needy is just.
33:15 [A] He who walks righteously and **speaks** what is right,
36:11 [D] "Please **speak** to your servants in Aramaic, since we
36:11 [D] Don't **speak** to us in Hebrew in the hearing of the people on
36:12 [D] and you that my master sent me to **say** these things,
37:22 [D] this is the word the LORD *has* **spoken** against him:
38:7 [D] sign to you that the LORD will do what *he has* **promised**:
38:15 [D] what *can I* **say**? He has spoken to me, and he himself has
39:8 [D] "The word of the LORD *you have* **spoken** is good,"
40:2 [D] **Speak** tenderly *to* Jerusalem, and proclaim to her that her
40:5 [D] will see it. For the mouth of the LORD *has* **spoken**."
40:27 [D] Why do you say, O Jacob, and **complain**, O Israel, "My way
41:1 [D] Let them come forward and **speak**; let us meet together at the
45:19 [D] *I have* not **spoken** in secret, from somewhere in a land of
45:19 [D] I, the LORD, **speak** the truth; I declare what is right.
46:11 [D] What *I have* **said**, that will I bring about; what I have
48:15 [D] I, even I, *have* **spoken**; yes, I have called him. I will bring
48:16 [D] "From the first announcement *I have* not **spoken** in secret;
52:6 [D] therefore in that day they will know that it is I who **foretold**
58:9 [D] of oppression, with the pointing finger and malicious **talk**,
58:13 [D] and not doing as you please or **speaking** idle words,
58:14 [D] of your father Jacob." The mouth of the LORD *has* **spoken**.
59:3 [D] Your lips *have* **spoken** lies, and your tongue mutters wicked

Isa 59: 4 [D] They rely on empty arguments and **speak** lies; they conceive
59: 13 [D] our backs on our God, **fomenting** oppression and revolt,
63: 1 [D] "It is I, **speaking** in righteousness, mighty to save."
65: 12 [D] but you did not answer, *I* **spoke** but you did not listen.
65: 24 [D] call I will answer; while they *are* still **speaking** I will hear.
66: 4 [D] I called, no one answered, *when I* **spoke**, no one listened.
Jer 1: 6 [D] Sovereign LORD," I said, "I do not know how *to* **speak**;
1: 7 [D] to everyone I send you to and **say** whatever I command you.
1: 16 [D] *I will* **pronounce** my judgments *on* my people because of
1: 17 [D] Stand up and **say** to them whatever I command you.
3: 5 [D] This is how *you* **talk**, but you do all the evil you can."
4: 12 [D] from me. Now I **pronounce** my judgments against them."
4: 28 [D] because *I have* **spoken** and will not relent, I have decided
5: 5 [D] So I will go to the leaders and **speak** *to* them; surely they
5: 14 [D] "Because the people *have* **spoken** these words, I will make
5: 15 [D] whose language you do not know, *whose* **speech** [+4537]
6: 10 [D] To whom *can I* **speak** and give warning? Who will listen to
7: 13 [D] declares the LORD, *I* **spoke** to you again and again, but you
7: 13 [D] spoke to you again and again, **[RPH]** but you did not listen;
7: 22 [D] I brought your forefathers out of Egypt and **spoke** *to* them,
7: 27 [D] "When *you* **tell** them all this, they will not listen to you;
8: 6 [D] I have listened attentively, but *they do* not **say** what is right.
9: 5 [9:4] [D] Friend deceives friend, and no *one* **speaks** the truth.
9: 5 [9:4] [D] They have taught their tongues *to* **lie** [+9214];
9: 8 [9:7] [D] Their tongue is a deadly arrow; *it* **speaks** *with* deceit.
9: 8 [9:7] [D] With his mouth *each* **speaks** cordially to his neighbor,
9: 12 [9:11] [D] Who *has been* **instructed** [+448+7023] *by* the
9: 22 [9:21] [D] **Say**, "This is what the LORD declares: " 'The dead
10: 1 [D] Hear what the LORD **says** to you, O house of Israel.
10: 5 [D] Like a scarecrow in a melon patch, their idols cannot **speak**;
11: 2 [D] **tell** them to the people of Judah and to those who live in
11: 17 [D] who planted you, *has* **decreed** disaster for you,
12: 1 [D] before you. Yet *I would* **speak** with you about your justice:
12: 6 [D] Do not trust them, though *they* **speak** well of you.
13: 15 [D] do not be arrogant, for the LORD *has* **spoken**.
14: 14 [D] I have not sent them or appointed them or **spoken** to them.
16: 10 [D] 'Why *has* the LORD **decreed** such a great disaster against
18: 7 [D] If at any time *I* **announce** that a nation or kingdom is to be
18: 8 [D] if that nation *I* **warned** repents of its evil, then I will relent
18: 9 [D] if at another time *I* **announce** that a nation or kingdom is to
18: 20 [D] and **spoke** in their behalf to turn your wrath away from them.
19: 2 [D] of the Potsherd Gate. There proclaim the words *I* **tell** you,
19: 5 [D] something I did not command or **mention**, nor did it enter
19: 15 [D] the villages around it every disaster *I* **pronounced** against
20: 8 [D] Whenever *I* **speak**, I cry out proclaiming violence
20: 9 [D] "I will not mention him or **speak** any more in his name,"
22: 1 [D] palace of the king of Judah and **proclaim** this message there:
22: 21 [A] *I* **warned** you when you felt secure, but you said, 'I will not
23: 16 [D] *They* **speak** visions from their own minds, not from the
23: 17 [D] keep saying to those who despise me, 'The LORD **says**:
23: 21 [D] *I did* not **speak** to them, yet they have prophesied.
23: 28 [D] but *let* the one who has my word **speak** it faithfully.
23: 35 [D] is the LORD's answer?' or 'What *has* the LORD **spoken**?'
23: 37 [D] LORD's answer to you?' or 'What *has* the LORD **spoken**?'
25: 2 [D] So Jeremiah the prophet **said** to all the people of Judah
25: 3 [D] has come to me and *I have* **spoken** to you again and again,
25: 3 [D] to you again and again, **[RPH]** but you have not listened.
25: 13 [D] I will bring upon that land all the things *I have* **spoken**
26: 2 [D] **speak** to all the people of the towns of Judah who come to
26: 2 [D] **Tell** them everything I command you; do not omit a word.
26: 7 [D] all the people heard Jeremiah **speak** these words in the house
26: 8 [D] as soon as Jeremiah finished **telling** all the people everything
26: 8 [D] people everything the LORD had commanded him to **say**,
26: 13 [D] and not bring the disaster *he has* **pronounced** against you.
26: 15 [D] for in truth the LORD has sent me to you to **speak** all these
26: 16 [D] *He has* **spoken** to us in the name of the LORD our God."
26: 19 [D] so that he did not bring the disaster *he* **pronounced** against
27: 12 [D] *I* **gave the** same **message** [+465+1821+2021+2021+3972] to
27: 13 [D] plague with which the LORD *has* **threatened** any nation
27: 16 [D] *I* **said** to the priests and all these people, "This is what the
28: 7 [A] listen to what I *have to* **say** in your hearing and in the
28: 16 [D] because *you have* **preached** rebellion against the LORD.' "
29: 23 [D] neighbors' wives and in my name *have* **spoken** [+1821] lies,
29: 32 [D] because *he has* **preached** rebellion against me.' "
30: 2 [D] says: 'Write in a book all the words *I have* **spoken** to you.
30: 4 [D] These are the words the LORD **spoke** concerning Israel
31: 20 [D] Though I often **speak** against him, I still remember him.
32: 4 [D] *will* **speak** *with* him face to face and see him with his own
32: 24 [D] attacking it. What *you* **said** has happened, as you now see.
32: 42 [A] so I will give them all the prosperity I *have* **promised** them.
33: 14 [D] 'when I will fulfill the gracious promise *I* **made** to the house
33: 24 [D] "Have you not noticed that these people *are* **saying**, 'The
34: 3 [D] with your own eyes, and he *will* **speak** *with* you face to face.
34: 5 [D] *I* myself **make** *this* **promise** [+1821], declares the
34: 6 [D] Jeremiah the prophet **told** all this to Zedekiah king of Judah,
35: 2 [D] **invite** them to come to one of the side rooms of the house of
35: 14 [D] I *have* **spoken** to you again and again, yet you have not
35: 14 [D] to you again and again, **[RPH]** yet you have not obeyed me.
35: 17 [D] on everyone living in Jerusalem every disaster *I* **pronounced**
35: 17 [D] *I* **spoke** to them, but they did not listen; I called to them,
36: 2 [D] write on it all the words *I have* **spoken** to you concerning
36: 2 [D] all the other nations from the time *I began* **speaking** to you
36: 4 [D] dictated all the words the LORD *had* **spoken** to him,
36: 7 [D] wrath **pronounced** against this people *by* the LORD are
36: 31 [D] the people of Judah every disaster *I* **pronounced** against
37: 2 [D] the LORD *had* **spoken** through Jeremiah the prophet.
38: 1 [D] Pashhur son of Malkijah heard what Jeremiah *was* **telling** all
38: 4 [D] as well as all the people, by the things he *is* **saying** to them.
38: 8 [D] Ebed-Melech went out of the palace and **said** to him,
38: 20 [A] "Obey the LORD by doing what I **tell** you.
38: 25 [D] If the officials hear that *I* **talked** with you, and they come to
38: 25 [D] 'Tell us what *you* **said** to the king and what the king said to
38: 25 [D] us what you said to the king and what the king **said** to you;
39: 5 [D] of Hamath, where *he* **pronounced** [+907] sentence **on** him.
39: 12 [D] after him; don't harm him but do for him whatever *he* **asks**."
40: 2 [D] "The LORD your God **decreed** this disaster for this place.
40: 3 [D] has brought it about; he has done just as *he* **said** he would.
40: 16 [A] a thing! *What* you *are* **saying** about Ishmael is not true."
42: 19 [D] of Judah, the LORD *has* **told** you, 'Do not go to Egypt.'
43: 1 [D] When Jeremiah finished **telling** the people all the words of
43: 2 [D] the arrogant men said to Jeremiah, "You *are* **lying** [+9214]!
44: 16 [D] "We will not listen to the message *you have* **spoken** to us in
44: 25 [D] actions what you **promised** [+928+7023] when you said,
45: 1 [D] This is what Jeremiah the prophet **told** Baruch son of Neriah
46: 13 [D] **spoke** to Jeremiah the prophet *about* the coming of
50: 1 [D] This is the word the LORD **spoke** through Jeremiah the
51: 12 [D] out his purpose, *his* **decree** against the people of Babylon.
51: 62 [D] 'O LORD, you *have* **said** you will destroy this place,
52: 9 [D] of Hamath, where *he* **pronounced** [+907] sentence **on** him.
52: 32 [D] *He* **spoke** kindly to him and gave him a seat of honor higher
Eze 1: 28 [D] I fell facedown, and I heard the voice of *one* **speaking**.
2: 1 [D] "Son of man, stand up on your feet and *I will* **speak** to you."
2: 2 [D] As *he* **spoke**, the Spirit came into me and raised me to my
2: 2 [F] and raised me to my feet, and I heard *him* **speaking** to me.
2: 7 [D] *You must* **speak** my words to them, whether they listen
2: 8 [D] you, son of man, listen to what I **say** to you. Do not rebel like
3: 1 [D] eat this scroll; then go and **speak** to the house of Israel."
3: 4 [D] go now to the house of Israel and **speak** my words to them.
3: 10 [D] listen carefully and take to heart all the words *I* **speak** to you.
3: 11 [D] Go now to your countrymen in exile and **speak** to them. Say
3: 18 [D] or **speak out** to dissuade him from his evil ways in order to
3: 22 [D] and go out to the plain, and there *I will* **speak** to you."
3: 24 [D] *He* **spoke** to me and said: "Go, shut yourself inside your
3: 27 [D] when I **speak** to you, I will open your mouth and you shall
5: 13 [D] they will know that I the LORD *have* **spoken** in my zeal.
5: 15 [D] and with stinging rebuke. I the LORD *have* **spoken**.
5: 17 [D] bring the sword against you. I the LORD *have* **spoken**."
6: 10 [D] *I did* not **threaten** in vain to bring this calamity on them.
10: 5 [D] outer court, like the voice of God Almighty when he **speaks**.
11: 25 [D] and *I* **told** the exiles everything the LORD had shown me.
12: 23 [D] **Say** to them, 'The days are near when every vision will be
12: 25 [D] I the LORD *will* **speak** what I will, and it shall be fulfilled
12: 25 [D] I the LORD will speak what *I* **will**[s] [+1821], and it shall be
12: 25 [D] you rebellious house, I will fulfill *whatever I* **say** [+1821],
12: 28 [D] whatever *I* **say** [+1821] will be fulfilled,
13: 7 [D] you say, "The LORD declares," though I *have* not **spoken**?
13: 8 [D] Because of your false **words** and lying visions, I am against
14: 4 [D] Therefore **speak** to them and tell them, 'This is what the
14: 9 [D] " 'And if the prophet is enticed *to* **utter** a prophecy,
17: 21 [D] Then you will know that I the LORD *have* **spoken**.
17: 24 [D] " 'I the LORD *have* **spoken**, and I will do it.' "
20: 3 [D] "Son of man, **speak** to the elders of Israel and say to them,
20: 27 [D] son of man, **speak** to the people of Israel and say to them,
21: 17 [21:22] [D] my wrath will subside. I the LORD *have* **spoken**."
21: 32 [21:37] [D] no more; for I the LORD *have* **spoken**.' "
22: 14 [D] I deal with you? I the LORD *have* **spoken**, and I will do it.
22: 28 [D] Sovereign LORD says'—when the LORD *has* not **spoken**.
23: 34 [D] your breasts. I *have* **spoken**, declares the Sovereign LORD.
24: 14 [D] " 'I the LORD *have* **spoken**. The time has come for me to
24: 18 [D] So *I* **spoke** to the people in the morning, and in the evening
24: 27 [D] *you will* **speak** with him and will no longer be silent.
26: 5 [D] for I *have* **spoken**, declares the Sovereign LORD.
26: 14 [D] You will never be rebuilt, for I the LORD *have* **spoken**,
28: 10 [D] I *have* **spoken**, declares the Sovereign LORD.' "
29: 3 [D] **Speak** to him and say: 'This is what the Sovereign LORD
30: 12 [D] the land and everything in it. I the LORD *have* **spoken**.
32: 21 [D] From within the grave the mighty leaders *will* **say** of Egypt
33: 2 [D] "Son of man, **speak** to your countrymen and say to them:

Eze 33: 8 [D] and *you do* not **speak out** to dissuade him from his ways,
33: 30 [C] your countrymen *are* **talking together** about you by the
33: 30 [D] **saying** to each other, 'Come and hear the message that has
34: 24 [D] will be prince among them. I the LORD *have* **spoken.**
36: 5 [D] In my burning zeal *I have* **spoken** against the rest of the
36: 6 [D] I **speak** in my jealous wrath because you have suffered the
36: 36 [D] was desolate. I the LORD *have* **spoken**, and I will do it.'
37: 14 [D] you will know that I the LORD *have* **spoken**, and I have
37: 19 [D] **say** to them, 'This is what the Sovereign LORD says: I am
37: 21 [D] and **say** to them, 'This is what the Sovereign LORD says:
38: 17 [D] Are you not the one *I* **spoke** *of* in former days by my
38: 19 [D] fiery wrath *I* **declare** that at that time there shall be a great
39: 5 [D] You will fall in the open field, for I *have* **spoken**,
39: 8 [D] the Sovereign LORD. This is the day *I have* **spoken** *of.*
40: 4 [D] The man **said** to me, "Son of man, look with your eyes
40: 45 [D] *He* **said** to me, "The room facing south is for the priests who
41: 22 [D] The man **said** to me, "This is the table that is before the
43: 6 [F] I heard *someone* **speaking** to me from inside the temple.
44: 5 [D] give attention to everything I **tell** you concerning all the
Da 1: 19 [D] The king **talked** with them, and he found none equal to
2: 4 [D] Then the astrologers **answered** the king in Aramaic, "O king,
8: 13 [D] I heard a holy one **speaking**, and another holy one said to
8: 13 [D] **[RPH]** "How long will it take for the vision to be fulfilled—
8: 18 [D] While he *was* **speaking** to me, I was in a deep sleep, with my
9: 6 [D] who **spoke** in your name to our kings, our princes and our
9: 12 [D] You have fulfilled the words **spoken** against us and against
9: 20 [D] While I *was* **speaking** and praying, confessing my sin
9: 21 [D] while I was still **[RPH]** in prayer, Gabriel, the man I had
9: 22 [D] He instructed me and **said** to me, "Daniel, I have now come
10: 11 [A] consider carefully the words I *am about to* **speak** to you,
10: 11 [D] to you." And when he **said** this to me, I stood up trembling.
10: 15 [D] While he *was* **saying** this to me, I bowed with my face
10: 16 [D] my lips, and I opened my mouth and *began to* **speak**.
10: 17 [D] How can I, your servant, **talk** with you, my lord? My
10: 19 [D] When he **spoke** to me, I was strengthened and said, "Speak,
10: 19 [D] spoke to me, I was strengthened and said, "**Speak**, my lord,
11: 27 [D] will sit at the same table and **lie** *to each* **other** [+3942],
11: 36 [D] and *will* **say** unheard-of things against the God of gods.
Hos 1: 2 [D] When the LORD began *to* **speak** through Hosea,
2: 14 [2:16] [D] lead her into the desert and **speak** tenderly *to* her.
7: 13 [D] I long to redeem them but they **speak** lies against me.
10: 4 [D] *They* **make many promises** [+1821], take false oaths
12: 4 [12:5] [D] He found him at Bethel and **talked** with him there—
12: 10 [12:11] [D] *I* **spoke** to the prophets, gave them many visions
13: 1 [D] When Ephraim **spoke**, men trembled; he was exalted in
Joel 3: 8 [4:8] [D] a nation far away." The LORD *has* **spoken**.
Am 3: 1 [D] Hear this word the LORD *has* **spoken** against you,
3: 8 [D] The Sovereign LORD *has* **spoken**—who can but prophesy?
5: 10 [A] who reproves in court and despise *him who* **tells** the truth.
Ob 1: 18 [D] survivors from the house of Esau." The LORD *has* **spoken**.
Jnh 3: 2 [A] city of Nineveh and proclaim to it the message I **give** you."
3: 10 [D] did not bring upon them the destruction *he had* **threatened**.
Mic 4: 4 [D] them afraid, for the LORD Almighty *has* **spoken** [+7023].
6: 12 [D] her people *are* **liars** [+9214] and their tongues speak
7: 3 [A] judge accepts bribes, the powerful **dictate** what they desire—
Hab 2: 1 [D] I will look to see what *he will* **say** to me, and what answer I
Zep 3: 13 [D] *they will* **speak** no lies, nor will deceit be found in their
Zec 1: 9 [A] The angel who *was* **talking** with me answered, "I will show
1: 13 [A] and comforting words to the angel who **talked** with me.
1: 14 [A] the angel who *was* **speaking** to me said, "Proclaim this word:
1: 19 [2:2] [A] I asked the angel who *was* **speaking** to me, "What are
2: 3 [2:7] [A] the angel who *was* **speaking** to me left, and another
2: 4 [2:8] [D] "Run, **tell** that young man, 'Jerusalem will be a city
4: 1 [A] the angel who **talked** with me returned and wakened me,
4: 4 [A] I asked the angel who **talked** with me, "What are these,
4: 5 [A] He **[RPH]** answered, "Do you not know what these are?"
5: 5 [A] the angel who *was* **speaking** to me came forward and said to
5: 10 [A] the basket?" I asked the angel who *was* **speaking** to me.
6: 4 [A] I asked the angel who *was* **speaking** to me, "What are these,
6: 8 [D] he called to me, **[NIE]** "Look, those going toward the north
8: 16 [D] **Speak** the truth to each other, and render true and sound
9: 10 [D] bow will be broken. *He will* **proclaim** peace to the nations.
10: 2 [D] The idols **speak** deceit, diviners see visions that lie; they tell
10: 2 [D] *they* **tell** dreams that are false, they give comfort in vain.
13: 3 [D] must die, because *you have* **told** lies in the LORD's name.'
Mal 3: 13 [C] the LORD. "Yet you ask, 'What *have we* **said** against you?'
3: 16 [C] Then those who feared the LORD **talked** with each other,

1820 ^{3}דָּבָר *dābar*^{3}, v. Not used in NIV/BHS

1821 דָּבָר *dābār*, n.m. [1440 / 1442] [√ 1819]

word [339], words [226], events [51], this^{s} [+2021+2021+2296] [44], annals [+3427] [37], *untranslated* [35], things [33], message [31], what^{s} [+2021] [31], thing [27], matter [24], what said [21], nothing [+4202] [18], promise [15], anything [14], say [13], this^{s} [+465+2021+2021] [12], command [11], everything [+2021+3972] [11], what^{s} [11], said [10], answer [9], report [8], what say [8], anything [+3972] [7], records [7], terms [7], because of [+6584] [6], case [6], commandments [6], it^{s} [+2021] [6], some time later [+339+465+2021+2021] [6], asked [5], cases [5], everything [+3972] [5], instructions [5], promises [5], reported [+906+8740] [5], this^{s} [+2021] [5], account [4], advice [4], answer [+906+8740] [4], commanded [4], it^{s} [+2021+2021+2296] [4], plan [4], promised [4], say [+1819] [4], sayings [4], something [4], told [4], affairs [3], annals [3], answer [+8740] [3], because [+6584] [3], commands [3], concerning [+6584] [3], conversation [3], instruction [3], lies [+9214] [3], questions [3], request [3], speak [3], way [3], what^{s} [+2021+2021+2296] [3], about [+6584] [2], achievements [2], affair [2], answered [+906+8740] [2], anything [+1821+2021+3972+4946] [2], bidding [2], charge [2], conduct [2], counsel [2], decree [2], deeds [2], dispute [2], doing [2], empty words [+8557] [2], for [+6584] [2], for each day [+928+3427+3427] [2], give answer [+448+1819] [2], nothing [+3972+4202] [2], nothing [+401] [2], occasion [2], order [2], predicting [2], regulations [2], relationship [2], required [2], requirement [2], requirements [2], saying [2], some [2], speaks [2], spoke [2], story [2], thoughts [2], verdict [+5477] [2], voice [2], what asks [2], what written [2], what^{s} [+465+2021+2021] [2], written [2], accusations [1], accuse [+928+8492] [1], activity [1], after [+928] [1], after a while [+339+465+2021+2021] [1], amount [1], animal^{s} [1], answer [+4200+8740] [1], answer [+6699] [1], answered [+8740] [1], answers [+8740] [1], anything [+2021+3972] [1], anything [+3972+4946] [1], as a result of [+6584] [1], ask [+2011+4946+6640] [1], at all [1], behavior [1], business [1], cases [+8191] [1], cause [1], charges [1], claims [1], compliments [+5833] [1], concerned [1], conferred [+2118] [1], conferred [1], consult [+928+2011] [1], curses [1], customary [+4027] [1], daily [+928+3427+3427] [1], danger [1], day by day [+928+2257+3427+3427] [1], day by day [+928+3427+3427] [1], decided [+6641] [1], decisions [1], deed [1], defiance [1], demand [1], details [1], directed [1], disease [1], disputes [1], done [1], duties [1], duty [1], edict [1], eloquent [+408] [1], else [1], enough [1], ever say [+906+1819] [1], everything [+465+2021+2021+3972] [1], feat [+1524] [1], flaw [+8273] [1], fulfilled [1], gave the message [+465+1819+2021+2021+3972] [1], harm [+8273] [1], how [1], idea [1], in behalf of [+6584] [1], inquires of [+928+8626] [1], instructed [1], it^{s} [1], language [1], later [+339+465+2021+2021] [1], lesson [1], lies [+3942] [1], make many promises [+1819] [1], make promise [+1819] [1], matters [1], mere talk [+8557] [1], mission [+889+8938] [1], need [1], news [1], nothing [+1524+2256+4202+7785] [1], nothing [+906+4202] [1], nothing whatever [+401+3972] [1], offering [1], one^{s} [1], ones^{s} [1], ordered [1], plans [1], plot [1], prediction [1], promise [+1819] [1], promises [+1819] [1], prophecy [1], proposal [1], proposed [1], question [1], record [1], refrain [1], reported [+906+906+8740] [1], reports [1], request [+906+1819] [1], requested [1], responded [1], revelation [1], rule [1], said [+1819] [1], said [+448+1819+2021] [1], say [+906+1819] [1], says [1], secret [1], sins [+6411] [1], situation [1], slandered [+6613+8492] [1], slanders [+4200+6613+8492] [1], something to say [1], songs [+8877] [1], speak up [1], speaking [+7754] [1], speaking [1], speech [1], speeches [1], spoken [+1819] [1], spoken [1], such^{s} [1], suggested [+2021+2021+2296] [1], suggestion [1], tell [+606] [1], text [1], that happened [+465+2021+2021] [1], that said [1], that^{s} [+465+2021+2021] [1], the word [1], them^{s} [+2021+2021+2296] [1], them^{s} [+3870] [1], theme [1], they^{s} [+3870] [1], this [+2021+2021+2296] [1], this is how [+465+2021+2021+3869] [1], this^{s} [+1821+2021+2296] [1], this^{s} [1], thought [1], threatened [1], threats [1], through [+3869] [1], times [1], transfer of property [+3972+9455] [1], trouble [1], what foretold [1], what happened [1], what have to say [1], what said [+7754] [1], what says [1], what spoke [1], what^{s} [+7754] [1], whatever [+4537] [1], whisper [1], why [1], will^{s} [+1819] [1], words [+7023] [1], work [1], year [+9102] [1]

Ge 11: 1 Now the whole world had one language and a common **speech**.
12: 17 and his household **because of** [+6584] Abram's wife Sarai.
15: 1 After **this**^{s} [+465+2021+2021], the word of the LORD came to
15: 1 After this, the **word** *of* the LORD came to Abram in a vision:
15: 4 the **word** *of* the LORD came to him: "This man will not be your
18: 14 Is **anything** too hard for the LORD? I will return to you at the
18: 25 Far be it from you to do such a **thing**—to kill the righteous with
19: 8 don't do **anything** to these men, for they have come under the
19: 21 He said to him, "Very well, I will grant this **request** too; I will not
19: 22 there quickly, because I cannot do **anything** until you reach it."
20: 8 and when he told them all **that** had **happened** [+465+2021+2021],
20: 10 "What was your reason for doing **this**^{s} [+2021+2021+2296]?"
20: 11 in this place, and they will kill me **because of** [+6584] my wife.'
20: 18 **because of** [+6584] Abraham's wife Sarah.
21: 11 The **matter** distressed Abraham greatly because it concerned his
21: 26 "I don't know who has done **this**^{s} [+2021+2021+2296].

Ge 22: 1 **Some time later** [+339+465+2021+2021] God tested Abraham.
22: 16 that because you have done **this**[s] [+2021+2021+2296] and have not
22: 20 **Some time later** [+339+465+2021+2021] Abraham was told,
24: 9 master Abraham and swore an oath to him concerning this **matter**.
24: 28 The girl ran and told her mother's household about these **things**.
24: 30 and had heard Rebekah **tell** [+606] what the man said to her,
24: 33 he said, "I will not eat until I have told you **what** I **have to say**."
24: 50 and Bethuel answered, "**This**[s] [+2021] is from the LORD;
24: 52 When Abraham's servant heard **what** they **said**, he bowed down to
24: 66 Then the servant told Isaac all **[NIE]** he had done.
27: 34 When Esau heard his father's **words**, he burst out with a loud
27: 42 When Rebekah was told **what** her older son Esau had **said**,
29: 13 brought him to his home, and there Jacob told him all these **things**.
30: 31 "But if you will do this *one* **thing** for me, I will go on tending your
30: 34 "Agreed," said Laban. "Let it be as you have **said**."
31: 1 Jacob heard that Laban's sons *were* **saying**, "Jacob has taken
32: 19 [32:20] "You are to say the same **thing** to Esau when you meet
34: 14 They said to them, "We can't do such a **thing**; we can't give our
34: 18 Their **proposal** seemed good to Hamor and his son Shechem.
34: 19 lost no time in doing what they **said**, because he was delighted
37: 8 hated him all the more because of his dream and **what** he had **said**.
37: 11 were jealous of him, but his father kept the **matter** in mind.
37: 14 your brothers and with the flocks, and bring **word** back to me."
39: 7 and **after a while** [+339+465+2021+2021] his master's wife took
39: 17 she told him this **story**: "That Hebrew slave you brought us came
39: 19 When his master heard the **story** his wife told him, saying,
39: 19 "**This is how** [+465+2021+2021+3869] your slave treated me,"
40: 1 **Some time later** [+339+465+2021+2021], the cupbearer and the
41: 28 "It is just as I said **[NIE]** to Pharaoh: God has shown Pharaoh
41: 32 in two forms is that the **matter** has been firmly decided by God,
41: 37 The **plan** seemed good to Pharaoh and to all his officials.
42: 16 so that your **words** may be tested to see if you are telling the truth.
42: 20 so that your **words** may be verified and that you may not die."
43: 7 'Do you have another brother?' We simply answered his **questions**.
43: 18 **because of** [+6584] the silver that was put back into our sacks the
44: 2 with the silver for his grain." And he did as Joseph said. **[NIE]**
44: 6 When he caught up with them, he repeated these **words** to them.
44: 7 But they said to him, "Why does my lord say such **things**?
44: 7 such things? Far be it from your servants to do **anything** like that!
44: 10 "Very well, then," he said, "let it be as you **say**. Whoever is found
44: 18 "Please, my lord, let your servant speak a **word** to my lord.
44: 24 to your servant my father, we told him **what** my lord had **said**.
45: 27 when they told him **everything** [+3972] Joseph had said to them,
47: 30 bury me where they are buried." "I will do as you **say**," he said.
48: 1 **Some time later** [+339+465+2021+2021] Joseph was told, "Your
Ex 1: 18 asked them, "Why have you done **this**[s] [+2021+2021+2296]?
2: 14 and thought, "**What**[s] [+2021] I did must have become known."
2: 15 When Pharaoh heard of **this**[s] [+2021+2021+2296], he tried to kill
4: 10 said to the LORD, "O Lord, I have never been **eloquent** [+408],
4: 15 You shall speak to him and put **words** in his mouth; I will help
4: 28 Moses told Aaron everything the LORD had sent him to **say**,
4: 30 Aaron told them **everything** [+3972] the LORD had said to
5: 9 so that they keep working and pay no attention to **lies** [+9214]."
5: 11 you can find it, but your work will not be reduced **at all**.' "
5: 13 the work required of you **for each day** [+928+3427+3427],
5: 19 of bricks required of you **for each day** [+928+3427+3427]."
8: 10 [8:6] Moses replied, "It will be as you **say**, so that you may know
8: 12 [8:8] Moses cried out to the LORD **about** [+6584] the frogs he
8: 13 [8:9] the LORD did what Moses **asked**. The frogs died in the
8: 31 [8:27] the LORD did what Moses **asked**: The flies left Pharaoh
9: 4 of Egypt, so that no **animal**[s] belonging to the Israelites will die.' "
9: 5 "Tomorrow the LORD will do **this**[s] [+2021+2021+2296] in the
9: 6 And the next day the LORD did **it**[s] [+2021+2021+2296]:
9: 20 Those officials of Pharaoh who feared the **word** *of* the LORD
9: 21 But those who ignored the **word** *of* the LORD left their slaves
12: 24 "Obey these **instructions** as a lasting ordinance for you and your
12: 35 The Israelites did as Moses **instructed** and asked the Egyptians for
14: 12 Didn't *we* **say** [+1819] to you in Egypt, 'Leave us alone; let us
16: 4 The people are to go out each day and gather **enough** for that day.
16: 16 This is **what**[s] [+2021] the LORD has commanded: 'Each one is to
16: 32 Moses said, "This is **what**[s] [+2021] the LORD has commanded:
18: 11 for he did **this**[s] [+2021] to those who had treated Israel
18: 14 "What is **this**[s] [+2021+2021+2296] you are doing for the people?
18: 16 Whenever they have a **dispute**, it is brought to me, and I decide
18: 17 Moses' father-in-law replied, "**What**[s] [+2021] you are doing is not
18: 18 The **work** is too heavy for you; you cannot handle it alone.
18: 19 people's representative before God and bring their **disputes** to him.
18: 22 people at all times, but have them bring every difficult **case** to you;
18: 22 difficult case to you; the simple **cases** they can decide themselves.
18: 23 If you do **this**[s] [+2021+2021+2296] and God so commands, you
18: 26 The difficult **cases** they brought to Moses, but the simple ones they
18: 26 brought to Moses, but the simple **ones**[s] they decided themselves.
19: 6 These are the **words** you are to speak to the Israelites."
19: 7 set before them all the **words** the LORD had commanded him to
19: 8 has said." So Moses brought their **answer** back to the LORD.
19: 9 in you." Then Moses told the LORD **what** the people had **said**.
20: 1 And God spoke all these **words**:
22: 9 [22:8] In all **cases** *of* illegal possession of an ox, a donkey, a
22: 9 [22:8] both parties are to bring their **cases** before the judges.
23: 7 Have nothing to do with a false **charge** and do not put an innocent
23: 8 a bribe blinds those who see and twists the **words** *of* the righteous.
24: 3 Moses went and told the people all the LORD's **words** and laws,
24: 3 "**Everything** [+2021+3972] the LORD has said we will do."
24: 4 Moses then wrote down everything the LORD had **said**. He got
24: 8 LORD has made with you in accordance with all these **words**."
24: 14 are with you, and anyone involved in a **dispute** can go to them."
29: 1 "This is **what**[s] [+2021] you are to do to consecrate them, so they
32: 28 The Levites did as Moses **commanded**, and that day about three
33: 4 When the people heard these distressing **words**, they began to
33: 17 "I will do the very **thing** you have asked, because I am pleased
34: 1 and I will write on them the **words** that were on the first tablets,
34: 27 Then the LORD said to Moses, "Write down these **words**,
34: 27 for in accordance with these **words** I have made a covenant with
34: 28 he wrote on the tablets the **words** *of* the covenant—the Ten
34: 28 the tablets the words of the covenant—the Ten **Commandments**.
35: 1 "These are the **things** the LORD has commanded you to do:
35: 4 "This is **what**[s] [+2021] the LORD has commanded:
Lev 4: 13 even though the community is unaware of the **matter**, they are
5: 2 " 'Or if a person touches **anything** [+3972] ceremonially unclean—
8: 5 "This is **what**[s] the LORD has commanded to be done."
8: 36 So Aaron and his sons did **everything** [+2021+3972] the LORD
9: 6 "This is **what**[s] [+2021] the LORD has commanded you to do,
10: 7 the LORD's anointing oil is on you." So they did as Moses **said**.
17: 2 say to them: 'This is **what**[s] [+2021] the LORD has commanded:
23: 37 sacrifices and drink offerings **required** *for* each day.
Nu 11: 23 will now see whether or not *what* I **say** will come true for you."
11: 24 So Moses went out and told the people **what** the LORD had **said**.
12: 6 he said, "Listen to my **words**: "When a prophet of the LORD is
13: 26 There *they* **reported** [+906+906+8740] *to* them and to the whole
14: 20 The LORD replied, "I have forgiven them, as you **asked**.
14: 39 When Moses reported **this**[s] [+465+2021+2021] to all the Israelites,
15: 31 Because he has despised the LORD's **word** and broken his
16: 31 As soon as he finished saying all **this**[s] [+465+2021+2021],
16: 49 [17:14] to those who had died **because of** [+6584] Korah.
18: 7 serve as priests in connection with **everything at** [+3972] the altar
20: 19 pay for it. We only want to pass through on foot—nothing **else**."
22: 7 When they came to Balaam, they told him **what** Balak had **said**.
22: 8 "and I will bring you back the **answer** the LORD gives me."
22: 20 summon you, go with them, but do only **what**[s] [+2021] I tell you."
22: 35 "Go with the men, but speak only **what**[s] [+2021] I tell you."
22: 38 I must speak only **what**[s] [+2021] God puts in my mouth."
23: 3 **Whatever** [+4537] he reveals to me I will tell you." Then he went
23: 5 The LORD put a **message** in Balaam's mouth and said, "Go back
23: 16 LORD met with Balaam and put a **message** in his mouth and said,
25: 18 you as enemies when they deceived you in the **affair** *of* Peor
25: 18 deceived you in the affair of Peor and **[RPH]** their sister Cozbi,
25: 18 was killed when the plague came **as a result** [+6584] **of** Peor."
30: 1 [30:2] of Israel: "This is **what**[s] [+2021] the LORD commands:
30: 2 [30:3] he must not break his **word** but must do everything he said.
31: 16 "They were the ones who followed Balaam's **advice** and were the
31: 16 the Israelites away from the LORD in **what happened** *at* Peor,
31: 23 **anything** [+3972] else that can withstand fire must be put through
32: 20 Then Moses said to them, "If you will do **this**[s] [+2021+2021+2296]
36: 6 This is **what**[s] [+2021] the LORD commands for Zelophehad's
Dt 1: 1 These are the **words** Moses spoke to all Israel in the desert east of
1: 14 You answered me, "**What**[s] [+2021] you propose to do is good."
1: 17 to God. Bring me any **case** too hard for you, and I will hear it.
1: 18 at that time I told you **everything** [+2021+3972] you were to do.
1: 22 bring back a **report** *about* the route we are to take and the towns
1: 23 The **idea** seemed good to me; so I selected twelve of you,
1: 25 of the land, they brought it down to us and **reported** [+906+8740],
1: 32 In spite of **this**[s] [+2021+2021+2296], you did not trust in the LORD
1: 34 When the LORD heard **what** you **said** [+7754], he was angry
2: 7 your God has been with you, and you have not lacked **anything**.
2: 26 I sent messengers to Sihon king of Heshbon **offering** peace
3: 26 the LORD said. "Do not speak to me anymore about this **matter**.
4: 2 Do not add to **what**[s] [+2021] I command you and do not subtract
4: 9 so that you do not forget the **things** your eyes have seen
4: 10 "Assemble the people before me to hear my **words** so that they
4: 12 You heard the sound of **words** but saw no form; there was only a
4: 13 He declared to you his covenant, the Ten **Commandments**,
4: 21 The LORD was angry with me **because of** [+6584] you,
4: 30 you are in distress and all these **things** have happened to you,
4: 32 Has **anything** so great as this ever happened, or has anything like it
4: 36 you his great fire, and you heard his **words** from out of the fire.
5: 5 the LORD and you to declare to you the **word** *of* the LORD,
5: 22 These are the **commandments** the LORD proclaimed in a loud
5: 28 The LORD heard **[RPH]** you when you spoke to me

Dt 5:28 said to me, "I have heard **what**[s] [+7754] this people said to you.
6: 6 These **commandments** that I give you today are to be upon your
9: 5 to accomplish **what**[s] [+2021] he swore to your fathers,
9:10 On them were all the **commandments** the LORD proclaimed to
10: 2 I will write on the tablets the **words** that were on the first tablets,
10: 4 the Ten **Commandments** he had proclaimed to you on the
11:18 Fix these **words** *of* mine in your hearts and minds; tie them as
12:28 Be careful to obey all these **regulations** I am giving you, so that it
12:32 [13:1] See that you do all **[NIE]** I command you; do not add to it
13: 3 [13:4] you must not listen to the **words** *of* that prophet
13:11 [13:12] and no one among you will do such an evil **thing** again.
13:14 [13:15] if **it**[s] [+2021] is true and it has been proved that this
15: 2 This is **how** it is to be done: Every creditor shall cancel the loan he
15: 9 Be careful not to harbor this wicked **thought**: "The seventh year,
15:10 because of **this**[s] [+2021+2021+2296] the LORD your God will bless
15:15 God redeemed you. That is why I give you this **command** today.
16:19 blinds the eyes of the wise and twists the **words** *of* the righteous.
17: 1 your God an ox or a sheep that has any defect or **flaw** [+8273] in it,
17: 4 If **it**[s] [+2021] is true and it has been proved that this detestable
17: 5 the man or woman who has done this evil **deed** to your city gate
17: 8 If **cases** [+8191] come before your courts that are too difficult for
17: 8 If cases **[RPH]** come before your courts that are too difficult for
17: 9 Inquire of them and they will give you the **verdict** [+5477].
17:10 You must act according to the **decisions** they give you at the place
17:11 Do not turn aside from **what**[s] [+2021] they tell you, to the right
17:19 and follow carefully all the **words** *of* this law and these decrees
18:18 I will put my **words** in his mouth, and he will tell them everything
18:19 If anyone does not listen to my **words** that the prophet speaks in
18:20 a prophet who presumes to speak in my name **anything** I have not
18:21 "How can we know when a **message** has not been spoken by the
18:22 the name of the LORD does not take place **[RPH]** or come true,
18:22 or come true, that is a **message** the LORD has not spoken.
19: 4 This is the **rule** *concerning* the man who kills another and flees
19:15 A **matter** must be established by the testimony of two or three
19:20 and never again will such an evil **thing** be done among you.
22:14 **slanders** [+4200+6613+8492] her and gives her a bad name,
22:17 Now he *has* **slandered** [+6613+8492] her and said, 'I did not find
22:20 the **charge** is true and no proof of the girl's virginity can be found,
22:24 the girl **because** [+6584] she was in a town and did not scream for
22:24 and the man **because** [+6584] he violated another man's wife.
22:26 Do **nothing** [+4202] to the girl; she has committed no sin
22:26 This **case** is like that of someone who attacks and murders his
23: 4 [23:5] **For** [+6584] they did not come to meet you with bread
23: 9 [23:10] keep away from **everything** [+3972] impure.
23:14 [23:15] so that he will not see among you **anything** indecent
23:19 [23:20] or food or **anything** [+3972] else that may earn interest.
24: 1 displeasing to him because he finds **something** indecent about her,
24: 5 he must not be sent to war or have any other **duty** laid on him.
24:18 That is why I command you to do **this**[s] [+2021+2021+2296].
24:22 That is why I command you to do **this**[s] [+2021+2021+2296].
27: 3 Write on them all the **words** *of* this law when you have crossed
27: 8 you shall write very clearly all the **words** *of* this law on these
27:26 "Cursed is the man who does not uphold the **words** *of* this law by
28:14 Do not turn aside from any of the **commands** I give you today,
28:58 If you do not carefully follow all the **words** *of* this law, which are
29: 1 [28:69] These are the **terms** *of* the covenant the LORD
29: 9 [29:8] Carefully follow the **terms** *of* this covenant, so that you
29:19 [29:18] When such a person hears the **words** *of* this oath, he
29:29 [29:28] that we may follow all the **words** *of* this law.
30: 1 When all these **[RPH]** blessings and curses I have set before you
30:14 No, the **word** is very near you; it is in your mouth and in your
31: 1 Then Moses went out and spoke these **words** to all Israel:
31:12 LORD your God and follow carefully all the **words** *of* this law.
31:24 After Moses finished writing in a book the **words** *of* this law from
31:28 so that I can speak these **words** in their hearing and call heaven
31:30 Moses recited the **words** *of* this song from beginning to end in the
32:44 and spoke all the **words** *of* this song in the hearing of the people.
32:45 When Moses finished reciting all these **words** to all Israel,
32:46 "Take to heart all the **words** I have solemnly declared to you this
32:46 command your children to obey carefully all the **words** *of* this law.
32:47 They are not just idle **words** for you—they are your life. By them
32:47 By **them**[s] [+2021+2021+2296] you will live long in the land
Jos 1:13 "Remember the **command** that Moses the servant of the LORD
1:18 Whoever rebels against your word and does not obey your **words**,
2:14 "If you don't tell what we are **doing**, we will treat you kindly
2:20 if you tell what we are **doing**, we will be released from the oath
2:21 "Agreed," she replied. "Let it be as you **say**." So she sent them
3: 9 "Come here and listen to the **words** *of* the LORD your God.
4:10 in the middle of the Jordan until **everything** [+2021+3972]
5: 4 Now this is **why** he did so: All those who came out of Egypt—
6:10 your voices, do not say a **word** until the day I tell you to shout.
8: 8 Do what the LORD has **commanded**. See to it; you have my
8:27 plunder of this city, as **[NIE]** the LORD had instructed Joshua.
8:34 Afterward, Joshua read all the **words** *of* the law—the blessings
8:35 There was not a **word** of all that Moses had commanded that
9:24 because of you, and that is why we did **this**[s] [+2021+2021+2296].
11:15 he left **nothing** [+4202] undone of all that the LORD commanded
14: 6 "You know **what**[s] [+2021] the LORD said to Moses the man of
14: 7 And I brought him back a **report** according to my convictions,
14:10 since the time he said **this**[s] [+2021+2021+2296] to Moses,
20: 4 of the city gate and state his **case** before the elders of that city.
21:45 Not **one**[s] of all the LORD's good promises to the house of Israel
21:45 Not one of all the LORD's good **promises** [+1819] to the house
22:24 We did it for fear **[NIE]** that some day your descendants might
22:30 heard **what**[s] [+2021] Reuben, Gad and Manasseh had to say,
22:32 and Gadites in Gilead and **reported** [+906+8740] *to* the Israelites.
22:33 They were glad to hear the **report** and praised God. And they
23:14 soul that not **[RPH]** one of all the good promises the LORD
23:14 soul that not one of all the good **promises** the LORD your God
23:14 has failed. Every **promise** has been fulfilled; not one has failed.
23:15 just as every good **promise** of the LORD your God has come
23:15 so the LORD will bring on you all the evil he has **threatened**,
24:26 And Joshua recorded these **things** in the Book of the Law of God.
24:29 After these **things**, Joshua son of Nun, the servant of the LORD,
Jdg 2: 4 When the angel of the LORD had spoken these **things** to all the
3:19 turned back and said, "I have a secret **message** for you, O king."
3:20 summer palace and said, "I have a **message** *from* God for you."
6:29 They asked each other, "Who did **this**[s] [+2021+2021+2296]?"
6:29 they were told, "Gideon son of Joash did **it**[s] [+2021+2021+2296]."
8: 1 "Why have you treated us like **this**[s] [+2021+2021+2296]?
8: 3 At **this**[s] [+2021+2021+2296], their resentment against him
9: 3 the brothers repeated all **this**[s] [+465+2021+2021] to the citizens of
9:30 Zebul the governor of the city heard **what** Gaal son of Ebed **said**,
11:10 "The LORD is our witness; we will certainly do as you **say**."
11:11 And he repeated all his **words** before the LORD in Mizpah.
11:28 however, paid no attention to the **message** Jephthah sent him.
11:37 grant me this one **request**," she said. "Give me two months to
13:12 So Manoah asked him, "When your **words** are fulfilled, what is to
13:17 so that we may honor you when your **word** comes true?"
16:16 With **such**[s] nagging she prodded him day after day until he was
18: 7 And since their land lacked **nothing** [+401], they were prosperous.
18: 7 way from the Sidonians and had no **relationship** with anyone else.
18:10 into your hands, a land that lacks **nothing whatever** [+401+3972]."
18:28 a long way from Sidon and had no **relationship** with anyone else.
19:19 and the young man with us. We don't need **anything** [+3972]."
19:24 you wish. But to this man, don't do such a disgraceful **thing**."
20: 7 Now, all you Israelites, **speak up** and give your verdict."
20: 9 now this is **what**[s] [+2021] we'll do to Gibeah: We'll go up against
21:11 "This is **what**[s] [+2021] you are to do," they said. "Kill every male
Ru 3:18 **[RPH]** For the man will not rest until the matter is settled today."
3:18 For the man will not rest until the **matter** is settled today."
4: 7 and **transfer of property** [+3972+9455] to become final,
1Sa 1:23 have weaned him; only may the LORD make good his **word**."
2:23 So he said to them, "Why do you do such **things**? I hear from all
2:23 I hear from all the people about these wicked **deeds** *of* yours.
3: 1 In those days the **word** *of* the LORD was rare; there were not
3: 7 The **word** *of* the LORD had not yet been revealed to him.
3:11 I am about to do **something** in Israel that will make the ears of
3:17 "What was **it**[s] [+2021] he said to you?" Eli asked. "Do not hide it
3:17 hide from me **anything** [+1821+2021+3972+4946] he told you."
3:17 hide from me **anything** [+1821+2021+3972+4946] he told you."
3:18 So Samuel told him **everything** [+2021+3972], hiding nothing
3:19 as he grew up, and he let none of his **words** fall to the ground.
3:21 and there he revealed himself to Samuel through his **word**.
4: 1 Samuel's **word** came to all Israel. Now the Israelites went out to
4:16 it this very day." Eli asked, "What happened, my son?" **[NIE]**
8: 6 "Give us a king to lead us," **this**[s] [+2021] displeased Samuel;
8:10 Samuel told all the **words** *of* the LORD to the people who were
8:21 When Samuel heard all **that** the people **said**, he repeated it before
9:10 "Good," **[NIE]** Saul said to his servant. "Come, let's go."
9:21 of the tribe of Benjamin? Why do you say such a **thing** to me?"
9:27 stay here awhile, so that I may give you a **message** *from* God."
10: 2 And now your father has stopped thinking about **[NIE]** them
10:16 he did not tell his uncle **what**[s] Samuel had said about the kingship.
11: 4 came to Gibeah of Saul and reported these **terms** to the people,
11: 5 Then they repeated to him **what** the men of Jabesh had **said**.
11: 6 When Saul heard their **words**, the Spirit of God came upon him in
12:16 see this great **thing** the LORD is about to do before your eyes!
14:12 his armor-bearer, "Come up to us and we'll teach you a **lesson**."
15: 1 his people Israel; so listen now to the **message** *from* the LORD.
15:10 Then the **word** *of* the LORD came to Samuel:
15:11 turned away from me and has not carried out my **instructions**."
15:13 LORD bless you! I have carried out the LORD's **instructions**."
15:23 Because you have rejected the **word** *of* the LORD, he has
15:24 I violated the LORD's command and your **instructions**.
15:26 You have rejected the **word** *of* the LORD, and the LORD has
16:18 and a warrior. He **speaks** well and is a fine-looking man.
17:11 On hearing the Philistine's **words**, Saul and all the Israelites were

1Sa 17:23 stepped out from his lines and shouted his usual **defiance**,
17:27 They repeated to him what they had been **saying** and told him,
17:29 "Now what have I done?" said David. "Can't I even **speak**?"
17:30 then turned away to someone else and brought up the same **matter**,
17:30 up the same matter, and the men **answered** [+8740] him as before.
17:30 up the same matter, and the men answered him as **[RPH]** before.
17:31 **What**[s] [+2021] David said was overheard and reported to Saul,
18:8 Saul was very angry; this **refrain** galled him. "They have credited
18:20 and when they told Saul about it, he was pleased. **[NIE]**
18:23 They repeated these **words** to David. But David said, "Do you
18:24 Saul's servants told him **what**[s] [+465+2021+2021] David had said,
18:26 When the attendants told David these **things**, he was pleased to
18:26 he was pleased **[RPH]** to become the king's son-in-law.
19:7 So Jonathan called David and told him the whole **conversation**.
20:2 Look, my father doesn't do **anything**, great or small, without
20:2 do anything, great or **[RPH]** small, without confiding in me.
20:2 Why would he hide **this**[s] [+2021+2021+2296] from me?
20:21 as surely as the LORD lives, you are safe; there is no **danger**.
20:23 about the **matter** you and I discussed—remember, the LORD is
20:39 (The boy knew nothing of all **this**[s]; only Jonathan and David
21:2 [21:3] "The king charged me with a *certain* **matter** and said to
21:2 [21:3] one is to know anything about your **mission** [+889+8938]
21:8 [21:9] other weapon, because the king's **business** was urgent."
21:12 [21:13] David took these **words** to heart and was very much
22:15 *Let* not the king **accuse** [+928+8492] your servant or any of his
22:15 for your servant knows nothing at all about this whole **affair**."
24:6 [24:7] "The LORD forbid that I should do such a **thing** to my
24:7 [24:8] With these **words** David rebuked his men and did not
24:9 [24:10] said to Saul, "Why do you listen **[NIE]** when men say,
24:16 [24:17] When David finished saying **this**[s] [+465+2021+2021],
25:9 men arrived, they gave Nabal this **message** in David's name.
25:12 and went back. When they arrived, they reported every **word**.
25:24 let your servant speak to you; hear **what** your servant has to **say**.
25:36 So she told him **nothing** [+1524+2256+4202+7785] until daybreak.
25:37 when Nabal was sober, his wife told him all these **things**,
26:16 **What**[s] [+2021+2021+2296] you have done is not good.
26:19 Now let my lord the king listen to his servant's **words**.
28:10 you will not be punished for **this**[s] [+2021+2021+2296]."
28:18 the LORD has done **this**[s] [+2021+2021+2296] to you today.
28:20 length on the ground, filled with fear because of Samuel's **words**.
28:21 I took my life in my hands and did **what**[s] you told me to do.
30:24 Who will listen to **what** you **say**? The share of the man who stayed
2Sa 1:4 "What **[NIE]** happened?" David asked. "Tell me." He said,
2:6 the same favor because you have done **this**[s] [+2021+2021+2296].
3:8 very angry because of **what** Ish-Bosheth **said** and he answered,
3:11 Ish-Bosheth did not dare to say another **word** to Abner, because he
3:13 will make an agreement with you. But I demand one **thing** of you:
3:17 Abner **conferred** with the elders of Israel and said, "For some time
7:4 That night the **word** *of* the LORD came to Nathan, saying:
7:7 *did I* **ever say to** [+906+1819] any of their rulers whom I
7:17 Nathan reported to David all the **words** of this entire revelation.
7:21 For the sake of your **word** and according to your will, you have
7:25 keep forever the **promise** you have made concerning your servant
7:28 Your **words** are trustworthy, and you have promised these good
11:11 with my wife? As surely as you live, I will not do such a **thing**!"
11:18 Joab sent David a full **account** *of* the battle.
11:19 "When you have finished giving the king this **account** *of* the
11:25 "Say this to Joab: 'Don't let **this**[s] [+2021+2021+2296] upset you;
11:27 him a son. But the **thing** David had done displeased the LORD.
12:6 four times over, because he did such a **thing** and had no pity."
12:9 Why did you despise the **word** *of* the LORD by doing what is evil
12:12 but I will do this **thing** in broad daylight before all Israel.' "
12:14 because by doing **this**[s] [+2021+2021+2296] you have made the
12:21 His servants asked him, "Why are you acting this **way**? While the
13:20 my sister; he is your brother. Don't take this **thing** to heart."
13:21 King David heard all **this**[s] [+465+2021+2021], he was furious.
13:22 hated Amnon **because** [+6584] he had disgraced his sister Tamar.
13:33 My lord the king should not be concerned about the **report** that all
13:35 the king's sons are here; it has happened just as your servant **said**."
14:3 go to the king and speak these **words** to him." And Joab put the
14:3 speak these words to him." And Joab put the **words** in her mouth.
14:12 woman said, "Let your servant speak a **word** to my lord the king."
14:13 When the king says **this**[s] [+2021+2021+2296], does he not convict
14:15 "And now I have come to say **this**[s] [+2021+2021+2296] to my lord
14:15 'I will speak to the king; perhaps he will do **what** his servant **asks**.
14:17 servant says, 'May the **word** *of* my lord the king bring me rest,
14:18 "Do not keep from me the **answer** to what I am going to ask you."
14:19 and who put all these **words** into the mouth of your servant.
14:20 Your servant Joab did **this**[s] [+2021+2021+2296] to change the
14:20 Your servant Joab did this to change the present **situation**.
14:21 king said to Joab, "Very well, I will do **it**[s] [+2021+2021+2296].
14:22 lord the king, because the king has granted his servant's **request**."
15:3 would say to him, "Look, your **claims** are valid and proper,
15:6 Absalom behaved in this **way** toward all the Israelites who came to
15:11 and went quite innocently, knowing nothing about the **matter**.
15:28 I will wait at the fords in the desert until **word** comes from you to
15:35 Tell them **anything** [+2021+3972] you hear in the king's palace.
15:36 with them. Send them to me with **anything** [+3972] you hear."
16:23 gave was like that of one *who* **inquires of** [+928+8626] God.
17:4 This **plan** seemed good to Absalom and to all the elders of Israel.
17:6 came to him, Absalom said, "Ahithophel has given this **advice**.
17:6 Should we do **what** he **says**? If not, give us your opinion."
17:19 and scattered grain over it. No one knew **anything** about it.
18:5 all the troops heard the king giving orders **concerning** [+6584]
18:13 in jeopardy—and **nothing** [+3972+4202] is hidden from the king—
19:11 [19:12] since **what** is being **said** throughout Israel has reached the
19:29 [19:30] The king said to him, "Why **say** [+1819] more? I order
19:42 [19:43] Why are you angry about **it**[s] [+2021+2021+2296]?
19:43 [19:44] Were we not the first to **speak** *of* bringing back our
19:43 [19:44] the men of Judah **responded** even more harshly than the
19:43 [19:44] even more harshly than **[RPH]** the men of Israel.
20:17 he answered. She said, "Listen to **what** your servant *has to* **say**."
20:21 That is not the **case**. A man named Sheba son of Bicri,
22:1 David sang to the LORD the **words** *of* this song when the
23:1 These are the last **words** *of* David: "The oracle of David son of
24:3 But why does my lord the king want to do such a **thing**?"
24:4 The king's **word**, however, overruled Joab and the army
24:11 the **word** *of* the LORD had come to Gad the prophet,
24:13 and decide how *I should* **answer** [+8740] the one who sent me."
24:19 went up, as the LORD had commanded **through** [+3869] Gad.
1Ki 1:7 Adonijah **conferred** [+2118] with Joab son of Zeruiah and with
1:14 to the king, I will come in and confirm **what** you have **said**."
1:27 Is this **something** my lord the king has done without letting his
2:4 and that the LORD may keep his **promise** [+1819] to me:
2:14 he added, "I have **something to say** to you." "You may say it,"
2:23 Adonijah does not pay with his life for this **request** [+906+1819]!
2:27 fulfilling the **word** the LORD had spoken at Shiloh about the
2:30 Benaiah **reported** [+906+8740] *to* the king, "This is how Joab
2:38 Shimei answered the king, "**What** you **say** is good. Your servant
2:42 At that time you said to me, '**What** you **say** is good. I will obey.'
3:10 The Lord was pleased **[RPH]** that Solomon had asked for this.
3:10 was pleased that Solomon had asked for **this**[s] [+2021+2021+2296].
3:11 said to him, "Since you have asked for **this**[s] [+2021+2021+2296]
3:12 I will do what you have **asked**. I will give you a wise
4:27 [5:7] They saw to it that **nothing** [+4202] was lacking.
5:7 [5:21] When Hiram heard Solomon's **message**, he was greatly
6:11 The **word** *of* the LORD came to Solomon:
6:12 I will fulfill through you the **promise** I gave to David your father.
6:38 the temple was finished in all its **details** according to its
8:20 "The LORD has kept the **promise** he made: I have succeeded
8:26 let your **word** that you promised your servant David my father
8:56 Not one **word** has failed of all the good promises he gave through
8:56 Not one word has failed of all the good **promises** he gave through
8:59 may these **words** *of* mine, which I have prayed before the LORD,
8:59 and the cause of his people Israel according to each day's **need**,
9:15 Here is the **account** *of* the forced labor King Solomon conscripted
10:3 Solomon answered all her **questions**; nothing was too hard for the
10:3 **nothing** [+4202] was too hard for the king to explain to her.
10:6 "The **report** I heard in my own country about your achievements
10:6 "The report I heard in my own country about your **achievements**
10:7 I did not believe these **things** until I came and saw with my own
10:25 Year **after** [+928] year, everyone who came brought a gift—
11:10 Although he had forbidden Solomon **[NIE]** to follow other gods,
11:27 Here is the **account** of how he rebelled against the king:
11:41 As for the other **events** *of* Solomon's reign—all he did
11:41 are they not written in the book of the **annals** *of* Solomon?
12:6 "How would you advise me to **answer** [+906+8740] these
12:7 and serve them and **give** them a favorable **answer** [+448+1819],
12:9 How *should we* **answer** [+906+8740] these people who say to me,
12:15 to fulfill the **word** the LORD had spoken to Jeroboam son of
12:16 refused to listen to them, they **answered** [+906+8740] the king:
12:22 But this **word** *of* God came to Shemaiah the man of God:
12:24 every one of you, for **this**[s] [+2021+2021+2296] is my doing.' "
12:24 for this is my doing.' " So they obeyed the **word** *of* the LORD
12:24 of the LORD and went home again, as the LORD had **ordered**.
12:30 this **thing** became a sin; the people went even as far as Dan to
13:1 By the **word** *of* the LORD a man of God came from Judah to
13:2 He cried out against the altar by the **word** *of* the LORD:
13:4 When King Jeroboam heard **what**[s] the man of God cried out
13:5 to the sign given by the man of God by the **word** *of* the LORD.
13:9 For I was commanded by the **word** *of* the LORD: 'You must not
13:11 They also told their father **what**[s] [+2021] he had said to the king.
13:17 I have been **told** by the word of the LORD: 'You must not eat
13:17 I have been told by the **word** *of* the LORD: 'You must not eat
13:18 as you are. And an angel said to me by the **word** *of* the LORD:
13:20 the **word** *of* the LORD came to the old prophet who had brought
13:26 and killed him, as the **word** *of* the LORD had warned him."
13:32 For the **message** he declared by the word of the LORD against

1Ki 13:32 For the message he declared by the **word** *of* the LORD against
13:33 Even after **this**[s] [+2021+2021+2296], Jeroboam did not change his
13:34 **This**[s] [+2021+2021+2296] was the sin of the house of Jeroboam
14: 5 "Jeroboam's wife is coming to **ask** [+2011+4946+6640] you about
14:13 in whom the LORD, the God of Israel, has found **anything** good.
14:18 as the LORD *had* **said** [+1819] through his servant the prophet
14:19 The other **events** *of* Jeroboam's reign, his wars and how he ruled,
14:19 are written in the book of the **annals** [+3427] of the kings of Israel.
14:29 As for the other **events** *of* Rehoboam's reign, and all he did,
14:29 are they not written in the book of the **annals** [+3427] of the kings
15: 5 all the days of his life—except in the **case** *of* Uriah the Hittite.
15: 7 As for the other **events** *of* Abijah's reign, and all he did, are they
15: 7 are they not written in the book of the **annals** [+3427] of the kings
15:23 As for all the other **events** *of* Asa's reign, all his achievements,
15:23 are they not written in the book of the **annals** [+3427] of the kings
15:29 according to the **word** *of* the LORD given through his servant
15:31 As for the other **events** *of* Nadab's reign, and all he did, are they
15:31 are they not written in the book of the **annals** [+3427] of the kings
16: 1 the **word** *of* the LORD came to Jehu son of Hanani against
16: 5 As for the other **events** *of* Baasha's reign, what he did and his
16: 5 are they not written in the book of the **annals** [+3427] of the kings
16: 7 the **word** *of* the LORD came through the prophet Jehu son of
16:12 in accordance with the **word** *of* the LORD spoken against Baasha
16:14 As for the other **events** *of* Elah's reign, and all he did, are they not
16:14 are they not written in the book of the **annals** [+3427] of the kings
16:20 As for the other **events** *of* Zimri's reign, and the rebellion he
16:20 are they not written in the book of the **annals** [+3427] of the kings
16:27 As for the other **events** *of* Omri's reign, what he did and the things
16:27 are they not written in the book of the **annals** [+3427] of the kings
16:34 in accordance with the **word** *of* the LORD spoken by Joshua son
17: 1 be neither dew nor rain in the next few years except at my **word**."
17: 2 Then the **word** *of* the LORD came to Elijah:
17: 5 So he did what the LORD had **told** him. He went to the Kerith
17: 8 Then the **word** *of* the LORD came to him:
17:13 said to her, "Don't be afraid. Go home and do as you have **said**.
17:15 She went away and did as Elijah had **told** her. So there was food
17:16 in keeping with the **word** *of* the LORD spoken by Elijah.
17:17 **Some time later** [+339+465+2021+2021] the son of the woman
17:24 and that the **word** *of* the LORD from your mouth is the truth."
18: 1 in the third year, the **word** *of* the LORD came to Elijah:
18:21 is God, follow him." But the people said **nothing** [+906+4202].
18:24 he is God." Then all the people said, "What you **say** is good."
18:31 to whom the **word** *of* the LORD had come, saying, "Your name
18:36 I am your servant and have done all these **things** at your command.
18:36 am your servant and have done all these things at your **command**.
19: 9 and spent the night. And the **word** *of* the LORD came to him:
20: 4 The king of Israel answered, "Just as you **say**, my lord the king.
20: 9 this **demand** I cannot meet.' " They left and took the answer back
20: 9 cannot meet.' " They left and took the **answer** back to Ben-Hadad.
20:12 Ben-Hadad heard this **message** while he and the kings were
20:24 Do **this**[s] [+2021+2021+2296]: Remove all the kings from their
20:35 By the **word** *of* the LORD one of the sons of the prophets said to
21: 1 **Some time later** [+339+465+2021+2021] there was an incident
21: 4 Naboth the Jezreelite *had* **said** [+448+1819+2021], "I will not give
21:17 Then the **word** *of* the LORD came to Elijah the Tishbite:
21:27 When Ahab heard these **words**, he tore his clothes, put on
21:28 Then the **word** *of* the LORD came to Elijah the Tishbite:
22: 5 said to the king of Israel, "First seek the **counsel** *of* the LORD."
22:13 as one man the other prophets are **predicting** success for the king.
22:13 the king. Let your **word** agree with theirs, and speak favorably."
22:13 Let your word agree **[RPH]** with theirs, and speak favorably."
22:19 Micaiah continued, "Therefore hear the **word** *of* the LORD:
22:38 dogs licked up his blood, as the **word** *of* the LORD had declared.
22:39 As for the other **events** *of* Ahab's reign, including all he did,
22:39 are they not written in the book of the **annals** [+3427] of the kings
22:45 [22:46] As for the other **events** *of* Jehoshaphat's reign, the things
22:45 [22:46] are they not written in the book of the **annals** [+3427] of
2Ki 1: 7 who came to meet you and told you **this**[s] [+465+2021+2021]?"
1:16 because there is no God in Israel for you to **consult** [+928+2011]
1:17 according to the **word** *of* the LORD that Elijah had spoken.
1:18 As for all the other **events** *of* Ahaziah's reign, and what he did,
1:18 are they not written in the book of the **annals** [+3427] of the kings
2:22 wholesome to this day, according to the **word** Elisha had spoken.
3:12 Jehoshaphat said, "The **word** *of* the LORD is with him."
4:41 people to eat." And there was **nothing** [+4202] harmful in the pot.
4:44 and had some left over, according to the **word** *of* the LORD.
5:13 "My father, if the prophet had told you to do *some* great **thing**,
5:14 as the man of God had **told** him, and his flesh was restored
5:18 But may the LORD forgive your servant for this one **thing**:
5:18 may the LORD forgive your servant for **this**[s] [+2021+2021+2296]."
6:11 **This**[s] [+2021+2021+2296] enraged the king of Aram.
6:12 tells the king of Israel the very **words** you speak in your bedroom."
6:18 So he struck them with blindness, as Elisha had **asked**.
6:30 When the king heard the woman's **words**, he tore his robes.
7: 1 Elisha said, "Hear the **word** *of* the LORD. This is what the
7: 2 floodgates of the heavens, could **this** [+2021+2021+2296] happen?"
7:16 and two seahs of barley sold for a shekel, as the LORD had **said**.
7:19 of the heavens, could **this**[s] [+2021+2021+2296] happen?"
8: 2 The woman proceeded to do as the man of God **said**. She and her
8:13 could your servant, a mere dog, accomplish such a **feat** [+1524]?"
8:23 As for the other **events** *of* Jehoram's reign, and all he did,
8:23 are they not written in the book of the **annals** [+3427] of the kings
9: 5 "I have a **message** for you, commander," he said. "For which of
9:26 him on that plot, in accordance with the **word** *of* the LORD."
9:36 "This is the **word** *of* the LORD that he spoke through his servant
10:10 that not a **word** the LORD has spoken against the house of Ahab
10:17 according to the **word** *of* the LORD spoken to Elijah.
10:34 As for the other **events** *of* Jehu's reign, all he did, and all his
10:34 are they not written in the book of the **annals** [+3427] of the kings
11: 5 commanded them, saying, "This is **what**[s] [+2021] you are to do:
12:19 [12:20] As for the other **events** *of* the reign of Joash, and all he
12:19 [12:20] are they not written in the book of the **annals** [+3427] of
13: 8 As for the other **events** *of* the reign of Jehoahaz, all he did
13: 8 are they not written in the book of the **annals** [+3427] of the kings
13:12 As for the other **events** *of* the reign of Jehoash, all he did and his
13:12 are they not written in the book of the **annals** [+3427] of the kings
14:15 As for the other **events** *of* the reign of Jehoash, what he did
14:15 are they not written in the book of the **annals** [+3427] of the kings
14:18 As for the other **events** *of* Amaziah's reign, are they not written in
14:18 are they not written in the book of the **annals** [+3427] of the kings
14:25 in accordance with the **word** *of* the LORD, the God of Israel,
14:28 As for the other **events** *of* Jeroboam's reign, all he did, and his
14:28 are they not written in the book of the **annals** [+3427] of the kings
15: 6 As for the other **events** *of* Azariah's reign, and all he did, are they
15: 6 are they not written in the book of the **annals** [+3427] of the kings
15:11 The other **events** *of* Zechariah's reign are written in the book of the
15:11 are written in the book of the **annals** [+3427] of the kings of Israel.
15:12 So the **word** *of* the LORD spoken to Jehu was fulfilled: "Your
15:15 The other **events** *of* Shallum's reign, and the conspiracy he led,
15:15 are written in the book of the **annals** [+3427] of the kings of Israel.
15:21 As for the other **events** *of* Menahem's reign, and all he did,
15:21 are they not written in the book of the **annals** [+3427] of the kings
15:26 The other **events** *of* Pekahiah's reign, and all he did, are written in
15:26 are written in the book of the **annals** [+3427] of the kings of Israel.
15:31 As for the other **events** *of* Pekah's reign, and all he did, are they
15:31 are they not written in the book of the **annals** [+3427] of the kings
15:36 As for the other **events** *of* Jotham's reign, and what he did,
15:36 are they not written in the book of the **annals** [+3427] of the kings
16:19 As for the other **events** *of* the reign of Ahaz, and what he did,
16:19 are they not written in the book of the **annals** [+3427] of the kings
17: 9 The Israelites secretly did **things** against the LORD their God that
17:11 They did wicked **things** that provoked the LORD to anger.
17:12 the LORD had said, "You shall not do **this**[s] [+2021+2021+2296]."
18:20 and military strength—but you speak only **empty words** [+8557].
18:27 to your master and you that my master sent me to say these **things**,
18:28 in Hebrew: "Hear the **word** *of* the great king, the king of Assyria!
18:36 But the people remained silent and said **nothing** [+4202] in reply,
18:37 clothes torn, and told him **what** the field commander had **said**.
19: 4 It may be that the LORD your God will hear all the **words** *of* the
19: 4 that he will rebuke him for the **words** the LORD your God has
19: 6 those **words** with which the underlings of the king of Assyria have
19:16 listen to the **words** Sennacherib has sent to insult the living God.
19:21 This is the **word** that the LORD has spoken against him:
20: 4 had left the middle court, the **word** *of* the LORD came to him:
20: 9 to you that the LORD will do **what**[s] [+2021] he has promised:
20:13 There was **nothing** [+4202] in his palace or in all his kingdom that
20:15 "There is **nothing** [+4202] among my treasures that I did not show
20:16 Then Isaiah said to Hezekiah, "Hear the **word** *of* the LORD:
20:17 off to Babylon. **Nothing** [+4202] will be left, says the LORD.
20:19 "The **word** *of* the LORD you have spoken is good,"
20:20 As for the other **events** *of* Hezekiah's reign, all his achievements
20:20 are they not written in the book of the **annals** [+3427] of the kings
21:17 As for the other **events** *of* Manasseh's reign, and all he did,
21:17 are they not written in the book of the **annals** [+3427] of the kings
21:25 As for the other **events** *of* Amon's reign, and what he did,
21:25 are they not written in the book of the **annals** [+3427] of the kings
22: 9 the secretary went to the king and **reported** [+906+8740] *to* him:
22:11 When the king heard the **words** *of* the Book of the Law, he tore his
22:13 for all Judah about **what is written** *in* this book that has been
22:13 because our fathers have not obeyed the **words** *of* this book;
22:13 according to everything **written** *in* the book the king of Judah has
22:18 the God of Israel, says concerning the **words** you heard:
22:20 to bring on this place.' " So they took her **answer** back to the king.
23: 2 He read in their hearing all the **words** *of* the Book of the Covenant,
23: 3 thus confirming the **words** *of* the covenant written in this book.
23:16 in accordance with the **word** *of* the LORD proclaimed by the man
23:16 LORD proclaimed by the man of God who foretold these **things**.
23:17 pronounced against the altar of Bethel the very **things** you have

2Ki 23:24 This he did to fulfill the **requirements** *of* the law written in the
23:28 As for the other **events** *of* Josiah's reign, and all he did, are they
23:28 are they not written in the book of the **annals** [+3427] of the kings
24: 2 in accordance with the **word** *of* the LORD proclaimed by his
24: 5 As for the other **events** *of* Jehoiakim's reign, and all he did,
24: 5 are they not written in the book of the **annals** [+3427] of the kings
25:30 **Day by day** [+928+2257+3427+3427] the king gave Jehoiachin a
1Ch 4:22 and Jashubi Lehem. (These **records** are from ancient times.)
10:13 he did not keep the **word** *of* the LORD and even consulted a
11: 3 king over Israel, as the LORD had **promised** through Samuel.
11:10 to extend it over the whole land, as the LORD had **promised**—
13: 4 to do this, because **it**[s] [+2021] seemed right to all the people.
15:15 as Moses had commanded in accordance with the **word** *of* the
16:15 the **word** he commanded, for a thousand generations,
16:37 to minister there regularly, according to each day's **requirements**.
17: 3 That night the **word** *of* God came to Nathan, saying:
17: 6 *did I ever* **say to** [+906+1819] any of their leaders whom I
17:15 Nathan reported to David all the **words** of this entire revelation.
17:23 let the **promise** you have made concerning your servant and his
21: 4 The king's **word**, however, overruled Joab; so Joab left and went
21: 6 the numbering, because the king's **command** was repulsive to him.
21: 7 This **command** was also evil in the sight of God; so he punished
21: 8 "I have sinned greatly by doing **this**[s] [+2021+2021+2296].
21:12 decide how *I should* **answer** [+906+8740] the one who sent me."
21:19 So David went up in obedience to the **word** that Gad had spoken in
22: 8 this **word** *of* the LORD came to me: 'You have shed much blood
23:27 According to the last **instructions** *of* David, the Levites were
25: 5 They were given him through the **promises** *of* God to exalt him.
26:32 and the half-tribe of Manasseh for every **matter** *pertaining to* God
26:32 for every matter pertaining to God and for the **affairs** *of* the king.
27: 1 who served the king in all *that* **concerned** the army divisions that
27:24 the number was not entered in the book of the **annals** [+3427] of
28:21 The officials and all the people will obey your every **command**."
29:29 As for the **events** *of* King David's reign, from beginning to end,
29:29 to end, they are written in the **records** *of* Samuel the seer,
29:29 the **records** *of* Nathan the prophet and the records of Gad the seer,
29:29 the records of Nathan the prophet and the **records** *of* Gad the seer,
2Ch 1: 9 LORD God, let your **promise** to my father David be confirmed,
6:10 "The LORD has kept the **promise** he made. I have succeeded
6:17 let your **word** that you promised your servant David come true.
8:13 according to the daily **requirement** for offerings commanded by
8:14 and to assist the priests according to each day's **requirement**.
8:15 the king's commands to the priests or to the Levites in any **matter**,
9: 2 Solomon answered all her **questions**; nothing was too hard for him
9: 2 **nothing** [+4202] was too hard for him to explain to her.
9: 5 "The **report** I heard in my own country about your achievements
9: 5 "The report I heard in my own country about your **achievements**
9: 6 I did not believe **what** they **said** until I came and saw with my own
9:24 **Year** [+9102] after year, everyone who came brought a gift—
9:29 As for the other **events** *of* Solomon's reign, from beginning to end,
9:29 are they not written in the **records** *of* Nathan the prophet,
10: 6 "How would you advise me to **answer** [+4200+8740] these
10: 7 and please them and **give** them a favorable **answer** [+448+1819],
10: 9 How *should we* **answer** [+906+8740] these people who say to me,
10:15 to fulfill the **word** the LORD had spoken to Jeroboam son of
11: 2 But this **word** *of* the LORD came to Shemaiah the man of God:
11: 4 for **this**[s] [+2021+2021+2296] is my doing.' " So they obeyed the
11: 4 for this is my doing.' " So they obeyed the **words** *of* the LORD
12: 7 humbled themselves, this **word** *of* the LORD came to Shemaiah:
12:12 was not totally destroyed. Indeed, there was **some** good in Judah.
12:15 As for the **events** *of* Rehoboam's reign, from beginning to end,
12:15 are they not written in the **records** *of* Shemaiah the prophet
13:22 The other **events** *of* Abijah's reign, what he did and what he said,
13:22 The other events of Abijah's reign, what he did and **what** he **said**,
15: 8 When Asa heard these **words** and the prophecy of Azariah son of
16:11 The **events** *of* Asa's reign, from beginning to end, are written in
18: 4 said to the king of Israel, "First seek the **counsel** *of* the LORD."
18:12 as one man the other prophets are **predicting** success for the king.
18:12 the king. Let your **word** agree with theirs, and speak favorably."
18:18 Micaiah continued, "Therefore hear the **word** *of* the LORD:
19: 3 There is, however, **some** good in you, for you have rid the land of
19: 6 who is with you whenever you give a **verdict** [+5477].
19:11 priest will be over you in any **matter** *concerning* the LORD,
19:11 of Judah, will be over you in any **matter** *concerning* the king,
20:34 The other **events** *of* Jehoshaphat's reign, from beginning to end,
20:34 beginning to end, are written in the **annals** *of* Jehu son of Hanani,
23: 4 Now this is **what**[s] [+2021] you are to do: A third of you priests
23:19 so that no one who was in any **way** unclean might enter.
24: 5 all Israel, to repair the temple of your God. Do **it**[s] [+2021] now."
25:26 As for the other **events** *of* Amaziah's reign, from beginning to end,
26:22 The other **events** *of* Uzziah's reign, from beginning to end,
27: 7 The other **events** *in* Jotham's reign, including all his wars
28:26 The other **events** *of* his reign and all his ways, from beginning to
29:15 as the king had ordered, following the **word** *of* the LORD.
29:30 ordered the Levites to praise the LORD with the **words** *of* David
29:36 about for his people, because **it**[s] [+2021] was done so quickly.
30: 4 The **plan** seemed right both to the king and to the whole assembly.
30: 5 *They* **decided** [+6641] to send a proclamation throughout Israel,
30:12 and his officials had ordered, following the **word** *of* the LORD.
31: 5 As soon as the **order** went out, the Israelites generously gave the
31:16 of the LORD to perform the daily **duties** of their various tasks,
32: 1 After *all* that Hezekiah had so faithfully **done**, Sennacherib king of
32: 8 gained confidence from **what** Hezekiah the king of Judah **said**.
32:32 The other **events** *of* Hezekiah's reign and his acts of devotion are
33:18 The other **events** *of* Manasseh's reign, including his prayer to his
33:18 and the **words** the seers spoke to him in the name of the LORD,
33:18 the God of Israel, are written in the **annals** *of* the kings of Israel.
33:19 he humbled himself—all are written in the **records** *of* the seers.
34:16 took the book to the king and **reported** [+906+8740] *to* him:
34:19 When the king heard the **words** *of* the Law, he tore his robes.
34:21 and Judah about **what** is **written** *in* this book that has been found.
34:21 because our fathers have not kept the **word** *of* the LORD;
34:26 the God of Israel, says concerning the **words** you heard:
34:27 before God when you heard **what** he **spoke** against this place and
34:28 on those who live here.' " So they took her **answer** back to the
34:30 He read in their hearing all the **words** *of* the Book of the Covenant,
34:31 and to obey the **words** *of* the covenant written in this book.
35: 6 doing what the LORD **commanded** through Moses."
35:22 He would not listen to **what** Neco had **said** at God's command
35:26 The other **events** *of* Josiah's reign and his acts of devotion,
35:27 all the **events**, from beginning to end, are written in the book of the
36: 8 The other **events** *of* Jehoiakim's reign, the detestable things he did
36:16 despised his **words** and scoffed at his prophets until the wrath of
36:21 in fulfillment of the **word** *of* the LORD spoken by Jeremiah.
36:22 in order to fulfill the **word** *of* the LORD spoken by Jeremiah,
Ezr 1: 1 in order to fulfill the **word** *of* the LORD spoken by Jeremiah,
3: 4 they celebrated the Feast of Tabernacles with the **required** number
7: 1 After these **things**, during the reign of Artaxerxes king of Persia,
7:11 a man learned in **matters** *concerning* the commands and decrees
8:17 I told them **what**[s] to say to Iddo and his kinsmen, the temple
9: 3 When I heard **this**[s] [+2021+2021+2296], I tore my tunic and cloak,
9: 4 everyone who trembled at the **words** *of* the God of Israel gathered
10: 4 Rise up; this **matter** is in your hands. We will support you,
10: 5 under oath to do what had been **suggested** [+2021+2021+2296].
10: 9 greatly distressed by the **occasion** and because of the rain.
10:12 with a loud voice: "You are right! We must do as you **say**.
10:13 of in a day or two, because we have sinned greatly in this **thing**.
10:14 until the fierce anger of our God in this **matter** is turned away
10:16 first day of the tenth month they sat down to investigate the **cases**,
Ne 1: 1 The **words** *of* Nehemiah son of Hacaliah: In the month of Kislev in
1: 4 When I heard these **things**, I sat down and wept. For some days I
1: 8 "Remember the **instruction** you gave your servant Moses,
2:18 hand of my God upon me and **what**[s] the king had said to me.
2:19 "What is **this**[s] [+2021+2021+2296] you are doing?" they asked.
2:20 *I* **answered** [+906+8740] them by saying, "The God of heaven will
5: 6 When I heard their outcry and these **charges**, I was very angry.
5: 8 to us!" They kept quiet, because they could find nothing to **say**.
5: 9 So I continued, "**What**[s] [+2021] you are doing is not right.
5:12 the nobles and officials take an oath to do what they had **promised**.
5:13 and possessions every man who does not keep this **promise**.
5:13 and praised the LORD. And the people did as they had **promised**.
6: 4 Four times they sent me the same **message**, and each time I gave
6: 4 me the same message, and each time I gave them the same **answer**.
6: 5 the fifth time, Sanballat sent his aide to me with the same **message**,
6: 6 according to these **reports** you are about to become their king
6: 7 Now this **report** will get back to the king; so come, let us confer
6: 8 "Nothing like **what**[s] [+465+2021+2021] you are saying is
6:19 reporting to me his good deeds and then telling him **what I said**.
8: 4 the scribe stood on a high wooden platform built for the **occasion**.
8: 9 people had been weeping as they listened to the **words** *of* the Law.
8:12 because they now understood the **words** that had been made
8:13 gathered around Ezra the scribe to give attention to the **words** *of*
9: 8 You have kept your **promise** because you are righteous.
11:23 were under the king's orders, which regulated their daily **activity**.
11:24 of Judah, was the king's agent in all **affairs** relating to the people.
12:23 son of Eliashib were recorded in the book of the **annals** [+3427].
12:47 all Israel contributed the **daily** [+928+3427+3427] portions for the
13:17 and said to them, "What is this wicked **thing** you are doing—
Est 1:12 when the attendants delivered the king's **command**, Queen Vashti
1:13 Since it was **customary** [+4027] *for* the king to consult experts in
1:17 For the queen's **conduct** will become known to all the women,
1:18 **conduct** will respond to all the king's nobles in the same way.
1:19 let him issue a royal **decree** and let it be written in the laws of
1:21 The king and his nobles were pleased with this **advice**, so the king
1:21 pleased with this advice, so the king did as Memucan **proposed**.
2: 1 **Later** [+339+465+2021+2021] when the anger of King Xerxes had
2: 4 of Vashti." This **advice** appealed to the king, and he followed it.
2: 8 When the king's **order** and edict had been proclaimed, many girls

[F] Hitpael (hitpoel, hitpoal, hitpolel, hitpolal, hitpalel, hitpalal, hitpalpel, hitpalpal, hotpael, hotpaal) [G] Hiphil (hiphtil) [H] Hophal [I] Hishtaphel

Est 2:15 to the king, she asked for **nothing** [+4202] other than what Hegai,
2:22 But Mordecai found out about the **plot** and told Queen Esther,
2:23 And when the **report** was investigated and found to be true,
2:23 All this was recorded in the book of the **annals** [+3427] in the
3: 1 After these **events**, King Xerxes honored Haman son of
3: 4 about it to see whether Mordecai's **behavior** would be tolerated,
3:15 Spurred on by the king's **command**, the couriers went out,
4: 3 In every province to which the **edict** and order of the king came,
4: 9 went back and reported to Esther **what** Mordecai had **said**.
4:12 When Esther's **words** were reported to Mordecai,
5: 5 at once," the king said, "so that we may do **what** Esther **asks**."
5: 8 I will prepare for them. Then I will answer the king's **question**."
5:14 This **suggestion** delighted Haman, and he had the gallows built.
6: 1 the **record** *of* his reign, to be brought in and read to him.
6: 3 "**Nothing** [+4202] has been done for him," his attendants
6:10 Do not neglect **anything** [+3972+4946] you have recommended."
7: 8 As soon as the **word** left the king's mouth, they covered Haman's
8: 5 "and if he regards me with favor and thinks it the right **thing** to do,
8:14 the royal horses, raced out, spurred on by the king's **command**.
8:17 wherever **[RPH]** the edict of the king went, there was joy
9: 1 of Adar, the edict **commanded** *by* the king was to be carried out.
9:20 Mordecai recorded these **events**, and he sent letters to all the Jews
9:26 Because of everything **written** *in* this letter and because of what
9:30 of the kingdom of Xerxes—**words** *of* goodwill and assurance—
9:31 their descendants in regard to their **times** *of* fasting
9:32 Esther's decree confirmed these **regulations** *about* Purim,
10: 2 are they not written in the book of the **annals** [+3427] of the kings
Job 2:13 No one said a **word** to him, because they saw how great his
4: 2 "If someone ventures a **word** with you, will you be impatient?
4:12 "A **word** was secretly brought to me, my ears caught a whisper of
6: 3 the sand of the seas—no wonder my **words** have been impetuous.
9:14 can I dispute with him? How can I find **words** to argue with him?
11: 2 "Are all these **words** to go unanswered? Is this talker to be
15: 3 Would he argue with useless **words**, with speeches that have no
15:11 consolations not enough for you, **words** *spoken* gently to you?
16: 3 Will your long-winded **speeches** never end? What ails you that you
19:28 'How we will hound him, since the root of the **trouble** lies in him,'
26:14 outer fringe of his works; how faint the **whisper** we hear of him!
29:22 After I had **spoken**, they spoke no more; my words fell gently on
31:40 and weeds instead of barley." The **words** *of* Job are ended.
32: 4 Now Elihu had waited before **speaking** to Job because they were
32:11 I waited while you **spoke**, I listened to your reasoning; while you
33: 1 Job, listen to my words; pay attention to everything I **say**.
33:13 do you complain to him that he answers none of man's **words**?
34:35 'Job speaks without knowledge; his **words** lack insight.'
41:12 [41:4] of his limbs, his **[NIE]** strength and his graceful form.
42: 7 After the LORD had said these **things** to Job, he said to Eliphaz
Ps 7: T [7:1] which he sang to the LORD **concerning** [+6584] Cush,
17: 4 by the **word** *of* your lips I have kept myself from the ways of the
18: T [18:1] He sang to the LORD the **words** *of* this song when the
19: 3 [19:4] is no speech or **language** where their voice is not heard.
22: 1 [22:2] far from saving me, so far from the **words** *of* my groaning?
33: 4 For the **word** *of* the LORD is right and true; he is faithful in all he
33: 6 By the **word** *of* the LORD were the heavens made, their starry
35:20 devise false **accusations** against those who live quietly in the land.
36: 3 [36:4] The **words** *of* his mouth are wicked and deceitful; he has
41: 8 [41:9] "A vile **disease** has beset him; he will never get up from
45: 1 [45:2] My heart is stirred by a noble **theme** as I recite my verses
45: 4 [45:5] In your majesty ride forth victoriously **in behalf** [+6584] **of**
50:17 You hate my instruction and cast my **words** behind you.
52: 4 [52:6] You love every harmful **word**, O you deceitful tongue!
55:21 [55:22] his **words** are more soothing than oil, yet they are drawn
56: 4 [56:5] In God, whose **word** I praise, in God I trust; I will not be
56: 5 [56:6] All day long they twist my **words**; they are always plotting
56:10 [56:11] In God, whose **word** I praise, in the LORD, whose word
56:10 [56:11] word I praise, in the LORD, whose **word** I praise—
59:12 [59:13] For the sins of their mouths, for the **words** *of* their lips, let
64: 3 [64:4] like swords and aim their **words** like deadly arrows.
64: 5 [64:6] They encourage each other in evil **plans**, they talk about
65: 3 [65:4] When we were overwhelmed by **sins** [+6411], you forgave
79: 9 Help us, O God our Savior, **for** [+6584] the glory of your name;
101: 3 I will set before my eyes no vile **thing**. The deeds of faithless men
103:20 the LORD, you his angels, you mighty ones who do his **bidding**,
103:20 you mighty ones who do his bidding, who obey his **word**.
105: 8 the **word** he commanded, for a thousand generations,
105:19 till **what** he **foretold** came to pass, till the word of the LORD
105:27 They performed his **[NIE]** miraculous signs among them,
105:28 for had they not rebelled against his **words**?
105:42 For he remembered his holy **promise** given to his servant
106:12 Then they believed his **promises** and sang his praise.
106:24 they despised the pleasant land; they did not believe his **promise**.
107:20 He sent forth his **word** and healed them; he rescued them from the
109: 3 With **words** *of* hatred they surround me; they attack me without
112: 5 is generous and lends freely, who conducts his **affairs** with justice.
119: 9 young man keep his way pure? By living according to your **word**.
119:16 I delight in your decrees; I will not neglect your **word**.
119:17 Do good to your servant, and I will live; I will obey your **word**.
119:25 I am laid low in the dust; preserve my life according to your **word**.
119:28 soul is weary with sorrow; strengthen me according to your **word**.
119:37 preserve my life according to your **word**. [BHS 2006]
119:42 *I will* **answer** [+6699] the one who taunts me, for I trust in your
119:42 then I will answer the one who taunts me, for I trust in your **word**.
119:43 Do not snatch the **word** *of* truth from my mouth, for I have put my
119:49 Remember your **word** to your servant, for you have given me
119:57 are my portion, O LORD; I have promised to obey your **words**.
119:65 Do good to your servant according to your **word**, O LORD.
119:74 rejoice when they see me, for I have put my hope in your **word**.
119:81 longing for your salvation, but I have put my hope in your **word**.
119:89 Your **word**, O LORD, is eternal; it stands firm in the heavens.
119:101 kept my feet from every evil path so that I might obey your **word**.
119:105 Your **word** is a lamp to my feet and a light for my path.
119:107 preserve my life, O LORD, according to your **word**.
119:114 are my refuge and my shield; I have put my hope in your **word**.
119:130 The unfolding of your **words** gives light; it gives understanding to
119:139 My zeal wears me out, for my enemies ignore your **words**.
119:147 before dawn and cry for help; I have put my hope in your **word**.
119:160 All your **words** are true; all your righteous laws are eternal.
119:161 persecute me without cause, but my heart trembles at your **word**.
119:169 O LORD; give me understanding according to your **word**.
130: 5 for the LORD, my soul waits, and in his **word** I put my hope.
137: 3 for there our captors asked us for **songs** [+8877], our tormentors
141: 4 Let not my heart be drawn to **what**ˢ is evil, to take part in wicked
145: 5 *They will* speak [BHS *On the word of*; NIV 1819] *of* the glorious
145:13 The LORD is faithful to all his **promises** [BHS-] and loving
147:15 He sends his command to the earth; his **word** runs swiftly.
147:18 He sends his **word** and melts them; he stirs up his breezes,
147:19 He has revealed his **word** to Jacob, his laws and decrees to Israel.
148: 8 and hail, snow and clouds, stormy winds that do his **bidding**,
Pr 1: 6 and parables, the **sayings** and riddles *of* the wise.
1:23 poured out my heart to you and made my **thoughts** known to you.
4: 4 he taught me and said, "Lay hold of my **words** with all your heart;
4:20 My son, pay attention to **what** I **say**; listen closely to my words.
10:19 When **words** are many, sin is not absent, but he who holds his
11:13 gossip betrays a confidence, but a trustworthy man keeps a **secret**.
12: 6 The **words** *of* the wicked lie in wait for blood, but the speech of
12:25 anxious heart weighs a man down, but a kind **word** cheers him up.
13: 5 The righteous hate **what**ˢ is false, but the wicked bring shame
13:13 He who scorns **instruction** will pay for it, but he who respects a
14:15 A simple man believes **anything** [+3972], but a prudent man gives
14:23 work brings a profit, but **mere talk** [+8557] leads only to poverty.
15: 1 A gentle answer turns away wrath, but a harsh **word** stirs up anger.
15:23 finds joy in giving an apt reply—and how good is a timely **word**!
16:20 Whoever gives heed to **instruction** prospers, and blessed is he who
17: 9 but whoever repeats the **matter** separates close friends.
18: 4 The **words** *of* a man's mouth are deep waters, but the fountain of
18: 8 The **words** *of* a gossip are like choice morsels; they go down to a
18:13 *He who* **answers** [+8740] before listening—that is his folly
22:12 over knowledge, but he frustrates the **words** *of* the unfaithful.
22:17 Pay attention and listen to the **sayings** *of* the wise; apply your heart
23: 8 you have eaten and will have wasted your **compliments** [+5833].
24:26 An honest **answer** [+8740] is like a kiss on the lips.
25: 2 It is the glory of God to conceal a **matter**; to search out a matter is
25: 2 to conceal a matter; to search out a **matter** is the glory of kings.
25:11 A **word** aptly spoken is like apples of gold in settings of silver.
26: 6 or drinking violence is the sending of a **message** by the hand of a
26:22 The **words** *of* a gossip are like choice morsels; they go down to a
27:11 then *I can* **answer** [+8740] anyone who treats me with contempt.
29:12 If a ruler listens to **lies** [+9214], all his officials become wicked.
29:19 A servant cannot be corrected by mere **words**; though he
29:20 Do you see a man who **speaks** in haste? There is more hope for a
30: 1 The **sayings** *of* Agur son of Jakeh—an oracle: This man declared
30: 6 Do not add to his **words**, or he will rebuke you and prove you a
30: 8 Keep falsehood and **lies** [+3942] far from me; give me neither
31: 1 The **sayings** *of* King Lemuel—an oracle his mother taught him:
Ecc 1: 1 The **words** *of* the Teacher, son of David, king in Jerusalem:
1: 8 All **things** are wearisome, more than one can say. The eye never
1:10 Is there **anything** of which one can say, "Look! This is something
5: 2 [5:1] do not be hasty in your heart to utter **anything** before God.
5: 2 [5:1] is in heaven and you are on earth, so let your **words** be few.
5: 3 [5:2] so the speech of a fool when there are many **words**.
5: 7 [5:6] Much dreaming and many **words** are meaningless.
6:11 The more the **words**, the less the meaning, and how does that
7: 8 The end of a **matter** is better than its beginning, and patience is
7:21 Do not pay attention to every **word** people say, or you may hear
8: 1 Who is like the wise man? Who knows the explanation of **things**?
8: 3 Do not stand up for a bad **cause**, for he will do whatever he
8: 4 Since a king's **word** is supreme, who can say to him, "What are
8: 5 Whoever obeys his command will come to no **harm** [+8273],

Ecc 9:16 man's wisdom is despised, and his **words** are no longer heeded.
9:17 The quiet **words** *of* the wise are more to be heeded than the shouts
10:12 **Words** *from* a wise man's mouth are gracious, but a fool is
10:13 At the beginning his **words** [+7023] are folly; at the end they are
10:14 and the fool multiplies **words**. No one knows what is coming—
10:20 carry your words, and a bird on the wing may report **what** you **say**.
12:10 The Teacher searched to find just the right **words**, and what he
12:10 find just the right words, and **what**[s] he wrote was upright and true.
12:11 The **words** *of* the wise are like goads, their collected sayings like
12:13 Now all has been heard; here is the conclusion of the **matter**:
Isa 1:10 Hear the **word** *of* the LORD, you rulers of Sodom; listen to the
2:1 **This**[s] [+2021] is what Isaiah son of Amoz saw concerning Judah
2:3 will go out from Zion, the **word** *of* the LORD from Jerusalem.
8:10 propose your **plan**, but it will not stand, for God is with us.
8:20 If they do not speak according to this **word**, they have no light of
9:8 [9:7] The Lord has sent a **message** against Jacob; it will fall on
16:13 This is the **word** the LORD has already spoken concerning Moab.
24:3 and totally plundered. The LORD has spoken this **word**.
28:13 So then, the **word** *of* the LORD to them will become: Do
28:14 Therefore hear the **word** *of* the LORD, you scoffers who rule this
29:11 For you this whole vision is nothing but **words** sealed *in* a scroll.
29:18 In that day the deaf will hear the **words** *of* the scroll, and out of
29:21 those who with a **word** make a man out to be guilty, who ensnare
30:12 "Because you have rejected this **message**, relied on oppression
30:21 or to the left, your ears will hear a **voice** behind you, saying,
31:2 too is wise and can bring disaster; he does not take back his **words**.
36:5 and military strength—but you speak only **empty words** [+8557].
36:12 to your master and you that my master sent me to say these **things**,
36:13 in Hebrew, "Hear the **words** *of* the great king, the king of Assyria!
36:21 But the people remained silent and said **nothing** [+4202] in reply,
36:22 clothes torn, and told him **what** the field commander had **said**.
37:4 It may be that the LORD your God will hear the **words** *of* the
37:4 that he will rebuke him for the **words** the LORD your God has
37:6 those **words** with which the underlings of the king of Assyria have
37:17 listen to all the **words** Sennacherib has sent to insult the living
37:22 this is the **word** the LORD has spoken against him: "The Virgin
38:4 Then the **word** *of* the LORD came to Isaiah:
38:7 the LORD will do **what**[s] [+2021+2021+2296] he has promised:
39:2 There was **nothing** [+4202] in his palace or in all his kingdom that
39:4 "There is **nothing** [+4202] among my treasures that I did not show
39:5 Isaiah said to Hezekiah, "Hear the **word** *of* the LORD Almighty:
39:6 off to Babylon. **Nothing** [+4202] will be left, says the LORD.
39:8 "The **word** *of* the LORD you have spoken is good,"
40:8 and the flowers fall, but the **word** *of* our God stands forever."
41:28 them to give counsel, no one to give **answer** when I ask them.
42:16 These are the **things** I will do; I will not forsake them.
44:26 who carries out the **words** *of* his servants and fulfills the
45:23 my mouth has uttered in all integrity a **word** that will not be
50:4 me an instructed tongue, to know the **word** that sustains the weary.
51:16 I have put my **words** in your mouth and covered you with the
55:11 so is my **word** that goes out from my mouth: It will not return to
58:13 your own way and not doing as you please or speaking idle **words**,
59:13 and revolt, uttering **lies** [+9214] our hearts have conceived.
59:21 my **words** that I have put in your mouth will not depart from your
66:2 he who is humble and contrite in spirit, and trembles at my **word**.
66:5 Hear the **word** *of* the LORD, you who tremble at his word:
66:5 Hear the word of the LORD, you who tremble at his **word**:
Jer 1:1 The **words** *of* Jeremiah son of Hilkiah, one of the priests at
1:2 The **word** *of* the LORD came to him in the thirteenth year of the
1:4 The **word** *of* the LORD came to me, saying,
1:9 and said to me, "Now, I have put my **words** in your mouth.
1:11 The **word** *of* the LORD came to me: "What do you see,
1:12 seen correctly, for I am watching to see that my **word** is fulfilled."
1:13 The **word** *of* the LORD came to me again: "What do you see?"
2:1 The **word** *of* the LORD came to me:
2:4 Hear the **word** *of* the LORD, O house of Jacob, all you clans of
2:31 "You of this generation, consider the **word** *of* the LORD:
3:12 Go, proclaim this **message** toward the north: " 'Return,
5:14 "Because the people have spoken these **words**, I will make my
5:14 I will make my **words** in your mouth a fire and these people the
5:28 Their evil **deeds** have no limit; they do not plead the case of the
6:10 The **word** *of* the LORD is offensive to them; they find no
6:19 because they have not listened to my **words** and have rejected my
7:1 This is the **word** that came to Jeremiah from the LORD:
7:2 at the gate of the LORD's house and there proclaim this **message**:
7:2 " 'Hear the **word** *of* the LORD, all you people of Judah who come
7:4 Do not trust in deceptive **words** and say, "This is the temple of the
7:8 But look, you are trusting in deceptive **words** that are worthless.
7:22 I did not just give them commands **about** [+6584] burnt offerings
7:23 **[RPH]** Obey me, and I will be your God and you will be my
7:27 "When you tell them all **this**[s] [+465+2021+2021], they will not
8:9 Since they have rejected the **word** *of* the LORD, what kind of
9:20 [9:19] Now, O women, hear the **word** *of* the LORD; open your
9:20 [9:19] of the LORD; open your ears to the **words** *of* his mouth.
10:1 Hear **what**[s] [+2021] the LORD says to you, O house of Israel.
11:1 This is the **word** that came to Jeremiah from the LORD:
11:2 "Listen to the **terms** *of* this covenant and tell them to the people of
11:3 'Cursed is the man who does not obey the **terms** *of* this covenant—
11:6 "Proclaim all these **words** in the towns of Judah and in the streets
11:6 'Listen to the **terms** *of* this covenant and follow them.
11:8 So I brought on them all the **curses** *of* the covenant I had
11:10 to the sins of their forefathers, who refused to listen to my **words**.
13:2 So I bought a belt, as the LORD **directed**, and put it around my
13:3 Then the **word** *of* the LORD came to me a second time:
13:8 Then the **word** *of* the LORD came to me:
13:10 These wicked people, who refuse to listen to my **words**,
13:12 to them: **[NIE]** 'This is what the LORD, the God of Israel, says:
14:1 This is the **word** *of* the LORD to Jeremiah concerning the
14:1 This is the word of the LORD to Jeremiah **concerning** [+6584]
14:17 "Speak this **word** to them: " 'Let my eyes overflow with tears night
15:16 When your **words** came, I ate them; they were my joy and my
15:16 **they**[s] [+3870] were my joy and my heart's delight, for I bear your
16:1 Then the **word** *of* the LORD came to me:
16:10 "When you tell these people all **this**[s] [+465+2021+2021] and they
17:15 They keep saying to me, "Where is the **word** *of* the LORD?
17:20 Say to them, 'Hear the **word** *of* the LORD, O kings of Judah
18:1 This is the **word** that came to Jeremiah from the LORD:
18:2 down to the potter's house, and there I will give you my **message**."
18:5 Then the **word** *of* the LORD came to me:
18:18 nor will counsel from the wise, nor the **word** from the prophets.
18:18 him with our tongues and pay no attention to anything he **says**."
19:2 entrance of the Potsherd Gate. There proclaim the **words** I tell you,
19:3 say, 'Hear the **word** *of* the LORD, O kings of Judah and people of
19:15 they were stiff-necked and would not listen to my **words**.' "
20:1 temple of the LORD, heard Jeremiah prophesying these **things**,
20:8 So the **word** *of* the LORD has brought me insult and reproach all
21:1 The **word** came to Jeremiah from the LORD when King
21:11 say to the royal house of Judah, 'Hear the **word** *of* the LORD;
22:1 to the palace of the king of Judah and proclaim this **message** there:
22:2 'Hear the **word** *of* the LORD, O king of Judah, you who sit on
22:4 For if you are careful to carry out these **commands**, then kings
22:5 But if you do not obey these **commands**, declares the LORD,
22:29 O land, land, land, hear the **word** *of* the LORD!
23:9 overcome by wine, because of the LORD and his holy **words**.
23:16 "Do not listen to **what**[s] the prophets are prophesying to you;
23:18 has stood in the council of the LORD to see or to hear his **word**?
23:18 or to hear his word? Who has listened and heard his **word**?
23:22 they would have proclaimed my **words** to my people and would
23:28 tell his dream, but let the one who has my **word** speak it faithfully.
23:28 tell his dream, but let the one who has my word speak **it**[s] faithfully.
23:29 "Is not my **word** like fire," declares the LORD, "and like a
23:30 prophets who steal from one another **words** supposedly *from* me.
23:36 because every man's own **word** becomes his oracle and so you
23:36 becomes his oracle and so you distort the **words** *of* the living God,
23:38 You used the **words**, 'This is the oracle of the LORD,'
24:4 Then the **word** *of* the LORD came to me:
25:1 The **word** came to Jeremiah concerning all the people of Judah in
25:3 the **word** *of* the LORD has come to me and I have spoken to you
25:8 Almighty says this: "Because you have not listened to my **words**,
25:13 I will bring upon that land all the **things** I have spoken against it,
25:30 "Now prophesy all these **words** against them and say to them:
26:1 son of Josiah king of Judah, this **word** came from the LORD:
26:2 Tell them **everything** [+2021+3972] I command you; do not omit
26:2 Tell them everything I command you; do not omit a **word**.
26:5 and if you do not listen to the **words** *of* my servants the prophets,
26:7 all the people heard Jeremiah speak these **words** in the house of
26:10 When the officials of Judah heard about these **things**, they went up
26:12 against this house and this city all the **things** you have heard.
26:15 for in truth the LORD has sent me to you to speak all these **words**
26:20 he prophesied the same **things** against this city and this land as
26:21 King Jehoiakim and all his officers and officials heard his **words**,
27:1 king of Judah, this **word** came to Jeremiah from the LORD:
27:12 ***I* gave the** same **message** [+465+1819+2021+2021+3972] to
27:14 Do not listen to the **words** *of* the prophets who say to you,
27:16 Do not listen to **[RPH]** the prophets who say, 'Very soon now the
27:18 If they are prophets and have the **word** *of* the LORD, let them
28:6 May the LORD fulfill the **words** you have prophesied by
28:7 listen to **what**[s] [+2021+2021+2296] I have to say in your hearing
28:9 as one truly sent by the LORD only if his **prediction** comes true."
28:12 the prophet Jeremiah, the **word** *of* the LORD came to Jeremiah:
29:1 This is the **text** *of* the letter that the prophet Jeremiah sent from
29:10 and fulfill my gracious **promise** to bring you back to this place.
29:19 For they have not listened to my **words**," declares the LORD,
29:20 Therefore, hear the **word** *of* the LORD, all you exiles whom I
29:23 their neighbors' wives and in my name *have* **spoken** [+1819] lies,
29:30 Then the **word** *of* the LORD came to Jeremiah:
30:1 This is the **word** that came to Jeremiah from the LORD:
30:2 says: 'Write in a book all the **words** I have spoken to you.

Jer 30: 4 These are the **words** the LORD spoke concerning Israel
31: 10 "Hear the **word** *of* the LORD, O nations; proclaim it in distant
31: 23 the land of Judah and in its towns will once again use these **words**:
32: 1 This is the **word** that came to Jeremiah from the LORD in the
32: 6 Jeremiah said, "The **word** *of* the LORD came to me:
32: 8 "Then, just as the LORD had **said**, my cousin Hanamel came to
32: 8 buy it for yourself.' "I knew that this was the **word** *of* the LORD;
32: 17 and outstretched arm. **Nothing** [+3972+4202] is too hard for you.
32: 26 Then the **word** *of* the LORD came to Jeremiah:
32: 27 the God of all mankind. Is **anything** [+3972] too hard for me?
33: 1 of the guard, the **word** *of* the LORD came to him a second time:
33: 14 'when I will fulfill the gracious **promise** I made to the house of
33: 19 The **word** *of* the LORD came to Jeremiah:
33: 23 The **word** *of* the LORD came to Jeremiah:
34: 1 surrounding towns, this **word** came to Jeremiah from the LORD:
34: 4 " 'Yet hear the **promise** *of* the LORD, O Zedekiah king of Judah.
34: 5 *I* myself **make** *this* **promise** [+1819], declares the LORD.' "
34: 6 Jeremiah the prophet told all **this**[s] [+465+2021+2021] to Zedekiah
34: 8 The **word** came to Jeremiah from the LORD after King Zedekiah
34: 12 Then the **word** *of* the LORD came to Jeremiah:
34: 18 have not fulfilled the **terms** *of* the covenant they made before me,
35: 1 This is the **word** that came to Jeremiah from the LORD during
35: 12 Then the **word** *of* the LORD came to Jeremiah, saying:
35: 13 of Jerusalem, 'Will you not learn a lesson and obey my **words**?'
35: 14 his sons not to drink wine and this **command** has been kept.
36: 1 king of Judah, this **word** came to Jeremiah from the LORD:
36: 2 write on it all the **words** I have spoken to you concerning Israel,
36: 4 while Jeremiah dictated all the **words** the LORD had spoken to
36: 6 read to the people from the scroll the **words** *of* the LORD that
36: 8 at the LORD's temple he read the **words** *of* the LORD from the
36: 10 Baruch read to all the people at the LORD's temple the **words** *of*
36: 11 son of Shaphan, heard all the **words** *of* the LORD from the scroll,
36: 13 After Micaiah told them **everything** [+2021+3972] he had heard
36: 16 When they heard all these **words**, they looked at each other in fear
36: 16 and said to Baruch, "We must report all these **words** to the king."
36: 17 "Tell us, how did you come to write all **this**[s] [+465+2021+2021]?
36: 18 "Yes," Baruch replied, "he dictated all these **words** to me,
36: 20 in the courtyard and reported **everything** [+2021+3972] to him.
36: 24 and all his attendants who heard all these **words** showed no fear,
36: 27 After the king burned the scroll containing the **words** that Baruch
36: 27 at Jeremiah's dictation, the **word** *of* the LORD came to Jeremiah:
36: 28 and write on it all the **words** that were on the first scroll,
36: 32 Baruch wrote on it all the **words** *of* the scroll that Jehoiakim king
36: 32 burned in the fire. And many similar **words** were added to them.
37: 2 the **words** the LORD had spoken through Jeremiah the prophet.
37: 6 Then the **word** *of* the LORD came to Jeremiah the prophet:
37: 17 he asked him privately, "Is there any **word** from the LORD?"
38: 1 Pashhur son of Malkijah heard **what**[s] [+2021] Jeremiah was telling
38: 4 as well as all the people, by the **things** he is saying to them.
38: 5 "The king can do **nothing** [+401] to oppose you."
38: 14 "I am going to ask you **something**," the king said to Jeremiah.
38: 14 the king said to Jeremiah. "Do not hide **anything** from me."
38: 21 to surrender, this is **what**[s] [+2021] the LORD has revealed to me:
38: 24 "Do not let anyone know about this **conversation**, or you may die.
38: 27 and he told them everything the king had ordered him to **say**.
38: 27 more to him, for no one had heard his **conversation** with the king.
39: 15 the courtyard of the guard, the **word** *of* the LORD came to him:
39: 16 I am about to fulfill my **words** against this city through disaster,
40: 1 The **word** came to Jeremiah from the LORD after Nebuzaradan
40: 3 *All* **this**[s] [+1821+2021+2296] happened because you people sinned
40: 16 of Ahikam said to Johanan son of Kareah, "Don't do such a **thing**!
42: 3 will tell us where we should go and **what**[s] [+2021] we should do."
42: 4 will certainly pray to the LORD your God as you have **requested**;
42: 4 I will tell you **everything** [+2021+3972] the LORD says and will
42: 4 the LORD says and will keep **nothing** [+4202] back from you."
42: 5 if we do not act in accordance with **everything** [+2021+3972]
42: 7 Ten days later the **word** *of* the LORD came to Jeremiah.
42: 15 hear the **word** *of* the LORD, O remnant of Judah. This is what the
43: 1 When Jeremiah finished telling the people all the **words** *of* the
43: 1 **everything** [+465+2021+2021+3972] the LORD had sent him to
43: 8 In Tahpanhes the **word** *of* the LORD came to Jeremiah:
44: 1 This **word** came to Jeremiah concerning all the Jews living in
44: 4 the prophets, who said, 'Do not do this detestable **thing** that I hate!'
44: 16 "We will not listen to the **message** you have spoken to us in the
44: 17 We will certainly do **everything** [+2021+3972] we said we would:
44: 20 both men and women, who were answering him, **[NIE]**
44: 24 including the women, "Hear the **word** *of* the LORD, all you
44: 26 But hear the **word** *of* the LORD, all Jews living in Egypt:
44: 28 who came to live in Egypt will know whose **word** will stand—
44: 29 'so that you will know that my **threats** of harm against you will
45: 1 This is **what**[s] Jeremiah the prophet told Baruch son of Neriah in
45: 1 after Baruch had written on a scroll the **words** Jeremiah was
46: 1 This is the **word** *of* the LORD that came to Jeremiah the prophet
46: 13 This is the **message** the LORD spoke to Jeremiah the prophet
47: 1 This is the **word** *of* the LORD that came to Jeremiah the prophet
48: 27 that you shake your head in scorn whenever you **speak** of her?
49: 34 This is the **word** *of* the LORD that came to Jeremiah the prophet
50: 1 This is the **word** the LORD spoke through Jeremiah the prophet
51: 59 This is the **message** Jeremiah gave to the staff officer Seraiah son
51: 60 all **that**[s] [+465+2021+2021] had been recorded concerning
51: 61 you get to Babylon, see that you read all these **words** aloud.
51: 64 And her people will fall.' " The **words** *of* Jeremiah end here.
52: 34 **Day by day** [+928+3427+3427] the king of Babylon gave
Eze 1: 3 the **word** *of* the LORD came to Ezekiel the priest, the son of
2: 6 And you, son of man, do not be afraid of them or their **words**.
2: 6 Do not be afraid of **what** they **say** or terrified by them, though they
2: 7 You must speak my **words** to them, whether they listen or fail to
3: 4 go now to the house of Israel and speak my **words** to them.
3: 6 and difficult language, whose **words** you cannot understand.
3: 10 listen carefully and take to heart all the **words** I speak to you.
3: 16 At the end of seven days the **word** *of* the LORD came to me:
3: 17 so hear the **word** I speak and give them warning from me.
6: 1 The **word** *of* the LORD came to me:
6: 3 'O mountains of Israel, hear the **word** *of* the Sovereign LORD.
7: 1 The **word** *of* the LORD came to me:
9: 11 the man in linen with the writing kit at his side brought back **word**,
11: 14 The **word** *of* the LORD came to me:
11: 25 I told the exiles **everything** [+3972] the LORD had shown me.
12: 1 The **word** *of* the LORD came to me:
12: 8 In the morning the **word** *of* the LORD came to me:
12: 17 The **word** *of* the LORD came to me:
12: 21 The **word** *of* the LORD came to me:
12: 23 Say to them, 'The days are near when every vision will be **fulfilled**.
12: 25 I the LORD will speak what *I* **will**[s] [+1819], and it shall be
12: 25 you rebellious house, I will fulfill *whatever I* **say** [+1819],
12: 26 The **word** *of* the LORD came to me:
12: 28 None of my **words** will be delayed any longer; whatever I say will
12: 28 whatever *I* **say** [+1819] will be fulfilled, declares the Sovereign
13: 1 The **word** *of* the LORD came to me:
13: 2 out of their own imagination: 'Hear the **word** *of* the LORD!
13: 6 has not sent them; yet they expect their **words** to be fulfilled.
14: 2 Then the **word** *of* the LORD came to me:
14: 9 " 'And if the prophet is enticed to utter a **prophecy**, I the LORD
14: 12 The **word** *of* the LORD came to me:
15: 1 The **word** *of* the LORD came to me:
16: 1 The **word** *of* the LORD came to me:
16: 35 " 'Therefore, you prostitute, hear the **word** *of* the LORD!
17: 1 The **word** *of* the LORD came to me:
17: 11 Then the **word** *of* the LORD came to me:
18: 1 The **word** *of* the LORD came to me:
20: 2 Then the **word** *of* the LORD came to me:
20: 45 [21:1] The **word** *of* the LORD came to me:
20: 47 [21:3] Say to the southern forest: 'Hear the **word** *of* the LORD.
21: 1 [21:6] The **word** *of* the LORD came to me:
21: 8 [21:13] The **word** *of* the LORD came to me:
21: 18 [21:23] The **word** *of* the LORD came to me:
22: 1 The **word** *of* the LORD came to me:
22: 17 Then the **word** *of* the LORD came to me:
22: 23 Again the **word** *of* the LORD came to me:
23: 1 The **word** *of* the LORD came to me:
24: 1 tenth month on the tenth day, the **word** *of* the LORD came to me:
24: 15 The **word** *of* the LORD came to me:
24: 20 So I said to them, "The **word** *of* the LORD came to me:
25: 1 The **word** *of* the LORD came to me:
25: 3 Say to them, 'Hear the **word** *of* the Sovereign LORD. This is
26: 1 on the first day of the month, the **word** *of* the LORD came to me:
27: 1 The **word** *of* the LORD came to me:
28: 1 The **word** *of* the LORD came to me:
28: 11 The **word** *of* the LORD came to me:
28: 20 The **word** *of* the LORD came to me:
29: 1 month on the twelfth day, the **word** *of* the LORD came to me:
29: 17 first month on the first day, the **word** *of* the LORD came to me:
30: 1 The **word** *of* the LORD came to me:
30: 20 month on the seventh day, the **word** *of* the LORD came to me:
31: 1 third month on the first day, the **word** *of* the LORD came to me:
32: 1 month on the first day, the **word** *of* the LORD came to me:
32: 17 fifteenth day of the month, the **word** *of* the LORD came to me:
33: 1 The **word** *of* the LORD came to me:
33: 7 so hear the **word** I speak and give them warning from me.
33: 23 Then the **word** *of* the LORD came to me:
33: 30 'Come and hear the **message** that has come from the LORD.'
33: 31 as they usually do, and sit before you to listen to your **words**,
33: 32 for they hear your **words** but do not put them into practice.
34: 1 The **word** *of* the LORD came to me:
34: 7 " 'Therefore, you shepherds, hear the **word** *of* the LORD:
34: 9 therefore, O shepherds, hear the **word** *of* the LORD:
35: 1 The **word** *of* the LORD came to me:
35: 13 You boasted against me and **spoke** against me without restraint,

Eze 36: 1 and say, 'O mountains of Israel, hear the **word** *of* the LORD.
36: 4 O mountains of Israel, hear the **word** *of* the Sovereign LORD:
36: 16 Again the **word** *of* the LORD came to me:
37: 4 and say to them, 'Dry bones, hear the **word** *of* the LORD!
37: 15 The **word** *of* the LORD came to me:
38: 1 The **word** *of* the LORD came to me:
38: 10 On that day **thoughts** will come into your mind and you will
Da 1: 5 The king assigned them a daily **amount** of food and wine from the
1: 14 he agreed to **this**[s] [+2021+2021+2296] and tested them for ten days.
1: 20 In every **matter** *of* wisdom and understanding about which the
9: 2 according to the **word** *of* the LORD given to Jeremiah the
9: 12 You have fulfilled the **words** spoken against us and against our
9: 23 As soon as you began to pray, an **answer** was given, which I have
9: 23 Therefore, consider the **message** and understand the vision:
9: 25 From the issuing of the **decree** to restore and rebuild Jerusalem
10: 1 a **revelation** was given to Daniel (who was called Belteshazzar).
10: 1 Its **message** was true and it concerned a great war. The
10: 1 The understanding of the **message** came to him in a vision.
10: 6 of burnished bronze, and his **voice** like the sound of a multitude.
10: 9 Then I heard him **speaking** [+7754], and as I listened to him,
10: 9 as I listened to **[RPH]** him, I fell into a deep sleep, my face to the
10: 11 consider carefully the **words** I am about to speak to you, and stand
10: 11 when he said **this**[s] [+2021+2021+2296] to me, I stood up trembling.
10: 12 your **words** were heard, and I have come in response to them.
10: 12 words were heard, and I have come in response to **them**[s] [+3870].
10: 15 While he was saying **this**[s] [+465+2021+2021] to me, I bowed with
12: 4 close up and seal the **words** of the scroll until the time of the end.
12: 9 because the **words** are closed up and sealed until the time of the
Hos 1: 1 The **word** *of* the LORD that came to Hosea son of Beeri during
4: 1 Hear the **word** *of* the LORD, you Israelites, because the LORD
10: 4 *They* **make many promises** [+1819], take false oaths and make
14: 2 [14:3] Take **words** with you and return to the LORD. Say to
Joel 1: 1 The **word** *of* the LORD that came to Joel son of Pethuel.
2: 11 are beyond number, and mighty are those who obey his **command**.
Am 1: 1 The **words** *of* Amos, one of the shepherds of Tekoa—what he saw
3: 1 Hear this **word** the LORD has spoken against you, O people of
3: 7 Surely the Sovereign LORD does **nothing** [+4202] without
4: 1 Hear this **word**, you cows of Bashan on Mount Samaria,
5: 1 Hear this **word**, O house of Israel, this lament I take up concerning
7: 10 you in the very heart of Israel. The land cannot bear all his **words**.
7: 16 Now then, hear the **word** *of* the LORD. You say, " 'Do not
8: 11 thirst for water, but a famine of hearing the **words** *of* the LORD.
8: 12 searching for the **word** *of* the LORD, but they will not find it.
Jnh 1: 1 The **word** *of* the LORD came to Jonah son of Amittai:
3: 1 Then the **word** *of* the LORD came to Jonah a second time:
3: 3 Jonah obeyed the **word** *of* the LORD and went to Nineveh.
3: 6 When the **news** reached the king of Nineveh, he rose from his
4: 2 "O LORD, is this not **what I said** when I was still at home?
Mic 1: 1 The **word** *of* the LORD that came to Micah of Moresheth during
2: 7 "Do not my **words** do good to him whose ways are upright?
4: 2 will go out from Zion, the **word** *of* the LORD from Jerusalem.
Zep 1: 1 The **word** *of* the LORD that came to Zephaniah son of Cushi,
2: 5 the **word** *of* the LORD is against you, O Canaan, land of the
Hag 1: 1 the **word** *of* the LORD came through the prophet Haggai to
1: 3 Then the **word** *of* the LORD came through the prophet Haggai:
1: 12 of the LORD their God and the **message** *of* the prophet Haggai,
2: 1 the **word** *of* the LORD came through the prophet Haggai:
2: 5 **'This**[s] [+2021] is what I covenanted with you when you came out
2: 10 of Darius, the **word** *of* the LORD came to the prophet Haggai:
2: 20 The **word** *of* the LORD came to Haggai a second time on the
Zec 1: 1 the **word** *of* the LORD came to the prophet Zechariah son of
1: 6 did not my **words** and my decrees, which I commanded my
1: 7 the **word** *of* the LORD came to the prophet Zechariah son of
1: 13 spoke kind and comforting **words** to the angel who talked with me.
1: 13 and comforting words **[RPH]** to the angel who talked with me.
4: 6 So he said to me, "This is the **word** *of* the LORD to Zerubbabel:
4: 8 Then the **word** *of* the LORD came to me:
6: 9 The **word** *of* the LORD came to me:
7: 1 the **word** *of* the LORD came to Zechariah on the fourth day of the
7: 4 Then the **word** *of* the LORD Almighty came to me:
7: 7 Are these not the **words** the LORD proclaimed through the earlier
7: 8 And the **word** *of* the LORD came again to Zechariah:
7: 12 or to the **words** that the LORD Almighty had sent by his Spirit
8: 1 Again the **word** *of* the LORD Almighty came to me.
8: 9 "You who now hear these **words** spoken by the prophets who were
8: 16 These are the **things** you are to do: Speak the truth to each other,
8: 18 Again the **word** *of* the LORD Almighty came to me.
9: 1 An Oracle The **word** *of* the LORD is against the land of Hadrach
11: 11 flock who were watching me knew it was the **word** *of* the LORD.
12: 1 An Oracle This is the **word** *of* the LORD concerning Israel.
Mal 1: 1 An oracle: The **word** *of* the LORD to Israel through Malachi.
2: 17 You have wearied the LORD with your **words**. "How have we
3: 13 "You *have* **said** harsh *things* against me," says the LORD.

1822 דֶּ֫בֶר[1] *deber*[1], n.m. [49] [√ 1818]

plague [43], plagues [3], pestilence [2], diseases [1]

Ex 5: 3 our God, or he may strike us with **plagues** or with the sword."
9: 3 the hand of the LORD will bring a terrible **plague** on your
9: 15 your people with a **plague** that would have wiped you off the earth.
Lev 26: 25 you withdraw into your cities, I will send a **plague** among you,
Nu 14: 12 I will strike them down with a **plague** and destroy them, but I will
Dt 28: 21 The LORD will plague you with **diseases** until he has destroyed
2Sa 24: 13 Or three days of **plague** in your land? Now then, think it over
24: 15 So the LORD sent a **plague** on Israel from that morning until the
1Ki 8: 37 "When famine or **plague** comes to the land, or blight or mildew,
1Ch 21: 12 days of **plague** in the land, with the angel of the LORD ravaging
21: 14 So the LORD sent a **plague** on Israel, and seventy thousand men
2Ch 6: 28 "When famine or **plague** comes to the land, or blight or mildew,
7: 13 locusts to devour the land or send a **plague** among my people,
20: 9 upon us, whether the sword of judgment, or **plague** or famine,
Ps 78: 50 he did not spare them from death but gave them over to the **plague**.
91: 3 save you from the fowler's snare and from the deadly **pestilence**.
91: 6 nor the **pestilence** that stalks in the darkness, nor the plague that
Jer 14: 12 Instead, I will destroy them with the sword, famine and **plague**."
21: 6 both men and animals—and they will die of a terrible **plague**.
21: 7 his officials and the people in this city who survive the **plague**,
21: 9 Whoever stays in this city will die by the sword, famine or **plague**.
24: 10 **plague** against them until they are destroyed from the land I gave
27: 8 famine and **plague**, declares the LORD, until I destroy it by his
27: 13 **plague** with which the LORD has threatened any nation that will
28: 8 disaster and **plague** against many countries and great kingdoms.
29: 17 famine and **plague** against them and I will make them like poor
29: 18 famine and **plague** and will make them abhorrent to all the
32: 24 Because of the sword, famine and **plague**, the city will be handed
32: 36 and **plague** it will be handed over to the king of Babylon';
34: 17 the LORD—'freedom' to fall by the sword, **plague** and famine.
38: 2 'Whoever stays in this city will die by the sword, famine or **plague**,
42: 17 to Egypt to settle there will die by the sword, famine and **plague**;
42: 22 famine and **plague** in the place where you want to go to settle."
44: 13 Egypt with the sword, famine and **plague**, as I punished Jerusalem.
Eze 5: 12 A third of your people will die of the **plague** or perish by famine
5: 17 **Plague** and bloodshed will sweep through you, and I will bring the
6: 11 house of Israel, for they will fall by the sword, famine and **plague**.
6: 12 He that is far away will die of the **plague**, and he that is near will
7: 15 "Outside is the sword, inside are **plague** and famine; those in the
7: 15 and those in the city will be devoured by famine and **plague**.
12: 16 But I will spare a few of them from the sword, famine and **plague**,
14: 19 "Or if I send a **plague** into that land and pour out my wrath upon it
14: 21 sword and famine and wild beasts and **plague**—to kill its men
28: 23 I will send a **plague** upon her and make blood flow in her streets.
33: 27 and those in strongholds and caves will die of a **plague**.
38: 22 I will execute judgment upon him with **plague** and bloodshed;
Hos 13: 14 Where, O death, are your **plagues**? Where, O grave, is your
Am 4: 10 "I sent **plagues** among you as I did to Egypt. I killed your young
Hab 3: 5 **Plague** went before him; pestilence followed his steps.

1823 דֶּ֫בֶר[2] *deber*[2], n.m. Not used in NIV/BHS [√ 1818]

1824 דֹּבֶר *dōber*, n.[m.]. [2] [√ 1818]

pasture [2]

Isa 5: 17 sheep will graze as in their own **pasture**; lambs will feed among
Mic 2: 12 bring them together like sheep in a pen, like a flock in its **pasture**;

1825 דִּבֵּר *dibbēr*, n.[m.]. [1] [√ 1819]

word [1]

Jer 5: 13 The prophets are but wind and the **word** is not in them; so let what

1826 דִּבְרָה *dibrâ*, n.f. [5] [√ 1819; Ar 10159]

as for [+6584] [1], because [+6584] [1], cause [1], order [1], therefore [+6584+8611] [1]

Job 5: 8 I would appeal to God; I would lay my **cause** before him.
Ps 110: 4 his mind: "You are a priest forever, in the **order** *of* Melchizedek."
Ecc 3: 18 I also thought, "**As for** [+6584] men, God tests them so that they
7: 14 **Therefore** [+6584+8611], a man cannot discover anything about
8: 2 I say, **because** [+6584] you took an oath before God.

1827 דֹּבְרוֹת *dōberôt*, n.f.pl. [1] [√ 1818]

rafts [1]

1Ki 5: 9 [5:23] I will float them in **rafts** by sea to the place you specify.

1828 דִּבְרִי *dibrî*, n.pr.m. [1]

Dibri [1]

Lev 24: 11 mother's name was Shelomith, the daughter of **Dibri** the Danite.)

1829 דָּבְרַת dāb^erat, n.pr.loc. [3] [√ 1818]
Daberath [3]

Jos 19:12 of Kisloth Tabor and went on to **Daberath** and up to Japhia.
21:28 from the tribe of Issachar, Kishion, **Daberath**,
1Ch 6:72 [6:57] from the tribe of Issachar they received Kedesh, **Daberath**,

1830 דַּבֶּרֶת dabberet, n.f. [1] [√ 1819]
instruction [1]

Dt 33:3 At your feet they all bow down, and from you receive **instruction**,

1831 דְּבַשׁ d^ebaš, n.m. [54] [→ 3340]
honey [52], honeycomb [+3626] [1], honeycomb [+7430] [1]

Ge 43:11 a little balm and a little **honey**, some spices and myrrh,
Ex 3:8 a good and spacious land, a land flowing with milk and **honey**—
3:17 Hivites and Jebusites—a land flowing with milk and **honey**.'
13:5 your forefathers to give you, a land flowing with milk and **honey**—
16:31 white like coriander seed and tasted like wafers made with **honey**.
33:3 Go up to the land flowing with milk and **honey**. But I will not go
Lev 2:11 burn any yeast or **honey** in an offering made to the LORD by fire.
20:24 it to you as an inheritance, a land flowing with milk and **honey**."
Nu 13:27 land to which you sent us, and it does flow with milk and **honey**!
14:8 a land flowing with milk and **honey**, and will give it to us.
16:13 out of a land flowing with milk and **honey** to kill us in the desert?
16:14 and **honey** or given us an inheritance of fields and vineyards.
Dt 6:3 you may increase greatly in a land flowing with milk and **honey**,
8:8 and barley, vines and fig trees, pomegranates, olive oil and **honey**;
11:9 and their descendants, a land flowing with milk and **honey**.
26:9 and gave us this land, a land flowing with milk and **honey**;
26:15 on oath to our forefathers, a land flowing with milk and **honey**."
27:3 a land flowing with milk and **honey**, just as the LORD, the God
31:20 I have brought them into the land flowing with milk and **honey**,
32:13 He nourished him with **honey** from the rock, and with oil from the
Jos 5:6 their fathers to give us, a land flowing with milk and **honey**.
Jdg 14:8 at the lion's carcass. In it was a swarm of bees and *some* **honey**,
14:9 he did not tell them that he had taken the **honey** from the lion's
14:18 day the men of the town said to him, "What is sweeter than **honey**?
1Sa 14:25 entire army entered the woods, and there was **honey** on the ground.
14:26 When they went into the woods, they saw the **honey** oozing out,
14:27 that was in his hand and dipped it into the **honeycomb** [+3626].
14:29 See how my eyes brightened when I tasted a little of this **honey**.
14:43 told him, "I merely tasted a little **honey** with the end of my staff.
2Sa 17:29 **honey** and curds, sheep, and cheese from cows' milk for David
1Ki 14:3 of bread with you, some cakes and a jar of **honey**, and go to him.
2Ki 18:32 a land of bread and vineyards, a land of olive trees and **honey**.
2Ch 31:5 new wine, oil and **honey** and all that the fields produced.
Job 20:17 not enjoy the streams, the rivers flowing with **honey** and cream.
Ps 19:10 [19:11] they are sweeter than **honey**, than honey from the comb.
81:16 [81:17] of wheat; with **honey** from the rock I would satisfy you."
119:103 are your words to my taste, sweeter than **honey** to my mouth!
Pr 16:24 Pleasant words are a **honeycomb** [+7430], sweet to the soul
24:13 Eat **honey**, my son, for it is good; honey from the comb is sweet to
25:16 If you find **honey**, eat just enough—too much of it, and you will
25:27 It is not good to eat too much **honey**, nor is it honorable to seek
SS 4:11 the honeycomb, my bride; milk and **honey** are under your tongue.
5:1 I have eaten my honeycomb and my **honey**; I have drunk my wine
Isa 7:15 eat curds and **honey** when he knows enough to reject the wrong
7:22 curds to eat. All who remain in the land will eat curds and **honey**.
Jer 11:5 to give them a land flowing with milk and **honey**'—
32:22 to give their forefathers, a land flowing with milk and **honey**.
41:8 We have wheat and barley, oil and **honey**, hidden in a field."
Eze 3:3 with it." So I ate it, and it tasted as sweet as **honey** in my mouth.
16:13 embroidered cloth. Your food was fine flour, **honey** and olive oil.
16:19 for you—the fine flour, olive oil and **honey** I gave you to eat—
20:6 a land flowing with milk and **honey**, the most beautiful of all
20:15 a land flowing with milk and **honey**, most beautiful of all lands—
27:17 from Minnith and confections, **honey**, oil and balm for your wares.

1832 דַּבֶּשֶׁת¹ dabbešet¹, n.f. [1] [→ 1833?]
humps [1]

Isa 30:6 their treasures on the **humps** *of* camels, to that unprofitable nation,

1833 דַּבֶּשֶׁת² dabbešet², n.pr.loc. [1] [√ 1832?]
Dabbesheth [1]

Jos 19:11 Going west it ran to Maralah, touched **Dabbesheth**, and extended

1834 דָּג dāg, n.m. [18] [→ 1794, 1835?, 1836, 1854, 1855, 1900; cf. 1899]
fish [17], fishing [1]

Ge 9:2 that moves along the ground, and upon all the **fish** *of* the sea;
Nu 11:22 Would they have enough if all the **fish** *in* the sea were caught for
1Ki 4:33 [5:13] He also taught about animals and birds, reptiles and **fish**.
2Ch 33:14 as far as the entrance of the **Fish** Gate and encircling the hill of
Ne 3:3 The **Fish** Gate was rebuilt by the sons of Hassenaah. They laid its
12:39 the Jeshanah Gate, the **Fish** Gate, the Tower of Hananel
Job 12:8 and it will teach you, or let the **fish** *of* the sea inform you.
41:7 [40:31] his hide with harpoons or his head with **fishing** spears?
Ps 8:8 [8:9] the birds of the air, and the **fish** *of* the sea, all that swim the
Ecc 9:12 As **fish** are caught in a cruel net, or birds are taken in a snare,
Eze 38:20 The **fish** *of* the sea, the birds of the air, the beasts of the field,
Hos 4:3 of the field and the birds of the air and the **fish** *of* the sea are dying.
Jnh 1:17 [2:1] the LORD provided a great **fish** to swallow Jonah,
1:17 [2:1] and Jonah was inside the **fish** three days and three nights.
2:10 [2:11] the LORD commanded the **fish**, and it vomited Jonah
Hab 1:14 You have made men like **fish** *in* the sea, like sea creatures that
Zep 1:3 I will sweep away the birds of the air and the **fish** *of* the sea.
1:10 declares the LORD, "a cry will go up from the **Fish** Gate,

1835 דָּגָה¹ dāgâ¹, v. [1] [√ 1834?]
increase [1]

Ge 48:16 [A] and Isaac, and *may they* **increase** greatly upon the earth."

1836 דָּגָה² dāgâ², n.f. [15] [√ 1834]
fish [15]

Ge 1:26 and let them rule over the **fish** *of* the sea and the birds of the air,
1:28 Rule over the **fish** *of* the sea and the birds of the air and over every
Ex 7:18 The **fish** in the Nile will die, and the river will stink; the Egyptians
7:21 The **fish** in the Nile died, and the river smelled so bad that the
Nu 11:5 We remember the **fish** we ate in Egypt at no cost—also the
Dt 4:18 that moves along the ground or any **fish** in the waters below.
Ps 105:29 He turned their waters into blood, causing their **fish** to die.
Isa 50:2 rivers into a desert; their **fish** rot for lack of water and die of thirst.
Eze 29:4 in your jaws and make the **fish** *of* your streams stick to your scales.
29:4 from among your streams, with all the **fish** sticking to your scales.
29:5 I will leave you in the desert, you and all the **fish** *of* your streams.
47:9 There will be large numbers of **fish**, because this water flows there
47:10 The **fish** will be of many kinds—like the fish of the Great Sea.
47:10 The fish will be of many kinds—like the **fish** *of* the Great Sea.
Jnh 2:1 [2:2] From inside the **fish** Jonah prayed to the LORD his God.

1837 דָּגוֹן dāgôn, n.pr.m. [13] [→ 1087, 1841]
Dagon [8], Dagon's [2], *untranslated* [1], his^s body [1], his^s [1]

Jdg 16:23 Philistines assembled to offer a great sacrifice to **Dagon** their god
1Sa 5:2 they carried the ark into **Dagon's** temple and set it beside Dagon.
5:2 they carried the ark into Dagon's temple and set it beside **Dagon**.
5:3 the people of Ashdod rose early the next day, there was **Dagon**,
5:3 of the LORD! They took **Dagon** and put him back in his place.
5:4 But the following morning when they rose, there was **Dagon**,
5:4 **His^s** head and hands had been broken off and were lying on the
5:4 and were lying on the threshold; only **his^s body** remained.
5:5 That is why to this day neither the priests of **Dagon** nor any others
5:5 others who enter **Dagon's** temple at Ashdod step on the threshold.
5:5 enter Dagon's temple at Ashdod step on the threshold. **[RPH]**
5:7 because his hand is heavy upon us and upon **Dagon** our god."
1Ch 10:10 temple of their gods and hung up his head in the temple of **Dagon**.

1838 דָּגַל¹ dāgal¹, v. [1] [√ 1840]
outstanding [1]

SS 5:10 [B] lover is radiant and ruddy, **outstanding** among ten thousand.

1839 דָּגַל² dāgal², v.den. [3] [√ 1840]
in procession [1], lift up banners [1], troops with banners [1]

Ps 20:5 [20:6] [A] and *will* **lift up** *our* **banners** in the name of our God.
SS 6:4 [C] lovely as Jerusalem, majestic as **troops with banners**.
6:10 [C] bright as the sun, majestic as the stars **in procession**?

1840 דֶּגֶל degel, n.m. [14] [→ 1838, 1839, 5609]
standard [11], standards [2], banner [1]

Nu 1:52 by divisions, each man in his own camp under his own **standard**.
2:2 each man under his **standard** with the banners of his family."
2:3 of the camp of Judah are to encamp under their **standard**.
2:10 will be the divisions of the camp of Reuben under their **standard**.
2:17 order as they encamp, each in his own place under his **standard**.
2:18 will be the divisions of the camp of Ephraim under their **standard**.
2:25 will be the divisions of the camp of Dan, under their **standard**.
2:31 Dan number 157,600. They will set out last, under their **standards**.
2:34 that is the way they encamped under their **standards**, and that is
10:14 divisions of the camp of Judah went first, under their **standard**.
10:18 divisions of the camp of Reuben went next, under their **standard**.

Nu 10:22 divisions of the camp of Ephraim went next, under their **standard**.
10:25 the divisions of the camp of Dan set out, under their **standard**.
SS 2:4 has taken me to the banquet hall, and his **banner** over me is love.

1841 דָּגָן *dāgān*, n.m. [40] [√ 1837]

grain [38], bread [1], threshing floor [+1755] [1]

Ge 27:28 and of earth's richness—an abundance of **grain** and new wine.
27:37 his servants, and I have sustained him with **grain** and new wine.
Nu 18:12 and **grain** they give the LORD as the firstfruits of their harvest.
18:27 Your offering will be reckoned to you as **grain** from the threshing
Dt 7:13 the crops of your land—your **grain**, new wine and oil—
11:14 so that you may gather in your **grain**, new wine and oil.
12:17 You must not eat in your own towns the tithe of your **grain**
14:23 Eat the tithe of your **grain**, new wine and oil, and the firstborn of
18:4 You are to give them the firstfruits of your **grain**, new wine
28:51 They will leave you no **grain**, new wine or oil, nor any calves of
33:28 Jacob's spring is secure in a land of **grain** and new wine, where the
2Ki 18:32 a land of **grain** and new wine, a land of bread and vineyards,
2Ch 31:5 the Israelites generously gave the firstfruits of their **grain**,
32:28 He also made buildings to store the harvest of **grain**, new wine
Ne 5:2 in order for us to eat and stay alive, we must get **grain**."
5:3 our vineyards and our homes to get **grain** during the famine."
5:10 and my men are also lending the people money and **grain**.
5:11 the hundredth part of the money, **grain**, new wine and oil."
10:39 [10:40] are to bring their contributions of **grain**, new wine and oil
13:5 also the tithes of **grain**, new wine and oil prescribed for the
13:12 All Judah brought the tithes of **grain**, new wine and oil into the
Ps 4:7 [4:8] have filled my heart with greater joy than when their **grain**
65:9 [65:10] are filled with water to provide the people with **grain**,
78:24 manna for the people to eat, he gave them the **grain** *of* heaven.
Isa 36:17 a land of **grain** and new wine, a land of bread and vineyards.
62:8 "Never again will I give your **grain** as food for your enemies,
Jer 31:12 the **grain**, the new wine and the oil, the young of the flocks
La 2:12 They say to their mothers, "Where is **bread** and wine?" as they
Eze 36:29 I will call for the **grain** and make it plentiful and will not bring
Hos 2:8 [2:10] acknowledged that I was the one who gave her the **grain**,
2:9 [2:11] "Therefore I will take away my **grain** when it ripens,
2:22 [2:24] the earth will respond to the **grain**, the new wine and oil,
7:14 They gather together for **grain** and new wine but turn away from
9:1 love the wages of a prostitute at every **threshing floor** [+1755].
14:7 [14:8] He will flourish like the **grain**. He will blossom like a vine,
Joel 1:10 the **grain** is destroyed, the new wine is dried up, the oil fails.
1:17 the granaries have been broken down, for the **grain** has dried up.
2:19 "I am sending you **grain**, new wine and oil, enough to satisfy you
Hag 1:11 on the **grain**, the new wine, the oil and whatever the ground
Zec 9:17 **Grain** will make the young men thrive, and new wine the young

1842 דָּגַר *dāgar*, v. [2]

care for young [1], hatches eggs [1]

Isa 34:15 [A] and **care for** *her* **young** under the shadow of her wings;
Jer 17:11 [A] Like a partridge *that* **hatches eggs** it did not lay is the man

1843 דַּד *dad*, n.m. [4]

bosom [2], bosoms [1], breasts [1]

Pr 5:19 may her **breasts** satisfy you always, may you ever be captivated by
Eze 23:3 land their breasts were fondled and their virgin **bosoms** caressed.
23:8 caressed her virgin **bosom** and poured out their lust upon her.
23:21 when in Egypt your **bosom** was caressed and your young breasts

1844 דָּדָה *dādâ*, v. [2]

leading [1], walk humbly [1]

Ps 42:4 [42:5] [F] **leading** the procession to the house of God,
Isa 38:15 [F] *I will* **walk humbly** all my years because of this anguish of

1845 דֹּדָוָהוּ *dōdāwāhû*, n.pr.m. [1]

Dodavahu [1]

2Ch 20:37 Eliezer son of **Dodavahu** of Mareshah prophesied against

1846 דֹּדִי *dōdî*, n.pr.m. Not used in NIV/BHS [√ 1856?]

1847 דְּדָן *dedān*, n.pr.loc. & g. [11 / 10] [→ 1848]

Dedan [10]

Ge 10:7 Raamah and Sabteca. The sons of Raamah: Sheba and **Dedan**.
25:3 Jokshan was the father of Sheba and **Dedan**; the descendants of
25:3 the descendants of **Dedan** were the Asshurites, the Letushites
1Ch 1:9 Raamah and Sabteca. The sons of Raamah: Sheba and **Dedan**.
1:32 Ishbak and Shuah. The sons of Jokshan: Sheba and **Dedan**.
Jer 25:23 **Dedan**, Tema, Buz and all who are in distant places;
49:8 Turn and flee, hide in deep caves, you who live in **Dedan**,
Eze 25:13 lay it waste, and from Teman to **Dedan** they will fall by the sword.
27:15 " 'The men of Rhodes [BHS *Dedan*; NIV 8102] traded with you,
27:20 " '**Dedan** traded in saddle blankets with you.
38:13 Sheba and **Dedan** and the merchants of Tarshish and all her

1848 דְּדָנִי *dedānî*, a.g. [1] [√ 1847]

Dedanites [1]

Isa 21:13 You caravans of **Dedanites**, who camp in the thickets of Arabia,

1849 דֹּדָנִים *dōdānim*, n.pr.g.pl. [1 / 0] [cf. 8102]

Ge 10:4 Tarshish, the Kittim and the Rodanim. [BHS *Dodanim*; NIV 8102]

1850 דָּהַם *dāham*, v. [1]

taken by surprise [1]

Jer 14:9 [C] Why are you like a man **taken by surprise**, like a warrior

1851 דָּהַר *dāhar*, v. [1] [→ 1852]

galloping [1]

Na 3:2 [A] the clatter of wheels, **galloping** horses and jolting chariots!

1852 דַּהֲרָה *dahărâ*, n.f. [2] [√ 1851]

galloping [2]

Jdg 5:22 the horses' hoofs—**galloping**, galloping go his mighty steeds.
5:22 the horses' hoofs—galloping, **galloping** go his mighty steeds.

1853 דּוּב *dûb*, v. [1] [cf. 2307]

drain away [1]

Lev 26:16 [G] fever that will destroy your sight and **drain away** your life.

1854 דַּוָּג *dawwāg*, n.m. [1] [√ 1834]

fishermen [1]

Jer 16:16 ["But now I will send for many **fishermen**," [K; see Q 1900] declares the LORD,]
Eze 47:10 **Fishermen** will stand along the shore; from En Gedi to En Eglaim

1855 דּוּגָה *dûgâ*, n.f. [1] [√ 1834]

fishhooks [+6106] [1]

Am 4:2 be taken away with hooks, the last of you with **fishhooks** [+6106].

1856 דּוֹד *dôd*, n.m. [61] [→ 455, 485, 1161, 1846?, 1858?, 1860, 1861?, 1862?]

lover [28], uncle [11], love [8], cousin [+1201] [3], beloved [2], others[s] [2], *untranslated* [1], cousin [+1426] [1], cousin [1], cousins on their father's side [+1201] [1], lover's [+4200] [1], lovers [1], relative [1]

Lev 10:4 summoned Mishael and Elzaphan, sons of Aaron's **uncle** Uzziel,
20:20 " 'If a man sleeps with his aunt, he has dishonored his **uncle**.
25:49 An **uncle** or a cousin or any blood relative in his clan may redeem
25:49 An uncle or a **cousin** [+1201] or any blood relative in his clan may
Nu 36:11 and Noah—married their **cousins on their father's side** [+1201].
1Sa 10:14 Now Saul's **uncle** asked him and his servant, "Where have you
10:15 Saul's **uncle** said, "Tell me what Samuel said to you."
10:16 he did not tell his **uncle** what Samuel had said about the kingship.
14:50 of Saul's army was Abner son of Ner, and Ner was Saul's **uncle**.
2Ki 24:17 Jehoiachin's **uncle**, king in his place and changed his name to
1Ch 27:32 Jonathan, David's **uncle**, was a counselor, a man of insight
Est 2:7 Mordecai had a **cousin** [+1426] named Hadassah, whom he had
2:15 (the girl Mordecai had adopted, the daughter of his **uncle** Abihail)
Pr 7:18 Come, let's drink deep of **love** till morning; let's enjoy ourselves
SS 1:2 kisses of his mouth—for your **love** is more delightful than wine.
1:4 and delight in you; we will praise your **love** more than wine.
1:13 My **lover** is to me a sachet of myrrh resting between my breasts.
1:14 My **lover** is to me a cluster of henna blossoms from the vineyards
1:16 How handsome you are, my **lover**! Oh, how charming! And our
2:3 Like an apple tree among the trees of the forest is my **lover** among
2:8 Listen! My **lover**! Look! Here he comes, leaping across the
2:9 My **lover** is like a gazelle or a young stag. Look! There he stands
2:10 My **lover** spoke and said to me, "Arise, my darling, my beautiful
2:16 My **lover** is mine and I am his; he browses among the lilies.
2:17 turn, my **lover**, and be like a gazelle or like a young stag on the
4:10 How delightful is your **love**, my sister, my bride! How much more
4:10 How much more pleasing is your **love** than wine, and the fragrance
4:16 Let my **lover** come into his garden and taste its choice fruits.
5:1 and my milk. Eat, O friends, and drink; drink your fill, O **lovers**.
5:2 Listen! My **lover** is knocking: "Open to me, my sister, my darling,
5:4 My **lover** thrust his hand through the latch-opening; my heart
5:5 I arose to open for my **lover**, and my hands dripped with myrrh,
5:6 I opened for my **lover**, but my lover had left; he was gone.

SS 5: 6 I opened for my lover, but my **lover** had left; he was gone.
5: 8 I charge you—if you find my **lover**, what will you tell him?
5: 9 How is your **beloved** better than others, most beautiful of women?
5: 9 How is your beloved better than **others**[s], most beautiful of
5: 9 How is your **beloved** better than others, that you charge us so?
5: 9 How is your beloved better than **others**[s], that you charge us so?
5: 10 My **lover** is radiant and ruddy, outstanding among ten thousand.
5: 16 This is my **lover**, this my friend, O daughters of Jerusalem.
6: 1 Where has your **lover** gone, most beautiful of women? Which way
6: 1 Which way did your **lover** turn, that we may look for him with
6: 2 My **lover** has gone down to his garden, to the beds of spices,
6: 3 I am my **lover's** [+4200] and my lover is mine; he browses among
6: 3 I am my lover's and my **lover** is mine; he browses among the
7: 9 [7:10] May the wine go straight to my **lover**, flowing gently over
7: 10 [7:11] I belong to my **lover**, and his desire is for me.
7: 11 [7:12] Come, my **lover**, let us go to the countryside, let us spend
7: 12 [7:13] pomegranates are in bloom—there I will give you my **love**.
7: 13 [7:14] both new and old, that I have stored up for you, my **lover**.
8: 5 Who is this coming up from the desert leaning on her **lover**?
8: 14 Come away, my **lover**, and be like a gazelle or like a young stag on
Isa 5: 1 I will sing for the one I love a song **[RPH]** about his vineyard:
Jer 32: 7 Hanamel son of Shallum your **uncle** is going to come to you
32: 8 my **cousin** [+1201] Hanamel came to me in the courtyard of the
32: 9 so I bought the field at Anathoth from my **cousin** [+1201] Hanamel
32: 12 in the presence of my **cousin** Hanamel and of the witnesses who
Eze 16: 8 when I looked at you and saw that you were old enough for **love**,
23: 17 came to her, to the bed of **love**, and in their lust they defiled her.
Am 6: 10 if a **relative** who is to burn the bodies comes to carry them out of

1857 דּוּד *dûd*, n.m. [8]

basket [3], baskets [2], caldrons [1], kettle [1], pot [1]

1Sa 2: 14 He would plunge it into the pan or **kettle** or caldron or pot,
2Ki 10: 7 They put their heads in **baskets** and sent them to Jehu in Jezreel.
2Ch 35: 13 **caldrons** and pans and served them quickly to all the people.
Job 41: 20 [41:12] Smoke pours from his nostrils as from a boiling **pot** over
Ps 81: 6 [81:7] their shoulders; their hands were set free from the **basket**.
Jer 24: 1 the LORD showed me two **baskets** *of* figs placed in front of the
24: 2 One **basket** had very good figs, like those that ripen early;
24: 2 the other **basket** had very poor figs, so bad they could not be eaten.

1858 דָּוִד *dāwid*, n.pr.m. [1075] [√ 1856?]

David [906], David's [69], he[s] [47], *untranslated* [21], him[s] [18], David's [+4200] [8], his[s] [4], David's line [1], you[s] [1]

Ru 4: 17 named him Obed. He was the father of Jesse, the father of **David**.
4: 22 Obed the father of Jesse, and Jesse the father of **David**.
1Sa 16: 13 from that day on the Spirit of the LORD came upon **David** in
16: 19 Saul sent messengers to Jesse and said, "Send me your son **David**,
16: 20 and a young goat and sent them with his son **David** to Saul.
16: 21 **David** came to Saul and entered his service. Saul liked him very
16: 22 saying, "Allow **David** to remain in my service, for I am pleased
16: 23 from God came upon Saul, **David** would take his harp and play.
17: 12 Now **David** was the son of an Ephrathite named Jesse, who was
17: 14 **David** was the youngest. The three oldest followed Saul,
17: 15 **David** went back and forth from Saul to tend his father's sheep at
17: 17 Now Jesse said to his son **David**, "Take this ephah of roasted grain
17: 20 Early in the morning **David** left the flock with a shepherd,
17: 22 **David** left his things with the keeper of supplies, ran to the battle
17: 23 from his lines and shouted his usual defiance, and **David** heard it.
17: 26 **David** asked the men standing near him, "What will be done for
17: 28 speaking with the men, he burned with anger at **him**[s] and asked,
17: 29 "Now what have I done?" said **David**. "Can't I even speak?"
17: 31 What **David** said was overheard and reported to Saul, and Saul
17: 32 **David** said to Saul, "Let no one lose heart on account of this
17: 33 **[RPH]** "You are not able to go out against this Philistine
17: 34 **David** said to Saul, "Your servant has been keeping his father's
17: 37 **[NIE]** The LORD who delivered me from the paw of the lion
17: 37 Saul said to **David**, "Go, and the LORD be with you."
17: 38 Saul dressed **David** in his own tunic. He put a coat of armor on
17: 39 **David** fastened on his sword over the tunic and tried walking
17: 39 "I cannot go in these," **he**[s] said to Saul, "because I am not used to
17: 39 to Saul, "because I am not used to them." So **he**[s] took them off.
17: 41 with his shield bearer in front of him, kept coming closer to **David**.
17: 42 He looked **David** over and saw that he was only a boy, ruddy
17: 43 He said to **David**, "Am I a dog, that you come at me with sticks?"
17: 43 at me with sticks?" And the Philistine cursed **David** by his gods.
17: 44 **[RPH]** "and I'll give your flesh to the birds of the air and the
17: 45 **David** said to the Philistine, "You come against me with sword
17: 48 As the Philistine moved closer to attack **him**[s], David ran quickly
17: 48 attack him, **David** ran quickly toward the battle line to meet him.
17: 49 **[RPH]** Reaching into his bag and taking out a stone, he slung it
17: 50 So **David** triumphed over the Philistine with a sling and a stone;
17: 50 without a sword in **his**[s] hand he struck down the Philistine
17: 51 **David** ran and stood over him. He took hold of the Philistine's
17: 54 **David** took the Philistine's head and brought it to Jerusalem,
17: 55 As Saul watched **David** going out to meet the Philistine, he said to
17: 57 As soon as **David** returned from killing the Philistine, Abner took
17: 58 **David** said, "I am the son of your servant Jesse of Bethlehem."
18: 1 Jonathan became one in spirit with **David**, and he loved him as
18: 3 Jonathan made a covenant with **David** because he loved him as
18: 4 Jonathan took off the robe he was wearing and gave it to **David**,
18: 5 **David** did it so successfully that Saul gave him a high rank in the
18: 6 When the men were returning home after **David** had killed the
18: 7 "Saul has slain his thousands, and **David** his tens of thousands."
18: 8 "They have credited **David** with tens of thousands," he thought,
18: 9 And from that time on Saul kept a jealous eye on **David**.
18: 10 in his house, while **David** was playing the harp, as he usually did.
18: 11 and he hurled it, saying to himself, "I'll pin **David** to the wall."
18: 11 "I'll pin David to the wall." But **David** eluded him twice.
18: 12 Saul was afraid of **David**, because the LORD was with David
18: 14 In everything he did **he**[s] had great success, because the LORD
18: 16 all Israel and Judah loved **David**, because he led them in their
18: 17 Saul said to **David**, "Here is my older daughter Merab. I will give
18: 18 But **David** said to Saul, "Who am I, and what is my family
18: 19 the time came for Merab, Saul's daughter, to be given to **David**,
18: 20 Now Saul's daughter Michal was in love with **David**, and when
18: 21 So Saul said to **David**, "Now you have a second opportunity to
18: 22 "Speak to **David** privately and say, 'Look, the king is pleased with
18: 23 They repeated these words to **David**. But David said, "Do you
18: 23 **David** said, "Do you think it is a small matter to become the king's
18: 24 When Saul's servants told him what **David** had said,
18: 25 Saul replied, "Say to **David**, 'The king wants no other price for the
18: 25 to take revenge on his enemies.' " Saul's plan was to have **David**
18: 26 When the attendants told **David** these things, he was pleased to
18: 26 these things, **he**[s] was pleased to become the king's son-in-law.
18: 27 **David** and his men went out and killed two hundred Philistines.
18: 27 **He**[s] brought their foreskins and presented the full number to the
18: 28 When Saul realized that the LORD was with **David** and that his
18: 29 Saul became still more afraid of **him**[s], and he remained his enemy
18: 29 afraid of him, and he remained **his**[s] enemy the rest of his days.
18: 30 **David** met with more success than the rest of Saul's officers,
19: 1 Saul told his son Jonathan and all the attendants to kill **David**.
19: 1 the attendants to kill David. But Jonathan was very fond of **David**
19: 2 warned **him**[s], "My father Saul is looking for a chance to kill you.
19: 4 Jonathan spoke well of **David** to Saul his father and said to him,
19: 4 and said to him, "Let not the king do wrong to his servant **David**;
19: 5 would you do wrong to an innocent man like **David** by killing him
19: 7 So Jonathan called **David** and told him the whole conversation.
19: 7 He brought him to Saul, and **David** was with Saul as before.
19: 8 more war broke out, and **David** went out and fought the Philistines.
19: 9 with his spear in his hand. While **David** was playing the harp,
19: 10 but **David** eluded him as Saul drove the spear into the wall.
19: 10 the spear into the wall. That night **David** made good his escape.
19: 11 Saul sent men to **David's** house to watch it and to kill him in the
19: 11 Michal, **David's** wife, warned him, "If you don't run for your life
19: 12 So Michal let **David** down through a window, and he fled
19: 14 When Saul sent the men to capture **David**, Michal said, "He is ill."
19: 15 Saul sent the men back to see **David** and told them, "Bring him up
19: 18 When **David** had fled and made his escape, he went to Samuel at
19: 19 Word came to Saul: "**David** is in Naioth at Ramah";
19: 20 so he sent men to capture **him**[s]. But when they saw a group of
19: 22 he asked, "Where are Samuel and **David**?" "Over in Naioth at
20: 1 Then **David** fled from Naioth at Ramah and went to Jonathan
20: 3 **David** took an oath and said, "Your father knows very well that I
20: 4 Jonathan said to **David**, "Whatever you want me to do, I'll do for
20: 5 So **David** said, "Look, tomorrow is the New Moon festival,
20: 6 '**David** earnestly asked my permission to hurry to Bethlehem,
20: 10 **David** asked, "Who will tell me if your father answers you
20: 11 "Come," Jonathan said, **[RPH]** "let's go out into the field."
20: 12 Then Jonathan said to **David**: "By the LORD, the God of Israel,
20: 12 If he is favorably disposed toward **you**[s], will I not send you word
20: 15 not even when the LORD has cut off every one of **David's**
20: 16 So Jonathan made a covenant with the house of **David**, saying,
20: 16 saying, "May the LORD call **David's** enemies to account."
20: 17 And Jonathan had **David** reaffirm his oath out of love for him,
20: 24 So **David** hid in the field, and when the New Moon festival came,
20: 25 and Abner sat next to Saul, but **David's** place was empty.
20: 27 the second day of the month, **David's** place was empty again.
20: 28 "**David** earnestly asked me for permission to go to Bethlehem.
20: 33 Then Jonathan knew that his father intended to kill **David**.
20: 34 he was grieved at his father's shameful treatment of **David**.
20: 35 morning Jonathan went out to the field for his meeting with **David**.
20: 39 (The boy knew nothing of all this; only Jonathan and **David** knew.)
20: 41 **David** got up from the south side ⌊of the stone⌋ and bowed down
20: 41 kissed each other and wept together—but **David** wept the most.
20: 42 Jonathan said to **David**, "Go in peace, for we have sworn
21: 1 [21:2] **David** went to Nob, to Ahimelech the priest. Ahimelech

1Sa 21: 1 [21:2] Ahimelech trembled when he met **him**[s], and asked, "Why
21: 2 [21:3] **David** answered Ahimelech the priest, "The king charged
21: 4 [21:5] the priest answered **David**, "I don't have any ordinary
21: 5 [21:6] **David** replied, "Indeed women have been kept from us,
21: 8 [21:9] **David** asked Ahimelech, "Don't you have a spear or a
21: 9 [21:10] **David** said, "There is none like it; give it to me."
21:10 [21:11] That day **David** fled from Saul and went to Achish king
21:11 [21:12] said to him, "Isn't this **David**, the king of the land?
21:11 [21:12] slain his thousands, and **David** his tens of thousands'?"
21:12 [21:13] **David** took these words to heart and was very much
22: 1 **David** left Gath and escaped to the cave of Adullam. When his
22: 3 From there **David** went to Mizpah in Moab and said to the king of
22: 4 and they stayed with him as long as **David** was in the stronghold.
22: 5 But the prophet Gad said to **David**, "Do not stay in the stronghold.
22: 5 the land of Judah." So **David** left and went to the forest of Hereth.
22: 6 Now Saul heard that **David** and his men had been discovered.
22:14 "Who of all your servants is as loyal as **David**, the king's
22:17 the priests of the LORD, because they too have sided with **David**.
22:20 a son of Ahimelech son of Ahitub, escaped and fled to join **David**.
22:21 He told **David** that Saul had killed the priests of the LORD.
22:22 **David** said to Abiathar: "That day, when Doeg the Edomite was
23: 1 When **David** was told, "Look, the Philistines are fighting against
23: 2 **he**[s] inquired of the LORD, saying, "Shall I go and attack these
23: 2 The LORD answered **him**[s], "Go, attack the Philistines and save
23: 3 But **David's** men said to him, "Here in Judah we are afraid.
23: 4 Once again **David** inquired of the LORD, and the LORD
23: 5 So **David** and his men went to Keilah, fought the Philistines
23: 5 **He**[s] inflicted heavy losses on the Philistines and saved the people
23: 6 the ephod down with him when he fled to **David** at Keilah.)
23: 7 Saul was told that **David** had gone to Keilah, and he said,
23: 8 for battle, to go down to Keilah to besiege **David** and his men.
23: 9 When **David** learned that Saul was plotting against him, he said to
23:10 **David** said, "O LORD, God of Israel, your servant has heard
23:12 Again **David** asked, "Will the citizens of Keilah surrender me
23:13 So **David** and his men, about six hundred in number, left Keilah
23:13 When Saul was told that **David** had escaped from Keilah,
23:14 **David** stayed in the desert strongholds and in the hills of the Desert
23:15 While **David** was at Horesh in the Desert of Ziph, he learned that
23:15 Desert of Ziph, **he**[s] learned that Saul had come out to take his life.
23:16 Saul's son Jonathan went to **David** at Horesh and helped him find
23:18 Then Jonathan went home, but **David** remained at Horesh.
23:19 "Is not **David** hiding among us in the strongholds at Horesh,
23:24 Now **David** and his men were in the Desert of Maon, in the Arabah
23:25 and when **David** was told about it, he went down to the rock
23:25 heard this, he went into the Desert of Maon in pursuit of **David**.
23:26 **David** and his men were on the other side, hurrying to get away
23:26 were on the other side, **[RPH]** hurrying to get away from Saul.
23:26 As Saul and his forces were closing in on **David** and his men to
23:28 Saul broke off his pursuit of **David** and went to meet the
23:29 [24:1] **David** went up from there and lived in the strongholds of
24: 1 [24:2] he was told, "**David** is in the Desert of En Gedi."
24: 2 [24:3] set out to look for **David** and his men near the Crags of the
24: 3 [24:4] **David** and his men were far back in the cave.
24: 4 [24:5] The men **[RPH]** said, "This is the day the LORD spoke
24: 4 [24:5] to deal with as you wish.' " Then **David** crept up unnoticed
24: 5 [24:6] **David** was conscience-stricken for having cut off a corner
24: 7 [24:8] With these words **David** rebuked his men and did not allow
24: 8 [24:9] **David** went out of the cave and called out to Saul, "My
24: 8 [24:9] **David** bowed down and prostrated himself with his face to
24: 9 [24:10] **He**[s] said to Saul, "Why do you listen when men say,
24: 9 [24:10] you listen when men say, '**David** is bent on harming you'?
24:16 [24:17] When **David** finished saying this, Saul asked, "Is that
24:16 [24:17] Saul asked, "Is that your voice, **David** my son?"
24:17 [24:18] **[RPH]** "You have treated me well, but I have treated
24:22 [24:23] So **David** gave his oath to Saul. Then Saul returned home,
24:22 [24:23] but **David** and his men went up to the stronghold.
25: 1 in Ramah. Then **David** moved down into the Desert of Maon.
25: 4 While **David** was in the desert, he heard that Nabal was shearing
25: 5 So **he**[s] sent ten young men and said to them, "Go up to Nabal at
25: 5 So he sent ten young men and **[RPH]** said to them, "Go up to
25: 8 and your son **David** whatever you can find for them.' "
25: 9 When **David's** men arrived, they gave Nabal this message in
25: 9 men arrived, they gave Nabal this message in **David's** name.
25:10 Nabal answered **David's** servants, "Who is this David? Who is this
25:10 Nabal answered David's servants, "Who is this **David**? Who is this
25:12 **David's** men turned around and went back. When they arrived,
25:13 **David** said to his men, "Put on your swords!" So they put on their
25:13 your swords!" So they put on their swords, and **David** put on his.
25:13 About four hundred men went up with **David**, while two hundred
25:14 "**David** sent messengers from the desert to give our master his
25:20 there were **David** and his men descending toward her, and she met
25:21 **David** had just said, "It's been useless—all my watching over this
25:22 May God deal with **David**, be it ever so severely, if by morning I
25:23 When Abigail saw **David**, she quickly got off her donkey
25:23 and bowed down before **David** with her face to the ground.
25:32 **David** said to Abigail, "Praise be to the LORD, the God of Israel,
25:35 Then **David** accepted from her hand what she had brought him
25:39 When **David** heard that Nabal was dead, he said, "Praise be to the
25:39 Then **David** sent word to Abigail, asking her to become his wife.
25:40 **His**[s] servants went to Carmel and said to Abigail, "David has sent
25:40 "**David** has sent us to you to take you to become his wife."
25:42 five maids, went with **David's** messengers and became his wife.
25:43 **David** had also married Ahinoam of Jezreel, and they both were
25:44 **David's** wife, to Paltiel son of Laish, who was from Gallim.
26: 1 at Gibeah and said, "Is not **David** hiding on the hill of Hakilah,
26: 2 his three thousand chosen men of Israel, to search there for **David**.
26: 3 the hill of Hakilah facing Jeshimon, but **David** stayed in the desert.
26: 4 **he**[s] sent out scouts and learned that Saul had definitely arrived.
26: 5 Then **David** set out and went to the place where Saul had camped.
26: 5 **He**[s] saw where Saul and Abner son of Ner, the commander of the
26: 6 **David** then asked Ahimelech the Hittite and Abishai son of
26: 7 So **David** and Abishai went to the army by night, and there was
26: 8 Abishai said to **David**, "Today God has delivered your enemy into
26: 9 **David** said to Abishai, "Don't destroy him! Who can lay a hand on
26:10 As surely as the LORD lives," **he**[s] said, "the LORD himself will
26:12 So **David** took the spear and water jug near Saul's head, and they
26:13 **David** crossed over to the other side and stood on top of the hill
26:14 **He**[s] called out to the army and to Abner son of Ner, "Aren't you
26:15 **David** said, "You're a man, aren't you? And who is like you in
26:17 Saul recognized **David's** voice and said, "Is that your voice,
26:17 David's voice and said, "Is that your voice, **David** my son?"
26:17 David my son?" **David** replied, "Yes it is, my lord the king."
26:21 Then Saul said, "I have sinned. Come back, **David** my son.
26:22 "Here is the king's spear," **David** answered. "Let one of your
26:25 Then Saul said to **David**, "May you be blessed, my son David;
26:25 Then Saul said to David, "May you be blessed, my son **David**;
26:25 So **David** went on his way, and Saul returned home.
27: 1 **David** thought to himself, "One of these days I will be destroyed
27: 2 So **David** and the six hundred men with him left and went over to
27: 3 **David** and his men settled in Gath with Achish. Each man had his
27: 3 Each man had his family with him, and **David** had his two wives:
27: 4 When Saul was told that **David** had fled to Gath, he no longer
27: 5 Then **David** said to Achish, "If I have found favor in your eyes,
27: 7 **David** lived in Philistine territory a year and four months.
27: 8 Now **David** and his men went up and raided the Geshurites,
27: 9 Whenever **David** attacked an area, he did not leave a man
27:10 **David** would say, "Against the Negev of Judah" or "Against the
27:11 **He**[s] did not leave a man or woman alive to be brought to Gath,
27:11 'This is what **David** did.' " And such was his practice as long as he
27:12 Achish trusted **David** and said to himself, "He has become
28: 1 Achish said to **David**, "You must understand that you and your
28: 2 **David** said, "Then you will see for yourself what your servant can
28: 2 Achish replied, **[RPH]** "Very well, I will make you my
28:17 out of your hands and given it to one of your neighbors—to **David**.
29: 2 **David** and his men were marching at the rear with Achish.
29: 3 Achish replied, "Is this not **David**, who was an officer of Saul king
29: 5 Isn't this the **David** they sang about in their dances: " 'Saul has
29: 5 " 'Saul has slain his thousands, and **David** his tens of thousands'?"
29: 6 So Achish called **David** and said to him, "As surely as the LORD
29: 8 "But what have I done?" asked **David**. "What have you found
29: 9 **[RPH]** "I know that you have been as pleasing in my eyes as an
29:11 So **David** and his men got up early in the morning to go back to the
30: 1 **David** and his men reached Ziklag on the third day.
30: 3 When **David** and his men came to Ziklag, they found it destroyed
30: 4 So **David** and his men wept aloud until they had no strength left to
30: 5 **David's** two wives had been captured—Ahinoam of Jezreel
30: 6 **David** was greatly distressed because the men were talking of
30: 6 and daughters. But **David** found strength in the LORD his God.
30: 7 Then **David** said to Abiathar the priest, the son of Ahimelech,
30: 7 of Ahimelech, "Bring me the ephod." Abiathar brought it to **him**[s],
30: 8 **David** inquired of the LORD, "Shall I pursue this raiding party?
30: 9 **David** and the six hundred men with him came to the Besor
30:10 the ravine. But **David** and four hundred men continued the pursuit.
30:11 They found an Egyptian in a field and brought him to **David**.
30:13 **David** asked him, "To whom do you belong, and where do you
30:15 **David** asked him, "Can you lead me down to this raiding party?"
30:17 **David** fought them from dusk until the evening of the next day,
30:18 **David** recovered everything the Amalekites had taken,
30:18 the Amalekites had taken, including his two wives. **[RPH]**
30:19 or anything else they had taken. **David** brought everything back.
30:20 **He**[s] took all the flocks and herds, and his men drove them ahead of
30:20 ahead of the other livestock, saying, "This is **David's** plunder."
30:21 **David** came to the two hundred men who had been too exhausted
30:21 the two hundred men who had been too exhausted to follow **him**[s]
30:21 They came out to meet **David** and the people with him. As David
30:21 with him. As **David** and his men approached, he greeted them.
30:22 all the evil men and troublemakers among **David's** followers said,
30:23 **David** replied, "No, my brothers, you must not do that with what

1Sa 30:26 When **David** arrived in Ziklag, he sent some of the plunder to the
30:31 to those in all the other places where **David** and his men had
2Sa 1: 1 **David** returned from defeating the Amalekites and stayed in Ziklag
1: 1 defeating the Amalekites and stayed **[RPH]** in Ziklag two days.
1: 2 When he came to **David**, he fell to the ground to pay him honor.
1: 3 **David** asked him. He answered, "I have escaped from the Israelite
1: 4 **David** asked. "Tell me." He said, "The men fled from the battle.
1: 5 Then **David** said to the young man who brought him the report,
1:11 Then **David** and all the men with him took hold of their clothes
1:13 **David** said to the young man who brought him the report,
1:14 **David** asked him, "Why were you not afraid to lift your hand to
1:15 **David** called one of his men and said, "Go, strike him down!"
1:16 For **David** had said to him, "Your blood be on your own head.
1:17 **David** took up this lament concerning Saul and his son Jonathan,
2: 1 In the course of time, **David** inquired of the LORD. "Shall I go up
2: 1 The LORD said, "Go up." **David** asked, "Where shall I go?"
2: 2 So **David** went up there with his two wives, Ahinoam of Jezreel
2: 3 **David** also took the men who were with him, each with his family,
2: 4 and there they anointed **David** king over the house of Judah.
2: 4 When **David** was told that it was the men of Jabesh Gilead who
2: 5 **he**[s] sent messengers to the men of Jabesh Gilead to say to them,
2:10 reigned two years. The house of Judah, however, followed **David**.
2:11 The length of time **David** was king in Hebron over the house of
2:13 Joab son of Zeruiah and **David's** men went out and met them at the
2:15 for Benjamin and Ish-Bosheth son of Saul, and twelve for **David**.
2:17 and Abner and the men of Israel were defeated by **David's** men.
2:30 Besides Asahel, nineteen of **David's** men were found missing.
2:31 **David's** men had killed three hundred and sixty Benjamites who
3: 1 the house of Saul and the house of **David** lasted a long time.
3: 1 **David** grew stronger and stronger, while the house of Saul grew
3: 2 Sons were born to **David** in Hebron: His firstborn was Amnon the
3: 5 the sixth, Ithream the son of **David's** wife Eglah. These were born
3: 5 son of David's wife Eglah. These were born to **David** in Hebron.
3: 6 During the war between the house of Saul and the house of **David**,
3: 8 and to his family and friends. I haven't handed you over to **David**.
3: 9 if I do not do for **David** what the LORD promised him on oath
3:10 establish **David's** throne over Israel and Judah from Dan to
3:12 Then Abner sent messengers on his behalf to say to **David**,
3:14 **David** sent messengers to Ish-Bosheth son of Saul, demanding,
3:17 "For some time you have wanted to make **David** your king.
3:18 For the LORD promised **David**, 'By my servant David I will
3:18 'By my servant **David** I will rescue my people Israel from the hand
3:19 Then he went to Hebron to tell **David** everything that Israel
3:20 came to **David** at Hebron, David prepared a feast for him and his
3:20 to David at Hebron, **David** prepared a feast for him and his men.
3:21 Abner said to **David**, "Let me go at once and assemble all Israel
3:21 heart desires." So **David** sent Abner away, and he went in peace.
3:22 Just then **David's** men and Joab returned from a raid and brought
3:22 Abner was no longer with **David** in Hebron, because David had
3:26 Joab then left **David** and sent messengers after Abner, and they
3:26 him back from the well of Sirah. But **David** did not know it.
3:28 Later, when **David** heard about this, he said, "I and my kingdom
3:31 **David** said to Joab and all the people with him, "Tear your clothes
3:31 in front of Abner." King **David** himself walked behind the bier.
3:35 all came and urged **David** to eat something while it was still day;
3:35 but **David** took an oath, saying, "May God deal with me, be it ever
4: 8 They brought the head of Ish-Bosheth to **David** at Hebron
4: 9 **David** answered Recab and his brother Baanah, the sons of
4:12 So **David** gave an order to his men, and they killed them. They cut
5: 1 All the tribes of Israel came to **David** at Hebron and said,
5: 3 When all the elders of Israel had come to King **David** at Hebron,
5: 3 before the LORD, and they anointed **David** king over Israel.
5: 4 **David** was thirty years old when he became king, and he reigned
5: 6 The Jebusites said to **David**, "You will not get in here; even the
5: 6 lame can ward you off." They thought, "**David** cannot get in here."
5: 7 Nevertheless, **David** captured the fortress of Zion, the City of
5: 7 David captured the fortress of Zion, the City of **David**.
5: 8 On that day, **David** said, "Anyone who conquers the Jebusites will
5: 8 shaft to reach those 'lame and blind' who are **David's** enemies."
5: 9 **David** then took up residence in the fortress and called it the City
5: 9 took up residence in the fortress and called it the City of **David**.
5: 9 **He**[s] built up the area around it, from the supporting terraces
5:10 **he**[s] became more and more powerful, because the LORD God
5:11 Now Hiram king of Tyre sent messengers to **David**, along with
5:11 and carpenters and stonemasons, and they built a palace for **David**.
5:12 **David** knew that the LORD had established him as king over
5:13 **David** took more concubines and wives in Jerusalem, and more
5:13 in Jerusalem, and more sons and daughters were born to **him**[s].
5:17 When the Philistines heard that **David** had been anointed king over
5:17 they went up in full force to search for **him**[s], but David heard
5:17 but **David** heard about it and went down to the stronghold.
5:19 so **David** inquired of the LORD, "Shall I go and attack the
5:19 The LORD answered **him**[s], "Go, for I will surely hand the
5:20 So **David** went to Baal Perazim, and there he defeated them.
5:20 So David went to Baal Perazim, and there **he**[s] defeated them.
5:21 their idols there, and **David** and his men carried them off.
5:23 so **David** inquired of the LORD, and he answered, "Do not go
5:25 So **David** did as the LORD commanded him, and he struck down
6: 1 **David** again brought together out of Israel chosen men,
6: 2 **He**[s] and all his men set out from Baalah of Judah to bring up from
6: 5 **David** and the whole house of Israel were celebrating with all their
6: 8 **David** was angry because the LORD's wrath had broken out
6: 9 **David** was afraid of the LORD that day and said, "How can the
6:10 **He**[s] was not willing to take the ark of the LORD to be with him
6:10 to take the ark of the LORD to be with him in the City of **David**.
6:10 Instead, **he**[s] took it aside to the house of Obed-Edom the Gittite.
6:12 Now King **David** was told, "The LORD has blessed the
6:12 So **David** went down and brought up the ark of God from the
6:12 from the house of Obed-Edom to the City of **David** with rejoicing.
6:14 **David**, wearing a linen ephod, danced before the LORD with all
6:14 David, **[RPH]** wearing a linen ephod, danced before the LORD
6:15 while **he**[s] and the entire house of Israel brought up the ark of the
6:16 As the ark of the LORD was entering the City of **David**,
6:16 when she saw King **David** leaping and dancing before the LORD,
6:17 and set it in its place inside the tent that **David** had pitched for it,
6:17 **David** sacrificed burnt offerings and fellowship offerings before
6:18 After **he**[s] had finished sacrificing the burnt offerings
6:20 When **David** returned home to bless his household, Michal
6:20 Michal daughter of Saul came out to meet **him**[s] and said,
6:21 **David** said to Michal, "It was before the LORD, who chose me
7: 5 "Go and tell my servant **David**, 'This is what the LORD says:
7: 8 "Now then, tell my servant **David**, 'This is what the LORD
7:17 Nathan reported to **David** all the words of this entire revelation.
7:18 Then King **David** went in and sat before the LORD, and he said:
7:20 "What more can **David** say to you? For you know your servant,
7:26 the house of your servant **David** will be established before you.
8: 1 course of time, **David** defeated the Philistines and subdued them,
8: 1 and **he**[s] took Metheg Ammah from the control of the Philistines.
8: 2 So the Moabites became subject to **David** and brought tribute.
8: 3 Moreover, **David** fought Hadadezer son of Rehob, king of Zobah,
8: 4 **David** captured a thousand of his chariots, seven thousand
8: 4 **He**[s] hamstrung all but a hundred of the chariot horses.
8: 5 king of Zobah, **David** struck down twenty-two thousand of them.
8: 6 **He**[s] put garrisons in the Aramean kingdom of Damascus,
8: 6 and the Arameans became subject to **him**[s] and brought tribute.
8: 6 The LORD gave **David** victory wherever he went.
8: 7 **David** took the gold shields that belonged to the officers of
8: 8 to Hadadezer, King **David** took a great quantity of bronze.
8: 9 When Tou king of Hamath heard that **David** had defeated the
8:10 he sent his son Joram to King **David** to greet him and congratulate
8:11 King **David** dedicated these articles to the LORD, as he had done
8:13 **David** became famous after he returned from striking down
8:14 throughout Edom, and all the Edomites became subject to **David**.
8:14 to David. The LORD gave **David** victory wherever he went.
8:15 **David** reigned over all Israel, doing what was just and right for all
8:15 all Israel, **[RPH]** doing what was just and right for all his people.
8:18 and Pelethites; and **David's** sons were royal advisers.
9: 1 **David** asked, "Is there anyone still left of the house of Saul to
9: 2 They called him to appear before **David**, and the king said to him,
9: 5 So King **David** had him brought from Lo Debar, from the house of
9: 6 the son of Saul, came to **David**, he bowed down to pay him honor.
9: 6 **David** said, "Mephibosheth!" "Your servant," he replied.
9: 7 "Don't be afraid," **David** said to him, "for I will surely show you
10: 2 **David** thought, "I will show kindness to Hanun son of Nahash,
10: 2 So **David** sent a delegation to express his sympathy to Hanun
10: 2 his father. When **David's** men came to the land of the Ammonites,
10: 3 "Do you think **David** is honoring your father by sending men to
10: 3 Hasn't **David** sent them to you to explore the city and spy it out
10: 4 So Hanun seized **David's** men, shaved off half of each man's
10: 5 When **David** was told about this, he sent messengers to meet the
10: 6 realized that they had become a stench in **David's** nostrils,
10: 7 **David** sent Joab out with the entire army of fighting men.
10:17 When **David** was told of this, he gathered all Israel, crossed the
10:17 The Arameans formed their battle lines to meet **David** and fought
10:18 **David** killed seven hundred of their charioteers and forty thousand
11: 1 **David** sent Joab out with the king's men and the whole Israelite
11: 1 and besieged Rabbah. But **David** remained in Jerusalem.
11: 2 One evening **David** got up from his bed and walked around on the
11: 3 and **David** sent someone to find out about her. The man said,
11: 4 Then **David** sent messengers to get her. She came to him,
11: 5 The woman conceived and sent word to **David**, saying, "I am
11: 6 So **David** sent this word to Joab: "Send me Uriah the Hittite."
11: 6 "Send me Uriah the Hittite." And Joab sent him to **David**.
11: 7 **David** asked him how Joab was, how the soldiers were and how
11: 8 **David** said to Uriah, "Go down to your house and wash your feet."
11:10 When **David** was told, "Uriah did not go home," he asked him,
11:10 When David was told, "Uriah did not go home," **he**[s] asked him,
11:11 Uriah said to **David**, "The ark and Israel and Judah are staying in

2Sa 11:12 **David** said to him, "Stay here one more day, and tomorrow I will
11:13 At **David's** invitation, he ate and drank with him, and David made
11:14 In the morning **David** wrote a letter to Joab and sent it with Uriah.
11:17 and fought against Joab, some of the men in **David's** army fell;
11:18 Joab sent **David** a full account of the battle.
11:22 when he arrived he told **David** everything Joab had sent him to
11:23 The messenger said to **David**, "The men overpowered us and came
11:25 **David** told the messenger, "Say this to Joab: 'Don't let this upset
11:27 **David** had her brought to his house, and she became his wife
11:27 him a son. But the thing **David** had done displeased the LORD.
12: 1 The LORD sent Nathan to **David**. When he came to him,
12: 5 **David** burned with anger against the man and said to Nathan,
12: 7 Nathan said to **David**, "You are the man! This is what the LORD,
12:13 Then **David** said to Nathan, "I have sinned against the LORD."
12:13 Nathan replied, **[RPH]** "The LORD has taken away your sin.
12:15 the LORD struck the child that Uriah's wife had borne to **David**,
12:16 **David** pleaded with God for the child. He fasted and went into his
12:16 **He**[s] fasted and went into his house and spent the nights lying on
12:18 **David's** servants were afraid to tell him that the child was dead,
12:19 **David** noticed that his servants were whispering among themselves
12:19 whispering among themselves and **he**[s] realized the child was dead.
12:19 "Is the child dead?" **he**[s] asked. "Yes," they replied, "he is dead."
12:20 Then **David** got up from the ground. After he had washed,
12:24 Then **David** comforted his wife Bathsheba, and he went to her
12:27 Joab then sent messengers to **David**, saying, "I have fought against
12:29 So **David** mustered the entire army and went to Rabbah,
12:30 was set with precious stones—and it was placed on **David's** head.
12:31 Then **David** and his entire army returned to Jerusalem.
13: 1 In the course of time, Amnon son of **David** fell in love with Tamar,
13: 1 in love with Tamar, the beautiful sister of Absalom son of **David**.
13: 3 had a friend named Jonadab son of Shimeah, **David's** brother.
13: 7 **David** sent word to Tamar at the palace: "Go to the house of your
13:21 When King **David** heard all this, he was furious.
13:30 While they were on their way, the report came to **David**: "Absalom
13:32 Jonadab son of Shimeah, **David's** brother, said, "My lord should
13:39 And the spirit of the king **[RPH]** longed to go to Absalom,
15:12 **David's** counselor, to come from Giloh, his hometown.
15:13 A messenger came and told **David**, "The hearts of the men of
15:14 **David** said to all his officials who were with him in Jerusalem,
15:22 **David** said to Ittai, "Go ahead, march on." So Ittai the Gittite
15:30 But **David** continued up the Mount of Olives, weeping as he went;
15:31 Now **David** had been told, "Ahithophel is among the conspirators
15:31 So **David** prayed, "O LORD, turn Ahithophel's counsel into
15:32 When **David** arrived at the summit, where people used to worship
15:33 **David** said to him, "If you go with me, you will be a burden to me.
15:37 So **David's** friend Hushai arrived at Jerusalem as Absalom was
16: 1 When **David** had gone a short distance beyond the summit,
16: 5 As King **David** approached Bahurim, a man from the same clan as
16: 6 He pelted **David** and all the king's officials with stones, though all
16: 6 He pelted David and all the king's **[RPH]** officials with stones,
16:10 said to him, 'Curse **David**,' who can ask, 'Why do you do this?' "
16:11 **David** then said to Abishai and all his officials, "My son, who is of
16:13 So **David** and his men continued along the road while Shimei was
16:16 **David's** friend, went to Absalom and said to him, "Long live the
16:23 That was how both **David** and Absalom regarded all of
17: 1 twelve thousand men and set out tonight in pursuit of **David**.
17:16 Now send a message immediately and tell **David**, 'Do not spend
17:17 and inform them, and they were to go and tell King **David**,
17:21 the two climbed out of the well and went to inform King **David**.
17:21 They said to **him**[s], "Set out and cross the river at once; Ahithophel
17:22 So **David** and all the people with him set out and crossed the
17:24 **David** went to Mahanaim, and Absalom crossed the Jordan with all
17:27 When **David** came to Mahanaim, Shobi son of Nahash from
17:29 and cheese from cows' milk for **David** and his people to eat.
18: 1 **David** mustered the men who were with him and appointed over
18: 2 **David** sent the troops out—a third under the command of Joab,
18: 7 There the army of Israel was defeated by **David's** men,
18: 9 Now Absalom happened to meet **David's** men. He was riding his
18:24 While **David** was sitting between the inner and outer gates,
19:11 [19:12] King **David** sent this message to Zadok and Abiathar,
19:16 [19:17] hurried down with the men of Judah to meet King **David**.
19:22 [19:23] **David** replied, "What do you and I have in common, you
19:41 [19:42] household across the Jordan, together with all **his**[s] men?"
19:43 [19:44] we have a greater claim on **David** than you have.
20: 1 He sounded the trumpet and shouted, "We have no share in **David**,
20: 2 So all the men of Israel deserted **David** to follow Sheba son of
20: 3 When **David** returned to his palace in Jerusalem, he took the ten
20: 6 **David** said to Abishai, "Now Sheba son of Bicri will do us more
20:11 favors Joab, and whoever is for **David**, let him follow Joab!"
20:21 of Ephraim, has lifted up his hand against the king, against **David**.
20:26 and Ira the Jairite was **David's** [+4200] priest.
21: 1 During the reign of **David**, there was a famine for three successive
21: 1 three successive years; so **David** sought the face of the LORD.
21: 3 **David** asked the Gibeonites, "What shall I do for you? How shall I
21: 7 because of the oath before the LORD between **David**
21:11 When **David** was told what Aiah's daughter Rizpah,
21:12 **he**[s] went and took the bones of Saul and his son Jonathan from the
21:15 **David** went down with his men to fight against the Philistines,
21:15 his men to fight against the Philistines, and **he**[s] became exhausted.
21:16 and who was armed with a new ⌞sword⌟, said he would kill **David**.
21:17 **David's** men swore to him, saying, "Never again will you go out
21:21 Jonathan son of Shimeah, **David's** brother, killed him.
21:22 of Rapha in Gath, and they fell at the hands of **David** and his men.
22: 1 **David** sang to the LORD the words of this song when the
22:51 kindness to his anointed, to **David** and his descendants forever."
23: 1 These are the last words of **David**: "The oracle of David son of
23: 1 "The oracle of **David** son of Jesse, the oracle of the man exalted by
23: 8 These are the names of **David's** [+4200] mighty men:
23: 9 he was with **David** when they taunted the Philistines gathered ⌞at
23:13 three of the thirty chief men came down to **David** at the cave of
23:14 At that time **David** was in the stronghold, and the Philistine
23:15 **David** longed for water and said, "Oh, that someone would get me
23:16 the well near the gate of Bethlehem and carried it back to **David**.
23:23 among the Three. And **David** put him in charge of his bodyguard.
24: 1 he incited **David** against them, saying, "Go and take a census of
24:10 **David** was conscience-stricken after he had counted the fighting
24:10 **he**[s] said to the LORD, "I have sinned greatly in what I have done.
24:11 Before **David** got up the next morning, the word of the LORD
24:11 word of the LORD had come to Gad the prophet, **David's** seer:
24:12 "Go and tell **David**, 'This is what the LORD says: I am giving
24:13 So Gad went to **David** and said to him, "Shall there come upon
24:14 **David** said to Gad, "I am in deep distress. Let us fall into the hands
24:17 When **David** saw the angel who was striking down the people,
24:18 On that day Gad went to **David** and said to him, "Go up and build
24:19 So **David** went up, as the LORD had commanded through Gad.
24:21 "To buy your threshing floor," **David** answered, "so I can build an
24:22 Araunah said to **David**, "Let my lord the king take whatever
24:24 So **David** bought the threshing floor and the oxen and paid fifty
24:25 **David** built an altar to the LORD there and sacrificed burnt
1Ki 1: 1 When King **David** was old and well advanced in years, he could
1: 8 and **David's** [+4200] special guard did not join Adonijah.
1:11 of Haggith, has become king without our lord **David's** knowing it?
1:13 Go in to King **David** and say to him, 'My lord the king, did you not
1:28 King **David** said, "Call in Bathsheba." So she came into the king's
1:31 before the king, said, "May my lord King **David** live forever!"
1:32 King **David** said, "Call in Zadok the priest, Nathan the prophet
1:37 his throne even greater than the throne of my lord King **David**!"
1:38 put Solomon on King **David's** mule and escorted him to Gihon.
1:43 "Our lord King **David** has made Solomon king.
1:47 the royal officials have come to congratulate our lord King **David**,
2: 1 When the time drew near for **David** to die, he gave a charge to
2:10 **David** rested with his fathers and was buried in the City of David.
2:10 David rested with his fathers and was buried in the City of **David**.
2:11 **He**[s] had reigned forty years over Israel—seven years in Hebron
2:12 So Solomon sat on the throne of his father **David**, and his rule was
2:24 who has established me securely on the throne of my father **David**
2:26 carried the ark of the Sovereign LORD before my father **David**
2:32 because without the knowledge of my father **David** he attacked
2:33 But on **David** and his descendants, his house and his throne,
2:44 "You know in your heart all the wrong you did to my father **David**.
2:45 and **David's** throne will remain secure before the LORD forever."
3: 1 He brought her to the City of **David** until he finished building his
3: 3 LORD by walking according to the statutes of his father **David**,
3: 6 my father **David**, because he was faithful to you and righteous
3: 7 you have made your servant king in place of my father **David**.
3:14 and obey my statutes and commands as **David** your father did,
5: 1 [5:15] because he had always been on friendly terms with **David**.
5: 3 [5:17] because of the wars waged against my father **David** from
5: 5 [5:19] as the LORD told my father **David**, when he said,
5: 7 [5:21] for he has given **David** a wise son to rule over this great
6:12 I will fulfill through you the promise I gave to **David** your father.
7:51 he brought in the things his father **David** had dedicated—
8: 1 up the ark of the LORD's covenant from Zion, the City of **David**.
8:15 fulfilled what he promised with his own mouth to my father **David**.
8:16 to be there, but I have chosen **David** to rule my people Israel.'
8:17 "My father **David** had it in his heart to build a temple for the Name
8:18 the LORD said to my father **David**, 'Because it was in your heart
8:20 I have succeeded **David** my father and now I sit on the throne of
8:24 You have kept your promise to your servant **David** my father;
8:25 keep for your servant **David** my father the promises you made to
8:26 let your word that you promised your servant **David** my father
8:66 for all the good things the LORD had done for his servant **David**
9: 4 me in integrity of heart and uprightness, as **David** your father did,
9: 5 over Israel forever, as I promised **David** your father when I said,
9:24 After Pharaoh's daughter had come up from the City of **David** to
11: 4 to the LORD his God, as the heart of **David** his father had been.
11: 6 not follow the LORD completely, as **David** his father had done.
11:12 Nevertheless, for the sake of **David** your father, I will not do it

1Ki 11: 13 but will give him one tribe for the sake of **David** my servant
11: 15 Earlier when **David** was fighting with Edom, Joab the commander
11: 21 Hadad heard that **David** rested with his fathers and that Joab the
11: 24 became the leader of a band of rebels when **David** destroyed the
11: 27 and had filled in the gap in the wall of the city of **David** his father.
11: 32 But for the sake of my servant **David** and the city of Jerusalem,
11: 33 nor kept my statutes and laws as **David**, Solomon's father,
11: 34 I have made him ruler all the days of his life for the sake of **David**
11: 36 so that **David** my servant may always have a lamp before me in
11: 38 by keeping my statutes and commands, as **David** my servant did,
11: 38 I will build you a dynasty as enduring as the one I built for **David**
11: 39 I will humble **David's** descendants because of this, but not
11: 43 with his fathers and was buried in the city of **David** his father.
12: 16 "What share do we have in **David**, what part in Jesse's son?
12: 16 To your tents, O Israel! Look after your own house, O **David**!"
12: 19 So Israel has been in rebellion against the house of **David** to this
12: 20 Only the tribe of Judah remained loyal to the house of **David**.
12: 26 "The kingdom will now likely revert to the house of **David**.
13: 2 'A son named Josiah will be born to the house of **David**.
14: 8 I tore the kingdom away from the house of **David** and gave it to
14: 8 and gave it to you, but you have not been like my servant **David**,
14: 31 with his fathers and was buried with them in the City of **David**.
15: 3 the LORD his God, as the heart of **David** his forefather had been.
15: 4 for **David's** sake the LORD his God gave him a lamp in
15: 5 For **David** had done what was right in the eyes of the LORD
15: 8 Abijah rested with his fathers and was buried in the City of **David**.
15: 11 was right in the eyes of the LORD, as his father **David** had done.
15: 24 and was buried with them in the city of his father **David**.
22: 50 [22:51] and was buried with them in the city of **David** his father.
2Ki 8: 19 Nevertheless, for the sake of his servant **David**, the LORD was
8: 24 with his fathers and was buried with them in the City of **David**.
9: 28 and buried him with his fathers in his tomb in the City of **David**.
11: 10 the spears and shields that had belonged to King **David**
12: 21 [12:22] and was buried with his fathers in the City of **David**.
14: 3 in the eyes of the LORD, but not as his father **David** had done.
14: 20 and was buried in Jerusalem with his fathers, in the City of **David**.
15: 7 with his fathers and was buried near them in the City of **David**.
15: 38 with his fathers and was buried with them in the City of **David**,
16: 2 Unlike **David** his father, he did not do what was right in the eyes of
16: 20 with his fathers and was buried with them in the City of **David**.
17: 21 When he tore Israel away from the house of **David**, they made
18: 3 right in the eyes of the LORD, just as his father **David** had done.
19: 34 and save it, for my sake and for the sake of **David** my servant."
20: 5 'This is what the LORD, the God of your father **David**, says:
20: 6 this city for my sake and for the sake of my servant **David**.' "
21: 7 of which the LORD had said to **David** and to his son Solomon,
22: 2 eyes of the LORD and walked in all the ways of his father **David**,
1Ch 2: 15 the sixth Ozem and the seventh **David**.
3: 1 These were the sons of **David** born to him in Hebron: The firstborn
3: 9 All these were the sons of **David**, besides his sons by his
4: 31 and Shaaraim. These were their towns until the reign of **David**.
6: 31 [6:16] These are the men **David** put in charge of the music in the
7: 2 During the reign of **David**, the descendants of Tola listed as
9: 22 gatekeepers had been assigned to their positions of trust by **David**
10: 14 him to death and turned the kingdom over to **David** son of Jesse.
11: 1 All Israel came together to **David** at Hebron and said, "We are
11: 3 When all the elders of Israel had come to King **David** at Hebron,
11: 3 they anointed **David** king over Israel, as the LORD had promised
11: 4 **David** and all the Israelites marched to Jerusalem (that is,
11: 5 said to **David**, "You will not get in here." Nevertheless,
11: 5 Nevertheless, **David** captured the fortress of Zion, the City of
11: 5 David captured the fortress of Zion, the City of **David**.
11: 6 **David** had said, "Whoever leads the attack on the Jebusites will
11: 7 **David** then took up residence in the fortress, and so it was called
11: 7 up residence in the fortress, and so it was called the City of **David**.
11: 9 **David** became more and more powerful, because the LORD
11: 10 These were the chiefs of **David's** [+4200] mighty men—they,
11: 11 this is the list of **David's** [+4200] mighty men: Jashobeam,
11: 13 He was with **David** at Pas Dammim when the Philistines gathered
11: 15 Three of the thirty chiefs came down to **David** to the rock at the
11: 16 At that time **David** was in the stronghold, and the Philistine
11: 17 **David** longed for water and said, "Oh, that someone would get me
11: 18 the well near the gate of Bethlehem and carried it back to **David**.
11: 18 **he**[s] refused to drink it; instead, he poured it out before the LORD.
11: 25 among the Three. And **David** put him in charge of his bodyguard.
12: 1 These were the men who came to **David** at Ziklag, while he was
12: 8 [12:9] Some Gadites defected to **David** at his stronghold in the
12: 16 [12:17] some men from Judah also came to **David** in his
12: 17 [12:18] **David** went out to meet them and said to them, "If you
12: 18 [12:19] chief of the Thirty, and he said: "We are yours, O **David**!
12: 18 [12:19] So **David** received them and made them leaders of his
12: 19 [12:20] Some of the men of Manasseh defected to **David** when he
12: 21 [12:22] They helped **David** against raiding bands, for all of them
12: 22 [12:23] Day after day men came to help **David**, until he had a
12: 23 [12:24] to **David** at Hebron to turn Saul's kingdom over to him,
12: 31 [12:32] designated by name to come and make **David** king—
12: 38 [12:39] They came to Hebron fully determined to make **David**
12: 38 [12:39] the Israelites were also of one mind to make **David** king.
12: 39 [12:40] The men spent three days there with **David**, eating
13: 1 **David** conferred with each of his officers, the commanders of
13: 2 **He**[s] then said to the whole assembly of Israel, "If it seems good to
13: 5 So **David** assembled all the Israelites, from the Shihor River in
13: 6 **David** and all the Israelites with him went to Baalah of Judah
13: 8 **David** and all the Israelites were celebrating with all their might
13: 11 **David** was angry because the LORD's wrath had broken out
13: 12 **David** was afraid of God that day and asked, "How can I ever
13: 13 **He**[s] did not take the ark to be with him in the City of David.
13: 13 He did not take the ark to be with him in the City of **David**.
14: 1 Now Hiram king of Tyre sent messengers to **David**, along with
14: 2 **David** knew that the LORD had established him as king over
14: 3 In Jerusalem **David** took more wives and became the father of
14: 3 and became the father of **[RPH]** more sons and daughters.
14: 8 When the Philistines heard that **David** had been anointed king over
14: 8 they went up in full force to search for **him**[s], but David heard
14: 8 for him, but **David** heard about it and went out to meet them.
14: 10 so **David** inquired of God: "Shall I go and attack the Philistines?
14: 11 So **David** and his men went up to Baal Perazim, and there he
14: 11 **He**[s] said, "As waters break out, God has broken out against my
14: 12 their gods there, and **David** gave orders to burn them in the fire.
14: 14 so **David** inquired of God again, and God answered him, "Do not
14: 16 So **David** did as God commanded him, and they struck down the
14: 17 So **David's** fame spread throughout every land, and the LORD
15: 1 David had constructed buildings for himself in the City of **David**,
15: 2 **David** said, "No one but the Levites may carry the ark of God,
15: 3 **David** assembled all Israel in Jerusalem to bring up the ark of the
15: 4 **He**[s] called together the descendants of Aaron and the Levites:
15: 11 Then **David** summoned Zadok and Abiathar the priests, and Uriel,
15: 16 **David** told the leaders of the Levites to appoint their brothers as
15: 25 So **David** and the elders of Israel and the commanders of units of a
15: 27 Now **David** was clothed in a robe of fine linen, as were all the
15: 27 charge of the singing of the choirs. **David** also wore a linen ephod.
15: 29 ark of the covenant of the LORD was entering the City of **David**,
15: 29 when she saw King **David** dancing and celebrating, she despised
16: 1 ark of God and set it inside the tent that **David** had pitched for it,
16: 2 After **David** had finished sacrificing the burnt offerings
16: 7 That day **David** first committed to Asaph and his associates this
16: 43 for his own home, and **David** returned home to bless his family.
17: 1 After **David** was settled in his palace, he said to Nathan the
17: 1 **he**[s] said to Nathan the prophet, "Here I am, living in a palace of
17: 2 Nathan replied to **David**, "Whatever you have in mind, do it,
17: 4 "Go and tell my servant **David**, 'This is what the LORD says:
17: 7 "Now then, tell my servant **David**, 'This is what the LORD
17: 15 Nathan reported to **David** all the words of this entire revelation.
17: 16 Then King **David** went in and sat before the LORD, and he said:
17: 18 "What more can **David** say to you for honoring your servant?
17: 24 the house of your servant **David** will be established before you.
18: 1 **David** defeated the Philistines and subdued them, and he took Gath
18: 2 **David** also defeated the Moabites, and they became subject to him
18: 3 Moreover, **David** fought Hadadezer king of Zobah, as far as
18: 4 **David** captured a thousand of his chariots, seven thousand
18: 4 **He**[s] hamstrung all but a hundred of the chariot horses.
18: 5 king of Zobah, **David** struck down twenty-two thousand of them.
18: 6 **He**[s] put garrisons in the Aramean kingdom of Damascus,
18: 6 and the Arameans became subject to **him**[s] and brought tribute.
18: 6 The LORD gave **David** victory everywhere he went.
18: 7 **David** took the gold shields carried by the officers of Hadadezer
18: 8 that belonged to Hadadezer, **David** took a great quantity of bronze,
18: 9 When Tou king of Hamath heard that **David** had defeated the
18: 10 he sent his son Hadoram to King **David** to greet him
18: 11 King **David** dedicated these articles to the LORD, as he had done
18: 13 garrisons in Edom, and all the Edomites became subject to **David**.
18: 13 to David. The LORD gave **David** victory everywhere he went.
18: 14 **David** reigned over all Israel, doing what was just and right for all
18: 17 and **David's** sons were chief officials at the king's side.
19: 2 **David** thought, "I will show kindness to Hanun son of Nahash,
19: 2 So **David** sent a delegation to express his sympathy to Hanun
19: 2 When **David's** men came to Hanun in the land of the Ammonites
19: 3 "Do you think **David** is honoring your father by sending men to
19: 4 So Hanun seized **David's** men, shaved them, cut off their garments
19: 5 When someone came and told **David** about the men, he sent
19: 6 realized that they had become a stench in **David's** nostrils,
19: 8 **David** sent Joab out with the entire army of fighting men.
19: 17 When **David** was told of this, he gathered all Israel and crossed the
19: 17 **David** formed his lines to meet the Arameans in battle, and they
19: 18 **David** killed seven thousand of their charioteers and forty thousand
19: 19 by Israel, they made peace with **David** and became subject to him.
20: 1 went to Rabbah and besieged it, but **David** remained in Jerusalem.
20: 2 **David** took the crown from the head of their king—its weight was

1Ch 20: 2 was set with precious stones—and it was placed on **David's** head.
20: 3 iron picks and axes. **David** did this to all the Ammonite towns.
20: 3 Then **David** and his entire army returned to Jerusalem.
20: 7 Jonathan son of Shimea, **David's** brother, killed him.
20: 8 of Rapha in Gath, and they fell at the hands of **David** and his men.
21: 1 rose up against Israel and incited **David** to take a census of Israel.
21: 2 So **David** said to Joab and the commanders of the troops, "Go
21: 5 Joab reported the number of the fighting men to **David**: In all
21: 8 Then **David** said to God, "I have sinned greatly by doing this.
21: 9 The LORD said to Gad, **David's** seer,
21: 10 "Go and tell **David**, 'This is what the LORD says: I am giving
21: 11 So Gad went to **David** and said to him, "This is what the LORD
21: 13 **David** said to Gad, "I am in deep distress. Let me fall into the
21: 16 **David** looked up and saw the angel of the LORD standing
21: 16 Then **David** and the elders, clothed in sackcloth, fell facedown.
21: 17 **David** said to God, "Was it not I who ordered the fighting men to
21: 18 Then the angel of the LORD ordered Gad to tell **David** to go up
21: 18 **[RPH]** and build an altar to the LORD on the threshing floor of
21: 19 So **David** went up in obedience to the word that Gad had spoken in
21: 21 Then **David** approached, and when Araunah looked and saw him,
21: 21 Then David approached, and when Araunah looked and saw **him**[s],
21: 21 and bowed down before **David** with his face to the ground.
21: 22 **David** said to him, "Let me have the site of your threshing floor
21: 23 Araunah said to **David**, "Take it! Let my lord the king do whatever
21: 24 King **David** replied to Araunah, "No, I insist on paying the full
21: 25 So **David** paid Araunah six hundred shekels of gold for the site.
21: 26 **David** built an altar to the LORD there and sacrificed burnt
21: 28 when **David** saw that the LORD had answered him on the
21: 30 **David** could not go before it to inquire of God, because he was
22: 1 Then **David** said, "The house of the LORD God is to be here,
22: 2 So **David** gave orders to assemble the aliens living in Israel,
22: 3 **He**[s] provided a large amount of iron to make nails for the doors of
22: 4 and Tyrians had brought large numbers of them to **David**.
22: 5 **David** said, "My son Solomon is young and inexperienced,
22: 5 for it." So **David** made extensive preparations before his death.
22: 7 **David** said to Solomon: "My son, I had it in my heart to build a
22: 17 **David** ordered all the leaders of Israel to help his son Solomon.
23: 1 When **David** was old and full of years, he made his son Solomon
23: 6 **David** divided the Levites into groups corresponding to the sons of
23: 25 For **David** had said, "Since the LORD, the God of Israel,
23: 27 According to the last instructions of **David**, the Levites were
24: 3 **David** separated them into divisions for their appointed order of
24: 31 in the presence of King **David** and of Zadok, Ahimelech,
25: 1 **David**, together with the commanders of the army, set apart some
26: 26 charge of all the treasuries for the things dedicated by King **David**,
26: 31 In the fortieth year of **David's** reign a search was made in the
26: 32 and King **David** put them in charge of the Reubenites, the Gadites
27: 18 over Judah: Elihu, a brother of **David**; over Issachar: Omri son of
27: 23 **David** did not take the number of the men twenty years old
27: 24 number was not entered in the book of the annals of King **David**.
27: 31 All these were the officials in charge of King **David's** [+4200]
27: 32 Jonathan, **David's** uncle, was a counselor, a man of insight
28: 1 **David** summoned all the officials of Israel to assemble at
28: 2 King **David** rose to his feet and said: "Listen to me, my brothers
28: 11 **David** gave his son Solomon the plans for the portico of the
28: 20 **David** also said to Solomon his son, "Be strong and courageous,
29: 1 Then King **David** said to the whole assembly: "My son Solomon,
29: 9 to the LORD. **David** the king also rejoiced greatly.
29: 10 **David** praised the LORD in the presence of the whole assembly,
29: 10 saying, **[RPH]** "Praise be to you, O LORD, God of our father
29: 20 **David** said to the whole assembly, "Praise the LORD your God."
29: 22 they acknowledged Solomon son of **David** as king a second time,
29: 23 on the throne of the LORD as king in place of his father **David**.
29: 24 the officers and mighty men, as well as all of King **David's** sons,
29: 26 **David** son of Jesse was king over all Israel.
29: 29 As for the events of King **David's** reign, from beginning to end,
2Ch 1: 1 Solomon son of **David** established himself firmly over his
1: 4 Now **David** had brought up the ark of God from Kiriath Jearim to
1: 4 ark of God from Kiriath Jearim to the place **he**[s] had prepared for it,
1: 8 "You have shown great kindness to **David** my father and have
1: 9 LORD God, let your promise to my father **David** be confirmed,
2: 3 [2:2] "Send me cedar logs as you did for my father **David** when
2: 7 [2:6] with my skilled craftsmen, whom my father **David** provided.
2: 12 [2:11] He has given King **David** a wise son, endowed with
2: 14 [2:13] and with those of my lord, **David** your father.
2: 17 [2:16] were in Israel, after the census his father **David** had taken;
3: 1 where the LORD had appeared to his father **David**.
3: 1 floor of Araunah the Jebusite, the place provided by **David**.
5: 1 he brought in the things his father **David** had dedicated—
5: 2 up the ark of the LORD's covenant from Zion, the City of **David**.
6: 4 has fulfilled what he promised with his mouth to my father **David**.
6: 6 to be there, and I have chosen **David** to rule my people Israel.'
6: 7 "My father **David** had it in his heart to build a temple for the Name
6: 8 the LORD said to my father **David**, 'Because it was in your heart
6: 10 I have succeeded **David** my father and now I sit on the throne of
6: 15 You have kept your promise to your servant **David** my father;
6: 16 keep for your servant **David** my father the promises you made to
6: 17 let your word that you promised your servant **David** come true.
6: 42 Remember the great love promised to **David** your servant."
7: 6 which King **David** had made for praising the LORD and which
7: 6 praising the LORD and which were used when **he**[s] gave thanks,
7: 10 glad in heart for the good things the LORD had done for **David**
7: 17 "As for you, if you walk before me as **David** your father did,
7: 18 royal throne, as I covenanted with **David** your father when I said,
8: 11 Solomon brought Pharaoh's daughter up from the City of **David** to
8: 11 "My wife must not live in the palace of **David** king of Israel,
8: 14 In keeping with the ordinance of his father **David**, he appointed the
8: 14 because this was what **David** the man of God had ordered.
9: 31 with his fathers and was buried in the city of **David** his father.
10: 16 "What share do we have in **David**, what part in Jesse's son?
10: 16 To your tents, O Israel! Look after your own house, O **David**!"
10: 19 So Israel has been in rebellion against the house of **David** to this
11: 17 walking in the ways of **David** and Solomon during this time.
11: 18 who was the daughter of **David's** son Jerimoth and of Abihail,
12: 16 rested with his fathers and was buried in the City of **David**.
13: 5 has given the kingship of Israel to **David** and his descendants
13: 6 an official of Solomon son of **David**, rebelled against his master.
13: 8 of the LORD, which is in the hands of **David's** descendants.
14: 1 [13:23] with his fathers and was buried in the City of **David**.
16: 14 in the tomb that he had cut out for himself in the City of **David**.
17: 3 because in his early years he walked in the ways his father **David**
21: 1 with his fathers and was buried with them in the City of **David**.
21: 7 because of the covenant the LORD had made with **David**,
21: 7 the LORD was not willing to destroy the house of **David**.
21: 12 "This is what the LORD, the God of your father **David**, says:
21: 20 to no one's regret, and was buried in the City of **David**,
23: 3 as the LORD promised concerning the descendants of **David**.
23: 9 and the large and small shields that had belonged to King **David**
23: 18 were Levites, to whom **David** had made assignments in the temple,
23: 18 Law of Moses, with rejoicing and singing, as **David** had ordered.
24: 16 He was buried with the kings in the City of **David**, because of the
24: 25 So he died and was buried in the City of **David**, but not in the
27: 9 Jotham rested with his fathers and was buried in the City of **David**.
28: 1 Unlike **David** his father, he did not do what was right in the eyes of
29: 2 right in the eyes of the LORD, just as his father **David** had done.
29: 25 harps and lyres in the way prescribed by **David** and Gad the king's
29: 26 So the Levites stood ready with **David's** instruments,
29: 27 by trumpets and the instruments of **David** king of Israel.
29: 30 ordered the Levites to praise the LORD with the words of **David**
30: 26 for since the days of Solomon son of **David** king of Israel there had
32: 5 and reinforced the supporting terraces of the City of **David**.
32: 30 channeled the water down to the west side of the City of **David**.
32: 33 was buried on the hill where the tombs of **David's** descendants are.
33: 7 of which God had said to **David** and to his son Solomon, "In this
33: 14 Afterward he rebuilt the outer wall of the City of **David**, west of
34: 2 eyes of the LORD and walked in the ways of his father **David**,
34: 3 he was still young, he began to seek the God of his father **David**.
35: 3 "Put the sacred ark in the temple that Solomon son of **David** king
35: 4 according to the directions written by **David** king of Israel
35: 15 were in the places prescribed by **David**, Asaph, Heman
Ezr 3: 10 places to praise the LORD, as prescribed by **David** king of Israel.
8: 2 of Ithamar, Daniel; of the descendants of **David**, Hattush
8: 20 a body that **David** and the officials had established to assist the
Ne 3: 15 as far as the steps going down from the City of **David**.
3: 16 made repairs up to a point opposite the tombs of **David**, as far as
12: 24 responding to the other, as prescribed by **David** the man of God.
12: 36 with musical instruments ⌊prescribed by⌋ **David** the man of God.
12: 37 directly up the steps of the City of **David** on the ascent to the wall
12: 37 passed above the house of **David** to the Water Gate on the east.
12: 45 according to the commands of **David** and his son Solomon.
12: 46 For long ago, in the days of **David** and Asaph, there had been
Ps 3: T [3:1] A psalm of **David**. When he fled from his son Absalom.
4: T [4:1] of music. With stringed instruments. A psalm of **David**.
5: T [5:1] For the director of music. For flutes. A psalm of **David**.
6: T [6:1] According to *sheminith.* A psalm of **David**.
7: T [7:1] A *shiggaion* of **David**, which he sang to the LORD
8: T [8:1] director of music. According to *gittith.* A psalm of **David**.
9: T [9:1] To ⌊the tune of⌋ "The Death of the Son." A psalm of **David**.
11: T [11:1] For the director of music. Of **David**.
12: T [12:1] of music. According to *sheminith.* A psalm of **David**.
13: T [13:1] For the director of music. A psalm of **David**.
14: T [14:1] For the director of music. Of **David**.
15: T [15:1] A psalm of **David**.
16: T [16:1] A *miktam* of **David**.
17: T [17:1] A prayer of **David**.
18: T [18:1] the director of music. Of **David** the servant of the LORD.
18: 50 [18:51] to his anointed, to **David** and his descendants forever.
19: T [19:1] For the director of music. A psalm of **David**.

Ps 20: T [20:1] For the director of music. A psalm of **David**.
21: T [21:1] For the director of music. A psalm of **David**.
22: T [22:1] ⌞the tune of⌟ "The Doe of the Morning." A psalm of **David**.
23: T [23:1] A psalm of **David**.
24: T [24:1] Of **David**. A psalm.
25: T [25:1] Of **David**.
26: T [26:1] Of **David**.
27: T [27:1] Of **David**.
28: T [28:1] Of **David**.
29: T [29:1] A psalm of **David**.
30: T [30:1] A song. For the dedication of the temple. Of **David**.
31: T [31:1] For the director of music. A psalm of **David**.
32: T [32:1] Of **David**. A *maskil*.
34: T [34:1] Of **David**. When he pretended to be insane before
35: T [35:1] Of **David**.
36: T [36:1] the director of music. Of **David** the servant of the LORD.
37: T [37:1] Of **David**.
38: T [38:1] A psalm of **David**. A petition.
39: T [39:1] For the director of music. For Jeduthun. A psalm of **David**.
40: T [40:1] For the director of music. Of **David**. A psalm.
41: T [41:1] For the director of music. A psalm of **David**.
51: T [51:1] For the director of music. A psalm of **David**.
52: T [52:1] For the director of music. A *maskil* of **David**.
52: T [52:2] and told him: "**David** has gone to the house of Ahimelech."
53: T [53:1] of music. According to *mahalath*. A *maskil* of **David**.
54: T [54:1] of music. With stringed instruments. A *maskil* of **David**.
54: T [54:2] gone to Saul and said, "Is not **David** hiding among us?"
55: T [55:1] of music. With stringed instruments. A *maskil* of **David**.
56: T [56:1] of⌟ "A Dove on Distant Oaks." Of **David**. A *miktam*.
57: T [57:1] the tune of⌟ "Do Not Destroy." Of **David**. A *miktam*.
58: T [58:1] the tune of⌟ "Do Not Destroy." Of **David**. A *miktam*.
59: T [59:1] the tune of⌟ "Do Not Destroy." Of **David**. A *miktam*.
60: T [60:1] A *miktam* of **David**. For teaching. When he fought Aram
61: T [61:1] the director of music. With stringed instruments. Of **David**.
62: T [62:1] For the director of music. For Jeduthun. A psalm of **David**.
63: T [63:1] A psalm of **David**. When he was in the Desert of Judah.
64: T [64:1] For the director of music. A psalm of **David**.
65: T [65:1] For the director of music. A psalm of **David**. A song.
68: T [68:1] For the director of music. Of **David**. A psalm. A song.
69: T [69:1] the director of music. To ⌞the tune of⌟ "Lilies." Of **David**.
70: T [70:1] For the director of music. Of **David**. A petition.
72: 20 This concludes the prayers of **David** son of Jesse.
78: 70 He chose **David** his servant and took him from the sheep pens;
86: T [86:1] A prayer of **David**.
89: 3 [89:4] with my chosen one, I have sworn to **David** my servant,
89: 20 [89:21] I have found **David** my servant; with my sacred oil I have
89: 35 [89:36] have sworn by my holiness—and I will not lie to **David**—
89: 49 [89:50] which in your faithfulness you swore to **David**?
101: T [101:1] Of **David**. A psalm.
103: T [103:1] Of **David**.
108: T [108:1] A song. A psalm of **David**.
109: T [109:1] For the director of music. Of **David**. A psalm.
110: T [110:1] Of **David**. A psalm.
122: T [122:1] A song of ascents. Of **David**.
122: 5 the thrones for judgment stand, the thrones of the house of **David**.
124: T [124:1] A song of ascents. Of **David**.
131: T [131:1] A song of ascents. Of **David**.
132: 1 O LORD, remember **David** and all the hardships he endured.
132: 10 For the sake of **David** your servant, do not reject your anointed
132: 11 The LORD swore an oath to **David**, a sure oath that he will not
132: 17 "Here I will make a horn grow for **David** and set up a lamp for my
133: T [133:1] A song of ascents. Of **David**.
138: T [138:1] Of **David**.
139: T [139:1] For the director of music. Of **David**. A psalm.
140: T [140:1] For the director of music. A psalm of **David**.
141: T [141:1] A psalm of **David**.
142: T [142:1] A *maskil* of **David**. When he was in the cave. A prayer.
143: T [143:1] A psalm of **David**.
144: T [144:1] Of **David**.
144: 10 to kings, who delivers his servant **David** from the deadly sword.
145: T [145:1] A psalm of praise. Of **David**.
Pr 1: 1 The proverbs of Solomon son of **David**, king of Israel:
Ecc 1: 1 The words of the Teacher, son of **David**, king in Jerusalem:
SS 4: 4 Your neck is like the tower of **David**, built with elegance;
Isa 7: 2 Now the house of **David** was told, "Aram has allied itself with
7: 13 Isaiah said, "Hear now, you house of **David**! Is it not enough to try
9: 7 [9:6] He will reign on **David's** throne and over his kingdom,
16: 5 one from the house of **David**—one who in judging seeks justice
22: 9 you saw that the City of **David** had many breaches in its defenses;
22: 22 I will place on his shoulder the key to the house of **David**;
29: 1 Woe to you, Ariel, Ariel, the city where **David** settled! Add year to
37: 35 and save it, for my sake and for the sake of **David** my servant!"
38: 5 'This is what the LORD, the God of your father **David**, says:
55: 3 everlasting covenant with you, my faithful love promised to **David**.
Jer 13: 13 including the kings who sit on **David's** [+4200] throne, the priests,
17: 25 kings who sit on **David's** throne will come through the gates of
21: 12 O house of **David**, this is what the LORD says:
22: 2 of the LORD, O king of Judah, you who sit on **David's** throne—
22: 4 kings who sit on **David's** [+4200] throne will come through the
22: 30 none will sit on the throne of **David** or rule anymore in Judah."
23: 5 the LORD, "when I will raise up to **David** a righteous Branch,
29: 16 this is what the LORD says about the king who sits on **David's**
30: 9 they will serve the LORD their God and **David** their king,
33: 15 that time I will make a righteous Branch sprout from **David's line**;
33: 17 '**David** will never fail to have a man to sit on the throne of the
33: 21 my covenant with **David** my servant—and my covenant with the
33: 22 I will make the descendants of **David** my servant and the Levites
33: 26 then I will reject the descendants of Jacob and **David** my servant
36: 30 He will have no one to sit on the throne of **David**; his body will be
Eze 34: 23 over them one shepherd, my servant **David**, and he will tend them;
34: 24 be their God, and my servant **David** will be prince among them.
37: 24 " 'My servant **David** will be king over them, and they will all have
37: 25 there forever, and **David** my servant will be their prince forever.
Hos 3: 5 will return and seek the LORD their God and **David** their king.
Am 6: 5 You strum away on your harps like **David** and improvise on
9: 11 "In that day I will restore **David's** fallen tent. I will repair its
Zec 12: 7 so that the honor of the house of **David** and of Jerusalem's
12: 8 so that the feeblest among them will be like **David**, and the house
12: 8 the house of **David** will be like God, like the Angel of the LORD
12: 10 "And I will pour out on the house of **David** and the inhabitants of
12: 12 the clan of the house of **David** and their wives, the clan of the
13: 1 "On that day a fountain will be opened to the house of **David**

1859 דּוּדָאִים *dûdā'îm*, n.m. [6] [√ 1863]

mandrakes [5], mandrake plants [1]

Ge 30: 14 Reuben went out into the fields and found *some* **mandrake plants**,
30: 14 said to Leah, "Please give me some of your son's **mandrakes**."
30: 15 Will you take my son's **mandrakes** too?" "Very well,"
30: 15 can sleep with you tonight in return for your son's **mandrakes**."
30: 16 with me," she said. "I have hired you with my son's **mandrakes**."
SS 7: 13 [7:14] The **mandrakes** send out their fragrance, and at our door is

1860 דּוֹדָה *dôdâ*, n.f. [3] [√ 1856]

aunt [2], father's sister [1]

Ex 6: 20 Amram married his **father's sister** Jochebed, who bore him Aaron
Lev 18: 14 by approaching his wife to have sexual relations; she is your **aunt**.
20: 20 " 'If a man sleeps with his **aunt**, he has dishonored his uncle.

1861 דּוֹדוֹ *dôdô*, n.pr.m. [3] [√ 1856?]

Dodo [3]

Jdg 10: 1 of Issachar, Tola son of Puah, the son of **Dodo**, rose to save Israel.
2Sa 23: 9 [Eleazar son of **Dodai** [Q; see K 1862] the Ahohite.]
23: 24 Asahel the brother of Joab, Elhanan son of **Dodo** *from* Bethlehem,
1Ch 11: 12 Eleazar son of <u>Dodai</u> [BHS *Dodo*; NIV 1862] the Ahohite,
11: 26 Asahel the brother of Joab, Elhanan son of **Dodo** from Bethlehem,

1862 דּוֹדַי *dôday*, n.pr.m. [2] [√ 1856?]

Dodai [2]

1Ch 11: 12 Next to him was Eleazar son of **Dodai** [K; see Q 1861] the Ahohite,
27: 4 In charge of the division for the second month was **Dodai** the

1863 דּוּדַי *dûday*, n.m. Not used in NIV/BHS [→ 1859]

1864 דָּוָה *dāwâ*, v. [1] [→ 1865, 1867, 1868, 1902?, 4504]

monthly period [+5614] [1]

Lev 12: 2 [A] just as she is unclean during her **monthly period** [+5614].

1865 דָּוֶה *dāweh*, a. [5] [√ 1864]

faint [2], menstrual cloth [1], monthly period [+5614] [1], monthly period [1]

Lev 15: 33 for a *woman* in her **monthly period** [+5614], for a man or a
20: 18 " 'If a man lies with a woman during her **monthly period**
Isa 30: 22 you will throw them away like a **menstrual cloth** and say to them,
La 1: 13 and turned me back. He made me desolate, **faint** all the day long.
5: 17 Because of this our hearts are **faint**, because of these things our

1866 דּוּחַ *dûaḥ*, v. [3] [cf. 5615]

cleanse [1], rinsed [1], washed [1]

2Ch 4: 6 [G] the things to be used for the burnt offerings *were* **rinsed**,
Isa 4: 4 [G] *he will* **cleanse** the bloodstains from Jerusalem by a spirit of
Eze 40: 38 [G] the inner gateways, where the burnt offerings *were* **washed**.

1867 דְּוַי **dᵉway**, n.[m.]. [2] [√ 1864]

ill [1], sickbed [+6911] [1]

Job 6: 7 I refuse to touch it; such food makes me **ill**.
Ps 41: 3 [41:4] The LORD will sustain him on his **sickbed** [+6911] and

1868 דַּוָּי **dawwāy**, a. [3] [√ 1864]

faint [2], afflicted [1]

Isa 1: 5 Your whole head is injured, your whole heart **afflicted**.
Jer 8: 18 O my Comforter in sorrow, my heart is **faint** within me.
La 1: 22 because of all my sins. My groans are many and my heart is **faint**."

1869 דּוֹיֵג **dôyēg**, n.pr.m. [0] [√ 1793]

1Sa 22: 18 [The king then ordered **Doeg**, [K; see Q 1795] "You turn and strike]

1870 דּוּךְ **dûk**, v. [1] [→ 4521; cf. 1916, 1917, 1920, 1990]

crushed [1]

Nu 11: 8 [A] and then ground it in a handmill or **crushed** it in a mortar.

1871 דּוּכִיפַת **dûkîpat**, n.f. [2]

hoopoe [2]

Lev 11: 19 the stork, any kind of heron, the **hoopoe** and the bat.
Dt 14: 18 the stork, any kind of heron, the **hoopoe** and the bat.

1872 ¹דּוּמָה **dûmâ¹**, n.f. [2] [√ 1957]

silence of death [1], silence [1]

Ps 94: 17 given me help, I would soon have dwelt in the **silence of death**.
115: 17 the dead who praise the LORD, those who go down to **silence**;

1873 ²דּוּמָה **dûmâ²**, n.pr.loc. [0 / 1]

Dumah [1]

Jos 15: 52 Arab, **Dumah**, [BHS 8126] Eshan,

1874 ³דּוּמָה **dûmâ³**, n.pr.loc. [3]

Dumah [3]

Ge 25: 14 Mishma, **Dumah**, Massa,
1Ch 1: 30 Mishma, **Dumah**, Massa, Hadad, Tema,
Isa 21: 11 An oracle concerning **Dumah**: Someone calls to me from Seir,

1875 דּוּמִיָּה **dûmiyyâ**, n.f. [4] [√ 1957; cf. 1949]

awaits [1], rest [1], silent [1], still [1]

Ps 22: 2 [22:3] by day, but you do not answer, by night, and am not **silent**.
39: 2 [39:3] when I was silent and **still**, not even saying anything good,
62: 1 [62:2] My soul finds **rest** in God alone; my salvation comes from
65: 1 [65:2] Praise **awaits** you, O God, in Zion; to you our vows will be

1876 דּוּמָם **dûmām**, n.[m.]. [3] [cf. 1957]

in silence [1], lifeless [1], quietly [1]

Isa 47: 5 "Sit **in silence**, go into darkness, Daughter of the Babylonians;
La 3: 26 it is good to wait **quietly** for the salvation of the LORD.
Hab 2: 19 who says to wood, 'Come to life!' Or to **lifeless** stone, 'Wake up!'

1877 דּוּמֶּשֶׂק **dûmmeśeq**, n.pr.loc. [1] [√ 1966]

Damascus [1]

2Ki 16: 10 King Ahaz went to **Damascus** to meet Tiglath-Pileser king of

1878 דּוֹן **dôn**, v. Not used in NIV/BHS

1879 דּוּן **dûn**, n.[m.]. [0] [√ 1906]

Job 19: 29 [and then you will know that there is **judgment**." [Q; see K 1907]]

1880 דּוֹנַג **dônag**, n.m. [4]

wax [4]

Ps 22: 14 [22:15] My heart has turned to **wax**; it has melted away within
68: 2 [68:3] as **wax** melts before the fire, may the wicked perish before
97: 5 The mountains melt like **wax** before the LORD, before the Lord
Mic 1: 4 beneath him and the valleys split apart, like **wax** before the fire,

1881 דּוּץ **dûṣ**, v. [1]

goes [1]

Job 41: 22 [41:14] [A] resides in his neck; dismay **goes** before him.

1882 דּוּק **dûq**, v. Not used in NIV/BHS [→ 1911]

1883 ¹דּוּר **dûr¹**, v. [1] [→ 4509; cf. 1799, 1884, 1888]

pile wood [1]

Eze 24: 5 [A] **Pile wood** beneath it *for* the bones; bring it to a boil and

1884 ²דּוּר **dûr²**, v. [1] [→ 126, 1885, 1886, 1887; cf. 1799, 1883, 1888; Ar 10163]

dwell [1]

Ps 84: 10 [84:11] [A] of my God than **dwell** in the tents of the wicked.

1885 ³דּוּר **dûr³**, n.[m.]. [2] [√ 1884; Ar 10753]

all around [+2021+3869] [1], ball [1]

Isa 22: 18 He will roll you up tightly like a **ball** and throw you into a large
29: 3 I will encamp against you **all around** [+2021+3869]; I will

1886 ¹דּוֹר **dôr¹**, n.m. [1] [√ 1884]

house [1]

Isa 38: 12 Like a shepherd's tent my **house** has been pulled down and taken

1887 ²דּוֹר **dôr²**, n.m. [166] [√ 1884; Ar 10183]

generation [44], generations to come [37], all generations [+1887+2256] [26], generations [12], descendants [6], generations [+1887+2256] [6], all generations [+1887] [5], those[s] [4], *untranslated* [2], age-old [+1887+2256] [2], all time [+1887+2256] [2], always [+1887+2256+4200] [2], endless generations [+1887+2256] [2], generations long past [+1887+2256+9102] [2], generations to come [+1887+2256] [2], many generations [+1887+2256] [2], through all generations [+1887] [2], to come [+1887+2256] [2], all generations [+1887+1887] [1], another[s] [1], children [+1201] [1], company [1], people of time [1], people [1]

Ge 6: 9 blameless among the **people of** his **time**, and he walked with God.
7: 1 because I have found you righteous in this **generation**.
9: 12 living creature with you, a covenant for all **generations** to come:
15: 16 In the fourth **generation** your descendants will come back here,
17: 7 and your descendants after you for the **generations to come**,
17: 9 and your descendants after you for the **generations to come**.
17: 12 For the **generations to come** every male among you who is eight
Ex 1: 6 Now Joseph and all his brothers and all that **generation** died,
3: 15 the name by which I am to be remembered *from* **generation** to
3: 15 by which I am to be remembered from generation to **generation**.
12: 14 for the **generations to come** you shall celebrate it as a festival to
12: 17 this day as a lasting ordinance for the **generations to come**.
12: 42 are to keep vigil to honor the LORD for the **generations to come**.
16: 32 'Take an omer of manna and keep it for the **generations to come**,
16: 33 it before the LORD to be kept for the **generations to come**."
17: 16 be at war against the Amalekites from **generation** *to* generation."
17: 16 be at war against the Amalekites from generation to **generation**."
27: 21 ordinance among the Israelites for the **generations to come**.
29: 42 "For the **generations to come** this burnt offering is to be made
30: 8 burn regularly before the LORD for the **generations to come**.
30: 10 the blood of the atoning sin offering for the **generations to come**.
30: 21 for Aaron and his descendants for the **generations to come**."
30: 31 'This is to be my sacred anointing oil for the **generations to come**.
31: 13 will be a sign between me and you for the **generations to come**,
31: 16 celebrating it for the **generations to come** as a lasting covenant.
40: 15 be to a priesthood that will continue for all **generations to come**."
Lev 3: 17 " 'This is a lasting ordinance for the **generations to come**,
6: 18 [6:11] made to the LORD by fire for the **generations to come**.
7: 36 this to them as their regular share for the **generations to come**.
10: 9 will die. This is a lasting ordinance for the **generations to come**.
17: 7 be a lasting ordinance for them and for the **generations to come**.'
21: 17 'For the **generations to come** none of your descendants who has a
22: 3 'For the **generations to come**, if any of your descendants is
23: 14 This is to be a lasting ordinance for the **generations to come**,
23: 21 This is to be a lasting ordinance for the **generations to come**,
23: 31 This is to be a lasting ordinance for the **generations to come**,
23: 41 This is to be a lasting ordinance for the **generations to come**;
23: 43 so your **descendants** will know that I had the Israelites live in
24: 3 This is to be a lasting ordinance for the **generations to come**.
25: 30 city shall belong permanently to the buyer and his **descendants**.
Nu 9: 10 'When any of you or your **descendants** are unclean because of a
10: 8 is to be a lasting ordinance for you and the **generations to come**.
15: 14 For the **generations to come**, whenever an alien or anyone else
15: 15 this is a lasting ordinance for the **generations to come**.
15: 21 Throughout the **generations to come** you are to give this offering
15: 23 gave them and continuing through the **generations to come**—
15: 38 'Throughout the **generations to come** you are to make tassels on
18: 23 against it. This is a lasting ordinance for the **generations to come**.
32: 13 until the whole **generation** *of* those who had done evil in his sight
35: 29 be legal requirements for you throughout the **generations to come**,
Dt 1: 35 "Not a man of this evil **generation** shall see the good land I swore

Dt 2: 14 that entire **generation** *of* fighting men had perished from the camp,
7: 9 keeping his covenant of love to a thousand **generations** of those
23: 2 [23:3] of the LORD, even down to the tenth **generation**.
23: 3 [23:4] of the LORD, even down to the tenth **generation**.
23: 8 [23:9] The third **generation** of children born to them may enter
29: 22 [29:21] Your children who follow you in later **generations**
32: 5 are no longer his children, but a warped and crooked **generation**.
32: 7 consider the **generations** [+1887+2256+9102] **long past**.
32: 7 consider the **generations long past** [+1887+2256+9102].
32: 20 for they are a perverse **generation**, children who are unfaithful.
Jos 22: 27 be a witness between us and you and the **generations** that follow,
22: 28 'If they ever say this to us, or to our **descendants**, we will answer:
Jdg 2: 10 After that whole **generation** had been gathered to their fathers,
2: 10 had been gathered to their fathers, another **generation** grew up,
3: 2 (he did this only to teach warfare to the **descendants** *of* the
1Ch 16: 15 the word he commanded, for a thousand **generations**,
Est 9: 28 be remembered and observed in every **generation** by every family,
9: 28 and observed in every generation **[RPH]** by every family,
Job 8: 8 "Ask the former **generations** and find out what their fathers
42: 16 he saw his children and their children to the fourth **generation**.
Ps 10: 6 I'll **always** [+1887+2256+4200] be happy and never have trouble."
10: 6 I'll **always** [+1887+2256+4200] be happy and never have trouble."
12: 7 [12:8] will keep us safe and protect us from such **people** forever.
14: 5 with dread, for God is present in the **company** *of* the righteous.
22: 30 [22:31] serve him; future **generations** will be told about the Lord.
24: 6 Such is the **generation** *of* those who seek him, who seek your face,
33: 11 the purposes of his heart through **all generations** [+1887+2256].
33: 11 the purposes of his heart through **all generations** [+1887+2256].
45: 17 [45:18] your memory through all **generations** [+1887+2256];
45: 17 [45:18] your memory through all **generations** [+1887+2256];
48: 13 [48:14] that you may tell of them to the next **generation**.
49: 11 [49:12] their dwellings for **endless generations** [+1887+2256],
49: 11 [49:12] their dwellings for **endless generations** [+1887+2256],
49: 19 [49:20] he will join the **generation** *of* his fathers, who will never
61: 6 [61:7] his years for **many generations** [+1887+2256].
61: 6 [61:7] his years for **many generations** [+1887+2256].
71: 18 O God, till I declare your power to the next **generation**,
72: 5 as the sun, as long as the moon, **through all generations** [+1887].
72: 5 as the sun, as long as the moon, **through all generations** [+1887].
73: 15 "I will speak thus," I would have betrayed your **children** [+1201].
77: 8 [77:9] Has his promise failed for **all time** [+1887+2256]?
77: 8 [77:9] Has his promise failed for **all time** [+1887+2256]?
78: 4 we will tell the next **generation** the praiseworthy deeds of the
78: 6 so the next **generation** would know them, even the children yet to
78: 8 a stubborn and rebellious **generation**, whose hearts were not loyal
78: 8 rebellious generation, **[RPH]** whose hearts were not loyal to God,
79: 13 from **generation** to generation we will recount your praise.
79: 13 from generation to **generation** we will recount your praise.
85: 5 [85:6] prolong your anger through **all generations** [+1887+2256]?
85: 5 [85:6] prolong your anger through **all generations** [+1887+2256]?
89: 1 [89:2] faithfulness known through **all generations** [+1887+2256].
89: 1 [89:2] faithfulness known through **all generations** [+1887+2256].
89: 4 [89:5] your throne firm through **all generations** [+1887+2256].' "
89: 4 [89:5] your throne firm through **all generations** [+1887+2256].' "
90: 1 our dwelling place throughout **all generations** [+1887+2256].
90: 1 our dwelling place throughout **all generations** [+1887+2256].
95: 10 For forty years I was angry with that **generation**; I said, "They are
100: 5 his faithfulness continues through **all generations** [+1887+2256].
100: 5 his faithfulness continues through **all generations** [+1887+2256].
102: 12 [102:13] renown endures through **all generations** [+1887+2256].
102: 12 [102:13] renown endures through **all generations** [+1887+2256].
102: 18 [102:19] Let this be written for a future **generation**, that a people
102: 24 [102:25] your years go on through **all generations** [+1887].
102: 24 [102:25] your years go on through **all generations** [+1887].
105: 8 the word he commanded, for a thousand **generations**,
106: 31 as righteousness for endless **generations** [+1887+2256] **to come**.
106: 31 as righteousness for endless **generations to come** [+1887+2256].
109: 13 be cut off, their names blotted out from the next **generation**.
112: 2 mighty in the land; the **generation** *of* the upright will be blessed.
119: 90 faithfulness continues through **all generations** [+1887+2256];
119: 90 faithfulness continues through **all generations** [+1887+2256];
135: 13 your renown, O LORD, through **all generations** [+1887+2256].
135: 13 your renown, O LORD, through **all generations** [+1887+2256].
145: 4 *One* **generation** will commend your works to another; they will
145: 4 One generation will commend your works to **another**[s]; they will
145: 13 your dominion endures through all **generations** [+1887+2256].
145: 13 your dominion endures through all **generations** [+1887+2256].
146: 10 your God, O Zion, for **all generations** [+1887+2256].
146: 10 your God, O Zion, for **all generations** [+1887+2256].
Pr 27: 24 and a crown is not secure for **all generations** [+1887+2256].
27: 24 and a crown is not secure for **all generations** [+1887+2256].
30: 11 "There are **those**[s] who curse their fathers and do not bless their
30: 12 **those**[s] who are pure in their own eyes and yet are not cleansed of
30: 13 **those**[s] whose eyes are ever so haughty, whose glances are
30: 14 **those**[s] whose teeth are swords and whose jaws are set with knives
Ecc 1: 4 **Generations** come and generations go, but the earth remains
1: 4 Generations come and **generations** go, but the earth remains
Isa 13: 20 be inhabited or lived in through **all generations** [+1887+2256];
13: 20 be inhabited or lived in through **all generations** [+1887+2256];
34: 10 From **generation** to generation it will lie desolate; no one will ever
34: 10 From generation to **generation** it will lie desolate; no one will ever
34: 17 possess it forever and dwell there from **generation** to generation.
34: 17 possess it forever and dwell there from generation to **generation**.
41: 4 it through, calling forth the **generations** from the beginning?
51: 8 will last forever, my salvation through **all generations** [+1887]."
51: 8 will last forever, my salvation through **all generations** [+1887]."
51: 9 the LORD; awake, as in days gone by, as in **generations** of old.
53: 8 he was taken away. And who can speak of his **descendants**?
58: 12 and will raise up the **age-old** [+1887+2256] foundations;
58: 12 and will raise up the **age-old** [+1887+2256] foundations;
60: 15 everlasting pride and the joy of **all generations** [+1887+2256].
60: 15 everlasting pride and the joy of **all generations** [+1887+2256].
61: 4 cities that have been devastated for **generations** [+1887+2256].
61: 4 cities that have been devastated for **generations** [+1887+2256].
Jer 2: 31 "You of this **generation**, consider the word of the LORD:
7: 29 and abandoned this **generation** *that* is *under* his wrath.
50: 39 never again be inhabited or lived in from **generation** to generation.
50: 39 never again be inhabited or lived in from generation to **generation**.
La 5: 19 reign forever; your throne endures from **generation** to generation.
5: 19 reign forever; your throne endures from generation to **generation**.
Joel 1: 3 tell it to their children, and their children to the next **generation**.
2: 2 never was of old nor ever will be in ages **to come** [+1887+2256].
2: 2 never was of old nor ever will be in ages **to come** [+1887+2256].
3: 20 [4:20] and Jerusalem through **all generations** [+1887+2256].
3: 20 [4:20] and Jerusalem through **all generations** [+1887+2256].

1888 ³דּוֹר **dôr³**, n.pr.loc. [3] [√ 1799; cf. 1883, 1884]

Dor [3]

Jos 12: 23 the king of **Dor** (in Naphoth Dor) one the king of Goyim in Gilgal
Jdg 1: 27 or Taanach or **Dor** or Ibleam or Megiddo and their surrounding
1Ch 7: 29 Taanach, Megiddo and **Dor**, together with their villages.

1889 דּוּשׁ **dûš**, v. [16] [→ 1912, 1913?, 4536; Ar 10165]

thresh [3], go on threshing [+1889] [2], threshed [2], be trampled [1], is threshed [1], is trampled down [1], tear [1], threshing grain [1], threshing time [1], threshing [1], trample [1], treading out grain [1]

Dt 25: 4 [A] Do not muzzle an ox while it *is* **treading out** *the* **grain**.
Jdg 8: 7 [A] *I will* **tear** your flesh with desert thorns and briers."
2Ki 13: 7 [A] the rest and made them like the dust at **threshing time**.
1Ch 21: 20 [A] While Araunah *was* **threshing** wheat, he turned and saw the
Job 39: 15 [A] may crush them, that some wild animal *may* **trample** them.
Isa 25: 10 [C] Moab *will* **be trampled** under him as straw is trampled down
25: 10 [C] Moab will be trampled under him as straw **is trampled down**
28: 27 [H] Caraway **is** not **threshed** with a sledge, nor is a cartwheel
28: 28 [A] so *one does* not **go on threshing** [+1889] it forever.
28: 28 [A] so *one does* not **go on threshing** [+1889] it forever.
41: 15 [A] *You will* **thresh** the mountains and crush them, and reduce
Jer 50: 11 [A] because you frolic like a heifer **threshing grain** and neigh
Hos 10: 11 [A] Ephraim is a trained heifer that loves to **thresh**; so I will put
Am 1: 3 [A] Because she **threshed** Gilead with sledges having iron teeth,
Mic 4: 13 [A] "Rise and **thresh**, O Daughter of Zion, for I will give you
Hab 3: 12 [A] through the earth and in anger *you* **threshed** the nations.

1890 דָּחָה **dāḥâ**, v. [8] [→ 1892, 4510; cf. 1891, 5615; Ar 10166]

was pushed back [+1890] [2], are brought down [1], be banished [1], driving away [1], thrown down [1], tottering [1], trip [1]

Ps 35: 5 [A] the wind, with the angel of the LORD **driving** them **away**;
36: 12 [36:13] [E] evildoers lie fallen—**thrown down**, not able to rise!
62: 3 [62:4] [B] him down—this leaning wall, this **tottering** fence?
118: 13 [C] *I* **was pushed** [+1890] **back** and about to fall,
118: 13 [A] *I* **was pushed back** [+1890] and about to fall,
140: 4 [140:5] [A] protect me from men of violence who plan to **trip**
Pr 14: 32 [C] When calamity comes, the wicked **are brought down**,
Jer 23: 12 [C] *they will* **be banished** to darkness and there they will fall.

1891 דָּחַח **dāḥaḥ**, v. Not used in NIV/BHS [cf. 1890, 5615]

1892 דְּחִי **dᵉḥî**, n.[m.]. [2] [√ 1890]

stumbling [2]

Ps 56: 13 [56:14] delivered me from death and my feet from **stumbling**,
116: 8 my soul from death, my eyes from tears, my feet from **stumbling**,

1893 דֹּחַן *dōḥan*, n.m. [1]
millet [1]
Eze 4: 9 "Take wheat and barley, beans and lentils, **millet** and spelt;

1894 דָּחַף *dāḥap*, v. [4] [→ 4511]
spurred on [2], eager [1], rushed [1]
2Ch 26:20 [C] Indeed, *he* himself *was* **eager** to leave, because the LORD
Est 3:15 [B] **Spurred on** by the king's command, the couriers went out,
6:12 [C] But Haman **rushed** home, with his head covered in grief,
8:14 [B] royal horses, raced out, **spurred on** by the king's command.

1895 דָּחַק *dāḥaq*, v. [2]
afflicted [1], jostle [1]
Jdg 2:18 [A] they groaned under those who oppressed and **afflicted** them.
Joel 2: 8 [A] *They do* not **jostle** each other; each marches straight ahead.

1896 דַּי *day*, subst. [39] [→ 972, 1973, 3904, 4514]
whenever [+4946] [5], enough [4], from [+4946] [3], as much as wanted [2], as often as [+4946] [2], for nothing [+928+8198] [2], afford [+3338+5162] [1], afford [+3338+5595] [1], after [+928+4946] [1], as far as possible [+3869] [1], at the blast [+928] [1], deserves [+3869] [1], due annually [+928+4946+9102+9102] [1], enough [+4200+4537] [1], fuel for fire [+836+928] [1], fuel for flames [+836+928] [1], just enough [1], means [1], no end [+3869] [1], often [+4946] [1], plenty [1], room enough [1], sufficient means [+3869] [1], sufficient [1], swarms [1], whatever [1], whenever [+3954+4946] [1]
Ex 36: 5 "The people are bringing more than **enough** *for* doing the work the
36: 7 because what they already had was more than **enough** to do all the
Lev 5: 7 " 'If he cannot **afford** [+3338+5595] a lamb, he is to bring two
12: 8 If she cannot **afford** [+3338+5162] a lamb, she is to bring two
25:26 and acquires **sufficient** [+3869] **means** *to* redeem it,
25:28 if he does not acquire the **means** to repay him, what he sold will
Dt 15: 8 Rather be openhanded and freely lend him **whatever** he needs.
25: 2 his presence with the number of lashes his crime **deserves** [+3869],
Jdg 6: 5 came up with their livestock and their tents like **swarms** *of* locusts.
1Sa 1: 7 **Whenever** [+4946] Hannah went up to the house of the LORD,
7:16 **From** [+4946] year to year he went on a circuit from Bethel to
18:30 continued to go out to battle, and **as often** [+4946] as they did,
1Ki 14:28 **Whenever** [+4946] the king went to the LORD's temple,
2Ki 4: 8 So **whenever** [+4946] he came by, he stopped there to eat.
2Ch 12:11 **Whenever** [+4946] the king went to the LORD's temple,
24: 5 the money **due annually** [+928+4946+9102+9102] from all Israel,
30: 3 because not **enough** [+4200+4537] priests had consecrated
Ne 5: 8 said: "**As far** [+3869] **as possible**, we have bought back our Jewish
Est 1:18 same way. There will be **no end** [+3869] *of* disrespect and discord.
Job 39:25 **At the blast of** [+928] the trumpet he snorts, 'Aha!' He catches the
Pr 25:16 If you find honey, eat **just enough**—too much of it, and you will
27:27 You will have **plenty** *of* goats' milk to feed you and your family
Isa 28:19 **As often** [+4946] **as** it comes it will carry you away; morning after
40:16 Lebanon is not **sufficient** *for* altar fires, nor its animals enough for
40:16 sufficient for altar fires, nor its animals **enough** *for* burnt offerings.
66:23 **From** [+4946] one New Moon to another and from one Sabbath to
66:23 New Moon to another and **from** [+4946] one Sabbath to another,
Jer 20: 8 **Whenever** [+3954+4946] I speak, I cry out proclaiming violence
31:20 Though I **often** [+4946] speak against him, I still remember him.
48:27 that you shake your head in scorn **whenever** [+4946] you speak of
49: 9 the night, would they not steal only **as much as** they **wanted**?
51:58 the peoples exhaust themselves **for nothing** [+928+8198],
51:58 the nations' labor is only **fuel for** the **flames** [+836+928]."
Ob 1: 5 awaits you—would they not steal only **as much as** they **wanted**?
Na 2:12 [2:13] The lion killed **enough** *for* his cubs and strangled the prey
Hab 2:13 that the people's labor is only **fuel for the fire** [+836+928],
2:13 that the nations exhaust themselves **for nothing** [+928+8198]?
Zec 14:16 will go up year **after** [+928+4946] year to worship the King,
Mal 3:10 so much blessing that you will not have **room enough** for it.

1897 דִּיבוֹן *dîbôn*, n.pr.loc. [9] [→ 1898; cf. 1904, 1905]
Dibon [9]
Nu 21:30 have overthrown them; Heshbon is destroyed all the way to **Dibon**.
32: 3 "Ataroth, **Dibon**, Jazer, Nimrah, Heshbon, Elealeh, Sebam,
32:34 The Gadites built up **Dibon**, Ataroth, Aroer,
Jos 13: 9 and included the whole plateau of Medeba as far as **Dibon**,
13:17 on the plateau, including **Dibon**, Bamoth Baal, Beth Baal Meon,
Ne 11:25 in **Dibon** and its settlements, in Jekabzeel and its villages,
Isa 15: 2 **Dibon** goes up to its temple, to its high places to weep; Moab wails
Jer 48:18 sit on the parched ground, O inhabitants of the Daughter of **Dibon**,
48:22 to **Dibon**, Nebo and Beth Diblathaim,

1898 דִּיבֹן גָּד *dîbôn gād*, n.pr.loc. [2] [√ 1897 + 1514]
Dibon Gad [2]
Nu 33:45 They left Iyim and camped at **Dibon Gad**.
33:46 They left **Dibon Gad** and camped at Almon Diblathaim.

1899 דִּיג *dîg*, v.den. [1] [cf. 1834]
catch [1]
Jer 16:16 [A] declares the LORD, "and *they will* **catch** them.

1900 דַּיָּג *dayyāg*, n.m. [2] [√ 1834]
fishermen [2]
Isa 19: 8 The **fishermen** will groan and lament, all who cast hooks into the
Jer 16:16 "But now I will send for many **fishermen**," [K 1854] declares the

1901 דַּיָּה *dayyâ*, n.f. [2] [cf. 1797]
falcon [1], falcons [1]
Dt 14:13 the red kite, the black kite, any kind of **falcon**,
Isa 34:15 of her wings; there also the **falcons** will gather, each with its mate.

1902 דְּיוֹ *d^{e}yô*, n.m. [1] [√ 1864?]
ink [1]
Jer 36:18 all these words to me, and I wrote them in **ink** on the scroll."

1903 דִּי זָהָב *dî zāhāb*, n.pr.loc. [1]
Dizahab [1]
Dt 1: 1 between Paran and Tophel, Laban, Hazeroth and **Dizahab**.

1904 דִּימוֹן *dîmôn*, n.pr.loc. [2] [cf. 1897]
Dimon [1], Dimon's [1]
Isa 15: 9 **Dimon's** waters are full of blood, but I will bring still more upon
15: 9 waters are full of blood, but I will bring still more upon **Dimon**—

1905 דִּימוֹנָה *dîmônâ*, n.pr.loc. [1] [cf. 1897]
Dimonah [1]
Jos 15:22 Kinah, **Dimonah**, Adadah,

1906 דִּין *dîn[1]*, v. [24] [→ 1879, 1907, 1908, 1909, 1968, 1969, 4506, 4507, 4519, 4528, 8723, 8726; Ar 10169; *also used with compound proper names*]
judge [8], contend [2], govern [2], plead [2], vindicate [2], administer [1], arguing with each other [1], defend rights [1], defended [1], governs [1], provide justice [1], punish [1], vindicated [1]
Ge 6: 3 [A] "My Spirit *will* not **contend** with man forever, for he is
15:14 [A] I *will* **punish** the nation they serve as slaves, and afterward
30: 6 [A] Rachel said, "God *has* **vindicated** me; he has listened to my
49:16 [A] "Dan *will* **provide justice** *for* his people as one of the tribes
Dt 32:36 [A] The LORD *will* **judge** his people and have compassion on
1Sa 2:10 [A] from heaven; the LORD *will* **judge** the ends of the earth.
2Sa 19: 9 [19:10] [C] people *were* all **arguing with each other**, saying,
Job 36:31 [A] This is the way *he* **governs** the nations and provides food in
Ps 7: 8 [7:9] [A] *let* the LORD **judge** the peoples. Judge me,
9: 8 [9:9] [A] *he will* **govern** the peoples with justice.
50: 4 [A] heavens above, and the earth, that he *may* **judge** his people:
54: 1 [54:3] [A] O God, by your name; **vindicate** me by your might.
72: 2 [A] *He will* **judge** your people in righteousness, your afflicted
96:10 [A] it cannot be moved; *he will* **judge** the peoples with equity.
110: 6 [A] *He will* **judge** the nations, heaping up the dead and crushing
135:14 [A] For the LORD *will* **vindicate** his people and have
Pr 31: 9 [A] and judge fairly; **defend** the **rights** *of* the poor and needy."
Ecc 6:10 [A] no man can **contend** with one who is stronger than he.
Isa 3:13 [A] LORD takes his place in court; he rises to **judge** the people.
Jer 5:28 [A] *they do* not **plead** the case of the fatherless to win it, they do
21:12 [A] " '**Administer** justice every morning; rescue from the hand
22:16 [A] *He* **defended** the cause of the poor and needy, and so all
30:13 [A] There is no *one to* **plead** your cause, no remedy for your
Zec 3: 7 [A] you *will* **govern** my house and have charge of my courts,

1907 [2]דִּין *dîn[2]*, n.[m.] [20] [√ 1906; Ar 10170]
judgment [4], cause [3], justice [3], rights [3], case [2], lawsuits [+1907+4200] [2], *untranslated* [1], judge [1], quarrels [1]
Dt 17: 8 whether bloodshed, **lawsuits** [+1907+4200] or assaults—take them
17: 8 whether bloodshed, **lawsuits** [+1907+4200] or assaults—take them
Est 1:13 for the king to consult experts in matters of law and **justice**,
Job 19:29 and then you will know that there is **judgment**." [Q 1879]
35:14 see him, that your **case** is before him and you must wait for him,
36:17 But now you are laden with the **judgment** *due* the wicked;

[F] Hitpael (hitpoel, hitpoal, hitpolel, hitpolal, hitpalel, hitpalal, hitpalpel, hitpalpal, hotpael, hotpaal) [G] Hiphil (hiphtil) [H] Hophal [I] Hishtaphel

Job 36: 17 due the wicked; **judgment** and justice have taken hold of you.
Ps 9: 4 [9:5] For you have upheld my right and my **cause**; you have sat
76: 8 [76:9] From heaven you pronounced **judgment**, and the land
140: 12 [140:13] I know that the LORD secures **justice** *for* the poor
Pr 20: 8 When a king sits on his throne to **judge**, he winnows out all evil
22: 10 out the mocker, and out goes strife; **quarrels** and insults are ended.
29: 7 The righteous care about **justice** *for* the poor, but the wicked have
31: 5 what the law decrees, and deprive all the oppressed of their **rights**.
31: 8 cannot speak for themselves, for the **rights** *of* all who are destitute.
Isa 10: 2 to deprive the poor of their **rights** and withhold justice from the
Jer 5: 28 they do not plead **[RPH]** the case of the fatherless to win it,
5: 28 they do not plead the **case** *of* the fatherless to win it, they do not
22: 16 He defended the **cause** *of* the poor and needy, and so all went well.
30: 13 There is no one to plead your **cause**, no remedy for your sore,

1908 דַּיָּן *dayyān*, n.m. [2] [√ 1906; Ar 10171]

defender [1], judge [1]

1Sa 24: 15 [24:16] May the LORD be our **judge** and decide between us.
Ps 68: 5 [68:6] A father to the fatherless, a **defender** *of* widows, is God in

1909 דִּינָה *dînâ*, n.pr.f. [8] [√ 1906]

Dinah [7], Dinah's [1]

Ge 30: 21 Some time later she gave birth to a daughter and named her **Dinah**.
34: 1 Now **Dinah**, the daughter Leah had borne to Jacob, went out to
34: 3 His heart was drawn to **Dinah** daughter of Jacob, and he loved the
34: 5 When Jacob heard that his daughter **Dinah** had been defiled,
34: 13 Because their sister **Dinah** had been defiled, Jacob's sons replied
34: 25 Simeon and Levi, **Dinah's** brothers, took their swords and attacked
34: 26 to the sword and took **Dinah** from Shechem's house and left.
46: 15 Leah bore to Jacob in Paddan Aram, besides his daughter **Dinah**.

1910 דִּיפַת *dîpat*, n.pr.m. [1 / 0] [cf. 8196]

1Ch 1: 6 Ashkenaz, Riphath [BHS *Diphath*; NIV 8196] and Togarmah.

1911 דָּיֵק *dāyēq*, n.m. [6] [√ 1882]

siege works [6]

2Ki 25: 1 He encamped outside the city and built **siege works** all around it.
Jer 52: 4 They camped outside the city and built **siege works** all around it.
Eze 4: 2 Erect **siege works** against it, build a ramp up to it, set up camps
17: 17 ramps are built and **siege works** erected to destroy many lives.
21: 22 [21:27] the gates, to build a ramp and to erect **siege works**.
26: 8 he will set up **siege works** against you, build a ramp up to your

1912 דַּיִשׁ *dayiš*, n.m. [1] [√ 1889]

threshing [1]

Lev 26: 5 Your **threshing** will continue until grape harvest and the grape

1913 דִּישׁוֹן *dîšôn*[1], n.[m.]. [1] [→ 1914?, 1915?; cf. 1889?]

ibex [1]

Dt 14: 5 the wild goat, the **ibex**, the antelope and the mountain sheep.

1914 דִּישׁוֹן *dîšôn*[2], n.pr.m. [7 / 8] [√ 1913?]

Dishon [7], Dishan [1]

Ge 36: 21 **Dishon**, Ezer and Dishan. These sons of Seir in Edom were Horite
36: 25 The children of Anah: **Dishon** and Oholibamah daughter of Anah.
36: 26 The sons of **Dishon**: [BHS 1915] Hemdan, Eshban, Ithran
36: 30 **Dishon**, Ezer and Dishan. These were the Horite chiefs,
1Ch 1: 38 of Seir: Lotan, Shobal, Zibeon, Anah, **Dishon**, Ezer and Dishan.
1: 41 The son of Anah: **Dishon**. The sons of Dishon: Hemdan, Eshban,
1: 41 Dishon. The sons of **Dishon**: Hemdan, Eshban, Ithran and Keran.
1: 42 Bilhan, Zaavan and Akan. The sons of **Dishan**: Uz and Aran.

1915 דִּישָׁן *dîšān*, n.pr.m. [5 / 4] [√ 1913?]

Dishan [4]

Ge 36: 21 Dishon, Ezer and **Dishan**. These sons of Seir in Edom were Horite
36: 26 The sons of Dishon: [BHS *Dishan*; NIV 1914] Hemdan, Eshban,
36: 28 The sons of **Dishan**: Uz and Aran.
36: 30 Dishon, Ezer and **Dishan**. These were the Horite chiefs,
1Ch 1: 38 of Seir: Lotan, Shobal, Zibeon, Anah, Dishon, Ezer and **Dishan**.

1916 דַּךְ *dak*, a. [4] [→ 1921; cf. 1870, 1917, 1920, 1990]

oppressed [3], hurts [1]

Ps 9: 9 [9:10] The LORD is a refuge for the **oppressed**, a stronghold in
10: 18 defending the fatherless and the **oppressed**, in order that man,
74: 21 Do not let the **oppressed** retreat in disgrace; may the poor
Pr 26: 28 A lying tongue hates *those* it **hurts**, and a flattering mouth works

1917 דָּכָא *dākā'*, v. [18] [→ 1918, 1919; cf. 1870, 1916, 1920, 1990]

crush [7], crushed [4], broke [1], contrite [1], crushes [1], crushing [1], dejected [1], humbled themselves [1], was crushed [1]

Job 4: 19 [D] are in the dust, who *are* **crushed** more readily than a moth!
5: 4 [F] are far from safety, **crushed** in court without a defender.
6: 9 [D] that God would be willing *to* **crush** me, to let loose his hand
19: 2 [D] "How long will you torment me and **crush** me with words?
22: 9 [E] away empty-handed and **broke** the strength of the fatherless.
34: 25 [F] he overthrows them in the night and *they are* **crushed**.
Ps 72: 4 [D] save the children of the needy; *he will* **crush** the oppressor.
89: 10 [89:11] [D] You **crushed** Rahab like one of the slain; with your
94: 5 [D] *They* **crush** your people, O LORD; they oppress your
143: 3 [D] The enemy pursues me, *he* **crushes** me to the ground;
Pr 22: 22 [D] because they are poor and *do* not **crush** the needy in court,
Isa 3: 15 [D] What do you mean by **crushing** my people and grinding the
19: 10 [E] The workers in cloth will be **dejected**, and all the wage
53: 5 [E] for our transgressions, *he* **was crushed** for our iniquities;
53: 10 [D] Yet it was the LORD's will *to* **crush** him and cause him to
57: 15 [C] the spirit of the lowly and to revive the heart of the **contrite**.
Jer 44: 10 [E] To this day *they have* not **humbled themselves** or shown
La 3: 34 [D] To **crush** underfoot all prisoners in the land,

1918 דַּכָּא *dakkā'*[1], a. [3] [√ 1917]

contrite [1], crushed [1], crushing [1]

Dt 23: 1 [23:2] No one who has been emasculated by **crushing** or cutting
Ps 34: 18 [34:19] and saves *those who* are **crushed** *in* spirit.
Isa 57: 15 holy place, but also with *him who* is **contrite** and lowly in spirit,

1919 דַּכָּא *dakkā'*[2], n.[m.]. [1] [√ 1917]

dust [1]

Ps 90: 3 You turn men back to **dust**, saying, "Return to dust, O sons of

1920 דָּכָה *dākâ*, v. [5] [→ 1922; cf. 1870, 1916, 1917, 1990]

crushed [4], contrite [1]

Ps 10: 10 [A] His victims *are* **crushed**, they collapse; they fall under his
38: 8 [38:9] [C] I am feeble and utterly **crushed**; I groan in anguish of
44: 19 [44:20] [D] *you* **crushed** us and made us a haunt for jackals
51: 8 [51:10] [D] let the bones *you have* **crushed** rejoice.
51: 17 [51:19] [C] and **contrite** heart, O God, you will not despise.

1921 דַּכָּה *dakkâ*, n.f. Not used in NIV/BHS [√ 1916]

1922 דֳּכִי *d^ekî*, n.[m.]. [1] [√ 1920]

pounding waves [1]

Ps 93: 3 lifted up their voice; the seas have lifted up their **pounding waves**.

1923 דַּל *dal*[1], n.[m.]. [1] [→ 1928, 1946]

door [1]

Ps 141: 3 over my mouth, O LORD; keep watch over the **door** *of* my lips.

1924 דַּל *dal*[2], a. [48] [→ 1930; cf. 1937]

poor [36], weak [4], grew weaker and weaker [+2143+2256] [1], haggard [1], helpless [1], humble [1], needy [1], poorest of the poor [+1147] [1], scrawny [1], weakest [1]

Ge 41: 19 seven other cows came up—**scrawny** and very ugly and lean.
Ex 23: 3 and do not show favoritism to a **poor** *man* in his lawsuit.
30: 15 the **poor** are not to give less when you make the offering to the
Lev 14: 21 "If, however, he is **poor** and cannot afford these, he must take one
19: 15 do not show partiality to the **poor** or favoritism to the great,
Jdg 6: 15 My clan is the **weakest** in Manasseh, and I am the least in my
Ru 3: 10 You have not run after the younger men, whether rich or **poor**.
1Sa 2: 8 He raises the **poor** from the dust and lifts the needy from the ash
2Sa 3: 1 while the house of Saul **grew weaker** [+2143+2256] **and weaker**.
13: 4 do you, the king's son, look so **haggard** morning after morning?
Job 5: 16 So the **poor** have hope, and injustice shuts its mouth.
20: 10 His children must make amends to the **poor**; his own hands must
20: 19 For he has oppressed the **poor** and left them destitute; he has
31: 16 "If I have denied the desires of the **poor** or let the eyes of the
34: 19 no partiality to princes and does not favor the rich over the **poor**,
34: 28 They caused the cry of the **poor** to come before him, so that he
Ps 41: 1 [41:2] Blessed is he who has regard for the **weak**; the LORD
72: 13 He will take pity on the **weak** and the needy and save the needy
82: 3 Defend the cause of the **weak** and fatherless; maintain the rights of
82: 4 Rescue the **weak** and needy; deliver them from the hand of the
113: 7 He raises the **poor** from the dust and lifts the needy from the ash
Pr 10: 15 of the rich is their fortified city, but poverty is the ruin of the **poor**.
14: 31 He who oppresses the **poor** shows contempt for their Maker,

Pr 19: 4 Wealth brings many friends, but a **poor** *man's* friend deserts him.
19: 17 He who is kind to the **poor** lends to the LORD, and he will
21: 13 If a man shuts his ears to the cry of the **poor**, he too will cry out
22: 9 man will himself be blessed, for he shares his food with the **poor**.
22: 16 He who oppresses the **poor** to increase his wealth and he who
22: 22 Do not exploit the **poor** because they are poor and do not crush the
22: 22 Do not exploit the poor because they are **poor** and do not crush the
28: 3 A ruler who oppresses the **poor** is like a driving rain that leaves no
28: 8 interest amasses it for another, who will be kind to the **poor**.
28: 11 own eyes, but a **poor** *man* who has discernment sees through him.
28: 15 or a charging bear is a wicked man ruling over a **helpless** people.
29: 7 The righteous care about justice for the **poor**, but the wicked have
29: 14 If a king judges the **poor** with fairness, his throne will always be
Isa 10: 2 to deprive the **poor** of their rights and withhold justice from the
11: 4 with righteousness he will judge the **needy**, with justice he will
14: 30 The **poorest of the poor** [+1147] will find pasture, and the needy
25: 4 You have been a refuge for the **poor**, a refuge for the needy in his
26: 6 it down—the feet of the oppressed, the footsteps of the **poor**.
Jer 5: 4 I thought, "These are only the **poor**; they are foolish, for they do
39: 10 the guard left behind in the land of Judah some of the **poor** people,
Am 2: 7 They trample on the heads of the **poor** as upon the dust of the
4: 1 you women who oppress the **poor** and crush the needy and say to
5: 11 You trample on the **poor** and force him to give you grain.
8: 6 buying the **poor** with silver and the needy for a pair of sandals,
Zep 3: 12 I will leave within you the meek and **humble**, who trust in the

1925 דָּלַג *dālag*, v. [5]

scale [2], avoid stepping [1], leap [1], leaping [1]

2Sa 22: 30 [D] can advance against a troop; with my God *I can* **scale** a wall.
Ps 18: 29 [18:30] [D] against a troop; with my God *I can* **scale** a wall.
SS 2: 8 [D] Here he comes, **leaping** across the mountains, bounding over
Isa 35: 6 [D] *will* the lame **leap** like a deer, and the mute tongue shout for
Zep 1: 9 [A] On that day I will punish all who **avoid stepping** on the

1926 ¹דָּלָה *dālâ¹*, v. [5] [→ 1932, 1933, 1934,; cf. 1927]

drew water [+1926] [2], draw water [1], draws out [1], lifted out of the depths [1]

Ex 2: 16 [A] they came *to* **draw water** and fill the troughs to water their
2: 19 [A] *He* even **drew** [+1926] **water** for us and watered the flock."
2: 19 [A] *He* even **drew water** [+1926] for us and watered the flock."
Ps 30: 1 [30:2] [D] for *you* **lifted** me **out of the depths** and did not let
Pr 20: 5 [A] are deep waters, but a man of understanding **draws** them **out**.

1927 ²דָּלָה *dālâ²*, v. [1] [→ 1936; cf. 1926]

hang limp [1]

Pr 26: 7 [A] Like a lame man's legs *that* **hang limp** is a proverb in the

1928 ³דָּלָה *dālâ³*, n.f. Not used in NIV/BHS [√ 1923]

1929 ¹דַּלָּה *dallâ¹*, n.f. [2] [√ 1938]

hair [+8031] [1], loom [1]

SS 7: 5 [7:6] Your **hair** [+8031] is like royal tapestry; the king is held
Isa 38: 12 I have rolled up my life, and he has cut me off from the **loom**;

1930 ²דַּלָּה *dallâ²*, n.f. [5] [√ 1924; cf. 1937]

poorest [5]

2Ki 24: 14 of ten thousand. Only the **poorest** people of the land were left.
25: 12 the commander left behind some of the **poorest** *people of* the land
Jer 40: 7 women and children who were the **poorest** *in* the land and who
52: 15 of the guard carried into exile some of the **poorest** people
52: 16 Nebuzaradan left behind the rest of the **poorest** *people of* the land

1931 דָּלַח *dālaḥ*, v. [3]

churning [1], muddied [1], stirred [1]

Eze 32: 2 [A] **churning** the water with your feet and muddying the
32: 13 [A] abundant waters no longer *to be* **stirred** *by* the foot of man
32: 13 [A] stirred by the foot of man or **muddied** *by* the hoofs of cattle.

1932 דְּלִי *dᵉlî*, n.[m.]. [2] [√ 1926]

bucket [1], buckets [1]

Nu 24: 7 Water will flow from their **buckets**; their seed will have abundant
Isa 40: 15 Surely the nations are like a drop in a **bucket**; they are regarded as

1933 דְּלָיָה *dᵉlāyâ*, n.pr.m. [4] [√ 1926 + 3378]

Delaiah [4]

1Ch 3: 24 Hodaviah, Eliashib, Pelaiah, Akkub, Johanan, **Delaiah** and Anani—
Ezr 2: 60 The descendants of **Delaiah**, Tobiah and Nekoda 652
Ne 6: 10 One day I went to the house of Shemaiah son of **Delaiah**,
7: 62 the descendants of **Delaiah**, Tobiah and Nekoda 642

1934 דְּלָיָהוּ *dᵉlāyāhû*, n.pr.m. [3] [√ 1926 + 3378]

Delaiah [3]

1Ch 24: 18 the twenty-third to **Delaiah** and the twenty-fourth to Maaziah.
Jer 36: 12 the secretary, **Delaiah** son of Shemaiah, Elnathan son of Acbor,
36: 25 **Delaiah** and Gemariah urged the king not to burn the scroll,

1935 דְּלִילָה *dᵉlîlâ*, n.pr.f. [6] [√ 1938]

Delilah [6]

Jdg 16: 4 with a woman in the Valley of Sorek whose name was **Delilah**.
16: 6 So **Delilah** said to Samson, "Tell me the secret of your great
16: 10 Then **Delilah** said to Samson, "You have made a fool of me;
16: 12 So **Delilah** took new ropes and tied him with them. Then,
16: 13 **Delilah** then said to Samson, "Until now, you have been making a
16: 18 When **Delilah** saw that he had told her everything, she sent word to

1936 דָּלִית *dālît*, n.f. [8] [√ 1927]

branches [6], boughs [2]

Jer 11: 16 mighty storm he will set it on fire, and its **branches** will be broken.
Eze 17: 6 Its **branches** turned toward him, but its roots remained under it.
17: 7 it was planted and stretched out its **branches** to him for water.
17: 23 will nest in it; they will find shelter in the shade of its **branches**.
19: 11 thick foliage, conspicuous for its height and for its many **branches**.
31: 7 It was majestic in beauty, with its spreading **boughs**, for its roots
31: 9 I made it beautiful with abundant **branches**, the envy of all the
31: 12 Its **boughs** fell on the mountains and in all the valleys; its branches

1937 ¹דָּלַל *dālal¹*, v. [7] [→ 1924, 1930; cf. 1938]

in need [2], dwindle [1], fade [1], impoverished [1], in great need [1], weak [1]

Jdg 6: 6 [A] so **impoverished** the Israelites that they cried out to the
Ps 79: 8 [A] come quickly to meet us, for *we are* **in** desperate **need**.
116: 6 [A] the simplehearted; *when I was* **in great need**, he saved me.
142: 6 [142:7] [A] Listen to my cry, for *I am* **in** desperate **need**;
Isa 17: 4 [A] "In that day the glory of Jacob *will* **fade**; the fat of his body
19: 6 [A] will stink; the streams of Egypt *will* **dwindle** and dry up.
38: 14 [A] My eyes *grew* **weak** as I looked to the heavens. I am

1938 ²דָּלַל *dālal²*, v. [1] [→ 1929, 1935; cf. 1937]

dangles [1]

Job 28: 4 [A] by the foot of man; far from men *he* **dangles** and sways.

1939 דִּלְעָן *dil'ān*, n.pr.loc. [1]

Dilean [1]

Jos 15: 38 **Dilean**, Mizpah, Joktheel,

1940 ¹דָּלַף *dālap¹*, v. [2] [→ 1942]

leaks [1], pour out tears [1]

Job 16: 20 [A] My intercessor is my friend *as* my eyes **pour out tears** to
Ecc 10: 18 [A] is lazy, the rafters sag; if his hands are idle, the house **leaks**.

1941 ²דָּלַף *dālap²*, v. [1] [→ 1943, 3358]

weary [1]

Ps 119: 28 [A] My soul *is* **weary** with sorrow; strengthen me according to

1942 דֶּלֶף *delep*, n.m. [2] [√ 1940]

constant dripping [+3265] [2]

Pr 19: 13 and a quarrelsome wife is like a **constant dripping** [+3265].
27: 15 A quarrelsome wife is like a **constant dripping** [+3265] on a rainy

1943 דַּלְפוֹן *dalpôn*, n.pr.m. [1] [√ 1941]

Dalphon [1]

Est 9: 7 They also killed Parshandatha, **Dalphon**, Aspatha,

1944 דָּלַק *dālaq*, v. [9] [→ 1945; Ar 10178]

chased [1], chasing [+339] [1], fervent [1], flaming [1], hunt down [1], hunts down [1], inflamed [1], kindle [1], set on fire [1]

Ge 31: 36 [A] "What sin have I committed that *you* **hunt** me **down**?
1Sa 17: 53 [A] When the Israelites returned from **chasing** [+339] the
Ps 7: 13 [7:14] [A] deadly weapons; he makes ready his **flaming** arrows.
10: 2 [A] In his arrogance the wicked man **hunts down** the weak,
Pr 26: 23 [A] Like a coating of glaze over earthenware are **fervent** lips
Isa 5: 11 [G] who stay up late at night *till* they *are* **inflamed** *with* wine.
La 4: 19 [A] *they* **chased** us over the mountains and lay in wait for us in
Eze 24: 10 [G] So heap on the wood and **kindle** the fire. Cook the meat well,

Ob 1:18 [A] will be stubble, and *they will* **set** it **on fire** and consume it.

1945 דַּלֶּקֶת ***dalleqet***, n.f. [1] [√ 1944]

inflammation [1]

Dt 28:22 with fever and **inflammation**, with scorching heat and drought,

1946 דֶּלֶת ***delet***, n.f. [& m.?]. [87] [√ 1923]

doors [46], door [21], gates [10], *untranslated* [3], leaves [2], columns [1], gate [1], it[s] [+2021] [1], lid [1], outside [+4946] [1]

Ge 19: 6 Lot went outside to meet them and shut the **door** behind him
19: 9 pressure on Lot and moved forward to break down the **door**.
19:10 reached out and pulled Lot back into the house and shut the **door**.
Ex 21: 6 He shall take him to the **door** or the doorpost and pierce his ear
Dt 3: 5 these cities were fortified with high walls and with **gates** and bars,
15:17 then take an awl and push it through his ear lobe into the **door**,
Jos 2:19 If anyone goes **outside** [+4946] your house into the street,
6:26 its foundations; at the cost of his youngest will he set up its **gates**."
Jdg 3:23 he shut the **doors** *of* the upper room behind him and locked them.
3:24 the servants came and found the **doors** *of* the upper room locked.
3:25 but when he did not open the **doors** *of* the room, they took a key
11:31 whatever comes out of the **door** *of* my house to meet me when I
16: 3 Then he got up and took hold of the **doors** *of* the city gate,
19:22 Pounding on the **door**, they shouted to the old man who owned the
19:27 her master got up in the morning and opened the **door** *of* the house
1Sa 3:15 and then opened the **doors** *of* the house of the LORD.
21:13 [21:14] making marks on the **doors** *of* the gate and letting saliva
23: 7 for David has imprisoned himself by entering a town with **gates**
2Sa 13:17 and said, "Get this woman out of here and bolt the **door** after her."
13:18 So his servant put her out and bolted the **door** after her. She was
1Ki 6:31 For the entrance of the inner sanctuary he made **doors** *of* olive
6:32 And on the two olive wood **doors** he carved cherubim, palm trees
6:34 He also made two pine **doors**, each having two leaves that turned
6:34 pine doors, each **[RPH]** having two leaves that turned in sockets.
6:34 pine doors, each having two leaves that turned in sockets. **[RPH]**
7:50 and the gold sockets for the **doors** *of* the innermost room,
7:50 Holy Place, and also for the **doors** of the main hall of the temple.
16:34 and he set up its **gates** at the cost of his youngest son Segub,
2Ki 4: 4 Then go inside and shut the **door** behind you and your sons.
4: 5 She left him and afterward shut the **door** behind her and her sons.
4:33 shut the **door** on the two of them and prayed to the LORD.
6:32 the messenger comes, shut the **door** and hold it shut against him.
6:32 shut the door and hold **it**[s] [+2021] shut against him.
9: 3 you king over Israel.' Then open the **door** and run; don't delay!"
9:10 and no one will bury her.' " Then he opened the **door** and ran.
12: 9 [12:10] Jehoiada the priest took a chest and bored a hole in its **lid**.
18:16 of Judah stripped off the gold with which he had covered the **doors**
1Ch 22: 3 He provided a large amount of iron to make nails for the **doors** *of*
2Ch 3: 7 doorframes, walls and **doors** *of* the temple with gold,
4: 9 the large court and the **doors** for the court, and overlaid the doors
4: 9 and the doors for the court, and overlaid the **doors** with bronze.
4:22 the inner **doors** to the Most Holy Place and the doors of the main
4:22 inner doors to the Most Holy Place and the **doors** of the main hall.
8: 5 Beth Horon as fortified cities, with walls and with **gates** and bars,
14: 7 [14:6] "and put walls around them, with towers, **gates** and bars.
28:24 He shut the **doors** *of* the LORD's temple and set up altars at
29: 3 he opened the **doors** *of* the temple of the LORD and repaired
29: 7 They also shut the **doors** *of* the portico and put out the lamps.
Ne 3: 1 They dedicated it and set its **doors** in place, building as far as the
3: 3 They laid its beams and put its **doors** and bolts and bars in place.
3: 6 They laid its beams and put its **doors** and bolts and bars in place.
3:13 They rebuilt it and put its **doors** and bolts and bars in place.
3:14 He rebuilt it and put its **doors** and bolts and bars in place.
3:15 roofing it over and putting its **doors** and bolts and bars in place.
6: 1 though up to that time I had not set the **doors** in the gates—
6:10 house of God, inside the temple, and let us close the temple **doors**,
7: 1 After the wall had been rebuilt and I had set the **doors** in place,
7: 3 are still on duty, have them shut the **doors** and bar them.
13:19 I ordered the **doors** to be shut and not opened until the Sabbath
Job 3:10 for it did not shut the **doors** *of* the womb on me to hide trouble
31:32 night in the street, for my **door** was always open to the traveler—
38: 8 "Who shut up the sea behind **doors** when it burst forth from the
38:10 when I fixed limits for it and set its **doors** and bars in place,
41:14 [41:6] Who dares open the **doors** *of* his mouth, ringed about with
Ps 78:23 command to the skies above and opened the **doors** *of* the heavens;
107:16 for he breaks down **gates** *of* bronze and cuts through bars of iron.
Pr 8:34 listens to me, watching daily at my **doors**, waiting at my doorway.
26:14 As a **door** turns on its hinges, so a sluggard turns on his bed.
Ecc 12: 4 when the **doors** to the street are closed and the sound of grinding
SS 8: 9 on her. If she is a **door**, we will enclose her with panels of cedar.
Isa 26:20 my people, enter your rooms and shut the **doors** behind you;
45: 1 to open **doors** before him so that gates will not be shut:
45: 2 I will break down **gates** *of* bronze and cut through bars of iron.
57: 8 Behind your **doors** and your doorposts you have put your pagan
Jer 36:23 Whenever Jehudi had read three or four **columns** of the scroll,
49:31 declares the LORD, "a nation that has neither **gates** nor bars;
Eze 26: 2 The **gate** *to* the nations is broken, and its doors have swung open
38:11 all of them living without walls and without **gates** and bars.
41:23 the outer sanctuary and the Most Holy Place had double **doors**.
41:24 Each **door** had two leaves—two hinged leaves for each door.
41:24 Each door had two **leaves**—two hinged leaves for each door.
41:24 Each door had two leaves—two hinged **leaves** for each door.
41:24 Each door had two leaves—two hinged leaves for each **door**.
41:24 door had two leaves—two hinged leaves for each door. **[RPH]**
41:25 And on the **doors** *of* the outer sanctuary were carved cherubim
Zec 11: 1 Open your **doors**, O Lebanon, so that fire may devour your cedars!
Mal 1:10 "Oh, that one of you would shut the temple **doors**, so that you

1947 דָּם ***dām***, n.m. [360 / 358] [cf. 1956?]

blood [282], bloodshed [17], bloodthirsty [6], bloodshed [+1947+4200] [4], guilty of bloodshed [4], it[s] [+2021] [4], guilt of blood [3], lifeblood [+5883] [3], bleeding [2], bloodguilt [2], bloodshed [+928+995] [2], guilt of bloodshed [2], guilt of shedding blood [2], *untranslated* [1], blood shed [1], blood vengeance [1], blood-stained [1], bloodshed [+5477] [1], bloodshed [+9161] [1], bloodstains [1], death [1], destruction [1], do anything that endangers life [+6584+6641] [1], flow [1], guilt of murder [+5883] [1], guilty of blood [1], guilty of murder [1], innocent man [+5929] [1], it[s] [+2023+4946] [1], it[s] [+2257] [1], it[s] [1], killing [1], massacre [1], murder [1], murdering [1], other[s] [1], person[s] [1], shedding of blood [1]

Ge 4:10 Listen! Your brother's **blood** cries out to me from the ground.
4:11 which opened its mouth to receive your brother's **blood** from your
9: 4 "But you must not eat meat that has its **lifeblood** [+5883] still in it.
9: 5 for your **lifeblood** [+5883] I will surely demand an accounting.
9: 6 "Whoever sheds the **blood** *of* man, by man shall his blood be shed;
9: 6 "Whoever sheds the blood of man, by man shall his **blood** be shed;
37:22 "Don't shed any **blood**. Throw him into this cistern here in the
37:26 "What will we gain if we kill our brother and cover up his **blood**?
37:31 Joseph's robe, slaughtered a goat and dipped the robe in the **blood**.
42:22 wouldn't listen! Now we must give an accounting for his **blood**."
49:11 he will wash his garments in wine, his robes in the **blood** *of* grapes.
Ex 4: 9 The water you take from the river will become **blood** on the
4:25 with it. "Surely you are a bridegroom of **blood** to me," she said.
4:26 (At that time she said "bridegroom of **blood**," referring to
7:17 will strike the water of the Nile, and it will be changed into **blood**.
7:19 over the ponds and all the reservoirs'—and they will turn to **blood**.
7:19 **Blood** will be everywhere in Egypt, even in the wooden buckets
7:20 the water of the Nile, and all the water was changed into **blood**.
7:21 could not drink its water. **Blood** was everywhere in Egypt.
12: 7 Then they are to take some of the **blood** and put it on the sides
12:13 The **blood** will be a sign for you on the houses where you are;
12:13 where you are; and when I see the **blood**, I will pass over you.
12:22 dip it into the **blood** in the basin and put some of the blood on the
12:22 it into the blood in the basin and put some of the **blood** on the top
12:23 he will see the **blood** on the top and sides of the doorframe
22: 2 [22:1] so that he dies, the defender is not **guilty of bloodshed**;
22: 3 [22:2] if it happens after sunrise, he is **guilty of bloodshed**. "A
23:18 "Do not offer the **blood** *of* a sacrifice to me along with anything
24: 6 Moses took half of the **blood** and put it in bowls, and the other half
24: 6 and put it in bowls, and the **other**[s] half he sprinkled on the altar.
24: 8 Moses then took the **blood**, sprinkled it on the people and said,
24: 8 "This is the **blood** *of* the covenant that the LORD has made with
29:12 Take some of the bull's **blood** and put it on the horns of the altar
29:12 and pour out the rest of **it**[s] [+2021] at the base of the altar.
29:16 Slaughter it and take the **blood** and sprinkle it against the altar on
29:20 take some of its **blood** and put it on the lobes of the right ears of
29:20 their right feet. Then sprinkle **blood** against the altar on all sides.
29:21 take some of the **blood** on the altar and some of the anointing oil
30:10 This annual atonement must be made with the **blood** *of* the atoning
34:25 "Do not offer the **blood** *of* a sacrifice to me along with anything
Lev 1: 5 then Aaron's sons the priests shall bring the **blood** and sprinkle it
1: 5 sprinkle **it**[s] [+2021] against the altar on all sides at the entrance to
1:11 Aaron's sons the priests shall sprinkle its **blood** against the altar on
1:15 it on the altar; its **blood** shall be drained out on the side of the altar.
3: 2 Aaron's sons the priests shall sprinkle the **blood** against the altar
3: 8 Aaron's sons shall sprinkle its **blood** against the altar on all sides.
3:13 Aaron's sons shall sprinkle its **blood** against the altar on all sides.
3:17 wherever you live: You must not eat any fat or any **blood**.' "
4: 5 Then the anointed priest shall take some of the bull's **blood**
4: 6 He is to dip his finger into the **blood** and sprinkle some of it seven
4: 6 and sprinkle some of **it**[s] [+2021] seven times before the LORD,
4: 7 put some of the **blood** on the horns of the altar of fragrant incense
4: 7 The rest of the bull's **blood** he shall pour out at the base of the altar
4:16 the anointed priest is to take some of the bull's **blood** into the Tent
4:17 He shall dip his finger into the **blood** and sprinkle it before the
4:18 He is to put some of the **blood** on the horns of the altar that is

Lev 4:18 The rest of the **blood** he shall pour out at the base of the altar of
4:25 the priest shall take some of the **blood** *of* the sin offering with his
4:25 and pour out the rest of the **blood** at the base of the altar.
4:30 Then the priest is to take some of the **blood** with his finger
4:30 and pour out the rest of the **blood** at the base of the altar.
4:34 the priest shall take some of the **blood** *of* the sin offering with his
4:34 and pour out the rest of the **blood** at the base of the altar.
5: 9 is to sprinkle some of the **blood** *of* the sin offering against the side
5: 9 the rest of the **blood** must be drained out at the base of the altar.
6:27 [6:20] if any of the **blood** is spattered on a garment, you must
6:30 [6:23] any sin offering whose **blood** is brought into the Tent of
7: 2 and its **blood** is to be sprinkled against the altar on all sides.
7:14 it belongs to the priest who sprinkles the **blood** *of* the fellowship
7:26 you live, you must not eat the **blood** of any bird or animal.
7:27 If anyone eats **blood**, that person must be cut off from his
7:33 The son of Aaron who offers the **blood** and the fat of the
8:15 Moses slaughtered the bull and took *some of* the **blood**, and with
8:15 He poured out the rest of the **blood** at the base of the altar.
8:19 the ram and sprinkled the **blood** against the altar on all sides.
8:23 Moses slaughtered the ram and took some of its **blood** and put it on
8:24 and put some of the **blood** on the lobes of their right ears,
8:24 right feet. Then he sprinkled **blood** against the altar on all sides.
8:30 and some of the **blood** from the altar and sprinkled them on Aaron
9: 9 His sons brought the **blood** to him, and he dipped his finger into
9: 9 he dipped his finger into the **blood** and put it on the horns of the
9: 9 the rest of the **blood** he poured out at the base of the altar.
9:12 His sons handed him the **blood**, and he sprinkled it against the altar
9:18 His sons handed him the **blood**, and he sprinkled it against the altar
10:18 Since its **blood** was not taken into the Holy Place, you should have
12: 4 must wait thirty-three days to be purified from her **bleeding**.
12: 5 she must wait sixty-six days to be purified from her **bleeding**.
12: 7 then she will be ceremonially clean from her flow of **blood**.
14: 6 into the **blood** *of* the bird that was killed over the fresh water.
14:14 The priest is to take some of the **blood** *of* the guilt offering
14:17 big toe of his right foot, on top of the **blood** *of* the guilt offering.
14:25 slaughter the lamb for the guilt offering and take some of its **blood**
14:28 is to put on the same places he put the **blood** *of* the guilt offering—
14:51 dip them into the **blood** *of* the dead bird and the fresh water,
14:52 He shall purify the house with the bird's **blood**, the fresh water,
15:19 " 'When a woman has her regular flow of **blood**, the impurity of
15:25 " 'When a woman has a discharge of **blood** for many days at a time
16:14 He is to take some of the bull's **blood** and with his finger sprinkle
16:14 he shall sprinkle some of **it**[s] [+2021] with his finger seven times
16:15 take its **blood** behind the curtain and do with it as he did with the
16:15 the curtain and do with **it**[s] [+2257] as he did with the bull's blood:
16:15 behind the curtain and do with it as he did with the bull's **blood**:
16:18 He shall take some of the bull's **blood** and some of the goat's
16:18 and some of the goat's **blood** and put it on all the horns of the altar.
16:19 He shall sprinkle some of the **blood** on it with his finger seven
16:27 whose **blood** was brought into the Most Holy Place to make
17: 4 that man shall be considered **guilty of bloodshed**; he has shed
17: 4 he has shed **blood** and must be cut off from his people.
17: 6 The priest is to sprinkle the **blood** against the altar of the LORD
17:10 or any alien living among them who eats any **blood**—
17:10 I will set my face against that person who eats **blood** and will cut
17:11 For the life of a creature is in the **blood**, and I have given it to you
17:11 on the altar; it is the **blood** that makes atonement for one's life.
17:12 Therefore I say to the Israelites, "None of you may eat **blood**,
17:12 you may eat blood, nor may an alien living among you eat **blood**."
17:13 or bird that may be eaten must drain out the **blood** and cover it
17:14 because the life of every creature is its **blood**. That is why I have
17:14 said to the Israelites, "You must not eat the **blood** *of* any creature,
17:14 of any creature, because the life of every creature is its **blood**;
19:16 " '*Do* not **do anything that endangers** your neighbor's **life**
[+6584+6641].
19:26 " 'Do not eat any meat with the **blood** still in it. " 'Do not practice
20: 9 his father or his mother, and his **blood** will be on his own head.
20:11 must be put to death; their **blood** will be on their own heads.
20:12 have done is a perversion; their **blood** will be on their own heads.
20:13 They must be put to death; their **blood** will be on their own heads.
20:16 They must be put to death; their **blood** will be on their own heads.
20:18 he has exposed the source of her **flow**, and she has also uncovered
20:27 You are to stone them; their **blood** will be on their own heads.' "
Nu 18:17 Sprinkle their **blood** on the altar and burn their fat as an offering
19: 4 Then Eleazar the priest is to take some of its **blood** on his finger
19: 4 sprinkle **it**[s] [+2023+4946] seven times toward the front of the Tent
19: 5 the heifer is to be burned—its hide, flesh, **blood** and offal.
23:24 rest till he devours his prey and drinks the **blood** *of* his victims."
35:19 The avenger of **blood** shall put the murderer to death; when he
35:21 The avenger of **blood** shall put the murderer to death when he
35:24 and the avenger of **blood** according to these regulations.
35:25 must protect the one accused of murder from the avenger of **blood**
35:27 the avenger of **blood** finds him outside the city, the avenger of
35:27 the avenger of **blood** may kill the accused without being guilty of
35:27 of blood may kill the accused without being **guilty of murder**.
35:33 **Bloodshed** pollutes the land, and atonement cannot be made for
35:33 atonement cannot be made for the land on which **blood** has been
35:33 blood has been shed, except by the **blood** *of* the one who shed it.
Dt 12:16 you must not eat the **blood**; pour it out on the ground like water.
12:23 But be sure you do not eat the **blood**, because the blood is the life,
12:23 But be sure you do not eat the blood, because the **blood** is the life,
12:27 on the altar of the LORD your God, both the meat and the **blood**.
12:27 The **blood** *of* your sacrifices must be poured beside the altar of the
15:23 you must not eat the **blood**; pour it out on the ground like water.
17: 8 to judge—whether **bloodshed** [+1947+4200], lawsuits or assaults
17: 8 to judge—whether **bloodshed** [+1947+4200], lawsuits or assaults
19: 6 Otherwise, the avenger of **blood** might pursue him in a rage,
19:10 Do this so that innocent **blood** will not be shed in your land,
19:10 your inheritance, and so that you will not be **guilty of bloodshed**.
19:12 from the city, and hand him over to the avenger of **blood** to die.
19:13 You must purge from Israel the **guilt of shedding** innocent **blood**,
21: 7 "Our hands did not shed this **blood**, nor did our eyes see it done.
21: 8 do not hold your people **guilty of** *the* **blood** *of* an innocent man."
21: 8 blood of an innocent man." And the **bloodshed** will be atoned for.
21: 9 will purge from yourselves the **guilt of shedding** innocent **blood**,
22: 8 so that you may not bring the **guilt of bloodshed** on your house if
27:25 is the man who accepts a bribe to kill an innocent **person**[s]."
32:14 finest kernels of wheat. You drank the foaming **blood** *of* the grape.
32:42 I will make my arrows drunk with **blood**, while my sword devours
32:42 the **blood** *of* the slain and the captives, the heads of the enemy
32:43 with his people, for he will avenge the **blood** *of* his servants;
Jos 2:19 your house into the street, his **blood** will be on his own head;
2:19 with you, his **blood** will be on our head if a hand is laid on him.
20: 3 may flee there and find protection from the avenger of **blood**.
20: 5 If the avenger of **blood** pursues him, they must not surrender the
20: 9 not be killed by the avenger of **blood** prior to standing trial before
Jdg 9:24 the **shedding of** their **blood**, might be avenged on their brother
1Sa 14:32 them on the ground and ate them, together with the **blood**.
14:33 sinning against the LORD by eating meat that has **blood** in it."
14:34 Do not sin against the LORD by eating meat with **blood** still in
19: 5 would you do wrong to an **innocent man** [+5929] like David by
25:26 from **bloodshed** [+928+995] and from avenging yourself with your
25:31 conscience the staggering burden of needless **bloodshed** [+9161]
25:33 and for keeping me from **bloodshed** [+928+995] this day
26:20 Now do not let my **blood** fall to the ground far from the presence
2Sa 1:16 For David had said to him, "Your **blood** be on your own head.
1:22 From the **blood** *of* the slain, from the flesh of the mighty, the bow
3:27 there, to avenge the **blood** *of* his brother Asahel, Joab stabbed him
3:28 before the LORD concerning the **blood** *of* Abner son of Ner.
4:11 should I not now demand his **blood** from your hand and rid the
14:11 to prevent the avenger of **blood** from adding to the destruction,
16: 7 As he cursed, Shimei said, "Get out, get out, you man of **blood**,
16: 8 The LORD has repaid you for all the **blood** you **shed** *in* the
16: 8 You have come to ruin because you are a man of **blood**!"
20:12 Amasa lay wallowing in his **blood** in the middle of the road,
21: 1 "It is on account of Saul and his **blood-stained** house;
23:17 "Is it not the **blood** *of* men who went at the risk of their lives?"
1Ki 2: 5 He killed them, shedding their **blood** in peacetime *as if in* battle,
2: 5 with that **blood** stained the belt around his waist and the sandals on
2: 9 to do to him. Bring his gray head down to the grave in **blood**."
2:31 my father's house of the **guilt of** the innocent **blood** that Joab shed.
2:32 The LORD will repay him for the **blood** he shed, because without
2:33 May the **guilt of** their **blood** rest on the head of Joab and his
2:37 can be sure you will die; your **blood** will be on your own head."
18:28 and spears, as was their custom, until their **blood** flowed.
21:19 In the place where dogs licked up Naboth's **blood**, dogs will lick
21:19 dogs licked up Naboth's blood, dogs will lick up your **blood**—
22:35 The **blood** *from* his wound ran onto the floor of the chariot,
22:38 the dogs licked up his **blood**, as the word of the LORD had
2Ki 3:22 To the Moabites across the way, the water looked red—like **blood**.
3:23 "That's **blood**!" they said. "Those kings must have fought
9: 7 I will avenge the **blood** *of* my servants the prophets and the blood
9: 7 and the **blood** *of* all the LORD's servants shed by Jezebel.
9:26 'Yesterday I saw the **blood** *of* Naboth and the blood of his sons,
9:26 'Yesterday I saw the blood of Naboth and the **blood** *of* his sons,
9:33 some of her **blood** spattered the wall and the horses as they
16:13 and sprinkled the **blood** *of* his fellowship offerings on the altar.
16:15 Sprinkle on the altar all the **blood** *of* the burnt offerings
16:15 the altar all the blood of the burnt offerings and **[RPH]** sacrifices.
21:16 so much innocent **blood** that he filled Jerusalem from end to end—
24: 4 including the shedding of innocent **blood**. For he had filled
24: 4 For he had filled Jerusalem with innocent **blood**, and the LORD
1Ch 11:19 "Should I drink the **blood** *of* these men who went at the risk of
22: 8 to me: 'You have shed much **blood** and have fought many wars.
22: 8 because you have shed much **blood** on the earth in my sight.
28: 3 for my Name, because you are a warrior and have shed **blood**.'
2Ch 19:10 whether **bloodshed** [+1947+4200] or other concerns of the law,
19:10 whether **bloodshed** [+1947+4200] or other concerns of the law,

2Ch 24:25 His officials conspired against him for **murdering** the son of
29:22 and the priests took the **blood** and sprinkled it on the altar;
29:22 they slaughtered the rams and sprinkled their **blood** on the altar;
29:22 they slaughtered the lambs and sprinkled their **blood** on the altar.
29:24 presented their **blood** on the altar for a sin offering to atone for all
30:16 The priests sprinkled the **blood** handed to them by the Levites.
Job 16:18 "O earth, do not cover my **blood**; may my cry never be laid to rest!
39:30 His young ones feast on **blood**, and where the slain are, there is
Ps 5:6 [5:7] tell lies; **bloodthirsty** and deceitful men the LORD abhors.
9:12 [9:13] For he who avenges **blood** remembers; he does not ignore
16:4 I will not pour out their libations of **blood** or take up their names
26:9 away my soul along with sinners, my life with **bloodthirsty** men,
30:9 [30:10] "What gain is there in my **destruction**, in my going down
50:13 Do I eat the flesh of bulls or drink the **blood** *of* goats?
51:14 [51:16] Save me from **bloodguilt**, O God, the God who saves me,
55:23 [55:24] **bloodthirsty** and deceitful men will not live out half their
58:10 [58:11] when they bathe their feet in the **blood** *of* the wicked.
59:2 [59:3] me from evildoers and save me from **bloodthirsty** men.
68:23 [68:24] that you may plunge your feet in the **blood** of your foes,
72:14 and violence, for precious is their **blood** in his sight.
78:44 He turned their rivers to **blood**; they could not drink from their
79:3 They have poured out **blood** like water all around Jerusalem,
79:10 the nations that you avenge the outpoured **blood** *of* your servants.
94:21 together against the righteous and condemn the innocent to **death**.
105:29 He turned their waters into **blood**, causing their fish to die.
106:38 They shed innocent **blood**, the blood of their sons and daughters,
106:38 They shed innocent blood, the **blood** *of* their sons and daughters,
106:38 to the idols of Canaan, and the land was desecrated by their **blood**.
139:19 slay the wicked, O God! Away from me, you **bloodthirsty** men!
Pr 1:11 let's lie in wait for someone's **blood**, let's waylay some harmless
1:16 for their feet rush into sin, they are swift to shed **blood**.
1:18 These men lie in wait for their own **blood**; they waylay only
6:17 haughty eyes, a lying tongue, hands that shed innocent **blood**,
12:6 The words of the wicked lie in wait for **blood**, but the speech of the
28:17 A man tormented by the **guilt of murder** [+5883] will be a
29:10 **Bloodthirsty** men hate a man of integrity and seek to kill the
30:33 as twisting the nose produces **blood**, so stirring up anger produces
Isa 1:11 I have no pleasure in the **blood** *of* bulls and lambs and goats.
1:15 offer many prayers, I will not listen. Your hands are full of **blood**;
4:4 he will cleanse the **bloodstains** from Jerusalem by a spirit of
9:5 [9:4] every garment rolled in **blood** will be destined for burning,
15:9 Dimon's waters are full of **blood**, but I will bring still more upon
26:21 The earth will disclose the **blood** *shed upon* her; she will conceal
33:15 who stops his ears against plots of **murder** and shuts his eyes
34:3 send up a stench; the mountains will be soaked with their **blood**.
34:6 The sword of the LORD is bathed in **blood**, it is covered with
34:6 the **blood** *of* lambs and goats, fat from the kidneys of rams.
34:7 Their land will be drenched with **blood**, and the dust will be
49:26 own flesh; they will be drunk on their own **blood**, as with wine.
59:3 For your hands are stained with **blood**, your fingers with guilt.
59:7 Their feet rush into sin; they are swift to shed innocent **blood**.
66:3 makes a grain offering is like one who presents pig's **blood**,
Jer 2:34 On your clothes men find the **lifeblood of** [+5883] the innocent
7:6 or the widow and do not shed innocent **blood** in this place,
19:4 and they have filled this place with the **blood** *of* the innocent.
22:3 or the widow, and do not shed innocent **blood** in this place.
22:17 on shedding innocent **blood** and on oppression and extortion."
26:15 you will bring the **guilt of** innocent **blood** on yourselves and on
46:10 devour till it is satisfied, till it has quenched its thirst with **blood**.
48:10 A curse on him who keeps his sword from **bloodshed**!
51:35 "May our **blood** be on those who live in Babylonia,"
La 4:13 of her priests, who shed within her the **blood** *of* the righteous.
4:14 so defiled with **blood** that no one dares to touch their garments.
Eze 3:18 will die for his sin, and I will hold you accountable for his **blood**.
3:20 not be remembered, and I will hold you accountable for his **blood**.
5:17 Plague and **bloodshed** will sweep through you, and I will bring the
7:23 because the land is full of **bloodshed** [+5477] and the city is full of
9:9 the land is full of **bloodshed** and the city is full of injustice.
14:19 into that land and pour out my wrath upon it through **bloodshed**,
16:6 " 'Then I passed by and saw you kicking about in your **blood**,
16:6 and as you lay there in your **blood** I said to you, "Live!"
16:6 and as you lay there in your blood I said to you, "Live!" [BHS+ *And as you lay there in your blood*]
16:9 " 'I bathed you with water and washed the **blood** from you
16:22 when you were naked and bare, kicking about in your **blood**.
16:36 detestable idols, and because you gave them your children's **blood**,
16:38 punishment of women who commit adultery and who shed **blood**;
16:38 I will bring upon you the **blood vengeance** *of* my wrath
18:10 a violent son, who sheds **blood** or does any of these other things
18:13 will surely be put to death and his **blood** will be on his own head.
19:10 mother was like a vine in your vineyard [BHS ***blood***; NIV 4142]
21:32 [21:37] be fuel for the fire, your **blood** will be shed in your land,
22:2 will you judge her? Will you judge this city of **bloodshed**?
22:3 O city that brings on herself doom by shedding **blood** in her midst
22:4 you have become guilty because of the **blood** you have shed
22:6 the princes of Israel who are in you uses his power to shed **blood**.
22:9 In you are slanderous men bent on shedding **blood**; in you are
22:12 In you men accept bribes to shed **blood**; you take usury
22:13 gain you have made and at the **blood** you have shed in your midst.
22:27 their prey; they shed **blood** and kill people to make unjust gain.
23:37 for they have committed adultery and **blood** is on their hands.
23:45 to the punishment of women who commit adultery and shed **blood**,
23:45 because they are adulterous and **blood** is on their hands.
24:6 " 'Woe to the city of **bloodshed**, to the pot now encrusted,
24:7 " 'For the **blood** she shed is in her midst: She poured it on the bare
24:8 To stir up wrath and take revenge I put her **blood** on the bare rock,
24:9 " 'Woe to the city of **bloodshed**! I, too, will pile the wood high.
28:23 I will send a plague upon her and make **blood** flow in her streets.
32:6 I will drench the land with your flowing **blood** all the way to the
33:4 sword comes and takes his life, his **blood** will be on his own head.
33:5 but did not take warning, his **blood** will be on his own head.
33:6 of his sin, but I will hold the watchman accountable for his **blood**.'
33:8 will die for his sin, and I will hold you accountable for his **blood**.
33:25 Since you eat meat with the **blood** still in it and look to your idols
33:25 with the blood still in it and look to your idols and shed **blood**,
35:6 I will give you over to **bloodshed** and it will pursue you.
35:6 I will give you over to bloodshed and **it**[s] will pursue you.
35:6 Since you did not hate **bloodshed**, bloodshed will pursue you.
35:6 Since you did not hate bloodshed, **bloodshed** will pursue you.
36:18 out my wrath on them because they had shed **blood** in the land and
38:22 I will execute judgment upon him with plague and **bloodshed**;
39:17 the mountains of Israel. There you will eat flesh and drink **blood**.
39:18 and drink the **blood** *of* the princes of the earth as if they were rams
39:19 will eat fat till you are glutted and drink **blood** till you are drunk.
43:18 burnt offerings and sprinkling **blood** upon the altar when it is built:
43:20 You are to take some of its **blood** and put it on the four horns of
44:7 you offered me food, fat and **blood**, and you broke my covenant.
44:15 they are to stand before me to offer sacrifices of fat and **blood**,
45:19 The priest is to take some of the **blood** *of* the sin offering and put it
Hos 1:4 because I will soon punish the house of Jehu for the **massacre** *at*
4:2 they break all bounds, and **bloodshed** follows bloodshed.
4:2 they break all bounds, and bloodshed follows **bloodshed**.
6:8 Gilead is a city of wicked men, stained with footprints of **blood**.
12:14 [12:15] his Lord will leave upon him the **guilt of** his **bloodshed**
Joel 2:30 [3:3] and on the earth, **blood** and fire and billows of smoke.
2:31 [3:4] the moon to **blood** before the coming of the great
3:19 [4:19] people of Judah, in whose land they shed innocent **blood**.
3:21 [4:21] Their **bloodguilt**, which I have not pardoned, I will
Jnh 1:14 Do not hold us accountable for **killing** an innocent man, for you,
Mic 3:10 who build Zion with **bloodshed**, and Jerusalem with wickedness.
7:2 All men lie in wait to shed **blood**; each hunts his brother with a net.
Na 3:1 Woe to the city of **blood**, full of lies, full of plunder, never without
Hab 2:8 For you have shed man's **blood**; you have destroyed lands
2:12 "Woe to him who builds a city with **bloodshed** and establishes a
2:17 For you have shed man's **blood**; you have destroyed lands
Zep 1:17 Their **blood** will be poured out like dust and their entrails like filth.
Zec 9:7 I will take the **blood** from their mouths, the forbidden food from
9:11 As for you, because of the **blood** *of* my covenant with you,

1948 דָּמָה I ***dāmâ***[1], v. [29] [→ 1952, 1953, 1955; Ar 10179] compare [4], compared [3], is like [3], be like [2], am like [1], are like [1], been like [1], equal [1], intending [1], intends [1], like [1], liken [1], make myself like [1], match [1], meditate [1], plan [1], planned [1], plotted [1], think [1], thought [1], told parables [1]

Nu 33:56 [D] And then I will do to you what *I* **plan** to do to them.' "
Jdg 20:5 [D] after me and surrounded the house, **intending** to kill me.
2Sa 21:5 [D] and **plotted** against us so that we have been decimated
Est 4:13 [D] "*Do* not **think** that because you are in the king's house you
Ps 48:9 [48:10] [D] O God, *we* **meditate** *on* your unfailing love.
50:21 [D] and I kept silent; *you* **thought** I was altogether like you.
89:6 [89:7] [A] *Who* **is like** the LORD among the heavenly beings?
102:6 [102:7] [A] *I* **am like** a desert owl, like an owl among the ruins.
144:4 [A] Man *is* **like** a breath; his days are like a fleeting shadow.
SS 1:9 [D] *I* **liken** you, my darling, to a mare harnessed to one of the
2:9 [A] My lover **is like** a gazelle or a young stag. Look! There he
2:17 [A] and **be like** a gazelle or like a young stag on the rugged hills.
7:7 [7:8] [A] stature **is like** that of the palm, and your breasts like
8:14 [A] **be like** a gazelle or like a young stag on the spice-laden
Isa 1:9 [A] become like Sodom, *we would have* **been like** Gomorrah.
10:7 [D] this is not what *he* **intends**, this is not what he has in mind;
14:14 [F] tops of the clouds; *I will* **make myself like** the Most High."
14:24 [D] "Surely, as *I have* **planned**, so it will be, and as I have
40:18 [D] To whom, then, *will you* **compare** God? What image will
40:25 [D] "To whom *will you* **compare** me? Or who is my equal?"
46:5 [D] "To whom *will you* **compare** me or count me equal? To
46:5 [A] To whom will you liken me that *we may be* **compared**?
La 2:13 [D] With what *can I* **compare** you, O Daughter of Jerusalem?

Eze 31: 2 [A] to his hordes: " 'Who *can be* **compared** with *you* in majesty?
31: 8 [A] could not rival it, nor *could* the pine trees **equal** its boughs,
31: 8 [A] no tree in the garden of God *could* **match** its beauty.
31: 18 [A] " 'Which of the trees of Eden *can be* **compared** with *you* in
32: 2 [C] " '*You* **are like** a lion among the nations; you are like a
Hos 12: 10 [12:11] [D] many visions and **told parables** through them."

1949 ²דָּמָה **dāmâ²**, v. [4] [→ 1950, 1951?, 1954; cf. 1875, 1957, 1958]

be silenced [1], ceasing [1], silence [1], unceasingly [+4202] [1]

Jer 14: 17 [A] my eyes overflow with tears night and day without **ceasing**;
47: 5 [C] will shave her head in mourning; Ashkelon *will* **be silenced**.
La 2: 10 [A] elders of the Daughter of Zion sit on the ground *in* **silence**;
3: 49 [A] My eyes will flow **unceasingly** [+4202], without relief,

1950 ³דָּמָה **dāmâ³**, v. [13] [√ 1949]

ruined [3], be completely destroyed [+1950] [2], destroy [2], perish [2], are destroyed [1], be wiped out [1], disaster awaits [1], float away [1]

Ps 49: 12 [49:13] [C] does not endure; he is like the beasts *that* **perish**.
49: 20 [49:21] [C] without understanding is like the beasts *that* **perish**.
Isa 6: 5 [C] "Woe to me!" I cried. "*I am* **ruined**! For I am a man of
15: 1 [C] Ar in Moab *is* **ruined**, destroyed in a night! Kir in Moab is
15: 1 [C] in a night! Kir in Moab *is* **ruined**, destroyed in a night!
Jer 6: 2 [A] *I will* **destroy** the Daughter of Zion, so beautiful
Hos 4: 5 [A] prophets stumble with you. So *I will* **destroy** your mother—
4: 6 [C] my people **are destroyed** from lack of knowledge.
10: 7 [C] its king *will* **float away** like a twig on the surface of the
10: 15 [C] the king of Israel *will* **be completely destroyed** [+1950].
10: 15 [C] the king of Israel *will* **be completely destroyed** [+1950].
Ob 1: 5 [C] if robbers in the night—Oh, what a **disaster awaits** *you*—
Zep 1: 11 [C] all your merchants *will* **be wiped out**, all who trade with

1951 ³דּוּמָה **dumâ**, n.f. [1] [√ 1949?]

silenced [1]

Eze 27: 32 "Who was ever **silenced** like Tyre, surrounded by the sea?"

1952 דְּמוּת **dᵉmût**, n.f. [25] [√ 1948]

likeness [5], like [4], looked like [4], looked [3], figure [2], *untranslated* [1], appearance [1], figures [1], form [1], image [1], like [+3869] [1], sketch [1]

Ge 1: 26 Then God said, "Let us make man in our image, in our **likeness**,
5: 1 When God created man, he made him in the **likeness** *of* God.
5: 3 130 years, he had a son in his own **likeness**, in his own image;
2Ki 16: 10 altar in Damascus and sent to Uriah the priest a **sketch** *of* the altar,
2Ch 4: 3 Below the rim, **figures** *of* bulls encircled it—ten to a cubit.
Ps 58: 4 [58:5] Their venom is **like** [+3869] the venom of a snake, like that
Isa 13: 4 Listen, a noise on the mountains, **like** *that of* a great multitude!
40: 18 will you compare God? What **image** will you compare him to?
Eze 1: 5 and in the fire was *what* **looked like** four living creatures.
1: 5 four living creatures. In appearance their **form** was that of a man,
1: 10 Their faces **looked like** this: Each of the four had the face of a
1: 13 The appearance of the living creatures was **like** burning coals of
1: 16 They sparkled like chrysolite, and all four **looked** alike.
1: 22 the heads of the living creatures was *what* **looked like** an expanse,
1: 26 Above the expanse over their heads was what looked **like** a throne
1: 26 high above on **[RPH]** the throne was a figure like that of a man.
1: 26 and high above on the throne was a **figure** like that of a man.
1: 28 This was the appearance of the **likeness** *of* the glory of the
8: 2 I looked, and I saw a **figure** like that of a man. From what
10: 1 I saw the **likeness** *of* a throne of sapphire above the expanse that
10: 10 As for their appearance, the four of them **looked** alike; each was
10: 21 and under their wings was *what* **looked like** the hands of a man.
10: 22 Their faces had the same **appearance** as those I had seen by the
23: 15 all of them looked **like** Babylonian chariot officers, natives of
Da 10: 16 one who **looked** like a man touched my lips, and I opened my

1953 דְּמִי **dᵉmî**, n.[m.]. [1] [√ 1948]

prime [1]

Isa 38: 10 "In the **prime** *of* my life must I go through the gates of death

1954 דֳּמִי **dᵒmî**, n.[m.]. [3] [√ 1949]

rest [2], silent [1]

Ps 83: 1 [83:2] O God, do not keep **silent**; be not quiet, O God, be not still.
Isa 62: 6 or night. You who call on the LORD, give yourselves no **rest**,
62: 7 give him no **rest** till he establishes Jerusalem and makes her the

1955 דִּמְיוֹן **dimyôn**, n.[m.]. [1] [√ 1948]

like [1]

Ps 17: 12 They are **like** a lion hungry for prey, like a great lion crouching in

1956 דַּמִּים **dammîm**, n.pr.loc. Not used in NIV/BHS [→ 702, 7169; cf. 1947?]

1957 ¹דָּמַם **dāmam¹**, v. [25] [→ 1872, 1875, 1960; cf. 1876, 1949, 1959]

silent [6], be silenced [3], be still [2], ceasing [1], find rest [1], keeps quiet [1], quieted [1], quietly [1], rest [1], silence [1], silenced [1], stand still [1], still [1], stood still [1], stops [1], wait [1], waiting in silence [1]

Ex 15: 16 [A] By the power of your arm *they will be* as **still** as a stone—
Lev 10: 3 [A] of all the people I will be honored.' " Aaron *remained* **silent**.
Jos 10: 12 [A] "O sun, **stand still** over Gibeon, O moon, over the Valley of
10: 13 [A] So the sun **stood still**, and the moon stopped, till the nation
1Sa 2: 9 [C] feet of his saints, but the wicked *will* **be silenced** in darkness.
14: 9 [A] If they say to us, '**Wait** there until we come to you,' we will
Job 29: 21 [A] to me expectantly, **waiting in silence** for my counsel.
30: 27 [A] The churning inside me never **stops**; days of suffering
31: 34 [A] and so dreaded the contempt of the clans that *I kept* **silent**
Ps 4: 4 [4:5] [A] you are on your beds, search your hearts and *be* **silent**.
30: 12 [30:13] [A] that my heart may sing to you and not *be* **silent**.
31: 17 [31:18] [A] wicked be put to shame and *lie* **silent** in the grave.
35: 15 [A] me when I was unaware. They slandered me without **ceasing**.
37: 7 [A] **Be still** before the LORD and wait patiently for him; do not
62: 5 [62:6] [A] **Find rest**, O my soul, in God alone; my hope comes
131: 2 [D] I have stilled and **quieted** my soul; like a weaned child with
Isa 23: 2 [A] *Be* **silent**, *you* people of the island and you merchants of
Jer 47: 6 [A] till you rest? Return to your scabbard; cease and **be still**.'
48: 2 [A] *You* too, O Madmen, *will be* **silenced**; the sword will pursue
49: 26 [C] all her soldiers *will* **be silenced** in that day,"
50: 30 [C] all her soldiers *will* **be silenced** in that day,"
La 2: 18 [A] river day and night; give yourself no relief, your eyes no **rest**.
3: 28 [A] Let him sit alone *in* **silence**, for the LORD has laid it on
Eze 24: 17 [A] Groan **quietly**; do not mourn for the dead. Keep your turban
Am 5: 13 [A] Therefore the prudent man **keeps quiet** in such times,

1958 ²דָּמַם **dāmam²**, v. Not used in NIV/BHS [cf. 1949]

1959 ³דָּמַם **dāmam³**, v. [4] [cf. 1957]

be destroyed [1], doomed to perish [1], perish [1], will be laid waste [1]

Jer 8: 14 [A] Let us flee to the fortified cities and **perish** there!
8: 14 [G] For the LORD our God *has* **doomed** us **to perish** and given
25: 37 [C] The peaceful meadows **will be laid waste** because of the
51: 6 [C] Run for your lives! *Do* not **be destroyed** because of her sins.

1960 דְּמָמָה **dᵉmāmâ**, n.f. [3] [√ 1957]

hushed [1], whisper [+7754] [1], whisper [1]

1Ki 19: 12 not in the fire. And after the fire came a gentle **whisper** [+7754].
Job 4: 16 A form stood before my eyes, and I heard a **hushed** voice:
Ps 107: 29 He stilled the storm to a **whisper**; the waves of the sea were

1961 דֹּמֶן **dōmen**, n.m. [6] [→ 4523]

refuse [6]

2Ki 9: 37 Jezebel's body will be like **refuse** on the ground in the plot at
Ps 83: 10 [83:11] perished at Endor and became like **refuse** on the ground.
Jer 8: 2 gathered up or buried, but will be like **refuse** lying on the ground.
9: 22 [9:21] " 'The dead bodies of men will lie like **refuse** on the open
16: 4 be mourned or buried but will be like **refuse** lying on the ground.
25: 33 gathered up or buried, but will be like **refuse** lying on the ground.

1962 דִּמְנָה **dimnâ**, n.pr.loc. [1]

Dimnah [1]

Jos 21: 35 **Dimnah** and Nahalal, together with their pasturelands—

1963 דָּמַע **dāma'**, v. [2] [→ 1964, 1965]

weep bitterly [+1963] [2]

Jer 13: 17 [A] my eyes *will* **weep** [+1963] **bitterly**, overflowing with tears,
13: 17 [A] my eyes *will* **weep bitterly** [+1963], overflowing with tears,

1964 דֶּמַע **dema'**, n.[m.]. [1] [√ 1963]

vats [1]

Ex 22: 29 [22:28] not hold back offerings from your granaries or your **vats**.

1965 דִּמְעָה dim'â, n.f. [23] [√ 1963]

tears [21], weeping [2]

2Ki 20: 5 I have heard your prayer and seen your **tears**; I will heal you.
Ps 6: 6 [6:7] my bed with weeping and drench my couch with **tears**.
39: 12 [39:13] listen to my cry for help; be not deaf to my **weeping**.
42: 3 [42:4] My **tears** have been my food day and night, while men say
56: 8 [56:9] Record my lament; list my **tears** on your scroll—are they
80: 5 [80:6] You have fed them with the bread of **tears**; you have made
80: 5 [80:6] of tears; you have made them drink **tears** by the bowlful.
116: 8 my soul from death, my eyes from **tears**, my feet from stumbling,
126: 5 Those who sow in **tears** will reap with songs of joy.
Ecc 4: 1 I saw the **tears** *of* the oppressed—and they have no comforter;
Isa 16: 9 vines of Sibmah. O Heshbon, O Elealeh, I drench you with **tears**!
25: 8 The Sovereign LORD will wipe away the **tears** from all faces;
38: 5 I have heard your prayer and seen your **tears**; I will add fifteen
Jer 9: 1 [8:23] were a spring of water and my eyes a fountain of **tears**!
9: 18 [9:17] and wail over us till our eyes overflow with **tears**
13: 17 my eyes will weep bitterly, overflowing with **tears**,
14: 17 " 'Let my eyes overflow with **tears** night and day without ceasing;
31: 16 "Restrain your voice from weeping and your eyes from **tears**,
La 1: 2 Bitterly she weeps at night, **tears** are upon her cheeks. Among all
2: 11 My eyes fail from **weeping**, I am in torment within, my heart is
2: 18 the Daughter of Zion, let your **tears** flow like a river day and night;
Eze 24: 16 delight of your eyes. Yet do not lament or weep or shed any **tears**.
Mal 2: 13 You flood the LORD's altar with **tears**. You weep and wail

1966 דַּמֶּשֶׂק dammeśeq, n.pr.loc. [38 / 39] [→ 1877, 1967?, 2008]

Damascus [37], *untranslated* [2]

Ge 14: 15 routed them, pursuing them as far as Hobah, north of **Damascus**.
15: 2 and the one who will inherit my estate is Eliezer *of* **Damascus**?"
2Sa 8: 5 When the Arameans of **Damascus** came to help Hadadezer king of
8: 6 He put garrisons in the Aramean kingdom of **Damascus**,
1Ki 11: 24 the rebels went to **Damascus**, where they settled and took control.
11: 24 went to Damascus, where they settled and took control. **[RPH]**
15: 18 the son of Hezion, the king of Aram, who was ruling in **Damascus**.
19: 15 "Go back the way you came, and go to the Desert of **Damascus**.
20: 34 "You may set up your own market areas in **Damascus**, as my
2Ki 5: 12 Are not Abana and Pharpar, the rivers of **Damascus**, better than
8: 7 Elisha went to **Damascus**, and Ben-Hadad king of Aram was ill.
8: 9 him as a gift forty camel-loads of all the finest wares of **Damascus**.
14: 28 including how he recovered for Israel both **Damascus** and Hamath,
16: 9 The king of Assyria complied by attacking **Damascus**
16: 10 He saw an altar in **Damascus** and sent to Uriah the priest a sketch
16: 11 with all the plans that King Ahaz had sent from **Damascus**
16: 11 and finished it before King Ahaz returned. **[RPH]**
16: 12 When the king came back from **Damascus** and saw the altar,
SS 7: 4 [7:5] is like the tower of Lebanon looking toward **Damascus**.
Isa 7: 8 for the head of Aram is **Damascus**, and the head of Damascus is
7: 8 of Aram is Damascus, and the head of **Damascus** is only Rezin.
8: 4 the wealth of **Damascus** and the plunder of Samaria will be carried
10: 9 Is not Hamath like Arpad, and Samaria like **Damascus**?
17: 1 An oracle concerning **Damascus**: "See, Damascus will no longer
17: 1 **Damascus** will no longer be a city but will become a heap of ruins.
17: 3 will disappear from Ephraim, and royal power from **Damascus**;
Jer 49: 23 Concerning **Damascus**: "Hamath and Arpad are dismayed,
49: 24 **Damascus** has become feeble, she has turned to flee and panic has
49: 27 "I will set fire to the walls of **Damascus**; it will consume the
Eze 27: 18 " '**Damascus**, because of your many products and great wealth of
47: 16 and Sibraim (which lies on the border between **Damascus**
47: 17 along the northern border of **Damascus**, with the border of Hamath
47: 18 east side the boundary will run between Hauran and **Damascus**,
48: 1 the northern border of **Damascus** next to Hamath will be part of its
Am 1: 3 "For three sins of **Damascus**, even for four, I will not turn back
1: 5 I will break down the gate of **Damascus**; I will destroy the king
3: 12 of their beds and in **Damascus** [BHS 1967] on their couches."
5: 27 Therefore I will send you into exile beyond **Damascus**,"
Zec 9: 1 is against the land of Hadrach and will rest upon **Damascus**—

1967 דְּמֶשֶׁק d^e^mešeq, n.[m.?]. [1 / 0] [√ 1966?]

Am 3: 12 and in Damascus [BHS *Damascus*?; NIV 1966] on their couches."

1968 דָּן dān[1], n.pr.m. [50] [→ 1970, 1974; cf. 1906]

Dan [33], Danites [+1201] [9], Dan [+1201] [4], *untranslated* [1], Danite [+4200+4751] [1], Danites [1], they[s] [+1201] [1]

Ge 30: 6 and given me a son." Because of this she named him **Dan**.
35: 25 The sons of Rachel's maidservant Bilhah: **Dan** and Naphtali.
46: 23 The son of **Dan**: Hushim.
49: 16 "**Dan** will provide justice for his people as one of the tribes of
49: 17 **Dan** will be a serpent by the roadside, a viper along the path,
Ex 1: 4 **Dan** and Naphtali; Gad and Asher.
31: 6 Oholiab son of Ahisamach, of the tribe of **Dan**, to help him.
35: 34 son of Ahisamach, of the tribe of **Dan**, the ability to teach others.
38: 23 with him was Oholiab son of Ahisamach, of the tribe of **Dan**—
Lev 24: 11 was Shelomith, the daughter of Dibri the **Danite** [+4200+4751].)
Nu 1: 12 from **Dan**, Ahiezer son of Ammishaddai;
1: 38 From the descendants of **Dan**: All the men twenty years old
1: 39 The number from the tribe of **Dan** was 62,700.
2: 25 On the north will be the divisions of the camp of **Dan**, under their
2: 25 The leader of the people of **Dan** is Ahiezer son of Ammishaddai.
2: 31 All the men assigned to the camp of **Dan** number 157,600.
7: 66 the leader of the people of **Dan**, brought his offering.
10: 25 the divisions of the camp of **Dan** [+1201] set out, under their
13: 12 from the tribe of **Dan**, Ammiel son of Gemalli;
26: 42 These were the descendants of **Dan** by their clans:
26: 42 the Shuhamite clan. These were the clans of **Dan**:
34: 22 Bukki son of Jogli, the leader from the tribe of **Dan** [+1201];
Dt 27: 13 Reuben, Gad, Asher, Zebulun, **Dan** and Naphtali.
33: 22 About **Dan** he said: "Dan is a lion's cub, springing out of Bashan."
33: 22 About Dan he said: "**Dan** is a lion's cub, springing out of Bashan."
34: 1 the LORD showed him the whole land—from Gilead to **Dan**,
Jos 19: 40 The seventh lot came out for the tribe of **Dan** [+1201], clan by
19: 47 (But the **Danites** [+1201] had difficulty taking possession of their
19: 47 so **they**[s] [+1201] went up and attacked Leshem, took it, put it to
19: 47 in Leshem and named it Dan after their forefather.) **[RPH]**
19: 48 and their villages were the inheritance of the tribe of **Dan** [+1201],
21: 5 from the clans of the tribes of Ephraim, **Dan** and half of Manasseh.
21: 23 Also from the tribe of **Dan** they received Eltekeh, Gibbethon,
Jdg 1: 34 The Amorites confined the **Danites** [+1201] to the hill country,
5: 17 **Dan**, why did he linger by the ships? Asher remained on the coast
18: 2 So the **Danites** [+1201] sent five warriors from Zorah and Eshtaol
18: 16 The six hundred **Danites** [+1201], armed for battle, stood at the
18: 22 Micah were called together and overtook the **Danites** [+1201].
18: 23 shouted after them, the **Danites** [+1201] turned and said to Micah,
18: 25 The **Danites** [+1201] answered, "Don't argue with us, or some
18: 26 So the **Danites** [+1201] went their way, and Micah, seeing that
18: 29 They named it Dan after their forefather **Dan**, who was born to
18: 30 There the **Danites** [+1201] set up for themselves the idols,
1Ch 2: 2 **Dan**, Joseph, Benjamin, Naphtali, Gad and Asher.
27: 22 over **Dan**: Azarel son of Jeroham. These were the officers over the
2Ch 2: 14 [2:13] whose mother was from **Dan** and whose father was from
Eze 27: 19 " '**Danites** and Greeks from Uzal bought your merchandise;
48: 1 At the northern frontier, **Dan** will have one portion; it will follow
48: 2 one portion; it will border the territory of **Dan** from east to west.
48: 32 the gate of Joseph, the gate of Benjamin and the gate of **Dan**.

1969 דָּן dān[2], n.pr.loc. [20] [√ 1906]

Dan [20]

Ge 14: 14 men born in his household and went in pursuit as far as **Dan**.
Jos 19: 47 They settled in Leshem and named it **Dan** after their forefather.)
Jdg 18: 29 They named it **Dan** after their forefather Dan, who was born to
20: 1 all the Israelites from **Dan** to Beersheba and from the land of
1Sa 3: 20 all Israel from **Dan** to Beersheba recognized that Samuel was
2Sa 3: 10 David's throne over Israel and Judah from **Dan** to Beersheba."
17: 11 Let all Israel, from **Dan** to Beersheba—as numerous as the sand on
24: 2 "Go throughout the tribes of Israel from **Dan** to Beersheba
24: 15 and seventy thousand of the people from **Dan** to Beersheba died.
1Ki 4: 25 [5:5] lifetime Judah and Israel, from **Dan** to Beersheba,
12: 29 One he set up in Bethel, and the other in **Dan**.
12: 30 the people went even as far as **Dan** to worship the one there.
15: 20 **Dan**, Abel Beth Maacah and all Kinnereth in addition to Naphtali.
2Ki 10: 29 to commit—the worship of the golden calves at Bethel and **Dan**.
1Ch 21: 2 of the troops, "Go and count the Israelites from Beersheba to **Dan**.
2Ch 16: 4 **Dan**, Abel Maim and all the store cities of Naphtali.
30: 5 from Beersheba to **Dan**, calling the people to come to Jerusalem
Jer 4: 15 A voice is announcing from **Dan**, proclaiming disaster from the
8: 16 The snorting of the enemy's horses is heard from **Dan**; at the
Am 8: 14 or say, 'As surely as your god lives, O **Dan**,' or, 'As surely as the

1970 דָּן יַעַן dān ya'an, n.pr.loc. [1] [√ 1968 + 3611]

Dan Jaan [1]

2Sa 24: 6 of Tahtim Hodshi, and on to **Dan Jaan** and around toward Sidon.

1971 דָּנִאֵל dāni'ēl, n.pr.m. [0] [√ 1906 + 446]

Eze 14: 14 [Noah, **Daniel** [K; see Q 1975] and Job—were in it, they could]
14: 20 [even if Noah, **Daniel** [K; see Q 1975] and Job were in it,]
28: 3 [Are you wiser than **Daniel**? [K; see Q 1975] Is no secret hidden]

1972 דַּנָּה dannâ, n.pr.loc. [1] [→ 4527]

Dannah [1]

Jos 15: 49 **Dannah**, Kiriath Sannah (that is, Debir),

1973 דִּנְהָבָה *dinhābâ*, n.pr.loc. [2] [√ 1896 + 5649]

Dinhabah [2]

Ge 36:32 son of Beor became king of Edom. His city was named **Dinhabah**.
1Ch 1:43 king reigned: Bela son of Beor, whose city was named **Dinhabah**.

1974 דָּנִי *dānî*, a.g. [5] [√ 1968]

Danites [3], Dan [1], men of Dan [1]

Jdg 13: 2 man of Zorah, named Manoah, from the clan of the **Danites**,
18: 1 in those days the tribe of the **Danites** was seeking a place of their
18:11 six hundred men from the clan of the **Danites**, armed for battle,
18:30 his sons were priests for the tribe of **Dan** until the time of the
1Ch 12:35 [12:36] **men of Dan**, ready for battle—28,600;

1975 דָּנִיֵּאל *dāniyyē'l*, n.pr.m. [29] [√ 1906 + 446; Ar 10181]

Daniel [29]

1Ch 3: 1 of Jezreel; the second, **Daniel** the son of Abigail of Carmel;
Ezr 8: 2 of Phinehas, Gershom; of the descendants of Ithamar, **Daniel**;
Ne 10: 6 [10:7] **Daniel**, Ginnethon, Baruch,
Eze 14:14 Noah, **Daniel** [K 1971] and Job—were in it, they could save only
14:20 even if Noah, **Daniel** [K 1971] and Job were in it,
28: 3 Are you wiser than **Daniel**? [K 1971] Is no secret hidden from
Da 1: 6 were some from Judah: **Daniel**, Hananiah, Mishael and Azariah.
1: 7 to **Daniel**, the name Belteshazzar; to Hananiah, Shadrach;
1: 8 But **Daniel** resolved not to defile himself with the royal food
1: 9 God had caused the official to show favor and sympathy to **Daniel**,
1:10 but the official told **Daniel**, "I am afraid of my lord the king,
1:11 **Daniel** then said to the guard whom the chief official had
1:11 to the guard whom the chief official had appointed over **Daniel**,
1:17 And **Daniel** could understand visions and dreams of all kinds.
1:19 he found none equal to **Daniel**, Hananiah, Mishael and Azariah;
1:21 And **Daniel** remained there until the first year of King Cyrus.
8: 1 the third year of King Belshazzar's reign, I, **Daniel**, had a vision,
8:15 While I, **Daniel**, was watching the vision and trying to understand
8:27 I, **Daniel**, was exhausted and lay ill for several days. Then I got up
9: 2 in the first year of his reign, I, **Daniel**, understood from the
9:22 He instructed me and said to me, "**Daniel**, I have now come to give
10: 1 a revelation was given to **Daniel** (who was called Belteshazzar).
10: 2 At that time I, **Daniel**, mourned for three weeks.
10: 7 I, **Daniel**, was the only one who saw the vision; the men with me
10:11 He said, "**Daniel**, you who are highly esteemed, consider carefully
10:12 he continued, "Do not be afraid, **Daniel**. Since the first day that
12: 4 **Daniel**, close up and seal the words of the scroll until the time of
12: 5 Then I, **Daniel**, looked, and there before me stood two others,
12: 9 He replied, "Go your way, **Daniel**, because the words are closed up

1976 דֵּעַ *dēa'*, n.[m.]. [5] [→ 1978; cf. 3359]

what know [3], knowledge [2]

Job 32: 6 that is why I was fearful, not daring to tell you **what I know**.
32:10 "Therefore I say: Listen to me; I too will tell you **what I know**.
32:17 I too will have my say; I too will tell **what I know**.
36: 3 I get my **knowledge** from afar; I will ascribe justice to my Maker.
37:16 hang poised, those wonders of him who is perfect in **knowledge**?

1977 דָּעָה *dā'â*, v. Not used in NIV/BHS [→ 456]

1978 דֵּעָה *dē'â*, n.f. [6] [√ 1976; cf. 3359]

knowledge [4], knows [1], teach [+906+3723] [1]

1Sa 2: 3 for the LORD is a God who **knows**, and by him deeds are
Job 36: 4 that my words are not false; one perfect in **knowledge** is with you.
Ps 73:11 "How can God know? Does the Most High have **knowledge**?"
Isa 11: 9 for the earth will be full of the **knowledge** *of* the LORD as the
28: 9 "Who is it *he is trying to* **teach** [+906+3723]? To whom is he
Jer 3:15 own heart, who will lead you with **knowledge** and understanding.

1979 דְּעוּאֵל *de'û'ēl*, n.pr.m. [4 / 5] [√ 3359 + 446]

Deuel [5]

Nu 1:14 from Gad, Eliasaph son of **Deuel**;
2:14 leader of the people of Gad is Eliasaph son of **Deuel**. [BHS 8294]
7:42 On the sixth day Eliasaph son of **Deuel**, the leader of the people of
7:47 This was the offering of Eliasaph son of **Deuel**.
10:20 Eliasaph son of **Deuel** was over the division of the tribe of Gad.

1980 דָּעַךְ *dā'ak*, v. [9] [cf. 2403]

snuffed out [5], died out [1], extinguished [1], goes out [1], vanish [1]

Job 6:17 [C] in the dry season, and in the heat **vanish** from their channels.
18: 5 [A] "The lamp of the wicked *is* **snuffed out**; the flame of his fire
18: 6 [A] light in his tent becomes dark; the lamp beside him **goes out**.
21:17 [A] "Yet how often *is* the lamp of the wicked **snuffed out**? How
Ps 118:12 [E] me like bees, but *they* **died out** as quickly as burning thorns;
Pr 13: 9 [A] shines brightly, but the lamp of the wicked is **snuffed out**.
20:20 [A] or mother, his lamp *will be* **snuffed out** in pitch darkness.
24:20 [A] future hope, and the lamp of the wicked *will be* **snuffed out**.
Isa 43:17 [A] they lay there, never to rise again, **extinguished**, snuffed out

1981 דַּעַת *da'at[1]*, n.f. & m. [91] [√ 3359]

knowledge [68], know [5], unintentionally [+928+1172] [4], acknowledgment [2], experienced [+2256+9312] [1], has knowledge [+3359] [1], have concern [+1067] [1], have knowledge [+3359] [1], it[s] [1], learning [1], man of knowledge [+3359] [1], notions [1], understanding [1], well informed [+3359] [1], what know [1], what teach [1]

Ge 2: 9 the tree of life and the tree of the **knowledge** *of* good and evil.
2:17 but you must not eat from the tree of the **knowledge** *of* good
Ex 31: 3 of God, with skill, ability and **knowledge** in all kinds of crafts—
35:31 of God, with skill, ability and **knowledge** in all kinds of crafts—
Nu 24:16 *who* **has knowledge from** [+3359] the Most High, who sees a
Dt 4:42 if he *had* **unintentionally** [+928+1172] killed his neighbor without
19: 4 one who kills his neighbor **unintentionally** [+928+1172], without
Jos 20: 3 who kills a person accidentally and **unintentionally** [+928+1172]
20: 5 because he killed his neighbor **unintentionally** [+928+1172]
1Ki 7:14 Huram was highly skilled and **experienced** [+2256+9312] in all
Job 10: 7 though you **know** that I am not guilty and that no one can rescue
13: 2 What you **know**, I also know; I am not inferior to you.
15: 2 "Would a wise man answer with empty **notions** or fill his belly
21:14 to God, 'Leave us alone! We have no desire to **know** your ways.
21:22 "Can anyone teach **knowledge** to God, since he judges even the
33: 3 come from an upright heart; my lips sincerely speak **what I know**.
34:35 'Job speaks without **knowledge**; his words lack insight.'
35:16 mouth with empty talk; without **knowledge** he multiplies words."
36:12 they will perish by the sword and die without **knowledge**.
38: 2 is this that darkens my counsel with words without **knowledge**?
42: 3 asked,⌟ 'Who is this that obscures my counsel without **knowledge**?'
Ps 19: 2 [19:3] forth speech; night after night they display **knowledge**.
94:10 nations not punish? Does he who teaches man lack **knowledge**?
119:66 Teach me **knowledge** and good judgment, for I believe in your
139: 6 *Such* **knowledge** is too wonderful for me, too lofty for me to
Pr 1: 4 prudence to the simple, **knowledge** and discretion to the young—
1: 7 The fear of the LORD is the beginning of **knowledge**, but fools
1:22 long will mockers delight in mockery and fools hate **knowledge**?
1:29 Since they hated **knowledge** and did not choose to fear the
2: 5 understand the fear of the LORD and find the **knowledge** *of* God.
2: 6 and from his mouth come **knowledge** and understanding.
2:10 will enter your heart, and **knowledge** will be pleasant to your soul.
3:20 by his **knowledge** the deeps were divided, and the clouds let drop
5: 2 may maintain discretion and your lips may preserve **knowledge**.
8: 9 of them are right; they are faultless to those who have **knowledge**.
8:10 instruction instead of silver, **knowledge** rather than choice gold,
8:12 dwell together with prudence; I possess **knowledge** and discretion.
9:10 of wisdom, and **knowledge** *of* the Holy One is understanding.
10:14 Wise men store up **knowledge**, but the mouth of a fool invites ruin.
11: 9 his neighbor, but through **knowledge** the righteous escape.
12: 1 Whoever loves discipline loves **knowledge**, but he who hates
12:23 A prudent man keeps his **knowledge** to himself, but the heart of
13:16 Every prudent man acts out of **knowledge**, but a fool exposes his
14: 6 and finds none, but **knowledge** comes easily to the discerning.
14: 7 from a foolish man, for you will not find **knowledge** on his lips.
14:18 simple inherit folly, but the prudent are crowned with **knowledge**.
15: 2 The tongue of the wise commends **knowledge**, but the mouth of
15: 7 The lips of the wise spread **knowledge**; not so the hearts of fools.
15:14 The discerning heart seeks **knowledge**, but the mouth of a fool
17:27 A **man of knowledge** [+3359] uses words with restraint, and a
18:15 The heart of the discerning acquires **knowledge**; the ears of the
18:15 discerning acquires knowledge; the ears of the wise seek **it**[s] out.
19: 2 It is not good to have zeal without **knowledge**, nor to be hasty
19:25 rebuke a discerning man, and he will gain **knowledge**.
19:27 my son, and you will stray from the words of **knowledge**.
20:15 in abundance, but lips that speak **knowledge** are a rare jewel.
21:11 gain wisdom; when a wise man is instructed, he gets **knowledge**.
22:12 The eyes of the LORD keep watch over **knowledge**, but he
22:17 listen to the sayings of the wise; apply your heart to **what I teach**,
22:20 written thirty sayings for you, sayings of counsel and **knowledge**,
23:12 your heart to instruction and your ears to words of **knowledge**.
24: 4 through **knowledge** its rooms are filled with rare and beautiful
24: 5 man has great power, and a man of **knowledge** increases strength;
29: 7 justice for the poor, but the wicked **have** no *such* **concern** [+1067].
30: 3 learned wisdom, nor **have** *I* **knowledge of** [+3359] the Holy One.
Ecc 1:16 before me; I have experienced much of wisdom and **knowledge**."
1:18 wisdom comes much sorrow; the more **knowledge**, the more grief.
2:21 **knowledge** and skill, and then he must leave all he owns to
2:26 who pleases him, God gives wisdom, **knowledge** and happiness,
7:12 as money is a shelter, but the advantage of **knowledge** is this:

Ecc 9:10 there is neither working nor planning nor **knowledge** nor wisdom.
12: 9 the Teacher wise, but also he imparted **knowledge** *to* the people.
Isa 5:13 Therefore my people will go into exile for lack of **understanding**;
11: 2 of power, the Spirit of **knowledge** and of the fear of the LORD—
33: 6 your times, a rich store of salvation and wisdom and **knowledge**;
40:14 Who was it that taught him **knowledge** or showed him the path of
44:19 stops to think, no one has the **knowledge** or understanding to say,
44:25 who overthrows the **learning** *of* the wise and turns it into
47:10 and **knowledge** mislead you when you say to yourself,
53:11 by his **knowledge** my righteous servant will justify many,
58: 2 they seem eager to **know** my ways, as if they were a nation that
Jer 10:14 Everyone is senseless and without **knowledge**; every goldsmith is
22:16 and so all went well. Is that not what it means to **know** me?"
51:17 "Every man is senseless and without **knowledge**; every goldsmith
Da 1: 4 **well informed** [+3359], quick to understand, and qualified to serve
12: 4 of the end. Many will go here and there to increase **knowledge**."
Hos 4: 1 no faithfulness, no love, no **acknowledgment** *of* God in the land.
4: 6 my people are destroyed from lack of **knowledge**. "Because you
4: 6 "Because you have rejected **knowledge**, I also reject you as my
6: 6 and **acknowledgment** *of* God rather than burnt offerings.
Mal 2: 7 "For the lips of a priest ought to preserve **knowledge**, and from his

1982 ²דַּעַת da'at², n.f. Not used in NIV/BHS [√ 3359]

1983 ³דַּעַת da'at³, n.f. Not used in NIV/BHS

1984 דֳּפִי d°pî, n.[m.]. [1]

slander [+928+5989] [1]

Ps 50:20 your brother and **slander** [+928+5989] your own mother's son.

1985 דָּפַק dāpaq, v. [3] [→ 1986]

driven hard [1], knocking [1], pounding [1]

Ge 33:13 [A] If they *are* **driven hard** just one day, all the animals will die.
Jdg 19:22 [F] **Pounding** on the door, they shouted to the old man who
SS 5: 2 [A] Listen! My lover *is* **knocking**: "Open to me, my sister,

1986 דָּפְקָה dopqâ, n.pr.loc. [2] [√ 1985]

Dophkah [2]

Nu 33:12 They left the Desert of Sin and camped at **Dophkah**.
33:13 They left **Dophkah** and camped at Alush.

1987 דַּק daq, a. [14] [√ 1990]

thin [6], fine [2], gaunt [+1414] [2], *untranslated* [1], dwarfed [1], finely ground [1], gentle [1]

Ge 41: 3 After them, seven other cows, ugly and **gaunt** [+1414], came up
41: 4 the cows that were ugly and **gaunt** [+1414] ate up the seven sleek,
41: 6 other heads of grain sprouted—**thin** and scorched by the east wind.
41: 7 The **thin** heads of grain swallowed up the seven healthy, full
41:23 heads sprouted—withered and **thin** and scorched by the east wind.
41:24 The **thin** heads of grain swallowed up the seven good heads.
Ex 16:14 **thin** flakes like frost on the ground appeared on the desert floor.
16:14 thin flakes **[RPH]** like frost on the ground appeared on the desert
Lev 13:30 to be more than skin deep and the hair in it is yellow and **thin**,
16:12 two handfuls of **finely ground** fragrant incense and take them
21:20 or who is hunchbacked or **dwarfed**, or who has any eye defect,
1Ki 19:12 was not in the fire. And after the fire came a **gentle** whisper.
Isa 29: 5 your many enemies will become like **fine** dust, the ruthless hordes
40:15 on the scales; he weighs the islands as though they were **fine** dust.

1988 דֹּק dōq, n.[m.]. [1] [√ 1990]

canopy [1]

Isa 40:22 He stretches out the heavens like a **canopy**, and spreads them out

1989 דִּקְלָה diqlâ, n.pr.m.[loc.]. [2]

Diklah [2]

Ge 10:27 Hadoram, Uzal, **Diklah**,
1Ch 1:21 Hadoram, Uzal, **Diklah**,

1990 דָּקַק dāqaq, v. [13] [→ 1987, 1988; cf. 1870, 1916, 1917, 1920; Ar 10182]

powder [3], ground [2], be ground [1], break to pieces [1], broke to pieces [1], broke up [1], crush [1], fine [1], grind [1], pounded [1]

Ex 30:36 [G] Grind some of it to **powder** and place it in front of the
32:20 [A] he ground it to **powder**, scattered it on the water and made
Dt 9:21 [A] I crushed it and ground it to powder as **fine** as dust and threw
2Sa 22:43 [G] *I* **pounded** and trampled them like mud in the streets.
2Ki 23: 6 [G] *He* **ground** it to powder and scattered the dust over the
23:15 [G] He burned the high place and **ground** it to powder,
2Ch 15:16 [G] pole down, **broke it up** and burned it in the Kidron Valley.
34: 4 [G] These *he* **broke to pieces** and scattered over the graves of
34: 7 [G] and the Asherah poles and crushed the idols to **powder**
Isa 28:28 [H] Grain *must* **be ground** to make bread; so one does not go on
28:28 [A] of his threshing cart over it, his horses *do* not **grind** it.
41:15 [A] You will thresh the mountains and **crush** them, and reduce
Mic 4:13 [G] hoofs of bronze and *you will* **break to pieces** many nations."

1991 דָּקַר dāqar, v. [11] [→ 1206, 1992, 4532]

run through [3], be thrust through [1], drove through [1], fatally wounded [1], pierced [1], racked with hunger [1], ran through [1], stab [1], wounded [1]

Nu 25: 8 [A] *He* **drove** the spear **through** both of them—through the
Jdg 9:54 [A] 'A woman killed him.' " So his servant **ran** him **through**,
1Sa 31: 4 [A] to his armor-bearer, "Draw your sword and **run me through**,
31: 4 [A] fellows will come and **run** me **through** and abuse me."
1Ch 10: 4 [A] to his armor-bearer, "Draw your sword and **run me through**,
Isa 13:15 [C] Whoever is captured *will* **be thrust through**; all who are
Jer 37:10 [E] attacking you and only **wounded** men were left in their tents,
51: 4 [E] fall down slain in Babylon, **fatally wounded** in her streets.
La 4: 9 [E] **racked with hunger**, they waste away for lack of food from
Zec 12:10 [A] They will look on me, the one *they have* **pierced**, and they
13: 3 [A] When he prophesies, his own parents *will* **stab** him.

1992 דֶּקֶר deqer, n.pr.m. Not used in NIV/BHS [√ 1991]

1993 דַּר dar, n.[m.]. [1]

mother-of-pearl [1]

Est 1: 6 of porphyry, marble, **mother-of-pearl** and other costly stones.

1994 דֵּרָאוֹן dērā'ôn, n.m. [2]

contempt [1], loathsome [1]

Isa 66:24 their fire be quenched, and they will be **loathsome** to all mankind."
Da 12: 2 some to everlasting life, others to shame and everlasting **contempt**.

1995 דָּרְבָן dorbān, n.[m.]. [1] [→ 1996]

goads [1]

1Sa 13:21 of a shekel for sharpening forks and axes and for repointing **goads**.

1996 דָּרְבֹנָה dorbōnâ, n.[f.]. [1] [√ 1995]

goads [1]

Ecc 12:11 The words of the wise are like **goads**, their collected sayings like

1997 דַּרְדַּע darda', n.pr.m. [1 / 2] [cf. 2009]

Darda [2]

1Ki 4:31 [5:11] wiser than Heman, Calcol and **Darda**, the sons of Mahol.
1Ch 2: 6 Zimri, Ethan, Heman, Calcol and **Darda**[BHS 2009]—five in all.

1998 דַּרְדַּר dardar, n.[m.]. [2]

thistles [2]

Ge 3:18 It will produce thorns and **thistles** for you, and you will eat the
Hos 10: 8 of Israel. Thorns and **thistles** will grow up and cover their altars.

1999 דָּרוֹם dārôm, n.m. [17 / 19]

south [17], south wind [1], southward [1]

Dt 33:23 and is full of his blessing; he will inherit **southward** to the lake."
Job 37:17 in your clothes when the land lies hushed under the **south wind**,
Ecc 1: 6 The wind blows to the **south** and turns to the north; round
11: 3 Whether a tree falls to the **south** or to the north, in the place where
Eze 20:46 [21:2] preach against the **south** and prophesy against the forest of
40:24 Then he led me to the **south** side and I saw a gate facing south.
40:24 Then he led me to the south side and I saw a gate facing **south**.
40:27 The inner court also had a gate facing **south**, and he measured
40:27 and he measured from this gate to the outer gate on the **south** side;
40:28 Then he brought me into the inner court through the **south** gate,
40:28 inner court through the south gate, and he measured the **south** gate;
40:44 were two rooms, one at the side of the north gate and facing **south**,
40:44 another at the side of the **south** [BHS 7708] gate and facing north.
40:45 "The room facing **south** is for the priests who have charge of the
41:11 from the open area, one on the north and another on the **south**;
42:10 On the **south** [BHS 7708] side along the length of the wall of the
42:12 were the doorways of the rooms on the **south**. There was a
42:13 and **south** rooms facing the temple courtyard are the priests' rooms,
42:18 He measured the **south** side; it was five hundred cubits by the

2000 ¹דְּרוֹר ***d^{e}rôr[1]***, n.f. [2]

swallow [2]

Ps 84: 3 [84:4] the **swallow** a nest for herself, where she may have her
Pr 26: 2 Like a fluttering sparrow or a darting **swallow**, an undeserved

2001 ²דְּרוֹר ***d^{e}rôr[2]***, n.[m.]. [1]

liquid [1]

Ex 30:23 500 shekels of **liquid** myrrh, half as much (that is, 250 shekels)

2002 ³דְּרוֹר ***d^{e}rôr[3]***, n.[m.]. [7]

freedom [5], freedom for slaves [1], liberty [1]

Lev 25:10 and proclaim **liberty** throughout the land to all its inhabitants.
Isa 61: 1 to proclaim **freedom** for the captives and release from darkness for
Jer 34: 8 all the people in Jerusalem to proclaim **freedom for** *the* **slaves**.
34:15 in my sight: Each of you proclaimed **freedom** to his countrymen.
34:17 you have not proclaimed **freedom** for your fellow countrymen.
34:17 So I now proclaim '**freedom**' for you, declares the LORD—
Eze 46:17 of his servants, the servant may keep it until the year of **freedom**;

2003 דָּרְיָוֶשׁ ***dār^{e}yāweš***, n.pr.m. [10] [→ Ar 10184]

Darius [10]

Ezr 4: 5 king of Persia and down to the reign of **Darius** king of Persia.
Ne 12:22 of the priests, were recorded in the reign of **Darius** the Persian.
Da 9: 1 In the first year of **Darius** son of Xerxes (a Mede by descent),
11: 1 in the first year of **Darius** the Mede, I took my stand to support
Hag 1: 1 In the second year of King **Darius**, on the first day of the sixth
1:15 day of the sixth month in the second year of King **Darius**.
2:10 day of the ninth month, in the second year of **Darius**,
Zec 1: 1 In the eighth month of the second year of **Darius**, the word of the
1: 7 eleventh month, the month of Shebat, in the second year of **Darius**,
7: 1 In the fourth year of King **Darius**, the word of the LORD came to

2004 דַּרְיוֹשׁ ***daryôš***, v. [1 / 0]

Ezr 10:16 they sat down to investigate [BHS ?; NIV 2011] the cases,

2005 דָּרַךְ ***dārak***, v. [63 / 62] [→ 2006, 4534]

bend [4], trampled [4], treads [4], draw [3], tread [3], treading [3], guide [2], marches [2], set [2], strung [2], trodden [2], *untranslated* [1], aim [1], archer [1], bent [1], come [1], cross over [1], direct [1], directs [1], draw the bow [1], drew [1], enables to go [1], go [1], guides [1], handle [1], lead [1], led [1], make ready to shoot [1], march on [1], overran [1], press [1], set feet [1], set foot on [1], step [1], string [1], trample down [1], treads out [1], trod [1], use [1], walked [1], walks [1], with bows [+8008] [1]

Nu 24:17 [A] A star *will* **come** out of Jacob; a scepter will rise out of
Dt 1:36 [A] will give him and his descendants the land *he* **set** *his* **feet** on,
11:24 [A] Every place where *you* **set** your foot will be yours:
11:25 [A] and fear of you on the whole land, wherever *you* **go**.
33:29 [A] before you, and you *will* **trample down** their high places."
Jos 1: 3 [A] I will give you every place where *you* **set** your foot, as I
14: 9 [A] 'The land on which your feet *have* **walked** will be your
Jdg 5:21 [A] the river Kishon. **March on**, my soul; be strong!
9:27 [A] out into the fields and gathered the grapes and **trodden** them,
20:43 [G] easily **overran** them in the vicinity of Gibeah on the east.
1Sa 5: 5 [A] who enter Dagon's temple at Ashdod **step** on the threshold.
1Ch 5:18 [A] who could handle shield and sword, *who could* **use** a bow,
8:40 [A] The sons of Ulam were brave warriors *who could* **handle** the
2Ch 14: 8 [14:7] [A] armed with small shields and **with bows** [+8008].
Ne 13:15 [A] In those days I saw *men* in Judah **treading** winepresses on
Job 9: 8 [A] stretches out the heavens and **treads** on the waves of the sea.
22:15 [A] Will you keep to the old path that evil men *have* **trod**?
24:11 [A] the terraces; *they* **tread** the winepresses, yet suffer thirst.
28: 8 [G] Proud beasts *do* not **set foot on** it, and no lion prowls there.
Ps 7:12 [7:13] [A] sharpen his sword; *he will* **bend** and string his bow.
11: 2 [A] For look, the wicked **bend** their bows; they set their arrows
25: 5 [G] **guide** me in your truth and teach me, for you are God my
25: 9 [G] *He* **guides** the humble in what is right and teaches them his
37:14 [A] and **bend** the bow to bring down the poor and needy,
58: 7 [58:8] [A] *when they* **draw the bow**, let their arrows be
64: 3 [64:4] [A] like swords and **aim** their words like deadly arrows.
91:13 [A] *You will* **tread** upon the lion and the cobra; you will trample
107: 7 [G] *He* **led** them by a straight way to a city where they could
119:35 [G] **Direct** me in the path of your commands, for there I find
Pr 4:11 [G] you in the way of wisdom and **lead** you along straight paths.
Isa 5:28 [B] Their arrows are sharp, all their bows *are* **strung**;
11:15 [G] up into seven streams so that *men can* **cross over** in sandals.
16:10 [A] no *one* **treads out** wine at the presses, for I have put an end
16:10 [A] no one treads out **[RPH]** wine at the presses, for I have put
21:15 [B] drawn sword, from the **bent** bow and from the heat of battle.
42:16 [G] have not known, along unfamiliar paths *I will* **guide** them;
48:17 [G] is best for you, *who* **directs** you in the way you should go.
59: 8 [A] crooked roads; no one *who* **walks** in them will know peace.
63: 2 [A] your garments red, like those of *one* **treading** the winepress?
63: 3 [A] "*I have* **trodden** the winepress alone; from the nations no
63: 3 [A] *I* **trampled** them in my anger and trod them down in my
Jer 9: 3 [9:2] [G] "*They* **make ready** their tongue like a bow, **to shoot**
25:30 [A] He will shout like *those who* **tread** the grapes, shout against
46: 9 [A] and Put who carry shields, men of Lydia *who* **draw** the bow.
48:33 [A] from the presses; no *one* **treads** them with shouts of joy.
50:14 [A] your positions around Babylon, all you *who* **draw** the bow.
50:29 [A] archers against Babylon, all *those who* **draw** the bow.
51: 3 [A] Let not the **archer** string his bow, nor let him put on his
51: 3 [A] *Let* not the archer **string** his bow, nor let him put on his
51: 3 [A] [not the archer string [BHS+ Q *let him string*; no K] his bow,]
51:33 [G] of Babylon is like a threshing floor at the time it *is* **trampled**;
La 1:15 [A] In his winepress the Lord *has* **trampled** the Virgin Daughter
2: 4 [A] Like an enemy *he has* **strung** his bow; his right hand is
3:12 [A] *He* **drew** his bow and made me the target for his arrows.
Am 4:13 [A] dawn to darkness, and **treads** the high places of the earth—
9:13 [A] by the plowman and the planter by the *one* **treading** grapes.
Mic 1: 3 [A] he comes down and **treads** the high places of the earth.
5: 5 [5:4] [A] invades our land and **marches** through our fortresses,
5: 6 [5:5] [A] he invades our land and **marches** into our borders.
6:15 [A] you *will* **press** olives but not use the oil on yourselves, you
Hab 3:15 [A] *You* **trampled** the sea with your horses, churning the great
3:19 [G] like the feet of a deer, he **enables** me **to go** on the heights.
Zec 9:13 [A] *I will* **bend** Judah as I bend my bow and fill it with Ephraim.

2006 דֶּרֶךְ ***derek***, n.m. [706] [√ 2005]

ways [180], way [177], road [61], *untranslated* [33], journey [30], path [21], conduct [18], toward [15], direction [9], roads [9], through [8], route [7], life [5], what done [5], pass by [+6296] [4], paths [4], side [4], to [4], as [+928] [3], by [3], highway [3], mission [3], on [3], roadside [3], wherever [+889+928+2021] [3], works [3], all do [2], course [2], distance [2], does [2], facing [2], go to [2], main road [+2006] [2], passageway [2], street [2], trackless [+4202] [2], what[s] [+2021] [2], action [1], along [1], at [+928+2021] [1], behavior [1], by way of [1], course of life [1], crossroads [1], custom [1], did [1], dispersed [+2143+4200] [1], distant [+2021+8049] [1], do so[s] [+4946+8740] [1], done [1], everything do [1], extending [1], fate [1], favors [1], follow [1], following [1], go [+928+2143] [1], god [1], how behaved [1], how live [1], in the way should go [+6584+7023] [1], justice [1], leads to [1], leads [1], let get away [+928+8938] [1], line [1], long [1], man of integrity [+9448] [1], march [1], missions [1], northward [+2021+7600] [1], on way [+6913] [1], path [+784] [1], period [+851] [1], place [1], room [1], routes [1], running here and there [+8592] [1], siege ramp [1], skilled [+3512] [1], streets [1], strength [1], teaching [1], that[s] [1], there[s] [+928+2021] [1], things did [1], toward [+448] [1], toward [+6584] [1], toward [+6584+7156] [1], travel [+6296] [1], traveled [+2143] [1], traveled [1], traveling [1], upright [+3838] [1], vigor [1], walk [+928+2143] [1], walk [1], walked [1], walking along [+928+2021] [1], waylaid [+928+2021+4200+8492] [1], what did [1], where[s] [+2021] [1], which way [+361+2021+2296] [1]

Ge 3:24 sword flashing back and forth to guard the **way** *to* the tree of life.
6:12 had become, for all the people on earth had corrupted their **ways**.
16: 7 in the desert; it was the spring that is beside the **road** *to* Shur.
18:19 his household after him to keep the **way** *of* the LORD by doing
19: 2 spend the night and then go on your **way** early in the morning."
19:31 man around here to lie with us, as is the **custom** all over the earth.
24:21 learn whether or not the LORD had made his **journey** successful.
24:27 the LORD has led me on the **journey** to the house of my master's
24:40 will send his angel with you and make your **journey** a success,
24:42 please grant success to the **journey** on which I have come.
24:48 who had led me on the right **road** to get the granddaughter of my
24:56 now that the LORD has granted success to my **journey**.
28:20 be with me and will watch over me on this **journey** I am taking
30:36 Then he put a three-day **journey** between himself and Jacob,
31:23 **[NIE]** and caught up with him in the hill country of Gilead.
31:35 I cannot stand up in your presence; I'm having my **period** [+851]."
32: 1 [32:2] Jacob also went on his **way**, and the angels of God met
33:16 So that day Esau started on his **way** back to Seir.
35: 3 who has been with me **wherever** [+889+928+2021] I have gone."
35:19 So Rachel died and was buried on the **way** to Ephrath (that is,
38:14 sat down at the entrance to Enaim, which is on the **road** to Timnah.
38:16 he went over to her by the **roadside** and said, "Come now,
38:21 "Where is the shrine prostitute who was beside the **road** at
42:25 back in his sack, and to give them provisions for their **journey**.
42:38 If harm comes to him on the **journey** you are taking, you will
45:21 and he also gave them provisions for their **journey**.
45:23 loaded with grain and bread and other provisions for his **journey**.
45:24 as they were leaving he said to them, "Don't quarrel on the **way**!"
48: 7 Rachel died in the land of Canaan while we were still on the **way**,
48: 7 So I buried her there beside the **road** *to* Ephrath" (that is,

Ge 49:17 Dan will be a serpent by the **roadside**, a viper along the path,
Ex 3:18 Let us take a three-day **journey** into the desert to offer sacrifices to
4:24 At a lodging place on the **way**, the LORD met ⌊Moses⌋ and was
5:3 Now let us take a three-day **journey** into the desert to offer
8:27 [8:23] We must take a three-day **journey** into the desert to offer
13:17 God did not lead them on the **road** *through* the Philistine country,
13:18 So God led the people around by the desert **road** toward the Red
13:21 went ahead of them in a pillar of cloud to guide them on their **way**
18:8 and about all the hardships they had met along the **way**
18:20 and show them the **way** to live and the duties they are to perform.
23:20 I am sending an angel ahead of you to guard you along the **way**
32:8 They have been quick to turn away from **what**° [+2021] I
33:3 you are a stiff-necked people and I might destroy you on the **way**."
33:13 teach me your **ways** so I may know you and continue to find favor
Lev 26:22 and make you so few in number that your **roads** will be deserted.
Nu 9:10 are unclean because of a dead body or are away on a **journey**,
9:13 and not on a **journey** fails to celebrate the Passover,
10:33 out from the mountain of the LORD and **traveled** *for* three days.
10:33 The ark of the covenant of the LORD went before them **[RPH]**
11:31 three feet above the ground, as far as a day's **walk** in any direction.
11:31 above the ground, as far as a day's walk in any direction. **[RPH]**
14:25 and set out toward the desert *along* the **route** *to* the Red Sea."
20:17 We will travel along the king's **highway** and not turn to the right
21:1 heard that Israel was coming along the **road** *to* Atharim,
21:4 They traveled from Mount Hor along the **route** *to* the Red Sea,
21:4 to go around Edom. But the people grew impatient on the **way**;
21:22 We will travel along the king's **highway** until we have passed
21:33 Then they turned and went up along the **road** *toward* Bashan,
22:22 and the angel of the LORD stood in the **road** to oppose him.
22:23 the LORD standing in the **road** with a drawn sword in his hand,
22:23 a drawn sword in his hand, she turned off the **road** into a field.
22:23 the road into a field. Balaam beat her to get her back on the **road**.
22:26 and stood in a narrow place where there was no **room** to turn,
22:31 he saw the angel of the LORD standing in the **road** with his
22:32 here to oppose you because your **path** is a reckless one before me.
22:34 I did not realize you were standing in the **road** to oppose me.
24:25 Balaam got up and returned home and Balak went his own **way**.
33:8 when *they had* **traveled** [+2143] for three days in the Desert of
Dt 1:2 days to go from Horeb to Kadesh Barnea by the Mount Seir **road**.)
1:19 went **toward** the hill country of the Amorites through all that vast
1:22 bring back a report about the **route** we are to take and the towns
1:31 carries his son, all the **way** you went until you reached this place."
1:33 who went ahead of you on your **journey**, in fire by night and in a
1:33 places for you to camp and to show you the **way** you should go.
1:40 and set out toward the desert along the **route** *to* the Red Sea."
2:1 and set out toward the desert along the **route** *to* the Red Sea,
2:8 We turned from the Arabah **road**, which comes up from Elath
2:8 and Ezion Geber, and traveled along the desert **road** *of* Moab.
2:27 We will stay on the **main road** [+2006]; we will not turn aside to
2:27 We will stay on the **main road** [+2006]; we will not turn aside to
3:1 Next we turned and went up along the **road** *toward* Bashan,
5:33 Walk in all the **way** that the LORD your God has commanded
6:7 them when you sit at home and when you walk along the **road**,
8:2 Remember how the LORD your God led you all the **way** in the
8:6 of the LORD your God, walking in his **ways** and revering him.
9:12 They have turned away quickly from **what**° [+2021] I commanded
9:16 You had turned aside quickly from the **way** that the LORD had
10:12 to fear the LORD your God, to walk in all his **ways**, to love him,
11:19 them when you sit at home and when you walk along the **road**,
11:22 LORD your God, to walk in all his **ways** and to hold fast to him—
11:28 turn from the **way** that I command you today by following other
11:30 west of the **road**, toward the setting sun, near the great trees of
13:5 [13:6] he has tried to turn you from the **way** the LORD your God
14:24 if that place *is* too **distant** [+2021+8049] and you have been
17:16 the LORD has told you, "You are not to go back that **way** again."
19:3 Build **roads** to them and divide into three parts the land the
19:6 pursue him in a rage, overtake him if the **distance** is too great,
19:9 to love the LORD your God and to walk always in his **ways**—
22:4 If you see your brother's donkey or his ox fallen on the **road**,
22:6 If you come across a bird's nest beside the **road**, either in a tree
23:4 [23:5] and water on your **way** when you came out of Egypt,
24:9 God did to Miriam along the **way** after you came out of Egypt.
25:17 Remember what the Amalekites did to you along the **way** when
25:18 they met you on your **journey** and cut off all who were lagging
26:17 that the LORD is your God and that you will walk in his **ways**,
27:18 "Cursed is the man who leads the blind astray on the **road**."
28:7 They will come at you from one **direction** but flee from you in
28:7 at you from one direction but flee from you in seven. **[RPH]**
28:9 keep the commands of the LORD your God and walk in his **ways**.
28:25 You will come at them from one **direction** but flee from them in
28:25 **[RPH]** and you will become a thing of horror to all the kingdoms
28:29 You will be unsuccessful in **everything** you **do**; day after day you
28:68 The LORD will send you back in ships to Egypt on a **journey** I
30:16 to walk in his **ways**, and to keep his commands, decrees and laws;
31:29 utterly corrupt and to turn from the **way** I have commanded you.
32:4 He is the Rock, his works are perfect, and all his **ways** are just.
Jos 1:8 written in it. Then you will be prosperous **[NIE]** and successful.
2:7 So the men set out in pursuit of the spies on the **road** that leads to
2:16 there three days until they return, and then go on your **way**."
2:22 until the pursuers had searched all along the **road** and returned
3:4 you will know which **way** to go, since you have never been this
3:4 know which way to go, since you have never been this **way** before.
5:4 of military age—died in the desert on the **way** after leaving Egypt.
5:5 all the people born in the desert during the **journey** from Egypt
5:7 because they had not been circumcised on the **way**.
8:15 be driven back before them, and they fled **toward** the desert.
9:11 living in our country said to us, 'Take provisions for your **journey**;
9:13 our clothes and sandals are worn out by the very long **journey**."
10:10 Israel pursued them along the **road** going up to Beth Horon
12:3 **to** Beth Jeshimoth, and then southward below the slopes of Pisgah.
22:5 to walk in all his **ways**, to obey his commands, to hold fast to him
23:14 "Now I am about to go the **way** *of* all the earth. You know with all
24:17 He protected us on our entire **journey** and among all the nations
Jdg 2:17 they quickly turned from the **way** in which their fathers had
2:19 They refused to give up their evil practices and stubborn **ways**.
2:22 to test Israel and see whether they will keep the **way** *of* the LORD
4:9 because of the **way** you are going about this, the honor will not be
5:10 your saddle blankets, and you who walk along the **road**, consider
8:11 Gideon went up by the **route** *of* the nomads east of Nobah
9:25 who passed by, **[NIE]** and this was reported to Abimelech.
9:37 a company is coming from the **direction** *of* the soothsayers' tree."
17:8 town in search of some other place to stay. **On** his **way** [+6913]
18:5 "Please inquire of God to learn whether our **journey** will be
18:6 "Go in peace. Your **journey** has the LORD's approval."
18:26 So the Danites went their **way**, and Micah, seeing that they were
19:9 tomorrow morning you can get up and be on your **way** home."
19:27 the door of the house and stepped out to continue on his **way**,
20:42 So they fled before the Israelites in the **direction** *of* the desert,
Ru 1:7 set out on the **road** that would take them back to the land of Judah.
1Sa 1:18 she went her **way** and ate something, and her face was no longer
4:13 there was Eli sitting on his chair by the side of the **road**, watching,
6:9 If it goes up **to** its own territory, toward Beth Shemesh, then the
6:12 Then the cows went straight **[RPH]** up toward Beth Shemesh,
6:12 Then the cows went straight up **toward** [+6584] Beth Shemesh,
8:3 his sons did not walk in his **ways**. They turned aside after dishonest
8:5 said to him, "You are old, and your sons do not walk in your **ways**;
9:6 Let's go there now. Perhaps he will tell us what **way** to take."
9:8 give it to the man of God so that he will tell us what **way** to take."
12:23 pray for you. And I will teach you the **way** that is good and right.
13:17 One turned **toward** [+448] Ophrah in the vicinity of Shual,
13:18 another **toward** Beth Horon, and the third toward the borderland
13:18 the third **toward** the borderland overlooking the Valley of Zeboim
15:2 'I will punish the Amalekites for what they did to Israel when *they* **waylaid** [+928+2021+4200+8492] them as they came up from
15:18 he sent you on a **mission**, saying, 'Go and completely destroy those
15:20 Saul said. "I went on the **mission** the LORD assigned me.
17:52 Their dead were strewn along the Shaaraim **road** to Gath
18:14 In everything he **did** he had great success, because the LORD was
21:5 [21:6] The men's things are holy even on **missions** that are not
24:3 [24:4] He came to the sheep pens along the **way**; a cave was
24:7 [24:8] to attack Saul. And Saul left the cave and went his **way**.
24:19 [24:20] *does he* **let** him **get away** [+928+8938] unharmed?
25:12 David's men turned around **[NIE]** and went back. When they
26:3 Saul made his camp beside the **road** on the hill of Hakilah facing
26:25 So David went on his **way**, and Saul returned home.
28:22 so you may eat and have the strength to go on your **way**."
30:2 none of them, but carried them off as they went on their **way**.
2Sa 2:24 hill of Ammah, near Giah on the **way** *to* the wasteland of Gibeon.
4:7 Taking it with them, they traveled all night **by way of** the Arabah.
11:10 go home," he asked him, "Haven't you just come from a **distance**?
13:30 While they were on their **way**, the report came to David: "Absalom
13:34 watch looked up and saw many people on the **road** west of him,
13:34 told the king, "I see men in the **direction** [BHS-] *of* Horonaim,
15:2 and stand by the side of the **road** *leading to* the city gate.
15:23 and all the people moved on **toward** [+6584+7156] the desert.
16:13 his men continued along the **road** while Shimei was going along
18:23 Then Ahimaaz ran *by* **way** *of* the plain and outran the Cushite.
22:22 For I have kept the **ways** *of* the LORD; I have not done evil by
22:31 "As for God, his **way** is perfect; the word of the LORD is
22:33 It is God who arms me with strength and makes my **way** perfect.
1Ki 1:49 all Adonijah's guests rose in alarm and **dispersed** [+2143+4200].
2:2 "I am about to go the **way** *of* all the earth," he said. "So be strong,
2:3 Walk in his **ways**, and keep his decrees and commands, his laws
2:4 'If your descendants watch **how** they **live**, and if they walk
3:14 if you walk in my **ways** and obey my statutes and commands as
8:25 if only your sons are careful **in all** they **do** to walk before me as
8:32 the guilty and bringing down on his own head **what** he has **done**.
8:36 Teach them the right **way** to live, and send rain on the land you

1Ki 8:39 deal with each man according to all he **does**, since you know his
8:44 against their enemies, **wherever** [+889+928+2021] you send them,
8:44 when they pray to the LORD **toward** the city you have chosen
8:48 pray to you **toward** the land you gave their fathers, toward the city
8:58 to walk in all his **ways** and to keep the commands, decrees
11:29 Ahijah the prophet of Shiloh met him on the **way**, wearing a new
11:33 have not walked in my **ways**, nor done what is right in my eyes,
11:38 If you do whatever I command you and walk in my **ways** and do
13: 9 not eat bread or drink water or return by the **way** you came.' "
13:10 So he took another **road** and did not return by the way he had
13:10 another road and did not return by the **way** he had come to Bethel.
13:12 Their father asked them, "Which **way** did he go?" And his sons
13:12 his sons showed him which **road** the man of God from Judah had
13:17 eat bread or drink water there or return by the **way** you came.' "
13:24 As he went on his way, a lion met him on the **road** and killed him,
13:24 and killed him, and his body was thrown down on the **road**,
13:25 who passed by saw the body thrown down **there**[s] [+928+2021],
13:26 When the prophet who had brought him back from his **journey**
13:28 Then he went out and found the body thrown down on the **road**,
13:33 Even after this, Jeroboam did not change his evil **ways**, but once
15:26 of the LORD, walking in the **ways** *of* his father and in his sin,
15:34 of the LORD, walking in the **ways** *of* Jeroboam and in his sin,
16: 2 you walked in the **ways** *of* Jeroboam and caused my people Israel
16:19 walking in the **ways** *of* Jeroboam and in the sin he had committed
16:26 He walked in all the **ways** *of* Jeroboam son of Nebat and in his sin,
18: 6 to cover, Ahab going in one **direction** and Obadiah in another.
18: 6 Ahab going in one direction and Obadiah in **[RPH]** another.
18: 7 As Obadiah was **walking along** [+928+2021], Elijah met him.
18:27 he is a god! Perhaps he is deep in thought, or busy, or **traveling**.
18:43 "Go and look **toward** the sea," he told his servant. And he went up
19: 4 while he himself went a day's **journey** into the desert. He came to
19: 7 and said, "Get up and eat, for the **journey** is too much for you."
19:15 The LORD said to him, "Go back the **way** you came, and go to
20:38 Then the prophet went and stood by the **road** waiting for the king.
22:43 In everything he walked in the **ways** *of* his father Asa and did not
22:52 [22:53] because he walked in the **ways** *of* his father and mother
22:52 [22:53] **[RPH]** mother and in the ways of Jeroboam son of
22:52 [22:53] and mother and in the **ways** *of* Jeroboam son of Nebat,
2Ki 2:23 As he was walking along the **road**, some youths came out of the
3: 8 "By what **route** shall we attack?" he asked. "Through the Desert of
3: 8 he asked. "**Through** the Desert of Edom," he answered.
3: 9 After a roundabout **march** *of* seven days, the army had no more
3:20 there it was—water flowing from the **direction** *of* Edom!
6:19 Elisha told them, "This is not the **road** and this is not the city.
7:15 they found the whole **road** strewn with the clothing and equipment
8:18 He walked in the **ways** *of* the kings of Israel, as the house of Ahab
8:27 He walked in the **ways** *of* the house of Ahab and did evil in the
9:27 saw what had happened, he fled up the **road** *to* Beth Haggan.
10:12 toward Samaria. **At** [+928+2021] Beth Eked of the Shepherds,
11:16 So they seized her as she reached the **place** *where* the horses enter
11:19 and went into the palace, entering *by* **way** *of* the gate of the guards.
16: 3 He walked in the **ways** *of* the kings of Israel and even sacrificed
17:13 through all his prophets and seers: "Turn from your evil **ways**.
19:28 in your mouth, and I will make you return by the **way** you came.'
19:33 By the **way** that he came he will return; he will not enter this city,
21:21 He walked in all the **ways** of his father; he worshiped the idols his
21:22 the God of his fathers, and did not walk in the **way** *of* the LORD.
22: 2 eyes of the LORD and walked in all the **ways** *of* his father David,
25: 4 the whole army fled at night **through** the gate between the two
25: 4 were surrounding the city. They fled **toward** the Arabah,
2Ch 6:16 if only your sons are careful in **all** they **do** to walk before me
6:23 the guilty by bringing down on his own head **what** he has **done**.
6:27 Teach them the right **way** to live, and send rain on the land you
6:30 Forgive, and deal with each man according to all he **does**,
6:31 walk in your **ways** all the time they live in the land you gave our
6:34 against their enemies, **wherever** [+889+928+2021] you send them,
6:34 and when they pray to you **toward** this city you have chosen
6:38 pray **toward** the land you gave their fathers, toward the city you
7:14 and pray and seek my face and turn from their wicked **ways**,
11:17 walking in the **ways** *of* David and Solomon during this time.
13:22 The other events of Abijah's reign, **what** he **did** and what he said,
17: 3 because in his early years he walked in the **ways** his father David
17: 6 His heart was devoted to the **ways** *of* the LORD; furthermore,
18:23 "**Which way** [+361+2021+2296] did the spirit from the LORD
20:32 He walked in the **ways** *of* his father Asa and did not stray from
21: 6 He walked in the **ways** *of* the kings of Israel, as the house of Ahab
21:12 'You have not walked in the **ways** *of* your father Jehoshaphat
21:12 ways of your father Jehoshaphat or **[RPH]** of Asa king of Judah.
21:13 you have walked in the **ways** *of* the kings of Israel, and you have
22: 3 He too walked in the **ways** *of* the house of Ahab, for his mother
27: 6 because he **walked** steadfastly before the LORD his God.
27: 7 Jotham's reign, including all his wars and the other **things** he **did**,
28: 2 He walked in the **ways** *of* the kings of Israel and also made cast
28:26 The other events of his reign and all his **ways**, from beginning to
34: 2 the eyes of the LORD and walked in the **ways** *of* his father David,
Ezr 8:21 our God and ask him for a safe **journey** for us and our children,
8:22 for soldiers and horsemen to protect us from enemies on the **road**,
8:31 and he protected us from enemies and bandits along the **way**.
Ne 9:12 by night with a pillar of fire to give them light on the **way** they
9:19 day the pillar of cloud did not cease to guide them on their **path**,
9:19 nor the pillar of fire by night to shine on the **way** they were to take.
Job 3:23 Why is life given to a man whose **way** is hidden, whom God has
4: 6 piety be your confidence and your blameless **ways** your hope?
6:18 Caravans turn aside from their **routes**; they go up into the
8:19 Surely its **life** withers away, and from the soil other plants grow.
12:24 he sends them wandering through a **trackless** [+4202] waste.
13:15 yet will I hope in him; I will surely defend my **ways** to his face.
17: 9 Nevertheless, the righteous will hold to their **ways**, and those with
19:12 they build a **siege ramp** against me and encamp around my tent.
21:14 to God, 'Leave us alone! We have no desire to know your **ways**.
21:29 Have you never questioned *those who* **travel** [+6296]? Have you
21:31 Who denounces his **conduct** to his face? Who repays him for what
22: 3 were righteous? What would he gain if your **ways** were blameless?
22:28 you decide on will be done, and light will shine on your **ways**.
23:10 he knows the **way** that I take; when he has tested me, I will come
23:11 followed his steps; I have kept to his **way** without turning aside.
24: 4 They thrust the needy from the **path** and force all the poor of the
24:13 against the light, who do not know its **ways** or stay in its paths.
24:18 portion of the land is cursed, so that no one goes **to** the vineyards.
24:23 let them rest in a feeling of security, but his eyes are on their **ways**.
26:14 these are but the outer fringe of his **works**; how faint the whisper
28:23 God understands the **way** *to* it and he alone knows where it dwells,
28:26 he made a decree for the rain and a **path** for the thunderstorm,
29:25 I chose the **way** *for* them and sat as their chief; I dwelt as a king
31: 4 Does he not see my **ways** and count my every step?
31: 7 if my steps have turned from the **path**, if my heart has been led by
34:21 "His eyes are on the **ways** *of* men; he sees their every step.
34:27 turned from following him and had no regard for any of his **ways**.
36:23 Who has prescribed his **ways** for him, or said to him, 'You have
38:19 "What is the **way** to the abode of light? And where does darkness
38:24 What is the **way** to the place where the lightning is dispersed,
38:25 a channel for the torrents of rain, and a **path** for the thunderstorm,
40:19 He ranks first among the **works** *of* God, yet his Maker can
Ps 1: 1 or stand in the **way** *of* sinners or sit in the seat of mockers.
1: 6 For the LORD watches over the **way** *of* the righteous, but the way
1: 6 the way of the righteous, but the **way** *of* the wicked will perish.
2:12 Kiss the Son, lest he be angry and you be destroyed *in* your **way**,
5: 8 [5:9] because of my enemies—make straight your **way** before me.
10: 5 His **ways** are always prosperous; he is haughty and your laws are
18:21 [18:22] For I have kept the **ways** *of* the LORD; I have not done
18:30 [18:31] As for God, his **way** is perfect; the word of the LORD is
18:32 [18:33] who arms me with strength and makes my **way** perfect.
25: 4 Show me your ways, O LORD, teach me your **paths**;
25: 8 upright is the LORD; therefore he instructs sinners in his **ways**.
25: 9 He guides the humble in what is right and teaches them his **way**.
25:12 fears the LORD? He will instruct him in the **way** chosen for him.
27:11 Teach me your **way**, O LORD; lead me in a straight path
32: 8 I will instruct you and teach you in the **way** you should go;
35: 6 may their **path** be dark and slippery, with the angel of the LORD
36: 4 [36:5] he commits himself to a sinful **course** and does not reject
37: 5 Commit your **way** to the LORD; trust in him and he will do this:
37: 7 do not fret when men succeed in their **ways**, when they carry out
37:14 down the poor and needy, to slay those whose **ways** are upright.
37:23 If the LORD delights in a man's **way**, he makes his steps firm;
37:34 Wait for the LORD and keep his **way**. He will exalt you to inherit
39: 1 [39:2] "I will watch my **ways** and keep my tongue from sin;
49:13 [49:14] This is the **fate** *of* those who trust in themselves, and of
50:23 he prepares the **way** so that I may show him the salvation of God."
51:13 [51:15] I will teach transgressors your **ways**, and sinners will turn
67: 2 [67:3] that your **ways** may be known on earth, your salvation
77:13 [77:14] Your **ways**, O God, are holy. What god is so great as our
77:19 [77:20] Your **path** led through the sea, your way through the
80:12 [80:13] its walls so that all *who* **pass by** [+6296] pick its grapes?
81:13 [81:14] but listen to me, if Israel would follow my **ways**,
85:13 [85:14] goes before him and prepares the **way** *for* his steps.
86:11 Teach me your **way**, O LORD, and I will walk in your truth;
89:41 [89:42] All *who* **pass by** [+6296] have plundered him; he has
91:11 command his angels concerning you to guard you in all your **ways**;
95:10 whose hearts go astray, and they have not known my **ways**."
101: 2 I will be careful to lead a blameless **life**—when will you come to
101: 6 *he whose* **walk is** [+928+2143] blameless will minister to me.
102:23 [102:24] In the **course of** my **life** he broke my strength; he cut
103: 7 He made known his **ways** to Moses, his deeds to the people of
107: 4 desert wastelands, finding no **way** *to* a city where they could settle.
107: 7 He led them by a straight **way** to a city where they could settle.
107:17 Some became fools through their rebellious **ways** and suffered
107:40 on nobles made them wander in a **trackless** [+4202] waste.
110: 7 He will drink from a brook beside the **way**; therefore he will lift up

Ps 119: 1 Blessed are they whose **ways** are blameless, who walk according to
119: 3 They do nothing wrong; they walk in his **ways**.
119: 5 Oh, that my **ways** were steadfast in obeying your decrees!
119: 14 I rejoice in **following** your statutes as one rejoices in great riches.
119: 26 I recounted my **ways** and you answered me; teach me your
119: 27 Let me understand the **teaching** *of* your precepts; then I will
119: 29 Keep me from deceitful **ways**; be gracious to me through your law.
119: 30 I have chosen the **way** *of* truth; I have set my heart on your laws.
119: 32 I run in the **path** *of* your commands, for you have set my heart
119: 33 Teach me, O LORD, to **follow** your decrees; then I will keep
119: 37 my life according to your word. [BHS *in your way*; NIV 1821]
119: 59 I have considered my **ways** and have turned my steps to your
119: 168 your precepts and your statutes, for all my **ways** are known to you.
128: 1 Blessed are all who fear the LORD, who walk in his **ways**.
138: 5 May they sing of the **ways** *of* the LORD, for the glory of the
139: 3 going out and my lying down; you are familiar with all my **ways**.
139: 24 See if there is any offensive **way** in me, and lead me in the way
139: 24 is any offensive way in me, and lead me in the **way** everlasting.
143: 8 Show me the **way** I should go, for to you I lift up my soul.
145: 17 The LORD is righteous in all his **ways** and loving toward all he
146: 9 and the widow, but he frustrates the **ways** *of* the wicked.
Pr 1: 15 my son, *do* not **go** [+928+2143] along with them, do not set foot
1: 31 they will eat the fruit of their **ways** and be filled with the fruit of
2: 8 the course of the just and protects the **way** *of* his faithful ones.
2: 12 Wisdom will save you from the **ways** *of* wicked men, from men
2: 13 who leave the straight paths to walk in dark **ways**,
2: 20 Thus you will walk in the **ways** *of* good men and keep to the paths
3: 6 in all your **ways** acknowledge him, and he will make your paths
3: 17 Her **ways** are pleasant ways, and all her paths are peace.
3: 17 Her ways are pleasant **ways**, and all her paths are peace.
3: 23 you will go on your **way** in safety, and your foot will not stumble;
3: 31 Do not envy a violent man or choose any of his **ways**,
4: 11 I guide you in the **way** *of* wisdom and lead you along straight
4: 14 set foot on the path of the wicked or walk in the **way** *of* evil men.
4: 19 the **way** *of* the wicked is like deep darkness; they do not know
4: 26 Make level paths for your feet and take only **ways** that are firm.
5: 8 Keep to a **path** far from her, do not go near the door of her house,
5: 21 For a man's **ways** are in full view of the LORD, and he examines
6: 6 Go to the ant, you sluggard; consider its **ways** and be wise!
6: 23 is a light, and the corrections of discipline are the **way** *to* life,
7: 8 street near her corner, walking along in the **direction** *of* her house
7: 19 My husband is not at home; he has gone on a long **journey**.
7: 25 Do not let your heart turn to her **ways** or stray into her paths.
7: 27 Her house is a **highway** *to* the grave, leading down to the
8: 2 On the heights along the **way**, where the paths meet, she takes her
8: 13 I hate pride and arrogance, evil **behavior** and perverse speech.
8: 22 "The LORD brought me forth as the first of his **works**, before his
8: 32 my sons, listen to me; blessed are those who keep my **ways**.
9: 6 simple ways and you will live; walk in the **way** *of* understanding.
9: 15 calling out to *those who* **pass by** [+6296], who go straight on their
10: 9 walks securely, but he who takes crooked **paths** will be found out.
10: 29 The **way** *of* the LORD is a refuge for the righteous, but it is the
11: 5 The righteousness of the blameless makes a straight **way** *for* them,
11: 20 perverse heart but he delights in those whose **ways** are blameless.
12: 15 The **way** *of* a fool seems right to him, but a wise man listens to
12: 26 cautious in friendship, but the **way** *of* the wicked leads them astray.
12: 28 way of righteousness there is life; **along** that path is immortality.
13: 6 Righteousness guards the **man of integrity** [+9448], but
13: 15 understanding wins favor, but the **way** *of* the unfaithful is hard.
14: 2 fears the LORD, but he whose **ways** are devious despises him.
14: 8 The wisdom of the prudent is to give thought to their **ways**,
14: 12 There is a **way** that seems right to a man, but in the end it leads to
14: 12 is a way that seems right to a man, but in the end it **leads to** death.
14: 14 The faithless will be fully repaid for their **ways**, and the good man
15: 9 The LORD detests the **way** *of* the wicked but he loves those who
15: 19 The **way** *of* the sluggard is blocked with thorns, but the path of the
16: 2 All a man's **ways** seem innocent to him, but motives are weighed
16: 7 When a man's **ways** are pleasing to the LORD, he makes even his
16: 9 In his heart a man plans his **course**, but the LORD determines his
16: 17 of the upright avoids evil; he who guards his **way** guards his life.
16: 25 There is a **way** that seems right to a man, but in the end it leads to
16: 25 is a way that seems right to a man, but in the end it **leads** *to* death.
16: 29 entices his neighbor and leads him down a **path** that is not good.
16: 31 Gray hair is a crown of splendor; it is attained by a righteous **life**.
19: 3 A man's own folly ruins his **life**, yet his heart rages against the
19: 16 guards his life, but he who is contemptuous of his **ways** will die.
20: 24 by the LORD. How then can anyone understand his own **way**?
21: 2 All a man's **ways** seem right to him, but the LORD weighs the
21: 8 The **way** *of* the guilty is devious, but the conduct of the innocent is
21: 16 A man who strays from the **path** *of* understanding comes to rest in
21: 29 puts up a bold front, but an upright man gives thought to his **ways**.
22: 5 In the **paths** *of* the wicked lie thorns and snares, but he who guards
22: 6 Train a child **in the way** [+6584+7023] he **should go**, and when he
23: 19 my son, and be wise, and keep your heart on the right **path**.
23: 26 My son, give me your heart and let your eyes keep to my **ways**,
26: 13 The sluggard says, "There is a lion in the **road**, a fierce lion
28: 6 whose walk is blameless than a rich man whose **ways** are perverse.
28: 10 He who leads the upright along an evil **path** will fall into his own
28: 18 is kept safe, but he whose **ways** are perverse will suddenly fall.
29: 27 detest the dishonest; the wicked detest the **upright** [+3838].
30: 19 the **way** *of* an eagle in the sky, the way of a snake on a rock,
30: 19 the way of an eagle in the sky, the **way** *of* a snake on a rock,
30: 19 the way of a snake on a rock, the **way** *of* a ship on the high seas,
30: 19 of a ship on the high seas, and the **way** *of* a man with a maiden.
30: 20 "This is the **way** *of* an adulteress: She eats and wipes her mouth
31: 3 your strength on women, your **vigor** on those who ruin kings.
Ecc 10: 3 Even as he walks along the **road**, the fool lacks sense and shows
11: 5 As you do not know the **path** *of* the wind, or how the body is
11: 9 Follow the **ways** *of* your heart and whatever your eyes see,
12: 5 when men are afraid of heights and of dangers in the **streets**;
Isa 2: 3 He will teach us his **ways**, so that we may walk in his paths."
3: 12 your guides lead you astray; they turn you from the **path** [+784].
8: 11 hand upon me, warning me not to follow the **way** *of* this people.
9: 1 [8:23] of the Gentiles, *by* the **way** *of* the sea, along the Jordan—
10: 24 you with a rod and lift up a club against you, **as** [+928] Egypt did.
10: 26 he will raise his staff over the waters, **as** [+928] he did in Egypt.
15: 5 as they go; on the **road** *to* Horonaim they lament their destruction.
30: 11 Leave this **way**, get off this path, and stop confronting us with the
30: 21 your ears will hear a voice behind you, saying, "This is the **way**;
35: 8 will be there; **[RPH]** it will be called the Way of Holiness.
35: 8 And a highway will be there; it will be called the **Way** *of* Holiness.
35: 8 will not journey on it; it will be for those who walk in that **Way**;
37: 29 in your mouth, and I will make you return by the **way** you came.
37: 34 By the **way** that he came he will return; he will not enter this city,"
40: 3 "In the desert prepare the **way** *for* the LORD; make straight in the
40: 14 taught him knowledge or showed him the **path** *of* understanding?
40: 27 and complain, O Israel, "My **way** is hidden from the LORD;
42: 16 I will lead the blind by **ways** they have not known,
42: 24 For they would not follow his **ways**; they did not obey his law.
43: 16 he who made a **way** through the sea, a path through the mighty
43: 19 I am making a **way** in the desert and streams in the wasteland.
45: 13 I will make all his **ways** straight. He will rebuild my city and set
48: 15 called him. I will bring him, and he will succeed in his **mission**.
48: 17 what is best for you, who directs you in the **way** you should go.
49: 9 "They will feed beside the **roads** and find pasture on every barren
49: 11 I will turn all my mountains into **roads**, and my highways will be
51: 10 who made a **road** in the depths of the sea so that the redeemed
53: 6 like sheep, have gone astray, each of us has turned to his own **way**;
55: 7 Let the wicked forsake his **way** and the evil man his thoughts.
55: 8 neither are your **ways** my ways," declares the LORD.
55: 8 neither are your ways my **ways**," declares the LORD.
55: 9 so are my **ways** higher than your ways and my thoughts than your
55: 9 so are my ways higher than your **ways** and my thoughts than your
56: 11 they all turn to their own **way**, each seeks his own gain.
57: 10 You were wearied by all your **ways**, but you would not say,
57: 14 And it will be said: "Build up, build up, prepare the **road**!
57: 14 the road! Remove the obstacles out of the **way** *of* my people."
57: 17 and hid my face in anger, yet he kept on in his willful **ways**.
57: 18 I have seen his **ways**, but I will heal him; I will guide him
58: 2 they seem eager to know my **ways**, as if they were a nation that
58: 13 if you honor it by not going your own **way** and not doing as you
59: 8 The **way** *of* peace they do not know; there is no justice in their
62: 10 Prepare the **way** *for* the people. Build up, build up the highway!
63: 17 do you make us wander from your **ways** and harden our hearts
64: 5 [64:4] of those who gladly do right, who remember your **ways**.
65: 2 who walk in **ways** not good, pursuing their own imaginations—
66: 3 They have chosen their own **ways**, and their souls delight in their
Jer 2: 17 by forsaking the LORD your God when he led you in the **way**?
2: 18 Now why **go to** Egypt to drink water from the Shihor? And why go
2: 18 the Shihor? And why **go to** Assyria to drink water from the River?
2: 23 See **how** you **behaved** in the valley; consider what you have done.
2: 23 You are a swift she-camel **running here and there** [+8592],
2: 33 How **skilled** *you* **are** [+3512] at pursuing love! Even the worst of
2: 33 Even the worst of women can learn from your **ways**.
2: 36 Why do you go about so much, changing your **ways**? You will be
3: 2 By the **roadside** you sat waiting for lovers, sat like a nomad in the
3: 13 you have scattered your **favors** to foreign gods under every
3: 21 because they have perverted their **ways** and have forgotten the
4: 11 from the barren heights in the desert blows **toward** my people,
4: 18 "Your own **conduct** and actions have brought this upon you.
5: 4 they are foolish, for they do not know the **way** *of* the LORD,
5: 5 surely they know the **way** *of* the LORD, the requirements of their
6: 16 "Stand at the **crossroads** and look; ask for the ancient paths,
6: 16 for the ancient paths, ask where the good **way** is, and walk in it,
6: 25 Do not go out to the fields or walk on the **roads**, for the enemy has
6: 27 and my people the ore, that you may observe and test their **ways**.
7: 3 Reform your **ways** and your actions, and I will let you live in this
7: 5 If you really change your **ways** and your actions and deal with

Jer 7:23 Walk in all the **ways** I command you, that it may go well with you.
10: 2 "Do not learn the **ways** *of* the nations or be terrified by signs in the
10:23 I know, O LORD, that a man's **life** is not his own; it is not for
12: 1 Why does the **way** *of* the wicked prosper? Why do all the faithless
12:16 if they learn well the **ways** *of* my people and swear by my name,
15: 7 destruction on my people, for they have not changed their **ways**.
16:17 My eyes are on all their **ways**; they are not hidden from me,
17:10 and examine the mind, to reward a man according to his **conduct**,
18:11 So turn from your evil **ways**, each one of you, and reform your
18:11 each one of you, and reform your **ways** and your actions.'
18:15 which made them stumble in their **ways** and in the ancient paths.
18:15 They made them walk in bypaths and on **roads** not built up.
21: 8 I am setting before you the **way** *of* life and the way of death.
21: 8 I am setting before you the way of life and the **way** *of* death.
22:21 This has been your **way** from your youth; you have not obeyed me.
23:12 "Therefore their **path** will become slippery; they will be banished
23:22 would have turned them from their evil **ways** and from their evil
25: 5 each of you, from your evil **ways** and your evil practices,
26: 3 Perhaps they will listen and each will turn from his evil **way**.
26:13 Now reform your **ways** and your actions and obey the LORD
28:11 within two years.' " At this, the prophet Jeremiah went on his **way**.
31: 9 I will lead them beside streams of water on a level **path** where they
31:21 Take note of the highway, the **road** *that* you take. Return,
32:19 Your eyes are open to all the **ways** *of* men; you reward everyone
32:19 you reward everyone according to his **conduct** and as his deeds
32:39 I will give them singleness of heart and **action**, so that they will
35:15 "Each of you must turn from your wicked **ways** and reform your
36: 3 to inflict on them, each of them will turn from his wicked **way**;
36: 7 each will turn from his wicked **ways**, for the anger and wrath
39: 4 they left the city at night *by* **way** *of* the king's garden,
39: 4 the gate between the two walls, and headed **toward** the Arabah.
42: 3 Pray that the LORD your God will tell us **where**[s] [+2021] we
48:19 Stand by the **road** and watch, you who live in Aroer. Ask the man
50: 5 They will ask the **way** to Zion and turn their faces toward it.
52: 7 They left the city at night **through** the gate between the two walls
52: 7 were surrounding the city. They fled **toward** the Arabah,
La 1: 4 The **roads** *to* Zion mourn, for no one comes to her appointed
1:12 "Is it nothing to you, all you *who* **pass by** [+6296]? Look around
2:15 All who pass your **way** clap their hands at you; they scoff
3: 9 He has barred my **way** with blocks of stone; he has made my paths
3:11 he dragged me from the **path** and mangled me and left me without
3:40 Let us examine our **ways** and test them, and let us return to the
Eze 3:18 or speak out to dissuade him from his evil **ways** in order to save his
3:19 and he does not turn from his wickedness or from his evil **ways**,
7: 3 I will judge you according to your **conduct** and repay you for all
7: 4 I will surely repay you for your **conduct** and the detestable
7: 8 I will judge you according to your **conduct** and repay you for all
7: 9 I will repay you in accordance with your **conduct**
7:27 I will deal with them according to their **conduct**, and by their own
8: 5 Then he said to me, "Son of man, look **toward** the north."
8: 5 **[RPH]** and in the entrance north of the gate of the altar I saw this
9: 2 And I saw six men coming from the **direction** *of* the upper gate,
9:10 but I will bring down on their own heads **what** they have **done**."
11:21 I will bring down on their own heads **what** they have **done**,
13:22 you encouraged the wicked not to turn from their evil **ways**
14:22 come to you, and when you see their **conduct** and their actions,
14:23 You will be consoled when you see their **conduct** and their
16:25 At the head of every **street** you built your lofty shrines
16:27 of the Philistines, who were shocked by your lewd **conduct**.
16:31 When you built your mounds at the head of every **street** and made
16:43 I will surely bring down on your head **what** you have **done**,
16:47 You not only walked in their **ways** and copied their detestable
16:47 but in all your **ways** you soon became more depraved than they.
16:61 you will remember your **ways** and be ashamed when you receive
18:23 am I not pleased when they turn from their **ways** and live?
18:25 "Yet you say, 'The **way** *of* the Lord is not just.' Hear, O house of
18:25 of the Lord is not just.' Hear, O house of Israel: Is my **way** unjust?
18:25 of Israel: Is my way unjust? Is it not your **ways** that are unjust?
18:29 Yet the house of Israel says, 'The **way** *of* the Lord is not just.'
18:29 of the Lord is not just.' Are my **ways** unjust, O house of Israel?
18:29 ways unjust, O house of Israel? Is it not your **ways** that are unjust?
18:30 O house of Israel, I will judge you, each one according to his **ways**,
20:30 Will you defile yourselves the **way** your fathers did and lust after
20:43 There you will remember your **conduct** and all the actions by
20:44 and not according to your evil **ways** and your corrupt practices,
20:46 [21:2] "Son of man, set your face **toward** the south; preach
21:19 [21:24] mark out two **roads** for the sword of the king of Babylon
21:19 [21:24] Make a signpost where the **road** branches off to the city.
21:20 [21:25] Mark out *one* **road** for the sword to come against Rabbah
21:21 [21:26] For the king of Babylon will stop at the fork in the **road**,
21:21 [21:26] at the junction of the two **roads**, to seek an omen:
22:31 bringing down on their own heads *all* they have **done**,
23:13 I saw that she too defiled herself; both of them went the same **way**.
23:31 You have gone the **way** *of* your sister; so I will put her cup into
24:14 You will be judged according to your **conduct** and your actions,
28:15 You were blameless in your **ways** from the day you were created
33: 8 and you do not speak out to dissuade him from his **ways**,
33: 9 But if you do warn the wicked man to turn from his **ways**
33: 9 man to turn from his ways and *he does* not **do**[s] **so** [+4946+8740],
33:11 of the wicked, but rather that they turn from their **ways** and live.
33:11 turn from their ways and live. Turn! Turn from your evil **ways**!
33:17 "Yet your countrymen say, 'The **way** *of* the Lord is not just.'
33:17 'The way of the Lord is not just.' But it is their **way** that is not just.
33:20 O house of Israel, you say, 'The **way** *of* the Lord is not just.'
33:20 not just.' But I will judge each of you according to his own **ways**."
36:17 in their own land, they defiled it by their **conduct** and their actions.
36:17 Their **conduct** was like a woman's monthly uncleanness in my
36:19 I judged them according to their **conduct** and their actions.
36:31 Then you will remember your evil **ways** and wicked deeds,
36:32 Be ashamed and disgraced for your **conduct**, O house of Israel!
40: 6 Then he went to the gate facing **[NIE]** east. He climbed its steps
40:10 Inside the **[NIE]** east gate were three alcoves on each side;
40:20 he measured the length and width of the gate facing **[NIE]** north,
40:22 the same measurements as those of the gate facing **[NIE]** east.
40:24 Then he led me to the south **side** and I saw a gate facing south.
40:24 Then he led me to the south side and I saw a gate **facing** south.
40:27 The inner court also had a gate **facing** south, and he measured from
40:27 and he measured from this gate to the outer gate on the south **side**;
40:32 he brought me to the inner court on the east **side**, and he measured
40:44 one at the side of the north gate and facing **[NIE]** south,
40:44 and another at the side of the south gate and facing **[NIE]** north.
40:45 "The room facing **[NIE]** south is for the priests who have charge
40:46 the room facing **[NIE]** north is for the priests who have charge of
41:11 from the open area, one **on** the north and another on the south;
41:12 The building facing the temple courtyard on the west side **[NIE]**
42: 1 the man led me **northward** [+2021+7600] into the outer court and
42: 1 **[RPH]** and brought me to the rooms opposite the temple
42: 4 an inner passageway ten cubits wide and a hundred cubits **long**.
42: 7 was an outer wall parallel to the rooms and **[NIE]** the outer court;
42:10 On the south **side** along the length of the wall of the outer court,
42:11 with a **passageway** in front of them. These were like the rooms on
42:11 These were like the rooms **on** the north; they had the same length
42:12 were the doorways of the rooms **on** the south. There was a
42:12 There was a doorway at the beginning of the **passageway** that was
42:12 There was a doorway at the beginning of the passageway **that**[s] was
42:12 that was parallel to the corresponding wall **extending** eastward,
42:15 he led me out **by** the east gate and measured the area all around:
42:15 me out by the east gate **[RPH]** and measured the area all around:
43: 1 Then the man brought me to the gate facing **[NIE]** east,
43: 2 I saw the glory of the God of Israel coming from **[NIE]** the east.
43: 4 The glory of the LORD entered the temple **through** the gate
43: 4 LORD entered the temple through the gate facing **[RPH]** east.
44: 1 Then the man brought me back **to** the outer gate of the sanctuary,
44: 3 He is to enter by **way** *of* the portico of the gateway and go out the
44: 3 by way of the portico of the gateway and go out the same **way**."
44: 4 the man brought me *by* **way** *of* the north gate to the front of the
46: 2 The prince is to enter from the outside **through** the portico of the
46: 8 the prince enters, he is to go in **through** the portico of the gateway,
46: 8 the portico of the gateway, and he is to come out the same **way**.
46: 9 whoever enters **by** the north gate to worship is to go out the south
46: 9 whoever enters by the north gate to worship is to go out **[RPH]**
46: 9 and whoever enters **by** the south gate is to go out the north gate.
46: 9 whoever enters by the south gate is to go out the **[RPH]** north
46: 9 No one is to return **through** the gate by which he entered,
47: 2 He then brought me out **through** the north gate and led me around
47: 2 and led me around **[RPH]** the outside to the outer gate facing east,
47: 2 and led me around the outside to the outer gate **[RPH]** facing east,
47:15 the Great Sea by the Hethlon **road** past Lebo Hamath to Zedad,
48: 1 it will follow the Hethlon **road** to Lebo Hamath; Hazar Enan
Hos 2: 6 [2:8] Therefore I will block her **path** with thornbushes; I will wall
4: 9 I will punish both of them for their **ways** and repay them for their
6: 9 they murder on the **road** to Shechem, committing shameful crimes.
9: 8 the watchman over Ephraim, yet snares await him on all his **paths**,
10:13 Because you have depended on your own **strength** and on your
12: 2 [12:3] he will punish Jacob according to his **ways** and repay him
13: 7 come upon them like a lion, like a leopard I will lurk by the **path**.
14: 9 [14:10] The **ways** *of* the LORD are right; the righteous walk in
Joel 2: 7 They all march in **line**, not swerving from their course.
Am 2: 7 as upon the dust of the ground and deny **justice** *to* the oppressed.
4:10 "I sent plagues among you **as** [+928] I did to Egypt. I killed your
8:14 god lives, O Dan,' or, 'As surely as the **god** *of* Beersheba lives'—
Jnh 3: 8 on God. Let them give up their evil **ways** and their violence.
3:10 God saw what they did and how they turned from their evil **ways**,
Mic 4: 2 He will teach us his **ways**, so that we may walk in his paths."
Na 1: 3 His **way** is in the whirlwind and the storm, and clouds are the dust
2: 1 [2:2] Guard the fortress, watch the **road**, brace yourselves,
Hag 1: 5 the LORD Almighty says: "Give careful thought to your **ways**.
1: 7 the LORD Almighty says: "Give careful thought to your **ways**.

Zec 1: 4 'Turn from your evil **ways** and your evil practices.' But they would
1: 6 'The LORD Almighty has done to us what our **ways** and practices
3: 7 'If you will walk in my **ways** and keep my requirements, then you
Mal 2: 8 you have turned from the **way** and by your teaching have caused
2: 9 because you have not followed my **ways** but have shown partiality
3: 1 I will send my messenger, who will prepare the **way** before me.

2007 דַּרְכְּמוֹנִים *dark^e môn^îm*, n.[m.]. [4] [→ 163]

drachmas [4]

Ezr 2: 69 they gave to the treasury for this work 61,000 **drachmas** of gold,
Ne 7: 70 [7:69] The governor gave to the treasury 1,000 **drachmas** of gold,
7: 71 [7:70] gave to the treasury for the work 20,000 **drachmas** of gold
7: 72 [7:71] by the rest of the people was 20,000 **drachmas** of gold,

2008 דַּרְמֶשֶׂק *darmeśeq*, n.pr.loc. [6] [√ 1966]

Damascus [6]

1Ch 18: 5 When the Arameans of **Damascus** came to help Hadadezer king of
18: 6 He put garrisons in the Aramean kingdom of **Damascus**,
2Ch 16: 2 sent it to Ben-Hadad king of Aram, who was ruling in **Damascus**.
24: 23 of the people. They sent all the plunder to their king in **Damascus**.
28: 5 many of his people as prisoners and brought them to **Damascus**.
28: 23 He offered sacrifices to the gods of **Damascus**, who had defeated

2009 דָּרַע *dāra'*, n.pr.m. [1 / 0] [cf. 1997]

1Ch 2: 6 Zimri, Ethan, Heman, Calcol and Darda—[BHS *Dara*; NIV 1997]

2010 דַּרְקוֹן *darqôn*, n.pr.m. [2]

Darkon [2]

Ezr 2: 56 Jaala, **Darkon**, Giddel,
Ne 7: 58 Jaala, **Darkon**, Giddel,

2011 דָּרַשׁ *dāraš*, v. [163] [→ 4535]

seek [34], inquire of [19], sought [11], consult [5], seeking [5], consult [+928] [4], call to account [3], demand an accounting [3], inquire of [+928] [3], cares for [2], certainly demand [+2011] [2], consults [2], inquired about [+906+2011] [2], investigate [2], let inquire of [+4200] [2], let inquire of at all [+2011+4200] [2], look [2], require [2], search for [2], searches [2], seek help [2], seek out [2], seeks [2], sought out [2], study [2], appeal [1], are pondered [1], ask [+1821+4946+6640] [1], ask [1], asked [1], avenges [1], call to account [+4946+6640] [1], care about [1], care for [1], carefully investigated [+1335+2256] [1], cares [1], comes looking for [1], consult [+928+1821] [1], consulted [1], find out [1], follow [1], give an accounting [1], guidance [1], hold accountable [+3338+4946] [1], hold accountable [+906+3338+4946] [1], inquire of [+4200] [1], inquire of [+448] [1], inquire of [+907+4946] [1], inquire of [+928+4200] [1], inquire [1], inquired of [1], inquiring [1], let inquire of [1], look for [1], look to [1], make investigation [1], probe [1], rally [1], required [+6584] [1], revealed myself [1], search was made [1], searched [1], searches for [1], seek will [1], selects [1], sought after [1], worked for [1], would [1], yield to the plea [1]

Ge 9: 5 [A] And for your lifeblood *I will* surely **demand an accounting**.
9: 5 [A] *I will* **demand an accounting** from every animal. And from
9: 5 [A] *I will* **demand an accounting** for the life of his fellow man.
25: 22 [A] happening to me?" So she went to **inquire of** the LORD.
42: 22 [A] Now *we must* **give an accounting** *for* his blood."
Ex 18: 15 [A] "Because the people come to me to **seek** God's **will**.
Lev 10: 16 [A] When Moses **inquired** [+906+2011] **about** the goat of the
10: 16 [A] When Moses **inquired about** [+906+2011] the goat of the
Dt 4: 29 [A] you will find him if *you* **look for** him with all your heart
11: 12 [A] It is a land the LORD your God **cares for**; the eyes of the
12: 5 [A] *you are to* **seek** the place the LORD your God will choose
12: 30 [A] be careful not to be ensnared *by* **inquiring** about their gods,
13: 14 [13:15] [A] *you must* **inquire**, probe and investigate it
17: 4 [A] to your attention, then *you must* **investigate** it thoroughly.
17: 9 [A] that time. **Inquire of** them and they will give you the verdict.
18: 11 [A] or who is a medium or spiritist or *who* **consults** the dead.
18: 19 [A] my name, *I* myself *will* **call** him **to account** [+4946+6640].
19: 18 [A] The judges *must* **make** *a* thorough **investigation**, and if the
22: 2 [A] it home with you and keep it until he **comes looking for** it.
23: 6 [23:7] [A] *Do* not **seek** a treaty of friendship with them as long
23: 21 [23:22] [A] your God *will* **certainly demand** [+2011] it of you
23: 21 [23:22] [A] your God *will* **certainly demand** [+2011] it of you
Jdg 6: 29 [A] When *they* **carefully investigated** [+1335+2256], they were
1Sa 9: 9 [A] if a man went to **inquire of** God, he would say, "Come,
28: 7 [A] who is a medium, so I may go and **inquire** [+928] **of** her."
2Sa 11: 3 [A] and David sent someone *to* **find out** about her. The man said,
1Ki 14: 5 [A] "Jeroboam's wife is coming to **ask** [+1821+4946+6640] you
22: 5 [A] to the king of Israel, "First **seek** the counsel of the LORD."
22: 7 [A] of the LORD here whom *we can* **inquire** [+907+4946] **of**?"
22: 8 [A] "There is still one man through whom we *can* **inquire of** the
2Ki 1: 2 [A] saying to them, "Go and **consult** [+928] Baal-Zebub, the god
1: 3 [A] in Israel that you are going off to **consult** [+928] Baal-Zebub,
1: 6 [A] that you are sending men to **consult** [+928] Baal-Zebub,
1: 16 [A] **consult** [+928+1821] that you have sent messengers to
1: 16 [A] that you have sent messengers to **consult** [+928] Baal-Zebub,
3: 11 [A] that *we may* **inquire of** the LORD through him?"
8: 8 [A] **Consult** the LORD through him; ask him, 'Will I recover
22: 13 [A] "Go and **inquire of** the LORD for me and for the people
22: 18 [A] the king of Judah, who sent you to **inquire of** the LORD,
1Ch 10: 13 [A] of the LORD and even consulted a medium for **guidance**,
10: 14 [A] *did* not **inquire** [+928] **of** the LORD. So the LORD put
13: 3 [A] to us, for *we did* not **inquire of** it during the reign of Saul."
15: 13 [A] *We did* not **inquire of** him *about* how to do it in the
16: 11 [A] **Look to** the LORD and his strength; seek his face always.
21: 30 [A] David could not go before it to **inquire of** God, because he
22: 19 [A] devote your heart and soul to **seeking** the LORD your God.
26: 31 [C] In the fortieth year of David's reign *a* **search was made** in
28: 8 [A] Be careful *to* **follow** all the commands of the LORD your
28: 9 [A] for the LORD **searches** every heart and understands every
28: 9 [A] If *you* **seek** him, he will be found by you; but if you forsake
2Ch 1: 5 [A] so Solomon and the assembly **inquired of** him there.
12: 14 [A] because he had not set his heart on **seeking** the LORD.
14: 4 [14:3] [A] He commanded Judah to **seek** the LORD, the God
14: 7 [14:6] [A] because *we have* **sought** the LORD our God;
14: 7 [14:6] [A] *we* **sought** him and he has given us rest on every
15: 2 [A] If *you* **seek** him, he will be found by you, but if you forsake
15: 12 [A] They entered into a covenant to **seek** the LORD, the God of
15: 13 [A] All who *would* not **seek** the LORD, the God of Israel,
16: 12 [A] even in his illness *he did* not **seek help** *from* the LORD,
17: 3 [A] his father David had followed. *He did* not **consult** the Baals
17: 4 [A] **sought** the God of his father and followed his commands
18: 4 [A] to the king of Israel, "First **seek** the counsel of the LORD."
18: 6 [A] not a prophet of the LORD here whom *we can* **inquire of**?"
18: 7 [A] "There is still one man through whom we *can* **inquire of** the
19: 3 [A] the Asherah poles and have set your heart on **seeking** God."
20: 3 [A] Jehoshaphat resolved to **inquire** [+4200] **of** the LORD,
22: 9 [A] of Jehoshaphat, who **sought** the LORD with all his heart."
24: 6 [A] "Why haven't *you* **required** [+6584] the Levites to bring in
24: 22 [A] "May the LORD see this and **call** you **to account**."
25: 15 [A] to him, who said, "Why *do you* **consult** this people's gods,
25: 20 [A] over to ⌊Jehoash⌋, because *they* **sought** the gods of Edom.
26: 5 [A] He **sought** God during the days of Zechariah, who instructed
26: 5 [A] As long as he **sought** the LORD, God gave him success.
30: 19 [A] who sets his heart *on* **seeking** God—the LORD, the God of
31: 9 [A] Hezekiah **asked** the priests and Levites about the heaps;
31: 21 [A] he **sought** his God and worked wholeheartedly.
32: 31 [A] **ask** him *about* the miraculous sign that had occurred in the
34: 3 [A] still young, he began to **seek** the God of his father David.
34: 21 [A] "Go and **inquire of** the LORD for me and for the remnant
34: 26 [A] of Judah, who sent you to **inquire** [+928] **of** the LORD,
Ezr 4: 2 [A] *we* **seek** your God and have been sacrificing to him since the
6: 21 [A] of their Gentile neighbors in order to **seek** the LORD,
7: 10 [A] For Ezra had devoted himself to the **study** and observance of
9: 12 [A] *Do* not **seek** a treaty of friendship with them at any time, that
10: 16 [A] month they sat down to **investigate** [BHS 2004] the cases,
Est 10: 3 [A] because *he* **worked for** the good of his people and spoke up
Job 3: 4 [A] may it turn to darkness; *may* God above not **care about** it;
5: 8 [A] "But if it were I, *I would* **appeal** to God; I would lay my
10: 6 [A] that you must search out my faults and **probe** after my sin—
39: 8 [A] the hills for his pasture and **searches** for any green thing.
Ps 9: 10 [9:11] [A] LORD, have never forsaken *those who* **seek** you.
9: 12 [9:13] [A] For *he who* **avenges** blood remembers; he does not
10: 4 [A] In his pride the wicked *does* not **seek** him; in all his thoughts
10: 13 [A] Why does he say to himself, "*He* won't **call** me **to account**"?
10: 15 [A] **call** him **to account** *for* his wickedness that would not be
14: 2 [A] to see if there are any who understand, *any who* **seek** God.
22: 26 [22:27] [A] *they who* **seek** the LORD will praise him—
24: 6 [A] Such is the generation of *those who* **seek** him, who seek your
34: 4 [34:5] [A] *I* **sought** the LORD, and he answered me; he
34: 10 [34:11] [A] but *those who* **seek** the LORD lack no good thing.
38: 12 [38:13] [A] *those who* **would** harm me talk of my ruin;
53: 2 [53:3] [A] if there are any who understand, *any who* **seek** God.
69: 32 [69:33] [A] be glad—you *who* **seek** God, may your hearts live!
77: 2 [77:3] [A] When I was in distress, *I* **sought** the Lord; at night I
78: 34 [A] Whenever God slew them, *they would* **seek** him; they
105: 4 [A] **Look** *to* the LORD and his strength; seek his face always.
109: 10 [e] *may they* **be driven** [BHS *sought*; NIV 1763] from their ruined
111: 2 [B] the LORD; *they* **are pondered** by all who delight in them.
119: 2 [A] they who keep his statutes and **seek** him with all their heart.
119: 10 [A] *I* **seek** you with all my heart; do not let me stray from your
119: 45 [A] walk about in freedom, for *I have* **sought out** your precepts.
119: 94 [A] Save me, for I am yours; *I have* **sought out** your precepts.
119: 155 [A] far from the wicked, for *they do* not **seek out** your decrees.

[A] Qal [B] Qal passive [C] Niphal [D] Piel (poel, polel, pilel, pilal, pealal, pilpel) [E] Pual (poal, polal, poalal, pulal, pualal)

Ps 142: 4 [142:5] [A] for me. I have no refuge; no *one* **cares for** my life.
Pr 11:27 [A] finds goodwill, but evil comes to him *who* **searches for** it.
31:13 [A] *She* **selects** wool and flax and works with eager hands.
Ecc 1:13 [A] I devoted myself to **study** and to explore by wisdom all that
Isa 1:17 [A] learn to do right! **Seek** justice, encourage the oppressed.
8:19 [A] When men tell you *to* **consult** mediums and spiritists,
8:19 [A] and mutter, *should* not a people **inquire** [+448] **of** their God?
9:13 [9:12] [A] nor *have they* **sought** the LORD Almighty.
11:10 [A] the nations *will* **rally** to him, and his place of rest will be
16: 5 [A] one who in judging **seeks** justice and speeds the cause of
19: 3 [A] *they will* **consult** the idols and the spirits of the dead,
31: 1 [A] to the Holy One of Israel, or **seek help** *from* the LORD.
34:16 [A] **Look** in the scroll of the LORD and read: None of these
55: 6 [A] **Seek** the LORD while he may be found; call on him while
58: 2 [A] For day after day *they* **seek** me **out**; they seem eager to know
62:12 [B] you will be called **Sought After**, the City No Longer
65: 1 [C] "*I* **revealed myself** to those who did not ask for me; I was
65:10 [A] Achor a resting place for herds, for my people who **seek** me.
Jer 8: 2 [A] and which they have followed and **consulted** and worshiped.
10:21 [A] shepherds are senseless and *do* not **inquire of** the LORD;
21: 2 [A] "**Inquire** now **of** the LORD for us because Nebuchadnezzar
29: 7 [A] **seek** the peace and prosperity of the city to which I have
29:13 [A] seek me and find me when *you* **seek** me with all your heart.
30:14 [A] your allies have forgotten you; *they* **care** nothing **for** you.
30:17 [A] you are called an outcast, Zion for whom no *one* **cares**.'
37: 7 [A] of Judah, who sent you to **inquire of** me, 'Pharaoh's army,
38: 4 [A] This man *is* not **seeking** the good of these people but their
La 3:25 [A] to those whose hope is in him, to the one *who* **seeks** him;
Eze 14: 3 [C] *Should I* **let** them **inquire** [+2011+4200] **of** *me* **at all**?
14: 3 [C] *Should I* **let** them **inquire of** *me* **at all** [+2011+4200]?
14: 7 [A] and then goes to a prophet to **inquire** [+928+4200] **of** me,
14:10 [A] the prophet will be as guilty as the *one who* **consults** him.
20: 1 [A] some of the elders of Israel came to **inquire of** the LORD,
20: 3 [A] Have you come to **inquire of** me? As surely as I live, I will
20: 3 [C] As surely as I live, *I will* not **let** you **inquire of** *me*, declares
20:31 [C] *Am* I *to* **let** you **inquire** [+4200] **of** *me*, O house of Israel?
20:31 [C] Sovereign LORD, *I will* not **let** you **inquire** [+4200] **of** *me*.
20:40 [A] There *I will* **require** your offerings and your choice gifts,
33: 6 [A] but *I will* **hold** the watchman **accountable** [+3338+4946] *for*
34: 6 [A] the whole earth, and no *one* **searched** or looked for them.
34: 8 [A] because my shepherds *did* not **search for** my flock but cared
34:10 [A] *will* **hold** them **accountable** [+906+3338+4946] *for* my flock.
34:11 [A] I myself *will* **search for** my sheep and look after them.
36:37 [C] Once again *I will* **yield to the plea** of the house of Israel
Hos 10:12 [A] for it is time to **seek** the LORD, until he comes and showers
Am 5: 4 [A] the LORD says to the house of Israel: "**Seek** me and live;
5: 5 [A] *do* not **seek** Bethel, do not go to Gilgal, do not journey to
5: 6 [A] **Seek** the LORD and live, or he will sweep through the
5:14 [A] **Seek** good, not evil, that you may live. Then the LORD
Mic 6: 8 [A] what *does* the LORD **require** of you? To act justly and to
Zep 1: 6 [A] the LORD and neither seek the LORD nor **inquire of** him.

2012 דָּשָׁא *dāšā'*, v. [2] [→ 2013]

green [1], produce [1]

Ge 1:11 [G] God said, "*Let* the land **produce** vegetation:
Joel 2:22 [A] O wild animals, for the open pastures *are becoming* **green**.

2013 דֶּשֶׁא *deše'*, n.m. [14] [√ 2012; Ar 10187]

grass [4], green [4], vegetation [3], grass [+4604] [1], new grass [1], new growth [1]

Ge 1:11 God said, "Let the land produce **vegetation**: seed-bearing plants
1:12 The land produced **vegetation**: plants bearing seed according to
Dt 32: 2 and my words descend like dew, like showers on **new grass**,
2Sa 23: 4 like the brightness after rain that brings the **grass** from the earth.'
2Ki 19:26 like tender **green** shoots, like grass sprouting on the roof, scorched
Job 6: 5 Does a wild donkey bray when it has **grass**, or an ox bellow when
38:27 a desolate wasteland and make it sprout with **grass** [+4604]?
Ps 23: 2 He makes me lie down in **green** pastures, he leads me beside quiet
37: 2 they will soon wither, like **green** plants they will soon die away.
Pr 27:25 When the hay is removed and **new growth** appears and the grass
Isa 15: 6 grass is withered; the **vegetation** is gone and nothing green is left.
37:27 like tender **green** shoots, like grass sprouting on the roof, scorched
66:14 see this, your heart will rejoice and you will flourish like **grass**;
Jer 14: 5 in the field deserts her newborn fawn because there is no **grass**.

2014 [1]דָּשֵׁן *dāšēn[1]*, v. [11] [→ 2015, 2016]

prosper [2], remove ashes [2], accept [1], anoint [1], are fully satisfied [1], be soaked [1], gives health [1], is covered [1], thrive [1]

Ex 27: 3 [D] its pots to **remove** the **ashes**, and its shovels, sprinkling
Nu 4:13 [D] "*They are to* **remove** the **ashes** *from* the bronze altar
Dt 31:20 [A] when they eat their fill and **thrive**, they will turn to other
Ps 20: 3 [20:4] [D] all your sacrifices and **accept** your burnt offerings.
23: 5 [D] *You* **anoint** my head with oil; my cup overflows.
Pr 11:25 [E] A generous man *will* **prosper**; he who refreshes others will
13: 4 [E] but the desires of the diligent **are fully satisfied**.
15:30 [D] joy to the heart, and good news **gives health** *to* the bones.
28:25 [E] up dissension, but he who trusts in the LORD *will* **prosper**.
Isa 34: 6 [F] of the LORD is bathed in blood, *it* **is covered** with fat—
34: 7 [E] be drenched with blood, and the dust *will* **be soaked** with fat.

2015 [2]דָּשֵׁן *dāšēn[2]*, a. [2] [√ 2014]

fresh [1], rich [1]

Ps 92:14 [92:15] still bear fruit in old age, they will stay **fresh** and green,
Isa 30:23 and the food that comes from the land will be **rich** and plentiful.

2016 דֶּשֶׁן *dešen*, n.m. [16] [√ 2014]

ashes [7], abundance [3], ash [1], choice food [1], oil [1], rich [1], richest of fare [1], richest of foods [+2256+2693] [1]

Lev 1:16 and throw it to the east side of the altar, where the **ashes** are.
4:12 where the **ashes** are thrown, and burn it in a wood fire on the ash
4:12 the ashes are thrown, and burn it in a wood fire on the **ash** heap.
6:10 [6:3] shall remove the **ashes** of the burnt offering that the fire has
6:11 [6:4] carry the **ashes** outside the camp to a place that is
Jdg 9: 9 'Should I give up my **oil**, by which both gods and men are honored,
1Ki 13: 3 The altar will be split apart and the **ashes** on it will be poured out."
13: 5 its **ashes** poured out according to the sign given by the man of God
Job 36:16 to the comfort of your table laden with **choice food**.
Ps 22:29 [22:30] All the **rich** *of* the earth will feast and worship; all who go
36: 8 [36:9] They feast on the **abundance** *of* your house; you give them
63: 5 [63:6] be satisfied as with the **richest** [+2256+2693] **of foods**;
65:11 [65:12] your bounty, and your carts overflow with **abundance**.
Isa 55: 2 eat what is good, and your soul will delight in the **richest of fare**.
Jer 31:14 I will satisfy the priests with **abundance**, and my people will be
31:40 The whole valley where dead bodies and **ashes** are thrown,

2017 דָּת *dāt*, n.f. [21] [→ Ar 10186]

edict [8], law [6], laws [2], command [1], customs [1], order [1], orders [1], prescribed [1]

Dt 33: 2 [the south, from his **mountain slopes**. [Q +836; see K 850]]
Ezr 8:36 They also delivered the king's **orders** to the royal satraps and to
Est 1: 8 By the king's **command** each guest was allowed to drink in his
1:13 it was customary for the king to consult experts in *matters of* **law**
1:15 "According to **law**, what must be done to Queen Vashti?'
1:19 a royal decree and let it be written in the **laws** *of* Persia and Media,
2: 8 When the king's order and **edict** had been proclaimed, many girls
2:12 twelve months of beauty treatments **prescribed** *for* the women,
3: 8 whose **customs** are different from those of all other people
3: 8 those of all other people and who do not obey the king's **laws**;
3:14 A copy of the text of the edict was to be issued as **law** in every
3:15 couriers went out, and the **edict** was issued in the citadel of Susa.
4: 3 In every province to which the edict and **order** *of* the king came,
4: 8 He also gave him a copy of the text of the **edict** for their
4:11 the inner court without being summoned the king has but one **law**:
4:16 this is done, I will go to the king, even though it is against the **law**.
8:13 A copy of the text of the edict was to be issued as **law** in every
8:14 And the **edict** was also issued in the citadel of Susa.
8:17 wherever the **edict** *of* the king went, there was joy and gladness
9: 1 of Adar, the **edict** commanded by the king was to be carried out.
9:13 "give the Jews in Susa permission to carry out this day's **edict**
9:14 An **edict** was issued in Susa, and they hanged the ten sons of

2018 דָּתָן *dātān*, n.pr.m. [10]

Dathan [10]

Nu 16: 1 **Dathan** and Abiram, sons of Eliab, and On son of Peleth—
16:12 Then Moses summoned **Dathan** and Abiram, the sons of Eliab.
16:24 'Move away from the tents of Korah, **Dathan** and Abiram.' "
16:25 Moses got up and went to **Dathan** and Abiram, and the elders of
16:27 So they moved away from the tents of Korah, **Dathan** and Abiram.
16:27 **Dathan** and Abiram had come out and were standing with their
26: 9 the sons of Eliab were Nemuel, **Dathan** and Abiram. The same
26: 9 The same **Dathan** and Abiram were the community officials who
Dt 11: 6 what he did to **Dathan** and Abiram, sons of Eliab the Reubenite,
Ps 106:17 The earth opened up and swallowed **Dathan**; it buried the

2019 דֹּתָן *dōtān*, n.pr.loc. [3]

Dothan [3]

Ge 37:17 'Let's go to **Dothan**.' " So Joseph went after his brothers and found
37:17 So Joseph went after his brothers and found them near **Dothan**.
2Ki 6:13 and capture him." The report came back: "He is in **Dothan**."

ה, *h*

2020 ה ***h***, letter. Not used in NIV/BHS [→ Ar 10189]

2021 -הַ ***ha-***, art.pref. [30393 / 30401] [→ Ar 10002; *also used with compound proper names*] Not indexed

the [16202], *untranslated* [9915], a [760], who [469], that [205], his[s] [157], this [150], those [145], today [+3427] [137], their[s] [95], this[s] [+1821+2021+2296] [88], an [78], today [+2021+2296+3427] [78], what [67], your[s] [59], these [54], he[s] [44], each [40], O [35], now [+2021+2296+3427] [34], my[s] [31], what[s] [+1821] [31], him[s] [+4889] [29], they[s] [+6639] [28], he[s] [+4889] [26], one [26], its[s] [25], this[s] [+465+1821+2021] [24], her[s] [22], any [21], them[s] [+6639] [19], always [+3427+3972] [18], anyone [18], they[s] [18], which [18], whoever [18], other[s] [17], he[s] [+3913] [16], now [+3427] [14], our[s] [14], you[s] [13], some time later [+339+465+1821+2021] [12], at twilight [+1068+6847] [11], everything [+1821+3972] [11], whatever [11], him[s] [10], it[s] [+6551] [10], tonight [+4326] [10], it[s] [+1473] [9], some[s] [9], they[s] [+408] [9], every morning [+928+928+1332+1332 +2021] [8], every [8], it[s] [+1821+2021+2296] [8], burn down [+836+928+8596] [7], everyone [+3972+5883] [7], it[s] [7], outside [+928+2575] [7], before [+928+8037] [6], ever since [+2021+2296 +3427+6330] [6], he[s] [+408] [6], her[s] [+851] [6], his[s] [+4889] [6], it[s] [+1821] [6], it[s] [+4640] [6], it[s] [+824] [6], prison [+1074+6045] [6], secretly [+928+6260] [6], set on fire [+836+906+928+3675] [6], she[s] [+851] [6], sunset [+995 +9087] [6], what[s] [+1821+2021+2296] [6], as long as [+3427+3972] [5], burned [+836+906+928+8596] [5], there[s] [+928+1195] [5], this[s] [+1821] [5], those[s] [+6639] [5], all day long [+928+2021+2085+3427] [4], allotted [+928+1598+4200] [4], be burned up [+836+928+8596] [4], burned down [+836+906+928 +8596] [4], day after day [+3427+3972] [4], falsely [+4200+9214] [4], first [+3427+3869] [4], he[s] [+2021+2085+5883] [4], here[s] [+2021+2296+5226] [4], his[s] own [4], in vain [+4200+8736] [4], it[s] [+1074] [4], it[s] [+1947] [4], it[s] [+3542] [4], it[s] [+778] [4], its[s] [+380] [4], now [+465+928+2021+3427] [4], prison [+1074+3975] [4], still [+2021+2296+3427+6330] [4], them[s] [+7931] [4], those[s] [+408] [4], Trans-Euphrates [+5643+6298] [4], what[s] [+465+1821+2021] [4], who[s] [+3913] [4], anyone [+408+4769] [3], burning [+836+6584] [3], daybreak [+240+1332] [3], east [+4667+9087] [3], first [+928+9378] [3], forever [+3427+3972] [3], he[s] [+7149] [3], him[s] [+408] [3], his own[s] [+4889] [3], it[s] [+185] [3], it[s] [+2215] [3], it[s] [+5438] [3], it[s] [+5596] [3], it[s] [+5999] [3], it[s] [+6219] [3], its[s] [+4640] [3], its[s] [+824] [3], men[s] [3], on high [+928+5294] [3], set on fire [+836+928+3675] [3], stone [+74+906+928+8083] [3], them[s] [+3913] [3], them[s] [+7971] [3], what[s] [+5126] [3], what[s] [3], wherever [+889+928+2006] [3], whose [3], wild [+928+8441] [3], after a while [+339+465+1821 +2021] [2], again [+928+1685+2021+2085+7193] [2], Amaziah [+4889] [2], angels [+466+1201] [2], anyone [+3972+5883] [2], anything [+3972+3998] [2], anything [2], at once [+928+2021+2085 +3427] [2], at once [+928+2021+2085+6961] [2], both[s] [+170+2021 +2256+8533] [2], burn down [+836+906+928+8596] [2], burn up [+836+906+928+8596] [2], burned [+836+928+8596] [2], certain [2], champion [+408+1227] [2], chief officer [+7372+8569] [2], completely [+3972+4200] [2], continual [+3427+3972] [2], continually [+3427+3972] [2], dawn [+240+1332] [2], daybreak [+6590+8840] [2], each day [+2021+3427+3427+4200+4200] [2], each morning [+1332+1332+2021+4200+4200] [2], each morning [+928+928+1332 +1332+2021] [2], earlier [+928+9378] [2], east [+2025+4667+9087] [2], evening [+928+928+2021+6847+6847] [2], every evening [+928+928+2021+6847+6847] [2], everyone [+3972+6639] [2], everything [+465+1821+2021+3972] [2], first [+928+8037] [2], forever [+6330+6409] [2], gave the message [+465+1819+1821 +2021+3972] [2], he[s] [+340+408+2021] [2], he[s] [+408+2021+6640 +8886] [2], he[s] [+466] [2], he[s] [+8357] [2], her[s] [+5855] [2], her[s] [+912] [2], here[s] [+928+2021+2296+5226] [2], him[s] [+5853] [2], his own[s] [+2021+2418+5566] [2], his own[s] [+3913] [2], in broad daylight [+2021+2296+4200+6524+9087] [2], in midair [+824+1068+1068 +2021+2256+9028] [2], inside [+928+1074] [2], it[s] [+2021+2085 +5226] [2], it[s] [+2021+2296+6551] [2], it[s] [+2021+2296 +8878] [2], it[s] [+2021+2645+7606] [2], it[s] [+380] [2], it[s] [+4966] [2], it[s] [+5577] [2], it[s] [+7228] [2], it[s] [+7339] [2], it[s] [+8120] [2], it[s] [+824+2021+2296] [2], it[s] [+836] [2], its[s] [+1074] [2], its[s] [+2958] [2], its[s] [+3284] [2], its[s] [+7228] [2], its[s] [+9133] [2], Judah [+824] [2], lasting [+2021+2296 +3427+6330] [2], later [+339+465+1821+2021] [2], misuse [+906+4200+5951+8736] [2], misuses [+906+4200+5951+8736] [2], never [+3427+3972+4202] [2], now [+3869+6961] [2], on each side [+2021+2296+2296+4946+4946+4946+4946+6298+6298] [2], one[s] [+6639] [2], one's [2], prison [+1074+3999] [2], privately [+928+6260] [2], quietly [+928+4319] [2], reflects a face [+2021+4200+7156 +7156] [2], Sabbath after Sabbath [+928+928+2021+3427+3427 +8701+8701] [2], set on fire [+836+906+928+8596] [2], set on fire [+836+928+8596] [2], she[s] [+5853] [2], someone [2], someone[s] [2], something[s] [2], still [+2021+2296+3427+3869] [2], stone [+74+928+6232] [2], stone [+74+928+8083] [2], suggested [+1821+2021+2296] [2], sunrise [+2436+9087] [2], sunset [+995+6961+9087] [2], that[s] [+1074+2021+2296] [2], that[s] [+465+1821+2021] [2], that happened [+465+1821+2021] [2], the other[s] [+824+7895] [2], their[s] [+6639] [2], their[s] [+964] [2], their[s] own [2], them[s] [+1821+2021+2296] [2], them[s] [+2021+2296+6639] [2], them[s] [+3051] [2], them[s] [+3192] [2], them[s] [+3338] [2], them[s] [+3972+6639] [2], them[s] [+408] [2], them[s] [+4131] [2], them[s] [+4291] [2], them[s] [+5853] [2], them[s] [+8993] [2], them[s] [2], then [+2021+2085 +6961] [2], then [+340+928] [2], then[s] [+928+2021+2085+3427] [2], there[s] [+824] [2], there[s] [+928+1074] [2], there[s] [+928+2215] [2], they[s] [+3913] [2], they[s] [+7366] [2], they[s] [+824+6639] [2], this [+2021+2296+5126] [2], this is how [+465+1821+2021+3869] [2], this very [2], those[s] [+5877] [2], two-horned [+1251+7967] [2], used to [+4200+8037] [2], what[s] [+2006] [2], what[s] [+2021+2296+5184] [2], when [+928+3427] [2], where[s] [+2021+2667+2958] [2], where[s] [+5226] [2], wherever [+889+928+3972+5226] [2], whoever [+408+4769] [2], whose[s] [+285+2021+9108] [2], whose[s] [2], yet [+2021+2085+3427+6330] [2], yet [+2021+2156+3427+6330] [2], above [+928+5294] [1], abroad [+2575+4200] [1], accuses [+907+4200+5477+7756] [1], afternoon [+3427+5742] [1], age of childbearing [+784+851+3869] [1], ago [+3427] [1], Ai [+6551] [1], all around [+1885+3869] [1], all men [+132+1201] [1], all night long [+928+4326] [1], all-night [+3972+4326] [1], allotted [+906+906+928 +1598+5989] [1], allotted [+906+928+1598+5989] [1], allotted [+928+1598+2118+4200] [1], already [+928+9378] [1], annual [+285+928+9102] [1], annual [+928+7193+9102] [1], anointed [+1201+3658] [1], another [+132] [1], another [+2215+2296+4946] [1], another [+9019] [1], another[s] [1], any man [+408+4769] [1], anyone [+408] [1], anyone [+408+3972] [1], anyone [+4637] [1], anything [+1821+1821+3972+4946] [1], anything [+1821+3972] [1], anything[s] [1], archers [+408+928+4619+8008] [1], archers [+928+4619+8008] [1], are burned up [+836+928+8596+8596] [1], around [+2575+4946] [1], as [+3869] [1], assemble [+928+6590 +7736] [1], at [+928+2006] [1], at last [+7193] [1], at once [+3427] [1], at once [+928+3427] [1], at this time [+3427] [1], away [+448+2025+2575] [1], awhile [+3427+3869] [1], banded together [+665+2653+4200] [1], be burned [+836+928+8596] [1], be burned down [+836+928+8596] [1], be taken captive [+928+4090+9530] [1], before [+928+9378] [1], below [+141+6584] [1], below deck [+3752+6208] [1], besiege [+928+995+4946+5189+7156] [1], blind [+928+5782+6427] [1], Boaz [+408] [1], bought [+928+4084+7864] [1], breeding [+3501+7366] [1], brings to ruin [+4200+6156+8273] [1], burn [+836+906+906+906+928+8596] [1], burn [+836+906+906 +928+8596] [1], burn [+836+906+928+8596] [1], burn [+836+928 +8596] [1], burn to death [+836+906+906+928+8596] [1], burn up [+836+928+8596] [1], burned [+836+906+906+928+8596] [1], burned [+836+928+8938] [1], burned to death [+836+906+906 +928+8596] [1], burned up [+836+906+906+906+906+928+8596] [1], burned up [+836+906+906+906+928+8596] [1], burned up [+836+906+906+928+8596] [1], burned up [+836+906+928+8596] [1], callous [+2693+3869] [1], captain [+2480+8042] [1], cargo [+641+889+928+3998] [1], carry off [+928+995+8660] [1], charred [+836+928+1277] [1], children [+1061+7262] [1], commander in chief [+6584+7372] [1], community [+824+6639] [1], crops [+141+7262] [1], daily [+3427+4200] [1], David's[s] [1], daybreak [+1332+7155] [1], daylight [+240+1332] [1], did so[s] [+906+6913+7175] [1], distant [+2006+8049] [1], doing this[s] [+3569+6894] [1], doubly [+928+9109] [1], dreamer [+1251+2706] [1], each [+4090] [1], each day [+3427+4200] [1], end [+340+928+2118] [1], enthrones [+3782+4058+4200] [1], especially bred [+1201+8247] [1], evening [+6847+6961] [1], ever [+3427+3972] [1], every day [+3427+4200] [1], everyone [+132+3972] [1], everyone [+408+3972] [1], everyone[s] [1], everything [+3972] [1], everything [+3972+4856] [1], everywhere [+3972+5226] [1], fiercely [+928+6677] [1], fifteen feet [+564+928+6924] [1], fight [+3655+4200+4878] [1], followers [+339+889+6639] [1], for life [+3427+3972] [1], foreigner [+1201+5797] [1], foreigners [+1201+5797] [1], forevermore [+6330+6409] [1], formerly [+928+8037] [1], from now on [+3427+3972] [1], furthermore [+2256+9108] [1], get out of here [+906+2025+2575+4946+6584+8938] [1], give in marriage [+851+4200+5989] [1], God-fearing [+466+3710] [1], hard [+3668+4200+4607] [1], he[s] [+3381+3913] [1], he[s] [+3758+5566] [1], he[s] [+408+5283] [1], he[s] [+466+824] [1], he[s] [+4855] [1], he[s] [+5853] [1], he[s] [+7595] [1], he himself[s] [+3913] [1], her[s] [+6320] [1], here [+5226] [1], here [+824] [1], here[s] [+824+928] [1], here[s] [+928+4497] [1], him[s] [+1201+3778] [1], him[s] [+132] [1], him[s] [+3450] [1], him[s] [+3759+5566] [1], him[s] [+466] [1], him[s] [+4889+6460] [1], him[s] [+5782] [1], him[s] [+5999] [1], him[s] [+7127] [1], him[s] [+7140] [1], him[s] [+7149] [1], him[s] [+8357] [1], himself[s] [+408] [1], his[s] [+132] [1], his[s] [+408] [1], his[s] [+4637] [1], his[s] [+5566] [1], his[s] [+928+4889] [1], his own[s] [+367] [1], immediately [+3427+3869] [1], imprisoned [+657+906+1074+5989] [1], in [+1074+2025] [1], in broad daylight [+5584+9087] [1], infamous [+3238+9005] [1], inside [+448+1074] [1], interwoven [+928+1808] [1], Israel's[s] [1], Israelite [+408+3778] [1], it[s] [+1352] [1], it[s] [+1580] [1], it[s] [+1946] [1], it[s] [+2162] [1], it[s] [+2570] [1], it[s] [+258] [1], it[s] [+2633] [1], it[s] [+2706] [1], it[s] [+2851] [1], it[s] [+3051] [1], it[s] [+3136] [1], it[s] [+3855] [1], it[s] [+4058] [1], it[s] [+4084] [1], it[s] [+4114] [1], it[s] [+4223] [1], it[s] [+4258] [1], it[s] [+466+778] [1], it[s] [+4722] [1], it[s] [+4784] [1], it[s] [+4889+9133] [1], it[s] [+4963] [1], it[s] [+5120] [1], it[s] [+5261] [1], it[s] [+6130] [1], it[s] [+616+1473] [1], it[s] [+6174] [1], it[s] [+6322] [1], it[s] [+6592] [1], it[s] [+6639] [1], it[s] [+6727] [1], it[s] [+6770] [1], it[s] [+680] [1], it[s] [+7498] [1], it[s] [+7663] [1], it[s] [+778+1382] [1], it[s] [+7815] [1], it[s] [+793+1581] [1], it[s] [+8288] [1], it[s] [+8367] [1], it[s] [+8385] [1], it[s] [+8407] [1], it[s] [+8441] [1], it[s] [+8538] [1], it[s] [+8701] [1], it[s] [+8947] [1], it[s] [+9024] [1], it[s] [+9043] [1], it[s] [+9310] [1], it's [+3427] [1], its[s] [+2633] [1], its[s] [+3720] [1], its[s] [+4058+4200] [1], its[s] [+6425] [1], its[s] [+6592] [1], its[s] [+7175] [1], its[s] [+871] [1], its[s] [+928+6551] [1], Jacob's[s] [1], Jether [+5853] [1], just [+3427] [1], just now [+3427] [1], laid siege [+928+995+5189] [1], lamb [+928+3897+8445] [1], lamb [+928+4166+8445] [1], last night [+4326] [1], last watch of the night [+874+1332] [1], later [+340+928] [1], leads [+928+8037] [1], leveled completely [+928+9164+9168] [1], likes [+928+3202+4200] [1], live [+928+2644] [1], lived [+928+1074] [1], long ago [+928+8037] [1], long life [+2644+4200] [1], man's[s] [1], mealtime [+431+6961] [1], men [+132+1201] [1], midnight [+2942+4326] [1], misuse [+4200+5951+8736] [1], mounted [+928+6061] [1], must sell [+928+4084+4835+4835] [1], Naomi [+851] [1], native-born [+275+824] [1], native-born [+824+928+3528] [1], natural [+132+3869+3972] [1], nightfall [+4326] [1], noon [+3427+4734] [1], northward [+2006+7600] [1], nothing [+3972+4202] [1], now [+7193] [1], on fire [+836+928+1277] [1], on foot [+824+6584] [1], on high [+4200+5294] [1], on high [+5294] [1], on the west [+4427+9087] [1], once again [+3869+8037] [1], once more [+421+7193] [1], one[s] [+4131] [1], one[s] [+5566] [1], one another [+6639] [1], oppressed [+928+4200+6913+6945] [1], other nationalities [+824+6639] [1], others[s] [+851] [1], others[s] [1], out here [+928+2575] [1], outdoor [+928+2575] [1], outer [+2575+4200] [1], outside the family [+2025+2424+2575] [1], overboard [+448+3542] [1], painted [+928+7037+8531] [1], penned up [+906+928+1074+3973] [1], people[s] [1], perjurers [+4200+8678+9214] [1], perjury [+4200+8678+9214] [1], permanently [+4200+7552] [1], places[s] [1], plotting [+3086+8288] [1], preserved [+928+2645+8492] [1], prison [+1074+4551] [1], prison [+1074+7213] [1], prison [+673+1074] [1], privately [+928+4319] [1], privately [+928+8952] [1], put out [+906+2575+3655] [1], ready for battle [+408+4200+4878+7372] [1], ready for battle [+928+4878+7372] [1], recently [+3427] [1], reflects the man [+132+4200] [1], regular [+3427+3972] [1], safely [+4200+8934] [1], said [+448+1819+1821] [1], sail [+641+928+2143] [1], sandaled [+928+5837] [1], Saul's[s] [1], scoundrel [+408+1175] [1], see [+906+4200+6524+8011] [1], set ablaze [+836+928+3675] [1], set farther back [+337+2958] [1], set fire to [+836+906+906+928+8596] [1], set fire to [+836+928+8938] [1], seven and a half feet [+564+928+2822] [1], seven-day periods [+3427+8679] [1], she [+4893] [1], she [+5855] [1], she [+912] [1], she[s] [1], shoot [+928+8008] [1], similar [+3869+5260] [1], sling stones [+74+928] [1], sober [+3516+3655+4946] [1], some distance [+824+3896] [1], someone [+285+6639] [1], someone[s] [+5877] [1], someone[s] [+8011] [1], southward [+448+3545] [1], spear [1], spreads feathers to run [+928+5257+5294] [1], spring [+4784+6524] [1], spring [+9102+9588] [1], steward [+408+889+1074+6584] [1], stoned [+74+906+928+6232] [1], stoned [+74+906+928+8083] [1], stoned [+74+928+6232] [1], stoning [+74+906+928+8083] [1], such[s] [+6913] [1], such [1], sunset [+995+3064] [1], tent-dwelling [+185+928] [1], the place[s] [1], their[s] [+1201+1769] [1], their[s] [+2498+4200] [1], their[s] [+3913] [1], their[s] [+408] [1], their[s] [+4131] [1], their[s] [+465] [1], their[s] [+824+6639] [1], their[s] [1], them[s] [+1522] [1], them[s] [+2143] [1], them[s] [+3192+9109] [1], them[s] [+4283] [1], them[s] [+466+1074+3998] [1], them[s] [+5566] [1], them[s] [+5987] [1], them[s] [+6109] [1], them[s] [+6296] [1], them[s] [+6929+7983] [1], them[s] [+7194] [1], them[s] [+74+9109] [1], them[s] [+74+928+4392] [1], them[s] [+7700] [1], them[s] [+7736] [1], them[s] [+7983] [1], them[s] [+824+6551] [1], them[s] [+912] [1], them[s] [+9149] [1], there[s] [+824+928] [1], there[s] [+8441] [1], there[s] [+928+1014] [1], there[s] [+928+1074+3752] [1], there[s] [+928+2006] [1], there[s] [+928+4722] [1], there[s] [+928+5207] [1], there[s] [+928+6551] [1], there[s] [+9399] [1], these [+2693] [1], these [+74] [1], these men[s] [+1201+5566] [1], these men[s] [+4856+6913] [1], they[s] [+132] [1], they[s] [+2256+2657+3405+8569] [1], they[s] [+3374] [1], they[s] [+3452] [1], they[s] [+3972+6639] [1], they[s] [+4291] [1], they[s] [+4619] [1], they[s] [+4784] [1], they[s] [+4855] [1], they[s] [+5954] [1], they[s] [+6296] [1], they[s] [+746] [1], they[s] [+7736] [1], they[s] [+8103] [1], they[s] [+851] [1], they[s] [+851+1201] [1], they[s] [+8569] [1], they[s] [+9133] [1], they[s] [+964] [1], thirty feet [+564+928+6929] [1], this [+1821+2296] [1], this [+2021+2296] [1], this [+9108] [1], this kind of sore [+5596+5999] [1], thoroughly purge away [+1342+3869+7671] [1], those[s] [+1583] [1], those[s] [+2651] [1], those[s] [+339+889+6639] [1], those[s] [+7156] [1], those[s] [+7239] [1], those[s] [+8599] [1], those[s] [+8636] [1], tomorrow[s] [1], two[s] [1], unnoticed [+928+4319] [1], useless [+4200+9214] [1], very old [+928+995+2416+3427] [1], wage war [+1741+4200+4878] [1], walking along [+928+2006] [1], waylaid [+928+2006+4200+8492] [1], what[s] [+4856] [1], what[s] [+995] [1], whatever[s] [+3655] [1], where[s] [+2006] [1], where[s] [+928+5226] [1], wherever [+285+889+928+5226] [1], wherever [+3972+4946+5226] [1], wherever [+889+3972+5226+6584] [1], wherever [+889+928+5226] [1], wherever [+928+3972+5226] [1], which[s] [+7366] [1], which[s] [+8965] [1], which way [+361+2006+2296] [1], who [+408+6504] [1], whoever [+132+3972] [1], whoever[s] [1], whom [1], without meaning [+928+2039] [1], woman's monthly uncleanness [+3240+5614] [1], workmen [+928+4856+6913] [1], year [+3427+4200] [1], years [+6961+9102] [1], yet [+3427] [1], Ziklag [+6551] [1]

2022 -הֲ ***hᵃ-***, inter.pt.pref. [743 / 742] [→ Ar 10190] Not indexed

untranslated [689], whether [12], if [11], not [8], when [4], don't [3], as you know [+4202] [2], or [2], rather [2], aren't [1], isn't [1], not only [1], only [+4202] [1], so [1], surely [1], unless [+4202] [1], what about [+4202] [1], whether [+561+4202] [1]

2023 הָ- ***-āh***, הָ- ***-hā***, [1]הָ- ***-â[1]***, הָא- ***-hā'***, p.f.s.suf. [3110 / 3115] [→ 2024, 2084, 2114, 2157, 2161, 2177, 2181, 2257, 4392, 4564, 5527, 5626, 5647] Not indexed

her [1135], *untranslated* [673], it[s] [539], its [257], the[s] [95], their [67], she [66], them [28], there[s] [+928] [26], his [13], the city[s] [12], the land[s] [12], whose [12], this [10], herself [8], herself [+5883] [7], which[s] [7], there[s] [+6584] [6], your [6], a[s] [5], her [+4200] [5], her own [5], there[s] [+928+9348] [4], him [3], one [3], that city[s] [3], there[s] [3], Hagar[s] [2], hers [2], its [+4200] [2], its [+928] [2], its land[s] [2], its[s] [2], Jerusalem[s] [2], land[s] [2], she [+5883] [2], that[s] [2], the town[s] [2], there[s] [+928] [2], where[s] [+928] [2], which [2], wisdom[s] [2], you [2], all this [1], an[s] [1], another[s] [1], city[s] [1], Dinah's[s] [1], Edom's[s] [1], Edom[s] [1], Egypt[s] [1], Hannah[s] [1], he[s] [+3] [1], here[s] [+928] [1], hers [+4200] [1], herself [+4222] [1], herself [+7931] [1], him[s] [+1201] [1], him[s] [+1251] [1], him[s] [+3] [1], his[s] [+3] [1], his former righteousness[s] [1], his nurse[s] [1], in [1], Israel's[s] [1], it[s] [+1947+4946] [1], its [+6584] [1], its inhabitants[s] [1], its own [1], its people[s] [1], Judah[s] [1], Moab[s] [1], my law[s] [1], Nineveh[s] [+5226] [1], piece[s] [1], that day[s] [1], that place[s] [1], that time[s] [1], that [1], that's [1], the courtyard[s] [1], the daughter's[s] [1], the dove[s] [1], the earth[s] [1], the fire[s] [1], the first woman[s] [1], the girl[s] [1], the goat[s] [1], the kingdom[s] [1], the lampstand[s] [1], the pit[s] [1], the place[s] [1], the plot[s] [1], the spring[s] [1], the sword[s] [1], the temple[s] [1], the [1], their land[s] [1], their lands[s] [1], them[s] [+1074] [1], themselves [1], there[s] [+5226] [1], there[s] [+928+8148] [1], these [1], this city[s] [1], this land[s] [1], those [1], tongue[s] [1], Tyre[s] [1], what[s] happened [1], whom [1], word[s] [1], your own [1], your wife[s] [1], yourself [+4222] [1], Zion[s] [1]

2024 הֹ- ***-ōh***, p.m.s.suf. [34 / 36] [√ 2023] Not indexed

untranslated [14], his [10], they [4], them [3], its [2], it [1], their [1], those [1]

2025 [2]הָ- ***-â[2]***, adv.suf. [1117] Not indexed

to [292], *untranslated* [112], on [95], at [58], there [+9004] [58], into [51], in [37], more [+5087] [36], west [+3542] [28], north [+7600] [26], toward [25], where [+625] [17], where [+9004] [16], east [+7708] [13], how long [+625+6330] [12], for [9], northern [+7600] [9], south [+5582] [9], outside [+2575] [8], east [+4667] [7], east [+7711] [7], upward [+4200+5087] [6], out [+2575] [5], south [+9402] [5], above [+4200+4946+5087] [4], anywhere else [+625+625+2025+2256] [4], reached [+995] [4], south [+2025+5582+9402] [4], the Jordan[s] [+9004] [4], above [+4200+5087] [3], eastern [+7711] [3], from [3], in it[s] [+9004] [3], on [+5087] [3], over [+4200+4946+5087] [3], south [+5582+9402] [3], southern [+5582] [3], toward [+995+3870] [3], westward [+3542] [3], after [2], anywhere [+625+625+2025+2256] [2], as far as [2], at each successive level [+2025+4200+4200+5087+5087] [2], each year [+3427+3427+4946] [2], east [+2021+4667+9087] [2], eastern [+4667] [2], eastward [+2025+4667+7711] [2], head [+2256+4946+5087+8900] [2], higher [+5087] [2], highly [+4200+5087] [2], in ascending stages [+2025+4200+4200+5087+5087] [2], in the presence of [+5584] [2], inside [+1074] [2], inside [2], it[s] [+9004] [2], outside [+2575+4946] [2], southeast [+2025+5582+7711] [2], top [+4200+4946+5087] [2], up [+4200+5087] [2], very [+4200+5087] [2], western [+3542] [2], wherever [+9004] [2], which way [+625] [2], across [1], advance [+7156] [1], against [1], along [1], among [1], annual

[+3427+3427+4946] [1], away [+448+2021+2575] [1], back[s] [+9004] [1], beyond [+5087] [1], deep [+5087] [1], depth [+4200+5087] [1], down [+824] [1], downstream [+4200+4946+5087] [1], east [+4667+6298] [1], east [+928+4667+6298] [1], east [+928+4667 +6298+9087] [1], eastern [+7708] [1], eastward [+4667] [1], eastward [+7708] [1], eastward [+7711] [1], entered [+995] [1], entering [+995] [1], enters [+995] [1], exceedingly [+4200+5087] [1], extend eastward [+7708] [1], extend out [+2575] [1], extend westward [+3542] [1], facing [1], fail [+824+4946+5877] [1], get out of here [+906+2021+2575+4946+6584+8938] [1], heights [+4200+5087] [1], here [+2178] [1], here[s] [+5213] [1], high above [+4200+4946+5087] [1], higher than [+4200+5087+8049] [1], in [+1074+2021] [1], inside[s] [+9004] [1], interior [+1074+4946] [1], invade [+995+9004] [1], inward [+1074] [1], join [1], magnificence [+5087] [1], more [+4200+5087] [1], more and more powerful [+1541+2143+2256 +4200+5087+6330] [1], northern [+4946+7600] [1], old [+5087] [1], older [+5087] [1], on to [1], onto [1], outer [+4200+4946+5087] [1], outside [+2667] [1], outside [+7339] [1], outside the family [+2021+2424+2575] [1], over and above [+4200+5087] [1], over [1], overturned [+2200+4200+5087] [1], pen up [+1074] [1], project upward [+4200+5087] [1], severe [+4200+5087] [1], southeast [+5582+7711] [1], the land[s] [+9004] [1], there[s] [+824+4046] [1], there[s] [+928+9463] [1], to [+9004] [1], top [+4200+5087] [1], top [+5087] [1], top of [+4200+4946+5087] [1], upstream [+4200+5087] [1], upward [+4200+4946+5087] [1], very [+4200+5087+6330] [1], west [+5115] [1], western[s] [+4667] [1], when [+625+6330] [1], where[s] [+7730] [1], where [1], wherever [+625] [1], wherever [+889+9004] [1], wielding [+995+4200+5087] [1]

2026 הֵא hē', interj. [2] [→ Ar 10194, 10195]

here [1], surely [1]

Ge 47:23 for Pharaoh, **here** is seed for you so you can plant the ground.
Eze 16:43 I will **surely** bring down on your head what you have done,

2027 הֶאָח he'āḥ, interj. [12]

aha [11], ah [1]

Job 39:25 At the blast of the trumpet he snorts, '**Aha**!' He catches the scent of
Ps 35:21 They gape at me and say, "**Aha**! Aha! With our own eyes we have
35:21 They gape at me and say, "Aha! **Aha**! With our own eyes we have
35:25 Do not let them think, "**Aha**, just what we wanted!" or say,
40:15 [40:16] May those who say to me, "**Aha**! Aha!" be appalled at
40:15 [40:16] May those who say to me, "Aha! **Aha**!" be appalled at
70:3 [70:4] May those who say to me, "**Aha**! Aha!" turn back because
70:3 [70:4] May those who say to me, "Aha! **Aha**!" turn back because
Isa 44:16 He also warms himself and says, "**Ah**! I am warm; I see the fire."
Eze 25:3 This is what the Sovereign LORD says: Because you said "**Aha**!"
26:2 "Son of man, because Tyre has said of Jerusalem, '**Aha**! The gate
36:2 is what the Sovereign LORD says: The enemy said of you, "**Aha**!

2028 הָאֲחַשְׁתָּרִי hā'ᵃḥaštārî, n.pr.m. *or* a.g. [1] [√ 349]

Haahashtari [1]

1Ch 4:6 Naarah bore him Ahuzzam, Hepher, Temeni and **Haahashtari**.

2029 הָאֱלִי hā'ᵉlî, a.g. Not used in NIV/BHS [cf. 1088]

2030 הָאֶלֶף hā'elep, n.pr.loc. [1]

Haeleph [1]

Jos 18:28 Zelah, **Haeleph**, the Jebusite city (that is, Jerusalem), Gibeah

2031 הָאַמָּה hā'ammâ, n.pr.loc. Not used in NIV/BHS [→ 1094]

2032 הָאֵצֶל hā'ēṣel, n.pr.loc. Not used in NIV/BHS [→ 1089]

2033 הָאַרְבַּע hā'arba', n.pr.loc. Not used in NIV/BHS [√ 752]

2034 הָאֲרָרִי hā'rārî, var. Not used in NIV/BHS [cf. 828]

2035 הַב¹ hab¹, v. [33] [cf. 3364]

give [12], ascribe [9], come [5], bring [2], appoint [1], choose [1], do [1], praise [1], put [1]

Ge 11:3 each other, "**Come**, let's make bricks and bake them thoroughly."
11:4 they said, "**Come**, let us build ourselves a city, with a tower that
11:7 **Come**, let us go down and confuse their language so they will not
29:21 Jacob said to Laban, "**Give** me my wife. My time is completed,
30:1 of her sister. So she said to Jacob, "**Give** me children, or I'll die!"
38:16 he went over to her by the roadside and said, "**Come** now,
47:15 was gone, all Egypt came to Joseph and said, "**Give** us food.
47:16 "Then **bring** your livestock," said Joseph. "I will sell you food in
Ex 1:10 **Come**, we must deal shrewdly with them or they will become even
Dt 1:13 **Choose** some wise, understanding and respected men from each of
32:3 the name of the LORD. Oh, **praise** the greatness of our God!
Jos 18:4 **Appoint** three men from each tribe. I will send them out to make a
Jdg 1:15 She replied, "**Do** me a special favor. Since you have given me land
20:7 Now, all you Israelites, speak up and **give** your verdict."
Ru 3:15 also said, "**Bring** me the shawl you are wearing and hold it out."
1Sa 14:41 to the LORD, the God of Israel, "**Give** me the right answer."
2Sa 11:15 he wrote, "**Put** Uriah in the front line where the fighting is fiercest.
16:20 Absalom said to Ahithophel, "**Give** us your advice. What should
1Ch 16:28 **Ascribe** to the LORD, O families of nations, ascribe to the
16:28 O families of nations, **ascribe** to the LORD glory and strength,
16:29 **ascribe** to the LORD the glory due his name. Bring an offering
Job 6:22 Have I ever said, '**Give** something on my behalf, pay a ransom for
Ps 29:1 **Ascribe** to the LORD, O mighty ones, ascribe to the LORD
29:1 O mighty ones, **ascribe** to the LORD glory and strength.
29:2 **Ascribe** to the LORD the glory due his name; worship the
60:11 [60:13] **Give** us aid against the enemy, for the help of man is
96:7 **Ascribe** to the LORD, O families of nations, ascribe to the
96:7 O families of nations, **ascribe** to the LORD glory and strength.
96:8 **Ascribe** to the LORD the glory due his name; bring an offering
108:12 [108:13] **Give** us aid against the enemy, for the help of man is
Pr 30:15 "The leech has two daughters. '**Give**! Give!' they cry. "There are
30:15 "The leech has two daughters. 'Give! **Give**!' they cry. "There are
Zec 11:12 I told them, "If you think it best, **give** me my pay; but if not,

2036 הַב² hab², n.m.?. Not used in NIV/BHS [→ 9105]

2037 הַבְהָב habhab, n.m. [1]

given [1]

Hos 8:13 They offer sacrifices **given** *to* me and they eat the meat,

2038 הָבַל hābal, v.den. [5] [√ 2039]

worthless [2], fill with false hopes [1], meaningless talk [+2039] [1], take pride [1]

2Ki 17:15 [A] followed worthless idols and *themselves became* **worthless**.
Job 27:12 [A] this yourselves. Why then this **meaningless** [+2039] **talk**?
Ps 62:10 [62:11] [A] Do not trust in extortion or **take pride** in stolen
Jer 2:5 [A] followed worthless idols and *became* **worthless** *themselves*.
23:16 [G] are prophesying to you; they **fill** you **with false hopes**.

2039 הֶבֶל¹ hebel¹, n.m. [73] [→ 2038; cf. 2040]

meaningless [34], worthless idols [9], breath [5], in vain [5], worthless [4], utterly meaningless [+2039] [2], dishonest [1], empty talk [1], fleeting [1], futile [1], futility [1], less meaning [+8049] [1], meaningless talk [+2038] [1], mere breath [1], no meaning [1], nonsense [1], utterly useless [+2256+8198] [1], vapor [1], without meaning [+928+2021] [1], worthless idols [+8736] [1]

Dt 32:21 by what is no god and angered me with their **worthless idols**.
1Ki 16:13 the LORD, the God of Israel, to anger by their **worthless idols**.
16:26 the LORD, the God of Israel, to anger by their **worthless idols**.
2Ki 17:15 They followed **worthless idols** and themselves became worthless.
Job 7:16 I would not live forever. Let me alone; my days have **no meaning**.
9:29 Since I am already found guilty, why should I struggle **in vain**?
21:34 "So how can you console me with your **nonsense**? Nothing is left
27:12 all seen this yourselves. Why then this **meaningless talk** [+2038]?
35:16 So Job opens his mouth with **empty talk**; without knowledge he
Ps 31:6 [31:7] I hate those who cling to **worthless** [+8736] **idols**; I trust in
39:5 [39:6] before you. Each man's life is but a **breath**. *Selah*
39:6 [39:7] He bustles about, but only **in vain**; he heaps up wealth, not
39:11 [39:12] their wealth like a moth—each man is but a **breath**.
62:9 [62:10] Lowborn men are but a **breath**, the highborn are but a lie;
62:9 [62:10] they are nothing; together they are only a **breath**.
78:33 So he ended their days in **futility** and their years in terror.
94:11 LORD knows the thoughts of man; he knows that they are **futile**.
144:4 Man is like a **breath**; his days are like a fleeting shadow.
Pr 13:11 **Dishonest** money dwindles away, but he who gathers money little
21:6 A fortune made by a lying tongue is a fleeting **vapor** and a deadly
31:30 Charm is deceptive, and beauty is **fleeting**; but a woman who fears
Ecc 1:2 "**Meaningless**! Meaningless!" says the Teacher. "Utterly
1:2 "Meaningless! **Meaningless**!" says the Teacher. "Utterly
1:2 Meaningless!" says the Teacher. "**Utterly meaningless** [+2039]!
1:2 Meaningless!" says the Teacher. "**Utterly meaningless** [+2039]!
1:2 the Teacher. "Utterly meaningless! Everything is **meaningless**."
1:14 the sun; all of them are **meaningless**, a chasing after the wind.
2:1 to find out what is good." But that also proved to be **meaningless**.
2:11 to achieve, everything was **meaningless**, a chasing after the wind;
2:15 gain by being wise?" I said in my heart, "This too is **meaningless**."
2:17 grievous to me. All of it is **meaningless**, a chasing after the wind.
2:19 poured my effort and skill under the sun. This too is **meaningless**.
2:21 not worked for it. This too is **meaningless** and a great misfortune.

Ecc 2:23 even at night his mind does not rest. This too is **meaningless**.
2:26 pleases God. This too is **meaningless**, a chasing after the wind.
3:19 man has no advantage over the animal. Everything is **meaningless**.
4:4 of his neighbor. This too is **meaningless**, a chasing after the wind.
4:7 Again I saw *something* **meaningless** under the sun:
4:8 of enjoyment?" This too is **meaningless**—a miserable business!
4:16 the successor. This too is **meaningless**, a chasing after the wind.
5:7 [5:6] Much dreaming and many words are **meaningless**.
5:10 [5:9] is never satisfied with his income. This too is **meaningless**.
6:2 stranger enjoys them instead. This is **meaningless**, a grievous evil.
6:4 It comes **without meaning** [+928+2021], it departs in darkness,
6:9 of the appetite. This too is **meaningless**, a chasing after the wind.
6:11 The more the words, the **less** the **meaning** [+8049], and how does
6:12 the few and **meaningless** days he passes through like a shadow?
7:6 under the pot, so is the laughter of fools. This too is **meaningless**.
7:15 In this **meaningless** life of mine I have seen both of these:
8:10 praise in the city where they did this. This too is **meaningless**.
8:14 There is something else **meaningless** that occurs on earth:
8:14 get what the righteous deserve. This too, I say, is **meaningless**.
9:9 all the days of this **meaningless** life that God has given you under
9:9 that God has given you under the sun—all your **meaningless** days.
11:8 for they will be many. Everything to come is **meaningless**.
11:10 off the troubles of your body, for youth and vigor are **meaningless**.
12:8 "**Meaningless**! Meaningless!" says the Teacher. "Everything is
12:8 "Meaningless! **Meaningless**!" says the Teacher. "Everything is
12:8 Meaningless!" says the Teacher. "Everything is **meaningless**!"
Isa 30:7 to Egypt, whose help is **utterly useless** [+2256+8198]. Therefore I
49:4 to no purpose; I have spent my strength **in vain** and for nothing.
57:13 will carry all of them off, a **mere breath** will blow them away.
Jer 2:5 They followed **worthless idols** and became worthless themselves.
8:19 me to anger with their images, with their **worthless** foreign **idols**?"
10:3 For the customs of the peoples are **worthless**; they cut a tree out of
10:8 and foolish; they are taught by **worthless** wooden **idols**.
10:15 They are **worthless**, the objects of mockery; when their judgment
14:22 Do any of the **worthless idols** *of* the nations bring rain? Do the
16:19 but false gods, **worthless idols** that did them no good.
51:18 They are **worthless**, the objects of mockery; when their judgment
La 4:17 Moreover, our eyes failed, looking **in vain** for help; from our
Jnh 2:8 [2:9] "Those who cling to **worthless** idols forfeit the grace that
Zec 10:2 that lie; they tell dreams that are false, they give comfort **in vain**.

2040 ²הֶבֶל hebel², n.pr.m. [8] [cf. 2039?]

Abel [8]

Ge 4:2 Later she gave birth to his brother **Abel**. Now Abel kept flocks,
4:2 his brother Abel. Now **Abel** kept flocks, and Cain worked the soil.
4:4 **Abel** brought fat portions from some of the firstborn of his flock.
4:4 his flock. The LORD looked with favor on **Abel** and his offering,
4:8 Now Cain said to his brother **Abel**, "Let's go out to the field."
4:8 were in the field, Cain attacked his brother **Abel** and killed him.
4:9 Then the LORD said to Cain, "Where is your brother **Abel**?"
4:25 saying, "God has granted me another child in place of **Abel**,

2041 הָבְנִים hobnîm, n.[m.]. [1]

ebony [1]

Eze 27:15 were your customers; they paid you with ivory tusks and **ebony**.

2042 הָבַר hābar, v. [1]

astrologers [+9028] [1]

Isa 47:13 [A] Let your **astrologers** [+9028] come forward, those stargazers

2043 הֵגֶא hēgē', n.pr.m. [1] [cf. 2051]

Hegai [1]

Est 2:3 Let them be placed under the care of **Hegai**, the king's eunuch,

2044 הַגִּדְגָּד haggidgād, n.pr.m. Not used in NIV/BHS [→ 2988; cf. 1515]

2045 הַגְּדוֹלִים haggᵉdôlîm, n.pr.m. [1] [√ 1524]

Haggedolim [1]

Ne 11:14 128. Their chief officer was Zabdiel son of **Haggedolim**.

2046 הַגּוֹיִם haggôyim, n.pr.loc. Not used in NIV/BHS [→ 3099]

2047 ¹הָגָה hāgâ¹, v. [25] [→ 2049, 2050, 2053]

meditate [3], plot [3], moan mournfully [+2047] [2], growls [1], lament [1], meditates [1], moan [1], moaned [1], mutter [1], mutters [1], ponder [1], speak [1], speaks [1], tell [1], think [1], utter a sound [1], utter [1], uttering [1], utters [1], weighs [1]

Jos 1:8 [A] **meditate** on it day and night, so that you may be careful to
Job 27:4 [A] not speak wickedness, and my tongue *will* **utter** no deceit.
Ps 1:2 [A] of the LORD, and on his law *he* **meditates** day and night.
2:1 [A] Why do the nations conspire and the peoples **plot** in vain?
35:28 [A] My tongue *will* **speak** *of* your righteousness and *of* your
37:30 [A] The mouth of the righteous man **utters** wisdom, and his
38:12 [38:13] [A] talk of my ruin; all day long *they* **plot** deception.
63:6 [63:7] [A] *I* **think** of you through the watches of the night.
71:24 [A] My tongue *will* **tell** *of* your righteous acts all day long,
77:12 [77:13] [A] *I will* **meditate** on all your works and consider all
115:7 [A] cannot walk; nor *can they* **utter a sound** with their throats.
143:5 [A] *I* **meditate** on all your works and consider what your hands
Pr 8:7 [A] My mouth **speaks** what is true, for my lips detest
15:28 [A] The heart of the righteous **weighs** its answers, but the mouth
24:2 [A] for their hearts **plot** violence, and their lips talk about making
Isa 8:19 [G] to consult mediums and spiritists, who whisper and **mutter**,
16:7 [A] for Moab. **Lament** and grieve for the men of Kir Hareseth.
31:4 [A] "As a lion **growls**, a great lion over his prey—and though a
33:18 [A] In your thoughts *you will* **ponder** the former terror:
38:14 [A] I cried like a swift or thrush, *I* **moaned** like a mourning dove.
59:3 [A] have spoken lies, and your tongue **mutters** wicked things.
59:11 [A] growl like bears; *we* **moan** [+2047] **mournfully** like doves.
59:11 [A] growl like bears; *we* **moan mournfully** [+2047] like doves.
59:13 [A] and revolt, **uttering** lies our hearts have conceived.
Jer 48:31 [A] for all Moab I cry out, *I* **moan** for the men of Kir Hareseth.

2048 ²הָגָה hāgâ², v. [3] [cf. 3325]

remove [2], drives out [1]

Pr 25:4 [A] **Remove** the dross from the silver, and out comes material for
25:5 [A] **remove** the wicked from the king's presence, and his throne
Isa 27:8 [A] with his fierce blast *he* **drives** her **out**, as on a day the east

2049 הֶגֶה hegeh, n.m. [3] [√ 2047]

moan [1], mourning [1], rumbling [1]

Job 37:2 the roar of his voice, to the **rumbling** that comes from his mouth.
Ps 90:9 pass away under your wrath; we finish our years with a **moan**.
Eze 2:10 sides of it were written words of lament and **mourning** and woe.

2050 הָגוּת hāgût, n.f. [1] [√ 2047]

utterance [1]

Ps 49:3 [49:4] the **utterance** *from* my heart will give understanding.

2051 הֵגַי hēgay, n.pr.m. [3] [cf. 2043]

Hegai [3]

Est 2:8 brought to the citadel of Susa and put under the care of **Hegai**.
2:8 Esther also was taken to the king's palace and entrusted to **Hegai**,
2:15 to go to the king, she asked for nothing other than what **Hegai**,

2052 הָגִיג hāgîg, n.m. [2]

meditated [1], sighing [1]

Ps 5:1 [5:2] Give ear to my words, O LORD, consider my **sighing**.
39:3 [39:4] grew hot within me, and as I **meditated**, the fire burned;

2053 הִגָּיוֹן higgāyôn, n.m. [4] [√ 2047]

higgaion [1], meditation [1], melody [1], mutter [1]

Ps 9:16 [9:17] ensnared by the work of their hands. ***Higgaion***. *Selah*
19:14 [19:15] and the **meditation** *of* my heart be pleasing in your sight,
92:3 [92:4] music of the ten-stringed lyre and the **melody** of the harp.
La 3:62 what my enemies whisper and **mutter** against me all day long.

2054 הָגִין hāgîn, a. [1]

corresponding [1]

Eze 42:12 that was parallel to the **corresponding** wall extending eastward,

2055 הַגִּלְגָּל haggilgāl, n.pr.loc. Not used in NIV/BHS [√ 1670]

2056 הַגָּן haggān, n.pr.loc.?. Not used in NIV/BHS [→ 1091]

2057 הָגָר hāgār, n.pr.f. [12] [→ 2058?]

Hagar [11], she[s] [1]

Ge 16:1 no children. But she had an Egyptian maidservant named **Hagar**;
16:3 Sarai his wife took her Egyptian maidservant **Hagar** and gave her
16:4 He slept with **Hagar**, and she conceived. When she knew she was
16:8 And he said, "**Hagar**, servant of Sarai, where have you come from,
16:15 So **Hagar** bore Abram a son, and Abram gave the name Ishmael to

Ge 16:15 and Abram gave the name Ishmael to the son she[s] had borne.
16:16 Abram was eighty-six years old when **Hagar** bore him Ishmael.
21: 9 Sarah saw that the son whom **Hagar** the Egyptian had borne to
21:14 took some food and a skin of water and gave them to **Hagar**.
21:17 and the angel of God called to **Hagar** from heaven and said to her,
21:17 to Hagar from heaven and said to her, "What is the matter, **Hagar**?
25:12 whom Sarah's maidservant, **Hagar** the Egyptian, bore to Abraham.

2058 הַגְרִי ***hagrî***, a.g. [& n.pr.m.?]. [6 / 7] [√ 2057?]

Hagrites [4], Hagri [2], Hagrite [1]

2Sa 23:36 Igal son of Nathan from Zobah, the son of **Hagri**, [BHS 1532]
1Ch 5:10 During Saul's reign they waged war against the **Hagrites**,
5:19 They waged war against the **Hagrites**, Jetur, Naphish and Nodab.
5:20 and God handed the **Hagrites** and all their allies over to them,
11:38 Joel the brother of Nathan, Mibhar son of **Hagri**,
27:31 Jaziz the **Hagrite** was in charge of the flocks. All these were the
Ps 83: 6 [83:7] of Edom and the Ishmaelites, of Moab and the **Hagrites**,

2059 הֵד ***hēd***, n.[m.]. [1] [√ 2116]

joy [1]

Eze 7: 7 the day is near; there is panic, not **joy**, *upon* the mountains.

2060 הֲדַד ***h^adad***, n.pr.m. [12 / 13] [→ 119, 1207, 2061, 2062, 2066, 2067, 2836]

Hadad [12], *untranslated* [1]

Ge 36:35 When Husham died, **Hadad** son of Bedad, who defeated Midian in
36:36 When **Hadad** died, Samlah from Masrekah succeeded him as king.
36:39 son of Acbor died, **Hadad** [BHS 2076] succeeded him as king.
1Ki 11:14 an adversary, **Hadad** the Edomite, from the royal line of Edom.
11:17 Hadad, **[RPH]** still only a boy, fled to Egypt with some Edomite
11:19 so pleased with **Hadad** that he gave him a sister of his own wife,
11:21 **Hadad** heard that David rested with his fathers and that Joab the
11:21 **Hadad** said to Pharaoh, "Let me go, that I may return to my own
11:25 as long as Solomon lived, adding to the trouble caused by **Hadad**.
1Ch 1:46 When Husham died, **Hadad** son of Bedad, who defeated Midian in
1:47 When **Hadad** died, Samlah from Masrekah succeeded him as king.
1:50 When Baal-Hanan died, **Hadad** succeeded him as king. His city
1:51 **Hadad** also died. The chiefs of Edom were: Timna, Alvah,

2061 הֲדַדְעֶזֶר ***h^adad'ezer***, n.pr.m. [21] [√ 2060 + 6469]

Hadadezer [17], Hadadezer's [2], who[s] [2]

2Sa 8: 3 Moreover, David fought **Hadadezer** son of Rehob, king of Zobah,
8: 5 When the Arameans of Damascus came to help **Hadadezer** king of
8: 7 took the gold shields that belonged to the officers of **Hadadezer**
8: 8 From Tebah and Berothai, towns that belonged to **Hadadezer**,
8: 9 heard that David had defeated the entire army of **Hadadezer**,
8:10 and congratulate him on his victory in battle over **Hadadezer**,
8:10 victory in battle over Hadadezer, **who**[s] had been at war with Tou.
8:12 He also dedicated the plunder taken from **Hadadezer** son of
10:16 **Hadadezer** had Arameans brought from beyond the River;
10:16 with Shobach the commander of **Hadadezer's** army leading them.
10:19 When all the kings who were vassals of **Hadadezer** saw that they
1Ki 11:23 who had fled from his master, **Hadadezer** king of Zobah.
1Ch 18: 3 Moreover, David fought **Hadadezer** king of Zobah, as far as
18: 5 When the Arameans of Damascus came to help **Hadadezer** king of
18: 7 David took the gold shields carried by the officers of **Hadadezer**
18: 8 From Tebah and Cun, towns that belonged to **Hadadezer**,
18: 9 David had defeated the entire army of **Hadadezer** king of Zobah,
18:10 and congratulate him on his victory in battle over **Hadadezer**,
18:10 victory in battle over Hadadezer, **who**[s] had been at war with Tou.
19:16 with Shophach the commander of **Hadadezer's** army leading
19:19 When the vassals of **Hadadezer** saw that they had been defeated

2062 הֲדַד־רִמּוֹן ***h^adad-rimmôn***, n.pr.m.[loc.?]. [1] [√ 2060 + 8235]

Hadad Rimmon [1]

Zec 12:11 like the weeping of **Hadad Rimmon** in the plain of Megiddo.

2063 הָדָה ***hādâ***, v. [1]

put [1]

Isa 11: 8 [A] and the young child **put** his hand into the viper's nest.

2064 הֹדּוּ ***hōddû***, n.pr.loc. [2]

India [2]

Est 1: 1 the Xerxes who ruled over 127 provinces stretching from **India** to
8: 9 and nobles of the 127 provinces stretching from **India** to Cush.

2065 הֲדוּרִים ***h^adûrîm***, n.[pl.m.]. [1]

mountains [1]

Isa 45: 2 I will go before you and will level the **mountains**; I will break

2066 הֲדוֹרָם ***h^adôrām[1]***, n.pr.m. [2] [√ 2060 + 8123]

Hadoram [2]

Ge 10:27 **Hadoram**, Uzal, Diklah,
1Ch 1:21 **Hadoram**, Uzal, Diklah,

2067 הֲדוֹרָם ***h^adôrām[2]***, n.pr.m. [2] [√ 2060 + 8123]

Adoniram [1], Hadoram [1]

1Ch 18:10 he sent his son **Hadoram** to King David to greet him
2Ch 10:18 King Rehoboam sent out **Adoniram**, who was in charge of forced

2068 הִדַּי ***hidday***, n.pr.m. [1] [cf. 2583]

Hiddai [1]

2Sa 23:30 Benaiah the Pirathonite, **Hiddai** from the ravines of Gaash,

2069 הֹדַיְוָהוּ ***hōdaywāhû***, n.pr.m. [0] [√ 2089]

1Ch 3:24 [The sons of Elioenai: **Hodaviah**, [K; see Q 2090] Eliashib, Pelaiah, Akkub, Johanan, Delaiah and Anani—seven in all.]

2070 הָדַךְ ***hādak***, v. [1]

crush [1]

Job 40:12 [A] and humble him, **crush** the wicked where they stand.

2071 הֲדֹם ***h^adōm***, n.m. [6]

footstool [+8079] [5], footstool [1]

1Ch 28: 2 for the **footstool** [+8079] *of* our God, and I made plans to build it.
Ps 99: 5 Exalt the LORD our God and worship at his **footstool** [+8079];
110: 1 "Sit at my right hand until I make your enemies a **footstool** for
132: 7 go to his dwelling place; let us worship at his **footstool** [+8079]—
Isa 66: 1 "Heaven is my throne, and the earth is my **footstool** [+8079].
La 2: 1 he has not remembered his **footstool** [+8079] in the day of his

2072 הֲדַס ***h^adas***, n.m. [6] [→ 2073]

myrtle trees [3], myrtle [2], myrtles [1]

Ne 8:15 and from **myrtles**, palms and shade trees, to make booths"—
Isa 41:19 put in the desert the cedar and the acacia, the **myrtle** and the olive.
55:13 will grow the pine tree, and instead of briers the **myrtle** will grow.
Zec 1: 8 He was standing among the **myrtle trees** in a ravine. Behind him
1:10 Then the man standing among the **myrtle trees** explained,
1:11 who was standing among the **myrtle trees**, "We have gone

2073 הֲדַסָּה ***h^adassâ***, n.pr.f. [1] [√ 2072]

Hadassah [1]

Est 2: 7 Mordecai had a cousin named **Hadassah**, whom he had brought up

2074 הָדַף ***hādap***, v. [11]

shoves [2], depose [1], drive out [1], driven out [1], driven [1], push away [1], push down [1], shove [1], thrusting out [1], thwarts [1]

Nu 35:20 [A] If *anyone* with malice aforethought **shoves** another or throws
35:22 [A] " 'But if without hostility *someone* suddenly **shoves** another
Dt 6:19 [A] **thrusting out** all your enemies before you, as the LORD
9: 4 [A] After the LORD your God has **driven** them **out** before you,
Jos 23: 5 [A] The LORD your God himself *will* **drive** them **out** of your
2Ki 4:27 [A] Gehazi came over to **push** her **away**, but the man of God
Job 18:18 [A] He *is* **driven** from light into darkness and is banished from
Pr 10: 3 [A] go hungry but *he* **thwarts** the craving of the wicked.
Isa 22:19 [A] *I will* **depose** you from your office, and you will be ousted
Jer 46:15 [A] They cannot stand, for the LORD *will* **push** them **down**.
Eze 34:21 [A] Because *you* **shove** with flank and shoulder, butting all the

2075 הָדַר ***hādar***, v. [6] [→ 2077, 2078, 2079; Ar 10198]

are shown respect [+7156] [1], exalt yourself [1], favoritism [+7156] [1], show favoritism [1], show respect [1], splendor [1]

Ex 23: 3 [A] and *do* not **show favoritism** *to* a poor man in his lawsuit.
Lev 19:15 [A] partiality to the poor or **favoritism** [+7156] *to* the great,
19:32 [A] the aged, **show respect** for the elderly and revere your God.
Pr 25: 6 [F] *Do* not **exalt yourself** in the king's presence, and do not
Isa 63: 1 [B] Who is this, robed in **splendor**, striding forward in the
La 5:12 [C] up by their hands; elders **are shown** no **respect** [+7156].

2076 הֲדַר ***h^adar***, n.pr.m. [1 / 0] [→ 2080]

Ge 36:39 Hadad [BHS *Hadar*; NIV 2060] succeeded him as king.

2077 הָדָר ***hādār***, n.m. [30] [√ 2075; Ar 10199]

splendor [12], majesty [10], majestic [2], blessing [1], choice [1], dignity [1], glory [1], honor [1], nobles [1]

Lev 23: 40 On the first day you are to take **choice** fruit from the trees,
Dt 33: 17 In **majesty** he is like a firstborn bull; his horns are the horns of a
1Ch 16: 27 Splendor and **majesty** are before him; strength and joy in his
Job 40: 10 with glory and splendor, and clothe yourself in honor and **majesty**.
Ps 8: 5 [8:6] the heavenly beings and crowned him with glory and **honor**.
21: 5 [21:6] is great; you have bestowed on him splendor and **majesty**.
29: 4 of the LORD is powerful; the voice of the LORD is **majestic**.
45: 3 [45:4] O mighty one; clothe yourself with splendor and **majesty**.
45: 4 [45:5] In your **majesty** ride forth victoriously in behalf of truth,
90: 16 deeds be shown to your servants, your **splendor** to their children.
96: 6 Splendor and **majesty** are before him; strength and glory are in his
104: 1 you are very great; you are clothed with splendor and **majesty**.
110: 3 Arrayed in holy **majesty**, from the womb of the dawn you will
111: 3 Glorious and **majestic** are his deeds, and his righteousness endures
145: 5 They will speak of the glorious **splendor** *of* your majesty,
145: 12 of your mighty acts and the glorious **splendor** *of* your kingdom.
149: 9 against them. This is the **glory** of all his saints. Praise the LORD.
Pr 20: 29 of young men is their strength, gray hair the **splendor** *of* the old.
31: 25 She is clothed with strength and **dignity**; she can laugh at the days
Isa 2: 10 ground from dread of the LORD and the **splendor** *of* his majesty!
2: 19 ground from dread of the LORD and the **splendor** *of* his majesty,
2: 21 crags from dread of the LORD and the **splendor** *of* his majesty,
5: 14 into it will descend their **nobles** and masses with all their brawlers
35: 2 of Lebanon will be given to it, the **splendor** *of* Carmel and Sharon;
35: 2 they will see the glory of the LORD, the **splendor** *of* our God.
53: 2 He had no beauty or **majesty** to attract us to him, nothing in his
La 1: 6 All the **splendor** has departed from the Daughter of Zion.
Eze 16: 14 because the **splendor** I had given you made your beauty perfect,
27: 10 their shields and helmets on your walls, bringing you **splendor**.
Mic 2: 9 You take away my **blessing** from their children forever.

2078 הֶדֶר ***heder***, n.[m.]. [1] [√ 2075; Ar 10199]

splendor [1]

Da 11: 20 will send out a tax collector to maintain the royal **splendor**.

2079 הֲדָרָה ***hᵃdārâ***, n.f. [5] [√ 2075]

splendor [4], glory [1]

1Ch 16: 29 before him; worship the LORD in the **splendor** *of* his holiness.
2Ch 20: 21 to praise him for the **splendor** *of* his holiness as they went out at
Ps 29: 2 due his name; worship the LORD in the **splendor** *of* his holiness.
96: 9 Worship the LORD in the **splendor** *of* his holiness;
Pr 14: 28 A large population is a king's **glory**, but without subjects a prince

2080 הֲדַרְעֶזֶר ***hᵃdarʿezer***, n.pr.m. Not used in NIV/BHS [√ 2076 + 6469]

2081 הָהּ ***hāh***, interj. [1]

alas [1]

Eze 30: 2 the Sovereign LORD says: " 'Wail and say, "**Alas** for that day!"

2082 הוֹ ***hô***, interj. [2] [→ 2098]

anguish [+2082] [2]

Am 5: 16 all the streets and cries of **anguish** [+2082] in every public square.
5: 16 all the streets and cries of **anguish** [+2082] in every public square.

2083 הוּ ***hû***, p.m.s. [1] [√ 2085]

it [1]

Nu 1: 50 all its furnishings; they are to take care of **it** and encamp around it.

2084 הוּ- ***-hû***, p.m.s.suf. [1081 / 1080] [√ 2023] Not indexed

him [484], it [147], *untranslated* [141], his [137], them [36], he [20], their [19], its [13], the[s] [10], his own [6], a[s] [4], David[s] [4], her [4], they [4], which [4], someone [3], each [2], Moses[s] [2], Pekahiah[s] [2], whose [2], your [2], Abram[s] [1], Asahel's[s] [1], Ben-Hadad[s] [1], both of you [+2256+3870] [1], Cyrus[s] [1], gave orders [1], God[s] [1], idol[s] [1], Joab[s] [1], meal[s] [1], my [1], Nadab[s] [1], one's [1], she [1], that day[s] [1], the altar[s] [1], the child[s] [1], the clouds[s] [1], the idol[s] [1], the inside[s] [1], the lamb[s] [1], the lion[s] [1], the manna[s] [1], the mountain[s] [1], the parties [+408+2256+8276] [1], the stand[s] [1], the water[s] [1], their own [1], theirs [1], this [1], together [+408+907+8276] [1], who [1], whom [1], you [1]

2085 הוּא ***hû'***, p.m.s. [1879] [→ 2083, 2115, 2156, 2160, 2179; Ar 10200, 10205; *also used with compound proper names*] Not indexed

he [438], *untranslated* [435], that [379], it [191], she [82], this [54], they [40], that is [34], who [32], himself [22], that same [19], one [11], same [10], which [9], him [7], his [6], those [6], these [4], Jotham[s] [3], the man[s] [3], this city[s] [3], Abram[s] [2], all day long [+928+2021+2021+3427] [2], far and wide [+2134+2256+4946] [2], he[s] [+2021+2021+5883] [2], her [2], its [2], only [2], that man[s] [2], that very [2], the animal[s] [2], the LORD[s] [2], them [2], what [2], you [2], again [+928+1685+2021+2021+7193] [1], any[s] [1], anyone [1], at once [+928+2021+2021+3427] [1], at once [+928+2021+2021+6961] [1], Baal[s] [1], Balaam[s] [1], Beerah[s] [1], daughter[s] [1], David[s] [1], death[s] [1], each of us [+638+2256] [1], Elah[s] [1], Elijah[s] [1], Elisha[s] [1], else [1], fire[s] [1], Gaal[s] [1], Gehazi[s] [1], Hannah[s] [1], he alone [1], he himself [1], herself [1], it[s] [+2021+2021+5226] [1], joy[s] [1], let it be [+4027] [1], man[s] [1], mine [1], my vow[s] [1], Naaman[s] [1], Naomi[s] [1], other[s] [1], priests[s] [1], regular[s] [1], Ruth[s] [1], she's [1], Shem[s] [1], something[s] [1], such [1], that part[s] [1], that person[s] [1], that slave[s] [1], that son[s] [1], that's [1], the city[s] [1], the father[s] [1], the key[s] [1], the Makirites[s] [1], the person[s] [1], the prophet[s] [1], the slave[s] [1], the woman[s] [1], then[s] [+2021+2021+6961] [1], then[s] [+928+2021+2021+3427] [1], things[s] [1], this man[s] [1], this same [1], very [1], which[s] [1], who[s] [1], whoever [1], whose [1], yet [+2021+2021+3427+6330] [1]

2086 הוֹד¹ ***hôd¹***, n.m. [24] [→ 2087, 6654; cf. 3344; *also used with compound proper names*]

splendor [10], majesty [3], glory [2], honor [2], proud [2], authority [1], best strength [1], face [1], glorious [1], majestic [1]

Nu 27: 20 Give him some of your **authority** so the whole Israelite
1Ch 16: 27 **Splendor** and majesty are before him; strength and joy in his
29: 11 and the power and the glory and the majesty and the **splendor**,
29: 25 bestowed on him royal **splendor** such as no king over Israel ever
Job 37: 22 he comes in golden splendor; God comes in awesome **majesty**.
39: 20 him leap like a locust, striking terror with his **proud** snorting?
40: 10 with glory and splendor, and clothe yourself in **honor** and majesty.
Ps 8: 1 [8:2] in all the earth! You have set your **glory** above the heavens.
21: 5 [21:6] is great; you have bestowed on him **splendor** and majesty.
45: 3 [45:4] O mighty one; clothe yourself with **splendor** and majesty.
96: 6 **Splendor** and majesty are before him; strength and glory are in his
104: 1 you are very great; you are clothed with **splendor** and majesty.
111: 3 **Glorious** and majestic are his deeds, and his righteousness endures
145: 5 They will speak of the glorious splendor of your **majesty**,
148: 13 alone is exalted; his **splendor** is above the earth and the heavens.
Pr 5: 9 lest you give your **best strength** to others and your years to one
Isa 30: 30 The LORD will cause men to hear his **majestic** voice and will
Jer 22: 18 will not mourn for him: 'Alas, my master! Alas, his **splendor**!'
Da 10: 8 no strength left, my **face** turned deathly pale and I was helpless.
11: 21 contemptible person who has not been given the **honor** *of* royalty.
Hos 14: 6 [14:7] His **splendor** will be like an olive tree, his fragrance like a
Hab 3: 3 *Selah* His **glory** covered the heavens and his praise filled the
Zec 6: 13 he will be clothed with **majesty** and will sit and rule on his throne.
10: 3 the house of Judah, and make them like a **proud** horse in battle.

2087 הוֹד² ***hôd²***, n.pr.m. [1] [√ 2086]

Hod [1]

1Ch 7: 37 Bezer, **Hod**, Shamma, Shilshah, Ithran and Beera.

2088 הוֹדְוָה ***hôdᵉwâ***, n.pr.m. [1 / 2] [→ 2089, 2090; cf. 3344 + 3378]

Hodaviah [2]

Ezr 3: 9 and Kadmiel and his sons (descendants of **Hodaviah**) [BHS 3373]
Ne 7: 43 of Jeshua (through Kadmiel through the line of **Hodaviah**)

2089 הוֹדַוְיָה ***hôdawyâ***, n.pr.m. [3] [→ 2069, 2088; cf. 3344 + 3378]

Hodaviah [3]

1Ch 5: 24 Epher, Ishi, Eliel, Azriel, Jeremiah, **Hodaviah** and Jahdiel.
9: 7 son of Meshullam, the son of **Hodaviah**, the son of Hassenuah;
Ezr 2: 40 descendants of Jeshua and Kadmiel (through the line of **Hodaviah**)

2090 הוֹדַוְיָהוּ ***hôdawyāhû***, n.pr.m. [1] [√ 2088; cf. 3344 + 3378]

Hodaviah [1]

1Ch 3:24 **Hodaviah**, [K 2069] Eliashib, Pelaiah, Akkub, Johanan, Delaiah

2091 הוֹדִיָּה ***hôdiyyâ***, n.pr.m. [6] [√ 2086 + 3378]

Hodiah [5], Hodiah's [1]

1Ch 4:19 The sons of **Hodiah's** wife, the sister of Naham: the father of
Ne 8: 7 **Hodiah**, Maaseiah, Kelita, Azariah, Jozabad, Hanan and Pelaiah—
9: 5 Hashabneiah, Sherebiah, **Hodiah**, Shebaniah and Pethahiah—
10:10 [10:11] Shebaniah, **Hodiah**, Kelita, Pelaiah, Hanan,
10:13 [10:14] **Hodiah**, Bani and Beninu.
10:18 [10:19] **Hodiah**, Hashum, Bezai,

2092 הָוָה ***hāwâ¹***, v. [1] [→ 2095, 2096, 2119; cf. 2093]

fall [1]

Job 37: 6 [A] He says to the snow, '**Fall** *on* the earth,' and to the rain

2093 הָוָה ***hāwâ²***, v. [5] [cf. 2092, 2118; Ar 10201]

be [2], become [1], get [1], lie [1]

Ge 27:29 [A] **Be** lord over your brothers, and may the sons of your mother
Ne 6: 6 [A] according to these reports you *are about to* **become** their
Ecc 2:22 [A] What *does* a man **get** for all the toil and anxious striving with
11: 3 [A] or to the north, in the place where it falls, there *will it* **lie**.
Isa 16: 4 [A] fugitives stay with you; **be** their shelter from the destroyer."

2094 הַוָּה ***hawwâ¹***, n.f. [3] [√ 205; cf. 203]

craving [1], desire [1], evil desires [1]

Pr 10: 3 the righteous go hungry but he thwarts the **craving** *of* the wicked.
11: 6 delivers them, but the unfaithful are trapped by **evil desires**.
Mic 7: 3 the judge accepts bribes, the powerful dictate what they **desire**—

2095 הַוָּה ***hawwâ²***, n.f. [13] [→ 2119; cf. 2092]

destroying [2], destruction [2], ruin [2], corrupt [1], deadly [1], destructive forces [1], disaster [1], malice [1], malicious [1], misery [1]

Job 6: 2 be weighed and all my **misery** [K 2119] be placed on the scales!
6:30 any wickedness on my lips? Can my mouth not discern **malice**?
30:13 They break up my road; they succeed in **destroying** me—
Ps 5: 9 [5:10] mouth can be trusted; their heart is filled with **destruction**.
38:12 [38:13] set their traps, those who would harm me talk of my **ruin**;
52: 2 [52:4] Your tongue plots **destruction**; it is like a sharpened razor,
52: 7 [52:9] in his great wealth and grew strong by **destroying** others!"
55:11 [55:12] **Destructive forces** are at work in the city; threats and lies
57: 1 [57:2] in the shadow of your wings until the **disaster** has passed.
91: 3 save you from the fowler's snare and from the **deadly** pestilence.
94:20 Can a **corrupt** throne be allied with you—one that brings on
Pr 17: 4 man listens to evil lips; a liar pays attention to a **malicious** tongue.
19:13 A foolish son is his father's **ruin**, and a quarrelsome wife is like a

2096 הֹוָה ***hōwâ***, n.f. [3] [√ 2092]

calamity [3]

Isa 47:11 A **calamity** will fall upon you that you cannot ward off with a
Eze 7:26 **Calamity** upon calamity will come, and rumor upon rumor.
7:26 Calamity upon **calamity** will come, and rumor upon rumor.

2097 הוֹהָם ***hôhām***, n.pr.m. [1]

Hoham [1]

Jos 10: 3 So Adoni-Zedek king of Jerusalem appealed to **Hoham** king of

2098 הוֹי ***hôy***, interj. [51] [√ 2082]

woe [36], alas [5], come [4], ah [3], oh [2], awful [+1524] [1]

1Ki 13:30 and they mourned over him and said, "**Oh**, my brother!"
Isa 1: 4 **Ah**, sinful nation, a people loaded with guilt, a brood of evildoers,
1:24 "**Ah**, I will get relief from my foes and avenge myself on my
5: 8 **Woe** *to* you who add house to house and join field to field till no
5:11 **Woe** to those who rise early in the morning to run after their
5:18 **Woe** *to* those who draw sin along with cords of deceit,
5:20 **Woe** *to* those who call evil good and good evil, who put darkness
5:21 **Woe** *to* those who are wise in their own eyes and clever in their
5:22 **Woe** *to* those who are heroes at drinking wine and champions at
10: 1 **Woe** *to* those who make unjust laws, to those who issue oppressive
10: 5 "**Woe** *to* the Assyrian, the rod of my anger, in whose hand is the
17:12 **Oh**, the raging of many nations—they rage like the raging sea!
18: 1 **Woe** *to* the land of whirring wings along the rivers of Cush,
28: 1 **Woe** *to* that wreath, the pride of Ephraim's drunkards, to the
29: 1 **Woe** *to* you, Ariel, Ariel, the city where David settled! Add year to
29:15 **Woe** *to* those who go to great depths to hide their plans from the
30: 1 "**Woe** *to* the obstinate children," declares the LORD, "to those
31: 1 **Woe** *to* those who go down to Egypt for help, who rely on horses,
33: 1 **Woe** *to* you, O destroyer, you who have not been destroyed!
45: 9 "**Woe** *to* him who quarrels with his Maker, to him who is
45:10 **Woe** *to* him who says to his father, 'What have you begotten?'
55: 1 "**Come**, all you who are thirsty, come to the waters; and you who
Jer 22:13 "**Woe** *to* him who builds his palace by unrighteousness, his upper
22:18 '**Alas**, my brother! Alas, my sister!' They will not mourn for him:
22:18 'Alas, my brother! **Alas**, my sister!' They will not mourn for him:
22:18 will not mourn for him: '**Alas**, my master! Alas, his splendor!'
22:18 will not mourn for him: 'Alas, my master! **Alas**, his splendor!'
23: 1 "**Woe** *to* the shepherds who are destroying and scattering the sheep
30: 7 How **awful** [+1524] that day will be! None will be like it.
34: 5 they will make a fire in your honor and lament, "**Alas**, O master!"
47: 6 " '**Ah**, sword of the LORD,' ⌊you cry,⌋ 'how long till you rest?
48: 1 the God of Israel, says: "**Woe** to Nebo, for it will be ruined.
50:27 **Woe** to them! For their day has come, the time for them to be
Eze 13: 3 **Woe** to the foolish prophets who follow their own spirit and have
13:18 **Woe** to the women who sew magic charms on all their wrists
34: 2 **Woe** *to* the shepherds of Israel who only take care of themselves!
Am 5:18 **Woe** to you who long for the day of the LORD! Why do you long
6: 1 **Woe** to you who are complacent in Zion, and to you who feel
Mic 2: 1 **Woe** to those who plan iniquity, to those who plot evil on their
Na 3: 1 **Woe** to the city of blood, full of lies, full of plunder, never without
Hab 2: 6 " '**Woe** to him who piles up stolen goods and makes himself
2: 9 "**Woe** to him who builds his realm by unjust gain to set his nest on
2:12 "**Woe** to him who builds a city with bloodshed and establishes a
2:15 "**Woe** to him who gives drink to his neighbors, pouring it from the
2:19 **Woe** to him who says to wood, 'Come to life!' Or to lifeless stone,
Zep 2: 5 **Woe** to you who live by the sea, O Kerethite people; the word of
3: 1 **Woe** to the city of oppressors, rebellious and defiled!
Zec 2: 6 [2:10] "**Come**! Come! Flee from the land of the north,"
2: 6 [2:10] "Come! **Come**! Flee from the land of the north,"
2: 7 [2:11] "**Come**, O Zion! Escape, you who live in the Daughter of
11:17 "**Woe** to the worthless shepherd, who deserts the flock!

2099 הוֹלֵלוֹת ***hôlēlôt***, n.f. [4] [√ 2147]

madness [4]

Ecc 1:17 and also of **madness** and folly, but I learned that this, too,
2:12 my thoughts to consider wisdom, and also **madness** and folly.
7:25 understand the stupidity of wickedness and the **madness** of folly.
9: 3 are full of evil and there is **madness** in their hearts while they live,

2100 הוֹלֵלוּת ***hôlēlût***, n.f. [1] [√ 2147]

madness [1]

Ecc 10:13 his words are folly; at the end they are wicked **madness**—

2101 הוּם ***hûm***, v. [4] [→ 4539; cf. 2159, 2169, 5637]

distraught [1], shook [1], stirred [1], throng [1]

Ru 1:19 [C] the whole town *was* **stirred** because of them, and the women
1Sa 4: 5 [C] all Israel raised such a great shout that the ground **shook**.
Ps 55: 2 [55:3] [G] My thoughts trouble me and *I am* **distraught**
Mic 2:12 [G] like a flock in its pasture; the place *will* **throng** with people.

2102 הוֹמָם ***hômām***, n.pr.m. [1] [→ 2123]

Homam [1]

1Ch 1:39 The sons of Lotan: Hori and **Homam**. Timna was Lotan's sister.

2103 הוּן ***hûn***, v. [1] [→ 2104]

thinking it easy [1]

Dt 1:41 [G] his weapons, **thinking it easy** to go up into the hill country.

2104 הוֹן ***hôn***, n.m. [26] [√ 2103]

wealth [15], enough [2], wealth of goods [2], money [1], pittance [+4202] [1], possessions [1], rich [1], riches [1], treasures [1], valuable things [+3701] [1]

Ps 44:12 [44:13] You sold your people for a **pittance** [+4202], gaining
112: 3 **Wealth** and riches are in his house, and his righteousness endures
119:14 I rejoice in following your statutes as one rejoices in great **riches**.
Pr 1:13 we will get all sorts of **valuable things** [+3701] and fill our houses
3: 9 Honor the LORD with your **wealth**, with the firstfruits of all your
6:31 pay sevenfold, though it costs him all the **wealth** *of* his house.
8:18 With me are riches and honor, enduring **wealth** and prosperity.
10:15 The **wealth** *of* the rich is their fortified city, but poverty is the ruin
11: 4 **Wealth** is worthless in the day of wrath, but righteousness delivers
12:27 not roast his game, but the diligent man prizes his **possessions**.
13: 7 yet has nothing; another pretends to be poor, yet has great **wealth**.
13:11 Dishonest **money** dwindles away, but he who gathers money little
18:11 The **wealth** *of* the rich is their fortified city; they imagine it an

Pr 19: 4 **Wealth** brings many friends, but a poor man's friend deserts him.
19: 14 Houses and **wealth** are inherited from parents, but a prudent wife
24: 4 knowledge its rooms are filled with rare and beautiful **treasures**.
28: 8 He who increases his **wealth** by exorbitant interest amasses it for
28: 22 A stingy man is eager to get **rich** and is unaware that poverty
29: 3 to his father, but a companion of prostitutes squanders his **wealth**.
30: 15 three things that are never satisfied, four that never say, '**Enough**!':
30: 16 is never satisfied with water, and fire, which never says, '**Enough**!'
SS 8: 7 If one were to give all the **wealth** *of* his house for love, it would be
Eze 27: 12 did business with you because of your great **wealth of goods**;
27: 18 because of your many products and great **wealth of goods**,
27: 27 Your **wealth**, merchandise and wares, your mariners, seamen
27: 33 with your great **wealth** and your wares you enriched the kings of

2105 הוֹר *hôr*, n.m. Not used in NIV/BHS [cf. 2215]

2106 הוֹשָׁמָע *hôšāmā'*, n.pr.m. [1] [√ 9048 + 3378]

Hoshama [1]

1Ch 3: 18 Shenazzar, Jekamiah, **Hoshama** and Nedabiah.

2107 הוֹשֵׁעַ *hôšēa'*, n.pr.m. [16] [√ 3828 + 446 *or* 3378]

Hoshea [12], Hosea [2], him[s] [1], Joshua [1]

Nu 13: 8 from the tribe of Ephraim, **Hoshea** son of Nun;
13: 16 the land. (Moses gave **Hoshea** son of Nun the name Joshua.)
Dt 32: 44 Moses came with **Joshua** son of Nun and spoke all the words of
2Ki 15: 30 **Hoshea** son of Elah conspired against Pekah son of Remaliah.
17: 1 **Hoshea** son of Elah became king of Israel in Samaria, and he
17: 3 Shalmaneser king of Assyria came up to attack **Hoshea**, who had
17: 4 But the king of Assyria discovered that **Hoshea** was a traitor,
17: 6 In the ninth year of **Hoshea**, the king of Assyria captured Samaria
18: 1 In the third year of **Hoshea** son of Elah king of Israel,
18: 9 which was the seventh year of **Hoshea** son of Elah king of Israel,
18: 10 sixth year, which was the ninth year of **Hoshea** king of Israel.
1Ch 27: 20 **Hoshea** son of Azaziah; over half the tribe of Manasseh: Joel son
Ne 10: 23 [10:24] **Hoshea**, Hananiah, Hasshub,
Hos 1: 1 The word of the LORD that came to **Hosea** son of Beeri during
1: 2 When the LORD began to speak through **Hosea**, the LORD said
1: 2 the LORD said to **him**[s], "Go, take to yourself an adulterous wife

2108 הוֹשַׁעְיָה *hôša'yâ*, n.pr.m. [3] [√ 3828 + 3378]

Hoshaiah [3]

Ne 12: 32 **Hoshaiah** and half the leaders of Judah followed them,
Jer 42: 1 including Johanan son of Kareah and Jezaniah son of **Hoshaiah**,
43: 2 Azariah son of **Hoshaiah** and Johanan son of Kareah and all the

2109 הות *hût*, v. [1] [cf. 2254]

assault [1]

Ps 62: 3 [62:4] [D] How long *will you* **assault** a man? Would all of you

2110 הוֹתִיר *hôtîr*, n.pr.m. [2] [√ 3855]

Hothir [2]

1Ch 25: 4 Joshbekashah, Mallothi, **Hothir** and Mahazioth.
25: 28 the twenty-first to **Hothir**, his sons and relatives, 12

2111 הָזָה *hāzâ*, v. [1]

dream [1]

Isa 56: 10 [A] cannot bark; they lie around and **dream**, they love to sleep.

2112 הַחִירֹת *haḥîrōt*, n.pr.loc. Not used in NIV/BHS [√ 2672]

2113 הִי *hî*, n.[m.]. [1]

woe [1]

Eze 2: 10 sides of it were written words of lament and mourning and **woe**.

2114 הִי- *-hî*, p.m.s.suf. [1] [√ 2023]

his [1]

Ps 116: 12 How can I repay the LORD for all **his** goodness to me?

2115 הִיא *hî'*, p.f.s. Not used in NIV/BHS [√ 2085; Ar 10205]

2116 הֵידָד *hêdād*, n.m. [7] [→ 2059]

shouts of joy [3], shout in triumph [+6702] [1], shout [1], shouting [1], shouts [1]

Isa 16: 9 The **shouts of joy** over your ripened fruit and over your harvests
16: 10 out wine at the presses, for I have put an end to the **shouting**.
Jer 25: 30 *He will* **shout** like those who tread the grapes, shout against all
48: 33 of wine from the presses; no one treads them with **shouts of joy**.
48: 33 shouts of joy. Although there are **shouts**, they are not shouts of joy.
48: 33 of joy. Although there are shouts, they are not **shouts of joy**.
51: 14 of locusts, and *they will* **shout in triumph** [+6702] over you.

2117 הֻיְּדוֹת *huyy[e]dôt*, n.f.pl. [1] [√ 3344]

songs of thanksgiving [1]

Ne 12: 8 with his associates, was in charge of the **songs of thanksgiving**.

2118 הָיָה *hāyâ*, v. [3561 / 3562] [→ 181; cf. 2093; Ar 10201]

untranslated [872], be [715], was [305], came [165], become [164], were [159], is [97], been [77], are [76], became [59], had [+4200] [50], have [+4200] [47], come [26], happened [26], will [19], am [17], had [16], happen [16], have [16], remain [14], lived [+3427] [12], belong to [+4200] [11], has [11], hold [10], becomes [9], fall [9], comes [8], lived [8], remained [8], set [8], go [7], bring [6], continue [6], done [6], fell [6], lie [6], made [6], serve [6], went [6], belonged to [+4200] [5], consider [+4200] [5], ended [+9362] [5], fallen [5], has [+4200] [5], has [+928] [5], left [5], stay [5], stayed [5], belongs to [+4200] [4], endure [4], included [4], keep [4], last [4], leave [4], numbered [4], one day [+2256] [4], rest [4], spread [4], took place [4], touch [+928] [4], appears [3], bring [+4200] [3], coming [3], end [+9362] [3], ending [+9362] [3], extend [3], given [3], keep [+4200] [3], kept [3], lay [3], make [3], marry [+851+4200+4200] [3], may [3], put [3], stand [3], taken [3], use [3], used [3], wear [+6584] [3], agree [+285+3869] [2], applies [2], arose [2], be [+2118] [2], bind [+3213+4200] [2], bring [+4200+4200] [2], brought [2], came [+2118] [2], certainly come true [+2118] [2], come into being [+2118] [2], come what may [+4537] [2], connecting [2], did [2], do [2], extended [2], follow [+339] [2], fulfilled [2], get [2], help [+6640] [2], lies [2], living [2], lying [2], married [+851+4200] [2], married [+851+4200+4200] [2], marries [+408+2118+4200] [2], marry [+851+4200] [2], occur [2], overwhelmed [+928+4202+6388+8120] [2], preceded [+4200+7156] [2], reached [2], receive [+4200] [2], regard as [+4200] [2], rule [+6584] [2], serve as [2], served [2], settled [2], sold for [+928] [2], spent [2], struck [+928] [2], surely become [+2118+4200] [2], take place [2], turn to [2], turned into [+4200] [2], use [+4200] [2], was altogether [+2118] [2], wear [2], abound [+7172] [1], acquired [+4200] [1], act [1], allotted [+1598] [1], allotted [+1598+4200] [1], allotted [+928+1598+2021+4200] [1], amount to [1], amounted to [1], appear [+928+3869+6524] [1], appear [1], appeared [1], apply [1], aroused [+4200+6584] [1], arranged [+4200+4595] [1], attach [1], be treated as [1], become [+4200] [1], becoming [1], began [1], beginning [1], being [1], belong to [+928] [1], belong [1], belonged to [+448] [1], belonging to [+4200] [1], belongs [1], bring about [+928] [1], brings [1], broke out [1], brought about [+4946] [1], brought with [+928+3338] [1], came into being [1], came on [1], came to be [1], came to [1], carried by [+6584] [1], caught [1], cause [+4946] [1], comes of [1], committed [1], company [+907] [1], compare with [+3869] [1], complete [+4200+4946+7891] [1], condemn [+2631+4200] [1], conferred [+1821] [1], consist of [1], continued [+2143] [1], controlled [+4200] [1], could not [+6584] [1], count [+4200+4200] [1], covered [+928] [1], decide [+6584+7023] [1], decided [+4213+6640] [1], designate [1], do[s] that [+928+2257+3338] [1], downcast [+4200] [1], drove back [+6584] [1], earlier [1], end [+340+928+2021] [1], ends [1], endure [+4200+4200] [1], engaged in [1], escapes [+4200+7129] [1], exhausted [1], exists [1], extending [1], fared [1], feared [+3007] [1], fighting with [+907] [1], filled [+928+3972] [1], find [1], follow [1], followed [+339] [1], formed [1], fulfilled [+4027] [1], future [+4537+8611] [1], gain support [+907+3338] [1], gained [1], give [+4200+4200] [1], give shelter [+6261+6584] [1], give [1], goes [+8079] [1], gone [+928+4202] [1], gone [1], got [+4200] [1], grew worse and worse [+2617+2716+4394] [1], had [+6584] [1], had [+928] [1], had chance [+928+3338] [1], had part in [+4946] [1], had to [+6584] [1], happening [1], happens [1], harbor [+4222+6640] [1], harbored [+4200] [1], has [+4200+4200] [1], has [+6640] [1], have [+1068] [1], have [+4200+4200] [1], have [+6584] [1], have [+928] [1], having [+4200] [1], help [+4200] [1], help [+907] [1], hold [+928+3338] [1], holds [+928+3338] [1], in office [1], inclined [+2296] [1], include [1], increase [1], incurs [1], inherit [+448] [1], into marry [+4200] [1], join [+928] [1], joined [1], lasted [1], led the way [+3338+8037] [1], left [+4200] [1], lend [1], let [1], life [+889+3427] [1], looked [+928+6524] [1], made angry [+906+7911] [1], made fall [+4200+4200+4842] [1], make sport of [+4200+4200+5442] [1], making [1], married to [+851+4200+4200] [1], marries [+408+4200] [1], marries [+4200] [1], marry [+408+4200] [1], marry into [+4200] [1], mattered [1], mount [+4853] [1], moved [1], observe [1], occurred [1], once [1], owes [1], own [+4200] [1], owned [+4200+5238] [1], owned [+5238] [1], participate in [+448] [1], passed [1], predecessor [+889+4200+7156] [1], prepare [+3922] [1], produced [1], proper place [+889+5226+9004] [1], property[s] [+889+4200] [1], prove to be [1], proved to be [1], provided for [+430+2256+4200+4312] [1], raise

[1], raised [1], reached [+928] [1], reaching [1], ready [1], rebel [+5308] [1], received [+4200] [1], received [1], regard [+4200+7156] [1], remain unmarried [+408+1194+4200+4200+6328] [1], remains [1], required [1], rested [1], restored [1], retains [+4200] [1], retains [1], ruled [+4889] [1], run [1], seem [+928+4200+6524] [1], seem [1], seemed [+928+6524] [1], seemed [1], sell for [+928] [1], serve [+4200] [1], serve [+4200+7156] [1], served [+4200+7156] [1], served as [1], serving [1], share [+4200] [1], shed [1], shine [+240] [1], show [+4200] [1], shows to be [+4200] [1], sprang up [1], standing [1], start [1], started [1], staying [1], steals forth [1], stretched [1], strike [+928] [1], strike [1], striking [+928] [1], suffer [1], suffered [+4200] [1], suffered [+928] [1], supply [+4200] [1], supported [+339] [1], supported [+907+3338] [1], surely take place [1], surround [+4946+6017+6584] [1], take [+4200] [1], take care of [+4200+4200+5466] [1], take care of [+4200+6125] [1], take command [+4200+5464] [1], take hold of [+928] [1], take the place of [+9393] [1], take [1], tasted [1], taught [+906+3723] [1], tend livestock [+408+5238] [1], tended livestock [+408+5238] [1], testify [+6332] [1], took care of [+4200+6125] [1], touches [+6584] [1], treated [+6640] [1], treated [1], treating [1], turn against [+4200+4200 +8477] [1], turned out [1], turned [1], unite [+3480+4200+4222+6584] [1], unmarried [+408+4200+4202] [1], used to [1], using [1], want[s] [1], was committed [1], wasn't [+4202] [1], weighed [1], went over [+6017] [1], when [+4946] [1], with [+928] [1], work [1], you [1]

Ge 1: 2 [A] Now the earth **was** formless and empty, darkness was over
1: 3 [A] And God said, "*Let there* **be** light," and there was light.
1: 3 [A] And God said, "Let there be light," and *there* **was** light.
1: 5 [A] *there* **was** evening, and there was morning—the first day.
1: 5 [A] there was evening, and *there* **was** morning—the first day.
1: 6 [A] "*Let there* **be** an expanse between the waters to separate
1: 6 [A] "Let there be an expanse between the waters **[NIE]** to
1: 7 [A] under the expanse from the water above it. And *it* **was** so.
1: 8 [A] *there* **was** evening, and there was morning—the second day.
1: 8 [A] there was evening, and *there* **was** morning—the second day.
1: 9 [A] to one place, and let dry ground appear." And *it* **was** so.
1: 11 [A] seed in it, according to their various kinds." And *it* **was** so.
1: 13 [A] *there* **was** evening, and there was morning—the third day.
1: 13 [A] there was evening, and *there* **was** morning—the third day.
1: 14 [A] "*Let there* **be** lights in the expanse of the sky to separate the
1: 14 [A] *let them* **serve** as signs to mark seasons and days and years,
1: 15 [A] *let them* **be** lights in the expanse of the sky to give light on
1: 15 [A] expanse of the sky to give light on the earth." And *it* **was** so.
1: 19 [A] *there* **was** evening, and there was morning—the fourth day.
1: 19 [A] there was evening, and *there* **was** morning—the fourth day.
1: 23 [A] *there* **was** evening, and there was morning—the fifth day.
1: 23 [A] there was evening, and *there* **was** morning—the fifth day.
1: 24 [A] and wild animals, each according to its kind." And *it* **was** so.
1: 29 [A] tree that has fruit with seed in it. *They will* **be** yours for food.
1: 30 [A] life in it—I give every green plant for food." And *it* **was** so.
1: 31 [A] *there* **was** evening, and there was morning—the sixth day.
1: 31 [A] there was evening, and *there* **was** morning—the sixth day.
2: 5 [A] no shrub of the field *had* yet **appeared** on the earth and no
2: 7 [A] nostrils the breath of life, and the man **became** a living being.
2: 10 [A] from there it was separated **[NIE]** into four headwaters.
2: 18 [A] LORD God said, "It is not good for the man *to* **be** alone.
2: 24 [A] and be united to his wife, and *they will* **become** one flesh.
2: 25 [A] The man and his wife **were** both naked, and they felt no
3: 1 [A] Now the serpent **was** more crafty than any of the wild
3: 5 [A] and *you will* **be** like God, knowing good and evil."
3: 20 [A] because she *would* **become** the mother of all the living.
3: 22 [A] "The man *has* now **become** like one of us, knowing good
4: 2 [A] Now **[NIE]** Abel kept flocks, and Cain worked the soil.
4: 2 [A] Now Abel kept flocks, and Cain **[NIE]** worked the soil.
4: 3 [A] **[NIE]** In the course of time Cain brought some of the fruits
4: 8 [A] **[NIE]** while they were in the field, Cain attacked his brother
4: 8 [A] while they **were** in the field, Cain attacked his brother Abel
4: 12 [A] crops for you. *You will* **be** a restless wanderer on the earth."
4: 14 [A] *I will* **be** a restless wanderer on the earth, and whoever finds
4: 14 [A] on the earth, and **[NIE]** whoever finds me will kill me."
4: 17 [A] Cain **was** then building a city, and he named it after his son
4: 20 [A] he **was** the father of those who live in tents and raise
4: 21 [A] he **was** the father of all who play the harp and flute.
5: 4 [A] Adam **lived** [+3427] 800 years and had other sons
5: 5 [A] **[NIE]** Altogether, Adam lived 930 years, and then he died.
5: 8 [A] Altogether, Seth **lived** [+3427] 912 years, and then he died.
5: 11 [A] Altogether, Enosh **lived** [+3427] 905 years, and then he died.
5: 14 [A] Altogether, Kenan **lived** [+3427] 910 years, and then he died.
5: 17 [A] Mahalalel **lived** [+3427] 895 years, and then he died.
5: 20 [A] Altogether, Jared **lived** [+3427] 962 years, and then he died.
5: 23 [A] Altogether, Enoch **lived** [+3427] 365 years.
5: 27 [A] Methuselah **lived** [+3427] 969 years, and then he died.
5: 31 [A] Lamech **lived** [+3427] 777 years, and then he died.
5: 32 [A] After Noah **was** 500 years old, he became the father of Shem,
6: 1 [A] **[NIE]** When men began to increase in number on the earth
6: 3 [A] he is mortal; his days *will* **be** a hundred and twenty years."
6: 4 [A] The Nephilim **were** on the earth in those days—and also
6: 9 [A] Noah **was** a righteous man, blameless among the people of
6: 19 [A] and female, **[NIE]** to keep them alive with you.
6: 21 [A] and store it away **[NIE]** as food for you and for them."
7: 6 [A] Noah was six hundred years old when the floodwaters **came**
7: 10 [A] **[NIE]** after the seven days the floodwaters came on the
7: 10 [A] And after the seven days the floodwaters **came** on the earth.
7: 12 [A] And rain **fell** on the earth forty days and forty nights.
7: 17 [A] For forty days the flood *kept* **coming** on the earth, and as the
8: 5 [A] The waters **continued** [+2143] to recede until the tenth
8: 6 [A] **[NIE]** After forty days Noah opened the window he had
8: 13 [A] **[NIE]** By the first day of the first month of Noah's six
9: 2 [A] and dread of you *will* **fall** upon all the beasts of the earth
9: 3 [A] Everything that lives and moves *will* **be** food for you. Just as
9: 11 [A] never again *will there* **be** a flood to destroy the earth."
9: 13 [A] *it will* **be** the sign of the covenant between me and the earth.
9: 14 [A] **[NIE]** Whenever I bring clouds over the earth
9: 15 [A] Never again *will* the waters **become** a flood to destroy all
9: 16 [A] Whenever the rainbow **appears** in the clouds, I will see it
9: 18 [A] The sons of Noah who came out of the ark **were** Shem, Ham
9: 25 [A] be Canaan! The lowest of slaves *will he* **be** to his brothers."
9: 26 [A] the God of Shem! *May* Canaan **be** the slave of Shem.
9: 27 [A] live in the tents of Shem, and *may* Canaan **be** his slave."
9: 29 [A] Altogether, Noah **lived** [+3427] 950 years, and then he died.
10: 8 [A] of Nimrod, who grew to **be** a mighty warrior on the earth.
10: 9 [A] He **was** a mighty hunter before the LORD; that is why it is
10: 10 [A] The first centers of his kingdom **were** Babylon, Erech,
10: 19 [A] the borders of Canaan **reached** from Sidon toward Gerar as
10: 30 [A] The region where they lived **stretched** from Mesha toward
11: 1 [A] Now the whole world **had** one language and a common
11: 2 [A] **[NIE]** As men moved eastward, they found a plain in Shinar
11: 3 [A] They **used** brick instead of stone, and tar for mortar.
11: 3 [A] They used brick instead of stone, and tar **[RPH]** for mortar.
11: 30 [A] Now Sarai **was** barren; she had no children.
11: 32 [A] Terah **lived** [+3427] 205 years, and he died in Haran.
12: 2 [A] I will make your name great, and *you will* **be** a blessing.
12: 10 [A] Now *there* **was** a famine in the land, and Abram went down
12: 11 [A] **[NIE]** As he was about to enter Egypt, he said to his wife
12: 12 [A] **[NIE]** When the Egyptians see you, they will say, 'This is
12: 14 [A] **[NIE]** When Abram came to Egypt, the Egyptians saw that
12: 16 [A] Abram **acquired** [+4200] sheep and cattle, male and female
13: 3 [A] place between Bethel and Ai where his tent *had* **been** earlier
13: 5 [A] with Abram, also **had** [+4200] flocks and herds and tents.
13: 6 [A] for their possessions **were** so great that they were not able to
13: 7 [A] quarreling **arose** between Abram's herdsmen and the
13: 8 [A] to Lot, "*Let's* not **have** any quarreling between you and me,
14: 1 [A] **[NIE]** At this time Amraphel king of Shinar, Arioch king of
15: 1 [A] the word of the LORD **came** to Abram in a vision:
15: 5 [A] Then he said to him, "So *shall* your offspring **be**."
15: 12 [A] **[NIE]** As the sun was setting, Abram fell into a deep sleep,
15: 13 [A] "Know for certain that your descendants *will* **be** strangers in
15: 17 [A] When **[NIE]** the sun had set and darkness had fallen, a
15: 17 [A] When the sun had set and darkness *had* **fallen**, a smoking
16: 12 [A] He *will* **be** a wild donkey of a man; his hand will be against
17: 1 [A] When Abram **was** ninety-nine years old, the LORD
17: 1 [A] "I am God Almighty; walk before me and **be** blameless.
17: 4 [A] covenant with you: *You will* **be** the father of many nations.
17: 5 [A] your name *will* **be** Abraham, for I have made you a father of
17: 7 [A] to **be** your God and the God of your descendants after you.
17: 8 [A] and your descendants after you; and *I will* **be** their God."
17: 11 [A] and *it will* **be** the sign of the covenant between me and you.
17: 13 [A] My covenant in your flesh **is** *to be* an everlasting covenant.
17: 16 [A] I will bless her so that *she will* **be** the mother of nations;
17: 16 [A] the mother of nations; kings of peoples *will* **come** from her."
18: 11 [A] in years, and Sarah **was** past the age of childbearing.
18: 12 [A] my master is old, *will* I *now* **have** [+4200] this pleasure?"
18: 18 [A] Abraham *will* **surely become** [+2118+4200] a great
18: 18 [A] Abraham *will* **surely become** [+2118+4200] a great
18: 25 [A] with the wicked, **treating** the righteous and the wicked alike.
19: 14 [A] destroy the city!" But his sons-in-law thought *he* **was** joking.
19: 17 [A] **[NIE]** As soon as they had brought them out, one of them
19: 26 [A] But Lot's wife looked back, and *she* **became** a pillar of salt.
19: 29 [A] So **[NIE]** when God destroyed the cities of the plain, he
19: 34 [A] **[NIE]** The next day the older daughter said to the younger,
20: 12 [A] father though not of my mother; and *she* **became** my wife.
20: 13 [A] **[NIE]** when God had me wander from my father's
21: 20 [A] God **was** with the boy as he grew up. He lived in the desert
21: 20 [A] as he grew up. He lived in the desert and **became** an archer.
21: 22 [A] **[NIE]** At that time Abimelech and Phicol the commander of
21: 30 [A] "Accept these seven lambs from my hand **[NIE]** as a
22: 1 [A] **[NIE]** Some time later God tested Abraham. He said to him,
22: 20 [A] **[NIE]** Some time later Abraham was told, "Milcah is also a

Ge 23: 1 [A] Sarah lived *to* **be** a hundred and twenty-seven years old.
24: 14 [A] *May it* **be** that when I say to a girl, 'Please let down your jar
24: 15 [A] **[NIE]** Before he had finished praying, Rebekah came out
24: 22 [A] **[NIE]** When the camels had finished drinking, the man took
24: 30 [A] **[NIE]** As soon as he had seen the nose ring, and the
24: 41 [A] to give her to you—*you will* **be** released from my oath.'
24: 43 [A] if **[NIE]** a maiden comes out to draw water and I say to her,
24: 51 [A] and go, and *let her* **become** the wife of your master's son,
24: 52 [A] **[NIE]** When Abraham's servant heard what they said, he
24: 60 [A] "Our sister, *may* you **increase** to thousands upon thousands;
24: 67 [A] So *she* **became** his wife, and he loved her; and Isaac was
25: 3 [A] the descendants of Dedan **were** the Asshurites, the Letushites
25: 11 [A] **[NIE]** After Abraham's death, God blessed his son Isaac,
25: 20 [A] Isaac **was** forty years old when he married Rebekah daughter
25: 27 [A] The boys grew up, and Esau **became** a skillful hunter, a man
26: 1 [A] Now *there* **was** a famine in the land—besides the earlier
26: 1 [A] besides the earlier famine **[NIE]** of Abraham's time—
26: 3 [A] land for a while, and *I will* **be** with you and will bless you.
26: 8 [A] **[NIE]** When Isaac had been there a long time, Abimelech
26: 14 [A] **[NIE]** He had so many flocks and herds and servants that
26: 28 [A] "We saw clearly that the LORD **was** with you;
26: 28 [A] '*There ought to* **be** a sworn agreement between us'—
26: 32 [A] **[NIE]** That day Isaac's servants came and told him about
26: 34 [A] When Esau **was** forty years old, he married Judith daughter
26: 35 [A] *They* **were** a source of grief to Isaac and Rebekah.
27: 1 [A] **[NIE]** When Isaac was old and his eyes were so weak that
27: 12 [A] *I would* **appear** [+928+3869+6524] to be tricking him and
27: 23 [A] for his hands **were** hairy like those of his brother Esau;
27: 30 [A] **[NIE]** After Isaac finished blessing him and Jacob had
27: 30 [A] and **[NIE]** Jacob had scarcely left his father's presence,
27: 33 [A] and I blessed him—and indeed *he* **will** be blessed!"
27: 39 [A] "Your dwelling *will* **be** away from the earth's richness,
27: 40 [A] **[NIE]** when you grow restless, you will throw his yoke
28: 3 [A] increase your numbers until *you* **become** a community of
28: 14 [A] Your descendants *will* **be** like the dust of the earth, and you
28: 20 [A] "If God *will* **be** with me and will watch over me on this
28: 21 [A] to my father's house, then the LORD *will* **be** my God
28: 22 [A] this stone that I have set up as a pillar *will* **be** God's house,
29: 10 [A] **[NIE]** When Jacob saw Rachel daughter of Laban,
29: 13 [A] **[NIE]** As soon as Laban heard the news about Jacob,
29: 17 [A] had weak eyes, but Rachel **was** lovely in form, and beautiful.
29: 20 [A] but *they* **seemed** like only a few days **to** [+928+6524] him
29: 23 [A] when evening **came**, he took his daughter Leah and gave her
29: 25 [A] When morning **came**, there was Leah! So Jacob said to
30: 25 [A] **[NIE]** After Rachel gave birth to Joseph, Jacob said to
30: 29 [A] for you and how your livestock *has* **fared** under my care.
30: 30 [A] The little you **had** [+4200] before I came has increased
30: 32 [A] and every spotted or speckled goat. *They will* **be** my wages.
30: 34 [A] "Agreed," said Laban. "Let *it* **be** as you have said."
30: 41 [A] **[NIE]** Whenever the stronger females were in heat, Jacob
30: 42 [A] So the weak animals **went** to Laban and the strong ones to
30: 43 [A] and *came to* **own** [+4200] large flocks,
31: 3 [A] of your fathers and to your relatives, and *I will* **be** with you."
31: 5 [A] it was before, but the God of my father *has* **been** with me.
31: 8 [A] If he said, 'The speckled ones *will* **be** your wages,' then all
31: 8 [A] if he said, 'The streaked ones *will* **be** your wages,' then all the
31: 10 [A] **[NIE]** "In breeding season I once had a dream in which I
31: 40 [A] *This* **was** *my situation*: The heat consumed me in the
31: 42 [A] of Abraham and the Fear of Isaac, *had* not **been** with me,
31: 44 [A] you and I, and *let it* **serve** as a witness between us."
32: 5 [32:6] [A] I **have** [+4200] cattle and donkeys, sheep and goats,
32: 8 [32:9] [A] attacks one group, the group that is left **may** escape."
32: 10 [32:11] [A] this Jordan, but now *I have* **become** two groups.
33: 9 [A] have plenty, my brother. **Keep** what you have for yourself."
34: 5 [A] been defiled, his sons **were** in the fields with his livestock;
34: 10 [A] You can settle among us; the land **is** open to you. Live in it,
34: 15 [A] that *you* **become** like us by circumcising all your males.
34: 16 [A] We'll settle among you and **become** one people with you.
34: 22 [A] the men will consent to live with us **[NIE]** as one people
34: 25 [A] **[NIE]** Three days later, while all of them were still in pain,
34: 25 [A] Three days later, while all of them **were** still in pain, two of
35: 3 [A] and *who has* **been** with me wherever I have gone."
35: 5 [A] the terror of God **fell** upon the towns all around them so that
35: 10 [A] will no longer be called Jacob; your name *will* **be** Israel."
35: 11 [A] A nation and a community of nations *will* **come** from you,
35: 16 [A] While *they* **were** still some distance from Ephrath, Rachel
35: 17 [A] And **[NIE]** as she was having great difficulty in childbirth,
35: 18 [A] **[NIE]** As she breathed her last—for she was dying—she
35: 22 [A] **[NIE]** While Israel was living in that region, Reuben went
35: 22 [A] and Israel heard of it. Jacob **had** twelve sons:
35: 28 [A] Isaac **lived** [+3427] a hundred and eighty years.
36: 7 [A] Their possessions **were** too great for them to remain together;
36: 11 [A] **[NIE]** The sons of Eliphaz: Teman, Omar, Zepho, Gatam
36: 12 [A] Esau's son Eliphaz also **had** [+4200] a concubine named
36: 13 [A] and Mizzah. These **were** grandsons of Esau's wife Basemath.
36: 14 [A] **[NIE]** The sons of Esau's wife Oholibamah daughter of
36: 22 [A] **[NIE]** The sons of Lotan: Hori and Homam. Timna was
37: 2 [A] **was** tending the flocks with his brothers, the sons of Bilhah
37: 20 [A] devoured him. Then we'll see what **comes of** his dreams."
37: 23 [A] So **[NIE]** when Joseph came to his brothers, they stripped
37: 27 [A] sell him to the Ishmaelites and not **lay** our hands on him;
38: 1 [A] **[NIE]** At that time, Judah left his brothers and went down to
38: 5 [A] him Shelah. *It* **was** at Kezib that she gave birth to him.
38: 7 [A] But Er, Judah's firstborn, **was** wicked in the LORD's sight;
38: 9 [A] Onan knew that the offspring *would* not **be** his; so whenever
38: 9 [A] so **[NIE]** whenever he lay with his brother's wife, he spilled
38: 21 [A] "*There* hasn't **been** any shrine prostitute here," they said.
38: 22 [A] there said, '*There* hasn't **been** any shrine prostitute here.' "
38: 23 [A] her keep what she has, or *we will* **become** a laughingstock.
38: 24 [A] **[NIE]** About three months later Judah was told, "Your
38: 27 [A] When the time **came** for her to give birth, there were twin
38: 28 [A] **[NIE]** As she was giving birth, one of them put out his
38: 29 [A] **[NIE]** when he drew back his hand, his brother came out,
39: 2 [A] The LORD **was** with Joseph and he prospered, and he lived
39: 2 [A] The LORD was with Joseph and **[NIE]** he prospered,
39: 2 [A] and *he* **lived** in the house of his Egyptian master.
39: 5 [A] **[NIE]** From the time he put him in charge of his household
39: 5 [A] The blessing of the LORD **was** on everything Potiphar had,
39: 6 [A] the food he ate. Now Joseph **was** well-built and handsome,
39: 7 [A] **[NIE]** after a while his master's wife took notice of Joseph
39: 10 [A] **[NIE]** though she spoke to Joseph day after day, he refused
39: 10 [A] he refused to go to bed with her or even **be** with her.
39: 11 [A] **[NIE]** One day he went into the house to attend to his
39: 13 [A] **[NIE]** When she saw that he had left his cloak in her hand
39: 15 [A] **[NIE]** When he heard me scream for help, he left his cloak
39: 18 [A] **[NIE]** as soon as I screamed for help, he left his cloak
39: 19 [A] **[NIE]** When his master heard the story his wife told him,
39: 20 [A] were confined. But while Joseph **was** there in the prison,
39: 21 [A] the LORD **was** with him; he showed him kindness
39: 22 [A] and he **was** made responsible for all that was done there.
40: 1 [A] **[NIE]** Some time later, the cupbearer and the baker of the
40: 4 [A] After *they had* **been** in custody for some time,
40: 13 [A] just as you used to do when *you* **were** his cupbearer.
40: 20 [A] Now the third day **was** Pharaoh's birthday, and he gave a
41: 1 [A] **[NIE]** When two full years had passed, Pharaoh had a
41: 8 [A] **[NIE]** In the morning his mind was troubled, so he sent for
41: 13 [A] And *things* **turned out** exactly as he interpreted them to us:
41: 13 [A] **[RPH]** I was restored to my position, and the other man was
41: 27 [A] scorched by the east wind: *They* **are** seven years of famine.
41: 36 [A] This food *should* **be** held in reserve for the country, to be
41: 36 [A] to be used during the seven years of famine that *will* **come**
41: 40 [A] You *shall* **be** in charge of my palace, and all my people are
41: 48 [A] Joseph collected all the food **produced** in those seven years
41: 53 [A] The seven years of abundance **[NIE]** in Egypt came to an
41: 54 [A] *There* **was** famine in all the other lands, but in the whole
41: 54 [A] other lands, but in the whole land of Egypt *there* **was** food.
41: 56 [A] When the famine *had* **spread** over the whole country, Joseph
42: 5 [A] to buy grain, for the famine **was** in the land of Canaan also.
42: 11 [A] sons of one man. Your servants **are** honest men, not spies."
42: 31 [A] But we said to him, 'We are honest men; *we* **are** not spies.
42: 35 [A] As they **were** emptying their sacks, there in each man's sack
42: 36 [A] now you want to take Benjamin. Everything **is** against me!"
43: 2 [A] So **[NIE]** when they had eaten all the grain they had brought
43: 21 [A] **[NIE]** at the place where we stopped for the night we
44: 9 [A] he will die; and the rest of us *will* **become** my lord's slaves."
44: 10 [A] Whoever is found to have it *will* **become** my slave; the rest
44: 10 [A] become my slave; the rest of you *will* **be** free from blame."
44: 17 [A] Only the man who was found to have the cup *will* **become**
44: 24 [A] **[NIE]** When we went back to your servant my father, we
44: 31 [A] **[NIE]** sees that the boy isn't there, he will die. Your
45: 10 [A] You shall live in the region of Goshen and **be** near me—you,
46: 12 [A] of Canaan). The sons of Perez: **[NIE]** Hezron and Hamul.
46: 32 [A] The men are shepherds; *they* **tend livestock** [+408+5238],
46: 33 [A] **[NIE]** When Pharaoh calls you in and asks, 'What is your
46: 34 [A] 'Your servants *have* **tended livestock** [+408+5238] from our
47: 9 [A] My years *have* **been** few and difficult, and they do not equal
47: 19 [A] and we with our land *will* **be** in bondage to Pharaoh.
47: 20 [A] famine was too severe for them. The land **became** Pharaoh's,
47: 24 [A] **[NIE]** when the crop comes in, give a fifth of it to Pharaoh.
47: 24 [A] The other four-fifths you *may* **keep** [+4200] as seed for the
47: 25 [A] in the eyes of our lord; *we will* **be** in bondage to Pharaoh."
47: 26 [A] It was only the land of the priests that *did* not **become**
47: 28 [A] and the years of his life **were** a hundred and forty-seven.
48: 1 [A] **[NIE]** Some time later Joseph was told, "Your father is ill."
48: 5 [A] Ephraim and Manasseh *will* **be** mine, just as Reuben
48: 6 [A] Any children born to you after them *will* **be** yours;
48: 19 [A] He too *will* **become** a people, and he too will become great.
48: 19 [A] and his descendants *will* **become** a group of nations."

Ge 48:21 [A] God *will* **be** with you and take you back to the land of your
49:15 [A] his shoulder to the burden and **[NIE]** submit to forced labor.
49:17 [A] Dan *will* **be** a serpent by the roadside, a viper along the path,
49:26 [A] *Let all these* **rest** on the head of Joseph, on the brow of the
50: 9 [A] also went up with him. *It* **was** a very large company.
Ex 1: 5 [A] The descendants of Jacob **numbered** seventy in all; Joseph
1: 5 [A] Jacob numbered seventy in all; Joseph **was** *already* in Egypt.
1:10 [A] **[NIE]** if war breaks out, will join our enemies, fight against
1:21 [A] **[NIE]** because the midwives feared God, he gave them
2:10 [A] she took him to Pharaoh's daughter and *he* **became** her son.
2:11 [A] **[NIE]** One day, after Moses had grown up, he went out to
2:22 [A] "*I have* **become** an alien in a foreign land."
2:23 [A] **[NIE]** During that long period, the king of Egypt died. The
3: 1 [A] Now Moses **was** tending the flock of Jethro his father-in-law,
3:12 [A] God said, "*I will* **be** with you. And this will be the sign to
3:14 [A] God said to Moses, "*I* **AM** WHO I AM. This is what you are
3:14 [A] God said to Moses, "I AM WHO *I* **AM**. This is what you are
3:14 [A] you are to say to the Israelites: '*I* **AM** has sent me to you.' "
3:21 [A] so that **[NIE]** when you leave you will not go
4: 3 [A] Moses threw it on the ground and *it* **became** a snake, and he
4: 4 [A] and *it* **turned** [+4200] *back* **into** a staff in his hand.
4: 8 [A] Then **[NIE]** the LORD said, "If they do not believe you
4: 9 [A] **[NIE]** if they do not believe these two signs or listen to you,
4: 9 [A] **[NIE]** The water you take from the river will become blood
4: 9 [A] The water you take from the river *will* **become** blood on the
4:12 [A] I *will* **help** [+6640] you speak and will teach you what to
4:15 [A] I *will* **help** [+6640] both of you speak and will teach you
4:16 [A] *it will* **be** as if he were your mouth and as if you were God to
4:16 [A] it will be as if he **were** your mouth and as if you were God to
4:16 [A] be as if he were your mouth and as if you **were** God to him.
4:24 [A] **[NIE]** At a lodging place on the way, the LORD met
5:13 [A] required of you for each day, just as when you **had** straw."
6: 7 [A] I will take you as my own people, and *I will* **be** your God.
6:28 [A] Now **[NIE]** when the LORD spoke to Moses in Egypt,
7: 1 [A] to Pharaoh, and your brother Aaron *will* **be** your prophet.
7: 9 [A] throw it down before Pharaoh,' and *it will* **become** a snake."
7:10 [A] in front of Pharaoh and his officials, and *it* **became** a snake.
7:12 [A] Each one threw down his staff and *it* **became** a snake.
7:19 [A] and all the reservoirs'—and *they will* **turn to** blood.
7:19 [A] Blood *will* **be** everywhere in Egypt, even in the wooden
7:21 [A] could not drink its water. Blood **was** everywhere in Egypt.
8:15 [8:11] [A] when Pharaoh saw that *there* **was** relief, he hardened
8:16 [8:12] [A] throughout the land of Egypt the dust *will* **become**
8:17 [8:13] [A] of the ground, gnats **came** upon men and animals.
8:17 [8:13] [A] the dust throughout the land of Egypt **became** gnats.
8:18 [8:14] [A] could not. And the gnats **were** on men and animals.
8:22 [8:18] [A] no swarms of flies *will* **be** there, so that you will
8:23 [8:19] [A] This miraculous sign *will* **occur** tomorrow.' "
9: 3 [A] the hand of the LORD *will* **bring** a terrible plague on your
9: 9 [A] *It will* **become** fine dust over the whole land of Egypt,
9: 9 [A] festering boils **will** break out on men and animals throughout
9:10 [A] and **[NIE]** festering boils broke out on men and animals.
9:11 [A] because of the boils that **were** on them and on all the
9:18 [A] I will send the worst hailstorm that *has* ever **fallen** on Egypt,
9:22 [A] hand toward the sky so that hail *will* **fall** all over Egypt—
9:24 [A] hail **fell** and lightning flashed back and forth. It was the worst
9:24 [A] *It* **was** the worst storm in all the land of Egypt since it had
9:24 [A] storm in all the land of Egypt since *it had* **become** a nation.
9:26 [A] The only place *it* **did** not hail was the land of Goshen,
9:28 [A] to the LORD, for we *have* **had** enough thunder and hail.
9:29 [A] The thunder will stop and *there will* **be** no more hail, so you
10: 6 [A] day they **settled** in this land till now.' " Then Moses turned
10: 7 [A] said to him, "How long *will* this man **be** a snare to us?
10:10 [A] Pharaoh said, "The LORD **be** with you—if I let you go,
10:13 [A] By morning **[NIE]** the wind had brought the locusts;
10:14 [A] Never before *had there* **been** such a plague of locusts, nor
10:14 [A] been such a plague of locusts, nor *will there ever* **be** again.
10:21 [A] toward the sky so that darkness *will* **spread** over Egypt—
10:22 [A] and total darkness **covered** [+928] all Egypt for three days.
10:23 [A] Yet all the Israelites **had** [+4200] light in the places where
11: 6 [A] *There will* **be** loud wailing throughout Egypt—worse than
11: 6 [C] worse than *there has ever* **been** or ever will be again.
12: 4 [A] If any household is too small **[NIE]** for a whole lamb, they
12: 5 [A] The animals you choose *must* **be** year-old males without
12: 6 [A] **Take care of** [+4200+4200+5466] them until the fourteenth
12:13 [A] The blood *will* **be** a sign for you on the houses where you
12:13 [A] No destructive plague *will* **touch** [+928] you when I strike
12:14 [A] "This **is** a day you are to commemorate; for the generations
12:16 [A] On the first day **hold** a sacred assembly, and another one on
12:25 [A] **[NIE]** When you enter the land that the LORD will give
12:26 [A] **[NIE]** when your children ask you, 'What does this
12:29 [A] **[NIE]** At midnight the LORD struck down all the firstborn
12:30 [A] got up during the night, and *there* **was** loud wailing in Egypt,
12:41 [A] **[NIE]** At the end of the 430 years, to the very day, all the
12:41 [A] At the end of the 430 years, **[NIE]** to the very day, all the
12:48 [A] then he may take part **[NIE]** like one born in the land.
12:49 [A] The same law **applies** to the native-born and to the alien
12:51 [A] **[NIE]** on that very day the LORD brought the Israelites
13: 5 [A] **[NIE]** When the LORD brings you into the land of the
13: 9 [A] This observance *will* **be** for you like a sign on your hand
13: 9 [A] forehead that the law of the LORD *is to* **be** on your lips.
13:11 [A] **[NIE]** "After the LORD brings you into the land of the
13:12 [A] All the firstborn males of your livestock **[NIE]** belong to the
13:14 [A] **[NIE]** "In days to come, when your son asks you, 'What
13:15 [A] **[NIE]** When Pharaoh stubbornly refused to let us go,
13:16 [A] *it will* **be** like a sign on your hand and a symbol on your
13:17 [A] **[NIE]** When Pharaoh let the people go, God did not lead
14:20 [A] Israel. Throughout the night the cloud **brought** darkness to
14:24 [A] **[NIE]** During the last watch of the night the LORD looked
15: 2 [A] is my strength and my song; *he has* **become** my salvation.
16: 5 [A] **[NIE]** On the sixth day they are to prepare what they bring
16: 5 [A] *that is to* **be** twice as much as they gather on the other days."
16:10 [A] **[NIE]** While Aaron was speaking to the whole Israelite
16:13 [A] **[NIE]** That evening quail came and covered the camp,
16:13 [A] in the morning *there* **was** a layer of dew around the camp.
16:22 [A] **[NIE]** On the sixth day, they gathered twice as much—two
16:24 [A] Moses commanded, and it did not stink or **get** maggots in it.
16:26 [A] but on the seventh day, the Sabbath, *there will* not **be** any."
16:27 [A] **[NIE]** some of the people went out on the seventh day to
17:11 [A] **[NIE]** As long as Moses held up his hands, the Israelites
17:12 [A] on the other—so that his hands **remained** steady till sunset.
18: 3 [A] for Moses said, "*I have* **become** an alien in a foreign land";
18:13 [A] **[NIE]** The next day Moses took his seat to serve as judge
18:16 [A] Whenever they **have** [+4200] a dispute, it is brought to me,
18:19 [A] and I will give you some advice, and *may* God **be** with you.
18:19 [A] You *must* **be** the people's representative before God
18:22 [A] but **[NIE]** have them bring every difficult case to you;
19: 5 [A] then out of all nations *you will* **be** my treasured possession.
19: 6 [A] you *will* **be** for me a kingdom of priests and a holy nation.'
19:11 [A] **be** ready by the third day, because on that day the LORD
19:15 [A] he said to the people, "**Prepare yourselves** [+3922] for the
19:16 [A] **[NIE]** On the morning of the third day there was thunder
19:16 [A] On **[NIE]** the morning of the third day there was thunder
19:16 [A] On the morning of the third day *there* **was** thunder
19:19 [A] and **[NIE]** the sound of the trumpet grew louder and louder.
20: 3 [A] "You *shall* **have** [+4200] no other gods before me.
20:20 [A] so that the fear of God *will* **be** with you to keep you from
21: 4 [A] and her children *shall* **belong** [+4200] **to** her master,
21:22 [A] she gives birth prematurely but *there* **is** no serious injury,
21:23 [A] But if *there* **is** serious injury, you are to take life for life,
21:34 [A] he must pay its owner, and the dead animal *will* **be** his.
21:36 [A] must pay, animal for animal, and the dead animal *will* **be** his.
22:11 [22:10] [A] the issue between them *will be* **settled** *by* the taking
22:21 [22:20] [A] or oppress him, for *you* **were** aliens in Egypt.
22:24 [22:23] [A] your wives *will* **become** widows and your children
22:25 [22:24] [A] you who is needy, *do* not **be** like a moneylender;
22:27 [22:26] [A] **[NIE]** When he cries out to me, I will hear, for I
22:30 [22:29] [A] *Let them* **stay** with their mothers for seven days,
22:31 [22:30] [A] "*You are to* **be** my holy people. So do not eat the
23: 1 [A] Do not help a wicked man by **being** a malicious witness.
23: 2 [A] "*Do* not **follow** [+339] the crowd in doing wrong. When you
23: 9 [A] how it feels to be aliens, because *you* **were** aliens in Egypt.
23:26 [A] none *will* miscarry or **be** barren in your land. I will give you
23:29 [A] because the land *would* **become** desolate and the wild
23:33 [A] because the worship of their gods *will* certainly **be** a snare to
24:12 [A] to Moses, "Come up to me on the mountain and **stay** here,
24:18 [A] And he **stayed** on the mountain forty days and forty nights.
25:15 [A] The poles *are to* **remain** in the rings of this ark; they are not
25:20 [A] The cherubim *are to* **have** their wings spread upward,
25:20 [A] The cherubim **are** *to* face each other, looking toward the
25:27 [A] The rings *are to* **be** close to the rim to hold the poles used in
25:31 [A] buds and blossoms *shall* **be** of one piece with it.
25:36 [A] and branches *shall* all **be** of one piece with the lampstand,
26: 3 [A] **[NIE]** Join five of the curtains together, and do the same
26: 6 [A] to fasten the curtains together so that the tabernacle **is** a unit.
26:11 [A] put them in the loops to fasten the tent together **[NIE]** as a
26:13 [A] The tent curtains *will* **be** a cubit longer on both sides; what is
26:24 [A] At these two corners **[RPH]** they must be double from the
26:24 [A] At these two corners *they must* **be** double from the bottom
26:24 [A] all the way to the top, and fitted **[RPH]** into a single ring;
26:24 [A] to the top, and fitted into a single ring; both *shall* **be** like that.
26:25 [A] So *there will* **be** eight frames and sixteen silver bases—two
27: 1 [A] it *is to* **be** square, five cubits long and five cubits wide.
27: 2 [A] so that the horns and the altar **are** of one piece, and overlay
27: 5 [A] it under the ledge of the altar so that it **is** halfway up the altar.
27: 7 [A] so they *will* **be** on two sides of the altar when it is carried.
28: 7 [A] It *is to* **have** [+4200] two shoulder pieces attached to two of
28: 8 [A] piece with the ephod and **made** *with* gold, and *with* blue,

Ex 28:16 [A] *It is to* **be** square—a span long and a span wide—and folded
28:20 [A] and a jasper. **Mount** [+4853] them in gold filigree settings.
28:21 [A] *There are to* **be** twelve stones, one for each of the names of
28:21 [A] like a seal with the name of one of the twelve tribes. **[RPH]**
28:28 [A] **connecting** it to the waistband, so that the breastpiece will
28:30 [A] so *they may* **be** over Aaron's heart whenever he enters the
28:32 [A] **[RPH]** with an opening for the head in its center.
28:32 [A] *There shall* **be** a woven edge like a collar around this
28:32 [A] a collar around this opening, so that **[RPH]** it will not tear.
28:35 [A] Aaron *must* **wear** [+6584] *it* when he ministers. The sound
28:37 [A] Fasten a blue cord to it *to* **attach** it to the turban; it is to be
28:37 [A] to attach it to the turban; *it is to* **be** on the front of the turban.
28:38 [A] *It will* **be** on Aaron's forehead, and he will bear the guilt
28:38 [A] *It will* **be** on Aaron's forehead continually so that they will
28:42 [A] a covering for the body, **reaching** from the waist to the thigh.
28:43 [A] his sons *must* **wear** [+6584] *them* whenever they enter the
29: 9 [A] and his sons. The priesthood **is** theirs by a lasting ordinance.
29:26 [A] the LORD as a wave offering, and *it will* **be** your share.
29:28 [A] *This is* always *to* **be** the regular share from the Israelites for
29:28 [A] It is the contribution the Israelites *are to* **make** to the
29:29 [A] "Aaron's sacred garments *will* **belong** [+4200] **to** his
29:37 [A] the altar *will* **be** most holy, and whatever touches it will be
29:45 [A] Then I will dwell among the Israelites and **be** their God.
30: 2 [A] *It is to* **be** square, a cubit long and a cubit wide, and two
30: 4 [A] on opposite sides—**[NIE]** to hold the poles used to carry it.
30:12 [A] Then no plague *will* **come** on them when you number them.
30:16 [A] *It will* **be** a memorial for the Israelites before the LORD,
30:21 [A] *This is to* **be** a lasting ordinance for Aaron and his
30:25 [A] the work of a perfumer. *It will* **be** the sacred anointing oil.
30:29 [A] You shall consecrate them so *they will* **be** most holy, and
30:31 [A] 'This *is to* **be** my sacred anointing oil for the generations to
30:32 [A] It is sacred, and you *are to* **consider** [+4200] *it* sacred.
30:34 [A] and pure frankincense, all in equal amounts, **[NIE]**
30:36 [A] where I will meet with you. *It shall* **be** most holy to you.
30:37 [A] for yourselves; **consider** [+4200] *it* holy to the LORD.
32: 1 [A] up out of Egypt, we don't know what *has* **happened** to him."
32:19 [A] **[NIE]** When Moses approached the camp and saw the calf
32:23 [A] up out of Egypt, we don't know what *has* **happened** to him.'
32:30 [A] **[NIE]** The next day Moses said to the people, "You have
33: 7 [A] **[NIE]** Anyone inquiring of the LORD would go to the tent
33: 8 [A] **[NIE]** whenever Moses went out to the tent, all the people
33: 9 [A] **[NIE]** As Moses went into the tent, the pillar of cloud
33:22 [A] **[NIE]** When my glory passes by, I will put you in a cleft in
34: 1 [A] I will write on them the words that **were** on the first tablets,
34: 2 [A] **Be** ready in the morning, and then come up on Mount Sinai.
34:12 [A] land where you are going, or *they will* **be** a snare among you.
34:28 [A] Moses **was** there with the LORD forty days and forty nights
34:29 [A] **[NIE]** When Moses came down from Mount Sinai with the
35: 2 [A] is to be done, but the seventh day *shall* **be** your holy day,
36: 7 [A] because what *they already* **had** was more than enough to do
36:13 [A] two sets of curtains together so that the tabernacle **was** a unit.
36:18 [A] bronze clasps to fasten the tent together as **[NIE]** a unit.
36:29 [A] At these two corners the frames **were** double from the
36:29 [A] all the way to the top and fitted **[RPH]** into a single ring;
36:30 [A] So *there* **were** eight frames and sixteen silver bases—two
37: 9 [A] The cherubim **had** their wings spread upward,
37: 9 [A] cherubim faced each other, **[NIE]** looking toward the cover.
37:14 [A] The rings **were** put close to the rim to hold the poles used in
37:17 [A] buds and blossoms **were** of one piece with it.
37:22 [A] and the branches **were** all of one piece with the lampstand,
37:25 [A] and two cubits high—its horns of one piece with it. **[NIE]**
38: 2 [A] so that the horns and the altar **were** of one piece, and they
38:24 [A] offering used for all the work on the sanctuary **was** 29 talents
38:27 [A] The 100 talents of silver *were* **used** to cast the bases for the
39: 9 [A] *It* **was** square—a span long and a span wide—and folded
39:21 [A] **connecting** it to the waistband so that the breastpiece would
40: 9 [A] in it; consecrate it and all its furnishings, and *it will* **be** holy.
40:10 [A] all its utensils; consecrate the altar, and it *will* **be** most holy.
40:15 [A] Their anointing *will* **be** to a priesthood that will continue for
40:15 [A] Their anointing will be **[RPH]** to a priesthood that will
40:17 [A] So **[NIE]** the tabernacle was set up on the first day of the
40:38 [A] fire **was** in the cloud by night, in the sight of all the house of
Lev 2: 1 [A] offering to the LORD, his offering *is to* **be** *of* fine flour.
2: 5 [A] *it* **is** to be made of fine flour mixed with oil, and without
5: 5 [A] **[NIE]** " 'When anyone is guilty in any of these ways, he
5:13 [A] The rest of the offering *will* **belong** [+4200] **to** the priest,
6: 4 [5:23] [A] **[NIE]** when he thus sins and becomes guilty, he
6:23 [6:16] [A] Every grain offering of a priest *shall* **be** burned
7: 7 [A] *They* **belong** [+4200] **to** the priest who makes atonement
7: 8 [A] The priest who offers a burnt offering for anyone *may* **keep**
7: 9 [A] or on a griddle **belongs** [+4200] **to** the priest who offers it,
7:10 [A] with oil or dry, **belongs** equally to all the sons of Aaron.
7:14 [A] *it* **belongs** [+4200] **to** the priest who sprinkles the blood of
7:18 [A] will not be credited to the one who offered it, for *it* **is** impure;
7:31 [A] but the breast **belongs** [+4200] **to** Aaron and his sons.
7:33 [A] the fat of the fellowship offering *shall* **have** [+4200] the right
8:29 [A] took the breast—Moses' **[NIE]** share of the ordination ram—
9: 1 [A] **[NIE]** On the eighth day Moses summoned Aaron and his
10:15 [A] *This will* **be** the regular share for you and your children, as
11:11 [A] since you **are** to detest *them*, you must not eat their meat
11:35 [A] are unclean, and you *are to* **regard** [+4200] them **as** unclean.
11:36 [A] however, or a cistern for collecting water **remains** clean,
11:44 [A] consecrate yourselves and **be** holy, because I am holy.
11:45 [A] I am the LORD who brought you up out of Egypt to **be** your
11:45 [A] Egypt to be your God; therefore **be** holy, because I am holy.
13: 2 [A] "When anyone **has** a swelling or a rash or a bright spot on his
13: 2 [A] or a bright spot on his skin that *may* **become** an infectious
13: 9 [A] "When anyone **has** [+928] an infectious skin disease, he
13:18 [A] "When someone **has** [+928] a boil on his skin and it heals,
13:19 [A] the boil was, a white swelling or reddish-white spot **appears**,
13:24 [A] "When someone **has** a burn on his skin and a reddish-white
13:24 [A] or white spot **appears** in the raw flesh of the burn,
13:29 [A] "If a man or woman **has** [+928] a sore on the head or on the
13:32 [A] and if the itch has not spread and *there* **is** no yellow hair in it
13:38 [A] "When a man or woman **has** white spots on the skin,
13:42 [A] if *he* **has** a reddish-white sore on his bald head or forehead,
13:45 [A] "The person with such an infectious disease *must* **wear** torn
13:45 [A] *let* his hair **be** unkempt, cover the lower part of his face
13:47 [A] "If any clothing **is** contaminated with mildew—any woolen
13:49 [A] knitted material, or any leather article, **is** greenish or reddish,
13:52 [A] or any leather article that **has** the contamination in it,
14: 2 [A] "These **are** the regulations for the diseased person at the time
14: 9 [A] **[NIE]** On the seventh day he must shave off all his hair;
14:22 [A] one for a **[NIE]** sin offering and the other for a burnt
15: 2 [A] 'When any man **has** a bodily discharge, the discharge is
15: 3 [A] This is how his discharge *will* **bring** [+928] **about**
15:10 [A] whoever touches any of the things that **were** under him will
15:17 [A] or leather that **has** semen on it must be washed with water,
15:19 [A] " 'When a woman **has** her regular flow of blood, the impurity
15:19 [A] **[RPH]** the impurity of her monthly period will last seven
15:19 [A] the impurity of her monthly period *will* **last** seven days,
15:24 [A] lies with her and her monthly flow **touches** [+6584] him,
15:25 [A] she *will* **be** unclean as long as she has the discharge, just as
15:26 [A] Any bed she lies on while her discharge continues *will* **be**
15:26 [A] as **is** her bed during her monthly period, and anything she sits
16: 4 [A] with linen undergarments **[NIE]** next to his body;
16:17 [A] No one *is to* **be** in the Tent of Meeting from the time Aaron
16:29 [A] "*This is to* **be** a lasting ordinance for you: On the tenth day
16:34 [A] "This *is to* **be** a lasting ordinance for you: Atonement is to be
17: 7 [A] This *is to* **be** a lasting ordinance for them and for the
19: 2 [A] to them: '**Be** holy because I, the LORD your God, am holy.
19:20 [A] or given her freedom, *there must* **be** due punishment.
19:23 [A] For three years you *are to* **consider** [+4200] it forbidden;
19:24 [A] In the fourth year all its fruit *will* **be** holy, an offering of
19:34 [A] The alien living with you *must be* **treated** as one of your
19:34 [A] Love him as yourself, for *you* **were** aliens in Egypt. I am the
19:36 [A] **Use** [+4200] honest scales and honest weights, an honest
20: 7 [A] " 'Consecrate yourselves and **be** holy, because I am the
20:14 [A] burned in the fire, so that no wickedness *will* **be** among you.
20:21 [A] he has dishonored his brother. *They will* **be** childless.
20:26 [A] *You are to* **be** holy to me because I, the LORD, am holy,
20:26 [A] and I have set you apart from the nations to **be** my own.
20:27 [A] " 'A man or woman *who* **is** a medium or spiritist among you
21: 3 [A] dependent on him since *she* **has** [+4200+4200] no husband—
21: 6 [A] *They must* **be** holy to their God and must not profane the
21: 6 [A] LORD by fire, the food of their God, *they are to* **be** holy.
21: 8 [A] **Consider** [+4200] *them* holy, because I the LORD am
21:17 [A] **has** [+928] a defect may come near to offer the food of his
21:19 [A] no man **with** [+928] a crippled foot or hand,
22:12 [A] If a priest's daughter **marries** [+408+4200] anyone other
22:13 [A] But if a priest's daughter **becomes** a widow or is divorced,
22:20 [A] with a defect, because *it will* not **be** accepted on your behalf.
22:21 [A] *it must* **be** without defect or blemish to be acceptable.
22:21 [A] must be without defect or blemish **[RPH]** to be acceptable.
22:27 [A] a goat is born, *it is to* **remain** with its mother for seven days.
22:33 [A] who brought you out of Egypt to **be** your God. I am the
23: 7 [A] On the first day **hold** a sacred assembly and do no regular
23:15 [A] of the wave offering, count off seven full weeks. **[NIE]**
23:17 [A] bring two loaves **made** *of* two-tenths of an ephah of fine
23:18 [A] *They will* **be** a burnt offering to the LORD, together with
23:20 [A] *They* **are** a sacred offering to the LORD for the priest.
23:21 [A] proclaim a sacred assembly **[NIE]** and do no regular work.
23:24 [A] of the seventh month you *are to* **have** [+4200] a day of rest,
23:27 [A] **Hold** a sacred assembly and deny yourselves, and present an
23:36 [A] on the eighth day **hold** a sacred assembly and present an
24: 5 [A] loaves of bread, **using** two-tenths of an ephah for each loaf.
24: 7 [A] the bread and *to* **be** an offering made to the LORD by fire.
24: 9 [A] *It* **belongs** [+4200] **to** Aaron and his sons, who are to eat it in

Lev 24:22 [A] You *are to* **have** [+4200] the same law for the alien and the
24:22 [A] and the native-born. **[RPH]** I am the LORD your God.' "
25: 4 [A] in the seventh year the land *is to* **have** [+4200] a sabbath of
25: 5 [A] untended vines. The land *is to* **have** [+4200] a year of rest.
25: 6 [A] Whatever the land yields during the sabbath year *will* **be**
25: 7 [A] in your land. Whatever the land produces *may* **be** eaten.
25: 8 [A] so that the seven sabbaths of years **amount to** a period of
25:10 [A] It *shall* **be** a jubilee for you; each one of you is to return to
25:11 [A] The fiftieth year *shall* **be** a jubilee for you; do not sow and do
25:12 [A] For it is a jubilee and *is to* **be** holy for you; eat only what is
25:26 [A] a man **has** [+4200] no one to redeem it for him but he
25:28 [A] what he sold *will* **remain** in the possession of the buyer until
25:29 [A] he **retains** the right of redemption a full year after its sale.
25:29 [A] a full year after its sale. During that time *he* **may** redeem it.
25:31 [A] They *can* **be** redeemed, and they are to be returned in the
25:32 [A] " 'The Levites always **have** [+4200] the right to redeem their
25:38 [A] of Egypt to give you the land of Canaan and to **be** your God.
25:40 [A] *He is to* **be** treated as a hired worker or a temporary resident
25:44 [A] and female slaves *are to* **come** from the nations around you;
25:45 [A] born in your country, and *they will* **become** your property.
25:48 [A] he **retains** [+4200] the right of redemption after he has sold
25:50 [A] The price for his release *is to* **be** based on the rate paid to a
25:50 [A] rate paid to a hired man for that number of years. **[RPH]**
25:53 [A] He *is to be* **treated** [+6640] as a man hired from year to year;
26:12 [A] I will walk among you and **be** your God, and you will be my
26:12 [A] among you and be your God, and you *will* **be** my people.
26:13 [A] so that you *would* no longer **be** slaves to the Egyptians;
26:33 [A] Your land *will* **be** laid waste, and your cities will lie in ruins.
26:33 [A] Your land will be laid waste, and your cities *will* **lie** in ruins.
26:37 [A] So you *will* not **be** able to stand before your enemies.
26:44 [A] in spite of this, when they **are** in the land of their enemies,
26:45 [A] out of Egypt in the sight of the nations to **be** their God.
27: 3 [A] **set** the value of a male between the ages of twenty and sixty
27: 3 [A] the ages of twenty and sixty **[RPH]** at fifty shekels of silver,
27: 4 [A] and if it is a female, **set** her value at thirty shekels.
27: 5 [A] **set** the value of a male at twenty shekels and of a female at
27: 6 [A] **set** the value of a male at five shekels of silver and that of a
27: 7 [A] **set** the value of a male at fifteen shekels and of a female at
27: 9 [A] such an animal given to the LORD **becomes** holy.
27:10 [A] for another, both **[RPH]** it and the substitute become holy.
27:10 [A] animal for another, both it and the substitute **become** holy.
27:12 [A] Whatever value the priest then sets, that *is what it will* **be**.
27:15 [A] add a fifth to its value, and the house *will again* **become** his.
27:16 [A] its value *is to be* **set** according to the amount of seed required
27:21 [A] it *will* **become** holy, like a field devoted to the LORD;
27:21 [A] to the LORD; *it will* **become** the property of the priests.
27:25 [A] Every value *is to be* **set** according to the sanctuary shekel,
27:25 [A] to the sanctuary shekel, twenty gerahs to **[NIE]** the shekel.
27:32 [A] under the shepherd's rod—*will* **be** holy to the LORD.
27:33 [A] both the animal and its substitute **become** holy and cannot
27:33 [A] both the animal and its substitute become **[RPH]** holy
Nu 1: 4 [A] each tribe, each the head of his family, *is to* **help** [+907] you.
1:20 [A] or more who were able to serve in the army **were** listed by
1:44 [A] leaders of Israel, each one representing his family. **[NIE]**
1:45 [A] or more who were able to serve in Israel's army **were**
1:46 [A] The total number **was** 603,550.
1:53 [A] so that wrath *will* not **fall** on the Israelite community.
3: 4 [A] They **had** [+4200] no sons; so only Eleazar and Ithamar
3:12 [A] offspring of every Israelite woman. The Levites **are** mine,
3:13 [A] in Israel, whether man or animal. *They are to* **be** mine.
3:17 [A] These **were** the names of the sons of Levi: Gershon, Kohath
3:43 [A] males a month old or more, listed by name, **was** 22,273.
3:45 [A] their livestock. The Levites *are to* **be** mine. I am the LORD.
4: 7 [A] the bread that is continually there *is to* **remain** on it.
4:27 [A] *is to be* **done** under the direction of Aaron and his sons.
4:36 [A] counted by clans, **were** 2,750.
4:40 [A] counted by their clans and families, **were** 2,630.
4:44 [A] counted by their clans, **were** 3,200.
4:48 [A] **[NIE]** numbered 8,580.
5: 9 [A] the Israelites bring to a priest *will* **belong** [+4200] **to** him.
5:10 [A] Each man's sacred gifts **are** his own, but what he gives to
5:10 [A] what he gives to the priest *will* **belong** [+4200] **to** the
5:17 [A] put some dust **[NIE]** from the tabernacle floor into the
5:18 [A] while he himself **holds** [+928+3338] the bitter water that
5:27 [A] **[NIE]** If she has defiled herself and been unfaithful to her
5:27 [A] and she *will* **become** accursed among her people.
6: 5 [A] *He must* **be** holy until the period of his separation to the
7: 1 [A] **[NIE]** When Moses finished setting up the tabernacle, he
7: 5 [A] that *they may* **be** used in the work at the Tent of Meeting.
7:12 [A] The one who brought his offering on the first day **was**
8:11 [A] so that *they may be* **ready** to do the work of the LORD.
8:14 [A] apart from the other Israelites, and the Levites *will* **be** mine.
8:19 [A] so that no plague *will* **strike** [+928] the Israelites when they
9: 6 [A] **[NIE]** some of them could not celebrate the Passover on
9: 6 [A] because *they* **were** ceremonially unclean on account of a
9:10 [A] 'When any of you or your descendants **are** unclean
9:13 [A] if a man who **is** ceremonially clean and not on a journey fails
9:14 [A] You *must* **have** [+4200] the same regulations for the alien
9:15 [A] the cloud above the tabernacle **[NIE]** looked like fire.
9:16 [A] That is how *it* continued *to* **be**; the cloud covered it, and at
9:20 [A] Sometimes the cloud **was** over the tabernacle only a few
9:21 [A] Sometimes the cloud **stayed** only from evening till morning,
10: 2 [A] use them **[NIE]** for calling the community together and for
10: 8 [A] *This is to* **be** a lasting ordinance for you and the generations
10:10 [A] and *they will* **be** a memorial for you before your God.
10:11 [A] **[NIE]** On the twentieth day of the second month of the
10:31 [A] we should camp in the desert, and *you can* **be** our eyes.
10:32 [A] **[NIE]** If you come with us, we will share with you whatever
10:32 [A] **[NIE]** we will share with you whatever good things the
10:35 [A] **[NIE]** Whenever the ark set out, Moses said, "Rise up,
11: 1 [A] Now **[NIE]** the people complained about their hardships in
11: 8 [A] And **[NIE]** it tasted like something made with olive oil.
11:20 [A] until it comes out of your nostrils and **[NIE]** you loathe it—
11:25 [A] **[NIE]** When the Spirit rested on them, they prophesied,
11:35 [A] Hattaavah the people traveled to Hazeroth and **stayed** there.
12: 6 [A] "When a prophet of the LORD **is** among you, I reveal
12:12 [A] *Do* not *let her* **be** like a stillborn infant coming from its
13:33 [A] *We* **seemed** like grasshoppers in our own eyes, and we
13:33 [A] own eyes, and *we* **looked** the same **to** [+928+6524] them."
14: 3 [A] Our wives and children *will be* **taken** as plunder. Wouldn't it
14:24 [A] But because my servant Caleb **has** [+6640] a different spirit
14:31 [A] As for your children that you said *would be* **taken** as
14:33 [A] Your children *will* **be** shepherds here for forty years,
14:43 [A] he *will* not **be** with you and you will fall by the sword."
15:15 [A] You and the alien *shall* **be** the same before the LORD:
15:16 [A] The same laws and regulations *will* **apply** both to you and to
15:19 [A] **[NIE]** you eat the food of the land, present a portion as an
15:24 [A] **[NIE]** if this is done unintentionally without the community
15:29 [A] the same law **applies** to everyone who sins unintentionally,
15:32 [A] While the Israelites **were** in the desert, a man was found
15:39 [A] You *will* **have** [+4200+4200] these tassels to look at and
15:40 [A] obey all my commands and *will* **be** consecrated to your God.
15:41 [A] your God, who brought you out of Egypt to **be** your God.
16: 7 [A] The man the LORD chooses *will* **be** the one who is holy.
16:16 [A] all your followers *are to* **appear** before the LORD
16:31 [A] **[NIE]** As soon as he finished saying all this, the ground
16:38 [17:3] [A] become holy. *Let them* **be** a sign to the Israelites."
16:40 [17:5] [A] or *he would* **become** like Korah and his followers.
16:42 [17:7] [A] **[NIE]** when the assembly gathered in opposition to
16:49 [17:14] [A] **[NIE]** 14,700 people died from the plague, in
17: 5 [17:20] [A] **[NIE]** The staff belonging to the man I choose will
17: 8 [17:23] [A] **[NIE]** The next day Moses entered the Tent of the
18: 5 [A] the altar, so that wrath *will* not **fall** on the Israelites again.
18: 9 [A] You *are to* **have** [+4200] the part of the most holy offerings
18:10 [A] every male shall eat it. You *must* **regard** [+4200] it **as** holy.
18:13 [A] All the land's firstfruits that they bring to the LORD *will* **be**
18:14 [A] "Everything in Israel that is devoted to the LORD **is** yours.
18:15 [A] both man and animal, that is offered to the LORD **is** yours.
18:18 [A] Their meat *is to* **be** yours, just as the breast of the wave
18:18 [A] the breast of the wave offering and the right thigh **are** yours.
18:20 [A] their land, nor *will* you **have** [+4200] any share among them;
19: 9 [A] *They shall be* **kept** by the Israelite community for use in the
19:10 [A] *This will* **be** a lasting ordinance both for the Israelites and for
19:13 [A] of cleansing has not been sprinkled on him, *he* **is** unclean;
19:18 [A] and all the furnishings and the people who **were** there.
19:21 [A] *This* **is** a lasting ordinance for them. "The man who sprinkles
20: 2 [A] Now *there* **was** no water for the community, and the people
21: 8 [A] a pole; **[NIE]** anyone who is bitten can look at it and live."
21: 9 [A] **[NIE]** when anyone was bitten by a snake and looked at the
22:41 [A] **[NIE]** The next morning Balak took Balaam up to Bamoth
23:10 [A] the death of the righteous, and *may* my end **be** like theirs!"
24: 2 [A] encamped tribe by tribe, the Spirit of God **came** upon him
24:18 [A] Edom *will* **be** conquered; Seir, his enemy, will be conquered,
24:18 [A] Seir, his enemy, *will* **be** conquered, but Israel will grow
24:22 [A] yet you Kenites *will* **be** destroyed when Asshur takes you
25: 9 [A] but those who died in the plague **numbered** 24,000.
25:13 [A] his descendants *will* **have** [+4200] a covenant of a lasting
26: 1 [25:19] [A] **[NIE]** After the plague the LORD said to Moses
26: 7 [A] were the clans of Reuben; those numbered **were** 43,730.
26:10 [A] devoured the 250 men. And *they* **served** as a warning sign.
26:20 [A] The descendants of Judah by their clans **were**:
26:21 [A] The descendants of Perez **were**: through Hezron,
26:33 [A] (Zelophehad son of Hepher **had** [+4200] no sons; he had
26:40 [A] The descendants of Bela through Ard and Naaman **were**:
26:62 [A] **[NIE]** All the male Levites a month old or more numbered
26:64 [A] Not one of them **was** among those counted by Moses
27: 3 [A] He **was** not among Korah's followers, who banded together
27: 3 [A] but he died for his own sin and **left** [+4200] no sons.

Nu 27:11 [A] *This is to* **be** a legal requirement for the Israelites, as the
27:17 [A] so the LORD's people *will* not **be** like sheep without a
28:14 [A] With each bull *there is to* **be** a drink offering of half a hin of
28:19 [A] and seven male lambs a year old, all without defect. **[NIE]**
28:25 [A] On the seventh day **hold** a sacred assembly and do no regular
28:26 [A] of Weeks, **hold** a sacred assembly and do no regular work.
28:31 [A] and its grain offering. Be sure the animals **are** without defect.
29: 1 [A] " 'On the first day of the seventh month **hold** a sacred
29: 1 [A] do no regular work. *It* **is** a day for you to sound the trumpets.
29: 7 [A] " 'On the tenth day of this seventh month **hold** a sacred
29: 8 [A] and seven male lambs a year old, all without defect. **[NIE]**
29:12 [A] **hold** a sacred assembly and do no regular work.
29:13 [A] fourteen male lambs a year old, all without defect. **[NIE]**
29:35 [A] " 'On the eighth day **hold** an assembly and do no regular
30: 6 [30:7] [A] "If *she* **marries** [+408+2118+4200] after she makes a
30: 6 [30:7] [A] "If *she* **marries** [+408+2118+4200] after she makes a
31: 3 [A] "Arm some of your men *to* **go** to war against the Midianites
31:16 [A] **were** the means of turning the Israelites away from the
31:16 [A] at Peor, so that a plague **struck** [+928] the LORD's people.
31:32 [A] plunder remaining from the spoils that the soldiers took **was**
31:36 [A] The half share of those who fought in the battle **was**:
31:37 [A] of which the tribute for the LORD **was** 675;
31:43 [A] the community's half—**was** 337,500 sheep,
31:52 [A] Eleazar presented as a gift to the LORD **weighed** 16,750
32: 1 [A] and Gadites, who **had** [+4200] very large herds and flocks,
32:22 [A] and **be** free from your obligation to the LORD and to Israel.
32:22 [A] And this land *will* **be** your possession before the LORD.
32:26 [A] our flocks and herds *will* **remain** here in the cities of Gilead.
33:14 [A] where *there* **was** no water for the people to drink.
33:54 [A] a smaller one. Whatever falls to them by lot *will* **be** theirs.
33:55 [A] you allow to remain *will* **become** barbs in your eyes and
33:56 [A] then **[NIE]** I will do to you what I plan to do to them.' "
34: 3 [A] " 'Your southern side *will* **include** some of the Desert of Zin
34: 3 [A] your southern boundary *will* **start** from the end of the Salt
34: 4 [A] continue on to Zin and **go** south of Kadesh Barnea.
34: 5 [A] will turn, join the Wadi of Egypt and **end** [+9362] at the Sea.
34: 6 [A] " 'Your western boundary *will* **be** the coast of the Great Sea.
34: 6 [A] of the Great Sea. This *will* **be** your boundary on the west.
34: 7 [A] **[NIE]** " 'For your northern boundary, run a line from the
34: 8 [A] Hor to Lebo Hamath. Then the boundary *will* **go** to Zedad,
34: 9 [A] continue to Ziphron and **end at** [+9362] Hazar Enan. This
34: 9 [A] end at Hazar Enan. This *will* **be** your boundary on the north.
34:12 [A] go down along the Jordan and **end at** [+9362] the Salt Sea.
34:12 [A] " 'This *will* **be** your land, with its boundaries on every
35: 3 [A] they *will* **have** [+4200] towns to live in and pasturelands for
35: 3 [A] have towns to live in and pasturelands **[NIE]** for their cattle,
35: 5 [A] They *will* **have** [+4200] this area as pastureland for the
35:11 [A] select some towns *to* **be** your cities of refuge, to which a
35:12 [A] *They will* **be** places of refuge from the avenger, so that a
35:13 [A] These six towns you give *will* **be** your cities of refuge.
35:14 [A] of the Jordan and three in Canaan as cities of refuge. **[NIE]**
35:15 [A] These six towns *will* **be** a place of refuge for Israelites, aliens
35:29 [A] " 'These *are to* **be** legal requirements for you throughout the
36: 3 [A] Now suppose *they* **marry** [+851+4200+4200] men from other
36: 3 [A] and added to that of the tribe *they* **marry** [+4200] **into**.
36: 4 [A] When the Year of Jubilee for the Israelites **comes**, their
36: 4 [A] be added to that of the tribe **into** which *they* **marry** [+4200],
36: 6 [A] *They may* **marry** [+851+4200] anyone they please as long
36: 6 [A] *they* **marry** [+851+4200] within the tribal clan of their
36: 8 [A] *must* **marry** [+851+4200+4200] someone in her father's tribal
36:11 [A] **married** [+851+4200+4200] their cousins on their father's side.
36:12 [A] *They* **married** [+851+4200] within the clans of the
36:12 [A] their inheritance **remained** in their father's clan and tribe.
Dt 1: 3 [A] **[NIE]** In the fortieth year, on the first day of the eleventh
1:39 [A] the little ones that you said *would* **be** taken captive, your
2:15 [A] The LORD's hand **was** against them until he had
2:16 [A] Now **[NIE]** when the last of these fighting men among the
2:36 [A] even as far as Gilead, not one town **was** too strong for us.
3: 4 [A] *There* **was** not one of the sixty cities that we did not take
4:20 [A] out of Egypt, to **be** the people of his inheritance, as you now
4:32 [A] now about the former days, **[NIE]** long before your time,
4:32 [C] *Has* anything so great as this *ever* **happened**, or has anything
5: 7 [A] "You *shall* **have** [+4200] no other gods before me.
5:15 [A] Remember that *you* **were** slaves in Egypt and that the
5:23 [A] **[NIE]** When you heard the voice out of the darkness,
5:29 [A] that their hearts *would be* **inclined** [+2296] to fear me
6: 6 [A] These commandments that I give you today *are to* **be** upon
6: 8 [A] your hands and **bind** [+3213+4200] them on your foreheads.
6:10 [A] **[NIE]** When the LORD your God brings you into the land
6:21 [A] "*We* **were** slaves of Pharaoh in Egypt, but the LORD
6:25 [A] as he has commanded us, *that will* **be** our righteousness."
7: 6 [A] out of all the peoples on the face of the earth to **be** his people,
7:12 [A] **[NIE]** If you pay attention to these laws and are careful to
7:14 [A] *You will* **be** blessed more than any other people; none of
7:14 [A] none of your men or women *will* **be** childless, nor any of
7:26 [A] your house or *you*, like it, *will* **be** set apart for destruction.
8:19 [A] **[NIE]** If you ever forget the LORD your God and follow
9: 7 [A] arrived here, *you have* **been** rebellious against the LORD.
9:11 [A] **[NIE]** At the end of the forty days and forty nights,
9:22 [A] *You* also **made** the LORD **angry** [+906+7911] at Taberah,
9:24 [A] *You have* **been** rebellious against the LORD ever since I
10: 2 [A] I will write on the tablets the words that **were** on the first
10: 5 [A] as the LORD commanded me, and *they* **are** there now.
10: 9 [A] That is why the Levites **have** [+4200] no share or inheritance
10:19 [A] who are aliens, for *you yourselves* **were** aliens in Egypt.
11:13 [A] So **[NIE]** if you faithfully obey the commands I am giving
11:17 [A] he will shut the heavens so that *it* **will** not rain
11:18 [A] your hands and **bind** [+3213+4200] them on your foreheads.
11:24 [A] Every place where you set your foot *will* **be** yours:
11:24 [A] Your territory *will* **extend** from the desert to Lebanon,
11:29 [A] **[NIE]** When the LORD your God has brought you into the
12:11 [A] **[NIE]** to the place the LORD your God will choose as a
12:26 [A] and whatever you **have** [+4200] vowed to give,
13: 9 [13:10] [A] Your hand *must* **be** the first in putting him to death,
13:16 [13:17] [A] *It is to* **remain** a ruin forever, never to be rebuilt.
14: 2 [A] the LORD has chosen you to **be** his treasured possession.
15: 3 [A] but you must cancel any debt your brother **owes** you.
15: 4 [A] However, *there should* **be** no poor among you, for in the
15: 7 [A] If *there* **is** a poor man among your brothers in any of the
15: 9 [A] Be careful not *to* **harbor** [+4222+6640] this wicked thought:
15: 9 [A] the LORD against you, and you *will* **be** found guilty of sin.
15:15 [A] Remember that *you* **were** slaves in Egypt and the LORD
15:16 [A] **[NIE]** if your servant says to you, "I do not want to leave
15:17 [A] lobe into the door, and *he will* **become** your servant for life.
15:21 [A] If an animal **has** [+928] a defect, is lame or blind, or has any
16:12 [A] Remember that *you* **were** slaves in Egypt, and follow
16:15 [A] in all the work of your hands, and your joy *will* **be** complete.
17: 1 [A] your God an ox or a sheep that **has** any defect or flaw in it,
17: 7 [A] The hands of the witnesses *must* **be** the first in putting him to
17: 9 [A] are Levites, and to the judge who **is** in office at that time.
17:18 [A] **[NIE]** When he takes the throne of his kingdom, he is to
17:19 [A] *It is to* **be** with him, and he is to read it all the days of his life
18: 1 [A] *are to* **have** [+4200] no allotment or inheritance with Israel.
18: 2 [A] They *shall* **have** [+4200] no inheritance among their
18: 3 [A] This **is** the share due the priests from the people who
18:13 [A] *You must* **be** blameless before the LORD your God.
18:19 [A] If **[NIE]** anyone does not listen to my words that the
18:22 [A] proclaims in the name of the LORD *does* not **take place**
19: 3 [A] so that **[NIE]** anyone who kills a man may flee there.
19:10 [A] and so that you *will* not **be** guilty of bloodshed.
19:11 [A] if **[NIE]** a man hates his neighbor and lies in wait for him,
19:17 [A] the priests and the judges who **are** in office at the time.
20: 2 [A] **[NIE]** When you are about to go into battle, the priest shall
20: 9 [A] **[NIE]** When the officers have finished speaking to the
20:11 [A] **[NIE]** If they accept and open their gates, all the people in it
20:11 [A] **[NIE]** all the people in it shall be subject to forced labor and
20:11 [A] all the people in it *shall* **be** subject to forced labor and shall
20:14 [A] the livestock and everything else **[NIE]** in the city,
21: 3 [A] **[NIE]** the elders of the town nearest the body shall take a
21: 5 [A] and to **decide** [+6584+7023] all cases of dispute and assault.
21:13 [A] go to her and be her husband and *she shall* **be** your wife.
21:14 [A] **[NIE]** If you are not pleased with her, let her go wherever
21:15 [A] If a man **has** [+4200] two wives, and he loves one but not the
21:15 [A] but the firstborn **is** the son of the wife he does not love,
21:16 [A] **[NIE]** when he wills his property to his sons, he must not
21:16 [A] when he wills his **property** [+889+4200] to his sons, he
21:18 [A] If a man **has** [+4200] a stubborn and rebellious son who does
21:22 [A] If a **[NIE]** man guilty of a capital offense is put to death
22: 2 [A] it home with you and **keep** it until he comes looking for it.
22: 5 [A] A woman *must* not **wear** [+6584] men's clothing, nor a man
22:19 [A] *She shall continue to* **be** his wife; he must not divorce her as
22:20 [A] the charge **is** true and no proof of the girl's virginity can be
22:23 [A] If **[NIE]** a man happens to meet in a town a virgin pledged
22:29 [A] He *must* **marry** [+851+4200+4200] the girl, for he has violated
23: 7 [23:8] [A] because *you* **lived** as an alien in his country.
23:10 [23:11] [A] If **[NIE]** one of your men is unclean because of a
23:10 [23:11] [A] If *one* of your men **is** unclean because of a nocturnal
23:11 [23:12] [A] **[NIE]** as evening approaches he is to wash
23:12 [23:13] [A] **Designate** a place outside the camp where you can
23:13 [23:14] [A] As part of your equipment **have** [+4200] something
23:13 [23:14] [A] **[NIE]** when you relieve yourself, dig a hole and
23:14 [23:15] [A] Your camp *must* **be** holy, so that he will not see
23:17 [23:18] [A] or woman *is to* **become** a shrine prostitute.
23:17 [23:18] [A] or woman is to become a shrine prostitute. **[RPH]**
23:21 [23:22] [A] demand it of you and you *will* **be** guilty of sin.
23:22 [23:23] [A] refrain from making a vow, you *will* not **be** guilty.
24: 1 [A] If a man marries a woman *who* **becomes** displeasing to him
24: 2 [A] if after she leaves his house *she* **becomes** the wife of another

Dt 24: 4 [A] is not allowed to marry her **[NIE]** again after she has been
24: 5 [A] For one year *he is to* **be** free to stay at home and bring
24: 13 [A] *it will* **be** regarded as a righteous act in the sight of the
24: 15 [A] cry to the LORD against you, and you *will* **be** guilty of sin.
24: 18 [A] Remember that *you* **were** slaves in Egypt and the LORD
24: 19 [A] **Leave** it for the alien, the fatherless and the widow, so that
24: 20 [A] **Leave** what remains for the alien, the fatherless and the
24: 21 [A] **Leave** what remains for the alien, the fatherless and the
24: 22 [A] Remember that *you* **were** slaves in Egypt. That is why I
25: 1 [A] When men **have** [+1068] a dispute, they are to take it to court
25: 2 [A] **[RPH]** If the guilty man deserves to be beaten, the judge
25: 5 [A] his widow *must* not **marry** [+408+4200] outside the family.
25: 6 [A] **[NIE]** The first son she bears shall carry on the name of the
25: 13 [A] *Do* not **have** [+4200] two differing weights in your bag—
25: 14 [A] *Do* not **have** [+4200] two differing measures in your house—
25: 15 [A] You *must* **have** [+4200] accurate and honest weights
25: 15 [A] **[RPH]** so that you may live long in the land the LORD
25: 19 [A] **[NIE]** When the LORD your God gives you rest from all
26: 1 [A] **[NIE]** When you have entered the land the LORD your
26: 3 [A] say to the priest **in office** at the time, "I declare today to the
26: 5 [A] with a few people and lived there and **became** a great nation,
26: 17 [A] You have declared this day that the LORD **is** your God
26: 18 [A] the LORD has declared this day that you **are** his people,
26: 19 [A] and that you *will* **be** a people holy to the LORD your God,
27: 2 [A] **[NIE]** When you have crossed the Jordan into the land the
27: 4 [A] **[NIE]** when you have crossed the Jordan, set up these
27: 9 [C] *You have* now **become** the people of the LORD your God.
28: 1 [A] **[NIE]** If you fully obey the LORD your God and carefully
28: 13 [A] *you will* always **be** at the top, never at the bottom.
28: 13 [A] you will always be at the top, never **[RPH]** at the bottom.
28: 15 [A] **[NIE]** if you do not obey the LORD your God and do not
28: 23 [A] The sky over your head *will* **be** bronze, the ground beneath
28: 25 [A] *you will* **become** a thing of horror to all the kingdoms on
28: 26 [A] Your carcasses *will* **be** food for all the birds of the air and the
28: 29 [A] **[NIE]** At midday you will grope about like a blind man in
28: 29 [A] day after day *you will* **be** oppressed and robbed, with no one
28: 33 [A] and *you will* **have** nothing but cruel oppression all your days.
28: 34 [A] The sights you see **will** drive you mad.
28: 37 [A] *You will* **become** a thing of horror and an object of scorn
28: 40 [A] You *will* **have** [+4200] olive trees throughout your country
28: 41 [A] have sons and daughters but you *will* not **keep** [+4200] them,
28: 44 [A] not lend to him. He *will* **be** the head, but you will be the tail.
28: 44 [A] not lend to him. He will be the head, but you *will* **be** the tail.
28: 46 [A] *They will* **be** a sign and a wonder to you and your
28: 62 [A] *You* who **were** as numerous as the stars in the sky will be left
28: 63 [A] **[NIE]** Just as it pleased the LORD to make you prosper
28: 65 [A] no repose, no **[NIE]** resting place for the sole of your foot.
28: 66 [A] You **will** live in constant suspense, filled with dread both
29: 13 [29:12] [A] that he *may* **be** your God as he promised you and as
29: 19 [29:18] [A] **[NIE]** When such a person hears the words of this
29: 19 [29:18] [A] on himself and therefore thinks, "I *will* **be** safe,
30: 1 [A] **[NIE]** When all these blessings and curses I have set before
30: 4 [A] Even if **[NIE]** you have been banished to the most distant
31: 8 [A] The LORD himself goes before you and *will* **be** with you;
31: 17 [A] I will hide my face from them, and *they will* **be** destroyed.
31: 19 [A] them sing it, so that it *may* **be** a witness for me against them.
31: 21 [A] **[NIE]** when many disasters and difficulties come upon
31: 23 [A] I promised them on oath, and *I* myself *will* **be** with you."
31: 24 [A] **[NIE]** After Moses finished writing in a book the words of
31: 26 [A] your God. There *it will* **remain** as a witness against you.
31: 27 [A] If *you have* **been** rebellious against the LORD while I am
32: 38 [A] up to help you! *Let them* **give** you **shelter** [+6261+6584]!
33: 5 [A] *He* **was** king over Jeshurun when the leaders of the people
33: 6 [A] "Let Reuben live and not die, nor his men **be** few."
33: 7 [A] hands he defends his cause. Oh, **be** his help against his foes!"
33: 24 [A] *let him* **be** favored by his brothers, and let him bathe his feet
Jos 1: 1 [A] **[NIE]** After the death of Moses the servant of the LORD,
1: 4 [A] Your territory *will* **extend** from the desert to Lebanon, and
1: 5 [A] As *I* **was** with Moses, so I will be with you; I will never
1: 5 [A] As I was with Moses, so *I will* **be** with you; I will never
1: 17 [A] Only *may* the LORD your God **be** with you as he was with
1: 17 [A] Only may the LORD your God be with you as *he* **was** with
2: 5 [A] At dusk, *when it* **was** time to close the city gate, the men left.
2: 14 [A] **[NIE]** we will treat you kindly and faithfully when the
2: 19 [A] **[NIE]** If anyone goes outside your house into the street,
2: 19 [A] As for anyone who **is** in the house with you, his blood will be
2: 19 [A] his blood will be on our head if a hand **is** laid on him.
2: 20 [A] *we will* **be** released from the oath you made us swear."
3: 2 [A] **[NIE]** After three days the officers went throughout the
3: 4 [A] But **keep** a distance of about a thousand yards between you
3: 7 [A] so they may know that *I* **am** with you as I was with Moses.
3: 7 [A] so they may know that I am with you as *I* **was** with Moses.
3: 13 [A] **[NIE]** as soon as the priests who carry the ark of the
3: 14 [A] So **[NIE]** when the people broke camp to cross the Jordan,
4: 1 [A] **[NIE]** When the whole nation had finished crossing the
4: 6 [A] to **serve as** a sign among you. In the future, when your
4: 7 [A] These stones *are to* **be** a memorial to the people of Israel
4: 9 [A] ark of the covenant had stood. And *they* **are** there to this day.
4: 11 [A] **[NIE]** as soon as all of them had crossed, the ark of the
4: 18 [A] **[NIE]** the priests came up out of the river carrying the ark
5: 1 [A] Now **[NIE]** when all the Amorite kings west of the Jordan
5: 1 [A] they no longer **had** [+928] the courage to face the Israelites.
5: 5 [A] All the people that came out **[NIE]** had been circumcised,
5: 7 [A] *They* **were** still uncircumcised because they had not been
5: 8 [A] And **[NIE]** after the whole nation had been circumcised,
5: 12 [A] *there* **was** no longer any manna for the Israelites, but that
5: 13 [A] Now **[NIE]** when Joshua was near Jericho, he looked up
5: 13 [A] Now when Joshua **was** near Jericho, he looked up and saw a
6: 5 [A] **[NIE]** When you hear them sound a long blast on the
6: 8 [A] **[NIE]** When Joshua had spoken to the people, the seven
6: 15 [A] **[NIE]** On the seventh day, they got up at daybreak
6: 16 [A] **[NIE]** The seventh time around, when the priests sounded
6: 17 [A] The city and all that is in it *are to* **be** devoted to the LORD.
6: 20 [A] the people shouted, and **[NIE]** at the sound of the trumpet,
6: 27 [A] So the LORD **was** with Joshua, and his fame spread
6: 27 [A] was with Joshua, and his fame **spread** throughout the land.
7: 5 [A] this the hearts of the people melted and **became** like water.
7: 12 [A] and run because *they have been* **made** liable to destruction.
7: 12 [A] *I will* not **be** with you anymore unless you destroy whatever
7: 14 [A] **[NIE]** The tribe that the LORD takes shall come forward
7: 15 [A] **[NIE]** He who is caught with the devoted things shall be
8: 4 [A] the city. Don't go very far from it. All of you **be** on the alert.
8: 5 [A] **[NIE]** when the men come out against us, as they did
8: 8 [A] **[NIE]** When you have taken the city, set it on fire. Do what
8: 14 [A] **[NIE]** When the king of Ai saw this, he and all the men of
8: 20 [A] they **had** [+928+3338] no **chance** to escape in any direction,
8: 22 [A] so that *they were* **caught** in the middle, with Israelites on
8: 24 [A] **[NIE]** When Israel had finished killing all the men of Ai in
8: 25 [A] **[NIE]** Twelve thousand men and women fell that day—
8: 35 [A] *There* **was** not a word of all that Moses had commanded that
9: 1 [A] Now **[NIE]** when all the kings west of the Jordan heard
9: 5 [A] All the bread of their food supply **was** dry and moldy.
9: 12 [A] we left to come to you. But now see how dry and moldy *it* **is**.
9: 16 [A] **[NIE]** Three days after they made the treaty with the
9: 20 [A] so that wrath *will* not **fall** on us for breaking the oath we
9: 21 [A] *let them* **be** woodcutters and water carriers for the entire
10: 1 [A] Now Adoni-Zedek **[NIE]** king of Jerusalem heard that
10: 1 [A] made a treaty of peace with Israel and *were* **living** near them.
10: 11 [A] **[NIE]** As they fled before Israel on the road down from
10: 14 [A] *There has* never **been** a day like it before or since, a day
10: 20 [A] So **[NIE]** Joshua and the Israelites destroyed them
10: 24 [A] **[NIE]** When they had brought these kings to Joshua, he
10: 26 [A] and *they* **were** left hanging on the trees until evening.
10: 27 [A] **[NIE]** At sunset Joshua gave the order and they took them
11: 1 [A] **[NIE]** When Jabin king of Hazor heard of this, he sent word
11: 19 [A] not **[NIE]** one city made a treaty of peace with the
11: 20 [A] For *it* **was** the LORD himself who hardened their hearts to
11: 20 [A] them totally, exterminating them without **[NIE]** mercy,
13: 16 [A] **[NIE]** The territory from Aroer on the rim of the Arnon
13: 23 [A] The boundary of the Reubenites **was** the bank of the Jordan.
13: 25 [A] **[NIE]** The territory of Jazer, all the towns of Gilead
13: 29 [A] *that* **is**, to half the family of the descendants of Manasseh,
13: 30 [A] The territory **extending** from Mahanaim and including all of
14: 4 [A] for the sons of Joseph *had* **become** two tribes—Manasseh
14: 9 [A] 'The land on which your feet have walked *will* **be** your
14: 14 [A] So Hebron *has* **belonged** [+4200] **to** Caleb son of Jephunneh
15: 1 [A] clan by clan, **extended** down to the territory of Edom,
15: 2 [A] Their southern boundary **started** from the bay at the southern
15: 4 [A] and joined the Wadi of Egypt, **ending** [+9362] at the sea.
15: 4 [A] of Egypt, ending at the sea. This **is** their southern boundary.
15: 7 [A] to the waters of En Shemesh and **came** out at En Rogel.
15: 11 [A] and reached Jabneel. The boundary **ended** [+9362] at the sea.
15: 18 [A] **One day** [+2256] when she came to Othniel, she urged him
15: 21 [A] of Judah in the Negev toward the boundary of Edom **were**:
16: 3 [A] Beth Horon and on to Gezer, **ending** [+9362] at the sea.
16: 5 [A] *This* **was** the territory of Ephraim, clan by clan: The
16: 5 [A] The boundary of their inheritance **went** from Ataroth Addar
16: 8 [A] went west to the Kanah Ravine and **ended** [+9362] at the sea.
16: 10 [A] the people of Ephraim but *are* **required** to do forced labor.
17: 1 [A] *This* **was** the allotment for the tribe of Manasseh as Joseph's
17: 1 [A] who *had* **received** [+4200] Gilead and Bashan
17: 1 [A] and Bashan because the Makirites **were** great soldiers.
17: 2 [A] So this allotment **was** for the rest of the people of
17: 3 [A] son of Manasseh, **had** [+4200] no sons but only daughters,
17: 6 [A] The land of Gilead **belonged** [+4200] **to** the rest of the
17: 7 [A] The territory of Manasseh **extended** from Asher to
17: 8 [A] (Manasseh **had** [+4200] the land of Tappuah, but Tappuah
17: 9 [A] the northern side of the ravine and **ended** [+9362] at the sea.

Jos 17:10 [A] The territory of Manasseh **reached** the sea and bordered
17:11 [A] Manasseh also **had** [+4200] Beth Shan, Ibleam and the
17:13 [A] However, **[NIE]** when the Israelites grew stronger, they
17:17 [A] You *will* **have** [+4200] not only one allotment
17:18 [A] **[RPH]** Clear it, and its farthest limits will be yours;
17:18 [A] Clear it, and its farthest limits *will* **be** yours;
18:12 [A] On the north side their boundary **began** at the Jordan, passed
18:12 [A] into the hill country, **coming** out at the desert of Beth Aven.
18:14 [A] along the western side and **came** out at Kiriath Baal (that is,
18:19 [A] and **came** out at the northern bay of the Salt Sea,
18:21 [A] of Benjamin, clan by clan, **had** [+4200] the following cities:
19: 1 [A] by clan. Their inheritance **lay** within the territory of Judah.
19: 2 [A] It **included**: Beersheba (or Sheba), Moladah,
19: 9 [A] because Judah's portion **was** more than they needed.
19:10 [A] The boundary of their inheritance **went** as far as Sarid.
19:14 [A] to Hannathon and **ended** [+9362] at the Valley of Iphtah El.
19:18 [A] Their territory **included**: Jezreel, Kesulloth, Shunem,
19:22 [A] and Beth Shemesh, and **ended** [+9362] at the Jordan.
19:25 [A] Their territory **included**: Helkath, Hali, Beten, Acshaph,
19:29 [A] toward Hosah and **came** out at the sea in the region of Aczib,
19:33 [A] Their boundary **went** from Heleph and the large tree in
19:33 [A] and Jabneel to Lakkum and **ending** [+9362] *at* the Jordan.
19:41 [A] The territory of their inheritance **included**: Zorah, Eshtaol,
20: 3 [A] may flee there and **find** protection from the avenger of blood.
20: 6 [A] until the death of the high priest who *is* **serving** at that time.
20: 9 [A] accidentally could flee to these **[NIE]** designated cities
21: 4 [A] of Aaron the priest *were* **allotted** [+928+1598+2021+4200]
21:10 [A] (these towns **were** assigned to the descendants of Aaron who
21:10 [A] clans of the Levites, because the first lot **fell** to them):
21:20 [A] *were* **allotted** [+1598+4200] towns from the tribe of
21:40 [A] All the towns **allotted** [+1598] to the Merarite clans, who
21:42 [A] Each of these towns **had** pasturelands surrounding it;
22:17 [A] even though a plague **fell** on the community of the LORD!
22:18 [A] " 'If **[NIE]** you rebel against the LORD today, tomorrow
22:20 [A] *did* not wrath **come** upon the whole community of Israel?
22:28 [A] "And we said, **[NIE]** 'If they ever say this to us, or to our
23: 1 [A] After a long time *had* **passed** and the LORD had given
23:13 [A] *they will* **become** snares and traps for you, whips on your
23:15 [A] **[NIE]** just as every good promise of the LORD your God
24:27 [A] to all the people. "This stone *will* **be** a witness against us.
24:27 [A] *It will* **be** a witness against you if you are untrue to your
24:29 [A] **[NIE]** After these things, Joshua son of Nun, the servant of
24:32 [A] *This* **became** the inheritance of Joseph's descendants.
Jdg 1: 1 [A] **[NIE]** After the death of Joshua, the Israelites asked the
1: 7 [A] big toes cut off **[NIE]** have picked up scraps under my
1:14 [A] **One day** [+2256] when she came to Othniel, she urged him
1:19 [A] The LORD **was** with the men of Judah. They took
1:28 [A] **[NIE]** When Israel became strong, they pressed the
1:30 [A] but **[NIE]** they did subject them to forced labor.
1:33 [A] and Beth Anath **became** forced laborers for them.
1:35 [A] of Joseph increased, *they* too **were** pressed into forced labor.
2: 3 [A] *they will* **be** ˻thorns˼ in your sides and their gods will be a
2: 3 [A] ˻thorns˼ in your sides and their gods *will* **be** a snare to you."
2: 4 [A] **[NIE]** When the angel of the LORD had spoken these
2:15 [A] the hand of the LORD **was** against them to defeat them,
2:18 [A] he **was** with the judge and saved them out of the hands of
2:19 [A] **[NIE]** when the judge died, the people returned to ways
3: 4 [A] *They were* **left** to test the Israelites to see whether they
3:10 [A] The Spirit of the LORD **came** upon him, so that he became
3:18 [A] **[NIE]** After Ehud had presented the tribute, he sent on their
3:27 [A] **[NIE]** When he arrived there, he blew a trumpet in the hill
3:31 [A] After Ehud **came** Shamgar son of Anath, who struck down
4: 9 [A] the way you are going about this, the honor *will* not **be** yours,
4:20 [A] **[NIE]** "If someone comes by and asks you, 'Is anyone here?'
6: 3 [A] **[NIE]** Whenever the Israelites planted their crops,
6: 7 [A] **[NIE]** When the Israelites cried to the LORD because of
6:16 [A] The LORD answered, "*I will* **be** with you, and you will
6:25 [A] **[NIE]** That same night the LORD said to him, "Take the
6:27 [A] **[NIE]** because he was afraid of his family and the men of
6:37 [A] If *there* **is** dew only on the fleece and all the ground is dry,
6:38 [A] And that *is what* **happened**. Gideon rose early the next day;
6:39 [A] This time **make** the fleece dry and the ground covered with
6:39 [A] the fleece dry and the ground **[RPH]** covered with dew."
6:40 [A] Only the fleece **was** dry; all the ground was covered with
6:40 [A] the fleece was dry; all the ground **was** covered with dew.
7: 1 [A] The camp of Midian **was** north of them in the valley near the
7: 4 [A] **[NIE]** If I say, 'This one shall go with you,' he shall go; but
7: 6 [A] **[NIE]** Three hundred men lapped with their hands to their
7: 8 [A] Now the camp of Midian **lay** below him in the valley.
7: 9 [A] **[NIE]** During that night the LORD said to Gideon,
7:15 [A] **[NIE]** When Gideon heard the dream and its interpretation,
7:17 [A] I get to the edge of the camp, **[NIE]** do exactly as I do.
8:11 [A] and Jogbehah and fell upon the unsuspecting army. **[NIE]**
8:26 [A] The weight of the gold rings he asked for **came to** seventeen
8:27 [A] it there, and *it* **became** a snare to Gideon and his family.
8:30 [A] He **had** [+4200] seventy sons of his own, for he had many
8:30 [A] seventy sons of his own, for he **had** [+4200] many wives.
8:33 [A] **[NIE]** No sooner had Gideon died than the Israelites again
9:33 [A] **[NIE]** In the morning at sunrise, advance against the city.
9:42 [A] **[NIE]** The next day the people of Shechem went out to the
9:51 [A] Inside the city, however, **was** a strong tower, to which all the
10: 4 [A] He **had** [+4200] thirty sons, who rode thirty donkeys. They
10:18 [A] Ammonites *will* **be** the head of all those living in Gilead."
11: 1 [A] Jephthah the Gileadite **was** a mighty warrior. His father was
11: 4 [A] **[NIE]** Some time later, when the Ammonites made war on
11: 5 [A] the **[NIE]** elders of Gilead went to get Jephthah from the
11: 6 [A] "Come," they said, "**be** our commander, so we can fight the
11: 8 [A] and *you will* **be** our head over all who live in Gilead."
11: 9 [A] the LORD gives them to me—*will* I *really* **be** your head?"
11:10 [A] The elders of Gilead replied, "The LORD **is** our witness;
11:29 [A] the Spirit of the LORD **came** upon Jephthah. He crossed
11:31 [A] **[NIE]** whatever comes out of the door of my house to meet
11:31 [A] return in triumph from the Ammonites *will* **be** the LORD's,
11:35 [A] **[NIE]** When he saw her, he tore his clothes and cried, "Oh!
11:35 [A] You have made me miserable and **[NIE]** wretched, because
11:39 [A] **[NIE]** After the two months, she returned to her father
11:39 [A] And she was a virgin. From this **comes** the Israelite custom
12: 2 [A] my people *were* **engaged in** a great struggle with the
12: 5 [A] **[NIE]** whenever a survivor of Ephraim said, "Let me cross
12: 9 [A] He **had** [+4200] thirty sons and thirty daughters. He gave his
12:14 [A] He **had** [+4200] forty sons and thirty grandsons, who rode on
13: 2 [A] **had** a wife who was sterile and remained childless.
13: 5 [A] because the boy *is to* **be** a Nazirite, set apart to God from
13: 7 [A] because the boy *will* **be** a Nazirite of God from birth until
13:12 [A] what *is to* **be** the rule for the boy's life and work?"
13:20 [A] **[NIE]** As the flame blazed up from the altar toward heaven,
14:11 [A] **[NIE]** When he appeared, he was given thirty companions.
14:11 [A] When he appeared, he was given thirty companions. **[NIE]**
14:15 [A] **[NIE]** On the fourth day, they said to Samson's wife,
14:17 [A] She cried the whole seven days **[NIE]** of the feast. So on the
14:17 [A] So **[NIE]** on the seventh day he finally told her, because she
14:20 [A] Samson's wife *was* **given** to the friend who had attended him
15: 1 [A] **[NIE]** Later on, at the time of wheat harvest, Samson took a
15: 2 [A] younger sister more attractive? **Take** [+4200] *her* instead."
15:14 [A] The ropes on his arms **became** like charred flax,
15:17 [A] **[NIE]** When he finished speaking, he threw away the
16: 4 [A] **[NIE]** Some time later, he fell in love with a woman in the
16: 7 [A] have not been dried, *I'll* **become** as weak as any other man."
16:11 [A] never been used, *I'll* **become** as weak as any other man."
16:13 [A] the pin, *I'll* **become** [BHS-] as weak as any other man."
16:16 [A] **[NIE]** With such nagging she prodded him day after day
16:17 [A] leave me, and *I would* **become** as weak as any other man."
16:21 [A] with bronze shackles, they **set** *him to* grinding in the prison.
16:25 [A] **[NIE]** While they were in high spirits, they shouted,
16:30 [A] Thus **[NIE]** he killed many more when he died than while
17: 1 [A] Now **[NIE]** a man named Micah from the hill country of
17: 4 [A] the image and the idol. And *they were* **put** in Micah's house.
17: 5 [A] some idols and installed one of his sons **[NIE]** as his priest.
17: 7 [A] **[NIE]** A young Levite from Bethlehem in Judah, who had
17:10 [A] said to him, "Live with me and **be** my father and priest,
17:11 [A] with him, and the young man **was** to him like one of his sons.
17:12 [A] and the young man **became** his priest and lived in his house.
17:12 [A] and the young man became his priest and **lived** in his house.
17:13 [A] will be good to me, since this Levite *has* **become** my priest."
18: 4 [A] for him, and said, "He has hired me and *I* **am** his priest."
18:19 [A] say a word. Come with us, and **be** our father and priest.
18:19 [A] Isn't it better that you **serve** [+4200] a tribe and clan in Israel
18:19 [A] as priest rather than just one man's household?" **[RPH]**
18:27 [A] **[NIE]** his priest, and went on to Laish, against a peaceful
18:30 [A] his sons **were** priests for the tribe of Dan until the time of the
18:31 [A] had made, all the time the house of God **was** in Shiloh.
19: 1 [A] **[NIE]** In those days Israel had no king. Now a Levite who
19: 1 [A] Now **[NIE]** a Levite who lived in a remote area in the hill
19: 2 [A] in Bethlehem, Judah. After *she had* **been** there four months,
19: 5 [A] **[NIE]** On the fourth day they got up early and he prepared
19:30 [A] **[NIE]** Everyone who saw it said, "Such a thing has never
19:30 [C] who saw it said, "Such a thing has never been seen or **done**,
20: 3 [C] the Israelites said, "Tell us how this awful thing **happened**."
20:12 [C] "What about this awful crime that **was committed** among
20:38 [A] The men of Israel *had* **arranged** [+4200+4595] with the
20:46 [A] **[NIE]** On that day twenty-five thousand Benjamite
21: 3 [A] God of Israel," they cried, "why *has* this **happened** to Israel?
21: 4 [A] **[NIE]** Early the next day the people built an altar
21: 5 [A] For they *had* **taken** a solemn oath that anyone who failed to
21:22 [A] **[NIE]** When their fathers or brothers complain to us, we
Ru 1: 1 [A] **[NIE]** In the days when the judges ruled, there was a famine
1: 1 [A] days when the judges ruled, *there* **was** a famine in the land,
1: 2 [A] Judah. And they went to Moab and **lived** there.

Ru 1: 7 [A] she left the place where *she had been* **living**
1: 11 [A] to have any more sons, *who could* **become** your husbands?
1: 12 [A] my daughters; I am too old *to* **have** [+4200] another husband.
1: 12 [A] even if *I* **had** [+4200] a husband tonight and then gave birth
1: 13 [A] *Would you* **remain unmarried** [+408+1194+4200+4200 +6328] for them?
1: 19 [A] **[NIE]** When they arrived in Bethlehem, the whole town was
2: 12 [A] *May* you **be** richly rewarded by the LORD, the God of
2: 13 [A] though I *do* not **have** the standing of one of your servant
2: 17 [A] barley she had gathered, and *it* **amounted to** about an ephah.
2: 19 [A] did you work? Blessed **be** the man who took notice of you!"
3: 2 [A] Is not Boaz, with whose servant girls *you have* **been**,
3: 4 [A] **[NIE]** When he lies down, note the place where he is lying.
3: 8 [A] **[NIE]** In the middle of the night something startled the man,
3: 13 [A] and **[NIE]** in the morning if he wants to redeem, good;
4: 12 [A] *may* your family **be** like that of Perez, whom Tamar bore to
4: 13 [A] So Boaz took Ruth and *she* **became** his wife. Then he went
4: 15 [A] *He* **will** renew your life and sustain you in your old age.
4: 16 [A] took the child, laid him in her lap and **[NIE]** cared for him.
1Sa 1: 1 [A] *There* **was** a certain man from Ramathaim, a Zuphite from
1: 2 [A] Peninnah **had** [+4200] children, but Hannah had none.
1: 4 [A] Whenever the day **came** for Elkanah to sacrifice, he would
1: 12 [A] **[NIE]** As she kept on praying to the LORD, Eli observed
1: 18 [A] and her face *was* no longer **downcast** [+4200].
1: 20 [A] So **[NIE]** in the course of time Hannah conceived and gave
1: 28 [A] *For* his whole **life** [+889+3427] he will be given over to the
2: 11 [A] the boy **[NIE]** ministered before the LORD under Eli the
2: 17 [A] This sin of the young men **was** very great in the LORD's
2: 27 [A] your father's house when they **were** in Egypt under Pharaoh?
2: 31 [A] so that *there will* not **be** an old man in your family line
2: 32 [A] to Israel, in your family line *there will* never **be** an old man.
2: 36 [A] **[NIE]** everyone left in your family line will come and bow
3: 1 [A] In those days the word of the LORD **was** rare; there were
3: 2 [A] **[NIE]** One night Eli, whose eyes were becoming so weak
3: 9 [A] lie down, and **[NIE]** if he calls you, say, 'Speak, LORD,
3: 19 [A] The LORD **was** with Samuel as he grew up, and he let none
4: 1 [A] Samuel's word **came** to all Israel. Now the Israelites went
4: 5 [A] **[NIE]** When the ark of the LORD's covenant came into
4: 7 [A] "We're in trouble! Nothing like this *has* **happened** before.
4: 9 [A] **Be** men, or you will be subject to the Hebrews, as they have
4: 9 [A] the Hebrews, as they have been to you. **Be** men, and fight!"
4: 10 [A] The slaughter **was** very great; Israel lost thirty thousand foot
4: 13 [A] because his heart **feared** [+3007] for the ark of God.
4: 16 [A] from it this very day." Eli asked, "What **happened**, my son?"
4: 17 [A] and the army *has* **suffered** [+928] heavy losses.
4: 18 [A] **[NIE]** When he mentioned the ark of God, Eli fell backward
5: 9 [A] **[NIE]** after they had moved it, the LORD's hand was
5: 9 [A] they had moved it, the LORD's hand **was** against that city,
5: 10 [A] **[NIE]** As the ark of God was entering Ekron, the people of
5: 11 [A] For death *had* **filled** [+928+3972] the city *with* panic; God's
6: 1 [A] When the ark of the LORD *had* **been** in Philistine territory
6: 9 [A] hand that struck us and that it **happened** to us by chance."
7: 2 [A] *It* **was** a long time, twenty years in all, that the ark remained
7: 2 [A] **[NIE]** and all the people of Israel mourned and sought after
7: 10 [A] While Samuel **was** sacrificing the burnt offering,
7: 13 [A] the hand of the LORD **was** against the Philistines.
7: 14 [A] And *there* **was** peace between Israel and the Amorites.
8: 1 [A] **[NIE]** When Samuel grew old, he appointed his sons as
8: 2 [A] The name of his firstborn **was** Joel and the name of his
8: 11 [A] "This **is** what the king who will reign over you will do:
8: 17 [A] of your flocks, and *you* yourselves *will* **become** his slaves.
8: 19 [A] listen to Samuel. "No!" they said. "We **want** a king over us.
8: 20 [A] we *will* **be** like all the other nations, with a king to lead us
9: 1 [A] *There* **was** a Benjamite, a man of standing, whose name was
9: 2 [A] He **had** [+4200] a son named Saul, an impressive young man
9: 26 [A] They rose **[NIE]** about daybreak and Samuel called to Saul
10: 5 [A] **[NIE]** As you approach the town, you will meet a
10: 7 [A] **[NIE]** Once these signs are fulfilled, do whatever your hand
10: 9 [A] **[NIE]** As Saul turned to leave Samuel, God changed Saul's
10: 11 [A] **[NIE]** When all those who had formerly known him saw
10: 11 [A] "What is this *that has* **happened** to the son of Kish?
10: 12 [A] "And who is their father?" So *it* **became** a saying:
10: 27 [A] despised him and brought him no gifts. But Saul **kept** silent.
11: 8 [A] the men of Israel **numbered** three hundred thousand
11: 9 [A] you *will* **be** delivered.' " When the messengers went
11: 11 [A] **[NIE]** The next day Saul separated his men into three
11: 11 [A] **[NIE]** Those who survived were scattered, so that no two of
12: 14 [A] the king who reigns over you **follow** [+339] the LORD your
12: 15 [A] his hand *will* **be** against you, as it was against your fathers.
13: 2 [A] two thousand **were** with him at Micmash and in the hill
13: 2 [A] and a thousand **were** with Jonathan at Gibeah in Benjamin.
13: 10 [A] **[NIE]** Just as he finished making the offering, Samuel
13: 21 [A] The price **was** two thirds of a shekel for sharpening
13: 22 [A] So **[NIE]** on the day of the battle not a soldier with Saul
14: 1 [A] **[NIE]** One day Jonathan son of Saul said to the young man
14: 14 [A] **[NIE]** In that first attack Jonathan and his armor-bearer
14: 15 [A] panic **struck** [+928] the whole army—those in the camp
14: 15 [A] and the ground shook. *It* **was** a panic sent by God.
14: 18 [A] the ark of God." (At that time it **was** with the Israelites.)
14: 19 [A] **[NIE]** While Saul was talking to the priest, the tumult in the
14: 20 [A] total confusion, **striking** [+928] each other with their swords.
14: 21 [A] Those Hebrews *who had* previously **been** with the
14: 21 [A] had gone up with them to their camp **went over** [+6017] to
14: 25 [A] army entered the woods, and *there* **was** honey on the ground.
14: 38 [A] and let us find out what sin *has been* **committed** today.
14: 40 [A] Saul then said to all the Israelites, "You **stand** over there;
14: 40 [A] over there; I and Jonathan my son *will* **stand** over here."
14: 49 [A] Saul's sons **were** Jonathan, Ishvi and Malki-Shua. The name
14: 52 [A] All the days of Saul *there* **was** bitter war with the Philistines,
15: 10 [A] Then the word of the LORD **came** to Samuel:
15: 26 [A] and the LORD has rejected you as **[NIE]** king over Israel!"
16: 6 [A] **[NIE]** When they arrived, Samuel saw Eliab and thought,
16: 16 [A] **[NIE]** He will play when the evil spirit from God comes
16: 16 [A] He will play when the evil spirit from God **comes** upon you,
16: 21 [A] him very much, and David **became** one of his armor-bearers.
16: 23 [A] **[NIE]** Whenever the spirit from God came upon Saul,
16: 23 [A] Whenever the spirit from God **came** upon Saul, David would
17: 9 [A] he is able to fight and kill me, *we will* **become** your subjects;
17: 9 [A] and kill him, *you will* **become** our subjects and serve us."
17: 25 [A] **[NIE]** The king will give great wealth to the man who kills
17: 34 [A] to Saul, "Your servant *has* **been** keeping his father's sheep.
17: 36 [A] this uncircumcised Philistine *will* **be** like one of them,
17: 37 [A] Saul said to David, "Go, and the LORD **be** with you."
17: 42 [A] He looked David over and saw that *he* **was** only a boy, ruddy
17: 48 [A] **[NIE]** As the Philistine moved closer to attack him, David
18: 1 [A] **[NIE]** After David had finished talking with Saul, Jonathan
18: 6 [A] **[NIE]** When the men were returning home after David had
18: 9 [A] **[NIE]** from that time on Saul kept a jealous eye on David.
18: 10 [A] **[NIE]** The next day an evil spirit from God came forcefully
18: 12 [A] because the LORD **was** with David but had left Saul.
18: 14 [A] **[NIE]** In everything he did he had great success,
18: 17 [A] only **serve** me bravely and fight the battles of the LORD."
18: 17 [A] For Saul said to himself, "I *will* not **raise** a hand against him.
18: 17 [A] *Let* the Philistines **do** [+928+2257+3338] **that**!"
18: 18 [A] clan in Israel, that *I should* **become** the king's son-in-law?"
18: 19 [A] So when the time **came** for Merab, Saul's daughter, to be
18: 21 [A] "so that *she may* **be** a snare to him and so that the hand of
18: 21 [A] and so that the hand of the Philistines *may* **be** against him."
18: 29 [A] of him, and he **remained** his enemy the rest of his days.
18: 30 [A] continued to go out to battle, and **[NIE]** as often as they did,
19: 7 [A] He brought him to Saul, and David **was** with Saul as before.
19: 8 [A] Once more war **broke out**, and David went out and fought
19: 9 [A] an evil spirit from the LORD **came** upon Saul as he was
19: 20 [A] the Spirit of God **came** upon Saul's men and they also
19: 23 [A] the Spirit of God **came** even upon him, and he walked along
20: 13 [A] *May* the LORD **be** with you as he has been with my father.
20: 13 [A] May the LORD be with you as *he has* **been** with my father.
20: 24 [A] when the New Moon festival **came**, the king sat down to eat.
20: 27 [A] **[NIE]** the next day, the second day of the month,
20: 35 [A] **[NIE]** In the morning Jonathan went out to the field for his
20: 42 [A] saying, 'The LORD **is** witness between you and me,
21: 5 [21:6] [A] The men's things **are** holy even on missions that are
21: 6 [21:7] [A] since *there* **was** no bread there except the bread of
21: 8 [21:9] [A] because the king's business **was** urgent."
22: 2 [A] gathered around him, and *he* **became** their leader.
22: 2 [A] became their leader. About four hundred men **were** with him.
22: 4 [A] they stayed with him as long as David **was** in the stronghold.
23: 6 [A] (Now **[NIE]** Abiathar son of Ahimelech had brought the
23: 17 [A] You will be king over Israel, and I *will* **be** second to you.
23: 22 [A] Find out where David *usually* **goes** [+8079] and who has
23: 23 [A] **[NIE]** if he is in the area, I will track him down among all
23: 26 [A] on the other side, **[NIE]** hurrying to get away from Saul.
24: 1 [24:2] [A] **[NIE]** After Saul returned from pursuing the
24: 5 [24:6] [A] **[NIE]** Afterward, David was conscience-stricken for
24: 12 [24:13] [A] done to me, but my hand *will* not **touch** [+928] you.
24: 13 [24:14] [A] evil deeds,' so my hand *will* not **touch** [+928] you.
24: 15 [24:16] [A] *May* the LORD **be** our judge and decide between
24: 16 [24:17] [A] **[NIE]** When David finished saying this, Saul
25: 2 [A] and three thousand sheep, which *he* **was** shearing in Carmel.
25: 7 [A] When your shepherds **were** with us, we did not mistreat
25: 7 [A] the whole time they **were** at Carmel nothing of theirs was
25: 15 [A] the whole time we **were** out in the fields near them nothing
25: 16 [A] day *they* **were** a wall around us all the time we were herding
25: 16 [A] day they were a wall around us all the time we **were** herding
25: 20 [A] As **[NIE]** she came riding her donkey into a mountain
25: 26 [A] *may* your enemies and all who intend to harm my master **be**
25: 29 [A] the life of my master *will* **be** bound securely in the bundle of
25: 30 [A] **[NIE]** When the LORD has done for my master every

1Sa 25:31 [A] my master *will* not **have** [+4200] on his conscience the
25:37 [A] **[NIE]** in the morning, when Nabal was sober, his wife told
25:37 [A] and his heart failed him and he **became** like a stone.
25:38 [A] **[NIE]** About ten days later, the LORD struck Nabal and he
25:42 [A] went with David's messengers and **became** his wife.
25:43 [A] married Ahinoam of Jezreel, and they both **were** his wives.
27: 6 [A] and it *has* **belonged** [+4200] **to** the kings of Judah ever since.
27: 7 [A] **[NIE]** David lived in Philistine territory a year and four
27:12 [A] his people, the Israelites, that *he will* **be** my servant forever."
28: 1 [A] **[NIE]** In those days the Philistines gathered their forces to
28:16 [A] LORD has turned away from you and **become** your enemy?
28:20 [A] His strength *was* **gone** [+928+4202], for he had eaten
28:22 [A] may eat and **have** [+928] the strength to go on your way."
29: 3 [A] He *has already* **been** with me for over a year, and from the
29: 4 [A] or *he will* **turn against** [+4200+4200+8477] us during the
29: 8 [A] against your servant from the day *I* **came** to you until now?
30: 1 [A] **[NIE]** David and his men reached Ziklag on the third day.
30:25 [A] **[NIE]** David made this a statute and ordinance for Israel
31: 8 [A] **[NIE]** The next day, when the Philistines came to strip the
2Sa 1: 1 [A] **[NIE]** After the death of Saul, David returned from
1: 2 [A] **[NIE]** On the third day a man arrived from Saul's camp,
1: 2 [A] **[NIE]** When he came to David, he fell to the ground to pay
1: 4 [A] "What **happened**?" David asked. "Tell me." He said, "The
2: 1 [A] **[NIE]** In the course of time, David inquired of the LORD.
2: 7 [A] Now then, be strong and **[NIE]** brave, for Saul your master
2:10 [A] The house of Judah, however, **followed** [+339] David.
2:11 [A] **[NIE]** The length of time David was king in Hebron over
2:11 [A] The length of time David **was** king in Hebron over the house
2:17 [A] The battle that day **was** very fierce, and Abner and the men
2:18 [A] The three sons of Zeruiah **were** there: Joab, Abishai
2:23 [A] **[NIE]** every man stopped when he came to the place where
2:25 [A] *They* **formed** *themselves* into a group and took their stand
2:26 [A] Don't you realize that *this will* **end in** [+340+928+2021]
3: 1 [A] the house of Saul and the house of David **lasted** a long time.
3: 2 [A] His firstborn **was** Amnon the son of Ahinoam of Jezreel;
3: 6 [A] **[NIE]** During the war between the house of Saul and the
3: 6 [A] During **[NIE]** the war between the house of Saul and the
3: 6 [A] Abner *had* **been** strengthening his own position in the house
3:17 [A] **[NIE]** Abner conferred with the elders of Israel and said,
3:17 [A] "For some time **[NIE]** you have wanted to make David your
3:37 [A] all Israel knew that the king **had** no **part in** [+4946] the
4: 2 [A] Now Saul's son **had** two men who were leaders of raiding
4: 3 [A] fled to Gittaim and *have* **lived** there as aliens to this day.
4: 4 [A] *He* **was** five years old when the news about Saul
4: 4 [A] **[NIE]** as she hurried to leave, he fell and became crippled.
4:10 [A] thought he **was** bringing good news, I seized him and put
5: 2 [A] In the past, while Saul **was** king over us, you were the one
5: 2 [A] you **were** the one who led Israel on their military campaigns.
5: 2 [A] my people Israel, and you *will* **become** their ruler.' "
5:24 [A] **[NIE]** As soon as you hear the sound of marching in the
6:13 [A] **[NIE]** When those who were carrying the ark of the LORD
6:16 [A] As **[NIE]** the ark of the LORD was entering the City of
6:22 [A] than this, and *I will* **be** humiliated in my own eyes.
6:23 [A] Michal daughter of Saul **had** [+4200] no children to the day
7: 1 [A] **[NIE]** After the king was settled in his palace
7: 4 [A] **[NIE]** That night the word of the LORD came to Nathan,
7: 4 [A] That night the word of the LORD **came** to Nathan, saying:
7: 6 [A] *I have* **been** moving from place to place with a tent as my
7: 8 [A] from following the flock to **be** ruler over my people Israel.
7: 9 [A] *I have* **been** with you wherever you have gone, and I have
7:14 [A] I *will* **be** his father, and he will be my son. When he does
7:14 [A] I will be his father, and he *will* **be** my son. When he does
7:16 [A] forever before me; your throne *will* **be** established forever.' "
7:24 [A] own forever, and you, O LORD, *have* **become** their God.
7:26 [A] the house of your servant David *will* **be** established before
7:28 [A] Your words **are** trustworthy, and you have promised these
7:29 [A] of your servant, that *it may* **continue** forever in your sight;
8: 1 [A] **[NIE]** In the course of time, David defeated the Philistines
8: 2 [A] So the Moabites **became** subject to David and brought
8: 6 [A] the Arameans **became** subject to him and brought tribute.
8: 7 [A] David took the gold shields that **belonged** [+448] **to** the
8:10 [A] in battle over Hadadezer, who *had* **been** at war with Tou.
8:10 [A] Joram **brought** [+928+3338] **with** him articles of silver
8:14 [A] and all the Edomites **became** subject to David.
8:15 [A] **[NIE]** doing what was just and right for all his people.
8:18 [A] and Pelethites; and David's sons **were** royal advisers.
9: 9 [A] master's grandson everything that **belonged** [+4200] **to** Saul
9:10 [A] grandson *may be* **provided** [+430+2256+4200+4312] **for**.
10: 1 [A] **[NIE]** In the course of time, the king of the Ammonites
10: 5 [A] to meet the men, for they **were** greatly humiliated.
10: 9 [A] Joab saw that *there* **were** battle lines in front of him and
10:11 [A] are too strong for me, then *you are to* **come** to my rescue;
11: 1 [A] **[NIE]** In the spring, at the time when kings go off to war,
11: 2 [A] **[NIE]** One evening David got up from his bed and walked
11:14 [A] **[NIE]** In the morning David wrote a letter to Joab and sent
11:16 [A] So **[NIE]** while Joab had the city under siege, he put Uriah
11:20 [A] **[NIE]** the king's anger may flare up, and he may ask you,
11:23 [A] *we* **drove** them **back** [+6584] to the entrance to the city gate.
11:27 [A] to his house, and *she* **became** his wife and bore him a son.
12: 1 [A] he said, "*There* **were** two men in a certain town, one rich
12: 2 [A] The rich man **had** [+4200] a very large number of sheep
12: 3 [A] and even slept in his arms. *It* **was** like a daughter to him.
12:10 [A] and took the wife of Uriah the Hittite to **be** your own.'
12:18 [A] **[NIE]** On the seventh day the child died. David's servants
12:18 [A] for they thought, "While the child **was** *still* living, we spoke
12:30 [A] set with precious stones—and *it* **was** placed on David's head.
13: 1 [A] **[NIE]** In the course of time, Amnon son of David fell in
13:13 [A] *You would* **be** like one of the wicked fools in Israel.
13:20 [A] said to her, "*Has* that Amnon, your brother, **been** with you?
13:23 [A] **[NIE]** Two years later, when Absalom's sheepshearers were
13:23 [A] when Absalom's sheepshearers **were** at Baal Hazor near the
13:28 [A] not I given you this order? Be strong and **[NIE]** brave."
13:30 [A] While they **were** on their way, the report came to David:
13:32 [A] *This has* **been** Absalom's expressed intention ever since the
13:35 [A] sons are here; *it has* **happened** just as your servant said."
13:36 [A] **[NIE]** As he finished speaking, the king's sons came in,
13:38 [A] and went to Geshur, *he* **stayed** there three years.
14: 2 [A] **Act** like a woman who has spent many days grieving for the
14:17 [A] '*May* the word of my lord the king **bring** [+4200] me rest,
14:17 [A] and evil. *May* the LORD your God **be** with you.' "
14:25 [A] In all Israel *there* **was** not a man so highly praised for his
14:25 [A] From the top of his head to the sole of his foot *there* **was** no
14:26 [A] *he* **used to** cut his hair from time to time when it became too
14:27 [A] name was Tamar, and she **became** a beautiful woman.
15: 1 [A] **[NIE]** In the course of time, Absalom provided himself with
15: 2 [A] Whenever **[NIE]** anyone came with a complaint to be
15: 2 [A] Whenever anyone **came** with a complaint to be placed before
15: 4 [A] everyone who **has** [+4200] a complaint or case could come
15: 5 [A] **[NIE]** whenever anyone approached him to bow down
15: 7 [A] **[NIE]** At the end of four years, Absalom said to the king,
15:12 [A] so the conspiracy **gained** strength, and Absalom's following
15:13 [A] "The hearts of the men of Israel **are** with Absalom."
15:14 [A] We must flee, or none of us **will** escape from Absalom.
15:21 [A] wherever my lord the king *may* **be**, whether it means life
15:21 [A] whether it means life or death, there *will* your servant **be**."
15:32 [A] When **[NIE]** David arrived at the summit, where people
15:33 [A] said to him, "If you go with me, *you will* **be** a burden to me.
15:34 [A] I **was** your father's servant in the past, but now I will be your
15:35 [A] **[NIE]** Tell them anything you hear in the king's palace.
16:16 [A] **[NIE]** Then Hushai the Arkite, David's friend, went to
16:18 [A] the men of Israel—his *I will* **be**, and I will remain with him.
16:19 [A] as I served your father, so *I will* **serve** [+4200+7156] you."
17: 3 [A] will mean the return of all; all the people *will* **be** unharmed."
17: 9 [A] If **[NIE]** he should attack your troops first, whoever hears
17: 9 [A] '*There has* **been** a slaughter among the troops who follow
17:21 [A] **[NIE]** After the men had gone, the two climbed out of the
17:27 [A] **[NIE]** When David came to Mahanaim, Shobi son of
18: 3 [A] *It would* **be** better now for you to give us support from the
18: 6 [A] and the battle **took place** in the forest of Ephraim.
18: 7 [A] by David's men, and the casualties that day **were** great—
18: 8 [A] **[NIE]** The battle spread out over the whole countryside,
18:22 [A] "**Come** [+4537] **what may**, please let me run behind the
18:23 [A] He said, "**Come** [+4537] **what may**, I want to run." So Joab
18:32 [A] and all who rise up to harm you **be**
19: 2 [19:3] [A] victory that day *was* **turned** [+4200] **into** mourning,
19: 9 [19:10] [A] **[NIE]** Throughout the tribes of Israel, the people
19:11 [19:12] [A] 'Why *should you* **be** the last to bring the king back
19:12 [19:13] [A] why *should you* **be** the last to bring back the king?'
19:13 [19:14] [A] if from now on *you* **are** not the commander of my
19:22 [19:23] [A] This day *you have* **become** my adversaries!
19:25 [19:26] [A] **[NIE]** When he came from Jerusalem to meet the
19:28 [19:29] [A] but death **[NIE]** from my lord the king,
19:35 [19:36] [A] Why *should* your servant **be** an added burden to my
19:43 [19:44] [A] **Were** we not the first to speak of bringing back our
20: 3 [A] *They* **were** kept in confinement till the day of their death,
20:26 [A] and Ira the Jairite **was** David's priest.
21: 1 [A] of David, *there* **was** a famine for three successive years;
21:15 [A] Once again *there* **was** a battle between the Philistines
21:18 [A] **[NIE]** In the course of time, there was another battle with
21:18 [A] of time, *there* **was** another battle with the Philistines, at Gob.
21:19 [A] **[NIE]** In another battle with the Philistines at Gob, Elhanan
21:20 [A] In still another battle, *which* **took place** at Gath, there was a
21:20 [A] *there* **was** a huge man with six fingers on each hand and six
22:19 [A] in the day of my disaster, but the LORD **was** my support.
22:24 [A] *I have* **been** blameless before him and have kept myself from
23:11 [A] together at a place where *there* **was** a field full of lentils,
23:19 [A] *He* **became** their commander, even though he was not
24: 9 [A] In Israel *there* **were** eight hundred thousand able-bodied men

2Sa 24: 11 [A] the word of the LORD *had* **come** to Gad the prophet,
24: 13 [A] Or **[NIE]** three days of plague in your land? Now then,
24: 16 [A] The angel of the LORD **was** then at the threshing floor of
24: 17 [A] have they done? *Let* your hand **fall** upon me and my family."
1Ki 1: 2 [A] virgin to attend the king and **take care of** [+4200+6125] him.
1: 4 [A] The girl was very beautiful; *she* **took care of** [+4200+6125]
1: 7 [A] Adonijah **conferred** [+1821] with Joab son of Zeruiah
1: 8 [A] and Rei and David's special guard **did** not join Adonijah.
1: 21 [A] **[NIE]** as soon as my lord the king is laid to rest with his
1: 21 [A] I and my son Solomon *will* **be treated as** criminals."
1: 27 [C] *Is* this something my lord the king *has* **done** without letting
1: 35 [A] I have appointed him **[NIE]** ruler over Israel and Judah."
1: 37 [A] As the LORD **was** with my lord the king, so may he be with
1: 37 [A] so *may he* **be** with Solomon to make his throne even greater
1: 52 [A] "If *he* **shows** [+4200] *himself* **to be** a worthy man,
2: 2 [A] he said. "So be strong, **show** [+4200] *yourself* a man,
2: 7 [A] of Gilead and *let them* **be** among those who eat at your table.
2: 15 [A] "As you know," he said, "the kingdom **was** mine. All Israel
2: 15 [A] things changed, and the kingdom *has* **gone** to my brother;
2: 15 [A] gone to my brother; for *it has* **come** to him from the LORD.
2: 27 [A] So Solomon removed Abiathar from **[NIE]** the priesthood
2: 33 [A] and his throne, *may there* **be** the LORD's peace forever."
2: 37 [A] **[NIE]** The day you leave and cross the Kidron Valley,
2: 37 [A] be sure you will die; your blood *will* **be** on your own head."
2: 39 [A] **[NIE]** three years later, two of Shimei's slaves ran off to
2: 45 [A] David's throne *will* **remain** secure before the LORD
3: 12 [A] so that *there will* never *have* **been** anyone like you,
3: 13 [A] so that in your lifetime you *will* **have** no equal among kings.
3: 18 [A] **[NIE]** The third day after my child was born, this woman
3: 21 [A] I saw that *it* **wasn't** [+4202] the son I had borne."
3: 26 [A] the other said, "Neither I nor you *shall* **have** [+4200] *him*.
4: 1 [A] So King Solomon **ruled** [+4889] over all Israel.
4: 7 [A] Each one **had** [+6584] **to** provide supplies for one month in
4: 11 [A] (he *was* **married** [+851+4200+4200] **to** Taphath daughter of
4: 21 [5:1] [A] Solomon **[NIE]** ruled over all the kingdoms from the
4: 22 [5:2] [A] Solomon's daily provisions **were** thirty cors of fine
4: 24 [5:4] [A] Tiphsah to Gaza, and **had** [+4200] peace on all sides.
4: 26 [5:6] [A] Solomon **had** [+4200] four thousand stalls for chariot
4: 28 [5:8] [A] to the **proper place** [+889+5226+9004] their quotas of
4: 31 [5:11] [A] And his fame **spread** to all the surrounding nations.
4: 32 [5:12] [A] and his songs **numbered** a thousand and five.
5: 1 [5:15] [A] because he *had* always **been** on friendly terms with
5: 6 [5:20] [A] My men *will* **work** with yours, and I will pay you for
5: 7 [5:21] [A] **[NIE]** When Hiram heard Solomon's message, he
5: 10 [5:24] [A] In this way **[NIE]** Hiram kept Solomon supplied
5: 12 [5:26] [A] *There* **were** peaceful relations between Hiram
5: 13 [5:27] [A] laborers from all Israel—**[NIE]** thirty thousand men.
5: 14 [5:28] [A] so that *they* **spent** one month in Lebanon and two
5: 15 [5:29] [A] Solomon **had** [+4200] seventy thousand carriers and
6: 1 [A] **[NIE]** In the four hundred and eightieth year after the
6: 11 [A] The word of the LORD **came** to Solomon:
6: 17 [A] The main hall in front of this room **was** forty cubits long.
7: 8 [A] which he was to live, set farther back, **was** similar in design.
8: 8 [A] from outside the Holy Place; and *they* **are** still there today.
8: 10 [A] **[NIE]** When the priests withdrew from the Holy Place,
8: 16 [A] tribe of Israel to have a temple built for my Name to **be** there,
8: 16 [A] but I have chosen David to **rule** [+6584] my people Israel.'
8: 17 [A] "My father David **had** *it* in his heart to build a temple for the
8: 18 [A] 'Because *it* **was** in your heart to build a temple for my Name,
8: 18 [A] temple for my Name, you did well *to* **have** this in your heart.
8: 29 [A] *May* your eyes **be** open toward this temple night and day,
8: 29 [A] this place of which you said, 'My Name *shall* **be** there,'
8: 35 [A] "When the heavens are shut up and *there* **is** no rain
8: 37 [A] "When famine or plague **comes** to the land, or blight
8: 37 [A] **[RPH]** or blight or mildew, locusts or grasshoppers,
8: 37 [A] in any of their cities, whatever disaster or disease *may* **come**,
8: 38 [A] when a prayer or plea *is* **made** by any of your people Israel—
8: 52 [A] "*May* your eyes **be** open to your servant's plea and to the
8: 54 [A] **[NIE]** When Solomon had finished all these prayers
8: 57 [A] *May* the LORD our God **be** with us as he was with our
8: 57 [A] May the LORD our God be with us as *he* **was** with our
8: 59 [A] *may* these words of mine, which I have prayed ... **be**
8: 61 [A] your hearts *must* **be** fully committed to the LORD our God,
9: 1 [A] **[NIE]** When Solomon had finished building the temple of
9: 3 [A] there forever. My eyes and my heart *will* always **be** there.
9: 7 [A] Israel *will* then **become** a byword and an object of ridicule
9: 8 [A] though this temple **is** *now* imposing, all who pass by will be
9: 10 [A] **[NIE]** At the end of twenty years, during which Solomon
9: 19 [A] **[NIE]** and the towns for his chariots and for his horses—
10: 2 [A] and talked with him about all that *she* **had** on her mind.
10: 3 [A] nothing **was** too hard for the king to explain to her.
10: 5 [A] she *was* **overwhelmed** [+928+4202+6388+8120].
10: 6 [A] country about your achievements and your wisdom **is** true.
10: 9 [A] Praise **be** to the LORD your God, who has delighted in you
10: 14 [A] The weight of the gold that Solomon received yearly **was**
10: 26 [A] he **had** [+4200] fourteen hundred chariots and twelve
11: 3 [A] He **had** [+4200] seven hundred wives of royal birth and three
11: 4 [A] **[NIE]** As Solomon grew old, his wives turned his heart after
11: 4 [A] and his heart **was** not fully devoted to the LORD his God,
11: 11 [A] "Since this **is** your attitude and you have not kept my
11: 15 [A] **Earlier** when David was fighting with Edom, Joab the
11: 15 [A] Earlier when David *was* **fighting** [+907] **with** Edom, Joab
11: 20 [A] There Genubath **lived** with Pharaoh's own children.
11: 24 [A] **became** the leader of a band of rebels when David destroyed
11: 25 [A] Rezon **was** Israel's adversary as long as Solomon lived,
11: 29 [A] **[NIE]** About that time Jeroboam was going out of
11: 32 [A] out of all the tribes of Israel, he *will* **have** [+4200] one tribe.
11: 36 [A] so that David my servant *may* always **have** [+4200] a lamp
11: 37 [A] over all that your heart desires; *you will* **be** king over Israel.
11: 38 [A] **[NIE]** If you do whatever I command you and walk in my
11: 38 [A] and commands, as David my servant did, *I will* **be** with you.
11: 40 [A] to Shishak the king, and **stayed** there until Solomon's death.
12: 2 [A] **[NIE]** When Jeroboam son of Nebat heard this (he was still
12: 6 [A] King Rehoboam consulted the elders who **[NIE]** had served
12: 6 [A] had served his father Solomon during **[NIE]** his lifetime.
12: 7 [A] "If today *you will* **be** a servant to these people and serve
12: 7 [A] them a favorable answer, *they will* always **be** your servants."
12: 15 [A] to the people, for this turn of events **was** from the LORD,
12: 20 [A] **[NIE]** When all the Israelites heard that Jeroboam had
12: 20 [A] Only the tribe of Judah **remained** loyal to the house of
12: 22 [A] But this word of God **came** to Shemaiah the man of God:
12: 24 [C] for this **is** my doing.' " So they obeyed the word of the
12: 30 [A] this thing **became** a sin; the people went even as far as Dan
12: 31 [A] from all sorts of people, even though *they* **were** not Levites.
13: 4 [A] **[NIE]** When King Jeroboam heard what the man of God
13: 6 [A] the king's hand was restored and **became** as it was before.
13: 20 [A] While they **were** sitting at the table, the word of the LORD
13: 20 [A] the word of the LORD **came** to the old prophet who had
13: 23 [A] When **[NIE]** the man of God had finished eating and
13: 24 [A] and killed him, and his body **was** thrown down on the road,
13: 31 [A] **[NIE]** After burying him, he said to his sons, "When I die,
13: 32 [A] in the towns of Samaria *will* **certainly come true** [+2118]."
13: 32 [A] in the towns of Samaria *will* **certainly come true** [+2118]."
13: 33 [A] Anyone who wanted *to* **become** a priest he consecrated for
13: 34 [A] This **was** the sin of the house of Jeroboam that led to its
14: 3 [A] and go to him. He will tell you what *will* **happen** to the boy."
14: 5 [A] **[NIE]** When she arrives, she will pretend to be someone
14: 6 [A] So **[NIE]** when Ahijah heard the sound of her footsteps at
14: 8 [A] gave it to you, but *you have* not **been** like my servant David,
14: 9 [A] You have done more evil than all who **lived** before you. You
14: 24 [A] *There* **were** even male shrine prostitutes in the land;
14: 25 [A] **[NIE]** In the fifth year of King Rehoboam, Shishak king of
14: 28 [A] **[NIE]** Whenever the king went to the LORD's temple,
14: 30 [A] *There* **was** continual warfare between Rehoboam
15: 3 [A] his heart **was** not fully devoted to the LORD his God,
15: 6 [A] *There* **was** war between Rehoboam and Jeroboam
15: 7 [A] of Judah? *There* **was** war between Abijah and Jeroboam.
15: 14 [A] Asa's heart **was** fully committed to the LORD all his life.
15: 16 [A] *There* **was** war between Asa and Baasha king of Israel
15: 21 [A] **[NIE]** When Baasha heard this, he stopped building Ramah
15: 29 [A] **[NIE]** As soon as he began to reign, he killed Jeroboam's
15: 32 [A] *There* **was** war between Asa and Baasha king of Israel
16: 1 [A] the word of the LORD **came** to Jehu son of Hanani against
16: 7 [A] the word of the LORD **came** through the prophet Jehu son
16: 7 [A] things he did, and **becoming** like the house of Jeroboam—
16: 11 [A] **[NIE]** As soon as he began to reign and was seated on the
16: 18 [A] **[NIE]** When Zimri saw that the city was taken, he went into
16: 21 [A] half **supported** [+339] Tibni son of Ginath for king, and the
16: 31 [A] **[NIE]** He not only considered it trivial to commit the sins of
16: 33 [A] to anger than did all the kings of Israel **[NIE]** before him.
17: 1 [A] *there will* **be** neither dew nor rain in the next few years
17: 2 [A] Then the word of the LORD **came** to Elijah:
17: 4 [A] **[NIE]** You will drink from the brook, and I have ordered
17: 7 [A] **[NIE]** Some time later the brook dried up because there had
17: 7 [A] brook dried up because *there had* **been** no rain in the land.
17: 8 [A] Then the word of the LORD **came** to him:
17: 17 [A] **[NIE]** Some time later the son of the woman who owned the
17: 17 [A] He **grew worse and worse** [+2617+2716+4394], and finally
18: 1 [A] **[NIE]** After a long time, in the third year, the word of the
18: 1 [A] in the third year, the word of the LORD **came** to Elijah:
18: 3 [A] of his palace. (Obadiah **was** a devout believer in the LORD.
18: 4 [A] **[NIE]** While Jezebel was killing off the LORD's prophets,
18: 7 [A] As Obadiah **was** walking along, Elijah met him. Obadiah
18: 12 [A] **[NIE]** I don't know where the Spirit of the LORD may
18: 17 [A] **[NIE]** When he saw Elijah, he said to him, "Is that you,
18: 24 [A] **[NIE]** The god who answers by fire—he is God." Then all
18: 27 [A] **[NIE]** At noon Elijah began to taunt them. "Shout louder!"
18: 29 [A] **[NIE]** Midday passed, and they continued their frantic

1Ki 18:31 [A] to whom the word of the LORD *had* **come**, saying,
18:31 [A] the LORD had come, saying, "Your name *shall* **be** Israel."
18:36 [A] **[NIE]** At the time of sacrifice, the prophet Elijah stepped
18:44 [A] **[NIE]** The seventh time the servant reported, "A cloud as
18:45 [A] **[NIE]** Meanwhile, the sky grew black with clouds, the wind
18:45 [A] a heavy rain **came on** and Ahab rode off to Jezreel.
18:46 [A] The power of the LORD **came** upon Elijah and, tucking his
19:13 [A] **[NIE]** When Elijah heard it, he pulled his cloak over his
19:17 [A] **[NIE]** Jehu will put to death any who escape the sword of
20: 6 [A] **[NIE]** They will seize everything you value and carry it
20:12 [A] **[NIE]** Ben-Hadad heard this message while he and the
20:15 [A] officers of the provincial commanders, **[NIE]** 232 men.
20:26 [A] **[NIE]** The next spring Ben-Hadad mustered the Arameans
20:29 [A] and **[NIE]** on the seventh day the battle was joined.
20:39 [A] As **[NIE]** the king passed by, the prophet called out to him,
20:39 [A] If he is missing, *it will* **be** your life for his life, or you must
20:40 [A] While your servant **was** busy here and there, the man
20:42 [A] Therefore *it* **is** your life for his life, your people for his
21: 1 [A] Some time later *there* **was** an incident involving a vineyard
21: 1 [A] a vineyard **belonging** [+4200] **to** Naboth the Jezreelite.
21: 2 [A] "Let me have your vineyard *to* **use** for a vegetable garden,
21:15 [A] **[NIE]** As soon as Jezebel heard that Naboth had been
21:16 [A] **[NIE]** When Ahab heard that Naboth was dead, he got up
21:17 [A] Then the word of the LORD **came** to Elijah the Tishbite:
21:25 [A] (*There* **was** never a man like Ahab, who sold himself to do
21:27 [A] **[NIE]** When Ahab heard these words, he tore his clothes,
21:28 [A] Then the word of the LORD **came** to Elijah the Tishbite:
22: 2 [A] **[NIE]** in the third year Jehoshaphat king of Judah went
22:13 [A] *Let* your word **agree** [+285+3869] with theirs, and speak
22:22 [A] go out and **be** a lying spirit in the mouths of all his prophets,'
22:32 [A] **[NIE]** When the chariot commanders saw Jehoshaphat, they
22:33 [A] **[NIE]** the chariot commanders saw that he was not the king
22:35 [A] the king **was** propped up in his chariot facing the Arameans.
2Ki 1:17 [A] Because Ahaziah **had** [+4200] no son, Joram succeeded him
2: 1 [A] **[NIE]** When the LORD was about to take Elijah up to
2: 9 [A] **[NIE]** When they had crossed, Elijah said to Elisha,
2: 9 [A] "*Let* me **inherit** [+448] a double portion of your spirit,"
2:10 [A] if you see me when I am taken from you, *it will* **be** yours—
2:10 [A] am taken from you, it will be yours—otherwise not." **[NIE]**
2:11 [A] As they **were** walking along and talking together, suddenly a
2:21 [A] Never again *will* it **cause** [+4946] death or make the land
3: 4 [A] Now Mesha king of Moab **[NIE]** raised sheep, and he had
3: 5 [A] **[NIE]** after Ahab died, the king of Moab rebelled against
3: 9 [A] the army **had** [+4200] no more water for themselves or for
3:15 [A] While the harpist **was** playing, the hand of the LORD came
3:15 [A] was playing, the hand of the LORD **came** upon Elisha
3:20 [A] **[NIE]** The next morning, about the time for offering the
3:27 [A] The fury against Israel **was** great; they withdrew and returned
4: 1 [A] is dead, and you know that he **[NIE]** revered the LORD.
4: 6 [A] **[NIE]** When all the jars were full, she said to her son,
4: 8 [A] **[NIE]** One day Elisha went to Shunem. And a well-to-do
4: 8 [A] So **[NIE]** whenever he came by, he stopped there to eat.
4:10 [A] Then **[NIE]** he can stay there whenever he comes to us."
4:11 [A] **[NIE]** One day when Elisha came, he went up to his room
4:18 [A] child grew, and one day **[NIE]** he went out to his father,
4:25 [A] **[NIE]** When he saw her in the distance, the man of God said
4:40 [A] **[NIE]** as they began to eat it, they cried out, "O man of
4:41 [A] the people to eat." And *there* **was** nothing harmful in the pot.
5: 1 [A] *He* **was** a great man in the sight of his master and highly
5: 1 [A] victory to Aram. He **was** a valiant soldier, but he had leprosy.
5: 2 [A] from Israel, and *she* **served** [+4200+7156] Naaman's wife.
5: 7 [A] **[NIE]** As soon as the king of Israel read the letter, he tore
5: 8 [A] **[NIE]** When Elisha the man of God heard that the king of
6: 5 [A] As one of them **was** cutting down a tree, the iron axhead fell
6: 8 [A] Now the king of Aram **was** at war with Israel.
6:20 [A] **[NIE]** After they entered the city, Elisha said, "LORD,
6:24 [A] **[NIE]** Some time later, Ben-Hadad king of Aram mobilized
6:25 [A] *There* **was** a great famine in the city; the siege lasted so long
6:25 [A] so long that a donkey's head **sold** [+928] **for** eighty shekels
6:26 [A] As the king of Israel **was** passing by on the wall, a woman
6:30 [A] **[NIE]** When the king heard the woman's words, he tore his
7: 2 [A] open the floodgates of the heavens, *could* this **happen**?"
7: 3 [A] Now *there* **were** four men with leprosy at the entrance of the
7:16 [A] So a seah of flour **sold** [+928] **for** a shekel, and two seahs of
7:18 [A] *It* **happened** as the man of God had said to the king: "About
7:18 [A] a seah of flour *will* **sell** [+928] **for** a shekel and two seahs of
7:19 [A] open the floodgates of the heavens, *could* this **happen**?"
7:20 [A] that is exactly *what* **happened** to him, for the people
8: 3 [A] **[NIE]** At the end of the seven years she came back from the
8: 5 [A] Just as Gehazi **was** telling the king how Elisha had restored
8:15 [A] **[NIE]** the next day he took a thick cloth, soaked it in water
8:17 [A] *He* **was** thirty-two years old when he became king, and he
8:18 [A] for *he* **married** [+851+4200+4200] a daughter of Ahab.
8:21 [A] but **[NIE]** he rose up and broke through by night;
9:14 [A] all Israel *had* **been** defending Ramoth Gilead against Hazael
9:22 [A] **[NIE]** When Joram saw Jehu he asked, "Have you come in
9:37 [A] Jezebel's body *will* **be** like refuse on the ground in the plot at
10: 7 [A] **[NIE]** When the letter arrived, these men took the princes
10: 9 [A] **[NIE]** The next morning Jehu went out. He stood before all
10:25 [A] **[NIE]** As soon as Jehu had finished making the burnt
11: 3 [A] *He* **remained** hidden with his nurse at the temple of the
11: 8 [A] be put to death. **Stay** close to the king wherever he goes."
11:17 [A] the king and people that *they would* **be** the LORD's people.
12: 6 [12:7] [A] **[NIE]** by the twenty-third year of King Joash the
12:10 [12:11] [A] **[NIE]** Whenever they saw that there was a large
12:16 [12:17] [A] of the LORD; *it* **belonged** [+4200] **to** the priests.
13:21 [A] **Once** while some Israelites were burying a man, suddenly
14: 2 [A] *He* **was** twenty-five years old when he became king, and he
14: 5 [A] **[NIE]** After the kingdom was firmly in his grasp, he
15: 2 [A] *He* **was** sixteen years old when he became king, and he
15: 5 [A] The LORD afflicted the king **[NIE]** with leprosy until the
15:12 [A] word of the LORD spoken to Jehu *was* **fulfilled** [+4027]:
15:19 [A] a thousand talents of silver to **gain** his **support** [+907+3338]
15:33 [A] *He* **was** twenty-five years old when he became king, and he
16:15 [A] But I *will* **use** [+4200] the bronze altar for seeking guidance."
17: 2 [A] not like the kings of Israel who **preceded** [+4200+7156] him.
17: 3 [A] who *had* **been** Shalmaneser's vassal and had paid him
17: 7 [A] *All this* **took place** because the Israelites had sinned against
17:25 [A] **[NIE]** When they first lived there, they did not worship the
17:25 [A] lions among them and **[NIE]** they killed some of the people.
17:28 [A] and **taught** [+906+3723] them how to worship the LORD.
17:29 [A] each national group **[NIE]** made its own gods in the several
17:32 [A] **[NIE]** They worshiped the LORD, but they also appointed
17:32 [A] they also appointed all sorts of their own people **[NIE]** to
17:33 [A] **[NIE]** They worshiped the LORD, but they also served
17:33 [A] **[NIE]** they also served their own gods in accordance with
17:41 [A] Even while these people **were** worshiping the LORD, they
17:41 [A] were worshiping the LORD, *they* **were** serving their idols.
18: 1 [A] **[NIE]** In the third year of Hoshea son of Elah king of Israel,
18: 2 [A] *He* **was** twenty-five years old when he became king, and he
18: 4 [A] for up to that time the Israelites *had* **been** burning incense to
18: 5 [A] *There* **was** no *one* like him among all the kings of Judah,
18: 5 [A] all the kings of Judah, either **[RPH]** before him or after him.
18: 7 [A] the LORD **was** with him; he was successful in whatever he
18: 9 [A] **[NIE]** In King Hezekiah's fourth year, which was the
19: 1 [A] **[NIE]** When King Hezekiah heard this, he tore his clothes
19:25 [A] that **[NIE]** you have turned fortified cities into piles of
19:26 [A] *They* **are** like plants in the field, like tender green shoots,
19:35 [A] **[NIE]** That night the angel of the LORD went out and put
19:37 [A] **One day** [+2256], while he was worshiping in the temple of
20: 4 [A] **[NIE]** Before Isaiah had left the middle court, the word of
20: 4 [A] left the middle court, the word of the LORD **came** to him:
20:13 [A] *There* **was** nothing in his palace or in all his kingdom that
20:15 [A] "*There* **is** nothing among my treasures that I did not show
20:18 [A] *they will* **become** eunuchs in the palace of the king of
20:19 [A] "*Will there* not **be** peace and security in my lifetime?"
21:14 [A] *They will* **be** looted and plundered by all their foes,
21:15 [A] **have** provoked me to anger from the day their forefathers
22: 3 [A] **[NIE]** In the eighteenth year of his reign, King Josiah sent
22:11 [A] **[NIE]** When the king heard the words of the Book of the
22:19 [A] that they *would* **become** accursed and laid waste, and
23:25 [A] Neither before nor after Josiah **was** *there* a king like him
23:27 [A] this temple, about which I said, 'There *shall* my Name **be**.' "
24: 1 [A] the land, and Jehoiakim **became** his vassal for three years.
24: 3 [A] Surely *these things* **happened** to Judah according to the
24: 7 [A] **[NIE]** from the Wadi of Egypt to the Euphrates River.
24:20 [A] because of the LORD's anger that *all this* **happened** to
25: 1 [A] So **[NIE]** in the ninth year of Zedekiah's reign, on the tenth
25: 3 [A] so severe that *there* **was** no food for the people to eat.
25:16 [A] the temple of the LORD, **was** more than could be weighed.
25:25 [A] **[NIE]** In the seventh month, however, Ishmael son of
25:25 [A] of Judah and the Babylonians who **were** with him at Mizpah.
25:27 [A] **[NIE]** In the thirty-seventh year of the exile of Jehoiachin
1Ch 1:10 [A] father of Nimrod, who grew to **be** a mighty warrior on earth.
1:51 [A] also died. The chiefs of Edom **were**: Timna, Alvah, Jetheth,
2: 3 [A] Er, Judah's firstborn, **was** wicked in the LORD's sight;
2:22 [A] who **controlled** [+4200] twenty-three towns in Gilead.
2:25 [A] **[NIE]** The sons of Jerahmeel the firstborn of Hezron:
2:26 [A] Jerahmeel **had** [+4200] another wife, whose name was
2:27 [A] **[NIE]** The sons of Ram the firstborn of Jerahmeel: Maaz,
2:28 [A] **[NIE]** The sons of Onam: Shammai and Jada. The sons of
2:33 [A] Peleth and Zaza. These **were** the descendants of Jerahmeel.
2:34 [A] Sheshan **had** [+4200] no sons—only daughters. He had an
2:50 [A] These **were** the descendants of Caleb. The sons of Hur the
2:52 [A] The descendants of Shobal the father of Kiriath Jearim **were**:
3: 1 [A] These **were** the sons of David born to him in Hebron:
4: 5 [A] Ashhur the father of Tekoa **had** [+4200] two wives, Helah
4: 9 [A] Jabez **was** more honorable than his brothers. His mother had

1Ch 4:10 [A] *Let* your hand **be** with me, and keep me from harm so that I
4:14 [A] It was called this because *its people* **were** craftsmen.
6:32 [6:17] [A] **[NIE]** They ministered with music before the
6:54 [6:39] [A] Kohathite clan, because the first lot **was** for them):
6:66 [6:51] [A] Some of the Kohathite clans *were* **given** as their
7:15 [A] was named Zelophehad, who **had** [+4200] only daughters.
7:19 [A] The sons of Shemida **were**: Ahian, Shechem, Likhi
7:23 [A] because *there had* **been** misfortune in his family.
8:3 [A] The sons of Bela **were**: Addar, Gera, Abihud,
8:40 [A] The sons of Ulam **were** brave warriors who could handle the
9:20 [A] In earlier times Phinehas son of Eleazar **was** in charge of the
9:24 [A] The gatekeepers **were** on the four sides: east, west, north and
9:26 [A] were entrusted with **[NIE]** the responsibility for the rooms
10:8 [A] **[NIE]** The next day, when the Philistines came to strip the
11:2 [A] In the past, even while Saul **was** king, you were the one who
11:2 [A] my people Israel, and you *will* **become** their ruler.' "
11:6 [A] "Whoever leads the attack on the Jebusites *will* **become**
11:6 [A] of Zeruiah went up first, and so *he* **received** the command.
11:13 [A] He **was** with David at Pas Dammim when the Philistines
11:13 [A] At a place where *there* **was** a field full of barley, the troops
11:20 [A] Abishai the brother of Joab **was** chief of the Three. He raised
11:21 [A] honored above the Three and **became** their commander,
12:17 [12:18] [A] *to have* you **unite** [+3480+4200+4222+6584] with me.
12:21 [12:22] [A] and *they* **were** commanders in his army.
12:39 [12:40] [A] *The men* **spent** three days there with David, eating
14:4 [A] These are the names of the children born **[NIE]** to him
14:15 [A] **[NIE]** As soon as you hear the sound of marching in the
15:25 [A] So **[NIE]** David and the elders of Israel
15:26 [A] **[NIE]** Because God had helped the Levites who were
15:29 [A] As the ark of the covenant of the LORD **was** entering the
16:19 [A] When they **were** but few in number, few indeed,
17:1 [A] **[NIE]** After David was settled in his palace, he said to
17:3 [A] **[NIE]** That night the word of God came to Nathan, saying:
17:3 [A] That night the word of God **came** to Nathan, saying:
17:5 [A] *I have* **moved** from one tent site to another, from one
17:7 [A] from following the flock, to **be** ruler over my people Israel.
17:8 [A] *I have* **been** with you wherever you have gone, and I have
17:11 [A] **[NIE]** When your days are over and you go to be with your
17:11 [A] **[NIE]** one of your own sons, and I will establish his
17:13 [A] I *will* **be** his father, and he will be my son. I will never take
17:13 [A] I will be his father, and he *will* **be** my son. I will never take
17:13 [A] as I took it away from your **predecessor** [+889+4200+7156].
17:14 [A] kingdom forever; his throne *will* **be** established forever.' "
17:22 [A] own forever, and you, O LORD, *have* **become** their God.
17:27 [A] of your servant, that *it may* **continue** forever in your sight;
18:1 [A] **[NIE]** In the course of time, David defeated the Philistines
18:2 [A] and they **became** subject to him and brought tribute.
18:6 [A] the Arameans **became** subject to him and brought tribute.
18:7 [A] David took the gold shields **carried by** [+6584] the officers
18:10 [A] in battle over Hadadezer, who *had* **been** at war with Tou.
18:13 [A] in Edom, and all the Edomites **became** subject to David.
18:14 [A] **[NIE]** doing what was just and right for all his people.
19:1 [A] **[NIE]** In the course of time, Nahash king of the Ammonites
19:5 [A] messengers to meet them, for they **were** greatly humiliated.
19:10 [A] Joab saw that *there* **were** battle lines in front of him
19:12 [A] Arameans are too strong for me, then *you* **are** *to* rescue me;
20:1 [A] **[NIE]** In the spring, at the time when kings go off to war,
20:2 [A] set with precious stones—and *it* **was** placed on David's head.
20:4 [A] **[NIE]** In the course of time, war broke out with the
20:5 [A] **[NIE]** In another battle with the Philistines, Elhanan son of
20:6 [A] In still another battle, *which* **took place** at Gath, there was a
20:6 [A] *there* **was** a huge man with six fingers on each hand and six
21:3 [A] to do this? Why *should he* **bring** [+4200] guilt on Israel?"
21:5 [A] In all Israel *there* **were** one million one hundred thousand
21:17 [A] LORD my God, *let* your hand **fall** upon me and my family,
22:7 [A] I **had** *it* in my heart to build a house for the Name of the
22:8 [A] this word of the LORD **came** to me: 'You have shed much
22:9 [A] But you will have a son who *will* **be** a man of peace and rest,
22:9 [A] His name *will* **be** Solomon, and I will grant Israel peace
22:10 [A] for my Name. He *will* **be** my son, and I will be his father.
22:11 [A] "Now, my son, the LORD **be** with you, and may you have
22:14 [A] quantities of bronze and iron too great *to* **be** weighed,
22:16 [A] Now begin the work, and the LORD **be** with you."
23:3 [A] and the total number of men **was** thirty-eight thousand.
23:11 [A] Jahath **was** the first and Ziza the second, but Jeush
23:11 [A] so *they* **were** counted as one family with one assignment.
23:17 [A] Rehabiah **was** the first. Eliezer had no other sons,
23:17 [A] Eliezer **had** [+4200] no other sons, but the sons of Rehabiah
23:22 [A] Eleazar died without **having** [+4200] sons: he had only
24:2 [A] died before their father did, and they **had** [+4200] no sons;
24:5 [A] for *there* **were** officials of the sanctuary and officials of God
24:28 [A] From Mahli: Eleazar, who **had** [+4200] no sons.
25:1 [A] *Here* **is** the list of the men who performed this service:
25:7 [A] in music for the LORD—they **[NIE]** numbered 288.
26:10 [A] Shimri the first (although *he* **was** not the firstborn, his father
27:24 [A] Wrath **came** on Israel on account of this numbering,
28:4 [A] chose me from my whole family to **be** king over Israel
28:6 [A] for I have chosen him to be my son, and I *will* **be** his father.
28:12 [A] He gave him the plans of all that the Spirit *had* **put** in his
29:25 [A] such as no king over Israel ever **had** [+6584] before.
2Ch 1:3 [A] high place at Gibeon, for God's Tent of Meeting **was** there,
1:11 [A] "Since this **is** your heart's desire and you have not asked for
1:12 [A] such as no king who was before you *ever* **had** and none after
1:12 [A] who was before you ever had and none after you *will* **have**."
1:14 [A] he **had** [+4200] fourteen hundred chariots and twelve
5:8 [A] **[NIE]** The cherubim spread their wings over the place of
5:9 [A] from outside the Holy Place; and *they* **are** still there today.
5:11 [A] The priests then **[NIE]** withdrew from the Holy Place. All
5:13 [A] The trumpeters and singers **joined** in unison, as with one
6:5 [A] tribe of Israel to have a temple built for my Name to **be** there,
6:5 [A] nor have I chosen anyone to **be** the leader over my people
6:6 [A] But now I have chosen Jerusalem for my Name to **be** there,
6:6 [A] and I have chosen David to **rule** [+6584] my people Israel.'
6:7 [A] "My father David **had** *it* in his heart to build a temple for the
6:8 [A] 'Because *it* **was** in your heart to build a temple for my Name,
6:8 [A] temple for my Name, you did well *to* **have** this in your heart.
6:20 [A] *May* your eyes **be** open toward this temple day and night,
6:26 [A] "When the heavens are shut up and *there* **is** no rain
6:28 [A] "When famine or plague **comes** to the land, or blight
6:28 [A] **[RPH]** or blight or mildew, locusts or grasshoppers,
6:28 [A] in any of their cities, whatever disaster or disease *may* **come**,
6:29 [A] when a prayer or plea *is* **made** by any of your people Israel—
6:40 [A] *may* your eyes **be** open and your ears attentive to the prayers
7:13 [A] "When I shut up the heavens so that *there* **is** no rain,
7:15 [A] Now my eyes *will* **be** open and my ears attentive to the
7:16 [A] this temple so that my Name *may* **be** there forever.
7:16 [A] be there forever. My eyes and my heart *will* always **be** there.
7:21 [A] though this temple **is** now so imposing, all who pass by will
8:1 [A] **[NIE]** At the end of twenty years, during which Solomon
8:6 [A] as well as Baalath and all **[NIE]** his store cities, and all the
9:1 [A] and talked with him about all *she* **had** on her mind.
9:4 [A] she *was* **overwhelmed** [+928+4202+6388+8120].
9:8 [A] Praise **be** to the LORD your God, who has delighted in you
9:9 [A] *There had* never **been** such spices as those the queen of
9:13 [A] The weight of the gold that Solomon received yearly **was**
9:25 [A] Solomon **had** [+4200] four thousand stalls for horses
9:26 [A] **[NIE]** He ruled over all the kings from the River to the land
10:2 [A] **[NIE]** When Jeroboam son of Nebat heard this (he was in
10:6 [A] King Rehoboam consulted the elders who **[NIE]** had served
10:6 [A] had served his father Solomon during **[NIE]** his lifetime.
10:7 [A] "If *you will* **be** kind to these people and please them and give
10:7 [A] them a favorable answer, *they will* always **be** your servants."
10:15 [A] not listen to the people, for this turn of events **was** from God,
11:2 [A] this word of the LORD **came** to Shemaiah the man of God:
11:4 [C] for this **is** my doing.' " So they obeyed the words of the
11:12 [A] made them very strong. So Judah and Benjamin **were** his.
12:1 [A] **[NIE]** After Rehoboam's position as king was established
12:2 [A] **[NIE]** Because they had been unfaithful to the LORD,
12:7 [A] this word of the LORD **came** to Shemaiah:
12:8 [A] *They will*, however, **become** subject to him, so that they may
12:11 [A] **[NIE]** Whenever the king went to the LORD's temple,
12:12 [A] not totally destroyed. Indeed, *there* **was** some good in Judah.
13:2 [A] of Gibeah. *There* **was** war between Abijah and Jeroboam.
13:7 [A] and opposed Rehoboam son of Solomon when he **was** young
13:9 [A] and seven rams *may* **become** a priest of what are not gods.
13:13 [A] so that *while he* **was** in front of Judah the ambush was
13:15 [A] **[NIE]** At the sound of their battle cry, God routed Jeroboam
14:8 [14:7] [A] Asa **had** [+4200] an army of three hundred thousand
14:14 [14:13] [A] for the terror of the LORD *had* **fallen** upon them.
14:14 [14:13] [A] all these villages, since *there* **was** much booty there.
15:1 [A] The Spirit of God **came** upon Azariah son of Oded.
15:2 [A] The LORD is with you when you **are** with him.
15:17 [A] Asa's heart **was** fully committed ˻to the LORD˼ all his life.
15:19 [A] *There* **was** no more war until the thirty-fifth year of Asa's
16:5 [A] **[NIE]** When Baasha heard this, he stopped building Ramah
16:8 [A] **Were** not the Cushites and Libyans a mighty army with great
17:3 [A] The LORD **was** with Jehoshaphat because in his early years
17:5 [A] so that he **had** [+4200] great wealth and honor.
17:10 [A] The fear of the LORD **fell** on all the kingdoms of the lands
17:12 [A] Jehoshaphat **became** more and more powerful; he built forts
17:13 [A] **had** [+4200] large supplies in the towns of Judah. He also
18:1 [A] Now Jehoshaphat **had** [+4200] great wealth and honor,
18:12 [A] *Let* your word **agree** [+285+3869] with theirs, and speak
18:21 [A] will go and **be** a lying spirit in the mouths of all his prophets,'
18:31 [A] **[NIE]** When the chariot commanders saw Jehoshaphat, they
18:32 [A] for **[NIE]** when the chariot commanders saw that he was not
18:32 [A] for when the chariot commanders saw that *he* **was** not the
18:34 [A] the king of Israel **[NIE]** propped himself up in his chariot

2Ch 19: 7 [A] Now *let* the fear of the LORD **be** upon you. Judge carefully,
19: 10 [A] otherwise his wrath *will* **come** on you and your brothers.
19: 11 [A] and *may* the LORD **be** with those who do well."
20: 1 [A] **[NIE]** After this, the Moabites and Ammonites with some
20: 14 [A] the Spirit of the LORD **came** upon Jahaziel son of
20: 25 [A] *There* **was** so much plunder that it took three days to collect
20: 29 [A] The fear of God **came** upon all the kingdoms of the countries
21: 6 [A] had done, for he **married** [+851+4200] a daughter of Ahab.
21: 9 [A] but **[NIE]** he rose up and broke through by night.
21: 19 [A] **[NIE]** In the course of time, at the end of the second year,
21: 20 [A] Jehoram **was** thirty-two years old when he became king,
22: 3 [A] for his mother **[NIE]** encouraged him in doing wrong.
22: 4 [A] for after his father's death they **became** his advisers, to his
22: 7 [A] to Joram, God **brought** [+4946] **about** Ahaziah's downfall.
22: 8 [A] While Jehu **was** executing judgment on the house of Ahab,
22: 11 [A] **was** Ahaziah's sister, she hid the child from Athaliah so she
22: 12 [A] *He* **remained** hidden with them at the temple of God for six
23: 7 [A] be put to death. **Stay** close to the king wherever he goes."
23: 16 [A] and the people and the king *would* **be** the LORD's people.
24: 4 [A] **[NIE]** Some time later Joash decided to restore the temple
24: 4 [A] Some time later Joash **decided** [+4213+6640] to restore the
24: 11 [A] **[NIE]** Whenever the chest was brought in by the Levites to
24: 12 [A] **[NIE]** They hired masons and carpenters to restore the
24: 14 [A] burnt offerings **were** presented continually in the temple of
24: 18 [A] of their guilt, God's anger **came** upon Judah and Jerusalem.
24: 23 [A] **[NIE]** At the turn of the year, the army of Aram marched
25: 3 [A] **[NIE]** After the kingdom was firmly in his control, he
25: 14 [A] **[NIE]** When Amaziah returned from slaughtering the
25: 16 [A] While he **was** still speaking, the king said to him, "Have we
26: 5 [A] **[NIE]** He sought God during the days of Zechariah,
26: 10 [A] because he **had** [+4200] much livestock in the foothills
26: 10 [A] the hills and in the fertile lands, for he loved the soil. **[NIE]**
26: 11 [A] Uzziah **had** [+4200] a well-trained army, ready to go out by
26: 15 [A] machines designed by skillful men for **use** on the towers
26: 21 [A] **[NIE]** King Uzziah had leprosy until the day he died. He
27: 8 [A] *He* **was** twenty-five years old when he became king, and he
28: 9 [A] a prophet of the LORD named Oded **was** there, and he went
28: 23 [A] But they **were** his downfall and the downfall of all Israel.
29: 8 [A] the anger of the LORD *has* **fallen** on Judah and Jerusalem;
29: 11 [A] to **[NIE]** minister before him and to burn incense."
29: 32 [A] The number of burnt offerings the assembly brought **was**
29: 34 [A] however, **were** too few to skin all the burnt offerings;
29: 36 [A] brought about for his people, because it *was* **done** so quickly.
30: 7 [A] *Do* not **be** like your fathers and brothers, who were unfaithful
30: 10 [A] **[NIE]** The couriers went from town to town in Ephraim
30: 10 [A] but **[NIE]** the people scorned and ridiculed them.
30: 12 [A] Also in Judah the hand of God **was** on the people to give
30: 26 [A] *There* **was** great joy in Jerusalem, for since the days of
32: 25 [A] therefore the LORD's wrath **was** on him and on Judah
32: 27 [A] Hezekiah **had** [+4200] very great riches and honor, and he
32: 31 [A] him about the miraculous sign that *had* **occurred** in the land,
33: 4 [A] had said, "My Name *will* **remain** in Jerusalem forever."
34: 19 [A] **[NIE]** When the king heard the words of the Law, he tore
36: 16 [A] **[NIE]** they mocked God's messengers, despised his words
36: 20 [A] *they* **became** servants to him and his sons until the kingdom
Ezr 1: 3 [A] *may* his God **be** with him, and let him go up to Jerusalem in
4: 4 [A] **[NIE]** the peoples around them set out to discourage the
8: 31 [A] The hand of our God **was** on us, and he protected us from
9: 2 [A] officials *have* **led the way** [+3338+8037] in this
9: 8 [A] the LORD our God *has* **been** gracious in leaving us a
Ne 1: 1 [A] **[NIE]** In the month of Kislev in the twentieth year, while I
1: 1 [A] in the twentieth year, while I **was** in the citadel of Susa,
1: 4 [A] **[NIE]** When I heard these things, I sat down and wept. For
1: 4 [A] For some days I mourned and **[NIE]** fasted and prayed
1: 6 [A] *let* your ear **be** attentive and your eyes open to hear the
1: 9 [A] then even if your exiled people **are** at the farthest horizon,
1: 11 [A] *let* your ear **be** attentive to the prayer of this your servant
1: 11 [A] in the presence of this man." I **was** cupbearer to the king.
2: 1 [A] **[NIE]** In the month of Nisan in the twentieth year of King
2: 1 [A] gave it to the king. *I had* not **been** sad in his presence before;
2: 6 [A] asked me, "How long *will* your journey **take**, and when will
2: 11 [A] I went to Jerusalem, and after **staying** there three days
2: 13 [A] the Dung Gate, **[NIE]** examining the walls of Jerusalem,
2: 15 [A] so **[NIE]** I went up the valley by night, examining the wall.
2: 15 [A] so I went up the valley by night, **[NIE]** examining the wall.
2: 17 [A] the wall of Jerusalem, and *we will* no longer **be** in disgrace."
3: 26 [A] the temple servants **[NIE]** living on the hill of Ophel made
4: 1 [3:33] [A] **[NIE]** When Sanballat heard that we were
4: 4 [3:36] [A] Hear us, O our God, for *we* **are** despised. Turn their
4: 6 [3:38] [A] for **[NIE]** the people worked with all their heart.
4: 7 [4:1] [A] **[NIE]** when Sanballat, Tobiah, the Arabs,
4: 12 [4:6] [A] **[NIE]** the Jews who lived near them came and told us
4: 15 [4:9] [A] **[NIE]** When our enemies heard that we were aware
4: 16 [4:10] [A] **[NIE]** From that day on, half of my men did the
4: 22 [4:16] [A] so *they can* **serve** us as guards by night
5: 1 [A] their wives **raised** a great outcry against their Jewish
5: 13 [A] So *may such a man* **be** shaken out and emptied!" At this the
5: 14 [A] when I was appointed to **be** their governor in the land of
5: 18 [A] **[NIE]** Each day one ox, six choice sheep and some poultry
6: 1 [A] **[NIE]** When word came to Sanballat, Tobiah, Geshem the
6: 8 [C] "Nothing like what you are saying *is* **happening**; you are just
6: 13 [A] they *would* **give** [+4200+4200] me a bad name to discredit
6: 14 [A] the rest of the prophets who *have* **been** trying to intimidate
6: 16 [A] **[NIE]** When all our enemies heard about this, all the
6: 19 [A] *they* **kept** reporting to me his good deeds and then telling
6: 19 [A] me his good deeds and then **[RPH]** telling him what I said.
7: 1 [A] **[NIE]** After the wall had been rebuilt and I had set the doors
8: 5 [A] people could see him because *he was* **standing** above them;
8: 17 [A] had not celebrated it like this. And their joy **was** very great.
10: 38 [10:39] [A] A priest descended from Aaron **is** to accompany the
12: 12 [A] of Joiakim, *these* **were** the heads of the priestly families:
13: 3 [A] **[NIE]** When the people heard this law, they excluded from
13: 5 [A] he had provided him with a large room formerly **used** to
13: 6 [A] while all this was going on, *I* **was** not in Jerusalem, for in the
13: 19 [A] **[NIE]** When evening shadows fell on the gates of Jerusalem
13: 22 [A] Then I commanded the Levites **[NIE]** to purify themselves
13: 26 [A] Among the many nations *there* **was** no king like him. He
13: 26 [A] by his God, **[NIE]** and God made him king over all Israel,
Est 1: 1 [A] *This is what* **happened** during the time of Xerxes,
1: 22 [A] that every man *should* **be** ruler over his own household.
2: 5 [A] Now *there* **was** in the citadel of Susa a Jew of the tribe of
2: 7 [A] **[NIE]** Mordecai had a cousin named Hadassah, whom he
2: 8 [A] **[NIE]** When the king's order and edict had been
2: 12 [A] she *had to* **complete** [+4200+4946+7891] twelve months of
2: 15 [A] And Esther **[NIE]** won the favor of everyone who saw her.
2: 20 [A] instructions as *she had* **done** when he was bringing her up.
3: 4 [A] **[NIE]** Day after day they spoke to him but he refused to
3: 14 [A] of every nationality so they *would* **be** ready for that day.
5: 1 [A] **[NIE]** On the third day Esther put on her royal robes
5: 2 [A] **[NIE]** When he saw Queen Esther standing in the court,
6: 1 [A] record of his reign, to be brought in and **[NIE]** read to him.
8: 13 [A] so that the Jews *would* **be** ready on that day to avenge
8: 16 [A] For the Jews *it* **was** a time of happiness and joy, gladness
9: 21 [A] to have them **[NIE]** celebrate annually the fourteenth and
9: 27 [A] all who join them should without fail **[NIE]** observe these
Job 1: 1 [A] In the land of Uz *there* **lived** a man whose name was Job.
1: 1 [A] This man **was** blameless and upright; he feared God
1: 3 [A] he **owned** [+5238] seven thousand sheep, three thousand
1: 3 [A] *He* **was** the greatest man among all the people of the East.
1: 5 [A] **[NIE]** When a period of feasting had run its course, Job
1: 6 [A] **[NIE]** One day the angels came to present themselves
1: 13 [A] **[NIE]** One day when Job's sons and daughters were
1: 14 [A] "The oxen **were** plowing and the donkeys were grazing
1: 21 [A] has taken away; *may* the name of the LORD **be** praised."
2: 1 [A] **[NIE]** On another day the angels came to present
3: 4 [A] That day—*may it* **turn to** darkness; may God above not care
3: 7 [A] *May* that night **be** barren; may no shout of joy be heard in it.
3: 16 [A] Or why **was** *I* not hidden in the ground like a stillborn child,
5: 16 [A] So the poor **have** [+4200] hope, and injustice shuts its mouth.
6: 10 [A] I *would* still **have** this consolation—my joy in unrelenting
6: 21 [A] Now *you* too *have* **proved to be** of no help; you see
6: 29 [A] Relent, *do* not **be** unjust; reconsider, for my integrity is at
7: 20 [A] you made me your target? *Have I* **become** a burden to you?
8: 7 [A] Your beginnings *will* **seem** humble, so prosperous will your
10: 19 [A] If only *I had* never **come into being** [+2118], or had been
10: 19 [A] If only *I had* never **come into being** [+2118], or had been
11: 4 [A] to God, 'My beliefs are flawless and *I* **am** pure in your sight.'
11: 15 [A] face without shame; *you will* **stand** firm and without fear.
11: 17 [A] than noonday, and darkness *will* **become** like morning.
12: 4 [A] "*I have* **become** a laughingstock to my friends, though I
13: 5 [A] would be altogether silent! For you, *that would* **be** wisdom.
15: 31 [A] trusting what is worthless, for he *will* **get** nothing in return.
16: 8 [A] *it has* **become** a witness; my gauntness rises up and testifies
16: 12 [A] All **was** well *with me*, but he shattered me; he seized me by
16: 18 [A] do not cover my blood; *may* my cry never **be** laid to rest!
17: 6 [A] to everyone, a man in whose face people spit. **[NIE]**
18: 12 [A] Calamity **is** hungry for him; disaster is ready for him when he
19: 15 [A] count me a stranger; they look upon me **[NIE]** as an alien.
20: 23 [A] When *he* **has** filled his belly, God will vent his burning anger
21: 2 [A] to my words; *let* this **be** the consolation you give me.
21: 18 [A] How often **are** *they* like straw before the wind, like chaff
22: 25 [A] the Almighty *will* **be** your gold, the choicest silver for you.
24: 13 [A] "*There* **are** those who rebel against the light, who do not
24: 14 [A] the poor and needy; in the night *he* **steals forth** like a thief.
27: 7 [A] "*May* my enemies **be** like the wicked, my adversaries like
29: 4 [A] Oh, for the days when *I* **was** in my prime, when God's
29: 15 [A] *I* **was** eyes to the blind and feet to the lame.
30: 9 [A] me in song; **[RPH]** I have become a byword among them.

Job 30: 9 [A] mock me in song; *I have* **become** a byword among them.
30:29 [A] *I have* **become** a brother of jackals, a companion of owls.
30:31 [A] My harp **is** tuned to mourning, and my flute to the sound of
38: 4 [A] "Where *were* **you** when I laid the earth's foundation?
42: 7 [A] **[NIE]** After the LORD had said these things to Job, he
42:12 [A] He **had** [+4200] fourteen thousand sheep, six thousand
42:13 [A] And he also **had** [+4200] seven sons and three daughters.
Ps 1: 3 [A] *He* **is** like a tree planted by streams of water, which yields its
9: 9 [9:10] [A] The LORD **is** a refuge for the oppressed,
10:14 [A] commits himself to you; you **are** the helper of the fatherless.
18:18 [18:19] [A] day of my disaster, but the LORD **was** my support.
18:23 [18:24] [A] *I have* **been** blameless before him and have kept
19:14 [19:15] [A] and the meditation of my heart **be**
22:14 [22:15] [A] My heart *has* **turned** to wax; it has melted away
27: 9 [A] turn your servant away in anger; *you have* **been** my helper.
30: 7 [30:8] [A] but when you hid your face, *I* **was** dismayed.
30:10 [30:11] [A] and be merciful to me; O LORD, **be** my help."
31: 2 [31:3] [A] **be** my rock of refuge, a strong fortress to save me.
31:11 [31:12] [A] *I* **am** the utter contempt of my neighbors;
31:12 [31:13] [A] I were dead; *I have* **become** like broken pottery.
32: 9 [A] *Do* not **be** like the horse or the mule, which have no
33: 9 [A] For he spoke, and *it* **came to be**; he commanded, and it stood
33:22 [A] *May* your unfailing love **rest** upon us, O LORD, even as we
35: 5 [A] *May they* **be** like chaff before the wind, with the angel of the
35: 6 [A] *may* their path **be** dark and slippery, with the angel of the
37:18 [A] to the LORD, and their inheritance *will* **endure** forever.
37:25 [A] *I* **was** young and now I am old, yet I have never seen the
38:14 [38:15] [A] *I have* **become** like a man who does not hear,
42: 3 [42:4] [A] My tears *have* **been** my food day and night,
45:16 [45:17] [A] Your sons *will* **take the place of** [+9393] your
50:21 [A] I kept silent; you thought *I* **was** [+2118] **altogether** like you.
50:21 [A] I kept silent; you thought *I* **was altogether** [+2118] like you.
53: 5 [53:6] [A] with dread, where *there* **was** nothing to dread.
55:18 [55:19] [A] against me, even though many **[NIE]** oppose me.
59:16 [59:17] [A] *you* **are** my fortress, my refuge in times of trouble.
61: 3 [61:4] [A] For *you have* **been** my refuge, a strong tower against
63: T [63:1] [A] psalm of David. When he **was** in the Desert of Judah.
63: 7 [63:8] [A] Because *you* **are** my help, I sing in the shadow of
63:10 [63:11] [A] over to the sword and **become** food for jackals.
64: 7 [64:8] [A] with arrows; suddenly they *will* **be** struck down.
69: 8 [69:9] [A] *I* **am** a stranger to my brothers, an alien to my own
69:10 [69:11] [A] and fast, I *must* **endure** [+4200+4200] scorn;
69:11 [69:12] [A] people **make sport of me** [+4200+4200+5442].
69:22 [69:23] [A] *May* the table set before them **become** a snare;
69:25 [69:26] [A] *May* their place **be** deserted; let there be no one to
69:25 [69:26] [A] *let there* **be** no one to dwell in their tents.
71: 3 [A] **Be** my rock of refuge, to which I can always go; give the
71: 7 [A] *I have* **become** like a portent to many, but you are my strong
72:16 [A] *Let* grain **abound** [+7172] throughout the land; on the tops
72:17 [A] *May* his name **endure** forever; may it continue as long as the
73:14 [A] All day long *I have* **been** plagued; I have been punished
73:19 [A] How suddenly **are** *they* destroyed, completely swept away
73:22 [A] I was senseless and ignorant; *I* **was** a brute beast before you.
76: 2 [76:3] [A] His tent **is** in Salem, his dwelling place in Zion.
78: 8 [A] *They would* not **be** like their forefathers—a stubborn
79: 4 [A] *We* **are** objects of reproach to our neighbors, of scorn
80:17 [80:18] [A] *Let* your hand **rest** on the man at your right hand,
81: 9 [81:10] [A] You *shall* **have** no foreign god among you; you
81:15 [81:16] [A] and their punishment *would* **last** forever.
83: 8 [83:9] [A] Even Assyria has joined them *to* **lend** strength to the
83:10 [83:11] [A] at Endor and **became** like refuse on the ground.
88: 4 [88:5] [A] go down to the pit; *I* **am** like a man without strength.
89:36 [89:37] [A] that his line *will* **continue** forever and his throne
89:41 [89:42] [A] *he has* **become** the scorn of his neighbors.
90: 1 [A] you *have* **been** our dwelling place throughout all generations.
90: 5 [A] sleep of death; *they* **are** like the new grass of the morning—
90:17 [A] *May* the favor of the Lord our God **rest** upon us; establish
92:14 [92:15] [A] bear fruit in old age, *they will* **stay** fresh and green,
94:22 [A] the LORD *has* **become** my fortress, and my God the rock in
99: 8 [A] *you* **were** to Israel a forgiving God, though you punished
102: 6 [102:7] [A] a desert owl, **[RPH]** like an owl among the ruins.
102: 7 [102:8] [A] *I have* **become** like a bird alone on a roof.
104:20 [A] You bring darkness, *it* **becomes** night, and all the beasts of
104:31 [A] *May* the glory of the LORD **endure** forever;
105:12 [A] When they **were** but few in number, few indeed,
106:36 [A] They worshiped their idols, *which* **became** a snare to them.
109: 7 [A] and *may* his prayers **condemn** [+2631+4200] him.
109: 8 [A] *May* his days **be** few; may another take his place of
109: 9 [A] *May* his children **be** fatherless and his wife a widow.
109:12 [A] **[NIE]** May no one extend kindness to him or take pity on
109:12 [A] to him or **[NIE]** take pity on his fatherless children.
109:13 [A] *May* his descendants **be** cut off, their names blotted out from
109:15 [A] *May* their sins always **remain** before the LORD, that he
109:19 [A] *May it* **be** like a cloak wrapped about him, like a belt tied
109:25 [A] **I am** an object of scorn to my accusers; when they see me,
112: 2 [A] His children *will* **be** mighty in the land; the generation of the
112: 6 [A] be shaken; a righteous man *will* **be** remembered forever.
113: 2 [A] *Let* the name of the LORD **be** praised, both now
114: 2 [A] Judah **became** God's sanctuary, Israel his dominion.
115: 8 [A] Those who make them *will* **be** like them, and so will all who
118:14 [A] is my strength and my song; *he has* **become** my salvation.
118:21 [A] for you answered me; *you have* **become** my salvation.
118:22 [A] The stone the builders rejected *has* **become** the capstone;
118:23 [A] the LORD *has* **done** this, and it is marvelous in our eyes.
119:54 [A] Your decrees **are** the theme of my song wherever I lodge.
119:56 [A] This *has* **been** my practice: I obey your precepts.
119:76 [A] *May* your unfailing love **be** my comfort, according to your
119:80 [A] *May* my heart **be** blameless toward your decrees, that I may
119:83 [A] Though *I* **am** like a wineskin in the smoke, I do not forget
119:173 [A] *May* your hand **be** ready to help me, for I have chosen your
122: 2 [A] Our feet **are** standing in your gates, O Jerusalem.
122: 7 [A] *May there* **be** peace within your walls and security within
124: 1 [A] If the LORD *had* not **been** on our side—let Israel say—
124: 2 [A] if the LORD *had* not **been** on our side when men attacked
126: 1 [A] back the captives to Zion, *we* **were** like men who dreamed.
126: 3 [A] has done great things for us, and *we* **are** filled with joy.
129: 6 [A] *May they* **be** like grass on the roof, which withers before it
130: 2 [A] my voice. *Let* your ears **be** attentive to my cry for mercy.
135:18 [A] Those who make them *will* **be** like them, and so will all who
139:22 [A] hatred for them; I **count** [+4200+4200] *them* my enemies.
142: T [142:1] [A] of David. When he **was** in the cave. A prayer.
Pr 1:14 [A] lot with us, and we *will* **share** [+4200] a common purse"—
3: 7 [A] *Do* not **be** wise in your own eyes; fear the LORD and shun
3: 8 [A] *This will* **bring** health to your body and nourishment to your
3:22 [A] *they will* **be** life for you, an ornament to grace your neck.
3:26 [A] for the LORD *will* **be** your confidence and will keep your
3:27 [A] from those who deserve it, when *it* **is** in your power to act.
4: 3 [A] When *I* **was** a boy in my father's house, still tender, and an
5:14 [A] *I have* **come** to the brink of utter ruin in the midst of the
5:17 [A] *Let them* **be** yours alone, never to be shared with strangers.
5:18 [A] *May* your fountain **be** blessed, and may you rejoice in the
8:30 [A] *I* **was** the craftsman at his side. I was filled with delight day
8:30 [A] *I* **was** filled with delight day after day, rejoicing always in his
12: 8 [A] to his wisdom, but men with warped minds **are** despised.
12:24 [A] Diligent hands will rule, but laziness **ends** in slave labor.
13:19 [C] A longing **fulfilled** is sweet to the soul, but fools detest
14:23 [A] All hard work **brings** a profit, but mere talk leads only to
14:26 [A] has a secure fortress, and for his children *it will* **be** a refuge.
14:35 [A] in a wise servant, but a shameful servant **incurs** his wrath.
22:19 [A] So that your trust *may* **be** in the LORD, I teach you today,
22:26 [A] *Do* not **be** a man who strikes hands in pledge or puts up
23:20 [A] *Do* not **join** [+928] those who drink too much wine or gorge
23:34 [A] *You will* **be** like one sleeping on the high seas, lying on top
24: 1 [A] not envy wicked men, do not desire their **company** [+907];
24:20 [A] for the evil man **has** [+4200] no future hope, and the lamp of
24:28 [A] *Do* not **testify** [+6332] against your neighbor without cause,
26: 5 [A] according to his folly, or *he will* **be** wise in his own eyes.
29:21 [A] his servant from youth, *he will* **bring** grief in the end.
31:14 [A] *She* **is** like the merchant ships, bringing her food from afar.
Ecc 1: 9 [A] What *has* **been** will be again, what has been done will be
1: 9 [A] What has been *will* **be** *again*, what has been done will be
1:10 [A] *It* **was** here already, long ago; it was here before our time.
1:10 [A] It was here already, long ago; it **was** here before our time.
1:11 [A] even those who **are** yet to come will not be remembered by
1:11 [A] even those who are yet to come *will* not **be** remembered by
1:11 [A] come will not be remembered by those who follow. **[RPH]**
1:12 [A] I, the Teacher, **was** king over Israel in Jerusalem.
1:16 [A] increased in wisdom more than anyone who **has** ruled over
2: 7 [A] and **had** [+4200] other slaves who were born in my house.
2: 7 [A] I also **owned** [+4200+5238] more herds and flocks than
2: 7 [A] and flocks than anyone in Jerusalem before me. **[NIE]**
2: 9 [A] I became greater by far than anyone **[NIE]** in Jerusalem
2:10 [A] in all my work, and this **was** the reward for all my labor.
2:18 [A] because I must leave them to the one who **comes** after me.
2:19 [A] And who knows whether *he will* **be** a wise man or a fool?
3:14 [A] I know that everything God does *will* **endure** forever;
3:15 [A] Whatever is *has* already **been**, and what will be has been
3:15 [A] is has already been, and what *will* **be** has been before;
3:15 [A] is has already been, and what will be *has* **been** before;
3:20 [A] to the same place; all **come** from dust, and to dust all return.
3:22 [A] For who can bring him to see what *will* **happen** after him?
4: 3 [A] better than both is *he* who *has* not yet **been**, who has not
4:16 [A] There was no end to all the people who **were** before them.
5: 2 [5:1] [A] and you are on earth, so *let* your words **be** few.
6: 3 [A] yet no matter how long **[NIE]** he lives, if he cannot enjoy
6: 3 [A] his prosperity and *does* not **receive** [+4200] proper burial,
6:10 [A] Whatever **exists** has already been named, and what man is
6:12 [A] Who can tell him what *will* **happen** under the sun after he is

Ecc 7:10 [A] Do not say, "Why **were** the old days better than these?"
7:10 [A] not say, "Why were the old days **[RPH]** better than these?"
7:14 [A] When times are good, **be** happy; but when times are bad,
7:16 [A] *Do* not **be** overrighteous, neither be overwise—why destroy
7:17 [A] Do not be overwicked, and *do* not **be** a fool—why die before
7:19 [A] one wise man more powerful than ten rulers **[NIE]** in a city.
7:24 [A] Whatever wisdom *may* **be**, it is far off and most profound—
8: 7 [A] Since no man knows the **future** [+4537+8611], who can tell
8: 7 [A] no man knows the future, who can tell him what *is to* **come**?
8:12 [A] long time, I know that *it will* **go** better with God-fearing men,
8:13 [A] the wicked do not fear God, *it will* not **go** well with them,
9: 8 [A] Always **be** clothed in white, and always anoint your head
10:14 [A] No one knows what *is* **coming**—who can tell him what will
10:14 [A] is coming—who can tell him what *will* **happen** after him?
11: 2 [A] for you do not know what disaster *may* **come** upon the land.
11: 8 [A] him remember the days of darkness, for *they will* **be** many.
12: 7 [A] the dust returns to the ground *it* **came** *from*, and the spirit
12: 9 [A] Not only **was** the Teacher wise, but also he imparted
SS 1: 7 [A] Why *should I* **be** like a veiled woman beside the flocks of
7: 8 [7:9] [A] *May* your breasts **be** like the clusters of the vine,
8:10 [A] Thus *I have* **become** in his eyes like one bringing
8:11 [A] Solomon **had** [+4200] a vineyard in Baal Hamon; he let out
Isa 1: 9 [A] *we would have* **become** like Sodom, we would have been
1:14 [A] *They have* **become** a burden to me; I am weary of bearing
1:18 [A] "Though your sins **are** like scarlet, they shall be as white as
1:18 [A] though they are red as crimson, *they shall* **be** like wool.
1:21 [A] See how the faithful city *has* **become** a harlot! She once was
1:22 [A] Your silver *has* **become** dross, your choice wine is diluted
1:30 [A] *You will* **be** like an oak with fading leaves, like a garden
1:31 [A] The mighty man *will* **become** tinder and his work a spark;
2: 2 [A] **[NIE]** In the last days the mountain of the LORD's temple
2: 2 [A] In the last days the mountain of the LORD's temple *will* **be**
3: 6 [A] and say, "You have a cloak, *you* **be** our leader;
3: 7 [A] in that day he will cry out, "*I* **have** no remedy. I have no food
3:24 [A] **[NIE]** Instead of fragrance there will be a stench; instead of
3:24 [A] Instead of fragrance *there will* **be** a stench; instead of a sash,
4: 2 [A] In that day the Branch of the LORD *will* **be** beautiful
4: 3 [A] **[NIE]** Those who are left in Zion, who remain in Jerusalem,
4: 6 [A] *It will* **be** a shelter and shade from the heat of the day, and a
5: 1 [A] My loved one **had** [+4200] a vineyard on a fertile hillside.
5: 5 [A] I will take away its hedge, and *it will* **be** destroyed; I will
5: 5 [A] I will break down its wall, and *it will* **be** trampled.
5: 9 [A] "Surely the great houses *will* **become** desolate, the fine
5:12 [A] *They* **have** harps and lyres at their banquets, tambourines
5:24 [A] so their roots **will** decay and their flowers blow away like
5:25 [A] and the dead bodies **are** like refuse in the streets.
6:13 [A] though a tenth remains in the land, it will again **be** laid waste.
7: 1 [A] **[NIE]** When Ahaz son of Jotham, the son of Uzziah,
7: 7 [A] LORD says: " 'It will not take place, *it will* not **happen**,
7:18 [A] **[NIE]** In that day the LORD will whistle for flies from the
7:21 [A] **[NIE]** In that day, a man will keep alive a young cow and
7:22 [A] And **[NIE]** because of the abundance of the milk they give,
7:23 [A] **[NIE]** In that day, in every place where there were a
7:23 [A] **[RPH]** in every place where there were a thousand vines
7:23 [A] in every place where *there* **were** a thousand vines worth a
7:23 [A] thousand silver shekels, *there will* **be** only briers and thorns.
7:24 [A] for the land *will* **be** covered with briers and thorns.
7:25 [A] *they will* **become** places where cattle are turned loose and
8: 8 [A] Its outspread wings **will** cover the breadth of your land,
8:14 [A] *he will* **be** a sanctuary; but for both houses of Israel he will be
8:21 [A] **[NIE]** when they are famished, they will become enraged
9: 5 [9:4] [A] every garment rolled in blood *will* **be** destined for
9: 6 [9:5] [A] is given, and the government *will* **be** on his shoulders.
9:16 [9:15] [A] **[NIE]** Those who guide this people mislead them,
9:19 [9:18] [A] be scorched and the people *will* **be** fuel for the fire;
10: 2 [A] **making** widows their prey and robbing the fatherless.
10:12 [A] **[NIE]** When the Lord has finished all his work against
10:14 [A] not **[NIE]** one flapped a wing, or opened its mouth to
10:17 [A] The Light of Israel *will* **become** a fire, their Holy One a
10:18 [A] completely destroy, **[NIE]** as when a sick man wastes away.
10:19 [A] the remaining trees of his forests *will* **be** so few that a child
10:20 [A] **[NIE]** In that day the remnant of Israel, the survivors of the
10:22 [A] Though your people, O Israel, **be** like the sand by the sea,
10:27 [A] **[NIE]** In that day their burden will be lifted from your
11: 5 [A] Righteousness *will* **be** his belt and faithfulness the sash
11:10 [A] **[NIE]** In that day the Root of Jesse will stand as a banner
11:10 [A] will rally to him, and his place of rest *will* **be** glorious.
11:11 [A] **[NIE]** In that day the Lord will reach out his hand a second
11:16 [A] *There will* **be** a highway for the remnant of his people that is
11:16 [A] as *there* **was** for Israel when they came up from Egypt.
12: 2 [A] is my strength and my song; *he has* **become** my salvation."
13:14 [A] **[NIE]** Like a hunted gazelle, like sheep without a shepherd,
13:19 [A] *will* **be** overthrown by God like Sodom and Gomorrah.
14: 2 [A] **[NIE]** They will make captives of their captors and rule
14: 3 [A] **[NIE]** On the day the LORD gives you relief from
14:24 [A] "Surely, as I have planned, so *it will* **be**, and as I have
14:28 [A] This oracle **came** in the year King Ahaz died:
15: 6 [A] The waters of Nimrim **are** dried up and the grass is withered;
15: 6 [A] is withered; the vegetation is gone and nothing green *is* **left**.
16: 2 [A] **[NIE]** Like fluttering birds pushed from the nest, so are the
16: 2 [A] so **are** the women of Moab at the fords of the Arnon.
16:12 [A] **[NIE]** When Moab appears at her high place, she only
17: 1 [A] will no longer be a city but *will* **become** a heap of ruins.
17: 2 [A] The cities of Aroer will be deserted and **left** to flocks, which
17: 3 [A] the remnant of Aram *will* **be** like the glory of the Israelites,"
17: 4 [A] **[NIE]** "In that day the glory of Jacob will fade; the fat of his
17: 5 [A] *It will* **be** as when a reaper gathers the standing grain
17: 5 [A] **[NIE]** as when a man gleans heads of grain in the Valley of
17: 9 [A] *will* **be** like places abandoned to thickets and undergrowth.
17: 9 [A] to thickets and undergrowth. And *all will* **be** desolation.
18: 5 [A] blossom is gone and the flower **becomes** a ripening grape,
19:10 [A] The workers in cloth *will* **be** dejected, and all the wage
19:15 [A] *There* **is** nothing Egypt can do—head or tail, palm branch
19:16 [A] In that day the Egyptians *will* **be** like women. They will
19:17 [A] the land of Judah *will* **bring** [+4200+4200] terror *to* the
19:18 [A] In that day **[NIE]** five cities in Egypt will speak the
19:19 [A] In that day *there will* **be** an altar to the LORD in the heart
19:20 [A] *It will* **be** a sign and witness to the LORD Almighty in the
19:23 [A] In that day *there will* **be** a highway from Egypt to Assyria.
19:24 [A] In that day Israel *will* **be** the third, along with Egypt
22: 7 [A] **[NIE]** Your choicest valleys are full of chariots,
22:20 [A] **[NIE]** "In that day I will summon my servant, Eliakim son
22:21 [A] *He will* **be** a father to those who live in Jerusalem and to the
22:23 [A] *he will* **be** a seat of honor for the house of his father.
23: 3 [A] of Tyre, and *she* **became** the marketplace of the nations.
23:13 [A] of the Babylonians, this people *that* **is** *now* of no account!
23:15 [A] **[NIE]** At that time Tyre will be forgotten for seventy years,
23:15 [A] *it will* **happen** to Tyre as in the song of the prostitute:
23:17 [A] **[NIE]** At the end of seventy years, the LORD will deal
23:18 [A] her profit and her earnings *will* **be** set apart for the LORD;
23:18 [A] Her profits *will* **go** to those who live before the LORD,
24: 2 [A] *it will* **be** the same for priest as for people, for master as for
24:13 [A] So *will it* **be** on the earth and among the nations, as when an
24:18 [A] **[NIE]** Whoever flees at the sound of terror will fall into a
24:21 [A] **[NIE]** In that day the LORD will punish the powers in the
25: 4 [A] *You have* **been** a refuge for the poor, a refuge for the needy
26:17 [A] out in her pain, so **were** *we* in your presence, O LORD.
27:12 [A] **[NIE]** In that day the LORD will thresh from the flowing
27:13 [A] **[NIE]** in that day a great trumpet will sound. Those who
28: 4 [A] head of a fertile valley, *will* **be** like a fig ripe before harvest—
28: 5 [A] In that day the LORD Almighty *will* **be** a glorious crown,
28:13 [A] So then, the word of the LORD to them *will* **become**: Do
28:18 [A] scourge sweeps by, *you will* **be** beaten down by it.
28:19 [A] The understanding of this message *will* **bring** sheer terror.
29: 2 [A] *she* **will** mourn and lament, she will be to me like an altar
29: 2 [A] will mourn and lament, *she will* **be** to me like an altar hearth.
29: 4 [A] Your voice *will* **come** ghostlike from the earth; out of the
29: 5 [A] your many enemies *will* **become** like fine dust, the ruthless
29: 5 [A] hordes like blown chaff. **[NIE]** Suddenly, in an instant,
29: 7 [A] and her fortress and besiege her, *will* **be** as it is with a dream,
29: 8 [A] **[NIE]** as when a hungry man dreams that he is eating,
29: 8 [A] So *will it* **be** with the hordes of all the nations that fight
29:11 [A] For you this whole vision **is** nothing but words sealed in a
29:13 [A] Their worship of me **is** *made up only of* rules taught by men.
29:15 [A] *who* **do** their work in darkness and think, "Who sees us?
30: 3 [A] Pharaoh's protection *will* **be** to your shame, Egypt's shade
30: 4 [A] Though they **have** officials in Zoan and their envoys have
30: 8 [A] that for the days to come *it may* **be** an everlasting witness.
30:13 [A] this sin *will* **become** for you like a high wall, cracked and
30:15 [A] rest is your salvation, in quietness and trust **is** your strength,
30:20 [A] no more; **[NIE]** with your own eyes you will see them.
30:23 [A] the food that comes from the land *will* **be** rich and plentiful.
30:25 [A] **[NIE]** In the day of great slaughter, when the towers fall,
30:26 [A] The moon *will* **shine** [+240] like the sun, and the sunlight
30:26 [A] the sunlight *will* **be** seven times brighter, like the light of
30:29 [A] you **will** sing as on the night you celebrate a holy festival;
30:32 [A] with his punishing rod *will* **be** to the music of tambourines
31: 8 [A] the sword and their young men *will be* **put** to forced labor.
32: 2 [A] Each man *will* **be** like a shelter from the wind and a refuge
32:14 [A] citadel and watchtower *will* **become** a wasteland forever,
32:15 [A] the desert **becomes** a fertile field, and the fertile field seems
32:17 [A] The fruit of righteousness *will* **be** peace; the effect of
33: 2 [A] **Be** our strength every morning, our salvation in time of
33: 6 [A] *He will* **be** the sure foundation for your times, a rich store of
33: 9 [A] Sharon **is** like the Arabah, and Bashan and Carmel drop their
33:12 [A] The peoples *will* **be** burned as if to lime; like cut thornbushes
34: 9 [A] dust into burning sulfur; her land *will* **become** blazing pitch!
34:12 [A] to be called a kingdom, all her princes **will** vanish away.

Isa 34:13 [A] *She will* **become** a haunt for jackals, a home for owls.
35: 7 [A] The burning sand *will* **become** a pool, the thirsty ground
35: 8 [A] a highway *will* **be** there; it will be called the Way of
35: 9 [A] No lion *will* **be** there, nor will any ferocious beast get up on
36: 1 [A] **[NIE]** In the fourteenth year of King Hezekiah's reign,
37: 1 [A] **[NIE]** When King Hezekiah heard this, he tore his clothes
37:26 [A] that **[NIE]** you have turned fortified cities into piles of
37:27 [A] *They* **are** like plants in the field, like tender green shoots,
37:38 [A] **One day** [+2256], while he was worshiping in the temple of
38: 4 [A] Then the word of the LORD **came** to Isaiah:
39: 2 [A] *There* **was** nothing in his palace or in all his kingdom that
39: 4 [A] "*There* **is** nothing among my treasures that I did not show
39: 7 [A] *they will* **become** eunuchs in the palace of the king of
39: 8 [A] "*There will* **be** peace and security in my lifetime."
40: 4 [A] the rough ground *shall* **become** level, the rugged places a
41:11 [A] those who oppose you *will* **be** as nothing and perish.
41:12 [A] Those who wage war against you *will* **be** as nothing at all.
42:22 [A] *They have* **become** plunder, with no one to rescue them;
43:10 [A] me no god was formed, nor *will there* **be** *one* after me.
44:15 [A] *It* **is** man's fuel for burning; some of it he takes and warms
45:14 [A] tall Sabeans—they will come over to you and *will* **be** yours;
46: 1 [A] Nebo stoops low; their idols **are** borne by beasts of burden.
47: 7 [A] You said, '*I will* **continue** forever—the eternal queen!'
47:14 [A] Surely *they* **are** like stubble; the fire will burn them up.
47:15 [A] That is all *they can* **do** for you—these you have labored with
48:16 [A] not spoken in secret; at the time it **happens**, I am there."
48:18 [A] your peace *would have* **been** like a river, your righteousness
48:19 [A] Your descendants *would have* **been** like the sand, your
49: 5 [A] the eyes of the LORD and my God *has* **been** my strength—
49: 6 [A] "It is too small a thing for you *to* **be** my servant to restore the
49: 6 [A] that you *may* **bring** my salvation to the ends of the earth."
49:23 [A] Kings *will* **be** your foster fathers, and their queens your
50:11 [A] This is what you *shall* **receive** [+4200] from my hand:
51: 6 [A] my salvation *will* **last** forever, my righteousness will never
51: 8 [A] my righteousness *will* **last** forever, my salvation through all
55: 6 [A] LORD while he may be found; call on him while he **is** near.
55:11 [A] so **is** my word that goes out from my mouth: It will not return
55:13 [A] *This will* **be** for the LORD's renown, for an everlasting
56: 6 [A] to love the name of the LORD, and **[NIE]** to worship him,
56:12 [A] of beer! And tomorrow *will* **be** like today, or even far better."
58: 5 [A] **Is** this the kind of fast I have chosen, only a day for a man to
58:11 [A] *You will* **be** like a well-watered garden, like a spring whose
59: 2 [A] your iniquities **[NIE]** have separated you from your God;
59: 6 [A] Their cobwebs **are** useless for clothing; they cannot cover
59:15 [A] Truth **is** nowhere to be found, and whoever shuns evil
60:15 [A] "Although you *have* **been** forsaken and hated, with no one
60:19 [A] The sun *will* no more **be** your light by day, nor will the
60:19 [A] for the LORD *will* **be** your everlasting light, and your God
60:20 [A] the LORD *will* **be** your everlasting light, and your days of
60:22 [A] The least of you *will* **become** a thousand, the smallest a
61: 7 [A] portion in their land, and everlasting joy *will* **be** theirs.
62: 3 [A] *You will* **be** a crown of splendor in the LORD's hand,
63: 8 [A] who will not be false to me"; and so *he* **became** their Savior.
63:19 [A] *We* **are** yours from of old; but you have not ruled over them,
64: 6 [64:5] [A] All of us *have* **become** like one who is unclean,
64:10 [64:9] [A] Your sacred cities *have* **become** a desert; even Zion
64:10 [64:9] [A] even Zion **is** a desert, Jerusalem a desolation.
64:11 [64:10] [A] our fathers praised you, *has* **been** burned with fire,
64:11 [64:10] [A] with fire, and all that we treasured **lies** in ruins.
65:10 [A] *will* **become** a pasture for flocks, and the Valley of Achor
65:20 [A] "Never again *will there* **be** in it an infant who lives but a few
65:24 [A] **[NIE]** Before they call I will answer; while they are still
66: 2 [A] hand made all these things, and so they **came into being**?"
66:23 [A] **[NIE]** From one New Moon to another and from one
66:24 [A] be quenched, and *they will* **be** loathsome to all mankind."
Jer 1: 2 [A] The word of the LORD **came** to him in the thirteenth year
1: 3 [A] **[NIE]** through the reign of Jehoiakim son of Josiah king of
1: 4 [A] The word of the LORD **came** to me, saying,
1:11 [A] The word of the LORD **came** to me: "What do you see,
1:13 [A] The word of the LORD **came** to me again: "What do you
2: 1 [A] The word of the LORD **came** to me:
2:10 [A] see if *there has ever* **been** anything like this:
2:14 [A] a slave by birth? Why then *has he* **become** plunder?
2:28 [A] For you **have** as many gods as you have towns, O Judah.
2:31 [A] "*Have I* **been** a desert to Israel or a land of great darkness?
3: 1 [A] and she leaves him and **marries** [+4200] another man,
3: 3 [A] showers have been withheld, and no spring rains *have* **fallen**.
3: 3 [A] Yet you **have** [+4200] the brazen look of a prostitute;
3: 9 [A] Because Israel's immorality **mattered** so little to her, she
3:16 [A] **[NIE]** In those days, when your numbers have increased
4: 9 [A] **[NIE]** "In that day," declares the LORD, "the king
4:10 [A] and Jerusalem by saying, 'You *will* **have** [+4200] peace,'
4:17 [A] *They* **surround** [+4946+6017+6584] her like men guarding a
4:27 [A] "The whole land *will* **be** ruined, though I will not destroy it
5: 8 [A] *They* **are** well-fed, lusty stallions, each neighing for another
5:13 [A] The prophets **are** but wind and the word is not in them; so let
5:19 [A] **[NIE]** when the people ask, 'Why has the LORD our God
5:23 [A] these people **have** [+4200] stubborn and rebellious hearts;
5:30 [C] "A horrible and shocking thing *has* **happened** in the land:
6:10 [A] The word of the LORD **is** offensive to them; they find no
7: 1 [A] This is the word that **came** to Jeremiah from the LORD:
7:11 [A] *Has* this house, which bears my Name, **become** a den of
7:23 [A] Obey me, and *I will* **be** your God and you will be my people.
7:23 [A] Obey me, and I will be your God and you *will* **be** my people.
7:24 [A] of their evil hearts. *They* **went** backward and not forward.
7:33 [A] the carcasses of this people *will* **become** food for the birds of
7:34 [A] the streets of Jerusalem, for the land *will* **become** desolate.
8: 2 [A] or buried, but *will* **be** like refuse lying on the ground.
11: 1 [A] This is the word that **came** to Jeremiah from the LORD:
11: 4 [A] and *you will* **be** my people, and I will be your God.
11: 4 [A] and you will be my people, and I *will* **be** your God.
11:13 [A] You **have** as many gods as you have towns, O Judah;
11:23 [A] Not even a remnant *will be* **left** to them, because I will bring
12: 8 [A] My inheritance *has* **become** to me like a lion in the forest.
12:15 [A] But **[NIE]** after I uproot them, I will again have compassion
12:16 [A] **[NIE]** if they learn well the ways of my people and swear
13: 3 [A] Then the word of the LORD **came** to me a second time:
13: 6 [A] **[NIE]** Many days later the LORD said to me, "Go now to
13: 8 [A] Then the word of the LORD **came** to me:
13:10 [A] other gods to serve and worship them, *will* **be** like this belt—
13:11 [A] 'to **be** my people for my renown and praise and honor.
14: 1 [A] This **is** the word of the LORD to Jeremiah concerning the
14: 4 [A] The ground is cracked because *there* **is** no rain in the land;
14: 5 [A] the field deserts her newborn fawn because *there* **is** no grass.
14: 8 [A] in times of distress, why **are** *you* like a stranger in the land,
14: 9 [A] Why **are** *you* like a man taken by surprise, like a warrior
14:13 [A] telling them, 'You will not see the sword or **suffer** famine.
14:15 [A] are saying, 'No sword or famine *will* **touch** [+928] this land.'
14:16 [A] the people they are prophesying to *will* **be** thrown out into
15: 2 [A] And **[NIE]** if they ask you, 'Where shall we go?' tell them,
15:16 [A] they **were** my joy and my heart's delight, for I bear your
15:18 [A] Why **is** my pain unending and my wound grievous
15:18 [A] *Will you* **be** [+2118] to me like a deceptive brook, like a
15:18 [A] *Will you* **be** [+2118] to me like a deceptive brook, like a
15:19 [A] not worthless, words, *you will* **be** my spokesman.
16: 1 [A] Then the word of the LORD **came** to me:
16: 2 [A] "You must not marry and **have** [+4200] sons or daughters in
16: 4 [A] or buried but will be like refuse **lying** on the ground.
16: 4 [A] their dead bodies *will* **become** food for the birds of the air
16:10 [A] **[NIE]** "When you tell these people all this and they ask you,
17: 6 [A] *He will* **be** like a bush in the wastelands; he will not see
17: 7 [A] man who trusts in the LORD, whose confidence **is** in him.
17: 8 [A] *He will* **be** like a tree planted by the water that sends out its
17: 8 [A] does not fear when heat comes; its leaves **are** *always* green.
17:11 [A] will desert him, and in the end *he will* **prove to be** a fool.
17:16 [A] the day of despair. What passes my lips **is** open before you.
17:17 [A] *Do* not **be** a terror to me; you are my refuge in the day of
17:24 [A] **[NIE]** if you are careful to obey me, declares the LORD,
18: 1 [A] This is the word that **came** to Jeremiah from the LORD:
18: 5 [A] Then the word of the LORD **came** to me:
18:21 [A] *Let* their wives **be** *made* childless and widows; let their men
18:21 [A] *let* their men **be** put to death, their young men slain by the
18:23 [A] *Let them* **be** overthrown before you; deal with them in the
19:13 [A] and those of the kings of Judah *will* **be** defiled like this place,
20: 3 [A] **[NIE]** The next day, when Pashhur released him from the
20: 7 [A] *I* **am** ridiculed all day long; everyone mocks me.
20: 8 [A] So the word of the LORD *has* **brought** me insult and
20: 9 [A] his word **is** in my heart like a fire, a fire shut up in my bones.
20:14 [A] I was born! *May* the day my mother bore me not **be** blessed!
20:16 [A] *May* that man **be** like the towns the LORD overthrew
20:17 [A] with **[NIE]** my mother as my grave, her womb enlarged
21: 1 [A] The word **came** to Jeremiah from the LORD when King
21: 9 [A] besieging you will live; **[NIE]** he will escape with his life.
22: 5 [A] I swear by myself that this palace *will* **become** a ruin.' "
22:24 [A] if *you*, Jehoiachin son of Jehoiakim king of Judah, **were**
23: 9 [A] *I* **am** like a drunken man, like a man overcome by wine,
23:10 [A] The ⌞prophets⌟ **follow** an evil course and use their power
23:12 [A] "Therefore their path *will* **become** slippery; they will be
23:14 [A] They **are** all like Sodom to me; the people of Jerusalem are
23:17 [A] 'The LORD says: You *will* **have** [+4200] peace.'
23:36 [A] because every man's own word **becomes** his oracle and
24: 4 [A] Then the word of the LORD **came** to me:
24: 7 [A] *They will* **be** my people, and I will be their God, for they will
24: 7 [A] They will be my people, and I *will* **be** their God, for they will
25: 1 [A] The word **came** to Jeremiah concerning all the people of
25: 3 [A] the word of the LORD *has* **come** to me and I have spoken
25:11 [A] This whole country *will* **become** a desolate wasteland,
25:12 [A] "But **[NIE]** when the seventy years are fulfilled, I will

Jer 25:28 [A] **[NIE]** if they refuse to take the cup from your hand
25:33 [A] At that time those slain by the LORD *will* **be** everywhere—
25:33 [A] or buried, but *will* **be** like refuse lying on the ground.
25:38 [A] their land *will* **become** desolate because of the sword of the
26: 1 [A] of Josiah king of Judah, this word **came** from the LORD:
26: 8 [A] **[NIE]** as soon as Jeremiah finished telling all the people
26: 9 [A] in the LORD's name that this house *will* **be** like Shiloh
26:18 [A] "Micah of Moresheth **[NIE]** prophesied in the days of
26:18 [A] Jerusalem *will* **become** a heap of rubble, the temple hill a
26:20 [A] (Now Uriah son of Shemaiah from Kiriath Jearim **was**
26:24 [A] Ahikam son of Shaphan **supported** [+907+3338] Jeremiah,
27: 1 [A] king of Judah, this word **came** to Jeremiah from the LORD:
27: 8 [A] **[NIE]** any nation or kingdom will not serve
27:17 [A] and you will live. Why *should* this city **become** a ruin?
27:22 [A] and there *they will* **remain** until the day I come for them,'
28: 1 [A] **[NIE]** In the fifth month of that same year, the fourth year,
28: 8 [A] From early times the prophets who **[NIE]** preceded you
28:12 [A] prophet Jeremiah, the word of the LORD **came** to Jeremiah:
29: 7 [A] LORD for it, because if it prospers, you too **will** prosper."
29:26 [A] place of Jehoiada to **be** in charge of the house of the LORD;
29:30 [A] Then the word of the LORD **came** to Jeremiah:
29:32 [A] He *will* **have** [+4200] no one left among this people, nor will
30: 1 [A] This is the word that **came** to Jeremiah from the LORD:
30: 8 [A] **[NIE]** " 'In that day,' declares the LORD Almighty, 'I will
30:16 [A] Those who plunder you *will* **be** plundered; all who make
30:20 [A] Their children *will* **be** as in days of old, and their community
30:21 [A] Their leader *will* **be** one of their own; their ruler will arise
30:22 [A] " 'So *you will* **be** my people, and I will be your God.' "
30:22 [A] " 'So you will be my people, and I *will* **be** your God.' "
31: 1 [A] the LORD, "*I will* **be** the God of all the clans of Israel,
31: 1 [A] God of all the clans of Israel, and they *will* **be** my people."
31: 9 [A] because *I* **am** Israel's father, and Ephraim is my firstborn
31:12 [A] They *will* **be** like a well-watered garden, and they will
31:28 [A] **[NIE]** Just as I watched over them to uproot and tear down,
31:33 [A] their hearts. *I will* **be** their God, and they will be my people.
31:33 [A] their hearts. I will be their God, and they *will* **be** my people.
31:36 [A] "will the descendants of Israel ever cease *to* **be** a nation
32: 1 [A] This is the word that **came** to Jeremiah from the LORD in
32: 2 [A] Jeremiah the prophet **was** confined in the courtyard of the
32: 5 [A] where *he will* **remain** until I deal with him,
32: 6 [A] Jeremiah said, "The word of the LORD **came** to me:
32:24 [A] attacking it. What you said *has* **happened**, as you now see.
32:26 [A] Then the word of the LORD **came** to Jeremiah:
32:30 [A] **[NIE]** "The people of Israel and Judah have done nothing
32:31 [A] this city *has* so **aroused** [+4200+6584] my anger and wrath
32:38 [A] *They will* **be** my people, and I will be their God.
32:38 [A] They will be my people, and I *will* **be** their God.
33: 1 [A] the word of the LORD **came** to him a second time:
33: 9 [A] this city *will* **bring** [+4200+4200] me renown, joy, praise
33:12 [A] in all its towns *there will* again **be** pastures for shepherds to
33:19 [A] The word of the LORD **came** to Jeremiah:
33:20 [A] so that day and night no *longer* **come** at their appointed time,
33:21 [A] David *will* no longer **have** [+4200] a descendant to reign on
33:23 [A] The word of the LORD **came** to Jeremiah:
33:24 [A] and no longer **regard** them **as** [+4200+7156] a nation.
34: 1 [A] this word **came** to Jeremiah from the LORD:
34: 5 [A] the former kings who **preceded** [+4200+7156] you, so they
34: 8 [A] The word **came** to Jeremiah from the LORD after King
34:12 [A] Then the word of the LORD **came** to Jeremiah:
34:16 [A] You have forced them to **become** your slaves again.
34:20 [A] Their dead bodies *will* **become** food for the birds of the air
35: 1 [A] This is the word that **came** to Jeremiah from the LORD
35: 7 [A] you *must* never **have** [+4200] any of these things, but must
35: 9 [A] or built houses to live in or **had** [+4200] vineyards, fields
35:11 [A] **[NIE]** when Nebuchadnezzar king of Babylon invaded this
35:12 [A] Then the word of the LORD **came** to Jeremiah, saying:
36: 1 [A] **[NIE]** In the fourth year of Jehoiakim son of Josiah king of
36: 1 [A] king of Judah, this word **came** to Jeremiah from the LORD:
36: 9 [A] **[NIE]** In the ninth month of the fifth year of Jehoiakim son
36:16 [A] **[NIE]** When they heard all these words, they looked at each
36:23 [A] **[NIE]** Whenever Jehudi had read three or four columns of
36:27 [A] the word of the LORD **came** to Jeremiah:
36:28 [A] and write on it all the words that **were** on the first scroll,
36:30 [A] *He will* **have** [+4200] no one to sit on the throne of David;
36:30 [A] his body *will* **be** thrown out and exposed to the heat by day
37: 6 [A] Then the word of the LORD **came** to Jeremiah the prophet:
37:11 [A] **[NIE]** After the Babylonian army had withdrawn from
37:13 [A] *when* he **reached** [+928] the Benjamin Gate, the captain of
38: 2 [A] will live. **[NIE]** He will escape with his life; he will live.'
38:28 [A] was captured. **[NIE]** This is how Jerusalem was taken:
39: 4 [A] **[NIE]** When Zedekiah king of Judah and all the soldiers
39:15 [A] While Jeremiah *had* **been** confined in the courtyard of the
39:15 [A] courtyard of the guard, the word of the LORD **came** to him:
39:16 [A] At that time *they will be* **fulfilled** before your eyes.
39:18 [A] not fall by the sword but **[NIE]** will escape with your life,
40: 1 [A] The word **came** to Jeremiah from the LORD after
40: 3 [A] All this **happened** because you people sinned against the
41: 1 [A] **[NIE]** In the seventh month Ishmael son of Nethaniah,
41: 2 [A] son of Nethaniah and the ten men who **were** with him got up
41: 3 [A] Ishmael also killed all the Jews who **were** with Gedaliah at
41: 4 [A] **[NIE]** The day after Gedaliah's assassination, before
41: 6 [A] **[NIE]** When he met them, he said, "Come to Gedaliah son
41: 7 [A] **[NIE]** When they went into the city, Ishmael son of
41:13 [A] **[NIE]** When all the people Ishmael had with him saw
42: 4 [A] **[NIE]** I will tell you everything the LORD says and will
42: 5 [A] "*May* the LORD **be** a true and faithful witness against us if
42: 7 [A] **[NIE]** Ten days later the word of the LORD came to
42: 7 [A] Ten days later the word of the LORD **came** to Jeremiah.
42:16 [A] **[NIE]** the sword you fear will overtake you there, and the
42:17 [A] **[NIE]** all who are determined to go to Egypt to settle there
42:17 [A] not *one* of them **will** survive or escape the disaster I will
42:18 [A] *You will* **be** an object of cursing and horror, of condemnation
43: 1 [A] **[NIE]** When Jeremiah finished telling the people all the
43: 8 [A] In Tahpanhes the word of the LORD **came** to Jeremiah:
44: 1 [A] This word **came** to Jeremiah concerning all the Jews living in
44: 6 [A] and made them the desolate ruins *they* **are** today.
44: 8 [A] **make** yourselves an object of cursing and reproach among all
44:12 [A] *They will* **become** an object of cursing and horror,
44:14 [A] remnant of Judah who have gone to live in Egypt **will** escape
44:17 [A] had plenty of food and **were** well off and suffered no harm.
44:22 [A] your land **became** an object of cursing and a desolate waste
44:26 [A] 'that no one from Judah living anywhere in Egypt **[NIE]**
46: 1 [A] This is the word of the LORD that **came** to Jeremiah the
46: 2 [A] which **was** defeated at Carchemish on the Euphrates River by
46:19 [A] for Memphis *will* **be** laid waste and lie in ruins without
47: 1 [A] This is the word of the LORD that **came** to Jeremiah the
47: 2 [A] rising in the north; *they will* **become** an overflowing torrent.
48: 6 [A] Flee! Run for your lives; **become** like a bush in the desert.
48: 9 [A] her towns *will* **become** desolate, with no one to live in them.
48:19 [C] and the woman escaping, ask them, 'What *has* **happened**?'
48:26 [A] Moab wallow in her vomit; *let* her **be** an object of ridicule.
48:27 [A] **Was** not Israel the object of your ridicule? Was she caught
48:28 [A] **Be** like a dove that makes its nest at the mouth of a cave.
48:34 [A] for even the waters of Nimrim **are** dried up.
48:39 [A] Moab *has* **become** an object of ridicule, an object of horror
48:41 [A] In that day the hearts of Moab's warriors *will* **be** like the
49: 2 [A] *it will* **become** a mound of ruins, and its surrounding villages
49:13 [A] *will* **become** a ruin and an object of horror, of reproach and
49:13 [A] and of cursing; and all its towns *will* **be** in ruins forever."
49:17 [A] "Edom *will* **become** an object of horror; all who pass by will
49:22 [A] In that day the hearts of Edom's warriors *will* **be** like the
49:32 [A] Their camels *will* **become** plunder, and their large herds will
49:33 [A] "Hazor *will* **become** a haunt of jackals, a desolate place
49:34 [A] This is the word of the LORD that **came** to Jeremiah the
49:36 [A] and *there will* not **be** a nation where Elam's exiles do not go.
49:39 [A] "Yet **[NIE]** I will restore the fortunes of Elam in days to
50: 3 [A] No **[NIE]** one will live in it; both men and animals will flee
50: 6 [A] "My people *have* **been** lost sheep; their shepherds have led
50: 8 [A] of the Babylonians, and **be** like the goats that lead the flock.
50:10 [A] So Babylonia *will* **be** plundered; all who plunder her will
50:13 [A] she will not be inhabited but *will* **be** completely desolate.
50:23 [A] the whole earth! How desolate **is** Babylon among the nations!
50:26 [A] of grain. Completely destroy her and **leave** her no remnant.
50:29 [A] Encamp all around her; **let** no one escape. Repay her for her
50:37 [A] *They will* **become** women. A sword against her treasures!
51: 2 [A] *they* **will** oppose her on every side in the day of her disaster.
51:26 [A] for *you will* **be** desolate forever," declares the LORD.
51:30 [A] Their strength is exhausted; *they have* **become** like women.
51:37 [A] Babylon *will* **be** a heap of ruins, a haunt of jackals, an object
51:41 [A] What a horror Babylon *will* **be** among the nations!
51:43 [A] Her towns *will* **be** desolate, a dry and desert land, a land
51:62 [A] so that neither man nor animal **[NIE]** will live in it;
51:62 [A] man nor animal will live in it; *it will* **be** desolate forever.'
51:63 [A] **[NIE]** When you finish reading this scroll, tie a stone to it
52: 3 [A] because of the LORD's anger that *all this* **happened** to
52: 4 [A] So **[NIE]** in the ninth year of Zedekiah's reign, on the tenth
52: 6 [A] so severe that *there* **was** no food for the people to eat.
52:20 [A] the temple of the LORD, **was** more than could be weighed.
52:23 [A] *There* **were** ninety-six pomegranates on the sides; the total
52:25 [A] he took the officer **[RPH]** in charge of the fighting men,
52:31 [A] **[NIE]** In the thirty-seventh year of the exile of Jehoiachin
La 1: 1 [A] How like a widow **is** *she*, who once was great among the
1: 1 [A] She who was queen among the provinces *has now* **become** a
1: 2 [A] friends have betrayed her; *they have* **become** her enemies.
1: 5 [A] Her foes *have* **become** her masters; her enemies are at ease.
1: 6 [A] Her princes **are** like deer that find no pasture; in weakness
1: 7 [A] wandering Jerusalem remembers all the treasures that **were**
1: 8 [A] Jerusalem has sinned greatly and so *has* **become** unclean.

La 1:11 [A] "Look, O LORD, and consider, for *I* **am** despised."
1:16 [A] My children **are** destitute because the enemy has prevailed."
1:17 [A] Jerusalem *has* **become** an unclean thing among them.
1:21 [A] the day you have announced so *they may* **become** like me.
2:5 [A] The Lord **is** like an enemy; he has swallowed up Israel.
2:22 [A] In the day of the LORD's anger no **[NIE]** one escaped
3:14 [A] *I* **became** the laughingstock of all my people; they mock me
3:37 [A] can speak and *have it* **happen** if the Lord has not decreed it?
3:47 [A] We *have* **suffered** [+4200] terror and pitfalls, ruin
4:8 [A] has shriveled on their bones; *it has* **become** as dry as a stick.
4:9 [A] Those killed by the sword **are** better off than those who die
4:10 [A] *who* **became** their food when my people were destroyed.
4:19 [A] Our pursuers **were** swifter than eagles in the sky; they chased
5:1 [A] Remember, O LORD, what *has* **happened** to us; look, and
5:3 [A] *We have* **become** orphans and fatherless, our mothers like
5:17 [A] Because of this our hearts **are** faint, because of these things
Eze 1:1 [A] **[NIE]** In the thirtieth year, in the fourth month on the fifth
1:3 [A] the word of the LORD **came** [+2118] to Ezekiel the priest,
1:3 [A] the word of the LORD **came** [+2118] to Ezekiel the priest,
1:3 [A] There the hand of the LORD **was** upon him.
1:12 [A] Wherever the spirit **[NIE]** would go, they would go,
1:16 [A] Each appeared to be made like **[NIE]** a wheel intersecting a
1:20 [A] **[NIE]** Wherever the spirit would go, they would go, and the
1:25 [A] *there* **came** a voice from above the expanse over their heads
1:28 [A] Like the appearance of a rainbow **[NIE]** in the clouds on a
2:5 [A] they will know that a prophet *has* **been** among them.
2:8 [A] listen to what I say to you. *Do* not **rebel** [+5308] like that
3:3 [A] So I ate it, and *it* **tasted** as sweet as honey in my mouth.
3:16 [A] **[NIE]** At the end of seven days the word of the LORD
3:16 [A] At the end of seven days the word of the LORD **came** to
3:22 [A] The hand of the LORD **was** upon me there, and he said to
3:26 [A] to rebuke them, **[NIE]** though they are a rebellious house.
4:3 [A] toward it. *It will* **be** under siege, and you shall besiege it.
5:15 [A] *You will* **be** a reproach and a taunt, a warning and an object
5:16 [A] with my deadly **[NIE]** and destructive arrows of famine,
6:1 [A] The word of the LORD **came** to me:
6:8 [A] for some of you **[NIE]** will escape the sword when you are
6:13 [A] when their people **lie** slain among their idols around their
7:1 [A] The word of the LORD **came** to me:
7:4 [A] **[NIE]** Then you will know that I am the LORD.
7:9 [A] **[NIE]** Then you will know that it is I the LORD who
7:16 [A] All who survive and escape *will* **be** in the mountains,
7:19 [A] silver into the streets, and their gold *will* **be** an unclean thing.
7:19 [A] their stomachs with it, for *it has* **made** them stumble into sin.
7:26 [A] **[NIE]** They will try to get a vision from the prophet;
8:1 [A] **[NIE]** In the sixth year, in the sixth month on the fifth day,
9:3 [A] where *it had* **been**, and moved to the threshold of the temple.
9:8 [A] **[NIE]** While they were killing and I was left alone, I fell
10:6 [A] **[NIE]** When the LORD commanded the man in linen,
10:10 [A] looked alike; *each* **was** like a wheel intersecting a wheel.
11:11 [A] This city *will* not **be** a pot for you, nor will you be the meat
11:11 [A] city will not be a pot for you, nor *will* you **be** the meat in it;
11:13 [A] Now **[NIE]** as I was prophesying, Pelatiah son of Benaiah
11:14 [A] The word of the LORD **came** to me:
11:16 [A] yet for a little while *I have* **been** a sanctuary for them in the
11:20 [A] my laws. *They will* **be** my people, and I will be their God.
11:20 [A] my laws. They will be my people, and I *will* **be** their God.
12:1 [A] The word of the LORD **came** to me:
12:8 [A] In the morning the word of the LORD **came** to me:
12:17 [A] The word of the LORD **came** to me:
12:20 [A] towns will be laid waste and the land *will* **be** desolate.
12:21 [A] The word of the LORD **came** to me:
12:24 [A] For *there will* **be** no more false visions or flattering
12:26 [A] The word of the LORD **came** to me:
13:1 [A] The word of the LORD **came** to me:
13:4 [A] Your prophets, O Israel, **are** like jackals among ruins.
13:9 [A] My hand *will* **be** against the prophets who see false visions
13:9 [A] *They will* not **belong** [+928] **to** the council of my people
13:11 [A] Rain *will* **come** in torrents, and I will send hailstones hurtling
13:13 [A] and torrents of rain *will* **fall** with destructive fury.
13:21 [A] your hands, and *they will* no longer **fall** prey to your power.
14:2 [A] Then the word of the LORD **came** to me:
14:10 [A] the prophet *will* **be** as guilty as the one who consults him.
14:11 [A] *They will* **be** my people, and I will be their God,
14:11 [A] They will be my people, and I *will* **be** their God,
14:12 [A] The word of the LORD **came** to me:
14:14 [A] **were** in it, they could save only themselves by their
14:15 [A] they leave it childless and *it* **becomes** desolate so that no one
14:16 [A] They alone would be saved, but the land *would* **be** desolate.
15:1 [A] The word of the LORD **came** to me:
15:2 [A] how **is** the wood of a vine better than that of a branch on any
15:2 [A] that of a branch **[RPH]** on any of the trees in the forest?
15:5 [A] If it was not useful for anything when it **was** whole,
16:1 [A] The word of the LORD **came** to me:
16:8 [A] declares the Sovereign LORD, and *you* **became** mine.
16:15 [A] on anyone who passed by and your beauty **became** his.
16:16 [A] Such things should not happen, nor *should they ever* **occur**.
16:19 [A] *That is what* **happened**, declares the Sovereign LORD.
16:22 [A] when you **were** naked and bare, kicking about in your blood.
16:22 [A] were naked and bare, kicking about in your blood. **[NIE]**
16:23 [A] **[NIE]** In addition to all your other wickedness,
16:31 [A] *you* **were** unlike a prostitute, because you scorned payment.
16:34 [A] So in your prostitution you **are** the opposite of others; no one
16:34 [A] *You* **are** the very opposite, for you give payment and none is
16:49 [A] " 'Now this **was** the sin of your sister Sodom: She and her
16:49 [A] She and her daughters **were** arrogant, overfed and
16:56 [A] You would not even mention **[NIE]** your sister Sodom in
16:63 [A] and be ashamed and never again **[NIE]** open your mouth
17:1 [A] The word of the LORD **came** to me:
17:6 [A] it sprouted and **became** a low, spreading vine. Its branches
17:6 [A] branches turned toward him, but its roots **remained** under it.
17:6 [A] So *it* **became** a vine and produced branches and put out leafy
17:7 [A] " 'But *there* **was** another great eagle with powerful wings
17:8 [A] produce branches, bear fruit and **become** a splendid vine.'
17:11 [A] Then the word of the LORD **came** to me:
17:14 [A] so that the kingdom *would* **be** brought low, unable to rise
17:23 [A] and bear fruit and **become** a splendid cedar.
18:1 [A] The word of the LORD **came** to me:
18:3 [A] **[NIE]** you will no longer quote this proverb in Israel.
18:5 [A] "Suppose *there* **is** a righteous man who does what is just
18:13 [A] surely be put to death and his blood *will* **be** on his own head.
18:20 [A] The righteousness of the righteous man *will* **be** credited to
18:20 [A] the wickedness of the wicked *will* **be** charged against him.
18:30 [A] from all your offenses; then sin *will* not **be** your downfall.
19:3 [A] She brought up one of her cubs, and *he* **became** a strong lion.
19:6 [A] He prowled among the lions, for *he* **was** now a strong lion.
19:10 [A] *it* **was** fruitful and full of branches because of abundant
19:11 [A] Its branches **were** strong, fit for a ruler's scepter. It towered
19:14 [A] No strong branch *is* **left** on it fit for a ruler's scepter.' This is
19:14 [A] This is a lament and *is to* **be** used as a lament."
20:1 [A] **[NIE]** In the seventh year, in the fifth month on the tenth
20:2 [A] Then the word of the LORD **came** to me:
20:12 [A] Also I gave them my Sabbaths **[NIE]** as a sign between us,
20:20 [A] Keep my Sabbaths holy, that *they may* **be** a sign between us.
20:24 [A] and their eyes ˛lusted˛ **[NIE]** after their fathers' idols.
20:32 [A] " 'You say, "*We want to* **be** like the nations, like the peoples
20:32 [A] But what you have in mind **[RPH]** will never happen.
20:32 [A] and stone." But what you have in mind *will* never **happen**.
20:45 [21:1] [A] The word of the LORD **came** to me:
21:1 [21:6] [A] The word of the LORD **came** to me:
21:7 [21:12] [A] **[NIE]** when they ask you, 'Why are you groaning?'
21:7 [21:12] [C] *It will* **surely take place**, declares the Sovereign
21:8 [21:13] [A] The word of the LORD **came** to me:
21:10 [21:15] [A] polished to **[NIE]** flash like lightning!
21:12 [21:17] [A] Cry out and wail, son of man, for it **is** against my
21:12 [21:17] [A] *They* **are** thrown to the sword along with my
21:13 [21:18] [A] which the sword despises, *does* not **continue**?
21:18 [21:23] [A] The word of the LORD **came** to me:
21:22 [21:27] [A] Into his right hand *will* **come** the lot for Jerusalem,
21:23 [21:28] [A] *It will* **seem** like a false omen **to** [+928+4200+6524]
21:27 [21:32] [A] It *will* not *be* **restored** until he comes to whom it
21:32 [21:37] [A] *You will* **be** fuel for the fire, your blood will be
21:32 [21:37] [A] for the fire, your blood *will* **be** shed in your land,
22:1 [A] The word of the LORD **came** to me:
22:6 [A] " 'See how each of the princes of Israel *who* **are** in you uses
22:9 [A] In you **are** slanderous men bent on shedding blood; in you
22:13 [A] have made and at the blood *you have* **shed** in your midst.
22:17 [A] Then the word of the LORD **came** to me:
22:18 [A] "Son of man, the house of Israel *has* **become** dross to me;
22:18 [A] lead left inside a furnace. *They* **are** but the dross of silver.
22:19 [A] 'Because you *have* all **become** dross, I will gather you into
22:23 [A] Again the word of the LORD **came** to me:
23:1 [A] The word of the LORD **came** to me:
23:2 [A] "Son of man, *there* **were** two women, daughters of the same
23:4 [A] *They* **were** mine and gave birth to sons and daughters.
23:10 [A] *She* **became** a byword among women, and punishment was
23:32 [A] *it will* **bring** [+4200] scorn and derision, for it holds
24:1 [A] month on the tenth day, the word of the LORD **came** to me:
24:7 [A] " 'For the blood she shed **is** in her midst: She poured it on the
24:15 [A] The word of the LORD **came** to me:
24:20 [A] So I said to them, "The word of the LORD **came** to me:
24:24 [A] Ezekiel *will* **be** a sign to you; you will do just as he has done.
24:27 [A] So *you will* **be** a sign to them, and they will know that I am
25:1 [A] The word of the LORD **came** to me:
26:1 [A] **[NIE]** In the eleventh year, on the first day of the month,
26:1 [A] first day of the month, the word of the LORD **came** to me:
26:5 [A] Out in the sea *she will* **become** a place to spread fishnets,
26:5 [A] Sovereign LORD. *She will* **become** plunder for the nations,

Eze 26:14 [A] a bare rock, and *you will* **become** a place to spread fishnets.
26:17 [A] *You* **were** a power on the seas, you and your citizens; you
27: 1 [A] The word of the LORD **came** to me:
27: 7 [A] Fine embroidered linen from Egypt **was** your sail and served
27: 7 [A] linen from Egypt was your sail and **served** as your banner;
27: 7 [A] your awnings **were** of blue and purple from the coasts of
27: 8 [A] Men of Sidon and Arvad **were** your oarsmen; your skilled
27: 8 [A] your skilled men, O Tyre, **were** aboard as your seamen.
27: 9 [A] Veteran craftsmen of Gebal **were** on board as shipwrights to
27: 9 [A] and their sailors **came** alongside to trade for your wares.
27:10 [A] of Persia, Lydia and Put **served as** soldiers in your army.
27:11 [A] walls on every side; men of Gammad **were** in your towers.
27:19 [A] wrought iron, cassia and calamus for your wares. **[NIE]**
27:36 [A] *you have* **come** *to* a horrible end and will be no more.' "
28: 1 [A] The word of the LORD **came** to me:
28:11 [A] The word of the LORD **came** to me:
28:13 [A] *You* **were** in Eden, the garden of God; every precious stone
28:14 [A] *You* **were** on the holy mount of God; you walked among the
28:19 [A] *you have* **come** *to* a horrible end and will be no more.' "
28:20 [A] The word of the LORD **came** to me:
28:24 [A] " 'No longer *will* the people of Israel **have** [+4200] malicious
29: 1 [A] on the twelfth day, the word of the LORD **came** to me:
29: 6 [A] " 'You *have* **been** a staff of reed for the house of Israel.
29: 9 [A] Egypt *will* **become** a desolate wasteland. Then they will
29:12 [A] her cities *will* **lie** desolate forty years among ruined cities.
29:14 [A] land of their ancestry. There *they will* **be** a lowly kingdom.
29:15 [A] *It will* **be** the lowliest of kingdoms and will never again exalt
29:16 [A] Egypt *will* no longer **be** a source of confidence for the people
29:17 [A] **[NIE]** In the twenty-seventh year, in the first month on the
29:17 [A] month on the first day, the word of the LORD **came** to me:
29:18 [A] his army **got** [+4200] no reward from the campaign he led
29:19 [A] He will loot and plunder the land **[NIE]** as pay for his army.
30: 1 [A] The word of the LORD **came** to me:
30: 3 [A] a day of clouds, a time of doom for the nations. **[NIE]**
30: 4 [A] will come against Egypt, and anguish *will* **come** upon Cush.
30: 7 [A] desolate lands, and their cities *will* **lie** among ruined cities.
30: 9 [A] Anguish *will* **take hold** [+928] **of** them on the day of Egypt's
30:13 [A] No longer *will there* **be** a prince in Egypt, and I will spread
30:16 [A] Thebes *will* **be** taken by storm; Memphis will be in constant
30:20 [A] **[NIE]** In the eleventh year, in the first month on the seventh
30:20 [A] on the seventh day, the word of the LORD **came** to me:
31: 1 [A] **[NIE]** In the eleventh year, in the third month on the first
31: 1 [A] month on the first day, the word of the LORD **came** to me:
31: 3 [A] it towered on high, its top **[NIE]** above the thick foliage.
31: 7 [A] for its roots **went** *down* to abundant waters.
31: 8 [A] nor *could* the plane trees **compare with** [+3869] its
31:13 [A] and all the beasts of the field **were** among its branches.
32: 1 [A] **[NIE]** In the twelfth year, in the twelfth month on the first
32: 1 [A] month on the first day, the word of the LORD **came** to me:
32:17 [A] **[NIE]** In the twelfth year, on the fifteenth day of the month,
32:17 [A] day of the month, the word of the LORD **came** to me:
32:23 [A] in the depths of the pit and her army **lies** around her grave.
32:27 [A] The punishment for their sins **rested** on their bones,
33: 1 [A] The word of the LORD **came** to me:
33: 4 [A] and takes his life, his blood *will* **be** on his own head.
33: 5 [A] but did not take warning, his blood *will* **be** on his own head.
33:21 [A] **[NIE]** In the twelfth year of our exile, in the tenth month on
33:22 [A] the man arrived, the hand of the LORD **was** upon me,
33:23 [A] Then the word of the LORD **came** to me:
33:24 [A] 'Abraham **was** only one man, yet he possessed the land.
33:33 [A] then they will know that a prophet *has* **been** among them."
34: 1 [A] The word of the LORD **came** to me:
34: 2 [A] Woe to the shepherds of Israel who **[NIE]** only take care of
34: 5 [A] when they were scattered *they* **became** food for all the wild
34: 8 [A] my flock lacks a shepherd and so *has* **been** plundered
34: 8 [A] and *has* **become** food for all the wild animals,
34:10 [A] from their mouths, and *it will* no longer **be** food for them.
34:12 [A] As a shepherd looks after his scattered flock when he **is** with
34:14 [A] and the mountain heights of Israel *will* **be** their grazing land.
34:22 [A] I will save my flock, and *they will* no longer **be** plundered.
34:23 [A] he will tend them; he will tend them and **be** their shepherd.
34:24 [A] I the LORD *will* **be** their God, and my servant David will be
34:26 [A] down showers in season; *there will* **be** showers of blessing.
34:27 [A] will yield its crops; *the people will* **be** secure in their land.
34:28 [A] *They will* no longer **be** plundered by the nations, nor will
34:29 [A] *they will* no longer **be** victims of famine in the land or bear
35: 1 [A] The word of the LORD **came** to me:
35: 4 [A] I will turn your towns into ruins and you *will* **be** desolate.
35: 5 [A] " 'Because you **harbored** [+4200] an ancient hostility
35:10 [A] "These two nations and countries *will* **be** ours and we will
35:10 [A] possession of them," even though I the LORD **was** there,
35:15 [A] *You will* **be** desolate, O Mount Seir, you and all of Edom.
36: 2 [A] "Aha! The ancient heights *have* **become** our possession." '
36: 3 [A] so that you **became** the possession of the rest of the nations
36: 4 [A] the deserted towns that *have* **been** plundered and ridiculed by
36:12 [A] They will possess you, and *you will* **be** their inheritance; you
36:13 [A] devour men and deprive your nation of its children," **[NIE]**
36:16 [A] Again the word of the LORD **came** to me:
36:17 [A] Their conduct **was** like a woman's monthly uncleanness in
36:28 [A] *you will* **be** my people, and I will be your God.
36:28 [A] you will be my people, and I *will* **be** your God.
36:34 [A] The desolate land will be cultivated instead of **lying** desolate
36:35 [A] "This land that was laid waste *has* **become** like the garden of
36:38 [A] So *will* the ruined cities **be** filled with flocks of people.
37: 1 [A] The hand of the LORD **was** upon me, and he brought me
37: 7 [A] as I was prophesying, *there* **was** a noise, a rattling sound,
37:15 [A] The word of the LORD **came** to me:
37:17 [A] into one stick so that *they will* **become** one in your hand.
37:19 [A] single stick of wood, and *they will* **become** one in my hand.'
37:20 [A] **Hold** [+928+3338] before their eyes the sticks you have
37:22 [A] *There will* **be** one king over all of them and they will never
37:22 [A] *they will* never again **be** two nations or be divided into two
37:23 [A] *They will* **be** my people, and I will be their God.
37:23 [A] They will be my people, and I *will* **be** their God.
37:24 [A] king over them, and they *will* all **have** [+4200] one shepherd.
37:26 [A] of peace with them; *it will* **be** an everlasting covenant.
37:27 [A] My dwelling place *will* **be** with them; I will be their God,
37:27 [A] with them; *I will* **be** their God, and they will be my people.
37:27 [A] with them; I will be their God, and they *will* **be** my people.
37:28 [A] Israel holy, when my sanctuary **is** among them forever.' "
38: 1 [A] The word of the LORD **came** to me:
38: 7 [A] and **take command** [+4200+5464] of them.
38: 8 [A] to the mountains of Israel, which *had* long **been** desolate.
38: 9 [A] like a storm; *you will* **be** like a cloud covering the land.
38:10 [A] **[NIE]** On that day thoughts will come into your mind
38:16 [A] In days to come, **[NIE]** O Gog, I will bring you against my
38:18 [A] *This is what will* **happen** in that day: When Gog attacks the
38:19 [A] fiery wrath I declare that at that time *there shall* **be** a great
38:21 [A] Every man's sword *will* **be** against his brother.
39: 8 [C] *It will* surely **take place**, declares the Sovereign LORD.
39:11 [A] **[NIE]** " 'On that day I will give Gog a burial place in Israel,
39:13 [A] and the day I am glorified *will* **be** a memorable day for them,
40: 1 [A] on that very day the hand of the LORD **was** upon me and he
40:21 [A] its portico **had** the same measurements as those of the first
41: 6 [A] wall of the temple to **serve as** supports for the side rooms,
41: 6 [A] so that the supports **were** not inserted into the wall of the
43: 6 [A] While the man **was** standing beside me, I heard someone
43:27 [A] At the end of these days, **[NIE]** from the eighth day on,
44: 2 [A] The LORD said to me, "This gate *is to* **remain** shut. It must
44: 2 [A] *It is to* **remain** shut because the LORD, the God of Israel,
44: 7 [A] uncircumcised in heart and **[NIE]** flesh into my sanctuary,
44:11 [A] *They may* **serve** in my sanctuary, having charge of the gates
44:12 [A] **made** the house of Israel **fall into** [+4200+4200+4842] sin,
44:17 [A] **[NIE]** " 'When they enter the gates of the inner court,
44:18 [A] *They are to* **wear** linen turbans on their heads and linen
44:18 [A] and linen undergarments **[RPH]** around their waists.
44:22 [A] only virgins of Israelite descent or widows **[NIE]** of priests.
44:25 [A] or daughter, brother or **unmarried** [+408+4200+4202] sister,
44:28 [A] **[NIE]** " 'I am to be the only inheritance the priests have.
44:29 [A] in Israel devoted to the LORD *will* **belong** [+4200] **to** them.
44:30 [A] of all your special gifts *will* **belong** [+4200] **to** the priests.
45: 2 [A] Of this, a section 500 cubits square *is to* **be** for the sanctuary,
45: 3 [A] cubits wide. In it *will* **be** the sanctuary, the Most Holy Place.
45: 4 [A] It *will* **be** the sacred portion of the land for the priests,
45: 4 [A] *It will* **be** a place for their houses as well as a holy place for
45: 5 [A] and 10,000 cubits wide *will* **belong** to the Levites,
45: 6 [A] *it will* **belong** [+4200] **to** the whole house of Israel.
45: 8 [A] This land *will* **be** his possession in Israel. And my princes
45:10 [A] You *are to* **use** accurate scales, an accurate ephah and an
45:11 [A] The ephah and the bath *are to* **be** the same size, the bath
45:11 [A] of a homer; the homer *is to* **be** the standard measure for both.
45:12 [A] The shekel *is to* **consist of** twenty gerahs. Twenty shekels
45:16 [A] All the people of the land *will* **participate** [+448] **in** this
45:17 [A] *It will* **be** the duty of the prince to provide the burnt
45:21 [A] " 'In the first month on the fourteenth day you *are to* **observe**
46: 1 [A] The gate of the inner court facing east *is to* **be** shut on the six
46: 6 [A] a young bull, six lambs and a ram, all without defect. **[NIE]**
46:11 [A] the grain offering *is to* **be** an ephah with a bull, an ephah
46:16 [A] of his sons, it *will* also **belong** [+4200] **to** his descendants;
46:17 [A] the servant *may* **keep** [+4200] it until the year of freedom;
46:17 [A] His inheritance belongs to his sons only; *it* **is** theirs.
47: 9 [A] **[NIE]** Swarms of living creatures will live wherever the
47: 9 [A] *There will* **be** large numbers of fish, because this water flows
47:10 [A] **[NIE]** Fishermen will stand along the shore; from En Gedi
47:10 [A] from En Gedi to En Eglaim *there will* **be** places for
47:10 [A] The fish *will* **be** of many kinds—like the fish of the Great
47:12 [A] Their fruit *will* **serve** for food and their leaves for healing."
47:17 [A] The boundary *will* **extend** from the sea to Hazar Enan, along

Eze 47:22 [A] **[NIE]** You are to allot it as an inheritance for yourselves
47:22 [A] You *are to* **consider** [+4200] them as native-born Israelites;
47:23 [A] **[NIE]** In whatever tribe the alien settles, there you are to
48: 1 [A] the northern border of Damascus next to Hamath *will* **be** part
48: 8 [A] "Bordering the territory of Judah from east to west *will* **be**
48: 8 [A] of the tribal portions; the sanctuary *will* **be** in the center of it.
48:10 [A] This *will* **be** the sacred portion for the priests. It will be
48:10 [A] In the center of it *will* **be** the sanctuary of the LORD.
48:12 [A] *It will* **be** a special gift to them from the sacred portion of the
48:15 [A] and for pastureland. The city *will* **be** in the center of it
48:17 [A] The pastureland for the city *will* **be** 250 cubits on the north,
48:18 [A] *will* **be** 10,000 cubits on the east side and 10,000 cubits on
48:18 [A] Its produce *will* **supply** [+4200] food for the workers of the
48:21 [A] the sacred portion with the temple sanctuary *will* **be** in the
48:22 [A] the property of the city *will* **lie** in the center of the area that
48:22 [A] The area belonging to the prince *will* **lie** between the border
48:28 [A] "The southern boundary of Gad *will* **run** south from Tamar
Da 1: 6 [A] Among these **were** some from Judah: Daniel, Hananiah,
1:16 [A] So **[NIE]** the guard took away their choice food
1:21 [A] Daniel **remained** there until the first year of King Cyrus.
2: 1 [C] his mind was troubled and he **could** [+6584] **not** sleep.
8: 2 [A] In my vision I saw **[NIE]** myself in the citadel of Susa in the
8: 2 [A] province of Elam; in the vision I **was** beside the Ulai Canal.
8: 5 [A] As I **was** thinking about this, suddenly a goat with a
8: 7 [A] The ram **was** powerless to stand against him; the goat
8: 7 [A] and none **[NIE]** could rescue the ram from his power.
8:15 [A] **[NIE]** While I, Daniel, was watching the vision and trying
8:19 [A] "I am going to tell you what *will* **happen** later in the time of
8:27 [C] I, Daniel, *was* **exhausted** and lay ill for several days. Then I
9: 2 [A] according to the word of the LORD **given** to Jeremiah the
10: 2 [A] At that time I, Daniel, **[NIE]** mourned for three weeks.
10: 4 [A] as I **was** standing on the bank of the great river, the Tigris,
10: 7 [A] the men **[NIE]** with me did not see it, but such terror
10: 9 [A] to him, I **[NIE]** fell into a deep sleep, my face to the ground.
11:17 [A] but his plans will not succeed or **help** [+4200] him.
11:29 [A] this time the outcome *will* **be** different from what it was
11:42 [A] extend his power over many countries; Egypt **will** not escape.
12: 1 [A] *There will* **be** a time of distress such as has not happened
12: 1 [C] There will be a time of distress such as *has* not **happened**
12: 1 [A] as has not happened from the **beginning** *of* nations until then.
Hos 1: 1 [A] The word of the LORD that **came** to Hosea son of Beeri
1: 5 [A] **[NIE]** In that day I will break Israel's bow in the Valley of
1: 9 [A] for you are not my people, and I **am** not your God.
1:10 [2:1] [A] "Yet the Israelites *will* **be** like the sand on the
1:10 [2:1] [A] **[NIE]** In the place where it was said to them,
2:16 [2:18] [A] **[NIE]** "In that day," declares the LORD, "you will
2:21 [2:23] [A] **[NIE]** "In that day I will respond,"
3: 3 [A] you must not be a prostitute or **be** intimate with any man, and
4: 9 [A] *it will* **be**: Like people, like priests. I will punish both of
5: 1 [A] *You have* **been** a snare at Mizpah, a net spread out on Tabor.
5: 9 [A] Ephraim *will* **be** laid waste on the day of reckoning.
5:10 [A] Judah's leaders **are** like those who move boundary stones.
7: 2 [A] Their sins engulf them; *they* **are** always before me.
7: 8 [A] with the nations; Ephraim **is** a flat cake not turned over.
7:11 [A] "Ephraim **is** like a dove, easily deceived and senseless—
7:16 [A] do not turn to the Most High; *they* **are** like a faulty bow.
8: 6 [A] it is not God. *It will* **be** broken in pieces, that calf of Samaria.
8: 8 [A] now *she* **is** among the nations like a worthless thing.
8:11 [A] altars for sin offerings, *these have* **become** altars for sinning.
9:10 [A] shameful idol and **became** as vile as the thing they loved.
9:17 [A] not obeyed him; *they will* **be** wanderers among the nations.
11: 4 [A] **[NIE]** I lifted the yoke from their neck and bent down to
12:11 [12:12] [A] Is Gilead wicked? *Its people* **are** worthless!
13: 3 [A] Therefore *they will* **be** like the morning mist, like the early
13: 7 [A] So *I will* **come** upon them like a lion, like a leopard I will
14: 5 [14:6] [A] *I will* **be** like the dew to Israel; he will blossom like a
14: 6 [14:7] [A] His splendor *will* **be** like an olive tree, his fragrance
Joel 1: 1 [A] The word of the LORD that **came** to Joel son of Pethuel.
1: 2 [A] *Has* anything like this *ever* **happened** in your days or in the
2: 2 [C] such as never **was** of old nor ever will be in ages to come.
2: 3 [A] a desert waste—nothing **escapes** [+4200+7129] them.
2:28 [3:1] [A] "And **[NIE]** afterward, I will pour out my Spirit on
2:32 [3:5] [A] **[NIE]** everyone who calls on the name of the LORD
2:32 [3:5] [A] and in Jerusalem *there will* **be** deliverance,
3:17 [4:17] [A] Jerusalem *will* **be** holy; never again will foreigners
3:18 [4:18] [A] **[NIE]** "In that day the mountains will drip new
3:19 [4:19] [A] Egypt *will* **be** desolate, Edom a desert waste, because
3:19 [4:19] [A] **[RPH]** because of violence done to the people of
Am 1: 1 [A] The words of Amos, **[NIE]** one of the shepherds of Tekoa—
3: 6 [A] When disaster **comes** to a city, has not the LORD caused it?
4:11 [A] *You* **were** like a burning stick snatched from the fire, yet you
5: 5 [A] surely go into exile, and Bethel *will* **be** reduced to nothing."
5:14 [A] the LORD God Almighty *will* **be** with you, just as you say
6: 9 [A] **[NIE]** If ten men are left in one house, they too will die.
7: 2 [A] **[NIE]** When they had stripped the land clean, I cried out,
7: 3 [A] LORD relented. "*This will* not **happen**," the LORD said.
7: 6 [A] "This *will* not **happen** either," the Sovereign LORD said.
8: 9 [A] **[NIE]** "In that day," declares the Sovereign LORD, "I will
Ob 1:16 [A] they will drink and drink and **be** as if they had never been.
1:16 [A] they will drink and drink and be as if *they had* never **been**.
1:17 [A] on Mount Zion *will* **be** deliverance; it will be holy,
1:17 [A] *it will* **be** holy, and the house of Jacob will possess its
1:18 [A] The house of Jacob *will* **be** a fire and the house of Joseph a
1:18 [A] *There will* **be** no survivors from the house of Esau."
1:21 [A] mountains of Esau. And the kingdom *will* **be** the LORD's.
Jnh 1: 1 [A] The word of the LORD **came** to Jonah son of Amittai:
1: 4 [A] such a violent storm **arose** that the ship threatened to break
1:17 [2:1] [A] Jonah **was** inside the fish three days and three nights.
3: 1 [A] Then the word of the LORD **came** to Jonah a second time:
3: 3 [A] Now Nineveh **was** a very important city—a visit required
4: 2 [A] "O LORD, is this not what I said *when* I **was** still at home?
4: 5 [A] in its shade and waited to see what *would* **happen** to the city.
4: 6 [A] made it grow up over Jonah to **give** shade for his head to ease
4: 8 [A] **[NIE]** When the sun rose, God provided a scorching east
4:10 [A] or make it grow. *It* **sprang up** overnight and died overnight.
Mic 1: 1 [A] The word of the LORD that **came** to Micah of Moresheth
1: 2 [A] in it, that the Sovereign LORD **may** witness against you,
2: 4 [C] **[NIE]** 'We are utterly ruined; my people's possession is
2: 5 [A] Therefore you *will* **have** [+4200] no one in the assembly of
2:11 [A] and beer,' *he would* **be** just the prophet for this people!
3:12 [A] plowed like a field, Jerusalem *will* **become** a heap of rubble,
4: 1 [A] **[NIE]** In the last days the mountain of the LORD's temple
4: 1 [A] In the last days the mountain of the LORD's temple *will* **be**
5: 2 [5:1] [A] though *you* **are** small among the clans of Judah,
5: 2 [5:1] [A] out of you will come for me *one who will* **be** ruler
5: 5 [5:4] [A] *he will* **be** their peace. When the Assyrian invades our
5: 7 [5:6] [A] The remnant of Jacob *will* **be** in the midst of many
5: 8 [5:7] [A] The remnant of Jacob *will* **be** among the nations,
5:10 [5:9] [A] "I will destroy **[NIE]** your horses from among you
5:12 [5:11] [A] your witchcraft and you **will** no longer cast spells.
7: 1 [A] *I* **am** like one who gathers summer fruit at the gleaning of the
7: 4 [A] the day God visits you. Now **is** the time of their confusion.
7:10 [A] even now *she will* **be** trampled underfoot like mire in the
7:13 [A] The earth *will* **become** desolate because of its inhabitants,
Na 3: 7 [A] **[NIE]** All who see you will flee from you and say,
3: 9 [A] her boundless strength; Put and Libya **were** among her allies.
3:11 [A] *you will* **go** *into* hiding and seek refuge from the enemy.
Hab 1: 3 [A] violence are before me; *there* **is** strife, and conflict abounds.
2: 7 [A] you tremble? Then *you will* **become** [+4200] their victim.
3: 4 [A] His splendor **was** like the sunrise; rays flashed from his hand,
Zep 1: 1 [A] The word of the LORD that **came** to Zephaniah son of
1: 8 [A] **[NIE]** On the day of the LORD's sacrifice I will punish the
1:10 [A] **[NIE]** "On that day," declares the LORD, "a cry will go up
1:12 [A] **[NIE]** At that time I will search Jerusalem with lamps
1:13 [A] Their wealth *will* **be** plundered, their houses demolished.
2: 4 [A] Gaza *will* **be** abandoned and Ashkelon left in ruins.
2: 6 [A] *will* **be** a place for shepherds and sheep pens.
2: 7 [A] It *will* **belong** [+4200] **to** the remnant of the house of Judah;
2: 9 [A] the God of Israel, "surely Moab *will* **become** like Sodom,
2:15 [A] What a ruin *she has* **become**, a lair for wild beasts! All who
3:18 [A] remove from you; *they* **are** a burden and a reproach to you.
Hag 1: 1 [A] the word of the LORD **came** through the prophet Haggai to
1: 3 [A] the word of the LORD **came** through the prophet Haggai:
2: 1 [A] the word of the LORD **came** through the prophet Haggai:
2: 9 [A] 'The glory of this present house *will* **be** greater than the glory
2:10 [A] the word of the LORD **came** to the prophet Haggai:
2:16 [A] **When** [+4946] anyone came to a heap of twenty measures,
2:16 [A] came to a heap of twenty measures, *there* **were** only ten.
2:16 [A] to a wine vat to draw fifty measures, *there* **were** only twenty.
2:20 [A] The word of the LORD **came** to Haggai a second time on
Zec 1: 1 [A] the word of the LORD **came** to the prophet Zechariah son
1: 4 [A] *Do* not **be** like your forefathers, to whom the earlier prophets
1: 7 [A] the word of the LORD **came** to the prophet Zechariah son
2: 5 [2:9] [A] *I* myself *will* **be** a wall of fire around it,'
2: 5 [2:9] [A] declares the LORD, 'and *I will* **be** its glory within.'
2: 9 [2:13] [A] against them so that their slaves **will** plunder them.
2:11 [2:15] [A] the LORD in that day and *will* **become** my people.
3: 3 [A] Now Joshua **was** dressed in filthy clothes as he stood before
4: 8 [A] Then the word of the LORD **came** to me:
6: 9 [A] The word of the LORD **came** to me:
6:13 [A] and rule on his throne. And *he will* **be** a priest on his throne.
6:13 [A] on his throne. And *there will* **be** harmony between the two.'
6:14 [A] The crown *will* **be** given to Heldai, Tobijah, Jedaiah and Hen
6:15 [A] *This will* **happen** if you diligently obey the LORD your
7: 1 [A] **[NIE]** In the fourth year of King Darius, the word of the
7: 1 [A] the word of the LORD **came** to Zechariah on the fourth day
7: 4 [A] Then the word of the LORD Almighty **came** to me:
7: 7 [A] and its surrounding towns **were** at rest and prosperous,

Zec 7: 8 [A] And the word of the LORD **came** again to Zechariah:
7: 12 [A] earlier prophets. So the LORD Almighty **was** very angry.
7: 13 [A] **[NIE]** " 'When I called, they did not listen; so when they
8: 1 [A] Again the word of the LORD Almighty **came** to me.
8: 8 [A] *they will* **be** my people, and I will be faithful and righteous
8: 8 [A] and I *will* **be** faithful and righteous to them as their God."
8: 10 [C] Before that time *there* **were** no wages for man or beast. No
8: 13 [A] **[RPH]** As you have been an object of cursing among the
8: 13 [A] As *you have* **been** an object of cursing among the nations,
8: 13 [A] and Israel, so will I save you, and *you will* **be** a blessing.
8: 18 [A] Again the word of the LORD Almighty **came** to me.
8: 19 [A] tenth months *will* **become** joyful and glad occasions and
9: 7 [A] are left will belong to our God and **become** leaders in Judah,
10: 5 [A] Together *they will* **be** like mighty men trampling the muddy
10: 6 [A] *They will* **be** as though I had not rejected them, for I am the
10: 7 [A] The Ephraimites *will* **become** like mighty men, and their
12: 2 [A] peoples reeling. Judah *will* **be** besieged as well as Jerusalem.
12: 3 [A] **[NIE]** On that day, when all the nations of the earth are
12: 8 [A] so that the feeblest among them *will* **be** like David,
12: 9 [A] **[NIE]** On that day I will set out to destroy all the nations
13: 1 [A] "On that day a fountain *will* **be** opened to the house of David
13: 2 [A] **[NIE]** "On that day, I will banish the names of the idols
13: 3 [A] And **[NIE]** if anyone still prophesies, his father and mother,
13: 4 [A] **[NIE]** "On that day every prophet will be ashamed of his
13: 8 [A] **[NIE]** In the whole land," declares the LORD, "two-thirds
14: 6 [A] **[NIE]** On that day there will be no light, no cold or frost.
14: 6 [A] On that day *there will* **be** no light, no cold or frost.
14: 7 [A] It *will* **be** a unique day, without daytime or nighttime—a day
14: 7 [A] to the LORD. When evening **comes**, there will be light.
14: 7 [A] to the LORD. When evening comes, *there will* **be** light.
14: 8 [A] **[NIE]** On that day living water will flow out from
14: 8 [A] and half to the western sea, in summer and in winter. **[NIE]**
14: 9 [A] The LORD *will* **be** king over the whole earth. On that day
14: 9 [A] On that day *there will* **be** one LORD, and his name the only
14: 11 [A] It will be inhabited; never again *will it* **be** destroyed.
14: 12 [A] This **is** the plague with which the LORD will strike all the
14: 13 [A] **[NIE]** On that day men will be stricken by the LORD with
14: 13 [A] On that day men *will* **be** stricken by the LORD with great
14: 15 [A] A similar plague *will* **strike** the horses and mules, the camels
14: 15 [A] and donkeys, and all the animals **[NIE]** in those camps.
14: 16 [A] **[NIE]** the survivors from all the nations that have attacked
14: 17 [A] **[NIE]** If any of the peoples of the earth do not go up to
14: 17 [A] the LORD Almighty, they *will* **have** [+6584] no rain.
14: 18 [A] The LORD *will* **bring** on them the plague he inflicts on the
14: 19 [A] This *will* **be** the punishment of Egypt and the punishment of
14: 20 [A] On that day HOLY TO THE LORD *will* **be** inscribed on the
14: 20 [A] the cooking pots in the LORD's house *will* **be** like the
14: 21 [A] in Jerusalem and Judah *will* **be** holy to the LORD Almighty,
14: 21 [A] on that day *there will* no longer **be** a Canaanite in the house
Mal 1: 9 [A] offerings from your hands, **[NIE]** will he accept you?"—
2: 4 [A] so that my covenant with Levi *may* **continue**,"
2: 5 [A] "My covenant **was** with him, a covenant of life and peace,
2: 6 [A] True instruction **was** in his mouth and nothing false was
3: 3 [A] the LORD *will* **have** [+4200] men who will bring offerings
3: 5 [A] *I will* **be** quick to testify against sorcerers, adulterers
3: 10 [A] into the storehouse, that *there may* **be** food in my house.
3: 12 [A] for yours *will* **be** a delightful land," says the LORD
3: 17 [A] "*They will* **be** mine," says the LORD Almighty, "in the day
4: 1 [3:19] [A] All the arrogant and every evildoer *will* **be** stubble,
4: 3 [3:21] [A] *they will* **be** ashes under the soles of your feet on the

2119 הַיָּה *hayyâ*, n.f. [0] [√ 2095; cf. 2092]

Job 6: 2 [and all my **misery** [K; see Q 2095] be placed on the scales!]

2120 הֵיךְ *hêk*, adv. [2] [cf. 375]

how [2]

1Ch 13: 12 that day and asked, "**How** can I ever bring the ark of God to me?"
Da 10: 17 **How** can I, your servant, talk with you, my lord? My strength is

2121 הֵיכָל *hêkāl*, n.m. [80] [→ Ar 10206]

temple [54], outer sanctuary [7], palace [7], main hall [6], palaces [4], sanctuary [1], temples [1]

1Sa 1: 9 was sitting on a chair by the doorpost of the LORD's **temple**.
3: 3 and Samuel was lying down in the **temple** *of* the LORD,
2Sa 22: 7 From his **temple** he heard my voice; my cry came to his ears.
1Ki 6: 3 The portico at the front of the **main hall** *of* the temple extended the
6: 5 Against the walls of the **main hall** and inner sanctuary he built a
6: 17 The **main hall** in front of this room was forty cubits long.
6: 33 four-sided jambs of olive wood for the entrance to the **main hall**.
7: 21 He erected the pillars at the portico of the **temple**. The pillar to the
7: 50 Holy Place, and also for the doors of the **main hall** of the temple.
21: 1 was in Jezreel, close to the **palace** *of* Ahab king of Samaria.
2Ki 18: 16 had covered the doors and doorposts of the **temple** *of* the LORD,
20: 18 they will become eunuchs in the **palace** *of* the king of Babylon."
23: 4 the doorkeepers to remove from the **temple** *of* the LORD all the
24: 13 Solomon king of Israel had made for the **temple** *of* the LORD.
2Ch 3: 17 He erected the pillars in the front of the **temple**, one to the south
4: 7 to the specifications for them and placed them in the **temple**,
4: 8 He made ten tables and placed them in the **temple**, five on the
4: 22 inner doors to the Most Holy Place and the doors of the **main hall**.
26: 16 entered the **temple** *of* the LORD to burn incense on the altar of
27: 2 but unlike him he did not enter the **temple** *of* the LORD.
29: 16 everything unclean that they found in the **temple** *of* the LORD.
36: 7 from the temple of the LORD and put them in his **temple** there.
Ezr 3: 6 though the foundation of the LORD's **temple** had not yet been
3: 10 When the builders laid the foundation of the **temple** *of* the
4: 1 Benjamin heard that the exiles were building a **temple** for the
Ne 6: 10 house of God, inside the **temple**, and let us close the temple doors,
6: 10 house of God, inside the temple, and let us close the **temple** doors,
6: 11 Or should one like me go into the **temple** to save his life?
Ps 5: 7 [5:8] in reverence will I bow down toward your holy **temple**.
11: 4 The LORD is in his holy **temple**; the LORD is on his heavenly
18: 6 [18:7] From his **temple** he heard my voice; my cry came before
27: 4 gaze upon the beauty of the LORD and to seek him in his **temple**.
29: 9 and strips the forests bare. And in his **temple** all cry, "Glory!"
45: 8 [45:9] from **palaces** *adorned with* ivory the music of the strings
45: 15 [45:16] with joy and gladness; they enter the **palace** *of* the king.
48: 9 [48:10] Within your **temple**, O God, we meditate on your
65: 4 [65:5] with the good things of your house, of your holy **temple**.
68: 29 [68:30] Because of your **temple** at Jerusalem kings will bring you
79: 1 they have defiled your holy **temple**, they have reduced Jerusalem
138: 2 I will bow down toward your holy **temple** and will praise your
144: 12 and our daughters will be like pillars carved to adorn a **palace**.
Pr 30: 28 lizard can be caught with the hand, yet it is found in kings' **palaces**.
Isa 6: 1 high and exalted, and the train of his robe filled the **temple**.
13: 22 will howl in her strongholds, jackals in her luxurious **palaces**.
39: 7 they will become eunuchs in the **palace** *of* the king of Babylon."
44: 28 he will say of Jerusalem, "Let it be rebuilt," and of the **temple**,
66: 6 Hear that uproar from the city, hear that noise from the **temple**!
Jer 7: 4 in deceptive words and say, "This is the **temple** *of* the LORD,
7: 4 the **temple** *of* the LORD, the temple of the LORD!"
7: 4 the temple of the LORD, the **temple** *of* the LORD!"
24: 1 two baskets of figs placed in front of the **temple** *of* the LORD.
50: 28 LORD our God has taken vengeance, vengeance for his **temple**.
51: 11 The LORD will take vengeance, vengeance for his **temple**.
Eze 8: 16 and there at the entrance to the **temple**, between the portico
8: 16 With their backs toward the **temple** *of* the LORD and their faces
41: 1 the man brought me to the **outer sanctuary** and measured the
41: 4 its width was twenty cubits across the end of the **outer sanctuary**.
41: 15 The **outer sanctuary**, the inner sanctuary and the portico facing
41: 20 and palm trees were carved on the wall of the **outer sanctuary**.
41: 21 The **outer sanctuary** had a rectangular doorframe, and the one at
41: 23 Both the **outer sanctuary** and the Most Holy Place had double
41: 25 And on the doors of the **outer sanctuary** were carved cherubim
42: 8 the row on the side nearest the **sanctuary** was a hundred cubits
Da 1: 4 quick to understand, and qualified to serve in the king's **palace**.
Hos 8: 14 Israel has forgotten his Maker and built **palaces**; Judah has
Joel 3: 5 [4:5] my gold and carried off my finest treasures to your **temples**.
Am 8: 3 Sovereign LORD, "the songs in the **temple** will turn to wailing.
Jnh 2: 4 [2:5] your sight; yet I will look again toward your holy **temple**.'
2: 7 [2:8] LORD, and my prayer rose to you, to your holy **temple**.
Mic 1: 2 LORD may witness against you, the Lord from his holy **temple**.
Na 2: 6 [2:7] The river gates are thrown open and the **palace** collapses.
Hab 2: 20 the LORD is in his holy **temple**; let all the earth be silent before
Hag 2: 15 were before one stone was laid on another in the LORD's **temple**.
2: 18 to the day when the foundation of the LORD's **temple** was laid.
Zec 6: 12 will branch out from his place and build the **temple** *of* the LORD.
6: 13 It is he who will build the **temple** *of* the LORD, and he will be
6: 14 Hen son of Zephaniah as a memorial in the **temple** *of* the LORD.
6: 15 far away will come and help to build the **temple** *of* the LORD,
8: 9 let your hands be strong so that the **temple** may be built.
Mal 3: 1 Then suddenly the Lord you are seeking will come to his **temple**;

2122 הֵילֵל *hêlēl*, n.m.[pr.?]. [1] [√ 2145]

morning star [1]

Isa 14: 12 you have fallen from heaven, O **morning star**, son of the dawn!

2123 הֵימָם *hêmām*, n.pr.m. [1] [√ 2102]

Homam [1]

Ge 36: 22 The sons of Lotan: Hori and **Homam**. Timna was Lotan's sister.

2124 הֵימָן *hêmān*, n.pr.m. [17] [√ 3545? *or* 586?]
Heman [16], his[s] [1]

1Ki 4: 31 [5:11] wiser than **Heman**, Calcol and Darda, the sons of Mahol.
1Ch 2: 6 of Zerah: Zimri, Ethan, **Heman**, Calcol and Darda—five in all.
6: 33 [6:18] **Heman**, the musician, the son of Joel, the son of Samuel,
15: 17 So the Levites appointed **Heman** son of Joel; from his brothers,
15: 19 The musicians **Heman**, Asaph and Ethan were to sound the bronze
16: 41 With them were **Heman** and Jeduthun and the rest of those chosen
16: 42 **Heman** and Jeduthun were responsible for the sounding of the
25: 1 **Heman** and Jeduthun for the ministry of prophesying,
25: 4 As for **Heman**, from his sons: Bukkiah, Mattaniah, Uzziel,
25: 4 As for Heman, from **his**[s] sons: Bukkiah, Mattaniah, Uzziel,
25: 5 All these were sons of **Heman** the king's seer. They were given
25: 5 to exalt him. God gave **Heman** fourteen sons and three daughters.
25: 6 Jeduthun and **Heman** were under the supervision of the king.
2Ch 5: 12 Asaph, **Heman**, Jeduthun and their sons and relatives—stood on
29: 14 from the descendants of **Heman**, Jehiel and Shimei; from the
35: 15 prescribed by David, Asaph, **Heman** and Jeduthun the king's seer.
Ps 88: T [88:1] A *maskil* of **Heman** the Ezrahite.

2125 הִין *hîn*, n.m. [22]
hin [22]

Ex 29: 40 fine flour mixed with a quarter of a **hin** *of* oil from pressed olives,
29: 40 pressed olives, and a quarter of a **hin** *of* wine as a drink offering.
30: 24 all according to the sanctuary shekel—and a **hin** *of* olive oil.
Lev 19: 36 and honest weights, an honest ephah and an honest **hin**.
23: 13 and its drink offering of a quarter of a **hin** of wine.
Nu 15: 4 tenth of an ephah of fine flour mixed with a quarter of a **hin** *of* oil.
15: 5 the sacrifice, prepare a quarter of a **hin** *of* wine as a drink offering.
15: 6 of an ephah of fine flour mixed with a third of a **hin** *of* oil,
15: 7 a third of a **hin** *of* wine as a drink offering. Offer it as an aroma
15: 9 three-tenths of an ephah of fine flour mixed with half a **hin** *of* oil.
15: 10 Also bring half a **hin** *of* wine as a drink offering. It will be an
28: 5 fine flour mixed with a quarter of a **hin** *of* oil from pressed olives.
28: 7 The accompanying drink offering is to be a quarter of a **hin** of
28: 14 With each bull there is to be a drink offering of half a **hin** of wine;
28: 14 with the ram, a third of a **hin**; and with each lamb, a quarter of a
28: 14 the ram, a third of a hin; and with each lamb, a quarter of a **hin**.
Eze 4: 11 Also measure out a sixth of a **hin** of water and drink it at set times.
45: 24 and an ephah for each ram, along with a **hin** *of* oil for each ephah.
46: 5 to be as much as he pleases, along with a **hin** *of* oil for each ephah.
46: 7 much as he wants to give, along with a **hin** of oil with each ephah.
46: 11 as much as one pleases, along with a **hin** of oil for each ephah.
46: 14 consisting of a sixth of an ephah with a third of a **hin** of oil to

2126 הַיַּרְקוֹן *hayyarqôn*, n.pr.loc. Not used in NIV/BHS [→ 4770]

2127 הַיְשִׁימוֹת *hay^e^šîmôt*, n.pr.loc. Not used in NIV/BHS [→ 1093; cf. 3811]

2128 הָכַר *hākar*, v. [1 / 0] [cf. 2686]

Job 19: 3 [a] shamelessly *you* attack [BHS ?: NIV 2686] me.

2129 הַכָּרָה *hakkārâ*, n.f. [1] [√ 5795]
look [1]

Isa 3: 9 The **look** *on* their faces testifies against them; they parade their sin

2130 הַכֶּרֶם *hakkerem*, n.pr.loc. Not used in NIV/BHS [→ 1094]

2131 הַל *hal*, l.inter. Not used in NIV/BHS [√ 2021 + 4200]

2132 הֲלֹא *h^a^lō'*, pt.inter.+adv. Not used in NIV/BHS [√ 2022 + 4202]

2133 הָלָא *hālā'*, v.den. [1]
driven away [1]

Mic 4: 7 [C] make the lame a remnant, those **driven away** a strong nation.

2134 הָלְאָה *hāl^e^'â*, adv. [16]
on [4], beyond [+2256+4946] [2], far and wide [+2085+2256+4946] [2], beyond [+4200+4946] [1], beyond [+4946] [1], continuing [1], forward [1], on the other side of [+2256+4946+6298] [1], outside [+4946] [1], some distance away [1], way [1]

Ge 19: 9 "Get out of our **way**," they replied. And they said, "This fellow
35: 21 moved on again and pitched his tent **beyond** [+4946] Migdal Eder.
Lev 22: 27 From the eighth day **on**, it will be acceptable as an offering made
Nu 15: 23 gave them and **continuing** through the generations to come—
16: 37 [17:2] and scatter the coals **some distance away**,
32: 19 with them **on the other side of** [+2256+4946+6298] the Jordan,
1Sa 10: 3 "Then you will go **on** from there until you reach the great tree of
18: 9 And from that time **on** Saul kept a jealous eye on David.
20: 22 'Look, the arrows are **beyond** [+2256+4946] you,' then you must
20: 37 called out after him, "Isn't the arrow **beyond** [+2256+4946] you?"
Isa 18: 2 to a people feared **far** [+2085+2256+4946] **and wide**,
18: 7 from a people feared **far** [+2085+2256+4946] **and wide**,
Jer 22: 19 dragged away and thrown **outside** [+4946] the gates of Jerusalem."
Eze 39: 22 From that day **forward** the house of Israel will know that I am the
43: 27 At the end of these days, from the eighth day **on**, the priests are to
Am 5: 27 Therefore I will send you into exile **beyond** [+4200+4946]

2135 הַלּוֹחֵשׁ *hallôḥēš*, n.pr.m. [2] [√ 2021 + 4317]
Hallohesh [2]

Ne 3: 12 Shallum son of **Hallohesh**, ruler of a half-district of Jerusalem,
10: 24 [10:25] **Hallohesh**, Pilha, Shobek,

2136 הִלּוּלִים *hillûlîm*, n.[m.]. [2] [√ 2146]
festival [1], offering of praise [1]

Lev 19: 24 year all its fruit will be holy, an **offering of praise** to the LORD.
Jdg 9: 27 and trodden them, they held a **festival** in the temple of their god.

2137 הַלָּז *hallāz*, p.com.s. [7] [√ 2138; cf. 4208]
this [3], that [2], the [1], there's [1]

Jdg 6: 20 place them on **this** rock, and pour out the broth."
1Sa 14: 1 "Come, let's go over to the Philistine outpost on **the** other side."
17: 26 "What will be done for the man who kills **this** Philistine
2Ki 4: 25 God said to his servant Gehazi, "Look! **There's** the Shunammite!
23: 17 The king asked, "What is **that** tombstone I see?" The men of the
Da 8: 16 the Ulai calling, "Gabriel, tell **this** *man* the meaning of the vision."
Zec 2: 4 [2:8] "Run, tell **that** young man, 'Jerusalem will be a city without

2138 הַלָּזֶה *hallāzeh*, p.m. [3] [→ 2137, 2139; cf. 2306]
that [2], this [1]

Ge 24: 65 the servant, "Who is **that** man in the field coming to meet us?"
37: 19 "Here comes **that** dreamer!" they said to each other.
Eze 36: 35 "**This** land that was laid waste has become like the garden of Eden;

2139 הַלֵּזוּ *hallēzû*, p.f. Not used in NIV/BHS [√ 2138]

2140 הַלַּחְמִי *hallaḥmî*, a.g. Not used in NIV/BHS [→ 1095]

2141 הָלִיךְ *hālîk*, n.[m.]. [1] [√ 2143]
path [1]

Job 29: 6 when my **path** was drenched with cream and the rock poured out

2142 הֲלִיכָה *h^a^lîkâ*, n.f. [6] [√ 2143]
procession [2], affairs [1], traveling merchants [1], way [1], ways [1]

Job 6: 19 look for water, the **traveling merchants** *of* Sheba look in hope.
Ps 68: 24 [68:25] Your **procession** has come into view, O God,
68: 24 [68:25] the **procession** *of* my God and King into the sanctuary.
Pr 31: 27 She watches over the **affairs** *of* her household and does not eat the
Na 2: 5 [2:6] summons his picked troops, yet they stumble on their **way**.
Hab 3: 6 and the age-old hills collapsed. His **ways** are eternal.

2143 הָלַךְ *hālak*, v. [1549 / 1551] [→ 2141, 2142, 2144, 2168, 4544, 4907, 9336, 9354; Ar 10207]
go [327], went [171], come [94], walk [87], *untranslated* [71], walked [38], left [32], gone [29], followed [+339] [27], follow [+928] [21], follow [+339] [20], going [15], moved [15], set out [15], led [14], came [11], went away [11], followed [+928] [10], take [10], walking [10], went out [9], walks [8], go about [7], go back [7], goes [7], leave [7], continue [6], continued [6], following [+339] [6], live [6], go out [5], left [+4946] [5], marched [5], returned [5], run [5], traveled [5], went off [5], went on [5], became more and more powerful [+1524+2143+2256] [4], brought [4], coming [4], fled [4], go [+2143] [4], go [+2256+4200+8740] [4], go away [4], go off [4], lead [4], left [+907+4946] [4], be [3], did[s] [3], follow [3], followed [3], follows [+928] [3], go ahead [3], going about [3], grow [3], leave [+4946] [3], on way [3], ran [3], taking [3], wandered [3], withdrew [3], advanced [2], away [2], bandit [2], be on way [2], been [2], began [2], carry [2], departs [2], disappears [2], do not know where am going [+889+2143+6584] [2], done[s] [2], flow [2], flowed [2], get out [2], get [2], go at once [+2143] [2], go now [+995] [2], go way [2], goes about [2], goes out [+2143] [2], going back and forth [2], going back [2],

gone [+2143] [2], gone off [+2143] [2], gossip [+8215] [2], increased more and more [+2143+2256+8041] [2], keeping all the way [+2143] [2], kept coming [+2143] [2], leader [+4200+7156] [2], leads away [2], leave [+907+4946] [2], make a survey of [+928] [2], march [2], marched out [2], marching [2], minister [2], move [2], moved about [2], moving from place to place [+889+928+2143] [2], remain [2], return [2], rode [2], sent [2], set sail [2], spread [2], stay [2], surely leave [+2143+4946+6584] [2], took [2], travel [2], very well go [+2143] [2], walk about [2], walked along [+2143] [2], walking along [+2143] [2], way [2], weak [2], went [+2143] [2], went along [+2143] [2], went on way [2], went out [+2143] [2], went over [2], went up [2], were on way [2], about [1], accompanied [+907] [1], accompanied by [+6640] [1], accompany [+4200+5584] [1], advances [1], all the way [1], all this time [1], associates [1], attended by [+4200+8079] [1], banish [1], be on way [+2256+5825] [1], became more and more powerful [+1524+2256] [1], blows [1], by all means go [+995] [1], came back [+995+2256] [1], cause to walk [1], climbed up [1], closer and closer [+2256+7929] [1], comes [1], commit [+928] [1], committed [+928] [1], concern [1], conduct [1], consult [+448] [1], continued [+2118] [1], continued to grow [1], course [1], crawl [1], depart [1], departed [1], deported [1], devoted to [+339] [1], devoted to [1], disappeared [+4946+6524] [1], dispersed [+2006+4200] [1], drive [1], driven [1], drove back [1], enabled to walk [1], entered [+6330] [1], escape [1], escorted [1], exiled [1], fade away [1], faithful [+622+928] [1], flashed back and forth [1], flashed down [1], fleeing [1], fleet of trading ships [+641+4200+9576] [1], fleet of trading ships [+641+9576] [1], floated [1], flowing [1], flows away [1], flows [1], flying [1], follow [+906+928] [1], follow [+928+8079] [1], follow along [1], followers [+339] [1], followers [+408+889+6640] [1], freely strut [1], get away [1], get back [1], get rid of [1], go [+928+2006] [1], go [+995] [1], go aside [1], go at once [+995+2256] [1], go forward [1], go in [+995+2256] [1], go on way [1], go on [1], go over [1], go to and fro [1], go up [1], goes down [1], goes to and fro [1], going around [1], going off [1], gone away [1], gone up [1], greedy [+339] [1], grew even wilder [+2256+6192+6584] [1], grew louder and louder [+2256+2618+4394] [1], grew stronger and stronger [+2256+2618] [1], grew stronger and stronger [+2256+7997] [1], grew weaker and weaker [+1924+2256] [1], have go [1], hurry [+4559] [1], invaded [+4200] [1], join [+6584] [1], join [+6640] [1], journey [1], journeyed [1], keep [+928] [1], keep on [1], kept [+928] [1], kept on [+8743] [1], kept on [1], kept [1], lead [+4200+7156] [1], lead life [+928] [1], lead on [+2256+5627] [1], leading [1], leads a life [1], leads [1], leave [+4200+4946] [1], leave [+4946+6640] [1], leave [+4946+6643] [1], leaves [+907+4946] [1], leaving [1], led [+339] [1], led life [+928] [1], left [+4946+6640] [1], live [+928] [1], lived [1], made walk [1], made way [1], make flow [1], man[s] [1], marches [1], melting away [+2256+4570] [1], more and more powerful [+1541+2025+2256 +4200+5087+6330] [1], moved back and forth [1], moves about [1], moves along [1], moves [1], moving about [1], moving from place to place [1], moving [1], near [+907] [1], neared [+725] [1], obey [+928] [1], off [1], passed away [1], passing [1], persisted [1], proceed [1], proceeded [1], prowled [1], prowling [1], pursue [+339] [1], pursued [+339] [1], pursuing [+339] [1], ran down [1], receded steadily [+2256+8740+8740] [1], rejoined [+448] [1], resort to [+4200+7925] [1], return [+2256+7155] [1], return [+8740] [1], return [+995] [1], ride [+928] [1], rides [1], roam [+2256+3718+6584] [1], roamed [1], rode off [1], rougher and rougher [+2256+6192] [1], roving [1], runs along [1], sail [+641+928+2021] [1], sending on [1], sending [1], set off [1], shining ever brighter [+239+2256] [1], slanderer [+8215] [1], stalks [1], stream [1], sweep [1], take back [1], take part [+6640] [1], take possession [1], take turns [+3427] [1], taken [1], them[s] [+2021] [1], took [+906+906+906+906+1583] [1], took to [1], travel along [1], traveled [+2006] [1], travelers [+5986] [1], traveling [1], tripping along with mincing steps [+2256+3262] [1], trudge [1], turned [1], turning [1], use [+448] [1], walk [+928+2006] [1], walk continually [1], walked along [1], walked around [1], walked back and forth [1], walked on [1], walking along [1], walking around [1], walks around [1], wanders [1], ways [1], went about [1], went around [1], went back [1], went down [1], went forth [1], went forward [1], went home [1], went in [1], will[s] [1], with [1], withdraw [1], withdrew [+4946] [1]

Ge 2:14 [A] third river is the Tigris; it **runs along** the east side of Asshur.
3: 8 [F] God *as he was* **walking** in the garden in the cool of the day,
3:14 [A] *You will* **crawl** on your belly and you will eat dust all the
4: 8 [A] said to his brother Abel, "*Let's* **go out** [BHS-] *to* the field."
5:22 [F] Enoch **walked** with God 300 years and had other sons
5:24 [F] Enoch **walked** with God; then he was no more, because God
6: 9 [F] among the people of his time, and he **walked** with God.
7:18 [A] on the earth, and the ark **floated** on the surface of the water.
8: 3 [A] The water **receded steadily** [+2256+8740+8740] from the
8: 5 [A] The waters **continued** [+2118] to recede until the tenth
9:23 [A] *they* **walked** *in* backward and covered their father's
11:31 [A] together they set out from Ur of the Chaldeans to **go** to
12: 1 [A] "**Leave** [+4200+4946] your country, your people and your
12: 4 [A] So Abram **left**, as the LORD had told him; and Lot went
12: 4 [A] as the LORD had told him; and Lot **went** with him.
12: 5 [A] they set out **[RPH]** for the land of Canaan, and they arrived
12: 9 [A] Then Abram set out and **continued** toward the Negev.
12:19 [A] be my wife? Now then, here is your wife. Take her and **go**!"
13: 3 [A] From the Negev *he* **went** from place to place until he came to
13: 5 [A] Now Lot, who *was* **moving about** with Abram, also had
13:17 [F] Go, **walk** through the length and breadth of the land, for I am
14:11 [A] and Gomorrah and all their food; then *they* **went away**.
14:12 [A] They also carried **off** Abram's nephew Lot and his
14:24 [A] and the share that belongs to the men who **went** with me—
15: 2 [A] what can you give me since I **remain** childless and the one
16: 8 [A] where have you come from, and where *are you* **going**?"
17: 1 [F] "I am God Almighty; **walk** before me and be blameless.
18:16 [A] Abraham **walked along** with them to see them on their way.
18:22 [A] The men turned away and **went** toward Sodom, but Abraham
18:33 [A] with Abraham, *he* **left**, and Abraham returned home.
19: 2 [A] the night and then **go** on your way early in the morning."
19:32 [A] **[NIE]** Let's get our father to drink wine and then lie with
21:14 [A] *She* **went on** *her* **way** and wandered in the desert of
21:16 [A] *she* **went off** and sat down nearby, about a bowshot away,
21:19 [A] So *she* **went** and filled the skin with water and gave the boy a
22: 2 [A] Isaac, whom you love, and **go** to the region of Moriah.
22: 3 [A] *he* **set out** for the place God had told him about.
22: 5 [A] "Stay here with the donkey while I and the boy **go** over there.
22: 6 [A] the fire and the knife. As the two of them **went on** together,
22: 8 [A] my son." And the two of them **went on** together.
22:13 [A] He **went over** and took the ram and sacrificed it as a burnt
22:19 [A] to his servants, and *they* **set off** together for Beersheba.
24: 4 [A] *will* **go** to my country and my own relatives and get a wife
24: 5 [A] "What if the woman is unwilling to **come** back with me to
24: 8 [A] If the woman is unwilling to **come** back with you, then you
24:10 [A] the servant took ten of his master's camels and **left**, taking
24:10 [A] for Aram Naharaim and **made** *his* **way** to the town of Nahor.
24:38 [A] **go** to my father's family and to my own clan, and get a wife
24:39 [A] my master, 'What if the woman *will* not **come** back with me?'
24:40 [F] "He replied, 'The LORD, before whom *I have* **walked**,
24:42 [A] please grant success to the journey on which I *have* **come**.
24:51 [A] take her and **go**, and let her become the wife of your master's
24:55 [A] the girl remain with us ten days or so; then *you may* **go**."
24:56 [A] my journey. Send me on my way so *I may* **go** to my master."
24:58 [A] called Rebekah and asked her, "*Will you* **go** with this man?"
24:58 [A] asked her, "Will you go with this man?" "*I will* **go**," she said.
24:61 [A] and mounted their camels and **went** back with the man.
24:61 [A] back with the man. So the servant took Rebekah and **left**.
24:65 [A] "Who is that man in the field **coming** to meet us?"
25:22 [A] happening to me?" So *she* **went** to inquire of the LORD.
25:32 [A] "Look, I *am* **about** to die," Esau said. "What good is the
25:34 [A] some lentil stew. He ate and drank, and then got up and **left**.
26: 1 [A] and Isaac **went** to Abimelech king of the Philistines in Gerar.
26:13 [A] his wealth **continued** to grow until he became very wealthy.
26:13 [A] his wealth continued *to* **grow** until he became very wealthy.
26:16 [A] Abimelech said to Isaac, "**Move** away from us; you have
26:17 [A] So Isaac **moved** away from there and encamped in the Valley
26:26 [A] Meanwhile, Abimelech *had* **come** to him from Gerar,
26:31 [A] Isaac sent them on their way, and *they* **left** him in peace.
27: 5 [A] When Esau **left** *for* the open country to hunt game and bring
27: 9 [A] **Go out** to the flock and bring me two choice young goats,
27:13 [A] curse fall on me. Just do what I say; **go** and get them for me."
27:14 [A] So *he* **went** and got them and brought them to his mother,
28: 2 [A] **Go** at once to Paddan Aram, to the house of your mother's
28: 5 [A] Isaac sent Jacob on his way, and *he* **went** to Paddan Aram,
28: 7 [A] obeyed his father and mother and *had* **gone** to Paddan Aram.
28: 9 [A] so he **went** to Ishmael and married Mahalath, the sister of
28:10 [A] Jacob left Beersheba and **set out** for Haran.
28:15 [A] I am with you and will watch over you wherever *you* **go**,
28:20 [A] with me and will watch over me on this journey I *am* **taking**
29: 1 [A] on his journey and **came** to the land of the eastern peoples.
29: 7 [A] Water the sheep and **take** them **back** *to* pasture."
30:14 [A] Reuben **went out** into the fields and found some mandrake
30:25 [A] "Send me on my way so *I can* **go back** to my own homeland.
30:26 [A] for whom I have served you, and *I will* **be on** *my* **way**.
31:19 [A] When Laban *had* **gone** to shear his sheep, Rachel stole her
31:30 [A] Now *you have* **gone** [+2143] **off** because you longed to
31:30 [A] Now *you have* **gone off** [+2143] because you longed to
31:44 [A] **Come** now, let's make a covenant, you and I, and let it serve
31:55 [32:1] [A] and blessed them. Then he **left** and returned home.
32: 1 [32:2] [A] Jacob also **went** on his way, and the angels of God
32: 6 [32:7] [A] brother Esau, and now *he is* **coming** to meet you,
32:17 [32:18] [A] 'To whom do you belong, and where *are you* **going**,
32:19 [32:20] [A] and all the *others who* **followed** [+339] the herds:
32:20 [32:21] [A] "I will pacify him with these gifts I *am* **sending on**
33:12 [A] Esau said, "*Let us* **be on** *our* **way** [+2256+5825]; I'll
33:12 [A] "Let us be on our way; *I'll* **accompany** [+4200+5584] you."

Ge 34:17 [A] not agree to be circumcised, we'll take our sister and **go**."
35: 3 [A] and who has been with me wherever *I have* **gone**."
35:22 [A] Reuben **went in** and slept with his father's concubine Bilhah,
36: 6 [A] and **moved** to a land some distance from his brother Jacob.
37:12 [A] Now his brothers *had* **gone** to graze their father's flocks near
37:13 [A] **Come**, I am going to send you to them." "Very well," he
37:14 [A] "**Go** and see if all is well with your brothers and with the
37:17 [A] '*Let's* **go** to Dothan.' " So Joseph went after his brothers
37:17 [A] 'Let's go to Dothan.' " So Joseph **went** after his brothers
37:20 [A] "**Come** now, let's kill him and throw him into one of these
37:25 [A] and *they* **were on** *their* **way** to take them down to Egypt.
37:27 [A] **Come**, let's sell him to the Ishmaelites and not lay our hands
38:11 [A] his brothers." So Tamar **went** to live in her father's house.
38:19 [A] After *she* **left**, she took off her veil and put on her widow's
41:55 [A] all the Egyptians, "**Go** to Joseph and do what he tells you."
42:19 [A] while the rest of you **go** and take grain back for your starving
42:26 [A] they loaded their grain on their donkeys and **left**.
42:33 [A] with me, and take food for your starving households and **go**.
42:38 [A] If harm comes to him on the journey *you are* **taking**, you
43: 8 [A] "Send the boy along with me and *we will* **go** at once, so that
45:17 [A] Load your animals and **return** [+995] to the land of Canaan,
45:24 [A] *as they were* **leaving** he said to them, "Don't quarrel on the
45:28 [A] son Joseph is still alive. *I will* **go** and see him before I die."
48:15 [F] the God before whom my fathers Abraham and Isaac **walked**,
50:18 [A] His brothers then **came** and threw themselves down before
Ex 2: 1 [A] Now **[NIE]** a man of the house of Levi married a Levite
2: 5 [A] and her attendants *were* **walking** along the river bank.
2: 7 [A] "*Shall I* **go** and get one of the Hebrew women to nurse the
2: 8 [A] "Yes, **go**," she answered. And the girl went and got the
2: 8 [A] she answered. And the girl **went** and got the baby's mother.
2: 9 [G] "**Take** this baby and nurse him for me, and I will pay you."
3:10 [A] So now, **go**. I am sending you to Pharaoh to bring my people
3:11 [A] that *I should* **go** to Pharaoh and bring the Israelites out of
3:16 [A] "**Go**, assemble the elders of Israel and say to them,
3:18 [A] *Let us* **take** a three-day journey into the desert to offer
3:19 [A] I know that the king of Egypt will not let you **go** unless a
3:21 [A] so that when *you* **leave** you will not go empty-handed.
3:21 [A] so that when you leave *you will* not **go** empty-handed.
4:12 [A] Now **go**; I will help you speak and will teach you what to
4:18 [A] Moses **went** back to Jethro his father-in-law and said to him,
4:18 [A] "*Let me* **go** back to my own people in Egypt to see if any of
4:18 [A] them are still alive." Jethro said, "**Go**, and I wish you well."
4:19 [A] the LORD had said to Moses in Midian, "**Go** back to Egypt,
4:21 [A] LORD said to Moses, "When you **return** [+8740] to Egypt,
4:27 [A] LORD said to Aaron, "**Go** into the desert to meet Moses."
4:27 [A] So **[RPH]** he met Moses at the mountain of God and kissed
4:29 [A] Aaron **[NIE]** brought together all the elders of the Israelites,
5: 3 [A] Now *let us* **take** a three-day journey into the desert to offer
5: 4 [A] the people away from their labor? **Get back** to your work!"
5: 7 [A] for making bricks; *let* them **go** and gather their own straw.
5: 8 [A] why they are crying out, '*Let us* **go** and sacrifice to our God.'
5:11 [A] **Go** and get your own straw wherever you can find it,
5:17 [A] you keep saying, '*Let us* **go** and sacrifice to the LORD.'
5:18 [A] Now **get** to work. You will not be given any straw, yet you
7:15 [A] **Go** to Pharaoh in the morning as he goes out to the water.
8:25 [8:21] [A] Pharaoh summoned Moses and Aaron and said, "**Go**,
8:27 [8:23] [A] *We must* **take** a three-day journey into the desert to
8:28 [8:24] [A] your God in the desert, but you must not **go** very far.
9:23 [A] and hail, and lightning **flashed down** to the ground.
10: 8 [A] "**Go**, worship the LORD your God," he said. "But just who
10: 8 [A] LORD your God," he said. "But just who *will be* **going**?"
10: 9 [A] "*We will* **go** with our young and old, with our sons
10: 9 [A] **[RPH]** because we are to celebrate a festival to the
10:11 [A] *Have* only the men **go**; and worship the LORD, since that's
10:24 [A] Pharaoh summoned Moses and said, "**Go**, worship the
10:24 [A] Even your women and children *may* **go** with you; only leave
10:26 [A] Our livestock too *must* **go** with us; not a hoof is to be left
10:28 [A] Pharaoh said to Moses, "**Get** out of my sight! Make sure you
12:28 [A] **[NIE]** The Israelites did just what the LORD commanded
12:31 [A] **Go**, worship the LORD as you have requested.
12:32 [A] Take your flocks and herds, as you have said, and **go**.
13:21 [A] By day the LORD **went** ahead of them in a pillar of cloud to
13:21 [A] to give them light, so that they *could* **travel** by day or night.
14:19 [A] who *had been* **traveling** in front of Israel's army, withdrew
14:19 [A] in front of Israel's army, withdrew and **went** behind them.
14:21 [G] all that night the LORD **drove** the sea **back** with a strong
14:29 [A] the Israelites **went** through the sea on dry ground, with a wall
15:19 [A] but the Israelites **walked** through the sea on dry ground.
15:22 [A] For three days *they* **traveled** in the desert without finding
16: 4 [A] and see whether *they will* **follow** [+928] my instructions.
17: 5 [A] in your hand the staff with which you struck the Nile, and **go**.
18:20 [A] show them the way *to* **live** and the duties they are to perform.
18:27 [A] on his way, and Jethro **returned** to his own country.
19:10 [A] "**Go** to the people and consecrate them today and tomorrow.
19:19 [A] of the trumpet **grew louder and louder** [+2256+2618+4394].
19:24 [A] LORD replied, "**Go** down and bring Aaron up with you.
21:19 [F] if the other gets up and **walks around** outside with his staff;
23:23 [A] My angel *will* **go** ahead of you and bring you into the land of
32: 1 [A] and said, "Come, make us gods who *will* **go** before us.
32: 7 [A] the LORD said to Moses, "**Go** down, because your people,
32:23 [A] They said to me, 'Make us gods who *will* **go** before us. As for
32:34 [A] Now **go**, lead the people to the place I spoke of, and my
32:34 [A] to the place I spoke of, and my angel *will* **go** before you.
33: 1 [A] "**Leave** [+4946] this place, you and the people you brought
33:14 [A] The LORD replied, "My Presence *will* **go** with you, and I
33:15 [A] Moses said to him, "If your Presence *does* not **go** with us,
33:16 [A] pleased with me and with your people unless you **go** with us?
34: 9 [A] favor in your eyes," he said, "then *let* the Lord **go** with us.
Lev 11:20 [A] " 'All flying insects that **walk** on all fours are to be detestable
11:21 [A] some winged creatures that **walk** on all fours that you may
11:27 [A] Of all the animals that **walk** on all fours, those that walk on
11:27 [A] all fours, those *that* **walk** on their paws are unclean for you;
11:42 [A] whether *it* **moves** on its belly or walks on all fours or on
11:42 [A] it moves on its belly or **walks** on all fours or on many feet;
18: 3 [A] where I am bringing you. *Do* not **follow** their practices.
18: 4 [A] You must obey my laws and be careful to **follow** my decrees.
19:16 [A] " '*Do* not **go about** spreading slander among your people.
20:23 [A] *You must* not **live** according to the customs of the nations I
26: 3 [A] " 'If *you* **follow** my decrees and are careful to obey my
26:12 [F] *I will* **walk** among you and be your God, and you will be my
26:13 [G] of your yoke and **enabled** you **to walk** with heads held high.
26:21 [A] " 'If *you* **remain** hostile toward me and refuse to listen to me,
26:23 [A] accept my correction but **continue** *to be* hostile toward me,
26:24 [A] *I* myself *will* **be** hostile toward you and will afflict you for
26:27 [A] still do not listen to me but **continue** *to be* hostile toward me,
26:28 [A] in my anger *I will* **be** hostile toward you, and I myself will
26:40 [A] treachery against me and **[NIE]** their hostility toward me,
26:41 [A] which made me **[NIE]** hostile toward them so that I sent
Nu 10:29 [A] **Come** with us and we will treat you well, for the LORD has
10:30 [A] He answered, "No, *I will* not **go**; I am going back to my own
10:30 [A] *I am* **going back** to my own land and my own people."
10:32 [A] If *you* **come** with us, we will share with you whatever good
12: 9 [A] anger of the LORD burned against them, and *he* **left** them.
13:26 [A] *They* **came** [+995+2256] **back** to Moses and Aaron and the
14:14 [A] that you **go** before them in a pillar of cloud by day and a
14:38 [A] Of the men who **went** to explore the land, only Joshua son of
16:25 [A] Moses got up and **went** to Dathan and Abiram, and the elders
16:25 [A] and Abiram, and the elders of Israel **followed** [+339] him.
16:46 [17:11] [A] **hurry** [+4559] to the assembly to make atonement
20:17 [A] *We will* **travel along** the king's highway and not turn to the
21:22 [A] *We will* **travel** along the king's highway until we have
22: 6 [A] Now **come** and put a curse on these people, because they are
22: 7 [A] The elders of Moab and Midian **left**, taking with them the fee
22:11 [A] Now **come** and put a curse on them for me. Perhaps then I
22:12 [A] God said to Balaam, "*Do* not **go** with them. You must not put
22:13 [A] and said to Balak's princes, "**Go back** to your own country,
22:13 [A] for the LORD has refused to let me **go** with you."
22:14 [A] to Balak and said, "Balaam refused *to* **come** with us."
22:16 [A] Do not let anything keep you from **coming** to me,
22:17 [A] you say. **Come** and put a curse on these people for me."
22:20 [A] to summon you, **go** with them, but do only what I tell you."
22:21 [A] saddled his donkey and **went** with the princes of Moab.
22:22 [A] God was very angry when he **went**, and the angel of the
22:23 [A] sword in his hand, she turned off the road **[NIE]** into a field.
22:35 [A] "**Go** with the men, but speak only what I tell you."
22:35 [A] what I tell you." So Balaam **went** with the princes of Balak.
22:37 [A] Why didn't *you* **come** to me? Am I really not able to reward
22:39 [A] Then Balaam **went** with Balak *to* Kiriath Huzoth.
23: 3 [A] to Balak, "Stay here beside your offering while *I* **go aside**.
23: 3 [A] to me I will tell you." Then *he* **went off** *to* a barren height.
23: 7 [A] '**Come**,' he said, 'curse Jacob for me; come, denounce Israel.'
23: 7 [A] 'Come,' he said, 'curse Jacob for me; **come**, denounce Israel.'
23:13 [A] "**Come** with me to another place where you can see them;
23:27 [A] Balak said to Balaam, "**Come**, let me take you to another
24: 1 [A] *he did* not **resort** [+4200+7925] **to** sorcery as at other times,
24:14 [A] Now I *am* **going back** to my people, but come, let me warn
24:14 [A] Now I am going back to my people, but **come**, let me warn
24:25 [A] Balaam got up **[NIE]** and returned home and Balak went his
24:25 [A] got up and returned home and Balak **went** his own way.
32:39 [A] The descendants of Makir son of Manasseh **went** to Gilead,
32:41 [A] **[NIE]** captured their settlements and called them Havvoth
32:42 [A] Nobah **[NIE]** captured Kenath and its surrounding
33: 8 [A] when *they had* **traveled** [+2006] for three days in the Desert
Dt 1:19 [A] **went** toward the hill country of the Amorites *through* all that
1:30 [A] your God, who *is* **going** before you, will fight for you,
1:31 [A] his son, all the way *you* **went** until you reached this place."
1:33 [A] who **went** ahead of you on your journey, in fire by night
1:33 [A] for you to camp and to show you the way *you should* **go**.

Dt 2: 7 [A] He has watched over your **journey** *through* this vast desert.
2: 14 [A] Thirty-eight years passed from the time *we* **left** [+4946]
2: 27 [A] *We will* **stay** on the main road; we will not turn aside to the
4: 3 [A] among you everyone who **followed** [+339] the Baal of Peor,
5: 30 [A] "**Go**, tell them to return to their tents.
5: 33 [A] **Walk** in all the way that the LORD your God has
6: 7 [A] when you sit at home and when you **walk** along the road,
6: 14 [A] *Do* not **follow** [+339] other gods, the gods of the peoples
8: 2 [G] Remember how the LORD your God **led** you all the way in
8: 6 [A] LORD your God, **walking** in his ways and revering him.
8: 15 [G] He **led** you through the vast and dreadful desert, that thirsty
8: 19 [A] **follow** [+339] other gods and worship and bow down to
10: 11 [A] "and **lead** [+4200+7156] the people on their way, so that they
10: 12 [A] the LORD your God, to **walk** in all his ways, to love him,
11: 19 [A] when you sit at home and when you **walk** along the road,
11: 22 [A] your God, to **walk** in all his ways and to hold fast to him—
11: 28 [A] that I command you today by **following** [+339] other gods,
13: 2 [13:3] [A] "*Let us* **follow** [+339] other gods" (gods you have
13: 4 [13:5] [A] It is the LORD your God *you must* **follow** [+339],
13: 5 [13:6] [A] LORD your God commanded you to **follow** [+928].
13: 6 [13:7] [A] "*Let us* **go** and worship other gods" (gods that
13: 13 [13:14] [A] "*Let us* **go** and worship other gods" (gods you have
14: 25 [A] and **go** to the place the LORD your God will choose.
16: 7 [A] Then in the morning **return** [+2256+7155] to your tents.
17: 3 [A] contrary to my command **[NIE]** has worshiped other gods,
19: 9 [A] love the LORD your God and to **walk** always in his ways—
20: 4 [A] For the LORD your God *is* the *one who* **goes** with you to
20: 5 [A] *Let him* **go** [+2256+4200+8740] home, or he may die in
20: 6 [A] *Let him* **go** [+2256+4200+8740] home, or he may die in
20: 7 [A] *Let him* **go** [+2256+4200+8740] home, or he may die in
20: 8 [A] *Let him* **go** [+2256+4200+8740] home so that his brothers
23: 14 [23:15] [F] For the LORD your God **moves about** in your
24: 2 [A] if after she leaves his house **[RPH]** she becomes the wife of
26: 2 [A] **go** to the place the LORD your God will choose as a
26: 17 [A] the LORD is your God and that you *will* **walk** in his ways,
28: 9 [A] commands of the LORD your God and **walk** in his ways.
28: 14 [A] or to the left, **following** [+339] other gods and serving them.
28: 36 [G] The LORD *will* **drive** you and the king you set over you to
28: 41 [A] you will not keep them, because *they will* **go** into captivity.
29: 5 [29:4] [G] During the forty years that *I* **led** you through the
29: 18 [29:17] [A] heart turns away from the LORD our God to **go**
29: 19 [29:18] [A] even though *I* persist in **going** my own way."
29: 26 [29:25] [A] *They* **went off** and worshiped other gods and bowed
30: 16 [A] to **walk** in his ways, and to keep his commands, decrees and
31: 1 [A] Then Moses **went out** and spoke these words to all Israel:
31: 6 [A] because of them, for the LORD your God **goes** with you;
31: 8 [A] The LORD himself **goes** before you and will be with you;
31: 14 [A] So Moses and Joshua **came** and presented themselves at the
Jos 1: 7 [A] or to the left, that you may be successful wherever *you* **go**.
1: 9 [A] for the LORD your God will be with you wherever *you* **go**."
1: 16 [A] us we will do, and wherever you send us *we will* **go**.
2: 1 [A] "**Go**, look over the land," he said, "especially Jericho."
2: 1 [A] So *they* **went** and entered the house of a prostitute named
2: 5 [A] city gate, the men left. I don't know which way they **went**.
2: 16 [A] to them, "**Go** to the hills so the pursuers will not find you.
2: 16 [A] there three days until they return, and then **go** on your way."
2: 21 [A] it be as you say." So she sent them away and *they* **departed**.
2: 22 [A] When *they* **left**, they went into the hills and stayed there
3: 3 [A] are to move out from your positions and **follow** [+339] it.
3: 4 [A] you will know which way *to* **go**, since you have never been
3: 6 [A] of the people." So they took it up and **went** ahead of them.
4: 18 [A] returned to their place and **ran** at flood stage as before.
5: 6 [A] The Israelites *had* **moved about** in the desert forty years
5: 13 [A] Joshua **went up** to him and asked, "Are you for us or for our
6: 8 [A] and the ark of the LORD's covenant **followed** [+339] them.
6: 9 [A] The armed guard **marched** ahead of the priests who blew the
6: 9 [A] the trumpets, and the rear guard **followed** [+339] the ark.
6: 9 [A] followed the ark. **All this time** the trumpets were sounding.
6: 13 [A] The seven priests carrying the seven trumpets **went forward**,
6: 13 [A] **marching** before the ark of the LORD and blowing the
6: 13 [A] The armed men **went** ahead of them and the rear guard
6: 13 [A] and the rear guard **followed** [+339] the ark of the LORD,
6: 13 [A] the ark of the LORD, while the trumpets **kept** sounding.
8: 9 [A] *they* **went** to the place of ambush and lay in wait between
8: 13 [A] to the west of it. That night Joshua **went** into the valley.
8: 35 [A] and children, and the aliens who **lived** among them.
9: 4 [A] *They* **went** as a delegation whose donkeys were loaded with
9: 6 [A] *they* **went** to Joshua in the camp at Gilgal and said to him
9: 11 [A] **go** and meet them and say to them, "We are your servants;
9: 12 [A] we packed it at home on the day we left to **come** to you.
10: 24 [A] and said to the army commanders who *had* **come** with him,
14: 10 [A] said this to Moses, while Israel **moved about** in the desert.
16: 8 [A] From Tappuah the border **went** west to the Kanah Ravine
17: 7 [A] The boundary **ran** southward from there to include the
18: 4 [F] I will send them out *to* **make a survey** [+928] **of** the land
18: 8 [A] As the men started **on** *their* **way** to map out the land, Joshua
18: 8 [A] Joshua instructed **them**[s] [+2021], "Go and make a survey of
18: 8 [A] "**Go** and make a survey of the land and write a description of
18: 8 [F] "Go and **make a survey** [+928] **of** the land and write a
18: 9 [A] So the men **left** and went through the land. They wrote its
22: 4 [A] return **[RPH]** to your homes in the land that Moses the
22: 5 [A] to **walk** in all his ways, to obey his commands, to hold fast to
22: 6 [A] and sent them away, and *they* **went** to their homes.
22: 9 [A] the half-tribe of Manasseh **left** [+907+4946] the Israelites at
22: 9 [A] the Israelites at Shiloh in Canaan to return **[RPH]** to Gilead,
23: 14 [A] "Now I *am about to* **go** the way of all the earth. You know
23: 16 [A] and **go** and serve other gods and bow down to them,
24: 3 [G] **led** him throughout Canaan and gave him many descendants.
24: 17 [A] **[NIE]** and among all the nations through which we traveled.
Jdg 1: 3 [A] the Canaanites. We in turn *will* **go** with you into yours."
1: 3 [A] go with you into yours." So the Simeonites **went** with them.
1: 10 [A] They **advanced** against the Canaanites living in Hebron
1: 11 [A] From there *they* **advanced** against the people living in Debir
1: 16 [A] of the Desert of Judah in the Negev near Arad. **[NIE]**
1: 17 [A] the men of Judah **went** with the Simeonites their brothers
1: 26 [A] He then **went** *to* the land of the Hittites, where he built a city
2: 6 [A] they **went** to take possession of the land, each to his own
2: 12 [A] *They* **followed** [+339] and worshiped various gods of the
2: 17 [A] turned from the way in which their fathers *had* **walked**,
2: 19 [A] **following** [+339] other gods and serving and worshiping
2: 22 [A] way of the LORD and **walk** in it as their forefathers did."
3: 13 [A] and Amalekites to join him, Eglon **came** and attacked Israel,
4: 6 [A] to him, "The LORD, the God of Israel, commands *you*: '**Go**,
4: 8 [A] Barak said to her, "If *you* **go** with me, I will go; but if you
4: 8 [A] Barak said to her, "If you go with me, *I will* **go**; but if you
4: 8 [A] with me, I will go; but if *you* don't **go** with me, I won't go."
4: 8 [A] with me, I will go; but if you don't go with me, *I* won't **go**."
4: 9 [A] "**Very well**," Deborah said, "*I will* **go** [+2143] with you. But
4: 9 [A] "**Very well**," Deborah said, "*I will* **go** [+2143] with you. But
4: 9 [A] because of the way you *are* **going about** this, the honor will
4: 9 [A] over to a woman." So Deborah **went** with Barak to Kedesh,
4: 22 [A] "**Come**," she said, "I will show you the man you're looking
4: 24 [A] the hand of the Israelites **[RPH]** grew stronger and stronger
4: 24 [A] of the Israelites **grew stronger and stronger** [+2256+7997]
5: 6 [A] were abandoned; **travelers** [+5986] took to winding paths.
5: 6 [A] the roads were abandoned; travelers **took to** winding paths.
5: 10 [A] saddle blankets, and *you who* **walk** along the road, consider
6: 14 [A] "**Go** in the strength you have and save Israel out of Midian's
6: 21 [A] And the angel of the LORD **disappeared** [+4946+6524].
7: 4 [A] If I say, 'This one *shall* **go** with you,' he shall go; but if I say,
7: 4 [A] If I say, 'This one shall go with you,' he *shall* **go**; but if I say,
7: 4 [A] but if I say, 'This one *shall* not **go** with you,' he shall not go."
7: 4 [A] but if I say, 'This one shall not go with you,' he *shall* not **go**."
7: 7 [A] your hands. *Let* all the other men **go**, each to his own place."
8: 1 [A] Why didn't you call us when *you* **went** to fight Midian?"
8: 29 [A] Jerub-Baal son of Joash **went back** home to live.
9: 1 [A] Abimelech son of Jerub-Baal **went** to his mother's brothers
9: 4 [A] hire reckless adventurers, *who became* his **followers** [+339].
9: 6 [A] at the pillar in Shechem **[NIE]** to crown Abimelech king.
9: 7 [A] *he* **climbed up** on the top of Mount Gerizim and shouted to
9: 8 [A] One day the trees **went** [+2143] **out** to anoint a king for
9: 8 [A] One day the trees **went out** [+2143] to anoint a king for
9: 9 [A] and men are honored, **[NIE]** to hold sway over the trees?'
9: 10 [A] "Next, the trees said to the fig tree, '**Come** and be our king.'
9: 11 [A] so good and sweet, **[NIE]** to hold sway over the trees?'
9: 12 [A] "Then the trees said to the vine, '**Come** and be our king.'
9: 13 [A] both gods and men, **[NIE]** to hold sway over the trees?'
9: 14 [A] all the trees said to the thornbush, '**Come** and be our king.'
9: 21 [A] escaping **[NIE]** to Beer, and he lived there because he was
9: 49 [A] So all the men cut branches and **followed** [+339] Abimelech.
9: 50 [A] Next Abimelech **went** to Thebez and besieged it
9: 55 [A] the Israelites saw that Abimelech was dead, they **went** home.
10: 14 [A] **Go** and cry out to the gods you have chosen. Let them save
11: 5 [A] the elders of Gilead **went** to get Jephthah from the land of
11: 6 [A] "**Come**," they said, "be our commander, so we can fight the
11: 8 [A] **come** with us to fight the Ammonites, and you will be our
11: 11 [A] So Jephthah **went** with the elders of Gilead, and the people
11: 16 [A] Israel **went** through the desert to the Red Sea and on to
11: 18 [A] "Next *they* **traveled** through the desert, skirted the lands of
11: 37 [A] "Give me two months *to* **roam** [+2256+3718+6584] the hills
11: 38 [A] "*You may* **go**," he said. And he let her go for two months.
11: 38 [A] She and the girls **went** into the hills and wept because she
11: 40 [A] that each year the young women of Israel **go** *out* for four
12: 1 [A] go to fight the Ammonites without calling us to **go** with you?
13: 11 [A] Manoah got up and **followed** [+339] his wife. When he came
14: 3 [A] *Must* you **go** to the uncircumcised Philistines to get a wife?"
14: 9 [A] out with his hands and ate as *he* **went** [+2143] **along**.
14: 9 [A] out with his hands and ate as *he* **went along** [+2143].

Jdg 14: 9 [A] When *he* **rejoined** [+448] his parents, he gave them some,
15: 4 [A] So he **went out** and caught three hundred foxes and tied them
16: 1 [A] One day Samson **went** to Gaza, where he saw a prostitute.
17: 8 [A] **left** [+4946] that town in search of some other place to stay.
17: 9 [A] he said, "and I'm looking for a place to stay." **[NIE]**
17:10 [A] shekels of silver a year, your clothes and your food." **[NIE]**
18: 2 [A] all their clans. They told them, "**Go**, explore the land."
18: 5 [A] to learn whether our journey will be successful." **[NIE]**
18: 6 [A] The priest answered them, "**Go** in peace. Your journey has
18: 6 [A] in peace. Your journey **[NIE]** has the LORD's approval."
18: 7 [A] So the five men **left** and came to Laish, where they saw that
18: 9 [A] to do something? Don't hesitate to **go** there and take it over.
18:14 [A] the five men who **[NIE]** had spied out the land of Laish said
18:17 [A] The five men who **[NIE]** had spied out the land went inside
18:19 [A] say a word. **Come** with us, and be our father and priest.
18:21 [A] their possessions in front of them, they turned away and **left**.
18:24 [A] "You took the gods I made, and my priest, and **went away**.
18:26 [A] So the Danites **went** their way, and Micah, seeing that they
19: 2 [A] *She* **left** [+907+4946] him and went back to her father's
19: 3 [A] her husband **went** to her to persuade her to return. He had
19: 5 [A] On the fourth day they got up early and he prepared to **leave**,
19: 5 [A] "Refresh yourself with something to eat; then *you can* **go**."
19: 7 [A] when the man got up to **go**, his father-in-law persuaded him,
19: 8 [A] when he rose to **go**, the girl's father said, "Refresh yourself.
19: 9 [A] with his concubine and his servant, got up to **leave**, his
19: 9 [A] morning you can get up and **be** on your way home."
19:10 [A] the man **left** and went toward Jebus (that is, Jerusalem), with
19:11 [A] day was almost gone, the servant said to his master, "**Come**,
19:13 [A] He added, "**Come**, let's try to reach Gibeah or Ramah
19:14 [A] and the sun set as *they* **neared** [+725] Gibeah in Benjamin.
19:17 [A] in the city square, the old man asked, "Where *are you* **going**?
19:18 [A] *I have* **been** to Bethlehem in Judah and now I am going to
19:18 [A] in Judah and now I *am* **going** *to* the house of the LORD.
19:27 [A] door of the house and stepped out to **continue** on his way,
19:28 [A] He said to her, "Get up; *let's* **go**." But there was no answer.
19:28 [A] Then the man put her on his donkey and **set out** for home.
20: 8 [A] people rose as one man, saying, "None of *us will* **go** home.
21:10 [A] fighting men with instructions *to* **go** *to* Jabesh Gilead
21:20 [A] the Benjamites, saying, "**Go** and hide in the vineyards
21:21 [A] wife from the girls of Shiloh and **go** *to* the land of Benjamin.
21:23 [A] **[NIE]** they returned to their inheritance and rebuilt the
21:24 [F] At that time the Israelites **left** [+4946] that place and went
Ru 1: 1 [A] two sons, **went** to live for a while in the country of Moab.
1: 7 [A] **set out** on the road that would take them back to the land of
1: 8 [A] "**Go** back, each of *you*, to your mother's home.
1:11 [A] my daughters. Why *would you* **come** with me?
1:12 [A] my daughters; **[RPH]** I am too old to have another husband.
1:16 [A] leave you or to turn back from you. Where *you* **go** I will go,
1:16 [A] Where you go *I will* **go**, and where you stay I will stay.
1:18 [A] When Naomi realized that Ruth was determined to **go** with
1:19 [A] So the two women **went on** until they came to Bethlehem.
1:21 [A] I **went away** full, but the LORD has brought me back
2: 2 [A] "*Let me* **go** *to* the fields and pick up the leftover grain
2: 2 [A] I find favor." Naomi said to her, "**Go ahead**, my daughter."
2: 3 [A] So *she* **went** out and began to glean in the fields behind the
2: 8 [A] Don't **go** and glean in another field and don't go away from
2: 9 [A] the men are harvesting, and **follow along** after the girls.
2: 9 [A] **go** and get a drink from the water jars the men have filled."
2:11 [A] and **came** to live with a people you did not know before.
3:10 [A] You *have* not **run** after the younger men, whether rich or
1Sa 1:17 [A] Eli answered, "**Go** in peace, and may the God of Israel grant
1:18 [A] she **went** her way and ate something, and her face was no
2:11 [A] Elkanah **went** home to Ramah, but the boy ministered before
2:20 [A] and gave to the LORD." Then *they would* **go** home.
2:26 [A] the boy Samuel **continued to grow** in stature and in favor
2:30 [F] and your father's house *would* **minister** before me forever.'
2:35 [F] and *he will* **minister** before my anointed one always.
3: 5 [A] not call; go back and lie down." So *he* **went** and lay down.
3: 6 [A] Samuel got up and **went** to Eli and said, "Here I am; you
3: 8 [A] and Samuel got up and **went** to Eli and said, "Here I am;
3: 9 [A] "**Go** and lie down, and if he calls you, say, 'Speak, LORD,
3: 9 [A] for your servant is listening.' " So Samuel **went** and lay down
6: 6 [A] not send the Israelites out so *they could* **go on** *their* **way**?
6: 8 [A] sending back to him as a guilt offering. Send it **on** *its* **way**,
6:12 [A] **keeping** [+2143] on the road and lowing **all the way**;
6:12 [A] **keeping** on the road and lowing **all the way** [+2143];
6:12 [A] The rulers of the Philistines **followed** [+339] them as far as
7:16 [A] From year to year *he* **went** on a circuit from Bethel to Gilgal
8: 3 [A] his sons *did* not **walk** in his ways. They turned aside after
8: 5 [A] "You are old, and your sons *do* not **walk** in your ways;
8:22 [A] said to the men of Israel, "Everyone **go back** to his town."
9: 3 [A] of the servants with you and **go** and look for the donkeys."
9: 5 [A] said to the servant who was with him, "**Come**, let's go back,
9: 6 [A] and everything he says comes true. *Let's* **go** there now.
9: 6 [A] go there now. Perhaps he will tell us what way *to* **take**."
9: 7 [A] Saul said to his servant, "If *we* **go**, what can we give the
9: 9 [A] if a man **went** to inquire of God, he would say, "Come,
9: 9 [A] inquire of God, he would say, "**Come**, let us go to the seer,"
9: 9 [A] inquire of God, he would say, "Come, *let us* **go** to the seer,"
9:10 [A] "Good," Saul said to his servant. "**Come**, let's go." So they
9:10 [A] "Good," Saul said to his servant. "Come, *let's* **go**." So they
9:10 [A] So *they* **set out** for the town where the man of God was.
10: 2 [A] When you **leave** [+4946+6643] me today, you will meet two
10: 2 [A] 'The donkeys *you* **set out** to look for have been found.
10: 7 [A] **[NIE]** do whatever your hand finds to do, for God is with
10: 9 [A] As Saul turned to **leave** [+4946+6640] Samuel, God changed
10:14 [A] uncle asked him and his servant, "Where *have you* **been**?"
10:26 [A] Saul also **went** to his home in Gibeah, accompanied by
10:26 [A] also went to his home in Gibeah, **accompanied by** [+6640]
11:14 [A] "**Come**, let us go to Gilgal and there reaffirm the kingship."
11:14 [A] "Come, *let us* **go** *to* Gilgal and there reaffirm the kingship."
11:15 [A] So all the people **went** *to* Gilgal and confirmed Saul as king
12: 2 [F] Now you have a king *as* your **leader** [+4200+7156]. As for
12: 2 [F] I *have been* your **leader** [+4200+7156] from my youth until
14: 1 [A] "**Come**, let's go over to the Philistine outpost on the other
14: 3 [A] priest in Shiloh. No one was aware that Jonathan *had* **left**.
14: 6 [A] Jonathan said to his young armor-bearer, "**Come**, let's go
14:16 [A] saw the army **melting away** [+2256+4570] in all directions.
14:17 [A] "Muster the forces and see who *has* **left** [+4946+6640] us."
14:19 [A] camp **increased** [+2143+2256+8041] **more and more**.
14:19 [A] camp **increased more and more** [+2143+2256+8041].
14:46 [A] the Philistines, and they **withdrew** to their own land.
15: 3 [A] Now **go**, attack the Amalekites and totally destroy everything
15: 6 [A] "**Go** away, leave the Amalekites so that I do not destroy you
15:18 [A] saying, '**Go** and completely destroy those wicked people,
15:20 [A] Saul said. "*I* **went** on the mission the LORD assigned me.
15:27 [A] As Samuel turned to **leave**, Saul caught hold of the hem of
15:32 [A] Agag **came** to him confidently, thinking, "Surely the
15:34 [A] Samuel **left** for Ramah, but Saul went up to his home in
16: 1 [A] Fill your horn with oil and **be on** *your* **way**; I am sending
16: 2 [A] Samuel said, "How *can I* **go**? Saul will hear about it and kill
16:13 [A] came upon David in power. Samuel then **went** to Ramah.
17: 7 [A] six hundred shekels. His shield bearer **went** ahead of him.
17:13 [A] Jesse's three oldest sons **[NIE]** had followed Saul to the
17:13 [A] Jesse's three oldest sons *had* **followed** [+339] Saul to the
17:13 [A] **[RPH]** The firstborn was Eliab; the second, Abinadab;
17:14 [A] was the youngest. The three oldest **followed** [+339] Saul,
17:15 [A] David **went** back and **forth** from Saul to tend his father's
17:20 [A] with a shepherd, loaded up and **set out**, as Jesse had directed.
17:32 [A] of this Philistine; your servant *will* **go** and fight him."
17:33 [A] "You are not able to **go out** against this Philistine and fight
17:37 [A] Saul said to David, "**Go**, and the LORD be with you."
17:39 [A] on his sword over the tunic and tried **walking around**,
17:39 [A] "I cannot **go** in these," he said to Saul, "because I am not
17:41 [A] bearer in front of him, **kept coming** [+2143] closer to David.
17:41 [A] bearer in front of him, **kept coming** [+2143] closer to David.
17:44 [A] "**Come** here," he said, "and I'll give your flesh to the birds of
17:48 [A] As the Philistine **moved** closer to attack him, David ran
18:27 [A] David and his men **went out** and killed two hundred
19:12 [A] down through a window, and **[RPH]** he fled and escaped.
19:18 [A] to him. Then he and Samuel **went** to Naioth and stayed there.
19:22 [A] *he* himself **left** for Ramah and went to the great cistern at
19:23 [A] So Saul **went** to Naioth at Ramah. But the Spirit of God
19:23 [A] *he* **walked** [+2143] **along** prophesying until he came to
19:23 [A] *he* **walked along** [+2143] prophesying until he came to
20:11 [A] "**Come**," Jonathan said, "let's go out into the field." So they
20:13 [A] if I do not let you know and send you **away** safely.
20:21 [A] I will send a boy and say, '**Go**, find the arrows.' If I say to
20:22 [A] 'Look, the arrows are beyond you,' then *you must* **go**,
20:40 [A] Then Jonathan gave his weapons to the boy and said, "**Go**,
20:42 [A] Jonathan said to David, "**Go** in peace, for we have sworn
20:42 [21:1] [A] and my descendants forever.' " Then David **left**,
22: 1 [A] David **left** [+4946] Gath and escaped to the cave of Adullam.
22: 3 [A] From there David **went** *to* Mizpah in Moab and said to the
22: 5 [A] **Go** into the land of Judah." So David left and went to the
22: 5 [A] of Judah." So David **left** and went to the forest of Hereth.
23: 2 [A] saying, "*Shall I* **go** and attack these Philistines?"
23: 2 [A] answered him, "**Go**, attack the Philistines and save Keilah."
23: 3 [A] then, if *we* **go** *to* Keilah against the Philistine forces!"
23: 5 [A] So David and his men **went** *to* Keilah, fought the Philistines
23:13 [F] and *kept* **moving** [+889+928+2143] **from place to place**.
23:13 [F] and *kept* **moving from place to place** [+889+928+2143].
23:16 [A] Saul's son Jonathan **went** to David at Horesh and helped him
23:18 [A] Then Jonathan **went** home, but David remained at Horesh.
23:22 [A] **Go** and make further preparation. Find out where David
23:23 [A] *I will* **go** with you; if he is in the area, I will track him down
23:24 [A] So they set out and **went** to Ziph ahead of Saul. Now David
23:25 [A] Saul and his men **began** the search, and when David was told

1Sa 23:26 [A] Saul *was* **going** along one side of the mountain, and David
23:26 [A] men were on the other side, hurrying to **get away** from Saul.
23:27 [A] a messenger came to Saul, saying, "**Come** quickly! The
23:28 [A] off his pursuit of David and **went** to meet the Philistines.
24: 2 [24:3] [A] **set out** to look for David and his men near the Crags
24: 7 [24:8] [A] attack Saul. And Saul left the cave and **went** his way.
24:22 [24:23] [A] Saul **returned** home, but David and his men went
25:15 [F] the whole time we were out in the fields **near** [+907] them
25:27 [F] be given to the men who **follow** [+928+8079] you.
25:42 [A] **attended** [+4200+8079] **by** her five maids, went with
25:42 [A] **went** with David's messengers and became his wife.
26:11 [A] the spear and water jug that are near his head, and *let's* **go**."
26:12 [A] took the spear and water jug near Saul's head, and *they* **left**.
26:19 [A] my share in the LORD's inheritance and have said, '**Go**,
26:25 [A] So David **went** on his way, and Saul returned home.
28: 7 [A] a woman who is a medium, so *I may* **go** and inquire of her."
28: 8 [A] and at night he and two men **[NIE]** went to the woman.
28:22 [A] so you may eat and have the strength *to* **go** on your way."
28:25 [A] his men, and they ate. That same night they got up and **left**.
29: 7 [A] Turn back and **go** in peace; do nothing to displease the
29:10 [A] with you, and **leave** in the morning as soon as it is light."
29:11 [A] his men got up early in the morning to **go** back to the land of
30: 2 [A] of them, but carried them off as *they* **went** on their way.
30: 9 [A] **[NIE]** David and the six hundred men with him came to the
30:21 [A] men who had been too exhausted *to* **follow** [+339] him
30:22 [A] troublemakers among David's **followers** [+408+889+6640]
30:22 [A] followers said, "Because *they did* not **go out** with us,
30:22 [A] However, each man may take his wife and children and **go**."
30:31 [F] in all the other places where David and his men *had* **roamed**.
31:12 [A] all their valiant men **journeyed** through the night to Beth
2Sa 2:19 [A] neither to the right nor to the left as he **pursued** [+339] him.
2:29 [A] that night Abner and his men **marched** through the Arabah.
2:29 [A] **continued** *through* the whole Bithron and came to
2:32 [A] Joab and his men **marched** all night and arrived at Hebron
3: 1 [A] David **grew stronger and stronger** [+2256+2618],
3: 1 [A] the house of Saul **grew weaker and weaker** [+1924+2256].
3:16 [A] Her husband, however, **went** with her, weeping behind her
3:16 [A] went with her, weeping behind her **all the way** to Bahurim.
3:16 [A] Then Abner said to him, "**Go** back home!" So he went back.
3:19 [A] Then he **went** to Hebron to tell David everything that Israel
3:21 [A] "*Let me* **go** at once and assemble all Israel for my lord the
3:21 [A] So David sent Abner away, and *he* **went** in peace.
3:22 [A] because David had sent him away, and *he had* **gone** in peace.
3:23 [A] the king had sent him away and that *he had* **gone** in peace.
3:24 [A] to you. Why did you let him go? Now *he is* **gone** [+2143]!
3:24 [A] to you. Why did you let him go? Now *he is* **gone** [+2143]!
3:31 [A] front of Abner." King David *himself* **walked** behind the bier.
4: 5 [A] Rimmon the Beerothite, **set out** for the house of Ish-Bosheth,
4: 7 [A] it with them, *they* **traveled** all night by way of the Arabah.
5: 6 [A] and his men **marched** *to* Jerusalem to attack the Jebusites,
5:10 [A] he **became more and more powerful** [+1524+2143+2256],
5:10 [A] he **became more and more powerful** [+1524+2143+2256],
6: 2 [A] all his men **set out** from Baalah of Judah to bring up from
6: 4 [A] the ark of God on it, and Ahio *was* **walking** in front of it.
6:12 [A] So David **went down** and brought up the ark of God from the
6:19 [A] and women. And all the people **went** to their homes.
7: 3 [A] in mind, **go ahead** and do it, for the LORD is with you."
7: 5 [A] "**Go** and tell my servant David, 'This is what the LORD
7: 6 [F] I have been **moving from place to place** with a tent as my
7: 7 [F] Wherever *I have* **moved** with all the Israelites, did I ever say
7: 9 [A] I have been with you wherever *you have* **gone**, and I have
7:23 [A] the one nation on earth that God **went out** to redeem as a
8: 3 [A] when he **went** to restore his control along the Euphrates
8: 6 [A] The LORD gave David victory wherever *he* **went**.
8:14 [A] to David. The LORD gave David victory wherever *he* **went**.
10:11 [A] are too strong for you, then *I will* **come** to rescue you.
11: 2 [F] from his bed and **walked around** on the roof of the palace.
11:22 [A] The messenger **set out**, and when he arrived he told David
12:15 [A] After Nathan *had* **gone** home, the LORD struck the child
12:23 [A] back again? I *will* **go** to him, but he will not return to me."
12:29 [A] So David mustered the entire army and **went** to Rabbah,
13: 7 [A] "**Go** *to* the house of your brother Amnon and prepare some
13: 8 [A] So Tamar **went** *to* the house of her brother Amnon, who was
13:13 [G] What about me? Where *could I* **get rid of** my disgrace?
13:15 [A] he had loved her. Amnon said to her, "Get up and **get out**!"
13:19 [A] She put her hand on her head and **went away**, weeping aloud
13:19 [A] on her head and went away, weeping aloud *as she* **went**.
13:24 [A] *Will* the king and his officials please **join** [+6640] me?"
13:25 [A] "All of us *should* not **go**; we would only be a burden to you."
13:25 [A] urged him, he still refused to **go**, but gave him his blessing.
13:26 [A] "If not, please *let* my brother Amnon **come** with us."
13:26 [A] The king asked him, "Why *should he* **go** with you?"
13:34 [A] on the road west of him, **coming** down the side of the hill.
13:37 [A] Absalom fled and **went** to Talmai son of Ammihud, the king
13:38 [A] After Absalom fled and **went** *to* Geshur, he stayed there
14: 8 [A] The king said to the woman, "**Go** home, and I will issue an
14:21 [A] I will do it. **Go**, bring back the young man Absalom."
14:23 [A] Joab **went** to Geshur and brought Absalom back to
14:30 [A] next to mine, and he has barley there. **Go** and set it on fire."
15: 7 [A] "*Let me* **go** to Hebron and fulfill a vow I made to the
15: 9 [A] The king said to him, "**Go** in peace." So he went to Hebron.
15: 9 [A] The king said to him, "Go in peace." So *he* **went** to Hebron.
15:11 [A] Two hundred men from Jerusalem *had* **accompanied** [+907]
15:11 [A] They had been invited as guests and **went** quite innocently,
15:12 [A] and Absalom's following **kept on** increasing.
15:14 [A] We must **leave** immediately, or he will move quickly to
15:19 [A] to Ittai the Gittite, "Why *should* you **come** along with us?
15:20 [A] with us, **[RPH]** when I do not know where I am going?
15:20 [A] when I **do not know where I am going** [+889+2143+6584]?
15:20 [A] when I **do not know where I am going** [+889+2143+6584]?
15:22 [A] David said to Ittai, "**Go ahead**, march on." So Ittai the Gittite
15:30 [A] he went; his head was covered and he was **[RPH]** barefoot.
16:13 [A] his men **continued** along the road while Shimei was going
16:13 [A] his men continued along the road while Shimei *was* **going**
16:13 [A] cursing as *he* **went** and throwing stones at him
16:17 [A] you show your friend? Why didn't *you* **go** with your friend?"
17:11 [A] gathered to you, with you yourself **leading** them into battle.
17:17 [A] A servant girl *was to* **go** and inform them, and they were to
17:17 [A] and inform them, and they *were to* **go** and tell King David,
17:18 [A] So the two of them **left** quickly and went to the house of a
17:21 [A] After the men *had* **gone**, the two climbed out of the well
17:21 [A] two climbed out of the well and **went** to inform King David.
17:23 [A] his donkey and **set out** for his house in his hometown.
18:21 [A] Joab said to a Cushite, "**Go**, tell the king what you have
18:24 [A] the watchman **went up** to the roof of the gateway by the
18:25 [A] must have good news." And the man **came** closer and closer.
18:25 [A] And the man came **closer and closer** [+2256+7929].
18:33 [19:1] [A] over the gateway and wept. As he **went**, he said:
19:15 [19:16] [A] Now the men of Judah had come to Gilgal to **go out**
19:24 [19:25] [A] or washed his clothes from the day the king **left**
19:25 [19:26] [A] "Why didn't *you* **go** with me, Mephibosheth?"
19:26 [19:27] [A] and will ride on it, so *I can* **go** with the king.'
20: 5 [A] when Amasa **went** to summon Judah, he took longer than the
20:21 [A] Hand over this one man, and *I'll* **withdraw** from the city."
21:12 [A] he **went** and took the bones of Saul and his son Jonathan
23:17 [A] "Is it not the blood of men who **went** at the risk of their
24: 1 [A] saying, "**Go** and take a census of Israel and Judah."
24:12 [A] "**Go** and tell David, 'This is what the LORD says: I am
1Ki 1:12 [A] **[NIE]** let me advise you how you can save your own life
1:13 [A] **Go** [+995+2256] **in** to King David and say to him, 'My lord
1:38 [G] Solomon on King David's mule and **escorted** him to Gihon.
1:49 [A] Adonijah's guests rose in alarm and **dispersed** [+2006+4200].
1:50 [A] fear of Solomon, **went** and took hold of the horns of the altar.
1:53 [A] to King Solomon, and Solomon said, "**Go** to your home."
2: 2 [A] "I *am about to* **go** the way of all the earth," he said. "So be
2: 3 [A] **Walk** in his ways, and keep his decrees and commands, his
2: 4 [A] if they **walk** faithfully before me with all their heart and soul,
2: 8 [A] who called down bitter curses on me the day I **went** *to*
2:26 [A] the priest the king said, "**Go back** to your fields in Anathoth.
2:29 [A] ordered Benaiah son of Jehoiada, "**Go**, strike him down!"
2:40 [A] and **went** to Achish at Gath in search of his slaves.
2:40 [A] So Shimei **went away** and brought the slaves back from
2:41 [A] was told that Shimei *had* **gone** from Jerusalem *to* Gath
2:42 [A] and warn you, 'On the day you leave *to* **go** anywhere else,
3: 3 [A] Solomon showed his love for the LORD by **walking**
3: 4 [A] The king **went** to Gibeon to offer sacrifices, for that was the
3: 6 [A] because *he was* **faithful** [+622+928] to you and righteous
3:14 [A] if *you* **walk** in my ways and obey my statutes and commands
3:14 [A] obey my statutes and commands as David your father **did**[s],
6:12 [A] if *you* **follow** [+928] my decrees, carry out my regulations
6:12 [A] and keep all my commands and **obey** [+928] them,
8:23 [A] your servants who **continue** wholeheartedly in your way.
8:25 [A] if only your sons are careful in all they do to **walk** before me
8:25 [A] careful in all they do to walk before me as *you have* **done**[s].'
8:36 [A] Teach them the right way *to* **live**, and send rain on the land
8:58 [A] to **walk** in all his ways and to keep the commands, decrees
8:61 [A] to **live** by his decrees and obey his commands, as at this
8:66 [A] They blessed the king and then **went** home, joyful and glad
9: 4 [A] if *you* **walk** before me in integrity of heart and uprightness,
9: 4 [A] integrity of heart and uprightness, as David your father **did**[s],
9: 6 [A] given you and **go off** to serve other gods and worship them,
10:13 [A] she left and **returned** with her retinue to her own country.
11: 5 [A] He **followed** [+339] Ashtoreth the goddess of the Sidonians,
11:10 [A] Although he had forbidden Solomon *to* **follow** [+339] other
11:21 [A] "Let me go, that *I may* **return** to my own country."
11:22 [A] "What have you lacked here that you want to **go back** to
11:24 [A] the rebels **went** *to* Damascus, where they settled and took
11:33 [A] *have* not **walked** in my ways, nor done what is right in my

1Ki 11:38 [A] If you do whatever I command you and **walk** in my ways
12: 1 [A] Rehoboam **went** *to* Shechem, for all the Israelites had gone
12: 5 [A] "**Go away** for three days and then come back to me."
12: 5 [A] and then come back to me." So the people **went away**.
12:16 [A] your own house, O David!" So the Israelites **went** home.
12:24 [A] they obeyed the word of the LORD and **went home** again,
12:30 [A] the people **went** even as far as Dan to worship the one there.
13: 9 [A] eat bread or drink water or return by the way *you* **came**.' "
13:10 [A] So *he* **took** another road and did not return by the way he had
13:12 [A] Their father asked them, "Which way *did he* **go**?" And his
13:12 [A] him which road the man of God from Judah *had* **taken**.
13:14 [A] **rode** after the man of God. He found him sitting under an
13:15 [A] So the prophet said to him, "**Come** home with me and eat."
13:17 [A] drink water there or return **[RPH]** by the way you came.' "
13:17 [A] or drink water there or return by the way *you* **came**.' "
13:24 [A] As *he* **went on** *his* **way**, a lion met him on the road and killed
13:28 [A] *he* **went out** and found the body thrown down on the road,
14: 2 [A] **go** *to* Shiloh. Ahijah the prophet is there—the one who told
14: 4 [A] wife did what he said and **went** *to* Ahijah's house in Shiloh.
14: 7 [A] **Go**, tell Jeroboam that this is what the LORD, the God of
14: 8 [A] my commands and **followed** [+339] me with all his heart,
14: 9 [A] **[NIE]** You have made for yourself other gods, idols made
14:12 [A] "As for you, **go back** home. When you set foot in your city,
14:17 [A] Then Jeroboam's wife got up and **left** and went to Tirzah.
15: 3 [A] *He* **committed** [+928] all the sins his father had done before
15:19 [A] Now **[NIE]** break your treaty with Baasha king of Israel
15:26 [A] the LORD, **walking** in the ways of his father and in his sin,
15:34 [A] the LORD, **walking** in the ways of Jeroboam and in his sin,
16: 2 [A] *you* **walked** in the ways of Jeroboam and caused my people
16:19 [A] **walking** in the ways of Jeroboam and in the sin he had
16:26 [A] *He* **walked** in all the ways of Jeroboam son of Nebat and in
16:31 [A] He not only considered it trivial *to* **commit** [+928] the sins of
16:31 [A] of the Sidonians, and **began** to serve Baal and worship him.
17: 3 [A] "**Leave** [+4946] here, turn eastward and hide in the Kerith
17: 5 [A] So **[RPH]** he did what the LORD had told him. He went to
17: 5 [A] *He* **went** to the Kerith Ravine, east of the Jordan, and stayed
17: 9 [A] "**Go** at once to Zarephath of Sidon and stay there. I have
17:10 [A] So *he* **went** to Zarephath. When he came to the town gate,
17:11 [A] As *she was* **going** to get it, he called, "And bring me, please,
17:15 [A] *She* **went away** and did as Elijah had told her. So there was
18: 1 [A] "**Go** and present yourself to Ahab, and I will send rain on the
18: 2 [A] So Elijah **went** to present himself to Ahab. Now the famine
18: 5 [A] "**Go** through the land to all the springs and valleys.
18: 6 [A] Ahab **going** in one direction and Obadiah in another.
18: 6 [A] Ahab going in one direction and Obadiah **[RPH]** in another.
18: 8 [A] "Yes," he replied. "**Go** tell your master, 'Elijah is here.' "
18:11 [A] now you tell me *to* **go** to my master and say, 'Elijah is here.'
18:12 [A] the LORD may carry you when I **leave** [+907+4946] you.
18:14 [A] now you tell me *to* **go** to my master and say, 'Elijah is here.'
18:16 [A] So Obadiah **went** to meet Ahab and told him, and Ahab went
18:16 [A] to meet Ahab and told him, and Ahab **went** to meet Elijah.
18:18 [A] LORD's commands and *have* **followed** [+339] the Baals.
18:21 [A] If the LORD is God, **follow** [+339] him; but if Baal is God,
18:21 [A] is God, follow him; but if Baal is God, **follow** [+339] him."
18:35 [A] The water **ran down** around the altar and even filled the
18:45 [A] a heavy rain came on and Ahab rode off **[NIE]** to Jezreel.
19: 3 [A] Elijah was afraid and **ran** for his life. When he came to
19: 4 [A] while *he* himself **went** a day's journey into the desert. He
19: 8 [A] *he* **traveled** forty days and forty nights until he reached
19:15 [A] The LORD said to him, "**Go** back the way you came,
19:19 [A] So Elijah **went** from there and found Elisha son of Shaphat.
19:20 [A] mother good-by," he said, "and then *I will* **come** with you."
19:20 [A] "and then I will come with you." "**Go** back," Elijah replied.
19:21 [A] he set out *to* **follow** [+339] Elijah and became his attendant.
20: 9 [A] this demand I cannot meet.' " They **left** and took the answer
20:22 [A] **[NIE]** "Strengthen your position and see what must be
20:27 [A] and given provisions, *they* **marched out** to meet them.
20:36 [A] as soon as you **leave** [+907+4946] me a lion will kill you."
20:36 [A] after the man **went** away, a lion found him and killed him.
20:38 [A] the prophet **went** and stood by the road waiting for the king.
20:43 [A] and angry, the king of Israel **went** to his palace in Samaria.
21:26 [A] He behaved in the vilest manner by **going** after idols, like the
21:27 [D] and fasted. He lay in sackcloth and **went around** meekly.
22: 4 [A] "*Will you* **go** with me to fight against Ramoth Gilead?"
22: 6 [A] and asked them, "*Shall I* **go** to war against Ramoth Gilead,
22:13 [A] The messenger who *had* **gone** to summon Micaiah said to
22:15 [A] "Micaiah, *shall we* **go** to war against Ramoth Gilead, or shall
22:43 [A] In everything *he* **walked** in the ways of his father Asa
22:48 [22:49] [A] Now Jehoshaphat built a fleet of trading ships to **go**
22:48 [22:49] [A] to go to Ophir for gold, but *they* never **set sail**—
22:49 [22:50] [A] "*Let* my men **sail** [+641+928+2021] with your
22:52 [22:53] [A] because *he* **walked** in the ways of his father
2Ki 1: 2 [A] saying to them, "**Go** and consult Baal-Zebub, the god of
1: 3 [A] because there is no God in Israel that you *are* **going off** to
1: 4 [A] you are lying on. You will certainly die!' " So Elijah **went**.
1: 6 [A] he said to us, '**Go** back to the king who sent you and tell him,
2: 1 [A] Elijah and Elisha **were on** *their* **way** from Gilgal.
2: 6 [A] I will not leave you." So the two of them **walked on**.
2: 7 [A] Fifty men of the company of the prophets **went** and stood at
2:11 [A] As they were **walking** [+2143] **along** and talking *together*,
2:11 [A] As they were **walking along** and talking **together** [+2143],
2:16 [A] have fifty able men. *Let them* **go** and look for your master.
2:18 [A] in Jericho, he said to them, "Didn't I tell you not *to* **go**?"
2:25 [A] *he* **went on** to Mount Carmel and from there returned to
3: 7 [A] **[NIE]** He also sent this message to Jehoshaphat king of
3: 7 [A] *Will you* **go** with me to fight against Moab?" "I will go with
3: 9 [A] So the king of Israel **set out** with the king of Judah
3:13 [A] **Go** to the prophets of your father and the prophets of your
4: 3 [A] "**Go** around and ask all your neighbors for empty jars.
4: 5 [A] *She* **left** [+907+4946] him and afterward shut the door
4: 7 [A] of God, and he said, "**Go**, sell the oil and pay your debts.
4:23 [A] "Why **go** to him today?" he asked. "It's not the New Moon
4:24 [A] the donkey and said to her servant, "**Lead on** [+2256+5627];
4:25 [A] So *she* **set out** and came to the man of God at Mount Carmel.
4:29 [A] your cloak into your belt, take my staff in your hand and **run**.
4:30 [A] I will not leave you." So he got up and **followed** [+339] her.
4:35 [A] Elisha turned away and **walked** back and forth in the room
5: 5 [A] "**By all means, go** [+995]," the king of Aram replied. "I will
5: 5 [A] So Naaman **left**, taking with him ten talents of silver, six
5:10 [A] Elisha sent a messenger to say to him, "**Go**, wash yourself
5:11 [A] Naaman **went away** angry and said, "I thought that he would
5:12 [A] and be cleansed?" So he turned and **went off** in a rage.
5:19 [A] "**Go** in peace," Elisha said. After Naaman had traveled some
5:19 [A] Elisha said. After Naaman *had* **traveled** some distance,
5:24 [A] them away in the house. He sent the men away and *they* **left**.
5:25 [A] "Your servant didn't **go** anywhere," Gehazi answered.
5:26 [A] "*Was* not my spirit **with** you when the man got down from
6: 2 [A] *Let us* **go** to the Jordan, where each of us can get a pole;
6: 2 [A] let us build a place there for us to live." And he said, "**Go**."
6: 3 [A] of them said, "*Won't you* please **come** with your servants?"
6: 3 [A] please come with your servants?" "I **will**," Elisha replied.
6: 4 [A] *he* **went** with them. They went to the Jordan and began to cut
6:13 [A] "**Go**, find out where he is," the king ordered, "so I can send
6:19 [A] **Follow** [+339] me, and I will lead you to the man you are
6:19 [G] and *I will* **lead** you to the man you are looking for."
6:19 [G] to the man you are looking for." And *he* **led** them to Samaria.
6:22 [A] they may eat and drink and then **go back** to their master."
6:23 [A] he sent them away, and *they* **returned** to their master.
7: 4 [A] So *let's* **go over** to the camp of the Arameans and surrender.
7: 8 [A] away silver, gold and clothes, and **went off** and hid them.
7: 8 [A] and took some things from it and **[RPH]** hid them also.
7: 9 [A] *Let's* **go** [+995+2256] **at once** and report this to the royal
7:14 [A] the drivers, "**Go** and find out what has happened."
7:15 [A] *They* **followed** [+339] them as far as the Jordan, and they
8: 1 [A] "**Go away** with your family and stay for a while wherever
8: 2 [A] She and her family **went away** and stayed in the land of the
8: 8 [A] "Take a gift with you and **go** to meet the man of God.
8: 9 [A] Hazael **went** to meet Elisha, taking with him as a gift forty
8:10 [A] Elisha answered, "**Go** and say to him, 'You will certainly
8:14 [A] Hazael **left** [+907+4946] Elisha and returned to his master.
8:18 [A] *He* **walked** in the ways of the kings of Israel, as the house of
8:27 [A] *He* **walked** in the ways of the house of Ahab and did evil in
8:28 [A] Ahaziah **went** with Joram son of Ahab to war against Hazael
9: 1 [A] take this flask of oil with you and **go** *to* Ramoth Gilead.
9: 4 [A] So the young man, the prophet, **went** *to* Ramoth Gilead.
9:15 [A] don't let anyone slip out of the city to **go** and tell the news in
9:16 [A] he got into his chariot and **rode** to Jezreel, because Joram
9:18 [A] The horseman **rode off** to meet Jehu and said, "This is what
9:35 [A] when *they* **went out** to bury her, they found nothing except
10:12 [A] Jehu then set out and **went** *toward* Samaria. At Beth Eked of
10:15 [A] After *he* **left** [+4946] there, he came upon Jehonadab son of
10:16 [A] Jehu said, "**Come** with me and see my zeal for the LORD."
10:25 [A] then **entered** [+6330] the inner shrine of the temple of Baal.
10:31 [A] Yet Jehu was not careful to **keep** [+928] the law of the
13: 2 [A] He did evil in the eyes of the LORD *by* **following** [+339]
13: 6 [A] he had caused Israel to commit; *they* **continued** in them.
13:11 [A] which he had caused Israel to commit; *he* **continued** in them.
13:21 [A] **[NIE]** When the body touched Elisha's bones, the man
14: 8 [A] of Israel, with the challenge: "**Come**, meet me face to face."
16: 3 [A] *He* **walked** in the ways of the kings of Israel and even
16:10 [A] King Ahaz **went** *to* Damascus to meet Tiglath-Pileser king of
17: 8 [A] **followed** [+928] the practices of the nations the LORD had
17:15 [A] *They* **followed** [+339] worthless idols and themselves
17:19 [A] *They* **followed** [+928] the practices Israel had introduced.
17:22 [A] The Israelites **persisted** in all the sins of Jeroboam and did
17:27 [G] "**Have** one of the priests you took captive from Samaria **go**
17:27 [A] you took captive from Samaria go back **[RPH]** to live there
19:36 [A] So Sennacherib king of Assyria broke camp and **withdrew**.

2Ki 20: 3 [F] how *I have* **walked** before you faithfully and with
20: 9 [A] *Shall* the shadow **go forward** ten steps, or shall it go back
21:21 [A] *He* **walked** in all the ways of his father; he worshiped the
21:21 [A] He walked in all the ways of **[RPH]** his father; he
21:22 [A] of his fathers, and *did* not **walk** in the way of the LORD.
22: 2 [A] the LORD and **walked** in all the ways of his father David,
22:13 [A] "**Go** and inquire of the LORD for me and for the people
22:14 [A] Shaphan and Asaiah **went** to speak to the prophetess Huldah,
23: 3 [A] to **follow** [+339] the LORD and keep his commands,
23:29 [A] King Josiah **marched out** to meet him in battle, but Neco
24:15 [G] *He* also **took** [+906+906+906+906+1583] from Jerusalem to
25: 4 [A] were surrounding the city. *They* **fled** toward the Arabah,
25:20 [G] them all and **brought** them to the king of Babylon at Riblah.
1Ch 4:39 [A] *they* **went** to the outskirts of Gedor to the east of the valley
4:42 [A] the sons of Ishi, **invaded** [+4200] the hill country of Seir.
6:15 [5:41] [A] Jehozadak *was* **deported** when the LORD sent
11: 4 [A] David and all the Israelites **marched** *to* Jerusalem (that is,
11: 9 [A] David **became more and more powerful** [+1524+2143+2256]
11: 9 [A] David **became more and more powerful** [+1524+2143+2256]
12:20 [12:21] [A] When David **went** to Ziklag, these were the men of
15:25 [A] the commanders of units of a thousand **went** to bring up the
16:20 [F] *they* **wandered** from nation to nation, from one kingdom to
16:43 [A] all the people **left**, each for his own home, and David
17: 4 [A] "**Go** and tell my servant David, 'This is what the LORD
17: 6 [F] Wherever *I have* **moved** with all the Israelites, did I ever say
17: 8 [A] I have been with you wherever *you have* **gone**, and I have
17:11 [A] When your days are over and you **go** to be with your fathers,
17:21 [A] the one nation on earth whose God **went out** to redeem a
18: 3 [A] when he **went** to establish his control along the Euphrates
18: 6 [A] The LORD gave David victory everywhere *he* **went**.
18:13 [A] The LORD gave David victory everywhere *he* **went**.
19: 5 [A] When *someone* **came** and told David about the men, he sent
21: 2 [A] "**Go** and count the Israelites from Beersheba to Dan.
21: 4 [F] so Joab left and **went** throughout Israel and then came back to
21:10 [A] "**Go** and tell David, 'This is what the LORD says: I am
21:30 [A] David could not **go** before it to inquire of God, because he
2Ch 1: 3 [A] and the whole assembly **went** to the high place at Gibeon,
6:14 [A] your servants who **continue** wholeheartedly in your way.
6:16 [A] if only your sons are careful in all they do to **walk** before me
6:16 [A] to walk before me according to my law, as *you have* **done**[s].'
6:27 [A] Teach them the right way *to* **live**, and send rain on the land
6:31 [A] **walk** in your ways all the time they live in the land you gave
7:17 [A] "As for you, if *you* **walk** before me as David your father did,
7:17 [A] for you, if you walk before me as David your father **did**[s],
7:19 [A] given you and **go off** to serve other gods and worship them,
8: 3 [A] Solomon then **went** *to* Hamath Zobah and captured it.
8:17 [A] Solomon **went** to Ezion Geber and Elath on the coast of
9:12 [A] she left and **returned** with her retinue to her own country.
9:21 [A] The king had a **fleet of trading ships** [+641+9576] manned
10: 1 [A] Rehoboam **went** to Shechem, for all the Israelites had gone
10: 5 [A] "Come back to me in three days." So the people **went away**.
10:16 [A] your own house, O David!" So all the Israelites **went** home.
11: 4 [A] and turned back from **marching** against Jeroboam.
11:14 [A] **came** to Judah and Jerusalem because Jeroboam and his sons
11:17 [A] **walking** in the ways of David and Solomon during this time.
16: 3 [A] Now **[NIE]** break your treaty with Baasha king of Israel
17: 3 [A] because in his early years *he* **walked** in the ways his father
17: 4 [A] **followed** [+928] his commands rather than the practices of
17:12 [A] Jehoshaphat became **more and more powerful**
[+1541+2025+2256+4200+5087+6330]; he built forts
18: 3 [A] of Judah, "*Will you* **go** with me *against* Ramoth Gilead?"
18: 5 [A] and asked them, "*Shall we* **go** to war against Ramoth Gilead,
18:12 [A] The messenger who *had* **gone** to summon Micaiah said to
18:14 [A] "Micaiah, *shall we* **go** to war against Ramoth Gilead, or shall
20:32 [A] *He* **walked** in the ways of his father Asa and did not stray
20:36 [A] to construct a **fleet of trading ships** [+641+4200+9576].
20:37 [A] The ships were wrecked and were not able to **set sail** to trade.
21: 6 [A] *He* **walked** in the ways of the kings of Israel, as the house of
21:12 [A] '*You have* not **walked** in the ways of your father
21:13 [A] *you have* **walked** in the ways of the kings of Israel, and you
21:20 [A] *He* **passed away**, to no one's regret, and was buried in the
22: 3 [A] He too **walked** in the ways of the house of Ahab, for his
22: 5 [A] *He* also **followed** [+928] their counsel when he went with
22: 5 [A] He also followed their counsel when *he* **went** with Joram son
24:25 [A] When the Arameans **withdrew** [+4946], they left Joash
25:10 [A] who had come to him from Ephraim and **sent** them home.
25:11 [A] his strength and led his army **[NIE]** to the Valley of Salt,
25:13 [A] *had* not *allowed to* **take part** [+6640] in the war raided
25:17 [A] king of Israel: "**Come**, [K 3870+4200] meet me face to face."
26: 8 [A] his fame **spread** as far as the border of Egypt, because he had
28: 2 [A] *He* **walked** in the ways of the kings of Israel and also made
30: 6 [A] couriers **went** throughout Israel and Judah with letters from
33:11 [G] bound him with bronze shackles and **took** him to Babylon.
34: 2 [A] of the LORD and **walked** in the ways of his father David,
34:21 [A] "**Go** and inquire of the LORD for me and for the remnant in
34:22 [A] those the king had sent with him **went** to speak to the
34:31 [A] to **follow** [+339] the LORD and keep his commands,
35:24 [G] in the other chariot he had and **brought** him *to* Jerusalem,
36: 6 [G] and bound him with bronze shackles to **take** him to Babylon.
Ezr 8:31 [A] month we set out from the Ahava Canal to **go** *to* Jerusalem.
10: 6 [A] of God and **went** to the room of Jehohanan son of Eliashib.
10: 6 [A] **[RPH]** While he was there, he ate no food and drank no
Ne 2:16 [A] The officials did not know where *I had* **gone** or what I was
2:17 [A] **Come**, let us rebuild the wall of Jerusalem, and we will no
5: 9 [A] Shouldn't *you* **walk** in the fear of our God to avoid the
6: 2 [A] "**Come**, let us meet together in one of the villages on the
6: 7 [A] will get back to the king; so **come**, let us confer together."
6:17 [A] in those days the nobles of Judah were **sending** many letters
8:10 [A] Nehemiah said, "**Go** and enjoy choice food and sweet drinks,
8:12 [A] all the people **went away** to eat and drink, to send portions of
9:12 [A] pillar of fire to give them light on the way *they were to* **take**.
9:19 [A] pillar of fire by night to shine on the way *they were to* **take**.
10:29 [10:30] [A] an oath to **follow** [+928] the Law of God given
12:31 [A] One *was to* **proceed** [BHS 9336] on top of the wall to the
12:32 [A] and half the leaders of Judah **followed** [+339] them,
12:38 [A] The second choir **proceeded** in the opposite direction. I
Est 2:11 [F] Every day he **walked back and forth** near the courtyard of
4:16 [A] "**Go**, gather together all the Jews who are in Susa, and fast
9: 4 [A] his reputation **spread** throughout the provinces, and he
9: 4 [A] and he **became more and more powerful** [+1524+2256].
Job 1: 4 [A] His sons *used to* **take turns** [+3427] holding feasts in their
1: 7 [F] roaming through the earth and **going back and forth** in it."
2: 2 [F] roaming through the earth and **going back and forth** in it."
7: 9 [A] As a cloud vanishes and *is* **gone**, so he who goes down to the
10:21 [A] before *I* **go** to the place of no return, to the land of gloom
12:17 [G] *He* **leads** counselors **away** stripped and makes fools of
12:19 [G] *He* **leads** priests **away** stripped and overthrows men long
14:20 [A] You overpower him once for all, and *he is* **gone**; you change
16: 6 [A] my pain is not relieved; and if I refrain, *it does* not **go** away.
16:22 [A] "Only a few years will pass before *I* **go** *on* the journey of no
18: 8 [F] His feet thrust him into a net and *he* **wanders** into its mesh.
19:10 [A] He tears me down on every side till *I am* **gone**; he uproots
20:25 [A] gleaming point out of his liver. Terrors *will* **come** over him;
22:14 [F] so he does not see us as *he* **goes about** *in* the vaulted
23: 8 [A] "But if *I* **go** *to* the east, he is not there; if I go to the west, I
24:10 [D] Lacking clothes, *they* **go about** naked; they carry the
27:21 [A] The east wind carries him off, and *he is* **gone**; it sweeps him
29: 3 [A] upon my head and by his light *I* **walked** *through* darkness!
30:28 [D] *I* **go about** blackened, but not by the sun; I stand up in the
31: 5 [A] "If *I have* **walked** in falsehood or my foot has hurried after
31: 7 [A] if my heart *has been* **led** [+339] *by* my eyes, or if my hands
31:26 [A] the sun in its radiance or the moon **moving** in splendor,
34: 8 [A] company with evildoers; he **associates** with wicked men.
34:23 [A] men further, that they *should* **come** before him for judgment.
38:16 [F] the springs of the sea or **walked** in the recesses of the deep?
38:35 [A] Do you send the lightning bolts **on** *their* **way**? Do they report
41:19 [41:11] [A] Firebrands **stream** from his mouth; sparks of fire
42: 8 [A] take seven bulls and seven rams and **go** to my servant Job
42: 9 [A] Zophar the Naamathite **[RPH]** did what the LORD told
Ps 1: 1 [A] Blessed is the man who *does* not **walk** in the counsel of the
12: 8 [12:9] [F] The wicked **freely strut** about when what is vile is
15: 2 [A] *He whose* **walk** *is* blameless and who does what is righteous,
23: 4 [A] Even though *I* **walk** through the valley of the shadow of
26: 1 [A] O LORD, for I *have* **led** [+928] a blameless **life**;
26: 3 [F] love is ever before me, and *I* **walk continually** in your truth.
26:11 [A] I **lead** [+928] a blameless **life**; redeem me and be merciful to
32: 8 [A] I will instruct you and teach you in the way *you should* **go**;
34: T [34:1] [A] before Abimelech, who drove him away, and *he* **left**.
34:11 [34:12] [A] **Come**, my children, listen to me; I will teach you
35:14 [F] *I* **went about** mourning as though for my friend or brother.
38: 6 [38:7] [D] brought very low; all day long *I* **go about** mourning.
39: 6 [39:7] [F] Man is a mere phantom *as he* **goes to and fro**:
39:13 [39:14] [A] that I may rejoice again before *I* **depart** and am no
42: 9 [42:10] [A] Why *must I* **go about** mourning, oppressed by the
43: 2 [F] Why *must I* **go about** mourning, oppressed by the enemy?
46: 8 [46:9] [A] **Come** and see the works of the LORD,
55:14 [55:15] [D] *as we* **walked** with the throng at the house of God.
56:13 [56:14] [F] that I *may* **walk** before God in the light of life.
58: 7 [58:8] [F] Let them vanish like water *that* **flows away**; when
58: 8 [58:9] [A] Like a slug melting away *as it* **moves along**, like a
66: 5 [A] **Come** and see what God has done, how awesome his works
66:16 [A] **Come** and listen, all you who fear God; let me tell you what
68:21 [68:22] [F] the hairy crowns of *those who* **go on** in their sins.
73: 9 [A] to heaven, and their tongues **take possession** of the earth.
77:17 [77:18] [F] with thunder; your arrows **flashed back and forth**.
78:10 [A] did not keep God's covenant and refused to **live** by his law.
78:39 [A] they were but flesh, a **passing** breeze that does not return.
80: 2 [80:3] [A] Awaken your might; **come** and save us.

[F] Hitpael (hitpoel, hitpoal, hitpolel, hitpolal, hitpalel, hitpalal, hitpalpel, hitpalpal, hotpael, hotpaal) [G] Hiphil (hiphtil) [H] Hophal [I] Hishtaphel

Ps 81:12 [81:13] [A] stubborn hearts *to* **follow** [+928] their own devices.
81:13 [81:14] [D] listen to me, if Israel *would* **follow** [+928] my ways,
82: 5 [F] *They* **walk about** in darkness; all the foundations of the earth
83: 4 [83:5] [A] "**Come**," they say, "let us destroy them as a nation,
84: 7 [84:8] [A] *They* **go** from strength to strength, till each appears
84:11 [84:12] [A] he withhold from those *whose* **walk** is blameless.
85:13 [85:14] [D] Righteousness **goes** before him and prepares the
86:11 [D] me your way, O LORD, and *I will* **walk** in your truth;
89:15 [89:16] [D] *who* **walk** in the light of your presence, O LORD.
89:30 [89:31] [A] my law and *do* not **follow** [+928] my statutes,
91: 6 [A] nor the pestilence *that* **stalks** in the darkness, nor the plague
95: 1 [A] **Come**, let us sing for joy to the LORD; let us shout aloud to
97: 3 [A] Fire **goes** before him and consumes his foes on every side.
101: 2 [F] come to me? *I will* **walk** in my house with blameless heart.
101: 6 [A] *he whose* **walk** [+928+2006] *is* blameless will minister to
104: 3 [D] the clouds his chariot and **rides** on the wings of the wind.
104:10 [D] pour water into the ravines; *it* **flows** between the mountains.
104:26 [D] There the ships **go to and fro**, and the leviathan, which you
105:13 [F] *they* **wandered** from nation to nation, from one kingdom to
105:41 [A] and water gushed out; like a river *it* **flowed** in the desert.
106: 9 [G] dried up; *he* **led** them through the depths as through a desert.
107: 7 [A] He led them by a straight way **[NIE]** to a city where they
109:23 [C] *I* **fade away** like an evening shadow; I am shaken off like a
115: 7 [D] they have hands, but cannot feel, feet, but *they* cannot **walk**;
116: 9 [F] that *I may* **walk** before the LORD in the land of the living.
119: 1 [A] are blameless, who **walk** according to the law of the LORD.
119: 3 [A] They do nothing wrong; *they* **walk** in his ways.
119:45 [F] *I will* **walk about** in freedom, for I have sought out your
122: 1 [A] who said to me, "*Let us* **go** *to* the house of the LORD."
125: 5 [G] those who turn to crooked ways the LORD *will* **banish** with
126: 6 [A] *He who* **goes** [+2143] **out** weeping, carrying seed to sow,
126: 6 [A] *He who* **goes out** [+2143] weeping, carrying seed to sow,
128: 1 [A] Blessed are all who fear the LORD, who **walk** in his ways.
131: 1 [D] *I do* not **concern** *myself* with great matters or things too
136:16 [G] to *him who* **led** his people through the desert, *His love*
138: 7 [A] Though *I* **walk** in the midst of trouble, you preserve my life;
139: 7 [A] Where *can I* **go** from your Spirit? Where can I flee from your
142: 3 [142:4] [D] In the path where *I* **walk** men have hidden a snare
143: 8 [A] Show me the way *I should* **go**, for to you I lift up my soul.
Pr 1:11 [A] If they say, "**Come** along with us; let's lie in wait for
1:15 [A] my son, *do* not **go** [+928+2006] along with them, do not set
2: 7 [A] the upright, he is a shield to *those whose* **walk** is blameless,
2:13 [A] who leave the straight paths to **walk** in dark ways,
2:20 [A] Thus *you will* **walk** in the ways of good men and keep to the
3:23 [A] *you will* **go** *on* your way in safety, and your foot will not
3:28 [A] Do not say to your neighbor, "**Come** back later; I'll give it
4:12 [A] When you **walk**, your steps will not be hampered; when you
4:18 [A] the first gleam of dawn, **shining ever brighter** [+239+2256]
6: 3 [A] **Go** and humble yourself; press your plea with your neighbor!
6: 6 [A] **Go** to the ant, *you* sluggard; consider its ways and be wise!
6:11 [D] poverty will come on you like a **bandit** and scarcity like an
6:12 [A] and villain, *who* **goes about** with a corrupt mouth,
6:22 [F] When you **walk**, they will guide you; when you sleep,
6:28 [D] Can a man **walk** on hot coals without his feet being
7:18 [A] **Come**, let's drink deep of love till morning; let's enjoy
7:19 [A] My husband is not at home; *he has* **gone** on a long journey.
7:22 [A] All at once *he* **followed** [+339] her like an ox going to the
8:20 [D] *I* **walk** in the way of righteousness, along the paths of justice,
9: 5 [A] "**Come**, eat my food and drink the wine I have mixed.
10: 9 [A] The **man**[s] of integrity walks securely, but he who takes
10: 9 [A] The man of integrity **walks** securely, but he who takes
11:13 [A] A **gossip** [+8215] betrays a confidence, but a trustworthy
13:20 [A] *He who* **walks** with the wise grows wise, but a companion of
14: 2 [A] *He* whose **walk** is upright fears the LORD, but he whose
14: 7 [A] **Stay** away from a foolish man, for you will not find
15:12 [A] resents correction; *he will* not **consult** [+448] the wise.
15:21 [A] but a man of understanding keeps a straight **course**.
16:29 [G] his neighbor and **leads** him down a path that is not good.
19: 1 [A] Better a poor man whose **walk** is blameless than a fool
20: 7 [F] The righteous man **leads a** blameless **life**; blessed are his
20:19 [A] A **gossip** [+8215] betrays a confidence; so avoid a man who
23:31 [F] when it sparkles in the cup, when *it* **goes down** smoothly!
24:34 [F] poverty will come on you like a **bandit** and scarcity like an
28: 6 [A] Better a poor man *whose* **walk** *is* blameless than a rich man
28:18 [A] *He whose* **walk** is blameless is kept safe, but he whose ways
28:26 [A] in himself is a fool, but *he who* **walks** in wisdom is kept safe.
30:29 [A] stately in their stride, four *that* **move** with stately bearing:
Ecc 1: 4 [A] Generations **come** and generations go, but the earth remains
1: 6 [A] The wind **blows** to the south and turns to the north; round
1: 6 [A] round and round *it* **goes**, ever returning on its course.
1: 7 [A] All streams **flow** into the sea, yet the sea is never full.
1: 7 [A] To the place the streams **come** from, there they return again.
1: 7 [A] To the place the streams come from, there they **return** again.
2: 1 [A] I thought in my heart, "**Come** now, I will test you with
2:14 [A] has eyes in his head, while the fool **walks** in the darkness;
3:20 [A] All **go** to the same place; all come from dust, and to dust all
4:15 [D] all who lived and **walked** under the sun followed the youth,
5: 1 [4:17] [A] Guard your steps when *you* **go** to the house of God.
5:15 [5:14] [A] **[NIE]** He takes nothing from his labor that he can
5:15 [5:14] [G] He takes nothing from his labor that *he can* **carry** in
5:16 [5:15] [A] As a man comes, so *he* **departs**, and what does he
6: 4 [A] It comes without meaning, *it* **departs** in darkness, and in
6: 6 [A] fails to enjoy his prosperity. *Do* not all **go** to the same place?
6: 8 [A] man gain by knowing how to **conduct** *himself* before others?
6: 9 [A] Better what the eye sees than the **roving** *of* the appetite.
7: 2 [A] It is better to **go** to a house of mourning than to go to a house
7: 2 [A] It is better to go to a house of mourning than *to* **go** to a house
8: 3 [A] Do not be in a hurry *to* **leave** [+4946] the king's presence.
8:10 [D] those who used to come and **go** from the holy place
9: 7 [A] **Go**, eat your food with gladness, and drink your wine with a
9:10 [A] it with all your might, for in the grave, where you *are* **going**,
10: 3 [A] Even as *he* **walks** along the road, the fool lacks sense and
10: 7 [A] slaves on horseback, while princes **go** on foot like slaves.
10:15 [A] fool's work wearies him; he does not know the **way** to town.
10:20 [G] because a bird of the air *may* **carry** your words,
11: 9 [D] **Follow** [+928] the ways of your heart and whatever your
12: 5 [A] man **goes** to his eternal home and mourners go about the
SS 2:10 [A] "Arise, my darling, my beautiful one, and **come** with me.
2:11 [A] See! The winter is past; the rains are over and **gone**.
2:13 [A] Arise, **come**, [Q 3871+4200] my darling; my beautiful one,
2:13 [A] Arise, come, my darling; my beautiful one, **come** with me."
4: 6 [A] *I will* **go** to the mountain of myrrh and to the hill of incense.
6: 1 [A] Where *has* your lover **gone**, most beautiful of women?
7: 9 [7:10] [A] *May* the wine **go** straight to my lover, flowing gently
7:11 [7:12] [A] **Come**, my lover, let us go to the countryside, let us
Isa 1:18 [A] "**Come** now, let us reason together," says the LORD.
2: 3 [A] Many peoples *will* **come** and say, "Come, let us go up to the
2: 3 [A] Many peoples will come and say, "**Come**, let us go up to the
2: 3 [A] He will teach us his ways, so that *we may* **walk** in his paths."
2: 5 [A] **Come**, O house of Jacob, let us walk in the light of the
2: 5 [A] O house of Jacob, *let us* **walk** in the light of the LORD.
3:16 [A] **walking along** with outstretched necks, flirting with their
3:16 [A] **tripping along with mincing steps** [+2256+3262],
3:16 [A] **[RPH]** with ornaments jingling on their ankles.
6: 8 [A] And who *will* **go** for us?" And I said, "Here am I. Send me!"
6: 9 [A] He said, "**Go** and tell this people: " 'Be ever hearing, but
8: 6 [A] "Because this people has rejected the gently **flowing** waters
8: 7 [A] It will overflow all its channels, **run** over all its banks
8:11 [A] warning me not *to* **follow** [+928] the way of this people.
9: 2 [9:1] [A] The people **walking** in darkness have seen a great
18: 2 [A] **Go**, swift messengers, to a people tall and smooth-skinned,
20: 2 [A] **[NIE]** "Take off the sackcloth from your body and the
20: 2 [A] And he did so, **going around** stripped and barefoot.
20: 3 [A] "Just as my servant Isaiah *has* **gone** stripped and barefoot for
21: 6 [A] to me: "**Go**, post a lookout and have him report what he sees.
22:15 [A] "**Go** [+995], say to this steward, to Shebna, who is in charge
26:20 [A] **Go**, my people, enter your rooms and shut the doors behind
28:13 [A] so that *they will* **go** and fall backward, be injured and snared
30: 2 [A] who **go** down to Egypt without consulting me; who look for
30:21 [A] a voice behind you, saying, "This is the way; **walk** in it."
30:29 [A] your hearts will rejoice as *when* people **go up** with flutes to
33:15 [A] *He who* **walks** righteously and speaks what is right,
33:21 [A] No galley with oars *will* **ride** [+928] them, no mighty ship
35: 8 [A] not journey on it; it will be for those *who* **walk** *in* that Way;
35: 9 [A] not be found there. But only the redeemed *will* **walk** there,
37:37 [A] So Sennacherib king of Assyria broke camp and **withdrew**.
38: 3 [F] how *I have* **walked** before you faithfully and with
38: 5 [A] "**Go** and tell Hezekiah, 'This is what the LORD, the God of
38:10 [A] "In the prime of my life *must I* **go** through the gates of death
40:31 [A] will run and not grow weary, *they will* **walk** and not be faint.
42: 5 [A] gives breath to its people, and life to those *who* **walk** on it:
42:16 [G] *I will* **lead** the blind by ways they have not known,
42:24 [A] For they would not **follow** [+928] his ways; they did not obey
43: 2 [A] When *you* **walk** through the fire, you will not be burned;
45: 2 [A] I *will* **go** before you and will level the mountains; I will break
45:14 [A] *they will* **trudge** behind you, coming over to you in chains.
45:16 [A] and disgraced; *they will* **go off** into disgrace together.
46: 2 [A] to rescue the burden, *they* themselves **go off** into captivity.
48:17 [A] is best for you, who directs you in the way *you should* **go**.
48:21 [G] They did not thirst *when he* **led** them through the deserts;
50:10 [A] Let *him* who **walks** *in* the dark, who has no light, trust in the
50:11 [A] *go*, **walk** in the light of your fires and of the torches you have
52:12 [A] you will not leave in haste or **go** in flight; for the LORD
52:12 [A] for the LORD *will* **go** before you, the God of Israel will be
55: 1 [A] "Come, all you who are thirsty, **come** to the waters; and you
55: 1 [A] the waters; and you who have no money, **come**, buy and eat!
55: 1 [A] **Come**, buy wine and milk without money and without cost.
55: 3 [A] Give ear and **come** to me; hear me, that your soul may live.

Isa 57: 2 [A] *Those who* **walk** uprightly enter into peace; they find rest as
57:17 [A] my face in anger, yet *he* **kept** [+8743] **on** in his willful ways.
58: 8 [A] your righteousness *will* **go** before you, and the glory of the
59: 9 [D] all is darkness; for brightness, but *we* **walk** in deep shadows.
60: 3 [A] Nations *will* **come** to your light, and kings to the brightness
60:14 [A] The sons of your oppressors *will* **come** bowing before you;
63:12 [G] *who* **sent** his glorious arm of power to be at Moses' right
63:13 [G] *who* **led** them through the depths? Like a horse in open
65: 2 [A] who **walk** *in* ways not good, pursuing their own
Jer 1: 7 [A] *You must* **go** to everyone I send you to and say whatever I
2: 2 [A] "**Go** and proclaim in the hearing of Jerusalem: " 'I remember
2: 2 [A] you loved me and **followed** [+339] me through the desert,
2: 5 [A] *They* **followed** [+339] worthless idols and became worthless
2: 6 [G] us up out of Egypt and **led** us through the barren wilderness,
2: 8 [A] prophesied by Baal, **following** [+339] worthless idols.
2:17 [G] forsaking the LORD your God when *he* **led** you in the way?
2:23 [A] you say, 'I am not defiled; *I have* not **run** after the Baals'?
2:25 [A] 'It's no use! I love foreign gods, and *I must* **go** after them.'
3: 1 [A] and *she* **leaves** [+907+4946] him and marries another man,
3: 6 [A] She *has* **gone up** on every high hill and under every
3: 8 [A] had no fear; she also **went out** and committed adultery.
3:12 [A] **Go**, proclaim this message toward the north: " 'Return,
3:17 [A] No longer *will they* **follow** [+339] the stubbornness of their
3:18 [A] In those days the house of Judah *will* **join** [+6584] the house
5: 5 [A] So *I will* **go** to the leaders and speak to them; surely they
5:23 [A] and rebellious hearts; they have turned aside and **gone away**.
6:16 [A] the ancient paths, ask where the good way is, and **walk** in it,
6:16 [A] find rest for your souls. But you said, '*We will* not **walk** in it.'
6:25 [A] Do not go out to the fields or **walk** on the roads,
6:28 [A] They are all hardened rebels, **going about** to slander.
7: 6 [A] if *you do* not **follow** [+339] other gods to your own harm,
7: 9 [A] to Baal and **follow** [+339] other gods you have not known,
7:12 [A] " '**Go** now to the place in Shiloh where I first made a
7:23 [A] **Walk** in all the ways I command you, that it may go well
7:24 [A] *they* **followed** [+928] the stubborn inclinations of their evil
8: 2 [A] served and which *they have* **followed** [+339] and consulted
9: 2 [9:1] [A] that I might leave my people and **go** away from them;
9: 4 [9:3] [A] is a deceiver, and every friend a **slanderer** [+8215].
9:10 [9:9] [A] birds of the air have fled and the animals *are* **gone**.
9:13 [9:12] [A] they have not obeyed me or **followed** [+928] my law.
9:14 [9:13] [A] *they have* **followed** [+339] the stubbornness of their
10:23 [A] life is not his own; it is not for man **[NIE]** to direct his steps.
11: 8 [A] they **followed** [+928] the stubbornness of their evil hearts.
11:10 [A] They *have* **followed** [+339] other gods to serve them.
11:12 [A] The towns of Judah and the people of Jerusalem *will* **go**
12: 2 [A] and they have taken root; *they* **grow** and bear fruit.
12: 9 [A] **Go** and gather all the wild beasts; bring them to devour.
13: 1 [A] "**Go** and buy a linen belt and put it around your waist, but do
13: 4 [A] **go** now to Perath and hide it there in a crevice in the rocks."
13: 5 [A] So *I* **went** and hid it at Perath, as the LORD told me.
13: 6 [A] "**Go** now to Perath and get the belt I told you to hide there."
13: 7 [A] So *I* **went** to Perath and dug up the belt and took it from the
13:10 [A] who **follow** [+928] the stubbornness of their hearts and go
13:10 [A] and **go** after other gods to serve and worship them,
15: 6 [A] declares the LORD. "*You* **keep on** backsliding.
16: 5 [A] *do* not **go** to mourn or show sympathy, because I have
16:11 [A] 'and **followed** [+339] other gods and served and worshiped
16:12 [A] See how each of you *is* **following** [+339] the stubbornness of
17:19 [A] "**Go** and stand at the gate of the people, through which the
18:12 [A] *We will* **continue** with our own plans; each of us will follow
18:15 [A] They *made* them **walk** *in* bypaths and on roads not built up.
18:18 [A] They said, "**Come**, let's make plans against Jeremiah;
18:18 [A] So **come**, let's attack him with our tongues and pay no
19: 1 [A] what the LORD says: "**Go** and buy a clay jar from a potter.
19:10 [A] "Then break the jar while those who **go** with you are
20: 6 [A] and all who live in your house *will* **go** into exile to Babylon.
22:10 [A] rather, weep bitterly for him *who is* **exiled**, because he will
22:22 [A] all your shepherds away, and your allies *will* **go** into exile.
23:14 [A] They commit adultery and **live** [+928] a lie. They strengthen
23:17 [A] to all *who* **follow** [+928] the stubbornness of their hearts they
25: 6 [A] *Do* not **follow** [+339] other gods to serve and worship them;
26: 4 [A] If you do not listen to me and **follow** [+928] my law, which I
28:11 [A] two years.' " At this, the prophet Jeremiah **went** on his way.
28:13 [A] "**Go** and tell Hananiah, 'This is what the LORD says:
29:12 [A] you will call upon me and **come** and pray to me, and I will
30:16 [A] you will be devoured; all your enemies *will* **go** into exile.
31: 2 [A] find favor in the desert; I *will* **come** to give rest to Israel."
31: 9 [G] *I will* **lead** them beside streams of water on a level path
31:21 [A] Take note of the highway, the road that *you* **take**. Return,
32: 5 [G] *He will* **take** Zedekiah *to* Babylon, where he will remain
32:23 [A] of it, but they did not obey you or **follow** [+928] your law;
34: 2 [A] **Go** to Zedekiah king of Judah and tell him, 'This is what the
35: 2 [A] "**Go** to the Recabite family and invite them to come to one of
35:13 [A] **Go** and tell the men of Judah and the people of Jerusalem,
35:15 [A] your actions; *do* not **follow** [+339] other gods to serve them.
36:14 [A] scroll from which you have read to the people and **come**."
36:19 [A] the officials said to Baruch, "You and Jeremiah, **go** and hide.
37: 9 [A] 'The Babylonians *will* **surely leave** [+2143+4946+6584] us.'
37: 9 [A] 'The Babylonians *will* **surely leave** [+2143+4946+6584] us.'
37: 9 [A] Babylonians will surely leave us.' They will not! **[RPH]**
37:12 [A] Jeremiah started to leave the city to **go** *to* the territory of
39:16 [A] "**Go** and tell Ebed-Melech the Cushite, 'This is what the
40: 4 [A] the whole country lies before you; **go** wherever you please."
40: 4 [A] country lies before you; go **[RPH]** wherever you please."
40: 5 [A] with him among the people, or **go** anywhere else you please."
40: 5 [A] **[RPH]** Then the commander gave him provisions and a
40:15 [A] "*Let me* **go** and kill Ishmael son of Nethaniah, and no one
41: 6 [A] out from Mizpah to meet them, weeping *as he* **went** [+2143].
41: 6 [A] out from Mizpah to meet them, weeping *as he* **went** [+2143].
41:10 [A] them captive and **set out** to cross over to the Ammonites.
41:12 [A] all their men and **went** to fight Ishmael son of Nethaniah.
41:14 [A] at Mizpah turned and **went over** to Johanan son of Kareah.
41:15 [A] of his men escaped from Johanan and **fled** to the Ammonites.
41:17 [A] *they* **went on**, stopping at Geruth Kimham near Bethlehem
41:17 [A] stopping at Geruth Kimham near Bethlehem *on their* **way** to
42: 3 [A] that the LORD your God will tell us where *we should* **go**
44: 3 [A] They provoked me to anger **[NIE]** by burning incense
44:10 [A] nor *have they* **followed** [+928] my law and the decrees I set
44:23 [A] or **followed** [+928] his law or his decrees or his stipulations,
45: 5 [A] but wherever *you* **go** I will let you escape with your life.' "
46:22 [A] Egypt will hiss like a **fleeing** serpent as the enemy advances
46:22 [A] Egypt will hiss like a fleeing serpent as the enemy **advances**
48: 2 [A] '**Come**, let us put an end to that nation.' You too, O Madmen,
48: 2 [A] will be silenced; the sword *will* **pursue** [+339] you.
48:11 [A] poured from one jar to another—*she has* not **gone** into exile.
49: 3 [A] for Molech *will* **go** into exile, together with his priests
50: 3 [A] No one will live in it; both men and animals will flee **away**.
50: 4 [A] the people of Judah together will go in tears **[RPH]** to seek
50: 4 [A] the people of Judah together will go in tears **[RPH]** to seek
50: 6 [A] *They* **wandered** over mountain and hill and forgot their own
51: 9 [A] let us leave her and each **go** to his own land, for her judgment
51:50 [A] You who have escaped the sword, **leave** and do not linger!
51:59 [A] when he **went** *to* Babylon with Zedekiah king of Judah in the
52: 7 [A] were surrounding the city. *They* **fled** toward the Arabah,
52:26 [G] them all and **brought** them to the king of Babylon at Riblah.
La 1: 5 [A] Her children *have* **gone** *into* exile, captive before the foe.
1: 6 [A] no pasture; in weakness *they have* **fled** before the pursuer.
1:18 [A] My young men and maidens *have* **gone** into exile.
3: 2 [G] me away and **made** me **walk** *in* darkness rather than light;
4:18 [A] stalked us at every step, so we *could* not **walk** in our streets.
5:18 [D] which lies desolate, with jackals **prowling** over it.
Eze 1: 9 [A] Each one **went** straight ahead; they did not turn as they
1: 9 [A] one went straight ahead; they did not turn as they **moved**.
1:12 [A] Each one **went** straight ahead. Wherever the spirit would go,
1:12 [A] Wherever the spirit *would* **go**, they would go,
1:12 [A] spirit would go, *they would* **go**, without turning as they went.
1:12 [A] spirit would go, they would go, without turning as they **went**.
1:13 [F] Fire **moved back and forth** among the creatures; it was
1:17 [A] As they **moved**, they would go in any one of the four
1:17 [A] *they would* **go** in any one of the four directions the creatures
1:17 [A] the wheels did not turn about as the creatures **went**.
1:19 [A] When the living creatures **moved**, the wheels beside them
1:19 [A] the living creatures moved, the wheels beside them **moved**;
1:20 [A] Wherever the spirit *would* **go**, they would go, and the wheels
1:20 [A] Wherever the spirit would go, *they would* **go**, and the wheels
1:20 [A] **[RPH]** and the wheels would rise along with them,
1:21 [A] When the creatures **moved**, they also moved; when the
1:21 [A] When the creatures moved, *they* also **moved**; when the
1:24 [A] When the creatures **moved**, I heard the sound of their wings,
3: 1 [A] eat this scroll; then **go** and speak to the house of Israel."
3: 4 [A] **go** [+995] **now** to the house of Israel and speak my words to
3:11 [A] **Go** [+995] **now** to your countrymen in exile and speak to
3:14 [A] and *I* **went** in bitterness and in the anger of my spirit,
5: 6 [A] She has rejected my laws and *has* not **followed** my decrees.
5: 7 [A] and *have* not **followed** my decrees or kept my laws.
7:14 [A] and get everything ready, no *one will* **go** into battle,
7:17 [A] will go limp, and every knee *will become as* **weak** *as* water.
10:11 [A] As they **moved**, they would go in any one of the four
10:11 [A] *they would* **go** in any one of the four directions the cherubim
10:11 [A] the wheels did not turn about as the cherubim **went**.
10:11 [A] The cherubim **went** *in* whatever direction the head faced,
10:11 [A] direction the head faced, without turning as they **went**.
10:16 [A] When the cherubim **moved**, the wheels beside them moved;
10:16 [A] When the cherubim moved, the wheels beside them **moved**;
10:22 [A] I had seen by the Kebar River. Each one **went** straight ahead.
11:12 [A] for *you have* not **followed** my decrees or kept my laws
11:20 [A] *they will* **follow** [+928] my decrees and be careful to keep
11:21 [A] as for those whose hearts *are* **devoted** to their vile images

[F] Hitpael (hitpoel, hitpoal, hitpolel, hitpolal, hitpalel, hitpalal, hitpalpel, hitpalpal, hotpael, hotpaal) [G] Hiphil (hiphtil) [H] Hophal [I] Hishtaphel

Eze 12: 11 [A] it will be done to them. *They will* **go** into exile as captives.
13: 3 [A] Woe to the foolish prophets who **follow** [+339] their own
16: 47 [A] *You* not only **walked** in their ways and copied their
18: 9 [D] *He* **follows** [+928] my decrees and faithfully keeps my laws.
18: 17 [A] He keeps my laws and **follows** [+928] my decrees.
19: 6 [F] *He* **prowled** among the lions, for he was now a strong lion.
20: 13 [A] *They did* not **follow** [+928] my decrees but rejected my
20: 16 [A] *did* not **follow** [+906+928] my decrees and desecrated my
20: 16 [A] For their hearts *were* **devoted** [+339] **to** their idols.
20: 18 [A] "*Do* not **follow** [+928] the statutes of your fathers or keep
20: 19 [A] **follow** [+928] my decrees and be careful to keep my laws.
20: 21 [A] *They did* not **follow** [+928] my decrees, they were not
20: 39 [A] LORD says: **Go** and serve your idols, every one of you!
21: 7 [21:12] [A] and every knee *become as* **weak** *as* water.'
23: 31 [A] *You have* **gone** the way of your sister; so I will put her cup
25: 3 [A] and over the people of Judah when *they* **went** into exile,
28: 14 [F] the holy mount of God; *you* **walked** among the fiery stones.
30: 17 [A] by the sword, and the cities themselves *will* **go** into captivity.
30: 18 [A] covered with clouds, and her villages *will* **go** into captivity.
31: 4 [A] their streams **flowed** all around its base and sent their
32: 14 [G] I will let her waters settle and **make** her streams **flow** like oil,
33: 15 [A] **follows** [+928] the decrees that give life, and does no evil,
33: 31 [A] but their hearts *are* **greedy** [+339] *for* unjust gain.
36: 12 [G] *I will* **cause** people, my people Israel, **to walk** upon you.
36: 27 [A] my Spirit in you and move *you to* **follow** [+928] my decrees
37: 21 [A] take the Israelites out of the nations where *they have* **gone**.
37: 24 [A] *They will* **follow** [+928] my laws and be careful to keep my
40: 24 [G] *he* **led** me *to* the south side and I saw a gate facing south.
43: 1 [G] Then the man **brought** me to the gate facing east,
47: 6 [G] you see this?" Then *he* **led** me back to the bank of the river.
Da 9: 10 [A] or **kept** [+928] the laws he gave us through his servants the
12: 9 [A] He replied, "**Go** *your* **way**, Daniel, because the words are
12: 13 [A] "As for you, **go** *your* **way** till the end. You will rest, and
Hos 1: 2 [A] the LORD said to him, "**Go**, take to yourself an adulterous
1: 3 [A] So **[NIE]** he married Gomer daughter of Diblaim, and she
2: 5 [2:7] [A] She said, '*I will* **go** after my lovers, who give me my
2: 7 [2:9] [A] '*I will* **go** back to my husband as at first, for then I was
2: 13 [2:15] [A] with rings and jewelry, and **went** after her lovers,
2: 14 [2:16] [G] *I will* **lead** her into the desert and speak tenderly to
3: 1 [A] The LORD said to me, "**Go**, show your love to your wife
5: 6 [A] *When they* **go** with their flocks and herds to seek the
5: 11 [A] trampled in judgment, intent on **pursuing** [+339] idols.
5: 13 [A] and Judah his sores, then Ephraim **turned** to Assyria,
5: 14 [A] I will tear them to pieces and **go away**; I will carry them off,
5: 15 [A] Then *I will* **go** back to my place until they admit their guilt.
6: 1 [A] "**Come**, let us return to the LORD. He has torn us to pieces
6: 4 [A] is like the morning mist, like the early dew *that* **disappears**.
7: 11 [A] now calling to Egypt, now **turning** *to* Assyria.
7: 12 [A] When *they* **go**, I will throw my net over them; I will pull
9: 6 [A] Even if *they* **escape** from destruction, Egypt will gather
11: 2 [A] But the more I called Israel, the further they **went** from me.
11: 10 [A] *They will* **follow** [+339] the LORD; he will roar like a lion.
13: 3 [A] like the early dew *that* **disappears**, like chaff swirling from a
14: 6 [14:7] [A] his young shoots *will* **grow**. His splendor will be like
14: 9 [14:10] [A] the righteous **walk** in them, but the rebellious
Joel 2: 7 [A] They all **march** in line, not swerving from their course.
2: 8 [A] They do not jostle each other; each **marches** straight ahead.
3: 18 [4:18] [A] will drip new wine, and the hills *will* **flow** *with* milk;
3: 18 [4:18] [A] all the ravines of Judah *will* **run** *with* water.
Am 1: 15 [A] Her king *will* **go** into exile, he and his officials together,"
2: 4 [A] by false gods, the gods their ancestors **followed** [+339],
2: 7 [A] Father and son **use** [+448] the same girl and so profane my
2: 10 [G] *I* **led** you forty years in the desert to give you the land of the
3: 3 [A] *Do* two **walk** together unless they have agreed to do so?
6: 2 [A] **go** from there *to* great Hamath, and then go down to Gath in
7: 12 [A] Amaziah said to Amos, "**Get out**, you seer! Go back to the
7: 15 [A] LORD took me from tending the flock and said to me, '**Go**,
9: 4 [A] Though *they are* **driven** into exile by their enemies, there I
Jnh 1: 2 [A] "**Go** to the great city of Nineveh and preach against it,
1: 7 [A] the sailors said to each other, "**Come**, let us cast lots to find
1: 11 [A] The sea *was getting* **rougher and rougher** [+2256+6192].
1: 13 [A] for the sea **grew even wilder** [+2256+6192+6584] than before.
3: 2 [A] "**Go** to the great city of Nineveh and proclaim to it the
3: 3 [A] Jonah obeyed the word of the LORD and **went** to Nineveh.
Mic 1: 8 [A] this I will weep and wail; *I will* **go about** barefoot and naked.
2: 3 [A] *You will* no longer **walk** proudly, for it will be a time of
2: 7 [A] "Do not my words do good to *him whose* **ways** are upright?
2: 10 [A] Get up, **go away**! For this is not your resting place, because it
2: 11 [A] If a liar and deceiver **comes** and says, 'I will prophesy for you
4: 2 [A] Many nations *will* **come** and say, "Come, let us go up to the
4: 2 [A] Many nations will come and say, "**Come**, let us go up to the
4: 2 [A] He will teach us his ways, so that *we may* **walk** in his paths."
4: 5 [A] All the nations *may* **walk** in the name of their gods; we will
4: 5 [A] we *will* **walk** in the name of the LORD our God for ever
6: 8 [A] and to love mercy and *to* **walk** humbly with your God.
6: 16 [A] Ahab's house, and *you have* **followed** [+928] their traditions.
Na 2: 11 [2:12] [A] where the lion and lioness **went**, and the cubs, with
3: 10 [A] Yet she was taken captive and **went** into exile. Her infants
Hab 1: 6 [A] who **sweep** across the whole earth to seize dwelling places
3: 5 [A] Plague **went** before him; pestilence followed his steps.
3: 11 [D] moon stood still in the heavens at the glint of your **flying**
Zep 1: 17 [A] distress on the people and *they will* **walk** like blind men,
Zec 1: 10 [F] "They are the ones the LORD has sent to **go** throughout the
1: 11 [F] "*We have* **gone** throughout the earth and found the whole
2: 2 [2:6] [A] I asked, "Where *are* you **going**?" He answered me,
3: 7 [A] 'If *you will* **walk** in my ways and keep my requirements, then
5: 10 [G] "Where *are* they **taking** the basket?" I asked the angel who
6: 7 [A] they were straining to **go** [+2143] throughout the earth.
6: 7 [F] they were straining to **go** [+2143] throughout the earth.
6: 7 [A] he said, "**Go** [+2143] throughout the earth!" So they went
6: 7 [F] he said, "**Go** [+2143] throughout the earth!" So they went
6: 7 [F] throughout the earth!" So *they* **went** throughout the earth.
8: 21 [A] the inhabitants of one city *will* **go** to another and say, 'Let us
8: 21 [A] '*Let us* **go** [+2143] **at once** to entreat the LORD and seek
8: 21 [A] '*Let us* **go at once** [+2143] to entreat the LORD and seek
8: 21 [A] and seek the LORD Almighty. *I* myself *am* **going**.'
8: 23 [A] one Jew by the hem of his robe and say, '*Let us* **go** with you,
9: 14 [A] sound the trumpet; *he will* **march** in the storms of the south,
10: 12 [F] them in the LORD and in his name *they will* **walk**,"
Mal 2: 6 [A] *He* **walked** with me in peace and uprightness, and turned
3: 14 [A] **going about** like mourners before the LORD Almighty?

2144 הֵלֶךְ hēlek, n.m. [2] [√ 2143]

oozing out [1], traveler [1]

1Sa 14: 26 When they went into the woods, they saw the honey **oozing out**,
2Sa 12: 4 "Now a **traveler** came to the rich man, but the rich man refrained

2145 ¹הָלַל hālal[1], v. [4] [→ 183, 2122]

radiance [1], shone [1], show [1], throws out flashes [1]

Job 29: 3 [G] when his lamp **shone** upon my head and by his light I walked
31: 26 [G] if I have regarded the sun in *its* **radiance** or the moon
41: 18 [41:10] [G] His snorting **throws out flashes** *of* light; his eyes
Isa 13: 10 [G] of heaven and their constellations *will* not **show** their light.

2146 ²הָלַל hālal[2], v. [146] [→ 2136, 2148, 2149, 4545, 9335; *also used with compound proper names*]

praise [89], boast [11], praised [7], worthy of praise [6], boasts [4], glory [4], give praise [3], praises [3], be praised [2], praising [2], bring praise [1], cheering [1], extol [1], exult [1], gave thanks [1], giving praise [1], had wedding songs [1], is praised [1], make boast [1], renown [1], sang praises [1], sang [1], sing praise [1], sing praises [1], that purpose[s] [1]

Ge 12: 15 [D] *they* **praised** her to Pharaoh, and she was taken into his
Jdg 16: 24 [D] When the people saw him, *they* **praised** their god, saying,
2Sa 14: 25 [D] so highly **praised** *for* his handsome appearance as Absalom.
22: 4 [E] I call to the LORD, *who is* **worthy of praise**, and I am
1Ki 20: 11 [F] 'One who puts on his armor *should* not **boast** like one who
1Ch 16: 4 [D] to make petition, to give thanks, and to **praise** the LORD,
16: 10 [F] **Glory** in his holy name; let the hearts of those who seek the
16: 25 [E] For great is the LORD and most **worthy of praise**; he is to
16: 36 [D] Then all the people said "Amen" and "**Praise** the LORD."
23: 5 [D] four thousand *are to* **praise** the LORD with the musical
23: 5 [D] the musical instruments I have provided for **that purpose**[s]."
23: 30 [D] also to stand every morning to thank and **praise** the LORD.
25: 3 [D] using the harp in thanking and **praising** the LORD.
29: 13 [D] our God, we give you thanks, and **praise** your glorious name.
2Ch 5: 13 [D] as with one voice, to **give praise** and thanks to the LORD.
5: 13 [D] they raised their voices in **praise** to the LORD and sang:
7: 6 [D] the LORD and which were used when he **gave thanks**,
8: 14 [D] the Levites to lead the **praise** and to assist the priests
20: 19 [D] and Korahites stood up and **praised** the LORD,
20: 21 [D] *to* **praise** him for the splendor of his holiness as they went
23: 12 [D] heard the noise of the people running and **cheering** the king,
23: 13 [D] singers with musical instruments were leading the **praises**.
29: 30 [D] his officials ordered the Levites to **praise** the LORD with
29: 30 [D] So *they* **sang praises** with gladness and bowed their heads
30: 21 [D] while the Levites and priests **sang** to the LORD every day,
31: 2 [D] and to **sing praises** at the gates of the LORD's dwelling.
Ezr 3: 10 [D] with cymbals, took their places to **praise** the LORD,
3: 11 [D] With **praise** and thanksgiving they sang to the LORD: "He
3: 11 [D] all the people gave a great shout of **praise** to the LORD,
Ne 5: 13 [D] the whole assembly said, "Amen," and **praised** the LORD.
12: 24 [D] who stood opposite them to **give praise** and thanksgiving,
Ps 10: 3 [D] He **boasts** of the cravings of his heart; he blesses the greedy
18: 3 [18:4] [E] I call to the LORD, *who is* **worthy of praise**, and I

Ps 22:22 [22:23] [D] my brothers; in the congregation *I will* **praise** you.
22:23 [22:24] [D] *You* who fear the LORD, **praise** him! All you
22:26 [22:27] [D] they who seek the LORD *will* **praise** him—
34:2 [34:3] [F] My soul *will* **boast** in the LORD; let the afflicted
35:18 [D] great assembly; among throngs of people *I will* **praise** you.
44:8 [44:9] [D] In God *we* **make** *our* **boast** all day long, and we will
48:1 [48:2] [E] Great is the LORD, and most **worthy of praise**,
49:6 [49:7] [F] trust in their wealth and **boast** of their great riches?
52:1 [52:3] [F] Why *do you* **boast** of evil, you mighty man? Why do
56:4 [56:5] [D] In God, whose word *I* **praise**, in God I trust; I will
56:10 [56:11] [D] In God, whose word *I* **praise**, in the LORD,
56:10 [56:11] [D] I praise, in the LORD, whose word *I* **praise**—
63:5 [63:6] [D] of foods; with singing lips my mouth *will* **praise** you.
63:11 [63:12] [F] all who swear by God's name *will* **praise** him,
64:10 [64:11] [F] refuge in him; *let* all the upright in heart **praise** him!
69:30 [69:31] [D] *I will* **praise** God's name in song and glorify him
69:34 [69:35] [D] *Let* heaven and earth **praise** him, the seas and all
74:21 [D] in disgrace; *may* the poor and needy **praise** your name.
78:63 [E] their young men, and their maidens **had** no **wedding songs**;
84:4 [84:5] [D] dwell in your house; *they are* ever **praising** you.
96:4 [E] For great is the LORD and most **worthy of praise**; he is to
97:7 [F] worship images are put to shame, those *who* **boast** in idols—
102:18 [102:19] [D] a people not yet created *may* **praise** the LORD:
104:35 [D] no more. Praise the LORD, O my soul. **Praise** the LORD.
105:3 [F] **Glory** in his holy name; let the hearts of those who seek the
105:45 [D] keep his precepts and observe his laws. **Praise** the LORD.
106:1 [D] **Praise** the LORD. Give thanks to the LORD, for he is
106:5 [F] joy of your nation and join your inheritance in **giving praise**.
106:48 [D] Let all the people say, "Amen!" **Praise** the LORD.
107:32 [D] of the people and **praise** him in the council of the elders.
109:30 [D] extol the LORD; in the great throng *I will* **praise** him.
111:1 [D] **Praise** the LORD. I will extol the LORD with all my heart
112:1 [D] **Praise** the LORD. Blessed is the man who fears the
113:1 [D] **Praise** the LORD. Praise, O servants of the LORD,
113:1 [D] **Praise**, O servants of the LORD, praise the name of the
113:1 [D] O servants of the LORD, **praise** the name of the LORD.
113:3 [E] place where it sets, the name of the LORD *is to* **be praised**.
113:9 [D] her home as a happy mother of children. **Praise** the LORD.
115:17 [D] It is not the dead *who* **praise** the LORD, those who go
115:18 [D] the LORD, both now and forevermore. **Praise** the LORD.
116:19 [D] in your midst, O Jerusalem. **Praise** the LORD.
117:1 [D] **Praise** the LORD, all *you* nations; extol him, all you
117:2 [D] of the LORD endures forever. **Praise** the LORD.
119:164 [D] Seven times a day *I* **praise** you for your righteous laws.
119:175 [D] Let me live that I *may* **praise** you, and may your laws sustain
135:1 [D] **Praise** the LORD. Praise the name of the LORD;
135:1 [D] **Praise** the name of the LORD; praise him, you servants of
135:1 [D] of the LORD; **praise** him, *you* servants of the LORD,
135:3 [D] **Praise** the LORD, for the LORD is good; sing praise to his
135:21 [D] to him who dwells in Jerusalem. **Praise** the LORD.
145:2 [D] day I will praise you and **extol** your name for ever and ever.
145:3 [E] Great is the LORD and most **worthy of praise**; his
146:1 [D] **Praise** the LORD. Praise the LORD, O my soul.
146:1 [D] Praise the LORD. **Praise** the LORD, O my soul.
146:2 [D] *I will* **praise** the LORD all my life; I will sing praise to my
146:10 [D] your God, O Zion, for all generations. **Praise** the LORD.
147:1 [D] **Praise** the LORD. How good it is to sing praises to our
147:12 [D] Extol the LORD, O Jerusalem; **praise** your God, O Zion,
147:20 [D] other nation; they do not know his laws. **Praise** the LORD.
148:1 [D] **Praise** the LORD. Praise the LORD from the heavens,
148:1 [D] **Praise** the LORD from the heavens, praise him in the
148:1 [D] LORD from the heavens, **praise** him in the heights above.
148:2 [D] **Praise** him, all his angels, praise him, all his heavenly hosts.
148:2 [D] Praise him, all his angels, **praise** him, all his heavenly hosts.
148:3 [D] **Praise** him, sun and moon, praise him, all you shining stars.
148:3 [D] Praise him, sun and moon, **praise** him, all you shining stars.
148:4 [D] **Praise** him, you highest heavens and you waters above the
148:5 [D] *Let them* **praise** the name of the LORD, for he commanded
148:7 [D] **Praise** the LORD from the earth, *you* great sea creatures
148:13 [D] *Let them* **praise** the name of the LORD, for his name alone
148:14 [D] of Israel, the people close to his heart. **Praise** the LORD.
149:1 [D] **Praise** the LORD. Sing to the LORD a new song,
149:3 [D] *Let them* **praise** his name with dancing and make music to
149:9 [D] This is the glory of all his saints. **Praise** the LORD.
150:1 [D] **Praise** the LORD. Praise God in his sanctuary; praise him
150:1 [D] **Praise** God in his sanctuary; praise him in his mighty
150:1 [D] God in his sanctuary; **praise** him in his mighty heavens.
150:2 [D] **Praise** him for his acts of power; praise him for his
150:2 [D] for his acts of power; **praise** him for his surpassing greatness.
150:3 [D] **Praise** him with the sounding of the trumpet, praise him with
150:3 [D] sounding of the trumpet, **praise** him with the harp and lyre,
150:4 [D] **praise** him with tambourine and dancing, praise him with the
150:4 [D] and dancing, **praise** him with the strings and flute,
150:5 [D] **praise** him with the clash of cymbals, praise him with
150:5 [D] the clash of cymbals, **praise** him with resounding cymbals.
150:6 [D] *Let* everything that has breath **praise** the LORD.
150:6 [D] that has breath praise the LORD. **Praise** the LORD.
Pr 12:8 [E] A man **is praised** according to his wisdom, but men with
20:14 [F] the buyer; then off he goes and **boasts** *about* his purchase.
25:14 [F] wind without rain is a man *who* **boasts** of gifts he does not
27:1 [F] *Do* not **boast** about tomorrow, for you do not know what a
27:2 [D] *Let* another **praise** you, and not your own mouth;
28:4 [D] Those who forsake the law **praise** the wicked, but those who
31:28 [D] and call her blessed; her husband also, and *he* **praises** her:
31:30 [F] but a woman who fears the LORD *is to* **be praised**.
31:31 [D] and *let* her works **bring** her **praise** at the city gate.
SS 6:9 [D] called her blessed; the queens and concubines **praised** her.
Isa 38:18 [D] the grave cannot praise you, death cannot **sing** your **praise**;
41:16 [F] rejoice in the LORD and **glory** in the Holy One of Israel.
45:25 [F] descendants of Israel will be found righteous and *will* **exult**.
62:9 [D] but those who harvest it will eat it and **praise** the LORD,
64:11 [64:10] [D] and glorious temple, where our fathers **praised** you,
Jer 4:2 [F] nations will be blessed by him and in him *they will* **glory**."
9:23 [9:22] [F] "*Let* not the wise man **boast** of his wisdom or the
9:23 [9:22] [F] or the strong man **boast** of his strength or the rich
9:23 [9:22] [F] of his strength or the rich man **boast** of his riches,
9:24 [9:23] [F] *let* him *who* **boasts** boast about this: that he
9:24 [9:23] [F] let him who boasts **boast** about this: that he
20:13 [D] Sing to the LORD! **Give praise** *to* the LORD! He rescues
31:7 [D] Make *your* **praises** heard, and say, 'O LORD, save your
49:4 [F] Why *do you* **boast** of your valleys, boast of your valleys
Eze 26:17 [E] " 'How you are destroyed, O city of **renown**, peopled by men
Joel 2:26 [D] and *you will* **praise** the name of the LORD your God,

2147 ³הָלַל hālal[3], v. [15 / 16] [→ 2099, 2100]

arrogant [3], go mad [2], makes fools of [2], acted like a madman [1], boast [1], drive furiously [1], foolish [1], gone mad [1], mock [1], rail [1], storm [1], turns into a fool [1]

1Sa 21:13 [21:14] [F] he was in their hands *he* **acted like a madman**,
Job 12:17 [D] leads counselors away stripped and **makes fools of** judges.
Ps 5:5 [5:6] [A] The **arrogant** cannot stand in your presence; you hate
73:3 [A] For I envied the **arrogant** when I saw the prosperity of the
75:4 [75:5] [A] To the **arrogant** I say, 'Boast no more,' and to the
75:4 [75:5] [A] To the arrogant I say, '**Boast** no more,' and to the
102:8 [102:9] [D] *those who* **rail** *against* me use my name as a curse.
Ecc 2:2 [D] "Laughter," I said, "*is* **foolish**. And what does pleasure
7:7 [D] Extortion **turns** a wise man **into a fool**, and a bribe corrupts
Isa 44:25 [D] foils the signs of false prophets and **makes fools of** diviners,
52:5 [D] those who rule them **mock**," [BHS 3536] declares the
Jer 25:16 [F] they will stagger and **go mad** because of the sword I will
46:9 [F] Charge, O horses! **Drive furiously**, O charioteers! March on,
50:38 [F] For it is a land of idols, idols *that will* **go mad** with terror.
51:7 [F] nations drank her wine; therefore they *have now* **gone mad**.
Na 2:4 [2:5] [F] The chariots **storm** through the streets, rushing back

2148 הִלֵּל hillēl, n.pr.m. [2] [√ 2146]

Hillel [2]

Jdg 12:13 After him, Abdon son of **Hillel**, from Pirathon, led Israel.
12:15 Abdon son of **Hillel** died, and was buried at Pirathon in Ephraim,

2149 הַלְלוּיָהּ halᵉlûyāh, v.+n.pr.m. *or* excl. Not used in NIV/BHS [√ 2146 + 3378]

2150 הָלַם hālam, v. [8] [→ 2153, 4547]

beat [1], laid low [1], smashed [1], strike [1], strikes [1], struck [1], thundered [1], trampled down [1]

Jdg 5:22 [A] **thundered** the horses' hoofs—galloping, galloping go his
5:26 [A] *She* **struck** Sisera, she crushed his head, she shattered
Ps 74:6 [A] *They* **smashed** all the carved paneling with their axes
141:5 [A] *Let* a righteous man **strike** me—it is a kindness; let him
Pr 23:35 [A] will say, "but I'm not hurt! *They* **beat** me, but I don't feel it!
Isa 16:8 [A] The rulers of the nations *have* **trampled down** the choicest
28:1 [B] to that city, the pride of *those* **laid low** *by* wine!
41:7 [A] he who smooths with the hammer spurs on *him who* **strikes**

2151 הֲלֹם hᵃlōm, adv. [12]

here [4], *untranslated* [2], this far [+6330] [2], in all directions [1], now [1], over here [1], to [1]

Ge 16:13 sees me," for she said, "I have **now** seen the One who sees me."
Ex 3:5 "Do not come any closer," **[NIE]** God said. "Take off your
Jdg 18:3 so they turned in there and asked him, "Who brought you **here**?
20:7 all you Israelites, speak up and give your verdict." **[NIE]**
Ru 2:14 At mealtime Boaz said to her, "Come **over here**. Have some bread
1Sa 10:22 inquired further of the LORD, "Has the man come **here** yet?"

[F] Hitpael (hitpoel, hitpoal, hitpolel, hitpolal, hitpalel, hitpalal, hitpalpel, hitpalpal, hotpael, hotpaal) [G] Hiphil (hiphtil) [H] Hophal [I] Hishtaphel

1Sa 14:16 Gibeah in Benjamin saw the army melting away **in all directions**.
14:36 they replied. But the priest said, "Let us inquire of God **here**."
14:38 Saul therefore said, "Come **here**, all you who are leaders of the
2Sa 7:18 and what is my family, that you have brought me **this far** [+6330]?
1Ch 17:16 and what is my family, that you have brought me **this far** [+6330]?
Ps 73:10 Therefore their people turn **to** them and drink up waters in

2152 הֶלֶם ***hēlem***, n.pr.m. [1]

Helem [1]

1Ch 7:35 The sons of his brother **Helem**: Zophah, Imna, Shelesh and Amal.

2153 הַלְמוּת ***halmût***, n.f. [1] [√ 2150]

hammer [1]

Jdg 5:26 for the tent peg, her right hand for the workman's **hammer**.

2154 הָם¹ ***hām¹***, n.pr.loc. [1]

Ham [1]

Ge 14:5 the Zuzites in **Ham**, the Emites in Shaveh Kiriathaim

2155 הָם² ***hām²***, n.[m.]. [1] [cf. 2166]

wealth [1]

Eze 7:11 will be left, none of that crowd—no **wealth**, nothing of value.

2156 הֵם ***hēm***, p.m.pl. [559 / 560] [√ 2085; Ar 10210] Not indexed

they [321], *untranslated* [120], those [39], them [14], these [13], that [10], who [6], it [5], themselves [4], things[s] [3], men[s] [2], such[s] [2], the gatekeepers[s] [2], this [2], all[s] [1], his net[s] [1], Israelites[s] [1], our[s] own [1], people[s] [1], the Benjamites[s] [1], the Israelites[s] [1], the others[s] [1], the people[s] [1], the places[s] [1], the priests[s] [1], the spies[s] [1], the [1], their idols[s] [1], those same [1], yet [+2021+2021+3427+6330] [1], you [1]

2157 הֶם- ***-hem***, הֵם- ***-hēm***, p.m.pl.suf. [3037 / 3038] [→ 4548; cf. 2023] Not indexed

them [1103], their [915], *untranslated* [557], they [116], the[s] [54], their [+4200] [35], themselves [27], their own [20], those [18], the people[s] [11], it [9], these [9], whose [7], men[s] [6], who [6], her [5], his [5], its [5], their own [+4200] [5], theirs [4], which [4], whom [4], him [3], Israel[s] [3], Moses[s] and Aaron [3], my people[s] [3], the idols[s] [3], the Israelites[s] [3], theirs [+4200] [3], a[s] [2], each [2], its own [2], people[s] [2], the Gibeonites[s] [2], the Hagrites[s] [2], the posts[s] [2], the [2], them[s] [+4053] [2], you [2], your [2], both[s] [1], doing so[s] [1], each other[s] [+9109] [1], Elijah and Elisha[s] [+9109] [1], enemies[s] [1], his descendants[s] [1], his followers[s] [1], his precepts[s] [1], Israelites[s] [1], it[s] [1], itself [1], lovers[s] [1], man's[s] [1], my accusers[s] [1], nephews [+1201] [1], officials[s] [1], one[s] [+4200] [1], one kind after another [+4200+5476] [1], others[s] [+4946] [1], people from Benjamin [+278] [1], people from Judah [+278] [1], priests[s] [+278] [1], related[s] [1], such things[s] [1], that [1], the Ammonites[s] [1], the bodies[s] [1], the brothers[s] [1], the cherubim[s] [1], the Egyptians[s] [1], the envoys[s] [1], the gatekeepers[s] [1], the heavens[s] [1], the Hebronites[s] [1], the Kohathite[s] [1], the Levites[s] [1], the man[s] and the woman [1], the men[s] [1], the messengers[s] [1], the Philistines[s] [1], the pots[s] [1], the procession[s] [1], the sea[s] [1], the shepherds[s] [1], the spies[s] [1], the stands[s] [1], the storehouses[s] [+889+928+3972] [1], the storerooms[s] [1], the waters [1], their [+448] [1], their [+4946] [1], their [+6584] [1], their own [+7156] [1], their[s] [+928+4090] [1], theirs [+4946] [1], them[s] [+466] [1], them[s] [+8533] [1], themselves [+7156] [1], there[s] [+6584] [1], there[s] [+928] [1], these days[s] [1], these men[s] [1], these things[s] [1], this threat[s] [1], thorns[s] [1], those Israelites[s] [1], us [+2256+3276] [1], where[s] [+6584] [1], women[s] [1], your troops[s] [1]

2158 הַמְּדָתָא ***hammᵉdātā'***, n.pr.m. [5]

Hammedatha [5]

Est 3:1 King Xerxes honored Haman son of **Hammedatha**, the Agagite,
3:10 ring from his finger and gave it to Haman son of **Hammedatha**,
8:5 overruling the dispatches that Haman son of **Hammedatha**,
9:10 the ten sons of Haman son of **Hammedatha**, the enemy of the
9:24 For Haman son of **Hammedatha**, the Agagite, the enemy of all the

2159 הָמָה ***hāmâ***, v. [34] [→ 2162, 2164?, 2166, 2167?; cf. 2101, 2169, 5637]

roar [5], disturbed [3], laments [3], loud [2], rage [2], roaring [2], snarling [2], astir [1], brawler [1], bustles about [1], cry out [1], groaned [1], growl [1], in uproar [1], moaning [1], noise [+7754] [1], noisy [1], pound [1], pounds [1], raging [1], tumult [1], yearns [1]

1Ki 1:41 [A] "What's the meaning of all the **noise in** [+7754] the city?"
Ps 39:6 [39:7] [A] *He* **bustles about**, but only in vain; he heaps up
42:5 [42:6] [A] O my soul? Why *so* **disturbed** within me?
42:11 [42:12] [A] O my soul? Why *so* **disturbed** within me?
43:5 [A] are you downcast, O my soul? Why *so* **disturbed** within me?
46:3 [46:4] [A] though its waters **roar** and foam and the mountains
46:6 [46:7] [A] Nations *are* **in uproar**, kingdoms fall; he lifts his
55:17 [55:18] [A] Evening, morning and noon *I* **cry out** in distress,
59:6 [59:7] [A] They return at evening, **snarling** like dogs, and prowl
59:14 [59:15] [A] They return at evening, **snarling** like dogs,
77:3 [77:4] [A] I remembered you, O God, and *I* **groaned**; I mused,
83:2 [83:3] [A] See how your enemies *are* **astir**, how your foes rear
Pr 1:21 [A] at the head of the **noisy** streets she cries out, in the gateways
7:11 [A] (She *is* **loud** and defiant, her feet never stay at home;
9:13 [A] The woman Folly *is* **loud**; she is undisciplined and without
20:1 [A] Wine is a mocker and beer a **brawler**; whoever is led astray
SS 5:4 [A] the latch-opening; my heart *began to* **pound** for him.
Isa 16:11 [A] My heart **laments** for Moab like a harp, my inmost being for
17:12 [A] the raging of many nations—*they* **rage** like the raging sea!
17:12 [A] the raging of many nations—they rage like the **raging** sea!
22:2 [A] O town full of commotion, O city of **tumult** and revelry?
51:15 [A] your God, who churns up the sea so that its waves **roar**—
59:11 [A] We all **growl** like bears; we moan mournfully like doves.
Jer 4:19 [A] my heart! My heart **pounds** within me, I cannot keep silent.
5:22 [A] they cannot prevail; *they may* **roar**, but they cannot cross it.
6:23 [A] They sound like the **roaring** sea as they ride on their horses;
31:20 [A] Therefore my heart **yearns** for him; I have great compassion
31:35 [A] shine by night, who stirs up the sea so that its waves **roar**—
48:36 [A] "So my heart **laments** for Moab like a flute; it laments like a
48:36 [A] a flute; it **laments** like a flute for the men of Kir Hareseth.
50:42 [A] They sound like the **roaring** sea as they ride on their horses;
51:55 [A] Waves ⌞of enemies⌟ *will* **rage** like great waters; the roar of
Eze 7:16 [A] **moaning** like doves of the valleys, each because of his sins.
Zec 9:15 [A] They will drink and **roar** as with wine; they will be full like a

2160 הֵמָּה ***hēmmâ***, p.m.pl. Not used in NIV/BHS [√ 2085; Ar 10210]

2161 הֵמָה- ***-hēmâ***, p.m.pl.suf. [1] [√ 2023]

the[s] [1]

Eze 40:16 **the**[s] projecting walls inside the gateway were surmounted by

2162 הָמוֹן ***hāmôn***, n.m. [82] [→ 1255, 2163, 2164; cf. 2159]

hordes [18], army [11], crowd [7], wealth [5], many [4], all [+3972] [2], commotion [2], masses [2], multitudes [2], noise [2], noisy [2], roar [2], vast army [2], abundance [1], army [+2657] [1], clamor [1], confusion [1], great amount [1], heavy [1], it[s] [+2021] [1], large [1], multitude [1], people [1], populace [1], raging [1], roaring [1], rumble [1], tenderness [+5055] [1], throng [1], thunder [1], troops [1], tumult [1], turmoil [1], uproar [+7754] [1]

Ge 17:4 is my covenant with you: You will be the father of **many** nations.
17:5 will be Abraham, for I have made you a father of **many** nations.
Jdg 4:7 with his chariots and his **troops** to the Kishon River and give him
1Sa 4:14 and asked, "What is the meaning of this **uproar** [+7754]?"
14:16 Saul's lookouts at Gibeah in Benjamin saw the **army** melting away
14:19 the **tumult** in the Philistine camp increased more and more.
2Sa 6:19 a cake of raisins to each person in the whole **crowd** *of* Israelites,
18:29 "I saw great **confusion** just as Joab was about to send the king's
1Ki 18:41 "Go, eat and drink, for there is the sound of a **heavy** rain."
20:13 "This is what the LORD says: 'Do you see this vast **army**?
20:28 a god of the valleys, I will deliver this vast **army** into your hands,
2Ki 7:13 Their plight will be like that of **all** [+3972] the Israelites left here—
7:13 they will only be like **all** [+3972] these Israelites who are doomed.
25:11 along with the rest of the **populace** and those who had gone over to
1Ch 29:16 as for all this **abundance** that we have provided for building you a
2Ch 11:23 He gave them abundant provisions and took **many** wives for them.
13:8 You are indeed a vast **army** and have with you the golden calves
14:11 [14:10] and in your name we have come against this **vast army**.
20:2 told Jehoshaphat, "A vast **army** is coming against you from Edom,
20:12 For we have no power to face this vast **army** that is attacking us.
20:15 'Do not be afraid or discouraged because of this vast **army**.
20:24 place that overlooks the desert and looked toward the **vast army**,
31:10 has blessed his people, and this **great amount** is left over."
32:7 because of the king of Assyria and the vast **army** with him,
Job 31:34 because I so feared the **crowd** and so dreaded the contempt of the
39:7 He laughs at the **commotion** *in* the town; he does not hear a
Ps 37:16 Better the little that the righteous have than the **wealth** *of* many
42:4 [42:5] shouts of joy and thanksgiving among the festive **throng**.
65:7 [65:8] the roaring of their waves, and the **turmoil** *of* the nations.
Ecc 5:10 [5:9] whoever loves **wealth** is never satisfied with his income.
Isa 5:13 will die of hunger and their **masses** will be parched with thirst.
5:14 their nobles and **masses** with all their brawlers and revelers.
13:4 Listen, a **noise** on the mountains, like that of a great multitude!

Isa 16:14 Moab's splendor and all her many **people** will be despised,
17:12 Oh, the **raging** *of* many nations—they rage like the raging sea!
29: 5 your **many** enemies will become like fine dust, the ruthless hordes
29: 5 will become like fine dust, the ruthless **hordes** like blown chaff.
29: 7 Then the **hordes** *of* all the nations that fight against Ariel,
29: 8 So will it be with the **hordes** *of* all the nations that fight against
31: 4 he is not frightened by their shouts or disturbed by their **clamor**—
32:14 The fortress will be abandoned, the **noisy** city deserted; citadel
33: 3 At the **thunder** *of* your voice, the peoples flee; when you rise up,
60: 5 the **wealth** *on* the seas will be brought to you, to you the riches of
63:15 Your **tenderness** [+5055] and compassion are withheld from us.
Jer 3:23 Surely the ˻idolatrous˼ **commotion** on the hills and mountains is a
10:13 When he thunders, the waters in the heavens **roar**; he makes
47: 3 at the noise of enemy chariots and the **rumble** *of* their wheels.
49:32 camels will become plunder, and their **large** herds will be booty.
51:16 When he thunders, the waters in the heavens **roar**; he makes
51:42 The sea will rise over Babylon; its **roaring** waves will cover her.
Eze 7:11 none of the people will be left, none of that **crowd**—no wealth,
7:12 rejoice nor the seller grieve, for wrath is upon the whole **crowd**.
7:13 for the vision concerning the whole **crowd** will not be reversed.
7:14 no one will go into battle, for my wrath is upon the whole **crowd**.
23:42 "The noise of a carefree **crowd** was around her; Sabeans were
26:13 I will put an end to your **noisy** songs, and the music of your harps
29:19 Nebuchadnezzar king of Babylon, and he will carry off its **wealth**.
30: 4 her **wealth** will be carried away and her foundations torn down.
30:10 " 'I will put an end to the **hordes** *of* Egypt by the hand of
30:15 the stronghold of Egypt, and cut off the **hordes** *of* Thebes.
31: 2 "Son of man, say to Pharaoh king of Egypt and to his **hordes**:
31:18 " 'This is Pharaoh and all his **hordes**, declares the Sovereign
32:12 I will cause your **hordes** to fall by the swords of mighty men—
32:12 shatter the pride of Egypt, and all her **hordes** will be overthrown.
32:16 for Egypt and all her **hordes** they will chant it,
32:18 wail for the **hordes** *of* Egypt and consign to the earth below both
32:20 The sword is drawn; let her be dragged off with all her **hordes**.
32:24 "Elam is there, with all her **hordes** around her grave. All of them
32:25 for her among the slain, with all her **hordes** around her grave.
32:26 and Tubal are there, with all their **hordes** around their graves.
32:31 he will be consoled for all his **hordes** that were killed by the
32:32 Pharaoh and all his **hordes** will be laid among the uncircumcised,
39:11 of travelers, because Gog and all his **hordes** will be buried there.
Da 10: 6 of burnished bronze, and his voice like the sound of a **multitude**.
11:10 His sons will prepare for war and assemble a great **army** [+2657],
11:11 of the North, who will raise a large **army**, but it will be defeated.
11:11 who will raise a large army, but **it**[s] [+2021] will be defeated.
11:12 When the **army** is carried off, the king of the South will be filled
11:13 For the king of the North will muster another **army**, larger than the
Joel 3:14 [4:14] **Multitudes**, multitudes in the valley of decision!
3:14 [4:14] Multitudes, **multitudes** in the valley of decision!
Am 5:23 Away with the **noise** *of* your songs! I will not listen to the music of

2163 הֲמוֹן גּוֹג hᵃmôn gôg, n.pr.loc. [2] [√ 2162 + 1573]

Hamon Gog [2]

Eze 39:11 will be buried there. So it will be called the Valley of **Hamon Gog**.
39:15 until the gravediggers have buried it in the Valley of **Hamon Gog**.

2164 הֲמוֹנָה hᵃmônâ, n.pr.loc. [1] [√ 2162?; cf. 2159]

Hamonah [1]

Eze 39:16 (Also a town called **Hamonah** will be there.) And so they will

2165 הַמַּחְלְקוֹת hammaḥlᵉqôt, n.pl.f. Not used in NIV/BHS [→ 6154; cf. 2745, 4712]

2166 הֶמְיָה hemyâ, n.f. [1] [√ 2159; cf. 2155]

noise [1]

Isa 14:11 brought down to the grave, along with the **noise** *of* your harps;

2167 הֲמֻלָּה hᵃmullâ, n.f. [2] [√ 2159?]

storm [1], tumult [+7754] [1]

Jer 11:16 with the roar of a mighty **storm** he will set it on fire, and its
Eze 1:24 like the voice of the Almighty, like the **tumult** [+7754] of an army.

2168 הַמֹּלֶכֶת hammōleket, n.pr.f. [1] [√ 2143; cf. 4907]

Hammoleketh [1]

1Ch 7:18 His sister **Hammoleketh** gave birth to Ishhod, Abiezer

2169 הָמַם¹ hāmam¹, v. [15] [cf. 2101, 2159, 5637]

routed [3], threw into confusion [2], drives over [1], eliminated [1], resounds [1], rout [1], ruin [1], threw into a panic [1], throw into confusion [1], throwing into confusion [+4539] [1], thrown into confusion [1], troubling [1]

Ex 14:24 [A] and cloud at the Egyptian army and **threw it into confusion**.
23:27 [A] and **throw into confusion** every nation you encounter.
Dt 2:15 [A] until he *had* completely **eliminated** them from the camp.
7:23 [A] **throwing** them **into** great **confusion** [+4539] until they are
Jos 10:10 [A] The LORD **threw** them **into confusion** before Israel, who
Jdg 4:15 [A] the LORD **routed** Sisera and all his chariots and army by
1Sa 7:10 [A] **threw** them **into** *such* **a panic** that they were routed before
2Sa 22:15 [A] scattered ˻the enemies˼, bolts of lightning and **routed** them.
1Ki 1:45 [C] they have gone up cheering, and the city **resounds** with it.
2Ch 15: 6 [A] because God *was* **troubling** them with every kind of distress.
Est 9:24 [A] cast the *pur* (that is, the lot) for their **ruin** and destruction.
Ps 18:14 [18:15] [A] great bolts of lightning and **routed** them.
144: 6 [A] and scatter ˻the enemies˼; shoot your arrows and **rout** them.
Isa 28:28 [A] Though *he* **drives** the wheels of his threshing cart **over** it,
Jer 51:34 [A] *he has* **thrown** us **into confusion**, he has made us an empty

2170 הָמַם² hāmam², v. Not used in NIV/BHS

2171 הָמַן hāman, v.den.?. [1]

unruly [1]

Eze 5: 7 [A] You *have been* more **unruly** than the nations around you

2172 הָמָן hāmān, n.pr.m. [54]

Haman [43], Haman's [5], he[s] [5], *untranslated* [1]

Est 3: 1 King Xerxes honored **Haman** son of Hammedatha, the Agagite,
3: 2 officials at the king's gate knelt down and paid honor to **Haman**,
3: 4 Therefore they told **Haman** about it to see whether Mordecai's
3: 5 When **Haman** saw that Mordecai would not kneel down or pay
3: 5 would not kneel down or pay him honor, **he**[s] was enraged.
3: 6 Instead **Haman** looked for a way to destroy all Mordecai's people,
3: 7 the lot) in the presence of **Haman** to select a day and month.
3: 8 **Haman** said to King Xerxes, "There is a certain people dispersed
3:10 ring from his finger and gave it to **Haman** son of Hammedatha,
3:11 "Keep the money," the king said to **Haman**, "and do with the
3:12 in the language of each people all **Haman's** orders to the king's
3:15 The king and **Haman** sat down to drink, but the city of Susa was
4: 7 including the exact amount of money **Haman** had promised to pay
5: 4 the king," replied Esther, "let the king, together with **Haman**,
5: 5 "Bring **Haman** at once," the king said, "so that we may do what
5: 5 So the king and **Haman** went to the banquet Esther had prepared.
5: 8 and **Haman** come tomorrow to the banquet I will prepare for them.
5: 9 **Haman** went out that day happy and in high spirits. But when he
5: 9 when **he**[s] saw Mordecai at the king's gate and observed that he
5: 9 fear in his presence, **he**[s] was filled with rage against Mordecai.
5:10 Nevertheless, **Haman** restrained himself and went home. Calling
5:11 **Haman** boasted to them about his vast wealth, his many sons,
5:12 "And that's not all," **Haman** added. "I'm the only person Queen
5:14 This suggestion delighted **Haman**, and he had the gallows built.
6: 4 Now **Haman** had just entered the outer court of the palace to speak
6: 5 His attendants answered, "**Haman** is standing in the court."
6: 6 When **Haman** entered, the king asked him, "What should be done
6: 6 Now **Haman** thought to himself, "Who is there that the king would
6: 7 So **he**[s] answered the king, "For the man the king delights to honor,
6:10 "Go at once," the king commanded **Haman**. "Get the robe
6:11 So **Haman** got the robe and the horse. He robed Mordecai,
6:12 But **Haman** rushed home, with his head covered in grief,
6:13 **[RPH]** told Zeresh his wife and all his friends everything that had
6:14 and hurried **Haman** away to the banquet Esther had prepared.
7: 1 So the king and **Haman** went to dine with Queen Esther,
7: 6 Esther said, "The adversary and enemy is this vile **Haman**."
7: 6 Then **Haman** was terrified before the king and queen.
7: 7 But **Haman**, realizing that the king had already decided his fate,
7: 8 **Haman** was falling on the couch where Esther was reclining.
7: 8 as the word left the king's mouth, they covered **Haman's** face.
7: 9 "A gallows seventy-five feet high stands by **Haman's** house.
7: 9 **He**[s] had it made for Mordecai, who spoke up to help the king."
7:10 So they hanged **Haman** on the gallows he had prepared for
8: 1 same day King Xerxes gave Queen Esther the estate of **Haman**,
8: 2 which he had reclaimed from **Haman**, and presented it to
8: 2 it to Mordecai. And Esther appointed him over **Haman's** estate.
8: 3 She begged him to put an end to the evil plan of **Haman** the
8: 5 let an order be written overruling the dispatches that **Haman** son of
8: 7 and to Mordecai the Jew, "Because **Haman** attacked the Jews,
9:10 the ten sons of **Haman** son of Hammedatha, the enemy of the
9:12 hundred men and the ten sons of **Haman** in the citadel of Susa.
9:13 tomorrow also, and let **Haman's** ten sons be hanged on gallows."
9:14 edict was issued in Susa, and they hanged the ten sons of **Haman**.
9:24 For **Haman** son of Hammedatha, the Agagite, the enemy of all the

2173 הֲמָסִים *hamāsîm*, n.[m.]. [1]

twigs [1]

Isa 64: 2 [64:1] As when fire sets **twigs** ablaze and causes water to boil,

2174 הַמִּצְפֶּה *hammiṣpeh*, n.pr.loc. Not used in NIV/BHS [→ 8256; cf. 5205, 7595]

2175 הַמַּרְכָּבוֹת *hammarkābôt*, n.pr.loc. Not used in NIV/BHS [→ 1096]

2176 הֵן¹ *hēn¹*, adv.demo. *or* interj. [99] [→ 434, 435, 2178, 2180, 6364; Ar 10213] See Select Index

untranslated [37], if [15], but [7], surely [7], see [6], look [4], now [4], when [4], since [2], though [2], yet [2], agreed [1], but if [1], even [1], for [1], full well [1], here [1], oh [1], only [1], what if [1]

2177 ²הֶן- *-hēn²*, הֶן- *-hen*, p.f.pl.suf. [183] [√ 2023] Not indexed

their [77], them [46], *untranslated* [30], they [8], the[s] [3], it [2], its [2], their [+4200] [2], their own [2], both[s] [1], lead to do the same[s] [+339+466+906+2388] [1], the girls[s] [1], the rooms[s] [1], the woman[s] and her sister [1], theirs [1], these [1], things [1], where[s] [+928] [1], which [1], which[s] [1]

2178 ¹הֵנָּה *hēnnâ¹*, adv. [51] [→ 6364; cf. 2176]

here [25], *untranslated* [2], back and forth [+285+285+2178+2256] [2], in any direction [+2178+2256] [2], left[s] [2], now [2], right[s] [2], here [+2025] [1], here [+6330] [1], nearby [1], on this side [1], opposite [1], since [+6330] [1], the present time [1], then [1], there [1], this day[s] [1], this [1], thus far [+6330] [1], toward it [1], yet [+6330] [1]

Ge 15: 16 fourth generation your descendants will come back **here** [+2025],
15: 16 for the sin of the Amorites has not **yet** [+6330] reached its full
21: 23 Now swear to me **here** before God that you will not deal falsely
42: 15 will not leave this place unless your youngest brother comes **here**.
44: 28 been torn to pieces." And I have not seen him **since** [+6330].
45: 5 and do not be angry with yourselves for selling me **here**,
45: 8 "So then, it was not you who sent me **here**, but God. He made me
45: 13 you have seen. And bring my father down **here** quickly."
Nu 14: 19 you have pardoned them from the time they left Egypt until **now**."
Dt 20: 15 are at a distance from you and do not belong to the nations **nearby**.
Jos 2: 2 Some of the Israelites have come **here** tonight to spy out the land."
3: 9 "Come **here** and listen to the words of the LORD your God.
8: 20 but they had no chance to escape **in any direction** [+2178+2256],
8: 20 but they had no chance to escape **in any direction** [+2178+2256],
18: 6 bring them **here** to me and I will cast lots for you in the presence
Jdg 16: 2 The people of Gaza were told, "Samson is **here**!" So they
16: 13 Delilah then said to Samson, "Until **now**, you have been making a
1Sa 1: 16 I have been praying **here** [+6330] out of my great anguish
7: 12 it Ebenezer, saying, "**Thus far** [+6330] has the LORD helped us."
20: 21 If I say to him, 'Look, the arrows are **on this side** of you;
2Sa 1: 10 and the band on his arm and have brought them **here** to my lord."
5: 6 The Jebusites said to David, "You will not get in **here**; even the
5: 6 lame can ward you off." They thought, "David cannot get in **here**."
14: 32 and said, 'Come **here** so I can send you to the king to ask,
20: 16 "Listen! Listen! Tell Joab to come **here** so I can speak to him."
1Ki 20: 40 While your servant was busy **here** and there, the man
20: 40 While your servant was busy here and **there**, the man
2Ki 2: 8 The water divided *to the* **right**[s] and to the left, and the two of them
2: 8 The water divided to the right and *to the* **left**[s], and the two of them
2: 14 it divided *to the* **right**[s] and to the left, and he crossed over.
2: 14 it divided to the right and *to the* **left**[s], and he crossed over.
4: 35 turned away and walked **back** [+285+285+2178+2256] **and forth**
4: 35 turned away and walked **back and forth** [+285+285+2178+2256]
8: 7 king was told, "The man of God has come all the way up **here**,"
1Ch 9: 18 stationed at the King's Gate on the east, up to **the present time**.
11: 5 said to David, "You will not get in **here**." Nevertheless,
12: 29 [12:30] of whom had remained loyal to Saul's house until **then**;
2Ch 28: 13 "You must not bring those prisoners **here**," they said, "or we will
Ps 71: 17 have taught me, and to **this day**[s] I declare your marvelous deeds.
Pr 9: 4 "Let all who are simple come in **here**!" she says to those who lack
9: 16 "Let all who are simple come in **here**!" she says to those who lack
25: 7 it is better for him to say to you, "Come up **here**," than for him to
Isa 57: 3 come **here**, you sons of a sorceress, you offspring of adulterers
Jer 5: 6 **[NIE]** for their rebellion is great and their backslidings many.
31: 8 and women in labor; a great throng will return. **[NIE]**
48: 47 to come," declares the LORD. **Here** ends the judgment on Moab.
50: 5 They will ask the way to Zion and turn their faces **toward it**.
51: 64 And her people will fall.' " The words of Jeremiah end **here**.
Eze 40: 4 am going to show you, for that is why you have been brought **here**.
Da 12: 5 one on **this** bank of the river and one on the opposite bank.
12: 5 one on this bank of the river and one on the **opposite** bank.

2179 ²הֵנָּה *hēnnâ²*, p.f.pl. [47] [√ 2085]

untranslated [16], they [8], these [5], them [4], given even more [+2179+2256+3578+3869+3869+4200] [2], things[s] [2], those [2], both [1], cows[s] [1], people[s] [1], plans[s] [1], such [1], their [+4200] [1], themselves [1], what is the meaning [+4537] [1]

Ge 6: 2 were beautiful, **[RPR]** and they married any of them they chose.
21: 29 "**What is the meaning of** [+4537] these seven ewe lambs you have
33: 6 **[RPR]** and their children approached and bowed down.
41: 19 I had never seen such ugly **cows**[s] in all the land of Egypt.
41: 26 **[RPR]** and the seven good heads of grain are seven years;
41: 26 of grain are seven years; **[RPR]** it is one and the same dream.
41: 27 **[RPR]** and so are the seven worthless heads of grain scorched by
Ex 1: 19 **they** are vigorous and give birth before the midwives arrive."
9: 32 and spelt, however, were not destroyed, because **they** ripen later.)
39: 14 **[RPR]** each engraved like a seal with the name of one of the
Lev 4: 2 what is forbidden in any of the LORD's commands—**[RPR]**
6: 3 [5:22] or if he commits any **such** sin that people may do—
18: 10 or your daughter's daughter; that would dishonor you. **[RPR]**
18: 17 or her daughter's daughter; **they** are her close relatives.
Nu 13: 19 of towns do they live in? **[RPR]** Are they unwalled or fortified?
31: 16 "**They** were the ones who followed Balaam's advice and were the
Jdg 19: 12 We won't go into an alien city, whose **people**[s] are not Israelites.
1Sa 17: 28 And with whom did you leave **those** few sheep in the desert?
27: 8 (From ancient times **these** *peoples* had lived in the land extending
2Sa 4: 6 **They** went into the inner part of the house as if to get some wheat,
12: 8 And if all this had been too little, *I would have* **given** you **even more** [+2179+2256+3578+3869+3869+4200].
12: 8 And if all this had been too little, *I would have* **given** you **even more** [+2179+2256+3578+3869+3869+4200].
1Ch 21: 10 Choose one of **them** for me to carry out against you.' "
Job 23: 14 his decree against me, and many such **plans**[s] he still has in store.
Ps 34: 20 [34:21] he protects all his bones, not one of **them** will be broken.
Pr 6: 16 There are six **things**[s] the LORD hates, seven that are detestable to
30: 15 "There are three **things**[s] that are never satisfied, four that never
Isa 34: 16 None of **these** will be missing, not one will lack her mate.
41: 22 **[RPR]** so that we may consider them and know their final
51: 19 **These** double calamities have come upon you—who can comfort
Jer 5: 17 they will destroy the fortified cities in which you trust. **[RPR]**
34: 7 and Azekah. **These** were the only fortified cities left in Judah.
38: 22 **Those** women will say to you: " 'They misled you and overcame
Eze 1: 5 In appearance **their** [+4200] form was that of a man,
1: 23 the other, and each had two wings covering **[RPR]** its body.
1: 23 the other, and each had two wings covering its body. **[RPR]**
16: 51 You have done more detestable things than **they**, and have made
18: 4 living soul belongs to me, **[RPR]** the father as well as the son—
18: 4 to me, the father as well as the son—**both** *alike* belong to me.
23: 45 because **they** are adulterous and blood is on their hands.
30: 17 fall by the sword, and the cities **themselves** will go into captivity.
42: 5 for the galleries took more space from **them** than from the rooms
42: 6 The rooms on the third floor **[RPR]** had no pillars, as the courts
42: 9 entrance on the east side as one enters **them** from the outer court.
42: 13 south rooms facing the temple courtyard **[RPR]** are the priests'
42: 14 behind the garments in which they minister, for **these** are holy.
Zec 5: 9 **They** had wings like those of a stork, and they lifted up the basket

2180 הִנֵּה *hinnēh*, pt.demo. [1060] [√ 2176] See Select Index

untranslated [549], see [81], look [61], here [57], there [57], saw [43], now [33], if [28], surely [24], found [12], yes [9], how [6], indeed [6], listen [6], suddenly [6], but [5], this [4], beware [3], even [3], that [3], already [2], appeared [2], as soon as [2], discovered [2], just then [+2256] [2], just [2], remember [2], so [2], suppose [2], very well then [2], very well [2], what [2], when [2], after all [1], all at once [+2296] [1], be sure [1], behold [1], certainly [1], come then [1], come [1], consider [1], for [1], heard [1], here now [1], it is still there [1], just as [1], meanwhile [1], nevertheless [1], not [1], now then [1], ready to do [1], ready [1], realized [1], right now [1], showed [1], since [1], soon [1], suddenly appeared [1], sure [1], surely [+3954] [1], then [1], therefore [1], think [1], this is how [1], this is why [1], though [1], too [1], unless [1], very well [+5528] [1], well [1], what can do [1]

2181 הָנָה- *-henâ*, הֶנָה- *-henâ*, p.f.pl.suf. [3] [√ 2023] Not indexed

its [1], them [1], they [1]

2182 הֲנָחָה *hanāḥâ*, n.f. [1] [√ 5663]

holiday [1]

Est 2: 18 He proclaimed a **holiday** throughout the provinces and distributed

2183 הִנֹּם hinnōm, n.pr.m. & loc. [3] [→ 1208]

Hinnom [3]

Jos 15: 8 From there it climbed to the top of the hill west of the **Hinnom**
18: 16 It continued down the **Hinnom** Valley along the southern slope of
Ne 11: 30 were living all the way from Beersheba to the Valley of **Hinnom**.

2184 הֵנַע hēna', n.pr.loc. [3]

Hena [3]

2Ki 18: 34 and Arpad? Where are the gods of Sepharvaim, **Hena** and Ivvah?
19: 13 the king of the city of Sepharvaim, or of **Hena** or Ivvah?"
Isa 37: 13 the king of the city of Sepharvaim, or of **Hena** or Ivvah?"

2185 הֲנָפָה hănāpâ, v. Not used in NIV/BHS [√ 5677]

2186 הַנֶּקֶב hanneqeb, n.pr.loc. Not used in NIV/BHS [→ 146; cf. 2021 + 5918]

2187 הַס has, interj. [7] [→ 2188]

be silent [2], be still [2], hush [1], quiet [1], silence [1]

Jdg 3: 19 "I have a secret message for you, O king." The king said, "**Quiet**!"
Ne 8: 11 calmed all the people, saying, "**Be still**, for this is a sacred day.
Am 6: 10 "Is anyone with you?" and he says, "No," then he will say, "**Hush**!
8: 3 turn to wailing. Many, many bodies—flung everywhere! **Silence**!"
Hab 2: 20 is in his holy temple; *let* all the earth **be silent** before him."
Zep 1: 7 **Be silent** before the Sovereign LORD, for the day of the LORD
Zec 2: 13 [2:17] **Be still** before the LORD, all mankind, because he has

2188 הָסָה hāsâ, v.den. [1] [√ 2187]

silenced [1]

Nu 13: 30 [A] Caleb **silenced** the people before Moses and said,

2189 הַסְּנָאָה hassᵉnā'â, n.pr.m. [1] [√ 2021 + 6171]

Hassenaah [1]

Ne 3: 3 The Fish Gate was rebuilt by the sons of **Hassenaah**. They laid its

2190 הַסְּנוּאָה hassᵉnu'â, n.pr.m. [2] [√ 2021 + 8533]

Hassenuah [2]

1Ch 9: 7 son of Meshullam, the son of Hodaviah, the son of **Hassenuah**;
Ne 11: 9 Judah son of **Hassenuah** was over the Second District of the city.

2191 הַסֹּפֶרֶת hassōperet, n.pr.m. [1] [√ 2021 + 6219]

Hassophereth [1]

Ezr 2: 55 of Solomon: the descendants of Sotai, **Hassophereth**, Peruda,

2192 הָעֲבָרִים hāᵃbārîm, n.pr.loc. Not used in NIV/BHS [→ 6516]

2193 הָעֵזֶר hā'ēzer, n.pr.loc. Not used in NIV/BHS [√ 6469]

2194 הָעַמֹּנִי hā'ammōnî, a.g. Not used in NIV/BHS [→ 4112; cf. 2021 + 6648, 6671]

2195 הָעֵמֶק hā'ēmeq, n.pr.loc. Not used in NIV/BHS [√ 6676]

2196 הָעֲרָבָה hāᵃrābâ, n.pr.loc. Not used in NIV/BHS [→ 1098]

2197 הָעֲרָלוֹת hāᵃrālôt, n.f. Not used in NIV/BHS [→ 1502; cf. 6889]

2198 הֲפֻגָה hăpugâ, n.f. [1] [√ 7028]

relief [1]

La 3: 49 My eyes will flow unceasingly, without **relief**,

2199 הַפּוּךְ happûk, n.pr.f. Not used in NIV/BHS [→ 7968]

2200 הָפַךְ hāpak, v. [94] [→ 2201, 2202, 2203, 4550, 4551, 9337; cf. 60]

turned [21], turn [8], overthrew [5], changed [4], overthrow [4], be changed [2], be turned [2], turned back [2], was changed [2], wheel around [+3338] [2], are [1], be brought [1], be overturned [1], been turned over [1], came tumbling [1], change [1], changed [+337+4200] [1], deceitful [1], devastate [1], distort [1], disturbed [1], flashing back and forth [1], got down [1], is transformed [1], lays bare [1], left [1], overcome [1], overthrown [1], overthrows [1], overturn [1], overturned [+2025+4200+5087] [1], overturns [1], overwhelm [1], purify [+448+1359] [1], restore [1], routed [+6902] [1], swirl [1], takes shape [1], the tables were turned [1], turn into [1], turned about [+3338] [1], turned and became [1], turned around [1], turned into [1], turned over [1], turning [1], turns [1], unreliable [1], was overcome [1], was overthrown [1], was sapped [1], was turned [1]

Ge 3: 24 [F] a flaming sword **flashing back and forth** to guard the way to
19: 21 [A] this request too; I *will* not **overthrow** the town you speak of.
19: 25 [A] *he* **overthrew** those cities and the entire plain, including
19: 29 [A] he brought Lot out of the catastrophe that **overthrew** the
Ex 7: 15 [C] take in your hand the staff that **was changed** into a snake.
7: 17 [C] the water of the Nile, and *it will* **be changed** into blood.
7: 20 [C] water of the Nile, and all the water **was changed** into blood.
10: 19 [A] the LORD **changed** the wind *to* a very strong west wind,
14: 5 [C] Pharaoh and his officials **changed** their minds about them
Lev 13: 3 [A] if the hair in the sore *has* **turned** white and the sore appears
13: 4 [A] more than skin deep and the hair in it *has* not **turned** white,
13: 10 [A] if there is a white swelling in the skin that *has* **turned** the
13: 13 [A] that person clean. Since it *has* all **turned** white, he is clean.
13: 16 [C] *Should* the raw flesh change and **turn** white, he must go to
13: 17 [C] priest is to examine him, and if the sores *have* **turned** white,
13: 20 [A] to be more than skin deep and the hair in it *has* **turned** white,
13: 25 [C] is to examine the spot, and if the hair in it *has* **turned** white,
13: 55 [A] and if the mildew *has* not **changed** its appearance,
Dt 23: 5 [23:6] [A] but **turned** the curse into a blessing for you,
29: 23 [29:22] [A] which the LORD **overthrew** in fierce anger.
Jos 7: 8 [A] now that Israel *has been* **routed** [+6902] by its enemies?
8: 20 [C] toward the desert *had* **turned back** against their pursuers.
Jdg 7: 13 [F] "A round loaf of barley bread **came tumbling** into the
7: 13 [A] with such force that the tent **overturned** [+2025+4200+5087]
20: 39 [A] then the men of Israel *would* **turn** in the battle. The
20: 41 [A] the men of Israel **turned** *on* them, and the men of Benjamin
1Sa 4: 19 [C] and gave birth, but **was overcome** *by* her labor pains.
10: 6 [C] with them; and *you will* **be changed** into a different person.
10: 9 [A] to leave Samuel, God **changed** [+337+4200] Saul's heart,
25: 12 [A] David's men **turned around** and went back. When they
2Sa 10: 3 [A] to you to explore the city and spy it out and **overthrow** it?"
1Ki 22: 34 [A] "**Wheel around** [+3338] and get me out of the fighting.
2Ki 5: 26 [A] "Was not my spirit with you when the man **got down** from
9: 23 [A] Joram **turned** [+3338] **about** and fled, calling out to
21: 13 [A] as one wipes a dish, wiping it and **turning** it upside down.
1Ch 19: 3 [A] to you to explore and spy out the country and **overthrow** it?"
2Ch 9: 12 [A] she **left** and returned with her retinue to her own country.
18: 33 [A] "**Wheel around** [+3338] and get me out of the fighting.
Ne 13: 2 [A] (Our God, however, **turned** the curse into a blessing.)
Est 9: 1 [C] now **the tables were turned** and the Jews got the upper hand
9: 22 [C] as the month when their sorrow **was turned** into joy and their
Job 9: 5 [A] without their knowing it and **overturns** them in his anger.
12: 15 [A] is drought; if he lets them loose, *they* **devastate** the land.
19: 19 [C] friends detest me; those I love *have* **turned** against me.
20: 14 [C] yet his food *will* **turn** sour in his stomach; it will become the
28: 5 [C] from which food comes, **is transformed** below as by fire;
28: 9 [A] the flinty rock and **lays bare** the roots of the mountains.
30: 15 [H] Terrors **overwhelm** me; my dignity is driven away as by the
30: 21 [C] *You* **turn** on me ruthlessly; with the might of your hand you
34: 25 [A] *he* **overthrows** them in the night and they are crushed.
37: 12 [F] At his direction they **swirl** around over the face of the whole
38: 14 [F] The earth **takes shape** like clay under a seal; its features
41: 28 [41:20] [C] not make him flee; slingstones **are** like chaff to him.
Ps 30: 11 [30:12] [A] *You* **turned** my wailing into dancing; you removed
32: 4 [C] upon me; my strength **was sapped** as in the heat of summer.
41: 3 [41:4] [A] his sickbed and **restore** him from his bed of illness.
66: 6 [A] *He* **turned** the sea into dry land, they passed through the
78: 9 [A] though armed with bows, **turned back** on the day of battle;
78: 44 [A] *He* **turned** their rivers to blood; they could not drink from
78: 57 [C] were disloyal and faithless, as **unreliable** as a faulty bow.
105: 25 [A] whose hearts *he* **turned** to hate his people, to conspire
105: 29 [A] *He* **turned** their waters into blood, causing their fish to die.
114: 8 [A] who **turned** the rock **into** a pool, the hard rock into springs
Pr 12: 7 [A] Wicked men *are* **overthrown** and are no more, but the house
17: 20 [C] not prosper; *he* whose tongue *is* **deceitful** falls into trouble.
Isa 34: 9 [C] Edom's streams *will* **be turned** into pitch, her dust into
60: 5 [C] the wealth on the seas *will* **be brought** to you, to you the
63: 10 [C] So *he* **turned and became** their enemy and he himself
Jer 2: 21 [C] How then *did you* **turn** against me **into** a corrupt, wild vine?
13: 23 [A] *Can* the Ethiopian **change** his skin or the leopard its spots?
20: 16 [A] May that man be like the towns the LORD **overthrew**
23: 36 [A] his oracle and so *you* **distort** the words of the living God,
30: 6 [C] like a woman in labor, every face **turned** deathly pale?
31: 13 [A] *I will* **turn** their mourning into gladness; I will give them
La 1: 20 [C] I am in torment within, and in my heart *I am* **disturbed**, for I
3: 3 [A] indeed, *he has* **turned** his hand against me again and again,

La 4: 6 [B] which **was overthrown** in a moment without a hand turned
5: 2 [C] Our inheritance *has* **been turned over** to aliens, our homes
5: 15 [C] gone from our hearts; our dancing *has* **turned** to mourning.
Eze 4: 8 [C] so that *you* cannot **turn** from one side to the other until you
Da 10: 8 [C] strength left, my face **turned** deathly pale and I was helpless.
10: 16 [C] "I *am* **overcome** *with* anguish because of the vision,
Hos 7: 8 [B] with the nations; Ephraim is a flat cake not **turned over**.
11: 8 [C] My heart *is* **changed** within me; all my compassion is
Joel 2: 31 [3:4] [C] The sun *will* **be turned** to darkness and the moon to
Am 4: 11 [A] "*I* **overthrew** some of you as I overthrew Sodom
5: 7 [A] *You who* **turn** justice into bitterness and cast righteousness
5: 8 [A] *who* **turns** blackness into dawn and darkens day into night,
6: 12 [A] *you have* **turned** justice into poison and the fruit of
8: 10 [A] *I will* **turn** your religious feasts into mourning and all your
Jnh 3: 4 [C] "Forty more days and Nineveh *will* **be overturned**."
Zep 3: 9 [A] "Then *will I* **purify** [+448+1359] the lips of the peoples,
Hag 2: 22 [A] *I will* **overturn** royal thrones and shatter the power of the
2: 22 [A] *I will* **overthrow** chariots and their drivers; horses and their

2201 הֵפֶךְ hēpek, n.m. [3] [√ 2200]

opposite [1], turn upside down [1], very opposite [1]

Isa 29: 16 You **turn** things **upside down**, as if the potter were thought to be
Eze 16: 34 So in your prostitution you are the **opposite** of others; no one runs
16: 34 You are the **very opposite**, for you give payment and none is given

2202 הֲפֵכָה h^apēkâ, n.f. [1] [√ 2200]

catastrophe [1]

Ge 19: 29 he brought Lot out of the **catastrophe** that overthrew the cities

2203 הֲפַכְפַּךְ h^apakpak, a. [1] [√ 2200]

devious [1]

Pr 21: 8 The way of the guilty is **devious**, but the conduct of the innocent is

2204 הַפִּצֵּץ happiṣṣēṣ, n.pr.m. [1] [√ 2021 + 7207; cf. 7209]

Happizzez [1]

1Ch 24: 15 the seventeenth to Hezir, the eighteenth to **Happizzez**,

2205 הֻצַּב huṣṣab, var. Not used in NIV/BHS [√ 5893]

2206 הַצֹּבֵבָה haṣṣōbēbâ, n.pr.m. [1] [√ 2021 + 7376]

Hazzobebah [1]

1Ch 4: 8 who was the father of Anub and **Hazzobebah** and of the clans of

2207 הַצְּבָיִים haṣṣ^ebāyim, n.pr.m. Not used in NIV/BHS [→ 7097]

2208 הַצָּלָה haṣṣālâ, n.f. [1] [√ 5911]

deliverance [1]

Est 4: 14 and **deliverance** for the Jews will arise from another place,

2209 הַצְלֶלְפּוֹנִי haṣṣ^elelpônî, n.pr.f. [1] [√ 2021 + 7511 + 7156 + 3276]

Hazzelelponi [1]

1Ch 4: 3 Jezreel, Ishma and Idbash. Their sister was named **Hazzelelponi**.

2210 הֹצֶן hōṣen, n.[m.]. [1]

weapons [1]

Eze 23: 24 They will come against you with **weapons**, chariots and wagons

2211 הַצֻּרִים haṣṣurîm, n.pr.loc. Not used in NIV/BHS [→ 2763]

2212 הַקּוֹץ haqqôṣ, n.pr.m. [5] [√ 2021 + 7764?]

Hakkoz [5]

1Ch 24: 10 the seventh to **Hakkoz**, the eighth to Abijah,
Ezr 2: 61 **Hakkoz** and Barzillai (a man who had married a daughter of
Ne 3: 4 Meremoth son of Uriah, the son of **Hakkoz**, repaired the next
3: 21 Next to him, Meremoth son of Uriah, the son of **Hakkoz**,
7: 63 **Hakkoz** and Barzillai (a man who had married a daughter of

2213 הַקֹּרֵא haqqôrē', n.pr.loc. Not used in NIV/BHS [→ 6530]

2214 הַקָּטָן haqqāṭān, n.pr.m. [1] [√ 2021 + 7783]

Hakkatan [1]

Ezr 8: 12 of Azgad, Johanan son of **Hakkatan**, and with him 110 men;

2215 הַר har, n.m. [558 / 560] [→ 2216; cf. 2105]

mountains [143], mount [119], mountain [114], hill country [82], hills [40], hill [32], *untranslated* [5], mountain shrines [4], mountaintops [+8031] [4], it[s] [+2021] [3], another[s] [+2021+2296+4946] [1], hillside [+7521] [1], hillside [1], hilltop [+8031] [1], hilltop [1], hilltops [+8031] [1], it[s] [+1628] [1], mountain clefts [1], mountain haunts [1], mountain regions [1], mountaintop [+8031] [1], range [1], there[s] [+928+2021] [1], there[s] [+928+2021] [1]

Ge 7: 19 and all the high **mountains** under the entire heavens were covered.
7: 20 and covered the **mountains** to a depth of more than twenty feet.
8: 4 the seventh month the ark came to rest on the **mountains** *of* Ararat.
8: 5 on the first day of the tenth month the tops of the **mountains**
10: 30 stretched from Mesha toward Sephar, in the eastern **hill country**.
12: 8 From there he went on toward the **hills** east of Bethel and pitched
14: 6 the Horites in the **hill country** *of* Seir, as far as El Paran near the
14: 10 some of the men fell into them and the rest fled to the **hills**.
19: 17 in the plain! Flee to the **mountains** or you will be swept away!"
19: 19 But I can't flee to the **mountains**; this disaster will overtake me,
19: 30 and his two daughters left Zoar and settled in the **mountains**,
22: 2 Sacrifice him there as a burnt offering on one of the **mountains** I
22: 14 it is said, "On the **mountain** *of* the LORD it will be provided."
31: 21 and crossing the River, he headed for the **hill country** *of* Gilead.
31: 23 seven days and caught up with him in the **hill country** *of* Gilead.
31: 25 Jacob had pitched his tent in the **hill country** *of* Gilead when
31: 25 and Laban and his relatives camped **there**[s] [+928+2021] too.
31: 54 He offered a sacrifice there in the **hill country** and invited his
31: 54 After they had eaten, they spent the night **there** [+928+2021].
36: 8 So Esau (that is, Edom) settled in the **hill country** *of* Seir.
36: 9 of Esau the father of the Edomites in the **hill country** *of* Seir.
49: 26 greater than the blessings of the ancient **mountains**, [BHS 2225]
Ex 3: 1 the far side of the desert and came to Horeb, the **mountain** *of* God.
3: 12 the people out of Egypt, you will worship God on this **mountain**."
4: 27 So he met Moses at the **mountain** *of* God and kissed him.
15: 17 them in and plant them on the **mountain** *of* your inheritance—
18: 5 in the desert, where he was camped near the **mountain** *of* God.
19: 2 and Israel camped there in the desert in front of the **mountain**.
19: 3 and the LORD called to him from the **mountain** and said,
19: 11 because on that day the LORD will come down on **Mount** Sinai
19: 12 'Be careful that you do not go up the **mountain** or touch the foot of
19: 12 Whoever touches the **mountain** shall surely be put to death.
19: 13 ram's horn sounds a long blast may they go up to the **mountain**."
19: 14 After Moses had gone down the **mountain** to the people, he
19: 16 was thunder and lightning, with a thick cloud over the **mountain**,
19: 17 to meet with God, and they stood at the foot of the **mountain**.
19: 18 **Mount** Sinai was covered with smoke, because the LORD
19: 18 smoke from a furnace, the whole **mountain** trembled violently,
19: 20 The LORD descended to the top of **Mount** Sinai and called
19: 20 Mount Sinai **[RPH]** and called Moses to the top of the mountain.
19: 20 top of Mount Sinai and called Moses to the top of the **mountain**.
19: 23 said to the LORD, "The people cannot come up **Mount** Sinai,
19: 23 'Put limits around the **mountain** and set it apart as holy.' "
20: 18 and heard the trumpet and saw the **mountain** in smoke,
24: 4 the next morning and built an altar at the foot of the **mountain**
24: 12 said to Moses, "Come up to me on the **mountain** and stay here,
24: 13 with Joshua his aide, and Moses went up on the **mountain** *of* God.
24: 15 When Moses went up on the **mountain**, the cloud covered it,
24: 15 Moses went up on the mountain, the cloud covered **it**[s] [+2021],
24: 16 the glory of the LORD settled on **Mount** Sinai. For six days the
24: 17 the LORD looked like a consuming fire on top of the **mountain**.
24: 18 Then Moses entered the cloud as he went on up the **mountain**.
24: 18 And he stayed on the **mountain** forty days and forty nights.
25: 40 make them according to the pattern shown you on the **mountain**.
26: 30 the tabernacle according to the plan shown you on the **mountain**.
27: 8 It is to be made just as you were shown on the **mountain**.
31: 18 When the LORD finished speaking to Moses on **Mount** Sinai,
32: 1 saw that Moses was so long in coming down from the **mountain**,
32: 12 to kill them in the **mountains** and to wipe them off the face of the
32: 15 went down the **mountain** with the two tablets of the Testimony in
32: 19 of his hands, breaking them to pieces at the foot of the **mountain**.
33: 6 So the Israelites stripped off their ornaments at **Mount** Horeb.
34: 2 Be ready in the morning, and then come up on **Mount** Sinai.
34: 2 Mount Sinai. Present yourself to me there on top of the **mountain**.
34: 3 No one is to come with you or be seen anywhere on the **mountain**;
34: 3 not even the flocks and herds may graze in front of the **mountain**."
34: 4 like the first ones and went up **Mount** Sinai early in the morning,
34: 29 When Moses came down from **Mount** Sinai with the two tablets of
34: 29 **[RPH]** he was not aware that his face was radiant because he had
34: 32 all the commands the LORD had given him on **Mount** Sinai.

Lev 7:38 which the LORD gave Moses on **Mount** Sinai on the day he
25: 1 The LORD said to Moses on **Mount** Sinai,
26:46 the regulations that the LORD established on **Mount** Sinai
27:34 These are the commands the LORD gave Moses on **Mount** Sinai
Nu 3: 1 Moses at the time the LORD talked with Moses on **Mount** Sinai.
10:33 So they set out from the **mountain** *of* the LORD and traveled for
13:17 he said, "Go up through the Negev and on into the **hill country**.
13:29 the Hittites, Jebusites and Amorites live in the **hill country**;
14:40 Early the next morning they went up toward the high **hill country**.
14:44 in their presumption they went up toward the high **hill country**,
14:45 and Canaanites who lived in that **hill country** came down
20:22 Israelite community set out from Kadesh and came to **Mount** Hor.
20:23 At **Mount** Hor, near the border of Edom, the LORD said to
20:25 Get Aaron and his son Eleazar and take them up **Mount** Hor.
20:27 They went up **Mount** Hor in the sight of the whole community.
20:28 And Aaron died there on top of the **mountain**. Then Moses
20:28 Then Moses and Eleazar came down from the **mountain**,
21: 4 They traveled from **Mount** Hor along the route to the Red Sea,
23: 7 me from Aram, the king of Moab from the eastern **mountains**.
27:12 "Go up this **mountain** *in* the Abarim range and see the land I have
28: 6 This is the regular burnt offering instituted at **Mount** Sinai as a
33:23 They left Kehelathah and camped at **Mount** Shepher.
33:24 They left **Mount** Shepher and camped at Haradah.
33:37 They left Kadesh and camped at **Mount** Hor, on the border of
33:38 At the LORD's command Aaron the priest went up **Mount** Hor,
33:39 a hundred and twenty-three years old when he died on **Mount** Hor.
33:41 They left **Mount** Hor and camped at Zalmonah.
33:47 left Almon Diblathaim and camped in the **mountains** *of* Abarim,
33:48 They left the **mountains** *of* Abarim and camped on the plains of
34: 7 northern boundary, run a line from the Great Sea to **Mount** Hor
34: 8 from **Mount** Hor to Lebo Hamath. Then the boundary will go to
Dt 1: 2 days to go from Horeb to Kadesh Barnea by the **Mount** Seir road.)
1: 6 to us at Horeb, "You have stayed long enough at this **mountain**.
1: 7 Break camp and advance into the **hill country** *of* the Amorites;
1: 7 in the **mountains**, in the western foothills, in the Negev and along
1:19 went toward the **hill country** *of* the Amorites through all that vast
1:20 I said to you, "You have reached the **hill country** *of* the Amorites,
1:24 They left and went up into the **hill country**, and came to the Valley
1:41 put on his weapons, thinking it easy to go up into the **hill country**.
1:43 and in your arrogance you marched up into the **hill country**.
1:44 The Amorites who lived in those **hills** came out against you;
2: 1 For a long time we made our way around the **hill country** *of* Seir.
2: 3 "You have made your way around this **hill country** long enough;
2: 5 your foot on. I have given Esau the **hill country** *of* Seir as his own.
2:37 the course of the Jabbok nor that around the towns in the **hills**.
3: 8 east of the Jordan, from the Arnon Gorge as far as **Mount** Hermon.
3:12 including half the **hill country** *of* Gilead, together with its towns.
3:25 land beyond the Jordan—that fine **hill country** and Lebanon."
4:11 stood at the foot of the **mountain** while it blazed with fire to the
4:11 stood at the foot of the mountain while **it**[s] [+2021] blazed with fire
4:48 from Aroer on the rim of the Arnon Gorge to **Mount** Siyon (that is,
5: 4 LORD spoke to you face to face out of the fire on the **mountain**.
5: 5 you were afraid of the fire and did not go up the **mountain**.)
5:22 to your whole assembly there on the **mountain** from out of the fire,
5:23 while the **mountain** was ablaze with fire, all the leading men of
8: 7 and pools of water, with springs flowing in the valleys and **hills**;
8: 9 where the rocks are iron and you can dig copper out of the **hills**.
9: 9 When I went up on the **mountain** to receive the tablets of stone,
9: 9 with you, I stayed on the **mountain** forty days and forty nights;
9:10 the LORD proclaimed to you on the **mountain** out of the fire,
9:15 and went down from the **mountain** while it was ablaze with fire.
9:15 went down from the mountain while **it**[s] [+2021] was ablaze with
9:21 and threw the dust into a stream that flowed down the **mountain**.
10: 1 tablets like the first ones and come up to me on the **mountain**.
10: 3 and I went up on the **mountain** with the two tablets in my hands.
10: 4 Ten Commandments he had proclaimed to you on the **mountain**,
10: 5 I came back down the **mountain** and put the tablets in the ark I had
10:10 Now I had stayed on the **mountain** forty days and nights,
11:11 crossing the Jordan to take possession of is a land of **mountains**
11:29 you are to proclaim on **Mount** Gerizim the blessings, and on
11:29 on Mount Gerizim the blessings, and on **Mount** Ebal the curses.
12: 2 Destroy completely all the places on the high **mountains** and on
27: 4 set up these stones on **Mount** Ebal, as I command you today,
27:12 these tribes shall stand on **Mount** Gerizim to bless the people:
27:13 And these tribes shall stand on **Mount** Ebal to pronounce curses:
32:22 and its harvests and set afire the foundations of the **mountains**.
32:49 "Go up into the Abarim **Range** to Mount Nebo in Moab, across
32:49 "Go up into the Abarim Range to **Mount** Nebo in Moab, across
32:50 There on the **mountain** that you have climbed you will die
32:50 just as your brother Aaron died on **Mount** Hor and was gathered to
33: 2 dawned over them from Seir; he shone forth from **Mount** Paran.
33:15 with the choicest gifts of the ancient **mountains** and the
33:19 They will summon peoples to the **mountain** and there offer
34: 1 Moses climbed **Mount** Nebo from the plains of Moab to the top of
Jos 2:16 had said to them, "Go to the **hills** so the pursuers will not find you.
2:22 When they left, they went into the **hills** and stayed there three days,
2:23 They went down out of the **hills**, forded the river and came to
8:30 Then Joshua built on **Mount** Ebal an altar to the LORD,
8:33 Half of the people stood in front of **Mount** Gerizim and half of
8:33 front of Mount Gerizim and half of them in front of **Mount** Ebal,
9: 1 those in the **hill country**, in the western foothills, and along the
10: 6 because all the Amorite kings from the **hill country** have joined
10:40 including the **hill country**, the Negev, the western foothills
11: 2 to the northern kings who were in the **mountains**, in the Arabah
11: 3 the Amorites, Hittites, Perizzites and Jebusites in the **hill country**;
11:16 the **hill country**, all the Negev, the whole region of Goshen,
11:16 the Arabah and the **mountains** *of* Israel with their foothills,
11:17 from **Mount** Halak, which rises toward Seir, to Baal Gad in the
11:17 to Baal Gad in the Valley of Lebanon below **Mount** Hermon.
11:21 Joshua went and destroyed the Anakites from the **hill country**:
11:21 from Hebron, Debir and Anab, from all the **hill country** *of* Judah,
11:21 all the hill country of Judah, and from all the **hill country** *of* Israel.
12: 1 from the Arnon Gorge to **Mount** Hermon, including all the eastern
12: 5 He ruled over **Mount** Hermon, Salecah, all of Bashan to the border
12: 7 from Baal Gad in the Valley of Lebanon to **Mount** Halak,
12: 8 the **hill country**, the western foothills, the Arabah, the mountain
13: 5 to the east, from Baal Gad below **Mount** Hermon to Lebo Hamath.
13: 6 "As for all the inhabitants of the **mountain regions** from Lebanon
13:11 all of **Mount** Hermon and all Bashan as far as Salecah—
13:19 Kiriathaim, Sibmah, Zereth Shahar on the **hill** *in* the valley,
14:12 Now give me this **hill country** that the LORD promised me that
15: 8 From there it climbed to the top of the **hill** west of the Hinnom
15: 9 From the **hilltop** [+8031] the boundary headed toward the spring
15: 9 came out at the towns of **Mount** Ephron and went down toward
15:10 it curved westward from Baalah to **Mount** Seir, ran along the
15:10 ran along the northern slope of **Mount** Jearim (that is, Kesalon),
15:11 passed along to **Mount** Baalah and reached Jabneel.
15:48 In the **hill country**: Shamir, Jattir, Socoh,
16: 1 went up from there through the desert into the **hill country** *of*
17:15 "and if the **hill country** *of* Ephraim is too small for you,
17:16 people of Joseph replied, "The **hill country** is not enough for us,
17:18 the forested **hill country** as well. Clear it, and its farthest limits
18:12 northern slope of Jericho and headed west into the **hill country**,
18:13 went down to Ataroth Addar on the **hill** south of Lower Beth
18:14 From the **hill** facing Beth Horon on the south the boundary turned
18:16 The boundary went down to the foot of the **hill** facing the Valley of
19:50 town he asked for—Timnath Serah in the **hill country** *of* Ephraim.
20: 7 So they set apart Kedesh in Galilee in the **hill country** *of* Naphtali,
20: 7 Shechem in the **hill country** *of* Ephraim, and Kiriath Arba (that is,
20: 7 and Kiriath Arba (that is, Hebron) in the **hill country** *of* Judah.
21:11 with its surrounding pastureland, in the **hill country** *of* Judah.
21:21 In the **hill country** *of* Ephraim they were given Shechem (a city of
24: 4 I assigned the **hill country** *of* Seir to Esau, but Jacob and his sons
24:30 at Timnath Serah in the **hill country** *of* Ephraim, north of Mount
24:30 Serah in the hill country of Ephraim, north of **Mount** Gaash.
24:33 which had been allotted to his son Phinehas in the **hill country** *of*
Jdg 1: 9 down to fight against the Canaanites living in the **hill country**,
1:19 They took possession of the **hill country**, but they were unable to
1:34 The Amorites confined the Danites to the **hill country**, not
1:35 the Amorites were determined also to hold out in **Mount** Heres,
2: 9 at Timnath Heres in the **hill country** *of* Ephraim, north of Mount
2: 9 Heres in the hill country of Ephraim, north of **Mount** Gaash.
3: 3 the Hivites living in the Lebanon **mountains** from Mount Baal
3: 3 the Hivites living in the Lebanon mountains from **Mount** Baal
3:27 he arrived there, he blew a trumpet in the **hill country** *of* Ephraim,
3:27 the Israelites went down with him from the **hills**, with him leading
4: 5 between Ramah and Bethel in the **hill country** *of* Ephraim,
4: 6 men of Naphtali and Zebulun and lead the way to **Mount** Tabor.
4:12 Sisera that Barak son of Abinoam had gone up to **Mount** Tabor,
4:14 So Barak went down **Mount** Tabor, followed by ten thousand men.
5: 5 The **mountains** quaked before the LORD, the One of Sinai,
6: 2 the Israelites prepared shelters for themselves in **mountain clefts**,
7: 3 and leave **Mount** Gilead.' " So twenty-two thousand men left,
7:24 Gideon sent messengers throughout the **hill country** *of* Ephraim,
9: 7 he climbed up on the top of **Mount** Gerizim and shouted to them,
9:25 citizens of Shechem set men on the **hilltops** [+8031] to ambush
9:36 people are coming down from the tops of the **mountains**!"
9:36 "You mistake the shadows of the **mountains** for men."
9:48 he and all his men went up **Mount** Zalmon. He took an ax
10: 1 to save Israel. He lived in Shamir, in the **hill country** *of* Ephraim.
11:37 "Give me two months to roam the **hills** and weep with my friends,
11:38 She and the girls went into the **hills** and wept because she would
12:15 at Pirathon in Ephraim, in the **hill country** *of* the Amalekites.
16: 3 and carried them to the top of the **hill** that faces Hebron.
17: 1 Now a man named Micah from the **hill country** *of* Ephraim
17: 8 On his way he came to Micah's house in the **hill country** *of*
18: 2 The men entered the **hill country** *of* Ephraim and came to the
18:13 From there they went on to the **hill country** *of* Ephraim and came

Jdg 19: 1 Now a Levite who lived in a remote area in the **hill country** *of*
19: 16 That evening an old man from the **hill country** *of* Ephraim,
19: 18 Judah to a remote area in the **hill country** *of* Ephraim where I live.
1Sa 1: 1 a Zuphite from the **hill country** *of* Ephraim, whose name was
9: 4 So he passed through the **hill country** *of* Ephraim and through the
13: 2 were with him at Micmash and in the **hill country** *of* Bethel,
14: 22 When all the Israelites who had hidden in the **hill country** *of*
17: 3 The Philistines occupied one **hill** and the Israelites another,
17: 3 occupied one hill and the Israelites **another**[s] [+2021+2296+4946],
23: 14 in the desert strongholds and in the **hills** of the Desert of Ziph.
23: 26 Saul was going along one side of the **mountain**, and David
23: 26 were on the other side, **[RPH]** hurrying to get away from Saul.
25: 20 As she came riding her donkey into a **mountain** ravine, there were
26: 13 to the other side and stood on top of the **hill** some distance away;
26: 20 out to look for a flea—as one hunts a partridge in the **mountains**."
31: 1 Israelites fled before them, and many fell slain on **Mount** Gilboa.
31: 8 they found Saul and his three sons fallen on **Mount** Gilboa.
2Sa 1: 6 "I happened to be on **Mount** Gilboa," the young man said,
1: 21 "O **mountains** of Gilboa, may you have neither dew nor rain,
13: 34 people on the road west of him, coming down the side of the **hill**.
13: 34 men in the direction of Horonaim, on the side of the **hill**." [BHS-]
16: 13 while Shimei was going along the **hillside** [+7521] opposite him,
20: 21 man named Sheba son of Bicri, from the **hill country** *of* Ephraim,
21: 9 who killed and exposed them on a **hill** before the LORD.
1Ki 4: 8 These are their names: Ben-Hur—in the **hill country** *of* Ephraim;
5: 15 [5:29] and eighty thousand stonecutters in the **hills**,
11: 7 On a **hill** east of Jerusalem, Solomon built a high place for
12: 25 Then Jeroboam fortified Shechem in the **hill country** *of* Ephraim
16: 24 He bought the **hill** *of* Samaria from Shemer for two talents of silver
16: 24 from Shemer for two talents of silver and built a city on the **hill**,
16: 24 it Samaria, after Shemer, the name of the former owner of the **hill**.
18: 19 the people from all over Israel to meet me on **Mount** Carmel.
18: 20 all Israel and assembled the prophets on **Mount** Carmel.
19: 8 and forty nights until he reached Horeb, the **mountain** *of* God.
19: 11 and stand on the **mountain** in the presence of the LORD,
19: 11 Then a great and powerful wind tore the **mountains** apart
20: 23 of the king of Aram advised him, "Their gods are gods of the **hills**.
20: 28 'Because the Arameans think the LORD is a god of the **hills**
22: 17 "I saw all Israel scattered on the **hills** like sheep without a
2Ki 1: 9 who was sitting on the top of a **hill**, and said to him, "Man of God,
2: 16 him up and set him down on some **mountain** or in some valley."
2: 25 he went on to **Mount** Carmel and from there returned to Samaria.
4: 25 So she set out and came to the man of God at **Mount** Carmel.
4: 27 When she reached the man of God at the **mountain**, she took hold
5: 22 prophets have just come to me from the **hill country** *of* Ephraim.
6: 17 he looked and saw the **hills** full of horses and chariots of fire all
19: 23 my many chariots I have ascended the heights of the **mountains**,
19: 31 will come a remnant, and out of **Mount** Zion a band of survivors.
23: 13 that were east of Jerusalem on the south of the **Hill** *of* Corruption—
23: 16 and when he saw the tombs that were there on the **hillside**,
1Ch 4: 42 and Uzziel, the sons of Ishi, invaded the **hill country** *of* Seir.
5: 23 from Bashan to Baal Hermon, that is, to Senir (**Mount** Hermon).
6: 67 [6:52] In the **hill country** *of* Ephraim they were given Shechem (a
10: 1 Israelites fled before them, and many fell slain on **Mount** Gilboa.
10: 8 the dead, they found Saul and his sons fallen on **Mount** Gilboa.
12: 8 [12:9] and they were as swift as gazelles in the **mountains**.
2Ch 2: 2 [2:1] eighty thousand as stonecutters in the **hills** and thirty-six
2: 18 [2:17] to be carriers and 80,000 to be stonecutters in the **hills**,
3: 1 to build the temple of the LORD in Jerusalem on **Mount** Moriah,
13: 4 Abijah stood on **Mount** Zemaraim, in the hill country of Ephraim,
13: 4 in the **hill country** *of* Ephraim, and said, "Jeroboam and all Israel,
15: 8 and from the towns he had captured in the **hills** *of* Ephraim.
18: 16 "I saw all Israel scattered on the **hills** like sheep without a
19: 4 among the people from Beersheba to the **hill country** *of* Ephraim
20: 10 "But now here are men from Ammon, Moab and **Mount** Seir,
20: 22 of Ammon and Moab and **Mount** Seir who were invading Judah,
20: 23 and Moab rose up against the men from **Mount** Seir to destroy
21: 11 He had also built high places on the **hills** *of* Judah and had caused
26: 10 working his fields and vineyards in the **hills** and in the fertile lands,
27: 4 He built towns in the Judean **hills** and forts and towers in the
33: 15 as well as all the altars he had built on the temple **hill** and in
Ne 8: 15 "Go out into the **hill country** and bring back branches from olive
9: 13 "You came down on **Mount** Sinai; you spoke to them from
Job 9: 5 He moves **mountains** without their knowing it and overturns them
14: 18 "But as a **mountain** erodes and crumbles and as a rock is moved
24: 8 They are drenched by **mountain** rains and hug the rocks for lack of
28: 9 assaults the flinty rock and lays bare the roots of the **mountains**.
39: 8 He ranges the **hills** for his pasture and searches for any green thing.
40: 20 The **hills** bring him their produce, and all the wild animals play
Ps 2: 6 "I have installed my King on Zion, my holy **hill**."
3: 4 [3:5] LORD I cry aloud, and he answers me from his holy **hill**.
11: 1 then can you say to me: "Flee like a bird to your **mountain**.
15: 1 may dwell in your sanctuary? Who may live on your holy **hill**?
18: 7 [18:8] and quaked, and the foundations of the **mountains** shook;
24: 3 Who may ascend the **hill** *of* the LORD? Who may stand in his
30: 7 [30:8] when you favored me, you made my **mountain** stand firm;
36: 6 [36:7] Your righteousness is like the mighty **mountains**,
42: 6 [42:7] of the Jordan, the heights of Hermon—from **Mount** Mizar.
43: 3 let them bring me to your holy **mountain**, to the place where you
46: 2 [46:3] give way and the **mountains** fall into the heart of the sea,
46: 3 [46:4] and foam and the **mountains** quake with their surging.
48: 1 [48:2] of praise, in the city of our God, his holy **mountain**.
48: 2 [48:3] Like the utmost heights of Zaphon is **Mount** Zion, the city
48: 11 [48:12] **Mount** Zion rejoices, the villages of Judah are glad
50: 10 animal of the forest is mine, and the cattle on a thousand **hills**.
50: 11 I know every bird in the **mountains**, and the creatures of the field
65: 6 [65:7] who formed the **mountains** by your power, having armed
68: 15 [68:16] The **mountains** *of* Bashan are majestic mountains;
68: 15 [68:16] The mountains of Bashan are majestic **mountains**;
68: 15 [68:16] rugged are **[RPH]** the mountains of Bashan.
68: 15 [68:16] majestic mountains; rugged are the **mountains** *of* Bashan.
68: 16 [68:17] Why gaze in envy, O rugged **mountains**, at the mountain
68: 16 [68:17] at the **mountain** where God chooses to reign,
72: 3 The **mountains** will bring prosperity to the people, the hills the
72: 16 abound throughout the land; on the tops of the **hills** may it sway.
74: 2 whom you redeemed—**Mount** Zion, where you dwelt.
76: 4 [76:5] with light, more majestic than **mountains** *rich with* game.
78: 54 of his holy land, to the **hill country** his right hand had taken.
78: 68 but he chose the tribe of Judah, **Mount** Zion, which he loved.
80: 10 [80:11] The **mountains** were covered with its shade, the mighty
83: 14 [83:15] consumes the forest or a flame sets the **mountains** ablaze,
87: 1 He has set his foundation on the holy **mountain**;
90: 2 Before the **mountains** were born or you brought forth the earth
95: 4 are the depths of the earth, and the **mountain** peaks belong to him.
97: 5 The **mountains** melt like wax before the LORD, before the Lord
98: 8 the rivers clap their hands, let the **mountains** sing together for joy;
99: 9 Exalt the LORD our God and worship at his holy **mountain**,
104: 6 the deep as with a garment; the waters stood above the **mountains**.
104: 8 they flowed over the **mountains**, they went down into the valleys,
104: 10 pour water into the ravines; it flows between the **mountains**.
104: 13 He waters the **mountains** from his upper chambers; the earth is
104: 18 The high **mountains** belong to the wild goats; the crags are a
104: 32 and it trembles, who touches the **mountains**, and they smoke.
114: 4 the **mountains** skipped like rams, the hills like lambs.
114: 6 you **mountains**, that you skipped like rams, you hills, like lambs?
121: 1 I lift up my eyes to the **hills**—where does my help come from?
125: 1 Those who trust in the LORD are like **Mount** Zion, which cannot
125: 2 As the **mountains** surround Jerusalem, so the LORD surrounds
133: 3 It is as if the dew of Hermon were falling on **Mount** Zion.
144: 5 and come down; touch the **mountains**, so that they smoke.
147: 8 he supplies the earth with rain and makes grass grow on the **hills**.
148: 9 you **mountains** and all hills, fruit trees and all cedars,
Pr 8: 25 before the **mountains** were settled in place, before the hills,
27: 25 and new growth appears and the grass from the **hills** is gathered in,
SS 2: 8 Here he comes, leaping across the **mountains**, bounding over the
2: 17 and be like a gazelle or like a young stag on the rugged **hills**.
4: 1 Your hair is like a flock of goats descending from **Mount** Gilead.
4: 6 I will go to the **mountain** *of* myrrh and to the hill of incense.
4: 8 from the lions' dens and the **mountain haunts** *of* the leopards.
8: 14 like a gazelle or like a young stag on the spice-laden **mountains**.
Isa 2: 2 In the last days the **mountain** *of* the LORD's temple will be
2: 2 temple will be established as chief among the **mountains**;
2: 3 and say, "Come, let us go up to the **mountain** *of* the LORD,
2: 14 for all the towering **mountains** and all the high hills,
4: 5 the LORD will create over all of **Mount** Zion and over those who
5: 25 The **mountains** shake, and the dead bodies are like refuse in the
7: 25 As for all the **hills** once cultivated by the hoe, you will no longer
8: 18 in Israel from the LORD Almighty, who dwells on **Mount** Zion.
10: 12 When the Lord has finished all his work against **Mount** Zion
10: 32 they will shake their fist at the **mount** *of* the Daughter of Zion,
11: 9 They will neither harm nor destroy on all my holy **mountain**,
13: 2 Raise a banner on a bare **hilltop**, shout to them; beckon to them to
13: 4 Listen, a noise on the **mountains**, like that of a great multitude!
14: 13 I will sit enthroned on the **mount** *of* assembly, on the utmost
14: 25 Assyrian in my land; on my **mountains** I will trample him down.
16: 1 from Sela, across the desert, to the **mount** *of* the Daughter of Zion.
17: 13 driven before the wind like chaff on the **hills**, like tumbleweed
18: 3 when a banner is raised on the **mountains**, you will see it,
18: 6 They will all be left to the **mountain** birds of prey and to the wild
18: 7 the gifts will be brought to **Mount** Zion, the place of the Name of
22: 5 a day of battering down walls and of crying out to the **mountains**.
24: 23 for the LORD Almighty will reign on **Mount** Zion and in
25: 6 On this **mountain** the LORD Almighty will prepare a feast of
25: 7 On this **mountain** he will destroy the shroud that enfolds all
25: 10 The hand of the LORD will rest on this **mountain**; but Moab will
27: 13 and worship the LORD on the holy **mountain** in Jerusalem.
28: 21 The LORD will rise up as he did at **Mount** Perazim, he will rouse
29: 8 be with the hordes of all the nations that fight against **Mount** Zion.

Isa 30: 17 till you are left like a flagstaff on a **mountaintop** [+8031],
30: 25 streams of water will flow on every high **mountain** and every lofty
30: 29 as when people go up with flutes to the **mountain** *of* the LORD,
31: 4 so the LORD Almighty will come down to do battle on **Mount**
34: 3 send up a stench; the **mountains** will be soaked with their blood.
37: 24 my many chariots I have ascended the heights of the **mountains**,
37: 32 will come a remnant, and out of **Mount** Zion a band of survivors.
40: 4 valley shall be raised up, every **mountain** and hill made low;
40: 9 You who bring good tidings to Zion, go up on a high **mountain**.
40: 12 or weighed the **mountains** on the scales and the hills in a balance?
41: 15 You will thresh the **mountains** and crush them, and reduce the
42: 11 Sela sing for joy; let them shout from the **mountaintops** [+8031].
42: 15 I will lay waste the **mountains** and hills and dry up all their
44: 23 Burst into song, you **mountains**, you forests and all your trees,
49: 11 I will turn all my **mountains** into roads, and my highways will be
49: 13 O heavens; rejoice, O earth; burst into song, O **mountains**!
52: 7 How beautiful on the **mountains** are the feet of those who bring
54: 10 Though the **mountains** be shaken and the hills be removed,
55: 12 the **mountains** and hills will burst into song before you, and all the
56: 7 these I will bring to my holy **mountain** and give them joy in my
57: 7 You have made your bed on a high and lofty **hill**; there you went
57: 13 his refuge will inherit the land and possess my holy **mountain**."
64: 1 [63:19] that the **mountains** would tremble before you!
64: 3 [64:2] you came down, and the **mountains** trembled before you.
65: 7 "Because they burned sacrifices on the **mountains** and defied me
65: 9 and from Judah those who will possess my **mountains**;
65: 11 as for you who forsake the LORD and forget my holy **mountain**,
65: 25 They will neither harm nor destroy on all my holy **mountain**,"
66: 20 to my holy **mountain** in Jerusalem as an offering to the LORD—
Jer 3: 6 She has gone up on every high **hill** and under every spreading tree
3: 23 ⌞idolatrous⌟ commotion on the hills and **mountains** is a deception;
4: 15 from Dan, proclaiming disaster from the **hills** *of* Ephraim.
4: 24 I looked at the **mountains**, and they were quaking; all the hills
9: 10 [9:9] I will weep and wail for the **mountains** and take up a lament
13: 16 the darkness, before your feet stumble on the darkening **hills**.
16: 16 and they will hunt them down on every **mountain** and hill
17: 3 My **mountain** in the land and your wealth and all your treasures I
17: 26 from the **hill country** and the Negev, bringing burnt offerings
26: 18 a heap of rubble, the temple **hill** a mound overgrown with thickets.'
31: 5 Again you will plant vineyards on the **hills** *of* Samaria; the farmers
31: 6 There will be a day when watchmen cry out on the **hills** *of*
31: 23 'The LORD bless you, O righteous dwelling, O sacred **mountain**.'
32: 44 in the towns of Judah and in the towns of the **hill country**,
33: 13 In the towns of the **hill country**, of the western foothills and of the
46: 18 "one will come who is like Tabor among the **mountains**, like
50: 6 have led them astray and caused them to roam on the **mountains**.
50: 6 They wandered over **mountain** and hill and forgot their own
50: 19 his appetite will be satisfied on the **hills** *of* Ephraim and Gilead.
51: 25 "I am against you, O destroying **mountain**, you who destroy the
51: 25 roll you off the cliffs, and make you a burned-out **mountain**.
La 4: 19 they chased us over the **mountains** and lay in wait for us in the
5: 18 for **Mount** Zion, which lies desolate, with jackals prowling over it.
Eze 6: 2 "Son of man, set your face against the **mountains** *of* Israel;
6: 3 'O **mountains** *of* Israel, hear the word of the Sovereign LORD.
6: 3 This is what the Sovereign LORD says to the **mountains**
6: 13 on every high hill and on all the **mountaintops** [+8031], under
7: 7 the day is near; there is panic, not joy, upon the **mountains**.
7: 16 All who survive and escape will be in the **mountains**,
11: 23 up from within the city and stopped above the **mountain** east of it.
17: 22 from its topmost shoots and plant it on a high and lofty **mountain**.
17: 23 On the **mountain** heights of Israel I will plant it; it will produce
18: 6 He does not eat at the **mountain shrines** or look to the idols of the
18: 11 "He eats at the **mountain shrines**. He defiles his neighbor's wife.
18: 15 "He does not eat at the **mountain shrines** or look to the idols of
19: 9 so his roar was heard no longer on the **mountains** *of* Israel.
20: 40 For on my holy **mountain**, the high mountain of Israel,
20: 40 For on my holy mountain, the high **mountain** *of* Israel,
22: 9 in you are those who eat at the **mountain shrines** and commit
28: 14 You were on the holy **mount** *of* God; you walked among the fiery
28: 16 So I drove you in disgrace from the **mount** *of* God, and I expelled
31: 12 Its boughs fell on the **mountains** and in all the valleys; its branches
32: 5 I will spread your flesh on the **mountains** and fill the valleys with
32: 6 the land with your flowing blood all the way to the **mountains**,
33: 28 the **mountains** *of* Israel will become desolate so that no one will
34: 6 My sheep wandered over all the **mountains** and on every high hill.
34: 13 I will pasture them on the **mountains** *of* Israel, in the ravines
34: 14 and the **mountain** heights of Israel will be their grazing land.
34: 14 there they will feed in a rich pasture on the **mountains** *of* Israel.
35: 2 "Son of man, set your face against **Mount** Seir; prophesy against
35: 3 I am against you, **Mount** Seir, and I will stretch out my hand
35: 7 I will make **Mount** Seir a desolate waste and cut off from it all
35: 8 I will fill your **mountains** with the slain; those killed by the sword
35: 12 contemptible things you have said against the **mountains** *of* Israel.
35: 15 You will be desolate, O **Mount** Seir, you and all of Edom.
36: 1 "Son of man, prophesy to the **mountains** *of* Israel and say,
36: 1 to the mountains of Israel and say, 'O **mountains** *of* Israel,
36: 4 therefore, O **mountains** *of* Israel, hear the word of the Sovereign
36: 4 This is what the Sovereign LORD says to the **mountains**
36: 6 concerning the land of Israel and say to the **mountains** and hills,
36: 8 " 'But you, O **mountains** *of* Israel, will produce branches and fruit
37: 22 will make them one nation in the land, on the **mountains** *of* Israel.
38: 8 were gathered from many nations to the **mountains** *of* Israel,
38: 20 The **mountains** will be overturned, the cliffs will crumble
38: 21 I will summon a sword against Gog on all my **mountains**,
39: 2 from the far north and send you against the **mountains** *of* Israel.
39: 4 On the **mountains** *of* Israel you will fall, you and all your troops
39: 17 preparing for you, the great sacrifice on the **mountains** *of* Israel.
40: 2 took me to the land of Israel and set me on a very high **mountain**,
43: 12 All the surrounding area on top of the **mountain** will be most holy.
Da 9: 16 and your wrath from Jerusalem, your city, your holy **hill**.
9: 20 and making my request to the LORD my God for his holy **hill**—
11: 45 his royal tents between the seas at the beautiful holy **mountain**.
Hos 4: 13 They sacrifice on the **mountaintops** [+8031] and burn offerings on
10: 8 Then they will say to the **mountains**, "Cover us!" and to the hills,
Joel 2: 1 Blow the trumpet in Zion; sound the alarm on my holy **hill**.
2: 2 Like dawn spreading across the **mountains** a large and mighty
2: 5 like that of chariots they leap over the **mountaintops** [+8031],
2: 32 [3:5] for on **Mount** Zion and in Jerusalem there will be
3: 17 [4:17] that I, the LORD your God, dwell in Zion, my holy **hill**.
3: 18 [4:18] "In that day the **mountains** will drip new wine,
Am 3: 9 "Assemble yourselves on the **mountains** *of* Samaria; see the great
4: 1 Hear this word, you cows of Bashan on **Mount** Samaria,
4: 13 He who forms the **mountains**, creates the wind, and reveals his
6: 1 to you who feel secure on **Mount** Samaria, you notable men of the
9: 13 New wine will drip from the **mountains** and flow from all the
Ob 1: 8 men of Edom, men of understanding in the **mountains** *of* Esau?
1: 9 everyone in Esau's **mountains** will be cut down in the slaughter.
1: 16 Just as you drank on my holy **hill**, so all the nations will drink
1: 17 on **Mount** Zion will be deliverance; it will be holy, and the house
1: 19 People from the Negev will occupy the **mountains** *of* Esau,
1: 21 Deliverers will go up on **Mount** Zion to govern the mountains of
1: 21 Deliverers will go up on Mount Zion to govern the **mountains** *of*
Jnh 2: 6 [2:7] To the roots of the **mountains** I sank down; the earth
Mic 1: 4 The **mountains** melt beneath him and the valleys split apart,
3: 12 a heap of rubble, the temple **hill** a mound overgrown with thickets.
4: 1 In the last days the **mountain** *of* the LORD's temple will be
4: 1 temple will be established as chief among the **mountains**;
4: 2 and say, "Come, let us go up to the **mountain** *of* the LORD,
4: 7 The LORD will rule over them in **Mount** Zion from that day
6: 1 "Stand up, plead your case before the **mountains**; let the hills hear
6: 2 Hear, O **mountains**, the LORD's accusation; listen,
7: 12 the Euphrates and from sea to sea and from **mountain** to mountain.
7: 12 the Euphrates and from sea to sea and from mountain to **mountain**.
Na 1: 5 The **mountains** quake before him and the hills melt away.
1: 15 [2:1] Look, there on the **mountains**, the feet of one who brings
3: 18 Your people are scattered on the **mountains** with no one to gather
Hab 3: 3 God came from Teman, the Holy One from **Mount** Paran.
3: 6 The ancient **mountains** crumbled and the age-old hills collapsed.
3: 10 the **mountains** saw you and writhed. Torrents of water swept by;
Zep 3: 11 in their pride. Never again will you be haughty on my holy **hill**.
Hag 1: 8 Go up into the **mountains** and bring down timber and build the
1: 11 I called for a drought on the fields and the **mountains**, on the
Zec 4: 7 "What are you, O mighty **mountain**? Before Zerubbabel you will
6: 1 me were four chariots coming out from between two **mountains**—
6: 1 out from between two mountains—**[RPH]** mountains of bronze!
6: 1 coming out from between two mountains—**mountains** *of* bronze!
8: 3 the **mountain** *of* the LORD Almighty will be called the Holy
8: 3 of the LORD Almighty will be called the Holy **Mountain**."
14: 4 On that day his feet will stand on the **Mount** *of* Olives, east of
14: 4 and the **Mount** *of* Olives will be split in two from east to west,
14: 4 with half of the **mountain** moving north and half moving south.
14: 5 You will flee by my **mountain** valley, for it will extend to Azel.
14: 5 flee by my mountain valley, for **it**[s] [+1628] will extend to Azel.
Mal 1: 3 I have turned his **mountains** into a wasteland and left his

2216 הֹר *hōr*, n.pr.loc. [12] [√ 2215]

Hor [12]

Nu 20: 22 Israelite community set out from Kadesh and came to Mount **Hor**.
20: 23 At Mount **Hor**, near the border of Edom, the LORD said to
20: 25 Get Aaron and his son Eleazar and take them up Mount **Hor**.
20: 27 They went up Mount **Hor** in the sight of the whole community.
21: 4 They traveled from Mount **Hor** along the route to the Red Sea,
33: 37 They left Kadesh and camped at Mount **Hor**, on the border of
33: 38 At the LORD's command Aaron the priest went up Mount **Hor**,
33: 39 a hundred and twenty-three years old when he died on Mount **Hor**.
33: 41 They left Mount **Hor** and camped at Zalmonah.
34: 7 northern boundary, run a line from the Great Sea to Mount **Hor**

Nu 34: 8 from Mount **Hor** to Lebo Hamath. Then the boundary will go to
Dt 32: 50 just as your brother Aaron died on Mount **Hor** and was gathered to

2217 הָרָא *hārā'*, n.pr.loc. [1]

Hara [1]

1Ch 5: 26 He took them to Halah, Habor, **Hara** and the river of Gozan,

2218 הָרֹאֶה *hārō'eh*, n.pr.m. [1] [√ 8011]

Haroeh [1]

1Ch 2: 52 the father of Kiriath Jearim were: **Haroeh**, half the Manahathites,

2219 הַרְאֵל *har'ēl*, n.[m.]. [1] [cf. 789]

altar hearth [1]

Eze 43: 15 The **altar hearth** is four cubits high, and four horns project

2220 הַרְבָּה *harbâ*, v. Not used in NIV/BHS [√ 8049]

2221 הַרְבֵּה *harbēh*, v.inf. (used as adv.). [50] [√ 8049]

much [10], many [8], great quantity [+4394] [4], great [4], more [3], quantities [2], abundance [+4394] [1], abundance [1], abundant supply [1], all [1], extensive [1], full [1], great [+4394] [1], great numbers [+4394] [1], greatly [+4394] [1], greatly [1], large amount [+4394] [1], large number [1], large [1], overrighteous [+7404] [1], overwicked [+8399] [1], seldom [+4202] [1], so much [1], very [+4394] [1], wept bitterly [+1134+1135] [1]

Ge 15: 1 not be afraid, Abram. I am your shield, your very **great** reward."
41: 49 Joseph stored up huge **quantities** of grain, like the sand of the sea;
Dt 3: 5 and bars, and there were also a great **many** unwalled villages.
Jos 13: 1 and there are still very **large** areas of land to be taken over.
22: 8 bronze and iron, and a **great** [+4394] **quantity** *of* clothing—
1Sa 26: 21 Surely I have acted like a fool and have erred **greatly** [+4394]."
2Sa 1: 4 **Many** of them fell and died. And Saul and his son Jonathan are
8: 8 King David took a **great** [+4394] **quantity** of bronze.
12: 2 The rich man had a very **large number** *of* sheep and cattle,
12: 30 He took a **great** [+4394] **quantity** *of* plunder from the city
1Ki 4: 29 [5:9] God gave Solomon wisdom and very **great** insight, and a
10: 10 120 talents of gold, large **quantities** of spices, and precious stones.
10: 11 and from there they brought **great** [+4394] *cargoes of* almugwood
2Ki 10: 18 said to them, "Ahab served Baal a little; Jehu will serve him **much**.
21: 16 so **much** innocent blood that he filled Jerusalem from end to end—
1Ch 20: 2 He took a **great** [+4394] **quantity** *of* plunder from the city
2Ch 11: 12 and spears in all the cities, and made them **very** [+4394] strong.
14: 13 [14:12] The men of Judah carried off a **large** [+4394] **amount** of
16: 8 Libyans a mighty army with **great** [+4394] **numbers** of chariots
25: 9 of God replied, "The LORD can give you **much** more than that."
32: 27 Hezekiah had very **great** riches and honor, and he made treasuries
Ezr 10: 1 gathered around him. They too **wept bitterly** [+1134+1135].
Ne 2: 2 This can be nothing but sadness of heart." I was very **much** afraid,
4: 1 [3:33] the wall, he became angry and was **greatly** incensed.
4: 10 [4:4] there is **so much** rubble that we cannot rebuild the wall."
4: 19 [4:13] rest of the people, "The work is **extensive** and spread out,
5: 18 and every ten days an **abundant supply** of wine of all kinds.
Ps 51: 2 [51:4] Wash away **all** [Q 8049] my iniquity and cleanse me from
130: 7 with the LORD is unfailing love and with him is **full** redemption.
Ecc 1: 16 before me; I have experienced **much** *of* wisdom and knowledge."
2: 7 I also owned **more** herds and flocks than anyone in Jerusalem
5: 7 [5:6] Much dreaming and **many** words are meaningless.
5: 12 [5:11] sleep of a laborer is sweet, whether he eats little or **much**,
5: 17 [5:16] in darkness, with **great** frustration, affliction and anger.
5: 20 [5:19] He **seldom** [+4202] reflects on the days of his life,
6: 11 The **more** the words, the less the meaning, and how does that
7: 16 Do not be **overrighteous** [+7404], neither be overwise—why
7: 17 *Do* not *be* **overwicked** [+8399], and do not be a fool—why die
9: 18 is better than weapons of war, but one sinner destroys **much** good.
11: 8 However **many** years a man may live, let him enjoy them all.
11: 8 But let him remember the days of darkness, for they will be **many**.
12: 9 He pondered and searched out and set in order **many** proverbs.
12: 12 Of making **many** books there is no end, and much study wearies
12: 12 many books there is no end, and **much** study wearies the body.
Isa 30: 33 been made deep and wide, with an **abundance** of fire and wood;
Jer 40: 12 they harvested an **abundance** [+4394] of wine and summer fruit.
42: 2 For as you now see, though we were once **many**, now only a few
Jnh 4: 11 Nineveh has **more** than a hundred and twenty thousand people
Hag 1: 6 You have planted **much**, but have harvested little. You eat,
1: 9 "You expected **much**, but see, it turned out to be little. What you

2222 הָרַג *hārag*, v. [167] [→ 2223, 2224]

killed [53], kill [46], slain [9], put to death [7], killing [6], murdered [4], slay [4], *untranslated* [3], kills [3], put [3], destroyed [2], must certainly put to death [+2222] [2], put to death [+2222] [2], slaughter [2], slayer [2], be killed [1], be ravaged [1], been killed [1], destroy [1], destroying [1], executed [1], face death [1], murder [1], murderer [1], murderers [1], murdering [1], murders [1], put to death [+4638] [1], ravage [1], slaughter [+4200+5422] [1], slaughter takes place [+2223] [1], slaughtered [1], slaughtering [1], slew [1]

Ge 4: 8 [A] in the field, Cain attacked his brother Abel and **killed** him.
4: 14 [A] wanderer on the earth, and whoever finds me *will* **kill** me."
4: 15 [A] if anyone **kills** Cain, he will suffer vengeance seven times
4: 23 [A] *I have* **killed** a man for wounding me, a young man for
4: 25 [A] me another child in place of Abel, since Cain **killed** him."
12: 12 [A] 'This is his wife.' Then *they will* **kill** me but will let you live.
20: 4 [A] so he said, "Lord, *will you* **destroy** an innocent nation?
20: 11 [A] God in this place, and *they will* **kill** me because of my wife.'
26: 7 [A] "The men of this place might **kill** me on account of Rebekah,
27: 41 [A] for my father are near; then *I will* **kill** my brother Jacob."
27: 42 [A] Esau is consoling himself with the thought of **killing** you.
34: 25 [A] and attacked the unsuspecting city, **killing** every male.
34: 26 [A] *They* **put** Hamor and his son Shechem to the sword and took
37: 20 [A] *let's* **kill** him and throw him into one of these cisterns
37: 26 [A] "What will we gain if *we* **kill** our brother and cover up his
49: 6 [A] for *they have* **killed** men in their anger and hamstrung oxen
Ex 2: 14 [A] Are you thinking of **killing** me as you killed the Egyptian?"
2: 14 [A] Are you thinking of killing me as *you* **killed** the Egyptian?"
2: 15 [A] When Pharaoh heard of this, he tried to **kill** Moses,
4: 23 [A] you refused to let him go; so I *will* **kill** your firstborn son.' "
5: 21 [A] his officials and have put a sword in their hand to **kill** us."
13: 15 [A] the LORD **killed** every firstborn in Egypt, both man
21: 14 [A] if a man schemes and **kills** another man deliberately,
22: 24 [22:23] [A] will be aroused, and *I will* **kill** you with the sword;
23: 7 [A] and *do* not **put** an innocent or honest person **to death**,
32: 12 [A] to **kill** them in the mountains and to wipe them off the face of
32: 27 [A] the other, each **killing** his brother and friend and neighbor.' "
Lev 20: 15 [A] he must be put to death, and *you must* **kill** the animal.
20: 16 [A] sexual relations with it, **kill** both the woman and the animal.
Nu 11: 15 [A] are going to treat me, **put** me **to death** [+2222] right now—
11: 15 [A] are going to treat me, **put** me **to death** [+2222] right now—
22: 29 [A] If I had a sword in my hand, *I would* **kill** you right now."
22: 33 [A] not turned away, *I would* certainly *have* **killed** you by now,
25: 5 [A] "Each of *you must* **put to death** those of your men who
31: 7 [A] as the LORD commanded Moses, and **killed** every man.
31: 8 [A] **[RPH]** Among their victims were Evi, Rekem, Zur, Hur
31: 8 [A] Zur, Hur and Reba—the five kings of Midian. *They* also **killed**
31: 17 [A] Now **kill** all the boys. And kill every woman who has slept
31: 17 [A] the boys. And **kill** every woman who has slept with a man,
31: 19 [A] "All of you *who have* **killed** anyone or touched anyone who
Dt 13: 9 [13:10] [A] *You* **must certainly put** him **to death** [+2222].
13: 9 [13:10] [A] *You* **must certainly put** him **to death** [+2222].
Jos 8: 24 [A] When Israel had finished **killing** all the men of Ai in the
9: 26 [A] saved them from the Israelites, and *they did* not **kill** them.
10: 11 [A] more of them died from the hailstones than *were* **killed** by
13: 22 [A] the Israelites *had* **put** to the sword Balaam son of Beor,
Jdg 7: 25 [A] *They* **killed** Oreb at the rock of Oreb, and Zeeb at the
7: 25 [A] the rock of Oreb, and **[RPH]** Zeeb at the winepress of Zeeb.
8: 17 [A] down the tower of Peniel and **killed** the men of the town.
8: 18 [A] and Zalmunna, "What kind of men *did you* **kill** at Tabor?"
8: 19 [A] if you had spared their lives, *I would* not **kill** you."
8: 20 [A] Turning to Jether, his oldest son, he said, "**Kill** them!"
8: 21 [A] his strength.' " So Gideon stepped forward and **killed** them,
9: 5 [A] in Ophrah and on one stone **murdered** his seventy brothers,
9: 18 [A] **murdered** his seventy sons on a single stone, and made
9: 24 [A] brother Abimelech **[RPH]** and on the citizens of Shechem,
9: 24 [A] of Shechem, who had helped him **murder** his brothers.
9: 45 [A] against the city until he had captured it and **killed** its people.
9: 54 [A] 'A woman **killed** him.' " So his servant ran him through,
9: 56 [A] had done to his father by **murdering** his seventy brothers.
16: 2 [A] no move during the night, saying, "At dawn *we'll* **kill** him."
20: 5 [A] after me and surrounded the house, intending to **kill** me.
1Sa 16: 2 [A] "How can I go? Saul will hear about it and **kill** me."
22: 21 [A] He told David that Saul *had* **killed** the priests of the LORD.
24: 10 [24:11] [A] Some urged me to **kill** you, but I spared you; I said,
24: 11 [24:12] [A] I cut off the corner of your robe but *did* not **kill** you.
24: 18 [24:19] [A] me into your hands, but *you did* not **kill** me.
2Sa 3: 30 [A] (Joab and his brother Abishai **murdered** Abner because he
4: 10 [A] good news, I seized him and **put** him **to death** in Ziklag.
4: 11 [A] when wicked men *have* **killed** an innocent man in his own
4: 12 [A] So David gave an order to his men, and *they* **killed** them.
10: 18 [A] David **killed** seven hundred of their charioteers and forty
12: 9 [A] your own. *You* **killed** him with the sword of the Ammonites.
14: 7 [A] put him to death for the life of his brother whom *he* **killed**;
23: 21 [A] from the Egyptian's hand and **killed** him with his own spear.
1Ki 2: 5 [A] *He* **killed** them, shedding their blood in peacetime as if in
2: 32 [A] **killed** them with the sword. Both of them—Abner son of Ner,
9: 16 [A] *He* **killed** its Canaanite inhabitants and then gave it as a

1Ki 11:24 [A] became the leader of a band of rebels when David **destroyed**
12:27 [A] of Judah. *They will* **kill** me and return to King Rehoboam."
18:12 [A] If I go and tell Ahab and he doesn't find you, *he will* **kill** me.
18:13 [A] what I did while Jezebel *was* **killing** the prophets of the
18:14 [A] to go to my master and say, 'Elijah is here.' *He will* **kill** me!"
19: 1 [A] and how *he had* **killed** all the prophets with the sword.
19:10 [A] your altars, and **put** your prophets **to death** with the sword.
19:14 [A] your altars, and **put** your prophets **to death** with the sword.
2Ki 8:12 [A] **kill** their young men with the sword, dash their little children
9:31 [A] you come in peace, Zimri, you **murderer** *of* your master?"
10: 9 [A] It was I who conspired against my master and **killed** him,
11:18 [A] and **killed** Mattan the priest of Baal in front of the altars.
17:25 [A] sent lions among them and *they* **killed** some of the people.
1Ch 7:21 [A] Ezer and Elead *were* **killed** *by* the native-born men of Gath,
11:23 [A] from the Egyptian's hand and **killed** him with his own spear.
19:18 [A] David **killed** seven thousand of their charioteers and forty
2Ch 21: 4 [A] *he* **put** all his brothers to the sword along with some of the
21:13 [A] *You have* also **murdered** your own brothers, members of
22: 1 [A] with the Arabs into the camp, *had* **killed** all the older sons.
22: 8 [A] who had been attending Ahaziah, and *he* **killed** them.
23:17 [A] and **killed** Mattan the priest of Baal in front of the altars.
24:22 [A] father Jehoiada had shown him but **killed** his son,
24:25 [A] the son of Jehoiada the priest, and *they* **killed** him in his bed.
25: 3 [A] *he* **executed** the officials who had murdered his father the
28: 6 [A] In one day Pekah son of Remaliah **killed** a hundred
28: 7 [A] **killed** Maaseiah the king's son, Azrikam the officer in charge
28: 9 [A] *you have* **slaughtered** them in a rage that reaches to heaven.
36:17 [A] *who* **killed** their young men with the sword in the sanctuary,
Ne 4:11 [4:5] [A] and *will* **kill** them and put an end to the work."
6:10 [A] close the temple doors, because men are coming to **kill** you—
6:10 [A] coming to kill you—by night they are coming to **kill** you."
9:26 [A] *They* **killed** your prophets, who had admonished them in
Est 3:13 [A] with the order to destroy, **kill** and annihilate all the Jews—
7: 4 [A] been sold for destruction and **slaughter** and annihilation.
8:11 [A] **kill** and annihilate any armed force of any nationality
9: 6 [A] of Susa, the Jews **killed** and destroyed five hundred men.
9: 7 [9:10] [A] *They* also **killed** Parshandatha, Dalphon, Aspatha,
9:11 [B] The number of those **slain** in the citadel of Susa was reported
9:12 [A] "The Jews *have* **killed** and destroyed five hundred men and
9:15 [A] *they* **put to death** in Susa three hundred men, but they did
9:16 [A] They **killed** seventy-five thousand of them but did not lay
Job 5: 2 [A] Resentment **kills** a fool, and envy slays the simple.
20:16 [A] the poison of serpents; the fangs of an adder *will* **kill** him.
Ps 10: 8 [A] from ambush *he* **murders** the innocent, watching in secret
44:22 [44:23] [E] Yet for your sake *we* **face death** all day long; we are
59:11 [59:12] [A] *do* not **kill** them, O Lord our shield, or my people
78:31 [A] *he* **put to death** the sturdiest among them, cutting down the
78:34 [A] Whenever God **slew** them, they would seek him; they eagerly
78:47 [A] *He* **destroyed** their vines with hail and their sycamore-figs
94: 6 [A] *They* **slay** the widow and the alien; they murder the
135:10 [A] He struck down many nations and **killed** mighty kings—
136:18 [A] **killed** mighty kings—*His love endures forever.*
Pr 1:32 [A] For the waywardness of the simple *will* **kill** them,
7:26 [B] victims she has brought down; her **slain** are a mighty throng.
Ecc 3: 3 [A] a time to **kill** and a time to heal, a time to tear down and a
Isa 10: 4 [B] but to cringe among the captives or fall among the **slain**.
14:19 [B] you are covered with the **slain**, with those pierced by the
14:20 [A] for you have destroyed your land and **killed** your people.
14:30 [A] root I will destroy by famine; *it will* **slay** your survivors.
22:13 [A] and revelry, **slaughtering** *of* cattle and killing of sheep,
26:21 [B] the blood shed upon her; she will conceal her **slain** no longer.
27: 1 [A] the coiling serpent; *he will* **slay** the monster of the sea.
27: 7 [E] *Has she* **been killed** as those were killed who killed her?
27: 7 [B] Has she been killed as *those* were killed *who* **killed** her?
Jer 4:31 [A] "Alas! I am fainting; my life is given over to **murderers**."
15: 3 [A] "the sword to **kill** and the dogs to drag away and the birds of
18:21 [B] let their men be **put to death** [+4638], their young men slain
La 2: 4 [A] Like a foe *he has* **slain** all who were pleasing to the eye;
2:20 [C] *Should* priest and prophet **be killed** in the sanctuary of the
2:21 [A] *You have* **slain** them in the day of your anger; you have
3:43 [A] with anger and pursued us; *you have* **slain** without pity.
Eze 9: 6 [A] **Slaughter** [+4200+5422] old men, young men and maidens,
21:11 [21:16] [A] and polished, made ready for the hand of the **slayer**.
23:10 [A] away her sons and daughters and **killed** her with the sword.
23:47 [A] *they will* **kill** their sons and daughters and burn down their
26: 6 [C] her settlements on the mainland *will* **be ravaged** by the
26: 8 [A] *He will* **ravage** your settlements on the mainland with the
26:11 [A] *he will* **kill** your people with the sword, and your strong
26:15 [C] and *the* **slaughter** [+2223] **takes place** in you?
28: 9 [A] "I am a god," in the presence of *those who* **kill** you?
37: 9 [B] O breath, and breathe into these **slain**, that they may live.' "
Hos 6: 5 [A] with my prophets, *I* **killed** you with the words of my mouth;
9:13 [A] But Ephraim will bring out their children to the **slayer**."
Am 2: 3 [A] I will destroy her ruler and **kill** all her officials with him,"
4:10 [A] *I* **killed** your young men with the sword, along with your
9: 1 [A] of all the people; those who are left *I will* **kill** with the sword.
9: 4 [A] their enemies, there I will command the sword *to* **slay** them.
Hab 1:17 [A] keep on emptying his net, **destroying** nations without mercy?
Zec 11: 5 [A] Their buyers **slaughter** them and go unpunished. Those who

2223 הֶרֶג *hereg*, n.m. [5] [√ 2222]

slaughter [2], killed [1], killing [1], slaughter takes place [+2222] [1]

Est 9: 5 all their enemies with the sword, **killing** and destroying them,
Pr 24:11 led away to death; hold back those staggering toward **slaughter**.
Isa 27: 7 Has she been killed as those were **killed** who killed her?
30:25 In the day of great **slaughter**, when the towers fall, streams of
Eze 26:15 the wounded groan and *the* **slaughter takes place** [+2222] in you?

2224 הֲרֵגָה *hărēgâ*, n.f. [5] [√ 2222]

slaughter [5]

Jer 7:32 or the Valley of Ben Hinnom, but the Valley of **Slaughter**,
12: 3 sheep to be butchered! Set them apart for the day of **slaughter**!
19: 6 or the Valley of Ben Hinnom, but the Valley of **Slaughter**.
Zec 11: 4 the LORD my God says: "Pasture the flock marked for **slaughter**.
11: 7 So I pastured the flock marked for **slaughter**, particularly the

2225 הָרָה *hārâ*, v. [46 / 45] [→ 2226, 2228, 2230, 2231]

conceived [16], pregnant [16], conceive [7], with child [2], *untranslated* [1], conceives [1], gave birth [1], is born [1]

Ge 4: 1 [A] wife Eve, and *she became* **pregnant** and gave birth to Cain.
4:17 [A] his wife, and *she became* **pregnant** and gave birth to Enoch.
16: 4 [A] He slept with Hagar, and *she* **conceived**. When she knew she
16: 4 [A] When she knew *she was* **pregnant**, she began to despise her
16: 5 [A] and now that she knows *she is* **pregnant**, she despises me.
19:36 [A] So both of Lot's daughters *became* **pregnant** by their father.
21: 2 [A] Sarah *became* **pregnant** and bore a son to Abraham in his
25:21 [A] his prayer, and his wife Rebekah *became* **pregnant**.
29:32 [A] Leah *became* **pregnant** and gave birth to a son. She named
29:33 [A] *She* **conceived** again, and when she gave birth to a son she
29:34 [A] Again *she* **conceived**, and when she gave birth to a son she
29:35 [A] *She* **conceived** again, and when she gave birth to a son she
30: 5 [A] and she *became* **pregnant** and bore him a son.
30: 7 [A] Rachel's servant Bilhah **conceived** again and bore Jacob a
30:17 [A] and *she became* **pregnant** and bore Jacob a fifth son.
30:19 [A] Leah **conceived** again and bore Jacob a sixth son.
30:23 [A] *She became* **pregnant** and gave birth to a son and said,
38: 3 [A] *she became* **pregnant** and gave birth to a son, who was
38: 4 [A] *She* **conceived** again and gave birth to a son and named him
38:18 [A] to her and slept with her, and *she became* **pregnant** by him.
49:26 [a] of the ancient <u>mountains</u>, [BHS *my* **progenitors**; NIV 2215]
Ex 2: 2 [A] she *became* **pregnant** and gave birth to a son. When she saw
Nu 11:12 [A] *Did* I **conceive** all these people? Did I give them birth?
Jdg 13: 3 [A] and childless, but *you are going to* **conceive** and have a son.
13: 5 [A] because you *will* **conceive** and give birth to a son. No razor
13: 7 [A] But he said to me, 'You *will* **conceive** and give birth to a son.
1Sa 1:20 [A] So in the course of time Hannah **conceived** and gave birth to
2:21 [A] *she* **conceived** and gave birth to three sons and two
2Sa 11: 5 [A] The woman **conceived** and sent word to David, saying, "I am
2Ki 4:17 [A] the woman *became* **pregnant**, and the next year about that
1Ch 4:17 [A] One of Mered's wives **gave birth** *to* Miriam, Shammai and
7:23 [A] and *she became* **pregnant** and gave birth to a son.
Job 3: 3 [E] of my birth perish, and the night it was said, 'A boy **is born**!'
15:35 [A] They **conceive** trouble and give birth to evil; their womb
Ps 7:14 [7:15] [A] and **conceives** trouble gives birth to disillusionment.
SS 3: 4 [A] mother's house, to the room of the *one who* **conceived** me.
Isa 8: 3 [A] to the prophetess, and *she* **conceived** and gave birth to a son.
26:17 [A] As a *woman* **with child** and about to give birth writhes
26:18 [A] *We were* **with child**, we writhed in pain, but we gave birth
33:11 [A] *You* **conceive** chaff, you give birth to straw; your breath is a
59: 4 [A] and speak lies; they **conceive** trouble and give birth to evil.
59:13 [A] and revolt, uttering lies our hearts *have* **conceived**.
Hos 1: 3 [A] daughter of Diblaim, and *she* **conceived** and bore him a son.
1: 6 [A] Gomer **conceived** again and gave birth to a daughter.
1: 8 [A] had weaned Lo-Ruhamah, Gomer **[RPH]** had another son.
2: 5 [2:7] [A] been unfaithful and *has* **conceived** them in disgrace.

2226 הָרֶה *hāreh*, a.f. [12] [√ 2225]

pregnant [7], with child [2], enlarged [1], expectant mothers [1], pregnant women [1]

Ge 16:11 "You are now **with child** and you will have a son. You shall name
38:24 is guilty of prostitution, and as a result *she* is now **pregnant**."
38:25 "I am **pregnant** by the man who owns these," she said. And she
Ex 21:22 "If men who are fighting hit a **pregnant** woman and she gives
1Sa 4:19 the wife of Phinehas, was **pregnant** and near the time of delivery.
2Sa 11: 5 and sent word to David, saying, "I am **pregnant**."

2Ki 8:12 little children to the ground, and rip open their **pregnant** *women*."
15:16 He sacked Tiphsah and ripped open all the **pregnant** *women*.
Isa 7:14 The virgin will be **with child** and will give birth to a son, and will
Jer 20:17 with my mother as my grave, her womb **enlarged** forever.
31:8 be the blind and the lame, **expectant mothers** and women in labor;
Am 1:13 Because he ripped open the **pregnant women** *of* Gilead in order to

2227 הָרוּם *hārûm*, n.pr.m. [1] [cf. 2235]
Harum [1]
1Ch 4:8 and Hazzobebah and of the clans of Aharhel son of **Harum**.

2228 הֵרוֹן *hērôn*, n.[m.]. [1] [√ 2225]
childbearing [1]
Ge 3:16 woman he said, "I will greatly increase your pains in **childbearing**;

2229 הֲרוֹרִי *h*ᵃ*rôrî*, a.g. [1]
Harorite [1]
1Ch 11:27 Shammoth the **Harorite**, Helez the Pelonite,

2230 הָרִיָּה *hāriyyâ*, a.f. [1] [√ 2225]
pregnant women [1]
Hos 13:16 [14:1] dashed to the ground, their **pregnant women** ripped open."

2231 הֵרָיוֹן *hērāyôn*, n.[m.]. [2] [√ 2225]
conceive [1], conception [1]
Ru 4:13 Then he went to her, and the LORD enabled her to **conceive**,
Hos 9:11 will fly away like a bird—no birth, no pregnancy, no **conception**.

2232 הֲרִיסָה *h*ᵃ*rîsâ*, n.f. [1] [√ 2238]
ruins [1]
Am 9:11 its broken places, restore its **ruins**, and build it as it used to be,

2233 הֲרִיסוּת *h*ᵃ*rîsût*, n.f. [1] [√ 2238]
waste [1]
Isa 49:19 you were ruined and made desolate and your land laid **waste**,

2234 הָרָם *hārām*, n.pr.loc. Not used in NIV/BHS [→ 1099]

2235 הֹרָם *hōrām*, n.pr.m. [1] [cf. 2227]
Horam [1]
Jos 10:33 Meanwhile, **Horam** king of Gezer had come up to help Lachish,

2236 הַרְמוֹן *harmôn*, n.pr.loc. [1]
Harmon [1]
Am 4:3 and you will be cast out toward **Harmon**," declares the LORD.

2237 הָרָן *hārān*, n.pr.m. [7] [→ 1100]
Haran [7]
Ge 11:26 lived 70 years, he became the father of Abram, Nahor and **Haran**.
11:27 of Terah. Terah became the father of Abram, Nahor and **Haran**.
11:27 of Abram, Nahor and Haran. And **Haran** became the father of Lot.
11:28 **Haran** died in Ur of the Chaldeans, in the land of his birth.
11:29 she was the daughter of **Haran**, the father of both Milcah
11:31 Terah took his son Abram, his grandson Lot son of **Haran**,
1Ch 23:9 The sons of Shimei: Shelomoth, Haziel and **Haran**—three in all.

2238 הָרַס *hāras*, v. [43] [→ 2232, 2233]
tear down [7], overthrow [3], tears down [3], broken down [2], destroyed [2], force way through [2], in ruins [2], must demolish [+2238] [2], torn down [2], are torn down [1], be overturned [1], been broken down [1], being destroyed [1], break down [1], break [1], demolish [1], demolished [1], destroy [1], is destroyed [1], laid waste [+2256+2990] [1], left in ruins [1], ousted [1], overthrew [1], overthrown [1], pull down [1], threw down [1], was destroyed [1]
Ex 15:7 [A] In the greatness of your majesty *you* **threw down** those who
19:21 [A] so *they do* not **force** *their* **way through** to see the LORD
19:24 [A] the people *must* not **force** *their* **way through** to come up to
23:24 [D] *You* **must demolish** [+2238] them and break their sacred
23:24 [D] *You* **must demolish** [+2238] them and break their sacred
Jdg 6:25 [A] **Tear down** your father's altar to Baal and cut down the
2Sa 11:25 [A] Press the attack against the city and **destroy** it.' Say this to
1Ki 18:30 [B] and he repaired the altar of the LORD, which *was* **in ruins**.
19:10 [A] have rejected your covenant, **broken down** your altars,
19:14 [A] have rejected your covenant, **broken down** your altars,
2Ki 3:25 [A] *They* **destroyed** the towns, and each man threw a stone on
1Ch 20:1 [A] in Jerusalem. Joab attacked Rabbah and **left it in ruins**.
Job 12:14 [A] What *he* **tears down** cannot be rebuilt; the man he imprisons
Ps 11:3 [C] When the foundations *are* **being destroyed**, what can the
28:5 [A] *he will* **tear** them **down** and never build them up again.
58:6 [58:7] [A] **Break** the teeth in their mouths, O God; tear out,
Pr 11:11 [C] is exalted, but by the mouth of the wicked *it* **is destroyed**.
14:1 [A] but with her own hands the foolish one **tears** hers **down**.
24:31 [C] was covered with weeds, and the stone wall *was* **in ruins**.
29:4 [A] but one who is greedy for bribes **tears** it **down**.
Isa 14:17 [A] *who* **overthrew** its cities and would not let his captives go
22:19 [A] from your office, and you *will be* **ousted** from your position.
49:17 [D] *those who* **laid** you **waste** [+2256+2990] depart from you.
Jer 1:10 [A] tear down, to destroy and **overthrow**, to build and to plant."
24:6 [A] I will build them up and not **tear** them **down**; I will plant
31:28 [A] and tear down, and to **overthrow**, destroy and bring disaster,
31:40 [C] The city will never again be uprooted or **demolished**."
42:10 [A] stay in this land, I will build you up and not **tear** you **down**;
45:4 [A] I *will* **overthrow** what I have built and uproot what I have
50:15 [C] She surrenders, her towers fall, her walls **are torn down**.
La 2:2 [A] in his wrath *he has* **torn down** the strongholds of the
2:17 [A] *He has* **overthrown** you without pity, he has let the enemy
Eze 13:14 [A] *I will* **tear down** the wall you have covered with whitewash
16:39 [A] *they will* **tear down** your mounds and destroy your lofty
26:4 [A] will destroy the walls of Tyre and **pull down** her towers;
26:12 [A] *they will* **break down** your walls and demolish your fine
30:4 [C] wealth will be carried away and her foundations **torn down**.
36:35 [C] desolate and **destroyed**, are now fortified and inhabited."
36:36 [C] know that I the LORD have rebuilt what **was destroyed**
38:20 [C] The mountains *will* **be overturned**, the cliffs will crumble
Joel 1:17 [C] the granaries *have* **been broken down**, for the grain has
Mic 5:11 [5:10] [A] of your land and **tear down** all your strongholds.
Mal 1:4 [A] "They may build, but I *will* **demolish**. They will be called the

2239 הֶרֶס *heres*, n.[m.]. [1] [→ 6556]
Destruction [1]
Isa 19:18 One of them will be called the City of **Destruction**.

2240 הֲרָרִי *h*ᵃ*rārî*, a.g. [5]
Hararite [5]
2Sa 23:11 Next to him was Shammah son of Agee the **Hararite**.
23:33 son of Shammah the **Hararite**, Ahiam son of Sharar the Hararite,
23:33 son of Shammah the Hararite, Ahiam son of Sharar the **Hararite**,
1Ch 11:34 of Hashem the Gizonite, Jonathan son of Shagee the **Hararite**,
11:35 Ahiam son of Sacar the **Hararite**, Eliphal son of Ur,

2241 הַשַּׁחַר *haššaḥar*, n.pr.loc. Not used in NIV/BHS [→ 7680]

2242 הַשִּׁטָּה *haššiṭṭâ*, n.pr.loc. Not used in NIV/BHS [→ 1101]

2243 הַשִּׁטִּים *haššiṭṭîm*, n.pr.loc. Not used in NIV/BHS [→ 69]

2244 הָשֵׁם *hāšēm*, n.pr.m. [1]
Hashem [1]
1Ch 11:34 the sons of **Hashem** the Gizonite, Jonathan son of Shagee the

2245 הַשְׁמָעוּת *hašmāʿût*, n.f. [1] [√ 9048]
news [+265] [1]
Eze 24:26 on that day a fugitive will come to tell you the **news** [+265].

2246 הַתַּאֲוָה *hattaʾᵃwâ*, n.pr.loc. Not used in NIV/BHS [→ 7701]

2247 הִתּוּךְ *hittûk*, n.[m.]. [1] [√ 5988]
melted [1]
Eze 22:22 As silver is **melted** in a furnace, so you will be melted inside her,

2248 הִתְחַבְּרוּת *hitḥabbᵉrût*, n. *or* v.ptcp. Not used in NIV/BHS [√ 2489]

2249 הִתְיַחֵשׂ *hityaḥēś*, v.den. Not used in NIV/BHS [√ 3509]

2250 הַתִּיכוֹן *hattîkôn*, n.pr.loc. Not used in NIV/BHS [→ 2962; cf. 2021 + 9348]

2251 הֲתָךְ *h*ᵃ*tāk*, n.pr.m. [4]
Hathach [3], him[s] [1]
Est 4:5 Esther summoned **Hathach**, one of the king's eunuchs assigned to

Est 4: 6 So **Hathach** went out to Mordecai in the open square of the city in
4: 9 **Hathach** went back and reported to Esther what Mordecai had
4: 10 Then she instructed **him**[s] to say to Mordecai,

2252 הָתַל ***hātal***, v. [1] [→ 2253; cf. 9438]

taunt [1]

1Ki 18: 27 [D] At noon Elijah *began to* **taunt** them. "Shout louder!"

2253 הֲתֻלִים ***hᵃtulîm***, n.[m.]pl. [1] [√ 2252]

mockers [1]

Job 17: 2 Surely **mockers** surround me; my eyes must dwell on their

2254 הָתַת ***hātat***, v. Not used in NIV/BHS [cf. 2109]

ו, *w*

2255 ו ***w***, letter. Not used in NIV/BHS [→ Ar 10220]

2256 -וְ ***wᵉ-***, c.pref. [50303 / 50284] [→ Ar 10221] Not indexed

untranslated [20020], and [19276], but [1877], then [1821], so [1179], or [931], when [596], with [333], also [251], now [246], so that [236], that [175], yet [143], while [113], nor [+4202] [109], and then [91], as [89], for [88], after [78], both and [76], however [73], together with [73], nor [70], and when [64], as for [61], if [60], therefore [58], and also [56], even [56], and [+1685] [53], along with [48], and so [44], as well as [41], because [41], including [40], though [39], also [+1685] [26], but when [25], twenty-five [+2822+6929] [23], even though [22], again [20], since [19], instead [18], in this way [17], meanwhile [17], until [17], even [+1685] [15], 24,000 [+547+752+6929] [14], 25,000 [+547+2822+6929] [14], at this [14], or [+4202] [14], twenty-two [+6929+9109] [14], all generations [+1887+1887] [13], nor [+440] [13], thus [13], both [12], but as for [12], although [11], and now [11], next [11], 250 [+2822+4395] [10], and yet [10], but also [10], include [10], on each side [+4946+4946+7024+7024] [10], only [10], till [10], whether or [10], 603,550 [+547+547+2256+2256+2822+2822 +4395+4395+8993+9252] [9], nevertheless [9], too [9], twenty-fourth [+752+6929] [9], 4,500 [+547+752+2822+4395] [8], and that [8], moreover [+1685] [8], moreover [8], and as well [7], and though [7], and too [7], either or [7], finally [7], twenty-third [+6929+8993] [7], uttered [+606+5951] [7], 1,775 [+547+2256+2256+2822+4395 +8679+8679] [6], 127 [+2256+4395+6929+8679] [6], 45,650 [+547+752+2256+2256+2822+2822+4395+9252] [6], 53,400 [+547+752+2256+2822+4395+8993] [6], and [+677] [6], besides [6], but now [6], but then [6], on both sides[s] [+2296+2296+4946+4946] [6], sent for [+4200+7924+8938] [6], thirty-three [+8993+8993] [6], thirty-two [+8993+9109] [6], twenty-seventh [+6929+8679] [6], twenty-three [+6929+8993] [6], whenever [6], 120 [+4395+6929] [5], even if [5], indeed [5], just as [5], or [+561] [5], to [5], twenty-four [+752+6929] [5], twenty-nine [+6929+9596] [5], 1,254 [+547+752 +2822+4395] [4], 128 [+4395+6929+9046] [4], 137 [+2256+4395 +8679+8993] [4], 151,450 [+285+547+547+752+2256 +2256+2256 +2822+2822+4395+4395] [4], 32,200 [+547+2256+4395+8993 +9109] [4], 35,400 [+547+752+2256+2822+4395+8993] [4], 41,500 [+285+547+752+2256+2822+4395] [4], 46,500 [+547+752+2256 +2822+4395+9252] [4], 54,400 [+547+752+752+2256+2822+4395] [4], 57,400 [+547+752+2256+2822+4395+8679] [4], 59,300 [+547+2256+2822+4395+8993+9596] [4], 62,700 [+547+2256+4395 +8679+9109+9252] [4], 74,600 [+547+752+2256+4395+8679+9252] [4], afterward [4], and after [4], before [4], eighty-five [+2822+9046] [4], forty-one [+285+752] [4], forty-two [+752+9109] [4], go [+2143+4200+8740] [4], nor [+401] [4], now that [4], on either side[s] [+4946+4946+7024+7024] [4], on [4], one day [+2118] [4], one day [4], or [+1685] [4], so when [4], that is why [4], that is [4], too [+1685] [4], twenty-eight [+6929+9046] [4], twenty-first [+285+6929] [4], twenty-one [+285+6929] [4], yes [4], 1,365 [+547+2256+2256 +2822+4395+8993+9252] [3], 153,600 [+547+547+2256+2256 +2822+4395+4395+8993+9252] [3], 157,600 [+547+547+2256+2256 +2822+4395+4395+8679+9252] [3], 186,400 [+547+547+547+752 +2256+2256+4395+4395+9046+9252] [3], 22,034 [+547+752+2256 +2256+6929+8993+9109] [3], 22,273 [+547+2256+2256+4395 +6929+8679+8993+9109] [3], 29 [+6929+9596] [3], 32 [+8993+9109] [3], 337,500 [+547+547+547+2256+2256+2822+4395 +4395+8679+8993+8993] [3], 36,000 [+547+8993+9252] [3], 40,500 [+547+752+2822+4395] [3], 43,730 [+547+752+2256+2256+4395 +8679+8993+8993] [3], 430 [+752+4395+8993] [3], 44,760 [+547+752+752+2256+2256+4395+8679+9252] [3], after that [3], and afterward [3], and even [3], and since [3], as soon as [3], as well as [+1685] [3], between [+4946+6330] [3], each people [+6639+6639] [3], each province [+4519+4519] [3], eleven hundred [+547+4395] [3], fifty-two [+2822+9109] [3], forty-five [+752+2822] [3], generations [+1887+1887] [3], in [3], neither [+4202] [3], now [+1685] [3], otherwise [3], parents [+3+562] [3], seventy-five [+2822+8679] [3], seventy-seven [+8679+8679] [3], so then [3], then [+1685] [3], then when [3], thirty-five [+2822+8993] [3], thirty-ninth [+8993+9596] [3], thirty-one [+285+8993] [3], thirty-seventh [+8679+8993] [3], twenty-fifth [+2822+6929] [3], 1,052 [+547+2822+9109] [2], 1,247 [+547+752+4395+8679] [2], 1,760 [+547+2256+4395+8679+9252] [2], 108,100 [+547+547+2256 +4395+4395+9046] [2], 112 [+4395+6925+9109] [2], 122 [+2256+4395+6929+9109] [2], 123 [+4395+6929+8993] [2], 130 [+4395+8993] [2], 133 [+2256+4395+8993+8993] [2], 150 [+2822+4395] [2], 162 [+2256+4395+9109+9252] [2], 182 [+2256+4395+9046+9109] [2], 187 [+2256+4395+8679+9046] [2], 2,172 [+547+2256+4395+8679+9109] [2], 2,630 [+547+2256+4395 +8993+9252] [2], 22,200 [+547+2256+4395+6929+9109] [2], 22,600 [+547+2256+4395+6929+9109+9252] [2], 220 [+4395+6929] [2], 223 [+4395+6929+8993] [2], 245 [+752+2256+2822+4395] [2], 25,100 [+547+2256+2822+4395+6929] [2], 273 [+2256+4395+8679 +8993] [2], 28,600 [+547+2256+4395+6929+9046+9252] [2], 3,023 [+547+2256+6929+8993+8993] [2], 3,630 [+547+2256+4395 +8993+8993+9252] [2], 30,500 [+547+2822+4395+8993] [2], 307,500 [+547+547+2256+2822+4395+4395+8679+8993] [2], 32,500 [+547+2256+2822+4395+8993+9109] [2], 320 [+4395+6929 +8993] [2], 337,500 [+547+547+547+2256+2822+4395+4395 +8679+8993+8993] [2], 345 [+752+2822+4395+8993] [2], 365 [+2256+2822+4395+8993+9252] [2], 372 [+4395+8679+8993+9109] [2], 390 [+4395+8993+9596] [2], 392 [+4395+8993+9109+9596] [2], 4,600 [+547+752+4395+9252] [2], 403 [+752+4395+8993] [2], 42 [+752+9109] [2], 435 [+752+2822+4395+8993] [2], 45,400 [+547+752+752+2256+2822+4395] [2], 45,600 [+547+752+2256 +2822+4395+9252] [2], 52 [+2822+9109] [2], 52,700 [+547+2256 +2822+4395+8679+9109] [2], 595 [+2256+2822+2822+4395+9596] [2], 6,720 [+547+4395+6929+8679+9252] [2], 601,730 [+547+547 +2256+4395+4395+8679+8993+9252] [2], 621 [+285+4395 +6929+9252] [2], 64,300 [+547+752+2256+4395+8993+9252] [2], 64,400 [+547+752+752+2256+4395+9252] [2], 642 [+752+2256 +4395+9109+9252] [2], 65 [+2822+9252] [2], 652 [+2822+4395 +9109+9252] [2], 666 [+2256+4395+9252+9252+9252] [2], 666 [+4395+9252+9252+9252] [2], 675,000 [+547+547+547+2256+2822 +4395+8679+9252] [2], 7,337 [+547+4395+8679+8679+8993+8993] [2], 721 [+285+2256+4395+6929+8679] [2], 74 [+752+8679] [2], 743 [+752+2256+4395+8679+8993] [2], 76,500 [+547+2256+2822+4395 +8679+9252] [2], 760 [+4395+8679+9252] [2], 777 [+2256+4395 +8679+8679+8679] [2], 782 [+2256+4395+8679+9046+9109] [2], 8,580 [+547+2256+2822+4395+9046+9046] [2], 895 [+2256+2822 +4395+9046+9596] [2], 945 [+752+2256+2822+4395+9596] [2], 95 [+2822+9596] [2], 956 [+2256+2822+4395+9252+9596] [2], 962 [+2256+4395+9109+9252+9596] [2], 969 [+2256+4395 +9252+9596+9596] [2], 973 [+4395+8679+8993+9596] [2], 98 [+9046+9596] [2], altogether [+465] [2], and because [2], and included [2], and so that [2], anywhere else [+625+625+2025+2025] [2], as surely as [2], at either end[s] [+2296+2296+4946+4946] [2], at that time [2], became more and more powerful [+1524+2143+2143] [2], besides [+1685] [2], beyond [+2134+4946] [2], but [+1685] [2], but even [2], called together [+665+906+8938] [2], differing weights [+74+74] [2], each dish [+4094+4094] [2], each gate [+9133+9133] [2], each lampstand [+4963+4963] [2], even when [2], far and wide [+2085+2134+4946] [2], fifty-five [+2822+2822] [2], find out [+3359+8011] [2], followed by [2], forty-eight [+752+9046] [2], fourteen hundred [+547+752+4395] [2], from [2], fully accomplishes [+6913+7756] [2], furthermore [2], head [+2025+4946+5087+8900] [2], here [2], how [2], imported [+3655+6590] [2], in turn [2], included [2], indeed [+1685] [2], just then [+2180] [2], led in campaigns [+995+3655+4200+7156] [2], led on military campaigns [+906+995+3655] [2], neither [2], ninety-nine [+9596+9596] [2], ninety-six [+9252+9596] [2], nor [+1153] [2], now when [2], or [+3954] [2], rather than [+4202] [2], rebuilt [+906+1215+8740] [2], see [+3359+8011] [2], seventeen hundred [+547+4395+8679] [2], sixty-six [+9252+9252] [2], sixty-two [+9109+9252] [2], slaves [+6269+9148] [2], so [+1685] [2], still [2], them[s] [+2286+7518] [2], therefore [+1685] [2], thirty-eight [+8993+9046] [2], thirty-eighth [+8993+9046] [2], thirty-second [+8993+9109] [2], thirty-seven [+8679+8993] [2], together with [+1685] [2], too [+677] [2], treaty of friendship [+3208+8934] [2], twenty-second [+6929+9109] [2], twenty-seven [+6929+8679] [2], us [+3276+3870] [2], various kinds of service [+6275+6275] [2], where [2], wherever goes [+928+928 +995+3655] [2], with the help of [2], yes [+1685] [2], yet [+1685] [2], 1,017 [+547+6925+8679] [1], 1,222 [+547+4395+6929+9109] [1], 1,290 [+547+4395+9596] [1], 1,335 [+547+2822+4395+8993+8993] [1], 105 [+2822+4395] [1], 110 [+4395+6927] [1], 119 [+4395+6926+9596] [1], 120,000 [+547+4395+6929] [1], 122 [+4395+6929+9109] [1], 138 [+4395+8993+9046] [1], 139 [+4395+8993+9596] [1], 14,700 [+547+752+4395+6925+8679] [1],

148 [+752+4395+9046] [1], 156 [+2822+4395+9252] [1], 16,750 [+547+2822+4395+6925+8679+9252] [1], 160 [+4395+9252] [1], 17,200 [+547+4395+6925+8679] [1], 172 [+4395+8679+9109] [1], 180 [+4395+9046] [1], 180,000 [+547+4395+9046] [1], 188 [+4395+9046+9046] [1], 2,056 [+547+2822+9252] [1], 2,067 [+547+8679+9252] [1], 2,172 [+547+4395+8679+9109] [1], 2,200 [+547+4395] [1], 2,300 [+547+4395+8993] [1], 2,322 [+547+4395 +6929+8993+9109] [1], 2,400 [+547+752+4395] [1], 2,600 [+547+4395+9252] [1], 2,750 [+547+2822+4395+8679] [1], 2,812 [+547+4395+6925+9046+9109] [1], 2,818 [+547+4395+6925 +9046+9046] [1], 20,200 [+547+4395+6929] [1], 20,800 [+547+4395+6929+9046] [1], 205 [+2822+4395] [1], 207 [+4395+8679] [1], 209 [+4395+9596] [1], 212 [+4395+6925+9109] [1], 218 [+4395+6925+9046] [1], 22 [+6929+9109] [1], 22,000 [+547+6929+9109] [1], 23,000 [+547+6929+8993] [1], 232 [+4395+8993+9109] [1], 242 [+752+4395+9109] [1], 245 [+752 +2822+4395] [1], 245 [1], 26,000 [+547+6929+9252] [1], 28 [+6929 +9046] [1], 280,000 [+547+4395+9046] [1], 284 [+752+4395+9046] [1], 288 [+4395+9046+9046] [1], 3,200 [+547+4395+8993] [1], 3,600 [+547+4395+8993+9252] [1], 3,700 [+547+4395+8679+8993] [1], 3,930 [+547+4395+8993+8993+9596] [1], 318 [+4395+6925 +8993+9046] [1], 32,000 [+547+8993+9109] [1], 323 [+4395+6929 +8993+8993] [1], 324 [+752+4395+6929+8993] [1], 328 [+4395+6929+8993+9046] [1], 34 [+752+8993] [1], 35 [+2822+8993] [1], 350 [+2822+4395+8993] [1], 37,000 [+547+8679+8993] [1], 410 [+752+4395+6927] [1], 42,360 [+547+752+4395+8052+8993+9252] [1], 420 [+752+4395+6929] [1], 454 [+752+752+2822+4395] [1], 468 [+752+4395+9046+9252] [1], 5,400 [+547+752+2822+4395] [1], 530 [+2822+4395+8993] [1], 550 [+2822+2822+4395] [1], 56 [+2822+9252] [1], 6,200 [+547+4395+9252] [1], 6,800 [+547+4395 +9046+9252] [1], 60,500 [+547+2822+4395+9252] [1], 61 [+285+9252] [1], 61,000 [+285+547+9252] [1], 61,000 [+547+8052 +9252] [1], 62 [+9109+9252] [1], 623 [+4395+6929+8993+9252] [1], 628 [+4395+6929+9046+9252] [1], 642 [+752+4395+9109+9252] [1], 648 [+752+4395+9046+9252] [1], 650 [+2822+4395+9252] [1], 655 [+2822+2822+4395+9252] [1], 667 [+4395+8679+9252+9252] [1], 67 [+8679+9252] [1], 675 [+2822+4395+8679+9252] [1], 690 [+4395+9252+9596] [1], 7,100 [+547+4395+8679] [1], 7,500 [+547+2822+4395+8679] [1], 72 [+8679+9109] [1], 72,000 [+547+8679+9109] [1], 725 [+2822+4395+6929+8679] [1], 730 [+4395+8679+8993] [1], 736 [+4395+8679+8993+9252] [1], 736 [1], 743 [+752+4395+8679+8993] [1], 745 [+752+2822+4395+8679] [1], 775 [+2822+4395+8679+8679] [1], 8,600 [+547+4395+9046+9252] [1], 807 [+4395+8679+9046] [1], 815 [+2822+4395+6926+9046] [1], 822 [+4395+6929+9046+9109] [1], 830 [+4395+8993+9046] [1], 832 [+4395+8993+9046+9109] [1], 840 [+752+4395+9046] [1], 845 [+752+2822+4395+9046] [1], 87,000 [+547+8679+9046] [1], 905 [+2822+4395+9596] [1], 910 [+4395+6924+9596] [1], 912 [+4395+6926+9109+9596] [1], 928 [+4395+6929+9046+9596] [1], 930 [+4395+8993+9596] [1], 950 [+2822+4395+9596] [1], accompanied by [1], adding to [+907] [1], after [+1685] [1], after this [1], again and again [+8899+8938] [1], age-old [+1887+1887] [1], all generations [+1887] [1], all time [+1887+1887] [1], along with [+1685] [1], also [+677] [1], also included [1], alternate[s] [+2298+7194+8232] [1], alternated[s] [+7194+8232] [1], always [+1887+1887+4200] [1], and [+255] [1], and [+6330] [1], and [+907] [1], and again [1], and alike [1], and as for [1], and as [1], and either [1], and even after [1], and even though [1], and likewise [1], and still [1], and that is why [1], and what about [1], and whenever [1], and with [1], annually [+928+3972+9102+9102] [1], anywhere [+625+625+2025+2025] [1], army [+6639+7736] [1], as far as [1], as surely as live [+2644+2644 +5883] [1], as well as [+3869] [1], as well [1], assassinated [+906+906+906+4637+5782] [1], at that [1], autumn [1], back and forth [+285+285+2178+2178] [1], be on way [+2143+5825] [1], bearing [1], beasts of burden [+989+2651] [1], became more and more powerful [+1524+2143] [1], because [+4202] [1], because [+928+3610+3610] [1], been brought to attention [+4200+5583 +9048] [1], belong [1], bless [1], bordering each side[s] [+2296+2296+4946+4946] [1], both[s] [+170+2021+2021+8533] [1], both of you [+2084+3870] [1], bring [+906+3655+4374] [1], but [+3463] [1], but [+8370] [1], but even [+1685] [1], but too [1], but while [1], by the time [1], by then [1], called together [+448+665+8938] [1], called together [+448+665+906+8938] [1], calling together [+906+906+995 +8938] [1], came back [+995+2143] [1], carefully investigated [+1335+2011] [1], carry out duties [+995+3655] [1], carry the battle [+1741+8740] [1], cities [+6551+6551] [1], closer and closer [+2143+7929] [1], commander-in-chief [+8031+8569] [1], completely [+1414+4946+5883+6330] [1], cover up [+906+4059+8740] [1], crushed completely [+430+4730] [1], deception [+4213+4213] [1], did so[s] [+448+2932+4374+8008] [1], differing measures [+406+406] [1], each of us [+638+2085] [1], each table [+8947+8947] [1], each town [+6551+6551] [1], eighteen thousand [+547+8052+9046] [1], eighty-six [+9046+9252] [1], eighty-three [+8993+9046] [1], endless generations [+1887+1887] [1], enslaved [+3899+4200+4200+6269 +9148] [1], especially [1], even [+677] [1], even [+677+3954] [1], even then [1], even while [1], every city [+6551+6551] [1], every day [+3427+3427+3972] [1], every family [+5476+5476] [1], every province [+4519+4519] [1], except for [+4202] [1], executed [+906+4637+5782] [1], exorbitant interest [+5968+9552] [1], experienced [+1981+9312] [1], feasting [+430+9272] [1], fifteen [+2822+6927] [1], fifty-second [+2822+9109] [1], finally [+1685] [1], find out [+906+3359+8011] [1], fine [+1524+3202] [1], fly off [1], for instance [1], forty [+9109] [1], forty-first [+285+752] [1], forty-nine [+752+9596] [1], forty-seven [+752+8679] [1], fully obeyed [+3869+6913+9048] [1], furthermore [+1685] [1], furthermore [+2021+9108] [1], furthermore [+6388] [1], furthermore [+6964] [1], generations long past [+1887+1887+9102] [1], generations to come [+1887+1887] [1], given even more [+2179+2179+3578+3869 +3869+4200] [1], go about business [+995+3655] [1], go at once [+995+2143] [1], go in [+995+2143] [1], grapes or raisins [+3313+4300+6694] [1], great wrath [+2405+7912] [1], grew even wilder [+2143+6192+6584] [1], grew louder and louder [+2143+2618+4394] [1], grew stronger and stronger [+2143+2618] [1], grew stronger and stronger [+2143+7997] [1], grew weaker and weaker [+1924+2143] [1], had brought [+4374+8938] [1], had executed [+906+4637+5782] [1], had removed [+906+4374+8938] [1], harem [+8721+8721] [1], have to do with [+4200+4200] [1], here is what [+2296+2296+3869+3869] [1], how much more [+677+3954] [1], if then [1], in addition to [1], in addition [1], in any direction [+2178+2178] [1], in any direction [+3907+3907] [1], in midair [+824+1068+2021+2021+9028] [1], in order for [1], including [+1685] [1], including and [1], increased more and more [+2143+2143+8041] [1], indeed [+677+3954] [1], instead [+1685] [1], interest of any kind [+5968+9552] [1], invite [+4200+7924+8938] [1], joined [+1685] [1], just who [+4769+4769] [1], kills [+4637+5782+5883] [1], kinds of cattle [+989+989] [1], laid waste [+2238+2990] [1], later [1], lead [+995+3655] [1], lead [+995+3655+4200+7156] [1], lead on [+2143+5627] [1], likewise [1], live [1], made good escape [+4880+5674] [1], man [+408+408] [1], many generations [+1887+1887] [1], many years [+3427+9102] [1], marauding [+6296+8740] [1], marries [+1249+4374] [1], meanwhile [+3907+3907+6330+6330] [1], melting away [+2143+4570] [1], more and more powerful [+1541+2025+2143+4200+5087+6330] [1], movements [+4569+4604] [1], much too numerous [+6786+8041] [1], neither [+440] [1], never [+1153+6329+6409] [1], nine-and-a-half [+2942+9596] [1], ninety-eight [+9046+9596] [1], no more than [1], nor [+1685] [1], nor [+1685+4202] [1], nor [+401+1685] [1], nor [+401+4946] [1], nor [+448] [1], nor [+561] [1], nothing [+1524+1821+4202+7785] [1], nothing at all [+401+700] [1], nothing but skin [+1414+6425] [1], now [+6964] [1], numbers increased greatly [+7238+8049] [1], obey [+906+6913+9068] [1], on both[s] [+2296+2296+4946+4946] [1], on both sides[s] [+2296+2296+4946] [1], on both sides[s] [+294+7156] [1], on duty [+995+3655] [1], on each side[s] [+2296+2296+4946+4946] [1], on the other side of [+2134+4946+6298] [1], once more [1], one of the other peoples [+6639+6639] [1], or [+401+561] [1], or [+440] [1], or [+700] [1], or even [1], otherwise [+4202] [1], over nine feet [+564+2455+9252] [1], over [1], pay close attention [+7992+9048] [1], please [+928+3202 +3838+6524] [1], provided for [+430+2118+4200+4312] [1], raised [+906+5951+5989] [1], raped [+906+6700+8886] [1], rapes [+2616+6640+8886] [1], rapes [+6640+8886+9530] [1], rather [+1685] [1], rather [1], realize [+3359+8011] [1], realized [+3359+8011] [1], reappears [+7255+8740] [1], rebuild [+1215+8740] [1], recaptured [+906+4374+8740] [1], receded steadily [+2143+8740+8740] [1], recite [+606+6699] [1], reentered [+995+8740] [1], reopened [+906+2916+8740] [1], return [+2143+7155] [1], richest of foods [+2016+2693] [1], roam [+2143+3718+6584] [1], rougher and rougher [+2143+6192] [1], ruined [+2472+2476] [1], saw [1], say [+606+6699] [1], scream for help [+7754+7924+8123] [1], screamed for help [+7754+7924+8123] [1], see [+906+3359+8011] [1], send for [+4374+8938] [1], send for [+906+4374+8938] [1], sent for [+906+4200+4200+4374+8938] [1], sent for [+906+7924+8938] [1], sent for [+906+906+7924+8938] [1], sent word [+5583+8938] [1], sent word [+7924+8938] [1], serve [+995+3655] [1], seventeen [+6927+8679] [1], shining ever brighter [+239+2143] [1], shouted [+5951+7754+7924] [1], similarly [1], sixty-eight [+9046+9252] [1], sixty-five [+2822+9252] [1], slaves [+563+6269] [1], square [+4946+4946+7024+7024] [1], square [+802] [1], staggering burden [+4842+7050] [1], stared with a fixed gaze [+906+6641+7156+8492] [1], stayed night [+3782+4328] [1], still [+1685] [1], strip off clothes [+6910+7320] [1], summon [+448+906+4374+8938] [1], summoned [+4200+4200+7924+8938] [1], summoned [+4200+7924+8938] [1], suppose [1], surely [1], than [+1685] [1], than [+4202] [1], that [+1685] [1], the parties [+408+2084+8276] [1], the two of them[s] [+1189+1192] [1], them[s] [+59+7401] [1], then [+339] [1], then [+6964] [1], they[s] [+1201+1201+1514+8017] [1], they[s] [+1770+5083] [1], they[s]

[+2021+2657+3405+8569] [1], thirty-fifth [+2822+8993] [1], thirty-first [+285+8993] [1], thirty-six [+8993+9252] [1], thirty-six hundred [+547+4395 +8993+9252] [1], thirty-sixth [+8993+9252] [1], thirty-three hundred [+547+4395+8993+8993] [1], through [1], tightly shut up [+6037+6037] [1], till [+677] [1], time and again [+285+4202 +4202+9109] [1], to come [+1887+1887] [1], together with [+6330] [1], together with [+677] [1], took back [+906+995+8938] [1], travel about [+995+3655] [1], tripping along with mincing steps [+2143+3262] [1], twelve hundred [+547+4395] [1], twenty-seven hundred [+547+4395+8679] [1], twenty-six [+6929+9252] [1], twenty-six hundred [+547+4395+9252] [1], twenty-sixth [+6929+9252] [1], twenty-two [+752+9109] [1], two differing measures [+406+406] [1], two differing weights [+74+74] [1], two men [+278+408+3481] [1], two-and-a-half [+2942+9109] [1], undivided loyalty [+4202+4213+4213] [1], upon [1], us [+2157+3276] [1], us [+3276+4013] [1], utterly useless [+2039+8198] [1], various gates [+9133+9133] [1], various peoples [+6639+6639] [1], various provinces [+4519+4519] [1], violated [+906+6700+8886] [1], what [+2296+2296+3869+3869] [1], what [+2296+2297+3869+3869] [1], what about [1], when also [1], whether [+700] [1], whether [1], who [1], whoever he may be [+6424+6699] [1], whole assembly [+6337+7736] [1], with [+1685] [1], with both [1], yet [+677] [1], yet [+6964] [1], yet also [1]

2257 וֹ- ***-ô***, ו- ***-w***, וּ- ***-û***, p.m.s.suf. [11878 / 11887] [√ 2023]
Not indexed

his [4457], him [2172], *untranslated* [1883], he [548], it [499], its [373], the[s] [336], their [285], them [182], his own [140], his [+4200] [79], whose [56], himself [55], a[s] [40], her [36], they [31], whom [26], your [26], himself [+5883] [18], his [+907] [13], one [13], who [13], David[s] [11], the altar[s] [11], himself [+1414] [10], himself [+4213] [10], its own [10], their own [10], each [9], them[s] [+3] [9], you [9], God[s] [8], his own [+4200] [8], he [+5883] [7], Moses[s] [7], the king's[s] [7], the king[s] [7], God's[s] [6], man's[s] [6], that [6], the LORD[s] [6], the man[s] [6], this [6], that[s] [5], the value[s] [5], their[s] [+1201] [5], Aaron[s] [4], an[s] [4], David's[s] [4], Elijah[s] [4], Elisha[s] [4], Gideon[s] [4], its [+4200] [4], Jacob[s] [4], Jehoram[s] [4], Jehu[s] [4], she [4], the gateway[s] [4], their [+4200] [4], there[s] [+928] [4], those [4], those[s] [4], which [4], Abram[s] [3], any[s] [3], anyone [3], Eliakim's[s] [3], Jehoiachin[s] [3], Joseph[s] [3], same[s] [3], Saul's[s] [3], Solomon[s] [3], there[s] [3], these [3], whose [+4200] [3], Aaron's[s] [2], Abraham[s] [2], Ahab[s] [2], Ahaziah[s] [2], alone [+928+1727] [2], Amnon[s] [2], Gehazi[s] [2], he [+3338] [2], here[s] [2], him[s] [+3] [2], his [+6640] [2], Hosea[s] [2], Isaac[s] [2], Israel's[s] [2], Jehoiachin's[s] [2], Jehoram's[s] [2], Jeremiah[s] [2], Joab[s] [2], Joash[s] [2], Job's[s] [2], Joseph's[s] [2], Josiah's[s] [2], Josiah[s] [2], man[s] [2], my [2], Nebuchadnezzar[s] [2], Noah[s] [2], own [2], owner [+4200] [2], Saul[s] [2], she[s] [+562] [2], Solomon's[s] [2], the area[s] [2], the ark[s] [2], the king[s] of the South [2], the lamps[s] [2], the LORD's[s] [2], the man himself [2], the man's[s] [2], the neighbor[s] [2], the person[s] [2], the table[s] [2], the [2], their own [+4200] [2], them[s] [+6269] [2], they[s] [+6269] [2], tribe[s] [2], your own [2], Zedekiah's[s] [2], Abijah's[s] [1], Abishai[s] [1], Abraham's[s] [1], Absalom's[s] [1], Achan[s] [1], Adonijah[s] [1], Ahab's[s] [1], Ahaz[s] [1], Amasa[s] [1], Amon's[s] [1], animal[s] [1], another[s] [1], any such thing[s] [1], Baal's[s] [1], Baruch[s] [1], Benaiah[s] [1], both[s] [1], by himself [+963+4200] [1], by itself [+963+4200] [1], consecrate himself [+3338+4848] [1], creditor [+1251+3338+5408] [1], daily [+928+3427+3427] [1], day by day [+928+1821+3427+3427] [1], did[s] [+3338+5989] [1], did this[s] [+3338+5742] [1], do that[s] [+928+2118+3338] [1], each [+278+408] [1], each day's [+928+3427+3427] [1], Egypt[s] [1], Ehud[s] [1], Eleazar[s] [1], Elisha's[s] [1], enemy[s] [1], equally [+278+408+3869] [1], equally among them [+278+408+3869] [1], every [1], every[s] [1], God's name[s] [1], Gog[s] [1], Hadad[s] [1], Haman[s] [1], hands [1], Hanun[s] [1], he himself [1], Heman's[s] [1], her[s] [+123+851] [1], her[s] [+851] [1], her husband[s] [1], her son[s] [1], herself [1], him[s] [+3162] [1], him [+3338] [1], him [+5883] [1], him[s] [+6660] [1], himself [+4222] [1], himself [+8031] [1], himself [+8638] [1], himself [+9005] [1], his[s] [+3] [1], his [+4202] [1], his [+6584] [1], his [+928] [1], his body[s] [1], his descendants[s] [1], his father's[s] [1], his father[s] [1], his neighbor[s] [1], his own [+5883] [1], his own [+963+4946] [1], inner[s] sanctuary [1], Israel[s] [1], it[s] [+1947] [1], it[s] [+2308] [1], it[s] [+2942] [1], it[s] [+3338] [1], it[s] [+623] [1], it[s] [+8031] [1], it[s] [+9005] [1], it[s] [1], its own [+5883] [1], itself [1], Jacob's[s] [1], Jehoahaz[s] [1], Jehoiakim's[s] [1], Jehu's[s] [1], Jeriah[s] [1], Jesse[s] [1], Jethro[s] [1], Joab's[s] [1], Job[s] [1], Joshua[s] [1], Judah's[s] [1], Laban[s] [1], Lot's[s] [1], Manasseh[s] [1], married [+851+906+4200+4200+4374] [1], my[s] [+1201] [1], my companion[s] [1], Naaman's[s] [1], Naboth's[s] [1], Neco[s] [1], not circumcised [+4200+6889] [1], Obed-Edom[s] [1], of his own [+3655+3751] [1], one's [1], one[s] [1], only [+928+1727] [1], only one [+963+4200] [1], opposite[s] [1], others[s] [1], Othniel[s] [1], out [1], person[s] [1], Pharaoh's[s] [1], pillar[s] [1], Potiphar[s] [1], Rehoboam[s] [1], relieve himself [+906+6114+8079] [1], relieving himself [+906+6114+8079] [1], riches[s] [1], royal[s] [1], Sennacherib's[s] [1], servant[s] [1], Shalmaneser's[s] [+4200] [1], Shaul's[s] [1], she[s] [+3304] [1], she[s] [+7108] [1], she[s] [+851] [1], Sheba[s] [1], Sherebiah's[s] [1], Shimei[s] [1], soldier[s] [1], someone [1], someone's [1], something[s] [1], stolen goods [+4200+4202] [1], such[s] [1], that man's line[s] [1], that month[s] [1], that nation[s] [1], that person[s] [1], the angel[s] [1], the animal[s] [1], the article[s] [1], the basket[s] [1], the bells[s] [1], the Benjamites[s] [1], the boy's[s] [1], the boy[s] [1], the bread[s] [1], the calf[s] [1], the captain[s] [1], the cloud[s] [1], the coming storm[s] [1], the contaminated[s] part [1], the country[s] [1], the defender[s] [1], the enemy's[s] [1], the ephod[s] [1], the gold[s] [1], the grapes[s] [1], the injured man[s] [1], the king [1], the king's [1], the lambs[s] [1], the offender[s] [1], the one [1], the other half of Manasseh[s] [1], the other man[s] [1], the people[s] [1], the person [1], the Philistine's[s] [1], the pillar[s] [1], the platform[s] [1], the pot[s] [1], the priest[s] [1], the rim[s] [1], the robe[s] [1], the scroll[s] [1], the servant[s] [1], the shore[s] [1], the slave[s] [1], the snake[s] [1], the successor[s] [1], the tribe[s] [1], the wicked[s] [1], the wood[s] [1], their[s] [1], theirs [+4200] [1], them[s] [+278] [1], them[s] [+6639] [1], them[s] [+7366] [1], themselves [+5883] [1], there[s] [+824+928] [1], there[s] [+928+7931] [1], there[s] [+928+9348] [1], they[s] [+1201] [1], they [+5883] [1], they[s] [1], this[s] [+3769+4202] [1], this altar[s] [1], this god's[s] [1], this matter[s] [1], Uzziah[s] [1], walled [+2570+4202] [1], where[s] [+928] [1], which[s] [+678] [1], which[s] [+7366] [1], who[s] [1], whose[s] [+465+1426] [1], your [+928] [1], your brother's[s] [1], your father[s] [1], your side[s] [1], your tithe[s] [1], yourself [+4213] [1], yourself [+5883] [1], yourself [1], Zechariah's[s] [1], Zechariah[s] [1]

2258 וְדָן ***wedān***, n.pr.loc.?. Not used in NIV/BHS

2259 וָהֵב ***wāhēb***, n.pr.loc.?. [1]
Waheb [1]

Nu 21:14 the LORD says: "**Waheb** in Suphah and the ravines, the Arnon

2260 וָו ***wāw***, n.[m.]. [13]
hooks [13]

Ex 26:32 Hang it with gold **hooks** on four posts of acacia wood overlaid
26:37 Make gold **hooks** for this curtain and five posts of acacia wood
27:10 twenty bronze bases and with silver **hooks** and bands *on* the posts.
27:11 twenty bronze bases and with silver **hooks** and bands *on* the posts.
27:17 the posts around the courtyard are to have silver bands and **hooks**,
36:36 They made gold **hooks** for them and cast their four silver bases.
36:38 they made five posts with **hooks** *for* them. They overlaid the tops
38:10 twenty bronze bases, and with silver **hooks** and bands *on* the posts.
38:11 and twenty bronze bases, with silver **hooks** and bands *on* the posts.
38:12 ten posts and ten bases, with silver **hooks** and bands *on* the posts.
38:17 The **hooks** and bands *on* the posts were silver, and their tops were
38:19 Their **hooks** and bands were silver, and their tops were overlaid
38:28 They used the 1,775 shekels to make the **hooks** for the posts,

2261 וָזָר ***wāzār***, a. [1]
guilty [1]

Pr 21:8 The way of the **guilty** is devious, but the conduct of the innocent is

2262 וַיְזָתָא ***wayezātā'***, n.pr.m. [1]
Vaizatha [1]

Est 9:9 Parmashta, Arisai, Aridai and **Vaizatha**,

2263 וָלָד ***wālād***, n.m. [1] [√ 3528]
children [1]

Ge 11:30 Now Sarai was barren; she had no **children**.

2264 וַנְיָה ***wanyâ***, n.pr.m. [1]
Vaniah [1]

Ezr 10:36 **Vaniah**, Meremoth, Eliashib,

2265 וָפְסִי ***wopsî***, n.pr.m. [1]
Vophsi [1]

Nu 13:14 from the tribe of Naphtali, Nahbi son of **Vophsi**;

2266 וַשְׁנִי ***wašnî***, n.pr.m.?. Not used in NIV/BHS

2267 וַשְׁתִּי ***waštî***, n.pr.f. [10]
Vashti [10]

Est 1:9 Queen **Vashti** also gave a banquet for the women in the royal
1:11 to bring before him Queen **Vashti**, wearing her royal crown,
1:12 delivered the king's command, Queen **Vashti** refused to come.
1:15 "According to law, what must be done to Queen **Vashti**?"
1:16 of the king and the nobles, "Queen **Vashti** has done wrong,
1:17 'King Xerxes commanded Queen **Vashti** to be brought before him,
1:19 that **Vashti** is never again to enter the presence of King Xerxes.

Est 2: 1 he remembered **Vashti** and what she had done and what he had
2: 4 Then let the girl who pleases the king be queen instead of **Vashti**."
2: 17 a royal crown on her head and made her queen instead of **Vashti**.

ז, Z

2268 ז *z*, letter. Not used in NIV/BHS [→ Ar 10222]

2269 זְאֵב¹ ***zᵉʾēb¹***, n.m. [7] [→ 2270]
wolf [4], wolves [3]
Ge 49: 27 "Benjamin is a ravenous **wolf**; in the morning he devours the prey,
Isa 11: 6 The **wolf** will live with the lamb, the leopard will lie down with the
65: 25 The **wolf** and the lamb will feed together, and the lion will eat
Jer 5: 6 forest will attack them, a **wolf** *from* the desert will ravage them,
Eze 22: 27 Her officials within her are like **wolves** tearing their prey;
Hab 1: 8 Their horses are swifter than leopards, fiercer than **wolves** *at* dusk.
Zep 3: 3 Her officials are roaring lions, her rulers are evening **wolves**,

2270 זְאֵב² ***zᵉʾēb²***, n.pr.m. [6] [√ 2269]
Zeeb [6]
Jdg 7: 25 They also captured two of the Midianite leaders, Oreb and **Zeeb**.
7: 25 killed Oreb at the rock of Oreb, and **Zeeb** at the winepress of Zeeb.
7: 25 killed Oreb at the rock of Oreb, and Zeeb at the winepress of **Zeeb**.
7: 25 the Midianites and brought the heads of Oreb and **Zeeb** to Gideon,
8: 3 God gave Oreb and **Zeeb**, the Midianite leaders, into your hands.
Ps 83: 11 [83:12] Make their nobles like Oreb and **Zeeb**, all their princes

2271 זֹאת ***zōʾt***, p.demo. & adv. Not used in NIV/BHS [√ 2296]

2272 זָבַד ***zābad***, v. [1] [→ 2273, 2274, 2275, 2280, 2281, 2288; *also used with compound proper names*]
presented [1]
Ge 30: 20 [A] Leah said, "God *has* **presented** me *with* a precious gift.

2273 זֵבֶד ***zēbed***, n.m. [1] [√ 2272]
gift [1]
Ge 30: 20 Then Leah said, "God has presented me with a precious **gift**.

2274 זָבָד ***zābād***, n.pr.m. [8] [√ 2272]
Zabad [8]
1Ch 2: 36 Attai was the father of Nathan, Nathan the father of **Zabad**,
2: 37 **Zabad** the father of Ephlal, Ephlal the father of Obed,
7: 21 **Zabad** his son and Shuthelah his son. Ezer and Elead were killed
11: 41 Uriah the Hittite, **Zabad** son of Ahlai,
2Ch 24: 26 Those who conspired against him were **Zabad**, son of Shimeath an
Ezr 10: 27 Elioenai, Eliashib, Mattaniah, Jeremoth, **Zabad** and Aziza.
10: 33 Mattattah, **Zabad**, Eliphelet, Jeremai, Manasseh and Shimei.
10: 43 Jeiel, Mattithiah, **Zabad**, Zebina, Jaddai, Joel and Benaiah.

2275 זַבְדִּי ***zabdî***, n.pr.m. [6 / 3] [√ 2272]
Zabdi [3]
Jos 7: 1 Achan son of Carmi, the son of Zimri, [BHS ***Zabdi***; NIV 2381]
7: 17 by families, and Zimri [BHS ***Zabdi***; NIV 2381] was taken.
7: 18 and Achan son of Carmi, the son of Zimri, [BHS ***Zabdi***; NIV 2381]
1Ch 8: 19 Jakim, Zicri, **Zabdi**,
27: 27 **Zabdi** the Shiphmite was in charge of the produce of the vineyards
Ne 11: 17 Mattaniah son of Mica, the son of **Zabdi**, the son of Asaph,

2276 זַבְדִּיאֵל ***zabdîʾēl***, n.pr.m. [2] [√ 2272 + 446]
Zabdiel [2]
1Ch 27: 2 first division, for the first month, was Jashobeam son of **Zabdiel**.
Ne 11: 14 128. Their chief officer was **Zabdiel** son of Haggedolim.

2277 זְבַדְיָה ***zᵉbadyâ***, n.pr.m. [6] [→ 2278; cf. 2272 + 3378]
Zebadiah [6]
1Ch 8: 15 **Zebadiah**, Arad, Eder,
8: 17 **Zebadiah**, Meshullam, Hizki, Heber,
12: 7 [12:8] and Joelah and **Zebadiah** the sons of Jeroham from Gedor.
27: 7 Asahel the brother of Joab; his son **Zebadiah** was his successor.
Ezr 8: 8 of Shephatiah, **Zebadiah** son of Michael, and with him 80 men;
10: 20 From the descendants of Immer: Hanani and **Zebadiah**.

2278 זְבַדְיָהוּ ***zᵉbadyāhû***, n.pr.m. [3] [√ 2277; cf. 2272 + 3378]
Zebadiah [3]
1Ch 26: 2 Jediael the second, **Zebadiah** the third, Jathniel the fourth,
2Ch 17: 8 Shemaiah, Nethaniah, **Zebadiah**, Asahel, Shemiramoth,
19: 11 and **Zebadiah** son of Ishmael, the leader of the tribe of Judah,

2279 זְבוּב ***zᵉbûb***, n.m. [2] [→ 1256]
flies [2]
Ecc 10: 1 As dead **flies** give perfume a bad smell, so a little folly outweighs
Isa 7: 18 In that day the LORD will whistle for **flies** from the distant

2280 זָבוּד ***zābûd***, n.pr.m. [1] [√ 2272]
Zabud [1]
1Ki 4: 5 **Zabud** son of Nathan—a priest and personal adviser to the king;
Ezr 8: 14 [Uthai and Zaccur, [K; see Q 2346] and with them 70 men.]

2281 זְבוּדָּה ***zᵉbûddâ***, n.pr.f. [0] [√ 2272; cf. 2288]
Zebidah [0]
2Ki 23: 36 [His mother's name was **Zebidah** [Q; see K 2288]]

2282 זְבוּלוּן ***zᵉbûlûn***, n.pr.m. [45] [→ 2283; cf. 2292]
Zebulun [40], Zebulun [+1201] [5]
Ge 30: 20 because I have borne him six sons." So she named him **Zebulun**.
35: 23 the firstborn of Jacob, Simeon, Levi, Judah, Issachar and **Zebulun**.
46: 14 The sons of **Zebulun**: Sered, Elon and Jahleel.
49: 13 "**Zebulun** will live by the seashore and become a haven for ships;
Ex 1: 3 Issachar, **Zebulun** and Benjamin;
Nu 1: 9 from **Zebulun**, Eliab son of Helon;
1: 30 From the descendants of **Zebulun**: All the men twenty years old
1: 31 The number from the tribe of **Zebulun** was 57,400.
2: 7 The tribe of **Zebulun** will be next. The leader of the people of
2: 7 The leader of the people of **Zebulun** is Eliab son of Helon.
7: 24 third day, Eliab son of Helon, the leader of the people of **Zebulun**,
10: 16 of Helon was over the division of the tribe of **Zebulun** [+1201].
13: 10 from the tribe of **Zebulun**, Gaddiel son of Sodi;
26: 26 The descendants of **Zebulun** by their clans were: through Sered,
34: 25 son of Parnach, the leader from the tribe of **Zebulun** [+1201];
Dt 27: 13 Reuben, Gad, Asher, **Zebulun**, Dan and Naphtali.
33: 18 About **Zebulun** he said: "Rejoice, Zebulun, in your going out,
33: 18 "Rejoice, **Zebulun**, in your going out, and you, Issachar, in your
Jos 19: 10 The third lot came up for **Zebulun** [+1201], clan by clan: The
19: 16 and their villages were the inheritance of **Zebulun** [+1201],
19: 27 touched **Zebulun** and the Valley of Iphtah El, and went north to
19: 34 It touched **Zebulun** on the south, Asher on the west and the Jordan
21: 7 twelve towns from the tribes of Reuben, Gad and **Zebulun**.
21: 34 were given: from the tribe of **Zebulun**, Jokneam, Kartah,
Jdg 1: 30 Neither did **Zebulun** drive out the Canaanites living in Kitron
4: 6 and **Zebulun** [+1201] and lead the way to Mount Tabor.
4: 10 where he summoned **Zebulun** and Naphtali. Ten thousand men
5: 14 came down, from **Zebulun** those who bear a commander's staff.
5: 18 The people of **Zebulun** risked their very lives; so did Naphtali on
6: 35 calling them to arms, and also into Asher, **Zebulun** and Naphtali,
12: 12 Then Elon died, and was buried in Aijalon in the land of **Zebulun**.
1Ch 2: 1 sons of Israel: Reuben, Simeon, Levi, Judah, Issachar, **Zebulun**,
6: 63 [6:48] twelve towns from the tribes of Reuben, Gad and **Zebulun**.
6: 77 [6:62] From the tribe of **Zebulun** they received Jokneam, Kartah,
12: 33 [12:34] men of **Zebulun**, experienced soldiers prepared for battle
12: 40 [12:41] **Zebulun** and Naphtali came bringing food on donkeys,
27: 19 over **Zebulun**: Ishmaiah son of Obadiah; over Naphtali:
2Ch 30: 10 from town to town in Ephraim and Manasseh, as far as **Zebulun**,
30: 11 Manasseh and **Zebulun** humbled themselves and went to
30: 18 Manasseh, Issachar and **Zebulun** had not purified themselves,
Ps 68: 27 [68:28] and there the princes of **Zebulun** and of Naphtali.
Isa 9: 1 [8:23] In the past he humbled the land of **Zebulun** and the land of
Eze 48: 26 "**Zebulun** will have one portion; it will border the territory of
48: 27 it will border the territory of **Zebulun** from east to west.
48: 33 the gate of Simeon, the gate of Issachar and the gate of **Zebulun**.

2283 זְבוּלֹנִי ***zᵉbûlōnî***, a.g. [3] [√ 2282; cf. 2292]
untranslated [1], Zebulun [1], Zebulunite [1]
Nu 26: 27 These were the clans of **Zebulun**; those numbered were 60,500.
Jdg 12: 11 After him, Elon the **Zebulunite** led Israel ten years.
12: 12 **[RPH]** and was buried in Aijalon in the land of Zebulun.

2284 זָבַח ***zābaḥ***, v. [134] [→ 2285, 2286, 4640; Ar 10156]
sacrifice [39], sacrificed [18], offer sacrifices [17], offered [10], offer [9], offered sacrifices [8], sacrificing [6], sacrifices [4], slaughter [3],

slaughtered [3], *untranslated* [2], made sacrifices [+2285] [2], preparing [2], sacrifice [+2285] [2], butchered [1], do[s] [1], making [1], offer sacrifice [1], offered a sacrifice [1], offering sacrifices [1], offering [1], offers [1], sacrifices offer [1]

Ge 31: 54 [A] He **offered** a sacrifice there in the hill country and invited his
46: 1 [A] *he* **offered** sacrifices to the God of his father Isaac.
Ex 3: 18 [A] into the desert *to* **offer sacrifices** to the LORD our God.'
5: 3 [A] into the desert *to* **offer sacrifices** to the LORD our God,
5: 8 [A] why they are crying out, 'Let us go and **sacrifice** to our God.'
5: 17 [A] you keep saying, 'Let us go and **sacrifice** to the LORD.'
8: 8 [8:4] [A] I will let your people go *to* **offer sacrifices** to the
8: 25 [8:21] [A] "Go, **sacrifice** to your God here in the land."
8: 26 [8:22] [A] *The* **sacrifices** *we* **offer** the LORD our God would
8: 26 [8:22] [A] if *we* **offer sacrifices** that are detestable in their eyes,
8: 27 [8:23] [A] the desert *to* **offer sacrifices** to the LORD our God,
8: 28 [8:24] [A] "I will let you go *to* **offer sacrifices** to the LORD
8: 29 [8:25] [A] the people go to **offer sacrifices** to the LORD."
13: 15 [A] This is why I **sacrifice** to the LORD the first male offspring
20: 24 [A] **sacrifice** on it your burnt offerings and fellowship offerings,
22: 20 [22:19] [A] "*Whoever* **sacrifices** to any god other than the
23: 18 [A] "*Do* not **offer** the blood of a sacrifice to me along with
24: 5 [A] **sacrificed** young bulls as fellowship offerings to the LORD.
32: 8 [A] have bowed down to it and **sacrificed** to it and have said,
34: 15 [A] prostitute themselves to their gods and **sacrifice** to them,
Lev 9: 4 [A] a ram for a fellowship offering to **sacrifice** before the
17: 5 [A] the sacrifices they *are now* **making** in the open fields.
17: 5 [A] Tent of Meeting and **sacrifice** them as fellowship offerings.
17: 7 [A] *They must* no longer **offer** any of their sacrifices to the goat
19: 5 [A] " 'When *you* **sacrifice** a fellowship offering to the LORD,
19: 5 [A] **sacrifice** it in such a way that it will be accepted on your
22: 29 [A] "When *you* **sacrifice** a thank offering to the LORD,
22: 29 [A] **sacrifice** it in such a way that it will be accepted on your
Nu 22: 40 [A] Balak **sacrificed** cattle and sheep, and gave some to Balaam
Dt 12: 15 [A] *you may* **slaughter** your animals in any of your towns
12: 21 [A] *you may* **slaughter** animals from the herds and flocks the
15: 21 [A] *you must* not **sacrifice** it to the LORD your God.
16: 2 [A] **Sacrifice** as the Passover to the LORD your God an animal
16: 4 [A] Do not let any of the meat *you* **sacrifice** on the evening of
16: 5 [A] You must not **sacrifice** the Passover in any town the LORD
16: 6 [A] There *you must* **sacrifice** the Passover in the evening,
17: 1 [A] *Do* not **sacrifice** to the LORD your God an ox or a sheep
18: 3 [A] due the priests from the people *who* **sacrifice** [+2285] a bull
27: 7 [A] **Sacrifice** fellowship offerings there, eating them
32: 17 [A] *They* **sacrificed** to demons, which are not God—gods they
33: 19 [A] to the mountain and there **offer** sacrifices of righteousness;
Jos 8: 31 [A] LORD burnt offerings and **sacrificed** fellowship offerings.
Jdg 2: 5 [A] place Bokim. There *they* **offered sacrifices** to the LORD.
16: 23 [A] Now the rulers of the Philistines assembled to **offer** a great
1Sa 1: 3 [A] to worship and **sacrifice** to the LORD Almighty at Shiloh,
1: 4 [A] Whenever the day came for Elkanah *to* **sacrifice**, he would
1: 21 [A] to **offer** the annual sacrifice to the LORD and to fulfill
2: 13 [A] with the people that whenever anyone **offered** a sacrifice
2: 15 [A] priest would come and say to the man who *was* **sacrificing**,
2: 19 [A] took it to him when she went up with her husband to **offer**
6: 15 [A] burnt offerings and **made sacrifices** [+2285] to the LORD.
10: 8 [A] to sacrifice burnt offerings and **[NIE]** fellowship offerings,
11: 15 [A] There *they* **sacrificed** fellowship offerings before the
15: 15 [A] of the sheep and cattle to **sacrifice** to the LORD your God,
15: 21 [A] in order to **sacrifice** them to the LORD your God at Gilgal."
16: 2 [A] with you and say, 'I have come to **sacrifice** to the LORD.'
16: 5 [A] "Yes, in peace; I have come to **sacrifice** to the LORD.
28: 24 [A] a fattened calf at the house, which *she* **butchered** at once.
2Sa 6: 13 [A] had taken six steps, *he* **sacrificed** a bull and a fattened calf.
15: 12 [A] While Absalom *was* **offering** sacrifices, he also sent for
1Ki 1: 9 [A] Adonijah then **sacrificed** sheep, cattle and fattened calves at
1: 19 [A] *He has* **sacrificed** great numbers of cattle, fattened calves,
1: 25 [A] he has gone down and **sacrificed** great numbers of cattle,
3: 2 [D] however, *were still* **sacrificing** at the high places,
3: 3 [D] except that he **offered sacrifices** and burned incense on the
3: 4 [A] The king went to Gibeon to **offer sacrifices**, for that was the
8: 5 [D] **sacrificing** so many sheep and cattle that they could not be
8: 62 [A] and all Israel with him **offered** sacrifices before the LORD.
8: 63 [A] Solomon **offered a sacrifice** of fellowship offerings to the
8: 63 [A] Solomon offered a sacrifice of fellowship offerings **[RPH]**
11: 8 [D] who burned incense and **offered sacrifices** to their gods.
12: 32 [D] This he did in Bethel, **sacrificing** to the calves he had made.
13: 2 [A] On you *he will* **sacrifice** the priests of the high places who
19: 21 [A] went back. He took his yoke of oxen and **slaughtered** them.
22: 43 [22:44] [D] the people continued *to* **offer sacrifices** and burn
2Ki 12: 3 [12:4] [D] the people continued *to* **offer sacrifices** and burn
14: 4 [D] the people continued *to* **offer sacrifices** and burn incense
15: 4 [D] the people continued *to* **offer sacrifices** and burn incense
15: 35 [D] the people continued *to* **offer sacrifices** and burn incense
16: 4 [D] *He* **offered sacrifices** and burned incense at the high places,
17: 35 [A] or bow down to them, serve them or **sacrifice** to them.
17: 36 [A] To him you shall bow down and to him **offer sacrifices**.
23: 20 [A] Josiah **slaughtered** all the priests of those high places on the
1Ch 15: 26 [A] of the LORD, seven bulls and seven rams *were* **sacrificed**.
21: 28 [A] floor of Araunah the Jebusite, *he* **offered sacrifices** there.
29: 21 [A] The next day *they* **made sacrifices** [+2285] to the LORD
2Ch 5: 6 [D] **sacrificing** so many sheep and cattle that they could not be
7: 4 [A] and all the people **offered** sacrifices before the LORD.
7: 5 [A] King Solomon **offered** a sacrifice of twenty-two thousand
11: 16 [A] followed the Levites to Jerusalem to **offer sacrifices** to the
15: 11 [A] At that time *they* **sacrificed** to the LORD seven hundred
18: 2 [A] Ahab **slaughtered** many sheep and cattle for him and the
28: 4 [D] *He* **offered sacrifices** and burned incense at the high places,
28: 23 [A] *He* **offered sacrifices** to the gods of Damascus, who had
28: 23 [D] helped them, *I will* **sacrifice** to them so they will help me."
30: 22 [D] and **offered** fellowship offerings and praised the LORD,
33: 16 [A] and **sacrificed** fellowship offerings and thank offerings on it,
33: 17 [A] however, continued *to* **sacrifice** at the high places,
33: 22 [D] and **offered sacrifices** to all the idols Manasseh had made.
34: 4 [A] scattered over the graves of those *who had* **sacrificed** to
Ezr 4: 2 [A] *have been* **sacrificing** to him since the time of Esarhaddon
Ne 4: 2 [3:34] [A] *Will they* **offer sacrifices**? Will they finish in a day?
12: 43 [A] on that day *they* **offered** great sacrifices, rejoicing
Ps 4: 5 [4:6] [A] **Offer** right sacrifices and trust in the LORD.
27: 6 [A] at his tabernacle *will I* **sacrifice** [+2285] *with* shouts of joy;
50: 14 [A] **Sacrifice** thank offerings to God, fulfill your vows to the
50: 23 [A] *He who* **sacrifices** thank offerings honors me, and he
54: 6 [54:8] [A] *I will* **sacrifice** a freewill offering to you; I will
106: 37 [A] *They* **sacrificed** their sons and their daughters to demons.
106: 38 [D] and daughters, whom *they* **sacrificed** to the idols of Canaan,
107: 22 [A] *Let them* **sacrifice** thank offerings and tell of his works with
116: 17 [A] *I will* **sacrifice** a thank offering to you and call on the name
Ecc 9: 2 [A] those *who* **offer sacrifices** and those who do not.
9: 2 [A] those who offer sacrifices and *those* who **do**[s] not.
Isa 57: 7 [A] and lofty hill; there you went up to **offer** your sacrifices.
65: 3 [A] **offering sacrifices** in gardens and burning incense on altars
66: 3 [A] *whoever* **offers** a lamb, like one who breaks a dog's neck;
Eze 16: 20 [A] you bore to me and **sacrificed** them as food to the idols.
20: 28 [A] high hill or any leafy tree, there *they* **offered** their sacrifices,
34: 3 [A] yourselves with the wool and **slaughter** the choice animals,
39: 17 [A] from all around to the sacrifice I *am* **preparing** for you,
39: 19 [A] At the sacrifice *I am* **preparing** for you, you will eat fat till
Hos 4: 13 [D] *They* **sacrifice** on the mountaintops and burn offerings on
4: 14 [D] consort with harlots and **sacrifice** with shrine prostitutes—
8: 13 [A] *They* **offer** sacrifices given to me and they eat the meat,
11: 2 [D] *They* **sacrificed** to the Baals and they burned incense to
12: 11 [12:12] [D] are worthless! *Do they* **sacrifice** bulls in Gilgal?
13: 2 [A] "*They* **offer** human **sacrifice** and kiss the calf-idols."
Jnh 1: 16 [A] *they* **offered** a sacrifice to the LORD and made vows to
2: 9 [2:10] [A] I, with a song of thanksgiving, *will* **sacrifice** to you.
Hab 1: 16 [D] Therefore *he* **sacrifices** to his net and burns incense to his
Zec 14: 21 [A] all who come to **sacrifice** will take some of the pots and cook
Mal 1: 8 [A] When you bring blind animals for **sacrifice**, is that not
1: 14 [A] to give it, but then **sacrifices** a blemished animal to the Lord.

2285 זֶבַח[1] *zebaḥ*[1], n.m. [162] [→ 2286; cf. 2284; Ar 10157]

sacrifices [57], sacrifice [47], offering [24], offerings [15], sacrificed [13], made sacrifices [+2284] [2], sacrifice [+2284] [2], feasting [1], it[s] [+8968] [1]

Ge 31: 54 He offered a **sacrifice** there in the hill country and invited his
46: 1 he offered **sacrifices** to the God of his father Isaac.
Ex 10: 25 "You must allow us to have **sacrifices** and burnt offerings to
12: 27 then tell them, 'It is the Passover **sacrifice** to the LORD,
18: 12 brought a burnt offering and other **sacrifices** to God,
23: 18 "Do not offer the blood of a **sacrifice** to me along with anything
24: 5 and sacrificed young bulls as fellowship **offerings** to the LORD.
29: 28 are to make to the LORD from their fellowship **offerings**.
34: 15 to them, they will invite you and you will eat their **sacrifices**.
34: 25 "Do not offer the blood of a **sacrifice** *to* me along with anything
34: 25 do not let any of the **sacrifice** *from* the Passover Feast remain until
Lev 3: 1 " 'If someone's offering is a fellowship **offering**, and he offers an
3: 3 From the fellowship **offering** he is to bring a sacrifice made to the
3: 6 " 'If he offers an animal from the flock as a fellowship **offering** to
3: 9 From the fellowship **offering** he is to bring a sacrifice made to the
4: 10 just as the fat is removed from the ox **sacrificed** *as* a fellowship
4: 26 the fat on the altar as he burned the fat of the fellowship **offering**.
4: 31 all the fat, just as the fat is removed from the fellowship **offering**,
4: 35 just as the fat is removed from the lamb of the fellowship **offering**,
7: 11 " 'These are the regulations for the fellowship **offering** a person
7: 12 along with this thank **offering** he is to offer cakes of bread made
7: 13 Along with his fellowship **offering** *of* thanksgiving he is to present
7: 15 The meat of his fellowship **offering** *of* thanksgiving must be eaten

Lev 7: 16 his offering is the result of a vow or is a freewill **offering**,
7: 16 the **sacrifice** shall be eaten on the day he offers it,
7: 17 Any meat of the **sacrifice** left over till the third day must be burned
7: 18 If any meat of the fellowship **offering** is eaten on the third day,
7: 20 if anyone who is unclean eats any meat of the fellowship **offering**
7: 21 eats any of the meat of the fellowship **offering** belonging to the
7: 29 'Anyone who brings a fellowship **offering** to the LORD is to
7: 29 is to bring part of **it**[s] [+8968] as his sacrifice to the LORD.
7: 32 You are to give the right thigh of your fellowship **offerings** to the
7: 34 From the fellowship **offerings** of the Israelites, I have taken the
7: 37 guilt offering, the ordination offering and the fellowship **offering**,
9: 18 the ox and the ram as the fellowship **offering** for the people.
10: 14 your children as your share of the Israelites' fellowship **offerings**.
17: 5 so the Israelites will bring to the LORD the **sacrifices** they are
17: 5 to the Tent of Meeting and sacrifice them as fellowship **offerings**.
17: 7 They must no longer offer any of their **sacrifices** to the goat idols
17: 8 alien living among them who offers a burnt offering or **sacrifice**
19: 5 " 'When you sacrifice a fellowship **offering** to the LORD,
19: 6 It shall be eaten on the day you **sacrifice** it or on the next day;
22: 21 or flock a fellowship **offering** to the LORD to fulfill a special
22: 29 "When you sacrifice a thank **offering** to the LORD, sacrifice it in
23: 19 and two lambs, each a year old, for a fellowship **offering**.
23: 37 **sacrifices** and drink offerings required for each day.
Nu 6: 17 and is to sacrifice the ram as a fellowship **offering** to the LORD,
6: 18 put it in the fire that is under the **sacrifice** *of* the fellowship
7: 17 male lambs a year old, to be **sacrificed** as a fellowship offering.
7: 23 male lambs a year old, to be **sacrificed** as a fellowship offering.
7: 29 male lambs a year old, to be **sacrificed** as a fellowship offering.
7: 35 male lambs a year old, to be **sacrificed** as a fellowship offering.
7: 41 male lambs a year old, to be **sacrificed** as a fellowship offering.
7: 47 male lambs a year old, to be **sacrificed** as a fellowship offering.
7: 53 male lambs a year old, to be **sacrificed** as a fellowship offering.
7: 59 male lambs a year old, to be **sacrificed** as a fellowship offering.
7: 65 male lambs a year old, to be **sacrificed** as a fellowship offering.
7: 71 male lambs a year old, to be **sacrificed** as a fellowship offering.
7: 77 male lambs a year old, to be **sacrificed** as a fellowship offering.
7: 83 male lambs a year old, to be **sacrificed** as a fellowship offering.
7: 88 The total number of animals for the **sacrifice** *of* the fellowship
10: 10 the trumpets over your burnt offerings and fellowship **offerings**,
15: 3 whether burnt offerings or **sacrifices**, for special vows or freewill
15: 5 With each lamb for the burnt offering or the **sacrifice**, prepare a
15: 8 " 'When you prepare a young bull as a burnt offering or **sacrifice**,
25: 2 who invited them to the **sacrifices** *to* their gods. The people ate
Dt 12: 6 there bring your burnt offerings and **sacrifices**, your tithes
12: 11 your burnt offerings and **sacrifices**, your tithes and special gifts,
12: 27 The blood of your **sacrifices** must be poured beside the altar of the
18: 3 share due the priests from the people *who* **sacrifice** [+2284] a bull
32: 38 the gods who ate the fat of their **sacrifices** and drank the wine of
33: 19 peoples to the mountain and there offer **sacrifices** *of* righteousness;
Jos 22: 23 and grain offerings, or to sacrifice fellowship **offerings** on it,
22: 26 and build an altar—but not for burnt offerings or **sacrifices**.'
22: 27 with our burnt offerings, **sacrifices** and fellowship offerings.
22: 28 which our fathers built, not for burnt offerings and **sacrifices**,
22: 29 building an altar for burnt offerings, grain offerings and **sacrifices**,
Jdg 16: 23 Philistines assembled to offer a great **sacrifice** to Dagon their god
1Sa 1: 21 up with all his family to offer the annual **sacrifice** to the LORD
2: 13 priests with the people that whenever anyone offered a **sacrifice**
2: 19 when she went up with her husband to offer the annual **sacrifice**.
2: 29 Why do you scorn my **sacrifice** and offering that I prescribed for
3: 14 'The guilt of Eli's house will never be atoned for by **sacrifice**
6: 15 burnt offerings and **made sacrifices** [+2284] to the LORD.
9: 12 to our town today, for the people have a **sacrifice** at the high place.
9: 13 begin eating until he comes, because he must bless the **sacrifice**;
10: 8 down to you to sacrifice burnt offerings and fellowship **offerings**,
11: 15 There they sacrificed fellowship **offerings** before the LORD,
15: 22 and **sacrifices** as much as in obeying the voice of the LORD?
15: 22 To obey is better than **sacrifice**, and to heed is better than the fat of
16: 3 Invite Jesse to the **sacrifice**, and I will show you what to do.
16: 5 Consecrate yourselves and come to the **sacrifice** with me."
16: 5 he consecrated Jesse and his sons and invited them to the **sacrifice**.
20: 6 because an annual **sacrifice** is being made there for his whole clan.'
20: 29 because our family is observing a **sacrifice** in the town and my
2Sa 15: 12 While Absalom was offering **sacrifices**, he also sent for
1Ki 8: 62 and all Israel with him offered **sacrifices** before the LORD.
8: 63 Solomon offered a sacrifice of fellowship **offerings** to the LORD:
12: 27 If these people go up to offer **sacrifices** at the temple of the
2Ki 5: 17 burnt offerings and **sacrifices** to any other god but the LORD.
10: 19 is missing, because I am going to hold a great **sacrifice** for Baal.
10: 24 So they went in to make **sacrifices** and burnt offerings. Now Jehu
16: 15 on the altar all the blood of the burnt offerings and **sacrifices**.
1Ch 29: 21 The next day *they* **made sacrifices** [+2284] to the LORD
29: 21 drink offerings, and other **sacrifices** in abundance for all Israel.
2Ch 7: 1 from heaven and consumed the burnt offering and the **sacrifices**,
7: 4 the king and all the people offered **sacrifices** before the LORD.
7: 5 King Solomon offered a **sacrifice** *of* twenty-two thousand head of
7: 12 and have chosen this place for myself as a temple for **sacrifices**.
29: 31 Come and bring **sacrifices** and thank offerings to the temple of the
29: 31 So the assembly brought **sacrifices** and thank offerings, and all
30: 22 and offered fellowship **offerings** and praised the LORD,
33: 16 and sacrificed fellowship **offerings** and thank offerings on it,
Ne 12: 43 on that day they offered great **sacrifices**, rejoicing because God
Ps 4: 5 [4:6] Offer right **sacrifices** and trust in the LORD.
27: 6 at his tabernacle *will I* **sacrifice with** [+2284] shouts of joy;
40: 6 [40:7] **Sacrifice** and offering you did not desire, but my ears you
50: 5 my consecrated ones, who made a covenant with me by **sacrifice**."
50: 8 I do not rebuke you for your **sacrifices** or your burnt offerings,
51: 16 [51:18] You do not delight in **sacrifice**, or I would bring it;
51: 17 [51:19] The **sacrifices** *of* God are a broken spirit; a broken
51: 19 [51:21] there will be righteous **sacrifices**, whole burnt offerings to
106: 28 to the Baal of Peor and ate **sacrifices** *offered to* lifeless gods;
107: 22 Let them sacrifice thank **offerings** and tell of his works with songs
116: 17 I will sacrifice a thank **offering** to you and call on the name of the
Pr 7: 14 "I have fellowship **offerings** at home; today I fulfilled my vows.
15: 8 The LORD detests the **sacrifice** *of* the wicked, but the prayer of
17: 1 a dry crust with peace and quiet than a house full of **feasting**,
21: 3 is right and just is more acceptable to the LORD than **sacrifice**.
21: 27 The **sacrifice** *of* the wicked is detestable—how much more
Ecc 5: 1 [4:17] Go near to listen rather than to offer the **sacrifice** of fools,
Isa 1: 11 "The multitude of your **sacrifices**—what are they to me?"
19: 21 They will worship with **sacrifices** and grain offerings; they will
34: 6 For the LORD has a **sacrifice** in Bozrah and a great slaughter in
43: 23 me sheep for burnt offerings, nor honored me with your **sacrifices**.
43: 24 calamus for me, or lavished on me the fat of your **sacrifices**.
56: 7 Their burnt offerings and **sacrifices** will be accepted on my altar;
57: 7 on a high and lofty hill; there you went up to offer your **sacrifices**.
Jer 6: 20 offerings are not acceptable; your **sacrifices** do not please me."
7: 21 add your burnt offerings to your other **sacrifices** and eat the meat
7: 22 not just give them commands about burnt offerings and **sacrifices**,
17: 26 hill country and the Negev, bringing burnt offerings and **sacrifices**,
33: 18 burnt offerings, to burn grain offerings and to present **sacrifices**.' "
46: 10 will offer **sacrifice** in the land of the north by the River Euphrates.
Eze 20: 28 any high hill or any leafy tree, there they offered their **sacrifices**,
39: 17 come together from all around to the **sacrifice** I am preparing for
39: 17 preparing for you, the great **sacrifice** on the mountains of Israel.
39: 19 At the **sacrifice** I am preparing for you, you will eat fat till you are
40: 42 for slaughtering the burnt offerings and the other **sacrifices**.
44: 11 **sacrifices** for the people and stand before the people and serve
46: 24 who minister at the temple will cook the **sacrifices** *of* the people."
Da 9: 27 In the middle of the 'seven' he will put an end to **sacrifice**
Hos 3: 4 days without king or prince, without **sacrifice** or sacred stones,
4: 19 will sweep them away, and their **sacrifices** will bring them shame.
6: 6 For I desire mercy, not **sacrifice**, and acknowledgment of God
8: 13 They offer **sacrifices** given to me and they eat the meat,
9: 4 wine offerings to the LORD, nor will their **sacrifices** please him.
Am 4: 4 Bring your **sacrifices** every morning, your tithes every three years.
5: 25 "Did you bring me **sacrifices** and offerings forty years in the
Jnh 1: 16 and they offered a **sacrifice** to the LORD and made vows to him.
Zep 1: 7 The LORD has prepared a **sacrifice**; he has consecrated those he
1: 8 On the day of the LORD's **sacrifice** I will punish the princes

2286 ²זֶבַח *zebaḥ²*, n.pr.m. [12] [√ 2285; cf. 2284]

Zebah [10], them[s] [+2256+7518] [2]

Jdg 8: 5 they are worn out, and I am still pursuing **Zebah** and Zalmunna,
8: 6 "Do you already have the hands of **Zebah** and Zalmunna in your
8: 7 when the LORD has given **Zebah** and Zalmunna into my hand,
8: 10 Now **Zebah** and Zalmunna were in Karkor with a force of about
8: 12 **Zebah** and Zalmunna, the two kings of Midian, fled, but he
8: 12 fled, but he pursued them and captured **them**[s] [+2256+7518],
8: 15 and said to the men of Succoth, "Here are **Zebah** and Zalmunna,
8: 15 'Do you already have the hands of **Zebah** and Zalmunna in your
8: 18 he asked **Zebah** and Zalmunna, "What kind of men did you kill at
8: 21 **Zebah** and Zalmunna said, "Come, do it yourself. 'As is the man,
8: 21 So Gideon stepped forward and killed **them**[s] [+2256+7518],
Ps 83: 11 [83:12] and Zeeb, all their princes like **Zebah** and Zalmunna,

2287 זַבַּי *zabbay*, n.pr.m. [2]

Zabbai [2]

Ezr 10: 28 descendants of Bebai: Jehohanan, Hananiah, **Zabbai** and Athlai.
Ne 3: 20 Baruch son of **Zabbai** [Q 2347] zealously repaired another

2288 זְבִידָה *zᵉbîdâ*, n.pr.f. [1] [√ 2272; cf. 2281]

Zebidah [1]

2Ki 23: 36 His mother's name was **Zebidah** [Q 2281] daughter of Pedaiah;

2289 זְבִינָא zᵉbînāʾ, n.pr.m. [1]

Zebina [1]

Ezr 10:43 Jeiel, Mattithiah, Zabad, **Zebina**, Jaddai, Joel and Benaiah.

2290 זָבַל zābal, v. [1] [cf. 2292, 6022]

treat with honor [1]

Ge 30:20 [A] This time my husband *will* **treat** me **with honor**, because I

2291 ¹זְבֻל zᵉbul¹, n.pr.m. [6] [√ 2292]

Zebul [6]

Jdg 9:28 Isn't he Jerub-Baal's son, and isn't **Zebul** his deputy? Serve the
9:30 When **Zebul** the governor of the city heard what Gaal son of Ebed
9:36 When Gaal saw them, he said to **Zebul**, "Look, people are coming
9:36 **Zebul** replied, "You mistake the shadows of the mountains for
9:38 **Zebul** said to him, "Where is your big talk now, you who said,
9:41 and **Zebul** drove Gaal and his brothers out of Shechem.

2292 ²זְבֻל zᵉbul², n.[m.]. [5] [→ 374?, 2282, 2290, 2291]

magnificent [2], heavens [1], lofty throne [1], princely mansions [1]

1Ki 8:13 I have indeed built a **magnificent** temple for you, a place for you
2Ch 6:2 I have built a **magnificent** temple for you, a place for you to dwell
Ps 49:14 [49:15] will decay in the grave, far from their **princely mansions**.
Isa 63:15 Look down from heaven and see from your **lofty throne**, holy
Hab 3:11 moon stood still in the **heavens** at the glint of your flying arrows,

2293 זָג zāg, n.[m.]. [1] [cf. 2423]

skins [1]

Nu 6:4 that comes from the grapevine, not even the seeds or **skins**.

2294 זֵד zēd, a. [13] [→ 2295; cf. 2326]

arrogant [10], haughty [1], proud [1], willful sins [1]

Ps 19:13 [19:14] Keep your servant also from **willful sins**; may they not
86:14 The **arrogant** are attacking me, O God; a band of ruthless men
119:21 You rebuke the **arrogant**, who are cursed and who stray from your
119:51 The **arrogant** mock me without restraint, but I do not turn from
119:69 Though the **arrogant** have smeared me with lies, I keep your
119:78 May the **arrogant** be put to shame for wronging me without cause;
119:85 The **arrogant** dig pitfalls for me, contrary to your law.
119:122 Ensure your servant's well-being; let not the **arrogant** oppress me.
Pr 21:24 The **proud** and arrogant man—"Mocker" is his name; he behaves
Isa 13:11 I will put an end to the arrogance of the **haughty** and will humble
Jer 43:2 Johanan son of Kareah and all the **arrogant** men said to Jeremiah,
Mal 3:15 now we call the **arrogant** blessed. Certainly the evildoers prosper,
4:1 [3:19] All the **arrogant** and every evildoer will be stubble,

2295 זָדוֹן zādôn, n.m. [11] [√ 2294]

pride [4], arrogant [2], arrogance [1], conceited [1], contempt [1], overweening pride [+6301] [1], presumptuously [+928] [1]

Dt 17:12 The man who shows **contempt** for the judge or for the priest who
18:22 That prophet has spoken **presumptuously** [+928]. Do not be afraid
1Sa 17:28 I know how **conceited** you are and how wicked your heart is;
Pr 11:2 When **pride** comes, then comes disgrace, but with humility comes
13:10 **Pride** only breeds quarrels, but wisdom is found in those who take
21:24 is his name; he behaves with **overweening pride** [+6301].
Jer 49:16 terror you inspire and the **pride** *of* your heart have deceived you,
50:31 "See, I am against you, O **arrogant** *one*," declares the Lord,
50:32 The **arrogant** *one* will stumble and fall and no one will help her
Eze 7:10 has burst forth, the rod has budded, **arrogance** has blossomed!
Ob 1:3 The **pride** *of* your heart has deceived you, you who live in the

2296 זֶה zeh, p.demo. & adv. [1781 / 1782] [→ 2271, 2297, 2305, 2306, 4208, 4643, 4644; cf. 2306] Not indexed

this [1082], *untranslated* [143], these [109], that [49], this[s] [+1821 +2021+2021] [44], today [+2021+2021+3427] [39], here [17], now [+2021+2021+3427] [17], one [17], such [16], it [13], here [+928] [12], on both sides [+2256+2296+4946+4946] [12], he [9], where [+361] [9], another[s] [7], this is how [+928] [6], this very [6], other[s] [5], what [5], at either end[s] [+2256+2296+4946+4946] [4], it[s] [+1821 +2021+2021] [4], side[s] [4], the other[s] [4], the [4], ever since [+2021+2021+3427+6330] [3], now [3], really [3], same [3], so [+6584] [3], such [+3869] [3], that same [3], thing[s] [3], those [3], very [3], what [+1821+2021+2021] [3], what [+361] [3], another messenger[s] [2], bordering each side[s] [+2256+2296+4946+4946] [2], here[s] [+2021+2021+5226] [2], here is what [+2256+2296+3869 +3869] [2], how [2], man[s] [2], on both [+2256+2296+4946+4946] [2], on both sides[s] [+2256+2296+4946] [2], on each side [+2021+2021 +2296+4946+4946+4946+4946+6298+6298] [2], on each side[s] [+2256+2296+4946+4946] [2], over a year [+196+2296+3427+9102] [2], she [2], so [+3869] [2], still [+2021+2021+3427+6330] [2], them [2], there [2], therefore [+6584] [2], this is how [2], what [+2256+2296 +3869+3869] [2], which [+361] [2], which [2], who [2], all at once [+2180] [1], an [1], another[s] [+2021+2215+4946] [1], another messenger [1], back[s] [1], by what [+361] [1], except for [1], from [+4946] [1], front[s] [1], he's [1], her [1], here[s] [+928+2021+2021+5226] [1], how [+4537] [1], in broad daylight [+2021+2021+4200 +6524+9087] [1], inclined [+2118] [1], it[s] [+2021+2021+6551] [1], it[s] [+2021+2021+8878] [1], it[s] [+824+2021+2021] [1], its[s] [1], just [+6964] [1], lasting [+2021+2021+3427+6330] [1], later [+339] [1], Leah[s] [1], long[s] for [1], neither [+4202] [1], now [+3954] [1], now [+6964] [1], of what use [+4200+4537] [1], on the condition that [+928] [1], once [1], one condition[s] [1], right where [1], same[s] amount [1], so [1], still [+2021+2021+3427+3869] [1], such [+1524] [1], such offerings[s] [1], such questions[s] [1], suggested [+1821+2021+2021] [1], that[s] [+1074+2021+2021] [1], that's [1], the condition[s] [1], the first[s] one [1], the younger[s] one [1], the[s] [1], them[s] [+1821+2021+2021] [1], them[s] [+2021+2021+6639] [1], then [+928] [1], then [1], this [+1821+2021] [1], this[s] [+2021+2021+5126] [1], this fellow's[s] [+4200] [1], this is what [1], today [+3427] [1], what[s] [+2021+2021+5184] [1], what[s] [+2256+2297+3869+3869] [1], what [+4769] [1], what do I care about [+3276+4200+4200+4537] [1], which way [+361] [1], which way [+361+2006+2021] [1], whom [1], why [+361+4200] [1], why [+6584] [1], woman [1], you[s] [1]

2297 זֹה zōh, p.demo. & adv. [11] [→ 2305; cf. 2296; Ar 10154] Not indexed

this [6], *untranslated* [2], one [1], such [+3869] [1], what [+2256+2296+3869+3869] [1]

2298 זָהָב zāhāb, n.m. [389] [→ 4771; cf. 7410; Ar 10160]

gold [367], golden [9], *untranslated* [7], pure gold [+2298] [4], alternate[s] [+2256+7194+8232] [1], nuggets of gold [1]

Ge 2:11 it winds through the entire land of Havilah, where there is **gold**.
2:12 (The **gold** *of* that land is good; aromatic resin and onyx are also
13:2 had become very wealthy in livestock and in silver and **gold**.
24:22 the man took out a **gold** nose ring weighing a beka and two gold
24:22 ring weighing a beka and two **gold** bracelets weighing ten shekels.
24:35 He has given him sheep and cattle, silver and **gold**, menservants
24:53 the servant brought out **gold** and silver jewelry and articles of
41:42 him in robes of fine linen and put a **gold** chain around his neck.
44:8 So why would we steal silver or **gold** from your master's house?
Ex 3:22 living in her house for articles of silver and **gold** and for clothing,
11:2 alike are to ask their neighbors for articles of silver and **gold**."
12:35 asked the Egyptians for articles of silver and **gold** and for clothing.
20:23 do not make for yourselves gods of silver or gods of **gold**.
25:3 the offerings you are to receive from them: **gold**, silver and bronze;
25:11 Overlay it with pure **gold**, both inside and out, and make a gold
25:11 pure gold, both inside and out, and make a **gold** molding around it.
25:12 Cast four **gold** rings for it and fasten them to its four feet, with two
25:13 Then make poles of acacia wood and overlay them with **gold**.
25:17 "Make an atonement cover of pure **gold**—two and a half cubits
25:18 make two cherubim out of hammered **gold** at the ends of the cover.
25:24 Overlay it with pure **gold** and make a gold molding around it.
25:24 Overlay it with pure gold and make a **gold** molding around it.
25:25 it a rim a handbreadth wide and put a **gold** molding on the rim.
25:26 Make four **gold** rings for the table and fasten them to the four
25:28 acacia wood, overlay them with **gold** and carry the table with them.
25:29 And make its plates and dishes of pure **gold**, as well as its pitchers
25:31 "Make a lampstand of pure **gold** and hammer it out, base and shaft;
25:36 all be of one piece with the lampstand, hammered out of pure **gold**.
25:38 Its wick trimmers and trays are to be of pure **gold**.
25:39 A talent of pure **gold** is to be used for the lampstand and all these
26:6 make fifty **gold** clasps and use them to fasten the curtains together
26:29 Overlay the frames with **gold** and make gold rings to hold the
26:29 the frames with gold and make **gold** rings to hold the crossbars.
26:29 rings to hold the crossbars. Also overlay the crossbars with **gold**.
26:32 Hang it with **gold** hooks on four posts of acacia wood overlaid
26:32 it with gold hooks on four posts of acacia wood overlaid with **gold**
26:37 Make **gold** hooks for this curtain and five posts of acacia wood
26:37 for this curtain and five posts of acacia wood overlaid with **gold**.
28:5 Have them use **gold**, and blue, purple and scarlet yarn, and fine
28:6 "Make the ephod of **gold**, and of blue, purple and scarlet yarn,
28:8 of one piece with the ephod and made with **gold**, and with blue,
28:11 engraves a seal. Then mount the stones in **gold** filigree settings
28:13 Make **gold** filigree settings
28:14 two braided chains of pure **gold**, like a rope, and attach the chains
28:15 of **gold**, and of blue, purple and scarlet yarn, and of finely twisted
28:20 an onyx and a jasper. Mount them in **gold** filigree settings.
28:22 "For the breastpiece make braided chains of pure **gold**, like a rope.
28:23 Make two **gold** rings for it and fasten them to two corners of the
28:24 Fasten the two **gold** chains to the rings at the corners of the

Ex 28:26 Make two **gold** rings and attach them to the other two corners of
28:27 Make two more **gold** rings and attach them to the bottom of the
28:33 yarn around the hem of the robe, with **gold** bells between them.
28:34 The **gold** bells and the pomegranates are to alternate around the
28:34 and the pomegranates *are to* **alternate** [+2256+7194+8232]
28:36 "Make a plate of pure **gold** and engrave on it as on a seal:
30: 3 Overlay the top and all the sides and the horns with pure **gold**,
30: 3 and the horns with pure gold, and make a **gold** molding around it.
30: 4 Make two **gold** rings for the altar below the molding—two on
30: 5 Make the poles of acacia wood and overlay them with **gold**.
31: 4 to make artistic designs for work in **gold**, silver and bronze,
32: 2 "Take off the **gold** earrings that your wives, your sons and your
32: 3 people took off their earrings **[RPH]** and brought them to Aaron.
32:24 So I told them, 'Whoever has any **gold** jewelry, take it off.'
32:31 people have committed! They have made themselves gods of **gold**.
35: 5 who is willing is to bring to the LORD an offering of **gold**,
35:22 and women alike, came and brought **gold** jewelry of all kinds:
35:22 They all presented their **gold** as a wave offering to the LORD.
35:32 to make artistic designs for work in **gold**, silver and bronze,
36:13 they made fifty **gold** clasps and used them to fasten the two sets of
36:34 They overlaid the frames with **gold** and made gold rings to hold
36:34 the frames with gold and made **gold** rings to hold the crossbars.
36:34 to hold the crossbars. They also overlaid the crossbars with **gold**.
36:36 made four posts of acacia wood for it and overlaid them with **gold**.
36:36 They made **gold** hooks for them and cast their four silver bases.
36:38 They overlaid the tops of the posts and their bands with **gold**
37: 2 He overlaid it with pure **gold**, both inside and out, and made a gold
37: 2 pure gold, both inside and out, and made a **gold** molding around it.
37: 3 He cast four **gold** rings for it and fastened them to its four feet,
37: 4 Then he made poles of acacia wood and overlaid them with **gold**.
37: 6 He made the atonement cover of pure **gold**—two and a half cubits
37: 7 he made two cherubim out of hammered **gold** at the ends of the
37:11 they overlaid it with pure **gold** and made a gold molding around it.
37:11 they overlaid it with pure gold and made a **gold** molding around it.
37:12 it a rim a handbreadth wide and put a **gold** molding on the rim.
37:13 They cast four **gold** rings for the table and fastened them to the
37:15 the table were made of acacia wood and were overlaid with **gold**.
37:16 And they made from pure **gold** the articles for the table—its plates
37:17 They made the lampstand of pure **gold** and hammered it out,
37:22 all of one piece with the lampstand, hammered out of pure **gold**.
37:23 seven lamps, as well as its wick trimmers and trays, of pure **gold**.
37:24 the lampstand and all its accessories from one talent of pure **gold**.
37:26 overlaid the top and all the sides and the horns with pure **gold**,
37:26 and the horns with pure gold, and made a **gold** molding around it.
37:27 They made two **gold** rings below the molding—two on opposite
37:28 They made the poles of acacia wood and overlaid them with **gold**.
38:24 The total amount of the **gold** *from* the wave offering used for all
38:24 The total amount of the gold from **[RPH]** the wave offering used
39: 2 They made the ephod of **gold**, and of blue, purple and scarlet yarn,
39: 3 They hammered out thin sheets of **gold** and cut strands to be
39: 5 of one piece with the ephod and made with **gold**, and with blue,
39: 6 They mounted the onyx stones in **gold** filigree settings
39: 8 of **gold**, and of blue, purple and scarlet yarn, and of finely twisted
39:13 and a jasper. They were mounted in **gold** filigree settings.
39:15 For the breastpiece they made braided chains of pure **gold**,
39:16 They made two **gold** filigree settings and two gold rings,
39:16 They made two gold filigree settings and two **gold** rings,
39:17 They fastened the two **gold** chains to the rings at the corners of the
39:19 They made two **gold** rings and attached them to the other two
39:20 they made two more **gold** rings and attached them to the bottom of
39:25 they made bells of pure **gold** and attached them around the hem
39:30 the plate, the sacred diadem, out of pure **gold** and engraved on it,
39:38 the **gold** altar, the anointing oil, the fragrant incense, and the
40: 5 Place the **gold** altar of incense in front of the ark of the Testimony
40:26 Moses placed the **gold** altar in the Tent of Meeting in front of the
Lev 8: 9 Then he placed the turban on Aaron's head and set the **gold** plate,
Nu 4:11 "Over the **gold** altar they are to spread a blue cloth and cover that
7:14 one **gold** dish weighing ten shekels, filled with incense;
7:20 one **gold** dish weighing ten shekels, filled with incense;
7:26 one **gold** dish weighing ten shekels, filled with incense;
7:32 one **gold** dish weighing ten shekels, filled with incense;
7:38 one **gold** dish weighing ten shekels, filled with incense;
7:44 one **gold** dish weighing ten shekels, filled with incense;
7:50 one **gold** dish weighing ten shekels, filled with incense;
7:56 one **gold** dish weighing ten shekels, filled with incense;
7:62 one **gold** dish weighing ten shekels, filled with incense;
7:68 one **gold** dish weighing ten shekels, filled with incense;
7:74 one **gold** dish weighing ten shekels, filled with incense;
7:80 one **gold** dish weighing ten shekels, filled with incense;
7:84 twelve silver sprinkling bowls and twelve **gold** dishes.
7:86 The twelve **gold** dishes filled with incense weighed ten shekels
7:86 Altogether, the **gold** dishes weighed a hundred and twenty shekels.
8: 4 It was made of hammered **gold**—from its base to its blossoms.
22:18 "Even if Balak gave me his palace filled with silver and **gold**,
24:13 'Even if Balak gave me his palace filled with silver and **gold**,
31:22 **Gold**, silver, bronze, iron, tin, lead
31:50 So we have brought as an offering to the LORD the **gold** articles
31:51 Moses and Eleazar the priest accepted from them the **gold**—
31:52 All the **gold** from the commanders of thousands and commanders
31:54 Eleazar the priest accepted the **gold** from the commanders of
Dt 7:25 Do not covet the silver and **gold** on them, and do not take it for
8:13 your herds and flocks grow large and your silver and **gold** increase
17:17 He must not accumulate large amounts of silver and **gold**.
29:17 [29:16] and idols of wood and stone, of silver and **gold**.
Jos 6:19 All the silver and **gold** and the articles of bronze and iron are
6:24 they put the silver and **gold** and the articles of bronze and iron into
7:21 shekels of silver and a wedge of **gold** weighing fifty shekels,
7:24 the robe, the **gold** wedge, his sons and daughters, his cattle,
22: 8 with large herds of livestock, with silver, **gold**, bronze and iron,
Jdg 8:24 (It was the custom of the Ishmaelites to wear **gold** earrings.)
8:26 The weight of the **gold** rings he asked for came to seventeen
8:26 **[RPH]** not counting the ornaments, the pendants and the purple
1Sa 6: 4 They replied, "Five **gold** tumors and five gold rats, according to
6: 4 They replied, "Five gold tumors and five **gold** rats, according to
6: 8 in a chest beside it put the **gold** objects you are sending back to
6:11 along with it the chest containing the **gold** rats and the models of
6:15 together with the chest containing the **gold** objects, and placed
6:17 These are the **gold** tumors the Philistines sent as a guilt offering to
6:18 the number of the **gold** rats was according to the number of
2Sa 1:24 and finery, who adorned your garments with ornaments of **gold**.
8: 7 David took the **gold** shields that belonged to the officers of
8:10 Joram brought with him articles of silver and **gold** and bronze.
8:11 done with the silver and **gold** from all the nations he had subdued:
12:30 its weight was a talent of **gold**, and it was set with precious
21: 4 have no right to demand silver or **gold** from Saul or his family,
1Ki 6:20 He overlaid the inside with pure **gold**, and he also overlaid the altar
6:21 Solomon covered the inside of the temple with pure **gold**,
6:21 and he extended **gold** chains across the front of the inner sanctuary,
6:21 the front of the inner sanctuary, which was overlaid with **gold**.
6:22 So he overlaid the whole interior with **gold**. He also overlaid with
6:22 He also overlaid with **gold** the altar that belonged to the inner
6:28 He overlaid the cherubim with **gold**.
6:30 floors of both the inner and outer rooms of the temple with **gold**.
6:32 and overlaid the cherubim and palm trees with beaten **gold**.
6:32 overlaid the cherubim and palm trees with beaten gold. **[RPH]**
6:35 and overlaid them with **gold** hammered evenly over the carvings.
7:48 the **golden** altar; the golden table on which was the bread of the
7:48 the **golden** table on which was the bread of the Presence;
7:49 the lampstands of pure **gold** (five on the right and five on the left,
7:49 of the inner sanctuary); the **gold** floral work and lamps and tongs;
7:50 the pure **gold** basins, wick trimmers, sprinkling bowls, dishes
7:50 the **gold** sockets for the doors of the innermost room, the Most
7:51 David had dedicated—the silver and **gold** and the furnishings—
9:11 had supplied him with all the cedar and pine and **gold** he wanted.
9:14 Now Hiram had sent to the king 120 talents of **gold**.
9:28 They sailed to Ophir and brought back 420 talents of **gold**,
10: 2 carrying spices, large quantities of **gold**, and precious stones—
10:10 she gave the king 120 talents of **gold**, large quantities of spices,
10:11 (Hiram's ships brought **gold** from Ophir; and from there they
10:14 The weight of the **gold** that Solomon received yearly was 666
10:14 of the gold that Solomon received yearly was 666 talents, **[RPH]**
10:16 King Solomon made two hundred large shields of hammered **gold**;
10:16 hammered gold; six hundred bekas of **gold** went into each shield.
10:17 He also made three hundred small shields of hammered **gold**,
10:17 shields of hammered gold, with three minas of **gold** in each shield.
10:18 made a great throne inlaid with ivory and overlaid with fine **gold**.
10:21 All King Solomon's goblets were **gold**, and all the household
10:21 articles in the Palace of the Forest of Lebanon were pure **gold**.
10:22 it returned, carrying **gold**, silver and ivory, and apes and baboons.
10:25 articles of silver and **gold**, robes, weapons and spices, and horses
12:28 After seeking advice, the king made two **golden** calves. He said to
14:26 took everything, including all the **gold** shields Solomon had made.
15:15 and **gold** and the articles that he and his father had dedicated.
15:18 and **gold** that was left in the treasuries of the LORD's temple
15:19 and your father. See, I am sending you a gift of silver and **gold**.
20: 3 'Your silver and **gold** are mine, and the best of your wives
20: 5 'I sent to demand your silver and **gold**, your wives and your
20: 7 he sent for my wives and my children, my silver and my **gold**,
22:48 [22:49] built a fleet of trading ships to go to Ophir for **gold**,
2Ki 5: 5 of silver, six thousand shekels of **gold** and ten sets of clothing.
7: 8 carried away silver, **gold** and clothes, and went off and hid them.
10:29 to commit—the worship of the **golden** calves at Bethel and Dan.
12:13 [12:14] trumpets or any other articles of **gold** or silver for the
12:18 [12:19] all the **gold** found in the treasuries of the temple of the
14:14 He took all the **gold** and silver and all the articles found in the
16: 8 Ahaz took the silver and **gold** found in the temple of the LORD
18:14 of Judah three hundred talents of silver and thirty talents of **gold**.
20:13 the silver, the **gold**, the spices and the fine oil—his armory

2Ki 23:33 on Judah a levy of a hundred talents of silver and a talent of **gold**.
23:35 Jehoiakim paid Pharaoh Neco the silver and **gold** he demanded.
23:35 **gold** from the people of the land according to their assessments.
24:13 took away all the **gold** articles that Solomon king of Israel had
25:15 all that were made of **pure gold** [+2298] or silver.
25:15 all that were made of **pure gold** [+2298] or silver.
1Ch 18: 7 David took the **gold** shields carried by the officers of Hadadezer
18:10 Hadoram brought all kinds of articles of **gold** and silver
18:11 done with the silver and **gold** he had taken from all these nations:
20: 2 its weight was found to be a talent of **gold**, and it was set with
21:25 So David paid Araunah six hundred shekels of **gold** for the site.
22:14 for the temple of the LORD a hundred thousand talents of **gold**,
22:16 in **gold** and silver, bronze and iron—craftsmen beyond number.
28:14 He designated the weight of **gold** for all the gold articles to be used
28:14 He designated the weight of gold for all the **gold** articles to be used
28:15 the weight of **gold** for the gold lampstands and their lamps,
28:15 the weight of gold for the **gold** lampstands and their lamps,
28:16 the weight of **gold** for each table for consecrated bread; the weight
28:17 the weight of pure **gold** for the forks, sprinkling bowls
28:17 and pitchers; the weight of **gold** for each gold dish;
28:18 and the weight of the refined **gold** for the altar of incense.
28:18 the cherubim of **gold** that spread their wings and shelter the ark of
29: 2 **gold** for the gold work, silver for the silver, bronze for the bronze,
29: 2 gold for the **gold** *work*, silver for the silver, bronze for the bronze,
29: 3 to the temple of my God I now give my personal treasures of **gold**
29: 4 three thousand talents of **gold** (gold of Ophir) and seven thousand
29: 4 three thousand talents of gold (**gold** *of* Ophir) and seven thousand
29: 5 for the **gold** *work* and the silver work, and for all the work to be
29: 5 for the gold work **[RPH]** and the silver work, and for all the work
29: 7 of God five thousand talents and ten thousand darics of **gold**,
2Ch 1:15 The king made silver and **gold** as common in Jerusalem as stones,
2: 7 [2:6] a man skilled to work in **gold** and silver, bronze and iron,
2:14 [2:13] He is trained to work in **gold** and silver, bronze and iron,
3: 4 and twenty cubits high. He overlaid the inside with pure **gold**.
3: 5 and covered it with fine **gold** and decorated it with palm tree
3: 6 with precious stones. And the **gold** he used was gold of Parvaim.
3: 6 with precious stones. And the gold he used was **gold** *of* Parvaim.
3: 7 doorframes, walls and doors of the temple with **gold**,
3: 8 He overlaid the inside with six hundred talents of fine **gold**.
3: 9 The **gold** nails weighed fifty shekels. He also overlaid the upper
3: 9 weighed fifty shekels. He also overlaid the upper parts with **gold**.
3:10 made a pair of sculptured cherubim and overlaid them with **gold**.
4: 7 He made ten **gold** lampstands according to the specifications for
4: 8 five on the north. He also made a hundred **gold** sprinkling bowls.
4:19 the **golden** altar; the tables on which was the bread of the Presence;
4:20 the lampstands of pure **gold** with their lamps, to burn in front of
4:21 the **gold** floral work and lamps and tongs (they were solid gold);
4:21 the gold floral work and lamps and tongs (they were solid **gold**);
4:22 the pure **gold** wick trimmers, sprinkling bowls, dishes and censers;
4:22 dishes and censers; and the **gold** doors of the temple:
5: 1 the silver and **gold** and all the furnishings—and he placed them in
8:18 to Ophir and brought back four hundred and fifty talents of **gold**,
9: 1 carrying spices, large quantities of **gold**, and precious stones—
9: 9 she gave the king 120 talents of **gold**, large quantities of spices,
9:10 men of Hiram and the men of Solomon brought **gold** from Ophir;
9:13 The weight of the **gold** that Solomon received yearly was 666
9:13 of the gold that Solomon received yearly was 666 talents, **[RPH]**
9:14 and the governors of the land brought **gold** and silver to Solomon.
9:15 King Solomon made two hundred large shields of hammered **gold**;
9:15 six hundred bekas of hammered **gold** went into each shield.
9:16 He also made three hundred small shields of hammered **gold**,
9:16 hammered gold, with three hundred bekas of **gold** in each shield.
9:17 made a great throne inlaid with ivory and overlaid with pure **gold**.
9:18 The throne had six steps, and a footstool of **gold** was attached to it.
9:20 All King Solomon's goblets were **gold**, and all the household
9:20 articles in the Palace of the Forest of Lebanon were pure **gold**.
9:21 it returned, carrying **gold**, silver and ivory, and apes and baboons.
9:24 articles of silver and **gold**, and robes, weapons and spices,
12: 9 He took everything, including the **gold** shields Solomon had made.
13: 8 have with you the **golden** calves that Jeroboam made to be your
13:11 and light the lamps on the **gold** lampstand every evening.
15:18 and **gold** and the articles that he and his father had dedicated.
16: 2 the silver and **gold** out of the treasuries of the LORD's temple
16: 3 my father and your father. See, I am sending you silver and **gold**.
21: 3 had given them many gifts of silver and **gold** and articles of value,
24:14 and also dishes and other objects of **gold** and silver.
25:24 He took all the **gold** and silver and all the articles found in the
32:27 made treasuries for his silver and **gold** and for his precious stones,
36: 3 on Judah a levy of a hundred talents of silver and a talent of **gold**.
Ezr 1: 4 may now be living are to provide him with silver and **gold**,
1: 6 All their neighbors assisted them with articles of silver and **gold**,
1: 9 the inventory: **gold** dishes 30 silver dishes 1,000 silver pans 29
1:10 **gold** bowls 30 matching silver bowls 410 other articles 1,000
1:11 In all, there were 5,400 articles of **gold** and of silver.
2:69 they gave to the treasury for this work 61,000 drachmas of **gold**,
8:25 them the offering of silver and **gold** and the articles that the king,
8:26 of silver, silver articles weighing 100 talents, 100 talents of **gold**,
8:27 20 bowls of **gold** valued at 1,000 darics, and two fine articles of
8:27 and two fine articles of polished bronze, as precious as **gold**.
8:28 The silver and **gold** are a freewill offering to the LORD,
8:30 the priests and Levites received the silver and **gold** and sacred
8:33 we weighed out the silver and **gold** and the sacred articles into the
Ne 7:70 [7:69] The governor gave to the treasury 1,000 drachmas of **gold**,
7:71 [7:70] gave to the treasury for the work 20,000 drachmas of **gold**
7:72 [7:71] by the rest of the people was 20,000 drachmas of **gold**,
Est 1: 6 There were couches of **gold** and silver on a mosaic pavement of
1: 7 Wine was served in goblets of **gold**, each one different from the
4:11 The only exception to this is for the king to extend the **gold** scepter
5: 2 with her and held out to her the **gold** scepter that was in his hand.
8: 4 Then the king extended the **gold** scepter to Esther and she arose
8:15 and white, a large crown of **gold** and a purple robe of fine linen.
Job 3:15 with rulers who had **gold**, who filled their houses with silver.
23:10 way that I take; when he has tested me, I will come forth as **gold**.
28: 1 "There is a mine for silver and a place where **gold** is refined.
28: 6 come from its rocks, and its dust contains **nuggets of gold**.
28:17 Neither **gold** nor crystal can compare with it, nor can it be had for
31:24 "If I have put my trust in **gold** or said to pure gold, 'You are my
37:22 Out of the north he comes in **golden** splendor; God comes in
42:11 upon him, and each one gave him a piece of silver and a **gold** ring.
Ps 19:10 [19:11] They are more precious than **gold**, than much pure gold;
45:13 [45:14] within ⌞her chamber⌟; her gown is interwoven with **gold**.
72:15 Long may he live! May **gold** *from* Sheba be given him. May
105:37 He brought out Israel, laden with silver and **gold**, and from among
115: 4 But their idols are silver and **gold**, made by the hands of men.
119:72 is more precious to me than thousands of pieces of silver and **gold**.
119:127 Because I love your commands more than **gold**, more than pure
135:15 The idols of the nations are silver and **gold**, made by the hands of
Pr 11:22 Like a **gold** ring in a pig's snout is a beautiful woman who shows
17: 3 The crucible for silver and the furnace for **gold**, but the LORD
20:15 **Gold** there is, and rubies in abundance, but lips that speak
22: 1 than great riches; to be esteemed is better than silver or **gold**.
25:11 A word aptly spoken is like apples of **gold** in settings of silver.
25:12 Like an earring of **gold** or an ornament of fine gold is a wise man's
27:21 The crucible for silver and the furnace for **gold**, but man is tested
Ecc 2: 8 I amassed silver and **gold** for myself, and the treasure of kings
12: 6 before the silver cord is severed, or the **golden** bowl is broken;
SS 1:11 We will make you earrings of **gold**, studded with silver.
3:10 Its posts he made of silver, its base of **gold**. Its seat was
5:14 His arms are rods of **gold** set with chrysolite. His body is like
Isa 2: 7 Their land is full of silver and **gold**; there is no end to their
2:20 away to the rodents and bats their idols of silver and idols of **gold**,
13:17 the Medes, who do not care for silver and have no delight in **gold**.
30:22 your idols overlaid with silver and your images covered with **gold**;
31: 7 will reject the idols of silver and **gold** your sinful hands have made.
39: 2 the silver, the **gold**, the spices, the fine oil, his entire armory
40:19 a goldsmith overlays it with **gold** and fashions silver chains for it.
46: 6 Some pour out **gold** from their bags and weigh out silver on the
60: 6 bearing **gold** and incense and proclaiming the praise of the
60: 9 bringing your sons from afar, with their silver and **gold**,
60:17 Instead of bronze I will bring you **gold**, and silver in place of iron.
Jer 4:30 Why dress yourself in scarlet and put on jewels of **gold**?
10: 4 They adorn it with silver and **gold**; they fasten it with hammer
10: 9 Hammered silver is brought from Tarshish and **gold** from Uphaz.
51: 7 Babylon was a **gold** cup in the LORD's hand; she made the whole
52:19 drink offerings—all that were made of **pure gold** [+2298] or silver.
52:19 drink offerings—all that were made of **pure gold** [+2298] or silver.
La 4: 1 How the **gold** has lost its luster, the fine gold become dull!
Eze 7:19 their silver into the streets, and their **gold** will be an unclean thing.
7:19 **gold** will not be able to save them in the day of the LORD's
16:13 So you were adorned with **gold** and silver; your clothes were of
16:17 the jewelry made of my **gold** and silver, and you made for yourself
27:22 the finest of all kinds of spices and precious stones, and **gold**.
28: 4 wealth for yourself and amassed **gold** and silver in your treasuries.
28:13 Your settings and mountings were made of **gold**; on the day you
38:13 to carry off silver and **gold**, to take away livestock and goods
Da 11: 8 valuable articles of silver and **gold** and carry them off to Egypt.
11:38 a god unknown to his fathers he will honor with **gold** and silver,
11:43 He will gain control of the treasures of **gold** and silver and all the
Hos 2: 8 [2:10] and oil, who lavished on her the silver and **gold**—
8: 4 and **gold** they make idols for themselves to their own destruction.
Joel 3: 5 [4:5] For you took my silver and my **gold** and carried off my
Na 2: 9 [2:10] Plunder the silver! Plunder the **gold**! The supply is endless,
Hab 2:19 It is covered with **gold** and silver; there is no breath in it.
Zep 1:18 Neither their silver nor their **gold** will be able to save them on the
Hag 2: 8 'The silver is mine and the **gold** is mine,' declares the LORD
Zec 4: 2 "I see a solid **gold** lampstand with a bowl at the top and seven
4:12 "What are these two olive branches beside the two **gold** pipes that
4:12 olive branches beside the two gold pipes that pour out **golden** *oil*?"

Zec 6:11 Take the silver and **gold** and make a crown, and set it on the head
13:9 into the fire; I will refine them like silver and test them like **gold**.
14:14 will be collected—great quantities of **gold** and silver and clothing.
Mal 3:3 he will purify the Levites and refine them like **gold** and silver.

2299 זָהַם *zāham*, v. [1] [→ 2300]

finds repulsive [1]

Job 33:20 [D] so that his very being **finds** food **repulsive** and his soul

2300 זַהַם *zaham*, n.pr.m. [1] [√ 2299]

Zaham [1]

2Ch 11:19 She bore him sons: Jeush, Shemariah and **Zaham**.

2301 ¹זָהַר *zāhar[1]*, v. [1] [→ 2303; cf. 7413, 7414]

shine [1]

Da 12:3 [G] Those who are wise *will* **shine** like the brightness of the

2302 ²זָהַר *zāhar[2]*, v. [21] [cf. 2319; Ar 10224]

warn [8], take warning [3], dissuade [2], give warning [2], be warned [1], is warned [1], taken warning [1], teach [1], took warning [1], warned [1]

Ex 18:20 [G] **Teach** them the decrees and laws, and show them the way to
2Ki 6:10 [G] Time and again Elisha **warned** the king, so that he was on
2Ch 19:10 [G] *you are to* **warn** them not to sin against the LORD;
Ps 19:11 [19:12] [C] By them **is** your servant **warned**; in keeping them
Ecc 4:13 [C] but foolish king who no longer knows how to **take warning**.
12:12 [C] **Be warned**, my son, *of* anything in addition to them.
Eze 3:17 [G] so hear the word I speak and **give** them **warning** from me.
3:18 [G] *you do* not **warn** him or speak out to dissuade him from his
3:18 [G] or speak out to **dissuade** him from his evil ways in order to
3:19 [G] if you *do* **warn** the wicked man and he does not turn from his
3:20 [G] will die. Since *you did* not **warn** him, he will die for his sin.
3:21 [G] if you *do* **warn** the righteous man not to sin and he does not
3:21 [C] he does not sin, he will surely live because *he* **took warning**,
33:3 [G] against the land and blows the trumpet *to* **warn** the people,
33:4 [C] *does* not **take warning** and the sword comes and takes his
33:5 [C] he heard the sound of the trumpet but *did* not **take warning**,
33:5 [C] If he *had* **taken warning**, he would have saved himself.
33:6 [C] does not blow the trumpet *to* **warn** the people and the sword
33:7 [G] so hear the word I speak and **give** them **warning** from me.
33:8 [G] and you do not speak out to **dissuade** him from his ways,
33:9 [G] But if you *do* **warn** the wicked man to turn from his ways

2303 זֹהַר *zōhar*, n.[m.]. [2] [√ 2301]

bright [1], brightness [1]

Eze 8:2 and from there up his appearance was as **bright** as glowing metal.
Da 12:3 Those who are wise will shine like the **brightness** *of* the heavens,

2304 זִו *ziw*, n.pr. [2] [→ Ar 10228]

Ziv [2]

1Ki 6:1 in the month of **Ziv**, the second month, he began to build the
6:37 of the LORD was laid in the fourth year, in the month of **Ziv**.

2305 זוֹ *zô*, p.demo. [2] [√ 2297; cf. 2296]

untranslated [1], for this [1]

Ps 132:12 your sons keep my covenant and the statutes **[NIE]** I teach them,
Hos 7:16 insolent words. **For this** they will be ridiculed in the land of Egypt.

2306 זוּ *zû*, p.demo. & rel. [15] [√ 2296; cf. 2138]

the [4], *untranslated* [3], as [1], it [1], such [1], that [1], things [1], where [1], who [1], whose [1]

Ex 15:13 "In your unfailing love you will lead the people **[NIE]** you have
15:16 pass by, O LORD, until the people **[NIE]** you bought pass by.
Ps 9:15 [9:16] have dug; their feet are caught in **the** net they have hidden.
10:2 hunts down the weak, who are caught in **the** schemes he devises.
12:7 [12:8] will keep us safe and protect us from **such** people forever.
17:9 from the wicked **who** assail me, from my mortal enemies who
31:4 [31:5] Free me from the trap **that** is set for me, for you are my
32:8 I will instruct you and teach you in **the** way you should go;
62:11 [62:12] One thing God has spoken, two **things** have I heard:
68:28 [68:29] show us your strength, O God, **as** you have done before.
142:3 [142:4] In the path **where** I walk men have hidden a snare for me.
143:8 Show me **the** way I should go, for to you I lift up my soul.
Isa 42:24 Was **it** not the LORD, against whom we have sinned?
43:21 the people **[RPR]** I formed for myself that they may proclaim my
Hab 1:11 and go on—guilty men, **whose** own strength is their god."

2307 זוּב *zûb*, v. [42] [→ 2308; cf. 1853]

flowing [19], discharge [9], gushed out [3], man[s] [3], bodily discharge [1], discharge [+906+2308] [1], flow [1], fruitful [1], has a discharge [+2308] [1], regular flow [+928+1414] [1], running sore [1], waste away [1]

Ex 3:8 [A] and spacious land, a land **flowing** *with* milk and honey—
3:17 [A] Hivites and Jebusites—a land **flowing** *with* milk and honey.'
13:5 [A] to give you, a land **flowing** *with* milk and honey—
33:3 [A] Go up to the land **flowing** *with* milk and honey. But I will
Lev 15:2 [A] 'When any man has a bodily **discharge**, the discharge is
15:4 [A] " 'Any bed the *man with a* **discharge** lies on will be unclean,
15:6 [A] Whoever sits on anything that the *man with a* **discharge** sat
15:7 [A] " 'Whoever touches the *man who has a* **discharge** must
15:8 [A] " 'If the *man with the* **discharge** spits on someone who is
15:9 [A] " 'Everything the **man**[s] sits on when riding will be unclean,
15:11 [A] " 'Anyone the *man with a* **discharge** touches without rinsing
15:12 [A] " 'A clay pot that the **man**[s] touches must be broken, and any
15:13 [A] " 'When a **man**[s] is cleansed from his discharge, he is to count
15:19 [A] " 'When a woman has her **regular flow** [+928+1414] *of*
15:25 [A] " 'When a woman **has a discharge** [+2308] *of* blood for
15:25 [A] or *has a* **discharge** that continues beyond her period,
15:32 [A] These are the regulations for a *man with a* **discharge**, for
15:33 [A] for a man or a woman *with a* **discharge** [+906+2308],
20:24 [A] you as an inheritance, a land **flowing** *with* milk and honey."
22:4 [A] Aaron has an infectious skin disease or a **bodily discharge**,
Nu 5:2 [A] has an infectious skin disease or a **discharge** of any kind,
13:27 [A] to which you sent us, and it *does* **flow** *with* milk and honey!
14:8 [A] a land **flowing** *with* milk and honey, and will give it to us.
16:13 [A] that you have brought us up out of a land **flowing** *with* milk
16:14 [A] you haven't brought us into a land **flowing** *with* milk
Dt 6:3 [A] that you may increase greatly in a land **flowing** *with* milk
11:9 [A] and their descendants, a land **flowing** *with* milk and honey.
26:9 [A] and gave us this land, a land **flowing** *with* milk and honey;
26:15 [A] oath to our forefathers, a land **flowing** *with* milk and honey."
27:3 [A] a land **flowing** *with* milk and honey, just as the LORD,
31:20 [A] When I have brought them into the land **flowing** *with* milk
Jos 5:6 [A] their fathers to give us, a land **flowing** *with* milk and honey.
2Sa 3:29 [A] house never be without *someone who has a* **running sore**
Ps 78:20 [A] When he struck the rock, water **gushed out**, and streams
105:41 [A] He opened the rock, and water **gushed out**; like a river it
Isa 48:21 [A] them from the rock; he split the rock and water **gushed out**.
Jer 11:5 [A] to give them a land **flowing** *with* milk and honey'—
32:22 [A] to give their forefathers, a land **flowing** *with* milk and honey.
49:4 [A] you boast of your valleys, boast of your valleys *so* **fruitful**?
La 4:9 [A] *they* **waste away** for lack of food from the field.
Eze 20:6 [A] a land **flowing** *with* milk and honey, the most beautiful of all
20:15 [A] a land **flowing** *with* milk and honey, most beautiful of all

2308 זוֹב *zôb*, n.m. [13] [√ 2307]

discharge [7], *untranslated* [2], discharge [+3240] [1], discharge [+906+2307] [1], has a discharge [+2307] [1], it[s] [+2257] [1]

Lev 15:2 'When any man has a bodily discharge, the **discharge** is unclean.
15:3 Whether **it**[s] [+2257] continues flowing from his body or is
15:3 from his body or is blocked, **[RPH]** it will make him unclean.
15:3 This is how his **discharge** will bring about uncleanness:
15:13 " 'When a man is cleansed from his **discharge**, he is to count off
15:15 before the LORD for the man because of his **discharge**.
15:19 **[RPH]** the impurity of her monthly period will last seven days,
15:25 " 'When a woman **has a discharge of** [+2307] blood for many
15:25 she will be unclean as long as she has the **discharge** [+3240],
15:26 Any bed she lies on while her **discharge** continues will be unclean,
15:28 " 'When she is cleansed from her **discharge**, she must count off
15:30 for her before the LORD for the uncleanness of her **discharge**.
15:33 for a man or a woman *with a* **discharge** [+906+2307],

2309 זוּזִים *zûzîm*, n.pr.g. [1]

Zuzites [1]

Ge 14:5 the **Zuzites** in Ham, the Emites in Shaveh Kiriathaim

2310 זוּחַ *zûaḥ*, v. Not used in NIV/BHS [cf. 2322]

2311 זוֹחֵת *zôḥēt*, n.pr.m. [1] [→ 1209]

Zoheth [1]

1Ch 4:20 and Tilon. The descendants of Ishi: **Zoheth** and Ben-Zoheth.

2312 זָוִית *zāwît*, n.f. [2] [cf. 4646]

corners [1], pillars [1]

Ps 144:12 and our daughters will be like **pillars** carved to adorn a palace.
Zec 9:15 they will be full like a bowl used for sprinkling the **corners** *of* the

2313 זוּל zûl, v. [1] [→ 2314]
pour out [1]
Isa 46: 6 [A] Some **pour out** gold from their bags and weigh out silver on

2314 זוּלָה zûlâ, n.[f.] pp.c. [16] [√ 2313]
but [6], except [4], besides [2], apart from [1], only [+4202] [1], only [+963+4200] [1], only [1]
Dt 1:36 **except** Caleb son of Jephunneh. He will see it, and I will give him
4:12 heard the sound of words but saw no form; there was **only** a voice.
Jos 11:13 cities built on their mounds—**except** Hazor, which Joshua burned.
Ru 4: 4 For no one has the right to do it **except** you, and I am next in line."
1Sa 21: 9 [21:10] you want it, take it; there is no sword here **but** that one."
2Sa 7:22 There is no one like you, and there is no God **but** you, as we have
1Ki 3:18 We were alone; there was no one in the house **but** the two of us.
12:20 made him king over all Israel. **Only** [+963+4200] the tribe of
2Ki 24:14 a total of ten thousand. **Only** [+4202] the poorest people of the
1Ch 17:20 "There is no one like you, O LORD, and there is no God **but** you,
Ps 18:31 [18:32] the LORD? And who is the Rock **except** our God?
Isa 26:13 O LORD, our God, other lords **besides** you have ruled over us,
45: 5 the LORD, and there is no other; **apart from** me there is no God.
45:21 apart from me, a righteous God and a Savior; there is none **but** me.
64: 4 [64:3] ear has perceived, no eye has seen any God **besides** you,
Hos 13: 4 You shall acknowledge no God **but** me, no Savior except me.

2315 זוּן zûn, v. Not used in NIV/BHS [→ 4648; Ar 10226, 10410]

2316 זוּעַ zûa', v. [3] [→ 2317; cf. 2398, 2400; Ar 10227]
make tremble [1], showed fear [1], tremble [1]
Est 5: 9 [A] observed that he neither rose nor **showed fear** in his
Ecc 12: 3 [A] when the keepers of the house **tremble**, and the strong men
Hab 2: 7 [D] Will they not wake up and **make** you **tremble**? Then you

2317 זְוָעָה zᵉwā'â, n.f. [6] [√ 2316]
abhorrent [4], object of dread [1], terror [1]
2Ch 29: 8 he has made them an **object of dread** [Q 2400] and horror
Isa 28:19 The understanding of this message will bring sheer **terror**.
Jer 15: 4 I will make them **abhorrent** [Q 2400] to all the kingdoms of the
24: 9 I will make them **abhorrent** [Q 2400] and an offense to all the
29:18 will make them **abhorrent** [Q 2400] to all the kingdoms of the
34:17 I will make you **abhorrent** [Q 2400] to all the kingdoms of the

2318 ¹זוּר zûr¹, v. [4]
broken [1], cleansed [1], crush [1], squeezed [1]
Jdg 6:38 [A] *he* **squeezed** the fleece and wrung out the dew—a bowlful of
Job 39:15 [A] unmindful that a foot *may* **crush** them, that some wild
Isa 1: 6 [A] open sores, not **cleansed** or bandaged or soothed with oil.
59: 5 [A] eggs will die, and *when* one *is* **broken**, an adder is hatched.

2319 ²זוּר zûr², v. [6] [→ 2424; cf. 2302]
turned [2], deserted [1], estranged [1], go astray [1], stranger [1]
Job 19:13 [A] my acquaintances *are* completely **estranged** from me.
Ps 58: 3 [58:4] [A] Even from birth the wicked **go astray**;
69: 8 [69:9] [H] I am a **stranger** to my brothers, an alien to my own
78:30 [A] before *they* **turned** from the food they craved, even while it
Isa 1: 4 [C] the Holy One of Israel and **turned** *their* backs on him.
Eze 14: 5 [C] people of Israel, who *have* all **deserted** me for their idols.'

2320 ³זוּר zûr³, v. [1]
offensive [1]
Job 19:17 [A] My breath *is* **offensive** to my wife; I am loathsome to my

2321 זָזָא zāzā', n.pr.m. [1]
Zaza [1]
1Ch 2:33 The sons of Jonathan: Peleth and **Zaza**. These were the

2322 זָחַח zāḥaḥ, v. [2] [cf. 2310]
swing out [2]
Ex 28:28 [C] so that the breastpiece *will* not **swing out** from the ephod.
39:21 [C] so that the breastpiece *would* not **swing out** from the ephod—

2323 ¹זָחַל zāḥal¹, v. [2] [→ 2325; cf. 2324]
crawl [1], glide [1]
Dt 32:24 [A] of wild beasts, the venom of vipers *that* **glide** *in* the dust.
Mic 7:17 [A] dust like a snake, like *creatures that* **crawl** *on* the ground.

2324 ²זָחַל zāḥal², v. [1] [cf. 2323; Ar 10167]
fearful [1]
Job 32: 6 [A] that is why *I was* **fearful**, not daring to tell you what I know.

2325 זֹחֶלֶת zōḥelet, n.pr.loc. [1] [√ 2323]
Zoheleth [1]
1Ki 1: 9 and fattened calves at the Stone of **Zoheleth** near En Rogel.

2326 זִיד zîd, v. [10] [→ 2327, 5686; cf. 2294; Ar 10225]
arrogant [2], arrogance [1], arrogantly treated [1], contemptuous [1], cooking [1], defied [1], presumes [1], schemes [1], treated arrogantly [1]
Ge 25:29 [G] Once when Jacob *was* **cooking** some stew, Esau came in
Ex 18:11 [A] for he did this to *those* who *had* **treated** Israel **arrogantly**."
21:14 [G] if a man **schemes** and kills another man deliberately,
Dt 1:43 [G] and *in your* **arrogance** you marched up into the hill country.
17:13 [G] will hear and be afraid, and *will* not *be* **contemptuous** again.
18:20 [G] a prophet who **presumes** to speak in my name anything I
Ne 9:10 [G] for you knew how **arrogantly** the Egyptians **treated** them.
9:16 [G] our forefathers, *became* **arrogant** and stiff-necked,
9:29 [G] but they *became* **arrogant** and disobeyed your commands.
Jer 50:29 [A] For *she has* **defied** the LORD, the Holy One of Israel.

2327 זֵידוֹן zêdôn, a. [1] [√ 2326]
raging [1]
Ps 124: 5 the **raging** waters would have swept us away.

2328 ¹זִיז zîz¹, n.m. [2]
creatures [2]
Ps 50:11 bird in the mountains, and the **creatures** *of* the field are mine.
80:13 [80:14] forest ravage it and the **creatures** *of* the field feed on it.

2329 ²זִיז zîz², n.[m.] [1]
overflowing [1]
Isa 66:11 you will drink deeply and delight in her **overflowing** abundance."

2330 זִיזָא zîzā', n.pr.m. [2 / 3] [√ 2331?]
Ziza [3]
1Ch 4:37 and **Ziza** son of Shiphi, the son of Allon, the son of Jedaiah,
23:10 the sons of Shimei: Jahath, **Ziza**, [BHS 2332] Jeush and Beriah.
2Ch 11:20 of Absalom, who bore him Abijah, Attai, **Ziza** and Shelomith.

2331 זִיזָה zîzâ, n.pr.m. [1] [√ 2330?]
Ziza [1]
1Ch 23:11 Jahath was the first and **Ziza** the second, but Jeush and Beriah did

2332 זִינָא zînā', n.pr.m. [1 / 0] [cf. 2330]
1Ch 23:10 sons of Shimei: Jahath, Ziza, [BHS *Zina*; NIV 2330]

2333 זִיעַ zîa', n.pr.m. [1]
Zia [1]
1Ch 5:13 Michael, Meshullam, Sheba, Jorai, Jacan, **Zia** and Eber—seven in

2334 ¹זִיף zîp¹, n.pr.loc. [8] [→ 2337]
Ziph [7], there[s] [+4497] [1]
Jos 15:24 **Ziph**, Telem, Bealoth,
15:55 Maon, Carmel, **Ziph**, Juttah,
1Sa 23:14 in the desert strongholds and in the hills of the Desert of **Ziph**.
23:15 While David was at Horesh in the Desert of **Ziph**, he learned that
23:24 So they set out and went to **Ziph** ahead of Saul. Now David
26: 2 So Saul went down to the Desert of **Ziph**, with his three thousand
26: 2 thousand chosen men of Israel, to search **there**[s] [+4497] for David.
2Ch 11: 8 Gath, Mareshah, **Ziph**,

2335 ²זִיף zîp², n.pr.m. [2]
Ziph [2]
1Ch 2:42 Mesha his firstborn, who was the father of **Ziph**, and his son
4:16 The sons of Jehallelel: **Ziph**, Ziphah, Tiria and Asarel.

2336 זִיפָה zîpâ, n.pr.m. [1]
Ziphah [1]
1Ch 4:16 The sons of Jehallelel: Ziph, **Ziphah**, Tiria and Asarel.

2337 זִיפִי *zîpî*, a.g. [3] [√ 2334]

Ziphites [3]

1Sa 23: 19 The **Ziphites** went up to Saul at Gibeah and said, "Is not David
26: 1 The **Ziphites** went to Saul at Gibeah and said, "Is not David hiding
Ps 54: T [54:2] When the **Ziphites** had gone to Saul and said, "Is not

2338 זִיקוֹת *zîqôt*, n.[m.]. [2] [→ 2415]

flaming torches [1], torches [1]

Isa 50: 11 you who light fires and provide yourselves with **flaming torches**,
50: 11 in the light of your fires and of the **torches** you have set ablaze.

2339 זַיִת *zayit*, n.m. [38] [→ 1364, 1365, 2340, 2457?]

olive [9], olive tree [8], olive groves [7], olives [7], olive trees [4], olive grove [1], olive trees [+3658] [1], olives from trees [1]

Ge 8: 11 in the evening, there in its beak was a freshly plucked **olive** leaf!
Ex 23: 11 they leave. Do the same with your vineyard and your **olive grove**.
27: 20 "Command the Israelites to bring you clear oil of pressed **olives** for
30: 24 all according to the sanctuary shekel—and a hin of **olive** oil.
Lev 24: 2 "Command the Israelites to bring you clear oil of pressed **olives** for
Dt 6: 11 you did not dig, and vineyards and **olive groves** you did not plant—
8: 8 and barley, vines and fig trees, pomegranates, **olive** oil and honey;
24: 20 When you beat the **olives from** your **trees**, do not go over the
28: 40 You will have **olive trees** throughout your country but you will not
28: 40 but you will not use the oil, because the **olives** will drop off.
Jos 24: 13 and eat from vineyards and **olive groves** that you did not plant.'
Jdg 9: 8 a king for themselves. They said to the **olive tree**, 'Be our king.'
9: 9 "But the **olive tree** answered, 'Should I give up my oil, by which
15: 5 and standing grain, together with the vineyards and **olive groves**.
1Sa 8: 14 and vineyards and **olive groves** and give them to his attendants.
2Sa 15: 30 But David continued up the Mount of **Olives**, weeping as he went;
2Ki 5: 26 **olive groves**, vineyards, flocks, herds, or menservants
18: 32 of bread and vineyards, a land of **olive** [+3658] **trees** and honey.
1Ch 27: 28 Baal-Hanan the Gederite was in charge of the **olive**
Ne 5: 11 vineyards, **olive groves** and houses, and also the usury you are
8: 15 and bring back branches from **olive** and wild olive trees,
9: 25 already dug, vineyards, **olive groves** and fruit trees in abundance.
Job 15: 33 of its unripe grapes, like an **olive tree** shedding its blossoms.
Ps 52: 8 [52:10] I am like an **olive tree** flourishing in the house of God;
128: 3 your house; your sons will be like **olive** shoots around your table.
Isa 17: 6 as when an **olive tree** is beaten, leaving two or three olives on the
24: 13 the earth and among the nations, as when an **olive tree** is beaten,
Jer 11: 16 The LORD called you a thriving **olive tree** with fruit beautiful in
Hos 14: 6 [14:7] His splendor will be like an **olive tree**, his fragrance like a
Am 4: 9 Locusts devoured your fig and **olive trees**, yet you have not
Mic 6: 15 you will press **olives** but not use the oil on yourselves, you will
Hab 3: 17 though the **olive** crop fails and the fields produce no food,
Hag 2: 19 fig tree, the pomegranate and the **olive** tree have not borne fruit.
Zec 4: 3 Also there are two **olive trees** by it, one on the right of the bowl
4: 11 "What are these two **olive trees** on the right and the left of the
4: 12 "What are these two **olive** branches beside the two gold pipes that
14: 4 On that day his feet will stand on the Mount of **Olives**, east of
14: 4 and the Mount of **Olives** will be split in two from east to west,

2340 זֵיתָן *zêtān*, n.pr.m. [1] [√ 2339]

Zethan [1]

1Ch 7: 10 Benjamin, Ehud, Kenaanah, **Zethan**, Tarshish and Ahishahar.

2341 זַךְ *zak*, a. [11] [√ 2348]

pure [6], clear [2], flawless [1], innocent [1], upright [1]

Ex 27: 20 "Command the Israelites to bring you **clear** oil of pressed olives
30: 34 and galbanum—and **pure** frankincense, all in equal amounts,
Lev 24: 2 "Command the Israelites to bring you **clear** oil of pressed olives
24: 7 Along each row put some **pure** incense as a memorial portion to
Job 8: 6 if you are **pure** and upright, even now he will rouse himself on
11: 4 say to God, 'My beliefs are **flawless** and I am pure in your sight.'
16: 17 yet my hands have been free of violence and my prayer is **pure**.
33: 9 'I am **pure** and without sin; I am clean and free from guilt.
Pr 16: 2 All a man's ways seem **innocent** to him, but motives are weighed
20: 11 is known by his actions, by whether his conduct is **pure** and right.
21: 8 of the guilty is devious, but the conduct of the innocent is **upright**.

2342 זָכָה *zākâ*, v. [8] [cf. 2348; Ar 10229]

kept pure [2], pure [2], acquit [1], justified [1], keep pure [1], make yourselves clean [1]

Job 15: 14 [A] "What is man, that *he could be* **pure**, or one born of woman,
25: 4 [A] before God? How *can* one born of woman *be* **pure**?
Ps 51: 4 [51:6] [A] right when you speak and **justified** when you judge.
73: 13 [D] Surely in vain *have I* **kept** my heart **pure**; in vain have I
119: 9 [D] How *can* a young man **keep** his way **pure**? By living
Pr 20: 9 [D] Who can say, "*I have* **kept** my heart **pure**; I am clean
Isa 1: 16 [F] wash and **make yourselves clean**. Take your evil deeds out
Mic 6: 11 [A] *Shall I* **acquit** a man with dishonest scales, with a bag of

2343 זְכוֹכִית *zᵉkôkît*, n.[f.]. [1] [√ 2348]

crystal [1]

Job 28: 17 Neither gold nor **crystal** can compare with it, nor can it be had for

2344 זְכוּר *zᵉkûr*, n.m. [4] [√ 2350]

men [4]

Ex 23: 17 "Three times a year all the **men** are to appear before the Sovereign
34: 23 Three times a year all your **men** are to appear before the Sovereign
Dt 16: 16 Three times a year all your **men** must appear before the LORD
20: 13 God delivers it into your hand, put to the sword all the **men** *in* it.

2345 זָכוּר *zākûr*, n.m. Not used in NIV/BHS [√ 2350]

2346 זַכּוּר *zakkûr*, n.pr.m. [10] [√ 2349]

Zaccur [10]

Nu 13: 4 their names: from the tribe of Reuben, Shammua son of **Zaccur**;
1Ch 4: 26 of Mishma: Hammuel his son, **Zaccur** his son and Shimei his son.
24: 27 The sons of Merari: from Jaaziah: Beno, Shoham, **Zaccur** and Ibri.
25: 2 From the sons of Asaph: **Zaccur**, Joseph, Nethaniah and Asarelah.
25: 10 the third to **Zaccur**, his sons and relatives, 12
Ezr 8: 14 of Bigvai, Uthai and **Zaccur**, [K 2280] and with them 70 men.
Ne 3: 2 the adjoining section, and **Zaccur** son of Imri built next to them.
10: 12 [10:13] **Zaccur**, Sherebiah, Shebaniah,
12: 35 the son of Micaiah, the son of **Zaccur**, the son of Asaph,
13: 13 in charge of the storerooms and made Hanan son of **Zaccur**,

2347 זַכַּי *zakkay*, n.pr.m. [2] [√ 2349 + 3378?]

Zaccai [2]

Ezr 2: 9 of **Zaccai** 760
Ne 3: 20 [Baruch son of **Zabbai** [Q; see K 2287] zealously repaired another]
7: 14 of **Zaccai** 760

2348 זָכַךְ *zākak*, v. [4] [→ 2341, 2343; cf. 2342]

pure [2], *untranslated* [1], brighter [1]

Job 9: 30 [G] myself with soap and my hands **[RPH]** with washing soda,
15: 15 [A] in his holy ones, if even the heavens *are* not **pure** in his eyes,
25: 5 [A] the moon is not bright and the stars *are* not **pure** in his eyes,
La 4: 7 [A] Their princes *were* **brighter** than snow and whiter than milk,

2349 זָכַר¹ *zākar¹*, v. [222] [→ 260, 2345, 2346, 2352, 2353, 2354, 2355, 4654; *also used with compound proper names*]

remember [116], remembered [23], be remembered [15], remembers [8], invoke [4], mention [4], consider [2], mentioned [2], petition [2], proclaim [2], recalled [2], remember [+2349] [2], remember well [+906+2349] [2], remind [2], tell [2], well remember [+2349] [2], *untranslated* [1], are remembered [1], be invoked [1], brought to mind [1], burns memorial [1], call on [1], carry on the memory [1], cause to be honored [1], commemorate [1], disregarding [+4202] [1], done[s] this [1], draw attention to [1], forget [+440] [1], hold [1], honor [1], made mention of [1], make petition [1], mindful [1], perpetuate memory [+9005] [1], praise [1], recalling [1], record [1], reflect on [1], reflects on [1], reminded [1], reminder [1], review the past [1], summons [1], think about [1], thought [1], trust [1], worthy of mention [1]

Ge 8: 1 [A] God **remembered** Noah and all the wild animals and the
9: 15 [A] *I will* **remember** my covenant between me and you and all
9: 16 [A] see it and **remember** the everlasting covenant between God
19: 29 [A] destroyed the cities of the plain, he **remembered** Abraham,
30: 22 [A] God **remembered** Rachel; he listened to her and opened her
40: 14 [A] goes well with you, **remember** me and show me kindness;
40: 14 [G] **mention** me to Pharaoh and get me out of this prison.
40: 23 [A] The chief cupbearer, however, *did* not **remember** Joseph;
41: 9 [G] said to Pharaoh, "Today I *am* **reminded** *of* my shortcomings.
42: 9 [A] he **remembered** his dreams about them and said to them,
Ex 2: 24 [A] and he **remembered** his covenant with Abraham,
6: 5 [A] are enslaving, and *I have* **remembered** my covenant.
13: 3 [A] Then Moses said to the people, "**Commemorate** this day,
20: 8 [A] "**Remember** the Sabbath day by keeping it holy.
20: 24 [G] Wherever *I* **cause** my name **to be honored**, I will come to
23: 13 [G] *Do* not **invoke** the names of other gods; do not let them be
32: 13 [A] **Remember** your servants Abraham, Isaac and Israel,
Lev 26: 42 [A] *I will* **remember** my covenant with Jacob and my covenant
26: 42 [A] with Abraham, **[RPH]** and I will remember the land.
26: 42 [A] my covenant with Abraham, and *I will* **remember** the land.
26: 45 [A] for their sake *I will* **remember** the covenant with their

Nu 5:15 [G] for jealousy, a reminder offering *to* **draw attention to** guilt.
10:9 [C] *you will* **be remembered** by the LORD your God
11:5 [A] *We* **remember** the fish we ate in Egypt at no cost—also the
15:39 [A] and so *you will* **remember** all the commands of the LORD,
15:40 [A] *you will* **remember** to obey all my commands and will be
Dt 5:15 [A] **Remember** that you were slaves in Egypt and that the
7:18 [A] **remember** [+906+2349] **well** what the LORD your God did
7:18 [A] **remember well** [+906+2349] what the LORD your God did
8:2 [A] **Remember** how the LORD your God led you all the way in
8:18 [A] **remember** the LORD your God, for it is he who gives you
9:7 [A] **Remember** this and never forget how you provoked the
9:27 [A] **Remember** your servants Abraham, Isaac and Jacob.
15:15 [A] **Remember** that you were slaves in Egypt and the LORD
16:3 [A] so that all the days of your life *you may* **remember** the time
16:12 [A] **Remember** that you were slaves in Egypt, and follow
24:9 [A] **Remember** what the LORD your God did to Miriam along
24:18 [A] **Remember** that you were slaves in Egypt and the LORD
24:22 [A] **Remember** that you were slaves in Egypt. That is why I
25:17 [A] **Remember** what the Amalekites did to you along the way
32:7 [A] **Remember** the days of old; consider the generations long
Jos 1:13 [A] "**Remember** the command that Moses the servant of the
23:7 [G] *do* not **invoke** the names of their gods or swear by them.
Jdg 8:34 [A] *did* not **remember** the LORD their God, who had rescued
9:2 [A] or just one man?' **Remember**, I am your flesh and blood."
16:28 [A] to the LORD, "O Sovereign LORD, **remember** me.
1Sa 1:11 [A] only look upon your servant's misery and **remember** me,
1:19 [A] lay with Hannah his wife, and the LORD **remembered** her.
4:18 [G] When he **mentioned** the ark of God, Eli fell backward off his
25:31 [A] has brought my master success, **remember** your servant."
2Sa 14:11 [A] "Then *let* the king **invoke** the LORD his God to prevent the
18:18 [G] "I have no son to **carry on the memory** *of* my name."
19:19 [19:20] [A] *Do* not **remember** how your servant did wrong on the
1Ki 17:18 [G] Did you come to **remind** me *of* my sin and kill my son?"
2Ki 9:25 [A] **Remember** how you and I were riding together in chariots
20:3 [A] "**Remember**, O LORD, how I have walked before you
1Ch 16:4 [G] to **make petition**, to give thanks, and to praise the LORD,
16:12 [A] **Remember** the wonders he has done, his miracles,
16:15 [A] *He* **remembers** his covenant forever, the word he
2Ch 6:42 [A] **Remember** the great love promised to David your servant."
24:22 [A] King Joash *did* not **remember** the kindness Zechariah's
Ne 1:8 [A] "**Remember** the instruction you gave your servant Moses,
4:14 [4:8] [A] **Remember** the Lord, who is great and awesome,
5:19 [A] **Remember** me with favor, O my God, *for* all I have done for
6:14 [A] **Remember** Tobiah and Sanballat, O my God, because of what
9:17 [A] failed *to* **remember** the miracles you performed among
13:14 [A] **Remember** me for this, O my God, and do not blot out what
13:22 [A] **Remember** me for this also, O my God, and show mercy to
13:29 [A] **Remember** them, O my God, because they defiled the
13:31 [A] and for the firstfruits. **Remember** me with favor, O my God.
Est 2:1 [A] *he* **remembered** Vashti and what she had done and what he
9:28 [C] These days *should* **be remembered** and observed in every
Job 4:7 [A] "**Consider** now: Who, being innocent, has ever perished?
7:7 [A] **Remember**, O God, that my life is but a breath; my eyes will
10:9 [A] **Remember** that you molded me like clay. Will you now turn
11:16 [A] forget your trouble, **recalling** it only as waters gone by.
14:13 [A] If only you would set me a time and then **remember** me!
21:6 [A] When *I* **think about** this, I am terrified; trembling seizes my
24:20 [C] evil men **are** no longer **remembered** but are broken like a
28:18 [C] Coral and jasper *are* not **worthy of mention**; the price of
36:24 [A] **Remember** to extol his work, which men have praised in
41:8 [40:32] [A] *you will* **remember** the struggle and never do it
Ps 8:4 [8:5] [A] what is man that *you are* **mindful** *of* him, the son of
9:12 [9:13] [A] For he who avenges blood **remembers**; he does not
20:3 [20:4] [A] *May he* **remember** all your sacrifices and accept
20:7 [20:8] [G] but we **trust** in the name of the LORD our God.
22:27 [22:28] [A] All the ends of the earth *will* **remember** and turn to
25:6 [A] **Remember**, O LORD, your great mercy and love, for they
25:7 [A] **Remember** not the sins of my youth and my rebellious ways;
25:7 [A] according to your love **remember** me, for you are good,
38:T [38:1] [G] A psalm of David. A **petition**.
42:4 [42:5] [A] These things *I* **remember** as I pour out my soul:
42:6 [42:7] [A] therefore *I will* **remember** you from the land of the
45:17 [45:18] [G] *I will* **perpetuate** your **memory** [+9005] through all
63:6 [63:7] [A] On my bed *I* **remember** you; I think of you through
70:T [70:1] [G] For the director of music. Of David. A **petition**.
71:16 [G] I will come and **proclaim** your mighty acts, O Sovereign
74:2 [A] **Remember** the people you purchased of old, the tribe of
74:18 [A] **Remember** how the enemy has mocked you, O LORD,
74:22 [A] your cause; **remember** how fools mock you all day long.
77:3 [77:4] [A] *I* **remembered** you, O God, and I groaned; I mused,
77:6 [77:7] [A] *I* **remembered** my songs in the night. My heart
77:11 [77:12] [A] *I will* **remember** the deeds of the LORD; yes,
77:11 [77:12] [A] yes, *I will* **remember** your miracles of long ago.
78:35 [A] *They* **remembered** that God was their Rock, that God Most
78:39 [A] *He* **remembered** that they were but flesh, a passing breeze
78:42 [A] *They did* not **remember** his power—the day he redeemed
79:8 [A] *Do* not **hold** against us the sins of the fathers; may your
83:4 [83:5] [C] that the name of Israel **be remembered** no more."
87:4 [G] "*I will* **record** Rahab and Babylon among those who
88:5 [88:6] [A] whom *you* **remember** no more, who are cut off from
89:47 [89:48] [A] **Remember** how fleeting is my life. For what
89:50 [89:51] [A] **Remember**, Lord, how your servant has been
98:3 [A] *He has* **remembered** his love and his faithfulness to the
103:14 [B] knows how we are formed, *he* **remembers** that we are dust.
103:18 [A] who keep his covenant and **remember** to obey his precepts.
105:5 [A] **Remember** the wonders he has done, his miracles,
105:8 [A] *He* **remembers** his covenant forever, the word he
105:42 [A] For *he* **remembered** his holy promise given to his servant
106:4 [A] **Remember** me, O LORD, when you show favor to your
106:7 [A] *they did* not **remember** your many kindnesses, and they
106:45 [A] for their sake *he* **remembered** his covenant and out of his
109:14 [C] *May* the iniquity of his fathers **be remembered** before the
109:16 [A] For *he* never **thought** *of* doing a kindness, but hounded to
111:5 [A] for those who fear him; *he* **remembers** his covenant forever.
115:12 [A] The LORD **remembers** us and will bless us: He will bless
119:49 [A] **Remember** your word to your servant, for you have given
119:52 [A] *I* **remember** your ancient laws, O LORD, and I find
119:55 [A] In the night *I* **remember** your name, O LORD, and I will
132:1 [A] **remember** David and all the hardships he endured.
136:23 [A] to the *One* who **remembered** us in our low estate *His*
137:1 [A] of Babylon we sat and wept when we **remembered** Zion.
137:6 [A] cling to the roof of my mouth if *I do* not **remember** you,
137:7 [A] **Remember**, O LORD, what the Edomites did on the day
143:5 [A] *I* **remember** the days of long ago; I meditate on all your
Pr 31:7 [A] forget their poverty and **remember** their misery no more.
Ecc 5:20 [5:19] [A] *He* seldom **reflects on** the days of his life,
9:15 [A] city by his wisdom. But nobody **remembered** that poor man.
11:8 [A] *let him* **remember** the days of darkness, for they will be
12:1 [A] **Remember** your Creator in the days of your youth,
SS 1:4 [G] and delight in you; *we will* **praise** your love more than wine.
Isa 12:4 [G] what he has done, and **proclaim** that his name is exalted.
17:10 [A] *you have* not **remembered** the Rock, your fortress.
19:17 [G] everyone to whom Judah *is* **mentioned** will be terrified,
23:16 [C] sing many a song, so that *you will* **be remembered**."
26:13 [G] you have ruled over us, but your name alone *do we* **honor**.
38:3 [A] "**Remember**, O LORD, how I have walked before you
43:18 [A] "**Forget** [+440] the former things; do not dwell on the past.
43:25 [A] for my own sake, and **remembers** your sins no more.
43:26 [G] **Review the past** *for* me, let us argue the matter together;
44:21 [A] "**Remember** these things, O Jacob, for you are my servant,
46:8 [A] "**Remember** this, fix it in mind, take it to heart, you rebels.
46:9 [A] **Remember** the former things, those of long ago; I am God,
47:7 [A] not consider these things or **reflect on** what might happen.
48:1 [G] in the name of the LORD and **invoke** the God of Israel—
49:1 [G] called me; from my birth *he has* **made mention of** my name.
54:4 [A] and **remember** no more the reproach of your widowhood.
57:11 [A] *have* neither **remembered** me nor pondered this in your
62:6 [G] You who **call on** the LORD, give yourselves no rest,
63:7 [G] *I will* **tell** *of* the kindnesses of the LORD, the deeds for
63:11 [A] Then *his people* **recalled** the days of old, the days of Moses
64:5 [64:4] [A] who gladly do right, *who* **remember** your ways.
64:9 [64:8] [A] O LORD; *do* not **remember** our sins forever.
65:17 [C] The former things *will* not **be remembered**, nor will they
66:3 [G] *whoever* **burns memorial** incense, like one who worships an
Jer 2:2 [A] " '*I* **remember** the devotion of your youth, how as a bride
3:16 [A] It will never enter their minds or *be* **remembered**; it will not
4:16 [G] "**Tell** this to the nations, proclaim it to Jerusalem:
11:19 [C] land of the living, that his name **be remembered** no more."
14:10 [A] *he will* now **remember** their wickedness and punish them for
14:21 [A] **Remember** your covenant with us and do not break it.
15:15 [A] You understand, O LORD; **remember** me and care for me.
17:2 [A] Even their children **remember** their altars and Asherah poles
18:20 [A] **Remember** that I stood before you and spoke in their behalf
20:9 [A] "*I will* not **mention** him or speak any more in his name,"
23:36 [A] But *you must* not **mention** 'the oracle of the LORD' again,
31:20 [A] I often speak against him, *I* still **remember** [+2349] him.
31:20 [A] I often speak against him, *I* still **remember** [+2349] him.
31:34 [A] their wickedness and *will* **remember** their sins no more."
44:21 [A] "*Did* not the LORD **remember** and think about the incense
51:50 [A] **Remember** the LORD in a distant land, and think on
La 1:7 [A] wandering Jerusalem **remembers** all the treasures that were
1:9 [A] filthiness clung to her skirts; *she did* not **consider** her future.
2:1 [A] *he has* not **remembered** his footstool in the day of his anger.
3:19 [A] I **remember** my affliction and my wandering, the bitterness
3:20 [A] *I* **well remember** [+2349] them, and my soul is downcast
3:20 [A] *I* **well remember** [+2349] them, and my soul is downcast
5:1 [A] **Remember**, O LORD, what has happened to us; look, and
Eze 3:20 [C] The righteous things he did *will* not **be remembered**, and I

Eze 6: 9 [A] been carried captive, those who escape *will* **remember** me—
16: 22 [A] your prostitution *you did* not **remember** the days of your
16: 43 [A] " 'Because *you did* not **remember** the days of your youth
16: 60 [A] Yet I *will* **remember** the covenant I made with you in the
16: 61 [A] *you will* **remember** your ways and be ashamed when you
16: 63 [A] *you will* **remember** and be ashamed and never again open
18: 22 [C] None of the offenses he has committed *will* **be remembered**
18: 24 [C] of the righteous things he has done *will* **be remembered**.
20: 43 [A] There *you will* **remember** your conduct and all the actions
21: 23 [21:28] [G] he *will* **remind** them *of* their guilt and take them
21: 24 [21:29] [G] 'Because you people *have* **brought to mind** your
21: 24 [21:29] [C] you *have* **done**' **this**, you will be taken captive.
21: 32 [21:37] [C] in your land, *you will* **be remembered** no more;
23: 19 [A] and more promiscuous as she **recalled** the days of her youth,
23: 27 [A] on these things with longing or **remember** Egypt anymore.
25: 10 [C] so that the Ammonites *will* not **be remembered** among the
29: 16 [G] but *will be a* **reminder** *of* their sin in turning to her for help.
33: 13 [C] of the righteous things he has done *will* **be remembered**;
33: 16 [C] None of the sins he has committed *will* **be remembered**
36: 31 [A] Then *you will* **remember** your evil ways and wicked deeds,
Hos 2: 17 [2:19] [C] from her lips; no longer *will* their names **be invoked**.
7: 2 [A] but they do not realize that *I* **remember** all their evil deeds.
8: 13 [A] Now *he will* **remember** their wickedness and punish their
9: 9 [A] God *will* **remember** their wickedness and punish them for
Am 1: 9 [A] communities of captives to Edom, **disregarding** [+4202]
6: 10 [G] "Hush! *We must* not **mention** the name of the LORD."
Jnh 2: 7 [2:8] [A] *I* **remembered** you, LORD, and my prayer rose to
Mic 6: 5 [A] **remember** what Balak king of Moab counseled and what
Na 2: 5 [2:6] [A] *He* **summons** his picked troops, yet they stumble on
Hab 3: 2 [A] in our time make them known; in wrath **remember** mercy.
Zec 10: 9 [A] the peoples, yet in distant lands *they will* **remember** me.
13: 2 [C] *they will* **be remembered** no more," declares the LORD
Mal 4: 4 [3:22] [A] "**Remember** the law of my servant Moses,

2350 ²זָכָר **zākar²**, n.m. & a. [1] [→ 2344, 2345, 2351]

males [1]

Ex 34: 19 [C] including all the firstborn **males** of your livestock,

2351 זָכָר **zākār**, n.m. & a. [82] [√ 2350; Ar 10175]

male [37], men [17], males [11], man [9], son [3], boy [1], boys [+3251] [1], not a virgin [+3359+5435] [1], slept with [+3359+4200+5435] [1], slept with [+3359+5435] [1]

Ge 1: 27 image of God he created him; **male** and female he created them.
5: 2 He created them **male** and female and blessed them. And when
6: 19 all living creatures, **male** and female, to keep them alive with you.
7: 3 also seven of every kind of bird, **male** and female, to keep their
7: 9 **male** and female, came to Noah and entered the ark, as God had
7: 16 The animals going in were **male** and female of every living thing,
17: 10 you are to keep: Every **male** among you shall be circumcised.
17: 12 For the generations to come every **male** among you who is eight
17: 14 Any uncircumcised **male**, who has not been circumcised in the
17: 23 every **male** in his household, and circumcised them, as God told
34: 15 that you become like us by circumcising all your **males**.
34: 22 as one people only on the condition that our **males** be circumcised,
34: 24 and his son Shechem, and every **male** in the city was circumcised.
34: 25 their swords and attacked the unsuspecting city, killing every **male**.
Ex 12: 5 The animals you choose must be year-old **males** without defect,
12: 48 Passover must have all the **males** in his household circumcised;
13: 12 All the firstborn **males** of your livestock belong to the LORD.
13: 15 This is why I sacrifice to the LORD the first **male** offspring of
Lev 1: 3 a burnt offering from the herd, he is to offer a **male** without defect.
1: 10 either the sheep or the goats, he is to offer a **male** without defect.
3: 1 and he offers an animal from the herd, whether **male** or female,
3: 6 to the LORD, he is to offer a **male** or female without defect.
4: 23 he must bring as his offering a **male** goat without defect.
6: 18 [6:11] Any **male** descendant of Aaron may eat it. It is his regular
6: 29 [6:22] Any **male** in a priest's family may eat it; it is most holy.
7: 6 Any **male** in a priest's family may eat it, but it must be eaten in a
12: 2 gives birth to a **son** will be ceremonially unclean for seven days,
12: 7 " 'These are the regulations for the woman who gives birth to a **boy**
15: 33 in her monthly period, for a **man** or a woman with a discharge,
18: 22 " 'Do not lie with a **man** as one lies with a woman; that is
20: 13 " 'If a man lies with a **man** as one lies with a woman, both of them
22: 19 you must present a **male** without defect from the cattle, sheep
27: 3 set the value of a **male** between the ages of twenty and sixty at
27: 5 set the value of a **male** at twenty shekels and of a female at ten
27: 6 set the value of a **male** at five shekels of silver and that of a female
27: 7 set the value of a **male** at fifteen shekels and of a female at ten
Nu 1: 2 by their clans and families, listing every **man** by name, one by one.
1: 20 All the **men** twenty years old or more who were able to serve in
1: 22 All the **men** twenty years old or more who were able to serve in
3: 15 their families and clans. Count every **male** a month old or more."
3: 22 The number of all the **males** a month old or more who were
3: 28 The number of all the **males** a month old or more was 8,600.
3: 34 The number of all the **males** a month old or more who were
3: 39 their clans, including every **male** a month old or more, was 22,000.
3: 40 "Count all the firstborn Israelite **males** who are a month old
3: 43 The total number of firstborn **males** a month old or more,
5: 3 Send away **male** and female alike; send them outside the camp
18: 10 Eat it as something most holy; every **male** shall eat it. You must
26: 62 All the **male** Levites a month old or more numbered 23,000.
31: 7 as the LORD commanded Moses, and killed every **man**.
31: 17 Now kill all the **boys** [+3251]. And kill every woman who has
31: 17 kill all the boys. And kill every woman who has slept with a **man**,
31: 18 but save for yourselves every girl who has never slept with a **man**.
31: 35 32,000 women who *had* never **slept with** [+3359+5435] a man.
Dt 4: 16 an image of any shape, whether formed like a **man** or a woman,
15: 19 Set apart for the LORD your God every firstborn **male** of your
Jos 5: 4 All those who came out of Egypt—all the **men** of military age—
17: 2 These are the other **male** descendants of Manasseh son of Joseph
Jdg 21: 11 they said. "Kill every **male** and every woman who is not a virgin."
21: 11 every male and every woman *who is* **not a virgin** [+3359+5435]."
21: 12 young women who *had* never **slept with** [+3359+4200+5435]
1Ki 11: 15 gone up to bury the dead, had struck down all the **men** in Edom.
11: 16 there for six months, until they had destroyed all the **men** in Edom.
2Ch 31: 16 they distributed to the **males** three years old or more whose names
31: 19 men were designated by name to distribute portions to every **male**
Ezr 8: 3 of Parosh, Zechariah, and with him were registered 150 **men**;
8: 4 Eliehoenai son of Zerahiah, and with him 200 **men**;
8: 5 of Zattu, Shecaniah son of Jahaziel, and with him 300 **men**;
8: 6 descendants of Adin, Ebed son of Jonathan, and with him 50 **men**;
8: 7 of Elam, Jeshaiah son of Athaliah, and with him 70 **men**;
8: 8 of Shephatiah, Zebadiah son of Michael, and with him 80 **men**;
8: 9 of Joab, Obadiah son of Jehiel, and with him 218 **men**;
8: 10 of Bani, Shelomith son of Josiphiah, and with him 160 **men**;
8: 11 of Bebai, Zechariah son of Bebai, and with him 28 **men**;
8: 12 of Azgad, Johanan son of Hakkatan, and with him 110 **men**;
8: 13 names were Eliphelet, Jeuel and Shemaiah, and with them 60 **men**;
8: 14 descendants of Bigvai, Uthai and Zaccur, and with them 70 **men**.
Isa 66: 7 she gives birth; before the pains come upon her, she delivers a **son**.
Jer 20: 15 who made him very glad, saying, "A child is born to you—a **son**!"
30: 6 Ask and see: Can a **man** bear children? Then why do I see every
Eze 16: 17 you made for yourself **male** idols and engaged in prostitution with
Mal 1: 14 "Cursed is the cheat who has an acceptable **male** in his flock

2352 זֵכֶר **zēker**, n.m. [23] [√ 2349]

memory [11], renown [3], name [2], remembered [2], celebrate [+5580] [1], fame [1], name by which remembered [1], name of renown [1], remembers [1]

Ex 3: 15 the **name by which** I *am to be* **remembered** from generation to
17: 14 because I will completely blot out the **memory** *of* Amalek from
Dt 25: 19 you shall blot out the **memory** *of* Amalek from under heaven.
32: 26 I would scatter them and blot out their **memory** from mankind,
Est 9: 28 nor should the **memory** *of* them die out among their descendants.
Job 18: 17 The **memory** *of* him perishes from the earth; he has no name in the
Ps 6: 5 [6:6] No one **remembers** you when he is dead. Who praises you
9: 6 [9:7] their cities; even the **memory** *of* them has perished.
30: 4 [30:5] to the LORD, you saints of his; praise his holy **name**.
34: 16 [34:17] do evil, to cut off the **memory** *of* them from the earth.
97: 12 in the LORD, you who are righteous, and praise his holy **name**.
102: 12 [102:13] your **renown** endures through all generations.
109: 15 that he may cut off the **memory** *of* them from the earth.
111: 4 He has caused his wonders to be **remembered**; the LORD is
112: 6 never be shaken; a righteous man will be **remembered** forever.
135: 13 Your name, O LORD, endures forever, your **renown**, O LORD,
145: 7 *They will* **celebrate** [+5580] your abundant goodness and joyfully
Pr 10: 7 The **memory** *of* the righteous will be a blessing, but the name of
Ecc 9: 5 have no further reward, and even the **memory** *of* them is forgotten.
Isa 26: 8 wait for you; your name and **renown** are the desire of our hearts.
26: 14 and brought them to ruin; you wiped out all **memory** of them.
Hos 12: 5 [12:6] God Almighty, the LORD is his **name of renown**!
14: 7 [14:8] a vine, and his **fame** will be like the wine from Lebanon.

2353 ¹זֶכֶר **zeker¹**, n.pr.m. [1] [√ 2349]

Zeker [1]

1Ch 8: 31 Gedor, Ahio, **Zeker**

2354 ²זֵכֶר **zeker²**, n.m. Not used in NIV/BHS [√ 2349]

2355 זִכָּרוֹן **zikkārôn**, n.m. [24] [√ 2349; Ar 10176]

memorial [9], reminder [3], remembered [2], remembrance [2], chronicles [1], commemorate [1], commemorated [1], historic right

[1], maxims [1], pagan symbols [1], remind [1], something remembered [1]

Ex 12:14 "This is a day you are to **commemorate**; for the generations to
13: 9 a **reminder** on your forehead that the law of the LORD is to be
17:14 "Write this on a scroll as **something** to be **remembered** and make
28:12 fasten them on the shoulder pieces of the ephod as **memorial**
28:12 Aaron is to bear the names on his shoulders as a **memorial** before
28:29 of decision as a continuing **memorial** before the LORD.
30:16 It will be a **memorial** for the Israelites before the LORD,
39: 7 pieces of the ephod as **memorial** stones for the sons of Israel,
Lev 23:24 of rest, a sacred assembly **commemorated** *with* trumpet blasts.
Nu 5:15 for jealousy, a **reminder** offering to draw attention to guilt.
5:18 shall loosen her hair and place in her hands the **reminder** offering,
10:10 and they will be a **memorial** for you before your God.
16:40 [17:5] This was to **remind** the Israelites that no one except a
31:54 brought it into the Tent of Meeting as a **memorial** for the Israelites
Jos 4: 7 These stones are to be a **memorial** to the people of Israel forever."
Ne 2:20 have no share in Jerusalem or any claim or **historic right** to it."
Est 6: 1 so he ordered the book of the **chronicles**, the record of his reign,
Job 13:12 Your **maxims** are proverbs of ashes; your defenses are defenses of
Ecc 1:11 There is no **remembrance** of men of old, and even those who are
1:11 even those who are yet to come will not be **remembered** by those
2:16 For the wise man, like the fool, will not be long **remembered**;
Isa 57: 8 your doors and your doorposts you have put your **pagan symbols**.
Zec 6:14 Hen son of Zephaniah as a **memorial** in the temple of the LORD.
Mal 3:16 A scroll of **remembrance** was written in his presence concerning

2356 זִכְרִי zikrî, n.pr.m. [12] [√ 2349? + 3378?]

Zicri [12]

Ex 6:21 The sons of Izhar were Korah, Nepheg and **Zicri**.
1Ch 8:19 Jakim, **Zicri**, Zabdi,
8:23 Abdon, **Zicri**, Hanan,
8:27 Jaareshiah, Elijah and **Zicri** were the sons of Jeroham.
9:15 and Mattaniah son of Mica, the son of **Zicri**, the son of Asaph;
26:25 his son, Joram his son, **Zicri** his son and Shelomith his son.
27:16 over the Reubenites: Eliezer son of **Zicri**; over the Simeonites:
2Ch 17:16 next, Amasiah son of **Zicri**, who volunteered himself for the
23: 1 son of Obed, Maaseiah son of Adaiah, and Elishaphat son of **Zicri**.
28: 7 **Zicri**, an Ephraimite warrior, killed Maaseiah the king's son,
Ne 11: 9 Joel son of **Zicri** was their chief officer, and Judah son of
12:17 of Abijah's, **Zicri**; of Miniamin's and of Moadiah's, Piltai;

2357 זְכַרְיָה zᵉkaryâ, n.pr.m. [25] [→ 2358; cf. 2349 + 3378; Ar 10230]

Zechariah [24], Zechariah's [1]

2Ki 14:29 the kings of Israel. And **Zechariah** his son succeeded him as king.
15:11 The other events of **Zechariah's** reign are written in the book of
18: 2 His mother's name was Abijah daughter of **Zechariah**.
1Ch 9:21 **Zechariah** son of Meshelemiah was the gatekeeper at the entrance
9:37 Gedor, Ahio, **Zechariah** and Mikloth.
15:20 **Zechariah**, Aziel, Shemiramoth, Jehiel, Unni, Eliab, Maaseiah
16: 5 **Zechariah** second, then Jeiel, Shemiramoth, Jehiel, Mattithiah,
2Ch 17: 7 **Zechariah**, Nethanel and Micaiah to teach in the towns of Judah.
24:20 the Spirit of God came upon **Zechariah** son of Jehoiada the priest.
34:12 and **Zechariah** and Meshullam, descended from Kohath.
Ezr 8: 3 of the descendants of Parosh, **Zechariah**, and with him were
8:11 of Bebai, **Zechariah** son of Bebai, and with him 28 men;
8:16 Elnathan, Jarib, Elnathan, Nathan, **Zechariah** and Meshullam,
10:26 Mattaniah, **Zechariah**, Jehiel, Abdi, Jeremoth and Elijah.
Ne 8: 4 Malkijah, Hashum, Hashbaddanah, **Zechariah** and Meshullam.
11: 4 the son of **Zechariah**, the son of Amariah, the son of Shephatiah,
11: 5 the son of Adaiah, the son of Joiarib, the son of **Zechariah**,
11:12 the son of Amzi, the son of **Zechariah**, the son of Pashhur,
12:16 of Iddo's, **Zechariah**; of Ginnethon's, Meshullam;
12:35 and also **Zechariah** son of Jonathan, the son of Shemaiah,
12:41 Micaiah, Elioenai, **Zechariah** and Hananiah with their trumpets—
Zec 1: 1 the word of the LORD came to the prophet **Zechariah** son of
1: 7 the word of the LORD came to the prophet **Zechariah** son of
7: 1 the word of the LORD came to **Zechariah** on the fourth day of
7: 8 And the word of the LORD came again to **Zechariah**:

2358 זְכַרְיָהוּ zᵉkaryāhû, n.pr.m. [16] [√ 2357; cf. 2349 + 3378]

Zechariah [16]

2Ki 15: 8 **Zechariah** son of Jeroboam became king of Israel in Samaria,
1Ch 5: 7 according to their genealogical records: Jeiel the chief, **Zechariah**,
15:18 **Zechariah**, Jaaziel, Shemiramoth, Jehiel, Unni, Eliab, Benaiah,
15:24 **Zechariah**, Benaiah and Eliezer the priests were to blow trumpets
24:25 brother of Micah: Isshiah; from the sons of Isshiah: **Zechariah**.
26: 2 **Zechariah** the firstborn, Jediael the second, Zebadiah the third,
26:11 Hilkiah the second, Tabaliah the third and **Zechariah** the fourth.
26:14 Then lots were cast for his son **Zechariah**, a wise counselor,
27:21 Iddo son of **Zechariah**; over Benjamin: Jaasiel son of Abner;
2Ch 20:14 the Spirit of the LORD came upon Jahaziel son of **Zechariah**,
21: 2 Jehiel, **Zechariah**, Azariahu, Michael and Shephatiah.
26: 5 He sought God during the days of **Zechariah**, who instructed him
29: 1 His mother's name was Abijah daughter of **Zechariah**.
29:13 from the descendants of Asaph, **Zechariah** and Mattaniah;
35: 8 Hilkiah, **Zechariah** and Jehiel, the administrators of God's temple,
Isa 8: 2 and **Zechariah** son of Jeberekiah as reliable witnesses for me."

2359 זֻלּוּת zullût, n.f. [1] [√ 2361]

what is vile [1]

Ps 12: 8 [12:9] The wicked freely strut about when **what is vile** is honored

2360 זַלְזַל zalzal, n.[m.] [1] [√ 2361; cf. 6149]

shoots [1]

Isa 18: 5 he will cut off the **shoots** with pruning knives, and cut down

2361 זָלַל¹ zālal¹, v. [7] [→ 2359, 2360; cf. 2362]

gluttons [2], despise [1], despised [1], gorge [1], profligate [1], worthless [1]

Dt 21:20 [A] He will not obey us. *He is a* **profligate** and a drunkard."
Pr 23:20 [A] who drink too much wine or **gorge** themselves *on* meat,
23:21 [A] for drunkards and **gluttons** become poor, and drowsiness
28: 7 [A] but a companion of **gluttons** disgraces his father.
Jer 15:19 [A] if you utter worthy, not **worthless**, words, you will be my
La 1: 8 [G] All who honored her **despise** her, for they have seen her
1:11 [A] "Look, O LORD, and consider, for I am **despised**."

2362 ²זָלַל zālal², v. [3] [cf. 2361]

quaked [1], tremble [1], trembled [1]

Jdg 5: 5 [C] The mountains **quaked** before the LORD, the One of Sinai,
Isa 64: 1 [63:19] [C] that the mountains *would* **tremble** before you!
64: 3 [64:2] [C] came down, and the mountains **trembled** before you.

2363 זַלְעָפָה zal'āpâ, n.f. [3] [√ 2406]

feverish [1], indignation [1], scorching [1]

Ps 11: 6 fiery coals and burning sulfur; a **scorching** wind will be their lot.
119:53 **Indignation** grips me because of the wicked, who have forsaken
La 5:10 Our skin is hot as an oven, **feverish** from hunger.

2364 זִלְפָּה zilpâ, n.pr.f. [7]

Zilpah [7]

Ge 29:24 Laban gave his servant girl **Zilpah** to his daughter as her
30: 9 she took her maidservant **Zilpah** and gave her to Jacob as a wife.
30:10 Leah's servant **Zilpah** bore Jacob a son.
30:12 Leah's servant **Zilpah** bore Jacob a second son.
35:26 The sons of Leah's maidservant **Zilpah**: Gad and Asher.
37: 2 the sons of Bilhah and the sons of **Zilpah**, his father's wives,
46:18 These were the children born to Jacob by **Zilpah**, whom Laban had

2365 ¹זִמָּה zimmâ¹, n.f. [29]

lewdness [6], wickedness [3], consequences of lewdness [2], lewd [2], wicked schemes [2], *untranslated* [1], evil intent [1], evil schemes [1], evil [1], lewd act [1], lewd acts [1], penalty for lewdness [1], plans [1], schemes [1], shameful crimes [1], shameful [1], shamefully [+928] [1], shameless [1], wicked [1]

Lev 18:17 they are her close relatives. That is **wickedness**.
19:29 or the land will turn to prostitution and be filled with **wickedness**.
20:14 " 'If a man marries both a woman and her mother, it is **wicked**.
20:14 be burned in the fire, so that no **wickedness** will be among you.
Jdg 20: 6 because they committed this **lewd** and disgraceful **act** in Israel.
Job 17:11 my **plans** are shattered, and so are the desires of my heart.
31:11 For that would have been **shameful**, a sin to be judged.
Ps 26:10 in whose hands are **wicked schemes**, whose right hands are full of
119:150 Those who devise **wicked schemes** are near, but they are far from
Pr 10:23 A fool finds pleasure in **evil** conduct, but a man of understanding
21:27 is detestable—how much more so when brought with **evil intent**!
24: 9 The **schemes** *of* folly are sin, and men detest a mocker.
Isa 32: 7 he makes up **evil schemes** to destroy the poor with lies,
Jer 13:27 your adulteries and lustful neighings, your **shameless** prostitution!
Eze 16:27 of the Philistines, who were shocked by your **lewd** conduct.
16:43 Did you not add **lewdness** to all your other detestable practices?
16:58 You will bear the **consequences of** your **lewdness** and your
22: 9 are those who eat at the mountain shrines and commit **lewd acts**.
22:11 another **shamefully** [+928] defiles his daughter-in-law,
23:21 So you longed for the **lewdness** *of* your youth, when in Egypt your
23:27 So I will put a stop to the **lewdness** and prostitution you began in

Eze 23:29 your prostitution will be exposed. Your **lewdness** and promiscuity
23:35 you must bear the **consequences of** your **lewdness**
23:44 so they slept with those **lewd** women, Oholah and Oholibah.
23:48 "So I will put an end to **lewdness** in the land, that all women may
23:48 that all women may take warning and not imitate **[RPH]** you.
23:49 You will suffer the **penalty for** your **lewdness** and bear the
24:13 " 'Now your impurity is **lewdness**. Because I tried to cleanse you
Hos 6: 9 murder on the road to Shechem, committing **shameful crimes**.

2366 ²זִמָּה zimmâ², n.pr.m. [3]

Zimmah [3]

1Ch 6:20 [6:5] Of Gershon: Libni his son, Jehath his son, **Zimmah** his son,
6:42 [6:27] the son of Ethan, the son of **Zimmah**, the son of Shimei,
2Ch 29:12 from the Gershonites, Joah son of **Zimmah** and Eden son of Joah;

2367 זְמוֹרָה zemôrâ, n.[f.]. [5] [√ 2377; cf. 2444]

branch [3], vines [2]

Nu 13:23 of Eshcol, they cut off a **branch** bearing a single cluster of grapes.
Isa 17:10 though you set out the finest plants and plant imported **vines**,
Eze 8:17 me to anger? Look at them putting the **branch** to their nose!
15: 2 how is the wood of a vine better than that of a **branch** on any of
Na 2: 2 [2:3] destroyers have laid them waste and have ruined their **vines**.

2368 זַמְזֻמִּים zamzummîm, n.pr.g. [1] [√ 2372?]

Zamzummites [1]

Dt 2:20 used to live there; but the Ammonites called them **Zamzummites**.

2369 ¹זָמִיר zāmîr¹, n.m. [7] [√ 2376]

singing [2], songs [2], music and song [1], song [1], theme of song [1]

2Sa 23: 1 the man anointed by the God of Jacob, Israel's singer of **songs**:
Job 35:10 one says, 'Where is God my Maker, who gives **songs** in the night,
Ps 95: 2 before him with thanksgiving and extol him with **music and song**.
119:54 Your decrees are the **theme of** my **song** wherever I lodge.
SS 2:12 the season of **singing** has come, the cooing of doves is heard in our
Isa 24:16 From the ends of the earth we hear **singing**: "Glory to the
25: 5 by the shadow of a cloud, so the **song** *of* the ruthless is stilled.

2370 ²זָמִיר zāmîr², n.[m.]. Not used in NIV/BHS [√ 2377]

2371 זְמִירָה zemîrâ, n.pr.m. [1] [√ 2379?; cf. 2376]

Zemirah [1]

1Ch 7: 8 **Zemirah**, Joash, Eliezer, Elioenai, Omri, Jeremoth, Abijah,

2372 זָמַם zāmam, v. [13] [→ 2368?, 2373, 4659]

determined [3], plot [2], carry out purpose [1], considers [1], decided [1], intended [1], plan [1], planned evil [1], planned [1], resolved [1]

Ge 11: 6 [A] then nothing *they* **plan** to do will be impossible for them.
Dt 19:19 [A] do to him as *he* **intended** to do to his brother. You must
Ps 17: 3 [A] find nothing; *I have* **resolved** that my mouth will not sin.
31:13 [31:14] [A] they conspire against me and **plot** to take my life.
37:12 [A] The wicked **plot** against the righteous and gnash their teeth at
Pr 30:32 [A] the fool and exalted yourself, or if *you have* **planned evil**,
31:16 [A] *She* **considers** a field and buys it; out of her earnings she
Jer 4:28 [A] and will not relent, *I have* **decided** and will not turn back."
51:12 [A] The LORD *will* **carry out** *his* **purpose**, his decree against
La 2:17 [A] The LORD has done what *he* **planned**; he has fulfilled his
Zec 1: 6 [A] and practices deserve, just as *he* **determined** to do.' "
8:14 [A] "Just as *I had* **determined** to bring disaster upon you
8:15 [A] "so now *I have* **determined** to do good again to Jerusalem

2373 זָמָם zāmām, n.[m.]. [1] [√ 2372]

plans [1]

Ps 140: 8 [140:9] do not let their **plans** succeed, or they will become proud.

2374 זָמַן zāman, v. [3] [√ 2375; Ar 10231]

set [2], designated [1]

Ezr 10:14 [E] towns who has married a foreign woman come at a **set** time,
Ne 10:34 [10:35] [E] **set** times each year a contribution of wood to burn
13:31 [E] provision for contributions of wood at **designated** times,

2375 זְמָן zemān, n.m. [4] [→ 2374; Ar 10232]

time [2], designated times [1], time appointed [1]

Ne 2: 6 will you get back?" It pleased the king to send me; so I set a **time**.
Est 9:27 days every year, in the way prescribed and at the **time appointed**.
9:31 to establish these days of Purim at their **designated times**,
Ecc 3: 1 There is a **time** for everything, and a season for every activity

2376 ¹זָמַר zāmar¹, v. [45] [→ 2369, 2371?, 2379, 2384, 4660; Ar 10233, 10234]

sing praise [18], make music [10], sing praises [8], sing [7], music [1], praise [1]

Jdg 5: 3 [D] *I will* **make music** to the LORD, the God of Israel.
2Sa 22:50 [D] among the nations; *I will* **sing praises** to your name.
1Ch 16: 9 [D] Sing to him, **sing praise** to him; tell of all his wonderful acts.
Ps 7:17 [7:18] [D] *will* **sing praise** *to* the name of the LORD Most
9: 2 [9:3] [D] in you; *I will* **sing praise** *to* your name, O Most High.
9:11 [9:12] [D] **Sing praises** to the LORD, enthroned in Zion;
18:49 [18:50] [D] O LORD; *I will* **sing praises** to your name.
21:13 [21:14] [D] your strength; we will sing and **praise** your might.
27: 6 [D] shouts of joy; I will sing and **make music** to the LORD.
30: 4 [30:5] [D] **Sing** to the LORD, you saints of his; praise his holy
30:12 [30:13] [D] that my heart *may* **sing** *to* you and not be silent.
33: 2 [D] with the harp; **make music** to him on the ten-stringed lyre.
47: 6 [47:7] [D] **Sing praises** *to* God, sing praises; sing praises to our
47: 6 [47:7] [D] Sing praises to God, **sing praises**; sing praises to our
47: 6 [47:7] [D] sing praises; **sing praises** to our King, sing praises.
47: 6 [47:7] [D] sing praises; sing praises to our King, **sing praises**.
47: 7 [47:8] [D] King of all the earth; **sing** to him a psalm of praise.
57: 7 [57:8] [D] my heart is steadfast; I will sing and **make music**.
57: 9 [57:10] [D] the nations; *I will* **sing** *of* you among the peoples.
59:17 [59:18] [D] O my Strength, *I* **sing praise** to you; you, O God,
61: 8 [61:9] [D] *will I* ever **sing praise** *to* your name and fulfill my
66: 2 [D] **Sing** the glory of his name; make his praise glorious!
66: 4 [D] *they* **sing praise** to you, they sing praise to your name."
66: 4 [D] they sing praise to you, *they* **sing praise** *to* your name."
68: 4 [68:5] [D] Sing to God, **sing praise** *to* his name, extol him who
68:32 [68:33] [D] of the earth, **sing praise** *to* the Lord, *Selah*
71:22 [D] *I will* **sing praise** to you with the lyre, O Holy One of Israel.
71:23 [D] My lips will shout for joy when *I* **sing praise** to you—I,
75: 9 [75:10] [D] this forever; *I will* **sing praise** to the God of Jacob.
92: 1 [92:2] [D] to praise the LORD and **make music** to your name,
98: 4 [D] all the earth, burst into jubilant song with **music**;
98: 5 [D] **make music** to the LORD with the harp, with the harp
101: 1 [D] your love and justice; to you, O LORD, *I will* **sing praise**.
104:33 [D] all my life; *I will* **sing praise** to my God as long as I live.
105: 2 [D] Sing to him, **sing praise** to him; tell of all his wonderful acts.
108: 1 [108:2] [D] I will sing and **make music** *with* all my soul.
108: 3 [108:4] [D] the nations; *I will* **sing** *of* you among the peoples.
135: 3 [D] LORD is good; **sing praise** to his name, for that is pleasant.
138: 1 [D] with all my heart; before the "gods" *I will* **sing** your **praise**.
144: 9 [D] O God; on the ten-stringed lyre *I will* **make music** to you,
146: 2 [D] all my life; *I will* **sing praise** to my God as long as I live.
147: 1 [D] How good it is *to* **sing praises** *to* our God, how pleasant
147: 7 [D] with thanksgiving; **make music** to our God on the harp.
149: 3 [D] and **make music** to him with tambourine and harp.
Isa 12: 5 [D] **Sing** *to* the LORD, for he has done glorious things; let this

2377 ²זָמַר zāmar², v. [3] [→ 2367, 2370, 4661, 4662]

prune [2], pruned [1]

Lev 25: 3 [A] for six years **prune** your vineyards and gather their crops.
25: 4 [A] Do not sow your fields or **prune** your vineyards.
Isa 5: 6 [C] neither **pruned** nor cultivated, and briers and thorns will

2378 זֶמֶר zemer, n.[m.]. [1] [cf. 2380?]

mountain sheep [1]

Dt 14: 5 the wild goat, the ibex, the antelope and the **mountain sheep**.

2379 ¹זִמְרָה zimrâ¹, n.f. [7] [→ 2371?; cf. 2376]

song [3], music [2], singing [2]

Ex 15: 2 The LORD is my strength and my **song**; he has become my
Ps 81: 2 [81:3] Begin the **music**, strike the tambourine, play the melodious
98: 5 the LORD with the harp, with the harp and the sound of **singing**,
118:14 The LORD is my strength and my **song**; he has become my
Isa 12: 2 The LORD, the LORD, is my strength and my **song**; he has
51: 3 will be found in her, thanksgiving and the sound of **singing**.
Am 5:23 the noise of your songs! I will not listen to the **music** *of* your harps.

2380 ²זִמְרָה zimrâ², n.f. [1] [→ 2381; cf. 2378?]

best products [1]

Ge 43:11 Put some of the **best products** *of* the land in your bags and take

2381 ¹זִמְרִי zimrî¹, n.pr.m. [14 / 17] [√ 2380]

Zimri [16], Zimri's [1]

Nu 25:14 who was killed with the Midianite woman was **Zimri** son of Salu,
Jos 7: 1 the son of **Zimri**, [BHS 2275] the son of Zerah, of the tribe of
7:17 come forward by families, and **Zimri** [BHS 2275] was taken.

Jos 7:18 the son of **Zimri**, [BHS 2275] the son of Zerah, of the tribe of
1Ki 16: 9 **Zimri**, one of his officials, who had command of half his chariots,
16:10 **Zimri** came in, struck him down and killed him in the
16:12 So **Zimri** destroyed the whole family of Baasha, in accordance
16:15 year of Asa king of Judah, **Zimri** reigned in Tirzah seven days.
16:16 When the Israelites in the camp heard that **Zimri** had plotted
16:18 When **Zimri** saw that the city was taken, he went into the citadel
16:20 As for the other events of **Zimri's** reign, and the rebellion he
2Ki 9:31 Jehu entered the gate, she asked, "Have you come in peace, **Zimri**,
1Ch 2: 6 of Zerah: **Zimri**, Ethan, Heman, Calcol and Darda—five in all.
8:36 Azmaveth and **Zimri**, and Zimri was the father of Moza.
8:36 Azmaveth and Zimri, and **Zimri** was the father of Moza.
9:42 of Jadah, Jadah was the father of Alemeth, Azmaveth and **Zimri**,
9:42 Azmaveth and Zimri, and **Zimri** was the father of Moza.

2382 ²זִמְרִי *zimrî²*, n.pr.loc. [1]

Zimri [1]

Jer 25:25 all the kings of **Zimri**, Elam and Media;

2383 זִמְרָן *zimrān*, n.pr.m. [2]

Zimran [2]

Ge 25: 2 She bore him **Zimran**, Jokshan, Medan, Midian, Ishbak
1Ch 1:32 **Zimran**, Jokshan, Medan, Midian, Ishbak and Shuah. The sons of

2384 זִמְרָת *zimrāt*, n.f. Not used in NIV/BHS [√ 2376?]

2385 זַן *zan*, n.[m.]. [3] [→ Ar 10235]

every kind [+448+2385+4946] [2], various [1]

2Ch 16:14 him on a bier covered with spices and **various** blended perfumes,
Ps 144:13 will be filled with **every kind** [+448+2385+4946] *of* provision.
144:13 Our barns will be filled with **every kind** *of* [+448+2385+4946]

2386 זָנַב *zānab*, v.den. [2] [√ 2387]

attack from the rear [1], cut off [1]

Dt 25:18 [D] on your journey and **cut off** all who were lagging behind;
Jos 10:19 [D] **attack** them **from the rear** and don't let them reach their

2387 זָנָב *zānāb*, n.m. [11] [→ 2386]

tail [9], stubs [1], tails [1]

Ex 4: 4 LORD said to him, "Reach out your hand and take it by the **tail**."
Dt 28:13 The LORD will make you the head, not the **tail**. If you pay
28:44 will not lend to him. He will be the head, but you will be the **tail**.
Jdg 15: 4 and caught three hundred foxes and tied them **tail** to tail in pairs.
15: 4 and caught three hundred foxes and tied them tail to **tail** in pairs.
15: 4 tail to tail in pairs. He then fastened a torch to every pair of **tails**,
Job 40:17 His **tail** sways like a cedar; the sinews of his thighs are close-knit.
Isa 7: 4 not lose heart because of these two smoldering **stubs** *of* firewood—
9:14 [9:13] So the LORD will cut off from Israel both head and **tail**,
9:15 [9:14] men are the head, the prophets who teach lies are the **tail**.
19:15 There is nothing Egypt can do—head or **tail**, palm branch or reed.

2388 ¹זָנָה *zānâ¹*, v. [61] [→ 2390, 2393, 2394, 9373]

prostitute [12], prostituted [5], unfaithful [5], engaged in prostitution [4], turn to prostitution [3], committed adultery [2], continue prostitution [+2388] [2], guilty of the vilest adultery [+2388] [2], prostitutes [2], *untranslated* [1], adulterous [1], carried on prostitution [1], caused to prostitute themselves [1], commit adultery [1], did[s] [1], engage in prostitution [1], engaging in prostitution [1], guilty of prostitution [1], indulge in sexual immorality [1], lead to do[s] the same [+339+466+906+2177] [1], led to prostitute themselves [1], lust after [+339] [1], lusted after [+339] [1], lusted [1], making a prostitute [1], ply her trade [1], promiscuous [1], prostituting [1], prostitution [1], runs after for favors [+339] [1], that[s] [+4392] [1], turned to prostitution [1], use as a prostitute [+9373] [1]

Ge 38:24 [A] "Your daughter-in-law Tamar *is* **guilty of prostitution**, and
Ex 34:15 [A] for when *they* **prostitute** *themselves* to their gods
34:16 [A] and those daughters **prostitute** *themselves* to their gods,
34:16 [G] *will* **lead** your sons **to do**[s] [+339+466+906+2177] **the same**.
Lev 17: 7 [A] to the goat idols to whom they **prostitute** *themselves*.
19:29 [G] " 'Do not degrade your daughter by **making** her **a prostitute**,
19:29 [A] or the land *will* **turn to prostitution** and be filled with
20: 5 [A] all who **[RPH]** follow him in prostituting themselves to
20: 5 [A] all who follow him in **prostituting** *themselves* to Molech.
20: 6 [A] and spiritists to **prostitute** *himself* by following them,
21: 9 [A] a priest's daughter defiles herself by *becoming a* **prostitute**,
Nu 15:39 [A] not **prostitute** yourselves by going after the lusts of your
25: 1 [A] the men began to **indulge in sexual immorality** with
Dt 22:21 [A] Israel by *being* **promiscuous** while still in her father's house.
31:16 [A] these people *will* soon **prostitute** *themselves* to the foreign
Jdg 2:17 [A] **prostituted** *themselves* to other gods and worshiped them.
8:27 [A] All Israel **prostituted** *themselves* by worshiping it there,
8:33 [A] than the Israelites again **prostituted** *themselves* to the Baals.
19: 2 [A] she *was* **unfaithful** to him. She left him and went back to her
1Ch 5:25 [A] **prostituted** *themselves* to the gods of the peoples of the
2Ch 21:11 [G] *had* **caused** the people of Jerusalem **to prostitute themselves**
21:13 [G] *you have* **led** Judah and the people of Jerusalem **to prostitute themselves**,
21:13 [G] to prostitute themselves, just as the house of Ahab **did**[s].
Ps 73:27 [A] you will perish; you destroy all *who are* **unfaithful** to you.
106:39 [A] what they did; by their deeds *they* **prostituted** *themselves*.
Isa 23:17 [A] *will* **ply her trade** with all the kingdoms on the face of the
57: 3 [A] of a sorceress, you offspring of adulterers and **prostitutes**!
Jer 3: 1 [A] you *have lived as a* **prostitute** with many lovers—
3: 6 [A] every spreading tree and *has* **committed adultery** there.
3: 8 [A] had no fear; she also went out and **committed adultery**.
Eze 6: 9 [A] how I have been grieved by their **adulterous** hearts,
6: 9 [A] and by their eyes, which *have* **lusted** after their idols.
16:15 [A] in your beauty and used your fame *to become a* **prostitute**.
16:16 [A] gaudy high places, where *you* **carried on** *your* **prostitution**.
16:17 [A] yourself male idols and **engaged in prostitution** with them.
16:26 [A] *You* **engaged in prostitution** with the Egyptians,
16:28 [A] *You* **engaged in prostitution** with the Assyrians too,
16:28 [A] and even after **that**[s] [+4392], you still were not satisfied.
16:34 [E] of others; no *one* **runs after** you **for** your **favors** [+339].
16:41 [A] I will put a stop to your **prostitution**, and you will no longer
20:30 [A] way your fathers did and **lust** [+339] **after** their vile images?
23: 3 [A] *They became* **prostitutes** in Egypt, engaging in prostitution
23: 3 [A] in Egypt, **engaging in prostitution** from their youth.
23: 5 [A] "Oholah **engaged in prostitution** while she was still mine;
23:19 [A] the days of her youth, when *she was a* **prostitute** in Egypt.
23:30 [A] because you **lusted** [+339] **after** the nations and defiled
23:43 [A] 'Now *let them* **use** her **as a prostitute** [+9373], for that is all
Hos 1: 2 [A] because the land *is* **guilty of the vilest adultery** [+2388] in
1: 2 [A] because the land *is* **guilty of the vilest adultery** [+2388] in
2: 5 [2:7] [A] Their mother *has been* **unfaithful** and has conceived
3: 3 [A] *you must* not *be a* **prostitute** or be intimate with any man,
4:10 [G] *they will* **engage in prostitution** but not increase,
4:12 [A] leads them astray; *they are* **unfaithful** to their God.
4:13 [A] Therefore your daughters **turn to prostitution** and your
4:14 [A] not punish your daughters when *they* **turn to prostitution**,
4:15 [A] "Though you **commit adultery**, O Israel, let not Judah
4:18 [G] drinks are gone, *they* **continue** *their* **prostitution** [+2388];
4:18 [G] drinks are gone, *they* **continue** *their* **prostitution** [+2388];
5: 3 [G] Ephraim, *you have* now **turned to prostitution**; Israel is
9: 1 [A] For *you have been* **unfaithful** to your God; you love the
Am 7:17 [A] " 'Your wife *will become a* **prostitute** in the city, and your

2389 ²זָנָה *zānâ²*, v. Not used in NIV/BHS

2390 זֹנָה *zōnâ*, n.f. *or* v. [33] [√ 2388]

prostitute [20], prostitutes [7], harlot [2], prostitution [2], harlots [1], prostitute's [1]

Ge 34:31 they replied, "Should he have treated our sister like a **prostitute**?"
38:15 When Judah saw her, he thought she *was a* **prostitute**, for she had
Lev 21: 7 " 'They must not marry women defiled by **prostitution** or divorced
21:14 a widow, a divorced woman, or a woman defiled by **prostitution**,
Dt 23:18 [23:19] You must not bring the earnings of a *female* **prostitute**
Jos 2: 1 So they went and entered the house of a **prostitute** named Rahab
6:17 Only Rahab the **prostitute** and all who are with her in her house
6:22 "Go into the **prostitute's** house and bring her out and all who
6:25 Joshua spared Rahab the **prostitute**, with her family and all who
Jdg 11: 1 His father was Gilead; his mother was a **prostitute**.
16: 1 One day Samson went to Gaza, where he saw a **prostitute**.
1Ki 3:16 Now two **prostitutes** came to the king and stood before him.
22:38 the chariot at a pool in Samaria (where the **prostitutes** bathed),
Pr 6:26 for the **prostitute** reduces you to a loaf of bread, and the adulteress
7:10 to meet him, dressed like a **prostitute** and with crafty intent.
23:27 for a **prostitute** is a deep pit and a wayward wife is a narrow well.
29: 3 to his father, but a companion of **prostitutes** squanders his wealth.
Isa 1:21 See how the faithful city has become a **harlot**! She once was full
23:15 it will happen to Tyre as in the song of the **prostitute**:
23:16 "Take up a harp, walk through the city, O **prostitute** forgotten;
Jer 2:20 and under every spreading tree you lay down as a **prostitute**.
3: 3 Yet you have the brazen look of a **prostitute**; you refuse to blush
5: 7 they committed adultery and thronged to the houses of **prostitutes**.
Eze 16:30 when you do all these things, acting like a brazen **prostitute**!
16:31 you were unlike a **prostitute**, because you scorned payment.
16:33 Every **prostitute** receives a fee, but you give gifts to all your
16:35 " 'Therefore, you **prostitute**, hear the word of the LORD!
23:44 As men sleep with a **prostitute**, so they slept with those lewd
Hos 4:14 because the men themselves consort with **harlots** and sacrifice
Joel 3: 3 [4:3] cast lots for my people and traded boys for **prostitutes**;

Mic 1: 7 Since she gathered her gifts from the wages of **prostitutes**,
1: 7 of prostitutes, as the wages of **prostitutes** they will again be used."
Na 3: 4 all because of the wanton lust of a **harlot**, alluring, the mistress of

2391 זָנוֹחַ¹ *zānôaḥ¹*, n.pr.loc. [4] [→ 2392; cf. 2395 *or* 2396]

Zanoah [4]

Jos 15: 34 **Zanoah**, En Gannim, Tappuah, Enam,
15: 56 Jezreel, Jokdeam, **Zanoah**,
Ne 3: 13 Valley Gate was repaired by Hanun and the residents of **Zanoah**.
11: 30 **Zanoah**, Adullam and their villages, in Lachish and its fields,

2392 זָנוֹחַ² *zānôaḥ²*, n.pr.m. [1] [√ 2391; cf. 2395 *or* 2396]

Zanoah [1]

1Ch 4: 18 Heber the father of Soco, and Jekuthiel the father of **Zanoah**.)

2393 זְנוּנִים *zenûnîm*, n.[m.]. [12] [√ 2388]

prostitution [4], *untranslated* [2], adulterous look [1], adulterous [1], adultery [1], idolatry [1], unfaithfulness [1], wanton lust [1]

Ge 38: 24 guilty of prostitution, and as a result **[RPH]** she is now pregnant."
2Ki 9: 22 "as long as all the **idolatry** and witchcraft of your mother Jezebel
Eze 23: 11 and prostitution she was more depraved than **[NIE]** her sister.
23: 29 and bare, and the shame of your **prostitution** will be exposed.
Hos 1: 2 take to yourself an **adulterous** wife and children of unfaithfulness,
1: 2 take to yourself an adulterous wife and children of **unfaithfulness**,
2: 2 [2:4] Let her remove the **adulterous look** from her face
2: 4 [2:6] to her children, because they are the children of **adultery**.
4: 12 A spirit of **prostitution** leads them astray; they are unfaithful to
5: 4 A spirit of **prostitution** is in their heart; they do not acknowledge
Na 3: 4 all because of the **wanton lust** *of* a harlot, alluring, the mistress of
3: 4 who enslaved nations by her **prostitution** and peoples by her

2394 זְנוּת *zenût*, n.f.abst. [9] [√ 2388]

prostitution [7], immorality [1], unfaithfulness [1]

Nu 14: 33 suffering for your **unfaithfulness**, until the last of your bodies lies
Jer 3: 2 You have defiled the land with your **prostitution** and wickedness.
3: 9 Because Israel's **immorality** mattered so little to her, she defiled
13: 27 your adulteries and lustful neighings, your shameless **prostitution**!
Eze 23: 27 put a stop to the lewdness and **prostitution** you began in Egypt.
43: 7 by their **prostitution** and the lifeless idols of their kings at their
43: 9 Now let them put away from me their **prostitution** and the lifeless
Hos 4: 11 to **prostitution**, to old wine and new, which take away the
6: 10 There Ephraim is given to **prostitution** and Israel is defiled.

2395 זָנַח¹ *zānaḥ¹*, v. [1] [→ 2391?, 2392?]

stink [1]

Isa 19: 6 [G] The canals *will* **stink**; the streams of Egypt will dwindle

2396 זָנַח² *zānaḥ²*, v. [19] [→ 2391?, 2392?]

rejected [11], reject [4], cast off [1], deprived [1], removed [1], throw out [1]

1Ch 28: 9 [G] by you; but if you forsake him, *he will* **reject** you forever.
2Ch 11: 14 [G] and his sons *had* **rejected** them as priests of the LORD.
29: 19 [G] consecrated all the articles that King Ahaz **removed** in his
Ps 43: 2 [A] You are God my stronghold. Why *have you* **rejected** me?
44: 9 [44:10] [A] now *you have* **rejected** and humbled us; you no
44: 23 [44:24] [A] Rouse yourself! *Do* not **reject** us forever.
60: 1 [60:3] [A] *You have* **rejected** us, O God, and burst forth upon
60: 10 [60:12] [A] *you who have* **rejected** us and no longer go out
74: 1 [A] Why *have you* **rejected** us forever, O God? Why does your
77: 7 [77:8] [A] "*Will* the Lord **reject** forever? Will he never show
88: 14 [88:15] [A] *do you* **reject** me and hide your face from me?
89: 38 [89:39] [A] you *have* **rejected**, you have spurned, you have
108: 11 [108:12] [A] *you who have* **rejected** us and no longer go out
La 2: 7 [A] The Lord *has* **rejected** his altar and abandoned his sanctuary.
3: 17 [A] I *have been* **deprived** of peace; I have forgotten what
3: 31 [A] For *men are* not **cast off** *by* the Lord forever.
Hos 8: 3 [A] Israel *has* **rejected** what is good; an enemy will pursue him.
8: 5 [A] **Throw out** your calf-idol, O Samaria! My anger burns
Zec 10: 6 [A] They will be as though *I had* not **rejected** them, for I am the

2397 זָנַק *zānaq*, v. [1]

springing out [1]

Dt 33: 22 [D] Dan he said: "Dan is a lion's cub, **springing out** of Bashan."

2398 זָעָה *zā'â*, v. Not used in NIV/BHS [cf. 2316]

2399 זֵעָה *zē'â*, n.f. [1] [√ 3472]

sweat [1]

Ge 3: 19 By the **sweat** *of* your brow you will eat your food until you return

2400 זַעֲוָה *za'awâ*, n.f. [2] [→ 2401; cf. 2316]

terror [1], thing of horror [1]

Dt 28: 25 you will become a **thing of horror** to all the kingdoms on earth.
2Ch 29: 8 [he has made them an **object of dread** [Q; see K 2317] and horror]
Jer 15: 4 [I will make them **abhorrent** [Q; see K 2317] to all the kingdoms]
24: 9 [I will make them **abhorrent** [Q; see K 2317] and an offense to all]
29: 18 [will make them **abhorrent** [Q; see K 2317] to all the kingdoms]
34: 17 [I will make you **abhorrent** [Q; see K 2317] to all the kingdoms]
Eze 23: 46 a mob against them and give them over to **terror** and plunder.

2401 זַעֲוָן *za'awān*, n.pr.m. [2] [√ 2400 + 5527?]

Zaavan [2]

Ge 36: 27 The sons of Ezer: Bilhan, **Zaavan** and Akan.
1Ch 1: 42 The sons of Ezer: Bilhan, **Zaavan** and Akan. The sons of Dishan:

2402 זְעֵיר *ze'êr*, n.[m.]. [6] [→ 4663; cf. 7592; Ar 10236]

little [5], little longer [1]

Job 36: 2 "Bear with me a **little longer** and I will show you that there is
Isa 28: 10 and do, rule on rule, rule on rule; a **little** here, a little there."
28: 10 and do, rule on rule, rule on rule; a little here, a **little** there."
28: 13 and do, rule on rule, rule on rule; a **little** here, a little there—
28: 13 and do, rule on rule, rule on rule; a little here, a **little** there—
Da 7: 8 me was another horn, a **little** *one*, which came up among them;

2403 זָעַךְ *zā'ak*, v. [1] [cf. 1980]

are cut short [1]

Job 17: 1 [C] My spirit is broken, my days **are cut short**, the grave awaits

2404 זָעַם *zā'am*, v. [12] [→ 2405]

denounce [3], angry [2], accursed [1], denounced [1], expresses wrath [1], fury shown [1], under the wrath [1], under wrath [1], vent fury [1]

Nu 23: 7 [A] 'Come,' he said, 'curse Jacob for me; come, **denounce** Israel.'
23: 8 [A] How *can I* **denounce** those whom the LORD has not
23: 8 [A] can I denounce those whom the LORD *has* not **denounced**?
Ps 7: 11 [7:12] [A] a God *who* **expresses** his **wrath** every day.
Pr 22: 14 [B] *he who is* **under** the LORD's **wrath** will fall into it.
24: 24 [A] peoples will curse him and nations **denounce** him.
25: 23 [C] a north wind brings rain, so a sly tongue brings **angry** looks.
Isa 66: 14 [A] to his servants, but *his* **fury** *will be* **shown** *to* his foes.
Da 11: 30 [A] will turn back and **vent** *his* **fury** against the holy covenant.
Mic 6: 10 [B] ill-gotten treasures and the short ephah, which *is* **accursed**?
Zec 1: 12 [A] which *you have been* **angry** *with* these seventy years?"
Mal 1: 4 [A] a people always **under the wrath** *of* the LORD.

2405 זַעַם *za'am*, n.m. [22] [√ 2404]

wrath [15], indignation [3], anger [1], fierce [1], great wrath [+2256+7912] [1], insolent [1]

Ps 38: 3 [38:4] Because of your **wrath** there is no health in my body;
69: 24 [69:25] Pour out your **wrath** on them; let your fierce anger
78: 49 against them his hot anger, his wrath, **indignation** and hostility—
102: 10 [102:11] because of your **great wrath** [+2256+7912], for you
Isa 10: 5 the rod of my anger, in whose hand is the club of my **wrath**!
10: 25 Very soon my **anger** against you will end and my wrath will be
13: 5 the LORD and the weapons of his **wrath**—to destroy the whole
26: 20 hide yourselves for a little while until his **wrath** has passed by.
30: 27 his lips are full of **wrath**, and his tongue is a consuming fire.
Jer 10: 10 is angry, the earth trembles; the nations cannot endure his **wrath**.
15: 17 your hand was on me and you had filled me with **indignation**.
50: 25 has opened his arsenal and brought out the weapons of his **wrath**,
La 2: 6 in his **fierce** anger he has spurned both king and priest.
Eze 21: 31 [21:36] I will pour out my **wrath** upon you and breathe out my
22: 24 are a land that has had no rain or showers in the day of **wrath**.'
22: 31 So I will pour out my **wrath** on them and consume them with my
Da 8: 19 "I am going to tell you what will happen later in the time of **wrath**,
11: 36 He will be successful until the time of **wrath** is completed,
Hos 7: 16 leaders will fall by the sword because of their **insolent** words.
Na 1: 6 Who can withstand his **indignation**? Who can endure his fierce
Hab 3: 12 In **wrath** you strode through the earth and in anger you threshed
Zep 3: 8 to gather the kingdoms and to pour out my **wrath** on them—

2406 זָעַף¹ *zā'ap¹*, v. [3] [→ 2363, 2408, 2409; cf. 2407]

angry [1], rages [1], raging [1]

2Ch 26: 19 [A] a censer in his hand ready to burn incense, *became* **angry**.

2Ch 26:19 [A] While he *was* **raging** at the priests in their presence before
Pr 19: 3 [A] folly ruins his life, yet his heart **rages** against the LORD.

2407 ²זָעַף **za'ap²**, v. [2] [cf. 2406]

dejected [1], looking worse [1]

Ge 40: 6 [A] to them the next morning, he saw that they *were* **dejected**.
Da 1:10 [A] Why should he see you **looking worse** than the other young

2408 זַעַף **za'ap**, n.m. [6] [√ 2406]

rage [2], raging [2], enraged [1], wrath [1]

2Ch 16:10 because of this; he was so **enraged** that he put him in prison.
28: 9 But you have slaughtered them in a **rage** that reaches to heaven.
Pr 19:12 A king's **rage** is like the roar of a lion, but his favor is like dew on
Isa 30:30 and will make them see his arm coming down with **raging** anger
Jnh 1:15 and threw him overboard, and the **raging** sea grew calm.
Mic 7: 9 I will bear the LORD's **wrath**, until he pleads my case

2409 זָעֵף **zā'ēp**, a. [2] [√ 2406]

angry [2]

1Ki 20:43 Sullen and **angry**, the king of Israel went to his palace in Samaria.
21: 4 sullen and **angry** because Naboth the Jezreelite had said,

2410 זָעַק **zā'aq**, v. [73] [→ 2411; cf. 7590; Ar 10237]

cry out [18], cried out [16], cried [5], cries out [4], called [3], cry [3], crying out [2], summon [2], assembled [1], call out [1], called out to fight [1], calling to arms [+339] [1], cried for help [1], cried out for help [1], cry for help [+7754] [1], cry out for help [1], gathered together [1], howl [1], issued a proclamation [1], make appeals [1], sent up a cry [1], summoned [1], summoning [1], wail [1], wailing [+2411] [1], weeping aloud [1], were called together [1], were called [1]

Ex 2:23 [A] The Israelites groaned in their slavery and **cried out**,
Jos 8:16 [C] All the men of Ai **were called** to pursue them, and they
Jdg 3: 9 [A] when they **cried out** to the LORD, he raised up for them a
3:15 [A] Again the Israelites **cried out** to the LORD, and he gave
4:10 [G] where he **summoned** Zebulun and Naphtali. Ten thousand
4:13 [G] Sisera **gathered together** his nine hundred iron chariots and
6: 6 [A] the Israelites that they **cried out** to the LORD **for help**.
6: 7 [A] When the Israelites **cried** to the LORD because of Midian,
6:34 [C] he blew a trumpet, **summoning** the Abiezrites to follow him.
6:35 [C] **calling** [+339] them **to arms**, and also into Asher, Zebulun
10:10 [A] the Israelites **cried out** to the LORD, "We have sinned
10:14 [A] Go and **cry out** to the gods you have chosen. Let them save
12: 2 [A] and *although I* **called**, you didn't save me out of their hands.
18:22 [C] the men who lived near Micah **were called together**
18:23 [C] the matter with you that *you* **called out** your men **to fight**?"
1Sa 4:13 [A] and told what had happened, the whole town **sent up a cry**.
5:10 [A] of God was entering Ekron, the people of Ekron **cried out**,
7: 8 [A] "Do not stop **crying out** to the LORD our God for us,
7: 9 [A] He **cried out** to the LORD on Israel's behalf,
8:18 [A] *you will* **cry out** for relief from the king you have chosen,
12: 8 [A] they **cried** to the LORD **for help**, and the LORD sent
12:10 [A] *They* **cried out** to the LORD and said, 'We have sinned;
14:20 [C] Then Saul and all his men **assembled** and went to the battle.
15:11 [A] was troubled, and *he* **cried out** to the LORD all that night.
28:12 [A] *she* **cried out** at the top of her voice and said to Saul, "Why
2Sa 13:19 [A] on her head and went away, **weeping aloud** as she went.
19: 4 [19:5] [A] The king covered his face and **cried** aloud, "O my
19:28 [19:29] [A] So what right do I have to **make** any more **appeals**
20: 4 [G] "**Summon** the men of Judah to come to me within three
20: 5 [G] when Amasa went to **summon** Judah, he took longer than the
1Ki 22:32 [A] they turned to attack him, but when Jehoshaphat **cried out**,
1Ch 5:20 [A] to them, because *they* **cried out** to him during the battle.
2Ch 18:31 [A] but Jehoshaphat **cried out**, and the LORD helped him.
20: 9 [C] that bears your Name and *will* **cry out** to you in our distress,
32:20 [A] the prophet Isaiah son of Amoz **cried out** in prayer to heaven
Ne 9: 4 [A] *who* **called** with loud voices to the LORD their God.
9:28 [A] when *they* **cried out** *to* you again, you heard from heaven,
Est 4: 1 [A] went out into the city, **wailing** [+2411] loudly and bitterly.
Job 31:38 [A] "if my land **cries out** against me and all its furrows are wet
35: 9 [G] "*Men* **cry out** under a load of oppression; they plead for
Ps 22: 5 [22:6] [A] *They* **cried** to you and were saved; in you they
107:13 [A] *they* **cried** to the LORD in their trouble, and he saved them
107:19 [A] *they* **cried** to the LORD in their trouble, and he saved them
142: 1 [142:2] [A] *I* **cry** aloud to the LORD; I lift up my voice to the
142: 5 [142:6] [A] *I* **cry** to you, O LORD; I say, "You are my refuge,
Isa 14:31 [A] Wail, O gate! **Howl**, O city! Melt away, all you Philistines!
15: 4 [A] Heshbon and Elealeh **cry out**, their voices are heard all the
15: 5 [A] My heart **cries out** over Moab; her fugitives flee as far as
26:17 [A] and about to give birth writhes and **cries out** in her pain,
30:19 [A] How gracious he will be when you **cry** [+7754] **for help**!
57:13 [A] When you **cry out for help**, let your collection ⌞of idols⌟
Jer 11:11 [A] Although *they* **cry out** to me, I will not listen to them.
11:12 [A] will go and **cry out** to the gods to whom they burn incense,
20: 8 [A] I speak, *I* **cry out** proclaiming violence and destruction.
25:34 [A] Weep and **wail**, *you* shepherds; roll in the dust, you leaders
30:15 [A] Why *do you* **cry out** over your wound, your pain that has no
47: 2 [A] The people *will* **cry out**; all who dwell in the land will wail
48:20 [A] Moab is disgraced, for she is shattered. Wail and **cry out**!
48:31 [A] Therefore I wail over Moab, for all Moab *I* **cry out**, I moan
La 3: 8 [A] Even when *I* **call out** or cry for help, he shuts out my prayer.
Eze 9: 8 [A] I fell facedown, **crying out**, "Ah, Sovereign LORD!
11:13 [A] I fell facedown and **cried out** in a loud voice, "Ah,
21:12 [21:17] [A] **Cry out** and wail, son of man, for it is against my
27:30 [A] They will raise their voice and **cry** bitterly over you; they
Hos 7:14 [A] *They do* not **cry out** to me from their hearts but wail upon
8: 2 [A] Israel **cries out** to me, 'O our God, we acknowledge you!'
Joel 1:14 [A] house of the LORD your God, and **cry out** to the LORD.
Jnh 1: 5 [A] All the sailors were afraid and each **cried out** to his own god.
3: 7 [G] *he* **issued a proclamation** in Nineveh: "By the decree of the
Mic 3: 4 [A] *they will* **cry out** to the LORD, but he will not answer
Hab 1: 2 [A] Or **cry out** to you, "Violence!" but you do not save?
2:11 [A] The stones of the wall *will* **cry out**, and the beams of the
Zec 6: 8 [G] *he* **called** to me, "Look, those going toward the north country

2411 זְעָקָה **zᵉ'āqâ**, n.f. [18] [√ 2410]

cry [7], outcry [3], cry out [+7754] [1], cry out [+9048] [1], crying [1], lament [+6424] [1], lamentation [1], shouts [1], wailing [+2410] [1], wailing [1]

Ge 18:20 "The **outcry** *against* Sodom and Gomorrah is so great and their sin
Ne 5: 6 When I heard their **outcry** and these charges, I was very angry.
9: 9 of our forefathers in Egypt; you heard their **cry** at the Red Sea.
Est 4: 1 and went out into the city, **wailing** [+2410] loudly and bitterly.
9:31 descendants in regard to their times of fasting and **lamentation**.
Job 16:18 "O earth, do not cover my blood; may my **cry** never be laid to rest!
Pr 21:13 If a man shuts his ears to the **cry** *of* the poor, he too will cry out
Ecc 9:17 the wise are more to be heeded than the **shouts** *of* a ruler of fools.
Isa 15: 5 on the road to Horonaim *they* **lament** [+6424] their destruction.
15: 8 Their **outcry** echoes along the border of Moab; their wailing
65:19 the sound of weeping and of **crying** will be heard in it no more.
Jer 18:22 Let a **cry** be heard from their houses when you suddenly bring
20:16 May he hear **wailing** in the morning, a battle cry at noon.
48: 4 Moab will be broken; her little ones *will* **cry** [+9048] **out**.
48:34 "The sound of their **cry** rises from Heshbon to Elealeh and Jahaz,
50:46 the earth will tremble; its **cry** will resound among the nations.
51:54 "The sound of a **cry** comes from Babylon, the sound of great
Eze 27:28 The shorelands will quake when your seamen **cry** [+7754] **out**.

2412 זִפְרֹן **ziprôn**, n.pr.loc. [1]

Ziphron [1]

Nu 34: 9 continue to **Ziphron** and end at Hazar Enan. This will be your

2413 זֶפֶת **zepet**, n.f. [3]

pitch [3]

Ex 2: 3 she got a papyrus basket for him and coated it with tar and **pitch**.
Isa 34: 9 Edom's streams will be turned into **pitch**, her dust into burning
34: 9 her dust into burning sulfur; her land will become blazing **pitch**!

2414 ¹זִק **zēq¹**, n.[m.]. [4] [cf. 272]

chains [2], fetters [1], were put in chains [+928+8415] [1]

Job 36: 8 But if men are bound in **chains**, held fast by cords of affliction,
Ps 149: 8 to bind their kings with **fetters**, their nobles with shackles of iron,
Isa 45:14 they will trudge behind you, coming over to you in **chains**.
Na 3:10 her nobles, and all her great men **were put in chains** [+928+8415].

2415 ²זִק **zēq²**, n.[m.]. [1] [√ 2338]

firebrands [1]

Pr 26:18 Like a madman shooting **firebrands** or deadly arrows

2416 ¹זָקֵן **zāqēn¹**, v. [26] [√ 2417]

old [22], aged [+4394] [1], grew old [1], grow old [1], very old [+928+995+2021+3427] [1]

Ge 18:12 [A] "After I am worn out and my master *is* **old**, will I now have
18:13 [A] and say, 'Will I really have a child, now that I *am* **old**?'
19:31 [A] "Our father *is* **old**, and there is no man around here to lie
24: 1 [A] Abraham *was* now **old** and well advanced in years,
27: 1 [A] When Isaac *was* **old** and his eyes were so weak that he could
27: 2 [A] "*I am* now *an* **old** *man* and don't know the day of my death.
Jos 13: 1 [A] When Joshua *was* **old** and well advanced in years,
13: 1 [A] said to him, "You *are* **very old** [+928+995+2021+3427],
23: 1 [A] around them, Joshua, by then **old** and well advanced in years,

Jos 23: 2 [A] and said to them: "I *am* **old** and well advanced in years.
Ru 1: 12 [A] my daughters; *I am* too **old** to have another husband.
1Sa 2: 22 [A] Now Eli, *who was* very **old**, heard about everything his sons
8: 1 [A] When Samuel **grew old**, he appointed his sons as judges for
8: 5 [A] They said to him, "You *are* **old**, and your sons do not walk in
12: 2 [A] As for me, *I am* **old** and gray, and my sons are here with
17: 12 [A] and in Saul's time he *was* **old** and well advanced in years.
2Sa 19: 32 [19:33] [A] Now Barzillai *was* a very **old** *man*, eighty years of
1Ki 1: 1 [A] When King David *was* **old** and well advanced in years, he
1: 15 [A] So Bathsheba went to see the **aged** [+4394] king in his room,
2Ki 4: 14 [A] Gehazi said, "Well, she has no son and her husband *is* **old**."
1Ch 23: 1 [A] When David *was* **old** and full of years, he made his son
2Ch 24: 15 [A] Now Jehoiada *was* **old** and full of years, and he died at the
Job 14: 8 [G] Its roots *may* **grow old** in the ground and its stump die in the
Ps 37: 25 [A] I was young and now *I am* **old**, yet I have never seen the
Pr 22: 6 [G] he should go, and when *he is* **old** he will not turn from it.
23: 22 [A] you life, and do not despise your mother when *she is* **old**.

2417 זָקָן **zāqān**, n.m. [19] [→ 2416, 2418, 2419, 2420, 2421]

beard [11], beards [5], chin [2], hair [1]

Lev 13: 29 "If a man or woman has a sore on the head or on the **chin**,
13: 30 it is an itch, an infectious disease of the head or **chin**.
14: 9 shave his head, his **beard**, his eyebrows and the rest of his hair.
19: 27 hair at the sides of your head or clip off the edges of your **beard**.
21: 5 or shave off the edges of their **beards** or cut their bodies.
1Sa 17: 35 When it turned on me, I seized it by its **hair**, struck it and killed it.
21: 13 [21:14] doors of the gate and letting saliva run down his **beard**.
2Sa 10: 4 Hanun seized David's men, shaved off half of each man's **beard**,
10: 5 "Stay at Jericho till your **beards** have grown, and then come back."
20: 9 Joab took Amasa by the **beard** with his right hand to kiss him.
1Ch 19: 5 "Stay at Jericho till your **beards** have grown, and then come back."
Ezr 9: 3 pulled hair from my head and **beard** and sat down appalled.
Ps 133: 2 running down on the **beard**, running down on Aaron's beard,
133: 2 running down on the beard, running down on Aaron's **beard**,
Isa 7: 20 and the hair of your legs, and to take off your **beards** also.
15: 2 and Medeba. Every head is shaved and every **beard** cut off.
Jer 41: 5 eighty men who had shaved off their **beards**, torn their clothes
48: 37 Every head is shaved and every **beard** cut off; every hand is
Eze 5: 1 and use it as a barber's razor to shave your head and your **beard**.

2418 ²זָקֵן **zāqēn²**, a. [179] [√ 2417; Ar 10675]

elders [122], old [32], aged [5], *untranslated* [4], dignitaries [2], leaders [2], leading [2], chief [1], elder [1], elderly [1], his own[s] [+2021+2021+5566] [1], of ripe old age [1], older [+3427+4200] [1], older [1], them[s] [+1680] [1], veteran [1], women[s] [1]

Ge 18: 11 Abraham and Sarah were already **old** and well advanced in years,
19: 4 of the city of Sodom—both young and **old**—surrounded the house.
24: 2 He said to the **chief** servant *in* his household, the one in charge of
25: 8 his last and died at a good old age, an **old** *man* and full of years;
35: 29 and died and was gathered to his people, **old** and full of years.
43: 27 then he said, "How is your **aged** father you told me about?
44: 20 we answered, 'We have an **aged** father, and there is a young son
50: 7 the **dignitaries** *of* his court and all the dignitaries of Egypt—
50: 7 the dignitaries of his court and all the **dignitaries** *of* Egypt—
Ex 3: 16 "Go, assemble the **elders** *of* Israel and say to them, 'The LORD,
3: 18 "The **elders** *of* Israel will listen to you. Then you and the elders are
4: 29 and Aaron brought together all the **elders** *of* the Israelites,
10: 9 "We will go with our young and **old**, with our sons and daughters,
12: 21 Then Moses summoned all the **elders** *of* Israel and said to them,
17: 5 Take with you some of the **elders** *of* Israel and take in your hand
17: 6 to drink." So Moses did this in the sight of the **elders** *of* Israel.
18: 12 Aaron came with all the **elders** *of* Israel to eat bread with Moses'
19: 7 So Moses went back and summoned the **elders** *of* the people
24: 1 and Aaron, Nadab and Abihu, and seventy of the **elders** *of* Israel.
24: 9 Nadab and Abihu, and the seventy **elders** *of* Israel went up
24: 14 He said to the **elders**, "Wait here for us until we come back to you.
Lev 4: 15 The **elders** *of* the community are to lay their hands on the bull's
9: 1 day Moses summoned Aaron and his sons and the **elders** *of* Israel.
19: 32 of the aged, show respect for the **elderly** and revere your God.
Nu 11: 16 "Bring me seventy of Israel's **elders** who are known to you as
11: 16 me seventy of Israel's elders who are known to you as **leaders**
11: 24 He brought together seventy of their **elders** and had them stand
11: 25 the Spirit that was on him and put the Spirit on the seventy **elders**.
11: 30 Then Moses and the **elders** *of* Israel returned to the camp.
16: 25 went to Dathan and Abiram, and the **elders** *of* Israel followed him.
22: 4 The Moabites said to the **elders** *of* Midian, "This horde is going to
22: 7 The **elders** *of* Moab and Midian left, taking with them the fee for
22: 7 The elders of Moab and **[RPH]** Midian left, taking with them the
Dt 5: 23 all the leading men of your tribes and your **elders** came to me.
19: 12 the **elders** *of* his town shall send for him, bring him back from the
21: 2 your **elders** and judges shall go out and measure the distance from
21: 3 the **elders** *of* the town nearest the body shall take a heifer that has
21: 4 and lead her down **[RPH]** to a valley that has not been plowed
21: 6 all the **elders** *of* the town nearest the body shall wash their hands
21: 19 hold of him and bring him to the **elders** at the gate of his town.
21: 20 They shall say to the **elders**, "This son of ours is stubborn
22: 15 mother shall bring proof that she was a virgin to the town **elders** at
22: 16 The girl's father will say to the **elders**, "I gave my daughter in
22: 17 her parents shall display the cloth before the **elders** *of* the town,
22: 18 and the **elders** shall take the man and punish him.
25: 7 brother's wife, she shall go to the **elders** at the town gate and say,
25: 8 Then the **elders** *of* his town shall summon him and talk to him.
25: 9 brother's widow shall go up to him in the presence of the **elders**,
27: 1 Moses and the **elders** *of* Israel commanded the people: "Keep all
28: 50 a fierce-looking nation without respect for the **old** or pity for the
29: 10 [29:9] your leaders and chief men, your **elders** and officials, and
31: 9 ark of the covenant of the LORD, and to all the **elders** *of* Israel.
31: 28 Assemble before me all the **elders** *of* your tribes and all your
32: 7 Ask your father and he will tell you, your **elders**, and they will
Jos 6: 21 men and women, young and **old**, cattle, sheep and donkeys.
7: 6 The **elders** *of* Israel did the same, and sprinkled dust on their
8: 10 and he and the **leaders** *of* Israel marched before them to Ai.
8: 33 aliens and citizens alike, with their **elders**, officials and judges,
9: 11 And our **elders** and all those living in our country said to us,
20: 4 of the city gate and state his case before the **elders** *of* that city.
23: 2 their **elders**, leaders, judges and officials—and said to them:
24: 1 He summoned the **elders**, leaders, judges and officials of Israel,
24: 31 the lifetime of Joshua and of the **elders** who outlived him
Jdg 2: 7 the lifetime of Joshua and of the **elders** who outlived him
8: 14 of the seventy-seven officials of Succoth, the **elders** *of* the town.
8: 16 He took the **elders** *of* the town and taught the men of Succoth a
11: 5 the **elders** *of* Gilead went to get Jephthah from the land of Tob.
11: 7 Jephthah said to **them**[s] [+1680], "Didn't you hate me and drive me
11: 8 The **elders** *of* Gilead said to him, "Nevertheless, we are turning to
11: 9 **[RPH]** "Suppose you take me back to fight the Ammonites
11: 10 The **elders** *of* Gilead replied, "The LORD is our witness;
11: 11 So Jephthah went with the **elders** *of* Gilead, and the people made
19: 16 That evening an **old** man from the hill country of Ephraim,
19: 17 in the city square, the **old** man asked, "Where are you going?
19: 20 "You are welcome at my house," the **old** man said. "Let me supply
19: 22 on the door, they shouted to the **old** man who owned the house,
21: 16 the **elders** *of* the assembly said, "With the women of Benjamin
Ru 4: 2 Boaz took ten of the **elders** *of* the town and said, "Sit here,"
4: 4 of these seated here and in the presence of the **elders** *of* my people.
4: 9 Boaz announced to the **elders** and all the people, "Today you are
4: 11 Then the **elders** and all those at the gate said, "We are witnesses.
1Sa 2: 31 so that there will not be an **old** *man* in your family line
2: 32 done to Israel, in your family line there will never be an **old** *man*.
4: 3 When the soldiers returned to camp, the **elders** *of* Israel asked,
4: 18 neck was broken and he died, for he was an **old** man and heavy.
8: 4 So all the **elders** *of* Israel gathered together and came to Samuel at
11: 3 The **elders** *of* Jabesh said to him, "Give us seven days so we can
15: 30 please honor me before the **elders** *of* my people and before Israel;
16: 4 at Bethlehem, the **elders** *of* the town trembled when they met him.
28: 14 he asked. "An **old** man wearing a robe is coming up," she said.
30: 26 he sent some of the plunder to the **elders** *of* Judah, who were his
2Sa 3: 17 Abner conferred with the **elders** *of* Israel and said, "For some time
5: 3 When all the **elders** *of* Israel had come to King David at Hebron,
12: 17 The **elders** *of* his household stood beside him to get him up from
17: 4 This plan seemed good to Absalom and to all the **elders** *of* Israel.
17: 15 has advised Absalom and the **elders** *of* Israel to do such and such,
19: 11 [19:12] "Ask the **elders** *of* Judah, 'Why should you be the last to
1Ki 8: 1 summoned into his presence at Jerusalem the **elders** *of* Israel,
8: 3 When all the **elders** *of* Israel had arrived, the priests took up the
12: 6 King Rehoboam consulted the **elders** who had served his father
12: 8 Rehoboam rejected the advice the **elders** gave him and consulted
12: 13 the people harshly. Rejecting the advice given him by the **elders**,
13: 11 Now there was a certain **old** prophet living in Bethel, whose sons
13: 25 they went and reported it in the city where the **old** prophet lived.
13: 29 and brought it back to **his**[s] **own** [+2021+2021+5566] city to mourn
20: 7 The king of Israel summoned all the **elders** *of* the land and said to
20: 8 The **elders** and the people all answered, "Don't listen to him
21: 8 sent them to the **elders** and nobles who lived in Naboth's city with
21: 11 So the **elders** and nobles who lived in Naboth's city did as Jezebel
2Ki 6: 32 was sitting in his house, and the **elders** were sitting with him.
6: 32 a messenger ahead, but before he arrived, Elisha said to the **elders**,
10: 1 of Jezreel, to the **elders** and to the guardians of Ahab's children.
10: 5 the **elders** and the guardians sent this message to Jehu:
19: 2 Shebna the secretary and the **leading** priests, all wearing sackcloth,
23: 1 the king called together all the **elders** *of* Judah and Jerusalem.
1Ch 11: 3 When all the **elders** *of* Israel had come to King David at Hebron,
15: 25 So David and the **elders** *of* Israel and the commanders of units of a
21: 16 Then David and the **elders**, clothed in sackcloth, fell facedown.
2Ch 5: 2 Then Solomon summoned to Jerusalem the **elders** *of* Israel,
5: 4 When all the **elders** *of* Israel had arrived, the Levites took up the
10: 6 King Rehoboam consulted the **elders** who had served his father

2Ch 10: 8 Rehoboam rejected the advice the **elders** gave him and consulted
10: 13 king answered them harshly. Rejecting the advice of the **elders**,
34: 29 the king called together all the **elders** *of* Judah and Jerusalem.
36: 17 and spared neither young man nor young woman, **old** *man* or aged.
Ezr 3: 12 But many of the **older** priests and Levites and family heads,
10: 8 in accordance with the decision of the officials and **elders**,
10: 14 along with the **elders** and judges of each town, until the fierce
Est 3: 13 young and **old**, women and little children—on a single day,
Job 12: 20 lips of trusted advisers and takes away the discernment of **elders**.
32: 4 speaking to Job because they were **older** [+3427+4200] than he.
32: 9 old who are wise, not only the **aged** who understand what is right.
42: 17 And so he died, **old** and full of years.
Ps 105: 22 to instruct his princes as he pleased and teach his **elders** wisdom.
107: 32 assembly of the people and praise him in the council of the **elders**.
119: 100 I have more understanding than the **elders**, for I obey your
148: 12 young men and maidens, **old** *men* and children.
Pr 17: 6 Children's children are a crown to the **aged**, and parents are the
20: 29 of young men is their strength, gray hair the splendor of the **old**.
31: 23 the city gate, where he takes his seat among the **elders** *of* the land.
Ecc 4: 13 Better a poor but wise youth than an **old** but foolish king who no
Isa 3: 2 and warrior, the judge and prophet, the soothsayer and **elder**,
3: 5 The young will rise up against the **old**, the base against the
3: 14 The LORD enters into judgment against the **elders** and leaders of
9: 15 [9:14] the **elders** and prominent men are the head, the prophets
20: 4 barefoot the Egyptian captives and Cushite exiles, young and **old**,
24: 23 on Mount Zion and in Jerusalem, and before its **elders**, gloriously.
37: 2 Shebna the secretary, and the **leading** priests, all wearing
47: 6 them no mercy. Even on the **aged** you laid a very heavy yoke.
65: 20 but a few days, or an **old** *man* who does not live out his years;
Jer 6: 11 both husband and wife will be caught in it, and the **old**,
19: 1 Take along some of the **elders** *of* the people and of the priests
19: 1 along some of the elders of the people and **[RPH]** of the priests
26: 17 Some of the **elders** *of* the land stepped forward and said to the
29: 1 sent from Jerusalem to the surviving **elders** *among* the exiles
31: 13 Then maidens will dance and be glad, young men and **old** as well.
51: 22 I shatter man and woman, with you I shatter **old** *man* and youth,
La 1: 19 my **elders** perished in the city while they searched for food to keep
2: 10 The **elders** *of* the Daughter of Zion sit on the ground in silence;
2: 21 "Young and **old** lie together in the dust of the streets; my young
4: 16 over them. The priests are shown no honor, the **elders** no favor.
5: 12 have been hung up by their hands; **elders** are shown no respect.
5: 14 The **elders** are gone from the city gate; the young men have
Eze 7: 26 the law by the priest will be lost, as will the counsel of the **elders**.
8: 1 sitting in my house and the **elders** *of* Judah were sitting before me,
8: 11 In front of them stood seventy **elders** *of* the house of Israel,
8: 12 have you seen what the **elders** *of* the house of Israel are doing in
9: 6 Slaughter **old** *men*, young men and maidens, women and children,
9: 6 So they began with the **elders** who were in front of the temple.
14: 1 Some of the **elders** *of* Israel came to me and sat down in front of
20: 1 some of the **elders** *of* Israel came to inquire of the LORD,
20: 3 "Son of man, speak to the **elders** *of* Israel and say to them,
27: 9 **Veteran** craftsmen of Gebal were on board as shipwrights to caulk
Joel 1: 2 Hear this, you **elders**; listen, all who live in the land. Has anything
1: 14 Summon the **elders** and all who live in the land to the house of the
2: 16 bring together the **elders**, gather the children, those nursing at the
2: 28 [3:1] daughters will prophesy, your **old** *men* will dream dreams,
Zec 8: 4 and **women**[s] of ripe old age will sit in the streets of Jerusalem,
8: 4 "Once again *men* and women **of ripe old age** will sit in the streets

2419 זֹקֶן zōqen, n.[m.]. [1] [√ 2417]

old age [1]

Ge 48: 10 Now Israel's eyes were failing because of **old age**, and he could

2420 זִקְנָה ziqnâ, n.f. [6] [√ 2417]

old age [3], old [2], grew old [1]

Ge 24: 36 My master's wife Sarah has borne him a son in her **old age**,
1Ki 11: 4 As Solomon **grew old**, his wives turned his heart after other gods,
15: 23 kings of Judah? In his **old age**, however, his feet became diseased.
Ps 71: 9 Do not cast me away when I am **old**; do not forsake me when my
71: 18 Even when I am **old** and gray, do not forsake me, O God, till I
Isa 46: 4 Even to your **old age** and gray hairs I am he, I am he who will

2421 זְקֻנִים z^equnîm, n.pl.[m.]. [4] [√ 2417]

old age [4]

Ge 21: 2 Sarah became pregnant and bore a son to Abraham in his **old age**,
21: 7 would nurse children? Yet I have borne him a son in his **old age**."
37: 3 of his other sons, because he had been born to him in his **old age**;
44: 20 an aged father, and there is a young son born to him in his **old age**.

2422 זָקַף zāqap, v. [2] [→ Ar 10238]

lifts up [2]

Ps 145: 14 [A] all those who fall and **lifts up** all who are bowed down.
146: 8 [A] the LORD **lifts up** those who are bowed down, the LORD

2423 זָקַק zāqaq, v. [7] [cf. 2293]

refined [3], distill [1], finest [1], purified [1], refine [1]

1Ch 28: 18 [E] and the weight of the **refined** gold for the altar of incense.
29: 4 [E] seven thousand talents of **refined** silver, for the overlaying of
Job 28: 1 [A] "There is a mine for silver and a place where gold *is* **refined**.
36: 27 [A] up the drops of water, *which* **distill** as rain to the streams;
Ps 12: 6 [12:7] [E] refined in a furnace of clay, **purified** seven times.
Isa 25: 6 [E] of aged wine—the best of meats and the **finest** of wines.
Mal 3: 3 [D] will purify the Levites and **refine** them like gold and silver.

2424 זָר zār, a. or v.ptcp. [70 / 71] [√ 2319]

foreigners [15], foreign [9], strangers [7], another [4], anyone else [4], adulteress [3], else [3], stranger [3], unauthorized [3], adulteress [+851] [2], alien [2], aliens [2], anyone other than a priest [2], strange [2], distant sources [1], enemies [1], illegitimate [1], imported [1], one[s] [+408] [1], one[s] [1], other [1], outside a priest's family [1], outside the family [+2021+2025+2575] [1], unauthorized person [1]

Ex 29: 33 But no one **else** may eat them, because they are sacred.
30: 9 Do not offer on this altar any **other** incense or any burnt offering
30: 33 whoever puts it on **anyone other than a priest** must be cut off
Lev 10: 1 they offered **unauthorized** fire before the LORD, contrary to his
22: 10 " 'No one **outside a priest's family** may eat the sacred offering,
22: 12 If a priest's daughter marries **anyone other than a priest**,
22: 13 No **unauthorized person**, however, may eat any of it.
Nu 1: 51 shall do it. **Anyone else** who goes near it shall be put to death.
3: 4 offering with **unauthorized** fire before him in the Desert of Sinai.
3: 10 **anyone else** who approaches the sanctuary must be put to death."
3: 38 **Anyone else** who approached the sanctuary was to be put to death.
16: 40 [17:5] This was to remind the Israelites that no **one**[s] [+408]
18: 4 work at the Tent—and no one **else** may come near where you are.
18: 7 **Anyone else** who comes near the sanctuary must be put to death."
26: 61 they made an offering before the LORD with **unauthorized** fire.)
Dt 25: 5 his widow must not marry **outside the family** [+2021+2025+2575].
32: 16 They made him jealous with their **foreign** gods and angered him
1Ki 3: 18 We were alone; there was no **one**[s] in the house but the two of us.
2Ki 19: 24 I have dug wells in **foreign** *lands* and drunk the water there.
Job 15: 19 (to whom alone the land was given when no **alien** passed among
19: 15 My guests and my maidservants count me a **stranger**; they look
19: 27 I myself will see him with my own eyes—I, and not **another**.
Ps 44: 20 [44:21] of our God or spread out our hands to a **foreign** god,
54: 3 [54:5] **Strangers** are attacking me; ruthless men seek my life—
81: 9 [81:10] You shall have no **foreign** god among you; you shall not
109: 11 seize all he has; may **strangers** plunder the fruits of his labor.
Pr 2: 16 It will save you also from the **adulteress** [+851],
5: 3 For the lips of an **adulteress** drip honey, and her speech is
5: 10 lest **strangers** feast on your wealth and your toil enrich another
5: 17 Let them be yours alone, never to be shared with **strangers**.
5: 20 Why be captivated, my son, by an **adulteress**? Why embrace the
6: 1 for your neighbor, if you have struck hands in pledge for **another**,
7: 5 they will keep you from the **adulteress** [+851], from the wayward
11: 15 He who puts up security for **another** will surely suffer, but
14: 10 heart knows its own bitterness, and no *one* **else** can share its joy.
20: 16 Take the garment of one who puts up security for a **stranger**;
22: 14 The mouth of an **adulteress** is a deep pit; he who is under the
23: 33 Your eyes will see **strange** sights and your mind imagine
27: 2 Let **another** praise you, and not your own mouth; someone else,
27: 13 Take the garment of one who puts up security for a **stranger**;
Isa 1: 7 your fields are being stripped by **foreigners** right before you,
1: 7 right before you, laid waste as when overthrown by **strangers**.
17: 10 though you set out the finest plants and plant **imported** vines,
25: 2 the fortified town a ruin, the **foreigners**' stronghold a city no more;
25: 5 You silence the uproar of **foreigners**; as heat is reduced by the
28: 21 to do his work, his **strange** work, and perform his task, his alien
29: 5 your many **enemies** will become like fine dust, the ruthless hordes
37: 25 I have dug wells in **foreign** [BHS-] *lands* and drunk the water
43: 12 and proclaimed—I, and not *some* **foreign** god among you.
61: 5 **Aliens** will shepherd your flocks; foreigners will work your fields
Jer 2: 25 'It's no use! I love **foreign** gods, and I must go after them.'
3: 13 you have scattered your favors to **foreign** gods under every
5: 19 so now you will serve **foreigners** in a land not your own.'
18: 14 Do its cool waters from **distant sources** ever cease to flow?
30: 8 will tear off their bonds; no longer will **foreigners** enslave them.
51: 2 I will send **foreigners** to Babylon to winnow her and to devastate
51: 51 because **foreigners** have entered the holy places of the LORD's
La 5: 2 Our inheritance has been turned over to **aliens**, our homes to
Eze 7: 21 I will hand it all over as plunder to **foreigners** and as loot to the

Eze 11: 9 I will drive you out of the city and hand you over to **foreigners**
16: 32 adulterous wife! You prefer **strangers** to your own husband!
28: 7 I am going to bring **foreigners** against you, the most ruthless of
28: 10 will die the death of the uncircumcised at the hands of **foreigners**.
30: 12 by the hand of **foreigners** I will lay waste the land and everything
31: 12 and the most ruthless of **foreign** nations cut it down and left it.
Hos 5: 7 unfaithful to the LORD; they give birth to **illegitimate** children.
7: 9 **Foreigners** sap his strength, but he does not realize it. His hair is
8: 7 no flour. Were it to yield grain, **foreigners** would swallow it up.
8: 12 things of my law, but they regarded them as *something* **alien**.
Joel 3: 17 [4:17] will be holy; never again will **foreigners** invade her.
Ob 1: 11 On the day you stood aloof while **strangers** carried off his wealth

2425 זֵר zēr, n.m. [10] [√ 2452]

molding [10]

Ex 25: 11 pure gold, both inside and out, and make a gold **molding** around it.
25: 24 Overlay it with pure gold and make a gold **molding** around it.
25: 25 it a rim a handbreadth wide and put a gold **molding** on the rim.
30: 3 and the horns with pure gold, and make a gold **molding** around it.
30: 4 Make two gold rings for the altar below the **molding**—two on
37: 2 pure gold, both inside and out, and made a gold **molding** around it.
37: 11 they overlaid it with pure gold and made a gold **molding** around it.
37: 12 it a rim a handbreadth wide and put a gold **molding** on the rim.
37: 26 and the horns with pure gold, and made a gold **molding** around it.
37: 27 They made two gold rings below the **molding**—two on opposite

2426 זָרָא zārā', n.[f.]. [1]

loathe [1]

Nu 11: 20 until it comes out of your nostrils and you **loathe** it—

2427 זָרַב zārab, v. [1]

dry [1]

Job 6: 17 [E] that cease to flow in the **dry** season, and in the heat vanish

2428 זְרֻבָּבֶל z^erubbābel, n.pr.m. [21] [√ 2445 + 951; Ar 10239]

Zerubbabel [21]

1Ch 3: 19 The sons of Pedaiah: **Zerubbabel** and Shimei. The sons of
3: 19 and Shimei. The sons of **Zerubbabel**: Meshullam and Hananiah.
Ezr 2: 2 in company with **Zerubbabel**, Jeshua, Nehemiah, Seraiah,
3: 2 of Jozadak and his fellow priests and **Zerubbabel** son of Shealtiel
3: 8 **Zerubbabel** son of Shealtiel, Jeshua son of Jozadak and the rest of
4: 2 they came to **Zerubbabel** and to the heads of the families
4: 3 **Zerubbabel**, Jeshua and the rest of the heads of the families of
Ne 7: 7 in company with **Zerubbabel**, Jeshua, Nehemiah, Azariah,
12: 1 and Levites who returned with **Zerubbabel** son of Shealtiel
12: 47 So in the days of **Zerubbabel** and of Nehemiah, all Israel
Hag 1: 1 came through the prophet Haggai to **Zerubbabel** son of Shealtiel,
1: 12 Then **Zerubbabel** son of Shealtiel, Joshua son of Jehozadak,
1: 14 So the LORD stirred up the spirit of **Zerubbabel** son of Shealtiel,
2: 2 "Speak to **Zerubbabel** son of Shealtiel, governor of Judah,
2: 4 now be strong, O **Zerubbabel**,' declares the LORD. 'Be strong,
2: 21 "Tell **Zerubbabel** governor of Judah that I will shake the heavens
2: 23 'I will take you, my servant **Zerubbabel** son of Shealtiel,'
Zec 4: 6 So he said to me, "This is the word of the LORD to **Zerubbabel**:
4: 7 Before **Zerubbabel** you will become level ground.
4: 9 "The hands of **Zerubbabel** have laid the foundation of this temple;
4: 10 rejoice when they see the plumb line in the hand of **Zerubbabel**.

2429 זֶרֶד zered, n.pr.loc. [4]

Zered [3], the^s [1]

Nu 21: 12 From there they moved on and camped in the **Zered** Valley.
Dt 2: 13 And the LORD said, "Now get up and cross the **Zered** Valley."
2: 13 get up and cross the Zered Valley." So we crossed **the**^s valley.
2: 14 the time we left Kadesh Barnea until we crossed the **Zered** Valley.

2430 זָרָה zārâ¹, v. [38] [→ 4665, 4668; cf. 4664]

scatter [18], scattered [5], winnow [4], spread [3], winnows out [2], are scattered [1], is scattered [1], spread out [1], throw away [1], were scattered [1], winnowing [1]

Ex 32: 20 [A] **scattered** it on the water and made the Israelites drink it.
Lev 26: 33 [D] *I will* **scatter** you among the nations and will draw out my
Nu 16: 37 [17:2] [A] and **scatter** the coals some distance away,
Ru 3: 2 [A] Tonight he *will be* **winnowing** barley *on* the threshing floor.
1Ki 14: 15 [D] gave to their forefathers and **scatter** them beyond the River,
Job 18: 15 [E] in his tent; burning sulfur **is scattered** over his dwelling.
Ps 44: 11 [44:12] [D] and *have* **scattered** us among the nations.
106: 27 [A] among the nations and **scatter** them throughout the lands.
Pr 1: 17 [E] How useless *to* **spread** a net in full view of all the birds!
15: 7 [D] The lips of the wise **spread** knowledge; not so the hearts of
20: 8 [D] on his throne to judge, *he* **winnows out** all evil with his eyes.
20: 26 [D] A wise king **winnows out** the wicked; he drives the threshing
Isa 30: 22 [A] *you will* **throw** them **away** like a menstrual cloth and say to
30: 24 [A] will eat fodder and mash, **spread out** with fork and shovel.
41: 16 [A] *You will* **winnow** them, the wind will pick them up, and a
Jer 4: 11 [A] blows toward my people, but not to **winnow** or cleanse;
15: 7 [A] *I will* **winnow** them with a winnowing fork at the city gates
31: 10 [D] '*He who* **scattered** Israel will gather them and will watch
49: 32 [D] *I will* **scatter** to the winds those who are in distant places
49: 36 [D] *I will* **scatter** them to the four winds, and there will not be a
51: 2 [D] I will send foreigners to Babylon *to* **winnow** her and to
Eze 5: 2 [A] **scatter** a third to the wind. For I will pursue them with drawn
5: 10 [D] on you and *will* **scatter** all your survivors to the winds.
5: 12 [A] a third *I will* **scatter** to the winds and pursue with drawn
6: 5 [A] their idols, and *I will* **scatter** your bones around your altars.
6: 8 [C] escape the sword when you **are scattered** among the lands
12: 14 [A] *I will* **scatter** to the winds all those around him—his staff
12: 15 [D] among the nations and **scatter** them through the countries.
20: 23 [B] among the nations and **scatter** them through the countries,
22: 15 [D] you among the nations and **scatter** you through the countries;
29: 12 [D] among the nations and **scatter** them through the countries.
30: 23 [D] among the nations and **scatter** them through the countries.
30: 26 [D] among the nations and **scatter** them through the countries.
36: 19 [C] the nations, and *they* **were scattered** through the countries;
Zec 1: 19 [2:2] [D] "These are the horns that **scattered** Judah, Israel
1: 21 [2:4] [D] "These are the horns that **scattered** Judah so that no
1: 21 [2:4] [D] horns against the land of Judah to **scatter** its people."
Mal 2: 3 [D] *I will* **spread** on your faces the offal from your festival

2431 זָרָה zārâ², v. [1] [√ 2455]

discern [1]

Ps 139: 3 [D] *You* **discern** my going out and my lying down; you are

2432 זְרוֹעַ z^erôa', n.f. [91 / 90] [cf. 274; Ar 10013, 10185]

arm [53], arms [15], strength [6], power [4], shoulder [2], allies [1], arm of power [1], armed forces [1], army [1], forces [1], power [+3946] [1], powerful [1], shoulders [1], strengthened [+2616] [1], strong arms [+3338] [1]

Ge 49: 24 his bow remained steady, his **strong arms** [+3338] stayed limber,
Ex 6: 6 I will redeem you with an outstretched **arm** and with mighty acts
15: 16 By the power of your **arm** they will be as still as a stone—
Nu 6: 19 the priest is to place in his hands a boiled **shoulder** of the ram,
Dt 4: 34 by war, by a mighty hand and an outstretched **arm**, or by great
5: 15 you out of there with a mighty hand and an outstretched **arm**.
7: 19 and wonders, the mighty hand and outstretched **arm**,
9: 29 you brought out by your great power and your outstretched **arm**."
11: 2 your God: his majesty, his mighty hand, his outstretched **arm**;
18: 3 a bull or a sheep: the **shoulder**, the jowls and the inner parts.
26: 8 us out of Egypt with a mighty hand and an outstretched **arm**,
33: 20 Gad's domain! Gad lives there like a lion, tearing at **arm** or head.
33: 27 God is your refuge, and underneath are the everlasting **arms**.
Jdg 15: 14 The ropes on his **arms** became like charred flax, and the bindings
16: 12 But he snapped the ropes off his **arms** as if they were threads.
1Sa 2: 31 The time is coming when I will cut short your **strength** and the
2: 31 cut short your strength and the **strength** *of* your father's house,
2Sa 1: 10 and the band on his **arm** and have brought them here to my lord."
22: 35 He trains my hands for battle; my **arms** can bend a bow of bronze.
1Ki 8: 42 great name and your mighty hand and your outstretched **arm**—
2Ki 9: 24 Then Jehu drew his bow and shot Joram between the **shoulders**.
17: 36 you up out of Egypt with mighty power and outstretched **arm**,
2Ch 6: 32 great name and your mighty hand and your outstretched **arm**—
32: 8 With him is only the **arm** *of* flesh, but with us is the LORD our
Job 22: 8 though you were a **powerful** man, owning land—an honored man,
22: 9 away empty-handed and broke the **strength** *of* the fatherless.
26: 2 helped the powerless! How you have saved the **arm** that is feeble!
35: 9 of oppression; they plead for relief from the **arm** *of* the powerful.
38: 15 wicked are denied their light, and their upraised **arm** is broken.
40: 9 Do you have an **arm** like God's, and can your voice thunder like
Ps 10: 15 Break the **arm** *of* the wicked and evil man; call him to account for
18: 34 [18:35] my hands for battle; my **arms** can bend a bow of bronze.
37: 17 for the **power** *of* the wicked will be broken, but the LORD
44: 3 [44:4] they won the land, nor did their **arm** bring them victory;
44: 3 [44:4] it was your right hand, your **arm**, and the light of your
71: 18 O God, till I declare your **power** to the next generation,
77: 15 [77:16] With your mighty **arm** you redeemed your people,
79: 11 by the strength of your **arm** preserve those condemned to die.
83: 8 [83:9] Even Assyria has joined them to lend **strength** to the
89: 10 [89:11] with your strong **arm** you scattered your enemies.
89: 13 [89:14] Your **arm** is endued with power; your hand is strong,
89: 21 [89:22] hand will sustain him; surely my **arm** will strengthen him.
98: 1 his right hand and his holy **arm** have worked salvation for him.

Ps 136: 12 with a mighty hand and outstretched **arm**; *His love endures*
Pr 31: 17 sets about her work vigorously; her **arms** are strong for her tasks.
SS 8: 6 Place me like a seal over your heart, like a seal on your **arm**;
Isa 9: 20 [9:19] Each will feed on the flesh of his own offspring: [BHS ***arm***; NIV 2446]
17: 5 gathers the standing grain and harvests the grain with his **arm**—
30: 30 and will make them see his **arm** coming down with raging anger
33: 2 Be our **strength** every morning, our salvation in time of distress.
40: 10 Sovereign LORD comes with power, and his **arm** rules for him.
40: 11 He gathers the lambs in his **arms** and carries them close to his
44: 12 an idol with hammers, he forges it with the might of his **arm**.
48: 14 purpose against Babylon; his **arm** will be against the Babylonians.
51: 5 is on the way, and my **arm** will bring justice to the nations.
51: 5 The islands will look to me and wait in hope for my **arm**.
51: 9 Clothe yourself with strength, O **arm** *of* the LORD; awake,
52: 10 The LORD will lay bare his holy **arm** in the sight of all the
53: 1 and to whom has the **arm** *of* the LORD been revealed?
59: 16 so his own **arm** worked salvation for him, and his own
62: 8 The LORD has sworn by his right hand and by his mighty **arm**:
63: 5 so my own **arm** worked salvation for me, and my own wrath
63: 12 who sent his glorious **arm of power** to be at Moses' right hand,
Jer 17: 5 who depends on flesh for his **strength** and whose heart turns away
21: 5 and a mighty **arm** in anger and fury and great wrath.
27: 5 great power and outstretched **arm** I made the earth and its people
32: 17 and the earth by your great power and outstretched **arm**.
48: 25 Moab's horn is cut off; her **arm** is broken," declares the LORD.
Eze 4: 7 the siege of Jerusalem and *with* bared **arm** prophesy against her.
13: 20 you ensnare people like birds and I will tear them from your **arms**;
17: 9 It will not take a strong **arm** or many people to pull it up by the
20: 33 a mighty hand and an outstretched **arm** and with outpoured wrath.
20: 34 with a mighty hand and an outstretched **arm** and with outpoured
22: 6 the princes of Israel who are in you uses his **power** to shed blood.
30: 21 "Son of man, I have broken the **arm** *of* Pharaoh king of Egypt.
30: 22 I will break *both* his **arms**, the good arm as well as the broken one,
30: 24 I will strengthen the **arms** *of* the king of Babylon and put my
30: 24 put my sword in his hand, but I will break the **arms** *of* Pharaoh,
30: 25 I will strengthen the **arms** *of* the king of Babylon, but the arms of
30: 25 of the king of Babylon, but the **arms** *of* Pharaoh will fall limp.
31: 17 Those who lived in its shade, its **allies** among the nations,
Da 10: 6 his **arms** and legs like the gleam of burnished bronze,
11: 6 she will not retain her **power** [+3946], and he and his power will
11: 6 she will not retain her power, and he and his **power** will not last.
11: 15 The **forces** *of* the South will be powerless to resist; even their best
11: 22 Then an overwhelming **army** will be swept away before him;
11: 31 "His **armed forces** will rise up to desecrate the temple fortress
Hos 7: 15 I trained them and **strengthened** [+2616] them, but they plot evil
11: 3 It was I who taught Ephraim to walk, taking them by the **arms**;
Zec 11: 17 deserts the flock! May the sword strike his **arm** and his right eye!
11: 17 May his **arm** be completely withered, his right eye totally

2433 זֵרוּעַ ***zērûa'***, n.[m.]. [2] [√ 2445]

seeds [+2446] [1], seeds [1]

Lev 11: 37 If a carcass falls on any **seeds** [+2446] that are to be planted,
Isa 61: 11 soil makes the sprout come up and a garden causes **seeds** to grow,

2434 זַרְזִיף ***zarzîp***, n.[m.]. Not used in NIV/BHS [√ 2449]

2435 זַרְזִיר ***zarzîr***, a. [1] [√ 2452?]

strutting rooster [+5516] [1]

Pr 30: 31 a **strutting rooster** [+5516], a he-goat, and a king with his army

2436 זָרַח ***zāraḥ***, v. [18] [→ 275, 276, 2437, 2438, 2439, 4667; *also used with compound proper names*]

rises [5], rise [2], rose [2], sunrise [+2021+9087] [2], appears [1], broke out [1], dawned [1], dawns [1], shine [1], shining [1], sunrise [+9087] [1]

Ge 32: 31 [32:32] [A] The sun **rose** above him as he passed Peniel, and he
Ex 22: 3 [22:2] [A] if it happens *after* **sunrise** [+2021+9087], he is guilty
Dt 33: 2 [A] LORD came from Sinai and **dawned** over them from Seir;
Jdg 9: 33 [A] In the morning at **sunrise** [+2021+9087], advance against the
2Sa 23: 4 [A] he is like the light of morning at **sunrise** [+9087] *on a*
2Ki 3: 22 [A] up early in the morning, the sun *was* **shining** on the water.
2Ch 26: 19 [A] in the LORD's temple, leprosy **broke out** on his forehead.
Job 9: 7 [A] He speaks to the sun and *it does* not **shine**; he seals off the
Ps 104: 22 [A] The sun **rises**, and they steal away; they return and lie down
112: 4 [A] Even in darkness light **dawns** for the upright, for the gracious
Ecc 1: 5 [A] The sun **rises** and the sun sets, and hurries back to where it
1: 5 [A] sun rises and the sun sets, and hurries back to where it **rises**.
Isa 58: 10 [A] of the oppressed, then your light *will* **rise** in the darkness,
60: 1 [A] light has come, and the glory of the LORD **rises** upon you.
60: 2 [A] the LORD **rises** upon you and his glory appears over you.
Jnh 4: 8 [A] When the sun **rose**, God provided a scorching east wind,
Na 3: 17 [A] when the sun **appears** they fly away, and no one knows
Mal 4: 2 [3:20] [A] the sun of righteousness *will* **rise** with healing in its

2437 זֶרַח ***zeraḥ[1]***, n.[m.]. [1] [→ 2438, 2439; cf. 2436]

dawn [1]

Isa 60: 3 will come to your light, and kings to the brightness of your **dawn**.

2438 זֶרַח ***zeraḥ[2]***, n.pr.m. [21] [→ 276; cf. 2436, 2437]

Zerah [20], Zerahites [+1201] [1]

Ge 36: 13 The sons of Reuel: Nahath, **Zerah**, Shammah and Mizzah.
36: 17 Esau's son Reuel: Chiefs Nahath, **Zerah**, Shammah and Mizzah.
36: 33 Jobab son of **Zerah** from Bozrah succeeded him as king.
38: 30 thread on his wrist, came out and he was given the name **Zerah**.
46: 12 Perez and **Zerah** (but Er and Onan had died in the land of Canaan).
Nu 26: 13 through **Zerah**, the Zerahite clan; through Shaul, the Shaulite clan.
26: 20 through Perez, the Perezite clan; through **Zerah**, the Zerahite clan.
Jos 7: 1 the son of Zimri, the son of **Zerah**, of the tribe of Judah, took some
7: 18 the son of Zimri, the son of **Zerah**, of the tribe of Judah,
7: 24 took Achan son of **Zerah**, the silver, the robe, the gold wedge,
22: 20 When Achan son of **Zerah** acted unfaithfully regarding the
1Ch 1: 37 The sons of Reuel: Nahath, **Zerah**, Shammah and Mizzah.
1: 44 Jobab son of **Zerah** from Bozrah succeeded him as king.
2: 4 Tamar, Judah's daughter-in-law, bore him Perez and **Zerah**.
2: 6 The sons of **Zerah**: Zimri, Ethan, Heman, Calcol and Darda—
4: 24 descendants of Simeon: Nemuel, Jamin, Jarib, **Zerah** and Shaul;
6: 21 [6:6] his son, Iddo his son, **Zerah** his son and Jeatherai his son.
6: 41 [6:26] the son of Ethni, the son of **Zerah**, the son of Adaiah,
9: 6 Of the **Zerahites** [+1201]: Jeuel. The people from Judah numbered
2Ch 14: 9 [14:8] **Zerah** the Cushite marched out against them with a vast
Ne 11: 24 son of Meshezabel, one of the descendants of **Zerah** son of Judah,

2439 זַרְחִי ***zarḥî***, a.g. [6] [√ 2438; cf. 2436, 2437]

Zerahite [4], Zerahites [2]

Nu 26: 13 through Zerah, the **Zerahite** clan; through Shaul, the Shaulite clan.
26: 20 through Perez, the Perezite clan; through Zerah, the **Zerahite** clan.
Jos 7: 17 The clans of Judah came forward, and he took the **Zerahites**.
7: 17 He had the clan of the **Zerahites** come forward by families,
1Ch 27: 11 for the eighth month, was Sibbecai the Hushathite, a **Zerahite**.
27: 13 for the tenth month, was Maharai the Netophathite, a **Zerahite**.

2440 זְרַחְיָה ***z[e]raḥyâ***, n.pr.m. [5] [√ 2436 + 3378]

Zerahiah [5]

1Ch 6: 6 [5:32] Uzzi the father of **Zerahiah**, Zerahiah the father of
6: 6 [5:32] the father of Zerahiah, **Zerahiah** the father of Meraioth,
6: 51 [6:36] Bukki his son, Uzzi his son, **Zerahiah** his son,
Ezr 7: 4 the son of **Zerahiah**, the son of Uzzi, the son of Bukki,
8: 4 Eliehoenai son of **Zerahiah**, and with him 200 men;

2441 זָרַם ***zāram[1]***, v. Not used in NIV/BHS [cf. 2442]

2442 זָרַם ***zāram[2]***, v. [2] [→ 2443; cf. 2441]

poured down [1], sweep away [1]

Ps 77: 17 [77:18] [D] The clouds **poured down** water, the skies
90: 5 [A] *You* **sweep** men **away** in the sleep of death; they are like the

2443 זֶרֶם ***zerem***, n.m. [9] [√ 2442]

storm [4], driving rain [+4784] [1], hailstorm [+1352] [1], rains [1], thunderstorm [1], torrents [1]

Job 24: 8 They are drenched by mountain **rains** and hug the rocks for lack of
Isa 4: 6 of the day, and a refuge and hiding place from the **storm** and rain.
25: 4 in his distress, a shelter from the **storm** and a shade from the heat.
25: 4 For the breath of the ruthless is like a **storm** *driving against* a
28: 2 Like a **hailstorm** [+1352] and a destructive wind, like a driving
28: 2 like a **driving rain** [+4784] and a flooding downpour,
30: 30 and consuming fire, with cloudburst, **thunderstorm** and hail.
32: 2 will be like a shelter from the wind and a refuge from the **storm**,
Hab 3: 10 **Torrents** *of* water swept by; the deep roared and lifted its waves

2444 זִרְמָה ***zirmâ***, n.f. [2] [cf. 2367]

emission [1], that[s] [1]

Eze 23: 20 like those of donkeys and whose **emission** was like that of horses.
23: 20 like those of donkeys and whose emission was like **that**[s] *of* horses.

2445 זָרַע ***zāra'***, v. [56] [→ 2433, 2446, 2447, 2448, 4669; Ar 10240; *also used with compound proper names*]

sow [16], plant [9], planted [4], sown [4], planted crops [2], seed-bearing [+2446] [2], sower [2], sows [2], be able to have children [+2446] [1], be planted [1], bearing [1], have descendants [1], is shed [1], plant [+2446] [1], plant seed [1], plant with seed [1], planting [1], pregnant [1], scatter [1], scattered [1], seed [+2446] [1], sowed [1], sowing seed [1]

Ge 1:11 [G] **seed-bearing** [+2446] plants and trees on the land that bear
1:12 [G] plants **bearing** seed according to their kinds and trees
1:29 [A] "I give you every **seed-bearing** [+2446] plant on the face of
1:29 [A] and every tree that has fruit with **seed** [+2446] in it.
26:12 [A] Isaac **planted crops** in that land and the same year reaped a
47:23 [A] here is seed for you so *you can* **plant** the ground.
Ex 23:10 [A] "For six years *you are to* **sow** your fields and harvest the
23:16 [A] Harvest with the firstfruits of the crops you **sow** in your field.
Lev 11:37 [C] If a carcass falls on any seeds that *are to* **be planted**,
12:2 [G] 'A woman *who becomes* **pregnant** and gives birth to a son
19:19 [A] of animals. " '*Do* not **plant** your field **with** two kinds of **seed**.
25:3 [A] For six years **sow** your fields, and for six years prune your
25:4 [A] the LORD. *Do* not **sow** your fields or prune your vineyards.
25:11 [A] *do* not **sow** and do not reap what grows of itself or harvest
25:20 [A] "What will we eat in the seventh year if *we do* not **plant**
25:22 [A] While *you* **plant** during the eighth year, you will eat from the
26:16 [A] *You will* **plant** seed in vain, because your enemies will eat it.
Nu 5:28 [C] cleared of guilt and *will* **be able to have children** [+2446].
Dt 11:10 [A] where *you* **planted** your seed and irrigated it by foot as in a
21:4 [C] been plowed or **planted** and where there is a flowing stream.
22:9 [A] *Do* not **plant** two kinds of **seed** in your vineyard; if you do,
22:9 [A] not only the crops *you* **plant** [+2446] but also the fruit of the
29:23 [29:22] [C] nothing **planted**, nothing sprouting, no vegetation
Jdg 6:3 [A] Whenever the Israelites **planted** *their* **crops**, the Midianites,
9:45 [A] Then he destroyed the city and **scattered** salt *over* it.
2Ki 19:29 [A] in the third year **sow** and reap, plant vineyards and eat their
Job 4:8 [A] those who plow evil and *those who* **sow** trouble reap it.
31:8 [A] may others eat what *I have* **sown**, and may my crops be
Ps 97:11 [B] Light **is shed** upon the righteous and joy on the upright in
107:37 [A] *They* **sowed** fields and planted vineyards that yielded a
126:5 [A] Those *who* **sow** in tears will reap with songs of joy.
Pr 11:18 [A] but *he who* **sows** righteousness reaps a sure reward.
22:8 [A] *He who* **sows** wickedness reaps trouble, and the rod of his
Ecc 11:4 [A] Whoever watches the wind *will* not **plant**; whoever looks at
11:6 [A] **Sow** your seed in the morning, and at evening let not your
Isa 17:10 [A] though you set out the finest plants and **plant** imported vines,
28:24 [A] When a farmer plows for **planting**, does he plow
30:23 [A] He will also send you rain for the seed *you* **sow** *in* the
32:20 [A] **sowing** *your* **seed** by every stream, and letting your cattle
37:30 [A] in the third year **sow** and reap, plant vineyards and eat their
40:24 [E] No sooner are they planted, no sooner *are they* **sown**, no
55:10 [A] so that it yields seed for the **sower** and bread for the eater,
Jer 2:2 [B] and followed me through the desert, through a land not **sown**.
4:3 [A] up your unplowed ground and *do* not **sow** among thorns.
12:13 [A] *They will* **sow** wheat but reap thorns; they will wear
31:27 [A] *I will* **plant** the house of Israel and the house of Judah *with*
35:7 [A] you must never build houses, **sow** seed or plant vineyards;
50:16 [A] Cut off from Babylon the **sower**, and the reaper with his
Eze 36:9 [C] will look on you with favor; you will be plowed and **sown**,
Hos 2:23 [2:25] [A] *I will* **plant** her for myself in the land; I will show
8:7 [A] "*They* **sow** the wind and reap the whirlwind. The stalk has
10:12 [A] **Sow** for yourselves righteousness, reap the fruit of unfailing
Mic 6:15 [A] You *will* **plant** but not harvest; you will press olives but not
Na 1:14 [C] "*You will* **have** no **descendants** to bear your name.
Hag 1:6 [A] *You have* **planted** much, but have harvested little. You eat,
Zec 10:9 [A] Though *I* **scatter** them among the peoples, yet in distant

2446 זֶרַע *zera'*, n.m. [229 / 230] [√ 2445; Ar 10240]

descendants [82], offspring [35], seed [25], children [20], family [5], grain [5], semen [5], line [4], people [4], descent [3], *untranslated* [2], blood [2], descendant [2], descended [2], family line [2], posterity [2], seed-bearing [+2445] [2], be able to have children [+2445] [1], brood [1], child [1], crops [1], descendant [+408+4946] [1], fertile [1], have sexual relations [+4200+5989+8888] [1], Jews[s] [1], origin [1], plant [+2445] [1], plant [1], planter [+5432] [1], planting [1], produce [+3655+9311] [1], race [1], righteous [+7404] [1], seed [+2445] [1], seed to sow [+5433] [1], seeds [+2433] [1], seedtime [1], sleeping with [+907+8886+8887] [1], sleeps with [+907+8886+8887] [1], son [+408] [1], sons [1], stock [1], their[s] [+3870] [1], them[s] [+906+3870] [1], various kinds [1]

Ge 1:11 **seed-bearing** [+2445] plants and trees on the land that bear fruit
1:11 and trees on the land that bear fruit with **seed** in it,
1:12 plants bearing **seed** according to their kinds and trees bearing fruit
1:12 and trees bearing fruit with **seed** in it according to their kinds.
1:29 "I give you every **seed-bearing** [+2445] plant on the face of the
1:29 whole earth and every tree that has fruit with **seed** [+2445] in it.
3:15 and the woman, and between your **offspring** and hers;
3:15 **[RPH]** he will crush your head, and you will strike his heel."
4:25 saying, "God has granted me another **child** in place of Abel,
7:3 and female, to keep their **various kinds** alive throughout the earth.
8:22 **seedtime** and harvest, cold and heat, summer and winter, day
9:9 my covenant with you and with your **descendants** after you
12:7 to Abram and said, "To your **offspring** I will give this land."
13:15 the land that you see I will give to you and your **offspring** forever.
13:16 I will make your **offspring** like the dust of the earth, so that if
13:16 anyone could count the dust, then your **offspring** could be counted.
15:3 Abram said, "You have given me no **children**; so a servant in my
15:5 count them." Then he said to him, "So shall your **offspring** be."
15:13 "Know for certain that your **descendants** will be strangers in a
15:18 with Abram and said, "To your **descendants** I give this land,
16:10 so increase your **descendants** that they will be too numerous to
17:7 and your **descendants** after you for the generations to come,
17:7 to be your God and the God of your **descendants** after you.
17:8 an everlasting possession to you and your **descendants** after you;
17:9 and your **descendants** after you for the generations to come.
17:10 This is my covenant with you and your **descendants** after you,
17:12 with money from a foreigner—those who are not your **offspring**.
17:19 with him as an everlasting covenant for his **descendants** after him.
19:32 then lie with him and preserve our **family line** through our father."
19:34 with him so we can preserve our **family line** through our father."
21:12 because it is through Isaac that your **offspring** will be reckoned.
21:13 the maidservant into a nation also, because he is your **offspring**."
22:17 and make your **descendants** as numerous as the stars in the sky
22:17 Your **descendants** will take possession of the cities of their
22:18 and through your **offspring** all nations on earth will be blessed,
24:7 me on oath, saying, 'To your **offspring** I will give this land'—
24:60 may your **offspring** possess the gates of their enemies."
26:3 For to you and your **descendants** I will give all these lands
26:4 I will make your **descendants** as numerous as the stars in the sky
26:4 stars in the sky and will give **them**[s] [+906+3870] all these lands,
26:4 and through your **offspring** all nations on earth will be blessed,
26:24 will increase the number of your **descendants** for the sake of my
28:4 he give you and your **descendants** the blessing given to Abraham,
28:13 give you and your **descendants** the land on which you are lying.
28:14 Your **descendants** will be like the dust of the earth, and you will
28:14 peoples on earth will be blessed through you and your **offspring**.
32:12 [32:13] and will make your **descendants** like the sand of the sea,
35:12 to you, and I will give this land to your **descendants** after you."
38:8 fulfill your duty to her as a brother-in-law to produce **offspring** for
38:9 Onan knew that the **offspring** would not be his; so whenever he
38:9 on the ground to keep from producing **offspring** for his brother.
46:6 acquired in Canaan, and Jacob and all his **offspring** went to Egypt.
46:7 and his daughters and granddaughters—all his **offspring**.
47:19 Give us **seed** so that we may live and not die, and that the land may
47:23 for Pharaoh, here is **seed** for you so you can plant the ground.
47:24 The other four-fifths you may keep as **seed** *for* the fields and as
48:4 land as an everlasting possession to your **descendants** after you.'
48:11 and now God has allowed me to see your **children** too."
48:19 than he, and his **descendants** will become a group of nations."
Ex 16:31 It was white like coriander **seed** and tasted like wafers made with
28:43 "This is to be a lasting ordinance for Aaron and his **descendants**.
30:21 for Aaron and his **descendants** for the generations to come."
32:13 'I will make your **descendants** as numerous as the stars in the sky
32:13 and I will give your **descendants** all this land I promised them,
33:1 Isaac and Jacob, saying, 'I will give it to your **descendants**.'
Lev 11:37 If a carcass falls on any **seeds** [+2433] that are to be planted,
11:38 But if water has been put on the **seed** and a carcass falls on it,
15:16 " 'When a man has an emission of **semen**, he must bathe his whole
15:17 or leather that has **semen** on it must be washed with water,
15:18 When a man lies with a woman and there is an emission of **semen**,
15:32 a discharge, for anyone made unclean by an emission of **semen**,
18:20 " '*Do* not **have sexual relations** [+4200+5989+8888] with your
18:21 " 'Do not give any of your **children** to be sacrificed to Molech,
19:20 " 'If a man **sleeps with** [+907+8886+8887] a woman who is a slave
20:2 or any alien living in Israel who gives any of his **children** to
20:3 for by giving his **children** to Molech, he has defiled my sanctuary
20:4 close their eyes when that man gives one of his **children** to Molech
21:15 so he will not defile his **offspring** among his people. I am the
21:17 'For the generations to come none of your **descendants** who has a
21:21 No **descendant** *of* Aaron the priest who has any defect is to come
22:3 if any of your **descendants** is ceremonially unclean and yet comes
22:4 " 'If a **descendant** [+408+4946] *of* Aaron has an infectious skin
22:4 defiled by a corpse or by anyone who has an emission of **semen**,
22:13 daughter becomes a widow or is divorced, yet has no **children**,
26:5 grape harvest and the grape harvest will continue until **planting**,
26:16 You will plant **seed** in vain, because your enemies will eat it.
27:16 its value is to be set according to the amount of **seed** *required for*
27:16 required for it—fifty shekels of silver to a homer of barley **seed**.
27:30 whether **grain** *from* the soil or fruit from the trees, belongs to the
Nu 5:13 *by* **sleeping with** [+907+8886+8887] another man, and this is
5:28 will be cleared of guilt and *will* **be able to have children** [+2445].
11:7 The manna was like coriander **seed** and looked like resin.
14:24 him into the land he went to, and his **descendants** will inherit it.

Nu 16:40 [17:5] **descendant** *of* Aaron should come to burn incense before
18:19 of salt before the LORD for both you and your **offspring**."
20: 5 It has no **grain** or figs, grapevines or pomegranates. And there is
24: 7 will flow from their buckets; their **seed** will have abundant water.
25:13 and his **descendants** will have a covenant of a lasting priesthood,
Dt 1: 8 Isaac and Jacob—and to their **descendants** after them."
4:37 he loved your forefathers and chose their **descendants** after them,
10:15 and loved them, and he chose you, their **descendants**,
11: 9 swore to your forefathers to give to them and their **descendants**,
11:10 where you planted your **seed** and irrigated it by foot as in a
14:22 a tenth of all that your fields **produce** [+3655+9311] each year.
22: 9 not only the crops *you* **plant** [+2445] but also the fruit of the
28:38 You will sow much **seed** in the field but you will harvest little,
28:46 will be a sign and a wonder to you and your **descendants** forever.
28:59 LORD will send fearful plagues on you and your **descendants**,
30: 6 will circumcise your hearts and the hearts of your **descendants**,
30:19 Now choose life, so that you and your **children** may live
31:21 against them, because it will not be forgotten by their **descendants**.
34: 4 and Jacob when I said, 'I will give it to your **descendants**.'
Jos 24: 3 and led him throughout Canaan and gave him many **descendants**.
Ru 4:12 Through the **offspring** the LORD gives you by this young
1Sa 1:11 and not forget your servant but give her a **son** [+408],
2:20 "May the LORD give you **children** by this woman to take the
8:15 He will take a tenth of your **grain** and of your vintage and give it
20:42 between your **descendants** and my descendants forever.' " Then
20:42 your descendants and my **descendants** forever.' " Then David left,
24:21 [24:22] by the LORD that you will not cut off my **descendants**
2Sa 4: 8 has avenged my lord the king against Saul and his **offspring**."
7:12 with your fathers, I will raise up your **offspring** to succeed you,
22:51 kindness to his anointed, to David and his **descendants** forever."
1Ki 2:33 their blood rest on the head of Joab and his **descendants** forever.
2:33 But on David and his **descendants**, his house and his throne,
11:14 an adversary, Hadad the Edomite, from the royal **line** of Edom.
11:39 I will humble David's **descendants** because of this, but not
18:32 he dug a trench around it large enough to hold two seahs of **seed**.
2Ki 5:27 leprosy will cling to you and to your **descendants** forever."
11: 1 her son was dead, she proceeded to destroy the whole royal **family**.
17:20 Therefore the LORD rejected all the **people** *of* Israel; he afflicted
25:25 who was of royal **blood**, came with ten men and assassinated
1Ch 16:13 O **descendants** *of* Israel his servant, O sons of Jacob, his chosen
17:11 I will raise up your **offspring** to succeed you, one of your own
2Ch 20: 7 and give it forever to the **descendants** *of* Abraham your friend?
22:10 she proceeded to destroy the whole royal **family** of the house of
Ezr 2:59 they could not show that their families were **descended** from
9: 2 and have mingled the holy **race** with the peoples around them.
Ne 7:61 they could not show that their families were **descended** from
9: 2 Those of Israelite **descent** had separated themselves from all
9: 8 you made a covenant with him to give to his **descendants** the land
Est 6:13 has started, is of Jewish **origin**, you cannot stand against him—
9:27 themselves to establish the custom that they and their **descendants**
9:28 nor should the memory of them die out among their **descendants**.
9:31 their **descendants** in regard to their times of fasting
10: 3 good of his people and spoke up for the welfare of all the **Jews**[s].
Job 5:25 You will know that your **children** will be many, and your
21: 8 They see their **children** established around them, their offspring
39:12 Can you trust him to bring in your **grain** and gather it to your
Ps 18:50 [18:51] to his anointed, to David and his **descendants** forever.
21:10 [21:11] descendants from the earth, their **posterity** from mankind.
22:23 [22:24] praise him! All you **descendants** *of* Jacob, honor him!
22:23 [22:24] honor him! Revere him, all you **descendants** *of* Israel!
22:30 [22:31] **Posterity** will serve him; future generations will be told
25:13 his days in prosperity, and his **descendants** will inherit the land.
37:25 never seen the righteous forsaken or their **children** begging bread.
37:26 are always generous and lend freely; their **children** will be blessed.
37:28 protected forever, but the **offspring** *of* the wicked will be cut off;
69:36 [69:37] the **children** *of* his servants will inherit it, and those who
89: 4 [89:5] 'I will establish your **line** forever and make your throne
89:29 [89:30] I will establish his **line** forever, his throne as long as the
89:36 [89:37] that his **line** will continue forever and his throne endure
102:28 [102:29] their **descendants** will be established before you."
105: 6 O **descendants** *of* Abraham his servant, O sons of Jacob,
106:27 make their **descendants** fall among the nations and scatter them
112: 2 His **children** will be mighty in the land; the generation of the
126: 6 He who goes out weeping, carrying **seed** [+5433] **to sow**,
Pr 11:21 go unpunished, but *those who* are **righteous** [+7404] will go free.
Ecc 11: 6 Sow your **seed** in the morning, and at evening let not your hands
Isa 1: 4 sinful nation, a people loaded with guilt, a **brood** *of* evildoers,
5:10 only a bath of wine, a homer of **seed** only an ephah of grain."
6:13 they are cut down, so the holy **seed** will be the stump in the land."
9:20 [9:19] will feed on the flesh of his own **offspring**: [BHS 2432]
14:20 The **offspring** *of* the wicked will never be mentioned again.
17:11 you make them grow, and on the morning when you **plant** them,
23: 3 On the great waters came the **grain** *of* the Shihor; the harvest of
30:23 He will also send you rain for the **seed** you sow in the ground,
41: 8 whom I have chosen, you **descendants** *of* Abraham my friend,
43: 5 I will bring your **children** from the east and gather you from the
44: 3 I will pour out my Spirit on your **offspring**, and my blessing on
45:19 I have not said to Jacob's **descendants**, 'Seek me in vain.'
45:25 in the LORD all the **descendants** *of* Israel will be found righteous
48:19 Your **descendants** would have been like the sand, your children
53:10 he will see his **offspring** and prolong his days, and the will of the
54: 3 your **descendants** will dispossess nations and settle in their
55:10 so that it yields **seed** for the sower and bread for the eater,
57: 3 sons of a sorceress, you **offspring** *of* adulterers and prostitutes!
57: 4 your tongue? Are you not a brood of rebels, the **offspring** *of* liars?
59:21 or from the mouths of your **children**, or from the mouths of their
59:21 or from the mouths of **their**[s] [+3870] descendants from this time
59:21 or from the mouths of their **descendants** from this time on
61: 9 Their **descendants** will be known among the nations and their
61: 9 All who see them will acknowledge that they are a **people** the
65: 9 I will bring forth **descendants** from Jacob, and from Judah those
65:23 for they will be a **people** blessed by the LORD, they and their
66:22 declares the LORD, "so will your name and **descendants** endure.
Jer 2:21 I had planted you like a choice vine of sound and reliable **stock**.
7:15 my presence, just as I did all your brothers, the **people** *of* Ephraim.'
22:28 Why will he and his **children** be hurled out, cast into a land they
22:30 for none of his **offspring** will prosper, none will sit on the throne
23: 8 who brought the **descendants** *of* Israel up out of the land of the
29:32 will surely punish Shemaiah the Nehelamite and his **descendants**.
30:10 of a distant place, your **descendants** from the land of their exile.
31:27 and the house of Judah with the **offspring** *of* men and of animals.
31:27 house of Judah with the offspring of men and **[RPH]** of animals.
31:36 "will the **descendants** *of* Israel ever cease to be a nation before
31:37 below be searched out will I reject all the **descendants** *of* Israel
33:22 I will make the **descendants** *of* David my servant and the Levites
33:26 then I will reject the **descendants** *of* Jacob and David my servant
33:26 will not choose one of his **sons** to rule over the descendants of
33:26 will not choose one of his sons to rule over the **descendants** *of*
35: 7 Also you must never build houses, sow **seed** or plant vineyards;
35: 9 or built houses to live in or had vineyards, fields or **crops**.
36:31 I will punish him and his **children** and his attendants for their
41: 1 who was of royal **blood** and had been one of the king's officers,
46:27 of a distant place, your **descendants** from the land of their exile.
49:10 His **children**, relatives and neighbors will perish, and he will be no
Eze 17: 5 " 'He took some of the **seed** *of* your land and put it in fertile soil.
17: 5 " 'He took some of the seed of your land and put it in **fertile** soil.
17:13 he took a member of the royal **family** and made a treaty with him,
20: 5 I swore with uplifted hand to the **descendants** *of* the house of
43:19 who are Levites, of the **family** *of* Zadok, who come near to
44:22 they may marry only virgins of Israelite **descent** or widows of
Da 1: 3 to bring in some of the Israelites from the royal **family** and the
9: 1 In the first year of Darius son of Xerxes (a Mede by **descent**),
Am 9:13 the plowman and the **planter** [+5432] by the one treading grapes.
Hag 2:19 Is there yet any **seed** left in the barn? Until now, the vine
Zec 8:12 "The **seed** will grow well, the vine will yield its fruit, the ground
Mal 2: 3 "Because of you I will rebuke your **descendants**; I will spread on
2:15 are his. And why one? Because he was seeking godly **offspring**.

2447 זֵרֹעִים **zērō'îm**, n.[m.]. [1] [→ 2448; cf. 2445]

vegetables [1]

Da 1:12 ten days: Give us nothing but **vegetables** to eat and water to drink.

2448 זֵרְעֹנִים **zēr'ōnîm**, n.[m.]. [1] [√ 2447; cf. 2445]

vegetables [1]

Da 1:16 and the wine they were to drink and gave them **vegetables** instead.

2449 זָרַף **zārap**, n.[m.]. [1] [→ 2434]

watering [1]

Ps 72: 6 [D] falling on a mown field, like showers **watering** the earth.

2450 זָרַק **zāraq[1]**, v. [35] [→ 4670]

sprinkled [15], sprinkle [11], been sprinkled [2], scatter [2], scattered [1], sprinkles [1], sprinkling [1], toss [1], tossed [1]

Ex 9: 8 [A] *have* Moses **toss** it into the air in the presence of Pharaoh.
9:10 [A] Moses **tossed** it into the air, and festering boils broke out on
24: 6 [A] put it in bowls, and the other half *he* **sprinkled** on the altar.
24: 8 [A] then took the blood, **sprinkled** it on the people and said,
29:16 [A] take the blood and **sprinkle** it against the altar on all sides.
29:20 [A] right feet. Then **sprinkle** blood against the altar on all sides.
Lev 1: 5 [A] **sprinkle** it against the altar on all sides at the entrance to the
1:11 [A] Aaron's sons the priests *shall* **sprinkle** its blood against the
3: 2 [A] Aaron's sons the priests *shall* **sprinkle** the blood against the
3: 8 [A] Aaron's sons *shall* **sprinkle** its blood against the altar on all
3:13 [A] Aaron's sons *shall* **sprinkle** its blood against the altar on all
7: 2 [A] and its blood *is to be* **sprinkled** against the altar on all sides.

Lev 7:14 [A] it belongs to the priest who **sprinkles** the blood of the
8:19 [A] the ram and **sprinkled** the blood against the altar on all sides.
8:24 [A] Then he **sprinkled** blood against the altar on all sides.
9:12 [A] the blood, and *he* **sprinkled** it against the altar on all sides.
9:18 [A] the blood, and *he* **sprinkled** it against the altar on all sides.
17:6 [A] The priest *is to* **sprinkle** the blood against the altar of the
Nu 18:17 [A] **Sprinkle** their blood on the altar and burn their fat as an
19:13 [E] Because the water of cleansing *has* not **been sprinkled** on
19:20 [E] The water of cleansing *has* not **been sprinkled** on him,
2Ki 16:13 [A] **sprinkled** the blood of his fellowship offerings on the altar.
16:15 [A] **Sprinkle** on the altar all the blood of the burnt offerings
2Ch 29:22 [A] and the priests took the blood and **sprinkled** it on the altar;
29:22 [A] slaughtered the rams and **sprinkled** their blood on the altar;
29:22 [A] slaughtered the lambs and **sprinkled** their blood on the altar.
30:16 [A] The priests **sprinkled** the blood handed to them by the
34:4 [A] **scattered** over the graves of those who had sacrificed to
35:11 [A] and the priests **sprinkled** the blood handed to them,
Job 2:12 [A] and they tore their robes and **sprinkled** dust on their heads.
Isa 28:25 [A] the surface, does he not sow caraway and **scatter** cummin?
Eze 10:2 [A] from among the cherubim and **scatter** them over the city."
36:25 [A] *I will* **sprinkle** clean water on you, and you will be clean;
43:18 [A] and **sprinkling** blood upon the altar when it is built:
Hos 7:9 [A] but he does not realize it. His hair *is* **sprinkled** *with* gray,

2451 ²זָרַק ***zāraq²***, v. Not used in NIV/BHS

2452 ¹זָרַר ***zārar¹***, v. Not used in NIV/BHS [→ 2425, 2435?; cf. 2453]

2453 ²זָרַר ***zārar²***, v. [1] [cf. 2452]

sneezed [1]

2Ki 4:35 [D] The boy **sneezed** seven times and opened his eyes.

2454 זֶרֶשׁ ***zereš***, n.pr.f. [4]

Zeresh [4]

Est 5:10 and went home. Calling together his friends and **Zeresh**, his wife,
5:14 His wife **Zeresh** and all his friends said to him, "Have a gallows
6:13 told **Zeresh** his wife and all his friends everything that had
6:13 His advisers and his wife **Zeresh** said to him, "Since Mordecai,

2455 זֶרֶת ***zeret***, n.f. [7] [→ 2431]

span [5], breadth of hand [1], over nine feet [+564+2256+9252] [1]

Ex 28:16 It is to be square—a **span** long and a span wide—and folded
28:16 It is to be square—a span long and a **span** wide—and folded
39:9 It was square—a **span** long and a span wide—and folded double.
39:9 It was square—a span long and a **span** wide—and folded double.
1Sa 17:4 Philistine camp. He was **over nine feet** [+564+2256+9252] tall.
Isa 40:12 his hand, or with the **breadth of** his **hand** marked off the heavens?
Eze 43:13 and a cubit wide, with a rim of one **span** around the edge.

2456 זַתּוּא ***zattû'***, n.pr.m. [4 / 5]

Zattu [5]

Ezr 2:8 of **Zattu** 945
8:5 of the descendants of **Zattu**, [BHS-] Shecaniah son of Jahaziel,
10:27 From the descendants of **Zattu**: Elioenai, Eliashib, Mattaniah,
Ne 7:13 of **Zattu** 845
10:14 [10:15] of the people: Parosh, Pahath-Moab, Elam, **Zattu**, Bani,

2457 זֵתָם ***zētām***, n.pr.m. [2] [√ 2339?]

Zetham [2]

1Ch 23:8 The sons of Ladan: Jehiel the first, **Zetham** and Joel—three in all.
26:22 the sons of Jehieli, **Zetham** and his brother Joel. They were in

2458 זֵתַר ***zētar***, n.pr.m. [1]

Zethar [1]

Est 1:10 Mehuman, Biztha, Harbona, Bigtha, Abagtha, **Zethar** and Carcas—

ח, *ḥ*

2459 ח ***ḥ***, letter. Not used in NIV/BHS [→ Ar 10241]

2460 חֹב ***ḥōb***, n.[m.] [1] [√ 2462; cf. 2461]

heart [1]

Job 31:33 have concealed my sin as men do, by hiding my guilt in my **heart**

2461 חָבָא ***ḥābā'***, v. [34] [→ 494, 4675, 4676; cf. 2460, 2463?, 2464, 2465?]

hid [7], hidden [7], hiding [5], hid themselves [2], be protected [1], become hard [1], force into hiding [1], hidden away [1], hidden himself [1], hide themselves [1], hide yourselves [1], hide [1], hushed [1], secretly [1], stay there [1], stepped aside [1], uses[s] [1]

Ge 3:8 [F] *they* **hid** from the LORD God among the trees of the
3:10 [C] the garden, and I was afraid because I was naked; so *I* **hid**."
31:27 [C] Why did you run off **secretly** and deceive me? Why didn't
Jos 2:16 [C] **Hide yourselves** there three days until they return, and
6:17 [G] her house shall be spared, because *she* **hid** the spies we sent.
6:25 [G] because *she* **hid** the men Joshua had sent as spies to Jericho—
10:16 [C] the five kings had fled and **hidden** in the cave at Makkedah.
10:17 [C] five kings had been found **hiding** in the cave at Makkedah,
10:27 [C] and threw them into the cave where *they had been* **hiding**.
Jdg 9:5 [C] the youngest son of Jerub-Baal, escaped by **hiding**.
1Sa 10:22 [C] "Yes, he *has* **hidden himself** among the baggage."
13:6 [F] they **hid** in caves and thickets, among the rocks, and in pits
14:11 [F] "The Hebrews are crawling out of the holes *they were* **hiding**
14:22 [F] When all the Israelites who *had* **hidden** in the hill country of
19:2 [C] your guard tomorrow morning; go into hiding and **stay there**.
23:23 [F] Find out about all the hiding places *he* **uses**[s] and come back
2Sa 17:9 [C] Even now, he *is* **hidden** in a cave or some other place. If he
1Ki 18:4 [G] had taken a hundred prophets and **hidden** them in two caves,
18:13 [G] *I* **hid** a hundred of the LORD's prophets in two caves,
2Ki 6:29 [G] up your son so we may eat him,' but *she had* **hidden** him."
11:3 [F] He remained **hidden** with his nurse at the temple of the
1Ch 21:20 [F] the angel; his four sons who were with him **hid themselves**.
2Ch 18:24 [C] "You will find out on the day you go to **hide** *in* an inner
22:9 [F] and his men captured him while he *was* **hiding** in Samaria.
22:12 [F] He remained **hidden** with them at the temple of God for six
Job 5:21 [C] *You will* **be protected** from the lash of the tongue, and need
24:4 [E] from the path and **force** all the poor of the land **into hiding**.
29:8 [C] the young men saw me and **stepped aside** and the old men
29:10 [C] the voices of the nobles *were* **hushed**, and their tongues
38:30 [F] *when* the waters **become hard** as stone, when the surface of
Isa 42:22 [H] all of them trapped in pits or **hidden away** in prisons.
49:2 [G] like a sharpened sword, in the shadow of his hand *he* **hid** me;
Da 10:7 [C] terror overwhelmed them that they fled and **hid themselves**.
Am 9:3 [C] Though *they* **hide themselves** on the top of Carmel, there I

2462 חָבַב ***ḥābab***, v. [1] [→ 2460, 2463?, 2465?]

love [1]

Dt 33:3 [A] Surely it is you *who* **love** the people; all the holy ones are in

2463 חֹבָב ***ḥōbāb***, n.pr.m. [2] [√ 2462?; cf. 2461?]

Hobab [2]

Nu 10:29 Now Moses said to **Hobab** son of Reuel the Midianite,
Jdg 4:11 other Kenites, the descendants of **Hobab**, Moses' brother-in-law,

2464 חָבָה ***ḥābâ***, v. [4] [→ 2469, 2470; cf. 2461]

hide [3], conceal himself [1]

1Ki 22:25 [C] "You will find out on the day you go to **hide** *in* an inner
2Ki 7:12 [C] so they have left the camp to **hide** in the countryside,
Isa 26:20 [A] **hide** *yourselves* for a little while until his wrath has passed
Jer 49:10 [C] uncover his hiding places, so that he cannot **conceal himself**.

2465 חֻבָּה ***ḥubbâ***, n.pr.m. [1] [√ 2462?; cf. 2461?, 3478]

Hubbah [1]

1Ch 7:34 The sons of Shomer: Ahi, Rohgah, **Hubbah** [K 3478] and Aram.

2466 חָבוֹר ***ḥābôr***, n.pr.loc. [3]

Habor [3]

2Ki 17:6 in Gozan on the **Habor** River and in the towns of the Medes.
18:11 in Halah, in Gozan on the **Habor** River and in towns of the Medes.
1Ch 5:26 He took them to Halah, **Habor**, Hara and the river of Gozan,

2467 חַבּוּרָה ***ḥabbûrâ***, n.f. [7] [√ 2488]

bruise [2], wounds [2], blows [1], injuring [1], welts [1]

Ge 4:23 have killed a man for wounding me, a young man for **injuring** me.
Ex 21:25 burn for burn, wound for wound, **bruise** for bruise.
21:25 burn for burn, wound for wound, bruise for **bruise**.
Ps 38:5 [38:6] My **wounds** fester and are loathsome because of my sinful
Pr 20:30 **Blows** and wounds cleanse away evil, and beatings purge the
Isa 1:6 only wounds and **welts** and open sores, not cleansed or bandaged
53:5 brought us peace was upon him, and by his **wounds** we are healed.

2468 חָבַט ḥābaṭ, v. [5]

beat [1], is beaten out [1], thresh [1], threshed [1], threshing [1]

Dt 24:20 [A] When *you* **beat** the olives from your trees, do not go over the
Jdg 6:11 [A] where his son Gideon *was* **threshing** wheat in a winepress to
Ru 2:17 [A] *she* **threshed** the barley she had gathered, and it amounted to
Isa 27:12 [A] In that day the LORD *will* **thresh** from the flowing
28:27 [C] caraway **is beaten out** with a rod, and cummin with a stick.

2469 חֳבַיָּה ḥᵒbayyâ, n.pr.m. [2] [√ 2464 + 3378]

Hobaiah [2]

Ezr 2:61 The descendants of **Hobaiah**, Hakkoz and Barzillai (a man who
Ne 7:63 the descendants of **Hobaiah**, Hakkoz and Barzillai (a man who had

2470 חֶבְיוֹן ḥebyôn, n.[m.]. [1] [√ 2464]

hidden [1]

Hab 3:4 rays flashed from his hand, where his power was **hidden**.

2471 ¹חָבַל ḥābal[1], v. [12] [→ 2478, 2481]

hold in pledge [2], take as a pledge [+2471] [2], demanded security [1], require a pledge for a loan [+2478] [1], seized for a debt [1], take as a pledge [1], take as security for a debt [1], take in pledge [1], taken in pledge [1], taking as security [1]

Ex 22:26 [22:25] [A] *you* **take** your neighbor's cloak **as a pledge** [+2471],
22:26 [22:25] [A] *you* **take** your neighbor's cloak **as a pledge** [+2471],
Dt 24:6 [A] *Do* not **take** a pair of millstones … **as security for a debt**,
24:6 [A] that *would be* **taking** a man's livelihood **as security**.
24:17 [A] of justice, or **take** the cloak of the widow **as a pledge**.
Job 22:6 [A] *You* **demanded security** *from* your brothers for no reason;
24:3 [A] the orphan's donkey and **take** the widow's ox **in pledge**.
24:9 [A] from the breast; the infant of the poor *is* **seized for a debt**.
Pr 20:16 [A] **hold** it **in pledge** if he does it for a wayward woman.
27:13 [A] **hold** it **in pledge** if he does it for a wayward woman.
Eze 18:16 [A] not oppress anyone or **require a pledge** [+2478] **for a loan**.
Am 2:8 [B] lie down beside every altar on garments **taken in pledge**.

2472 ²חָבַל ḥābal[2], v. [12] [→ 2476; Ar 10243]

destroy [3], acted very wickedly [+2472] [2], be broken [1], is broken [1], offend [1], pay for it [1], ruin [1], ruined [+2256+2476] [1], work havoc [1]

Ne 1:7 [A] *We have* **acted very wickedly** [+2472] toward you. We have
1:7 [A] *We have* **acted very wickedly** [+2472] toward you. We have
Job 17:1 [E] My spirit **is broken**, my days are cut short, the grave awaits
34:31 [A] a man says to God, 'I am guilty but *will* **offend** no more.
Pr 13:13 [C] He who scorns instruction *will* **pay for it**, but he who
Ecc 5:6 [5:5] [D] at what you say and **destroy** the work of your hands?
SS 2:15 [D] for us the foxes, the little foxes *that* **ruin** the vineyards,
Isa 10:27 [E] the yoke *will* **be broken** because you have grown so fat.
13:5 [D] and the weapons of his wrath—to **destroy** the whole country.
32:7 [D] he makes up evil schemes to **destroy** the poor with lies,
54:16 [D] And it is I who have created the destroyer to **work havoc**;
Mic 2:10 [D] it is defiled, *it is* **ruined** [+2256+2476], beyond all remedy.

2473 ³חָבַל ḥābal[3], v. [3] [→ 2477]

conceived [1], in labor [1], pregnant [1]

Ps 7:14 [7:15] [D] *He who is* **pregnant** *with* evil and conceives trouble
SS 8:5 [D] there your mother **conceived** you, there she who was in labor
8:5 [D] conceived you, there *she who was* **in labor** gave you birth.

2474 ¹חֶבֶל ḥebel[1], n.m. [2] [cf. 2475, 2480, 2482]

procession [2]

1Sa 10:5 you will meet a **procession** *of* prophets coming down from the
10:10 When they arrived at Gibeah, a **procession** *of* prophets met him;

2475 ²חֶבֶל ḥebel[2], n.m. [49] [cf. 2474, 2479, 2480, 2482]

cords [11], ropes [9], region [4], portion [3], land [2], rope [2], share [2], allotted [1], boundary lines [1], by [1], cord [1], district [1], fate [1], it[s] [1], lands [1], length of cord [1], length [1], lengths [1], line [1], measured [1], noose [1], portions [1], rigging [1]

Dt 3:4 from them—the whole **region** *of* Argob, Og's kingdom in Bashan.
3:13 (The whole **region** *of* Argob in Bashan used to be known as a land
3:14 took the whole **region** *of* Argob as far as the border of the
32:9 the LORD's portion is his people, Jacob his **allotted** inheritance.
Jos 2:15 So she let them down by a **rope** through the window, for the house
17:5 Manasseh's **share** consisted of ten tracts of land besides Gilead
17:14 given us only one allotment and one **portion** for an inheritance?
19:9 The inheritance of the Simeonites was taken from the **share** *of*
19:29 toward Hosah and came out at the sea in the **region** *of* Aczib,
2Sa 8:2 down on the ground and measured them off with a **length of cord**.
8:2 Every two **lengths** of them were put to death, and the third length
8:2 of them were put to death, and the third **length** was allowed to live.
17:13 withdraws into a city, then all Israel will bring **ropes** to that city,
22:6 The **cords** *of* the grave coiled around me; the snares of death
1Ki 4:13 as well as the **district** *of* Argob in Bashan and its sixty large walled
20:31 with sackcloth around our waists and **ropes** around our heads.
20:32 sackcloth around their waists and **ropes** around their heads,
1Ch 16:18 "To you I will give the land of Canaan as the **portion** you will
Est 1:6 fastened with **cords** *of* white linen and purple material to silver
Job 18:10 A **noose** is hidden *for* him on the ground; a trap lies in his path.
21:17 does calamity come upon them, the **fate** God allots in his anger?
36:8 But if men are bound in chains, held fast by **cords** *of* affliction,
41:1 [40:25] with a fishhook or tie down his tongue with a **rope**?
Ps 16:6 The **boundary lines** have fallen for me in pleasant places;
18:4 [18:5] The **cords** *of* death entangled me; the torrents of
18:5 [18:6] The **cords** *of* the grave coiled around me; the snares of
78:55 before them and allotted their **lands** to them as an inheritance;
105:11 "To you I will give the land of Canaan as the **portion** you will
116:3 The **cords** *of* death entangled me, the anguish of the grave came
119:61 Though the wicked bind me with **ropes**, I will not forget your law.
140:5 [140:6] they have spread out the **cords** of their net and have set
Pr 5:22 of a wicked man ensnare him; the **cords** *of* his sin hold him fast.
Ecc 12:6 before the silver **cord** is severed, or the golden bowl is broken;
Isa 5:18 Woe to those who draw sin along with **cords** *of* deceit,
33:20 its stakes will never be pulled up, nor any of its **ropes** broken.
33:23 Your **rigging** hangs loose: The mast is not held secure, the sail is
Jer 38:6 They lowered Jeremiah by **ropes** into the cistern; it had no water in
38:11 from there and let them down with **ropes** to Jeremiah in the cistern.
38:12 old rags and worn-out clothes under your arms to pad the **ropes**."
38:13 they pulled him up with the **ropes** and lifted him out of the cistern.
Eze 27:24 embroidered work and multicolored rugs with **cords** twisted
47:13 among the twelve tribes of Israel, with *two* **portions** for Joseph.
Hos 11:4 I led them with **cords** *of* human kindness, with ties of love;
Am 7:17 Your land will be **measured** and divided up, and you yourself will
Mic 2:5 no one in the assembly of the LORD to divide the **land** by lot.
Zep 2:5 Woe to you who live **by** the sea, O Kerethite people; the word of
2:6 The **land** *by* the sea, where the Kerethites dwell, will be a place for
2:7 **It[s]** will belong to the remnant of the house of Judah; there they will
Zec 2:1 [2:5] there before me was a man with a measuring **line** in his

2476 ³חֶבֶל ḥebel[3], n.m. [1] [√ 2472]

ruined [+2256+2472] [1]

Mic 2:10 it is defiled, *it is* **ruined** [+2256+2472], beyond all remedy.

2477 חֵבֶל ḥēbel, n.m. [8] [√ 2473]

pain [3], pains [2], anguish [1], labor pains [1], pangs [1]

Job 39:3 and bring forth their young; their **labor pains** are ended.
Isa 13:8 Terror will seize them, pain and **anguish** will grip them; they will
26:17 with child and about to give birth writhes and cries out in her **pain**,
66:7 she gives birth; before the **pains** come upon her, she delivers a son.
Jer 13:21 Will not **pain** grip you like that of a woman in labor?
22:23 how you will groan when **pangs** come upon you, pain like that of a
49:24 anguish and **pain** have seized her, pain like that of a woman in
Hos 13:13 **Pains** *as of* a woman in childbirth come to him, but he is a child

2478 חֲבֹל ḥᵃbōl, n.[m.]. [3] [√ 2471]

require a pledge for a loan [+2471] [1], what took in pledge for a loan [1], what took in pledge [1]

Eze 18:12 He commits robbery. He does not return **what** he **took in pledge**.
18:16 does not oppress anyone or **require a pledge for a loan** [+2471].
33:15 if he gives back **what** he **took in pledge for a loan**, returns what

2479 חִבֵּל ḥibbēl, n.[m.]. [1] [√ 2475]

rigging [1]

Pr 23:34 be like one sleeping on the high seas, lying on top of the **rigging**.

2480 חֹבֵל ḥōbēl, n.m. [5] [cf. 2474, 2475, 2482]

seamen [3], captain [+2021+8042] [1], seamen [+3542] [1]

Eze 27:8 your skilled men, O Tyre, were aboard as your **seamen**.
27:27 merchandise and wares, your mariners, **seamen** and shipwrights,
27:28 The shorelands will quake when your **seamen** cry out.
27:29 the mariners and all the **seamen** [+3542] will stand on the shore.
Jnh 1:6 The **captain** [+2021+8042] went to him and said, "How can you

2481 חֲבֹלָה ḥᵃbōlâ, n.f. [1] [√ 2471]

what took in pledge [1]

Eze 18:7 not oppress anyone, but returns **what** he **took in pledge** *for* a loan.

2482 חֹבְלִים ḥōbᵉlîm, n.[m.]pl. [2] [cf. 2474, 2475, 2480]

Union [2]

Zec 11: 7 Then I took two staffs and called one Favor and the other **Union**,
11: 14 I broke my second staff called **Union**, breaking the brotherhood

2483 חֲבַצֶּלֶת ḥᵃbaṣṣelet, n.f. [2]

crocus [1], rose [1]

SS 2: 1 I am a **rose** *of* Sharon, a lily of the valleys.
Isa 35: 1 be glad; the wilderness will rejoice and blossom. Like the **crocus**,

2484 חֲבַצִּנְיָה ḥᵃbaṣṣinyâ, n.pr.m. [1]

Habazziniah [1]

Jer 35: 3 the son of **Habazziniah**, and his brothers and all his sons—

2485 חָבַק ḥābaq, v. [13] [→ 2486]

embrace [3], embraced [3], embraces [2], *untranslated* [1], folds [1], hold in arms [1], hug [1], lie [1]

Ge 29: 13 [D] *He* **embraced** him and kissed him and brought him to his
33: 4 [D] Esau ran to meet Jacob and **embraced** him; he threw his
48: 10 [D] close to him, and his father kissed them and **embraced** them.
2Ki 4: 16 [A] next year," Elisha said, "you *will* **hold** a son **in** your **arms**."
Job 24: 8 [D] by mountain rains and **hug** the rocks for lack of shelter.
Pr 4: 8 [D] and she will exalt you; **embrace** her, and she will honor you.
5: 20 [D] Why **embrace** the bosom of another man's wife?
Ecc 3: 5 [A] time to gather them, a time to **embrace** and a time to refrain,
3: 5 [D] a time to embrace and a time to refrain, **[RPH]**
4: 5 [A] The fool **folds** his hands and ruins himself.
SS 2: 6 [D] left arm is under my head, and his right arm **embraces** me.
8: 3 [D] left arm is under my head and his right arm **embraces** me.
La 4: 5 [D] in the streets. Those nurtured in purple now **lie** *on* ash heaps.

2486 חִבֻּק ḥibbuq, n.[m.]. [2] [√ 2485]

folding [2]

Pr 6: 10 A little sleep, a little slumber, a little **folding** *of* the hands to rest—
24: 33 A little sleep, a little slumber, a little **folding** *of* the hands to rest—

2487 חֲבַקּוּק ḥᵃbaqqûq, n.pr.m. [2]

Habakkuk [2]

Hab 1: 1 The oracle that **Habakkuk** the prophet received.
3: 1 A prayer of **Habakkuk** the prophet. On *shigionoth*.

2488 [1]חָבַר ḥābar[1], v. [1] [→ 2467, 2494]

make fine speeches [+928+4863] [1]

Job 16: 4 [G] *I could* **make fine speeches** [+928+4863] against you

2489 [2]חָבַר ḥābar[2], v. [28] [→ 2248, 2490, 2491, 2492, 2493, 2495, 2496, 2497, 2498, 2499, 2500, 2501, 4677, 4678]

attached [2], be fastened [2], fasten together [2], fasten [2], joined [2], made an alliance [2], agreed [1], allied with [1], allies [1], among [1], casts spells [+2490] [1], coming to an agreement [1], did[s] the same [+285+285+448] [1], do[s] the same [1], enchanter [+2490] [1], is closely compacted [1], join together [1], join [1], joined forces [1], joined to [1], touched [1], touching [1]

Ge 14: 3 [A] All these latter kings **joined forces** in the Valley of Siddim
Ex 26: 3 [A] **Join** five of the curtains together, and do the same with the
26: 3 [A] the curtains together, and **do[s] the same** *with* the other five.
26: 6 [D] fifty gold clasps and use them *to* **fasten** the curtains together
26: 9 [D] **Join** five of the curtains **together** into one set and the other
26: 11 [D] put them in the loops *to* **fasten** the tent **together** as a unit.
28: 7 [A] It is to have two shoulder pieces **attached** to two of its
28: 7 [E] pieces attached to two of its corners, so *it can* **be fastened**.
36: 10 [D] *They* **joined** five of the curtains together and did the same
36: 10 [D] and **did[s]** [+285+285+448] **the same** *with* the other five.
36: 13 [D] used them *to* **fasten** the two sets of curtains together so that
36: 16 [D] *They* **joined** five of the curtains into one set and the other six
36: 18 [D] They made fifty bronze clasps to **fasten** the tent **together** as
39: 4 [A] *which were* **attached** to two of its corners, so it could be
39: 4 [E] were attached to two of its corners, so *it could* **be fastened**.
Dt 18: 11 [A] or **casts spells** [+2490], or who is a medium or spiritist
2Ch 20: 35 [F] Jehoshaphat king of Judah **made an alliance** with Ahaziah
20: 36 [D] *He* **agreed** with him to construct a fleet of trading ships.
20: 37 [F] saying, "Because you *have* **made an alliance** with Ahaziah,
Ps 58: 5 [58:6] [A] however skillful the **enchanter** [+2490] *may be*.
94: 20 [A] *Can* a corrupt throne *be* **allied with** you—one that brings on
122: 3 [E] Jerusalem is built like a city that **is closely compacted**
Ecc 9: 4 [E] Anyone who *is* **among** [K 1047] the living has hope—even a
Eze 1: 9 [A] their wings **touched** one another. Each one went straight
1: 11 [A] *one* **touching** the wing of another creature on either side,
Da 11: 6 [F] After some years, *they will become* **allies**. The daughter of
11: 23 [F] After **coming to an agreement** with him, he will act
Hos 4: 17 [B] Ephraim *is* **joined to** idols; leave him alone!

2490 [1]חֶבֶר ḥeber[1], n.[m.]. [7] [√ 2489]

bands [1], casts spells [+2489] [1], enchanter [+2489] [1], magic spells [1], share with [1], share [1], spells [1]

Dt 18: 11 or **casts spells** [+2489], or who is a medium or spiritist or who
Ps 58: 5 [58:6] however skillful the **enchanter** *may* **be** [+2489].
Pr 21: 9 Better to live on a corner of the roof than **share** a house **with** a
25: 24 Better to live on a corner of the roof than **share** a house *with* a
Isa 47: 9 in spite of your many sorceries and all your potent **spells**.
47: 12 then, with your **magic spells** and with your many sorceries,
Hos 6: 9 As marauders lie in ambush for a man, so do **bands** *of* priests;

2491 [2]חֶבֶר ḥeber[2], n.pr.m. [11] [→ 2499; cf. 2489]

Heber [10], Heber's [1]

Ge 46: 17 Their sister was Serah. The sons of Beriah: **Heber** and Malkiel.
Nu 26: 45 through **Heber**, the Heberite clan; through Malkiel, the Malkielite
Jdg 4: 11 Now **Heber** the Kenite had left the other Kenites, the descendants
4: 17 fled on foot to the tent of Jael, the wife of **Heber** the Kenite,
4: 17 between Jabin king of Hazor and the clan of **Heber** the Kenite.
4: 21 But Jael, **Heber's** wife, picked up a tent peg and a hammer
5: 24 "Most blessed of women be Jael, the wife of **Heber** the Kenite,
1Ch 4: 18 **Heber** the father of Soco, and Jekuthiel the father of Zanoah.)
7: 31 sons of Beriah: **Heber** and Malkiel, who was the father of Birzaith.
7: 32 **Heber** was the father of Japhlet, Shomer and Hotham and of their
8: 17 Zebadiah, Meshullam, Hizki, **Heber**,

2492 חָבֵר ḥābēr, a. & n.m. [12] [√ 2489; Ar 10245, 10246]

associated with [3], companions [2], friend [2], friends [2], kind [1], partner [1], united [1]

Jdg 20: 11 men of Israel got together and **united** as one man against the city.
Ps 45: 7 [45:8] has set you above your **companions** by anointing you with
119: 63 I am a **friend** to all who fear you, to all who follow your precepts.
Pr 28: 24 and says, "It's not wrong"—he is **partner** to him who destroys.
Ecc 4: 10 If one falls down, his **friend** can help him up. But pity the man
SS 1: 7 should I be like a veiled woman beside the flocks of your **friends**?
8: 13 You who dwell in the gardens with **friends** in attendance,
Isa 1: 23 Your rulers are rebels, **companions** *of* thieves; they all love bribes
44: 11 He and his **kind** will be put to shame; craftsmen are nothing
Eze 37: 16 'Belonging to Judah and the Israelites **associated with** him.'
37: 16 to Joseph and all the house of Israel **associated with** him.'
37: 19 of the Israelite tribes **associated with** him, and join it to Judah's

2493 חַבָּר ḥabbār, n.m. [1] [√ 2489]

traders [1]

Job 41: 6 [40:30] Will **traders** barter for him? Will they divide him up

2494 חֲבַרְבֻּרוֹת ḥᵃbarburôt, n.f. [1] [√ 2488]

spots [1]

Jer 13: 23 Can the Ethiopian change his skin or the leopard its **spots**?

2495 חֶבְרָה ḥebrâ, n.f. [1] [√ 2489]

keeps company [+782+4200] [1]

Job 34: 8 *He* **keeps company** [+782+4200] with evildoers; he associates

2496 [1]חֶבְרוֹן ḥebrôn[1], n.pr.loc. [62 / 63] [√ 2489]

Hebron [62], *untranslated* [1]

Ge 13: 18 and went to live near the great trees of Mamre at **Hebron**,
23: 2 She died at Kiriath Arba (that is, **Hebron**) in the land of Canaan,
23: 19 cave in the field of Machpelah near Mamre (which is at **Hebron**)
35: 27 Arba (that is, **Hebron**), where Abraham and Isaac had stayed.
37: 14 back to me." Then he sent him off from the Valley of **Hebron**.
Nu 13: 22 They went up through the Negev and came to **Hebron**, where
13: 22 (**Hebron** had been built seven years before Zoan in Egypt.)
Jos 10: 3 king of Jerusalem appealed to Hoham king of **Hebron**,
10: 5 the kings of Jerusalem, **Hebron**, Jarmuth, Lachish and Eglon—
10: 23 the kings of Jerusalem, **Hebron**, Jarmuth, Lachish and Eglon.
10: 36 and all Israel with him went up from Eglon to **Hebron**
10: 39 its king as they had done to Libnah and its king and to **Hebron**.
11: 21 from **Hebron**, Debir and Anab, from all the hill country of Judah,
12: 10 the king of Jerusalem one the king of **Hebron** one
14: 13 Caleb son of Jephunneh and gave him **Hebron** as his inheritance.
14: 14 So **Hebron** has belonged to Caleb son of Jephunneh the Kenizzite
14: 15 (**Hebron** used to be called Kiriath Arba after Arba, who was the
15: 13 of Jephunneh a portion in Judah—Kiriath Arba, that is, **Hebron**.
15: 54 Humtah, Kiriath Arba (that is, **Hebron**) and Zior—nine towns

Jos 20: 7 in the hill country of Ephraim, and Kiriath Arba (that is, **Hebron**)
21: 11 **Hebron**), with its surrounding pastureland, in the hill country of
21: 13 So to the descendants of Aaron the priest they gave **Hebron** (a city
Jdg 1: 10 They advanced against the Canaanites living in **Hebron** (formerly
1: 10 They advanced against the Canaanites living in Hebron **[RPH]**
1: 20 As Moses had promised, **Hebron** was given to Caleb, who drove
16: 3 and carried them to the top of the hill that faces **Hebron**.
1Sa 30: 31 and **Hebron**; and to those in all the other places where David
2Sa 2: 1 "Where shall I go?" "To **Hebron**," the LORD answered.
2: 3 each with his family, and they settled in **Hebron** and its towns.
2: 11 The length of time David was king in **Hebron** over the house of
2: 32 and his men marched all night and arrived at **Hebron** by daybreak.
3: 2 Sons were born to David in **Hebron**: His firstborn was Amnon the
3: 5 son of David's wife Eglah. These were born to David in **Hebron**.
3: 19 Then he went to **Hebron** to tell David everything that Israel
3: 20 came to David at **Hebron**, David prepared a feast for him
3: 22 Abner was no longer with David in **Hebron**, because David had
3: 27 Now when Abner returned to **Hebron**, Joab took him aside into the
3: 32 They buried Abner in **Hebron**, and the king wept aloud at Abner's
4: 1 Ish-Bosheth son of Saul heard that Abner had died in **Hebron**,
4: 8 They brought the head of Ish-Bosheth to David at **Hebron**
4: 12 their hands and feet and hung the bodies by the pool in **Hebron**.
4: 12 the head of Ish-Bosheth and buried it in Abner's tomb at **Hebron**.
5: 1 All the tribes of Israel came to David at **Hebron** and said,
5: 3 When all the elders of Israel had come to King David at **Hebron**,
5: 3 the king made a compact with them at **Hebron** before the LORD,
5: 5 In **Hebron** he reigned over Judah seven years and six months,
5: 13 After he left **Hebron**, David took more concubines and wives in
15: 7 "Let me go to **Hebron** and fulfill a vow I made to the LORD.
15: 8 to Jerusalem, I will worship the LORD in **Hebron**.' " [BHS-]
15: 9 The king said to him, "Go in peace." So he went to **Hebron**.
15: 10 sound of the trumpets, then say, 'Absalom is king in **Hebron**.' "
1Ki 2: 11 over Israel—seven years in **Hebron** and thirty-three in Jerusalem.
1Ch 3: 1 These were the sons of David born to him in **Hebron**:
3: 4 These six were born to David in **Hebron**, where he reigned seven
6: 55 [6:40] They were given **Hebron** in Judah with its surrounding
6: 57 [6:42] So the descendants of Aaron were given **Hebron** (a city of
11: 1 All Israel came together to David at **Hebron** and said, "We are
11: 3 When all the elders of Israel had come to King David at **Hebron**,
11: 3 he made a compact with them at **Hebron** before the LORD,
12: 23 [12:24] to David at **Hebron** to turn Saul's kingdom over to him,
12: 38 [12:39] They came to **Hebron** fully determined to make David
29: 27 Israel forty years—seven in **Hebron** and thirty-three in Jerusalem.
2Ch 11: 10 Zorah, Aijalon and **Hebron**. These were fortified cities in Judah

2497 ²חֶבְרוֹן ḥebrôn², n.pr.m. [9 / 10] [→ 2498; cf. 2489, 2496?]

Hebron [10]

Ex 6: 18 The sons of Kohath were Amram, Izhar, **Hebron** and Uzziel.
Nu 3: 19 The Kohathite clans: Amram, Izhar, **Hebron** and Uzziel.
1Ch 2: 42 of Ziph, and his son Mareshah, who was the father of **Hebron**.
2: 43 The sons of **Hebron**: Korah, Tappuah, Rekem and Shema.
6: 2 [5:28] The sons of Kohath: Amram, Izhar, **Hebron** and Uzziel.
6: 18 [6:3] The sons of Kohath: Amram, Izhar, **Hebron** and Uzziel.
15: 9 from the descendants of **Hebron**, Eliel the leader and 80 relatives;
23: 12 sons of Kohath: Amram, Izhar, **Hebron** and Uzziel—four in all.
23: 19 The sons of **Hebron**: Jeriah the first, Amariah the second,
24: 23 The sons of **Hebron**: [BHS-] Jeriah the first, Amariah the second,

2498 חֶבְרוֹנִי ḥebrônî, a.g. [6] [√ 2497; cf. 2489, 2496]

Hebronites [4], Hebronite [1], their[s] [+2021+4200] [1]

Nu 3: 27 the clans of the Amramites, Izharites, **Hebronites** and Uzzielites;
26: 58 the Libnite clan, the **Hebronite** clan, the Mahlite clan, the Mushite
1Ch 26: 23 the Amramites, the Izharites, the **Hebronites** and the Uzzielites:
26: 30 From the **Hebronites**: Hashabiah and his relatives—seventeen
26: 31 As for the **Hebronites**, Jeriah was their chief according to the
26: 31 Jeriah was **their**[s] [+2021+4200] chief according to the

2499 חֶבְרִי ḥebrî, a.g. [1] [√ 2491; cf. 2489]

Heberite [1]

Nu 26: 45 through Heber, the **Heberite** clan; through Malkiel, the Malkielite

2500 חֲבֶרֶת ḥ[a]beret, n.f. [1] [√ 2489]

partner [1]

Mal 2: 14 though she is your **partner**, the wife of your marriage covenant.

2501 חֹבֶרֶת ḥōberet, n.f. [4] [√ 2489]

set [4]

Ex 26: 4 loops of blue material along the edge of the end curtain in one **set**,
26: 10 Make fifty loops along the edge of the end curtain in one **set**
26: 10 and also along the edge of the end curtain in the other **set**.
36: 17 and also along the edge of the end curtain in the other **set**.

2502 חָבַשׁ ḥābaš, v. [33 / 32] [cf. 3109]

saddled [9], bind up [3], binds up [3], put [2], saddle [2], *untranslated* [1], bandaged [1], been bound up [1], bound up [1], did[s] so [1], dressed [1], fastened [1], govern [1], have saddled [1], remedy [1], shroud [1], twisted [1], wrapped around [1]

Ge 22: 3 [A] the next morning Abraham got up and **saddled** his donkey.
Ex 29: 9 [A] **put** headbands on them. Then tie sashes on Aaron and his
Lev 8: 13 [A] tied sashes around them and **put** headbands on them,
Nu 22: 21 [A] **saddled** his donkey and went with the princes of Moab.
Jdg 19: 10 [B] Jerusalem), with his two **saddled** donkeys and his concubine.
2Sa 16: 1 [B] He had a string of donkeys **saddled** and loaded with two
17: 23 [A] *he* **saddled** his donkey and set out for his house in his
19: 26 [19:27] [A] '*I will* **have** my donkey **saddled** and will ride on it,
1Ki 2: 40 [A] he **saddled** his donkey and went to Achish at Gath in search
13: 13 [A] So he said to his sons, "**Saddle** the donkey for me."
13: 13 [A] when *they had* **saddled** the donkey for him, he mounted it
13: 23 [A] the prophet who had brought him back **saddled** his donkey
13: 27 [A] to his sons, "**Saddle** the donkey for me," and they did so.
13: 27 [A] to his sons, "Saddle the donkey for me," and *they* **did**[s] **so**.
2Ki 4: 24 [A] *She* **saddled** the donkey and said to her servant, "Lead on;
Job 5: 18 [A] For he wounds, but *he* also **binds up**; he injures,
28: 11 [d] *He* searches [BHS ***dams up***; NIV 2924] the sources of the
34: 17 [A] Can he who hates justice **govern**? Will you condemn the just
40: 13 [A] them all in the dust together; **shroud** their faces in the grave.
Ps 147: 3 [D] He heals the brokenhearted and **binds up** their wounds.
Isa 1: 6 [E] open sores, not cleansed or **bandaged** or soothed with oil.
3: 7 [A] in that day he will cry out, "I have no **remedy**. I have no
30: 26 [A] when the LORD **binds up** the bruises of his people
61: 1 [A] He has sent me to **bind up** the brokenhearted, to proclaim
Eze 16: 10 [A] *I* **dressed** you in fine linen and covered you with costly
24: 17 [A] *Keep* your turban **fastened** and your sandals on your feet;
27: 24 [B] embroidered work and multicolored rugs with cords **twisted**
30: 21 [E] *It has* not **been bound up** for healing or put in a splint so as
30: 21 [A] so as **[RPH]** to become strong enough to hold a sword.
34: 4 [A] the weak or healed the sick or **bound up** the injured.
34: 16 [A] *I will* **bind up** the injured and strengthen the weak, but the
Hos 6: 1 [A] heal us; he has injured us but *he will* **bind up** our wounds.
Jnh 2: 5 [2:6] [B] seaweed *was* **wrapped around** my head.

2503 חֲבִתִּים ḥ[a]bittîm, n.[m.]pl. [1] [→ 4679]

offering bread [1]

1Ch 9: 31 entrusted with the responsibility for baking the **offering bread**.

2504 חַג ḥag, n.m. [62] [√ 2510]

feast [33], festival [19], festivals [4], religious feasts [2], festal procession [1], festival offerings [1], festival sacrifices [1], yearly festivals [1]

Ex 10: 9 and herds, because we are to celebrate a **festival** *to* the LORD."
12: 14 for the generations to come you shall celebrate it as a **festival** to
13: 6 without yeast and on the seventh day hold a **festival** to the LORD.
23: 15 "Celebrate the **Feast** of Unleavened Bread; for seven days eat
23: 16 "Celebrate the **Feast** *of* Harvest with the firstfruits of the crops you
23: 16 "Celebrate the **Feast** *of* Ingathering at the end of the year,
23: 18 "The fat of my **festival offerings** must not be kept until morning.
32: 5 "Tomorrow there will be a **festival** to the LORD."
34: 18 "Celebrate the **Feast** *of* Unleavened Bread. For seven days eat
34: 22 "Celebrate the **Feast** *of* Weeks with the firstfruits of the wheat
34: 22 wheat harvest, and the **Feast** *of* Ingathering at the turn of the year.
34: 25 do not let any of the sacrifice from the Passover **Feast** remain until
Lev 23: 6 On the fifteenth day of that month the LORD's **Feast** *of*
23: 34 'On the fifteenth day of the seventh month the LORD's **Feast** *of*
23: 39 of the land, celebrate the **festival** *to* the LORD for seven days;
23: 41 Celebrate this as a **festival** to the LORD for seven days each year.
Nu 28: 17 On the fifteenth day of this month there is to be a **festival**;
29: 12 no regular work. Celebrate a **festival** to the LORD for seven days.
Dt 16: 10 celebrate the **Feast** *of* Weeks to the LORD your God by giving a
16: 13 Celebrate the **Feast** *of* Tabernacles for seven days after you have
16: 14 Be joyful at your **Feast**—you, your sons and daughters, your
16: 16 at the **Feast** *of* Unleavened Bread, the Feast of Weeks and the
16: 16 the **Feast** *of* Weeks and the Feast of Tabernacles.
16: 16 the Feast of Weeks and the **Feast** *of* Tabernacles.
31: 10 in the year for canceling debts, during the **Feast** *of* Tabernacles,
Jdg 21: 19 But look, there is the annual **festival** *of* the LORD in Shiloh,
1Ki 8: 2 King Solomon at the time of the **festival** in the month of Ethanim,
8: 65 So Solomon observed the **festival** at that time, and all Israel with
12: 32 He instituted a **festival** on the fifteenth day of the eighth month,
12: 32 like the **festival** held in Judah, and offered sacrifices on the altar.
12: 33 So he instituted the **festival** for the Israelites and went up to the

2Ch 5: 3 together to the king at the time of the **festival** in the seventh month.
7: 8 So Solomon observed the **festival** at that time for seven days,
7: 9 of the altar for seven days and the **festival** for seven days more.
8: 13 the **Feast** *of* Unleavened Bread, the Feast of Weeks and the Feast
8: 13 the **Feast** *of* Weeks and the Feast of Tabernacles.
8: 13 the Feast of Weeks and the **Feast** *of* Tabernacles.
30: 13 to celebrate the **Feast** *of* Unleavened Bread in the second month.
30: 21 the **Feast** *of* Unleavened Bread for seven days with great rejoicing,
35: 17 and observed the **Feast** *of* Unleavened Bread for seven days.
Ezr 3: 4 they celebrated the **Feast** *of* Tabernacles with the required number
6: 22 For seven days they celebrated with joy the **Feast** *of* Unleavened
Ne 8: 14 that the Israelites were to live in booths during the **feast** of the
8: 18 They celebrated the **feast** for seven days, and on the eighth day,
Ps 81: 3 [81:4] and when the moon is full, on the day of our **Feast**;
118: 27 in hand, join in the **festal procession** up to the horns of the altar.
Isa 29: 1 Add year to year and let your cycle of **festivals** go on.
30: 29 And you will sing as on the night you celebrate a holy **festival**;
Eze 45: 17 grain offerings and drink offerings at the **festivals**, the New Moons
45: 21 a **feast** *lasting* seven days, during which you shall eat bread made
45: 23 Every day during the seven days of the **Feast** he is to provide
45: 25 " 'During the seven days of the **Feast**, which begins in the seventh
46: 11 " 'At the **festivals** and the appointed feasts, the grain offering is to
Hos 2: 11 [2:13] her **yearly festivals**, her New Moons, her Sabbath days—
9: 5 day of your appointed feasts, on the **festival** days of the LORD?
Am 5: 21 "I hate, I despise your **religious feasts**; I cannot stand your
8: 10 I will turn your **religious feasts** into mourning and all your singing
Na 1: 15 [2:1] Celebrate your **festivals**, O Judah, and fulfill your vows.
Zec 14: 16 the LORD Almighty, and to celebrate the **Feast** *of* Tabernacles.
14: 18 the nations that do not go up to celebrate the **Feast** *of* Tabernacles.
14: 19 the nations that do not go up to celebrate the **Feast** *of* Tabernacles.
Mal 2: 3 I will spread on your faces the offal from your **festival sacrifices**,

2505 חָגָּא ḥoggā', n.[f.]. [1]

terror [1]

Isa 19: 17 the land of Judah will bring **terror** to the Egyptians; everyone to

2506 ¹חָגָב ḥāgāb¹, n.m. [5] [→ 2507, 2508, 2509]

grasshopper [2], grasshoppers [2], locusts [1]

Lev 11: 22 you may eat any kind of locust, katydid, cricket or **grasshopper**.
Nu 13: 33 We seemed like **grasshoppers** in our own eyes, and we looked the
2Ch 7: 13 or command **locusts** to devour the land or send a plague among my
Ecc 12: 5 the **grasshopper** drags himself along and desire no longer is
Isa 40: 22 above the circle of the earth, and its people are like **grasshoppers**.

2507 ²חָגָב ḥāgāb², n.pr.m. [1] [→ 2508, 2509; cf. 2506]

Hagab [1]

Ezr 2: 46 **Hagab**, Shalmai, Hanan,

2508 חֲגָבָא ḥªgābā', n.pr.m. Not used in NIV/BHS [√ 2507; cf. 2506]

2509 חֲגָבָה ḥªgābâ, n.pr.m. [2] [√ 2507; cf. 2506]

Hagaba [1], Hagabah [1]

Ezr 2: 45 Lebanah, **Hagabah**, Akkub,
Ne 7: 48 Lebana, **Hagaba**, Shalmai,

2510 חָגַג ḥāgag, v. [16] [→ 2504, 2515, 2516, 2517, 2518; cf. 2552]

celebrate [9], *untranslated* [1], celebrate a festival [1], celebrate the feast [1], festive [1], hold a festival [1], reeled [1], reveling [1]

Ex 5: 1 [A] so that *they may* **hold a festival** to me in the desert.' "
12: 14 [A] for the generations to come *you shall* **celebrate** it as a
12: 14 [A] it as a festival to the LORD—a lasting ordinance. **[RPH]**
23: 14 [A] "Three times a year *you are to* **celebrate a festival** to me.
Lev 23: 39 [A] the land, **celebrate** the festival to the LORD for seven days;
23: 41 [A] **Celebrate** this as a festival to the LORD for seven days
23: 41 [A] the generations to come; **celebrate** it in the seventh month.
Nu 29: 12 [A] **Celebrate** a festival to the LORD for seven days.
Dt 16: 15 [A] For seven days **celebrate the Feast** to the LORD your God
1Sa 30: 16 [A] drinking and **reveling** because of the great amount of plunder
Ps 42: 4 [42:5] [A] of joy and thanksgiving among the **festive** throng.
107: 27 [A] *They* **reeled** and staggered like drunken men; they were at
Na 1: 15 [2:1] [A] **Celebrate** your festivals, O Judah, and fulfill your
Zec 14: 16 [A] LORD Almighty, and to **celebrate** the Feast of Tabernacles.
14: 18 [A] that do not go up to **celebrate** the Feast of Tabernacles.
14: 19 [A] that do not go up to **celebrate** the Feast of Tabernacles.

2511 חָגוּ ḥāgû, n.m.pl. [3]

clefts [3]

SS 2: 14 My dove in the **clefts** *of* the rock, in the hiding places on the
Jer 49: 16 you who live in the **clefts** *of* the rocks, who occupy the heights of
Ob 1: 3 you who live in the **clefts** *of* the rocks and make your home on the

2512 חֲגוֹר ḥªgôr, n.[m.]. [3] [√ 2520]

belt [2], sashes [1]

1Sa 18: 4 along with his tunic, and even his sword, his bow and his **belt**.
2Sa 20: 8 strapped over it at his waist was a **belt** with a dagger in its sheath.
Pr 31: 24 and sells them, and supplies the merchants with **sashes**.

2513 חָגוֹר ḥāgôr, a. [1] [√ 2520]

belts [+258] [1]

Eze 23: 15 with **belts** [+258] around their waists and flowing turbans on their

2514 חֲגוֹרָה ḥªgôrâ, n.f. [5] [√ 2520]

bear arms [+2520] [1], belt [1], coverings [1], sash [1], warrior's belt [1]

Ge 3: 7 they sewed fig leaves together and made **coverings** for themselves.
2Sa 18: 11 have had to give you ten shekels of silver and a **warrior's belt**."
1Ki 2: 5 with that blood stained the **belt** around his waist and the sandals on
2Ki 3: 21 *who could* **bear arms** [+2520] was called up and stationed on the
Isa 3: 24 instead of a **sash**, a rope; instead of well-dressed hair, baldness;

2515 חַגִּי ḥaggî, n.pr.m. & a.g. [3] [√ 2510]

Haggi [2], Haggite [1]

Ge 46: 16 sons of Gad: Zephon, **Haggi**, Shuni, Ezbon, Eri, Arodi and Areli.
Nu 26: 15 through **Haggi**, the Haggite clan; through Shuni, the Shunite clan;
26: 15 through Haggi, the **Haggite** clan; through Shuni, the Shunite clan;

2516 חַגַּי ḥaggay, n.pr.m. [9] [√ 2510; Ar 10247]

Haggai [9]

Hag 1: 1 the word of the LORD came through the prophet **Haggai** to
1: 3 Then the word of the LORD came through the prophet **Haggai**:
1: 12 of the LORD their God and the message of the prophet **Haggai**,
1: 13 **Haggai**, the LORD's messenger, gave this message of the
2: 1 the word of the LORD came through the prophet **Haggai**:
2: 10 of Darius, the word of the LORD came to the prophet **Haggai**:
2: 13 **Haggai** said, "If a person defiled by contact with a dead body
2: 14 **Haggai** said, " 'So it is with this people and this nation in my
2: 20 The word of the LORD came to **Haggai** a second time on the

2517 חַגִּיָּה ḥaggiyyâ, n.pr.m. [1] [√ 2510 + 3378]

Haggiah [1]

1Ch 6: 30 [6:15] Shimea his son, **Haggiah** his son and Asaiah his son.

2518 חַגִּית ḥaggît, n.pr.f. [5] [√ 2510]

Haggith [5]

2Sa 3: 4 the fourth, Adonijah the son of **Haggith**; the fifth,
1Ki 1: 5 Now Adonijah, whose mother was **Haggith**, put himself forward
1: 11 "Have you not heard that Adonijah, the son of **Haggith**,
2: 13 Now Adonijah, the son of **Haggith**, went to Bathsheba, Solomon's
1Ch 3: 2 of Talmai king of Geshur; the fourth, Adonijah the son of **Haggith**;

2519 חָגְלָה ḥoglâ, n.pr.f. [4] [→ 1102; cf. 3005]

Hoglah [4]

Nu 26: 33 whose names were Mahlah, Noah, **Hoglah**, Milcah and Tirzah.)
27: 1 of the daughters were Mahlah, Noah, **Hoglah**, Milcah and Tirzah.
36: 11 Mahlah, Tirzah, **Hoglah**, Milcah and Noah—
Jos 17: 3 whose names were Mahlah, Noah, **Hoglah**, Milcah and Tirzah.

2520 חָגַר ḥāgar, v. [44 / 43] [→ 2512, 2513, 2514, 4680]

put on [13], wearing [4], armed [+3998] [3], tied around [3], tuck cloak into belt [+5516] [2], wear [2], bear arms [+2514] [1], belt [1], cloak tucked into belt [+5516] [1], clothed [1], fastened on [1], gird [1], in [1], put sackcloth around [1], puts on armor [1], restrained [1], sets about work [+5516] [1], strapped [1], tie around [1], tie [1], tied [1], was armed [1]

Ex 12: 11 [B] with your **cloak tucked** [+5516] **into** your **belt**, your sandals
29: 9 [A] headbands on them. Then **tie** sashes *on* Aaron and his sons.
Lev 8: 7 [A] **tied** the sash **around** him, clothed him with the robe and put
8: 7 [A] *He* also **tied** the ephod *to* him by its skillfully woven
8: 13 [A] **tied** sashes **around** them and put headbands on them,
16: 4 [A] *he is to* **tie** the linen sash **around** him and put on the linen
Dt 1: 41 [A] So every one of *you* **put on** his weapons, thinking it easy to
Jdg 3: 16 [A] which *he* **strapped** to his right thigh under his clothing.

Jdg 18: 11 [B] **armed** [+3998] *for* battle, set out from Zorah and Eshtaol.
18: 16 [B] The six hundred Danites, **armed** [+3998] *for* battle, stood at
18: 17 [B] the six hundred **armed** [+3998] men stood at the entrance to
1Sa 2: 18 [B] before the LORD—a boy **wearing** a linen ephod.
17: 39 [A] David **fastened on** his sword over the tunic and tried walking
25: 13 [A] David said to his men, "**Put on** your swords!" So they put on
25: 13 [A] So they **put on** their swords, and David put on his.
25: 13 [A] So they put on their swords, and David **put on** his.
2Sa 3: 31 [A] "Tear your clothes and **put on** sackcloth and walk in
6: 14 [B] David, **wearing** a linen ephod, danced before the LORD
20: 8 [B] Joab *was* **wearing** his military tunic, and strapped over it at
21: 16 [B] hundred shekels and who **was armed** *with* a new ⌊sword⌋,
22: 46 [a] *they* **come** trembling [BHS *arm themselves*; NIV 3004] from
1Ki 20: 11 [A] '*One who* **puts on** *his* **armor** should not boast like one who
20: 32 [A] **Wearing** sackcloth around their waists and ropes around
2Ki 3: 21 [A] *who could* **bear** [+2514] **arms** was called up and stationed
4: 29 [A] said to Gehazi, "**Tuck** [+5516] your **cloak into** your **belt**,
9: 1 [A] and said to him, "**Tuck** [+5516] *your* **cloak into** your **belt**,
Ps 45: 3 [45:4] [A] **Gird** your sword upon your side, O mighty one;
65: 12 [65:13] [A] desert overflow; the hills *are* **clothed** *with* gladness.
76: 10 [76:11] [A] and the survivors of your wrath *are* **restrained**.
109: 19 [A] wrapped about him, like a belt **tied** forever **around** him.
Pr 31: 17 [A] *She* **sets** [+5516] **about** her **work** vigorously; her arms are
Isa 15: 3 [A] In the streets *they* **wear** sackcloth; on the roofs and in the
22: 12 [A] and to wail, to tear out your hair and **put on** sackcloth.
32: 11 [A] Strip off your clothes, **put sackcloth around** your waists.
Jer 4: 8 [A] So **put on** sackcloth, lament and wail, for the fierce anger of
6: 26 [A] O my people, **put on** sackcloth and roll in ashes; mourn with
49: 3 [A] **Put on** sackcloth and mourn; rush here and there inside the
La 2: 10 [A] they have sprinkled dust on their heads and **put on** sackcloth.
Eze 7: 18 [A] *They will* **put on** sackcloth and be clothed with terror. Their
27: 31 [A] shave their heads because of you and *will* **put on** sackcloth.
44: 18 [A] *They must* not **wear** anything that makes them perspire.
Da 10: 5 [B] in linen, with a **belt** of the finest gold around his waist.
Joel 1: 8 [B] Mourn like a virgin **in** sackcloth grieving for the husband of
1: 13 [A] **Put on** sackcloth, O priests, and mourn; wail, you who

2521 ¹חַד **ḥad¹**, a. [4] [√ 2523]

sharp [3], sharpened [1]

Ps 57: 4 [57:5] are spears and arrows, whose tongues are **sharp** swords.
Pr 5: 4 but in the end she is bitter as gall, **sharp** as a double-edged sword.
Isa 49: 2 He made my mouth like a **sharpened** sword, in the shadow of his
Eze 5: 1 take a **sharp** sword and use it as a barber's razor to shave your

2522 ²חַד **ḥad²**, a. [1] [cf. 285]

each [1]

Eze 33: 30 saying to **each** other, 'Come and hear the message that has come

2523 חָדַד **ḥādad**, v. [6] [→ 2521, 2529, 2531]

sharpened [2], sharpens [2], fiercer [1], is sharpened [1]

Pr 27: 17 [G] As iron **sharpens** iron, so one man sharpens another.
27: 17 [G] As iron sharpens iron, so one man **sharpens** another.
Eze 21: 9 [21:14] [H] " 'A sword, a sword, **sharpened** and polished—
21: 10 [21:15] [H] **sharpened** for the slaughter, polished to flash like
21: 11 [21:16] [H] it **is sharpened** and polished, made ready for the
Hab 1: 8 [A] horses are swifter than leopards, **fiercer** than wolves at dusk.

2524 חֲדַד **ḥ^adad**, n.pr.m. [2]

Hadad [2]

Ge 25: 15 **Hadad**, Tema, Jetur, Naphish and Kedemah.
1Ch 1: 30 Mishma, Dumah, Massa, **Hadad**, Tema,

2525 ¹חָדָה **ḥādâ¹**, v. [2] [→ 2530, 3484, 3485; cf. 2526, 2527]

delighted [1], made glad [1]

Ex 18: 9 [A] Jethro *was* **delighted** to hear about all the good things the
Ps 21: 6 [21:7] [D] and **made** him **glad** with the joy of your presence.

2526 ²חָדָה **ḥādâ²**, v. [1] [cf. 2525]

be included [1]

Job 3: 6 [C] *may it* not **be included** among the days of the year nor be

2527 ³חָדָה **ḥādâ³**, v. Not used in NIV/BHS [cf. 2525]

2528 חַדָּה **ḥaddâ**, n.pr.loc. Not used in NIV/BHS [→ 6532]

2529 חַדּוּד **ḥaddûd**, a. [1] [√ 2523]

jagged [1]

Job 41: 30 [41:22] His undersides are **jagged** potsherds, leaving a trail in the

2530 חֶדְוָה **ḥedwâ**, n.f. [2] [√ 2525; Ar 10250]

joy [2]

1Ch 16: 27 and majesty are before him; strength and **joy** in his dwelling place.
Ne 8: 10 Do not grieve, for the **joy** *of* the LORD is your strength."

2531 חָדִיד **ḥādîd**, n.pr.loc. [3] [√ 2523]

Hadid [3]

Ezr 2: 33 of Lod, **Hadid** and Ono 725
Ne 7: 37 of Lod, **Hadid** and Ono 721
11: 34 in **Hadid**, Zeboim and Neballat,

2532 ¹חָדַל **ḥādal¹**, v. [58] [→ 2534, 2536?; cf. 2533]

stopped [10], stop [8], refrain [5], fail [4], ceased [3], give up [3], let alone [3], not [2], abandoned [1], absent [1], always be [+4202] [1], cease [1], do not [1], don't [1], failing [1], fails [1], gone away [1], keep [1], leave alone [+4946] [1], no enough [1], no more [1], over [1], past [1], refrain from [1], refuse [1], show restraint [1], silent [1], stop trusting in [+4200+4946] [1]

Ge 11: 8 [A] there over all the earth, and *they* **stopped** building the city.
18: 11 [A] in years, and Sarah was **past** the age of childbearing.
41: 49 [A] it was so much that *he* **stopped** keeping records because it
Ex 9: 29 [A] The thunder *will* **stop** and there will be no more hail, so you
9: 33 [A] the thunder and hail **stopped**, and the rain no longer poured
9: 34 [A] Pharaoh saw that the rain and hail and thunder *had* **stopped**,
14: 12 [A] Didn't we say to you in Egypt, '**Leave** us **alone** [+4946]; let
23: 5 [A] hates you fallen down under its load, **do not** leave it there;
Nu 9: 13 [A] and not on a journey **fails** to celebrate the Passover,
Dt 15: 11 [A] *There will* **always** [+4202] **be** poor people in the land.
23: 22 [23:23] [A] if *you* **refrain from** making a vow, you will not be
Jdg 5: 6 [A] son of Anath, in the days of Jael, the roads *were* **abandoned**;
5: 7 [A] Village life in Israel **ceased**, ceased until I, Deborah, arose,
5: 7 [A] **ceased** until I, Deborah, arose, arose a mother in Israel.
9: 9 [A] '*Should I* **give up** my oil, by which both gods and men are
9: 11 [A] tree replied, '*Should I* **give up** my fruit, so good and sweet,
9: 13 [A] '*Should I* **give up** my wine, which cheers both gods and men,
15: 7 [A] acted like this, *I* won't **stop** until I get my revenge on you."
20: 28 [A] we go up again to battle with Benjamin our brother, or **not**?"
Ru 1: 18 [A] Ruth was determined to go with her, *she* **stopped** urging her.
1Sa 2: 5 [A] out for food, but those who were hungry hunger **no more**.
9: 5 [A] or my father *will* **stop** thinking about the donkeys and start
12: 23 [A] I should sin against the LORD by **failing** to pray for you.
23: 13 [A] told that David had escaped from Keilah, he did **not** go there.
1Ki 15: 21 [A] *he* **stopped** building Ramah and withdrew to Tirzah.
22: 6 [A] I go to war against Ramoth Gilead, or *shall I* **refrain**?"
22: 15 [A] we go to war against Ramoth Gilead, or *shall I* **refrain**?"
2Ch 16: 5 [A] *he* **stopped** building Ramah and abandoned his work.
18: 5 [A] we go to war against Ramoth Gilead, or *shall I* **refrain**?"
18: 14 [A] we go to war against Ramoth Gilead, or *shall I* **refrain**?"
25: 16 [A] **Stop**! Why be struck down?" So the prophet stopped
25: 16 [A] So the prophet **stopped** but said, "I know that God has
35: 21 [A] so **stop** opposing God, who is with me, or he will destroy
Job 3: 17 [A] There the wicked **cease** *from* turmoil, and there the weary
7: 16 [A] not live forever. **Let** me **alone**; my days have no meaning.
10: 20 [A] *Are* not my few days *almost* **over**? Turn away from me so I
14: 6 [A] So look away from him and **let** him **alone**, till he has put in
14: 7 [A] it will sprout again, and its new shoots *will* not **fail**.
16: 6 [A] my pain is not relieved; and if *I* **refrain**, it does not go away.
19: 14 [A] My kinsmen *have* **gone away**; my friends have forgotten me.
Ps 36: 3 [36:4] [A] *he has* **ceased** to be wise and to do good.
49: 8 [49:9] [A] for a life is costly, **no** payment *is* ever **enough**—
Pr 10: 19 [A] When words are many, sin *is* not **absent**, but he who holds
19: 27 [A] **Stop** listening to instruction, my son, and you will stray from
23: 4 [A] yourself out to get rich; have the wisdom *to* **show restraint**.
Isa 1: 16 [A] Take your evil deeds out of my sight! **Stop** doing wrong,
2: 22 [A] **Stop** [+4200+4946] **trusting in** man, who has but a breath in
24: 8 [A] the noise of the revelers has stopped, the joyful harp *is* **silent**.
Jer 40: 4 [A] look after you; but if you do not want to, then **don't** come.
41: 8 [A] So *he* **let** them **alone** and did not kill them with the others.
44: 18 [A] ever since *we* **stopped** burning incense to the Queen of
51: 30 [A] Babylon's warriors *have* **stopped** fighting; they remain in
Eze 2: 5 [A] whether they listen or **fail** to listen—for they are a rebellious
2: 7 [A] whether they listen or **fail** to listen, for they are rebellious.
3: 11 [A] Sovereign LORD says,' whether they listen or **fail** to listen."
3: 27 [A] listen let him listen, and whoever will refuse *let him* **refuse**;
Am 7: 5 [A] I cried out, "Sovereign LORD, I beg you, **stop**! How can
Zec 11: 12 [A] "If you think it best, give me my pay; but if not, **keep** it."

2533 ²חָדַל **ḥādal²**, v. Not used in NIV/BHS [cf. 2532, 2536?]

2534 חָדֵל ḥādēl, a. [3] [√ 2532]

fleeting [1], refuse [1], rejected [1]

Ps 39: 4 [39:5] number of my days; let me know how **fleeting** is my life.
Isa 53: 3 He was despised and **rejected** *by* men, a man of sorrows,
Eze 3: 27 will listen let him listen, and whoever will **refuse** let him refuse;

2535 חֶדֶל ḥedel, n.[m.]. [1 / 0]

Isa 38: 11 now dwell in this world. [BHS *in the place of cessation*; NIV 2698]

2536 חַדְלָי ḥadlāy, n.pr.m. [1] [√ 2432 *or* 2533]

Hadlai [1]

2Ch 28: 12 Jehizkiah son of Shallum, and Amasa son of **Hadlai**—

2537 חֵדֶק ḥēdeq, n.[m.]. [2]

brier [1], thorns [1]

Pr 15: 19 The way of the sluggard is blocked with **thorns**, but the path of the
Mic 7: 4 The best of them is like a **brier**, the most upright worse than a

2538 חִדֶּקֶל ḥiddeqel, n.pr.loc. [2]

Tigris [2]

Ge 2: 14 The name of the third river is the **Tigris**; it runs along the east side
Da 10: 4 as I was standing on the bank of the great river, the **Tigris**,

2539 חָדַר ḥādar, v. [1] [→ 2540]

closing in from every side [1]

Eze 21: 14 [21:19] [A] great slaughter, **closing in** on them **from every side**.

2540 חֶדֶר ḥeder, n.m. [38] [√ 2539]

inner room [+928+2540] [8], room [6], bedroom [+5435] [4], rooms [3], bedroom [+4753] [2], bedroom [2], chambers [2], inmost being [+1061] [2], inmost parts [+1061] [2], bedrooms [1], chamber [1], constellations [1], homes [1], inner room [1], private room [1], shrine [1]

Ge 43: 30 for a place to weep. He went into his **private room** and wept there.
Ex 8: 3 [7:28] your palace and your **bedroom** [+5435] and onto your bed,
Dt 32: 25 sword will make them childless; in their **homes** terror will reign.
Jdg 3: 24 "He must be relieving himself in the **inner room** *of* the house."
15: 1 went to visit his wife. He said, "I'm going to my wife's **room**."
16: 9 With men hidden in the **room**, she called to him, "Samson,
16: 12 Then, with men hidden in the **room**, she called to him, "Samson,
2Sa 4: 7 the house while he was lying on the bed in his **bedroom** [+5435].
13: 10 "Bring the food here into my **bedroom** so I may eat from your
13: 10 had prepared and brought it to her brother Amnon in his **bedroom**.
1Ki 1: 15 So Bathsheba went to see the aged king in his **room**, where
20: 30 Ben-Hadad fled to the city and hid in an **inner room** [+928+2540].
20: 30 Ben-Hadad fled to the city and hid in an **inner room** [+928+2540].
22: 25 out on the day you go to hide in an **inner room** [+928+2540]."
22: 25 out on the day you go to hide in an **inner room** [+928+2540]."
2Ki 6: 12 of Israel the very words you speak in your **bedroom** [+5435]."
9: 2 his companions and take him into an **inner room** [+928+2540].
9: 2 his companions and take him into an **inner room** [+928+2540].
11: 2 and his nurse in a **bedroom** [+4753] to hide him from Athaliah;
1Ch 28: 11 its upper parts, its inner **rooms** and the place of atonement.
2Ch 18: 24 out on the day you go to hide in an **inner room** [+928+2540]."
18: 24 out on the day you go to hide in an **inner room** [+928+2540]."
22: 11 to be murdered and put him and his nurse in a **bedroom** [+4753].
Job 9: 9 and Orion, the Pleiades and the **constellations** *of* the south.
37: 9 The tempest comes out from its **chamber**, the cold from the
Ps 105: 30 with frogs, which went up into the **bedrooms** *of* their rulers.
Pr 7: 27 is a highway to the grave, leading down to the **chambers** *of* death.
18: 8 choice morsels; they go down to a man's **inmost parts** [+1061].
20: 27 the spirit of a man; it searches out his **inmost being** [+1061].
20: 30 cleanse away evil, and beatings purge the **inmost being** [+1061].
24: 4 through knowledge its **rooms** are filled with rare and beautiful
26: 22 choice morsels; they go down to a man's **inmost parts** [+1061].
Ecc 10: 20 even in your thoughts, or curse the rich in your **bedroom** [+5435],
SS 1: 4 Let the king bring me into his **chambers**. We rejoice and delight in
3: 4 to my mother's house, to the **room** *of* the one who conceived me.
Isa 26: 20 my people, enter your **rooms** and shut the doors behind you;
Eze 8: 12 Israel are doing in the darkness, each at the **shrine** *of* his own idol?
Joel 2: 16 Let the bridegroom leave his **room** and the bride her chamber.

2541 חַדְרָךְ ḥadrāk, n.pr.loc. [1]

Hadrach [1]

Zec 9: 1 An Oracle The word of the LORD is against the land of **Hadrach**

2542 חָדַשׁ ḥādaš, v. [10] [→ 2543, 2544, 2545, 2546, 2548]

renew [4], restore [2], bring new [1], is renewed [1], reaffirm [1], repaired [1]

1Sa 11: 14 [D] "Come, let us go to Gilgal and there **reaffirm** the kingship."
2Ch 15: 8 [D] *He* **repaired** the altar of the LORD that was in front of the
24: 4 [D] Some time later Joash decided to **restore** the temple of the
24: 12 [D] hired masons and carpenters to **restore** the LORD's temple,
Job 10: 17 [D] *You* **bring new** witnesses against me and increase your
Ps 51: 10 [51:12] [D] O God, and **renew** a steadfast spirit within me.
103: 5 [F] good things so that your youth **is renewed** like the eagle's.
104: 30 [D] they are created, and *you* **renew** the face of the earth.
Isa 61: 4 [D] *they will* **renew** the ruined cities that have been devastated
La 5: 21 [D] O LORD, that we may return; **renew** our days as of old

2543 חָדָשׁ ḥādāš, a. [53] [√ 2542; Ar 10251]

new [50], fresh [1], recently [+4946+7940] [1], recently [1]

Ex 1: 8 a **new** king, who did not know about Joseph, came to power in
Lev 23: 16 and then present an offering of **new** grain to the LORD.
26: 10 when you will have to move it out to make room for the **new**.
Nu 28: 26 when you present to the LORD an offering of **new** grain during
Dt 20: 5 "Has anyone built a **new** house and not dedicated it? Let him go
22: 8 When you build a **new** house, make a parapet around your roof
24: 5 If a man has **recently** married, he must not be sent to war or have
32: 17 they had not known, gods that **recently** [+4946+7940] appeared,
Jos 9: 13 these wineskins that we filled were **new**, but see how cracked they
Jdg 5: 8 When they chose **new** gods, war came to the city gates, and not a
15: 13 So they bound him with two **new** ropes and led him up from the
16: 11 "If anyone ties me securely with **new** ropes that have never been
16: 12 So Delilah took **new** ropes and tied him with them. Then,
1Sa 6: 7 "Now then, get a **new** cart ready, with two cows that have calved
2Sa 6: 3 They set the ark of God on a **new** cart and brought it from the
6: 3 Uzzah and Ahio, sons of Abinadab, were guiding the **new** cart
21: 16 three hundred shekels and who was armed with a **new** ⌞sword⌟,
1Ki 11: 29 the prophet of Shiloh met him on the way, wearing a **new** cloak.
11: 30 Ahijah took hold of the **new** cloak he was wearing and tore it into
2Ki 2: 20 "Bring me a **new** bowl," he said, "and put salt in it." So they
1Ch 13: 7 They moved the ark of God from Abinadab's house on a **new** cart,
2Ch 20: 5 Jerusalem at the temple of the LORD in the front of the **new**
Job 29: 20 My glory will remain **fresh** in me, the bow ever new in my hand.'
32: 19 inside I am like bottled-up wine, like **new** wineskins ready to burst.
Ps 33: 3 Sing to him a **new** song; play skillfully, and shout for joy.
40: 3 [40:4] He put a **new** song in my mouth, a hymn of praise to our
96: 1 Sing to the LORD a **new** song; sing to the LORD, all the earth.
98: 1 Sing to the LORD a **new** song, for he has done marvelous things;
144: 9 I will sing a **new** song to you, O God; on the ten-stringed lyre I
149: 1 Sing to the LORD a **new** song, his praise in the assembly of the
Ecc 1: 9 been done will be done again; there is nothing **new** under the sun.
1: 10 anything of which one can say, "Look! This is something **new**"?
SS 7: 13 [7:14] both **new** and old, that I have stored up for you, my lover.
Isa 41: 15 make you into a threshing sledge, **new** and sharp, with many teeth.
42: 9 the former things have taken place, and **new** *things* I declare;
42: 10 Sing to the LORD a **new** song, his praise from the ends of the
43: 19 See, I am doing a **new** *thing*! Now it springs up; do you not
48: 6 "From now on I will tell you of **new** *things*, of hidden things
62: 2 you will be called by a **new** name that the mouth of the LORD
65: 17 "Behold, I will create **new** heavens and a new earth. The former
65: 17 "Behold, I will create new heavens and a **new** earth. The former
66: 22 "As the **new** heavens and the new earth that I make will endure
66: 22 new heavens and the **new** earth that I make will endure before me,"
Jer 26: 10 took their places at the entrance of the **New** Gate of the LORD's
31: 22 The LORD will create a **new** *thing* on earth—a woman will
31: 31 "when I will make a **new** covenant with the house of Israel
36: 10 which was in the upper courtyard at the entrance of the **New** Gate
La 3: 23 *They* are **new** every morning; great is your faithfulness.
Eze 11: 19 I will give them an undivided heart and put a **new** spirit in them;
18: 31 offenses you have committed, and get a **new** heart and a new spirit.
18: 31 offenses you have committed, and get a new heart and a **new** spirit.
36: 26 I will give you a **new** heart and put a new spirit in you; I will
36: 26 I will give you a new heart and put a **new** spirit in you; I will

2544 חֹדֶשׁ ḥōdeš[1], n.m. [& f.?]. [283] [→ 2545; cf. 2542]

month [193], *untranslated* [31], months [30], new moon [8], New Moons [7], New Moon festivals [4], New Moon festival [3], monthly [+928+2544] [2], another[s] [1], mating time [1], monthly [1], New Moon festivals [+8031] [1], whole month [+3427] [1]

Ge 7: 11 year of Noah's life, on the seventeenth day of the second **month**—
7: 11 **[RPH]** on that day all the springs of the great deep burst forth,
8: 4 on the seventeenth day of the seventh **month** the ark came to rest
8: 4 on the seventeenth day of the seventh month **[RPH]** the ark came
8: 5 The waters continued to recede until the tenth **month**, and on the
8: 5 on the first day of the tenth **month** the tops of the mountains

Ge 8:13 By the first day of the first **month** of Noah's six hundred and first
8:14 By the twenty-seventh day of the second **month** the earth was
8:14 By the twenty-seventh day of the second month **[RPH]** the earth
29:14 After Jacob had stayed with him for a **whole month** [+3427],
38:24 About three **months** later Judah was told, "Your daughter-in-law
Ex 12:2 "This **month** is to be for you the first month, the first month of
12:2 "This month is to be for you the first **month**, the first month of
12:2 month is to be for you the first month, the first **month** *of* your year.
12:3 tenth day of this **month** each man is to take a lamb for his family,
12:6 Take care of them until the fourteenth day of the **month**, when all
12:18 In the first **month** you are to eat bread made without yeast,
12:18 fourteenth day until the evening of the twenty-first day. **[RPH]**
13:4 Today, in the **month** *of* Abib, you are leaving.
13:5 and honey—you are to observe this ceremony in this **month**:
16:1 on the fifteenth day of the second **month** after they had come out
19:1 In the third **month** after the Israelites left Egypt—on the very
23:15 Do this at the appointed time in the **month** *of* Abib, for in that
34:18 Do this at the appointed time in the **month** *of* Abib, for in that
34:18 in the month of Abib, for in that **month** you came out of Egypt.
40:2 the Tent of Meeting, on the first day of the first **month**.
40:2 the Tent of Meeting, on the first day of the first month. **[RPH]**
40:17 So the tabernacle was set up on the first day of the first **month** in
40:17 up on the first day of the first month in the second year. **[RPH]**
Lev 16:29 On the tenth day of the seventh **month** you must deny yourselves
16:29 On the tenth day of the seventh month **[RPH]** you must deny
23:5 begins at twilight on the fourteenth day of the first **month**.
23:5 begins at twilight on the fourteenth day of the first month. **[RPH]**
23:6 On the fifteenth day of that **month** the LORD's Feast of
23:24 'On the first day of the seventh **month** you are to have a day of
23:24 'On the first day of the seventh month **[RPH]** you are to have a
23:27 "The tenth day of this seventh **month** is the Day of Atonement.
23:32 From the evening of the ninth day of the **month** until the following
23:34 'On the fifteenth day of the seventh **month** the LORD's Feast of
23:39 " 'So beginning with the fifteenth day of the seventh **month**,
23:41 for the generations to come; celebrate it in the seventh **month**.
25:9 sounded everywhere on the tenth day of the seventh **month**;
25:9 **[RPH]** on the Day of Atonement sound the trumpet throughout
27:6 If it is a person between *one* **month** and five years, set the value of
Nu 1:1 **month** of the second year after the Israelites came out of Egypt.
1:18 whole community together on the first day of the second **month**.
3:15 their families and clans. Count every male a **month** old or more."
3:22 The number of all the males a **month** old or more who were
3:28 The number of all the males a **month** old or more was 8,600.
3:34 The number of all the males a **month** old or more who were
3:39 their clans, including every male a **month** old or more, was 22,000.
3:40 "Count all the firstborn Israelite males who are a **month** old
3:43 The total number of firstborn males a **month** old or more,
9:1 in the first **month** of the second year after they came out of Egypt.
9:3 at twilight on the fourteenth day of this **month**, in accordance with
9:5 Desert of Sinai at twilight on the fourteenth day of the first **month**.
9:11 They are to celebrate it on the fourteenth day of the second **month**
9:22 cloud stayed over the tabernacle for two days or a **month** or a year,
10:10 your appointed feasts and **New** [+8031] **Moon festivals**—
10:11 On the twentieth day of the second **month** of the second year,
10:11 On the twentieth day of the second month **[RPH]** of the second
11:20 but *for* a whole **month**—until it comes out of your nostrils
11:21 and you say, 'I will give them meat to eat *for* a whole **month**!'
18:16 When they are a **month** old, you must redeem them at the
20:1 In the first **month** the whole Israelite community arrived at the
26:62 All the male Levites a **month** old or more numbered 23,000.
28:11 " 'On the first of every **month**, present to the LORD a burnt
28:14 This is the **monthly** [+928+2544] burnt offering to be made at each
28:14 This is the **monthly** [+928+2544] burnt offering to be made at each
28:14 burnt offering to be made at each **new moon** *during* the year.
28:16 " 'On the fourteenth day of the first **month** the LORD's Passover
28:16 " 'On the fourteenth day of the first month **[RPH]** the LORD's
28:17 On the fifteenth day of this **month** there is to be a festival;
29:1 " 'On the first day of the seventh **month** hold a sacred assembly
29:1 " 'On the first day of the seventh month **[RPH]** hold a sacred
29:6 These are in addition to the **monthly** and daily burnt offerings with
29:7 " 'On the tenth day of this seventh **month** hold a sacred assembly.
29:12 " 'On the fifteenth day of the seventh **month**, hold a sacred
33:3 set out from Rameses on the fifteenth day of the first **month**,
33:3 fifteenth day of the first month, **[RPH]** the day after the Passover.
33:38 where he died on the first day of the fifth **month** of the fortieth
33:38 where he died on the first day of the fifth **month [RPH]** of the
Dt 1:3 In the fortieth year, on the first day of the eleventh **month**,
1:3 **[RPH]** Moses proclaimed to the Israelites all that the LORD had
16:1 Observe the **month** *of* Abib and celebrate the Passover of the
16:1 because in the **month** *of* Abib he brought you out of Egypt by
Jos 4:19 On the tenth day of the first **month** the people went up from the
5:10 On the evening of the fourteenth day of the **month**, while camped
Jdg 11:37 "Give me two **months** to roam the hills and weep with my friends,
11:38 he let her go *for* two **months**. She and the girls went into the hills
11:39 After the two **months**, she returned to her father and he did to her
19:2 house in Bethlehem, Judah. After she had been there four **months**,
20:47 the desert to the rock of Rimmon, where they stayed four **months**.
1Sa 6:1 ark of the LORD had been in Philistine territory seven **months**,
20:5 So David said, "Look, tomorrow is the **New Moon festival**,
20:18 "Tomorrow is the **New Moon festival**. You will be missed,
20:24 and when the **New Moon festival** came, the king sat down to eat.
20:27 the next day, the second day of the **month**, David's place was
20:34 on that second day of the **month** he did not eat, because he was
27:7 David lived in Philistine territory a year and four **months**.
2Sa 2:11 Hebron over the house of Judah was seven years and six **months**.
5:5 In Hebron he reigned over Judah seven years and six **months**,
6:11 remained in the house of Obed-Edom the Gittite *for* three **months**,
24:8 they came back to Jerusalem at the end of nine **months** and twenty
24:13 Or three **months** of fleeing from your enemies while they pursue
1Ki 4:7 Each one had to provide supplies for one **month** in the year.
4:27 [5:7] The district officers, each in his **month**, supplied provisions
5:14 [5:28] sent them off to Lebanon in shifts of ten thousand a **month**,
5:14 [5:28] so that they spent one **month** in Lebanon and two months
5:14 [5:28] spent one month in Lebanon and two **months** at home.
6:1 in the **month** *of* Ziv, the second month, he began to build the
6:1 in the month of Ziv, the second **month**, he began to build the
6:38 In the eleventh year in the month of Bul, the eighth **month**,
8:2 time of the festival in the month of Ethanim, the seventh **month**.
11:16 Joab and all the Israelites stayed there *for* six **months**, until they
12:32 He instituted a festival on the fifteenth day of the eighth **month**,
12:32 **[RPH]** like the festival held in Judah, and offered sacrifices on
12:33 On the fifteenth day of the eighth **month**, a month of his own
12:33 fifteenth day of the eighth month, a **month** of his own choosing,
2Ki 4:23 he asked. "It's not the **New Moon** or the Sabbath." "It's all right,"
15:8 became king of Israel in Samaria, and he reigned six **months**.
23:31 when he became king, and he reigned in Jerusalem three **months**.
24:8 when he became king, and he reigned in Jerusalem three **months**.
25:1 year of Zedekiah's reign, on the tenth day of the tenth **month**,
25:1 **[RPH]** Nebuchadnezzar king of Babylon marched against
25:3 By the ninth day of the ⌊fourth⌋ **month** the famine in the city had
25:8 On the seventh day of the fifth **month**, in the nineteenth year of
25:8 **[RPH]** in the nineteenth year of Nebuchadnezzar king of
25:25 In the seventh **month**, however, Ishmael son of Nethaniah,
25:27 from prison on the twenty-seventh day of the twelfth **month**.
25:27 prison on the twenty-seventh day of the twelfth month. **[RPH]**
1Ch 3:4 to David in Hebron, where he reigned seven years and six **months**.
12:15 [12:16] It was they who crossed the Jordan in the first **month**
13:14 with the family of Obed-Edom in his house *for* three **months**,
21:12 of famine, three **months** of being swept away before your enemies,
23:31 on Sabbaths and at **New Moon festivals** and at appointed feasts.
27:1 divisions that were on duty **month** by month throughout the year.
27:1 divisions that were on duty month by **month** throughout the year.
27:1 that were on duty month by month throughout **[RPH]** the year.
27:2 In charge of the first division, for the first **month**, was Jashobeam
27:3 of Perez and chief of all the army officers for the first **month**.
27:4 In charge of the division for the second **month** was Dodai the
27:5 The third army commander, for the third **month**, was Benaiah son
27:7 The fourth, for the fourth **month**, was Asahel the brother of Joab;
27:8 The fifth, for the fifth **month**, was the commander Shamhuth the
27:9 The sixth, for the sixth **month**, was Ira the son of Ikkesh the
27:10 The seventh, for the seventh **month**, was Helez the Pelonite,
27:11 The eighth, for the eighth **month**, was Sibbecai the Hushathite,
27:12 The ninth, for the ninth **month**, was Abiezer the Anathothite,
27:13 The tenth, for the tenth **month**, was Maharai the Netophathite,
27:14 The eleventh, for the eleventh **month**, was Benaiah the Pirathonite,
27:15 The twelfth, for the twelfth **month**, was Heldai the Netophathite,
2Ch 2:4 [2:3] and evening and on Sabbaths and **New Moons**
3:2 He began building on the second day of the second **month** in the
5:3 to the king at the time of the festival in the seventh **month**.
7:10 On the twenty-third day of the seventh **month** he sent the people to
8:13 by Moses for Sabbaths, **New Moons** and the three annual feasts—
15:10 They assembled at Jerusalem in the third **month** of the fifteenth
29:3 In the first **month** of the first year of his reign, he opened the doors
29:17 They began the consecration on the first day of the first **month**,
29:17 by the eighth day of the **month** they reached the portico of the
29:17 the LORD itself, finishing on the sixteenth day of the first **month**.
30:2 Jerusalem decided to celebrate the Passover in the second **month**.
30:13 to celebrate the Feast of Unleavened Bread in the second **month**.
30:15 the Passover lamb on the fourteenth day of the second **month**.
31:3 **New Moons** and appointed feasts as written in the Law of the
31:7 They began doing this in the third **month** and finished in the
31:7 doing this in the third month and finished in the seventh **month**.
35:1 lamb was slaughtered on the fourteenth day of the first **month**.
36:2 when he became king, and he reigned in Jerusalem three **months**.
36:9 and he reigned in Jerusalem three **months** and ten days.
Ezr 3:1 When the seventh **month** came and the Israelites had settled in
3:5 the **New Moon** sacrifices and the sacrifices for all the appointed
3:6 On the first day of the seventh **month** they began to offer burnt

Ezr 3: 8 In the second **month** of the second year after their arrival at the
6: 19 On the fourteenth day of the first **month**, the exiles celebrated the
7: 8 Ezra arrived in Jerusalem in the fifth **month** of the seventh year of
7: 9 begun his journey from Babylon on the first day of the first **month**,
7: 9 and he arrived in Jerusalem on the first day of the fifth **month**,
8: 31 On the twelfth day of the first **month** we set out from the Ahava
10: 9 on the twentieth day of the ninth **month**, all the people were sitting
10: 9 **[RPH]** all the people were sitting in the square before the house
10: 16 On the first day of the tenth **month** they sat down to investigate the
10: 17 by the first day of the first **month** they finished dealing with all the
Ne 1: 1 In the **month** *of* Kislev in the twentieth year, while I was in the
2: 1 In the **month** *of* Nisan in the twentieth year of King Artaxerxes,
7: 73 [7:72] When the seventh **month** came and the Israelites had
8: 2 So on the first day of the seventh **month** Ezra the priest brought
8: 14 were to live in booths during the feast of the seventh **month**
9: 1 On the twenty-fourth day of the same **month**, the Israelites
10: 33 [10:34] the Sabbaths, **New Moon festivals** and appointed feasts;
Est 2: 12 she had to complete twelve **months** of beauty treatments
2: 12 six **months** with oil of myrrh and six with perfumes and cosmetics.
2: 12 with oil of myrrh and six **[RPH]** with perfumes and cosmetics.
2: 16 taken to King Xerxes in the royal residence in the tenth **month**,
2: 16 tenth month, the **month** *of* Tebeth, in the seventh year of his reign.
3: 7 in the first **month**, the month of Nisan, they cast the *pur* (that is,
3: 7 in the first month, the **month** *of* Nisan, they cast the *pur* (that is,
3: 7 the lot) in the presence of Haman to select a day and **month**.
3: 7 And the lot fell on the twelfth **month**, the month of Adar.
3: 7 And the lot fell on the twelfth month, the **month** *of* Adar.
3: 12 on the thirteenth day of the first **month** the royal secretaries were
3: 13 on a single day, the thirteenth day of the twelfth **month**, the month
3: 13 the twelfth month, the **month** *of* Adar, and to plunder their goods.
8: 9 on the twenty-third day of the third **month**, the month of Sivan.
8: 9 on the twenty-third day of the third month, the **month** *of* Sivan.
8: 12 of King Xerxes was the thirteenth day of the twelfth **month**,
8: 12 was the thirteenth day of the twelfth month, the **month** *of* Adar.
9: 1 On the thirteenth day of the twelfth **month**, the month of Adar,
9: 1 On the thirteenth day of the twelfth month, the **month** *of* Adar,
9: 15 in Susa came together on the fourteenth day of the **month** *of* Adar,
9: 17 This happened on the thirteenth day of the **month** *of* Adar,
9: 19 observe the fourteenth of the **month** *of* Adar as a day of joy
9: 21 annually the fourteenth and fifteenth days of the **month** *of* Adar
9: 22 as the **month** when their sorrow was turned into joy and their
Job 14: 5 you have decreed the number of his **months** and have set limits he
21: 21 family he leaves behind when his allotted **months** come to an end?
Ps 81: 3 [81:4] Sound the ram's horn at the **New Moon**, and when the
Isa 1: 13 **New Moons**, Sabbaths and convocations—I cannot bear your evil
1: 14 Your **New Moon festivals** and your appointed feasts my soul
47: 13 those stargazers who make predictions month by **month**,
66: 23 From *one* **New Moon** to another and from one Sabbath to another,
66: 23 From one New Moon to **another**ˢ and from one Sabbath to
Jer 1: 3 down to the fifth **month** of the eleventh year of Zedekiah son of
2: 24 her need not tire themselves; at **mating time** they will find her.
28: 1 In the fifth **month** of that same year, the fourth year, early in the
28: 17 In the seventh **month** of that same year, Hananiah the prophet
36: 9 In the ninth **month** of the fifth year of Jehoiakim son of Josiah
36: 22 It was the ninth **month** and the king was sitting in the winter
39: 1 In the ninth year of Zedekiah king of Judah, in the tenth **month**,
39: 2 on the ninth day **[RPH]** of the fourth month of Zedekiah's
39: 2 on the ninth day of the fourth **month** of Zedekiah's eleventh year,
41: 1 In the seventh **month** Ishmael son of Nethaniah, the son of
52: 4 year of Zedekiah's reign, on the tenth day of the tenth **month**,
52: 4 **[RPH]** Nebuchadnezzar king of Babylon marched against
52: 6 By the ninth day of the fourth **month** the famine in the city had
52: 6 By the ninth day of the fourth month **[RPH]** the famine in the city
52: 12 On the tenth day of the fifth **month**, in the nineteenth year of
52: 12 **[RPH]** in the nineteenth year of Nebuchadnezzar king of
52: 31 him from prison on the twenty-fifth day of the twelfth **month**.
52: 31 from prison on the twenty-fifth day of the twelfth month. **[RPH]**
Eze 1: 1 In the thirtieth year, in the fourth **month** on the fifth day, while I
1: 2 On the fifth of the **month**—it was the fifth year of the exile of
8: 1 In the sixth year, in the sixth **month** on the fifth day, while I was
20: 1 In the seventh year, in the fifth **month** on the tenth day, some of
24: 1 In the ninth year, in the tenth **month** on the tenth day, the word of
24: 1 on the tenth day, **[RPH]** the word of the LORD came to me:
26: 1 In the eleventh year, on the first day of the **month**, the word of the
29: 1 In the tenth year, in the tenth **month** on the twelfth day, the word
29: 17 In the twenty-seventh year, in the first **month** on the first day,
30: 20 In the eleventh year, in the first **month** on the seventh day,
31: 1 In the eleventh year, in the third **month** on the first day, the word
32: 1 In the twelfth year, in the twelfth **month** on the first day, the word
32: 1 on the first day, **[RPH]** the word of the LORD came to me:
32: 17 In the twelfth year, on the fifteenth day of the **month**, the word of
33: 21 In the twelfth year of our exile, in the tenth **month** on the fifth day,
39: 12 " '*For* seven **months** the house of Israel will be burying them in
39: 14 At the end of the seven **months** they will begin their search.
40: 1 our exile, at the beginning of the year, on the tenth of the **month**,
45: 17 drink offerings at the festivals, the **New Moons** and the Sabbaths—
45: 18 In the first **month** on the first day you are to take a young bull
45: 20 You are to do the same on the seventh day of the **month** for
45: 21 " 'In the first **month** on the fourteenth day you are to observe the
45: 25 the Feast, which begins in the seventh **month** on the fifteenth day,
46: 1 Sabbath day and on the day of the **New Moon** it is to be opened.
46: 3 **New Moons** the people of the land are to worship in the presence
46: 6 On the day of the **New Moon** he is to offer a young bull, six lambs
47: 12 Every **month** they will bear, because the water from the sanctuary
Da 10: 4 On the twenty-fourth day of the first **month**, as I was standing on
Hos 2: 11 [2:13] her yearly festivals, her **New Moons**, her Sabbath days—
5: 7 Now their **New Moon festivals** will devour them and their fields.
Am 4: 7 rain from you when the harvest was still three **months** away.
8: 5 "When will the **New Moon** be over that we may sell grain,
Hag 1: 1 the second year of King Darius, on the first day of the sixth **month**,
1: 1 **[RPH]** the word of the LORD came through the prophet Haggai
1: 15 on the twenty-fourth day of the sixth **month** in the second year of
2: 1 On the twenty-first day of the seventh **month**, the word of the
2: 20 to Haggai a second time on the twenty-fourth day of the **month**:
Zec 1: 1 In the eighth **month** of the second year of Darius, the word of the
1: 7 On the twenty-fourth day of the eleventh **month**, the month of
1: 7 eleventh month, the **month** *of* Shebat, in the second year of Darius,
7: 1 LORD came to Zechariah on the fourth day of the ninth **month**,
7: 3 and the prophets, "Should I mourn and fast in the fifth **month**,

2545 ²חֹדֶשׁ ḥōdeš², n.pr.f. [1] [√ 2544; cf. 2542]

Hodesh [1]

1Ch 8: 9 By his wife **Hodesh** he had Jobab, Zibia, Mesha, Malcam,

2546 חֲדָשָׁה ḥᵃdāšâ, n.pr.loc. [1] [√ 2542]

Hadashah [1]

Jos 15: 37 Zenan, **Hadashah**, Migdal Gad,

2547 חָדְשִׁי ḥodšî, n.pr.loc. Not used in NIV/BHS [→ 9398]

2548 חֲדַתָּה ḥᵃdattâ, n.pr.loc. Not used in NIV/BHS [√ 2542]

2549 חוּב ḥûb, v. [1] [→ 2550]

because of [1]

Da 1: 10 [D] The king would then have my head **because of** *you*."

2550 חוֹב ḥôb, n.[m.]. [1] [√ 2549]

loan [1]

Eze 18: 7 not oppress anyone, but returns what he took in pledge for a **loan**.

2551 חוֹבָה ḥôbâ, n.pr.loc. [1]

Hobah [1]

Ge 14: 15 routed them, pursuing them as far as **Hobah**, north of Damascus.

2552 ¹חוּג ḥûg¹, v. [1] [→ 2553, 4684; cf. 2510]

marks out [1]

Job 26: 10 [A] *He* **marks out** the horizon on the face of the waters for a

2553 ²חוּג ḥûg², n.[m.]. [3] [√ 2552]

circle [1], horizon [1], vaulted [1]

Job 22: 14 so he does not see us as he goes about in the **vaulted** heavens.'
Pr 8: 27 in place, when he marked out the **horizon** on the face of the deep,
Isa 40: 22 He sits enthroned above the **circle** *of* the earth, and its people are

2554 חוּד ḥûd, v.den. [4] [√ 2648; cf. 284]

tell [2], given [1], set forth [1]

Jdg 14: 12 [A] "*Let me* **tell** you a riddle," Samson said to them. "If you can
14: 13 [A] of clothes." "**Tell** us your riddle," they said. "Let's hear it."
14: 16 [A] *You've* **given** my people a riddle, but you haven't told me
Eze 17: 2 [A] **set forth** an allegory and tell the house of Israel a parable.

2555 ¹חוה ḥāwâ¹, v. [6] [→ 289; Ar 10018, 10252]

tell [3], display [1], explain [1], show [1]

Job 15: 17 [D] "Listen to me and *I will* **explain** *to* you; let me tell you what
32: 6 [D] that is why I was fearful, not daring *to* **tell** you what I know.
32: 10 [D] I say: Listen to me; I too *will* **tell** you what I know.
32: 17 [D] I too will have my say; I too *will* **tell** what I know.
36: 2 [D] *I will* **show** you that there is more to be said in God's behalf.
Ps 19: 2 [19:3] [D] night after night *they* **display** knowledge.

2556 ²חָוָה **ḥāwâ²**, v. [170] [cf. 8817]
worship [39], bow down [33], bowed down [30], worshiped [23], pay honor [7], worshiping [7], bowed [6], bowing down [5], bowed in worship [2], prostrated himself [2], worships [2], bow down to worship [1], bow [1], bowed low [1], bows down [1], fell facedown [+678+4200] [1], fell prostrate [1], honor [1], humbly bow [1], kneeling [1], knelt [1], paid homage [1], paid honor [1], reverence [1], worshiped leaned [1]

Ge 18: 2 [I] of his tent to meet them and **bowed low** to the ground.
19: 1 [I] up to meet them and **bowed down** *with* his face to the ground.
22: 5 [I] *We will* **worship** and then we will come back to you."
23: 7 [I] Abraham rose and **bowed down** before the people of the land,
23: 12 [I] Again Abraham **bowed down** before the people of the land
24: 26 [I] Then the man bowed down and **worshiped** the LORD,
24: 48 [I] I bowed down and **worshiped** the LORD. I praised the
24: 52 [I] they said, *he* **bowed down** to the ground before the LORD.
27: 29 [I] May nations serve you and peoples **bow down** to you. Be lord
27: 29 [I] and *may* the sons of your mother **bow down** to you.
33: 3 [I] **bowed down** to the ground seven times as he approached his
33: 6 [I] and their children approached and **bowed down**.
33: 7 [I] Next, Leah and her children came and **bowed down**. Last of
33: 7 [I] of all came Joseph and Rachel, and *they* too **bowed down**.
37: 7 [I] your sheaves gathered around mine and **bowed down** to it."
37: 9 [I] and moon and eleven stars *were* **bowing down** to me."
37: 10 [I] actually come and **bow down** to the ground before you?"
42: 6 [I] *they* **bowed down** to him *with* their faces to the ground.
43: 26 [I] the house, and *they* **bowed down** before him to the ground.
43: 28 [I] still alive and well." And they bowed low *to* **pay** him **honor**.
47: 31 [I] and Israel **worshiped** *as he* **leaned** on the top of his staff.
48: 12 [I] Israel's knees and **bowed down** *with* his face to the ground.
49: 8 [I] of your enemies; your father's sons *will* **bow down** to you.
Ex 4: 31 [I] and had seen their misery, they bowed down and **worshiped**.
11: 8 [I] **bowing down** before me and saying, 'Go, you and all the
12: 27 [I] Egyptians.' " Then the people bowed down and **worshiped**.
18: 7 [I] to meet his father-in-law and **bowed down** and kissed him.
20: 5 [I] *You shall* not **bow down** to them or worship them; for I,
23: 24 [I] *Do* not **bow down** before their gods or worship them
24: 1 [I] of the elders of Israel. *You are to* **worship** at a distance,
32: 8 [I] *They have* **bowed down** to it and sacrificed to it and have
33: 10 [I] they all stood and **worshiped**, each at the entrance to his tent.
34: 8 [I] Moses bowed to the ground at once and **worshiped**.
34: 14 [I] *Do* not **worship** any other god, for the LORD, whose name
Lev 26: 1 [I] do not place a carved stone in your land to **bow down** before
Nu 22: 31 [I] So he bowed low and **fell** [+678+4200] **facedown**.
25: 2 [I] The people ate and **bowed down** before these gods.
Dt 4: 19 [I] do not be enticed into **bowing down** to them and worshiping
5: 9 [I] *You shall* not **bow down** to them or worship them; for I,
8: 19 [I] and follow other gods and worship and **bow down** to them,
11: 16 [I] to turn away and worship other gods and **bow down** to them.
17: 3 [I] **bowing down** to them or to the sun or the moon or the stars of
26: 10 [I] before the LORD your God and **bow down** before him.
29: 26 [29:25] [I] and worshiped other gods and **bowed down** to them,
30: 17 [I] if you are drawn away *to* **bow down** to other gods
Jos 5: 14 [I] Joshua fell facedown to the ground *in* **reverence**, and asked
23: 7 [I] by them. You must not serve them or **bow down** to them.
23: 16 [I] and go and serve other gods and **bow down** to them,
Jdg 2: 12 [I] and **worshiped** various gods of the peoples around them.
2: 17 [I] but prostituted themselves to other gods and **worshiped** them.
2: 19 [I] following other gods and serving and **worshiping** them.
7: 15 [I] heard the dream and its interpretation, *he* **worshiped** God.
Ru 2: 10 [I] At this, *she* **bowed** down with her face to the ground. She
1Sa 1: 3 [I] Year after year this man went up from his town to **worship**
1: 19 [I] morning they arose and **worshiped** before the LORD and
1: 28 [I] over to the LORD." And *he* **worshiped** the LORD there.
2: 36 [I] **bow down** before him for a piece of silver and a crust of
15: 25 [I] and come back with me, so that *I may* **worship** the LORD."
15: 30 [I] back with me, so that *I may* **worship** the LORD your God."
15: 31 [I] went back with Saul, and Saul **worshiped** the LORD.
20: 41 [I] ⌞of the stone⌟ and **bowed** down *before* Jonathan three times,
24: 8 [24:9] [I] and **prostrated himself** with his face to the ground.
25: 23 [I] and **bowed** down before David with her face to the ground.
25: 41 [I] *She* **bowed down** with her face to the ground and said,
28: 14 [I] and **prostrated himself** with his face to the ground.
2Sa 1: 2 [I] he came to David, he fell to the ground *to* **pay** him **honor**.
9: 6 [I] of Saul, came to David, he bowed down *to* **pay** him **honor**.
9: 8 [I] Mephibosheth **bowed down** and said, "What is your servant,
12: 20 [I] he went into the house of the LORD and **worshiped**.
14: 4 [I] she fell with her face to the ground *to* **pay** him **honor**, and she
14: 22 [I] Joab fell with his face to the ground *to* **pay** him **honor**, and he
14: 33 [I] and **bowed down** with his face to the ground before the king.
15: 5 [I] whenever anyone approached him to **bow down** before him,
15: 32 [I] arrived at the summit, where *people used to* **worship** God,
16: 4 [I] "*I* **humbly bow**," Ziba said. "May I find favor in your eyes,
18: 21 [I] The Cushite **bowed down** before Joab and ran off.
18: 28 [I] *He* **bowed down** before the king with his face to the ground
24: 20 [I] and **bowed down** before the king with his face to the ground.
1Ki 1: 16 [I] Bathsheba bowed low and **knelt** before the king. "What is it
1: 23 [I] went before the king and **bowed** with his face to the ground.
1: 31 [I] **kneeling** before the king, said, "May my lord King David live
1: 47 [I] than yours!' And the king **bowed in worship** on his bed
1: 53 [I] Adonijah came and **bowed down** to King Solomon,
2: 19 [I] to meet her, **bowed down** to her and sat down on his throne.
9: 6 [I] given you and go off to serve other gods and **worship** them,
9: 9 [I] have embraced other gods, **worshiping** and serving them—
11: 33 [I] **worshiped** Ashtoreth the goddess of the Sidonians, Chemosh
16: 31 [I] of the Sidonians, and began to serve Baal and **worship** him.
22: 53 [22:54] [I] He served and **worshiped** Baal and provoked the
2Ki 2: 15 [I] they went to meet him and **bowed** to the ground before him.
4: 37 [I] She came in, fell at his feet and **bowed** to the ground.
5: 18 [I] When my master enters the temple of Rimmon to **bow down**
5: 18 [I] bow down and he is leaning on my arm and *I* **bow** there also—
5: 18 [I] when I **bow down** *in* the temple of Rimmon, may the LORD
17: 16 [I] *They* **bowed down** to all the starry hosts, and they worshiped
17: 35 [I] "Do not worship any other gods or **bow down** to them, serve
17: 36 [I] To him *you shall* **bow down** and to him offer sacrifices.
18: 22 [I] "*You must* **worship** before this altar in Jerusalem"?
19: 37 [I] *while* he *was* **worshiping** in the temple of his god Nisroch,
21: 3 [I] *He* **bowed down** to all the starry hosts and worshiped them.
21: 21 [I] the idols his father had worshiped, and **bowed down** to them.
1Ch 16: 29 [I] **worship** the LORD in the splendor of his holiness.
21: 21 [I] and **bowed down** before David with his face to the ground.
29: 20 [I] bowed low and **fell prostrate** before the LORD and the king.
2Ch 7: 3 [I] and *they* **worshiped** and gave thanks to the LORD, saying,
7: 19 [I] given you and go off to serve other gods and **worship** them,
7: 22 [I] have embraced other gods, **worshiping** and serving them—
20: 18 [I] and Jerusalem fell down in **worship** before the LORD.
24: 17 [I] the officials of Judah came and **paid homage** to the king,
25: 14 [I] **bowed down** to them and burned sacrifices to them.
29: 28 [I] The whole assembly **bowed in worship**, while the singers
29: 29 [I] and everyone present with him knelt down and **worshiped**.
29: 30 [I] praises with gladness and bowed their heads and **worshiped**.
32: 12 [I] '*You must* **worship** before one altar and burn sacrifices on it'?
33: 3 [I] *He* **bowed down** to all the starry hosts and worshiped them.
Ne 8: 6 [I] and **worshiped** the LORD with their faces to the ground.
9: 3 [I] in confession and *in* **worshiping** the LORD their God.
9: 6 [I] life to everything, and the multitudes of heaven **worship** you.
Est 3: 2 [I] at the king's gate knelt down and **paid honor** to Haman,
3: 2 [I] But Mordecai would not kneel down or **pay** him **honor**.
3: 5 [I] saw that Mordecai would not kneel down or **pay** him **honor**,
Job 1: 20 [I] and shaved his head. Then he fell to the ground *in* **worship**
Ps 5: 7 [5:8] [I] in reverence *will I* **bow down** toward your holy temple.
22: 27 [22:28] [I] all the families of the nations *will* **bow down** before
22: 29 [22:30] [I] All the rich of the earth will feast and **worship**;
29: 2 [I] his name; **worship** the LORD in the splendor of his holiness.
45: 11 [45:12] [I] by your beauty; **honor** him, for he is your lord.
66: 4 [I] All the earth **bows down** to you; they sing praise to you,
72: 11 [I] All kings *will* **bow down** to him and all nations will serve
81: 9 [81:10] [I] among you; *you shall* not **bow down** to an alien god.
86: 9 [I] the nations you have made will come and **worship** before you,
95: 6 [I] Come, let us bow down *in* **worship**, let us kneel before the
96: 9 [I] **Worship** the LORD in the splendor of his holiness;
97: 7 [I] those who boast in idols—**worship** him, all *you* gods!
99: 5 [I] Exalt the LORD our God and **worship** at his footstool; he is
99: 9 [I] Exalt the LORD our God and **worship** at his holy mountain,
106: 19 [I] they made a calf and **worshiped** an idol cast from metal.
132: 7 [I] us go to his dwelling place; *let us* **worship** at his footstool—
138: 2 [I] *I will* **bow down** toward your holy temple and will praise
Isa 2: 8 [I] *they* **bow down** to the work of their hands, to what their
2: 20 [I] idols of silver and idols of gold, which they made to **worship**.
27: 13 [I] and **worship** the LORD on the holy mountain in Jerusalem.
36: 7 [I] and Jerusalem, "*You must* **worship** before this altar"?
37: 38 [I] *while* he *was* **worshiping** in the temple of his god Nisroch,
44: 15 [I] But he also fashions a god and **worships** it; he makes an idol
44: 17 [I] he makes a god, his idol; he bows down to it and **worships**.
45: 14 [I] *They will* **bow down** before you and plead with you, saying,
46: 6 [I] to make it into a god, and they bow down and **worship** it.
49: 7 [I] will see you and rise up, princes will see and **bow down**,
49: 23 [I] *They will* **bow down** before you *with* their faces *to* the
60: 14 [I] all who despise you *will* **bow down** at your feet and will call
66: 23 [I] all mankind will come and **bow down** before me,"
Jer 1: 16 [I] to other gods and *in* **worshiping** what their hands have made.
7: 2 [I] Judah who come through these gates to **worship** the LORD.
8: 2 [I] and which they have followed and consulted and **worshiped**.
13: 10 [I] and go after other gods to serve and **worship** them,
16: 11 [I] 'and followed other gods and served and **worshiped** them.
22: 9 [I] their God and *have* **worshiped** and served other gods.' "
25: 6 [I] Do not follow other gods to serve and **worship** them; do not

Jer 26: 2 [I] of Judah who come to **worship** *in* the house of the LORD.
Eze 8: 16 [I] the east, they *were* **bowing down** to the sun in the east.
46: 2 [I] *He is to* **worship** at the threshold of the gateway and then go
46: 3 [I] New Moons the people of the land *are to* **worship** in the
46: 9 [I] whoever enters by the north gate to **worship** is to go out the
Mic 5: 13 [5:12] [I] *you will* no longer **bow down** to the work of your
Zep 1: 5 [I] those *who* **bow down** on the roofs **to worship** the starry host,
1: 5 [I] those *who* **bow down** and swear by the LORD and who also
2: 11 [I] The nations on every shore *will* **worship** him, every one in its
Zec 14: 16 [I] Jerusalem will go up year after year to **worship** the King,
14: 17 [I] of the earth do not go up to Jerusalem to **worship** the King,

2557 ¹חַוָּה ḥawwâ[1], n.f. [3]

settlements [3]

Nu 32: 41 captured their **settlements** and called them Havvoth Jair.
Jos 13: 30 king of Bashan—all the **settlements** *of* Jair in Bashan, sixty towns,
1Ki 4: 13 in Ramoth Gilead (the **settlements** *of* Jair son of Manasseh in

2558 ²חַוָּה ḥawwâ[2], n.pr.f. [2] [cf. 2649]

Eve [2]

Ge 3: 20 Adam named his wife **Eve**, because she would become the mother
4: 1 Adam lay with his wife **Eve**, and she became pregnant and gave

2559 חוֹזָי ḥôzāy, n.m. [1 / 0] [√ 2602; cf. 2600]

2Ch 33: 19 all are written in the records of the seers. [BHS *Hozai* ?; NIV 2602]

2560 ¹חוֹחַ ḥôaḥ[1], n.m. [12] [cf. 2626]

thistle [4], hook [2], thorns [2], brambles [1], briers [1], thickets [1], thornbush [1]

1Sa 13: 6 they hid in caves and **thickets**, among the rocks, and in pits
2Ki 14: 9 "A **thistle** in Lebanon sent a message to a cedar in Lebanon,
14: 9 beast in Lebanon came along and trampled the **thistle** underfoot.
2Ch 25: 18 "A **thistle** in Lebanon sent a message to a cedar in Lebanon,
25: 18 beast in Lebanon came along and trampled the **thistle** underfoot.
33: 11 who took Manasseh prisoner, put a **hook** in his nose, bound him
Job 31: 40 let **briers** come up instead of wheat and weeds instead of barley."
41: 2 [40:26] put a cord through his nose or pierce his jaw with a **hook**?
Pr 26: 9 Like a **thornbush** in a drunkard's hand is a proverb in the mouth
SS 2: 2 Like a lily among **thorns** is my darling among the maidens.
Isa 34: 13 will overrun her citadels, nettles and **brambles** her strongholds.
Hos 9: 6 will be taken over by briers, and **thorns** will overrun their tents.

2561 ²חוֹחַ ḥôaḥ[2], n.m. Not used in NIV/BHS

2562 חוּט ḥûṭ, n.m. [7] [→ Ar 10253]

circumference [+6015] [1], cord [+9535] [1], cord [1], line [1], ribbon [1], thread [1], threads [1]

Ge 14: 23 not even a **thread** or the thong of a sandal, so that you will never
Jos 2: 18 you have tied this scarlet **cord** [+9535] in the window through
Jdg 16: 12 But he snapped the ropes off his arms as if they were **threads**.
1Ki 7: 15 each eighteen cubits high and twelve cubits around, *by* **line**.
Ecc 4: 12 defend themselves. A **cord** of three strands is not quickly broken.
SS 4: 3 Your lips are like a scarlet **ribbon**; your mouth is lovely.
Jer 52: 21 eighteen cubits high and twelve cubits *in* **circumference** [+6015];

2563 חִוִּי ḥiwwî, a.g. [25]

Hivites [23], Hivite [2]

Ge 10: 17 **Hivites**, Arkites, Sinites,
34: 2 When Shechem son of Hamor the **Hivite**, the ruler of that area,
36: 2 daughter of Anah and granddaughter of Zibeon the **Hivite**—
Ex 3: 8 Hittites, Amorites, Perizzites, **Hivites** and Jebusites.
3: 17 Hittites, Amorites, Perizzites, **Hivites** and Jebusites—
13: 5 land of the Canaanites, Hittites, Amorites, **Hivites** and Jebusites—
23: 23 Hittites, Perizzites, Canaanites, **Hivites** and Jebusites, and I will
23: 28 I will send the hornet ahead of you to drive the **Hivites**, Canaanites
33: 2 Amorites, Hittites, Perizzites, **Hivites** and Jebusites.
34: 11 Canaanites, Hittites, Perizzites, **Hivites** and Jebusites.
Dt 7: 1 Canaanites, Perizzites, **Hivites** and Jebusites,
20: 17 Amorites, Canaanites, Perizzites, **Hivites** and Jebusites—
Jos 3: 10 Hittites, **Hivites**, Perizzites, Girgashites, Amorites and Jebusites.
9: 1 Amorites, Canaanites, Perizzites, **Hivites** and Jebusites)—
9: 7 The men of Israel said to the **Hivites**, "But perhaps you live near
11: 3 and to the **Hivites** below Hermon in the region of Mizpah.
11: 19 Except for the **Hivites** living in Gibeon, not one city made a treaty
12: 8 Amorites, Canaanites, Perizzites, **Hivites** and Jebusites):
24: 11 Perizzites, Canaanites, Hittites, Girgashites, **Hivites** and Jebusites,
Jdg 3: 3 the **Hivites** living in the Lebanon mountains from Mount Baal
3: 5 Hittites, Amorites, Perizzites, **Hivites** and Jebusites.
2Sa 24: 7 fortress of Tyre and all the towns of the **Hivites** and Canaanites.
1Ki 9: 20 **Hivites** and Jebusites (these peoples were not Israelites),
1Ch 1: 15 **Hivites**, Arkites, Sinites,
2Ch 8: 7 **Hivites** and Jebusites (these peoples were not Israelites),

2564 חֲוִילָה ḥ[a]wîlâ, n.pr.loc. [7] [√ 2567]

Havilah [7]

Ge 2: 11 it winds through the entire land *of* **Havilah**, where there is gold.
10: 7 The sons of Cush: Seba, **Havilah**, Sabtah, Raamah and Sabteca.
10: 29 Ophir, **Havilah** and Jobab. All these were sons of Joktan.
25: 18 His descendants settled in the area from **Havilah** to Shur,
1Sa 15: 7 Saul attacked the Amalekites all the way from **Havilah** to Shur,
1Ch 1: 9 The sons of Cush: Seba, **Havilah**, Sabta, Raamah and Sabteca.
1: 23 Ophir, **Havilah** and Jobab. All these were sons of Joktan.

2565 ¹חוּל ḥûl[1], v. [10] [→ 4688, 4689, 4703, 4714?; cf. 2658]

swirling down [2], *untranslated* [1], dancing [1], fall [1], flash [1], join [1], turned [1], wait patiently [1], wait [1]

Jdg 21: 21 [A] When the girls of Shiloh come out to **join** in the dancing,
21: 23 [D] While the *girls were* **dancing**, each man caught one
2Sa 3: 29 [A] *May* his blood **fall** upon the head of Joab and upon all his
Job 35: 14 [D] that your case is before him and *you must* **wait** for him,
Ps 37: 7 [F] Be still before the LORD and **wait patiently** for him; do not
Jer 23: 19 [F] a whirlwind **swirling down** on the heads of the wicked.
23: 19 [A] swirling down on the heads of the wicked. **[RPH]**
30: 23 [A] a driving wind **swirling down** on the heads of the wicked.
La 4: 6 [A] overthrown in a moment without a hand **turned** to help her.
Hos 11: 6 [A] Swords *will* **flash** in their cities, will destroy the bars of their

2566 ²חוּל ḥûl[2], n.pr.m. [2]

Hul [2]

Ge 10: 23 The sons of Aram: Uz, **Hul**, Gether and Meshech.
1Ch 1: 17 and Aram. The sons of Aram: Uz, **Hul**, Gether and Meshech.

2567 ¹חוֹל ḥôl[1], n.m. [23] [→ 2564]

sand [21], grains of sand [2]

Ge 22: 17 as numerous as the stars in the sky and as the **sand** on the seashore.
32: 12 [32:13] and will make your descendants like the **sand** *of* the sea,
41: 49 Joseph stored up huge quantities of grain, like the **sand** *of* the sea;
Ex 2: 12 and seeing no one, he killed the Egyptian and hid him in the **sand**.
Dt 33: 19 on the abundance of the seas, on the treasures hidden in the **sand**."
Jos 11: 4 a huge army, as numerous as the **sand** on the seashore.
Jdg 7: 12 Their camels could no more be counted than the **sand** on the
1Sa 13: 5 and soldiers as numerous as the **sand** on the seashore.
2Sa 17: 11 as numerous as the **sand** on the seashore—be gathered to you,
1Ki 4: 20 of Judah and Israel were as numerous as the **sand** on the seashore;
4: 29 [5:9] a breadth of understanding as measureless as the **sand** on the
Job 6: 3 It would surely outweigh the **sand** *of* the seas—no wonder my
29: 18 die in my own house, my days as numerous as the **grains of sand**.
Ps 78: 27 down on them like dust, flying birds like **sand** *on* the seashore.
139: 18 Were I to count them, they would outnumber the **grains of sand**.
Pr 27: 3 Stone is heavy and **sand** a burden, but provocation by a fool is
Isa 10: 22 Though your people, O Israel, be like the **sand** *by* the sea,
48: 19 Your descendants would have been like the **sand**, your children
Jer 5: 22 I made the **sand** a boundary for the sea, an everlasting barrier it
15: 8 I will make their widows more numerous than the **sand** *of* the sea.
33: 22 stars of the sky and as measureless as the **sand** *on* the seashore.' "
Hos 1: 10 [2:1] "Yet the Israelites will be like the **sand** *on* the seashore,
Hab 1: 9 hordes advance like a desert wind and gather prisoners like **sand**.

2568 ²חוֹל ḥôl[2], n.m. Not used in NIV/BHS

2569 חוּם ḥûm, a. [4] [√ 2801]

dark-colored [4]

Ge 30: 32 every **dark-colored** lamb and every spotted or speckled goat.
30: 33 is not speckled or spotted, or any lamb that is not **dark-colored**,
30: 35 all the **dark-colored** lambs, and he placed them in the care of his
30: 40 the streaked and **dark-colored** animals that belonged to Laban.

2570 חוֹמָה ḥômâ, n.f. [133] [→ 3503]

wall [81], walls [43], *untranslated* [3], city wall [2], walled [2], it[s] [+2021] [1], walled [+4202] [1]

Ex 14: 22 on dry ground, with a **wall** *of* water on their right and on their left.
14: 29 on dry ground, with a **wall** *of* water on their right and on their left.
Lev 25: 29 " 'If a man sells a house in a **walled** city, he retains the right of
25: 30 the house in the **walled** [+4202] city shall belong permanently to
25: 31 houses in villages without **walls** around them are to be considered
Dt 3: 5 All these cities were fortified with high **walls** and with gates
28: 52 land until the high fortified **walls** in which you trust fall down.
Jos 2: 15 the window, for the house she lived in was part of the city **wall**.
2: 15 for the house she lived in was part of the city wall. **[RPH]**

Jos 6: 5 then the **wall** *of* the city will collapse and the people will go up,
6: 20 the trumpet, when the people gave a loud shout, the **wall** collapsed;
1Sa 25: 16 day they were a **wall** around us all the time we were herding our
31: 10 of the Ashtoreths and fastened his body to the **wall** *of* Beth Shan.
31: 12 and his sons from the **wall** *of* Beth Shan and went to Jabesh,
2Sa 11: 20 Didn't you know they would shoot arrows from the **wall**?
11: 21 Didn't a woman throw an upper millstone on him from the **wall**,
11: 21 Why did you get so close to the **wall**?' If he asks you this,
11: 24 Then the archers shot arrows at your servants from the **wall**,
18: 24 the watchman went up to the roof of the gateway by the **wall**.
20: 15 While they were battering the **wall** to bring it down,
20: 21 said to Joab, "His head will be thrown to you from the **wall**."
1Ki 3: 1 and the temple of the LORD, and the **wall** around Jerusalem.
4: 13 in Bashan and its sixty large **walled** cities with bronze gate bars);
9: 15 the **wall** *of* Jerusalem, and Hazor, Megiddo and Gezer.
20: 30 where the **wall** collapsed on twenty-seven thousand of them.
2Ki 3: 27 him as king, and offered him as a sacrifice on the **city wall**.
6: 26 As the king of Israel was passing by on the **wall**, a woman cried to
6: 30 As he went along the **wall**, the people looked, and there,
14: 13 broke down the **wall** *of* Jerusalem from the Ephraim Gate to the
18: 26 speak to us in Hebrew in the hearing of the people on the **wall**."
18: 27 sent me to say these things, and not to the men sitting on the **wall**—
25: 4 through the gate between the *two* **walls** near the king's garden,
25: 10 of the imperial guard, broke down the **walls** around Jerusalem.
2Ch 8: 5 Beth Horon as fortified cities, with **walls** and with gates and bars,
14: 7 [14:6] "and put **walls** around them, with towers, gates and bars.
25: 23 broke down the **wall** *of* Jerusalem from the Ephraim Gate to the
26: 6 to war against the Philistines and broke down the **walls** *of* Gath,
26: 6 and broke down the walls of Gath, **[RPH]** Jabneh and Ashdod.
26: 6 and broke down the walls of Gath, Jabneh and **[RPH]** Ashdod.
27: 3 and did extensive work on the **wall** *at* the hill of Ophel.
32: 5 Then he worked hard repairing all the broken sections of the **wall**
32: 5 He built another **wall** outside that one and reinforced the
32: 18 out in Hebrew to the people of Jerusalem who were on the **wall**,
33: 14 Afterward he rebuilt the outer **wall** of the City of David, west of
36: 19 set fire to God's temple and broke down the **wall** *of* Jerusalem;
Ne 1: 3 The **wall** *of* Jerusalem is broken down, and its gates have been
2: 8 and for the city **wall** and for the residence I will occupy?"
2: 13 Jackal Well and the Dung Gate, examining the **walls** *of* Jerusalem,
2: 15 so I went up the valley by night, examining the **wall**. Finally,
2: 17 Come, let us rebuild the **wall** *of* Jerusalem, and we will no longer
3: 8 next to that. They restored Jerusalem as far as the Broad **Wall**.
3: 13 They also repaired five hundred yards of the **wall** as far as the
3: 15 He also repaired the **wall** *of* the Pool of Siloam, by the King's
3: 27 from the great projecting tower to the **wall** *of* Ophel.
4: 1 [3:33] When Sanballat heard that we were rebuilding the **wall**, he
4: 3 [3:35] up on it, he would break down their **wall** *of* stones!"
4: 6 [3:38] So we rebuilt the **wall** till all of it reached half its height,
4: 6 [3:38] So we rebuilt the wall till all of **it**[s] [+2021] reached half its
4: 7 [4:1] heard that the repairs to Jerusalem's **walls** had gone ahead
4: 10 [4:4] and there is so much rubble that we cannot rebuild the **wall**."
4: 13 [4:7] behind the lowest points of the **wall** at the exposed places,
4: 15 [4:9] we all returned to the **wall**, each to his own work.
4: 17 [4:11] who were building the **wall**. Those who carried materials
4: 19 [4:13] we are widely separated from each other along the **wall**.
5: 16 Instead, I devoted myself to the work on this **wall**. All my men
6: 1 the Arab and the rest of our enemies that I had rebuilt the **wall**
6: 6 Jews are plotting to revolt, and therefore you are building the **wall**.
6: 15 So the **wall** was completed on the twenty-fifth of Elul, in fifty-two
7: 1 After the **wall** had been rebuilt and I had set the doors in place,
12: 27 At the dedication of the **wall** *of* Jerusalem, the Levites were sought
12: 30 they purified the people, the gates and the **wall**.
12: 31 I had the leaders of Judah go up on top of the **wall**. I also assigned
12: 31 One was to proceed on top of the **wall** to the right,
12: 37 directly up the steps of the City of David on the ascent to the **wall**
12: 38 I followed them on top of the **wall**, together with half the people—
12: 38 half the people—past the Tower of the Ovens to the Broad **Wall**,
13: 21 I warned them and said, "Why do you spend the night by the **wall**?
Ps 51: 18 [51:20] make Zion prosper; build up the **walls** *of* Jerusalem.
55: 10 [55:11] Day and night they prowl about on its **walls**; malice
Pr 18: 11 of the rich is their fortified city; they imagine it an unscalable **wall**.
25: 28 Like a city whose **walls** are broken down is a man who lacks
SS 5: 7 they took away my cloak, those watchmen of the **walls**!
8: 9 If she is a **wall**, we will build towers of silver on her. If she is a
8: 10 I am a **wall**, and my breasts are like towers. Thus I have become in
Isa 2: 15 for every lofty tower and every fortified **wall**,
22: 10 in Jerusalem and tore down houses to strengthen the **wall**.
22: 11 You built a reservoir between the *two* **walls** for the water of the
25: 12 He will bring down your high fortified **walls** and lay them low;
26: 1 We have a strong city; God makes salvation its **walls** and ramparts.
30: 13 this sin will become for you like a high **wall**, cracked and bulging,
36: 11 speak to us in Hebrew in the hearing of the people on the **wall**."
36: 12 sent me to say these things, and not to the men sitting on the **wall**—
49: 16 you on the palms of my hands; your **walls** are ever before me.
56: 5 its **walls** a memorial and a name better than sons and daughters;
60: 10 "Foreigners will rebuild your **walls**, and their kings will serve you.
60: 18 but you will call your **walls** Salvation and your gates Praise.
62: 6 I have posted watchmen on your **walls**, O Jerusalem; they will
Jer 1: 15 they will come against all her surrounding **walls** and against all the
1: 18 an iron pillar and a bronze **wall** to stand against the whole land—
15: 20 I will make you a **wall** to this people, a fortified wall of bronze;
21: 4 and the Babylonians who are outside the **wall** besieging you.
39: 4 through the gate between the *two* **walls**, and headed toward the
39: 8 the houses of the people and broke down the **walls** *of* Jerusalem.
49: 27 "I will set fire to the **walls** *of* Damascus; it will consume the
50: 15 She surrenders, her towers fall, her **walls** are torn down.
51: 12 Lift up a banner against the **walls** *of* Babylon! Reinforce the guard,
51: 44 will no longer stream to him. And the **wall** *of* Babylon will fall.
51: 58 "Babylon's thick **wall** will be leveled and her high gates set on
52: 7 They left the city at night through the gate between the *two* **walls**
52: 14 of the imperial guard broke down all the **walls** around Jerusalem.
La 2: 7 He has handed over to the enemy the **walls** *of* her palaces;
2: 8 The LORD determined to tear down the **wall** *around* the
2: 8 He made ramparts and **walls** lament; together they wasted away.
2: 18 O **wall** *of* the Daughter of Zion, let your tears flow like a river day
Eze 26: 4 They will destroy the **walls** *of* Tyre and pull down her towers;
26: 9 He will direct the blows of his battering rams against your **walls**
26: 10 Your **walls** will tremble at the noise of the war horses, wagons
26: 12 they will break down your **walls** and demolish your fine houses
27: 11 Men of Arvad and Helech manned your **walls** on every side;
27: 11 They hung their shields around your **walls**; they brought your
38: 11 all of them living without **walls** and without gates and bars.
38: 20 the cliffs will crumble and every **wall** will fall to the ground.
40: 5 I saw a **wall** completely surrounding the temple area. The length of
42: 20 It had a **wall** around it, five hundred cubits long and five hundred
Joel 2: 7 They charge like warriors; they scale **walls** like soldiers. They all
2: 9 They rush upon the city; they run along the **wall**. They climb into
Am 1: 7 I will send fire upon the **walls** *of* Gaza that will consume her
1: 10 I will send fire upon the **walls** *of* Tyre that will consume her
1: 14 I will set fire to the **walls** *of* Rabbah that will consume her
7: 7 The Lord was standing by a **wall** that had been built true to plumb,
Na 2: 5 [2:6] They dash to the **city wall**; the protective shield is put in
3: 8 water around her? The river was her defense, the waters her **wall**.
Zec 2: 5 [2:9] I myself will be a **wall** *of* fire around it,'

2571 חוּס *ḥûs*, v. [24]

look with pity [+6524] [6], concerned [2], looked with pity [+6524] [2], show mercy [2], show pity [+6524] [2], show pity [+6524+6584] [2], have pity [1], look with compassion [+6524] [1], mercy [1], mind [1], showing pity [+6524] [1], spare [1], spared [1], take pity [1]

Ge 45: 20 [A] Never **mind** about your belongings, because the best of all
Dt 7: 16 [A] *Do* not **look** on them **with pity** [+6524] and do not serve
13: 8 [13:9] [A] or listen to him. **Show** him no **pity** [+6524+6584].
19: 13 [A] **Show** him no **pity** [+6524+6584]. You must purge from
19: 21 [A] **Show** no **pity** [+6524]: life for life, eye for eye, tooth for
25: 12 [A] you shall cut off her hand. **Show** her no **pity** [+6524].
1Sa 24: 10 [24:11] [A] Some urged me to kill you, but I **spared** you; I said,
Ne 13: 22 [A] and **show mercy** to me according to your great love.
Ps 72: 13 [A] *He will* **take pity** on the weak and the needy and save the
Isa 13: 18 [A] nor *will* they **look with compassion** [+6524] on children.
Jer 13: 14 [A] I will allow no pity or **mercy** or compassion to keep me
21: 7 [A] *he will* **show** them no **mercy** or pity or compassion.'
Eze 5: 11 [A] I *will* not **look** *on* you **with pity** [+6524] or spare you.
7: 4 [A] I *will* not **look** on you **with pity** [+6524] or spare you; I will
7: 9 [A] I *will* not **look** *on* you **with pity** [+6524] or spare you; I will
8: 18 [A] I *will* not **look** *on* them **with pity** [+6524] or spare them.
9: 5 [A] and kill, without **showing pity** [+6524] or compassion.
9: 10 [A] So I *will* not **look** on them **with pity** [+6524] or spare them,
16: 5 [A] No *one* **looked** on you **with pity** [+6524] or had compassion
20: 17 [A] Yet I **looked** on them **with pity** [+6524] and did not destroy
24: 14 [A] I will not hold back; *I will* not **have pity**, nor will I relent.
Joel 2: 17 [A] and the altar. Let them say, "**Spare** your people, O LORD.
Jnh 4: 10 [A] LORD said, "You *have been* **concerned** about this vine,
4: 11 [A] as well. *Should* I not *be* **concerned** about that great city?"

2572 חוֹף *ḥôp*, n.[m.]. [7] [√ 2910]

coast [+3542] [4], coast [1], haven [1], seashore [+3542] [1]

Ge 49: 13 "Zebulun will live by the **seashore** [+3542] and become a haven
49: 13 "Zebulun will live by the seashore and become a **haven** *for* ships;
Dt 1: 7 in the western foothills, in the Negev and along the **coast** [+3542],
Jos 9: 1 along the entire **coast** *of* the Great Sea as far as Lebanon (the kings
Jdg 5: 17 Asher remained on the **coast** [+3542] and stayed in his coves.
Jer 47: 7 when he has ordered it to attack Ashkelon and the **coast** [+3542]?"
Eze 25: 16 and destroy those remaining along the **coast** [+3542].

2573 חוּפָם *ḥûpām*, n.pr.m. [1] [→ 2574]

Hupham [1]

Nu 26:39 the Shuphamite clan; through **Hupham**, the Huphamite clan.

2574 חוּפָמִי *ḥûpāmî*, a.g. [1] [√ 2573]

Huphamite [1]

Nu 26:39 the Shuphamite clan; through Hupham, the **Huphamite** clan.

2575 חוּץ *ḥûṣ*, n.[m.]. [164] [→ 2667; cf. 2666]

outside [+4946] [49], streets [38], street [13], outside [+2025] [8], outside [8], *untranslated* [7], outside [+928+2021] [7], out [+2025] [5], out [+4946] [4], outer [3], fields [2], outside [+2025+4946] [2], abroad [+2021+4200] [1], area [+4946] [1], around [+2021+4946] [1], away [+448+2021+2025] [1], countryside [1], elsewhere [1], extend out [+2025] [1], get out of here [+906+2021+2025+4946+6584+8938] [1], land [1], market areas [1], out here [+928+2021] [1], out [1], outdoor [+928+2021] [1], outer [+2021+4200] [1], outside the family [+2021+2025+2424] [1], put out [+906+2021+3655] [1], relieve yourself [+3782] [1], without [+4946] [1]

Ge 6:14 make rooms in it and coat it with pitch inside and **out** [+4946].
9:22 father's nakedness and told his two brothers **outside** [+928+2021].
15:5 He took him **outside** [+2025] and said, "Look up at the heavens
19:16 of his two daughters and led them safely **out** [+4946] of the city,
19:17 As soon as they had brought them **out** [+2025], one of them said,
24:11 He had the camels kneel down near the well **outside** [+4946] the
24:29 named Laban, and he hurried **out** [+2025] to the man at the spring.
24:31 he said. "Why are you standing **out** [+928+2021] **here**?
39:12 But he left his cloak in her hand and ran out **[RPH]** of the house.
39:13 left his cloak in her hand and had run **out** [+2025] of the house,
39:15 he left his cloak beside me and ran out **[RPH]** of the house."
39:18 he left his cloak beside me and ran **out** [+2025] of the house."
Ex 12:46 inside one house; take none of the meat **outside** [+2025] the house.
21:19 gets up and walks around **outside** [+928+2021] with his staff;
25:11 Overlay it with pure gold, both inside and **out** [+4946], and make a
26:35 Place the table **outside** [+4946] the curtain on the north side of the
27:21 In the Tent of Meeting, **outside** [+4946] the curtain that is in front
29:14 the bull's flesh and its hide and its offal **outside** [+4946] the camp.
33:7 and pitch it **outside** [+4946] the camp some distance away,
33:7 LORD would go to the tent of meeting **outside** [+4946] the camp.
37:2 He overlaid it with pure gold, both inside and **out** [+4946],
40:22 on the north side of the tabernacle **outside** [+4946] the curtain
Lev 4:12 he must take **outside** [+4946] the camp to a place ceremonially
4:21 he shall take the bull **outside** [+4946] the camp and burn it as he
6:11 [6:4] carry the ashes **outside** [+4946] the camp to a place that is
8:17 and its flesh and its offal he burned up **outside** [+4946] the camp,
9:11 the flesh and the hide he burned up **outside** [+4946] the camp.
10:4 carry your cousins **outside** [+4946] the camp, away from the front
10:5 and carried them, still in their tunics, **outside** [+4946] the camp,
13:46 He must live alone; he must live **outside** [+4946] the camp.
14:3 The priest is to go **outside** [+4946] the camp and examine him.
14:8 the camp, but he must stay **outside** [+4946] his tent for seven days.
14:40 and thrown into an unclean place **outside** [+4946] the town.
14:41 off dumped into an unclean place **outside** [+4946] the town.
14:45 the plaster—and taken out **[RPH]** of the town to an unclean place.
14:53 he is to release the live bird in the open fields **outside** [+4946] the
16:27 Place to make atonement, must be taken **outside** [+4946] the camp;
17:3 an ox, a lamb or a goat in the camp or **outside** [+4946] of it
18:9 whether she was born in the same home or **elsewhere**.
24:3 **Outside** [+4946] the curtain of the Testimony in the Tent of
24:14 "Take the blasphemer **outside** [+4946] the camp. All those who
24:23 they took the blasphemer **outside** [+4946] the camp and stoned
Nu 5:3 send them **outside** [+4946] the camp so they will not defile their
5:4 The Israelites did this; they sent them **outside** [+4946] the camp.
12:14 Confine her **outside** [+4946] the camp for seven days; after that
12:15 So Miriam was confined **outside** [+4946] the camp for seven days,
15:35 The whole assembly must stone him **outside** [+4946] the camp."
15:36 So the assembly took him **outside** [+4946] the camp and stoned
19:3 it is to be taken **outside** [+4946] the camp and slaughtered in his
19:9 put them in a ceremonially clean place **outside** [+4946] the camp.
31:13 of the community went to meet them **outside** [+4946] the camp.
31:19 or touched anyone who was killed must stay **outside** [+4946] the
35:4 will **extend out** [+2025] fifteen hundred feet from the town wall.
35:5 **Outside** [+4946] the town, measure three thousand feet on the east
35:27 and the avenger of blood finds him **outside** [+4946] the city,
Dt 23:10 [23:11] he is to go **outside** [+4946] the camp and stay there.
23:12 [23:13] Designate a place **outside** [+4946] the camp where you
23:12 [23:13] Designate a place outside the camp where **[RPH]** you
23:13 [23:14] when you **relieve yourself** [+3782], dig a hole and cover
24:11 Stay **outside** and let the man to whom you are making the loan
24:11 you are making the loan bring the pledge out to you. **[RPH]**
25:5 his widow must not marry **outside** [+2021+2025+2424] **the family**.
32:25 In the **street** the sword will make them childless; in their homes
Jos 2:19 If anyone goes outside your house into the **street**, his blood will be
6:23 and put them in a place **outside** [+4946] the camp of Israel.
Jdg 12:9 He gave his daughters away in marriage to those **outside** his *clan*,
12:9 he brought in thirty young women as wives from **outside** his *clan*.
19:25 So the man took his concubine and sent her **outside** to them,
1Sa 9:26 Saul got ready, he and Samuel went **outside** [+2025] together.
2Sa 1:20 "Tell it not in Gath, proclaim it not in the **streets** *of* Ashkelon,
13:17 **"Get** this woman **out of here** [+906+2021+2025+4946+6584+8938]
13:18 So his servant **put** her **out** [+906+2021+3655] and bolted the door
22:43 of the earth; I pounded and trampled them like mud in the **streets**.
1Ki 6:6 He made offset ledges around the **outside** [+2025] of the temple
7:9 from the **outside** to the great courtyard and from foundation to
7:9 cut to size and trimmed with a saw on their inner and **outer** *faces*.
8:8 the inner sanctuary, but not from **outside** [+2025] the Holy Place;
20:34 "You may set up your own **market areas** in Damascus, as my
21:13 So they took him **outside** [+4946] the city and stoned him to death.
2Ki 4:3 "Go **around** [+2021+4946] and ask all your neighbors for empty
10:24 Now Jehu had posted eighty men **outside** [+928+2021] with this
23:4 He burned them **outside** [+4946] Jerusalem in the fields of the
23:6 of the LORD to the Kidron Valley **outside** [+4946] Jerusalem
2Ch 5:9 the inner sanctuary, but not from **outside** [+2025] the Holy Place;
24:8 king's command, a chest was made and placed **outside** [+2025],
29:16 The Levites took it and carried it out **[OBJ]** to the Kidron Valley.
32:3 blocking off the water from the springs **outside** [+4946] the city,
32:5 He built another wall **outside** [+2025] that one and reinforced the
33:15 and in Jerusalem; and he threw them **out** [+2025] of the city.
Ezr 10:13 it is the rainy season; so we cannot stand **outside** [+928+2021].
Ne 13:8 and threw all Tobiah's household goods **out** of the room.
13:20 sellers of all kinds of goods spent the night **outside** [+4946]
Job 5:10 bestows rain on the earth; he sends water upon the **countryside**.
18:17 of him perishes from the earth; he has no name in the **land**.
31:32 no stranger had to spend the night in the **street**, for my door was
Ps 18:42 [18:43] on the wind; I poured them out like mud in the **streets**.
31:11 [31:12] those who see me on the **street** flee from me.
41:6 [41:7] then he goes out and spreads it **abroad** [+2021+4200].
144:13 will increase by thousands, by tens of thousands in our **fields**;
Pr 1:20 Wisdom calls aloud in the **street**, she raises her voice in the public
5:16 Should your springs overflow in the **streets**, your streams of water
7:12 now in the **street**, now in the squares, at every corner she lurks.)
8:26 before he made the earth or its **fields** or any of the dust of the
22:13 The sluggard says, "There is a lion **outside** [+928+2021]!"
24:27 Finish your **outdoor** [+928+2021] work and get your fields ready;
Ecc 2:25 for **without** [+4946] him, who can eat or find enjoyment?
SS 8:1 Then, if I found you **outside** [+928+2021], I would kiss you,
Isa 5:25 mountains shake, and the dead bodies are like refuse in the **streets**.
10:6 snatch plunder, and to trample them down like mud in the **streets**.
15:3 In the **streets** they wear sackcloth; on the roofs and in the public
24:11 In the **streets** they cry out for wine; all joy turns to gloom,
33:7 Look, their brave men cry aloud in the **streets**; the envoys of peace
42:2 He will not shout or cry out, or raise his voice in the **streets**.
51:20 they lie at the head of every **street**, like antelope caught in a net.
51:23 made your back like the ground, like a **street** to be walked over."
Jer 5:1 "Go up and down the **streets** *of* Jerusalem, look around and
6:11 "Pour it out on the children in the **street** and on the young men
7:17 are doing in the towns of Judah and in the **streets** *of* Jerusalem?
7:34 and bridegroom in the towns of Judah and the **streets** *of* Jerusalem,
9:21 [9:20] it has cut off the children from the **streets** and the young
11:6 these words in the towns of Judah and in the **streets** *of* Jerusalem:
11:13 to that shameful god Baal are as many as the **streets** *of* Jerusalem.'
14:16 are prophesying to will be thrown out into the **streets** *of* Jerusalem
21:4 the Babylonians who are **outside** [+4946] the wall besieging you.
33:10 the towns of Judah and the **streets** *of* Jerusalem that are deserted,
37:21 given bread from the **street** *of* the bakers each day until all the
44:6 it raged against the towns of Judah and the **streets** *of* Jerusalem
44:9 and your wives in the land of Judah and the **streets** *of* Jerusalem?
44:17 officials did in the towns of Judah and in the **streets** *of* Jerusalem.
44:21 of Judah and the **streets** *of* Jerusalem by you and your fathers,
51:4 will fall down slain in Babylon, fatally wounded in her **streets**.
La 1:20 for I have been most rebellious. **Outside** [+4946], the sword
2:19 of your children, who faint from hunger at the head of every **street**.
2:21 "Young and old lie together in the dust of the **streets**; my young
4:1 The sacred gems are scattered at the head of every **street**.
4:5 Those who once ate delicacies are destitute in the **streets**.
4:8 they are blacker than soot; they are not recognized in the **streets**.
4:14 Now they grope through the **streets** like men who are blind.
Eze 7:15 **"Outside** [+928+2021] is the sword, inside are plague and famine;
7:19 They will throw their silver into the **streets**, and their gold will be
11:6 killed many people in this city and filled its **streets** with the dead.
26:11 The hoofs of his horses will trample all your **streets**; he will kill
28:23 I will send a plague upon her and make blood flow in her **streets**.
34:21 your horns until you have driven them **away** [+448+2021+2025],
40:5 I saw a wall completely surrounding the temple **area** [+4946].
40:19 of the lower gateway to the **outside** [+4946] of the inner court;

Eze 40:40 By the **outside** [+2025+4946] wall of the portico of the gateway,
40:44 **Outside** [+2025+4946] the inner gate, within the inner court,
41: 9 The **outer** wall of the side rooms was five cubits thick. The open
41:17 In the space above the **outside** of the entrance to the inner
41:25 there was a wooden overhang on the front of the portico. **[NIE]**
42: 7 There was an **outer** [+2021+4200] wall parallel to the rooms
43:21 burn it in the designated part of the temple area **outside** [+4946]
46: 2 The prince is to enter from the **outside** through the portico of the
47: 2 and led me around the **outside** to the outer gate facing east,
47: 2 and led me around the outside to the **outer** gate facing east,
Hos 7: 1 thieves break into houses, bandits rob in the **streets**;
Am 5:16 "There will be wailing in all the **streets** and cries of anguish in
Mic 7:10 even now she will be trampled underfoot like mire in the **streets**.
Na 2: 4 [2:5] The chariots storm through the **streets**, rushing back
3:10 Her infants were dashed to pieces at the head of every **street**.
Zep 3: 6 I have left their **streets** deserted, with no one passing through.
Zec 9: 3 has heaped up silver like dust, and gold like the dirt of the **streets**.
10: 5 they will be like mighty men trampling the muddy **streets**

2576 חוֹק ***ḥôq***, n.[m.]. Not used in NIV/BHS [√ 2980]

2577 חוּקֹק ***ḥûqōq***, n.pr.loc. [1]

Hukok [1]

1Ch 6:75 [6:60] **Hukok** and Rehob, together with their pasturelands;

2578 חָוַר¹ ***ḥāwar¹***, v. [1] [→ 2580, 2583, 3035; Ar 10254]

grow pale [1]

Isa 29:22 [A] will Jacob be ashamed; no longer *will* their faces **grow pale**.

2579 חָוַר² ***ḥāwar²***, v. Not used in NIV/BHS

2580 חוּר¹ ***ḥûr¹***, n.[m.]. [2] [√ 2578]

white [2]

Est 1: 6 The garden had hangings of **white** and blue linen, fastened with
8:15 left the king's presence wearing royal garments of blue and **white**,

2581 חוּר² ***ḥûr²***, n.pr.m. [15] [→ 1210, 6656?]

Hur [15]

Ex 17:10 had ordered, and Moses, Aaron and **Hur** went to the top of the hill.
17:12 Aaron and **Hur** held his hands up—one on one side, one on the
24:14 Aaron and **Hur** are with you, and anyone involved in a dispute can
31: 2 chosen Bezalel son of Uri, the son of **Hur**, of the tribe of Judah,
35:30 chosen Bezalel son of Uri, the son of **Hur**, of the tribe of Judah,
38:22 (Bezalel son of Uri, the son of **Hur**, of the tribe of Judah,
Nu 31: 8 Among their victims were Evi, Rekem, Zur, **Hur** and Reba—
Jos 13:21 and the Midianite chiefs, Evi, Rekem, Zur, **Hur** and Reba—
1Ch 2:19 When Azubah died, Caleb married Ephrath, who bore him **Hur**.
2:20 **Hur** was the father of Uri, and Uri the father of Bezalel.
2:50 The sons of **Hur** the firstborn of Ephrathah: Shobal the father of
4: 1 The descendants of Judah: Perez, Hezron, Carmi, **Hur** and Shobal.
4: 4 These were the descendants of **Hur**, the firstborn of Ephrathah
2Ch 1: 5 But the bronze altar that Bezalel son of Uri, the son of **Hur**,
Ne 3: 9 Rephaiah son of **Hur**, ruler of a half-district of Jerusalem,

2582 חוֹרוֹן ***ḥôrôn***, n.pr.loc. Not used in NIV/BHS [→ 1103]

2583 חוֹרָי ***ḥôrāy***, n.m. [1] [√ 2578]

fine linen [1]

Isa 19: 9 combed flax will despair, the weavers of **fine linen** will lose hope.

2584 חוּרַי ***ḥûray***, n.pr.m. [1]

Hurai [1]

1Ch 11:32 **Hurai** from the ravines of Gaash, Abiel the Arbathite,

2585 חוּרִי ***ḥûrî***, n.pr.m. [1]

Huri [1]

1Ch 5:14 These were the sons of Abihail son of **Huri**, the son of Jaroah,

2586 חוּרָם ***ḥûrām***, n.pr.m. [10] [√ 325?]

Hiram [6], Huram [2], he[s] [1], Hiram's [1]

1Ch 8: 5 Gera, Shephuphan and **Huram**.
14: 1 [Now **Hiram** [Q; see K 2671] king of Tyre sent messengers]
2Ch 2: 3 [2:2] Solomon sent this message to **Hiram** king of Tyre:
2:11 [2:10] **Hiram** king of Tyre replied by letter to Solomon:
2:12 [2:11] **Hiram** added: "Praise be to the LORD, the God of Israel,
4:11 **He**[s] also made the pots and shovels and sprinkling bowls.
4:11 So **Huram** [K 2671] finished the work he had undertaken for King
8: 2 Solomon rebuilt the villages that **Hiram** had given him, and settled
8:18 And **Hiram** sent him ships commanded by his own officers,
9:10 (The men of **Hiram** [K 2671] and the men of Solomon brought
9:21 The king had a fleet of trading ships manned by **Hiram's** men.

2587 חוּרָם אָבִי ***ḥûrām 'ābî***, n.pr.m. [2] [√ 325? + 3]

Huram-Abi [2]

2Ch 2:13 [2:12] "I am sending you **Huram-Abi**, a man of great skill,
4:16 All the objects that **Huram-Abi** made for King Solomon for the

2588 חַוְרָן ***ḥawrān***, n.pr.loc. [2]

Hauran [2]

Eze 47:16 as far as Hazer Hatticon, which is on the border of **Hauran**.
47:18 "On the east side the boundary will run between **Hauran**

2589 חוֹרֹנַיִם ***ḥôrōnayim***, n.pr.loc. [4 / 5]

Horonaim [5]

2Sa 13:34 told the king, "I see men in the direction of **Horonaim**, [BHS-]
Isa 15: 5 as they go; on the road to **Horonaim** they lament their destruction.
Jer 48: 3 Listen to the cries from **Horonaim**, cries of great havoc
48: 5 on the road down to **Horonaim** anguished cries over the
48:34 and Jahaz, from Zoar as far as **Horonaim** and Eglath Shelishiyah,

2590 חוּשׁ¹ ***ḥûš¹***, v. [17] [→ 2673, 4561; cf. 2591]

come quickly [7], hasten [2], do swiftly [1], go quickly [1], hurried [1], hurry [1], ready [1], rushes [1], sudden [1], swooping [1]

Nu 32:17 [B] we *are* **ready** to arm ourselves and go ahead of the Israelites
Dt 32:35 [A] day of disaster is near and their doom **rushes** upon them."
Jdg 20:37 [G] The men who had been in ambush made a **sudden** dash into
1Sa 20:38 [A] he shouted, "Hurry! **Go quickly**! Don't stop!" The boy
Job 31: 5 [G] walked in falsehood or my foot *has* **hurried** after deceit—
Ps 22:19 [22:20] [A] far off; O my Strength, **come quickly** to help me.
38:22 [38:23] [A] **Come quickly** to help me, O Lord my Savior.
40:13 [40:14] [A] to save me; O LORD, **come quickly** to help me.
55: 8 [55:9] [G] *I would* **hurry** *to* my place of shelter, far from the
70: 1 [70:2] [A] to save me; O LORD, **come quickly** to help me.
70: 5 [70:6] [A] Yet I am poor and needy; **come quickly** to me,
71:12 [A] far from me, O God; **come quickly**, O my God, to help me.
119:60 [A] *I will* **hasten** and not delay to obey your commands.
141: 1 [A] O LORD, I call to you; **come quickly** to me. Hear my voice
Isa 5:19 [G] "Let God hurry, *let him* **hasten** his work so we may see it.
60:22 [G] I am the LORD; in its time *I will* **do** this **swiftly**."
Hab 1: 8 [A] come from afar. They fly like a vulture **swooping** to devour;

2591 חוּשׁ² ***ḥûš²***, v. [3] [cf. 2590]

dismayed [1], find enjoyment [1], greatly disturbed [1]

Job 20: 2 [A] prompt me to answer because I am **greatly disturbed**.
Ecc 2:25 [A] for without him, who can eat or **find enjoyment**?
Isa 28:16 [G] sure foundation; the one who trusts *will* never *be* **dismayed**.

2592 חוּשָׁה ***ḥûšâ***, n.pr.m. [1] [→ 3144]

Hushah [1]

1Ch 4: 4 Penuel was the father of Gedor, and Ezer the father of **Hushah**.

2593 חוּשַׁי ***ḥûšay***, n.pr.m. [14] [cf. 8856?]

Hushai [12], *untranslated* [2]

2Sa 15:32 **Hushai** the Arkite was there to meet him, his robe torn and dust on
15:37 So David's friend **Hushai** arrived at Jerusalem as Absalom was
16:16 Then **Hushai** the Arkite, David's friend, went to Absalom
16:16 David's friend, went to Absalom and said **[RPH]** to him,
16:17 Absalom asked **Hushai**, "Is this the love you show your friend?
16:18 **Hushai** said to Absalom, "No, the one chosen by the LORD,
17: 5 Absalom said, "Summon also **Hushai** the Arkite, so we can hear
17: 6 When **Hushai** came to him, Absalom said, "Ahithophel has given
17: 7 **Hushai** replied to Absalom, "The advice Ahithophel has given is
17: 8 **[RPH]** You know your father and his men; they are fighters,
17:14 "The advice of **Hushai** the Arkite is better than that of
17:15 **Hushai** told Zadok and Abiathar, the priests, "Ahithophel has
1Ki 4:16 Baana son of **Hushai**—in Asher and in Aloth;
1Ch 27:33 was the king's counselor. **Hushai** the Arkite was the king's friend.

2594 חוּשִׁים ***ḥûšîm***, n.pr.f. [2] [cf. 3123]

Hushim [2]

1Ch 8: 8 to Shaharaim in Moab after he had divorced his wives **Hushim**
8:11 By **Hushim** he had Abitub and Elpaal.

2595 חוּשָׁם ḥûšām, n.pr.m. [4] [cf. 3130]
Husham [4]

Ge 36:34 **Husham** from the land of the Temanites succeeded him as king.
36:35 When **Husham** died, Hadad son of Bedad, who defeated Midian in
1Ch 1:45 **Husham** from the land of the Temanites succeeded him as king.
1:46 When **Husham** died, Hadad son of Bedad, who defeated Midian in

2596 חַוֹּת יָאִיר ḥawwōt yā'îr, n.pr.m. & n.f. [4] [cf. 3281]
Havvoth Jair [4]

Nu 32:41 captured their settlements and called them **Havvoth Jair**.
Dt 3:14 after him, so that to this day Bashan is called **Havvoth Jair**.)
Jdg 10:4 thirty towns in Gilead, which to this day are called **Havvoth Jair**.
1Ch 2:23 (But Geshur and Aram captured **Havvoth Jair**, as well as Kenath

2597 חוֹתָם[1] ḥôtām[1], n.m. [14] [→ 2598; cf. 3159]
seal [10], signet ring [2], placed seal [+928+3159] [1], sealed together [+6037] [1]

Ge 38:18 "Your **seal** and its cord, and the staff in your hand," she answered.
Ex 28:11 of Israel on the two stones the way a gem cutter engraves a **seal**.
28:21 each engraved like a **seal** with the name of one of the twelve tribes.
28:36 "Make a plate of pure gold and engrave on it as on a **seal**:
39:6 and engraved them like a **seal** with the names of the sons of Israel.
39:14 each engraved like a **seal** with the name of one of the twelve tribes.
39:30 out of pure gold and engraved on it, like an inscription on a **seal**:
1Ki 21:8 **placed** his **seal on** [+928+3159] them, and sent them to the elders
Job 38:14 The earth takes shape like clay under a **seal**; its features stand out
41:15 [41:7] back has rows of shields tightly **sealed** [+6037] **together**;
SS 8:6 Place me like a **seal** over your heart, like a seal on your arm;
8:6 Place me like a seal over your heart, like a **seal** on your arm;
Jer 22:24 were a **signet ring** on my right hand, I would still pull you off.
Hag 2:23 declares the LORD, 'and I will make you like my **signet ring**,

2598 חוֹתָם[2] ḥôtām[2], n.pr.m. [2] [√ 2597; cf. 3159]
Hotham [2]

1Ch 7:32 the father of Japhlet, Shomer and **Hotham** and of their sister Shua.
11:44 the Ashterathite, Shama and Jeiel the sons of **Hotham** the Aroerite,

2599 חֲזָאֵל ḥ[a]zā'ēl, n.pr.m. [23] [√ 2600 + 446]
Hazael [21], he[s] [1], his[s] [1]

1Ki 19:15 of Damascus. When you get there, anoint **Hazael** king over Aram.
19:17 Jehu will put to death any who escape the sword of **Hazael**,
2Ki 8:8 he said to **Hazael**, "Take a gift with you and go to meet the man of
8:9 **Hazael** went to meet Elisha, taking with him as a gift forty
8:12 "Why is my lord weeping?" asked **Hazael**. "Because I know the
8:13 **Hazael** said, "How could your servant, a mere dog,
8:15 king's face, so that he died. Then **Hazael** succeeded him as king.
8:28 Ahaziah went with Joram son of Ahab to war against **Hazael** king
8:29 inflicted on him at Ramoth in his battle with **Hazael** king of Aram.
9:14 all Israel had been defending Ramoth Gilead against **Hazael** king
9:15 had inflicted on him in the battle with **Hazael** king of Aram.)
10:32 **Hazael** overpowered the Israelites throughout their territory
12:17 [12:18] About this time **Hazael** king of Aram went up
12:17 [12:18] and captured it. Then **he**[s] turned to attack Jerusalem.
12:18 [12:19] he sent them to **Hazael** king of Aram, who then withdrew
13:3 for a long time he kept them under the power of **Hazael** king of
13:3 under the power of Hazael king of Aram and Ben-Hadad **his**[s] son.
13:22 **Hazael** king of Aram oppressed Israel throughout the reign of
13:24 **Hazael** king of Aram died, and Ben-Hadad his son succeeded him
13:25 son of Jehoahaz recaptured from Ben-Hadad son of **Hazael**
2Ch 22:5 of Israel to war against **Hazael** king of Aram at Ramoth Gilead.
22:6 inflicted on him at Ramoth in his battle with **Hazael** king of Aram.
Am 1:4 I will send fire upon the house of **Hazael** that will consume the

2600 חָזָה ḥāzâ, v. [55] [→ 2559, 2602, 2606, 2607, 2608, 2612, 4690, 4691, 4692; Ar 10255; *also used with compound proper names*]
see [14], saw [5], seen [5], visions [5], gaze [3], look [3], see visions [3], sees [3], are[s] [1], gave [1], give visions [1], gloat [1], looked [1], looks [1], observed [1], observes [1], prophesy [1], received [1], saw visions [+2606] [1], select [1], stargazers [+928+3919] [1], vision saw [1]

Ex 18:21 [A] **select** capable men from all the people—men who fear God,
24:11 [A] of the Israelites; *they* **saw** God, and they ate and drank.
Nu 24:4 [A] who **sees** a vision from the Almighty, who falls prostrate,
24:16 [A] *who* **sees** a vision from the Almighty, who falls prostrate,
Job 8:17 [A] a pile of rocks and **looks** *for* a place among the stones.
15:17 [A] and I will explain to you; let me tell you what *I have* **seen**,
19:26 [A] my skin has been destroyed, yet in my flesh *I will* **see** God;
19:27 [A] I myself *will* **see** him with my own eyes—I, and not another.
23:9 [A] When he is at work in the north, *I do* not **see** him; when he
24:1 [A] Why *must* those who know him **look** in vain *for* such days?
27:12 [A] You *have* all **seen** this yourselves. Why then this
34:32 [A] Teach me what *I* cannot **see**; if I have done wrong, I will not
36:25 [A] All mankind *has* **seen** it; men gaze on it from afar.
Ps 11:4 [A] He **observes** the sons of men; his eyes examine them.
11:7 [A] is righteous, he loves justice; upright men *will* **see** his face.
17:2 [A] vindication come from you; *may* your eyes **see** what is right.
17:15 [A] And I—in righteousness *I will* **see** your face; when I awake,
27:4 [A] to **gaze** upon the beauty of the LORD and to seek him in his
46:8 [46:9] [A] Come and **see** the works of the LORD,
58:8 [58:9] [A] like a stillborn child, *may they* not **see** the sun.
58:10 [58:11] [A] The righteous will be glad when *they* **are**[s] avenged,
63:2 [63:3] [A] *I have* **seen** you in the sanctuary and beheld your
Pr 22:29 [A] *Do you* **see** a man skilled in his work? He will serve before
24:32 [A] I applied my heart to what *I* **observed** and learned a lesson
29:20 [A] *Do you* **see** a man who speaks in haste? There is more hope
SS 6:13 [7:1] [A] come back, come back, that *we may* **gaze** on you!
6:13 [7:1] [A] Why *would you* **gaze** on the Shulammite as on the
Isa 1:1 [A] Jerusalem that Isaiah son of Amoz **saw** during the reigns of
2:1 [A] This is what Isaiah son of Amoz **saw** concerning Judah
13:1 [A] An oracle concerning Babylon that Isaiah son of Amoz **saw**:
26:11 [A] O LORD, your hand is lifted high, but *they do* not **see** it.
26:11 [A] *Let them* **see** your zeal for your people and be put to shame;
30:10 [A] to the prophets, "**Give** us no *more* **visions** *of* what is right!
30:10 [A] of what is right! Tell us pleasant things, **prophesy** illusions.
33:17 [A] Your eyes *will* **see** the king in his beauty and view a land that
33:20 [A] **Look** *upon* Zion, the city of our festivals; your eyes will see
47:13 [A] those **stargazers** [+928+3919] who make predictions month
48:6 [A] You have heard these things; **look** *at* them all. Will you not
57:8 [A] whose beds you love, and *you* **looked** *on* their nakedness.
La 2:14 [A] *The* **visions** of your prophets were false and worthless; they
2:14 [A] The oracles *they* **gave** you were false and misleading.
Eze 12:27 [A] is saying, 'The vision he **sees** is for many years from now,
13:6 [A] *Their* **visions** *are* false and their divinations a lie. They say,
13:7 [A] *Have you* not **seen** false visions and uttered lying divinations
13:8 [A] Because of your false words and lying **visions**, I am against
13:9 [A] My hand will be against the prophets who **see** false **visions**
13:16 [A] **saw visions** [+2606] *of* peace for her when there was no
13:23 [A] therefore *you will* no longer **see** false **visions** or practice
21:29 [21:34] [A] Despite false **visions** concerning you and lying
22:28 [A] prophets whitewash these deeds for them by false **visions**
Am 1:1 [A] what *he* **saw** concerning Israel two years before the
Mic 1:1 [A] the **vision** *he* **saw** concerning Samaria and Jerusalem.
4:11 [A] They say, "Let her be defiled, *let* our eyes **gloat** over Zion!"
Hab 1:1 [A] The oracle that Habakkuk the prophet **received**.
Zec 10:2 [A] The idols speak deceit, diviners **see visions** that lie; they tell

2601 חָזֶה ḥāzeh, n.m. [13] [→ Ar 10249]
breast [11], breasts [2]

Ex 29:26 After you take the **breast** of the ram for Aaron's ordination,
29:27 the **breast** that was waved and the thigh that was presented.
Lev 7:30 he is to bring the fat, together with the **breast**, and wave the breast
7:30 and wave the **breast** before the LORD as a wave offering.
7:31 the fat on the altar, but the **breast** belongs to Aaron and his sons.
7:34 I have taken the **breast** that is waved and the thigh that is presented
8:29 He also took the **breast**—Moses' share of the ordination ram—
9:20 these they laid on the **breasts**, and then Aaron burned the fat on the
9:21 Aaron waved the **breasts** and the right thigh before the LORD as
10:14 your sons and your daughters may eat the **breast** that was waved
10:15 the **breast** that was waved must be brought with the fat portions of
Nu 6:20 together with the **breast** that was waved and the thigh that was
18:18 just as the **breast** *of* the wave offering and the right thigh are

2602 חֹזֶה[1] ḥōzeh[1], n.m. [16 / 17] [→ 2559, 3997; cf. 2600]
seer [11], seers [5], prophets [1]

2Sa 24:11 word of the LORD had come to Gad the prophet, David's **seer**:
2Ki 17:13 warned Israel and Judah through all his prophets and **seers**:
1Ch 21:9 The LORD said to Gad, David's **seer**,
25:5 All these were sons of Heman the king's **seer**. They were given
29:29 the records of Nathan the prophet and the records of Gad the **seer**,
2Ch 9:29 in the visions of Iddo the **seer** concerning Jeroboam son of Nebat?
12:15 the prophet and of Iddo the **seer** that deal with genealogies?
19:2 Jehu the **seer**, the son of Hanani, went out to meet him and said to
29:25 by David and Gad the king's **seer** and Nathan the prophet;
29:30 praise the LORD with the words of David and of Asaph the **seer**.
33:18 and the words the **seers** spoke to him in the name of the LORD,
33:19 all are written in the records of the **seers**. [BHS 2559]
35:15 prescribed by David, Asaph, Heman and Jeduthun the king's **seer**.
Isa 29:10 your eyes (the prophets); he has covered your heads (the **seers**).
30:10 and to the **prophets**, "Give us no more visions of what is right!
Am 7:12 Amaziah said to Amos, "Get out, you **seer**! Go back to the land of

Mic 3: 7 The **seers** will be ashamed and the diviners disgraced. They will all

2603 חֹזֶה² ḥōzeh², n.m. [1]

agreement [1]

Isa 28: 15 covenant with death, with the grave we have made an **agreement**.

2604 חֲזָהאֵל ḥᵃzāh'ēl, n.pr.m. Not used in NIV/BHS [√ 2600 + 446]

2605 חֲזוֹ ḥᵃzô, n.pr.m. [1]

Hazo [1]

Ge 22: 22 Kesed, **Hazo**, Pildash, Jidlaph and Bethuel."

2606 חָזוֹן ḥāzôn, n.m. [35] [√ 2600]

vision [22], visions [8], revelation [4], saw visions [+2600] [1]

1Sa 3: 1 the word of the LORD was rare; there were not many **visions**.
1Ch 17: 15 Nathan reported to David all the words of this entire **revelation**.
2Ch 32: 32 his acts of devotion are written in the **vision** *of* the prophet Isaiah
Ps 89: 19 [89:20] Once you spoke in a **vision**, to your faithful people you
Pr 29: 18 Where there is no **revelation**, the people cast off restraint;
Isa 1: 1 The **vision** concerning Judah and Jerusalem that Isaiah son of
29: 7 will be as it is with a dream, with a **vision** *in* the night—
Jer 14: 14 They are prophesying to you false **visions**, divinations, idolatries
23: 16 They speak **visions** *from* their own minds, not from the mouth of
La 2: 9 and her prophets no longer find **visions** from the LORD.
Eze 7: 13 for the **vision** concerning the whole crowd will not be reversed.
7: 26 They will try to get a **vision** from the prophet; the teaching of the
12: 22 land of Israel: 'The days go by and every **vision** comes to nothing'?
12: 23 Say to them, 'The days are near when every **vision** will be fulfilled.
12: 24 For there will be no more false **visions** or flattering divinations
12: 27 of Israel is saying, 'The **vision** he sees is for many years from now,
13: 16 and **saw visions of** [+2600] peace for her when there was no peace,
Da 1: 17 And Daniel could understand **visions** and dreams of all kinds.
8: 1 the third year of King Belshazzar's reign, I, Daniel, had a **vision**,
8: 2 In my **vision** I saw myself in the citadel of Susa in the province of
8: 2 in the province of Elam; in the **vision** I was beside the Ulai Canal.
8: 13 said to him, "How long will it take for the **vision** to be fulfilled—
8: 15 Daniel, was watching the **vision** and trying to understand it,
8: 17 "understand that the **vision** concerns the time of the end."
8: 26 is true, but seal up the **vision**, for it concerns the distant future."
9: 21 was still in prayer, Gabriel, the man I had seen in the earlier **vision**,
9: 24 to seal up **vision** and prophecy and to anoint the most holy.
10: 14 people in the future, for the **vision** concerns a time yet to come."
11: 14 men among your own people will rebel in fulfillment of the **vision**,
Hos 12: 10 [12:11] gave them many **visions** and told parables through them."
Ob 1: 1 The **vision** *of* Obadiah. This is what the Sovereign LORD says
Mic 3: 6 come over you, without **visions**, and darkness, without divination.
Na 1: 1 The book of the **vision** *of* Nahum the Elkoshite.
Hab 2: 2 "Write down the **revelation** and make it plain on tablets so that a
2: 3 For the **revelation** awaits an appointed time; it speaks of the end

2607 חָזוּת ḥāzût, n.f. [5] [√ 2600]

prominent [2], vision [2], agreement [1]

Isa 21: 2 A dire **vision** has been shown to me: The traitor betrays, the looter
28: 18 will be annulled; your **agreement** with the grave will not stand.
29: 11 For you this whole **vision** is nothing but words sealed in a scroll.
Da 8: 5 suddenly a goat with a **prominent** horn between his eyes came
8: 8 in its place four **prominent** horns grew up toward the four winds

2608 חֲזוֹת ḥᵃzôt, n.[f.]. [1] [√ 2600]

visions [1]

2Ch 9: 29 in the **visions** *of* Iddo the seer concerning Jeroboam son of Nebat?

2609 חֲזִיאֵל ḥᵃzî'ēl, n.pr.m. [1] [√ 2600 + 446]

Haziel [1]

1Ch 23: 9 The sons of Shimei: Shelomoth, **Haziel** and Haran—three in all.

2610 חֲזָיָה ḥᵃzāyâ, n.pr.m. [1] [√ 2600 + 3378]

Hazaiah [1]

Ne 11: 5 the son of **Hazaiah**, the son of Adaiah, the son of Joiarib,

2611 חֶזְיוֹן ḥezyôn, n.pr.m. [1]

Hezion [1]

1Ki 15: 18 the son of **Hezion**, the king of Aram, who was ruling in Damascus.

2612 חִזָּיוֹן ḥizzāyôn, n.m. [9] [√ 2600]

vision [5], visions [2], dreams [1], revelation [1]

2Sa 7: 17 Nathan reported to David all the words of this entire **revelation**.
Job 4: 13 Amid disquieting **dreams** *in* the night, when deep sleep falls on
7: 14 then you frighten me with dreams and terrify me with **visions**,
20: 8 no more to be found, banished like a **vision** *of* the night.
33: 15 In a dream, in a **vision** *of* the night, when deep sleep falls on men
Isa 22: 1 An oracle concerning the Valley of **Vision**: What troubles you
22: 5 a day of tumult and trampling and terror in the Valley of **Vision**,
Joel 2: 28 [3:1] men will dream dreams, your young men will see **visions**.
Zec 13: 4 that day every prophet will be ashamed of his prophetic **vision**.

2613 חֲזִיז ḥᵃzîz, n.[m.]. [3]

thunderstorm [+7754] [2], storm clouds [1]

Job 28: 26 a decree for the rain and a path for the **thunderstorm** [+7754],
38: 25 for the torrents of rain, and a path for the **thunderstorm** [+7754],
Zec 10: 1 in the springtime; it is the LORD who makes the **storm clouds**.

2614 חֲזִיר ḥᵃzîr, n.m. [7] [→ 2615, 3492]

pig [2], pig's [2], pigs [2], boars [1]

Lev 11: 7 And the **pig**, though it has a split hoof completely divided,
Dt 14: 8 The **pig** is also unclean; although it has a split hoof, it does not
Ps 80: 13 [80:14] **Boars** from the forest ravage it and the creatures of the
Pr 11: 22 Like a gold ring in a **pig's** snout is a beautiful woman who shows
Isa 65: 4 who eat the flesh of **pigs**, and whose pots hold broth of unclean
66: 3 whoever makes a grain offering is like one who presents **pig's**
66: 17 following the one in the midst of those who eat the flesh of **pigs**

2615 חֵזִיר ḥēzîr, n.pr.m. [2] [√ 2614]

Hezir [2]

1Ch 24: 15 the seventeenth to **Hezir**, the eighteenth to Happizzez,
Ne 10: 20 [10:21] Magpiash, Meshullam, **Hezir**,

2616 חָזַק ḥāzaq, v. [290] [→ 2617, 2618, 2619, 2620, 2621, 2622; *also used with compound proper names*]

strong [41], repaired [18], made repairs [14], strengthen [12], repair [10], took hold [7], hardened [6], severe [5], strengthened [5], stronger [5], encourage [4], firmly [4], hard [4], repairs made [4], take hold [4], took [4], *untranslated* [3], gripped [3], harden [3], hold fast [3], powerful [3], seizes [3], armed [2], embraced [2], encouraged [+3338] [2], encouraged [2], established himself firmly [2], fasten [2], fight bravely [2], grabbed [2], held [2], help [2], holds fast [2], seize [2], take [2], took courage [2], urged [2], assisted [+3338] [1], assisted [+928+3338] [1], be sure [1], began [+3338+4200] [1], brace yourselves [+5516] [1], captured [1], carried out repairs [1], caught hold [1], caught [1], caulk [1], cling [1], clings [1], come [1], conquered [+6584] [1], courage [1], courageously [1], devote [1], devoted [1], do best [1], embrace [1], encourages [1], equipped [1], fortified [1], found strength [1], gave power [1], gave strength [1], gave strong support [+928+6640] [1], give strength [1], given strength [1], gone[s] [1], grasped [1], grasping [1], grew in strength [1], grips [1], harsh [1], have strength [1], heavier [1], held secure [1], help [+3338] [1], helped [+906+3338] [1], helped find strength [+906+3338] [1], helped [1], hold back [1], hold on [1], holding on [1], holding [1], join [+6584] [1], kept [1], lay hold [1], leans [1], made harder [1], made strong [1], maintain [1], maintains [1], marshaled strength [1], nails down [+928+5021] [1], overpowered [1], overruled [+448+6584] [1], overruled [+6584] [1], preserve [1], press [1], prevailed upon [+928] [1], proved stronger [1], rallied strength [1], rapes [+2256+6640+8886] [1], recovery [1], reinforce [1], reinforced [1], repair [+981] [1], repairing [1], resist [1], restored [1], restoring [1], seized [1], shipwrights [+981] [1], showed strength [1], stay [1], strengthen position [1], strengthened [+2432] [1], strengthened himself [1], strengthening his own position [1], strengthens [1], strong [+3338] [1], support [1], supported [1], supports [+6640] [1], take courage [1], take firm hold [1], take up [1], takes hold [1], triumphed [1], unswerving [1], victorious [1], was strengthened [1], worked hard [1]

Ge 19: 16 [G] the men **grasped** his hand and the hands of his wife and of
21: 18 [G] Lift the boy up and **take** him by the hand, for I will make
41: 56 [A] the Egyptians, for the famine *was* **severe** throughout Egypt.
41: 57 [A] from Joseph, because the famine *was* **severe** in all the world.
47: 20 [A] sold their fields, because the famine *was too* **severe** for them.
48: 2 [F] to you," Israel **rallied** *his* **strength** and sat up on the bed.
Ex 4: 4 [G] So Moses reached out and **took hold** of the snake and it
4: 21 [D] I *will* **harden** his heart so that he will not let the people go.
7: 13 [A] Yet Pharaoh's heart *became* **hard** and he would not listen to
7: 22 [A] things by their secret arts, and Pharaoh's heart *became* **hard**;
8: 19 [8:15] [A] Pharaoh's heart *was* **hard** and he would not listen,
9: 2 [G] If you refuse to let them go and continue *to* **hold** them **back**,
9: 12 [D] the LORD **hardened** Pharaoh's heart and he would not

Ex 9:35 [A] So Pharaoh's heart *was* **hard** and he would not let the
10:20 [D] the LORD **hardened** Pharaoh's heart, and he would not let
10:27 [D] the LORD **hardened** Pharaoh's heart, and he was not
11:10 [D] the LORD **hardened** Pharaoh's heart, and he would not let
12:33 [A] The Egyptians **urged** the people to hurry and leave the
14: 4 [D] And *I will* **harden** Pharaoh's heart, and he will pursue them.
14: 8 [D] The LORD **hardened** the heart of Pharaoh king of Egypt,
14:17 [D] I *will* **harden** the hearts of the Egyptians so that they will go
Lev 25:35 [G] **help** him as you would an alien or a temporary resident,
Nu 13:20 [F] **Do** *your* **best** to bring back some of the fruit of the land."
Dt 1:38 [D] **Encourage** him, because he will lead Israel to inherit it.
3:28 [D] But commission Joshua, and **encourage** and strengthen him,
11: 8 [A] so that *you may* **have** *the* **strength** *to* go in and take over the
12:23 [A] **be sure** you do not eat the blood, because the blood is the
22:25 [G] pledged to be married and **rapes** [+2256+6640+8886] her,
25:11 [G] and she reaches out and **seizes** him by his private parts,
31: 6 [A] *Be* **strong** and courageous. Do not be afraid or terrified
31: 7 [A] him in the presence of all Israel, "*Be* **strong** and courageous,
31:23 [A] "*Be* **strong** and courageous, for you will bring the Israelites
Jos 1: 6 [A] "*Be* **strong** and courageous, because you will lead these
1: 7 [A] *Be* **strong** and very courageous. Be careful to obey all the
1: 9 [A] *Be* **strong** and courageous. Do not be terrified; do not be
1:18 [A] will be put to death. Only *be* **strong** and courageous!"
10:25 [A] be afraid; do not be discouraged. *Be* **strong** and courageous.
11:20 [D] For it was the LORD himself *who* **hardened** their hearts to
17:13 [A] However, when the Israelites *grew* **stronger**, they subjected
23: 6 [A] "*Be* very **strong**; be careful to obey all that is written in the
Jdg 1:28 [A] When Israel *became* **strong**, they pressed the Canaanites into
3:12 [D] evil the LORD **gave** Eglon king of Moab **power** over Israel.
7: 8 [G] rest of the Israelites to their tents but **kept** the three hundred,
7:11 [A] you *will be* **encouraged** [+3338] to attack the camp."
7:20 [G] **Grasping** the torches in their left hands and holding in their
9:24 [D] who *had* **helped** [+906+3338] him murder his brothers.
16:26 [G] Samson said to the servant who **held** his hand, "Put me
16:28 [D] O God, please **strengthen** me just once more, and let me
19: 4 [G] the girl's father, **prevailed** [+928] **upon** him to stay;
19:25 [G] So the man **took** his concubine and sent her outside to them,
19:29 [G] he took a knife **[NIE]** and cut up his concubine, limb by
20:22 [F] the men of Israel **encouraged** one another and again took up
1Sa 4: 9 [F] *Be* **strong**, Philistines! Be men, or you will be subject to the
15:27 [G] to leave, Saul **caught hold** of the hem of his robe, and it tore.
17:35 [G] it turned on me, *I* **seized** it by its hair, struck it and killed it.
17:50 [A] So David **triumphed** over the Philistine with a sling and a
23:16 [D] and **helped** him **find strength** [+906+3338] in God.
30: 6 [F] But David **found strength** in the LORD his God.
2Sa 1:11 [G] and all the men with him **took hold** of their clothes
2: 7 [A] Now then, *be* **strong** [+3338] and brave, for Saul your
2:16 [G] each man **grabbed** his opponent by the head and thrust his
3: 6 [F] Abner had been **strengthening his own position** in the house
3:29 [G] or leprosy or *who* **leans** on a crutch or who falls by the sword
10:11 [A] Joab said, "If the Arameans *are* too **strong** for me, then you
10:11 [A] if the Ammonites *are* too **strong** for you, then I will come to
10:12 [A] *Be* **strong** and let us fight bravely for our people and the
10:12 [F] Be strong and *let us* **fight bravely** for our people and the
11:25 [G] **Press** the attack against the city and destroy it.' Say this to
11:25 [D] against the city and destroy it.' Say this *to* **encourage** Joab."
13:11 [G] *he* **grabbed** her and said, "Come to bed with me, my sister."
13:14 [A] to her, and since *he was* **stronger** than she, he raped her.
13:28 [A] Have not I given you this order? *Be* **strong** and brave."
15: 5 [G] would reach out his hand, **take hold** of him and kiss him.
16:21 [A] and the hands of everyone with you *will be* **strengthened**."
18: 9 [A] of a large oak, Absalom's head *got* **caught** in the tree.
24: 4 [A] **overruled** [+448+6584] Joab and the army commanders;
1Ki 1:50 [G] of Solomon, went and **took hold** of the horns of the altar.
2: 2 [A] all the earth," he said. "So *be* **strong**, show yourself a man,
2:28 [G] tent of the LORD and **took hold** of the horns of the altar.
9: 9 [G] *have* **embraced** other gods, worshiping and serving them—
16:22 [A] Omri's followers **proved stronger** *than* those of Tibni son
20:22 [F] "**Strengthen** *your* **position** and see what must be done,
20:23 [A] gods of the hills. That is why *they were* too **strong** for us.
20:23 [A] them on the plains, surely *we will be* **stronger** than they.
20:25 [A] surely *we will be* **stronger** than they." He agreed with them
2Ki 2:12 [G] Then *he* **took hold** of his own clothes and tore them apart.
3:26 [A] When the king of Moab saw that the battle *had* **gone**ˢ against
4: 8 [G] woman was there, *who* **urged** him to stay for a meal.
4:27 [G] the man of God at the mountain, *she* **took hold** of his feet.
12: 5 [12:6] [D] *let it be used to* **repair** whatever damage is found in
12: 6 [12:7] [D] Joash the priests *still had* not **repaired** the temple.
12: 7 [12:8] [D] "Why aren't you **repairing** the damage done to the
12: 8 [12:9] [D] that they *would* not **repair** the temple themselves.
12:12 [12:13] [D] dressed stone for the **repair** *of* the temple of the
12:12 [12:13] [A] met all the other expenses of **restoring** the temple.
12:14 [12:15] [D] to the workmen, *who* used it *to* **repair** the temple.
14: 5 [A] After the kingdom *was* **firmly** in his grasp, he executed the
15:19 [G] his support and **strengthen** his own hold on the kingdom.
22: 5 [D] have these men pay the workers who **repair** [+981] the
22: 6 [D] them purchase timber and dressed stone to **repair** the temple.
25: 3 [A] ⌊fourth⌋ month the famine in the city *had become so* **severe**
1Ch 11:10 [F] **gave** his kingship **strong** [+928+6640] **support** to extend it
19:12 [A] Joab said, "If the Arameans *are* too **strong** for me, then you
19:12 [A] if the Ammonites *are* too **strong** for you, then I will rescue
19:13 [A] *Be* **strong** and let us fight bravely for our people and the
19:13 [F] Be strong and *let us* **fight bravely** for our people and the
21: 4 [A] The king's word, however, **overruled** [+6584] Joab; so Joab
22:13 [A] *Be* **strong** and courageous. Do not be afraid or discouraged.
26:27 [D] they dedicated for the **repair** of the temple of the LORD.
28: 7 [A] I will establish his kingdom forever if *he is* **unswerving** in
28:10 [A] to build a temple as a sanctuary. *Be* **strong** and do the work."
28:20 [A] his son, "*Be* **strong** and courageous, and do the work.
29:12 [D] are strength and power to exalt and **give strength** to all.
2Ch 1: 1 [F] Solomon son of David **established himself firmly** over his
4: 5 [G] like a lily blossom. It held **[RPH]** three thousand baths.
7:22 [G] *have* **embraced** other gods, worshiping and serving them—
8: 3 [A] Solomon then went to Hamath Zobah and **captured** it.
11:11 [D] *He* **strengthened** their defenses and put commanders in
11:12 [D] and spears in all the cities, and **made** them very **strong**.
11:17 [D] *They* **strengthened** the kingdom of Judah and supported
12:13 [F] King Rehoboam **established himself firmly** in Jerusalem
13: 7 [F] and indecisive and not **strong** *enough* to resist them.
13: 8 [F] "And now you plan to **resist** the kingdom of the LORD,
13:21 [F] Abijah **grew in strength**. He married fourteen wives and had
15: 7 [A] as for you, *be* **strong** and do not give up, for your work will
15: 8 [F] of Azariah son of Oded the prophet, *he* **took courage**.
16: 9 [F] to **strengthen** those whose hearts are fully committed to him.
17: 1 [F] him as king and **strengthened himself** against Israel.
19:11 [A] Act *with* **courage**, and may the LORD be with those who
21: 4 [F] When Jehoram established himself **firmly** over his father's
23: 1 [F] In the seventh year Jehoiada **showed** *his* **strength**. He made a
24: 5 [D] annually from all Israel, to **repair** the temple of your God.
24:12 [D] and also workers in iron and bronze to **repair** the temple.
25: 3 [A] After the kingdom *was* **firmly** in his control, he executed the
25: 8 [A] Even if you go and fight **courageously** in battle, God will
25:11 [F] Amaziah then **marshaled** *his* **strength** and led his army to
26: 8 [G] the border of Egypt, because *he had become* very **powerful**.
26: 9 [D] and at the angle of the wall, and *he* **fortified** them.
26:15 [A] for he was greatly helped until *he became* **powerful**.
27: 5 [A] on the king of the Ammonites and **conquered** [+6584] them.
27: 6 [F] Jotham *grew* **powerful** because he walked steadfastly before
28:15 [G] The men designated by name **took** the prisoners, and from
28:20 [A] came to him, but he gave him trouble instead of **help**.
29: 3 [D] the doors of the temple of the LORD and **repaired** them.
29:34 [D] so their kinsmen the Levites **helped** them until the task was
31: 4 [A] so *they could* **devote** *themselves* to the Law of the LORD.
32: 5 [F] *he* **worked hard** repairing all the broken sections of the wall
32: 5 [D] and **reinforced** the supporting terraces of the City of David.
32: 7 [A] "*Be* **strong** and courageous. Do not be afraid or discouraged
34: 8 [D] the recorder, to **repair** the temple of the LORD his God.
34:10 [D] men paid the workers who repaired and **restored** the temple.
35: 2 [D] and **encouraged** them in the service of the LORD's temple.
Ezr 1: 6 [D] All their neighbors **assisted** [+928+3338] them with articles
6:22 [D] so that he **assisted** [+3338] them in the work on the house of
7:28 [F] I **took courage** and gathered leading men from Israel to go up
9:12 [A] that *you may be* **strong** and eat the good things of the land
10: 4 [A] your hands. We will support you, so **take courage** and do it."
Ne 2:18 [D] So they **began** [+3338+4200] this good work.
3: 4 [G] son of Uriah, the son of Hakkoz, **repaired** the next section.
3: 4 [G] son of Berekiah, the son of Meshezabel, **made repairs**,
3: 4 [G] and next to him Zadok son of Baana also **made repairs**.
3: 5 [G] The next section *was* **repaired** *by* the men of Tekoa,
3: 6 [G] The Jeshanah Gate *was* **repaired** *by* Joiada son of Paseah
3: 7 [G] **repairs** *were* **made** *by* men from Gibeon and Mizpah—
3: 8 [G] one of the goldsmiths, **repaired** the next section;
3: 8 [G] one of the perfume-makers, **made repairs** next to that.
3: 9 [G] of a half-district of Jerusalem, **repaired** the next section.
3:10 [G] Jedaiah son of Harumaph **made repairs** opposite his house,
3:10 [G] and Hattush son of Hashabneiah **made repairs** next to him.
3:11 [G] Hasshub son of Pahath-Moab **repaired** another section and
3:12 [G] **repaired** the next section with the help of his daughters.
3:13 [G] The Valley Gate *was* **repaired** *by* Hanun and the residents of
3:14 [G] The Dung Gate *was* **repaired** *by* Malkijah son of Recab,
3:15 [G] *was* **repaired** *by* Shallun son of Col-Hozeh, ruler of the district
3:16 [G] **made repairs** up to a point opposite the tombs of David, as
3:17 [G] *the* **repairs** *were* **made** *by* the Levites under Rehum son of
3:17 [G] the district of Keilah, **carried out repairs** for his district.
3:18 [G] *the* **repairs** *were* **made** *by* their countrymen under Binnui
3:19 [D] son of Jeshua, ruler of Mizpah, **repaired** another section,
3:20 [G] Baruch son of Zabbai zealously **repaired** another section,
3:21 [G] son of Uriah, the son of Hakkoz, **repaired** another section,

Ne 3:22 [G] *The* **repairs** next to him *were* **made** *by* the priests from the
3:23 [G] Benjamin and Hasshub **made repairs** in front of their house;
3:23 [G] the son of Ananiah, **made repairs** beside his house.
3:24 [G] to him, Binnui son of Henadad **repaired** another section,
3:27 [G] Next to them, the men of Tekoa **repaired** another section,
3:28 [G] Above the Horse Gate, the priests **made repairs**, each in
3:29 [G] Zadok son of Immer **made repairs** opposite his house.
3:29 [G] son of Shecaniah, the guard at the East Gate, **made repairs**.
3:30 [G] the sixth son of Zalaph, **repaired** another section.
3:30 [G] Meshullam son of Berekiah **made repairs** opposite his living
3:31 [G] **made repairs** as far as the house of the temple servants
3:32 [G] the Sheep Gate the goldsmiths and merchants **made repairs**.
4:16 [4:10] [G] while the other half *were* **equipped** *with* spears,
4:17 [4:11] [G] work with one hand and **held** a weapon in the other,
4:21 [4:15] [G] So we continued the work with half the men **holding**
5:16 [G] Instead, *I* **devoted** *myself* to the work on this wall. All my
6:9 [D] be completed." ⌊But I prayed,⌋ "Now **strengthen** my hands."
10:29 [10:30] [G] all *these* now **join** [+6584] their brothers the nobles,
Job 2:3 [G] he still **maintains** his integrity, though you incited me
2:9 [G] wife said to him, "*Are* you still **holding on** to your integrity?
4:3 [D] instructed many, how *you have* **strengthened** feeble hands.
8:15 [G] his web, but it gives way; *he* **clings** to it, but it does not hold.
8:20 [G] reject a blameless man or **strengthen** the hands of evildoers.
18:9 [D] A trap seizes him by the heel; a snare **holds** him **fast**.
27:6 [G] *I will* **maintain** my righteousness and never let go of it;
Ps 27:14 [A] *be* **strong** and take heart and wait for the LORD.
31:24 [31:25] [A] *Be* **strong** and take heart, all you who hope in the
35:2 [G] **Take up** shield and buckler; arise and come to my aid.
64:5 [64:6] [D] *They* **encourage** each other in evil plans, they talk
147:13 [D] for *he* **strengthens** the bars of your gates and blesses your
Pr 3:18 [G] She is a tree of life to those *who* **embrace** her; those who lay
4:13 [G] **Hold on** to instruction, do not let it go; guard it well, for it is
7:13 [G] *She* **took hold** of him and kissed him and with a brazen face
26:17 [G] Like *one who* **seizes** a dog by the ears is a passer-by who
Isa 4:1 [G] In that day seven women *will* **take hold** of one man and say,
22:21 [D] clothe him with your robe and **fasten** your sash *around* him
27:5 [G] Or else *let them* **come** *to* me for refuge; let them make peace
28:22 [A] stop your mocking, or your chains *will become* **heavier**;
33:23 [D] The mast *is* not **held secure**, the sail is not spread.
35:3 [D] **Strengthen** the feeble hands, steady the knees that give way;
35:4 [A] say to those with fearful hearts, "*Be* **strong**, do not fear; your
39:1 [A] and a gift, because he had heard of his illness and **recovery**.
41:6 [A] each helps the other and says to his brother, "*Be* **strong**!"
41:7 [D] **encourages** the goldsmith, and he who smooths with the
41:7 [D] "It is good." *He* **nails down** [+928+5021] the idol so it will
41:9 [G] *I* **took** you from the ends of the earth, from its farthest
41:13 [G] *who* **takes hold** *of* your right hand and says to you,
42:6 [G] called you in righteousness; *I will* **take hold** of your hand.
45:1 [G] whose right hand *I* **take hold** *of* to subdue nations before him
51:18 [G] of all the sons she reared there was none *to* **take** her by the
54:2 [D] not hold back; lengthen your cords, **strengthen** your stakes.
56:2 [G] Blessed is the man who does this, the man *who* **holds** it **fast**,
56:4 [G] who choose what pleases me and **hold fast** to my covenant—
56:6 [G] without desecrating it and *who* **hold fast** to my covenant—
64:7 [64:6] [G] No one calls on your name or strives to **lay hold** of
Jer 5:3 [D] *They* **made** their faces **harder** than stone and refused to
6:23 [G] *They are* **armed** *with* bow and spear; they are cruel
6:24 [G] Anguish *has* **gripped** us, pain like that of a woman in labor.
8:5 [G] always turn away? *They* **cling** to deceit; they refuse to return.
8:21 [G] are crushed, I am crushed; I mourn, and horror **grips** me.
10:4 [D] *they* **fasten** it with hammer and nails so it will not totter.
20:7 [A] and I was deceived; *you* **overpowered** me and prevailed.
23:14 [D] *They* **strengthen** the hands of evildoers, so that no one turns
31:32 [G] when *I* **took** them by the hand to lead them out of Egypt,
49:24 [G] she has turned to flee and panic *has* **gripped** her;
50:33 [G] All their captors **hold** them **fast**, refusing to let them go.
50:42 [G] *They are* **armed** *with* bows and spears; they are cruel
50:43 [G] Anguish *has* **gripped** him, pain like that of a woman in
51:12 [G] **Reinforce** the guard, station the watchmen, prepare an
52:6 [A] fourth month the famine in the city *had become so* **severe**
Eze 7:13 [F] Because of their sins, not one of them *will* **preserve** his life.
13:22 [D] because you **encouraged** [+3338] the wicked not to turn
16:49 [G] *they did* not **help** [+3338] the poor and needy.
22:14 [A] or your hands *be* **strong** in the day I deal with you?
27:9 [G] of Gebal were on board as shipwrights *to* **caulk** your seams.
27:27 [G] and wares, your mariners, seamen and **shipwrights** [+981],
30:21 [A] in a splint so as to *become* **strong** *enough* to hold a sword.
30:24 [D] *I will* **strengthen** the arms of the king of Babylon and put
30:25 [G] *I will* **strengthen** the arms of the king of Babylon,
34:4 [D] *You have* not **strengthened** the weak or healed the sick
34:16 [D] I will bind up the injured and **strengthen** the weak, but the
Da 10:18 [D] who looked like a man touched me and **gave** me **strength**.
10:19 [A] he said. "Peace! *Be* **strong** now; be strong."
10:19 [A] he said. "Peace! Be strong now; *be* **strong**."
10:19 [F] spoke to me, *I* **was strengthened** and said, "Speak, my lord,
10:19 [D] "Speak, my lord, since *you have* **given** me **strength**."
10:21 [F] (No one **supports** [+6640] me against them except Michael,
11:1 [G] the Mede, I took my stand to **support** and protect him.)
11:5 [A] "The king of the South *will become* **strong**, but one of his
11:5 [A] one of his commanders *will become even* **stronger** than he
11:6 [G] royal escort and her father and the *one who* **supported** her.
11:7 [G] his fortress; he will fight against them and *be* **victorious**.
11:21 [G] its people feel secure, and *he will* **seize** it through intrigue.
11:32 [G] but the people who know their God will **firmly** resist him.
Hos 7:15 [D] I trained them and **strengthened** [+2432] them, but they plot
Mic 4:9 [G] that pain **seizes** you like that of a woman in labor?
7:18 [G] *You do* not **stay** angry forever but delight to show mercy.
Na 2:1 [2:2] [D] watch the road, **brace** [+5516] **yourselves**,
3:14 [D] Draw water for the siege, **strengthen** your defenses!
3:14 [G] Work the clay, tread the mortar, **repair** the brickwork!
Hag 2:4 [A] now *be* **strong**, O Zerubbabel,' declares the LORD. 'Be
2:4 [A] '*Be* **strong**, O Joshua son of Jehozadak, the high priest. Be
2:4 [A] *Be* **strong**, all you people of the land,' declares the LORD,
Zec 8:9 [A] *let* your hands *be* **strong** so that the temple may be built.
8:13 [A] a blessing. Do not be afraid, but *let* your hands *be* **strong**."
8:23 [G] nations *will* **take firm hold** *of* one Jew by the hem of his
8:23 [G] nations will take firm hold **[RPH]** of one Jew by the hem of
14:13 [G] Each man *will* **seize** the hand of another, and they will attack
Mal 3:13 [A] "You have said **harsh** things against me," says the LORD.

2617 חָזָק *ḥāzāq*, a. [57] [√ 2616]

mighty [23], strong [12], powerful [6], hardened [+5195] [2], power [2], stronger [2], bitter [1], fiercest [1], good [1], grew worse and worse [+2118+2716+4394] [1], hard [1], harder [1], loud [1], severe [1], stubborn [+4213] [1], unyielding [+7156] [1]

Ex 3:19 I know that the king of Egypt will not let you go unless a **mighty**
6:1 Because of my **mighty** hand he will let them go; because of my
6:1 because of my **mighty** hand he will drive them out of his country."
10:19 And the LORD changed the wind to a very **strong** west wind,
13:9 For the LORD brought you out of Egypt with his **mighty** hand.
19:16 a thick cloud over the mountain, and a very **loud** trumpet blast.
32:11 you brought out of Egypt with great power and a **mighty** hand?
Nu 13:18 and whether the people who live there are **strong** or weak,
13:31 "We can't attack those people; they are **stronger** than we are."
20:20 Edom came out against them with a large and **powerful** army.
Dt 3:24 to show to your servant your greatness and your **strong** hand.
4:34 by war, by a **mighty** hand and an outstretched arm, or by great
5:15 that the LORD your God brought you out of there with a **mighty**
6:21 but the LORD brought us out of Egypt with a **mighty** hand.
7:8 to your forefathers that he brought you out with a **mighty** hand
7:19 and wonders, the **mighty** hand and outstretched arm,
9:26 by your great power and brought out of Egypt with a **mighty** hand.
11:2 your God: his majesty, his **mighty** hand, his outstretched arm;
26:8 So the LORD brought us out of Egypt with a **mighty** hand
34:12 For no one has ever shown the **mighty** power or performed the
Jos 4:24 of the earth might know that the hand of the LORD is **powerful**
14:11 I am still as **strong** today as the day Moses sent me out; I'm just as
17:18 the Canaanites have iron chariots and though they are **strong**,
Jdg 18:26 and Micah, seeing that they were too **strong** for him, turned around
1Sa 14:52 All the days of Saul there was **bitter** war with the Philistines,
2Sa 11:15 he wrote, "Put Uriah in the front line where the fighting is **fiercest**.
1Ki 8:42 great name and your **mighty** hand and your outstretched arm—
17:17 He **grew worse and worse** [+2118+2716+4394], and finally
18:2 present himself to Ahab. Now the famine was **severe** in Samaria,
19:11 a great and **powerful** wind tore the mountains apart and shattered
2Ch 6:32 because of your great name and your **mighty** hand and your
Ne 1:10 whom you redeemed by your great strength and your **mighty** hand.
Job 5:15 in their mouth; he saves them from the clutches of the **powerful**.
37:18 him in spreading out the skies, **hard** as a mirror of cast bronze?
Ps 35:10 You rescue the poor from *those* too **strong** for them, the poor
136:12 with a **mighty** hand and outstretched arm; *His love endures*
Pr 23:11 for their Defender is **strong**; he will take up their case against you.
Isa 27:1 his fierce, great and **powerful** sword, Leviathan the gliding
28:2 See, the Lord has *one who* is **powerful** and strong. Like a
40:10 See, the Sovereign LORD comes with **power**, and his arm rules
Jer 21:5 and a **mighty** arm in anger and fury and great wrath.
31:11 and redeem them from the hand of *those* **stronger** than they.
32:21 by a **mighty** hand and an outstretched arm and with great terror.
50:34 Yet their Redeemer is **strong**; the LORD Almighty is his name.
Eze 2:4 to whom I am sending you are obstinate and **stubborn** [+4213].
3:7 for the whole house of Israel is **hardened** [+5195] and obstinate.
3:8 I will make you as **unyielding** [+7156] and hardened as they are.
3:8 I will make you as unyielding and **hardened** [+5195] as they are.
3:9 I will make your forehead like the hardest stone, **harder** than flint.
3:14 anger of my spirit, with the **strong** hand of the LORD upon me.
20:33 I will rule over you with a **mighty** hand and an outstretched arm
20:34 with a **mighty** hand and an outstretched arm and with outpoured

Eze 26:17 You were a **power** on the seas, you and your citizens; you put your
30:22 I will break both his arms, the **good** arm as well as the broken one,
34:16 strengthen the weak, but the sleek and the **strong** I will destroy.
Da 9:15 who brought your people out of Egypt with a **mighty** hand
Am 2:14 The swift will not escape, the **strong** will not muster their strength,

2618 חָזֵק *ḥāzēq*, a.vbl. [2] [√ 2616]

grew louder and louder [+2143+2256+4394] [1], grew stronger and stronger [+2143+2256] [1]

Ex 19:19 and the sound of the trumpet **grew louder** [+2143+2256+4394] **and louder**. Then Moses spoke and the voice of God answered him.
2Sa 3:1 David **grew stronger** [+2143+2256] **and stronger**,

2619 חֵזֶק *ḥēzeq*, n.[m.]. [1] [√ 2616]

strength [1]

Ps 18:1 [18:2] I love you, O LORD, my **strength**.

2620 חֹזֶק *ḥōzeq*, n.m. [5] [√ 2616]

mighty [3], power [1], strength [1]

Ex 13:3 because the LORD brought you out of it with a **mighty** hand.
13:14 'With a **mighty** hand the LORD brought us out of Egypt,
13:16 that the LORD brought us out of Egypt with his **mighty** hand."
Am 6:13 and say, "Did we not take Karnaim by our own **strength**?"
Hag 2:22 royal thrones and shatter the **power** *of* the foreign kingdoms.

2621 חֶזְקָה *ḥezqâ*, n.f. [4] [√ 2616]

became powerful [1], become strong [1], gained power [1], strong [1]

2Ch 12:1 position as king was established and he had **become strong**,
26:16 But after Uzziah **became powerful**, his pride led to his downfall.
Isa 8:11 The LORD spoke to me with his **strong** hand upon me, warning
Da 11:2 When he has **gained power** by his wealth, he will stir up everyone

2622 חָזְקָה *ḥozqâ*, n.f. [5] [√ 2616]

cruelly [+928] [1], force [1], harshly [+928] [1], sharply [+928] [1], urgently [+928] [1]

Jdg 4:3 and had **cruelly** [+928] oppressed the Israelites for twenty years,
8:1 went to fight Midian?" And they criticized him **sharply** [+928].
1Sa 2:16 "No, hand it over now; if you don't, I'll take it by **force**."
Eze 34:4 for the lost. You have ruled them **harshly** [+928] and brutally.
Jnh 3:8 Let everyone call **urgently** [+928] on God. Let them give up their

2623 חִזְקִי *ḥizqî*, n.pr.m. [1] [√ 2616 + 3378]

Hizki [1]

1Ch 8:17 Zebadiah, Meshullam, **Hizki**, Heber,

2624 חִזְקִיָּה *ḥizqiyyâ*, n.pr.m. [13] [√ 2616 + 3378]

Hezekiah [9], he[s] [1], Hezekiah's [+4200] [1], Hezekiah's [1], Hizkiah [1]

2Ki 18:1 king of Israel, **Hezekiah** son of Ahaz king of Judah began to reign.
18:10 So Samaria was captured in **Hezekiah's** [+4200] sixth year,
18:13 In the fourteenth year of King **Hezekiah's** reign, Sennacherib king
18:14 So **Hezekiah** king of Judah sent this message to the king of
18:14 The king of Assyria exacted from **Hezekiah** king of Judah three
18:15 So **Hezekiah** gave him all the silver that was found in the temple
18:16 At this time **Hezekiah** king of Judah stripped off the gold with
18:16 Judah stripped off the gold with which **he**[s] had covered the doors
1Ch 3:23 The sons of Neariah: Elioenai, **Hizkiah** and Azrikam—three in all.
Ne 7:21 of Ater (through **Hezekiah**) 98
10:17 [10:18] Ater, **Hezekiah**, Azzur,
Pr 25:1 of Solomon, copied by the men of **Hezekiah** king of Judah:
Zep 1:1 the son of Gedaliah, the son of Amariah, the son of **Hezekiah**,

2625 חִזְקִיָּהוּ *ḥizqiyyāhû*, n.pr.m. [74] [√ 2616 + 3378]

Hezekiah [66], Hezekiah's [5], he[s] [2], Hezekiah's [+4200] [1]

2Ki 16:20 the City of David. And **Hezekiah** his son succeeded him as king.
18:9 In King **Hezekiah's** [+4200] fourth year, which was the seventh
18:17 with a large army, from Lachish to King **Hezekiah** at Jerusalem.
18:19 The field commander said to them, "Tell **Hezekiah**: " 'This is what
18:22 isn't he the one whose high places and altars **Hezekiah** removed,
18:29 This is what the king says: Do not let **Hezekiah** deceive you.
18:30 Do not let **Hezekiah** persuade you to trust in the LORD when he
18:31 "Do not listen to **Hezekiah**. This is what the king of Assyria says:
18:32 "Do not listen to **Hezekiah**, for he is misleading you when he says,
18:37 and Joah son of Asaph the recorder went to **Hezekiah**,
19:1 When King **Hezekiah** heard this, he tore his clothes and put on
19:3 They told him, "This is what **Hezekiah** says: This day is a day of
19:5 When King **Hezekiah's** officials came to Isaiah,
19:9 So he again sent messengers to **Hezekiah** with this word:
19:10 "Say to **Hezekiah** king of Judah: Do not let the god you depend on
19:14 **Hezekiah** received the letter from the messengers and read it.
19:14 **he**[s] went up to the temple of the LORD and spread it out before
19:15 And **Hezekiah** prayed to the LORD: "O LORD, God of Israel,
19:20 Isaiah son of Amoz sent a message to **Hezekiah**: "This is what the
20:1 In those days **Hezekiah** became ill and was at the point of death.
20:3 done what is good in your eyes." And **Hezekiah** wept bitterly.
20:5 "Go back and tell **Hezekiah**, the leader of my people, 'This is what
20:8 **Hezekiah** had asked Isaiah, "What will be the sign that the
20:12 son of Baladan king of Babylon sent **Hezekiah** letters
20:12 and a gift, because he had heard of **Hezekiah's** illness.
20:13 **Hezekiah** received the messengers and showed them all that was
20:13 his palace or in all his kingdom that **Hezekiah** did not show them.
20:14 Then Isaiah the prophet went to King **Hezekiah** and asked,
20:14 "From a distant land," **Hezekiah** replied. "They came from
20:15 your palace?" "They saw everything in my palace," **Hezekiah** said.
20:16 Then Isaiah said to **Hezekiah**, "Hear the word of the LORD:
20:19 word of the LORD you have spoken is good," **Hezekiah** replied.
20:20 As for the other events of **Hezekiah's** reign, all his achievements
20:21 **Hezekiah** rested with his fathers. And Manasseh his son succeeded
21:3 He rebuilt the high places his father **Hezekiah** had destroyed;
1Ch 3:13 Ahaz his son, **Hezekiah** his son, Manasseh his son,
2Ch 29:18 they went in to King **Hezekiah** and reported: "We have purified
29:27 **Hezekiah** gave the order to sacrifice the burnt offering on the altar.
30:24 **Hezekiah** king of Judah provided a thousand bulls and seven
32:15 Now do not let **Hezekiah** deceive you and mislead you like this.
Isa 36:1 In the fourteenth year of King **Hezekiah's** reign, Sennacherib king
36:2 with a large army from Lachish to King **Hezekiah** at Jerusalem.
36:4 "Tell **Hezekiah**, " 'This is what the great king, the king of Assyria,
36:7 isn't he the one whose high places and altars **Hezekiah** removed,
36:14 Do not let **Hezekiah** deceive you. He cannot deliver you!
36:15 Do not let **Hezekiah** persuade you to trust in the LORD when he
36:16 "Do not listen to **Hezekiah**. This is what the king of Assyria says:
36:18 "Do not let **Hezekiah** mislead you when he says, 'The LORD will
36:22 and Joah son of Asaph the recorder went to **Hezekiah**,
37:1 When King **Hezekiah** heard this, he tore his clothes and put on
37:3 They told him, "This is what **Hezekiah** says: This day is a day of
37:5 When King **Hezekiah's** officials came to Isaiah,
37:9 When he heard it, he sent messengers to **Hezekiah** with this word:
37:10 "Say to **Hezekiah** king of Judah: Do not let the god you depend on
37:14 **Hezekiah** received the letter from the messengers and read it.
37:14 **he**[s] went up to the temple of the LORD and spread it out before
37:15 And **Hezekiah** prayed to the LORD:
37:21 Isaiah son of Amoz sent a message to **Hezekiah**: "This is what the
38:1 In those days **Hezekiah** became ill and was at the point of death.
38:2 **Hezekiah** turned his face to the wall and prayed to the LORD,
38:3 done what is good in your eyes." And **Hezekiah** wept bitterly.
38:5 "Go and tell **Hezekiah**, 'This is what the LORD, the God of your
38:9 A writing of **Hezekiah** king of Judah after his illness and recovery:
38:22 **Hezekiah** had asked, "What will be the sign that I will go up to the
39:1 son of Baladan king of Babylon sent **Hezekiah** letters
39:2 **Hezekiah** received the envoys gladly and showed them what was
39:2 his palace or in all his kingdom that **Hezekiah** did not show them.
39:3 Then Isaiah the prophet went to King **Hezekiah** and asked,
39:3 did they come from?" "From a distant land," **Hezekiah** replied.
39:4 your palace?" "They saw everything in my palace," **Hezekiah** said.
39:5 Isaiah said to **Hezekiah**, "Hear the word of the LORD Almighty:
39:8 word of the LORD you have spoken is good," **Hezekiah** replied.
Jer 26:18 "Micah of Moresheth prophesied in the days of **Hezekiah** king of
26:19 "Did **Hezekiah** king of Judah or anyone else in Judah put him to

2626 חָח *ḥāḥ*, n.m. [7] [cf. 2560]

hooks [4], hook [2], brooches [1]

Ex 35:22 gold jewelry of all kinds: **brooches**, earrings, rings and ornaments.
2Ki 19:28 I will put my **hook** in your nose and my bit in your mouth,
Isa 37:29 I will put my **hook** in your nose and my bit in your mouth,
Eze 19:4 trapped in their pit. They led him with **hooks** to the land of Egypt.
19:9 With **hooks** they pulled him into a cage and brought him to the
29:4 I will put **hooks** in your jaws and make the fish of your streams
38:4 put **hooks** in your jaws and bring you out with your whole army—

2627 חָטָא *ḥāṭā'*, v. [237] [→ 2628, 2629, 2630, 2631, 2632, 2633]

sinned [68], committed [23], sin [23], caused to commit [20], sins [19], purify [9], sinning [6], sinner [5], caused to sin [4], wronged [4], *untranslated* [3], purify himself [3], bear the blame [2], do wrong [2], done wrong [2], led into sin [2], purified [2], sinful [2], wrongs [2], a sin committed [+2631] [1], be purified [1], bore the loss [1], bring sin [1], cause to sin [1], cleanse [1], commit a sin [1], commit [1], commits sin [1], committed [+2628] [1], committed a sin [+2631] [1], crime committed [1], failed to do [1], fails to find [1], fails to reach [1], fault [1], find missing [1], forfeiting [1], forfeits [1], lead into sin [1], make out to be guilty [1], make sin [1], miss the way [1], miss [1], offended [1], offered for a sin offering [1], offers [1], presented for a sin offering [1], purified themselves [1], purify yourselves [1], purifying [1], retreat [1], sin offerings [1], sinned greatly [+2628] [1], sinner's [1], wicked [1]

Ge 20: 6 [A] and so I have kept you from **sinning** against me.
20: 9 [A] How *have I* **wronged** you that you have brought such great
31:39 [D] you animals torn by wild beasts; I **bore the loss** myself.
39: 9 [A] then could I do such a wicked thing and **sin** against God?"
40: 1 [A] and the baker of the king of Egypt **offended** their master,
42:22 [A] Reuben replied, "Didn't I tell you not *to* **sin** against the boy?
43: 9 [A] before you, *I will* **bear the blame** before you all my life.
44:32 [A] *I will* **bear the blame** before you, my father, all my life!'
Ex 5:16 [A] are being beaten, but *the* **fault** *is with* your own people."
9:27 [A] and Aaron. "This time *I have* **sinned**," he said to them.
9:34 [A] the rain and hail and thunder had stopped, *he* **sinned** again:
10:16 [A] "*I have* **sinned** against the LORD your God and against
20:20 [A] the fear of God will be with you to keep *you* from **sinning**."
23:33 [G] live in your land, or *they will* **cause** you **to sin** against me,
29:36 [D] **Purify** the altar by making atonement for it, and anoint it to
32:30 [A] to the people, "You *have* **committed** a great **sin** [+2631].
32:31 [A] "Oh, what a great **sin** [+2631] these people *have* **committed**!
32:33 [A] "Whoever *has* **sinned** against me I will blot out of my book.
Lev 4: 2 [A] 'When anyone **sins** unintentionally and does what is
4: 3 [A] " 'If the anointed priest **sins**, bringing guilt on the people, he
4: 3 [A] defect as a sin offering for the sin *he has* **committed**.
4:14 [A] When they become aware of the sin *they* **committed**, the
4:22 [A] " 'When a leader **sins** unintentionally and does what is
4:23 [A] When he is made aware of the sin *he* **committed**, he must
4:27 [A] " 'If a member of the community **sins** unintentionally and
4:28 [A] When he is made aware of the sin *he* **committed**, he must
4:28 [A] he must bring as his offering for the sin *he* **committed** a
4:35 [A] will make atonement for him for the sin *he has* **committed**,
5: 1 [A] " 'If a person **sins** because he does not speak up when he
5: 5 [A] of these ways, he must confess in what way *he has* **sinned**
5: 6 [A] and, as a penalty for the sin *he has* **committed**, he must
5: 7 [A] or two young pigeons to the LORD as a penalty for his **sin**—
5:10 [A] and make atonement for him for the sin *he has* **committed**,
5:11 [A] he is to bring as an offering for his **sin** a tenth of an ephah of
5:13 [A] atonement for him for any of these sins *he has* **committed**,
5:15 [A] **sins** unintentionally in regard to any of the LORD's holy
5:16 [A] He must make restitution for what *he has* **failed to do** in
5:17 [A] "If a person **sins** and does what is forbidden in any of the
6: 2 [5:21] [A] "If anyone **sins** and is unfaithful to the LORD by
6: 3 [5:22] [A] or if he **commits** any such **sin** that people may do—
6: 4 [5:23] [A] when *he* thus **sins** and becomes guilty, he must return
6:26 [6:19] [D] The priest who **offers** it shall eat it; it is to be eaten in
8:15 [D] with his finger he put it on all the horns of the altar *to* **purify**
9:15 [D] and **offered** it **for a sin offering** as he did with the first one.
14:49 [D] To **purify** the house he is to take two birds and some cedar
14:52 [D] *He shall* **purify** the house with the bird's blood, the fresh
19:22 [A] for him before the LORD for the sin *he has* **committed**,
19:22 [A] sin he has committed, and his sin **[RPH]** will be forgiven.
Nu 6:11 [A] because *he* **sinned** by being in the presence of the dead body.
8:21 [F] The Levites **purified themselves** and washed their clothes.
12:11 [A] not hold against us the sin *we have* so foolishly **committed**.
14:40 [A] "We *have* **sinned**," they said. "We will go up to the place the
15:27 [A] " 'But if just one person **sins** unintentionally, he must bring a
16:22 [A] be angry with the entire assembly when only one man **sins**?"
19:12 [F] He *must* **purify** himself with the water on the third day
19:12 [F] if *he does* not **purify himself** on the third and seventh days,
19:13 [F] and fails *to* **purify himself** defiles the LORD's tabernacle.
19:19 [D] seventh days, and on the seventh day *he is to* **purify** him.
19:20 [F] if a person who is unclean *does* not **purify himself**, he must
21: 7 [A] "*We* **sinned** when we spoke against the LORD and against
22:34 [A] Balaam said to the angel of the LORD, "*I have* **sinned**. I
31:19 [F] On the third and seventh days you *must* **purify yourselves**
31:20 [F] **Purify** every garment as well as everything made of leather,
31:23 [F] But *it must* also **be purified** with the water of cleansing.
32:23 [A] if you fail to do this, *you will be* **sinning** against the LORD;
Dt 1:41 [A] you replied, "*We have* **sinned** against the LORD. We will
9:16 [A] I saw that *you had* **sinned** against the LORD your God;
9:18 [A] drank no water, because of all the sin *you had* **committed**,
19:15 [A] of any crime or offense *he may have* **committed** [+2628].
20:18 [A] their gods, and *you will* **sin** against the LORD your God.
24: 4 [G] *Do* not **bring sin** *upon* the land the LORD your God is
Jos 7:11 [A] Israel *has* **sinned**; they have violated my covenant, which I
7:20 [A] is true! I *have* **sinned** against the LORD, the God of Israel.
Jdg 10:10 [A] "*We have* **sinned** against you, forsaking our God
10:15 [A] the Israelites said to the LORD, "*We have* **sinned**. Do with
11:27 [A] I *have* not **wronged** you, but you are doing me wrong by
20:16 [G] each of whom could sling a stone at a hair and not **miss**.
1Sa 2:25 [A] If a man **sins** against another man, God may mediate for him;
2:25 [A] if a man **sins** against the LORD, who will intercede for
7: 6 [A] there they confessed, "*We have* **sinned** against the LORD."
12:10 [A] They cried out to the LORD and said, '*We have* **sinned**;
12:23 [A] far be it from me that I *should* **sin** against the LORD by
14:33 [A] the men *are* **sinning** against the LORD by eating meat that
14:34 [A] *Do* not **sin** against the LORD by eating meat with blood still
15:24 [A] Saul said to Samuel, "*I have* **sinned**. I violated the LORD's
15:30 [A] Saul replied, "*I have* **sinned**. But please honor me before the
19: 4 [A] said to him, "*Let* not the king **do wrong** to his servant David;
19: 4 [A] *he has* not **wronged** you, and what he has done has benefited
19: 5 [A] *would you* **do wrong** to an innocent man like David by
24:11 [24:12] [A] *I have* not **wronged** you, but you are hunting me
26:21 [A] Then Saul said, "*I have* **sinned**. Come back, David my son.
2Sa 12:13 [A] David said to Nathan, "*I have* **sinned** against the LORD."
19:20 [19:21] [A] For I your servant know that I *have* **sinned**,
24:10 [A] to the LORD, "*I have* **sinned** greatly in what I have done.
24:17 [A] the LORD, "I *am the one who has* **sinned** and done wrong.
1Ki 8:31 [A] "When a man **wrongs** his neighbor and is required to take an
8:33 [A] defeated by an enemy because *they have* **sinned** against you,
8:35 [A] is no rain because your people *have* **sinned** against you,
8:46 [A] "When *they* **sin** against you—for there is no one who does
8:46 [A] they sin against you—for there is no one who *does* not **sin**—
8:47 [A] in the land of their conquerors and say, '*We have* **sinned**,
8:50 [A] forgive your people, who *have* **sinned** against you; forgive
14:16 [A] give Israel up because of the sins Jeroboam *has* **committed**
14:16 [G] Jeroboam has committed and *has* **caused** Israel **to commit**."
14:22 [A] By the sins *they* **committed** they stirred up his jealous anger
15:26 [G] and in his sin, which *he had* **caused** Israel **to commit**.
15:30 [A] because of the sins Jeroboam *had* **committed** and had caused
15:30 [G] Jeroboam had committed and *had* **caused** Israel **to commit**,
15:34 [G] and in his sin, which *he had* **caused** Israel **to commit**.
16: 2 [G] in the ways of Jeroboam and **caused** my people Israel **to sin**
16:13 [A] of all the sins Baasha and his son Elah *had* **committed**
16:13 [G] son Elah had committed and *had* **caused** Israel **to commit**,
16:19 [A] because of the sins *he had* **committed**, doing evil in the eyes
16:19 [G] the sin he had committed and *had* **caused** Israel **to commit**.
16:26 [G] and in his sin, which *he had* **caused** Israel **to commit**,
18: 9 [A] "What *have I* **done wrong**," asked Obadiah, "that you are
21:22 [G] have provoked me to anger and *have* **caused** Israel **to sin**.'
22:52 [22:53] [G] of Jeroboam son of Nebat, who **caused** Israel **to sin**.
2Ki 3: 3 [G] son of Nebat, which *he had* **caused** Israel **to commit**;
10:29 [G] son of Nebat, which *he had* **caused** Israel **to commit**—
10:31 [G] sins of Jeroboam, which *he had* **caused** Israel **to commit**.
13: 2 [G] which *he had* **caused** Israel **to commit**, and he did not turn
13: 6 [G] house of Jeroboam, which *he had* **caused** Israel **to commit**;
13:11 [G] son of Nebat, which *he had* **caused** Israel **to commit**.
14:24 [G] son of Nebat, which *he had* **caused** Israel **to commit**.
15: 9 [G] son of Nebat, which *he had* **caused** Israel **to commit**.
15:18 [G] son of Nebat, which *he had* **caused** Israel **to commit**.
15:24 [G] son of Nebat, which *he had* **caused** Israel **to commit**.
15:28 [G] son of Nebat, which *he had* **caused** Israel **to commit**.
17: 7 [A] because the Israelites *had* **sinned** against the LORD their
17:21 [G] the LORD and **caused** them **to commit** a great sin.
18:14 [A] "*I have* **done wrong**. Withdraw from me, and I will pay
21:11 [G] who preceded him and *has* **led** Judah **into sin** with his idols.
21:16 [G] besides the sin that *he had* **caused** Judah **to commit**, so that
21:17 [A] and all he did, including the sin *he* **committed**,
23:15 [G] by Jeroboam son of Nebat, who *had* **caused** Israel **to sin**—
1Ch 21: 8 [A] David said to God, "*I have* **sinned** greatly by doing this.
21:17 [A] I am the one who *has* **sinned** and done wrong. These are
2Ch 6:22 [A] "When a man **wrongs** his neighbor and is required to take an
6:24 [A] because *they have* **sinned** against you and when they turn
6:26 [A] is no rain because your people *have* **sinned** against you,
6:36 [A] "When *they* **sin** against you—for there is no one who does
6:36 [A] they sin against you—for there is no one who *does* not **sin**—
6:37 [A] you in the land of their captivity and say, '*We have* **sinned**,
6:39 [A] And forgive your people, who *have* **sinned** against you.
29:24 [D] **presented** their blood on the altar **for a sin offering** to atone
Ne 1: 6 [A] including myself and my father's house, *have* **committed**
1: 6 [A] and my father's house, have committed against you. **[RPH]**
6:13 [A] to intimidate me so that *I would* **commit a sin** by doing this,
9:29 [A] *They* **sinned** against your ordinances, by which a man will
13:26 [A] of marriages like these that Solomon king of Israel **sinned**?
13:26 [G] all Israel, but even he *was* **led into sin** *by* foreign women.
Job 1: 5 [A] "Perhaps my children *have* **sinned** and cursed God in their
1:22 [A] In all this, Job *did* not **sin** by charging God with wrongdoing.
2:10 [A] and not trouble?" In all this, Job *did* not **sin** in what he said.
5:24 [A] will take stock of your property and **find** nothing **missing**.
7:20 [A] If *I have* **sinned**, what have I done to you, O watcher of
8: 4 [A] When your children **sinned** against him, he gave them over
10:14 [A] If *I* **sinned**, you would be watching me and would not let my
24:19 [A] so the grave snatches away *those who have* **sinned**.
31:30 [A] I have not allowed my mouth to **sin** by invoking a curse
33:27 [A] he comes to men and says, '*I* **sinned**, and perverted what was

Job 35: 6 [A] If *you* **sin**, how does that affect him? If your sins are many,
41:25 [41:17] [F] are terrified; *they* **retreat** before his thrashing.
Ps 4: 4 [4:5] [A] In your anger *do* not **sin**; when you are on your beds,
39: 1 [39:2] [A] "I will watch my ways and keep my tongue from **sin**;
41: 4 [41:5] [A] on me; heal me, for *I have* **sinned** against you."
51: 4 [51:6] [A] *have I* **sinned** and done what is evil in your sight,
51: 7 [51:9] [D] **Cleanse** me with hyssop, and I will be clean;
78:17 [A] they continued to **sin** against him, rebelling in the desert
78:32 [A] In spite of all this, *they* kept on **sinning**; in spite of his
106: 6 [A] *We have* **sinned**, even as our fathers did; we have done
119:11 [A] I have hidden your word in my heart that *I might* not **sin**
Pr 8:36 [A] *whoever* **fails to find** me harms himself; all who hate me
11:31 [A] due on earth, how much more the ungodly and the **sinner**!
13:22 [A] but a **sinner's** wealth is stored up for the righteous.
14:21 [A] He who despises his neighbor **sins**, but blessed is he who is
19: 2 [A] zeal without knowledge, nor to be hasty and **miss the way**.
20: 2 [A] is like the roar of a lion; he who angers him **forfeits** his life.
Ecc 2:26 [A] to the **sinner** he gives the task of gathering and storing up
5: 6 [5:5] [G] Do not let your mouth **lead** you **into sin**. And do not
7:20 [A] man on earth who does what is right and never **sins**.
7:26 [A] pleases God will escape her, but the **sinner** she will ensnare.
8:12 [A] Although a **wicked** *man* commits a hundred crimes and still
9: 2 [A] As it is with the good man, so with the **sinner**; as it is with
9:18 [A] than weapons of war, but one **sinner** destroys much good.
Isa 1: 4 [A] Ah, **sinful** nation, a people loaded with guilt, a brood of
29:21 [G] *those who* with a word **make** a man **out to be guilty**, who
42:24 [A] Was it not the LORD, against whom *we have* **sinned**?
43:27 [A] Your first father **sinned**; your spokesmen rebelled against
64: 5 [64:4] [A] when *we* continued *to* **sin** against them, you were
65:20 [A] he *who* **fails to reach** a hundred will be considered accursed.
Jer 2:35 [A] pass judgment on you because you say, '*I have* not **sinned**.'
3:25 [A] *We have* **sinned** against the LORD our God, both we
8:14 [A] water to drink, because *we have* **sinned** against him.
14: 7 [A] For our backsliding is great; *we have* **sinned** against you.
14:20 [A] the guilt of our fathers; *we have* indeed **sinned** against you.
16:10 [A] What sin *have* we **committed** against the LORD our God?'
32:35 [G] should do such a detestable thing and so **make** Judah **sin**.
33: 8 [A] I will cleanse them from all the sin *they have* **committed**
33: 8 [A] and will forgive all their sins **[RPH]** of rebellion against me.
37:18 [A] "What **crime** *have I* **committed** against you or your officials
40: 3 [A] because *you people* **sinned** against the LORD
44:23 [A] *have* **sinned** against the LORD and have not obeyed him
50: 7 [A] for *they* **sinned** against the LORD, their true pasture,
50:14 [A] Spare no arrows, for *she has* **sinned** against the LORD.
La 1: 8 [A] Jerusalem *has* **sinned** [+2628] **greatly** and so has become
5: 7 [A] Our fathers **sinned** and are no more, and we bear their
5:16 [A] has fallen from our head. Woe to us, for *we have* **sinned**!
Eze 3:21 [A] if you do warn the righteous man not to **sin** and he does not
3:21 [A] you do warn the righteous man not to sin and he *does* not **sin**,
14:13 [A] if a country **sins** against me by being unfaithful and I stretch
16:51 [A] Samaria *did* not **commit** half the sins you did. You have
18: 4 [A] belong to me. The soul who **sins** is the one who will die.
18:20 [A] The soul who **sins** is the one who will die. The son will not
18:24 [A] he is guilty of and because of the sins *he has* **committed**,
28:16 [A] trade you were filled with violence, and *you* **sinned**.
33:12 [A] The righteous man, if he **sins**, will not be allowed to live
33:16 [A] None of the sins *he has* **committed** will be remembered
37:23 [A] for I will save them from all their **sinful** backsliding, and I
43:20 [D] the rim, and so **purify** the altar and make atonement for it.
43:22 [D] and the altar *is to be* **purified** as it was purified with the bull.
43:22 [D] and the altar is to be purified as *it was* **purified** with the bull.
43:23 [D] When you have finished **purifying** it, you are to offer a
45:18 [D] to take a young bull without defect and **purify** the sanctuary.
Da 9: 5 [A] *we have* **sinned** and done wrong. We have been wicked and
9: 8 [A] are covered with shame because *we have* **sinned** against you.
9:11 [A] been poured out on us, because *we have* **sinned** against you.
9:15 [A] endures to this day, *we have* **sinned**, we have done wrong.
Hos 4: 7 [A] more the priests increased, the more *they* **sinned** against me;
8:11 [A] "Though Ephraim built many altars for **sin offerings**,
8:11 [A] altars for sin offerings, these have become altars for **sinning**.
10: 9 [A] "Since the days of Gibeah, *you have* **sinned**, O Israel,
13: 2 [A] Now *they* **sin** more and more; they make idols for
Mic 7: 9 [A] Because *I have* **sinned** against him, I will bear the LORD's
Hab 2:10 [A] shaming your own house and **forfeiting** your life.
Zep 1:17 [A] blind men, because *they have* **sinned** against the LORD.

2628 חֵטְא *ḥēṭ'*, n.m. [33] [√ 2627; Ar 10259]

sins [8], sin [5], guilty of sin [3], consequences of sin [2], guilty [2], held responsible [+5951] [2], sinful [2], become guilty [+5951+6584] [1], committed [+2627] [1], consequences of sins [1], errors [1], guilt [1], guilty [+5951] [1], punished for sins [1], shortcomings [1], sinned greatly [+2627] [1]

Ge 41: 9 said to Pharaoh, "Today I am reminded of my **shortcomings**.
Lev 19:17 Rebuke your neighbor frankly so you will not share in his **guilt**.
20:20 They *will be* **held responsible** [+5951]; they will die childless.
22: 9 so that they *do* not **become guilty** [+5951+6584] and die for
24:15 'If anyone curses his God, he *will be* **held responsible** [+5951];
Nu 9:13 appointed time. That man will bear the **consequences of** his **sin**.
18:22 or they will bear the **consequences of** their **sin** and will die.
18:32 By presenting the best part of it *you will* not *be* **guilty** [+5951] in
27: 3 against the LORD, but he died for his own **sin** and left no sons.
Dt 15: 9 to the LORD against you, and you will be found **guilty of sin**.
19:15 accused of any crime or offense *he may have* **committed** [+2627].
21:22 If a man **guilty** *of* a capital offense is put to death and his body is
22:26 Do nothing to the girl; she has committed no **sin** *deserving* death.
23:21 [23:22] certainly demand it of you and you will be **guilty of sin**.
23:22 [23:23] if you refrain from making a vow, you will not be **guilty**.
24:15 may cry to the LORD against you, and you will be **guilty of sin**.
24:16 children put to death for their fathers; each is to die for his own **sin**.
2Ki 10:29 he did not turn away from the **sins** *of* Jeroboam son of Nebat,
14: 6 put to death for their fathers; each is to die for his own **sins**."
2Ch 25: 4 put to death for their fathers; each is to die for his own **sins**."
Ps 51: 5 [51:7] at birth, **sinful** from the time my mother conceived me.
51: 9 [51:11] Hide your face from my **sins** and blot out all my iniquity.
103:10 he does not treat us as our **sins** deserve or repay us according to
Ecc 10: 4 do not leave your post; calmness can lay great **errors** to rest.
Isa 1:18 "Though your **sins** are like scarlet, they shall be as white as snow;
31: 7 reject the idols of silver and gold your **sinful** hands have made.
38:17 the pit of destruction; you have put all my **sins** behind your back.
53:12 For he bore the **sin** *of* many, and made intercession for the
La 1: 8 Jerusalem *has* **sinned greatly** [+2627] and so has become unclean.
3:39 Why should any living man complain when **punished for** his **sins**?
Eze 23:49 your lewdness and bear the **consequences of** your **sins** *of* idolatry.
Da 9:16 Our **sins** and the iniquities of our fathers have made Jerusalem
Hos 12: 8 [12:9] all my wealth they will not find in me any iniquity or **sin**."

2629 חַטָּא *ḥaṭṭā'*, a. & n.m. [19] [√ 2627]

sinners [13], criminals [1], sinful [1], sinned [1], sinner [1], sinning [1], wicked people [1]

Ge 13:13 Sodom were wicked and were **sinning** greatly against the LORD.
Nu 16:38 [17:3] the censers of the men who **sinned** at the cost of their lives.
32:14 "And here you are, a brood of **sinners**, standing in the place of
1Sa 15:18 saying, 'Go and completely destroy those **wicked people**,
1Ki 1:21 his fathers, I and my son Solomon will be treated as **criminals**."
Ps 1: 1 or stand in the way of **sinners** or sit in the seat of mockers.
1: 5 stand in the judgment, nor **sinners** in the assembly of the righteous.
25: 8 upright is the LORD; therefore he instructs **sinners** in his ways.
26: 9 Do not take away my soul along with **sinners**, my life with
51:13 [51:15] your ways, and **sinners** will turn back to you.
104:35 But may **sinners** vanish from the earth and the wicked be no more.
Pr 1:10 My son, if **sinners** entice you, do not give in to them.
13:21 Misfortune pursues the **sinner**, but prosperity is the reward of the
23:17 Do not let your heart envy **sinners**, but always be zealous for the
Isa 1:28 rebels and **sinners** will both be broken, and those who forsake the
13: 9 to make the land desolate and destroy the **sinners** within it.
33:14 The **sinners** in Zion are terrified; trembling grips the godless:
Am 9: 8 "Surely the eyes of the Sovereign LORD are on the **sinful**
9:10 All the **sinners** *among* my people will die by the sword, all those

2630 חֶטְאָה *ḥeṭ'â*, n.[f.]. [1] [√ 2627]

sinning [1]

Nu 15:28 the LORD for the one who erred by **sinning** unintentionally,

2631 חֲטָאָה *ḥ^a^ṭā'â*, n.f. [8] [√ 2627]

sin [2], a sin committed [+2627] [1], committed a sin [+2627] [1], condemn [+2118+4200] [1], guilt [1], sin offerings [1], sins [1]

Ge 20: 9 How have I wronged you that you have brought such great **guilt**
Ex 32:21 did these people do to you, that you led them into such great **sin**?"
32:30 said to the people, "You *have* **committed a** great **sin** [+2627].
32:31 "Oh, what a great **sin** these people *have* **committed** [+2627]!
2Ki 17:21 from following the LORD and caused them to commit a great **sin**.
Ps 32: 1 is he whose transgressions are forgiven, whose **sins** are covered.
40: 6 [40:7] burnt offerings and **sin offerings** you did not require.
109: 7 be found guilty, and *may* his prayers **condemn** [+2118+4200] him.

2632 חַטָּאָה *ḥaṭṭā'â*, n.f. [2] [√ 2627]

sin [1], wickedness [1]

Ex 34: 7 love to thousands, and forgiving wickedness, rebellion and **sin**.
Ezr 6:17 [as a **sin offering** [Q; see K 10260] for all Israel,]
Isa 5:18 sin along with cords of deceit, and **wickedness** as with cart ropes,

2633 חַטָּאת *ḥaṭṭā't*, n.f. [293] [√ 2627; Ar 10258, 10260]
sin offering [105], sin [85], sins [74], sin offerings [8], *untranslated* [3], punishment [3], cleansing [1], iniquities [1], it[s] [+2021] [1], its[s] [+2021] [1], offense [1], purification from sin [1], purification offering [1], sinful thing [1], sinner [1], sinning [1], that[s] [1], wickedness [1], wronged [1], wrongs [+6913] [1], wrongs [1]

Ge 4: 7 But if you do not do what is right, **sin** is crouching at your door;
18:20 against Sodom and Gomorrah is so great and their **sin** so grievous
31:36 "What **sin** *have* I *committed* that you hunt me down?
50:17 the sins and the **wrongs** they committed in treating you so badly.'
Ex 10:17 Now forgive my **sin** once more and pray to the LORD your God
29:14 and its hide and its offal outside the camp. It is a **sin offering**.
29:36 Sacrifice a bull each day as a **sin offering** to make atonement.
30:10 the blood of the atoning **sin offering** for the generations to come.
32:30 go up to the LORD; perhaps I can make atonement for your **sin**."
32:32 now, please forgive their **sin**—but if not, then blot me out of the
32:34 the time comes for me to punish, I will punish them for their **sin**."
34: 9 forgive our wickedness and our **sin**, and take us as your
Lev 4: 3 bull without defect as a **sin offering** for the sin he has committed.
4: 3 bull without defect as a sin offering for the **sin** he has committed.
4: 8 He shall remove all the fat from the bull of the **sin offering**—
4:14 When they become aware of the **sin** they committed, the assembly
4:14 the assembly must bring a young bull as a **sin offering** and present
4:20 do with this bull just as he did with the bull for the **sin offering**.
4:21 he burned the first bull. This is the **sin offering** *for* the community.
4:23 When he is made aware of the **sin** he committed, he must bring as
4:24 offering is slaughtered before the LORD. It is a **sin offering**.
4:25 the priest shall take some of the blood of the **sin offering** with his
4:26 In this way the priest will make atonement for the man's **sin**,
4:28 When he is made aware of the **sin** he committed, he must bring as
4:28 he must bring as his offering for the **sin** he committed a female
4:29 He is to lay his hand on the head of the **sin offering** and slaughter
4:29 and slaughter **it**[s] [+2021] at the place of the burnt offering.
4:32 " 'If he brings a lamb as his **sin** offering, he is to bring a female
4:33 He is to lay his hand on **its**[s] [+2021] head and slaughter it for a sin
4:33 slaughter it for a **sin offering** at the place where the burnt offering
4:34 the priest shall take some of the blood of the **sin offering** with his
4:35 In this way the priest will make atonement for him for the **sin** he
5: 6 and, as a penalty for the **sin** he has committed, he must bring to the
5: 6 the LORD a female lamb or goat from the flock as a **sin offering**;
5: 6 and the priest shall make atonement for him for his **sin**.
5: 7 his sin—one for a **sin offering** and the other for a burnt offering.
5: 8 them to the priest, who shall first offer the one for the **sin offering**.
5: 9 is to sprinkle some of the blood of the **sin offering** against the side
5: 9 must be drained out at the base of the altar. It is a **sin offering**.
5:10 and make atonement for him for the **sin** he has committed,
5:11 for his sin a tenth of an ephah of fine flour for a **sin offering**.
5:11 He must not put oil or incense on it, because it is a **sin offering**.
5:12 of the offerings made to the LORD by fire. It is a **sin offering**.
5:13 make atonement for him for any of these **sins** he has committed,
6:17 [6:10] Like the **sin offering** and the guilt offering, it is most holy.
6:25 [6:18] and his sons: 'These are the regulations for the **sin offering**:
6:25 [6:18] The **sin offering** is to be slaughtered before the LORD in
6:30 [6:23] any **sin offering** whose blood is brought into the Tent of
7: 7 " 'The same law applies to both the **sin offering** and the guilt
7:37 the grain offering, the **sin offering**, the guilt offering, the
8: 2 the bull for the **sin offering**, the two rams and the basket
8:14 He then presented the bull for the **sin offering**, and Aaron
8:14 and Aaron and his sons laid their hands on its head. **[RPH]**
9: 2 "Take a bull calf for your **sin offering** and a ram for your burnt
9: 3 'Take a male goat for a **sin offering**, a calf and a lamb—both a year
9: 7 "Come to the altar and sacrifice your **sin offering** and your burnt
9: 8 to the altar and slaughtered the calf as a **sin offering** for himself.
9:10 the kidneys and the covering of the liver from the **sin offering**,
9:15 He took the goat for the people's **sin offering** and slaughtered it
9:22 having sacrificed the **sin offering**, the burnt offering
10:16 When Moses inquired about the goat of the **sin offering** and found
10:17 "Why didn't you eat the **sin offering** in the sanctuary area?
10:19 "Today they sacrificed their **sin offering** and their burnt offering
10:19 the LORD have been pleased if I had eaten the **sin offering**
12: 6 a burnt offering and a young pigeon or a dove for a **sin offering**.
12: 8 one for a burnt offering and the other for a **sin offering**.
14:13 He is to slaughter the lamb in the holy place where the **sin offering**
14:13 Like the **sin offering**, the guilt offering belongs to the priest;
14:19 "Then the priest is to sacrifice the **sin offering** and make
14:22 can afford, one for a **sin offering** and the other for a burnt offering.
14:31 one as a **sin offering** and the other as a burnt offering,
15:15 the one for a **sin offering** and the other for a burnt offering.
15:30 The priest is to sacrifice one for a **sin offering** and the other for a
16: 3 with a young bull for a **sin offering** and a ram for a burnt offering.
16: 5 Israelite community he is to take two male goats for a **sin offering**
16: 6 "Aaron is to offer the bull for his own **sin offering** to make
16: 9 whose lot falls to the LORD and sacrifice it for a **sin offering**.
16:11 "Aaron shall bring the bull for his own **sin offering** to make
16:11 and he is to slaughter the bull for his own **sin offering**.
16:15 "He shall then slaughter the goat for the **sin offering** for the people
16:16 and rebellion of the Israelites, whatever their **sins** have been.
16:21 it all the wickedness and rebellion of the Israelites—all their **sins**—
16:25 He shall also burn the fat of the **sin offering** on the altar.
16:27 The bull and the goat for the **sin offerings**, whose blood was
16:27 **[RPH]** whose blood was brought into the Most Holy Place to
16:30 Then, before the LORD, you will be clean from all your **sins**.
16:34 Atonement is to be made once a year for all the **sins** *of* the
19:22 for him before the LORD for the **sin** he has committed,
19:22 LORD for the sin he has committed, and his **sin** will be forgiven.
23:19 Then sacrifice one male goat for a **sin offering** and two lambs,
26:18 not listen to me, I will punish you for your **sins** seven times over.
26:21 multiply your afflictions seven times over, as your **sins** deserve.
26:24 toward you and will afflict you for your **sins** seven times over.
26:28 and I myself will punish you for your **sins** seven times over.
Nu 5: 6 'When a man or woman **wrongs** [+6913] another in any way and
5: 7 must confess the **sin** he has committed. He must make full
6:11 The priest is to offer one as a **sin offering** and the other as a burnt
6:14 a year-old ewe lamb without defect for a **sin offering**, a ram
6:16 the LORD and make the **sin offering** and the burnt offering.
7:16 one male goat for a **sin offering**;
7:22 one male goat for a **sin offering**;
7:28 one male goat for a **sin offering**;
7:34 one male goat for a **sin offering**;
7:40 one male goat for a **sin offering**;
7:46 one male goat for a **sin offering**;
7:52 one male goat for a **sin offering**;
7:58 one male goat for a **sin offering**;
7:64 one male goat for a **sin offering**;
7:70 one male goat for a **sin offering**;
7:76 one male goat for a **sin offering**;
7:82 one male goat for a **sin offering**;
7:87 grain offering. Twelve male goats were used for the **sin offering**.
8: 7 Sprinkle the water of **cleansing** on them; then have them shave
8: 8 then you are to take a second young bull for a **sin offering**.
8:12 use the one for a **sin offering** to the LORD and the other for a
12:11 do not hold against us the **sin** we have so foolishly committed.
15:24 and drink offering, and a male goat for a **sin offering**.
15:25 for their wrong an offering made by fire and a **sin offering**.
15:27 he must bring a year-old female goat for a **sin offering**.
16:26 to them, or you will be swept away because of all their **sins**."
18: 9 whether grain or **sin** or guilt offerings, that part belongs to you
19: 9 for use in the water of cleansing; it is for **purification from sin**.
19:17 put some ashes from the burned **purification offering** into a jar
28:15 one male goat is to be presented to the LORD as a **sin offering**.
28:22 Include one male goat as a **sin offering** to make atonement for you.
29: 5 Include one male goat as a **sin offering** to make atonement for you.
29:11 Include one male goat as a **sin offering**, in addition to the sin
29:11 in addition to the **sin offering** *for* atonement and the regular burnt
29:16 Include one male goat as a **sin offering**, in addition to the regular
29:19 Include one male goat as a **sin offering**, in addition to the regular
29:22 Include one male goat as a **sin offering**, in addition to the regular
29:25 Include one male goat as a **sin offering**, in addition to the regular
29:28 Include one male goat as a **sin offering**, in addition to the regular
29:31 Include one male goat as a **sin offering**, in addition to the regular
29:34 Include one male goat as a **sin offering**, in addition to the regular
29:38 Include one male goat as a **sin offering**, in addition to the regular
32:23 the LORD; and you may be sure that your **sin** will find you out.
Dt 9:18 and drank no water, because of all the **sin** you had committed,
9:21 Also I took that **sinful thing** *of* yours, the calf you had made,
9:27 the stubbornness of this people, their wickedness and their **sin**.
19:15 a man accused of any crime or **offense** he may have committed.
Jos 24:19 is a jealous God. He will not forgive your rebellion and your **sins**.
1Sa 2:17 This **sin** *of* the young men was very great in the LORD's sight,
12:19 for we have added to all our other **sins** the evil of asking for a
14:38 of the army, and let us find out what **sin** has been committed today.
15:23 For rebellion is like the **sin** *of* divination, and arrogance like the
15:25 Now I beg you, forgive my **sin** and come back with me, so that I
20: 1 How have I **wronged** your father, that he is trying to take my life?"
2Sa 12:13 Nathan replied, "The LORD has taken away your **sin**. You are not
1Ki 8:34 then hear from heaven and forgive the **sin** *of* your people Israel
8:35 confess your name and turn from their **sin** because you have
8:36 then hear from heaven and forgive the **sin** *of* your servants,
12:30 this thing became a **sin**; the people went even as far as Dan to
13:34 This was the **sin** *of* the house of Jeroboam that led to its downfall
14:16 he will give Israel up because of the **sins** Jeroboam has committed
14:22 By the **sins** they committed they stirred up his jealous anger more
15: 3 He committed all the **sins** his father had done before him;
15:26 of the LORD, walking in the ways of his father and in his **sin**,
15:30 because of the **sins** Jeroboam had committed and had caused Israel
15:34 of the LORD, walking in the ways of Jeroboam and in his **sin**,
16: 2 my people Israel to sin and to provoke me to anger by their **sins**.

1Ki 16:13 because of all the **sins** Baasha and his son Elah had committed
16:13 of all the sins Baasha and **[RPH]** his son Elah had committed
16:19 because of the **sins** he had committed, doing evil in the eyes of the
16:19 and in the **sin** he had committed and had caused Israel to commit.
16:26 He walked in all the ways of Jeroboam son of Nebat and in his **sin**,
16:31 He not only considered it trivial to commit the **sins** *of* Jeroboam
2Ki 3:3 Nevertheless he clung to the **sins** *of* Jeroboam son of Nebat,
10:31 He did not turn away from the **sins** *of* Jeroboam, which he had
12:16 [12:17] **sin offerings** was not brought into the temple of the
13:2 He did evil in the eyes of the LORD by following the **sins** *of*
13:6 But they did not turn away from the **sins** *of* the house of Jeroboam,
13:11 did not turn away from any of the **sins** *of* Jeroboam son of Nebat,
14:24 did not turn away from any of the **sins** *of* Jeroboam son of Nebat,
15:9 He did not turn away from the **sins** *of* Jeroboam son of Nebat,
15:18 During his entire reign he did not turn away from the **sins** *of*
15:24 He did not turn away from the **sins** *of* Jeroboam son of Nebat,
15:28 He did not turn away from the **sins** *of* Jeroboam son of Nebat,
17:22 The Israelites persisted in all the **sins** *of* Jeroboam and did not turn
21:16 besides the **sin** that he had caused Judah to commit, so that they
21:17 Manasseh's reign, and all he did, including the **sin** he committed,
24:3 his presence because of the **sins** *of* Manasseh and all he had done,
2Ch 6:25 then hear from heaven and forgive the **sin** *of* your people Israel
6:26 confess your name and turn from their **sin** because you have
6:27 then hear from heaven and forgive the **sin** *of* your servants,
7:14 hear from heaven and will forgive their **sin** and will heal their land.
28:13 Do you intend to add to our **sin** and guilt? For our guilt is already
29:21 and seven male goats as a **sin offering** for the kingdom,
29:23 The goats for the **sin offering** were brought before the king
29:24 had ordered the burnt offering and the **sin offering** for all Israel.
33:19 as well as all his **sins** and unfaithfulness, and the sites where he
Ezr 8:35 male lambs and, as a **sin offering**, twelve male goats.
Ne 1:6 I confess the **sins** we Israelites, including myself and my father's
4:5 [3:37] cover up their guilt or blot out their **sins** from your sight,
9:2 They stood in their places and confessed their **sins**
9:37 Because of our **sins**, its abundant harvest goes to the kings you
10:33 [10:34] for **sin offerings** to make atonement for Israel;
Job 10:6 that you must search out my faults and probe after my **sin**—
13:23 How many wrongs and **sins** have I committed? Show me my
13:23 and sins have I committed? Show me my offense and my **sin**.
14:16 then you will count my steps but not keep track of my **sin**.
34:37 To his **sin** he adds rebellion; scornfully he claps his hands among
35:3 'What profit is it to me, and what do I gain by not **sinning**?'
Ps 25:7 Remember not the **sins** *of* my youth and my rebellious ways;
25:18 upon my affliction and my distress and take away all my **sins**.
32:5 I acknowledged my **sin** to you and did not cover up my iniquity.
32:5 to the LORD"—and you forgave the guilt of my **sin**.
38:3 [38:4] my body; my bones have no soundness because of my **sin**.
38:18 [38:19] I confess my iniquity; I am troubled by my **sin**.
51:2 [51:4] Wash away all my iniquity and cleanse me from my **sin**.
51:3 [51:5] I know my transgressions, and my **sin** is always before me.
59:3 [59:4] men conspire against me for no offense or **sin** *of* mine,
59:12 [59:13] For the **sins** *of* their mouths, for the words of their lips, let
79:9 of your name; deliver us and forgive our **sins** for your name's sake.
85:2 [85:3] the iniquity of your people and covered all their **sins**.
109:14 before the LORD; may the **sin** *of* his mother never be blotted out.
Pr 5:22 of a wicked man ensnare him; the cords of his **sin** hold him fast.
10:16 them life, but the income of the wicked brings them **punishment**.
13:6 guards the man of integrity, but wickedness overthrows the **sinner**.
14:34 Righteousness exalts a nation, but **sin** is a disgrace to any people.
20:9 can say, "I have kept my heart pure; I am clean and without **sin**"?
21:4 Haughty eyes and a proud heart, the lamp of the wicked, are **sin**!
24:9 The schemes of folly are **sin**, and men detest a mocker.
Isa 3:9 against them; they parade their **sin** like Sodom; they do not hide it.
6:7 your lips; your guilt is taken away and your **sin** atoned for."
27:9 and this will be the full fruitage of the removal of his **sin**:
30:1 forming an alliance, but not by my Spirit, heaping **sin** upon sin;
30:1 forming an alliance, but not by my Spirit, heaping sin upon **sin**;
40:2 she has received from the LORD's hand double for all her **sins**.
43:24 you have burdened me with your **sins** and wearied me with your
43:25 for my own sake, and remembers your **sins** no more.
44:22 away your offenses like a cloud, your **sins** like the morning mist.
58:1 to my people their rebellion and to the house of Jacob their **sins**.
59:2 your **sins** have hidden his face from you, so that he will not hear.
59:12 our offenses are many in your sight, and our **sins** testify against us.
Jer 5:25 have kept these away; your **sins** have deprived you of good.
14:10 now remember their wickedness and punish them for their **sins**."
15:13 without charge, because of all your **sins** throughout your country.
16:10 What **sin** have we committed against the LORD our God?'
16:18 I will repay them double for their wickedness and their **sin**,
17:1 "Judah's **sin** is engraved with an iron tool, inscribed with a flint
17:3 with your high places, because of **sin** throughout your country.
18:23 Do not forgive their crimes or blot out their **sins** from your sight.
30:14 the cruel, because your guilt is so great and your **sins** so many.
30:15 of your great guilt and many **sins** I have done these things to you.
31:34 forgive their wickedness and will remember their **sins** no more."
36:3 his wicked way; then I will forgive their wickedness and their **sin**."
50:20 there will be none, and for the **sins** *of* Judah, but none will be
La 4:6 The punishment of my people is greater than **that**[s] *of* Sodom,
4:13 it happened because of the **sins** *of* her prophets and the iniquities of
4:22 of Edom, he will punish your sin and expose your **wickedness**.
Eze 3:20 he will die. Since you did not warn him, he will die for his **sin**.
16:51 Samaria did not commit half the **sins** you did. You have done more
16:52 Because your **sins** were more vile than theirs, they appear more
18:14 "But suppose this son has a son who sees all the **sins** his father
18:21 "But if a wicked man turns away from all the **sins** he has
18:24 he is guilty of and because of the **sins** he has committed,
21:24 [21:29] open rebellion, revealing your **sins** in all that you do—
33:10 "Our offenses and **sins** weigh us down, and we are wasting away
33:14 he then turns away from his **sin** and does what is just and right—
33:16 None of the **sins** he has committed will be remembered against
40:39 burnt offerings, **sin offerings** and guilt offerings were slaughtered.
42:13 the grain offerings, the **sin offerings** and the guilt offerings—
43:19 You are to give a young bull as a **sin offering** to the priests,
43:21 You are to take the bull for the **sin offering** and burn it in the
43:22 day you are to offer a male goat without defect for a **sin offering**,
43:25 seven days you are to provide a male goat daily for a **sin offering**;
44:27 he is to offer a **sin offering** for himself, declares the Sovereign
44:29 eat the grain offerings, the **sin offerings** and the guilt offerings;
45:17 He will provide the **sin offerings**, grain offerings, burnt offerings
45:19 The priest is to take some of the blood of the **sin offering**
45:22 On that day the prince is to provide a bull as a **sin offering** for
45:23 a burnt offering to the LORD, and a male goat for a **sin offering**.
45:25 he is to make the same provision for **sin offerings**, burnt offerings,
46:20 the guilt offering and the **sin offering** and bake the grain offering,
Da 9:20 confessing my **sin** and the sin of my people Israel and making my
9:20 confessing my sin and the **sin** *of* my people Israel and making my
9:24 to put an end to **sin**, to atone for wickedness, to bring in everlasting
Hos 4:8 They feed on the **sins** *of* my people and relish their wickedness.
8:13 Now he will remember their wickedness and punish their **sins**:
9:9 will remember their wickedness and punish them for their **sins**.
10:8 high places of wickedness will be destroyed—it is the **sin** *of* Israel.
13:12 The guilt of Ephraim is stored up, his **sins** are kept on record.
Am 5:12 For I know how many are your offenses and how great your **sins**.
Mic 1:5 of Jacob's transgression, because of the **sins** *of* the house of Israel.
1:13 You were the beginning of **sin** to the Daughter of Zion,
3:8 and might, to declare to Jacob his transgression, to Israel his **sin**.
6:7 for my transgression, the fruit of my body for the **sin** *of* my soul?
6:13 I have begun to destroy you, to ruin you because of your **sins**.
7:19 sins underfoot and hurl all our **iniquities** into the depths of the sea.
Zec 13:1 inhabitants of Jerusalem, to cleanse them from **sin** and impurity.
14:19 This will be the **punishment** *of* Egypt and the punishment of all
14:19 the **punishment** *of* all the nations that do not go up to celebrate the

2634 חָטַב *ḥāṭab*, v. [9]

woodcutters [+6770] [3], cut [2], carved [1], chop [1], cut down [1], woodsmen [1]

Dt 19:5 [A] a man may go into the forest with his neighbor to **cut** wood,
29:11 [29:10] [A] the aliens living in your camps *who* **chop** your
Jos 9:21 [A] let them be **woodcutters** [+6770] and water carriers for the
9:23 [A] You will never cease to serve as **woodcutters** [+6770] and
9:27 [A] That day he made the Gibeonites **woodcutters** [+6770] and
2Ch 2:10 [2:9] [A] give your servants, the **woodsmen** who cut the timber,
Ps 144:12 [E] our daughters will be like pillars **carved** to adorn a palace.
Jer 46:22 [A] come against her with axes, like *men who* **cut down** trees.
Eze 39:10 [A] need to gather wood from the fields or **cut** it from the forests,

2635 חֲטֻבוֹת *ḥaṭubôt*, n.f.pl. [1]

colored [1]

Pr 7:16 I have covered my bed with **colored** linens from Egypt.

2636 חִטָּה *ḥiṭṭâ*, n.f. [30] [√ 2845; Ar 10272]

wheat [30]

Ge 30:14 During **wheat** harvest, Reuben went out into the fields and found
Ex 9:32 The **wheat** and spelt, however, were not destroyed, because they
29:2 from fine **wheat** flour, without yeast, make bread, and cakes mixed
34:22 "Celebrate the Feast of Weeks with the firstfruits of the **wheat**
Dt 8:8 a land with **wheat** and barley, vines and fig trees, pomegranates,
32:14 with choice rams of Bashan and the finest kernels of **wheat**.
Jdg 6:11 where his son Gideon was threshing **wheat** in a winepress to keep
15:1 Later on, at the time of **wheat** harvest, Samson took a young goat
Ru 2:23 of Boaz to glean until the barley and **wheat** harvests were finished.
1Sa 6:13 Now the people of Beth Shemesh were harvesting their **wheat** in
12:17 Is it not **wheat** harvest now? I will call upon the LORD to send
2Sa 4:6 They went into the inner part of the house as if to get *some* **wheat**,
17:28 They also brought **wheat** and barley, flour and roasted grain,

1Ki 5:11 [5:25] Solomon gave Hiram twenty thousand cors of **wheat** as
1Ch 21:20 While Araunah was threshing **wheat**, he turned and saw the angel;
21:23 sledges for the wood, and the **wheat** for the grain offering.
2Ch 2:10 [2:9] twenty thousand cors of ground **wheat**, twenty thousand
2:15 [2:14] "Now let my lord send his servants the **wheat** and barley
27:5 ten thousand cors of **wheat** and ten thousand cors of barley.
Job 31:40 let briers come up instead of **wheat** and weeds instead of barley."
Ps 81:16 [81:17] you would be fed with the finest of **wheat**; with honey
147:14 peace to your borders and satisfies you with the finest of **wheat**.
SS 7:2 [7:3] Your waist is a mound of **wheat** encircled by lilies.
Isa 28:25 Does he not plant **wheat** in its place, barley in its plot, and spelt in
Jer 12:13 They will sow **wheat** but reap thorns; they will wear themselves
41:8 We have **wheat** and barley, oil and honey, hidden in a field."
Eze 4:9 "Take **wheat** and barley, beans and lentils, millet and spelt;
27:17 they exchanged **wheat** *from* Minnith and confections, honey,
45:13 a sixth of an ephah from each homer of **wheat** and a sixth of an
Joel 1:11 grieve for the **wheat** and the barley, because the harvest of the field

2637 חַטּוּשׁ *ḥaṭṭûš*, n.pr.m. [5]

Hattush [5]

1Ch 3:22 his sons: **Hattush**, Igal, Bariah, Neariah and Shaphat—six in all.
Ezr 8:2 of Ithamar, Daniel; of the descendants of David, **Hattush**
Ne 3:10 and **Hattush** son of Hashabneiah made repairs next to him.
10:4 [10:5] **Hattush**, Shebaniah, Malluch,
12:2 Amariah, Malluch, **Hattush**,

2638 חֲטִיטָא *ḥᵃṭîṭā'*, n.pr.m. [2]

Hatita [2]

Ezr 2:42 of Shallum, Ater, Talmon, Akkub, **Hatita** and Shobai 139
Ne 7:45 of Shallum, Ater, Talmon, Akkub, **Hatita** and Shobai 138

2639 חַטִּיל *ḥaṭṭîl*, n.pr.m. [2]

Hattil [2]

Ezr 2:57 Shephatiah, **Hattil**, Pokereth-Hazzebaim and Ami
Ne 7:59 Shephatiah, **Hattil**, Pokereth-Hazzebaim and Amon

2640 חֲטִיפָא *ḥᵃṭîpā'*, n.pr.m. [2] [√ 2642]

Hatipha [2]

Ezr 2:54 Neziah and **Hatipha**
Ne 7:56 Neziah and **Hatipha**

2641 חָטַם *ḥāṭam*, v. [1] [→ 3033]

hold back [1]

Isa 48:9 [A] for the sake of my praise *I* **hold** it **back** from you, so as not

2642 חָטַף *ḥāṭap*, v. [3] [→ 2640]

catch [1], catches [1], seize [1]

Jdg 21:21 [A] and each of you **seize** a wife from the girls of Shiloh
Ps 10:9 [A] he lies in wait to **catch** the helpless; he catches the helpless
10:9 [A] *he* **catches** the helpless and drags them off in his net.

2643 חֹטֶר *ḥōṭer*, n.m. [2]

rod [1], shoot [1]

Pr 14:3 A fool's talk brings a **rod** *to* his back, but the lips of the wise
Isa 11:1 A **shoot** will come up from the stump of Jesse; from his roots a

2644 חַי *ḥay*[1], n.m. [235] [→ 2652; cf. 2649]

life [108], as surely as lives [46], as surely as live [23], live [12], lived [9], as live [6], lives [6], *untranslated* [5], as lives [3], living [3], as surely as live [+2256+2644+5883] [2], as surely as live [+5883] [2], lifetime [2], creature [1], life will not be worth living [+4200+4537] [1], life-giving [1], lifetime [+3427] [1], live [+928+2021] [1], long life [+2021+4200] [1], nourish [1], old [+3427+9102] [1]

Ge 2:7 dust of the ground and breathed into his nostrils the breath of **life**,
2:9 In the middle of the garden were the tree of **life** and the tree of the
3:14 crawl on your belly and you will eat dust all the days of your **life**.
3:17 through painful toil you will eat of it all the days of your **life**.
3:22 to reach out his hand and take also from the tree of **life** and eat,
3:24 sword flashing back and forth to guard the way to the tree of **life**.
6:17 under the heavens, every creature that has the breath of **life** in it.
6:19 You are to bring into the ark two of all **living** creatures, male
7:11 In the six hundredth year of Noah's **life**, on the seventeenth day of
7:15 Pairs of all creatures that have the breath of **life** in them came to
7:22 Everything on dry land that had the breath of **life** in its nostrils
23:1 Sarah **lived** to be a hundred and twenty-seven years old.
23:1 Sarah lived to be a hundred and twenty-seven years old. **[RPH]**
25:7 **[RPH]** Abraham lived a hundred and seventy-five years.
25:17 Altogether, Ishmael **lived** a hundred and thirty-seven years.
27:46 "I'm disgusted with **living** because of these Hittite women.
27:46 like these, my **life** [+4200+4537] **will not be worth living**."
42:15 **As surely as** Pharaoh **lives**, you will not leave this place unless
42:16 If you are not, then **as surely as** Pharaoh **lives**, you are spies!"
47:8 Pharaoh asked him, "How **old** [+3427+9102] are you?"
47:9 My years **[RPH]** have been few and difficult, and they do not
47:9 they do not equal the years of **[RPH]** the pilgrimage of my
47:28 and the years of his **life** were a hundred and forty-seven.
Ex 1:14 They made their **lives** bitter with hard labor in brick and mortar
6:16 their records: Gershon, Kohath and Merari. Levi **lived** 137 years.
6:18 were Amram, Izhar, Hebron and Uzziel. Kohath **lived** 133 years.
6:20 who bore him Aaron and Moses. Amram **lived** 137 years.
Lev 18:18 and have sexual relations with her while your wife is **living**.
Nu 14:21 **as surely as** I **live** and as surely as the glory of the LORD fills the
14:28 So tell them, '**As surely as** I **live**, declares the LORD, I will do to
Dt 4:9 eyes have seen or let them slip from your heart as long as you **live**.
6:2 the LORD your God as long as you **live** by keeping all his decrees
16:3 so that all the days of your **life** you may remember the time of your
17:19 he is to read it all the days of his **life** so that he may learn to revere
28:66 You will **live** in constant suspense, filled with dread both night
28:66 filled with dread both night and day, never sure of your **life**.
30:6 may love him with all your heart and with all your soul, and **live**.
30:15 See, I set before you today **life** and prosperity, death
30:19 and earth as witnesses against you that I have set before you **life**
30:19 Now choose **life**, so that you and your children may live
30:20 For the LORD is your **life**, and he will give you many years in the
32:47 They are not just idle words for you—they are your **life**. By them
Jos 1:5 one will be able to stand up against you all the days of your **life**.
4:14 they revered him all the days of his **life**, just as they had revered
Jdg 8:19 **As surely as** the LORD **lives**, if you had spared their lives,
16:30 Thus he killed many more when he died than while he **lived**.
Ru 3:13 But if he is not willing, **as surely as** the LORD **lives** I will do it.
1Sa 1:11 then I will give him to the LORD for all the days of his **life**,
1:26 and she said to him, "**As surely as** you **live** [+5883], my lord,
7:15 Samuel continued as judge over Israel all the days of his **life**.
14:39 **As surely as** the LORD who rescues Israel **lives**, even if it lies
14:45 **As surely as** the LORD **lives**, not a hair of his head will fall to the
17:55 Abner replied, "**As surely as** you **live**, O king, I don't know."
19:6 "**As surely as** the LORD **lives**, David will not be put to death."
20:3 Yet **as surely as** the LORD **lives** and as you live, there is only a
20:3 Yet as surely as the LORD lives and **as** you **live**, there is only a
20:14 me unfailing kindness like that of the LORD as long as I **live**,
20:21 then come, because, **as surely as** the LORD **lives**, you are safe;
20:31 As long as the son of Jesse **lives** on this earth, neither you nor your
25:6 Say to him: '**Long life** [+2021+4200] to you! Good health to you
25:26 **as surely as** the LORD **lives** and as you live, may your enemies
25:26 as surely as the LORD lives and **as** you **live**, may your enemies
25:34 Otherwise, **as surely as** the LORD, the God of Israel, **lives**,
26:10 **As surely as** the LORD **lives**," he said, "the LORD himself will
26:16 **As surely as** the LORD **lives**, you and your men deserve to die,
28:10 Saul swore to her by the LORD, "**As surely as** the LORD **lives**,
29:6 called David and said to him, "**As surely as** the LORD **lives**,
2Sa 1:23 in **life** they were loved and gracious, and in death they were not
2:27 Joab answered, "**As surely as** God **lives**, if you had not spoken,
4:9 sons of Rimmon the Beerothite, "**As surely as** the LORD **lives**,
11:11 **As surely as** you **live** [+2256+2644+5883], I will not do such a
11:11 **As surely as** you **live** [+2256+2644+5883], I will not do such a
12:5 the man and said to Nathan, "**As surely as** the LORD **lives**,
14:11 "**As surely as** the LORD **lives**," he said, "not one hair of your
14:19 "**As surely as** you **live** [+5883], my lord the king,
15:21 But Ittai replied to the king, "**As surely as** the LORD **lives**,
15:21 "As surely as the LORD lives, and **as** my lord the king **lives**,
15:21 whether it means **life** or death, there will your servant be."
18:18 During his **lifetime** Absalom had taken a pillar and erected it in the
19:34 [19:35] answered the king, "How many more years will I **live**,
22:47 "The LORD **lives**! Praise be to my Rock! Exalted be God,
23:20 [Benaiah son of Jehoiada was a **valiant fighter** [K; see Q 2657]]
1Ki 1:29 "**As surely as** the LORD **lives**, who has delivered me out of every
2:24 now, **as surely as** the LORD **lives**—he who has established me
4:21 [5:1] brought tribute and were Solomon's subjects all his **life**.
11:34 I have made him ruler all the days of his **life** for the sake of David
15:5 to keep any of the LORD's commands all the days of his **life**—
15:6 and Jeroboam throughout ⌞Abijah's⌟ **lifetime** [+3427].
17:1 said to Ahab, "**As** the LORD, the God of Israel, **lives**, whom I
17:12 "**As surely as** the LORD your God **lives**," she replied, "I don't
18:10 **As surely as** the LORD your God **lives**, there is not a nation
18:15 Elijah said, "**As** the LORD Almighty **lives**, whom I serve,
22:14 Micaiah said, "**As surely as** the LORD **lives**, I can tell him only
2Ki 2:2 But Elisha said, "**As surely as** the LORD **lives** and as you live,
2:2 But Elisha said, "As surely as the LORD lives and **as** you **live**,
2:4 And he replied, "**As surely as** the LORD **lives** and as you live,
2:4 And he replied, "As surely as the LORD lives and **as** you **live**,
2:6 And he replied, "**As surely as** the LORD **lives** and as you live,
2:6 And he replied, "As surely as the LORD lives and **as** you **live**,

2Ki 3:14 Elisha said, "**As surely as** the LORD Almighty **lives**, whom I
4:30 "**As surely as** the LORD **lives** and as you live, I will not leave
4:30 "As surely as the LORD lives and **as** you **live**, I will not leave
5:16 prophet answered, "**As surely as** the LORD **lives**, whom I serve,
5:20 **As surely as** the LORD **lives**, I will run after him and get
25:29 and for the rest of his **life** ate regularly at the king's table.
25:30 the king gave Jehoiachin a regular allowance as long as he **lived**.
2Ch 18:13 Micaiah said, "**As surely as** the LORD **lives**, I can tell him only
Job 3:20 "Why is light given to those in misery, and **life** to the bitter of soul,
7:7 Remember, O God, that my **life** is but a breath; my eyes will never
9:21 am blameless, I have no concern for myself; I despise my own **life**.
10:1 "I loathe my very **life**; therefore I will give free rein to my
10:12 You gave me **life** and showed me kindness, and in your providence
12:10 In his hand is the life of every **creature** and the breath of all
24:22 though they become established, they have no assurance of **life**.
27:2 "**As surely as** God **lives**, who has denied me justice, the Almighty,
33:30 back his soul from the pit, that the light of **life** may shine on him.
Ps 7:5 [7:6] let him trample my **life** to the ground and make me sleep in
16:11 You have made known to me the path of **life**; you will fill me with
18:46 [18:47] The LORD **lives**! Praise be to my Rock! Exalted be God
21:4 [21:5] He asked you for **life**, and you gave it to him—length of
23:6 Surely goodness and love will follow me all the days of my **life**,
26:9 away my soul along with sinners, my **life** with bloodthirsty men,
27:1 The LORD is the stronghold of my **life**—of whom shall I be
27:4 that I may dwell in the house of the LORD all the days of my **life**,
30:5 [30:6] anger lasts only a moment, but his favor lasts a **lifetime**;
31:10 [31:11] My **life** is consumed by anguish and my years by
34:12 [34:13] Whoever of you loves **life** and desires to see many good
36:9 [36:10] For with you is the fountain of **life**; in your light we see
42:8 [42:9] night his song is with me—a prayer to the God of my **life**.
49:18 [49:19] Though while he **lived** he counted himself blessed—and
56:13 [56:14] that I may walk before God in the light of **life**.
63:3 [63:4] Because your love is better than **life**, my lips will glorify
63:4 [63:5] I will praise you as long as **I live**, and in your name I will
64:1 [64:2] my complaint; protect my **life** from the threat of the enemy.
69:28 [69:29] May they be blotted out of the book of **life** and not be
88:3 [88:4] my soul is full of trouble and my **life** draws near the grave.
103:4 who redeems your **life** from the pit and crowns you with love
104:33 I will sing to the LORD all my **life**; I will sing praise to my God
128:5 May the LORD bless you from Zion all the days of your **life**;
133:3 For there the LORD bestows his blessing, even **life** forevermore.
146:2 I will praise the LORD all my **life**; I will sing praise to my God as
Pr 2:19 None who go to her return or attain the paths of **life**.
3:2 for they will prolong your **life** many years and bring you
3:18 She is a tree of **life** to those who embrace her; those who lay hold
3:22 they will be **life** for you, an ornament to grace your neck.
4:10 accept what I say, and the years of your **life** will be many.
4:13 on to instruction, do not let it go; guard it well, for it is your **life**.
4:22 for they are **life** to those who find them and health to a man's
4:23 Above all else, guard your heart, for it is the wellspring of **life**.
5:6 She gives no thought to the way of **life**; her paths are crooked,
6:23 is a light, and the corrections of discipline are the way to **life**,
8:35 For whoever finds me finds **life** and receives favor from the
9:11 me your days will be many, and years will be added to your **life**.
10:11 The mouth of the righteous is a fountain of **life**, but violence
10:16 The wages of the righteous bring them **life**, but the income of the
10:17 He who heeds discipline shows the way to **life**, but whoever
11:19 The truly righteous man attains **life**, but he who pursues evil goes
11:30 The fruit of the righteous is a tree of **life**, and he who wins souls is
12:28 In the way of righteousness there is **life**; along that path is
13:12 makes the heart sick, but a longing fulfilled is a tree of **life**.
13:14 The teaching of the wise is a fountain of **life**, turning a man from
14:27 The fear of the LORD is a fountain of **life**, turning a man from the
14:30 A heart at peace gives **life** *to* the body, but envy rots the bones.
15:4 The tongue that brings healing is a tree of **life**, but a deceitful
15:24 The path of **life** leads upward for the wise to keep him from going
15:31 He who listens to a **life-giving** rebuke will be at home among the
16:15 When a king's face brightens, it means **life**; his favor is like a rain
16:22 Understanding is a fountain of **life** to those who have it, but folly
18:21 The tongue has the power of **life** and death, and those who love it
19:23 The fear of the LORD leads to **life**: Then one rests content,
21:21 He who pursues righteousness and love finds **life**, prosperity
22:4 and the fear of the LORD bring wealth and honor and **life**.
27:27 milk to feed you and your family and to **nourish** your servant girls.
31:12 She brings him good, not harm, all the days of her **life**.
Ecc 2:3 for men to do under heaven during the few days of their **lives**.
2:17 So I hated **life**, because the work that is done under the sun was
3:12 better for men than to be happy and do good while they **live**.
5:18 [5:17] the sun during the few days of **life** God has given him—
5:20 [5:19] He seldom reflects on the days of his **life**, because God
6:12 For who knows what is good for a man in **life**, during the few
6:12 and meaningless days **[RPH]** he passes through like a shadow?
8:15 joy will accompany him in his work all the days of the **life** God has
9:3 are full of evil and there is madness in their hearts while they **live**,
9:9 Enjoy **life** with your wife, whom you love, all the days of this
9:9 all the days of this meaningless **life** that God has given you under
9:9 For this is your lot in **life** and in your toilsome labor under the sun.
10:19 A feast is made for laughter, and wine makes **life** merry,
Isa 38:12 Like a weaver I have rolled up my **life**, and he has cut me off from
38:16 by such things men live; and my spirit finds **life** in them too.
38:20 we will sing with stringed instruments all the days of our **lives** in
49:18 **As surely as I live**," declares the LORD, "you will wear them all
Jer 4:2 and righteous way you swear, '**As surely as** the LORD **lives**,'
5:2 Although they say, '**As surely as** the LORD **lives**,' still they are
8:3 all the survivors of this evil nation will prefer death to **life**,
12:16 and swear by my name, saying, '**As surely as** the LORD **lives**'—
16:14 "when men will no longer say, '**As surely as** the LORD **lives**,
16:15 they will say, '**As surely as** the LORD **lives**, who brought the
21:8 I am setting before you the way of **life** and the way of death.
22:24 "**As surely as I live**," declares the LORD, "even if you,
23:7 "when people will no longer say, '**As surely as** the LORD **lives**,
23:8 they will say, '**As surely as** the LORD **lives**, who brought the
38:16 "**As surely as** the LORD **lives**, who has given us breath,
44:26 my name or swear, "**As surely as** the Sovereign LORD **lives**."
46:18 "**As surely as I live**," declares the King, whose name is the
52:33 and for the rest of his **life** ate regularly at the king's table.
52:34 Babylon gave Jehoiachin a regular allowance as long as he **lived**,
La 3:53 They tried to end my **life** in a pit and threw stones at me;
3:58 O Lord, you took up my case; you redeemed my **life**.
Eze 5:11 Therefore **as surely as I live**, declares the Sovereign LORD,
7:13 the land he has sold as long as both of them **live** [+928+2021],
14:16 **as surely as I live**, declares the Sovereign LORD, even if these
14:18 **as surely as I live**, declares the Sovereign LORD, even if these
14:20 **as surely as I live**, declares the Sovereign LORD, even if Noah,
16:48 **As surely as I live**, declares the Sovereign LORD, your sister
17:16 " '**As surely as I live**, declares the Sovereign LORD, he shall die
17:19 **As surely as I live**, I will bring down on his head my oath that he
18:3 "**As surely as I live**, declares the Sovereign LORD, you will no
20:3 **As surely as I live**, I will not let you inquire of me, declares the
20:31 **As surely as I live**, declares the Sovereign LORD, I will not let
20:33 **As surely as I live**, declares the Sovereign LORD, I will rule over
33:11 Say to them, '**As surely as I live**, declares the Sovereign LORD,
33:15 follows the decrees that give **life**, and does no evil, he will surely
33:27 **As surely as I live**, those who are left in the ruins will fall by the
34:8 **As surely as I live**, declares the Sovereign LORD, because my
35:6 therefore **as surely as I live**, declares the Sovereign LORD,
35:11 therefore **as surely as I live**, declares the Sovereign LORD,
47:9 the salt water fresh; so where the river flows everything *will* **live**.
Da 12:2 some to everlasting **life**, others to shame and everlasting contempt.
Hos 4:15 to Beth Aven. And do not swear, '**As surely as** the LORD **lives**!'
Am 8:14 or say, '**As surely as** your god **lives**, O Dan,' or, 'As surely as the
8:14 god lives, O Dan,' or, '**As surely as** the god of Beersheba **lives**'—
Jnh 2:6 [2:7] But you brought my **life** up from the pit, O LORD my God.
4:3 take away my life, for it is better for me to die than to **live**."
4:8 to die, and said, "It would be better for me to die than to **live**."
Zep 2:9 Therefore, **as surely as I live**," declares the LORD Almighty,
Mal 2:5 with him, a covenant of **life** and peace, and I gave them to him;

2645 חַי hay[2], a. [146] [√ 2649; Ar 10261]

living [62], alive [34], live [15], fresh [8], raw [5], lives [3], life [2], lifetime [2], next year [+6961] [2], next year [2], as surely as live [1], flowing [1], green [1], it[s] [+2021+2021+7606] [1], lived [1], living creatures [1], living thing [1], others[s] [1], preserved [+928+2021+8492] [1], raw [+4695] [1], vigorous [1]

Ge 1:20 God said, "Let the water teem with **living** creatures, and let birds
1:21 So God created the great creatures of the sea and every **living**
1:24 "Let the land produce **living** creatures according to their kinds:
1:30 everything that has the breath of **life** in it—I give every green plant
2:7 his nostrils the breath of life, and the man became a **living** being.
2:19 whatever the man called each **living** creature, that was its name.
3:20 wife Eve, because she would become the mother of all the **living**.
8:21 And never again will I destroy all **living creatures**, as I have done.
9:3 Everything that **lives** and moves will be food for you. Just as I gave
18:10 LORD said, "I will surely return to you about this time **next year**,
18:14 I will return to you at the appointed time **next year** and Sarah will
25:6 while he was still **living**, he gave gifts to the sons of his concubines
26:19 dug in the valley and discovered a well of **fresh** water there.
43:7 and our family. 'Is your father still **living**?' he asked us.
43:27 "How is your aged father you told me about? Is he still **living**?"
43:28 They replied, "Your servant our father is still **alive** and well."
45:3 Joseph said to his brothers, "I am Joseph! Is my father still **living**?"
45:26 They told him, "Joseph is still **alive**! In fact, he is ruler of all
45:28 My son Joseph is still **alive**. I will go and see him before I die."
46:30 ready to die, since I have seen for myself that you are still **alive**."
Ex 4:18 to my own people in Egypt to see if any of them are still **alive**."
21:35 they are to sell the **live** one and divide both the money and the dead
22:4 [22:3] "If the stolen animal is found **alive** in his possession—

Lev 13: 10 the hair white and if there is **raw** [+4695] flesh in the swelling,
13: 14 But whenever **raw** flesh appears on him, he will be unclean.
13: 15 When the priest sees the **raw** flesh, he shall pronounce him
13: 15 The **raw** flesh is unclean; he has an infectious disease.
13: 16 Should the **raw** flesh change and turn white, he must go to the
14: 4 the priest shall order that two **live** clean birds and some cedar
14: 5 the priest shall order that one of the birds be killed over **fresh**
14: 6 He is then to take the **live** bird and dip it, together with the cedar
14: 6 then to take the live bird and dip **it**[s] [+2021+2021+7606],
14: 6 into the blood of the bird that was killed over the **fresh** water.
14: 7 him clean. Then he is to release the **live** bird in the open fields.
14: 50 He shall kill one of the birds over **fresh** water in a clay pot.
14: 51 take the cedar wood, the hyssop, the scarlet yarn and the **live** bird,
14: 51 dip them into the blood of the dead bird and the **fresh** water,
14: 52 the **fresh** water, the live bird, the cedar wood, the hyssop and the
14: 52 the fresh water, the **live** bird, the cedar wood, the hyssop and the
14: 53 he is to release the **live** bird in the open fields outside the town.
15: 13 he must wash his clothes and bathe himself with **fresh** water,
16: 10 the goat chosen by lot as the scapegoat shall be presented **alive**
16: 20 Tent of Meeting and the altar, he shall bring forward the **live** goat.
16: 21 He is to lay both hands on the head of the **live** goat and confess
Nu 16: 30 that belongs to them, and they go down **alive** into the grave,
16: 33 They went down **alive** into the grave, with everything they owned;
16: 48 [17:13] He stood between the **living** and the dead, and the plague
19: 17 purification offering into a jar and pour **fresh** water over them.
Dt 4: 4 all of you who held fast to the LORD your God are still **alive**
4: 10 so that they may learn to revere me as long as they **live** in the land
5: 3 this covenant, but with us, with all of us who are **alive** here today.
5: 26 For what mortal man has ever heard the voice of the **living** God
12: 1 has given you to possess—as long as you **live** in the land.
31: 13 learn to fear the LORD your God as long as you **live** in the land
31: 27 you have been rebellious against the LORD while I am still **alive**
32: 40 I lift my hand to heaven and declare: **As surely as** I **live** forever,
Jos 3: 10 This is how you will know that the **living** God is among you
8: 23 But they took the king of Ai **alive** and brought him to Joshua.
Ru 2: 20 "He has not stopped showing his kindness to the **living** and the
1Sa 2: 15 to roast; he won't accept boiled meat from you, but only **raw**."
15: 8 He took Agag king of the Amalekites **alive**, and all his people he
17: 26 Philistine that he should defy the armies of the **living** God?"
17: 36 one of them, because he has defied the armies of the **living** God.
25: 29 securely in the bundle of the **living** by the LORD your God.
2Sa 12: 18 for they thought, "While the child was still **living**, we spoke to
12: 21 While the child was **alive**, you fasted and wept, but now that the
12: 22 He answered, "While the child was still **alive**, I fasted and wept.
18: 14 plunged them into Absalom's heart while Absalom was still **alive**
19: 6 [19:7] I see that you would be pleased if Absalom were **alive**
1Ki 3: 22 "No! The **living** *one* is my son; the dead one is yours."
3: 22 The dead one is yours; the **living** *one* is mine." And so they argued
3: 23 king said, "This one says, 'My son is **alive** and your son is dead,'
3: 23 while that one says, 'No! Your son is dead and mine is **alive**.' "
3: 25 "Cut the **living** child in two and give half to one and half to the
3: 26 The woman whose son was **alive** was filled with compassion for
3: 26 and said to the king, "Please, my lord, give her the **living** baby!
3: 27 "Give the **living** baby to the first woman. Do not kill him;
8: 40 so that they will fear you all the time they **live** in the land you gave
12: 6 the elders who had served his father Solomon during his **lifetime**.
17: 23 He gave him to his mother and said, "Look, your son is **alive**!"
20: 18 He said, "If they have come out for peace, take them **alive**;
20: 18 take them alive; if they have come out for war, take them **alive**."
20: 32 'Please let me live.' " The king answered, "Is he still **alive**?
21: 15 that he refused to sell you. He is no longer **alive**, but dead."
2Ki 4: 16 "About this time **next year** [+6961]," Elisha said, "you will hold a
4: 17 the **next year** [+6961] about that same time she gave birth to a son,
7: 12 come out, and then we will take them **alive** and get into the city.' "
10: 14 "Take them **alive**!" he ordered. So they took them alive
10: 14 So they took them **alive** and slaughtered them by the well of Beth
19: 4 his master, the king of Assyria, has sent to ridicule the **living** God,
19: 16 listen to the words Sennacherib has sent to insult the **living** God.
2Ch 6: 31 walk in your ways all the time they **live** in the land you gave our
10: 6 the elders who had served his father Solomon during his **lifetime**.
25: 12 The army of Judah also captured ten thousand *men* **alive**,
Job 19: 25 I know that my Redeemer **lives**, and that in the end he will stand
28: 13 comprehend its worth; it cannot be found in the land of the **living**.
28: 21 It is hidden from the eyes of every **living thing**, concealed even
30: 23 bring me down to death, to the place appointed for all the **living**.
Ps 17: 14 such men, from men of this world whose reward is in this **life**.
27: 13 I will see the goodness of the LORD in the land of the **living**.
38: 19 [38:20] Many are those who are my **vigorous** enemies; those who
42: 2 [42:3] My soul thirsts for God, for the **living** God. When can I go
52: 5 [52:7] your tent; he will uproot you from the land of the **living**.
55: 15 [55:16] let them go down **alive** to the grave, for evil finds lodging
58: 9 [58:10] whether they be **green** or dry—the wicked will be swept
66: 9 he *has* **preserved** [+928+2021+8492] our lives and kept our feet
84: 2 [84:3] my heart and my flesh cry out for the **living** God.
116: 9 that I may walk before the LORD in the land of the **living**.
124: 3 their anger flared against us, they would have swallowed us **alive**;
142: 5 [142:6] "You are my refuge, my portion in the land of the **living**."
143: 2 servant into judgment, for no one **living** is righteous before you.
145: 16 You open your hand and satisfy the desires of every **living** *thing*.
Pr 1: 12 let's swallow them **alive**, like the grave, and whole, like those who
Ecc 4: 2 had already died, are happier than the **living**, who are still alive.
4: 2 had already died, are happier than the living, who are still **alive**.
4: 15 I saw that all who **lived** and walked under the sun followed the
6: 8 poor man gain by knowing how to conduct himself before **others**[s]?
7: 2 is the destiny of every man; the **living** should take this to heart.
9: 4 Anyone who is among the **living** has hope—even a live dog is
9: 4 the living has hope—even a **live** dog is better off than a dead lion!
9: 5 For the **living** know that they will die, but the dead know nothing;
SS 4: 15 a well of **flowing** water streaming down from Lebanon.
Isa 4: 3 be called holy, all who are recorded among the **living** in Jerusalem.
8: 19 inquire of their God? Why consult the dead on behalf of the **living**?
37: 4 his master, the king of Assyria, has sent to ridicule the **living** God,
37: 17 listen to all the words Sennacherib has sent to insult the **living**
38: 11 not again see the LORD, the LORD, in the land of the **living**;
38: 19 The **living**, the living—they praise you, as I am doing today;
38: 19 The living, the **living**—they praise you, as I am doing today;
53: 8 For he was cut off from the land of the **living**; for the transgression
Jer 2: 13 They have forsaken me, the spring of **living** water, and have dug
10: 10 the LORD is the true God; he is the **living** God, the eternal King.
11: 19 let us cut him off from the land of the **living**, that his name be
17: 13 because they have forsaken the LORD, the spring of **living** water.
23: 36 becomes his oracle and so you distort the words of the **living** God,
La 3: 39 Why should any **living** man complain when punished for his sins?
Eze 26: 20 and you will not return or take your place in the land of the **living**.
32: 23 All who had spread terror in the land of the **living** are slain,
32: 24 All who had spread terror in the land of the **living** went down
32: 25 Because their terror had spread in the land of the **living**, they bear
32: 26 the sword because they spread their terror in the land of the **living**.
32: 27 terror of these warriors had stalked through the land of the **living**.
32: 32 Although I had him spread terror in the land of the **living**,
Da 12: 7 I heard him swear by *him who* **lives** forever, saying, "It will be for
Hos 1: 10 [2:1] not my people,' they will be called 'sons of the **living** God.'
Zec 14: 8 On that day **living** water will flow out from Jerusalem, half to the

2646 חַי[3] *ḥay*[3], n.[m.]. [1] [√ 2649; Ar 10261]

family [1]

1Sa 18: 18 "Who am I, and what is my **family** or my father's clan in Israel,

2647 חִיאֵל *ḥî'ēl*, n.pr.m. [1] [√ 278 + 446]

Hiel [1]

1Ki 16: 34 In Ahab's time, **Hiel** of Bethel rebuilt Jericho. He laid its

2648 חִידָה *ḥîdâ*, n.f. [17] [→ 2554; Ar 10019]

riddle [8], hard questions [2], riddles [2], allegory [1], answer [1], hidden things [1], intrigue [1], scorn [1]

Nu 12: 8 With him I speak face to face, clearly and not in **riddles**; he sees
Jdg 14: 12 "Let me tell you a **riddle**," Samson said to them. "If you can give
14: 13 sets of clothes." "Tell us your **riddle**," they said. "Let's hear it."
14: 14 something sweet." For three days they could not give the **answer**.
14: 15 "Coax your husband into explaining the **riddle** for us, or we will
14: 16 You've given my people a **riddle**, but you haven't told me the
14: 17 to press him. She in turn explained the **riddle** to her people.
14: 18 not plowed with my heifer, you would not have solved my **riddle**."
14: 19 and gave their clothes to those who had explained the **riddle**.
1Ki 10: 1 name of the LORD, she came to test him with **hard questions**.
2Ch 9: 1 she came to Jerusalem to test him with **hard questions**.
Ps 49: 4 [49:5] ear to a proverb; with the harp I will expound my **riddle**:
78: 2 mouth in parables, I will utter **hidden things**, things from of old—
Pr 1: 6 and parables, the sayings and **riddles** of the wise.
Eze 17: 2 set forth an **allegory** and tell the house of Israel a parable.
Da 8: 23 a stern-faced king, a master of **intrigue**, will arise.
Hab 2: 6 "Will not all of them taunt him with ridicule and **scorn**, saying,

2649 חָיָה *ḥāyâ*, v. [281 / 280] [→ 2644, 2645, 2646, 2650, 2651, 2652, 2653, 2654, 4695; cf. 2558; Ar 10262; *also used with compound proper names*]

live [90], lived [43], surely live [+2649] [18], preserve life [12], spared [10], long live [9], keep alive [7], let live [7], recover [6], revive [5], save life [5], certainly recover [+2649] [4], kept alive [3], leave alive [3], preserve [3], restored to life [3], allowed to live [2], bring back to life [2], came to life [2], come to life [2], preserves life [2], revived [2], save lives [2], save [2], spare [2], survive [2], survived [2], *untranslated* [1], allow to live [1], bring to life [1], brought back to life [1], choose life [1], die [+4202] [1], flourish [1], give life [1], gives life

[1], healed [1], live again [1], live on [1], lives [1], makes alive [1], preserved life [1], protect lives [1], raised [1], recovered [1], recovery [+2716+4946] [1], renew [1], restore life [1], restored [1], saved lives [1], saving [1], spare life [1], spare lives [1], spared lives [1], sparing [1], stay alive [1], will[s] [1]

Ge 3:22 [A] and take also from the tree of life and eat, and **live** forever."
5:3 [A] When Adam *had* **lived** 130 years, he had a son in his own
5:5 [A] Altogether, Adam **lived** 930 years, and then he died.
5:6 [A] When Seth *had* **lived** 105 years, he became the father of
5:7 [A] Seth **lived** 807 years and had other sons and daughters.
5:9 [A] When Enosh *had* **lived** 90 years, he became the father of
5:10 [A] Enosh **lived** 815 years and had other sons and daughters.
5:12 [A] When Kenan *had* **lived** 70 years, he became the father of
5:13 [A] Kenan **lived** 840 years and had other sons and daughters.
5:15 [A] When Mahalalel *had* **lived** 65 years, he became the father of
5:16 [A] Mahalalel **lived** 830 years and had other sons and daughters.
5:18 [A] When Jared *had* **lived** 162 years, he became the father of
5:19 [A] Jared **lived** 800 years and had other sons and daughters.
5:21 [A] When Enoch *had* **lived** 65 years, he became the father of
5:25 [A] When Methuselah *had* **lived** 187 years, he became the father
5:26 [A] Methuselah **lived** 782 years and had other sons
5:28 [A] When Lamech *had* **lived** 182 years, he had a son.
5:30 [A] Lamech **lived** 595 years and had other sons and daughters.
6:19 [G] male and female, to **keep** them **alive** with you.
6:20 [G] moves along the ground will come to you to *be* **kept alive**.
7:3 [D] to **keep** their various kinds **alive** throughout the earth.
9:28 [A] After the flood Noah **lived** 350 years.
11:11 [A] Shem **lived** 500 years and had other sons and daughters.
11:12 [A] When Arphaxad *had* **lived** 35 years, he became the father of
11:13 [A] Arphaxad **lived** 403 years and had other sons and daughters.
11:14 [A] When Shelah *had* **lived** 30 years, he became the father of
11:15 [A] Shelah **lived** 403 years and had other sons and daughters.
11:16 [A] When Eber *had* **lived** 34 years, he became the father of
11:17 [A] Eber **lived** 430 years and had other sons and daughters.
11:18 [A] When Peleg *had* **lived** 30 years, he became the father of Reu.
11:19 [A] Peleg **lived** 209 years and had other sons and daughters.
11:20 [A] When Reu *had* **lived** 32 years, he became the father of
11:21 [A] Reu **lived** 207 years and had other sons and daughters.
11:22 [A] When Serug *had* **lived** 30 years, he became the father of
11:23 [A] Serug **lived** 200 years and had other sons and daughters.
11:24 [A] When Nahor *had* **lived** 29 years, he became the father of
11:25 [A] Nahor **lived** 119 years and had other sons and daughters.
11:26 [A] After Terah *had* **lived** 70 years, he became the father of
12:12 [D] 'This is his wife.' Then they will kill me but *will* **let** you **live**.
12:13 [A] for your sake and my life *will be* **spared** because of you."
17:18 [A] to God, "If only Ishmael *might* **live** under your blessing!"
19:19 [G] and you have shown great kindness to me in **sparing** my life.
19:20 [A] to it—it is very small, isn't it? Then my life *will be* **spared**."
19:32 [D] with him and **preserve** our family line through our father."
19:34 [D] so *we can* **preserve** our family line through our father."
20:7 [A] he is a prophet, and he will pray for you and *you will* **live**.
25:7 [A] Altogether, Abraham **lived** a hundred and seventy-five years.
27:40 [A] *You will* **live** by the sword and you will serve your brother.
31:32 [A] But if you find anyone who has your gods, *he shall* not **live**.
42:2 [A] and buy some for us, so that *we may* **live** and not die."
42:18 [A] said to them, "Do this and *you will* **live**, for I fear God:
43:8 [A] so that we and you and our children *may* **live** and not die.
45:7 [G] on earth and to **save** your **lives** by a great deliverance.
45:27 [A] to carry him back, the spirit of their father Jacob **revived**.
47:19 [A] Give us seed so that *we may* **live** and not die, and that the
47:25 [G] "*You have* **saved** our **lives**," they said. "May we find favor
47:28 [A] Jacob **lived** in Egypt seventeen years, and the years of his life
50:20 [G] what is now being done, the **saving** *of* many lives.
50:22 [A] with all his father's family. He **lived** a hundred and ten years

Ex 1:16 [A] if it is a boy, kill him; but if it is a girl, *let her* **live**."
1:17 [D] the king of Egypt had told them to do; *they* **let** the boys **live**.
1:18 [D] "Why have you done this? Why *have you* **let** the boys **live**?"
1:22 [D] is born you must throw into the Nile, but **let** every girl **live**."
19:13 [A] Whether man or animal, *he shall* not *be permitted to* **live**.'
22:18 [22:17] [D] "*Do* not **allow** a sorceress **to live**.
33:20 [A] "you cannot see my face, for no one may see me and **live**."

Lev 18:5 [A] and laws, for the man who obeys them *will* **live** by them.
25:35 [A] a temporary resident, so *he can continue to* **live** among you.
25:36 [A] so that your countryman *may continue to* **live** among you.

Nu 4:19 [A] So that *they may* **live** and not die when they come near the
14:38 [A] Joshua son of Nun and Caleb son of Jephunneh **survived**.
21:8 [A] it up on a pole; anyone who is bitten can look at it and **live**."
21:9 [A] bitten by a snake and looked at the bronze snake, *he* **lived**.
22:33 [G] certainly have killed you by now, but *I would have* **spared**
24:23 [A] he uttered his oracle: "Ah, who *can* **live** when God does this?
31:15 [D] "*Have you* **allowed** all the women **to live**?" he asked them.
31:18 [G] **save** for yourselves every girl who has never slept with a

Dt 4:1 [A] Follow them so that *you may* **live** and may go in and take
4:33 [A] the voice of God speaking out of fire, as you have, and **lived**?
4:42 [A] He could flee into one of these cities and **save** *his* **life**.
5:24 [A] Today we have seen that a man *can* **live** even if God speaks
5:26 [A] living God speaking out of fire, as we have, and **survived**?
5:33 [A] so that *you may* **live** and prosper and prolong your days in
6:24 [D] so that we might always prosper and *be* **kept alive**, as is the
8:1 [A] so that *you may* **live** and increase and may enter and possess
8:3 [A] to teach you that man *does* not **live** on bread alone but on
8:3 [A] word that comes from the mouth of the LORD. **[RPH]**
16:20 [A] so that *you may* **live** and possess the land the LORD your
19:4 [A] the man who kills another and flees there *to* **save** *his* **life**—
19:5 [A] That man may flee to one of these cities and **save** *his* **life**.
20:16 [D] as an inheritance, *do* not **leave alive** anything that breathes.
30:16 [A] *you will* **live** and increase, and the LORD your God will
30:19 [A] Now choose life, so that you and your children *may* **live**
32:39 [D] I put to death and *I* **bring to life**, I have wounded and I will
33:6 [A] "*Let* Reuben **live** and not die, nor his men be few."

Jos 2:13 [G] *you will* **spare** *the* **lives** *of* my father and mother, my brothers
5:8 [A] remained where they were in camp until they *were* **healed**.
6:17 [A] and all who are with her in her house *shall be* **spared**,
6:25 [G] Joshua **spared** Rahab the prostitute, with her family and all
9:15 [D] Joshua made a treaty of peace with them to **let** them **live**,
9:20 [G] *We will* **let** them **live**, so that wrath will not fall on us for
9:21 [A] They continued, "*Let them* **live**, but let them be woodcutters
14:10 [G] *he has* **kept** me **alive** for forty-five years since the time he

Jdg 8:19 [G] if *you had* **spared** their **lives**, I would not kill you."
15:19 [A] When Samson drank, his strength returned and *he* **revived**.
21:14 [D] given the women of Jabesh Gilead who *had been* **spared**.

1Sa 2:6 [D] "The LORD brings death and **makes alive**; he brings down
10:24 [A] the people." Then the people shouted, "**Long live** the king!"
27:9 [D] *he did* not **leave** a man or woman **alive**, but took sheep
27:11 [D] He *did* not **leave** a man or woman **alive** to be brought to

2Sa 1:10 [A] because I knew that after he had fallen *he could* not **survive**.
8:2 [G] were put to death, and the third length *was* **allowed to live**.
12:3 [D] *He* **raised** it, and it grew up with him and his children. It
12:22 [A] The LORD may be gracious to me and *let* the child **live**.'
16:16 [A] went to Absalom and said to him, "**Long live** the king!
16:16 [A] and said to him, "Long live the king! **Long live** the king!"

1Ki 1:25 [A] drinking with him and saying, '**Long live** King Adonijah!'
1:31 [A] the king, said, "*May* my lord King David **live** forever!"
1:34 [A] Blow the trumpet and shout, '**Long live** King Solomon!'
1:39 [A] and all the people shouted, "**Long live** King Solomon!"
17:22 [A] Elijah's cry, and the boy's life returned to him, and *he* **lived**.
18:5 [D] we can find some grass *to* **keep** the horses and mules **alive**
20:31 [D] and ropes around our heads. Perhaps *he will* **spare** your life."
20:32 [A] 'Please *let* me **live**.'" The king answered, "Is he still alive?

2Ki 1:2 [A] the god of Ekron, to see if *I will* **recover** from this injury."
4:7 [A] pay your debts. You and your sons *can* **live** on what is left."
5:7 [G] and said, "Am I God? Can I kill and **bring back to life**?
7:4 [D] If *they* **spare** us, we live; if they kill us, then we die."
7:4 [A] If they spare us, *we* **live**; if they kill us, then we die."
8:1 [G] had said to the woman whose son *he had* **restored to life**,
8:5 [G] telling the king how Elisha *had* **restored** the dead **to life**,
8:5 [G] the woman whose son Elisha *had* **brought back to life** came
8:5 [G] the king, and this is her son whom Elisha **restored to life**."
8:8 [A] through him; ask him, '*Will I* **recover** from this illness?' "
8:9 [A] has sent me to ask, '*Will I* **recover** from this illness?' "
8:10 [A] "Go and say to him, '*You will* **certainly recover** [+2649]';
8:10 [A] "Go and say to him, '*You will* **certainly recover** [+2649]';
8:14 [A] "He told me that *you would* **certainly recover** [+2649]."
8:14 [A] "He told me that *you would* **certainly recover** [+2649]."
10:19 [A] for Baal. Anyone who fails to come *will* no *longer* **live**."
11:12 [A] clapped their hands and shouted, "**Long live** the king!"
13:21 [A] Elisha's bones, the man **came to life** and stood up on his feet.
14:17 [A] Amaziah son of Joash king of Judah **lived** for fifteen years
18:32 [A] a land of olive trees and honey. **Choose life** and not death!
20:1 [A] in order, because you are going to die; *you will* not **recover**."
20:7 [A] They did so and applied it to the boil, and *he* **recovered**.

1Ch 11:8 [D] the surrounding wall, while Joab **restored** the rest of the city.

2Ch 23:11 [A] They anointed him and shouted, "**Long live** the king!"
25:25 [A] Amaziah son of Joash king of Judah **lived** for fifteen years

Ne 2:3 [A] I said to the king, "*May* the king **live** forever! Why should
4:2 [3:34] [D] *Can they* **bring** the stones **back to life** from those
5:2 [A] in order for us to eat and **stay alive**, we must get grain."
6:11 [A] Or should one like me go into the temple *to* **save** *his* **life**?
9:6 [D] You **give life** *to* everything, and the multitudes of heaven
9:29 [A] your ordinances, by which a man *will* **live** if he obeys them.

Est 4:11 [A] the king to extend the gold scepter to him and **spare** *his* **life**.

Job 7:16 [A] I despise my life; *I would* not **live** forever. Let me alone; my
14:14 [A] If a man dies, *will he* **live again**? All the days of my hard
21:7 [A] Why *do* the wicked **live on**, growing old and increasing in
33:4 [D] God has made me; the breath of the Almighty **gives** me **life**.
36:6 [D] *He does* not **keep** the wicked **alive** but gives the afflicted
42:16 [A] After this, Job **lived** a hundred and forty years; he saw his

Ps 22:26 [22:27] [A] will praise him—*may* your hearts **live** forever!
22:29 [22:30] [D] *those who* cannot **keep** themselves **alive**.
30: 3 [30:4] [D] *you* **spared** me from going down into the pit.
33:19 [D] to deliver them from death and **keep** them **alive** in famine.
41: 2 [41:3] [D] The LORD will protect him and **preserve** his **life**;
49: 9 [49:10] [A] that *he should* **live** on forever and not see decay.
69:32 [69:33] [A] be glad—you who seek God, *may* your hearts **live**!
71:20 [D] see troubles, many and bitter, *you will* **restore** my **life** again;
72:15 [A] **Long** *may he* **live**! May gold from Sheba be given him. May
80:18 [80:19] [D] from you; **revive** us, and we will call on your name.
85: 6 [85:7] [D] *Will* you not **revive** us again, that your people may
89:48 [89:49] [A] What man *can* **live** and not see death, or save
118:17 [A] I will not die but **live**, and will proclaim what the LORD has
119:17 [A] Do good to your servant, and *I will* **live**; I will obey your
119:25 [D] low in the dust; **preserve** my **life** according to your word.
119:37 [D] worthless things; **preserve** my **life** according to your word.
119:40 [D] for your precepts! **Preserve** my **life** in your righteousness.
119:50 [D] in my suffering is this: Your promise **preserves** my **life**.
119:77 [A] Let your compassion come to me that *I may* **live**, for your
119:88 [D] **Preserve** my **life** according to your love, and I will obey the
119:93 [D] your precepts, for by them *you have* **preserved** my **life**.
119:107 [D] **preserve** my **life**, O LORD, according to your word.
119:116 [A] Sustain me according to your promise, and *I will* **live**; do not
119:144 [A] are forever right; give me understanding that *I may* **live**.
119:149 [D] **preserve** my **life**, O LORD, according to your laws.
119:154 [D] and redeem me; **preserve** my **life** according to your promise.
119:156 [D] is great, O LORD; **preserve** my **life** according to your laws.
119:159 [D] **preserve** my **life**, O LORD, according to your love.
119:175 [A] *Let* me **live** that I may praise you, and may your laws sustain
138: 7 [D] Though I walk in the midst of trouble, *you* **preserve** my **life**;
143:11 [D] For your name's sake, O LORD, **preserve** my **life**; in your
Pr 4: 4 [A] with all your heart; keep my commands and *you will* **live**.
7: 2 [A] Keep my commands and *you will* **live**; guard my teachings
9: 6 [A] Leave your simple ways and *you will* **live**; walk in the way
15:27 [A] brings trouble to his family, but he who hates bribes *will* **live**.
Ecc 6: 3 [A] A man may have a hundred children and **live** many years;
6: 6 [A] even if *he* **lives** a thousand years twice over but fails to enjoy
7:12 [D] is this: that wisdom **preserves** *the* **life** *of* its possessor.
11: 8 [A] However many years a man *may* **live**, let him enjoy them all.
Isa 7:21 [D] that day, a man *will* **keep alive** a young cow and two goats.
26:14 [A] They are now dead, *they* **live** no more; those departed spirits
26:19 [A] your dead *will* **live**; their bodies will rise. You who dwell in
38: 1 [A] in order, because you are going to die; *you will* not **recover**."
38: 9 [A] king of Judah after his illness and **recovery** [+2716+4946]:
38:16 [A] Lord, by such things *men* **live**; and my spirit finds life in
38:16 [G] life in them too. You restored me to health and **let** me **live**.
38:21 [A] poultice of figs and apply it to the boil, and *he will* **recover**."
55: 3 [A] Give ear and come to me; hear me, that your soul *may* **live**.
57:15 [G] to **revive** the spirit of the lowly and to revive the heart of the
57:15 [G] the spirit of the lowly and to **revive** the heart of the contrite.
Jer 21: 9 [A] to the Babylonians who are besieging you *will* **live**;
27:12 [A] king of Babylon; serve him and his people, and *you will* **live**.
27:17 [A] listen to them. Serve the king of Babylon, and *you will* **live**.
35: 7 [A] *you will* **live** a long time in the land where you are nomads.'
38: 2 [A] but whoever goes over to the Babylonians *will* **live**.
38: 2 [A] will live. He will escape with his life; *he will* **live**.'
38:17 [A] your life *will be* **spared** and this city will not be burned
38:17 [A] city will not be burned down; you and your family *will* **live**.
38:20 [A] Then it will go well with you, and your life *will be* **spared**.
49:11 [D] Leave your orphans; I *will* **protect** their **lives**. Your widows
La 4:20 [A] We thought that under his shadow *we would* **live** among the
Eze 3:18 [D] to dissuade him from his evil ways in order to **save** his **life**,
3:21 [A] not sin, *he will* **surely live** [+2649] because he took warning,
3:21 [A] not sin, *he will* **surely live** [+2649] because he took warning,
13:18 [D] you ensnare the lives of my people but **preserve** your own?
13:19 [D] not have died and *have* **spared** those who should not live.
13:19 [A] not have died and have spared those who *should* not **live**.
13:22 [G] not to turn from their evil ways and so **save** their **lives**,
16: 6 [A] and as you lay there in your blood I said to you, "**Live**!"
16: 6 [A] I said to you, "Live!" [BHS+ *And as you lay there in your blood I said to you, "**Live**!"*]
18: 9 [A] *he will* **surely live** [+2649], declares the Sovereign LORD.
18: 9 [A] *he will* **surely live** [+2649], declares the Sovereign LORD.
18:13 [A] takes excessive interest. *Will such a man* **live**? He will not!
18:13 [A] takes excessive interest. Will such a man live? *He* **will**[s] not!
18:17 [A] will not die for his father's sin; *he will* **surely live** [+2649].
18:17 [A] will not die for his father's sin; *he will* **surely live** [+2649].
18:19 [A] careful to keep all my decrees, *he will* **surely live** [+2649].
18:19 [A] careful to keep all my decrees, *he will* **surely live** [+2649].
18:21 [A] and does what is just and right, *he will* **surely live** [+2649];
18:21 [A] and does what is just and right, *he will* **surely live** [+2649];
18:22 [A] Because of the righteous things he has done, *he will* **live**.
18:23 [A] am I not pleased when they turn from their ways and **live**?
18:24 [A] the same detestable things the wicked man does, *will he* **live**?
18:27 [D] and does what is just and right, he *will* **save** his life.
18:28 [A] and turns away from them, *he will* **surely live** [+2649];
18:28 [A] and turns away from them, *he will* **surely live** [+2649];
18:32 [A] of anyone, declares the Sovereign LORD. Repent and **live**!
20:11 [A] my laws, for the man who obeys them *will* **live** by them.
20:13 [A] although the man who obeys them *will* **live** by them—
20:21 [A] although the man who obeys them *will* **live** by them—
20:25 [A] statutes that were not good and laws *they could* not **live** by;
33:10 [A] are wasting away because of them. How then *can we* **live**?" '
33:11 [A] the wicked, but rather that they turn from their ways and **live**.
33:12 [A] will not be allowed to **live** because of his former
33:13 [A] If I tell the righteous man that *he will* **surely live** [+2649],
33:13 [A] If I tell the righteous man that *he will* **surely live** [+2649],
33:15 [A] that give life, and does no evil, *he will* **surely live** [+2649];
33:15 [A] that give life, and does no evil, *he will* **surely live** [+2649];
33:16 [A] has done what is just and right; *he will* **surely live** [+2649].
33:16 [A] has done what is just and right; *he will* **surely live** [+2649].
33:19 [A] and does what is just and right, *he will* **live** by doing so.
37: 3 [A] He asked me, "Son of man, *can* these bones **live**?" I said,
37: 5 [A] I will make breath enter you, and *you will* **come to life**.
37: 6 [A] with skin; I will put breath in you, and *you will* **come to life**.
37: 9 [A] O breath, and breathe into these slain, that *they may* **live**.' "
37:10 [A] *they* **came to life** and stood up on their feet—a vast army.
37:14 [A] I will put my Spirit in you and *you will* **live**, and I will settle
47: 9 [A] Swarms of living creatures *will* **live** wherever the river flows.
Hos 6: 2 [D] After two days *he will* **revive** us; on the third day he will
6: 2 [A] third day he will restore us, that *we may* **live** in his presence.
14: 7 [14:8] [D] *He will* **flourish** like the grain. He will blossom like
Am 5: 4 [A] the LORD says to the house of Israel: "Seek me and **live**;
5: 6 [A] Seek the LORD and **live**, or he will sweep through the
5:14 [A] Seek good, not evil, that *you may* **live**. Then the LORD
Hab 2: 4 [A] are not upright—but the righteous *will* **live** by his faith—
3: 2 [D] **Renew** them in our day, in our time make them known;
Zec 1: 5 [A] forefathers now? And the prophets, *do they* **live** forever?
10: 9 [A] *They* and their children *will* **survive**, and they will return.
13: 3 [A] whom he was born, will say to him, '*You must* **die** [+4202],

2650 חָיֶה ***ḥāyeh***, a. [1] [√ 2649]

vigorous [1]

Ex 1:19 they are **vigorous** and give birth before the midwives arrive."

2651 חַיָּה[1] ***ḥayyâ[1]***, n.f. [103] [√ 2649; Ar 10263]

animals [25], beasts [25], living creatures [13], living [8], animal [7], wild animals [6], beast [4], creatures [3], living creature [2], wild beasts [2], animal [+7473] [1], beasts of burden [+989+2256] [1], creature [1], livestock [1], living things [1], ones[s] [1], those[s] [+2021] [1], wild animal [1]

Ge 1:24 along the ground, and wild **animals**, each according to its kind."
1:25 God made the wild **animals** according to their kinds, the livestock
1:28 and over every **living creature** that moves on the ground."
1:30 And to all the **beasts** *of* the earth and all the birds of the air
2:19 God had formed out of the ground all the **beasts** *of* the field
2:20 all the livestock, the birds of the air and all the **beasts** *of* the field.
3: 1 Now the serpent was more crafty than any of the wild **animals** the
3:14 "Cursed are you above all the livestock and all the wild **animals**!
7:14 They had with them every **wild animal** according to its kind,
7:21 birds, livestock, **wild animals**, all the creatures that swarm over the
8: 1 God remembered Noah and all the **wild animals** and the livestock
8:17 Bring out every kind of **living** creature that is with you—the birds,
8:19 All the **animals** and all the creatures that move along the ground
9: 2 The fear and dread of you will fall upon all the **beasts** *of* the earth
9: 5 I will demand an accounting from every **animal**. And from each
9:10 and with every **living** creature that was with you—the birds,
9:10 the birds, the livestock and all the wild **animals**, all those that
9:10 that came out of the ark with you—every **living creature** *on* earth.
9:12 making between me and you and every **living** creature with you,
9:15 between me and you and all **living** creatures of every kind.
9:16 between God and all **living** creatures of every kind on the earth."
37:20 of these cisterns and say that a ferocious **animal** devoured him.
37:33 "It is my son's robe! Some ferocious **animal** has devoured him.
Ex 23:11 get food from it, and the wild **animals** may eat what they leave.
23:29 become desolate and the wild **animals** too numerous for you.
Lev 5: 2 whether the carcasses of unclean **wild animals** or of unclean
11: 2 all the animals that live on land, these are the **ones**[s] you may eat:
11:10 or among all the other **living** creatures in the water—
11:27 Of all the **animals** that walk on all fours, those that walk on their
11:46 every **living** thing that moves in the water and every creature that
11:47 between **living creatures** that may be eaten and those that may
11:47 that may be eaten and **those**[s] [+2021] that may not be eaten.' "
17:13 or any alien living among you who hunts any **animal** [+7473]
25: 7 as well as for your livestock and the **wild animals** in your land.
26: 6 I will remove savage **beasts** from the land, and the sword will not

Lev 26:22 I will send wild **animals** against you, and they will rob you of your
Nu 35: 3 pasturelands for their cattle, flocks and all their *other* **livestock**.
Dt 7:22 them all at once, or the wild **animals** will multiply around you.
1Sa 17:46 Philistine army to the birds of the air and the **beasts** *of* the earth,
2Sa 21:10 the birds of the air touch them by day or the wild **animals** by night.
2Ki 14: 9 a wild **beast** in Lebanon came along and trampled the thistle
2Ch 25:18 a wild **beast** in Lebanon came along and trampled the thistle
Job 5:22 at destruction and famine, and need not fear the **beasts** *of* the earth.
5:23 stones of the field, and the wild **animals** will be at peace with you.
37: 8 The **animals** take cover; they remain in their dens.
39:15 a foot may crush them, that some wild **animal** may trample them.
40:20 hills bring him their produce, and all the wild **animals** play nearby.
Ps 50:10 for every **animal** *of* the forest is mine, and the cattle on a thousand
68:30 [68:31] Rebuke the **beast** *among* the reeds, the herd of bulls
74:19 Do not hand over the life of your dove to **wild beasts**; do not
79: 2 birds of the air, the flesh of your saints to the **beasts** *of* the earth.
104:11 They give water to all the **beasts** *of* the field; the wild donkeys
104:20 it becomes night, and all the **beasts** *of* the forest prowl.
104:25 with creatures beyond number—**living things** both large and small.
148:10 **wild animals** and all cattle, small creatures and flying birds,
Isa 35: 9 No lion will be there, nor will *any* ferocious **beast** get up on it;
40:16 sufficient for altar fires, nor its **animals** enough for burnt offerings.
43:20 The wild **animals** honor me, the jackals and the owls, because I
46: 1 their idols are borne by **beasts** [+989+2256] **of burden**.
56: 9 Come, all you **beasts** *of* the field, come and devour, all you beasts
56: 9 beasts of the field, come and devour, all you **beasts** of the forest!
Jer 12: 9 Go and gather all the wild **beasts**; bring them to devour.
27: 6 king of Babylon; I will make even the wild **animals** subject to him.
28:14 serve him. I will even give him control over the wild **animals**.' "
Eze 1: 5 and in the fire was what looked like four **living creatures**.
1:13 The appearance of the **living creatures** was like burning coals of
1:13 Fire moved back and forth among the **creatures**; it was bright,
1:14 The **creatures** sped back and forth like flashes of lightning.
1:15 As I looked at the **living creatures**, I saw a wheel on the ground
1:15 I saw a wheel on the ground beside each **creature** with its four
1:19 When the **living creatures** moved, the wheels beside them moved;
1:19 when the **living creatures** rose from the ground, the wheels also
1:20 because the spirit of the **living creatures** was in the wheels.
1:21 because the spirit of the **living creatures** was in the wheels.
1:22 Spread out above the heads of the **living creatures** was what
3:13 the sound of the wings of the **living creatures** brushing against
5:17 I will send famine and wild **beasts** against you, and they will leave
10:15 These were the **living creatures** I had seen by the Kebar River.
10:17 with them, because the spirit of the **living creatures** was in them.
10:20 These were the **living creatures** I had seen beneath the God of
14:15 "Or if I send wild **beasts** through that country and they leave it
14:15 so that no one can pass through it because of the **beasts**,
14:21 sword and famine and wild **beasts** and plague—to kill its men
29: 5 I will give you as food to the **beasts** *of* the earth and the birds of
31: 6 its boughs, all the **beasts** *of* the field gave birth under its branches;
31:13 fallen tree, and all the **beasts** *of* the field were among its branches.
32: 4 on you and all the **beasts** *of* the earth gorge themselves on you.
33:27 those out in the country I will give to the **wild animals** to be
34: 5 they were scattered they became food for all the wild **animals**.
34: 8 has been plundered and has become food for all the wild **animals**,
34:25 and rid the land of wild **beasts** so that they may live in the desert
34:28 be plundered by the nations, nor will wild **animals** devour them.
38:20 The fish of the sea, the birds of the air, the **beasts** *of* the field,
39: 4 you as food to all kinds of carrion birds and to the wild **animals**.
39:17 Call out to every kind of bird and all the wild **animals**: 'Assemble
47: 9 Swarms of **living** creatures will live wherever the river flows.
Da 8: 4 No **animal** could stand against him, and none could rescue from
Hos 2:12 [2:14] make them a thicket, and wild **animals** will devour them.
2:18 [2:20] I will make a covenant for them with the **beasts** *of* the field
4: 3 the **beasts** *of* the field and the birds of the air and the fish of the sea
13: 8 Like a lion I will devour them; a wild **animal** will tear them apart.
Zep 2:14 Flocks and herds will lie down there, **creatures** *of* every kind.
2:15 What a ruin she has become, a lair for **wild beasts**! All who pass

2652 ²חַיָּה ḥayyâ², n.f. [12] [√ 2644; cf. 2649]

life [3], *untranslated* [2], hunger [1], live [1], lives [1], me [+3276] [1], renewal [1], them [+4392] [1], very being [1]

Job 33:18 preserve his soul from the pit, his **life** from perishing by the sword.
33:20 so that his **very being** finds food repulsive and his soul loathes the
33:22 soul draws near to the pit, and his **life** to the messengers of death.
33:28 soul from going down to the pit, and I will **live** to enjoy the light.'
36:14 die in their youth, **[RPH]** among male prostitutes of the shrines.
38:39 hunt the prey for the lioness and satisfy the **hunger** *of* the lions
Ps 74:19 wild beasts; do not forget the **lives** *of* your afflicted people forever.
78:50 spare them from death but gave **them** [+4392] over to the plague.
143: 3 The enemy pursues me, he crushes **me** [+3276] to the ground;
Isa 57:10 You found **renewal** *of* your strength, and so you did not faint.
Eze 7:13 **[RPH]** for the vision concerning the whole crowd will not be
7:13 Because of their sins, not one of them will preserve his **life**.

2653 ³חַיָּה ḥayyâ³, n.f. [3] [√ 2649]

band [1], banded together [+665+2021+4200] [1], people [1]

2Sa 23:11 When the Philistines **banded together** [+665+2021+4200] at a place where there was a field full of lentils, Israel's troops fled from
23:13 while a **band** *of* Philistines was encamped in the Valley of
Ps 68:10 [68:11] Your **people** settled in it, and from your bounty, O God,

2654 חַיּוּת ḥayyût, n.f.abst. [1] [√ 2649]

living [1]

2Sa 20: 3 kept in confinement till the day of their death, **living** *as* widows.

2655 ¹חִיל ḥîl¹, v. [48 / 46] [→ 2659, 2660, 2714]

in anguish [4], in labor [4], tremble [4], gave birth [2], shakes [2], was given birth [2], wounded [2], writhe in agony [+2655] [2], writhe in pain [2], writhe [2], writhed [2], writhes [2], at birth [1], be born [1], bears [1], brings [1], brought forth [1], brought to birth [1], felt pain [1], goes into labor [1], in deep anguish [1], in distress [1], suffers torment [1], trembles [1], twists [1], were brought forth [1], writhe in agony [+4394] [1], writhed in pain [1]

Ge 8:10 [d] *He* waited [BHS ***trembled***; NIV 3498] seven more days
Dt 2:25 [A] of you and will tremble and *be* **in anguish** because of you."
32:18 [D] who fathered you; you forgot the God *who* **gave** you **birth**.
Jdg 3:25 [g] *They* waited [BHS ***trembled***; NIV 3498] to the point of
1Sa 31: 3 [A] the archers overtook him, they **wounded** *him* critically.
1Ch 10: 3 [A] and when the archers overtook him, they **wounded** *him*.
16:30 [A] **Tremble** before him, all the earth! The world is firmly
Est 4: 4 [F] and told her about Mordecai, she *was* **in** great **distress**.
Job 15: 7 [E] man ever born? **Were** *you* **brought forth** before the hills?
15:20 [F] All his days the wicked man **suffers torment**, the ruthless
26: 5 [D] "The dead *are* **in deep anguish**, those beneath the waters
39: 1 [D] give birth? Do you watch when the doe **bears** her fawn?
Ps 29: 8 [G] The voice of the LORD **shakes** the desert; the LORD
29: 8 [G] shakes the desert; the LORD **shakes** the Desert of Kadesh.
29: 9 [D] The voice of the LORD **twists** the oaks and strips the
51: 5 [51:7] [E] Surely *I was* sinful **at birth**, sinful from the time my
55: 4 [55:5] [A] My heart *is* **in anguish** within me; the terrors of
77:16 [77:17] [A] saw you, O God, the waters saw you and **writhed**;
90: 2 [D] were born or *you* **brought forth** the earth and the world,
96: 9 [A] splendor of his holiness; **tremble** before him, all the earth.
97: 4 [A] lightning lights up the world; the earth sees and **trembles**.
114: 7 [A] **Tremble**, O earth, at the presence of the Lord,
Pr 8:24 [D] When there were no oceans, *I* **was given birth**, when there
8:25 [E] were settled in place, before the hills, *I* **was given birth**,
25:23 [D] As a north wind **brings** rain, so a sly tongue brings angry
Isa 13: 8 [A] will grip them; *they will* **writhe** like a woman in labor.
23: 4 [A] "*I have* neither *been* **in labor** nor given birth; I have neither
23: 5 [A] to Egypt, *they will be* **in anguish** at the report from Tyre.
26:17 [A] As a woman with child and about to give birth **writhes**
26:18 [A] We were with child, *we* **writhed in pain**, but we gave birth
45:10 [A] or to his mother, 'What *have you* **brought to birth**?'
51: 2 [D] to Abraham, your father, and to Sarah, *who* **gave** you **birth**.
54: 1 [A] burst into song, shout for joy, you *who were* never **in labor**;
66: 7 [A] "Before *she* **goes into labor**, she gives birth; before the pains
66: 8 [H] *Can a* country **be born** in a day or a nation be brought forth
66: 8 [A] Yet no sooner *is* Zion **in labor** than she gives birth to her
Jer 4:19 [A] *I* **writhe** [Q 3498] **in pain**. Oh, the agony of my heart!
4:31 [A] I hear a cry as of a *woman* **in labor**, a groan as of one
5: 3 [A] You struck them, but *they* **felt** no **pain**; you crushed them,
5:22 [A] the LORD. "*Should you* not **tremble** in my presence?
51:29 [A] The land trembles and **writhes**, for the LORD's purposes
Eze 30:16 [A] set fire to Egypt; Pelusium *will* **writhe** [+2655] **in agony**.
30:16 [A] set fire to Egypt; Pelusium *will* **writhe in agony** [+2655].
Joel 2: 6 [A] At the sight of them, nations *are* **in anguish**; every face turns
Mic 1:12 [A] Those who live in Maroth **writhe in pain**, waiting for relief,
4:10 [A] **Writhe** in agony, O Daughter of Zion, like a woman in labor,
Hab 3:10 [A] the mountains saw you and **writhed**. Torrents of water swept
Zec 9: 5 [A] Gaza *will* **writhe** [+4394] **in agony**, and Ekron too, for her

2656 ²חִיל ḥîl², v. [2] [→ 2657]

endure [1], prosperous [1]

Job 20:21 [A] is left for him to devour; his prosperity *will* not **endure**.
Ps 10: 5 [A] His ways *are* always **prosperous**; he is haughty and your

2657 חַיִל ḥayil, n.m. [245] [→ 35, 38, 1211; cf. 2656; Ar 10264]

army [77], wealth [25], fighting men [+1475] [12], strength [11], brave warriors [+1475] [6], riches [5], able men [+1201] [4], brave [+1201] [4], force [4], troops [4], valiant [4], capable [3], forces [3], noble character [3], soldiers [3], strong [3], *untranslated* [2], able men [+1475] [2], able-bodied [2], best fighting men [+1475] [2], caravan [2], might [2], mighty things [2], power [2], standing [+1475] [2], standing [2], valiant fighter [+408+1201] [2], valiant fighters [+408] [2], valiant soldier [+1475] [2], victory [2], warriors [+408] [2], worthy [2], able [+1201] [1], able [1], able-bodied [+1201] [1], armed force [1], armed forces [+7372] [1], armies [1], army [+2162] [1], army [+7372] [1], battle [1], brave fighting men [+1475] [1], brave man [+1475] [1], brave warrior [+1475] [1], brave [1], bravely [+1201+4200] [1], bravest soldier [+1201] [1], capable men [+1475] [1], champions [+408] [1], company [1], courageous [+1201] [1], experienced fighting men [+408+1475+4878] [1], fighting [+1201] [1], fighting [1], goods [1], mighty men [+1475] [1], mighty warrior [+1475] [1], mighty [1], military leaders [1], military [1], noble [1], one[s] [1], profit [1], skills [1], soldiers [+1201] [1], special ability [1], strongest defenders [+408] [1], they[s] [+2021+2256+3405+8569] [1], troops [+1475] [1], valiantly [1], very capable men [+1475] [1], warriors [+1201] [1], warriors [+1475] [1], wealthy [1]

Ge 34:29 They carried off all their **wealth** and all their women and children,
47: 6 And if you know of any among them with **special ability**,
Ex 14: 4 But I will gain glory for myself through Pharaoh and all his **army**,
14: 9 all Pharaoh's horses and chariots, horsemen and **troops**—
14:17 I will gain glory through Pharaoh and all his **army**, through his
14:28 the entire **army** *of* Pharaoh that had followed the Israelites into the
15: 4 Pharaoh's chariots and his **army** he has hurled into the sea.
18:21 But select **capable** men from all the people—men who fear God,
18:25 He chose **capable** men from all Israel and made them leaders of
Nu 24:18 his enemy, will be conquered, but Israel will grow **strong**.
31: 9 and took all the Midianite herds, flocks and **goods** as plunder.
31:14 Moses was angry with the officers of the **army**—the commanders
Dt 3:18 all your **able-bodied** men, armed for battle, must cross over ahead
8:17 and the strength of my hands have produced this **wealth** for me."
8:18 for it is he who gives you the ability to produce **wealth**, and
11: 4 what he did to the Egyptian **army**, to its horses and chariots,
33:11 Bless all his **skills**, O LORD, and be pleased with the work of his
Jos 1:14 all your **fighting** [+1475] **men**, fully armed, must cross over ahead
6: 2 into your hands, along with its king and its **fighting** [+1475] **men**.
8: 3 He chose thirty thousand of his **best fighting** [+1475] **men**
10: 7 with his entire army, including all the **best fighting** [+1475] **men**.
Jdg 3:29 struck down about ten thousand Moabites, all vigorous and **strong**;
6:12 to Gideon, he said, "The LORD is with you, **mighty** warrior."
11: 1 Jephthah the Gileadite was a **mighty warrior** [+1475]. His father
18: 2 So the Danites sent five **warriors** [+1201] from Zorah and Eshtaol
20:44 thousand Benjamites fell, all of them **valiant fighters** [+408].
20:46 Benjamite swordsmen fell, all of them **valiant fighters** [+408].
21:10 So the assembly sent twelve thousand **fighting** [+1201] men with
Ru 2: 1 of Elimelech, a man of **standing** [+1475], whose name was Boaz.
3:11 fellow townsmen know that you are a woman of **noble character**.
4:11 May you have **standing** in Ephrathah and be famous in Bethlehem.
1Sa 2: 4 are broken, but those who stumbled are armed with **strength**.
9: 1 There was a Benjamite, a man of **standing**, whose name was Kish
10:26 accompanied by **valiant** *men* whose hearts God had touched.
14:48 He fought **valiantly** and defeated the Amalekites, delivering Israel
14:52 whenever Saul saw a mighty or **brave** [+1201] man, he took him
16:18 He is a **brave** [+1475] **man** and a warrior. He speaks well
17:20 He reached the camp as the **army** was going out to its battle
18:17 only serve me **bravely** [+1201+4200] and fight the battles of the
31:12 all their **valiant** men journeyed through the night to Beth Shan.
2Sa 2: 7 Now then, be strong and **brave** [+1201], for Saul your master is
8: 9 heard that David had defeated the entire **army** *of* Hadadezer,
11:16 at a place where he knew the **strongest** [+408] **defenders** were.
13:28 Have not I given you this order? Be strong and **brave** [+1201]."
17:10 even the **bravest** [+1201] **soldier**, whose heart is like the heart of a
17:10 your father is a fighter and that those with him are **brave** [+1201].
22:33 It is God who arms me with **strength** and makes my way perfect.
22:40 You armed me with **strength** for battle; you made my adversaries
23:20 son of Jehoiada was a **valiant fighter** [+408+1201] [K 2644]
24: 2 So the king said to Joab and the **army** commanders with him,
24: 4 king's word, however, overruled Joab and the **army** commanders;
24: 4 so **they**[s] [+2021+2256+3405+8569] left the presence of the king to
24: 9 In Israel there were eight hundred thousand **able-bodied** men who
1Ki 1:42 "Come in. A **worthy** man like you must be bringing good news."
1:52 Solomon replied, "If he shows himself to be a **worthy** man,
10: 2 Arriving at Jerusalem with a very great **caravan**—with camels
11:28 Now Jeroboam was a man of **standing** [+1475], and when
15:20 and sent the commanders of his **forces** against the towns of Israel.
20: 1 Now Ben-Hadad king of Aram mustered his entire **army**.
20:19 commanders marched out of the city with the **army** behind them
20:25 You must also raise an **army** like the one you lost—horse for horse
20:25 You must also raise an army like the **one**[s] you lost—horse for
2Ki 2:16 they said, "we your servants have fifty **able** [+1201] men.
5: 1 to Aram. He was a **valiant** [+1475] **soldier**, but he had leprosy.
6:14 Then he sent horses and chariots and a strong **force** there.
6:15 an **army** with horses and chariots had surrounded the city.
7: 6 to hear the sound of chariots and horses and a great **army**,
9: 5 When he arrived, he found the **army** officers sitting together.
11:15 of units of a hundred, who were in charge of the **troops**:
15:20 Every **wealthy** man had to contribute fifty shekels of silver to be
18:17 his chief officer and his field commander with a large **army**,
24:14 all the officers and **fighting** [+1475] **men**, and all the craftsmen
24:16 to Babylon the entire force of seven thousand **fighting** men,
25: 1 king of Babylon marched against Jerusalem with his whole **army**.
25: 5 the Babylonian **army** pursued the king and overtook him in the
25: 5 of Jericho. All his **soldiers** were separated from him and scattered,
25:10 The whole Babylonian **army**, under the commander of the imperial
25:23 When all the **army** officers and their men heard that the king of
25:26 together with the **army** officers, fled to Egypt for fear of the
1Ch 5:18 had 44,760 men ready for military service—**able-bodied** [+1201]
5:24 They were **brave** warriors, famous men, and heads of their
7: 2 the descendants of Tola listed as **fighting** [+1475] **men** in their
7: 5 The relatives who were **fighting** [+1475] **men** belonging to all the
7: 7 Their genealogical record listed 22,034 **fighting** [+1475] **men**.
7: 9 listed the heads of families and 20,200 **fighting** [+1475] **men**.
7:11 There were 17,200 **fighting** [+1475] **men** ready to go out to war.
7:40 choice men, **brave** [+1475] **warriors** and outstanding leaders.
8:40 The sons of Ulam were **brave** [+1475] **warriors** who could handle
9:13 They were **able** [+1475] **men**, responsible for ministering in the
10:12 all their **valiant** men went and took the bodies of Saul and his sons
11:22 Benaiah son of Jehoiada was a **valiant** [+408+1201] **fighter** from
11:26 The **mighty men** [+1475] were: Asahel the brother of Joab,
12: 8 [12:9] They were **brave** [+1475] **warriors**, ready for battle
12:21 [12:22] for all of them were **brave** [+1475] **warriors**, and they
12:25 [12:26] men of Simeon, **warriors** [+1475] ready for battle—
12:28 [12:29] Zadok, a **brave** [+1475] young **warrior**, with 22 officers
12:30 [12:31] men of Ephraim, **brave** [+1475] **warriors**, famous in
18: 9 David had defeated the entire **army** *of* Hadadezer king of Zobah,
20: 1 when kings go off to war, Joab led out the **armed forces** [+7372].
26: 6 father's family because they were **very capable** [+1475] **men**.
26: 7 his relatives Elihu and Semakiah were also **able** [+1201] **men**.
26: 8 their relatives were **capable** men with the strength to do the work—
26: 9 had sons and relatives, who were **able** [+1201] **men**—
26:30 and his relatives—seventeen hundred **able** [+1201] **men**—
26:31 **capable** [+1475] **men** among the Hebronites were found at Jazer in
26:32 who were **able** [+1201] **men** and heads of families,
28: 1 the mighty men and all the **brave** [+1475] **warriors**.
2Ch 9: 1 Arriving with a very great **caravan**—with camels carrying spices,
13: 3 Abijah went into battle with a **force** of four hundred thousand able
13: 3 line against him with eight hundred thousand able **troops** [+1475].
14: 8 [14:7] Asa had an **army** of three hundred thousand men from
14: 8 [14:7] with bows. All these were **brave fighting** [+1475] **men**.
14: 9 [14:8] the Cushite marched out against them with a vast **army**
16: 4 and sent the commanders of his **forces** against the towns of Israel.
16: 7 the **army** *of* the king of Aram has escaped from your hand.
16: 8 and Libyans a mighty **army** with great numbers of chariots
17: 2 He stationed **troops** in all the fortified cities of Judah and put
17:13 He also kept **experienced fighting** [+408+1475+4878] **men** in
17:14 Adnah the commander, with 300,000 **fighting** [+1475] **men**;
17:16 himself for the service of the LORD, with 200,000. **[RPH]**
17:17 Eliada, a **valiant** [+1475] **soldier**, with 200,000 men armed with
23:14 of a hundred, who were in charge of the **troops**, and said to them:
24:23 At the turn of the year, the **army** *of* Aram marched against Joash;
24:24 Although the Aramean **army** had come with only a few men,
24:24 the LORD delivered into their hands a much larger **army**.
25: 6 He also hired a hundred thousand **fighting** [+1475] **men** from
26:11 Uzziah had a well-trained **army**, ready to go out by divisions
26:12 The total number of family leaders over the **fighting** [+1475] **men**
26:13 Under their command was an **army** [+7372] of 307,500 men
26:13 for war, a powerful **force** to support the king against his enemies.
26:17 Azariah the priest with eighty other **courageous** [+1201] priests of
28: 6 killed a hundred and twenty thousand **soldiers** [+1201] in Judah—
32:21 who annihilated all the **fighting** [+1475] **men** and the leaders
33:14 He stationed **military** commanders in all the fortified cities in
Ezr 8:22 I was ashamed to ask the king for **soldiers** and horsemen to protect
Ne 2: 9 The king had also sent **army** officers and cavalry with me.
4: 2 [3:34] in the presence of his associates and the **army** *of* Samaria,
11: 6 The descendants of Perez who lived in Jerusalem totaled 468 **able**
11:14 his associates, who were **able** [+1475] **men**—128. Their chief
Est 1: 3 The **military leaders** *of* Persia and Media, the princes,
8:11 kill and annihilate any **armed force** *of* any nationality or province
Job 5: 5 it even from among thorns, and the thirsty pant after his **wealth**.
15:29 He will no longer be rich and his **wealth** will not endure, nor will
20:15 He will spit out the **riches** he swallowed; God will make his
20:18 give back uneaten; he will not enjoy the **profit** *from* his trading.
21: 7 Why do the wicked live on, growing old and increasing in **power**?
31:25 if I have rejoiced over my great **wealth**, the fortune my hands had
Ps 10:10 [His **victims** [Q +3875; see K 2724] are crushed, they collapse;]
18:32 [18:33] It is God who arms me with **strength** and makes my way

Ps 18:39 [18:40] You armed me with **strength** for battle; you made my
33:16 No king is saved by the size of his **army**; no warrior escapes by his
33:17 hope for deliverance; despite all its great **strength** it cannot save.
49:6 [49:7] those who trust in their **wealth** and boast of their great
49:10 [49:11] the senseless alike perish and leave their **wealth** to others.
59:11 [59:12] In your **might** make them wander about, and bring them
60:12 [60:14] With God we will gain the **victory**, and he will trample
62:10 [62:11] though your **riches** increase, do not set your heart on
73:12 the wicked are like—always carefree, they increase in **wealth**.
76:5 [76:6] not one of the **warriors** [+408] can lift his hands.
84:7 [84:8] They go from **strength** to strength, till each appears before
84:7 [84:8] They go from strength to **strength**, till each appears before
108:13 [108:14] With God we will gain the **victory**, and he will trample
110:3 Your troops will be willing on your day of **battle**. Arrayed in holy
118:15 the righteous: "The LORD's right hand has done **mighty things**!
118:16 is lifted high; the LORD's right hand has done **mighty things**!"
136:15 swept Pharaoh and his **army** into the Red Sea; *His love*
Pr 12:4 A wife of **noble character** is her husband's crown, but a
13:22 but a sinner's **wealth** is stored up for the righteous.
31:3 do not spend your **strength** on women, your vigor on those who
31:10 A wife of **noble character** who can find? She is worth far more
31:29 "Many women do **noble** *things*, but you surpass them all."
Ecc 10:10 *more* **strength** is needed but skill will bring success.
12:3 the **strong** men stoop, when the grinders cease because they are
Isa 5:22 heroes at drinking wine and **champions** [+408] at mixing drinks,
8:4 the **wealth** *of* Damascus and the plunder of Samaria will be carried
10:14 into a nest, so my hand reached for the **wealth** *of* the nations;
30:6 darting snakes, the envoys carry their **riches** on donkeys' backs,
36:2 the king of Assyria sent his field commander with a large **army**
43:17 out the chariots and horses, the **army** and reinforcements together,
60:5 will be brought to you, to you the **riches** *of* the nations will come.
60:11 or night, so that men may bring you the **wealth** *of* the nations—
61:6 You will feed on the **wealth** *of* nations, and in their riches you will
Jer 15:13 Your **wealth** and your treasures I will give as plunder, without
17:3 My mountain in the land and your **wealth** and all your treasures I
32:2 The **army** *of* the king of Babylon was then besieging Jerusalem,
34:1 king of Babylon and all his **army** and all the kingdoms
34:7 while the **army** *of* the king of Babylon was fighting against
34:21 to the **army** *of* the king of Babylon, which has withdrawn from
35:11 go to Jerusalem to escape the Babylonian and Aramean **armies**.'
35:11 and Aramean armies.' **[RPH]** So we have remained in Jerusalem."
37:5 Pharaoh's **army** had marched out of Egypt, and when the
37:7 the king of Judah, who sent you to inquire of me, 'Pharaoh's **army**,
37:10 Even if you were to defeat the entire Babylonian **army** that is
37:11 After the Babylonian **army** had withdrawn from Jerusalem
37:11 army had withdrawn from Jerusalem because of Pharaoh's **army**,
38:3 'This city will certainly be handed over to the **army** *of* the king of
39:1 king of Babylon marched against Jerusalem with his whole **army**
39:5 the Babylonian **army** pursued them and overtook Zedekiah in the
40:7 When all the **army** officers and their men who were still in the
40:13 all the **army** officers still in the open country came to Gedaliah at
41:11 all the **army** officers who were with him heard about all the crimes
41:13 Johanan son of Kareah and the **army** officers who were with him,
41:16 all the **army** officers who were with him led away all the survivors
42:1 Then all the **army** officers, including Johanan son of Kareah
42:8 son of Kareah and all the **army** officers who were with him
43:4 So Johanan son of Kareah and all the **army** officers and all the
43:5 all the **army** officers led away all the remnant of Judah who had
46:2 This is the message against the **army** *of* Pharaoh Neco king of
46:22 will hiss like a fleeing serpent as the enemy advances in **force**;
48:14 "How can you say, 'We are warriors, men **valiant** in battle'?
52:4 king of Babylon marched against Jerusalem with his whole **army**.
52:8 the Babylonian **army** pursued King Zedekiah and overtook him in
52:8 of Jericho. All his **soldiers** were separated from him and scattered,
52:14 The whole Babylonian **army** under the commander of the imperial
Eze 17:17 Pharaoh with his mighty **army** and great horde will be of no help
26:12 They will plunder your **wealth** and loot your merchandise;
27:10 " 'Men of Persia, Lydia and Put served as soldiers in your **army**.
28:4 and understanding you have gained **wealth** for yourself
28:5 By your great skill in trading you have increased your **wealth**,
28:5 and because of your **wealth** your heart has grown proud.
29:18 Nebuchadnezzar king of Babylon drove his **army** in a hard
29:18 his **army** got no reward from the campaign he led against Tyre.
29:19 its wealth. He will loot and plunder the land as pay for his **army**.
32:31 "Pharaoh—he and all his **army**—will see them and he will be
37:10 they came to life and stood up on their feet—a vast **army**.
38:4 put hooks in your jaws and bring you out with your whole **army**—
38:15 all of them riding on horses, a great horde, a mighty **army**.
Da 11:7 He will attack the **forces** of the king of the North and enter his
11:10 His sons will prepare for war and assemble a great **army** [+2162],
11:13 several years, he will advance with a huge **army** fully equipped.
11:25 "With a large **army** he will stir up his strength and courage against
11:25 of the South will wage war with a large and very powerful **army**,
11:26 his **army** will be swept away, and many will fall in battle.
Joel 2:11 The LORD thunders at the head of his **army**; his forces are
2:22 are bearing their fruit; the fig tree and the vine yield their **riches**.
2:25 and the locust swarm—my great **army** that I sent among you.
Ob 1:11 On the day you stood aloof while strangers carried off his **wealth**
1:13 of their disaster, nor seize their **wealth** in the day of their disaster.
1:20 This **company** of Israelite exiles who are in Canaan will possess
Mic 4:13 gains to the LORD, their **wealth** to the Lord of all the earth.
Na 2:3 [2:4] his soldiers are red; the **warriors** [+408] are clad in scarlet.
Hab 3:19 The Sovereign LORD is my **strength**; he makes my feet like the
Zep 1:13 Their **wealth** will be plundered, their houses demolished. They will
Zec 4:6 'Not by **might** nor by power, but by my Spirit,' says the LORD
9:4 will take away her possessions and destroy her **power** on the sea,
14:14 The **wealth** *of* all the surrounding nations will be collected—

2658 חֵיל ḥêl, n.m. [7] [cf. 2565]

ramparts [3], defense [1], outer fortifications [1], wall [1], walls [1]

2Sa 20:15 ramp up to the city, and it stood against the **outer fortifications**.
1Ki 21:23 the LORD says: 'Dogs will devour Jezebel by the **wall** *of* Jezreel.'
Ps 48:13 [48:14] consider well her **ramparts**, view her citadels, that you
122:7 May there be peace within your **walls** and security within your
Isa 26:1 have a strong city; God makes salvation its walls and **ramparts**.
La 2:8 He made **ramparts** and walls lament; together they wasted away.
Na 3:8 water around her? The river was her **defense**, the waters her wall.

2659 ³חִיל ḥîl³, n.m. [6] [√ 2655]

pain [5], anguish [1]

Ex 15:14 will hear and tremble; **anguish** will grip the people of Philistia.
Ps 48:6 [48:7] seized them there, **pain** like that of a woman in labor.
Jer 6:24 Anguish has gripped us, **pain** like that of a woman in labor.
22:23 when pangs come upon you, **pain** like that of a woman in labor!
50:43 Anguish has gripped him, **pain** like that of a woman in labor.
Mic 4:9 that **pain** seizes you like that of a woman in labor?

2660 חִילָה ḥîlâ, n.f. [1] [√ 2655]

pain [1]

Job 6:10 I would still have this consolation—my joy in unrelenting **pain**—

2661 חִילֵז ḥîlēz, n.pr.loc. [1 / 0] [cf. 2664]

1Ch 6:58 [6:43] Hilen, [BHS *Hilez*; NIV 2664] Debir,

2662 חֵלֶךְ ḥêlēk, n.pr.loc. [1]

Helech [1]

Eze 27:11 Men of Arvad and **Helech** manned your walls on every side;

2663 חֵילָם ḥêlām, n.pr.loc. [2] [cf. 2691]

Helam [2]

2Sa 10:16 they went to **Helam**, with Shobach the commander of Hadadezer's
10:17 he gathered all Israel, crossed the Jordan and went to **Helam**.

2664 חִילֵן ḥîlēn, n.pr.loc. [0 / 1] [cf. 2661]

Hilen [1]

1Ch 6:58 [6:43] **Hilen**, [BHS 2661] Debir,

2665 חִין ḥîn, n.[m.]. [1] [√ 2858]

graceful [1]

Job 41:12 [41:4] to speak of his limbs, his strength and his **graceful** form.

2666 חַיִץ ḥayiṣ, n.[m.]. [1] [cf. 2575]

flimsy wall [1]

Eze 13:10 when there is no peace, and because, when a **flimsy wall** is built,

2667 חִיצוֹן ḥîṣôn, a. [25] [√ 2575]

outer [20], away from [1], both outer [1], outside [+2025] [1], outside [1], where[s] [+2021+2021+2958] [1]

1Ki 6:29 in both the inner and **outer** *rooms*, he carved cherubim, palm trees
6:30 He also covered the floors of **both** the inner and **outer** *rooms* of
2Ki 16:18 removed the royal entryway **outside** [+2025] the temple of the
1Ch 26:29 Kenaniah and his sons were assigned duties **away from** the temple,
2Ch 33:14 Afterward he rebuilt the **outer** wall of the City of David, west of
Ne 11:16 who had charge of the **outside** work of the house of God;
Est 6:4 Now Haman had just entered the **outer** court of the palace to speak
Eze 10:5 of the cherubim could be heard as far away as the **outer** court,
40:17 Then he brought me into the **outer** court. There I saw some rooms
40:20 and width of the gate facing north, leading into the **outer** court.
40:31 Its portico faced the **outer** court; palm trees decorated its jambs,
40:34 Its portico faced the **outer** court; palm trees decorated the jambs on
40:37 Its portico faced the **outer** court; palm trees decorated the jambs on

Eze 41:17 walls at regular intervals all around the inner and **outer** sanctuary
42: 1 the man led me northward into the **outer** court and brought me to
42: 3 and in the section opposite the pavement of the **outer** court,
42: 7 There was an outer wall parallel to the rooms and the **outer** court;
42: 8 While the row of rooms on the side next to the **outer** court was
42: 9 entrance on the east side as one enters them from the **outer** court.
42:14 they are not to go into the **outer** court until they leave behind the
44: 1 Then the man brought me back to the **outer** gate of the sanctuary,
44:19 When they go out into the **outer** court where the people are,
44:19 out into the outer court **where**[s] [+2021+2021+2958] the people are,
46:20 to avoid bringing them into the **outer** court and consecrating the
46:21 He then brought me to the **outer** court and led me around to its

2668 חֵיק ḥêq, n.[m.]. [38]

arms [6], cloak [5], lap [4], laps [4], gutter [3], breast [2], heart [2], loves [2], *untranslated* [1], beside [+928] [1], bosom [1], embrace [1], floor [1], garment [1], love [1], returned unanswered [+8740] [1], secret [1], within [+928] [1]

Ge 16: 5 I put my servant in your **arms**, and now that she knows she is
Ex 4: 6 Then the LORD said, "Put your hand inside your **cloak**."
4: 6 So Moses put his hand into his **cloak**, and when he took it out,
4: 7 "Now put it back into your **cloak**," he said. So Moses put his hand
4: 7 So Moses put his hand back into his **cloak**, and when he took it
4: 7 he took it out, **[RPH]** it was restored, like the rest of his flesh.
Nu 11:12 Why do you tell me to carry them in my **arms**, as a nurse carries
Dt 13: 6 [13:7] own brother, or your son or daughter, or the wife you **love**,
28:54 on his own brother or the wife he **loves** or his surviving children,
28:56 will begrudge the husband she **loves** and her own son or daughter
Ru 4:16 Then Naomi took the child, laid him in her **lap** and cared for him.
2Sa 12: 3 It shared his food, drank from his cup and even slept in his **arms**.
12: 8 master's house to you, and your master's wives into your **arms**.
1Ki 1: 2 She can lie **beside** [+928] him so that our lord the king may keep
3:20 She put him by her **breast** and put her dead son by my breast.
3:20 She put him by her breast and put her dead son by my **breast**.
17:19 He took him from her **arms**, carried him to the upper room where
22:35 The blood from his wound ran onto the **floor** *of* the chariot,
Job 19:27 and not another. How my heart yearns **within** [+928] me!
Ps 35:13 When my prayers **returned** to me **unanswered** [+8740],
74:11 Take it from the folds of your **garment** and destroy them!
79:12 Pay back into the **laps** *of* our neighbors seven times the reproach
89:50 [89:51] how I bear in my **heart** the taunts of all the nations,
Pr 5:20 by an adulteress? Why embrace the **bosom** *of* another man's wife?
6:27 Can a man scoop fire into his **lap** without his clothes being
16:33 The lot is cast into the **lap**, but its every decision is from the
17:23 A wicked man accepts a bribe in **secret** to pervert the course of
21:14 and a bribe concealed in the **cloak** pacifies great wrath.
Ecc 7: 9 provoked in your spirit, for anger resides in the **lap** *of* fools.
Isa 40:11 gathers the lambs in his arms and carries them close to his **heart**;
65: 6 but will pay back in full; I will pay it back into their **laps**—
65: 7 I will measure into their **laps** the full payment for their former
Jer 32:18 bring the punishment for the fathers' sins into the **laps** *of* their
La 2:12 streets of the city, as their lives ebb away in their mothers' **arms**.
Eze 43:13 Its **gutter** is a cubit deep and a cubit wide, with a rim of one span
43:14 From the **gutter** *on* the ground up to the lower ledge it is two
43:17 with a rim of half a cubit and a **gutter** of a cubit all around.
Mic 7: 5 Even with her who lies in your **embrace** be careful of your words.

2669 חִירָה ḥîrâ, n.pr.m. [2]

Hirah [2]

Ge 38: 1 and went down to stay with a man of Adullam named **Hirah**.
38:12 his sheep, and his friend **Hirah** the Adullamite went with him.

2670 חִירוֹם ḥîrôm, n.pr.m. [3] [√ 325?]

Hiram [2], he[s] [1]

1Ki 5:10 [5:24] In this way **Hiram** kept Solomon supplied with all the
5:18 [5:32] **Hiram** and the men of Gebal cut and prepared the timber
7:40 **He**[s] also made the basins and shovels and sprinkling bowls.

2671 חִירָם ḥîrām, n.pr.m. [20] [√ 325?]

Hiram [15], Huram [3], he[s] [1], Hiram's [1]

2Sa 5:11 Now **Hiram** king of Tyre sent messengers to David, along with
1Ki 5: 1 [5:15] When **Hiram** king of Tyre heard that Solomon had been
5: 1 [5:15] because **he**[s] had always been on friendly terms with David.
5: 2 [5:16] Solomon sent back this message to **Hiram**:
5: 7 [5:21] When **Hiram** heard Solomon's message, he was greatly
5: 8 [5:22] So **Hiram** sent word to Solomon: "I have received the
5:11 [5:25] Solomon gave **Hiram** twenty thousand cors of wheat as
5:11 [5:25] Solomon continued to do this for **Hiram** year after year.
5:12 [5:26] There were peaceful relations between **Hiram**
7:13 King Solomon sent to Tyre and brought **Huram**,
7:40 So **Huram** finished all the work he had undertaken for King
7:45 All these objects that **Huram** made for King Solomon for the
9:11 King Solomon gave twenty towns in Galilee to **Hiram** king of
9:11 because **Hiram** had supplied him with all the cedar and pine
9:12 when **Hiram** went from Tyre to see the towns that Solomon had
9:14 Now **Hiram** had sent to the king 120 talents of gold.
9:27 **Hiram** sent his men—sailors who knew the sea—to serve in the
10:11 (**Hiram's** ships brought gold from Ophir; and from there they
10:22 had a fleet of trading ships at sea along with the ships of **Hiram**.
1Ch 14: 1 Now **Hiram** [Q 2586] king of Tyre sent messengers to David,
2Ch 4:11 [So **Huram** [K; see Q 2586] finished the work he had undertaken]
9:10 [(The men of **Hiram** [K; see Q 2586] and the men of Solomon]

2672 חִירֹת ḥîrōt, n.pr.loc. Not used in NIV/BHS [→ 2112, 7084]

2673 חִישׁ ḥîš, adv. [1] [√ 2590]

quickly [1]

Ps 90:10 yet their span is but trouble and sorrow, for they **quickly** pass,

2674 חֵךְ ḥēk, n.m. [18]

mouth [6], roof of mouth [3], taste [3], tongue [2], lips [1], on the tip of tongue [+928+4383] [1], roof of mouths [1], speech [1]

Job 6:30 any wickedness on my lips? Can my **mouth** not discern malice?
12:11 Does not the ear test words as the **tongue** tastes food?
20:13 though he cannot bear to let it go and keeps it in his **mouth**,
29:10 were hushed, and their tongues stuck to the **roof of** their **mouths**.
31:30 I have not allowed my **mouth** to sin by invoking a curse against his
33: 2 my mouth; my words are **on the tip of** my **tongue** [+928+4383].
34: 3 For the ear tests words as the **tongue** tastes food.
Ps 119:103 How sweet are your words to my **taste**, sweeter than honey to my
137: 6 May my tongue cling to the **roof of** my **mouth** if I do not
Pr 5: 3 of an adulteress drip honey, and her **speech** is smoother than oil;
8: 7 My **mouth** speaks what is true, for my lips detest wickedness.
24:13 for it is good; honey from the comb is sweet to your **taste**.
SS 2: 3 I delight to sit in his shade, and his fruit is sweet to my **taste**.
5:16 His **mouth** is sweetness itself; he is altogether lovely. This is my
7: 9 [7:10] your **mouth** like the best wine. May the wine go straight to
La 4: 4 of thirst the infant's tongue sticks to the **roof of** its **mouth**;
Eze 3:26 I will make your tongue stick to the **roof of** your **mouth** so that
Hos 8: 1 "Put the trumpet to your **lips**! An eagle is over the house of the

2675 חָכָה ḥākâ, v. [14]

wait [7], delay [1], lie in ambush [1], long for [1], longs [1], wait in hope [1], waited [1], waits for [1]

2Ki 7: 9 [D] If *we* **wait** until daylight, punishment will overtake us. Let's
9: 3 [D] king over Israel.' Then open the door and run; don't **delay**!"
Job 3:21 [D] to those *who* **long for** death that does not come, who search
32: 4 [D] Now Elihu *had* **waited** before speaking to Job because they
Ps 33:20 [D] We **wait in hope** for the LORD; he is our help and our
106:13 [D] forgot what he had done and *did* not **wait** for his counsel.
Isa 8:17 [D] *I will* **wait** for the LORD, who is hiding his face from the
30:18 [D] Yet the LORD **longs** to be gracious to you; he rises to show
30:18 [A] is a God of justice. Blessed are all *who* **wait** for him!
64: 4 [64:3] [D] who acts on behalf of *those who* **wait** for him.
Da 12:12 [D] Blessed is the *one who* **waits for** and reaches the end of the
Hos 6: 9 [D] As marauders **lie in ambush** *for* a man, so do bands of
Hab 2: 3 [D] Though it linger, **wait** for it; it will certainly come and will
Zep 3: 8 [D] Therefore **wait** for me," declares the LORD, "for the day I

2676 חַכָּה ḥakkâ, n.f. [3]

hooks [2], fishhook [1]

Job 41: 1 [40:25] "Can you pull in the leviathan with a **fishhook** or tie
Isa 19: 8 fishermen will groan and lament, all who cast **hooks** into the Nile;
Hab 1:15 The wicked foe pulls all of them up with **hooks**, he catches them in

2677 חֲכִילָה ḥ[a]kîlâ, n.pr.loc. [3] [√ 2679]

Hakilah [3]

1Sa 23:19 strongholds at Horesh, on the hill of **Hakilah**, south of Jeshimon?
26: 1 at Gibeah and said, "Is not David hiding on the hill of **Hakilah**,
26: 3 Saul made his camp beside the road on the hill of **Hakilah** facing

2678 חֲכַלְיָה ḥ[a]kalyâ, n.pr.m. [2] [√ 2679 + 3378]

Hacaliah [2]

Ne 1: 1 The words of Nehemiah son of **Hacaliah**: In the month of Kislev
10: 1 [10:2] Nehemiah the governor, the son of **Hacaliah**. Zedekiah,

2679 חַכְלִילִי ḥaklîlî, a. [1] [→ 2677, 2678, 2680]

darker [1]

Ge 49:12 His eyes will be **darker** than wine, his teeth whiter than milk.

2680 חַכְלִלוּת ḥaklilût, n.f. [1] [√ 2679]
bloodshot [1]

Pr 23:29 Who has needless bruises? Who has **bloodshot** eyes?

2681 חָכַם ḥākam, v. [27] [→ 2682, 2683, 2684, 2685?; Ar 10265]
wise [13], skillful [2], wisdom [2], wiser [2], deal shrewdly [1], extremely wise [+2682] [1], make wiser [1], makes wiser [1], making wise [1], overwise [+3463] [1], skill [1], teach wisdom [1]

Ex 1:10 [F] *we must* **deal shrewdly** with them or they will become even
Dt 32:29 [A] If only *they were* **wise** and would understand this
1Ki 4:31 [5:11] [A] *He was* **wiser** than any other man, including Ethan
Job 32: 9 [A] It is not only the old *who are* **wise**, not only the aged who
35:11 [D] of the earth and **makes** us **wiser** than the birds of the air?'
Ps 19: 7 [19:8] [G] the LORD are trustworthy, **making wise** the simple.
58: 5 [58:6] [E] the charmer, however **skillful** the enchanter may be.
105:22 [D] his princes as he pleased and **teach** his elders **wisdom**.
119:98 [D] Your commands **make** me **wiser** than my enemies, for they
Pr 6: 6 [A] Go to the ant, you sluggard; consider its ways and *be* **wise**!
8:33 [A] Listen to my instruction and *be* **wise**; do not ignore it.
9: 9 [A] Instruct a wise man and *he will be* **wiser** still; teach a
9:12 [A] If *you are* **wise**, your wisdom will reward you; if you are a
9:12 [A] If you are wise, *your* **wisdom** will reward you; if you are a
13:20 [A] He who walks with the wise *grows* **wise**, but a companion of
19:20 [A] and accept instruction, and in the end *you will be* **wise**.
20: 1 [A] and beer a brawler; whoever is led astray by them *is* not **wise**.
21:11 [A] When a mocker is punished, the simple *gain* **wisdom**; when
23:15 [A] My son, if your heart *is* **wise**, then my heart will be glad;
23:19 [A] Listen, my son, and *be* **wise**, and keep your heart on the right
27:11 [A] *Be* **wise**, my son, and bring joy to my heart; then I can
30:24 [E] on earth are small, yet they *are* **extremely wise** [+2682]:
Ecc 2:15 [A] What then do I gain *by being* **wise**?" I said in my heart,
2:19 [A] into which I have poured my effort and **skill** under the sun.
7:16 [F] Do not be overrighteous, neither *be* **overwise** [+3463]—why
7:23 [A] by wisdom and I said, "*I am determined to be* **wise**"—
Zec 9: 2 [A] and upon Tyre and Sidon, though *they are* very **skillful**.

2682 חָכָם ḥākām, a. [138] [√ 2681; Ar 10265]
wise [105], skilled [7], skilled [+4213] [6], wisdom [4], craftsmen [2], skilled craftsmen [2], wiser [2], advisers [1], craftsmen [+4213] [1], extremely wise [+2681] [1], great skill [+1069+3359] [1], shrewd [1], skillful [1], those[s] [1], unwise [+4202] [1], wise [+4213] [1], wisest [1]

Ge 41: 8 so he sent for all the magicians and **wise** *men of* Egypt.
41:33 and **wise** man and put him in charge of the land of Egypt.
41:39 this known to you, there is no one so discerning and **wise** as you.
Ex 7:11 Pharaoh then summoned **wise** *men* and sorcerers, and the Egyptian
28: 3 Tell all the **skilled** [+4213] *men* to whom I have given wisdom in
31: 6 Also I have given skill to all the **craftsmen** [+4213] to make
35:10 "All *who* are **skilled** [+4213] among you are to come and make
35:25 Every **skilled** [+4213] woman spun with her hands and brought
36: 1 every **skilled** [+4213] person to whom the LORD has given skill
36: 2 every **skilled** [+4213] person to whom the LORD had given
36: 4 So all the **skilled craftsmen** who were doing all the work on the
36: 8 All the **skilled** [+4213] *men* among the workmen made the
Dt 1:13 Choose *some* **wise**, understanding and respected men from each of
1:15 So I took the leading men of your tribes, **wise** and respected men,
4: 6 "Surely this great nation is a **wise** and understanding people."
16:19 for a bribe blinds the eyes of the **wise** and twists the words of the
32: 6 way you repay the LORD, O foolish and **unwise** [+4202] people?
Jdg 5:29 The **wisest** *of* her ladies answer her; indeed, she keeps saying to
2Sa 13: 3 son of Shimeah, David's brother. Jonadab was a very **shrewd** man.
14: 2 sent someone to Tekoa and had a **wise** woman brought from there.
14:20 My lord has **wisdom** like that of an angel of God—he knows
20:16 a **wise** woman called from the city, "Listen! Listen! Tell Joab to
1Ki 2: 9 You are a man of **wisdom**; you will know what to do to him.
3:12 I will give you a **wise** and discerning heart, so that there will never
5: 7 [5:21] for he has given David a **wise** son to rule over this great
1Ch 22:15 and carpenters, as well as men **skilled** in every kind of work
2Ch 2: 7 [2:6] a man **skilled** to work in gold and silver, bronze and iron,
2: 7 [2:6] to work in Judah and Jerusalem with my **skilled craftsmen**,
2:12 [2:11] He has given King David a **wise** son, endowed with
2:13 [2:12] you Huram-Abi, a man of **great skill** [+1069+3359],
2:14 [2:13] He will work with your **craftsmen** and with those of my
2:14 [2:13] will work with your craftsmen and with **those**[s] *of* my lord,
Est 1:13 and justice, he spoke with the **wise** *men* who understood the times
6:13 His **advisers** and his wife Zeresh said to him, "Since Mordecai,
Job 5:13 He catches the **wise** in their craftiness, and the schemes of the wily
9: 4 His **wisdom** is profound, his power is vast. Who has resisted him
15: 2 "Would a **wise** *man* answer with empty notions or fill his belly
15:18 what **wise** *men* have declared, hiding nothing received from their
17:10 all of you, try again! I will not find a **wise** *man* among you.
34: 2 "Hear my words, you **wise** *men*; listen to me, you men of learning.
34:34 "Men of understanding declare, **wise** men who hear me say to me,
37:24 revere him, for does he not have regard for all the **wise** *in* heart?"
Ps 49:10 [49:11] For all can see that **wise** *men* die; the foolish
107:43 Whoever is **wise**, let him heed these things and consider the great
Pr 1: 5 let the **wise** listen and add to their learning, and let the discerning
1: 6 and parables, the sayings and riddles of the **wise**.
3: 7 Do not be **wise** in your own eyes; fear the LORD and shun evil.
3:35 The **wise** inherit honor, but fools he holds up to shame.
9: 8 or he will hate you; rebuke a **wise** *man* and he will love you.
9: 9 Instruct a **wise** *man* and he will be wiser still; teach a righteous
10: 1 A **wise** son brings joy to his father, but a foolish son grief to his
10: 8 The **wise** *in* heart accept commands, but a chattering fool comes to
10:14 **Wise** *men* store up knowledge, but the mouth of a fool invites ruin.
11:29 inherit only wind, and the fool will be servant to the **wise** [+4213].
11:30 of the righteous is a tree of life, and he who wins souls is **wise**.
12:15 way of a fool seems right to him, but a **wise** *man* listens to advice.
12:18 pierce like a sword, but the tongue of the **wise** brings healing.
13: 1 A **wise** son heeds his father's instruction, but a mocker does not
13:14 The teaching of the **wise** is a fountain of life, turning a man from
13:20 He who walks with the **wise** grows wise, but a companion of fools
14: 1 The **wise** woman builds her house, but with her own hands the
14: 3 talk brings a rod to his back, but the lips of the **wise** protect them.
14:16 A **wise** *man* fears the LORD and shuns evil, but a fool is
14:24 The wealth of the **wise** is their crown, but the folly of fools yields
15: 2 The tongue of the **wise** commends knowledge, but the mouth of the
15: 7 The lips of the **wise** spread knowledge; not so the hearts of fools.
15:12 A mocker resents correction; he will not consult the **wise**.
15:20 A **wise** son brings joy to his father, but a foolish man despises his
15:31 who listens to a life-giving rebuke will be at home among the **wise**.
16:14 wrath is a messenger of death, but a **wise** man will appease it.
16:21 The **wise** *in* heart are called discerning, and pleasant words
16:23 A **wise** *man's* heart guides his mouth, and his lips promote
17:28 Even a fool is thought **wise** if he keeps silent, and discerning if he
18:15 the discerning acquires knowledge; the ears of the **wise** seek it out.
20:26 A **wise** king winnows out the wicked; he drives the threshing
21:11 gain wisdom; when a **wise** *man* is instructed, he gets knowledge.
21:20 In the house of the **wise** are stores of choice food and oil, but a
21:22 A **wise** *man* attacks the city of the mighty and pulls down the
22:17 Pay attention and listen to the sayings of the **wise**; apply your heart
23:24 righteous man has great joy; he who has a **wise** son delights in him.
24: 5 A **wise** man has great power, and a man of knowledge increases
24:23 These also are sayings of the **wise**: To show partiality in judging is
25:12 or an ornament of fine gold is a **wise** *man's* rebuke to a listening
26: 5 a fool according to his folly, or he will be **wise** in his own eyes.
26:12 Do you see a man **wise** in his own eyes? There is more hope for a
26:16 The sluggard is **wiser** in his own eyes than seven men who answer
28:11 A rich man may be **wise** in his own eyes, but a poor man who has
29: 8 Mockers stir up a city, but **wise** *men* turn away anger.
29: 9 If a **wise** man goes to court with a fool, the fool rages and scoffs,
29:11 full vent to his anger, but a **wise** *man* keeps himself under control.
30:24 things on earth are small, yet they *are* **extremely wise** [+2681]:
Ecc 2:14 The **wise** *man* has eyes in his head, while the fool walks in the
2:16 For the **wise** *man*, like the fool, will not be long remembered;
2:16 both will be forgotten. Like the fool, the **wise** *man* too must die!
2:19 And who knows whether he will be a **wise** *man* or a fool?
4:13 Better a poor but **wise** youth than an old but foolish king who no
6: 8 What advantage has a **wise** *man* over a fool? What does a poor
7: 4 The heart of the **wise** is in the house of mourning, but the heart of
7: 5 It is better to heed a **wise** *man's* rebuke than to listen to the song of
7: 7 Extortion turns a **wise** *man* into a fool, and a bribe corrupts the
7:19 Wisdom makes one **wise** *man* more powerful than ten rulers in a
8: 1 Who is like the **wise** *man*? Who knows the explanation of things?
8: 5 and the **wise** heart will know the proper time and procedure.
8:17 Even if a **wise** *man* claims he knows, he cannot really comprehend
9: 1 I reflected on all this and concluded that the righteous and the **wise**
9:11 nor does food come to the **wise** or wealth to the brilliant or favor to
9:15 Now there lived in that city a man poor but **wise**, and he saved the
9:17 The quiet words of the **wise** are more to be heeded than the shouts
10: 2 The heart of the **wise** inclines to the right, but the heart of the fool
10:12 Words from a **wise** *man's* mouth are gracious, but a fool is
12: 9 Not only was the Teacher **wise**, but also he imparted knowledge to
12:11 The words of the **wise** are like goads, their collected sayings like
Isa 3: 3 man of rank, the counselor, **skilled** craftsman and clever enchanter.
5:21 Woe to *those who* are **wise** in their own eyes and clever in their
19:11 but fools; the **wise** counselors of Pharaoh give senseless advice.
19:11 How can you say to Pharaoh, "I am one of the **wise** *men*, a disciple
19:12 Where are your **wise** *men* now? Let them show you and make
29:14 the wisdom of the **wise** will perish, the intelligence of the
31: 2 Yet he too is **wise** and can bring disaster; he does not take back his
40:20 He looks for a **skilled** craftsman to set up an idol that will not
44:25 who overthrows the learning of the **wise** and turns it into nonsense,
Jer 4:22 They are **skilled** in doing evil; they know not how to do good."
8: 8 " 'How can you say, "We are **wise**, for we have the law of the

[A] Qal [B] Qal passive [C] Niphal [D] Piel (poel, polel, pilel, pilal, pealal, pilpel) [E] Pual (poal, polal, poalal, pulal, pualal)

Jer 8: 9 The **wise** will be put to shame; they will be dismayed and trapped.
9: 12 [9:11] What man is **wise** *enough* to understand this? Who has
9: 17 [9:16] women to come; send for the *most* **skillful** *of them*.
9: 23 [9:22] "Let not the **wise** *man* boast of his wisdom or the strong
10: 7 Among all the **wise** *men of* the nations and in all their kingdoms,
10: 9 then dressed in blue and purple—all made by **skilled** *workers*.
18: 18 nor will counsel from the **wise**, nor the word from the prophets.
50: 35 those who live in Babylon and against her officials and **wise** *men*!
51: 57 I will make her officials and **wise** *men* drunk, her governors,
Eze 27: 8 your **skilled** *men*, O Tyre, were aboard as your seamen.
27: 9 Veteran **craftsmen** *of* Gebal were on board as shipwrights to caulk
28: 3 Are you **wiser** than Daniel? Is no secret hidden from you?
Hos 13: 13 in childbirth come to him, but he is a child without **wisdom**;
14: 9 [14:10] Who is **wise**? He will realize these things. Who is
Ob 1: 8 declares the LORD, "will I not destroy the **wise** *men* of Edom,

2683 חָכְמָה חָכְמָה ḥokmâ, n.f. [149] [√ 2681; Ar 10266]

wisdom [131], skill [7], learning [2], skilled [2], ability [+928+4213] [1], at wits end [+1182+3972] [1], skill [+4213] [1], that[s] [1], wisdom [+8120] [1], wise advice [1], wise [1]

Ex 28: 3 Tell all the skilled men to whom I have given **wisdom** [+8120] in
31: 3 of God, with **skill**, ability and knowledge in all kinds of crafts—
31: 6 Also I have given **skill** to all the craftsmen to make everything I
35: 26 the women who were willing and had the **skill** spun the goat hair.
35: 31 of God, with **skill**, ability and knowledge in all kinds of crafts—
35: 35 He has filled them with **skill** [+4213] to do all kinds of work as
36: 1 and every skilled person to whom the LORD has given **skill**
36: 2 skilled person to whom the LORD had given **ability** [+928+4213]
Dt 4: 6 for this will show your **wisdom** and understanding to the nations,
34: 9 Now Joshua son of Nun was filled with the spirit of **wisdom**
2Sa 14: 20 My lord has wisdom like **that**[s] *of* an angel of God—he knows
20: 22 Then the woman went to all the people with her **wise advice**,
1Ki 2: 6 Deal with him according to your **wisdom**, but do not let his gray
3: 28 because they saw that he had **wisdom** *from* God to administer
4: 29 [5:9] God gave Solomon **wisdom** and very great insight, and a
4: 30 [5:10] Solomon's **wisdom** was greater than the wisdom of all the
4: 30 [5:10] Solomon's wisdom was greater than the **wisdom** *of* all the
4: 30 [5:10] men of the East, and greater than all the **wisdom** *of* Egypt.
4: 34 [5:14] Men of all nations came to listen to Solomon's **wisdom**,
4: 34 [5:14] all the kings of the world, who had heard of his **wisdom**.
5: 12 [5:26] The LORD gave Solomon **wisdom**, just as he had
7: 14 Huram was highly **skilled** and experienced in all kinds of bronze
10: 4 When the queen of Sheba saw all the **wisdom** *of* Solomon
10: 6 own country about your achievements and your **wisdom** is true.
10: 7 in **wisdom** and wealth you have far exceeded the report I heard.
10: 8 who continually stand before you and hear your **wisdom**!
10: 23 greater in riches and **wisdom** than all the other kings of the earth.
10: 24 with Solomon to hear the **wisdom** God had put in his heart.
11: 41 of Solomon's reign—all he did and the **wisdom** he displayed—
1Ch 28: 21 every willing man **skilled** in any craft will help you in all the work.
2Ch 1: 10 Give me **wisdom** and knowledge, that I may lead this people,
1: 11 and since you have not asked for a long life but for **wisdom**
1: 12 therefore **wisdom** and knowledge will be given you. And I will
9: 3 When the queen of Sheba saw the **wisdom** *of* Solomon, as well as
9: 5 own country about your achievements and your **wisdom** is true.
9: 6 Indeed, not even half the greatness of your **wisdom** was told me;
9: 7 who continually stand before you and hear your **wisdom**!
9: 22 greater in riches and **wisdom** than all the other kings of the earth.
9: 23 with Solomon to hear the **wisdom** God had put in his heart.
Job 4: 21 the cords of their tent pulled up, so that they die without **wisdom**?'
11: 6 disclose to you the secrets of **wisdom**, for true wisdom has two
12: 2 "Doubtless you are the people, and **wisdom** will die with you!
12: 12 Is not **wisdom** found among the aged? Does not long life bring
12: 13 "To God belong **wisdom** and power; counsel and understanding
13: 5 you would be altogether silent! For you, that would be **wisdom**.
15: 8 you listen in on God's council? Do you limit **wisdom** to yourself?
26: 3 What advice you have offered to one without **wisdom**! And what
28: 12 "But where can **wisdom** be found? Where does understanding
28: 18 are not worthy of mention; the price of **wisdom** is beyond rubies.
28: 20 "Where then does **wisdom** come from? Where does understanding
28: 28 of the Lord—that is **wisdom**, and to shun evil is understanding.' "
32: 7 'Age should speak; advanced years should teach **wisdom**.'
32: 13 Do not say, 'We have found **wisdom**; let God refute him, not man.'
33: 33 then listen to me; be silent, and I will teach you **wisdom**."
38: 36 Who endowed the heart with **wisdom** or gave understanding to the
38: 37 Who has the **wisdom** to count the clouds? Who can tip over the
39: 17 for God did not endow her with **wisdom** or give her a share of
Ps 37: 30 The mouth of the righteous man utters **wisdom**, and his tongue
51: 6 [51:8] the inner parts; you teach me **wisdom** in the inmost place.
90: 12 us to number our days aright, that we may gain a heart of **wisdom**.
104: 24 In **wisdom** you made them all; the earth is full of your creatures.
107: 27 like drunken men; they *were* **at** their **wits' end** [+1182+3972].
111: 10 The fear of the LORD is the beginning of **wisdom**; all who follow
Pr 1: 2 for attaining **wisdom** and discipline; for understanding words of
1: 7 beginning of knowledge, but fools despise **wisdom** and discipline.
2: 2 turning your ear to **wisdom** and applying your heart to
2: 6 For the LORD gives **wisdom**, and from his mouth come
2: 10 For **wisdom** will enter your heart, and knowledge will be pleasant
3: 13 Blessed is the man who finds **wisdom**, the man who gains
3: 19 By **wisdom** the LORD laid the earth's foundations,
4: 5 Get **wisdom**, get understanding; do not forget my words or swerve
4: 7 **Wisdom** is supreme; therefore get wisdom. Though it cost all you
4: 7 Wisdom is supreme; therefore get **wisdom**. Though it cost all you
4: 11 I guide you in the way of **wisdom** and lead you along straight
5: 1 My son, pay attention to my **wisdom**, listen well to my words of
7: 4 Say to **wisdom**, "You are my sister," and call understanding your
8: 1 Does not **wisdom** call out? Does not understanding raise her
8: 11 for **wisdom** is more precious than rubies, and nothing you desire
8: 12 "I, **wisdom**, dwell together with prudence; I possess knowledge
9: 10 "The fear of the LORD is the beginning of **wisdom**,
10: 13 **Wisdom** is found on the lips of the discerning, but a rod is for the
10: 23 in evil conduct, but a man of understanding delights in **wisdom**.
10: 31 The mouth of the righteous brings forth **wisdom**, but a perverse
11: 2 then comes disgrace, but with humility comes **wisdom**.
13: 10 breeds quarrels, but **wisdom** is found in those who take advice.
14: 6 The mocker seeks **wisdom** and finds none, but knowledge comes
14: 8 The **wisdom** *of* the prudent is to give thought to their ways,
14: 33 **Wisdom** reposes in the heart of the discerning and even among
15: 33 The fear of the LORD teaches a man **wisdom**, and humility
16: 16 How much better to get **wisdom** than gold, to choose
17: 16 money in the hand of a fool, since he has no desire to get **wisdom**?
17: 24 A discerning man keeps **wisdom** in view, but a fool's eyes wander
18: 4 are deep waters, but the fountain of **wisdom** is a bubbling brook.
21: 30 There is no **wisdom**, no insight, no plan that can succeed against
23: 23 and do not sell it; get **wisdom**, discipline and understanding.
24: 3 By **wisdom** a house is built, and through understanding it is
24: 14 Know also that **wisdom** is sweet to your soul; if you find it,
28: 26 trusts in himself is a fool, but he who walks in **wisdom** is kept safe.
29: 3 A man who loves **wisdom** brings joy to his father, but a companion
29: 15 The rod of correction imparts **wisdom**, but a child left to himself
30: 3 I have not learned **wisdom**, nor have I knowledge of the Holy One.
31: 26 She speaks with **wisdom**, and faithful instruction is on her tongue.
Ecc 1: 13 to study and to explore by **wisdom** all that is done under heaven.
1: 16 increased in **wisdom** more than anyone who has ruled over
1: 16 before me; I have experienced much of **wisdom** and knowledge."
1: 17 I applied myself to the understanding of **wisdom**, and also of
1: 18 For with much **wisdom** comes much sorrow; the more knowledge,
2: 3 and embracing folly—my mind still guiding me with **wisdom**.
2: 9 in Jerusalem before me. In all this my **wisdom** stayed with me.
2: 12 Then I turned my thoughts to consider **wisdom**, and also madness
2: 13 I saw that **wisdom** is better than folly, just as light is better than
2: 21 For a man may do his work with **wisdom**, knowledge and skill,
2: 26 who pleases him, God gives **wisdom**, knowledge and happiness,
7: 10 old days better than these?" For it is not **wise** to ask such questions.
7: 11 **Wisdom**, like an inheritance, is a good thing and benefits those
7: 12 **Wisdom** is a shelter as money is a shelter, but the advantage of
7: 12 knowledge is this: that **wisdom** preserves the life of its possessor.
7: 19 **Wisdom** makes one wise man more powerful than ten rulers in a
7: 23 All this I tested by **wisdom** and I said, "I am determined to be
7: 25 to investigate and to search out **wisdom** and the scheme of things
8: 1 **Wisdom** brightens a man's face and changes its hard appearance.
8: 16 When I applied my mind to know **wisdom** and to observe man's
9: 10 there is neither working nor planning nor knowledge nor **wisdom**.
9: 13 I also saw under the sun this example of **wisdom** that greatly
9: 15 that city a man poor but wise, and he saved the city by his **wisdom**.
9: 16 So I said, "**Wisdom** is better than strength." But the poor man's
9: 16 the poor man's **wisdom** is despised, and his words are no longer
9: 18 **Wisdom** is better than weapons of war, but one sinner destroys
10: 1 perfume a bad smell, so a little folly outweighs **wisdom** and honor.
10: 10 more strength is needed but **skill** will bring success.
Isa 10: 13 have done this, and by my **wisdom**, because I have understanding.
11: 2 the Spirit of **wisdom** and of understanding, the Spirit of counsel
29: 14 the **wisdom** *of* the wise will perish, the intelligence of the
33: 6 your times, a rich store of salvation and **wisdom** and knowledge;
47: 10 Your **wisdom** and knowledge mislead you when you say to
Jer 8: 9 the word of the LORD, what kind of **wisdom** do they have?
9: 23 [9:22] "Let not the wise man boast of his **wisdom** or the strong
10: 12 he founded the world by his **wisdom** and stretched out the heavens
49: 7 "Is there no longer **wisdom** in Teman? Has counsel perished from
49: 7 counsel perished from the prudent? Has their **wisdom** decayed?
51: 15 he founded the world by his **wisdom** and stretched out the heavens
Eze 28: 4 By your **wisdom** and understanding you have gained wealth for
28: 5 By your great **skill** in trading you have increased your wealth,
28: 7 against your beauty and **wisdom** and pierce your shining splendor.
28: 12 were the model of perfection, full of **wisdom** and perfect in beauty.
28: 17 and you corrupted your **wisdom** because of your splendor.
Da 1: 4 handsome, showing aptitude for every kind of **learning**, well

Da 1:17 and understanding of all kinds of literature and **learning**.
1:20 In every matter of **wisdom** and understanding about which the king

2684 חָכְמוֹת *ḥokmôt*, n.f.pl.abst. [4] [√ 2681]

wisdom [4]

Ps 49: 3 [49:4] My mouth will speak *words of* **wisdom**; the utterance from
Pr 1:20 **Wisdom** calls aloud in the street, she raises her voice in the public
9: 1 **Wisdom** has built her house; she has hewn out its seven pillars.
24: 7 **Wisdom** is too high for a fool; in the assembly at the gate he has

2685 חַכְמֹנִי *ḥakmōnî*, n.pr.m.[g.?]. [2] [√ 2681?]

Hacmoni [1], Hacmonite [+1201] [1]

1Ch 11:11 Jashobeam, a **Hacmonite** [+1201], was chief of the officers;
27:32 and a scribe. Jehiel son of **Hacmoni** took care of the king's sons.

2686 הָכַר *hākar*, v. [0 / 1] [cf. 2128]

attack [1]

Job 19: 3 [A] reproached me; shamelessly *you* **attack** [BHS 2128] me.

2687 חֹל *ḥōl*, n.[m.]. [7] [√ 2725]

common [4], common use [1], not holy [1], ordinary [1]

Lev 10:10 You must distinguish between the holy and the **common**, between
1Sa 21: 4 [21:5] "I don't have any **ordinary** bread on hand;
21: 5 [21:6] men's things are holy even on missions that are **not holy**.
Eze 22:26 they do not distinguish between the holy and the **common**;
42:20 five hundred cubits wide, to separate the holy from the **common**.
44:23 the **common** and show them how to distinguish between the
48:15 will be for the **common use** of the city, for houses and for

2688 חָלָא *ḥālā'*, v. [1] [→ 2689, 2690, 9377; cf. 2703]

afflicted with a disease [1]

2Ch 16:12 [A] year of his reign Asa *was* **afflicted with a disease** in his feet.

2689 חֶלְאָה¹ *ḥel'â¹*, n.f. [5] [→ 2690; cf. 2688]

deposit [3], *untranslated* [1], encrusted [1]

Eze 24: 6 " 'Woe to the city of bloodshed, to the pot now **encrusted**,
24: 6 to the pot now encrusted, whose **deposit** will not go away!
24:11 so its impurities may be melted and its **deposit** burned away.
24:12 its heavy **deposit** has not been removed, not even by fire.
24:12 its heavy deposit has not been removed, not even by fire. **[RPH]**

2690 חֶלְאָה² *ḥel'â²*, n.pr.f. [2] [√ 2689; cf. 2688]

Helah [2]

1Ch 4: 5 Ashhur the father of Tekoa had two wives, **Helah** and Naarah.
4: 7 The sons of **Helah**: Zereth, Zohar, Ethnan,

2691 חֶלְאָם *ḥēlā'm*, n.pr.loc. Not used in NIV/BHS [cf. 2663]

2692 חָלָב *ḥālāb*, n.m. [44 / 45] [→ 2697]

milk [41], cheeses [+3043] [1], curds [1], suckling [1], well nourished [+4848] [1]

Ge 18: 8 He then brought some curds and **milk** and the calf that had been
49:12 His eyes will be darker than wine, his teeth whiter than **milk**.
Ex 3: 8 a good and spacious land, a land flowing with **milk** and honey—
3:17 Hivites and Jebusites—a land flowing with **milk** and honey.'
13: 5 your forefathers to give you, a land flowing with **milk** and honey—
23:19 your God. "Do not cook a young goat in its mother's **milk**.
33: 3 Go up to the land flowing with **milk** and honey. But I will not go
34:26 your God. "Do not cook a young goat in its mother's **milk**."
Lev 20:24 it to you as an inheritance, a land flowing with **milk** and honey."
Nu 13:27 land to which you sent us, and it does flow with **milk** and honey!
14: 8 a land flowing with **milk** and honey, and will give it to us.
16:13 that you have brought us up out of a land flowing with **milk**
16:14 you haven't brought us into a land flowing with **milk** and honey
Dt 6: 3 and that you may increase greatly in a land flowing with **milk**
11: 9 and their descendants, a land flowing with **milk** and honey.
14:21 LORD your God. Do not cook a young goat in its mother's **milk**.
26: 9 and gave us this land, a land flowing with **milk** and honey;
26:15 on oath to our forefathers, a land flowing with **milk** and honey."
27: 3 a land flowing with **milk** and honey, just as the LORD, the God
31:20 When I have brought them into the land flowing with **milk**
32:14 with curds and **milk** *from* herd and flock and with fattened lambs
Jos 5: 6 their fathers to give us, a land flowing with **milk** and honey.
Jdg 4:19 She opened a skin of **milk**, gave him a drink, and covered him up.
5:25 He asked for water, and she gave him **milk**; in a bowl fit for nobles
1Sa 7: 9 Samuel took a **suckling** lamb and offered it up as a whole burnt
17:18 Take along these ten **cheeses** [+3043] to the commander of their
Job 10:10 Did you not pour me out like **milk** and curdle me like cheese,
21:24 his body **well nourished** [+4848], his bones rich with marrow.
Pr 27:27 You will have plenty of goats' **milk** to feed you and your family
30:33 For as churning the **milk** produces butter, and as twisting the nose
SS 4:11 the honeycomb, my bride; **milk** and honey are under your tongue.
5: 1 and my honey; I have drunk my wine and my **milk**.
5:12 doves by the water streams, washed in **milk**, mounted like jewels.
Isa 7:22 because of the abundance of the **milk** they give, he will have curds
28: 9 To children weaned from their **milk**, to those just taken from the
55: 1 Come, buy wine and **milk** without money and without cost.
60:16 You will drink the **milk** *of* nations and be nursed at royal breasts.
Jer 11: 5 to give them a land flowing with **milk** and honey'—
32:22 to give their forefathers, a land flowing with **milk** and honey.
La 4: 7 Their princes were brighter than snow and whiter than **milk**,
Eze 20: 6 a land flowing with **milk** and honey, the most beautiful of all
20:15 a land flowing with **milk** and honey, most beautiful of all lands—
25: 4 their tents among you; they will eat your fruit and drink your **milk**.
34: 3 You eat the **curds**, [BHS 2693] clothe yourselves with the wool
Joel 3:18 [4:18] will drip new wine, and the hills will flow with **milk**;

2693 חֵלֶב¹ *ḥēleb¹*, n.m. [92 / 91]

fat [64], fat portions [7], *untranslated* [5], finest [5], best [3], callous hearts [2], callous [+2021+3869] [1], fattened [1], flesh [1], richest of foods [+2016+2256] [1], these[s] [+2021] [1]

Ge 4: 4 Abel brought **fat portions** from some of the firstborn of his flock.
45:18 the best of the land of Egypt and you can enjoy the **fat** *of* the land.'
Ex 23:18 "The **fat** *of* my festival offerings must not be kept until morning.
29:13 take all the **fat** around the inner parts, the covering of the liver,
29:13 the covering of the liver, and both kidneys with the **fat** on them,
29:22 "Take from this ram the **fat**, the fat tail, the fat around the inner
29:22 the fat tail, the **fat** around the inner parts, the covering of the liver,
29:22 of the liver, both kidneys with the **fat** on them, and the right thigh.
Lev 3: 3 all the **fat** that covers the inner parts or is connected to them,
3: 3 the fat that covers the inner parts or **[RPH]** is connected to them,
3: 4 both kidneys with the **fat** on them near the loins, and the covering
3: 9 its **fat**, the entire fat tail cut off close to the backbone, all the fat
3: 9 all the **fat** that covers the inner parts or is connected to them,
3: 9 the fat that covers the inner parts or **[RPH]** is connected to them,
3:10 both kidneys with the **fat** on them near the loins, and the covering
3:14 all the **fat** that covers the inner parts or is connected to them,
3:14 the fat that covers the inner parts or **[RPH]** is connected to them,
3:15 both kidneys with the **fat** on them near the loins, and the covering
3:16 made by fire, a pleasing aroma. All the **fat** is the LORD's.
3:17 wherever you live: You must not eat any **fat** or any blood.' "
4: 8 He shall remove all the **fat** from the bull of the sin offering—
4: 8 the **fat** that covers the inner parts or is connected to them,
4: 8 the fat that covers the inner parts or **[RPH]** is connected to them,
4: 9 both kidneys with the **fat** on them near the loins, and the covering
4:19 He shall remove all the **fat** from it and burn it on the altar,
4:26 He shall burn all the **fat** on the altar as he burned the fat of the
4:26 He shall burn all the fat on the altar as he burned the **fat** *of* the
4:31 He shall remove all the **fat**, just as the fat is removed from the
4:31 all the fat, just as the **fat** is removed from the fellowship offering,
4:35 He shall remove all the **fat**, just as the fat is removed from the
4:35 just as the **fat** is removed from the lamb of the fellowship offering,
6:12 [6:5] on the fire and burn the **fat** *of* the fellowship offerings on it.
7: 3 All its **fat** shall be offered: the fat tail and the fat that covers the
7: 3 shall be offered: the fat tail and the **fat** that covers the inner parts,
7: 4 both kidneys with the **fat** on them near the loins, and the covering
7:23 to the Israelites: 'Do not eat any of the **fat** *of* cattle, sheep or goats.
7:24 The **fat** *of* an animal found dead or torn by wild animals may be
7:24 or **[RPH]** torn by wild animals may be used for any other
7:25 Anyone who eats the **fat** of an animal from which an offering by
7:30 he is to bring the **fat**, together with the breast, and wave the breast
7:31 The priest shall burn the **fat** on the altar, but the breast belongs to
7:33 the **fat** *of* the fellowship offering shall have the right thigh as his
8:16 Moses also took all the **fat** around the inner parts, the covering of
8:16 the covering of the liver, and both kidneys and their **fat**,
8:25 He took the **fat**, the fat tail, all the fat around the inner parts,
8:25 He took the fat, the fat tail, all the **fat** around the inner parts,
8:25 covering of the liver, both kidneys and their **fat** and the right thigh.
8:26 and a wafer; he put these on the **fat portions** and on the right thigh.
9:10 On the altar he burned the **fat**, the kidneys and the covering of the
9:19 the **fat portions** of the ox and the ram—the fat tail, the layer of fat,
9:20 **these**[s] [+2021] they laid on the breasts, and then Aaron burned the
9:20 they laid on the breasts, and then Aaron burned the **fat** on the altar.
9:24 and consumed the burnt offering and the **fat portions** on the altar.
10:15 the breast that was waved must be brought with the **fat portions** *of*
16:25 He shall also burn the **fat** *of* the sin offering on the altar.
17: 6 of Meeting and burn the **fat** as an aroma pleasing to the LORD.
Nu 18:12 "I give you all the **finest** olive oil and all the finest new wine
18:12 "I give you all the finest olive oil and all the **finest** new wine
18:17 blood on the altar and burn their **fat** as an offering made by fire,
18:29 You must present as the LORD's portion the **best** and holiest part

Nu 18:30 'When you present the **best** part, it will be reckoned to you as the
18:32 By presenting the **best** part of it you will not be guilty in this
Dt 32:14 and milk from herd and flock and with **fattened** lambs and goats,
32:14 with choice rams of Bashan and the **finest** kernels of wheat.
32:38 the gods who ate the **fat** *of* their sacrifices and drank the wine of
Jdg 3:22 Ehud did not pull the sword out, and the **fat** closed in over it.
1Sa 2:15 even before the **fat** was burned, the servant of the priest would
2:16 "Let the **fat** be burned up first, and then take whatever you want,"
15:22 is better than sacrifice, and to heed is better than the **fat** *of* rams.
2Sa 1:22 From the blood of the slain, from the **flesh** *of* the mighty, the bow
1Ki 8:64 grain offerings and the **fat** *of* the fellowship offerings,
8:64 the grain offerings and the **fat** *of* the fellowship offerings.
2Ch 7:7 he offered burnt offerings and the **fat** *of* the fellowship offerings,
7:7 hold the burnt offerings, the grain offerings and the **fat portions**.
29:35 together with the **fat** *of* the fellowship offerings and the drink
35:14 sacrificing the burnt offerings and the **fat portions** until nightfall.
Job 15:27 "Though his face is covered with **fat** and his waist bulges with
Ps 17:10 They close up their **callous hearts**, and their mouths speak with
63:5 [63:6] be satisfied as with the **richest of foods** [+2016+2256];
73:7 From their **callous hearts** comes iniquity; the evil conceits of their
81:16 [81:17] you would be fed with the **finest** *of* wheat; with honey
119:70 Their hearts are **callous** [+2021+3869] and unfeeling, but I delight
147:14 peace to your borders and satisfies you with the **finest** *of* wheat.
Isa 1:11 enough of burnt offerings, of rams and the **fat** *of* fattened animals;
34:6 sword of the LORD is bathed in blood, it is covered with **fat**—
34:6 the blood of lambs and goats, **fat** *from* the kidneys of rams.
34:7 will be drenched with blood, and the dust will be soaked with **fat**.
43:24 calamus for me, or lavished on me the **fat** *of* your sacrifices.
Eze 34:3 You eat the curds, [BHS *fat*; NIV 2692] clothe yourselves with the
39:19 you will eat **fat** till you are glutted and drink blood till you are
44:7 you offered me food, **fat** and blood, and you broke my covenant.
44:15 they are to stand before me to offer sacrifices of **fat** and blood,

2694 ²חֵלֶב ***ḥēleb²***, n.pr.m. [1 / 0] [cf. 2699]

2Sa 23:29 Heled [BHS ***Heleb***; NIV 2699] son of Baanah the Netophathite,

2695 חֶלְבָּה ***ḥelbâ***, n.pr.loc. [1]

Helbah [1]

Jdg 1:31 or Sidon or Ahlab or Aczib or **Helbah** or Aphek or Rehob,

2696 חֶלְבּוֹן ***ḥelbôn***, n.pr.loc. [1]

Helbon [1]

Eze 27:18 did business with you in wine from **Helbon** and wool from Zahar.

2697 חֶלְבְּנָה ***ḥelbᵉnâ***, n.f. [1] [√ 2692]

galbanum [1]

Ex 30:34 gum resin, onycha and **galbanum**—and pure frankincense,

2698 חֶלֶד ***ḥeled***, n.[m.]. [5 / 6] [→ 2699, 2702]

world [3], fleeting life [1], life [1], span of years [1]

Job 11:17 **Life** will be brighter than noonday, and darkness will become like
Ps 17:14 such men, from men of this **world** whose reward is in this life.
39:5 [39:6] the **span of** my **years** is as nothing before you.
49:1 [49:2] Hear this, all you peoples; listen, all who live in this **world**,
89:47 [89:48] Remember how **fleeting** is my **life**. For what futility you
Isa 38:11 or be with those who now dwell in this **world**. [BHS 2535]

2699 חֵלֶד ***ḥēled***, n.pr.m. [1 / 2] [√ 2698]

Heled [2]

2Sa 23:29 **Heled** [BHS 2694] son of Baanah the Netophathite, Ithai son of
1Ch 11:30 Maharai the Netophathite, **Heled** son of Baanah the Netophathite,

2700 חֹלֶד ***ḥōled***, n.[m.]. [1] [→ 2701]

weasel [1]

Lev 11:29 are unclean for you: the **weasel**, the rat, any kind of great lizard,

2701 חֻלְדָּה ***ḥuldâ***, n.pr.m. [2] [√ 2700]

Huldah [2]

2Ki 22:14 Shaphan and Asaiah went to speak to the prophetess **Huldah**,
2Ch 34:22 king had sent with him went to speak to the prophetess **Huldah**,

2702 חֶלְדַּי ***ḥelday***, n.pr.m. [2 / 3] [√ 2698]

Heldai [3]

1Ch 27:15 The twelfth, for the twelfth month, was **Heldai** the Netophathite,
Zec 6:10 "Take ⌞silver and gold⌟ from the exiles **Heldai**, Tobijah
6:14 The crown will be given to **Heldai**, [BHS 2732] Tobijah,

2703 ¹חָלָה ***ḥālâ¹***, v. [56] [→ 2716, 4700, 4701, 4705?, 4706?, 4707?, 4708, 5710; cf. 2688, 2704]

ill [13], weak [8], illness [4], diseased [3], faint [3], wounded [3], been wounded [2], grievous [2], afflicted [1], beyond healing [1], cause to suffer [1], concerned [1], crushing [+4394] [1], fatal [1], grieve [1], hurt [1], incurable [1], inflamed [+2779] [1], injured [1], lay ill [1], makes sick [1], pretend to be ill [1], pretended to be ill [1], sick [1], suffering [1], wear themselves out [1]

Ge 48:1 [A] Some time later Joseph was told, "Your father *is* **ill**." So he
Dt 29:22 [29:21] [D] the diseases with which the LORD *has* **afflicted** it.
Jdg 16:7 [A] have not been dried, I'll become as **weak** as any other man."
16:11 [A] never been used, I'll become as **weak** as any other man."
16:13 [A] the pin, I'll become as **weak** [BHS-] as any other man."
16:17 [A] leave me, and I would become as **weak** as any other man."
1Sa 19:14 [A] Saul sent the men to capture David, Michal said, "He *is* **ill**."
22:8 [A] None of you *is* **concerned** about me or tells me that my son
30:13 [A] My master abandoned me when *I became* **ill** three days ago.
2Sa 13:2 [F] Amnon became frustrated to the point of **illness** on account of
13:5 [F] "Go to bed and **pretend to be ill**," Jonadab said. "When your
13:6 [F] So Amnon lay down and **pretended to be ill**. When the king
1Ki 14:1 [A] At that time Abijah son of Jeroboam *became* **ill**,
14:5 [A] for he *is* **ill**, and you are to give her such and such an answer.
15:23 [A] of Judah? In his old age, however, his feet *became* **diseased**.
17:17 [A] later the son of the woman who owned the house *became* **ill**.
22:34 [H] and get me out of the fighting. *I've* **been wounded**."
2Ki 1:2 [A] the lattice of his upper room in Samaria and **injured** *himself*.
8:7 [A] went to Damascus, and Ben-Hadad king of Aram *was* **ill**.
8:29 [A] to see Joram son of Ahab, because he *had been* **wounded**.
13:14 [A] Now Elisha *was* **suffering** *from* the illness from which he
20:1 [A] In those days Hezekiah *became* **ill** and was at the point of
20:12 [A] and a gift, because he had heard of Hezekiah's **illness**.
2Ch 18:33 [H] and get me out of the fighting. *I've* **been wounded**."
22:6 [A] to see Joram son of Ahab because he *had been* **wounded**.
32:24 [A] In those days Hezekiah *became* **ill** and was at the point of
35:23 [H] he told his officers, "Take me away; *I am* badly **wounded**."
Ne 2:2 [A] "Why does your face look so sad when you *are* not **ill**?
Ps 35:13 [A] Yet when they *were* **ill**, I put on sackcloth and humbled
Pr 13:12 [G] Hope deferred **makes** the heart **sick**, but a longing fulfilled is
23:35 [A] "They hit me," you will say, "but *I'm* not **hurt**! They beat
Ecc 5:13 [5:12] [A] I have seen a **grievous** evil under the sun:
5:16 [5:15] [A] This too *is* a **grievous** evil: As a man comes, so he
SS 2:5 [A] with raisins, refresh me with apples, for I *am* **faint** *with* love.
5:8 [A] what will you tell him? Tell him I *am* **faint** *with* love.
Isa 14:10 [E] will say to you, "You also *have become* **weak**, as we are;
33:24 [A] No one living in Zion will say, "*I am* **ill**"; and the sins of
38:1 [A] In those days Hezekiah *became* **ill** and was at the point of
38:9 [A] A writing of Hezekiah king of Judah after his **illness**
39:1 [A] and a gift, because he had heard of *his* **illness** and recovery.
53:10 [G] was the LORD's will to crush him and **cause** him **to suffer**,
57:10 [A] found renewal of your strength, and so *you did* not **faint**.
Jer 10:19 [C] My wound *is* **incurable**! Yet I said to myself, "This is my
12:13 [C] reap thorns; *they will* **wear themselves out** but gain nothing.
14:17 [C] has suffered a grievous wound, a **crushing** [+4394] blow.
30:12 [C] " 'Your wound is incurable, your injury **beyond healing**.
Eze 34:4 [C] You have not strengthened the **weak** or healed the sick
34:4 [A] the weak or healed the **sick** or bound up the injured.
34:16 [A] I will bind up the injured and strengthen the **weak**, but the
34:21 [C] butting all the **weak** sheep with your horns until you have
Da 8:27 [C] I, Daniel, was exhausted and **lay ill** for several days. Then I
Hos 7:5 [G] of our king the princes *become* **inflamed** [+2779] with wine,
Am 6:6 [C] finest lotions, but *you do* not **grieve** over the ruin of Joseph.
Mic 6:13 [g] I *have* begun [BHS *will make you sick*; NIV 2725] to destroy
Na 3:19 [C] Nothing can heal your wound; your injury *is* **fatal**.
Mal 1:8 [A] When you sacrifice crippled or **diseased** *animals*, is that not
1:13 [A] crippled or **diseased** *animals* and offer them as sacrifices,

2704 ²חָלָה ***ḥālâ²***, v. [17] [→ 4714?; cf. 2703]

entreat [+906+7156] [3], sought the favor of [+906+7156] [3], appeal [1], court favor [+7156] [1], curry favor with [+7156] [1], implore [+7156] [1], intercede with [+906+7156] [1], interceded with [+906+7156] [1], seek favor [+7156] [1], seek favor [+906+7156] [1], sought favor [+7156] [1], sought favor [+906+7156] [1], sought [1]

Ex 32:11 [D] Moses **sought** [+906+7156] **the favor of** the LORD his
1Sa 13:12 [D] and *I have* not **sought** [+7156] the LORD's **favor**.'
1Ki 13:6 [D] to the man of God, "**Intercede** [+906+7156] **with** the LORD
13:6 [D] So the man of God **interceded** [+906+7156] **with** the LORD,
2Ki 13:4 [D] Then Jehoahaz **sought** [+906+7156] the LORD's **favor**,
2Ch 33:12 [D] In his distress *he* **sought** [+906+7156] **the favor of** the
Job 11:19 [D] to make you afraid, and many *will* **court** your **favor** [+7156].
Ps 45:12 [45:13] [D] a gift, men of wealth *will* **seek** your **favor** [+7156].
77:10 [77:11] [D] I thought, "*To* this I *will* **appeal**: the years of the
119:58 [D] *I have* **sought** your face with all my heart; be gracious to me

[F] Hitpael (hitpoel, hitpoal, hitpolel, hitpolal, hitpalel, hitpalal, hitpalpel, hitpalpal, hotpael, hotpaal) [G] Hiphil (hiphtil) [H] Hophal [I] Hishtaphel

Pr 19: 6 [D] Many **curry favor** [+7156] **with** a ruler, and everyone is the
Jer 26: 19 [D] Hezekiah fear the LORD and **seek** his **favor** [+906+7156]?
Da 9: 13 [D] yet *we have* not **sought the favor** [+906+7156] **of** the
Zec 7: 2 [D] together with their men, to **entreat** [+906+7156] the LORD
8: 21 [D] 'Let us go at once to **entreat** [+906+7156] the LORD
8: 22 [D] the LORD Almighty and to **entreat** [+906+7156] him."
Mal 1: 9 [D] "Now **implore** [+7156] God to be gracious to us. With such

2705 חַלָּה **ḥallâ**, n.f. [14] [√ 2726]

cakes [6], cake [3], loaf [2], *untranslated* [1], cake [+4312] [1], loaves of bread [1]

Ex 29: 2 without yeast, make bread, and **cakes** mixed with oil, and wafers
29: 23 take a loaf, and a **cake** [+4312] *made with* oil, and a wafer.
Lev 2: 4 **cakes** *made* without yeast and mixed with oil, or wafers made
7: 12 along with this thank offering he is to offer **cakes** *of* bread made
7: 12 with oil, and **cakes** *of* fine flour well-kneaded and mixed with oil.
7: 13 he is to present an offering with **cakes** *of* bread made with yeast.
8: 26 he took a **cake** *of* bread, and one made with oil, and a wafer;
8: 26 took a cake of bread, and **[RPH]** one made with oil, and a wafer;
24: 5 "Take fine flour and bake twelve **loaves of bread**, using two-tenths
24: 5 twelve loaves of bread, using two-tenths of an ephah for each **loaf**.
Nu 6: 15 **cakes** *made of* fine flour mixed with oil, and wafers spread with
6: 19 and a **cake** and a wafer from the basket, both made without yeast.
15: 20 Present a **cake** from the first of your ground meal and present it as
2Sa 6: 19 he gave a **loaf** *of* bread, a cake of dates and a cake of raisins to

2706 חֲלוֹם **ḥ^a^lôm**, n.m. [65] [√ 2731; Ar 10267]

dream [28], dreams [14], had a dream [+2731] [6], dream had [+2731] [2], dreamer [+2731] [2], had dream [+2731] [2], had dreams [+2731] [2], *untranslated* [1], dreamed [1], dreamer [+1251+2021] [1], dreaming [1], dreams [+2731] [1], dreams encourage to have [+2731] [1], foretells by dreams [+2731] [1], interpreters of dreams [1], it[s] [+2021] [1]

Ge 20: 3 But God came to Abimelech in a **dream** one night and said to him,
20: 6 God said to him in the **dream**, "Yes, I know you did this with a
31: 10 "In breeding season I once had a **dream** in which I looked up
31: 11 The angel of God said to me in the **dream**, 'Jacob.' I answered,
31: 24 Then God came to Laban the Aramean in a **dream** *at* night
37: 5 Joseph **had a dream** [+2731], and when he told it to his brothers,
37: 6 He said to them, "Listen to this **dream** *I* **had** [+2731]:
37: 8 hated him all the more because of his **dream** and what he had said.
37: 9 Then *he* **had** another **dream** [+2731], and he told it to his brothers.
37: 9 "Listen," he said, "*I* **had** another **dream** [+2731], and this time the
37: 10 rebuked him and said, "What is this **dream** *you* **had** [+2731]?
37: 19 "Here comes that **dreamer** [+1251+2021]!" they said to each other.
37: 20 animal devoured him. Then we'll see what comes of his **dreams**."
40: 5 **had a dream** [+2731] the same night, and each dream had a
40: 5 had a dream **[RPH]** the same night, and each dream had a
40: 5 a dream the same night, and each **dream** had a meaning of its own.
40: 8 "*We both* **had dreams** [+2731]," they answered, "but there is no
40: 9 So the chief cupbearer told Joseph his **dream**. He said to him,
40: 9 He said to him, "In my **dream** I saw a vine in front of me,
40: 16 a favorable interpretation, he said to Joseph, "I too had a **dream**:
41: 7 full heads. Then Pharaoh woke up; it had been a **dream**.
41: 8 Pharaoh told them his **dreams**, but no one could interpret them for
41: 11 Each of us **had a dream** [+2731] the same night, and each dream
41: 11 a dream the same night, and each **dream** had a meaning of its own.
41: 12 We told him our **dreams**, and he interpreted them for us,
41: 12 them for us, giving each man the interpretation of his **dream**.
41: 15 Pharaoh said to Joseph, "*I* **had a dream** [+2731], and no one can
41: 15 I have heard it said of you that when you hear a **dream** you can
41: 17 to Joseph, "In my **dream** I was standing on the bank of the Nile,
41: 22 "In my **dreams** I also saw seven heads of grain, full and good,
41: 25 said to Pharaoh, "The **dreams** *of* Pharaoh are one and the same.
41: 26 good heads of grain are seven years; it is one and the same **dream**.
41: 32 The reason the **dream** was given to Pharaoh in two forms is that
42: 9 he remembered his **dreams** [+2731] about them and said to them,
Nu 12: 6 I reveal myself to him in visions, I speak to him in **dreams**.
Dt 13: 1 [13:2] If a prophet, or *one who* **foretells by dreams** [+2731],
13: 3 [13:4] not listen to the words of that prophet or **dreamer** [+2731].
13: 5 [13:6] That prophet or **dreamer** [+2731] must be put to death,
Jdg 7: 13 Gideon arrived just as a man was telling a friend his **dream**.
7: 13 a friend his dream. "*I* **had a dream** [+2731]," he was saying.
7: 15 When Gideon heard the **dream** and its interpretation, he worshiped
1Sa 28: 6 the LORD did not answer him by **dreams** or Urim or prophets.
28: 15 He no longer answers me, either by prophets or by **dreams**.
1Ki 3: 5 the LORD appeared to Solomon during the night in a **dream**,
3: 15 Then Solomon awoke—and he realized it had been a **dream**.
Job 7: 14 even then you frighten me with **dreams** and terrify me with
20: 8 Like a **dream** he flies away, no more to be found, banished like a
33: 15 In a **dream**, in a vision of the night, when deep sleep falls on men
Ps 73: 20 As a **dream** when one awakes, so when you arise, O Lord,
Ecc 5: 3 [5:2] As a **dream** comes when there are many cares, so the speech
5: 7 [5:6] Much **dreaming** and many words are meaningless.
Isa 29: 7 and her fortress and besiege her, will be as it is with a **dream**,
Jer 23: 27 They think the **dreams** they tell one another will make my people
23: 28 Let the prophet who has a **dream** tell his dream, but let the one
23: 28 Let the prophet who has a dream tell his **dream**, but let the one
23: 32 Indeed, I am against those who prophesy false **dreams**,"
27: 9 your diviners, your **interpreters of dreams**, your mediums
29: 8 Do not listen to the **dreams** you **encourage** them **to have** [+2731].
Da 1: 17 And Daniel could understand visions and **dreams** of all kinds.
2: 1 second year of his reign, Nebuchadnezzar **had dreams** [+2731];
2: 2 sorcerers and astrologers to tell him *what* he had **dreamed**.
2: 3 "*I have* **had a dream** [+2731] that troubles me and I want to know
2: 3 that troubles me and I want to know what **it**[s] [+2021] means."
Joel 2: 28 [3:1] daughters will prophesy, your old men will dream **dreams**,
Zec 10: 2 that lie; they tell **dreams** that are false, they give comfort in vain.

2707 חַלּוֹן **ḥallôn**, n.m. & f. [31] [√ 2726]

window [13], windows [10], openings [7], parapet openings [1]

Ge 8: 6 After forty days Noah opened the **window** he had made *in* the ark
26: 8 Abimelech king of the Philistines looked down from a **window**
Jos 2: 15 So she let them down by a rope through the **window**, for the house
2: 18 you have tied this scarlet cord in the **window** through which you
2: 21 and they departed. And she tied the scarlet cord in the **window**.
Jdg 5: 28 "Through the **window** peered Sisera's mother; behind the lattice
1Sa 19: 12 So Michal let David down through a **window**, and he fled
2Sa 6: 16 City of David, Michal daughter of Saul watched from a **window**.
1Ki 6: 4 He made narrow clerestory **windows** in the temple.
2Ki 9: 30 painted her eyes, arranged her hair and looked out of a **window**.
9: 32 He looked up at the **window** and called out, "Who is on my side?
13: 17 "Open the east **window**," he said, and he opened it. "Shoot!"
1Ch 15: 29 City of David, Michal daughter of Saul watched from a **window**.
Pr 7: 6 At the **window** *of* my house I looked out through the lattice.
SS 2: 9 our wall, gazing through the **windows**, peering through the lattice.
Jer 9: 21 [9:20] Death has climbed in through our **windows** and has entered
22: 14 So he makes large **windows** in it, panels it with cedar
Eze 40: 16 gateway were surmounted by narrow **parapet openings** all around,
40: 16 as was the portico; the **openings** all around faced inward.
40: 22 Its **openings**, its portico and its palm tree decorations had the same
40: 25 The gateway and its portico had narrow **openings** all around,
40: 25 had narrow openings all around, like the **openings** of the others.
40: 29 The gateway and its portico had **openings** all around. It was fifty
40: 33 The gateway and its portico had **openings** all around. It was fifty
40: 36 its projecting walls and its portico, and it had **openings** all around.
41: 16 as well as the thresholds and the narrow **windows** and galleries
41: 16 The floor, the wall up to the **windows**, and the windows were
41: 16 the wall up to the windows, and the **windows** were covered.
41: 26 On the sidewalls of the portico were narrow **windows** with palm
Joel 2: 9 climb into the houses; like thieves they enter through the **windows**.
Zep 2: 14 Their calls will echo through the **windows**, rubble will be in the

2708 חֹלוֹן **ḥōlôn**, n.pr.loc. [3]

Holon [3]

Jos 15: 51 Goshen, **Holon** and Giloh—eleven towns and their villages.
21: 15 **Holon**, Debir,
Jer 48: 21 has come to the plateau—to **Holon**, Jahzah and Mephaath,

2709 חַלּוֹנָי **ḥallônāy**, n.m. & f. Not used in NIV/BHS

2710 חֲלוֹף **ḥ^a^lôp**, n.m. [1] [√ 2736]

destitute [+1201] [1]

Pr 31: 8 for themselves, for the rights of all *who* are **destitute** [+1201].

2711 חֲלוּשָׁה **ḥ^a^lûšâ**, n.f. [1] [√ 2765]

defeat [1]

Ex 32: 18 "It is not the sound of victory, it is not the sound of **defeat**;

2712 חֲלַח **ḥ^a^laḥ**, n.pr.loc. [3]

Halah [3]

2Ki 17: 6 He settled them in **Halah**, in Gozan on the Habor River and in the
18: 11 of Assyria deported Israel to Assyria and settled them in **Halah**,
1Ch 5: 26 He took them to **Halah**, Habor, Hara and the river of Gozan,

2713 חַלְחוּל **ḥalḥûl**, n.pr.loc. [1]

Halhul [1]

Jos 15: 58 **Halhul**, Beth Zur, Gedor,

2714 חַלְחָלָה ḥalḥālâ, n.f. [4] [√ 2655]
anguish [2], pain [1], tremble [1]

Isa 21: 3 At this my body is racked with **pain**, pangs seize me, like those of
Eze 30: 4 sword will come against Egypt, and **anguish** will come upon Cush.
30: 9 **Anguish** will take hold of them on the day of Egypt's doom,
Na 2: 10 [2:11] Hearts melt, knees give way, bodies **tremble**, every face

2715 חָלַט ḥālaṭ, v. [1]
pick up [1]

1Ki 20: 33 [A] took this as a good sign and were quick *to* **pick up** his word.

2716 חֳלִי ḥ[o]lî, n.m. [24] [√ 2703]
disease [5], illness [5], sickness [4], affliction [1], evil [1], grew worse and worse [+2118+2617+4394] [1], ill [1], illnesses [1], infirmities [1], injured [1], injury [1], recovery [+2649+4946] [1], suffering [1]

Dt 7: 15 The LORD will keep you free from every **disease**. He will not
28: 59 and prolonged disasters, and severe and lingering **illnesses**.
28: 61 The LORD will also bring on you every kind of **sickness**
1Ki 17: 17 He **grew worse** [+2118+2617+4394] **and worse**, and finally
2Ki 1: 2 the god of Ekron, to see if I will recover from this **injury**."
8: 8 LORD through him; ask him, 'Will I recover from this **illness**?' "
8: 9 of Aram has sent me to ask, 'Will I recover from this **illness**?' "
13: 14 Now Elisha was suffering from the **illness** from which he died.
2Ch 16: 12 Though his **disease** was severe, even in his illness he did not seek
16: 12 even in his **illness** he did not seek help from the LORD, but only
21: 15 You yourself will be very **ill** with a lingering disease of the bowels,
21: 15 of the bowels, until the **disease** causes your bowels to come out.' "
21: 18 the LORD afflicted Jehoram with an incurable **disease** of the
21: 19 his bowels came out because of the **disease**, and he died in great
Ps 41: 3 [41:4] him on his sickbed and restore him from his bed of **illness**.
Ecc 5: 17 [5:16] in darkness, with great frustration, **affliction** and anger.
6: 2 stranger enjoys them instead. This is meaningless, a grievous **evil**.
Isa 1: 5 Your whole head is **injured**, your whole heart afflicted.
38: 9 king of Judah after his illness and **recovery** [+2649+4946]:
53: 3 rejected by men, a man of sorrows, and familiar with **suffering**.
53: 4 Surely he took up our **infirmities** and carried our sorrows,
Jer 6: 7 resound in her; her **sickness** and wounds are ever before me.
10: 19 Yet I said to myself, "This is my **sickness**, and I must endure it."
Hos 5: 13 "When Ephraim saw his **sickness**, and Judah his sores,

2717 ¹חֲלִי ḥ[a]lî[1], n.m. [2] [→ 2719]
jewels [1], ornament [1]

Pr 25: 12 or an **ornament** *of* fine gold is a wise man's rebuke to a listening
SS 7: 1 [7:2] Your graceful legs are like **jewels**, the work of a craftsman's

2718 ²חֲלִי ḥ[a]lî[2], n.pr.loc. [1]
Hali [1]

Jos 19: 25 Their territory included: Helkath, **Hali**, Beten, Acshaph,

2719 חֶלְיָה ḥelyâ, n.f. [1] [√ 2717]
jewelry [1]

Hos 2: 13 [2:15] she decked herself with rings and **jewelry**, and went after

2720 ¹חָלִיל ḥālîl[1] n.m. [6] [→ 2727, 5704?; cf. 2726]
flutes [4], flute [2]

1Sa 10: 5 tambourines, **flutes** and harps being played before them, and they
1Ki 1: 40 the people went up after him, playing **flutes** and rejoicing greatly,
Isa 5: 12 and lyres at their banquets, tambourines and **flutes** and wine,
30: 29 your hearts will rejoice as when people go up with **flutes** to the
Jer 48: 36 "So my heart laments for Moab like a **flute**; it laments like a flute
48: 36 like a flute; it laments like a **flute** for the men of Kir Hareseth.

2721 ²חָלִילָה ḥālîl[2], subst. [21] [√ 2725]
far be it [12], forbid [4], never [3], never [+561+4200] [1], of course not [1]

Ge 18: 25 **Far be it** from you to do such a thing—to kill the righteous with
18: 25 treating the righteous and the wicked alike. **Far be it** from you!
44: 7 such things? **Far be it** from your servants to do anything like that!
44: 17 Joseph said, "**Far be it** from me to do such a thing! Only the man
Jos 22: 29 "**Far be it** from us to rebel against the LORD and turn away from
24: 16 "**Far be it** from us to forsake the LORD to serve other gods!
1Sa 2: 30 now the LORD declares: '**Far be it** from me! Those who honor
12: 23 **far be it** from me that I should sin against the LORD by failing to
14: 45 **Never**! As surely as the LORD lives, not a hair of his head will
20: 2 "**Never**!" Jonathan replied. "You are not going to die! Look,
20: 9 "**Never**!" Jonathan said. "If I had the least inkling that my father
22: 15 **Of course not**! Let not the king accuse your servant or any of his
24: 6 [24:7] "The LORD **forbid** that I should do such a thing to my
26: 11 the LORD **forbid** that I should lay a hand on the LORD's
2Sa 20: 20 "**Far be it** from me!" Joab replied, "Far be it from me to swallow
20: 20 Joab replied, "**Far be it** from me to swallow up or destroy!
23: 17 "**Far be it** from me, O LORD, to do this!" he said. "Is it not the
1Ki 21: 3 "The LORD **forbid** that I should give you the inheritance of my
1Ch 11: 19 "God **forbid** that I should do this!" he said. "Should I drink the
Job 27: 5 I will **never** [+561+4200] admit you are in the right; till I die,
34: 10 **Far be it** from God to do evil, from the Almighty to do wrong.

2722 חֲלִיפָה ḥ[a]lîpâ, n.f. [12] [√ 2736]
sets [6], change [1], clothes [1], new [1], renewal [1], shifts [1], wave upon wave [1]

Ge 45: 22 To each of them he gave **new** clothing, but to Benjamin he gave
45: 22 he gave three hundred shekels of silver and five **sets** *of* clothes.
Jdg 14: 12 I will give you thirty linen garments and thirty **sets** *of* clothes.
14: 13 you must give me thirty linen garments and thirty **sets** *of* clothes."
14: 19 and gave their **clothes** to those who had explained the riddle.
1Ki 5: 14 [5:28] He sent them off to Lebanon in **shifts** of ten thousand a
2Ki 5: 5 of silver, six thousand shekels of gold and ten **sets** *of* clothing.
5: 22 Please give them a talent of silver and two **sets** *of* clothing.' "
5: 23 up the two talents of silver in two bags, with two **sets** *of* clothing.
Job 10: 17 anger toward me; your forces come against me **wave upon wave**.
14: 14 All the days of my hard service I will wait for my **renewal** to
Ps 55: 19 [55:20] *Selah* men who never **change** their ways and have no

2723 חֲלִיצָה ḥ[a]lîṣâ, n.f. [2] [√ 2741]
belongings [1], weapons [1]

Jdg 14: 19 stripped them of their **belongings** and gave their clothes to those
2Sa 2: 21 take on one of the young men and strip him of his **weapons**."

2724 חֵלְכָה ḥēlkâ, a. [3]
victims [2], victim [1]

Ps 10: 8 he murders the innocent, watching in secret for his **victims**.
10: 10 His **victims** [Q 2657+3875] are crushed, they collapse; they fall
10: 14 The **victim** commits himself to you; you are the helper of the

2725 ¹חָלַל ḥālal[1], v. [133 / 134] [→ 2687, 2721, 9378]
began [25], desecrated [11], profane [11], begin [8], desecrate [7], profaned [7], begun [6], defile [5], defiled [5], desecrating [5], enjoy [4], started [4], beginning [3], being profaned [3], *untranslated* [2], first time [2], grew [2], violate [2], am profaned [1], be defamed [1], be desecrated [1], becoming [1], been defiled [1], been profaned [1], break [1], bring low [1], defiles herself [1], degrade [1], desecrates [1], disgrace [1], disgraces [1], dishonor [1], drove in disgrace [1], launch [1], let be profaned [1], proceeded [1], treating with contempt [1], undertook [1], violates [1], was desecrated [1]

Ge 4: 26 [H] At that time *men* **began** to call on the name of the LORD.
6: 1 [G] When men **began** to increase in number on the earth
9: 20 [G] Noah, a man of the soil, **proceeded** to plant a vineyard.
10: 8 [G] of Nimrod, who **grew** to be a mighty warrior on the earth.
11: 6 [G] speaking the same language they *have* **begun** to do this,
41: 54 [G] and the seven years of famine **began**, just as Joseph had said.
44: 12 [G] **beginning** with the oldest and ending with the youngest.
49: 4 [D] went up onto your father's bed, onto my couch and **defiled** it.
Ex 20: 25 [D] dressed stones, for *you will* **defile** it if you use a tool on it.
31: 14 [D] *Anyone who* **desecrates** it must be put to death; whoever
Lev 18: 21 [D] to Molech, for *you must* not **profane** the name of your God.
19: 8 [D] because *he has* **desecrated** what is holy to the LORD;
19: 12 [D] falsely by my name and so **profane** the name of your God.
19: 29 [D] " '*Do* not **degrade** your daughter by making her a prostitute,
20: 3 [D] he has defiled my sanctuary and **profaned** my holy name.
21: 4 [C] for people related to him by marriage, and so **defile** himself.
21: 6 [D] to their God and *must* not **profane** the name of their God.
21: 9 [C] " 'If a priest's daughter **defiles herself** by becoming a
21: 9 [D] herself by becoming a prostitute, she **disgraces** her father;
21: 12 [D] nor leave the sanctuary of his God or **desecrate** it,
21: 15 [D] so *he will* not **defile** his offspring among his people. I am the
21: 23 [D] or approach the altar, and so **desecrate** my sanctuary.
22: 2 [D] consecrate to me, so *they will* not **profane** my holy name.
22: 9 [D] not become guilty and die for **treating** them **with contempt**.
22: 15 [D] *must* not **desecrate** the sacred offerings the Israelites
22: 32 [D] *Do* not **profane** my holy name. I must be acknowledged as
Nu 16: 46 [17:11] [G] out from the LORD; the plague *has* **started**."
16: 47 [17:12] [G] The plague *had already* **started** among the people,
18: 32 [D] then *you will* not **defile** the holy offerings of the Israelites,
25: 1 [G] the men **began** to indulge in sexual immorality with Moabite
30: 2 [30:3] [G] *he must* not **break** his word but must do everything
Dt 2: 24 [G] **Begin** to take possession of it and engage him in battle.
2: 25 [G] This very day *I will* **begin** to put the terror and fear of you on
2: 31 [G] *I have* **begun** to deliver Sihon and his country over to you.
2: 31 [G] over to you. Now **begin** to conquer and possess his land."

[F] Hitpael (hitpoel, hitpoal, hitpolel, hitpolal, hitpalel, hitpalal, hitpalpel, hitpalpal, hotpael, hotpaal) [G] Hiphil (hiphtil) [H] Hophal [I] Hishtaphel

Dt 3:24 [G] you *have* **begun** to show to your servant your greatness
16: 9 [G] Count off seven weeks from the time you **begin** to put the
16: 9 [G] you begin to put the sickle to the standing grain. **[RPH]**
20: 6 [D] Has anyone planted a vineyard and not *begun to* **enjoy** it?
20: 6 [D] go home, or he may die in battle and someone else **enjoy** it.
28:30 [D] a vineyard, but *you will* not *even begin to* **enjoy** its fruit.
Jos 3: 7 [G] "Today *I will* **begin** to exalt you in the eyes of all Israel,
Jdg 10:18 [G] "Whoever *will* **launch** the attack against the Ammonites will
13: 5 [G] he *will* **begin** the deliverance of Israel from the hands of the
13:25 [G] the Spirit of the LORD **began** to stir him while he was in
16:19 [G] off the seven braids of his hair, and so **began** to subdue him.
16:22 [G] the hair on his head **began** to grow *again* after it had been
20:31 [G] *They* **began** to inflict casualties on the Israelites as before,
20:39 [G] The Benjamites *had* **begun** to inflict casualties on the men of
20:40 [G] But when the column of smoke **began** to rise from the city,
1Sa 3: 2 [G] whose eyes *were* **becoming** so weak that he could barely see,
3:12 [G] I spoke against his family—from **beginning** to end.
14:35 [G] an altar to the LORD; it *was the* **first time** he had done this.
22:15 [G] *Was* that day *the* **first time** I inquired of God for him?
2Ki 10:32 [G] In those days the LORD **began** to reduce the size of Israel.
15:37 [G] (In those days the LORD **began** to send Rezin king of Aram
1Ch 1:10 [G] father of Nimrod, who **grew** to be a mighty warrior on earth.
5: 1 [D] the firstborn, but when he **defiled** his father's marriage bed,
27:24 [G] Joab son of Zeruiah **began** to count the men but did not
2Ch 3: 1 [G] Solomon **began** to build the temple of the LORD in
3: 2 [G] *He* **began** building on the second day of the second month in
20:22 [G] As *they* **began** to sing and praise, the LORD set ambushes
29:17 [G] *They* **began** the consecration on the first day of the first
29:27 [G] As the offering **began**, singing to the LORD began also,
29:27 [G] As the offering began, singing to the LORD **began** also,
31: 7 [G] *They* **began** doing this in the third month and finished in the
31:10 [G] "Since the people **began** to bring their contributions to the
31:21 [G] In everything that *he* **undertook** in the service of God's
34: 3 [G] still young, *he* **began** to seek the God of his father David.
34: 3 [G] In his twelfth year *he* **began** to purge Judah and Jerusalem of
Ezr 3: 6 [G] On the first day of the seventh month *they* **began** to offer
3: 8 [G] **began** the work, appointing Levites twenty years of age and
Ne 4: 7 [4:1] [G] and that the gaps **[NIE]** were being closed,
13:17 [D] wicked thing you are doing—**desecrating** the Sabbath day?
13:18 [D] up more wrath against Israel by **desecrating** the Sabbath."
Est 6:13 [G] "Since Mordecai, before whom your downfall *has* **started**,
9:23 [G] the Jews agreed to continue the celebration *they had* **begun**,
Ps 55:20 [55:21] [D] attacks his friends; *he* **violates** his covenant.
74: 7 [D] to the ground; *they* **defiled** the dwelling place of your Name.
89:31 [89:32] [D] if *they* **violate** my decrees and fail to keep my
89:34 [89:35] [D] *I will* not **violate** my covenant or alter what my lips
89:39 [89:40] [D] your servant and *have* **defiled** his crown in the dust.
Isa 23: 9 [D] to **bring low** the pride of all glory and to humble all who are
43:28 [D] So *I will* **disgrace** the dignitaries of your temple, and I will
47: 6 [D] I was angry with my people and **desecrated** my inheritance;
48:11 [C] my own sake, I do this. How *can* I *let* myself **be defamed**?
56: 2 [D] holds it fast, who keeps the Sabbath without **desecrating** it,
56: 6 [D] all who keep the Sabbath without **desecrating** it and who
Jer 16:18 [D] because they *have* **defiled** my land with the lifeless forms of
25:29 [G] I am **beginning** to bring disaster on the city that bears my
31: 5 [D] of Samaria; the farmers will plant them and **enjoy** their fruit.
34:16 [D] But now you have turned around and **profaned** my name;
La 2: 2 [D] her kingdom and its princes down to the ground *in* **dishonor**.
Eze 7:21 [D] and as loot to the wicked of the earth, and *they will* **defile** it.
7:22 [D] from them, and *they will* **desecrate** my treasured place;
7:22 [D] my treasured place; robbers will enter it and **desecrate** it.
7:24 [C] pride of the mighty, and their sanctuaries *will* **be desecrated**.
9: 6 [G] not touch anyone who has the mark. **Begin** at my sanctuary."
9: 6 [G] So *they* **began** with the elders who were in front of the
13:19 [D] *You have* **profaned** me among my people for a few handfuls
20: 9 [C] **being profaned** in the eyes of the nations they lived among
20:13 [D] will live by them—and *they* utterly **desecrated** my Sabbaths.
20:14 [C] **being profaned** in the eyes of the nations in whose sight I
20:16 [D] and did not follow my decrees and **desecrated** my Sabbaths.
20:21 [D] them will live by them—and *they* **desecrated** my Sabbaths.
20:22 [C] **being profaned** in the eyes of the nations in whose sight I
20:24 [D] but had rejected my decrees and **desecrated** my Sabbaths,
20:39 [D] no longer **profane** my holy name with your gifts and idols.
22: 8 [D] have despised my holy things and **desecrated** my Sabbaths.
22:16 [C] When *you have* **been defiled** in the eyes of the nations, you
22:26 [D] priests do violence to my law and **profane** my holy things;
22:26 [C] keeping of my Sabbaths, so that *I* **am profaned** among them.
23:38 [D] time they defiled my sanctuary and **desecrated** my Sabbaths.
23:39 [D] to their idols, they entered my sanctuary and **desecrated** it.
24:21 [D] I *am about to* **desecrate** my sanctuary—the stronghold in
25: 3 [C] over my sanctuary when *it* **was desecrated** and over the land
28:16 [D] So *I* **drove** you **in disgrace** from the mount of God, and I
28:18 [D] and dishonest trade you *have* **desecrated** your sanctuaries.
36:20 [D] wherever they went among the nations *they* **profaned** my
36:21 [D] which the house of Israel **profaned** among the nations where
36:22 [D] which *you have* **profaned** among the nations where you
36:23 [E] which *has* **been profaned** among the nations, the name you
36:23 [D] the nations, the name *you have* **profaned** among them.
39: 7 [G] *I will* no longer **let** my holy name **be profaned**, and the
44: 7 [D] **desecrating** my temple while you offered me food, fat
Da 11:31 [D] "His armed forces will rise up *to* **desecrate** the temple
Hos 8:10 [G] *They will* **begin** *to* waste away under the oppression of the
Am 2: 7 [D] and son use the same girl and so **profane** my holy name.
Jnh 3: 4 [G] On the first day, Jonah **started** into the city. He proclaimed:
Mic 6:13 [G] Therefore, I *have* **begun** [BHS 2703] to destroy you, to ruin
Zep 3: 4 [D] Her priests **profane** the sanctuary and do violence to the law.
Mal 1:12 [D] "But you **profane** it by saying of the Lord's table, 'It is
2:10 [D] Why *do we* **profane** the covenant of our fathers by breaking
2:11 [D] Judah *has* **desecrated** the sanctuary the LORD loves, by

2726 ²חָלַל **ḥālal[2]**, v. [8] [→ 2705, 2707, 2720, 2727, 2728, 2729, 4704, 5704?]

killed [1], pierce [1], pierced through [1], pierced [1], slay [1], was pierced [1], wounded [1], wounds [1]

Job 26:13 [D] the skies became fair; his hand **pierced** the gliding serpent.
Ps 109:22 [A] I am poor and needy, and my heart *is* **wounded** within me.
Pr 26:10 [D] Like an archer *who* **wounds** at random is he who hires a fool
Isa 51: 9 [D] cut Rahab to pieces, *who* **pierced** that monster **through**?
53: 5 [E] he **was pierced** for our transgressions, he was crushed for our
Eze 28: 7 [D] your beauty and wisdom and **pierce** your shining splendor.
28: 9 [D] but a man, not a god, in the hands of *those who* **slay** you.
32:26 [E] **killed** *by* the sword because they spread their terror in the

2727 ³חָלַל **ḥālal[3]**, v.den. [2] [√ 2720; cf. 2726]

make music [1], playing [1]

1Ki 1:40 [D] went up after him, **playing** flutes and rejoicing greatly,
Ps 87: 7 [A] As *they* **make music** they will sing, "All my fountains are in

2728 ¹חָלָל **ḥālāl[1]**, n.m. [91] [√ 2726]

slain [38], killed [21], dead [6], wounded [5], casualties [4], body [3], victims [3], slaughter [2], bodies [1], dead bodies [1], die [1], fall in battle [+5877] [1], hurt [1], mortally wounded man [1], people [1], slain in battle [1], violent [1]

Ge 34:27 The sons of Jacob came upon the **dead bodies** and looted the city
Nu 19:16 the open who touches someone *who* has been **killed** *with* a sword
19:18 or a grave or someone who has been **killed** or someone who has
23:24 rest till he devours his prey and drinks the blood of his **victims**."
31: 8 Among their **victims** were Evi, Rekem, Zur, Hur and Reba—
31:19 or touched anyone who was **killed** must stay outside the camp
Dt 21: 1 If a man is found **slain**, lying in a field in the land the LORD your
21: 2 and measure the distance from the **body** to the neighboring towns.
21: 3 the elders of the town nearest the **body** shall take a heifer that has
21: 6 all the elders of the town nearest the **body** shall wash their hands
32:42 the blood of the **slain** and the captives, the heads of the enemy
Jos 11: 6 by this time tomorrow I will hand all of them over to Israel, **slain**.
13:22 In addition to *those* **slain in battle**, the Israelites had put to the
Jdg 9:40 Abimelech chased him, and many fell **wounded** in the flight—
16:24 the one who laid waste our land and multiplied our **slain**."
20:31 They began to inflict **casualties** on the Israelites as before,
20:39 The Benjamites had begun to inflict **casualties** on the men of Israel
1Sa 17:52 Their **dead** were strewn along the Shaaraim road to Gath
31: 1 Israelites fled before them, and many fell **slain** on Mount Gilboa.
31: 8 The next day, when the Philistines came to strip the **dead**,
2Sa 1:19 "Your glory, O Israel, lies **slain** on your heights. How the mighty
1:22 From the blood of the **slain**, from the flesh of the mighty, the bow
1:25 mighty have fallen in battle! Jonathan lies **slain** on your heights.
23: 8 spear against eight hundred men, whom he **killed** in one encounter.
23:18 whom he **killed**, and so he became as famous as the Three.
1Ki 11:15 the commander of the army, who had gone up to bury the **dead**,
1Ch 5:22 many others fell **slain**, because the battle was God's. And they
10: 1 Israelites fled before them, and many fell **slain** on Mount Gilboa.
10: 8 The next day, when the Philistines came to strip the **dead**,
11:11 he raised his spear against three hundred *men*, whom he **killed** in
11:20 He raised his spear against three hundred *men*, *whom* he **killed**,
2Ch 13:17 so that there were five hundred thousand **casualties** among Israel's
Job 24:12 rise from the city, and the souls of the **wounded** cry out for help.
39:30 young ones feast on blood, and where the **slain** are, there is he."
Ps 69:26 [69:27] you wound and talk about the pain of *those* you **hurt**.
88: 5 [88:6] set apart with the dead, like the **slain** who lie in the grave,
89:10 [89:11] You crushed Rahab like *one of* the **slain**; with your strong
Pr 7:26 Many are the **victims** she has brought down; her slain are a mighty
Isa 22: 2 Your **slain** were not killed by the sword, nor did they die in battle.
22: 2 Your slain were not **killed** *by* the sword, nor did they die in battle.
34: 3 Their **slain** will be thrown out, their dead bodies will send up a
66:16 upon all men, and many will be *those* **slain** *by* the LORD.

Jer 9: 1 [8:23] I would weep day and night for the **slain** *of* my people.
14: 18 If I go into the country, I see *those* **slain** *by* the sword; if I go into
25: 33 At that time *those* **slain** *by* the LORD will be everywhere—
41: 9 king of Israel. Ishmael son of Nethaniah filled it with the **dead**.
51: 4 They will fall down **slain** in Babylon, fatally wounded in her
51: 47 land will be disgraced and her **slain** will all lie fallen within her.
51: 49 "Babylon must fall because of Israel's **slain**, just as the slain in all
51: 49 just as the **slain** *in* all the earth have fallen because of Babylon.
51: 52 punish her idols, and throughout her land the **wounded** will groan.
La 2: 12 as they faint like **wounded** *men* in the streets of the city, as their
4: 9 *Those* **killed** *by* the sword are better off than those who die of
4: 9 Those killed by the sword are better off than *those who* **die** *of*
Eze 6: 4 will be smashed; and I will slay your **people** in front of your idols.
6: 7 Your people will fall **slain** among you, and you will know that I
6: 13 when their *people* lie **slain** among their idols around their altars,
9: 7 said to them, "Defile the temple and fill the courts with the **slain**.
11: 6 You have **killed** many *people* in this city and filled its streets with
11: 6 killed many people in this city and filled its streets with the **dead**.
11: 7 The **bodies** you have thrown there are the meat and this city is the
21: 14 [21:19] It is a sword for **slaughter**—a sword for great slaughter,
21: 14 [21:19] a sword for great **slaughter**, closing in on them from
21: 29 [21:34] be laid on the necks of the wicked who are to be **slain**,
26: 15 when the **wounded** groan and the slaughter takes place in you?
28: 8 to the pit, and you will die a **violent** death in the heart of the seas.
28: 23 The **slain** will fall within her, with the sword against her on every
30: 4 When the **slain** fall in Egypt, her wealth will be carried away
30: 11 draw their swords against Egypt and fill the land with the **slain**.
30: 24 and he will groan before him like a **mortally wounded man**.
31: 17 gone down to the grave with it, joining *those* **killed** *by* the sword.
31: 18 will lie among the uncircumcised, with *those* **killed** *by* the sword.
32: 20 They will fall among *those* **killed** *by* the sword. The sword is
32: 21 they lie with the uncircumcised, with *those* **killed** *by* the sword.'
32: 22 she is surrounded by the graves of all her **slain**, all who have fallen
32: 23 All who had spread terror in the land of the living are **slain**,
32: 24 hordes around her grave. All of them are **slain**, fallen by the sword.
32: 25 A bed is made for her among the **slain**, with all her hordes around
32: 25 her grave. All of them are uncircumcised, **killed** *by* the sword.
32: 25 with those who go down to the pit; they are laid among the **slain**.
32: 28 will lie among the uncircumcised, with *those* **killed** *by* the sword.
32: 29 despite their power, they are laid with *those* **killed** *by* the sword.
32: 30 they went down with the **slain** in disgrace despite the terror caused
32: 30 They lie uncircumcised with *those* **killed** *by* the sword and bear
32: 31 he will be consoled for all his hordes *that* were **killed** *by* the
32: 32 with *those* **killed** *by* the sword, declares the Sovereign LORD."
35: 8 I will fill your mountains with the **slain**; those killed by the sword
35: 8 *those* **killed** *by* the sword will fall on your hills and in your valleys
Da 11: 26 his army will be swept away, and many *will* **fall in battle** [+5877].
Na 3: 3 Many **casualties**, piles of dead, bodies without number, people
Zep 2: 12 "You too, O Cushites, will be **slain** *by* my sword."

2729 חָלָל² ḥālāl[2], a. [3] [√ 2726]

defiled [2], profane [1]

Lev 21: 7 " 'They must not marry women **defiled** *by* prostitution or divorced
21: 14 a widow, a divorced woman, or a *woman* **defiled** *by* prostitution,
Eze 21: 25 [21:30] " 'O **profane** and wicked prince of Israel, whose day has

2730 חָלַם¹ ḥālam[1], v. [2] [cf. 2731]

grow strong [1], restored to health [1]

Job 39: 4 [A] Their young thrive and **grow strong** in the wilds; they leave
Isa 38: 16 [G] life in them too. *You* **restored** me **to health** and let me live.

2731 חָלַם² ḥālam[2], v. [27] [→ 2706; cf. 2730]

had a dream [+2706] [6], had a dream [5], dream had [+2706] [2], dreamer [+2706] [2], dreams [2], had dream [+2706] [2], had dreams [+2706] [2], *untranslated* [1], dream [1], dreamed [1], dreams [+2706] [1], dreams encourage to have [+2706] [1], foretells by dreams [+2706] [1]

Ge 28: 12 [A] *He* **had a dream** in which he saw a stairway resting on the
37: 5 [A] Joseph **had a dream** [+2706], and when he told it to his
37: 6 [A] He said to them, "Listen to this **dream** [+2706] *I* **had**:
37: 9 [A] *he* **had** another **dream** [+2706], and he told it to his brothers.
37: 9 [A] "Listen," he said, "*I* **had** another **dream** [+2706], and this
37: 10 [A] and said, "What is this **dream** [+2706] *you* **had**?
40: 5 [A] **had a dream** [+2706] the same night, and each dream had a
40: 8 [A] "*We both* **had dreams** [+2706]," they answered, "but there
41: 1 [A] When two full years had passed, Pharaoh **had a dream**: He
41: 5 [A] He fell asleep again and **had** a second **dream**: Seven heads
41: 11 [A] Each of us **had a dream** [+2706] the same night, and each
41: 11 [A] and each dream had a meaning of its own. **[RPH]**
41: 15 [A] Pharaoh said to Joseph, "*I* **had a dream** [+2706], and no one
42: 9 [A] he remembered his **dreams** [+2706] about them and said to
Dt 13: 1 [13:2] [A] a prophet, or *one who* **foretells by dreams** [+2706],
13: 3 [13:4] [A] to the words of that prophet or **dreamer** [+2706].
13: 5 [13:6] [A] That prophet or **dreamer** [+2706] must be put to
Jdg 7: 13 [A] a friend his dream. "*I* **had a dream** [+2706]," he was saying.
Ps 126: 1 [A] back the captives to Zion, we were like *men who* **dreamed**.
Isa 29: 8 [A] as *when* a hungry man **dreams** that he is eating, but he
29: 8 [A] as *when* a thirsty man **dreams** that he is drinking, but he
Jer 23: 25 [A] lies in my name. They say, '*I* **had a dream**! I had a dream!'
23: 25 [A] lies in my name. They say, 'I had a dream! *I* **had a dream**!'
29: 8 [G] listen to the **dreams** [+2706] you **encourage** them **to have**.
Da 2: 1 [A] year of his reign, Nebuchadnezzar **had dreams** [+2706];
2: 3 [A] "*I have* **had a dream** [+2706] that troubles me and I want to
Joel 2: 28 [3:1] [A] will prophesy, your old men *will* **dream** dreams,

2732 חֵלֶם ḥēlem, n.pr.m. [1 / 0] [cf. 2702]

Zec 6: 14 The crown will be given to Heldai, [BHS ***Helem***; NIV 2702]

2733 חַלָּמוּת ḥallāmût, n.f. [1]

egg [1]

Job 6: 6 food eaten without salt, or is there flavor in the white of an **egg**?

2734 חַלָּמִישׁ ḥallāmîš, n.m. [5]

flint [1], flinty rock [1], flinty [1], hard rock [1], hard [1]

Dt 8: 15 and scorpions. He brought you water out of **hard** rock.
32: 13 him with honey from the rock, and with oil from the **flinty** crag,
Job 28: 9 Man's hand assaults the **flinty rock** and lays bare the roots of the
Ps 114: 8 turned the rock into a pool, the **hard rock** into springs of water.
Isa 50: 7 Therefore have I set my face like **flint**, and I know I will not be put

2735 חֵלֹן ḥēlōn, n.pr.m. [5]

Helon [5]

Nu 1: 9 from Zebulun, Eliab son of **Helon**;
2: 7 The leader of the people of Zebulun is Eliab son of **Helon**.
7: 24 On the third day, Eliab son of **Helon**, the leader of the people of
7: 29 a fellowship offering. This was the offering of Eliab son of **Helon**.
10: 16 Eliab son of **Helon** was over the division of the tribe of Zebulun.

2736 חָלַף¹ ḥālap[1], v. [26] [→ 2710, 2722, 2739, 4709?, 4710; Ar 10268]

changed [3], new [3], change [2], changing [1], comes along [1], disappear [1], discarded [1], exchange [1], glided past [1], go [1], goes by [1], let renew [1], over [1], renew [1], replace [1], skim past [1], sprout [1], sweep on [1], sweep past [1], sweeping [1], violated [1]

Ge 31: 7 [G] yet your father has cheated me *by* **changing** my wages ten
31: 41 [G] years for your flocks, and *you* **changed** my wages ten times.
35: 2 [G] with you, and purify yourselves and **change** your clothes.
41: 14 [D] When he had shaved and **changed** his clothes, he came
Lev 27: 10 [G] *He must* not **exchange** it or substitute a good one for a bad
1Sa 10: 3 [A] "Then *you will* **go** on from there until you reach the great
2Sa 12: 20 [D] After he had washed, put on lotions and **changed** his clothes,
Job 4: 15 [A] A spirit **glided past** my face, and the hair on my body stood
9: 11 [A] I cannot see him; when *he* **goes by**, I cannot perceive him.
9: 26 [A] *They* **skim past** like boats of papyrus, like eagles swooping
11: 10 [A] "If *he* **comes along** and confines you in prison and convenes
14: 7 [G] If it is cut down, *it will* **sprout** again, and its new shoots will
29: 20 [G] glory will remain fresh in me, the bow *ever* **new** in my hand.'
Ps 90: 5 [A] sleep of death; they are like the **new** grass of the morning—
90: 6 [A] though in the morning it springs up **new**, by evening it is dry
102: 26 [102:27] [G] Like clothing *you will* **change** them and they will
102: 26 [102:27] [A] you will change them and *they will be* **discarded**.
SS 2: 11 [A] See! The winter is past; the rains *are* **over** and gone.
Isa 2: 18 [A] and the idols *will* totally **disappear**.
8: 8 [A] and **sweep on** into Judah, swirling over it, passing through it
9: 10 [9:9] [G] been felled, but *we will* **replace** them *with* cedars."
21: 1 [A] Like whirlwinds **sweeping** through the southland, an invader
24: 5 [A] **violated** the statutes and broken the everlasting covenant.
40: 31 [G] but those who hope in the LORD *will* **renew** their strength.
41: 1 [G] before me, you islands! **Let** the nations **renew** their strength!
Hab 1: 11 [A] Then *they* **sweep past** like the wind and go on—guilty men,

2737 חָלַף² ḥālap[2], v. [2] [→ 2738?]

pierced [1], pierces [1]

Jdg 5: 26 [A] she crushed his head, she shattered and **pierced** his temple.
Job 20: 24 [A] from an iron weapon, a bronze-tipped arrow **pierces** him.

2738 חֵלֶף¹ ḥēlep[1], n.pr.loc. [1] [√ 2737?]

Heleph [1]

Jos 19: 33 Their boundary went from **Heleph** and the large tree in

2739 ²חֵלֶף ***ḥēlep²***, n.[m.]. [2] [√ 2736]

for [1], in return for [1]

Nu 18:21 **in return for** the work they do while serving at the Tent of
18:31 for it is your wages **for** your work at the Tent of Meeting.

2740 ¹חָלַץ ***ḥālaṣ¹***, v. [23] [→ 4711; cf. 2741, 2742]

deliver [4], rescued [3], be delivered [2], delivers [2], torn out [2], *untranslated* [1], delivered [1], escape [1], is rescued [1], offer [1], rescue [1], robbed [1], take off [1], unsandaled [+5837] [1], withdrawn [1]

Lev 14:40 [D] he is to order that the contaminated stones *be* **torn out** and
14:43 [D] reappears in the house after the stones *have been* **torn out**
Dt 25: 9 [A] **take off** one of his sandals, spit in his face and say,
25:10 [B] known in Israel as The Family of the **Unsandaled** [+5837].
2Sa 22:20 [D] a spacious place; *he* **rescued** me because he delighted in me.
Job 36:15 [D] those who suffer *he* **delivers** in their suffering; he speaks to
Ps 6: 4 [6:5] [D] Turn, O LORD, and **deliver** me; save me because of
7: 4 [7:5] [D] peace with me or without cause *have* **robbed** my foe—
18:19 [18:20] [D] *he* **rescued** me because he delighted in me.
34: 7 [34:8] [D] around those who fear him, and *he* **delivers** them.
50:15 [D] day of trouble; *I will* **deliver** you, and you will honor me."
60: 5 [60:7] [C] right hand, that those you love *may* **be delivered**.
81: 7 [81:8] [D] In your distress you called and *I* **rescued** you,
91:15 [D] be with him in trouble, *I will* **deliver** him and honor him.
108: 6 [108:7] [C] right hand, that those you love *may* **be delivered**.
116: 8 [D] For *you*, O LORD, *have* **delivered** my soul from death, my
119:153 [D] Look upon my suffering and **deliver** me, for I have not
140: 1 [140:2] [D] **Rescue** me, O LORD, from evil men; protect me
Pr 11: 8 [C] The righteous man **is rescued** from trouble, and it comes on
11: 9 [C] his neighbor, but through knowledge the righteous **escape**.
Isa 20: 2 [A] from your body and **[RPH]** the sandals from your feet."
La 4: 3 [A] Even jackals **offer** their breasts to nurse their young, but my
Hos 5: 6 [A] will not find him; *he has* **withdrawn** *himself* from them.

2741 ²חָלַץ ***ḥālaṣ²***, v. [21] [→ 2723, 2742; cf. 2740]

armed [12], armed guard [2], arm ourselves [1], arm yourselves [1], arm [1], armed for battle [1], army [1], soldiers [1], strengthen [1]

Nu 31: 3 [C] "**Arm** some of your men to go to war against the Midianites
31: 5 [B] So twelve thousand *men* **armed** *for* battle, a thousand from
32:17 [C] we are ready *to* **arm ourselves** and go ahead of the Israelites
32:20 [C] if *you will* **arm yourselves** before the LORD for battle,
32:21 [B] if all of you will go **armed** over the Jordan before the
32:27 [B] your servants, every *man* **armed** *for* battle, will cross over to
32:29 [B] "If the Gadites and Reubenites, every *man* **armed** for battle,
32:30 [B] if they do not cross over with you **armed**, they must accept
32:32 [B] We will cross over before the LORD into Canaan **armed**,
Dt 3:18 [B] all your able-bodied men, **armed for battle**, must cross over
Jos 4:13 [B] About forty thousand **armed** *for* battle crossed over before
6: 7 [B] with the **armed guard** going ahead of the ark of the
6: 9 [B] The **armed guard** marched ahead of the priests who blew the
6:13 [B] The **armed** *men* went ahead of them and the rear guard
1Ch 12:23 [12:24] [B] These are the numbers of the men **armed** for battle
12:24 [12:25] [B] carrying shield and spear—6,800 **armed** *for* battle;
2Ch 17:18 [B] next, Jehozabad, with 180,000 *men* **armed** *for* battle.
20:21 [B] of his holiness as they went out at the head of the **army**,
28:14 [B] So the **soldiers** gave up the prisoners and plunder in the
Isa 15: 4 [B] Therefore the **armed** *men of* Moab cry out, and their hearts
58:11 [G] in a sun-scorched land and *will* **strengthen** your frame.

2742 חֶלֶץ ***ḥeleṣ***, n.pr.m. [5] [√ 2740 *or* 2741]

Helez [5]

2Sa 23:26 **Helez** the Paltite, Ira son of Ikkesh from Tekoa,
1Ch 2:39 Azariah the father of **Helez**, Helez the father of Eleasah,
2:39 Azariah the father of Helez, **Helez** the father of Eleasah,
11:27 Shammoth the Harorite, **Helez** the Pelonite,
27:10 for the seventh month, was **Helez** the Pelonite, an Ephraimite.

2743 חֲלָצַיִם ***ḥᵃlāṣayim***, n.[f.]. [10] [→ Ar 10284]

brace [+273] [2], flesh and blood [+3655+4946] [2], waist [2], body [1], heart [1], stomach [1], waists [1]

Ge 35:11 nations will come from you, and kings will come from your **body**.
1Ki 8:19 but your son, who *is* your own **flesh** [+3655+4946] **and blood**—
2Ch 6: 9 but your son, who *is* your own **flesh** [+3655+4946] **and blood**—
Job 31:20 his **heart** did not bless me for warming him with the fleece from
38: 3 **Brace** [+273] yourself like a man; I will question you, and you
40: 7 "**Brace** [+273] yourself like a man; I will question you, and you
Isa 5:27 not a belt is loosened at the **waist**, not a sandal thong is broken.
11: 5 will be his belt and faithfulness the sash around his **waist**.
32:11 Strip off your clothes, put sackcloth around your **waists**.
Jer 30: 6 why do I see every strong man with his hands on his **stomach** like

2744 ¹חָלַק ***ḥālaq¹***, v. [9] [→ 2747, 2748, 2749, 2752, 2753, 2756, 2761, 4712]

flatters [2], seductive [2], deceitful [1], flattering [1], smooth [1], smooths [1], speak deceit [1]

Ps 5: 9 [5:10] [G] an open grave; *with* their tongue *they* **speak deceit**.
36: 2 [36:3] [G] For in his own eyes *he* **flatters** himself *too much* to
55:21 [55:22] [A] His speech *is* **smooth** as butter, yet war is in his
Pr 2:16 [G] from the wayward wife with her **seductive** words,
7: 5 [G] from the wayward wife with her **seductive** words.
28:23 [G] end gain more favor than *he who has a* **flattering** tongue.
29: 5 [G] Whoever **flatters** his neighbor is spreading a net for his feet.
Isa 41: 7 [G] *he who* **smooths** *with* the hammer spurs on him who strikes
Hos 10: 2 [A] Their heart *is* **deceitful**, and now they must bear their guilt.

2745 ²חָלַק ***ḥālaq²***, v. [56] [→ 2165, 2750, 2754, 2755, 2758, 2759, 2760, 2762, 4713]

divide [9], divided [6], dividing [3], share [3], be divided [2], distribute [2], gave [2], parcel out [2], accomplice [+6640] [1], allots [1], allotting [1], apportioned [1], assigns [1], be allotted [1], be distributed [1], be divided up [1], distributed [1], distributes [1], distributing supplies [1], divide up [1], divided up [1], divides [1], get share of property [1], give a portion [1], give a share [1], given [1], is dispersed [1], is distributed [1], made assignments [1], received [1], scatter [1], scattered [1], separated into divisions [1], took some of the things [1], were split [1]

Ge 14:15 [C] During the night Abram **divided** his men to attack them
49: 7 [D] *I will* **scatter** them in Jacob and disperse them in Israel.
49:27 [D] he devours the prey, in the evening *he* **divides** the plunder."
Ex 15: 9 [D] *I will* **divide** the spoils; I will gorge myself on them.
Nu 26:53 [C] "The land *is to* **be allotted** to them as an inheritance based on
26:55 [C] Be sure that the land **is distributed** by lot. What each group
26:56 [C] Each inheritance *is to* **be distributed** by lot among the larger
Dt 4:19 [A] worshiping things the LORD your God *has* **apportioned** to
29:26 [29:25] [A] they did not know, gods *he had* not **given** them.
Jos 13: 7 [D] **divide** it as an inheritance among the nine tribes and half of
14: 5 [A] So the Israelites **divided** the land, just as the LORD had
18: 2 [A] Israelite tribes who *had* not *yet* **received** their inheritance.
18: 5 [F] *You are to* **divide** the land into seven parts. Judah is to
18:10 [D] there he **distributed** the land to the Israelites according to
19:51 [D] the Tent of Meeting. And so they finished **dividing** the land.
22: 8 [A] **divide** with your brothers the plunder from your enemies."
Jdg 5:30 [D] 'Are they not finding and **dividing** the spoils: a girl or two for
1Sa 30:24 [A] of him who went down to the battle. *All will* **share** alike."
2Sa 6:19 [D] *he* **gave** a loaf of bread, a cake of dates and a cake of raisins
19:29 [19:30] [A] I order you and Ziba *to* **divide** the fields."
1Ki 16:21 [C] the people of Israel **were split** into two factions;
18: 6 [D] So *they* **divided** the land they were to cover, Ahab going in
1Ch 16: 3 [D] *he* **gave** a loaf of bread, a cake of dates and a cake of raisins
23: 6 [A] David **divided** the Levites *into* groups corresponding to the
24: 3 [A] David **separated** them **into divisions** for their appointed
24: 4 [A] than among Ithamar's, and they *were* **divided** *accordingly*:
24: 5 [A] *They* **divided** them impartially by drawing lots, for there
2Ch 23:18 [A] *to* whom David *had* **made assignments** in the temple,
28:21 [A] **took some of the things** *from* the temple of the LORD and from
Ne 9:22 [A] and nations, **allotting** *to* them even the remotest frontiers.
13:13 [A] They were made responsible for **distributing** *the* **supplies** to
Job 21:17 [D] calamity come upon them, the fate God **allots** in his anger?
27:17 [A] righteous will wear, and the innocent *will* **divide** his silver.
38:24 [C] is the way to the place where the lightning **is dispersed**,
39:17 [A] endow her with wisdom or **give** her **a share** of good sense.
Ps 22:18 [22:19] [D] *They* **divide** my garments among them and cast lots
60: 6 [60:8] [D] "In triumph *I will* **parcel out** Shechem and measure
68:12 [68:13] [D] flee in haste; in the camps *men* **divide** the plunder.
108: 7 [108:8] [D] "In triumph *I will* **parcel out** Shechem and measure
Pr 16:19 [D] among the oppressed than *to* **share** plunder with the proud.
17: 2 [A] and *will* **share** the inheritance as one of the brothers.
29:24 [A] The **accomplice** [+6640] *of* a thief is his own enemy; he is
Isa 9: 3 [9:2] [D] the harvest, as men rejoice when **dividing** the plunder.
33:23 [E] an abundance of spoils *will* **be divided** and even the lame
34:17 [D] allots their portions; his hand **distributes** them by measure.
53:12 [D] Therefore *I will* **give** him **a portion** among the great, and he
53:12 [D] *he will* **divide** the spoils with the strong, because he poured
Jer 37:12 [G] to **get** *his* **share of** *the* **property** among the people there.
La 4:16 [D] The LORD himself *has* **scattered** them; he no longer
Eze 5: 1 [D] your beard. Then take a set of scales and **divide up** the hair.
47:21 [D] "*You are to* **distribute** this land among yourselves
Da 11:39 [D] over many people and *will* **distribute** the land at a price.
Joel 3: 2 [4:2] [D] my people among the nations and **divided up** my land.
Am 7:17 [E] Your land *will* **be** measured and **divided up**, and you
Mic 2: 4 [D] He takes it from me! *He* **assigns** our fields to traitors.' "
Zec 14: 1 [E] is coming when your plunder *will* **be divided** among you.

2746 [3]חָלַק **ḥālaq[3]**, v. Not used in NIV/BHS

2747 [1]חָלָק **ḥālāq[1]**, a. [10] [√ 2744]

flattering [4], smooth [2], flattery [1], pleasant [1], slippery [1], smoother [1]

Ge 27:11 my brother Esau is a hairy man, and I'm a man *with* **smooth** *skin*.
Ps 12: 2 [12:3] to his neighbor; their **flattering** lips speak with deception.
12: 3 [12:4] May the LORD cut off all **flattering** lips and every
73:18 Surely you place them on **slippery** *ground*; you cast them down to
Pr 5: 3 of an adulteress drip honey, and her speech is **smoother** than oil;
26:28 tongue hates those it hurts, and a **flattering** mouth works ruin.
Isa 30:10 of what is right! Tell us **pleasant** *things*, prophesy illusions.
57: 6 ⌞The idols⌟ among the **smooth** stones *of* the ravines are your
Eze 12:24 false visions or **flattering** divinations among the people of Israel.
Da 11:32 With **flattery** he will corrupt those who have violated the

2748 [2]חָלָק **ḥālāq[2]**, n.pr.loc. [2] [√ 2744]

Halak [2]

Jos 11:17 from Mount **Halak**, which rises toward Seir, to Baal Gad in the
12: 7 from Baal Gad in the Valley of Lebanon to Mount **Halak**,

2749 [1]חֵלֶק **ḥēleq[1]**, n.[m.]. [1] [√ 2744]

smooth [1]

Pr 7:21 words she led him astray; she seduced him with her **smooth** talk.

2750 [2]חֵלֶק **ḥēleq[2]**, n.m. [66] [→ 2754, 2762; cf. 2745; Ar 10269; *also used with compound proper names*]

share [16], portion [14], lot [6], allotment [4], portions [4], parts [3], reward [3], fate [2], plot of ground [2], *untranslated* [1], benefits [1], fields [1], have say [+6699] [1], inheritance [1], land [1], lives [1], owns [1], part [1], plot [1], possession [1], that[s] [1]

Ge 14:24 and the **share** *that belongs to* the men who went with me—
14:24 with me—to Aner, Eshcol and Mamre. Let them have their **share**."
31:14 "Do we still have any **share** in the inheritance of our father's
Lev 6:17 [6:10] I have given it as their **share** of the offerings made to me
Nu 18:20 inheritance in their land, nor will you have any **share** among them;
18:20 I am your **share** and your inheritance among the Israelites.
31:36 The half **share** *of* those who fought in the battle was:
Dt 10: 9 That is why the Levites have no **share** or inheritance among their
12:12 your towns, who have no **allotment** or inheritance of their own.
14:27 your towns, for they have no **allotment** or inheritance of their own.
14:29 so that the Levites (who have no **allotment** or inheritance of their
18: 1 tribe of Levi—are to have no **allotment** or inheritance with Israel.
18: 8 He is to share equally in their **benefits**, even though he has
18: 8 **[RPH]** even though he has received money from the sale of
32: 9 For the LORD's **portion** is his people, Jacob his allotted
Jos 14: 4 The Levites received no **share** of the land but only towns to live in,
15:13 Joshua gave to Caleb son of Jephunneh a **portion** in Judah—
18: 5 You are to divide the land into seven **parts**. Judah is to remain in
18: 6 After you have written descriptions of the seven **parts** of the land,
18: 7 The Levites, however, do not get a **portion** among you,
18: 9 wrote its description on a scroll, town by town, in seven **parts**,
19: 9 of Judah, because Judah's **portion** was more than they needed.
22:25 you Reubenites and Gadites! You have no **share** in the LORD.'
22:27 will not be able to say to ours, 'You have no **share** in the LORD.'
1Sa 30:24 The **share** *of* the man who stayed with the supplies is to be the
30:24 is to be the same as **that**[s] *of* him who went down to the battle.
2Sa 20: 1 He sounded the trumpet and shouted, "We have no **share** in David,
1Ki 12:16 "What **share** do we have in David, what part in Jesse's son?
2Ki 9:10 for Jezebel, dogs will devour her on the **plot of ground** *at* Jezreel,
9:36 On the **plot of ground** *at* Jezreel dogs will devour Jezebel's flesh.
9:37 Jezebel's body will be like refuse on the ground in the **plot** *at*
2Ch 10:16 "What **share** do we have in David, what part in Jesse's son?
Ne 2:20 you have no **share** in Jerusalem or any claim or historic right to it."
Job 17: 5 If a man denounces his friends for **reward**, the eyes of his children
20:29 Such is the **fate** God allots the wicked, the heritage appointed for
27:13 "Here is the **fate** God allots to the wicked, the heritage a ruthless
31: 2 For what is man's **lot** *from* God above, his heritage from the
32:17 I too *will* **have** my **say** [+6699]; I too will tell what I know.
Ps 16: 5 LORD, you have assigned me my **portion** and my cup; you have
17:14 such men, from men of this world whose **reward** is in this life.
50:18 a thief, you join with him; you throw in your **lot** with adulterers.
73:26 but God is the strength of my heart and my **portion** forever.
119:57 You are my **portion**, O LORD; I have promised to obey your
142: 5 [142:6] are my refuge, my **portion** in the land of the living."
Ecc 2:10 delight in all my work, and this was the **reward** for all my labor.
2:21 he must leave *all* he **owns** to someone who has not worked for it.
3:22 better for a man than to enjoy his work, because that is his **lot**.
5:18 [5:17] the few days of life God has given him—for this is his **lot**.
5:19 [5:18] to enjoy them, to accept his **lot** and be happy in his work—
9: 6 never again will they have a **part** in anything that happens under
9: 9 For this is your **lot** in life and in your toilsome labor under the sun.
11: 2 Give **portions** to seven, yes to eight, for you do not know what
Isa 17:14 This is the **portion** *of* those who loot us, the lot of those who
57: 6 idols⌟ among the smooth stones of the ravines are your **portion**;
61: 7 and instead of disgrace they will rejoice in their **inheritance**;
Jer 10:16 He who is the **Portion** *of* Jacob is not like these, for he is the
51:19 He who is the **Portion** *of* Jacob is not like these, for he is the
La 3:24 I say to myself, "The LORD is my **portion**; therefore I will wait
Eze 45: 7 western to the eastern border parallel to one of the tribal **portions**.
48: 8 its length from east to west will equal one of the tribal **portions**;
48:21 Both these areas running the length of the tribal **portions** will
Hos 5: 7 Now their New Moon festivals will devour them and their **fields**.
Am 7: 4 judgment by fire; it dried up the great deep and devoured the **land**.
Mic 2: 4 'We are utterly ruined; my people's **possession** is divided up.
Hab 1:16 for by his net he **lives** in luxury and enjoys the choicest food.
Zec 2:12 [2:16] The LORD will inherit Judah as his **portion** in the holy

2751 [3]חֵלֶק **ḥēleq[3]**, n.pr.m. [2] [→ 2757; cf. 2759?, 2760?]

Helek [2]

Nu 26:30 through Iezer, the Iezerite clan; through **Helek**, the Helekite clan;
Jos 17: 2 clans of Abiezer, **Helek**, Asriel, Shechem, Hepher and Shemida.

2752 חַלֻּק **ḥalluq**, a. [1] [√ 2744]

smooth [1]

1Sa 17:40 his staff in his hand, chose five **smooth** stones from the stream,

2753 [1]חֶלְקָה **ḥelqâ[1]**, n.f. [2] [√ 2744]

smooth [2]

Ge 27:16 his hands and the **smooth** *part of* his neck with the goatskins.
Pr 6:24 immoral woman, from the **smooth** tongue of the wayward wife.

2754 [2]חֶלְקָה **ḥelqâ[2]**, n.f. [23] [√ 2750; cf. 2745]

field [10], field [+8441] [4], plot of ground [2], plot [2], portion [2], another[s] [1], piece [1], tract [1]

Ge 33:19 father of Shechem, the **plot** *of* ground where he pitched his tent.
Dt 33:21 the best land for himself; the leader's **portion** was kept for him.
Jos 24:32 were buried at Shechem in the **tract** *of* land that Jacob bought for a
Ru 2: 3 she found herself working in a **field** [+8441] belonging to Boaz,
4: 3 is selling the **piece** *of* land that belonged to our brother Elimelech.
2Sa 14:30 "Look, Joab's **field** is next to mine, and he has barley there.
14:30 and set it on fire." So Absalom's servants set the **field** on fire.
14:31 and he said to him, "Why have your servants set my **field** on fire?"
23:11 together at a place where there was a **field** [+8441] full of lentils,
23:12 Shammah took his stand in the middle of the **field**. He defended it
2Ki 3:19 stop up all the springs, and ruin every good **field** with stones."
3:25 each man threw a stone on every good **field** until it was covered.
9:21 They met him at the **plot of ground** *that had belonged to* Naboth
9:25 throw him on the **field** *that belonged* **to** [+8441] Naboth the
9:26 and I will surely make you pay for it on this **plot of ground**,
9:26 Now then, pick him up and throw him on that **plot**, in accordance
1Ch 11:13 At a place where there was a **field** [+8441] full of barley,
11:14 they took their stand in the middle of the **field**. They defended it
Job 24:18 their **portion** of the land is cursed, so that no one goes to the
Jer 12:10 Many shepherds will ruin my vineyard and trample down my **field**;
12:10 they will turn my pleasant **field** into a desolate wasteland.
Am 4: 7 it from another. One **field** had rain; another had none and dried up.
4: 7 from another. One field had rain; **another**[s] had none and dried up.

2755 חֲלֻקָּה **ḥ[a]luqqâ**, n.f. [1] [√ 2745]

group [+3+1074] [1]

2Ch 35: 5 "Stand in the holy place with a **group** [+3+1074] of Levites for

2756 חֲלַקָּה **ḥ[a]laqqâ**, n.f. Not used in NIV/BHS [√ 2744]

2757 חֶלְקִי **ḥelqî**, a.g. [1] [√ 2751]

Helekite [1]

Nu 26:30 through Iezer, the Iezerite clan; through Helek, the **Helekite** clan;

2758 חֶלְקָי **ḥelqāy**, n.pr.m. [1] [√ 2750 + 3378?]

Helkai [1]

Ne 12:15 of Harim's, Adna; of Meremoth's, **Helkai**;

2759 חִלְקִיָּה **ḥilqiyyâ**, n.pr.m. [15] [→ 2760; cf. 2750 + 3378, 2751?]

Hilkiah [13], he[s] [1], Hilkiah's [1]

2Ki 18:37 Eliakim son of **Hilkiah** the palace administrator, Shebna the

2Ki 22: 8 in the temple of the LORD." **He**[s] gave it to Shaphan, who read it.
22: 10 informed the king, "**Hilkiah** the priest has given me a book."
22: 12 He gave these orders to **Hilkiah** the priest, Ahikam son of
1Ch 6: 13 [5:39] Shallum the father of Hilkiah, Hilkiah the father of
6: 13 [5:39] the father of Hilkiah, **Hilkiah** the father of Azariah,
6: 45 [6:30] son of Hashabiah, the son of Amaziah, the son of **Hilkiah**,
9: 11 Azariah son of **Hilkiah**, the son of Meshullam, the son of Zadok,
2Ch 35: 8 **Hilkiah**, Zechariah and Jehiel, the administrators of God's temple,
Ezr 7: 1 Ezra son of Seraiah, the son of Azariah, the son of **Hilkiah**,
Ne 8: 4 stood Mattithiah, Shema, Anaiah, Uriah, **Hilkiah** and Maaseiah;
11: 11 Seraiah son of **Hilkiah**, the son of Meshullam, the son of Zadok,
12: 7 Sallu, Amok, **Hilkiah** and Jedaiah. These were the leaders of the
12: 21 of **Hilkiah's**, Hashabiah; of Jedaiah's, Nethanel.
Jer 29: 3 letter to Elasah son of Shaphan and to Gemariah son of **Hilkiah**,

2760 חִלְקִיָּהוּ *ḥilqiyyāhû*, n.pr.m. [19] [√ 2759; cf. 2750 + 3378, 2751?]

Hilkiah [18], he[s] [1]

2Ki 18: 18 Eliakim son of **Hilkiah** the palace administrator, Shebna the
18: 26 Eliakim son of **Hilkiah**, and Shebna and Joah said to the field
22: 4 "Go up to **Hilkiah** the high priest and have him get ready the
22: 8 **Hilkiah** the high priest said to Shaphan the secretary, "I have
22: 14 **Hilkiah** the priest, Ahikam, Acbor, Shaphan and Asaiah went to
23: 4 The king ordered **Hilkiah** the high priest, the priests next in rank
23: 24 that **Hilkiah** the priest had discovered in the temple of the LORD.
1Ch 26: 11 **Hilkiah** the second, Tabaliah the third and Zechariah the fourth.
2Ch 34: 9 They went to **Hilkiah** the high priest and gave him the money that
34: 14 **Hilkiah** the priest found the Book of the Law of the LORD that
34: 15 **Hilkiah** said to Shaphan the secretary, "I have found the Book of
34: 15 of the Law in the temple of the LORD." **He**[s] gave it to Shaphan.
34: 18 informed the king, "**Hilkiah** the priest has given me a book."
34: 20 He gave these orders to **Hilkiah**, Ahikam son of Shaphan,
34: 22 **Hilkiah** and those the king had sent with him went to speak to the
Isa 22: 20 "In that day I will summon my servant, Eliakim son of **Hilkiah**.
36: 3 Eliakim son of **Hilkiah** the palace administrator, Shebna the
36: 22 Eliakim son of **Hilkiah** the palace administrator, Shebna the
Jer 1: 1 The words of Jeremiah son of **Hilkiah**, one of the priests at

2761 חֲלַקְלַק *ḥ[a]laqlaq*, n.f.abst. [4] [√ 2744]

slippery [2], intrigue [1], not sincere [1]

Ps 35: 6 may their path be dark and **slippery**, with the angel of the LORD
Jer 23: 12 "Therefore their path will become **slippery**; they will be banished
Da 11: 21 when its people feel secure, and he will seize it through **intrigue**.
11: 34 receive a little help, and many who are **not sincere** will join them.

2762 חֶלְקַת *ḥelqat*, n.pr.loc. [2] [→ 2763; cf. 2745, 2750]

Helkath [2]

Jos 19: 25 Their territory included: **Helkath**, Hali, Beten, Acshaph,
21: 31 **Helkath** and Rehob, together with their pasturelands—four towns;

2763 חֶלְקַת הַצֻּרִים *ḥelqat haṣṣurîm*, n.pr.loc. [1] [√ 2762 + 2211]

Helkath Hazzurim [1]

2Sa 2: 16 So that place in Gibeon was called **Helkath Hazzurim**.

2764 ¹חָלַשׁ *ḥālaš[1]*, v. [1] [→ 2766; cf. 2765]

laid low [1]

Job 14: 10 [A] man dies and *is* **laid low**; he breathes his last and is no more.

2765 ²חָלַשׁ *ḥālaš[2]*, v. [2] [→ 2711; cf. 2764]

laid low [1], overcame [1]

Ex 17: 13 [A] So Joshua **overcame** the Amalekite army with the sword.
Isa 14: 12 [A] cast down to the earth, *you who once* **laid low** the nations!

2766 חַלָּשׁ *ḥallāš*, a. [1] [√ 2764]

weakling [1]

Joel 3: 10 [4:10] hooks into spears. Let the **weakling** say, "I am strong!"

2767 ¹חָם *ḥām[1]*, n.m. [4] [→ 2782, 2792]

father-in-law [4]

Ge 38: 13 "Your **father-in-law** is on his way to Timnah to shear his sheep,"
38: 25 was being brought out, she sent a message to her **father-in-law**.
1Sa 4: 19 and that her **father-in-law** and her husband were dead,
4: 21 ark of God and the deaths of her **father-in-law** and her husband.

2768 ²חָם *ḥām[2]*, a. [2] [√ 2801]

swelter [1], warm [1]

Jos 9: 12 This bread of ours was **warm** when we packed it at home on the
Job 37: 17 You who **swelter** in your clothes when the land lies hushed under

2769 ³חָם *ḥām[3]*, n.pr.m. & loc. [16] [→ 2781, 2795]

Ham [15], Hamites [1]

Ge 5: 32 500 years old, he became the father of Shem, **Ham** and Japheth.
6: 10 Noah had three sons: Shem, **Ham** and Japheth.
7: 13 On that very day Noah and his sons, Shem, **Ham** and Japheth,
9: 18 of Noah who came out of the ark were Shem, **Ham** and Japheth.
9: 18 were Shem, Ham and Japheth. (**Ham** was the father of Canaan.)
9: 22 **Ham**, the father of Canaan, saw his father's nakedness and told his
10: 1 This is the account of Shem, **Ham** and Japheth, Noah's sons,
10: 6 The sons of **Ham**: Cush, Mizraim, Put and Canaan.
10: 20 These are the sons of **Ham** by their clans and languages, in their
1Ch 1: 4 The sons of Noah: Shem, **Ham** and Japheth.
1: 8 The sons of **Ham**: Cush, Mizraim, Put and Canaan.
4: 40 peaceful and quiet. Some **Hamites** had lived there formerly.
Ps 78: 51 firstborn of Egypt, the firstfruits of manhood in the tents of **Ham**.
105: 23 Israel entered Egypt; Jacob lived as an alien in the land of **Ham**.
105: 27 his miraculous signs among them, his wonders in the land of **Ham**.
106: 22 miracles in the land of **Ham** and awesome deeds by the Red Sea.

2770 חֹם *ḥōm*, n.m. [9] [√ 2801]

heat [8], hot [1]

Ge 8: 22 cold and **heat**, summer and winter, day and night will never
18: 1 he was sitting at the entrance to his tent in the **heat** *of* the day.
1Sa 11: 11 of the Ammonites and slaughtered them until the **heat** *of* the day.
21: 6 [21:7] and replaced by **hot** bread on the day it was taken away.
2Sa 4: 5 they arrived there in the **heat** *of* the day while he was taking his
Job 24: 19 As **heat** and drought snatch away the melted snow, so the grave
Isa 18: 4 on from my dwelling place, like shimmering **heat** in the sunshine,
18: 4 heat in the sunshine, like a cloud of dew in the **heat** *of* harvest."
Jer 17: 8 It does not fear when **heat** comes; its leaves are always green.

2771 חֵמָא *ḥēmā'*, n.f. Not used in NIV/BHS [√ 3501; cf. 2779]

2772 חֶמְאָה *ḥem'â*, n.f. [10] [cf. 4717]

curds [6], cream [2], butter [1], curdled milk [1]

Ge 18: 8 He then brought *some* **curds** and milk and the calf that had been
Dt 32: 14 with **curds** and milk from herd and flock and with fattened lambs
Jdg 5: 25 him milk; in a bowl fit for nobles she brought him **curdled milk**.
2Sa 17: 29 honey and **curds**, sheep, and cheese from cows' milk for David
Job 20: 17 not enjoy the streams, the rivers flowing with honey and **cream**.
29: 6 when my path was drenched with **cream** and the rock poured out
Pr 30: 33 For as churning the milk produces **butter**, and as twisting the nose
Isa 7: 15 He will eat **curds** and honey when he knows enough to reject the
7: 22 of the abundance of the milk they give, he will have **curds** to eat.
7: 22 curds to eat. All who remain in the land will eat **curds** and honey.

2773 חָמַד *ḥāmad*, v. [21] [→ 2774, 2775, 2776, 2777, 4718, 4719]

covet [6], desire [2], treasure [2], choice [1], chooses [1], coveted [1], delight in [1], delight [1], delighted [1], desirable [1], lust after [1], pleasing [1], precious [1], wealth [1]

Ge 2: 9 [C] trees *that were* **pleasing** to the eye and good for food.
3: 6 [C] also **desirable** for gaining wisdom, she took some and ate it.
Ex 20: 17 [A] "*You shall* not **covet** your neighbor's house. You shall not
20: 17 [A] *You shall* not **covet** your neighbor's wife, or his manservant
34: 24 [A] no one *will* **covet** your land when you go up three times each
Dt 5: 21 [A] "*You shall* not **covet** your neighbor's wife. You shall not set
7: 25 [A] *Do* not **covet** the silver and gold on them, and do not take it
Jos 7: 21 [A] gold weighing fifty shekels, *I* **coveted** them and took them.
Job 20: 20 [B] from his craving; he cannot save himself by his **treasure**.
Ps 19: 10 [19:11] [C] They *are* more **precious** than gold, than much pure
39: 11 [39:12] [B] you consume their **wealth** like a moth—each man is
68: 16 [68:17] [A] at the mountain where God **chooses** to reign,
Pr 1: 22 [A] How long *will* mockers **delight in** mockery and fools hate
6: 25 [A] *Do* not **lust** in your heart **after** her beauty or let her captivate
12: 12 [A] The wicked **desire** the plunder of evil men, but the root of
21: 20 [C] In the house of the wise are stores of **choice** *food* and oil,
SS 2: 3 [D] *I* **delight** to sit in his shade, and his fruit is sweet to my taste.
Isa 1: 29 [A] because of the sacred oaks *in* which *you have* **delighted**;
44: 9 [B] idols are nothing, and the *things* they **treasure** are worthless.
53: 2 [A] to him, nothing in his appearance that *we should* **desire** him.
Mic 2: 2 [A] *They* **covet** fields and seize them, and houses, and take them.

[A] Qal [B] Qal passive [C] Niphal [D] Piel (poel, polel, pilel, pilal, pealal, pilpel) [E] Pual (poal, polal, poalal, pulal, pualal)

2774 חֶמֶד *ḥemed*, n.[m.]. [6] [√ 2773]

handsome [3], fruitful [1], lush [1], pleasant [1]

Isa 27: 2 In that day—"Sing about a **fruitful** vineyard:
32: 12 Beat your breasts for the **pleasant** fields, for the fruitful vines
Eze 23: 6 governors and commanders, all of them **handsome** young men,
23: 12 in full dress, mounted horsemen, all **handsome** young men.
23: 23 **handsome** young men, all of them governors and commanders,
Am 5: 11 though you have planted **lush** vineyards, you will not drink their

2775 חֶמְדָּה *ḥemdâ*, n.f. [16] [√ 2773]

pleasant [3], desired [2], fine [2], treasures [+3998] [2], desirable [1], desire [1], regret [1], stately [1], valuable [1], valuables [1], value [1]

1Sa 9: 20 And to whom is all the **desire** *of* Israel turned, if not to you
2Ch 21: 20 He passed away, to no one's **regret**, and was buried in the City of
32: 27 for his precious stones, spices, shields and all kinds of **valuables**.
36: 10 together with articles of **value** *from* the temple of the LORD,
Ps 106: 24 they despised the **pleasant** land; they did not believe his promise.
Isa 2: 16 for every trading ship and every **stately** vessel.
Jer 3: 19 gladly would I treat you like sons and give you a **desirable** land,
12: 10 they will turn my **pleasant** field into a desolate wasteland.
25: 34 has come; you will fall and be shattered like **fine** pottery.
Eze 26: 12 your walls and demolish your **fine** houses and throw your stones,
Da 11: 8 their metal images and their **valuable** articles of silver and gold
11: 37 regard for the gods of his fathers or for the *one* **desired** *by* women,
Hos 13: 15 His storehouse will be plundered of all its **treasures** [+3998].
Na 2: 9 [2:10] is endless, the wealth from all its **treasures** [+3998]!
Hag 2: 7 I will shake all nations, and the **desired** *of* all nations will come,
Zec 7: 14 or go. This is how they made the **pleasant** land desolate.' "

2776 חֲמֻדוֹת *ḥ^amudôt*, n.f. [9] [√ 2773]

highly esteemed [3], best [1], choice [1], costly gifts [1], precious [1], riches [1], value [1]

Ge 27: 15 Then Rebekah took the **best** clothes of Esau her older son,
2Ch 20: 25 amount of equipment and clothing and also articles of **value**—
Ezr 8: 27 and two fine articles of polished bronze, as **precious** as gold.
Da 9: 23 which I have come to tell you, for you are **highly esteemed**.
10: 3 I ate no **choice** food; no meat or wine touched my lips; and I used
10: 11 He said, "Daniel, you who are **highly esteemed**, consider carefully
10: 19 "Do not be afraid, O man **highly esteemed**," he said. "Peace!
11: 38 honor with gold and silver, with precious stones and **costly gifts**.
11: 43 of the treasures of gold and silver and all the **riches** *of* Egypt,

2777 חֶמְדָּן *ḥemdān*, n.pr.m. [1 / 2] [√ 2773; cf. 2820]

Hemdan [2]

Ge 36: 26 The sons of Dishon: **Hemdan**, Eshban, Ithran and Keran.
1Ch 1: 41 sons of Dishon: **Hemdan**, [BHS 2820] Eshban, Ithran and Keran.

2778 חָמָה *ḥāmâ*, n.f. [0 / 1]

careful [1]

Job 36: 18 [A] *Be* **careful** [BHS 2779] that no one entices you by riches;

2779 חֵמָה *ḥēmâ*, n.f. [124 / 123] [√ 3501; cf. 2771; Ar 10270]

wrath [75], anger [12], fury [8], rage [5], venom [4], angry [2], burning [2], fierce [2], furious [2], poison [2], easily angered [1], enraged [+4848] [1], hot [1], hot-tempered [+1251] [1], hot-tempered [+1754] [1], hot-tempered [1], indignation [1], inflamed [+2703] [1], stinging [1]

Ge 27: 44 Stay with him for a while until your brother's **fury** subsides.
Lev 26: 28 in my **anger** I will be hostile toward you, and I myself will punish
Nu 25: 11 of Aaron, the priest, has turned my **anger** away from the Israelites;
Dt 9: 19 I feared the anger and **wrath** of the LORD, for he was angry
29: 23 [29:22] which the LORD overthrew in **fierce** anger.
29: 28 [29:27] In **furious** anger and in great wrath the LORD uprooted
32: 24 the fangs of wild beasts, the **venom** *of* vipers that glide in the dust.
32: 33 Their wine is the **venom** *of* serpents, the deadly poison of cobras.
2Sa 11: 20 the king's **anger** may flare up, and he may ask you, 'Why did you
2Ki 5: 12 in them and be cleansed?" So he turned and went off in a **rage**.
22: 13 Great is the LORD's **anger** that burns against us because our
22: 17 my **anger** will burn against this place and will not be quenched.'
2Ch 12: 7 My **wrath** will not be poured out on Jerusalem through Shishak.
28: 9 the LORD, the God of your fathers, was **angry** with Judah,
34: 21 Great is the LORD's **anger** that is poured out on us because our
34: 25 my **anger** will be poured out on this place and will not be
36: 16 scoffed at his prophets until the **wrath** *of* the LORD was aroused
Est 1: 12 to come. Then the king became furious and burned with **anger**.
2: 1 Later when the **anger** *of* King Xerxes had subsided,
3: 5 would not kneel down or pay him honor, he *was* **enraged** [+4848].
5: 9 fear in his presence, he was filled with **rage** against Mordecai.
7: 7 The king got up in a **rage**, left his wine and went out into the
7: 10 he had prepared for Mordecai. Then the king's **fury** subsided.
Job 6: 4 arrows of the Almighty are in me, my spirit drinks in their **poison**;
19: 29 for **wrath** will bring punishment by the sword, and then you will
21: 20 see his destruction; let him drink of the **wrath** *of* the Almighty.
36: 18 *Be* careful [BHS *Because of wrath*; NIV 2778] that no one entices
Ps 6: 1 [6:2] not rebuke me in your anger or discipline me in your **wrath**.
37: 8 Refrain from anger and turn from **wrath**; do not fret—it leads only
38: 1 [38:2] rebuke me in your anger or discipline me in your **wrath**.
58: 4 [58:5] Their **venom** is like the venom of a snake, like that of a
58: 4 [58:5] Their venom is like the **venom** *of* a snake, like that of a
59: 13 [59:14] consume them in **wrath**, consume them till they are no
76: 10 [76:11] Surely your **wrath** *against* men brings you praise,
76: 10 [76:11] and the survivors of your **wrath** are restrained.
78: 38 after time he restrained his anger and did not stir up his full **wrath**.
79: 6 Pour out your **wrath** on the nations that do not acknowledge you,
88: 7 [88:8] Your **wrath** lies heavily upon me; you have overwhelmed
89: 46 [89:47] How long will your **wrath** burn like fire?
90: 7 We are consumed by your anger and terrified by your **indignation**.
106: 23 stood in the breach before him to keep his **wrath** from destroying
140: 3 [140:4] sharp as a serpent's; the **poison** *of* vipers is on their lips.
Pr 6: 34 for jealousy arouses a husband's **fury**, and he will show no mercy
15: 1 A gentle answer turns away **wrath**, but a harsh word stirs up anger.
15: 18 A **hot-tempered** man stirs up dissension, but a patient man calms a
16: 14 A king's **wrath** is a messenger of death, but a wise man will
19: 19 A **hot-tempered** [+1754] *man* must pay the penalty; if you rescue
21: 14 and a bribe concealed in the cloak pacifies great **wrath**.
22: 24 a hot-tempered man, do not associate with one **easily angered**,
27: 4 **Anger** is cruel and fury overwhelming, but who can stand before
29: 22 and a **hot-tempered** [+1251] *one* commits many sins.
Isa 27: 4 I am not **angry**. If only there were briers and thorns confronting
34: 2 is angry with all nations; his **wrath** is upon all their armies.
42: 25 So he poured out on them his **burning** anger, the violence of war.
51: 13 in constant terror every day because of the **wrath** *of* the oppressor,
51: 13 is bent on destruction? For where is the **wrath** *of* the oppressor?
51: 17 have drunk from the hand of the LORD the cup of his **wrath**,
51: 20 They are filled with the **wrath** *of* the LORD and the rebuke of
51: 22 from that cup, the goblet of my **wrath**, you will never drink again.
59: 18 so will he repay **wrath** to his enemies and retribution to his foes;
63: 3 I trampled them in my anger and trod them down in my **wrath**;
63: 5 arm worked salvation for me, and my own **wrath** sustained me.
63: 6 in my **wrath** I made them drunk and poured their blood on the
66: 15 he will bring down his anger with **fury**, and his rebuke with flames
Jer 4: 4 or my **wrath** will break out and burn like fire because of the evil
6: 11 But I am full of the **wrath** *of* the LORD, and I cannot hold it in.
7: 20 My anger and my **wrath** will be poured out on this place,
10: 25 Pour out your **wrath** on the nations that do not acknowledge you,
18: 20 and spoke in their behalf to turn your **wrath** away from them.
21: 5 and a mighty arm in anger and **fury** and great wrath.
21: 12 or my **wrath** will break out and burn like fire because of the evil
23: 19 See, the storm of the LORD will burst out in **wrath**, a whirlwind
25: 15 "Take from my hand this cup filled with the wine of my **wrath**
30: 23 See, the storm of the LORD will burst out in **wrath**, a driving
32: 31 aroused my anger and **wrath** that I must remove it from my sight.
32: 37 them from all the lands where I banish them in my **furious** anger
33: 5 with the dead bodies of the men I will slay in my anger and **wrath**.
36: 7 **wrath** pronounced against this people by the LORD are great."
42: 18 and **wrath** have been poured out on those who lived in Jerusalem,
42: 18 so will my **wrath** be poured out on you when you go to Egypt.
44: 6 Therefore, my **fierce** anger was poured out; it raged against the
La 2: 4 he has poured out his **wrath** like fire on the tent of the Daughter of
4: 11 The LORD has given full vent to his **wrath**; he has poured out his
Eze 3: 14 me away, and I went in bitterness and in the **anger** *of* my spirit,
5: 13 my anger will cease and my **wrath** against them will subside,
5: 13 when I have spent my **wrath** upon them, they will know that I the
5: 15 on you in anger and in **wrath** and with stinging rebuke.
5: 15 punishment on you in anger and in wrath and with **stinging** rebuke.
6: 12 is spared will die of famine. So will I spend my **wrath** upon them.
7: 8 I am about to pour out my **wrath** on you and spend my anger
8: 18 Therefore I will deal with them in **anger**; I will not look on them
9: 8 remnant of Israel in this outpouring of your **wrath** on Jerusalem?"
13: 13 In my **wrath** I will unleash a violent wind, and in my anger
13: 13 anger hailstones and torrents of rain will fall with destructive **fury**.
13: 15 So I will spend my **wrath** against the wall and against those who
14: 19 into that land and pour out my **wrath** upon it through bloodshed,
16: 38 I will bring upon you the blood vengeance of my **wrath**
16: 42 my **wrath** against you will subside and my jealous anger will turn
19: 12 it was uprooted in **fury** and thrown to the ground. The east wind
20: 8 So I said I would pour out my **wrath** on them and spend my anger
20: 13 So I said I would pour out my **wrath** on them and destroy them in
20: 21 So I said I would pour out my **wrath** on them and spend my anger
20: 33 a mighty hand and an outstretched arm and with outpoured **wrath**.
20: 34 a mighty hand and an outstretched arm and with outpoured **wrath**.
21: 17 [21:22] will strike my hands together, and my **wrath** will subside.
22: 20 my anger and my **wrath** and put you inside the city and melt you.
22: 22 you will know that I the LORD have poured out my **wrath** upon

Eze 23:25 my jealous anger against you, and they will deal with you in **fury**.
24: 8 To stir up **wrath** and take revenge I put her blood on the bare rock,
24:13 you will not be clean again until my **wrath** against you has
25:14 will deal with Edom in accordance with my anger and my **wrath**;
25:17 carry out great vengeance on them and punish them in my **wrath**.
30:15 I will pour out my **wrath** on Pelusium, the stronghold of Egypt,
36: 6 I speak in my jealous **wrath** because you have suffered the scorn
36:18 So I poured out my **wrath** on them because they had shed blood in
38:18 my **hot** anger will be aroused, declares the Sovereign LORD.
Da 8: 6 seen standing beside the canal and charged at him in great **rage**.
9:16 turn away your anger and your **wrath** from Jerusalem, your city,
11:44 and he will set out in a great **rage** to destroy and annihilate many.
Hos 7: 5 of our king the princes *become* **inflamed** [+2703] with wine,
Mic 5:15 [5:14] and **wrath** upon the nations that have not obeyed me."
Na 1: 2 the LORD takes vengeance and is filled with **wrath**.
1: 6 His **wrath** is poured out like fire; the rocks are shattered before
Zec 8: 2 "I am very jealous for Zion; I am **burning** *with* jealousy for her."

2780 חַמָּה ḥammâ, n.f. [6] [√ 2801]

sun [4], heat [1], sunlight [+240] [1]

Job 30:28 I go about blackened, but not by the **sun**; I stand up in the
Ps 19: 6 [19:7] its circuit to the other; nothing is hidden from its **heat**.
SS 6:10 fair as the moon, bright as the **sun**, majestic as the stars in
Isa 24:23 The moon will be abashed, the **sun** ashamed; for the LORD
30:26 The moon will shine like the **sun**, and the sunlight will be seven
30:26 the **sunlight** [+240] will be seven times brighter, like the light of

2781 חַמּוּאֵל ḥammû'ēl, n.pr.m. [1] [√ 2769 + 446; cf. 2795]

Hammuel [1]

1Ch 4:26 of Mishma: **Hammuel** his son, Zaccur his son and Shimei his son.

2782 חֲמוּטַל ḥ^{a}mûṭal, n.pr.f. [3] [√ 2767 + 3228]

Hamutal [3]

2Ki 23:31 His mother's name was **Hamutal** daughter of Jeremiah; she was
24:18 His mother's name was **Hamutal** [K 2795] daughter of Jeremiah;
Jer 52: 1 His mother's name was **Hamutal** [K 2795] daughter of Jeremiah;

2783 חָמוּל ḥāmûl, n.pr.m. [3] [→ 2784; cf. 2798]

Hamul [3]

Ge 46:12 in the land of Canaan). The sons of Perez: Hezron and **Hamul**.
Nu 26:21 the Hezronite clan; through **Hamul**, the Hamulite clan.
1Ch 2: 5 The sons of Perez: Hezron and **Hamul**.

2784 חָמוּלִי ḥāmûlî, a.g. [1] [√ 2783; cf. 2798]

Hamulite [1]

Nu 26:21 the Hezronite clan; through Hamul, the **Hamulite** clan.

2785 חַמּוֹן ḥammôn, n.pr.loc. [2] [√ 2801]

Hammon [2]

Jos 19:28 It went to Abdon, Rehob, **Hammon** and Kanah, as far as Greater
1Ch 6:76 [6:61] **Hammon** and Kiriathaim, together with their pasturelands.

2786 חָמוּץ ḥāmûṣ, a. Not used in NIV/BHS [√ 2808]

2787 חָמוֹץ ḥāmôṣ, n.[m.]. [1] [√ 2807]

oppressed [1]

Isa 1:17 learn to do right! Seek justice, encourage the **oppressed**. Defend

2788 חַמּוּק ḥammûq, n.m. [1] [√ 2811]

graceful [1]

SS 7: 1 [7:2] Your **graceful** legs are like jewels, the work of a

2789 חֲמוֹר ḥ^{a}môr^{1}, n.m. [98] [→ 2791; cf. 2790, 2813]

donkey [47], donkeys [45], donkey's [3], donkeys [+2789] [2], male donkeys [1]

Ge 12:16 and Abram acquired sheep and cattle, **male** and female **donkeys**,
22: 3 Early the next morning Abraham got up and saddled his **donkey**.
22: 5 "Stay here with the **donkey** while I and the boy go over there.
24:35 and gold, menservants and maidservants, and camels and **donkeys**.
30:43 and maidservants and menservants, and camels and **donkeys**.
32: 5 [32:6] I have cattle and **donkeys**, sheep and goats, menservants
34:28 They seized their flocks and herds and **donkeys** and everything
36:24 the desert while he was grazing the **donkeys** of his father Zibeon.
42:26 they loaded their grain on their **donkeys** and left.
42:27 the night one of them opened his sack to get feed for his **donkey**,
43:18 and overpower us and seize us as slaves and take our **donkeys**."
43:24 water to wash their feet and provided fodder for their **donkeys**.
44: 3 the men were sent on their way with their **donkeys**.
44:13 Then they all loaded their **donkeys** and returned to the city.
45:23 ten **donkeys** loaded with the best things of Egypt, and ten female
47:17 for their horses, their sheep and goats, their cattle and **donkeys**.
49:14 "Issachar is a rawboned **donkey** lying down between two
Ex 4:20 and sons, put them on a **donkey** and started back to Egypt.
9: 3 on your horses and **donkeys** and camels and on your cattle
13:13 Redeem with a lamb every firstborn **donkey**, but if you do not
20:17 or his manservant or maidservant, his ox or **donkey**,
21:33 or digs one and fails to cover it and an ox or a **donkey** falls into it,
22: 4 [22:3] whether ox or **donkey** or sheep—he must pay back double.
22: 9 [22:8] illegal possession of an ox, a **donkey**, a sheep, a garment,
22:10 [22:9] "If a man gives a **donkey**, an ox, a sheep or any other
23: 4 "If you come across your enemy's ox or **donkey** wandering off,
23: 5 If you see the **donkey** *of* someone who hates you fallen down
23:12 so that your ox and your **donkey** may rest and the slave born in
34:20 Redeem the firstborn **donkey** with a lamb, but if you do not
Nu 16:15 I have not taken so much as a **donkey** from them, nor have I
31:28 five hundred, whether persons, cattle, **donkeys**, sheep or goats.
31:30 whether persons, cattle, **donkeys**, sheep, goats or other animals.
31:34 61,000 **donkeys**
31:39 30,500 **donkeys**, of which the tribute for the LORD was 61;
31:45 30,500 **donkeys**
Dt 5:14 or maidservant, nor your ox, your **donkey** or any of your animals,
5:21 or land, his manservant or maidservant, his ox or **donkey**,
22: 3 Do the same if you find your brother's **donkey** or his cloak
22: 4 If you see your brother's **donkey** or his ox fallen on the road,
22:10 Do not plow with an ox and a **donkey** yoked together.
28:31 Your **donkey** will be forcibly taken from you and will not be
Jos 6:21 men and women, young and old, cattle, sheep and **donkeys**.
7:24 his cattle, **donkeys** and sheep, his tent and all that he had,
9: 4 They went as a delegation whose **donkeys** were loaded with
15:18 When she got off her **donkey**, Caleb asked her, "What can I do for
Jdg 1:14 When she got off her **donkey**, Caleb asked her, "What can I do for
6: 4 spare a living thing for Israel, neither sheep nor cattle nor **donkeys**.
15:15 Finding a fresh jawbone of a **donkey**, he grabbed it and struck
15:16 "With a **donkey's** jawbone I have made donkeys of them.
15:16 "With a donkey's jawbone I have made **donkeys** [+2789] of them.
15:16 "With a donkey's jawbone I have made **donkeys** [+2789] of them.
15:16 of them. With a **donkey's** jawbone I have killed a thousand men."
19: 3 He had with him his servant and two **donkeys**. She took him into
19:10 Jerusalem), with his two saddled **donkeys** and his concubine.
19:19 We have both straw and fodder for our **donkeys** and bread
19:21 So he took him into his house and fed his **donkeys**. After they had
19:28 Then the man put her on his **donkey** and set out for home.
1Sa 8:16 the best of your cattle and **donkeys** he will take for his own use.
12: 3 have I taken? Whose **donkey** have I taken? Whom have I cheated?
15: 3 children and infants, cattle and sheep, camels and **donkeys**.' "
16:20 So Jesse took a **donkey** *loaded with* bread, a skin of wine
22:19 its children and infants, and its cattle, **donkeys** and sheep.
25:18 two hundred cakes of pressed figs, and loaded them on **donkeys**.
25:20 As she came riding her **donkey** into a mountain ravine, there were
25:23 she quickly got off her **donkey** and bowed down before David with
25:42 Abigail quickly got on a **donkey** and, attended by her five maids,
27: 9 but took sheep and cattle, **donkeys** and camels, and clothes.
2Sa 16: 1 He had a string of **donkeys** saddled and loaded with two hundred
16: 2 "The **donkeys** are for the king's household to ride on, the bread
17:23 he saddled his **donkey** and set out for his house in his hometown.
19:26 [19:27] I said, 'I will have my **donkey** saddled and will ride on it,
1Ki 2:40 he saddled his **donkey** and went to Achish at Gath in search of his
13:13 So he said to his sons, "Saddle the **donkey** for me." And when they
13:13 And when they had saddled the **donkey** for him, he mounted it
13:23 the prophet who had brought him back saddled his **donkey** for
13:24 on the road, with both the **donkey** and the lion standing beside it.
13:27 said to his sons, "Saddle the **donkey** for me," and they did so.
13:28 down on the road, with the **donkey** and the lion standing beside it.
13:28 The lion had neither eaten the body nor mauled the **donkey**.
13:29 laid it on the **donkey**, and brought it back to his own city to mourn
2Ki 6:25 so long that a **donkey's** head sold for eighty shekels of silver,
7: 7 the dusk and abandoned their tents and their horses and **donkeys**.
7:10 only tethered horses and **donkeys**, and the tents left just as they
1Ch 5:21 two hundred fifty thousand sheep and two thousand **donkeys**.
12:40 [12:41] Zebulun and Naphtali came bringing food on **donkeys**,
2Ch 28:15 and healing balm. All those who were weak they put on **donkeys**.
Ezr 2:67 435 camels and 6,720 **donkeys**.
Ne 7:69 [7:68] 435 camels and 6,720 **donkeys**.
13:15 on the Sabbath and bringing in grain and loading it on **donkeys**,
Job 24: 3 They drive away the orphan's **donkey** and take the widow's ox in
Pr 26: 3 A whip for the horse, a halter for the **donkey**, and a rod for the
Isa 1: 3 the **donkey** his owner's manger, but Israel does not know,
21: 7 riders on **donkeys** or riders on camels, let him be alert, fully alert."
32:20 by every stream, and letting your cattle and **donkeys** range free.
Jer 22:19 He will have the burial of a **donkey**—dragged away and thrown
Eze 23:20 whose genitals were like those of **donkeys** and whose emission

Zec 9: 9 gentle and riding on a **donkey**, on a colt, the foal of a donkey.
14: 15 plague will strike the horses and mules, the camels and **donkeys**,

2790 ²חֲמוֹר **ḥ^a^môr²**, n.[m.]. Not used in NIV/BHS [√ 2813; cf. 2789]

2791 ³חֲמוֹר **ḥ^a^môr³**, n.pr.m. [13] [√ 2789; cf. 2813]

Hamor [12], his[s] [1]

Ge 33: 19 he bought from the sons of **Hamor**, the father of Shechem,
34: 2 When Shechem son of **Hamor** the Hivite, the ruler of that area,
34: 4 Shechem said to his father **Hamor**, "Get me this girl as my wife."
34: 6 Then Shechem's father **Hamor** went out to talk with Jacob.
34: 8 **Hamor** said to them, "My son Shechem has his heart set on your
34: 13 deceitfully as they spoke to Shechem and his father **Hamor**.
34: 18 Their proposal seemed good to **Hamor** and his son Shechem.
34: 18 Their proposal seemed good to Hamor and **his**[s] son Shechem.
34: 20 So **Hamor** and his son Shechem went to the gate of their city to
34: 24 All the men who went out of the city gate agreed with **Hamor**
34: 26 They put **Hamor** and his son Shechem to the sword and took
Jos 24: 32 bought for a hundred pieces of silver from the sons of **Hamor**,
Jdg 9: 28 Zebul his deputy? Serve the men of **Hamor**, Shechem's father!

2792 חָמוֹת **ḥāmôt**, n.f. [11] [√ 2767]

mother-in-law [11]

Ru 1: 14 Orpah kissed her **mother-in-law** good-by, but Ruth clung to her.
2: 11 done for your **mother-in-law** since the death of your husband—
2: 18 to town, and her **mother-in-law** saw how much she had gathered.
2: 19 Her **mother-in-law** asked her, "Where did you glean today?
2: 19 Ruth told her **mother-in-law** about the one at whose place she had
2: 23 harvests were finished. And she lived with her **mother-in-law**.
3: 1 One day Naomi her **mother-in-law** said to her, "My daughter,
3: 6 and did everything her **mother-in-law** told her to do.
3: 16 When Ruth came to her **mother-in-law**, Naomi asked, "How did it
3: 17 saying, 'Don't go back to your **mother-in-law** empty-handed.' "
Mic 7: 6 against her mother, a daughter-in-law against her **mother-in-law**—

2793 חֹמֶט **ḥōmeṭ**, n.[m.]. [1]

skink [1]

Lev 11: 30 the monitor lizard, the wall lizard, the **skink** and the chameleon.

2794 חֻמְטָה **ḥumṭâ**, n.pr.loc. [1]

Humtah [1]

Jos 15: 54 **Humtah**, Kiriath Arba (that is, Hebron) and Zior—nine towns

2795 חֲמִיטַל **ḥ^a^mîṭal**, n.pr.f. [0] [√ 2769; cf. 2782]

2Ki 24: 18 [His mother's name was **Hamutal** [K; see Q 2782] daughter of Jeremiah;]
Jer 52: 1 [His mother's name was **Hamutal** [K; see Q 2782] daughter of Jeremiah;]

2796 חָמִיץ **ḥāmîṣ**, a. [1] [√ 2806]

mash [1]

Isa 30: 24 The oxen and donkeys that work the soil will eat fodder and **mash**,

2797 חֲמִישִׁי חֲמִשִׁי **ḥ^a^mîšî**, a.num.ord. [45] [√ 2822]

fifth [43], five-sided [1], one fifth [1]

Ge 1: 23 And there was evening, and there was morning—the **fifth** day.
30: 17 to Leah, and she became pregnant and bore Jacob a **fifth** son.
47: 24 when the crop comes in, give a **fifth** of it to Pharaoh. The other
Lev 5: 16 add a **fifth** *of* the value to that and give it all to the priest, who will
6: 5 [5:24] add a **fifth** *of* the value to it and give it all to the owner on
19: 25 in the **fifth** year you may eat its fruit. In this way your harvest will
22: 14 to the priest for the offering and add a **fifth** *of* the value to it.
27: 13 wishes to redeem the animal, he must add a **fifth** to its value.
27: 15 he must add a **fifth** to its value, and the house will again become
27: 19 he must add a **fifth** to its value, and the field will again become his.
27: 27 he may buy it back at its set value, adding a **fifth** *of* the value to it.
27: 31 man redeems any of his tithe, he must add a **fifth** *of* the value to it.
Nu 5: 7 add **one fifth** to it and give it all to the person he has wronged.
7: 36 On the **fifth** day Shelumiel son of Zurishaddai, the leader of the
29: 26 " 'On the **fifth** day prepare nine bulls, two rams and fourteen male
33: 38 where he died on the first day of the **fifth** month of the fortieth
Jos 19: 24 The **fifth** lot came out for the tribe of Asher, clan by clan.
Jdg 19: 8 On the morning of the **fifth** day, when he rose to go, the girl's
2Sa 3: 4 the son of Haggith; the **fifth**, Shephatiah the son of Abital;
1Ki 6: 31 sanctuary he made doors of olive wood with **five-sided** jambs.
14: 25 In the **fifth** year of King Rehoboam, Shishak king of Egypt
2Ki 25: 8 On the seventh day of the **fifth** month, in the nineteenth year of
1Ch 2: 14 the fourth Nethanel, the **fifth** Raddai,
3: 3 the **fifth**, Shephatiah the son of Abital; and the sixth, Ithream,
8: 2 Nohah the fourth and Rapha the **fifth**.
12: 10 [12:11] Mishmannah the fourth, Jeremiah the **fifth**,
24: 9 the **fifth** to Malkijah, the sixth to Mijamin,
25: 12 the **fifth** to Nethaniah, his sons and relatives, 12
26: 3 Elam the **fifth**, Jehohanan the sixth and Eliehoenai the seventh.
26: 4 the second, Joah the third, Sacar the fourth, Nethanel the **fifth**,
27: 8 The **fifth**, for the fifth month, was the commander Shamhuth the
27: 8 The fifth, for the **fifth** month, was the commander Shamhuth the
2Ch 12: 2 Shishak king of Egypt attacked Jerusalem in the **fifth** year of King
Ezr 7: 8 Ezra arrived in Jerusalem in the **fifth** month of the seventh year of
7: 9 and he arrived in Jerusalem on the first day of the **fifth** month,
Ne 6: 5 Then, the **fifth** time, Sanballat sent his aide to me with the same
Jer 1: 3 down to the **fifth** month of the eleventh year of Zedekiah son of
28: 1 In the **fifth** month of that same year, the fourth year, early in the
36: 9 In the ninth month of the **fifth** year of Jehoiakim son of Josiah king
52: 12 On the tenth day of the **fifth** month, in the nineteenth year of
Eze 1: 2 the month—it was the **fifth** year of the exile of King Jehoiachin—
20: 1 In the seventh year, in the **fifth** month on the tenth day, some of
Zec 7: 3 and the prophets, "Should I mourn and fast in the **fifth** month,
7: 5 'When you fasted and mourned in the **fifth** and seventh months for
8: 19 **fifth**, seventh and tenth months will become joyful and glad

2798 חָמַל **ḥāmal**, v. [41] [→ 2783, 2784, 2799, 2800, 2857, 4720?]

spare [12], pity [6], spared [4], had pity [2], have pity [2], mercy [2], allow pity [1], bear [1], compassion [1], concern [1], felt sorry [1], had compassion [1], had concern [1], in compassion spares [1], mercilessly [+4202] [1], refrained [1], show mercy [1], take pity [1], unrelenting [+4202] [1]

Ex 2: 6 [A] and saw the baby. He was crying, and *she* **felt sorry** for him.
Dt 13: 8 [13:9] [A] Show him no pity. *Do* not **spare** him or shield him.
1Sa 15: 3 [A] *Do* not **spare** them; put to death men and women, children
15: 9 [A] **spared** Agag and the best of the sheep and cattle, the fat calves
15: 15 [A] *they* **spared** the best of the sheep and cattle to sacrifice to the
23: 21 [A] "The LORD bless you for *your* **concern** for me.
2Sa 12: 4 [A] but the rich man **refrained** *from* taking one of his own sheep
12: 6 [A] times over, because he did such a thing and **had** no **pity**."
21: 7 [A] The king **spared** Mephibosheth son of Jonathan, the son of
2Ch 36: 15 [A] because *he* **had pity** on his people and on his dwelling place.
36: 17 [A] and **spared** neither young man nor young woman, old man
Job 6: 10 [A] have this consolation—my joy in **unrelenting** [+4202] pain—
16: 13 [A] Without **pity**, he pierces my kidneys and spills my gall on the
20: 13 [A] though *he* cannot **bear** to let it go and keeps it in his mouth,
27: 22 [A] It hurls itself against him without **mercy** as he flees headlong
Pr 6: 34 [A] and *he will* **show** no **mercy** when he takes revenge.
Isa 9: 19 [9:18] [A] will be fuel for the fire; no one *will* **spare** his brother.
30: 14 [A] shattered *so* **mercilessly** [+4202] that among its pieces not a
Jer 13: 14 [A] *I will* **allow** no **pity** or mercy or compassion to keep me
15: 5 [A] "Who *will* **have pity** on you, O Jerusalem? Who will mourn
21: 7 [A] he will show them no mercy or **pity** or compassion.'
50: 14 [A] **Spare** no arrows, for she has sinned against the LORD.
51: 3 [A] *Do* not **spare** her young men; completely destroy her army.
La 2: 2 [A] Without **pity** the Lord has swallowed up all the dwellings of
2: 17 [A] He has overthrown you without **pity**, he has let the enemy
2: 21 [A] day of your anger; you have slaughtered them without **pity**.
3: 43 [A] with anger and pursued us; you have slain without **pity**.
Eze 5: 11 [A] my favor; I will not look on you with pity or **spare** you.
7: 4 [A] I will not look on you with pity or **spare** you; I will surely
7: 9 [A] I will not look on you with pity or **spare** you; I will repay
8: 18 [A] in anger; I will not look on them with pity or **spare** them.
9: 5 [A] the city and kill, without showing pity or **compassion**.
9: 10 [A] So I will not look on them with pity or **spare** them, but I will
16: 5 [A] or **had compassion** *enough* to do any of these things for
36: 21 [A] *I* **had concern** for my holy name, which the house of Israel
Joel 2: 18 [A] will be jealous for his land and **take pity** on his people.
Hab 1: 17 [A] keep on emptying his net, destroying nations without **mercy**?
Zec 11: 5 [A] I am rich!' Their own shepherds *do* not **spare** them.
11: 6 [A] For *I will* no longer **have pity** on the people of the land,"
Mal 3: 17 [A] *I will* **spare** them, just as in compassion a man spares his son
3: 17 [A] just as **in compassion** a man **spares** his son who serves him.

2799 חֶמְלָה **ḥemlâ**, n.f. [2] [√ 2798]

merciful [1], mercy [1]

Ge 19: 16 them safely out of the city, for the LORD was **merciful** to them.
Isa 63: 9 In his love and **mercy** he redeemed them; he lifted them up

2800 חֻמְלָה **ḥumlâ**, n.[f.] *or* v.inf. Not used in NIV/BHS [√ 2798]

[F] Hitpael (hitpoel, hitpoal, hitpolel, hitpolal, hitpalel, hitpalal, hitpalpel, hitpalpal, hotpael, hotpaal) [G] Hiphil (hiphtil) [H] Hophal [I] Hishtaphel

2801 חָמַם ***ḥāmam***, v. [22] [→ 2569, 2768, 2770, 2780, 2785, 2802, 2829, 2832, 2833; cf. 3501]

warm [8], hot [6], warms [2], aroused [1], burn with lust [1], heat [1], in a rage [+4222] [1], lets warm [1], warming [1]

Ex 16:21 [A] as he needed, and when the sun *grew* **hot**, it melted away.
Dt 19: 6 [A] the avenger of blood might pursue him **in a rage** [+4222],
1Sa 11: 9 [A] men of Jabesh Gilead, 'By the time the sun *is* **hot** tomorrow,
1Ki 1: 1 [A] he *could* not *keep* **warm** even when they put covers over
1: 2 [A] lie beside him so that our lord the king *may keep* **warm**."
2Ki 4:34 [A] stretched himself out upon him, the boy's body *grew* **warm**.
Ne 7: 3 [A] gates of Jerusalem are not to be opened until the sun *is* **hot**.
Job 6:17 [A] in the dry season, and in the **heat** vanish from their channels.
31:20 [F] his heart did not bless me for **warming** him with the fleece
39:14 [D] lays her eggs on the ground and **lets** them **warm** in the sand,
Ps 39: 3 [39:4] [A] My heart *grew* **hot** within me, and as I meditated,
Ecc 4:11 [A] Also, if two lie down together, they will *keep* **warm**. But
4:11 [A] they will keep warm. But how *can* one *keep* **warm** alone?
Isa 44:15 [A] some of it he takes and **warms** *himself*, he kindles a fire
44:16 [A] *He* also **warms** *himself* and says, "Ah! I am warm; I see the
44:16 [A] warms himself and says, "Ah! *I am* **warm**; I see the fire."
47:14 [A] Here are no coals to **warm** anyone; here is no fire to sit by.
57: 5 [C] You **burn with lust** among the oaks and under every
Jer 51:39 [A] But while they *are* **aroused**, I will set out a feast for them
Eze 24:11 [A] set the empty pot on the coals till *it becomes* **hot** and its
Hos 7: 7 [A] All of them *are* **hot** as an oven; they devour their rulers.
Hag 1: 6 [A] You put on clothes, but *are* not **warm**. You earn wages, only

2802 חַמָּן ***ḥammān***, n.m. [8] [√ 2801]

incense altars [8]

Lev 26:30 cut down your **incense altars** and pile your dead bodies on the
2Ch 14: 5 [14:4] the high places and **incense altars** in every town in Judah,
34: 4 he cut to pieces the **incense altars** that were above them,
34: 7 and cut to pieces all the **incense altars** throughout Israel.
Isa 17: 8 the Asherah poles and the **incense altars** their fingers have made.
27: 9 to pieces, no Asherah poles or **incense altars** will be left standing.
Eze 6: 4 altars will be demolished and your **incense altars** will be smashed;
6: 6 your idols smashed and ruined, your **incense altars** broken down,

2803 ¹חָמַס ***ḥāmas[1]***, v. [8] [→ 2805, 9379?; cf. 2804]

do violence [2], harms [1], laid waste [1], mistreated [1], stripped [1], violence [1], wrong [1]

Job 15:33 [A] He will be like a vine **stripped** *of* its unripe grapes, like an
21:27 [A] are thinking, the schemes by which *you would* **wrong** me.
Pr 8:36 [A] whoever fails to find me **harms** himself; all who hate me
Jer 13:22 [C] that your skirts have been torn off and your body **mistreated**.
22: 3 [A] Do no wrong or **violence** *to* the alien, the fatherless
La 2: 6 [A] *He has* **laid waste** his dwelling like a garden; he has
Eze 22:26 [A] Her priests **do violence** *to* my law and profane my holy
Zep 3: 4 [A] Her priests profane the sanctuary and **do violence** *to* the law.

2804 ²חָמַס ***ḥāmas[2]***, v. Not used in NIV/BHS [cf. 2803]

2805 חָמָס ***ḥāmās***, n.m. [60] [√ 2803]

violence [43], violent [5], destroyed [2], malicious [2], crime [1], fiercely [1], plunder [1], ruthless [1], terror [1], violent [+4848] [1], wrong [1], wronged [1]

Ge 6:11 Now the earth was corrupt in God's sight and was full of **violence**.
6:13 to all people, for the earth is filled with **violence** because of them.
16: 5 said to Abram, "You are responsible for the **wrong** I am *suffering*.
49: 5 and Levi are brothers—their swords are weapons of **violence**.
Ex 23: 1 Do not help a wicked man by being a **malicious** witness.
Dt 19:16 If a **malicious** witness takes the stand to accuse a man of a crime,
Jdg 9:24 God did this in order that the **crime** *against* Jerub-Baal's seventy
2Sa 22: 3 my refuge and my savior—from **violent** *men* you save me.
22:49 You exalted me above my foes; from **violent** men you rescued me.
1Ch 12:17 [12:18] me to my enemies when my hands are free from **violence**,
Job 16:17 yet my hands have been free of **violence** and my prayer is pure.
19: 7 "Though I cry, 'I've been **wronged**!' I get no response; though I
Ps 7:16 [7:17] on himself; his **violence** comes down on his own head.
11: 5 but the wicked and those who love **violence** his soul hates.
18:48 [18:49] me above my foes; from **violent** men you rescued me.
25:19 how my enemies have increased and how **fiercely** they hate me!
27:12 for false witnesses rise up against me, breathing out **violence**.
35:11 **Ruthless** witnesses come forward; they question me on things I
55: 9 [55:10] their speech, for I see **violence** and strife in the city.
58: 2 [58:3] and your hands mete out **violence** on the earth.
72:14 He will rescue them from oppression and **violence**, for precious is
73: 6 pride is their necklace; they clothe themselves with **violence**.
74:20 because haunts of **violence** fill the dark places of the land.
140: 1 [140:2] from evil men; protect me from men of **violence**,
140: 4 [140:5] protect me from men of **violence** who plan to trip my feet.
140:11 [140:12] in the land; may disaster hunt down men of **violence**.
Pr 3:31 Do not envy a **violent** man or choose any of his ways,
4:17 They eat the bread of wickedness and drink the wine of **violence**.
10: 6 the righteous, but **violence** overwhelms the mouth of the wicked.
10:11 fountain of life, but **violence** overwhelms the mouth of the wicked.
13: 2 enjoys good things, but the unfaithful have a craving for **violence**.
16:29 A **violent** man entices his neighbor and leads him down a path that
26: 6 or drinking **violence** is the sending of a message by the hand of a
Isa 53: 9 and with the rich in his death, though he had done no **violence**,
59: 6 Their deeds are evil deeds, and acts of **violence** are in their hands.
60:18 No longer will **violence** be heard in your land, nor ruin
Jer 6: 7 **Violence** and destruction resound in her; her sickness and wounds
20: 8 Whenever I speak, I cry out proclaiming **violence** and destruction.
51:35 May the **violence** done to our flesh be upon Babylon,"
51:46 the next, rumors of **violence** in the land and of ruler against ruler.
Eze 7:11 **Violence** has grown into a rod to punish wickedness; none of the
7:23 the land is full of bloodshed and the city is full of **violence**.
8:17 Must they also fill the land with **violence** and continually provoke
12:19 of everything in it because of the **violence** *of* all who live there.
28:16 Through your widespread trade you were filled with **violence**,
45: 9 Give up your **violence** and oppression and do what is just
Joel 3:19 [4:19] because of **violence** *done to* the people of Judah,
Am 3:10 the LORD, "who hoard **plunder** and loot in their fortresses."
6: 3 You put off the evil day and bring near a reign of **terror**.
Ob 1:10 Because of the **violence** *against* your brother Jacob, you will be
Jnh 3: 8 on God. Let them give up their evil ways and their **violence**.
Mic 6:12 Her rich men *are* **violent** [+4848]; her people are liars and their
Hab 1: 2 do not listen? Or cry out to you, "**Violence**!" but you do not save?
1: 3 Destruction and **violence** are before me; there is strife, and conflict
1: 9 they all come bent on **violence**. Their hordes advance like a desert
2: 8 you have **destroyed** lands and cities and everyone in them.
2:17 The **violence** you have done *to* Lebanon will overwhelm you,
2:17 you have **destroyed** lands and cities and everyone in them.
Zep 1: 9 who fill the temple of their gods with **violence** and deceit.
Mal 2:16 "and I hate a man's covering himself with **violence** as well as with

2806 ¹חָמֵץ ***ḥāmēṣ[1]***, v. [4] [→ 2786, 2796, 2809, 2810, 4721]

rises [1], was grieved [1], yeast added [1], yeast [1]

Ex 12:34 [A] So the people took their dough before *the* **yeast** *was* **added**,
12:39 [A] The dough *was* without **yeast** because they had been driven
Ps 73:21 [F] When my heart **was grieved** and my spirit embittered,
Hos 7: 4 [A] need not stir from the kneading of the dough till it **rises**.

2807 ²חָמֵץ ***ḥāmēṣ[2]***, v. [1] [→ 2787]

cruel [1]

Ps 71: 4 [A] hand of the wicked, from the grasp of evil and **cruel** *men*.

2808 ³חָמֵץ ***ḥāmēṣ[3]***, v. [1] [→ 2786]

stained crimson [1]

Isa 63: 1 [B] from Bozrah, with his garments **stained crimson**?

2809 ⁴חָמֵץ ***ḥāmēṣ[4]***, n.m. [11] [√ 2806]

yeast [3], anything containing yeast [2], anything with yeast in it [1], bread made with yeast [1], containing yeast [1], leavened bread [1], made with yeast [1], with yeast in it [1]

Ex 12:15 for whoever eats **anything with yeast in it** from the first day
13: 3 you out of it with a mighty hand. Eat nothing **containing yeast**.
13: 7 nothing **with yeast in it** is to be seen among you, nor shall any
23:18 blood of a sacrifice to me along with **anything containing yeast**.
34:25 blood of a sacrifice to me along with **anything containing yeast**,
Lev 2:11 offering you bring to the LORD must be made without **yeast**,
6:17 [6:10] It must not be baked with **yeast**; I have given it as their
7:13 he is to present an offering with cakes of bread **made with yeast**.
23:17 baked with **yeast**, as a wave offering of firstfruits to the LORD.
Dt 16: 3 Do not eat it with **bread made with yeast**, but for seven days eat
Am 4: 5 Burn **leavened bread** as a thank offering and brag about your

2810 חֹמֶץ ***ḥōmeṣ***, n.m. [6] [√ 2806]

vinegar [4], *untranslated* [1], wine vinegar [1]

Nu 6: 3 fermented drink and must not drink **vinegar** *made from* wine
6: 3 vinegar made from wine or **[RPH]** from other fermented drink.
Ru 2:14 over here. Have some bread and dip it in the **wine vinegar**."
Ps 69:21 [69:22] put gall in my food and gave me **vinegar** for my thirst.
Pr 10:26 As **vinegar** to the teeth and smoke to the eyes, so is a sluggard to
25:20 or like **vinegar** poured on soda, is one who sings songs to a heavy

2811 חָמַק ***ḥāmaq***, v. [2] [→ 2788]

left [1], wander [1]

SS 5: 6 [A] I opened for my lover, but my lover *had* **left**; he was gone.
Jer 31: 22 [F] How long *will you* **wander**, O unfaithful daughter? The

2812 [1]חָמַר ***ḥāmar[1]***, v. [2] [→ 2815, 2816, 2819; cf. 2814]

foam [1], foaming [1]

Ps 46: 3 [46:4] [A] though its waters roar and **foam** and the mountains
75: 8 [75:9] [A] In the hand of the LORD is a cup full of **foaming**

2813 [2]חָמַר ***ḥāmar[2]***, v. [3] [→ 2789, 2790, 2791, 2817, 3502]

in torment [2], red [1]

Job 16: 16 [D] My face *is* **red** with weeping, deep shadows ring my eyes;
La 1: 20 [D] I *am* **in torment** within, and in my heart I am disturbed, for I
2: 11 [E] My eyes fail from weeping, I *am* **in torment** within,

2814 [3]חָמַר ***ḥāmar[3]***, v.den. [1] [cf. 2812]

coated [1]

Ex 2: 3 [A] got a papyrus basket for him and **coated** it with tar and pitch.

2815 חֶמֶר ***ḥemer***, n.[m.]. [1] [√ 2812; Ar 10271]

foaming [1]

Dt 32: 14 finest kernels of wheat. You drank the **foaming** blood of the grape.

2816 [1]חֹמֶר ***ḥōmer[1]***, n.[m.]. [1] [√ 2812]

churning [1]

Hab 3: 15 You trampled the sea with your horses, **churning** the great waters.

2817 [2]חֹמֶר ***ḥōmer[2]***, n.m. [17] [√ 2813]

clay [11], mortar [4], mud [2]

Ge 11: 3 They used brick instead of stone, and tar for **mortar**.
Ex 1: 14 labor in brick and **mortar** and with all kinds of work in the fields;
Job 4: 19 how much more those who live in houses of **clay**,
10: 9 Remember that you molded me like **clay**. Will you now turn me to
13: 12 maxims are proverbs of ashes; your defenses are defenses of **clay**.
27: 16 Though he heaps up silver like dust and clothes like piles of **clay**,
30: 19 He throws me into the **mud**, and I am reduced to dust and ashes.
33: 6 I am just like you before God; I too have been taken from **clay**.
38: 14 The earth takes shape like **clay** *under* a seal; its features stand out
Isa 10: 6 snatch plunder, and to trample them down like **mud** *in* the streets.
29: 16 upside down, as if the potter were thought to be like the **clay**!
41: 25 He treads on rulers as if they were **mortar**, as if he were a potter
45: 9 Does the **clay** say to the potter, 'What are you making?' Does your
64: 8 [64:7] We are the **clay**, you are the potter; we are all the work of
Jer 18: 4 But the pot he was shaping from the **clay** was marred in his hands;
18: 6 "Like **clay** in the hand of the potter, so are you in my hand,
Na 3: 14 Work the clay, tread the **mortar**, repair the brickwork!

2818 [3]חֹמֶר ***ḥōmer[3]***, n.m. [13]

homer [10], heaps [+2818] [2], homers [1]

Ex 8: 14 [8:10] They were piled into **heaps** [+2818], and the land reeked of
8: 14 [8:10] They were piled into **heaps** [+2818], and the land reeked of
Lev 27: 16 required for it—fifty shekels of silver to a **homer** *of* barley seed.
Nu 11: 32 and gathered quail. No one gathered less than ten **homers**.
Isa 5: 10 only a bath of wine, a **homer** of seed only an ephah of grain."
Eze 45: 11 the bath containing a tenth of a **homer** and the ephah a tenth of a
45: 11 containing a tenth of a homer and the ephah a tenth of a **homer**;
45: 11 tenth of a homer; the **homer** is to be the standard measure for both.
45: 13 a sixth of an ephah from each **homer** *of* wheat and a sixth of an
45: 13 of wheat and a sixth of an ephah from each **homer** *of* barley.
45: 14 of a bath from each cor (which consists of ten baths or one **homer**,
45: 14 of ten baths or one homer, for ten baths are equivalent to a **homer**).
Hos 3: 2 fifteen shekels of silver and about a **homer** and a lethek of barley.

2819 חֵמָר ***ḥēmār***, n.[m.]. [3] [√ 2812]

tar [3]

Ge 11: 3 They used brick instead of stone, and **tar** for mortar.
14: 10 Now the Valley of Siddim was full of **tar** pits, and when the kings
Ex 2: 3 she got a papyrus basket for him and coated it with **tar** and pitch.

2820 חַמְרָן ***ḥamrān***, n.pr.m. [1 / 0] [cf. 2777]

1Ch 1: 41 The sons of Dishon: Hemdan, [BHS ***Hamran***; NIV 2777] Eshban,

2821 חָמַשׁ ***ḥāmaš***, v.den. [5] [→ 2826; cf. 2822]

armed for battle [1], armed [1], fully armed [1], outposts [+7895] [1], take a fifth [1]

Ge 41: 34 [D] *to* **take a fifth** *of* the harvest of Egypt during the seven years
Ex 13: 18 [B] The Israelites went up out of Egypt **armed for battle**.
Jos 1: 14 [B] all your fighting men, **fully armed**, must cross over ahead of
4: 12 [B] **armed**, in front of the Israelites, as Moses had directed them.
Jdg 7: 11 [B] Purah his servant went down to the **outposts** [+7895] of the

2822 חָמֵשׁ ***ḥāmēš***, n.m. & f. [507] [→ 2797, 2821, 2823, 2825, 2826]

five [164], fifty [77], twenty-five [+2256+6929] [23], fifteenth [+6925] [15], 25,000 [+547+2256+6929] [14], *untranslated* [11], 250 [+2256+4395] [10], 4,500 [+547+752+2256+4395] [8], fifteen [+6926] [8], 603,550 [+547+547+2256+2256+2256+2822+4395+4395+8993+9252] [6], fifteen [+6925] [6], 500 [+4395] [5], captain [+8569] [5], fifth [5], 1,254 [+547+752+2256+4395] [4], 45,650 [+547+752+2256+2256+2256+2822+4395+9252] [4], eighty-five [+2256+9046] [4], fifties [4], fifty-five [+2256+2822] [4], 40,500 [+547+752+2256+4395] [3], 5,000 [+547] [3], 50 [3], 53,400 [+547+752+2256+2256+4395+8993] [3], fiftieth [3], fifty-two [+2256+9109] [3], forty-five [+752+2256] [3], seventy-five [+2256+8679] [3], thirty-five [+2256+8993] [3], twenty-fifth [+2256+6929] [3], 1,052 [+547+2256+9109] [2], 1,775 [+547+2256+2256+2256+4395+8679+8679] [2], 150 [+2256+4395] [2], 151,450 [+285+547+547+752+2256+2256+2256+2256+2822+4395+4395] [2], 245 [+752+2256+4395] [2], 30,500 [+547+2256+4395+8993] [2], 345 [+752+2256+4395+8993] [2], 35,400 [+547+752+2256+2256+4395+8993] [2], 41,500 [+285+547+752+2256+2256+4395] [2], 435 [+752+2256+4395+8993] [2], 46,500 [+547+752+2256+2256+4395+9252] [2], 52 [+2256+9109] [2], 54,400 [+547+752+752+2256+2256+4395] [2], 550 [+2256+2822+4395] [2], 57,400 [+547+752+2256+2256+4395+8679] [2], 59,300 [+547+2256+2256+4395+8993+9596] [2], 595 [+2256+2256+2822+4395+9596] [2], 65 [+2256+9252] [2], 652 [+2256+4395+9109+9252] [2], 655 [+2256+2822+4395+9252] [2], 95 [+2256+9596] [2], fifteenth [+6926] [2], men[s] [2], seventy-five feet [+564] [2], 1,335 [+547+2256+4395+8993+8993] [1], 1,365 [+547+2256+2256+2256+4395+8993+9252] [1], 105 [+2256+4395] [1], 153,600 [+547+547+2256+2256+2256+4395+4395+8993+9252] [1], 156 [+2256+4395+9252] [1], 157,600 [+547+547+2256+2256+2256+4395+4395+8679+9252] [1], 16,750 [+547+2256+4395+6925+8679+9252] [1], 2,056 [+547+2256+9252] [1], 2,750 [+547+2256+4395+8679] [1], 205 [+2256+4395] [1], 245 [+752+2256+2256+4395] [1], 25,100 [+547+2256+2256+4395+6929] [1], 307,500 [+547+547+2256+2256+4395+4395+8679+8993] [1], 32,500 [+547+2256+2256+4395+8993+9109] [1], 337,500 [+547+547+547+2256+2256+2256+4395+4395+8679+8993+8993] [1], 337,500 [+547+547+547+2256+2256+4395+4395+8679+8993+8993] [1], 35 [+2256+8993] [1], 350 [+2256+4395+8993] [1], 365 [+2256+2256+4395+8993+9252] [1], 45,400 [+547+752+752+2256+2256+4395] [1], 45,600 [+547+752+2256+2256+4395+9252] [1], 454 [+752+752+2256+4395] [1], 5,400 [+547+752+2256+4395] [1], 50,000 [+547] [1], 52,700 [+547+2256+2256+4395+8679+9109] [1], 530 [+2256+4395+8993] [1], 56 [+2256+9252] [1], 60,500 [+547+2256+4395+9252] [1], 650 [+2256+4395+9252] [1], 675 [+2256+4395+8679+9252] [1], 675,000 [+547+547+547+2256+2256+4395+8679+9252] [1], 7,500 [+547+2256+4395+8679] [1], 725 [+2256+4395+6929+8679] [1], 745 [+752+2256+4395+8679] [1], 75 feet [+564] [1], 76,500 [+547+2256+2256+4395+8679+9252] [1], 775 [+2256+4395+8679+8679] [1], 8,580 [+547+2256+2256+4395+9046+9046] [1], 815 [+2256+4395+6926+9046] [1], 845 [+752+2256+4395+9046] [1], 895 [+2256+2256+4395+9046+9596] [1], 905 [+2256+4395+9596] [1], 945 [+752+2256+2256+4395+9596] [1], 950 [+2256+4395+9596] [1], 956 [+2256+2256+4395+9252+9596] [1], captains [+8569] [1], fifteen [+2256+6927] [1], fifty-second [+2256+9109] [1], seven and a half feet [+564+928+2021] [1], sixty-five [+2256+9252] [1], thirty-fifth [+2256+8993] [1], twenty feet [+564+6926] [1]

Ge 5: 6 When Seth had lived **105** [+2256+4395] years, he became the
5: 10 Enosh lived **815** [+2256+4395+6926+9046] years and had other
5: 11 Enosh lived **905** [+2256+4395+9596] years, and then he died.
5: 15 When Mahalalel had lived **65** [+2256+9252] years, he became the
5: 17 Mahalalel lived **895** [+2256+2256+4395+9046+9596] years, and
5: 21 When Enoch had lived **65** [+2256+9252] years, he became the
5: 23 Enoch lived **365** [+2256+2256+4395+8993+9252] years.
5: 30 Lamech lived **595** [+2256+2256+2822+4395+9596] years and had
5: 30 Lamech lived **595** [+2256+2256+2822+4395+9596] years and had
5: 32 After Noah was **500** [+4395] years old, he became the father of
6: 15 The ark is to be 450 feet long, **75 feet** [+564] wide and 45 feet
7: 20 the mountains to a depth of more than **twenty feet** [+564+6926].
7: 24 The waters flooded the earth for a hundred and **fifty** days.
8: 3 At the end of the hundred and **fifty** days the water had gone down,

Ge 9:28 After the flood Noah lived **350** [+2256+4395+8993] years.
9:29 Noah lived **950** [+2256+4395+9596] years, and then he died.
11:11 Shem lived **500** [+4395] years and had other sons and daughters.
11:12 When Arphaxad had lived **35** [+2256+8993] years, he became the
11:32 Terah lived **205** [+2256+4395] years, and he died in Haran.
12: 4 Abram was **seventy-five** [+2256+8679] years old when he set out
14: 9 king of Shinar and Arioch king of Ellasar—four kings against **five**.
18:24 What if there are **fifty** righteous people in the city? Will you really
18:24 not spare the place for the sake of the **fifty** righteous people in it?
18:26 LORD said, "If I find **fifty** righteous people in the city of Sodom,
18:28 what if the number of the righteous is **five** less than fifty? Will you
18:28 what if the number of the righteous is five less than **fifty**?
18:28 Will you destroy the whole city because of **five** *people*?" "If I find
18:28 "If I find **forty-five** [+752+2256] there," he said, "I will not
25: 7 Abraham lived a hundred and **seventy-five** [+2256+8679] years.
43:34 Benjamin's portion was **five** times as much as anyone else's.
45: 6 and for the next **five** years there will not be plowing and reaping.
45:11 for you there, because **five** years of famine are still to come.
45:22 he gave three hundred shekels of silver and **five** sets of clothes.
47: 2 He chose **five** of his brothers and presented them before Pharaoh.
Ex 16: 1 on the **fifteenth** [+6925] day of the second month after they had
18:21 appoint them as officials over thousands, hundreds, **fifties** and tens.
18:25 of the people, officials over thousands, hundreds, **fifties** and tens.
22: 1 [21:37] he must pay back **five** head of cattle for the ox and four
26: 3 Join **five** *of* the curtains together, and do the same with the other
26: 3 five of the curtains together, and do the same with the other **five**.
26: 5 Make **fifty** loops on one curtain and fifty loops on the end curtain
26: 5 on one curtain and **fifty** loops on the end curtain of the other set,
26: 6 make **fifty** gold clasps and use them to fasten the curtains together
26: 9 Join **five** *of* the curtains together into one set and the other six into
26:10 Make **fifty** loops along the edge of the end curtain in one set
26:10 and also **[RPH]** along the edge of the end curtain in the other set.
26:11 make **fifty** bronze clasps and put them in the loops to fasten the
26:26 of acacia wood: **five** for the frames on one side of the tabernacle,
26:27 **five** for those on the other side, and five for the frames on the west,
26:27 and **five** for the frames on the west, at the far end of the tabernacle.
26:37 for this curtain and **five** posts of acacia wood overlaid with gold.
26:37 wood overlaid with gold. And cast **five** bronze bases for them.
27: 1 cubits high; it is to be square, **five** cubits long and five cubits wide.
27: 1 cubits high; it is to be square, five cubits long and **five** cubits wide.
27:12 "The west end of the courtyard shall be **fifty** cubits wide and have
27:13 toward the sunrise, the courtyard shall also be **fifty** cubits wide.
27:14 Curtains **fifteen** [+6926] cubits long are to be on one side of the
27:15 and curtains **fifteen** [+6926] cubits long are to be on the other side,
27:18 The courtyard shall be a hundred cubits long and **fifty** cubits wide,
27:18 **[RPH]** with curtains of finely twisted linen five cubits high,
27:18 cubits wide, with curtains of finely twisted linen **five** cubits high,
30:23 **500** [+4395] shekels of liquid myrrh, half as much (that is,
30:23 of liquid myrrh, half as much (that is, **250** [+2256+4395] shekels)
30:23 of fragrant cinnamon, **250** [+2256+4395] shekels of fragrant cane,
30:24 **500** [+4395] shekels of cassia—all according to the sanctuary
36:10 They joined **five** *of* the curtains together and did the same with the
36:10 five of the curtains together and did the same with the other **five**.
36:12 They also made **fifty** loops on one curtain and fifty loops on the
36:12 on one curtain and **fifty** loops on the end curtain of the other set,
36:13 they made **fifty** gold clasps and used them to fasten the two sets of
36:16 They joined **five** *of* the curtains into one set and the other six into
36:17 they made **fifty** loops along the edge of the end curtain in one set
36:17 and also **[RPH]** along the edge of the end curtain in the other set.
36:18 They made **fifty** bronze clasps to fasten the tent together as a unit.
36:31 of acacia wood: **five** for the frames on one side of the tabernacle,
36:32 **five** for those on the other side, and five for the frames on the west,
36:32 and **five** for the frames on the west, at the far end of the tabernacle.
36:38 they made **five** posts with hooks for them. They overlaid the tops
36:38 and their bands with gold and made their **five** bases of bronze.
38: 1 cubits high; it was square, **five** cubits long and five cubits wide.
38: 1 cubits high; it was square, five cubits long and **five** cubits wide.
38:12 The west end was **fifty** cubits wide and had curtains, with ten posts
38:13 The east end, toward the sunrise, was also **fifty** cubits wide.
38:14 Curtains **fifteen** [+6926] cubits long were on one side of the
38:15 curtains **fifteen** [+6926] cubits long were on the other side of the
38:18 cubits long and, like the curtains of the courtyard, **five** cubits high,
38:25 and **1,775** [+547+2256+2256+2256+4395+8679+8679] shekels,
38:26 twenty years old or more, a total of **603,550** [+547+547+2256 +2256+2256+2822+4395+4395+8993+9252] men.
38:26 twenty years old or more, a total of **603,550** [+547+547+2256 +2256+2256+2822+4395+4395+8993+9252] men.
38:28 the **1,775** [+547+2256+2256+2256+4395+8679+8679] shekels
Lev 23: 6 On the **fifteenth** [+6925] day of that month the LORD's Feast of
23:16 Count off **fifty** days up to the day after the seventh Sabbath,
23:34 'On the **fifteenth** [+6925] day of the seventh month the LORD's
23:39 " 'So beginning with the **fifteenth** [+6925] day of the seventh
25:10 Consecrate the **fiftieth** year and proclaim liberty throughout the
25:11 The **fiftieth** year shall be a jubilee for you; do not sow and do not
26: 8 **Five** of you will chase a hundred, and a hundred of you will chase
27: 3 male between the ages of twenty and sixty at **fifty** shekels of silver,
27: 5 If it is a person between the ages of **five** and twenty, set the value
27: 6 If it is a person between one month and **five** years, set the value of
27: 6 set the value of a male at **five** shekels of silver and that of a female
27: 7 set the value of a male at **fifteen** [+6925] shekels and of a female at
27:16 required for it—**fifty** shekels of silver to a homer of barley seed.
Nu 1:21 tribe of Reuben was **46,500** [+547+752+2256+2256+4395+9252].
1:23 tribe of Simeon was **59,300** [+547+2256+2256+4395+8993+9596].
1:25 Gad was **45,650** [+547+752+2256+2256+2256+2822+4395+9252].
1:25 Gad was **45,650** [+547+752+2256+2256+2256+2822+4395+9252].
1:29 tribe of Issachar was **54,400** [+547+752+752+2256+2256+4395].
1:31 tribe of Zebulun was **57,400** [+547+752+2256+2256+4395+8679].
1:33 from the tribe of Ephraim was **40,500** [+547+752+2256+4395].
1:37 of Benjamin was **35,400** [+547+752+2256+2256+4395+8993].
1:41 the tribe of Asher was **41,500** [+285+547+752+2256+2256+4395].
1:43 tribe of Naphtali was **53,400** [+547+752+2256+2256+4395+8993].
1:46 The total number was **603,550** [+547+547+2256+2256+2256 +2822+4395+4395+8993+9252].
1:46 The total number was **603,550** [+547+547+2256+2256+2256 +2822+4395+4395+8993+9252].
2: 6 His division numbers **54,400** [+547+752+752+2256+2256+4395].
2: 8 His division numbers **57,400** [+547+752+2256+2256+4395+8679].
2:11 His division numbers **46,500** [+547+752+2256+2256+4395+9252].
2:13 division numbers **59,300** [+547+2256+2256+4395+8993+9596].
2:15 numbers **45,650** [+547+752+2256+2256+2256+2822+4395+9252].
2:15 numbers **45,650** [+547+752+2256+2256+2256+2822+4395+9252].
2:16 the camp of Reuben, according to their divisions, number **151,450** [+285+547+547+752+2256+2256+2256+2256+2822+4395+4395].
2:16 the camp of Reuben, according to their divisions, number **151,450** [+285+547+547+752+2256+2256+2256+2256+2822+4395+4395].
2:19 His division numbers **40,500** [+547+752+2256+4395].
2:23 His division numbers **35,400** [+547+752+2256+2256+4395+8993].
2:28 His division numbers **41,500** [+285+547+752+2256+2256+4395].
2:30 His division numbers **53,400** [+547+752+2256+2256+4395+8993].
2:31 All the men assigned to the camp of Dan number **157,600** [+547+547+2256+2256+2256+4395+4395+8679+9252].
2:32 All those in the camps, by their divisions, number **603,550** [+547+547+2256+2256+2256+2822+4395+4395+8993+9252].
2:32 All those in the camps, by their divisions, number **603,550** [+547+547+2256+2256+2256+2822+4395+4395+8993+9252].
3:22 who were counted was **7,500** [+547+2256+4395+8679].
3:47 collect **five** shekels for each one, according to the sanctuary shekel,
3:47 collect five **[RPH]** shekels for each one, according to the
3:50 **1,365** [+547+2256+2256+2256+4395+8993+9252] shekels,
4: 3 Count all the men from thirty to **fifty** years of age who come to
4:23 Count all the men from thirty to **fifty** years of age who come to
4:30 Count all the men from thirty to **fifty** years of age who come to
4:35 All the men from thirty to **fifty** years of age who came to serve in
4:36 counted by clans, were **2,750** [+547+2256+4395+8679].
4:39 All the men from thirty to **fifty** years of age who came to serve in
4:43 All the men from thirty to **fifty** years of age who came to serve in
4:47 All the men from thirty to **fifty** years of age who came to do the
4:48 numbered **8,580** [+547+2256+2256+4395+9046+9046].
7:17 two oxen, **five** rams, five male goats and five male lambs a year
7:17 five rams, **five** male goats and five male lambs a year old,
7:17 five rams, five male goats and **five** male lambs a year old,
7:23 two oxen, **five** rams, five male goats and five male lambs a year
7:23 five rams, **five** male goats and five male lambs a year old,
7:23 five rams, five male goats and **five** male lambs a year old,
7:29 two oxen, **five** rams, five male goats and five male lambs a year
7:29 five rams, **five** male goats and five male lambs a year old,
7:29 five rams, five male goats and **five** male lambs a year old,
7:35 two oxen, **five** rams, five male goats and five male lambs a year
7:35 five rams, **five** male goats and five male lambs a year old,
7:35 five rams, five male goats and **five** male lambs a year old,
7:41 two oxen, **five** rams, five male goats and five male lambs a year
7:41 five rams, **five** male goats and five male lambs a year old,
7:41 five rams, five male goats and **five** male lambs a year old,
7:47 two oxen, **five** rams, five male goats and five male lambs a year
7:47 five rams, **five** male goats and five male lambs a year old,
7:47 five rams, five male goats and **five** male lambs a year old,
7:53 two oxen, **five** rams, five male goats and five male lambs a year
7:53 five rams, **five** male goats and five male lambs a year old,
7:53 five rams, five male goats and **five** male lambs a year old,
7:59 two oxen, **five** rams, five male goats and five male lambs a year
7:59 five rams, **five** male goats and five male lambs a year old,
7:59 five rams, five male goats and **five** male lambs a year old,
7:65 two oxen, **five** rams, five male goats and five male lambs a year
7:65 five rams, **five** male goats and five male lambs a year old,
7:65 five rams, five male goats and **five** male lambs a year old,
7:71 two oxen, **five** rams, five male goats and five male lambs a year
7:71 five rams, **five** male goats and five male lambs a year old,
7:71 five rams, five male goats and **five** male lambs a year old,

Nu 7:77 two oxen, **five** rams, five male goats and five male lambs a year
7:77 five rams, **five** male goats and five male lambs a year old,
7:77 five rams, five male goats and **five** male lambs a year old,
7:83 two oxen, **five** rams, five male goats and five male lambs a year
7:83 five rams, **five** male goats and five male lambs a year old,
7:83 five rams, five male goats and **five** male lambs a year old,
8:24 the Levites: Men **twenty-five** [+2256+6929] years old or more
8:25 but at the age of **fifty**, they must retire from their regular service
11:19 not eat it for just one day, or two days, or **five**, ten or twenty days,
16:2 With them were **250** [+2256+4395] Israelite men, well-known
16:17 his censer and put incense in it—**250** [+2256+4395] censers in all—
16:35 consumed the **250** [+2256+4395] men who were offering the
18:16 redeem them at the redemption price set at **five** shekels *of* silver,
26:10 followers died when the fire devoured the **250** [+2256+4395] men.
26:18 of Gad; those numbered were **40,500** [+547+752+2256+4395].
26:22 numbered were **76,500** [+547+2256+2256+4395+8679+9252].
26:27 Zebulun; those numbered were **60,500** [+547+2256+4395+9252].
26:34 numbered were **52,700** [+547+2256+2256+4395+8679+9109].
26:37 numbered were **32,500** [+547+2256+2256+4395+8993+9109].
26:41 those numbered were **45,600** [+547+752+2256+2256+4395+9252].
26:47 those numbered were **53,400** [+547+752+2256+2256+4395+8993].
26:50 those numbered were **45,400** [+547+752+752+2256+2256+4395].
28:17 On the **fifteenth** [+6925] day of this month there is to be a festival;
29:12 " 'On the **fifteenth** [+6925] day of the seventh month, hold a
31:8 were Evi, Rekem, Zur, Hur and Reba—the **five** kings of Midian.
31:28 set apart as tribute for the LORD one out of every **five** hundred,
31:30 select one out of every **fifty**, whether persons, cattle, donkeys,
31:32 **675,000** [+547+547+547+2256+2256+4395+8679+9252] sheep,
31:36 share of those who fought in the battle was: **337,500** [+547+547 +547+2256+2256+2256+4395+4395+8679+8993+8993] sheep,
31:37 the tribute for the LORD was **675** [+2256+4395+8679+9252];
31:39 **30,500** [+547+2256+4395+8993] donkeys, of which the tribute for
31:43 the community's half—was **337,500** [+547+547+547+2256+2256 +4395+4395+8679+8993+8993] sheep,
31:45 **30,500** [+547+2256+4395+8993] donkeys
31:47 Moses selected one out of every **fifty** persons and animals,
31:52 weighed **16,750** [+547+2256+4395+6925+8679+9252] shekels.
33:3 The Israelites set out from Rameses on the **fifteenth** [+6925] day
Dt 1:15 of hundreds, of **fifties** and of tens and as tribal officials.
22:29 he shall pay the girl's father **fifty** shekels of silver. He must marry
Jos 7:21 shekels of silver and a wedge of gold weighing **fifty** shekels,
8:12 Joshua had taken about **five** thousand men and set them in ambush
10:5 Then the **five** kings of the Amorites—the kings of Jerusalem,
10:16 Now the **five** kings had fled and hidden in the cave at Makkedah.
10:17 When Joshua was told that the **five** kings had been found hiding in
10:22 "Open the mouth of the cave and bring those **five** kings out to me."
10:23 So they brought the **five** kings out of the cave—the kings of
10:26 Joshua struck and killed the kings and hung them on **five** trees,
13:3 all of it counted as Canaanite (the territory of the **five** Philistine
14:10 he has kept me alive for **forty-five** [+752+2256] years since the
14:10 So here I am today, **eighty-five** [+2256+9046] years old!
Jdg 3:3 the **five** rulers of the Philistines, all the Canaanites, the Sidonians,
8:10 Zalmunna were in Karkor with a force of about **fifteen** [+6925]
18:2 So the Danites sent **five** warriors from Zorah and Eshtaol to spy
18:7 So the **five** men left and came to Laish, where they saw that the
18:14 the **five** men who had spied out the land of Laish said to their
18:17 The **five** men who had spied out the land went inside and took the
20:35 struck down **25,100** [+547+2256+2256+4395+6929] Benjamites,
20:45 the Israelites cut down **five** thousand men along the roads.
20:46 **twenty-five** [+2256+6929] thousand Benjamite swordsmen fell,
1Sa 6:4 They replied, "**Five** gold tumors and five gold rats, according to
6:4 They replied, "Five gold tumors and **five** gold rats, according to the
6:16 The **five** rulers of the Philistines saw all this and then returned that
6:18 to the number of Philistine towns belonging to the **five** rulers—
6:19 putting seventy [BHS+ *50,070*] of them to death because they had
8:12 assign to be commanders of thousands and commanders of **fifties**,
17:5 wore a coat of scale armor of bronze weighing **five** thousand
17:40 his staff in his hand, chose **five** smooth stones from the stream,
21:3 [21:4] Give me **five** loaves of bread, or whatever you can find."
22:18 That day he killed **eighty-five** [+2256+9046] men who wore the
25:18 two skins of wine, **five** dressed sheep, five seahs of roasted grain,
25:18 two skins of wine, five dressed sheep, **five** seahs of roasted grain,
25:42 attended by her **five** maids, went with David's messengers
2Sa 4:4 He was **five** years old when the news about Saul and Jonathan
9:10 (Now Ziba had **fifteen** [+6925] sons and twenty servants.)
15:1 with a chariot and horses and with **fifty** men to run ahead of him.
19:17 [19:18] and his **fifteen** [+6925] sons and twenty servants.
21:8 to Saul, together with the **five** sons of Saul's daughter Merab,
24:9 who could handle a sword, and in Judah **five** hundred thousand.
24:24 and the oxen and paid **fifty** shekels of silver for them.
1Ki 1:5 got chariots and horses ready, with **fifty** men to run ahead of him.
4:32 [5:12] and his songs numbered a thousand and **five**.
6:6 The lowest floor was **five** cubits wide, the middle floor six cubits
6:10 The height of each was **five** cubits, and they were attached to the
6:24 One wing of the first cherub was **five** cubits long, and the other
6:24 first cherub was five cubits long, and the other wing **five** cubits—
7:2 **fifty** wide and thirty high, with four rows of cedar columns
7:3 on the columns—**forty-five** [+752+2256] beams, fifteen to a row.
7:3 rested on the columns—forty-five beams, **fifteen** [+6925] to a row.
7:6 He made a colonnade **fifty** cubits long and thirty wide. In front of
7:16 to set on the tops of the pillars; each capital was **five** cubits high.
7:16 the tops of the pillars; each capital was five cubits high. **[RPH]**
7:23 measuring ten cubits from rim to rim and **five** cubits high.
7:39 He placed **five** of the stands on the south side of the temple
7:39 of the stands on the south side of the temple and **five** on the north.
7:49 the lampstands of pure gold (**five** on the right and five on the left,
7:49 the lampstands of pure gold (five on the right and **five** on the left,
9:23 **550** [+2256+2822+4395] officials supervising the men who did the
9:23 **550** [+2256+2822+4395] officials supervising the men who did the
10:29 six hundred shekels of silver, and a horse for a hundred and **fifty**.
12:32 He instituted a festival on the **fifteenth** [+6925] day of the eighth
12:33 On the **fifteenth** [+6925] day of the eighth month, a month of his
18:4 a hundred prophets and hidden them in two caves, **fifty** in each,
18:13 in two caves, **fifty** in each, and supplied them with food and water.
18:13 fifty **[RPH]** in each, and supplied them with food and water.
18:19 bring the four hundred and **fifty** prophets of Baal and the four
18:22 prophets left, but Baal has four hundred and **fifty** prophets.
22:42 Jehoshaphat was **thirty-five** [+2256+8993] years old when he
22:42 and he reigned in Jerusalem **twenty-five** [+2256+6929] years.
2Ki 1:9 he sent to Elijah a **captain** [+8569] with his company of fifty men.
1:9 Then he sent to Elijah a captain with his *company of* **fifty** *men*.
1:10 Elijah answered the **captain** [+8569], "If I am a man of God,
1:10 come down from heaven and consume you and your **fifty** *men*!"
1:10 Then fire fell from heaven and consumed the captain and his **men**[s].
1:11 At this the king sent to Elijah another **captain** [+8569] with his
1:11 At this the king sent to Elijah another captain with his **fifty** *men*.
1:12 come down from heaven and consume you and your **fifty** *men*!"
1:12 fire of God fell from heaven and consumed him and his **fifty** *men*.
1:13 So the king sent a third **captain** [+8569] with his fifty men.
1:13 So the king sent a third captain with his **fifty** *men*. This third
1:13 This third **captain** [+8569] went up and fell on his knees before
1:13 "please have respect for my life and the lives of these **fifty** *men*,
1:14 and consumed the first two **captains** [+8569] and all their men.
1:14 and consumed the first two captains and *all* their **men**[s].
2:7 **Fifty** men of the company of the prophets went and stood at a
2:16 "Look," they said, "we your servants have **fifty** able men.
2:17 they sent **fifty** men, who searched for three days but did not find
6:25 of silver, and a quarter of a cab of seed pods for **five** shekels.
7:13 "Have some men take **five** of the horses that are left in the city.
8:16 In the **fifth** year of Joram son of Ahab king of Israel,
13:7 Nothing had been left of the army of Jehoahaz except **fifty**
13:19 and said, "You should have struck the ground **five** or six times;
14:2 He was **twenty-five** [+2256+6929] years old when he became
14:17 Amaziah son of Joash king of Judah lived for **fifteen** [+6926] years
14:23 In the **fifteenth** [+6926] year of Amaziah son of Joash king of
15:2 and he reigned in Jerusalem **fifty-two** [+2256+9109] years.
15:20 Every wealthy man had to contribute **fifty** shekels of silver to be
15:23 In the **fiftieth** year of Azariah king of Judah, Pekahiah son of
15:25 Taking **fifty** men of Gilead with him, he assassinated Pekahiah,
15:27 In the **fifty-second** [+2256+9109] year of Azariah king of Judah,
15:33 He was **twenty-five** [+2256+6929] years old when he became
18:2 He was **twenty-five** [+2256+6929] years old when he became
19:35 and **eighty-five** [+2256+9046] thousand men in the Assyrian camp.
20:6 I will add **fifteen** [+6926] years to your life. And I will deliver you
21:1 and he reigned in Jerusalem **fifty-five** [+2256+2822] years.
21:1 and he reigned in Jerusalem **fifty-five** [+2256+2822] years.
23:36 Jehoiakim was **twenty-five** [+2256+6929] years old when he
25:19 the officer in charge of the fighting men and **five** royal advisers.
1Ch 2:4 bore him Perez and Zerah. Judah had **five** sons in all.
2:6 of Zerah: Zimri, Ethan, Heman, Calcol and Darda—**five** in all.
3:20 There were also **five** others: Hashubah, Ohel, Berekiah, Hasadiah
4:32 were Etam, Ain, Rimmon, Token and Ashan—**five** towns—
4:42 And **five** hundred of these Simeonites, led by Pelatiah, Neariah,
5:21 **fifty** thousand camels, two hundred fifty thousand sheep and two
5:21 two hundred **fifty** thousand sheep and two thousand donkeys.
7:3 Michael, Obadiah, Joel and Isshiah. All **five** of them were chiefs.
7:7 Uzzi, Uzziel, Jerimoth and Iri, heads of families—**five** in all.
8:40 They had many sons and grandsons—**150** [+2256+4395] in all.
9:9 their genealogy, numbered **956** [+2256+2256+4395+9252+9596].
11:23 an Egyptian who was **seven and a half feet** [+564+928+2021]
12:33 [12:34] to help David with undivided loyalty—**50,000** [+547];
24:14 the **fifteenth** [+6925] to Bilgah, the sixteenth to Immer,
25:22 the **fifteenth** [+6925] to Jerimoth, his sons and relatives, 12
29:7 They gave toward the work on the temple of God **five** thousand
2Ch 1:17 six hundred shekels of silver, and a horse for a hundred and **fifty**.
2:17 [2:16] his father David had taken; and they were found to be **153,600** [+547+547+2256+2256+2256+4395+4395+8993+9252].
3:9 The gold nails weighed **fifty** shekels. He also overlaid the upper

2Ch 3:11 One wing of the first cherub was **five** cubits long and touched the
3:11 touched the temple wall, while its other wing, also **five** cubits long,
3:12 Similarly one wing of the second cherub was **five** cubits long
3:12 the other temple wall, and its other wing, also **five** cubits long,
3:15 **thirty-five** [+2256+8993] cubits long, each with a capital on top
3:15 cubits long, each with a capital on top measuring **five** cubits.
4:2 measuring ten cubits from rim to rim and **five** cubits high.
4:6 for washing and placed **five** on the south side and five on the north.
4:6 for washing and placed five on the south side and **five** on the north.
4:7 them in the temple, **five** on the south side and five on the north.
4:7 them in the temple, five on the south side and **five** on the north.
4:8 them in the temple, **five** on the south side and five on the north.
4:8 them in the temple, five on the south side and **five** on the north.
6:13 **five** cubits long, five cubits wide and three cubits high,
6:13 five cubits long, **five** cubits wide and three cubits high,
8:10 two hundred and **fifty** officials supervising the men.
8:18 to Ophir and brought back four hundred and **fifty** talents of gold,
13:17 so that there were **five** hundred thousand casualties among Israel's
15:10 in the third month of the **fifteenth** [+6926] year of Asa's reign.
15:19 no more war until the **thirty-fifth** [+2256+8993] year of Asa's
20:31 He was **thirty-five** [+2256+8993] years old when he became king
20:31 and he reigned in Jerusalem **twenty-five** [+2256+6929] years.
25:1 Amaziah was **twenty-five** [+2256+6929] years old when he
25:25 Amaziah son of Joash king of Judah lived for **fifteen** [+6926] years
26:3 and he reigned in Jerusalem **fifty-two** [+2256+9109] years.
26:13 of **307,500** [+547+547+2256+2256+4395+4395+8679+8993] men
27:1 Jotham was **twenty-five** [+2256+6929] years old when he became
27:8 He was **twenty-five** [+2256+6929] years old when he became
29:1 Hezekiah was **twenty-five** [+2256+6929] years old when he
33:1 and he reigned in Jerusalem **fifty-five** [+2256+2822] years.
33:1 and he reigned in Jerusalem **fifty-five** [+2256+2822] years.
35:9 provided **five** thousand Passover offerings and five hundred head
35:9 Passover offerings and **five** hundred head of cattle for the Levites.
36:5 Jehoiakim was **twenty-five** [+2256+6929] years old when he
Ezr 1:11 In all, there were **5,400** [+547+752+2256+4395] articles of gold
2:5 of Arah **775** [+2256+4395+8679+8679]
2:7 of Elam **1,254** [+547+752+2256+4395]
2:8 of Zattu **945** [+752+2256+2256+4395+9596]
2:14 of Bigvai **2,056** [+547+2256+9252]
2:15 of Adin **454** [+752+752+2256+4395]
2:20 of Gibbar **95** [+2256+9596]
2:22 of Netophah **56** [+2256+9252]
2:29 of Nebo **52** [+2256+9109]
2:30 of Magbish **156** [+2256+4395+9252]
2:31 of the other Elam **1,254** [+547+752+2256+4395]
2:33 of Lod, Hadid and Ono **725** [+2256+4395+6929+8679]
2:34 of Jericho **345** [+752+2256+4395+8993]
2:37 of Immer **1,052** [+547+2256+9109]
2:60 of Delaiah, Tobiah and Nekoda **652** [+2256+4395+9109+9252]
2:66 They had 736 horses, **245** [+752+2256+4395] mules,
2:67 **435** [+752+2256+4395+8993] camels and 6,720 donkeys.
2:69 of gold, **5,000** [+547] minas of silver and 100 priestly garments.
8:3 Zechariah, and with him were registered **150** [+2256+4395] men;
8:6 descendants of Adin, Ebed son of Jonathan, and with him **50** men;
8:26 I weighed out to them **650** [+2256+4395+9252] talents of silver,
Ne 5:17 Furthermore, a hundred and **fifty** Jews and officials ate at my table,
6:15 the wall was completed on the **twenty-fifth** [+2256+6929] of Elul,
6:15 on the twenty-fifth of Elul, in **fifty-two** [+2256+9109] days.
7:10 of Arah **652** [+2256+4395+9109+9252]
7:12 of Elam **1,254** [+547+752+2256+4395]
7:13 of Zattu **845** [+752+2256+4395+9046]
7:20 of Adin **655** [+2256+2822+4395+9252]
7:20 of Adin **655** [+2256+2822+4395+9252]
7:25 of Gibeon **95** [+2256+9596]
7:33 of the other Nebo **52** [+2256+9109]
7:34 of the other Elam **1,254** [+547+752+2256+4395]
7:36 of Jericho **345** [+752+2256+4395+8993]
7:40 of Immer **1,052** [+547+2256+9109]
7:67 also had **245** [+752+2256+2256+4395] men and women singers.
7:68 [7:67] 736 horses, **245** [+752+2256+4395] [BHS-] mules,
7:69 [7:68] **435** [+752+2256+4395+8993] camels and 6,720 donkeys.
7:70 [7:69] drachmas of gold, **50** bowls and 530 garments for priests.
7:70 [7:69] 50 bowls and **530** [+2256+4395+8993] garments for priests.
Est 5:14 said to him, "Have a gallows built, **seventy-five feet** [+564] high,
7:9 "A gallows **seventy-five feet** [+564] high stands by Haman's
9:6 citadel of Susa, the Jews killed and destroyed **five** hundred men.
9:12 "The Jews have killed and destroyed **five** hundred men and the ten
9:16 They killed **seventy-five** [+2256+8679] thousand of them but did
9:18 then on the **fifteenth** [+6925] they rested and made it a day of
9:21 the fourteenth and **fifteenth** [+6925] days of the month of Adar
Job 1:3 **five** hundred yoke of oxen and five hundred donkeys,
1:3 five hundred yoke of oxen and **five** hundred donkeys,
Isa 3:3 the captain of **fifty** and man of rank, the counselor, skilled
7:8 Within **sixty-five** [+2256+9252] years Ephraim will be too
17:6 four or **five** on the fruitful boughs," declares the LORD, the God
19:18 In that day **five** cities in Egypt will speak the language of Canaan
30:17 at the threat of **five** you will all flee away, till you are left like a
37:36 and **eighty-five** [+2256+9046] thousand men in the Assyrian camp.
38:5 and seen your tears; I will add **fifteen** [+6926] years to your life.
Jer 52:22 The bronze capital on top of the one pillar was **five** cubits high
52:30 **745** [+752+2256+4395+8679] Jews taken into exile by
52:31 on the **twenty-fifth** [+2256+6929] day of the twelfth month.
Eze 1:1 In the thirtieth year, in the fourth month on the **fifth** day, while I
1:2 On the **fifth** of the month—it was the fifth year of the exile of King
8:1 In the sixth year, in the sixth month on the **fifth** day, while I was
8:16 and the altar, were about **twenty-five** [+2256+6929] men.
11:1 at the entrance to the gate were **twenty-five** [+2256+6929] men,
32:17 In the twelfth year, on the **fifteenth** [+6925] day of the month,
33:21 In the twelfth year of our exile, in the tenth month on the **fifth** day,
40:1 In the **twenty-fifth** [+2256+6929] year of our exile, at the
40:7 and the projecting walls between the alcoves were **five** cubits thick.
40:13 distance was **twenty-five** [+2256+6929] cubits from one parapet
40:15 of the gateway to the far end of its portico was **fifty** cubits.
40:21 first gateway. It was **fifty** cubits long and twenty-five cubits wide.
40:21 It was fifty cubits long and **twenty-five** [+2256+6929] cubits wide.
40:25 It was **fifty** cubits long and twenty-five cubits wide.
40:25 It was fifty cubits long and **twenty-five** [+2256+6929] cubits wide.
40:29 It was **fifty** cubits long and twenty-five cubits wide.
40:29 It was fifty cubits long and **twenty-five** [+2256+6929] cubits wide.
40:30 were **twenty-five** [+2256+6929] cubits wide and five cubits deep.)
40:30 the inner court were twenty-five cubits wide and **five** cubits deep.)
40:33 It was **fifty** cubits long and twenty-five cubits wide.
40:33 It was fifty cubits long and **twenty-five** [+2256+6929] cubits wide.
40:36 It was **fifty** cubits long and twenty-five cubits wide.
40:36 It was fifty cubits long and **twenty-five** [+2256+6929] cubits wide.
40:48 the jambs of the portico; they were **five** cubits wide on either side.
40:48 **[RPH]** The width of the entrance was fourteen cubits and its
41:2 and the projecting walls on each side of it were **five** cubits wide.
41:2 **[RPH]** He also measured the outer sanctuary; it was forty cubits
41:9 The outer wall of the side rooms was **five** cubits thick. The open
41:11 the base adjoining the open area was **five** cubits wide all around.
41:12 The wall of the building was **five** cubits thick all around, and its
42:2 door faced north was a hundred cubits long and **fifty** cubits wide.
42:7 the outer court; it extended in front of the rooms for **fifty** cubits.
42:8 of rooms on the side next to the outer court was **fifty** cubits long,
42:16 the east side with the measuring rod; it was **five** hundred cubits.
42:17 the north side; it was **five** hundred cubits by the measuring rod.
42:18 the south side; it was **five** hundred cubits by the measuring rod.
42:19 and measured; it was **five** hundred cubits by the measuring rod.
42:20 around it, **five** hundred cubits long and five hundred cubits wide,
42:20 around it, five hundred cubits long and **five** hundred cubits wide,
45:1 **25,000** [+547+2256+6929] cubits long and 20,000 cubits wide;
45:2 a section **500** [+4395] cubits square is to be for the sanctuary,
45:2 for the sanctuary, **[RPH]** with 50 cubits around it for open land.
45:2 is to be for the sanctuary, with **50** cubits around it for open land.
45:3 measure off a section **25,000** [+547+2256+6929] cubits long and
45:5 An area **25,000** [+547+2256+6929] cubits long and 10,000 cubits
45:6 " 'You are to give the city as its property an area **5,000** [+547]
45:6 area 5,000 cubits wide and **25,000** [+547+2256+6929] cubits long,
45:12 Twenty shekels plus **twenty-five** [+2256+6929] shekels plus
45:12 shekels plus **fifteen** [+2256+6927] shekels equal one mina.
45:25 which begins in the seventh month on the **fifteenth** [+6925] day,
48:8 It will be **25,000** [+547+2256+6929] cubits wide, and its length
48:9 be **25,000** [+547+2256+6929] cubits long and 10,000 cubits wide.
48:10 It will be **25,000** [+547+2256+6929] cubits long on the north side,
48:10 and **25,000** [+547+2256+6929] cubits long on the south side.
48:13 will have an allotment **25,000** [+547+2256+6929] cubits long and
48:13 Its total length will be **25,000** [+547+2256+6929] cubits and its
48:15 remaining area, **5,000** [+547] cubits wide and 25,000 cubits long,
48:15 area, 5,000 cubits wide and **25,000** [+547+2256+6929] cubits long,
48:16 the north side **4,500** [+547+752+2256+4395] cubits, the south side
48:16 the south side **4,500** [+547+752+2256+4395] cubits, the east side
48:16 [south side 4,500 cubits, [K without Q] the east side 4,500 cubits,]
48:16 the east side **4,500** [+547+752+2256+4395] cubits, and the west
48:16 and the west side **4,500** [+547+752+2256+4395] cubits.
48:17 The pastureland for the city will be **250** [+2256+4395] cubits on
48:17 **250** [+2256+4395] cubits on the south, 250 cubits on the east,
48:17 250 cubits on the south, **250** [+2256+4395] cubits on the east,
48:17 250 cubits on the east, and **250** [+2256+4395] cubits on the west.
48:20 a square, **25,000** [+547+2256+6929] cubits on each side.
48:20 **[RPH]** As a special gift you will set aside the sacred portion,
48:21 It will extend eastward from the **25,000** [+547+2256+6929] cubits
48:21 and westward from the **25,000** [+547+2256+6929] cubits to the
48:30 north side, which is **4,500** [+547+752+2256+4395] cubits long,
48:32 "On the east side, which is **4,500** [+547+752+2256+4395] cubits
48:33 south side, which measures **4,500** [+547+752+2256+4395] cubits,
48:34 the west side, which is **4,500** [+547+752+2256+4395] cubits long,
Da 12:12 reaches the end of the **1,335** [+547+2256+4395+8993+8993] days.

Hos 3: 2 So I bought her for **fifteen** [+6925] shekels *of* silver and about a
Hag 2: 16 When anyone went to a wine vat to draw **fifty** measures, there

2823 ¹חֹמֶשׁ **ḥōmeš[1]**, n.[m.]. [1] [√ 2822]

fifth [1]

Ge 47: 26 still in force today—that a **fifth** of the produce belongs to Pharaoh.

2824 ²חֹמֶשׁ **ḥōmeš[2]**, n.m. [4]

stomach [3], belly [1]

2Sa 2: 23 so Abner thrust the butt of his spear into Asahel's **stomach**,
3: 27 his brother Asahel, Joab stabbed him in the **stomach**, and he died.
4: 6 as if to get some wheat, and they stabbed him in the **stomach**.
20: 10 Joab plunged it into his **belly**, and his intestines spilled out on the

2825 חֲמִשִּׁים **ḥamiššîm**, n.pl. Not used in NIV/BHS [√ 2822]

2826 חֲמֻשִׁים **ḥamušîm**, a.pl. Not used in NIV/BHS [√ 2821; cf. 2822]

2827 חֵמֶת **ḥēmet**, n.[m.]. [4]

skin [3], wineskin [1]

Ge 21: 14 took some food and a **skin** *of* water and gave them to Hagar.
21: 15 When the water in the **skin** was gone, she put the boy under one of
21: 19 So she went and filled the **skin** with water and gave the boy a
Hab 2: 15 pouring it from the **wineskin** till they are drunk, so that he can

2828 חֲמָת **ḥamāt**, n.pr.loc. [24] [→ 2832, 2833, 4217]

Hamath [24]

2Sa 8: 9 When Tou king of **Hamath** heard that David had defeated the
2Ki 14: 28 how he recovered for Israel both Damascus and **Hamath**,
17: 24 **Hamath** and Sepharvaim and settled them in the towns of Samaria
17: 30 Cuthah made Nergal, and the men from **Hamath** made Ashima;
18: 34 Where are the gods of **Hamath** and Arpad? Where are the gods of
19: 13 Where is the king of **Hamath**, the king of Arpad, the king of the
23: 33 Pharaoh Neco put him in chains at Riblah in the land of **Hamath**
25: 21 There at Riblah, in the land of **Hamath**, the king had them
1Ch 18: 3 David fought Hadadezer king of Zobah, as far as **Hamath**,
18: 9 When Tou king of **Hamath** heard that David had defeated the
2Ch 8: 4 in the desert and all the store cities he had built in **Hamath**.
Isa 10: 9 Is not **Hamath** like Arpad, and Samaria like Damascus?
11: 11 from Babylonia, from **Hamath** and from the islands of the sea.
36: 19 Where are the gods of **Hamath** and Arpad? Where are the gods of
37: 13 Where is the king of **Hamath**, the king of Arpad, the king of the
Jer 39: 5 Nebuchadnezzar king of Babylon at Riblah in the land of **Hamath**,
49: 23 "**Hamath** and Arpad are dismayed, for they have heard bad news.
52: 9 was taken to the king of Babylon at Riblah in the land of **Hamath**,
52: 27 There at Riblah, in the land of **Hamath**, the king had them
Eze 47: 16 (which lies on the border between Damascus and **Hamath**),
47: 17 border of Damascus, with the border of **Hamath** to the north.
48: 1 the northern border of Damascus next to **Hamath** will be part of its
Am 6: 2 go from there to great **Hamath**, and then go down to Gath in
Zec 9: 2 and upon **Hamath** too, which borders on it, and upon Tyre

2829 ¹חַמַּת **ḥammat[1]**, n.pr.loc. [1] [→ 2831; cf. 2801]

Hammath [1]

Jos 19: 35 fortified cities were Ziddim, Zer, **Hammath**, Rakkath, Kinnereth,

2830 ²חַמַּת **ḥammat[2]**, n.pr.m. [1]

Hammath [1]

1Ch 2: 55 These are the Kenites who came from **Hammath**, the father of the

2831 חַמֹּת דֹּאר **ḥammōt dō'r**, n.pr.loc. [1] [√ 2829 + 1799]

Hammoth Dor [1]

Jos 21: 32 **Hammoth Dor** and Kartan, together with their pasturelands—

2832 חֲמַת צוֹבָה **ḥamāt ṣôbâ**, n.pr.loc. [1] [√ 2828 + 7420]

Hamath Zobah [1]

2Ch 8: 3 Solomon then went to **Hamath Zobah** and captured it.

2833 חֲמָתִי **ḥamātî**, a.g. [2] [√ 2828; cf. 2801]

Hamathites [2]

Ge 10: 18 Arvadites, Zemarites and **Hamathites**. Later the Canaanite clans
1Ch 1: 16 Arvadites, Zemarites and **Hamathites**.

2834 ¹חֵן **ḥēn[1]**, n.m. [69] [→ 2836, 2839, 2855; cf. 2858; *also used with compound proper names*]

favor [41], grace [5], pleased with [+928+5162+6524] [5], favorably disposed toward [+928+6524] [3], bless [2], gracious [2], alluring [+3202] [1], charm [+74] [1], charm [1], displease [+928+4202+5162+6524] [1], displeasing [+928+4202+5162+6524] [1], esteemed [1], favorable toward [+928+5162+6524] [1], graceful [1], kindhearted [1], ornament to grace [1], pleased with [+928+5951+6524] [1]

Ge 6: 8 But Noah found **favor** in the eyes of the LORD.
18: 3 He said, "If I have found **favor** in your eyes, my lord, do not pass
19: 19 Your servant has found **favor** in your eyes, and you have shown
30: 27 Laban said to him, "If I have found **favor** in your eyes, please stay.
32: 5 [32:6] message to my lord, that I may find **favor** in your eyes.' "
33: 8 droves I met?" "To find **favor** in your eyes, my lord," he said.
33: 10 "If I have found **favor** in your eyes, accept this gift from me.
33: 15 Jacob asked. "Just let me find **favor** in the eyes of my lord."
34: 11 to Dinah's father and brothers, "Let me find **favor** in your eyes,
39: 4 Joseph found **favor** in his eyes and became his attendant. Potiphar
39: 21 and granted him **favor** in the eyes of the prison warden.
47: 25 "May we find **favor** in the eyes of our lord; we will be in bondage
47: 29 his son Joseph and said to him, "If I have found **favor** in your eyes,
50: 4 "If I have found **favor** in your eyes, speak to Pharaoh for me.
Ex 3: 21 Egyptians **favorably** [+928+6524] **disposed toward** this people,
11: 3 Egyptians **favorably** [+928+6524] **disposed toward** the people,
12: 36 Egyptians **favorably** [+928+6524] **disposed toward** the people,
33: 12 'I know you by name and you have found **favor** with me.'
33: 13 If you *are* **pleased** [+928+5162+6524] **with** *me*, teach me your
33: 13 your ways so I may know you and continue to find **favor** with you.
33: 16 anyone know that you *are* **pleased** [+928+5162+6524] **with** me
33: 17 because I *am* **pleased** [+928+5162+6524] **with** *you* and I know
34: 9 "O Lord, if I have found **favor** in your eyes," he said, "then let the
Nu 11: 11 What *have I done to* **displease** [+928+4202+5162+6524] you that
11: 15 put me to death right now—if I have found **favor** in your eyes—
32: 5 If we have found **favor** in your eyes," they said, "let this land be
Dt 24: 1 who becomes **displeasing** [+928+4202+5162+6524] *to* him
Jdg 6: 17 Gideon replied, "If now I have found **favor** in your eyes, give me a
Ru 2: 2 up the leftover grain behind anyone in whose eyes I find **favor**."
2: 10 "Why have I found such **favor** in your eyes that you notice me—
2: 13 "May I continue to find **favor** in your eyes, my lord," she said.
1Sa 1: 18 She said, "May your servant find **favor** in your eyes." Then she
16: 22 in my service, for I *am* **pleased with him** [+928+5162+6524]."
20: 3 "Your father knows very well that I have found **favor** in your eyes,
20: 29 If I have found **favor** in your eyes, let me get away to see my
25: 8 Therefore *be* **favorable** [+928+5162+6524] **toward** my young
27: 5 Then David said to Achish, "If I have found **favor** in your eyes,
2Sa 14: 22 "Today your servant knows that he has found **favor** in your eyes,
15: 25 If I find **favor** in the LORD's eyes, he will bring me back
16: 4 Ziba said. "May I find **favor** in your eyes, my lord the king."
1Ki 11: 19 Pharaoh *was* so **pleased** [+928+5162+6524] **with** Hadad that he
Est 2: 15 suggested. And Esther won the **favor** of everyone who saw her.
2: 17 she won his **favor** and approval more than any of the other virgins.
5: 2 he *was* **pleased** [+928+5951+6524] **with** *her* and held out to her
5: 8 If the king regards me with **favor** and if it pleases the king to grant
7: 3 "If I have found **favor** with you, O king, and if it pleases your
8: 5 "and if he regards me with **favor** and thinks it the right thing to do,
Ps 45: 2 [45:3] of men and your lips have been anointed with **grace**,
84: 11 [84:12] is a sun and shield; the LORD bestows **favor** and honor;
Pr 1: 9 They will be a garland to **grace** your head and a chain to adorn
3: 4 Then you will win **favor** and a good name in the sight of God
3: 22 they will be life for you, an **ornament to grace** your neck.
3: 34 He mocks proud mockers but gives **grace** to the humble.
4: 9 She will set a garland of **grace** on your head and present you with
5: 19 A loving doe, a **graceful** deer—may her breasts satisfy you
11: 16 A **kindhearted** woman gains respect, but ruthless men gain only
13: 15 Good understanding wins **favor**, but the way of the unfaithful is
17: 8 A bribe is a **charm** [+74] to the one who gives it; wherever he
22: 1 than great riches; to be **esteemed** is better than silver or gold.
22: 11 and whose speech is **gracious** will have the king for his friend.
28: 23 He who rebukes a man will in the end gain more **favor** than he
31: 30 **Charm** is deceptive, and beauty is fleeting; but a woman who fears
Ecc 9: 11 come to the wise or wealth to the brilliant or **favor** to the learned;
10: 12 Words from a wise man's mouth are **gracious**, but a fool is
Jer 31: 2 "The people who survive the sword will find **favor** in the desert;
Na 3: 4 all because of the wanton lust of a harlot, **alluring** [+3202],
Zec 4: 7 Then he will bring out the capstone to shouts of 'God **bless** it!
4: 7 bring out the capstone to shouts of 'God **bless** it! God **bless** it!' "
12: 10 and the inhabitants of Jerusalem a spirit of **grace** and supplication.

2835 ²חֵן **ḥēn[2]**, n.pr.m. [1] [√ 2858]

Hen [1]

Zec 6: 14 **Hen** son of Zephaniah as a memorial in the temple of the LORD.

[F] Hitpael (hitpoel, hitpoal, hitpolel, hitpolal, hitpalel, hitpalal, hitpalpel, hitpalpal, hotpael, hotpaal) [G] Hiphil (hiphtil) [H] Hophal [I] Hishtaphel

2836 חֲנָדָד ḥēnādād, n.pr.m. [4] [√ 2834 + 2060]

Henadad [4]

Ezr 3: 9 the sons of **Henadad** and their sons and brothers—all Levites—
Ne 3: 18 were made by their countrymen under Binnui son of **Henadad**,
3: 24 Next to him, Binnui son of **Henadad** repaired another section,
10: 9 [10:10] son of Azaniah, Binnui of the sons of **Henadad**, Kadmiel,

2837 חָנָה¹ ḥānâ¹, v. [143] [→ 2844, 4722, 4724, 9381, 9386?]

camped [77], encamped [12], camp [11], encamp [9], *untranslated* [4], set up camp [4], took up positions [3], besiege [+6584] [2], made camp [2], pitched camp [2], set up tents [2], attacked [1], besieged [+6584] [1], besieged [+928] [1], camping [1], defend [1], encamps [1], laid siege to [+6584] [1], living [1], nearly over [1], remain in camp [1], remained in camp [1], set up [1], settle [1], settled [1], stay [1]

Ge 26: 17 [A] and **encamped** in the Valley of Gerar and settled there.
33: 18 [A] of Shechem in Canaan and **camped** within sight of the city.
Ex 13: 20 [A] After leaving Succoth *they* **camped** at Etham on the edge of
14: 2 [A] the Israelites to turn back and **encamp** near Pi Hahiroth,
14: 2 [A] *They are to* **encamp** by the sea, directly opposite Baal
14: 9 [A] overtook them *as they* **camped** by the sea near Pi Hahiroth,
15: 27 [A] seventy palm trees, and *they* **camped** there near the water.
17: 1 [A] *They* **camped** at Rephidim, but there was no water for the
18: 5 [A] the desert, where he *was* **camped** near the mountain of God.
19: 2 [A] Israel **camped** there in the desert in front of the mountain.
19: 2 [A] Israel camped there in the desert **[RPH]** in front of the
Nu 1: 50 [A] they are to take care of it and **encamp** around it.
1: 51 [A] whenever the tabernacle *is to be* **set up**, the Levites shall do
1: 52 [A] The Israelites *are to* **set up** their **tents** by divisions,
1: 53 [A] *are to* **set up** their **tents** around the tabernacle of the
2: 2 [A] "The Israelites *are to* **camp** around the Tent of Meeting
2: 2 [A] around the Tent of Meeting **[RPH]** some distance from it,
2: 3 [A] the divisions of the camp of Judah *are to* **encamp** under their
2: 5 [A] The tribe of Issachar *will* **camp** next to them. The leader of
2: 12 [A] The tribe of Simeon *will* **camp** next to them. The leader of
2: 17 [A] They will set out in the same order as *they* **encamp**, each in
2: 27 [A] The tribe of Asher *will* **camp** next to them. The leader of the
2: 34 [A] that is the way *they* **encamped** under their standards,
3: 23 [A] The Gershonite clans *were to* **camp** on the west,
3: 29 [A] The Kohathite clans *were to* **camp** on the south side of the
3: 35 [A] *they were to* **camp** on the north side of the tabernacle.
3: 38 [A] and his sons *were to* **camp** to the east of the tabernacle,
9: 17 [A] set out; wherever the cloud settled, the Israelites **encamped**.
9: 18 [A] the Israelites set out, and at his command *they* **encamped**.
9: 18 [A] cloud stayed over the tabernacle, *they* **remained in camp**.
9: 20 [A] at the LORD's command *they would* **encamp**, and then at
9: 22 [A] a year, the Israelites *would* **remain in camp** and not set out;
9: 23 [A] At the LORD's command *they* **encamped**, and at the
10: 5 [A] blast is sounded, the tribes **camping** on the east are to set out.
10: 6 [A] a second blast, the camps **[RPH]** on the south are to set out.
10: 31 [A] You know where we *should* **camp** in the desert, and you can
12: 16 [A] people left Hazeroth and **encamped** in the Desert of Paran.
21: 10 [A] The Israelites moved on and **camped** at Oboth.
21: 11 [A] Then they set out from Oboth and **camped** in Iye Abarim,
21: 12 [A] From there they moved on and **camped** in the Zered Valley.
21: 13 [A] They set out from there and **camped** alongside the Arnon,
22: 1 [A] of Moab and **camped** along the Jordan across from Jericho.
31: 19 [A] or touched anyone who was killed *must* **stay** outside the
33: 5 [A] The Israelites left Rameses and **camped** at Succoth.
33: 6 [A] They left Succoth and **camped** at Etham, on the edge of the
33: 7 [A] to the east of Baal Zephon, and **camped** near Migdol.
33: 8 [A] three days in the Desert of Etham, *they* **camped** at Marah.
33: 9 [A] and seventy palm trees, and *they* **camped** there.
33: 10 [A] They left Elim and **camped** by the Red Sea.
33: 11 [A] They left the Red Sea and **camped** in the Desert of Sin.
33: 12 [A] They left the Desert of Sin and **camped** at Dophkah.
33: 13 [A] They left Dophkah and **camped** at Alush.
33: 14 [A] They left Alush and **camped** at Rephidim, where there was
33: 15 [A] They left Rephidim and **camped** in the Desert of Sinai.
33: 16 [A] left the Desert of Sinai and **camped** at Kibroth Hattaavah.
33: 17 [A] They left Kibroth Hattaavah and **camped** at Hazeroth.
33: 18 [A] They left Hazeroth and **camped** at Rithmah.
33: 19 [A] They left Rithmah and **camped** at Rimmon Perez.
33: 20 [A] They left Rimmon Perez and **camped** at Libnah.
33: 21 [A] They left Libnah and **camped** at Rissah.
33: 22 [A] They left Rissah and **camped** at Kehelathah.
33: 23 [A] They left Kehelathah and **camped** at Mount Shepher.
33: 24 [A] They left Mount Shepher and **camped** at Haradah.
33: 25 [A] They left Haradah and **camped** at Makheloth.
33: 26 [A] They left Makheloth and **camped** at Tahath.
33: 27 [A] They left Tahath and **camped** at Terah.
33: 28 [A] They left Terah and **camped** at Mithcah.
33: 29 [A] They left Mithcah and **camped** at Hashmonah.
33: 30 [A] They left Hashmonah and **camped** at Moseroth.
33: 31 [A] They left Moseroth and **camped** at Bene Jaakan.
33: 32 [A] They left Bene Jaakan and **camped** at Hor Haggidgad.
33: 33 [A] They left Hor Haggidgad and **camped** at Jotbathah.
33: 34 [A] They left Jotbathah and **camped** at Abronah.
33: 35 [A] They left Abronah and **camped** at Ezion Geber.
33: 36 [A] They left Ezion Geber and **camped** at Kadesh, in the Desert
33: 37 [A] They left Kadesh and **camped** at Mount Hor, on the border
33: 41 [A] They left Mount Hor and **camped** at Zalmonah.
33: 42 [A] They left Zalmonah and **camped** at Punon.
33: 43 [A] They left Punon and **camped** at Oboth.
33: 44 [A] They left Oboth and **camped** at Iye Abarim, on the border of
33: 45 [A] They left Iyim and **camped** at Dibon Gad.
33: 46 [A] They left Dibon Gad and **camped** at Almon Diblathaim.
33: 47 [A] Almon Diblathaim and **camped** in the mountains of Abarim,
33: 48 [A] **camped** on the plains of Moab by the Jordan across from
33: 49 [A] There on the plains of Moab *they* **camped** along the Jordan
Dt 1: 33 [A] to search out places for you to **camp** and to show you the
Jos 4: 19 [A] and **camped** at Gilgal on the eastern border of Jericho.
5: 10 [A] *while* **camped** at Gilgal on the plains of Jericho,
8: 11 [A] *They* **set up camp** north of Ai, with the valley between them
10: 5 [A] and **took up positions** against Gibeon and attacked it.
10: 31 [A] to Lachish; *he* **took up positions** against it and attacked it.
10: 34 [A] to Eglon; *they* **took up positions** against it and attacked it.
11: 5 [A] and **made camp** together at the Waters of Merom,
Jdg 6: 4 [A] *They* **camped** on the land and ruined the crops all the way to
6: 33 [A] crossed over the Jordan and **camped** in the Valley of Jezreel.
7: 1 [A] Gideon) and all his men **camped** at the spring of Harod.
9: 50 [A] went to Thebez and **besieged** [+928] it and captured it.
10: 17 [A] the Ammonites were called to arms and **camped** in Gilead,
10: 17 [A] in Gilead, the Israelites assembled and **camped** at Mizpah.
11: 18 [A] of Moab, and **camped** on the other side of the Arnon.
11: 20 [A] all his men and **encamped** at Jahaz and fought with Israel.
15: 9 [A] The Philistines went up and **camped** in Judah, spreading out
18: 12 [A] On their way *they* **set up camp** near Kiriath Jearim in Judah.
19: 9 [A] Spend the night here; the day *is* **nearly over**. Stay and enjoy
20: 19 [A] morning the Israelites got up and **pitched camp** near Gibeah.
1Sa 4: 1 [A] The Israelites **camped** at Ebenezer, and the Philistines at
4: 1 [A] camped at Ebenezer, and the Philistines **[RPH]** at Aphek.
11: 1 [A] the Ammonite went up and **besieged** [+6584] Jabesh Gilead.
13: 5 [A] They went up and **camped** at Micmash, east of Beth Aven.
13: 16 [A] in Benjamin, while the Philistines **camped** at Micmash.
17: 1 [A] *They* **pitched camp** at Ephes Dammim, between Socoh
17: 2 [A] the Israelites assembled and **camped** in the Valley of Elah
26: 3 [A] Saul **made** *his* **camp** beside the road on the hill of Hakilah
26: 5 [A] David set out and went to the place where Saul *had* **camped**.
26: 5 [A] lying inside the camp, with the army **encamped** around him.
28: 4 [A] Philistines assembled and came and **set up camp** at Shunem,
28: 4 [A] Saul gathered all the Israelites and **set up camp** at Gilboa.
29: 1 [A] forces at Aphek, and Israel **camped** by the spring in Jezreel.
2Sa 11: 11 [A] and my lord's men *are* **camped** in the open fields.
12: 28 [A] rest of the troops and **besiege** [+6584] the city and capture it.
17: 26 [A] The Israelites and Absalom **camped** *in* the land of Gilead.
23: 13 [A] while a band of Philistines *was* **encamped** in the Valley of
24: 5 [A] After crossing the Jordan, *they* **camped** near Aroer, south of
1Ki 16: 15 [A] The army *was* **encamped** near Gibbethon, a Philistine town.
16: 16 [A] When the Israelites in the **camp** heard that Zimri had plotted
20: 27 [A] The Israelites **camped** opposite them like two small flocks of
20: 29 [A] For seven days they **camped** opposite each other, and on the
2Ki 25: 1 [A] *He* **encamped** outside the city and built siege works all
1Ch 11: 15 [A] while a band of Philistines *was* **encamped** in the Valley of
19: 7 [A] with his troops, who came and **camped** near Medeba,
2Ch 32: 1 [A] *He* **laid siege** [+6584] **to** the fortified cities, thinking to
Ezr 8: 15 [A] that flows toward Ahava, and *we* **camped** there three days.
Ne 11: 30 [A] So *they were* **living** all the way from Beersheba to the
Job 19: 12 [A] build a siege ramp against me and **encamp** around my tent.
Ps 27: 3 [A] Though an army **besiege** [+6584] me, my heart will not fear;
34: 7 [34:8] [A] The angel of the LORD **encamps** around those who
53: 5 [53:6] [A] God scattered the bones of *those who* **attacked** you;
Isa 29: 1 [A] Woe to you, Ariel, Ariel, the city where David **settled**!
29: 3 [A] *I will* **encamp** against you all around; I will encircle you
Jer 50: 29 [A] **Encamp** all around her; let no one escape. Repay her for her
52: 4 [A] *They* **camped** outside the city and built siege works all
Na 3: 17 [A] your officials like swarms of locusts that **settle** in the walls
Zec 9: 8 [A] *I will* **defend** my house against marauding forces. Never

2838 חָנָה² ḥānâ², v. Not used in NIV/BHS

2839 חַנָּה ḥannâ, n.pr.f. [13] [√ 2834; cf. 2858]

Hannah [12], her[s] [1]

1Sa 1: 2 He had two wives; one was called **Hannah** and the other Peninnah.
1: 2 the other Peninnah. Peninnah had children, but **Hannah** had none.
1: 5 But to **Hannah** he gave a double portion because he loved her,

1Sa 1: 5 But to Hannah he gave a double portion because he loved **her**[s],
1: 8 her husband would say to her, "**Hannah**, why are you weeping?
1: 9 they had finished eating and drinking in Shiloh, **Hannah** stood up.
1: 13 **Hannah** was praying in her heart, and her lips were moving
1: 15 "Not so, my lord," **Hannah** replied, "I am a woman who is deeply
1: 19 Elkanah lay with **Hannah** his wife, and the LORD remembered
1: 20 So in the course of time **Hannah** conceived and gave birth to a
1: 22 **Hannah** did not go. She said to her husband, "After the boy is
2: 1 Then **Hannah** prayed and said: "My heart rejoices in the LORD;
2: 21 And the LORD was gracious to **Hannah**; she conceived

2840 [1]חֲנוֹךְ ***ḥᵃnôk***[1], n.pr.m. [16] [→ 2841, 2854; cf. 2849, 2852]

Enoch [10], Hanoch [6]

Ge 4: 17 with his wife, and she became pregnant and gave birth to **Enoch**.
4: 17 Cain was then building a city, and he named it after his son **Enoch**.
4: 18 To **Enoch** was born Irad, and Irad was the father of Mehujael,
5: 18 When Jared had lived 162 years, he became the father of **Enoch**.
5: 19 And after he became the father of **Enoch**, Jared lived 800 years
5: 21 When **Enoch** had lived 65 years, he became the father of
5: 22 **Enoch** walked with God 300 years and had other sons
5: 23 Altogether, **Enoch** lived 365 years.
5: 24 **Enoch** walked with God; then he was no more, because God took
25: 4 sons of Midian were Ephah, Epher, **Hanoch**, Abida and Eldaah.
46: 9 The sons of Reuben: **Hanoch**, Pallu, Hezron and Carmi.
Ex 6: 14 The sons of Reuben the firstborn son of Israel were **Hanoch**
Nu 26: 5 through **Hanoch**, the Hanochite clan; through Pallu, the Palluite
1Ch 1: 3 **Enoch**, Methuselah, Lamech, Noah.
1: 33 The sons of Midian: Ephah, Epher, **Hanoch**, Abida and Eldaah.
5: 3 Reuben the firstborn of Israel: **Hanoch**, Pallu, Hezron and Carmi.

2841 [2]חֲנוֹךְ ***ḥᵃnôk***[2], n.pr.loc. Not used in NIV/BHS [√ 2840; cf. 2852]

2842 חָנוּן ***ḥānûn***, n.pr.m. [11] [√ 2858]

Hanun [11]

2Sa 10: 1 of the Ammonites died, and his son **Hanun** succeeded him as king.
10: 2 David thought, "I will show kindness to **Hanun** son of Nahash,
10: 3 the Ammonite nobles said to **Hanun** their lord, "Do you think
10: 4 So **Hanun** seized David's men, shaved off half of each man's
1Ch 19: 2 David thought, "I will show kindness to **Hanun** son of Nahash,
19: 2 When David's men came to **Hanun** in the land of the Ammonites
19: 3 the Ammonite nobles said to **Hanun**, "Do you think David is
19: 4 So **Hanun** seized David's men, shaved them, cut off their
19: 6 **Hanun** and the Ammonites sent a thousand talents of silver to hire
Ne 3: 13 The Valley Gate was repaired by **Hanun** and the residents of
3: 30 and **Hanun**, the sixth son of Zalaph, repaired another section.

2843 חַנּוּן ***ḥannûn***, a. [13] [√ 2858]

gracious [12], compassionate [1]

Ex 22: 27 [22:26] he cries out to me, I will hear, for I am **compassionate**.
34: 6 the LORD, the compassionate and **gracious** God, slow to anger,
2Ch 30: 9 for the LORD your God is **gracious** and compassionate.
Ne 9: 17 **gracious** and compassionate, slow to anger and abounding in love.
9: 31 or abandon them, for you are a **gracious** and merciful God.
Ps 86: 15 you, O Lord, are a compassionate and **gracious** God, slow to
103: 8 The LORD is compassionate and **gracious**, slow to anger,
111: 4 to be remembered; the LORD is **gracious** and compassionate.
112: 4 for the **gracious** and compassionate and righteous man.
116: 5 The LORD is **gracious** and righteous; our God is full of
145: 8 The LORD is **gracious** and compassionate, slow to anger
Joel 2: 13 for he is **gracious** and compassionate, slow to anger and abounding
Jnh 4: 2 I knew that you are a **gracious** and compassionate God, slow to

2844 חָנוּת ***ḥānût***, n.f. [1] [√ 2837]

vaulted cell [1]

Jer 37: 16 Jeremiah was put into a **vaulted cell** in a dungeon, where he

2845 [1]חָנַט ***ḥānaṭ***[1], v. [1] [→ 2636]

forms [1]

SS 2: 13 [A] The fig tree **forms** its early fruit; the blossoming vines spread

2846 [2]חָנַט ***ḥānaṭ***[2], v. [3] [→ 2847]

embalmed [2], embalm [1]

Ge 50: 2 [A] Joseph directed the physicians in his service to **embalm** his
50: 2 [A] embalm his father Israel. So the physicians **embalmed** him,
50: 26 [A] after *they* **embalmed** him, he was placed in a coffin in

2847 חֲנֻטִים ***ḥᵃnuṭîm***, n.[m.]pl.abst. [1] [√ 2846]

embalming [1]

Ge 50: 3 a full forty days, for that was the time required for **embalming**.

2848 חַנִּיאֵל ***ḥannî'ēl***, n.pr.m. [2] [√ 2858 + 446]

Hanniel [2]

Nu 34: 23 **Hanniel** son of Ephod, the leader from the tribe of Manasseh son
1Ch 7: 39 The sons of Ulla: Arah, **Hanniel** and Rizia.

2849 חָנִיךְ ***ḥānîk***, a. [1] [√ 2852; cf. 2840]

trained men [1]

Ge 14: 14 he called out the 318 **trained men** born in his household and went

2850 חֲנִינָה ***ḥᵃnînâ***, n.f. [1] [√ 2858]

favor [1]

Jer 16: 13 will serve other gods day and night, for I will show you no **favor**.'

2851 חֲנִית ***ḥᵃnît***, n.f. [48]

spear [38], spears [8], it[s] [+2021] [1], its[s] [1]

1Sa 13: 19 had said, "Otherwise the Hebrews will make swords or **spears**!"
13: 22 a soldier with Saul and Jonathan had a sword or **spear** in his hand;
17: 7 His **spear** shaft was like a weaver's rod, and its iron point weighed
17: 7 a weaver's rod, and **its**[s] iron point weighed six hundred shekels.
17: 45 "You come against me with sword and **spear** and javelin,
17: 47 will know that it is not by sword or **spear** that the LORD saves;
18: 10 playing the harp, as he usually did. Saul had a **spear** in his hand
18: 11 he hurled **it**[s] [+2021], saying to himself, "I'll pin David to the
19: 9 upon Saul as he was sitting in his house with his **spear** in his hand.
19: 10 Saul tried to pin him to the wall with his **spear**, but David eluded
19: 10 but David eluded him as Saul drove the **spear** into the wall.
20: 33 Saul hurled his **spear** at him to kill him. Then Jonathan knew that
21: 8 [21:9] "Don't you have a **spear** or a sword here?
22: 6 Saul, **spear** in hand, was seated under the tamarisk tree on the hill
26: 7 lying asleep inside the camp with his **spear** stuck in the ground
26: 8 Now let me pin him to the ground with one thrust of my **spear**;
26: 11 Now get the **spear** and water jug that are near his head, and let's
26: 12 So David took the **spear** and water jug near Saul's head, and they
26: 16 Where are the king's **spear** and water jug that were near his head?"
26: 22 "Here is the king's **spear**," David answered.
2Sa 1: 6 leaning on his **spear**, with the chariots and riders almost upon him.
2: 23 so Abner thrust the butt of his **spear** into Asahel's stomach,
2: 23 into Asahel's stomach, and the **spear** came out through his back.
21: 19 the Gittite, who had a **spear** with a shaft like a weaver's rod.
23: 7 Whoever touches thorns uses a tool of iron or the shaft of a **spear**;
23: 8 he raised his **spear** against eight hundred men, whom he killed in
23: 18 He raised his **spear** against three hundred men, whom he killed,
23: 21 Although the Egyptian had a **spear** in his hand, Benaiah went
23: 21 He snatched the **spear** from the Egyptian's hand and killed him
23: 21 spear from the Egyptian's hand and killed him with his own **spear**.
2Ki 11: 10 he gave the commanders the **spears** and shields that had belonged
1Ch 11: 11 he raised his **spear** against three hundred men, whom he killed in
11: 20 He raised his **spear** against three hundred men, whom he killed,
11: 23 Although the Egyptian had a **spear** like a weaver's rod in his hand,
11: 23 He snatched the **spear** from the Egyptian's hand and killed him
11: 23 spear from the Egyptian's hand and killed him with his own **spear**.
12: 34 [12:35] together with 37,000 men carrying shields and **spears**;
20: 5 the Gittite, who had a **spear** with a shaft like a weaver's rod.
2Ch 23: 9 Then he gave the commanders of units of a hundred the **spears**
Job 39: 23 rattles against his side, along with the flashing **spear** and lance.
41: 26 [41:18] has no effect, nor does the **spear** or the dart or the javelin.
Ps 35: 3 Brandish **spear** and javelin against those who pursue me. Say to
46: 9 [46:10] he breaks the bow and shatters the **spear**, he burns the
57: 4 [57:5] men whose teeth are **spears** and arrows, whose tongues are
Isa 2: 4 their swords into plowshares and their **spears** into pruning hooks.
Mic 4: 3 their swords into plowshares and their **spears** into pruning hooks.
Na 3: 3 Charging cavalry, flashing swords and glittering **spears**! Many
Hab 3: 11 glint of your flying arrows, at the lightning of your flashing **spear**.

2852 חָנַךְ ***ḥānak***, v. [5] [→ 2840, 2841, 2849, 2853, 2854]

dedicated [3], dedicate [1], train [1]

Dt 20: 5 [A] "Has anyone built a new house and not **dedicated** it? Let him
20: 5 [A] or he may die in battle and someone else *may* **dedicate** it.
1Ki 8: 63 [A] and all the Israelites **dedicated** the temple of the LORD.
2Ch 7: 5 [A] So the king and all the people **dedicated** the temple of God.
Pr 22: 6 [A] **Train** a child in the way he should go, and when he is old he

2853 חֲנֻכָּה ***ḥᵃnukkâ***, n.f. [8] [√ 2852; Ar 10273]

dedication [6], offerings for dedication [2]

Nu 7: 10 the leaders brought their offerings for its **dedication** and presented

Nu 7:11 "Each day one leader is to bring his offering for the **dedication** *of*
7:84 **offerings** of the Israelite leaders **for** the **dedication** *of* the altar
7:88 These were the **offerings for** the **dedication** *of* the altar after it
2Ch 7:9 for they had celebrated the **dedication** *of* the altar for seven days
Ne 12:27 At the **dedication** *of* the wall of Jerusalem, the Levites were
12:27 were brought to Jerusalem to celebrate joyfully the **dedication**
Ps 30:T [30:1] A psalm. A song. For the **dedication** *of* the temple.

2854 חֲנֹכִי ḥᵃnōkî, a.g. [1] [√ 2840; cf. 2852]

Hanochite [1]

Nu 26:5 through Hanoch, the **Hanochite** clan; through Pallu, the Palluite

2855 חִנָּם ḥinnām, subst.adv. [32] [√ 2834; cf. 2858]

without cause [7], for nothing [5], for no reason [4], needless [2], useless [2], without reason [2], at no cost [1], cost nothing [1], costs nothing [1], harmless soul [+5929] [1], in vain [+448] [1], innocent [1], undeserved [1], without any payment [+401] [1], without any reason [1], without paying anything [1]

Ge 29:15 you are a relative of mine, should you work for me **for nothing**?
Ex 21:2 in the seventh year, he shall go free, **without paying anything**.
21:11 she is to go free, **without** [+401] **any payment** of money.
Nu 11:5 We remember the fish we ate in Egypt **at no cost**—also the
1Sa 19:5 to an innocent man like David by killing him **for no reason**?"
25:31 on his conscience the staggering burden of **needless** bloodshed
2Sa 24:24 to the LORD my God burnt offerings that **cost** me **nothing**."
1Ki 2:31 my father's house of the guilt of the **innocent** blood that Joab shed.
1Ch 21:24 what is yours, or sacrifice a burnt offering that **costs** me **nothing**."
Job 1:9 "Does Job fear God **for nothing**?" Satan replied.
2:3 you incited me against him to ruin him **without any reason**."
9:17 crush me with a storm and multiply my wounds **for no reason**.
22:6 You demanded security from your brothers **for no reason**;
Ps 35:7 Since they hid their net for me **without cause** and without cause
35:7 their net for me without cause and **without cause** dug a pit for me,
35:19 let not those who hate me **without reason** maliciously wink the
69:4 [69:5] Those who hate me **without reason** outnumber the hairs of
109:3 words of hatred they surround me; they attack me **without cause**.
119:161 Rulers persecute me **without cause**, but my heart trembles at your
Pr 1:11 for someone's blood, let's waylay some **harmless soul** [+5929];
1:17 How **useless** to spread a net in full view of all the birds!
3:30 Do not accuse a man **for no reason**—when he has done you no
23:29 Who has strife? Who has complaints? Who has **needless** bruises?
24:28 Do not testify against your neighbor **without cause**, or use your
26:2 or a darting swallow, an **undeserved** curse does not come to rest.
Isa 52:3 "You were sold **for nothing**, and without money you will be
52:5 "For my people have been taken away **for nothing**, and those who
Jer 22:13 rooms by injustice, making his countrymen work **for nothing**,
La 3:52 Those who were my enemies **without cause** hunted me like a bird.
Eze 6:10 I did not threaten **in vain** [+448] to bring this calamity on them.
14:23 for you will know that I have done nothing in it **without cause**,
Mal 1:10 temple doors, so that you would not light **useless** fires on my altar!

2856 חֲנַמְאֵל ḥᵃnam'ēl, n.pr.m. [4] [√ 2834 + 446]

Hanamel [4]

Jer 32:7 **Hanamel** son of Shallum your uncle is going to come to you
32:8 my cousin **Hanamel** came to me in the courtyard of the guard
32:9 so I bought the field at Anathoth from my cousin **Hanamel**
32:12 in the presence of my cousin **Hanamel** and of the witnesses who

2857 חֲנָמָל ḥᵃnāmal, n.[m.] [1] [√ 2798]

sleet [1]

Ps 78:47 destroyed their vines with hail and their sycamore-figs with **sleet**.

2858 ¹חָנַן ḥānan¹, v. [78 / 77] [→ 2665, 2834, 2835, 2839, 2842, 2843, 2850, 2855, 2860, 9380?, 9382, 9383, 9384, 9385?; Ar 10274; *also used with compound proper names*]

have mercy [14], gracious [13], merciful [8], kind [4], plead [3], begged [2], generous [2], gracious [+2858] [2], have pity [2], making supplication [2], pleaded [2], show mercy [2], beg for mercy [1], beg [1], begged for favor [1], charming [1], cried for mercy [1], do a kindness [1], favor [1], generously [1], gets mercy [1], grace is shown [1], graciously given [1], lift up for mercy [1], made[s] [1], moves to pity [1], pity [1], plead for mercy [1], prayed [1], show favor [1], shows favor [1], shows mercy [1], take pity [1]

Ge 33:5 [A] "They are the children God *has* **graciously given** your
33:11 [A] for God *has been* **gracious** *to* me and I have all I need."
42:21 [F] We saw how distressed he was when he **pleaded** with us *for*
43:29 [A] me about?" And he said, "God *be* **gracious** *to* you, my son."
Ex 33:19 [A] *I will* **have mercy** *on* whom I will have mercy, and I will
33:19 [A] I will have mercy on whom *I will* **have mercy**, and I will
Nu 6:25 [A] make his face shine upon you and *be* **gracious** *to* you;
Dt 3:23 [F] At that time *I* **pleaded** with the LORD:
7:2 [A] Make no treaty with them, and **show** them no **mercy**.
28:50 [A] nation without respect for the old or **pity** *for* the young.
Jdg 21:22 [A] we will say to them, '**Do us a kindness** by helping them,
2Sa 12:22 [A] The LORD *may be* **gracious** *to* me and let the child live.'
1Ki 8:33 [F] and **making supplication** to you in this temple,
8:47 [F] and **plead** with you in the land of their conquerors and say,
8:59 [F] words of mine, which *I have* **prayed** before the LORD,
9:3 [F] "I have heard the prayer and plea *you have* **made**[s] before me;
2Ki 1:13 [F] "Man of God," *he* **begged**, "please have respect for my life
13:23 [A] But the LORD *was* **gracious** *to* them and had compassion
2Ch 6:24 [F] praying and **making supplication** before you in this temple,
6:37 [F] and **plead** with you in the land of their captivity and say,
Est 4:8 [F] to urge her to go into the king's presence to **beg for mercy**
8:3 [F] *She* **begged** him to put an end to the evil plan of Haman the
Job 8:5 [F] But if you will look to God and **plead** with the Almighty,
9:15 [F] answer him; *I could* only **plead** with my Judge **for mercy**.
19:16 [F] he does not answer, though *I* **beg** him with my own mouth.
19:21 [A] "**Have pity** *on* me, my friends, have pity, for the hand of
19:21 [A] "Have pity on me, my friends, **have pity**, for the hand of God
33:24 [A] *to be* **gracious** *to* him and say, 'Spare him from going down
Ps 4:1 [4:2] [A] my distress; *be* **merciful** *to* me and hear my prayer.
6:2 [6:3] [A] *Be* **merciful** *to* me, LORD, for I am faint; O LORD,
9:13 [9:14] [A] **Have mercy** and lift me up from the gates of death,
25:16 [A] Turn to me and *be* **gracious** *to* me, for I am lonely
26:11 [A] I lead a blameless life; redeem me and *be* **merciful** *to* me.
27:7 [A] when I call, O LORD; *be* **merciful** *to* me and answer me.
30:8 [30:9] [F] O LORD, I called; to the Lord *I* **cried for mercy**:
30:10 [30:11] [A] Hear, O LORD, and *be* **merciful** *to* me;
31:9 [31:10] [A] *Be* **merciful** *to* me, O LORD, for I am in distress;
37:21 [A] and do not repay, but the righteous give **generously**;
37:26 [A] *They are* always **generous** and lend freely; their children
41:4 [41:5] [A] I said, "O LORD, **have mercy** *on* me; heal me, for I
41:10 [41:11] [A] you, O LORD, **have mercy** *on* me; raise me up,
51:1 [51:3] [A] **Have mercy** *on* me, O God, according to your
56:1 [56:2] [A] *Be* **merciful** *to* me, O God, for men hotly pursue me;
57:1 [57:2] [A] **Have mercy** *on* me, O God, have mercy on me,
57:1 [57:2] [A] Have mercy on me, O God, **have mercy** *on* me,
59:5 [59:6] [A] all the nations; **show** no **mercy** *to* wicked traitors.
67:1 [67:2] [A] *May* God *be* **gracious** *to* us and bless us and make
77:9 [77:10] [A] Has God forgotten *to be* **merciful**? Has he in anger
86:3 [A] **Have mercy** *on* me, O Lord, for I call to you all day long.
86:16 [A] Turn to me and **have mercy** *on* me; grant your strength to
102:13 [102:14] [A] on Zion, for it is time to **show favor** *to* her;
102:14 [102:15] [D] your servants; her very dust **moves** *them* **to pity**.
109:12 [A] kindness to him or **take pity** on his fatherless children.
112:5 [A] Good will come to him *who is* **generous** and lends freely,
119:29 [A] from deceitful ways; *be* **gracious** *to* me through your law.
119:58 [A] all my heart; *be* **gracious** *to* me according to your promise.
119:132 [A] Turn to me and **have mercy** *on* me, as you always do to
123:2 [A] look to the LORD our God, till *he* **shows** us *his* **mercy**.
123:3 [A] **Have mercy** *on* us, O LORD, have mercy on us, for we
123:3 [A] Have mercy on us, O LORD, **have mercy** *on* us, for we
142:1 [142:2] [F] *I* **lift up** my voice to the LORD **for mercy**.
Pr 14:21 [D] his neighbor sins, but blessed is he *who is* **kind** *to* the needy.
14:31 [A] their Maker, but *whoever is* **kind** *to* the needy honors God.
19:17 [A] *He who is* **kind** *to* the poor lends to the LORD, and he will
21:10 [H] man craves evil; his neighbor **gets** no **mercy** from him.
26:25 [D] Though his speech *is* **charming**, do not believe him,
28:8 [A] interest amasses it for *another, who will be* **kind** *to*
Isa 26:10 [H] Though **grace is shown** *to* the wicked, they do not learn
27:11 [A] compassion on them, and their Creator **shows** them no **favor**.
30:18 [A] Yet the LORD longs to *be* **gracious** *to* you; he rises to
30:19 [A] *How* **gracious** [+2858] *he will be* when you cry for help!
30:19 [A] *How* **gracious** *he will* **be** [+2858] when you cry for help!
33:2 [A] O LORD, *be* **gracious** *to* us; we long for you. Be our
Jer 22:23 [c] how *you will* groan [BHS **be gracious**; NIV 634] when pangs
La 4:16 [A] The priests are shown no honor, the elders no **favor**.
Hos 12:4 [12:5] [F] and overcame him; he wept and **begged for** his **favor**.
Am 5:15 [A] Perhaps the LORD God Almighty *will* **have mercy** *on* the
Mal 1:9 [A] "Now implore God *to be* **gracious** *to* us. With such offerings

2859 ²חָנַן ḥānan², v. [1]

loathsome [1]

Job 19:17 [A] is offensive to my wife; *I am* **loathsome** to my own brothers.

2860 חָנָן ḥānān, n.pr.m. [12] [√ 2858; *also used with compound proper names*]

Hanan [12]

1Ch 8:23 Abdon, Zicri, **Hanan**,
8:38 Azrikam, Bokeru, Ishmael, Sheariah, Obadiah and **Hanan**.

1Ch 9:44 Azrikam, Bokeru, Ishmael, Sheariah, Obadiah and **Hanan**.
11:43 **Hanan** son of Maacah, Joshaphat the Mithnite,
Ezr 2:46 Hagab, Shalmai, **Hanan**,
Ne 7:49 **Hanan**, Giddel, Gahar,
8: 7 Maaseiah, Kelita, Azariah, Jozabad, **Hanan** and Pelaiah—
10:10 [10:11] Shebaniah, Hodiah, Kelita, Pelaiah, **Hanan**,
10:22 [10:23] Pelatiah, **Hanan**, Anaiah,
10:26 [10:27] Ahiah, **Hanan**, Anan,
13:13 in charge of the storerooms and made **Hanan** son of Zaccur,
Jer 35: 4 into the room of the sons of **Hanan** son of Igdaliah the man of

2861 חֲנַנְאֵל ḥ[a]nan'ēl, n.pr.m. [4] [√ 2858 + 446]

Hananel [4]

Ne 3: 1 which they dedicated, and as far as the Tower of **Hananel**.
12:39 Fish Gate, the Tower of **Hananel** and the Tower of the Hundred,
Jer 31:38 "when this city will be rebuilt for me from the Tower of **Hananel**
Zec 14:10 and from the Tower of **Hananel** to the royal winepresses.

2862 חֲנָנִי ḥ[a]nānî, n.pr.m. [11] [√ 2858 + 3378]

Hanani [11]

1Ki 16: 1 the word of the LORD came to Jehu son of **Hanani** against
16: 7 LORD came through the prophet Jehu son of **Hanani** to Baasha
1Ch 25: 4 Hananiah, **Hanani**, Eliathah, Giddalti and Romamti-Ezer;
25:25 the eighteenth to **Hanani**, his sons and relatives, 12
2Ch 16: 7 At that time **Hanani** the seer came to Asa king of Judah and said to
19: 2 Jehu the seer, the son of **Hanani**, went out to meet him and said to
20:34 beginning to end, are written in the annals of Jehu son of **Hanani**,
Ezr 10:20 From the descendants of Immer: **Hanani** and Zebadiah.
Ne 1: 2 **Hanani**, one of my brothers, came from Judah with some other
7: 2 I put in charge of Jerusalem my brother **Hanani**, along with
12:36 Azarel, Milalai, Gilalai, Maai, Nethanel, Judah and **Hanani**—

2863 חֲנַנְיָה ḥ[a]nanyâ, n.pr.m. [25] [√ 2858 + 3378; Ar 10275]

Hananiah [24], he[s] [1]

1Ch 3:19 and Shimei. The sons of Zerubbabel: Meshullam and **Hananiah**.
3:21 The descendants of **Hananiah**: Pelatiah and Jeshaiah, and the sons
8:24 **Hananiah**, Elam, Anthothijah,
25: 4 **Hananiah**, Hanani, Eliathah, Giddalti and Romamti-Ezer;
Ezr 10:28 descendants of Bebai: Jehohanan, **Hananiah**, Zabbai and Athlai.
Ne 3: 8 **Hananiah**, one of the perfume-makers, made repairs next to that.
3:30 Next to him, **Hananiah** son of Shelemiah, and Hanun, the sixth
7: 2 along with **Hananiah** the commander of the citadel, because he
10:23 [10:24] Hoshea, **Hananiah**, Hasshub,
12:12 of Seraiah's family, Meraiah; of Jeremiah's, **Hananiah**;
12:41 Micaiah, Elioenai, Zechariah and **Hananiah** with their trumpets—
Jer 28: 1 the prophet **Hananiah** son of Azzur, who was from Gibeon,
28: 5 the prophet Jeremiah replied to the prophet **Hananiah** before the
28:10 the prophet **Hananiah** took the yoke off the neck of the prophet
28:11 and **he**[s] said before all the people, "This is what the LORD says:
28:12 Shortly after the prophet **Hananiah** had broken the yoke off the
28:13 "Go and tell **Hananiah**, 'This is what the LORD says: You have
28:15 Then the prophet Jeremiah said to **Hananiah** the prophet,
28:15 Jeremiah said to Hananiah the prophet, "Listen, **Hananiah**!
28:17 the seventh month of that same year, **Hananiah** the prophet died.
37:13 the son of **Hananiah**, arrested him and said, "You are deserting to
Da 1: 6 were some from Judah: Daniel, **Hananiah**, Mishael and Azariah.
1: 7 to **Hananiah**, Shadrach; to Mishael, Meshach; and to Azariah,
1:11 had appointed over Daniel, **Hananiah**, Mishael and Azariah,
1:19 he found none equal to Daniel, **Hananiah**, Mishael and Azariah;

2864 חֲנַנְיָהוּ ḥ[a]nanyāhû, n.pr.m. [3] [√ 2858 + 3378]

Hananiah [3]

1Ch 25:23 the sixteenth to **Hananiah**, his sons and relatives, 12
2Ch 26:11 and Maaseiah the officer under the direction of **Hananiah**,
Jer 36:12 of Shaphan, Zedekiah son of **Hananiah**, and all the other officials.

2865 חָנֵס ḥānēs, n.pr.loc. [1]

Hanes [1]

Isa 30: 4 they have officials in Zoan and their envoys have arrived in **Hanes**,

2866 [1]חָנֵף ḥānēp[1], v. [11] [→ 2868, 2869, 2870]

defiled [4], completely defiled [+2866] [2], corrupt [1], desecrated [1], godless [1], pollute [1], pollutes [1]

Nu 35:33 [G] " '*Do* not **pollute** the land where you are. Bloodshed pollutes
35:33 [G] Bloodshed **pollutes** the land, and atonement cannot be made
Ps 106:38 [A] idols of Canaan, and the land *was* **desecrated** by their blood.
Isa 24: 5 [A] The earth *is* **defiled** by its people; they have disobeyed the
Jer 3: 1 [A] *Would* not the land *be* **completely defiled** [+2866]?
3: 1 [A] *Would* not the land *be* **completely defiled** [+2866]?
3: 2 [G] *You have* **defiled** the land with your prostitution
3: 9 [A] *she* **defiled** the land and committed adultery with stone
23:11 [A] "Both prophet and priest *are* **godless**; even in my temple I
Da 11:32 [G] With flattery *he will* **corrupt** those who have violated the
Mic 4:11 [A] They say, "*Let her be* **defiled**, let our eyes gloat over Zion!"

2867 [2]חָנֵף ḥānēp[2], a. Not used in NIV/BHS

2868 [3]חָנֵף ḥānēp[3], a. [13] [√ 2866]

godless [10], ungodly [3]

Job 8:13 destiny of all who forget God; so perishes the hope of the **godless**.
13:16 my deliverance, for no **godless** *man* would dare come before him!
15:34 For the company of the **godless** will be barren, and fire will
17: 8 are appalled at this; the innocent are aroused against the **ungodly**.
20: 5 of the wicked is brief, the joy of the **godless** lasts but a moment.
27: 8 For what hope has the **godless** when he is cut off, when God takes
34:30 to keep a **godless** man from ruling, from laying snares for the
36:13 "The **godless** *in* heart harbor resentment; even when he fetters
Ps 35:16 Like the **ungodly** they maliciously mocked; they gnashed their
Pr 11: 9 With his mouth the **godless** destroys his neighbor, but through
Isa 9:17 [9:16] and widows, for everyone is **ungodly** and wicked,
10: 6 I send him against a **godless** nation, I dispatch him against a people
33:14 The sinners in Zion are terrified; trembling grips the **godless**:

2869 חֹנֶף ḥōnep, n.[m.] [1] [√ 2866]

ungodliness [1]

Isa 32: 6 He practices **ungodliness** and spreads error concerning the

2870 חֲנֻפָּה ḥ[a]nuppâ, n.f. [1] [√ 2866]

ungodliness [1]

Jer 23:15 because from the prophets of Jerusalem **ungodliness** has spread

2871 חָנַק ḥānaq, v. [2] [→ 4725]

hanged himself [1], strangled [1]

2Sa 17:23 [C] He put his house in order and then **hanged himself**. So he
Na 2:12 [2:13] [D] for his cubs and **strangled** the prey for his mate,

2872 חַנָּתֹון ḥannātôn, n.pr.loc. [1]

Hannathon [1]

Jos 19:14 There the boundary went around on the north to **Hannathon**

2873 [1]חָסַד ḥāsad[1], v. [1] [→ 2875]

shame [1]

Pr 25:10 [D] or he who hears it *may* **shame** you and you will never lose

2874 [2]חָסַד ḥāsad[2], v. [2] [→ 1213, 2876, 2877, 2883, 2884]

show yourself faithful [2]

2Sa 22:26 [F] "To the faithful *you* **show yourself faithful**, to the blameless
Ps 18:25 [18:26] [F] To the faithful *you* **show yourself faithful**,

2875 [1]חֶסֶד ḥesed[1], n.m. [3] [√ 2873]

disgrace [3]

Lev 20:17 or his mother, and they have sexual relations, it is a **disgrace**.
Ps 52: 1 [52:3] all day long, you who are a **disgrace** *in the eyes of* God?
Pr 14:34 Righteousness exalts a nation, but sin is a **disgrace** *to* any people.

2876 [2]חֶסֶד ḥesed[2], n.m. [244] [→ 1213, 2877, 2878?, 2883; cf. 2874]

love [129], kindness [41], unfailing love [32], great love [6], mercy [6], loving [5], kindnesses [3], unfailing kindness [3], acts of devotion [2], devotion [2], favor [2], approval [1], devout [1], faithful [1], faithfully [1], glory [1], good favor [1], grace [1], kind [1], kindly [1], loving-kindness [1], loyal [1], merciful [1], well [1]

Ge 19:19 and you have shown great **kindness** to me in sparing my life.
20:13 I said to her, 'This is how you can show your **love** to me:
21:23 the country where you are living as an alien the same **kindness** I
24:12 give me success today, and show **kindness** to my master Abraham.
24:14 By this I will know that you have shown **kindness** to my master."
24:27 who has not abandoned his **kindness** and faithfulness to my
24:49 Now if you will show **kindness** and faithfulness to my master,
32:10 [32:11] I am unworthy of all the **kindness** and faithfulness you
39:21 he showed him **kindness** and granted him favor in the eyes of the
40:14 all goes well with you, remember me and show me **kindness**;
47:29 and promise that you will show me **kindness** and faithfulness.
Ex 15:13 "In your **unfailing love** you will lead the people you have
20: 6 but showing **love** to a thousand ⌞generations⌟ of those who love me
34: 6 gracious God, slow to anger, abounding in **love** and faithfulness,

Ex 34: 7 maintaining **love** to thousands, and forgiving wickedness,
Nu 14: 18 is slow to anger, abounding in **love** and forgiving sin and rebellion.
14: 19 In accordance with your great **love**, forgive the sin of these people,
Dt 5: 10 but showing **love** to a thousand ⌞generations⌟ of those who love me
7: 9 keeping his covenant of **love** to a thousand generations of those
7: 12 then the LORD your God will keep his covenant of **love** with you,
Jos 2: 12 please swear to me by the LORD that you will show **kindness** to
2: 12 kindness to my family, because I have shown **kindness** to you.
2: 14 we will treat you **kindly** and faithfully when the LORD gives us
Jdg 1: 24 how to get into the city and we will see that you are treated **well**."
8: 35 They also failed to show **kindness** to the family of Jerub-Baal (that
Ru 1: 8 May the LORD show **kindness** to you, as you have shown to
2: 20 "He has not stopped showing his **kindness** to the living and the
3: 10 "This **kindness** is greater than that which you showed earlier:
1Sa 15: 6 for you showed **kindness** to all the Israelites when they came up
20: 8 As for you, show **kindness** to your servant, for you have brought
20: 14 show me **unfailing kindness** *like that of* the LORD as long as I
20: 15 do not ever cut off your **kindness** from my family—not even when
2Sa 2: 5 "The LORD bless you for showing this **kindness** to Saul your
2: 6 May the LORD now show you **kindness** and faithfulness,
3: 8 This very day I am **loyal** to the house of your father Saul and to his
7: 15 my **love** will never be taken away from him, as I took it away from
9: 1 house of Saul to whom I can show **kindness** for Jonathan's sake?"
9: 3 left of the house of Saul to whom I can show God's **kindness**?"
9: 7 "for I will surely show you **kindness** for the sake of your father
10: 2 David thought, "I will show **kindness** to Hanun son of Nahash,
10: 2 Hanun son of Nahash, just as his father showed **kindness** to me."
15: 20 your countrymen. May **kindness** and faithfulness be with you."
16: 17 Absalom asked Hushai, "Is this the **love** you show your friend?
22: 51 he shows **unfailing kindness** to his anointed, to David and his
1Ki 2: 7 "But show **kindness** to the sons of Barzillai of Gilead and let them
3: 6 "You have shown great **kindness** to your servant, my father David,
3: 6 You have continued this great **kindness** to him and have given him
8: 23 you who keep your covenant of **love** with your servants who
20: 31 we have heard that the kings of the house of Israel are **merciful**.
1Ch 16: 34 thanks to the LORD, for he is good; his **love** endures forever.
16: 41 name to give thanks to the LORD, "for his **love** endures forever."
17: 13 I will never take my **love** away from him, as I took it away from
19: 2 David thought, "I will show **kindness** to Hanun son of Nahash,
19: 2 Hanun son of Nahash, because his father showed **kindness** to me."
2Ch 1: 8 "You have shown great **kindness** to David my father and have
5: 13 to the LORD and sang: "He is good; his **love** endures forever."
6: 14 you who keep your covenant of **love** with your servants who
6: 42 Remember the **great love** *promised to* David your servant."
7: 3 to the LORD, saying, "He is good; his **love** endures forever."
7: 6 used when he gave thanks, saying, "His **love** endures forever."
20: 21 "Give thanks to the LORD, for his **love** endures forever."
24: 22 King Joash did not remember the **kindness** Zechariah's father
32: 32 his **acts of devotion** are written in the vision of the prophet Isaiah
35: 26 The other events of Josiah's reign and his **acts of devotion**,
Ezr 3: 11 to the LORD: "He is good; his **love** to Israel endures forever."
7: 28 and who has extended his **good favor** to me before the king
9: 9 He has shown us **kindness** in the sight of the kings of Persia:
Ne 1: 5 who keeps his covenant of **love** with those who love him and obey
9: 17 gracious and compassionate, slow to anger and abounding in **love**.
9: 32 mighty and awesome God, who keeps his covenant of **love**,
13: 14 *so* **faithfully** done for the house of my God and its services.
13: 22 O my God, and show mercy to me according to your great **love**.
Est 2: 9 The girl pleased him and won his **favor**. Immediately he provided
2: 17 she won his favor and **approval** more than any of the other virgins.
Job 6: 14 "A despairing man should have the **devotion** of his friends,
10: 12 You gave me life and showed me **kindness**, and in your
37: 13 the clouds to punish men, or to water his earth and show his **love**.
Ps 5: 7 [5:8] I, by your great **mercy**, will come into your house;
6: 4 [6:5] and deliver me; save me because of your **unfailing love**.
13: 5 [13:6] I trust in your **unfailing love**; my heart rejoices in your
17: 7 Show the wonder of your **great love**, you who save by your right
18: 50 [18:51] he shows **unfailing kindness** to his anointed, to David
21: 7 [21:8] through the **unfailing love** *of* the Most High he will not be
23: 6 Surely goodness and **love** will follow me all the days of my life,
25: 6 Remember, O LORD, your great mercy and **love**, for they are
25: 7 according to your **love** remember me, for you are good, O LORD.
25: 10 All the ways of the LORD are **loving** and faithful for those who
26: 3 for your **love** is ever before me, and I walk continually in your
31: 7 [31:8] I will be glad and rejoice in your **love**, for you saw my
31: 16 [31:17] shine on your servant; save me in your **unfailing love**.
31: 21 [31:22] for he showed his wonderful **love** to me when I was in a
32: 10 the LORD's **unfailing love** surrounds the man who trusts in him.
33: 5 and justice; the earth is full of his **unfailing love**.
33: 18 those who fear him, on those whose hope is in his **unfailing love**,
33: 22 May your **unfailing love** rest upon us, O LORD, even as we put
36: 5 [36:6] Your **love**, O LORD, reaches to the heavens,
36: 7 [36:8] How priceless is your **unfailing love**! Both high and low
36: 10 [36:11] Continue your **love** to those who know you, your
40: 10 [40:11] I do not conceal your **love** and your truth from the great
40: 11 [40:12] may your **love** and your truth always protect me.
42: 8 [42:9] By day the LORD directs his **love**, at night his song is
44: 26 [44:27] and help us; redeem us because of your **unfailing love**.
48: 9 [48:10] your temple, O God, we meditate on your **unfailing love**.
51: 1 [51:3] mercy on me, O God, according to your **unfailing love**;
52: 8 [52:10] of God; I trust in God's **unfailing love** for ever and ever.
57: 3 [57:4] *Selah* God sends his **love** and his faithfulness.
57: 10 [57:11] For great is your **love**, reaching to the heavens; your
59: 10 [59:11] my **loving** God. God will go before me and will let me
59: 16 [59:17] of your strength, in the morning I will sing of your **love**;
59: 17 [59:18] to you; you, O God, are my fortress, my **loving** God.
61: 7 [61:8] appoint your **love** and faithfulness to protect him.
62: 12 [62:13] that you, O Lord, are **loving**. Surely you will reward each
63: 3 [63:4] Because your **love** is better than life, my lips will glorify
66: 20 who has not rejected my prayer or withheld his **love** from me!
69: 13 [69:14] in your great **love**, O God, answer me with your sure
69: 16 [69:17] Answer me, O LORD, out of the goodness of your **love**;
77: 8 [77:9] Has his **unfailing love** vanished forever? Has his promise
85: 7 [85:8] Show us your **unfailing love**, O LORD, and grant us your
85: 10 [85:11] **Love** and faithfulness meet together; righteousness
86: 5 and good, O Lord, abounding in **love** to all who call to you.
86: 13 For great is your **love** toward me; you have delivered me from the
86: 15 gracious God, slow to anger, abounding in **love** and faithfulness.
88: 11 [88:12] Is your **love** declared in the grave, your faithfulness in
89: 1 [89:2] I will sing of the LORD's **great love** forever; with my
89: 2 [89:3] I will declare that your **love** stands firm forever, that you
89: 14 [89:15] of your throne; **love** and faithfulness go before you.
89: 24 [89:25] My faithful **love** will be with him, and through my name
89: 28 [89:29] I will maintain my **love** to him forever, and my covenant
89: 33 [89:34] I will not take my **love** from him, nor will I ever betray
89: 49 [89:50] O Lord, where is your former **great love**, which in your
90: 14 Satisfy us in the morning with your **unfailing love**, that we may
92: 2 [92:3] to proclaim your **love** in the morning and your faithfulness
94: 18 "My foot is slipping," your **love**, O LORD, supported me.
98: 3 He has remembered his **love** and his faithfulness to the house of
100: 5 For the LORD is good and his **love** endures forever; his
101: 1 I will sing of your **love** and justice; to you, O LORD, I will sing
103: 4 your life from the pit and crowns you with **love** and compassion,
103: 8 is compassionate and gracious, slow to anger, abounding in **love**.
103: 11 are above the earth, so great is his **love** for those who fear him;
103: 17 from everlasting to everlasting the LORD's **love** is with those
106: 1 thanks to the LORD, for he is good; his **love** endures forever.
106: 7 they did not remember your many **kindnesses**, and they rebelled
106: 45 he remembered his covenant and out of his great **love** he relented.
107: 1 thanks to the LORD, for he is good; his **love** endures forever.
107: 8 Let them give thanks to the LORD for his **unfailing love**
107: 15 Let them give thanks to the LORD for his **unfailing love**
107: 21 Let them give thanks to the LORD for his **unfailing love**
107: 31 Let them give thanks to the LORD for his **unfailing love**
107: 43 him heed these things and consider the **great love** *of* the LORD.
108: 4 [108:5] For great is your **love**, higher than the heavens; your
109: 12 May no one extend **kindness** to him or take pity on his fatherless
109: 16 For he never thought of doing a **kindness**, but hounded to death the
109: 21 for your name's sake; out of the goodness of your **love**, deliver me.
109: 26 O LORD my God; save me in accordance with your **love**.
115: 1 to your name be the glory, because of your **love** and faithfulness.
117: 2 For great is his **love** toward us, and the faithfulness of the LORD
118: 1 thanks to the LORD, for he is good; his **love** endures forever.
118: 2 Let Israel say: "His **love** endures forever."
118: 3 Let the house of Aaron say: "His **love** endures forever."
118: 4 Let those who fear the LORD say: "His **love** endures forever."
118: 29 thanks to the LORD, for he is good; his **love** endures forever.
119: 41 May your **unfailing love** come to me, O LORD, your salvation
119: 64 The earth is filled with your **love**, O LORD; teach me your
119: 76 May your **unfailing love** be my comfort, according to your
119: 88 Preserve my life according to your **love**, and I will obey the
119: 124 Deal with your servant according to your **love** and teach me your
119: 149 Hear my voice in accordance with your **love**; preserve my life,
119: 159 your precepts; preserve my life, O LORD, according to your **love**.
130: 7 for with the LORD is **unfailing love** and with him is full
136: 1 to the LORD, for he is good. *His* **love** *endures forever.*
136: 2 thanks to the God of gods. *His* **love** *endures forever.*
136: 3 thanks to the Lord of lords: *His* **love** *endures forever.*
136: 4 who alone does great wonders, *His* **love** *endures forever.*
136: 5 made the heavens, *His* **love** *endures forever.*
136: 6 out the earth upon the waters, *His* **love** *endures forever.*
136: 7 who made the great lights—*His* **love** *endures forever.*
136: 8 the sun to govern the day, *His* **love** *endures forever.*
136: 9 and stars to govern the night; *His* **love** *endures forever.*
136: 10 to him who struck down the firstborn of Egypt *His* **love**
136: 11 brought Israel out from among them *His* **love** *endures*
136: 12 and outstretched arm; *His* **love** *endures forever.*
136: 13 to him who divided the Red Sea asunder *His* **love** *endures*

Ps 136:14 Israel through the midst of it, *His* **love** *endures forever.*
136:15 and his army into the Red Sea; *His* **love** *endures forever.*
136:16 his people through the desert, *His* **love** *endures forever.*
136:17 who struck down great kings, *His* **love** *endures forever.*
136:18 and killed mighty kings—*His* **love** *endures forever.*
136:19 Sihon king of the Amorites *His* **love** *endures forever.*
136:20 and Og king of Bashan—*His* **love** *endures forever.*
136:21 their land as an inheritance, *His* **love** *endures forever.*
136:22 to his servant Israel; *His* **love** *endures forever.*
136:23 to the One who remembered us in our low estate *His* **love**
136:24 and freed us from our enemies, *His* **love** *endures forever.*
136:25 gives food to every creature. *His* **love** *endures forever.*
136:26 thanks to the God of heaven. *His* **love** *endures forever.*
138: 2 and will praise your name for your **love** and your faithfulness,
138: 8 your **love**, O LORD, endures forever—do not abandon the works
141: 5 it is a **kindness**; let him rebuke me—it is oil on my head.
143: 8 Let the morning bring me word of your **unfailing love**, for I have
143:12 In your **unfailing love**, silence my enemies; destroy all my foes,
144: 2 He is my **loving** God and my fortress, my stronghold and my
145: 8 is gracious and compassionate, slow to anger and rich in **love**.
147:11 in those who fear him, who put their hope in his **unfailing love**.
Pr 3: 3 Let **love** and faithfulness never leave you; bind them around your
11:17 A **kind** man benefits himself, but a cruel man brings trouble on
14:22 But those who plan what is good find **love** and faithfulness.
16: 6 Through **love** and faithfulness sin is atoned for; through the fear of
19:22 What a man desires is **unfailing love**; better to be poor than a liar.
20: 6 Many a man claims to have **unfailing love**, but a faithful man who
20:28 **Love** and faithfulness keep a king safe; through love his throne is
20:28 keep a king safe; through **love** his throne is made secure.
21:21 He who pursues righteousness and **love** finds life, prosperity
31:26 She speaks with wisdom, and **faithful** instruction is on her tongue.
Isa 16: 5 In **love** a throne will be established; in faithfulness a man will sit
40: 6 are like grass, and all their **glory** is like the flowers of the field.
54: 8 but with everlasting **kindness** I will have compassion on you,"
54:10 yet my **unfailing love** for you will not be shaken nor my covenant
55: 3 covenant with you, my faithful **love** *promised to* David.
57: 1 **devout** men are taken away, and no one understands that the
63: 7 I will tell of the **kindnesses** *of* the LORD, the deeds for which he
63: 7 house of Israel, according to his compassion and many **kindnesses**.
Jer 2: 2 " 'I remember the **devotion** *of* your youth, how as a bride you
9:24 [9:23] who exercises **kindness**, justice and righteousness on earth,
16: 5 my **love** and my pity from this people," declares the LORD.
31: 3 with an everlasting love; I have drawn you with **loving-kindness**.
32:18 You show **love** to thousands but bring the punishment for the
33:11 for the LORD is good; his **love** endures forever."
La 3:22 Because of the LORD's **great love** we are not consumed,
3:32 he will show compassion, so great is his **unfailing love**.
Da 1: 9 Now God had caused the official to show **favor** and sympathy to
9: 4 who keeps his covenant of **love** with all who love him and obey his
Hos 2:19 [2:21] you in righteousness and justice, in **love** and compassion.
4: 1 "There is no faithfulness, no **love**, no acknowledgment of God in
6: 4 Your **love** is like the morning mist, like the early dew that
6: 6 For I desire **mercy**, not sacrifice, and acknowledgment of God
10:12 Sow for yourselves righteousness, reap the fruit of **unfailing love**,
12: 6 [12:7] maintain **love** and justice, and wait for your God always.
Joel 2:13 and compassionate, slow to anger and abounding in **love**,
Jnh 2: 8 [2:9] "Those who cling to worthless idols forfeit the **grace** that
4: 2 and compassionate God, slow to anger and abounding in **love**,
Mic 6: 8 To act justly and to love **mercy** and to walk humbly with your
7:18 You do not stay angry forever but delight to show **mercy**.
7:20 You will be true to Jacob, and show **mercy** to Abraham, as you
Zec 7: 9 true justice; show **mercy** and compassion to one another.

2877 [3]חֶסֶד ***ḥesed*[3]**, n.pr.m. Not used in NIV/BHS [√ 2876; cf. 2874]

2878 חֲסַדְיָה ***ḥ[a]sadyâ***, n.pr.m. [1] [√ 2876 + 3378]

Hasadiah [1]

1Ch 3:20 Hashubah, Ohel, Berekiah, **Hasadiah** and Jushab-Hesed.

2879 חָסָה ***ḥāsâ***, v. [37] [→ 335, 2882, 4726; *also used with compound proper names*]

take refuge [23], find refuge [3], takes refuge [3], taken refuge [2], trust [2], have a refuge [1], makes refuge [1], refuge [1], took refuge [1]

Dt 32:37 [A] "Now where are their gods, the rock *they* **took refuge** in,
Jdg 9:15 [A] anoint me king over you, come and **take refuge** in my shade;
Ru 2:12 [A] of Israel, under whose wings you have come to **take refuge**."
2Sa 22: 3 [A] in whom *I* **take refuge**, my shield and the horn of my
22:31 [A] is flawless. He is a shield for all who **take refuge** in him.
Ps 2:12 [A] up in a moment. Blessed are all *who* **take refuge** in him.
5:11 [5:12] [A] let all *who* **take refuge** in you be glad; let them ever
7: 1 [7:2] [A] O LORD my God, *I* **take refuge** in you; save and
11: 1 [A] In the LORD *I* **take refuge**. How then can you say to me:
16: 1 [A] Keep me safe, O God, for in you *I* **take refuge**.
17: 7 [A] you who save by your right hand *those who* **take refuge** in
18: 2 [18:3] [A] my God is my rock, in whom *I* **take refuge**.
18:30 [18:31] [A] He is a shield for all who **take refuge** in him.
25:20 [A] let me not be put to shame, for *I* **take refuge** in you.
31: 1 [31:2] [A] In you, O LORD, *I have* **taken refuge**; let me never
31:19 [31:20] [A] the sight of men on those *who* **take refuge** in you.
34: 8 [34:9] [A] is good; blessed is the man *who* **takes refuge** in him.
34:22 [34:23] [A] no one will be condemned who **takes refuge** in him.
36: 7 [36:8] [A] low among men **find refuge** in the shadow of your
37:40 [A] the wicked and saves them, because *they* **take refuge** in him.
57: 1 [57:2] [A] have mercy on me, for in you my soul **takes refuge**.
57: 1 [57:2] [A] *I will* **take refuge** in the shadow of your wings until
61: 4 [61:5] [A] and **take refuge** in the shelter of your wings.
64:10 [64:11] [A] rejoice in the LORD and **take refuge** in him;
71: 1 [A] In you, O LORD, *I have* **taken refuge**; let me never be put
91: 4 [A] with his feathers, and under his wings *you will* **find refuge**;
118: 8 [A] It is better to **take refuge** in the LORD than to trust in man.
118: 9 [A] It is better to **take refuge** in the LORD than to trust in
141: 8 [A] fixed on you, O Sovereign LORD; in you *I* **take refuge**—
144: 2 [A] and my deliverer, my shield, in whom *I* **take refuge**,
Pr 14:32 [A] brought down, but even in death the righteous **have a refuge**.
30: 5 [A] is flawless; he is a shield to those *who* **take refuge** in him.
Isa 14:32 [A] and in her his afflicted people *will* **find refuge**."
30: 2 [A] for help to Pharaoh's protection, to Egypt's shade *for* **refuge**.
57:13 [A] But the *man who* **makes** me *his* **refuge** will inherit the land
Na 1: 7 [A] in times of trouble. He cares for *those who* **trust** in him,
Zep 3:12 [A] the meek and humble, *who* **trust** in the name of the LORD.

2880 [1]חֹסָה ***ḥōsâ*[1]**, n.pr.m. [4]

Hosah [4]

1Ch 16:38 Obed-Edom son of Jeduthun, and also **Hosah**, were gatekeepers.
26:10 **Hosah** the Merarite had sons: Shimri the first (although he was not
26:11 the fourth. The sons and relatives of **Hosah** were 13 in all.
26:16 the Shalleketh Gate on the upper road fell to Shuppim and **Hosah**.

2881 [2]חֹסָה ***ḥōsâ*[2]**, n.pr.loc. [1]

Hosah [1]

Jos 19:29 turned toward **Hosah** and came out at the sea in the region of

2882 חָסוּת ***ḥāsût***, n.f. [1] [√ 2879]

untranslated [1]

Isa 30: 3 be to your shame, **[RPH]** Egypt's shade will bring you disgrace.

2883 חָסִיד ***ḥāsîd***, a.m. [32 / 33] [→ 2884; cf. 2874, 2876]

saints [15], faithful [6], godly [4], loving [2], consecrated [1], devoted [1], favored [1], holy [1], merciful [1], ungodly [+4202] [1]

Dt 33: 8 "Your Thummim and Urim belong to the man you **favored**.
1Sa 2: 9 He will guard the feet of his **saints**, but the wicked will be silenced
2Sa 22:26 "To the **faithful** you show yourself faithful, to the blameless you
2Ch 6:41 clothed with salvation, may your **saints** rejoice in your goodness.
Ps 4: 3 [4:4] Know that the LORD has set apart the **godly** for himself;
12: 1 [12:2] Help, LORD, for the **godly** are no more; the faithful have
16:10 me to the grave, nor will you let your **Holy** *One* see decay.
18:25 [18:26] To the **faithful** you show yourself faithful,
30: 4 [30:5] Sing to the LORD, you **saints** *of* his; praise his holy
31:23 [31:24] Love the LORD, all his **saints**! The LORD preserves
32: 6 Therefore let everyone *who* is **godly** pray to you while you may be
37:28 the LORD loves the just and will not forsake his **faithful** *ones*.
43: 1 O God, and plead my cause against an **ungodly** [+4202] nation;
50: 5 "Gather to me my **consecrated** *ones*, who made a covenant with
52: 9 [52:11] is good. I will praise you in the presence of your **saints**.
79: 2 birds of the air, the flesh of your **saints** to the beasts of the earth.
85: 8 [85:9] he promises peace to his people, his **saints**—but let them
86: 2 Guard my life, for I am **devoted** to you. You are my God;
89:19 [89:20] you spoke in a vision, to your **faithful** *people* you said:
97:10 for he guards the lives of his **faithful** *ones* and delivers them from
116:15 Precious in the sight of the LORD is the death of his **saints**.
132: 9 be clothed with righteousness; may your **saints** sing for joy."
132:16 her priests with salvation, and her **saints** will ever sing for joy.
145:10 have made will praise you, O LORD; your **saints** will extol you.
145:13 to all his promises and **loving** [BHS-] toward all he has made.
145:17 is righteous in all his ways and **loving** toward all he has made.
148:14 the praise of all his **saints**, of Israel, the people close to his heart.
149: 1 to the LORD a new song, his praise in the assembly of the **saints**.
149: 5 Let the **saints** rejoice in this honor and sing for joy on their beds.
149: 9 against them. This is the glory of all his **saints**. Praise the LORD.
Pr 2: 8 the course of the just and protects the way of his **faithful** *ones*.

Jer 3:12 for I am **merciful**,' declares the LORD, 'I will not be angry
Mic 7: 2 The **godly** have been swept from the land; not one upright man

2884 חֲסִידָה ***ḥ*ᵃ*sîdâ***, n.f. [6] [√ 2883; cf. 2874]
stork [6]
Lev 11:19 the **stork**, any kind of heron, the hoopoe and the bat.
Dt 14:18 the **stork**, any kind of heron, the hoopoe and the bat.
Job 39:13 but they cannot compare with the pinions and feathers of the **stork**.
Ps 104:17 the birds make their nests; the **stork** has its home in the pine trees.
Jer 8: 7 Even the **stork** in the sky knows her appointed seasons,
Zec 5: 9 They had wings like those of a **stork**, and they lifted up the basket

2885 חָסִיל ***ḥāsîl***, n.m. [6] [√ 2887]
grasshoppers [2], locusts [2], grasshopper [1], young locusts [1]
1Ki 8:37 comes to the land, or blight or mildew, locusts or **grasshoppers**,
2Ch 6:28 comes to the land, or blight or mildew, locusts or **grasshoppers**,
Ps 78:46 He gave their crops to the **grasshopper**, their produce to the locust.
Isa 33: 4 Your plunder, O nations, is harvested as by **young locusts**;
Joel 1: 4 what the young locusts have left other **locusts** have eaten.
2:25 and the young locust, the other **locusts** and the locust swarm—

2886 חֲסִין ***ḥ*ᵃ*sîn***, a. [1] [→ 2891]
mighty [1]
Ps 89: 8 [89:9] You are **mighty**, O LORD, and your faithfulness

2887 חָסַל ***ḥāsal***, v. [1] [→ 2885]
devour [1]
Dt 28:38 [G] but you will harvest little, because locusts *will* **devour** it.

2888 חָסַם ***ḥāsam***, v. [2] [→ 4727]
block the way [1], muzzle [1]
Dt 25: 4 [A] *Do* not **muzzle** an ox while it is treading out the grain.
Eze 39:11 [A] It *will* **block the way** *of* travelers, because Gog and all his

2889 חָסַן ***ḥāsan***, v.den. [1] [→ 2890; Ar 10277]
hoarded [1]
Isa 23:18 [C] apart for the LORD; they will not be stored up or **hoarded**.

2890 חֹסֶן ***ḥōsen***, n.m. [5] [√ 2889; Ar 10278]
rich store [1], riches [1], treasure [1], treasures [1], wealth [1]
Pr 15: 6 The house of the righteous contains great **treasure**, but the income
27:24 for **riches** do not endure forever, and a crown is not secure for all
Isa 33: 6 your times, a **rich store** *of* salvation and wisdom and knowledge;
Jer 20: 5 I will hand over to their enemies all the **wealth** *of* this city—
Eze 22:25 take **treasures** and precious things and make many widows within

2891 חָסֹן ***ḥāsōn***, a. [2] [√ 2886]
mighty [1], strong [1]
Isa 1:31 The **mighty** *man* will become tinder and his work a spark;
Am 2: 9 though he was tall as the cedars and **strong** as the oaks.

2892 חַסְפַּס ***ḥaspas***, v. [1]
flakes [1]
Ex 16:14 [E] thin **flakes** like frost on the ground appeared on the desert

2893 ¹חָסֵר ***ḥāsēr***¹, v. [23] [→ 2894, 2895, 2896, 2898, 4728]
lack [3], lacks [3], lacked [2], run dry [2], always [+440] [1], depriving [1], goes hungry [1], gone down [1], had nothing [+3972] [1], have too little [1], in want [1], made lower [1], needs [+4728] [1], number is less than [1], recede [1], scarce [1], withholds [1]
Ge 8: 3 [A] end of the hundred and fifty days the water *had* **gone down**,
8: 5 [A] The waters continued *to* **recede** until the tenth month, and on
18:28 [A] what if the **number** of the righteous **is** five **less than** fifty?
Ex 16:18 [G] too much, and he who gathered little *did* not **have too little**.
Dt 2: 7 [A] God has been with you, and *you have* not **lacked** anything.
8: 9 [A] where bread will not be scarce and *you will* **lack** nothing;
15: 8 [A] and freely lend him whatever he **needs** [+4728].
1Ki 17:14 [A] the jug of oil *will* not **run dry** until the day the LORD
17:16 [A] of flour was not used up and the jug of oil *did* not **run dry**,
Ne 9:21 [A] *they* **lacked** nothing, their clothes did not wear out nor did
Ps 8: 5 [8:6] [D] *You* **made** him a little **lower** than the heavenly beings
23: 1 [A] The LORD is my shepherd, *I shall* not be **in want**.
34:10 [34:11] [A] but those who seek the LORD **lack** no good thing.
Pr 13:25 [A] hearts' content, but the stomach of the wicked **goes hungry**.
31:11 [A] has full confidence in her and **lacks** nothing of value.
Ecc 4: 8 [D] he asked, "and why *am* I **depriving** myself of enjoyment?"
9: 8 [A] in white, and **always** [+440] anoint your head with oil.
10: 3 [A] the fool **lacks** sense and shows everyone how stupid he is.
SS 7: 2 [7:3] [A] Your navel is a rounded goblet *that* never **lacks**
Isa 32: 6 [G] he leaves empty and *from* the thirsty *he* **withholds** water.
51:14 [A] they will not die in their dungeon, nor *will they* **lack** bread.
Jer 44:18 [A] *we have* **had nothing** [+3972] and have been perishing by
Eze 4:17 [A] for food and water *will be* **scarce**. They will be appalled at

2894 ²חָסֵר ***ḥāsēr***², a. [17] [√ 2893]
lacks [9], lack [3], lacked [2], have no [1], lacking [1], short [1]
1Sa 21:15 [21:16] *so* **short** *of* madmen that you have to bring this fellow
2Sa 3:29 leans on a crutch or who falls by the sword or who **lacks** food."
1Ki 11:22 "What *have* you **lacked** here that you want to go back to your own
Pr 6:32 But a man who commits adultery **lacks** judgment; whoever does
7: 7 I noticed among the young men, a youth who **lacked** judgment.
9: 4 are simple come in here!" she says to those who **lack** judgment.
9:16 are simple come in here!" she says to those *who* **lack** judgment.
10:13 but a rod is for the back of him who **lacks** judgment.
10:21 of the righteous nourish many, but fools die for **lack** *of* judgment.
11:12 A man who **lacks** judgment derides his neighbor, but a man of
12: 9 yet have a servant than pretend to be somebody and **have no** food.
12:11 have abundant food, but he who chases fantasies **lacks** judgment.
15:21 Folly delights a *man who* **lacks** judgment, but a man of
17:18 A man **lacking** *in* judgment strikes hands in pledge and puts up
24:30 of the sluggard, past the vineyard of the man who **lacks** judgment;
28:16 A tyrannical ruler **lacks** judgment, but he who hates ill-gotten gain
Ecc 6: 2 possessions and honor, so that he **lacks** nothing his heart desires,

2895 חֶסֶר ***ḥeser***, n.m. [2] [√ 2893]
poverty [1], want [1]
Job 30: 3 Haggard from **want** and hunger, they roamed the parched land in
Pr 28:22 man is eager to get rich and is unaware that **poverty** awaits him.

2896 חֹסֶר ***ḥōser***, n.[m.]. [3] [√ 2893]
untranslated [1], lack [1], poverty [1]
Dt 28:48 therefore in hunger and thirst, in nakedness and dire **poverty**,
28:57 For she intends to eat them secretly **[RPH]** during the siege
Am 4: 6 you empty stomachs in every city and **lack** *of* bread in every town,

2897 חַסְרָה ***ḥasrâ***, n.pr.m. [1] [cf. 3030]
Hasrah [1]
2Ch 34:22 son of Tokhath, the son of **Hasrah**, keeper of the wardrobe.

2898 חֶסְרוֹן ***ḥesrôn***, n.m. [1] [√ 2893]
lacking [1]
Ecc 1:15 twisted cannot be straightened; *what* is **lacking** cannot be counted.

2899 ¹חַף ***ḥap***¹, a. [1] [√ 2910]
clean [1]
Job 33: 9 'I am pure and without sin; I am **clean** and free from guilt.

2900 ²חַף ***ḥap***², n.pr.m. Not used in NIV/BHS

2901 חָפָא ***ḥāpā'***, v. [1]
secretly did [1]
2Ki 17: 9 [D] The Israelites **secretly did** things against the LORD their

2902 חָפָה ***ḥāpâ***, v. [12] [→ 2903, 2904; cf. 2910]
covered [4], overlaid [3], cover [2], are sheathed [1], paneled [1], was covered [1]
2Sa 15:30 [B] as he went; his head **was covered** and he was barefoot.
15:30 [A] All the people with him **covered** their heads too and were
2Ch 3: 5 [D] *He* **paneled** the main hall *with* pine and covered it with fine
3: 5 [D] and **covered** it *with* fine gold and decorated it with palm tree
3: 7 [D] *He* **overlaid** the ceiling beams, doorframes, walls and doors of the temple *with*
3: 8 [D] *He* **overlaid** the inside with six hundred talents of fine gold.
3: 9 [D] fifty shekels. *He* also **overlaid** the upper parts *with* gold.
Est 6:12 [B] But Haman rushed home, with his head **covered** *in* grief,
7: 8 [A] the word left the king's mouth, *they* **covered** Haman's face.
Ps 68:13 [68:14] [C] the wings of ⌞my⌟ dove **are sheathed** with silver, its
Jer 14: 3 [A] dismayed and despairing, *they* **cover** their heads.
14: 4 [A] in the land; the farmers are dismayed and **cover** their heads.

2903 ¹חֻפָּה ***ḥuppâ***¹, n.f. [3] [→ 2904; cf. 2902]
canopy [1], chamber [1], pavilion [1]
Ps 19: 5 [19:6] which is like a bridegroom coming forth from his **pavilion**,
Isa 4: 5 a glow of flaming fire by night; over all the glory will be a **canopy**.

Joel 2:16 Let the bridegroom leave his room and the bride her **chamber**.

2904 ²חֻפָּה **ḥuppâ²**, n.pr.m. [1] [√ 2903; cf. 2902]

Huppah [1]

1Ch 24:13 the thirteenth to **Huppah**, the fourteenth to Jeshebeab,

2905 חָפַז **ḥāpaz**, v. [9] [→ 2906]

alarm [1], alarmed [1], dismay [1], fled [1], headlong flight [1], hurried [1], hurrying [1], terrified [1], took to flight [1]

Dt 20:3 [A] *do* not *be* **terrified** or give way to panic before them.
1Sa 23:26 [C] men were on the other side, **hurrying** to get away from Saul.
2Sa 4:4 [A] but as she **hurried** to leave, he fell and became crippled.
2Ki 7:15 [A] the Arameans had thrown away in their **headlong flight**.
Job 40:23 [A] When the river rages, *he is* not **alarmed**; he is secure,
Ps 31:22 [31:23] [A] In my **alarm** I said, "I am cut off from your sight!"
48:5 [48:6] [C] saw ⌞her⌟ and were astounded; *they* **fled** in terror.
104:7 [C] waters fled, at the sound of your thunder *they* **took to flight**;
116:11 [A] And in my **dismay** I said, "All men are liars."

2906 חִפָּזוֹן **ḥippāzôn**, n.[m.]. [3] [√ 2905]

haste [3]

Ex 12:11 your staff in your hand. Eat it in **haste**; it is the LORD's Passover.
Dt 16:3 the bread of affliction, because you left Egypt in **haste**—
Isa 52:12 you will not leave in **haste** or go in flight; for the LORD will go

2907 חֻפִּים **ḥuppîm**, n.pr.m. & a.g. [3]

Huppites [2], Huppim [1]

Ge 46:21 Ashbel, Gera, Naaman, Ehi, Rosh, Muppim, **Huppim** and Ard.
1Ch 7:12 The Shuppites and **Huppites** were the descendants of Ir,
7:15 Makir took a wife from among the **Huppites** and Shuppites.

2908 חֹפֶן **ḥōpen**, n.[m.]. [6]

handfuls [+4850] [2], hands [2], hollow of hands [1], two handfuls [+4850] [1]

Ex 9:8 "Take **handfuls** [+4850] *of* soot from a furnace and have Moses
Lev 16:12 and **two handfuls** [+4850] *of* finely ground fragrant incense
Pr 30:4 Who has gathered up the wind in the **hollow** of his **hands**?
Ecc 4:6 Better one handful with tranquillity than *two* **handfuls** [+4850]
Eze 10:2 Fill your **hands** with burning coals from among the cherubim
10:7 He took up some of it and put it into the **hands** *of* the man in linen,

2909 חָפְנִי **ḥopnî**, n.pr.m. [5]

Hophni [5]

1Sa 1:3 where **Hophni** and Phinehas, the two sons of Eli, were priests of
2:34 to your two sons, **Hophni** and Phinehas, will be a sign to you—
4:4 Eli's two sons, **Hophni** and Phinehas, were there with the ark of
4:11 God was captured, and Eli's two sons, **Hophni** and Phinehas, died.
4:17 Also your two sons, **Hophni** and Phinehas, are dead, and the ark of

2910 חָפַף **ḥāpap**, v. [1] [→ 2572, 2899; cf. 2902]

shields [1]

Dt 33:12 [A] LORD rest secure in him, for *he* **shields** him all day long,

2911 ¹חָפֵץ **ḥāpēṣ¹**, v. [74] [→ 2913, 2914, 2915]

pleased [9], desire [7], delights [6], delighted [5], pleases [5], want [5], delight [4], desires [3], delight in [2], displeases [+4202] [2], eager [2], take any pleasure in [+2911] [2], take pleasure [2], will [2], delights in [1], desired [+3139] [1], favors [1], find delight [1], find pleasure [1], finds delight [1], finds pleasure [1], fond [1], found pleasure [1], have delight [1], have desire [1], have pleasure [1], meant [1], pleasure [1], rather [1], take delight [1], willing [1], wished [1]

Ge 34:19 [A] they said, because *he was* **delighted** with Jacob's daughter.
Nu 14:8 [A] If the LORD *is* **pleased** with us, he will lead us into that
Dt 21:14 [A] If *you are* not **pleased** with her, let her go wherever she
25:7 [A] However, if a man *does* not **want** to marry his brother's wife,
25:8 [A] to him. If he persists in saying, "*I do* not **want** to marry her,"
Jdg 13:23 [A] But his wife answered, "If the LORD *had* **meant** to kill us,
Ru 3:13 [A] if *he is* not **willing**, as surely as the LORD lives I will do it.
1Sa 2:25 [A] for *it was* the LORD's **will** to put them to death.
18:22 [A] David privately and say, 'Look, the king *is* **pleased** with you,
19:1 [A] to kill David. But Jonathan *was* very **fond** of David
2Sa 15:26 [A] But if he says, '*I am* not **pleased** with you,' then I am ready;
20:11 [A] men stood beside Amasa and said, "Whoever **favors** Joab,
22:20 [A] a spacious place; he rescued me because *he* **delighted** in me.
24:3 [A] But why *does* my lord the king **want** to do such a thing?"
1Ki 9:1 [A] and had achieved all he had **desired** [+3139] to do,
10:9 [A] who *has* **delighted** in you and placed you on the throne of
2Ch 9:8 [A] who *has* **delighted** in you and placed you on his throne as
Est 2:14 [A] She would not return to the king unless he *was* **pleased** with
6:6 [A] "What should be done for the man the king **delights** to
6:6 [A] "Who is there that the king *would* **rather** honor than me?"
6:7 [A] answered the king, "For the man the king **delights** to honor,
6:9 [A] Let them robe the man the king **delights** to honor, and lead
6:9 [A] 'This is what is done for the man the king **delights** to
6:11 [A] "This is what is done for the man the king **delights** to
Job 9:3 [A] Though *one* **wished** to dispute with him, he could not answer
13:3 [A] **I desire** to speak to the Almighty and to argue my case with
21:14 [A] 'Leave us alone! *We* **have** no **desire** to know your ways.
33:32 [A] to say, answer me; speak up, for *I* **want** you to be cleared.
Ps 18:19 [18:20] [A] he rescued me because *he* **delighted** in me.
22:8 [22:9] [A] Let him deliver him, since *he* **delights** in him."
37:23 [A] If the LORD **delights in** a man's way, he makes his steps
40:6 [40:7] [A] Sacrifice and offering *you did* not **desire**, but my
40:8 [40:9] [A] *I* **desire** to do your will, O my God; your law is
41:11 [41:12] [A] I know that *you are* **pleased** with me, for my enemy
51:6 [51:8] [A] Surely *you* **desire** truth in the inner parts; you teach
51:16 [51:18] [A] *You do* not **delight in** sacrifice, or I would bring it;
51:19 [51:21] [A] whole burnt offerings *to* **delight** *you*;
68:30 [68:31] [A] of silver. Scatter the nations *who* **delight in** war.
73:25 [A] but you? And earth has nothing *I* **desire** besides you.
109:17 [A] may it come on him; *he* **found** no **pleasure** in blessing—may
112:1 [A] fears the LORD, *who* **finds** great **delight** in his commands.
115:3 [A] Our God is in heaven; he does whatever **pleases** *him*.
119:35 [A] me in the path of your commands, for there *I* **find delight**.
135:6 [A] The LORD does whatever **pleases** *him*, in the heavens
147:10 [A] *His* **pleasure** *is* not in the strength of the horse, nor his
Pr 18:2 [A] A fool **finds** no **pleasure** in understanding but delights in
21:1 [A] he directs it like a watercourse wherever *he* **pleases**.
Ecc 8:3 [A] stand up for a bad cause, for he will do whatever *he* **pleases**.
SS 2:7 [A] of the field: Do not arouse or awaken love until *it so* **desires**.
3:5 [A] of the field: Do not arouse or awaken love until *it so* **desires**.
8:4 [A] charge you: Do not arouse or awaken love until *it so* **desires**.
Isa 1:11 [A] *I* **have** no **pleasure** *in* the blood of bulls and lambs
13:17 [A] who do not care for silver and **have** no **delight** in gold.
42:21 [A] *It* **pleased** the LORD for the sake of his righteousness to
53:10 [A] Yet *it was* the LORD's **will** to crush him and cause him to
55:11 [A] will accomplish what *I* **desire** and achieve the purpose for
56:4 [A] who choose what **pleases** me and hold fast to my covenant—
58:2 [A] *they seem* **eager** to know my ways, as if they were a nation
58:2 [A] just decisions and *seem* **eager** *for* God to come near them.
62:4 [A] for the LORD *will* **take delight** in you, and your land will
65:12 [A] did evil in my sight and chose what **displeases** [+4202] *me*."
66:3 [A] their own ways, and their souls **delight** in their abominations;
66:4 [A] did evil in my sight and chose what **displeases** [+4202] *me*."
Jer 6:10 [A] the LORD is offensive to them; *they* **find** no **pleasure** in it.
9:24 [9:23] [A] on earth, for in these *I* **delight**," declares the LORD.
42:22 [A] and plague in the place where *you* **want** to go to settle."
Eze 18:23 [A] *Do I* **take any pleasure** [+2911] **in** the death of the wicked?
18:23 [A] *Do I* **take any pleasure in** [+2911] the death of the wicked?
18:32 [A] For *I* **take** no **pleasure** in the death of anyone,
33:11 [A] *I* **take** no **pleasure** in the death of the wicked,
Hos 6:6 [A] For *I* **desire** mercy, not sacrifice, and acknowledgment of
Jnh 1:14 [A] for you, O LORD, have done as *you* **pleased**."
Mic 7:18 [A] You do not stay angry forever but **delight** to show mercy.
Mal 2:17 [A] he *is* **pleased** with them" or "Where is the God of justice?"

2912 ²חָפֵץ **ḥāpaṣ²**, v. [1]

sways [1]

Job 40:17 [A] His tail **sways** like a cedar; the sinews of his thighs are

2913 ³חָפֵץ **ḥāpēṣ³**, a.vbl. [12] [√ 2911]

desire [3], delight [2], delight in [1], delights in [1], loves [1], prefer [1], takes pleasure in [1], wanted [1], willing [1]

1Ki 13:33 Anyone *who* **wanted** to become a priest he consecrated for the
21:6 or if you **prefer**, I will give you another vineyard in its place.'
1Ch 28:9 serve him with wholehearted devotion and with a **willing** mind,
Ne 1:11 to the prayer of your servants who **delight** in revering your name.
Ps 5:4 [5:5] You are not a God *who* **takes pleasure in** evil; with you the
34:12 [34:13] Whoever of you **loves** life and desires to see many good
35:27 May *those who* **delight in** my vindication shout for joy
35:27 LORD be exalted, who **delights in** the well-being of his servant."
40:14 [40:15] may *all who* **desire** my ruin be turned back in disgrace.
70:2 [70:3] may *all who* **desire** my ruin be turned back in disgrace.
111:2 of the LORD; they are pondered by all *who* **delight** *in* them.
Mal 3:1 whom you **desire**, will come," says the LORD Almighty.

2914 חֵפֶץ **ḥēpeṣ**, n.m. [38] [√ 2911]

please [5], delight [3], desire [3], desired [3], pleasure [3], wants [3], activity [2], wanted [2], care [1], delightful [1], desires [1], eager [1], just right [1], matter [1], pleased [1], precious [1], purpose [1], such things[s] [1], want [1], will [1], wish [1], worthless [+401] [1]

1Sa 15: 22 "Does the LORD **delight** in burnt offerings and sacrifices as
18: 25 'The king **wants** no other price for the bride than a hundred
2Sa 23: 5 not bring to fruition my salvation and grant me my every **desire**?
1Ki 5: 8 [5:22] will do all you **want** in providing the cedar and pine logs.
5: 9 [5:23] you are to grant my **wish** by providing food for my royal
5: 10 [5:24] supplied with all the cedar and pine logs he **wanted**,
9: 11 had supplied him with all the cedar and pine and gold he **wanted**.
10: 13 King Solomon gave the queen of Sheba all she **desired** and asked
2Ch 9: 12 King Solomon gave the queen of Sheba all she **desired** and asked
Job 21: 21 For what does he **care** about the family he leaves behind when his
22: 3 What **pleasure** would it give the Almighty if you were righteous?
31: 16 "If I have denied the **desires** *of* the poor or let the eyes of the
Ps 1: 2 his **delight** is in the law of the LORD, and on his law he
16: 3 in the land, they are the glorious ones in whom is all my **delight**.
107: 30 when it grew calm, and he guided them to their **desired** haven.
Pr 3: 15 precious than rubies; nothing you **desire** can compare with her.
8: 11 precious than rubies, and nothing you **desire** can compare with her.
31: 13 She selects wool and flax and works with **eager** hands.
Ecc 3: 1 time for everything, and a season for every **activity** under heaven:
3: 17 and the wicked, for there will be a time for every **activity**,
5: 4 [5:3] in fulfilling it. He has no **pleasure** in fools; fulfill your vow.
5: 8 [5:7] and rights denied, do not be surprised at **such things**[s];
8: 6 For there is a proper time and procedure for every **matter**,
12: 1 years approach when you will say, "I find no **pleasure** in them"—
12: 10 The Teacher searched to find **just** the **right** words, and what he
Isa 44: 28 of Cyrus, 'He is my shepherd and will accomplish all *that* I **please**;
46: 10 I say: My purpose will stand, and I will do all *that* I **please**.
48: 14 The LORD's chosen ally will carry out his **purpose** against
53: 10 his days, and the **will** *of* the LORD will prosper in his hand.
54: 12 gates of sparkling jewels, and all your walls of **precious** stones.
58: 3 of your fasting, you do as you **please** and exploit all your workers.
58: 13 the Sabbath and from doing *as* you **please** on my holy day,
58: 13 your own way and not doing *as* you **please** or speaking idle words,
Jer 22: 28 man Jehoiachin a despised, broken pot, an object no one **wants**?
48: 38 for I have broken Moab like a jar that no one **wants**,"
Hos 8: 8 now she is among the nations like a **worthless** [+401] thing.
Mal 1: 10 that you would not light useless fires on my altar! I am not **pleased**
3: 12 for yours will be a **delightful** land," says the LORD Almighty.

2915 חֶפְצִי־בָהּ *ḥepṣî-bāh*, n.pr.f. [2] [√ 2911 + 928 + 2023]

Hephzibah [2]

2Ki 21: 1 in Jerusalem fifty-five years. His mother's name was **Hephzibah**.
Isa 62: 4 But you will be called **Hephzibah**, and your land Beulah;

2916 חָפַר¹ *ḥāpar¹*, v. [23 / 22] [→ 1783, 2919, 2921, 2923, 7249]

dug [10], spy out [3], dig a hole [1], digs [1], dug up [1], look about [1], paws [1], reopened [+906+2256+8740] [1], scoops out [1], search for [1], seeks out [1]

Ge 21: 30 [A] seven lambs from my hand as a witness that *I* **dug** this well."
26: 15 [A] So all the wells that his father's servants *had* **dug** in the time
26: 18 [A] Isaac **reopened** [+906+2256+8740] the wells that had been dug
26: 18 [A] Isaac reopened the wells that *had been* **dug** in the time of his
26: 19 [A] Isaac's servants **dug** in the valley and discovered a well of
26: 21 [A] *they* **dug** another well, but they quarreled over that one also;
26: 22 [A] He moved on from there and **dug** another well, and no one
26: 32 [A] servants came and told him about the well *they had* **dug**.
Ex 7: 24 [A] all the Egyptians **dug** along the Nile to get drinking water,
Nu 21: 18 [A] about the well that the princes **dug**, that the nobles of the
Dt 1: 22 [A] "Let us send men ahead *to* **spy out** the land for us and bring
23: 13 [23:14] [A] **dig a hole** and cover up your excrement.
Jos 2: 2 [A] Some of the Israelites have come here tonight to **spy out** the
2: 3 [A] because they have come to **spy out** the whole land."
Job 3: 21 [A] not come, *who* **search for** it more than for hidden treasure,
11: 18 [A] is hope; *you will* **look about** you and take your rest in safety.
39: 21 [A] *He* **paws** fiercely, rejoicing in his strength, and charges into
39: 29 [A] From there *he* **seeks out** his food; his eyes detect it from afar.
Ps 7: 15 [7:16] [A] and **scoops** it **out** falls into the pit he has made.
35: 7 [A] net for me without cause and without cause **dug** a pit for me,
Ecc 10: 8 [A] *Whoever* **digs** a pit may fall into it; whoever breaks through
Isa 2: 20 [a] men will throw away to the <u>rodents</u> [BHS *to dig*?; NIV 2923]
Jer 13: 7 [A] So I went to Perath and **dug up** the belt and took it from the

2917 חָפֵר² *ḥāpar²*, v. [17]

confusion [4], disgrace [3], disgraced [3], humiliated [2], abashed [1], ashamed [1], covered with shame [1], disappointed [1], dismay [1]

Job 6: 20 [A] been confident; they arrive there, only *to be* **disappointed**.
Ps 34: 5 [34:6] [A] their faces *are* never **covered with shame**.
35: 4 [A] may those who plot my ruin be turned back *in* **dismay**.
35: 26 [A] who gloat over my distress be put to shame and **confusion**;
40: 14 [40:15] [A] seek to take my life be put to shame and **confusion**;
70: 2 [70:3] [A] who seek my life be put to shame and **confusion**;
71: 24 [A] wanted to harm me have been put to shame and **confusion**.
83: 17 [83:18] [A] and dismayed; may they perish *in* **disgrace**.
Pr 13: 5 [G] hate what is false, but the wicked bring shame and **disgrace**.
19: 26 [G] out his mother is a son who brings shame and **disgrace**.
Isa 1: 29 [A] *you will be* **disgraced** because of the gardens that you have
24: 23 [A] The moon *will be* **abashed**, the sun ashamed; for the LORD
33: 9 [G] and wastes away, Lebanon *is* **ashamed** and withers;
54: 4 [G] Do not fear disgrace; *you will* not *be* **humiliated**.
Jer 15: 9 [A] set while it is still day; she will be disgraced and **humiliated**.
50: 12 [A] greatly ashamed; she who gave you birth *will be* **disgraced**.
Mic 3: 7 [A] The seers will be ashamed and the diviners **disgraced**. They

2918 חֵפֶר¹ *ḥēper¹*, n.pr.m. [7] [→ 2920]

Hepher [7]

Nu 26: 32 the Shemidaite clan; through **Hepher**, the Hepherite clan.
26: 33 (Zelophehad son of **Hepher** had no sons; he had only daughters,
27: 1 The daughters of Zelophehad son of **Hepher**, the son of Gilead,
Jos 17: 2 clans of Abiezer, Helek, Asriel, Shechem, **Hepher** and Shemida.
17: 3 Now Zelophehad son of **Hepher**, the son of Gilead, the son of
1Ch 4: 6 Naarah bore him Ahuzzam, **Hepher**, Temeni and Haahashtari.
11: 36 **Hepher** the Mekerathite, Ahijah the Pelonite,

2919 חֵפֶר² *ḥēper²*, n.pr.loc. [2] [→ 1783; cf. 2916]

Hepher [2]

Jos 12: 17 the king of Tappuah one the king of **Hepher** one
1Ki 4: 10 in Arubboth (Socoh and all the land of **Hepher** were his);

2920 חֶפְרִי *ḥeprî*, a.g. [1] [√ 2918]

Hepherite [1]

Nu 26: 32 the Shemidaite clan; through Hepher, the **Hepherite** clan.

2921 חֲפָרַיִם *ḥ^a^pārayim*, n.pr.loc. [1] [√ 2916]

Hapharaim [1]

Jos 19: 19 **Hapharaim**, Shion, Anaharath,

2922 חָפְרַע *ḥopra'*, n.pr.m. [1]

Hophra [1]

Jer 44: 30 'I am going to hand Pharaoh **Hophra** king of Egypt over to his

2923 חֲפַרְפָּרָה *ḥ^a^parpārâ*, n.f. [0 / 1] [√ 2916]

rodents [1]

Isa 2: 20 In that day men will throw away to the **rodents** [BHS 2916]

2924 חָפַשׂ *ḥāpaś*, v. [23 / 24] [→ 2925]

disguised himself [5], search [3], in disguise [2], searches [2], be ransacked [1], becomes like [1], devised [1], examine [1], go into hiding [1], hunt down [1], inquired [1], look around [1], plot [1], search for [1], searched [1], track down [1]

Ge 31: 35 [D] So *he* **searched** but could not find the household gods.
44: 12 [D] the steward *proceeded to* **search**, beginning with the oldest
1Sa 23: 23 [D] *I will* **track** him **down** among all the clans of Judah."
28: 8 [F] So Saul **disguised himself**, putting on other clothes, and at
1Ki 20: 6 [D] I am going to send my officials *to* **search** your palace and
20: 38 [F] *He* **disguised himself** with his headband down over his eyes.
22: 30 [F] "I will enter the battle **in disguise**, but you wear your royal
22: 30 [F] So the king of Israel **disguised himself** and went into battle.
2Ki 10: 23 [D] "**Look around** and see that no servants of the LORD are
2Ch 18: 29 [F] "I will enter the battle **in disguise**, but you wear your royal
18: 29 [F] So the king of Israel **disguised himself** and went into battle.
35: 22 [F] from him, but **disguised himself** to engage him in battle.
Job 28: 11 [D] *He* **searches** [BHS 2502] the sources of the rivers and brings
30: 18 [F] In his great power ⌞God⌟ **becomes like** clothing to me;
Ps 64: 6 [64:7] [A] *They* **plot** injustice and say, "We have devised a
64: 6 [64:7] [E] and say, "We have **devised** a perfect plan!"
77: 6 [77:7] [D] in the night. My heart mused and my spirit **inquired**:
Pr 2: 4 [A] for it as for silver and **search for** it as for hidden treasure,
20: 27 [A] The lamp of the LORD **searches** the spirit of a man;
28: 12 [E] but when the wicked rise to power, men **go into hiding**.
La 3: 40 [A] *Let us* **examine** our ways and test them, and let us return to
Am 9: 3 [D] top of Carmel, there *I will* **hunt** them **down** and seize them.
Ob 1: 6 [C] how Esau *will* **be ransacked**, his hidden treasures pillaged!
Zep 1: 12 [D] At that time *I will* **search** Jerusalem with lamps and punish

2925 חֵפֶשׂ ḥēpeś, n.[m.]. [1] [√ 2924]

plan [1]

Ps 64: 6 [64:7] plot injustice and say, "We have devised a perfect **plan**!"

2926 חָפַשׁ ḥāpaš, v. [1] [√ 2930]

been freed [1]

Lev 19: 20 [E] are not to be put to death, because *she had* not **been freed**.

2927 חֹפֶשׁ ḥōpeš, n.[m.]. [1]

blankets [+955] [1]

Eze 27: 20 " 'Dedan traded in saddle **blankets** [+955] with you.

2928 חֻפְשָׁה ḥupšâ, n.f. [1] [√ 2930]

freedom [1]

Lev 19: 20 another man but who has not been ransomed or given her **freedom**,

2929 חָפְשׁוּת ḥopšût, n.f. [0] [√ 2930]

2Ch 26: 21 [He lived in a **separate** [K; see Q 2931] house—leprous,]

2930 חָפְשִׁי ḥopšî, a. [17] [→ 2926, 2928, 2929, 2931]

free [9], free [+906+906+8938] [2], *untranslated* [1], exempt from taxes [+906+6913] [1], freed [+8938] [1], freed [1], set apart [1], set free [+906+4946+6640+8938] [1]

Ex 21: 2 But in the seventh year, he shall go **free**, without paying anything.
21: 5 my master and my wife and children and do not want to go **free**,'
21: 26 he must let the servant go **free** to compensate for the eye.
21: 27 he must let the servant go **free** to compensate for the tooth.
Dt 15: 12 serves you six years, in the seventh year you must let him go **free**.
15: 13 you release him, do not send him **[RPH]** away empty-handed.
15: 18 a hardship *to* **set** your servant **free** [+906+4946+6640+8938],
1Sa 17: 25 *will* **exempt** [+906+6913] his father's family **from taxes** in Israel."
Job 3: 19 and the great are there, and the slave is **freed** from his master.
39: 5 "Who let the wild donkey go **free**? Who untied his ropes?
Ps 88: 5 [88:6] I am **set apart** with the dead, like the slain who lie in the
Isa 58: 6 cords of the yoke, to set the oppressed **free** and break every yoke?
Jer 34: 9 was to **free** [+906+906+8938] his Hebrew slaves, both male and
34: 10 covenant agreed that they *would* **free** [+906+906+8938] their male
34: 11 took back the slaves *they had* **freed** [+8938] and enslaved them
34: 14 After he has served you six years, you must let him go **free**.'
34: 16 and female slaves you had set **free** to go where they wished.

2931 חָפְשִׁית ḥopšît, n.f. [2] [√ 2930]

separate [2]

2Ki 15: 5 leprosy until the day he died, and he lived in a **separate** house.
2Ch 26: 21 He lived in a **separate** [K 2929] house—leprous, and excluded

2932 חֵץ ḥēṣ, n.m. [52] [→ 2943]

arrows [38], arrow [12], archers [+1251] [1], did so[s] [+448+2256+4374+8008] [1]

Ge 49: 23 With bitterness **archers** [+1251] attacked him; they shot at him
Nu 24: 8 break their bones in pieces; with their **arrows** they pierce them.
Dt 32: 23 heap calamities upon them and spend my **arrows** against them.
32: 42 I will make my **arrows** drunk with blood, while my sword devours
1Sa 17: 7 [His spear **shaft** [K; see Q 6770] was like a weaver's rod,]
20: 20 I will shoot three **arrows** to the side of it, as though I were
20: 21 I will send a boy and say, 'Go, find the **arrows**.' If I say to him,
20: 21 If I say to him, 'Look, the **arrows** are on this side of you;
20: 22 to the boy, 'Look, the **arrows** are beyond you,' then you must go,
20: 36 and he said to the boy, "Run and find the **arrows** I shoot."
20: 38 [The boy picked up the **arrow** [Q; see K 2943] and returned to his]
2Sa 22: 15 He shot **arrows** and scattered ⌊the enemies⌋, bolts of lightning
2Ki 13: 15 Elisha said, "Get a bow and *some* **arrows**," and he did so.
13: 15 and some arrows," and *he* **did**[s] **so** [+448+2256+4374+8008].
13: 17 "The LORD's **arrow** *of* victory, the arrow of victory over Aram!"
13: 17 "The LORD's arrow of victory, the **arrow** *of* victory over Aram!"
13: 18 Then he said, "Take the **arrows**," and the king took them.
19: 32 "He will not enter this city or shoot an **arrow** here. He will not
1Ch 12: 2 they were armed with bows and were able to shoot **arrows**
2Ch 26: 15 and on the corner defenses to shoot **arrows** and hurl large stones.
Job 6: 4 The **arrows** *of* the Almighty are in me, my spirit drinks in their
34: 6 although I am guiltless, his **arrow** inflicts an incurable wound.'
Ps 7: 13 [7:14] his deadly weapons; he makes ready his flaming **arrows**.
11: 2 they set their **arrows** against the strings to shoot from the shadows
18: 14 [18:15] He shot his **arrows** and scattered ⌊the enemies⌋, great
38: 2 [38:3] For your **arrows** have pierced me, and your hand has come
45: 5 [45:6] Let your sharp **arrows** pierce the hearts of the king's
57: 4 [57:5] men whose teeth are spears and **arrows**, whose tongues are
58: 7 [58:8] when they draw the bow, let their **arrows** be blunted.
64: 3 [64:4] like swords and aim their words like deadly **arrows**.
64: 7 [64:8] God will shoot them with **arrows**; suddenly they will be
77: 17 [77:18] with thunder; your **arrows** flashed back and forth.
91: 5 will not fear the terror of night, nor the **arrow** that flies by day,
120: 4 He will punish you with a warrior's sharp **arrows**, with burning
127: 4 Like **arrows** in the hands of a warrior are sons born in one's youth.
144: 6 and scatter ⌊the enemies⌋; shoot your **arrows** and rout them.
Pr 7: 23 till an **arrow** pierces his liver, like a bird darting into a snare,
25: 18 or a sharp **arrow** is the man who gives false testimony against his
26: 18 Like a madman shooting firebrands or deadly **arrows**
Isa 5: 28 Their **arrows** are sharp, all their bows are strung; their horses'
7: 24 Men will go there with bow and **arrow**, for the land will be
37: 33 "He will not enter this city or shoot an **arrow** here. He will not
49: 2 he made me into a polished **arrow** and concealed me in his quiver.
Jer 9: 8 [9:7] Their tongue is a deadly **arrow**; it speaks with deceit.
50: 9 Their **arrows** will be like skilled warriors who do not return
50: 14 at her! Spare no **arrows**, for she has sinned against the LORD.
51: 11 "Sharpen the **arrows**, take up the shields! The LORD has stirred
La 3: 12 He drew his bow and made me the target for his **arrows**.
Eze 5: 16 I shoot at you with my deadly and destructive **arrows** *of* famine,
21: 21 [21:26] He will cast lots with **arrows**, he will consult his idols,
39: 3 your left hand and make your **arrows** drop from your right hand.
39: 9 and large shields, the bows and **arrows**, the war clubs and spears.
Hab 3: 11 moon stood still in the heavens at the glint of your flying **arrows**,
Zec 9: 14 LORD will appear over them; his **arrow** will flash like lightning.

2933 ¹חָצַב ḥāṣēb¹, v. [16] [→ 2935, 4732; cf. 2934]

dug [3], cut out [2], dig [2], *untranslated* [1], cut in pieces [1], cut to pieces [1], engraved [1], hewing [1], hewn out [1], prepare [1], swings [1], were cut [1]

Dt 6: 11 [B] wells **[RPH]** you did not dig, and vineyards and olive
6: 11 [A] wells *you did* not **dig**, and vineyards and olive groves you
8: 9 [A] the rocks are iron and *you can* **dig** copper out of the hills.
1Ch 22: 2 [A] from among them he appointed stonecutters to **prepare**
2Ch 26: 10 [A] He also built towers in the desert and **dug** many cisterns,
Ne 9: 25 [B] wells *already* **dug**, vineyards, olive groves and fruit trees in
Job 19: 24 [C] with an iron tool on lead, or **engraved** in rock forever!
Pr 9: 1 [A] has built her house; *she has* **hewn out** its seven pillars.
Isa 5: 2 [A] He built a watchtower in it and **cut out** a winepress as well.
10: 15 [A] Does the ax raise itself above him *who* **swings** it, or the saw
22: 16 [A] who gave you permission *to* **cut out** a grave for yourself
22: 16 [A] **hewing** your grave on the height and chiseling your resting
51: 1 [E] Look to the rock from which *you* **were cut** and to the quarry
51: 9 [G] Was it not you who **cut** Rahab **to pieces**, who pierced that
Jer 2: 13 [A] the spring of living water, and *have* **dug** their own cisterns,
Hos 6: 5 [A] Therefore *I* **cut** you **in pieces** with my prophets, I killed you

2934 ²חָצַב ḥāṣab², v. [1] [cf. 2933]

strikes [1]

Ps 29: 7 [A] The voice of the LORD **strikes** with flashes of lightning.

2935 חֹצֵב ḥōṣēb, n.[m.] *or* v.ptcp. [8] [√ 2933]

stonecutters [5], masons [2], stonecutters [+74] [1]

1Ki 5: 15 [5:29] and eighty thousand **stonecutters** in the hills,
2Ki 12: 12 [12:13] the masons and **stonecutters** [+74]. They purchased
1Ch 22: 2 from among them he appointed **stonecutters** to prepare dressed
22: 15 **stonecutters**, masons and carpenters, as well as men skilled in
2Ch 2: 2 [2:1] eighty thousand as **stonecutters** in the hills and thirty-six
2: 18 [2:17] to be carriers and 80,000 to be **stonecutters** in the hills,
24: 12 They hired **masons** and carpenters to restore the LORD's temple,
Ezr 3: 7 they gave money to the **masons** and carpenters, and gave food

2936 חָצָה ḥāṣâ, v. [15] [→ 2940, 2942, 2944, 3505, 3507, 4733, 4734; cf. 2951, 2952, 2953]

divided [5], *untranslated* [1], be divided [1], divide equally [1], divide up [1], divide [1], dividing [1], live out half [1], parceled out [1], rising up [1], set apart [1]

Ge 32: 7 [32:8] [A] **divided** the people who were with him into two groups,
33: 1 [A] so *he* **divided** the children among Leah, Rachel and the two
Ex 21: 35 [A] and **divide** both the money and the dead animal **equally**.
21: 35 [A] divide both the money and the dead animal equally. **[RPH]**
Nu 31: 27 [A] **Divide** the spoils between the soldiers who took part in the
31: 42 [A] which Moses **set apart** from that of the fighting men—
Jdg 7: 16 [A] **Dividing** the three hundred men into three companies, he
9: 43 [A] **divided** them into three companies and set an ambush in the
2Ki 2: 8 [C] The water **divided** to the right and to the left, and the two of
2: 14 [C] *it* **divided** to the right and to the left, and he crossed over.
Job 41: 6 [40:30] [A] *Will they* **divide** him **up** among the merchants?
Ps 55: 23 [55:24] [A] and deceitful men *will* not **live out half** their days.
Isa 30: 28 [A] His breath is like a rushing torrent, **rising up** to the neck.

Eze 37:22 [C] never again be two nations or **be divided** into two kingdoms.
Da 11: 4 [C] broken up and **parceled out** toward the four winds of heaven.

2937 חָצוֹר **ḥāṣôr[1]**, n.pr.loc. [15] [→ 6533; cf. 2958]

Hazor [15]

Jos 11: 1 When Jabin king of **Hazor** heard of this, he sent word to Jobab
11:10 turned back and captured **Hazor** and put its king to the sword.
11:10 to the sword. (**Hazor** had been the head of all these kingdoms.)
11:11 not sparing anything that breathed, and he burned up **Hazor** itself.
11:13 cities built on their mounds—except **Hazor**, which Joshua burned.
12:19 the king of Madon one the king of **Hazor** one
15:23 Kedesh, **Hazor**, Ithnan,
15:25 Hazor Hadattah, Kerioth Hezron (that is, **Hazor**),
19:36 Adamah, Ramah, **Hazor**,
Jdg 4: 2 into the hands of Jabin, a king of Canaan, who reigned in **Hazor**.
4:17 because there were friendly relations between Jabin king of **Hazor**
1Sa 12: 9 the commander of the army of **Hazor**, and into the hands of the
1Ki 9:15 the wall of Jerusalem, and **Hazor**, Megiddo and Gezer.
2Ki 15:29 and took Ijon, Abel Beth Maacah, Janoah, Kedesh and **Hazor**.
Ne 11:33 in **Hazor**, Ramah and Gittaim,

2938 חָצוֹר[2] **ḥāṣôr[2]**, n.pr.loc. [3] [√ 2958]

Hazor [3]

Jer 49:28 Concerning Kedar and the kingdoms of **Hazor**,
49:30 Stay in deep caves, you who live in **Hazor**," declares the LORD.
49:33 "**Hazor** will become a haunt of jackals, a desolate place forever.

2939 חָצוֹר חֲדַתָּה **ḥāṣôr ḥ[a]dattâ**, n.pr.loc. [1] [√ 2958]

Hazor Hadattah [1]

Jos 15:25 **Hazor Hadattah**, Kerioth Hezron (that is, Hazor),

2940 חֲצוֹת **ḥ[a]ṣôt**, n.f. [3] [√ 2936]

midnight [+4326] [2], middle [1]

Ex 11: 4 'About **midnight** [+4326] I will go throughout Egypt.
Job 34:20 They die in an instant, in the **middle** *of* the night; the people are
Ps 119:62 *At* **midnight** [+4326] I rise to give you thanks for your righteous

2941 חֻצוֹת **ḥuṣôt**, n.pr.loc. Not used in NIV/BHS [→ 7960]

2942 חֵצִי **ḥ[e]ṣî**, n.m. [125] [√ 2936]

half [79], half-tribe [+8657] [18], middle [6], half-tribe [+4751] [5], half-district [+7135] [4], *untranslated* [3], halfway [2], two [2], half-tribe [1], it[s] [+2257] [1], midnight [+2021+4326] [1], midst [1], nine-and-a-half [+2256+9596] [1], two-and-a-half [+2256+9109] [1]

Ex 12:29 At **midnight** [+2021+4326] the LORD struck down all the
24: 6 Moses took **half** *of* the blood and put it in bowls, and the other half
24: 6 and put it in bowls, and the other **half** he sprinkled on the altar.
25:10 two and a **half** cubits long, a cubit and a half wide, and a cubit
25:10 cubits long, a cubit and a **half** wide, and a cubit and a half high.
25:10 cubits long, a cubit and a half wide, and a cubit and a **half** high.
25:17 pure gold—two and a **half** cubits long and a cubit and a half wide.
25:17 pure gold—two and a half cubits long and a cubit and a **half** wide.
25:23 two cubits long, a cubit wide and a cubit and a **half** high.
26:12 the **half** curtain that is left over is to hang down at the rear of the
26:16 Each frame is to be ten cubits long and a cubit and a **half** wide,
27: 5 Put it under the ledge of the altar so that it is **halfway** up the altar.
36:21 Each frame was ten cubits long and a cubit and a **half** wide,
37: 1 two and a **half** cubits long, a cubit and a half wide, and a cubit
37: 1 cubits long, a cubit and a **half** wide, and a cubit and a half high.
37: 1 cubits long, a cubit and a half wide, and a cubit and a **half** high.
37: 6 pure gold—two and a **half** cubits long and a cubit and a half wide.
37: 6 pure gold—two and a half cubits long and a cubit and a **half** wide.
37:10 two cubits long, a cubit wide, and a cubit and a **half** high.
38: 4 a bronze network, to be under its ledge, **halfway** up the altar.
Nu 12:12 coming from its mother's womb with its flesh **half** eaten away."
15: 9 three-tenths of an ephah of fine flour mixed with **half** a hin of oil.
15:10 Also bring **half** a hin of wine as a drink offering. It will be an
28:14 With each bull there is to be a drink offering of **half** a hin of wine;
32:33 the **half-tribe** [+8657] *of* Manasseh son of Joseph the kingdom of
34:13 LORD has ordered that it be given to the nine and a **half** tribes,
34:14 the **half-tribe** [+4751] *of* Manasseh have received their
34:15 a **half** tribes have received their inheritance on the east side of the
Dt 3:12 including **half** the hill country of Gilead, together with its towns.
3:13 the kingdom of Og, I gave to the **half** tribe of Manasseh.
29: 8 [29:7] the Gadites and the **half-tribe** [+8657] *of* Manasseh.
Jos 1:12 the Gadites and the **half-tribe** [+8657] *of* Manasseh, Joshua said,
4:12 Gad and the **half-tribe** [+8657] *of* Manasseh crossed over,
8:33 **Half** *of* the people stood in front of Mount Gerizim and half of
8:33 in front of Mount Gerizim and **half** *of* them in front of Mount Ebal,
10:13 The sun stopped in the **middle** *of* the sky and delayed going down
12: 2 is the border of the Ammonites. This included **half** *of* Gilead.
12: 5 and **half** *of* Gilead to the border of Sihon king of Heshbon.
12: 6 and the **half-tribe** [+8657] *of* Manasseh to be their possession.
13: 7 among the nine tribes and **half** *of* the tribe of Manasseh."
13:25 towns of Gilead and **half** the Ammonite country as far as Aroer,
13:29 This is what Moses had given to the **half-tribe** [+8657] *of*
13:29 that is, to **half** the family of the descendants of Manasseh,
13:31 **half** *of* Gilead, and Ashtaroth and Edrei (the royal cities of Og in
13:31 son of Manasseh—for **half** *of* the sons of Makir, clan by clan.
14: 2 were assigned by lot to the **nine-and-a-half** [+2256+9596] tribes,
14: 3 granted the **two-and-a-half** [+2256+9109] tribes their inheritance
18: 7 the **half-tribe** [+8657] *of* Manasseh have already received their
21: 5 from the clans of the tribes of Ephraim, Dan and **half** *of* Manasseh.
21: 6 Naphtali and the **half-tribe** [+4751] *of* Manasseh in Bashan.
21:27 from the **half-tribe** [+4751] *of* Manasseh, Golan in Bashan (a city
22: 1 the Gadites and the **half-tribe** [+4751] *of* Manasseh
22: 7 (To the **half-tribe** [+8657] *of* Manasseh Moses had given land in
22: 7 to the other **half** *of* the tribe Joshua gave land on the west side of
22: 9 the **half-tribe** [+8657] *of* Manasseh left the Israelites at Shiloh in
22:10 the **half-tribe** [+8657] *of* Manasseh built an imposing altar there
22:11 of Canaan at Geliloth **[RPH]** near the Jordan on the Israelite side,
22:13 to Reuben, Gad and the **half-tribe** [+8657] *of* Manasseh.
22:15 to Reuben, Gad and the **half-tribe** [+8657] *of* Manasseh—
22:21 the **half-tribe** [+8657] *of* Manasseh replied to the heads of the
Jdg 16: 3 Samson lay there only until the **middle** *of* the night. Then he got
16: 3 Then he got up **[RPH]** and took hold of the doors of the city gate,
Ru 3: 8 In the **middle** *of* the night something startled the man, and he
1Sa 14:14 his armor-bearer killed some twenty men in an area of about **half**
2Sa 10: 4 Hanun seized David's men, shaved off **half** *of* each man's beard,
10: 4 cut off their garments in the **middle** at the buttocks, and sent them
18: 3 Even if **half** *of* us die, they won't care; but you are worth ten
19:40 [19:41] and **half** the troops of Israel had taken the king over.
1Ki 3:25 the living child in two and give **half** to one and half to the other."
3:25 the living child in two and give half to one and **half** to the other."
7:31 was round, and with its basework it measured a cubit and a **half**.
7:32 to the stand. The diameter of each wheel was a cubit and a **half**.
7:35 At the top of the stand there was a circular band **half** a cubit deep.
10: 7 Indeed, not even **half** was told me; in wisdom and wealth you have
13: 8 "Even if you were to give me **half** your possessions, I would not
16:21 the people of Israel were split into **two** *factions*; half supported
16:21 **half** supported Tibni son of Ginath for king, and the other half
16:21 Tibni son of Ginath for king, and the other **half** supported Omri.
1Ch 2:52 the father of Kiriath Jearim were: Haroeh, **half** the Manahathites,
2:54 Atroth Beth Joab, **half** the Manahathites, the Zorites,
5:18 the **half-tribe** [+8657] *of* Manasseh had 44,760 men ready for
5:23 The people of the **half-tribe** [+8657] *of* Manasseh were numerous;
5:26 the Gadites and the **half-tribe** [+8657] *of* Manasseh into exile.
6:61 [6:46] towns from the clans of half the tribe of **[RPH]** Manasseh.
6:71 [6:56] From the clan of the **half-tribe** [+4751] *of* Manasseh they
12:31 [12:32] men of **half** the tribe of Manasseh, designated by name to
12:37 [12:38] of Reuben, Gad and the **half-tribe** [+8657] *of* Manasseh,
19: 4 shaved them, cut off their garments in the **middle** at the buttocks,
26:32 the **half-tribe** [+8657] *of* Manasseh for every matter pertaining to
27:20 Hoshea son of Azaziah; over **half** the tribe of Manasseh: Joel son
27:21 over the **half-tribe** *of* Manasseh in Gilead: Iddo son of Zechariah;
2Ch 9: 6 Indeed, not even **half** the greatness of your wisdom was told me;
Ne 3: 9 Rephaiah son of Hur, ruler of a **half-district** [+7135] *of* Jerusalem,
3:12 son of Hallohesh, ruler of a **half-district** [+7135] *of* Jerusalem,
3:16 son of Azbuk, ruler of a **half-district** [+7135] *of* Beth Zur,
3:17 Beside him, Hashabiah, ruler of **half** the district of Keilah,
3:18 son of Henadad, ruler of the other **half-district** [+7135] *of* Keilah.
4: 6 [3:38] So we rebuilt the wall till all of it reached **half** its height,
4:16 [4:10] From that day on, **half** *of* my men did the work,
4:16 [4:10] while the other **half** were equipped with spears, shields,
4:21 [4:15] So we continued the work with **half** the men holding
12:32 Hoshaiah and **half** the leaders of Judah followed them,
12:38 I followed them on top of the wall, together with **half** the people—
12:40 in the house of God; so did I, together with **half** the officials,
13:24 **Half** *of* their children spoke the language of Ashdod or the
Est 5: 3 your request? Even up to **half** the kingdom, it will be given you."
5: 6 is your request? Even up to **half** the kingdom, it will be granted."
7: 2 is your request? Even up to **half** the kingdom, it will be granted."
Ps 102:24 [102:25] not take me away, O my God, in the **midst** *of* my days;
Isa 44:16 **Half** *of* the wood he burns in the fire; over it he prepares his meal,
44:16 over **it**[s] [+2257] he prepares his meal, he roasts his meat and eats
44:19 the knowledge or understanding to say, "**Half** *of* it I used for fuel;
Jer 17:11 When his life is **half** *gone*, they will desert him, and in the end he
Eze 16:51 Samaria did not commit **half** the sins you did. You have done more
40:42 each a cubit and a **half** long, a cubit and a half wide and a cubit
40:42 a cubit and a half long, a cubit and a **half** wide and a cubit high.
43:17 with a rim of **half** a cubit and a gutter of a cubit all around.
Da 9:27 *In* the **middle** *of* the 'seven' he will put an end to sacrifice
12: 7 lives forever, saying, "It will be for a time, times and **half** a time.
Zec 14: 2 **Half** *of* the city will go into exile, but the rest of the people will not

Zec 14: 4 and the Mount of Olives will be split in **two** from east to west,
14: 4 with **half** *of* the mountain moving north and half moving south.
14: 4 with half of the mountain moving north and **half** moving south.
14: 8 **half** to the eastern sea and half to the western sea, in summer
14: 8 half to the eastern sea and **half** to the western sea, in summer

2943 ¹חֵצִי **חֵ֫צִי** ***ḥēṣî¹***, n.m. [5] [√ 2932]

arrow [5]

1Sa 20: 36 the arrows I shoot." As the boy ran, he shot an **arrow** beyond him.
20: 37 When the boy came to the place where Jonathan's **arrow** had
20: 37 Jonathan called out after him, "Isn't the **arrow** beyond you?"
20: 38 The boy picked up the **arrow** [Q 2932] and returned to his master.
2Ki 9: 24 The **arrow** pierced his heart and he slumped down in his chariot.

2944 ²חֵצִי **חֵ֫צִי** ***ḥēṣî²***, n.m. Not used in NIV/BHS [√ 2936]

2945 ¹חָצִיר **חָצִיר** ***ḥāṣîr¹***, n.m. [20]

grass [19], hay [1]

1Ki 18: 5 Maybe we can find *some* **grass** to keep the horses and mules alive
2Ki 19: 26 like tender green shoots, like **grass** *sprouting on* the roof,
Job 8: 12 still growing and uncut, they wither more quickly than **grass**.
40: 15 which I made along with you and which feeds on **grass** like an ox.
Ps 37: 2 for like the **grass** they will soon wither, like green plants they will
90: 5 in the sleep of death; they are like the new **grass** of the morning—
103: 15 As for man, his days are like **grass**, he flourishes like a flower of
104: 14 He makes **grass** grow for the cattle, and plants for man to
129: 6 May they be like **grass** *on* the roof, which withers before it can
147: 8 he supplies the earth with rain and makes **grass** grow on the hills.
Pr 27: 25 When the **hay** is removed and new growth appears and the grass
Isa 15: 6 The waters of Nimrim are dried up and the **grass** is withered;
35: 7 where jackals once lay, **grass** and reeds and papyrus will grow.
37: 27 like tender green shoots, like **grass** *sprouting on* the roof,
40: 6 "All men are like **grass**, and all their glory is like the flowers of the
40: 7 The **grass** withers and the flowers fall, because the breath of the
40: 7 breath of the LORD blows on them. Surely the people are **grass**.
40: 8 The **grass** withers and the flowers fall, but the word of our God
44: 4 They will spring up like **grass** in a meadow, like poplar trees by
51: 12 you that you fear mortal men, the sons of men, who are but **grass**,

2946 ²חָצִיר **חָצִיר** ***ḥāṣîr²***, n.m. [1] [→ 2947, 2955, 2956, 2968, 2969, 2974]

leeks [1]

Nu 11: 5 at no cost—also the cucumbers, melons, **leeks**, onions and garlic.

2947 ³חָצִיר **חָצִיר** ***ḥāṣîr³***, n.[m.] & n.m. Not used in NIV/BHS [√ 2946]

2948 ⁴חָצִיר **חָצִיר** ***ḥāṣîr⁴***, n.[m.]. [1]

home [1]

Isa 34: 13 She will become a haunt for jackals, a **home** for owls.

2949 חֵצֶן **חֵ֫צֶן** ***ḥēṣen***, n.m. Not used in NIV/BHS [→ 2950, 3079?]

2950 חֹצֶן **חֹ֫צֶן** ***ḥōṣen***, n.m. [3] [√ 2949]

arms [2], folds of robe [1]

Ne 5: 13 I also shook out the **folds of** my **robe** and said, "In this way may
Ps 129: 7 reaper cannot fill his hands, nor the one who gathers fill his **arms**.
Isa 49: 22 they will bring your sons in their **arms** and carry your daughters on

2951 ¹חָצַץ **חָצַץ** ***ḥāṣaṣ¹***, v. [2] [cf. 2936]

come to an end [1], in ranks [1]

Job 21: 21 [E] he leaves behind when his allotted months **come to an end**?
Pr 30: 27 [A] locusts have no king, yet they advance together **in ranks**;

2952 ²חָצַץ **חָצַץ** ***ḥāṣaṣ²***, v.den. [1] [cf. 2936]

singers [1]

Jdg 5: 11 [D] the voice of the **singers** at the watering places. They recite

2953 חָצָץ **חָצָץ** ***ḥāṣāṣ***, n.[m.]. [2] [cf. 2936]

gravel [2]

Pr 20: 17 tastes sweet to a man, but he ends up with a mouth full of **gravel**.
La 3: 16 He has broken my teeth with **gravel**; he has trampled me in the

2954 חַצְצוֹן תָּמָר **חַֽצְצ֫וֹן תָּמָר** ***haṣᵉṣôn tāmār***, n.pr.loc. [2] [cf. 9469]

Hazazon Tamar [2]

Ge 14: 7 as well as the Amorites who were living in **Hazazon Tamar**.
2Ch 20: 2 of the Sea. It is already in **Hazazon Tamar**" (that is, En Gedi).

2955 חצצר **חָצַר** ***ḥaṣṣar***, v.den. [6] [√ 2956; cf. 2946]

blew trumpets [1], blew [1], blow [1], played [1], sounding [1], trumpeters [1]

1Ch 15: 24 [D] Eliezer the priests *were to* **blow** trumpets before the ark of
2Ch 5: 12 [D] They were accompanied by 120 priests **sounding** trumpets.
5: 13 [D] The **trumpeters** and singers joined in unison, as with one
7: 6 [D] Opposite the Levites, the priests **blew** *their* **trumpets**, and
13: 14 [D] cried out to the LORD. The priests **blew** their trumpets
29: 28 [D] in worship, while the singers sang and the trumpeters **played**.

2956 חֲצֹצְרָה **חֲצֹצְרָה** ***hᵃṣōṣᵉrâ***, n.f. [29] [→ 2955, 2957; cf. 2946]

trumpets [25], trumpeters [3], horn [1]

Nu 10: 2 "Make two **trumpets** *of* hammered silver, and use them for calling
10: 8 "The sons of Aaron, the priests, are to blow the **trumpets**.
10: 9 an enemy who is oppressing you, sound a blast on the **trumpets**.
10: 10 you are to sound the **trumpets** over your burnt offerings
31: 6 him articles from the sanctuary and the **trumpets** *for* signaling.
2Ki 11: 14 The officers and the **trumpeters** were beside the king, and all the
11: 14 all the people of the land were rejoicing and blowing **trumpets**.
12: 13 [12:14] **trumpets** or any other articles of gold or silver for the
1Ch 13: 8 and with harps, lyres, tambourines, cymbals and **trumpets**.
15: 24 Eliezer the priests were to blow **trumpets** before the ark of God.
15: 28 with the sounding of rams' horns and **trumpets**, and of cymbals,
16: 6 Jahaziel the priests were to blow the **trumpets** regularly before the
16: 42 and Jeduthun were responsible for the sounding of the **trumpets**
2Ch 5: 12 They were accompanied by 120 priests sounding **trumpets**.
5: 13 Accompanied by **trumpets**, cymbals and other instruments,
13: 12 His priests with their **trumpets** will sound the battle cry against
13: 14 they cried out to the LORD. The priests blew their **trumpets**
15: 14 loud acclamation, with shouting and with **trumpets** and horns.
20: 28 to the temple of the LORD with harps and lutes and **trumpets**.
23: 13 The officers and the **trumpeters** were beside the king, and all the
23: 13 all the people of the land were rejoicing and blowing **trumpets**,
29: 26 with David's instruments, and the priests with their **trumpets**.
29: 27 accompanied by **trumpets** and the instruments of David king of
29: 28 in worship, while the singers sang and the **trumpeters** played.
Ezr 3: 10 the priests in their vestments and with **trumpets**, and the Levites
Ne 12: 35 as well as some priests with **trumpets**, and also Zechariah son of
12: 41 Micaiah, Elioenai, Zechariah and Hananiah with their **trumpets**—
Ps 98: 6 with **trumpets** and the blast of the ram's horn—shout for joy
Hos 5: 8 "Sound the trumpet in Gibeah, the **horn** in Ramah. Raise the battle

2957 חָצַר **חָצַר** ***ḥāṣar***, v. Not used in NIV/BHS [√ 2956]

2958 ¹חָצֵר **חָצֵר** ***ḥāṣēr¹***, n.m. [191] [→ 2937, 2938, 2939, 2959, 2962, 2973]

courtyard [59], court [48], villages [45], courts [21], *untranslated* [6], courtyards [4], its[s] [+2021] [2], settlements [2], enclosed [1], set farther back [+337+2021] [1], surrounding villages [1], where[s] [+2021+2021+2667] [1]

Ge 25: 16 the names of the twelve tribal rulers according to their **settlements**
Ex 8: 13 [8:9] frogs died in the houses, in the **courtyards** and in the fields.
27: 9 "Make a **courtyard** *for* the tabernacle. The south side shall be a
27: 9 cubits long and is to have **[RPH]** curtains of finely twisted linen,
27: 12 "The west end of the **courtyard** shall be fifty cubits wide
27: 13 toward the sunrise, the **courtyard** shall also be fifty cubits wide.
27: 16 "For the entrance to the **courtyard**, provide a curtain twenty cubits
27: 17 All the posts around the **courtyard** are to have silver bands
27: 18 The **courtyard** shall be a hundred cubits long and fifty cubits
27: 19 including all the tent pegs for it and those for the **courtyard**,
35: 17 the curtains of the **courtyard** with its posts and bases, and the
35: 17 and bases, and the curtain for the entrance to the **courtyard**;
35: 18 the tent pegs for the tabernacle and for the **courtyard**, and their
38: 9 Next they made the **courtyard**. The south side was a hundred
38: 9 cubits long and had curtains **[RPH]** of finely twisted linen,
38: 15 cubits long were on the other side of the entrance to the **courtyard**,
38: 16 All the curtains around the **courtyard** were of finely twisted linen.
38: 17 with silver; so all the posts of the **courtyard** had silver bands.
38: 18 The curtain for the entrance to the **courtyard** was of blue,
38: 18 long and, like the curtains of the **courtyard**, five cubits high,
38: 20 of the tabernacle and of the surrounding **courtyard** were bronze.
38: 31 the bases for the surrounding **courtyard** and those for its entrance
38: 31 those for **its**[s] [+2021] entrance and all the tent pegs for the
38: 31 pegs for the tabernacle and those for the surrounding **courtyard**.
39: 40 the curtains of the **courtyard** with its posts and bases, and the
39: 40 and bases, and the curtain for the entrance to the **courtyard**;
40: 8 Set up the **courtyard** around it and put the curtain at the entrance
40: 8 around it and put the curtain at the entrance to the **courtyard**.
40: 33 Then Moses set up the **courtyard** around the tabernacle and altar

Ex 40:33 and altar and put up the curtain at the entrance to the **courtyard**.
Lev 6:16 [6:9] they are to eat it in the **courtyard** *of* the Tent of Meeting.
6:26 [6:19] in a holy place, in the **courtyard** *of* the Tent of Meeting.
25:31 houses in **villages** without walls around them are to be considered
Nu 3:26 the curtains of the **courtyard**, the curtain at the entrance to the
3:26 the curtain at the entrance to the **courtyard** surrounding the
3:37 as well as the posts of the surrounding **courtyard** with their bases,
4:26 the curtains of the **courtyard** surrounding the tabernacle and altar,
4:26 **[RPH]** the ropes and all the equipment used in its service.
4:32 as well as the posts of the surrounding **courtyard** with their bases,
Dt 2:23 And as for the Avvites who lived in **villages** as far as Gaza,
Jos 13:23 and their **villages** were the inheritance of the Reubenites,
13:28 These towns and their **villages** were the inheritance of the Gadites,
15:32 and Rimmon—a total of twenty-nine towns and their **villages**.
15:36 and Gederah (or Gederothaim)—fourteen towns and their **villages**.
15:41 Naamah and Makkedah—sixteen towns and their **villages**.
15:44 Keilah, Aczib and Mareshah—nine towns and their **villages**.
15:45 Ekron, with its surrounding settlements and **villages**;
15:46 all that were in the vicinity of Ashdod, together with their **villages**;
15:47 Ashdod, its surrounding settlements and **villages**; and Gaza,
15:47 and Gaza, its settlements and **villages**, as far as the Wadi of Egypt
15:51 Goshen, Holon and Giloh—eleven towns and their **villages**.
15:54 Arba (that is, Hebron) and Zior—nine towns and their **villages**.
15:57 Kain, Gibeah and Timnah—ten towns and their **villages**.
15:59 Maarath, Beth Anoth and Eltekon—six towns and their **villages**.
15:60 Kiriath Jearim) and Rabbah—two towns and their **villages**.
15:62 the City of Salt and En Gedi—six towns and their **villages**.
16:9 their **villages** that were set aside for the Ephraimites within the
18:24 Ophni and Geba—twelve towns and their **villages**.
18:28 Jerusalem), Gibeah and Kiriath—fourteen towns and their **villages**.
19:6 Beth Lebaoth and Sharuhen—thirteen towns and their **villages**;
19:7 Rimmon, Ether and Ashan—four towns and their **villages**—
19:8 all the **villages** around these towns as far as Baalath Beer (Ramah
19:15 and Bethlehem. There were twelve towns and their **villages**.
19:16 These towns and their **villages** were the inheritance of Zebulun,
19:22 ended at the Jordan. There were sixteen towns and their **villages**.
19:23 and their **villages** were the inheritance of the tribe of Issachar,
19:30 and Rehob. There were twenty-two towns and their **villages**.
19:31 and their **villages** were the inheritance of the tribe of Asher,
19:38 and Beth Shemesh. There were nineteen towns and their **villages**.
19:39 and their **villages** were the inheritance of the tribe of Naphtali,
19:48 and their **villages** were the inheritance of the tribe of Dan,
21:12 **villages** *around* the city they had given to Caleb son of Jephunneh
2Sa 17:18 He had a well in his **courtyard**, and they climbed down into it.
1Ki 6:36 And he built the inner **courtyard** of three courses of dressed stone
7:8 the palace in which he was to live, **set farther back** [+337+2021],
7:9 from the outside to the great **courtyard** and from foundation to
7:12 The great **courtyard** was surrounded by a wall of three courses of
7:12 as was the inner **courtyard** *of* the temple of the LORD with its
8:64 middle part of the **courtyard** in front of the temple of the LORD,
2Ki 20:4 Before Isaiah had left the middle **court**, [K 2021+6551]
21:5 In both **courts** *of* the temple of the LORD, he built altars to all the
23:12 the altars Manasseh had built in the two **courts** *of* the temple of the
1Ch 4:32 Their **surrounding villages** were Etam, Ain, Rimmon, Token
4:33 all the **villages** around these towns as far as Baalath. These were
6:56 [6:41] **villages** *around* the city were given to Caleb son of
9:16 the son of Elkanah, who lived in the **villages** *of* the Netophathites.
9:22 They were registered by genealogy in their **villages**.
9:25 Their brothers in their **villages** had to come from time to time
23:28 to be in charge of the **courtyards**, the side rooms, the purification
28:6 your son is the one who will build my house and my **courts**,
28:12 had put in his mind for the **courts** *of* the temple of the LORD
2Ch 4:9 He made the **courtyard** *of* the priests, and the large court
7:7 Solomon consecrated the middle part of the **courtyard** in front of
20:5 at the temple of the LORD in the front of the new **courtyard**
23:5 all the other men are to be in the **courtyards** *of* the temple of the
24:21 by order of the king they stoned him to death in the **courtyard** *of*
29:16 They brought out to the **courtyard** *of* the LORD's temple
33:5 In both **courts** *of* the temple of the LORD, he built altars to all the
Ne 3:25 the tower projecting from the upper palace near the **court** *of* the
8:16 in their **courtyards**, in the courts of the house of God and in the
8:16 in the **courts** *of* the house of God and in the square by the Water
11:25 As for the **villages** with their fields, some of the people of Judah
11:25 in Dibon and its settlements, in Jekabzeel and its **villages**,
11:30 Zanoah, Adullam and their **villages**, in Lachish and its fields,
12:28 region around Jerusalem—from the **villages** *of* the Netophathites,
12:29 for the singers had built **villages** for themselves around Jerusalem.
13:7 in providing Tobiah a room in the **courts** *of* the house of God.
Est 1:5 lasting seven days, in the **enclosed** garden of the king's palace,
2:11 forth near the **courtyard** *of* the harem to find out how Esther was
4:11 or woman who approaches the king in the inner **court** without
5:1 put on her royal robes and stood in the inner **court** *of* the palace,
5:2 When he saw Queen Esther standing in the **court**, he was pleased
6:4 The king said, "Who is in the **court**?" Now Haman had just
6:4 Now Haman had just entered the outer **court** *of* the palace to speak
6:5 His attendants answered, "Haman is standing in the **court**."
Ps 10:8 He lies in wait near the **villages**; from ambush he murders the
65:4 [65:5] are those you choose and bring near to live in your **courts**!
84:2 [84:3] My soul yearns, even faints, for the **courts** *of* the LORD;
84:10 [84:11] Better is one day in your **courts** than a thousand
92:13 [92:14] the LORD, they will flourish in the **courts** *of* our God.
96:8 the glory due his name; bring an offering and come into his **courts**.
100:4 Enter his gates with thanksgiving and his **courts** with praise;
116:19 in the **courts** *of* the house of the LORD—in your midst,
135:2 in the house of the LORD, in the **courts** *of* the house of our God.
Isa 1:12 before me, who has asked this of you, this trampling of my **courts**?
42:11 raise their voices; let the **settlements** where Kedar lives rejoice.
62:9 those who gather the grapes will drink it in the **courts** *of* my
Jer 19:14 stood in the **court** *of* the LORD's temple and said to all the
26:2 Stand in the **courtyard** *of* the LORD's house and speak to all the
32:2 Jeremiah the prophet was confined in the **courtyard** *of* the guard
32:8 my cousin Hanamel came to me in the **courtyard** *of* the guard
32:12 the deed and of all the Jews sitting in the **courtyard** *of* the guard.
33:1 While Jeremiah was still confined in the **courtyard** *of* the guard,
36:10 which was in the upper **courtyard** at the entrance of the New Gate
36:20 they went to the king in the **courtyard** and reported everything to
37:21 gave orders for Jeremiah to be placed in the **courtyard** *of* the
37:21 was gone. So Jeremiah remained in the **courtyard** *of* the guard.
38:6 the king's son, which was in the **courtyard** *of* the guard.
38:13 the cistern. And Jeremiah remained in the **courtyard** *of* the guard.
38:28 Jeremiah remained in the **courtyard** *of* the guard until the day
39:14 and had Jeremiah taken out of the **courtyard** *of* the guard.
39:15 While Jeremiah had been confined in the **courtyard** *of* the guard,
Eze 8:7 Then he brought me to the entrance to the **court**. I looked,
8:16 then brought me into the inner **court** *of* the house of the LORD,
9:7 said to them, "Defile the temple and fill the **courts** with the slain.
10:3 temple when the man went in, and a cloud filled the inner **court**.
10:4 and the **court** was full of the radiance of the glory of the LORD.
10:5 of the cherubim could be heard as far away as the outer **court**,
40:14 The measurement was up to the portico facing the **courtyard**.
40:17 Then he brought me into the outer **court**. There I saw some rooms
40:17 and a pavement that had been constructed all around the **court**;
40:19 the inside of the lower gateway to the outside of the inner **court**;
40:20 and width of the gate facing north, leading into the outer **court**.
40:23 There was a gate to the inner **court** facing the north gate, just as
40:27 The inner **court** also had a gate facing south, and he measured
40:28 Then he brought me into the inner **court** through the south gate,
40:31 Its portico faced the outer **court**; palm trees decorated its jambs,
40:32 he brought me to the inner **court** *on* the east side, and he measured
40:34 Its portico faced the outer **court**; palm trees decorated the jambs on
40:37 Its portico faced the outer **court**; palm trees decorated the jambs on
40:44 Outside the inner gate, within the inner **court**, were two rooms,
40:47 Then he measured the **court**: It was square—a hundred cubits long
41:15 the inner sanctuary and the portico facing the **court**,
42:1 the man led me northward into the outer **court** and brought me to
42:3 Both in the section twenty cubits from the inner **court** and in the
42:3 and in the section opposite the pavement of the outer **court**,
42:6 The rooms on the third floor had no pillars, as the **courts** had;
42:7 There was an outer wall parallel to the rooms and the outer **court**;
42:8 While the row of rooms on the side next to the outer **court** was
42:9 entrance on the east side as one enters them from the outer **court**.
42:10 On the south side along the length of the wall of the outer **court**,
42:14 they are not to go into the outer **court** until they leave behind the
43:5 Then the Spirit lifted me up and brought me into the inner **court**,
44:17 " 'When they enter the gates of the inner **court**, they are to wear
44:17 woolen garment while ministering at the gates of the inner **court**
44:19 When they go out into the outer **court** where the people are,
44:19 out into the outer court **where**[s] [+2021+2021+2667] the people are,
44:21 No priest is to drink wine when he enters the inner **court**.
44:27 On the day he goes into the inner **court** of the sanctuary to minister
45:19 the upper ledge of the altar and on the gateposts of the inner **court**.
46:1 The gate of the inner **court** facing east is to be shut on the six
46:20 to avoid bringing them into the outer **court** and consecrating the
46:21 He then brought me to the outer **court** and led me around to its
46:21 to the outer court and led me around to **its**[s] [+2021] four corners,
46:21 around to its four corners, and I saw in each corner another **court**.
46:21 to its four corners, and I saw in each corner another court. **[RPH]**
46:21 to its four corners, and I saw in each corner another court. **[RPH]**
46:21 to its four corners, and I saw in each corner another court. **[RPH]**
46:22 In the four corners of the outer **court** were enclosed courts,
46:22 In the four corners of the outer court were enclosed **courts**,
Zec 3:7 then you will govern my house and have charge of my **courts**,

2959 2חָצֵר ***ḥāṣēr***[2], n.m. Not used in NIV/BHS [→ 1258, 2960, 2961, 2963, 2964, 2965, 2966, 2967, 2975; cf. 2958]

2960 חֲצַר־אַדָּר ḥ^a sar-'addār, n.pr.loc. [1] [√ 162 + 2959]

Hazar Addar [1]

Nu 34: 4 Then it will go to **Hazar Addar** and over to Azmon,

2961 חֲצַר גַּדָּה ḥ^a sar gaddâ, n.pr.loc. [1] [√ 2959 + 1520]

Hazar Gaddah [1]

Jos 15: 27 **Hazar Gaddah**, Heshmon, Beth Pelet,

2962 חָצֵר הַתִּיכוֹן ḥāṣēr hattîkôn, n.pr.loc. [1] [√ 2958 + 2250]

Hazer Hatticon [1]

Eze 47: 16 border between Damascus and Hamath), as far as **Hazer Hatticon**,

2963 חֲצַר סוּסָה ḥ^a sar sûsâ, n.pr.loc. [1] [√ 2959 + 6063]

Hazar Susah [1]

Jos 19: 5 Ziklag, Beth Marcaboth, **Hazar Susah**,

2964 חֲצַר סוּסִים ḥ^a sar sûsîm, n.pr.loc. [1] [√ 2959 + 6065]

Hazar Susim [1]

1Ch 4: 31 Beth Marcaboth, **Hazar Susim**, Beth Biri and Shaaraim.

2965 חֲצַר עֵינוֹן ḥ^a sar 'ênôn, n.pr.loc. [1] [√ 2959 + 6541]

Hazar Enan [1]

Eze 47: 17 The boundary will extend from the sea to **Hazar Enan**, along the

2966 חֲצַר עֵינָן ḥ^a sar 'ênān, n.pr.loc. [3] [√ 2959 + 6544]

Hazar Enan [3]

Nu 34: 9 continue to Ziphron and end at **Hazar Enan**. This will be your
34: 10 your eastern boundary, run a line from **Hazar Enan** to Shepham.
Eze 48: 1 **Hazar Enan** and the northern border of Damascus next to Hamath

2967 חֲצַר שׁוּעָל ḥ^a sar šû'āl, n.pr.loc. [4] [√ 2959 + 8785]

Hazar Shual [4]

Jos 15: 28 **Hazar Shual**, Beersheba, Biziothiah,
19: 3 **Hazar Shual**, Balah, Ezem,
1Ch 4: 28 They lived in Beersheba, Moladah, **Hazar Shual**,
Ne 11: 27 in **Hazar Shual**, in Beersheba and its settlements,

2968 חֶצְרוֹ ḥeṣrô, n.pr.m. [2] [√ 2946; cf. 2974]

Hezro [2]

2Sa 23: 35 **Hezro** [Q 2974] the Carmelite, Paarai the Arbite,
1Ch 11: 37 **Hezro** the Carmelite, Naarai son of Ezbai,

2969 ¹חֶצְרוֹן ḥeṣrôn¹, n.pr.m. [16] [→ 2971; cf. 2946, 2970]

Hezron [16]

Ge 46: 9 The sons of Reuben: Hanoch, Pallu, **Hezron** and Carmi.
46: 12 in the land of Canaan). The sons of Perez: **Hezron** and Hamul.
Ex 6: 14 firstborn son of Israel were Hanoch and Pallu, **Hezron** and Carmi.
Nu 26: 6 through **Hezron**, the Hezronite clan; through Carmi, the Carmite
26: 21 through **Hezron**, the Hezronite clan; through Hamul, the Hamulite
Ru 4: 18 is the family line of Perez: Perez was the father of **Hezron**,
4: 19 **Hezron** the father of Ram, Ram the father of Amminadab,
1Ch 2: 5 The sons of Perez: **Hezron** and Hamul.
2: 9 The sons born to **Hezron** were: Jerahmeel, Ram and Caleb.
2: 18 Caleb son of **Hezron** had children by his wife Azubah (and by
2: 21 **Hezron** lay with the daughter of Makir the father of Gilead (he had
2: 24 After **Hezron** died in Caleb Ephrathah, Abijah the wife of Hezron
2: 24 Abijah the wife of **Hezron** bore him Ashhur the father of Tekoa.
2: 25 The sons of Jerahmeel the firstborn of **Hezron**: Ram his firstborn,
4: 1 The descendants of Judah: Perez, **Hezron**, Carmi, Hur and Shobal.
5: 3 Reuben the firstborn of Israel: Hanoch, Pallu, **Hezron** and Carmi.

2970 ²חֶצְרוֹן ḥeṣrôn², n.pr.loc. [1] [√ 7955; cf. 2969]

Hezron [1]

Jos 15: 3 Then it ran past **Hezron** up to Addar and curved around to Karka.

2971 חֶצְרוֹנִי ḥeṣrônî, a.g. [2] [√ 2969; cf. 2946]

Hezronite [2]

Nu 26: 6 through Hezron, the **Hezronite** clan; through Carmi, the Carmite
26: 21 through Hezron, the **Hezronite** clan; through Hamul, the Hamulite

2972 חֲצֵרוֹת ḥ^a sērôt, n.pr.loc. [6]

Hazeroth [5], there[s] [+928] [1]

Nu 11: 35 From Kibroth Hattaavah the people traveled to **Hazeroth**
11: 35 the people traveled to Hazeroth and stayed **there**[s] [+928].
12: 16 the people left **Hazeroth** and encamped in the Desert of Paran.
33: 17 They left Kibroth Hattaavah and camped at **Hazeroth**.
33: 18 They left **Hazeroth** and camped at Rithmah.
Dt 1: 1 between Paran and Tophel, Laban, **Hazeroth** and Dizahab.

2973 חֲצֵרִים ḥ^a sērîm, n.pr.loc. Not used in NIV/BHS [√ 2958]

2974 חֶצְרַי ḥeṣray, n.pr.m. [0] [√ 2946; cf. 2968]

2Sa 23: 35 [**Hezro** [Q; see K 2968] the Carmelite, Paarai the Arbite,]

2975 חֲצַרְמָוֶת ḥ^a sarmāwet, n.pr.m. [2] [√ 2959 + 4638]

Hazarmaveth [2]

Ge 10: 26 Joktan was the father of Almodad, Sheleph, **Hazarmaveth**, Jerah,
1Ch 1: 20 Joktan was the father of Almodad, Sheleph, **Hazarmaveth**, Jerah,

2976 חֹק ḥōq, n.m. [129 / 128] [→ 2978, 2981; cf. 2980]

decrees [75], share [11], decree [8], statutes [4], limits [2], ordinance [2], *untranslated* [1], allotment [1], appointed time [1], barrier [1], boundaries [1], boundary [1], conditions [1], custom [1], daily bread [+4312] [1], daily bread [1], horizon [1], law [1], laws [1], limit [1], make laws [+2980] [1], portions [1], precepts [1], prescribed portion [1], quota [1], regular allotment [1], regular share [1], regulations [1], statute [1], territory [1], time [1], tradition [1]

Ge 47: 22 because they received a **regular allotment** from Pharaoh and had
47: 22 and had food enough from the **allotment** Pharaoh gave them.
47: 26 So Joseph established it as a **law** concerning land in Egypt—
Ex 5: 14 "Why didn't you meet your **quota** *of* bricks yesterday or today,
12: 24 "Obey these instructions as a lasting **ordinance** for you and your
15: 25 There the LORD made a **decree** and a law for them, and there he
15: 26 if you pay attention to his commands and keep all his **decrees**,
18: 16 between the parties and inform them of God's **decrees** and laws."
18: 20 Teach them the **decrees** and laws, and show them the way to live
29: 28 This is always to be the **regular share** from the Israelites for
30: 21 This is to be a lasting **ordinance** for Aaron and his descendants for
Lev 6: 18 [6:11] It is his regular **share** of the offerings made to the LORD
6: 22 [6:15] It is the LORD's regular **share** and is to be burned
7: 34 the priest and his sons as their regular **share** from the Israelites.' "
10: 11 you must teach the Israelites all the **decrees** the LORD has given
10: 13 because it is your **share** and your sons' share of the offerings made
10: 13 and your sons' **share** of the offerings made to the LORD by fire;
10: 14 your children as your **share** of the Israelites' fellowship offerings.
10: 14 your children as your share **[RPH]** of the Israelites' fellowship
10: 15 This will be the regular **share** for you and your children, as the
24: 9 because it is a most holy part of their regular **share** *of* the offerings
26: 46 These are the **decrees**, the laws and the regulations that the
Nu 18: 8 me I give to you and your sons as your portion and regular **share**.
18: 11 give this to you and your sons and daughters as your regular **share**.
18: 19 I give to you and your sons and daughters as your regular **share**.
30: 16 [30:17] These are the **regulations** the LORD gave Moses
Dt 4: 1 Hear now, O Israel, the **decrees** and laws I am about to teach you.
4: 5 I have taught you **decrees** and laws as the LORD my God
4: 6 to the nations, who will hear about all these **decrees** and say,
4: 8 And what other nation is so great as to have such righteous **decrees**
4: 14 And the LORD directed me at that time to teach you the **decrees**
4: 40 Keep his **decrees** and commands, which I am giving you today,
4: 45 **decrees** and laws Moses gave them when they came out of Egypt
5: 1 O Israel, the **decrees** and laws I declare in your hearing today.
5: 31 **decrees** and laws you are to teach them to follow in the land I am
6: 1 **decrees** and laws the LORD your God directed me to teach you
6: 17 your God and the stipulations and **decrees** he has given you.
6: 20 **decrees** and laws the LORD our God has commanded you?"
6: 24 The LORD commanded us to obey all these **decrees** and to fear
7: 11 care to follow the commands, **decrees** and laws I give you today.
11: 32 be sure that you obey all the **decrees** and laws I am setting before
12: 1 These are the **decrees** and laws you must be careful to follow in
16: 12 that you were slaves in Egypt, and follow carefully these **decrees**.
17: 19 and follow carefully all the words of this law and these **decrees**
26: 16 LORD your God commands you this day to follow these **decrees**
26: 17 that you will keep his **decrees**, commands and laws, and that you
27: 10 and follow his commands and **decrees** that I give you today."
Jos 24: 25 and there at Shechem he drew up for them **decrees** and laws.
Jdg 5: 15 there was much searching [BHS ***decrees***; NIV 2984] *of* heart.
11: 39 And she was a virgin. From this comes the Israelite **custom**
1Sa 30: 25 David made this a **statute** and ordinance for Israel from that day to
1Ki 3: 14 if you walk in my ways and obey my **statutes** and commands as
8: 58 keep the commands, **decrees** and regulations he gave our fathers.
8: 61 to live by his **decrees** and obey his commands, as at this time."
9: 4 and do all I command and observe my **decrees** and laws,
2Ki 17: 15 They rejected his **decrees** and the covenant he had made with their
17: 37 You must always be careful to keep the **decrees** and ordinances,
1Ch 16: 17 He confirmed it to Jacob as a **decree**, to Israel as an everlasting

1Ch 22:13 you will have success if you are careful to observe the **decrees**
29:19 requirements and **decrees** and to do everything to build the palatial
2Ch 7:17 and do all I command, and observe my **decrees** and laws,
19:10 or other concerns of the law, commands, **decrees** or ordinances—
33: 8 all the laws, **decrees** and ordinances given through Moses."
34:31 regulations and **decrees** with all his heart and all his soul,
35:25 These became a **tradition** in Israel and are written in the Laments.
Ezr 7:10 Law of the LORD, and to teaching its **decrees** and laws in Israel.
7:11 concerning the commands and **decrees** *of* the LORD for Israel:
Ne 1: 7 the commands, **decrees** and laws you gave your servant Moses.
9:13 that are just and right, and **decrees** and commands that are good.
9:14 them commands, **decrees** and laws through your servant Moses.
10:29 [10:30] and **decrees** *of* the LORD our Lord.
Job 14: 5 the number of his months and have set **limits** he cannot exceed.
14:13 If only you would set me a **time** and then remember me!
23:12 I have treasured the words of his mouth more than my **daily bread**.
23:14 He carries out his **decree** *against* me, and many such plans he still
26:10 He marks out the **horizon** on the face of the waters for a boundary
28:26 when he made a **decree** for the rain and a path for the
38:10 when I fixed **limits** for it and set its doors and bars in place,
Ps 2: 7 I will proclaim the **decree** *of* the LORD: He said to me, "You are
50:16 "What right have you to recite my **laws** or take my covenant on
81: 4 [81:5] this is a **decree** for Israel, an ordinance of the God of
94:20 be allied with you—one that brings on misery by its **decrees**?
99: 7 pillar of cloud; they kept his statutes and the **decrees** he gave them.
105:10 He confirmed it to Jacob as a **decree**, to Israel as an everlasting
105:45 that they might keep his **precepts** and observe his laws.
119: 5 Oh, that my ways were steadfast in obeying your **decrees**!
119: 8 I will obey your **decrees**; do not utterly forsake me.
119:12 Praise be to you, O LORD; teach me your **decrees**.
119:23 and slander me, your servant will meditate on your **decrees**.
119:26 recounted my ways and you answered me; teach me your **decrees**.
119:33 Teach me, O LORD, to follow your **decrees**; then I will keep
119:48 to your commands, which I love, and I meditate on your **decrees**.
119:54 Your **decrees** are the theme of my song wherever I lodge.
119:64 earth is filled with your love, O LORD; teach me your **decrees**.
119:68 You are good, and what you do is good; teach me your **decrees**.
119:71 was good for me to be afflicted so that I might learn your **decrees**.
119:80 May my heart be blameless toward your **decrees**, that I may not be
119:83 I am like a wineskin in the smoke, I do not forget your **decrees**.
119:112 My heart is set on keeping your **decrees** to the very end.
119:117 and I will be delivered; I will always have regard for your **decrees**.
119:118 You reject all who stray from your **decrees**, for their deceitfulness
119:124 your servant according to your love and teach me your **decrees**.
119:135 your face shine upon your servant and teach me your **decrees**.
119:145 all my heart; answer me, O LORD, and I will obey your **decrees**.
119:155 is far from the wicked, for they do not seek out your **decrees**.
119:171 May my lips overflow with praise, for you teach me your **decrees**.
147:19 He has revealed his word to Jacob, his laws and **decrees** to Israel.
148: 6 for ever and ever; he gave a **decree** that will never pass away.
Pr 8:29 when he gave the sea its **boundary** so the waters would not
30: 8 poverty nor riches, but give me only my **daily bread** [+4312].
31:15 she provides food for her family and **portions** for her servant girls.
Isa 5:14 the grave enlarges its appetite and opens its mouth without **limit**;
10: 1 Woe to those *who* **make** unjust **laws** [+2980], to those who issue
24: 5 violated the **statutes** and broken the everlasting covenant.
Jer 5:22 sand a boundary for the sea, an everlasting **barrier** it cannot cross.
31:36 "Only if these **decrees** vanish from my sight,"
32:11 the sealed copy containing the terms and **conditions**, as well as the
Eze 11:12 for you have not followed my **decrees** or kept my laws but have
16:27 So I stretched out my hand against you and reduced your **territory**;
20:18 "Do not follow the **statutes** *of* your fathers or keep their laws
20:25 I also gave them over to **statutes** that were not good and laws they
36:27 I will put my Spirit in you and move you to follow my **decrees**
45:14 The **prescribed portion** *of* oil, measured by the bath, is a tenth of
Am 2: 4 have rejected the law of the LORD and have not kept his **decrees**,
Mic 7:11 your walls will come, the day for extending your **boundaries**.
Zep 2: 2 before the **appointed time** arrives and that day sweeps on like
Zec 1: 6 did not my words and my **decrees**, which I commanded my
Mal 3: 7 time of your forefathers you have turned away from my **decrees**
4: 4 [3:22] the **decrees** and laws I gave him at Horeb for all Israel.

2977 חָקָה *ḥāqâ*, v. [4] [cf. 2980]

portrayed [2], carvings [1], putting marks [1]

1Ki 6:35 [E] overlaid them with gold hammered evenly over the **carvings**.
Job 13:27 [F] you keep close watch on all my paths *by* **putting marks** on
Eze 8:10 [E] I saw **portrayed** all over the walls all kinds of crawling
23:14 [E] She saw men **portrayed** on a wall, figures of Chaldeans

2978 חֻקָּה *ḥuqqâ*, n.f. [104] [√ 2976; cf. 2980]

decrees [52], ordinance [23], regulations [7], statutes [5], customs [3], practices [3], requirement [3], rules [3], fixed laws [1], laws [1], regular [1], requirements [1], share [1]

Ge 26: 5 kept my requirements, my commands, my **decrees** and my laws."
Ex 12:14 shall celebrate it as a festival to the LORD—a lasting **ordinance**.
12:17 Celebrate this day as a lasting **ordinance** for the generations to
12:43 to Moses and Aaron, "These are the **regulations** *for* the Passover:
13:10 You must keep this **ordinance** at the appointed time year after
27:21 This is to be a lasting **ordinance** among the Israelites for the
28:43 "This is to be a lasting **ordinance** for Aaron and his descendants.
29: 9 and his sons. The priesthood is theirs by a lasting **ordinance**.
Lev 3:17 " 'This is a lasting **ordinance** for the generations to come,
7:36 give this to them as their regular **share** for the generations to come.
10: 9 will die. This is a lasting **ordinance** for the generations to come.
16:29 "This is to be a lasting **ordinance** for you: On the tenth day of the
16:31 of rest, and you must deny yourselves; it is a lasting **ordinance**.
16:34 "This is to be a lasting **ordinance** for you: Atonement is to be
17: 7 This is to be a lasting **ordinance** for them and for the generations
18: 3 of Canaan, where I am bringing you. Do not follow their **practices**.
18: 4 You must obey my laws and be careful to follow my **decrees**.
18: 5 Keep my **decrees** and laws, for the man who obeys them will live
18:26 But you must keep my **decrees** and my laws. The native-born
18:30 do not follow any of the detestable **customs** that were practiced
19:19 " 'Keep my **decrees**. " 'Do not mate different kinds of animals.
19:37 " 'Keep all my **decrees** and all my laws and follow them. I am the
20: 8 Keep my **decrees** and follow them. I am the LORD, who makes
20:22 " 'Keep all my **decrees** and laws and follow them, so that the land
20:23 You must not live according to the **customs** *of* the nations I am
23:14 This is to be a lasting **ordinance** for the generations to come,
23:21 This is to be a lasting **ordinance** for the generations to come,
23:31 This is to be a lasting **ordinance** for the generations to come,
23:41 This is to be a lasting **ordinance** for the generations to come;
24: 3 This is to be a lasting **ordinance** for the generations to come.
25:18 " 'Follow my **decrees** and be careful to obey my laws, and you will
26: 3 " 'If you follow my **decrees** and are careful to obey my commands,
26:15 if you reject my **decrees** and abhor my laws and fail to carry out all
26:43 their sins because they rejected my laws and abhorred my **decrees**.
Nu 9: 3 day of this month, in accordance with all its **rules** and regulations."
9:12 they celebrate the Passover, they must follow all the **regulations**.
9:14 Passover must do so in accordance with its **rules** and regulations.
9:14 You must have the same **regulations** for the alien and the
10: 8 This is to be a lasting **ordinance** for you and the generations to
15:15 The community is to have the same **rules** for you and for the alien
15:15 among you; this is a lasting **ordinance** for the generations to come.
18:23 against it. This is a lasting **ordinance** for the generations to come.
19: 2 "This is a **requirement** *of* the law that the LORD has
19:10 This will be a lasting **ordinance** both for the Israelites and for the
19:21 This is a lasting **ordinance** for them. "The man who sprinkles the
27:11 This is to be a legal **requirement** for the Israelites, as the LORD
31:21 "This is the **requirement** *of* the law that the LORD gave Moses:
35:29 " 'These are to be legal **requirements** for you throughout the
Dt 6: 2 LORD your God as long as you live by keeping all his **decrees**
8:11 his laws and his **decrees** that I am giving you this day.
10:13 and **decrees** that I am giving you today for your own good?
11: 1 his requirements, his **decrees**, his laws and his commands always.
28:15 follow all his commands and **decrees** I am giving you today,
28:45 your God and observe the commands and **decrees** he gave you.
30:10 his commands and **decrees** that are written in this Book of the Law
30:16 to walk in his ways, and to keep his commands, **decrees** and laws;
2Sa 22:23 his laws are before me; I have not turned away from his **decrees**.
1Ki 2: 3 and keep his **decrees** and commands, his laws and requirements,
3: 3 LORD by walking according to the **statutes** *of* his father David,
6:12 if you follow my **decrees**, carry out my regulations and keep all
9: 6 and **decrees** I have given you and go off to serve other gods
11:11 your attitude and you have not kept my covenant and my **decrees**,
11:33 nor kept my **statutes** and laws as David, Solomon's father,
11:34 whom I chose and who observed my commands and **statutes**.
11:38 do what is right in my eyes by keeping my **statutes**
2Ki 17: 8 followed the **practices** *of* the nations the LORD had driven out
17:13 Observe my commands and **decrees**, in accordance with the entire
17:19 their God. They followed the **practices** Israel had introduced.
17:34 They neither worship the LORD nor adhere to the **decrees**
23: 3 regulations and **decrees** with all his heart and all his soul,
2Ch 7:19 "But if you turn away and forsake the **decrees** and commands I
Job 38:33 Do you know the **laws** *of* the heavens? Can you set up ⌞God's⌟
Ps 18:22 [18:23] are before me; I have not turned away from his **decrees**.
89:31 [89:32] if they violate my **decrees** and fail to keep my commands,
119:16 I delight in your **decrees**; I will not neglect your word.
Jer 5:24 rains in season, who assures us of the **regular** weeks of harvest.'
10: 3 For the **customs** *of* the peoples are worthless; they cut a tree out of
31:35 who **decrees** the moon and stars to shine by night, who stirs up the
33:25 with day and night and the **fixed laws** *of* heaven and earth,

Jer 44: 10 followed my law and the **decrees** I set before you and your fathers.
44: 23 obeyed him or followed his law or his **decrees** or his stipulations,
Eze 5: 6 and **decrees** more than the nations and countries around her.
5: 6 She has rejected my laws and has not followed my **decrees**.
5: 7 around you and have not followed my **decrees** or kept my laws.
11: 20 Then they will follow my **decrees** and be careful to keep my laws.
18: 9 He follows my **decrees** and faithfully keeps my laws. That man is
18: 17 or excessive interest. He keeps my laws and follows my **decrees**.
18: 19 what is just and right and has been careful to keep all my **decrees**,
18: 21 and keeps all my **decrees** and does what is just and right,
20: 11 I gave them my **decrees** and made known to them my laws,
20: 13 They did not follow my **decrees** but rejected my laws—
20: 16 and did not follow my **decrees** and desecrated my Sabbaths.
20: 19 your God; follow my **decrees** and be careful to keep my laws.
20: 21 They did not follow my **decrees**, they were not careful to keep my
20: 24 but had rejected my **decrees** and desecrated my Sabbaths,
33: 15 follows the **decrees** *that give* life, and does no evil, he will surely
37: 24 They will follow my laws and be careful to keep my **decrees**.
43: 11 and entrances—its whole design and all its **regulations** and laws.
43: 11 they may be faithful to its design and follow all its **regulations**.
43: 18 These will be the **regulations** *for* sacrificing burnt offerings
44: 5 all the **regulations** *regarding* the temple of the LORD.
44: 24 are to keep my laws and my **decrees** for all my appointed feasts,
46: 14 of this grain offering to the LORD is a lasting **ordinance**.
Mic 6: 16 You have observed the **statutes** *of* Omri and all the practices of

2979 חֲקוּפָא *hᵃqûpā'*, n.pr.m. [2]

Hakupha [2]

Ezr 2: 51 Bakbuk, **Hakupha**, Harhur,
Ne 7: 53 Bakbuk, **Hakupha**, Harhur,

2980 חָקַק *ḥāqaq*, v. [19] [→ 2576, 2976, 2978; cf. 2977]

marked out [2], scepter [2], captains [1], chiseling [1], decrees [1], draw [1], engraved [1], inscribe [1], lawgiver [1], leader's [1], make laws [+2976] [1], make laws [1], portrayed [1], princes [1], ruler's staff [1], scepters [1], were written [1]

Ge 49: 10 [D] nor the **ruler's staff** from between his feet, until he comes to
Nu 21: 18 [D] of the people sank—the nobles with **scepters** and staffs."
Dt 33: 21 [D] best land for himself; the **leader's** portion was kept for him.
Jdg 5: 9 [A] My heart is with Israel's **princes**, with the willing volunteers
5: 14 [D] From Makir **captains** came down, from Zebulun those who
Job 19: 23 [H] my words were recorded, that *they* **were written** on a scroll,
Ps 60: 7 [60:9] [D] is mine; Ephraim is my helmet, Judah my **scepter**.
108: 8 [108:9] [D] is mine; Ephraim is my helmet, Judah my **scepter**.
Pr 8: 15 [D] By me kings reign and rulers **make laws** that are just;
8: 27 [A] when he **marked out** the horizon on the face of the deep,
8: 29 [A] and when he **marked out** the foundations of the earth.
31: 5 [E] lest they drink and forget what the law **decrees**, and deprive
Isa 10: 1 [A] Woe to those *who* **make** unjust **laws** [+2976], to those who
22: 16 [A] on the height and **chiseling** your resting place in the rock?
30: 8 [A] Go now, write it on a tablet for them, **inscribe** it on a scroll,
33: 22 [D] the LORD *is* our **lawgiver**, the LORD is our king;
49: 16 [A] See, *I have* **engraved** you on the palms of my hands;
Eze 4: 1 [A] put it in front of you and **draw** the city of Jerusalem on it.
23: 14 [B] portrayed on a wall, figures of Chaldeans **portrayed** in red,

2981 חֵקֶק *ḥēqeq*, var. Not used in NIV/BHS [√ 2976]

2982 חֻקֹּק *ḥuqqōq*, n.pr.loc. [1]

Hukkok [1]

Jos 19: 34 ran west through Aznoth Tabor and came out at **Hukkok**.

2983 חָקַר *ḥāqar*, v. [27] [→ 2984, 4736]

explore [4], search [3], examined [2], was determined [2], be searched out [1], dense [+4202] [1], discovered [1], probe [1], questions [1], sample [1], search out [1], searched out [1], searched [1], searches for [1], searching for [1], sees through [1], sound out [1], test [1], tested [1], took up [1]

Dt 13: 14 [13:15] [A] must inquire, **probe** and investigate it thoroughly.
Jdg 18: 2 [A] from Zorah and Eshtaol to spy out the land and **explore** it.
18: 2 [A] all their clans. They told them, "Go, **explore** the land."
1Sa 20: 12 [A] *I will* surely **sound out** my father by this time the day after
2Sa 10: 3 [A] Hasn't David sent them to you to **explore** the city and spy it
1Ki 7: 47 [C] so many; the weight of the bronze **was** not **determined**.
1Ch 19: 3 [A] Haven't his men come to you to **explore** and spy out the
2Ch 4: 18 [C] so much that the weight of the bronze **was** not **determined**.
Job 5: 27 [A] "*We have* **examined** this, and it is true. So hear it and apply
13: 9 [A] Would it turn out well if *he* **examined** you? Could you
28: 3 [A] he **searches** the farthest recesses **for** ore in the blackest
28: 27 [A] at wisdom and appraised it; he confirmed it and **tested** it.
29: 16 [A] I was a father to the needy; *I* **took up** the case of the stranger.
32: 11 [A] to your reasoning; while *you were* **searching for** words,
Ps 44: 21 [44:22] [A] *would* not God *have* **discovered** it, since he knows
139: 1 [A] O LORD, *you have* **searched** me and you know me.
139: 23 [A] **Search** me, O God, and know my heart; test me and know
Pr 18: 17 [A] seems right, till another comes forward and **questions** him.
23: 30 [A] linger over wine, who go to **sample** bowls of mixed wine.
25: 2 [A] conceal a matter; *to* **search out** a matter is the glory of kings.
28: 11 [A] but a poor man who has discernment **sees through** him.
Ecc 12: 9 [D] He pondered and **searched out** and set in order many
Jer 17: 10 [A] "I the LORD **search** the heart and examine the mind, to
31: 37 [C] the foundations of the earth below **be searched out** will I
46: 23 [C] declares the LORD, "**dense** [+4202] though *it be*.
La 3: 40 [A] Let us examine our ways and **test** them, and let us return to
Eze 39: 14 [A] At the end of the seven months *they will begin their* **search**.

2984 חֵקֶר *ḥēqer*, n.m. [12 / 13] [√ 2983]

fathom [2], fathomed [2], searching [2], finding out [1], inquiry [1], mysteries [1], recesses [1], seek [1], unsearchable [+401] [1], what learned [1]

Jdg 5: 15 of Reuben there was much **searching** [BHS 2976] *of* heart.
5: 16 In the districts of Reuben there was much **searching** *of* heart.
Job 5: 9 He performs wonders that cannot be **fathomed**, miracles that
8: 8 the former generations and find out **what** their fathers **learned**,
9: 10 He performs wonders that cannot be **fathomed**, miracles that
11: 7 "Can you fathom the **mysteries** *of* God? Can you probe the limits
34: 24 Without **inquiry** he shatters the mighty and sets up others in their
36: 26 our understanding! The number of his years is past **finding out**.
38: 16 to the springs of the sea or walked in the **recesses** *of* the deep?
Ps 145: 3 and most worthy of praise; his greatness no one can **fathom**.
Pr 25: 3 the earth is deep, so the hearts of kings are **unsearchable** [+401].
25: 27 to eat too much honey, nor is it honorable to **seek** one's own honor.
Isa 40: 28 not grow tired or weary, and his understanding no one can **fathom**.

2985 חֹרִי¹ *ḥōr¹*, n.m. [13]

nobles [12], noble [1]

1Ki 21: 8 them to the elders and **nobles** who lived in Naboth's city with him.
21: 11 **nobles** who lived in Naboth's city did as Jezebel directed in the
Ne 2: 16 or the priests or **nobles** or officials or any others who would be
4: 14 [4:8] I stood up and said to the **nobles**, the officials and the rest of
4: 19 [4:13] I said to the **nobles**, the officials and the rest of the people,
5: 7 them in my mind and then accused the **nobles** and officials.
6: 17 in those days the **nobles** *of* Judah were sending many letters to
7: 5 So my God put it into my heart to assemble the **nobles**, the
13: 17 I rebuked the **nobles** *of* Judah and said to them, "What is this
Ecc 10: 17 O land whose king is of **noble** birth and whose princes eat at a
Isa 34: 12 Her **nobles** will have nothing there to be called a kingdom,
Jer 27: 20 to Babylon, along with all the **nobles** *of* Judah and Jerusalem—
39: 6 of Zedekiah before his eyes and also killed all the **nobles** *of* Judah.

2986 ²חֹר *ḥōr²*, n.[m.] [7] [→ 2987, 2988]

hole [2], holes [2], lairs [1], latch-opening [1], sockets [1]

1Sa 14: 11 "The Hebrews are crawling out of the **holes** they were hiding in."
2Ki 12: 9 [12:10] Jehoiada the priest took a chest and bored a **hole** in its lid.
Job 30: 6 in the dry stream beds, among the rocks and in **holes** *in* the ground.
SS 5: 4 My lover thrust his hand through the **latch-opening**; my heart
Eze 8: 7 to the entrance to the court. I looked, and I saw a **hole** in the wall.
Na 2: 12 [2:13] filling his **lairs** with the kill and his dens with the prey.
Zec 14: 12 their eyes will rot in their **sockets**, and their tongues will rot in

2987 חֻר *ḥur*, n.[m.] [2] [√ 2986]

hole [1], pits [1]

Isa 11: 8 The infant will play near the **hole** *of* the cobra, and the young child
42: 22 and looted, all of them trapped in **pits** or hidden away in prisons.

2988 חֹר הַגִּדְגָּד *ḥōr haggidgād*, n.pr.loc. [2] [√ 2986 + 2044]

Hor Haggidgad [2]

Nu 33: 32 They left Bene Jaakan and camped at **Hor Haggidgad**.
33: 33 They left **Hor Haggidgad** and camped at Jotbathah.

2989 חֲרָאִים *hᵃrā'îm*, n.[m.] [2] [→ 4738; cf. 3039]

filth [2]

2Ki 6: 25 [a quarter of a cab of **seed pods** [K; see Q 1807] for five shekels.]
18: 27 will have to eat their own **filth** [Q 7363] and drink their own
Isa 36: 12 will have to eat their own **filth** [Q 7363] and drink their own

2990 [1]חָרֵב ***ḥārēb***[1], v. [36 / 37] [→ 2992, 2993, 2994, 2996, 2997, 2998?, 2999, 3000, 3001; Ar 10281]

laid waste [6], dried up [5], dry up [5], desolate [3], ruined [3], been dried [2], dry [2], parched [2], utterly ruined [+2990] [2], devastated [1], horror [1], laid waste [+2238+2256] [1], lay waste [1], left deserted [1], lies in ruins [1], makes run dry [1]

Ge 8:13 [A] and first year, the water *had* **dried up** from the earth.
8:13 [A] from the ark and saw that the surface of the ground *was* **dry**.
Jdg 16:7 [E] ties me with seven fresh thongs that *have* not **been dried**,
16:8 [E] brought her seven fresh thongs that *had* not **been dried**,
16:24 [G] the *one who* **laid waste** our land and multiplied our slain."
2Ki 19:17 [G] that the Assyrian kings *have* **laid waste** these nations and
19:24 [G] With the soles of my feet *I have* **dried up** all the streams of
Job 14:11 [A] from the sea or a riverbed *becomes* **parched** and dry,
Ps 106:9 [A] He rebuked the Red Sea, and *it* **dried up**; he led them
Isa 11:15 [G] The LORD *will* **dry** [BHS 3049] **up** the gulf of the
19:5 [A] river will dry up, and the riverbed *will be* **parched** and dry.
19:6 [A] will stink; the streams of Egypt will dwindle and **dry up**.
34:10 [A] From generation to generation *it will lie* **desolate**; no one
37:18 [G] that the Assyrian kings *have* **laid waste** all these peoples and
37:25 [G] With the soles of my feet *I have* **dried up** all the streams of
42:15 [G] *I will* **lay waste** the mountains and hills and dry up all their
44:27 [A] who says to the watery deep, '*Be* **dry**, and I will dry up your
49:17 [G] *those who* **laid** you **waste** [+2238+2256] depart from you.
50:2 [G] By a mere rebuke *I* **dry up** the sea, I turn rivers into a desert;
51:10 [G] Was it not you who **dried up** the sea, the waters of the great
60:12 [A] not serve you will perish; it *will be* **utterly ruined** [+2990].
60:12 [A] not serve you will perish; it *will be* **utterly ruined** [+2990].
Jer 2:12 [A] appalled at this, O heavens, and shudder with great **horror**,"
26:9 [A] be like Shiloh and this city *will be* **desolate** and deserted?"
51:36 [G] avenge you; *I will* **dry up** her sea and make her springs dry.
Eze 6:6 [A] the towns *will be* **laid waste** and the high places demolished,
6:6 [A] so that your altars *will be* **laid waste** and devastated, your
12:20 [A] The inhabited towns *will be* **laid waste** and the land will be
19:7 [G] He broke down their strongholds and **devastated** their towns.
26:2 [H] swung open to me; now that *she* **lies in ruins** I will prosper,'
26:19 [C] When I make you a **desolate** city, like cities no longer
29:12 [H] her cities will lie desolate forty years among **ruined** cities.
30:7 [C] desolate lands, and their cities will lie among **ruined** cities.
Hos 13:15 [A] in from the desert; his spring will fail and his well **dry up**.
Am 7:9 [A] be destroyed and the sanctuaries of Israel *will be* **ruined**;
Na 1:4 [G] the sea and dries it up; *he* **makes** all the rivers **run dry**.
Zep 3:6 [G] *I have* **left** their streets **deserted**, with no one passing

2991 [2]חָרֵב ***ḥārēb***[2], v. [4] [√ 2995]

kill [2], must have fought [+2991] [2]

2Ki 3:23 [C] "Those kings **must have fought** [+2991] and slaughtered
3:23 [H] "Those kings **must have fought** [+2991] and slaughtered
Jer 50:21 [A] Pursue, **kill** and completely destroy them,"
50:27 [A] **Kill** all her young bulls; let them go down to the slaughter!

2992 [3]חָרֵב ***ḥārēb***[3], a. [10] [√ 2990]

in ruins [3], dry [2], ruin [2], desolate waste [1], desolate [1], ruined [1]

Lev 7:10 every grain offering, whether mixed with oil or **dry**,
Ne 2:3 look sad when the city where my fathers are buried lies **in ruins**,
2:17 Jerusalem lies **in ruins**, and its gates have been burned with fire.
Pr 17:1 Better a **dry** crust with peace and quiet than a house full of
Jer 33:10 about this place, "It is a **desolate waste**, without men or animals."
33:12 'In this place, **desolate** and without men or animals—in all its
Eze 36:35 the cities that were lying **in ruins**, desolate and destroyed,
36:38 So will the **ruined** cities be filled with flocks of people. Then they
Hag 1:4 living in your paneled houses, while this house remains a **ruin**?"
1:9 "Because of my house, which remains a **ruin**, while each of you is

2993 [4]חָרֵב ***ḥārēb***[4], v. Not used in NIV/BHS [√ 2990]

2994 [5]חָרֵב ***ḥārēb***[5], a. Not used in NIV/BHS [√ 2990]

2995 חֶרֶב ***ḥereb***, n.f. [412] [→ 2991]

sword [362], swords [31], swordsmen [+408+8990] [5], *untranslated* [4], dagger [3], knives [2], war [2], killed [+906+4200+5782+7023] [1], tool [1], weapons [1]

Ge 3:24 a flaming **sword** flashing back and forth to guard the way to the
27:40 You will live by the **sword** and you will serve your brother.
31:26 and you've carried off my daughters like captives in **war**.
34:25 took their **swords** and attacked the unsuspecting city,
34:26 They put Hamor and his son Shechem to the **sword** and took
48:22 I give the ridge of land I took from the Amorites with my **sword**
Ex 5:3 our God, or he may strike us with plagues or with the **sword**."
5:21 and his officials and have put a **sword** in their hand to kill us."
15:9 on them. I will draw my **sword** and my hand will destroy them.'
17:13 So Joshua overcame the Amalekite army with the **sword**.
18:4 God was my helper; he saved me from the **sword** *of* Pharaoh."
20:25 it with dressed stones, for you will defile it if you use a **tool** on it.
22:24 [22:23] anger will be aroused, and I will kill you with the **sword**;
32:27 the God of Israel, says: 'Each man strap a **sword** to his side.
Lev 26:6 from the land, and the **sword** will not pass through your country.
26:7 pursue your enemies, and they will fall by the **sword** before you.
26:8 ten thousand, and your enemies will fall by the **sword** before you.
26:25 I will bring the **sword** upon you to avenge the breaking of the
26:33 among the nations and will draw out my **sword** and pursue you.
26:36 They will run as though fleeing from the **sword**, and they will fall,
26:37 will stumble over one another as though fleeing from the **sword**,
Nu 14:3 LORD bringing us to this land only to let us fall by the **sword**?
14:43 he will not be with you and you will fall by the **sword**."
19:16 the open who touches someone who has been killed with a **sword**
20:18 if you try, we will march out and attack you with the **sword**."
21:24 put him to the **sword** and took over his land from the Arnon to the
22:23 the LORD standing in the road with a drawn **sword** in his hand,
22:29 of me! If I had a **sword** in my hand, I would kill you right now."
22:31 angel of the LORD standing in the road with his **sword** drawn.
31:8 of Midian. They also killed Balaam son of Beor with the **sword**.
Dt 13:15 [13:16] you must certainly put to the **sword** all who live in that
13:15 [13:16] it completely, both its people and its livestock. **[RPH]**
20:13 God delivers it into your hand, put to the **sword** all the men in it.
28:22 with scorching heat and drought, [BHS *sword*; NIV 2996]
32:25 In the street the **sword** will make them childless; in their homes
32:41 when I sharpen my flashing **sword** and my hand grasps it in
32:42 make my arrows drunk with blood, while my **sword** devours flesh:
33:29 He is your shield and helper and your glorious **sword**.
Jos 5:2 to Joshua, "Make flint **knives** and circumcise the Israelites again."
5:3 So Joshua made flint **knives** and circumcised the Israelites at
5:13 saw a man standing in front of him with a drawn **sword** in his
6:21 the LORD and destroyed with the **sword** every living thing in it—
8:24 when every one of them had been put to the **sword**, all the
8:24 to Ai and **killed** [+906+4200+5782+7023] those who were in it.
10:11 from the hailstones than were killed by the **swords** of the Israelites.
10:28 He put the city and its king to the **sword** and totally destroyed
10:30 The city and everyone in it Joshua put to the **sword**. He left no
10:32 The city and everyone in it he put to the **sword**, just as he had done
10:35 They captured it that same day and put it to the **sword** and totally
10:37 They took the city and put it to the **sword**, together with its king,
10:39 took the city, its king and its villages, and put them to the **sword**.
11:10 turned back and captured Hazor and put its king to the **sword**.
11:11 Everyone in it they put to the **sword**. They totally destroyed them,
11:12 all these royal cities and their kings and put them to the **sword**.
11:14 all the people they put to the **sword** until they completely
13:22 the Israelites had put to the **sword** Balaam son of Beor,
19:47 and attacked Leshem, took it, put it to the **sword** and occupied it.
24:12 Amorite kings. You did not do it with your own **sword** and bow.
Jdg 1:8 and took it. They put the city to the **sword** and set it on fire.
1:25 they put the city to the **sword** but spared the man and his whole
3:16 Now Ehud had made a double-edged **sword** about a foot and a half
3:21 drew the **sword** from his right thigh and plunged it into the king's
3:22 Ehud did not pull the **sword** out, and the fat closed in over it.
4:15 LORD routed Sisera and all his chariots and army by the **sword**,
4:16 All the troops of Sisera fell by the **sword**; not a man was left.
7:14 "This can be nothing other than the **sword** *of* Gideon son of Joash,
7:20 they shouted, "A **sword** for the LORD and for Gideon!"
7:22 men throughout the camp to turn on each other with their **swords**.
8:10 hundred and twenty thousand **swordsmen** [+408+8990] had fallen.
8:20 But Jether did not draw his **sword**, because he was only a boy
9:54 "Draw your **sword** and kill me, so that they can't say,
18:27 They attacked them with the **sword** and burned down their city.
20:2 people of God, four hundred thousand soldiers armed with **swords**.
20:15 twenty-six thousand **swordsmen** [+408+8990] from their towns,
20:17 mustered four hundred thousand **swordsmen** [+408+8990],
20:25 eighteen thousand Israelites, all of them armed with **swords**.
20:35 Israelites struck down 25,100 Benjamites, all armed with **swords**.
20:37 dash into Gibeah, spread out and put the whole city to the **sword**.
20:46 twenty-five thousand Benjamite **swordsmen** [+408+8990] fell,
20:48 of Israel went back to Benjamin and put all the towns to the **sword**,
21:10 to go to Jabesh Gilead and put to the **sword** those living there,
1Sa 13:19 had said, "Otherwise the Hebrews will make **swords** or spears!"
13:22 a soldier with Saul and Jonathan had a **sword** or spear in his hand;
14:20 Philistines in total confusion, striking each other with their **swords**.
15:8 and all his people he totally destroyed with the **sword**.
15:33 But Samuel said, "As your **sword** has made women childless,
17:39 David fastened on his **sword** over the tunic and tried walking
17:45 "You come against me with **sword** and spear and javelin,
17:47 All those gathered here will know that it is not by **sword** or spear
17:50 without a **sword** in his hand he struck down the Philistine
17:51 He took hold of the Philistine's **sword** and drew it from the
18:4 along with his tunic, and even his **sword**, his bow and his belt.

1Sa 21: 8 [21:9] "Don't you have a spear or a **sword** here?
21: 8 [21:9] I haven't brought my **sword** or any other weapon, because
21: 9 [21:10] The priest replied, "The **sword** *of* Goliath the Philistine,
22: 10 also gave him provisions and the **sword** *of* Goliath the Philistine."
22: 13 giving him bread and a **sword** and inquiring of God for him,
22: 19 He also put to the **sword** Nob, the town of the priests, with its men
22: 19 its children and infants, and its cattle, donkeys and sheep. **[RPH]**
25: 13 David said to his men, "Put on your **swords**!" So they put on their
25: 13 your swords!" So they put on their **swords**, and David put on his.
25: 13 **[RPH]** About four hundred men went up with David, while two
31: 4 said to his armor-bearer, "Draw your **sword** and run me through,
31: 4 and would not do it; so Saul took his own **sword** and fell on it.
31: 5 that Saul was dead, he too fell on his **sword** and died with him.
2Sa 1: 12 and the house of Israel, because they had fallen by the **sword**.
1: 22 did not turn back, the **sword** *of* Saul did not return unsatisfied.
2: 16 by the head and thrust his **dagger** into his opponent's side,
2: 26 Abner called out to Joab, "Must the **sword** devour forever?
3: 29 leans on a crutch or who falls by the **sword** or who lacks food."
11: 25 'Don't let this upset you; the **sword** devours one as well as another.
12: 9 You struck down Uriah the Hittite with the **sword** and took his
12: 9 to be your own. You killed him with the **sword** *of* the Ammonites.
12: 10 Now, therefore, the **sword** will never depart from your house,
15: 14 overtake us and bring ruin upon us and put the city to the **sword**."
18: 8 and the forest claimed more lives that day than the **sword**.
20: 8 strapped over it at his waist was a belt with a **dagger** in its sheath.
20: 10 Amasa was not on his guard against the **dagger** in Joab's hand,
23: 10 down the Philistines till his hand grew tired and froze to the **sword**.
24: 9 hundred thousand able-bodied men who could handle a **sword**,
1Ki 1: 51 today that he will not put his servant to death with the **sword**.' "
2: 8 to him by the LORD: 'I will not put you to death by the **sword**.'
2: 32 father David he attacked two men and killed them with the **sword**.
3: 24 the king said, "Bring me a **sword**." So they brought a sword for the
3: 24 "Bring me a sword." So they brought a **sword** for the king.
18: 28 shouted louder and slashed themselves with **swords** and spears,
19: 1 had done and how he had killed all the prophets with the **sword**.
19: 10 down your altars, and put your prophets to death with the **sword**.
19: 14 down your altars, and put your prophets to death with the **sword**.
19: 17 Jehu will put to death any who escape the **sword** *of* Hazael,
19: 17 and Elisha will put to death any who escape the **sword** *of* Jehu.
2Ki 3: 26 he took with him seven hundred **swordsmen** [+408+8990] to break
6: 22 "Would you kill men you have captured with your own **sword**
8: 12 kill their young men with the **sword**, dash their little children to the
10: 25 So they cut them down with the **sword**. The guards and officers
11: 15 between the ranks and put to the **sword** anyone who follows her."
11: 20 because Athaliah had been slain with the **sword** at the palace.
19: 7 and there I will have him cut down with the **sword**.' "
19: 37 his sons Adrammelech and Sharezer cut him down with the **sword**,
1Ch 5: 18 able-bodied men who could handle shield and **sword**, who could
10: 4 said to his armor-bearer, "Draw your **sword** and run me through,
10: 4 and would not do it; so Saul took his own **sword** and fell on it.
10: 5 saw that Saul was dead, he too fell on his **sword** and died.
21: 5 one million one hundred thousand men who could handle a **sword**,
21: 5 including four hundred and seventy thousand in Judah. **[RPH]**
21: 12 with their **swords** overtaking you, or three days of the sword of the
21: 12 swords overtaking you, or three days of the **sword** *of* the LORD—
21: 16 with a drawn **sword** in his hand extended over Jerusalem.
21: 27 spoke to the angel, and he put his **sword** back into its sheath.
21: 30 because he was afraid of the **sword** *of* the angel of the LORD.
2Ch 20: 9 upon us, whether the **sword** *of* judgment, or plague or famine,
21: 4 he put all his brothers to the **sword** along with some of the princes
23: 14 between the ranks and put to the **sword** anyone who follows her."
23: 21 the city was quiet, because Athaliah had been slain with the **sword**.
29: 9 This is why our fathers have fallen by the **sword** and why our sons
32: 21 temple of his god, some of his sons cut him down with the **sword**.
36: 17 who killed their young men with the **sword** in the sanctuary,
36: 20 who escaped from the **sword**, and they became servants to him
Ezr 9: 7 and our priests have been subjected to the **sword** and captivity,
Ne 4: 13 [4:7] them by families, with their **swords**, spears and bows.
4: 18 [4:12] each of the builders wore his **sword** at his side as he
Est 9: 5 The Jews struck down all their enemies with the **sword**, killing
Job 1: 15 They put the servants to the **sword**, and I am the only one who has
1: 17 They put the servants to the **sword**, and I am the only one who has
5: 15 He saves the needy from the **sword** in their mouth; he saves them
5: 20 ransom you from death, and in battle from the stroke of the **sword**.
15: 22 He despairs of escaping the darkness; he is marked for the **sword**.
19: 29 you should fear the **sword** yourselves; for wrath will bring
19: 29 for wrath will bring punishment by the **sword**, and then you will
27: 14 However many his children, their fate is the **sword**; his offspring
39: 22 at fear, afraid of nothing; he does not shy away from the **sword**.
40: 19 the works of God, yet his Maker can approach him with his **sword**.
41: 26 [41:18] The **sword** that reaches him has no effect, nor does the
Ps 7: 12 [7:13] If he does not relent, he will sharpen his **sword**; he will
17: 13 bring them down; rescue me from the wicked by your **sword**.
22: 20 [22:21] Deliver my life from the **sword**, my precious life from the
37: 14 The wicked draw the **sword** and bend the bow to bring down the
37: 15 their **swords** will pierce their own hearts, and their bows will be
44: 3 [44:4] It was not by their **sword** that they won the land, nor did
44: 6 [44:7] not trust in my bow, my **sword** does not bring me victory;
45: 3 [45:4] Gird your **sword** upon your side, O mighty one;
57: 4 [57:5] are spears and arrows, whose tongues are sharp **swords**.
59: 7 [59:8] they spew out **swords** from their lips, and they say, "Who
63: 10 [63:11] They will be given over to the **sword** and become food
64: 3 [64:4] They sharpen their tongues like **swords** and aim their
76: 3 [76:4] the shields and the **swords**, the weapons of war.
78: 62 He gave his people over to the **sword**; he was very angry with his
78: 64 their priests were put to the **sword**, and their widows could not
89: 43 [89:44] You have turned back the edge of his **sword** and have not
144: 10 to kings, who delivers his servant David from the deadly **sword**.
149: 6 God be in their mouths and a double-edged **sword** in their hands,
Pr 5: 4 but in the end she is bitter as gall, sharp as a double-edged **sword**.
12: 18 Reckless words pierce like a **sword**, but the tongue of the wise
25: 18 Like a club or a **sword** or a sharp arrow is the man who gives false
30: 14 those whose teeth are **swords** and whose jaws are set with knives
SS 3: 8 all of them wearing the **sword**, all experienced in battle, each with
3: 8 all experienced in battle, each with his **sword** at his side,
Isa 1: 20 but if you resist and rebel, you will be devoured by the **sword**."
2: 4 They will beat their **swords** into plowshares and their spears into
2: 4 Nation will not take up **sword** against nation, nor will they train for
3: 25 Your men will fall by the **sword**, your warriors in battle.
13: 15 will be thrust through; all who are caught will fall by the **sword**.
14: 19 you are covered with the slain, with those pierced by the **sword**,
21: 15 They flee from the **sword**, from the drawn sword, from the bent
21: 15 from the drawn **sword**, from the bent bow and from the heat of
22: 2 Your slain were not killed by the **sword**, nor did they die in battle.
27: 1 the LORD will punish with his **sword**, his fierce, great
31: 8 "Assyria will fall by a **sword** that is not of man; a sword, not of
31: 8 that is not of man; a **sword**, not of mortals, will devour them.
31: 8 They will flee before the **sword** and their young men will be put to
34: 5 My **sword** has drunk its fill in the heavens; see, it descends in
34: 6 The **sword** of the LORD is bathed in blood, it is covered with
37: 7 and there I will have him cut down with the **sword**.' "
37: 38 his sons Adrammelech and Sharezer cut him down with the **sword**,
41: 2 He turns them to dust with his **sword**, to windblown chaff with his
49: 2 He made my mouth like a sharpened **sword**, in the shadow of his
51: 19 ruin and destruction, famine and **sword**—who can console you?
65: 12 I will destine you for the **sword**, and you will all bend down for the
66: 16 with his **sword** the LORD will execute judgment upon all men,
Jer 2: 30 Your **sword** has devoured your prophets like a ravening lion.
4: 10 'You will have peace,' when the **sword** is at our throats."
5: 12 No harm will come to us; we will never see **sword** or famine.
5: 17 With the **sword** they will destroy the fortified cities in which you
6: 25 out to the fields or walk on the roads, for the enemy has a **sword**,
9: 16 [9:15] I will pursue them with the **sword** until I have destroyed
11: 22 Their young men will die by the **sword**, their sons and daughters
12: 12 for the **sword** of the LORD will devour from one end of the land
14: 12 Instead, I will destroy them with the **sword**, famine and plague."
14: 13 keep telling them, 'You will not see the **sword** or suffer famine.
14: 15 yet they are saying, 'No **sword** or famine will touch this land.'
14: 15 this land.' Those same prophets will perish by **sword** and famine.
14: 16 out into the streets of Jerusalem because of the famine and **sword**.
14: 18 If I go into the country, I see those slain by the **sword**; if I go into
15: 2 destined for death, to death; those for the **sword**, to the sword;
15: 2 destined for death, to death; those for the sword, to the **sword**;
15: 3 "the **sword** to kill and the dogs to drag away and the birds of the
15: 9 I will put the survivors to the **sword** before their enemies,"
16: 4 They will perish by **sword** and famine, and their dead bodies will
18: 21 children over to famine; hand them over to the power of the **sword**.
18: 21 men be put to death, their young men slain by the **sword** in battle.
19: 7 I will make them fall by the **sword** before their enemies, at the
20: 4 with your own eyes you will see them fall by the **sword** *of* their
20: 4 who will carry them away to Babylon or put them to the **sword**.
21: 7 **sword** and famine, to Nebuchadnezzar king of Babylon and to
21: 7 He will put them to the **sword**; he will show them no mercy
21: 9 Whoever stays in this city will die by the **sword**, famine or plague.
24: 10 I will send the **sword**, famine and plague against them until they
25: 16 and go mad because of the **sword** I will send among them."
25: 27 fall to rise no more because of the **sword** I will send among you.'
25: 29 for I am calling down a **sword** upon all who live on the earth,
25: 31 and put the wicked to the **sword**,' " declares the LORD.
25: 38 because of the **sword** [BHS 3019] *of* the oppressor and
26: 23 who had him struck down with a **sword** and his body thrown into
27: 8 I will punish that nation with the **sword**, famine and plague,
27: 13 Why will you and your people die by the **sword**, famine
29: 17 "I will send the **sword**, famine and plague against them and I will
29: 18 I will pursue them with the **sword**, famine and plague and will
31: 2 "The people who survive the **sword** will find favor in the desert;
32: 24 Because of the **sword**, famine and plague, the city will be handed
32: 36 'By the **sword**, famine and plague it will be handed over to the

Jer 33: 4 been torn down to be used against the siege ramps and the **sword**
34: 4 the LORD says concerning you: You will not die by the **sword**;
34: 17 the LORD—'freedom' to fall by the **sword**, plague and famine.
38: 2 'Whoever stays in this city will die by the **sword**, famine or plague,
39: 18 you will not fall by the **sword** but will escape with your life,
41: 2 Gedaliah son of Ahikam, the son of Shaphan, with the **sword**,
42: 16 the **sword** you fear will overtake you there, and the famine you
42: 17 are determined to go to Egypt to settle there will die by the **sword**,
42: 22 You will die by the **sword**, famine and plague in the place where
43: 11 for captivity, and the **sword** to those destined for the sword.
43: 11 for captivity, and the sword to those destined for the **sword**.
44: 12 all perish in Egypt; they will fall by the **sword** or die from famine.
44: 12 From the least to the greatest, they will die by **sword** or famine.
44: 13 I will punish those who live in Egypt with the **sword**, famine
44: 18 have had nothing and have been perishing by **sword** and famine."
44: 27 the Jews in Egypt will perish by **sword** and famine until they are
44: 28 Those who escape the **sword** and return to the land of Judah from
46: 10 The **sword** will devour till it is satisfied, till it has quenched its
46: 14 and get ready, for the **sword** devours those around you.'
46: 16 and our native lands, away from the **sword** *of* the oppressor.'
47: 6 " 'Ah, **sword** of the LORD,' ⌊you cry,⌋ 'how long till you rest?
48: 2 You too, O Madmen, will be silenced; the **sword** will pursue you.
48: 10 A curse on him who keeps his **sword** from bloodshed!
49: 37 "I will pursue them with the **sword** until I have made an end of
50: 16 Because of the **sword** *of* the oppressor let everyone return to his
50: 35 "A **sword** against the Babylonians!" declares the LORD—
50: 36 A **sword** against her false prophets! They will become fools.
50: 36 They will become fools. A **sword** against her warriors! They will
50: 37 A **sword** against her horses and chariots and all the foreigners in
50: 37 A **sword** against her treasures! They will be plundered.
51: 50 You who have escaped the **sword**, leave and do not linger!
La 1: 20 Outside, the **sword** bereaves; inside, there is only death.
2: 21 the streets; my young men and maidens have fallen by the **sword**.
4: 9 Those killed by the **sword** are better off than those who die of
5: 9 bread at the risk of our lives because of the **sword** *in* the desert.
Eze 5: 1 take a sharp **sword** and use it as a barber's razor to shave your
5: 2 Take a third and strike it with the **sword** all around the city.
5: 2 a third to the wind. For I will pursue them with drawn **sword**.
5: 12 inside you; a third will fall by the **sword** outside your walls;
5: 12 a third I will scatter to the winds and pursue with drawn **sword**.
5: 17 will sweep through you, and I will bring the **sword** against you.
6: 3 I am about to bring a **sword** against you, and I will destroy your
6: 8 for some of you will escape the **sword** when you are scattered
6: 11 house of Israel, for they will fall by the **sword**, famine and plague.
6: 12 and he that is near will fall by the **sword**, and he that survives
7: 15 "Outside is the **sword**, inside are plague and famine; those in the
7: 15 those in the country will die by the **sword**, and those in the city
11: 8 You fear the **sword**, and the sword is what I will bring against you,
11: 8 You fear the sword, and the **sword** is what I will bring against you,
11: 10 You will fall by the **sword**, and I will execute judgment on you at
12: 14 and all his troops—and I will pursue them with drawn **sword**.
12: 16 But I will spare a few of them from the **sword**, famine and plague,
14: 17 "Or if I bring a **sword** against that country and say, 'Let the sword
14: 17 that country and say, 'Let the **sword** pass throughout the land,'
14: 21 **sword** and famine and wild beasts and plague—to kill its men
16: 40 who will stone you and hack you to pieces with their **swords**.
17: 21 All his fleeing troops will fall by the **sword**, and the survivors will
21: 3 [21:8] I will draw my **sword** from its scabbard and cut off from
21: 4 [21:9] my **sword** will be unsheathed against everyone from south
21: 5 [21:10] I the LORD have drawn my **sword** from its scabbard;
21: 9 [21:14] Lord says: " 'A **sword**, a sword, sharpened and polished—
21: 9 [21:14] Lord says: " 'A sword, a **sword**, sharpened and polished—
21: 11 [21:16] " 'The **sword** is appointed to be polished, to be grasped
21: 12 [21:17] They are thrown to the **sword** along with my people.
21: 14 [21:19] Let the **sword** strike twice, even three times. It is a sword
21: 14 [21:19] It is a **sword** *for* slaughter—a sword for great slaughter,
21: 14 [21:19] a **sword** *for* great slaughter, closing in on them from
21: 15 [21:20] I have stationed the **sword** for slaughter at all their gates.
21: 19 [21:24] mark out two roads for the **sword** *of* the king of Babylon
21: 20 [21:25] Mark out one road for the **sword** to come against Rabbah
21: 28 [21:33] " 'A **sword**, a sword, drawn for the slaughter, polished to
21: 28 [21:33] " 'A sword, a **sword**, drawn for the slaughter, polished to
23: 10 took away her sons and daughters and killed her with the **sword**.
23: 25 and your ears, and those of you who are left will fall by the **sword**.
23: 47 The mob will stone them and cut them down with their **swords**;
24: 21 The sons and daughters you left behind will fall by the **sword**.
25: 13 lay it waste, and from Teman to Dedan they will fall by the **sword**.
26: 6 and her settlements on the mainland will be ravaged by the **sword**.
26: 8 He will ravage your settlements on the mainland with the **sword**;
26: 9 against your walls and demolish your towers with his **weapons**.
26: 11 he will kill your people with the **sword**, and your strong pillars will
28: 7 they will draw their **swords** against your beauty and wisdom
28: 23 slain will fall within her, with the **sword** against her on every side.
29: 8 I will bring a **sword** against you and kill your men and their
30: 4 A **sword** will come against Egypt, and anguish will come upon
30: 5 the people of the covenant land will fall by the **sword** along with
30: 6 From Migdol to Aswan they will fall by the **sword** within her,
30: 11 They will draw their **swords** against Egypt and fill the land with
30: 17 The young men of Heliopolis and Bubastis will fall by the **sword**,
30: 21 or put in a splint so as to become strong enough to hold a **sword**.
30: 22 as well as the broken one, and make the **sword** fall from his hand.
30: 24 the arms of the king of Babylon and put my **sword** in his hand,
30: 25 when I put my **sword** into the hand of the king of Babylon
31: 17 gone down to the grave with it, joining those killed by the **sword**.
31: 18 will lie among the uncircumcised, with those killed by the **sword**.
32: 10 because of you when I brandish my **sword** before them.
32: 11 " 'The **sword** *of* the king of Babylon will come against you.
32: 12 I will cause your hordes to fall by the **swords** *of* mighty men—
32: 20 They will fall among those killed by the **sword**. The sword is
32: 20 The **sword** is drawn; let her be dragged off with all her hordes.
32: 21 they lie with the uncircumcised, with those killed by the **sword**.'
32: 22 by the graves of all her slain, all who have fallen by the **sword**.
32: 23 spread terror in the land of the living are slain, fallen by the **sword**.
32: 24 hordes around her grave. All of them are slain, fallen by the **sword**.
32: 25 her grave. All of them are uncircumcised, killed by the **sword**.
32: 26 killed by the **sword** because they spread their terror in the land of
32: 27 weapons of war, whose **swords** were placed under their heads?
32: 28 will lie among the uncircumcised, with those killed by the **sword**.
32: 29 despite their power, they are laid with those killed by the **sword**.
32: 30 They lie uncircumcised with those killed by the **sword** and bear
32: 31 will be consoled for all his hordes that were killed by the **sword**,
32: 32 with those killed by the **sword**, declares the Sovereign LORD."
33: 2 'When I bring the **sword** against a land, and the people of the land
33: 3 he sees the **sword** coming against the land and blows the trumpet
33: 4 but does not take warning and the **sword** comes and takes his life,
33: 6 if the watchman sees the **sword** coming and does not blow the
33: 6 the people and the **sword** comes and takes the life of one of them,
33: 26 You rely on your **sword**, you do detestable things, and each of you
33: 27 as I live, those who are left in the ruins will fall by the **sword**,
35: 5 delivered the Israelites over to the **sword** at the time of their
35: 8 those killed by the **sword** will fall on your hills and in your valleys
38: 4 with large and small shields, all of them brandishing their **swords**.
38: 8 In future years you will invade a land that has recovered from **war**,
38: 21 I will summon a **sword** against Gog on all my mountains,
38: 21 Sovereign LORD. Every man's **sword** will be against his brother.
39: 23 handed them over to their enemies, and they all fell by the **sword**.
Da 11: 33 though for a time they will fall by the **sword** or be burned
Hos 1: 7 not by bow, **sword** or battle, or by horses and horsemen, but by the
2: 18 [2:20] Bow and **sword** and battle I will abolish from the land,
7: 16 Their leaders will fall by the **sword** because of their insolent
11: 6 **Swords** will flash in their cities, will destroy the bars of their gates
13: 16 [14:1] They will fall by the **sword**; their little ones will be dashed
Joel 3: 10 [4:10] Beat your plowshares into **swords** and your pruning hooks
Am 1: 11 Because he pursued his brother with a **sword**, stifling all
4: 10 I killed your young men with the **sword**, along with your captured
7: 9 with my **sword** I will rise against the house of Jeroboam."
7: 11 " 'Jeroboam will die by the **sword**, and Israel will surely go into
7: 17 in the city, and your sons and daughters will fall by the **sword**.
9: 1 of all the people; those who are left I will kill with the **sword**.
9: 4 by their enemies, there I will command the **sword** to slay them.
9: 10 All the sinners among my people will die by the **sword**, all those
Mic 4: 3 They will beat their **swords** into plowshares and their spears into
4: 3 Nation will not take up **sword** against nation, nor will they train for
5: 6 [5:5] They will rule the land of Assyria with the **sword**, the land
6: 14 but save nothing, because what you save I will give to the **sword**.
Na 2: 13 [2:14] in smoke, and the **sword** will devour your young lions.
3: 3 Charging cavalry, flashing **swords** and glittering spears! Many
3: 15 the **sword** will cut you down and, like grasshoppers, consume you.
Zep 2: 12 "You too, O Cushites, will be slain by my **sword**."
Hag 2: 22 and their riders will fall, each by the **sword** *of* his brother.
Zec 9: 13 against your sons, O Greece, and make you like a warrior's **sword**.
11: 17 deserts the flock! May the **sword** strike his arm and his right eye!
13: 7 "Awake, O **sword**, against my shepherd, against the man who is

2996 חֹרֶב ḥōreb¹, n.m. [12 / 13] [√ 2990]

heat [6], drought [3], dry [3], fever [1]

Ge 31: 40 The **heat** consumed me in the daytime and the cold at night,
Dt 28: 22 with scorching heat and **drought**, [BHS 2995] with blight
Jdg 6: 37 If there is dew only on the fleece and all the ground is **dry**,
6: 39 This time make the fleece **dry** and the ground covered with dew."
6: 40 Only the fleece was **dry**; all the ground was covered with dew.
Job 30: 30 My skin grows black and peels; my body burns with **fever**.
Isa 4: 6 It will be a shelter and shade from the **heat** of the day, and a refuge
25: 4 in his distress, a shelter from the storm and a shade from the **heat**.
25: 5 like the **heat** of the desert. You silence the uproar of foreigners;
25: 5 as **heat** is reduced by the shadow of a cloud, so the song of the
Jer 36: 30 thrown out and exposed to the **heat** by day and the frost by night.

Jer 50:38 A **drought** on her waters! They will dry up. For it is a land of
Hag 1:11 I called for a **drought** on the fields and the mountains, on the

2997 ²חֹרֶב **ḥōreb²**, n.[m.]. [4] [√ 2990]

object of horror [1], rubble [1], ruined [1], waste [1]

Isa 61: 4 they will renew the **ruined** cities that have been devastated for
Jer 49:13 "that Bozrah will become a ruin and an **object of horror**,
Eze 29:10 land of Egypt a ruin and a desolate **waste** from Migdol to Aswan,
Zep 2:14 **rubble** will be in the doorways, the beams of cedar will be

2998 חֹרֵב **ḥōrēb**, n.pr.loc. [17] [√ 2990?]

Horeb [17]

Ex 3: 1 he led the flock to the far side of the desert and came to **Horeb**,
17: 6 I will stand there before you by the rock at **Horeb**. Strike the rock,
33: 6 So the Israelites stripped off their ornaments at Mount **Horeb**.
Dt 1: 2 (It takes eleven days to go from **Horeb** to Kadesh Barnea by the
1: 6 The LORD our God said to us at **Horeb**, "You have stayed long
1:19 we set out from **Horeb** and went toward the hill country of the
4:10 the day you stood before the LORD your God at **Horeb**,
4:15 any kind the day the LORD spoke to you at **Horeb** out of the fire.
5: 2 The LORD our God made a covenant with us at **Horeb**.
9: 8 At **Horeb** you aroused the LORD's wrath so that he was angry
18:16 For this is what you asked of the LORD your God at **Horeb** on
29: 1 [28:69] to the covenant he had made with them at **Horeb**.
1Ki 8: 9 except the two stone tablets that Moses had placed in it at **Horeb**,
19: 8 he traveled forty days and forty nights until he reached **Horeb**,
2Ch 5:10 the ark except the two tablets that Moses had placed in it at **Horeb**,
Ps 106:19 At **Horeb** they made a calf and worshiped an idol cast from metal.
Mal 4: 4 [3:22] the decrees and laws I gave him at **Horeb** for all Israel.

2999 חָרְבָּה **ḥorbâ**, n.f. [43] [√ 2990]

ruins [21], ruin [7], desolate [5], in ruins [3], deserts [1], desolation [1], places lying in ruins [1], ruined homes [1], ruined [1], waste [1], wasteland [1]

Lev 26:31 I will turn your cities into **ruins** and lay waste your sanctuaries,
26:33 Your land will be laid waste, and your cities will lie **in ruins**.
2Ch 34: 6 as far as Naphtali, and in the **ruins** [K 1074] around them,
Ezr 9: 9 us new life to rebuild the house of our God and repair its **ruins**,
Job 3:14 of the earth, who built for themselves **places** now **lying in ruins**,
Ps 9: 6 [9:7] Endless **ruin** has overtaken the enemy, you have uprooted
102: 6 [102:7] I am like a desert owl, like an owl among the **ruins**.
109:10 wandering beggars; may they be driven from their **ruined homes**.
Isa 5:17 in their own pasture; lambs will feed among the **ruins** *of* the rich.
44:26 'They shall be built,' and of their **ruins**, 'I will restore them,'
48:21 They did not thirst when he led them through the **deserts**;
49:19 "Though you *were* **ruined** and made desolate and your land laid
51: 3 comfort Zion and will look with compassion on all her **ruins**;
52: 9 Burst into songs of joy together, you **ruins** *of* Jerusalem,
58:12 Your people will rebuild the ancient **ruins** and will raise up the
61: 4 They will rebuild the ancient **ruins** and restore the places long
64:11 [64:10] burned with fire, and all that we treasured lies in **ruins**.
Jer 7:34 and the streets of Jerusalem, for the land will become **desolate**.
22: 5 I swear by myself that this palace will become a **ruin**.' "
25: 9 make them an object of horror and scorn, and an everlasting **ruin**.
25:11 This whole country will become a **desolate** wasteland, and these
25:18 to make them a **ruin** and an object of horror and scorn and cursing,
27:17 and you will live. Why should this city become a **ruin**?
44: 2 on all the towns of Judah. Today they lie deserted and **in ruins**
44: 6 of Jerusalem and made them the **desolate** ruins they are today.
44:22 an object of cursing and a **desolate** waste without inhabitants,
49:13 and of cursing; and all its towns will be **in ruins** forever."
Eze 5:14 "I will make you a **ruin** and a reproach among the nations around
13: 4 Your prophets, O Israel, are like jackals among **ruins**.
25:13 I will lay it **waste**, and from Teman to Dedan they will fall by the
26:20 as in ancient **ruins**, with those who go down to the pit, and you
29: 9 Egypt will become a desolate **wasteland**. Then they will know that
29:10 I will make the land of Egypt a **ruin** and a desolate waste from
33:24 the people living in those **ruins** in the land of Israel are saying,
33:27 as I live, those who are left in the **ruins** will fall by the sword,
35: 4 I will turn your towns into **ruins** and you will be desolate.
36: 4 to the desolate **ruins** and the deserted towns that have been
36:10 house of Israel. The towns will be inhabited and the **ruins** rebuilt.
36:33 your sins, I will resettle your towns, and the **ruins** will be rebuilt.
38: 8 nations to the mountains of Israel, which had long been **desolate**.
38:12 I will plunder and loot and turn my hand against the resettled **ruins**
Da 9: 2 that the **desolation** *of* Jerusalem would last seventy years.
Mal 1: 4 "Though we have been crushed, we will rebuild the **ruins**."

3000 חָרָבָה **ḥārābâ**, n.f. [8] [√ 2990]

dry ground [4], dry land [3], dry up [+5989] [1]

Ge 7:22 Everything on **dry land** that had the breath of life in its nostrils
Ex 14:21 the sea back with a strong east wind and turned it into **dry land**.
Jos 3:17 the LORD stood firm on **dry ground** in the middle of the Jordan,
3:17 until the whole nation had completed the crossing on **dry ground**.
4:18 No sooner had they set their feet on the **dry ground** than the
2Ki 2: 8 and to the left, and the two of them crossed over on **dry ground**.
Eze 30:12 *I will* **dry** [+5989] **up** the streams of the Nile and sell the land to
Hag 2: 6 more shake the heavens and the earth, the sea and the **dry land**.

3001 חֲרָבוֹן **ḥ^arābôn**, n.m. [1] [√ 2990]

heat [1]

Ps 32: 4 heavy upon me; my strength was sapped as in the **heat** *of* summer.

3002 חַרְבוֹנָא **ḥarbônā'**, n.pr.m. [1] [cf. 3003]

Harbona [1]

Est 1:10 Biztha, **Harbona**, Bigtha, Abagtha, Zethar and Carcas—

3003 חַרְבוֹנָה **ḥarbônâ**, n.pr.m. [1] [cf. 3002]

Harbona [1]

Est 7: 9 Then **Harbona**, one of the eunuchs attending the king, said,

3004 חָרַג **ḥārag**, v. [1 / 2]

come trembling [2]

2Sa 22:46 [A] *they* **come trembling** [BHS 2520] from their strongholds.
Ps 18:45 [18:46] [A] *they* **come trembling** from their strongholds.

3005 חַרְגֹּל **ḥargōl**, n.[m.]. [1] [cf. 2519]

cricket [1]

Lev 11:22 you may eat any kind of locust, katydid, **cricket** or grasshopper.

3006 חָרַד **ḥārad**, v. [39] [→ 3007, 3008?, 3009, 3010, 3011?, 3012?]

make afraid [9], tremble [5], trembled [4], come trembling [2], frighten away [2], trembling [2], *untranslated* [1], alarm [1], fear [1], frighten [1], gone to trouble [+906+3010] [1], pounds [1], quaking with fear [1], routing [1], shudder [1], startled [1], strike with terror [1], terrify [1], terror filled [+4394] [1], trembled violently [+1524+3010+4394+6330] [1], trembles [1]

Ge 27:33 [A] Isaac **trembled** [+1524+3010+4394+6330] **violently** and said,
42:28 [A] and *they turned* to each other **trembling** and said,
Ex 19:16 [A] a very loud trumpet blast. Everyone in the camp **trembled**.
19:18 [A] from a furnace, the whole mountain **trembled** violently,
Lev 26: 6 [G] and you will lie down and no *one will* **make** you **afraid**.
Dt 28:26 [G] of the earth, and there will be no *one to* **frighten** them **away**.
Jdg 8:12 [G] pursued them and captured them, **routing** their entire army.
Ru 3: 8 [A] In the middle of the night *something* **startled** the man,
1Sa 13: 7 [A] and all the troops with him *were* **quaking with fear**.
14:15 [A] and raiding parties—**[RPH]** and the ground shook.
16: 4 [A] the elders of the town **trembled** when they met him.
21: 1 [21:2] [A] Ahimelech **trembled** when he met him, and asked,
28: 5 [A] he was afraid; **terror** [+4394] **filled** his heart.
2Sa 17: 2 [G] *I would* **strike** him **with terror**, and then all the people with
1Ki 1:49 [A] At this, all Adonijah's guests rose *in* **alarm** and dispersed.
2Ki 4:13 [A] '*You have* **gone to** all this **trouble** [+906+3010] for us.
Job 11:19 [G] You will lie down, with no *one to* **make** you **afraid**,
37: 1 [A] "At this my heart **pounds** and leaps from its place.
Isa 10:29 [A] overnight at Geba." Ramah **trembles**; Gibeah of Saul flees.
17: 2 [G] which will lie down, with no *one to* **make** them **afraid**.
19:16 [A] *They will* **shudder** with fear at the uplifted hand that the
32:11 [A] **Tremble**, *you* complacent women; shudder, you daughters
41: 5 [A] islands have seen it and fear; the ends of the earth **tremble**.
Jer 7:33 [G] of the earth, and there will be no *one to* **frighten** them **away**.
30:10 [G] have peace and security, and no *one will* **make** him **afraid**.
46:27 [G] have peace and security, and no *one will* **make** him **afraid**.
Eze 26:16 [A] sit on the ground, **trembling** every moment, appalled at you.
26:18 [A] Now the coastlands **tremble** on the day of your fall;
30: 9 [G] from me in ships to **frighten** Cush *out of* her complacency.
32:10 [A] On the day of your downfall each of them *will* **tremble** every
34:28 [G] They will live in safety, and no *one will* **make** them **afraid**.
39:26 [G] in safety in their land with no *one to* **make** them **afraid**.
Hos 11:10 [A] he roars, his children *will* **come trembling** from the west.
11:11 [A] *They will* **come trembling** like birds from Egypt, like doves
Am 3: 6 [A] When a trumpet sounds in a city, *do* not the people **tremble**?
Mic 4: 4 [G] under his own fig tree, and no *one will* **make** them **afraid**,
Na 2:11 [2:12] [G] and lioness went, and the cubs, with nothing *to* **fear**?
Zep 3:13 [G] will eat and lie down and no *one will* **make** them **afraid**."
Zec 1:21 [2:4] [G] the craftsmen have come to **terrify** them and throw

3007 חָרֵד **ḥārēd**, a.vbl. [6] [√ 3006]

trembles [2], fear [1], feared [+2118] [1], tremble [1], trembled [1]

Jdg 7: 3 'Anyone *who* **trembles** with fear may turn back and leave Mount
1Sa 4: 13 watching, because his heart **feared** [+2118] for the ark of God.
Ezr 9: 4 everyone *who* **trembled** at the words of the God of Israel gathered
10: 3 of my lord and of those *who* **fear** the commands of our God.
Isa 66: 2 he who is humble and contrite in spirit, and **trembles** at my word.
66: 5 Hear the word of the LORD, you who **tremble** at his word:

3008 ¹חֲרֹד **ḥ^{a}rōd^{1}**, n.pr.loc. [1] [→ 3009?, 3012, 6534; cf. 3006?]

Harod [1]

Jdg 7: 1 (that is, Gideon) and all his men camped at the spring of **Harod**.

3009 ²חֲרֹד **ḥ^{a}rōd^{2}**, a.g. *or* n.pr. Not used in NIV/BHS [√ 3006?; cf. 3008?]

3010 ¹חֲרָדָה **ḥ^{a}rādâ^{1}**, n.f. [9] [√ 3006]

fear [2], panic [2], terror [2], gone to trouble [+906+3006] [1], horror [1], trembled violently [+1524+3006+4394+6330] [1]

Ge 27: 33 Isaac **trembled violently** [+1524+3006+4394+6330] and said, "Who was it, then, that hunted game and brought it to me? I ate it just
1Sa 14: 15 Then **panic** struck the whole army—those in the camp and field,
14: 15 and the ground shook. It was a **panic** *sent by* God.
2Ki 4: 13 "Tell her, '*You have* **gone to** all this **trouble** [+906+3006] for us.
Pr 29: 25 **Fear** *of* man will prove to be a snare, but whoever trusts in the
Isa 21: 4 me tremble; the twilight I longed for has become a **horror** to me.
Jer 30: 5 the LORD says: " 'Cries of **fear** are heard—terror, not peace.
Eze 26: 16 Clothed with **terror**, they will sit on the ground, trembling every
Da 10: 7 such **terror** overwhelmed them that they fled and hid themselves.

3011 ²חֲרָדָה **ḥ^{a}rādâ^{2}**, n.pr.loc. [2] [√ 3006?]

Haradah [2]

Nu 33: 24 They left Mount Shepher and camped at **Haradah**.
33: 25 They left **Haradah** and camped at Makheloth.

3012 חֲרֹדִי **ḥ^{a}rōdî**, a.loc. [2] [√ 3008; cf. 3006?]

Harodite [2]

2Sa 23: 25 Shammah the **Harodite**, Elika the Harodite,
23: 25 Shammah the Harodite, Elika the **Harodite**,

3013 ¹חָרָה **ḥārâ^{1}**, v. [92] [→ 3019, 3034; cf. 3081]

angry [22], burned [18], angry [+678] [11], burn [6], aroused [4], burns [4], fret [4], very angry [+678] [4], burned [+4394] [2], loses temper [+3013+4200] [2], *untranslated* [1], anger [+678] [1], angry [+928+6524] [1], burning [1], compete [1], flared up [1], flared [1], furious [+4200+4394] [1], furious [+678+4394] [1], fury [+4200+4394] [1], have more and more [1], rage [1], raged [1], troubled [1], zealously [1]

Ge 4: 5 [A] So Cain *was* very **angry**, and his face was downcast.
4: 6 [A] the LORD said to Cain, "Why *are* you **angry**? Why is your
18: 30 [A] Then he said, "*May* the Lord not *be* **angry**, but let me speak.
18: 32 [A] he said, "*May* the Lord not *be* **angry**, but let me speak just
30: 2 [A] Jacob *became* **angry** [+678] with her and said, "Am I in the
31: 35 [A] said to her father, "Don't *be* **angry** [+928+6524], my lord,
31: 36 [A] Jacob *was* **angry** and took Laban to task. "What is my
34: 7 [A] They were filled with grief and **fury** [+4200+4394], because
39: 19 [A] "This is how your slave treated me," he **burned** *with* anger.
44: 18 [A] *Do* not *be* **angry** [+678] with your servant, though you are
45: 5 [A] and *do* not *be* **angry** with yourselves for selling me here,
Ex 4: 14 [A] Then the LORD's anger **burned** against Moses and he said,
22: 24 [22:23] [A] My anger *will be* **aroused**, and I will kill you with
32: 10 [A] leave me alone so that my anger *may* **burn** against them
32: 11 [A] he said, "why *should* your anger **burn** against your people,
32: 19 [A] his anger **burned** and he threw the tablets out of his hands,
32: 22 [A] "*Do* not *be* **angry** [+678], my lord," Aaron answered.
Nu 11: 1 [A] the LORD, and when he heard them his anger *was* **aroused**.
11: 10 [A] The LORD *became* exceedingly **angry** [+678], and Moses
11: 33 [A] the anger of the LORD **burned** against the people,
12: 9 [A] The anger of the LORD **burned** against them, and he left
16: 15 [A] Moses *became* very **angry** and said to the LORD, "Do not
22: 22 [A] God *was* **very angry** [+678] when he went, and the angel of
22: 27 [A] and he *was* **angry** [+678] and beat her with his staff.
24: 10 [A] Balak's anger **burned** against Balaam. He struck his hands
25: 3 [A] Baal of Peor. And the LORD's anger **burned** against them.
32: 10 [A] The LORD's anger *was* **aroused** that day and he swore this
32: 13 [A] The LORD's anger **burned** against Israel and he made them
Dt 6: 15 [A] is a jealous God and his anger *will* **burn** against you,
7: 4 [A] the LORD's anger *will* **burn** against you and will quickly
11: 17 [A] the LORD's anger *will* **burn** against you, and he will shut
29: 27 [29:26] [A] Therefore the LORD's anger **burned** against this
31: 17 [A] On that day I *will become* **angry** [+678] with them
Jos 7: 1 [A] some of them. So the LORD's anger **burned** against Israel.
23: 16 [A] down to them, the LORD's anger *will* **burn** against you,
Jdg 2: 14 [A] *In his* **anger** [+678] against Israel the LORD handed them
2: 20 [A] Therefore the LORD *was* **very angry** [+678] with Israel
3: 8 [A] The anger of the LORD **burned** against Israel so that he
6: 39 [A] Then Gideon said to God, "*Do* not *be* **angry** [+678] with me.
9: 30 [A] what Gaal son of Ebed said, he *was* **very angry** [+678].
10: 7 [A] he *became* **angry** [+678] with them. He sold them into the
14: 19 [A] **Burning** *with* anger, he went up to his father's house.
1Sa 11: 6 [A] came upon him in power, and he **burned** [+4394] with anger.
15: 11 [A] has not carried out my instructions." Samuel *was* **troubled**,
17: 28 [A] with the men, he **burned** *with* anger at him and asked,
18: 8 [A] Saul *was* very **angry**; this refrain galled him. "They have
20: 7 [A] if *he* **loses** his **temper** [+3013+4200], you can be sure that he
20: 7 [A] if *he* **loses** his **temper** [+3013+4200], you can be sure that he
20: 30 [A] Saul's anger **flared up** at Jonathan and he said to him,
2Sa 3: 8 [A] Abner *was* very **angry** because of what Ish-Bosheth said
6: 7 [A] The LORD's anger **burned** against Uzzah because of his
6: 8 [A] David *was* **angry** because the LORD's wrath had broken
12: 5 [A] David **burned** [+4394] *with* anger against the man and said
13: 21 [A] King David heard all this, he *was* **furious** [+4200+4394].
19: 42 [19:43] [A] closely related to us. Why *are* you **angry** about it?
22: 8 [A] of the heavens shook; they trembled because he *was* **angry**.
24: 1 [A] Again the anger of the LORD **burned** against Israel, and he
2Ki 13: 3 [A] So the LORD's anger **burned** against Israel, and for a long
23: 26 [A] which **burned** against Judah because of all that Manasseh
1Ch 13: 10 [A] The LORD's anger **burned** against Uzzah, and he struck
13: 11 [A] David *was* **angry** because the LORD's wrath had broken
2Ch 25: 10 [A] They *were* **furious** [+678+4394] with Judah and left for
25: 15 [A] The anger of the LORD **burned** against Amaziah, and he
Ne 3: 20 [G] Baruch son of Zabbai **zealously** repaired another section,
4: 1 [3:33] [A] the wall, he *became* **angry** and was greatly incensed.
4: 7 [4:1] [A] the gaps were being closed, they *were* very **angry**.
5: 6 [A] I heard their outcry and these charges, I *was* very **angry**.
Job 19: 11 [A] His anger **burns** against me; he counts me among his
32: 2 [A] *became* **very angry** [+678] with Job for justifying himself
32: 2 [A] became very angry with Job **[RPH]** for justifying himself
32: 3 [A] He *was* also **angry** [+678] with the three friends,
32: 5 [A] three men had nothing more to say, his anger *was* **aroused**.
42: 7 [A] "I *am* **angry** [+678] with you and your two friends,
Ps 18: 7 [18:8] [A] they trembled because he *was* **angry**.
37: 1 [F] *Do* not **fret** because of evil men or be envious of those who
37: 7 [F] *do* not **fret** when men succeed in their ways, when they carry
37: 8 [F] and turn from wrath; *do* not **fret**—it leads only to evil.
106: 40 [A] Therefore the LORD *was* **angry** [+678] with his people
124: 3 [A] when their anger **flared** against us, they would have
Pr 24: 19 [F] *Do* not **fret** because of evil men or be envious of the wicked,
Isa 5: 25 [A] Therefore the LORD's anger **burns** against his people; his
41: 11 [C] "All who **rage** against you will surely be ashamed
45: 24 [C] strength.' " All who *have* **raged** against him will come to him
Jer 12: 5 [G] they have worn you out, how *can you* **compete** with horses?
22: 15 [G] "Does it make you a king *to* **have more and more** cedar?
Hos 8: 5 [A] out your calf-idol, O Samaria! My anger **burns** against them.
Jnh 4: 1 [A] But Jonah was greatly displeased and *became* **angry**.
4: 4 [A] But the LORD replied, "Have you any right *to be* **angry**?"
4: 9 [A] to Jonah, "Do you have a right *to be* **angry** about the vine?"
4: 9 [A] about the vine?" "I do," he said. "I *am* **angry** enough to die."
Hab 3: 8 [A] *Were you* **angry** with the rivers, O LORD? Was your wrath
Zec 10: 3 [A] "My anger **burns** against the shepherds, and I will punish the

3014 ²חָרָה **ḥārâ^{2}**, v. Not used in NIV/BHS

3015 חַרְהֲיָה **ḥarh^{a}yâ**, n.pr.m. [1] [cf. 3029]

Harhaiah [1]

Ne 3: 8 Uzziel son of **Harhaiah**, one of the goldsmiths, repaired the next

3016 חֲרוּזִים **ḥ^{a}rûzîm**, n.[m.]pl. [1]

strings of jewels [1]

SS 1: 10 are beautiful with earrings, your neck with **strings of jewels**.

3017 חָרוּל **ḥārûl**, n.[m.]. [3]

weeds [2], undergrowth [1]

Job 30: 7 They brayed among the bushes and huddled in the **undergrowth**.
Pr 24: 31 the ground was covered with **weeds**, and the stone wall was in
Zep 2: 9 a place of **weeds** and salt pits, a wasteland forever.

3018 חֲרוּמַף **ḥ^a^rûmap**, n.pr.m. [1] [√ 3050 + 678]

Harumaph [1]

Ne 3:10 Jedaiah son of **Harumaph** made repairs opposite his house,

3019 חָרוֹן **ḥārôn**, n.m. [41 / 40] [√ 3013]

fierce [28], wrath [5], burning [2], angry [+678] [1], burning anger [1], dry [1], heat [1], hot [1]

Ex 15:7 You unleashed your **burning anger**; it consumed them like
32:12 Turn from your **fierce** anger; relent and do not bring disaster on
Nu 25:4 so that the LORD's **fierce** anger may turn away from Israel."
32:14 and making the LORD even more **angry** [+678] with Israel.
Dt 13:17 [13:18] so that the LORD will turn from his **fierce** anger;
Jos 7:26 remains to this day. Then the LORD turned from his **fierce** anger.
1Sa 28:18 the LORD or carry out his **fierce** wrath against the Amalekites,
2Ki 23:26 the LORD did not turn away from the **heat** *of* his fierce anger,
2Ch 28:11 taken as prisoners, for the LORD's **fierce** anger rests on you."
28:13 For our guilt is already great, and his **fierce** anger rests on Israel."
29:10 the God of Israel, so that his **fierce** anger will turn away from us.
30:8 your God, so that his **fierce** anger will turn away from you.
Ezr 10:14 until the **fierce** anger of our God in this matter is turned away from
Ne 13:18 Now you are stirring up more **wrath** against Israel by desecrating
Job 20:23 God will vent his **burning** anger against him and rain down his
Ps 2:5 Then he rebukes them in his anger and terrifies them in his **wrath**,
58:9 [58:10] whether they be green or **dry**—the wicked will be swept
69:24 [69:25] your wrath on them; let your **fierce** anger overtake them.
78:49 He unleashed against them his **hot** anger, his wrath, indignation
85:3 [85:4] set aside all your wrath and turned from your **fierce** anger.
88:16 [88:17] Your **wrath** has swept over me; your terrors have
Isa 13:9 a cruel day, with wrath and **fierce** anger—to make the land
13:13 wrath of the LORD Almighty, in the day of his **burning** anger.
Jer 4:8 for the **fierce** anger of the LORD has not turned away from us.
4:26 its towns lay in ruins before the LORD, before his **fierce** anger.
12:13 the shame of your harvest because of the LORD's **fierce** anger."
25:37 will be laid waste because of the **fierce** anger of the LORD.
25:38 because of the sword [BHS *anger*; NIV 2995] *of* the oppressor
25:38 sword of the oppressor and because of the LORD's **fierce** anger.
30:24 The **fierce** anger of the LORD will not turn back until he fully
49:37 disaster upon them, even my **fierce** anger," declares the LORD.
51:45 Run for your lives! Run from the **fierce** anger of the LORD.
La 1:12 that the LORD brought on me in the day of his **fierce** anger?
4:11 has given full vent to his wrath; he has poured out his **fierce** anger.
Eze 7:12 rejoice nor the seller grieve, for **wrath** is upon the whole crowd.
7:14 no one will go into battle, for my **wrath** is upon the whole crowd.
Hos 11:9 I will not carry out my **fierce** anger, nor will I turn and devastate
Jnh 3:9 God may yet relent and with compassion turn from his **fierce** anger
Na 1:6 Who can endure his **fierce** anger? His wrath is poured out like fire;
Zep 2:2 like chaff, before the **fierce** anger of the LORD comes upon you,
3:8 and to pour out my wrath on them—all my **fierce** anger.

3020 חֲרוּפִי **ḥ^a^rûpî**, a.g. [1] [cf. 3042]

Haruphite [1]

1Ch 12:5 [12:6] and Shephatiah the **Haruphite**; [K 3042]

3021 ¹חָרוּץ **ḥārûṣ¹**, n.m. [6]

gold [5], *untranslated* [1]

Ps 68:13 [68:14] are sheathed with silver, its feathers with shining **gold**."
Pr 3:14 is more profitable than silver and yields better returns than **gold**.
8:10 instruction instead of silver, knowledge rather than choice **gold**,
8:19 better than fine gold; **[RPH]** what I yield surpasses choice silver.
16:16 How much better to get wisdom than **gold**, to choose
Zec 9:3 has heaped up silver like dust, and **gold** like the dirt of the streets.

3022 ²חָרוּץ **ḥārûṣ²**, n.[m.]. [1] [√ 3076]

trench [1]

Da 9:25 It will be rebuilt with streets and a **trench**, but in times of trouble.

3023 ³חָרוּץ **ḥārûṣ³**, a. [4] [√ 3076]

sharp [1], sledge [1], sledges [1], threshing sledge [1]

Job 41:30 [41:22] leaving a trail in the mud like a **threshing sledge**.
Isa 28:27 Caraway is not threshed with a **sledge**, nor is a cartwheel rolled
41:15 make you into a threshing sledge, new and **sharp**, with many teeth.
Am 1:3 Because she threshed Gilead with **sledges** *having* iron teeth,

3024 ⁴חָרוּץ **ḥārûṣ⁴**, v. [1] [√ 3076]

maimed [1]

Lev 22:22 the injured or the **maimed**, or anything with warts or festering

3025 ⁵חָרוּץ **ḥārûṣ⁵**, n.[m.]. [2] [√ 3076]

decision [2]

Joel 3:14 [4:14] Multitudes, multitudes in the valley of **decision**!
3:14 [4:14] For the day of the LORD is near in the valley of **decision**.

3026 ⁶חָרוּץ **ḥārûṣ⁶**, a. [5] [√ 3077]

diligent [5]

Pr 10:4 Lazy hands make a man poor, but **diligent** hands bring wealth.
12:24 **Diligent** hands will rule, but laziness ends in slave labor.
12:27 not roast his game, but the **diligent** man prizes his possessions.
13:4 and gets nothing, but the desires of the **diligent** are fully satisfied.
21:5 The plans of the **diligent** lead to profit as surely as haste leads to

3027 ⁷חָרוּץ **ḥārûṣ⁷**, n.pr.m. [1] [√ 3077?]

Haruz [1]

2Ki 21:19 His mother's name was Meshullemeth daughter of **Haruz**;

3028 חַרְחוּר **ḥarḥûr**, n.pr.m. [2] [√ 3031; cf. 3081]

Harhur [2]

Ezr 2:51 Bakbuk, Hakupha, **Harhur**,
Ne 7:53 Bakbuk, Hakupha, **Harhur**,

3029 חַרְהֲיָה **ḥarh^a^yâ**, n.pr.m. Not used in NIV/BHS [cf. 3015]

3030 חַרְחַס **ḥarḥas**, n.pr.m. [1] [cf. 2897]

Harhas [1]

2Ki 22:14 Shallum son of Tikvah, the son of **Harhas**, keeper of the wardrobe.

3031 חַרְחֻר **ḥarḥur**, n.m. [1] [→ 3028; cf. 3081]

scorching heat [1]

Dt 28:22 with **scorching heat** and drought, with blight and mildew,

3032 חֶרֶט **ḥereṭ**, n.[m.]. [2]

pen [1], tool [1]

Ex 32:4 it into an idol cast in the shape of a calf, fashioning it with a **tool**.
Isa 8:1 to me, "Take a large scroll and write on it with an ordinary **pen**:

3033 חַרְטֹם **ḥarṭōm**, n.m. [11] [√ 2641; Ar 10282]

magicians [10], them^s^ [1]

Ge 41:8 so he sent for all the **magicians** and wise men of Egypt.
41:24 I told this to the **magicians**, but none could explain it to me."
Ex 7:11 the Egyptian **magicians** also did the same things by their secret
7:22 the Egyptian **magicians** did the same things by their secret arts,
8:7 [8:3] But the **magicians** did the same things by their secret arts;
8:18 [8:14] when the **magicians** tried to produce gnats by their secret
8:19 [8:15] The **magicians** said to Pharaoh, "This is the finger of
9:11 The **magicians** could not stand before Moses because of the boils
9:11 because of the boils that were on **them**^s^ and on all the Egyptians.
Da 1:20 he found them ten times better than all the **magicians**
2:2 So the king summoned the **magicians**, enchanters, sorcerers

3034 חֳרִי **ḥ^o^rî**, n.m. [6] [√ 3013]

fierce [3], burning [1], great rage [+678] [1], hot [1]

Ex 11:8 After that I will leave." Then Moses, **hot** with anger, left Pharaoh.
Dt 29:24 [29:23] done this to this land? Why this fierce, **burning** anger?"
1Sa 20:34 Jonathan got up from the table in **fierce** anger; on that second day
2Ch 25:10 were furious with Judah and left for home in a **great rage** [+678].
Isa 7:4 because of the **fierce** anger of Rezin and Aram and of the son of
La 2:3 In **fierce** anger he has cut off every horn of Israel. He has

3035 ¹חֹרִי **ḥōrî¹**, n.[m.]. [1] [√ 2578]

bread [1]

Ge 40:16 "I too had a dream: On my head were three baskets of **bread**.

3036 ²חֹרִי **ḥōrî²**, n.pr.m. [3]

Hori [3]

Ge 36:22 The sons of Lotan: **Hori** and Homam. Timna was Lotan's sister.
Nu 13:5 from the tribe of Simeon, Shaphat son of **Hori**;
1Ch 1:39 The sons of Lotan: **Hori** and Homam. Timna was Lotan's sister.

3037 ³חֹרִי **ḥōrî³**, a.g. [7]

Horite [4], Horites [3]

Ge 14:6 the **Horites** in the hill country of Seir, as far as El Paran near the
36:20 These were the sons of Seir the **Horite**, who were living in the
36:21 and Dishan. These sons of Seir in Edom were **Horite** chiefs.

Ge 36:29 These were the **Horite** chiefs: Lotan, Shobal, Zibeon, Anah,
36:30 These were the **Horite** chiefs, according to their divisions,
Dt 2:12 **Horites** used to live in Seir, but the descendants of Esau drove
2:22 lived in Seir, when he destroyed the **Horites** from before them.

3038 חָרִיט *ḥārîṭ*, n.m. [2]

bags [1], purses [1]

2Ki 5:23 then tied up the two talents of silver in two **bags**, with two sets of
Isa 3:22 the fine robes and the capes and cloaks, the **purses**

3039 חִרְיוֹנִים *ḥiryyônîm*, n.[m.]. Not used in NIV/BHS [cf. 2989 + 3433]

3040 חָרִיף *ḥārîp*, n.pr.m. [2] [→ 3042; cf. 3069]

Hariph [2]

Ne 7:24 of **Hariph** 112
10:19 [10:20] **Hariph**, Anathoth, Nebai,

3041 חֲרִיפוֹת *ḥ[a]rîpôt*, n.[f.]. Not used in NIV/BHS [√ 3070]

3042 חֲרִיפִי *ḥ[a]rîpî*, a.g. [0] [√ 3040; cf. 3020, 3069, 3070?]

1Ch 12:5 [12:6] [Shemariah and Shephatiah the **Haruphite**; [K; see Q 3020]]

3043 ¹חָרִיץ *ḥārîṣ¹*, n.m. [1] [√ 3076]

cheeses [+2692] [1]

1Sa 17:18 Take along these ten **cheeses** [+2692] to the commander of their

3044 ²חָרִיץ *ḥārîṣ²*, n.m. [2] [√ 3076]

picks [2]

2Sa 12:31 consigning them to labor with saws and with iron **picks** and axes,
1Ch 20:3 consigning them to labor with saws and with iron **picks** and axes.

3045 חָרִישׁ *ḥārîš*, n.m. [3] [√ 3086]

ground [1], plowing season [1], plowing [1]

Ge 45:6 and for the next five years there will not be **plowing** and reaping.
Ex 34:21 even during the **plowing season** and harvest you must rest.
1Sa 8:12 of fifties, and others to plow his **ground** and reap his harvest,

3046 חֲרִישִׁי *ḥ[a]rîšî*, a. [1] [√ 3086?]

scorching [1]

Jnh 4:8 When the sun rose, God provided a **scorching** east wind,

3047 חָרַךְ *ḥārak*, v. [1]

roast [1]

Pr 12:27 [A] The lazy man *does* not **roast** his game, but the diligent man

3048 חֲרַכִּים *ḥ[a]rakkîm*, n.[m.]pl. [1]

lattice [1]

SS 2:9 our wall, gazing through the windows, peering through the **lattice**.

3049 ¹חָרַם *ḥāram¹*, v. [51 / 50] [→ 1259, 3051, 3055, 3056, 3057]

totally destroyed [13], completely destroyed [6], completely destroy [5], totally destroy [3], completely destroy [+3049] [2], destroy completely [2], destroyed [2], destroying completely [2], must destroy totally [+906+3049] [2], annihilate [1], be destroyed [1], bring about destruction [1], destroy totally [1], destroy [1], destroying [1], devote [1], devoted and destroyed [1], devoted to destruction [+3051] [1], devotes [1], exterminate [1], forfeit [1], kill [1]

Ex 22:20 [22:19] [H] any god other than the LORD *must* **be destroyed.**
Lev 27:28 [G] " 'But nothing that a man owns and **devotes** to the LORD—
27:29 [H] " 'No person **devoted** [+3051] **to destruction** may be
Nu 21:2 [G] people into our hands, *we will* **totally destroy** their cities."
21:3 [G] *They* **completely destroyed** them and their towns;
Dt 2:34 [G] time we took all his towns and **completely destroyed** them—
3:6 [G] *We* **completely destroyed** them, as we had done with Sihon
3:6 [G] done with Sihon king of Heshbon, **destroying** every city—
7:2 [G] then *you* **must destroy** [+906+3049] them **totally.**
7:2 [G] then *you* **must destroy** them **totally** [+906+3049].
13:15 [13:16] [G] **Destroy** it **completely**, both its people and its
20:17 [G] **Completely destroy** [+3049] them—the Hittites, Amorites,
20:17 [G] **Completely destroy** [+3049] them—the Hittites, Amorites,
Jos 2:10 [G] east of the Jordan, whom *you* **completely destroyed**.
6:18 [G] so that *you will* not **bring about** *your own* **destruction** by
6:21 [G] *They* **devoted** the city to the LORD **and destroyed** with
8:26 [G] out his javelin until *he had* **destroyed** all who lived in Ai.
10:1 [G] heard that Joshua had taken Ai and **totally destroyed** it,
10:28 [G] its king to the sword and **totally destroyed** everyone in it.
10:35 [G] and put it to the sword and **totally destroyed** everyone in it,
10:37 [G] Just as at Eglon, *they* **totally destroyed** it and everyone in it.
10:39 [G] Everyone in it *they* **totally destroyed**. They left no
10:40 [G] *He* **totally destroyed** all who breathed, just as the LORD,
11:11 [G] *They* **totally destroyed** them, not sparing anything that
11:12 [G] *He* **totally destroyed** them, as Moses the servant of the
11:20 [G] so that *he might* **destroy** them **totally**, exterminating them
11:21 [G] of Israel. Joshua **totally destroyed** them and their towns.
Jdg 1:17 [G] living in Zephath, and *they* **totally destroyed** the city.
21:11 [G] "**Kill** every male and every woman who is not a virgin."
1Sa 15:3 [G] and **totally destroy** everything that belongs to them.
15:8 [G] and all his people *he* **totally destroyed** with the sword.
15:9 [G] These they were unwilling *to* **destroy completely**,
15:9 [G] that was despised and weak *they* **totally destroyed.**
15:15 [G] to the LORD your God, but *we* **totally destroyed** the rest."
15:18 [G] saying, 'Go and **completely destroy** those wicked people,
15:20 [G] *I* **completely destroyed** the Amalekites and brought back
1Ki 9:21 [G] in the land, whom the Israelites could not **exterminate**—
2Ki 19:11 [G] have done to all the countries, **destroying** them **completely**.
1Ch 4:41 [G] Meunites who were there and **completely destroyed** them,
2Ch 20:23 [G] Moab rose up against the men from Mount Seir to **destroy**
32:14 [G] of all the gods of these nations that my fathers **destroyed**
Ezr 10:8 [H] Anyone who failed to appear within three days *would* **forfeit**
Isa 11:15 [g] The LORD *will* dry **up** [BHS *destroy*; NIV 2990] the gulf
34:2 [G] *He will* **totally destroy** them, he will give them over to
37:11 [G] have done to all the countries, **destroying** them **completely**.
Jer 25:9 [G] *I will* **completely destroy** them and make them an object of
50:21 [G] Pursue, kill and **completely destroy** them,"
50:26 [G] of grain. **Completely destroy** her and leave her no remnant.
51:3 [G] Do not spare her young men; **completely destroy** her army.
Da 11:44 [G] will set out in a great rage to destroy and **annihilate** many.
Mic 4:13 [G] *You will* **devote** their ill-gotten gains to the LORD, their

3050 ²חָרַם *ḥāram²*, v. [1] [→ 3018, 3052, 3053?]

disfigured [1]

Lev 21:18 [B] no man who is blind or lame, **disfigured** or deformed;

3051 ¹חֵרֶם *ḥērem¹*, n.m. [29] [√ 3049]

devoted things [6], devoted [4], destruction [3], set apart for destruction [2], them[s] [+2021] [2], *untranslated* [1], condemned things [1], curse [1], destroyed [1], determined should die [1], devoted to destruction [+3049] [1], devoted to destruction [1], devoted to God [1], devoted to the LORD [1], it[s] [+2021] [1], that which is devoted [1], totally destroyed [1]

Lev 27:21 it will become holy, like a field **devoted** to the LORD;
27:28 " 'But **[RPH]** nothing that a man owns and devotes to the
27:28 or redeemed; everything so **devoted** is most holy to the LORD.
27:29 " 'No person **devoted to destruction** [+3049] may be ransomed;
Nu 18:14 "Everything in Israel that is **devoted to the LORD** is yours.
Dt 7:26 into your house or you, like it, will be **set apart for destruction**.
7:26 Utterly abhor and detest it, for it is **set apart for destruction.**
13:17 [13:18] None of those **condemned things** shall be found in your
Jos 6:17 The city and all that is in it are to be **devoted** to the LORD.
6:18 keep away from the **devoted things**, so that you will not bring
6:18 bring about your own destruction by taking any of **them**[s] [+2021].
6:18 Otherwise you will make the camp of Israel liable to **destruction**
7:1 the Israelites acted unfaithfully in regard to the **devoted things**;
7:1 son of Zerah, of the tribe of Judah, took some of **them**[s] [+2021].
7:11 They have taken some of the **devoted things**; they have stolen,
7:12 and run because they have been made liable to **destruction.**
7:12 unless you destroy whatever among you is **devoted to destruction.**
7:13 God of Israel, says: **That which is devoted** is among you, O Israel.
7:13 cannot stand against your enemies until you remove **it**[s] [+2021].
7:15 He who is caught with the **devoted things** shall be destroyed by
22:20 son of Zerah acted unfaithfully regarding the **devoted things**,
1Sa 15:21 and cattle from the plunder, the best of what was **devoted to God**,
1Ki 20:42 'You have set free a man I had **determined should die**.
1Ch 2:7 trouble on Israel by violating the ban on taking **devoted things**.
Isa 34:5 in judgment on Edom, the people I have **totally destroyed.**
43:28 and I will consign Jacob to **destruction** and Israel to scorn.
Eze 44:29 everything in Israel **devoted** to the LORD will belong to them.
Zec 14:11 It will be inhabited; never again will it be **destroyed**. Jerusalem
Mal 4:6 [3:24] or else I will come and strike the land with a **curse**."

3052 ²חֵרֶם *ḥērem²*, n.m. [9] [√ 3050]

net [5], fishnets [2], nets [1], trap [1]

Ecc 7:26 who is a snare, whose heart is a **trap** and whose hands are chains.
Eze 26:5 Out in the sea she will become a place to spread **fishnets**,
26:14 you a bare rock, and you will become a place to spread **fishnets**.

Eze 32: 3 I will cast my net over you, and they will haul you up in my **net**.
47: 10 from En Gedi to En Eglaim there will be places for spreading **nets**.
Mic 7: 2 All men lie in wait to shed blood; each hunts his brother with a **net**.
Hab 1: 15 he catches them in his **net**, he gathers them up in his dragnet;
1: 16 Therefore he sacrifices to his **net** and burns incense to his dragnet,
1: 17 Is he to keep on emptying his **net**, destroying nations without

3053 חָרִם *ḥārim*, n.pr.m. [11] [√ 3050?]

Harim [10], Harim's [1]

1Ch 24: 8 the third to **Harim**, the fourth to Seorim,
Ezr 2: 32 of **Harim** 320
2: 39 of **Harim** 1,017
10: 21 From the descendants of **Harim**: Maaseiah, Elijah, Shemaiah,
10: 31 From the descendants of **Harim**: Eliezer, Ishijah, Malkijah,
Ne 3: 11 Malkijah son of **Harim** and Hasshub son of Pahath-Moab repaired
7: 35 of **Harim** 320
7: 42 of **Harim** 1,017
10: 5 [10:6] **Harim**, Meremoth, Obadiah,
10: 27 [10:28] Malluch, **Harim** and Baanah.
12: 15 of **Harim's**, Adna; of Meremoth's, Helkai;

3054 חֹרֵם *ḥ^orēm*, n.pr.loc. [1]

Horem [1]

Jos 19: 38 Iron, Migdal El, **Horem**, Beth Anath and Beth Shemesh. There

3055 חָרְמָה *ḥormâ*, n.pr.loc. [9] [√ 3049]

Hormah [9]

Nu 14: 45 and attacked them and beat them down all the way to **Hormah**.
21: 3 destroyed them and their towns; so the place was named **Hormah**.
Dt 1: 44 of bees and beat you down from Seir all the way to **Hormah**.
Jos 12: 14 the king of **Hormah** one the king of Arad one
15: 30 Eltolad, Kesil, **Hormah**,
19: 4 Eltolad, Bethul, **Hormah**,
Jdg 1: 17 they totally destroyed the city. Therefore it was called **Hormah**.
1Sa 30: 30 to those in **Hormah**, Bor Ashan, Athach
1Ch 4: 30 Bethuel, **Hormah**, Ziklag,

3056 חֶרְמוֹן *ḥermôn*, n.pr.loc. [14] [→ 1259, 3057; cf. 3049]

Hermon [13], heights of Hermon [1]

Dt 3: 8 east of the Jordan, from the Arnon Gorge as far as Mount **Hermon**.
3: 9 (**Hermon** is called Sirion by the Sidonians; the Amorites call it
4: 48 on the rim of the Arnon Gorge to Mount Siyon (that is, **Hermon**),
Jos 11: 3 and to the Hivites below **Hermon** in the region of Mizpah.
11: 17 to Baal Gad in the Valley of Lebanon below Mount **Hermon**.
12: 1 from the Arnon Gorge to Mount **Hermon**, including all the eastern
12: 5 He ruled over Mount **Hermon**, Salecah, all of Bashan to the border
13: 5 to the east, from Baal Gad below Mount **Hermon** to Lebo Hamath.
13: 11 all of Mount **Hermon** and all Bashan as far as Salecah—
1Ch 5: 23 from Bashan to Baal Hermon, that is, to Senir (Mount **Hermon**).
Ps 42: 6 [42:7] you from the land of the Jordan, the **heights of Hermon**—
89: 12 [89:13] the south; Tabor and **Hermon** sing for joy at your name.
133: 3 It is as if the dew of **Hermon** were falling on Mount Zion.
SS 4: 8 the summit of **Hermon**, from the lions' dens and the mountain

3057 חֶרְמֹנִים *ḥermōnîm*, n.pr.loc. Not used in NIV/BHS [√ 3056; cf. 3049]

3058 חֶרְמֵשׁ *ḥermēš*, n.[m.]. [2 / 3]

sickle [2], sickles [1]

Dt 16: 9 Count off seven weeks from the time you begin to put the **sickle** to
23: 25 [23:26] but you must not put a **sickle** to his standing grain.
1Sa 13: 20 mattocks, axes and **sickles** [BHS 4739] sharpened.

3059 ¹חָרָן *ḥārān¹*, n.pr.loc. [10]

Haran [10]

Ge 11: 31 to go to Canaan. But when they came to **Haran**, they settled there.
11: 32 Terah lived 205 years, and he died in **Haran**.
12: 4 Abram was seventy-five years old when he set out from **Haran**.
12: 5 they had accumulated and the people they had acquired in **Haran**,
27: 43 do what I say: Flee at once to my brother Laban in **Haran**.
28: 10 Jacob left Beersheba and set out for **Haran**.
29: 4 where are you from?" "We're from **Haran**," they replied.
2Ki 19: 12 **Haran**, Rezeph and the people of Eden who were in Tel Assar?
Isa 37: 12 **Haran**, Rezeph and the people of Eden who were in Tel Assar?
Eze 27: 23 " '**Haran**, Canneh and Eden and merchants of Sheba, Asshur

3060 ²חָרָן *ḥārān²*, n.pr.m. [2]

Haran [2]

1Ch 2: 46 Caleb's concubine Ephah was the mother of **Haran**, Moza
2: 46 of Haran, Moza and Gazez. **Haran** was the father of Gazez.

3061 חֹרֹנִי *ḥōrōnî*, a.g. [3]

Horonite [3]

Ne 2: 10 When Sanballat the **Horonite** and Tobiah the Ammonite official
2: 19 But when Sanballat the **Horonite**, Tobiah the Ammonite official
13: 28 Eliashib the high priest was son-in-law to Sanballat the **Horonite**.

3062 חַרְנֶפֶר *ḥarneper*, n.pr.m. *or* loc. [1]

Harnepher [1]

1Ch 7: 36 The sons of Zophah: Suah, **Harnepher**, Shual, Beri, Imrah,

3063 ¹חֶרֶס *ḥeres¹*, n.[m.]. [1]

itch [1]

Dt 28: 27 the boils of Egypt and with tumors, festering sores and the **itch**,

3064 ²חֶרֶס *ḥeres²*, n.m. [2] [→ 3065, 3066, 6557, 9467]

sun [1], sunset [+995+2021] [1]

Jdg 14: 18 Before **sunset** [+995+2021] on the seventh day the men of the
Job 9: 7 He speaks to the **sun** and it does not shine; he seals off the light of

3065 ³חֶרֶס *ḥeres³*, n.pr.loc. [2] [√ 3064, 9466]

Heres [2]

Jdg 1: 35 the Amorites were determined also to hold out in Mount **Heres**,
8: 13 son of Joash then returned from the battle by the Pass of **Heres**.

3066 חַרְסָה *ḥar^esâ*, n.m. Not used in NIV/BHS [√ 3064]

3067 חַרְסוּת *ḥarsût*, n.f.col. [0] [√ 3084]

Jer 19: 2 [near the entrance of the **Potsherd** [K; see Q 3068] Gate.]

3068 חַרְסִית *ḥarsît*, n.f.col. [1] [√ 3084]

Potsherd [1]

Jer 19: 2 of Ben Hinnom, near the entrance of the **Potsherd** [K 3067] Gate.

3069 ¹חָרַף *ḥārap¹*, v.den. [1] [→ 3040, 3042, 3073, 3074; cf. 3072]

all winter [1]

Isa 18: 6 [A] will feed on them all summer, the wild animals **all winter**.

3070 ²חָרַף *ḥārap²*, v. [39] [→ 3041, 3075; cf. 3042?]

taunted [4], defied [3], defy [3], insult [3], insulted [3], insulting [3], mocked [3], heaped insults on [2], reproach [2], ridicule [2], shows contempt [2], taunt [2], discredit [1], hurled [1], mock [1], rebuking [1], risked [+4200+4637] [1], taunts [1], treats with contempt [1]

Jdg 5: 18 [D] The people of Zebulun **risked** [+4200+4637] their very lives;
8: 15 [D] and Zalmunna, about whom *you* **taunted** me by saying,
1Sa 17: 10 [D] Then the Philistine said, "This day I **defy** the ranks of Israel!
17: 25 [D] this man keeps coming out? He comes out to **defy** Israel.
17: 26 [D] Who is this uncircumcised Philistine that *he should* **defy** the
17: 36 [D] of them, because *he has* **defied** the armies of the living God.
17: 45 [D] the God of the armies of Israel, whom *you have* **defied**.
2Sa 21: 21 [D] When *he* **taunted** Israel, Jonathan son of Shimeah, David's
23: 9 [D] he was with David when they **taunted** the Philistines
2Ki 19: 4 [D] the king of Assyria, has sent to **ridicule** the living God,
19: 16 [D] listen to the words Sennacherib has sent to **insult** the living
19: 22 [D] Who is it *you have* **insulted** and blasphemed? Against whom
19: 23 [D] By your messengers *you have* **heaped insults on** the Lord.
1Ch 20: 7 [D] When *he* **taunted** Israel, Jonathan son of Shimea,
2Ch 32: 17 [D] The king also wrote letters **insulting** the LORD, the God of
Ne 6: 13 [D] and then they would give me a bad name to **discredit** me.
Job 27: 6 [A] of it; my conscience *will* not **reproach** me as long as I live.
Ps 42: 10 [42:11] [D] My bones suffer mortal agony *as* my foes **taunt** me,
44: 16 [44:17] [D] at the taunts of *those who* **reproach** and revile me,
55: 12 [55:13] [D] If an enemy *were* **insulting** me, I could endure it;
57: 3 [57:4] [D] and saves me, **rebuking** those who hotly pursue me;
69: 9 [69:10] [A] and the insults of *those who* **insult** you fall on me.
74: 10 [D] How long *will* the enemy **mock** you, O God? Will the foe
74: 18 [D] Remember how the enemy *has* **mocked** you, O LORD, how
79: 12 [D] neighbors seven times the reproach *they have* **hurled** *at* you,
89: 51 [89:52] [D] the taunts with which your enemies *have* **mocked**,
89: 51 [89:52] [D] with which *they have* **mocked** every step of your
102: 8 [102:9] [D] All day long my enemies **taunt** me; those who rail

Ps 119:42 [A] I will answer the *one who* **taunts** me, for I trust in your
Pr 14:31 [D] He who oppresses the poor **shows contempt** *for* their Maker,
17: 5 [D] He who mocks the poor **shows contempt** *for* their Maker;
27:11 [A] then I can answer *anyone who* **treats** me **with contempt**.
Isa 37: 4 [D] the king of Assyria, has sent to **ridicule** the living God,
37:17 [D] listen to all the words Sennacherib has sent to **insult** the
37:23 [D] Who is it *you have* **insulted** and blasphemed? Against whom
37:24 [D] By your messengers *you have* **heaped insults on** the Lord.
65: 7 [D] sacrifices on the mountains and **defied** me on the hills,
Zep 2: 8 [D] who **insulted** my people and made threats against their land.
2:10 [D] for **insulting** and mocking the people of the LORD

3071 ³חָרַף ḥārap³, v. Not used in NIV/BHS

3072 ⁴חָרַף ḥārap⁴, v. [1] [cf. 3069]

promised [1]

Lev 19:20 [C] " 'If a man sleeps with a woman who is a slave girl **promised**

3073 חָרֵף ḥārēp, n.pr.m. [1] [√ 3069]

Hareph [1]

1Ch 2:51 the father of Bethlehem, and **Hareph** the father of Beth Gader.

3074 חֹרֶף ḥōrep, n.m. [7] [√ 3069]

winter [5], prime [1], season [1]

Ge 8:22 and heat, summer and **winter**, day and night will never cease."
Job 29: 4 Oh, for the days when I was in my **prime**, when God's intimate
Ps 74:17 all the boundaries of the earth; you made both summer and **winter**.
Pr 20: 4 A sluggard does not plow in **season**; so at harvest time he looks
Jer 36:22 the ninth month and the king was sitting in the **winter** apartment,
Am 3:15 I will tear down the **winter** house along with the summer house;
Zec 14: 8 eastern sea and half to the western sea, in summer and in **winter**.

3075 חֶרְפָּה ḥerpâ, n.f. [73] [√ 3070]

disgrace [17], reproach [16], scorn [10], insults [5], object of scorn [5], shame [4], contempt [3], scorned [3], insolence [2], humiliation [1], insult [1], insulted [1], mock [1], mocked [1], objects of reproach [1], offensive [1], slur [1]

Ge 30:23 gave birth to a son and said, "God has taken away my **disgrace**."
34:14 to a man who is not circumcised. That would be a **disgrace** to us.
Jos 5: 9 "Today I have rolled away the **reproach** *of* Egypt from you."
1Sa 11: 2 right eye of every one of you and so bring **disgrace** on all Israel."
17:26 who kills this Philistine and removes this **disgrace** from Israel?
25:39 has upheld my cause against Nabal for treating me with **contempt**.
2Sa 13:13 What about me? Where could I get rid of my **disgrace**? And what
Ne 1: 3 and are back in the province are in great trouble and **disgrace**.
2:17 the wall of Jerusalem, and we will no longer be *in* **disgrace**."
4: 4 [3:36] are despised. Turn their **insults** back on their own heads.
5: 9 Shouldn't you walk in the fear of our God to avoid the **reproach** *of*
Job 16:10 they strike my cheek in **scorn** and unite together against me.
19: 5 exalt yourselves above me and use my **humiliation** against me,
Ps 15: 3 does his neighbor no wrong and casts no **slur** on his fellowman,
22: 6 [22:7] not a man, **scorned** *by* men and despised by the people.
31:11 [31:12] all my enemies, I am the utter **contempt** of my neighbors;
39: 8 [39:9] all my transgressions; do not make me the **scorn** *of* fools.
44:13 [44:14] You have made us a **reproach** to our neighbors, the scorn
69: 7 [69:8] For I endure **scorn** for your sake, and shame covers my
69: 9 [69:10] and the **insults** *of* those who insult you fall on me.
69:10 [69:11] When I weep and fast, I must endure **scorn**;
69:19 [69:20] You know how I am **scorned**, disgraced and shamed; all
69:20 [69:21] **Scorn** has broken my heart and has left me helpless; I
71:13 may those who want to harm me be covered with **scorn**
74:22 defend your cause; remember how fools **mock** you all day long.
78:66 He beat back his enemies; he put them to everlasting **shame**.
79: 4 We are **objects of reproach** to our neighbors, of scorn
79:12 Pay back into the laps of our neighbors seven times the **reproach**
89:41 [89:42] plundered him; he has become the **scorn** of his neighbors.
89:50 [89:51] Remember, Lord, how your servant has been **mocked**,
109:25 I am an **object of scorn** to my accusers; when they see me,
119:22 Remove from me **scorn** and contempt, for I keep your statutes.
119:39 Take away the **disgrace** I dread, for your laws are good.
Pr 6:33 and disgrace are his lot, and his **shame** will never be wiped away;
18: 3 so does contempt, and with shame comes **disgrace**.
Isa 4: 1 only let us be called by your name. Take away our **disgrace**!"
25: 8 he will remove the **disgrace** *of* his people from all the earth.
30: 5 bring neither help nor advantage, but only shame and **disgrace**."
47: 3 Your nakedness will be exposed and your **shame** uncovered.
51: 7 Do not fear the **reproach** *of* men or be terrified by their insults.
54: 4 and remember no more the **reproach** *of* your widowhood.
Jer 6:10 The word of the LORD is **offensive** to them; they find no
15:15 do not take me away; think of how I suffer **reproach** for your sake.
20: 8 So the word of the LORD has brought me **insult** and reproach all
23:40 I will bring upon you everlasting **disgrace**—everlasting shame that
24: 9 a **reproach** and a byword, an object of ridicule and cursing,
29:18 and an object of cursing and horror, of scorn and **reproach**,
31:19 and humiliated because I bore the **disgrace** *of* my youth.'
42:18 be an object of cursing and horror, of condemnation and **reproach**;
44: 8 an object of cursing and **reproach** among all the nations on earth.
44:12 an object of cursing and horror, of condemnation and **reproach**.
49:13 become a ruin and an object of horror, of **reproach** and of cursing;
51:51 for we have been **insulted** and shame covers our faces,
La 3:30 to one who would strike him, and let him be filled with **disgrace**.
3:61 O LORD, you have heard their **insults**, all their plots against me—
5: 1 O LORD, what has happened to us; look, and see our **disgrace**.
Eze 5:14 make you a ruin and a **reproach** among the nations around you,
5:15 You will be a **reproach** and a taunt, a warning and an object of
16:57 *you are* now **scorned** *by* the daughters of Edom and all her
21:28 [21:33] LORD says about the Ammonites and their **insults**:
22: 4 Therefore I will make you an **object of scorn** to the nations
36:15 no longer will you suffer the **scorn** *of* the peoples or cause your
36:30 you will no longer suffer **disgrace** among the nations *because of*
Da 9:16 and your people an **object of scorn** to all those around us.
11:18 a commander will put an end to his **insolence** and will turn his
11:18 an end to his insolence and will turn his **insolence** back upon him.
12: 2 some to everlasting life, others to **shame** and everlasting contempt.
Hos 12:14 [12:15] of his bloodshed and will repay him for his **contempt**.
Joel 2:17 Do not make your inheritance an **object of scorn**, a byword among
2:19 never again will I make you an **object of scorn** to the nations.
Mic 6:16 your people to derision; you will bear the **scorn** *of* the nations."
Zep 2: 8 "I have heard the **insults** *of* Moab and the taunts of the
3:18 I will remove from you; they are a burden and a **reproach** to you.

3076 ¹חָרַץ ḥāraṣ¹, v. [10] [→ 3022, 3023, 3024, 3025, 3043, 3044]

been decreed [2], decreed [2], bark [+4383] [1], been determined [1], determined [1], is decreed [1], pronounced [1], uttered a word [+906+4383] [1]

Ex 11: 7 [A] among the Israelites not a dog *will* **bark** [+4383] at any man
Jos 10:21 [A] no one **uttered** [+906+4383] **a word** against the Israelites.
1Ki 20:40 [A] the king of Israel said. "*You have* **pronounced** it yourself."
Job 14: 5 [B] Man's days *are* **determined**; you have decreed the number
Isa 10:22 [B] Destruction *has* **been decreed**, overwhelming and righteous.
10:23 [C] will carry out the destruction **decreed** upon the whole land.
28:22 [C] has told me of the destruction **decreed** against the whole
Da 9:26 [C] continue until the end, and desolations *have* **been decreed**.
9:27 [C] until the end *that* **is decreed** is poured out on him."
11:36 [C] for *what has* **been determined** must take place.

3077 ²חָרַץ ḥāraṣ², v. [1] [√ 3026 *or* 3027?]

move quickly [1]

2Sa 5:24 [A] of marching in the tops of the balsam trees, **move quickly**,

3078 חַרְצֹב ḥarṣōb, n.[f.]. [2]

chains [1], struggles [1]

Ps 73: 4 They have no **struggles**; their bodies are healthy and strong.
Isa 58: 6 to loose the **chains** *of* injustice and untie the cords of the yoke,

3079 חַרְצָן ḥarṣān, n.m.pl. [1] [√ 2949?]

seeds [1]

Nu 6: 4 that comes from the grapevine, not even the **seeds** or skins.

3080 חָרַק ḥāraq, v. [5]

gnash [3], gnashed [1], gnashes [1]

Job 16: 9 [A] and tears me in his anger and **gnashes** his teeth at me;
Ps 35:16 [A] they maliciously mocked; *they* **gnashed** their teeth at me.
37:12 [A] plot against the righteous and **gnash** their teeth at them;
112:10 [A] and be vexed, *he will* **gnash** his teeth and waste away;
La 2:16 [A] they scoff and **gnash** their teeth and say, "We have

3081 ¹חָרַר ḥārar¹, v. [9] [→ 3028, 3031, 3083; cf. 3013]

be charred [1], burn [1], burned up [1], burns [1], chars [1], glows [1], is charred [1], kindling [1], parched [1]

Job 30:30 [A] My skin grows black and peels; my body **burns** with fever.
Ps 69: 3 [69:4] [C] I am worn out calling for help; my throat *is* **parched**.
102: 3 [102:4] [C] like smoke; my bones **burn** like glowing embers.
Pr 26:21 [D] as wood to fire, so is a quarrelsome man for **kindling** strife.
Isa 24: 6 [A] Therefore earth's inhabitants *are* **burned up**, and very few
Eze 15: 4 [C] fire as fuel and the fire burns both ends and **chars** the middle,
15: 5 [C] useful when the fire has burned it and *it* **is charred**?
24:10 [C] mixing in the spices; and *let* the bones **be charred**.
24:11 [A] its copper **glows** so its impurities may be melted and its

3082 ²חָרַר **ḥarar²**, v. Not used in NIV/BHS

3083 חֲרֵרִים **ḥ^a^rērîm**, n.[m.]. [1] [√ 3081]

parched places [1]

Jer 17: 6 He will dwell in the **parched places** of the desert, in a salt land

3084 חֶרֶשׂ **ḥereś**, n.[m.]. [17] [→ 3067, 3068, 3085, 7818, 7819]

clay [9], potsherd [2], potsherds [2], earthenware [1], fragment [1], piece of broken pottery [1], pieces [1]

Lev 6: 28 [6:21] The **clay** pot the meat is cooked in must be broken; but if it
11: 33 If one of them falls into a **clay** pot, everything in it will be unclean,
14: 5 order that one of the birds be killed over fresh water in a **clay** pot.
14: 50 He shall kill one of the birds over fresh water in a **clay** pot.
15: 12 " 'A **clay** pot that the man touches must be broken, and any
Nu 5: 17 he shall take some holy water in a **clay** jar and put some dust from
Job 2: 8 Job took a **piece of broken pottery** and scraped himself with it as
41: 30 [41:22] His undersides are jagged **potsherds**, leaving a trail in the
Ps 22: 15 [22:16] My strength is dried up like a **potsherd**, and my tongue
Pr 26: 23 Like a coating of glaze over **earthenware** are fervent lips with an
Isa 30: 14 so mercilessly that among its pieces not a **fragment** will be found
45: 9 to him who is but a **potsherd** among the potsherds on the ground.
45: 9 to him who is but a potsherd among the **potsherds** *on* the ground.
Jer 19: 1 is what the LORD says: "Go and buy a **clay** jar from a potter.
32: 14 of purchase, and put them in a **clay** jar so they will last a long time.
La 4: 2 are now considered as pots of **clay**, the work of a potter's hands!
Eze 23: 34 and drain it dry; you will dash it to **pieces** and tear your breasts.

3085 חֲרֶשֶׂת **ḥ^a^reśet**, n.pr.loc. Not used in NIV/BHS [√ 3084]

3086 ¹חָרַשׁ **ḥāraš¹**, v. [27] [→ 3045, 3046?, 3088, 3093, 3096, 3098, 4739]

plow [6], plot [3], be plowed [2], plowed [2], plowing [2], craftsman [1], devises [1], farmer [1], inscribed [1], plan [1], planted [1], plots [1], plotting [+2021+8288] [1], plowman [1], plowmen [1], plows [1], tools [1]

Ge 4: 22 [A] who forged all kinds of **tools** out of bronze and iron.
Dt 22: 10 [A] *Do* not **plow** with an ox and a donkey yoked together.
Jdg 14: 18 [A] said to them, "If *you had* not **plowed** with my heifer,
1Sa 8: 12 [A] of fifties, and others to **plow** his ground and reap his harvest,
23: 9 [G] When David learned that Saul *was* **plotting** [+2021+8288]
1Ki 7: 14 [A] whose father was a man of Tyre and a **craftsman** *in* bronze.
19: 19 [A] He *was* **plowing** *with* twelve yoke of oxen, and he himself
Job 1: 14 [A] "The oxen were **plowing** and the donkeys were grazing
4: 8 [A] *those who* **plow** evil and those who sow trouble reap it.
Ps 129: 3 [A] **Plowmen** have plowed my back and made their furrows
129: 3 [A] Plowmen *have* **plowed** my back and made their furrows
Pr 3: 29 [A] *Do* not **plot** harm against your neighbor, who lives trustfully
6: 14 [A] *who* **plots** evil with deceit in his heart—he always stirs up
6: 18 [A] a heart *that* **devises** wicked schemes, feet that are quick to
12: 20 [A] There is deceit in the hearts of *those who* **plot** evil, but joy
14: 22 [A] Do not *those who* **plot** evil go astray? But those who plan
14: 22 [A] But *those who* **plan** what is good find love and faithfulness.
20: 4 [A] A sluggard *does* not **plow** in season; so at harvest time he
Isa 28: 24 [A] When a **farmer** plows for planting, does he plow
28: 24 [A] When a farmer **plows** for planting, does he plow continually?
Jer 17: 1 [B] **inscribed** with a flint point, on the tablets of their hearts
26: 18 [C] " 'Zion *will* **be plowed** like a field, Jerusalem will become a
Hos 10: 11 [A] I will drive Ephraim, Judah *must* **plow**, and Jacob must
10: 13 [A] *you have* **planted** wickedness, you have reaped evil,
Am 6: 12 [A] run on the rocky crags? *Does one* **plow** there with oxen?
9: 13 [A] "when the reaper will be overtaken by the **plowman**
Mic 3: 12 [C] Therefore because of you, Zion *will* **be plowed** like a field,

3087 ²חָרֵשׁ **ḥārēš²**, v. [47] [→ 3089, 3090?, 3094, 3095?]

silent [15], quiet [8], says nothing [3], altogether silent [+3087] [2], deaf [2], remain silent [+3087] [2], says nothing [+3087] [2], fail to speak [1], holds tongue [1], keeps silent [1], kept quiet [1], made no move [1], reduce to silence [1], said no more [1], say nothing [1], saying nothing [1], still [1], stop [1], turn a deaf ear [1], without saying a word [1]

Ge 24: 21 [G] **Without saying a word**, the man watched her closely to
34: 5 [G] so he **kept quiet** *about* it until they came home.
Ex 14: 14 [G] The LORD will fight for you; you *need only to be* **still**."
Nu 30: 4 [30:5] [G] about her vow or pledge but **says nothing** to her,
30: 7 [30:8] [G] her husband hears about it but **says nothing** to her,
30: 11 [30:12] [G] but **says nothing** to her and does not forbid her,
30: 14 [30:15] [G] if her husband **says** [+3087] **nothing** to her *about* it
30: 14 [30:15] [G] if her husband **says nothing** to her **about** [+3087] it
30: 14 [30:15] [G] He confirms them by **saying nothing** to her when
Jdg 16: 2 [F] *They* **made no move** during the night, saying, "At dawn
18: 19 [G] They answered him, "*Be* **quiet**! Don't say a word. Come
1Sa 7: 8 [G] "*Do* not **stop** crying out to the LORD our God for us,
10: 27 [G] despised him and brought him no gifts. But Saul kept **silent**.
2Sa 13: 20 [G] been with you? *Be* **quiet** now, my sister; he is your brother.
19: 10 [19:11] [G] So why *do* you **say nothing** *about* bringing the
2Ki 18: 36 [G] But the people *remained* **silent** and said nothing in reply,
Ne 5: 8 [G] *They kept* **quiet**, because they could find nothing to say.
Est 4: 14 [G] For if *you* **remain silent** [+3087] at this time, relief
4: 14 [G] For if *you* **remain silent** [+3087] at this time, relief
7: 4 [G] sold as male and female slaves, *I would have kept* **quiet**,
Job 6: 24 [G] "Teach me, and I *will be* **quiet**; show me where I have been
11: 3 [G] *Will* your idle talk **reduce** men **to silence**? Will no one
13: 5 [G] If only *you would be* **altogether silent** [+3087]! For you,
13: 5 [G] If only *you would be* **altogether silent** [+3087]! For you,
13: 13 [G] "*Keep* **silent** and let me speak; then let come to me what
13: 19 [G] bring charges against me? If so, *I will be* **silent** and die.
33: 31 [G] Job, and listen to me; *be* **silent**, and I will speak.
33: 33 [G] then listen to me; *be* **silent**, and I will teach you wisdom."
41: 12 [41:4] [G] "*I will* not **fail to speak** *of* his limbs, his strength
Ps 28: 1 [A] I call, O LORD my Rock; *do* not **turn a deaf ear** to me.
32: 3 [G] When *I kept* **silent**, my bones wasted away through my
35: 22 [A] O LORD, you have seen this; *be* not **silent**. Do not be far
39: 12 [39:13] [A] to my cry for help; *be* not **deaf** to my weeping.
50: 3 [A] Our God comes and *will* not *be* **silent**; a fire devours before
50: 21 [G] These things you have done and *I kept* **silent**; you thought I
83: 1 [83:2] [A] do not keep silent; *be* not **quiet**, O God, be not still.
109: 1 [A] O God, whom I praise, *do* not *remain* **silent**,
Pr 11: 12 [G] his neighbor, but a man of understanding **holds** *his* **tongue**.
17: 28 [G] Even a fool is thought wise if *he* **keeps silent**, and discerning
Isa 36: 21 [G] But *the people remained* **silent** and said nothing in reply,
41: 1 [G] "*Be* **silent** before me, you islands! Let the nations renew their
42: 14 [G] I have kept silent, *I have been* **quiet** and held myself back.
Jer 4: 19 [G] my heart! My heart pounds within me, *I* cannot *keep* **silent**.
38: 27 [G] So *they* **said no more** to him, for no one had heard his
Mic 7: 16 [A] their hands on their mouths and their ears *will become* **deaf**.
Hab 1: 13 [G] Why *are you* **silent** while the wicked swallow up those more
Zep 3: 17 [G] will take great delight in you, *he will* **quiet** you with his love,

3088 ¹חֶרֶשׁ **ḥereš¹**, n.[m.]. Not used in NIV/BHS [√ 3086]

3089 ²חֶרֶשׁ **ḥereš²**, n.[m.] (used as adv.). [1] [√ 3087]

secretly [1]

Jos 2: 1 Then Joshua son of Nun **secretly** sent two spies from Shittim.

3090 ³חֶרֶשׁ **ḥereš³**, n.pr.m. [1] [√ 3087?]

Heresh [1]

1Ch 9: 15 Bakbakkar, **Heresh**, Galal and Mattaniah son of Mica, the son of

3091 ¹חֹרֶשׁ **ḥōreš¹**, n.m. [3] [→ 3092?; cf. 3099]

forest [1], thickets [1], wooded areas [1]

2Ch 27: 4 in the Judean hills and forts and towers in the **wooded areas**.
Isa 17: 9 will be like places abandoned to **thickets** and undergrowth.
Eze 31: 3 in Lebanon, with beautiful branches overshadowing the **forest**;

3092 ²חֹרֶשׁ **ḥōreš²**, n.pr.loc. [4] [√ 3091? *or* 3093?]

Horesh [4]

1Sa 23: 15 While David was at **Horesh** in the Desert of Ziph, he learned that
23: 16 Saul's son Jonathan went to David at **Horesh** and helped him find
23: 18 Then Jonathan went home, but David remained at **Horesh**.
23: 19 "Is not David hiding among us in the strongholds at **Horesh**,

3093 חָרָשׁ **ḥārāš**, n.m. [38] [√ 3086, 3092?]

craftsmen [11], craftsman [8], carpenters [4], carpenters [+6770] [3], blacksmith [2], blacksmith [+1366] [1], carpenter [+6770] [1], craftsman's [1], cutter [1], makers [1], masons [+74] [1], skilled [1], stonemasons [+74+7815] [1], stonemasons [+7815] [1], workers [1]

Ex 28: 11 of Israel on the two stones the way a gem **cutter** engraves a seal.
35: 35 He has filled them with skill to do all kinds of work as **craftsmen**,
38: 23 a **craftsman** and designer, and an embroiderer in blue, purple
Dt 27: 15 detestable to the LORD, the work of the **craftsman's** hands—
1Sa 13: 19 Not a **blacksmith** could be found in the whole land of Israel,
2Sa 5: 11 along with cedar logs and **carpenters** [+6770] and stonemasons,
5: 11 and **stonemasons** [+74+7815], and they built a palace for David.
2Ki 12: 11 [12:12] of the LORD—the **carpenters** [+6770] and builders,
22: 6 the **carpenters**, the builders and the masons. Also have them
24: 14 the officers and fighting men, and all the **craftsmen** and artisans—
24: 16 strong and fit for war, and a thousand **craftsmen** and artisans.
1Ch 4: 14 It was called this because its people were **craftsmen**.
14: 1 **stonemasons** [+7815] and carpenters to build a palace for him.

1Ch 14: 1 stonemasons and **carpenters** [+6770] to build a palace for him.
22: 15 stonecutters, **masons** [+74] and carpenters, as well as men skilled
29: 5 the silver work, and for all the work to be done by the **craftsmen**.
2Ch 24: 12 They hired masons and **carpenters** to restore the LORD's temple,
24: 12 and also **workers** *in* iron and bronze to repair the temple.
34: 11 They also gave money to the **carpenters** and builders to purchase
Ezr 3: 7 they gave money to the masons and **carpenters**, and gave food
Ne 11: 35 in Lod and Ono, and in the Valley of the **Craftsmen**.
Isa 3: 3 of rank, the counselor, skilled **craftsman** and clever enchanter.
40: 19 As for an idol, a **craftsman** casts it, and a goldsmith overlays it
40: 20 He looks for a skilled **craftsman** to set up an idol that will not
41: 7 The **craftsman** encourages the goldsmith, and he who smooths
44: 11 and his kind will be put to shame; **craftsmen** are nothing but men.
44: 12 The **blacksmith** [+1366] takes a tool and works with it in the
44: 13 The **carpenter** [+6770] measures with a line and makes an outline
45: 16 All the **makers** *of* idols will be put to shame and disgraced;
54: 16 it is I who created the **blacksmith** who fans the coals into flame
Jer 10: 3 a tree out of the forest, and a **craftsman** shapes it with his chisel.
10: 9 What the **craftsman** and goldsmith have made is then dressed in
24: 1 the **craftsmen** and the artisans of Judah were carried into exile
29: 2 the **craftsmen** and the artisans had gone into exile from
Eze 21: 31 [21:36] hand you over to brutal men, *men* **skilled** *in* destruction.
Hos 8: 6 are from Israel! This calf—a **craftsman** has made it; it is not God.
13: 2 cleverly fashioned images, all of them the work of **craftsmen**.
Zec 1: 20 [2:3] Then the LORD showed me four **craftsmen**.

3094 חֵרֵשׁ *ḥērēš*, a. [9] [√ 3087]

deaf [8], *untranslated* [1]

Ex 4: 11 Who makes him **deaf** or mute? Who gives him sight or makes him
Lev 19: 14 " 'Do not curse the **deaf** or put a stumbling block in front of the
Ps 38: 13 [38:14] I am like a **deaf** *man*, who cannot hear, like a mute,
58: 4 [58:5] like that of a cobra **[NIE]** that has stopped its ears,
Isa 29: 18 In that day the **deaf** will hear the words of the scroll, and out of
35: 5 the eyes of the blind be opened and the ears of the **deaf** unstopped.
42: 18 "Hear, you **deaf**; look, you blind, and see!
42: 19 Who is blind but my servant, and **deaf** like the messenger I send?
43: 8 out those who have eyes but are blind, who have ears but are **deaf**.

3095 חַרְשָׁא *ḥaršā'*, n.pr.m. [2] [→ 9426; cf. 3087?]

Harsha [2]

Ezr 2: 52 Bazluth, Mehida, **Harsha**,
Ne 7: 54 Bazluth, Mehida, **Harsha**,

3096 חֲרָשִׁים *ḥ^a^rāšîm*, n.pr.loc. Not used in NIV/BHS [→ 1629; cf. 3086]

3097 חֲרֶשֶׁת *ḥ^a^rešet*, n.pr.loc. Not used in NIV/BHS [√ 7819]

3098 חֲרֹשֶׁת *ḥ^a^rōšet*[1], n.f. [4] [√ 3086]

cut [2], work [2]

Ex 31: 5 to **cut** and set stones, to work in wood, and to engage in all kinds
31: 5 to cut and set stones, to **work** *in* wood, and to engage in all kinds
35: 33 to **cut** and set stones, to work in wood and to engage in all kinds of
35: 33 to **work** *in* wood and to engage in all kinds of artistic

3099 חֲרֹשֶׁת הַגּוֹיִם *ḥ^a^rōšet haggôyim*, n.pr.loc. [3] [√ 2046; cf. 2046, 3091]

Harosheth Haggoyim [3]

Jdg 4: 2 of his army was Sisera, who lived in **Harosheth Haggoyim**.
4: 13 men with him, from **Harosheth Haggoyim** to the Kishon River.
4: 16 pursued the chariots and army as far as **Harosheth Haggoyim**.

3100 חָרַת *ḥārat*, v. [1]

engraved [1]

Ex 32: 16 [B] the writing was the writing of God, **engraved** on the tablets.

3101 חֶרֶת *ḥeret*, n.pr.loc. [1]

Hereth [1]

1Sa 22: 5 the land of Judah." So David left and went to the forest of **Hereth**.

3102 חֲשׂוּפָא *ḥ^a^śûpā'*, n.pr.m. [2]

Hasupha [2]

Ezr 2: 43 The temple servants: the descendants of Ziha, **Hasupha**, Tabbaoth,
Ne 7: 46 The temple servants: the descendants of Ziha, **Hasupha**, Tabbaoth,

3103 חֲשׂוּפַי *ḥ^a^śûpay*, v. Not used in NIV/BHS [√ 3106]

3104 חָשַׂךְ *ḥāśak*, v. [28 / 27]

hold back [3], withheld [3], kept [2], bring relief [1], halted [1], hesitate [1], holds [1], is relieved [1], is spared [1], keep silent [+7023] [1], keep [1], preserve [1], punished less [+4200+4752] [1], relentless [+1172] [1], reserve [1], restrain [1], spare [1], spares [1], sparing [1], too easy on [1], uses with restraint [1], withholds [1]

Ge 20: 6 [A] and so I *have* **kept** you from sinning against me.
22: 12 [A] because *you have* not **withheld** from me your son, your only
22: 16 [A] because you have done this and *have* not **withheld** your son,
39: 9 [A] My master *has* **withheld** nothing from me except you,
1Sa 25: 39 [A] *He has* **kept** his servant from doing wrong and has brought
2Sa 18: 16 [A] and the troops stopped pursuing Israel, for Joab **halted** them.
2Ki 5: 20 [A] "My master *was* **too easy on** Naaman, this Aramean,
Ezr 9: 13 [A] you *have* **punished** us **less** [+4200+4752] than our sins have
Job 7: 11 [A] "Therefore I *will* not **keep** [+7023] **silent**; I will speak out in
16: 5 [A] comfort from my lips *would* **bring** you **relief**.
16: 6 [C] "Yet if I speak, my pain **is** not **relieved**; and if I refrain,
21: 30 [C] that the evil man **is spared** from the day of calamity, that he
30: 10 [A] keep their distance; *they do* not **hesitate** to spit in my face.
33: 18 [A] *to* **preserve** his soul from the pit, his life from perishing by
38: 23 [A] which *I* **reserve** for times of trouble, for days of war
Ps 19: 13 [19:14] [A] **Keep** your servant also from willful sins; may they
78: 50 [A] *he did* not **spare** them from death but gave them over to the
Pr 10: 19 [A] sin is not absent, but *he who* **holds** his tongue is wise.
11: 24 [A] even more; *another* **withholds** unduly, but comes to poverty.
13: 24 [A] *He who* **spares** the rod hates his son, but he who loves him is
17: 27 [A] A man of knowledge **uses** words **with restraint**, and a man
21: 26 [A] he craves for more, but the righteous give without **sparing**.
24: 11 [A] away to death; **hold back** those staggering toward slaughter.
Isa 14: 6 [A] in fury subdued nations with **relentless** [+1172] aggression.
54: 2 [A] your tent, stretch your tent curtains wide, *do* not **hold back**;
58: 1 [A] "Shout it aloud, *do* not **hold back**. Raise your voice like a
Jer 14: 10 [A] "They greatly love to wander; *they do* not **restrain** their feet.
Eze 30: 18 [a] Dark *will be* [BHS *He will* **hold back**; NIV 3124] the day at

3105 חָשִׂף *ḥāśip*, n.m. [1] [√ 3107]

small flocks [1]

1Ki 20: 27 The Israelites camped opposite them like two **small flocks** *of*

3106 חָשַׂף *ḥāśap*[1], v. [11] [→ 3103, 4741]

bared [2], stripped off bark [+3106] [2], draw [1], lay bare [1], lift up [1], pull up [1], scooping [1], strip bare [1], strips bare [1]

Ps 29: 9 [A] of the LORD twists the oaks and **strips** the forests **bare**.
Isa 20: 4 [B] and Cushite exiles, young and old, with buttocks **bared**—
30: 14 [A] coals from a hearth or **scooping** water out of a cistern."
47: 2 [A] **Lift up** *your* skirts, bare your legs, and wade through the
52: 10 [A] The LORD *will* **lay bare** his holy arm in the sight of all the
Jer 13: 26 [A] I *will* **pull up** your skirts over your face that your shame may
49: 10 [A] But I *will* **strip** Esau **bare**; I will uncover his hiding places,
Eze 4: 7 [B] siege of Jerusalem and with **bared** arm prophesy against her.
Joel 1: 7 [A] *It has* **stripped** [+3106] **off** their **bark** and thrown it away,
1: 7 [A] *It has* **stripped off** their **bark** [+3106] and thrown it away,
Hag 2: 16 [A] When anyone went to a wine vat to **draw** fifty measures,

3107 חָשַׂף *ḥāśap*[2], v. Not used in NIV/BHS [→ 3105]

3108 חָשַׁב *ḥāšab*, v. [112] [→ 3110, 3112, 3113, 3114, 3115, 3116, 3117, 3121, 4742; Ar 10285]

think [6], devised [5], plot [5], plan [4], plots [4], are regarded [3], count [3], devise [3], plotting [3], thought [3], was considered [3], are considered [2], be considered [2], be reckoned [2], considered [2], determine [2], devises [2], intended [2], make [2], planning [2], purposed [+4742] [2], seem [2], seems [2], were considered [2], account for [+907] [1], account [1], am counted [1], be credited [1], be taken [1], care for [1], compute [1], consider themselves [1], consider [1], considers [1], counted [1], counts [1], credited [1], determine the value [1], determined [1], devise plans [1], devising [1], esteemed [1], execute [1], has in mind [+4222] [1], hold [1], honored [1], imagine [1], improvise [1], is considered [1], is thought [1], make plans [+4742] [1], mean [1], planned [1], plans have [+4742] [1], plans [1], plot against [+906+928+4222] [1], plotted [+4742] [1], plotted [1], regard [1], regarded [1], require an accounting [1], respected [1], scheming [1], threatened [1], treats [1], tried [1], was credited [1], were thought [1]

Ge 15: 6 [A] the LORD, and *he* **credited** it to him *as* righteousness.
31: 15 [C] *Does* he not **regard** *us as* foreigners? Not only has he sold
38: 15 [A] When Judah saw her, *he* **thought** she was a prostitute,
50: 20 [A] You **intended** *to* harm me, but God intended it for good to
50: 20 [A] God **intended** it for good to accomplish what is now being
Ex 31: 4 [A] to **make** artistic designs for work in gold, silver and bronze,

Ex 35:32 [A] to **make** artistic designs for work in gold, silver and bronze,
Lev 7:18 [C] *It will* not **be credited** to the one who offered it, for it is
17: 4 [C] the tabernacle of the LORD—that man *shall* **be considered**
25:27 [D] *he is to* **determine the value** *for* the years since he sold it
25:31 [C] walls around them *are to* **be considered** as open country.
25:50 [D] *He* and his buyer *are to* **count** the time from the year he sold
25:52 [D] *he is to* **compute** that and pay for his redemption
27:18 [D] the priest *will* **determine** the value according to the number
27:23 [D] the priest *will* **determine** its value up to the Year of Jubilee,
Nu 18:27 [C] Your offering *will* **be reckoned** to you as grain from the
18:30 [C] *it will* **be reckoned** to you as the product of the threshing
23: 9 [F] live apart and *do* not **consider themselves** one of the nations.
Dt 2:11 [C] Like the Anakites, they too **were considered** Rephaites,
2:20 [C] (That too **was considered** a land of the Rephaites, who used
Jos 13: 3 [C] all of *it* **counted** as Canaanite (the territory of the five
1Sa 1:13 [A] but her voice was not heard. Eli **thought** she was drunk
18:25 [A] to take revenge on his enemies.' " Saul's **plan** *was* to have
2Sa 4: 2 [C] tribe of Benjamin—Beeroth **is considered** part of Benjamin,
14:13 [A] *have you* **devised** a thing like this against the people of God?
14:14 [A] *he* **devises** ways so that a banished person may not remain
19:19 [19:20] [A] said to him, "*May* my lord not **hold** me guilty. Do
1Ki 10:21 [C] because silver **was considered** of little value in Solomon's
2Ki 12:15 [12:16] [D] *They did* not **require an accounting** *from* those to
22: 7 [C] they *need* not **account** [+907] **for** the money entrusted to
2Ch 2:14 [2:13] [A] and *can* **execute** any design given to him.
9:20 [C] because silver **was considered** of little value in Solomon's
Ne 6: 2 [A] on the plain of Ono." But they *were* **scheming** to harm me;
6: 6 [A] that you and the Jews *are* **plotting** to revolt, and therefore
13:13 [C] because *these men* **were considered** trustworthy.
Est 8: 3 [A] Haman the Agagite, which *he had* **devised** against the Jews.
9:24 [A] *had* **plotted** against the Jews to destroy them and had cast
9:25 [A] *had* **devised** against the Jews should come back onto his own
Job 6:26 [A] *Do you* **mean** to correct what I say, and treat the words of a
13:24 [A] Why do you hide your face and **consider** me your enemy?
18: 3 [C] Why **are** *we* **regarded** as cattle and considered stupid in your
19:11 [A] anger burns against me; *he* **counts** me among his enemies.
19:15 [A] My guests and my maidservants **count** me a stranger;
33:10 [A] God has found fault with me; *he* **considers** me his enemy.
35: 2 [A] "*Do you* **think** this is just? You say, 'I will be cleared by
41:27 [41:19] [A] Iron *he* **treats** like straw and bronze like rotten
41:29 [41:21] [C] A club **seems** to him but a piece of straw; he laughs
41:32 [41:24] [A] *one would* **think** the deep had white hair.
Ps 10: 2 [A] down the weak, who are caught in the schemes *he* **devises**.
21:11 [21:12] [A] plot evil against you and **devise** wicked schemes,
32: 2 [A] Blessed is the man whose sin the LORD *does* not **count**
35: 4 [A] may *those who* **plot** my ruin be turned back in dismay.
35:20 [A] **devise** false accusations against those who live quietly in the
36: 4 [36:5] [A] Even on his bed *he* **plots** evil; he commits himself to
40:17 [40:18] [A] Yet I am poor and needy; *may* the Lord **think** **of** me.
41: 7 [41:8] [A] against me; *they* **imagine** the worst for me, saying,
44:22 [44:23] [C] *we* **are considered** as sheep to be slaughtered.
52: 2 [52:4] [A] Your tongue **plots** destruction; it is like a sharpened
73:16 [D] When *I* **tried** to understand all this, it was oppressive to me
77: 5 [77:6] [D] *I* **thought** *about* the former days, the years of long
88: 4 [88:5] [C] *I* **am counted** among those who go down to the pit;
106:31 [C] *This* **was credited** to him as righteousness for endless
119:59 [D] *I have* **considered** my ways and have turned my steps to
140: 2 [140:3] [A] who **devise** evil **plans** in their hearts and stir up war
140: 4 [140:5] [A] protect me from men of violence who **plan** to trip
144: 3 [D] that you care for him, the son of man that *you* **think** *of* him?
Pr 16: 9 [D] In his heart a man **plans** his course, but the LORD
16:30 [A] He who winks with his eye *is* **plotting** perversity; he who
17:28 [C] Even a fool **is thought** wise if he keeps silent, and discerning
24: 8 [D] *He who* **plots** evil will be known as a schemer.
27:14 [C] his neighbor early in the morning, *it will* **be taken** as a curse.
Isa 2:22 [C] who has but a breath in his nostrils. Of what **account** is he?
5:28 [C] their horses' hoofs **seem** like flint, their chariot wheels like a
10: 7 [A] not what he intends, this is not what he **has in mind** [+4222];
13:17 [A] who *do* not **care for** silver and have no delight in gold.
29:16 [C] as if the potter **were thought** to be like the clay!
29:17 [C] into a fertile field and the fertile field **seem** like a forest?
32:15 [C] a fertile field, and the fertile field **seems** like a forest.
33: 8 [A] is broken, its witnesses are despised, no one *is* **respected**.
40:15 [C] a drop in a bucket; *they* **are regarded** as dust on the scales;
40:17 [C] *they* **are regarded** by him as worthless and less than
53: 3 [A] hide their faces he was despised, and *we* **esteemed** him not.
53: 4 [A] yet we **considered** him stricken by God, smitten by him,
Jer 11:19 [A] I did not realize that *they had* **plotted** [+4742] against me,
18: 8 [A] I will relent and not inflict on it the disaster *I had* **planned**.
18:11 [A] preparing a disaster for you and **devising** a plan against you.
18:18 [A] "Come, *let's* **make plans** [+4742] against Jeremiah;
23:27 [A] They **think** the dreams they tell one another will make my
26: 3 [A] will relent and not bring on them the disaster I *was* **planning**
29:11 [A] For I know the **plans** [+4742] **I have** for you,"
36: 3 [A] of Judah hear about every disaster I **plan** to inflict on them,
48: 2 [A] be praised no more; in Heshbon *men will* **plot** her downfall:
49:20 [A] what *he has* **purposed** [+4742] against those who live in
49:30 [A] has plotted against you; *he has* **devised** a plan against you.
50:45 [A] what *he has* **purposed** [+4742] against the land of the
La 2: 8 [A] The LORD **determined** to tear down the wall around the
4: 2 [C] **are** now **considered** as pots of clay, the work of a potter's
Eze 11: 2 [A] these are the men who *are* **plotting** evil and giving wicked
38:10 [A] come into your mind and *you will* **devise** an evil scheme.
Da 11:24 [D] *He will* **plot** the overthrow of fortresses—but only for a time.
11:25 [A] not be able to stand because of the plots **devised** against him.
Hos 7:15 [D] and strengthened them, but *they* **plot** evil against me.
8:12 [C] of my law, but *they* **regarded** *them* as something alien.
Am 6: 5 [A] your harps like David and **improvise** on musical instruments.
Jnh 1: 4 [D] such a violent storm arose that the ship **threatened** to break
Mic 2: 1 [A] Woe to *those who* **plan** iniquity, to those who plot evil on
2: 3 [A] "I *am* **planning** disaster against this people, from which you
Na 1: 9 [D] Whatever *they* **plot** against the LORD he will bring to an
1:11 [A] ⌞O Nineveh,⌟ has one come forth *who* **plots** evil against the
Zec 7:10 [A] or the poor. In your hearts *do* not **think** evil of each other.'
8:17 [A] *do* not **plot** [+906+928+4222] evil **against** your neighbor,
Mal 3:16 [A] those who feared the LORD and **honored** his name.

3109 חֵשֶׁב ḥēšeb, n.m. [8] [cf. 2502]

waistband [7], skillfully woven waistband [1]

Ex 28: 8 Its skillfully woven **waistband** is to be like it—of one piece with
28:27 close to the seam just above the **waistband** *of* the ephod.
28:28 connecting it to the **waistband**, so that the breastpiece will not
29: 5 Fasten the ephod on him by its skillfully woven **waistband**.
39: 5 Its skillfully woven **waistband** was like it—of one piece with the
39:20 close to the seam just above the **waistband** *of* the ephod.
39:21 connecting it to the **waistband** so that the breastpiece would not
Lev 8: 7 He also tied the ephod to him by its **skillfully woven waistband**;

3110 חֹשֵׁב ḥōšēb, n.[m.] *or* v.ptcp. [12] [√ 3108]

skilled craftsman [8], designer [1], designers [+4742] [1], designers [1], skillful men [1]

Ex 26: 1 with cherubim worked into them by a **skilled craftsman**.
26:31 with cherubim worked into it by a **skilled craftsman**.
28: 6 and of finely twisted linen—the work of a **skilled craftsman**.
28:15 for making decisions—the work of a **skilled craftsman**.
35:35 **designers**, embroiderers in blue, purple and scarlet yarn and fine
35:35 all of them master craftsmen and **designers** [+4742].
36: 8 with cherubim worked into them by a **skilled craftsman**.
36:35 with cherubim worked into it by a **skilled craftsman**.
38:23 a craftsman and **designer**, and an embroiderer in blue, purple
39: 3 and scarlet yarn and fine linen—the work of a **skilled craftsman**.
39: 8 They fashioned the breastpiece—the work of a **skilled craftsman**.
2Ch 26:15 In Jerusalem he made machines designed by **skillful men** for use

3111 חַשְׁבַּדָּנָה ḥašbaddānâ, n.pr.m. [1] [cf. 3116]

Hashbaddanah [1]

Ne 8: 4 Mishael, Malkijah, Hashum, **Hashbaddanah**, Zechariah

3112 חֲשֻׁבָה ḥᵃšubâ, n.pr.m. [1] [√ 3108]

Hashubah [1]

1Ch 3:20 **Hashubah**, Ohel, Berekiah, Hasadiah and Jushab-Hesed.

3113 ¹חֶשְׁבּוֹן ḥešbôn¹, n.m. [3] [√ 3108]

scheme of things [2], planning [1]

Ecc 7:25 to investigate and to search out wisdom and the **scheme of things**
7:27 "Adding one thing to another to discover the **scheme of things**—
9:10 there is neither working nor **planning** nor knowledge nor wisdom.

3114 ²חֶשְׁבּוֹן ḥešbôn², n.pr.loc. [38] [√ 3108]

Heshbon [38]

Nu 21:25 including **Heshbon** and all its surrounding settlements.
21:26 **Heshbon** was the city of Sihon king of the Amorites, who had
21:27 "Come to **Heshbon** and let it be rebuilt; let Sihon's city be
21:28 "Fire went out from **Heshbon**, a blaze from the city of Sihon.
21:30 have overthrown them; **Heshbon** is destroyed all the way to Dibon.
21:34 you did to Sihon king of the Amorites, who reigned in **Heshbon**."
32: 3 Jazer, Nimrah, **Heshbon**, Elealeh, Sebam, Nebo and Beon—
32:37 And the Reubenites rebuilt **Heshbon**, Elealeh and Kiriathaim,
Dt 1: 4 who reigned in **Heshbon**, and at Edrei had defeated Og king of
2:24 your hand Sihon the Amorite, king of **Heshbon**, and his country.
2:26 I sent messengers to Sihon king of **Heshbon** offering peace
2:30 But Sihon king of **Heshbon** refused to let us pass through.
3: 2 you did to Sihon king of the Amorites, who reigned in **Heshbon**."

Dt 3: 6 as we had done with Sihon king of **Heshbon**, destroying every
4:46 who reigned in **Heshbon** and was defeated by Moses
29: 7 [29:6] Sihon king of **Heshbon** and Og king of Bashan came out to
Jos 9:10 Sihon king of **Heshbon**, and Og king of Bashan, who reigned in
12: 2 Sihon king of the Amorites, who reigned in **Heshbon**. He ruled
12: 5 and half of Gilead to the border of Sihon king of **Heshbon**.
13:10 who ruled in **Heshbon**, out to the border of the Ammonites.
13:17 to **Heshbon** and all its towns on the plateau, including Dibon,
13:21 entire realm of Sihon king of the Amorites, who ruled at **Heshbon**.
13:26 from **Heshbon** to Ramath Mizpah and Betonim, and from
13:27 Zaphon with the rest of the realm of Sihon king of **Heshbon** (the
21:39 **Heshbon** and Jazer, together with their pasturelands—four towns
Jdg 11:19 who ruled in **Heshbon**, and said to him, 'Let us pass through your
11:26 For three hundred years Israel occupied **Heshbon**, Aroer, the
1Ch 6:81 [6:66] **Heshbon** and Jazer, together with their pasturelands.
Ne 9:22 They took over the country of Sihon king of **Heshbon** and the
SS 7: 4 [7:5] Your eyes are the pools of **Heshbon** by the gate of Bath
Isa 15: 4 **Heshbon** and Elealeh cry out, their voices are heard all the way to
16: 8 The fields of **Heshbon** wither, the vines of Sibmah also. The rulers
16: 9 vines of Sibmah. O **Heshbon**, O Elealeh, I drench you with tears!
Jer 48: 2 will be praised no more; in **Heshbon** men will plot her downfall:
48:34 "The sound of their cry rises from **Heshbon** to Elealeh and Jahaz,
48:45 "In the shadow of **Heshbon** the fugitives stand helpless, for a fire
48:45 for a fire has gone out from **Heshbon**, a blaze from the midst of
49: 3 "Wail, O **Heshbon**, for Ai is destroyed! Cry out, O inhabitants of

3115 חִשָּׁבוֹן **ḥiššābôn**, n.m. [2] [√ 3108]

machines [1], schemes [1]

2Ch 26:15 In Jerusalem he made **machines** designed by skillful men for use
Ecc 7:29 mankind upright, but men have gone in search of many **schemes**."

3116 חֲשַׁבְיָה **ḥ^{a}šabyâ**, n.pr.m. [12] [√ 3108 + 3378; cf. 3111]

Hashabiah [12]

1Ch 6:45 [6:30] the son of **Hashabiah**, the son of Amaziah, the son of
9:14 of Hasshub, the son of Azrikam, the son of **Hashabiah**, a Merarite;
25:19 the twelfth to **Hashabiah**, his sons and relatives, 12
27:17 over Levi: **Hashabiah** son of Kemuel; over Aaron: Zadok;
Ezr 8:19 **Hashabiah**, together with Jeshaiah from the descendants of
8:24 together with Sherebiah, **Hashabiah** and ten of their brothers,
Ne 3:17 Beside him, **Hashabiah**, ruler of half the district of Keilah,
10:11 [10:12] Mica, Rehob, **Hashabiah**,
11:15 the son of Azrikam, the son of **Hashabiah**, the son of Bunni;
11:22 the son of **Hashabiah**, the son of Mattaniah, the son of Mica.
12:21 of Hilkiah's, **Hashabiah**; of Jedaiah's, Nethanel.
12:24 And the leaders of the Levites were **Hashabiah**, Sherebiah,

3117 חֲשַׁבְיָהוּ **ḥ^{a}šabyāhû**, n.pr.m. [3] [√ 3108 + 3378]

Hashabiah [3]

1Ch 25: 3 Zeri, Jeshaiah, Shimei, **Hashabiah** and Mattithiah, six in all,
26:30 **Hashabiah** and his relatives—seventeen hundred able men—
2Ch 35: 9 and Nethanel, his brothers, and **Hashabiah**, Jeiel and Jozabad,

3118 חֲשַׁבְנָה **ḥ^{a}šabnâ**, n.pr.m. [1]

Hashabnah [1]

Ne 10:25 [10:26] Rehum, **Hashabnah**, Maaseiah,

3119 חֲשַׁבְנְיָה **ḥ^{a}šabn^{e}yâ**, n.pr.m. [2]

Hashabneiah [2]

Ne 3:10 and Hattush son of **Hashabneiah** made repairs next to him.
9: 5 Jeshua, Kadmiel, Bani, **Hashabneiah**, Sherebiah, Hodiah,

3120 חָשָׁה **ḥāšâ**, v. [16]

silent [8], not speak [2], aren't do something [1], calmed [1], doing nothing [1], hushed [1], keeping it to ourselves [1], not saying [1]

Jdg 18: 9 [G] **Aren't** you *going to* **do something**? Don't hesitate to go
1Ki 22: 3 [G] yet we *are* **doing nothing** to retake it from the king of
2Ki 2: 3 [G] I know," Elisha replied, "but *do* **not speak** *of* it."
2: 5 [G] "Yes, I know," he replied, "but *do* **not speak** *of* it."
7: 9 [G] is a day of good news and we *are* **keeping it to ourselves**.
Ne 8:11 [G] The Levites **calmed** all the people, saying, "Be still, for this
Ps 28: 1 [A] For if *you remain* **silent**, I will be like those who have gone
39: 2 [39:3] [G] I was silent and still, **not** *even* **saying** anything good,
107:29 [A] the storm to a whisper; the waves of the sea *were* **hushed**.
Ecc 3: 7 [A] and a time to mend, a time to *be* **silent** and a time to speak,
Isa 42:14 [G] "For a long time *I have kept* **silent**, I have been quiet
57:11 [G] because I *have* long *been* **silent** that you do not fear me?
62: 1 [A] For Zion's sake *I will* not *keep* **silent**, for Jerusalem's sake I
62: 6 [A] O Jerusalem; *they will* never *be* **silent** day or night.
64:12 [64:11] [A] *Will you keep* **silent** and punish us beyond
65: 6 [A] *I will* not *keep* **silent** but will pay back in full; I will pay it

3121 חַשּׁוּב **ḥaššûb**, n.pr.m. [5] [√ 3108]

Hasshub [5]

1Ch 9:14 Shemaiah son of **Hasshub**, the son of Azrikam, the son of
Ne 3:11 and **Hasshub** son of Pahath-Moab repaired another section
3:23 Benjamin and **Hasshub** made repairs in front of their house;
10:23 [10:24] Hoshea, Hananiah, **Hasshub**,
11:15 Shemaiah son of **Hasshub**, the son of Azrikam, the son of

3122 חָשׁוּק **ḥāšûq**, n.[m.]. [8] [√ 3138]

bands [8]

Ex 27:10 twenty bronze bases and with silver hooks and **bands** on the posts.
27:11 twenty bronze bases and with silver hooks and **bands** on the posts.
36:38 They overlaid the tops of the posts and their **bands** with gold
38:10 twenty bronze bases, and with silver hooks and **bands** on the posts.
38:11 and twenty bronze bases, with silver hooks and **bands** on the posts.
38:12 ten posts and ten bases, with silver hooks and **bands** on the posts.
38:17 The hooks and **bands** on the posts were silver, and their tops were
38:19 Their hooks and **bands** were silver, and their tops were overlaid

3123 חֻשִׁים **ḥušîm**, n.pr.m. [1] [cf. 2594]

Hushim [1]

Ge 46:23 The son of Dan: **Hushim**.

3124 חָשַׁךְ **ḥāšak**, v. [16 / 17] [→ 3125, 3126, 3127, 3128, 4743]

dark [5], darkened [3], darkens [2], dim [2], black [1], blacker [1], brings darkness [1], darken [1], made dark [1]

Ex 10:15 [A] They covered all the ground until it *was* **black**. They
Job 3: 9 [A] *May* its morning stars *become* **dark**; may it wait for daylight
18: 6 [A] The light in his tent *becomes* **dark**; the lamp beside him goes
38: 2 [G] "Who is this *that* **darkens** my counsel with words without
Ps 69:23 [69:24] [A] *May* their eyes *be* **darkened** so they cannot see,
105:28 [G] He sent darkness and **made** the land **dark**—for had they not
139:12 [G] even the darkness *will* not *be* **dark** to you; the night will
Ecc 12: 2 [A] the sun and the light and the moon and the stars *grow* **dark**,
12: 3 [A] are few, and those looking through the windows *grow* **dim**;
Isa 5:30 [A] and distress; even the light *will be* **darkened** by the clouds.
13:10 [A] The rising sun *will be* **darkened** and the moon will not give
Jer 13:16 [G] to the LORD your God before *he* **brings** *the* **darkness**,
La 4: 8 [A] now they *are* **blacker** than soot; they are not recognized in
5:17 [A] hearts are faint, because of these things our eyes *grow* **dim**
Eze 30:18 [A] **Dark** [BHS 3104] *will be* the day at Tahpanhes when I
Am 5: 8 [G] who turns blackness into dawn and **darkens** day *into* night,
8: 9 [G] sun go down at noon and **darken** the earth in broad daylight.

3125 חֹשֶׁךְ **ḥōšek**, n.m. [80] [√ 3124; Ar 10286]

darkness [70], dark [4], black [1], dark place [1], dusk [1], gloom [1], pitch darkness [+413] [1], total darkness [+696] [1]

Ge 1: 2 and empty, **darkness** was over the surface of the deep,
1: 4 the light was good, and he separated the light from the **darkness**.
1: 5 God called the light "day," and the **darkness** he called "night."
1:18 govern the day and the night, and to separate light from **darkness**.
Ex 10:21 hand toward the sky so that **darkness** will spread over Egypt—
10:21 that darkness will spread over Egypt—**darkness** that can be felt."
10:22 and **total darkness** [+696] covered all Egypt for three days.
14:20 Throughout the night the cloud brought **darkness** to the one side
Dt 4:11 with fire to the very heavens, with **black** clouds and deep darkness.
5:23 When you heard the voice out of the **darkness**, while the mountain
Jos 2: 5 At **dusk**, when it was time to close the city gate, the men left.
1Sa 2: 9 the feet of his saints, but the wicked will be silenced in **darkness**.
2Sa 22:12 He made **darkness** his canopy around him—the dark rain clouds
22:29 are my lamp, O LORD; the LORD turns my **darkness** into light.
Job 3: 4 That day—may it turn to **darkness**; may God above not care about
3: 5 May **darkness** and deep shadow claim it once more; may a cloud
5:14 **Darkness** comes upon them in the daytime; at noon they grope as
10:21 go to the place of no return, to the land of **gloom** and deep shadow,
12:22 He reveals the deep things of **darkness** and brings deep shadows
12:25 They grope in **darkness** with no light; he makes them stagger like
15:22 He despairs of escaping the **darkness**; he is marked for the sword.
15:23 food for vultures; he knows the day of **darkness** is at hand.
15:30 He will not escape the **darkness**; a flame will wither his shoots,
17:12 turn night into day; in the face of **darkness** they say, 'Light is near.'
17:13 home I hope for is the grave, if I spread out my bed in **darkness**,
18:18 He is driven from light into **darkness** and is banished from the
19: 8 my way so I cannot pass; he has shrouded my paths in **darkness**.
20:26 total **darkness** lies in wait for his treasures. A fire unfanned will
22:11 why it is so **dark** you cannot see, and why a flood of water covers
23:17 Yet I am not silenced by the **darkness**, by the thick darkness that

Job 24: 16 In the **dark**, men break into houses, but by day they shut
26: 10 the face of the waters for a boundary between light and **darkness**.
28: 3 Man puts an end to the **darkness**; he searches the farthest recesses
29: 3 shone upon my head and by his light I walked through **darkness**!
34: 22 There is no **dark place**, no deep shadow, where evildoers can hide.
37: 19 say to him; we cannot draw up our case because of our **darkness**.
38: 19 is the way to the abode of light? And where does **darkness** reside?
Ps 18: 11 [18:12] He made **darkness** his covering, his canopy around him—
18: 28 [18:29] my lamp burning; my God turns my **darkness** into light.
35: 6 may their path be **dark** and slippery, with the angel of the LORD
88: 12 [88:13] Are your wonders known in the *place of* **darkness**,
104: 20 You bring **darkness**, it becomes night, and all the beasts of the
105: 28 He sent **darkness** and made the land dark—for had they not
107: 10 Some sat in **darkness** and the deepest gloom, prisoners suffering in
107: 14 He brought them out of **darkness** and the deepest gloom and broke
112: 4 Even in **darkness** light dawns for the upright, for the gracious
139: 11 "Surely the **darkness** will hide me and the light become night
139: 12 even the **darkness** will not be dark to you; the night will shine like
Pr 2: 13 who leave the straight paths to walk in **dark** ways,
20: 20 or mother, his lamp will be snuffed out in **pitch darkness** [+413].
Ecc 2: 13 wisdom is better than folly, just as light is better than **darkness**.
2: 14 man has eyes in his head, while the fool walks in the **darkness**;
5: 17 [5:16] All his days he eats in **darkness**, with great frustration,
6: 4 It comes without meaning, it departs in **darkness**, and in darkness
6: 4 it departs in darkness, and in **darkness** its name is shrouded.
11: 8 But let him remember the days of **darkness**, for they will be many.
Isa 5: 20 and good evil, who put **darkness** for light and light for darkness,
5: 20 and good evil, who put darkness for light and light for **darkness**,
5: 30 And if one looks at the land, he will see **darkness** and distress;
9: 2 [9:1] The people walking in **darkness** have seen a great light;
29: 18 and out of gloom and **darkness** the eyes of the blind will see.
42: 7 and to release from the dungeon those who sit in **darkness**.
45: 3 I will give you the treasures of **darkness**, riches stored in secret
45: 7 I form the light and create **darkness**, I bring prosperity and create
45: 19 have not spoken in secret, from somewhere in a land of **darkness**;
47: 5 "Sit in silence, go into **darkness**, Daughter of the Babylonians;
49: 9 say to the captives, 'Come out,' and to those in **darkness**, 'Be free!'
58: 10 needs of the oppressed, then your light will rise in the **darkness**,
59: 9 We look for light, but all is **darkness**; for brightness, but we walk
60: 2 **darkness** covers the earth and thick darkness is over the peoples,
La 3: 2 driven me away and made me walk in **darkness** rather than light;
Eze 8: 12 what the elders of the house of Israel are doing in the **darkness**,
32: 8 I will bring **darkness** over your land, declares the Sovereign
Joel 2: 2 a day of **darkness** and gloom, a day of clouds and blackness.
2: 31 [3:4] The sun will be turned to **darkness** and the moon to blood
Am 5: 18 for the day of the LORD? That day will be **darkness**, not light.
5: 20 Will not the day of the LORD be **darkness**, not light—pitch-dark,
Mic 7: 8 I will rise. Though I sit in **darkness**, the LORD will be my light.
Na 1: 8 make an end of ⌞Nineveh⌟; he will pursue his foes into **darkness**.
Zep 1: 15 a day of trouble and ruin, a day of **darkness** and gloom,

3126 חָשֹׁךְ ḥāšōk, a. [1] [√ 3124]

obscure [1]

Pr 22: 29 He will serve before kings; he will not serve before **obscure** *men*.

3127 חָשְׁכָה ḥoškâ, n.f. [1] [√ 3124]

darkness [1]

Mic 3: 6 come over you, without visions, and **darkness**, without divination.

3128 חֲשֵׁכָה ḥ^ašēkâ, n.f. [6 / 7] [√ 3124]

darkness [4], dark [3]

Ge 15: 12 a deep sleep, and a thick and dreadful **darkness** came over him.
2Sa 22: 12 canopy around him—the **dark** [BHS 3142] rain clouds of the sky.
Ps 18: 11 [18:12] his canopy around him—the **dark** rain clouds of the sky.
82: 5 They walk about in **darkness**; all the foundations of the earth are
139: 12 the night will shine like the day, for **darkness** is as light to you.
Isa 8: 22 the earth and see only distress and **darkness** and fearful gloom,
50: 10 Let him who walks in the **dark**, who has no light, trust in the name

3129 חָשַׁל ḥāšal, v. [1]

lagging [1]

Dt 25: 18 [C] on your journey and cut off all who *were* **lagging** behind;

3130 חָשֻׁם ḥāšum, n.pr.m. [5] [→ 3131, 3132, 3135; cf. 2595]

Hashum [5]

Ezr 2: 19 of **Hashum** 223
10: 33 From the descendants of **Hashum**: Mattenai, Mattattah, Zabad,
Ne 7: 22 of **Hashum** 328
8: 4 Mishael, Malkijah, **Hashum**, Hashbaddanah, Zechariah
10: 18 [10:19] Hodiah, **Hashum**, Bezai,

3131 חֻשִׁם ḥušim, n.pr.m.[g.]. [1] [√ 3130]

Hushites [1]

1Ch 7: 12 the descendants of Ir, and the **Hushites** the descendants of Aher.

3132 חֶשְׁמוֹן ḥešmôn, n.pr.loc. [1] [√ 3130]

Heshmon [1]

Jos 15: 27 Hazar Gaddah, **Heshmon**, Beth Pelet,

3133 חַשְׁמַל ḥašmal, n.[m.]. [3]

glowing metal [3]

Eze 1: 4 by brilliant light. The center of the fire looked like **glowing metal**,
1: 27 what appeared to be his waist up he looked like **glowing metal**,
8: 2 and from there up his appearance was as bright as **glowing metal**.

3134 חַשְׁמַן ḥašman, n.m. [1]

envoys [1]

Ps 68: 31 [68:32] **Envoys** will come from Egypt; Cush will submit herself

3135 חַשְׁמֹנָה ḥašmōnâ, n.pr.loc. [2] [√ 3130]

Hashmonah [2]

Nu 33: 29 They left Mithcah and camped at **Hashmonah**.
33: 30 They left **Hashmonah** and camped at Moseroth.

3136 חֹשֶׁן ḥōšen, n.m. [25]

breastpiece [23], *untranslated* [1], it [+2021] [1]

Ex 25: 7 and other gems to be mounted on the ephod and **breastpiece**.
28: 4 a **breastpiece**, an ephod, a robe, a woven tunic, a turban and a
28: 15 "Fashion a **breastpiece** *for* making decisions—the work of a
28: 22 "For the **breastpiece** make braided chains of pure gold, like a rope.
28: 23 Make two gold rings for **it** [+2021] and fasten them to two corners
28: 23 gold rings for it and fasten them to two corners of the **breastpiece**.
28: 24 the two gold chains to the rings at the corners of the **breastpiece**,
28: 26 attach them to the other two corners of the **breastpiece** on the
28: 28 The rings of the **breastpiece** are to be tied to the rings of the ephod
28: 28 so that the **breastpiece** will not swing out from the ephod.
28: 29 **breastpiece** *of* decision as a continuing memorial before the
28: 30 Also put the Urim and the Thummim in the **breastpiece**, so they
29: 5 the robe of the ephod, the ephod itself and the **breastpiece**.
35: 9 and other gems to be mounted on the ephod and **breastpiece**.
35: 27 and other gems to be mounted on the ephod and **breastpiece**.
39: 8 They fashioned the **breastpiece**—the work of a skilled craftsman.
39: 9 a span long and a span wide—and folded double. **[RPH]**
39: 15 For the **breastpiece** they made braided chains of pure gold,
39: 16 and fastened the rings to two of the corners of the **breastpiece**.
39: 17 the two gold chains to the rings at the corners of the **breastpiece**,
39: 19 attached them to the other two corners of the **breastpiece** on the
39: 21 They tied the rings of the **breastpiece** to the rings of the ephod
39: 21 so that the **breastpiece** would not swing out from the ephod—
Lev 8: 8 He placed the **breastpiece** on him and put the Urim and Thummim
8: 8 on him and put the Urim and Thummim in the **breastpiece**.

3137 [1]חָשַׁק ḥāšaq[1], v. [8] [→ 3139; cf. 3138]

desired [+3139] [2], set affection [2], attracted [1], in love kept [1], loves [1], set [1]

Ge 34: 8 [A] "My son Shechem *has* his heart **set** on your daughter.
Dt 7: 7 [A] The LORD *did* not **set** *his* **affection** on you and choose you
10: 15 [A] Yet the LORD **set** *his* **affection** on your forefathers
21: 11 [A] the captives a beautiful woman and *are* **attracted** to her,
1Ki 9: 19 [A] whatever he **desired** [+3139] to build in Jerusalem, in
2Ch 8: 6 [A] whatever he **desired** [+3139] to build in Jerusalem, in
Ps 91: 14 [A] "Because *he* **loves** me," says the LORD, "I will rescue him;
Isa 38: 17 [A] **In** *your* **love** you **kept** me from the pit of destruction; you

3138 [2]חָשַׁק ḥāšaq[2], v.den. [3] [→ 3122, 3140; cf. 3137]

bands [2], make bands [1]

Ex 27: 17 [E] All the posts around the courtyard *are to have* silver **bands**
38: 17 [E] with silver; so all the posts of the courtyard *had* silver **bands**.
38: 28 [D] to overlay the tops of the posts, and *to* **make** their **bands**.

3139 חֵשֶׁק ḥēšeq, n.m. [4] [√ 3137]

desired [+3137] [2], desired [+2911] [1], longed for [1]

1Ki 9: 1 royal palace, and had achieved all he had **desired** [+2911] to do,
9: 19 whatever he **desired** [+3137] to build in Jerusalem, in Lebanon
2Ch 8: 6 whatever he **desired** [+3137] to build in Jerusalem, in Lebanon
Isa 21: 4 me tremble; the twilight I **longed for** has become a horror to me.

3140 חִשֻּׁק ḥiššuq, n.[m.]. [1] [√ 3138]

spokes [1]

1Ki 7:33 the axles, rims, **spokes** and hubs were all of cast metal.

3141 חִשֻּׁר ḥiššur, n.[m.]. [1] [→ 3142]

hubs [1]

1Ki 7:33 the axles, rims, spokes and **hubs** were all of cast metal.

3142 חַשְׁרָה ḥašrâ, n.f. [1 / 0] [√ 3141]

2Sa 22:12 the dark [BHS *massed*; NIV 3128] rain clouds of the sky.

3143 חֲשַׁשׁ ḥᵃšaš, n.m. [2]

chaff [1], dry grass [1]

Isa 5:24 of fire lick up straw and as **dry grass** sinks down in the flames,
33:11 You conceive **chaff**, you give birth to straw; your breath is a fire

3144 חֻשָׁתִי ḥušātî, a.g. [5] [√ 2592]

Hushathite [5]

2Sa 21:18 At that time Sibbecai the **Hushathite** killed Saph, one of the
23:27 Abiezer from Anathoth, Mebunnai the **Hushathite**,
1Ch 11:29 Sibbecai the **Hushathite**, Ilai the Ahohite,
20:4 At that time Sibbecai the **Hushathite** killed Sippai, one of the
27:11 for the eighth month, was Sibbecai the **Hushathite**, a Zerahite.

3145 חַת ḥat¹, n.m. [2] [√ 3169]

dread [1], fear [1]

Ge 9:2 The fear and **dread** *of* you will fall upon all the beasts of the earth
Job 41:33 [41:25] Nothing on earth is his equal—a creature without **fear**.

3146 ²חַת ḥat², a. [2] [√ 3169]

broken [1], terrified [1]

1Sa 2:4 "The bows of the warriors are **broken**, but those who stumbled are
Jer 46:5 They are **terrified**, they are retreating, their warriors are defeated.

3147 חֵת ḥēt, n.pr.m. [14] [→ 3153]

Hittites [+1201] [9], Hittite [2], Hittites [2], his people[s] [+1201] [1]

Ge 10:15 Canaan was the father of Sidon his firstborn, and of the **Hittites**,
23:3 rose from beside his dead wife and spoke to the **Hittites** [+1201].
23:5 The **Hittites** [+1201] replied to Abraham,
23:7 bowed down before the people of the land, the **Hittites** [+1201].
23:10 Ephron the Hittite was sitting among **his people**[s] [+1201]
23:10 he replied to Abraham in the hearing of all the **Hittites** [+1201]
23:16 him the price he had named in the hearing of the **Hittites** [+1201]:
23:18 of all the **Hittites** [+1201] who had come to the gate of the city.
23:20 the cave in it were deeded to Abraham by the **Hittites** [+1201] as a
25:10 the field Abraham had bought from the **Hittites** [+1201].
27:46 "I'm disgusted with living because of these **Hittite** women.
27:46 from **Hittite** women like these, my life will not be worth living."
49:32 and the cave in it were bought from the **Hittites** [+1201]."
1Ch 1:13 Canaan was the father of Sidon his firstborn, and of the **Hittites**,

3148 חָטָא ḥāṭā', v. Not used in NIV/BHS

3149 חָתָה ḥātâ, v. [4] [→ 4746]

heap [1], scoop [1], snatch up [1], taking [1]

Ps 52:5 [52:7] [A] *He will* **snatch** you **up** and tear you from your tent;
Pr 6:27 [A] *Can* a man **scoop** fire into his lap without his clothes being
25:22 [A] In doing this, you *will* **heap** burning coals on his head,
Isa 30:14 [A] not a fragment will be found for **taking** coals from a hearth

3150 חִתָּה ḥittâ, n.f. [1] [√ 3169]

terror [1]

Ge 35:5 and the **terror** *of* God fell upon the towns all around them

3151 חִתּוּל ḥittûl, n.[m.]. [1] [√ 3156]

splint [1]

Eze 30:21 It has not been bound up for healing or put in a **splint** so as to

3152 חַתְחַת ḥatḥat, n.[m.]. [1] [√ 3169]

dangers [1]

Ecc 12:5 when men are afraid of heights and of **dangers** in the streets;

3153 חִתִּי ḥittî, a.g. [48] [√ 3147]

Hittites [25], Hittite [23]

Ge 15:20 **Hittites**, Perizzites, Rephaites,
23:10 Ephron the **Hittite** was sitting among his people and he replied to
25:9 near Mamre, in the field of Ephron son of Zohar the **Hittite**,
26:34 forty years old, he married Judith daughter of Beeri the **Hittite**,
26:34 Beeri the Hittite, and also Basemath daughter of Elon the **Hittite**.
36:2 Adah daughter of Elon the **Hittite**, and Oholibamah daughter of
49:29 me with my fathers in the cave in the field of Ephron the **Hittite**,
49:30 which Abraham bought as a burial place from Ephron the **Hittite**,
50:13 Abraham had bought as a burial place from Ephron the **Hittite**,
Ex 3:8 **Hittites**, Amorites, Perizzites, Hivites and Jebusites.
3:17 **Hittites**, Amorites, Perizzites, Hivites and Jebusites—
13:5 land of the Canaanites, **Hittites**, Amorites, Hivites and Jebusites—
23:23 **Hittites**, Perizzites, Canaanites, Hivites and Jebusites, and I will
23:28 you to drive the Hivites, Canaanites and **Hittites** out of your way.
33:2 Amorites, **Hittites**, Perizzites, Hivites and Jebusites.
34:11 Canaanites, **Hittites**, Perizzites, Hivites and Jebusites.
Nu 13:29 the **Hittites**, Jebusites and Amorites live in the hill country;
Dt 7:1 the **Hittites**, Girgashites, Amorites, Canaanites, Perizzites,
20:17 the **Hittites**, Amorites, Canaanites, Perizzites, Hivites
Jos 1:4 and from the great river, the Euphrates—all the **Hittite** country—
3:10 **Hittites**, Hivites, Perizzites, Girgashites, Amorites and Jebusites.
9:1 coast of the Great Sea as far as Lebanon (the kings of the **Hittites**,
11:3 the Amorites, **Hittites**, Perizzites and Jebusites in the hill country;
12:8 the lands of the **Hittites**, Amorites, Canaanites, Perizzites,
24:11 Perizzites, Canaanites, **Hittites**, Girgashites, Hivites and Jebusites,
Jdg 1:26 He then went to the land of the **Hittites**, where he built a city
3:5 **Hittites**, Amorites, Perizzites, Hivites and Jebusites.
1Sa 26:6 David then asked Ahimelech the **Hittite** and Abishai son of
2Sa 11:3 the daughter of Eliam and the wife of Uriah the **Hittite**?"
11:6 "Send me Uriah the **Hittite**." And Joab sent him to David.
11:17 of the men in David's army fell; moreover, Uriah the **Hittite** died.
11:21 then say to him, 'Also, your servant Uriah the **Hittite** is dead.' "
11:24 men died. Moreover, your servant Uriah the **Hittite** is dead."
12:9 You struck down Uriah the **Hittite** with the sword and took his
12:10 despised me and took the wife of Uriah the **Hittite** to be your own.'
23:39 and Uriah the **Hittite**. There were thirty-seven in all.
1Ki 9:20 **Hittites**, Perizzites, Hivites and Jebusites (these peoples were not
10:29 They also exported them to all the kings of the **Hittites** and of the
11:1 Moabites, Ammonites, Edomites, Sidonians and **Hittites**.
15:5 all the days of his life—except in the case of Uriah the **Hittite**.
2Ki 7:6 the king of Israel has hired the **Hittite** and Egyptian kings to attack
1Ch 11:41 Uriah the **Hittite**, Zabad son of Ahlai,
2Ch 1:17 They also exported them to all the kings of the **Hittites** and of the
8:7 All the people left from the **Hittites**, Amorites, Perizzites,
Ezr 9:1 **Hittites**, Perizzites, Jebusites, Ammonites, Moabites, Egyptians
Ne 9:8 **Hittites**, Amorites, Perizzites, Jebusites and Girgashites.
Eze 16:3 your father was an Amorite and your mother a **Hittite**.
16:45 Your mother was a **Hittite** and your father an Amorite.

3154 חִתִּית ḥittît, n.f. [8] [√ 3169]

terror [8]

Eze 26:17 and your citizens; you put your **terror** on all who lived there.
32:23 All who had spread **terror** in the land of the living are slain,
32:24 All who had spread **terror** in the land of the living went down
32:25 Because their **terror** had spread in the land of the living, they bear
32:26 the sword because they spread their **terror** in the land of the living.
32:27 though the **terror** *of* these warriors had stalked through the land of
32:30 they went down with the slain in disgrace despite the **terror** caused
32:32 Although I had him spread **terror** in the land of the living,

3155 חָתַךְ ḥātak, v. [1]

are decreed [1]

Da 9:24 [C] "Seventy 'sevens' **are decreed** for your people and your holy

3156 חָתַל ḥātal, v. [2] [→ 3151, 3157]

wrapped in cloths [+3156] [2]

Eze 16:4 [E] nor were you rubbed with salt or **wrapped** [+3156] **in cloths**.
16:4 [H] nor were you rubbed with salt or **wrapped in cloths** [+3156].

3157 חֲתֻלָּה ḥᵃtullâ, n.f. [1] [√ 3156]

wrapped [1]

Job 38:9 I made the clouds its garment and **wrapped** it in thick darkness,

3158 חֶתְלוֹן ḥetlôn, n.pr.loc. [2]

Hethlon [2]

Eze 47:15 "On the north side it will run from the Great Sea by the **Hethlon**
48:1 it will follow the **Hethlon** road to Lebo Hamath; Hazar Enan

3159 חָתַם ḥātam, v. [26 / 25] [→ 2597, 2598, 3160; Ar 10291]

sealed [12], seal up [2], seal [2], affixing seals [1], be sealed up [1], blocked [1], enclosed [1], model [1], placed seal [+928+2597] [1], seals off [+1237] [1], shut in [1], stops [1]

Lev 15: 3 [G] Whether it continues flowing from his body or *is* **blocked**,
Dt 32: 34 [B] "Have I not kept this in reserve and **sealed** it in my vaults?
1Ki 21: 8 [A] **placed** his **seal** [+928+2597] *on* them, and sent them to the
Ne 9: 38 [10:1] [B] and our priests *are* **affixing** their **seals** to it."
10: 1 [10:2] [B] Those *who* **sealed** it were: Nehemiah the governor,
Est 3: 12 [C] name of King Xerxes himself and **sealed** with his own ring.
8: 8 [A] as seems best to you, and **seal** it with the king's signet ring—
8: 8 [C] in the king's name and **sealed** with his ring can be revoked."
8: 10 [A] **sealed** the dispatches with the king's signet ring, and sent
Job 9: 7 [A] it does not shine; *he* **seals** [+1237] **off** the light of the stars.
14: 17 [B] My offenses *will* **be sealed up** in a bag; you will cover over
24: 16 [D] men break into houses, but by day *they* **shut** themselves **in**;
33: 16 [g] and terrify [BHS *seal*; NIV 3169] them with warnings,
37: 7 [A] may know his work, *he* **stops** every man from his labor.
SS 4: 12 [B] my bride; you are a spring **enclosed**, a sealed fountain.
Isa 8: 16 [A] up the testimony and **seal up** the law among my disciples.
29: 11 [B] you this whole vision is nothing but words **sealed** in a scroll.
29: 11 [B] "Read this, please," he will answer, "I can't; it *is* **sealed**."
Jer 32: 10 [A] I signed and **sealed** the deed, had it witnessed, and weighed
32: 11 [B] the **sealed** *copy* containing the terms and conditions, as well
32: 14 [B] both the **sealed** and unsealed copies of the deed of purchase,
32: 44 [A] be signed, **sealed** and witnessed in the territory of Benjamin,
Eze 28: 12 [A] " 'You were the **model** *of* perfection, full of wisdom
Da 9: 24 [g] [to **put an end** [K; see Q 9462] *to* sin, to atone for]
9: 24 [A] to **seal up** vision and prophecy and to anoint the most holy.
12: 4 [A] and **seal** the words of the scroll until the time of the end.
12: 9 [B] the words are closed up and **sealed** until the time of the end.

3160 חֹתֶמֶת ḥōtemet, n.f. [1] [√ 3159]

seal [1]

Ge 38: 25 "See if you recognize whose **seal** and cord and staff these are."

3161 חָתַן ḥātan, v.den. [11] [√ 3163]

son-in-law [5], intermarry [4], allied himself by marriage [1], made an alliance [1]

Ge 34: 9 [F] **Intermarry** *with* us; give us your daughters and take our
Dt 7: 3 [F] *Do* not **intermarry** with them. Do not give your daughters to
Jos 23: 12 [F] and if *you* **intermarry** with them and associate with them,
1Sa 18: 21 [F] *you have* a second opportunity *to become* my **son-in-law**."
18: 22 [F] his attendants all like you; now *become* his **son-in-law**.' "
18: 23 [F] think it is a small matter *to become* the king's **son-in-law**?
18: 26 [F] he was pleased to *become* the king's **son-in-law**.
18: 27 [F] to the king so that *he might become* the king's **son-in-law**.
1Ki 3: 1 [F] Solomon **made an alliance** with Pharaoh king of Egypt
2Ch 18: 1 [F] and honor, and *he* **allied himself** with Ahab **by marriage**.
Ezr 9: 14 [F] **intermarry** with the peoples who commit such detestable

3162 חֹתֵן ḥōtēn, n.vbl. [21] [√ 3163]

father-in-law [19], brother-in-law [1], him[s] [+2257] [1]

Ex 3: 1 Now Moses was tending the flock of Jethro his **father-in-law**,
4: 18 Then Moses went back to Jethro his **father-in-law** and said to him,
18: 1 Now Jethro, the priest of Midian and **father-in-law** *of* Moses,
18: 2 sent away his wife Zipporah, his **father-in-law** Jethro received her
18: 5 Jethro, Moses' **father-in-law**, together with Moses' sons and wife,
18: 6 Jethro had sent word to him, "I, your **father-in-law** Jethro,
18: 7 So Moses went out to meet his **father-in-law** and bowed down
18: 8 Moses told his **father-in-law** about everything the LORD had
18: 12 Then Jethro, Moses' **father-in-law**, brought a burnt offering
18: 12 to eat bread with Moses' **father-in-law** in the presence of God.
18: 14 When his **father-in-law** saw all that Moses was doing for the
18: 15 Moses answered **him**[s] [+2257], "Because the people come to me to
18: 17 Moses' **father-in-law** replied, "What you are doing is not good.
18: 24 Moses listened to his **father-in-law** and did everything he said.
18: 27 Moses sent his **father-in-law** on his way, and Jethro returned to his
Nu 10: 29 said to Hobab son of Reuel the Midianite, Moses' **father-in-law**,
Jdg 1: 16 The descendants of Moses' **father-in-law**, the Kenite, went up
4: 11 other Kenites, the descendants of Hobab, Moses' **brother-in-law**,
19: 4 His **father-in-law**, the girl's father, prevailed upon him to stay;
19: 7 his **father-in-law** persuaded him, so he stayed there that night.
19: 9 his concubine and his servant, got up to leave, his **father-in-law**,

3163 חָתָן ḥātān, n.m. [20] [→ 3161, 3162, 3164, 3165]

bridegroom [10], son-in-law [6], sons-in-law [3], related by marriage [1]

Ge 19: 12 **sons-in-law**, sons or daughters, or anyone else in the city who
19: 14 So Lot went out and spoke to his **sons-in-law**, who were pledged
19: 14 to destroy the city!" But his **sons-in-law** thought he was joking.
Ex 4: 25 with it. "Surely you are a **bridegroom** *of* blood to me," she said.
4: 26 (At that time she said "**bridegroom** *of* blood," referring to
Jdg 15: 6 they were told, "Samson, the Timnite's **son-in-law**, because his
19: 5 he prepared to leave, but the girl's father said to his **son-in-law**,
1Sa 18: 18 clan in Israel, that I should become the king's **son-in-law**?"
22: 14 the king's **son-in-law**, captain of your bodyguard and highly
2Ki 8: 27 Ahab had done, for he was **related by marriage** *to* Ahab's family.
Ne 6: 18 oath to him, since he was **son-in-law** to Shecaniah son of Arah,
13: 28 Eliashib the high priest was **son-in-law** to Sanballat the Horonite.
Ps 19: 5 [19:6] which is like a **bridegroom** coming forth from his
Isa 61: 10 of righteousness, as a **bridegroom** adorns his head like a priest,
62: 5 as a **bridegroom** rejoices over his bride, so will your God rejoice
Jer 7: 34 and to the voices of bride and **bridegroom** in the towns of Judah
16: 9 and to the voices of bride and **bridegroom** in this place.
25: 10 sounds of joy and gladness, the voices of bride and **bridegroom**,
33: 11 sounds of joy and gladness, the voices of bride and **bridegroom**,
Joel 2: 16 Let the **bridegroom** leave his room and the bride her chamber.

3164 חֲתֻנָּה ḥ[a]tunnâ, n.f. [1] [√ 3163]

wedding [1]

SS 3: 11 with which his mother crowned him on the day of his **wedding**,

3165 חֹתֶנֶת ḥōtenet, n.f.vbl. [1] [√ 3163]

mother-in-law [1]

Dt 27: 23 "Cursed is the man who sleeps with his **mother-in-law**." Then all

3166 חָתַף ḥātap, v. [1] [→ 3167]

snatches away [1]

Job 9: 12 [A] If *he* **snatches away**, who can stop him? Who can say to

3167 חֶתֶף ḥetep, n.[m.]. [1] [√ 3166]

bandit [1]

Pr 23: 28 Like a **bandit** she lies in wait, and multiplies the unfaithful among

3168 חָתַר ḥātar, v. [8] [→ 4747]

dug [3], dig [2], break into [1], dig down [1], row [1]

Job 24: 16 [A] In the dark, *men* **break into** houses, but by day they shut
Eze 8: 8 [A] He said to me, "Son of man, now **dig** into the wall." So I dug
8: 8 [A] the wall." So *I* **dug** into the wall and saw a doorway there.
12: 5 [A] **dig** through the wall and take your belongings out through it.
12: 7 [A] Then in the evening *I* **dug** through the wall with my hands.
12: 12 [A] and a hole *will be* **dug** in the wall for him to go through.
Am 9: 2 [A] Though *they* **dig down** to the depths of the grave, from there
Jnh 1: 13 [A] Instead, the men *did their best to* **row** back to land. But they

3169 חָתַת ḥātat, v. [53 / 54] [→ 3145, 3146, 3150, 3152, 3154, 3170, 3171?, 4744?, 4745]

discouraged [10], terrified [9], dismayed [7], shattered [7], filled with terror [3], terrify [3], afraid [2], be shattered [2], shatter [2], broken [1], cracked [1], dreaded [1], fail [1], frighten [1], frightened [1], panic [1], stood in awe [1], terror [1]

Dt 1: 21 [C] told you. Do not be afraid; *do* not *be* **discouraged**."
31: 8 [C] nor forsake you. Do not be afraid; *do* not *be* **discouraged**."
Jos 1: 9 [C] *do* not *be* **discouraged**, for the LORD your God will be
8: 1 [C] said to Joshua, "Do not be afraid; *do* not *be* **discouraged**.
10: 25 [C] said to them, "Do not be afraid; *do* not *be* **discouraged**.
1Sa 2: 10 [C] those who oppose the LORD *will* **be shattered**. He will
17: 11 [C] Saul and all the Israelites *were* **dismayed** and terrified.
2Ki 19: 26 [A] drained of power, *are* **dismayed** and put to shame.
1Ch 22: 13 [C] Be strong and courageous. Do not be afraid or **discouraged**.
28: 20 [C] Do not be afraid or **discouraged**, for the LORD God,
2Ch 20: 15 [C] 'Do not be afraid or **discouraged** because of this vast army.
20: 17 [C] and Jerusalem. Do not be afraid; *do* not *be* **discouraged**.
32: 7 [C] Do not be afraid or **discouraged** because of the king of
Job 7: 14 [D] even then *you* **frighten** me with dreams and terrify me with
31: 34 [G] and so **dreaded** the contempt of the clans that I kept silent
32: 15 [A] "*They are* **dismayed** and have no more to say; words have
33: 16 [G] in their ears and **terrify** [BHS 3159] them with warnings,
39: 22 [C] He laughs at fear, **afraid** *of* nothing; he does not shy away
Isa 7: 8 [C] Within sixty-five years Ephraim *will* **be** too **shattered** to be a
8: 9 [A] Raise the war cry, you nations, and *be* **shattered**! Listen,
8: 9 [A] Prepare for battle, and *be* **shattered**! Prepare for battle,
8: 9 [A] and be shattered! Prepare for battle, and *be* **shattered**!
9: 4 [9:3] [G] *you have* **shattered** the yoke that burdens them, the
20: 5 [A] and boasted in Egypt *will be* **afraid** and put to shame.
30: 31 [C] The voice of the LORD *will* **shatter** Assyria; with his
31: 4 [C] *he is* not **frightened** by their shouts or disturbed by their
31: 9 [A] at sight of the battle standard their commanders *will* **panic**,"

Isa 37:27 [A] drained of power, *are* **dismayed** and put to shame.
51: 6 [C] salvation will last forever, my righteousness *will* never **fail**.
51: 7 [C] not fear the reproach of men or *be* **terrified** by their insults.
Jer 1:17 [C] *Do* not *be* **terrified** by them, or I will terrify you before
1:17 [G] not be terrified by them, or *I will* **terrify** you before them.
8: 9 [A] will be put to shame; *they will be* **dismayed** and trapped.
10: 2 [C] the ways of the nations or *be* **terrified** by signs in the sky,
10: 2 [C] by signs in the sky, though the nations *are* **terrified** by them.
14: 4 [A] The ground *is* **cracked** because there is no rain in the land;
17:18 [C] from shame; *let* them *be* **terrified**, but keep me from terror.
17:18 [C] from shame; let them be terrified, but *keep* me from **terror**.
23: 4 [C] they will no longer be afraid or **terrified**, nor will any be
30:10 [C] *do* not *be* **dismayed**, O Israel,' declares the LORD.
46:27 [C] not fear, O Jacob my servant; *do* not *be* **dismayed**, O Israel.
48: 1 [A] and captured; the stronghold will be disgraced and **shattered**.
48:20 [A] Moab is disgraced, for *she is* **shattered**. Wail and cry out!
48:39 [A] "How **shattered** *she is*! How they wail! How Moab turns her
49:37 [G] *I will* **shatter** Elam before their foes, before those who seek
50: 2 [A] Bel will be put to shame, Marduk **filled with terror**.
50: 2 [A] images will be put to shame and her idols **filled with terror**.'
50:36 [A] sword against her warriors! *They will be* **filled with terror**.
51:56 [D] her warriors will be captured, and their bows *will be* **broken**.
Eze 2: 6 [C] Do not be afraid of what they say or **terrified** by them,
3: 9 [C] Do not be afraid of them or **terrified** by them, though they
Ob 1: 9 [A] Your warriors, O Teman, *will be* **terrified**, and everyone in
Hab 2:17 [G] and your destruction of animals *will* **terrify** you.
Mal 2: 5 [C] and he revered me and **stood in awe** of my name.

3170 חֲתַתִי **ḥ*a*tat[1]**, n.[m.]. [1] [→ 3170; cf. 3169]

something dreadful [1]

Job 6:21 to be of no help; you see **something dreadful** and are afraid.

3171 חֲתַת² **ḥ*a*tat[2]**, n.pr.m. [1] [√ 3170?; cf. 3169?]

Hathath [1]

1Ch 4:13 and Seraiah. The sons of Othniel: **Hathath** and Meonothai.

ט, ṭ

3172 ט **ṭ**, letter. Not used in NIV/BHS [→ Ar 10292]

3173 טֵאטֵא **ṭēʼṭēʼ**, v. [1] [→ 4748; cf. 3226]

sweep [1]

Isa 14:23 [D] *I will* **sweep** her with the broom of destruction,"

3174 טָבְאַל **ṭāb*e*ʼal**, n.pr.m. [1] [√ 3202 + 446]

Tabeel [1]

Isa 7: 6 it among ourselves, and make the son of **Tabeel** king over it."

3175 טָבְאֵל **ṭāb*e*ʼēl**, n.pr.m. [1] [√ 3202 + 446]

Tabeel [1]

Ezr 4: 7 **Tabeel** and the rest of his associates wrote a letter to Artaxerxes.

3176 טבב **ṭābab**, v. Not used in NIV/BHS [√ 3201]

3177 טִבָּה **ṭibbâ**, n.f. Not used in NIV/BHS

3178 טְבוּלִים **ṭ*e*bûlîm**, n.m. [1]

turbans [1]

Eze 23:15 with belts around their waists and flowing **turbans** on their heads;

3179 טַבּוּר **ṭabbûr**, n.[m.]. [2]

center [2]

Jdg 9:37 "Look, people are coming down from the **center** *of* the land,
Eze 38:12 rich in livestock and goods, living at the **center** *of* the land."

3180 טבח **ṭābaḥ**, v. [11] [→ 3181, 3184, 3185, 3186, 4749]

slaughter [3], slaughtered [3], be slaughtered [1], prepared [1], slaughter [+3181] [1], slaughters [1], slay [1]

Ge 43:16 [A] men to my house, **slaughter** an animal and prepare dinner;
Ex 22: 1 [21:37] [A] steals an ox or a sheep and **slaughters** it or sells it,
Dt 28:31 [B] Your ox *will* **be slaughtered** before your eyes, but you will
1Sa 25:11 [A] and water, and the meat *I have* **slaughtered** for my shearers,
Ps 37:14 [A] the poor and needy, to **slay** those whose ways are upright.
Pr 9: 2 [A] *She has* **prepared** her meat and mixed her wine; she has also
Jer 11:19 [A] I had been like a gentle lamb led to the **slaughter**; I did not
25:34 [A] For your time to *be* **slaughtered** has come; you will fall
51:40 [A] "I will bring them down like lambs to the **slaughter**,
La 2:21 [A] day of your anger; *you have* **slaughtered** them without pity.
Eze 21:10 [21:15] [A] sharpened for the **slaughter** [+3181], polished to

3181 טֶבַח¹ **ṭebaḥ[1]**, n.m. [12] [→ 3182; cf. 18, 3180]

slaughter [9], animal [1], meat [1], slaughter [+3180] [1]

Ge 43:16 these men to my house, slaughter an **animal** and prepare dinner;
Pr 7:22 All at once he followed her like an ox going to the **slaughter**,
9: 2 She has prepared her **meat** and mixed her wine; she has also set
Isa 34: 2 He will totally destroy them, he will give them over to **slaughter**.
34: 6 LORD has a sacrifice in Bozrah and a great **slaughter** in Edom.
53: 7 he was led like a lamb to the **slaughter**, and as a sheep before her
65:12 you for the sword, and you will all bend down for the **slaughter**;
Jer 48:15 her finest young men will go down in the **slaughter**,"
50:27 Kill all her young bulls; let them go down to the **slaughter**!
Eze 21:10 [21:15] sharpened for the **slaughter** [+3180], polished to flash
21:15 [21:20] is made to flash like lightning, it is grasped for **slaughter**.
21:28 [21:33] " 'A sword, a sword, drawn for the **slaughter**, polished to

3182 טֶבַח² **ṭebaḥ[2]**, n.pr.m. [1] [√ 3181]

Tebah [1]

Ge 22:24 was Reumah, also had sons: **Tebah**, Gaham, Tahash and Maacah.

3183 טֶבַח³ **ṭebaḥ[3]**, n.pr.loc. [0 / 1] [cf. 3187]

Tebah [1]

2Sa 8: 8 From **Tebah** [BHS 1056] and Berothai, towns that belonged to

3184 טַבָּח **ṭabbāḥ**, n.m. [32] [→ 3185; cf. 3180; Ar 10295]

guard [13], imperial guard [12], *untranslated* [5], cook [2]

Ge 37:36 to Potiphar, one of Pharaoh's officials, the captain of the **guard**.
39: 1 who was one of Pharaoh's officials, the captain of the **guard**,
40: 3 and put them in custody in the house of the captain of the **guard**,
40: 4 The captain of the **guard** assigned them to Joseph, and he attended
41:10 and the chief baker in the house of the captain of the **guard**.
41:12 Hebrew was there with us, a servant of the captain of the **guard**.
1Sa 9:23 Samuel said to the **cook**, "Bring the piece of meat I gave you,
9:24 So the **cook** took up the leg with what was on it and set it in front
2Ki 25: 8 Nebuzaradan commander of the **imperial guard**, an official of the
25:10 Babylonian army, under the commander of the **imperial guard**,
25:11 Nebuzaradan the commander of the **guard** carried into exile the
25:12 the commander **[RPH]** left behind some of the poorest people of
25:15 The commander of the **imperial guard** took away the censers
25:18 The commander of the **guard** took as prisoners Seraiah the chief
25:20 Nebuzaradan the commander **[RPH]** took them all and brought
Jer 39: 9 Nebuzaradan commander of the **imperial guard** carried into exile
39:10 Nebuzaradan the commander of the **guard** left behind in the land
39:11 Jeremiah through Nebuzaradan commander of the **imperial guard**:
39:13 So Nebuzaradan the commander of the **guard**, Nebushazban a
40: 1 commander of the **imperial guard** had released him at Ramah.
40: 2 When the commander of the **guard** found Jeremiah, he said to him,
40: 5 Then the commander **[RPH]** gave him provisions and a present
41:10 over whom Nebuzaradan commander of the **imperial guard** had
43: 6 of the **imperial guard** had left with Gedaliah son of Ahikam,
52:12 Nebuzaradan commander of the **imperial guard**, who served the
52:14 of the **imperial guard** broke down all the walls around Jerusalem.
52:15 Nebuzaradan the commander of the **guard** carried into exile some
52:16 Nebuzaradan **[RPH]** left behind the rest of the poorest people of
52:19 The commander of the **imperial guard** took away the basins,
52:24 The commander of the **guard** took as prisoners Seraiah the chief
52:26 Nebuzaradan the commander **[RPH]** took them all and brought
52:30 into exile by Nebuzaradan the commander of the **imperial guard**.

3185 טַבָּחָה **ṭabbāḥâ**, n.f. [1] [√ 3184; cf. 3180]

cooks [1]

1Sa 8:13 He will take your daughters to be perfumers and **cooks** and bakers.

3186 טִבְחָה **ṭibḥâ**, n.f. [3] [√ 3180]

butchered [1], meat [1], slaughtered [1]

1Sa 25:11 and water, and the **meat** I have slaughtered for my shearers,
Ps 44:22 [44:23] day long; we are considered as sheep to be **slaughtered**.
Jer 12: 3 my thoughts about you. Drag them off like sheep to be **butchered**!

3187 טִבְחַת **ṭibḥat**, n.pr.loc. [1] [cf. 1056, 3183]

Tebah [1]

1Ch 18: 8 From **Tebah** and Cun, towns that belonged to Hadadezer,

3188 טָבַל ṭābal, v. [16]

dip [8], dipped [4], bathe [1], plunge [1], soaked [1], touched [1]

Ge 37:31 [A] slaughtered a goat and **dipped** the robe in the blood.
Ex 12:22 [A] **dip** it into the blood in the basin and put some of the blood
Lev 4: 6 [A] He *is to* **dip** his finger into the blood and sprinkle some of it
4:17 [A] He *shall* **dip** his finger into the blood and sprinkle it before
9: 9 [A] *he* **dipped** his finger into the blood and put it on the horns of
14: 6 [A] He is then to take the live bird and **dip** it, together with the
14:16 [A] **dip** his right forefinger into the oil in his palm, and with his
14:51 [A] **dip** them into the blood of the dead bird and the fresh water,
Nu 19:18 [A] **dip** it in the water and sprinkle the tent and all the
Dt 33:24 [A] be favored by his brothers, and *let him* **bathe** his feet in oil.
Jos 3:15 [C] reached the Jordan and their feet **touched** the water's edge,
Ru 2:14 [A] over here. Have some bread and **dip** it in the wine vinegar."
1Sa 14:27 [A] staff that was in his hand and **dipped** it into the honeycomb.
2Ki 5:14 [A] he went down and **dipped** *himself* in the Jordan seven times,
8:15 [A] **soaked** it in water and spread it over the king's face, so that
Job 9:31 [A] *you would* **plunge** me into a slime pit so that even my

3189 טְבַלְיָהוּ ṭ[e]balyāhû, n.pr.m. [1] [√ 3228 + 4200? + 3378?]

Tabaliah [1]

1Ch 26:11 Hilkiah the second, **Tabaliah** the third and Zechariah the fourth.

3190 טָבַע ṭābaʿ, v. [10] [→ 3191, 3192]

sink [2], sunk [2], are drowned [1], fallen [1], sank down [1], sank [1], were set [1], were settled in place [1]

Ex 15: 4 [E] The best of Pharaoh's officers **are drowned** in the Red Sea.
1Sa 17:49 [A] The stone **sank** into his forehead, and he fell facedown on
Job 38: 6 [H] On what **were** its footings **set**, or who laid its cornerstone—
Ps 9:15 [9:16] [A] The nations *have* **fallen** into the pit they have dug;
69: 2 [69:3] [A] *I* **sink** in the miry depths, where there is no foothold.
69:14 [69:15] [A] Rescue me from the mire, *do* not *let me* **sink**;
Pr 8:25 [H] before the mountains **were settled in place**, before the hills,
Jer 38: 6 [A] water in it, only mud, and Jeremiah **sank down** into the mud.
38:22 [H] Your feet *are* **sunk** in the mud; your friends have deserted
La 2: 9 [A] Her gates *have* **sunk** into the ground; their bars he has

3191 טַבָּעוֹת ṭabbāʿôt, n.pr.m. [2] [√ 3192; cf. 3190]

Tabbaoth [2]

Ezr 2:43 The temple servants: the descendants of Ziha, Hasupha, **Tabbaoth**,
Ne 7:46 The temple servants: the descendants of Ziha, Hasupha, **Tabbaoth**,

3192 טַבַּעַת ṭabbaʿat, n.f. [49] [→ 3191; cf. 3190]

rings [34], ring [5], signet ring [5], signet rings [2], them[s] [+2021] [1], them[s] [+2021] [1], them[s] [+2021+9109] [1]

Ge 41:42 Pharaoh took his **signet ring** from his finger and put it on Joseph's
Ex 25:12 Cast four gold **rings** for it and fasten them to its four feet,
25:12 its four feet, with two **rings** on one side and two rings on the other.
25:12 its four feet, with two rings on one side and two **rings** on the other.
25:14 Insert the poles into the **rings** on the sides of the chest to carry it.
25:15 The poles are to remain in the **rings** *of* this ark; they are not to be
25:26 Make four gold **rings** for the table and fasten them to the four
25:26 rings for the table and fasten **them**[s] [+2021] to the four corners,
25:27 The **rings** are to be close to the rim to hold the poles used in
26:24 from the bottom all the way to the top, and fitted into a single **ring**;
26:29 the frames with gold and make gold **rings** to hold the crossbars.
27: 4 and make a bronze **ring** at each of the four corners of the network.
27: 7 The poles are to be inserted into the **rings** so they will be on two
28:23 Make two gold **rings** for it and fasten them to two corners of the
28:23 and fasten **them**[s] [+2021+9109] to two corners of the breastpiece.
28:24 Fasten the two gold chains to the **rings** at the corners of the
28:26 Make two gold **rings** and attach them to the other two corners of
28:27 Make two more gold **rings** and attach them to the bottom of the
28:28 The **rings** *of* the breastpiece are to be tied to the rings of the ephod
28:28 The rings of the breastpiece are to be tied to the **rings** *of* the ephod
30: 4 Make two gold **rings** for the altar below the molding—two on
35:22 gold jewelry of all kinds: brooches, earrings, **rings** and ornaments.
36:29 from the bottom all the way to the top and fitted into a single **ring**;
36:34 the frames with gold and made gold **rings** to hold the crossbars.
37: 3 He cast four gold **rings** for it and fastened them to its four feet,
37: 3 its four feet, with two **rings** on one side and two rings on the other.
37: 3 its four feet, with two rings on one side and two **rings** on the other.
37: 5 he inserted the poles into the **rings** on the sides of the ark to carry
37:13 They cast four gold **rings** for the table and fastened them to the
37:13 rings for the table and fastened **them**[s] [+2021] to the four corners,
37:14 The **rings** were put close to the rim to hold the poles used in
37:27 They made two gold **rings** below the molding—two on opposite
38: 5 They cast bronze **rings** to hold the poles for the four corners of the
38: 7 They inserted the poles into the **rings** so they would be on the sides
39:16 They made two gold filigree settings and two gold **rings**,
39:16 and fastened the **rings** to two of the corners of the breastpiece.
39:17 They fastened the two gold chains to the **rings** at the corners of the
39:19 They made two gold **rings** and attached them to the other two
39:20 they made two more gold **rings** and attached them to the bottom of
39:21 They tied the **rings** *of* the breastpiece to the rings of the ephod with
39:21 They tied the rings of the breastpiece to the **rings** *of* the ephod with
Nu 31:50 armlets, bracelets, **signet rings**, earrings and necklaces—to make
Est 3:10 So the king took his **signet ring** from his finger and gave it to
3:12 in the name of King Xerxes himself and sealed with his own **ring**.
8: 2 The king took off his **signet ring**, which he had reclaimed from
8: 8 Jews as seems best to you, and seal it with the king's **signet ring**—
8: 8 in the king's name and sealed with his **ring** can be revoked."
8:10 sealed the dispatches with the king's **signet ring**, and sent them by
Isa 3:21 the **signet rings** and nose rings,

3193 טַבְרִמֹּן ṭabrimmōn, n.pr.m. [1] [√ 3202 + 8235]

Tabrimmon [1]

1Ki 15:18 it to his officials and sent them to Ben-Hadad son of **Tabrimmon**,

3194 טֵבֵת ṭēbēt, n.pr. [1]

Tebeth [1]

Est 2:16 tenth month, the month of **Tebeth**, in the seventh year of his reign.

3195 טַבָּת ṭabbāt, n.pr.loc. [1]

Tabbath [1]

Jdg 7:22 Zererah as far as the border of Abel Meholah near **Tabbath**.

3196 טָהוֹר ṭāhôr, a. [95] [√ 3197]

pure [42], clean [33], ceremonially clean [13], unclean [+4202] [3], ceremonially unclean [+1194] [1], flawless [1], free from impurity [1], unclean [+401] [1]

Ge 7: 2 Take with you seven of every kind of **clean** animal, a male
7: 2 and two of every kind of **unclean** [+4202] animal, a male
7: 8 Pairs of **clean** and unclean animals, of birds and of all creatures
7: 8 Pairs of clean and **unclean** [+401] animals, of birds and of all
8:20 taking some of all the **clean** animals and clean birds, he sacrificed
8:20 taking some of all the clean animals and **clean** birds, he sacrificed
Ex 25:11 Overlay it with **pure** gold, both inside and out, and make a gold
25:17 "Make an atonement cover of **pure** gold—two and a half cubits
25:24 Overlay it with **pure** gold and make a gold molding around it.
25:29 And make its plates and dishes of **pure** gold, as well as its pitchers
25:31 "Make a lampstand of **pure** gold and hammer it out, base and
25:36 be of one piece with the lampstand, hammered out of **pure** gold.
25:38 Its wick trimmers and trays are to be of **pure** gold.
25:39 A talent of **pure** gold is to be used for the lampstand and all these
28:14 two braided chains of **pure** gold, like a rope, and attach the chains
28:22 "For the breastpiece make braided chains of **pure** gold, like a rope.
28:36 "Make a plate of **pure** gold and engrave on it as on a seal:
30: 3 Overlay the top and all the sides and the horns with **pure** gold,
30:35 the work of a perfumer. It is to be salted and **pure** and sacred.
31: 8 and its articles, the **pure** gold lampstand and all its accessories,
37: 2 He overlaid it with **pure** gold, both inside and out, and made a gold
37: 6 He made the atonement cover of **pure** gold—two and a half cubits
37:11 they overlaid it with **pure** gold and made a gold molding around it.
37:16 And they made from **pure** gold the articles for the table—
37:17 They made the lampstand of **pure** gold and hammered it out,
37:22 all of one piece with the lampstand, hammered out of **pure** gold.
37:23 seven lamps, as well as its wick trimmers and trays, of **pure** gold.
37:24 the lampstand and all its accessories from one talent of **pure** gold.
37:26 overlaid the top and all the sides and the horns with **pure** gold,
37:29 They also made the sacred anointing oil and the **pure**,
39:15 For the breastpiece they made braided chains of **pure** gold,
39:25 they made bells of **pure** gold and attached them around the hem
39:30 the plate, the sacred diadem, out of **pure** gold and engraved on it,
39:37 the **pure** gold lampstand with its row of lamps and all its
Lev 4:12 he must take outside the camp to a place **ceremonially clean**,
6:11 [6:4] outside the camp to a place that is **ceremonially clean**.
7:19 As for other meat, anyone **ceremonially clean** may eat it.
10:10 the holy and the common, between the unclean and the **clean**,
10:14 Eat them in a **ceremonially clean** place; they have been given to
11:36 A spring, however, or a cistern for collecting water remains **clean**,
11:37 carcass falls on any seeds that are to be planted, they remain **clean**.
11:47 You must distinguish between the unclean and the **clean**, between
13:13 that person clean. Since it has all turned white, he is **clean**.
13:17 shall pronounce the infected person clean; then he will be **clean**.
13:37 is healed. He is **clean**, and the priest shall pronounce him clean.
13:39 harmless rash that has broken out on the skin; that person is **clean**.
13:40 "When a man has lost his hair and is bald, he is **clean**.
13:41 hair from the front of his scalp and has a bald forehead, he is **clean**.
14: 4 the priest shall order that two live **clean** birds and some cedar

[F] Hitpael (hitpoel, hitpoal, hitpolel, hitpolal, hitpalel, hitpalal, hitpalpel, hitpalpal, hotpael, hotpaal) [G] Hiphil (hiphtil) [H] Hophal [I] Hishtaphel

Lev 14:57 to determine when something is **clean** or unclean. These are the
15: 8 " 'If the man with the discharge spits on someone who is **clean**,
20:25 " 'You must therefore make a distinction between **clean**
20:25 and unclean animals and between unclean and **clean** birds.
24: 4 The lamps on the **pure** gold lampstand before the LORD must be
24: 6 six in each row, on the table of **pure** gold before the LORD.
Nu 5:28 the woman has not defiled herself and is **free from impurity**,
9:13 if a man who is **ceremonially clean** and not on a journey fails to
18:11 Everyone in your household who is **ceremonially clean** may eat it.
18:13 Everyone in your household who is **ceremonially clean** may eat it.
19: 9 "A man who is **clean** shall gather up the ashes of the heifer
19: 9 and put them in a **ceremonially clean** place outside the camp.
19:18 Then a man who is **ceremonially clean** is to take some hyssop,
19:19 The *man* who is **clean** is to sprinkle the unclean person on the
Dt 12:15 gives you. Both the ceremonially unclean and the **clean** may eat it.
12:22 or deer. Both the ceremonially unclean and the **clean** may eat.
14:11 You may eat any **clean** bird.
14:20 But any winged creature that is **clean** you may eat.
15:22 Both the ceremonially unclean and the **clean** may eat it, as if it
23:10 [23:11] If one of your men is **unclean** [+4202] because of a
1Sa 20:26 happened to David to make him **ceremonially unclean** [+1194]—
20:26 make him ceremonially unclean—surely he is **unclean** [+4202]."
1Ch 28:17 the weight of **pure** gold for the forks, sprinkling bowls
2Ch 3: 4 and twenty cubits high. He overlaid the inside with **pure** gold.
9:17 made a great throne inlaid with ivory and overlaid with **pure** gold.
13:11 They set out the bread on the **ceremonially clean** table and light
30:17 the Passover lambs for all *those who* were not **ceremonially clean**
Ezr 6:20 Levites had purified themselves and were all **ceremonially clean**.
Job 14: 4 Who can bring *what* is **pure** from the impure? No one!
17: 9 hold to their ways, and those with **clean** hands will grow stronger.
28:19 Cush cannot compare with it; it cannot be bought with **pure** gold.
Ps 12: 6 [12:7] the words of the LORD are **flawless**, like silver refined in
19: 9 [19:10] The fear of the LORD is **pure**, enduring forever. The
51:10 [51:12] Create in me a **pure** heart, O God, and renew a steadfast
Pr 15:26 thoughts of the wicked, but those of the **pure** are pleasing to him.
22:11 He who loves a **pure** heart and whose speech is gracious will have
30:12 those who are **pure** in their own eyes and yet are not cleansed of
Ecc 9: 2 and the wicked, the good and the bad, the **clean** and the unclean,
Isa 66:20 to the temple of the LORD in **ceremonially clean** vessels.
Eze 22:26 teach that there is no difference between the unclean and the **clean**;
36:25 I will sprinkle **clean** water on you, and you will be clean; I will
44:23 show them how to distinguish between the unclean and the **clean**.
Hab 1:13 Your eyes are too **pure** to look on evil; you cannot tolerate wrong.
Zec 3: 5 I said, "Put a **clean** turban on his head." So they put a clean turban
3: 5 So they put a **clean** turban on his head and clothed him,
Mal 1:11 place incense and **pure** offerings will be brought to my name,

3197 טָהֵר ***ṭāhēr***, v. [94 / 93] [→ 3196, 3198, 3199, 3200, 4756]

clean [23], be cleansed [12], cleanse [12], pronounce clean [9], cleansed [8], purify [7], purified [4], ceremonially clean [3], purify themselves [3], purified themselves [2], make ceremonially clean [1], pronounces clean [1], pronouncing clean [1], pure [1], purge [1], purged [1], purified themselves ceremonially [1], purifier [1], purify yourselves [1], unclean [+4202] [1]

Ge 35: 2 [F] with you, and **purify yourselves** and change your clothes.
Lev 11:32 [A] it will be unclean till evening, and then *it will be* **clean**.
12: 7 [A] then *she will be* **ceremonially clean** from her flow of blood.
12: 8 [A] priest will make atonement for her, and *she will be* **clean**.' "
13: 6 [D] not spread in the skin, the priest *shall* **pronounce** him **clean**;
13: 6 [A] a rash. The man must wash his clothes, and *he will be* **clean**.
13:13 [D] his whole body, *he shall* **pronounce** that person **clean**.
13:17 [D] the priest *shall* **pronounce** the infected person **clean**;
13:23 [D] scar from the boil, and the priest *shall* **pronounce** him **clean**.
13:28 [D] from the burn, and the priest *shall* **pronounce** him **clean**;
13:34 [D] more than skin deep, the priest *shall* **pronounce** him **clean**.
13:34 [A] him clean. He must wash his clothes, and *he will be* **clean**.
13:37 [D] He is clean, and the priest *shall* **pronounce** him **clean**.
13:58 [A] of the mildew, must be washed again, and *it will be* **clean**."
13:59 [D] any leather article, for **pronouncing** them **clean** or unclean.
14: 4 [F] and hyssop be brought for the *one to* **be cleansed**.
14: 7 [F] Seven times he shall sprinkle the *one to* **be cleansed** of the
14: 7 [D] cleansed of the infectious disease and **pronounce** him **clean**.
14: 8 [F] "The *person to* **be cleansed** must wash his clothes, shave off
14: 8 [A] and bathe with water; then *he will be* **ceremonially clean**.
14: 9 [A] and bathe himself with water, and *he will be* **clean**.
14:11 [D] The priest who **pronounces** him **clean** shall present both the
14:11 [F] him clean shall present both the one *to* **be cleansed**
14:14 [F] put it on the lobe of the right ear of the *one to* **be cleansed**,
14:17 [F] palm on the lobe of the right ear of the *one to* **be cleansed**,
14:18 [F] the priest shall put on the head of the *one to* **be cleansed**
14:19 [F] make atonement for the *one to* **be cleansed** from his
14:20 [A] and make atonement for him, and *he will be* **clean**.
14:25 [F] put it on the lobe of the right ear of the *one to* **be cleansed**,
14:28 [F] on the lobe of the right ear of the *one to* **be cleansed**, on the
14:29 [F] the priest shall put on the head of the *one to* **be cleansed**,
14:31 [F] before the LORD on behalf of the *one to* **be cleansed**."
14:48 [D] he *shall* **pronounce** the house **clean**, because the mildew is
14:53 [A] he will make atonement for the house, and *it will be* **clean**."
15:13 [A] " 'When a man *is* **cleansed** from his discharge, he is to count
15:13 [A] and bathe himself with fresh water, and *he will be* **clean**.
15:28 [A] " 'When *she is* **cleansed** from her discharge, she must count
15:28 [A] seven days, and after that *she will be* **ceremonially clean**.
16:19 [D] of the blood on it with his finger seven times *to* **cleanse** it
16:30 [D] on this day atonement will be made for you, to **cleanse** you.
16:30 [A] before the LORD, *you will be* **clean** from all your sins.
17:15 [A] be ceremonially unclean till evening; then *he will be* **clean**.
22: 4 [A] he may not eat the sacred offerings until *he is* **cleansed**.
22: 7 [A] When the sun goes down, *he will be* **clean**, and after that he
Nu 8: 6 [D] the other Israelites and **make** them **ceremonially clean**.
8: 7 [D] To **purify** them, do this: Sprinkle the water of cleansing on
8: 7 [F] and wash their clothes, and so **purify themselves**.
8:15 [D] "After *you have* **purified** the Levites and presented them as
8:21 [D] the LORD and made atonement for them to **purify** them.
19:12 [A] the third day and on the seventh day; then *he will be* **clean**.
19:12 [A] himself on the third and seventh days, *he will* not *be* **clean**.
19:19 [A] and bathe with water, and that evening *he will be* **clean**.
31:23 [A] fire must be put through the fire, and then *it will be* **clean**.
31:24 [A] On the seventh day wash your clothes and *you will be* **clean**.
Jos 22:17 [F] Up to this very day *we have* not **cleansed** ourselves from that
2Ki 5:10 [A] and your flesh will be restored and *you will be* **cleansed**."
5:12 [A] Couldn't I wash in them and *be* **cleansed**?" So he turned
5:13 [A] then, when he tells you, 'Wash and *be* **cleansed**'!"
5:14 [A] was restored and *became* **clean** like that of a young boy.
2Ch 29:15 [D] they went in to **purify** the temple of the LORD, as the king
29:16 [D] The priests went into the sanctuary of the LORD to **purify**
29:18 [A] "*We have* **purified** the entire temple of the LORD, the altar of
30:18 [F] Issachar and Zebulun *had* not **purified themselves**,
34: 3 [D] In his twelfth year he began to **purge** Judah and Jerusalem of
34: 5 [D] on their altars, and so *he* **purged** Judah and Jerusalem.
34: 8 [D] to **purify** the land and the temple, he sent Shaphan son of
Ezr 6:20 [F] The priests and Levites *had* **purified themselves** and were all
Ne 12:30 [F] and Levites *had* **purified themselves ceremonially**,
12:30 [D] *they* **purified** the people, the gates and the wall.
13: 9 [D] I gave orders *to* **purify** the rooms, and then I put back into
13:22 [F] Then I commanded the Levites *to* **purify themselves** and go
13:30 [D] So *I* **purified** the priests and the Levites of everything
Job 4:17 [A] than God? *Can* a man *be* more **pure** than his Maker?
37:21 [D] as it is in the skies after the wind has swept them **clean**.
Ps 51: 2 [51:4] [D] away all my iniquity and **cleanse** me from my sin.
51: 7 [51:9] [A] Cleanse me with hyssop, and *I will be* **clean**;
Pr 20: 9 [A] "I have kept my heart pure; *I am* **clean** and without sin"?
Isa 66:17 [F] who consecrate and **purify themselves** to go into the gardens,
Jer 13:27 [A] O Jerusalem! How long *will you be* **unclean** [+4202]?"
33: 8 [D] *I will* **cleanse** them from all the sin they have committed
Eze 22:24 [h] that *has* **had** no <u>rain</u> [BHS *has not been cleansed*; NIV 4763]
24:13 [D] Because *I tried to* **cleanse** you but you would not be
24:13 [A] but *you would* not *be* **cleansed** from your impurity,
24:13 [A] *you will* not *be* **clean** again until my wrath against you has
36:25 [A] I will sprinkle clean water on you, and *you will be* **clean**;
36:25 [D] *I will* **cleanse** you from all your impurities and from all your
36:33 [D] On the day I **cleanse** you from all your sins, I will resettle
37:23 [D] from all their sinful backsliding, and *I will* **cleanse** them.
39:12 [D] of Israel will be burying them in order to **cleanse** the land.
39:14 [D] " 'Men will be regularly employed to **cleanse** the land.
39:16 [D] Hamonah will be there.) And so *they will* **cleanse** the land.'
43:26 [D] days they are to make atonement for the altar and **cleanse** it;
Mal 3: 3 [D] He will sit as a refiner and **purifier** *of* silver; he will purify
3: 3 [D] *he will* **purify** the Levites and refine them like gold

3198 טֹהַר ***ṭōhar***, n.[m.]. [3] [√ 3197]

purification [2], clear [1]

Ex 24:10 like a pavement made of sapphire, **clear** as the sky itself.
Lev 12: 4 or go to the sanctuary until the days of her **purification** are over.
12: 6 " 'When the days of her **purification** for a son or daughter are

3199 טְהָר ***ṭᵉhār***, n.[m.]. [1] [√ 3197]

splendor [1]

Ps 89:44 [89:45] You have put an end to his **splendor** and cast his throne

3200 טָהֳרָה ***ṭohᵒrâ***, n.f. [13] [√ 3197]

cleansing [3], ceremonial cleansing [2], pronounced clean [2], purification [2], purified [2], clean [1], cleansed [1]

Lev 12: 4 the woman must wait thirty-three days to be **purified** from her

Lev 12: 5 she must wait sixty-six days to be **purified** from her bleeding.
13: 7 after he has shown himself to the priest to be **pronounced clean**,
13:35 if the itch does spread in the skin after he is **pronounced clean**,
14: 2 for the diseased person at the time of his **ceremonial cleansing**,
14:23 "On the eighth day he must bring them for his **cleansing** to the
14:32 and who cannot afford the regular offerings for his **cleansing**.
15:13 he is to count off seven days for his **ceremonial cleansing**;
Nu 6: 9 has dedicated, he must shave his head on the day of his **cleansing**—
1Ch 23:28 the **purification** of all sacred things and the performance of other
2Ch 30:19 even if he is not **clean** according to the rules of the sanctuary."
Ne 12:45 performed the service of their God and the service of **purification**,
Eze 44:26 After he is **cleansed**, he must wait seven days.

3201 ¹טוֹב *ṭôb¹*, v. [28] [→ 3176, 3202, 3203, 3204, 3205, 3206, 3208; cf. 3512; Ar 10293, 10320]

pleases [7], in high spirits [+4213] [5], better [+3201] [2], did well [2], feel better [2], beautiful [1], doing good [1], done well [1], favorably disposed [1], go well [1], make prosper [1], pleased [+928+6524] [1], pleasing [1], prosper [1], well off [1]

Nu 24: 1 [A] Now when Balaam saw that *it* **pleased** [+928+6524] the
24: 5 [A] "How **beautiful** *are* your tents, O Jacob, your dwelling
Dt 5:33 [A] so that you may live and **prosper** and prolong your days in
15:16 [A] he loves you and your family and *is* **well off** with you,
19:13 [A] of shedding innocent blood, so that *it may* **go well** with you.
Jdg 11:25 [A] Are you **better** [+3201] than Balak son of Zippor, king of
11:25 [A] Are you **better** [+3201] than Balak son of Zippor, king of
16:25 [A] While they *were* **in high** [+4213] **spirits**, they shouted,
1Sa 16:16 [A] spirit from God comes upon you, and you *will* **feel better**."
16:23 [A] he *would* **feel better**, and the evil spirit would leave him.
20:12 [A] If *he is* **favorably disposed** toward you, will I not send you
25:36 [A] He *was* **in high** [+4213] **spirits** and very drunk. So she told
2Sa 13:28 [A] When Amnon *is* **in high** [+4213] **spirits** from drinking wine
1Ki 8:18 [G] temple for my Name, *you* **did well** to have this in your heart.
2Ki 10:30 [G] "Because *you have* **done well** in accomplishing what is right
2Ch 6: 8 [G] temple for my Name, *you* **did well** to have this in your heart.
Ne 2: 5 [A] "If *it* **pleases** the king and if your servant has found favor in
2: 7 [A] I also said to him, "If *it* **pleases** the king, may I have letters
Est 1:10 [A] when King Xerxes *was* **in high** [+4213] **spirits** from wine,
1:19 [A] "Therefore, if *it* **pleases** the king, let him issue a royal decree
3: 9 [A] If *it* **pleases** the king, let a decree be issued to destroy them,
5: 4 [A] "If *it* **pleases** the king," replied Esther, "let the king,
5: 8 [A] if *it* **pleases** the king to grant my petition and fulfill my
5: 9 [A] Haman went out that day happy and **in high** [+4213] **spirits**.
7: 3 [A] O king, and if *it* **pleases** your majesty, grant me my life—
SS 4:10 [A] How much more **pleasing** *is* your love than wine,
Jer 32:41 [G] I will rejoice in **doing** them **good** and will assuredly plant
Eze 36:11 [G] as in the past and *will* **make** you **prosper** more than before.

3202 ²טוֹב *ṭôb²*, a. & n.m. [489] [→ 3204, 3208; cf. 3201; Ar 10294; *also used with compound proper names*]

good [241], better [64], best [17], well [10], fine [9], prosperity [9], right [7], better off [6], gracious [6], pleases [6], beautiful [+5260] [5], pleases [+928+6524] [5], favorable [4], goodness [4], precious [4], choice [3], kind [3], like [+928+6524] [3], *untranslated* [2], beautiful [2], favorably [2], glad [2], happy [2], please [+928+6524] [2], please [2], pleased [+928+6524] [2], pleasing [2], prospers [+5162] [2], rich [2], satisfaction [2], success [2], very well [2], alluring [+2834] [1], approve of [+928+6524] [1], attractive [1], benefited [1], better [+4946] [1], bounty [1], celebrating [+3427] [1], celebration [1], cheerful [1], delightful [1], favor [1], festive [1], fine [+1524+2256] [1], finest [1], flourishing [1], generous man [+6524] [1], graciously [1], handsome [+5260] [1], handsome [+9307] [1], handsome [1], happiness [1], healthier [1], help [1], impressive [1], intelligent [+8507] [1], joyful [1], likes [+928+2021+4200] [1], lovely [1], mean more [1], noble [1], pleasant [1], please [+928+2256+3838+6524] [1], pleased with [+928+6524] [1], prefer [+928+6524] [1], profitable [+6087] [1], profitable [1], prosper [+5162] [1], prosper [1], prospered [1], prosperous [1], relief [1], sinful [+4202] [1], sound [1], the other[s] [1], valid [1], wanted to do [+928+6524] [1], wealth [1], well off [1], well-being [1], wicked [+4202] [1], wish [+928+6524] [1], wished [+928+6524] [1], without equal [+401+4946] [1], worthwhile [1], wrong [+4202] [1]

Ge 1: 4 God saw that the light was **good**, and he separated the light from
1:10 gathered waters he called "seas." And God saw that it was **good**.
1:12 seed in it according to their kinds. And God saw that it was **good**.
1:18 and to separate light from darkness. And God saw that it was **good**.
1:21 winged bird according to its kind. And God saw that it was **good**.
1:25 the ground according to their kinds. And God saw that it was **good**.
1:31 God saw all that he had made, and it was very **good**. And there was
2: 9 the ground—trees that were pleasing to the eye and **good** for food.
2: 9 were the tree of life and the tree of the knowledge of **good** and evil.
2:12 (The gold of that land is **good**; aromatic resin and onyx are also
2:17 but you must not eat from the tree of the knowledge of **good**
2:18 The LORD God said, "It is not **good** for the man to be alone.
3: 5 will be opened, and you will be like God, knowing **good** and evil."
3: 6 When the woman saw that the fruit of the tree was **good** for food
3:22 "The man has now become like one of us, knowing **good** and evil.
6: 2 the sons of God saw that the daughters of men were **beautiful**,
15:15 will go to your fathers in peace and be buried at a **good** old age.
16: 6 your hands," Abram said. "Do with her whatever you think **best**."
18: 7 he ran to the herd and selected a **choice**, tender calf and gave it to a
19: 8 out to you, and you can do what you **like** [+928+6524] with them.
20:15 "My land is before you; live wherever you **like** [+928+6524]."
24:16 The girl was very **beautiful** [+5260], a virgin; no man had ever
24:50 the LORD; we can say nothing to you one way or **the other[s]**.
25: 8 Then Abraham breathed his last and died at a **good** old age,
26: 7 kill me on account of Rebekah, because she is **beautiful** [+5260]."
26:29 but always treated you **well** and sent you away in peace.
27: 9 Go out to the flock and bring me two **choice** young goats,
29:19 "It's **better** that I give her to you than to some other man.
30:20 Then Leah said, "God has presented me with a **precious** gift.
31:24 "Be careful not to say anything to Jacob, either **good** or bad."
31:29 'Be careful not to say anything to Jacob, either **good** or bad.'
40:16 When the chief baker saw that Joseph had given a **favorable**
41: 5 Seven heads of grain, healthy and **good**, were growing on a single
41:22 saw seven heads of grain, full and **good**, growing on a single stalk.
41:24 The thin heads of grain swallowed up the seven **good** heads.
41:26 The seven **good** cows are seven years, and the seven good heads of
41:26 are seven years, and the seven **good** heads of grain are seven years;
41:35 They should collect all the food of these **good** years that are
49:15 When he sees how **good** is his resting place and how pleasant is his
Ex 2: 2 When she saw that he was a **fine** *child*, she hid him for three
3: 8 to bring them up out of that land into a **good** and spacious land,
14:12 It would have been **better** for us to serve the Egyptians than to die
18:17 Moses' father-in-law replied, "What you are doing is not **good**.
Lev 27:10 He must not exchange it or substitute a **good** one for a bad one,
27:10 or substitute a good one for a bad one, or a bad one for a **good** *one*;
27:12 who will judge its quality as **good** or bad. Whatever value the
27:14 holy to the LORD, the priest will judge its quality as **good** or bad.
27:33 He must not pick out the **good** from the bad or make any
Nu 10:29 treat you well, for the LORD has promised **good** *things* to Israel."
10:32 we will share with you whatever **good** things the LORD gives
11:18 "If only we had meat to eat! We were **better off** in Egypt!"
13:19 What kind of land do they live in? Is it **good** or bad? What kind of
14: 3 as plunder. Wouldn't it be **better** for us to go back to Egypt?"
14: 7 "The land we passed through and explored is exceedingly **good**.
36: 6 They may marry anyone they **please** [+928+6524] as long as they
Dt 1:14 You answered me, "What you propose to do is **good**."
1:25 "It is a **good** land that the LORD our God is giving us."
1:35 "Not a man of this evil generation shall see the **good** land I swore
1:39 taken captive, your children who do not yet know **good** from bad—
3:25 Let me go over and see the **good** land beyond the Jordan—
3:25 good land beyond the Jordan—that **fine** hill country and Lebanon."
4:21 enter the **good** land the LORD your God is giving you as your
4:22 you are about to cross over and take possession of that **good** land.
6:10 give you—a land with large, **flourishing** cities you did not build,
6:18 Do what is right and **good** in the LORD's sight, so that it may go
6:18 take over the **good** land that the LORD promised on oath to your
6:24 so that we might always **prosper** and be kept alive, as is the case
8: 7 For the LORD your God is bringing you into a **good** land—
8:10 praise the LORD your God for the **good** land he has given you.
8:12 and are satisfied, when you build **fine** houses and settle down,
9: 6 that the LORD your God is giving you this **good** land to possess,
10:13 and decrees that I am giving you today for your own **good**?
11:17 you will soon perish from the **good** land the LORD is giving you.
12:28 because you will be doing what is **good** and right in the eyes of the
23:16 [23:17] live among you wherever he **likes** [+928+2021+4200] and
26:11 the aliens among you shall rejoice in all the **good** *things* the
28:12 the storehouse of his **bounty**, to send rain on your land in season
30: 9 The LORD will again delight in you and make you **prosperous**,
30:15 See, I set before you today life and **prosperity**, death
Jos 7:21 When I saw in the plunder a **beautiful** robe from Babylonia,
9:25 in your hands. Do to us whatever seems **good** and right to you."
21:45 Not one of all the LORD's **good** promises to the house of Israel
23:13 and thorns in your eyes, until you perish from this **good** land,
23:14 soul that not one of all the **good** promises the LORD your God
23:15 just as every **good** promise of the LORD your God has come true,
23:15 until he has destroyed you from this **good** land he has given you.
23:16 and you will quickly perish from the **good** land he has given you."
Jdg 8: 2 Aren't the gleanings of Ephraim's grapes **better** than the full grape
8:32 Gideon son of Joash died at a **good** old age and was buried in the
9: 2 "Ask all the citizens of Shechem, 'Which is **better** for you:
9:11 the fig tree replied, 'Should I give up my fruit, so **good** and sweet,
10:15 Do with us whatever you think **best**, but please rescue us now."
15: 2 Isn't her younger sister more **attractive**? Take her instead."

Jdg 18: 9 let's attack them! We have seen that the land is very **good**.
18:19 Isn't it **better** that you serve a tribe and clan in Israel as priest
19:24 you can use them and do to them whatever you **wish** [+928+6524].
Ru 2:22 "It will be **good** for you, my daughter, to go with his girls,
3:13 here for the night, and in the morning if he wants to redeem, **good**;
4:15 who loves you and who is **better** to you than seven sons, has given
1Sa 1: 8 are you downhearted? Don't I **mean more** to you than ten sons?"
1:23 "Do what seems **best** to you," Elkanah her husband told her.
2:24 it is not a **good** report that I hear spreading among the LORD's
2:26 to grow in stature and *in* **favor** with the LORD and with men.
3:18 Eli said, "He is the LORD; let him do what is **good** in his eyes."
8:14 He will take the **best** of your fields and vineyards and olive groves
8:16 Your menservants and maidservants and the **best** of your cattle
9: 2 an **impressive** young man without equal among the Israelites—
9: 2 an impressive young man **without equal** [+401+4946] among the
9:10 "**Good**," Saul said to his servant. "Come, let's go." So they set out
11:10 to you, and you can do to us whatever seems **good** to you."
14:36 "Do whatever seems **best** to you," they replied. But the priest said,
14:40 stand over here." "Do what seems **best** to you," the men replied.
15: 9 and cattle, the fat calves and lambs—everything that was **good**.
15:22 To obey is **better** than sacrifice, and to heed is better than the fat of
15:28 and has given it to one of your neighbors—to one **better** than you.
16:12 He was ruddy, with a fine appearance and **handsome** features.
19: 4 Jonathan spoke **well** of David to Saul his father and said to him,
19: 4 not wronged you, and what he has done has **benefited** you greatly.
20: 7 If he says, '**Very well**,' then your servant is safe. But if he loses his
25: 3 She was an **intelligent** [+8507] and beautiful woman, but her
25: 8 favorable toward my young men, since we come at a **festive** time.
25:15 Yet these men were very **good** to us. They did not mistreat us,
26:16 What you have done is not **good**. As surely as the LORD lives,
27: 1 The **best** *thing* I can do is to escape to the land of the Philistines.
29: 6 I would be **pleased** [+928+6524] to have you serve with me in the
29: 6 no fault in you, but the rulers don't **approve** [+928+6524] **of** you.
29: 9 "I know that you have been as **pleasing** in my eyes as an angel of
2Sa 3:13 "**Good**," said David. "I will make an agreement with you.
3:19 and the whole house of Benjamin **wanted** [+928+6524] **to do**.
3:36 indeed, everything the king did **pleased** [+928+6524] them.
10:12 cities of our God. The LORD will do what is **good** in his sight."
11: 2 he saw a woman bathing. The woman was very **beautiful** [+5260],
13:22 Absalom never said a word to Amnon, either **good** or bad;
14:17 for my lord the king is like an angel of God in discerning **good**
14:32 It would be **better** for me if I were still there!" ' Now then,
15: 3 would say to him, "Look, your claims are **valid** and proper,
15:26 then I am ready; let him do to me whatever seems **good** to him."
17: 7 "The advice Ahithophel has given is not **good** this time.
17:14 "The advice of Hushai the Arkite is **better** than that of
17:14 For the LORD had determined to frustrate the **good** advice of
18: 3 It would be **better** now for you to give us support from the city."
18:27 "He's a **good** man," the king said. "He comes with good news."
18:27 "He's a good man," the king said. "He comes with **good** news."
19:18 [19:19] and to do whatever he **wished** [+928+6524].
19:27 [19:28] angel of God; so do whatever **pleases** [+928+6524] you.
19:35 [19:36] Can I tell the difference between what is **good** and what is
19:37 [19:38] the king. Do for him whatever **pleases** [+928+6524] you."
19:38 [19:39] and I will do for him whatever **pleases** [+928+6524] you.
24:22 "Let my lord the king take whatever **pleases** [+928+6524] him
1Ki 1: 6 He was also very **handsome** [+9307] and was born next after
1:42 "Come in. A worthy man like you must be bringing **good** news."
2:18 "**Very well**," Bathsheba replied, "I will speak to the king for you."
2:32 of Judah's army—were **better** *men* and more upright than he.
2:38 Shimei answered the king, "What you say is **good**. Your servant
2:42 At that time you said to me, 'What you say is **good**. I will obey.'
3: 9 to govern your people and to distinguish between **right** and wrong.
8:36 Teach them the **right** way to live, and send rain on the land you
8:56 Not one word has failed of all the **good** promises he gave through
8:66 **glad** *in* heart for all the good things the LORD had done for his
10: 7 in wisdom and **wealth** you have far exceeded the report I heard.
12: 7 to these people and serve them and give them a **favorable** answer,
14:13 in whom the LORD, the God of Israel, has found anything **good**.
14:15 He will uproot Israel from this **good** land that he gave to their
18:24 he is God." Then all the people said, "What you say is **good**."
19: 4 he said. "Take my life; I am no **better** than my ancestors."
20: 3 gold are mine, and the **best** of your wives and children are mine.' "
21: 2 In exchange I will give you a **better** [+4946] vineyard or,
21: 2 if you **prefer** [+928+6524], I will pay you whatever it is worth."
22: 8 I hate him because he never prophesies *anything* **good** about me,
22:13 as one man the other prophets are predicting **success** for the king.
22:13 the king. Let your word agree with theirs, and speak **favorably**."
22:18 "Didn't I tell you that he never prophesies *anything* **good** about
2Ki 2:19 "Look, our lord, this town is **well** situated, as you can see,
3:19 You will cut down every **good** tree, stop up all the springs,
3:19 stop up all the springs, and ruin every **good** field with stones."
3:25 each man threw a stone on every **good** field until it was covered.
3:25 They stopped up all the springs and cut down every **good** tree.
5:12 the rivers of Damascus, **better** than any of the waters of Israel?
10: 3 choose the **best** and most worthy of your master's sons and set him
10: 5 will not appoint anyone as king; you do whatever you think **best**."
20: 3 wholehearted devotion and have done what is **good** in your eyes."
20:13 the silver, the gold, the spices and the **fine** oil—his armory
20:19 "The word of the LORD you have spoken is **good**,"
1Ch 4:40 They found rich, **good** pasture, and the land was spacious,
13: 2 "If it seems **good** to you and if it is the will of the LORD our
16:34 Give thanks to the LORD, for he is **good**; his love endures
19:13 cities of our God. The LORD will do what is **good** in his sight."
21:23 Let my lord the king do whatever **pleases** [+928+6524] him.
28: 8 that you may possess this **good** land and pass it on as an
29:28 He died at a **good** old age, having enjoyed long life, wealth
2Ch 3: 5 and covered it with **fine** gold and decorated it with palm tree
3: 8 He overlaid the inside with six hundred talents of **fine** gold.
5:13 to the LORD and sang: "He is **good**; his love endures forever."
6:27 Teach them the **right** way to live, and send rain on the land you
6:41 clothed with salvation, may your saints rejoice in your **goodness**.
7: 3 and gave thanks to the LORD, saying, "He is **good**;
7:10 **glad** *in* heart for the good things the LORD had done for David
10: 7 "If you will be **kind** to these people and please them and give them
10: 7 to these people and please them and give them a **favorable** answer,
12:12 was not totally destroyed. Indeed, there was some **good** in Judah.
14: 2 [14:1] Asa did what was **good** and right in the eyes of the LORD
18:12 as one man the other prophets are predicting **success** for the king.
18:12 the king. Let your word agree with theirs, and speak **favorably**."
18:17 "Didn't I tell you that he never prophesies *anything* **good** about
19: 3 There is, however, some **good** in you, for you have rid the land of
19:11 with courage, and may the LORD be with those who do **well**."
21:13 members of your father's house, men *who* were **better** than you.
30:18 saying, "May the LORD, who is **good**, pardon everyone
30:22 who showed **good** understanding of the service of the LORD.
31:20 doing what was **good** and right and faithful before the LORD his
Ezr 3:11 to the LORD: "He is **good**; his love to Israel endures forever."
7: 9 of the fifth month, for the **gracious** hand of his God was on him.
8:18 Because the **gracious** hand of our God was on us, they brought us
8:27 and two **fine** articles of polished bronze, as precious as gold.
Ne 2: 8 And because the **gracious** hand of my God was upon me,
2:18 I also told them about the **gracious** hand of my God upon me
5: 9 So I continued, "What you are doing is not **right**. Shouldn't you
9:13 that are just and right, and decrees and commands that are **good**.
9:20 You gave your **good** Spirit to instruct them. You did not withhold
Est 1:11 her beauty to the people and nobles, for she was **lovely** to look at.
1:19 give her royal position to someone else who is **better** than she.
2: 2 "Let a search be made for **beautiful** [+5260] young virgins for the
2: 3 these **beautiful** [+5260] girls into the harem at the citadel of Susa.
2: 7 also known as Esther, was lovely in form and **[RPH]** features,
2: 9 and moved her and her maids into the **best** *place in* the harem.
3:11 to Haman, "and do with the people as you **please** [+928+6524]."
7: 9 He had it made for Mordecai, who spoke up to **help** the king."
8: 5 "If it **pleases** the king," she said, "and if he regards me with favor
8: 5 it the right thing to do, and if he is **pleased** [+928+6524] **with** me,
8: 8 in the king's name in behalf of the Jews as seems **best** to you,
8:17 gladness among the Jews, with feasting and **celebrating** [+3427].
9:13 "If it **pleases** the king," Esther answered, "give the Jews in Susa
9:19 and feasting, a day **[RPH]** for giving presents to each other.
9:22 was turned into joy and their mourning into a day of **celebration**.
10: 3 because he worked for the **good** of his people and spoke up for the
Job 2:10 Shall we accept **good** from God, and not trouble?" In all this,
7: 7 my life is but a breath; my eyes will never see **happiness** again.
10: 3 Does it **please** you to oppress me, to spurn the work of your hands,
13: 9 Would it turn out **well** if he examined you? Could you deceive him
21:13 They spend their years in **prosperity** and go down to the grave in
22:18 Yet it was he who filled their houses with **good** *things*, so I stand
30:26 Yet when I hoped for **good**, evil came; when I looked for light,
34: 4 for ourselves what is right; let us learn together what is **good**.
36:11 they will spend the rest of their days in **prosperity** and their years
Ps 4: 6 [4:7] Many are asking, "Who can show us any **good**?"
14: 1 are corrupt, their deeds are vile; there is no one who does **good**.
14: 3 become corrupt; there is no one who does **good**, not even one.
21: 3 [21:4] You welcomed him with **rich** blessings and placed a crown
23: 6 Surely **goodness** and love will follow me all the days of my life,
25: 8 **Good** and upright is the LORD; therefore he instructs sinners in
25:13 He will spend his days in **prosperity**, and his descendants will
34: 8 [34:9] Taste and see that the LORD is **good**; blessed is the man
34:10 [34:11] but those who seek the LORD lack no **good** *thing*.
34:12 [34:13] of you loves life and desires to see many **good** days,
34:14 [34:15] Turn from evil and do **good**; seek peace and pursue it.
36: 4 [36:5] he commits himself to a **sinful** [+4202] course and does not
37: 3 Trust in the LORD and do **good**; dwell in the land and enjoy safe
37:16 **Better** the little that the righteous have than the wealth of many
37:27 Turn from evil and do **good**; then you will dwell in the land
38:20 [38:21] good with evil slander me when I pursue *what* is **good**.
39: 2 [39:3] when I was silent and still, not even saying *anything* **good**,

Ps 45: 1 [45:2] My heart is stirred by a **noble** theme as I recite my verses
52: 3 [52:5] You love evil rather than **good**, falsehood rather than
52: 9 [52:11] in your name I will hope, for your name is **good**.
53: 1 [53:2] and their ways are vile; there is no one who does **good**.
53: 3 [53:4] there is no one who does **good**, not even one.
54: 6 [54:8] to you; I will praise your name, O LORD, for it is **good**.
63: 3 [63:4] Because your love is **better** than life, my lips will glorify
69: 16 [69:17] Answer me, O LORD, out of the **goodness** *of* your love;
73: 1 Surely God is **good** to Israel, to those who are pure in heart.
73: 28 as for me, it is **good** to be near God. I have made the Sovereign
84: 10 [84:11] **Better** is one day in your courts than a thousand
84: 11 [84:12] no **good** *thing* does he withhold from those whose walk is
85: 12 [85:13] The LORD will indeed give what is **good**, and our land
86: 5 You are forgiving and **good**, O Lord, abounding in love to all who
92: 1 [92:2] It is **good** to praise the LORD and make music to your
100: 5 For the LORD is **good** and his love endures forever; his
103: 5 who satisfies your desires with **good** *things* so that your youth is
104: 28 when you open your hand, they are satisfied with **good** *things*.
106: 1 Give thanks to the LORD, for he is **good**; his love endures
107: 1 Give thanks to the LORD, for he is **good**; his love endures
107: 9 for he satisfies the thirsty and fills the hungry with **good** *things*.
109: 21 for your name's sake; out of the **goodness** *of* your love, deliver me.
111: 10 of wisdom; all who follow his precepts have **good** understanding.
112: 5 **Good** will come to him who is generous and lends freely,
118: 1 Give thanks to the LORD, for he is **good**; his love endures
118: 8 It is **better** to take refuge in the LORD than to trust in man.
118: 9 It is **better** to take refuge in the LORD than to trust in princes.
118: 29 Give thanks to the LORD, for he is **good**; his love endures
119: 39 Take away the disgrace I dread, for your laws are **good**.
119: 65 Do **good** to your servant according to your word, O LORD.
119: 68 You are **good**, and what you do is good; teach me your decrees.
119: 71 It was **good** for me to be afflicted so that I might learn your
119: 72 The law from your mouth is more **precious** to me than thousands
119: 122 Ensure your servant's **well-being**; let not the arrogant oppress me.
122: 9 of the house of the LORD our God, I will seek your **prosperity**.
125: 4 Do good, O LORD, to those *who* are **good**, to those who are
128: 2 eat the fruit of your labor; blessings and **prosperity** will be yours.
133: 1 How **good** and pleasant it is when brothers live together in unity!
133: 2 It is like **precious** oil poured on the head, running down on the
135: 3 Praise the LORD, for the LORD is **good**; sing praise to his
136: 1 Give thanks to the LORD, for he is **good**. *His love*
143: 10 you are my God; may your **good** Spirit lead me on level ground.
145: 9 The LORD is **good** to all; he has compassion on all he has made.
147: 1 How **good** it is to sing praises to our God, how pleasant and fitting
Pr 2: 9 will understand what is right and just and fair—every **good** path.
2: 20 Thus you will walk in the ways of **good** *men* and keep to the paths
3: 4 you will win favor and a **good** name in the sight of God and man.
3: 14 for she is more **profitable** [+6087] than silver and yields better
3: 27 Do not withhold **good** from those who deserve it, when it is in your
4: 2 I give you **sound** learning, so do not forsake my teaching.
8: 11 for wisdom is more **precious** than rubies, and nothing you desire
8: 19 My fruit is **better** than fine gold; what I yield surpasses choice
11: 23 The desire of the righteous ends only in **good**, but the hope of the
11: 27 He who seeks **good** finds goodwill, but evil comes to him who
12: 2 A **good** *man* obtains favor from the LORD, but the LORD
12: 9 **Better** to be a nobody and yet have a servant than pretend to be
12: 14 From the fruit of his lips a man is filled with **good** *things* as surely
12: 25 anxious heart weighs a man down, but a **kind** word cheers him up.
13: 2 From the fruit of his lips a man enjoys **good** *things*,
13: 15 **Good** understanding wins favor, but the way of the unfaithful is
13: 21 pursues the sinner, but **prosperity** is the reward of the righteous.
13: 22 A **good** *man* leaves an inheritance for his children's children,
14: 14 be fully repaid for their ways, and the **good** man rewarded for his.
14: 19 Evil men will bow down in the presence of the **good**,
14: 22 But those who plan *what* is **good** find love and faithfulness.
15: 3 are everywhere, keeping watch on the wicked and the **good**.
15: 15 are wretched, but the **cheerful** heart has a continual feast.
15: 16 **Better** a little with the fear of the LORD than great wealth with
15: 17 **Better** a meal of vegetables where there is love than a fattened calf
15: 23 finds joy in giving an apt reply—and how **good** is a timely word!
15: 30 brings joy to the heart, and **good** news gives health to the bones.
16: 8 **Better** a little with righteousness than much gain with injustice.
16: 16 How much **better** to get wisdom than gold, to choose
16: 19 **Better** to be lowly in spirit and among the oppressed than to share
16: 20 Whoever gives heed to instruction **prospers** [+5162], and blessed
16: 29 entices his neighbor and leads him down a path that is not **good**.
16: 32 **Better** a patient man than a warrior, a man who controls his temper
17: 1 **Better** a dry crust with peace and quiet than a house full of
17: 20 A man of perverse heart *does* not **prosper** [+5162]; he whose
17: 26 It is not **good** to punish an innocent man, or to flog officials for
18: 5 It is not **good** to be partial to the wicked or to deprive the innocent
18: 22 He who finds a wife finds *what* is **good** and receives favor from
19: 1 **Better** a poor man whose walk is blameless than a fool whose lips
19: 2 It is not **good** to have zeal without knowledge, nor to be hasty
19: 8 his own soul; he who cherishes understanding **prospers** [+5162].
19: 22 What a man desires is unfailing love; **better** to be poor than a liar.
20: 23 detests differing weights, and dishonest scales do not **please** him.
21: 9 **Better** to live on a corner of the roof than share a house with a
21: 19 **Better** to live in a desert than with a quarrelsome and ill-tempered
22: 1 than great riches; to be esteemed is **better** than silver or gold.
22: 9 A **generous** [+6524] **man** will himself be blessed, for he shares his
24: 13 Eat honey, my son, for it is **good**; honey from the comb is sweet to
24: 23 are sayings of the wise: To show partiality in judging is not **good**:
24: 25 who convict the guilty, and **rich** blessing will come upon them.
25: 7 it is **better** for him to say to you, "Come up here," than for him to
25: 24 **Better** to live on a corner of the roof than share a house with a
25: 25 Like cold water to a weary soul is **good** news from a distant land.
25: 27 It is not **good** to eat too much honey, nor is it honorable to seek
27: 5 **Better** is open rebuke than hidden love.
27: 10 strikes you—**better** a neighbor nearby than a brother far away.
28: 6 **Better** a poor man whose walk is blameless than a rich man whose
28: 10 his own trap, but the blameless will receive a **good** inheritance.
28: 21 To show partiality is not **good**—yet a man will do wrong for a
31: 12 She brings him **good**, not harm, all the days of her life.
31: 18 She sees that her trading is **profitable**, and her lamp does not go
Ecc 2: 1 I will test you with pleasure to find out *what* is **good**."
2: 3 I wanted to see what was **worthwhile** for men to do under heaven
2: 24 A man can do nothing **better** than to eat and drink and find
2: 24 better than to eat and drink and find **satisfaction** in his work.
2: 26 To the man who **pleases** him, God gives wisdom, knowledge
2: 26 and storing up wealth to hand it over to the *one who* **pleases** God.
3: 12 I know that there is nothing **better** for men than to be happy
3: 12 better for men than to be happy and do **good** while they live.
3: 13 everyone may eat and drink, and find **satisfaction** in all his toil—
3: 22 So I saw that there is nothing **better** for a man than to enjoy his
4: 3 **better** than both is he who has not yet been, who has not seen the
4: 6 **Better** one handful with tranquillity than two handfuls with toil
4: 9 Two are **better** than one, because they have a good return for their
4: 9 are better than one, because they have a **good** return for their work:
4: 13 **Better** a poor but wise youth than an old but foolish king who no
5: 5 [5:4] It is **better** not to vow than to make a vow and not fulfill it.
5: 18 [5:17] I realized that it is **good** and proper for a man to eat
6: 3 proper burial, I say that a stillborn child is **better off** than he.
6: 9 **Better** what the eye sees than the roving of the appetite. This too is
6: 12 For who knows what is **good** for a man in life, during the few
7: 1 A **good** name is better than fine perfume, and the day of death
7: 1 A good name is **better** than fine perfume, and the day of death
7: 2 It is **better** to go to a house of mourning than to go to a house of
7: 3 Sorrow is **better** than laughter, because a sad face is good for the
7: 5 It is **better** to heed a wise man's rebuke than to listen to the song
7: 8 The end of a matter is **better** than its beginning, and patience is
7: 8 is better than its beginning, and patience is **better** than pride.
7: 10 Do not say, "Why were the old days **better** than these?" For it is
7: 11 an inheritance, is a **good** *thing* and benefits those who see the sun.
7: 14 When times are good, be **happy**; but when times are bad, consider:
7: 18 It is **good** to grasp the one and not let go of the other. The man who
7: 20 There is not a righteous man on earth who does *what* is **right**
7: 26 The *man who* **pleases** God will escape her, but the sinner she will
8: 12 a long time, I know that it will go **better** with God-fearing men,
8: 13 because the wicked do not fear God, it will not go **well** with them,
8: 15 because nothing is **better** for a man under the sun than to eat
9: 2 and the wicked, the **good** and the bad, the clean and the unclean,
9: 2 As it is with the **good** *man*, so with the sinner; as it is with those
9: 4 the living has hope—even a live dog is **better off** than a dead lion!
9: 7 your food with gladness, and drink your wine with a **joyful** heart,
9: 16 So I said, "Wisdom is **better** than strength." But the poor man's
9: 18 Wisdom is **better** than weapons of war, but one sinner destroys
11: 6 whether this or that, or whether both will do equally **well**.
11: 7 Light is sweet, and it **pleases** the eyes to see the sun.
12: 14 including every hidden thing, whether it is **good** or evil.
SS 1: 2 kisses of his mouth—for your love is more **delightful** than wine.
1: 3 **Pleasing** is the fragrance of your perfumes; your name is like
7: 9 [7:10] your mouth like the **best** wine. May the wine go straight to
Isa 3: 10 Tell the righteous it will be **well** with them, for they will enjoy the
5: 9 the **fine** [+1524+2256] mansions left without occupants.
5: 20 Woe to those who call evil **good** and good evil, who put darkness
5: 20 Woe to those who call evil good and **good** evil, who put darkness
7: 15 when he knows enough to reject the wrong and choose the **right**.
7: 16 the boy knows enough to reject the wrong and choose the **right**,
38: 3 wholehearted devotion and have done what is **good** in your eyes."
39: 2 the silver, the gold, the spices, the **fine** oil, his entire armory
39: 8 "The word of the LORD you have spoken is **good**,"
41: 7 He says of the welding, "It is **good**." He nails down the idol
52: 7 who proclaim peace, who bring **good** tidings, who proclaim
55: 2 Listen, listen to me, and eat *what* is **good**, and your soul will
56: 5 its walls a memorial and a name **better** than sons and daughters;
65: 2 who walk in ways not **good**, pursuing their own imaginations—
Jer 5: 25 have kept these away; your sins have deprived you of **good**.

Jer 6:16 for the ancient paths, ask where the **good** way is, and walk in it,
8:15 We hoped for peace but no **good** has come, for a time of healing
14:19 We hoped for peace but no **good** has come, for a time of healing
15:11 The LORD said, "Surely I will deliver you for a **good** *purpose*;
17:6 a bush in the wastelands; he will not see **prosperity** when it comes.
22:15 He did what was right and just, so all went **well** with him.
22:16 He defended the cause of the poor and needy, and so all went **well**.
24:2 One basket had very **good** figs, like those that ripen early;
24:3 "The **good** ones are very good, but the poor ones are so bad they
24:3 "The good ones are very **good**, but the poor ones are so bad they
24:5 'Like these **good** figs, I regard as good the exiles from Judah,
26:14 in your hands; do with me whatever you think is **good** and right.
29:10 and fulfill my **gracious** promise to bring you back to this place.
29:32 nor will he see the **good** *things* I will do for my people,
32:39 so that they will always fear me for their own **good** and the good of
33:11 "Give thanks to the LORD Almighty, for the LORD is **good**;
33:14 'when I will fulfill the **gracious** promise I made to the house of
40:4 me to Babylon, if you **like** [+928+6524], and I will look after you;
40:4 go wherever you **please** [+928+2256+3838+6524]."
42:6 Whether it is **favorable** or unfavorable, we will obey the LORD
44:17 we had plenty of food and were **well off** and suffered no harm.
La 3:25 The LORD is **good** to those whose hope is in him, to the one who
3:26 it is **good** to wait quietly for the salvation of the LORD.
3:27 It is **good** for a man to bear the yoke while he is young.
3:38 of the Most High that both calamities and **good** *things* come?
4:1 How the gold has lost its luster, the **fine** gold become dull!
4:9 Those killed by the sword are **better off** than those who die of
Eze 17:8 It had been planted in **good** soil by abundant water so that it would
18:18 his brother and did what was **wrong** [+4202] among his people.
20:25 I also gave them over to statutes that were not **good** and laws they
24:4 Put into it the pieces of meat, all the **choice** pieces—the leg
31:16 Then all the trees of Eden, the choicest and **best** *of* Lebanon,
34:14 I will tend them in a **good** pasture, and the mountain heights of
34:14 There they will lie down in **good** grazing land, and there they will
34:18 Is it not enough for you to feed on the **good** pasture? Must you also
36:31 you will remember your evil ways and **wicked** [+4202] deeds,
Da 1:4 young men without any physical defect, **handsome** [+5260],
1:15 At the end of the ten days they looked **healthier** and better
Hos 2:7 [2:9] my husband as at first, for then I was **better off** than now.'
4:13 under oak, poplar and terebinth, where the shade is **pleasant**.
8:3 But Israel has rejected what is **good**; an enemy will pursue him.
10:1 more altars; as his land **prospered**, he adorned his sacred stones.
14:2 [14:3] "Forgive all our sins and receive us **graciously**, that we
Joel 3:5 [4:5] my gold and carried off my **finest** treasures to your temples.
Am 5:14 Seek **good**, not evil, that you may live. Then the LORD God
5:15 Hate evil, love **good**; maintain justice in the courts.
6:2 Are *they* **better off** than your two kingdoms? Is their land larger
Jnh 4:3 take away my life, for it is **better** for me to die than to live."
4:8 to die, and said, "It would be **better** for me to die than to live."
Mic 1:12 Those who live in Maroth writhe in pain, waiting for **relief**,
3:2 you who hate **good** and love evil; who tear the skin from my
6:8 He has showed you, O man, what is **good**. And what does the
7:4 The **best** *of* them is like a brier, the most upright worse than a
Na 1:7 The LORD is **good**, a refuge in times of trouble. He cares for
3:4 all because of the wanton lust of a harlot, **alluring** [+2834],
Zec 1:13 So the LORD spoke **kind** and comforting words to the angel who
1:17 'My towns will again overflow with **prosperity**, and the LORD
8:19 become joyful and glad occasions and **happy** festivals for Judah.
11:12 I told them, "If you think it **best**, give me my pay; but if not,
Mal 2:17 By saying, "All who do evil are **good** in the eyes of the LORD,

3203 ³טוֹב ṭôb³, a. [1] [√ 3201]

sweet [1]

Jer 6:20 about incense from Sheba or **sweet** calamus from a distant land?

3204 ⁴טוֹב ṭôb⁴, n.pr.loc. [4] [√ 3202; cf. 3201]

Tob [4]

Jdg 11:3 So Jephthah fled from his brothers and settled in the land of **Tob**,
11:5 the elders of Gilead went to get Jephthah from the land of **Tob**.
2Sa 10:6 with a thousand men, and also twelve thousand men from **Tob**.
10:8 while the Arameans of Zobah and Rehob and the men of **Tob**

3205 ⁵טוֹב ṭôb⁵, n.m. Not used in NIV/BHS [√ 3201]

3206 טוּב ṭûb, n.m. [32] [√ 3201]

good things [7], goodness [6], best [3], prosperity [3], bounty [2], good [2], attractive [1], best things [1], blessings [1], fair [1], finest wares [1], gladly [+928+4222] [1], joy [1], prosper [1], rich produce [1]

Ge 24:10 taking with him all kinds of **good things** *from* his master.
45:18 I will give you the **best** *of* the land of Egypt and you can enjoy the
45:20 your belongings, because the **best** *of* all Egypt will be yours.' "
45:23 ten donkeys loaded with the **best things** *of* Egypt, and ten female
Ex 33:19 LORD said, "I will cause all my **goodness** to pass in front of you,
Dt 6:11 houses filled with all kinds of **good things** you did not provide,
28:47 God joyfully and **gladly** [+928+4222] in the time of prosperity,
2Ki 8:9 as a gift forty camel-loads of all the **finest wares** *of* Damascus.
Ezr 9:12 that you may be strong and eat the **good things** *of* the land
Ne 9:25 they took possession of houses filled with all kinds of **good things**,
9:25 and were well-nourished; they reveled in your great **goodness**.
9:35 enjoying your great **goodness** to them in the spacious and fertile
9:36 so they could eat its fruit and the other **good things** it *produces*.
Job 20:21 Nothing is left for him to devour; his **prosperity** will not endure.
21:16 their **prosperity** is not in their own hands, so I stand aloof from the
Ps 25:7 according to your love remember me, for you are **good**, O LORD.
27:13 I will see the **goodness** *of* the LORD in the land of the living.
31:19 [31:20] How great is your **goodness**, which you have stored up
65:4 [65:5] We are filled with the **good things** *of* your house, *of* your
119:66 Teach me knowledge and **good** judgment, for I believe in your
128:5 all the days of your life; may you see the **prosperity** *of* Jerusalem,
145:7 They will celebrate your abundant **goodness** and joyfully sing of
Pr 11:10 When the righteous **prosper**, the city rejoices; when the wicked
Isa 1:19 you are willing and obedient, you will eat the **best** *from* the land;
63:7 the many **good things** he has done for the house of Israel,
65:14 My servants will sing out of the **joy** *of* their hearts, but you will cry
Jer 2:7 I brought you into a fertile land to eat its fruit and **rich produce**.
31:12 they will rejoice in the **bounty** *of* the LORD—the grain,
31:14 my people will be filled with my **bounty**," declares the LORD.
Hos 3:5 come trembling to the LORD and to his **blessings** in the last days.
10:11 heifer that loves to thresh; so I will put a yoke on her **fair** neck.
Zec 9:17 How **attractive** and beautiful they will be! Grain will make the

3207 טוֹב אֲדוֹנִיָּה ṭôb ᵓădôniyyâ, n.pr.m. [1] [√ 3204 + 125]

Tob-Adonijah [1]

2Ch 17:8 Shemiramoth, Jehonathan, Adonijah, Tobijah and **Tob-Adonijah**—

3208 טוֹבָה ṭôbâ, n.f. [67] [√ 3202; cf. 3201]

good [22], prosperity [9], good things [7], favor [3], well [3], bounty [2], good thing [2], kindly [2], treaty of friendship [+2256+8934] [2], enjoyment [1], fair [1], good deeds [1], good do [+906+3512] [1], good work [1], goodness [1], goods [1], gracious [1], in behalf [+6584] [1], joy [1], prosperous [1], satisfaction [1], unharmed [1], welfare [1], well-being [1]

Ge 44:4 up with them, say to them, 'Why have you repaid **good** with evil?
50:20 God intended it for **good** to accomplish what is now being done,
Ex 18:9 Jethro was delighted to hear about all the **good things** the LORD
Nu 24:13 and gold, I could not do *anything* of my own accord, **good** or bad,
Dt 23:6 [23:7] Do not seek a **treaty of friendship with** [+2256+8934]
28:11 The LORD will grant you abundant **prosperity**—in the fruit of
30:9 the LORD your God will make you most **prosperous** in all the
Jdg 8:35 (that is, Gideon) for all the **good things** he had done for them.
9:16 if you have been **fair** to Jerub-Baal and his family, and if you have
1Sa 12:23 pray for you. And I will teach you the way that is **good** and right.
24:17 [24:18] "You have treated me **well**, but I have treated you badly.
24:18 [24:19] You have just now told me of the **good** you did to me; the
24:19 [24:20] finds his enemy, does he let him get away **unharmed**?
24:19 [24:20] May the LORD reward you **well** for the way you treated
25:21 that nothing of his was missing. He has paid me back evil for **good**.
25:30 When the LORD has done for my master every **good thing** he
2Sa 2:6 I too will show you the same **favor** because you have done this.
7:28 and you have promised these **good things** to your servant.
16:12 and repay me with **good** for the cursing I am receiving today."
1Ki 8:66 glad in heart for all the **good things** the LORD had done for his
2Ki 25:28 He spoke **kindly** to him and gave him a seat of honor higher than
1Ch 17:26 are God! You have promised these **good things** to your servant.
2Ch 7:10 glad in heart for the **good things** the LORD had done for David
18:7 I hate him because he never prophesies *anything* **good** about me,
24:16 because of the **good** he had done in Israel for God and his temple.
Ezr 8:22 "The **gracious** hand of our God is on everyone who looks to him,
9:12 Do not seek a **treaty of friendship with** [+2256+8934] them at
Ne 2:10 that someone had come to promote the **welfare** of the Israelites.
2:18 "Let us start rebuilding." So they began this **good work**.
5:19 Remember me with **favor**, O my God, for all I have done for these
6:19 they kept reporting to me his **good deeds** and then telling him what
13:31 and for the firstfruits. Remember me with **favor**, O my God.
Job 9:25 are swifter than a runner; they fly away without a glimpse of **joy**.
21:25 dies in bitterness of soul, never having enjoyed anything **good**.
22:21 and be at peace with him; in this way **prosperity** will come to you.
Ps 16:2 "You are my Lord; apart from you I have no **good thing**."
35:12 They repay me evil for **good** and leave my soul forlorn.
38:20 [38:21] Those who repay my **good** with evil slander me when I
65:11 [65:12] You crown the year with your **bounty**, and your carts
68:10 [68:11] Your people settled in it, and from your **bounty**, O God,
86:17 Give me a sign of your **goodness**, that my enemies may see it

Ps 106: 5 that I may enjoy the **prosperity** *of* your chosen ones, that I may
109: 5 They repay me evil for **good**, and hatred for my friendship.
Pr 17:13 If a man pays back evil for **good**, evil will never leave his house.
Ecc 4: 8 he asked, "and why am I depriving myself of **enjoyment**?"
5:11 [5:10] As **goods** increase, so do those who consume them.
5:18 [5:17] to find **satisfaction** in his toilsome labor under the sun
6: 3 if he cannot enjoy his **prosperity** and does not receive proper
6: 6 lives a thousand years twice over but fails to enjoy his **prosperity**.
7:14 When times are **good**, be happy; but when times are bad, consider:
9:18 is better than weapons of war, but one sinner destroys much **good**.
Jer 12: 6 cry against you. Do not trust them, though they speak **well** of you.
14:11 LORD said to me, "Do not pray for the **well-being** of this people.
18:10 I will reconsider the **good** [+906+3512] I had intended to **do** *for* it.
18:20 Should **good** be repaid with evil? Yet they have dug a pit for me.
18:20 spoke **in** their **behalf** [+6584] to turn your wrath away from them.
21:10 I have determined to do this city harm and not **good**,
24: 5 'Like these good figs, I regard as **good** the exiles from Judah,
24: 6 My eyes will watch over them for their **good**, and I will bring them
32:42 so I will give them all the **prosperity** I have promised them.
33: 9 honor before all nations on earth that hear of all the **good things** I
33: 9 they will be in awe and will tremble at the abundant **prosperity**
39:16 fulfill my words against this city through disaster, not **prosperity**.
44:27 For I am watching over them for harm, not for **good**; the Jews in
52:32 He spoke **kindly** to him and gave him a seat of honor higher than
La 3:17 I have been deprived of peace; I have forgotten what **prosperity** is.
Am 9: 4 slay them. I will fix my eyes upon them for evil and not for **good**."

3209 טוֹבִיָּה ***ṭôbiyyâ***, n.pr.m. [17] [√ 3202 + 3378]

Tobiah [14], Tobijah [2], Tobiah's [1]

Ezr 2:60 The descendants of Delaiah, **Tobiah** and Nekoda 652
Ne 2:10 the Horonite and **Tobiah** the Ammonite official heard about this,
2:19 **Tobiah** the Ammonite official and Geshem the Arab heard about
4: 3 [3:35] **Tobiah** the Ammonite, who was at his side, said, "What
4: 7 [4:1] **Tobiah**, the Arabs, the Ammonites and the men of Ashdod
6: 1 **Tobiah**, Geshem the Arab and the rest of our enemies that I had
6:12 against me because **Tobiah** and Sanballat had hired him.
6:14 Remember **Tobiah** and Sanballat, O my God, because of what they
6:17 days the nobles of Judah were sending many letters to **Tobiah**,
6:17 letters to Tobiah, and replies from **Tobiah** kept coming to them.
6:19 telling him what I said. And **Tobiah** sent letters to intimidate me.
7:62 the descendants of Delaiah, **Tobiah** and Nekoda 642
13: 4 of the house of our God. He was closely associated with **Tobiah**,
13: 7 in providing **Tobiah** a room in the courts of the house of God.
13: 8 and threw all **Tobiah's** household goods out of the room.
Zec 6:10 **Tobijah** and Jedaiah, who have arrived from Babylon.
6:14 **Tobijah**, Jedaiah and Hen son of Zephaniah as a memorial in the

3210 טוֹבִיָּהוּ ***ṭôbiyyāhû***, n.pr.m. [1] [√ 3202 + 3378]

Tobijah [1]

2Ch 17: 8 Shemiramoth, Jehonathan, Adonijah, **Tobijah** and Tob-Adonijah—

3211 טָוָה ***ṭāwâ***, v. [2] [→ 4757]

spun [2]

Ex 35:25 [A] Every skilled woman **spun** with her hands and brought what
35:26 [A] who were willing and had the skill **spun** the goat hair.

3212 טוּחַ ***ṭûaḥ***, v. [11] [→ 3225; cf. 3220]

covered [3], cover [2], been plastered [1], overlaying [1], plaster [1], plastered [1], whitewash [+9521] [1], whitewashed [1]

Lev 14:42 [A] to replace these and take new clay and **plaster** the house.
14:43 [C] have been torn out and the house scraped and **plastered**,
14:48 [C] mildew has not spread after the house *has* **been plastered**,
1Ch 29: 4 [A] for the **overlaying** *of* the walls of the buildings,
Eze 13:10 [A] when a flimsy wall is built, they **cover** it *with* whitewash,
13:11 [A] therefore tell *those who* **cover** it *with* whitewash that it is
13:12 [A] not ask you, "Where is the whitewash *you* **covered** it *with*?"
13:14 [A] I will tear down the wall *you have* **covered** *with* whitewash
13:15 [A] the wall and against those *who* **covered** it *with* whitewash.
13:15 [A] "The wall is gone and so are those *who* **whitewashed** it,
22:28 [A] Her prophets **whitewash** [+9521] these deeds for them by

3213 טוֹטָפֹת ***ṭôṭāpōt***, n.f.pl. [3] [√ 5752]

bind [+2118+4200] [2], symbol [1]

Ex 13:16 a **symbol** on your forehead that the LORD brought us out of
Dt 6: 8 on your hands and **bind** [+2118+4200] them on your foreheads.
11:18 on your hands and **bind** [+2118+4200] them on your foreheads.

3214 טוּל ***ṭûl***, v. [14] [→ 3232]

hurl [2], hurled [2], threw [2], throw [2], be hurled out [1], fall [1], hurl away [+3232] [1], is cast [1], overpowering [1], sent [1]

1Sa 18:11 [G] he **hurled** it, saying to himself, "I'll pin David to the wall."
20:33 [G] Saul **hurled** his spear at him to kill him. Then Jonathan knew
Job 41: 9 [41:1] [H] him is false; the mere sight of him *is* **overpowering**.
Ps 37:24 [H] though he stumble, *he will* not **fall**, for the LORD upholds
Pr 16:33 [H] The lot **is cast** into the lap, but its every decision is from the
Isa 22:17 [D] is about to take firm hold of you and **hurl** [+3232] you **away**,
Jer 16:13 [G] So *I will* **throw** you out of this land into a land neither you
22:26 [G] *I will* **hurl** you and the mother who gave you birth into
22:28 [H] Why *will* he and his children **be hurled out**, cast into a land
Eze 32: 4 [G] I will throw you on the land and **hurl** you on the open field.
Jnh 1: 4 [G] the LORD **sent** a great wind on the sea, and such a violent
1: 5 [G] And *they* **threw** the cargo into the sea to lighten the ship.
1:12 [G] "Pick me up and **throw** me into the sea," he replied, "and it
1:15 [G] they took Jonah and **threw** him overboard, and the raging sea

3215 טוּר ***ṭûr***, n.m. [26] [→ 3227]

row [9], rows [9], *untranslated* [2], course [2], courses [2], ledge of stone [1], sets [1]

Ex 28:17 mount four **rows** of precious stones on it. In the first row there
28:17 on it. In the first **row** there shall be a ruby, a topaz and a beryl;
28:17 In the first row **[RPH]** there shall be a ruby, a topaz and a beryl;
28:18 in the second **row** a turquoise, a sapphire and an emerald;
28:19 in the third **row** a jacinth, an agate and an amethyst;
28:20 in the fourth **row** a chrysolite, an onyx and a jasper. Mount them in
39:10 they mounted four **rows** *of* precious stones on it. In the first row
39:10 stones on it. In the first **row** there was a ruby, a topaz and a beryl;
39:10 In the first row **[RPH]** there was a ruby, a topaz and a beryl;
39:11 in the second **row** a turquoise, a sapphire and an emerald;
39:12 in the third **row** a jacinth, an agate and an amethyst;
39:13 in the fourth **row** a chrysolite, an onyx and a jasper. They were
1Ki 6:36 And he built the inner courtyard of three **courses** *of* dressed stone
6:36 courses of dressed stone and one **course** *of* trimmed cedar beams.
7: 2 with four **rows** *of* cedar columns supporting trimmed cedar beams.
7: 3 that rested on the columns—forty-five beams, fifteen to a **row**.
7: 4 Its windows were placed high in **sets** *of* three, facing each other.
7:12 The great courtyard was surrounded by a wall of three **courses** of
7:12 courses of dressed stone and one **course** *of* trimmed cedar beams,
7:18 He made pomegranates in two **rows** encircling each network to
7:20 were the two hundred pomegranates in **rows** all around.
7:24 The gourds were cast in two **rows** in one piece with the Sea.
7:42 two sets of network (two **rows** of pomegranates for each network,
2Ch 4: 3 The bulls were cast in two **rows** in one piece with the Sea.
4:13 two sets of network (two **rows** of pomegranates for each network,
Eze 46:23 Around the inside of each of the four courts was a **ledge of stone**,

3216 טוּשׂ ***ṭûś***, v. [1]

swooping down [1]

Job 9:26 [A] boats of papyrus, like eagles **swooping down** on their prey.

3217 טָחָה ***ṭāḥâ***, v. [1]

bowshot [+8008] [1]

Ge 21:16 [D] about a **bowshot** [+8008] away, for she thought,

3218 טְחוֹן ***ṭᵉḥôn***, n.[m.]. [1] [√ 3221]

millstones [1]

La 5:13 Young men toil at the **millstones**; boys stagger under loads of

3219 טֻחוֹת ***ṭuḥôt***, n.f.pl. [2]

heart [1], inner parts [1]

Job 38:36 Who endowed the **heart** with wisdom or gave understanding to the
Ps 51: 6 [51:8] Surely you desire truth in the **inner parts**; you teach me

3220 טָחַח ***ṭāḥaḥ***, v. [1] [cf. 3212]

plastered over [1]

Isa 44:18 [A] their eyes *are* **plastered over** so they cannot see, and their

3221 טָחַן ***ṭāḥan***, v. [7] [→ 3218, 3222, 3223]

grinding [2], ground [2], grind grain [1], grind [1], ground to powder [+3512] [1]

Ex 32:20 [A] *he* **ground** it to powder, scattered it on the water and made
Nu 11: 8 [A] and then **ground** it in a handmill or crushed it in a mortar.
Dt 9:21 [A] I crushed it and **ground** [+3512] it **to powder** as fine as dust
Jdg 16:21 [A] with bronze shackles, they set him to **grinding** in the prison.
Job 31:10 [A] *may* my wife **grind** another man's **grain**, and may other men
Isa 3:15 [A] by crushing my people and **grinding** the faces of the poor?"

Isa 47: 2 [A] Take millstones and **grind** flour; take off your veil. Lift up

3222 טַחֲנָה ṭaḥanâ, n.f. [1] [√ 3221]

grinding [1]

Ecc 12: 4 the doors to the street are closed and the sound of **grinding** fades;

3223 טֹחֲנָה ṭōḥanâ, n.f. [1] [√ 3221]

grinders [1]

Ecc 12: 3 strong men stoop, when the **grinders** cease because they are few,

3224 טְחֹרִים ṭehōrîm, n.m. [2]

tumors [2]

Dt 28:27 [boils of Egypt and with **tumors**, [Q; see K 6754] festering sores]
1Sa 5: 6 [and afflicted them with **tumors**. [Q; see K 6754]]
5: 9 [both young and old, with an outbreak of **tumors**. [Q; see K 6754]]
5:12 [who did not die were afflicted with **tumors**, [Q; see K 6754]]
6: 4 ["Five gold **tumors** [Q; see K 6754] and five gold rats,]
6: 5 [Make models of the **tumors** [Q; see K 6754] and of the rats that]
6:11 it the chest containing the gold rats and the models of the **tumors**.
6:17 These are the gold **tumors** the Philistines sent as a guilt offering to

3225 טִיחַ ṭîaḥ, n.[m.]. [1] [√ 3212]

whitewash [1]

Eze 13:12 not ask you, "Where is the **whitewash** you covered it with?"

3226 טִיט ṭîṭ, n.m. [13] [→ 3173, 4748; Ar 10298]

mud [7], clay [2], mire [2], dirt [1], muddy [1]

2Sa 22:43 of the earth; I pounded and trampled them like **mud** *in* the streets.
Job 41:30 [41:22] leaving a trail in the **mud** like a threshing sledge.
Ps 18:42 [18:43] on the wind; I poured them out like **mud** *in* the streets.
40: 2 [40:3] He lifted me out of the slimy pit, out of the **mud** and mire;
69:14 [69:15] Rescue me from the **mire**, do not let me sink; deliver me
Isa 41:25 as if they were mortar, as if he were a potter treading the **clay**.
57:20 tossing sea, which cannot rest, whose waves cast up mire and **mud**.
Jer 38: 6 it had no water in it, only **mud**, and Jeremiah sank down into the
38: 6 no water in it, only mud, and Jeremiah sank down into the **mud**.
Mic 7:10 even now she will be trampled underfoot like **mire** *in* the streets.
Na 3:14 Work the **clay**, tread the mortar, repair the brickwork!
Zec 9: 3 has heaped up silver like dust, and gold like the **dirt** *of* the streets.
10: 5 Together they will be like mighty men trampling the **muddy**

3227 טִירָה ṭîrâ, n.f. [7] [√ 3215; cf. 3515?, 7652]

camps [3], ledge [1], locations [1], place [1], towers [1]

Ge 25:16 the twelve tribal rulers according to their settlements and **camps**.
Nu 31:10 towns where the Midianites had settled, as well as all their **camps**.
1Ch 6:54 [6:39] These were the **locations** *of* their settlements allotted as
Ps 69:25 [69:26] May their **place** be deserted; let there be no one to dwell
SS 8: 9 If she is a wall, we will build **towers** *of* silver on her. If she is a
Eze 25: 4 They will set up their **camps** and pitch their tents among you;
46:23 ledge of stone, with places for fire built all around under the **ledge**.

3228 טַל ṭal, n.m. [31] [→ 40, 2782, 3189; Ar 10299]

dew [31]

Ge 27:28 May God give you of heaven's **dew** and of earth's richness—
27:39 from the earth's richness, away from the **dew** *of* heaven above.
Ex 16:13 and in the morning there was a layer of **dew** around the camp.
16:14 When the **dew** was gone, thin flakes like frost on the ground
Nu 11: 9 When the **dew** settled on the camp at night, the manna also came
Dt 32: 2 Let my teaching fall like rain and my words descend like **dew**,
33:13 "May the LORD bless his land with the precious **dew** from
33:28 in a land of grain and new wine, where the heavens drop **dew**.
Jdg 6:37 If there is **dew** only on the fleece and all the ground is dry,
6:38 he squeezed the fleece and wrung out the **dew**—a bowlful of
6:39 This time make the fleece dry and the ground covered with **dew**."
6:40 Only the fleece was dry; all the ground was covered with **dew**.
2Sa 1:21 "O mountains of Gilboa, may you have neither **dew** nor rain,
17:12 be found, and we will fall on him as **dew** settles on the ground.
1Ki 17: 1 there will be neither **dew** nor rain in the next few years except at
Job 29:19 reach to the water, and the **dew** will lie all night on my branches.
38:28 Does the rain have a father? Who fathers the drops of **dew**?
Ps 110: 3 from the womb of the dawn you will receive the **dew** *of* your
133: 3 It is as if the **dew** *of* Hermon were falling on Mount Zion.
Pr 3:20 the deeps were divided, and the clouds let drop the **dew**.
19:12 rage is like the roar of a lion, but his favor is like **dew** on the grass.
SS 5: 2 My head is drenched with **dew**, my hair with the dampness of the
Isa 18: 4 heat in the sunshine, like a cloud of **dew** in the heat of harvest."
26:19 Your **dew** is like the dew of the morning; the earth will give birth
26:19 Your dew is like the **dew** *of* the morning; the earth will give birth
Hos 6: 4 love is like the morning mist, like the early **dew** that disappears.
13: 3 like the early **dew** that disappears, like chaff swirling from a
14: 5 [14:6] I will be like the **dew** to Israel; he will blossom like a lily.
Mic 5: 7 [5:6] be in the midst of many peoples like **dew** from the LORD,
Hag 1:10 because of you the heavens have withheld their **dew** and the earth
Zec 8:12 ground will produce its crops, and the heavens will drop their **dew**.

3229 טָלָא ṭālā', v. [8]

spotted [6], gaudy [1], patched [1]

Ge 30:32 [B] and remove from them every speckled or **spotted** sheep,
30:32 [B] every dark-colored lamb and every **spotted** or speckled goat.
30:33 [B] Any goat in my possession that is not speckled or **spotted**,
30:35 [B] he removed all the male goats that were streaked or **spotted**,
30:35 [B] or **spotted** *female* goats (all that had white on them)
30:39 [B] they bore young that were streaked or speckled or **spotted**.
Jos 9: 5 [E] The men put worn and **patched** sandals on their feet
Eze 16:16 [B] You took some of your garments to make **gaudy** high places,

3230 טְלָאִים ṭelā'îm, n.pr.loc. [1] [√ 3231]

Telaim [1]

1Sa 15: 4 So Saul summoned the men and mustered them at **Telaim**—

3231 טָלֶה ṭāleh, n.m. [3] [√ 3230]

lamb [2], lambs [1]

1Sa 7: 9 Samuel took a suckling **lamb** and offered it up as a whole burnt
Isa 40:11 He gathers the **lambs** in his arms and carries them close to his
65:25 The wolf and the **lamb** will feed together, and the lion will eat

3232 טַלְטֵלָה ṭalṭēlâ, n.f. [1] [√ 3214]

hurl away [+3214] [1]

Isa 22:17 is about to take firm hold of you and **hurl** you **away** [+3214],

3233 טָלַל ṭālal, v. [1] [cf. 7511]

roofing over [1]

Ne 3:15 [D] **roofing** it **over** and putting its doors and bolts and bars in

3234 טֶלֶם ṭelem[1], n.pr.loc. [1] [√ 3235; cf. 3236]

Telem [1]

Jos 15:24 Ziph, **Telem**, Bealoth,

3235 טֶלֶם ṭelem[2], n.pr.m. [1] [→ 3234; cf. 3236]

Telem [1]

Ezr 10:24 Eliashib. From the gatekeepers: Shallum, **Telem** and Uri.

3236 טַלְמוֹן ṭalmôn, n.pr.m. [5] [cf. 3234, 3235]

Talmon [5]

1Ch 9:17 Shallum, Akkub, **Talmon**, Ahiman and their brothers,
Ezr 2:42 of Shallum, Ater, **Talmon**, Akkub, Hatita and Shobai 139
Ne 7:45 of Shallum, Ater, **Talmon**, Akkub, Hatita and Shobai 138
11:19 Akkub, **Talmon** and their associates, who kept watch at the gates—
12:25 **Talmon** and Akkub were gatekeepers who guarded the storerooms

3237 טָמֵא ṭāmē'[1], v. [163] [→ 3238, 3239, 3240, 3241?]

unclean [62], defiled [28], defile [12], pronounce unclean [8], defile yourselves [6], defiles [5], defiled herself [4], ceremonially unclean [3], defiling [3], desecrated [3], make himself unclean [3], defile themselves [2], defiled yourself [2], impure [2], make himself ceremonially unclean [2], make yourselves unclean [2], pronounce unclean [+3237] [2], be made unclean [1], became defiled [1], been defiled [1], corrupt [1], defile himself [1], defiled yourselves [1], defiles herself [1], desecrate [1], impurity [1], let become defiled [1], make unclean [1], pronounce ceremonially unclean [1], pronounced unclean [1], remains unclean [+3238] [1]

Ge 34: 5 [D] When Jacob heard that his daughter Dinah *had been* **defiled**,
34:13 [D] Because their sister Dinah *had been* **defiled**, Jacob's sons
34:27 [D] and looted the city where their sister *had been* **defiled**.
Lev 5: 2 [A] he is unaware of it, he *has become* **unclean** and is guilty.
5: 3 [A] anything that *would make him* **unclean**—even though he is
11:24 [F] "*You will* **make yourselves unclean** by these;
11:24 [A] whoever touches their carcasses *will be* **unclean** till evening.
11:25 [A] must wash his clothes, and *he will be* **unclean** till evening.
11:26 [A] touches ⌞the carcass of⌟ any of them *will be* **unclean**.
11:27 [A] whoever touches their carcasses *will be* **unclean** till evening.
11:28 [A] must wash his clothes, and *he will be* **unclean** till evening.
11:31 [A] Whoever touches them when they are dead *will be* **unclean**
11:32 [A] on something, that article, whatever its use, *will be* **unclean**,
11:32 [A] *it will be* **unclean** till evening, and then it will be clean.
11:33 [A] everything in it *will be* **unclean**, and you must break the pot.

Lev 11:34 [A] could be eaten but has water on it from such a pot *is* **unclean**,
11:34 [A] and any liquid that could be drunk from it *is* **unclean**.
11:35 [A] that one of their carcasses falls on *becomes* **unclean**;
11:36 [A] but anyone who touches one of these carcasses *is* **unclean**.
11:39 [A] anyone who touches the carcass *will be* **unclean** till evening.
11:40 [A] must wash his clothes, and *he will be* **unclean** till evening.
11:40 [A] must wash his clothes, and *he will be* **unclean** till evening.
11:43 [F] *Do* not **make yourselves unclean** by means of them or be
11:43 [C] unclean by means of them or **be made unclean** by them.
11:44 [D] *Do* not **make** yourselves **unclean** by any creature that moves
12: 2 [A] gives birth to a son *will be* **ceremonially unclean** for seven
12: 2 [A] seven days, just as *she is* **unclean** during her monthly period.
12: 5 [A] for two weeks the woman *will be* **unclean**, as during her
13: 3 [D] *he shall* **pronounce** him **ceremonially unclean**.
13: 8 [D] rash has spread in the skin, he *shall* **pronounce** him **unclean**;
13:11 [D] skin disease and the priest *shall* **pronounce** him **unclean**.
13:14 [A] But whenever raw flesh appears on him, *he will be* **unclean**.
13:15 [D] priest sees the raw flesh, *he shall* **pronounce** him **unclean**.
13:20 [D] it has turned white, the priest *shall* **pronounce** him **unclean**.
13:22 [D] in the skin, the priest *shall* **pronounce** him **unclean**;
13:25 [D] The priest *shall* **pronounce** him **unclean**; it is an infectious
13:27 [D] in the skin, the priest *shall* **pronounce** him **unclean**;
13:30 [D] and thin, the priest *shall* **pronounce** that person **unclean**;
13:44 [D] The priest *shall* **pronounce** him **unclean** [+3237] because of
13:44 [D] The priest *shall* **pronounce** him **unclean** [+3237] because of
13:46 [A] As long as he has the infection he **remains unclean** [+3238].
13:59 [D] any leather article, for pronouncing them clean or **unclean**.
14:36 [A] so that nothing in the house *will be* **pronounced unclean**.
14:46 [A] the house while it is closed up *will be* **unclean** till evening.
15: 4 [A] " 'Any bed the man with a discharge lies on *will be* **unclean**,
15: 4 [A] on will be unclean, and anything he sits on *will be* **unclean**.
15: 5 [A] and bathe with water, and *he will be* **unclean** till evening.
15: 6 [A] and bathe with water, and *he will be* **unclean** till evening.
15: 7 [A] and bathe with water, and *he will be* **unclean** till evening.
15: 8 [A] and bathe with water, and *he will be* **unclean** till evening.
15: 9 [A] " 'Everything the man sits on when riding *will be* **unclean**,
15:10 [A] the things that were under him *will be* **unclean** till evening;
15:10 [A] and bathe with water, and *he will be* **unclean** till evening.
15:11 [A] and bathe with water, and *he will be* **unclean** till evening.
15:16 [A] whole body with water, and *he will be* **unclean** till evening.
15:17 [A] be washed with water, and *it will be* **unclean** till evening.
15:18 [A] must bathe with water, and *they will be* **unclean** till evening.
15:19 [A] and anyone who touches her *will be* **unclean** till evening.
15:20 [A] " 'Anything she lies on during her period *will be* **unclean**,
15:20 [A] will be unclean, and anything she sits on *will be* **unclean**.
15:21 [A] and bathe with water, and *he will be* **unclean** till evening.
15:22 [A] and bathe with water, and *he will be* **unclean** till evening.
15:23 [A] when anyone touches it, *he will be* **unclean** till evening.
15:24 [A] flow touches him, *he will be* **unclean** for seven days;
15:24 [A] unclean for seven days; any bed he lies on *will be* **unclean**.
15:27 [A] Whoever touches them *will be* **unclean**; he must wash his
15:27 [A] and bathe with water, and *he will be* **unclean** till evening.
15:31 [D] so they will not die in their uncleanness for **defiling** my
15:32 [A] for *anyone made* **unclean** by an emission of semen,
17:15 [A] and *he will be* **ceremonially unclean** till evening;
18:20 [A] with your neighbor's wife and **defile** *yourself* with her.
18:23 [A] sexual relations with an animal and **defile** *yourself* with it.
18:24 [F] " '*Do* not **defile yourselves** in any of these ways, because this
18:24 [C] that I am going to drive out before you **became defiled**.
18:25 [A] Even the land *was* **defiled**; so I punished it for its sin,
18:27 [A] lived in the land before you, and the land *became* **defiled**.
18:28 [D] if you **defile** the land, it will vomit you out as it vomited out
18:30 [F] before you came and *do* not **defile yourselves** with them.
19:31 [A] or seek out spiritists, for you *will be* **defiled** by them.
20: 3 [D] *he has* **defiled** my sanctuary and profaned my holy name.
20:25 [D] the ground—those which I have set apart as **unclean** for you.
21: 1 [F] *must* not **make himself ceremonially unclean** for any of his
21: 3 [F] she has no husband—for her *he may* **make himself unclean**.
21: 4 [F] *He must* not **make himself unclean** for people related to him
21:11 [F] *He must* not **make himself unclean**, even for his father
22: 5 [A] or if he touches any crawling thing that *makes* him **unclean**,
22: 5 [A] or any person who *makes* him **unclean**, whatever the
22: 6 [A] The one who touches any such thing *will be* **unclean** till
22: 8 [A] or torn by wild animals, and so *become* **unclean** through it.
Nu 5: 3 [D] them outside the camp so *they will* not **defile** their camp,
5:13 [C] *her* **impurity** is undetected (since there is no witness against
5:14 [C] her husband and he suspects his wife and she *is* **impure**—
5:14 [C] is jealous and suspects her even though she *is* not **impure**—
5:20 [C] *you have* **defiled yourself** by sleeping with a man other than
5:27 [C] If *she has* **defiled herself** and been unfaithful to her husband,
5:28 [C] the woman *has* not **defiled herself** and is free from impurity,
5:29 [C] goes astray and **defiles herself** while married to her husband,
6: 7 [F] *he must* not **make himself ceremonially unclean** on account
6: 9 [D] in his presence, thus **defiling** the hair he has dedicated,
6:12 [A] not count, because *he became* **defiled** during his separation.
19: 7 [A] the camp, but he *will be* **ceremonially unclean** till evening.
19: 8 [A] bathe with water, and *he* too *will be* **unclean** till evening.
19:10 [A] wash his clothes, and *he* too *will be* **unclean** till evening.
19:11 [A] "Whoever touches the dead body of anyone *will be* **unclean**
19:13 [D] and fails to purify himself **defiles** the LORD's tabernacle.
19:14 [A] and anyone who is in it *will be* **unclean** for seven days,
19:16 [A] a human bone or a grave, *will be* **unclean** for seven days.
19:20 [A] if a person who *is* **unclean** does not purify himself, he must
19:20 [D] because *he has* **defiled** the sanctuary of the LORD.
19:21 [A] anyone who touches the water of cleansing *will be* **unclean**
19:22 [A] Anything that an unclean person touches *becomes* **unclean**,
19:22 [A] and anyone who touches it *becomes* **unclean** till evening."
35:34 [D] *Do* not **defile** the land where you live and where I dwell, for
Dt 21:23 [D] *You must* not **desecrate** the land the LORD your God is
24: 4 [F] is not allowed to marry her again after *she has* **been defiled**.
2Ki 23: 8 [D] from the towns of Judah and **desecrated** the high places,
23:10 [D] *He* **desecrated** Topheth, which was in the Valley of Ben
23:13 [D] The king also **desecrated** the high places that were east of
23:16 [D] removed from them and burned on the altar *to* **defile** it,
2Ch 36:14 [D] of the nations and **defiling** the temple of the LORD,
Ps 79: 1 [D] *they have* **defiled** your holy temple, they have reduced
106:39 [A] *They* **defiled** *themselves* by what they did; by their deeds
Isa 30:22 [D] *you will* **defile** your idols overlaid with silver and your
Jer 2: 7 [D] you came and **defiled** my land and made my inheritance
2:23 [C] "How can you say, '*I am* not **defiled**; I have not run after the
7:30 [D] idols in the house that bears my Name and *have* **defiled** it.
32:34 [D] idols in the house that bears my Name and **defiled** it.
Eze 4:14 [E] "Not so, Sovereign LORD! *I have* never **defiled** myself.
5:11 [D] because *you have* **defiled** my sanctuary with all your vile
9: 7 [D] to them, "**Defile** the temple and fill the courts with the slain.
14:11 [F] nor *will they* **defile themselves** anymore with all their sins.
18: 6 [D] *He does* not **defile** his neighbor's wife or lie with a woman
18:11 [D] eats at the mountain shrines. *He* **defiles** his neighbor's wife.
18:15 [D] of the house of Israel. *He does* not **defile** his neighbor's wife.
20: 7 [F] eyes on, and *do* not **defile yourselves** with the idols of Egypt.
20:18 [F] or keep their laws or **defile yourselves** with their idols.
20:26 [D] *I* **let** them **become defiled** through their gifts—the sacrifice
20:30 [C] *Will* you **defile yourselves** the way your fathers did and lust
20:31 [C] you *continue to* **defile yourselves** with all your idols to this
20:43 [C] and all the actions by which *you have* **defiled yourselves**,
22: 3 [A] blood in her midst and **defiles** herself by making idols,
22: 4 [A] and *have become* **defiled** by the idols you have made.
22:11 [D] another shamefully **defiles** his daughter-in-law, and another
23: 7 [C] **defiled herself** with all the idols of everyone she lusted after.
23:13 [C] I saw that *she* too **defiled herself**; both of them went the
23:17 [D] to her, to the bed of love, and in their lust *they* **defiled** her.
23:17 [A] After *she had been* **defiled** by them, she turned away from
23:30 [C] lusted after the nations and **defiled yourself** with their idols.
23:38 [D] At that same time *they* **defiled** my sanctuary and desecrated
33:26 [D] and each of you **defiles** his neighbor's wife.
36:17 [D] own land, *they* **defiled** it by their conduct and their actions.
36:18 [D] in the land and because *they had* **defiled** it with their idols.
37:23 [F] *They will* no longer **defile themselves** with their idols
43: 7 [D] The house of Israel *will* never again **defile** my holy name—
43: 8 [D] *they* **defiled** my holy name by their detestable practices.
44:25 [A] " 'A priest *must* not **defile** *himself* by going near a dead
44:25 [F] or unmarried sister, then *he may* **defile himself**.
Hos 5: 3 [C] you have now turned to prostitution; Israel *is* **corrupt**.
6:10 [C] There Ephraim is given to prostitution and Israel *is* **defiled**.
9: 4 [F] like the bread of mourners; all who eat them *will be* **unclean**.
Mic 2:10 [A] because *it is* **defiled**, it is ruined, beyond all remedy.
Hag 2:13 [A] body touches one of these things, *does it become* **defiled**?"
2:13 [A] "Yes," the priests replied, "*it becomes* **defiled**."

3238 ²טָמֵא *ṭāmē'²*, a. [87] [√ 3237]

unclean [64], ceremonially unclean [12], defiled [7], impure [1], infamous [+2021+9005] [1], pagan [1], remains unclean [+3237] [1]

Lev 5: 2 " 'Or if a person touches anything **ceremonially unclean**—
5: 2 whether the carcasses of **unclean** wild animals or of unclean
5: 2 the carcasses of unclean wild animals or of **unclean** livestock
5: 2 or of **unclean** creatures that move along the ground—
7:19 " 'Meat that touches anything **ceremonially unclean** must not be
7:21 If anyone touches something **unclean**—whether human
7:21 whether human uncleanness or an **unclean** animal or any unclean,
7:21 whether human uncleanness or an unclean animal or any **unclean**,
10:10 the holy and the common, between the **unclean** and the clean,
11: 4 does not have a split hoof; it is **ceremonially unclean** for you.
11: 5 it chews the cud, does not have a split hoof; it is **unclean** for you.
11: 6 it chews the cud, does not have a split hoof; it is **unclean** for you.
11: 7 completely divided, does not chew the cud; it is **unclean** for you.
11: 8 eat their meat or touch their carcasses; they are **unclean** for you.
11:26 or that does not chew the cud is **unclean** for you;

Lev 11:27 on all fours, those that walk on their paws are **unclean** for you;
11:28 and he will be unclean till evening. They are **unclean** for you.
11:29 animals that move about on the ground, these are **unclean** for you:
11:31 Of all those that move along the ground, these are **unclean** for you.
11:35 They are **unclean**, and you are to regard them as unclean.
11:35 They are unclean, and you are to regard them as **unclean**.
11:38 been put on the seed and a carcass falls on it, it is **unclean** for you.
11:47 You must distinguish between the **unclean** and the clean, between
13:11 He is not to put him in isolation, because he is already **unclean**.
13:15 The raw flesh is **unclean**; he has an infectious disease.
13:36 priest does not need to look for yellow hair; the person is **unclean**.
13:44 the man is diseased and is **unclean**. The priest shall pronounce him
13:45 be unkempt, cover the lower part of his face and cry out, '**Unclean**!
13:45 cover the lower part of his face and cry out, 'Unclean! **Unclean**!'
13:46 As long as he has the infection he **remains unclean** [+3237].
13:51 whatever its use, it is a destructive mildew; the article is **unclean**.
13:55 its appearance, even though it has not spread, it is **unclean**.
14:40 be torn out and thrown into an **unclean** place outside the town.
14:41 the material that is scraped off dumped into an **unclean** place
14:44 in the house, it is a destructive mildew; the house is **unclean**.
14:45 and all the plaster—and taken out of the town to an **unclean** place.
14:57 to determine when something is clean or **unclean**. These are the
15: 2 'When any man has a bodily discharge, the discharge is **unclean**.
15:25 she will be **unclean** as long as she has the discharge, just as in the
15:26 and anything she sits on will be **unclean**, as during her period.
15:33 for a man who lies with a *woman who is* **ceremonially unclean**.
20:25 and **unclean** animals and between unclean and clean birds.
20:25 and unclean animals and between **unclean** and clean birds.
22: 4 He will also be unclean if he touches something **defiled** *by* a
27:11 If what he vowed is a **ceremonially unclean** animal—one that is
27:27 If it is one of the **unclean** animals, he may buy it back at its set
Nu 5: 2 any kind, or who is **ceremonially unclean** because of a dead body.
9: 6 because they were **ceremonially unclean** on account of a dead
9: 7 said to Moses, "We have become **unclean** because of a dead body,
9:10 'When any of you or your descendants are **unclean** because of a
18:15 every firstborn son and every firstborn male of **unclean** animals.
19:13 water of cleansing has not been sprinkled on him, he is **unclean**;
19:15 every open container without a lid fastened on it will be **unclean**.
19:17 "For the **unclean** *person*, put some ashes from the burned
19:19 The man who is clean is to sprinkle the **unclean** *person* on the
19:20 of cleansing has not been sprinkled on him, and he is **unclean**.
19:22 Anything that an **unclean** *person* touches becomes unclean,
Dt 12:15 Both the **ceremonially unclean** and the clean may eat it.
12:22 or deer. Both the **ceremonially unclean** and the clean may eat.
14: 7 do not have a split hoof; they are **ceremonially unclean** for you.
14: 8 The pig is also **unclean**; although it has a split hoof, it does not
14:10 not have fins and scales you may not eat; for you it is **unclean**.
14:19 All flying insects that swarm are **unclean** to you; do not eat them.
15:22 Both the **ceremonially unclean** and the clean may eat it, as if it
26:14 nor have I removed any of it while I was **unclean**, nor have I
Jos 22:19 If the land you possess is **defiled**, come over to the LORD's land,
Jdg 13: 4 or other fermented drink and that you do not eat anything **unclean**,
2Ch 23:19 so that no *one who* was in any way **unclean** might enter.
Job 14: 4 Who can bring what is pure from the **impure**? No one!
Ecc 9: 2 and the wicked, the good and the bad, the clean and the **unclean**,
Isa 6: 5 For I am a man of **unclean** lips, and I live among a people of
6: 5 a man of unclean lips, and I live among a people of **unclean** lips,
35: 8 The **unclean** will not journey on it; it will be for those who walk in
52: 1 holy city. The uncircumcised and **defiled** will not enter you again.
52:11 Touch no **unclean** *thing*! Come out from it and be pure, you who
64: 6 [64:5] All of us have become like one *who* is **unclean**, and all our
Jer 19:13 and those of the kings of Judah will be **defiled** like this place,
La 4:15 "Go away! You are **unclean**!" men cry to them. "Away! Away!
Eze 4:13 "In this way the people of Israel will eat **defiled** food among the
22: 5 will mock you, O **infamous** [+2021+9005] city, full of turmoil.
22:10 women during their period, when they are **ceremonially unclean**.
22:26 they teach that there is no difference between the **unclean**
44:23 show them how to distinguish between the **unclean** and the clean.
Hos 9: 3 Ephraim will return to Egypt and eat **unclean** food in Assyria.
Am 7:17 and divided up, and you yourself will die in a **pagan** country.
Hag 2:13 "If a *person* **defiled** *by contact with* a dead body touches one of
2:14 'Whatever they do and whatever they offer there is **defiled**.

3239 טֻמְאָה ṭom'â, n.f. Not used in NIV/BHS [√ 3237]

3240 טֻמְאָה ṭum'â, n.f. [36] [√ 3237]

uncleanness [16], unclean [6], impurity [4], impurities [2], *untranslated* [1], ceremonially unclean [1], discharge [+2308] [1], filthiness [1], impure [1], things that make unclean [1], unclean practices [1], woman's monthly uncleanness [+2021+5614] [1]

Lev 5: 3 " 'Or if he touches human **uncleanness**—anything that would
5: 3 anything **[RPH]** that would make him unclean—even though he
7:20 if anyone who is **unclean** eats any meat of the fellowship offering
7:21 whether human **uncleanness** or an unclean animal or any unclean,
14:19 make atonement for the one to be cleansed from his **uncleanness**.
15: 3 flowing from his body or is blocked, it will make him **unclean**.
15: 3 This is how his discharge will bring about **uncleanness**:
15:25 she will be unclean as long as she has the **discharge** [+2308],
15:26 Any bed she lies on while her discharge continues will be **unclean**,
15:30 for her before the LORD for the **uncleanness** *of* her discharge.
15:31 keep the Israelites separate from **things that make** them **unclean**,
15:31 so they will not die in their **uncleanness** for defiling my dwelling
16:16 because of the **uncleanness** and rebellion of the Israelites,
16:16 which is among them in the midst of their **uncleanness**.
16:19 and to consecrate it from the **uncleanness** *of* the Israelites.
18:19 sexual relations during the **uncleanness** *of* her monthly period.
22: 3 if any of your descendants is **ceremonially unclean** and yet comes
22: 5 person who makes him unclean, whatever the **uncleanness** may be.
Nu 5:19 gone astray and become **impure** while married to your husband,
19:13 sprinkled on him, he is unclean; his **uncleanness** remains on him.
Jdg 13: 7 or other fermented drink and do not eat anything **unclean**,
13:14 drink any wine or other fermented drink nor eat anything **unclean**.
2Sa 11: 4 (She had purified herself from her **uncleanness**.) Then she went
2Ch 29:16 everything **unclean** that they found in the temple of the LORD.
Ezr 6:21 **unclean practices** *of* their Gentile neighbors in order to seek the
9:11 By their detestable practices they have filled it with their **impurity**
La 1: 9 Her **filthiness** clung to her skirts; she did not consider her future.
Eze 22:15 through the countries; and I will put an end to your **uncleanness**.
24:11 its copper glows so its **impurities** may be melted and its deposit
24:13 " 'Now your **impurity** is lewdness. Because I tried to cleanse you
24:13 to cleanse you but you would not be cleansed from your **impurity**,
36:17 like a **woman's monthly uncleanness** [+2021+5614] in my sight.
36:25 I will cleanse you from all your **impurities** and from all your idols.
36:29 I will save you from all your **uncleanness**. I will call for the grain
39:24 I dealt with them according to their **uncleanness** and their
Zec 13: 2 remove both the prophets and the spirit of **impurity** from the land.

3241 טָמָה ṭāmâ, v. [1] [√ 3237?]

considered stupid [1]

Job 18: 3 [C] we regarded as cattle and **considered stupid** in your sight?

3242 טָמַם ṭāmam, v. Not used in NIV/BHS

3243 טָמַן ṭāman, v. [31] [→ 4759]

hidden [10], hid [6], hide [3], buried [2], buries [2], bury [2], hiding [2], grave [1], lies in wait [1], set [1], treasures hidden [+8561] [1]

Ge 35: 4 [A] their ears, and Jacob **buried** them under the oak at Shechem.
Ex 2:12 [A] no one, he killed the Egyptian and **hid** him in the sand.
Dt 33:19 [B] of the seas, on the **treasures hidden** [+8561] *in* the sand."
Jos 2: 6 [A] **hidden** them under the stalks of flax she had laid out on the
7:21 [B] They *are* **hidden** in the ground inside my tent, with the silver
7:22 [B] and they ran to the tent, and there it was, **hidden** in his tent,
2Ki 7: 8 [G] away silver, gold and clothes, and went off and **hid** them.
7: 8 [G] another tent and took some things from it and **hid** them also.
Job 3:16 [B] Or why was I not **hidden** in the ground like a stillborn child,
18:10 [B] A noose *is* **hidden** for him on the ground; a trap lies in his
20:26 [B] total darkness **lies in wait** for his treasures. A fire unfanned
31:33 [A] concealed my sin as men do, by **hiding** my guilt in my heart
40:13 [A] **Bury** them all in the dust together; shroud their faces in the
40:13 [B] them all in the dust together; shroud their faces in the **grave**.
Ps 9:15 [9:16] [A] their feet are caught in the net *they have* **hidden**.
31: 4 [31:5] [A] Free me from the trap that *is* **set** for me, for you are
35: 7 [A] Since *they* **hid** their net for me without cause and without
35: 8 [A] may the net *they* **hid** entangle them, may they fall into the
64: 5 [64:6] [A] in evil plans, they talk about **hiding** their snares;
140: 5 [140:6] [A] Proud men *have* **hidden** a snare for me; they have
142: 3 [142:4] [A] In the path where I walk *men have* **hidden** a snare
Pr 19:24 [A] The sluggard **buries** his hand in the dish; he will not even
26:15 [A] The sluggard **buries** his hand in the dish; he is too lazy to
Isa 2:10 [C] **hide** in the ground from dread of the LORD and the
Jer 13: 4 [A] go now to Perath and **hide** it there in a crevice in the rocks."
13: 5 [A] So I went and **hid** it at Perath, as the LORD told me.
13: 6 [A] "Go now to Perath and get the belt I told you to **hide** there."
13: 7 [A] up the belt and took it from the place where *I had* **hidden** it,
18:22 [A] dug a pit to capture me and *have* **hidden** snares for my feet.
43: 9 [A] **bury** them in clay in the brick pavement at the entrance to
43:10 [A] I will set his throne over these stones *I have* **buried** here;

3244 טֶנֶא ṭene', n.m. [4]

basket [4]

Dt 26: 2 land the LORD your God is giving you and put them in a **basket**.
26: 4 The priest shall take the **basket** from your hands and set it down in
28: 5 Your **basket** and your kneading trough will be blessed.
28:17 Your **basket** and your kneading trough will be cursed.

3245 טָנַף *ṭānap*, v. [1]
soil [1]
SS 5: 3 [D] it on again? I have washed my feet—*must I* **soil** them again?

3246 טָעָה *ṭā'â*, v. [1] [cf. 9494]
lead astray [1]
Eze 13: 10 [G] " 'Because *they* **lead** my people **astray**, saying, "Peace,"

3247 טָעַם *ṭā'am*, v. [11] [→ 3248, 4761; Ar 10301]
taste [4], merely tasted [+3247] [2], tasted [2], tastes [2], sees [1]
1Sa 14: 24 [A] myself on my enemies!" So none of the troops **tasted** food.
14: 29 [A] See how my eyes brightened when *I* **tasted** a little of this
14: 43 [A] "*I* **merely tasted** [+3247] a little honey with the end of my
14: 43 [A] "*I* **merely tasted** [+3247] a little honey with the end of my
2Sa 3: 35 [A] if *I* **taste** bread or anything else before the sun sets!"
19: 35 [19:36] [A] *Can* your servant **taste** what he eats and drinks?
Job 12: 11 [A] Does not the ear test words as the tongue **tastes** food?
34: 3 [A] For the ear tests words as the tongue **tastes** food.
Ps 34: 8 [34:9] [A] **Taste** and see that the LORD is good; blessed is the
Pr 31: 18 [A] *She* **sees** that her trading is profitable, and her lamp does not
Jnh 3: 7 [A] *Do* not *let* any man or beast, herd or flock, **taste** anything;

3248 טַעַם *ṭa'am*, n.m. [13] [√ 3247; Ar 10302]
pretended to be insane [+906+9101] [2], tasted [2], *untranslated* [1], decree [1], discernment [1], discreetly [1], discretion [1], flavor [1], good judgment [1], judgment [1], tastes [1]
Ex 16: 31 white like coriander seed and **tasted** like wafers made with honey.
Nu 11: 8 it into cakes. And it **tasted** like something made with olive oil.
11: 8 And it tasted like **[RPH]** something made with olive oil.
1Sa 21: 13 [21:14] So *he* **pretended to be insane** [+906+9101] in their
25: 33 May you be blessed for your **good judgment** and for keeping me
Job 6: 6 food eaten without salt, or is there **flavor** in the white of an egg?
12: 20 lips of trusted advisers and takes away the **discernment** *of* elders.
Ps 34: T [34:1] When he **pretended to be insane** [+906+9101] before
119: 66 Teach me knowledge and good **judgment**, for I believe in your
Pr 11: 22 in a pig's snout is a beautiful woman who shows no **discretion**.
26: 16 is wiser in his own eyes than seven men who answer **discreetly**.
Jer 48: 11 into exile. So she **tastes** as she did, and her aroma is unchanged.
Jnh 3: 7 "By the **decree** *of* the king and his nobles: Do not let any man

3249 ¹טָעַן *ṭā'an*[1], v. [1]
pierced [1]
Isa 14: 19 [E] are covered with the slain, with *those* **pierced** *by* the sword,

3250 ²טָעַן *ṭā'an*[2], v. [1]
load [1]
Ge 45: 17 [A] 'Do this: **Load** your animals and return to the land of Canaan,

3251 ¹טַף *ṭap*[1], n.m. [42] [→ 3262; cf. 3252]
children [27], women and children [6], little ones [4], little children [2], boys [+2351] [1], families [1], girl [+851] [1]
Ge 34: 29 They carried off all their wealth and all their women and **children**,
43: 8 so that we and you and our **children** may live and not die.
45: 19 Take some carts from Egypt for your **children** and your wives,
46: 5 and Israel's sons took their father Jacob and their **children**
47: 12 household with food, according to the number of their **children**.
47: 24 as food for yourselves and your households and your **children**."
50: 8 Only their **children** and their flocks and herds were left in Goshen.
50: 21 don't be afraid. I will provide for you and your **children**."
Ex 10: 10 with you—if I let you go, along with your **women and children**!
10: 24 Even your **women and children** may go with you; only leave your
12: 37 six hundred thousand men on foot, besides **women and children**.
Nu 14: 3 Our wives and **children** will be taken as plunder. Wouldn't it be
14: 31 As for your **children** that you said would be taken as plunder,
16: 27 their wives, children and **little ones** at the entrances to their tents.
31: 9 Midianite women and **children** and took all the Midianite herds,
31: 17 Now kill all the **boys** [+2351]. And kill every woman who has
31: 18 save for yourselves every **girl** [+851] who has never slept with a
32: 16 pens here for our livestock and cities for our **women and children**.
32: 17 Meanwhile our **women and children** will live in fortified cities,
32: 24 Build cities for your **women and children**, and pens for your
32: 26 Our **children** and wives, our flocks and herds will remain here in
Dt 1: 39 the **little ones** that you said would be taken captive, your children
2: 34 and completely destroyed them—men, women and **children**.
3: 6 of Heshbon, destroying every city—men, women and **children**.
3: 19 your **children** and your livestock (I know you have much
20: 14 the **children**, the livestock and everything else in the city,
29: 11 [29:10] together with your **children** and your wives,
31: 12 men, women and **children**, and the aliens living in your towns—
Jos 1: 14 your **children** and your livestock may stay in the land that Moses
8: 35 including the women and **children**, and the aliens who lived
Jdg 18: 21 Putting their **little children**, their livestock and their possessions in
21: 10 to the sword those living there, including the women and **children**.
2Sa 15: 22 marched on with all his men and the **families** that were with him.
2Ch 20: 13 All the men of Judah, with their wives and children and **little ones**,
31: 18 They included all the **little ones**, the wives, and the sons
Ezr 8: 21 our God and ask him for a safe journey for us and our **children**,
Est 3: 13 young and old, women and **little children**—on a single day,
8: 11 or province that might attack them and their women and **children**;
Jer 40: 7 women and **children** who were the poorest in the land and who
41: 16 women, **children** and court officials he had brought from Gibeon.
43: 6 women and **children** and the king's daughters whom Nebuzaradan
Eze 9: 6 Slaughter old men, young men and maidens, women and **children**,

3252 ²טַף *ṭap*[2], n.m. Not used in NIV/BHS [cf. 3251]

3253 ¹טָפַח *ṭāpaḥ*[1], v. [1] [→ 3255, 3256, 3257, 3258; cf. 3254?]
spread out [1]
Isa 48: 13 [D] of the earth, and my right hand **spread out** the heavens;

3254 ²טָפַח *ṭāpaḥ*[2], v.den. [1] [→ 3259, 4762; cf. 3253?]
cared for [1]
La 2: 22 [D] those *I* **cared for** and reared, my enemy has destroyed."

3255 טֶפַח *ṭepaḥ*, n.[m.]. [2] [→ 3256; cf. 3253]
handbreadth [2]
1Ki 7: 26 It was a **handbreadth** in thickness, and its rim was like the rim of
2Ch 4: 5 It was a **handbreadth** in thickness, and its rim was like the rim of

3256 טֹפַח *ṭōpaḥ*, n.m. [5] [√ 3255; cf. 3253]
handbreadth [5]
Ex 25: 25 Also make around it a rim a **handbreadth** *wide* and put a gold
37: 12 They also made around it a rim a **handbreadth** wide and put a
Eze 40: 5 was six long cubits, each of which was a cubit and a **handbreadth**.
40: 43 double-pronged hooks, each a **handbreadth** long, were attached to
43: 13 altar in long cubits, that cubit being a cubit and a **handbreadth**:

3257 ¹טְפָחָה *ṭapḥâ*[1], n.[m.]. [1] [√ 3253]
handbreadth [1]
Ps 39: 5 [39:6] You have made my days a mere **handbreadth**; the span of

3258 ²טְפָחָה *ṭapḥâ*[2], n.[m.]. [1] [√ 3253]
eaves [1]
1Ki 7: 9 the outside to the great courtyard and from foundation to **eaves**,

3259 טִפֻּחִים *ṭippuḥîm*, n.[m.]pl.abst. [1] [√ 3254]
cared for [1]
La 2: 20 women eat their offspring, the children they have **cared for**?

3260 טָפַל *ṭāpal*, v. [3] [cf. 9521]
cover [1], smear [1], smeared [1]
Job 13: 4 [A] You, however, **smear** me *with* lies; you are worthless
14: 17 [A] will be sealed up in a bag; *you will* **cover** over my sin.
Ps 119: 69 [A] Though the arrogant *have* **smeared** me *with* lies, I keep your

3261 טִפְסָר *ṭipsār*, n.[m.]. [2]
commander [1], officials [1]
Jer 51: 27 Appoint a **commander** against her; send up horses like a swarm of
Na 3: 17 your **officials** like swarms of locusts that settle in the walls on a

3262 טָפַף *ṭāpap*, v. [1] [√ 3251]
tripping along with mincing steps [+2143+2256] [1]
Isa 3: 16 [A] **tripping** [+2143+2256] **along with mincing steps**,

3263 טָפַשׁ *ṭāpaš*, v. [1]
unfeeling [1]
Ps 119: 70 [A] Their hearts *are* callous and **unfeeling**, but I delight in your

3264 טָפַת *ṭāpat*, n.pr.f. [1]
Taphath [1]
1Ki 4: 11 in Naphoth Dor (he was married to **Taphath** daughter of

3265 טרד טָרַד ṭārad, v. [2] [→ 4765; Ar 10304]

constant dripping [+1942] [2]

Pr 19: 13 [A] and a quarrelsome wife is like a **constant dripping** [+1942].
27: 15 [A] A quarrelsome wife is like a **constant dripping** [+1942] on a

3266 טרום טְרוֹם ṭerôm, adv.temp. [0] [→ 3269, 3270]

Ru 3: 14 **[before** [+928] [K; see Q 3270] anyone could be recognized;]

3267 טרח טָרַח ṭāraḥ, v. [1] [→ 3268]

loads [1]

Job 37: 11 [G] *He* **loads** the clouds with moisture; he scatters his lightning

3268 טרח טֹרַח ṭōraḥ, n.m. [2] [√ 3267]

burden [1], problems [1]

Dt 1: 12 how can I bear your **problems** and your burdens and your disputes
Isa 1: 14 They have become a **burden** to me; I am weary of bearing them.

3269 טרי טָרִי ṭārî, a. [2] [√ 3266]

fresh [1], open [1]

Jdg 15: 15 Finding a **fresh** jawbone of a donkey, he grabbed it and struck
Isa 1: 6 only wounds and welts and **open** sores, not cleansed or bandaged

3270 טרם טֶרֶם ṭerem, adv.temp. & c. [56] [√ 3266]

before [+928] [36], before [9], not yet [4], before [+928+4202] [2], before [+4946] [1], just before [+928] [1], no yet [+3972] [1], no yet [1], still not [1]

Ge 2: 5 **no** shrub of the field had **yet** appeared on the earth and no plant of
2: 5 on the earth and **no** [+3972] plant of the field had **yet** sprung up,
19: 4 **Before** they had gone to bed, all the men from every part of the
24: 15 **Before** he had finished praying, Rebekah came out with her jar on
24: 45 "**Before** I finished praying in my heart, Rebekah came out,
27: 4 me to eat, so that I may give you my blessing **before** [+928] I die."
27: 33 I ate it **just before** [+928] you came and I blessed him—
37: 18 and **before** [+928] he reached them, they plotted to kill him.
41: 50 **Before** [+928] the years of famine came, two sons were born to
45: 28 son Joseph is still alive. I will go and see him **before** [+928] I die."
Ex 1: 19 are vigorous and give birth **before** [+928] the midwives arrive."
9: 30 that you and your officials **still** do **not** fear the LORD God."
10: 7 LORD their God. Do you **not yet** realize that Egypt is ruined?"
12: 34 So the people took their dough **before** the yeast was added,
Lev 14: 36 The priest is to order the house to be emptied **before** [+928] he
Nu 11: 33 was still between their teeth and **before** it could be consumed,
Dt 31: 21 even **before** [+928] I bring them into the land I promised them on
Jos 2: 8 **Before** the spies lay down for the night, she went up on the roof
3: 1 and went to the Jordan, where they camped **before** crossing over.
Jdg 14: 18 **Before** [+928] sunset on the seventh day the men of the town said
Ru 3: 14 but got up **before** [+928] [K 3266] anyone could be recognized;
1Sa 2: 15 even **before** [+928] the fat was burned, the servant of the priest
3: 3 The lamp of God had **not yet** gone out, and Samuel was lying
3: 7 Now Samuel did **not yet** know the LORD: The word of the
3: 7 The word of the LORD had **not yet** been revealed to him.
9: 13 you will find him **before** [+928] he goes up to the high place to eat.
2Ki 2: 9 what can I do for you **before** [+928] I am taken from you?"
6: 32 but **before** [+928] he arrived, Elisha said to the elders,
Job 10: 21 **before** [+928] I go to the place of no return, to the land of gloom
Ps 39: 13 [39:14] that I may rejoice again **before** [+928] I depart and am no
58: 9 [58:10] **Before** [+928] your pots can feel the heat of the thorns—
90: 2 **Before** [+928] the mountains were born or you brought forth the
119: 67 **Before** I was afflicted I went astray, but now I obey your word.
Pr 8: 25 **before** [+928] the mountains were settled in place, before the hills,
18: 13 He who answers **before** [+928] listening—that is his folly
30: 7 I ask of you, O LORD; do not refuse me **before** [+928] I die:
Isa 7: 16 But **before** [+928] the boy knows enough to reject the wrong
8: 4 **Before** [+928] the boy knows how to say 'My father' or 'My
17: 14 sudden terror! **Before** [+928] the morning, they are gone!
28: 4 of a fertile valley, will be like a fig ripe **before** [+928] harvest—
42: 9 new things I declare; **before** [+928] they spring into being I
48: 5 Therefore I told you these things long ago; **before** [+928] they
65: 24 **Before** they call I will answer; while they are still speaking I will
66: 7 "**Before** [+928] she goes into labor, she gives birth; before the
66: 7 she gives birth; **before** [+928] the pains come upon her, she
Jer 1: 5 "**Before** [+928] I formed you in the womb I knew you, before you
1: 5 "Before I formed you in the womb I knew you, **before** [+928] you
13: 16 Give glory to the LORD your God **before** [+928] he brings the
13: 16 the LORD your God before he brings the darkness, **before** [+928]
38: 10 lift Jeremiah the prophet out of the cistern **before** [+928] he dies."
47: 1 concerning the Philistines **before** [+928] Pharaoh attacked Gaza:
Eze 16: 57 **before** [+928] your wickedness was uncovered. Even so, you are
Zep 2: 2 **before** [+928] the appointed time arrives and that day sweeps on
2: 2 that day sweeps on like chaff, **before** [+928+4202] the fierce anger
2: 2 fierce anger of the LORD comes upon you, **before** [+928+4202]
Hag 2: 15 consider how things were **before** [+4946] one stone was laid on

3271 טרף טָרַף ṭārap, v. [25] [→ 3272, 3273, 3274]

tear to pieces [4], tear [3], tearing [3], been torn to pieces [+3271] [2], surely been torn to pieces [+3271] [2], was torn to pieces by a wild animal [+3271] [2], give [1], killed [1], mangles [1], prey [1], raged [1], ravenous [1], tearing prey [1], tears [1], torn to pieces [1]

Ge 37: 33 [E] Joseph *has* **surely been torn** [+3271] **to pieces**."
37: 33 [A] Joseph *has* **surely been torn to pieces** [+3271]."
44: 28 [E] and I said, "*He has* surely **been torn** [+3271] **to pieces**."
44: 28 [A] and I said, "*He has* surely **been torn to pieces** [+3271]."
49: 27 [A] "Benjamin *is* a **ravenous** wolf; in the morning he devours the
Ex 22: 13 [22:12] [C] If *it* **was torn** [+3271] **to pieces by a wild animal**,
22: 13 [22:12] [A] If *it* **was torn to pieces by a wild animal** [+3271],
Dt 33: 20 [A] Gad lives there like a lion, **tearing** *at* arm or head.
Job 16: 9 [A] God assails me and **tears** me in his anger and gnashes his
18: 4 [A] You *who* **tear** yourself **to pieces** in your anger, is the earth to
Ps 7: 2 [7:3] [A] or *they will* **tear** me like a lion and rip me to pieces
17: 12 [A] They are like a lion hungry for **prey**, like a great lion
22: 13 [22:14] [A] Roaring lions **tearing** their **prey** open their mouths
50: 22 [A] forget God, or *I will* **tear** you **to pieces**, with none to rescue:
Pr 30: 8 [G] neither poverty nor riches, but **give** me only my daily bread.
Jer 5: 6 [C] a leopard will lie in wait near their towns *to* **tear to pieces**
Eze 19: 3 [A] He learned to **tear** the prey and he devoured men.
19: 6 [A] He learned to **tear** the prey and he devoured men.
22: 25 [A] of her princes within her like a roaring lion **tearing** its prey;
22: 27 [A] Her officials within her are like wolves **tearing** their prey;
Hos 5: 14 [A] I *will* **tear** them **to pieces** and go away; I will carry them off,
6: 1 [A] He *has* **torn** us **to pieces** but he will heal us; he has injured
Am 1: 11 [A] because his anger **raged** continually and his fury flamed
Mic 5: 8 [5:7] [A] which mauls and **mangles** as it goes, and no one can
Na 2: 12 [2:13] [A] The lion **killed** enough for his cubs and strangled the

3272 טרף טֶרֶף ṭerep, n.m. [22] [√ 3271]

prey [13], food [4], victims [2], game [1], kill [1], torn [1]

Ge 49: 9 You are a lion's cub, O Judah; you return from the **prey**, my son.
Nu 23: 24 themselves like a lion that does not rest till he devours his **prey**
Job 4: 11 The lion perishes for lack of **prey**, and the cubs of the lioness are
24: 5 in the desert, the poor go about their labor of foraging **food**;
29: 17 the fangs of the wicked and snatched the **victims** from their teeth.
38: 39 "Do you hunt the **prey** for the lioness and satisfy the hunger of the
Ps 76: 4 [76:5] with light, more majestic than mountains rich with **game**.
104: 21 The lions roar for their **prey** and seek their food from God.
111: 5 He provides **food** for those who fear him; he remembers his
124: 6 Praise be to the LORD, who has not let us be **torn** by their teeth.
Pr 31: 15 she provides **food** for her family and portions for her servant girls.
Isa 5: 29 they growl as they seize their **prey** and carry it off with no one to
31: 4 "As a lion growls, a great lion over his **prey**—and though a whole
Eze 19: 3 a strong lion. He learned to tear the **prey** and he devoured men.
19: 6 a strong lion. He learned to tear the **prey** and he devoured men.
22: 25 of her princes within her like a roaring lion tearing its **prey**;
22: 27 Her officials within her are like wolves tearing their **prey**;
Am 3: 4 Does a lion roar in the thicket when he has no **prey**? Does he
Na 2: 12 [2:13] filling his lairs with the **kill** and his dens with the prey.
2: 13 [2:14] your young lions. I will leave you no **prey** on the earth.
3: 1 city of blood, full of lies, full of plunder, never without **victims**!
Mal 3: 10 tithe into the storehouse, that there may be **food** in my house.

3273 טרף טָרָף ṭārāp, a. [2] [√ 3271]

freshly plucked [1], new [1]

Ge 8: 11 in the evening, there in its beak was a **freshly plucked** olive leaf!
Eze 17: 9 of its fruit so that it withers? All its **new** growth will wither.

3274 טרפה טְרֵפָה ṭerēpâ, n.f. [9] [√ 3271]

torn by wild animals [5], animal torn by beasts [1], animals torn by wild beasts [1], prey [1], remains [1]

Ge 31: 39 I did not bring you **animals torn by wild beasts**; I bore the loss
Ex 22: 13 [22:12] he shall bring in the **remains** as evidence and he will not
22: 31 [22:30] So do not eat the meat of an **animal torn by** wild **beasts**;
Lev 7: 24 or **torn by wild animals** may be used for any other purpose,
17: 15 or **torn by wild animals** must wash his clothes and bathe with
22: 8 He must not eat anything found dead or **torn by wild animals**,
Eze 4: 14 I have never eaten anything found dead or **torn by wild animals**.
44: 31 eat anything, bird or animal, found dead or **torn by wild animals**.
Na 2: 12 [2:13] filling his lairs with the kill and his dens with the **prey**.

י, y

3275 י y, letter. Not used in NIV/BHS [→ Ar 10306]

3276 ִי- -î, p.s.com.suf. [6484 / 6477] [→ 483, 5646, 5761] Not indexed

my [3488], me [1800], I [381], *untranslated* [340], my [+4200] [77], the[s] [52], my own [43], me [+5883] [35], mine [+4200] [33], I [+5883] [29], myself [26], our [25], us [18], mine [16], a[s] [9], myself [+5883] [9], I'm [4], my [+5883] [4], my own [+4200] [4], his [3], me [+7156] [3], myself [+4213] [3], we [3], you[s] [+123] [3], her [2], here[s] [2], him [2], I've [2], me [+3883] [2], my [+928+8079] [2], this [2], us [+2256+3870] [2], you [2], all by myself [+963+4200] [1], an[s] [1], by myself [+907+4769] [1], by myself [+963+4200] [1], he[s] [+123] [1], he[s] [+3] [1], her [+4200] [1], her own [1], her[s] [1], here[s] [+6640] [1], here[s] [+6584] [1], him[s] [+123] [1], him[s] [+3] [1], his[s] [+466] [1], I [+4213] [1], I [+5055] [1], I [+7023] [1], I [+8120] [1], it[s] [+1460] [1], it[s] [+274] [1], it[s] [+4213] [1], it[s] [+7754] [1], its [1], me [+2652] [1], me [+8120] [1], me alone [+638] [1], mine [+4200+8611] [1], mine [+6643] [1], mine [+9393] [1], my [+4200+7156] [1], my [+6640] [1], my [+7156] [1], my [+907] [1], my [+928] [1], my life [1], my life's [1], my own [+4200+8611] [1], myself [+1414] [1], myself [+3338] [1], myself [+963] [1], our own [1], ours [+4200] [1], their[s] [+3776+6639] [1], them[s] [+6639] [1], they[s] [+7366] [1], thought [+448+606] [1], us [+2157+2256] [1], us [+2256+4013] [1], what do I care about [+2296+4200+4200+4537] [1], your[s] [+123] [1], your [1]

3277 יָאַב yā'ab, v. [1] [→ 95?, 3365?; cf. 14?, 9289?]

longing for [1]

Ps 119:131 [A] I open my mouth and pant, **longing for** your commands.

3278 יָאָה yā'â, v. [1]

due [1]

Jer 10: 7 [A] not revere you, O King of the nations? This is your **due**.

3279 יַאֲזַנְיָה ya'^{a}zanyâ, n.pr.m. [2] [→ 3280; cf. 263 + 3378]

Jaazaniah [2]

Jer 35: 3 So I went to get **Jaazaniah** son of Jeremiah, the son of
Eze 11: 1 I saw among them **Jaazaniah** son of Azzur and Pelatiah son of

3280 יַאֲזַנְיָהוּ ya'^{a}zanyāhû, n.pr.m. [2] [√ 3279; cf. 263 + 3378]

Jaazaniah [2]

2Ki 25:23 **Jaazaniah** the son of the Maacathite, and their men.
Eze 8:11 and **Jaazaniah** son of Shaphan was standing among them.

3281 יָאִיר yā'îr, n.pr.m. [8] [→ 2596, 3285]

Jair [8]

Nu 32:41 **Jair**, a descendant of Manasseh, captured their settlements
Dt 3:14 **Jair**, a descendant of Manasseh, took the whole region of Argob as
Jos 13:30 king of Bashan—all the settlements of **Jair** in Bashan, sixty towns,
Jdg 10: 3 He was followed by **Jair** of Gilead, who led Israel twenty-two
10: 5 When **Jair** died, he was buried in Kamon.
1Ki 4:13 in Ramoth Gilead (the settlements of **Jair** son of Manasseh in
1Ch 2:22 Segub was the father of **Jair**, who controlled twenty-three towns in
Est 2: 5 named Mordecai son of **Jair**, the son of Shimei, the son of Kish,

3282 יָאַל¹ yā'al[1], v. [4] [cf. 211]

become fools [2], foolish [1], foolishly [1]

Nu 12:11 [C] not hold against us the sin we have *so* **foolishly** committed.
Isa 19:13 [C] The officials of Zoan *have* **become fools**, the leaders of
Jer 5: 4 [C] *they are* **foolish**, for they do not know the way of the
50:36 [C] *They will* **become fools**. A sword against her warriors! They

3283 יָאַל² yā'al[2], v. [19] [cf. 215, 4578]

determined [3], pleased [3], agreed [2], bold [2], *untranslated* [1], be so kind as [1], began [1], by all means [1], content [1], intent on [1], please [+5528] [1], tried [1], willing [1]

Ge 18:27 [G] "Now *that I have been so* **bold** *as* to speak to the Lord,
18:31 [G] "Now *that I have been so* **bold** *as* to speak to the Lord,
Ex 2:21 [G] Moses **agreed** to stay with the man, who gave his daughter
Dt 1: 5 [G] territory of Moab, Moses **began** to expound this law, saying:
Jos 7: 7 [G] If only *we had been* **content** to stay on the other side of the
17:12 [G] for the Canaanites *were* **determined** to live in that region.
Jdg 1:27 [G] for the Canaanites *were* **determined** to live in that land.
1:35 [G] the Amorites *were* **determined** also to hold out in Mount
17:11 [G] So the Levite **agreed** to live with him, and the young man
19: 6 [G] father said, **[NIE]** "Please stay tonight and enjoy yourself."
1Sa 12:22 [G] because the LORD *was* **pleased** to make you his own.
17:39 [G] on his sword over the tunic and **tried** walking around,
2Sa 7:29 [G] Now *be* **pleased** to bless the house of your servant, that it
2Ki 5:23 [G] "**By all means**, take two talents," said Naaman. He urged
6: 3 [G] "Won't you **please** [+5528] come with your servants?"
1Ch 17:27 [G] Now *you have been* **pleased** to bless the house of your
Job 6: 9 [G] that God *would be* **willing** to crush me, to let loose his hand
6:28 [G] "But now **be so kind as** to look at me. Would I lie to your
Hos 5:11 [G] is oppressed, trampled in judgment, **intent on** pursuing idols.

3284 יְאֹר y^e'ōr, n.m. [65]

Nile [31], river [13], streams [10], *untranslated* [3], canals [2], its[s] [+2021] [2], riverbank [+8557] [1], rivers [1], streams of the Nile [1], tunnels [+1324] [1]

Ge 41: 1 had passed, Pharaoh had a dream: He was standing by the **Nile**,
41: 2 when out of the **river** there came up seven cows, sleek and fat,
41: 3 came up out of the **Nile** and stood beside those on the riverbank.
41: 3 out of the Nile and stood beside those on the **riverbank** [+8557].
41:17 to Joseph, "In my dream I was standing on the bank of the **Nile**,
41:18 when out of the **river** there came up seven cows, fat and sleek,
Ex 1:22 "Every boy that is born you must throw into the **Nile**, but let every
2: 3 child in it and put it among the reeds along the bank of the **Nile**.
2: 5 Pharaoh's daughter went down to the **Nile** to bathe, and her
2: 5 to bathe, and her attendants were walking along the **river** bank.
4: 9 take some water from the **Nile** and pour it on the dry ground.
4: 9 The water you take from the **river** will become blood on the
7:15 Wait on the bank of the **Nile** to meet him, and take in your hand
7:17 With the staff that is in my hand I will strike the water of the **Nile**,
7:18 The fish in the **Nile** will die, and the river will stink; the Egyptians
7:18 The fish in the Nile will die, and the **river** will stink;
7:18 the Egyptians will not be able to drink **its**[s] [+2021] water.' "
7:19 over the streams and **canals**, over the ponds and all the
7:20 of Pharaoh and his officials and struck the water of the **Nile**,
7:20 of the Nile, and all the water **[RPH]** was changed into blood.
7:21 The fish in the **Nile** died, and the river smelled so bad that the
7:21 the **river** smelled so bad that the Egyptians could not drink its
7:21 so bad that the Egyptians could not drink **its**[s] [+2021] water.
7:24 And all the Egyptians dug along the **Nile** to get drinking water,
7:24 drinking water, because they could not drink the water of the **river**.
7:25 Seven days passed after the LORD struck the **Nile**.
8: 3 [7:28] The **Nile** will teem with frogs. They will come up into your
8: 5 [8:1] hand with your staff over the streams and **canals** and ponds,
8: 9 [8:5] be rid of the frogs, except for those that remain in the **Nile**."
8:11 [8:7] and your people; they will remain only in the **Nile**."
17: 5 and take in your hand the staff with which you struck the **Nile**,
2Ki 19:24 With the soles of my feet I have dried up all the **streams** *of*
Job 28:10 *He* **tunnels** [+1324] through the rock; his eyes see all its treasures.
Ps 78:44 He turned their **rivers** to blood; they could not drink from their
Isa 7:18 the LORD will whistle for flies from the distant **streams** *of* Egypt
19: 6 canals will stink; the **streams** *of* Egypt will dwindle and dry up.
19: 7 also the plants along the **Nile**, at the mouth of the river. Every
19: 7 also the plants along the Nile, at the mouth of the **river**. Every
19: 7 Every sown field along the **Nile** will become parched, will blow
19: 8 fishermen will groan and lament, all who cast hooks into the **Nile**;
23: 3 the harvest of the **Nile** was the revenue of Tyre, and she became
23:10 Till your land as along the **Nile**, O Daughter of Tarshish, for you
33:21 It will be like a place of broad rivers and **streams**. No galley with
37:25 With the soles of my feet I have dried up all the **streams** *of* Egypt.'
Jer 46: 7 "Who is this that rises like the **Nile**, like rivers of surging waters?
46: 8 Egypt rises like the **Nile**, like rivers of surging waters. She says,
Eze 29: 3 king of Egypt, you great monster lying among your **streams**.
29: 3 your streams. You say, "The **Nile** is mine; I made it for myself."
29: 4 your jaws and make the fish of your **streams** stick to your scales.
29: 4 I will pull you out from among your **streams**, with all the fish
29: 4 your streams, with all the fish **[RPH]** sticking to your scales.
29: 5 I will leave you in the desert, you and all the fish of your **streams**.
29: 9 am the LORD. " 'Because you said, "The **Nile** is mine; I made it,"
29:10 therefore I am against you and against your **streams**, and I will
30:12 I will dry up the **streams of the Nile** and sell the land to evil men;
Da 12: 5 one on this bank of the **river** and one on the opposite bank.
12: 5 on this bank of the river and one on the opposite bank. **[RPH]**
12: 6 to the man clothed in linen, who was above the waters of the **river**,
12: 7 who was above the waters of the **river**, lifted his right hand
Am 8: 8 The whole land will rise like the **Nile**; it will be stirred up
8: 8 the Nile; it will be stirred up and then sink like the **river** *of* Egypt.
9: 5 the whole land rises like the **Nile**, then sinks like the river of
9: 5 whole land rises like the Nile, then sinks like the **river** *of* Egypt—
Na 3: 8 better than Thebes, situated on the **Nile**, with water around her?
Zec 10:11 sea will be subdued and all the depths of the **Nile** will dry up.

[F] Hitpael (hitpoel, hitpoal, hitpolel, hitpolal, hitpalel, hitpalal, hitpalpel, hitpalpal, hotpael, hotpaal) [G] Hiphil (hiphtil) [H] Hophal [I] Hishtaphel

3285 יָאִרִי *yā'îrî*, a.g. [1] [√ 3281]
Jairite [1]
2Sa 20:26 and Ira the **Jairite** was David's priest.

3286 יָאַשׁ *yā'aš*, v. [6]
despair [1], despairing [1], give up [1], hopeless [1], no use [1], use [1]
1Sa 27: 1 [C] Then Saul *will* **give up** searching for me anywhere in Israel,
Job 6:26 [C] what I say, and treat the words of a **despairing** *man* as wind?
Ecc 2:20 [D] So my heart began to **despair** over all my toilsome labor
Isa 57:10 [C] by all your ways, but you would not say, '*It is* **hopeless**.'
Jer 2:25 [C] you said, '*It's* no **use**! I love foreign gods, and I must go after
18:12 [C] they will reply, '*It's* **no use**. We will continue with our own

3287 יֹאשִׁיָּה *yō'šiyyâ*, n.pr.m. [1] [→ 3288 [+ 3378]]
Josiah [1]
Zec 6:10 Go the same day to the house of **Josiah** son of Zephaniah.

3288 יֹאשִׁיָּהוּ *yō'šiyyāhû*, n.pr.m. [52] [√ 3287 [+ 3378]]
Josiah [47], Josiah's [3], *untranslated* [1], him[s] [1]
1Ki 13: 2 'A son named **Josiah** will be born to the house of David.
2Ki 21:24 King Amon, and they made **Josiah** his son king in his place.
21:26 in the garden of Uzza. And **Josiah** his son succeeded him as king.
22: 1 **Josiah** was eight years old when he became king, and he reigned in
22: 3 King **Josiah** sent the secretary, Shaphan son of Azaliah, the son of
23:16 **Josiah** looked around, and when he saw the tombs that were there
23:19 **Josiah** removed and defiled all the shrines at the high places that
23:23 in the eighteenth year of King **Josiah**, this Passover was celebrated
23:24 Furthermore, **Josiah** got rid of the mediums and spiritists,
23:28 As for the other events of **Josiah's** reign, and all he did, are they
23:29 King **Josiah** marched out to meet him in battle, but Neco faced
23:30 the people of the land took Jehoahaz son of **Josiah** and anointed
23:34 Pharaoh Neco made Eliakim son of **Josiah** king in place of his
23:34 Neco made Eliakim son of Josiah king in place of his father **Josiah**
1Ch 3:14 Amon his son, **Josiah** his son.
3:15 The sons of **Josiah**: Johanan the firstborn, Jehoiakim the second
2Ch 33:25 King Amon, and they made **Josiah** his son king in his place.
34: 1 **Josiah** was eight years old when he became king, and he reigned in
34:33 **Josiah** removed all the detestable idols from all the territory
35: 1 **Josiah** celebrated the Passover to the LORD in Jerusalem,
35: 7 **Josiah** provided for all the lay people who were there a total of
35:16 offerings on the altar of the LORD, as King **Josiah** had ordered.
35:18 kings of Israel had ever celebrated such a Passover as did **Josiah**,
35:19 This Passover was celebrated in the eighteenth year of **Josiah's**
35:20 After all this, when **Josiah** had set the temple in order, Neco king
35:20 on the Euphrates, and **Josiah** marched out to meet him in battle.
35:22 **Josiah**, however, would not turn away from him, but disguised
35:23 Archers shot King **Josiah**, and he told his officers, "Take me away;
35:24 of his fathers, and all Judah and Jerusalem mourned for **him**[s].
35:25 Jeremiah composed laments for **Josiah**, and to this day all the men
35:25 the men and women singers commemorate **Josiah** in the laments.
35:26 The other events of **Josiah's** reign and his acts of devotion,
36: 1 the people of the land took Jehoahaz son of **Josiah** and made him
Jer 1: 2 thirteenth year of the reign of **Josiah** son of Amon king of Judah,
1: 3 and through the reign of Jehoiakim son of **Josiah** king of Judah,
1: 3 of the eleventh year of Zedekiah son of **Josiah** king of Judah,
3: 6 During the reign of King **Josiah**, the LORD said to me, "Have
22:11 For this is what the LORD says about Shallum son of **Josiah**,
22:11 his father as king of Judah **[RPH]** but has gone from this place:
22:18 the LORD says about Jehoiakim son of **Josiah** king of Judah:
25: 1 Judah in the fourth year of Jehoiakim son of **Josiah** king of Judah,
25: 3 from the thirteenth year of **Josiah** son of Amon king of Judah until
26: 1 Early in the reign of Jehoiakim son of **Josiah** king of Judah,
27: 1 Early in the reign of Zedekiah son of **Josiah** king of Judah,
35: 1 LORD during the reign of Jehoiakim son of **Josiah** king of Judah:
36: 1 In the fourth year of Jehoiakim son of **Josiah** king of Judah,
36: 2 the time I began speaking to you in the reign of **Josiah** till now.
36: 9 In the ninth month of the fifth year of Jehoiakim son of **Josiah**
37: 1 Zedekiah son of **Josiah** was made king of Judah by
45: 1 Neriah in the fourth year of Jehoiakim son of **Josiah** king of Judah,
46: 2 in the fourth year of Jehoiakim son of **Josiah** king of Judah:
Zep 1: 1 during the reign of **Josiah** son of Amon king of Judah:

3289 יִאתוֹן *yi'tôn*, n.m. Not used in NIV/BHS [cf. 415]

3290 יְאָתְרַי *y^e'āt^{e}ray*, n.pr.m. [1]
Jeatherai [1]
1Ch 6:21 [6:6] his son, Iddo his son, Zerah his son and **Jeatherai** his son.

3291 יָבַב *yābab*, v. [1] [√ 3412]
cried out [1]
Jdg 5:28 [D] behind the lattice *she* **cried out**, 'Why is his chariot so long

3292 יְבוּל *y^{e}bûl*, n.m. [13 / 12] [√ 3297]
crops [7], harvest [2], grapes [1], harvests [1], produce [1]
Lev 26: 4 the ground will yield its **crops** and the trees of the field their fruit.
26:20 will be spent in vain, because your soil will not yield its **crops**,
Dt 11:17 so that it will not rain and the ground will yield no **produce**,
32:22 It will devour the earth and its **harvests** and set afire the
Jdg 6: 4 They camped on the land and ruined the **crops** all the way to Gaza
Job 20:28 A flood [BHS ***possessions*** *will be carried off*; NIV 3298] will carry
Ps 67: 6 [67:7] the land will yield its **harvest**, and God, our God, will bless
78:46 He gave their **crops** to the grasshopper, their produce to the locust.
85:12 [85:13] give what is good, and our land will yield its **harvest**.
Eze 34:27 of the field will yield their fruit and the ground will yield its **crops**;
Hab 3:17 the fig tree does not bud and there are no **grapes** on the vines,
Hag 1:10 of you the heavens have withheld their dew and the earth its **crops**.
Zec 8:12 the vine will yield its fruit, the ground will produce its **crops**,

3293 יְבוּס *y^{e}bûs*, n.pr.loc. [4] [→ 3294]
Jebus [3], *untranslated* [1]
Jdg 19:10 the man left and went toward **Jebus** (that is, Jerusalem), with his
19:11 When they were near **Jebus** and the day was almost gone,
1Ch 11: 4 and all the Israelites marched to Jerusalem (that is, **Jebus**).
11: 5 **[RPH]** said to David, "You will not get in here." Nevertheless,

3294 יְבוּסִי *y^{e}bûsî*, a.g. [41] [√ 3293]
Jebusites [32], Jebusite [9]
Ge 10:16 **Jebusites**, Amorites, Girgashites,
15:21 Amorites, Canaanites, Girgashites and **Jebusites**."
Ex 3: 8 Hittites, Amorites, Perizzites, Hivites and **Jebusites**.
3:17 Hittites, Amorites, Perizzites, Hivites and **Jebusites**—
13: 5 land of the Canaanites, Hittites, Amorites, Hivites and **Jebusites**—
23:23 Hittites, Perizzites, Canaanites, Hivites and **Jebusites**, and I will
33: 2 Amorites, Hittites, Perizzites, Hivites and **Jebusites**.
34:11 Canaanites, Hittites, Perizzites, Hivites and **Jebusites**.
Nu 13:29 the Hittites, **Jebusites** and Amorites live in the hill country;
Dt 7: 1 Canaanites, Perizzites, Hivites and **Jebusites**,
20:17 Amorites, Canaanites, Perizzites, Hivites and **Jebusites**—
Jos 3:10 Hittites, Hivites, Perizzites, Girgashites, Amorites and **Jebusites**.
9: 1 Amorites, Canaanites, Perizzites, Hivites and **Jebusites**)—
11: 3 the Amorites, Hittites, Perizzites and **Jebusites** in the hill country;
12: 8 Amorites, Canaanites, Perizzites, Hivites and **Jebusites**):
15: 8 Ben Hinnom along the southern slope of the **Jebusite** city (that is,
15:63 Judah could not dislodge the **Jebusites**, who were living in
15:63 to this day the **Jebusites** live there with the people of Judah.
18:16 the Hinnom Valley along the southern slope of the **Jebusite** *city*
18:28 Zelah, Haeleph, the **Jebusite** *city* (that is, Jerusalem), Gibeah
24:11 Perizzites, Canaanites, Hittites, Girgashites, Hivites and **Jebusites**,
Jdg 1:21 The Benjamites, however, failed to dislodge the **Jebusites**,
1:21 to this day the **Jebusites** live there with the Benjamites.
3: 5 Hittites, Amorites, Perizzites, Hivites and **Jebusites**.
19:11 let's stop at this city of the **Jebusites** and spend the night."
2Sa 5: 6 and his men marched to Jerusalem to attack the **Jebusites**,
5: 8 "Anyone who conquers the **Jebusites** will have to use the water
24:16 LORD was then at the threshing floor of Araunah the **Jebusite**.
24:18 to the LORD on the threshing floor of Araunah the **Jebusite**."
1Ki 9:20 and **Jebusites** (these peoples were not Israelites),
1Ch 1:14 **Jebusites**, Amorites, Girgashites,
11: 4 to Jerusalem (that is, Jebus). The **Jebusites** who lived there
11: 6 "Whoever leads the attack on the **Jebusites** will become
21:15 then standing at the threshing floor of Araunah the **Jebusite**.
21:18 altar to the LORD on the threshing floor of Araunah the **Jebusite**.
21:28 had answered him on the threshing floor of Araunah the **Jebusite**,
2Ch 3: 1 It was on the threshing floor of Araunah the **Jebusite**, the place
8: 7 and **Jebusites** (these peoples were not Israelites),
Ezr 9: 1 Hittites, Perizzites, **Jebusites**, Ammonites, Moabites, Egyptians
Ne 9: 8 Amorites, Perizzites, **Jebusites** and Girgashites.
Zec 9: 7 and become leaders in Judah, and Ekron will be like the **Jebusites**.

3295 יִבְחָר *yibḥār*, n.pr.m. [3] [√ 1047]
Ibhar [3]
2Sa 5:15 **Ibhar**, Elishua, Nepheg, Japhia,
1Ch 3: 6 There were also **Ibhar**, Elishua, Eliphelet,
14: 5 **Ibhar**, Elishua, Elpelet,

3296 יָבִין ***yābîn***, n.pr.m. [8] [√ 1067]

Jabin [6], him[s] [+4046+4889] [1], Jabin's [1]

Jos 11: 1 When **Jabin** king of Hazor heard of this, he sent word to Jobab
Jdg 4: 2 So the LORD sold them into the hands of **Jabin**, a king of
4: 7 the commander of **Jabin's** army, with his chariots and his troops to
4: 17 because there were friendly relations between **Jabin** king of Hazor
4: 23 On that day God subdued **Jabin**, the Canaanite king, before the
4: 24 the hand of the Israelites grew stronger and stronger against **Jabin**,
4: 24 the Canaanite king, until they destroyed **him**[s] [+4046+4889].
Ps 83: 9 [83:10] as you did to Sisera and **Jabin** at the river Kishon,

3297 יָבַל ***yābal***, v. [18] [→ 64, 201, 3292, 3298, 3299, 3414; Ar 10308]

bring [5], are led in [1], be brought [1], be carried [1], be led forth [1], been carried [1], bring back [1], is carried [1], is delivered [1], is led [1], led [1], sends [1], taken [1], was led [1]

Job 10: 19 [H] or *had* **been carried** straight from the womb to the grave!
21: 30 [H] day of calamity, that *he* **is delivered** from the day of wrath?
21: 32 [H] He **is carried** to the grave, and watch is kept over his tomb.
Ps 45: 14 [45:15] [H] In embroidered garments *she* **is led** to the king;
45: 15 [45:16] [H] *They* **are led in** with joy and gladness; they enter
60: 9 [60:11] [G] Who *will* **bring** me to the fortified city? Who will
68: 29 [68:30] [G] your temple at Jerusalem kings *will* **bring** you gifts.
76: 11 [76:12] [G] *let* all the neighboring lands **bring** gifts to the One
108: 10 [108:11] [G] Who *will* **bring** me *to* the fortified city? Who will
Isa 18: 7 [H] *will* **be brought** to the LORD Almighty *from* a people tall
23: 7 [G] old city, whose feet *have* **taken** her to settle in far-off lands?
53: 7 [H] *he* **was led** like a lamb to the slaughter, and as a sheep before
55: 12 [H] You will go out in joy and **be led forth** in peace;
Jer 11: 19 [H] I had been like a gentle lamb **led** to the slaughter; I did not
31: 9 [G] come with weeping; they will pray *as I* **bring** them **back**.
Hos 10: 6 [H] It *will* **be carried** to Assyria as tribute for the great king.
12: 1 [12:2] [H] a treaty with Assyria and **sends** olive oil to Egypt.
Zep 3: 10 [G] my worshipers, my scattered people, *will* **bring** me offerings.

3298 ¹יָבָל ***yābāl*[1]**, n.[m.]. [2 / 3] [√ 3297]

flood [1], flow [1], flowing streams [+4784] [1]

Job 20: 28 A **flood** [BHS 3292] will carry off his house, rushing waters on
Isa 30: 25 streams of water will **flow** on every high mountain and every lofty
44: 4 grass in a meadow, like poplar trees by **flowing streams** [+4784].

3299 ²יָבָל ***yābāl*[2]**, n.pr.m. [1] [√ 3297]

Jabal [1]

Ge 4: 20 Adah gave birth to **Jabal**; he was the father of those who live in

3300 יִבְלְעָם ***yiblᵉʿām***, n.pr.loc. [3] [√ 1180? *or* 1181? *or* 1182?]

Ibleam [3]

Jos 17: 11 **Ibleam** and the people of Dor, Endor, Taanach and Megiddo,
Jdg 1: 27 or Taanach or Dor or **Ibleam** or Megiddo and their surrounding
2Ki 9: 27 wounded him in his chariot on the way up to Gur near **Ibleam**,

3301 יַבֶּלֶת ***yabbelet***, a. [1] [→ 3413]

anything with warts [1]

Lev 22: 22 the maimed, or **anything with warts** or festering or running sores.

3302 יָבַם ***yābam***, v.den. [3] [√ 3303]

fulfill the duty of a brother-in-law [2], fulfill duty as a brother-in-law [1]

Ge 38: 8 [D] **fulfill** *your* **duty** *to* her **as a brother-in-law** to produce
Dt 25: 5 [D] marry her and **fulfill the duty of a brother-in-law** *to* her.
25: 7 [D] He will not **fulfill the duty of a brother-in-law** *to* me."

3303 יָבָם ***yābām***, n.m. [2] [→ 3302, 3304]

husband's brother [2]

Dt 25: 5 Her **husband's brother** shall take her and marry her and fulfill the
25: 7 "My **husband's brother** refuses to carry on his brother's name in

3304 יְבָמָה ***yᵉbāmâ***, n.f. [5] [√ 3303]

brother's widow [1], brother's wife [1], her[s] [+3871] [1], she[s] [+2257] [1], sister-in-law [1]

Dt 25: 7 However, if a man does not want to marry his **brother's wife**,
25: 7 **she**[s] [+2257] shall go to the elders at the town gate and say,
25: 9 his **brother's widow** shall go up to him in the presence of the
Ru 1: 15 "your **sister-in-law** is going back to her people and her gods.
1: 15 back to her people and her gods. Go back with **her**[s] [+3871]."

3305 יַבְנְאֵל ***yabnᵉʾēl***, n.pr.loc. [2] [√ 1215 + 446; cf. 3306]

Jabneel [2]

Jos 15: 11 passed along to Mount Baalah and reached **Jabneel**.
19: 33 passing Adami Nekeb and **Jabneel** to Lakkum and ending at the

3306 יַבְנֶה ***yabnēh***, n.pr.loc. [1] [cf. 3305]

Jabneh [1]

2Ch 26: 6 and broke down the walls of Gath, **Jabneh** and Ashdod.

3307 יִבְנְיָה ***yibnᵉyâ***, n.pr.m. [1] [√ 1215 + 3378]

Ibneiah [1]

1Ch 9: 8 **Ibneiah** son of Jeroham; Elah son of Uzzi, the son of Micri;

3308 יִבְנִיָּה ***yibniyyâ***, n.pr.m. [1] [√ 1215 + 3378]

Ibnijah [1]

1Ch 9: 8 son of Shephatiah, the son of Reuel, the son of **Ibnijah**.

3309 יַבֹּק ***yabbōq***, n.pr.loc. [7] [√ 1327? *or* 84?]

Jabbok [7]

Ge 32: 22 [32:23] and his eleven sons and crossed the ford of the **Jabbok**.
Nu 21: 24 to the sword and took over his land from the Arnon to the **Jabbok**,
Dt 2: 37 neither the land along the course of the **Jabbok** nor that around the
3: 16 out to the **Jabbok** River, which is the border of the Ammonites.
Jos 12: 2 to the **Jabbok** River, which is the border of the Ammonites.
Jdg 11: 13 they took away my land from the Arnon to the **Jabbok**, all the way
11: 22 capturing all of it from the Arnon to the **Jabbok** and from the

3310 יְבֶרֶכְיָהוּ ***yᵉberekyāhû***, n.pr.m. [1] [√ 1385 + 3378]

Jeberekiah [1]

Isa 8: 2 and Zechariah son of **Jeberekiah** as reliable witnesses for me."

3311 יִבְשָׂם ***yibśām***, n.pr.m. [1] [√ 1411]

Ibsam [1]

1Ch 7: 2 Uzzi, Rephaiah, Jeriel, Jahmai, **Ibsam** and Samuel—heads of their

3312 ¹יָבֵשׁ ***yābēš*[1]**, v. [62 / 63] [→ 3313, 3314?, 3315?, 3316, 3317, 3318]

dried up [15], withered [8], dry up [7], wither [6], dry [5], withers [5], completely withered [+3312] [2], dries up [2], wither away [2], wither completely [+3312] [2], completely dry [1], drought [1], fail [1], made shrivel [1], make dry [1], overthrow [1], parched [1], shriveled up [1], withered away [1]

Ge 8: 7 [A] and forth until the water *had* **dried up** from the earth.
8: 14 [A] day of the second month the earth *was* **completely dry**.
Jos 2: 10 [G] We have heard how the LORD **dried up** the water of the
4: 23 [G] For the LORD your God **dried up** the Jordan before you
4: 23 [G] Sea when *he* **dried** it **up** before us until we had crossed over.
5: 1 [G] *had* **dried up** the Jordan before the Israelites until we had
9: 5 [A] All the bread of their food supply was **dry** and moldy.
9: 12 [A] we left to come to you. But now see how **dry** and moldy it is.
1Ki 13: 4 [A] But the hand he stretched out toward the man **shriveled up**,
17: 7 [A] Some time later the brook **dried up** because there had been
Job 8: 12 [A] still growing and uncut, *they* **wither** more quickly than grass.
12: 15 [A] If he holds back the waters, *there is* **drought**; if he lets them
14: 11 [A] from the sea or a riverbed becomes parched and **dry**,
15: 30 [D] a flame *will* **wither** his shoots, and the breath of God's
18: 16 [A] His roots **dry up** below and his branches wither above.
Ps 22: 15 [22:16] [A] My strength *is* **dried up** like a potsherd, and my
37: 19 [A] In times of disaster *they will* not **wither**; in days of famine
74: 15 [G] up springs and streams; you **dried up** the ever flowing rivers.
90: 6 [A] morning it springs up new, by evening it is dry and **withered**.
102: 4 [102:5] [A] My heart is blighted and **withered** like grass; I
102: 11 [102:12] [A] like the evening shadow; I **wither away** like grass.
129: 6 [A] be like grass on the roof, which **withers** before it can grow;
Pr 17: 22 [D] is good medicine, but a crushed spirit **dries up** the bones.
Isa 15: 6 [A] The waters of Nimrim are dried up and the grass *is* **withered**;
19: 5 [A] river will dry up, and the riverbed will be parched and **dry**.
19: 7 [A] Every sown field along the Nile *will become* **parched**,
27: 11 [A] When its twigs *are* **dry**, they are broken off and women
40: 7 [A] The grass **withers** and the flowers fall, because the breath of
40: 8 [A] The grass **withers** and the flowers fall, but the word of our
40: 24 [A] root in the ground, than he blows on them and *they* **wither**,
42: 15 [G] waste the mountains and hills and **dry up** all their vegetation;
42: 15 [G] I will turn rivers into islands and **dry up** the pools.
44: 27 [G] to the watery deep, 'Be dry, and *I will* **dry up** your streams,'
Jer 12: 4 [A] the land lie parched and the grass in every field *be* **withered**?
23: 10 [A] land lies parched and the pastures in the desert *are* **withered**.

Jer 50:38 [A] *They will* **dry up**. For it is a land of idols, idols that will go
51:36 [G] avenge you; I will dry up her sea and **make** her springs **dry**.
Eze 17: 9 [A] it not be uprooted and stripped of its fruit so that *it* **withers**?
17: 9 [A] of its fruit so that it withers? All its new growth *will* **wither**.
17:10 [A] *Will it* not **wither** [+3312] **completely** when the east wind
17:10 [A] *Will it* not **wither completely** [+3312] when the east wind
17:10 [A] wind strikes it—**wither away** in the plot where it grew?' "
17:24 [G] *I* **dry up** the green tree and make the dry tree flourish.
19:12 [G] The east wind **made** *it* **shrivel**, it was stripped of its fruit;
19:12 [A] its strong branches **withered** and fire consumed them.
37:11 [A] They say, 'Our bones *are* **dried up** and our hope is gone;
Hos 9:16 [A] is blighted, their root *is* **withered**, they yield no fruit.
13:15 [A] his spring *will* **fail** [BHS 1017] and his well dry up.
Joel 1:10 [G] the grain is destroyed, the new wine *is* **dried up**, the oil fails.
1:12 [G] The vine *is* **dried up** and the fig tree is withered;
1:12 [A] and the apple tree—all the trees of the field—*are* **dried up**.
1:12 [G] are dried up. Surely the joy of mankind *is* **withered away**.
1:17 [G] have been broken down, for the grain *has* **dried up**.
1:20 [A] the streams of water *have* **dried up** and fire has devoured the
Am 1: 2 [A] of the shepherds dry up, and the top of Carmel **withers**."
4: 7 [A] One field had rain; another had none and **dried up**.
Jnh 4: 7 [A] provided a worm, which chewed the vine so that *it* **withered**.
Na 1: 4 [D] He rebukes the sea and **dries it up**; he makes all the rivers
Zec 9: 5 [G] writhe in agony, and Ekron too, for her hope *will* **wither**.
10: 5 [G] is with them, they will fight and **overthrow** the horsemen.
10:11 [G] will be subdued and all the depths of the Nile *will* **dry up**.
11:17 [A] *May* his arm *be* **completely withered** [+3312], his right eye
11:17 [A] *May* his arm *be* **completely withered** [+3312], his right eye

3313 [2]יָבֵשׁ *yābēš*[2], a.vbl. *or* v.ptcp. [10] [√ 3312]

dry [8], grapes or raisins [+2256+4300+6694] [1], lost [1]

Nu 6: 3 not drink grape juice or eat **grapes or raisins** [+2256+4300+6694].
11: 6 But now we *have* **lost** our appetite; we never see anything
Job 13:25 you torment a windblown leaf? Will you chase after **dry** chaff?
Isa 56: 3 And let not any eunuch complain, "I am only a **dry** tree."
La 4: 8 skin has shriveled on their bones; it has become as **dry** as a stick.
Eze 17:24 I dry up the green tree and make the **dry** tree flourish.
20:47 [21:3] and it will consume all your trees, both green and **dry**.
37: 2 many bones on the floor of the valley, bones *that* were very **dry**.
37: 4 said to me, "Prophesy to these bones and say to them, '**Dry** bones,
Na 1:10 and drunk from their wine; they will be consumed like **dry** stubble.

3314 [3]יָבֵשׁ *yābēš*[3], n.pr.m. [3] [√ 3312?]

Jabesh [3]

2Ki 15:10 Shallum son of **Jabesh** conspired against Zechariah. He attacked
15:13 Shallum son of **Jabesh** became king in the thirty-ninth year of
15:14 He attacked Shallum son of **Jabesh** in Samaria, assassinated him

3315 [4]יָבֵשׁ *yābēš*[4], n.pr.loc. [9] [√ 3312?]

Jabesh [8], they[s] [+408] [1]

1Sa 11: 1 And all the men of **Jabesh** said to him, "Make a treaty with us,
11: 3 The elders of **Jabesh** said to him, "Give us seven days so we can
11: 5 Then they repeated to him what the men of **Jabesh** had said.
11: 9 When the messengers went and reported this to the men of **Jabesh**,
11:10 **They**[s] [+408] said to the Ammonites, "Tomorrow we will
31:12 and his sons from the wall of Beth Shan and went to **Jabesh**,
31:13 took their bones and buried them under a tamarisk tree at **Jabesh**,
1Ch 10:12 took the bodies of Saul and his sons and brought them to **Jabesh**.
10:12 Then they buried their bones under the great tree in **Jabesh**,

3316 יָבֵשׁ גִּלְעָד *yābēš gil'ād*, n.pr.loc. [12] [√ 3312 + 1680]

Jabesh Gilead [12]

Jdg 21: 8 They discovered that no one from **Jabesh Gilead** had come to the
21: 9 they found that none of the people of **Jabesh Gilead** were there.
21:10 thousand fighting men with instructions to go to **Jabesh Gilead**
21:12 They found among the people living in **Jabesh Gilead** four
21:14 were given the women of **Jabesh Gilead** who had been spared.
1Sa 11: 1 Nahash the Ammonite went up and besieged **Jabesh Gilead**.
11: 9 "Say to the men of **Jabesh Gilead**, 'By the time the sun is hot
31:11 When the people of **Jabesh Gilead** heard of what the Philistines
2Sa 2: 4 When David was told that it was the men of **Jabesh Gilead** who
2: 5 he sent messengers to the men of **Jabesh Gilead** to say to them,
21:12 of Saul and his son Jonathan from the citizens of **Jabesh Gilead**.
1Ch 10:11 When all the inhabitants of **Jabesh Gilead** heard of everything the

3317 יַבָּשָׁה *yabbāšâ*, n.f. [14] [√ 3312; Ar 10309]

dry ground [10], dry land [2], land [2]

Ge 1: 9 the sky be gathered to one place, and let **dry ground** appear."
1:10 God called the **dry ground** "land," and the gathered waters he
Ex 4: 9 take some water from the Nile and pour it on the **dry ground**.
14:16 so that the Israelites can go through the sea on **dry ground**.
14:22 the Israelites went through the sea on **dry ground**, with a wall of
14:29 the Israelites went through the sea on **dry ground**, with a wall of
15:19 but the Israelites walked through the sea on **dry ground**.
Jos 4:22 tell them, 'Israel crossed the Jordan on **dry ground**.'
Ne 9:11 the sea before them, so that they passed through it on **dry ground**,
Ps 66: 6 He turned the sea into **dry land**, they passed through the waters on
Isa 44: 3 will pour water on the thirsty land, and streams on the **dry ground**;
Jnh 1: 9 the LORD, the God of heaven, who made the sea and the **land**."
1:13 Instead, the men did their best to row back to **land**. But they could
2:10 [2:11] commanded the fish, and it vomited Jonah onto **dry land**.

3318 יַבֶּשֶׁת *yabbešet*, n.f. [2] [√ 3312]

dry land [1], ground [1]

Ex 4: 9 water you take from the river will become blood on the **ground**."
Ps 95: 5 The sea is his, for he made it, and his hands formed the **dry land**.

3319 יִגְאָל *yig'āl*, n.pr.m. [3] [√ 1457]

Igal [3]

Nu 13: 7 from the tribe of Issachar, **Igal** son of Joseph;
2Sa 23:36 **Igal** son of Nathan from Zobah, the son of Hagri,
1Ch 3:22 his sons: Hattush, **Igal**, Bariah, Neariah and Shaphat—six in all.

3320 יָגַב *yāgab*, v. [2] [→ 3321]

fields [2]

2Ki 25:12 [A] poorest people of the land to work the vineyards and **fields**.
Jer 52:16 [A] poorest people of the land to work the vineyards and **fields**.

3321 יָגֵב *yāgēb*, n.m. [1] [√ 3320]

fields [1]

Jer 39:10 owned nothing; and at that time he gave them vineyards and **fields**.

3322 יָגְבְּהָה *yogbᵉhâ*, n.pr.loc. [2] [√ 1467]

Jogbehah [2]

Nu 32:35 Atroth Shophan, Jazer, **Jogbehah**,
Jdg 8:11 east of Nobah and **Jogbehah** and fell upon the unsuspecting army.

3323 יְגַדַּלְיָהוּ *yigdalyāhû*, n.pr.m. [1] [√ 1540 + 3378]

Igdaliah [1]

Jer 35: 4 into the room of the sons of Hanan son of **Igdaliah** the man of

3324 [1]יָגָה *yāgâ*[1], v. [7] [→ 3326, 9342; cf. 3325]

brings grief [1], brought grief [1], brought [1], grief [1], grieve [1], torment [1], tormentors [1]

Job 19: 2 [G] "How long *will you* **torment** me and crush me with words?
Isa 51:23 [G] I will put it into the hands of your **tormentors**, who said to
La 1: 4 [C] her priests groan, her maidens **grieve**, and she is in bitter
1: 5 [G] The LORD *has* **brought** her **grief** because of her many
1:12 [G] that the LORD **brought** on me in the day of his fierce
3:32 [G] Though *he* **brings grief**, he will show compassion, so great
3:33 [D] not willingly bring affliction or **grief** *to* the children of men.

3325 [2]יָגָה *yāgâ*[2], v. [1] [cf. 2048, 3324]

been removed [1]

2Sa 20:13 [G] After Amasa *had* **been removed** from the road, all the men

3326 יָגוֹן *yāgôn*, n.[m.]. [14] [√ 3324]

sorrow [13], anguish [1]

Ge 42:38 you will bring my gray head down to the grave in **sorrow**."
44:31 will bring the gray head of our father down to the grave in **sorrow**.
Est 9:22 as the month when their **sorrow** was turned into joy and their
Ps 13: 2 [13:3] with my thoughts and every day have **sorrow** in my heart?
31:10 [31:11] My life is consumed by **anguish** and my years by
107:39 and they were humbled by oppression, calamity and **sorrow**;
116: 3 the grave came upon me; I was overcome by trouble and **sorrow**.
Isa 35:10 and joy will overtake them, and **sorrow** and sighing will flee away.
51:11 and joy will overtake them, and **sorrow** and sighing will flee away.
Jer 8:18 O my Comforter in **sorrow**, my heart is faint within me.
20:18 the womb to see trouble and **sorrow** and to end my days in shame?
31:13 into gladness; I will give them comfort and joy instead of **sorrow**.
45: 3 The LORD has added **sorrow** to my pain; I am worn out with
Eze 23:33 You will be filled with drunkenness and **sorrow**, the cup of ruin

3327 יָגוּר *yāgûr*, n.pr.loc. [1] [cf. 1597]

Jagur [1]

Jos 15:21 Negev toward the boundary of Edom were: Kabzeel, Eder, **Jagur**,

3328 יָגוֹר *yāgôr*, a.vbl. [2] [√ 3336]

fear [2]

Jer 22:25 I will hand you over to those who seek your life, those you **fear**—
39:17 the LORD; you will not be handed over to those you **fear**.

3329 יָגִיעַ *yāgîa'*, a. [1] [√ 3333]

weary [+3946] [1]

Job 3:17 cease from turmoil, and there the **weary** [+3946] are at rest.

3330 יְגִיעַ *y^egîa'*, n.m. [16] [√ 3333]

labor [4], fruits of labor [2], products [2], fruit of labor [+4090] [1], heavy work [1], possessions [1], produce [1], toil [1], wealth [1], work [1], worked [1]

Ge 31:42 God has seen my hardship and the **toil** *of* my hands, and last night
Dt 28:33 that you do not know will eat what your land and **labor** produce,
Ne 5:13 and **possessions** every man who does not keep this promise.
Job 10:3 Does it please you to oppress me, to spurn the **work** *of* your hands,
39:11 for his great strength? Will you leave your **heavy work** to him?
39:16 as if they were not hers; she cares not that her **labor** was in vain,
Ps 78:46 He gave their crops to the grasshopper, their **produce** to the locust.
109:11 seize all he has; may strangers plunder the **fruits of** his **labor**.
128:2 You will eat the **fruit of** your **labor** [+4090]; blessings and
Isa 45:14 "The **products** *of* Egypt and the merchandise of Cush, and those
55:2 on what is not bread, and your **labor** on what does not satisfy?
Jer 3:24 shameful gods have consumed the **fruits of** our fathers' **labor**—
20:5 all its **products**, all its valuables and all the treasures of the kings
Eze 23:29 with you in hatred and take away everything you have **worked** *for*.
Hos 12:8 [12:9] With all my **wealth** they will not find in me any iniquity
Hag 1:11 on men and cattle, and on the **labor** *of* your hands."

3331 יְגִיעָה *y^egî'â*, n.f. [1] [√ 3333]

wearies [1]

Ecc 12:12 many books there is no end, and much study **wearies** the body.

3332 יָגְלִי *yoglî*, n.pr.m. [1]

Jogli [1]

Nu 34:22 Bukki son of **Jogli**, the leader from the tribe of Dan;

3333 יָגַע *yāga'*, v. [26] [→ 3329, 3330, 3331, 3334, 3335]

wearied [6], weary [5], labored [3], worn out [3], toil [2], exhaust [1], labor [1], struggle [1], tired [1], toiled [1], wear out [1], wearies [1]

Jos 7:3 [D] thousand men to take it and *do* not **weary** all the people,
24:13 [A] So I gave you a land on which *you did* not **toil** and cities you
2Sa 23:10 [A] struck down the Philistines till his hand *grew* **tired** and froze
Job 9:29 [A] I am already found guilty, why *should I* **struggle** in vain?
Ps 6:6 [6:7] [A] *I am* **worn out** from groaning; all night long I flood
69:3 [69:4] [A] *I am* **worn out** calling for help; my throat is parched.
Pr 23:4 [A] *Do* not **wear** *yourself* **out** to get rich; have the wisdom to
Ecc 10:15 [D] A fool's work **wearies** him; he does not know the way to
Isa 40:28 [A] He will not grow tired or **weary**, and his understanding no
40:30 [A] Even youths grow tired and **weary**, and young men stumble
40:31 [A] they will run and not *grow* **weary**, they will walk and not be
43:22 [A] O Jacob, *you have* not **wearied** *yourselves* for me, O Israel.
43:23 [G] I have not burdened you with grain offerings nor **wearied**
43:24 [G] me with your sins and **wearied** me with your offenses.
47:12 [A] many sorceries, which *you have* **labored** at since childhood.
47:15 [A] these *you have* **labored** *with* and trafficked with since
49:4 [A] I said, "*I have* **labored** to no purpose; I have spent my
57:10 [A] *You were* **wearied** by all your ways, but you would not say,
62:8 [A] foreigners drink the new wine for which *you have* **toiled**;
65:23 [A] *They will* not **toil** in vain or bear children doomed to
Jer 45:3 [A] to my pain; *I am* **worn out** with groaning and find no rest.' "
51:58 [A] the peoples **exhaust** *themselves* for nothing, the nations'
La 5:5 [A] pursue us are at our heels; *we are* **weary** and find no rest.
Hab 2:13 [A] determined that the people's **labor** is only fuel for the fire,
Mal 2:17 [G] *You have* **wearied** the LORD with your words. "How have
2:17 [G] "How *have we* **wearied** him?" you ask. By saying, "All who

3334 יָגָע *yāgā'*, n.[m.] [1] [√ 3333]

what toiled for [1]

Job 20:18 **What** he **toiled for** he must give back uneaten; he will not enjoy

3335 יָגֵעַ *yāgēa'*, a. [3] [√ 3333]

wearisome [1], weary [1], worn out [1]

Dt 25:18 When you were weary and **worn out**, they met you on your
2Sa 17:2 I would attack him while he is **weary** and weak. I would strike him
Ecc 1:8 All things are **wearisome**, more than one can say. The eye never

3336 יָגֹר *yāgōr*, v. [5] [→ 3328; cf. 1593]

dread [2], dreaded [2], feared [1]

Dt 9:19 [A] *I* **feared** the anger and wrath of the LORD, for he was
28:60 [A] bring upon you all the diseases of Egypt that *you* **dreaded**,
Job 3:25 [A] has come upon me; what *I* **dreaded** has happened to me.
9:28 [A] *I still* **dread** all my sufferings, for I know you will not hold
Ps 119:39 [A] Take away the disgrace *I* **dread**, for your laws are good.

3337 יְגַר שָׂהֲדוּתָא *y^egar śāh^adûtā'*, n.[m.] & n.m. [1] [→ Ar 10310 + 10679]

Jegar Sahadutha [1]

Ge 31:47 Laban called it **Jegar Sahadutha**, and Jacob called it Galeed.

3338 יָד *yād*, n.f. & m. [1617 / 1616] [→ Ar 10311]

hand [538], hands [348], through [+928] [62], *untranslated* [61], power [34], from [+4946] [33], with [+928] [20], by [+928] [18], hand over [+906+928+5989] [18], to [+928] [15], care [14], hand over [+928+5989] [14], handed over [+928+5989] [13], to [+6584] [12], be handed over [+928+5989] [8], arm [7], handed over [+906+928 +5989] [7], next to [+6584] [7], afford [+5952] [6], arms [6], command [6], control [5], direction [5], next section [+6584] [5], side [5], supervision [5], against [+4946+9393] [4], be sure of this [+3338+4200] [4], finger [4], have [+928] [4], possession [4], spacious [+8146] [4], clutches [3], fist [3], hands [+4090] [3], hold accountable [+1335+4946] [3], next [+6584] [3], ordained [+906+4848] [3], power [+445] [3], special gifts [+9556] [3], strength [3], under [+928] [3], along [+6584] [2], armrests [2], as much as pleases [+5522] [2], assassinate [+928+8938] [2], authority [2], axles [2], bank [2], boldly [+928+8123] [2], by [+6584] [2], certainly be handed over [+928+5989+5989] [2], encouraged [+2616] [2], grasp [2], guilty [+928] [2], had [+928] [2], hand over [+906+906+906+906 +928+5989] [2], hand over [+928+6037] [2], handed over [+906+906+906+928+5989] [2], handed over [+928+6037] [2], handed [2], he [+2257] [2], installed [+906+4848] [2], left-handed [+360+3545] [2], liberality [2], monument [2], next to [+448] [2], ordain [+4848] [2], ordination [+906+4848] [2], paw [2], place [2], play [+928+5594] [2], playing the harp [+928+5594] [2], projection [2], projections [2], prospers [+5952] [2], rebelled [+8123] [2], seized [+4200+8492] [2], supports [2], taking with [+928] [2], them[s] [+2021] [2], thumbs [+984] [2], times [2], wheel around [+2200] [2], wrist [2], you [+3870] [2], abandon [+4946+8332] [1], accompanied by [+6584] [1], actions [1], adjoining [+6584] [1], adjoining section [+6584] [1], afford [+1896+5162] [1], afford [+1896+5595] [1], afford [+4200+4200+5952] [1], against [+4946] [1], agent [+4200] [1], along [+4200] [1], along with [+928] [1], along [1], arms [+723] [1], as a direct result [+9393] [1], as prescribed by [+6584] [1], assistant [+6584] [1], assisted [+2616] [1], assisted [+6584] [1], assisted [+928+2616] [1], attack [+6584+6590] [1], attack [+928+8938] [1], attacked [+928+8938] [1], attacks [+928+8938] [1], be defeated [+928+5989] [1], because of [+928] [1], beckon [+5677] [1], beckon [+5951] [1], been handed over [+928+5989] [1], began [+2616+4200] [1], beside [+4200] [1], beside [+448] [1], beside [+6584] [1], beside [+928] [1], body [1], border [1], borders [1], bounty [1], bracelets [+6584+7543] [1], broad [+8146] [1], brought [+928] [1], brought with [+928+2118] [1], call to account [+1335 +4946] [1], carried [+906+906+928+4374] [1], cause [+928] [1], commanded [1], companies [1], consecrate himself [+2257+4848] [1], consecrate himself [+4848] [1], consecrated [+906+4848] [1], creditor [+1251+2257+5408] [1], custody [1], customers [+6086] [1], customers [+6088] [1], debts [+5391] [1], dedicate [+4848] [1], dedicated [+4848] [1], delegation [+928+6269] [1], delivered [+928] [1], deserves [+1691] [1], did[s] [+2257+5989] [1], did this[s] [+2257+5742] [1], discourage [+8332] [1], discouraging [+906+906+8332] [1], do [+5126] [1], do that[s] [+928+2118+2257] [1], don't say a word [+6584+7023+8492] [1], done by [+928] [1], drew [+928+4848] [1], entrusted to [+448] [1], entrusted to [+928] [1], fists [1], follow [+448] [1], for [+6584] [1], for [+928] [1], force [1], forcefully [+928] [1], four-fifths [+752] [1], from [+928] [1], gain support [+907+2118] [1], gave victory [+928+5989] [1], give [+928+5989] [1], give up [+8332] [1], given over [+5599+6584] [1], had chance [+928+2118] [1], hand over [+906+906+928+5989] [1], hand over [+906+928+4835] [1], hand over [+906+928+5162] [1], hand over to [+906+928+5989] [1], handed [+4946] [1], handed [+906+906+928+5989] [1], handed over [+906+906+928+5989] [1], handed over [+906+928+5796] [1], handed over [+928+5162] [1], handing over [+906+928+5989] [1], handing over [+928+6037] [1], handiwork [+5126] [1], has [+928] [1], have [+3780+9393] [1], have [+928+5162] [1], have on hand [+3780+9393] [1], have on hand [+448+9393] [1], help [+2616] [1], help [+4200] [1], help [+6640] [1], help [+6640+8883] [1], helped [+906+2616] [1], helped find strength [+906+2616] [1], him [+2257] [1], hold [+928+2118] [1], hold accountable [+2011+4946] [1], hold accountable [+906+2011+4946] [1], hold responsible [+1335+4946] [1], hold [1], holding [+928] [1], holds [+928+2118] [1], in charge of [+928] [1], it[s] [+2257] [1], it[s] [+3870] [1], killing [+928+8938] [1], labor [1], large [+8146] [1], leadership [1], led the way [+2118+8037] [1], let go [+906+5663] [1], lets happen [+628+4200] [1], little by little [+6584] [1], lost courage [+8332] [1], made subject to [+4044+9393] [1], man-made [+132 +5126] [1], marched past [+6296+6584] [1], memorial [1], myself [+3276] [1], nakedness [1], near [+6584] [1], nearby [+6584] [1], of [+4946] [1], openhanded [+906+4200+7337+7337] [1], openhanded [+906+7337+7337] [1], ordain [+906+4848] [1], ordained [+4848] [1], ordered [1], overpowered [+6451+6584] [1], pledged [+5989] [1], plenty of room [+8146] [1], portion [1], powerless [+401+445+4200] [1], put in charge [+6584+6641] [1], put up security [+4200+9546] [1], reached out [+906+8938] [1], reaches out [+8938] [1], reaching [+906+8938] [1], remaining [1], reward earned [+7262] [1], rich [+5952] [1], ruled [+4939] [1], seize [+928+8492] [1], set apart [+4848] [1], set free [+906+4946+8938] [1], shapes [+5126] [1], shares [1], shed by [+4946] [1], shores [1], sided with [+6640] [1], signpost [1], sins defiantly [+928+6913+8123] [1], snare [1], someone[s] else [+928] [1], stroke [1], strong [+2616] [1], strong arms [+2432] [1], submit [+5989] [1], submit [+8132] [1], submitted [+5989] [1], supported [+907+2118] [1], surely hand over [+906+928 +5989+5989] [1], surrender [+906+928+6037] [1], surrenders [+5989] [1], swore [+5951] [1], sworn [+906+5951] [1], take charge of [+9393] [1], taken [+928] [1], things did [+5126] [1], those[s] [1], tightfisted [+906+7890] [1], to [+9393] [1], took with [+928] [1], turned about [+2200] [1], unable to support [+4572] [1], under [+4946] [1], under care [1], used [+928] [1], uses [+928] [1], vicinity [1], wants to give [+5952] [1], war clubs [+5234] [1], waves [1], weak [+8333] [1], with [+4200] [1], with [+6584] [1], wrists [+723] [1], wrists [1]

Ge 3:22 He must not be allowed to reach out his **hand** and take also from
4:11 opened its mouth to receive your brother's blood from your **hand**.
5:29 painful toil of our **hands** caused by the ground the LORD has
8: 9 He reached out his **hand** and took the dove and brought it back to
9: 2 and upon all the fish of the sea; they are given into your **hands**.
9: 5 I will demand an accounting **from** [+4946] every animal.
9: 5 **from** [+4946] each man, too, I will demand an accounting for the
9: 5 from **[RPH]** each man, too, I will demand an accounting for the
14:20 be God Most High, who delivered your enemies into your **hand**."
14:22 "I have raised my **hand** to the LORD, God Most High, Creator of
16: 6 "Your servant is in your **hands**," Abram said. "Do with her
16: 9 told her, "Go back to your mistress and submit **to** [+9393] her."
16:12 his **hand** will be against everyone and everyone's hand against
16:12 hand will be against everyone and everyone's **hand** against him,
19:10 the men inside **reached out** [+906+8938] and pulled Lot back into
19:16 the men grasped his **hand** and the hands of his wife and of his two
19:16 his hand and the **hands** *of* his wife and of his two daughters
19:16 and the hands of his wife and **[RPH]** of his two daughters
21:18 Lift the boy up and take him by the **hand**, for I will make him into
21:30 "Accept these seven lambs from my **hand** as a witness that I dug
22: 6 *he* himself **carried** [+906+906+928+4374] the fire and the knife.
22:10 Then he reached out his **hand** and took the knife to slay his son.
22:12 "Do not lay a **hand** on the boy," he said. "Do not do anything to
24: 2 one in charge of all that he had, "Put your **hand** under my thigh.
24: 9 So the servant put his **hand** under the thigh of his master Abraham
24:10 left, **taking** [+928] **with** him all kinds of good things from his
24:18 and quickly lowered the jar to her **hands** and gave him a drink.
24:22 and two gold **bracelets** [+6584+7543] weighing ten shekels.
24:30 as he had seen the nose ring, and the bracelets on his sister's **arms**,
24:47 "Then I put the ring in her nose and the bracelets on her **arms**,
25:26 his brother came out, with his **hand** grasping Esau's heel;
27:16 She also covered his **hands** and the smooth part of his neck with
27:17 Then *she* **handed** [+906+906+928+5989] *to* her son Jacob the tasty
27:22 voice is the voice of Jacob, but the **hands** are the hands of Esau."
27:22 voice is the voice of Jacob, but the hands are the **hands** *of* Esau."
27:23 for his **hands** were hairy like those of his brother Esau;
27:23 for his hands were hairy like **those**[s] *of* his brother Esau;
30:35 the dark-colored lambs, and he placed them in the **care** *of* his sons.
31:29 I have the **power** [+445] to harm you; but last night the God of
31:39 you animals torn by wild beasts; I bore the loss **myself** [+3276].
32:11 [32:12] Save me, I pray, from the **hand** *of* my brother Esau, for I
32:11 [32:12] I pray, from the hand of my brother **[RPH]** Esau,
32:13 [32:14] from what he **had with** [+928] him he selected a gift for
32:16 [32:17] He put them in the **care** *of* his servants, each herd by
33:10 I have found favor in your eyes, accept this gift **from** [+4946] me.
33:19 he bought **from** [+4946] the sons of Hamor, the father of Shechem,
34:21 and trade in it; the land has **plenty of room** [+8146] for them.
35: 4 So they gave Jacob all the foreign gods they **had** [+928] and the
37:21 When Reuben heard this, he tried to rescue him from their **hands**.
37:22 into this cistern here in the desert, but don't lay a **hand** on him."
37:22 Reuben said this to rescue him **from** [+4946] them and take him
37:27 let's sell him to the Ishmaelites and not lay our **hands** on him;
38:18 "Your seal and its cord, and the staff in your **hand**," she answered.
38:20 Meanwhile Judah sent the young goat **by** [+928] his friend the
38:20 in order to get his pledge back **from** [+4946] the woman,
38:28 As she was giving birth, one of them put out his **hand**;
38:28 the midwife took a scarlet thread and tied it on his **wrist** and said,
38:29 when he drew back his **hand**, his brother came out, and she said,
38:30 who had the scarlet thread on his **wrist**, came out and he was given
39: 1 bought him **from** [+4946] the Ishmaelites who had taken him
39: 3 that the LORD gave **him** [+2257] success in everything he did,
39: 4 his household, and he entrusted to his **care** everything he owned.
39: 6 So he left in Joseph's **care** everything he had; with Joseph in
39: 8 in the house; everything he owns he has entrusted to my **care**.
39:12 But he left his cloak in her **hand** and ran out of the house.
39:13 When she saw that he had left his cloak in her **hand** and had run
39:22 So the warden put Joseph **in charge** [+928] **of** all those held in the
39:23 The warden paid no attention to anything under Joseph's **care**,
40:11 Pharaoh's cup was in my **hand**, and I took the grapes, squeezed
40:13 you to your position, and you will put Pharaoh's cup in his **hand**,
41:35 are coming and store up the grain under the **authority** *of* Pharaoh,
41:42 Pharaoh took his signet ring from his **finger** and put it on Joseph's
41:42 took his signet ring from his finger and put it on Joseph's **finger**.
41:44 but without your word no one will lift **hand** or foot in all Egypt."
42:37 back to you. Entrust him to my **care**, and I will bring him back."
43: 9 *you can* **hold** me personally **responsible for** [+1335+4946] him.
43:12 Take double the amount of silver **with** [+928] you, for you must
43:12 for you must return the silver **[RPH]** that was put back into the
43:15 and double the amount of silver, **[RPH]** and Benjamin also.
43:21 the mouth of his sack. So we have brought it back **with** [+928] us.
43:22 We have also brought additional silver **with** [+928] us to buy food.
43:26 they presented to him the gifts they had **brought** [+928] into the
43:34 Benjamin's portion was five **times** as much as anyone else's.
44:16 we ourselves and the one who was found to **have** [+928] the cup."
44:17 Only the man who was found to **have** [+928] the cup will become
46: 4 you back again. And Joseph's own **hand** will close your eyes."
47:24 The *other* **four-fifths** [+752] you may keep as seed for the fields
47:29 put your **hand** under my thigh and promise that you will show me
48:14 though he was the younger, and crossing his **arms**,
48:17 When Joseph saw his father placing his right **hand** on Ephraim's
48:17 so he took hold of his father's **hand** to move it from Ephraim's
48:22 I give the ridge of land I took **from** [+4946] the Amorites with my
49: 8 will praise you; your **hand** will be on the neck of your enemies;
49:24 his bow remained steady, his **strong arms** [+2432] stayed limber,
49:24 because of the **hand** *of* the Mighty One of Jacob, because of the
Ex 2: 5 to bathe, and her attendants were walking along the river **bank**.
2:19 "An Egyptian rescued us **from** [+4946] the shepherds.
3: 8 So I have come down to rescue them from the **hand** *of* the
3:19 of Egypt will not let you go unless a mighty **hand** compels him.
3:20 So I will stretch out my **hand** and strike the Egyptians with all the
4: 2 Then the LORD said to him, "What is that in your **hand**?"
4: 4 LORD said to him, "Reach out your **hand** and take it by the tail."
4: 4 So Moses reached out **[RPH]** and took hold of the snake
4: 6 Then the LORD said, "Put your **hand** inside your cloak."
4: 6 So Moses put his **hand** into his cloak, and when he took it out,
4: 6 and when he took it out, **it**[s] [+2257] was leprous, like snow.
4: 7 "Now put **it**[s] [+3870] back into your cloak," he said. So Moses put
4: 7 So Moses put his **hand** back into his cloak, and when he took it
4:13 Moses said, "O Lord, please send **someone**[s] [+928] **else** to do it."
4:17 take this staff in your **hand** so you can perform miraculous signs
4:20 started back to Egypt. And he took the staff of God in his **hand**.
4:21 before Pharaoh all the wonders I have given you the **power** to do.
5:21 and his officials and have put a sword in their **hand** to kill us."
6: 1 Because of my mighty **hand** he will let them go; because of my
6: 1 because of my mighty **hand** he will drive them out of his country."
6: 8 I will bring you to the land I swore with uplifted **hand** to give to
7: 4 I will lay my **hand** on Egypt and with mighty acts of judgment I
7: 5 that I am the LORD when I stretch out my **hand** against Egypt
7:15 and take in your **hand** the staff that was changed into a snake.
7:17 With the staff that is in my **hand** I will strike the water of the Nile,
7:19 your staff and stretch out your **hand** over the waters of Egypt—
8: 5 [8:1] 'Stretch out your **hand** with your staff over the streams
8: 6 [8:2] So Aaron stretched out his **hand** over the waters of Egypt,
8:17 [8:13] when Aaron stretched out his **hand** with the staff
9: 3 the **hand** *of* the LORD will bring a terrible plague on your
9:15 For by now I could have stretched out my **hand** and struck you
9:22 "Stretch out your **hand** toward the sky so that hail will fall all over
9:35 Israelites go, just as the LORD had said **through** [+928] Moses.
10:12 "Stretch out your **hand** over Egypt so that locusts will swarm over
10:21 "Stretch out your **hand** toward the sky so that darkness will spread
10:22 So Moses stretched out his **hand** toward the sky, and total darkness
10:25 "You must allow us to **have** [+928] sacrifices and burnt offerings
12:11 your belt, your sandals on your feet and your staff in your **hand**.
13: 3 because the LORD brought you out of it with a mighty **hand**.
13: 9 This observance will be for you like a sign on your **hand** and a
13: 9 For the LORD brought you out of Egypt with his mighty **hand**.

Ex 13:14 'With a mighty **hand** the LORD brought us out of Egypt,
13:16 it will be like a sign on your **hand** and a symbol on your forehead
13:16 that the LORD brought us out of Egypt with his mighty **hand**."
14: 8 the Israelites, who were marching out **boldly** [+928+8123].
14:16 and stretch out your **hand** over the sea to divide the water
14:21 Moses stretched out his **hand** over the sea, and all that night the
14:26 "Stretch out your **hand** over the sea so that the waters may flow
14:27 Moses stretched out his **hand** over the sea, and at daybreak the sea
14:30 That day the LORD saved Israel from the **hands** *of* the Egyptians,
14:31 when the Israelites saw the great **power** the LORD displayed
15: 9 on them. I will draw my sword and my **hand** will destroy them.'
15:17 for your dwelling, the sanctuary, O Lord, your **hands** established.
15:20 the prophetess, Aaron's sister, took a tambourine in her **hand**,
16: 3 said to them, "If only we had died by the LORD's **hand** in Egypt!
17: 5 and take in your **hand** the staff with which you struck the Nile,
17: 9 I will stand on top of the hill with the staff of God in my **hands**."
17:11 As long as Moses held up his **hands**, the Israelites were winning,
17:11 the Israelites were winning, but whenever he lowered his **hands**,
17:12 When Moses' **hands** grew tired, they took a stone and put it under
17:12 Aaron and Hur held his **hands** up—one on one side, one on the
17:12 one on the other—so that his **hands** remained steady till sunset.
17:16 He said, "For **hands** were lifted up to the throne of the LORD.
18: 9 done for Israel in rescuing them from the **hand** *of* the Egyptians.
18:10 who rescued you from the **hand** *of* the Egyptians and of Pharaoh,
18:10 you from the hand of the Egyptians and **[RPH]** of Pharaoh,
18:10 and who rescued the people from the **hand** *of* the Egyptians.
19:13 be stoned or shot with arrows; not a **hand** is to be laid on him.
21:13 does not do it intentionally, but God **lets** *it* **happen** [+628+4200],
21:16 or still **has** [+928] him when he is caught must be put to death.
21:20 slave with a rod and the slave dies **as a direct result** [+9393],
21:24 eye for eye, tooth for tooth, **hand** for hand, foot for foot,
21:24 eye for eye, tooth for tooth, hand for **hand**, foot for foot,
22: 4 [22:3] "If the stolen animal is found alive in his **possession**—
22: 8 [22:7] whether he has laid his **hands** on the other man's property.
22:11 [22:10] did not lay **hands** on the other person's property.
23: 1 *Do* not **help** [+6640+8883] a wicked man by being a malicious
23:31 *I will* **hand** [+906+928+5989] **over to** you the people who live in
24:11 God did not raise his **hand** against these leaders of the Israelites;
26:17 with two **projections** set parallel to each other. Make all the
26:19 under them—two bases for each frame, one under each **projection**.
26:19 two bases for each frame, one under each projection. **[RPH]**
28:41 brother Aaron and his sons, anoint and **ordain** [+906+4848] them.
29: 9 In this way *you shall* **ordain** [+4848] Aaron and his sons.
29: 9 In this way you shall ordain Aaron and **[RPH]** his sons.
29:10 and Aaron and his sons shall lay their **hands** on its head.
29:15 the rams, and Aaron and his sons shall lay their **hands** on its head.
29:19 other ram, and Aaron and his sons shall lay their **hands** on its head.
29:20 ears of Aaron and his sons, on the thumbs of their right **hands**,
29:25 take them from their **hands** and burn them on the altar along with
29:29 so that they can be anointed and **ordained** [+906+4848] in them.
29:33 by which atonement was made for their **ordination** [+906+4848]
29:35 have commanded you, taking seven days *to* **ordain** [+4848] them.
30:19 Aaron and his sons are to wash their **hands** and feet with water
30:21 they shall wash their **hands** and feet so that they will not die.
32: 4 He took what they **handed** him and made it into an idol cast in the
32:11 you brought out of Egypt with great power and a mighty **hand**?
32:15 the mountain with the two tablets of the Testimony in his **hands**.
32:19 his anger burned and he threw the tablets out of his **hands**,
32:29 "You *have been* **set apart** [+4848] to the LORD today,
34: 4 commanded him; and he carried the two stone tablets in his **hands**.
34:29 Mount Sinai with the two tablets of the Testimony in his **hands**,
35:25 Every skilled woman spun with her **hands** and brought what she
35:29 the LORD **through** [+928] Moses had commanded them to do.
36:22 with two **projections** set parallel to each other. They made all the
36:24 under them—two bases for each frame, one under each **projection**.
36:24 two bases for each frame, one under each projection. **[RPH]**
38:21 by the Levites under the **direction** *of* Ithamar son of Aaron,
40:31 and Aaron and his sons used it to wash their **hands** and feet.
Lev 1: 4 He is to lay his **hand** on the head of the burnt offering, and it will
3: 2 He is to lay his **hand** on the head of his offering and slaughter it at
3: 8 He is to lay his **hand** on the head of his offering and slaughter it in
3:13 He is to lay his **hand** on its head and slaughter it in front of the
4: 4 He is to lay his **hand** on its head and slaughter it before the
4:15 The elders of the community are to lay their **hands** on the bull's
4:24 He is to lay his **hand** on the goat's head and slaughter it at the
4:29 He is to lay his **hand** on the head of the sin offering and slaughter
4:33 He is to lay his **hand** on its head and slaughter it for a sin offering
5: 7 " 'If he cannot **afford** [+1896+5595] a lamb, he is to bring two
5:11 " 'If, however, he cannot **afford** [+4200+4200+5952] two doves or
6: 2 [5:21] something entrusted to him or left in his **care** or stolen,
7:30 With his own **hands** he is to bring the offering made to the LORD
8:14 sin offering, and Aaron and his sons laid their **hands** on its head.
8:18 burnt offering, and Aaron and his sons laid their **hands** on its head.
8:22 the ordination, and Aaron and his sons laid their **hands** on its head.
8:23 on the thumb of his right **hand** and on the big toe of his right foot.
8:24 on the thumbs of their right **hands** and on the big toes of their right
8:33 completed, for your **ordination** [+906+4848] will last seven days.
8:36 his sons did everything the LORD commanded **through** [+928]
9:22 Then Aaron lifted his **hands** toward the people and blessed them.
10:11 the decrees the LORD has given them **through** [+928] Moses."
12: 8 If she cannot **afford** [+1896+5162] a lamb, she is to bring two
14:14 on the thumb of his right **hand** and on the big toe of his right foot.
14:17 on the thumb of his right **hand** and on the big toe of his right foot,
14:21 "If, however, he is poor and cannot **afford** [+5952] these,
14:22 which he *can* **afford** [+5952], one for a sin offering and the other
14:25 on the thumb of his right **hand** and on the big toe of his right foot.
14:28 on the thumb of his right **hand** and on the big toe of his right foot.
14:30 or the young pigeons, which the person *can* **afford** [+5952],
14:31 [BHS+ *such as the person can **afford*** +5952] one as a sin offering
14:32 who cannot **afford** [+5952] the regular offerings for his cleansing.
15:11 without rinsing his **hands** with water must wash his clothes
16:21 He is to lay both **hands** on the head of the live goat and confess
16:21 He shall send the goat away into the desert in the **care** *of* a man
16:32 **ordained** [+906+4848] to succeed his father as high priest is to
21:10 *who has been* **ordained** [+906+4848] to wear the priestly
21:19 no man with a crippled foot or **hand**,
22:25 and you must not accept such animals from the **hand** *of* a foreigner
24:14 All those who heard him are to lay their **hands** on his head,
25:14 sell land to one of your countrymen or buy any **from** [+4946] him,
25:26 has no one to redeem it for him but *he* himself **prospers** [+5952]
25:28 But if **he** [+2257] does not acquire the means to repay him,
25:28 what he sold will remain in the **possession** *of* the buyer until the
25:35 and *is* **unable to support** [+4572] himself among you,
25:47 or a temporary resident among you *becomes* **rich** [+5952]
25:49 redeem him. Or if he **prospers** [+5952], he may redeem himself.
26:25 a plague among you, and you will be given into enemy **hands**.
26:46 Sinai between himself and the Israelites **through** [+928] Moses.
27: 8 according to what the man making the vow *can* **afford** [+5952].
Nu 2:17 order as they encamp, each in his own **place** under his standard.
3: 3 anointed priests, who *were* **ordained** [+4848] to serve as priests.
4:28 Their duties are to be under the **direction** *of* Ithamar son of Aaron,
4:33 the Tent of Meeting under the **direction** *of* Ithamar son of Aaron,
4:37 them according to the LORD's command **through** [+928] Moses.
4:45 them according to the LORD's command **through** [+928] Moses.
4:49 At the LORD's command **through** [+928] Moses, each was
5:18 while he himself **holds** [+928+2118] the bitter water that brings a
5:25 The priest is to take from her **hands** the grain offering for jealousy,
6:21 his separation, in addition to whatever else he *can* **afford** [+5952].
7: 8 They were all under the **direction** *of* Ithamar son of Aaron,
8:10 the LORD, and the Israelites are to lay their **hands** on them.
8:12 "After the Levites lay their **hands** on the heads of the bulls,
9:23 in accordance with his command **through** [+928] Moses.
10:13 this first time, at the LORD's command **through** [+928] Moses.
11:23 The LORD answered Moses, "Is the LORD's **arm** too short?
13:29 the Canaanites live near the sea and **along** [+6584] the Jordan."
14:30 Not one of you will enter the land I swore with uplifted **hand** to
15:23 any of the LORD's commands to you **through** [+928] him,
15:30 " 'But anyone who **sins defiantly** [+928+6913+8123], whether
16:40 [17:5] as the LORD directed him **through** [+928] Moses.
20:11 Then Moses raised his **arm** and struck the rock twice with his staff.
20:20 came out against them with a large and powerful army. **[NIE]**
21: 2 "If you will deliver these people into our **hands**, we will totally
21:26 and had taken **from** [+4946] him all his land as far as the Arnon.
21:34 for *I have* **handed** [+906+906+906+928+5989] him **over** *to* you,
22: 7 and Midian left, **taking** [+928] **with** them the fee for divination.
22:23 the LORD standing in the road with a drawn sword in his **hand**,
22:29 If I had a sword in my **hand**, I would kill you right now."
22:31 his sword drawn. **[RPH]** So he bowed low and fell facedown.
24:24 Ships will come from the **shores** *of* Kittim; they will subdue
25: 7 the priest, saw this, he left the assembly, took a spear in his **hand**
27:18 of Nun, a man in whom is the spirit, and lay your **hand** on him.
27:23 he laid his **hands** on him and commissioned him, as the LORD
27:23 as the LORD instructed **through** [+928] Moses.
31: 6 who **took with** [+928] him articles from the sanctuary
31:49 "Your servants have counted the soldiers under our **command**,
33: 1 came out of Egypt by divisions under the **leadership** *of* Moses
33: 3 They marched out **boldly** [+928+8123] in full view of all the
34: 3 will include some of the Desert of Zin along the **border** *of* Edom.
35:17 Or if anyone has a stone in his **hand** that could kill, and he strikes
35:18 Or if anyone has a wooden object in his **hand** that could kill,
35:21 or if in hostility he hits him with his **fist** so that he dies, that person
35:25 the one accused of murder **from** [+4946] the avenger of blood
36:13 regulations the LORD gave **through** [+928] Moses to the
Dt 1:25 Taking **with** [+928] them some of the fruit of the land, they
1:27 so he brought us out of Egypt to deliver us into the **hands** *of* the
2: 7 LORD your God has blessed you in all the work of your **hands**.
2:15 The LORD's **hand** was against them until he had completely
2:24 See, I have given into your **hand** Sihon the Amorite, king of

Dt 2:30 and his heart obstinate in order to give him into your **hands**,
2:37 neither the land **along** the course of the Jabbok nor that around the
3: 2 for *I have* **handed** [+906+906+906+928+5989] him **over** *to* you
3: 3 So the LORD our God also gave into our **hands** Og king of
3: 8 So at that time we took **from** [+4946] these two kings of the
3:24 to show to your servant your greatness and your strong **hand**.
4:28 There you will worship **man-made** [+132+5126] gods of wood
4:34 by war, by a mighty **hand** and an outstretched arm, or by great
5:15 the LORD your God brought you out of there with a mighty **hand**
6: 8 Tie them as symbols on your **hands** and bind them on your
6:21 but the LORD brought us out of Egypt with a mighty **hand**.
7: 8 to your forefathers that he brought you out with a mighty **hand**
7: 8 the land of slavery, from the **power** *of* Pharaoh king of Egypt.
7:19 and wonders, the mighty **hand** and outstretched arm,
7:24 He will give their kings into your **hand**, and you will wipe out
8:17 and the strength of my **hands** have produced this wealth for me."
9:15 with fire. And the two tablets of the covenant were in my **hands**.
9:17 So I took the two tablets and threw them out of my **hands**,
9:26 by your great power and brought out of Egypt with a mighty **hand**.
10: 3 and I went up on the mountain with the two tablets in my **hands**.
11: 2 your God: his majesty, his mighty **hand**, his outstretched arm;
11:18 tie them as symbols on your **hands** and bind them on your
12: 6 and sacrifices, your tithes and **special gifts** [+9556],
12: 7 and shall rejoice in everything you have put your **hand** to,
12:11 and sacrifices, your tithes and **special gifts** [+9556],
12:17 vowed to give, or your freewill offerings or **special gifts** [+9556].
12:18 before the LORD your God in everything you put your **hand** to.
13: 9 [13:10] Your **hand** must be the first in putting him to death, and
13: 9 [13:10] putting him to death, and then the **hands** *of* all the people.
13:17 [13:18] of those condemned things shall be found in your **hands**,
14:25 take the silver **with** [+928] you and go to the place the LORD
14:29 the LORD your God may bless you in all the work of your **hands**.
15: 2 Every **creditor** [+1251+2257+5408] shall cancel the loan he has
15: 3 but **you** [+3870] must cancel any debt your brother owes you.
15: 7 or **tightfisted** [+906+7890] toward your poor brother.
15: 8 Rather *be* **openhanded** [+906+4200+7337+7337] and freely lend
15:10 bless you in all your work and in everything you put your **hand** to.
15:11 Therefore I command you *to be* **openhanded** [+906+7337+7337]
16:10 **[NIE]** in proportion to the blessings the LORD your God has
16:15 will bless you in all your harvest and in all the work of your **hands**,
16:17 Each of you must bring a gift **[NIE]** in proportion to the way the
17: 7 The **hands** *of* the witnesses must be the first in putting him to
17: 7 first in putting him to death, and then the **hands** *of* all the people.
19: 5 and as **he** [+2257] swings his ax to fell a tree, the head may fly off
19:12 **hand** [+906+928+5989] him **over** *to* the avenger of blood to die.
19:21 for life, eye for eye, tooth for tooth, **hand** for hand, foot for foot.
19:21 for life, eye for eye, tooth for tooth, hand for **hand**, foot for foot.
20:13 When the LORD your God delivers it into your **hand**, put to the
21: 6 all the elders of the town nearest the body shall wash their **hands**
21: 7 "Our **hands** did not shed this blood, nor did our eyes see it done.
21:10 the LORD your God delivers them into your **hands** and you take
23:12 [23:13] Designate a **place** outside the camp where you can go to
23:20 [23:21] put your **hand** to in the land you are entering to possess.
23:25 [23:26] you may pick kernels with your **hands**,
24: 1 of divorce, gives it **to** [+928] her and sends her from his house,
24: 3 gives it **to** [+928] her and sends her from his house, or if he dies,
24:19 the LORD your God may bless you in all the work of your **hands**.
25:11 the wife of one of them comes to rescue her husband **from** [+4946]
25:11 and *she* **reaches out** [+8938] and seizes him by his private parts,
26: 4 The priest shall take the basket from your **hands** and set it down in
26: 8 So the LORD brought us out of Egypt with a mighty **hand**
27:15 detestable to the LORD, the work of the craftsman's **hands**—
28: 8 a blessing on your barns and on everything you put your **hand** to.
28:12 rain on your land in season and to bless all the work of your **hands**.
28:20 confusion and rebuke in everything you put your **hand** to,
28:32 eyes watching for them day after day, powerless to lift a **hand**.
30: 9 God will make you most prosperous in all the work of your **hands**
31:29 and provoke him to anger by what your **hands** have made."
32:27 the adversary misunderstand and say, 'Our **hand** has triumphed;
32:36 have compassion on his servants when he sees their **strength** is
32:39 and I will heal, and no one can deliver out of my **hand**.
32:40 I lift my **hand** to heaven and declare: As surely as I live forever,
32:41 I sharpen my flashing sword and my **hand** grasps it in judgment,
33: 3 it is you who love the people; all the holy ones are in your **hand**.
33: 7 With his own **hands** he defends his cause. Oh, be his help against
33:11 his skills, O LORD, and be pleased with the work of his **hands**.
34: 9 the spirit of wisdom because Moses had laid his **hands** on him.
34:12 For no one has ever shown the mighty **power** or performed the
Jos 2:19 with you, his blood will be on our head if a **hand** is laid on him.
2:24 "The LORD has surely given the whole land into our **hands**;
4:24 so that all the peoples of the earth might know that the **hand** *of* the
5:13 a man standing in front of him with a drawn sword in his **hand**.
6: 2 "See, I have delivered Jericho into your **hands**, along with its king
7: 7 Jordan to deliver us into the **hands** *of* the Amorites to destroy us?
8: 1 For I have delivered into your **hands** the king of Ai, his people,
8: 7 take the city. The LORD your God will give it into your **hand**.
8:18 to Joshua, "Hold out toward Ai the javelin that is in your **hand**,
8:18 that is in your hand, for into your **hand** I will deliver the city."
8:18 deliver the city." So Joshua held out his javelin **[RPH]** toward Ai.
8:19 As soon as *he* **did**[s] **this** [+2257+5742], the men in the ambush rose
8:20 but they **had** no **chance** [+928+2118] to escape in any direction,
8:26 For Joshua did not draw back the **hand** that held out his javelin
9:11 our country said to us, 'Take **[OBJ]** provisions for your journey;
9:25 We are now in your **hands**. Do to us whatever seems good
9:26 So Joshua saved them **from** [+4946] the Israelites, and they did not
10: 6 "*Do* not **abandon** [+4946+8332] your servants. Come up to us
10: 8 "Do not be afraid of them; I have given them into your **hand**.
10:19 for the LORD your God has given them into your **hand**."
10:30 The LORD also gave that city and its king into Israel's **hand**.
10:32 The LORD **handed** [+906+928+5989] Lachish **over** *to* Israel,
11: 8 the LORD gave them into the **hand** *of* Israel. They defeated them
14: 2 as the LORD had commanded **through** [+928] Moses.
15:46 west of Ekron, all that were in the **vicinity** *of* Ashdod,
20: 2 the cities of refuge, as I instructed you **through** [+928] Moses,
20: 5 *they must* not **surrender** [+906+928+6037] the one accused,
20: 9 not be killed **by** [+928] the avenger of blood prior to standing trial
21: 2 "The LORD commanded **through** [+928] Moses that you give us
21: 8 as the LORD had commanded **through** [+928] Moses.
21:44 LORD **handed** [+906+928+5989] all their enemies **over** *to* them.
22: 9 with the command of the LORD **through** [+928] Moses.
22:31 Now you have rescued the Israelites from the LORD's **hand**."
24: 8 They fought against you, but I gave them into your **hands**.
24:10 blessed you again and again, and I delivered you out of his **hand**.
24:11 and Jebusites, but I gave them into your **hands**.
Jdg 1: 2 "Judah is to go; I have given the land into their **hands**."
1: 4 the LORD gave the Canaanites and Perizzites into their **hands**
1: 6 and caught him, and cut off his **thumbs** [+984] and big toes.
1: 7 "Seventy kings with their **thumbs** [+984] and big toes cut off have
1:35 but when the **power** *of* the house of Joseph increased,
2:14 **handed** [+928+5989] them **over** *to* raiders who plundered them.
2:14 He sold them **to** [+928] their enemies all around, whom they were
2:15 the **hand** *of* the LORD was against them to defeat them,
2:16 raised up judges, who saved them out of the **hands** *of* these raiders.
2:18 saved them out of the **hands** *of* their enemies as long as the judge
2:23 he did not drive them out at once by giving them into the **hands** *of*
3: 4 which he had given their forefathers **through** [+928] Moses.
3: 8 so that he sold them into the **hands** *of* Cushan-Rishathaim king of
3:10 gave Cushan-Rishathaim king of Aram into the **hands** *of* Othniel,
3:10 into the hands of Othniel, who **overpowered** [+6451+6584] him.
3:15 Ehud, a **left-handed** [+360+3545] man, the son of Gera
3:15 The Israelites sent him **with** [+928] tribute to Eglon king of Moab.
3:21 Ehud reached with his left **hand**, drew the sword from his right
3:28 "for the LORD has given Moab, your enemy, into your **hands**."
3:30 That day Moab *was* **made subject to** [+4044+9393] Israel,
4: 2 So the LORD sold them into the **hands** *of* Jabin, a king of
4: 7 his troops to the Kishon River and give him into your **hands**.' "
4: 9 for the LORD *will* **hand** [+906+928+4835] Sisera **over** *to* a
4:14 This is the day the LORD has given Sisera into your **hands**.
4:21 a hammer **[NIE]** and went quietly to him while he lay fast asleep,
4:24 the **hand** *of* the Israelites grew stronger and stronger against Jabin,
5:26 Her **hand** reached for the tent peg, her right hand for the
6: 1 and for seven years he gave them into the **hands** *of* the Midianites.
6: 2 Because the **power** *of* Midian was so oppressive, the Israelites
6: 9 I snatched you from the **power** *of* Egypt and from the hand of all
6: 9 from the power of Egypt and from the **hand** *of* all your oppressors.
6:21 With the tip of the staff that was in his **hand**, the angel of the
6:36 "If you will save Israel by my **hand** as you have promised—
6:37 I will know that you will save Israel by my **hand**, as you said."
7: 2 have too many men for me to deliver Midian into their **hands**.
7: 2 In order that Israel may not boast against me that her own **strength**
7: 6 Three hundred men lapped with their **hands** to their mouths.
7: 7 lapped I will save you and give the Midianites into your **hands**.
7: 8 who took over the provisions **[NIE]** and trumpets of the others.
7: 9 against the camp, because I am going to give it into your **hands**.
7:11 Afterward, you *will be* **encouraged** [+2616] to attack the camp."
7:14 God has given the Midianites and the whole camp into his **hands**."
7:15 The LORD has given the Midianite camp into your **hands**."
7:16 he placed trumpets and empty jars in the **hands** *of* all of them,
7:19 blew their trumpets and broke the jars that were in their **hands**.
7:20 Grasping the torches in their left **hands** and holding in their right
7:20 and holding in their right **hands** the trumpets they were to blow,
8: 3 God gave Oreb and Zeeb, the Midianite leaders, into your **hands**.
8: 6 have the hands of Zebah and Zalmunna in your **possession**?
8: 7 when the LORD has given Zebah and Zalmunna into my **hand**,
8:15 have the hands of Zebah and Zalmunna in your **possession**?
8:22 because you have saved us out of the **hand** *of* Midian."
8:34 who had rescued them from the **hands** *of* all their enemies on
9:16 his family, and if you have treated him as he **deserves** [+1691]—

Jdg 9:17 for you, risked his life to rescue you from the **hand** *of* Midian
9:24 who *had* **helped** [+906+2616] him murder his brothers.
9:29 If only this people were under my **command**! Then I would get rid
9:33 men come out against you, do whatever your **hand** finds to do."
9:48 He took an ax **[NIE]** and cut off some branches, which he lifted to
10: 7 He sold them into the **hands** *of* the Philistines and the Ammonites,
10: 7 them into the hands of the Philistines and **[RPH]** the Ammonites,
10:12 and you cried to me for help, did I not save you from their **hands**?
11:21 the God of Israel, gave Sihon and all his men into Israel's **hands**,
11:26 and all the towns **along** [+6584] the Arnon.
11:30 a vow to the LORD: "If you give the Ammonites into my **hands**,
11:32 to fight the Ammonites, and the LORD gave them into his **hands**.
12: 2 and although I called, you didn't save me out of their **hands**.
12: 3 and the LORD **gave** me the **victory over** [+928+5989] them.
13: 1 so the LORD delivered them into the **hands** *of* the Philistines for
13: 5 he will begin the deliverance of Israel from the **hands** *of* the
13:23 have accepted a burnt offering and grain offering from our **hands**,
14: 6 so that he tore the lion apart with his bare **hands** as he might have
15:12 to tie you up and **hand** [+928+5989] you **over** *to* the Philistines."
15:13 will only tie you up and **hand** [+928+5989] you **over** *to* them.
15:14 like charred flax, and the bindings dropped from his **hands**.
15:15 a donkey, **[NIE]** he grabbed it and struck down a thousand men.
15:17 away the jawbone; **[NIE]** and the place was called Ramath Lehi.
15:18 "You have given **[NIE]** your servant this great victory.
15:18 I now die of thirst and fall into the **hands** *of* the uncircumcised?"
16:18 the rulers of the Philistines returned with the silver in their **hands**.
16:23 "Our god has delivered Samson, our enemy, into our **hands**."
16:24 saying, "Our god has delivered our enemy into our **hands**,
16:26 Samson said to the servant who held his **hand**, "Put me where I
17: 3 "I solemnly consecrate my silver to the LORD **[NIE]** for my son
17: 5 some idols and **installed** [+906+4848] one of his sons as his priest.
17:12 Micah **installed** [+906+4848] the Levite, and the young man
18:10 and a **spacious** [+8146] land that God has put into your hands,
18:10 and a spacious land that God has put into your **hands**,
18:19 answered him, "Be quiet! **Don't say a word** [+6584+7023+8492].
19:27 in the doorway of the house, with her **hands** on the threshold.
20:16 seven hundred chosen men who were **left-handed** [+360+3545],
20:28 "Go, for tomorrow I will give them into your **hands**."
Ru 1:13 for you, because the LORD's **hand** has gone out against me!"
4: 5 "On the day you buy the land **from** [+4946] Naomi and from Ruth
4: 9 "Today you are witnesses that I have bought **from** [+4946] Naomi
1Sa 2:13 of the priest would come with a three-pronged fork in his **hand**.
4: 8 Who will deliver us from the **hand** *of* these mighty gods?
4:13 there was Eli sitting on his chair by the **side** *of* the road, watching,
4:18 ark of God, Eli fell backward off his chair by the **side** *of* the gate.
5: 4 His head and **hands** [+4090] had been broken off and were lying
5: 6 The LORD's **hand** was heavy upon the people of Ashdod
5: 7 because his **hand** is heavy upon us and upon Dagon our god."
5: 9 after they had moved it, the LORD's **hand** was against that city,
5:11 had filled the city with panic; God's **hand** was very heavy upon it.
6: 3 and you will know why his **hand** has not been lifted from you."
6: 5 Perhaps he will lift his **hand** from you and your gods and your
6: 9 we will know that it was not his **hand** that struck us and that it
7: 3 and he will deliver you out of the **hand** *of* the Philistines."
7: 8 for us, that he may rescue us from the **hand** *of* the Philistines."
7:13 the **hand** *of* the LORD was against the Philistines.
7:14 Israel delivered the neighboring territory from the **power** *of* the
9: 8 he said, "I **have** [+928+5162] a quarter of a shekel of silver.
9:16 he will deliver my people from the **hand** *of* the Philistines.
10: 4 two loaves of bread, which you will accept **from** [+4946] them.
10: 7 do whatever your **hand** finds to do, for God is with you.
10:18 I delivered you from the **power** *of* Egypt and all the kingdoms that
10:18 power of Egypt and **[RPH]** all the kingdoms that oppressed you.'
11: 7 and sent the pieces **by** [+928] messengers throughout Israel,
12: 3 From whose **hand** have I accepted a bribe to make me shut my
12: 4 they replied. "You have not taken anything from anyone's **hand**."
12: 5 is witness this day, that you have not found anything in my **hand**."
12: 9 so he sold them into the **hand** *of* Sisera, the commander of the
12: 9 and into the **hands** *of* the Philistines and the king of Moab,
12: 9 and into the hands of the Philistines and **[RPH]** the king of Moab,
12:10 now deliver us from the **hands** *of* our enemies, and we will serve
12:11 he delivered you from the **hands** *of* your enemies on every side,
12:15 his **hand** will be against you, as it was against your fathers.
13:22 a soldier with Saul and Jonathan had a sword or spear in his **hand**;
14:10 will be our sign that the LORD has given them into our **hands**."
14:12 up after me; the LORD has given them into the **hand** *of* Israel."
14:13 Jonathan climbed up, using his **hands** and feet, with his
14:19 and more. So Saul said to the priest, "Withdraw your **hand**."
14:26 yet no one put his **hand** to his mouth, because they feared the oath.
14:27 so he reached out the end of the staff that was in his **hand**
14:27 He raised his **hand** to his mouth, and his eyes brightened.
14:34 blood still in it.' " So everyone brought his ox **[NIE]** that night
14:37 Will you give them into Israel's **hand**?" But God did not answer
14:43 little honey with the end of my staff. **[NIE]** And now must I die?"
14:48 delivering Israel from the **hands** *of* those who had plundered them.
15:12 There he has set up a **monument** in his own honor and has turned
16: 2 The LORD said, "Take a heifer **with** [+928] you and say,
16:16 He *will* **play** [+928+5594] when the evil spirit from God comes
16:20 and a young goat and sent them **with** [+928] his son David to Saul.
16:23 came upon Saul, David would take his harp and **play** [+928+5594].
17:22 David left his things **with** [+6584] the keeper of supplies,
17:37 The LORD who delivered me from the **paw** *of* the lion and the
17:37 the **paw** *of* the bear will deliver me from the hand of this
17:37 the paw of the bear will deliver me from the **hand** *of* this
17:40 he took his staff in his **hand**, chose five smooth stones from the
17:40 bag and, with his sling in his **hand**, approached the Philistine.
17:46 This day the LORD *will* **hand** [+928+6037] you **over** *to* me,
17:47 battle is the LORD's, and he will give all of you into our **hands**."
17:49 **Reaching** [+906+8938] into his bag and taking out a stone,
17:50 without a sword in his **hand** he struck down the Philistine
17:57 before Saul, with David still **holding** [+928] the Philistine's head.
18:10 while David *was* **playing the harp** [+928+5594], as he usually
18:10 playing the harp, as he usually did. Saul had a spear in his **hand**
18:17 For Saul said to himself, "I will not raise a **hand** against him.
18:17 *Let* the Philistines **do**[s] **that** [+928+2118+2257]!"
18:21 and so that the **hand** *of* the Philistines may be against him."
18:25 Saul's plan was to have David fall by the **hands** *of* the Philistines.
19: 3 and stand **with** [+4200] my father in the field where you are.
19: 9 upon Saul as he was sitting in his house with his spear in his **hand**.
19: 9 in his hand. While David *was* **playing the harp** [+928+5594],
20:16 "*May* the LORD **call** David's enemies **to account** [+1335+4946]."
21: 3 [21:4] Now then, what *do* you **have on hand** [+3780+9393]?
21: 3 [21:4] **Give** [+928+5989] me five loaves of bread, or whatever
21: 4 [21:5] "I don't **have** any ordinary bread **on hand** [+448+9393];
21: 8 [21:9] "Don't you **have** [+3780+9393] a spear or a sword here?
21: 8 [21:9] I haven't brought **[OBJ]** my sword or any other weapon,
21:13 [21:14] while he was in their **hands** he acted like a madman,
22: 6 Saul, spear in **hand**, was seated under the tamarisk tree on the hill
22:17 of the LORD, because they too have **sided** [+6640] **with** David.
22:17 the king's officials were not willing to raise a **hand** to strike the
23: 4 to Keilah, for I am going to give the Philistines into your **hand**."
23: 6 the ephod down **with** [+928] him when he fled to David at Keilah.)
23: 7 he said, "God *has* **handed** [+906+928+5796] him **over** *to* me,
23:11 Will the citizens of Keilah surrender me **to** [+928] him? Will Saul
23:12 the citizens of Keilah surrender me and my men **to** [+928] Saul?"
23:14 Saul searched for him, but God did not give David into his **hands**.
23:16 at Horesh and **helped** him **find strength** [+906+2616] in God.
23:17 be afraid," he said. "My father Saul will not lay a **hand** on you.
23:20 we will be responsible for **handing** [+928+6037] him **over** *to* the
24: 4 [24:5] 'I will give your enemy into your **hands** for you to deal
24: 6 [24:7] the LORD's anointed, or lift my **hand** against him;
24:10 [24:11] how the LORD delivered you into my **hands** in the cave.
24:10 [24:11] I said, 'I will not lift my **hand** against my master,
24:11 [24:12] my father, look at this piece of your robe in my **hand**!
24:11 [24:12] recognize that I am not **guilty** [+928] *of* wrongdoing
24:12 [24:13] you have done to me, but my **hand** will not touch you.
24:13 [24:14] come evil deeds,' so my **hand** will not touch you.
24:15 [24:16] may he vindicate me by delivering me from your **hand**."
24:18 [24:19] the LORD delivered me into your **hands**, but you did
24:20 [24:21] the kingdom of Israel will be established in your **hands**.
25: 8 and your son David whatever **you** [+3870] can find for them.' "
25:26 from bloodshed and from avenging yourself with your own **hands**,
25:33 bloodshed this day and from avenging myself with my own **hands**.
25:35 Then David accepted from her **hand** what she had brought him
25:39 who has upheld my cause **against** [+4946] Nabal for treating me
26: 8 to David, "Today God has delivered your enemy into your **hands**.
26: 9 Who can lay a **hand** on the LORD's anointed and be guiltless?
26:11 the LORD forbid that I should lay a **hand** on the LORD's
26:18 What have I done, and what wrong am I **guilty of** [+928]?
26:23 The LORD delivered you into my **hands** today, but I would not
26:23 hands today, but I would not lay a **hand** on the LORD's anointed.
27: 1 "One of these days I will be destroyed by the **hand** *of* Saul.
27: 1 for me anywhere in Israel, and I will slip out of his **hand**."
28:15 He no longer answers me, either **by** [+928] prophets or by dreams.
28:17 The LORD has done what he predicted **through** [+928] me.
28:17 The LORD has torn the kingdom out of your **hands** and given it
28:19 LORD *will* **hand** [+906+928+5989] **over** both Israel and you *to*
28:19 *will* also **hand** [+906+928+5989] **over** the army of Israel *to* the
30:15 you will not kill me or **hand** [+928+6037] me **over** *to* my master,
30:23 He has protected us and **handed** [+906+928+5989] **over** *to* us the
2Sa 1:14 "Why were you not afraid to lift your **hand** to destroy the
2: 7 Now then, *be* **strong** [+2616] and brave, for Saul your master is
3: 8 and friends. *I* haven't **handed** [+928+5162] you **over** *to* David.
3:12 with me, and I will **help** [+6640] you bring all Israel over to you."
3:18 '**By** [+928] my servant David I will rescue my people Israel from
3:18 I will rescue my people Israel from the **hand** *of* the Philistines
3:18 hand of the Philistines and from the **hand** *of* all their enemies.' "
3:34 Your **hands** were not bound, your feet were not fettered. You fell

[F] Hitpael (hitpoel, hitpoal, hitpolel, hitpolal, hitpalel, hitpalal, hitpalpel, hitpalpal, hotpael, hotpaal) [G] Hiphil (hiphtil) [H] Hophal [I] Hishtaphel

2Sa 4: 1 in Hebron, he **lost courage** [+8332], and all Israel became alarmed.
4: 11 should I not now demand his blood from your **hand** and rid the
4: 12 They cut off their **hands** and feet and hung the bodies by the pool
5: 19 attack the Philistines? *Will you* **hand** [+928+5989] them **over** *to*
5: 19 *I will* **surely hand** [+906+928+5989+5989] the Philistines **over** *to*
8: 1 and he took Metheg Ammah from the **control** *of* the Philistines.
8: 3 when he went to restore his **control** along the Euphrates River.
8: 10 Joram **brought with** [+928+2118] him articles of silver and gold
10: 2 So David sent a **delegation** [+928+6269] to express his sympathy
10: 10 He put the rest of the men under the **command** *of* Abishai his
11: 14 morning David wrote a letter to Joab and sent it **with** [+928] Uriah.
12: 7 you king over Israel, and I delivered you from the **hand** *of* Saul.
12: 25 he sent word **through** [+928] Nathan the prophet to name him
13: 5 in my sight so I may watch her and then eat it from her **hand**.' "
13: 6 make some special bread in my sight, so I may eat from her **hand**."
13: 10 the food here into my bedroom so I may eat from your **hand**."
13: 19 She put her **hand** on her head and went away, weeping aloud as
14: 19 The king asked, "Isn't the **hand** *of* Joab with you in all this?"
14: 30 "Look, Joab's field is **next** [+448] **to** mine, and he has barley there.
15: 2 up early and stand by the **side** *of* the road leading to the city gate.
15: 5 Absalom would reach out his **hand**, take hold of him and kiss him.
15: 18 All his men **marched past** [+6296+6584] him, along with all the
15: 36 there with them. Send them to me **with** [+928] anything you hear."
16: 8 The LORD *has* **handed** [+906+928+5989] the kingdom **over** *to*
16: 21 and the **hands** *of* everyone with you will be strengthened."
17: 2 I would attack him while he is weary and **weak** [+8333]. I would
18: 2 a third under the **command** *of* Joab, a third under Joab's brother
18: 2 a third **under** [+928] Joab's brother Abishai son of Zeruiah,
18: 2 Abishai son of Zeruiah, and a third **under** [+928] Ittai the Gittite.
18: 4 So the king stood **beside** [+448] the gate while all the men
18: 12 out into my hands, I would not lift my **hand** against the king's son.
18: 18 after himself, and it is called Absalom's **Monument** to this day.
18: 19 that the LORD has delivered him from the **hand** *of* his enemies."
18: 28 He has delivered up the men who lifted their **hands** against my
18: 31 The LORD has delivered you today **from** [+4946] all who rose up
19: 43 [19:44] the men of Judah, "We have ten **shares** in the king;
20: 9 Joab took Amasa by the beard with his right **hand** to kiss him.
20: 10 Amasa was not on his guard against the dagger in Joab's **hand**,
20: 21 of Ephraim, has lifted up his **hand** against the king, against David.
21: 9 *He* **handed** [+928+5989] them **over** *to* the Gibeonites, who killed
21: 20 there was a huge man with six fingers on each **hand** and six toes
21: 22 of Rapha in Gath, and they fell at the **hands** *of* David and his men.
21: 22 in Gath, and they fell at the hands of David and **[RPH]** his men.
22: 21 according to the cleanness of my **hands** he has rewarded me.
22: 35 He trains my **hands** for battle; my arms can bend a bow of bronze.
23: 6 to be cast aside like thorns, which are not gathered with the **hand**.
23: 10 struck down the Philistines till his **hand** grew tired and froze to the
23: 10 Philistines till his hand grew tired and froze **[RPH]** to the sword.
23: 21 Although the Egyptian had a spear in his **hand**, Benaiah went
23: 21 He snatched the spear from the Egyptian's **hand** and killed him
24: 14 Let us fall into the **hands** *of* the LORD, for his mercy is great;
24: 14 his mercy is great; but do not let me fall into the **hands** *of* men."
24: 16 When the angel stretched out his **hand** to destroy Jerusalem,
24: 16 who was afflicting the people, "Enough! Withdraw your **hand**."
24: 17 have they done? Let your **hand** fall upon me and my family."
1Ki 2: 25 So King Solomon gave orders **to** [+928] Benaiah son of Jehoiada,
2: 46 The kingdom was now firmly established in Solomon's **hands**.
7: 32 the panels, and the **axles** *of* the wheels were attached to the stand.
7: 33 the **axles**, rims, spokes and hubs were all of cast metal.
7: 35 The **supports** and panels were attached to the top of the stand.
7: 36 lions and palm trees on the surfaces of the **supports** and on the
8: 15 who with his own **hand** has fulfilled what he promised with his
8: 24 you have promised and with your **hand** you have fulfilled it—
8: 42 great name and your mighty **hand** and your outstretched arm—
8: 53 just as you declared **through** [+928] your servant Moses when
8: 56 all the good promises he gave **through** [+928] his servant Moses.
10: 13 asked for, besides what he had given her out of his royal **bounty**.
10: 19 On both sides of the seat were **armrests**, with a lion standing
10: 19 were armrests, with a lion standing beside each of **them**ˢ [+2021].
10: 29 **[NIE]** They also exported them to all the kings of the Hittites
11: 12 do it during your lifetime. I will tear it out of the **hand** *of* your son.
11: 26 Jeroboam son of Nebat **rebelled** [+8123] against the king.
11: 27 Here is the account of how *he* **rebelled** [+8123] against the king:
11: 31 I am going to tear the kingdom out of Solomon's **hand** and give
11: 34 " 'But I will not take the whole kingdom out of Solomon's **hand**;
11: 35 I will take the kingdom from his son's **hands** and give you ten
12: 15 to Jeroboam son of Nebat **through** [+928] Ahijah the Shilonite.
13: 4 he stretched out his **hand** from the altar and said, "Seize him!"
13: 4 But the **hand** he stretched out toward the man shriveled up,
13: 6 LORD your God and pray for me that my **hand** may be restored."
13: 6 and the king's **hand** was restored and became as it was before.
13: 33 become a priest *he* **consecrated** [+906+4848] for the high places.
14: 3 Take ten loaves of bread **with** [+928] you, some cakes and a jar of
14: 18 as the LORD had said **through** [+928] his servant the prophet
14: 27 assigned these **to** [+6584] the commanders of the guard on duty at
15: 18 He entrusted it **to** [+928] his officials and sent them to Ben-Hadad
15: 29 according to the word of the LORD given **through** [+928] his
16: 7 the word of the LORD came **through** [+928] the prophet Jehu
16: 7 provoking him to anger by the **things** he **did** [+5126], and
16: 12 LORD spoken against Baasha **through** [+928] the prophet Jehu—
16: 34 in accordance with the word of the LORD spoken **by** [+928]
17: 11 he called, "And bring me, please, a piece of bread." **[OBJ]**
17: 16 in keeping with the word of the LORD spoken **by** [+928] Elijah.
18: 9 you *are* **handing** [+906+928+5989] your servant **over** *to* Ahab to
18: 46 The **power** *of* the LORD came upon Elijah and, tucking his cloak
20: 6 *They will* **seize** [+928+8492] everything you value and carry it
20: 13 I will give it into your **hand** today, and then you will know that I
20: 28 a god of the valleys, I will deliver this vast army into your **hands**,
20: 42 '*You have* **set free** [+906+4946+8938] a man I had determined
22: 3 yet we are doing nothing to retake it **from** [+4946] the king of
22: 6 they answered, "for the Lord will give it into the king's **hand**."
22: 12 they said, "for the LORD will give it into the king's **hand**."
22: 15 he answered, "for the LORD will give it into the king's **hand**."
22: 34 "**Wheel around** [+2200] and get me out of the fighting.
2Ki 3: 10 kings together only to **hand** [+906+928+5989] us **over** *to* Moab?"
3: 11 of Shaphat is here. He used to pour water on the **hands** *of* Elijah."
3: 13 three kings together to **hand** [+906+928+5989] us **over** *to* Moab."
3: 15 the harpist was playing, the **hand** *of* the LORD came upon Elisha
3: 18 of the LORD; *he will* also **hand** [+906+928+5989] Moab **over** *to*
4: 29 your cloak into your belt, take my staff in your **hand** and run.
5: 5 So Naaman left, taking **with** [+928] him ten talents of silver,
5: 11 his God, wave his **hand** over the spot and cure me of my leprosy.
5: 18 to bow down and he is leaning on my **arm** and I bow there also—
5: 20 by not accepting **from** [+4946] him what he brought.
5: 24 he took the things **from** [+4946] the servants and put them away in
6: 7 it out," he said. Then the man reached out his **hand** and took it.
7: 2 The officer on whose **arm** the king was leaning said to the man of
7: 17 Now the king had put the officer on whose **arm** he leaned in
8: 8 "Take a gift **with** [+928] you and go to meet the man of God.
8: 9 taking **with** [+928] him as a gift forty camel-loads of all the finest
8: 20 Edom rebelled **against** [+4946+9393] Judah and set up its own
8: 22 To this day Edom has been in rebellion **against** [+4946+9393]
9: 1 take this flask of oil **with** [+928] you and go to Ramoth Gilead.
9: 7 the blood of all the LORD's servants **shed by** [+4946] Jezebel.
9: 23 Joram **turned about** [+2200] and fled, calling out to Ahaziah,
9: 24 Jehu **drew** [+928+4848] his bow and shot Joram between the
9: 35 found nothing except her skull, her feet and her **hands** [+4090].
9: 36 "This is the word of the LORD that he spoke **through** [+928] his
10: 10 The LORD has done what he promised **through** [+928] his
10: 15 "If so," said Jehu, "give me your **hand**." So he did, and Jehu
10: 15 So *he* **did**ˢ [+2257+5989], and Jehu helped him up into the chariot.
10: 24 "If one of you lets any of the men I am placing in your **hands**
11: 7 you who are in the other two **companies** that normally go off
11: 8 yourselves around the king, each man with his weapon in his **hand**.
11: 11 The guards, each with his weapon in his **hand**,
11: 16 So *they* **seized** [+4200+8492] her as she reached the place where
12: 11 [12:12] they gave the money **to** [+6584] the men appointed to
12: 15 [12:16] They did not require an accounting from those **to** [+6584]
13: 3 for a long time he kept them under the **power** *of* Hazael king of
13: 3 the power of Hazael king of Aram and **[RPH]** Ben-Hadad his son.
13: 5 a deliverer for Israel, and they escaped from the **power** *of* Aram.
13: 16 "Take the bow in your **hands**," he said to the king of Israel.
13: 16 he had taken it, **[RPH]** Elisha put his hands on the king's hands.
13: 16 When he had taken it, Elisha put his **hands** on the king's hands.
13: 16 When he had taken it, Elisha put his hands on the king's **hands**.
13: 25 Jehoash son of Jehoahaz recaptured **from** [+4946] Ben-Hadad son
13: 25 the towns he had taken in battle **from** [+4946] his father Jehoahaz.
14: 5 After the kingdom was firmly in his **grasp**, he executed the
14: 25 of Israel, spoken **through** [+928] his servant Jonah son of Amittai,
14: 27 he saved them by the **hand** *of* Jeroboam son of Jehoash.
15: 19 him a thousand talents of silver to **gain** his **support** [+907+2118]
15: 19 to gain his support and strengthen his own **hold** on the kingdom.
17: 7 who had brought them up out of Egypt from under the **power** *of*
17: 13 warned Israel and Judah **through** [+928] all his prophets and seers:
17: 13 that I delivered to you **through** [+928] my servants the prophets."
17: 20 he afflicted them and gave them into the **hands** *of* plunderers,
17: 23 as he had warned **through** [+928] all his servants the prophets.
17: 39 it is he who will deliver you from the **hand** *of* all your enemies."
18: 29 let Hezekiah deceive you. He cannot deliver you from my **hand**.
18: 30 this city will not be given into the **hand** *of* the king of Assyria.'
18: 33 Has the god of any nation ever delivered his land from the **hand** *of*
18: 34 Hena and Ivvah? Have they rescued Samaria from my **hand**?
18: 35 of these countries has been able to save his land **from** [+4946] me?
18: 35 How then can the LORD deliver Jerusalem from my **hand**?"
19: 10 'Jerusalem *will* not **be handed** [+928+5989] **over** *to* the king of
19: 14 Hezekiah received the letter **from** [+4946] the messengers
19: 18 not gods but only wood and stone, fashioned by men's **hands**.
19: 19 Now, O LORD our God, deliver us from his **hand**, so that all

2Ki 19:23 **By** [+928] your messengers you have heaped insults on the Lord.
19:26 Their people, drained of **power**, are dismayed and put to shame.
21:10 The LORD said **through** [+928] his servants the prophets:
21:14 my inheritance and **hand** [+928+5989] them **over** *to* their enemies.
22:5 Have them entrust it **to** [+6584] the men appointed to supervise the
22:7 they need not account for the money entrusted **to** [+6584] them,
22:9 have entrusted it **to** [+6584] the workers and supervisors at the
22:17 and provoked me to anger by all the idols their **hands** have made,
24:2 in accordance with the word of the LORD proclaimed **by** [+928]
1Ch 4:10 Let your **hand** be with me, and keep me from harm so that I will
4:40 and the land was **spacious** [+8146], peaceful and quiet.
5:10 waged war against the Hagrites, who were defeated at their **hands**;
5:20 God **handed** [+928+5989] the Hagrites and all their allies **over** *to*
6:15 [5:41] and Jerusalem into exile by the **hand** *of* Nebuchadnezzar.
6:31 [6:16] These are the men David **put in charge of** [+6584+6641]
7:29 Along the **borders** *of* Manasseh were Beth Shan, Taanach,
11:3 over Israel, as the LORD had promised **through** [+928] Samuel.
11:23 Although the Egyptian had a spear like a weaver's rod in his **hand**,
11:23 He snatched the spear from the Egyptian's **hand** and killed him
13:9 Uzzah reached out his **hand** to steady the ark, because the oxen
13:10 and he struck him down because he had put his **hand** on the ark.
14:10 attack the Philistines? *Will you* **hand** [+928+5989] them **over** *to*
14:10 answered him, "Go, *I will* **hand** [+928+5989] them **over** *to* you."
14:11 break out, God has broken out against my enemies by my **hand**."
16:7 That day David first committed **to** [+928] Asaph and his associates
18:1 and its surrounding villages from the **control** *of* the Philistines.
18:3 when he went to establish his **control** along the Euphrates River.
18:17 and David's sons were chief officials at the king's **side**.
19:11 He put the rest of the men under the **command** *of* Abishai his
20:8 of Rapha in Gath, and they fell at the **hands** *of* David and his men.
20:8 in Gath, and they fell at the hands of David and **[RPH]** his men.
21:13 Let me fall into the **hands** *of* the LORD, for his mercy is very
21:13 mercy is very great; but do not let me fall into the **hands** *of* men."
21:15 who was destroying the people, "Enough! Withdraw your **hand**."
21:16 with a drawn sword in his **hand** extended over Jerusalem.
21:17 O LORD my God, let your **hand** fall upon me and my family,
22:18 *he has* **handed** [+906+928+5989] the inhabitants of the land **over**
23:28 The duty of the Levites was to **help** [+4200] Aaron's descendants
24:19 according to the regulations prescribed for them **by** [+928] their
25:2 The sons of Asaph were under the **supervision** *of* Asaph,
25:2 of Asaph, who prophesied under the king's **supervision**.
25:3 six in all, under the **supervision** *of* their father Jeduthun,
25:6 All these men were under the **supervision** *of* their fathers for the
25:6 Jeduthun and Heman were under the **supervision** *of* the king.
26:28 and all the other dedicated things were in the **care** *of* Shelomith
28:19 "I have in writing from the **hand** *of* the LORD upon me,
29:5 and for all the work to be **done by** [+928] the craftsmen.
29:5 who is willing to **consecrate himself** [+2257+4848] today to the
29:8 the temple of the LORD in the **custody** *of* Jehiel the Gershonite.
29:12 In your **hands** are strength and power to exalt and give strength to
29:12 are strength and power **[RPH]** to exalt and give strength to all.
29:14 and we have given you only what comes from your **hand**.
29:16 Holy Name, it comes from your **hand**, and all of it belongs to you.
29:24 David's sons, **pledged** [+5989] their submission to King Solomon.
2Ch 1:17 **[NIE]** They also exported them to all the kings of the Hittites
6:4 who with his **hands** has fulfilled what he promised with his mouth
6:15 you have promised and with your **hand** you have fulfilled it—
6:32 because of your great name and your mighty **hand** and your
7:6 the LORD and which were **used** [+928] when he gave thanks,
8:18 And Hiram sent him ships **commanded** by his own officers,
9:18 On both sides of the seat were **armrests**, with a lion standing
9:18 were armrests, with a lion standing beside each of **them**[s] [+2021].
10:15 to Jeroboam son of Nebat **through** [+928] Ahijah the Shilonite.
12:5 abandoned me; therefore, I now abandon you **to** [+928] Shishak.' "
12:7 My wrath will not be poured out on Jerusalem **through** [+928]
12:10 assigned these **to** [+6584] the commanders of the guard on duty at
13:8 of the LORD, which is in the **hands** *of* David's descendants.
13:9 Whoever comes to **consecrate himself** [+4848] with a young bull
13:16 fled before Judah, and God delivered them into their **hands**.
15:7 as for you, be strong and *do* not **give up** [+8332], for your work
16:7 the army of the king of Aram has escaped from your **hand**.
16:8 when you relied on the LORD, he delivered them into your **hand**.
17:5 The LORD established the kingdom under his **control**; and all
17:15 **next** [+6584], Jehohanan the commander, with 280,000;
17:16 **next** [+6584], Amasiah son of Zicri, who volunteered himself for
17:18 **next** [+6584], Jehozabad, with 180,000 men armed for battle.
18:5 they answered, "for God will give it into the king's **hand**."
18:11 they said, "for the LORD will give it into the king's **hand**."
18:14 he answered, "for they will be given into your **hand**."
18:33 "**Wheel around** [+2200] and get me out of the fighting.
20:6 Power and might are in your **hand**, and no one can withstand you.
21:8 Edom rebelled **against** [+4946+9393] Judah and set up its own
21:10 To this day Edom has been in rebellion **against** [+4946+9393]
21:10 **[RPH]** because Jehoram had forsaken the LORD, the God of his
21:16 and of the Arabs who lived **near** [+6584] the Cushites.
23:7 around the king, each man with his weapons in his **hand**.
23:10 all the men, each with his weapon in his **hand**, around the king—
23:15 So *they* **seized** [+4200+8492] her as she reached the entrance of
23:18 oversight of the temple of the LORD in the **hands** *of* the priests,
23:18 Law of Moses, with rejoicing and singing, as David had **ordered**.
24:11 Whenever the chest was brought in **by** [+928] the Levites to the
24:13 work were diligent, and the repairs progressed **under** [+928] them.
24:24 the LORD delivered into their **hands** a much larger army.
25:15 which could not save their own people from your **hand**?"
25:20 so worked that he *might* **hand** [+928+5989] them **over** to
26:11 to their numbers as mustered **by** [+928] Jeiel the secretary
26:11 and Maaseiah the officer under the **direction** *of* Hananiah,
26:13 Under their **command** was an army of 307,500 men trained for
26:19 Uzziah, who had a censer in his **hand** ready to burn incense,
28:5 Therefore the LORD his God **handed** [+928+5989] him **over** *to*
28:5 He was also given into the **hands** *of* the king of Israel, who
28:9 your fathers, was angry with Judah, he gave them into your **hand**.
29:23 the king and the assembly, and they laid their **hands** on them.
29:25 this was commanded **by** [+928] the LORD through his prophets.
29:25 this was commanded by the LORD **through** [+928] his prophets.
29:27 **accompanied by** [+6584] trumpets and the instruments of David
29:31 "*You have* now **dedicated** [+4848] yourselves to the LORD.
30:6 Judah with letters **from** [+4946] the king and from his officials,
30:8 as your fathers were; **submit** [+5989] to the LORD.
30:12 Also in Judah the **hand** *of* God was on the people to give them
30:16 The priests sprinkled the blood **handed** to them by the Levites.
31:13 Mahath and Benaiah were supervisors **under** [+4946] Conaniah
31:15 Shecaniah **assisted** [+6584] him faithfully in the towns of the
32:13 of those nations ever able to deliver their land from my **hand**?
32:14 **[RPH]** How then can your god deliver you from my hand?
32:14 from me? How then can your god deliver you from my **hand**?
32:15 or kingdom has been able to deliver his people from my **hand**
32:15 able to deliver his people from my hand or the **hand** *of* my fathers.
32:15 How much less will your god deliver you from my **hand**!"
32:17 of the other lands did not rescue their people from my **hand**,
32:17 so the god of Hezekiah will not rescue his people from my **hand**."
32:19 gods of the other peoples of the world—the work of men's **hands**.
32:22 the people of Jerusalem from the **hand** *of* Sennacherib king of
32:22 of Sennacherib king of Assyria and from the **hand** *of* all others.
33:8 all the laws, decrees and ordinances given **through** [+928] Moses."
34:9 doorkeepers had collected **from** [+4946] the people of Manasseh,
34:10 they entrusted it **to** [+6584] the men appointed to supervise the
34:14 Law of the LORD that had been given **through** [+928] Moses.
34:16 are doing everything that has been committed **to** [+928] them.
34:17 and have entrusted it **to** [+6584] the supervisors and workers."
34:17 and have entrusted it to the supervisors and **[RPH]** workers."
34:25 and provoked me to anger by all that their **hands** have made,
35:6 doing what the LORD commanded **through** [+928] Moses."
35:11 and the priests sprinkled the blood **handed** [+4946] *to* them,
36:15 sent word to them **through** [+928] his messengers again and again,
36:17 God **handed** [+928+5989] all of them **over** *to* Nebuchadnezzar.
Ezr 1:6 All their neighbors **assisted** [+928+2616] them with articles of
1:8 Cyrus king of Persia had them brought **by** [+6584] Mithredath the
3:10 praise the LORD, **as prescribed by** [+6584] David king of Israel.
4:4 the peoples around them *set out to* **discourage** [+8332] the people
6:22 so that he **assisted** [+2616] them in the work on the house of God,
7:6 he asked, for the **hand** *of* the LORD his God was on him.
7:9 of the fifth month, for the gracious **hand** *of* his God was on him.
7:28 Because the **hand** *of* the LORD my God was on me, I took
8:18 Because the gracious **hand** *of* our God was on us, they brought us
8:22 "The gracious **hand** *of* our God is on everyone who looks to him,
8:26 I weighed out **to** [+6584] them 650 talents of silver, silver articles
8:31 The **hand** *of* our God was on us, and he protected us from enemies
8:33 and the sacred articles into the **hands** *of* Meremoth son of Uriah,
9:2 officials *have* **led the way** [+2118+8037] in this unfaithfulness."
9:7 to pillage and humiliation at the **hand** *of* foreign kings, as it is
9:11 you gave **through** [+928] your servants the prophets when you
10:19 (They all gave their **hands** in pledge to put away their wives,
Ne 1:10 whom you redeemed by your great strength and your mighty **hand**.
2:8 And because the gracious **hand** *of* my God was upon me,
2:18 I also told them about the gracious **hand** *of* my God upon me
2:18 us start rebuilding." So they **began** [+2616+4200] this good work.
3:2 The men of Jericho built the **adjoining section** [+6584], and
3:2 and Zaccur son of Imri built **next to** [+6584] them.
3:4 of Uriah, the son of Hakkoz, repaired the **next section** [+6584].
3:4 **Next to** [+6584] him Meshullam son of Berekiah, the son of
3:4 and **next to** [+6584] him Zadok son of Baana also made repairs.
3:5 The **next section** [+6584] was repaired by the men of Tekoa,
3:7 **Next to** [+6584] them, repairs were made by men from Gibeon
3:8 one of the goldsmiths, repaired the **next section** [+6584];
3:8 one of the perfume-makers, made repairs **next to** [+6584] that.
3:9 of a half-district of Jerusalem, repaired the **next section** [+6584].
3:10 **Adjoining** [+6584] this, Jedaiah son of Harumaph made repairs

Ne 3:10 and Hattush son of Hashabneiah made repairs **next to** [+6584] him.
3:12 repaired the **next section** [+6584] with the help of his daughters.
3:17 **Beside** [+6584] him, Hashabiah, ruler of half the district of Keilah,
3:19 **Next to** [+6584] him, Ezer son of Jeshua, ruler of Mizpah,
4:17 [4:11] Those who carried materials did their work with one **hand**
5:5 but we are **powerless** [+401+445+4200], because our fields and
6:5 me with the same message, and in his **hand** was an unsealed letter
6:9 thinking, "Their **hands** will get too weak for the work, and it will
6:9 not be completed." ⌞But I prayed,⌟ "Now strengthen my **hands**."
7:4 Now the city was large and **spacious** [+8146], but there were few
8:6 and all the people lifted their **hands** and responded, "Amen!
8:14 which the LORD had commanded **through** [+928] Moses,
9:14 decrees and laws **through** [+928] your servant Moses.
9:15 take possession of the land you had sworn with uplifted **hand** to
9:24 *you* **handed** [+906+906+928+5989] the Canaanites **over** *to* them,
9:27 So *you* **handed** [+928+5989] them **over** *to* their enemies,
9:27 them deliverers, who rescued them from the **hand** *of* their enemies.
9:28 you abandoned them to the **hand** *of* their enemies so that they
9:30 By your Spirit you admonished them **through** [+928] your
9:30 so *you* **handed** [+928+5989] them **over** *to* the neighboring
10:29 [10:30] an oath to follow the Law of God given **through** [+928]
10:31 [10:32] forgo working the land and will cancel all **debts** [+5391].
11:1 while the **remaining** nine were to stay in their own towns.
11:24 was the king's **agent** [+4200] in all affairs relating to the people.
13:13 son of Zaccur, the son of Mattaniah, their **assistant** [+6584],
13:21 night by the wall? If you do this again, I will lay **hands** on you."
Est 1:7 the royal wine was abundant, in keeping with the king's **liberality**.
1:12 But when the attendants **delivered** [+928] the king's command,
1:15 of King Xerxes that the eunuchs have **taken** [+928] to her."
2:3 Let them be placed under the **care** *of* Hegai, the king's eunuch,
2:8 brought to the citadel of Susa and put under the **care** *of* Hegai.
2:8 also was taken to the king's palace and **entrusted to** [+448] Hegai,
2:14 in the morning return to another part of the harem to the **care** *of*
2:18 throughout the provinces and distributed gifts with royal **liberality**.
2:21 angry and conspired to **assassinate** [+928+8938] King Xerxes.
3:6 he scorned the idea of **killing** [+928+8938] only Mordecai.
3:9 royal treasury **for** [+6584] the men who carry out this business."
3:10 So the king took his signet ring from his **finger** and gave it to
3:13 Dispatches were sent **by** [+928] couriers to all the king's provinces
5:2 with her and held out to her the gold scepter that was in his **hand**.
6:2 who had conspired to **assassinate** [+928+8938] King Xerxes.
6:9 horse be entrusted **to** [+6584] one of the king's most noble princes.
8:7 the Jew, "Because Haman **attacked** [+928+8938] the Jews,
8:10 the king's signet ring, and sent them **by** [+928] mounted couriers,
9:2 Xerxes to **attack** [+928+8938] those seeking their destruction.
9:10 enemy of the Jews. But they did not lay their **hands** on the plunder.
9:15 three hundred men, but they did not lay their **hands** on the plunder.
9:16 thousand of them but did not lay their **hands** on the plunder.
Job 1:10 You have blessed the work of his **hands**, so that his flocks
1:11 stretch out your **hand** and strike everything he has, and he will
1:12 said to Satan, "Very well, then, everything he has is in your **hands**,
1:12 has is in your hands, but on the man himself do not lay a **finger**."
1:14 oxen were plowing and the donkeys were grazing **nearby** [+6584],
2:5 stretch out your **hand** and strike his flesh and bones, and he will
2:6 The LORD said to Satan, "Very well, then, he is in your **hands**;
4:3 have instructed many, how you have strengthened feeble **hands**.
5:12 the plans of the crafty, so that their **hands** achieve no success.
5:15 in their mouth; he saves them from the **clutches** *of* the powerful.
5:18 but he also binds up; he injures, but his **hands** also heal.
5:20 ransom you from death, and in battle from the **stroke** *of* the sword.
6:9 would be willing to crush me, to let loose his **hand** and cut me off!
6:23 deliver me from the **hand** *of* the enemy, ransom me from the
6:23 hand of the enemy, ransom me from the **clutches** *of* the ruthless'?
8:4 against him, he gave them over **to** [+928] the penalty of their sin.
8:20 not reject a blameless man or strengthen the **hands** *of* evildoers.
9:24 When a land falls into the **hands** *of* the wicked, he blindfolds its
9:33 someone to arbitrate between us, to lay his **hand** upon us both,
10:7 I am not guilty and that no one can rescue me from your **hand**?
10:8 "Your **hands** shaped me and made me. Will you now turn
11:14 if you put away the sin that is in your **hand** and allow no evil to
12:6 provoke God are secure—those who carry their god in their **hands**.
12:9 Which of all these does not know that the **hand** *of* the LORD has
12:10 In his **hand** is the life of every creature and the breath of all
14:15 answer you; you will long for the creature your **hands** have made.
15:23 food for vultures; he knows the day of darkness is at **hand**.
15:25 because he shakes his **fist** at God and vaunts himself against the
16:11 over to evil men and thrown me into the **clutches** *of* the wicked.
17:3 Who else *will* **put up security for** [+4200+9546] me?
17:9 hold to their ways, and those with clean **hands** will grow stronger.
19:21 my friends, have pity, for the **hand** *of* God has struck me.
20:10 amends to the poor; his own **hands** must give back his wealth.
20:22 will overtake him; the full **force** *of* misery will come upon him.
21:5 Look at me and be astonished; clap your **hand** over your mouth.
21:16 their prosperity is not in their own **hands**, so I stand aloof from the
23:2 my complaint is bitter; his **hand** is heavy in spite of my groaning.
26:13 breath the skies became fair; his **hand** pierced the gliding serpent.
27:11 "I will teach you about the **power** *of* God; the ways of the
27:22 against him without mercy as he flees headlong from its **power**.
28:9 Man's **hand** assaults the flinty rock and lays bare the roots of the
29:20 My glory will remain fresh in me, the bow ever new in my **hand**.'
30:2 Of what use was the strength of their **hands** to me, since their
30:21 turn on me ruthlessly; with the might of your **hand** you attack me.
30:24 "Surely no one lays a **hand** on a broken man when he cries for
31:21 if I have raised my **hand** against the fatherless, knowing that I had
31:25 rejoiced over my great wealth, the fortune my **hands** had gained,
31:27 was secretly enticed and my **hand** offered them a kiss of homage,
34:19 favor the rich over the poor, for they are all the work of his **hands**?
34:20 and they pass away; the mighty are removed without human **hand**.
35:7 what do you give to him, or what does he receive from your **hand**?
37:7 has made may know his work, he stops every man from his **labor**.
40:4 how can I reply to you? I put my **hand** over my mouth.
Ps 8:6 [8:7] You made him ruler over the works of your **hands**; you put
10:12 Arise, LORD! Lift up your **hand**, O God. Do not forget the
10:14 do see trouble and grief; you consider it to take it in **hand**.
17:14 O LORD, by your **hand** save me from such men, from men of
18:T [18:1] the hand of all his enemies and from the **hand** *of* Saul.
18:20 [18:21] according to the cleanness of my **hands** he has rewarded
18:24 [18:25] according to the cleanness of my **hands** in his sight.
18:34 [18:35] He trains my **hands** for battle; my arms can bend a bow
19:1 [19:2] the glory of God; the skies proclaim the work of his **hands**.
21:8 [21:9] Your **hand** will lay hold on all your enemies; your right
22:16 [22:17] encircled me, they have pierced my **hands** and my feet.
22:20 [22:21] the sword, my precious life from the **power** *of* the dogs.
26:10 in whose **hands** are wicked schemes, whose right hands are full of
28:2 you for help, as I lift up my **hands** toward your Most Holy Place.
28:4 repay them for what their **hands** have done and bring back upon
28:5 regard for the works of the LORD and what his **hands** have done,
31:5 [31:6] Into your **hands** I commit my spirit; redeem me,
31:8 [31:9] *You have* not **handed** [+928+6037] me **over** *to* the enemy
31:15 [31:16] My times are in your **hands**; deliver me from my enemies
31:15 [31:16] deliver me **from** [+4946] my enemies and from those who
32:4 For day and night your **hand** was heavy upon me; my strength was
36:11 [36:12] against me, nor the **hand** *of* the wicked drive me away.
37:24 he will not fall, for the LORD upholds him with his **hand**.
37:33 the LORD will not leave them in their **power** or let them be
38:2 [38:3] have pierced me, and your **hand** has come down upon me.
39:10 [39:11] from me; I am overcome by the blow of your **hand**.
44:2 [44:3] With your **hand** you drove out the nations and planted our
49:15 [49:16] God will redeem my life **from** [+4946] the grave; he will
55:20 [55:21] My companion **attacks** [+928+8938] his friends;
58:2 [58:3] and your **hands** mete out violence on the earth.
63:10 [63:11] They *will be* **given over to** [+5599+6584] the sword
68:31 [68:32] from Egypt; Cush *will* **submit** [+8132] herself to God.
71:4 Deliver me, O my God, from the **hand** *of* the wicked,
73:23 Yet I am always with you; you hold me by my right **hand**.
74:11 Why do you hold back your **hand**, your right hand? Take it from
75:8 [75:9] In the **hand** *of* the LORD is a cup full of foaming wine
76:5 [76:6] their last sleep; not one of the warriors can lift his **hands**.
77:2 [77:3] at night I stretched out untiring **hands** and my soul refused
77:20 [77:21] You led your people like a flock by the **hand** *of* Moses
78:42 They did not remember his **power**—the day he redeemed them
78:61 his might into captivity, his splendor into the **hands** *of* the enemy.
80:17 [80:18] Let your **hand** rest on the man at your right hand, the son
81:14 [81:15] subdue their enemies and turn my **hand** against their foes!
82:4 the weak and needy; deliver them from the **hand** *of* the wicked.
88:5 [88:6] you remember no more, who are cut off from your **care**.
89:13 [89:14] with power; your **hand** is strong, your right hand exalted.
89:21 [89:22] My **hand** will sustain him; surely my arm will strengthen
89:25 [89:26] I will set his **hand** over the sea, his right hand over the
89:48 [89:49] see death, or save himself from the **power** *of* the grave?
90:17 establish the work of our **hands** for us—yes, establish the work of
90:17 work of our hands for us—yes, establish the work of our **hands**.
92:4 [92:5] O LORD; I sing for joy at the works of your **hands**.
95:4 In his **hand** are the depths of the earth, and the mountain peaks
95:5 The sea is his, for he made it, and his **hands** formed the dry land.
95:7 and we are the people of his pasture, the flock **under** his **care**.
97:10 of his faithful ones and delivers them from the **hand** *of* the wicked.
102:25 [102:26] the earth, and the heavens are the work of your **hands**.
104:25 There is the sea, vast and **spacious** [+8146], teeming with creatures
104:28 when you open your **hand**, they are satisfied with good things.
106:10 He saved them from the **hand** *of* the foe; from the hand of the
106:10 hand of the foe; from the **hand** *of* the enemy he redeemed them.
106:26 So he swore to them with uplifted **hand** that he would make them
106:41 *He* **handed** [+928+5989] them **over** *to* the nations, and their foes
106:42 Their enemies oppressed them and subjected them to their **power**.
107:2 the LORD say this—those he redeemed from the **hand** *of* the foe,
109:27 Let them know that it is your **hand**, that you, O LORD,
111:7 The works of his **hands** are faithful and just; all his precepts are

Ps 115: 4 But their idols are silver and gold, made by the **hands** *of* men.
115: 7 they have **hands**, but cannot feel, feet, but they cannot walk;
119: 73 Your **hands** made me and formed me; give me understanding to
119:173 May your **hand** be ready to help me, for I have chosen your
121: 5 watches over you—the LORD is your shade at your right **hand**;
123: 2 As the eyes of slaves look to the **hand** *of* their master, as the eyes
123: 2 as the eyes of a maid look to the **hand** *of* her mistress, so our eyes
125: 3 for then the righteous might use their **hands** to do evil.
127: 4 Like arrows in the **hands** *of* a warrior are sons born in one's youth.
134: 2 Lift up your **hands** in the sanctuary and praise the LORD.
135: 15 idols of the nations are silver and gold, made by the **hands** *of* men.
136: 12 with a mighty **hand** and outstretched arm; *His love endures*
138: 7 you stretch out your **hand** against the anger of my foes, with your
138: 8 endures forever—do not abandon the works of your **hands**.
139: 10 even there your **hand** will guide me, your right hand will hold me
140: 4 [140:5] Keep me, O LORD, from the **hands** *of* the wicked;
140: 5 [140:6] their net and have set traps for me **along** [+4200] my path.
141: 6 their rulers will be thrown down **from** [+928] the cliffs,
141: 9 Keep me **from** [+4946] the snares they have laid for me, from the
143: 5 on all your works and consider what your **hands** have done.
143: 6 I spread out my **hands** to you; my soul thirsts for you like a
144: 1 my Rock, who trains my **hands** for war, my fingers for battle.
144: 7 Reach down your **hand** from on high; deliver me and rescue me
144: 7 rescue me from the mighty waters, from the **hands** *of* foreigners
144: 11 rescue me from the **hands** *of* foreigners whose mouths are full of
145: 16 You open your **hand** and satisfy the desires of every living thing.
149: 6 God be in their mouths and a double-edged sword in their **hands**,
Pr 1: 24 when I called and no one gave heed when I stretched out my **hand**,
3: 27 from those who deserve it, when it is in your **power** [+445] to act.
6: 5 Free yourself, like a gazelle from the **hand** of the hunter, like a
6: 5 the hand of the hunter, like a bird from the **snare** *of* the fowler.
6: 10 A little sleep, a little slumber, a little folding of the **hands** to rest—
6: 17 haughty eyes, a lying tongue, **hands** that shed innocent blood,
7: 20 He took **[OBJ]** his purse filled with money and will not be home
8: 3 **beside** [+4200] the gates leading into the city, at the entrances,
10: 4 Lazy hands make a man poor, but diligent **hands** bring wealth.
11: 21 **Be sure** [+3338+4200] **of this**: The wicked will not go
11: 21 **Be sure of this** [+3338+4200]: The wicked will not go
12: 14 with good things as surely as the work of his **hands** rewards him.
12: 24 Diligent **hands** will rule, but laziness ends in slave labor.
13: 11 but he who gathers money **little** [+6584] **by little** makes it grow.
14: 1 her house, but with her own **hands** the foolish one tears hers down.
16: 5 **Be sure** [+3338+4200] **of this**: They will not go unpunished.
16: 5 **Be sure of this** [+3338+4200]: They will not go unpunished.
17: 16 Of what use is money in the **hand** *of* a fool, since he has no desire
18: 21 The tongue has the **power** *of* life and death, and those who love it
19: 24 The sluggard buries his **hand** in the dish; he will not even bring it
21: 1 The king's heart is in the **hand** *of* the LORD; he directs it like a
21: 25 craving will be the death of him, because his **hands** refuse to work.
24: 33 A little sleep, a little slumber, a little folding of the **hands** to rest—
26: 6 or drinking violence is the sending of a message by the **hand** *of* a
26: 9 Like a thornbush in a drunkard's **hand** is a proverb in the mouth of
26: 15 The sluggard buries his **hand** in the dish; he is too lazy to bring it
30: 28 a lizard can be caught with the **hand**, yet it is found in kings'
30: 32 or if you have planned evil, clap your **hand** over your mouth!
31: 19 In her **hand** she holds the distaff and grasps the spindle with her
31: 20 opens her arms to the poor and extends her **hands** to the needy.
31: 31 Give her the **reward** she has **earned** [+7262], and let her works
Ecc 2: 11 Yet when I surveyed all that my **hands** had done and what I had
2: 24 satisfaction in his work. This too, I see, is from the **hand** *of* God,
4: 1 power was on the **side** *of* their oppressors—and they have no
4: 5 The fool folds his **hands** and ruins himself.
5: 6 [5:5] angry at what you say and destroy the work of your **hands**?
5: 14 [5:13] so that when he has a son there is nothing left **for** [+928]
5: 15 [5:14] takes nothing from his labor that he can carry in his **hand**.
7: 18 It is good to grasp the one and not **let go** [+906+5663] of the other.
7: 26 who is a snare, whose heart is a trap and whose **hands** are chains.
9: 1 the righteous and the wise and what they do are in God's **hands**,
9: 10 Whatever your **hand** finds to do, do it with all your might,
10: 18 a man is lazy, the rafters sag; if his **hands** are idle, the house leaks.
11: 6 seed in the morning, and at evening let not your **hands** be idle,
SS 5: 4 My lover thrust his **hand** through the latch-opening; my heart
5: 5 I arose to open for my lover, and my **hands** dripped with myrrh,
5: 14 His **arms** are rods of gold set with chrysolite. His body is like
7: 1 [7:2] legs are like jewels, the work of a craftsman's **hands**.
Isa 1: 12 who has asked this **of** [+4946] you, this trampling of my courts?
1: 15 offer many prayers, I will not listen. Your **hands** are full of blood;
1: 25 I will turn my **hand** against you; I will thoroughly purge away
2: 8 they bow down to the work of their **hands**, to what their fingers
3: 6 you be our leader; **take charge of** [+9393] this heap of ruins!"
3: 11 They will be paid back for what their **hands** have done.
5: 12 for the deeds of the LORD, no respect for the work of his **hands**.
5: 25 against his people; his **hand** is raised and he strikes them down.
5: 25 for all this, his anger is not turned away, his **hand** is still upraised.
6: 6 Then one of the seraphs flew to me with a live coal in his **hand**,
8: 11 The LORD spoke to me with his strong **hand** upon me, warning
9: 12 [9:11] his anger is not turned away, his **hand** is still upraised.
9: 17 [9:16] his anger is not turned away, his **hand** is still upraised.
9: 21 [9:20] his anger is not turned away, his **hand** is still upraised.
10: 4 for all this, his anger is not turned away, his **hand** is still upraised.
10: 5 the rod of my anger, in whose **hand** is the club of my wrath!
10: 10 As my **hand** seized the kingdoms of the idols, kingdoms whose
10: 13 " 'By the strength of my **hand** I have done this, and by my wisdom,
10: 14 into a nest, so my **hand** reached for the wealth of the nations;
10: 32 they will shake their **fist** at the mount of the Daughter of Zion,
11: 8 of the cobra, and the young child put his **hand** into the viper's nest.
11: 11 In that day the Lord will reach out his **hand** a second time to
11: 14 They will lay **hands** on Edom and Moab, and the Ammonites will
11: 15 with a scorching wind he will sweep his **hand** over the Euphrates
13: 2 to them; **beckon to** [+5677] them to enter the gates of the nobles.
13: 7 Because of this, all **hands** will go limp, every man's heart will
14: 26 for the whole world; this is the **hand** stretched out over all nations.
14: 27 thwart him? His **hand** is stretched out, and who can turn it back?
17: 8 They will not look to the altars, the work of their **hands**, and they
19: 4 I will hand the Egyptians over to the **power** *of* a cruel master,
19: 16 They will shudder with fear at the uplifted **hand** that the LORD
19: 25 Assyria my **handiwork** [+5126], and Israel my inheritance."
20: 2 at that time the LORD spoke **through** [+928] Isaiah son of Amoz.
22: 18 up tightly like a ball and throw you into a **large** [+8146] country.
22: 21 around him and **hand** [+928+5989] your authority **over** *to* him.
23: 11 The LORD has stretched out his **hand** over the sea and made its
25: 10 The **hand** *of* the LORD will rest on this mountain; but Moab will
25: 11 They will spread out their **hands** in it, as a swimmer spreads out
25: 11 will bring down their pride despite the cleverness of their **hands**.
26: 11 O LORD, your **hand** is lifted high, but they do not see it.
28: 2 he will throw it **forcefully** [+928] to the ground.
29: 23 the work of my **hands**, they will keep my name holy;
31: 3 When the LORD stretches out his **hand**, he who helps will
31: 7 reject the idols of silver and gold your sinful **hands** have made.
33: 21 It will be like a place of **broad** [+8146] rivers and streams.
34: 17 He allots their portions; his **hand** distributes them by measure.
35: 3 Strengthen the feeble **hands**, steady the knees that give way;
36: 15 this city will not be given into the **hand** *of* the king of Assyria.'
36: 18 Has the god of any nation ever delivered his land from the **hand** *of*
36: 19 gods of Sepharvaim? Have they rescued Samaria from my **hand**?
36: 20 of these countries has been able to save his land **from** [+4946] me?
36: 20 How then can the LORD deliver Jerusalem from my **hand**?"
37: 10 'Jerusalem *will* not **be handed** [+928+5989] **over** *to* the king of
37: 14 Hezekiah received the letter **from** [+4946] the messengers
37: 19 not gods but only wood and stone, fashioned by human **hands**.
37: 20 Now, O LORD our God, deliver us from his **hand**, so that all
37: 24 **By** [+928] your messengers you have heaped insults on the Lord.
37: 27 Their people, drained of **power**, are dismayed and put to shame.
40: 2 that she has received from the LORD's **hand** double for all her
41: 20 and understand, that the **hand** *of* the LORD has done this,
42: 6 have called you in righteousness; I will take hold of your **hand**.
43: 13 No one can deliver out of my **hand**. When I act, who can reverse
44: 5 still another will write on his **hand**, 'The LORD's,' and will take
45: 9 'What are you making?' Does your work say, 'He has no **hands**'?
45: 11 about my children, or give me orders about the work of my **hands**?
45: 12 My own **hands** stretched out the heavens; I marshaled their starry
47: 6 I gave them into your **hand**, and you showed them no mercy.
47: 14 They cannot even save themselves from the **power** *of* the flame.
48: 13 My own **hand** laid the foundations of the earth, and my right hand
49: 2 like a sharpened sword, in the shadow of his **hand** he hid me;
49: 22 "See, I *will* **beckon** [+5951] to the Gentiles, I will lift up my
50: 2 there no one to answer? Was my **arm** too short to ransom you?
50: 11 This is what you shall receive from my **hand**: You will lie down in
51: 16 in your mouth and covered you with the shadow of my **hand**—
51: 17 you who have drunk from the **hand** *of* the LORD the cup of his
51: 18 of all the sons she reared there was none to take her by the **hand**.
51: 22 I have taken out of your **hand** the cup that made you stagger;
51: 23 I will put it into the **hands** *of* your tormentors, who said to you,
53: 10 his days, and the will of the LORD will prosper in his **hand**.
56: 2 without desecrating it, and keeps his **hand** from doing any evil."
56: 5 its walls a **memorial** and a name better than sons and daughters;
57: 8 those whose beds you love, and you looked on their **nakedness**.
57: 10 You found renewal of your **strength**, and so you did not faint.
59: 1 Surely the **arm** *of* the LORD is not too short to save, nor his ear
60: 21 the work of my **hands**, for the display of my splendor.
62: 3 You will be a crown of splendor in the LORD's **hand**, a royal
64: 7 [64:6] and made us waste away **because of** [+928] our sins.
64: 8 [64:7] you are the potter; we are all the work of your **hand**.
65: 2 All day long I have held out my **hands** to an obstinate people,
65: 22 my chosen ones will long enjoy the works of their **hands**.
66: 2 Has not my **hand** made all these things, and so they came into
66: 14 the **hand** *of* the LORD will be made known to his servants,
Jer 1: 9 Then the LORD reached out his **hand** and touched my mouth

Jer 1:16 to other gods and in worshiping what their **hands** have made.
2:37 You will also leave that place with your **hands** on your head,
5:31 The prophets prophesy lies, the priests rule by their own **authority**,
6: 3 will pitch their tents around her, each tending his own **portion**."
6: 9 pass your **hand** over the branches again, like one gathering
6:12 when I stretch out my **hand** against those who live in the land,"
6:24 We have heard reports about them, and our **hands** hang limp.
10: 3 out of the forest, and a craftsman **shapes** [+5126] it with his chisel.
10: 9 What the craftsman and goldsmith have made **[NIE]** is
11:21 in the name of the LORD or you will die by our **hands**'—
15: 6 So I will lay **hands** on you and destroy you; I can no longer show
15:17 I sat alone because your **hand** was on me and you had filled me
15:21 "I will save you from the **hands** *of* the wicked and redeem you
16:21 will teach them—this time I will teach them my **power** and might.
18: 4 But the pot he was shaping from the clay was marred in his **hands**;
18: 6 "Like clay in the **hand** *of* the potter, so are you in my hand,
18: 6 in the hand of the potter, so are you in my **hand**, O house of Israel.
18:21 children over to famine; hand them over to the **power** *of* the sword.
19: 7 before their enemies, at the **hands** *of* those who seek their lives,
20: 4 of their enemies. *I will* **hand** [+906+928+5989] all Judah **over** *to*
20: 5 *I will* **hand** [+906+906+906+906+928+5989] **over** *to* their
20:13 He rescues the life of the needy from the **hands** *of* the wicked.
21: 4 to turn against you the weapons of war that are in your **hands**,
21: 5 I myself will fight against you with an outstretched **hand** and a
21: 7 *I will* **hand** [+906+906+906+906+928+5989] **over** Zedekiah king
21: 7 king of Babylon and to **[RPH]** their enemies who seek their lives.
21: 7 king of Babylon and to their enemies **[RPH]** who seek their lives.
21:10 It will be given into the **hands** *of* the king of Babylon, and he will
21:12 rescue from the **hand** *of* his oppressor the one who has been
22: 3 Rescue from the **hand** *of* his oppressor the one who has been
22:24 were a signet ring on my right **hand**, I would still pull you off.
22:25 *I will* **hand** [+928+5989] you **over** *to* those who seek your life,
22:25 you over to those who seek your life, **[RPH]** those you fear—
22:25 to **[RPH]** Nebuchadnezzar king of Babylon and to the
22:25 Nebuchadnezzar king of Babylon and **to** [+928] the Babylonians.
23:14 They strengthen the **hands** *of* evildoers, so that no one turns from
25: 6 do not provoke me to anger with what your **hands** have made.
25: 7 "and you have provoked me with what your **hands** have made,
25:14 repay them according to their deeds and the work of their **hands**."
25:15 "Take from my **hand** this cup filled with the wine of my wrath
25:17 So I took the cup from the LORD's **hand** and made all the
25:28 But if they refuse to take the cup from your **hand** and drink,
26:14 As for me, I am in your **hands**; do with me whatever you think is
26:24 Ahikam son of Shaphan **supported** [+907+2118] Jeremiah,
26:24 and so he *was* not **handed** [+906+928+5989] **over** *to* the people to
27: 3 Sidon **through** [+928] the envoys who have come to Jerusalem to
27: 6 Now I *will* **hand** [+906+928+5989] all your countries **over** *to* my
27: 8 and plague, declares the LORD, until I destroy it by his **hand**.
29: 3 He **entrusted** the letter **to** [+928] Elasah son of Shaphan and to
29:21 "I *will* **hand** [+906+928+5989] them **over** *to* Nebuchadnezzar king
30: 6 why do I see every strong man with his **hands** on his stomach like
31:11 and redeem them from the **hand** *of* those stronger than they.
31:32 when I took them by the **hand** to lead them out of Egypt,
32: 3 I *am about to* **hand** [+906+928+5989] this city **over** *to* the king of
32: 4 Zedekiah king of Judah will not escape out of the **hands** *of* the
32: 4 but *will* **certainly be handed** [+928+5989+5989] **over** *to* the king
32:21 by a mighty **hand** and an outstretched arm and with great terror.
32:24 the city *will* **be handed** [+928+5989] **over** *to* the Babylonians who
32:25 though the city *will* **be handed** [+928+5989] **over** *to* the
32:28 I *am about to* **hand** [+906+928+5989] this city **over** *to* the
32:28 the Babylonians and to **[RPH]** Nebuchadnezzar king of Babylon,
32:30 done nothing but provoke me with what their **hands** have made,
32:36 plague *it will* **be handed** [+928+5989] **over** *to* the king of
32:43 for *it has* **been handed** [+928+5989] **over** *to* the Babylonians.'
33:13 flocks will again pass under the **hand** *of* the one who counts them,'
34: 1 peoples in the empire he **ruled** [+4939] were fighting against
34: 2 I *am about to* **hand** [+906+928+5989] this city **over** *to* the king of
34: 3 You will not escape from his **grasp** but will surely be captured
34: 3 but will surely be captured and **handed** [+928+5989] **over** *to* him.
34:20 *I will* **hand** [+906+928+5989] **over** *to* their enemies who seek
34:20 I will hand over to their enemies **[RPH]** who seek their lives.
34:21 "*I will* **hand** [+906+906+928+5989] Zedekiah king of Judah and his officials **over** *to* their enemies who seek their lives,
34:21 and his officials over to their enemies **[RPH]** who seek their lives,
34:21 **[RPH]** to the army of the king of Babylon, which has withdrawn
36:14 "Bring **[RPH]** the scroll from which you have read to the people
36:14 So Baruch son of Neriah went to them with the scroll in his **hand**.
37: 2 the LORD had spoken **through** [+928] Jeremiah the prophet.
37:17 Jeremiah replied, "*you will* **be handed** [+928+5989] **over** *to* the
38: 3 'This city *will* **certainly be handed** [+928+5989+5989] **over** *to* the
38: 4 He *is* **discouraging** [+906+906+8332] the soldiers who are left in
38: 4 as well as **[RPH]** all the people, by the things he is saying to
38: 5 "He is in your **hands**," King Zedekiah answered. "The king can do
38:10 "Take thirty men from here **with** [+928] you and lift Jeremiah the
38:11 So Ebed-Melech took the men **with** [+928] him and went to a
38:12 and worn-out clothes under your **arms** [+723] to pad the ropes."
38:16 I will neither kill you nor **hand** [+928+5989] you **over** *to* those
38:18 this city *will* **be handed** [+928+5989] **over** *to* the Babylonians
38:18 burn it down; you yourself will not escape from their **hands**.' "
38:19 for the Babylonians *may* **hand** [+906+928+5989] me **over** *to* them
38:23 You yourself will not escape from their **hands** but will be captured
38:23 their hands but will be captured **by** [+928] the king of Babylon;
39:11 **through** [+928] Nebuzaradan commander of the imperial guard:
39:17 the LORD; *you will* not **be handed** [+928+5989] **over** *to*
40: 4 But today I am freeing you from the chains on your **wrists**.
41: 5 and incense **with** [+928] them to the house of the LORD.
41: 9 **along with** [+928] Gedaliah was the one King Asa had made as
42:11 I am with you and will save you and deliver you from his **hands**.
43: 3 against us to **hand** [+906+928+5989] us **over** *to* the Babylonians,
43: 9 take some large stones **with** [+928] you and bury them in clay in
44: 8 Why provoke me to anger with what your **hands** have made,
44:25 your wives have shown by your **actions** what you promised when
44:30 'I *am going to* **hand** [+906+928+5989] Pharaoh Hophra king of Egypt **over** *to* his enemies
44:30 king of Egypt over to his enemies **[RPH]** who seek his life,
44:30 just as *I* **handed** [+906+928+5989] Zedekiah king of Judah **over** *to*
46: 6 In the north **by** [+6584] the River Euphrates they stumble
46:24 of Egypt will be put to shame, **handed** [+928+5989] **over** *to*
46:26 *I will* **hand** [+928+5989] them **over** *to* those who seek their lives,
46:26 to **[RPH]** Nebuchadnezzar king of Babylon and his officers.
46:26 to Nebuchadnezzar king of Babylon and **[RPH]** his officers.
47: 3 will not turn to help their children; their **hands** will hang limp.
48:37 every **hand** is slashed and every waist is covered with sackcloth.
50: 1 This is the word the LORD spoke **through** [+928] Jeremiah the
50:15 *She* **surrenders** [+5989], her towers fall, her walls are torn down.
50:43 of Babylon has heard reports about them, and his **hands** hang limp.
51: 7 Babylon was a gold cup in the LORD's **hand**; she made the
51:25 "I will stretch out my **hand** against you, roll you off the cliffs,

La 1: 7 When her people fell into enemy **hands**, there was no one to help
1:10 The enemy laid **hands** on all her treasures; she saw pagan nations
1:14 been bound into a yoke; by his **hands** they were woven together.
1:14 has sapped my strength. *He has* **handed** [+928+5989] me **over** *to*
1:17 Zion stretches out her **hands**, but there is no one to comfort her.
2: 7 abandoned his sanctuary. *He has* **handed** [+928+6037] **over** *to* the
2: 8 a measuring line and did not withhold his **hand** from destroying.
3: 3 indeed, he has turned his **hand** against me again and again,
3:64 what they deserve, O LORD, for what their **hands** have done.
4: 2 are now considered as pots of clay, the work of a potter's **hands**!
4: 6 which was overthrown in a moment without a **hand** turned to help
4:10 With their own **hands** compassionate women have cooked their
5: 6 *We* **submitted to** [+5989] Egypt and Assyria to get enough bread.
5: 8 Slaves rule over us, and there is none to free us from their **hands**.
5:12 Princes have been hung up by their **hands**; elders are shown no

Eze 1: 3 of the Babylonians. There the **hand** *of* the LORD was upon him.
2: 9 I looked, and I saw a **hand** stretched out to me. In it was a scroll,
3:14 anger of my spirit, with the strong **hand** *of* the LORD upon me.
3:18 and *I will* **hold** you **accountable for** [+1335+4946] his blood.
3:20 and *I will* **hold** you **accountable for** [+1335+4946] his blood.
3:22 The **hand** *of* the LORD was upon me there, and he said to me,
6:14 I will stretch out my **hand** against them and make the land a
7:17 Every **hand** will go limp, and every knee will become as weak as
7:21 *I will* **hand** [+928+5989] it all **over** as plunder *to* foreigners
7:27 with despair, and the **hands** *of* the people of the land will tremble.
8: 1 the **hand** *of* the Sovereign LORD came upon me there.
8: 3 He stretched out what looked like a **hand** and took me by the hair
8:11 Each had a censer in his **hand**, and a fragrant cloud of incense was
9: 1 the guards of the city here, each with a weapon in his **hand**."
9: 2 which faces north, each with a deadly weapon in his **hand**.
10: 7 one of the cherubim reached out his **hand** to the fire that was
10: 8 the cherubim could be seen what looked like the **hands** *of* a man.)
10:12 entire bodies, including their backs, their **hands** and their wings,
10:21 and under their wings was what looked like the **hands** *of* a man.
11: 9 out of the city and **hand** [+906+928+5989] you **over** *to* foreigners
12: 7 Then in the evening I dug through the wall with my **hands**.
13: 9 My **hand** will be against the prophets who see false visions
13:18 to the women who sew magic charms on all their **wrists** [+723]
13:21 I will tear off your veils and save my people from your **hands**,
13:21 from your hands, and they will no longer fall prey to your **power**.
13:22 because you **encouraged** [+2616] the wicked not to turn from their
13:23 I will save my people from your **hands**. And then you will know
14: 9 I will stretch out my **hand** against him and destroy him from
14:13 and I stretch out my **hand** against it to cut off its food supply
16:11 I put bracelets on your **arms** and a necklace around your neck,
16:27 So I stretched out my **hand** against you and reduced your territory;
16:39 Then *I will* **hand** [+906+928+5989] you **over** *to* your lovers,
16:49 and unconcerned; *they did* not **help** [+2616] the poor and needy.
17:18 Because he had given his **hand** in pledge and yet did all these
18: 8 He withholds his **hand** from doing wrong and judges fairly

Eze 18:17 He withholds his **hand** from sin and takes no usury or excessive
20: 5 I swore with uplifted **hand** to the descendants of the house of
20: 5 With uplifted **hand** I said to them, "I am the LORD your God."
20: 6 On that day *I* **swore** [+5951] to them that I would bring them out
20:15 Also with uplifted **hand** I swore to them in the desert that I would
20:22 I withheld my **hand**, and for the sake of my name I did what would
20:23 Also with uplifted **hand** I swore to them in the desert that I would
20:28 When I brought them into the land I *had* **sworn** [+906+5951] to
20:33 I will rule over you with a mighty **hand** and an outstretched arm
20:34 with a mighty **hand** and an outstretched arm and with outpoured
20:42 the land I had sworn with uplifted **hand** to give to your fathers.
21: 7 [21:12] Every heart will melt and every **hand** go limp; every
21:11 [21:16] and polished, made ready for the **hand** *of* the slayer.
21:19 [21:24] Make a **signpost** where the road branches off to the city.
21:31 [21:36] anger against you; *I will* **hand** [+928+5989] you **over** *to*
22:14 courage endure or your **hands** be strong in the day I deal with you?
23: 9 "Therefore *I* **handed** [+928+5989] her **over** *to* her lovers,
23: 9 her over to her lovers, **[RPH]** the Assyrians, for whom she lusted.
23:28 I *am about to* **hand** [+928+5989] you **over** *to* those you hate,
23:28 those you hate, **[RPH]** to those you turned away from in disgust.
23:31 gone the way of your sister; so I will put her cup into your **hand**.
23:37 for they have committed adultery and blood is on their **hands**.
23:42 and they put bracelets on the **arms** *of* the woman and her sister
23:45 because they are adulterous and blood is on their **hands**.
25: 6 Because you have clapped your **hands** and stamped your feet,
25: 7 therefore I will stretch out my **hand** against you and give you as
25:13 I will stretch out my **hand** against Edom and kill its men and their
25:14 I will take vengeance on Edom by the **hand** *of* my people Israel,
25:16 I am about to stretch out my **hand** against the Philistines, and I will
27:15 with you, and many coastlands were your **customers** [+6088];
27:21 and all the princes of Kedar were your **customers** [+6086];
28: 9 but a man, not a god, in the **hands** *of* those who slay you.
28:10 You will die the death of the uncircumcised at the **hands** *of*
30:10 " 'I will put an end to the hordes of Egypt by the **hand** *of*
30:12 dry up the streams of the Nile and sell the land **to** [+928] evil men;
30:12 by the **hand** *of* foreigners I will lay waste the land and everything
30:22 as well as the broken one, and make the sword fall from his **hand**.
30:24 the arms of the king of Babylon and put my sword in his **hand**,
30:25 when I put my sword into the **hand** *of* the king of Babylon
31:11 I handed it over **to** [+928] the ruler of the nations, for him to deal
33: 6 *I will* **hold** the watchman **accountable for** [+2011+4946] his
33: 8 and *I will* **hold** you **accountable for** [+1335+4946] his blood.
33:22 before the man arrived, the **hand** *of* the LORD was upon me,
34:10 and *will* **hold** them **accountable for** [+906+2011+4946] my flock.
34:27 and rescue them from the **hands** *of* those who enslaved them.
35: 3 I will stretch out my **hand** against you and make you a desolate
35: 5 delivered the Israelites over **to** [+6584] the sword at the time of
36: 7 I swear with uplifted **hand** that the nations around you will also
37: 1 The **hand** *of* the LORD was upon me, and he brought me out by
37:17 together into one stick so that they will become one in your **hand**.
37:19 going to take the stick of Joseph—which is in Ephraim's **hand**—
37:19 a single stick of wood, and they will become one in my **hand**.'
37:20 **Hold** [+928+2118] before their eyes the sticks you have written on
38:12 I will plunder and loot and turn my **hand** against the resettled ruins
38:17 Are you not the one I spoke of in former days **by** [+928] my
39: 3 I will strike your bow from your left **hand** and make your arrows
39: 3 your left hand and make your arrows drop from your right **hand**.
39: 9 the bows and arrows, the **war clubs** [+5234] and spears.
39:21 will see the punishment I inflict and the **hand** I lay upon them.
39:23 from them and **handed** [+928+5989] them **over** *to* their enemies,
40: 1 on that very day the **hand** *of* the LORD was upon me and he took
40: 3 in the gateway with a linen cord and a measuring rod in his **hand**.
40: 5 The length of the measuring rod in the man's **hand** was six long
43:26 for the altar and cleanse it; thus *they will* **dedicate** [+4848] it.
44:12 therefore I have sworn with uplifted **hand** that they must bear the
46: 5 offering with the lambs is to be **as much as** he **pleases** [+5522],
46: 7 the ram, and with the lambs as much as he **wants to give** [+5952],
46:11 with a ram, and with the lambs **as much as** one **pleases** [+5522],
47: 3 As the man went eastward with a measuring line in his **hand**,
47:14 Because I swore with uplifted **hand** to give it to your forefathers,
48: 1 it will **follow** [+448] the Hethlon road to Lebo Hamath; Hazar
48: 1 the northern border of Damascus **next to** [+448] Hamath will be
Da 1: 2 And the Lord delivered Jehoiakim king of Judah into his **hand**,
1:20 he found them ten **times** better than all the magicians
8: 4 could stand against him, and none could rescue from his **power**.
8: 7 trampled on him, and none could rescue the ram from his **power**.
8:25 He will **cause** [+928] deceit to prosper, and he will consider
8:25 of princes. Yet he will be destroyed, but not by human **power**.
9:10 or kept the laws he gave us **through** [+928] his servants the
9:15 who brought your people out of Egypt with a mighty **hand**
10: 4 as I was standing on the **bank** *of* the great river, the Tigris,
10:10 A **hand** touched me and set me trembling on my hands and knees.
10:10 touched me and set me trembling on my **hands** [+4090] and knees.
11:11 who will raise a large army, but it *will* **be defeated** [+928+5989].
11:16 in the Beautiful Land and will **have** [+928] the power to destroy it.
11:41 and the leaders of Ammon will be delivered from his **hand**.
11:42 He will extend his **power** over many countries; Egypt will not
12: 7 When the **power** *of* the holy people has been finally broken,
Hos 2:10 [2:12] eyes of her lovers; no one will take her out of my **hands**.
7: 5 become inflamed with wine, and he joins **hands** with the mockers.
12: 7 [12:8] The merchant **uses** [+928] dishonest scales; he loves to
12:10 [12:11] many visions and told parables **through** [+928] them."
13:14 "I will ransom them from the **power** *of* the grave; I will redeem
14: 3 [14:4] We will never again say 'Our gods' to what our own **hands**
Joel 3: 8 [4:8] sell your sons and daughters **to** [+928] the people of Judah,
Am 1: 8 I will turn my **hand** against Ekron, till the last of the Philistines is
5:19 and rested his **hand** on the wall only to have a snake bite him.
7: 7 that had been built true to plumb, with a plumb line in his **hand**.
9: 2 to the depths of the grave, from there my **hand** will take them.
Mic 2: 1 light they carry it out because it is in their **power** [+445] to do it.
5: 9 [5:8] Your **hand** will be lifted up in triumph over your enemies,
5:12 [5:11] I will destroy **[NIE]** your witchcraft and you will no
5:13 [5:12] you will no longer bow down to the work of your **hands**.
7:16 They will lay their **hands** on their mouths and their ears will
Hab 3: 4 rays flashed from his **hand**, where his power was hidden.
3:10 of water swept by; the deep roared and lifted its **waves** on high.
Zep 1: 4 "I will stretch out my **hand** against Judah and against all who live
2:13 He will stretch out his **hand** against the north and destroy Assyria,
2:15 lair for wild beasts! All who pass by her scoff and shake their **fists**.
3:16 "Do not fear, O Zion; do not let your **hands** hang limp.
Hag 1: 1 the word of the LORD came **through** [+928] the prophet Haggai
1: 3 the word of the LORD came **through** [+928] the prophet Haggai:
2: 1 the word of the LORD came **through** [+928] the prophet Haggai:
2:14 'Whatever they **do** [+5126] and whatever they offer there is defiled.
2:17 I struck all the work of your **hands** with blight, mildew and hail,
Zec 2: 1 [2:5] before me was a man with a measuring line in his **hand**!
2: 9 [2:13] I will surely raise my **hand** against them so that their
4: 9 "The **hands** *of* Zerubbabel have laid the foundation of this temple;
4: 9 laid the foundation of this temple; his **hands** will also complete it.
4:10 Men will rejoice when they see the plumb line in the **hand** *of*
4:12 "What are these two olive branches **beside** [+928] the two gold
7: 7 Are these not the words the LORD proclaimed **through** [+928]
7:12 had sent by his Spirit **through** [+928] the earlier prophets.
8: 4 streets of Jerusalem, each with cane in **hand** because of his age.
8: 9 let your **hands** be strong so that the temple may be built.
8:13 will be a blessing. Do not be afraid, but let your **hands** be strong."
11: 6 "I *will* **hand** [+906+928+5162] everyone **over** *to* his neighbor
11: 6 "I will hand everyone over to his neighbor and **[RPH]** his king.
11: 6 will oppress the land, and I will not rescue them from their **hands**."
13: 6 If someone asks him, 'What are these wounds on your **body**?'
13: 7 will be scattered, and I will turn my **hand** against the little ones.
14:13 Each man will seize the **hand** *of* another, and they will attack each
14:13 hand of another, and they *will* **attack** [+6584+6590] each other.
14:13 seize the hand of another, and they will attack each other. **[RPH]**
Mal 1: 1 The word of the LORD to Israel **through** [+928] Malachi.
1: 9 With such offerings from your **hands**, will he accept you?"—
1:10 LORD Almighty, "and I will accept no offering from your **hands**.
1:13 offer them as sacrifices, should I accept them from your **hands**?"
2:13 to your offerings or accepts them with pleasure from your **hands**.

3339 יִדְאֲלָה *yid'ᵃlâ*, n.pr.loc. [1]

Idalah [1]

Jos 19:15 Included were Kattath, Nahalal, Shimron, **Idalah** and Bethlehem.

3340 יִדְבָּשׁ *yidbāš*, n.pr.m. [1] [√ 1831]

Idbash [1]

1Ch 4: 3 These were the sons of Etam: Jezreel, Ishma and **Idbash**. Their

3341 יָדַד *yādad*, v. [3] [cf. 3343]

cast [3]

Joel 3: 3 [4:3] [A] *They* **cast** lots for my people and traded boys for
Ob 1:11 [A] and foreigners entered his gates and **cast** lots for Jerusalem,
Na 3:10 [A] Lots *were* **cast** for her nobles, and all her great men were put

3342 יְדִדוּת *yᵉdidût*, n.f. [1] [√ 3351]

love [1]

Jer 12: 7 I will give the *one* I **love** into the hands of her enemies.

3343 יָדָה *yādâ*[1], v. [3] [cf. 3341]

shoot [1], threw [1], throw down [1]

Jer 50:14 [A] **Shoot** at her! Spare no arrows, for she has sinned against the
La 3:53 [D] They tried to end my life in a pit and **threw** stones at me;
Zec 1:21 [2:4] [D] **throw down** these horns of the nations who lifted up

3344 ²יָדָה yādâ², v. [111] [→ 2086, 2088, 2089, 2090, 2117, 9343; Ar 10312]
praise [44], give thanks [35], confess [10], thanksgiving [3], confessed [2], confessing [2], extol [2], admit [1], brings praise [1], confesses [1], confession [1], gave thanks [1], led in thanksgiving [+4200+9378] [1], praised [1], praises [1], praising [1], psalm of thanks [1], thank [1], thanking [1], thanks [1]

Ge 29:35 [G] birth to a son she said, "This time *I will* **praise** the LORD."
49: 8 [G] "Judah, your brothers *will* **praise** you; your hand will be on
Lev 5: 5 [F] of these ways, *he must* **confess** in what way he has sinned
16:21 [F] **confess** over it all the wickedness and rebellion of the
26:40 [F] " 'But if *they will* **confess** their sins and the sins of their
Nu 5: 7 [F] *must* **confess** the sin he has committed. He must make full
2Sa 22:50 [G] Therefore *I will* **praise** you, O LORD, among the nations;
1Ki 8:33 [G] when they turn back to you and **confess** your name, praying
8:35 [G] **confess** your name and turn from their sin because you have
1Ch 16: 4 [G] to make petition, to **give thanks**, and to praise the LORD,
16: 7 [G] and his associates *this* **psalm of thanks** to the LORD:
16: 8 [G] **Give thanks** to the LORD, call on his name; make known
16:34 [G] **Give thanks** to the LORD, for he is good; his love endures
16:35 [G] the nations, that we *may* **give thanks** to your holy name,
16:41 [G] and designated by name to **give thanks** to the LORD,
23:30 [G] They were also to stand every morning to **thank** and praise
25: 3 [G] using the harp in **thanking** and praising the LORD.
29:13 [G] Now, our God, we **give** you **thanks**, and praise your glorious
2Ch 5:13 [G] as with one voice, to give praise and **thanks** to the LORD.
6:24 [G] against you and when they turn back and **confess** your name,
6:26 [G] **confess** your name and turn from their sin because you have
7: 3 [G] and they worshiped and **gave thanks** to the LORD, saying,
7: 6 [G] which King David had made for **praising** the LORD
20:21 [G] "**Give thanks** to the LORD, for his love endures forever."
30:22 [F] and offered fellowship offerings and **praised** the LORD,
31: 2 [G] to **give thanks** and to sing praises at the gates of the
Ezr 3:11 [G] With praise and **thanksgiving** they sang to the LORD: "He
10: 1 [F] While Ezra was praying and **confessing**, weeping
Ne 1: 6 [F] *I* **confess** the sins we Israelites, including myself and my
9: 2 [F] They stood in their places and **confessed** their sins
9: 3 [F] *spent* another quarter *in* **confession** and in worshiping the
11:17 [G] the director *who* **led in thanksgiving** [+4200+9378] and prayer;
12:24 [G] who stood opposite them to give praise and **thanksgiving**,
12:46 [G] and for the songs of praise and **thanksgiving** to God.
Job 40:14 [G] *I* myself *will* **admit** *to* you that your own right hand can save
Ps 6: 5 [6:6] [G] when he is dead. Who **praises** you from the grave?
7:17 [7:18] [G] *I will* **give thanks** *to* the LORD because of his
9: 1 [9:2] [G] *I will* **praise** you, O LORD, with all my heart; I will
18:49 [18:50] [G] Therefore *I will* **praise** you among the nations,
28: 7 [G] My heart leaps for joy and *I will* **give thanks** *to* him in song.
30: 4 [30:5] [G] the LORD, you saints of his; **praise** his holy name.
30: 9 [30:10] [G] going down into the pit? *Will* the dust **praise** you?
30:12 [30:13] [G] O LORD my God, *I will* **give** you **thanks** forever.
32: 5 [G] I said, "*I will* **confess** my transgressions to the LORD"—
33: 2 [G] **Praise** the LORD with the harp; make music to him on the
35:18 [G] *I will* **give** you **thanks** in the great assembly; among throngs
42: 5 [42:6] [G] in God, for *I will* yet **praise** him, my Savior and
42:11 [42:12] [G] for *I will* yet **praise** him, my Savior and my God.
43: 4 [G] my delight. *I will* **praise** you with the harp, O God, my God.
43: 5 [G] in God, for *I will* yet **praise** him, my Savior and my God.
44: 8 [44:9] [G] all day long, and *we will* **praise** your name forever.
45:17 [45:18] [G] the nations *will* **praise** you for ever and ever.
49:18 [49:19] [G] and *men* **praise** you when you prosper—
52: 9 [52:11] [G] *I will* **praise** you forever for what you have done; in
54: 6 [54:8] [G] *I will* **praise** your name, O LORD, for it is good.
57: 9 [57:10] [G] *I will* **praise** you, O Lord, among the nations; I will
67: 3 [67:4] [G] *May* the peoples **praise** you, O God; may all the
67: 3 [67:4] [G] praise you, O God; *may* all the peoples **praise** you.
67: 5 [67:6] [G] *May* the peoples **praise** you, O God; may all the
67: 5 [67:6] [G] praise you, O God; *may* all the peoples **praise** you.
71:22 [G] I *will* **praise** you with the harp *for* your faithfulness, O my
75: 1 [75:2] [G] *We* **give thanks** to you, O God, we give thanks,
75: 1 [75:2] [G] O God, *we* **give thanks**, for your Name is near;
76:10 [76:11] [G] Surely your wrath against men **brings** you **praise**,
79:13 [G] the sheep of your pasture, *will* **praise** you forever;
86:12 [G] *I will* **praise** you, O Lord my God, with all my heart; I will
88:10 [88:11] [G] those who are dead rise up and **praise** you? *Selah*
89: 5 [89:6] [G] The heavens **praise** your wonders, O LORD,
92: 1 [92:2] [G] It is good to **praise** the LORD and make music to
97:12 [G] you who are righteous, and **praise** his holy name.
99: 3 [G] *Let them* **praise** your great and awesome name—he is holy.
100: 4 [G] courts with praise; **give thanks** to him and praise his name.
105: 1 [G] **Give thanks** to the LORD, call on his name; make known
106: 1 [G] **Give thanks** to the LORD, for he is good; his love endures
106:47 [G] that we *may* **give thanks** to your holy name and glory in
107: 1 [G] **Give thanks** to the LORD, for he is good; his love endures
107: 8 [G] *Let them* **give thanks** to the LORD *for* his unfailing love
107:15 [G] *Let them* **give thanks** to the LORD *for* his unfailing love
107:21 [G] *Let them* **give thanks** to the LORD *for* his unfailing love
107:31 [G] *Let them* **give thanks** to the LORD *for* his unfailing love
108: 3 [108:4] [G] *I will* **praise** you, O LORD, among the nations; I
109:30 [G] With my mouth *I will* greatly **extol** the LORD; in the great
111: 1 [G] *I will* **extol** the LORD with all my heart in the council of
118: 1 [G] **Give thanks** to the LORD, for he is good; his love endures
118:19 [G] of righteousness; I will enter and **give thanks** *to* the LORD.
118:21 [G] *I will* **give** you **thanks**, for you answered me; you have
118:28 [G] You are my God, and *I will* **give** you **thanks**; you are my
118:29 [G] **Give thanks** to the LORD, for he is good; his love endures
119: 7 [G] *I will* **praise** you with an upright heart as I learn your
119:62 [G] At midnight I rise to **give** you **thanks** for your righteous
122: 4 [G] to **praise** the name of the LORD according to the statute
136: 1 [G] **Give thanks** to the LORD, for he is good. *His love*
136: 2 [G] **Give thanks** to the God of gods. *His love endures*
136: 3 [G] **Give thanks** to the Lord of lords: *His love endures*
136:26 [G] **Give thanks** to the God of heaven. *His love endures*
138: 1 [G] *I will* **praise** you, O LORD, with all my heart;
138: 2 [G] *will* **praise** your name for your love and your faithfulness,
138: 4 [G] *May* all the kings of the earth **praise** you, O LORD,
139:14 [G] *I* **praise** you because I am fearfully and wonderfully made;
140:13 [140:14] [G] Surely the righteous *will* **praise** your name
142: 7 [142:8] [G] free from my prison, that I *may* **praise** your name.
145:10 [G] All you have made *will* **praise** you, O LORD; your saints
Pr 28:13 [G] but *whoever* **confesses** and renounces them finds mercy.
Isa 12: 1 [G] In that day you will say: "*I will* **praise** you, O LORD.
12: 4 [G] "**Give thanks** to the LORD, call on his name; make known
25: 1 [G] **praise** your name, for *in* perfect faithfulness you have done
38:18 [G] For the grave cannot **praise** you, death cannot sing your
38:19 [G] The living, the living—they **praise** you, as I am doing today;
Jer 33:11 [G] saying, "**Give thanks** *to* the LORD Almighty,
Da 9: 4 [F] I prayed to the LORD my God and **confessed**: "O Lord,
9:20 [F] **confessing** my sin and the sin of my people Israel and making

3345 יַדַּו yaddaw, n.pr.m. [0] [√ 3351?]

Ezr 10:43 [Zabad, Zebina, **Jaddai**, [K; see Q 3350] Joel and Benaiah.]

3346 יִדּוֹ yiddô, n.pr.m. [1] [√ 3351; cf. 3350]
Iddo [1]

1Ch 27:21 **Iddo** son of Zechariah; over Benjamin: Jaasiel son of Abner;

3347 יָדוֹן yādôn, n.pr.m. [1]
Jadon [1]

Ne 3: 7 and Mizpah—Melatiah of Gibeon and **Jadon** of Meronoth—

3348 יַדּוּעַ yaddûaʿ, n.pr.m. [3] [√ 3359]
Jaddua [3]

Ne 10:21 [10:22] Meshezabel, Zadok, **Jaddua**,
12:11 Joiada the father of Jonathan, and Jonathan the father of **Jaddua**.
12:22 Joiada, Johanan and **Jaddua**, as well as those of the priests,

3349 יְדוּתוּן yᵉdûtûn, n.pr.m. [16] [→ 3357]
Jeduthun [15], his[s] [1]

1Ch 9:16 Obadiah son of Shemaiah, the son of Galal, the son of **Jeduthun**;
16:41 With them were Heman and **Jeduthun** and the rest of those chosen
16:42 and **Jeduthun** were responsible for the sounding of the trumpets
16:42 for sacred song. The sons of **Jeduthun** were stationed at the gate.
25: 1 Heman and **Jeduthun** for the ministry of prophesying,
25: 3 As for **Jeduthun**, from his sons: Gedaliah, Zeri, Jeshaiah,
25: 3 As for Jeduthun, from **his**[s] sons: Gedaliah, Zeri, Jeshaiah,
25: 3 six in all, under the supervision of their father **Jeduthun**,
25: 6 **Jeduthun** and Heman were under the supervision of the king.
2Ch 5:12 Asaph, Heman, **Jeduthun** and their sons and relatives—stood on
29:14 from the descendants of **Jeduthun**, Shemaiah and Uzziel.
35:15 prescribed by David, Asaph, Heman and **Jeduthun** the king's seer.
Ne 11:17 son of Shammua, the son of Galal, the son of **Jeduthun**. [K 3357]
Ps 39: T [39:1] of music. For **Jeduthun**. [K 3357] A psalm of David.
62: T [62:1] the director of music. For **Jeduthun**. A psalm of David.
77: T [77:1] of music. For **Jeduthun**. [K 3357] Of Asaph. A psalm.

3350 יַדַּי yadday, n.pr.m. [1] [cf. 3346]
Jaddai [1]

Ezr 10:43 Mattithiah, Zabad, Zebina, **Jaddai**, [K 3345] Joel and Benaiah.

3351 יָדִיד yādîd, a. [8] [→ 3342, 3345?, 3346, 3352, 3353, 3354]
love [3], beloved [2], loved one [1], lovely [1], loves [1]

Dt 33:12 "Let the **beloved** *of* the LORD rest secure in him, for he shields
Ps 60: 5 [60:7] with your right hand, that *those* you **love** may be delivered.
84: 1 [84:2] How **lovely** is your dwelling place, O LORD Almighty!
108: 6 [108:7] your right hand, that *those* you **love** may be delivered.
127: 2 toiling for food to eat—for he grants sleep to *those* he **loves**.
Isa 5: 1 I will sing for the *one* I **love** a song about his vineyard: My loved
5: 1 his vineyard: My **loved one** had a vineyard on a fertile hillside.
Jer 11:15 "What is my **beloved** doing in my temple as she works out her evil

3352 יְדִידָה yedîdâ, n.pr.f. [1] [√ 3351]
Jedidah [1]

2Ki 22: 1 His mother's name was **Jedidah** daughter of Adaiah; she was from

3353 יְדִידֹת yedîdôt, a. [1] [√ 3351]
wedding [1]

Ps 45: T [45:1] Of the Sons of Korah. A *maskil*. A **wedding** song.

3354 יְדִידְיָהּ yedîdeyāh, n.pr.m. [1] [√ 3351 + 3378]
Jedidiah [1]

2Sa 12:25 he sent word through Nathan the prophet to name him **Jedidiah**.

3355 יְדָיָה yedāyâ, n.pr.m. [2]
Jedaiah [2]

1Ch 4:37 the son of Allon, the son of **Jedaiah**, the son of Shimri, the son of
Ne 3:10 **Jedaiah** son of Harumaph made repairs opposite his house,

3356 יְדִיעֲאֵל yedî'a'ēl, n.pr.m. [6] [√ 3359 + 446]
Jediael [6]

1Ch 7: 6 Three sons of Benjamin: Bela, Beker and **Jediael**.
7:10 The son of **Jediael**: Bilhan. The sons of Bilhan: Jeush, Benjamin,
7:11 All these sons of **Jediael** were heads of families. There were
11:45 **Jediael** son of Shimri, his brother Joha the Tizite,
12:20 [12:21] Adnah, Jozabad, **Jediael**, Michael, Jozabad, Elihu
26: 2 **Jediael** the second, Zebadiah the third, Jathniel the fourth,

3357 יְדִיתוּן yedîtûn, n.pr.m. [1] [√ 3349]
Jeduthun [1]

1Ch 16:38 Obed-Edom son of **Jeduthun**, and also Hosah, were gatekeepers.
Ne 11:17 [the son of Galal, the son of **Jeduthun**. [K; see Q 3349]]
Ps 39: T [39:1] [For the director of music. For **Jeduthun**. [K; see Q 3349]]
77: T [77:1] [For the director of music. For **Jeduthun**. [K; see Q 3349]]

3358 יִדְלָף yidlāp, n.pr.m. [1] [√ 1941]
Jidlaph [1]

Ge 22:22 Kesed, Hazo, Pildash, **Jidlaph** and Bethuel."

3359 יָדַע yāda', v. [947 / 946] [→ 1976, 1978, 1981, 1982, 3348, 3362, 4529, 4530, 4531; cf. 1983; Ar 10313; *also used with compound proper names*]
know [422], knows [43], knew [39], known [23], acknowledge [21], understand [15], teach [13], realize [12], make known [11], tell [11], be sure [+3359] [10], made known [10], learned [9], aware [8], find out [8], know how [8], show [7], know [+3359] [6], know about [6], knowing [6], learn [6], *untranslated* [5], knew about [5], knowledge [5], realized [5], be known [4], experienced [4], knows how [4], lay with [4], see [4], understanding [4], acknowledged [3], answer [3], be sure [3], confront [3], consider [3], is known [3], make myself known [3], observe [3], skilled [3], unknown [+4202] [3], assured [+3359] [2], be sure know [+3359] [2], cares for [2], chosen [2], concern [2], concerned about [2], find out [+2256+8011] [2], found out [2], friends [2], gain [2], had the least inkling [+3359] [2], have sex with [2], have [2], ignorant [+4202] [2], is made aware [2], know for certain [+3359] [2], knows very well [+3359] [2], learns [2], let know [2], must understand [+3359] [2], recognized [2], respected [2], revealed myself [2], see [+2256+8011] [2], take notice [2], unaware [+4202] [2], understood [2], able [1], acknowledges [1], acquaintances [1], agreed [1], apply [1], approval [1], are known [1], assured [1], attaining [1], be found out [1], be made known [1], be recognized [1], be remembered [1], become aware [1], become known [1], been discovered [1], been known [1], behaved [1], by surprise [+4202] [1], can read [+6219] [1], can [1], cannot read [+4202+6219] [1], care about [1], care for [1], cared for [1], close friend [1], close friends [1], closest friend [1], closest friends [1], come to [1], comprehend [1], decide [1], display [1], displayed [1], endowed with [1], enjoy [1], experts [1], familiar with [1], feel [1], find out [+906+2256+8011] [1], find [1], foresee [1], great skill [+1069+2682] [1], had experience [1], had intimate relations with [1], had regard for [1], has knowledge [+1981] [1], have concern for [1], have knowledge [+1981] [1], have to do with [1], ignorant [+1153] [1], inform [1], instructed [1], is respected [1], know all about [1], know how to read [+6219] [1], know what it is like [1], know what means [1], knowing about [1], knowing how [1], lain with [1], leading [1], learn the difference between [1], learned about [1], learning [1], lets be known [1], letting know [1], made himself known [1], make himself known [1], make predictions [1], makes known [1], man of knowledge [+1981] [1], mourners [+5631] [1], not a virgin [+2351+5435] [1], note [1], notice [1], noticed [1], perceive [1], perceiving [1], proclaim [1], raped [1], realize [+2256+8011] [1], realized [+2256+8011] [1], realizing [1], recognizes [1], remember [1], reveal myself [1], revealed [1], see [+906+2256+8011] [1], show how to distinguish [1], showed [1], shown himself [1], shown [1], shows [1], skillful [1], sleep with [1], slept with [+2351+4200+5435] [1], slept with [+2351+5435] [1], slept with [+408+4200+5435] [1], slept with [+5435] [1], slept with [1], stranger [+4202] [1], strangers [+4202] [1], suffer [1], taught a lesson [1], teaching [1], tell the difference [1], think it over [1], think over [1], think [1], told [1], trained [1], understand [+1069] [1], understands [1], understood [+1069+4200] [1], unfamiliar [+4202] [1], virgin [+408+4202] [1], want to do with [1], was discovered [1], was known [1], watched over [1], watches over [1], well informed [+1981] [1], were seen [1]

Ge 3: 5 [A] "For God **knows** that when you eat of it your eyes will be
3: 5 [A] and you will be like God, **knowing** good and evil."
3: 7 [A] of them were opened, and *they* **realized** they were naked;
3:22 [A] man has now become like one of us, **knowing** good and evil.
4: 1 [A] Adam **lay with** his wife Eve, and she became pregnant
4: 9 [A] "*I* don't **know**," he replied. "Am I my brother's keeper?"
4:17 [A] Cain **lay with** his wife, and she became pregnant and gave
4:25 [A] Adam **lay with** his wife again, and she gave birth to a son
8:11 [A] Then Noah **knew** that the water had receded from the earth.
9:24 [A] and **found out** what his youngest son had done to him,
12:11 [A] to his wife Sarai, "*I* **know** what a beautiful woman you are.
15: 8 [A] how *can I* **know** that I will gain possession of it?"
15:13 [A] "**Know** [+3359] **for certain** that your descendants will be
15:13 [A] "**Know for certain** [+3359] that your descendants will be
18:19 [A] For *I have* **chosen** him, so that he will direct his children
18:21 [A] bad as the outcry that has reached me. If not, *I will* **know**."
19: 5 [A] Bring them out to us so that *we can* **have sex with** them."
19: 8 [A] I have two daughters who *have* never **slept with** a man.
19:33 [A] *He was* not **aware** *of it* when she lay down or when she got
19:35 [A] Again *he was* not **aware** *of it* when she lay down or when
20: 6 [A] I **know** you did this with a clear conscience, and so I have
20: 7 [A] return her, *you may* **be sure** that you and all yours will die."
21:26 [A] Abimelech said, "*I* don't **know** who has done this. You did
22:12 [A] Now *I* **know** that you fear God, because you have not
24:14 [A] By this *I will* **know** that you have shown kindness to my
24:16 [A] was very beautiful, a virgin; no man *had ever* **lain with** her.
24:21 [A] the man watched her closely to **learn** whether or not the
25:27 [A] The boys grew up, and Esau became a **skillful** hunter, a man
27: 2 [A] "I am now an old man and don't **know** the day of my death.
28:16 [A] the LORD is in this place, and I *was* not **aware** *of* it."
29: 5 [A] He said to them, "*Do you* **know** Laban, Nahor's grandson?"
29: 5 [A] Nahor's grandson?" "Yes, *we* **know** him," they answered.
30:26 [A] on my way. You **know** how much work I've done for you."
30:29 [A] "You **know** how I have worked for you and how your
31: 6 [A] You **know** that I've worked for your father with all my
31:32 [A] Now Jacob *did* not **know** that Rachel had stolen the gods.
33:13 [A] "My lord **knows** that the children are tender and that I must
38: 9 [A] Onan **knew** that the offspring would not be his; so whenever
38:16 [A] Not **realizing** that she was his daughter-in-law, he went over
38:26 [A] her to my son Shelah." And *he did* not **sleep with** her again.
39: 6 [A] *he did* not **concern** *himself with* anything except the food he
39: 8 [A] "my master *does* not **concern** *himself with* anything in the
41:21 [C] after they ate them, no *one could* **tell** that they had done so;
41:31 [C] The abundance in the land *will* not **be remembered**,
41:39 [G] "Since God *has* **made** all this **known** *to* you, there is no one
42:23 [A] They *did* not **realize** that Joseph could understand them,
42:33 [A] to us, 'This is how *I will* **know** whether you are honest men:
42:34 [A] to me so *I will* **know** that you are not spies but honest men.
43: 7 [A] *How were we to* **know** [+3359] he would say, 'Bring your
43: 7 [A] *How were we to* **know** [+3359] he would say, 'Bring your
43:22 [A] buy food. *We* don't **know** who put our silver in our sacks."
44:15 [A] Don't *you* **know** that a man like me can find things out by
44:27 [A] father said to us, 'You **know** that my wife bore me two sons.
45: 1 [F] with Joseph when he **made himself known** to his brothers.
47: 6 [A] And if *you* **know** *of* any among them with special ability,
48:19 [A] But his father refused and said, "*I* **know**, my son, I know.

Ge 48:19 [A] But his father refused and said, "I know, my son, *I* **know**.
Ex 1:8 [A] a new king, who *did* not **know about** Joseph, came to power
2:4 [A] His sister stood at a distance to **see** what would happen to
2:14 [C] and thought, "What I did *must have* **become known**."
2:25 [A] God looked on the Israelites and *was* **concerned about** them.
3:7 [A] slave drivers, and *I am* **concerned about** their suffering.
3:19 [A] I **know** that the king of Egypt will not let you go unless a
4:14 [A] your brother, Aaron the Levite? *I* **know** he can speak well.
5:2 [A] *I do* not **know** the LORD and I will not let Israel go."
6:3 [C] by my name the LORD *I did* not **make myself known** to
6:7 [A] *you will* **know** that I am the LORD your God, who brought
7:5 [A] the Egyptians *will* **know** that I am the LORD when I stretch
7:17 [A] LORD says: By this *you will* **know** that I am the LORD:
8:10 [8:6] [A] so that *you may* **know** there is no one like the LORD
8:22 [8:18] [A] so that *you will* **know** that I, the LORD, am in this
9:14 [A] so *you may* **know** that there is no one like me in all the earth.
9:29 [A] more hail, so *you may* **know** that the earth is the LORD's.
9:30 [A] *I* **know** that you and your officials still do not fear the
10:2 [A] among them, and that *you may* **know** that I am the LORD."
10:7 [A] their God. *Do you* not yet **realize** that Egypt is ruined?"
10:26 [A] until we get there we *will* not **know** what we are to use to
11:7 [A] *you will* **know** that the LORD makes a distinction between
14:4 [A] and the Egyptians *will* **know** that I am the LORD."
14:18 [A] The Egyptians *will* **know** that I am the LORD when I gain
16:6 [A] "In the evening *you will* **know** that it was the LORD who
16:12 [A] Then *you will* **know** that I am the LORD your God.' "
16:15 [A] each other, "What is it?" For *they did* not **know** what it was.
18:11 [A] Now *I* **know** that the LORD is greater than all other gods,
18:16 [G] the parties and **inform** them *of* God's decrees and laws."
18:20 [G] **show** them the way to live and the duties they are to perform.
21:36 [C] if *it* **was known** that the bull had the habit of goring,
23:9 [A] *you* yourselves **know** how it feels to be aliens, because you
29:46 [A] *They will* **know** that I am the LORD their God,
31:13 [A] so *you may* **know** that I am the LORD, who makes you
32:1 [A] up out of Egypt, *we* don't **know** what has happened to him."
32:22 [A] "You **know** how prone these people are to evil.
32:23 [A] up out of Egypt, *we* don't **know** what has happened to him.'
33:5 [A] off your ornaments and *I will* **decide** what to do with you.' "
33:12 [G] but you *have* not **let** me **know** whom you will send with me.
33:12 [A] '*I* **know** you by name and you have found favor with me.'
33:13 [G] **teach** me your ways so I may know you and continue to find
33:13 [A] teach me your ways so *I may* **know** you and continue to find
33:16 [C] How *will anyone* **know** that you are pleased with me and
33:17 [A] because I am pleased with you and *I* **know** you by name."
34:29 [A] he *was* not **aware** that his face was radiant because he had
36:1 [A] ability to **know how** to carry out all the work of constructing
Lev 4:14 [C] When *they* **become aware** *of* the sin they committed, the
4:23 [H] When he **is made aware** *of* the sin he committed, he must
4:28 [H] When he **is made aware** *of* the sin he committed, he must
5:1 [A] to testify regarding something he has seen or **learned about**,
5:3 [A] he is unaware of it, when he **learns** of it he will be guilty.
5:4 [A] of it, in any case when he **learns** of it he will be guilty.
5:17 [A] even though *he does* not **know** it, he is guilty and will be
5:18 [A] committed unintentionally, **[RPH]** and he will be forgiven.
23:43 [A] so your descendants *will* **know** that I had the Israelites live in
Nu 10:31 [A] *You* **know** where we should camp in the desert, and you can
11:16 [A] "Bring me seventy of Israel's elders who *are* **known** *to you*
12:6 [F] *I* **reveal myself** to him in visions, I speak to him in dreams.
14:31 [A] I will bring them in *to* **enjoy** the land you have rejected.
14:34 [A] your sins and **know what it is like** to have me against you.'
16:5 [G] the morning the LORD *will* **show** who belongs to him and
16:28 [A] "This is how *you will* **know** that the LORD has sent me to
16:30 [A] *you will* **know** that these men have treated the LORD with
20:14 [A] You **know about** all the hardships that have come upon us.
22:6 [A] For *I* **know** that those you bless are blessed, and those you
22:19 [A] and *I will* **find out** what else the LORD will tell me."
22:34 [A] *I did* not **realize** you were standing in the road to oppose me.
24:16 [A] *who* **has knowledge** [+1981] *from* the Most High, who sees
31:17 [A] every woman *who has* **slept** [+408+4200+5435] **with** a man,
31:18 [A] every girl who *has* never **slept** [+5435] **with** a man.
31:35 [A] 32,000 women who *had* never **slept** [+2351+5435] **with** a
32:23 [A] and *you may* **be sure** that your sin will find you out.
Dt 1:13 [B] understanding and **respected** men from each of your tribes,
1:15 [B] took the leading men of your tribes, wise and **respected** men,
1:39 [A] your children who *do* not yet **know** good from bad—
2:7 [A] *He has* **watched over** your journey through this vast desert.
3:19 [A] and your livestock (*I* **know** you have much livestock)
4:9 [G] **Teach** them to your children and to their children after them.
4:35 [A] these things so that *you might* **know** that the LORD is God;
4:39 [A] **Acknowledge** and take to heart this day that the LORD is
7:9 [A] **Know** therefore that the LORD your God is God; he is the
7:15 [A] He will not inflict on you the horrible diseases *you* **knew** in
8:2 [A] and to test you in order to **know** what was in your heart,
8:3 [A] with manna, which neither *you* nor your fathers *had* **known**,
8:3 [A] **[RPH]** to teach you that man does not live on bread alone
8:3 [G] to **teach** you that man does not live on bread alone but on
8:5 [A] **Know** then in your heart that as a man disciplines his son,
8:16 [A] something your fathers *had* never **known**, to humble and to
9:2 [A] You **know about** them and have heard it said:
9:3 [A] *be* **assured** today that the LORD your God is the one who
9:6 [A] **Understand**, then, that it is not because of your
9:24 [A] rebellious against the LORD ever since I *have* **known** you.
11:2 [A] **Remember** today that your children were not the ones who
11:2 [A] **experienced** the discipline of the LORD your God: his
11:28 [A] today by following other gods, which *you have* not **known**.
13:2 [13:3] [A] us follow other gods" (gods *you have* not **known**)
13:3 [13:4] [A] The LORD your God is testing you to **find out**
13:6 [13:7] [A] (gods that neither you nor your fathers *have* **known**,
13:13 [13:14] [A] worship other gods" (gods *you have* not **known**),
18:21 [A] "How *can we* **know** when a message has not been spoken by
20:20 [A] you may cut down trees that *you* **know** are not fruit trees and
21:1 [C] is giving you to possess, and *it* **is** not **known** who killed him,
22:2 [A] does not live near you or if *you do* not **know** who he is,
28:33 [A] A people that *you do* not **know** will eat what your land
28:36 [A] the king you set over you to a nation **unknown** [+4202] *to*
28:64 [A] and stone, which neither you nor your fathers *have* **known**.
29:4 [29:3] [A] LORD has not given you a mind that **understands**
29:6 [29:5] [A] *you might* **know** that I am the LORD your God.
29:16 [29:15] [A] *You* yourselves **know** how we lived in Egypt and
29:26 [29:25] [A] and bowed down to them, gods *they did* not **know**,
31:13 [A] who *do* not **know** this law, must hear it and learn to fear the
31:21 [A] *I* **know** what they are disposed to do, even before I bring
31:27 [A] For I **know** how rebellious and stiff-necked you are. If you
31:29 [A] For *I* **know** that after my death you are sure to become
32:17 [A] gods *they had* not **known**, gods that recently appeared,
33:9 [A] not recognize his brothers or **acknowledge** his own children,
34:6 [A] Beth Peor, but to this day no one **knows** where his grave is.
34:10 [A] in Israel like Moses, whom the LORD **knew** face to face,
Jos 2:4 [A] came to me, but *I did* not **know** where they had come from.
2:5 [A] city gate, the men left. *I* don't **know** which way they went.
2:9 [A] "*I* **know** that the LORD has given this land to you and that
3:4 [A] *you will* **know** which way to go, since you have never been
3:7 [A] so *they may* **know** that I am with you as I was with Moses.
3:10 [A] This is how *you will* **know** that the living God is among you
4:22 [G] **tell** them, 'Israel crossed the Jordan on dry ground.'
4:24 [A] so that all the peoples of the earth *might* **know** that the hand
8:14 [A] he *did* not **know** that an ambush had been set against him
14:6 [A] "You **know** what the LORD said to Moses the man of God
22:22 [A] the LORD! The Mighty One, God, the LORD! He **knows**!
22:22 [A] God, the LORD! He knows! And *let* Israel **know**!
22:31 [A] and Manasseh, "Today *we* **know** that the LORD is with us,
23:13 [A] *you may* **be sure** [+3359] that the LORD your God will no
23:13 [A] *you may* **be sure** [+3359] that the LORD your God will no
23:14 [A] *You* **know** with all your heart and soul that not one of all the
24:31 [A] who *had* **experienced** everything the LORD had done for
Jdg 2:10 [A] who **knew** neither the LORD nor what he had done for
3:1 [A] who *had* not **experienced** any of the wars in Canaan
3:2 [A] the Israelites who *had* not **had** previous battle **experience**):
3:2 [A] who had not had previous battle experience): **[RPH]**
3:4 [A] They were left to test the Israelites to **see** whether they would
6:37 [A] *I will* **know** that you will save Israel by my hand, as you
8:16 [G] **taught** the men of Succoth **a lesson** by punishing them with
11:39 [A] to her as he had vowed. And she *was a* **virgin** [+408+4202].
13:16 [A] (Manoah *did* not **realize** that it was the angel of the
13:21 [A] Manoah **realized** that it was the angel of the LORD.
14:4 [A] (His parents *did* not **know** that this was from the LORD,
15:11 [A] "Don't *you* **realize** that the Philistines are rulers over us?
16:9 [C] to a flame. So the secret of his strength **was** not **discovered**.
16:20 [A] But he *did* not **know** that the LORD had left him.
17:13 [A] "Now *I* **know** that the LORD will be good to me,
18:5 [A] "Please inquire of God *to* **learn** whether our journey will be
18:14 [A] "*Do you* **know** that one of these houses has an ephod, other
18:14 [A] a carved image and a cast idol? Now *you* **know** what to do."
19:22 [A] man who came to your house so *we can* **have sex with** him."
19:25 [A] *they* **raped** her and abused her throughout the night, and at
20:34 [A] so heavy that the Benjamites *did* not **realize** how near
21:11 [A] and every woman *who is* **not a virgin** [+2351+5435]."
21:12 [A] women who *had* never **slept** [+2351+4200+5435] **with** a man,
Ru 2:1 [e] [Naomi had a **relative** [K; see Q 4530] on her husband's side,]
2:11 [A] and came to live with a people *you did* not **know** before.
3:3 [C] don't **let** him **know** *you* are there until he has finished eating
3:4 [A] When he lies down, **note** the place where he is lying.
3:11 [A] All my fellow townsmen **know** that you are a woman of
3:14 [C] "Don't *let it* **be known** that a woman came to the threshing
3:18 [A] "Wait, my daughter, until *you* **find out** what happens.
4:4 [A] redeem it, do so. But if you will not, tell me, so *I will* **know**.
1Sa 1:19 [A] Elkanah **lay with** Hannah his wife, and the LORD
2:12 [A] sons were wicked men; *they* **had** no **regard for** the LORD.

1Sa 3: 7 [A] Now Samuel *did* not yet **know** the LORD: The word of the
3: 13 [A] judge his family forever because of the sin *he* **knew about**;
3: 20 [A] all Israel from Dan to Beersheba **recognized** that Samuel was
4: 6 [A] When *they* **learned** that the ark of the LORD had come into
6: 2 [G] **Tell** us how we should send it back to its place."
6: 3 [C] you *will* **know** why his hand has not been lifted from you."
6: 9 [A] *we will* **know** that it was not his hand that struck us and that
10: 8 [G] days until I come to you and **tell** you what you are to do."
10: 11 [A] When all *those who had* formerly **known** him saw him
12: 17 [A] *you will* **realize** [+2256+8011] what an evil thing you did in
14: 3 [A] priest in Shiloh. No one *was* **aware** that Jonathan had left.
14: 12 [G] "Come up to us and *we'll* **teach** you a lesson."
14: 38 [A] *let us* **find** [+2256+8011] **out** what sin has been committed
16: 3 [G] Invite Jesse to the sacrifice, and I *will* **show** you what to do.
16: 16 [A] servants here to search for someone *who* **can** play the harp.
16: 18 [A] "I have seen a son of Jesse of Bethlehem *who* **knows how** to
17: 28 [A] I **know** how conceited you are and how wicked your heart is;
17: 46 [A] and the whole world *will* **know** that there is a God in Israel.
17: 47 [A] All those gathered here *will* **know** that it is not by sword
17: 55 [A] Abner replied, "As surely as you live, O king, *I* don't **know**."
18: 28 [A] When Saul **realized** [+2256+8011] that the LORD was with
20: 3 [A] "Your father **knows** [+3359] **very well** that I have found
20: 3 [A] "Your father **knows very well** [+3359] that I have found
20: 3 [A] 'Jonathan *must* not **know** this or he will be grieved.'
20: 7 [A] *you can* **be sure** that he is determined to harm me.
20: 9 [A] "If *I* **had the least inkling** [+3359] that my father was
20: 9 [A] "If *I* **had the least inkling** [+3359] that my father was
20: 30 [A] Don't *I* **know** that you have sided with the son of Jesse to
20: 33 [A] Then Jonathan **knew** that his father intended to kill David.
20: 39 [A] (The boy **knew** nothing *of* all this; only Jonathan and David
20: 39 [A] knew nothing of all this; only Jonathan and David **knew**.)
21: 2 [21:3] [A] 'No one *is to* **know** anything **about** your mission and
21: 2 [21:3] [G] *I have* **told** them to meet me at a certain place.
22: 3 [A] and stay with you until *I* **learn** what God will do for me?"
22: 6 [C] Saul heard that David and his men *had* **been discovered**.
22: 15 [A] for your servant **knows** nothing at all about this whole
22: 17 [A] *They* **knew** he was fleeing, yet they did not tell me."
22: 22 [A] the Edomite was there, *I* **knew** he would be sure to tell Saul.
23: 9 [A] When David **learned** that Saul was plotting against him, he
23: 17 [A] I will be second to you. Even my father Saul **knows** this."
23: 22 [A] **Find** [+906+2256+8011] **out** where David usually goes and
23: 23 [A] **Find out** [+2256+8011] about all the hiding places he uses
24: 11 [24:12] [A] Now **understand** and recognize that I am not guilty
24: 20 [24:21] [A] *I* **know** that you will surely be king and that the
25: 11 [A] and give it to men coming from who **knows** where?"
25: 17 [A] Now **think it over** and see what you can do, because disaster
26: 4 [A] sent out scouts and **learned** that Saul had definitely arrived.
26: 12 [A] No one saw or **knew about** it, nor did anyone wake up.
28: 1 [A] "*You* **must understand** [+3359] that you and your men will
28: 1 [A] "*You* **must understand** [+3359] that you and your men will
28: 2 [A] "Then *you will* **see** for yourself what your servant can do."
28: 9 [A] woman said to him, "Surely you **know** what Saul has done.
28: 14 [A] Saul **knew** it was Samuel, and he bowed down and prostrated
28: 15 [G] or by dreams. So I have called on you to **tell** me what to do."
29: 9 [A] "*I* **know** that you have been as pleasing in my eyes as an
2Sa 1: 5 [A] "How *do you* **know** that Saul and his son Jonathan are
1: 10 [A] because *I* **knew** that after he had fallen he could not survive.
2: 26 [A] Don't *you* **realize** that this will end in bitterness?
3: 25 [A] *You* **know** Abner son of Ner; he came to deceive you
3: 25 [A] **observe** your movements and find out everything you are
3: 25 [A] your movements and **find out** everything you are doing."
3: 26 [A] him back from the well of Sirah. But David *did* not **know** it.
3: 37 [A] all Israel **knew** that the king had no part in the murder of
3: 38 [A] "*Do you* not **realize** that a prince and a great man has fallen
5: 12 [A] David **knew** that the LORD had established him as king
7: 20 [A] to you? For you **know** your servant, O Sovereign LORD.
7: 21 [G] done this great thing and **made** it **known** *to* your servant.
11: 16 [A] he put Uriah at a place where *he* **knew** the strongest
11: 20 [A] Didn't *you* **know** they would shoot arrows from the wall?
12: 22 [A] was still alive, I fasted and wept. I thought, 'Who **knows**?
14: 1 [A] Joab son of Zeruiah **knew** that the king's heart longed for
14: 20 [A] of God—he **knows** everything that happens in the land."
14: 22 [A] "Today your servant **knows** that he has found favor in your
15: 11 [A] went quite innocently, **knowing** nothing **about** the matter.
17: 8 [A] You **know** your father and his men; they are fighters, and as
17: 10 [A] for all Israel **knows** that your father is a fighter and that those
17: 19 [C] and scattered grain over it. No *one* **knew** anything **about** it.
18: 29 [A] and me, your servant, but *I* don't **know** what it was."
19: 6 [19:7] [A] *I* **see** that you would be pleased if Absalom were
19: 20 [19:21] [A] For I your servant **know** that I have sinned,
19: 22 [19:23] [A] *Do I* not **know** that today I am king over Israel?"
19: 35 [19:36] [A] *Can I* **tell the difference** between what is good and
22: 44 [A] the head of nations. People *I did* not **know** are subject to me,
24: 2 [A] the fighting men, so that *I may* **know** how many there are."
24: 13 [A] **think** *it* **over** and decide how I should answer the one who
1Ki 1: 4 [A] on him, but the king **had** no **intimate relations with** her.
1: 11 [A] has become king without our lord David's **knowing** it?
1: 18 [A] and *you*, my lord the king, *do* not **know about** it.
1: 27 [G] **letting** his servants **know** who should sit on the throne of my
2: 5 [A] "Now *you* yourself **know** what Joab son of Zeruiah did to
2: 9 [A] You are a man of wisdom; *you will* **know** what to do to him.
2: 15 [A] "*As* you **know**," he said, "the kingdom was mine. All Israel
2: 32 [A] because without the **knowledge** *of* my father David he
2: 37 [A] the Kidron Valley, *you can* **be sure** [+3359] you will die;
2: 37 [A] the Kidron Valley, *you can* **be sure** [+3359] you will die;
2: 42 [A] to go anywhere else, *you can* **be sure** [+3359] you will die'?
2: 42 [A] to go anywhere else, *you can* **be sure** [+3359] you will die'?
2: 44 [A] "You **know** in your heart all the wrong you did to my father
2: 44 [A] "You know **[RPH]** in your heart all the wrong you did to
3: 7 [A] a little child and *do* not **know how** to carry out my duties.
5: 3 [5:17] [A] "You **know** that because of the wars waged against
5: 6 [5:20] [A] You **know** that we have no one so skilled in felling
5: 6 [5:20] [A] no one *so* **skilled** *in* felling timber as the Sidonians."
8: 38 [A] each one **aware** *of* the afflictions of his own heart,
8: 39 [A] since *you* **know** his heart (for you alone know the hearts of
8: 39 [A] since you know his heart (for you alone **know** the hearts of
8: 43 [A] so that all the peoples of the earth *may* **know** your name
8: 43 [A] and *may* **know** that this house I have built bears your Name.
8: 60 [A] so that all the peoples of the earth *may* **know** that the
9: 27 [A] Hiram sent his men—sailors *who* **knew** the sea—to serve in
14: 2 [A] so you won't *be* **recognized** as the wife of Jeroboam.
17: 24 [A] "Now *I* **know** that you are a man of God and that the word of
18: 12 [A] *I* don't **know** where the Spirit of the LORD may carry you
18: 36 [C] *let it* **be known** today that you are God in Israel and that I am
18: 37 [A] so these people *will* **know** that you, O LORD, are God,
20: 7 [A] "**See** [+2256+8011] how this man is looking for trouble!
20: 13 [A] hand today, and then *you will* **know** that I am the LORD.' "
20: 22 [A] your position and **see** [+906+2256+8011] what must be done,
20: 28 [A] into your hands, and *you will* **know** that I am the LORD.' "
22: 3 [A] "Don't *you* **know** that Ramoth Gilead belongs to us and yet
2Ki 2: 3 [A] "*Do you* **know** that the LORD is going to take your master
2: 3 [A] I **know**," Elisha replied, "but do not speak of it."
2: 5 [A] "*Do you* **know** that the LORD is going to take your master
2: 5 [A] "Yes, I **know**," he replied, "but do not speak of it."
4: 1 [A] husband is dead, and you **know** that he revered the LORD.
4: 9 [A] "*I* **know** that this man who often comes our way is a holy
4: 39 [A] up into the pot of stew, though no *one* **knew** what they were.
5: 7 [A] someone to me to be cured of his leprosy? **See** [+2256+8011]
5: 8 [A] to me and *he will* **know** that there is a prophet in Israel."
5: 15 [A] "Now *I* **know** that there is no God in all the world except in
7: 12 [A] *They* **know** we are starving; so they have left the camp to
8: 12 [A] "Because *I* **know** the harm you will do to the Israelites,"
9: 11 [A] "You **know** the man and the sort of things he says,"
10: 10 [A] **Know** then, that not a word the LORD has spoken against
10: 11 [E] his **close friends** and his priests, leaving him no survivor.
17: 26 [A] resettled in the towns of Samaria *do* not **know** what the god
17: 26 [A] them off, because the people *do* not **know** what he requires."
19: 19 [A] so that all kingdoms on earth *may* **know** that you alone, O
19: 27 [A] *I* **know** where you stay and when you come and go and
1Ch 12: 32 [12:33] [A] *who* **understood** [+1069+4200] the times and knew
12: 32 [12:33] [A] the times and **knew** what Israel should do—
14: 2 [A] David **knew** that the LORD had established him as king
16: 8 [G] his name; **make known** among the nations what he has done.
17: 18 [A] you for honoring your servant? For you **know** your servant,
17: 19 [G] this great thing and **made known** all these great promises.
21: 2 [A] report back to me so that *I may* **know** how many there are."
28: 9 [A] my son Solomon, **acknowledge** the God of your father,
29: 17 [A] *I* **know**, my God, that you test the heart and are pleased with
2Ch 2: 7 [2:6] [A] blue yarn, and **experienced** in the art of engraving,
2: 8 [2:7] [A] for I **know** that your men are skilled in cutting timber
2: 8 [2:7] [A] for I know that your men *are* **skilled** *in* cutting timber
2: 12 [2:11] [A] **endowed with** intelligence and discernment,
2: 13 [2:12] [A] you Huram-Abi, a man of **great skill** [+1069+2682],
2: 14 [2:13] [A] *He is* **trained** to work in gold and silver, bronze
6: 29 [A] each one **aware** *of* his afflictions and pains, and spreading
6: 30 [A] since *you* **know** his heart (for you alone know the hearts of
6: 30 [A] since you know his heart (for you alone **know** the hearts of
6: 33 [A] so that all the peoples of the earth *may* **know** your name
6: 33 [A] and *may* **know** that this house I have built bears your Name.
8: 18 [A] commanded by his own officers, men *who* **knew** the sea.
12: 8 [A] so that *they may* **learn the difference between** serving me
13: 5 [A] Don't you **know** that the LORD, the God of Israel,
20: 12 [A] We *do* not **know** what to do, but our eyes are upon you."
23: 13 [G] singers with musical instruments *were* **leading** the praises.
25: 16 [A] but said, "*I* **know** that God has determined to destroy you,
32: 13 [A] "*Do you* not **know** what I and my fathers have done to all the
32: 31 [A] him to test him and to **know** everything that was in his heart.
33: 13 [A] his kingdom. Then Manasseh **knew** that the LORD is God.

Ne 2:16 [A] The officials *did* not **know** where I had gone or what I was
4:11 [4:5] [A] Also our enemies said, "Before *they* **know** it or see us,
4:15 [4:9] [C] When our enemies heard that we *were* **aware** *of* their
6:16 [A] because *they* **realized** that this work had been done with the
8:12 [G] understood the words that *had been* **made known** to them.
9:10 [A] for *you* **knew** how arrogantly the Egyptians treated them.
9:14 [G] *You* **made known** to them your holy Sabbath and gave them
10:28 [10:29] [A] and daughters *who are* **able** to understand—
13:10 [A] *I* also **learned** that the portions assigned to the Levites had
Est 1:13 [A] Since it was customary for the king to consult **experts** *in*
1:13 [A] he spoke with the wise men *who* **understood** the times
2:11 [A] forth near the courtyard of the harem to **find out** how Esther
2:22 [C] Mordecai **found out** *about* the plot and told Queen Esther,
4:1 [A] When Mordecai **learned** *of* all that had been done, he tore
4:5 [A] and ordered him to **find out** what was troubling Mordecai
4:11 [A] and the people of the royal provinces **know** that for any man
4:14 [A] who **knows** but that you have come to royal position for such
Job 5:24 [A] *You will* **know** that your tent is secure; you will take stock of
5:25 [A] *You will* **know** that your children will be many, and your
5:27 [A] and it is true. So hear it and **apply** it to yourself."
8:9 [A] for we were born only yesterday and **know** nothing, and our
9:2 [A] "Indeed, *I* **know** that this is true. But how can a mortal be
9:5 [A] He moves mountains without *their* **knowing** it and overturns
9:21 [A] "Although I am blameless, *I* **have** no **concern for** myself;
9:28 [A] all my sufferings, for *I* **know** you will not hold me innocent.
10:2 [G] condemn me, but **tell** me what charges you have against me.
10:13 [A] in your heart, and *I* **know** that this was in your mind:
11:6 [A] of wisdom, for true wisdom has two sides. **Know** this:
11:8 [A] deeper than the depths of the grave—what *can you* **know**?
11:11 [A] Surely he **recognizes** deceitful men; and when he sees evil,
12:9 [A] Which of all these *does* not **know** that the hand of the
13:2 [A] What you know, I also **know**; I am not inferior to you.
13:18 [A] that I have prepared my case, *I* **know** I will be vindicated.
13:23 [G] and sins have I committed? **Show** me my offense and my sin.
14:21 [A] If his sons are honored, *he does* not **know** it; if they are
15:9 [A] What *do you* **know** that we do not know? What insights do
15:9 [A] What do you know that *we do* not **know**? What insights do
15:23 [A] food for vultures; *he* **knows** the day of darkness is at hand.
18:21 [A] an evil man; such is the place of *one who* **knows** not God."
19:6 [A] **know** that God has wronged me and drawn his net around
19:13 [A] my **acquaintances** are completely estranged from me.
19:14 [E] My kinsmen have gone away; my **friends** have forgotten me.
19:25 [A] I **know** that my Redeemer lives, and that in the end he will
19:29 [A] the sword, and then *you will* **know** that there is judgment."
20:4 [A] "Surely *you* **know** how it has been from of old, ever since
20:20 [A] "Surely *he will* **have** no respite from his craving; he cannot
21:19 [A] Let him repay the man himself, so that *he will* **know** it!
21:27 [A] "*I* **know** full well what you are thinking, the schemes by
22:13 [A] Yet you say, 'What *does* God **know**? Does he judge through
23:3 [A] If only *I* **knew** where to find him; if only I could go to his
23:5 [A] *I would* **find out** what he would answer me, and consider
23:10 [A] But *he* **knows** the way that I take; when he has tested me,
24:1 [A] Why must *those who* **know** him look in vain for such days?
24:16 [A] shut themselves in; *they* **want** nothing **to do with** the light.
26:3 [G] And what great insight *you have* **displayed**!
28:7 [A] No bird of prey **knows** that hidden path, no falcon's eye has
28:13 [A] Man *does* not **comprehend** its worth; it cannot be found in
28:23 [A] the way to it and he alone **knows** where it dwells,
29:16 [A] to the needy; I took up the case of the **stranger** [+4202].
30:23 [A] *I* **know** you will bring me down to death, to the place
31:6 [A] me in honest scales and *he will* **know** that I am blameless—
32:7 [G] 'Age should speak; advanced years *should* **teach** wisdom.'
32:22 [A] for if *I were* **skilled** *in* flattery, my Maker would soon take
34:2 [A] my words, you wise men; listen to me, you *men of* **learning**.
34:4 [A] ourselves what is right; *let* us **learn** together what is good.
34:33 [A] to repent? You must decide, not I; so tell me what *you* **know**.
35:15 [A] and *he does* not **take** the least **notice** of wickedness.
36:26 [A] How great is God—beyond *our* **understanding**! The number
37:5 [A] he does great things beyond *our* **understanding**.
37:7 [A] So that all men he has made *may* **know** his work, he stops
37:15 [A] *Do you* **know** how God controls the clouds and makes his
37:16 [A] *Do you* **know** how the clouds hang poised, those wonders of
37:19 [G] "**Tell** us what we should say to him; we cannot draw up our
38:3 [G] like a man; I will question you, and *you shall* **answer** me.
38:4 [A] the earth's foundation? Tell me, if *you* **understand** [+1069].
38:5 [A] Who marked off its dimensions? Surely *you* **know**! Who
38:12 [D] given orders to the morning, or **shown** the dawn its place,
38:18 [A] the vast expanses of the earth? Tell me, if *you* **know** all this.
38:21 [A] Surely *you* **know**, for you were already born! You have lived
38:33 [A] *Do you* **know** the laws of the heavens? Can you set up
39:1 [A] "*Do you* **know** when the mountain goats give birth? Do you
39:2 [A] months till they bear? *Do you* **know** the time they give birth?
40:7 [G] like a man; I will question you, and *you shall* **answer** me.
42:2 [A] "*I* **know** that you can do all things; no plan of yours can be
42:3 [A] I did not understand, things too wonderful for me *to* **know**.
42:4 [G] I will speak; I will question you, and *you shall* **answer** me.'
42:11 [A] and sisters and everyone *who had* **known** him before came
Ps 1:6 [A] For the LORD **watches over** the way of the righteous,
4:3 [4:4] [A] **Know** that the LORD has set apart the godly for
9:10 [9:11] [A] *Those who* **know** your name will trust in you,
9:16 [9:17] [C] The LORD **is known** *by* his justice; the wicked are
9:20 [9:21] [A] O LORD; *let* the nations **know** they are but men.
14:4 [A] *Will* evildoers never **learn**—those who devour my people as
16:11 [G] *You have* **made known** *to* me the path of life; you will fill
18:43 [18:44] [A] of nations; people *I did* not **know** are subject to me.
20:6 [20:7] [A] Now *I* **know** that the LORD saves his anointed;
25:4 [G] **Show** me your ways, O LORD, teach me your paths;
25:14 [G] those who fear him; he **makes** his covenant **known** *to* them.
31:7 [31:8] [A] saw my affliction and **knew** the anguish of my soul.
31:11 [31:12] [E] of my neighbors; I am a dread to my **friends**—
32:5 [G] *I* **acknowledged** my sin *to* you and did not cover up my
35:8 [A] may ruin overtake them **by surprise** [+4202]—may the net
35:11 [A] they question me on things *I* **know** nothing **about**.
35:15 [A] attackers gathered against me when *I was* **unaware** [+4202].
36:10 [36:11] [A] Continue your love to *those who* **know** you, your
37:18 [A] The days of the blameless *are* **known** *to* the LORD,
39:4 [39:5] [G] "**Show** me, O LORD, my life's end and the number
39:4 [39:5] [A] of my days; *let me* **know** how fleeting is my life.
39:6 [39:7] [A] he heaps up wealth, not **knowing** who will get it.
40:9 [40:10] [A] I do not seal my lips, *as* you **know**, O LORD.
41:11 [41:12] [A] *I* **know** that you are pleased with me, for my enemy
44:21 [44:22] [A] since he **knows** the secrets of the heart?
46:10 [46:11] [A] "Be still, and **know** that I am God; I will be exalted
48:3 [48:4] [C] her citadels; *he has* **shown himself** to be her fortress.
50:11 [A] *I* **know** every bird in the mountains, and the creatures of the
51:3 [51:5] [A] For I **know** my transgressions, and my sin is always
51:6 [51:8] [G] *you* **teach** me wisdom in the inmost place.
53:4 [53:5] [A] *Will* the evildoers never **learn**—those who devour
55:13 [55:14] [E] a man like myself, my companion, my **close friend**,
56:9 [56:10] [A] call for help. By this *I will* **know** that God is for me.
59:13 [59:14] [A] *it will be* **known** to the ends of the earth that God
67:2 [67:3] [A] that your ways *may be* **known** on earth,
69:5 [69:6] [A] You **know** my folly, O God; my guilt is not hidden
69:19 [69:20] [A] You **know** how I am scorned, disgraced and
71:15 [A] your salvation all day long, though *I* **know** not its measure.
73:11 [A] They say, "How *can* God **know**? Does the Most High have
73:16 [A] When I tried to **understand** all this, it was oppressive to me
73:22 [A] I was senseless and **ignorant** [+4202]; I was a brute beast
74:5 [C] *They* **behaved** like men wielding axes to cut through a
74:9 [A] are left, and none of us **knows** how long this will be.
76:1 [76:2] [C] In Judah God **is known**; his name is great in Israel.
77:14 [77:15] [G] *you* **display** your power among the peoples.
77:19 [77:20] [C] though your footprints **were** not **seen**.
78:3 [A] what we have heard and **known**, what our fathers have told
78:5 [G] which he commanded our forefathers to **teach** their children,
78:6 [A] so the next generation *would* **know** them, even the children
79:6 [A] Pour out your wrath on the nations that *do* not **acknowledge**
79:10 [C] **make known** among the nations that you avenge the
81:5 [81:6] [A] where we heard a language *we did* not **understand**.
82:5 [A] "*They* **know** nothing, they understand nothing. They walk
83:18 [83:19] [A] *Let them* **know** that you, whose name is the
87:4 [A] and Babylon among *those who* **acknowledge** me—
88:8 [88:9] [E] You have taken from me my **closest friends** and have
88:12 [88:13] [C] **Are** your wonders **known** in the place of darkness,
88:18 [88:19] [E] ones from me; the darkness *is* my **closest friend**.
89:1 [89:2] [G] with my mouth *I will* **make** your faithfulness **known**
89:15 [89:16] [A] Blessed are those *who have* **learned** to acclaim
90:11 [A] Who **knows** the power of your anger? For your wrath is as
90:12 [G] **Teach** us to number our days aright, that we may gain a heart
91:14 [A] I will protect him, for *he* **acknowledges** my name.
92:6 [92:7] [A] The senseless man *does* not **know**, fools do not
94:11 [A] The LORD **knows** the thoughts of man; he knows that they
95:10 [A] whose hearts go astray, and they *have* not **known** my ways."
98:2 [G] The LORD *has* **made** his salvation **known** and revealed his
100:3 [A] **Know** that the LORD is God. It is he who made us, and we
101:4 [A] shall be far from me; *I will* **have** nothing **to do with** evil.
103:7 [G] *He* **made known** his ways to Moses, his deeds to the people
103:14 [A] for he **knows how** we are formed, he remembers that we are
104:19 [A] marks off the seasons, and the sun **knows** when to go down.
105:1 [G] his name; **make known** among the nations what he has done.
106:8 [G] them for his name's sake, to **make** his mighty power **known**.
109:27 [A] *Let them* **know** that it is your hand, that you, O LORD,
119:75 [A] *I* **know**, O LORD, that your laws are righteous, and in
119:79 [A] fear you turn to me, *those who* **understand** your statutes.
119:125 [A] give me discernment that *I may* **understand** your statutes.
119:152 [A] Long ago *I* **learned** from your statutes that you established
135:5 [A] I **know** that the LORD is great, that our Lord is greater than
138:6 [A] he looks upon the lowly, but the proud *he* **knows** from afar.

Ps 139: 1 [A] O LORD, you have searched me and *you* **know** me.
139: 2 [A] You **know** when I sit and when I rise; you perceive my
139: 4 [A] Before a word is on my tongue *you* **know** it completely,
139: 14 [A] your works are wonderful, I **know** that full well.
139: 23 [A] Search me, O God, and **know** my heart; test me and know
139: 23 [A] and know my heart; test me and **know** my anxious thoughts.
140: 12 [140:13] [A] *I* **know** that the LORD secures justice for the
142: 3 [142:4] [A] grows faint within me, it is you *who* **know** my way.
143: 8 [G] **Show** me the way I should go, for to you I lift up my soul.
144: 3 [A] O LORD, what is man that *you* **care for** him, the son of
145: 12 [G] so that all men *may* **know** *of* your mighty acts
147: 20 [A] has done this for no other nation; *they do* not **know** his laws.
Pr 1: 2 [A] for **attaining** wisdom and discipline; for understanding
1: 23 [G] out my heart to you and **made** my thoughts **known** *to* you.
3: 6 [A] in all your ways **acknowledge** him, and he will make your
4: 1 [A] a father's instruction; pay attention and **gain** understanding.
4: 19 [A] deep darkness; *they do* not **know** what makes them stumble.
5: 6 [A] the way of life; her paths are crooked, but *she* **knows** it not.
7: 23 [A] darting into a snare, little **knowing** it will cost him his life.
9: 9 [G] **teach** a righteous man and he will add to his learning.
9: 13 [A] Folly is loud; she is undisciplined and without **knowledge**.
9: 18 [A] little *do they* **know** that the dead are there, that her guests are
10: 9 [C] but he who takes crooked paths *will* **be found out**.
10: 32 [A] The lips of the righteous **know** what is fitting, but the mouth
12: 10 [A] A righteous man **cares for** the needs of his animal,
12: 16 [C] A fool **shows** his annoyance at once, but a prudent man
14: 7 [A] a foolish man, for *you will* not **find** knowledge on his lips.
14: 10 [A] Each heart **knows** its own bitterness, and no one else can
14: 33 [C] and even among fools *she* **lets** *herself* **be known**.
17: 27 [A] A **man of knowledge** [+1981] uses words with restraint, and
22: 19 [G] trust may be in the LORD, *I* **teach** you today, even you.
22: 21 [G] **teaching** you true and reliable words, so that you can give
23: 35 [A] will say, "but I'm not hurt! They beat me, but *I* don't **feel** it!
24: 12 [A] If you say, "But *we* **knew** nothing **about** this," does not he
24: 12 [A] heart perceive it? *Does* not he who guards your life **know** it?
24: 14 [A] **Know** also that wisdom is sweet to your soul; if you find it,
24: 22 [A] upon them, and who **knows** what calamities they can bring?
27: 1 [A] for *you do* not **know** what a day may bring forth.
27: 23 [A] **Be sure** *you* **know** [+3359] the condition of your flocks,
27: 23 [A] **Be sure** *you* **know** [+3359] the condition of your flocks,
28: 2 [A] but a man of understanding and **knowledge** maintains order.
28: 22 [A] to get rich and *is* **unaware** [+4202] that poverty awaits him.
29: 7 [A] The righteous **care about** justice for the poor, but the wicked
30: 3 [A] nor **have** *I* **knowledge** [+1981] *of* the Holy One.
30: 4 [A] is his name, and the name of his son? Tell me if *you* **know**!
30: 18 [A] that are too amazing for me, four *that I do* not **understand**:
31: 23 [C] Her husband **is respected** at the city gate, where he takes his
Ecc 1: 17 [A] I applied myself to the **understanding** *of* wisdom, and also
1: 17 [A] and also **[RPH]** of madness and folly, but I learned that this,
1: 17 [A] and also of madness and folly, but *I* **learned** that this, too,
2: 14 [A] but I *came to* **realize** that the same fate overtakes them both.
2: 19 [A] And who **knows** whether he will be a wise man or a fool?
3: 12 [A] *I* **know** that there is nothing better for men than to be happy
3: 14 [A] *I* **know** that everything God does will endure forever;
3: 21 [A] Who **knows** if the spirit of man rises upward and if the spirit
4: 13 [A] but foolish king who no longer **knows how** to take warning.
5: 1 [4:17] [A] of fools, who *do* not **know** that they do wrong.
6: 5 [A] Though it never saw the sun or **knew** anything, it has more
6: 8 [A] What does a poor man gain *by* **knowing how** to conduct
6: 10 [C] has already been named, and what man is *has* **been known**;
6: 12 [A] For who **knows** what is good for a man in life,
7: 22 [A] for *you* **know** in your heart that many times you yourself
7: 25 [A] So I turned my mind to **understand**, to investigate and to
7: 25 [A] of things and to **understand** the stupidity of wickedness
8: 1 [A] is like the wise man? Who **knows** the explanation of things?
8: 5 [A] Whoever obeys his command *will* **come to** no harm,
8: 5 [A] and the wise heart *will* **know** the proper time and procedure.
8: 7 [A] Since no man **knows** the future, who can tell him what is to
8: 12 [A] I **know** that it will go better with God-fearing men,
8: 16 [A] When I applied my mind to **know** wisdom and to observe
8: 17 [A] Even if a wise man claims he **knows**, he cannot really
9: 1 [A] but no man **knows** whether love or hate awaits him.
9: 5 [A] For the living **know** that they will die, but the dead know
9: 5 [A] living know that they will die, but the dead **know** nothing;
9: 11 [A] to the wise or wealth to the brilliant or favor to the **learned**;
9: 12 [A] Moreover, no man **knows** when his hour will come: As fish
10: 14 [A] No one **knows** what is coming—who can tell him what will
10: 15 [A] fool's work wearies him; *he does* not **know** the way to town.
11: 2 [A] for *you do* not **know** what disaster may come upon the land.
11: 5 [A] As you *do* not **know** the path of the wind, or how the body is
11: 5 [A] so *you* cannot **understand** the work of God, the Maker of all
11: 6 [A] for you *do* not **know** which will succeed, whether this
11: 9 [A] **know** that for all these things God will bring you to
SS 1: 8 [A] If *you do* not **know**, most beautiful of women, follow the
6: 12 [A] Before *I* **realized** it, my desire set me among the royal
Isa 1: 3 [A] The ox **knows** his master, the donkey his owner's manger,
1: 3 [A] but Israel *does* not **know**, my people do not understand."
5: 5 [G] Now *I will* **tell** you what I am going to do to my vineyard:
5: 19 [A] plan of the Holy One of Israel come, so *we may* **know** it."
6: 9 [A] never understanding; be ever seeing, but never **perceiving**.'
7: 15 [A] and honey when he **knows** *enough* to reject the wrong
7: 16 [A] before the boy **knows** *enough* to reject the wrong and choose
8: 4 [A] Before the boy **knows how** to say 'My father' or 'My mother,'
9: 9 [9:8] [A] All the people *will* **know** it—Ephraim
12: 4 [G] **make known** among the nations what he has done,
12: 5 [H] has done glorious things; *let* this **be known** to all the world.
19: 12 [A] **make known** what the LORD Almighty has planned
19: 21 [C] So the LORD *will* **make himself known** to the Egyptians,
19: 21 [A] and in that day they *will* **acknowledge** the LORD.
29: 11 [A] if you give the scroll to *someone who* **can read** [+6219],
29: 12 [A] give the scroll to someone *who* **cannot read** [+4202+6219],
29: 12 [A] he will answer, "*I* don't **know how to read** [+6219]."
29: 15 [A] work in darkness and think, "Who sees us? Who *will* **know**?"
29: 24 [A] Those who are wayward in spirit *will* **gain** understanding;
32: 4 [A] The mind of the rash *will* **know** and understand,
33: 13 [A] I have done; you who are near, **acknowledge** my power!
37: 20 [A] so that all kingdoms on earth *may* **know** that you alone, O
37: 28 [A] "But *I* **know** where you stay and when you come and go and
38: 19 [G] fathers **tell** their children about your faithfulness.
40: 13 [G] the mind of the LORD, or **instructed** him as his counselor?
40: 14 [G] him knowledge or **showed** him the path of understanding?
40: 21 [A] *Do you* not **know**? Have you not heard? Has it not been told
40: 28 [A] *Do you* not **know**? Have you not heard? The LORD is the
41: 20 [A] so that people may see and **know**, may consider
41: 22 [A] so that we may consider them and **know** their final outcome.
41: 23 [A] us what the future holds, so *we may* **know** that you are gods.
41: 26 [A] so *we could* **know**, or beforehand, so we could say, 'He was
42: 16 [A] I will lead the blind by ways *they have* not **known**,
42: 16 [A] along **unfamiliar** [+4202] paths I will guide them;
42: 25 [A] It enveloped them in flames, yet *they did* not **understand**;
43: 10 [A] so that *you may* **know** and believe me and understand that I
43: 19 [A] a new thing! Now it springs up; *do you* not **perceive** it?
44: 8 [A] besides me? No, there is no other Rock; *I* **know** not one."
44: 9 [A] speak up for them are blind; *they are* **ignorant** [+1153],
44: 18 [A] *They* **know** nothing, they understand nothing; their eyes are
45: 3 [A] so that *you may* **know** that I am the LORD, the God of
45: 4 [A] on you a title of honor, though *you do* not **acknowledge** me.
45: 5 [A] will strengthen you, though *you have* not **acknowledged** me,
45: 6 [A] place of its setting *men may* **know** there is none besides me.
45: 20 [A] you fugitives from the nations. **Ignorant** [+4202] *are* those
47: 8 [A] I will never be a widow or **suffer** the loss of children.'
47: 11 [A] upon you, and *you will* not **know how** to conjure it away.
47: 11 [A] a catastrophe *you* cannot **foresee** will suddenly come upon
47: 13 [G] those stargazers *who* **make predictions** month by month,
48: 4 [A] For I **knew** how stubborn you were; the sinews of your neck
48: 6 [A] of new things, of hidden things **unknown** [+4202] *to you*.
48: 7 [A] them before today. So you cannot say, 'Yes, *I* **knew** *of* them.'
48: 8 [A] You have neither heard nor **understood**; from of old your ear
48: 8 [A] Well *do I* **know** how treacherous you are; you were called a
49: 23 [A] *you will* **know** that I am the LORD; those who hope in me
49: 26 [A] all mankind *will* **know** that I, the LORD, am your Savior,
50: 4 [A] instructed tongue, to **know** the word that sustains the weary.
50: 7 [A] I set my face like flint, and *I* **know** I will not be put to shame.
51: 7 [A] "Hear me, *you who* **know** what is right, you people who
52: 6 [A] Therefore my people *will* **know** my name; therefore in that
53: 3 [A] by men, a man of sorrows, and **familiar with** suffering.
55: 5 [A] Surely you will summon nations *you* **know** not, and nations
55: 5 [A] nations *that do* not **know** you will hasten to you, because of
56: 10 [A] Israel's watchmen are blind, they all lack **knowledge**;
56: 11 [A] are dogs with mighty appetites; *they* never **have** enough.
56: 11 [A] They are shepherds *who* lack **understanding**; they all turn to
58: 3 [A] have we humbled ourselves, and *you have* not **noticed**?'
59: 8 [A] The way of peace *they do* not **know**; there is no justice in
59: 8 [A] crooked roads; no one who walks in them *will* **know** peace.
59: 12 [A] are ever with us, and *we* **acknowledge** our iniquities:
60: 16 [A] *you will* **know** that I, the LORD, am your Savior, your
61: 9 [C] Their descendants *will* **be known** among the nations
63: 16 [A] though Abraham *does* not **know** us or Israel acknowledge us;
64: 2 [64:1] [G] come down to **make** your name **known** to your
66: 14 [C] the hand of the LORD *will* **be made known** *to* his servants,
Jer 1: 5 [A] "Before I formed you in the womb *I* **knew** you, before you
1: 6 [A] Sovereign LORD," I said, "*I do* not **know how** to speak;
2: 8 [A] Those who deal with the law *did* not **know** me; the leaders
2: 19 [A] **Consider** then and realize how evil and bitter it is for you
2: 23 [A] you behaved in the valley; **consider** what you have done.
3: 13 [A] Only **acknowledge** your guilt—you have rebelled against the
4: 22 [A] "My people are fools; *they do* not **know** me. They are
4: 22 [A] are skilled in doing evil; *they* **know** not **how** to do good."

Jer 5: 1 [A] look around and **consider**, search through her squares.
5: 4 [A] are foolish, for *they do* not **know** the way of the LORD,
5: 5 [A] surely they **know** the way of the LORD, the requirements of
5: 15 [A] enduring nation, a people whose language *you do* not **know**,
6: 15 [A] have no shame at all; *they do* not even **know how** to blush.
6: 18 [A] O nations; **observe**, O witnesses, what will happen to them.
6: 27 [A] my people the ore, that *you may* **observe** and test their ways.
7: 9 [A] incense to Baal and follow other gods *you have* not **known**,
8: 7 [A] Even the stork in the sky **knows** her appointed seasons,
8: 7 [A] But my people *do* not **know** the requirements of the LORD.
8: 12 [A] have no shame at all; *they do* not even **know how** to blush.
9: 3 [9:2] [A] *they do* not **acknowledge** me," declares the LORD.
9: 6 [9:5] [A] in their deceit they refuse *to* **acknowledge** me,"
9: 16 [9:15] [A] that neither they nor their fathers *have* **known**,
9: 24 [9:23] [A] that he understands and **knows** me, that I am the
10: 23 [A] *I* **know**, O LORD, that a man's life is not his own; it is not
10: 25 [A] Pour out your wrath on the nations that *do* not **acknowledge**
11: 18 [G] Because the LORD **revealed** their plot *to* me, I knew it,
11: 18 [A] Because the LORD revealed their plot to me, *I* **knew** it,
11: 19 [A] *I did* not **realize** that they had plotted against me, saying,
12: 3 [A] Yet you **know** me, O LORD; you see me and test my
13: 12 [A] 'Don't *we* **know** [+3359] that every wineskin should be filled
13: 12 [A] 'Don't *we* **know** [+3359] that every wineskin should be filled
14: 18 [A] and priest have gone to a land *they* **know** not.' "
14: 20 [A] *we* **acknowledge** our wickedness and the guilt of our fathers;
15: 14 [A] will enslave you to your enemies in a land *you do* not **know**,
15: 15 [A] You **understand**, O LORD; remember me and care for me.
15: 15 [A] take me away; **think** *of* how I suffer reproach for your sake.
16: 13 [A] land into a land neither you nor your fathers *have* **known**,
16: 21 [G] "Therefore I *will* **teach** them—this time I will teach them my
16: 21 [G] this time *I will* **teach** them my power and might.
16: 21 [A] Then *they will* **know** that my name is the LORD.
17: 4 [A] will enslave you to your enemies in a land *you do* not **know**,
17: 9 [A] above all things and beyond cure. Who *can* **understand** it?
17: 16 [A] you **know** I have not desired the day of despair.
18: 23 [A] you **know**, O LORD, all their plots to kill me. Do not
19: 4 [A] they nor their fathers nor the kings of Judah *ever* **knew**,
22: 28 [A] his children be hurled out, cast into a land *they do* not **know**?
24: 7 [A] I will give them a heart to **know** me, that I am the LORD.
26: 15 [A] *Be* **assured** [+3359], however, that if you put me to death,
26: 15 [A] *Be* **assured** [+3359], however, that if you put me to death,
28: 9 [C] the prophet who prophesies peace *will* **be recognized** as one
29: 11 [A] For I **know** the plans I have for you," declares the LORD,
29: 23 [A] to do. I **know** it and am a witness to it," declares the LORD.
31: 19 [C] I repented; after I *came to* **understand**, I beat my breast.
31: 34 [A] or a man his brother, saying, '**Know** the LORD,'
31: 34 [A] saying, 'Know the LORD,' because they *will* all **know** me,
32: 8 [A] for yourself.' "*I* **knew** that this was the word of the LORD;
33: 3 [A] and tell you great and unsearchable things *you do* not **know**.'
36: 19 [A] go and hide. Don't *let* anyone **know** where you are."
38: 24 [A] "*Do* not *let* anyone **know** about this conversation, or you
40: 14 [A] "Don't *you* **know** [+3359] that Baalis king of the Ammonites
40: 14 [A] "Don't *you* **know** [+3359] that Baalis king of the Ammonites
40: 15 [A] and kill Ishmael son of Nethaniah, and no one *will* **know** it.
41: 4 [A] after Gedaliah's assassination, before anyone **knew about** it,
42: 19 [A] not go to Egypt.' **Be sure** [+3359] *of* this: I warn you today
42: 19 [A] not go to Egypt.' **Be sure of** [+3359] this: I warn you today
42: 22 [A] So now, **be sure** [+3359] *of* this: You will die by the sword,
42: 22 [A] So now, **be sure of** [+3359] this: You will die by the sword,
44: 3 [A] gods that neither they nor you nor your fathers *ever* **knew**.
44: 15 [A] all the men who **knew** that their wives were burning incense
44: 28 [A] came to live in Egypt *will* **know** whose word will stand—
44: 29 [A] 'so that *you will* **know** that my threats of harm against you
48: 17 [A] for her, all who live around her, all *who* **know** her fame;
48: 30 [A] I **know** her insolence but it is futile," declares the LORD,
50: 24 [A] O Babylon, and you were caught before you **knew** it;
Eze 2: 5 [A] *they will* **know** that a prophet has been among them.
5: 13 [A] *they will* **know** that I the LORD have spoken in my zeal.
6: 7 [A] slain among you, and *you will* **know** that I am the LORD.
6: 10 [A] *they will* **know** that I am the LORD; I did not threaten in
6: 13 [A] *they will* **know** that I am the LORD, when their people lie
6: 14 [A] they live. Then *they will* **know** that I am the LORD.' "
7: 4 [A] among you. Then *you will* **know** that I am the LORD.
7: 9 [A] *you will* **know** that it is I the LORD who strikes the blow.
7: 27 [A] judge them. Then *they will* **know** that I am the LORD."
10: 20 [A] by the Kebar River, and *I* **realized** that they were cherubim.
11: 5 [A] house of Israel, but I **know** what is going through your mind.
11: 10 [A] borders of Israel. Then *you will* **know** that I am the LORD.
11: 12 [A] *you will* **know** that I am the LORD, for you have not
12: 15 [A] "*They will* **know** that I am the LORD, when I disperse
12: 16 [A] Then *they will* **know** that I am the LORD."
12: 20 [A] be desolate. Then *you will* **know** that I am the LORD.' "
13: 9 [A] Then *you will* **know** that I am the Sovereign LORD.
13: 14 [A] be destroyed in it; and *you will* **know** that I am the LORD.
13: 21 [A] to your power. Then *you will* **know** that I am the LORD.
13: 23 [A] And then *you will* **know** that I am the LORD.' "
14: 8 [A] from my people. Then *you will* **know** that I am the LORD.
14: 23 [A] for *you will* **know** that I have done nothing in it without
15: 7 [A] my face against them, *you will* **know** that I am the LORD.
16: 2 [G] of man, **confront** Jerusalem *with* her detestable practices
16: 62 [A] covenant with you, and *you will* **know** that I am the LORD.
17: 12 [A] rebellious house, '*Do you* not **know** what these things mean?'
17: 21 [A] Then *you will* **know** that I the LORD have spoken.
17: 24 [A] All the trees of the field *will* **know** that I the LORD bring
19: 7 [a] *He* broke down [BHS *knew*; NIV 1548] their strongholds
20: 4 [G] **confront** them *with* the detestable practices of their fathers
20: 5 [C] of the house of Jacob and **revealed myself** to them in Egypt.
20: 9 [C] in whose sight *I had* **revealed myself** to the Israelites by
20: 11 [G] I gave them my decrees and **made known** *to* them my laws,
20: 12 [A] so they *would* **know** that I the LORD made them holy.
20: 20 [A] Then *you will* **know** that I am the LORD your God."
20: 26 [A] them with horror so *they would* **know** that I am the LORD.'
20: 38 [A] the land of Israel. Then *you will* **know** that I am the LORD.
20: 42 [A] *you will* **know** that I am the LORD, when I bring you into
20: 44 [A] *You will* **know** that I am the LORD, when I deal with you
21: 5 [21:10] [A] all people *will* **know** that I the LORD have drawn
22: 2 [G] Then **confront** her *with* all her detestable practices
22: 16 [A] eyes of the nations, *you will* **know** that I am the LORD.' "
22: 22 [A] *you will* **know** that I the LORD have poured out my wrath
22: 26 [G] *they* **teach** that there is no difference between the unclean
23: 49 [A] Then *you will* **know** that I am the Sovereign LORD."
24: 24 [A] *you will* **know** that I am the Sovereign LORD.'
24: 27 [A] be a sign to them, and *they will* **know** that I am the LORD."
25: 5 [A] place for sheep. Then *you will* **know** that I am the LORD.
25: 7 [A] destroy you, and *you will* **know** that I am the LORD.' "
25: 11 [A] on Moab. Then *they will* **know** that I am the LORD.' "
25: 14 [A] *they will* **know** my vengeance, declares the Sovereign
25: 17 [A] *they will* **know** that I am the LORD, when I take
26: 6 [A] by the sword. Then *they will* **know** that I am the LORD.
28: 19 [A] All the nations *who* **knew** you are appalled at you; you have
28: 22 [A] *They will* **know** that I am the LORD, when I inflict
28: 23 [A] on every side. Then *they will* **know** that I am the LORD.
28: 24 [A] Then *they will* **know** that I am the Sovereign LORD.
28: 26 [A] Then *they will* **know** that I am the LORD their God.' "
29: 6 [A] Then all who live in Egypt *will* **know** that I am the LORD.
29: 9 [A] *they will* **know** that I am the LORD. " 'Because you said,
29: 16 [A] Then *they will* **know** that I am the Sovereign LORD.' "
29: 21 [A] among them. Then *they will* **know** that I am the LORD."
30: 8 [A] *they will* **know** that I am the LORD, when I set fire to
30: 19 [A] on Egypt, and *they will* **know** that I am the LORD.' "
30: 25 [A] *they will* **know** that I am the LORD, when I put my sword
30: 26 [A] the countries. Then *they will* **know** that I am the LORD."
32: 9 [A] among the nations, among lands *you have* not **known**.
32: 15 [A] who live there, then *they will* **know** that I am the LORD.'
33: 29 [A] *they will* **know** that I am the LORD, when I have made the
33: 33 [A] then *they will* **know** that a prophet has been among them."
34: 27 [A] *They will* **know** that I am the LORD, when I break the bars
34: 30 [A] *they will* **know** that I, the LORD their God, am with them
35: 4 [A] will be desolate. Then *you will* **know** that I am the LORD.
35: 9 [A] not be inhabited. Then *you will* **know** that I am the LORD.
35: 11 [C] *I will* **make myself known** among them when I judge you.
35: 12 [A] *you will* **know** that I the LORD have heard all the
35: 15 [A] all of Edom. Then *they will* **know** that I am the LORD.' "
36: 11 [A] more than before. Then *you will* **know** that I am the LORD.
36: 23 [A] the nations *will* **know** that I am the LORD,
36: 32 [C] *I want* you *to* **know** that I am not doing this for your sake,
36: 36 [A] the nations around you that remain *will* **know** that I the
36: 38 [A] of people. Then *they will* **know** that I am the LORD."
37: 3 [A] bones live?" I said, "O Sovereign LORD, you alone **know**."
37: 6 [A] come to life. Then *you will* **know** that I am the LORD.' "
37: 13 [A] *you*, my people, *will* **know** that I am the LORD, when I
37: 14 [A] *you will* **know** that I the LORD have spoken, and I have
37: 28 [A] the nations *will* **know** that I the LORD make Israel holy,
38: 14 [A] Israel are living in safety, *will you* not **take notice** *of* it?
38: 16 [A] so that the nations *may* **know** me when I show myself holy
38: 23 [C] and *I will* **make myself known** in the sight of many nations.
38: 23 [A] of many nations. Then *they will* **know** that I am the LORD.'
39: 6 [A] in the coastlands, and *they will* **know** that I am the LORD.
39: 7 [G] " '*I will* **make known** my holy name among my people
39: 7 [A] the nations *will* **know** that I the LORD am the Holy One in
39: 22 [A] From that day forward the house of Israel *will* **know** that I
39: 23 [A] the nations *will* **know** that the people of Israel went into exile
39: 28 [A] *they will* **know** that I am the LORD their God, for though I
43: 11 [G] **make known** *to* them the design of the temple—its
44: 23 [G] **show** them **how to distinguish** between the unclean and the
Da 1: 4 [A] **well informed** [+1981], quick to understand, and qualified to
2: 3 [A] dream that troubles me and I want to **know what** it **means**."
8: 19 [G] "I *am going to* **tell** you what will happen later in the time of

Da 9:25 [A] "**Know** and understand this: From the issuing of the decree
10:20 [A] So he said, "*Do you* **know** why I have come to you? Soon I
11:32 [A] but the people *who* **know** their God will firmly resist him.
11:38 [A] a god **unknown** [+4202] *to* his fathers he will honor with
Hos 2: 8 [2:10] [A] She *has* not **acknowledged** that I was the one who
2:20 [2:22] [A] and *you will* **acknowledge** the LORD.
5: 3 [A] I **know all about** Ephraim; Israel is not hidden from me.
5: 4 [A] is in their heart; *they do* not **acknowledge** the LORD.
5: 9 [G] Among the tribes of Israel *I* **proclaim** what is certain.
6: 3 [A] *Let us* **acknowledge** the LORD; let us press on to
6: 3 [A] the LORD; let us press on to **acknowledge** him.
7: 9 [A] Foreigners sap his strength, but he *does* not **realize** it. His
7: 9 [A] His hair is sprinkled with gray, but he *does* not **notice**.
8: 2 [A] Israel cries out to me, 'O our God, *we* **acknowledge** you!'
8: 4 [A] my consent; they choose princes without *my* **approval**.
9: 7 [A] *Let* Israel **know** this. Because your sins are so many
11: 3 [A] the arms; but *they did* not **realize** it was I who healed them.
13: 4 [A] *You shall* **acknowledge** no God but me, no Savior except
13: 5 [A] I **cared for** you in the desert, in the land of burning heat.
14: 9 [14:10] [A] Who is discerning? *He will* **understand** them.
Joel 2:14 [A] Who **knows**? He may turn and have pity and leave behind a
2:27 [A] *you will* **know** that I am in Israel, that I am the LORD your
3:17 [4:17] [A] "Then *you will* **know** that I, the LORD your God,
Am 3: 2 [A] "You only *have I* **chosen** of all the families of the earth;
3: 3 [C] Do two walk together unless *they have* **agreed** to do so?
3:10 [A] "*They do* not **know how** to do right," declares the LORD,
5:12 [A] For *I* **know** how many are your offenses and how great your
5:16 [A] be summoned to weep and the **mourners** [+5631] to wail.
Jnh 1: 7 [A] let us cast lots *to* **find out** who is responsible for this
1:10 [A] (They **knew** he was running away from the LORD,
1:12 [A] I **know** that it is my fault that this great storm has come upon
3: 9 [A] Who **knows**? God may yet relent and with compassion turn
4: 2 [A] *I* **knew** that you are a gracious and compassionate God,
4:11 [A] twenty thousand people who cannot **tell** their right hand from
Mic 3: 1 [A] rulers of the house of Israel. *Should* you not **know** justice,
4:12 [A] they *do* not **know** the thoughts of the LORD; they do not
6: 5 [A] that *you may* **know** the righteous acts of the LORD."
Na 1: 7 [A] in times of trouble. *He* **cares for** those who trust in him,
3:17 [C] the sun appears they fly away, and no *one* **knows** where.
Hab 2:14 [A] For the earth will be filled with the **knowledge** *of* the glory
3: 2 [G] Renew them in our day, in our time **make** them **known**;
Zep 3: 5 [A] day he does not fail, yet the unrighteous **know** no shame.
Zec 2: 9 [2:13] [A] *you will* **know** that the LORD Almighty has sent
2:11 [2:15] [A] *you will* **know** that the LORD Almighty has sent
4: 5 [A] He answered, "*Do you* not **know** what these are?" "No,
4: 9 [A] *you will* **know** that the LORD Almighty has sent me to you.
4:13 [A] He replied, "*Do you* not **know** what these are?" "No,
6:15 [A] *you will* **know** that the LORD Almighty has sent me to you.
7:14 [A] among all the nations, where they *were* **strangers** [+4202].
11:11 [A] so the afflicted of the flock who were watching me **knew** it
14: 7 [C] without daytime or nighttime—a day **known** to the LORD.
Mal 2: 4 [A] *you will* **know** that I have sent you this admonition so that

3360 יָדָע *yādā'*, n.pr.m. [2]

Jada [2]

1Ch 2:28 The sons of Onam: Shammai and **Jada**. The sons of Shammai:
2:32 The sons of **Jada**, Shammai's brother: Jether and Jonathan.

3361 יְדַעְיָה *y^eda'yâ*, n.pr.m. [11] [√ 3359 + 3378]

Jedaiah [9], Jedaiah's [2]

1Ch 9:10 Of the priests: **Jedaiah**; Jehoiarib; Jakin;
24: 7 The first lot fell to Jehoiarib, the second to **Jedaiah**,
Ezr 2:36 the descendants of **Jedaiah** (through the family of Jeshua)
Ne 7:39 the descendants of **Jedaiah** (through the family of Jeshua)
11:10 From the priests: **Jedaiah**; the son of Joiarib; Jakin;
12: 6 Shemaiah, Joiarib, **Jedaiah**,
12: 7 Sallu, Amok, Hilkiah and **Jedaiah**. These were the leaders of the
12:19 of Joiarib's, Mattenai; of **Jedaiah's**, Uzzi;
12:21 of Hilkiah's, Hashabiah; of **Jedaiah's**, Nethanel.
Zec 6:10 Tobijah and **Jedaiah**, who have arrived from Babylon.
6:14 **Jedaiah** and Hen son of Zephaniah as a memorial in the temple of

3362 יִדְּעֹנִי *yidd^e'ōnî*, n.m. [11] [√ 3359]

spiritists [9], spiritist [2]

Lev 19:31 " 'Do not turn to mediums or seek out **spiritists**, for you will be
20: 6 to mediums and **spiritists** to prostitute himself by following them,
20:27 who is a medium or **spiritist** among you must be put to death.
Dt 18:11 or who is a medium or **spiritist** or who consults the dead.
1Sa 28: 3 Saul had expelled the mediums and **spiritists** from the land.
28: 9 has done. He has cut off the mediums and **spiritists** from the land.
2Ki 21: 6 and divination, and consulted mediums and **spiritists**.
23:24 Furthermore, Josiah got rid of the mediums and **spiritists**,
2Ch 33: 6 divination and witchcraft, and consulted mediums and **spiritists**.
Isa 8:19 When men tell you to consult mediums and **spiritists**, who whisper
19: 3 and the spirits of the dead, the mediums and the **spiritists**.

3363 יָהּ *yāh*, n.pr.m. [49] [√ 3378]

the LORD [44], LORD [4], he[s] [1]

Ex 15: 2 **The LORD** is my strength and my song; he has become my
17:16 He said, "For hands were lifted up to the throne of **the LORD**.
Ps 68: 4 [68:5] his name is **the LORD**—and rejoice before him.
68:18 [68:19] that you, O **LORD** God, might dwell there.
77:11 [77:12] I will remember the deeds of **the LORD**; yes, I will
89: 8 [89:9] You are mighty, O **LORD**, and your faithfulness
94: 7 They say, "**The LORD** does not see; the God of Jacob pays no
94:12 man you discipline, O **LORD**, the man you teach from your law;
102:18 [102:19] that a people not yet created may praise **the LORD**:
104:35 be no more. Praise the LORD, O my soul. Praise **the LORD**.
105:45 might keep his precepts and observe his laws. Praise **the LORD**.
106: 1 Praise **the LORD**. Give thanks to the LORD, for he is good;
106:48 to everlasting. Let all the people say, "Amen!" Praise **the LORD**.
111: 1 Praise **the LORD**. I will extol the LORD with all my heart in
112: 1 Praise **the LORD**. Blessed is the man who fears the LORD,
113: 1 Praise **the LORD**. Praise, O servants of the LORD, praise the
113: 9 in her home as a happy mother of children. Praise **the LORD**.
115:17 It is not the dead who praise **the LORD**, those who go down to
115:18 it is we who extol **the LORD**, both now and forevermore.
115:18 extol the LORD, both now and forevermore. Praise **the LORD**.
116:19 of the LORD—in your midst, O Jerusalem. Praise **the LORD**.
117: 2 faithfulness of the LORD endures forever. Praise **the LORD**.
118: 5 In my anguish I cried to **the LORD**, and he answered by setting
118: 5 I cried to the LORD, and **he**[s] answered by setting me free.
118:14 **The LORD** is my strength and my song; he has become my
118:17 will not die but live, and will proclaim what **the LORD** has done.
118:18 **The LORD** has chastened me severely, but he has not given me
118:19 gates of righteousness; I will enter and give thanks to **the LORD**.
122: 4 That is where the tribes go up, the tribes of **the LORD**, to praise
130: 3 If you, O **LORD**, kept a record of sins, O Lord, who could stand?
135: 1 Praise **the LORD**. Praise the name of the LORD; praise him,
135: 3 Praise **the LORD**, for the LORD is good; sing praise to his
135: 4 For **the LORD** has chosen Jacob to be his own, Israel to be his
135:21 from Zion, to him who dwells in Jerusalem. Praise **the LORD**.
146: 1 Praise **the LORD**. Praise the LORD, O my soul.
146:10 your God, O Zion, for all generations. Praise **the LORD**.
147: 1 Praise **the LORD**. How good it is to sing praises to our God,
147:20 for no other nation; they do not know his laws. Praise **the LORD**.
148: 1 Praise **the LORD**. Praise the LORD from the heavens,
148:14 of Israel, the people close to his heart. Praise **the LORD**.
149: 1 Praise **the LORD**. Sing to the LORD a new song, his praise in
149: 9 against them. This is the glory of all his saints. Praise **the LORD**.
150: 1 Praise **the LORD**. Praise God in his sanctuary; praise him in his
150: 6 Let everything that has breath praise **the LORD**.
150: 6 everything that has breath praise the LORD. Praise **the LORD**.
Isa 12: 2 **The LORD**, the LORD, is my strength and my song; he has
26: 4 LORD forever, for **the LORD**, the LORD, is the Rock eternal.
38:11 I said, "I will not again see **the LORD**, the LORD, in the land of
38:11 not again see the LORD, **the LORD**, in the land of the living;

3364 יָהַב *yāhab*, v. Not used in NIV/BHS [cf. 2035; Ar 10314]

3365 יְהָב *y^ehāb*, n.[m.]. [1] [√ 3277?]

cares [1]

Ps 55:22 [55:23] Cast your **cares** on the LORD and he will sustain you;

3366 יָהַד *yāhad*, v.den. [1] [√ 3374; cf. 3373]

became Jews [1]

Est 8:17 [F] many people of other nationalities **became Jews** because fear

3367 יָהְדַי *yāhday*, n.pr.m. [1]

Jahdai [1]

1Ch 2:47 The sons of **Jahdai**: Regem, Jotham, Geshan, Pelet, Ephah

3368 יְהוּדִיָּה *y^ehudiyyâ*, a.g. Not used in NIV/BHS [√ 3373]

3369 יֵהוּא *yēhû'*, n.pr.m. [58] [√ 3378 + 2085]

Jehu [52], he[s] [4], Jehu's [2]

1Ki 16: 1 the word of the LORD came to **Jehu** son of Hanani against
16: 7 the word of the LORD came through the prophet **Jehu** son of
16:12 of the LORD spoken against Baasha through the prophet **Jehu**—
19:16 Also, anoint **Jehu** son of Nimshi king over Israel, and anoint
19:17 **Jehu** will put to death any who escape the sword of Hazael,

1Ki 19:17 and Elisha will put to death any who escape the sword of **Jehu**.
2Ki 9: 2 you get there, look for **Jehu** son of Jehoshaphat, the son of Nimshi.
9: 5 "For which of us?" asked **Jehu**. "For you, commander," he replied.
9:11 When **Jehu** went out to his fellow officers, one of them asked him,
9:13 Then they blew the trumpet and shouted, "**Jehu** is king!"
9:14 So **Jehu** son of Jehoshaphat, the son of Nimshi, conspired against
9:15 **Jehu** said, "If this is the way you feel, don't let anyone slip out of
9:16 **he**[s] got into his chariot and rode to Jezreel, because Joram was
9:17 When the lookout standing on the tower in Jezreel saw **Jehu's**
9:18 **Jehu** replied. "Fall in behind me." The lookout reported, "The
9:19 'Do you come in peace?' " **Jehu** replied, "What do you have to do
9:20 The driving is like that of **Jehu** son of Nimshi—he drives like a
9:21 king of Judah rode out, each in his own chariot, to meet **Jehu**.
9:22 When Joram saw **Jehu** he asked, "Have you come in peace,
9:22 When Joram saw Jehu he asked, "Have you come in peace, **Jehu**?"
9:24 Then **Jehu** drew his bow and shot Joram between the shoulders.
9:27 road to Beth Haggan. **Jehu** chased him, shouting, "Kill him too!"
9:30 **Jehu** went to Jezreel. When Jezebel heard about it, she painted her
9:31 As **Jehu** entered the gate, she asked, "Have you come in peace,
10: 1 So **Jehu** wrote letters and sent them to Samaria: to the officials of
10: 5 the elders and the guardians sent this message to **Jehu**:
10:11 So **Jehu** killed everyone in Jezreel who remained of the house of
10:13 **he**[s] met some relatives of Ahaziah king of Judah and asked,
10:18 Then **Jehu** brought all the people together and said to them,
10:18 said to them, "Ahab served Baal a little; **Jehu** will serve him much.
10:19 **Jehu** was acting deceptively in order to destroy the ministers of
10:20 **Jehu** said, "Call an assembly in honor of Baal." So they
10:21 **he**[s] sent word throughout Israel, and all the ministers of Baal
10:23 **Jehu** and Jehonadab son of Recab went into the temple of Baal.
10:24 Now **Jehu** had posted eighty men outside with this warning:
10:25 As soon as **Jehu** had finished making the burnt offering, he
10:28 So **Jehu** destroyed Baal worship in Israel.
10:29 **he**[s] did not turn away from the sins of Jeroboam son of Nebat,
10:30 The LORD said to **Jehu**, "Because you have done well in
10:31 Yet **Jehu** was not careful to keep the law of the LORD, the God
10:34 As for the other events of **Jehu's** reign, all he did, and all his
10:35 **Jehu** rested with his fathers and was buried in Samaria.
10:36 The time that **Jehu** reigned over Israel in Samaria was
12: 1 [12:2] In the seventh year of **Jehu**, Joash became king, and he
13: 1 Jehoahaz son of **Jehu** became king of Israel in Samaria, and he
14: 8 of Jehoahaz, the son of **Jehu**, king of Israel, with the challenge:
15:12 So the word of the LORD spoken to **Jehu** was fulfilled: "Your
1Ch 2:38 Obed the father of **Jehu**, Jehu the father of Azariah,
2:38 Obed the father of Jehu, **Jehu** the father of Azariah,
4:35 Joel, **Jehu** son of Joshibiah, the son of Seraiah, the son of Asiel,
12: 3 and Pelet the sons of Azmaveth; Beracah, **Jehu** the Anathothite,
2Ch 19: 2 **Jehu** the seer, the son of Hanani, went out to meet him and said to
20:34 beginning to end, are written in the annals of **Jehu** son of Hanani,
22: 7 he went out with Joram to meet **Jehu** son of Nimshi,
22: 8 While **Jehu** was executing judgment on the house of Ahab,
22: 9 He was brought to **Jehu** and put to death. They buried him,
25:17 to Jehoash son of Jehoahaz, the son of **Jehu**, king of Israel:
Hos 1: 4 because I will soon punish the house of **Jehu** for the massacre at

3370 יְהוֹאָחָז *yᵉhô'āḥāz*, n.pr.m. [20] [√ 3378 + 296]

Jehoahaz [18], Ahaziah [2]

2Ki 10:35 buried in Samaria. And **Jehoahaz** his son succeeded him as king.
13: 1 **Jehoahaz** son of Jehu became king of Israel in Samaria, and he
13: 4 **Jehoahaz** sought the LORD's favor, and the LORD listened to
13: 7 Nothing had been left of the army of **Jehoahaz** except fifty
13: 8 As for the other events of the reign of **Jehoahaz**, all he did
13: 9 **Jehoahaz** rested with his fathers and was buried in Samaria.
13:10 Jehoash son of **Jehoahaz** became king of Israel in Samaria,
13:22 king of Aram oppressed Israel throughout the reign of **Jehoahaz**.
13:25 Jehoash son of **Jehoahaz** recaptured from Ben-Hadad son of
13:25 Hazael the towns he had taken in battle from his father **Jehoahaz**.
14: 8 Then Amaziah sent messengers to Jehoash son of **Jehoahaz**,
14:17 years after the death of Jehoash son of **Jehoahaz** king of Israel.
23:30 the people of the land took **Jehoahaz** son of Josiah and anointed
23:31 **Jehoahaz** was twenty-three years old when he became king,
23:34 he took **Jehoahaz** and carried him off to Egypt, and there he died.
2Ch 21:17 Not a son was left to him except **Ahaziah**, the youngest.
25:17 he sent this challenge to Jehoash son of **Jehoahaz**, the son of Jehu,
25:23 of Judah, the son of Joash, the son of **Ahaziah**, at Beth Shemesh.
25:25 years after the death of Jehoash son of **Jehoahaz** king of Israel.
36: 1 the people of the land took **Jehoahaz** son of Josiah and made him

3371 יְהוֹאָשׁ *yᵉhô'āš*, n.pr.m. [17] [√ 3378 + 408]

Jehoash [9], Joash [8]

2Ki 11:21 [12:1] **Joash** was seven years old when he began to reign.
12: 1 [12:2] In the seventh year of Jehu, **Joash** became king, and he
12: 2 [12:3] **Joash** did what was right in the eyes of the LORD all the
12: 4 [12:5] **Joash** said to the priests, "Collect all the money that is
12: 6 [12:7] by the twenty-third year of King **Joash** the priests still had
12: 7 [12:8] Therefore King **Joash** summoned Jehoiada the priest
12:18 [12:19] **Joash** king of Judah took all the sacred objects dedicated
13:10 **Jehoash** son of Jehoahaz became king of Israel in Samaria,
13:25 **Jehoash** son of Jehoahaz recaptured from Ben-Hadad son of
14: 8 Then Amaziah sent messengers to **Jehoash** son of Jehoahaz,
14: 9 But **Jehoash** king of Israel replied to Amaziah king of Judah:
14:11 however, would not listen, so **Jehoash** king of Israel attacked.
14:13 **Jehoash** king of Israel captured Amaziah king of Judah, the son of
14:13 of Judah, the son of **Joash**, the son of Ahaziah, at Beth Shemesh.
14:15 As for the other events of the reign of **Jehoash**, what he did
14:16 **Jehoash** rested with his fathers and was buried in Samaria with the
14:17 years after the death of **Jehoash** son of Jehoahaz king of Israel.

3372 יְהוּד *yᵉhûd*, n.pr.loc. [1]

Jehud [1]

Jos 19:45 **Jehud**, Bene Berak, Gath Rimmon,

3373 יְהוּדָה *yᵉhûdâ*, n.pr.m. & loc. [820 / 817] [→ 3366, 3368, 3374, 3375, 3376, 3377; Ar 10315]

Judah [772], Judah [+1201] [11], Judah's [11], Judah [+824] [6], *untranslated* [4], Judah [+1074] [4], Jews [3], Judean [2], Judah's [+1201] [1], of Judah [+1201] [1], their[s] [+408] [1], they[s] [1]

Ge 29:35 So she named him **Judah**. Then she stopped having children.
35:23 the firstborn of Jacob, Simeon, Levi, **Judah**, Issachar and Zebulun.
37:26 **Judah** said to his brothers, "What will we gain if we kill our
38: 1 **Judah** left his brothers and went down to stay with a man of
38: 2 There **Judah** met the daughter of a Canaanite man named Shua.
38: 6 **Judah** got a wife for Er, his firstborn, and her name was Tamar.
38: 7 But Er, **Judah's** firstborn, was wicked in the LORD's sight;
38: 8 **Judah** said to Onan, "Lie with your brother's wife and fulfill your
38:11 **Judah** then said to his daughter-in-law Tamar, "Live as a widow in
38:12 After a long time **Judah's** wife, the daughter of Shua, died.
38:12 When **Judah** had recovered from his grief, he went up to Timnah,
38:15 When **Judah** saw her, he thought she was a prostitute, for she had
38:20 Meanwhile **Judah** sent the young goat by his friend the Adullamite
38:22 So he went back to **Judah** and said, "I didn't find her. Besides,
38:23 **Judah** said, "Let her keep what she has, or we will become a
38:24 About three months later **Judah** was told, "Your daughter-in-law
38:24 **Judah** said, "Bring her out and have her burned to death!"
38:26 **Judah** recognized them and said, "She is more righteous than I,
43: 3 **Judah** said to him, "The man warned us solemnly, 'You will not
43: 8 Then **Judah** said to Israel his father, "Send the boy along with me
44:14 Joseph was still in the house when **Judah** and his brothers came in,
44:16 "What can we say to my lord?" **Judah** replied. "What can we say?
44:18 **Judah** went up to him and said: "Please, my lord, let your servant
46:12 The sons of **Judah**: Er, Onan, Shelah, Perez and Zerah (but Er
46:28 Now Jacob sent **Judah** ahead of him to Joseph to get directions to
49: 8 "**Judah**, your brothers will praise you; your hand will be on the
49: 9 You are a lion's cub, O **Judah**; you return from the prey, my son.
49:10 The scepter will not depart from **Judah**, nor the ruler's staff from
Ex 1: 2 Reuben, Simeon, Levi and **Judah**;
31: 2 chosen Bezalel son of Uri, the son of Hur, of the tribe of **Judah**,
35:30 chosen Bezalel son of Uri, the son of Hur, of the tribe of **Judah**,
38:22 (Bezalel son of Uri, the son of Hur, of the tribe of **Judah**,
Nu 1: 7 from **Judah**, Nahshon son of Amminadab;
1:26 From the descendants of **Judah**: All the men twenty years old
1:27 The number from the tribe of **Judah** was 74,600.
2: 3 the divisions of the camp of **Judah** are to encamp under their
2: 3 The leader of the people of **Judah** is Nahshon son of Amminadab.
2: 9 All the men assigned to the camp of **Judah**, according to their
7:12 first day was Nahshon son of Amminadab of the tribe of **Judah**.
10:14 The divisions of the camp of **Judah** [+1201] went first, under their
13: 6 from the tribe of **Judah**, Caleb son of Jephunneh;
26:19 Er and Onan were sons of **Judah**, but they died in Canaan.
26:20 The descendants of **Judah** by their clans were: through Shelah,
26:22 These were the clans of **Judah**; those numbered were 76,500.
34:19 are their names: Caleb son of Jephunneh, from the tribe of **Judah**;
Dt 27:12 the people: Simeon, Levi, **Judah**, Issachar, Joseph and Benjamin.
33: 7 And this he said about **Judah**: "Hear, O LORD, the cry of Judah;
33: 7 "Hear, O LORD, the cry of **Judah**; bring him to his people.
34: 2 and Manasseh, all the land of **Judah** as far as the western sea,
Jos 7: 1 the son of Zimri, the son of Zerah, of the tribe of **Judah**, took some
7:16 Joshua had Israel come forward by tribes, and **Judah** was taken.
7:17 The clans of **Judah** came forward, and he took the Zerahites.
7:18 son of Zimri, the son of Zerah, of the tribe of **Judah**, was taken.
11:21 from Hebron, Debir and Anab, from all the hill country of **Judah**,
14: 6 Now the men of **Judah** approached Joshua at Gilgal, and Caleb
15: 1 The allotment for the tribe of **Judah** [+1201], clan by clan,
15:12 These are the boundaries around the people of **Judah** by their
15:13 gave to Caleb son of Jephunneh a portion in **Judah** [+1201]—

Jos 15:20 This is the inheritance of the tribe of **Judah** [+1201], clan by clan:
15:21 The southernmost towns of the tribe of **Judah** [+1201] in the
15:63 **Judah** [+1201] could not dislodge the Jebusites, who were living
15:63 to this day the Jebusites live there with the people of **Judah**.
18: 5 **Judah** is to remain in its territory on the south and the house of
18:11 Their allotted territory lay between the tribes of **Judah** and Joseph:
18:14 Baal (that is, Kiriath Jearim), a town of the people of **Judah**.
19: 1 Their inheritance lay within the territory of **Judah** [+1201].
19: 9 of the Simeonites was taken from the share of **Judah** [+1201],
19: 9 because **Judah's** [+1201] portion was more than they needed.
19:34 Asher on the west and [BHS+ ***Judah***] the Jordan on the east.
20: 7 and Kiriath Arba (that is, Hebron) in the hill country of **Judah**.
21: 4 the priest were allotted thirteen towns from the tribes of **Judah**,
21: 9 From the tribes of **Judah** [+1201] and Simeon they allotted the
21:11 with its surrounding pastureland, in the hill country of **Judah**.
Jdg 1: 2 The LORD answered, "**Judah** is to go; I have given the land into
1: 3 Then the men of **Judah** said to the Simeonites their brothers,
1: 4 When **Judah** attacked, the LORD gave the Canaanites
1: 8 The men of **Judah** attacked Jerusalem also and took it. They put
1: 9 the men of **Judah** went down to fight against the Canaanites living
1:10 **They**[s] advanced against the Canaanites living in Hebron (formerly
1:16 went up from the City of Palms with the men of **Judah** to live
1:16 among the people of the Desert of **Judah** in the Negev near Arad.
1:17 Then the men of **Judah** went with the Simeonites their brothers
1:18 The men of **Judah** also took Gaza, Ashkelon and Ekron—
1:19 The LORD was with the men of **Judah**. They took possession of
10: 9 The Ammonites also crossed the Jordan to fight against **Judah**,
15: 9 The Philistines went up and camped in **Judah**, spreading out near
15:10 The men of **Judah** asked, "Why have you come to fight us?"
15:11 three thousand men from **Judah** went down to the cave in the rock
17: 7 A young Levite from Bethlehem in **Judah**, who had been living
17: 7 Bethlehem in Judah, who had been living within the clan of **Judah**,
17: 8 left that town **[RPH]** in search of some other place to stay.
17: 9 "I'm a Levite from Bethlehem in **Judah**," he said, "and I'm
18:12 On their way they set up camp near Kiriath Jearim in **Judah**.
19: 1 country of Ephraim took a concubine from Bethlehem in **Judah**.
19: 2 and went back to her father's house in Bethlehem, **Judah**.
19:18 "We are on our way from Bethlehem in **Judah** to a remote area in
19:18 I have been to Bethlehem in **Judah** and now I am going to the
20:18 the Benjamites?" The LORD replied, "**Judah** shall go first."
Ru 1: 1 and a man from Bethlehem in **Judah**, together with his wife
1: 2 and Kilion. They were Ephrathites from Bethlehem, **Judah**.
1: 7 set out on the road that would take them back to the land of **Judah**.
4:12 your family be like that of Perez, whom Tamar bore to **Judah**."
1Sa 11: 8 three hundred thousand and the men of **Judah** thirty thousand.
15: 4 hundred thousand foot soldiers and ten thousand men from **Judah**.
17: 1 gathered their forces for war and assembled at Socoh in **Judah**.
17:12 of an Ephrathite named Jesse, who was from Bethlehem in **Judah**.
17:52 Then the men of Israel and **Judah** surged forward with a shout
18:16 all Israel and **Judah** loved David, because he led them in their
22: 5 Go into the land of **Judah**." So David left and went to the forest of
23: 3 But David's men said to him, "Here in **Judah** we are afraid.
23:23 is in the area, I will track him down among all the clans of **Judah**."
27: 6 him Ziklag, and it has belonged to the kings of **Judah** ever since.
27:10 "Against the Negev of **Judah**" or "Against the Negev of
30:14 and the territory belonging to **Judah** and the Negev of Caleb.
30:16 they had taken from the land of the Philistines and from **Judah**.
30:26 he sent some of the plunder to the elders of **Judah**, who were his
2Sa 1:18 ordered that the men of **Judah** be taught this lament of the bow (it
2: 1 "Shall I go up to one of the towns of **Judah**?" he asked. The
2: 4 the men of **Judah** came to Hebron and there they anointed David
2: 4 and there they anointed David king over the house of **Judah**.
2: 7 and the house of **Judah** has anointed me king over them."
2:10 reigned two years. The house of **Judah**, however, followed David.
2:11 was king in Hebron over the house of **Judah** was seven years
3: 8 and he answered, "Am I a dog's head—on **Judah's** side?
3:10 David's throne over Israel and **Judah** from Dan to Beersheba."
5: 5 In Hebron he reigned over **Judah** seven years and six months,
5: 5 Jerusalem he reigned over all Israel and **Judah** thirty-three years.
6: 2 all his men set out from Baalah of **Judah** to bring up from there
11:11 "The ark and Israel and **Judah** are staying in tents, and my master
12: 8 I gave you the house of Israel and **Judah**. And if all this had been
19:11 [19:12] "Ask the elders of **Judah**, 'Why should you be the last to
19:14 [19:15] He won over the hearts of all the men of **Judah** as though
19:15 [19:16] Now the men of **Judah** had come to Gilgal to go out
19:16 [19:17] hurried down with the men of **Judah** to meet King David.
19:40 [19:41] All the troops of **Judah** and half the troops of Israel had
19:41 [19:42] the men of **Judah**, steal the king away and bring him
19:42 [19:43] All the men of **Judah** answered the men of Israel,
19:43 [19:44] the men of Israel answered the men of **Judah**, "We have
19:43 [19:44] the men of **Judah** responded even more harshly than the
20: 2 the men of **Judah** stayed by their king all the way from the Jordan
20: 4 "Summon the men of **Judah** to come to me within three days,
20: 5 when Amasa went to summon **Judah**, he took longer than the time
21: 2 Saul in his zeal for Israel and **Judah** had tried to annihilate them.)
24: 1 against them, saying, "Go and take a census of Israel and **Judah**."
24: 7 Finally, they went on to Beersheba in the Negev of **Judah**.
24: 9 who could handle a sword, and in **Judah** five hundred thousand.
1Ki 1: 9 the king's sons, and all the men of **Judah** who were royal officials,
1:35 in my place. I have appointed him ruler over Israel and **Judah**."
2:32 and Amasa son of Jether, commander of **Judah's** army—
4:20 The people of **Judah** and Israel were as numerous as the sand on
4:25 [5:5] During Solomon's lifetime **Judah** and Israel, from Dan to
12:17 But as for the Israelites who were living in the towns of **Judah**,
12:20 Only the tribe of **Judah** remained loyal to the house of David.
12:21 he mustered the whole house of **Judah** and the tribe of Benjamin—
12:23 "Say to Rehoboam son of Solomon king of **Judah**, to the whole
12:23 to the whole house of **Judah** and Benjamin, and to the rest of the
12:27 again give their allegiance to their lord, Rehoboam king of **Judah**.
12:27 They will kill me and return to King Rehoboam." **[RPH]**
12:32 like the festival held in **Judah**, and offered sacrifices on the altar.
13: 1 By the word of the LORD a man of God came from **Judah** to
13:12 his sons showed him which road the man of God from **Judah** had
13:14 and asked, "Are you the man of God who came from **Judah**?"
13:21 He cried out to the man of God who had come from **Judah**,
14:21 Rehoboam son of Solomon was king in **Judah**. He was forty-one
14:22 **Judah** did evil in the eyes of the LORD. By the sins they
14:29 they not written in the book of the annals of the kings of **Judah**?
15: 1 the reign of Jeroboam son of Nebat, Abijah became king of **Judah**,
15: 7 they not written in the book of the annals of the kings of **Judah**?
15: 9 year of Jeroboam king of Israel, Asa became king of **Judah**,
15:17 Baasha king of Israel went up against **Judah** and fortified Ramah
15:17 from leaving or entering the territory of Asa king of **Judah**.
15:22 King Asa issued an order to all **Judah**—no one was exempt—
15:23 they not written in the book of the annals of the kings of **Judah**?
15:25 became king of Israel in the second year of Asa king of **Judah**,
15:28 Baasha killed Nadab in the third year of Asa king of **Judah**
15:33 In the third year of Asa king of **Judah**, Baasha son of Ahijah
16: 8 In the twenty-sixth year of Asa king of **Judah**, Elah son of Baasha
16:10 and killed him in the twenty-seventh year of Asa king of **Judah**.
16:15 In the twenty-seventh year of Asa king of **Judah**, Zimri reigned in
16:23 In the thirty-first year of Asa king of **Judah**, Omri became king of
16:29 In the thirty-eighth year of Asa king of **Judah**, Ahab son of Omri
19: 3 When he came to Beersheba in **Judah**, he left his servant there,
22: 2 in the third year Jehoshaphat king of **Judah** went down to see the
22:10 Jehoshaphat king of **Judah** were sitting on their thrones at the
22:29 and Jehoshaphat king of **Judah** went up to Ramoth Gilead.
22:41 Jehoshaphat son of Asa became king of **Judah** in the fourth year of
22:45 [22:46] written in the book of the annals of the kings of **Judah**?
22:51 [22:52] in the seventeenth year of Jehoshaphat king of **Judah**,
2Ki 1:17 in the second year of Jehoram son of Jehoshaphat king of **Judah**.
3: 1 in Samaria in the eighteenth year of Jehoshaphat king of **Judah**,
3: 7 He also sent this message to Jehoshaphat king of **Judah**: "The king
3: 9 So the king of Israel set out with the king of **Judah** and the king of
3:14 not have respect for the presence of Jehoshaphat king of **Judah**,
8:16 son of Ahab king of Israel, when Jehoshaphat was king of **Judah**,
8:16 Jehoram son of Jehoshaphat began his reign as king of **Judah**.
8:19 his servant David, the LORD was not willing to destroy **Judah**.
8:20 of Jehoram, Edom rebelled against **Judah** and set up its own king.
8:22 To this day Edom has been in rebellion against **Judah**. Libnah
8:23 they not written in the book of the annals of the kings of **Judah**?
8:25 of Israel, Ahaziah son of Jehoram king of **Judah** began to reign.
8:29 Ahaziah son of Jehoram king of **Judah** went down to Jezreel to see
9:16 and Ahaziah king of **Judah** had gone down to see him.
9:21 Joram king of Israel and Ahaziah king of **Judah** rode out,
9:27 When Ahaziah king of **Judah** saw what had happened, he fled up
9:29 year of Joram son of Ahab, Ahaziah had become king of **Judah**.)
10:13 he met some relatives of Ahaziah king of **Judah** and asked,
12:18 [12:19] Joash king of **Judah** took all the sacred objects dedicated
12:18 [12:19] Jehoshaphat, Jehoram and Ahaziah, the kings of **Judah**—
12:19 [12:20] written in the book of the annals of the kings of **Judah**?
13: 1 In the twenty-third year of Joash son of Ahaziah king of **Judah**,
13:10 In the thirty-seventh year of Joash king of **Judah**, Jehoash son of
13:12 including his war against Amaziah king of **Judah**,
14: 1 king of Israel, Amaziah son of Joash king of **Judah** began to reign.
14: 9 But Jehoash king of Israel replied to Amaziah king of **Judah**:
14:10 for trouble and cause your own downfall and that of **Judah** also?"
14:11 Amaziah king of **Judah** faced each other at Beth Shemesh in
14:11 king of Judah faced each other at Beth Shemesh in **Judah**.
14:12 **Judah** was routed by Israel, and every man fled to his home.
14:13 Jehoash king of Israel captured Amaziah king of **Judah**, the son of
14:15 including his war against Amaziah king of **Judah**,
14:17 Amaziah son of Joash king of **Judah** lived for fifteen years after
14:18 they not written in the book of the annals of the kings of **Judah**?
14:21 all the people of **Judah** took Azariah, who was sixteen years old,
14:22 and restored it to **Judah** after Amaziah rested with his fathers.
14:23 In the fifteenth year of Amaziah son of Joash king of **Judah**,
14:28 which had belonged to Yaudi, [BHS *Judah*; NIV 3375]

2Ki 15: 1 of Israel, Azariah son of Amaziah king of **Judah** began to reign.
15: 6 they not written in the book of the annals of the kings of **Judah**?
15: 8 In the thirty-eighth year of Azariah king of **Judah**, Zechariah son
15: 13 became king in the thirty-ninth year of Uzziah king of **Judah**,
15: 17 In the thirty-ninth year of Azariah king of **Judah**, Menahem son of
15: 23 In the fiftieth year of Azariah king of **Judah**, Pekahiah son of
15: 27 In the fifty-second year of Azariah king of **Judah**, Pekah son of
15: 32 king of Israel, Jotham son of Uzziah king of **Judah** began to reign.
15: 36 they not written in the book of the annals of the kings of **Judah**?
15: 37 Rezin king of Aram and Pekah son of Remaliah against **Judah**.)
16: 1 of Remaliah, Ahaz son of Jotham king of **Judah** began to reign.
16: 19 they not written in the book of the annals of the kings of **Judah**?
17: 1 In the twelfth year of Ahaz king of **Judah**, Hoshea son of Elah
17: 13 warned Israel and **Judah** through all his prophets and seers:
17: 18 removed them from his presence. Only the tribe of **Judah** was left,
17: 19 even **Judah** did not keep the commands of the LORD their God.
18: 1 king of Israel, Hezekiah son of Ahaz king of **Judah** began to reign.
18: 5 There was no one like him among all the kings of **Judah**,
18: 13 king of Assyria attacked all the fortified cities of **Judah**
18: 14 So Hezekiah king of **Judah** sent this message to the king of
18: 14 The king of Assyria exacted from Hezekiah king of **Judah** three
18: 16 At this time Hezekiah king of **Judah** stripped off the gold with
18: 22 and altars Hezekiah removed, saying to **Judah** and Jerusalem,
19: 10 "Say to Hezekiah king of **Judah**: Do not let the god you depend on
19: 30 Once more a remnant of the house of **Judah** will take root below
20: 20 they not written in the book of the annals of the kings of **Judah**?
21: 11 "Manasseh king of **Judah** has committed these detestable sins.
21: 11 who preceded him and has led **Judah** into sin with his idols.
21: 12 and **Judah** that the ears of everyone who hears of it will tingle.
21: 16 besides the sin that he had caused **Judah** to commit, so that they
21: 17 they not written in the book of the annals of the kings of **Judah**?
21: 25 they not written in the book of the annals of the kings of **Judah**?
22: 13 for all **Judah** about what is written in this book that has been
22: 16 according to everything written in the book the king of **Judah** has
22: 18 Tell the king of **Judah**, who sent you to inquire of the LORD,
23: 1 the king called together all the elders of **Judah** and Jerusalem.
23: 2 He went up to the temple of the LORD with the men of **Judah**,
23: 5 of **Judah** to burn incense on the high places of the towns of Judah
23: 5 of Judah to burn incense on the high places of the towns of **Judah**
23: 8 Josiah brought all the priests from the towns of **Judah**
23: 11 the horses that the kings of **Judah** had dedicated to the sun.
23: 12 He pulled down the altars the kings of **Judah** had erected on the
23: 17 "It marks the tomb of the man of God who came from **Judah**
23: 22 throughout the days of the kings of Israel and the kings of **Judah**,
23: 24 the idols and all the other detestable things seen in **Judah** [+824]
23: 26 which burned against **Judah** because of all that Manasseh had
23: 27 "I will remove **Judah** also from my presence as I removed Israel,
23: 28 they not written in the book of the annals of the kings of **Judah**?
24: 2 He sent them to destroy **Judah**, in accordance with the word of the
24: 3 Surely these things happened to **Judah** according to the LORD's
24: 5 they not written in the book of the annals of the kings of **Judah**?
24: 12 Jehoiachin king of **Judah**, his mother, his attendants, his nobles
24: 20 the LORD's anger that all this happened to Jerusalem and **Judah**,
25: 21 them executed. So **Judah** went into captivity, away from her land.
25: 22 to be over the people he had left behind in **Judah** [+824].
25: 27 In the thirty-seventh year of the exile of Jehoiachin king of **Judah**,
25: 27 he released Jehoiachin **[RPH]** from prison on the twenty-seventh
1Ch 2: 1 sons of Israel: Reuben, Simeon, Levi, **Judah**, Issachar, Zebulun,
2: 3 The sons of **Judah**: Er, Onan and Shelah. These three were born to
2: 3 Er, **Judah's** firstborn, was wicked in the LORD's sight;
2: 4 bore him Perez and Zerah. **Judah** had five sons in all.
2: 10 the father of Nahshon, the leader of the people of **Judah**.
4: 1 The descendants of **Judah**: Perez, Hezron, Carmi, Hur and Shobal.
4: 21 The sons of Shelah son of **Judah**: Er the father of Lecah, Laadah
4: 27 entire clan did not become as numerous as the people of **Judah**.
4: 41 names were listed came in the days of Hezekiah king of **Judah**.
5: 2 though **Judah** was the strongest of his brothers and a ruler came
5: 17 the genealogical records during the reigns of Jotham king of **Judah**
6: 15 [5:41] Jehozadak was deported when the LORD sent **Judah**
6: 55 [6:40] They were given Hebron in **Judah** [+824] with its
6: 65 [6:50] From the tribes of **Judah** [+1201], Simeon and Benjamin
9: 1 The people of **Judah** were taken captive to Babylon because of
9: 3 Those from **Judah** [+1201], from Benjamin, and from Ephraim
9: 4 son of Imri, the son of Bani, a descendant of Perez son of **Judah**.
12: 16 [12:17] some men from **Judah** also came to David in his
12: 24 [12:25] men of **Judah**, carrying shield and spear—6,800 armed
13: 6 all the Israelites with him went to Baalah of **Judah** (Kiriath
21: 5 a sword, including four hundred and seventy thousand in **Judah**.
27: 18 over **Judah**: Elihu, a brother of David; over Issachar: Omri son of
28: 4 He chose **Judah** as leader, and from the house of Judah he chose
28: 4 Judah as leader, and from the house of **Judah** he chose my family,
2Ch 2: 7 [2:6] to work in **Judah** and Jerusalem with my skilled craftsmen,
9: 11 Nothing like them had ever been seen in **Judah** [+824].)
10: 17 But as for the Israelites who were living in the towns of **Judah**,
11: 1 in Jerusalem, he mustered the house of **Judah** and Benjamin—
11: 3 "Say to Rehoboam son of Solomon king of **Judah** and to all the
11: 3 king of Judah and to all the Israelites in **Judah** and Benjamin,
11: 5 lived in Jerusalem and built up towns for defense in **Judah**:
11: 10 and Hebron. These were fortified cities in **Judah** and Benjamin.
11: 12 and made them very strong. So **Judah** and Benjamin were his.
11: 14 came to **Judah** and Jerusalem because Jeroboam and his sons had
11: 17 They strengthened the kingdom of **Judah** and supported
11: 23 dispersing some of his sons throughout the districts of **Judah**
12: 4 he captured the fortified cities of **Judah** and came as far as
12: 5 to the leaders of **Judah** who had assembled in Jerusalem for fear of
12: 12 was not totally destroyed. Indeed, there was some good in **Judah**.
13: 1 year of the reign of Jeroboam, Abijah became king of **Judah**,
13: 13 so that while he was in front of **Judah** the ambush was behind
13: 14 **Judah** turned and saw that they were being attacked at both front
13: 15 the men of **Judah** raised the battle cry. At the sound of their battle
13: 15 At the sound of **their**[s] [+408] battle cry, God routed Jeroboam
13: 15 God routed Jeroboam and all Israel before Abijah and **Judah**.
13: 16 The Israelites fled before **Judah**, and God delivered them into their
13: 18 the men of **Judah** were victorious because they relied on the
14: 4 [14:3] He commanded **Judah** to seek the LORD, the God of
14: 5 [14:4] the high places and incense altars in every town in **Judah**,
14: 6 [14:5] He built up the fortified cities of **Judah**, since the land was
14: 7 [14:6] he said to **Judah**, "and put walls around them, with towers,
14: 8 [14:7] had an army of three hundred thousand men from **Judah**,
14: 12 [14:11] LORD struck down the Cushites before Asa and **Judah**.
15: 2 and said to him, "Listen to me, Asa and all **Judah** and Benjamin.
15: 8 He removed the detestable idols from the whole land of **Judah**
15: 9 he assembled all **Judah** and Benjamin and the people from
15: 15 All **Judah** rejoiced about the oath because they had sworn it
16: 1 year of Asa's reign Baasha king of Israel went up against **Judah**
16: 1 from leaving or entering the territory of Asa king of **Judah**.
16: 6 King Asa brought all the men of **Judah**, and they carried away
16: 7 At that time Hanani the seer came to Asa king of **Judah** and said
16: 11 to end, are written in the book of the kings of **Judah** and Israel.
17: 2 He stationed troops in all the fortified cities of **Judah** and put
17: 2 all the fortified cities of Judah and put garrisons in **Judah** [+824]
17: 5 all **Judah** brought gifts to Jehoshaphat, so that he had great wealth
17: 6 he removed the high places and the Asherah poles from **Judah**.
17: 7 Zechariah, Nethanel and Micaiah to teach in the towns of **Judah**.
17: 9 They taught throughout **Judah**, taking with them the Book of the
17: 9 they went around to all the towns of **Judah** and taught the people.
17: 10 LORD fell on all the kingdoms of the lands surrounding **Judah**,
17: 12 and more powerful; he built forts and store cities in **Judah**
17: 13 had large supplies in the towns of **Judah**. He also kept experienced
17: 14 From **Judah**, commanders of units of 1,000:
17: 19 besides those he stationed in the fortified cities throughout **Judah**.
18: 3 Ahab king of Israel asked Jehoshaphat king of **Judah**, "Will you
18: 9 Jehoshaphat king of **Judah** were sitting on their thrones at the
18: 28 and Jehoshaphat king of **Judah** went up to Ramoth Gilead.
19: 1 When Jehoshaphat king of **Judah** returned safely to his palace in
19: 5 judges in the land, in each of the fortified cities of **Judah**.
19: 11 and Zebadiah son of Ishmael, the leader of the tribe of **Judah**,
20: 3 to inquire of the LORD, and he proclaimed a fast for all **Judah**.
20: 4 The people of **Judah** came together to seek help from the LORD;
20: 4 indeed, they came from every town in **Judah** to seek him.
20: 5 Jehoshaphat stood up in the assembly of **Judah** and Jerusalem at
20: 13 All the men of **Judah**, with their wives and children and little ones,
20: 15 King Jehoshaphat and all who live in **Judah** and Jerusalem!
20: 17 the deliverance the LORD will give you, O **Judah** and Jerusalem.
20: 18 all the people of **Judah** and Jerusalem fell down in worship before
20: 20 and said, "Listen to me, **Judah** and people of Jerusalem!
20: 22 of Ammon and Moab and Mount Seir who were invading **Judah**,
20: 24 When the men of **Judah** came to the place that overlooks the
20: 27 all the men of **Judah** and Jerusalem returned joyfully to Jerusalem,
20: 31 So Jehoshaphat reigned over **Judah**. He was thirty-five years old
20: 35 Jehoshaphat king of **Judah** made an alliance with Ahaziah king of
21: 3 and gold and articles of value, as well as fortified cities in **Judah**,
21: 8 of Jehoram, Edom rebelled against **Judah** and set up its own king.
21: 10 To this day Edom has been in rebellion against **Judah**. Libnah
21: 11 He had also built high places on the hills of **Judah** and had caused
21: 11 of Jerusalem to prostitute themselves and had led **Judah** astray.
21: 12 in the ways of your father Jehoshaphat or of Asa king of **Judah**.
21: 13 you have led **Judah** and the people of Jerusalem to prostitute
21: 17 They attacked **Judah**, invaded it and carried off all the goods
22: 1 So Ahaziah son of Jehoram king of **Judah** began to reign.
22: 6 Ahaziah son of Jehoram king of **Judah** went down to Jezreel to see
22: 8 he found the princes of **Judah** and the sons of Ahaziah's relatives,
22: 10 to destroy the whole royal family of the house of **Judah**.
23: 2 They went throughout **Judah** and gathered the Levites
23: 2 families from all the towns. **[RPH]** When they came to Jerusalem,
23: 8 and all the men of **Judah** did just as Jehoiada the priest ordered.
24: 5 "Go to the towns of **Judah** and collect the money due annually
24: 6 "Why haven't you required the Levites to bring in from **Judah**

2Ch 24: 9 A proclamation was then issued in **Judah** and Jerusalem that they
24: 17 the officials of **Judah** came and paid homage to the king, and he
24: 18 of their guilt, God's anger came upon **Judah** and Jerusalem.
24: 23 it invaded **Judah** and Jerusalem and killed all the leaders of the
25: 5 Amaziah called the people of **Judah** together and assigned them
25: 5 and commanders of hundreds for all **Judah** and Benjamin.
25: 10 They were furious with **Judah** and left for home in a great rage.
25: 12 The army of **Judah** also captured ten thousand men alive,
25: 13 had not allowed to take part in the war raided **Judean** towns from
25: 17 After Amaziah king of **Judah** consulted his advisers, he sent this
25: 18 But Jehoash king of Israel replied to Amaziah king of **Judah**:
25: 19 for trouble and cause your own downfall and that of **Judah** also?"
25: 21 Amaziah king of **Judah** faced each other at Beth Shemesh in
25: 21 king of Judah faced each other at Beth Shemesh in **Judah**.
25: 22 **Judah** was routed by Israel, and every man fled to his home.
25: 23 Jehoash king of Israel captured Amaziah king of **Judah**, the son of
25: 25 Amaziah son of Joash king of **Judah** lived for fifteen years after
25: 26 are they not written in the book of the kings of **Judah** and Israel?
25: 28 back by horse and was buried with his fathers in the City of **Judah**.
26: 1 all the people of **Judah** took Uzziah, who was sixteen years old,
26: 2 and restored it to **Judah** after Amaziah rested with his fathers.
27: 4 He built towns in the **Judean** hills and forts and towers in the
27: 7 he did, are written in the book of the kings of Israel and **Judah**.
28: 6 killed a hundred and twenty thousand soldiers in **Judah**—
28: 9 the LORD, the God of your fathers, was angry with **Judah**,
28: 10 and women **of Judah** [+1201] and Jerusalem your slaves.
28: 17 had again come and attacked **Judah** and carried away prisoners,
28: 18 had raided towns in the foothills and in the Negev of **Judah**.
28: 19 The LORD had humbled **Judah** because of Ahaz king of Israel,
28: 19 for he had promoted wickedness in **Judah** and had been most
28: 25 In every town in **Judah** he built high places to burn sacrifices to
28: 26 to end, are written in the book of the kings of **Judah** and Israel.
29: 8 the anger of the LORD has fallen on **Judah** and Jerusalem;
29: 21 as a sin offering for the kingdom, for the sanctuary and for **Judah**.
30: 1 Hezekiah sent word to all Israel and **Judah** and also wrote letters
30: 6 and **Judah** with letters from the king and from his officials,
30: 12 Also in **Judah** the hand of God was on the people to give them
30: 24 Hezekiah king of **Judah** provided a thousand bulls and seven
30: 25 The entire assembly of **Judah** rejoiced, along with the priests
30: 25 the aliens who had come from Israel and those who lived in **Judah**.
31: 1 the Israelites who were there went out to the towns of **Judah**,
31: 1 and the altars throughout **Judah** and Benjamin and in Ephraim
31: 6 **Judah** who lived in the towns of Judah also brought a tithe of their
31: 6 Judah who lived in the towns of **Judah** also brought a tithe of their
31: 20 This is what Hezekiah did throughout **Judah**, doing what was good
32: 1 Sennacherib king of Assyria came and invaded **Judah**.
32: 8 gained confidence from what Hezekiah the king of **Judah** said.
32: 9 to Jerusalem with this message for Hezekiah king of **Judah**
32: 9 king of Judah and for all the people of **Judah** who were there:
32: 12 this god's high places and altars, saying to **Judah** and Jerusalem,
32: 23 for the LORD and valuable gifts for Hezekiah king of **Judah**.
32: 25 the LORD's wrath was on him and on **Judah** and Jerusalem.
32: 32 the prophet Isaiah son of Amoz in the book of the kings of **Judah**
32: 33 All **Judah** and the people of Jerusalem honored him when he died.
33: 9 But Manasseh led **Judah** and the people of Jerusalem astray,
33: 14 stationed military commanders in all the fortified cities in **Judah**.
33: 16 on it, and told **Judah** to serve the LORD, the God of Israel.
34: 3 In his twelfth year he began to purge **Judah** and Jerusalem of high
34: 5 the priests on their altars, and so he purged **Judah** and Jerusalem.
34: 9 remnant of Israel and from all the people of **Judah** and Benjamin
34: 11 beams for the buildings that the kings of **Judah** had allowed to fall
34: 21 and **Judah** about what is written in this book that has been found.
34: 24 in the book that has been read in the presence of the king of **Judah**.
34: 26 Tell the king of **Judah**, who sent you to inquire of the LORD,
34: 29 the king called together all the elders of **Judah** and Jerusalem.
34: 30 He went up to the temple of the LORD with the men of **Judah**,
35: 18 the Levites and all **Judah** and Israel who were there with the
35: 21 "What quarrel is there between you and me, O king of **Judah**?
35: 24 of his fathers, and all **Judah** and Jerusalem mourned for him.
35: 27 to end, are written in the book of the kings of Israel and **Judah**.
36: 4 king over **Judah** and Jerusalem and changed Eliakim's name to
36: 8 are written in the book of the kings of Israel and **Judah**.
36: 10 Jehoiachin's uncle, Zedekiah, king over **Judah** and Jerusalem.
36: 23 has appointed me to build a temple for him at Jerusalem in **Judah**.
Ezr 1: 2 has appointed me to build a temple for him at Jerusalem in **Judah**.
1: 3 let him go up to Jerusalem in **Judah** and build the temple of the
1: 5 Then the family heads of **Judah** and Benjamin, and the priests
1: 8 who counted them out to Sheshbazzar the prince of **Judah**.
2: 1 taken captive to Babylon (they returned to Jerusalem and **Judah**,
3: 9 and his sons (descendants of Hodaviah) [BHS ***Yehudah***; NIV 2088]
4: 1 When the enemies of **Judah** and Benjamin heard that the exiles
4: 4 the peoples around them set out to discourage the people of **Judah**
4: 6 they lodged an accusation against the people of **Judah**
9: 9 and he has given us a wall of protection in **Judah** and Jerusalem.
10: 7 A proclamation was then issued throughout **Judah** and Jerusalem
10: 9 all the men of **Judah** and Benjamin had gathered in Jerusalem.
10: 23 Shimei, Kelaiah (that is, Kelita), Pethahiah, **Judah** and Eliezer.
Ne 1: 2 one of my brothers, came from **Judah** with some other men,
2: 5 let him send me to the city in **Judah** where my fathers are buried
2: 7 so that they will provide me safe-conduct until I arrive in **Judah**?
4: 10 [4:4] Meanwhile, the people in **Judah** said, "The strength of the
4: 16 [4:10] officers posted themselves behind all the people of **Judah**
5: 14 when I was appointed to be their governor in the land of **Judah**,
6: 7 'There is a king in **Judah**!' Now this report will get back to the
6: 17 in those days the nobles of **Judah** were sending many letters to
6: 18 For many in **Judah** were under oath to him, since he was
7: 6 Babylon had taken captive (they returned to Jerusalem and **Judah**,
11: 3 descendants of Solomon's servants lived in the towns of **Judah**,
11: 4 while other people from both **Judah** and Benjamin lived in
11: 4 From the descendants of **Judah**: Athaiah son of Uzziah, the son of
11: 9 **Judah** son of Hassenuah was over the Second District of the city.
11: 20 with the priests and Levites, were in all the towns of **Judah**,
11: 24 son of Meshezabel, one of the descendants of Zerah son of **Judah**,
11: 25 some of the people of **Judah** lived in Kiriath Arba and its
11: 36 Some of the divisions of the Levites of **Judah** settled in Benjamin.
12: 8 Binnui, Kadmiel, Sherebiah, **Judah**, and also Mattaniah, who,
12: 31 I had the leaders of **Judah** go up on top of the wall. I also assigned
12: 32 Hoshaiah and half the leaders of **Judah** followed them,
12: 34 **Judah**, Benjamin, Shemaiah, Jeremiah,
12: 36 Azarel, Milalai, Gilalai, Maai, Nethanel, **Judah** and Hanani—
12: 44 for **Judah** was pleased with the ministering priests and Levites.
13: 12 All **Judah** brought the tithes of grain, new wine and oil into the
13: 15 In those days I saw men in **Judah** treading winepresses on the
13: 16 selling them in Jerusalem on the Sabbath to the people of **Judah**.
13: 17 I rebuked the nobles of **Judah** and said to them, "What is this
Est 2: 6 among those taken captive with Jehoiachin king of **Judah**.
Ps 48: 11 [48:12] the villages of **Judah** are glad because of your judgments.
60: 7 [60:9] is mine; Ephraim is my helmet, **Judah** my scepter.
63: T [63:1] A psalm of David. When he was in the Desert of **Judah**.
68: 27 [68:28] leading them, there the great throng of **Judah's** princes,
69: 35 [69:36] for God will save Zion and rebuild the cities of **Judah**.
76: 1 [76:2] In **Judah** God is known; his name is great in Israel.
78: 68 but he chose the tribe of **Judah**, Mount Zion, which he loved.
97: 8 Zion hears and rejoices and the villages of **Judah** are glad
108: 8 [108:9] is mine; Ephraim is my helmet, **Judah** my scepter.
114: 2 **Judah** became God's sanctuary, Israel his dominion.
Pr 25: 1 of Solomon, copied by the men of Hezekiah king of **Judah**:
Isa 1: 1 The vision concerning **Judah** and Jerusalem that Isaiah son of
1: 1 the reigns of Uzziah, Jotham, Ahaz and Hezekiah, kings of **Judah**.
2: 1 This is what Isaiah son of Amoz saw concerning **Judah**
3: 1 about to take from Jerusalem and **Judah** both supply and support:
3: 8 Jerusalem staggers, **Judah** is falling; their words and deeds are
5: 3 "Now you dwellers in Jerusalem and men of **Judah**, judge between
5: 7 house of Israel, and the men of **Judah** are the garden of his delight.
7: 1 the son of Uzziah, was king of **Judah**, King Rezin of Aram
7: 6 "Let us invade **Judah**; let us tear it apart and divide it among
7: 17 father a time unlike any since Ephraim broke away from **Judah**—
8: 8 and sweep on into **Judah**, swirling over it, passing through it
9: 21 [9:20] on Manasseh; together they will turn against **Judah**.
11: 12 he will assemble the scattered people of **Judah** from the four
11: 13 jealousy will vanish, and **Judah's** enemies will be cut off;
11: 13 Ephraim will not be jealous of **Judah**, nor Judah hostile toward
11: 13 will not be jealous of Judah, nor **Judah** hostile toward Ephraim.
19: 17 the land of **Judah** will bring terror to the Egyptians; everyone to
22: 8 the defenses of **Judah** are stripped away. And you looked in that
22: 21 a father to those who live in Jerusalem and to the house of **Judah**.
26: 1 In that day this song will be sung in the land of **Judah**: We have a
36: 1 king of Assyria attacked all the fortified cities of **Judah**
36: 7 and altars Hezekiah removed, saying to **Judah** and Jerusalem,
37: 10 "Say to Hezekiah king of **Judah**: Do not let the god you depend on
37: 31 Once more a remnant of the house of **Judah** will take root below
38: 9 A writing of Hezekiah king of **Judah** after his illness and recovery:
40: 9 do not be afraid; say to the towns of **Judah**, "Here is your God!"
44: 26 of the towns of **Judah**, 'They shall be built,' and of their ruins,
48: 1 are called by the name of Israel and come from the line of **Judah**,
65: 9 and from **Judah** those who will possess my mountains;
Jer 1: 2 thirteenth year of the reign of Josiah son of Amon king of **Judah**,
1: 3 and through the reign of Jehoiakim son of Josiah king of **Judah**,
1: 3 of the eleventh year of Zedekiah son of Josiah king of **Judah**,
1: 15 all her surrounding walls and against all the towns of **Judah**.
1: 18 against the kings of **Judah**, its officials, its priests and the people
2: 28 For you have as many gods as you have towns, O **Judah**.
3: 7 return to me but she did not, and her unfaithful sister **Judah** saw it.
3: 8 Yet I saw that her unfaithful sister **Judah** had no fear; she also
3: 10 her unfaithful sister **Judah** did not return to me with all her heart,
3: 11 "Faithless Israel is more righteous than unfaithful **Judah**.
3: 18 In those days the house of **Judah** will join the house of Israel,
4: 3 This is what the LORD says to the men of **Judah** and to

Jer 4: 4 your hearts, you men of **Judah** and people of Jerusalem,
4: 5 "Announce in **Judah** and proclaim in Jerusalem and say: 'Sound
4: 16 from a distant land, raising a war cry against the cities of **Judah**.
5: 11 and the house of **Judah** have been utterly unfaithful to me,"
5: 20 "Announce this to the house of Jacob and proclaim it in **Judah**:
7: 2 all you people of **Judah** who come through these gates to worship
7: 17 Do you not see what they are doing in the towns of **Judah**
7: 30 " 'The people of **Judah** have done evil in my eyes,
7: 34 and to the voices of bride and bridegroom in the towns of **Judah**
8: 1 declares the LORD, the bones of the kings and officials of **Judah**,
9: 11 [9:10] I will lay waste the towns of **Judah** so no one can live
9: 26 [9:25] Egypt, **Judah**, Edom, Ammon, Moab and all who live in
10: 22 It will make the towns of **Judah** desolate, a haunt of jackals.
11: 2 tell them to the people of **Judah** and to those who live in
11: 6 "Proclaim all these words in the towns of **Judah** and in the streets
11: 9 "There is a conspiracy among the people of **Judah** and those who
11: 10 the house of **Judah** have broken the covenant I made with their
11: 12 The towns of **Judah** and the people of Jerusalem will go and cry
11: 13 You have as many gods as you have towns, O **Judah**;
11: 17 because the house of Israel and the house of **Judah** have done evil
12: 14 their lands and I will uproot the house of **Judah** from among them.
13: 9 'In the same way I will ruin the pride of **Judah** and the great pride
13: 11 the whole house of Israel and the whole house of **Judah** to me,'
13: 19 All **Judah** will be carried into exile, carried completely away.
14: 2 "**Judah** mourns, her cities languish; they wail for the land,
14: 19 Have you rejected **Judah** completely? Do you despise Zion?
15: 4 because of what Manasseh son of Hezekiah king of **Judah** did in
17: 1 "**Judah's** sin is engraved with an iron tool, inscribed with a flint
17: 19 of the people, through which the kings of **Judah** go in and out;
17: 20 O kings of **Judah** and all people of Judah and everyone living in
17: 20 O kings of Judah and all people of **Judah** and everyone living in
17: 25 accompanied by the men of **Judah** and those living in Jerusalem,
17: 26 People will come from the towns of **Judah** and the villages around
18: 11 "Now therefore say to the people of **Judah** and those living in
19: 3 word of the LORD, O kings of **Judah** and people of Jerusalem.
19: 4 neither they nor their fathers nor the kings of **Judah** ever knew,
19: 7 " 'In this place I will ruin the plans of **Judah** and Jerusalem.
19: 13 and those of the kings of **Judah** will be defiled like this place,
20: 4 I will hand all **Judah** over to the king of Babylon, who will carry
20: 5 all its valuables and all the treasures of the kings of **Judah**.
21: 7 I will hand over Zedekiah king of **Judah**, his officials
21: 11 "Moreover, say to the royal house of **Judah**, 'Hear the word of the
22: 1 "Go down to the palace of the king of **Judah** and proclaim this
22: 2 'Hear the word of the LORD, O king of **Judah**, you who sit on
22: 6 is what the LORD says about the palace of the king of **Judah**:
22: 11 who succeeded his father as king of **Judah** but has gone from this
22: 18 the LORD says about Jehoiakim son of Josiah king of **Judah**:
22: 24 "even if you, Jehoiachin son of Jehoiakim king of **Judah**,
22: 30 none will sit on the throne of David or rule anymore in **Judah**."
23: 6 In his days **Judah** will be saved and Israel will live in safety.
24: 1 After Jehoiachin son of Jehoiakim king of **Judah** and the officials,
24: 1 the artisans of **Judah** were carried into exile from Jerusalem to
24: 5 'Like these good figs, I regard as good the exiles from **Judah**,
24: 8 'so will I deal with Zedekiah king of **Judah**, his officials and the
25: 1 The word came to Jeremiah concerning all the people of **Judah** in
25: 1 Judah in the fourth year of Jehoiakim son of Josiah king of **Judah**,
25: 2 So Jeremiah the prophet said to all the people of **Judah** and to all
25: 3 from the thirteenth year of Josiah son of Amon king of **Judah** until
25: 18 Jerusalem and the towns of **Judah**, its kings and officials,
26: 1 Early in the reign of Jehoiakim son of Josiah king of **Judah**,
26: 2 speak to all the people of the towns of **Judah** who come to worship
26: 10 When the officials of **Judah** heard about these things, they went up
26: 18 of Moresheth prophesied in the days of Hezekiah king of **Judah**.
26: 18 He told all the people of **Judah**, 'This is what the LORD
26: 19 "Did Hezekiah king of **Judah** or anyone else in Judah put him to
26: 19 Hezekiah king of Judah or anyone else in **Judah** put him to death?
27: 1 Early in the reign of Zedekiah son of Josiah king of **Judah**,
27: 3 envoys who have come to Jerusalem to Zedekiah king of **Judah**.
27: 12 I gave the same message to Zedekiah king of **Judah**. I said,
27: 18 in the palace of the king of **Judah** and in Jerusalem not be taken to
27: 20 of Jehoiakim king of **Judah** into exile from Jerusalem to Babylon,
27: 20 to Babylon, along with all the nobles of **Judah** and Jerusalem—
27: 21 and in the palace of the king of **Judah** and in Jerusalem:
28: 1 the fourth year, early in the reign of Zedekiah king of **Judah**,
28: 4 bring back to this place Jehoiachin son of Jehoiakim king of **Judah**
28: 4 and all the other exiles from **Judah** who went to Babylon,'
29: 2 the court officials and the leaders of **Judah** and Jerusalem,
29: 3 whom Zedekiah king of **Judah** sent to King Nebuchadnezzar in
29: 22 all the exiles from **Judah** who are in Babylon will use this curse:
30: 3 'when I will bring my people Israel and **Judah** back from captivity
30: 4 are the words the LORD spoke concerning Israel and **Judah**:
31: 23 the people in the land of **Judah** and in its towns will once again
31: 24 People will live together in **Judah** and all its towns—farmers
31: 27 and the house of **Judah** with the offspring of men and of animals.
31: 31 covenant with the house of Israel and with the house of **Judah**.
32: 1 from the LORD in the tenth year of Zedekiah king of **Judah**,
32: 2 confined in the courtyard of the guard in the royal palace of **Judah**.
32: 3 Now Zedekiah king of **Judah** had imprisoned him there, saying,
32: 4 Zedekiah king of **Judah** will not escape out of the hands of the
32: 30 "The people of Israel and **Judah** have done nothing but evil in my
32: 32 and **Judah** have provoked me by all the evil they have done—
32: 32 and prophets, the men of **Judah** and the people of Jerusalem.
32: 35 that they should do such a detestable thing and so make **Judah** sin.
32: 44 in the towns of **Judah** and in the towns of the hill country,
33: 4 the royal palaces of **Judah** that have been torn down to be used
33: 7 I will bring **Judah** and Israel back from captivity and will rebuild
33: 10 Yet in the towns of **Judah** and the streets of Jerusalem that are
33: 13 in the villages around Jerusalem and in the towns of **Judah**,
33: 14 promise I made to the house of Israel and to the house of **Judah**.
33: 16 In those days **Judah** will be saved and Jerusalem will live in
34: 2 Go to Zedekiah king of **Judah** and tell him, 'This is what the
34: 4 " 'Yet hear the promise of the LORD, O Zedekiah king of **Judah**.
34: 6 Then Jeremiah the prophet told all this to Zedekiah king of **Judah**,
34: 7 and the other cities of **Judah** that were still holding out—
34: 7 and Azekah. These were the only fortified cities left in **Judah**.
34: 19 The leaders of **Judah** and Jerusalem, the court officials, the priests
34: 21 "I will hand Zedekiah king of **Judah** and his officials over to their
34: 22 And I will lay waste the towns of **Judah** so no one can live there."
35: 1 during the reign of Jehoiakim son of Josiah king of **Judah**:
35: 13 Go and tell the men of **Judah** and the people of Jerusalem,
35: 17 I am going to bring on **Judah** and on everyone living in Jerusalem
36: 1 In the fourth year of Jehoiakim son of Josiah king of **Judah**,
36: 2 **Judah** and all the other nations from the time I began speaking to
36: 3 Perhaps when the people of **Judah** hear about every disaster I plan
36: 6 Read them to all the people of **Judah** who come in from their
36: 9 month of the fifth year of Jehoiakim son of Josiah king of **Judah**,
36: 9 in Jerusalem and those who had come from the towns of **Judah**.
36: 28 were on the first scroll, which Jehoiakim king of **Judah** burned up.
36: 29 Also tell Jehoiakim king of **Judah**, 'This is what the LORD says:
36: 30 this is what the LORD says about Jehoiakim king of **Judah**:
36: 31 and the people of **Judah** every disaster I pronounced against them,
36: 32 of the scroll that Jehoiakim king of **Judah** had burned in the fire.
37: 1 Zedekiah son of Josiah was made king of **Judah** [+824] by
37: 7 Tell the king of **Judah**, who sent you to inquire of me,
38: 22 All the women left in the palace of the king of **Judah** will be
39: 1 In the ninth year of Zedekiah king of **Judah**, in the tenth month,
39: 4 When Zedekiah king of **Judah** and all the soldiers saw them,
39: 6 of Zedekiah before his eyes and also killed all the nobles of **Judah**.
39: 10 the guard left behind in the land of **Judah** some of the poor people,
40: 1 and **Judah** who were being carried into exile to Babylon.
40: 5 whom the king of Babylon has appointed over the towns of **Judah**,
40: 11 heard that the king of Babylon had left a remnant in **Judah**
40: 12 they all came back to the land of **Judah**, to Gedaliah at Mizpah,
40: 15 and cause all the **Jews** who are gathered around you to be scattered
40: 15 around you to be scattered and the remnant of **Judah** to perish?"
42: 15 hear the word of the LORD, O remnant of **Judah**. This is what
42: 19 "O remnant of **Judah**, the LORD has told you, 'Do not go to
43: 4 disobeyed the LORD's command to stay in the land of **Judah**.
43: 5 all the army officers led away all the remnant of **Judah** who had
43: 5 land of **Judah** from all the nations where they had been scattered.
44: 2 disaster I brought on Jerusalem and on all the towns of **Judah**.
44: 6 it raged against the towns of **Judah** and the streets of Jerusalem
44: 7 great disaster on yourselves by cutting off from **Judah** the men
44: 9 by the kings and queens of **Judah** and the wickedness committed
44: 9 and your wives in the land of **Judah** and the streets of Jerusalem?
44: 11 I am determined to bring disaster on you and to destroy all **Judah**.
44: 12 I will take away the remnant of **Judah** who were determined to go
44: 14 None of the remnant of **Judah** who have gone to live in Egypt will
44: 14 live in Egypt will escape or survive to return to the land of **Judah**,
44: 17 our kings and our officials did in the towns of **Judah** and in the
44: 21 and think about the incense burned in the towns of **Judah**
44: 24 "Hear the word of the LORD, all you people of **Judah** in Egypt.
44: 26 But hear the word of the LORD, all **Jews** living in Egypt:
44: 26 'that no one from **Judah** living anywhere in Egypt will ever again
44: 27 the **Jews** in Egypt will perish by sword and famine until they are
44: 28 and return to the land of **Judah** from Egypt will be very few.
44: 28 the whole remnant of **Judah** who came to live in Egypt will know
44: 30 just as I handed Zedekiah king of **Judah** over to Nebuchadnezzar
45: 1 in the fourth year of Jehoiakim son of Josiah king of **Judah**,
46: 2 in the fourth year of Jehoiakim son of Josiah king of **Judah**:
49: 34 concerning Elam, early in the reign of Zedekiah king of **Judah**:
50: 4 the people of **Judah** together will go in tears to seek the LORD
50: 20 there will be none, and for the sins of **Judah**, but none will be
50: 33 people of Israel are oppressed, and the people of **Judah** as well.
51: 5 For Israel and **Judah** have not been forsaken by their God,
51: 59 when he went to Babylon with Zedekiah king of **Judah** in the
52: 3 the LORD's anger that all this happened to Jerusalem and **Judah**,
52: 10 Zedekiah before his eyes; he also killed all the officials of **Judah**.

Jer 52:27 them executed. So **Judah** went into captivity, away from her land.
52:31 In the thirty-seventh year of the exile of Jehoiachin king of **Judah**,
52:31 he released Jehoiachin king of **Judah** and freed him from prison on
La 1: 3 After affliction and harsh labor, **Judah** has gone into exile.
1:15 his winepress the Lord has trampled the Virgin Daughter of **Judah**.
2: 2 wrath he has torn down the strongholds of the Daughter of **Judah**.
2: 5 multiplied mourning and lamentation for the Daughter of **Judah**.
5:11 have been ravished in Zion, and virgins in the towns of **Judah**.
Eze 4: 6 this time on your right side, and bear the sin of the house of **Judah**.
8: 1 sitting in my house and the elders of **Judah** were sitting before me,
8:17 Is it a trivial matter for the house of **Judah** to do the detestable
9: 9 "The sin of the house of Israel and **Judah** is exceedingly great;
21:20 [21:25] and another against **Judah** and fortified Jerusalem.
25: 3 laid waste and over the people of **Judah** when they went into exile,
25: 8 the house of **Judah** has become like all the other nations,"
25:12 'Because Edom took revenge on the house of **Judah** and became
27:17 " '**Judah** and Israel traded with you; they exchanged wheat from
37:16 'Belonging to **Judah** and the Israelites associated with him.'
37:19 and join it to **Judah's** stick, making them a single stick of wood,
48: 7 "**Judah** will have one portion; it will border the territory of Reuben
48: 8 "Bordering the territory of **Judah** from east to west will be the
48:22 area belonging to the prince will lie between the border of **Judah**
48:31 will be the gate of Reuben, the gate of **Judah** and the gate of Levi.
Da 1: 1 In the third year of the reign of Jehoiakim king of **Judah**,
1: 2 And the Lord delivered Jehoiakim king of **Judah** into his hand,
1: 6 Among these were some from **Judah**: Daniel, Hananiah, Mishael
9: 7 the men of **Judah** and people of Jerusalem and all Israel, both near
Hos 1: 1 Jotham, Ahaz and Hezekiah, kings of **Judah**, and during the reign
1: 7 Yet I will show love to the house of **Judah**; and I will save them—
1:11 [2:2] The people of **Judah** and the people of Israel will be
4:15 you commit adultery, O Israel, let not **Judah** become guilty.
5: 5 stumble in their sin; **Judah** also stumbles with them.
5:10 **Judah's** leaders are like those who move boundary stones.
5:12 I am like a moth to Ephraim, like rot to the people of **Judah**.
5:13 his sickness, and **Judah** his sores, then Ephraim turned to Assyria,
5:14 I will be like a lion to Ephraim, like a great lion to **Judah** [+1074].
6: 4 can I do with you, Ephraim? What can I do with you, **Judah**?
6:11 "Also for you, **Judah**, a harvest is appointed. "Whenever I would
8:14 his Maker and built palaces; **Judah** has fortified many towns.
10:11 I will drive Ephraim, **Judah** must plow, and Jacob must break up
11:12 [12:1] **Judah** is unruly against God, even against the faithful Holy
12: 2 [12:3] The LORD has a charge to bring against **Judah**; he will
Joel 3: 1 [4:1] when I restore the fortunes of **Judah** and Jerusalem,
3: 6 [4:6] You sold the people of **Judah** and Jerusalem to the Greeks,
3: 8 [4:8] I will sell your sons and daughters to the people of **Judah**,
3:18 [4:18] with milk; all the ravines of **Judah** will run with water.
3:19 [4:19] because of violence done to the people of **Judah**,
3:20 [4:20] **Judah** will be inhabited forever and Jerusalem through all
Am 1: 1 when Uzziah was king of **Judah** and Jeroboam son of Jehoash was
2: 4 "For three sins of **Judah**, even for four, I will not turn back ⌞my
2: 5 I will send fire upon **Judah** that will consume the fortresses of
7:12 said to Amos, "Get out, you seer! Go back to the land of **Judah**.
Ob 1:12 nor rejoice over the people of **Judah** in the day of their destruction,
Mic 1: 1 during the reigns of Jotham, Ahaz and Hezekiah, kings of **Judah**—
1: 5 Is it not Samaria? What is **Judah's** high place? Is it not Jerusalem?
1: 9 For her wound is incurable; it has come to **Judah**. It has reached
5: 2 [5:1] though you are small among the clans of **Judah**,
Na 1:15 [2:1] Celebrate your festivals, O **Judah**, and fulfill your vows.
Zep 1: 1 during the reign of Josiah son of Amon king of **Judah**:
1: 4 "I will stretch out my hand against **Judah** and against all who live
2: 7 It will belong to the remnant of the house of **Judah**; there they will
Hag 1: 1 governor of **Judah**, and to Joshua son of Jehozadak, the high
1:14 governor of **Judah**, and the spirit of Joshua son of Jehozadak,
2: 2 governor of **Judah**, to Joshua son of Jehozadak, the high priest,
2:21 "Tell Zerubbabel governor of **Judah** that I will shake the heavens
Zec 1:12 you withhold mercy from Jerusalem and from the towns of **Judah**,
1:19 [2:2] "These are the horns that scattered **Judah**, Israel
1:21 [2:4] "These are the horns that scattered **Judah** so that no one
1:21 [2:4] their horns against the land of **Judah** to scatter its people."
2:12 [2:16] The LORD will inherit **Judah** as his portion in the holy
8:13 O **Judah** [+1074] and Israel, so will I save you, and you will be a
8:15 determined to do good again to Jerusalem and **Judah** [+1074].
8:19 and glad occasions and happy festivals for **Judah** [+1074].
9: 7 who are left will belong to our God and become leaders in **Judah**,
9:13 I will bend **Judah** as I bend my bow and fill it with Ephraim.
10: 3 the house of **Judah**, and make them like a proud horse in battle.
10: 6 "I will strengthen the house of **Judah** and save the house of
11:14 called Union, breaking the brotherhood between **Judah** and Israel.
12: 2 peoples reeling. **Judah** will be besieged as well as Jerusalem.
12: 4 "I will keep a watchful eye over the house of **Judah**, but I will
12: 5 the leaders of **Judah** will say in their hearts, 'The people of
12: 6 "On that day I will make the leaders of **Judah** like a firepot in a
12: 7 "The LORD will save the dwellings of **Judah** first, so that the
12: 7 of Jerusalem's inhabitants may not be greater than that of **Judah**.
14: 5 you fled from the earthquake in the days of Uzziah king of **Judah**.
14:14 **Judah** too will fight at Jerusalem. The wealth of all the
14:21 pot in Jerusalem and **Judah** will be holy to the LORD Almighty,
Mal 2:11 **Judah** has broken faith. A detestable thing has been committed in
2:11 **Judah** has desecrated the sanctuary the LORD loves, by marrying
3: 4 the offerings of **Judah** and Jerusalem will be acceptable to the

3374 יְהוּדִי *yᵉhûdî*[1], a.g. [76] [→ 3366, 3375, 3377; cf. 3373; Ar 10316]

Jews [57], Jew [10], Jewish [4], men of Judah [3], Judean [1], they[s] [+2021] [1]

2Ki 16: 6 Aram recovered Elath for Aram by driving out the **men of Judah**.
25:25 with ten men and assassinated Gedaliah and also the **men of Judah**
1Ch 4:18 (His **Judean** wife gave birth to Jered the father of Gedor, Heber
Ne 1: 2 I questioned them about the **Jewish** remnant that survived the
2:16 because as yet I had said nothing to the **Jews** or the priests
4: 1 [3:33] and was greatly incensed. He ridiculed the **Jews**,
4: 2 [3:34] of Samaria, he said, "What are those feeble **Jews** doing?
4:12 [4:6] the **Jews** who lived near them came and told us ten times
5: 1 and their wives raised a great outcry against their **Jewish** brothers.
5: 8 we have bought back our **Jewish** brothers who were sold to the
5:17 Furthermore, a hundred and fifty **Jews** and officials ate at my table,
6: 6 that you and the **Jews** are plotting to revolt, and therefore you are
13:23 in those days I saw **men of Judah** who had married women from
Est 2: 5 Now there was in the citadel of Susa a **Jew** of the tribe of
3: 4 behavior would be tolerated, for he had told them he was a **Jew**.
3: 6 the **Jews**, throughout the whole kingdom of Xerxes.
3:10 Haman son of Hammedatha, the Agagite, the enemy of the **Jews**.
3:13 with the order to destroy, kill and annihilate all the **Jews**—
4: 3 there was great mourning among the **Jews**, with fasting, weeping
4: 7 to pay into the royal treasury for the destruction of the **Jews**.
4:13 because you are in the king's house you alone of all the **Jews** will
4:14 and deliverance for the **Jews** will arise from another place,
4:16 "Go, gather together all the **Jews** who are in Susa, and fast for me.
5:13 all this gives me no satisfaction as long as I see that **Jew** Mordecai
6:10 the horse and do just as you have suggested for Mordecai the **Jew**,
6:13 has started, is of **Jewish** origin, you cannot stand against him—
8: 1 gave Queen Esther the estate of Haman, the enemy of the **Jews**.
8: 3 of Haman the Agagite, which he had devised against the **Jews**.
8: 5 devised and wrote to destroy the **Jews** in all the king's provinces.
8: 7 King Xerxes replied to Queen Esther and to Mordecai the **Jew**,
8: 7 and to Mordecai the Jew, "Because Haman attacked the **Jews**,
8: 8 Now write another decree in the king's name in behalf of the **Jews**
8: 9 They wrote out all Mordecai's orders to the **Jews**, and to the
8: 9 each people and also to the **Jews** in their own script and language.
8:11 The king's edict granted the **Jews** in every city the right to
8:13 so that the **Jews** would be ready on that day to avenge themselves
8:16 For the **Jews** it was a time of happiness and joy, gladness
8:17 there was joy and gladness among the **Jews**, with feasting
8:17 became Jews because fear of the **Jews** had seized them.
9: 1 On this day the enemies of the **Jews** had hoped to overpower them,
9: 1 and the **Jews** got the upper hand over those who hated them.
9: 2 The **Jews** assembled in their cities in all the provinces of King
9: 3 the governors and the king's administrators helped the **Jews**,
9: 5 The **Jews** struck down all their enemies with the sword, killing
9: 6 citadel of Susa, the **Jews** killed and destroyed five hundred men.
9:10 the ten sons of Haman son of Hammedatha, the enemy of the **Jews**.
9:12 "The **Jews** have killed and destroyed five hundred men and the ten
9:13 "give the **Jews** in Susa permission to carry out this day's edict
9:15 The **Jews** in Susa came together on the fourteenth day of the
9:16 the remainder of the **Jews** who were in the king's provinces also
9:18 The **Jews** in Susa, however, had assembled on the thirteenth
9:19 That is why rural **Jews**—those living in villages—observe the
9:20 he sent letters to all the **Jews** throughout the provinces of King
9:22 as the time when the **Jews** got relief from their enemies, and as the
9:23 So the **Jews** agreed to continue the celebration they had begun,
9:24 son of Hammedatha, the Agagite, the enemy of all the **Jews**,
9:24 had plotted against the **Jews** to destroy them and had cast the *pur*
9:25 had devised against the **Jews** should come back onto his own head,
9:27 the **Jews** took it upon themselves to establish the custom that they
9:28 days of Purim should never cease to be celebrated by the **Jews**,
9:29 Queen Esther, daughter of Abihail, along with Mordecai the **Jew**,
9:30 Mordecai sent letters to all the **Jews** in the 127 provinces of the
9:31 as Mordecai the **Jew** and Queen Esther had decreed for them,
10: 3 Mordecai the **Jew** was second in rank to King Xerxes, preeminent
10: 3 preeminent among the **Jews**, and held in high esteem by his many
Jer 32:12 the deed and of all the **Jews** sitting in the courtyard of the guard.
34: 9 and female; no one was to hold a fellow **Jew** in bondage.
38:19 "I am afraid of the **Jews** who have gone over to the Babylonians,
40:11 When all the **Jews** in Moab, Ammon, Edom and all the other
40:12 **they**[s] [+2021] all came back to the land of Judah, to Gedaliah at
41: 3 Ishmael also killed all the **Jews** who were with Gedaliah at
43: 9 "While the **Jews** are watching, take some large stones with you

Jer 44: 1 This word came to Jeremiah concerning all the **Jews** living in
52: 28 carried into exile: in the seventh year, 3,023 **Jews**;
52: 30 745 **Jews** taken into exile by Nebuzaradan the commander of the
Zec 8: 23 and nations will take firm hold of one **Jew** by the hem of his robe

3375 יְהוּדִי² ***y^ehûdî²***, n.pr.m. [4 / 5] [√ 3374; cf. 3373]

Jehudi [4], Yaudi [1]

2Ki 14: 28 and Hamath, which had belonged to **Yaudi**, [BHS 3373]
Jer 36: 14 all the officials sent **Jehudi** son of Nethaniah, the son of
36: 21 The king sent **Jehudi** to get the scroll, and Jehudi brought it from
36: 21 and **Jehudi** brought it from the room of Elishama the secretary
36: 23 Whenever **Jehudi** had read three or four columns of the scroll,

3376 יְהוּדִית ***y^ehûdît¹***, a.g.f. (used as adv.). [6] [√ 3373]

in Hebrew [5], language of Judah [1]

2Ki 18: 26 Don't speak to us **in Hebrew** in the hearing of the people on the
18: 28 the commander stood and called out **in Hebrew**: "Hear the word of
2Ch 32: 18 they called out **in Hebrew** to the people of Jerusalem who were on
Ne 13: 24 and did not know how to speak the **language of Judah**.
Isa 36: 11 Don't speak to us **in Hebrew** in the hearing of the people on the
36: 13 the commander stood and called out **in Hebrew**, "Hear the words

3377 יְהוּדִית² ***y^ehûdît²***, n.pr.f. [1] [√ 3374; cf. 3373]

Judith [1]

Ge 26: 34 forty years old, he married **Judith** daughter of Beeri the Hittite,

3378 יהוה ***yhwh***, יְהוִה ***yehwih***, n.pr.m. [6828 / 6829]
[→ 3363; *also used with compound proper names*]

the LORD [6030], LORD [399], the LORD's [242], *untranslated* [38], he[s] [35], the LORD's [+4200] [27], him[s] [16], his[s] [13], he[s] [+466 +3870] [7], him[s] [+466+3870] [3], the LORD's [+907+4946] [3], his[s] [+466+3870] [2], its[s] [+1074] [2], me[s] [2], done this[s] [+1215+4200 +4640] [1], he[s] [+4855] [1], he[s] [+466] [1], he[s] [+466+5646] [1], him[s] [+466+4013] [1], it[s] [+1074] [1], LORD's [1], the angel [+4855] [1], the LORD's [+4946+6640] [1], the LORD himself [+7156] [1]

Ge 2: 4 When **the LORD** God made the earth and the heavens—
2: 5 for **the LORD** God had not sent rain on the earth and there was
2: 7 **the LORD** God formed the man from the dust of the ground
2: 8 Now **the LORD** God had planted a garden in the east, in Eden;
2: 9 **the LORD** God made all kinds of trees grow out of the ground—
2: 15 **The LORD** God took the man and put him in the Garden of Eden
2: 16 **the LORD** God commanded the man, "You are free to eat from
2: 18 **The LORD** God said, "It is not good for the man to be alone.
2: 19 Now **the LORD** God had formed out of the ground all the beasts
2: 21 So **the LORD** God caused the man to fall into a deep sleep;
2: 22 **the LORD** God made a woman from the rib he had taken out of
3: 1 crafty than any of the wild animals **the LORD** God had made.
3: 8 his wife heard the sound of **the LORD** God as he was walking in
3: 8 and they hid from **the LORD** God among the trees of the garden.
3: 9 But **the LORD** God called to the man, "Where are you?"
3: 13 **the LORD** God said to the woman, "What is this you have
3: 14 So **the LORD** God said to the serpent, "Because you have done
3: 21 **The LORD** God made garments of skin for Adam and his wife
3: 22 **the LORD** God said, "The man has now become like one of us,
3: 23 So **the LORD** God banished him from the Garden of Eden to
4: 1 "With the help of **the LORD** I have brought forth a man."
4: 3 brought some of the fruits of the soil as an offering to **the LORD**.
4: 4 his flock. **The LORD** looked with favor on Abel and his offering,
4: 6 **the LORD** said to Cain, "Why are you angry? Why is your face
4: 9 Then **the LORD** said to Cain, "Where is your brother Abel?"
4: 13 Cain said to **the LORD**, "My punishment is more than I can bear.
4: 15 But **the LORD** said to him, "Not so; if anyone kills Cain,
4: 15 **the LORD** put a mark on Cain so that no one who found him
4: 16 So Cain went out from **the LORD's** presence and lived in the
4: 26 At that time men began to call on the name of **the LORD**.
5: 29 painful toil of our hands caused by the ground **the LORD** has
6: 3 **the LORD** said, "My Spirit will not contend with man forever,
6: 5 **The LORD** saw how great man's wickedness on the earth had
6: 6 **The LORD** was grieved that he had made man on the earth,
6: 7 So **the LORD** said, "I will wipe mankind, whom I have created,
6: 8 But Noah found favor in the eyes of **the LORD**.
7: 1 **The LORD** then said to Noah, "Go into the ark, you and your
7: 5 And Noah did all that **the LORD** commanded him.
7: 16 as God had commanded Noah. Then **the LORD** shut him in.
8: 20 Noah built an altar to **the LORD** and, taking some of all the clean
8: 21 **The LORD** smelled the pleasing aroma and said in his heart:
8: 21 LORD smelled the pleasing aroma and **[RPH]** said in his heart:
9: 26 He also said, "Blessed be **the LORD**, the God of Shem!
10: 9 He was a mighty hunter before **the LORD**; that is why it is said,
10: 9 why it is said, "Like Nimrod, a mighty hunter before **the LORD**."
11: 5 **the LORD** came down to see the city and the tower that the men
11: 6 **The LORD** said, "If as one people speaking the same language
11: 8 So **the LORD** scattered them from there over all the earth,
11: 9 because there **the LORD** confused the language of the whole
11: 9 From there **the LORD** scattered them over the face of the whole
12: 1 **The LORD** had said to Abram, "Leave your country, your people
12: 4 So Abram left, as **the LORD** had told him; and Lot went with
12: 7 **The LORD** appeared to Abram and said, "To your offspring I
12: 7 So he built an altar there to **the LORD**, who had appeared to him.
12: 8 There he built an altar to **the LORD** and called on the name of
12: 8 an altar to the LORD and called on the name of **the LORD**.
12: 17 **the LORD** inflicted serious diseases on Pharaoh and his
13: 4 built an altar. There Abram called on the name of **the LORD**.
13: 10 like the garden of **the LORD**, like the land of Egypt,
13: 10 (This was before **the LORD** destroyed Sodom and Gomorrah.)
13: 13 Sodom were wicked and were sinning greatly against **the LORD**.
13: 14 **The LORD** said to Abram after Lot had parted from him,
13: 18 trees of Mamre at Hebron, where he built an altar to **the LORD**.
14: 22 "I have raised my hand to **the LORD**, God Most High, Creator of
15: 1 After this, the word of **the LORD** came to Abram in a vision:
15: 2 Abram said, "O Sovereign **LORD**, what can you give me since I
15: 4 the word of **the LORD** came to him: "This man will not be your
15: 6 Abram believed **the LORD**, and he credited it to him as
15: 7 He also said to him, "I am **the LORD**, who brought you out of Ur
15: 8 Abram said, "O Sovereign **LORD**, how can I know that I will
15: 18 On that day **the LORD** made a covenant with Abram and said,
16: 2 said to Abram, "**The LORD** has kept me from having children.
16: 5 she despises me. May **the LORD** judge between you and me."
16: 7 The angel of **the LORD** found Hagar near a spring in the desert;
16: 9 Then the angel of **the LORD** told her, "Go back to your mistress
16: 10 **The angel** [+4855] added, "I will so increase your descendants that
16: 11 The angel of **the LORD** also said to her: "You are now with child
16: 11 shall name him Ishmael, for **the LORD** has heard of your misery.
16: 13 She gave this name to **the LORD** who spoke to her: "You are the
17: 1 **the LORD** appeared to him and said, "I am God Almighty;
18: 1 **The LORD** appeared to Abraham near the great trees of Mamre
18: 13 Then **the LORD** said to Abraham, "Why did Sarah laugh
18: 14 Is anything too hard for **the LORD**? I will return to you at the
18: 17 **the LORD** said, "Shall I hide from Abraham what I am about to
18: 19 his household after him to keep the way of **the LORD** by doing
18: 19 so that **the LORD** will bring about for Abraham what he has
18: 20 **the LORD** said, "The outcry against Sodom and Gomorrah is
18: 22 but Abraham remained standing before **the LORD**.
18: 26 **The LORD** said, "If I find fifty righteous people in the city of
18: 33 When **the LORD** had finished speaking with Abraham, he left,
19: 13 The outcry to **the LORD** against its people is so great that he has
19: 13 against its people is so great that **he**[s] has sent us to destroy it."
19: 14 out of this place, because **the LORD** is about to destroy the city!"
19: 16 them safely out of the city, for **the LORD** was merciful to them.
19: 24 **the LORD** rained down burning sulfur on Sodom
19: 24 on Sodom and Gomorrah—from **the LORD** out of the heavens.
19: 27 and returned to the place where he had stood before **the LORD**.
20: 18 for **the LORD** had closed up every womb in Abimelech's
21: 1 Now **the LORD** was gracious to Sarah as he had said,
21: 1 he had said, and **the LORD** did for Sarah what he had promised.
21: 33 there he called upon the name of **the LORD**, the Eternal God.
22: 11 But the angel of **the LORD** called out to him from heaven,
22: 14 So Abraham called that place **The LORD** Will Provide. And to
22: 14 it is said, "On the mountain of **the LORD** it will be provided."
22: 15 The angel of **the LORD** called to Abraham from heaven a
22: 16 declares **the LORD**, that because you have done this and have
24: 1 advanced in years, and **the LORD** had blessed him in every way.
24: 3 I want you to swear by **the LORD**, the God of heaven
24: 7 "**The LORD**, the God of heaven, who brought me out of my
24: 12 Then he prayed, "O **LORD**, God of my master Abraham,
24: 21 learn whether or not **the LORD** had made his journey successful.
24: 26 Then the man bowed down and worshiped **the LORD**,
24: 27 saying, "Praise be to **the LORD**, the God of my master Abraham,
24: 27 **the LORD** has led me on the journey to the house of my master's
24: 31 "Come, you who are blessed by **the LORD**," he said. "Why are
24: 35 **The LORD** has blessed my master abundantly, and he has
24: 40 "He replied, '**The LORD**, before whom I have walked, will send
24: 42 I said, 'O **LORD**, God of my master Abraham, if you will,
24: 44 let her be the one **the LORD** has chosen for my master's son.'
24: 48 I bowed down and worshiped **the LORD**. I praised the LORD,
24: 48 I praised **the LORD**, the God of my master Abraham, who had
24: 50 Laban and Bethuel answered, "This is from **the LORD**; we can
24: 51 the wife of your master's son, as **the LORD** has directed."
24: 52 what they said, he bowed down to the ground before **the LORD**.
24: 56 now that **the LORD** has granted success to my journey.
25: 21 Isaac prayed to **the LORD** on behalf of his wife, because she was
25: 21 **The LORD** answered his prayer, and his wife Rebekah became
25: 22 is this happening to me?" So she went to inquire of **the LORD**.
25: 23 **The LORD** said to her, "Two nations are in your womb,

Ge 26: 2 **The LORD** appeared to Isaac and said, "Do not go down to
26: 12 same year reaped a hundredfold, because **the LORD** blessed him.
26: 22 "Now **the LORD** has given us room and we will flourish in the
26: 24 That night **the LORD** appeared to him and said, "I am the God of
26: 25 Isaac built an altar there and called on the name of **the LORD**.
26: 28 They answered, "We saw clearly that **the LORD** was with you;
26: 29 you away in peace. And now you are blessed by **the LORD**."
27: 7 so that I may give you my blessing in the presence of **the LORD**
27: 20 my son?" "**The LORD** your God gave me success," he replied.
27: 27 the smell of my son is like the smell of a field that **the LORD** has
28: 13 There above it stood **the LORD**, and he said: "I am the LORD,
28: 13 "I am **the LORD**, the God of your father Abraham and the God
28: 16 he thought, "Surely **the LORD** is in this place, and I was not
28: 21 safely to my father's house, then **the LORD** will be my God
29: 31 When **the LORD** saw that Leah was not loved, he opened her
29: 32 for she said, "It is because **the LORD** has seen my misery.
29: 33 "Because **the LORD** heard that I am not loved, he gave me this
29: 35 gave birth to a son she said, "This time I will praise **the LORD**."
30: 24 him Joseph, and said, "May **the LORD** add to me another son."
30: 27 I have learned by divination that **the LORD** has blessed me
30: 30 and **the LORD** has blessed you wherever I have been.
31: 3 **the LORD** said to Jacob, "Go back to the land of your fathers
31: 49 "May **the LORD** keep watch between you and me when we are
32: 9 [32:10] God of my father Isaac, O **LORD**, who said to me,
38: 7 But Er, Judah's firstborn, was wicked in **the LORD's** sight;
38: 7 wicked in the LORD's sight; so **the LORD** put him to death.
38: 10 What he did was wicked in **the LORD's** sight; so he put him to
39: 2 **The LORD** was with Joseph and he prospered, and he lived in
39: 3 When his master saw that **the LORD** was with him and that the
39: 3 and that **the LORD** gave him success in everything he did,
39: 5 **the LORD** blessed the household of the Egyptian because of
39: 5 The blessing of **the LORD** was on everything Potiphar had,
39: 21 **the LORD** was with him; he showed him kindness and granted
39: 23 because **the LORD** was with Joseph and gave him success in
39: 23 with Joseph and gave him success in whatever he did. **[RPH]**
49: 18 "I look for your deliverance, O **LORD**.
Ex 3: 2 There the angel of **the LORD** appeared to him in flames of fire
3: 4 When **the LORD** saw that he had gone over to look, God called
3: 7 **The LORD** said, "I have indeed seen the misery of my people in
3: 15 God also said to Moses, "Say to the Israelites, '**The LORD**,
3: 16 assemble the elders of Israel and say to them, '**The LORD**,
3: 18 elders are to go to the king of Egypt and say to him, '**The LORD**,
3: 18 journey into the desert to offer sacrifices to **the LORD** our God.'
4: 1 or listen to me and say, '**The LORD** did not appear to you'?"
4: 2 Then **the LORD** said to him, "What is that in your hand?"
4: 4 **the LORD** said to him, "Reach out your hand and take it by the
4: 5 said the LORD, "is so that they may believe that **the LORD**,
4: 6 Then **the LORD** said, "Put your hand inside your cloak."
4: 10 Moses said to **the LORD**, "O Lord, I have never been eloquent,
4: 11 **The LORD** said to him, "Who gave man his mouth? Who makes
4: 11 Who gives him sight or makes him blind? Is it not I, **the LORD**?
4: 14 Then **the LORD's** anger burned against Moses and he said,
4: 19 Now **the LORD** had said to Moses in Midian, "Go back to Egypt,
4: 21 **The LORD** said to Moses, "When you return to Egypt, see that
4: 22 say to Pharaoh, 'This is what **the LORD** says: Israel is my
4: 24 on the way, **the LORD** met ⌊Moses⌋ and was about to kill him.
4: 27 **The LORD** said to Aaron, "Go into the desert to meet Moses."
4: 28 Moses told Aaron everything **the LORD** had sent him to say,
4: 30 and Aaron told them everything **the LORD** had said to Moses.
4: 31 And when they heard that **the LORD** was concerned about them
5: 1 and Aaron went to Pharaoh and said, "This is what **the LORD**,
5: 2 Pharaoh said, "Who is **the LORD**, that I should obey him
5: 2 Israel go? I do not know **the LORD** and I will not let Israel go."
5: 3 journey into the desert to offer sacrifices to **the LORD** our God,
5: 17 is why you keep saying, 'Let us go and sacrifice to **the LORD**.'
5: 21 and they said, "May **the LORD** look upon you and judge you!
5: 22 Moses returned to **the LORD** and said, "O Lord, why have you
6: 1 **the LORD** said to Moses, "Now you will see what I will do to
6: 2 God also said to Moses, "I am **the LORD**.
6: 3 by my name **the LORD** I did not make myself known to them.
6: 6 'I am **the LORD**, and I will bring you out from under the yoke of
6: 7 you will know that I am **the LORD** your God, who brought you
6: 8 to Jacob. I will give it to you as a possession. I am **the LORD**.' "
6: 10 Then **the LORD** said to Moses,
6: 12 Moses said to **the LORD**, "If the Israelites will not listen to me,
6: 13 Now **the LORD** spoke to Moses and Aaron about the Israelites
6: 26 It was this same Aaron and Moses to whom **the LORD** said,
6: 28 Now when **the LORD** spoke to Moses in Egypt,
6: 29 **he**[s] said to him, "I am the LORD. Tell Pharaoh king of Egypt
6: 29 he said to him, "I am **the LORD**. Tell Pharaoh king of Egypt
6: 30 But Moses said to **the LORD**, "Since I speak with faltering lips,
7: 1 **the LORD** said to Moses, "See, I have made you like God to
7: 5 the Egyptians will know that I am **the LORD** when I stretch out
7: 6 Moses and Aaron did just as **the LORD** commanded them.
7: 8 **The LORD** said to Moses and Aaron,
7: 10 Aaron went to Pharaoh and did just as **the LORD** commanded.
7: 13 and he would not listen to them, just as **the LORD** had said.
7: 14 Then **the LORD** said to Moses, "Pharaoh's heart is unyielding;
7: 16 say to him, '**The LORD**, the God of the Hebrews, has sent me to
7: 17 This is what **the LORD** says: By this you will know that I am the
7: 17 the LORD says: By this you will know that I am **the LORD**:
7: 19 **The LORD** said to Moses, "Tell Aaron, 'Take your staff
7: 20 Moses and Aaron did just as **the LORD** had commanded.
7: 22 would not listen to Moses and Aaron, just as **the LORD** had said.
7: 25 Seven days passed after **the LORD** struck the Nile.
8: 1 [7:26] **the LORD** said to Moses, "Go to Pharaoh and say to him,
8: 1 [7:26] to Pharaoh and say to him, 'This is what **the LORD** says:
8: 5 [8:1] **the LORD** said to Moses, "Tell Aaron, 'Stretch out your
8: 8 [8:4] "Pray to **the LORD** to take the frogs away from me
8: 8 [8:4] I will let your people go to offer sacrifices to **the LORD**."
8: 10 [8:6] so that you may know there is no one like **the LORD** our
8: 12 [8:8] Moses cried out to **the LORD** about the frogs he had
8: 13 [8:9] **the LORD** did what Moses asked. The frogs died in the
8: 15 [8:11] listen to Moses and Aaron, just as **the LORD** had said.
8: 16 [8:12] **the LORD** said to Moses, "Tell Aaron, 'Stretch out your
8: 19 [8:15] and he would not listen, just as **the LORD** had said.
8: 20 [8:16] **the LORD** said to Moses, "Get up early in the morning
8: 20 [8:16] to the water and say to him, 'This is what **the LORD** says:
8: 22 [8:18] so that you will know that I, **the LORD**, am in this land.
8: 24 [8:20] **the LORD** did this. Dense swarms of flies poured into
8: 26 [8:22] The sacrifices we offer **the LORD** our God would be
8: 27 [8:23] into the desert to offer sacrifices to **the LORD** our God,
8: 28 [8:24] "I will let you go to offer sacrifices to **the LORD** your
8: 29 [8:25] "As soon as I leave you, I will pray to **the LORD**,
8: 29 [8:25] letting the people go to offer sacrifices to **the LORD**."
8: 30 [8:26] Then Moses left Pharaoh and prayed to **the LORD**,
8: 31 [8:27] **the LORD** did what Moses asked: The flies left Pharaoh
9: 1 Then **the LORD** said to Moses, "Go to Pharaoh and say to him,
9: 1 "Go to Pharaoh and say to him, 'This is what **the LORD**,
9: 3 the hand of **the LORD** will bring a terrible plague on your
9: 4 **the LORD** will make a distinction between the livestock of Israel
9: 5 **The LORD** set a time and said, "Tomorrow the LORD will do
9: 5 and said, "Tomorrow **the LORD** will do this in the land."
9: 6 the next day **the LORD** did it: All the livestock of the Egyptians
9: 8 **the LORD** said to Moses and Aaron, "Take handfuls of soot from
9: 12 **the LORD** hardened Pharaoh's heart and he would not listen to
9: 12 listen to Moses and Aaron, just as **the LORD** had said to Moses.
9: 13 Then **the LORD** said to Moses, "Get up early in the morning,
9: 13 confront Pharaoh and say to him, 'This is what **the LORD**,
9: 20 Those officials of Pharaoh who feared the word of **the LORD**
9: 21 But those who ignored the word of **the LORD** left their slaves
9: 22 **the LORD** said to Moses, "Stretch out your hand toward the sky
9: 23 **the LORD** sent thunder and hail, and lightning flashed down to
9: 23 to the ground. So **the LORD** rained hail on the land of Egypt;
9: 27 "**The LORD** is in the right, and I and my people are in the wrong.
9: 28 Pray to **the LORD**, for we have had enough thunder and hail.
9: 29 of the city, I will spread out my hands in prayer to **the LORD**.
9: 29 so you may know that the earth is **the LORD's** [+4200].
9: 30 that you and your officials still do not fear **the LORD** God."
9: 33 He spread out his hands toward **the LORD**; the thunder and hail
9: 35 let the Israelites go, just as **the LORD** had said through Moses.
10: 1 **the LORD** said to Moses, "Go to Pharaoh, for I have hardened
10: 2 signs among them, and that you may know that I am **the LORD**."
10: 3 Aaron went to Pharaoh and said to him, "This is what **the LORD**,
10: 7 the people go, so that they may worship **the LORD** their God.
10: 8 "Go, worship **the LORD** your God," he said. "But just who will
10: 9 and herds, because we are to celebrate a festival to **the LORD**."
10: 10 Pharaoh said, "**The LORD** be with you—if I let you go,
10: 11 worship **the LORD**, since that's what you have been asking for."
10: 12 And **the LORD** said to Moses, "Stretch out your hand over Egypt
10: 13 **the LORD** made an east wind blow across the land all that day
10: 16 "I have sinned against **the LORD** your God and against you.
10: 17 pray to **the LORD** your God to take this deadly plague away
10: 18 Moses then left Pharaoh and prayed to **the LORD**.
10: 19 And **the LORD** changed the wind to a very strong west wind,
10: 20 **the LORD** hardened Pharaoh's heart, and he would not let the
10: 21 **the LORD** said to Moses, "Stretch out your hand toward the sky
10: 24 Pharaoh summoned Moses and said, "Go, worship **the LORD**.
10: 25 and burnt offerings to present to **the LORD** our God.
10: 26 We have to use some of them in worshiping **the LORD** our God,
10: 26 we will not know what we are to use to worship **the LORD**."
10: 27 **the LORD** hardened Pharaoh's heart, and he was not willing to
11: 1 Now **the LORD** had said to Moses, "I will bring one more plague
11: 3 (**The LORD** made the Egyptians favorably disposed toward the
11: 4 So Moses said, "This is what **the LORD** says: 'About midnight I
11: 7 you will know that **the LORD** makes a distinction between Egypt
11: 9 **The LORD** had said to Moses, "Pharaoh will refuse to listen to
11: 10 **the LORD** hardened Pharaoh's heart, and he would not let the

Ex 12: 1 **The LORD** said to Moses and Aaron in Egypt,
12: 11 in your hand. Eat it in haste; it is **the LORD's** [+4200] Passover.
12: 12 I will bring judgment on all the gods of Egypt. I am **the LORD**.
12: 14 to come you shall celebrate it as a festival to **the LORD**—
12: 23 When **the LORD** goes through the land to strike down the
12: 23 and **he**[s] will not permit the destroyer to enter your houses
12: 25 When you enter the land that **the LORD** will give you as he
12: 27 then tell them, 'It is the Passover sacrifice to **the LORD**,
12: 28 The Israelites did just what **the LORD** commanded Moses
12: 29 At midnight **the LORD** struck down all the firstborn in Egypt,
12: 31 and the Israelites! Go, worship **the LORD** as you have requested.
12: 36 **The LORD** had made the Egyptians favorably disposed toward
12: 41 430 years, to the very day, all **the LORD's** divisions left Egypt.
12: 42 Because **the LORD** kept vigil that night to bring them out of
12: 42 are to keep vigil to honor **the LORD** for the generations to come.
12: 43 **The LORD** said to Moses and Aaron, "These are the regulations
12: 48 **the LORD's** [+4200] Passover must have all the males in his
12: 50 All the Israelites did just what **the LORD** had commanded Moses
12: 51 on that very day **the LORD** brought the Israelites out of Egypt by
13: 1 **The LORD** said to Moses,
13: 3 because **the LORD** brought you out of it with a mighty hand.
13: 5 When **the LORD** brings you into the land of the Canaanites,
13: 6 and on the seventh day hold a festival to **the LORD**.
13: 8 because of what **the LORD** did for me when I came out of
13: 9 a reminder on your forehead that the law of **the LORD** is to be on
13: 9 For **the LORD** brought you out of Egypt with his mighty hand.
13: 11 "After **the LORD** brings you into the land of the Canaanites
13: 12 you are to give over to **the LORD** the first offspring of every
13: 12 All the firstborn males of your livestock belong to **the LORD**.
13: 14 'With a mighty hand **the LORD** brought us out of Egypt,
13: 15 **the LORD** killed every firstborn in Egypt, both man and animal.
13: 15 This is why I sacrifice to **the LORD** the first male offspring of
13: 16 a symbol on your forehead that **the LORD** brought us out of
13: 21 By day **the LORD** went ahead of them in a pillar of cloud to
14: 1 Then **the LORD** said to Moses,
14: 4 all his army, and the Egyptians will know that I am **the LORD**."
14: 8 **The LORD** hardened the heart of Pharaoh king of Egypt,
14: 10 after them. They were terrified and cried out to **the LORD**.
14: 13 and you will see the deliverance **the LORD** will bring you today.
14: 14 **The LORD** will fight for you; you need only to be still."
14: 15 Then **the LORD** said to Moses, "Why are you crying out to me?
14: 18 The Egyptians will know that I am **the LORD** when I gain glory
14: 21 all that night **the LORD** drove the sea back with a strong east
14: 24 During the last watch of the night **the LORD** looked down from
14: 25 the Israelites! **The LORD** is fighting for them against Egypt."
14: 26 **the LORD** said to Moses, "Stretch out your hand over the sea
14: 27 were fleeing toward it, and **the LORD** swept them into the sea.
14: 30 That day **the LORD** saved Israel from the hands of the
14: 31 when the Israelites saw the great power **the LORD** displayed
14: 31 the people feared **the LORD** and put their trust in him and in
14: 31 the LORD and put their trust in **him**[s] and in Moses his servant.
15: 1 Then Moses and the Israelites sang this song to **the LORD**:
15: 1 "I will sing to **the LORD**, for he is highly exalted. The horse
15: 3 **The LORD** is a warrior; the LORD is his name.
15: 3 The LORD is a warrior; **the LORD** is his name.
15: 6 "Your right hand, O **LORD**, was majestic in power. Your right
15: 6 in power. Your right hand, O **LORD**, shattered the enemy.
15: 11 "Who among the gods is like you, O **LORD**? Who is like you—
15: 16 until your people pass by, O **LORD**, until the people you bought
15: 17 the place, O **LORD**, you made for your dwelling, the sanctuary,
15: 18 **The LORD** will reign for ever and ever."
15: 19 **the LORD** brought the waters of the sea back over them,
15: 21 "Sing to **the LORD**, for he is highly exalted. The horse and its
15: 25 Moses cried out to **the LORD**, and the LORD showed him a
15: 25 out to the LORD, and **the LORD** showed him a piece of wood.
15: 26 "If you listen carefully to the voice of **the LORD** your God
15: 26 I brought on the Egyptians, for I am **the LORD**, who heals you."
16: 3 said to them, "If only we had died by **the LORD's** hand in Egypt!
16: 4 **the LORD** said to Moses, "I will rain down bread from heaven
16: 6 "In the evening you will know that it was **the LORD** who
16: 7 and in the morning you will see the glory of **the LORD**,
16: 7 of the LORD, because he has heard your grumbling against **him**[s].
16: 8 "You will know that it was **the LORD** when he gives you meat to
16: 8 in the morning, because **he**[s] has heard your grumbling against him.
16: 8 You are not grumbling against us, but against **the LORD**."
16: 9 'Come before **the LORD**, for he has heard your grumbling.' "
16: 10 and there was the glory of **the LORD** appearing in the cloud.
16: 11 **The LORD** said to Moses,
16: 12 Then you will know that I am **the LORD** your God.' "
16: 15 said to them, "It is the bread **the LORD** has given you to eat.
16: 16 This is what **the LORD** has commanded: 'Each one is to gather as
16: 23 He said to them, "This is what **the LORD** commanded:
16: 23 'Tomorrow is to be a day of rest, a holy Sabbath to **the LORD**.
16: 25 it today," Moses said, "because today is a Sabbath to **the LORD**.
16: 28 **the LORD** said to Moses, "How long will you refuse to keep my
16: 29 Bear in mind that **the LORD** has given you the Sabbath;
16: 32 Moses said, "This is what **the LORD** has commanded: 'Take an
16: 33 place it before **the LORD** to be kept for the generations to come."
16: 34 As **the LORD** commanded Moses, Aaron put the manna in front
17: 1 traveling from place to place as **the LORD** commanded.
17: 2 do you quarrel with me? Why do you put **the LORD** to the test?"
17: 4 Moses cried out to **the LORD**, "What am I to do with these
17: 5 **The LORD** answered Moses, "Walk on ahead of the people.
17: 7 Israelites quarreled and because they tested **the LORD** saying,
17: 7 they tested the LORD saying, "Is **the LORD** among us or not?"
17: 14 **the LORD** said to Moses, "Write this on a scroll as something to
17: 15 Moses built an altar and called it **The LORD** is my Banner.
17: 16 **The LORD** will be at war against the Amalekites from
18: 1 and how **the LORD** had brought Israel out of Egypt.
18: 8 Moses told his father-in-law about everything **the LORD** had
18: 8 they had met along the way and how **the LORD** had saved them.
18: 9 Jethro was delighted to hear about all the good things **the LORD**
18: 10 He said, "Praise be to **the LORD**, who rescued you from the hand
18: 11 Now I know that **the LORD** is greater than all other gods,
19: 3 and **the LORD** called to him from the mountain and said,
19: 7 set before them all the words **the LORD** had commanded him to
19: 8 responded together, "We will do everything **the LORD** has said."
19: 8 has said." So Moses brought their answer back to **the LORD**.
19: 9 **The LORD** said to Moses, "I am going to come to you in a dense
19: 9 in you." Then Moses told **the LORD** what the people had said.
19: 10 **the LORD** said to Moses, "Go to the people and consecrate them
19: 11 because on that day **the LORD** will come down on Mount Sinai
19: 18 covered with smoke, because **the LORD** descended on it in fire.
19: 20 **The LORD** descended to the top of Mount Sinai and called
19: 20 Mount Sinai and **[RPH]** called Moses to the top of the mountain.
19: 21 and **the LORD** said to him, "Go down and warn the people
19: 21 so they do not force their way through to see **the LORD**
19: 22 Even the priests, who approach **the LORD**, must consecrate
19: 22 or **the LORD** will break out against them."
19: 23 Moses said to **the LORD**, "The people cannot come up Mount
19: 24 **The LORD** replied, "Go down and bring Aaron up with you.
19: 24 must not force their way through to come up to **the LORD**,
20: 2 "I am **the LORD** your God, who brought you out of Egypt,
20: 5 for I, **the LORD** your God, am a jealous God, punishing the
20: 7 "You shall not misuse the name of **the LORD** your God,
20: 7 for **the LORD** will not hold anyone guiltless who misuses his
20: 10 but the seventh day is a Sabbath to **the LORD** your God.
20: 11 For in six days **the LORD** made the heavens and the earth,
20: 11 Therefore **the LORD** blessed the Sabbath day and made it holy.
20: 12 so that you may live long in the land **the LORD** your God is
20: 22 **the LORD** said to Moses, "Tell the Israelites this: 'You have seen
22: 11 [22:10] **the LORD** that the neighbor did not lay hands on the
22: 20 [22:19] "Whoever sacrifices to any god other than **the LORD**
23: 17 a year all the men are to appear before the Sovereign **LORD**.
23: 19 of the firstfruits of your soil to the house of **the LORD** your God.
23: 25 Worship **the LORD** your God, and his blessing will be on your
24: 1 "Come up to **the LORD**, you and Aaron, Nadab and Abihu,
24: 2 Moses alone is to approach **the LORD**; the others must not come
24: 3 Moses went and told the people all **the LORD's** words and laws,
24: 3 with one voice, "Everything **the LORD** has said we will do."
24: 4 Moses then wrote down everything **the LORD** had said.
24: 5 and sacrificed young bulls as fellowship offerings to **the LORD**.
24: 7 They responded, "We will do everything **the LORD** has said;
24: 8 "This is the blood of the covenant that **the LORD** has made with
24: 12 **The LORD** said to Moses, "Come up to me on the mountain
24: 16 the glory of **the LORD** settled on Mount Sinai. For six days the
24: 17 To the Israelites the glory of **the LORD** looked like a consuming
25: 1 **The LORD** said to Moses,
27: 21 his sons are to keep the lamps burning before **the LORD** from
28: 12 bear the names on his shoulders as a memorial before **the LORD**.
28: 29 of decision as a continuing memorial before **the LORD**.
28: 30 Aaron's heart whenever he enters the presence of **the LORD**.
28: 30 decisions for the Israelites over his heart before **the LORD**.
28: 35 will be heard when he enters the Holy Place before **the LORD**
28: 36 pure gold and engrave on it as on a seal: HOLY TO **THE LORD**.
28: 38 so that they will be acceptable to **the LORD**.
29: 11 Slaughter it in **the LORD's** presence at the entrance to the Tent
29: 18 It is a burnt offering to **the LORD**, a pleasing aroma, an offering
29: 18 a pleasing aroma, an offering made to **the LORD** by fire.
29: 23 which is before **the LORD**, take a loaf, and a cake made with oil,
29: 24 his sons and wave them before **the LORD** as a wave offering.
29: 25 along with the burnt offering for a pleasing aroma to **the LORD**,
29: 25 aroma to the LORD, an offering made to **the LORD** by fire.
29: 26 wave it before **the LORD** as a wave offering, and it will be your
29: 28 It is the contribution the Israelites are to make to **the LORD** from
29: 41 a pleasing aroma, an offering made to **the LORD** by fire.
29: 42 at the entrance to the Tent of Meeting before **the LORD**.
29: 46 They will know that I am **the LORD** their God, who brought

Ex 29:46 so that I might dwell among them. I am **the LORD** their God.
30:8 so incense will burn regularly before **the LORD** for the
30:10 for the generations to come. It is most holy to **the LORD**."
30:11 Then **the LORD** said to Moses,
30:12 each one must pay **the LORD** a ransom for his life at the time he
30:13 twenty gerahs. This half shekel is an offering to **the LORD**.
30:14 twenty years old or more, are to give an offering to **the LORD**.
30:15 when you make the offering to **the LORD** to atone for your lives.
30:16 It will be a memorial for the Israelites before **the LORD**,
30:17 Then **the LORD** said to Moses,
30:20 to minister by presenting an offering made to **the LORD** by fire,
30:22 Then **the LORD** said to Moses,
30:34 **the LORD** said to Moses, "Take fragrant spices—gum resin,
30:37 with this formula for yourselves; consider it holy to **the LORD**.
31:1 Then **the LORD** said to Moses,
31:12 Then **the LORD** said to Moses,
31:13 so you may know that I am **the LORD**, who makes you holy.
31:15 but the seventh day is a Sabbath of rest, holy to **the LORD**.
31:17 for in six days **the LORD** made the heavens and the earth,
32:5 "Tomorrow there will be a festival to **the LORD**."
32:7 Then **the LORD** said to Moses, "Go down, because your people,
32:9 "I have seen these people," **the LORD** said to Moses, "and they
32:11 But Moses sought the favor of **the LORD** his God. "O LORD,"
32:11 "O **LORD**," he said, "why should your anger burn against your
32:14 **the LORD** relented and did not bring on his people the disaster
32:26 at the entrance to the camp and said, "Whoever is for **the LORD**,
32:27 he said to them, "This is what **the LORD**, the God of Israel, says:
32:29 Then Moses said, "You have been set apart to **the LORD** today,
32:30 now I will go up to **the LORD**; perhaps I can make atonement for
32:31 So Moses went back to **the LORD** and said, "Oh, what a great sin
32:33 **The LORD** replied to Moses, "Whoever has sinned against me I
32:35 **the LORD** struck the people with a plague because of what they
33:1 **the LORD** said to Moses, "Leave this place, you and the people
33:5 For **the LORD** had said to Moses, "Tell the Israelites, 'You are a
33:7 Anyone inquiring of **the LORD** would go to the tent of meeting
33:11 **The LORD** would speak to Moses face to face, as a man speaks
33:12 Moses said to **the LORD**, "You have been telling me, 'Lead these
33:17 **the LORD** said to Moses, "I will do the very thing you have
33:19 and I will proclaim my name, **the LORD**, in your presence.
33:21 **the LORD** said, "There is a place near me where you may stand
34:1 **The LORD** said to Moses, "Chisel out two stone tablets like the
34:4 Sinai early in the morning, as **the LORD** had commanded him;
34:5 **the LORD** came down in the cloud and stood there with him
34:5 and stood there with him and proclaimed his name, **the LORD**.
34:6 And **he**[s] passed in front of Moses, proclaiming, "The LORD,
34:6 proclaiming, "**The LORD**, the LORD, the compassionate
34:6 proclaiming, "The LORD, **the LORD**, the compassionate
34:10 see how awesome is the work that I, **the LORD**, will do for you.
34:14 for **the LORD**, whose name is Jealous, is a jealous God.
34:23 a year all your men are to appear before the Sovereign **LORD**,
34:24 up three times each year to appear before **the LORD** your God.
34:26 of the firstfruits of your soil to the house of **the LORD** your God.
34:27 Then **the LORD** said to Moses, "Write down these words,
34:28 Moses was there with **the LORD** forty days and forty nights
34:32 he gave them all the commands **the LORD** had given him on
34:34 whenever he entered **the LORD's** presence to speak with him,
35:1 "These are the things **the LORD** has commanded you to do:
35:2 day shall be your holy day, a Sabbath of rest to **the LORD**.
35:4 Israelite community, "This is what **the LORD** has commanded:
35:5 From what you have, take an offering for **the LORD**.
35:5 Everyone who is willing is to bring to **the LORD** an offering of
35:10 are to come and make everything **the LORD** has commanded:
35:21 brought an offering to **the LORD** for the work on the Tent of
35:22 They all presented their gold as a wave offering to **the LORD**.
35:24 of silver or bronze brought it as an offering to **the LORD**,
35:29 women who were willing brought to **the LORD** freewill offerings
35:29 the work **the LORD** through Moses had commanded them to do.
35:30 "See, **the LORD** has chosen Bezalel son of Uri, the son of Hur,
36:1 and every skilled person to whom **the LORD** has given skill
36:1 sanctuary are to do the work just as **the LORD** has commanded."
36:2 and every skilled person to whom **the LORD** had given ability
36:5 enough for doing the work **the LORD** commanded to be done."
38:22 tribe of Judah, made everything **the LORD** commanded Moses;
39:1 sacred garments for Aaron, as **the LORD** commanded Moses.
39:5 and with finely twisted linen, as **the LORD** commanded Moses.
39:7 stones for the sons of Israel, as **the LORD** commanded Moses.
39:21 swing out from the ephod—as **the LORD** commanded Moses.
39:26 to be worn for ministering, as **the LORD** commanded Moses.
39:29 the work of an embroiderer—as **the LORD** commanded Moses.
39:30 on it, like an inscription on a seal: HOLY TO **THE LORD**.
39:31 to it to attach it to the turban, as **the LORD** commanded Moses.
39:32 The Israelites did everything just as **the LORD** commanded
39:42 The Israelites had done all the work just as **the LORD** had
39:43 and saw that they had done it just as **the LORD** had commanded.
40:1 Then **the LORD** said to Moses:
40:16 Moses did everything just as **the LORD** commanded him.
40:19 put the covering over the tent, as **the LORD** commanded him.
40:21 the ark of the Testimony, as **the LORD** commanded him.
40:23 set out the bread on it before **the LORD**, as the LORD
40:23 bread on it before the LORD, as **the LORD** commanded him.
40:25 set up the lamps before **the LORD**, as the LORD commanded
40:25 up the lamps before the LORD, as **the LORD** commanded him.
40:27 and burned fragrant incense on it, as **the LORD** commanded him.
40:29 and grain offerings, as **the LORD** commanded him.
40:32 or approached the altar, as **the LORD** commanded Moses.
40:34 Tent of Meeting, and the glory of **the LORD** filled the tabernacle.
40:35 settled upon it, and the glory of **the LORD** filled the tabernacle.
40:38 So the cloud of **the LORD** was over the tabernacle by day,
Lev 1:1 **The LORD** called to Moses and spoke to him from the Tent of
1:2 'When any of you brings an offering to **the LORD**, bring as your
1:3 to the Tent of Meeting so that it will be acceptable to **the LORD**.
1:5 He is to slaughter the young bull before **the LORD**, and
1:9 an offering made by fire, an aroma pleasing to **the LORD**.
1:11 is to slaughter it at the north side of the altar before **the LORD**,
1:13 an offering made by fire, an aroma pleasing to **the LORD**.
1:14 " 'If the offering to **the LORD** is a burnt offering of birds,
1:17 an offering made by fire, an aroma pleasing to **the LORD**.
2:1 " 'When someone brings a grain offering to **the LORD**,
2:2 an offering made by fire, an aroma pleasing to **the LORD**.
2:3 it is a most holy part of the offerings made to **the LORD** by fire.
2:8 Bring the grain offering made of these things to **the LORD**;
2:9 as an offering made by fire, an aroma pleasing to **the LORD**.
2:10 it is a most holy part of the offerings made to **the LORD** by fire.
2:11 " 'Every grain offering you bring to **the LORD** must be made
2:11 any yeast or honey in an offering made to **the LORD** by fire.
2:12 You may bring them to **the LORD** as an offering of the
2:14 " 'If you bring a grain offering of firstfruits to **the LORD**,
2:16 with all the incense, as an offering made to **the LORD** by fire.
3:1 he is to present before **the LORD** an animal without defect.
3:3 offering he is to bring a sacrifice made to **the LORD** by fire:
3:5 as an offering made by fire, an aroma pleasing to **the LORD**.
3:6 an animal from the flock as a fellowship offering to **the LORD**,
3:7 If he offers a lamb, he is to present it before **the LORD**.
3:9 offering he is to bring a sacrifice made to **the LORD** by fire:
3:11 them on the altar as food, an offering made to **the LORD** by fire.
3:12 " 'If his offering is a goat, he is to present it before **the LORD**.
3:14 From what he offers he is to make this offering to **the LORD** by
3:16 by fire, a pleasing aroma. All the fat is **the LORD's** [+4200].
4:1 **The LORD** said to Moses,
4:2 and does what is forbidden in any of **the LORD's** commands—
4:3 he must bring to **the LORD** a young bull without defect as a sin
4:4 the bull at the entrance to the Tent of Meeting before **the LORD**.
4:4 is to lay his hand on its head and slaughter it before **the LORD**.
4:6 the blood and sprinkle some of it seven times before **the LORD**,
4:7 fragrant incense that is before **the LORD** in the Tent of Meeting.
4:13 and does what is forbidden in any of **the LORD's** commands,
4:15 are to lay their hands on the bull's head before **the LORD**,
4:15 the LORD, and the bull shall be slaughtered before **the LORD**.
4:17 sprinkle it before **the LORD** seven times in front of the curtain.
4:18 horns of the altar that is before **the LORD** in the Tent of Meeting.
4:22 does what is forbidden in any of the commands of **the LORD** his
4:24 place where the burnt offering is slaughtered before **the LORD**.
4:27 and does what is forbidden in any of **the LORD's** commands,
4:31 shall burn it on the altar as an aroma pleasing to **the LORD**.
4:35 it on the altar on top of the offerings made to **the LORD** by fire.
5:6 he must bring to **the LORD** a female lamb or goat from the flock
5:7 or two young pigeons to **the LORD** as a penalty for his sin—
5:12 burn it on the altar on top of the offerings made to **the LORD** by
5:14 **The LORD** said to Moses:
5:15 sins unintentionally in regard to any of **the LORD's** holy things,
5:15 he is to bring to **the LORD** as a penalty a ram from the flock,
5:17 and does what is forbidden in any of **the LORD's** commands,
5:19 he has been guilty of wrongdoing against **the LORD**."
6:1 [5:20] **The LORD** said to Moses:
6:2 [5:21] is unfaithful to **the LORD** by deceiving his neighbor
6:6 [5:25] that is, to **the LORD**, his guilt offering, a ram from the
6:7 [5:26] the priest will make atonement for him before **the LORD**,
6:8 [6:1] **The LORD** said to Moses:
6:14 [6:7] Aaron's sons are to bring it before **the LORD**, in front of
6:15 [6:8] portion on the altar as an aroma pleasing to **the LORD**.
6:18 [6:11] It is his regular share of the offerings made to **the LORD**
6:19 [6:12] **The LORD** also said to Moses,
6:20 [6:13] his sons are to bring to **the LORD** on the day he is
6:21 [6:14] broken in pieces as an aroma pleasing to **the LORD**.
6:22 [6:15] It is **the LORD's** [+4200] regular share and is to be
6:24 [6:17] **The LORD** said to Moses,
6:25 [6:18] The sin offering is to be slaughtered before **the LORD** in
7:5 burn them on the altar as an offering made to **the LORD** by fire.

[F] Hitpael (hitpoel, hitpoal, hitpolel, hitpolal, hitpalel, hitpalal, hitpalpel, hitpalpal, hotpael, hotpaal) [G] Hiphil (hiphtil) [H] Hophal [I] Hishtaphel

Lev 7: 11 for the fellowship offering a person may present to **the LORD**:
7: 14 one of each kind as an offering, a contribution to **the LORD**;
7: 20 eats any meat of the fellowship offering belonging to **the LORD**,
7: 21 of the meat of the fellowship offering belonging to **the LORD**,
7: 22 **The LORD** said to Moses,
7: 25 fire may be made to **the LORD** must be cut off from his people.
7: 28 **The LORD** said to Moses,
7: 29 'Anyone who brings a fellowship offering to **the LORD** is to
7: 29 to the LORD is to bring part of it as his sacrifice to **the LORD**.
7: 30 own hands he is to bring the offering made to **the LORD** by fire;
7: 30 and wave the breast before **the LORD** as a wave offering.
7: 35 This is the portion of the offerings made to **the LORD** by fire that
7: 35 his sons on the day they were presented to serve **the LORD** as
7: 36 **the LORD** commanded that the Israelites give this to them as
7: 38 which **the LORD** gave Moses on Mount Sinai on the day he
7: 38 commanded the Israelites to bring their offerings to **the LORD**,
8: 1 **The LORD** said to Moses,
8: 4 Moses did as **the LORD** commanded him, and the assembly
8: 5 "This is what **the LORD** has commanded to be done."
8: 9 on the front of it, as **the LORD** commanded Moses.
8: 13 and put headbands on them, as **the LORD** commanded Moses.
8: 17 burned up outside the camp, as **the LORD** commanded Moses.
8: 21 a pleasing aroma, an offering made to **the LORD** by fire,
8: 21 made to the LORD by fire, as **the LORD** commanded Moses.
8: 26 which was before **the LORD**, he took a cake of bread, and one
8: 27 his sons and waved them before **the LORD** as a wave offering.
8: 28 a pleasing aroma, an offering made to **the LORD** by fire.
8: 29 waved it before **the LORD** as a wave offering, as the LORD
8: 29 LORD as a wave offering, as **the LORD** commanded Moses.
8: 34 What has been done today was commanded by **the LORD** to
8: 35 and night for seven days and do what **the LORD** requires,
8: 36 his sons did everything **the LORD** commanded through Moses.
9: 2 both without defect, and present them before **the LORD**.
9: 4 and a ram for a fellowship offering to sacrifice before **the LORD**,
9: 4 mixed with oil. For today **the LORD** will appear to you.' "
9: 5 and the entire assembly came near and stood before **the LORD**.
9: 6 Moses said, "This is what **the LORD** has commanded you to do,
9: 6 you to do, so that the glory of **the LORD** may appear to you."
9: 7 and make atonement for them, as **the LORD** has commanded."
9: 10 the liver from the sin offering, as **the LORD** commanded Moses;
9: 21 and the right thigh before **the LORD** as a wave offering,
9: 23 the people; and the glory of **the LORD** appeared to all the people.
9: 24 Fire came out from the presence of **the LORD** and consumed the
10: 1 they offered unauthorized fire before **the LORD**, contrary to his
10: 2 So fire came out from the presence of **the LORD** and consumed
10: 2 and consumed them, and they died before **the LORD**.
10: 3 said to Aaron, "This is what **the LORD** spoke of when he said:
10: 6 of Israel, may mourn for those **the LORD** has destroyed by fire.
10: 7 or you will die, because **the LORD's** anointing oil is on you."
10: 8 Then **the LORD** said to Aaron,
10: 11 you must teach the Israelites all the decrees **the LORD** has given
10: 12 offering left over from the offerings made to **the LORD** by fire
10: 13 and your sons' share of the offerings made to **the LORD** by fire;
10: 15 made by fire, to be waved before **the LORD** as a wave offering.
10: 15 share for you and your children, as **the LORD** has commanded."
10: 17 the community by making atonement for them before **the LORD**.
10: 19 their sin offering and their burnt offering before **the LORD**,
10: 19 Would **the LORD** have been pleased if I had eaten the sin
11: 1 **The LORD** said to Moses and Aaron,
11: 44 I am **the LORD** your God; consecrate yourselves and be holy,
11: 45 I am **the LORD** who brought you up out of Egypt to be your
12: 1 **The LORD** said to Moses,
12: 7 He shall offer them before **the LORD** to make atonement for her,
13: 1 **The LORD** said to Moses and Aaron,
14: 1 **The LORD** said to Moses,
14: 11 his offerings before **the LORD** at the entrance to the Tent of
14: 12 he shall wave them before **the LORD** as a wave offering.
14: 16 with his finger sprinkle some of it before **the LORD** seven times.
14: 18 to be cleansed and make atonement for him before **the LORD**.
14: 23 priest at the entrance to the Tent of Meeting, before **the LORD**.
14: 24 log of oil, and wave them before **the LORD** as a wave offering.
14: 27 some of the oil from his palm seven times before **the LORD**.
14: 29 one to be cleansed, to make atonement for him before **the LORD**.
14: 31 In this way the priest will make atonement before **the LORD** on
14: 33 **The LORD** said to Moses and Aaron,
15: 1 **The LORD** said to Moses and Aaron,
15: 14 come before **the LORD** to the entrance to the Tent of Meeting
15: 15 In this way he will make atonement before **the LORD** for the
15: 30 In this way he will make atonement for her before **the LORD** for
16: 1 **The LORD** spoke to Moses after the death of the two sons of
16: 1 two sons of Aaron who died when they approached **the LORD**.
16: 2 **The LORD** said to Moses: "Tell your brother Aaron not to come
16: 7 present them before **the LORD** at the entrance to the Tent of
16: 8 one lot for **the LORD** and the other for the scapegoat.
16: 9 Aaron shall bring the goat whose lot falls to **the LORD**
16: 10 **the LORD** to be used for making atonement by sending it into
16: 12 a censer full of burning coals from the altar before **the LORD**
16: 13 He is to put the incense on the fire before **the LORD**,
16: 18 "Then he shall come out to the altar that is before **the LORD**
16: 30 Then, before **the LORD**, you will be clean from all your sins.
16: 34 And it was done, as **the LORD** commanded Moses.
17: 1 **The LORD** said to Moses,
17: 2 and say to them: 'This is what **the LORD** has commanded:
17: 4 offering to **the LORD** in front of the tabernacle of the LORD—
17: 4 offering to the LORD in front of the tabernacle of **the LORD**—
17: 5 so the Israelites will bring to **the LORD** the sacrifices they are
17: 5 They must bring them to the priest, that is, to **the LORD**,
17: 6 The priest is to sprinkle the blood against the altar of **the LORD**
17: 6 of Meeting and burn the fat as an aroma pleasing to **the LORD**.
17: 9 the entrance to the Tent of Meeting to sacrifice it to **the LORD**—
18: 1 **The LORD** said to Moses,
18: 2 to the Israelites and say to them: 'I am **the LORD** your God.
18: 4 and be careful to follow my decrees. I am **the LORD** your God.
18: 5 for the man who obeys them will live by them. I am **the LORD**.
18: 6 any close relative to have sexual relations. I am **the LORD**.
18: 21 for you must not profane the name of your God. I am **the LORD**.
18: 30 do not defile yourselves with them. I am **the LORD** your God.' "
19: 1 **The LORD** said to Moses,
19: 2 say to them: 'Be holy because I, **the LORD** your God, am holy.
19: 3 and you must observe my Sabbaths. I am **the LORD** your God.
19: 4 gods of cast metal for yourselves. I am **the LORD** your God.
19: 5 " 'When you sacrifice a fellowship offering to **the LORD**,
19: 8 because he has desecrated what is holy to **the LORD**;
19: 10 Leave them for the poor and the alien. I am **the LORD** your God.
19: 12 my name and so profane the name of your God. I am **the LORD**.
19: 14 block in front of the blind, but fear your God. I am **the LORD**.
19: 16 do anything that endangers your neighbor's life. I am **the LORD**.
19: 18 your people, but love your neighbor as yourself. I am **the LORD**.
19: 21 entrance to the Tent of Meeting for a guilt offering to **the LORD**.
19: 22 for him before **the LORD** for the sin he has committed,
19: 24 year all its fruit will be holy, an offering of praise to **the LORD**.
19: 25 way your harvest will be increased. I am **the LORD** your God.
19: 28 for the dead or put tattoo marks on yourselves. I am **the LORD**.
19: 30 and have reverence for my sanctuary. I am **the LORD**.
19: 31 for you will be defiled by them. I am **the LORD** your God.
19: 32 respect for the elderly and revere your God. I am **the LORD**.
19: 34 for you were aliens in Egypt. I am **the LORD** your God.
19: 36 I am **the LORD** your God, who brought you out of Egypt.
19: 37 my decrees and all my laws and follow them. I am **the LORD**.' "
20: 1 **The LORD** said to Moses,
20: 7 and be holy, because I am **the LORD** your God.
20: 8 and follow them. I am **the LORD**, who makes you holy.
20: 24 I am **the LORD** your God, who has set you apart from the
20: 26 You are to be holy to me because I, **the LORD**, am holy,
21: 1 **The LORD** said to Moses, "Speak to the priests, the sons of
21: 6 Because they present the offerings made to **the LORD** by fire,
21: 8 Consider them holy, because I **the LORD** am holy—I who make
21: 12 been dedicated by the anointing oil of his God. I am **the LORD**.
21: 15 among his people. I am **the LORD**, who makes him holy.' "
21: 16 **The LORD** said to Moses,
21: 21 to come near to present the offerings made to **the LORD** by fire.
21: 23 my sanctuary. I am **the LORD**, who makes them holy.' "
22: 1 **The LORD** said to Moses,
22: 2 so they will not profane my holy name. I am **the LORD**.
22: 3 the sacred offerings that the Israelites consecrate to **the LORD**,
22: 3 that person must be cut off from my presence. I am **the LORD**.
22: 8 wild animals, and so become unclean through it. I am **the LORD**.
22: 9 them with contempt. I am **the LORD**, who makes them holy.
22: 15 desecrate the sacred offerings the Israelites present to **the LORD**
22: 16 requiring payment. I am **the LORD**, who makes them holy.' "
22: 17 **The LORD** said to Moses,
22: 18 presents a gift for a burnt offering to **the LORD**, either to fulfill a
22: 21 or flock a fellowship offering to **the LORD** to fulfill a special
22: 22 Do not offer to **the LORD** the blind, the injured or the maimed,
22: 22 of these on the altar as an offering made to **the LORD** by fire.
22: 24 You must not offer to **the LORD** an animal whose testicles are
22: 26 **The LORD** said to Moses,
22: 27 it will be acceptable as an offering made to **the LORD** by fire.
22: 29 "When you sacrifice a thank offering to **the LORD**, sacrifice it in
22: 30 that same day; leave none of it till morning. I am **the LORD**.
22: 31 "Keep my commands and follow them. I am **the LORD**.
22: 32 as holy by the Israelites. I am **the LORD**, who makes you holy
22: 33 who brought you out of Egypt to be your God. I am **the LORD**."
23: 1 **The LORD** said to Moses,
23: 2 are my appointed feasts, the appointed feasts of **the LORD**,
23: 3 to do any work; wherever you live, it is a Sabbath to **the LORD**.
23: 4 " 'These are **the LORD's** appointed feasts, the sacred assemblies
23: 5 **The LORD's** [+4200] Passover begins at twilight on the

Lev 23: 6 On the fifteenth day of that month **the LORD's** [+4200] Feast of
23: 8 For seven days present an offering made to **the LORD** by fire.
23: 9 **The LORD** said to Moses,
23: 11 He is to wave the sheaf before **the LORD** so it will be accepted
23: 12 you must sacrifice as a burnt offering to **the LORD** a lamb a year
23: 13 an offering made to **the LORD** by fire, a pleasing aroma—
23: 16 and then present an offering of new grain to **the LORD**.
23: 17 baked with yeast, as a wave offering of firstfruits to **the LORD**.
23: 18 They will be a burnt offering to **the LORD**, together with their
23: 18 an offering made by fire, an aroma pleasing to **the LORD**.
23: 20 The priest is to wave the two lambs before **the LORD** as a wave
23: 20 They are a sacred offering to **the LORD** for the priest.
23: 22 them for the poor and the alien. I am **the LORD** your God.' "
23: 23 **The LORD** said to Moses,
23: 25 but present an offering made to **the LORD** by fire.' "
23: 26 **The LORD** said to Moses,
23: 27 and present an offering made to **the LORD** by fire.
23: 28 when atonement is made for you before **the LORD** your God.
23: 33 **The LORD** said to Moses,
23: 34 'On the fifteenth day of the seventh month **the LORD's** [+4200]
23: 36 For seven days present offerings made to **the LORD** by fire,
23: 36 and present an offering made to **the LORD** by fire.
23: 37 (" 'These are **the LORD's** appointed feasts, which you are to
23: 37 assemblies for bringing offerings made to **the LORD** by fire—
23: 38 These offerings are in addition to those for **the LORD's** Sabbaths
23: 38 have vowed and all the freewill offerings you give to **the LORD**.)
23: 39 of the land, celebrate the festival to **the LORD** for seven days;
23: 40 and rejoice before **the LORD** your God for seven days.
23: 41 Celebrate this as a festival to **the LORD** for seven days each
23: 43 when I brought them out of Egypt. I am **the LORD** your God.' "
23: 44 announced to the Israelites the appointed feasts of **the LORD**.
24: 1 **The LORD** said to Moses,
24: 3 Aaron is to tend the lamps before **the LORD** from evening till
24: 4 The lamps on the pure gold lampstand before **the LORD** must be
24: 6 six in each row, on the table of pure gold before **the LORD**.
24: 7 the bread and to be an offering made to **the LORD** by fire.
24: 8 This bread is to be set out before **the LORD** regularly, Sabbath
24: 9 of their regular share of the offerings made to **the LORD** by fire."
24: 12 They put him in custody until the will of **the LORD** should be
24: 13 Then **the LORD** said to Moses:
24: 16 anyone who blasphemes the name of **the LORD** must be put to
24: 22 for the alien and the native-born. I am **the LORD** your God.' "
24: 23 stoned him. The Israelites did as **the LORD** commanded Moses.
25: 1 **The LORD** said to Moses on Mount Sinai,
25: 2 to give you, the land itself must observe a sabbath to **the LORD**.
25: 4 year the land is to have a sabbath of rest, a sabbath to **the LORD**.
25: 17 of each other, but fear your God. I am **the LORD** your God.
25: 38 I am **the LORD** your God, who brought you out of Egypt to give
25: 55 whom I brought out of Egypt. I am **the LORD** your God.
26: 1 in your land to bow down before it. I am **the LORD** your God.
26: 2 and have reverence for my sanctuary. I am **the LORD**.
26: 13 I am **the LORD** your God, who brought you out of Egypt
26: 44 breaking my covenant with them. I am **the LORD** their God.
26: 45 in the sight of the nations to be their God. I am **the LORD**.' "
26: 46 the regulations that **the LORD** established on Mount Sinai
27: 1 **The LORD** said to Moses,
27: 2 'If anyone makes a special vow to dedicate persons to **the LORD**
27: 9 is an animal that is acceptable as an offering to **the LORD**,
27: 9 to the LORD, such an animal given to **the LORD** becomes holy.
27: 11 one that is not acceptable as an offering to **the LORD**—the
27: 14 " 'If a man dedicates his house as something holy to **the LORD**,
27: 16 " 'If a man dedicates to **the LORD** part of his family land,
27: 21 it will become holy, like a field devoted to **the LORD**;
27: 22 " 'If a man dedicates to **the LORD** a field he has bought,
27: 23 must pay its value on that day as something holy to **the LORD**.
27: 26 of an animal, since the firstborn already belongs to **the LORD**;
27: 26 the LORD; whether an ox or a sheep, it is **the LORD's** [+4200].
27: 28 " 'But nothing that a man owns and devotes to **the LORD**—
27: 28 or redeemed; everything so devoted is most holy to **the LORD**.
27: 30 grain from the soil or fruit from the trees, belongs to **the LORD**;
27: 30 from the trees, belongs to the LORD; it is holy to **the LORD**.
27: 32 that passes under the shepherd's rod—will be holy to **the LORD**.
27: 34 These are the commands **the LORD** gave Moses on Mount Sinai
Nu 1: 1 **The LORD** spoke to Moses in the Tent of Meeting in the Desert
1: 19 as **the LORD** commanded Moses. And so he counted them in the
1: 48 **The LORD** had said to Moses:
1: 54 The Israelites did all this just as **the LORD** commanded Moses.
2: 1 **The LORD** said to Moses and Aaron:
2: 33 along with the other Israelites, as **the LORD** commanded Moses.
2: 34 So the Israelites did everything **the LORD** commanded Moses;
3: 1 Moses at the time **the LORD** talked with Moses on Mount Sinai.
3: 4 fell dead before **the LORD** when they made an offering with
3: 4 offering with unauthorized fire before **him**[s] in the Desert of Sinai.
3: 5 **The LORD** said to Moses,
3: 11 **The LORD** also said to Moses,
3: 13 whether man or animal. They are to be mine. I am **the LORD**."
3: 14 **The LORD** said to Moses in the Desert of Sinai,
3: 16 counted them, as he was commanded by the word of **the LORD**.
3: 39 The total number of Levites counted at **the LORD's** command by
3: 40 **The LORD** said to Moses, "Count all the firstborn Israelite males
3: 41 the firstborn of the livestock of the Israelites. I am **the LORD**."
3: 42 all the firstborn of the Israelites, as **the LORD** commanded him.
3: 44 **The LORD** also said to Moses,
3: 45 of their livestock. The Levites are to be mine. I am **the LORD**.
3: 51 and his sons, as he was commanded by the word of **the LORD**.
3: 51 as he was commanded by the word of the LORD. **[RPH]**
4: 1 **The LORD** said to Moses and Aaron:
4: 17 **The LORD** said to Moses and Aaron,
4: 21 **The LORD** said to Moses,
4: 37 Aaron counted them according to **the LORD's** command through
4: 41 and Aaron counted them according to **the LORD's** command.
4: 45 Aaron counted them according to **the LORD's** command through
4: 49 At **the LORD's** command through Moses, each was assigned his
4: 49 Thus they were counted, as **the LORD** commanded Moses.
5: 1 **The LORD** said to Moses,
5: 4 the camp. They did just as **the LORD** had instructed Moses.
5: 5 **The LORD** said to Moses,
5: 6 wrongs another in any way and so is unfaithful to **the LORD**,
5: 8 the restitution belongs to **the LORD** and must be given to the
5: 11 Then **the LORD** said to Moses,
5: 16 " 'The priest shall bring her and have her stand before **the LORD**.
5: 18 After the priest has had the woman stand before **the LORD**,
5: 21 "may **the LORD** cause your people to curse and denounce you
5: 21 and denounce you when **he**[s] causes your thigh to waste away
5: 25 for jealousy, wave it before **the LORD** and bring it to the altar.
5: 30 The priest is to have her stand before **the LORD** and is to apply
6: 1 **The LORD** said to Moses,
6: 2 a special vow, a vow of separation to **the LORD** as a Nazirite,
6: 5 He must be holy until the period of his separation to **the LORD** is
6: 6 Throughout the period of his separation to **the LORD** he must not
6: 8 the period of his separation he is consecrated to **the LORD**.
6: 12 He must dedicate himself to **the LORD** for the period of his
6: 14 There he is to present his offerings to **the LORD**: a year-old male
6: 16 " 'The priest is to present them before **the LORD** and make the
6: 17 and is to sacrifice the ram as a fellowship offering to **the LORD**,
6: 20 priest shall then wave them before **the LORD** as a wave offering;
6: 21 his offering to **the LORD** in accordance with his separation,
6: 22 **The LORD** said to Moses,
6: 24 " ' "**The LORD** bless you and keep you;
6: 25 **the LORD** make his face shine upon you and be gracious to you;
6: 26 **the LORD** turn his face toward you and give you peace." '
7: 3 They brought as their gifts before **the LORD** six covered carts
7: 4 **The LORD** said to Moses,
7: 11 For **the LORD** had said to Moses, "Each day one leader is to
8: 1 **The LORD** said to Moses,
8: 3 forward on the lampstand, just as **the LORD** commanded Moses.
8: 4 The lampstand was made exactly like the pattern **the LORD** had
8: 5 **The LORD** said to Moses:
8: 10 You are to bring the Levites before **the LORD**, and the Israelites
8: 11 Aaron is to present the Levites before **the LORD** as a wave
8: 11 so that they may be ready to do the work of **the LORD**.
8: 12 use the one for a sin offering to **the LORD** and the other for a
8: 13 his sons and then present them as a wave offering to **the LORD**.
8: 20 did with the Levites just as **the LORD** commanded Moses.
8: 21 Then Aaron presented them as a wave offering before **the LORD**
8: 22 They did with the Levites just as **the LORD** commanded Moses.
8: 23 **The LORD** said to Moses,
9: 1 **The LORD** spoke to Moses in the Desert of Sinai in the first
9: 5 The Israelites did everything just as **the LORD** commanded
9: 7 why should we be kept from presenting **the LORD's** offering
9: 8 "Wait until I find out what **the LORD** commands concerning
9: 9 Then **the LORD** said to Moses,
9: 10 a journey, they may still celebrate **the LORD's** [+4200] Passover.
9: 13 because he did not present **the LORD's** offering at the appointed
9: 14 who wants to celebrate **the LORD's** [+4200] Passover must do
9: 18 At **the LORD's** command the Israelites set out, and at his
9: 18 the Israelites set out, and at **his**[s] command they encamped.
9: 19 the Israelites obeyed **the LORD's** order and did not set out.
9: 20 at **the LORD's** command they would encamp, and then at his
9: 20 they would encamp, and then at **his**[s] command they would set out.
9: 23 At **the LORD's** command they encamped, and at the LORD's
9: 23 they encamped, and at **the LORD's** command they set out.
9: 23 They obeyed **the LORD's** order, in accordance with his
9: 23 LORD's order, in accordance with **his**[s] command through Moses.
10: 1 **The LORD** said to Moses:
10: 9 you will be remembered by **the LORD** your God and rescued
10: 10 a memorial for you before your God. I am **the LORD** your God."
10: 13 this first time, at **the LORD's** command through Moses.

Nu 10:29 "We are setting out for the place about which **the LORD** said,
10:29 you well, for **the LORD** has promised good things to Israel."
10:32 we will share with you whatever good things **the LORD** gives
10:33 So they set out from the mountain of **the LORD** and traveled for
10:33 The ark of the covenant of **the LORD** went before them during
10:34 The cloud of **the LORD** was over them by day when they set out
10:35 Whenever the ark set out, Moses said, "Rise up, O **LORD**!
10:36 Whenever it came to rest, he said, "Return, O **LORD**,
11: 1 complained about their hardships in the hearing of **the LORD**,
11: 1 of the LORD, and when **he**[s] heard them his anger was aroused.
11: 1 fire from **the LORD** burned among them and consumed some of
11: 2 out to Moses, he prayed to **the LORD** and the fire died down.
11: 3 because fire from **the LORD** had burned among them.
11:10 **The LORD** became exceedingly angry, and Moses was troubled.
11:11 He asked **the LORD**, "Why have you brought this trouble on
11:16 **The LORD** said to Moses: "Bring me seventy of Israel's elders
11:18 **The LORD** heard you when you wailed, "If only we had meat to
11:18 Now **the LORD** will give you meat, and you will eat it.
11:20 because you have rejected **the LORD**, who is among you,
11:23 **The LORD** answered Moses, "Is the LORD's arm too short?
11:23 The LORD answered Moses, "Is **the LORD's** arm too short?
11:24 So Moses went out and told the people what **the LORD** had said.
11:25 Then **the LORD** came down in the cloud and spoke with him,
11:29 I wish that all **the LORD's** people were prophets and that the
11:29 were prophets and that **the LORD** would put his Spirit on them!"
11:31 Now a wind went out from **the LORD** and drove quail in from
11:33 be consumed, the anger of **the LORD** burned against the people,
11:33 against the people, and **he**[s] struck them with a severe plague.
12: 2 "Has **the LORD** spoken only through Moses?" they asked.
12: 2 "Hasn't he also spoken through us?" And **the LORD** heard this.
12: 4 At once **the LORD** said to Moses, Aaron and Miriam, "Come out
12: 5 **the LORD** came down in a pillar of cloud; he stood at the
12: 6 "When a prophet of **the LORD** is among you, I reveal myself to
12: 8 clearly and not in riddles; he sees the form of **the LORD**.
12: 9 The anger of **the LORD** burned against them, and he left them.
12:13 So Moses cried out to **the LORD**, "O God, please heal her!"
12:14 **The LORD** replied to Moses, "If her father had spit in her face,
13: 1 **The LORD** said to Moses,
13: 3 So at **the LORD's** command Moses sent them out from the
14: 3 Why is **the LORD** bringing us to this land only to let us fall by
14: 8 If **the LORD** is pleased with us, he will lead us into that land,
14: 9 Only do not rebel against **the LORD**. And do not be afraid of the
14: 9 Their protection is gone, but **the LORD** is with us. Do not be
14:10 the glory of **the LORD** appeared at the Tent of Meeting to all the
14:11 **The LORD** said to Moses, "How long will these people treat me
14:13 Moses said to **the LORD**, "Then the Egyptians will hear about it!
14:14 O **LORD**, are with these people and that you, O LORD,
14:14 O LORD, are with these people and that you, O **LORD**,
14:16 '**The LORD** was not able to bring these people into the land he
14:18 '**The LORD** is slow to anger, abounding in love and forgiving sin
14:20 **The LORD** replied, "I have forgiven them, as you asked.
14:21 and as surely as the glory of **the LORD** fills the whole earth,
14:26 **The LORD** said to Moses and Aaron:
14:28 So tell them, 'As surely as I live, declares **the LORD**, I will do to
14:35 I, **the LORD**, have spoken, and I will surely do these things to
14:37 land were struck down and died of a plague before **the LORD**.
14:40 they said. "We will go up to the place **the LORD** promised."
14:41 Moses said, "Why are you disobeying **the LORD's** command?
14:42 Do not go up, because **the LORD** is not with you. You will be
14:43 Because you have turned away from **the LORD**, he will not be
14:43 **he**[s] will not be with you and you will fall by the sword."
14:44 though neither Moses nor the ark of **the LORD's** covenant
15: 1 **The LORD** said to Moses,
15: 3 you present to **the LORD** offerings made by fire, from the herd
15: 3 from the herd or the flock, as an aroma pleasing to **the LORD**—
15: 4 the one who brings his offering shall present to **the LORD** a
15: 7 as a drink offering. Offer it as an aroma pleasing to **the LORD**.
15: 8 for a special vow or a fellowship offering to **the LORD**,
15:10 will be an offering made by fire, an aroma pleasing to **the LORD**.
15:13 an offering made by fire as an aroma pleasing to **the LORD**.
15:14 an offering made by fire as an aroma pleasing to **the LORD**,
15:15 to come. You and the alien shall be the same before **the LORD**:
15:17 **The LORD** said to Moses,
15:19 food of the land, present a portion as an offering to **the LORD**.
15:21 this offering to **the LORD** from the first of your ground meal.
15:22 fail to keep any of these commands **the LORD** gave Moses—
15:23 any of **the LORD's** commands to you through him, from the day
15:23 from the day **the LORD** gave them and continuing through the
15:24 bull for a burnt offering as an aroma pleasing to **the LORD**,
15:25 they have brought to **the LORD** for their wrong an offering made
15:25 for their wrong an offering made by fire **[RPH]** and a sin offering.
15:28 The priest is to make atonement before **the LORD** for the one
15:30 whether native-born or alien, blasphemes **the LORD**,
15:31 Because he has despised **the LORD's** word and broken his
15:35 **the LORD** said to Moses, "The man must die. The whole
15:36 and stoned him to death, as **the LORD** commanded Moses.
15:37 **The LORD** said to Moses,
15:39 and so you will remember all the commands of **the LORD**,
15:41 I am **the LORD** your God, who brought you out of Egypt to be
15:41 you out of Egypt to be your God. I am **the LORD** your God.' "
16: 3 is holy, every one of them, and **the LORD** is with them.
16: 3 then do you set yourselves above **the LORD's** assembly?"
16: 5 "In the morning **the LORD** will show who belongs to him
16: 7 and tomorrow put fire and incense in them before **the LORD**.
16: 7 The man **the LORD** chooses will be the one who is holy.
16: 9 brought you near himself to do the work at **the LORD's**
16:11 It is against **the LORD** that you and all your followers have
16:15 Moses became very angry and said to **the LORD**, "Do not accept
16:16 all your followers are to appear before **the LORD** tomorrow—
16:17 in it—250 censers in all—and present it before **the LORD**.
16:19 the glory of **the LORD** appeared to the entire assembly.
16:20 **The LORD** said to Moses and Aaron,
16:23 Then **the LORD** said to Moses,
16:28 "This is how you will know that **the LORD** has sent me to do all
16:29 what usually happens to men, then **the LORD** has not sent me.
16:30 if **the LORD** brings about something totally new, and the earth
16:30 you will know that these men have treated **the LORD** with
16:35 fire came out from **the LORD** and consumed the 250 men who
16:36 [17:1] **The LORD** said to Moses,
16:38 [17:3] for they were presented before **the LORD** and have
16:40 [17:5] as **the LORD** directed him through Moses. This was to
16:40 [17:5] of Aaron should come to burn incense before **the LORD**,
16:41 [17:6] "You have killed **the LORD's** people," they said.
16:42 [17:7] the cloud covered it and the glory of **the LORD** appeared.
16:44 [17:9] and **the LORD** said to Moses,
16:46 [17:11] Wrath has come out from **the LORD**; the plague has
17: 1 [17:16] **The LORD** said to Moses,
17: 7 [17:22] Moses placed the staffs before **the LORD** in the Tent of
17: 9 [17:24] Moses brought out all the staffs from **the LORD's**
17:10 [17:25] **The LORD** said to Moses, "Put back Aaron's staff in
17:11 [17:26] Moses did just as **the LORD** commanded him.
17:13 [17:28] even comes near the tabernacle of **the LORD** will die.
18: 1 **The LORD** said to Aaron, "You, your sons and your father's
18: 6 dedicated to **the LORD** to do the work at the Tent of Meeting.
18: 8 **the LORD** said to Aaron, "I myself have put you in charge of the
18:12 and grain they give **the LORD** as the firstfruits of their harvest.
18:13 All the land's firstfruits that they bring to **the LORD** will be
18:15 both man and animal, that is offered to **the LORD** is yours.
18:17 fat as an offering made by fire, an aroma pleasing to **the LORD**.
18:19 holy offerings the Israelites present to **the LORD** I give to you
18:19 It is an everlasting covenant of salt before **the LORD** for both
18:20 **The LORD** said to Aaron, "You will have no inheritance in their
18:24 the tithes that the Israelites present as an offering to **the LORD**.
18:25 **The LORD** said to Moses,
18:26 you must present a tenth of that tithe as **the LORD's** offering.
18:28 In this way you also will present an offering to **the LORD** from
18:28 From these tithes you must give **the LORD's** portion to Aaron
18:29 You must present as **the LORD's** portion the best and holiest part
19: 1 **The LORD** said to Moses and Aaron:
19: 2 "This is a requirement of the law that **the LORD** has
19:13 and fails to purify himself defiles **the LORD's** tabernacle.
19:20 because he has defiled the sanctuary of **the LORD**.
20: 3 only we had died when our brothers fell dead before **the LORD**!
20: 4 Why did you bring **the LORD's** community into this desert,
20: 6 and fell facedown, and the glory of **the LORD** appeared to them.
20: 7 **The LORD** said to Moses,
20: 9 So Moses took the staff from **the LORD's** presence, just as he
20:12 **the LORD** said to Moses and Aaron, "Because you did not trust
20:13 where the Israelites quarreled with **the LORD** and where he
20:16 when we cried out to **the LORD**, he heard our cry and sent an
20:23 near the border of Edom, **the LORD** said to Moses and Aaron,
20:27 Moses did as **the LORD** commanded: They went up Mount Hor
21: 2 Israel made this vow to **the LORD**: "If you will deliver these
21: 3 **The LORD** listened to Israel's plea and gave the Canaanites over
21: 6 **the LORD** sent venomous snakes among them; they bit the
21: 7 "We sinned when we spoke against **the LORD** and against you.
21: 7 Pray that **the LORD** will take the snakes away from us."
21: 8 **The LORD** said to Moses, "Make a snake and put it up on a pole;
21:14 That is why the Book of the Wars of **the LORD** says: "Waheb in
21:16 the well where **the LORD** said to Moses, "Gather the people
21:34 **The LORD** said to Moses, "Do not be afraid of him, for I have
22: 8 "and I will bring you back the answer **the LORD** gives me."
22:13 own country, for **the LORD** has refused to let me go with you."
22:18 or small to go beyond the command of **the LORD** my God.
22:19 others did, and I will find out what else **the LORD** will tell me."
22:22 and the angel of **the LORD** stood in the road to oppose him.
22:23 When the donkey saw the angel of **the LORD** standing in the
22:24 the angel of **the LORD** stood in a narrow path between two

Nu 22:25 When the donkey saw the angel of **the LORD**, she pressed close
22:26 the angel of **the LORD** moved on ahead and stood in a narrow
22:27 When the donkey saw the angel of **the LORD**, she lay down
22:28 **the LORD** opened the donkey's mouth, and she said to Balaam,
22:31 **the LORD** opened Balaam's eyes, and he saw the angel of the
22:31 he saw the angel of **the LORD** standing in the road with his
22:32 The angel of **the LORD** asked him, "Why have you beaten your
22:34 Balaam said to the angel of **the LORD**, "I have sinned. I did not
22:35 The angel of **the LORD** said to Balaam, "Go with the men,
23: 3 Perhaps **the LORD** will come to meet with me. Whatever he
23: 5 **The LORD** put a message in Balaam's mouth and said, "Go back
23: 8 How can I denounce those whom **the LORD** has not denounced?
23:12 "Must I not speak what **the LORD** puts in my mouth?"
23:16 **The LORD** met with Balaam and put a message in his mouth
23:17 princes of Moab. Balak asked him, "What did **the LORD** say?"
23:21 **The LORD** their God is with them; the shout of the King is
23:26 "Did I not tell you I must do whatever **the LORD** says?"
24: 1 Now when Balaam saw that it pleased **the LORD** to bless Israel,
24: 6 like gardens beside a river, like aloes planted by **the LORD**,
24:11 but **the LORD** has kept you from being rewarded."
24:13 good or bad, to go beyond the command of **the LORD**—
24:13 of the LORD—and I must say only what **the LORD** says'?
25: 3 the Baal of Peor. And **the LORD's** anger burned against them.
25: 4 **The LORD** said to Moses, "Take all the leaders of these people,
25: 4 kill them and expose them in broad daylight before **the LORD**,
25: 4 so that **the LORD's** fierce anger may turn away from Israel."
25:10 **The LORD** said to Moses,
25:16 **The LORD** said to Moses,
26: 1 After the plague **the LORD** said to Moses and Eleazar son of
26: 4 twenty years old or more, as **the LORD** commanded Moses."
26: 9 among Korah's followers when they rebelled against **the LORD**.
26:52 **The LORD** said to Moses,
26:61 Abihu died when they made an offering before **the LORD** with
26:65 For **the LORD** had told those Israelites they would surely die in
27: 3 who banded together against **the LORD**, but he died for his own
27: 5 So Moses brought their case before **the LORD**
27: 6 and **the LORD** said to him,
27:11 for the Israelites, as **the LORD** commanded Moses.' "
27:12 **the LORD** said to Moses, "Go up this mountain in the Abarim
27:15 Moses said to **the LORD**,
27:16 "May **the LORD**, the God of the spirits of all mankind, appoint a
27:17 so **the LORD's** people will not be like sheep without a
27:18 So **the LORD** said to Moses, "Take Joshua son of Nun, a man in
27:21 decisions for him by inquiring of the Urim before **the LORD**.
27:22 Moses did as **the LORD** commanded him. He took Joshua
27:23 and commissioned him, as **the LORD** instructed through Moses.
28: 1 **The LORD** said to Moses,
28: 3 is the offering made by fire that you are to present to **the LORD**:
28: 6 Sinai as a pleasing aroma, an offering made to **the LORD** by fire.
28: 7 Pour out the drink offering to **the LORD** at the sanctuary.
28: 8 This is an offering made by fire, an aroma pleasing to **the LORD**.
28:11 present to **the LORD** a burnt offering of two young bulls,
28:13 a pleasing aroma, an offering made to **the LORD** by fire.
28:15 one male goat is to be presented to **the LORD** as a sin offering.
28:16 " 'On the fourteenth day of the first month **the LORD's** [+4200]
28:19 Present to **the LORD** an offering made by fire, a burnt offering of
28:24 fire every day for seven days as an aroma pleasing to **the LORD**;
28:26 when you present to **the LORD** an offering of new grain during
28:27 seven male lambs a year old as an aroma pleasing to **the LORD**.
29: 2 As an aroma pleasing to **the LORD**, prepare a burnt offering of
29: 6 They are offerings made to **the LORD** by fire—a pleasing aroma.
29: 8 Present as an aroma pleasing to **the LORD** a burnt offering of
29:12 regular work. Celebrate a festival to **the LORD** for seven days.
29:13 an offering made by fire as an aroma pleasing to **the LORD**,
29:36 an offering made by fire as an aroma pleasing to **the LORD**,
29:39 prepare these for **the LORD** at your appointed feasts:
29:40 [30:1] Moses told the Israelites all that **the LORD** commanded
30: 1 [30:2] the tribes of Israel: "This is what **the LORD** commands:
30: 2 [30:3] When a man makes a vow to **the LORD** or takes an oath
30: 3 [30:4] living in her father's house makes a vow to **the LORD**
30: 5 [30:6] **the LORD** will release her because her father has
30: 8 [30:9] she obligates herself, and **the LORD** will release her.
30:12 [30:13] has nullified them, and **the LORD** will release her.
30:16 [30:17] These are the regulations **the LORD** gave Moses
31: 1 **The LORD** said to Moses,
31: 3 the Midianites and to carry out **the LORD's** vengeance on them.
31: 7 as **the LORD** commanded Moses, and killed every man.
31:16 were the means of turning the Israelites away from **the LORD** in
31:16 happened at Peor, so that a plague struck **the LORD's** people.
31:21 "This is the requirement of the law that **the LORD** gave Moses:
31:25 **The LORD** said to Moses,
31:28 set apart as tribute for **the LORD** one out of every five hundred,
31:29 half share and give it to Eleazar the priest as **the LORD's** part.
31:30 who are responsible for the care of **the LORD's** tabernacle."
31:31 and Eleazar the priest did as **the LORD** commanded Moses.
31:37 of which the tribute for **the LORD** was 675;
31:38 36,000 cattle, of which the tribute for **the LORD** was 72;
31:39 30,500 donkeys, of which the tribute for **the LORD** was 61;
31:40 16,000 people, of which the tribute for **the LORD** was 32.
31:41 Moses gave the tribute to Eleazar the priest as **the LORD's** part,
31:41 priest as the LORD's part, as **the LORD** commanded Moses.
31:47 every fifty persons and animals, as **the LORD** commanded him,
31:47 who were responsible for the care of **the LORD's** tabernacle.
31:50 So we have brought as an offering to **the LORD** the gold articles
31:50 to make atonement for ourselves before **the LORD**."
31:52 Eleazar presented as a gift to **the LORD** weighed 16,750 shekels.
31:54 of Meeting as a memorial for the Israelites before **the LORD**.
32: 4 the land **the LORD** subdued before the people of Israel—
32: 7 from going over into the land **the LORD** has given them?
32: 9 they discouraged the Israelites from entering the land **the LORD**
32:10 **The LORD's** anger was aroused that day and he swore this oath:
32:12 Joshua son of Nun, for they followed **the LORD** wholeheartedly.'
32:13 **The LORD's** anger burned against Israel and he made them
32:13 until the whole generation of those who had done evil in **his**[s] sight
32:14 your fathers and making **the LORD** even more angry with Israel.
32:20 do this—if you will arm yourselves before **the LORD** for battle,
32:21 if all of you will go armed over the Jordan before **the LORD** until
32:22 then when the land is subdued before **the LORD**, you may return
32:22 and be free from your obligation to **the LORD** and to Israel.
32:22 And this land will be your possession before **the LORD**.
32:23 "But if you fail to do this, you will be sinning against **the LORD**;
32:27 will cross over to fight before **the LORD**, just as our lord says."
32:29 for battle, cross over the Jordan with you before **the LORD**,
32:31 "Your servants will do what **the LORD** has said.
32:32 We will cross over before **the LORD** into Canaan armed,
33: 2 At **the LORD's** command Moses recorded the stages in their
33: 4 their firstborn, whom **the LORD** had struck down among them;
33: 4 among them; for **the LORD** had brought judgment on their gods.
33:38 At **the LORD's** command Aaron the priest went up Mount Hor,
33:50 by the Jordan across from Jericho **the LORD** said to Moses,
34: 1 **The LORD** said to Moses,
34:13 **The LORD** has ordered that it be given to the nine and a half
34:16 **The LORD** said to Moses,
34:29 These are the men **the LORD** commanded to assign the
35: 1 by the Jordan across from Jericho, **the LORD** said to Moses,
35: 9 Then **the LORD** said to Moses:
35:34 the land where you live and where I dwell, for I, **the LORD**,
36: 2 "When **the LORD** commanded my lord to give the land as an
36: 2 **he**[s] ordered you to give the inheritance of our brother Zelophehad
36: 5 at **the LORD's** command Moses gave this order to the Israelites:
36: 6 This is what **the LORD** commands for Zelophehad's daughters:
36:10 So Zelophehad's daughters did as **the LORD** commanded Moses.
36:13 regulations **the LORD** gave through Moses to the Israelites on
Dt 1: 3 Moses proclaimed to the Israelites all that **the LORD** had
1: 6 **The LORD** our God said to us at Horeb, "You have stayed long
1: 8 take possession of the land that **the LORD** swore he would give
1:10 **The LORD** your God has increased your numbers so that today
1:11 May **the LORD**, the God of your fathers, increase you a thousand
1:19 Then, as **the LORD** our God commanded us, we set out from
1:20 country of the Amorites, which **the LORD** our God is giving us.
1:21 See, **the LORD** your God has given you the land. Go up
1:21 Go up and take possession of it as **the LORD**, the God of your
1:25 "It is a good land that **the LORD** our God is giving us."
1:26 you rebelled against the command of **the LORD** your God.
1:27 You grumbled in your tents and said, "**The LORD** hates us;
1:30 **The LORD** your God, who is going before you, will fight for
1:31 There you saw how **the LORD** your God carried you, as a father
1:32 In spite of this, you did not trust in **the LORD** your God,
1:34 When **the LORD** heard what you said, he was angry
1:36 set his feet on, because he followed **the LORD** wholeheartedly."
1:37 Because of you **the LORD** became angry with me also and said,
1:41 you replied, "We have sinned against **the LORD**. We will go up
1:41 We will go up and fight, as **the LORD** our God commanded us."
1:42 But **the LORD** said to me, "Tell them, 'Do not go up and fight,
1:43 You rebelled against **the LORD's** command and in your
1:45 You came back and wept before **the LORD**, but he paid no
1:45 **he**[s] paid no attention to your weeping and turned a deaf ear to you.
2: 1 along the route to the Red Sea, as **the LORD** had directed me.
2: 2 Then **the LORD** said to me,
2: 7 **The LORD** your God has blessed you in all the work of your
2: 7 These forty years **the LORD** your God has been with you,
2: 9 Then **the LORD** said to me, "Do not harass the Moabites
2:12 just as Israel did in the land **the LORD** gave them as their
2:14 had perished from the camp, as **the LORD** had sworn to them.
2:15 **The LORD's** hand was against them until he had completely
2:17 **the LORD** said to me,
2:21 **The LORD** destroyed them from before the Ammonites,
2:29 until we cross the Jordan into the land **the LORD** our God is

Dt 2:30 For **the LORD** your God had made his spirit stubborn and his
2:31 **The LORD** said to me, "See, I have begun to deliver Sihon
2:33 **the LORD** our God delivered him over to us and we struck him
2:36 was too strong for us. **The LORD** our God gave us all of them.
2:37 But in accordance with the command of **the LORD** our God,
3: 2 **The LORD** said to me, "Do not be afraid of him, for I have
3: 3 So **the LORD** our God also gave into our hands Og king of
3:18 "**The LORD** your God has given you this land to take possession
3:20 until **the LORD** gives rest to your brothers as he has to you,
3:20 they too have taken over the land that **the LORD** your God is
3:21 "You have seen with your own eyes all that **the LORD** your God
3:21 **The LORD** will do the same to all the kingdoms over there
3:22 afraid of them; **the LORD** your God himself will fight for you."
3:23 At that time I pleaded with **the LORD**:
3:24 "O Sovereign **LORD**, you have begun to show to your servant
3:26 because of you **the LORD** was angry with me and would not
3:26 and would not listen to me. "That is enough," **the LORD** said.
4: 1 and may go in and take possession of the land that **the LORD**,
4: 2 but keep the commands of **the LORD** your God that I give you.
4: 3 You saw with your own eyes what **the LORD** did at Baal Peor.
4: 3 **The LORD** your God destroyed from among you everyone who
4: 4 all of you who held fast to **the LORD** your God are still alive
4: 5 you decrees and laws as **the LORD** my God commanded me,
4: 7 so great as to have their gods near them the way **the LORD** our
4:10 Remember the day you stood before **the LORD** your God at
4:10 when **he**[s] said to me, "Assemble the people before me to hear my
4:12 **the LORD** spoke to you out of the fire. You heard the sound of
4:14 And **the LORD** directed me at that time to teach you the decrees
4:15 You saw no form of any kind the day **the LORD** spoke to you at
4:19 worshiping things **the LORD** your God has apportioned to all the
4:20 **the LORD** took you and brought you out of the iron-smelting
4:21 **The LORD** was angry with me because of you, and he solemnly
4:21 enter the good land **the LORD** your God is giving you as your
4:23 Be careful not to forget the covenant of **the LORD** your God that
4:23 idol in the form of anything **the LORD** your God has forbidden.
4:24 For **the LORD** your God is a consuming fire, a jealous God.
4:25 doing evil in the eyes of **the LORD** your God and provoking him
4:27 **The LORD** will scatter you among the peoples, and only a few of
4:27 survive among the nations to which **the LORD** will drive you.
4:29 if from there you seek **the LORD** your God, you will find him if
4:30 then in later days you will return to **the LORD** your God
4:31 For **the LORD** your God is a merciful God; he will not abandon
4:34 like all the things **the LORD** your God did for you in Egypt
4:35 these things so that you might know that **the LORD** is God;
4:39 and take to heart this day that **the LORD** is God in heaven above
4:40 that you may live long in the land **the LORD** your God gives you
5: 2 **The LORD** our God made a covenant with us at Horeb.
5: 3 It was not with our fathers that **the LORD** made this covenant,
5: 4 **The LORD** spoke to you face to face out of the fire on the
5: 5 (At that time I stood between **the LORD** and you to declare to
5: 5 the LORD and you to declare to you the word of **the LORD**,
5: 6 "I am **the LORD** your God, who brought you out of Egypt,
5: 9 for I, **the LORD** your God, am a jealous God, punishing the
5:11 "You shall not misuse the name of **the LORD** your God,
5:11 for **the LORD** will not hold anyone guiltless who misuses his
5:12 by keeping it holy, as **the LORD** your God has commanded you.
5:14 but the seventh day is a Sabbath to **the LORD** your God.
5:15 that **the LORD** your God brought you out of there with a mighty
5:15 Therefore **the LORD** your God has commanded you to observe
5:16 and your mother, as **the LORD** your God has commanded you,
5:16 that it may go well with you in the land **the LORD** your God is
5:22 These are the commandments **the LORD** proclaimed in a loud
5:24 "**The LORD** our God has shown us his glory and his majesty,
5:25 we will die if we hear the voice of **the LORD** our God any
5:27 Go near and listen to all that **the LORD** our God says. Then tell
5:27 tell us whatever **the LORD** our God tells you. We will listen
5:28 **The LORD** heard you when you spoke to me and the LORD
5:28 heard you when you spoke to me and **the LORD** said to me,
5:32 So be careful to do what **the LORD** your God has commanded
5:33 Walk in all the way that **the LORD** your God has commanded
6: 1 laws **the LORD** your God directed me to teach you to observe in
6: 2 their children after them may fear **the LORD** your God as long as
6: 3 greatly in a land flowing with milk and honey, just as **the LORD**,
6: 4 Hear, O Israel: **The LORD** our God, the LORD is one.
6: 4 Hear, O Israel: The LORD our God, **the LORD** is one.
6: 5 Love **the LORD** your God with all your heart and with all your
6:10 When **the LORD** your God brings you into the land he swore to
6:12 be careful that you do not forget **the LORD**, who brought you out
6:13 Fear **the LORD** your God, serve him only and take your oaths in
6:15 for **the LORD** your God, who is among you, is a jealous God
6:15 is a jealous God and **his**[s] [+466+3870] anger will burn against you,
6:16 Do not test **the LORD** your God as you did at Massah.
6:17 Be sure to keep the commands of **the LORD** your God
6:18 Do what is right and good in **the LORD's** sight, so that it may go
6:18 take over the good land that **the LORD** promised on oath to your
6:19 thrusting out all your enemies before you, as **the LORD** said.
6:20 decrees and laws **the LORD** our God has commanded you?"
6:21 but **the LORD** brought us out of Egypt with a mighty hand.
6:22 Before our eyes **the LORD** sent miraculous signs and wonders—
6:24 **The LORD** commanded us to obey all these decrees and to fear
6:24 us to obey all these decrees and to fear **the LORD** our God,
6:25 if we are careful to obey all this law before **the LORD** our God,
7: 1 When **the LORD** your God brings you into the land you are
7: 2 and when **the LORD** your God has delivered them over to you
7: 4 **the LORD's** anger will burn against you and will quickly destroy
7: 6 For you are a people holy to **the LORD** your God. The LORD
7: 6 **The LORD** your God has chosen you out of all the peoples on
7: 7 **The LORD** did not set his affection on you and choose you
7: 8 it was because **the LORD** loved you and kept the oath he swore
7: 8 kept the oath he swore to your forefathers that **he**[s] brought you out
7: 9 Know therefore that **the LORD** your God is God; he is the
7:12 **the LORD** your God will keep his covenant of love with you,
7:15 **The LORD** will keep you free from every disease. He will not
7:16 You must destroy all the peoples **the LORD** your God gives over
7:18 remember well what **the LORD** your God did to Pharaoh
7:19 with which **the LORD** your God brought you out.
7:19 **The LORD** your God will do the same to all the peoples you now
7:20 **the LORD** your God will send the hornet among them until even
7:21 for **the LORD** your God, who is among you, is a great
7:22 **The LORD** your God will drive out those nations before you,
7:23 **the LORD** your God will deliver them over to you, throwing
7:25 will be ensnared by it, for it is detestable to **the LORD** your God.
8: 1 possess the land that **the LORD** promised on oath to your
8: 2 Remember how **the LORD** your God led you all the way in the
8: 3 but on every word that comes from the mouth of **the LORD**.
8: 5 man disciplines his son, so **the LORD** your God disciplines you.
8: 6 Observe the commands of **the LORD** your God, walking in his
8: 7 For **the LORD** your God is bringing you into a good land—
8:10 praise **the LORD** your God for the good land he has given you.
8:11 Be careful that you do not forget **the LORD** your God, failing to
8:14 will become proud and you will forget **the LORD** your God,
8:18 remember **the LORD** your God, for it is he who gives you the
8:19 If you ever forget **the LORD** your God and follow other gods
8:20 Like the nations **the LORD** destroyed before you, so you will be
8:20 so you will be destroyed for not obeying **the LORD** your God.
9: 3 be assured today that **the LORD** your God is the one who goes
9: 3 and annihilate them quickly, as **the LORD** has promised you.
9: 4 After **the LORD** your God *has* driven them out before you,
9: 4 "**The LORD** has brought me here to take possession of this land
9: 4 it is on account of the wickedness of these nations that **the LORD**
9: 5 **the LORD** your God will drive them out before you, to
9: 5 to accomplish what **he**[s] swore to your fathers, to Abraham,
9: 6 because of your righteousness that **the LORD** your God is giving
9: 7 never forget how you provoked **the LORD** your God to anger in
9: 7 you arrived here, you have been rebellious against **the LORD**.
9: 8 At Horeb you aroused **the LORD's** wrath so that he was angry
9: 8 the LORD's wrath so that **he**[s] was angry enough to destroy you.
9: 9 the tablets of the covenant that **the LORD** had made with you,
9:10 **The LORD** gave me two stone tablets inscribed by the finger of
9:10 On them were all the commandments **the LORD** proclaimed to
9:11 and forty nights, **the LORD** gave me the two stone tablets,
9:12 **the LORD** told me, "Go down from here at once, because your
9:13 **the LORD** said to me, "I have seen this people, and they are a
9:16 I looked, I saw that you had sinned against **the LORD** your God;
9:16 You had turned aside quickly from the way that **the LORD** had
9:18 Then once again I fell prostrate before **the LORD** for forty days
9:18 doing what was evil in **the LORD's** sight and so provoking him
9:19 I feared the anger and wrath of **the LORD**, for he was angry
9:19 with you to destroy you. But again **the LORD** listened to me.
9:20 And **the LORD** was angry enough with Aaron to destroy him,
9:22 You also made **the LORD** angry at Taberah, at Massah and at
9:23 And when **the LORD** sent you out from Kadesh Barnea,
9:23 But you rebelled against the command of **the LORD** your God.
9:24 You have been rebellious against **the LORD** ever since I have
9:25 I lay prostrate before **the LORD** those forty days and forty nights
9:25 forty nights because **the LORD** had said he would destroy you.
9:26 I prayed to **the LORD** and said, "O Sovereign LORD, do not
9:26 I prayed to the LORD and said, "O Sovereign **LORD**, do not
9:28 'Because **the LORD** was not able to take them into the land he
10: 1 At that time **the LORD** said to me, "Chisel out two stone tablets
10: 4 **The LORD** wrote on these tablets what he had written before,
10: 4 on the day of the assembly. And **the LORD** gave them to me.
10: 5 had made, as **the LORD** commanded me, and they are there now.
10: 8 At that time **the LORD** set apart the tribe of Levi to carry the ark
10: 8 the tribe of Levi to carry the ark of the covenant of **the LORD**,
10: 8 to stand before **the LORD** to minister and to pronounce blessings
10: 9 **the LORD** is their inheritance, as the LORD your God told
10: 9 LORD is their inheritance, as **the LORD** your God told them.)

Dt 10:10 did the first time, and **the LORD** listened to me at this time also.
10:10 listened to me at this time also. It was not **his**[s] will to destroy you.
10:11 "Go," **the LORD** said to me, "and lead the people on their way,
10:12 what does **the LORD** your God ask of you but to fear the LORD
10:12 LORD your God ask of you but to fear **the LORD** your God,
10:12 to serve **the LORD** your God with all your heart and with all
10:13 to observe **the LORD's** commands and decrees that I am giving
10:14 To **the LORD** your God belong the heavens, even the highest
10:15 Yet **the LORD** set his affection on your forefathers and loved
10:17 For **the LORD** your God is God of gods and Lord of lords,
10:20 Fear **the LORD** your God and serve him. Hold fast to him
10:22 now **the LORD** your God has made you as numerous as the stars
11: 1 Love **the LORD** your God and keep his requirements, his
11: 2 who saw and experienced the discipline of **the LORD** your God:
11: 4 pursuing you, and how **the LORD** brought lasting ruin on them.
11: 7 it was your own eyes that saw all these great things **the LORD**
11: 9 so that you may live long in the land that **the LORD** swore to
11:12 It is a land **the LORD** your God cares for; the eyes of the LORD
11:12 the eyes of **the LORD** your God are continually on it from the
11:13 to love **the LORD** your God and to serve him with all your heart
11:17 **the LORD's** anger will burn against you, and he will shut the
11:17 you will soon perish from the good land **the LORD** is giving you.
11:21 days of your children may be many in the land that **the LORD**
11:22 to love **the LORD** your God, to walk in all his ways and to hold
11:23 then **the LORD** will drive out all these nations before you,
11:25 **The LORD** your God, as he promised you, will put the terror
11:27 the blessing if you obey the commands of **the LORD** your God
11:28 the curse if you disobey the commands of **the LORD** your God
11:29 When **the LORD** your God has brought you into the land you are
11:31 take possession of the land **the LORD** your God is giving you.
12: 1 laws you must be careful to follow in the land that **the LORD**,
12: 4 You must not worship **the LORD** your God in their way.
12: 5 you are to seek the place **the LORD** your God will choose from
12: 7 in the presence of **the LORD** your God, you and your families
12: 7 put your hand to, because **the LORD** your God has blessed you.
12: 9 and the inheritance **the LORD** your God is giving you.
12:10 settle in the land **the LORD** your God is giving you as an
12:11 to the place **the LORD** your God will choose as a dwelling for
12:11 and all the choice possessions you have vowed to **the LORD**.
12:12 And there rejoice before **the LORD** your God, you, your sons
12:14 Offer them only at the place **the LORD** will choose in one of
12:15 according to the blessing **the LORD** your God gives you.
12:18 you are to eat them in the presence of **the LORD** your God at the
12:18 LORD your God at the place **the LORD** your God will choose—
12:18 you are to rejoice before **the LORD** your God in everything you
12:20 When **the LORD** your God has enlarged your territory as he
12:21 If the place where **the LORD** your God chooses to put his Name
12:21 animals from the herds and flocks **the LORD** has given you,
12:25 because you will be doing what is right in the eyes of **the LORD**.
12:26 have vowed to give, and go to the place **the LORD** will choose.
12:27 Present your burnt offerings on the altar of **the LORD** your God,
12:27 must be poured beside the altar of **the LORD** your God,
12:28 doing what is good and right in the eyes of **the LORD** your God.
12:29 **The LORD** your God will cut off before you the nations you are
12:31 You must not worship **the LORD** your God in their way,
12:31 their gods, they do all kinds of detestable things **the LORD** hates.
13: 3 [13:4] **The LORD** your God is testing you to find out whether
13: 3 [13:4] whether you love **him**[s] [+466+4013] with all your heart
13: 4 [13:5] It is **the LORD** your God you must follow, and him you
13: 5 [13:6] because he preached rebellion against **the LORD** your
13: 5 [13:6] he has tried to turn you from the way **the LORD** your
13:10 [13:11] because he tried to turn you away from **the LORD** your
13:12 [13:13] If you hear it said about one of the towns **the LORD**
13:16 [13:17] all its plunder as a whole burnt offering to **the LORD**
13:17 [13:18] so that **the LORD** will turn from his fierce anger;
13:18 [13:19] because you obey **the LORD** your God, keeping all his
13:18 [13:19] and doing what is right in **his**[s] [+466+3870] eyes.
14: 1 You are the children of **the LORD** your God. Do not cut
14: 2 for you are a people holy to **the LORD** your God. Out of all the
14: 2 **the LORD** has chosen you to be his treasured possession.
14:21 to a foreigner. But you are a people holy to **the LORD** your God.
14:23 flocks in the presence of **the LORD** your God at the place he will
14:23 so that you may learn to revere **the LORD** your God always.
14:24 you have been blessed by **the LORD** your God and cannot carry
14:24 (because the place where **the LORD** will choose to put his Name
14:25 with you and go to the place **the LORD** your God will choose.
14:26 your household shall eat there in the presence of **the LORD** your
14:29 so that **the LORD** your God may bless you in all the work of
15: 2 because **the LORD's** [+4200] time for canceling debts has been
15: 4 for in the land **the LORD** your God is giving you to possess as
15: 4 giving you to possess as your inheritance, **he**[s] will richly bless you,
15: 5 if only you fully obey **the LORD** your God and are careful to
15: 6 For **the LORD** your God will bless you as he has promised,
15: 7 of the towns of the land that **the LORD** your God is giving you,
15: 9 He may then appeal to **the LORD** against you, and you will be
15:10 because of this **the LORD** your God will bless you in all your
15:14 Give to him as **the LORD** your God has blessed you.
15:15 were slaves in Egypt and **the LORD** your God redeemed you.
15:18 And **the LORD** your God will bless you in everything you do.
15:19 Set apart for **the LORD** your God every firstborn male of your
15:20 your family are to eat them in the presence of **the LORD** your
15:20 the presence of the LORD your God at the place **he**[s] will choose.
15:21 serious flaw, you must not sacrifice it to **the LORD** your God.
16: 1 of Abib and celebrate the Passover of **the LORD** your God,
16: 1 because in the month of Abib **he**[s] [+466+3870] brought you out of
16: 2 Sacrifice as the Passover to **the LORD** your God an animal from
16: 2 or herd at the place **the LORD** will choose as a dwelling for his
16: 5 You must not sacrifice the Passover in any town **the LORD** your
16: 6 except in the place **he**[s] [+466+3870] will choose as a dwelling for
16: 7 Roast it and eat it at the place **the LORD** your God will choose.
16: 8 and on the seventh day hold an assembly to **the LORD** your God
16:10 celebrate the Feast of Weeks to **the LORD** your God by giving a
16:10 in proportion to the blessings **the LORD** your God has given you.
16:11 rejoice before **the LORD** your God at the place he will choose as
16:11 rejoice before the LORD your God at the place **he**[s] [+466+3870]
16:15 For seven days celebrate the Feast to **the LORD** your God at the
16:15 to the LORD your God at the place **the LORD** will choose.
16:15 For **the LORD** your God will bless you in all your harvest
16:16 Three times a year all your men must appear before **the LORD**
16:16 No man should appear before **the LORD** empty-handed:
16:17 Each of you must bring a gift in proportion to the way **the LORD**
16:18 officials for each of your tribes in every town **the LORD** your
16:20 and possess the land **the LORD** your God is giving you.
16:21 Asherah pole beside the altar you build to **the LORD** your God,
16:22 do not erect a sacred stone, for these **the LORD** your God hates.
17: 1 Do not sacrifice to **the LORD** your God an ox or a sheep that has
17: 1 or flaw in it, for that would be detestable to **him**[s] [+466+3870].
17: 2 or woman living among you in one of the towns **the LORD** gives
17: 2 in the eyes of **the LORD** your God in violation of his covenant,
17: 8 take them to the place **the LORD** your God will choose.
17:10 to the decisions they give you at the place **the LORD** will choose.
17:12 or for the priest who stands ministering there to **the LORD** your
17:14 When you enter the land **the LORD** your God is giving you
17:15 be sure to appoint over you the king **the LORD** your God
17:16 for **the LORD** has told you, "You are not to go back that way
17:19 days of his life so that he may learn to revere **the LORD** his God
18: 1 They shall live on the offerings made to **the LORD** by fire,
18: 2 **the LORD** is their inheritance, as he promised them.
18: 5 for **the LORD** your God has chosen them and their descendants
18: 5 all your tribes to stand and minister in **the LORD's** name always.
18: 6 and comes in all earnestness to the place **the LORD** will choose,
18: 7 he may minister in the name of **the LORD** his God like all his
18: 7 his fellow Levites who serve there in the presence of **the LORD**.
18: 9 When you enter the land **the LORD** your God is giving you,
18:12 Anyone who does these things is detestable to **the LORD**,
18:12 because of these detestable practices **the LORD** your God will
18:13 You must be blameless before **the LORD** your God.
18:14 as for you, **the LORD** your God has not permitted you to do so.
18:15 **The LORD** your God will raise up for you a prophet like me
18:16 For this is what you asked of **the LORD** your God at Horeb on
18:16 "Let us not hear the voice of **the LORD** our God nor see this
18:17 **The LORD** said to me: "What they say is good.
18:21 we know when a message has not been spoken by **the LORD**?"
18:22 If what a prophet proclaims in the name of **the LORD** does not
18:22 or come true, that is a message **the LORD** has not spoken.
19: 1 When **the LORD** your God has destroyed the nations whose land
19: 1 destroyed the nations whose land **he**[s] [+466+3870] is giving you,
19: 2 located in the land **the LORD** your God is giving you to possess.
19: 3 divide into three parts the land **the LORD** your God is giving you
19: 8 If **the LORD** your God enlarges your territory, as he promised on
19: 9 to love **the LORD** your God and to walk always in his ways—
19:10 which **the LORD** your God is giving you as your inheritance,
19:14 receive in the land **the LORD** your God is giving you to possess.
19:17 must stand in the presence of **the LORD** before the priests
20: 1 do not be afraid of them, because **the LORD** your God,
20: 4 For **the LORD** your God is the one who goes with you to fight
20:13 When **the LORD** your God delivers it into your hand, put to the
20:14 you may use the plunder **the LORD** your God gives you from
20:16 in the cities of the nations **the LORD** your God is giving you as
20:17 and Jebusites—as **the LORD** your God has commanded you.
20:18 their gods, and you will sin against **the LORD** your God.
21: 1 lying in a field in the land **the LORD** your God is giving you to
21: 5 for **the LORD** your God has chosen them to minister and to
21: 5 to pronounce blessings in the name of **the LORD** and to decide
21: 8 for your people Israel, whom you have redeemed, O **LORD**,
21: 9 since you have done what is right in the eyes of **the LORD**.
21:10 **the LORD** your God delivers them into your hands and you take
21:23 You must not desecrate the land **the LORD** your God is giving

Dt 22: 5 for **the LORD** your God detests anyone who does this.
23: 1 [23:2] or cutting may enter the assembly of **the LORD**.
23: 2 [23:3] of his descendants may enter the assembly of **the LORD**,
23: 2 [23:3] of the LORD, **[RPH]** even down to the tenth generation.
23: 3 [23:4] of his descendants may enter the assembly of **the LORD**,
23: 3 [23:4] of the LORD, **[RPH]** even down to the tenth generation.
23: 5 [23:6] **the LORD** your God would not listen to Balaam
23: 5 [23:6] but **[RPH]** turned the curse into a blessing for you,
23: 5 [23:6] blessing for you, because **the LORD** your God loves you.
23: 8 [23:9] born to them may enter the assembly of **the LORD**.
23: 14 [23:15] For **the LORD** your God moves about in your camp to
23: 18 [23:19] or of a male prostitute into the house of **the LORD** your
23: 18 [23:19] because **the LORD** your God detests them both.
23: 20 [23:21] so that **the LORD** your God may bless you in
23: 21 [23:22] If you make a vow to **the LORD** your God, do not be
23: 21 [23:22] for **the LORD** your God will certainly demand it of you
23: 23 [23:24] because you made your vow freely to **the LORD** your
24: 4 been defiled. That would be detestable in the eyes of **the LORD**.
24: 4 Do not bring sin upon the land **the LORD** your God is giving you
24: 9 Remember what **the LORD** your God did to Miriam along the
24: 13 it will be regarded as a righteous act in the sight of **the LORD**
24: 15 Otherwise he may cry to **the LORD** against you, and you will be
24: 18 in Egypt and **the LORD** your God redeemed you from there.
24: 19 so that **the LORD** your God may bless you in all the work of
25: 15 so that you may live long in the land **the LORD** your God is
25: 16 For **the LORD** your God detests anyone who does these things,
25: 19 When **the LORD** your God gives you rest from all the enemies
25: 19 land **he**[s] [+466+3870] is giving you to possess as an inheritance,
26: 1 When you have entered the land **the LORD** your God is giving
26: 2 from the soil of the land **the LORD** your God is giving you
26: 2 go to the place **the LORD** your God will choose as a dwelling
26: 3 "I declare today to **the LORD** your God that I have come to the
26: 3 come to the land **the LORD** swore to our forefathers to give us."
26: 4 and set it down in front of the altar of **the LORD** your God.
26: 5 you shall declare before **the LORD** your God: "My father was a
26: 7 Then we cried out to **the LORD**, the God of our fathers,
26: 7 and **the LORD** heard our voice and saw our misery, toil
26: 8 So **the LORD** brought us out of Egypt with a mighty hand
26: 10 the firstfruits of the soil that you, O **LORD**, have given me."
26: 10 Place the basket before **the LORD** your God and bow down
26: 10 the LORD your God and bow down before **him**[s] [+466+3870].
26: 11 in all the good things **the LORD** your God has given to you
26: 13 say to **the LORD** your God: "I have removed from my house the
26: 14 I have obeyed **the LORD** my God; I have done everything you
26: 16 **The LORD** your God commands you this day to follow these
26: 17 You have declared this day that **the LORD** is your God and that
26: 18 And **the LORD** has declared this day that you are his people,
26: 19 and that you will be a people holy to **the LORD** your God,
27: 2 When you have crossed the Jordan into the land **the LORD** your
27: 3 crossed over to enter the land **the LORD** your God is giving you,
27: 3 a land flowing with milk and honey, just as **the LORD**, the God
27: 5 Build there an altar to **the LORD** your God, an altar of stones.
27: 6 Build the altar of **the LORD** your God with fieldstones and offer
27: 6 and offer burnt offerings on it to **the LORD** your God.
27: 7 and rejoicing in the presence of **the LORD** your God.
27: 9 You have now become the people of **the LORD** your God.
27: 10 Obey **the LORD** your God and follow his commands and decrees
27: 15 a thing detestable to **the LORD**, the work of the craftsman's
28: 1 If you fully obey **the LORD** your God and carefully follow all
28: 1 **the LORD** your God will set you high above all the nations on
28: 2 upon you and accompany you if you obey **the LORD** your God:
28: 7 **The LORD** will grant that the enemies who rise up against you
28: 8 **The LORD** will send a blessing on your barns and on everything
28: 8 **The LORD** your God will bless you in the land he is giving you.
28: 9 **The LORD** will establish you as his holy people, as he promised
28: 9 if you keep the commands of **the LORD** your God and walk in
28: 10 on earth will see that you are called by the name of **the LORD**,
28: 11 **The LORD** will grant you abundant prosperity—in the fruit of
28: 11 in the land **he**[s] swore to your forefathers to give you.
28: 12 **The LORD** will open the heavens, the storehouse of his bounty,
28: 13 **The LORD** will make you the head, not the tail. If you pay
28: 13 If you pay attention to the commands of **the LORD** your God
28: 15 if you do not obey **the LORD** your God and do not carefully
28: 20 **The LORD** will send on you curses, confusion and rebuke in
28: 21 **The LORD** will plague you with diseases until he has destroyed
28: 22 **The LORD** will strike you with wasting disease, with fever
28: 24 **The LORD** will turn the rain of your country into dust
28: 25 **The LORD** will cause you to be defeated before your enemies.
28: 27 **The LORD** will afflict you with the boils of Egypt and with
28: 28 **The LORD** will afflict you with madness, blindness
28: 35 **The LORD** will afflict your knees and legs with painful boils that
28: 36 **The LORD** will drive you and the king you set over you to a
28: 37 and ridicule to all the nations where **the LORD** will drive you.
28: 45 because you did not obey **the LORD** your God and observe the
28: 47 Because you did not serve **the LORD** your God joyfully
28: 48 you will serve the enemies **the LORD** sends against you.
28: 49 **The LORD** will bring a nation against you from far away,
28: 52 They will besiege all the cities throughout the land **the LORD**
28: 53 of the sons and daughters **the LORD** your God has given you.
28: 58 revere this glorious and awesome name—**the LORD** your God—
28: 59 **the LORD** will send fearful plagues on you and your
28: 61 **The LORD** will also bring on you every kind of sickness
28: 62 few in number, because you did not obey **the LORD** your God.
28: 63 Just as it pleased **the LORD** to make you prosper and increase in
28: 63 increase in number, so it will please **him**[s] to ruin and destroy you.
28: 64 **the LORD** will scatter you among all nations, from one end of
28: 65 There **the LORD** will give you an anxious mind, eyes weary with
28: 68 **The LORD** will send you back in ships to Egypt on a journey I
29: 1 [28:69] These are the terms of the covenant **the LORD**
29: 2 [29:1] Your eyes have seen all that **the LORD** did in Egypt to
29: 4 [29:3] to this day **the LORD** has not given you a mind that
29: 6 [29:5] so that you might know that I am **the LORD** your God.
29: 10 [29:9] standing today in the presence of **the LORD** your God—
29: 12 [29:11] order to enter into a covenant with **the LORD** your God,
29: 12 [29:11] a covenant **the LORD** is making with you this day
29: 15 [29:14] with us today in the presence of **the LORD** our God
29: 18 [29:17] whose heart turns away from **the LORD** our God to go
29: 20 [29:19] **The LORD** will never be willing to forgive him; his
29: 20 [29:19] **his**[s] wrath and zeal will burn against that man.
29: 20 [29:19] **the LORD** will blot out his name from under heaven.
29: 21 [29:20] **The LORD** will single him out from all the tribes of
29: 22 [29:21] and the diseases with which **the LORD** has afflicted it.
29: 23 [29:22] which **the LORD** overthrew in fierce anger.
29: 24 [29:23] "Why has **the LORD** done this to this land? Why this
29: 25 [29:24] this people abandoned the covenant of **the LORD**,
29: 27 [29:26] Therefore **the LORD's** anger burned against this land,
29: 28 [29:27] in great wrath **the LORD** uprooted them from their land
29: 29 [29:28] The secret things belong to **the LORD** our God,
30: 1 you take them to heart wherever **the LORD** your God disperses
30: 2 and when you and your children return to **the LORD** your God
30: 3 **the LORD** your God will restore your fortunes and have
30: 3 gather you again from all the nations where **he**[s] [+466+3870]
30: 4 from there **the LORD** your God will gather you and bring you
30: 5 **He**[s] [+466+3870] will bring you to the land that belonged to your
30: 6 **The LORD** your God will circumcise your hearts and the hearts
30: 6 so that you may love **him**[s] [+466+3870] with all your heart
30: 7 **The LORD** your God will put all these curses on your enemies
30: 8 You will again obey **the LORD** and follow all his commands I
30: 9 **the LORD** your God will make you most prosperous in all the
30: 9 **The LORD** will again delight in you and make you prosperous,
30: 10 if you obey **the LORD** your God and keep his commands
30: 10 turn to **the LORD** your God with all your heart and with all your
30: 16 For I command you today to love **the LORD** your God, to walk
30: 16 **the LORD** your God will bless you in the land you are entering
30: 20 and that you may love **the LORD** your God, listen to his voice,
30: 20 For **the LORD** is your life, and he will give you many years in
31: 2 **The LORD** has said to me, 'You shall not cross the Jordan.'
31: 3 **The LORD** your God himself will cross over ahead of you.
31: 3 Joshua also will cross over ahead of you, as **the LORD** said.
31: 4 And **the LORD** will do to them what he did to Sihon and Og,
31: 5 **The LORD** will deliver them to you, and you must do to them all
31: 6 because of them, for **the LORD** your God goes with you;
31: 7 for you must go with this people into the land that **the LORD**
31: 8 **The LORD** himself goes before you and will be with you;
31: 9 sons of Levi, who carried the ark of the covenant of **the LORD**,
31: 11 when all Israel comes to appear before **the LORD** your God at
31: 12 so they can listen and learn to fear **the LORD** your God
31: 13 learn to fear **the LORD** your God as long as you live in the land
31: 14 **The LORD** said to Moses, "Now the day of your death is near.
31: 15 Then **the LORD** appeared at the Tent in a pillar of cloud,
31: 16 **the LORD** said to Moses: "You are going to rest with your
31: 25 to the Levites who carried the ark of the covenant of **the LORD**:
31: 26 place it beside the ark of the covenant of **the LORD** your God.
31: 27 If you have been rebellious against **the LORD** while I am still
31: 29 fall upon you because you will do evil in the sight of **the LORD**
32: 3 I will proclaim the name of **the LORD**. Oh, praise the greatness
32: 6 Is this the way you repay **the LORD**, O foolish and unwise
32: 9 For **the LORD's** portion is his people, Jacob his allotted
32: 12 **The LORD** alone led him; no foreign god was with him.
32: 19 **The LORD** saw this and rejected them because he was angered
32: 27 'Our hand has triumphed; **the LORD** has not done all this.' "
32: 30 their Rock had sold them, unless **the LORD** had given them up?
32: 36 **The LORD** will judge his people and have compassion on his
32: 48 On that same day **the LORD** told Moses,
33: 2 "**The LORD** came from Sinai and dawned over them from Seir;
33: 7 "Hear, O **LORD**, the cry of Judah; bring him to his people.
33: 11 Bless all his skills, O **LORD**, and be pleased with the work of his
33: 12 "Let the beloved of **the LORD** rest secure in him, for he shields

Dt 33:13 "May **the LORD** bless his land with the precious dew from
33:21 he carried out **the LORD's** righteous will, and his judgments
33:23 "Naphtali is abounding with the favor of **the LORD** and is full of
33:29 O Israel! Who is like you, a people saved by **the LORD**?
34: 1 There **the LORD** showed him the whole land—from Gilead to
34: 4 **the LORD** said to him, "This is the land I promised on oath to
34: 5 And Moses the servant of **the LORD** died there in Moab,
34: 5 of the LORD died there in Moab, as **the LORD** had said.
34: 9 listened to him and did what **the LORD** had commanded Moses.
34:10 risen in Israel like Moses, whom **the LORD** knew face to face,
34:11 and wonders **the LORD** sent him to do in Egypt—
Jos 1: 1 After the death of Moses the servant of **the LORD**, the LORD
1: 1 the LORD, **the LORD** said to Joshua son of Nun, Moses' aide:
1: 9 for **the LORD** your God will be with you wherever you go."
1:11 take possession of the land **the LORD** your God is giving you
1:13 "Remember the command that Moses the servant of **the LORD**
1:13 '**The LORD** your God is giving you rest and has granted you this
1:15 until **the LORD** gives them rest, as he has done for you,
1:15 until they too have taken possession of the land that **the LORD**
1:15 which Moses the servant of **the LORD** gave you east of the
1:17 Only may **the LORD** your God be with you as he was with
2: 9 "I know that **the LORD** has given this land to you and that a
2:10 We have heard how **the LORD** dried up the water of the Red Sea
2:11 for **the LORD** your God is God in heaven above and on the earth
2:12 please swear to me by **the LORD** that you will show kindness to
2:14 you kindly and faithfully when **the LORD** gives us the land."
2:24 "**The LORD** has surely given the whole land into our hands;
3: 3 "When you see the ark of the covenant of **the LORD** your God,
3: 5 for tomorrow **the LORD** will do amazing things among you."
3: 7 **the LORD** said to Joshua, "Today I will begin to exalt you in the
3: 9 "Come here and listen to the words of **the LORD** your God.
3:13 And as soon as the priests who carry the ark of **the LORD**—
3:17 The priests who carried the ark of the covenant of **the LORD**
4: 1 had finished crossing the Jordan, **the LORD** said to Joshua,
4: 5 "Go over before the ark of **the LORD** your God into the middle
4: 7 Jordan was cut off before the ark of the covenant of **the LORD**.
4: 8 of the tribes of the Israelites, as **the LORD** had told Joshua;
4:10 **the LORD** had commanded Joshua was done by the people,
4:11 the ark of **the LORD** and the priests came to the other side while
4:13 crossed over before **the LORD** to the plains of Jericho for war.
4:14 That day **the LORD** exalted Joshua in the sight of all Israel;
4:15 Then **the LORD** said to Joshua,
4:18 up out of the river carrying the ark of the covenant of **the LORD**.
4:23 For **the LORD** your God dried up the Jordan before you until you
4:23 **The LORD** your God did to the Jordan just what he had done to
4:24 of the earth might know that the hand of **the LORD** is powerful
4:24 and so that you might always fear **the LORD** your God."
5: 1 all the Canaanite kings along the coast heard how **the LORD** had
5: 2 At that time **the LORD** said to Joshua, "Make flint knives
5: 6 they left Egypt had died, since they had not obeyed **the LORD**.
5: 6 For **the LORD** had sworn to them that they would not see the
5: 6 the land that **he**[s] had solemnly promised their fathers to give us,
5: 9 **the LORD** said to Joshua, "Today I have rolled away the
5:14 "but as commander of the army of **the LORD** I have now come."
5:15 The commander of **the LORD's** army replied, "Take off your
6: 2 **the LORD** said to Joshua, "See, I have delivered Jericho into
6: 6 "Take up the ark of the covenant of **the LORD** and have seven
6: 7 with the armed guard going ahead of the ark of **the LORD**."
6: 8 the seven priests carrying the seven trumpets before **the LORD**
6: 8 and the ark of **the LORD's** covenant followed them.
6:11 So he had the ark of **the LORD** carried around the city, circling it
6:12 the next morning and the priests took up the ark of **the LORD**.
6:13 marching before the ark of **the LORD** and blowing the trumpets.
6:13 ahead of them and the rear guard followed the ark of **the LORD**,
6:16 the people, "Shout! For **the LORD** has given you the city!
6:17 The city and all that is in it are to be devoted to **the LORD**.
6:19 and the articles of bronze and iron are sacred to **the LORD**
6:19 and iron are sacred to the LORD and must go into **his**[s] treasury."
6:24 of bronze and iron into the treasury of **the LORD's** house.
6:26 "Cursed before **the LORD** is the man who undertakes to rebuild
6:27 So **the LORD** was with Joshua, and his fame spread throughout
7: 1 took some of them. So **the LORD's** anger burned against Israel.
7: 6 and fell facedown to the ground before the ark of **the LORD**,
7: 7 Joshua said, "Ah, Sovereign **LORD**, why did you ever bring this
7:10 **The LORD** said to Joshua, "Stand up! What are you doing down
7:13 for tomorrow; for this is what **the LORD**, the God of Israel, says:
7:14 The tribe that **the LORD** takes shall come forward clan by clan;
7:14 the clan that **the LORD** takes shall come forward family by
7:14 the family that **the LORD** takes shall come forward man by man.
7:15 He has violated the covenant of **the LORD** and has done a
7:19 "My son, give glory to **the LORD**, the God of Israel, and give
7:20 "It is true! I have sinned against **the LORD**, the God of Israel.
7:23 and all the Israelites and spread them out before **the LORD**.
7:25 **The LORD** will bring trouble on you today." Then all Israel
7:26 remains to this day. Then **the LORD** turned from his fierce anger.
8: 1 **the LORD** said to Joshua, "Do not be afraid; do not be
8: 7 take the city. **The LORD** your God will give it into your hand.
8: 8 Do what **the LORD** has commanded. See to it; you have my
8:18 **the LORD** said to Joshua, "Hold out toward Ai the javelin that is
8:27 and plunder of this city, as **the LORD** had instructed Joshua.
8:30 Then Joshua built on Mount Ebal an altar to **the LORD**,
8:31 as Moses the servant of **the LORD** had commanded the Israelites.
8:31 On it they offered to **the LORD** burnt offerings and sacrificed
8:33 standing on both sides of the ark of the covenant of **the LORD**,
8:33 as Moses the servant of **the LORD** had formerly commanded
9: 9 very distant country because of the fame of **the LORD** your God.
9:14 Israel sampled their provisions but did not inquire of **the LORD**.
9:18 leaders of the assembly had sworn an oath to them by **the LORD**,
9:19 "We have given them our oath by **the LORD**, the God of Israel,
9:24 "Your servants were clearly told how **the LORD** your God had
9:27 for the altar of **the LORD** at the place the LORD would choose.
10: 8 **The LORD** said to Joshua, "Do not be afraid of them; I have
10:10 **The LORD** threw them into confusion before Israel, who
10:11 **the LORD** hurled large hailstones down on them from the sky,
10:12 On the day **the LORD** gave the Amorites over to Israel,
10:12 over to Israel, Joshua said to **the LORD** in the presence of Israel:
10:14 like it before or since, a day when **the LORD** listened to a man.
10:14 listened to a man. Surely **the LORD** was fighting for Israel!
10:19 for **the LORD** your God has given them into your hand."
10:25 This is what **the LORD** will do to all the enemies you are going
10:30 **The LORD** also gave that city and its king into Israel's hand.
10:32 **The LORD** handed Lachish over to Israel, and Joshua took it on
10:40 just as **the LORD**, the God of Israel, had commanded.
10:42 because **the LORD**, the God of Israel, fought for Israel.
11: 6 **The LORD** said to Joshua, "Do not be afraid of them, because by
11: 8 **the LORD** gave them into the hand of Israel. They defeated them
11: 9 Joshua did to them as **the LORD** had directed: He hamstrung
11:12 as Moses the servant of **the LORD** had commanded.
11:15 As **the LORD** commanded his servant Moses, so Moses
11:15 he left nothing undone of all that **the LORD** commanded Moses.
11:20 For it was **the LORD** *himself* who hardened their hearts to wage
11:20 them without mercy, as **the LORD** had commanded Moses.
11:23 took the entire land, just as **the LORD** had directed Moses,
12: 6 Moses, the servant of **the LORD**, and the Israelites conquered
12: 6 Moses the servant of **the LORD** gave their land to the
13: 1 advanced in years, **the LORD** said to him, "You are very old,
13: 8 as he, the servant of **the LORD**, had assigned it to them.
13:14 since the offerings made by fire to **the LORD**, the God of Israel,
13:33 **the LORD**, the God of Israel, is their inheritance, as he promised
14: 2 as **the LORD** had commanded through Moses.
14: 5 divided the land, just as **the LORD** had commanded Moses.
14: 6 "You know what **the LORD** said to Moses the man of God at
14: 7 I was forty years old when Moses the servant of **the LORD** sent
14: 8 I, however, followed **the LORD** my God wholeheartedly.
14: 9 because you have followed **the LORD** my God wholeheartedly.'
14:10 "Now then, just as **the LORD** promised, he has kept me alive for
14:10 he has kept me alive for forty-five years since the time **he**[s] said this
14:12 Now give me this hill country that **the LORD** promised me that
14:12 their cities were large and fortified, but, **the LORD** helping me,
14:12 the LORD helping me, I will drive them out just as **he**[s] said."
14:14 because he followed **the LORD**, the God of Israel,
15:13 In accordance with **the LORD's** command to him, Joshua gave to
17: 4 "**The LORD** commanded Moses to give us an inheritance among
17: 4 the brothers of their father, according to **the LORD's** command.
17:14 a numerous people and **the LORD** has blessed us abundantly."
18: 3 before you begin to take possession of the land that **the LORD**,
18: 6 and I will cast lots for you in the presence of **the LORD** our God.
18: 7 because the priestly service of **the LORD** is their inheritance.
18: 7 of the Jordan. Moses the servant of **the LORD** gave it to them."
18: 8 cast lots for you here at Shiloh in the presence of **the LORD**."
18:10 then cast lots for them in Shiloh in the presence of **the LORD**,
19:50 as **the LORD** had commanded. They gave him the town he asked
19:51 the presence of **the LORD** at the entrance to the Tent of Meeting.
20: 1 Then **the LORD** said to Joshua:
21: 2 "**The LORD** commanded through Moses that you give us towns
21: 3 So, as **the LORD** had commanded, the Israelites gave the Levites
21: 8 their pasturelands, as **the LORD** had commanded through Moses.
21:43 So **the LORD** gave Israel all the land he had sworn to give their
21:44 **The LORD** gave them rest on every side, just as he had sworn to
21:44 **the LORD** handed all their enemies over to them.
21:45 Not one of all **the LORD's** good promises to the house of Israel
22: 2 "You have done all that Moses the servant of **the LORD**
22: 3 but have carried out the mission **the LORD** your God gave you.
22: 4 Now that **the LORD** your God has given your brothers rest as he
22: 4 servant of **the LORD** gave you on the other side of the Jordan.
22: 5 and the law that Moses the servant of **the LORD** gave you:
22: 5 to love **the LORD** your God, to walk in all his ways, to obey his
22: 9 in accordance with the command of **the LORD** through Moses.

[F] Hitpael (hitpoel, hitpoal, hitpolel, hitpolal, hitpalel, hitpalal, hitpalpel, hitpalpal, hotpael, hotpaal) [G] Hiphil (hiphtil) [H] Hophal [I] Hishtaphel

Jos 22:16 "The whole assembly of **the LORD** says: 'How could you break
22:16 How could you turn away from **the LORD** and build yourselves
22:16 and build yourselves an altar in rebellion against **him**[s] now?
22:17 even though a plague fell on the community of **the LORD**!
22:18 are you now turning away from **the LORD**? " 'If you rebel
22:18 " 'If you rebel against **the LORD** today, tomorrow he will be
22:19 If the land you possess is defiled, come over to **the LORD's** land,
22:19 where **the LORD's** tabernacle stands, and share the land with us.
22:19 do not rebel against **the LORD** or against us by building an altar
22:19 altar for yourselves, other than the altar of **the LORD** our God.
22:22 "The Mighty One, God, **the LORD**! The Mighty One, God,
22:22 the LORD! The Mighty One, God, **the LORD**! He knows!
22:22 If this has been in rebellion or disobedience to **the LORD**,
22:23 If we have built our own altar to turn away from **the LORD**
22:23 offerings on it, may **the LORD** himself call us to account.
22:24 'What do you have to do with **the LORD**, the God of Israel?
22:25 **The LORD** has made the Jordan a boundary between us
22:25 you Reubenites and Gadites! You have no share in **the LORD**.'
22:25 So your descendants might cause ours to stop fearing **the LORD**.
22:27 that we will worship **the LORD** at his sanctuary with our burnt
22:27 will not be able to say to ours, 'You have no share in **the LORD**.'
22:28 Look at the replica of **the LORD's** altar, which our fathers built,
22:29 "Far be it from us to rebel against **the LORD** and turn away from
22:29 turn away from **him**[s] today by building an altar for burnt offerings,
22:29 other than the altar of **the LORD** our God that stands before his
22:31 and Manasseh, "Today we know that **the LORD** is with us,
22:31 because you have not acted unfaithfully toward **the LORD** in this
22:31 Now you have rescued the Israelites from **the LORD's** hand."
22:34 altar this name: A Witness Between Us that **the LORD** is God.
23: 1 **the LORD** had given Israel rest from all their enemies around
23: 3 You yourselves have seen everything **the LORD** your God has
23: 3 for your sake; it was **the LORD** your God who fought for you.
23: 5 **The LORD** your God himself will drive them out of your way.
23: 5 possession of their land, as **the LORD** your God promised you.
23: 8 you are to hold fast to **the LORD** your God, as you have until
23: 9 "**The LORD** has driven out before you great and powerful
23:10 because **the LORD** your God fights for you, just as he promised.
23:11 So be very careful to love **the LORD** your God.
23:13 you may be sure that **the LORD** your God will no longer drive
23:13 from this good land, which **the LORD** your God has given you.
23:14 soul that not one of all the good promises **the LORD** your God
23:15 just as every good promise of **the LORD** your God has come
23:15 so **the LORD** will bring on you all the evil he has threatened,
23:15 until he has destroyed you from this good land **he**[s] [+466] has
23:16 If you violate the covenant of **the LORD** your God, which he
23:16 and bow down to them, **the LORD's** anger will burn against you,
24: 2 all the people, "This is what **the LORD**, the God of Israel, says:
24: 7 they cried to **the LORD** for help, and he put darkness between
24:14 "Now fear **the LORD** and serve him with all faithfulness.
24:14 worshiped beyond the River and in Egypt, and serve **the LORD**.
24:15 if serving **the LORD** seems undesirable to you, then choose for
24:15 But as for me and my household, we will serve **the LORD**."
24:16 "Far be it from us to forsake **the LORD** to serve other gods!
24:17 It was **the LORD** our God himself who brought us and our
24:18 **the LORD** drove out before us all the nations, including the
24:18 the land. We too will serve **the LORD**, because he is our God."
24:19 Joshua said to the people, "You are not able to serve **the LORD**.
24:20 If you forsake **the LORD** and serve foreign gods, he will turn
24:21 But the people said to Joshua, "No! We will serve **the LORD**."
24:22 against yourselves that you have chosen to serve **the LORD**."
24:23 gods that are among you and yield your hearts to **the LORD**,
24:24 to Joshua, "We will serve **the LORD** our God and obey him."
24:26 set it up there under the oak near the holy place of **the LORD**.
24:27 against us. It has heard all the words **the LORD** has said to us.
24:29 After these things, Joshua son of Nun, the servant of **the LORD**,
24:31 Israel served **the LORD** throughout the lifetime of Joshua
24:31 who had experienced everything **the LORD** had done for Israel.
Jdg 1: 1 After the death of Joshua, the Israelites asked **the LORD**,
1: 2 **The LORD** answered, "Judah is to go; I have given the land into
1: 4 **the LORD** gave the Canaanites and Perizzites into their hands
1:19 **The LORD** was with the men of Judah. They took possession of
1:22 house of Joseph attacked Bethel, and **the LORD** was with them.
2: 1 The angel of **the LORD** went up from Gilgal to Bokim and said,
2: 4 When the angel of **the LORD** had spoken these things to all the
2: 5 that place Bokim. There they offered sacrifices to **the LORD**.
2: 7 The people served **the LORD** throughout the lifetime of Joshua
2: 7 who had seen all the great things **the LORD** had done for Israel.
2: 8 Joshua son of Nun, the servant of **the LORD**, died at the age of a
2:10 who knew neither **the LORD** nor what he had done for Israel.
2:11 the Israelites did evil in the eyes of **the LORD** and served the
2:12 They forsook **the LORD**, the God of their fathers, who had
2:12 of the peoples around them. They provoked **the LORD** to anger
2:13 because they forsook **him**[s] and served Baal and the Ashtoreths.
2:14 In his anger against Israel **the LORD** handed them over to raiders
2:15 the hand of **the LORD** was against them to defeat them,
2:15 was against them to defeat them, just as **he**[s] had sworn to them.
2:15 just as he had sworn to them. **[RPH]** They were in great distress.
2:16 **the LORD** raised up judges, who saved them out of the hands of
2:17 had walked, the way of obedience to **the LORD's** commands.
2:18 Whenever **the LORD** raised up a judge for them, he was with the
2:18 **he**[s] was with the judge and saved them out of the hands of their
2:18 for **the LORD** had compassion on them as they groaned under
2:20 Therefore **the LORD** was very angry with Israel and said,
2:22 test Israel and see whether they will keep the way of **the LORD**
2:23 **The LORD** had allowed those nations to remain; he did not drive
3: 1 These are the nations **the LORD** left to test all those Israelites
3: 4 to see whether they would obey **the LORD's** commands,
3: 7 The Israelites did evil in the eyes of **the LORD**; they forgot the
3: 7 they forgot **the LORD** their God and served the Baals and the
3: 8 The anger of **the LORD** burned against Israel so that he sold
3: 9 when they cried out to **the LORD**, he raised up for them a
3: 9 **he**[s] raised up for them a deliverer, Othniel son of Kenaz,
3:10 The Spirit of **the LORD** came upon him, so that he became
3:10 **The LORD** gave Cushan-Rishathaim king of Aram into the
3:12 Once again the Israelites did evil in the eyes of **the LORD**,
3:12 because they did this evil **[RPH]** the LORD gave Eglon king of
3:12 because they did this evil **the LORD** gave Eglon king of Moab
3:15 Again the Israelites cried out to **the LORD**, and he gave them a
3:15 Israelites cried out to the LORD, and **he**[s] gave them a deliverer—
3:28 he ordered, "for **the LORD** has given Moab, your enemy,
4: 1 the Israelites once again did evil in the eyes of **the LORD**.
4: 2 So **the LORD** sold them into the hands of Jabin, a king of
4: 3 the Israelites for twenty years, they cried to **the LORD** for help.
4: 6 Abinoam from Kedesh in Naphtali and said to him, "**The LORD**,
4: 9 not be yours, for **the LORD** will hand Sisera over to a woman."
4:14 This is the day **the LORD** has given Sisera into your hands.
4:14 Has not **the LORD** gone ahead of you?" So Barak went down
4:15 **the LORD** routed Sisera and all his chariots and army by the
5: 2 when the people willingly offer themselves—praise **the LORD**!
5: 3 I will sing to **the LORD**, I will sing; I will make music to the
5: 3 I will sing; I will make music to **the LORD**, the God of Israel.
5: 4 "O **LORD**, when you went out from Seir, when you marched
5: 5 The mountains quaked before **the LORD**, the One of Sinai,
5: 5 the One of Sinai, before **the LORD**, the God of Israel.
5: 9 with the willing volunteers among the people. Praise **the LORD**!
5:11 They recite the righteous acts of **the LORD**, the righteous acts of
5:11 "Then the people of **the LORD** went down to the city gates.
5:13 the nobles; the people of **the LORD** came to me with the mighty.
5:23 'Curse Meroz,' said the angel of **the LORD**. 'Curse its people
5:23 its people bitterly, because they did not come to help **the LORD**,
5:23 come to help the LORD, to help **the LORD** against the mighty.'
5:31 "So may all your enemies perish, O **LORD**! But may they who
6: 1 Again the Israelites did evil in the eyes of **the LORD**, and for
6: 1 and for seven years **he**[s] gave them into the hands of the Midianites.
6: 6 so impoverished the Israelites that they cried out to **the LORD**
6: 7 When the Israelites cried to **the LORD** because of Midian,
6: 8 **he**[s] sent them a prophet, who said, "This is what the LORD,
6: 8 who said, "This is what **the LORD**, the God of Israel, says:
6:10 I said to you, 'I am **the LORD** your God; do not worship the gods
6:11 The angel of **the LORD** came and sat down under the oak in
6:12 When the angel of **the LORD** appeared to Gideon, he said,
6:12 to Gideon, he said, "**The LORD** is with you, mighty warrior."
6:13 "But sir," Gideon replied, "if **the LORD** is with us, why has all
6:13 when they said, 'Did not **the LORD** bring us up out of Egypt?'
6:13 now **the LORD** has abandoned us and put us into the hand of
6:14 **The LORD** turned to him and said, "Go in the strength you have
6:16 **The LORD** answered, "I will be with you, and you will strike
6:21 the angel of **the LORD** touched the meat and the unleavened
6:21 and the bread. And the angel of **the LORD** disappeared.
6:22 When Gideon realized that it was the angel of **the LORD**,
6:22 the angel of the LORD, he exclaimed, "Ah, Sovereign **LORD**!
6:22 I have seen the angel of **the LORD** face to face!"
6:23 **the LORD** said to him, "Peace! Do not be afraid. You are not
6:24 So Gideon built an altar to **the LORD** there and called it The
6:24 an altar to the LORD there and called it **The LORD** is Peace.
6:25 That same night **the LORD** said to him, "Take the second bull
6:26 build a proper kind of altar to **the LORD** your God on the top of
6:27 Gideon took ten of his servants and did as **the LORD** told him.
6:34 the Spirit of **the LORD** came upon Gideon, and he blew a
7: 2 **The LORD** said to Gideon, "You have too many men for me to
7: 4 But **the LORD** said to Gideon, "There are still too many men.
7: 5 There **the LORD** told him, "Separate those who lap the water
7: 7 **The LORD** said to Gideon, "With the three hundred men that
7: 9 During that night **the LORD** said to Gideon, "Get up, go down
7:15 **The LORD** has given the Midianite camp into your hands."
7:18 camp blow yours and shout, 'For **the LORD** and for Gideon.' "
7:20 they shouted, "A sword for **the LORD** and for Gideon!"
7:22 **the LORD** caused the men throughout the camp to turn on each

Jdg 8: 7 when **the LORD** has given Zebah and Zalmunna into my hand,
8: 19 As surely as **the LORD** lives, if you had spared their lives,
8: 23 nor will my son rule over you. **The LORD** will rule over you."
8: 34 did not remember **the LORD** their God, who had rescued them
10: 6 Again the Israelites did evil in the eyes of **the LORD**. They
10: 6 because the Israelites forsook **the LORD** and no longer served
10: 7 **he**[s] became angry with them. He sold them into the hands of the
10: 10 the Israelites cried out to **the LORD**, "We have sinned against
10: 11 **The LORD** replied, "When the Egyptians, the Amorites,
10: 15 the Israelites said to **the LORD**, "We have sinned. Do with us
10: 16 got rid of the foreign gods among them and served **the LORD**.
11: 9 back to fight the Ammonites and **the LORD** gives them to me—
11: 10 The elders of Gilead replied, "**The LORD** is our witness;
11: 11 And he repeated all his words before **the LORD** in Mizpah.
11: 21 "Then **the LORD**, the God of Israel, gave Sihon and all his men
11: 23 "Now since **the LORD**, the God of Israel, has driven the
11: 24 Likewise, whatever **the LORD** our God has given us, we will
11: 27 Let **the LORD**, the Judge, decide the dispute this day between the
11: 29 the Spirit of **the LORD** came upon Jephthah. He crossed Gilead
11: 30 Jephthah made a vow to **the LORD**: "If you give the Ammonites
11: 31 in triumph from the Ammonites will be **the LORD's** [+4200],
11: 32 to fight the Ammonites, and **the LORD** gave them into his hands.
11: 35 because I have made a vow to **the LORD** that I cannot break."
11: 36 she replied, "you have given your word to **the LORD**.
11: 36 now that **the LORD** has avenged you of your enemies,
12: 3 the Ammonites, and **the LORD** gave me the victory over them.
13: 1 Again the Israelites did evil in the eyes of **the LORD**,
13: 1 so **the LORD** delivered them into the hands of the Philistines for
13: 3 The angel of **the LORD** appeared to her and said, "You are
13: 8 Then Manoah prayed to **the LORD**: "O Lord, I beg you,
13: 13 The angel of **the LORD** answered, "Your wife must do all that I
13: 15 Manoah said to the angel of **the LORD**, "We would like you to
13: 16 The angel of **the LORD** replied, "Even though you detain me,
13: 16 But if you prepare a burnt offering, offer it to **the LORD**."
13: 16 (Manoah did not realize that it was the angel of **the LORD**.)
13: 17 Manoah inquired of the angel of **the LORD**, "What is your name,
13: 18 **He**[s] [+4855] replied, "Why do you ask my name? It is beyond
13: 19 with the grain offering, and sacrificed it on a rock to **the LORD**.
13: 20 toward heaven, the angel of **the LORD** ascended in the flame.
13: 21 When the angel of **the LORD** did not show himself again to
13: 21 and his wife, Manoah realized that it was the angel of **the LORD**.
13: 23 But his wife answered, "If **the LORD** had meant to kill us,
13: 24 and named him Samson. He grew and **the LORD** blessed him,
13: 25 the Spirit of **the LORD** began to stir him while he was in
14: 4 (His parents did not know that this was from **the LORD**,
14: 6 The Spirit of **the LORD** came upon him in power so that he tore
14: 19 the Spirit of **the LORD** came upon him in power. He went down
15: 14 him shouting. The Spirit of **the LORD** came upon him in power.
15: 18 Because he was very thirsty, he cried out to **the LORD**, "You
16: 20 myself free." But he did not know that **the LORD** had left him.
16: 28 Then Samson prayed to **the LORD**, "O Sovereign LORD,
16: 28 prayed to the LORD, "O Sovereign **LORD**, remember me.
17: 2 I took it." Then his mother said, "**The LORD** bless you, my son!"
17: 3 "I solemnly consecrate my silver to **the LORD** for my son to
17: 13 Micah said, "Now I know that **the LORD** will be good to me,
18: 6 "Go in peace. Your journey has **the LORD's** approval."
19: 18 in Judah and now I am going to the house of **the LORD**.
20: 1 out as one man and assembled before **the LORD** in Mizpah.
20: 18 the Benjamites?" **The LORD** replied, "Judah shall go first."
20: 23 The Israelites went up and wept before **the LORD** until evening,
20: 23 the LORD until evening, and they inquired of **the LORD**.
20: 23 our brothers?" **The LORD** answered, "Go up against them."
20: 26 went up to Bethel, and there they sat weeping before **the LORD**.
20: 26 presented burnt offerings and fellowship offerings to **the LORD**.
20: 27 the Israelites inquired of **the LORD**. (In those days the ark of the
20: 28 **The LORD** responded, "Go, for tomorrow I will give them into
20: 35 **The LORD** defeated Benjamin before Israel, and on that day the
21: 3 "O **LORD**, the God of Israel," they cried, "why has this happened
21: 5 all the tribes of Israel has failed to assemble before **the LORD**?"
21: 5 before **the LORD** at Mizpah should certainly be put to death.
21: 7 since we have taken an oath by **the LORD** not to give them any
21: 8 tribes of Israel failed to assemble before **the LORD** at Mizpah?"
21: 15 because **the LORD** had made a gap in the tribes of Israel.
21: 19 But look, there is the annual festival of **the LORD** in Shiloh,
Ru 1: 6 When she heard in Moab that **the LORD** had come to the aid of
1: 8 May **the LORD** show kindness to you, as you have shown to
1: 9 May **the LORD** grant that each of you will find rest in the home
1: 13 for you, because **the LORD's** hand has gone out against me!"
1: 17 May **the LORD** deal with me, be it ever so severely, if anything
1: 21 I went away full, but **the LORD** has brought me back empty.
1: 21 **The LORD** has afflicted me; the Almighty has brought
2: 4 and greeted the harvesters, "**The LORD** be with you!"
2: 4 LORD be with you!" "**The LORD** bless you!" they called back.
2: 12 May **the LORD** repay you for what you have done. May you be
2: 12 May you be richly rewarded by **the LORD**, the God of Israel,
2: 20 "**The LORD** bless him!" Naomi said to her daughter-in-law.
3: 10 "**The LORD** bless you, my daughter," he replied. "This kindness
3: 13 But if he is not willing, as surely as **the LORD** lives I will do it.
4: 11 May **the LORD** make the woman who is coming into your home
4: 12 Through the offspring **the LORD** gives you by this young
4: 13 Then he went to her, and **the LORD** enabled her to conceive,
4: 14 "Praise be to **the LORD**, who this day has not left you without a
1Sa 1: 3 town to worship and sacrifice to **the LORD** Almighty at Shiloh,
1: 3 and Phinehas, the two sons of Eli, were priests of **the LORD**.
1: 5 because he loved her, and **the LORD** had closed her womb.
1: 6 because **the LORD** had closed her womb, her rival kept
1: 7 Whenever Hannah went up to the house of **the LORD**, her rival
1: 9 was sitting on a chair by the doorpost of **the LORD's** temple.
1: 10 bitterness of soul Hannah wept much and prayed to **the LORD**.
1: 11 she made a vow, saying, "O **LORD** Almighty, if you will only
1: 11 then I will give him to **the LORD** for all the days of his life,
1: 12 As she kept on praying to **the LORD**, Eli observed her mouth.
1: 15 drinking wine or beer; I was pouring out my soul to **the LORD**.
1: 19 the next morning they arose and worshiped before **the LORD** and
1: 19 lay with Hannah his wife, and **the LORD** remembered her.
1: 20 him Samuel, saying, "Because I asked **the LORD** for him."
1: 21 up with all his family to offer the annual sacrifice to **the LORD**
1: 22 boy is weaned, I will take him and present him before **the LORD**,
1: 23 have weaned him; only may **the LORD** make good his word."
1: 24 of wine, and brought him to the house of **the LORD** at Shiloh.
1: 26 am the woman who stood here beside you praying to **the LORD**.
1: 27 for this child, and **the LORD** has granted me what I asked of him.
1: 28 So now I give him to **the LORD**. For his whole life he will be
1: 28 For his whole life he will be given over to **the LORD**."
1: 28 given over to the LORD." And he worshiped **the LORD** there.
2: 1 "My heart rejoices in **the LORD**; in the LORD my horn is lifted
2: 1 heart rejoices in the LORD; in **the LORD** my horn is lifted high.
2: 2 "There is no one holy like **the LORD**; there is no one besides
2: 3 for **the LORD** is a God who knows, and by him deeds are
2: 6 "**The LORD** brings death and makes alive; he brings down to the
2: 7 **The LORD** sends poverty and wealth; he humbles and he exalts.
2: 8 "For the foundations of the earth are **the LORD's** [+4200];
2: 10 those who oppose **the LORD** will be shattered. He will thunder
2: 10 them from heaven; **the LORD** will judge the ends of the earth.
2: 11 but the boy ministered before **the LORD** under Eli the priest.
2: 12 Eli's sons were wicked men; they had no regard for **the LORD**.
2: 17 This sin of the young men was very great in **the LORD's** sight,
2: 17 for they were treating **the LORD's** offering with contempt.
2: 18 Samuel was ministering before **the LORD**—a boy wearing a
2: 20 "May **the LORD** give you children by this woman to take the
2: 20 take the place of the one she prayed for and gave to **the LORD**."
2: 21 **the LORD** was gracious to Hannah; she conceived and gave birth
2: 21 the boy Samuel grew up in the presence of **the LORD**.
2: 24 it is not a good report that I hear spreading among **the LORD's**
2: 25 but if a man sins against **the LORD**, who will intercede for him?"
2: 25 father's rebuke, for it was **the LORD's** will to put them to death.
2: 26 to grow in stature and in favor with **the LORD** and with men.
2: 27 God came to Eli and said to him, "This is what **the LORD** says:
2: 30 "Therefore **the LORD**, the God of Israel, declares: 'I promised
2: 30 now **the LORD** declares: 'Far be it from me! Those who honor
3: 1 The boy Samuel ministered before **the LORD** under Eli.
3: 1 In those days the word of **the LORD** was rare; there were not
3: 3 and Samuel was lying down in the temple of **the LORD**,
3: 4 Then **the LORD** called Samuel. Samuel answered, "Here I am."
3: 6 Again **the LORD** called, "Samuel!" And Samuel got up
3: 7 Now Samuel did not yet know **the LORD**: The word of the
3: 7 The word of **the LORD** had not yet been revealed to him.
3: 8 **The LORD** called Samuel a third time, and Samuel got up
3: 8 called me." Then Eli realized that **the LORD** was calling the boy.
3: 9 "Go and lie down, and if he calls you, say, 'Speak, **LORD**,
3: 10 **The LORD** came and stood there, calling as at the other times,
3: 11 **the LORD** said to Samuel: "See, I am about to do something in
3: 15 and then opened the doors of the house of **the LORD**.
3: 18 Eli said, "He is **the LORD**; let him do what is good in his eyes."
3: 19 **The LORD** was with Samuel as he grew up, and he let none of
3: 20 recognized that Samuel was attested as a prophet of **the LORD**.
3: 21 **The LORD** continued to appear at Shiloh, and there he revealed
3: 21 and there **he**[s] revealed himself to Samuel through his word.
3: 21 and there he revealed himself to Samuel through **his**[s] word.
4: 3 "Why did **the LORD** bring defeat upon us today before the
4: 3 Let us bring the ark of the **LORD's** covenant from Shiloh,
4: 4 they brought back the ark of the covenant of **the LORD**
4: 5 When the ark of **the LORD's** covenant came into the camp,
4: 6 When they learned that the ark of **the LORD** had come into the
5: 3 fallen on his face on the ground before the ark of **the LORD**!
5: 4 fallen on his face on the ground before the ark of **the LORD**!
5: 6 **The LORD's** hand was heavy upon the people of Ashdod
5: 9 after they had moved it, **the LORD's** hand was against that city,

1Sa 6: 1 When the ark of **the LORD** had been in Philistine territory seven
6: 2 and said, "What shall we do with the ark of **the LORD**?
6: 8 Take the ark of **the LORD** and put it on the cart, and in a chest
6: 11 They placed the ark of **the LORD** on the cart and along with it
6: 14 and sacrificed the cows as a burnt offering to **the LORD**.
6: 15 The Levites took down the ark of **the LORD**, together with the
6: 15 offered burnt offerings and made sacrifices to **the LORD**.
6: 17 gold tumors the Philistines sent as a guilt offering to **the LORD**—
6: 18 The large rock, on which they set the ark of **the LORD**, is a
6: 19 them to death because they had looked into the ark of **the LORD**.
6: 19 because of the heavy blow **the LORD** had dealt them,
6: 20 "Who can stand in the presence of **the LORD**, this holy God?
6: 21 saying, "The Philistines have returned the ark of **the LORD**.
7: 1 men of Kiriath Jearim came and took up the ark of **the LORD**.
7: 1 and consecrated Eleazar his son to guard the ark of **the LORD**.
7: 2 and all the people of Israel mourned and sought after **the LORD**.
7: 3 "If you are returning to **the LORD** with all your hearts, then rid
7: 3 and the Ashtoreths and commit yourselves to **the LORD**
7: 4 put away their Baals and Ashtoreths, and served **the LORD** only.
7: 5 all Israel at Mizpah and I will intercede with **the LORD** for you."
7: 6 at Mizpah, they drew water and poured it out before **the LORD**.
7: 6 and there they confessed, "We have sinned against **the LORD**."
7: 8 to Samuel, "Do not stop crying out to **the LORD** our God for us,
7: 9 and offered it up as a whole burnt offering to **the LORD**.
7: 9 He cried out to **the LORD** on Israel's behalf, and the LORD
7: 9 to the LORD on Israel's behalf, and **the LORD** answered him.
7: 10 that day **the LORD** thundered with loud thunder against the
7: 12 named it Ebenezer, saying, "Thus far has **the LORD** helped us."
7: 13 the hand of **the LORD** was against the Philistines.
7: 17 he also judged Israel. And he built an altar there to **the LORD**.
8: 6 to lead us," this displeased Samuel; so he prayed to **the LORD**.
8: 7 **the LORD** told him: "Listen to all that the people are saying to
8: 10 Samuel told all the words of **the LORD** to the people who were
8: 18 have chosen, and **the LORD** will not answer you in that day."
8: 21 heard all that the people said, he repeated it before **the LORD**.
8: 22 **The LORD** answered, "Listen to them and give them a king."
9: 15 day before Saul came, **the LORD** had revealed this to Samuel:
9: 17 When Samuel caught sight of Saul, **the LORD** said to him,
10: 1 "Has not **the LORD** anointed you leader over his inheritance?
10: 6 The Spirit of **the LORD** will come upon you in power, and you
10: 17 Samuel summoned the people of Israel to **the LORD** at Mizpah
10: 18 and said to them, "This is what **the LORD**, the God of Israel,
10: 19 So now present yourselves before **the LORD** by your tribes
10: 22 So they inquired further of **the LORD**, "Has the man come here
10: 22 **the LORD** said, "Yes, he has hidden himself among the
10: 24 to all the people, "Do you see the man **the LORD** has chosen?
10: 25 wrote them down on a scroll and deposited it before **the LORD**.
11: 7 the terror of **the LORD** fell on the people, and they turned out as
11: 13 be put to death today, for this day **the LORD** has rescued Israel."
11: 15 and confirmed Saul as king in the presence of **the LORD**.
11: 15 There they sacrificed fellowship offerings before **the LORD**,
12: 3 Testify against me in the presence of **the LORD** and his anointed.
12: 5 Samuel said to them, "**The LORD** is witness against you,
12: 6 "It is **the LORD** who appointed Moses and Aaron and brought
12: 7 **the LORD** as to all the righteous acts performed by the LORD
12: 7 as to all the righteous acts performed by **the LORD** for you
12: 8 they cried to **the LORD** for help, and the LORD sent Moses
12: 8 to the LORD for help, and **the LORD** sent Moses and Aaron,
12: 9 "But they forgot **the LORD** their God; so he sold them into the
12: 10 They cried out to **the LORD** and said, 'We have sinned; we have
12: 10 we have forsaken **the LORD** and served the Baals and the
12: 11 Then **the LORD** sent Jerub-Baal, Barak, Jephthah and Samuel,
12: 12 rule over us'—even though **the LORD** your God was your king.
12: 13 the one you asked for; see, **the LORD** has set a king over you.
12: 14 If you fear **the LORD** and serve and obey him and do not rebel
12: 14 and serve and obey him and do not rebel against **his**[s] commands,
12: 14 and the king who reigns over you follow **the LORD** your God—
12: 15 if you do not obey **the LORD**, and if you rebel against his
12: 15 if you rebel against **his**[s] commands, his hand will be against you,
12: 15 **his**[s] hand will be against you, as it was against your fathers.
12: 16 see this great thing **the LORD** is about to do before your eyes!
12: 17 harvest now? I will call upon **the LORD** to send thunder and rain.
12: 17 you did in the eyes of **the LORD** when you asked for a king."
12: 18 Samuel called upon **the LORD**, and that same day the LORD
12: 18 the LORD, and that same day **the LORD** sent thunder and rain.
12: 18 So all the people stood in awe of **the LORD** and of Samuel.
12: 19 "Pray to **the LORD** your God for your servants so that we will
12: 20 yet do not turn away from **the LORD**, but serve the LORD with
12: 20 away from the LORD, but serve **the LORD** with all your heart.
12: 22 For the sake of his great name **the LORD** will not reject his
12: 22 his people, because **the LORD** was pleased to make you his own.
12: 23 far be it from me that I should sin against **the LORD** by failing to
12: 24 be sure to fear **the LORD** and serve him faithfully with all your
13: 12 against me at Gilgal, and I have not sought **the LORD's** favor.'
13: 13 "You have not kept the command **the LORD** your God gave you;
13: 13 **he**[s] would have established your kingdom over Israel for all time.
13: 14 **the LORD** has sought out a man after his own heart
13: 14 after his own heart and **[RPH]** appointed him leader of his people,
13: 14 his people, because you have not kept **the LORD's** command."
14: 3 son of Phinehas, the son of Eli, **the LORD's** priest in Shiloh.
14: 6 Perhaps **the LORD** will act in our behalf. Nothing can hinder the
14: 6 Nothing can hinder **the LORD** from saving, whether by many
14: 10 because that will be our sign that **the LORD** has given them into
14: 12 up after me; **the LORD** has given them into the hand of Israel."
14: 23 So **the LORD** rescued Israel that day, and the battle moved on
14: 33 the men are sinning against **the LORD** by eating meat that has
14: 34 Do not sin against **the LORD** by eating meat with blood still in
14: 35 Saul built an altar to **the LORD**; it was the first time he had done
14: 35 it was the first time *he had* **done**[s] **this** [+1215+4200+4640].
14: 39 As surely as **the LORD** who rescues Israel lives, even if it lies
14: 41 Saul prayed to **the LORD**, the God of Israel, "Give me the right
14: 45 As surely as **the LORD** lives, not a hair of his head will fall to
15: 1 "I am the one **the LORD** sent to anoint you king over his people
15: 1 his people Israel; so listen now to the message from **the LORD**.
15: 2 This is what **the LORD** Almighty says: 'I will punish the
15: 10 Then the word of **the LORD** came to Samuel:
15: 11 was troubled, and he cried out to **the LORD** all that night.
15: 13 When Samuel reached him, Saul said, "**The LORD** bless you!
15: 13 LORD bless you! I have carried out **the LORD's** instructions."
15: 15 best of the sheep and cattle to sacrifice to **the LORD** your God,
15: 16 "Let me tell you what **the LORD** said to me last night." "Tell
15: 17 of the tribes of Israel? **The LORD** anointed you king over Israel.
15: 18 **he**[s] sent you on a mission, saying, 'Go and completely destroy
15: 19 Why did you not obey **the LORD**? Why did you pounce on the
15: 19 pounce on the plunder and do evil in the eyes of **the LORD**?"
15: 20 "But I did obey **the LORD**," Saul said. "I went on the mission the
15: 20 Saul said. "I went on the mission **the LORD** assigned me.
15: 21 in order to sacrifice them to **the LORD** your God at Gilgal."
15: 22 "Does **the LORD** delight in burnt offerings and sacrifices as
15: 22 and sacrifices as much as in obeying the voice of **the LORD**?
15: 23 Because you have rejected the word of **the LORD**, he has
15: 24 I violated **the LORD's** command and your instructions.
15: 25 and come back with me, so that I may worship **the LORD**."
15: 26 You have rejected the word of **the LORD**, and the LORD has
15: 26 the LORD, and **the LORD** has rejected you as king over Israel!"
15: 28 "**The LORD** has torn the kingdom of Israel from you today
15: 30 come back with me, so that I may worship **the LORD** your God."
15: 31 So Samuel went back with Saul, and Saul worshiped **the LORD**.
15: 33 And Samuel put Agag to death before **the LORD** at Gilgal.
15: 35 **the LORD** was grieved that he had made Saul king over Israel.
16: 1 **The LORD** said to Samuel, "How long will you mourn for Saul,
16: 2 **The LORD** said, "Take a heifer with you and say, 'I have come to
16: 2 a heifer with you and say, 'I have come to sacrifice to **the LORD**.'
16: 4 Samuel did what **the LORD** said. When he arrived at Bethlehem,
16: 5 "Yes, in peace; I have come to sacrifice to **the LORD**.
16: 6 "Surely the LORD's anointed stands here before **the LORD**."
16: 7 But **the LORD** said to Samuel, "Do not consider his appearance
16: 7 at the outward appearance, but **the LORD** looks at the heart."
16: 8 But Samuel said, "**The LORD** has not chosen this one either."
16: 9 pass by, but Samuel said, "Nor has **the LORD** chosen this one."
16: 10 but Samuel said to him, "**The LORD** has not chosen these."
16: 12 Then **the LORD** said, "Rise and anoint him; he is the one."
16: 13 from that day on the Spirit of **the LORD** came upon David in
16: 14 Now the Spirit of **the LORD** had departed from Saul, and an evil
16: 14 from Saul, and an evil spirit from **the LORD** tormented him.
16: 18 and is a fine-looking man. And **the LORD** is with him."
17: 37 **The LORD** who delivered me from the paw of the lion and the
17: 37 Saul said to David, "Go, and **the LORD** be with you."
17: 45 but I come against you in the name of **the LORD** Almighty,
17: 46 This day **the LORD** will hand you over to me, and I'll strike you
17: 47 will know that it is not by sword or spear that **the LORD** saves;
17: 47 for the battle is **the LORD's** [+4200], and he will give all of you
18: 12 of David, because **the LORD** was with David but had left Saul.
18: 14 he did he had great success, because **the LORD** was with him.
18: 17 only serve me bravely and fight the battles of **the LORD**."
18: 28 When Saul realized that **the LORD** was with David and that his
19: 5 **The LORD** won a great victory for all Israel, and you saw it
19: 6 "As surely as **the LORD** lives, David will not be put to death."
19: 9 an evil spirit from **the LORD** came upon Saul as he was sitting in
20: 3 Yet as surely as **the LORD** lives and as you live, there is only a
20: 8 have brought him into a covenant with you before **the LORD**.
20: 12 "*By* **the LORD**, the God of Israel, I will surely sound out my
20: 13 may **the LORD** deal with me, be it ever so severely, if I do not let
20: 13 May **the LORD** be with you as he has been with my father.
20: 14 show me unfailing kindness like that of **the LORD** as long as I
20: 15 not even when **the LORD** has cut off every one of David's
20: 16 saying, "May **the LORD** call David's enemies to account."
20: 21 then come, because, as surely as **the LORD** lives, you are safe;

1Sa 20:22 then you must go, because **the LORD** has sent you away.
20:23 remember, **the LORD** is witness between you and me forever."
20:42 have sworn friendship with each other in the name of **the LORD**,
20:42 saying, '**The LORD** is witness between you and me, and between
21: 6 [21:7] Presence that had been removed from before **the LORD**
21: 7 [21:8] servants was there that day, detained before **the LORD**;
22:10 Ahimelech inquired of **the LORD** for him; he also gave him
22:17 "Turn and kill the priests of **the LORD**, because they too have
22:17 were not willing to raise a hand to strike the priests of **the LORD**.
22:21 He told David that Saul had killed the priests of **the LORD**.
23: 2 he inquired of **the LORD**, saying, "Shall I go and attack these
23: 2 **The LORD** answered him, "Go, attack the Philistines and save
23: 4 Once again David inquired of **the LORD**, and the LORD
23: 4 the LORD, and **the LORD** answered him, "Go down to Keilah,
23:10 David said, "O **LORD**, God of Israel, your servant has heard
23:11 O **LORD**, God of Israel, tell your servant." And the LORD said,
23:11 God of Israel, tell your servant." And **the LORD** said, "He will."
23:12 and my men to Saul?" And **the LORD** said, "They will."
23:18 The two of them made a covenant before **the LORD**.
23:21 Saul replied, "**The LORD** bless you for your concern for me.
24: 4 [24:5] "This is the day **the LORD** spoke of when he said to you,
24: 6 [24:7] "**The LORD** forbid that I should do such a thing to my
24: 6 [24:7] **the LORD's** anointed, or lift my hand against him;
24: 6 [24:7] hand against him; for he is the anointed of **the LORD**."
24:10 [24:11] **the LORD** delivered you into my hands in the cave.
24:10 [24:11] against my master, because he is **the LORD's** anointed.'
24:12 [24:13] May **the LORD** judge between you and me. And may
24:12 [24:13] may **the LORD** avenge the wrongs you have done to
24:15 [24:16] May **the LORD** be our judge and decide between us.
24:18 [24:19] **the LORD** delivered me into your hands, but you did
24:19 [24:20] May **the LORD** reward you well for the way you treated
24:21 [24:22] Now swear to me by **the LORD** that you will not cut off
25:26 "Now since **the LORD** has kept you, my master, from bloodshed
25:26 as surely as **the LORD** lives and as you live, may your enemies
25:28 for **the LORD** will certainly make a lasting dynasty for my
25:28 dynasty for my master, because he fights **the LORD's** battles.
25:29 securely in the bundle of the living by **the LORD** your God.
25:30 When **the LORD** has done for my master every good thing he
25:31 when **the LORD** has brought my master success, remember your
25:32 David said to Abigail, "Praise be to **the LORD**, the God of Israel,
25:34 Otherwise, as surely as **the LORD**, the God of Israel, lives,
25:38 About ten days later, **the LORD** struck Nabal and he died.
25:39 heard that Nabal was dead, he said, "Praise be to **the LORD**,
25:39 **[RPH]** Then David sent word to Abigail, asking her to become
26: 9 Who can lay a hand on **the LORD's** anointed and be guiltless?
26:10 As surely as **the LORD** lives," he said, "the LORD himself will
26:10 the LORD lives," he said, "**the LORD** himself will strike him;
26:11 **the LORD** forbid that I should lay a hand on the LORD's
26:11 the LORD forbid that I should lay a hand on **the LORD's**
26:12 all sleeping, because **the LORD** had put them into a deep sleep.
26:16 As surely as **the LORD** lives, you and your men deserve to die,
26:16 because you did not guard your master, **the LORD's** anointed.
26:19 If **the LORD** has incited you against me, then may he accept an
26:19 men have done it, may they be cursed before **the LORD**!
26:19 They have now driven me from my share in **the LORD's**
26:20 my blood fall to the ground far from the presence of **the LORD**.
26:23 **The LORD** rewards every man for his righteousness
26:23 **The LORD** delivered you into my hands today, but I would not
26:23 hands today, but I would not lay a hand on **the LORD's** anointed.
26:24 so may **the LORD** value my life and deliver me from all trouble."
28: 6 He inquired of **the LORD**, but the LORD did not answer him by
28: 6 **the LORD** did not answer him by dreams or Urim or prophets.
28:10 Saul swore to her by **the LORD**, "As surely as the LORD lives,
28:10 Saul swore to her by the LORD, "As surely as **the LORD** lives,
28:16 now that **the LORD** has turned away from you and become your
28:17 **The LORD** has done what he predicted through me. The LORD
28:17 **The LORD** has torn the kingdom out of your hands and given it
28:18 Because you did not obey **the LORD** or carry out his fierce wrath
28:18 against the Amalekites, **the LORD** has done this to you today.
28:19 **The LORD** will hand over both Israel and you to the Philistines,
28:19 **The LORD** will also hand over the army of Israel to the
29: 6 called David and said to him, "As surely as **the LORD** lives,
30: 6 and daughters. But David found strength in **the LORD** his God.
30: 8 David inquired of **the LORD**, "Shall I pursue this raiding party?
30:23 you must not do that with what **the LORD** has given us.
30:26 "Here is a present for you from the plunder of **the LORD's**
2Sa 1:12 and for the army of **the LORD** and the house of Israel,
1:14 not afraid to lift your hand to destroy **the LORD's** anointed?"
1:16 against you when you said, 'I killed **the LORD's** anointed.' "
2: 1 In the course of time, David inquired of **the LORD**. "Shall I go
2: 1 he asked. **The LORD** said, "Go up." David asked, "Where shall I
2: 5 "**The LORD** bless you for showing this kindness to Saul your
2: 6 May **the LORD** now show you kindness and faithfulness,
3: 9 if I do not do for David what **the LORD** promised him on oath
3:18 For **the LORD** promised David, 'By my servant David I will
3:28 my kingdom are forever innocent before **the LORD** concerning
3:39 May **the LORD** repay the evildoer according to his evil deeds!"
4: 8 This day **the LORD** has avenged my lord the king against Saul
4: 9 sons of Rimmon the Beerothite, "As surely as **the LORD** lives,
5: 2 And **the LORD** said to you, 'You will shepherd my people Israel,
5: 3 the king made a compact with them at Hebron before **the LORD**,
5:10 more powerful, because **the LORD** God Almighty was with him.
5:12 David knew that **the LORD** had established him as king over
5:19 so David inquired of **the LORD**, "Shall I go and attack the
5:19 **The LORD** answered him, "Go, for I will surely hand the
5:20 **the LORD** has broken out against my enemies before me."
5:23 so David inquired of **the LORD**, and he answered, "Do not go
5:24 because that will mean **the LORD** has gone out in front of you to
5:25 So David did as **the LORD** commanded him, and he struck down
6: 2 which is called by the Name, the name of **the LORD** Almighty,
6: 5 of Israel were celebrating with all their might before **the LORD**,
6: 7 **The LORD's** anger burned against Uzzah because of his
6: 8 because **the LORD's** wrath had broken out against Uzzah,
6: 9 David was afraid of **the LORD** that day and said, "How can the
6: 9 and said, "How can the ark of **the LORD** ever come to me?"
6:10 He was not willing to take the ark of **the LORD** to be with him in
6:11 The ark of **the LORD** remained in the house of Obed-Edom the
6:11 and **the LORD** blessed him and his entire household.
6:12 "**The LORD** has blessed the household of Obed-Edom and
6:13 When those who were carrying the ark of **the LORD** had taken
6:14 a linen ephod, danced before **the LORD** with all his might,
6:15 the entire house of Israel brought up the ark of **the LORD** with
6:16 As the ark of **the LORD** was entering the City of David,
6:16 she saw King David leaping and dancing before **the LORD**,
6:17 They brought the ark of **the LORD** and set it in its place inside
6:17 burnt offerings and fellowship offerings before **the LORD**.
6:18 he blessed the people in the name of **the LORD** Almighty.
6:21 David said to Michal, "It was before **the LORD**, who chose me
6:21 when he appointed me ruler over **the LORD's** people Israel—
6:21 the LORD's people Israel—I will celebrate before **the LORD**.
7: 1 **the LORD** had given him rest from all his enemies around him,
7: 3 have in mind, go ahead and do it, for **the LORD** is with you."
7: 4 That night the word of **the LORD** came to Nathan, saying:
7: 5 and tell my servant David, 'This is what **the LORD** says:
7: 8 tell my servant David, 'This is what **the LORD** Almighty says:
7:11 " '**The LORD** declares to you that the LORD himself will
7:11 " 'The LORD declares to you that **the LORD** himself will
7:18 Then King David went in and sat before **the LORD**, and he said:
7:18 "Who am I, O Sovereign **LORD**, and what is my family,
7:19 And as if this were not enough in your sight, O Sovereign **LORD**,
7:19 Is this your usual way of dealing with man, O Sovereign **LORD**?
7:20 say to you? For you know your servant, O Sovereign **LORD**.
7:22 "How great you are, O Sovereign **LORD**! There is no one like
7:24 very own forever, and you, O **LORD**, have become their God.
7:25 "And now, **LORD** God, keep forever the promise you have made
7:26 Then men will say, '**The LORD** Almighty is God over Israel!'
7:27 "O **LORD** Almighty, God of Israel, you have revealed this to
7:28 O Sovereign **LORD**, you are God! Your words are trustworthy,
7:29 for you, O Sovereign **LORD**, have spoken, and with your
8: 6 **The LORD** gave David victory wherever he went.
8:11 King David dedicated these articles to **the LORD**, as he had done
8:14 to David. **The LORD** gave David victory wherever he went.
10:12 cities of our God. **The LORD** will do what is good in his sight."
11:27 him a son. But the thing David had done displeased **the LORD**.
12: 1 **The LORD** sent Nathan to David. When he came to him,
12: 5 the man and said to Nathan, "As surely as **the LORD** lives,
12: 7 are the man! This is what **the LORD**, the God of Israel, says:
12: 9 Why did you despise the word of **the LORD** by doing what is
12:11 "This is what **the LORD** says: 'Out of your own household I am
12:13 Then David said to Nathan, "I have sinned against **the LORD**."
12:13 Nathan replied, "**The LORD** has taken away your sin. You are
12:14 because by doing this you have made the enemies of **the LORD**
12:15 **the LORD** struck the child that Uriah's wife had borne to David,
12:20 his clothes, he went into the house of **the LORD** and worshiped.
12:22 **The LORD** may be gracious to me and let the child live.'
12:24 to a son, and they named him Solomon. **The LORD** loved him;
12:25 because **the LORD** loved him, he sent word through Nathan the
14:11 "Then let the king invoke **the LORD** his God to prevent the
14:11 "As surely as **the LORD** lives," he said, "not one hair of your
14:17 and evil. May **the LORD** your God be with you.' "
15: 7 "Let me go to Hebron and fulfill a vow I made to **the LORD**.
15: 8 'If **the LORD** takes me back to Jerusalem, I will worship the
15: 8 me back to Jerusalem, I will worship **the LORD** in Hebron.' "
15:21 But Ittai replied to the king, "As surely as **the LORD** lives,
15:25 If I find favor in **the LORD's** eyes, he will bring me back
15:31 So David prayed, "O **LORD**, turn Ahithophel's counsel into
16: 8 **The LORD** has repaid you for all the blood you shed in the
16: 8 **The LORD** has handed the kingdom over to your son Absalom.

2Sa 16:10 If he is cursing because **the LORD** said to him, 'Curse David,'
16:11 Leave him alone; let him curse, for **the LORD** has told him to.
16:12 It may be that **the LORD** will see my distress and repay me with
16:12 **[RPH]** repay me with good for the cursing I am receiving today."
16:18 to Absalom, "No, the one chosen by **the LORD**, by these people,
17:14 For **the LORD** had determined to frustrate the good advice of
17:14 of Ahithophel in order to bring **[RPH]** disaster on Absalom.
18:19 take the news to the king that **the LORD** has delivered him from
18:28 face to the ground and said, "Praise be to **the LORD** your God!
18:31 **The LORD** has delivered you today from all who rose up against
19: 7 [19:8] I swear by **the LORD** that if you don't go out, not a man
19:21 [19:22] put to death for this? He cursed **the LORD's** anointed."
20:19 Why do you want to swallow up **the LORD's** inheritance?"
21: 1 three successive years; so David sought the face of **the LORD**.
21: 1 **The LORD** said, "It is on account of Saul and his blood-stained
21: 3 I make amends so that you will bless **the LORD's** inheritance?"
21: 6 us to be killed and exposed before **the LORD** at Gibeah of Saul—
21: 6 before the LORD at Gibeah of Saul—**the LORD's** chosen one."
21: 7 because of the oath before **the LORD** between David
21: 9 who killed and exposed them on a hill before **the LORD**.
22: 1 David sang to **the LORD** the words of this song when the
22: 1 sang to the LORD the words of this song when **the LORD**
22: 2 He said: "**The LORD** is my rock, my fortress and my deliverer;
22: 4 I call to **the LORD**, who is worthy of praise, and I am saved from
22: 7 In my distress I called to **the LORD**; I called out to my God.
22:14 **The LORD** thundered from heaven; the voice of the Most High
22:16 the foundations of the earth laid bare at the rebuke of **the LORD**,
22:19 me in the day of my disaster, but **the LORD** was my support.
22:21 "**The LORD** has dealt with me according to my righteousness;
22:22 For I have kept the ways of **the LORD**; I have not done evil by
22:25 **The LORD** has rewarded me according to my righteousness,
22:29 You are my lamp, O **LORD**; the LORD turns my darkness into
22:29 are my lamp, O LORD; **the LORD** turns my darkness into light.
22:31 for God, his way is perfect; the word of **the LORD** is flawless.
22:32 For who is God besides **the LORD**? And who is the Rock except
22:42 was no one to save them—to **the LORD**, but he did not answer.
22:47 "**The LORD** lives! Praise be to my Rock! Exalted be God,
22:50 Therefore I will praise you, O **LORD**, among the nations;
23: 2 "The Spirit of **the LORD** spoke through me; his word was on my
23:10 to the sword. **The LORD** brought about a great victory that day.
23:12 Philistines down, and **the LORD** brought about a great victory.
23:16 he refused to drink it; instead, he poured it out before **the LORD**.
23:17 "Far be it from me, O **LORD**, to do this!" he said. "Is it not the
24: 1 Again the anger of **the LORD** burned against Israel, and he
24: 3 "May **the LORD** your God multiply the troops a hundred times
24:10 he said to **the LORD**, "I have sinned greatly in what I have done.
24:10 Now, O **LORD**, I beg you, take away the guilt of your servant.
24:11 the word of **the LORD** had come to Gad the prophet,
24:12 "Go and tell David, 'This is what **the LORD** says: I am giving
24:14 Let us fall into the hands of **the LORD**, for his mercy is great;
24:15 So **the LORD** sent a plague on Israel from that morning until the
24:16 **the LORD** was grieved because of the calamity and said to the
24:16 The angel of **the LORD** was then at the threshing floor of
24:17 he said to **the LORD**, "I am the one who has sinned and done
24:18 build an altar to **the LORD** on the threshing floor of Araunah the
24:19 So David went up, as **the LORD** had commanded through Gad.
24:21 David answered, "so I can build an altar to **the LORD**,
24:23 also said to him, "May **the LORD** your God accept you."
24:24 I will not sacrifice to **the LORD** my God burnt offerings that cost
24:25 David built an altar to **the LORD** there and sacrificed burnt
24:25 **the LORD** answered prayer in behalf of the land, and the plague
1Ki 1:17 you yourself swore to me your servant by **the LORD** your God:
1:29 "As surely as **the LORD** lives, who has delivered me out of every
1:30 I will surely carry out today what I swore to you by **the LORD**,
1:36 May **the LORD**, the God of my lord the king, so declare it.
1:37 As **the LORD** was with my lord the king, so may he be with
1:48 said, 'Praise be to **the LORD**, the God of Israel, who has allowed
2: 3 observe what **the LORD** your God requires: Walk in his ways,
2: 4 that **the LORD** may keep his promise to me: 'If your descendants
2: 8 down to meet me at the Jordan, I swore to him by **the LORD**:
2:15 has gone to my brother; for it has come to him from **the LORD**.
2:23 King Solomon swore by **the LORD**: "May God deal with me,
2:24 now, as surely as **the LORD** lives—he who has established me
2:26 because you carried the ark of **the** Sovereign **LORD** before my
2:27 Solomon removed Abiathar from the priesthood of **the LORD**,
2:27 fulfilling the word **the LORD** had spoken at Shiloh about the
2:28 he fled to the tent of **the LORD** and took hold of the horns of the
2:29 Solomon was told that Joab had fled to the tent of **the LORD**
2:30 So Benaiah entered the tent of **the LORD** and said to Joab,
2:32 **The LORD** will repay him for the blood he shed,
2:33 But on David and his descendants, his house and his throne, may
there be **the LORD's** [+4946+6640] peace forever."
2:42 "Did I not make you swear by **the LORD** and warn you,
2:43 Why then did you not keep your oath to **the LORD** and obey the
2:44 Now **the LORD** will repay you for your wrongdoing.
2:45 David's throne will remain secure before **the LORD** forever."
3: 1 until he finished building his palace and the temple of **the LORD**,
3: 2 a temple had not yet been built for the Name of **the LORD**.
3: 3 Solomon showed his love for **the LORD** by walking according to
3: 5 At Gibeon **the LORD** appeared to Solomon during the night in a
3: 7 "Now, O **LORD** my God, you have made your servant king in
5: 3 [5:17] he could not build a temple for the Name of **the LORD**
5: 3 [5:17] his God until **the LORD** put his enemies under his feet.
5: 4 [5:18] now **the LORD** my God has given me rest on every side,
5: 5 [5:19] to build a temple for the Name of **the LORD** my God,
5: 5 [5:19] as **the LORD** told my father David, when he said,
5: 7 [5:21] greatly pleased and said, "Praise be to **the LORD** today,
5:12 [5:26] **The LORD** gave Solomon wisdom, just as he had
6: 1 the second month, he began to build the temple of **the LORD**.
6: 2 The temple that King Solomon built for **the LORD** was sixty
6:11 The word of **the LORD** came to Solomon:
6:19 the temple to set the ark of the covenant of **the LORD** there.
6:37 The foundation of the temple of **the LORD** was laid in the fourth
7:12 as was the inner courtyard of the temple of **the LORD** with its
7:40 he had undertaken for King Solomon in the temple of **the LORD**:
7:45 Solomon for the temple of **the LORD** were of burnished bronze.
7:48 Solomon also made all the furnishings that were in **the LORD's**
7:51 Solomon had done for the temple of **the LORD** was finished,
7:51 and he placed them in the treasuries of **the LORD's** temple.
8: 1 to bring up the ark of **the LORD's** covenant from Zion, the City
8: 4 they brought up the ark of **the LORD** and the Tent of Meeting
8: 6 brought the ark of **the LORD's** covenant to its place in the inner
8: 9 where **the LORD** made a covenant with the Israelites after they
8:10 from the Holy Place, the cloud filled the temple of **the LORD**.
8:11 because of the cloud, for the glory of **the LORD** filled his temple.
8:11 of the cloud, for the glory of the LORD filled **his**[s] temple.
8:12 "**The LORD** has said that he would dwell in a dark cloud;
8:15 "Praise be to **the LORD**, the God of Israel, who with his own
8:17 had it in his heart to build a temple for the Name of **the LORD**,
8:18 **the LORD** said to my father David, 'Because it was in your heart
8:20 "**The LORD** has kept the promise he made: I have succeeded
8:20 and now I sit on the throne of Israel, just as **the LORD** promised,
8:20 I have built the temple for the Name of **the LORD**, the God of
8:21 in which is the covenant of **the LORD** that he made with our
8:22 Solomon stood before the altar of **the LORD** in front of the
8:23 "O **LORD**, God of Israel, there is no God like you in heaven
8:25 "Now **LORD**, God of Israel, keep for your servant David my
8:28 your servant's prayer and his plea for mercy, O **LORD** my God.
8:44 when they pray to **the LORD** toward the city you have chosen
8:53 O Sovereign **LORD**, brought our fathers out of Egypt."
8:54 had finished all these prayers and supplications to **the LORD**,
8:54 to the LORD, he rose from before the altar of **the LORD**,
8:56 "Praise be to **the LORD**, who has given rest to his people Israel
8:57 May **the LORD** our God be with us as he was with our fathers;
8:59 may these words of mine, which I have prayed before **the LORD**,
8:59 before the LORD, be near to **the LORD** our God day and night,
8:60 so that all the peoples of the earth may know that **the LORD** is
8:61 But your hearts must be fully committed to **the LORD** our God,
8:62 and all Israel with him offered sacrifices before **the LORD**.
8:63 Solomon offered a sacrifice of fellowship offerings to **the LORD**:
8:63 and all the Israelites dedicated the temple of **the LORD**.
8:64 middle part of the courtyard in front of the temple of **the LORD**,
8:64 because the bronze altar before **the LORD** was too small to hold
8:65 They celebrated it before **the LORD** our God for seven days
8:66 glad in heart for all the good things **the LORD** had done for his
9: 1 When Solomon had finished building the temple of **the LORD**
9: 2 **the LORD** appeared to him a second time, as he had appeared to
9: 3 **The LORD** said to him: "I have heard the prayer and plea you
9: 8 'Why has **the LORD** done such a thing to this land and to this
9: 9 will answer, 'Because they have forsaken **the LORD** their God,
9: 9 that is why **the LORD** brought all this disaster on them.' "
9:10 two buildings—the temple of **the LORD** and the royal palace—
9:15 labor King Solomon conscripted to build **the LORD's** temple,
9:25 and fellowship offerings on the altar he had built for **the LORD**,
9:25 burning incense before **the LORD** along with them, and
10: 1 the fame of Solomon and his relation to the name of **the LORD**,
10: 5 and the burnt offerings he made at the temple of **the LORD**,
10: 9 Praise be to **the LORD** your God, who has delighted in you
10: 9 Because of **the LORD's** eternal love for Israel, he has made you
10:12 the almugwood to make supports for the temple of **the LORD**
11: 2 They were from nations about which **the LORD** had told the
11: 4 and his heart was not fully devoted to **the LORD** his God,
11: 6 So Solomon did evil in the eyes of **the LORD**; he did not follow
11: 6 he did not follow **the LORD** completely, as David his father had
11: 9 **The LORD** became angry with Solomon because his heart had
11: 9 because his heart had turned away from **the LORD**,
11:10 follow other gods, Solomon did not keep **the LORD's** command.
11:11 So **the LORD** said to Solomon, "Since this is your attitude

1Ki 11:14 Then **the LORD** raised up against Solomon an adversary,
11:31 for yourself, for this is what **the LORD**, the God of Israel, says:
12:15 listen to the people, for this turn of events was from **the LORD**,
12:15 to fulfill the word **the LORD** had spoken to Jeroboam son of
12:24 'This is what **the LORD** says: Do not go up to fight against your
12:24 for this is my doing.' " So they obeyed the word of **the LORD**
12:24 of the LORD and went home again, as **the LORD** had ordered.
12:27 go up to offer sacrifices at the temple of **the LORD** in Jerusalem,
13: 1 By the word of **the LORD** a man of God came from Judah to
13: 2 He cried out against the altar by the word of **the LORD**:
13: 2 "O altar, altar! This is what **the LORD** says: 'A son named Josiah
13: 3 "This is the sign **the LORD** has declared: The altar will be split
13: 5 to the sign given by the man of God by the word of **the LORD**.
13: 6 "Intercede with **the LORD** your God and pray for me that my
13: 6 So the man of God interceded with **the LORD**, and the king's
13: 9 For I was commanded by the word of **the LORD**: 'You must not
13:17 I have been told by the word of **the LORD**: 'You must not eat
13:18 as you are. And an angel said to me by the word of **the LORD**:
13:20 the word of **the LORD** came to the old prophet who had brought
13:21 of God who had come from Judah, "This is what **the LORD** says:
13:21 'You have defied the word of **the LORD** and have not kept the
13:21 and have not kept the command **the LORD** your God gave you.
13:26 "It is the man of God who defied the word of **the LORD**.
13:26 **The LORD** has given him over to the lion, which has mauled him
13:26 and killed him, as the word of **the LORD** had warned him."
13:32 For the message he declared by the word of **the LORD** against
14: 5 **the LORD** had told Ahijah, "Jeroboam's wife is coming to ask
14: 7 Go, tell Jeroboam that this is what **the LORD**, the God of Israel,
14:11 feed on those who die in the country. **The LORD** has spoken!'
14:13 he is the only one in the house of Jeroboam in whom **the LORD**,
14:14 "**The LORD** will raise up for himself a king over Israel who will
14:15 **the LORD** will strike Israel, so that it will be like a reed swaying
14:15 because they provoked **the LORD** to anger by making Asherah
14:18 as **the LORD** had said through his servant the prophet Ahijah.
14:21 the city **the LORD** had chosen out of all the tribes of Israel in
14:22 Judah did evil in the eyes of **the LORD**. By the sins they
14:24 of the nations **the LORD** had driven out before the Israelites.
14:26 He carried off the treasures of the temple of **the LORD** and the
14:28 Whenever the king went to **the LORD's** temple, the guards bore
15: 3 his heart was not fully devoted to **the LORD** his God, as the heart
15: 4 for David's sake **the LORD** his God gave him a lamp in
15: 5 For David had done what was right in the eyes of **the LORD**
15:11 Asa did what was right in the eyes of **the LORD**, as his father
15:14 Asa's heart was fully committed to **the LORD** all his life.
15:15 He brought into the temple of **the LORD** the silver and gold
15:18 and gold that was left in the treasuries of **the LORD's** temple
15:26 He did evil in the eyes of **the LORD**, walking in the ways of his
15:29 according to the word of **the LORD** given through his servant
15:30 and because he provoked **the LORD**, the God of Israel, to anger.
15:34 He did evil in the eyes of **the LORD**, walking in the ways of
16: 1 the word of **the LORD** came to Jehu son of Hanani against
16: 7 the word of **the LORD** came through the prophet Jehu son of
16: 7 because of all the evil he had done in the eyes of **the LORD**,
16:12 in accordance with the word of **the LORD** spoken against Baasha
16:13 so that they provoked **the LORD**, the God of Israel, to anger by
16:19 doing evil in the eyes of **the LORD** and walking in the ways of
16:25 Omri did evil in the eyes of **the LORD** and sinned more than all
16:26 so that they provoked **the LORD**, the God of Israel, to anger by
16:30 Ahab son of Omri did more evil in the eyes of **the LORD** than
16:33 also made an Asherah pole and did more to provoke **the LORD**,
16:34 in accordance with the word of **the LORD** spoken by Joshua son
17: 1 said to Ahab, "As **the LORD**, the God of Israel, lives, whom I
17: 2 Then the word of **the LORD** came to Elijah:
17: 5 So he did what **the LORD** had told him. He went to the Kerith
17: 8 Then the word of **the LORD** came to him:
17:12 "As surely as **the LORD** your God lives," she replied, "I don't
17:14 For this is what **the LORD**, the God of Israel, says: 'The jar of
17:14 the jug of oil will not run dry until the day **the LORD** gives rain
17:16 in keeping with the word of **the LORD** spoken by Elijah.
17:20 he cried out to **the LORD**, "O LORD my God, have you
17:20 he cried out to the LORD, "O **LORD** my God, have you brought
17:21 himself out on the boy three times and cried to **the LORD**,
17:21 the boy three times and cried to the LORD, "O **LORD** my God,
17:22 **The LORD** heard Elijah's cry, and the boy's life returned to him,
17:24 and that the word of **the LORD** from your mouth is the truth."
18: 1 in the third year, the word of **the LORD** came to Elijah:
18: 3 of his palace. (Obadiah was a devout believer in **the LORD**.
18: 4 While Jezebel was killing off **the LORD's** prophets, Obadiah had
18:10 As surely as **the LORD** your God lives, there is not a nation
18:12 I don't know where the Spirit of **the LORD** may carry you when
18:12 Yet I your servant have worshiped **the LORD** since my youth.
18:13 what I did while Jezebel was killing the prophets of **the LORD**?
18:13 I hid a hundred of **the LORD's** prophets in two caves, fifty in
18:15 Elijah said, "As **the LORD** Almighty lives, whom I serve,
18:18 You have abandoned **the LORD's** commands and have followed
18:21 If **the LORD** is God, follow him; but if Baal is God, follow him."
18:22 "I am the only one of **the LORD's** [+4200] prophets left,
18:24 the name of your god, and I will call on the name of **the LORD**.
18:30 They came to him, and he repaired the altar of **the LORD**,
18:31 to whom the word of **the LORD** had come, saying, "Your name
18:32 With the stones he built an altar in the name of **the LORD**,
18:36 "O **LORD**, God of Abraham, Isaac and Israel, let it be known
18:37 Answer me, O **LORD**, answer me, so these people will know that
18:37 so these people will know that you, O **LORD**, are God,
18:38 Then the fire of **the LORD** fell and burned up the sacrifice,
18:39 the people saw this, they fell prostrate and cried, "**The LORD**—
18:39 and cried, "The LORD—he is God! **The LORD**—he is God!"
18:46 The power of **the LORD** came upon Elijah and, tucking his cloak
19: 4 "I have had enough, **LORD**," he said. "Take my life; I am no
19: 7 The angel of **the LORD** came back a second time and touched
19: 9 and spent the night. And the word of **the LORD** came to him:
19:10 "I have been very zealous for **the LORD** God Almighty.
19:11 and stand on the mountain in the presence of **the LORD**,
19:11 the presence of the LORD, for **the LORD** is about to pass by."
19:11 the mountains apart and shattered the rocks before **the LORD**,
19:11 the rocks before the LORD, but **the LORD** was not in the wind.
19:11 was an earthquake, but **the LORD** was not in the earthquake.
19:12 the earthquake came a fire, but **the LORD** was not in the fire.
19:14 "I have been very zealous for **the LORD** God Almighty.
19:15 **The LORD** said to him, "Go back the way you came, and go to
20:13 king of Israel and announced, "This is what **the LORD** says:
20:13 your hand today, and then you will know that I am **the LORD**.' "
20:14 asked Ahab. The prophet replied, "This is what **the LORD** says:
20:28 and told the king of Israel, "This is what **the LORD** says:
20:28 'Because the Arameans think **the LORD** is a god of the hills
20:28 army into your hands, and you will know that I am **the LORD**.' "
20:35 By the word of **the LORD** one of the sons of the prophets said to
20:36 So the prophet said, "Because you have not obeyed **the LORD**,
20:42 He said to the king, "This is what **the LORD** says: 'You have set
21: 3 "**The LORD** forbid that I should give you the inheritance of my
21:17 Then the word of **the LORD** came to Elijah the Tishbite:
21:19 Say to him, 'This is what **the LORD** says: Have you not
21:19 his property?' Then say to him, 'This is what **the LORD** says:
21:20 you have sold yourself to do evil in the eyes of **the LORD**.
21:23 "And also concerning Jezebel **the LORD** says: 'Dogs will devour
21:25 who sold himself to do evil in the eyes of **the LORD**, urged on by
21:26 after idols, like the Amorites **the LORD** drove out before Israel.)
21:28 Then the word of **the LORD** came to Elijah the Tishbite:
22: 5 said to the king of Israel, "First seek the counsel of **the LORD**."
22: 7 "Is there not a prophet of **the LORD** here whom we can inquire
22: 8 is still one man through whom we can inquire of **the LORD**,
22:11 made iron horns and he declared, "This is what **the LORD** says:
22:12 they said, "for **the LORD** will give it into the king's hand."
22:14 Micaiah said, "As surely as **the LORD** lives, I can tell him only
22:14 the LORD lives, I can tell him only what **the LORD** tells me."
22:15 he answered, "for **the LORD** will give it into the king's hand."
22:16 swear to tell me nothing but the truth in the name of **the LORD**?"
22:17 a shepherd, and **the LORD** said, 'These people have no master.
22:19 Micaiah continued, "Therefore hear the word of **the LORD**:
22:19 I saw **the LORD** sitting on his throne with all the host of heaven
22:20 **the LORD** said, 'Who will entice Ahab into attacking Ramoth
22:21 stood before **the LORD** and said, 'I will entice him.'
22:22 [22:21] **the LORD** asked. " 'I will go out and be a lying spirit in
22:23 "So now **the LORD** has put a lying spirit in the mouths of all
22:23 prophets of yours. **The LORD** has decreed disaster for you."
22:24 "Which way did the spirit from **the LORD** go when he went from
22:28 you ever return safely, **the LORD** has not spoken through me."
22:38 dogs licked up his blood, as the word of **the LORD** had declared.
22:43 stray from them; he did what was right in the eyes of **the LORD**.
22:52 [22:53] He did evil in the eyes of **the LORD**, because he walked
22:53 [22:54] and worshiped Baal and provoked **the LORD**,
2Ki 1: 3 But the angel of **the LORD** said to Elijah the Tishbite, "Go up
1: 4 Therefore this is what **the LORD** says: 'You will not leave the
1: 6 king who sent you and tell him, "This is what **the LORD** says:
1:15 The angel of **the LORD** said to Elijah, "Go down with him;
1:16 He told the king, "This is what **the LORD** says: Is it
1:17 according to the word of **the LORD** that Elijah had spoken.
2: 1 When **the LORD** was about to take Elijah up to heaven in a
2: 2 said to Elisha, "Stay here; **the LORD** has sent me to Bethel."
2: 2 But Elisha said, "As surely as **the LORD** lives and as you live,
2: 3 "Do you know that **the LORD** is going to take your master from
2: 4 to him, "Stay here, Elisha; **the LORD** has sent me to Jericho."
2: 4 And he replied, "As surely as **the LORD** lives and as you live,
2: 5 "Do you know that **the LORD** is going to take your master from
2: 6 said to him, "Stay here; **the LORD** has sent me to the Jordan."
2: 6 And he replied, "As surely as **the LORD** lives and as you live,
2:14 "Where now is **the LORD**, the God of Elijah?" he asked.
2:16 Perhaps the Spirit of **the LORD** has picked him up and set him

2Ki 2:21 and threw the salt into it, saying, "This is what **the LORD** says:
2:24 and called down a curse on them in the name of **the LORD**.
3: 2 He did evil in the eyes of **the LORD**, but not as his father
3:10 "Has **the LORD** called us three kings together only to hand us
3:11 But Jehoshaphat asked, "Is there no prophet of **the LORD** here,
3:11 LORD here, that we may inquire of **the LORD** through him?"
3:12 Jehoshaphat said, "The word of **the LORD** is with him."
3:13 "because it was **the LORD** who called us three kings together to
3:14 Elisha said, "As surely as **the LORD** Almighty lives, whom I
3:15 harpist was playing, the hand of **the LORD** came upon Elisha
3:16 he said, "This is what **the LORD** says: Make this valley full of
3:17 For this is what **the LORD** says: You will see neither wind nor
3:18 This is an easy thing in the eyes of **the LORD**; he will also hand
4: 1 my husband is dead, and you know that he revered **the LORD**.
4:27 but **the LORD** has hidden it from me and has not told me why."
4:30 "As surely as **the LORD** lives and as you live, I will not leave
4:33 shut the door on the two of them and prayed to **the LORD**.
4:43 For this is what **the LORD** says: 'They will eat and have some
4:44 and had some left over, according to the word of **the LORD**.
5: 1 because through him **the LORD** had given victory to Aram.
5:11 out to me and stand and call on the name of **the LORD** his God,
5:16 prophet answered, "As surely as **the LORD** lives, whom I serve,
5:17 burnt offerings and sacrifices to any other god but **the LORD**.
5:18 But may **the LORD** forgive your servant for this one thing:
5:18 of Rimmon, may **the LORD** forgive your servant for this."
5:20 As surely as **the LORD** lives, I will run after him and get
6:17 And Elisha prayed, "O **LORD**, open his eyes so he may see."
6:17 Then **the LORD** opened the servant's eyes, and he looked
6:18 Elisha prayed to **the LORD**, "Strike these people with blindness."
6:20 After they entered the city, Elisha said, "**LORD**, open the eyes of
6:20 **the LORD** opened their eyes and they looked, and there they
6:27 The king replied, "If **the LORD** does not help you, where can I
6:33 to him. And ⌊the king⌋ said, "This disaster is from **the LORD**.
6:33 from the LORD. Why should I wait for **the LORD** any longer?"
7: 1 Elisha said, "Hear the word of **the LORD**. This is what the
7: 1 This is what **the LORD** says: About this time tomorrow,
7: 2 even if **the LORD** should open the floodgates of the heavens,
7:16 and two seahs of barley sold for a shekel, as **the LORD** had said.
7:19 even if **the LORD** should open the floodgates of the heavens,
8: 1 because **the LORD** has decreed a famine in the land that will last
8: 8 Consult **the LORD** through him; ask him, 'Will I recover from
8:10 but **the LORD** has revealed to me that he will in fact die."
8:13 "**The LORD** has shown me that you will become king of Aram,"
8:18 a daughter of Ahab. He did evil in the eyes of **the LORD**.
8:19 of his servant David, **the LORD** was not willing to destroy Judah.
8:27 ways of the house of Ahab and did evil in the eyes of **the LORD**,
9: 3 the oil on his head and declare, 'This is what **the LORD** says:
9: 6 the oil on Jehu's head and declared, "This is what **the LORD**,
9: 6 of Israel, says: 'I anoint you king over **the LORD's** people Israel.
9: 7 and the blood of all **the LORD's** servants shed by Jezebel.
9:12 "Here is what he told me: 'This is what **the LORD** says:
9:25 Ahab his father when **the LORD** made this prophecy about him:
9:26 blood of Naboth and the blood of his sons, declares **the LORD**,
9:26 make you pay for it on this plot of ground, declares **the LORD**.'
9:26 him on that plot, in accordance with the word of **the LORD**."
9:36 "This is the word of **the LORD** that he spoke through his servant
10:10 that not a word **the LORD** has spoken against the house of Ahab
10:10 that not a word the LORD has spoken **[RPH]** against the house
10:10 **The LORD** has done what he promised through his servant
10:16 Jehu said, "Come with me and see my zeal for **the LORD**."
10:17 according to the word of **the LORD** spoken to Elijah.
10:23 and see that no servants of **the LORD** are here with you—
10:30 **The LORD** said to Jehu, "Because you have done well in
10:31 Yet Jehu was not careful to keep the law of **the LORD**, the God
10:32 In those days **the LORD** began to reduce the size of Israel.
11: 3 He remained hidden with his nurse at the temple of **the LORD**
11: 4 and had them brought to him at the temple of **the LORD**.
11: 4 with them and put them under oath at the temple of **the LORD**.
11: 7 off Sabbath duty are all to guard the temple **[RPH]** for the king.
11:10 to King David and that were in the temple of **the LORD**.
11:13 the people, she went to the people at the temple of **the LORD**.
11:15 "She must not be put to death in the temple of **the LORD**."
11:17 Jehoiada then made a covenant between **the LORD** and the king
11:17 and people that they would be **the LORD's** [+4200] people.
11:18 Jehoiada the priest posted guards at the temple of **the LORD**.
11:19 they brought the king down from the temple of **the LORD**
12: 2 [12:3] Joash did what was right in the eyes of **the LORD** all the
12: 4 [12:5] brought as sacred offerings to the temple of **the LORD**—
12: 4 [12:5] and the money brought voluntarily to the temple. **[RPH]**
12: 9 [12:10] on the right side as one enters the temple of **the LORD**.
12: 9 [12:10] the money that was brought to the temple of **the LORD**.
12:10 [12:11] that had been brought into the temple of **the LORD**
12:11 [12:12] **[RPH]** With it they paid those who worked on the
12:11 [12:12] paid those who worked on the temple of **the LORD**—
12:12 [12:13] dressed stone for the repair of the temple of **the LORD**,
12:13 [12:14] The money brought into the temple **[RPH]** was not spent
12:13 [12:14] articles of gold or silver for the temple of **the LORD**;
12:14 [12:15] the workmen, who used it to repair the temple. **[RPH]**
12:16 [12:17] offerings was not brought into the temple of **the LORD**;
12:18 [12:19] gold found in the treasuries of the temple of **the LORD**
13: 2 He did evil in the eyes of **the LORD** by following the sins of
13: 3 So **the LORD's** anger burned against Israel, and for a long time
13: 4 Jehoahaz sought **the LORD's** favor, and the LORD listened to
13: 4 sought the LORD's favor, and **the LORD** listened to him,
13: 5 **The LORD** provided a deliverer for Israel, and they escaped from
13:11 He did evil in the eyes of **the LORD** and did not turn away from
13:17 Elisha said, and he shot. "**The LORD's** [+4200] arrow of victory,
13:23 But **the LORD** was gracious to them and had compassion
14: 3 He did what was right in the eyes of **the LORD**, but not as his
14: 6 in the Book of the Law of Moses where **the LORD** commanded:
14:14 and silver and all the articles found in the temple of **the LORD**
14:24 He did evil in the eyes of **the LORD** and did not turn away from
14:25 in accordance with the word of **the LORD**, the God of Israel,
14:26 **The LORD** had seen how bitterly everyone in Israel, whether
14:27 since **the LORD** had not said he would blot out the name of
15: 3 He did what was right in the eyes of **the LORD**, just as his father
15: 5 **The LORD** afflicted the king with leprosy until the day he died,
15: 9 He did evil in the eyes of **the LORD**, as his fathers had done.
15:12 So the word of **the LORD** spoken to Jehu was fulfilled: "Your
15:18 He did evil in the eyes of **the LORD**. During his entire reign he
15:24 Pekahiah did evil in the eyes of **the LORD**. He did not turn away
15:28 He did evil in the eyes of **the LORD**. He did not turn away from
15:34 He did what was right in the eyes of **the LORD**, just as his father
15:35 Jotham rebuilt the Upper Gate of the temple of **the LORD**.
15:37 (In those days **the LORD** began to send Rezin king of Aram
16: 2 he did not do what was right in the eyes of **the LORD** his God.
16: 3 following the detestable ways of the nations **the LORD** had
16: 8 Ahaz took the silver and gold found in the temple of **the LORD**
16:14 The bronze altar that stood before **the LORD** he brought from the
16:14 from between the new altar and the temple of **the LORD**—
16:18 removed the royal entryway outside the temple of **the LORD**,
17: 2 He did evil in the eyes of **the LORD**, but not like the kings of
17: 7 because the Israelites had sinned against **the LORD** their God,
17: 8 followed the practices of the nations **the LORD** had driven out
17: 9 The Israelites secretly did things against **the LORD** their God
17:11 as the nations whom **the LORD** had driven out before them had
17:11 They did wicked things that provoked **the LORD** to anger.
17:12 They worshiped idols, though **the LORD** had said, "You shall
17:13 **The LORD** warned Israel and Judah through all his prophets
17:14 as their fathers, who did not trust in **the LORD** their God.
17:15 They imitated the nations around them although **the LORD** had
17:16 They forsook all the commands of **the LORD** their God
17:17 and sold themselves to do evil in the eyes of **the LORD**,
17:18 So **the LORD** was very angry with Israel and removed them from
17:19 even Judah did not keep the commands of **the LORD** their God.
17:20 Therefore **the LORD** rejected all the people of Israel; he afflicted
17:21 Jeroboam enticed Israel away from following **the LORD**
17:23 until **the LORD** removed them from his presence, as he had
17:25 When they first lived there, they did not worship **the LORD**;
17:25 so **he**[s] sent lions among them and they killed some of the people.
17:28 to live in Bethel and taught them how to worship **the LORD**.
17:32 They worshiped **the LORD**, but they also appointed all sorts of
17:33 They worshiped **the LORD**, but they also served their own gods
17:34 They neither worship **the LORD** nor adhere to the decrees
17:34 and commands that **the LORD** gave the descendants of Jacob,
17:35 When **the LORD** made a covenant with the Israelites, he
17:36 **the LORD**, who brought you up out of Egypt with mighty power
17:39 Rather, worship **the LORD** your God; it is he who will deliver
17:41 Even while these people were worshiping **the LORD**, they were
18: 3 He did what was right in the eyes of **the LORD**, just as his father
18: 5 Hezekiah trusted in **the LORD**, the God of Israel. There was no
18: 6 He held fast to **the LORD** and did not cease to follow him;
18: 6 follow him; he kept the commands **the LORD** had given Moses.
18: 7 **the LORD** was with him; he was successful in whatever he
18:12 because they had not obeyed **the LORD** their God,
18:12 all that Moses the servant of **the LORD** commanded.
18:15 gave him all the silver that was found in the temple of **the LORD**
18:16 had covered the doors and doorposts of the temple of **the LORD**,
18:22 if you say to me, "We are depending on **the LORD** our God"—
18:25 to attack and destroy this place without word from **the LORD**?
18:25 **The LORD** himself told me to march against this country
18:30 Do not let Hezekiah persuade you to trust in **the LORD** when he
18:30 in the LORD when he says, '**The LORD** will surely deliver us;
18:32 he is misleading you when he says, '**The LORD** will deliver us.'
18:35 How then can **the LORD** deliver Jerusalem from my hand?"
19: 1 and put on sackcloth and went into the temple of **the LORD**.
19: 4 It may be that **the LORD** your God will hear all the words of the
19: 4 that he will rebuke him for the words **the LORD** your God has

2Ki 19: 6 said to them, "Tell your master, 'This is what **the LORD** says:
19: 14 he went up to the temple of **the LORD** and spread it out before
19: 14 to the temple of the LORD and spread it out before **the LORD**.
19: 15 And Hezekiah prayed to **the LORD**: "O LORD, God of Israel,
19: 15 "O **LORD**, God of Israel, enthroned between the cherubim,
19: 16 Give ear, O **LORD**, and hear; open your eyes, O LORD,
19: 16 O LORD, and hear; open your eyes, O **LORD**, and see;
19: 17 "It is true, O **LORD**, that the Assyrian kings have laid waste
19: 19 Now, O **LORD** our God, deliver us from his hand, so that all
19: 19 on earth may know that you alone, O **LORD**, are God."
19: 20 to Hezekiah: "This is what **the LORD**, the God of Israel, says:
19: 21 This is the word that **the LORD** has spoken against him:
19: 31 The zeal of **the LORD** Almighty will accomplish this.
19: 32 "Therefore this is what **the LORD** says concerning the king of
19: 33 he will return; he will not enter this city, declares **the LORD**.
19: 35 That night the angel of **the LORD** went out and put to death a
20: 1 of Amoz went to him and said, "This is what **the LORD** says:
20: 2 Hezekiah turned his face to the wall and prayed to **the LORD**,
20: 3 "Remember, O **LORD**, how I have walked before you faithfully
20: 4 had left the middle court, the word of **the LORD** came to him:
20: 5 tell Hezekiah, the leader of my people, 'This is what **the LORD**,
20: 5 third day from now you will go up to the temple of **the LORD**.
20: 8 "What will be the sign that **the LORD** will heal me and that I will
20: 8 that I will go up to the temple of **the LORD** on the third day from
20: 9 "This is **the LORD's** [+907+4946] sign to you that the LORD
20: 9 "This is the LORD's sign to you that **the LORD** will do what he
20: 11 the prophet Isaiah called upon **the LORD**, and the LORD made
20: 16 Then Isaiah said to Hezekiah, "Hear the word of **the LORD**:
20: 17 be carried off to Babylon. Nothing will be left, says **the LORD**.
20: 19 "The word of **the LORD** you have spoken is good,"
21: 2 He did evil in the eyes of **the LORD**, following the detestable
21: 2 following the detestable practices of the nations **the LORD** had
21: 4 He built altars in the temple of **the LORD**, of which the LORD
21: 4 of which **the LORD** had said, "In Jerusalem I will put my
21: 5 In both courts of the temple of **the LORD**, he built altars to all
21: 6 He did much evil in the eyes of **the LORD**, provoking him to
21: 7 of which **the LORD** had said to David and to his son Solomon,
21: 9 so that they did more evil than the nations **the LORD** had
21: 10 **The LORD** said through his servants the prophets:
21: 12 Therefore this is what **the LORD**, the God of Israel, says:
21: 16 Judah to commit, so that they did evil in the eyes of **the LORD**.
21: 20 He did evil in the eyes of **the LORD**, as his father Manasseh had
21: 22 He forsook **the LORD**, the God of his fathers, and did not walk
21: 22 the God of his fathers, and did not walk in the way of **the LORD**.
22: 2 He did what was right in the eyes of **the LORD** and walked in all
22: 3 of Azaliah, the son of Meshullam, to the temple of **the LORD**.
22: 4 the money that has been brought into the temple of **the LORD**,
22: 5 **[RPH]** And have these men pay the workers who repair the
22: 5 these men pay the workers who repair the temple of **the LORD**—
22: 8 "I have found the Book of the Law in the temple of **the LORD**."
22: 9 have paid out the money that was in the temple of **the LORD**
22: 13 "Go and inquire of **the LORD** for me and for the people
22: 13 Great is **the LORD's** anger that burns against us because our
22: 15 She said to them, "This is what **the LORD**, the God of Israel,
22: 16 'This is what **the LORD** says: I am going to bring disaster on this
22: 18 Tell the king of Judah, who sent you to inquire of **the LORD**,
22: 18 'This is what **the LORD**, the God of Israel, says concerning the
22: 19 you humbled yourself before **the LORD** when you heard what I
22: 19 and wept in my presence, I have heard you, declares **the LORD**.
23: 2 He went up to the temple of **the LORD** with the men of Judah,
23: 2 the Covenant, which had been found in the temple of **the LORD**.
23: 3 and renewed the covenant in the presence of **the LORD**—
23: 3 to follow **the LORD** and keep his commands, regulations
23: 4 the doorkeepers to remove from the temple of **the LORD** all the
23: 6 He took the Asherah pole from the temple of **the LORD** to the
23: 7 which were in the temple of **the LORD** and where women did
23: 9 high places did not serve at the altar of **the LORD** in Jerusalem,
23: 11 He removed from the entrance to the temple of **the LORD** the
23: 12 Manasseh had built in the two courts of the temple of **the LORD**.
23: 16 in accordance with the word of **the LORD** proclaimed by the
23: 21 "Celebrate the Passover to **the LORD** your God, as it is written in
23: 23 this Passover was celebrated to **the LORD** in Jerusalem.
23: 24 that Hilkiah the priest had discovered in the temple of **the LORD**.
23: 25 was there a king like him who turned to **the LORD** as he did—
23: 26 **the LORD** did not turn away from the heat of his fierce anger,
23: 27 So **the LORD** said, "I will remove Judah also from my presence
23: 32 He did evil in the eyes of **the LORD**, just as his fathers had done.
23: 37 he did evil in the eyes of **the LORD**, just as his fathers had done.
24: 2 **The LORD** sent Babylonian, Aramean, Moabite and Ammonite
24: 2 in accordance with the word of **the LORD** proclaimed by his
24: 3 Surely these things happened to Judah according to **the LORD's**
24: 4 with innocent blood, and **the LORD** was not willing to forgive.
24: 9 He did evil in the eyes of **the LORD**, just as his father had done.
24: 13 As **the LORD** had declared, Nebuchadnezzar removed all the
24: 13 removed all the treasures from the temple of **the LORD**
24: 13 Solomon king of Israel had made for the temple of **the LORD**.
24: 19 He did evil in the eyes of **the LORD**, just as Jehoiakim had done.
24: 20 because of **the LORD's** anger that all this happened to Jerusalem
25: 9 He set fire to the temple of **the LORD**, the royal palace and all
25: 13 **[RPH]** the movable stands and the bronze Sea that were at the
25: 13 and the bronze Sea that were at the temple of **the LORD**
25: 16 which Solomon had made for the temple of **the LORD**,
1Ch 2: 3 Er, Judah's firstborn, was wicked in **the LORD's** sight;
6: 15 [5:41] Jehozadak was deported when **the LORD** sent Judah
6: 31 [6:16] in the house of **the LORD** after the ark came to rest there.
6: 32 [6:17] until Solomon built the temple of **the LORD** in
9: 19 for guarding the entrance to the dwelling of **the LORD**.
9: 20 was in charge of the gatekeepers, and **the LORD** was with him.
9: 23 were in charge of guarding the gates of the house of **the LORD**—
10: 13 Saul died because he was unfaithful to **the LORD**; he did not
10: 13 he did not keep the word of **the LORD** and even consulted a
10: 14 did not inquire of **the LORD**. So the LORD put him to death
11: 2 **the LORD** your God said to you, 'You will shepherd my people
11: 3 he made a compact with them at Hebron before **the LORD**,
11: 3 king over Israel, as **the LORD** had promised through Samuel.
11: 9 and more powerful, because **the LORD** Almighty was with him.
11: 10 to extend it over the whole land, as **the LORD** had promised—
11: 14 Philistines down, and **the LORD** brought about a great victory.
11: 18 he refused to drink it; instead, he poured it out before **the LORD**.
12: 23 [12:24] Saul's kingdom over to him, as **the LORD** had said:
13: 2 it seems good to you and if it is the will of **the LORD** our God,
13: 6 to bring up from there the ark of God **the LORD**, who is
13: 10 **The LORD's** anger burned against Uzzah, and he struck him
13: 11 because **the LORD's** wrath had broken out against Uzzah,
13: 14 and **the LORD** blessed his household and everything he had.
14: 2 David knew that **the LORD** had established him as king over
14: 10 **The LORD** answered him, "Go, I will hand them over to you."
14: 17 every land, and **the LORD** made all the nations fear him.
15: 2 because **the LORD** chose them to carry the ark of the LORD
15: 2 because the LORD chose them to carry the ark of **the LORD**
15: 3 bring up the ark of **the LORD** to the place he had prepared for it.
15: 12 are to consecrate yourselves and bring up the ark of **the LORD**,
15: 13 did not bring it up the first time that **the LORD** our God broke
15: 14 consecrated themselves in order to bring up the ark of **the LORD**,
15: 15 had commanded in accordance with the word of **the LORD**.
15: 25 ark of the covenant of **the LORD** from the house of Obed-Edom,
15: 26 Levites who were carrying the ark of the covenant of **the LORD**,
15: 28 So all Israel brought up the ark of the covenant of **the LORD**
15: 29 As the ark of the covenant of **the LORD** was entering the City of
16: 2 he blessed the people in the name of **the LORD**.
16: 4 some of the Levites to minister before the ark of **the LORD**,
16: 4 to make petition, to give thanks, and to praise **the LORD**,
16: 7 to Asaph and his associates this psalm of thanks to **the LORD**:
16: 8 Give thanks to **the LORD**, call on his name; make known among
16: 10 holy name; let the hearts of those who seek **the LORD** rejoice.
16: 11 Look to **the LORD** and his strength; seek his face always.
16: 14 He is **the LORD** our God; his judgments are in all the earth.
16: 23 Sing to **the LORD**, all the earth; proclaim his salvation day after
16: 25 For great is **the LORD** and most worthy of praise; he is to be
16: 26 gods of the nations are idols, but **the LORD** made the heavens.
16: 28 Ascribe to **the LORD**, O families of nations, ascribe to the
16: 28 O families of nations, ascribe to **the LORD** glory and strength,
16: 29 ascribe to **the LORD** the glory due his name. Bring an offering
16: 29 before him; worship **the LORD** in the splendor of his holiness.
16: 31 be glad; let them say among the nations, "**The LORD** reigns!"
16: 33 they will sing for joy before **the LORD**, for he comes to judge
16: 34 Give thanks to **the LORD**, for he is good; his love endures
16: 36 Praise be to **the LORD**, the God of Israel, from everlasting to
16: 36 Then all the people said "Amen" and "Praise **the LORD**."
16: 37 his associates before the ark of the covenant of **the LORD** to
16: 39 his fellow priests before the tabernacle of **the LORD** at the high
16: 40 to present burnt offerings to **the LORD** on the altar of burnt
16: 40 in accordance with everything written in the Law of **the LORD**,
16: 41 and designated by name to give thanks to **the LORD**,
17: 1 while the ark of the covenant of **the LORD** is under a tent."
17: 4 and tell my servant David, 'This is what **the LORD** says:
17: 7 tell my servant David, 'This is what **the LORD** Almighty says:
17: 10 " 'I declare to you that **the LORD** will build a house for you:
17: 16 Then King David went in and sat before **the LORD**, and he said:
17: 16 "Who am I, O **LORD** God, and what is my family, that you have
17: 17 on me as though I were the most exalted of men, O **LORD** God.
17: 19 O **LORD**. For the sake of your servant and according to your
17: 20 "There is no one like you, O **LORD**, and there is no God but you,
17: 22 very own forever, and you, O **LORD**, have become their God.
17: 23 "And now, **LORD**, let the promise you have made concerning
17: 24 Then men will say, '**The LORD** Almighty, the God over Israel,
17: 26 O **LORD**, you are God! You have promised these good things to
17: 27 for you, O **LORD**, have blessed it, and it will be blessed forever."

1Ch 18: 6 **The LORD** gave David victory everywhere he went.
18: 11 King David dedicated these articles to **the LORD**, as he had done
18: 13 to David. **The LORD** gave David victory everywhere he went.
19: 13 cities of our God. **The LORD** will do what is good in his sight."
21: 3 "May **the LORD** multiply his troops a hundred times over.
21: 9 **The LORD** said to Gad, David's seer,
21: 10 "Go and tell David, 'This is what **the LORD** says: I am giving
21: 11 went to David and said to him, "This is what **the LORD** says:
21: 12 overtaking you, or three days of the sword of **the LORD**—
21: 12 with the angel of **the LORD** ravaging every part of Israel.'
21: 13 Let me fall into the hands of **the LORD**, for his mercy is very
21: 14 So **the LORD** sent a plague on Israel, and seventy thousand men
21: 15 **the LORD** saw it and was grieved because of the calamity
21: 15 The angel of **the LORD** was then standing at the threshing floor
21: 16 and saw the angel of **the LORD** standing between heaven
21: 17 O **LORD** my God, let your hand fall upon me and my family,
21: 18 Then the angel of **the LORD** ordered Gad to tell David to go up
21: 18 build an altar to **the LORD** on the threshing floor of Araunah the
21: 19 to the word that Gad had spoken in the name of **the LORD**.
21: 22 site of your threshing floor so I can build an altar to **the LORD**,
21: 24 I will not take for **the LORD** what is yours, or sacrifice a burnt
21: 26 David built an altar to **the LORD** there and sacrificed burnt
21: 26 He called on **the LORD**, and the LORD answered him with fire
21: 27 **the LORD** spoke to the angel, and he put his sword back into its
21: 28 when David saw that **the LORD** had answered him on the
21: 29 The tabernacle of **the LORD**, which Moses had made in the
21: 30 because he was afraid of the sword of the angel of **the LORD**.
22: 1 Then David said, "The house of **the LORD** God is to be here,
22: 5 the house to be built for **the LORD** should be of great
22: 6 son Solomon and charged him to build a house for **the LORD**,
22: 7 I had it in my heart to build a house for the Name of **the LORD**
22: 8 this word of **the LORD** came to me: 'You have shed much blood
22: 11 "Now, my son, **the LORD** be with you, and may you have
22: 11 you have success and build the house of **the LORD** your God,
22: 12 May **the LORD** give you discretion and understanding when he
22: 12 over Israel, so that you may keep the law of **the LORD** your God.
22: 13 the decrees and laws that **the LORD** gave Moses for Israel.
22: 14 "I have taken great pains to provide for the temple of **the LORD**
22: 16 Now begin the work, and **the LORD** be with you."
22: 18 He said to them, "Is not **the LORD** your God with you?
22: 18 to me, and the land is subject to **the LORD** and to his people.
22: 19 Now devote your heart and soul to seeking **the LORD** your God.
22: 19 Begin to build the sanctuary of **the LORD** God, so that you may
22: 19 so that you may bring the ark of the covenant of **the LORD**
22: 19 into the temple that will be built for the Name of **the LORD**."
23: 4 thousand are to supervise the work of the temple of **the LORD**
23: 5 four thousand are to praise **the LORD** with the musical
23: 13 to offer sacrifices before **the LORD**, to minister before him
23: 24 twenty years old or more who served in the temple of **the LORD**.
23: 25 For David had said, "Since **the LORD**, the God of Israel,
23: 28 Aaron's descendants in the service of the temple of **the LORD**:
23: 30 were also to stand every morning to thank and praise **the LORD**.
23: 31 whenever burnt offerings were presented to **the LORD** on
23: 31 They were to serve before **the LORD** regularly in the proper
23: 32 descendants of Aaron, for the service of the temple of **the LORD**.
24: 19 order of ministering when they entered the temple of **the LORD**,
24: 19 as **the LORD**, the God of Israel, had commanded him.
25: 3 using the harp in thanking and praising **the LORD**.
25: 6 of their fathers for the music of the temple of **the LORD**,
25: 7 all of them trained and skilled in music for **the LORD**—
26: 12 chief men, had duties for ministering in the temple of **the LORD**,
26: 22 They were in charge of the treasuries of the temple of **the LORD**.
26: 27 in battle they dedicated for the repair of the temple of **the LORD**.
26: 30 in Israel west of the Jordan for all the work of **the LORD**
27: 23 because **the LORD** had promised to make Israel as numerous as
28: 2 house as a place of rest for the ark of the covenant of **the LORD**,
28: 4 "Yet **the LORD**, the God of Israel, chose me from my whole
28: 5 Of all my sons—and **the LORD** has given me many—he has
28: 5 to sit on the throne of the kingdom of **the LORD** over Israel.
28: 8 you in the sight of all Israel and of the assembly of **the LORD**,
28: 8 Be careful to follow all the commands of **the LORD** your God,
28: 9 for **the LORD** searches every heart and understands every motive
28: 10 for **the LORD** has chosen you to build a temple as a sanctuary.
28: 12 had put in his mind for the courts of the temple of **the LORD**
28: 13 and for all the work of serving in the temple of **the LORD**,
28: 13 as well as for all the articles to be used in **its**[s] [+1074] service.
28: 18 their wings and shelter the ark of the covenant of **the LORD**.
28: 19 "I have in writing from the hand of **the LORD** upon me,
28: 20 or discouraged, for **the LORD** God, my God, is with you.
28: 20 the work for the service of the temple of **the LORD** is finished.
29: 1 this palatial structure is not for man but for **the LORD** God.
29: 5 who is willing to consecrate himself today to **the LORD**?"
29: 8 the temple of **the LORD** in the custody of Jehiel the Gershonite.
29: 9 for they had given freely and wholeheartedly to **the LORD**.
29: 10 David praised **the LORD** in the presence of the whole assembly,
29: 10 saying, "Praise be to you, O **LORD**, God of our father Israel,
29: 11 Yours, O **LORD**, is the greatness and the power and the glory
29: 11 Yours, O **LORD**, is the kingdom; you are exalted as head over
29: 16 O **LORD** our God, as for all this abundance that we have
29: 18 O **LORD**, God of our fathers Abraham, Isaac and Israel,
29: 20 David said to the whole assembly, "Praise **the LORD** your God."
29: 20 So they all praised **the LORD**, the God of their fathers; they
29: 20 they bowed low and fell prostrate before **the LORD** and the king.
29: 21 The next day they made sacrifices to **the LORD** and presented
29: 21 sacrifices to the LORD and presented burnt offerings to **him**[s]:
29: 22 and drank with great joy in the presence of **the LORD** that day.
29: 22 anointing him before **the LORD** to be ruler and Zadok to be
29: 23 So Solomon sat on the throne of **the LORD** as king in place of
29: 25 **The LORD** highly exalted Solomon in the sight of all Israel
2Ch 1: 1 for **the LORD** his God was with him and made him exceedingly
1: 3 which Moses **the LORD's** servant had made in the desert.
1: 5 had made was in Gibeon in front of the tabernacle of **the LORD**;
1: 6 Solomon went up to the bronze altar before **the LORD** in the
1: 9 Now, **LORD** God, let your promise to my father David be
2: 1 [1:18] gave orders to build a temple for the Name of **the LORD**
2: 4 [2:3] to build a temple for the Name of **the LORD** my God
2: 4 [2:3] and at the appointed feasts of **the LORD** our God.
2: 11 [2:10] "Because **the LORD** loves his people, he has made you
2: 12 [2:11] "Praise be to **the LORD**, the God of Israel, who made
2: 12 [2:11] who will build a temple for **the LORD** and a palace for
3: 1 Solomon began to build the temple of **the LORD** in Jerusalem on
4: 16 Solomon for the temple of **the LORD** were of polished bronze.
5: 1 Solomon had done for the temple of **the LORD** was finished,
5: 2 to bring up the ark of **the LORD's** covenant from Zion, the City
5: 7 brought the ark of **the LORD's** covenant to its place in the inner
5: 10 where **the LORD** made a covenant with the Israelites after they
5: 13 as with one voice, to give praise and thanks to **the LORD**.
5: 13 they raised their voices in praise to **the LORD** and sang:
5: 13 Then the temple of **the LORD** was filled with a cloud,
5: 14 of the cloud, for the glory of **the LORD** filled the temple of God.
6: 1 "**The LORD** has said that he would dwell in a dark cloud;
6: 4 "Praise be to **the LORD**, the God of Israel, who with his hands
6: 7 had it in his heart to build a temple for the Name of **the LORD**,
6: 8 **the LORD** said to my father David, 'Because it was in your heart
6: 10 "**The LORD** has kept the promise he made. I have succeeded
6: 10 and now I sit on the throne of Israel, just as **the LORD** promised,
6: 10 I have built the temple for the Name of **the LORD**, the God of
6: 11 in which is the covenant of **the LORD** that he made with the
6: 12 Solomon stood before the altar of **the LORD** in front of the
6: 14 "O **LORD**, God of Israel, there is no God like you in heaven
6: 16 "Now **LORD**, God of Israel, keep for your servant David my
6: 17 now, O **LORD**, God of Israel, let your word that you promised
6: 19 your servant's prayer and his plea for mercy, O **LORD** my God.
6: 41 "Now arise, O **LORD** God, and come to your resting place,
6: 41 May your priests, O **LORD** God, be clothed with salvation,
6: 42 O **LORD** God, do not reject your anointed one. Remember the
7: 1 and the sacrifices, and the glory of **the LORD** filled the temple.
7: 2 The priests could not enter the temple of **the LORD**
7: 2 temple of the LORD because the glory of **the LORD** filled it.
7: 2 of the LORD because the glory of the LORD filled **it**[s] [+1074].
7: 3 fire coming down and the glory of **the LORD** above the temple,
7: 3 and they worshiped and gave thanks to **the LORD**, saying,
7: 4 the king and all the people offered sacrifices before **the LORD**.
7: 6 as did the Levites with **the LORD's** musical instruments,
7: 6 which King David had made for praising **the LORD** and which
7: 7 middle part of the courtyard in front of the temple of **the LORD**,
7: 10 glad in heart for the good things **the LORD** had done for David
7: 11 When Solomon had finished the temple of **the LORD** and the
7: 11 carrying out all he had in mind to do in the temple of **the LORD**
7: 12 **the LORD** appeared to him at night and said: "I have heard your
7: 21 'Why has **the LORD** done such a thing to this land and to this
7: 22 People will answer, 'Because they have forsaken **the LORD**,
8: 1 during which Solomon built the temple of **the LORD** and his
8: 11 because the places the ark of **the LORD** has entered are holy."
8: 12 On the altar of **the LORD** that he had built in front of the portico,
8: 12 of the portico, Solomon sacrificed burnt offerings to **the LORD**,
8: 16 from the day the foundation of the temple of **the LORD** was laid
8: 16 until its completion. So the temple of **the LORD** was finished.
9: 4 and the burnt offerings he made at the temple of **the LORD**,
9: 8 Praise be to **the LORD** your God, who has delighted in you
9: 8 placed you on his throne as king to rule for **the LORD** your God.
9: 11 used the algumwood to make steps for the temple of **the LORD**
10: 15 to fulfill the word **the LORD** had spoken to Jeroboam son of
11: 2 But this word of **the LORD** came to Shemaiah the man of God:
11: 4 'This is what **the LORD** says: Do not go up to fight against your
11: 4 for this is my doing.' " So they obeyed the words of **the LORD**
11: 14 and his sons had rejected them as priests of **the LORD**.
11: 16 every tribe of Israel who set their hearts on seeking **the LORD**,

2Ch 11: 16 the Levites to Jerusalem to offer sacrifices to **the LORD**,
12: 1 and all Israel with him abandoned the law of **the LORD**.
12: 2 Because they had been unfaithful to **the LORD**, Shishak king of
12: 5 he said to them, "This is what **the LORD** says, 'You have
12: 6 and the king humbled themselves and said, "**The LORD** is just."
12: 7 When **the LORD** saw that they humbled themselves, this word of
12: 7 humbled themselves, this word of **the LORD** came to Shemaiah:
12: 9 he carried off the treasures of the temple of **the LORD** and the
12: 11 Whenever the king went to **the LORD's** temple, the guards went
12: 12 **the LORD's** anger turned from him, and he was not totally
12: 13 the city **the LORD** had chosen out of all the tribes of Israel in
12: 14 did evil because he had not set his heart on seeking **the LORD**.
13: 5 Don't you know that **the LORD**, the God of Israel, has given the
13: 8 "And now you plan to resist the kingdom of **the LORD**,
13: 9 didn't you drive out the priests of **the LORD**, the sons of Aaron,
13: 10 "As for us, **the LORD** is our God, and we have not forsaken him.
13: 10 The priests who serve **the LORD** are sons of Aaron,
13: 11 they present burnt offerings and fragrant incense to **the LORD**.
13: 11 We are observing the requirements of **the LORD** our God.
13: 12 Men of Israel, do not fight against **the LORD**, the God of your
13: 14 attacked at both front and rear. Then they cried out to **the LORD**.
13: 18 men of Judah were victorious because they relied on **the LORD**,
13: 20 the time of Abijah. And **the LORD** struck him down and he died.
14: 2 [14:1] was good and right in the eyes of **the LORD** his God.
14: 4 [14:3] He commanded Judah to seek **the LORD**, the God of
14: 6 [14:5] him during those years, for **the LORD** gave him rest.
14: 7 [14:6] is still ours, because we have sought **the LORD** our God;
14: 11 [14:10] Asa called to **the LORD** his God and said, "LORD,
14: 11 [14:10] Asa called to the LORD his God and said, "**LORD**,
14: 11 [14:10] Help us, O **LORD** our God, for we rely on you, and in
14: 11 [14:10] O **LORD**, you are our God; do not let man prevail
14: 12 [14:11] **The LORD** struck down the Cushites before Asa
14: 13 [14:12] they were crushed before **the LORD** and his forces.
14: 14 [14:13] for the terror of **the LORD** had fallen upon them.
15: 2 and Benjamin. **The LORD** is with you when you are with him.
15: 4 But in their distress they turned to **the LORD**, the God of Israel,
15: 8 He repaired the altar of **the LORD** that was in front of the portico
15: 8 LORD that was in front of the portico of **the LORD's** temple.
15: 9 from Israel when they saw that **the LORD** his God was with him.
15: 11 At that time they sacrificed to **the LORD** seven hundred head of
15: 12 They entered into a covenant to seek **the LORD**, the God of their
15: 13 All who would not seek **the LORD**, the God of Israel, were to be
15: 14 They took an oath to **the LORD** with loud acclamation, with
15: 15 was found by them. So **the LORD** gave them rest on every side.
16: 2 the silver and gold out of the treasuries of **the LORD's** temple
16: 7 you relied on the king of Aram and not on **the LORD** your God,
16: 8 Yet when you relied on **the LORD**, he delivered them into your
16: 9 For the eyes of **the LORD** range throughout the earth to
16: 12 even in his illness he did not seek help from **the LORD**,
17: 3 **The LORD** was with Jehoshaphat because in his early years he
17: 5 **The LORD** established the kingdom under his control; and all
17: 6 His heart was devoted to the ways of **the LORD**; furthermore,
17: 9 taking with them the Book of the Law of **the LORD**;
17: 10 The fear of **the LORD** fell on all the kingdoms of the lands
17: 16 who volunteered himself for the service of **the LORD**, with
18: 4 said to the king of Israel, "First seek the counsel of **the LORD**."
18: 6 "Is there not a prophet of **the LORD** here whom we can inquire
18: 7 is still one man through whom we can inquire of **the LORD**,
18: 10 made iron horns, and he declared, "This is what **the LORD** says:
18: 11 they said, "for **the LORD** will give it into the king's hand."
18: 13 Micaiah said, "As surely as **the LORD** lives, I can tell him only
18: 15 swear to tell me nothing but the truth in the name of **the LORD**?"
18: 16 a shepherd, and **the LORD** said, 'These people have no master.
18: 18 Micaiah continued, "Therefore hear the word of **the LORD**:
18: 18 I saw **the LORD** sitting on his throne with all the host of heaven
18: 19 **the LORD** said, 'Who will entice Ahab king of Israel into
18: 20 stood before **the LORD** and said, 'I will entice him.'
18: 20 'I will entice him.' " 'By what means?' **the LORD** asked.
18: 22 "So now **the LORD** has put a lying spirit in the mouths of these
18: 22 prophets of yours. **The LORD** has decreed disaster for you."
18: 23 "Which way did the spirit from **the LORD** go when he went from
18: 27 you ever return safely, **the LORD** has not spoken through me."
18: 31 attack him, but Jehoshaphat cried out, and **the LORD** helped him.
19: 2 you help the wicked and love those who hate **the LORD**?
19: 2 Because of this, the wrath of **the LORD** is upon you.
19: 4 the hill country of Ephraim and turned them back to **the LORD**,
19: 6 because you are not judging for man but for **the LORD**,
19: 7 Now let the fear of **the LORD** be upon you. Judge carefully,
19: 7 for with **the LORD** our God there is no injustice or partiality
19: 8 and heads of Israelite families to administer the law of **the LORD**
19: 9 serve faithfully and wholeheartedly in the fear of **the LORD**.
19: 10 you are to warn them not to sin against **the LORD**;
19: 11 chief priest will be over you in any matter concerning **the LORD**,
19: 11 with courage, and may **the LORD** be with those who do well."
20: 3 Alarmed, Jehoshaphat resolved to inquire of **the LORD**,
20: 4 The people of Judah came together to seek help from **the LORD**;
20: 4 indeed, they came from every town in Judah to seek **him**[s].
20: 5 Jerusalem at the temple of **the LORD** in the front of the new
20: 6 "O **LORD**, God of our fathers, are you not the God who is in
20: 13 and children and little ones, stood there before **the LORD**.
20: 14 the Spirit of **the LORD** came upon Jahaziel son of Zechariah,
20: 15 live in Judah and Jerusalem! This is what **the LORD** says to you:
20: 17 stand firm and see the deliverance **the LORD** will give you,
20: 17 out to face them tomorrow, and **the LORD** will be with you.' "
20: 18 of Judah and Jerusalem fell down in worship before **the LORD**.
20: 18 and Jerusalem fell down in worship before the LORD. **[RPH]**
20: 19 the Kohathites and Korahites stood up and praised **the LORD**,
20: 20 Have faith in **the LORD** your God and you will be upheld;
20: 21 Jehoshaphat appointed men to sing to **the LORD** and to praise
20: 21 "Give thanks to **the LORD**, for his love endures forever."
20: 22 **the LORD** set ambushes against the men of Ammon and Moab
20: 26 in the Valley of Beracah, where they praised **the LORD**.
20: 27 for **the LORD** had given them cause to rejoice over their
20: 28 and went to the temple of **the LORD** with harps and lutes
20: 29 heard how **the LORD** had fought against the enemies of Israel.
20: 32 stray from them; he did what was right in the eyes of **the LORD**.
20: 37 with Ahaziah, **the LORD** will destroy what you have made."
21: 6 a daughter of Ahab. He did evil in the eyes of **the LORD**.
21: 7 because of the covenant **the LORD** had made with David,
21: 10 because Jehoram had forsaken **the LORD**, the God of his fathers.
21: 12 "This is what **the LORD**, the God of your father David, says:
21: 14 So now **the LORD** is about to strike your people, your sons,
21: 16 **The LORD** aroused against Jehoram the hostility of the
21: 18 **the LORD** afflicted Jehoram with an incurable disease of the
22: 4 He did evil in the eyes of **the LORD**, as the house of Ahab had
22: 7 whom **the LORD** had anointed to destroy the house of Ahab.
22: 9 a son of Jehoshaphat, who sought **the LORD** with all his heart."
23: 3 as **the LORD** promised concerning the descendants of David.
23: 5 other men are to be in the courtyards of the temple of **the LORD**.
23: 6 No one is to enter the temple of **the LORD** except the priests
23: 6 all the other men are to guard what **the LORD** has assigned to
23: 12 cheering the king, she went to them at the temple of **the LORD**.
23: 14 had said, "Do not put her to death at the temple of **the LORD**."
23: 16 the people and the king would be **the LORD's** [+4200] people.
23: 18 Jehoiada placed the oversight of the temple of **the LORD** in the
23: 18 **[RPH]** to present the burnt offerings of the LORD as written in
23: 18 to present the burnt offerings of **the LORD** as written in the Law
23: 19 He also stationed doorkeepers at the gates of **the LORD's** temple
23: 20 and brought the king down from the temple of **the LORD**.
24: 2 Joash did what was right in the eyes of **the LORD** all the years of
24: 4 time later Joash decided to restore the temple of **the LORD**.
24: 6 Jerusalem the tax imposed by Moses the servant of **the LORD**
24: 7 and had used even **its**[s] [+1074] sacred objects for the Baals.
24: 8 and placed outside, at the gate of the temple of **the LORD**.
24: 9 Jerusalem that they should bring to **the LORD** the tax that Moses
24: 12 who carried out the work required for the temple of **the LORD**.
24: 12 They hired masons and carpenters to restore **the LORD's** temple,
24: 12 and also workers in iron and bronze to repair the temple. **[RPH]**
24: 14 and with it were made articles for **the LORD's** temple:
24: 14 offerings were presented continually in the temple of **the LORD**.
24: 18 They abandoned the temple of **the LORD**, the God of their
24: 19 Although **the LORD** sent prophets to the people to bring them
24: 20 'Why do you disobey **the LORD's** commands? You will not
24: 20 Because you have forsaken **the LORD**, he has forsaken you.' "
24: 21 they stoned him to death in the courtyard of **the LORD's** temple.
24: 22 he lay dying, "May **the LORD** see this and call you to account."
24: 24 **the LORD** delivered into their hands a much larger army.
24: 24 Because Judah had forsaken **the LORD**, the God of their fathers,
25: 2 He did what was right in the eyes of **the LORD**, but not
25: 4 in the Law, in the Book of Moses, where **the LORD** commanded:
25: 7 must not march with you, for **the LORD** is not with Israel—
25: 9 of God replied, "**The LORD** can give you much more than that."
25: 15 The anger of **the LORD** burned against Amaziah, and he sent a
25: 27 the time that Amaziah turned away from following **the LORD**,
26: 4 He did what was right in the eyes of **the LORD**, just as his father
26: 5 As long as he sought **the LORD**, God gave him success.
26: 16 He was unfaithful to **the LORD** his God, and entered the temple
26: 16 entered the temple of **the LORD** to burn incense on the altar of
26: 17 eighty other courageous priests of **the LORD** followed him in.
26: 18 "It is not right for you, Uzziah, to burn incense to **the LORD**.
26: 18 been unfaithful; and you will not be honored by **the LORD** God."
26: 19 in their presence before the incense altar in **the LORD's** temple,
26: 20 himself was eager to leave, because **the LORD** had afflicted him.
26: 21 leprous, and excluded from the temple of **the LORD**.
27: 2 He did what was right in the eyes of **the LORD**, just as his father
27: 2 but unlike him he did not enter the temple of **the LORD**.
27: 3 Jotham rebuilt the Upper Gate of the temple of **the LORD**
27: 6 because he walked steadfastly before **the LORD** his God.

2Ch 28: 1 his father, he did not do what was right in the eyes of **the LORD**.
28: 3 following the detestable ways of the nations **the LORD** had
28: 5 Therefore **the LORD** his God handed him over to the king of
28: 6 because Judah had forsaken **the LORD**, the God of their fathers.
28: 9 a prophet of **the LORD** named Oded was there, and he went out
28: 9 He said to them, "Because **the LORD**, the God of your fathers,
28: 10 But aren't you also guilty of sins against **the LORD** your God?
28: 11 taken as prisoners, for **the LORD's** fierce anger rests on you."
28: 13 they said, "or we will be guilty before **the LORD**.
28: 19 **The LORD** had humbled Judah because of Ahaz king of Israel,
28: 19 wickedness in Judah and had been most unfaithful to **the LORD**.
28: 21 Ahaz took some of the things from the temple of **the LORD**
28: 22 of trouble King Ahaz became even more unfaithful to **the LORD**.
28: 24 He shut the doors of **the LORD's** temple and set up altars at
28: 25 places to burn sacrifices to other gods and provoked **the LORD**,
29: 2 He did what was right in the eyes of **the LORD**, just as his father
29: 3 he opened the doors of the temple of **the LORD** and repaired
29: 5 yourselves now and consecrate the temple of **the LORD**,
29: 6 they did evil in the eyes of **the LORD** our God and forsook him.
29: 6 They turned their faces away from **the LORD's** dwelling place
29: 8 the anger of **the LORD** has fallen on Judah and Jerusalem;
29: 10 Now I intend to make a covenant with **the LORD**, the God of
29: 11 for **the LORD** has chosen you to stand before him and serve him,
29: 15 they went in to purify the temple of **the LORD**, as the king had
29: 15 as the king had ordered, following the word of **the LORD**.
29: 16 The priests went into the sanctuary of **the LORD** to purify it.
29: 16 They brought out to the courtyard of **the LORD's** temple
29: 16 everything unclean that they found in the temple of **the LORD**.
29: 17 eighth day of the month they reached the portico of **the LORD**.
29: 17 For eight more days they consecrated the temple of **the LORD**
29: 18 "We have purified the entire temple of **the LORD**, the altar of
29: 19 while he was king. They are now in front of **the LORD's** altar."
29: 20 city officials together and went up to the temple of **the LORD**.
29: 21 descendants of Aaron, to offer these on the altar of **the LORD**.
29: 25 He stationed the Levites in the temple of **the LORD** with
29: 25 this was commanded by **the LORD** through his prophets.
29: 27 As the offering began, singing to **the LORD** began also,
29: 30 his officials ordered the Levites to praise **the LORD** with the
29: 31 "You have now dedicated yourselves to **the LORD**.
29: 31 bring sacrifices and thank offerings to the temple of **the LORD**."
29: 32 male lambs—all of them for burnt offerings to **the LORD**.
29: 35 So the service of the temple of **the LORD** was reestablished.
30: 1 inviting them to come to the temple of **the LORD** in Jerusalem
30: 1 LORD in Jerusalem and celebrate the Passover to **the LORD**,
30: 5 to come to Jerusalem and celebrate the Passover to **the LORD**,
30: 6 "People of Israel, return to **the LORD**, the God of Abraham,
30: 7 like your fathers and brothers, who were unfaithful to **the LORD**,
30: 8 not be stiff-necked, as your fathers were; submit to **the LORD**.
30: 8 Serve **the LORD** your God, so that his fierce anger will turn
30: 9 If you return to **the LORD**, then your brothers and your children
30: 9 for **the LORD** your God is gracious and compassionate.
30: 12 and his officials had ordered, following the word of **the LORD**.
30: 15 and brought burnt offerings to the temple of **the LORD**.
30: 17 and could not consecrate ⌊their lambs⌋ to **the LORD**.
30: 18 saying, "May **the LORD**, who is good, pardon everyone
30: 19 his heart on seeking God—**the LORD**, the God of his fathers—
30: 20 And **the LORD** heard Hezekiah and healed the people.
30: 21 while the Levites and priests sang to **the LORD** every day,
30: 21 accompanied by **the LORD's** [+4200] instruments of praise.
30: 22 who showed good understanding of the service of **the LORD**.
30: 22 and offered fellowship offerings and praised **the LORD**,
31: 2 and to sing praises at the gates of **the LORD's** dwelling.
31: 3 and appointed feasts as written in the Law of **the LORD**.
31: 4 so they could devote themselves to the Law of **the LORD**.
31: 6 and a tithe of the holy things dedicated to **the LORD** their God,
31: 8 the heaps, they praised **the LORD** and blessed his people Israel.
31: 10 began to bring their contributions to the temple of **the LORD**,
31: 10 and plenty to spare, because **the LORD** has blessed his people,
31: 11 gave orders to prepare storerooms in the temple of **the LORD**,
31: 14 distributing the contributions made to **the LORD** and also the
31: 16 all who would enter the temple of **the LORD** to perform the daily
31: 20 what was good and right and faithful before **the LORD** his God.
32: 8 with us is **the LORD** our God to help us and to fight our battles."
32: 11 '**The LORD** our God will save us from the hand of the king of
32: 16 Sennacherib's officers spoke further against **the LORD** God
32: 17 The king also wrote letters insulting **the LORD**, the God of
32: 21 **the LORD** sent an angel, who annihilated all the fighting men
32: 22 So **the LORD** saved Hezekiah and the people of Jerusalem from
32: 23 Many brought offerings to Jerusalem for **the LORD** and valuable
32: 24 He prayed to **the LORD**, who answered him and gave him a
32: 26 therefore **the LORD's** wrath did not come upon them during the
33: 2 He did evil in the eyes of **the LORD**, following the detestable
33: 2 following the detestable practices of the nations **the LORD** had
33: 4 He built altars in the temple of **the LORD**, of which the LORD
33: 4 altars in the temple of the LORD, of which **the LORD** had said,
33: 5 In both courts of the temple of **the LORD**, he built altars to all
33: 6 He did much evil in the eyes of **the LORD**, provoking him to
33: 9 so that they did more evil than the nations **the LORD** had
33: 10 **The LORD** spoke to Manasseh and his people, but they paid no
33: 11 So **the LORD** brought against them the army commanders of the
33: 12 In his distress he sought the favor of **the LORD** his God
33: 13 and to his kingdom. Then Manasseh knew that **the LORD** is God.
33: 15 and removed the image from the temple of **the LORD**,
33: 15 as well as all the altars he had built on the temple **[RPH]** hill
33: 16 he restored the altar of **the LORD** and sacrificed fellowship
33: 16 on it, and told Judah to serve **the LORD**, the God of Israel.
33: 17 to sacrifice at the high places, but only to **the LORD** their God.
33: 18 and the words the seers spoke to him in the name of **the LORD**,
33: 22 He did evil in the eyes of **the LORD**, as his father Manasseh had
33: 23 father Manasseh, he did not humble himself before **the LORD**;
34: 2 He did what was right in the eyes of **the LORD** and walked in the
34: 8 the recorder, to repair the temple of **the LORD** his God.
34: 10 the men appointed to supervise the work on **the LORD's** temple.
34: 10 These men paid the workers **[RPH]** who repaired and restored the
34: 14 out the money that had been taken into the temple of **the LORD**,
34: 14 Hilkiah the priest found the Book of the Law of **the LORD** that
34: 15 "I have found the Book of the Law in the temple of **the LORD**."
34: 17 have paid out the money that was in the temple of **the LORD**
34: 21 "Go and inquire of **the LORD** for me and for the remnant in
34: 21 Great is **the LORD's** anger that is poured out on us because our
34: 21 because our fathers have not kept the word of **the LORD**;
34: 23 She said to them, "This is what **the LORD**, the God of Israel,
34: 24 'This is what **the LORD** says: I am going to bring disaster on this
34: 26 Tell the king of Judah, who sent you to inquire of **the LORD**,
34: 26 'This is what **the LORD**, the God of Israel, says concerning the
34: 27 and wept in my presence, I have heard you, declares **the LORD**.
34: 30 He went up to the temple of **the LORD** with the men of Judah,
34: 30 the Covenant, which had been found in the temple of **the LORD**.
34: 31 and renewed the covenant in the presence of **the LORD**—
34: 31 to follow **the LORD** and keep his commands, regulations
34: 33 he had all who were present in Israel serve **the LORD** their God.
34: 33 As long as he lived, they did not fail to follow **the LORD**,
35: 1 Josiah celebrated the Passover to **the LORD** in Jerusalem,
35: 2 and encouraged them in the service of **the LORD's** temple.
35: 3 instructed all Israel and who had been consecrated to **the LORD**:
35: 3 Now serve **the LORD** your God and his people Israel.
35: 6 doing what **the LORD** commanded through Moses."
35: 12 subdivisions of the families of the people to offer to **the LORD**,
35: 16 So at that time the entire service of **the LORD** was carried out for
35: 16 and the offering of burnt offerings on the altar of **the LORD**,
35: 26 according to what is written in the Law of **the LORD**—
36: 5 eleven years. He did evil in the eyes of **the LORD** his God.
36: 7 also took to Babylon articles from the temple of **the LORD**
36: 9 three months and ten days. He did evil in the eyes of **the LORD**.
36: 10 together with articles of value from the temple of **the LORD**,
36: 12 He did evil in the eyes of **the LORD** his God and did not humble
36: 12 before Jeremiah the prophet, who spoke the word of **the LORD**.
36: 13 and hardened his heart and would not turn to **the LORD**,
36: 14 practices of the nations and defiling the temple of **the LORD**,
36: 15 **The LORD**, the God of their fathers, sent word to them through
36: 16 scoffed at his prophets until the wrath of **the LORD** was aroused
36: 18 the treasures of **the LORD's** temple and the treasures of the king
36: 21 in fulfillment of the word of **the LORD** spoken by Jeremiah.
36: 22 in order to fulfill the word of **the LORD** spoken by Jeremiah,
36: 22 **the LORD** moved the heart of Cyrus king of Persia to make a
36: 23 " '**The LORD**, the God of heaven, has given me all the kingdoms
36: 23 may **the LORD** his God be with him, and let him go up.' "
Ezr 1: 1 in order to fulfill the word of **the LORD** spoken by Jeremiah,
1: 1 **the LORD** moved the heart of Cyrus king of Persia to make a
1: 2 " '**The LORD**, the God of heaven, has given me all the kingdoms
1: 3 go up to Jerusalem in Judah and build the temple of **the LORD**,
1: 5 prepared to go up and build the house of **the LORD** in Jerusalem.
1: 7 brought out the articles belonging to the temple of **the LORD**,
2: 68 When they arrived at the house of **the LORD** in Jerusalem,
3: 3 its foundation and sacrificed burnt offerings on it to **the LORD**,
3: 5 the sacrifices for all the appointed sacred feasts of **the LORD**,
3: 5 as well as those brought as freewill offerings to **the LORD**.
3: 6 seventh month they began to offer burnt offerings to **the LORD**,
3: 6 though the foundation of **the LORD's** temple had not yet been
3: 8 and older to supervise the building of the house of **the LORD**.
3: 10 the builders laid the foundation of the temple of **the LORD**,
3: 10 with cymbals, took their places to praise **the LORD**,
3: 11 With praise and thanksgiving they sang to **the LORD**: "He is
3: 11 And all the people gave a great shout of praise to **the LORD**,
3: 11 because the foundation of the house of **the LORD** was laid.
4: 1 heard that the exiles were building a temple for **the LORD**,
4: 3 We alone will build it for **the LORD**, the God of Israel, as King
6: 21 practices of their Gentile neighbors in order to seek **the LORD**,

Ezr 6:22 because **the LORD** had filled them with joy by changing the
7:6 Law of Moses, which **the LORD**, the God of Israel, had given.
7:6 he asked, for the hand of **the LORD** his God was on him.
7:10 himself to the study and observance of the Law of **the LORD**,
7:11 concerning the commands and decrees of **the LORD** for Israel:
7:27 Praise be to **the LORD**, the God of our fathers, who has put it
7:27 bring honor to the house of **the LORD** in Jerusalem in this way
7:28 Because the hand of **the LORD** my God was on me, I took
8:28 "You as well as these articles are consecrated to **the LORD**.
8:28 The silver and gold are a freewill offering to **the LORD**,
8:29 of the house of **the LORD** in Jerusalem before the leading priests
8:35 twelve male goats. All this was a burnt offering to **the LORD**.
9:5 fell on my knees with my hands spread out to **the LORD** my
9:8 **the LORD** our God has been gracious in leaving us a remnant
9:15 O **LORD**, God of Israel, you are righteous! We are left this day
10:11 Now make confession to **the LORD**, the God of your fathers,
Ne 1:5 "O **LORD**, God of heaven, the great and awesome God,
5:13 this the whole assembly said, "Amen," and praised **the LORD**.
8:1 the Law of Moses, which **the LORD** had commanded for Israel.
8:6 Ezra praised **the LORD**, the great God; and all the people lifted
8:6 and worshiped **the LORD** with their faces to the ground.
8:9 said to them all, "This day is sacred to **the LORD** your God.
8:10 Do not grieve, for the joy of **the LORD** is your strength."
8:14 in the Law, which **the LORD** had commanded through Moses,
9:3 read from the Book of the Law of **the LORD** their God for a
9:3 quarter in confession and in worshiping **the LORD** their God.
9:4 who called with loud voices to **the LORD** their God.
9:5 "Stand up and praise **the LORD** your God, who is from
9:6 You alone are **the LORD**. You made the heavens,
9:7 "You are **the LORD** God, who chose Abram and brought him out
10:29 [10:30] and decrees of **the LORD** our Lord.
10:34 [10:35] of wood to burn on the altar of **the LORD** our God,
10:35 [10:36] house of **the LORD** each year the firstfruits of our crops
Job 1:6 day the angels came to present themselves before **the LORD**,
1:7 **The LORD** said to Satan, "Where have you come from?"
1:7 Satan answered **the LORD**, "From roaming through the earth
1:8 **the LORD** said to Satan, "Have you considered my servant Job?
1:9 "Does Job fear God for nothing?" Satan replied. **[RPH]**
1:12 **The LORD** said to Satan, "Very well, then, everything he has is
1:12 a finger." Then Satan went out from the presence of **the LORD**.
1:21 **The LORD** gave and the LORD has taken away; may the name
1:21 The LORD gave and **the LORD** has taken away; may the name
1:21 has taken away; may the name of **the LORD** be praised."
2:1 day the angels came to present themselves before **the LORD**,
2:1 and Satan also came with them to present himself before **him**[s].
2:2 And **the LORD** said to Satan, "Where have you come from?"
2:2 Satan answered **the LORD**, "From roaming through the earth
2:3 **the LORD** said to Satan, "Have you considered my servant Job?
2:4 Satan replied. **[RPH]** "A man will give all he has for his own life.
2:6 **The LORD** said to Satan, "Very well, then, he is in your hands;
2:7 So Satan went out from the presence of **the LORD** and afflicted
12:9 Which of all these does not know that the hand of **the LORD** has
38:1 Then **the LORD** answered Job out of the storm. He said:
40:1 **The LORD** said to Job:
40:3 Then Job answered **the LORD**:
40:6 Then **the LORD** spoke to Job out of the storm:
42:1 Then Job replied to **the LORD**:
42:7 After **the LORD** had said these things to Job, he said to Eliphaz
42:7 **he**[s] said to Eliphaz the Temanite, "I am angry with you and your
42:9 and Zophar the Naamathite did what **the LORD** told them;
42:9 the LORD told them; and **the LORD** accepted Job's prayer.
42:10 **the LORD** made him prosperous again and gave him twice as
42:10 and gave **[RPH]** him twice as much as he had before.
42:11 consoled him over all the trouble **the LORD** had brought upon
42:12 **The LORD** blessed the latter part of Job's life more than the first.
Ps 1:2 his delight is in the law of **the LORD**, and on his law he
1:6 For **the LORD** watches over the way of the righteous,
2:2 the rulers gather together against **the LORD** and against his
2:7 I will proclaim the decree of **the LORD**: He said to me, "You are
2:11 Serve **the LORD** with fear and rejoice with trembling.
3:1 [3:2] O **LORD**, how many are my foes! How many rise up
3:3 [3:4] you are a shield around me, O **LORD**; you bestow glory on
3:4 [3:5] To **the LORD** I cry aloud, and he answers me from his
3:5 [3:6] and sleep; I wake again, because **the LORD** sustains me.
3:7 [3:8] Arise, O **LORD**! Deliver me, O my God! Strike all my
3:8 [3:9] From **the LORD** comes deliverance. May your blessing be
4:3 [4:4] Know that **the LORD** has set apart the godly for himself;
4:3 [4:4] godly for himself; **the LORD** will hear when I call to him.
4:5 [4:6] Offer right sacrifices and trust in **the LORD**.
4:6 [4:7] Let the light of your face shine upon us, O **LORD**.
4:8 [4:9] I will lie down and sleep in peace, for you alone, O **LORD**,
5:1 [5:2] Give ear to my words, O **LORD**, consider my sighing.
5:3 [5:4] In the morning, O **LORD**, you hear my voice;
5:6 [5:7] tell lies; bloodthirsty and deceitful men **the LORD** abhors.
5:8 [5:9] Lead me, O **LORD**, in your righteousness because of my
5:12 [5:13] For surely, O **LORD**, you bless the righteous;
6:1 [6:2] O **LORD**, do not rebuke me in your anger or discipline me
6:2 [6:3] Be merciful to me, **LORD**, for I am faint; O LORD,
6:2 [6:3] I am faint; O **LORD**, heal me, for my bones are in agony.
6:3 [6:4] My soul is in anguish. How long, O **LORD**, how long?
6:4 [6:5] Turn, O **LORD**, and deliver me; save me because of your
6:8 [6:9] all you who do evil, for **the LORD** has heard my weeping.
6:9 [6:10] **The LORD** has heard my cry for mercy; the LORD
6:9 [6:10] heard my cry for mercy; **the LORD** accepts my prayer.
7:T [7:1] which he sang to **the LORD** concerning Cush,
7:1 [7:2] O **LORD** my God, I take refuge in you; save and deliver
7:3 [7:4] O **LORD** my God, if I have done this and there is guilt on
7:6 [7:7] Arise, O **LORD**, in your anger; rise up against the rage of
7:8 [7:9] let **the LORD** judge the peoples. Judge me, O LORD,
7:8 [7:9] Judge me, O **LORD**, according to my righteousness,
7:17 [7:18] I will give thanks to **the LORD** because of his
7:17 [7:18] and will sing praise to the name of **the LORD** Most High.
8:1 [8:2] O **LORD**, our Lord, how majestic is your name in all the
8:9 [8:10] O **LORD**, our Lord, how majestic is your name in all the
9:1 [9:2] I will praise you, O **LORD**, with all my heart; I will tell of
9:7 [9:8] **The LORD** reigns forever; he has established his throne
9:9 [9:10] **The LORD** is a refuge for the oppressed, a stronghold in
9:10 [9:11] for you, **LORD**, have never forsaken those who seek you.
9:11 [9:12] Sing praises to **the LORD**, enthroned in Zion;
9:13 [9:14] O **LORD**, see how my enemies persecute me!
9:16 [9:17] **The LORD** is known by his justice; the wicked are
9:19 [9:20] Arise, O **LORD**, let not man triumph; let the nations be
9:20 [9:21] Strike them with terror, O **LORD**; let the nations know
10:1 Why, O **LORD**, do you stand far off? Why do you hide yourself
10:3 of his heart; he blesses the greedy and reviles **the LORD**.
10:12 Arise, **LORD**! Lift up your hand, O God. Do not forget the
10:16 **The LORD** is King for ever and ever; the nations will perish
10:17 You hear, O **LORD**, the desire of the afflicted; you encourage
11:1 In **the LORD** I take refuge. How then can you say to me:
11:4 **The LORD** is in his holy temple; the LORD is on his heavenly
11:4 is in his holy temple; **the LORD** is on his heavenly throne.
11:5 **The LORD** examines the righteous, but the wicked and those
11:7 For **the LORD** is righteous, he loves justice; upright men will see
12:1 [12:2] Help, **LORD**, for the godly are no more; the faithful have
12:3 [12:4] May **the LORD** cut off all flattering lips and every
12:5 [12:6] groaning of the needy, I will now arise," says **the LORD**.
12:6 [12:7] the words of **the LORD** are flawless, like silver refined in
12:7 [12:8] O **LORD**, you will keep us safe and protect us from such
13:1 [13:2] How long, O **LORD**? Will you forget me forever? How
13:3 [13:4] Look on me and answer, O **LORD** my God. Give light to
13:6 I will sing to **the LORD**, for he has been good to me.
14:2 **The LORD** looks down from heaven on the sons of men to see if
14:4 my people as men eat bread and who do not call on **the LORD**?
14:6 frustrate the plans of the poor, but **the LORD** is their refuge.
14:7 When **the LORD** restores the fortunes of his people, let Jacob
15:1 **LORD**, who may dwell in your sanctuary? Who may live on your
15:4 who despises a vile man but honors those who fear **the LORD**,
16:2 I said to **the LORD**, "You are my Lord; apart from you I have no
16:5 **LORD**, you have assigned me my portion and my cup; you have
16:7 I will praise **the LORD**, who counsels me; even at night my heart
16:8 I have set **the LORD** always before me. Because he is at my right
17:1 Hear, O **LORD**, my righteous plea; listen to my cry. Give ear to
17:13 Rise up, O **LORD**, confront them, bring them down; rescue me
17:14 O **LORD**, by your hand save me from such men, from men of
18:T [18:1] the director of music. Of David the servant of **the LORD**.
18:T [18:1] He sang to **the LORD** the words of this song when the
18:T [18:1] **the LORD** delivered him from the hand of all his enemies
18:1 [18:2] I love you, O **LORD**, my strength.
18:2 [18:3] **The LORD** is my rock, my fortress and my deliverer;
18:3 [18:4] I call to **the LORD**, who is worthy of praise, and I am
18:6 [18:7] In my distress I called to **the LORD**; I cried to my God
18:13 [18:14] **The LORD** thundered from heaven; the voice of the
18:15 [18:16] O **LORD**, at the blast of breath from your nostrils.
18:18 [18:19] the day of my disaster, but **the LORD** was my support.
18:20 [18:21] **The LORD** has dealt with me according to my
18:21 [18:22] For I have kept the ways of **the LORD**; I have not done
18:24 [18:25] **The LORD** has rewarded me according to my
18:28 [18:29] You, O **LORD**, keep my lamp burning; my God turns
18:30 [18:31] his way is perfect; the word of **the LORD** is flawless.
18:31 [18:32] For who is God besides **the LORD**? And who is the
18:41 [18:42] one to save them—to **the LORD**, but he did not answer.
18:46 [18:47] **The LORD** lives! Praise be to my Rock! Exalted be God
18:49 [18:50] I will praise you among the nations, O **LORD**;
19:7 [19:8] The law of **the LORD** is perfect, reviving the soul.
19:7 [19:8] The statutes of **the LORD** are trustworthy, making wise
19:8 [19:9] The precepts of **the LORD** are right, giving joy to the
19:8 [19:9] The commands of **the LORD** are radiant, giving light to
19:9 [19:10] The fear of **the LORD** is pure, enduring forever. The

Ps 19: 9 [19:10] The ordinances of **the LORD** are sure and altogether
19: 14 [19:15] in your sight, O **LORD**, my Rock and my Redeemer.
20: 1 [20:2] May **the LORD** answer you when you are in distress;
20: 5 [20:6] name of our God. May **the LORD** grant all your requests.
20: 6 [20:7] Now I know that **the LORD** saves his anointed;
20: 7 [20:8] in horses, but we trust in the name of **the LORD** our God.
20: 9 [20:10] O **LORD**, save the king! Answer us when we call!
21: 1 [21:2] O **LORD**, the king rejoices in your strength. How great is
21: 7 [21:8] For the king trusts in **the LORD**; through the unfailing
21: 9 [21:10] In his wrath **the LORD** will swallow them up, and his
21: 13 [21:14] Be exalted, O **LORD**, in your strength; we will sing
22: 8 [22:9] "He trusts in **the LORD**; let the LORD rescue him.
22: 19 [22:20] you, O **LORD**, be not far off; O my Strength,
22: 23 [22:24] You who fear **the LORD**, praise him! All you
22: 26 [22:27] be satisfied; they who seek **the LORD** will praise him—
22: 27 [22:28] ends of the earth will remember and turn to **the LORD**,
22: 28 [22:29] for dominion belongs to **the LORD** and he rules over
23: 1 **The LORD** is my shepherd, I shall not be in want.
23: 6 of my life, and I will dwell in the house of **the LORD** forever.
24: 1 The earth is **the LORD's** [+4200], and everything in it, the world,
24: 3 Who may ascend the hill of **the LORD**? Who may stand in his
24: 5 He will receive blessing from **the LORD** and vindication from
24: 8 **The LORD** strong and mighty, the LORD mighty in battle.
24: 8 The LORD strong and mighty, **the LORD** mighty in battle.
24: 10 **The LORD** Almighty—he is the King of glory. *Selah*
25: 1 To you, O **LORD**, I lift up my soul;
25: 4 Show me your ways, O **LORD**, teach me your paths;
25: 6 Remember, O **LORD**, your great mercy and love, for they are
25: 7 to your love remember me, for you are good, O **LORD**.
25: 8 Good and upright is **the LORD**; therefore he instructs sinners in
25: 10 All the ways of **the LORD** are loving and faithful for those who
25: 11 of your name, O **LORD**, forgive my iniquity, though it is great.
25: 12 Who, then, is the man that fears **the LORD**? He will instruct him
25: 14 **The LORD** confides in those who fear him; he makes his
25: 15 My eyes are ever on **the LORD**, for only he will release my feet
26: 1 Vindicate me, O **LORD**, for I have led a blameless life; I have
26: 1 a blameless life; I have trusted in **the LORD** without wavering.
26: 2 Test me, O **LORD**, and try me, examine my heart and my mind;
26: 6 I wash my hands in innocence, and go about your altar, O **LORD**,
26: 8 I love the house where you live, O **LORD**, the place where your
26: 12 on level ground; in the great assembly I will praise **the LORD**.
27: 1 **The LORD** is my light and my salvation—whom shall I fear?
27: 1 **The LORD** is the stronghold of my life—of whom shall I be
27: 4 One thing I ask of **the LORD**, this is what I seek: that I may
27: 4 that I may dwell in the house of **the LORD** all the days of my
27: 4 to gaze upon the beauty of **the LORD** and to seek him in his
27: 6 with shouts of joy; I will sing and make music to **the LORD**.
27: 7 Hear my voice when I call, O **LORD**; be merciful to me
27: 8 heart says of you, "Seek his face!" Your face, **LORD**, I will seek.
27: 10 my father and mother forsake me, **the LORD** will receive me.
27: 11 Teach me your way, O **LORD**; lead me in a straight path
27: 13 I will see the goodness of **the LORD** in the land of the living.
27: 14 Wait for **the LORD**; be strong and take heart and wait for the
27: 14 for the LORD; be strong and take heart and wait for **the LORD**.
28: 1 To you I call, O **LORD** my Rock; do not turn a deaf ear to me.
28: 5 Since they show no regard for the works of **the LORD** and what
28: 6 Praise be to **the LORD**, for he has heard my cry for mercy.
28: 7 **The LORD** is my strength and my shield; my heart trusts in him,
28: 8 **The LORD** is the strength of his people, a fortress of salvation
29: 1 Ascribe to **the LORD**, O mighty ones, ascribe to the LORD
29: 1 O mighty ones, ascribe to **the LORD** glory and strength.
29: 2 Ascribe to **the LORD** the glory due his name; worship the
29: 2 due his name; worship **the LORD** in the splendor of his holiness.
29: 3 The voice of **the LORD** is over the waters; the God of glory
29: 3 of glory thunders, **the LORD** thunders over the mighty waters.
29: 4 The voice of **the LORD** is powerful; the voice of the LORD is
29: 4 of the LORD is powerful; the voice of **the LORD** is majestic.
29: 5 The voice of **the LORD** breaks the cedars; the LORD breaks in
29: 5 the cedars; **the LORD** breaks in pieces the cedars of Lebanon.
29: 7 The voice of **the LORD** strikes with flashes of lightning.
29: 8 The voice of **the LORD** shakes the desert; the LORD shakes the
29: 8 shakes the desert; **the LORD** shakes the Desert of Kadesh.
29: 9 The voice of **the LORD** twists the oaks and strips the forests
29: 10 **The LORD** sits enthroned over the flood; the LORD is
29: 10 over the flood; **the LORD** is enthroned as King forever.
29: 11 **The LORD** gives strength to his people; the LORD blesses his
29: 11 strength to his people; **the LORD** blesses his people with peace.
30: 1 [30:2] I will exalt you, O **LORD**, for you lifted me out of the
30: 2 [30:3] O **LORD** my God, I called to you for help and you healed
30: 3 [30:4] O **LORD**, you brought me up from the grave; you spared
30: 4 [30:5] Sing to **the LORD**, you saints of his; praise his holy
30: 7 [30:8] O **LORD**, when you favored me, you made my mountain
30: 8 [30:9] To you, O **LORD**, I called; to the Lord I cried for mercy:
30: 10 [30:11] Hear, O **LORD**, and be merciful to me; O LORD,
30: 10 [30:11] and be merciful to me; O **LORD**, be my help."
30: 12 [30:13] O **LORD** my God, I will give you thanks forever.
31: 1 [31:2] In you, O **LORD**, I have taken refuge; let me never be put
31: 5 [31:6] commit my spirit; redeem me, O **LORD**, the God of truth.
31: 6 [31:7] those who cling to worthless idols; I trust in **the LORD**.
31: 9 [31:10] Be merciful to me, O **LORD**, for I am in distress; my
31: 14 [31:15] But I trust in you, O **LORD**; I say, "You are my God."
31: 17 [31:18] be put to shame, O **LORD**, for I have cried out to you;
31: 21 [31:22] Praise be to **the LORD**, for he showed his wonderful
31: 23 [31:24] Love **the LORD**, all his saints! The LORD preserves
31: 23 [31:24] **The LORD** preserves the faithful, but the proud he pays
31: 24 [31:25] and take heart, all you who hope in **the LORD**.
32: 2 Blessed is the man whose sin **the LORD** does not count against
32: 5 I said, "I will confess my transgressions to **the LORD**"—
32: 10 **the LORD's** unfailing love surrounds the man who trusts in him.
32: 11 Rejoice in **the LORD** and be glad, you righteous; sing, all you
33: 1 Sing joyfully to **the LORD**, you righteous; it is fitting for the
33: 2 Praise **the LORD** with the harp; make music to him on the
33: 4 For the word of **the LORD** is right and true; he is faithful in all
33: 5 **The LORD** loves righteousness and justice; the earth is full of his
33: 6 By the word of **the LORD** were the heavens made, their starry
33: 8 Let all the earth fear **the LORD**; let all the people of the world
33: 10 **The LORD** foils the plans of the nations; he thwarts the purposes
33: 11 the plans of **the LORD** stand firm forever, the purposes of his
33: 12 Blessed is the nation whose God is **the LORD**, the people he
33: 13 From heaven **the LORD** looks down and sees all mankind;
33: 18 the eyes of **the LORD** are on those who fear him, on those whose
33: 20 We wait in hope for **the LORD**; he is our help and our shield.
33: 22 love rest upon us, O **LORD**, even as we put our hope in you.
34: 1 [34:2] I will extol **the LORD** at all times; his praise will always
34: 2 [34:3] My soul will boast in **the LORD**; let the afflicted hear
34: 3 [34:4] Glorify **the LORD** with me; let us exalt his name
34: 4 [34:5] I sought **the LORD**, and he answered me; he delivered
34: 6 [34:7] This poor man called, and **the LORD** heard him; he
34: 7 [34:8] The angel of **the LORD** encamps around those who fear
34: 8 [34:9] Taste and see that **the LORD** is good; blessed is the man
34: 9 [34:10] Fear **the LORD**, you his saints, for those who fear him
34: 10 [34:11] but those who seek **the LORD** lack no good thing.
34: 11 [34:12] listen to me; I will teach you the fear of **the LORD**.
34: 15 [34:16] The eyes of **the LORD** are on the righteous and his ears
34: 16 [34:17] the face of **the LORD** is against those who do evil,
34: 17 [34:18] The righteous cry out, and **the LORD** hears them; he
34: 18 [34:19] **The LORD** is close to the brokenhearted and saves
34: 19 [34:20] but **the LORD** delivers him from them all;
34: 22 [34:23] **The LORD** redeems his servants; no one will be
35: 1 Contend, O **LORD**, with those who contend with me;
35: 5 before the wind, with the angel of **the LORD** driving them away;
35: 6 and slippery, with the angel of **the LORD** pursuing them.
35: 9 my soul will rejoice in **the LORD** and delight in his salvation.
35: 10 My whole being will exclaim, "Who is like you, O **LORD**?
35: 22 O **LORD**, you have seen this; be not silent. Do not be far from
35: 24 Vindicate me in your righteousness, O **LORD** my God; do not let
35: 27 may they always say, "**The LORD** be exalted, who delights in the
36: T [36:1] the director of music. Of David the servant of **the LORD**.
36: 5 [36:6] Your love, O **LORD**, reaches to the heavens,
36: 6 [36:7] great deep. O **LORD**, you preserve both man and beast.
37: 3 Trust in **the LORD** and do good; dwell in the land and enjoy safe
37: 4 Delight yourself in **the LORD** and he will give you the desires of
37: 5 Commit your way to **the LORD**; trust in him and he will do this:
37: 7 Be still before **the LORD** and wait patiently for him; do not fret
37: 9 be cut off, but those who hope in **the LORD** will inherit the land.
37: 17 the wicked will be broken, but **the LORD** upholds the righteous.
37: 18 The days of the blameless are known to **the LORD**, and their
37: 20 **The LORD's** enemies will be like the beauty of the fields,
37: 23 If **the LORD** delights in a man's way, he makes his steps firm;
37: 24 he will not fall, for **the LORD** upholds him with his hand.
37: 28 For **the LORD** loves the just and will not forsake his faithful
37: 33 **the LORD** will not leave them in their power or let them be
37: 34 Wait for **the LORD** and keep his way. He will exalt you to
37: 39 The salvation of the righteous comes from **the LORD**; he is their
37: 40 **The LORD** helps them and delivers them; he delivers them from
38: 1 [38:2] O **LORD**, do not rebuke me in your anger or discipline
38: 15 [38:16] I wait for you, O **LORD**; you will answer, O Lord my
38: 21 [38:22] O **LORD**, do not forsake me; be not far from me, O my
39: 4 [39:5] "Show me, O **LORD**, my life's end and the number of
39: 12 [39:13] "Hear my prayer, O **LORD**, listen to my cry for help;
40: 1 [40:2] I waited patiently for **the LORD**; he turned to me
40: 3 [40:4] Many will see and fear and put their trust in **the LORD**.
40: 4 [40:5] Blessed is the man who makes **the LORD** his trust, who
40: 5 [40:6] Many, O **LORD** my God, are the wonders you have done.
40: 9 [40:10] I do not seal my lips, as you know, O **LORD**.
40: 11 [40:12] Do not withhold your mercy from me, O **LORD**;
40: 13 [40:14] Be pleased, O **LORD**, to save me; O LORD,
40: 13 [40:14] to save me; O **LORD**, come quickly to help me.

Ps 40:16 [40:17] your salvation always say, "**The LORD** be exalted!"
41: 1 [41:2] for the weak; **the LORD** delivers him in times of trouble.
41: 2 [41:3] **The LORD** will protect him and preserve his life; he will
41: 3 [41:4] **The LORD** will sustain him on his sickbed and restore
41: 4 [41:5] I said, "O **LORD**, have mercy on me; heal me, for I have
41:10 [41:11] you, O **LORD**, have mercy on me; raise me up, that I
41:13 [41:14] Praise be to **the LORD**, the God of Israel,
42: 8 [42:9] By day **the LORD** directs his love, at night his song is
46: 7 [46:8] **The LORD** Almighty is with us; the God of Jacob is our
46: 8 [46:9] Come and see the works of **the LORD**, the desolations he
46:11 [46:12] **The LORD** Almighty is with us; the God of Jacob is our
47: 2 [47:3] How awesome is **the LORD** Most High, the great King
47: 5 [47:6] shouts of joy, **the LORD** amid the sounding of trumpets.
48: 1 [48:2] Great is **the LORD**, and most worthy of praise, in the city
48: 8 [48:9] so have we seen in the city of **the LORD** Almighty,
50: 1 God, **the LORD**, speaks and summons the earth from the rising
54: 6 [54:8] to you; I will praise your name, O **LORD**, for it is good.
55:16 [55:17] But I call to God, and **the LORD** saves me.
55:22 [55:23] Cast your cares on **the LORD** and he will sustain you;
56:10 [56:11] In God, whose word I praise, in **the LORD**, whose word
58: 6 [58:7] O God; tear out, O **LORD**, the fangs of the lions!
59: 3 [59:4] against me for no offense or sin of mine, O **LORD**.
59: 5 [59:6] O **LORD** God Almighty, the God of Israel, rouse yourself
59: 8 [59:9] you, O **LORD**, laugh at them; you scoff at all those
64:10 [64:11] Let the righteous rejoice in **the LORD** and take refuge
68:16 [68:17] to reign, where **the LORD** *himself* will dwell forever?
68:20 [68:21] from **the** Sovereign **LORD** comes escape from death.
68:26 [68:27] praise **the LORD** in the assembly of Israel.
69: 6 [69:7] because of me, O Lord, **the LORD** Almighty;
69:13 [69:14] I pray to you, O **LORD**, in the time of your favor;
69:16 [69:17] Answer me, O **LORD**, out of the goodness of your love;
69:31 [69:32] This will please **the LORD** more than an ox, more than
69:33 [69:34] **The LORD** hears the needy and does not despise his
70: 1 [70:2] O God, to save me; O **LORD**, come quickly to help me.
70: 5 [70:6] are my help and my deliverer; O **LORD**, do not delay.
71: 1 In you, O **LORD**, I have taken refuge; let me never be put to
71: 5 For you have been my hope, O Sovereign **LORD**, my confidence
71:16 I will come and proclaim your mighty acts, O Sovereign **LORD**;
72:18 Praise be to **the LORD** God, the God of Israel, who alone does
73:28 I have made **the** Sovereign **LORD** my refuge; I will tell of all
74:18 O **LORD**, how foolish people have reviled your name.
75: 8 [75:9] In the hand of **the LORD** is a cup full of foaming wine
76:11 [76:12] Make vows to **the LORD** your God and fulfill them;
78: 4 will tell the next generation the praiseworthy deeds of **the LORD**,
78:21 When **the LORD** heard them, he was very angry; his fire broke
79: 5 How long, O **LORD**? Will you be angry forever? How long will
80: 4 [80:5] O **LORD** God Almighty, how long will your anger
80:19 [80:20] Restore us, O **LORD** God Almighty; make your face
81:10 [81:11] I am **the LORD** your God, who brought you up out of
81:15 [81:16] Those who hate **the LORD** would cringe before him,
83:16 [83:17] with shame so that men will seek your name, O **LORD**.
83:18 [83:19] Let them know that you, whose name is **the LORD**—
84: 1 [84:2] How lovely is your dwelling place, O **LORD** Almighty!
84: 2 [84:3] My soul yearns, even faints, for the courts of **the LORD**;
84: 3 [84:4] your altar, O **LORD** Almighty, my King and my God.
84: 8 [84:9] Hear my prayer, O **LORD** God Almighty; listen to me,
84:11 [84:12] For **the LORD** God is a sun and shield; the LORD
84:11 [84:12] is a sun and shield; **the LORD** bestows favor and honor;
84:12 [84:13] O **LORD** Almighty, blessed is the man who trusts in
85: 1 [85:2] You showed favor to your land, O **LORD**; you restored
85: 7 [85:8] unfailing love, O **LORD**, and grant us your salvation.
85: 8 [85:9] I will listen to what God **the LORD** will say; he promises
85:12 [85:13] **The LORD** will indeed give what is good, and our land
86: 1 Hear, O **LORD**, and answer me, for I am poor and needy.
86: 6 Hear my prayer, O **LORD**; listen to my cry for mercy.
86:11 Teach me your way, O **LORD**, and I will walk in your truth;
86:17 to shame, for you, O **LORD**, have helped me and comforted me.
87: 2 **the LORD** loves the gates of Zion more than all the dwellings of
87: 6 **The LORD** will write in the register of the peoples: "This one
88: 1 [88:2] O **LORD**, the God who saves me, day and night I cry out
88: 9 [88:10] I call to you, O **LORD**, every day; I spread out my
88:13 [88:14] I cry to you for help, O **LORD**; in the morning my
88:14 [88:15] Why, O **LORD**, do you reject me and hide your face
89: 1 [89:2] I will sing of **the LORD's** great love forever; with my
89: 5 [89:6] O **LORD**, your faithfulness too, in the assembly of the
89: 6 [89:7] For who in the skies above can compare with **the LORD**?
89: 6 [89:7] Who is like **the LORD** among the heavenly beings?
89: 8 [89:9] O **LORD** God Almighty, who is like you? You are
89:15 [89:16] who walk in the light of your presence, O **LORD**.
89:18 [89:19] Indeed, our shield belongs to **the LORD**, our king to the
89:46 [89:47] How long, O **LORD**? Will you hide yourself forever?
89:51 [89:52] taunts with which your enemies have mocked, O **LORD**,
89:52 [89:53] Praise be to **the LORD** forever! Amen and Amen.
90:13 Relent, O **LORD**! How long will it be? Have compassion on your
91: 2 I will say of **the LORD**, "He is my refuge and my fortress,
91: 9 Most High your dwelling—even **the LORD**, who is my refuge—
92: 1 [92:2] It is good to praise **the LORD** and make music to your
92: 4 [92:5] For you make me glad by your deeds, O **LORD**; I sing
92: 5 [92:6] How great are your works, O **LORD**, how profound your
92: 8 [92:9] But you, O **LORD**, are exalted forever.
92: 9 [92:10] For surely your enemies, O **LORD**, surely your enemies
92:13 [92:14] planted in the house of **the LORD**, they will flourish in
92:15 [92:16] proclaiming, "**The LORD** is upright; he is my Rock,
93: 1 **The LORD** reigns, he is robed in majesty; the LORD is robed in
93: 1 **the LORD** is robed in majesty and is armed with strength.
93: 3 The seas have lifted up, O **LORD**, the seas have lifted up their
93: 4 than the breakers of the sea—**the LORD** on high is mighty.
93: 5 holiness adorns your house for endless days, O **LORD**.
94: 1 O **LORD**, the God who avenges, O God who avenges,
94: 3 How long will the wicked, O **LORD**, how long will the wicked
94: 5 They crush your people, O **LORD**; they oppress your inheritance.
94:11 **The LORD** knows the thoughts of man; he knows that they are
94:14 For **the LORD** will not reject his people; he will never forsake
94:17 Unless **the LORD** had given me help, I would soon have dwelt in
94:18 "My foot is slipping," your love, O **LORD**, supported me.
94:22 **the LORD** has become my fortress, and my God the rock in
94:23 them for their wickedness; **the LORD** our God will destroy them.
95: 1 Come, let us sing for joy to **the LORD**; let us shout aloud to the
95: 3 For **the LORD** is the great God, the great King above all gods.
95: 6 bow down in worship, let us kneel before **the LORD** our Maker;
96: 1 Sing to **the LORD** a new song; sing to the LORD, all the earth.
96: 1 Sing to the LORD a new song; sing to **the LORD**, all the earth.
96: 2 Sing to **the LORD**, praise his name; proclaim his salvation day
96: 4 For great is **the LORD** and most worthy of praise; he is to be
96: 5 gods of the nations are idols, but **the LORD** made the heavens.
96: 7 Ascribe to **the LORD**, O families of nations, ascribe to the
96: 7 O families of nations, ascribe to **the LORD** glory and strength.
96: 8 Ascribe to **the LORD** the glory due his name; bring an offering
96: 9 Worship **the LORD** in the splendor of his holiness;
96:10 Say among the nations, "**The LORD** reigns." The world is firmly
96:13 they will sing before **the LORD**, for he comes, he comes to judge
97: 1 **The LORD** reigns, let the earth be glad; let the distant shores
97: 5 The mountains melt like wax before **the LORD**, before the Lord
97: 8 villages of Judah are glad because of your judgments, O **LORD**.
97: 9 For you, O **LORD**, are the Most High over all the earth;
97:10 Let those who love **the LORD** hate evil, for he guards the lives of
97:12 Rejoice in **the LORD**, you who are righteous, and praise his holy
98: 1 Sing to **the LORD** a new song, for he has done marvelous things;
98: 2 **The LORD** has made his salvation known and revealed his
98: 4 Shout for joy to **the LORD**, all the earth, burst into jubilant song
98: 5 make music to **the LORD** with the harp, with the harp
98: 6 of the ram's horn—shout for joy before **the LORD**, the King.
98: 9 let them sing before **the LORD**, for he comes to judge the earth.
99: 1 **The LORD** reigns, let the nations tremble; he sits enthroned
99: 2 Great is **the LORD** in Zion; he is exalted over all the nations.
99: 5 Exalt **the LORD** our God and worship at his footstool; he is holy.
99: 6 on his name; they called on **the LORD** and he answered them.
99: 8 O **LORD** our God, you answered them; you were to Israel a
99: 9 Exalt **the LORD** our God and worship at his holy mountain,
99: 9 and worship at his holy mountain, for **the LORD** our God is holy.
100: 1 Shout for joy to **the LORD**, all the earth.
100: 2 Worship **the LORD** with gladness; come before him with joyful
100: 3 Know that **the LORD** is God. It is he who made us, and we are
100: 5 For **the LORD** is good and his love endures forever; his
101: 1 sing of your love and justice; to you, O **LORD**, I will sing praise.
101: 8 I will cut off every evildoer from the city of **the LORD**.
102: T [102:1] he is faint and pours out his lament before **the LORD**.
102: 1 [102:2] Hear my prayer, O **LORD**; let my cry for help come to
102:12 [102:13] you, O **LORD**, sit enthroned forever; your renown
102:15 [102:16] The nations will fear the name of **the LORD**, all the
102:16 [102:17] For **the LORD** will rebuild Zion and appear in his
102:19 [102:20] "**The LORD** looked down from his sanctuary on high,
102:21 [102:22] So the name of **the LORD** will be declared in Zion
102:22 [102:23] and the kingdoms assemble to worship **the LORD**.
103: 1 Praise **the LORD**, O my soul; all my inmost being, praise his
103: 2 Praise **the LORD**, O my soul, and forget not all his benefits—
103: 6 **The LORD** works righteousness and justice for all the oppressed.
103: 8 **The LORD** is compassionate and gracious, slow to anger,
103:13 so **the LORD** has compassion on those who fear him;
103:17 from everlasting to everlasting **the LORD's** love is with those
103:19 **The LORD** has established his throne in heaven, and his
103:20 Praise **the LORD**, you his angels, you mighty ones who do his
103:21 Praise **the LORD**, all his heavenly hosts, you his servants who do
103:22 Praise **the LORD**, all his works everywhere in his dominion.
103:22 works everywhere in his dominion. Praise **the LORD**, O my soul.
104: 1 Praise **the LORD**, O my soul. O LORD my God, you are very
104: 1 O **LORD** my God, you are very great; you are clothed with
104:16 The trees of **the LORD** are well watered, the cedars of Lebanon

[F] Hitpael (hitpoel, hitpoal, hitpolel, hitpolal, hitpalel, hitpalal, hitpalpel, hitpalpal, hotpael, hotpaal) [G] Hiphil (hiphtil) [H] Hophal [I] Hishtaphel

Ps 104:24 How many are your works, O **LORD**! In wisdom you made them
104:31 May the glory of **the LORD** endure forever; may the LORD
104:31 LORD endure forever; may **the LORD** rejoice in his works—
104:33 I will sing to **the LORD** all my life; I will sing praise to my God
104:34 May my meditation be pleasing to him, as I rejoice in **the LORD**.
104:35 be no more. Praise **the LORD**, O my soul. Praise the LORD.
105: 1 Give thanks to **the LORD**, call on his name; make known among
105: 3 holy name; let the hearts of those who seek **the LORD** rejoice.
105: 4 Look to **the LORD** and his strength; seek his face always.
105: 7 He is **the LORD** our God; his judgments are in all the earth.
105:19 came to pass, till the word of **the LORD** proved him true.
106: 1 Give thanks to **the LORD**, for he is good; his love endures
106: 2 Who can proclaim the mighty acts of **the LORD** or fully declare
106: 4 Remember me, O **LORD**, when you show favor to your people,
106:16 of Moses and of Aaron, who was consecrated to **the LORD**.
106:25 They grumbled in their tents and did not obey **the LORD**.
106:34 They did not destroy the peoples as **the LORD** had commanded
106:40 Therefore **the LORD** was angry with his people and abhorred his
106:47 Save us, O **LORD** our God, and gather us from the nations,
106:48 Praise be to **the LORD**, the God of Israel, from everlasting to
107: 1 Give thanks to **the LORD**, for he is good; his love endures
107: 2 Let the redeemed of **the LORD** say this—those he redeemed
107: 6 they cried out to **the LORD** in their trouble, and he delivered
107: 8 Let them give thanks to **the LORD** for his unfailing love
107:13 they cried to **the LORD** in their trouble, and he saved them from
107:15 Let them give thanks to **the LORD** for his unfailing love
107:19 they cried to **the LORD** in their trouble, and he saved them from
107:21 Let them give thanks to **the LORD** for his unfailing love
107:24 They saw the works of **the LORD**, his wonderful deeds in the
107:28 they cried out to **the LORD** in their trouble, and he brought them
107:31 Let them give thanks to **the LORD** for his unfailing love
107:43 him heed these things and consider the great love of **the LORD**.
108: 3 [108:4] I will praise you, O **LORD**, among the nations; I will
109:14 May the iniquity of his fathers be remembered before **the LORD**;
109:15 May their sins always remain before **the LORD**, that he may cut
109:20 May this be **the LORD's** [+907+4946] payment to my accusers,
109:21 you, O Sovereign **LORD**, deal well with me for your name's
109:26 Help me, O **LORD** my God; save me in accordance with your
109:27 them know that it is your hand, that you, O **LORD**, have done it.
109:30 With my mouth I will greatly extol **the LORD**; in the great
110: 1 **The LORD** says to my Lord: "Sit at my right hand until I make
110: 2 **The LORD** will extend your mighty scepter from Zion; you will
110: 4 **The LORD** has sworn and will not change his mind: "You are a
111: 1 I will extol **the LORD** with all my heart in the council of the
111: 2 Great are the works of **the LORD**; they are pondered by all who
111: 4 to be remembered; **the LORD** is gracious and compassionate.
111:10 The fear of **the LORD** is the beginning of wisdom; all who
112: 1 Blessed is the man who fears **the LORD**, who finds great delight
112: 7 no fear of bad news; his heart is steadfast, trusting in **the LORD**.
113: 1 Praise, O servants of **the LORD**, praise the name of the LORD.
113: 1 O servants of the LORD, praise the name of **the LORD**.
113: 2 Let the name of **the LORD** be praised, both now
113: 3 to the place where it sets, the name of **the LORD** is to be praised.
113: 4 **The LORD** is exalted over all the nations, his glory above the
113: 5 Who is like **the LORD** our God, the One who sits enthroned on
115: 1 Not to us, O **LORD**, not to us but to your name be the glory,
115: 9 O house of Israel, trust in **the LORD**—he is their help and shield.
115:10 O house of Aaron, trust in **the LORD**—he is their help
115:11 You who fear **him**[s], trust in the LORD—he is their help
115:11 You who fear him, trust in **the LORD**—he is their help
115:12 **The LORD** remembers us and will bless us: He will bless the
115:13 he will bless those who fear **the LORD**—small and great alike.
115:14 May **the LORD** make you increase, both you and your children.
115:15 May you be blessed by **the LORD**, the Maker of heaven
115:16 The highest heavens belong to **the LORD**, but the earth he has
116: 1 I love **the LORD**, for he heard my voice; he heard my cry for
116: 4 Then I called on the name of **the LORD**: "O LORD, save me!"
116: 4 Then I called on the name of the LORD: "O **LORD**, save me!"
116: 5 **The LORD** is gracious and righteous; our God is full of
116: 6 **The LORD** protects the simplehearted; when I was in great need,
116: 7 rest once more, O my soul, for **the LORD** has been good to you.
116: 9 that I may walk before **the LORD** in the land of the living.
116:12 How can I repay **the LORD** for all his goodness to me?
116:13 lift up the cup of salvation and call on the name of **the LORD**.
116:14 I will fulfill my vows to **the LORD** in the presence of all his
116:15 Precious in the sight of **the LORD** is the death of his saints.
116:16 O **LORD**, truly I am your servant; I am your servant, the son of
116:17 a thank offering to you and call on the name of **the LORD**.
116:18 I will fulfill my vows to **the LORD** in the presence of all his
116:19 in the courts of the house of **the LORD**—in your midst,
117: 1 Praise **the LORD**, all you nations; extol him, all you peoples.
117: 2 toward us, and the faithfulness of **the LORD** endures forever.
118: 1 Give thanks to **the LORD**, for he is good; his love endures
118: 4 Let those who fear **the LORD** say: "His love endures forever."
118: 6 **The LORD** is with me; I will not be afraid. What can man do to
118: 7 **The LORD** is with me; he is my helper. I will look in triumph on
118: 8 It is better to take refuge in **the LORD** than to trust in man.
118: 9 It is better to take refuge in **the LORD** than to trust in princes.
118:10 surrounded me, but in the name of **the LORD** I cut them off.
118:11 me on every side, but in the name of **the LORD** I cut them off.
118:12 as burning thorns; in the name of **the LORD** I cut them off.
118:13 I was pushed back and about to fall, but **the LORD** helped me.
118:15 the righteous: "**The LORD's** right hand has done mighty things!
118:16 **The LORD's** right hand is lifted high; the LORD's right hand
118:16 is lifted high; **the LORD's** right hand has done mighty things!"
118:20 This is the gate of **the LORD** through which the righteous may
118:23 **the LORD** has done this, and it is marvelous in our eyes.
118:24 This is the day **the LORD** has made; let us rejoice and be glad in
118:25 O **LORD**, save us; O LORD, grant us success.
118:25 O LORD, save us; O **LORD**, grant us success.
118:26 Blessed is he who comes in the name of **the LORD**.
118:26 name of the LORD. From the house of **the LORD** we bless you.
118:27 **The LORD** is God, and he has made his light shine upon us.
118:29 Give thanks to **the LORD**, for he is good; his love endures
119: 1 are blameless, who walk according to the law of **the LORD**.
119:12 Praise be to you, O **LORD**; teach me your decrees.
119:31 I hold fast to your statutes, O **LORD**; do not let me be put to
119:33 Teach me, O **LORD**, to follow your decrees; then I will keep
119:41 May your unfailing love come to me, O **LORD**, your salvation
119:52 your ancient laws, O **LORD**, and I find comfort in them.
119:55 night I remember your name, O **LORD**, and I will keep your law.
119:57 You are my portion, O **LORD**; I have promised to obey your
119:64 The earth is filled with your love, O **LORD**; teach me your
119:65 Do good to your servant according to your word, O **LORD**.
119:75 I know, O **LORD**, that your laws are righteous, and in
119:89 Your word, O **LORD**, is eternal; it stands firm in the heavens.
119:107 preserve my life, O **LORD**, according to your word.
119:108 Accept, O **LORD**, the willing praise of my mouth, and teach me
119:126 It is time for you to act, O **LORD**; your law is being broken.
119:137 Righteous are you, O **LORD**, and your laws are right.
119:145 all my heart; answer me, O **LORD**, and I will obey your decrees.
119:149 your love; preserve my life, O **LORD**, according to your laws.
119:151 Yet you are near, O **LORD**, and all your commands are true.
119:156 Your compassion is great, O **LORD**; preserve my life according
119:159 preserve my life, O **LORD**, according to your love.
119:166 I wait for your salvation, O **LORD**, and I follow your commands.
119:169 May my cry come before you, O **LORD**; give me understanding
119:174 I long for your salvation, O **LORD**, and your law is my delight.
120: 1 I call on **the LORD** in my distress, and he answers me.
120: 2 Save me, O **LORD**, from lying lips and from deceitful tongues.
121: 2 My help comes from **the LORD**, the Maker of heaven and earth.
121: 5 **The LORD** watches over you—the LORD is your shade at your
121: 5 watches over you—**the LORD** is your shade at your right hand;
121: 7 **The LORD** will keep you from all harm—he will watch over
121: 8 **the LORD** will watch over your coming and going both now
122: 1 those who said to me, "Let us go to the house of **the LORD**."
122: 4 to praise the name of **the LORD** according to the statute given to
122: 9 For the sake of the house of **the LORD** our God, I will seek your
123: 2 so our eyes look to **the LORD** our God, till he shows us his
123: 3 Have mercy on us, O **LORD**, have mercy on us, for we have
124: 1 If **the LORD** had not been on our side—let Israel say—
124: 2 if **the LORD** had not been on our side when men attacked us,
124: 6 Praise be to **the LORD**, who has not let us be torn by their teeth.
124: 8 Our help is in the name of **the LORD**, the Maker of heaven
125: 1 Those who trust in **the LORD** are like Mount Zion, which cannot
125: 2 so **the LORD** surrounds his people both now and forevermore.
125: 4 Do good, O **LORD**, to those who are good, to those who are
125: 5 those who turn to crooked ways **the LORD** will banish with the
126: 1 When **the LORD** brought back the captives to Zion, we were like
126: 2 among the nations, "**The LORD** has done great things for them."
126: 3 **The LORD** has done great things for us, and we are filled with
126: 4 Restore our fortunes, O **LORD**, like streams in the Negev.
127: 1 Unless **the LORD** builds the house, its builders labor in vain.
127: 1 Unless **the LORD** watches over the city, the watchmen stand
127: 3 Sons are a heritage from **the LORD**, children a reward from him.
128: 1 Blessed are all who fear **the LORD**, who walk in his ways.
128: 4 Thus is the man blessed who fears **the LORD**.
128: 5 May **the LORD** bless you from Zion all the days of your life;
129: 4 **the LORD** is righteous; he has cut me free from the cords of the
129: 8 who pass by not say, "The blessing of **the LORD** be upon you;
129: 8 LORD be upon you; we bless you in the name of **the LORD**."
130: 1 Out of the depths I cry to you, O **LORD**;
130: 5 I wait for **the LORD**, my soul waits, and in his word I put my
130: 7 O Israel, put your hope in **the LORD**, for with the LORD is
130: 7 for with **the LORD** is unfailing love and with him is full
131: 1 My heart is not proud, O **LORD**, my eyes are not haughty;
131: 3 O Israel, put your hope in **the LORD** both now and forevermore.
132: 1 O **LORD**, remember David and all the hardships he endured.

Ps 132: 2 He swore an oath to **the LORD** and made a vow to the Mighty
132: 5 till I find a place for **the LORD**, a dwelling for the Mighty One of
132: 8 arise, O **LORD**, and come to your resting place, you and the ark
132: 11 **The LORD** swore an oath to David, a sure oath that he will not
132: 13 For **the LORD** has chosen Zion, he has desired it for his
133: 3 For there **the LORD** bestows his blessing, even life forevermore.
134: 1 Praise **the LORD**, all you servants of the LORD who minister
134: 1 all you servants of **the LORD** who minister by night in the house
134: 1 of the LORD who minister by night in the house of **the LORD**.
134: 2 Lift up your hands in the sanctuary and praise **the LORD**.
134: 3 May **the LORD**, the Maker of heaven and earth, bless you from
135: 1 Praise the name of **the LORD**; praise him, you servants of the
135: 1 the name of the LORD; praise him, you servants of **the LORD**,
135: 2 you who minister in the house of **the LORD**, in the courts of the
135: 3 Praise the LORD, for **the LORD** is good; sing praise to his
135: 5 I know that **the LORD** is great, that our Lord is greater than all
135: 6 **The LORD** does whatever pleases him, in the heavens and on the
135: 13 Your name, O **LORD**, endures forever, your renown, O LORD,
135: 13 Your name, O LORD, endures forever, your renown, O **LORD**,
135: 14 For **the LORD** will vindicate his people and have compassion on
135: 19 O house of Israel, praise **the LORD**; O house of Aaron, praise the
135: 19 praise the LORD; O house of Aaron, praise **the LORD**;
135: 20 O house of Levi, praise **the LORD**; you who fear him, praise the
135: 20 praise the LORD; you who fear **him**[s], praise the LORD.
135: 20 praise the LORD; you who fear him, praise **the LORD**.
135: 21 Praise be to **the LORD** from Zion, to him who dwells in
136: 1 Give thanks to **the LORD**, for he is good. *His love*
137: 4 How can we sing the songs of **the LORD** while in a foreign land?
137: 7 Remember, O **LORD**, what the Edomites did on the day
138: 4 May all the kings of the earth praise you, O **LORD**, when they
138: 5 May they sing of the ways of **the LORD**, for the glory of the
138: 5 of the ways of the LORD, for the glory of **the LORD** is great.
138: 6 Though **the LORD** is on high, he looks upon the lowly,
138: 8 **The LORD** will fulfill ⌊his purpose⌋ for me; your love,
138: 8 your love, O **LORD**, endures forever—do not abandon the works
139: 1 O **LORD**, you have searched me and you know me.
139: 4 a word is on my tongue you know it completely, O **LORD**.
139: 21 Do I not hate those who hate you, O **LORD**, and abhor those who
140: 1 [140:2] Rescue me, O **LORD**, from evil men; protect me from
140: 4 [140:5] Keep me, O **LORD**, from the hands of the wicked;
140: 6 [140:7] O **LORD**, I say to you, "You are my God." Hear,
140: 6 [140:7] "You are my God." Hear, O **LORD**, my cry for mercy.
140: 7 [140:8] O Sovereign **LORD**, my strong deliverer, who shields
140: 8 [140:9] do not grant the wicked their desires, O **LORD**; do not
140: 12 [140:13] I know that **the LORD** secures justice for the poor
141: 1 O **LORD**, I call to you; come quickly to me. Hear my voice when
141: 3 Set a guard over my mouth, O **LORD**; keep watch over the door
141: 8 my eyes are fixed on you, O Sovereign **LORD**; in you I take
142: 1 [142:2] I cry aloud to **the LORD**; I lift up my voice to the
142: 1 [142:2] the LORD; I lift up my voice to **the LORD** for mercy.
142: 5 [142:6] I cry to you, O **LORD**; I say, "You are my refuge,
143: 1 O **LORD**, hear my prayer, listen to my cry for mercy; in your
143: 7 Answer me quickly, O **LORD**; my spirit fails. Do not hide your
143: 9 Rescue me from my enemies, O **LORD**, for I hide myself in you.
143: 11 For your name's sake, O **LORD**, preserve my life; in your
144: 1 Praise be to **the LORD** my Rock, who trains my hands for war,
144: 3 O **LORD**, what is man that you care for him, the son of man that
144: 5 Part your heavens, O **LORD**, and come down; touch the
144: 15 this is true; blessed are the people whose God is **the LORD**.
145: 3 Great is **the LORD** and most worthy of praise; his greatness no
145: 8 **The LORD** is gracious and compassionate, slow to anger
145: 9 **The LORD** is good to all; he has compassion on all he has made.
145: 10 All you have made will praise you, O **LORD**; your saints will
145: 13 **The LORD** [BHS-] is faithful to all his promises and loving
145: 14 **The LORD** upholds all those who fall and lifts up all who are
145: 17 **The LORD** is righteous in all his ways and loving toward all he
145: 18 **The LORD** is near to all who call on him, to all who call on him
145: 20 **The LORD** watches over all who love him, but all the wicked he
145: 21 My mouth will speak in praise of **the LORD**. Let every creature
146: 1 Praise the LORD. Praise **the LORD**, O my soul.
146: 2 I will praise **the LORD** all my life; I will sing praise to my God
146: 5 help is the God of Jacob, whose hope is in **the LORD** his God,
146: 7 and gives food to the hungry. **The LORD** sets prisoners free,
146: 8 **the LORD** gives sight to the blind, the LORD lifts up those who
146: 8 **the LORD** lifts up those who are bowed down, the LORD loves
146: 8 up those who are bowed down, **the LORD** loves the righteous.
146: 9 **The LORD** watches over the alien and sustains the fatherless
146: 10 **The LORD** reigns forever, your God, O Zion, for all generations.
147: 2 **The LORD** builds up Jerusalem; he gathers the exiles of Israel.
147: 6 **The LORD** sustains the humble but casts the wicked to the
147: 7 Sing to **the LORD** with thanksgiving; make music to our God on
147: 11 **the LORD** delights in those who fear him, who put their hope in
147: 12 Extol **the LORD**, O Jerusalem; praise your God, O Zion,
148: 1 Praise **the LORD** from the heavens, praise him in the heights
148: 5 Let them praise the name of **the LORD**, for he commanded
148: 7 Praise **the LORD** from the earth, you great sea creatures
148: 13 Let them praise the name of **the LORD**, for his name alone is
149: 1 Sing to **the LORD** a new song, his praise in the assembly of the
149: 4 For **the LORD** takes delight in his people; he crowns the humble
Pr 1: 7 The fear of **the LORD** is the beginning of knowledge, but fools
1: 29 they hated knowledge and did not choose to fear **the LORD**,
2: 5 you will understand the fear of **the LORD** and find the
2: 6 For **the LORD** gives wisdom, and from his mouth come
3: 5 Trust in **the LORD** with all your heart and lean not on your own
3: 7 Do not be wise in your own eyes; fear **the LORD** and shun evil.
3: 9 Honor **the LORD** with your wealth, with the firstfruits of all your
3: 11 do not despise **the LORD's** discipline and do not resent his
3: 12 because **the LORD** disciplines those he loves, as a father the son
3: 19 By wisdom **the LORD** laid the earth's foundations,
3: 26 for **the LORD** will be your confidence and will keep your foot
3: 32 for **the LORD** detests a perverse man but takes the upright into
3: 33 **The LORD's** curse is on the house of the wicked, but he blesses
5: 21 For a man's ways are in full view of **the LORD**, and he examines
6: 16 There are six things **the LORD** hates, seven that are detestable to
8: 13 To fear **the LORD** is to hate evil; I hate pride and arrogance,
8: 22 "**The LORD** brought me forth as the first of his works, before his
8: 35 whoever finds me finds life and receives favor from **the LORD**.
9: 10 "The fear of **the LORD** is the beginning of wisdom,
10: 3 **The LORD** does not let the righteous go hungry but he thwarts
10: 22 The blessing of **the LORD** brings wealth, and he adds no trouble
10: 27 The fear of **the LORD** adds length to life, but the years of the
10: 29 The way of **the LORD** is a refuge for the righteous, but it is the
11: 1 **The LORD** abhors dishonest scales, but accurate weights are his
11: 20 **The LORD** detests men of perverse heart but he delights in those
12: 2 A good man obtains favor from **the LORD**, but the LORD
12: 22 **The LORD** detests lying lips, but he delights in men who are
14: 2 He whose walk is upright fears **the LORD**, but he whose ways
14: 26 He who fears **the LORD** has a secure fortress, and for his
14: 27 The fear of **the LORD** is a fountain of life, turning a man from
15: 3 The eyes of **the LORD** are everywhere, keeping watch on the
15: 8 **The LORD** detests the sacrifice of the wicked, but the prayer of
15: 9 **The LORD** detests the way of the wicked but he loves those who
15: 11 Death and Destruction lie open before **the LORD**—how much
15: 16 Better a little with the fear of **the LORD** than great wealth with
15: 25 **The LORD** tears down the proud man's house but he keeps the
15: 26 **The LORD** detests the thoughts of the wicked, but those of the
15: 29 **The LORD** is far from the wicked but he hears the prayer of the
15: 33 The fear of **the LORD** teaches a man wisdom, and humility
16: 1 of the heart, but from **the LORD** comes the reply of the tongue.
16: 2 seem innocent to him, but motives are weighed by **the LORD**.
16: 3 Commit to **the LORD** whatever you do, and your plans will
16: 4 **The LORD** works out everything for his own ends—even the
16: 5 **The LORD** detests all the proud of heart. Be sure of this:
16: 6 is atoned for; through the fear of **the LORD** a man avoids evil.
16: 7 When a man's ways are pleasing to **the LORD**, he makes even
16: 9 heart a man plans his course, but **the LORD** determines his steps.
16: 11 Honest scales and balances are from **the LORD**; all the weights
16: 20 instruction prospers, and blessed is he who trusts in **the LORD**.
16: 33 lot is cast into the lap, but its every decision is from **the LORD**.
17: 3 for silver and the furnace for gold, but **the LORD** tests the heart.
17: 15 and condemning the innocent—**the LORD** detests them both.
18: 10 The name of **the LORD** is a strong tower; the righteous run to it
18: 22 a wife finds what is good and receives favor from **the LORD**.
19: 3 own folly ruins his life, yet his heart rages against **the LORD**.
19: 14 are inherited from parents, but a prudent wife is from **the LORD**.
19: 17 He who is kind to the poor lends to **the LORD**, and he will
19: 21 in a man's heart, but it is **the LORD's** purpose that prevails.
19: 23 The fear of **the LORD** leads to life: Then one rests content,
20: 10 and differing measures—**the LORD** detests them both.
20: 12 Ears that hear and eyes that see—**the LORD** has made them both.
20: 22 for this wrong!" Wait for **the LORD**, and he will deliver you.
20: 23 **The LORD** detests differing weights, and dishonest scales do not
20: 24 A man's steps are directed by **the LORD**. How then can anyone
20: 27 The lamp of **the LORD** searches the spirit of a man; it searches
21: 1 The king's heart is in the hand of **the LORD**; he directs it like a
21: 2 a man's ways seem right to him, but **the LORD** weighs the heart.
21: 3 is right and just is more acceptable to **the LORD** than sacrifice.
21: 30 no insight, no plan that can succeed against **the LORD**.
21: 31 ready for the day of battle, but victory rests with **the LORD**.
22: 2 poor have this in common: **The LORD** is the Maker of them all.
22: 4 Humility and the fear of **the LORD** bring wealth and honor
22: 12 The eyes of **the LORD** keep watch over knowledge, but he
22: 14 is a deep pit; he who is under **the LORD's** wrath will fall into it.
22: 19 So that your trust may be in **the LORD**, I teach you today,
22: 23 for **the LORD** will take up their case and will plunder those who
23: 17 envy sinners, but always be zealous for the fear of **the LORD**.
24: 18 or **the LORD** will see and disapprove and turn his wrath away
24: 21 Fear **the LORD** and the king, my son, and do not join with the

Pr 25:22 heap burning coals on his head, and **the LORD** will reward you.
28: 5 but those who seek **the LORD** understand it fully.
28:25 stirs up dissension, but he who trusts in **the LORD** will prosper.
29:13 have this in common: **The LORD** gives sight to the eyes of both.
29:25 prove to be a snare, but whoever trusts in **the LORD** is kept safe.
29:26 with a ruler, but it is from **the LORD** that man gets justice.
30: 9 have too much and disown you and say, 'Who is **the LORD**?'
31:30 is fleeting; but a woman who fears **the LORD** is to be praised.
Isa 1: 2 Hear, O heavens! Listen, O earth! For **the LORD** has spoken:
1: 4 They have forsaken **the LORD**; they have spurned the Holy One
1: 9 Unless **the LORD** Almighty had left us some survivors,
1:10 Hear the word of **the LORD**, you rulers of Sodom; listen to the
1:11 of your sacrifices—what are they to me?" says **the LORD**.
1:18 "Come now, let us reason together," says **the LORD**.
1:20 devoured by the sword." For the mouth of **the LORD** has spoken.
1:24 Therefore the Lord, **the LORD** Almighty, the Mighty One of
1:28 both be broken, and those who forsake **the LORD** will perish.
2: 2 In the last days the mountain of **the LORD's** temple will be
2: 3 and say, "Come, let us go up to the mountain of **the LORD**,
2: 3 will go out from Zion, the word of **the LORD** from Jerusalem.
2: 5 Come, O house of Jacob, let us walk in the light of **the LORD**.
2:10 hide in the ground from dread of **the LORD** and the splendor of
2:11 of men brought low; **the LORD** alone will be exalted in that day.
2:12 **The LORD** Almighty has a day in store for all the proud
2:17 of men humbled; **the LORD** alone will be exalted in that day,
2:19 to holes in the ground from dread of **the LORD** and the splendor
2:21 to the overhanging crags from dread of **the LORD** and the
3: 1 See now, the Lord, **the LORD** Almighty, is about to take from
3: 8 their words and deeds are against **the LORD**, defying his glorious
3:13 **The LORD** takes his place in court; he rises to judge the people.
3:14 **The LORD** enters into judgment against the elders and leaders of
3:15 the faces of the poor?" declares the Lord, **the LORD** Almighty.
3:16 **The LORD** says, "The women of Zion are haughty, walking
3:17 of the women of Zion; **the LORD** will make their scalps bald."
4: 2 In that day the Branch of **the LORD** will be beautiful
4: 5 **the LORD** will create over all of Mount Zion and over those who
5: 7 The vineyard of **the LORD** Almighty is the house of Israel,
5: 9 **The LORD** Almighty has declared in my hearing: "Surely the
5:12 and wine, but they have no regard for the deeds of **the LORD**,
5:16 **the LORD** Almighty will be exalted by his justice, and the holy
5:24 for they have rejected the law of **the LORD** Almighty
5:25 Therefore **the LORD's** anger burns against his people; his hand
6: 3 "Holy, holy, holy is **the LORD** Almighty; the whole earth is full
6: 5 and my eyes have seen the King, **the LORD** Almighty."
6:12 until **the LORD** has sent everyone far away and the land is
7: 3 **the LORD** said to Isaiah, "Go out, you and your son
7: 7 Yet this is what **the** Sovereign **LORD** says: " 'It will not take
7:10 Again **the LORD** spoke to Ahaz,
7:11 "Ask **the LORD** your God for a sign, whether in the deepest
7:12 Ahaz said, "I will not ask; I will not put **the LORD** to the test."
7:17 **The LORD** will bring on you and on your people and on the
7:18 In that day **the LORD** will whistle for flies from the distant
8: 1 **The LORD** said to me, "Take a large scroll and write on it with
8: 3 And **the LORD** said to me, "Name him Maher-Shalal-Hash-Baz.
8: 5 **The LORD** spoke to me again:
8:11 **The LORD** spoke to me with his strong hand upon me, warning
8:13 **The LORD** Almighty is the one you are to regard as holy,
8:17 I will wait for **the LORD**, who is hiding his face from the house
8:18 Here am I, and the children **the LORD** has given me. We are
8:18 We are signs and symbols in Israel from **the LORD** Almighty,
9: 7 [9:6] The zeal of **the LORD** Almighty will accomplish this.
9:11 [9:10] **the LORD** has strengthened Rezin's foes against them
9:13 [9:12] struck them, nor have they sought **the LORD** Almighty.
9:14 [9:13] So **the LORD** will cut off from Israel both head and tail,
9:19 [9:18] By the wrath of **the LORD** Almighty the land will be
10:16 Therefore, the Lord, **the LORD** Almighty, will send a wasting
10:20 on him who struck them down but will truly rely on **the LORD**,
10:23 The Lord, **the LORD** Almighty, will carry out the destruction
10:24 Therefore, this is what the Lord, **the LORD** Almighty, says:
10:26 **The LORD** Almighty will lash them with a whip, as when he
10:33 See, the Lord, **the LORD** Almighty, will lop off the boughs with
11: 2 The Spirit of **the LORD** will rest on him—the Spirit of wisdom
11: 2 of power, the Spirit of knowledge and of the fear of **the LORD**—
11: 3 he will delight in the fear of **the LORD**. He will not judge by
11: 9 for the earth will be full of the knowledge of **the LORD** as the
11:15 **The LORD** will dry up the gulf of the Egyptian sea; with a
12: 1 In that day you will say: "I will praise you, O **LORD**.
12: 2 The LORD, **the LORD**, is my strength and my song; he has
12: 4 "Give thanks to **the LORD**, call on his name; make known
12: 5 Sing to **the LORD**, for he has done glorious things; let this be
13: 4 **The LORD** Almighty is mustering an army for war.
13: 5 **the LORD** and the weapons of his wrath—to destroy the whole
13: 6 Wail, for the day of **the LORD** is near; it will come like
13: 9 See, the day of **the LORD** is coming—a cruel day, with wrath
13:13 the earth will shake from its place at the wrath of **the LORD**
14: 1 **The LORD** will have compassion on Jacob; once again he will
14: 2 nations as menservants and maidservants in **the LORD's** land.
14: 3 On the day **the LORD** gives you relief from suffering and turmoil
14: 5 **The LORD** has broken the rod of the wicked, the scepter of the
14:22 "I will rise up against them," declares **the LORD** Almighty.
14:22 her offspring and descendants," declares **the LORD**.
14:23 with the broom of destruction," declares **the LORD** Almighty.
14:24 **The LORD** Almighty has sworn, "Surely, as I have planned,
14:27 For **the LORD** Almighty has purposed, and who can thwart him?
14:32 "**The LORD** has established Zion, and in her his afflicted people
16:13 This is the word **the LORD** has already spoken concerning
16:14 now **the LORD** says: "Within three years, as a servant bound by
17: 3 be like the glory of the Israelites," declares **the LORD** Almighty.
17: 6 on the fruitful boughs," declares **the LORD**, the God of Israel.
18: 4 This is what **the LORD** says to me: "I will remain quiet and will
18: 7 At that time gifts will be brought to **the LORD** Almighty from a
18: 7 to Mount Zion, the place of the Name of **the LORD** Almighty.
19: 1 **the LORD** rides on a swift cloud and is coming to Egypt.
19: 4 will rule over them," declares the Lord, **the LORD** Almighty.
19:12 make known what **the LORD** Almighty has planned against
19:14 **The LORD** has poured into them a spirit of dizziness; they make
19:16 They will shudder with fear at the uplifted hand that **the LORD**
19:17 because of what **the LORD** Almighty is planning against them.
19:18 of Canaan and swear allegiance to **the LORD** Almighty.
19:19 In that day there will be an altar to **the LORD** in the heart of
19:19 in the heart of Egypt, and a monument to **the LORD** at its border.
19:20 and witness to **the LORD** Almighty in the land of Egypt.
19:20 When they cry out to **the LORD** because of their oppressors,
19:21 So **the LORD** will make himself known to the Egyptians,
19:21 the Egyptians, and in that day they will acknowledge **the LORD**.
19:21 they will make vows to **the LORD** and keep them.
19:22 **The LORD** will strike Egypt with a plague; he will strike them
19:22 They will turn to **the LORD**, and he will respond to their pleas
19:25 **The LORD** Almighty will bless them, saying, "Blessed be Egypt
20: 2 at that time **the LORD** spoke through Isaiah son of Amoz.
20: 3 **the LORD** said, "Just as my servant Isaiah has gone stripped
21:10 I tell you what I have heard from **the LORD** Almighty,
21:17 will be few." **The LORD**, the God of Israel, has spoken.
22: 5 The Lord, **the LORD** Almighty, has a day of tumult
22:12 The Lord, **the LORD** Almighty, called you on that day to weep
22:14 **The LORD** Almighty has revealed this in my hearing: "Till your
22:14 sin will not be atoned for," says the Lord, **the LORD** Almighty.
22:15 This is what the Lord, **the LORD** Almighty, says: "Go, say to
22:17 **the LORD** is about to take firm hold of you and hurl you away,
22:25 "In that day," declares **the LORD** Almighty, "the peg driven into
22:25 the load hanging on it will be cut down." **The LORD** has spoken.
23: 9 **The LORD** Almighty planned it, to bring low the pride of all
23:11 **The LORD** has stretched out his hand over the sea and made its
23:17 At the end of seventy years, **the LORD** will deal with Tyre.
23:18 Yet her profit and her earnings will be set apart for **the LORD**;
23:18 Her profits will go to those who live before **the LORD**,
24: 1 **the LORD** is going to lay waste the earth and devastate it;
24: 3 and totally plundered. **The LORD** has spoken this word.
24:14 shout for joy; from the west they acclaim **the LORD's** majesty.
24:15 Therefore in the east give glory to **the LORD**; exalt the name of
24:15 exalt the name of **the LORD**, the God of Israel, in the islands of
24:21 In that day **the LORD** will punish the powers in the heavens
24:23 for **the LORD** Almighty will reign on Mount Zion and in
25: 1 O **LORD**, you are my God; I will exalt you and praise your name,
25: 6 On this mountain **the LORD** Almighty will prepare a feast of rich
25: 8 **The** Sovereign **LORD** will wipe away the tears from all faces;
25: 8 disgrace of his people from all the earth. **The LORD** has spoken.
25: 9 This is **the LORD**, we trusted in him; let us rejoice and be glad in
25:10 The hand of **the LORD** will rest on this mountain; but Moab will
26: 4 Trust in **the LORD** forever, for the LORD, the LORD,
26: 4 LORD forever, for the LORD, **the LORD**, is the Rock eternal.
26: 8 Yes, **LORD**, walking in the way of your laws, we wait for you;
26:10 they go on doing evil and regard not the majesty of **the LORD**.
26:11 O **LORD**, your hand is lifted high, but they do not see it.
26:12 **LORD**, you establish peace for us; all that we have accomplished
26:13 O **LORD**, our God, other lords besides you have ruled over us,
26:15 You have enlarged the nation, O **LORD**; you have enlarged the
26:16 **LORD**, they came to you in their distress; when you disciplined
26:17 and cries out in her pain, so were we in your presence, O **LORD**.
26:21 **the LORD** is coming out of his dwelling to punish the people of
27: 1 **the LORD** will punish with his sword, his fierce, great
27: 3 I, **the LORD**, watch over it; I water it continually. I guard it day
27:12 In that day **the LORD** will thresh from the flowing Euphrates to
27:13 and worship **the LORD** on the holy mountain in Jerusalem.
28: 5 In that day **the LORD** Almighty will be a glorious crown,
28:13 So then, the word of **the LORD** to them will become: Do
28:14 Therefore hear the word of **the LORD**, you scoffers who rule this
28:16 So this is what **the** Sovereign **LORD** says: "See, I lay a stone in

Isa 28:21 **The LORD** will rise up as he did at Mount Perazim, he will rouse
28:22 the Lord, **the LORD** Almighty, has told me of the destruction
28:29 All this also comes from **the LORD** Almighty, wonderful in
29: 6 **the LORD** Almighty will come with thunder and earthquake
29:10 **The LORD** has brought over you a deep sleep: He has sealed
29:15 those who go to great depths to hide their plans from **the LORD**,
29:19 Once more the humble will rejoice in **the LORD**; the needy will
29:22 Therefore this is what **the LORD**, who redeemed Abraham,
30: 1 "Woe to the obstinate children," declares **the LORD**, "to those
30: 9 children unwilling to listen to **the LORD's** instruction.
30:15 This is what **the** Sovereign **LORD**, the Holy One of Israel,
30:18 Yet **the LORD** longs to be gracious to you; he rises to show you
30:18 For **the LORD** is a God of justice. Blessed are all who wait for
30:26 when **the LORD** binds up the bruises of his people and heals the
30:27 See, the Name of **the LORD** comes from afar, with burning anger
30:29 as when people go up with flutes to the mountain of **the LORD**,
30:30 **The LORD** will cause men to hear his majestic voice and will
30:31 The voice of **the LORD** will shatter Assyria; with his scepter he
30:32 Every stroke **the LORD** lays on them with his punishing rod will
30:33 the breath of **the LORD**, like a stream of burning sulfur,
31: 1 not look to the Holy One of Israel, or seek help from **the LORD**.
31: 3 When **the LORD** stretches out his hand, he who helps will
31: 4 This is what **the LORD** says to me: "As a lion growls, a great
31: 4 so **the LORD** Almighty will come down to do battle on Mount
31: 5 hovering overhead, **the LORD** Almighty will shield Jerusalem;
31: 9 declares **the LORD**, whose fire is in Zion, whose furnace is in
32: 6 practices ungodliness and spreads error concerning **the LORD**;
33: 2 O **LORD**, be gracious to us; we long for you. Be our strength
33: 5 **The LORD** is exalted, for he dwells on high; he will fill Zion
33: 6 and knowledge; the fear of **the LORD** is the key to this treasure.
33:10 "Now will I arise," says **the LORD**. "Now will I be exalted;
33:21 There **the LORD** will be our Mighty One. It will be like a place
33:22 For **the LORD** is our judge, the LORD is our lawgiver,
33:22 is our judge, **the LORD** is our lawgiver, the LORD is our king;
33:22 is our judge, the LORD is our lawgiver, **the LORD** is our king;
34: 2 **The LORD** is angry with all nations; his wrath is upon all their
34: 6 The sword of **the LORD** is bathed in blood, it is covered with
34: 6 For **the LORD** has a sacrifice in Bozrah and a great slaughter in
34: 8 For **the LORD** has a day of vengeance, a year of retribution,
34:16 Look in the scroll of **the LORD** and read: None of these will be
35: 2 they will see the glory of **the LORD**, the splendor of our God.
35:10 the ransomed of **the LORD** will return. They will enter Zion with
36: 7 if you say to me, "We are depending on **the LORD** our God"—
36:10 have I come to attack and destroy this land without **the LORD**?
36:10 **The LORD** himself told me to march against this country
36:15 Do not let Hezekiah persuade you to trust in **the LORD** when he
36:15 in the LORD when he says, '**The LORD** will surely deliver us;
36:18 Hezekiah mislead you when he says, '**The LORD** will deliver us.'
36:20 How then can **the LORD** deliver Jerusalem from my hand?"
37: 1 and put on sackcloth and went into the temple of **the LORD**.
37: 4 It may be that **the LORD** your God will hear the words of the
37: 4 that he will rebuke him for the words **the LORD** your God has
37: 6 said to them, "Tell your master, 'This is what **the LORD** says:
37:14 he went up to the temple of **the LORD** and spread it out before
37:14 to the temple of the LORD and spread it out before **the LORD**.
37:15 And Hezekiah prayed to **the LORD**:
37:16 "O **LORD** Almighty, God of Israel, enthroned between the
37:17 Give ear, O **LORD**, and hear; open your eyes, O LORD,
37:17 O LORD, and hear; open your eyes, O **LORD**, and see;
37:18 "It is true, O **LORD**, that the Assyrian kings have laid waste all
37:20 Now, O **LORD** our God, deliver us from his hand, so that all
37:20 on earth may know that you alone, O **LORD**, are God."
37:21 to Hezekiah: "This is what **the LORD**, the God of Israel, says:
37:22 this is the word **the LORD** has spoken against him: "The Virgin
37:32 The zeal of **the LORD** Almighty will accomplish this.
37:33 "Therefore this is what **the LORD** says concerning the king of
37:34 he will return; he will not enter this city," declares **the LORD**.
37:36 Then the angel of **the LORD** went out and put to death a hundred
38: 1 of Amoz went to him and said, "This is what **the LORD** says:
38: 2 Hezekiah turned his face to the wall and prayed to **the LORD**,
38: 3 "Remember, O **LORD**, how I have walked before you faithfully
38: 4 Then the word of **the LORD** came to Isaiah:
38: 5 "Go and tell Hezekiah, 'This is what **the LORD**, the God of your
38: 7 " 'This is **the LORD's** [+907+4946] sign to you that the LORD
38: 7 " 'This is the LORD's sign to you that **the LORD** will do what
38:20 **The LORD** will save me, and we will sing with stringed
38:20 instruments all the days of our lives in the temple of **the LORD**.
38:22 will be the sign that I will go up to the temple of **the LORD**?"
39: 5 Isaiah said to Hezekiah, "Hear the word of **the LORD** Almighty:
39: 6 be carried off to Babylon. Nothing will be left, says **the LORD**.
39: 8 "The word of **the LORD** you have spoken is good,"
40: 2 that she has received from **the LORD's** hand double for all her
40: 3 "In the desert prepare the way for **the LORD**; make straight in
40: 5 the glory of **the LORD** will be revealed, and all mankind together
40: 5 together will see it. For the mouth of **the LORD** has spoken."
40: 7 the flowers fall, because the breath of **the LORD** blows on them.
40:10 See, **the** Sovereign **LORD** comes with power, and his arm rules
40:13 Who has understood the mind of **the LORD**, or instructed him as
40:27 and complain, O Israel, "My way is hidden from **the LORD**;
40:28 **The LORD** is the everlasting God, the Creator of the ends of the
40:31 but those who hope in **the LORD** will renew their strength.
41: 4 I, **the LORD**—with the first of them and with the last—I am he."
41:13 For I am **the LORD**, your God, who takes hold of your right hand
41:14 declares **the LORD**, your Redeemer, the Holy One of Israel.
41:16 you will rejoice in **the LORD** and glory in the Holy One of
41:17 I **the LORD** will answer them; I, the God of Israel, will not
41:20 and understand, that the hand of **the LORD** has done this,
41:21 "Present your case," says **the LORD**. "Set forth your arguments,"
42: 5 This is what God **the LORD** says—he who created the heavens
42: 6 "I, **the LORD**, have called you in righteousness; I will take hold
42: 8 "I am **the LORD**; that is my name! I will not give my glory to
42:10 Sing to **the LORD** a new song, his praise from the ends of the
42:12 Let them give glory to **the LORD** and proclaim his praise in the
42:13 **The LORD** will march out like a mighty man, like a warrior he
42:19 the one committed to me, blind like the servant of **the LORD**?
42:21 It pleased **the LORD** for the sake of his righteousness to make
42:24 Was it not **the LORD**, against whom we have sinned?
43: 1 But now, this is what **the LORD** says—he who created you,
43: 3 For I am **the LORD**, your God, the Holy One of Israel,
43:10 "You are my witnesses," declares **the LORD**, "and my servant
43:11 I, even I, am **the LORD**, and apart from me there is no savior.
43:12 You are my witnesses," declares **the LORD**, "that I am God.
43:14 This is what **the LORD** says—your Redeemer, the Holy One of
43:15 I am **the LORD**, your Holy One, Israel's Creator, your King."
43:16 This is what **the LORD** says—he who made a way through the
44: 2 This is what **the LORD** says—he who made you, who formed
44: 5 One will say, 'I belong to **the LORD**'; another will call himself by
44: 5 still another will write on his hand, '**The LORD's** [+4200],'
44: 6 "This is what **the LORD** says—Israel's King and Redeemer,
44: 6 Israel's King and Redeemer, **the LORD** Almighty:
44:23 Sing for joy, O heavens, for **the LORD** has done this;
44:23 you forests and all your trees, for **the LORD** has redeemed Jacob,
44:24 "This is what **the LORD** says—your Redeemer, who formed you
44:24 I am **the LORD**, who has made all things, who alone stretched
45: 1 "This is what **the LORD** says to his anointed, to Cyrus,
45: 3 so that you may know that I am **the LORD**, the God of Israel,
45: 5 I am **the LORD**, and there is no other; apart from me there is no
45: 6 there is none besides me. I am **the LORD**, and there is no other.
45: 7 and create disaster; I, **the LORD**, do all these things.
45: 8 let righteousness grow with it; I, **the LORD**, have created it.
45:11 "This is what **the LORD** says—the Holy One of Israel, and its
45:13 but not for a price or reward, says **the LORD** Almighty."
45:14 This is what **the LORD** says: "The products of Egypt
45:17 Israel will be saved by **the LORD** with an everlasting salvation;
45:18 For this is what **the LORD** says—he who created the heavens,
45:18 to be inhabited—he says: "I am **the LORD**, and there is no other.
45:19 me in vain.' I, **the LORD**, speak the truth; I declare what is right.
45:21 Was it not I, **the LORD**? And there is no God apart from me,
45:24 'In **the LORD** alone are righteousness and strength.' " All who
45:25 in **the LORD** all the descendants of Israel will be found righteous
47: 4 Our Redeemer—**the LORD** Almighty is his name—is the Holy
48: 1 you who take oaths in the name of **the LORD** and invoke the
48: 2 and rely on the God of Israel—**the LORD** Almighty is his name:
48:14 **The LORD's** chosen ally will carry out his purpose against
48:16 And now **the** Sovereign **LORD** has sent me, with his Spirit.
48:17 This is what **the LORD** says—your Redeemer, the Holy One of
48:17 "I am **the LORD** your God, who teaches you what is best for
48:20 of the earth; say, "**The LORD** has redeemed his servant Jacob."
48:22 "There is no peace," says **the LORD**, "for the wicked."
49: 1 Before I was born **the LORD** called me; from my birth he has
49: 4 Yet what is due me is in **the LORD's** hand, and my reward is
49: 5 now **the LORD** says—he who formed me in the womb to be his
49: 5 for I am honored in the eyes of **the LORD** and my God has been
49: 7 This is what **the LORD** says—the Redeemer and Holy One of
49: 7 will see and bow down, because of **the LORD**, who is faithful,
49: 8 This is what **the LORD** says: "In the time of my favor I will
49:13 For **the LORD** comforts his people and will have compassion on
49:14 Zion said, "**The LORD** has forsaken me, the Lord has forgotten
49:18 As surely as I live," declares **the LORD**, "you will wear them all
49:22 This is what **the** Sovereign **LORD** says: "See, I will beckon to
49:23 you will know that I am **the LORD**; those who hope in me will
49:25 this is what **the LORD** says: "Yes, captives will be taken from
49:26 **the LORD**, am your Savior, your Redeemer, the Mighty One of
50: 1 This is what **the LORD** says: "Where is your mother's certificate
50: 4 **The** Sovereign **LORD** has given me an instructed tongue,
50: 5 **The** Sovereign **LORD** has opened my ears, and I have not been
50: 7 Because **the** Sovereign **LORD** helps me, I will not be disgraced.
50: 9 It is **the** Sovereign **LORD** who helps me. Who is he that will

Isa 50: 10 Who among you fears **the LORD** and obeys the word of his
50: 10 has no light, trust in the name of **the LORD** and rely on his God.
51: 1 you who pursue righteousness and who seek **the LORD**:
51: 3 **The LORD** will surely comfort Zion and will look with
51: 3 deserts like Eden, her wastelands like the garden of **the LORD**.
51: 9 Clothe yourself with strength, O arm of **the LORD**; awake,
51: 11 The ransomed of **the LORD** will return. They will enter Zion
51: 13 that you forget **the LORD** your Maker, who stretched out the
51: 15 For I am **the LORD** your God, who churns up the sea so that its
51: 15 so that its waves roar—**the LORD** Almighty is his name.
51: 17 you who have drunk from the hand of **the LORD** the cup of his
51: 20 They are filled with the wrath of **the LORD** and the rebuke of
51: 22 This is what your Sovereign **LORD** says, your God, who defends
52: 3 For this is what **the LORD** says: "You were sold for nothing,
52: 4 For this is what **the** Sovereign **LORD** says: "At first my people
52: 5 "And now what do I have here?" declares **the LORD**. "For my
52: 5 for nothing, and those who rule them mock," declares **the LORD**.
52: 8 When **the LORD** returns to Zion, they will see it with their own
52: 9 you ruins of Jerusalem, for **the LORD** has comforted his people,
52: 10 **The LORD** will lay bare his holy arm in the sight of all the
52: 11 out from it and be pure, you who carry the vessels of **the LORD**.
52: 12 for **the LORD** will go before you, the God of Israel will be your
53: 1 and to whom has the arm of **the LORD** been revealed?
53: 6 own way; and **the LORD** has laid on him the iniquity of us all.
53: 10 Yet it was **the LORD's** will to crush him and cause him to suffer,
53: 10 his days, and the will of **the LORD** will prosper in his hand.
54: 1 desolate woman than of her who has a husband," says **the LORD**.
54: 5 your Maker is your husband—**the LORD** Almighty is his name—
54: 6 **The LORD** will call you back as if you were a wife deserted
54: 8 I will have compassion on you," says **the LORD** your Redeemer.
54: 10 be removed," says **the LORD**, who has compassion on you.
54: 13 All your sons will be taught by **the LORD**, and great will be your
54: 17 This is the heritage of the servants of the **LORD**, and this is their
54: 17 and this is their vindication from me," declares **the LORD**.
55: 5 because of **the LORD** your God, the Holy One of Israel,
55: 6 Seek **the LORD** while he may be found; call on him while he is
55: 7 Let him turn to **the LORD**, and he will have mercy on him,
55: 8 neither are your ways my ways," declares **the LORD**.
55: 13 This will be for **the LORD's** [+4200] renown, for an everlasting
56: 1 This is what **the LORD** says: "Maintain justice and do what is
56: 3 Let no foreigner who has bound himself to **the LORD** say,
56: 3 "**The LORD** will surely exclude me from his people."
56: 4 For this is what **the LORD** says: "To the eunuchs who keep my
56: 6 And foreigners who bind themselves to **the LORD** to serve him,
56: 6 to love the name of **the LORD**, and to worship him, all who keep
56: 8 **The** Sovereign **LORD** declares—he who gathers the exiles of
57: 19 Peace, peace, to those far and near," says **the LORD**. "And I will
58: 5 Is that what you call a fast, a day acceptable to **the LORD**?
58: 8 before you, and the glory of **the LORD** will be your rear guard.
58: 9 you will call, and **the LORD** will answer; you will cry for help,
58: 11 **The LORD** will guide you always; he will satisfy your needs in a
58: 13 call the Sabbath a delight and **the LORD's** holy day honorable,
58: 14 you will find your joy in **the LORD**, and I will cause you to ride
58: 14 of your father Jacob." The mouth of **the LORD** has spoken.
59: 1 Surely the arm of **the LORD** is not too short to save, nor his ear
59: 13 rebellion and treachery against **the LORD**, turning our backs on
59: 15 **The LORD** looked and was displeased that there was no justice.
59: 19 From the west, men will fear the name of **the LORD**, and from
59: 19 like a pent-up flood that the breath of **the LORD** drives along.
59: 20 to those in Jacob who repent of their sins," declares **the LORD**.
59: 21 "As for me, this is my covenant with them," says **the LORD**.
59: 21 descendants from this time on and forever," says **the LORD**.
60: 1 your light has come, and the glory of **the LORD** rises upon you.
60: 2 but **the LORD** rises upon you and his glory appears over you.
60: 6 and incense and proclaiming the praise of **the LORD**.
60: 9 with their silver and gold, to the honor of **the LORD** your God,
60: 14 bow down at your feet and will call you the City of **the LORD**,
60: 16 **the LORD**, am your Savior, your Redeemer, the Mighty One of
60: 19 for **the LORD** will be your everlasting light, and your God will
60: 20 **the LORD** will be your everlasting light, and your days of sorrow
60: 22 mighty nation. I am **the LORD**; in its time I will do this swiftly."
61: 1 The Spirit of **the** Sovereign **LORD** is on me, because the LORD
61: 1 because **the LORD** has anointed me to preach good news to the
61: 2 to proclaim the year of **the LORD's** [+4200] favor and the day of
61: 3 a planting of **the LORD** for the display of his splendor.
61: 6 you will be called priests of **the LORD**, you will be named
61: 8 "For I, **the LORD**, love justice; I hate robbery and iniquity.
61: 9 will acknowledge that they are a people **the LORD** has blessed."
61: 10 I delight greatly in **the LORD**; my soul rejoices in my God.
61: 11 so **the** Sovereign **LORD** will make righteousness and praise
62: 2 you will be called by a new name that the mouth of **the LORD**
62: 3 You will be a crown of splendor in **the LORD's** hand, a royal
62: 4 for **the LORD** will take delight in you, and your land will be
62: 6 or night. You who call on **the LORD**, give yourselves no rest,
62: 8 **The LORD** has sworn by his right hand and by his mighty arm:
62: 9 but those who harvest it will eat it and praise **the LORD**,
62: 11 **The LORD** has made proclamation to the ends of the earth:
62: 12 will be called the Holy People, the Redeemed of **the LORD**;
63: 7 I will tell of the kindnesses of **the LORD**, the deeds for which he
63: 7 kindnesses of the LORD, the deeds for which **he**' is to be praised,
63: 7 he is to be praised, according to all **the LORD** has done for us—
63: 14 to the plain, they were given rest by the Spirit of **the LORD**.
63: 16 you, O **LORD**, are our Father, our Redeemer from of old is your
63: 17 Why, O **LORD**, do you make us wander from your ways
64: 8 [64:7] Yet, O **LORD**, you are our Father. We are the clay, you
64: 9 [64:8] Do not be angry beyond measure, O **LORD**; do not
64: 12 [64:11] After all this, O **LORD**, will you hold yourself back?
65: 7 both your sins and the sins of your fathers," says **the LORD**.
65: 8 This is what **the LORD** says: "As when juice is still found in a
65: 11 "But as for you who forsake **the LORD** and forget my holy
65: 13 Therefore this is what **the** Sovereign **LORD** says: "My servants
65: 15 **the** Sovereign **LORD** will put you to death, but to his servants he
65: 23 for they will be a people blessed by **the LORD**, they and their
65: 25 harm nor destroy on all my holy mountain," says **the LORD**.
66: 1 This is what **the LORD** says: "Heaven is my throne, and the earth
66: 2 declares **the LORD**. "This is the one I esteem: he who is humble
66: 5 Hear the word of **the LORD**, you who tremble at his word:
66: 5 because of my name, have said, 'Let **the LORD** be glorified,
66: 6 It is the sound of **the LORD** repaying his enemies all they
66: 9 to the moment of birth and not give delivery?" says **the LORD**.
66: 12 For this is what **the LORD** says: "I will extend peace to her like a
66: 14 the hand of **the LORD** will be made known to his servants,
66: 15 See, **the LORD** is coming with fire, and his chariots are like a
66: 16 with his sword **the LORD** will execute judgment upon all men,
66: 16 upon all men, and many will be those slain by **the LORD**.
66: 17 they will meet their end together," declares **the LORD**.
66: 20 to my holy mountain in Jerusalem as an offering to **the LORD**—
66: 20 and wagons, and on mules and camels," says **the LORD**.
66: 20 to the temple of **the LORD** in ceremonially clean vessels.
66: 21 some of them also to be priests and Levites," says **the LORD**.
66: 22 declares **the LORD**, "so will your name and descendants endure.
66: 23 mankind will come and bow down before me," says **the LORD**.
Jer 1: 2 The word of **the LORD** came to him in the thirteenth year of the
1: 4 The word of **the LORD** came to me, saying,
1: 6 "Ah, Sovereign **LORD**," I said, "I do not know how to speak;
1: 7 But **the LORD** said to me, "Do not say, 'I am only a child.'
1: 8 for I am with you and will rescue you," declares **the LORD**.
1: 9 Then **the LORD** reached out his hand and touched my mouth
1: 9 out his hand and touched my mouth and said **[RPH]** to me,
1: 11 The word of **the LORD** came to me: "What do you see,
1: 12 **The LORD** said to me, "You have seen correctly, for I am
1: 13 The word of **the LORD** came to me again: "What do you see?"
1: 14 **The LORD** said to me, "From the north disaster will be poured
1: 15 all the peoples of the northern kingdoms," declares **the LORD**.
1: 19 for I am with you and will rescue you," declares **the LORD**.
2: 1 The word of **the LORD** came to me:
2: 2 **[RPH]** " 'I remember the devotion of your youth, how as a bride
2: 3 Israel was holy to **the LORD**, the firstfruits of his harvest;
2: 3 held guilty, and disaster overtook them,' " declares **the LORD**.
2: 4 Hear the word of **the LORD**, O house of Jacob, all you clans of
2: 5 This is what **the LORD** says: "What fault did your fathers find in
2: 6 They did not ask, 'Where is **the LORD**, who brought us up out of
2: 8 The priests did not ask, 'Where is **the LORD**?' Those who deal
2: 9 I bring charges against you again," declares **the LORD**.
2: 12 O heavens, and shudder with great horror," declares **the LORD**.
2: 17 Have you not brought this on yourselves by forsaking **the LORD**
2: 19 and bitter it is for you when you forsake **the LORD** your God
2: 19 and have no awe of me," declares the Lord, **the LORD** Almighty.
2: 22 of your guilt is still before me," declares **the** Sovereign **LORD**.
2: 29 You have all rebelled against me," declares **the LORD**.
2: 31 "You of this generation, consider the word of **the LORD**:
2: 37 hands on your head, for **the LORD** has rejected those you trust;
3: 1 would you now return to me?" declares **the LORD**.
3: 6 During the reign of King Josiah, **the LORD** said to me, "Have
3: 10 me with all her heart, but only in pretense," declares **the LORD**.
3: 11 **The LORD** said to me, "Faithless Israel is more righteous than
3: 12 " 'Return, faithless Israel,' declares **the LORD**, 'I will frown on
3: 12 for I am merciful,' declares **the LORD**, 'I will not be angry
3: 13 you have rebelled against **the LORD** your God, you have
3: 13 spreading tree, and have not obeyed me,' " declares **the LORD**.
3: 14 "Return, faithless people," declares **the LORD**, "for I am your
3: 16 declares **the LORD**, "men will no longer say, 'The ark of the
3: 16 "men will no longer say, 'The ark of the covenant of **the LORD**.'
3: 17 At that time they will call Jerusalem The Throne of **the LORD**,
3: 17 nations will gather in Jerusalem to honor the name of **the LORD**.
3: 20 been unfaithful to me, O house of Israel," declares **the LORD**.
3: 21 perverted their ways and have forgotten **the LORD** their God.
3: 22 "Yes, we will come to you, for you are **the LORD** our God.

Jer 3:23 surely in **the LORD** our God is the salvation of Israel.
3:25 We have sinned against **the LORD** our God, both we and our
3:25 from our youth till this day we have not obeyed **the LORD** our
4: 1 "If you will return, O Israel, return to me," declares **the LORD**.
4: 2 and righteous way you swear, 'As surely as **the LORD** lives,'
4: 3 This is what **the LORD** says to the men of Judah and to
4: 4 Circumcise yourselves to **the LORD**, circumcise your hearts,
4: 8 for the fierce anger of **the LORD** has not turned away from us.
4: 9 declares **the LORD**, "the king and the officials will lose heart,
4:10 I said, "Ah, Sovereign **LORD**, how completely you have
4:17 because she has rebelled against me,' " declares **the LORD**.
4:26 all its towns lay in ruins before **the LORD**, before his fierce
4:27 This is what **the LORD** says: "The whole land will be ruined,
5: 2 Although they say, 'As surely as **the LORD** lives,' still they are
5: 3 O **LORD**, do not your eyes look for truth? You struck them,
5: 4 they are foolish, for they do not know the way of **the LORD**,
5: 5 surely they know the way of **the LORD**, the requirements of their
5: 9 Should I not punish them for this?" declares **the LORD**.
5:10 off her branches, for these people do not belong to **the LORD**.
5:11 of Judah have been utterly unfaithful to me," declares **the LORD**.
5:12 They have lied about **the LORD**; they said, "He will do nothing!
5:14 Therefore this is what **the LORD** God Almighty says:
5:15 O house of Israel," declares **the LORD**, "I am bringing a distant
5:18 "Yet even in those days," declares **the LORD**, "I will not destroy
5:19 the people ask, 'Why has **the LORD** our God done all this to us?'
5:22 Should you not fear me?" declares **the LORD**. "Should you not
5:24 'Let us fear **the LORD** our God, who gives autumn and spring
5:29 Should I not punish them for this?" declares **the LORD**.
6: 6 This is what **the LORD** Almighty says: "Cut down the trees
6: 9 This is what **the LORD** Almighty says: "Let them glean the
6:10 The word of **the LORD** is offensive to them; they find no
6:11 But I am full of the wrath of **the LORD**, and I cannot hold it in.
6:12 my hand against those who live in the land," declares **the LORD**.
6:15 they will be brought down when I punish them," says **the LORD**.
6:16 This is what **the LORD** says: "Stand at the crossroads and look;
6:21 Therefore this is what **the LORD** says: "I will put obstacles
6:22 This is what **the LORD** says: "Look, an army is coming from the
6:30 are called rejected silver, because **the LORD** has rejected them."
7: 1 This is the word that came to Jeremiah from **the LORD**:
7: 2 "Stand at the gate of **the LORD's** house and there proclaim this
7: 2 " 'Hear the word of **the LORD**, all you people of Judah who
7: 2 of Judah who come through these gates to worship **the LORD**.
7: 3 This is what **the LORD** Almighty, the God of Israel, says:
7: 4 in deceptive words and say, "This is the temple of **the LORD**,
7: 4 the temple of **the LORD**, the temple of the LORD!"
7: 4 the temple of the LORD, the temple of **the LORD**!"
7:11 robbers to you? But I have been watching! declares **the LORD**.
7:13 declares **the LORD**, I spoke to you again and again, but you did
7:19 But am I the one they are provoking? declares **the LORD**.
7:20 " 'Therefore this is what **the** Sovereign **LORD** says: My anger
7:21 " 'This is what **the LORD** Almighty, the God of Israel, says:
7:28 'This is the nation that has not obeyed **the LORD** its God
7:29 for **the LORD** has rejected and abandoned this generation that is
7:30 people of Judah have done evil in my eyes, declares **the LORD**.
7:32 So beware, the days are coming, declares **the LORD**,
8: 1 " 'At that time, declares **the LORD**, the bones of the kings
8: 3 nation will prefer death to life, declares **the LORD** Almighty.'
8: 4 "Say to them, 'This is what **the LORD** says: " 'When men fall
8: 7 But my people do not know the requirements of **the LORD**.
8: 8 can you say, "We are wise, for we have the law of **the LORD**,"
8: 9 Since they have rejected the word of **the LORD**, what kind of
8:12 will be brought down when they are punished, says **the LORD**.
8:13 " 'I will take away their harvest, declares **the LORD**. There will
8:14 For **the LORD** our God has doomed us to perish and given us
8:14 us poisoned water to drink, because we have sinned against **him**[s].
8:17 cannot be charmed, and they will bite you," declares **the LORD**.
8:19 "Is **the LORD** not in Zion? Is her King no longer there?"
9: 3 [9:2] they do not acknowledge me," declares **the LORD**.
9: 6 [9:5] they refuse to acknowledge me," declares **the LORD**.
9: 7 [9:6] Therefore this is what **the LORD** Almighty says: "See,
9: 9 [9:8] Should I not punish them for this?" declares **the LORD**.
9:12 [9:11] Who has been instructed by **the LORD** and can explain
9:13 [9:12] **The LORD** said, "It is because they have forsaken my
9:15 [9:14] Therefore, this is what **the LORD** Almighty, the God of
9:17 [9:16] This is what **the LORD** Almighty says: "Consider now!
9:20 [9:19] Now, O women, hear the word of **the LORD**; open your
9:22 [9:21] Say, "This is what **the LORD** declares: " 'The dead
9:23 [9:22] This is what **the LORD** says: "Let not the wise man boast
9:24 [9:23] that he understands and knows me, that I am **the LORD**,
9:24 [9:23] on earth, for in these I delight," declares **the LORD**.
9:25 [9:24] "The days are coming," declares **the LORD**, "when I will
10: 1 Hear what **the LORD** says to you, O house of Israel.
10: 2 This is what **the LORD** says: "Do not learn the ways of the
10: 6 No one is like you, O **LORD**; you are great, and your name is
10:10 **the LORD** is the true God; he is the living God, the eternal King.
10:16 the tribe of his inheritance—**the LORD** Almighty is his name.
10:18 For this is what **the LORD** says: "At this time I will hurl out
10:21 The shepherds are senseless and do not inquire of **the LORD**;
10:23 I know, O **LORD**, that a man's life is not his own; it is not for
10:24 Correct me, **LORD**, but only with justice—not in your anger,
11: 1 This is the word that came to Jeremiah from **the LORD**:
11: 3 Tell them that this is what **the LORD**, the God of Israel,
11: 5 the land you possess today." I answered, "Amen, **LORD**."
11: 6 **The LORD** said to me, "Proclaim all these words in the towns of
11: 9 **the LORD** said to me, "There is a conspiracy among the people
11:11 Therefore this is what **the LORD** says: 'I will bring on them a
11:16 **The LORD** called you a thriving olive tree with fruit beautiful in
11:17 **The LORD** Almighty, who planted you, has decreed disaster for
11:18 Because **the LORD** revealed their plot to me, I knew it, for at that
11:20 But, O **LORD** Almighty, you who judge righteously and test the
11:21 "Therefore this is what **the LORD** says about the men of
11:21 'Do not prophesy in the name of **the LORD** or you will die by our
11:22 therefore this is what **the LORD** Almighty says: 'I will punish
12: 1 You are always righteous, O **LORD**, when I bring a case before
12: 3 Yet you know me, O **LORD**; you see me and test my thoughts
12:12 for the sword of **the LORD** will devour from one end of the land
12:13 the shame of your harvest because of **the LORD's** fierce anger."
12:14 This is what **the LORD** says: "As for all my wicked neighbors
12:16 and swear by my name, saying, 'As surely as **the LORD** lives'—
12:17 I will completely uproot and destroy it," declares **the LORD**.
13: 1 This is what **the LORD** said to me: "Go and buy a linen belt
13: 2 So I bought a belt, as **the LORD** directed, and put it around my
13: 3 Then the word of **the LORD** came to me a second time:
13: 5 So I went and hid it at Perath, as **the LORD** told me.
13: 6 Many days later **the LORD** said to me, "Go now to Perath
13: 8 Then the word of **the LORD** came to me:
13: 9 "This is what **the LORD** says: 'In the same way I will ruin the
13:11 declares **the LORD**, 'to be my people for my renown and praise
13:12 "Say to them: 'This is what **the LORD**, the God of Israel, says:
13:13 tell them, 'This is what **the LORD** says: I am going to fill with
13:14 one against the other, fathers and sons alike, declares **the LORD**.
13:15 and pay attention, do not be arrogant, for **the LORD** has spoken.
13:16 Give glory to **the LORD** your God before he brings the darkness,
13:17 with tears, because **the LORD's** flock will be taken captive.
13:25 declares **the LORD**, "because you have forgotten me and trusted
14: 1 This is the word of **the LORD** to Jeremiah concerning the
14: 7 Although our sins testify against us, O **LORD**, do something for
14: 9 You are among us, O **LORD**, and we bear your name; do not
14:10 This is what **the LORD** says about this people: "They greatly
14:10 So **the LORD** does not accept them; he will now remember their
14:11 **the LORD** said to me, "Do not pray for the well-being of this
14:13 I said, "Ah, Sovereign **LORD**, the prophets keep telling them,
14:14 **the LORD** said to me, "The prophets are prophesying lies in my
14:15 this is what **the LORD** says about the prophets who are
14:20 O **LORD**, we acknowledge our wickedness and the guilt of our
14:22 No, it is you, O **LORD** our God. Therefore our hope is in you,
15: 1 **the LORD** said to me: "Even if Moses and Samuel were to stand
15: 2 'Where shall we go?' tell them, 'This is what **the LORD** says:
15: 3 declares **the LORD**, "the sword to kill and the dogs to drag away
15: 6 You have rejected me," declares **the LORD**. "You keep on
15: 9 survivors to the sword before their enemies," declares **the LORD**.
15:11 **The LORD** said, "Surely I will deliver you for a good purpose;
15:15 You understand, O **LORD**; remember me and care for me.
15:16 heart's delight, for I bear your name, O **LORD** God Almighty.
15:19 Therefore this is what **the LORD** says: "If you repent, I will
15:20 for I am with you to rescue and save you," declares **the LORD**.
16: 1 Then the word of **the LORD** came to me:
16: 3 For this is what **the LORD** says about the sons and daughters
16: 5 For this is what **the LORD** says: "Do not enter a house where
16: 5 my love and my pity from this people," declares **the LORD**.
16: 9 For this is what **the LORD** Almighty, the God of Israel,
16:10 'Why has **the LORD** decreed such a great disaster against us?
16:10 What sin have we committed against **the LORD** our God?'
16:11 declares **the LORD**, 'and followed other gods and served
16:14 "However, the days are coming," declares **the LORD**,
16:14 "when men will no longer say, 'As surely as **the LORD** lives,
16:15 they will say, 'As surely as **the LORD** lives, who brought the
16:16 many fishermen," declares **the LORD**, "and they will catch them.
16:19 O **LORD**, my strength and my fortress, my refuge in time of
16:21 and might. Then they will know that my name is **the LORD**.
17: 5 This is what **the LORD** says: "Cursed is the one who trusts in
17: 5 for his strength and whose heart turns away from **the LORD**.
17: 7 "But blessed is the man who trusts in **the LORD**, whose
17: 7 is the man who trusts in the LORD, whose confidence is in **him**[s].
17:10 "I **the LORD** search the heart and examine the mind, to reward a
17:13 O **LORD**, the hope of Israel, all who forsake you will be put to
17:13 will be written in the dust because they have forsaken **the LORD**,
17:14 Heal me, O **LORD**, and I will be healed; save me and I will be

Jer 17:15 They keep saying to me, "Where is the word of **the LORD**?
17:19 This is what **the LORD** said to me: "Go and stand at the gate of
17:20 Say to them, 'Hear the word of **the LORD**, O kings of Judah
17:21 This is what **the LORD** says: Be careful not to carry a load on the
17:24 if you are careful to obey me, declares **the LORD**, and bring no
17:26 incense and thank offerings to the house of **the LORD**.
18: 1 This is the word that came to Jeremiah from **the LORD**:
18: 5 Then the word of **the LORD** came to me:
18: 6 declares **the LORD**. "Like clay in the hand of the potter,
18:11 and those living in Jerusalem, 'This is what **the LORD** says:
18:13 Therefore this is what **the LORD** says: "Inquire among the
18:19 Listen to me, O **LORD**; hear what my accusers are saying!
18:23 you know, O **LORD**, all their plots to kill me. Do not forgive
19: 1 This is what **the LORD** says: "Go and buy a clay jar from a
19: 3 and say, 'Hear the word of **the LORD**, O kings of Judah
19: 3 This is what **the LORD** Almighty, the God of Israel, says:
19: 6 So beware, the days are coming, declares **the LORD**,
19:11 and say to them, 'This is what **the LORD** Almighty says:
19:12 do to this place and to those who live here, declares **the LORD**.
19:14 from Topheth, where **the LORD** had sent him to prophesy,
19:14 stood in the court of **the LORD's** temple and said to all the
19:15 "This is what **the LORD** Almighty, the God of Israel, says:
20: 1 son of Immer, the chief officer in the temple of **the LORD**,
20: 2 put in the stocks at the Upper Gate of Benjamin at **the LORD's**
20: 3 "**The LORD's** name for you is not Pashhur, but Magor-Missabib.
20: 4 For this is what **the LORD** says: 'I will make you a terror to
20: 7 O **LORD**, you deceived me, and I was deceived;
20: 8 So the word of **the LORD** has brought me insult and reproach all
20:11 **the LORD** is with me like a mighty warrior; so my persecutors
20:12 O **LORD** Almighty, you who examine the righteous and probe
20:13 Sing to **the LORD**! Give praise to the LORD! He rescues the
20:13 Sing to the LORD! Give praise to **the LORD**! He rescues the
20:16 May that man be like the towns **the LORD** overthrew without
21: 1 The word came to Jeremiah from **the LORD** when King
21: 2 "Inquire now of **the LORD** for us because Nebuchadnezzar king
21: 2 Perhaps **the LORD** will perform wonders for us as in times past
21: 4 'This is what **the LORD**, the God of Israel, says: I am about to
21: 7 After that, declares **the LORD**, I will hand over Zedekiah king of
21: 8 "Furthermore, tell the people, 'This is what **the LORD** says:
21:10 to do this city harm and not good, declares **the LORD**.
21:11 say to the royal house of Judah, 'Hear the word of **the LORD**;
21:12 O house of David, this is what **the LORD** says:
21:13 live above this valley on the rocky plateau, declares **the LORD**—
21:14 I will punish you as your deeds deserve, declares **the LORD**.
22: 1 This is what **the LORD** says: "Go down to the palace of the king
22: 2 'Hear the word of **the LORD**, O king of Judah, you who sit on
22: 3 This is what **the LORD** says: Do what is just and right. Rescue
22: 5 But if you do not obey these commands, declares **the LORD**,
22: 6 For this is what **the LORD** says about the palace of the king of
22: 8 'Why has **the LORD** done such a thing to this great city?'
22: 9 'Because they have forsaken the covenant of **the LORD** their God
22:11 For this is what **the LORD** says about Shallum son of Josiah,
22:16 Is that not what it means to know me?" declares **the LORD**.
22:18 Therefore this is what **the LORD** says about Jehoiakim son of
22:24 "As surely as I live," declares **the LORD**, "even if you,
22:29 O land, land, land, hear the word of **the LORD**!
22:30 This is what **the LORD** says: "Record this man as if childless,
23: 1 and scattering the sheep of my pasture!" declares **the LORD**.
23: 2 Therefore this is what **the LORD**, the God of Israel, says to the
23: 2 on you for the evil you have done," declares **the LORD**.
23: 4 or terrified, nor will any be missing," declares **the LORD**.
23: 5 "The days are coming," declares **the LORD**, "when I will raise
23: 6 name by which he will be called: **The LORD** Our Righteousness.
23: 7 "So then, the days are coming," declares **the LORD**,
23: 7 "when people will no longer say, 'As surely as **the LORD** lives,
23: 8 they will say, 'As surely as **the LORD** lives, who brought the
23: 9 overcome by wine, because of **the LORD** and his holy words.
23:11 even in my temple I find their wickedness," declares **the LORD**.
23:12 on them in the year they are punished," declares **the LORD**.
23:15 this is what **the LORD** Almighty says concerning the prophets:
23:16 This is what **the LORD** Almighty says: "Do not listen to what the
23:16 visions from their own minds, not from the mouth of **the LORD**.
23:17 They keep saying to those who despise me, '**The LORD** says:
23:18 But which of them has stood in the council of **the LORD** to see
23:19 See, the storm of **the LORD** will burst out in wrath, a whirlwind
23:20 The anger of **the LORD** will not turn back until he fully
23:23 a God nearby," declares **the LORD**, "and not a God far away?
23:24 declares **the LORD**. "Do not I fill heaven and earth?"
23:24 "Do not I fill heaven and earth?" declares **the LORD**.
23:28 For what has straw to do with grain?" declares **the LORD**.
23:29 "Is not my word like fire," declares **the LORD**, "and like a
23:30 "Therefore," declares **the LORD**, "I am against the prophets who
23:31 Yes," declares **the LORD**, "I am against the prophets who wag
23:32 against those who prophesy false dreams," declares **the LORD**.
23:32 do not benefit these people in the least," declares **the LORD**.
23:33 a prophet or a priest, ask you, 'What is the oracle of **the LORD**?'
23:33 to them, 'What oracle? I will forsake you, declares **the LORD**.'
23:34 'This is the oracle of **the LORD**,' I will punish that man and his
23:35 on saying to his friend or relative: 'What is **the LORD's** answer?'
23:35 'What is the LORD's answer?' or 'What has **the LORD** spoken?'
23:36 But you must not mention 'the oracle of **the LORD**' again,
23:36 the words of the living God, **the LORD** Almighty, our God.
23:37 'What is **the LORD's** answer to you?' or 'What has the LORD
23:37 is the LORD's answer to you?' or 'What has **the LORD** spoken?'
23:38 Although you claim, 'This is the oracle of **the LORD**,' this is
23:38 'This is the oracle of the LORD,' this is what **the LORD** says:
23:38 You used the words, 'This is the oracle of **the LORD**,'
23:38 you that you must not claim, 'This is the oracle of **the LORD**.'
24: 1 **the LORD** showed me two baskets of figs placed in front of the
24: 1 two baskets of figs placed in front of the temple of **the LORD**.
24: 3 Then **the LORD** asked me, "What do you see, Jeremiah?"
24: 4 Then the word of **the LORD** came to me:
24: 5 "This is what **the LORD**, the God of Israel, says: 'Like these
24: 7 I will give them a heart to know me, that I am **the LORD**.
24: 8 which are so bad they cannot be eaten,' says **the LORD**,
25: 3 the word of **the LORD** has come to me and I have spoken to you
25: 4 though **the LORD** has sent all his servants the prophets to you
25: 5 you can stay in the land **the LORD** gave to you and your fathers
25: 7 "But you did not listen to me," declares **the LORD**, "and you
25: 8 Therefore **the LORD** Almighty says this: "Because you have not
25: 9 declares **the LORD**, "and I will bring them against this land
25:12 the land of the Babylonians, for their guilt," declares **the LORD**,
25:15 This is what **the LORD**, the God of Israel, said to me:
25:17 So I took the cup from **the LORD's** hand and made all the
25:17 and made all the nations to whom **he**[s] sent me drink it:
25:27 "Then tell them, 'This is what **the LORD** Almighty, the God of
25:28 and drink, tell them, 'This is what **the LORD** Almighty says:
25:29 upon all who live on the earth, declares **the LORD** Almighty.'
25:30 " '**The LORD** will roar from on high; he will thunder from his
25:31 of the earth, for **the LORD** will bring charges against the nations;
25:31 and put the wicked to the sword,' " declares **the LORD**.
25:32 This is what **the LORD** Almighty says: "Look! Disaster is
25:33 At that time those slain by **the LORD** will be everywhere—
25:36 the leaders of the flock, for **the LORD** is destroying their pasture.
25:37 will be laid waste because of the fierce anger of **the LORD**.
26: 1 son of Josiah king of Judah, this word came from **the LORD**:
26: 2 "This is what **the LORD** says: Stand in the courtyard of the
26: 2 Stand in the courtyard of **the LORD's** house and speak to all the
26: 2 towns of Judah who come to worship in the house of **the LORD**.
26: 4 Say to them, 'This is what **the LORD** says: If you do not listen to
26: 7 heard Jeremiah speak these words in the house of **the LORD**.
26: 8 all the people everything **the LORD** had commanded him to say,
26: 9 Why do you prophesy in **the LORD's** name that this house will
26: 9 the people crowded around Jeremiah in the house of **the LORD**.
26:10 they went up from the royal palace to the house of **the LORD**
26:10 took their places at the entrance of the New Gate of **the LORD's**
26:12 "**The LORD** sent me to prophesy against this house and this city
26:13 your ways and your actions and obey **the LORD** your God.
26:13 **the LORD** will relent and not bring the disaster he has
26:15 for in truth **the LORD** has sent me to you to speak all these
26:16 He has spoken to us in the name of **the LORD** our God."
26:18 all the people of Judah, 'This is what **the LORD** Almighty says:
26:19 Did not Hezekiah fear **the LORD** and seek his favor? And did
26:19 Did not Hezekiah fear the LORD and seek **his**[s] favor? And did
26:19 did not **the LORD** relent, so that he did not bring the disaster he
26:20 was another man who prophesied in the name of **the LORD**;
27: 1 king of Judah, this word came to Jeremiah from **the LORD**:
27: 2 This is what **the LORD** said to me: "Make a yoke out of straps
27: 4 for their masters and say, 'This is what **the LORD** Almighty,
27: 8 famine and plague, declares **the LORD**, until I destroy it by his
27:11 in its own land to till it and to live there, declares **the LORD**." ' "
27:13 plague with which **the LORD** has threatened any nation that will
27:15 'I have not sent them,' declares **the LORD**. 'They are prophesying
27:16 to the priests and all these people, "This is what **the LORD** says:
27:16 'Very soon now the articles from **the LORD's** house will be
27:18 If they are prophets and have the word of **the LORD**, let them
27:18 let them plead with **the LORD** Almighty that the furnishings
27:18 that the furnishings remaining in the house of **the LORD**
27:19 For this is what **the LORD** Almighty says about the pillars,
27:21 yes, this is what **the LORD** Almighty, the God of Israel,
27:21 says about the things that are left in the house of **the LORD**
27:22 will remain until the day I come for them,' declares **the LORD**.
28: 1 said to me in the house of **the LORD** in the presence of the
28: 2 "This is what **the LORD** Almighty, the God of Israel, says:
28: 3 **the LORD's** house that Nebuchadnezzar king of Babylon
28: 4 declares **the LORD**, 'for I will break the yoke of the king of
28: 5 and all the people who were standing in the house of **the LORD**.
28: 6 He said, "Amen! May **the LORD** do so! May the LORD fulfill

Jer 28: 6 May **the LORD** fulfill the words you have prophesied by
28: 6 have prophesied by bringing the articles of **the LORD's** house
28: 9 as one truly sent by **the LORD** only if his prediction comes true."
28: 11 and he said before all the people, "This is what **the LORD** says:
28: 12 the prophet Jeremiah, the word of **the LORD** came to Jeremiah:
28: 13 "Go and tell Hananiah, 'This is what **the LORD** says: You have
28: 14 This is what **the LORD** Almighty, the God of Israel, says:
28: 15 **The LORD** has not sent you, yet you have persuaded this nation
28: 16 Therefore, this is what **the LORD** says: 'I am about to remove
28: 16 because you have preached rebellion against **the LORD**.' "
29: 4 This is what **the LORD** Almighty, the God of Israel, says to all
29: 7 Pray to **the LORD** for it, because if it prospers, you too will
29: 8 Yes, this is what **the LORD** Almighty, the God of Israel,
29: 9 to you in my name. I have not sent them," declares **the LORD**.
29: 10 This is what **the LORD** says: "When seventy years are completed
29: 11 declares **the LORD**, "plans to prosper you and not to harm you,
29: 14 I will be found by you," declares **the LORD**, "and will bring you
29: 14 and places where I have banished you," declares **the LORD**,
29: 15 may say, "**The LORD** has raised up prophets for us in Babylon,"
29: 16 this is what **the LORD** says about the king who sits on David's
29: 17 yes, this is what **the LORD** Almighty says: "I will send the
29: 19 declares **the LORD**, "words that I sent to them again and again
29: 19 And you exiles have not listened either," declares **the LORD**.
29: 20 Therefore, hear the word of **the LORD**, all you exiles whom I
29: 21 This is what **the LORD** Almighty, the God of Israel, says about
29: 22 '**The LORD** treat you like Zedekiah and Ahab, whom the king of
29: 23 them to do. I know it and am a witness to it," declares **the LORD**.
29: 25 "This is what **the LORD** Almighty, the God of Israel, says:
29: 26 '**The LORD** has appointed you priest in place of Jehoiada to be in
29: 26 in place of Jehoiada to be in charge of the house of **the LORD**;
29: 30 Then the word of **the LORD** came to Jeremiah:
29: 31 'This is what **the LORD** says about Shemaiah the Nehelamite:
29: 32 this is what **the LORD** says: I will surely punish Shemaiah the
29: 32 declares **the LORD**, because he has preached rebellion against
29: 32 the LORD, because he has preached rebellion against **me**[s].' "
30: 1 This is the word that came to Jeremiah from **the LORD**:
30: 2 "This is what **the LORD**, the God of Israel, says: 'Write in a book
30: 3 The days are coming,' declares **the LORD**, 'when I will bring my
30: 3 to the land I gave their forefathers to possess,' says **the LORD**."
30: 4 These are the words **the LORD** spoke concerning Israel
30: 5 "This is what **the LORD** says: " 'Cries of fear are heard—
30: 8 " 'In that day,' declares **the LORD** Almighty, 'I will break the
30: 9 they will serve **the LORD** their God and David their king,
30: 10 my servant; do not be dismayed, O Israel,' declares **the LORD**.
30: 11 I am with you and will save you,' declares **the LORD**. 'Though I
30: 12 "This is what **the LORD** says: " 'Your wound is incurable,
30: 17 restore you to health and heal your wounds,' declares **the LORD**,
30: 18 "This is what **the LORD** says: " 'I will restore the fortunes of
30: 21 who will devote himself to be close to me?' declares **the LORD**.
30: 23 See, the storm of **the LORD** will burst out in wrath, a driving
30: 24 The fierce anger of **the LORD** will not turn back until he fully
31: 1 "At that time," declares **the LORD**, "I will be the God of all the
31: 2 This is what **the LORD** says: "The people who survive the sword
31: 3 **The LORD** appeared to us in the past, saying: "I have loved you
31: 6 'Come, let us go up to Zion, to **the LORD** our God.' "
31: 7 This is what **the LORD** says: "Sing with joy for Jacob; shout for
31: 7 and say, 'O **LORD**, save your people, the remnant of Israel.'
31: 10 "Hear the word of **the LORD**, O nations; proclaim it in distant
31: 11 For **the LORD** will ransom Jacob and redeem them from the
31: 12 they will rejoice in the bounty of **the LORD**—the grain,
31: 14 my people will be filled with my bounty," declares **the LORD**.
31: 15 This is what **the LORD** says: "A voice is heard in Ramah,
31: 16 This is what **the LORD** says: "Restrain your voice from weeping
31: 16 from tears, for your work will be rewarded," declares **the LORD**.
31: 17 So there is hope for your future," declares **the LORD**. "Your
31: 18 and I will return, because you are **the LORD** my God.
31: 20 for him; I have great compassion for him," declares **the LORD**.
31: 22 **The LORD** will create a new thing on earth—a woman will
31: 23 This is what **the LORD** Almighty, the God of Israel, says:
31: 23 '**The LORD** bless you, O righteous dwelling, O sacred mountain.'
31: 27 "The days are coming," declares **the LORD**, "when I will plant
31: 28 will watch over them to build and to plant," declares **the LORD**.
31: 31 "The time is coming," declares **the LORD**, "when I will make a
31: 32 though I was a husband to them," declares **the LORD**.
31: 33 with the house of Israel after that time," declares **the LORD**.
31: 34 or a man his brother, saying, 'Know **the LORD**,' because they
31: 34 from the least of them to the greatest," declares **the LORD**.
31: 35 This is what **the LORD** says, he who appoints the sun to shine by
31: 35 so that its waves roar—**the LORD** Almighty is his name:
31: 36 if these decrees vanish from my sight," declares **the LORD**,
31: 37 This is what **the LORD** says: "Only if the heavens above can be
31: 37 of Israel because of all they have done," declares **the LORD**.
31: 38 "The days are coming," declares **the LORD**, "when this city will
31: 38 "when this city will be rebuilt for **me**[s] from the Tower of Hananel
31: 40 as far as the corner of the Horse Gate, will be holy to **the LORD**.
32: 1 This is the word that came to Jeremiah from **the LORD** in the
32: 3 you prophesy as you do? You say, 'This is what **the LORD** says:
32: 5 where he will remain until I deal with him, declares **the LORD**.
32: 6 Jeremiah said, "The word of **the LORD** came to me:
32: 8 "Then, just as **the LORD** had said, my cousin Hanamel came to
32: 8 buy it for yourself.' "I knew that this was the word of **the LORD**;
32: 14 'This is what **the LORD** Almighty, the God of Israel, says:
32: 15 For this is what **the LORD** Almighty, the God of Israel,
32: 16 deed of purchase to Baruch son of Neriah, I prayed to **the LORD**:
32: 17 "Ah, Sovereign **LORD**, you have made the heavens and the earth
32: 18 and powerful God, whose name is **the LORD** Almighty,
32: 25 you, O Sovereign **LORD**, say to me, 'Buy the field with silver
32: 26 Then the word of **the LORD** came to Jeremiah:
32: 27 "I am **the LORD**, the God of all mankind. Is anything too hard
32: 28 Therefore, this is what **the LORD** says: I am about to hand this
32: 30 me with what their hands have made, declares **the LORD**.
32: 36 of Babylon'; but this is what **the LORD**, the God of Israel, says:
32: 42 "This is what **the LORD** says: As I have brought all this great
32: 44 because I will restore their fortunes, declares **the LORD**."
33: 1 of the guard, the word of **the LORD** came to him a second time:
33: 2 "This is what **the LORD** says, he who made the earth,
33: 2 made the earth, **the LORD** who formed it and established it—
33: 2 who formed it and established it—**the LORD** is his name:
33: 4 For this is what **the LORD**, the God of Israel, says about the
33: 10 "This is what **the LORD** says: 'You say about this place,
33: 11 of those who bring thank offerings to the house of **the LORD**,
33: 11 saying, "Give thanks to **the LORD** Almighty, for the LORD is
33: 11 "Give thanks to the LORD Almighty, for **the LORD** is good;
33: 11 the fortunes of the land as they were before,' says **the LORD**.
33: 12 "This is what **the LORD** Almighty says: 'In this place, desolate
33: 13 under the hand of the one who counts them,' says **the LORD**.
33: 14 " 'The days are coming,' declares **the LORD**, 'when I will fulfill
33: 16 name by which it will be called: **The LORD** Our Righteousness.'
33: 17 For this is what **the LORD** says: 'David will never fail to have a
33: 19 The word of **the LORD** came to Jeremiah:
33: 20 "This is what **the LORD** says: 'If you can break my covenant
33: 23 The word of **the LORD** came to Jeremiah:
33: 24 are saying, '**The LORD** has rejected the two kingdoms he chose'?
33: 25 This is what **the LORD** says: 'If I have not established my
34: 1 surrounding towns, this word came to Jeremiah from **the LORD**:
34: 2 "This is what **the LORD**, the God of Israel, says: Go to Zedekiah
34: 2 king of Judah and tell him, 'This is what **the LORD** says:
34: 4 " 'Yet hear the promise of **the LORD**, O Zedekiah king of Judah.
34: 4 king of Judah. This is what **the LORD** says concerning you:
34: 5 O master!" I myself make this promise, declares **the LORD**.' "
34: 8 The word came to Jeremiah from **the LORD** after King Zedekiah
34: 12 Then the word of **the LORD** came to Jeremiah:
34: 12 Then the word of the LORD came to Jeremiah: **[RPH]**
34: 13 "This is what **the LORD**, the God of Israel, says: I made a
34: 17 "Therefore, this is what **the LORD** says: You have not obeyed
34: 17 So I now proclaim 'freedom' for you, declares **the LORD**—
34: 22 I am going to give the order, declares **the LORD**, and I will bring
35: 1 This is the word that came to Jeremiah from **the LORD** during
35: 2 them to come to one of the side rooms of the house of **the LORD**
35: 4 I brought them into the house of **the LORD**, into the room of the
35: 12 Then the word of **the LORD** came to Jeremiah, saying:
35: 13 "This is what **the LORD** Almighty, the God of Israel, says:
35: 13 you not learn a lesson and obey my words?' declares **the LORD**.
35: 17 "Therefore, this is what **the LORD** God Almighty, the God of
35: 18 "This is what **the LORD** Almighty, the God of Israel, says:
35: 19 Therefore, this is what **the LORD** Almighty, the God of Israel,
36: 1 king of Judah, this word came to Jeremiah from **the LORD**:
36: 4 while Jeremiah dictated all the words **the LORD** had spoken to
36: 5 told Baruch, "I am restricted; I cannot go to **the LORD's** temple.
36: 6 So you go to the house of **the LORD** on a day of fasting
36: 6 read to the people from the scroll the words of **the LORD** that
36: 7 Perhaps they will bring their petition before **the LORD**, and each
36: 7 wrath pronounced against this people by **the LORD** are great."
36: 8 at **the LORD's** temple he read the words of the LORD from the
36: 8 at the LORD's temple he read the words of **the LORD** from the
36: 9 a time of fasting before **the LORD** was proclaimed for all the
36: 10 Baruch **[RPH]** read to all the people at the LORD's temple the
36: 10 Baruch read to all the people at **the LORD's** temple the words of
36: 11 son of Shaphan, heard all the words of **the LORD** from the scroll,
36: 26 and Jeremiah the prophet. But **the LORD** had hidden them.
36: 27 at Jeremiah's dictation, the word of **the LORD** came to Jeremiah:
36: 29 Also tell Jehoiakim king of Judah, 'This is what **the LORD** says:
36: 30 this is what **the LORD** says about Jehoiakim king of Judah:
37: 2 the words **the LORD** had spoken through Jeremiah the prophet.
37: 3 with this message: "Please pray to **the LORD** our God for us."
37: 6 Then the word of **the LORD** came to Jeremiah the prophet:
37: 7 "This is what **the LORD**, the God of Israel, says: Tell the king of
37: 9 "This is what **the LORD** says: Do not deceive yourselves,

[F] Hitpael (hitpoel, hitpoal, hitpolel, hitpolal, hitpalel, hitpalal, hitpalpel, hitpalpal, hotpael, hotpaal) [G] Hiphil (hiphtil) [H] Hophal [I] Hishtaphel

Jer 37:17 he asked him privately, "Is there any word from **the LORD**?"
38: 2 "This is what **the LORD** says: 'Whoever stays in this city will die
38: 3 this is what **the LORD** says: 'This city will certainly be handed
38:14 had him brought to the third entrance to the temple of **the LORD**.
38:16 "As surely as **the LORD** lives, who has given us breath,
38:17 "This is what **the LORD** God Almighty, the God of Israel,
38:20 Jeremiah replied. "Obey **the LORD** by doing what I tell you.
38:21 refuse to surrender, this is what **the LORD** has revealed to me:
39:15 the courtyard of the guard, the word of **the LORD** came to him:
39:16 'This is what **the LORD** Almighty, the God of Israel, says:
39:17 I will rescue you on that day, declares **the LORD**; you will not be
39:18 with your life, because you trust in me, declares **the LORD**.' "
40: 1 The word came to Jeremiah from **the LORD** after Nebuzaradan
40: 2 "**The LORD** your God decreed this disaster for this place.
40: 3 now **the LORD** has brought it about; he has done just as he said
40: 3 All this happened because you people sinned against **the LORD**
41: 5 grain offerings and incense with them to the house of **the LORD**.
42: 2 and pray to **the LORD** your God for this entire remnant.
42: 3 Pray that **the LORD** your God will tell us where we should go
42: 4 "I will certainly pray to **the LORD** your God as you have
42: 4 I will tell you everything **the LORD** says and will keep nothing
42: 5 "May **the LORD** be a true and faithful witness against us if we
42: 5 with everything **the LORD** your God sends you to tell us.
42: 6 it is favorable or unfavorable, we will obey **the LORD** our God,
42: 6 it will go well with us, for we will obey **the LORD** our God."
42: 7 Ten days later the word of **the LORD** came to Jeremiah.
42: 9 He said to them, "This is what **the LORD**, the God of Israel,
42:11 declares **the LORD**, for I am with you and will save you
42:13 will not stay in this land,' and so disobey **the LORD** your God,
42:15 hear the word of **the LORD**, O remnant of Judah. This is what
42:15 This is what **the LORD** Almighty, the God of Israel, says:
42:18 This is what **the LORD** Almighty, the God of Israel, says:
42:19 remnant of Judah, **the LORD** has told you, 'Do not go to Egypt.'
42:20 that you made a fatal mistake when you sent me to **the LORD**
42:20 LORD your God and said, 'Pray to **the LORD** our God for us;
42:20 tell us everything **he**[s] [+466+5646] says and we will do it.'
42:21 you still have not obeyed **the LORD** your God in all he sent me
43: 1 finished telling the people all the words of **the LORD** their God—
43: 1 their God—everything **the LORD** had sent him to tell them—
43: 2 **The LORD** our God has not sent you to say, 'You must not go to
43: 4 all the people disobeyed **the LORD's** command to stay in the
43: 7 So they entered Egypt in disobedience to **the LORD** and went as
43: 8 In Tahpanhes the word of **the LORD** came to Jeremiah:
43:10 'This is what **the LORD** Almighty, the God of Israel, says:
44: 2 "This is what **the LORD** Almighty, the God of Israel, says:
44: 7 "Now this is what **the LORD** God Almighty, the God of Israel,
44:11 "Therefore, this is what **the LORD** Almighty, the God of Israel,
44:16 to the message you have spoken to us in the name of **the LORD**!
44:21 "Did not **the LORD** remember and think about the incense
44:22 When **the LORD** could no longer endure your wicked actions
44:23 and have sinned against **the LORD** and have not obeyed him
44:23 and have not obeyed **him**[s] or followed his law or his decrees
44:24 including the women, "Hear the word of **the LORD**, all you
44:25 This is what **the LORD** Almighty, the God of Israel, says:
44:26 But hear the word of **the LORD**, all Jews living in Egypt:
44:26 'I swear by my great name,' says **the LORD**, 'that no one from
44:26 my name or swear, "As surely as the Sovereign **LORD** lives."
44:29 to you that I will punish you in this place,' declares **the LORD**,
44:30 This is what **the LORD** says: 'I am going to hand Pharaoh
45: 2 "This is what **the LORD**, the God of Israel, says to you,
45: 3 **The LORD** has added sorrow to my pain; I am worn out with
45: 4 'This is what **the LORD** says: I will overthrow what I have built
45: 5 For I will bring disaster on all people, declares **the LORD**,
46: 1 This is the word of **the LORD** that came to Jeremiah the prophet
46: 5 and there is terror on every side," declares **the LORD**.
46:10 But that day belongs to the Lord, **the LORD** Almighty—
46:10 For the Lord, **the LORD** Almighty, will offer sacrifice in the land
46:13 This is the message **the LORD** spoke to Jeremiah the prophet
46:15 They cannot stand, for **the LORD** will push them down.
46:18 I live," declares the King, whose name is **the LORD** Almighty,
46:23 chop down her forest," declares **the LORD**, "dense though it be.
46:25 **The LORD** Almighty, the God of Israel, says: "I am about to
46:26 Egypt will be inhabited as in times past," declares **the LORD**.
46:28 O Jacob my servant, for I am with you," declares **the LORD**.
47: 1 This is the word of **the LORD** that came to Jeremiah the prophet
47: 2 This is what **the LORD** says: "See how the waters are rising in
47: 4 **The LORD** is about to destroy the Philistines, the remnant from
47: 6 " 'Ah, sword of **the LORD**,' ⌞you cry,⌟ 'how long till you rest?
47: 7 how can it rest when **the LORD** has commanded it, when he has
48: 1 This is what **the LORD** Almighty, the God of Israel, says:
48: 8 and the plateau destroyed, because **the LORD** has spoken.
48:10 "A curse on him who is lax in doing **the LORD's** work!
48:12 days are coming," declares **the LORD**, "when I will send men
48:15 declares the King, whose name is **the LORD** Almighty.
48:25 Moab's horn is cut off; her arm is broken," declares **the LORD**.
48:26 "Make her drunk, for she has defied **the LORD**. Let Moab
48:30 I know her insolence but it is futile," declares **the LORD**,
48:35 high places and burn incense to their gods," declares **the LORD**.
48:38 broken Moab like a jar that no one wants," declares **the LORD**.
48:40 This is what **the LORD** says: "Look! An eagle is swooping
48:42 will be destroyed as a nation because she defied **the LORD**.
48:43 and snare await you, O people of Moab," declares **the LORD**.
48:44 upon Moab the year of her punishment," declares **the LORD**.
48:47 the fortunes of Moab in days to come," declares **the LORD**.
49: 1 This is what **the LORD** says: "Has Israel no sons? Has she no
49: 2 the days are coming," declares **the LORD**, "when I will sound
49: 2 Israel will drive out those who drove her out," says **the LORD**.
49: 5 all those around you," declares the Lord, **the LORD** Almighty.
49: 6 will restore the fortunes of the Ammonites," declares **the LORD**.
49: 7 Concerning Edom: This is what **the LORD** Almighty says:
49:12 This is what **the LORD** says: "If those who do not deserve to
49:13 I swear by myself," declares **the LORD**, "that Bozrah will
49:14 I have heard a message from **the LORD**: An envoy was sent to
49:16 from there I will bring you down," declares **the LORD**.
49:18 neighboring towns," says **the LORD**, "so no one will live there;
49:20 Therefore, hear what **the LORD** has planned against Edom,
49:26 will be silenced in that day," declares **the LORD** Almighty.
49:28 This is what **the LORD** says: "Arise, and attack Kedar
49:30 Stay in deep caves, you who live in Hazor," declares **the LORD**.
49:31 a nation at ease, which lives in confidence," declares **the LORD**,
49:32 will bring disaster on them from every side," declares **the LORD**.
49:34 This is the word of **the LORD** that came to Jeremiah the prophet
49:35 This is what **the LORD** Almighty says: "See, I will break the
49:37 disaster upon them, even my fierce anger," declares **the LORD**.
49:38 and destroy her king and officials," declares **the LORD**.
49:39 the fortunes of Elam in days to come," declares **the LORD**.
50: 1 This is the word **the LORD** spoke through Jeremiah the prophet
50: 4 "In those days, at that time," declares **the LORD**, "the people of
50: 4 the people of Judah together will go in tears to seek **the LORD**
50: 5 bind themselves to **the LORD** in an everlasting covenant that will
50: 7 for they sinned against **the LORD**, their true pasture, the LORD,
50: 7 their true pasture, **the LORD**, the hope of their fathers.'
50:10 all who plunder her will have their fill," declares **the LORD**.
50:13 Because of **the LORD's** anger she will not be inhabited but will
50:14 at her! Spare no arrows, for she has sinned against **the LORD**.
50:15 Since this is the vengeance of **the LORD**, take vengeance on her;
50:18 Therefore this is what **the LORD** Almighty, the God of Israel,
50:20 In those days, at that time," declares **the LORD**, "search will be
50:21 Pursue, kill and completely destroy them," declares **the LORD**.
50:24 you were found and captured because you opposed **the LORD**.
50:25 **The LORD** has opened his arsenal and brought out the weapons
50:25 for **the** Sovereign **LORD** Almighty has work to do in the land of
50:28 refugees from Babylon declaring in Zion how **the LORD** our
50:29 has done. For she has defied **the LORD**, the Holy One of Israel.
50:30 all her soldiers will be silenced in that day," declares **the LORD**.
50:31 O arrogant one," declares the Lord, **the LORD** Almighty,
50:33 This is what **the LORD** Almighty says: "The people of Israel are
50:34 Yet their Redeemer is strong; **the LORD** Almighty is his name.
50:35 declares **the LORD**—"against those who live in Babylon
50:40 declares **the LORD**, "so no one will live there;
50:45 Therefore, hear what **the LORD** has planned against Babylon,
51: 1 This is what **the LORD** says: "See, I will stir up the spirit of a
51: 5 Judah have not been forsaken by their God, **the LORD** Almighty,
51: 6 It is time for **the LORD's** [+4200] vengeance; he will pay her
51: 7 Babylon was a gold cup in **the LORD's** hand; she made the
51:10 " '**The LORD** has vindicated us; come, let us tell in Zion what the
51:10 come, let us tell in Zion what **the LORD** our God has done.'
51:11 **The LORD** has stirred up the kings of the Medes, because his
51:11 **The LORD** will take vengeance, vengeance for his temple.
51:12 **The LORD** will carry out his purpose, his decree against the
51:14 **The LORD** Almighty has sworn by himself: I will surely fill you
51:19 the tribe of his inheritance—**the LORD** Almighty is his name.
51:24 for all the wrong they have done in Zion," declares **the LORD**.
51:25 you who destroy the whole earth," declares **the LORD**.
51:26 for you will be desolate forever," declares **the LORD**.
51:29 and writhes, for **the LORD's** purposes against Babylon stand—
51:33 This is what **the LORD** Almighty, the God of Israel, says:
51:36 Therefore, this is what **the LORD** says: "See, I will defend your
51:39 then sleep forever and not awake," declares **the LORD**.
51:45 Run for your lives! Run from the fierce anger of **the LORD**.
51:48 out of the north destroyers will attack her," declares **the LORD**.
51:50 Remember **the LORD** in a distant land, and think on Jerusalem."
51:51 because foreigners have entered the holy places of **the LORD's**
51:52 "But days are coming," declares **the LORD**, "when I will punish
51:53 I will send destroyers against her," declares **the LORD**.
51:55 **The LORD** will destroy Babylon; he will silence her noisy din.
51:56 For **the LORD** is a God of retribution; he will repay in full.
51:57 declares the King, whose name is **the LORD** Almighty.

[A] Qal [B] Qal passive [C] Niphal [D] Piel (poel, polel, pilel, pilal, pealal, pilpel) [E] Pual (poal, polal, poalal, pulal, pualal)

Jer 51:58 This is what **the LORD** Almighty says: "Babylon's thick wall
51:62 Then say, 'O **LORD**, you have said you will destroy this place,
52: 2 He did evil in the eyes of **the LORD**, just as Jehoiakim had done.
52: 3 because of **the LORD's** anger that all this happened to Jerusalem
52:13 He set fire to the temple of **the LORD**, the royal palace and all
52:17 and the bronze Sea that were at the temple of **the LORD**
52:17 of the LORD **[RPH]** and they carried all the bronze to Babylon.
52:20 which King Solomon had made for the temple of **the LORD**,
La 1: 5 **The LORD** has brought her grief because of her many sins.
1: 9 "Look, O **LORD**, on my affliction, for the enemy has
1:11 "Look, O **LORD**, and consider, for I am despised."
1:12 that **the LORD** brought on me in the day of his fierce anger?
1:17 **The LORD** has decreed for Jacob that his neighbors become his
1:18 "**The LORD** is righteous, yet I rebelled against his command.
1:20 "See, O **LORD**, how distressed I am! I am in torment within,
2: 6 **The LORD** has made Zion forget her appointed feasts and her
2: 7 they have raised a shout in the house of **the LORD** as on the day
2: 8 **The LORD** determined to tear down the wall around the
2: 9 and her prophets no longer find visions from **the LORD**.
2:17 **The LORD** has done what he planned; he has fulfilled his word,
2:20 "Look, O **LORD**, and consider: Whom have you ever treated like
2:22 In the day of **the LORD's** anger no one escaped or survived;
3:18 "My splendor is gone and all that I had hoped from **the LORD**."
3:22 Because of **the LORD's** great love we are not consumed,
3:24 I say to myself, "**The LORD** is my portion; therefore I will wait
3:25 **The LORD** is good to those whose hope is in him, to the one who
3:26 it is good to wait quietly for the salvation of **the LORD**.
3:40 examine our ways and test them, and let us return to **the LORD**.
3:50 until **the LORD** looks down from heaven and sees.
3:55 I called on your name, O **LORD**, from the depths of the pit.
3:59 You have seen, O **LORD**, the wrong done to me. Uphold my
3:61 O **LORD**, you have heard their insults, all their plots against me—
3:64 what they deserve, O **LORD**, for what their hands have done.
3:66 and destroy them from under the heavens of **the LORD**.
4:11 **The LORD** has given full vent to his wrath; he has poured out his
4:16 **The LORD** [+7156] **himself** has scattered them; he no longer
4:20 **The LORD's** anointed, our very life breath, was caught in their
5: 1 Remember, O **LORD**, what has happened to us; look, and see our
5:19 You, O **LORD**, reign forever; your throne endures from
5:21 Restore us to yourself, O **LORD**, that we may return; renew our
Eze 1: 3 the word of **the LORD** came to Ezekiel the priest, the son of
1: 3 of the Babylonians. There the hand of **the LORD** was upon him.
1:28 was the appearance of the likeness of the glory of **the LORD**.
2: 4 Say to them, 'This is what **the** Sovereign **LORD** says.'
3:11 Say to them, 'This is what **the** Sovereign **LORD** says,'
3:12 May the glory of **the LORD** be praised in his dwelling place!—
3:14 anger of my spirit, with the strong hand of **the LORD** upon me.
3:16 At the end of seven days the word of **the LORD** came to me:
3:22 The hand of **the LORD** was upon me there, and he said to me,
3:23 the glory of **the LORD** was standing there, like the glory I had
3:27 you shall say to them, 'This is what **the** Sovereign **LORD** says.'
4:13 **The LORD** said, "In this way the people of Israel will eat defiled
4:14 I said, "Not so, Sovereign **LORD**! I have never defiled myself.
5: 5 "This is what **the** Sovereign **LORD** says: This is Jerusalem,
5: 7 "Therefore this is what **the** Sovereign **LORD** says: You have
5: 8 "Therefore this is what **the** Sovereign **LORD** says: I myself am
5:11 Therefore as surely as I live, declares **the** Sovereign **LORD**,
5:13 they will know that I **the LORD** have spoken in my zeal.
5:15 and in wrath and with stinging rebuke. I **the LORD** have spoken.
5:17 I will bring the sword against you. I **the LORD** have spoken."
6: 1 The word of **the LORD** came to me:
6: 3 'O mountains of Israel, hear the word of **the** Sovereign **LORD**.
6: 3 This is what **the** Sovereign **LORD** says to the mountains
6: 7 fall slain among you, and you will know that I am **the LORD**.
6:10 they will know that I am **the LORD**; I did not threaten in vain to
6:11 " 'This is what **the** Sovereign **LORD** says: Strike your hands
6:13 they will know that I am **the LORD**, when their people lie slain
6:14 wherever they live. Then they will know that I am **the LORD**.' "
7: 1 The word of **the LORD** came to me:
7: 2 this is what **the** Sovereign **LORD** says to the land of Israel:
7: 4 practices among you. Then you will know that I am **the LORD**.
7: 5 "This is what **the** Sovereign **LORD** says: Disaster!
7: 9 Then you will know that it is I **the LORD** who strikes the blow.
7:19 gold will not be able to save them in the day of **the LORD's**
7:27 I will judge them. Then they will know that I am **the LORD**."
8: 1 the hand of **the** Sovereign **LORD** came upon me there.
8:12 They say, '**The LORD** does not see us; the LORD has forsaken
8:12 LORD does not see us; **the LORD** has forsaken the land.' "
8:14 me to the entrance to the north gate of the house of **the LORD**,
8:16 then brought me into the inner court of the house of **the LORD**,
8:16 **[RPH]** between the portico and the altar, were about twenty-five
8:16 With their backs toward the temple of **the LORD** and their faces
9: 4 and said **[RPH]** to him, "Go throughout the city of Jerusalem
9: 8 left alone, I fell facedown, crying out, "Ah, Sovereign **LORD**!
9: 9 They say, '**The LORD** has forsaken the land; the LORD does
9: 9 'The LORD has forsaken the land; **the LORD** does not see.'
10: 4 Then the glory of **the LORD** rose from above the cherubim
10: 4 and the court was full of the radiance of the glory of **the LORD**.
10:18 the glory of **the LORD** departed from over the threshold of the
10:19 They stopped at the entrance to the east gate of **the LORD's**
11: 1 brought me to the gate of the house of **the LORD** that faces east.
11: 5 the Spirit of **the LORD** came upon me, and he told me to say:
11: 5 upon me, and he told me to say: "This is what **the LORD** says:
11: 7 "Therefore this is what **the** Sovereign **LORD** says: The bodies
11: 8 is what I will bring against you, declares **the** Sovereign **LORD**.
11:10 at the borders of Israel. Then you will know that I am **the LORD**.
11:12 you will know that I am **the LORD**, for you have not followed
11:13 and cried out in a loud voice, "Ah, Sovereign **LORD**!
11:14 The word of **the LORD** came to me:
11:15 of Jerusalem have said, 'They are far away from **the LORD**;
11:16 "Therefore say: 'This is what **the** Sovereign **LORD** says:
11:17 "Therefore say: 'This is what **the** Sovereign **LORD** says:
11:21 own heads what they have done, declares **the** Sovereign **LORD**."
11:23 The glory of **the LORD** went up from within the city and stopped
11:25 and I told the exiles everything **the LORD** had shown me.
12: 1 The word of **the LORD** came to me:
12: 8 In the morning the word of **the LORD** came to me:
12:10 "Say to them, 'This is what **the** Sovereign **LORD** says: This
12:15 "They will know that I am **the LORD**, when I disperse them
12:16 detestable practices. Then they will know that I am **the LORD**."
12:17 The word of **the LORD** came to me:
12:19 'This is what **the** Sovereign **LORD** says about those living in
12:20 will be desolate. Then you will know that I am **the LORD**.' "
12:21 The word of **the LORD** came to me:
12:23 Say to them, 'This is what **the** Sovereign **LORD** says: I am going
12:25 I **the LORD** will speak what I will, and it shall be fulfilled
12:25 I will fulfill whatever I say, declares **the** Sovereign **LORD**.' "
12:26 The word of **the LORD** came to me:
12:28 "Therefore say to them, 'This is what **the** Sovereign **LORD** says:
12:28 whatever I say will be fulfilled, declares **the** Sovereign **LORD**.' "
13: 1 The word of **the LORD** came to me:
13: 2 out of their own imagination: 'Hear the word of **the LORD**!
13: 3 This is what **the** Sovereign **LORD** says: Woe to the foolish
13: 5 so that it will stand firm in the battle on the day of **the LORD**.
13: 6 They say, "**The LORD** declares," when the LORD has not sent
13: 6 "The LORD declares," when **the LORD** has not sent them;
13: 7 when you say, "**The LORD** declares," though I have not spoken?
13: 8 " 'Therefore this is what **the** Sovereign **LORD** says: Because of
13: 8 lying visions, I am against you, declares **the** Sovereign **LORD**.
13: 9 of Israel. Then you will know that I am **the** Sovereign **LORD**.
13:13 " 'Therefore this is what **the** Sovereign **LORD** says: In my wrath
13:14 will be destroyed in it; and you will know that I am **the LORD**.
13:16 her when there was no peace, declares **the** Sovereign **LORD**." '
13:18 say, 'This is what **the** Sovereign **LORD** says: Woe to the women
13:20 " 'Therefore this is what **the** Sovereign **LORD** says: I am against
13:21 prey to your power. Then you will know that I am **the LORD**.
13:23 your hands. And then you will know that I am **the LORD**.' "
14: 2 Then the word of **the LORD** came to me:
14: 4 to them and tell them, 'This is what **the** Sovereign **LORD** says:
14: 4 I **the LORD** will answer him myself in keeping with his great
14: 6 to the house of Israel, 'This is what **the** Sovereign **LORD** says:
14: 7 a prophet to inquire of me, I **the LORD** will answer him myself.
14: 8 off from my people. Then you will know that I am **the LORD**.
14: 9 I **the LORD** have enticed that prophet, and I will stretch out my
14:11 and I will be their God, declares **the** Sovereign **LORD**.' "
14:12 The word of **the LORD** came to me:
14:14 themselves by their righteousness, declares **the** Sovereign **LORD**.
14:16 as surely as I live, declares **the** Sovereign **LORD**, even if these
14:18 as surely as I live, declares **the** Sovereign **LORD**, even if these
14:20 declares **the** Sovereign **LORD**, even if Noah, Daniel and Job
14:21 "For this is what **the** Sovereign **LORD** says: How much worse
14:23 done nothing in it without cause, declares **the** Sovereign **LORD**."
15: 1 The word of **the LORD** came to me:
15: 6 "Therefore this is what **the** Sovereign **LORD** says: As I have
15: 7 I set my face against them, you will know that I am **the LORD**.
15: 8 they have been unfaithful, declares **the** Sovereign **LORD**."
16: 1 The word of **the LORD** came to me:
16: 3 and say, 'This is what **the** Sovereign **LORD** says to Jerusalem:
16: 8 with you, declares **the** Sovereign **LORD**, and you became mine.
16:14 you made your beauty perfect, declares **the** Sovereign **LORD**.
16:19 That is what happened, declares **the** Sovereign **LORD**.
16:23 " 'Woe! Woe to you, declares **the** Sovereign **LORD**. In addition
16:30 " 'How weak-willed you are, declares **the** Sovereign **LORD**,
16:35 " 'Therefore, you prostitute, hear the word of **the LORD**!
16:36 This is what **the** Sovereign **LORD** says: Because you poured out
16:43 your head what you have done, declares **the** Sovereign **LORD**.
16:48 declares **the** Sovereign **LORD**, your sister Sodom and her
16:58 your lewdness and your detestable practices, declares **the LORD**.

Eze 16:59 " 'This is what **the** Sovereign **LORD** says: I will deal with you as
16:62 my covenant with you, and you will know that I am **the LORD**.
16:63 because of your humiliation, declares **the** Sovereign **LORD**.' "
17: 1 The word of **the LORD** came to me:
17: 3 Say to them, 'This is what **the** Sovereign **LORD** says: A great
17: 9 "Say to them, 'This is what **the** Sovereign **LORD** says: Will it
17:11 Then the word of **the LORD** came to me:
17:16 " 'As surely as I live, declares **the** Sovereign **LORD**, he shall die
17:19 " 'Therefore this is what **the** Sovereign **LORD** says: As surely as
17:21 to the winds. Then you will know that I **the LORD** have spoken.
17:22 " 'This is what **the** Sovereign **LORD** says: I myself will take a
17:24 All the trees of the field will know that I **the LORD** bring down
17:24 dry tree flourish. " 'I **the LORD** have spoken, and I will do it.' "
18: 1 The word of **the LORD** came to me:
18: 3 "As surely as I live, declares **the** Sovereign **LORD**, you will no
18: 9 is righteous; he will surely live, declares **the** Sovereign **LORD**.
18:23 declares **the** Sovereign **LORD**. Rather, am I not pleased when
18:30 each one according to his ways, declares **the** Sovereign **LORD**.
18:32 pleasure in the death of anyone, declares **the** Sovereign **LORD**.
20: 1 some of the elders of Israel came to inquire of **the LORD**,
20: 2 Then the word of **the LORD** came to me:
20: 3 and say to them, 'This is what **the** Sovereign **LORD** says:
20: 3 I will not let you inquire of me, declares **the** Sovereign **LORD**.'
20: 5 and say to them: 'This is what **the** Sovereign **LORD** says:
20: 5 With uplifted hand I said to them, "I am **the LORD** your God."
20: 7 yourselves with the idols of Egypt. I am **the LORD** your God."
20:12 so they would know that I **the LORD** made them holy.
20:19 I am **the LORD** your God; follow my decrees and be careful to
20:20 between us. Then you will know that I am **the LORD** your God."
20:26 fill them with horror so they would know that I am **the LORD**.'
20:27 and say to them, 'This is what **the** Sovereign **LORD** says:
20:30 to the house of Israel: 'This is what **the** Sovereign **LORD** says:
20:31 As surely as I live, declares **the** Sovereign **LORD**, I will not let
20:33 As surely as I live, declares **the** Sovereign **LORD**, I will rule over
20:36 land of Egypt, so I will judge you, declares **the** Sovereign **LORD**.
20:38 enter the land of Israel. Then you will know that I am **the LORD**.
20:39 O house of Israel, this is what **the** Sovereign **LORD** says:
20:40 the high mountain of Israel, declares **the** Sovereign **LORD**,
20:42 you will know that I am **the LORD**, when I bring you into the
20:44 You will know that I am **the LORD**, when I deal with you for my
20:44 O house of Israel, declares **the** Sovereign **LORD**.' "
20:45 [21:1] The word of **the LORD** came to me:
20:47 [21:3] Say to the southern forest: 'Hear the word of **the LORD**.
20:47 [21:3] This is what **the** Sovereign **LORD** says: I am about to set
20:48 [21:4] Everyone will see that I **the LORD** have kindled it;
20:49 [21:5] I said, "Ah, Sovereign **LORD**! They are saying of me,
21: 1 [21:6] The word of **the LORD** came to me:
21: 3 [21:8] say to her: 'This is what **the LORD** says: I am against
21: 5 [21:10] all people will know that I **the LORD** have drawn my
21: 7 [21:12] It will surely take place, declares **the** Sovereign **LORD**."
21: 8 [21:13] The word of **the LORD** came to me:
21:13 [21:18] does not continue? declares **the** Sovereign **LORD**.'
21:17 [21:22] and my wrath will subside. I **the LORD** have spoken."
21:18 [21:23] The word of **the LORD** came to me:
21:24 [21:29] "Therefore this is what **the** Sovereign **LORD** says:
21:26 [21:31] this is what **the** Sovereign **LORD** says: Take off the
21:28 [21:33] 'This is what **the** Sovereign **LORD** says about the
21:32 [21:37] remembered no more; for I **the LORD** have spoken.' "
22: 1 The word of **the LORD** came to me:
22: 3 say: 'This is what **the** Sovereign **LORD** says: O city that brings
22:12 And you have forgotten me, declares **the** Sovereign **LORD**.
22:14 day I deal with you? I **the LORD** have spoken, and I will do it.
22:16 in the eyes of the nations, you will know that I am **the LORD**.' "
22:17 Then the word of **the LORD** came to me:
22:19 Therefore this is what **the** Sovereign **LORD** says: 'Because you
22:22 you will know that I **the LORD** have poured out my wrath upon
22:23 Again the word of **the LORD** came to me:
22:28 They say, 'This is what **the** Sovereign **LORD** says'—
22:28 the Sovereign LORD says'—when **the LORD** has not spoken.
22:31 own heads all they have done, declares **the** Sovereign **LORD**."
23: 1 The word of **the LORD** came to me:
23:22 "Therefore, Oholibah, this is what **the** Sovereign **LORD** says:
23:28 "For this is what **the** Sovereign **LORD** says: I am about to hand
23:32 "This is what **the** Sovereign **LORD** says: "You will drink your
23:34 tear your breasts. I have spoken, declares **the** Sovereign **LORD**.
23:35 "Therefore this is what **the** Sovereign **LORD** says: Since you
23:36 **The LORD** said to me: "Son of man, will you judge Oholah
23:46 "This is what **the** Sovereign **LORD** says: Bring a mob against
23:49 of idolatry. Then you will know that I am **the** Sovereign **LORD**."
24: 1 tenth month on the tenth day, the word of **the LORD** came to me:
24: 3 and say to them: 'This is what **the** Sovereign **LORD** says:
24: 6 " 'For this is what **the** Sovereign **LORD** says: " 'Woe to the city
24: 9 " 'Therefore this is what **the** Sovereign **LORD** says: " 'Woe to the
24:14 " 'I **the LORD** have spoken. The time has come for me to act.
24:14 your conduct and your actions, declares **the** Sovereign **LORD**.' "
24:15 The word of **the LORD** came to me:
24:20 So I said to them, "The word of **the LORD** came to me:
24:21 to the house of Israel, 'This is what **the** Sovereign **LORD** says:
24:24 this happens, you will know that I am **the** Sovereign **LORD**.'
24:27 will be a sign to them, and they will know that I am **the LORD**."
25: 1 The word of **the LORD** came to me:
25: 3 Say to them, 'Hear the word of **the** Sovereign **LORD**. This is
25: 3 This is what **the** Sovereign **LORD** says: Because you said "Aha!"
25: 5 resting place for sheep. Then you will know that I am **the LORD**.
25: 6 For this is what **the** Sovereign **LORD** says: Because you have
25: 7 I will destroy you, and you will know that I am **the LORD**.' "
25: 8 "This is what **the** Sovereign **LORD** says: 'Because Moab
25:11 on Moab. Then they will know that I am **the LORD**.' "
25:12 "This is what **the** Sovereign **LORD** says: 'Because Edom took
25:13 therefore this is what **the** Sovereign **LORD** says: I will stretch out
25:14 they will know my vengeance, declares **the** Sovereign **LORD**.' "
25:15 "This is what **the** Sovereign **LORD** says: 'Because the Philistines
25:16 therefore this is what **the** Sovereign **LORD** says: I am about to
25:17 they will know that I am **the LORD**, when I take vengeance on
26: 1 on the first day of the month, the word of **the LORD** came to me:
26: 3 therefore this is what **the** Sovereign **LORD** says: I am against
26: 5 spread fishnets, for I have spoken, declares **the** Sovereign **LORD**.
26: 6 ravaged by the sword. Then they will know that I am **the LORD**.
26: 7 "For this is what **the** Sovereign **LORD** says: From the north I am
26:14 You will never be rebuilt, for I **the LORD** have spoken,
26:14 for I the LORD have spoken, declares **the** Sovereign **LORD**.
26:15 "This is what **the** Sovereign **LORD** says to Tyre: Will not the
26:19 "This is what **the** Sovereign **LORD** says: When I make you a
26:21 you will never again be found, declares **the** Sovereign **LORD**."
27: 1 The word of **the LORD** came to me:
27: 3 peoples on many coasts, 'This is what **the** Sovereign **LORD** says:
28: 1 The word of **the LORD** came to me:
28: 2 say to the ruler of Tyre, 'This is what **the** Sovereign **LORD** says:
28: 6 " 'Therefore this is what **the** Sovereign **LORD** says:
28:10 of foreigners. I have spoken, declares **the** Sovereign **LORD**.' "
28:11 The word of **the LORD** came to me:
28:12 and say to him: 'This is what **the** Sovereign **LORD** says:
28:20 The word of **the LORD** came to me:
28:22 say: 'This is what **the** Sovereign **LORD** says: " 'I am against you,
28:22 They will know that I am **the LORD**, when I inflict punishment
28:23 her on every side. Then they will know that I am **the LORD**.
28:24 Then they will know that I am **the** Sovereign **LORD**.
28:25 " 'This is what **the** Sovereign **LORD** says: When I gather the
28:26 Then they will know that I am **the LORD** their God.' "
29: 1 month on the twelfth day, the word of **the LORD** came to me:
29: 3 Speak to him and say: 'This is what **the** Sovereign **LORD** says:
29: 6 Then all who live in Egypt will know that I am **the LORD**.
29: 8 " 'Therefore this is what **the** Sovereign **LORD** says: I will bring a
29: 9 Then they will know that I am **the LORD**. " 'Because you said,
29:13 " 'Yet this is what **the** Sovereign **LORD** says: At the end of forty
29:16 Then they will know that I am **the** Sovereign **LORD**.' "
29:17 first month on the first day, the word of **the LORD** came to me:
29:19 Therefore this is what **the** Sovereign **LORD** says: I am going to
29:20 and his army did it for me, declares **the** Sovereign **LORD**.
29:21 mouth among them. Then they will know that I am **the LORD**."
30: 1 The word of **the LORD** came to me:
30: 2 'This is what **the** Sovereign **LORD** says: " 'Wail and say,
30: 3 For the day is near, the day of **the LORD** is near—a day of
30: 6 " 'This is what **the LORD** says: " 'The allies of Egypt will fall
30: 6 will fall by the sword within her, declares **the** Sovereign **LORD**.
30: 8 they will know that I am **the LORD**, when I set fire to Egypt
30:10 " 'This is what **the** Sovereign **LORD** says: " 'I will put an end to
30:12 lay waste the land and everything in it. I **the LORD** have spoken.
30:13 " 'This is what **the** Sovereign **LORD** says: " 'I will destroy the
30:19 on Egypt, and they will know that I am **the LORD**.' "
30:20 month on the seventh day, the word of **the LORD** came to me:
30:22 Therefore this is what **the** Sovereign **LORD** says: I am against
30:25 they will know that I am **the LORD**, when I put my sword into
30:26 through the countries. Then they will know that I am **the LORD**."
31: 1 third month on the first day, the word of **the LORD** came to me:
31:10 " 'Therefore this is what **the** Sovereign **LORD** says: Because it
31:15 " 'This is what **the** Sovereign **LORD** says: On the day it was
31:18 is Pharaoh and all his hordes, declares **the** Sovereign **LORD**.' "
32: 1 month on the first day, the word of **the LORD** came to me:
32: 3 " 'This is what **the** Sovereign **LORD** says: " 'With a great throng
32: 8 bring darkness over your land, declares **the** Sovereign **LORD**.
32:11 " 'For this is what **the** Sovereign **LORD** says: " 'The sword of the
32:14 make her streams flow like oil, declares **the** Sovereign **LORD**.
32:15 all who live there, then they will know that I am **the LORD**.'
32:16 all her hordes they will chant it, declares **the** Sovereign **LORD**."
32:17 fifteenth day of the month, the word of **the LORD** came to me:
32:31 that were killed by the sword, declares **the** Sovereign **LORD**.
32:32 with those killed by the sword, declares **the** Sovereign **LORD**."

Eze 33: 1 The word of **the LORD** came to me:
33: 11 Say to them, 'As surely as I live, declares **the** Sovereign **LORD**,
33: 22 before the man arrived, the hand of **the LORD** was upon me,
33: 23 Then the word of **the LORD** came to me:
33: 25 Therefore say to them, 'This is what **the** Sovereign **LORD** says:
33: 27 "Say this to them: 'This is what **the** Sovereign **LORD** says:
33: 29 they will know that I am **the LORD**, when I have made the land a
33: 30 'Come and hear the message that has come from **the LORD**.'
34: 1 The word of **the LORD** came to me:
34: 2 and say to them: 'This is what **the** Sovereign **LORD** says:
34: 7 " 'Therefore, you shepherds, hear the word of **the LORD**:
34: 8 As surely as I live, declares **the** Sovereign **LORD**, because my
34: 9 therefore, O shepherds, hear the word of **the LORD**:
34: 10 This is what **the** Sovereign **LORD** says: I am against the
34: 11 " 'For this is what **the** Sovereign **LORD** says: I myself will search
34: 15 and have them lie down, declares **the** Sovereign **LORD**.
34: 17 " 'As for you, my flock, this is what **the** Sovereign **LORD** says:
34: 20 " 'Therefore this is what **the** Sovereign **LORD** says to them:
34: 24 I **the LORD** will be their God, and my servant David will be
34: 24 David will be prince among them. I **the LORD** have spoken.
34: 27 They will know that I am **the LORD**, when I break the bars of
34: 30 **the LORD** their God, am with them and that they, the house of
34: 30 house of Israel, are my people, declares **the** Sovereign **LORD**.
34: 31 are people, and I am your God, declares **the** Sovereign **LORD**.' "
35: 1 The word of **the LORD** came to me:
35: 3 say: 'This is what **the** Sovereign **LORD** says: I am against you,
35: 4 you will be desolate. Then you will know that I am **the LORD**.
35: 6 therefore as surely as I live, declares **the** Sovereign **LORD**,
35: 9 will not be inhabited. Then you will know that I am **the LORD**.
35: 10 take possession of them," even though I **the LORD** was there,
35: 11 therefore as surely as I live, declares **the** Sovereign **LORD**,
35: 12 you will know that I **the LORD** have heard all the contemptible
35: 14 This is what **the** Sovereign **LORD** says: While the whole earth
35: 15 and all of Edom. Then they will know that I am **the LORD**.' "
36: 1 and say, 'O mountains of Israel, hear the word of **the LORD**.
36: 2 This is what **the** Sovereign **LORD** says: The enemy said of you,
36: 3 and say, 'This is what **the** Sovereign **LORD** says:
36: 4 O mountains of Israel, hear the word of **the** Sovereign **LORD**:
36: 4 This is what **the** Sovereign **LORD** says to the mountains
36: 5 this is what **the** Sovereign **LORD** says: In my burning zeal I have
36: 6 the ravines and valleys: 'This is what **the** Sovereign **LORD** says:
36: 7 Therefore this is what **the** Sovereign **LORD** says: I swear with
36: 11 more than before. Then you will know that I am **the LORD**.
36: 13 " 'This is what **the** Sovereign **LORD** says: Because people say to
36: 14 or make your nation childless, declares **the** Sovereign **LORD**.
36: 15 or cause your nation to fall, declares **the** Sovereign **LORD**.' "
36: 16 Again the word of **the LORD** came to me:
36: 20 for it was said of them, 'These are **the LORD's** people, and yet
36: 22 to the house of Israel, 'This is what **the** Sovereign **LORD** says:
36: 23 the nations will know that I am **the LORD**,
36: 23 will know that I am the LORD, declares **the** Sovereign **LORD**,
36: 32 I am not doing this for your sake, declares **the** Sovereign **LORD**.
36: 33 " 'This is what **the** Sovereign **LORD** says: On the day I cleanse
36: 36 the nations around you that remain will know that I **the LORD**
36: 36 what was desolate. I **the LORD** have spoken, and I will do it.'
36: 37 "This is what **the** Sovereign **LORD** says: Once again I will yield
36: 38 with flocks of people. Then they will know that I am **the LORD**."
37: 1 The hand of **the LORD** was upon me, and he brought me out by
37: 1 he brought me out by the Spirit of **the LORD** and set me in the
37: 3 these bones live?" I said, "O Sovereign **LORD**, you alone know."
37: 4 and say to them, 'Dry bones, hear the word of **the LORD**!
37: 5 This is what **the** Sovereign **LORD** says to these bones: I will
37: 6 will come to life. Then you will know that I am **the LORD**.' "
37: 9 of man, and say to it, 'This is what **the** Sovereign **LORD** says:
37: 12 'This is what **the** Sovereign **LORD** says: O my people, I am
37: 13 you, my people, will know that I am **the LORD**, when I open
37: 14 you will know that I **the LORD** have spoken, and I have done it,
37: 14 LORD have spoken, and I have done it, declares **the LORD**.' "
37: 15 The word of **the LORD** came to me:
37: 19 say to them, 'This is what **the** Sovereign **LORD** says: I am going
37: 21 and say to them, 'This is what **the** Sovereign **LORD** says:
37: 28 Then the nations will know that I **the LORD** make Israel holy,
38: 1 The word of **the LORD** came to me:
38: 3 say: 'This is what **the** Sovereign **LORD** says: I am against you,
38: 10 " 'This is what **the** Sovereign **LORD** says: On that day thoughts
38: 14 'This is what **the** Sovereign **LORD** says: In that day, when my
38: 17 " 'This is what **the** Sovereign **LORD** says: Are you not the one I
38: 18 my hot anger will be aroused, declares **the** Sovereign **LORD**.
38: 21 against Gog on all my mountains, declares **the** Sovereign **LORD**.
38: 23 sight of many nations. Then they will know that I am **the LORD**.'
39: 1 against Gog and say: 'This is what **the** Sovereign **LORD** says:
39: 5 the open field, for I have spoken, declares **the** Sovereign **LORD**.
39: 6 safety in the coastlands, and they will know that I am **the LORD**.
39: 7 the nations will know that I **the LORD** am the Holy One in
39: 8 It will surely take place, declares **the** Sovereign **LORD**.
39: 10 and loot those who looted them, declares **the** Sovereign **LORD**.
39: 13 be a memorable day for them, declares **the** Sovereign **LORD**.
39: 17 "Son of man, this is what **the** Sovereign **LORD** says: Call out to
39: 20 and soldiers of every kind,' declares **the** Sovereign **LORD**.
39: 22 the house of Israel will know that I am **the LORD** their God.
39: 25 "Therefore this is what **the** Sovereign **LORD** says: I will now
39: 28 they will know that I am **the LORD** their God, for though I sent
39: 29 my Spirit on the house of Israel, declares **the** Sovereign **LORD**."
40: 1 on that very day the hand of **the LORD** was upon me and he took
40: 46 who are the only Levites who may draw near to **the LORD** to
41: 22 The man said to me, "This is the table that is before **the LORD**."
42: 13 where the priests who approach **the LORD** will eat the most holy
43: 4 The glory of **the LORD** entered the temple through the gate
43: 5 into the inner court, and the glory of **the LORD** filled the temple.
43: 18 said to me, "Son of man, this is what **the** Sovereign **LORD** says:
43: 19 come near to minister before me, declares **the** Sovereign **LORD**.
43: 24 You are to offer them before **the LORD**, and the priests are to
43: 24 salt on them and sacrifice them as a burnt offering to **the LORD**.
43: 27 Then I will accept you, declares **the** Sovereign **LORD**."
44: 2 **The LORD** said to me, "This gate is to remain shut. It must not
44: 2 It is to remain shut because **the LORD**, the God of Israel,
44: 3 may sit inside the gateway to eat in the presence of **the LORD**.
44: 4 and saw the glory of **the LORD** filling the temple of the LORD,
44: 4 and saw the glory of the LORD filling the temple of **the LORD**,
44: 5 **The LORD** said to me, "Son of man, look carefully, listen
44: 5 concerning all the regulations regarding the temple of **the LORD**.
44: 6 house of Israel, 'This is what **the** Sovereign **LORD** says:
44: 9 This is what **the** Sovereign **LORD** says: No foreigner
44: 12 the consequences of their sin, declares **the** Sovereign **LORD**.
44: 15 offer sacrifices of fat and blood, declares **the** Sovereign **LORD**.
44: 27 to offer a sin offering for himself, declares **the** Sovereign **LORD**.
45: 1 you are to present to **the LORD** a portion of the land as a sacred
45: 4 the sanctuary and who draw near to minister before **the LORD**.
45: 9 " 'This is what **the** Sovereign **LORD** says: You have gone far
45: 9 Stop dispossessing my people, declares **the** Sovereign **LORD**.
45: 15 to make atonement for the people, declares **the** Sovereign **LORD**.
45: 18 " 'This is what **the** Sovereign **LORD** says: In the first month on
45: 23 and seven rams without defect as a burnt offering to **the LORD**,
46: 1 " 'This is what **the** Sovereign **LORD** says: The gate of the inner
46: 3 in the presence of **the LORD** at the entrance to that gateway.
46: 4 The burnt offering the prince brings to **the LORD** on the Sabbath
46: 9 " 'When the people of the land come before **the LORD** at the
46: 12 When the prince provides a freewill offering to **the LORD**—
46: 13 a year-old lamb without defect for a burnt offering to **the LORD**;
46: 14 The presenting of this grain offering to **the LORD** is a lasting
46: 16 " 'This is what **the** Sovereign **LORD** says: If the prince makes a
47: 13 This is what **the** Sovereign **LORD** says: "These are the
47: 23 are to give him his inheritance," declares **the** Sovereign **LORD**.
48: 9 "The special portion you are to offer to **the LORD** will be 25,000
48: 10 south side. In the center of it will be the sanctuary of **the LORD**.
48: 14 must not pass into other hands, because it is holy to **the LORD**.
48: 29 and these will be their portions," declares **the** Sovereign **LORD**.
48: 35 of the city from that time on will be: **THE LORD** IS THERE."
Da 9: 2 according to the word of **the LORD** given to Jeremiah the
9: 4 I prayed to **the LORD** my God and confessed: "O Lord,
9: 8 O **LORD**, we and our kings, our princes and our fathers are
9: 10 we have not obeyed **the LORD** our God or kept the laws he gave
9: 13 yet we have not sought the favor of **the LORD** our God by
9: 14 **The LORD** did not hesitate to bring the disaster upon us,
9: 14 for **the LORD** our God is righteous in everything he does;
9: 20 and making my request to **the LORD** my God for his holy hill—
Hos 1: 1 The word of **the LORD** that came to Hosea son of Beeri during
1: 2 When **the LORD** began to speak through Hosea, the LORD said
1: 2 **the LORD** said to him, "Go, take to yourself an adulterous wife
1: 2 land is guilty of the vilest adultery in departing from **the LORD**."
1: 4 **the LORD** said to Hosea, "Call him Jezreel, because I will soon
1: 7 or by horses and horsemen, but by **the LORD** their God."
2: 13 [2:15] after her lovers, but me she forgot," declares **the LORD**.
2: 16 [2:18] "In that day," declares **the LORD**, "you will call me 'my
2: 20 [2:22] in faithfulness, and you will acknowledge **the LORD**.
2: 21 [2:23] "In that day I will respond," declares **the LORD**—"I will
3: 1 **The LORD** said to me, "Go, show your love to your wife again,
3: 1 Love her as **the LORD** loves the Israelites, though they turn to
3: 5 will return and seek **the LORD** their God and David their king.
3: 5 They will come trembling to **the LORD** and to his blessings in
4: 1 Hear the word of **the LORD**, you Israelites, because the LORD
4: 1 because **the LORD** has a charge to bring against you who live in
4: 10 because they have deserted **the LORD** to give themselves
4: 15 to Beth Aven. And do not swear, 'As surely as **the LORD** lives!'
4: 16 then can **the LORD** pasture them like lambs in a meadow?
5: 4 prostitution is in their heart; they do not acknowledge **the LORD**.
5: 6 When they go with their flocks and herds to seek **the LORD**,
5: 7 They are unfaithful to **the LORD**; they give birth to illegitimate

Hos 6: 1 "Come, let us return to **the LORD**. He has torn us to pieces
6: 3 Let us acknowledge **the LORD**; let us press on to acknowledge
7: 10 but despite all this he does not return to **the LORD** his God
8: 1 An eagle is over the house of **the LORD** because the people have
8: 13 and they eat the meat, but **the LORD** is not pleased with them.
9: 3 They will not remain in **the LORD's** land; Ephraim will return to
9: 4 They will not pour out wine offerings to **the LORD**, nor will their
9: 4 be for themselves; it will not come into the temple of **the LORD**.
9: 5 day of your appointed feasts, on the festival days of **the LORD**?
9: 14 Give them, O **LORD**—what will you give them? Give them
10: 3 "We have no king because we did not revere **the LORD**.
10: 12 for it is time to seek **the LORD**, until he comes and showers
11: 10 They will follow **the LORD**; he will roar like a lion. When he
11: 11 I will settle them in their homes," declares **the LORD**.
12: 2 [12:3] **The LORD** has a charge to bring against Judah; he will
12: 5 [12:6] **the LORD** God Almighty, the LORD is his name of
12: 5 [12:6] God Almighty, **the LORD** is his name of renown!
12: 9 [12:10] "I am **the LORD** your God, ⌊who brought you⌋ out of
12: 13 [12:14] **The LORD** used a prophet to bring Israel up from
13: 4 "But I am **the LORD** your God, ⌊who brought you⌋ out of Egypt.
13: 15 An east wind from **the LORD** will come, blowing in from the
14: 1 [14:2] Return, O Israel, to **the LORD** your God. Your sins have
14: 2 [14:3] Take words with you and return to **the LORD**. Say to
14: 9 [14:10] The ways of **the LORD** are right; the righteous walk in
Joel 1: 1 The word of **the LORD** that came to Joel son of Pethuel.
1: 9 and drink offerings are cut off from the house of **the LORD**.
1: 9 priests are in mourning, those who minister before **the LORD**.
1: 14 and all who live in the land to the house of **the LORD** your God,
1: 14 to the house of the LORD your God, and cry out to **the LORD**.
1: 15 For the day of **the LORD** is near; it will come like destruction
1: 19 To you, O **LORD**, I call, for fire has devoured the open pastures
2: 1 who live in the land tremble, for the day of **the LORD** is coming.
2: 11 **The LORD** thunders at the head of his army; his forces are
2: 11 The day of **the LORD** is great; it is dreadful. Who can endure it?
2: 12 "Even now," declares **the LORD**, "return to me with all your
2: 13 Return to **the LORD** your God, for he is gracious
2: 14 grain offerings and drink offerings for **the LORD** your God.
2: 17 Let the priests, who minister before **the LORD**, weep between
2: 17 and the altar. Let them say, "Spare your people, O **LORD**.
2: 18 **the LORD** will be jealous for his land and take pity on his
2: 19 **The LORD** will reply to them: "I am sending you grain,
2: 21 be glad and rejoice. Surely **the LORD** has done great things.
2: 23 Be glad, O people of Zion, rejoice in **the LORD** your God,
2: 26 are full, and you will praise the name of **the LORD** your God,
2: 27 that I am **the LORD** your God, and that there is no other;
2: 31 [3:4] the coming of the great and dreadful day of **the LORD**.
2: 32 [3:5] everyone who calls on the name of **the LORD** will be
2: 32 [3:5] Jerusalem there will be deliverance, as **the LORD** has said,
2: 32 [3:5] has said, among the survivors whom **the LORD** calls.
3: 8 [4:8] to the Sabeans, a nation far away." **The LORD** has spoken.
3: 11 [4:11] and assemble there. Bring down your warriors, O **LORD**!
3: 14 [4:14] For the day of **the LORD** is near in the valley of decision.
3: 16 [4:16] **The LORD** will roar from Zion and thunder from
3: 16 [4:16] **the LORD** will be a refuge for his people, a stronghold
3: 17 [4:17] that I, **the LORD** your God, dwell in Zion, my holy hill.
3: 18 [4:18] A fountain will flow out of **the LORD's** house and will
3: 21 [4:21] not pardoned, I will pardon." **The LORD** dwells in Zion!
Am 1: 2 "**The LORD** roars from Zion and thunders from Jerusalem;
1: 3 This is what **the LORD** says: "For three sins of Damascus,
1: 5 The people of Aram will go into exile to Kir," says **the LORD**.
1: 6 This is what **the LORD** says: "For three sins of Gaza, even for
1: 8 till the last of the Philistines is dead," says **the** Sovereign **LORD**.
1: 9 This is what **the LORD** says: "For three sins of Tyre, even for
1: 11 This is what **the LORD** says: "For three sins of Edom, even for
1: 13 This is what **the LORD** says: "For three sins of Ammon,
1: 15 will go into exile, he and his officials together," says **the LORD**.
2: 1 This is what **the LORD** says: "For three sins of Moab, even for
2: 3 her ruler and kill all her officials with him," says **the LORD**.
2: 4 This is what **the LORD** says: "For three sins of Judah, even for
2: 4 Because they have rejected the law of **the LORD** and have not
2: 6 This is what **the LORD** says: "For three sins of Israel, even for
2: 11 Is this not true, people of Israel?" declares **the LORD**.
2: 16 warriors will flee naked on that day," declares **the LORD**.
3: 1 Hear this word **the LORD** has spoken against you, O people of
3: 6 When disaster comes to a city, has not **the LORD** caused it?
3: 7 Surely **the** Sovereign **LORD** does nothing without revealing his
3: 8 **The** Sovereign **LORD** has spoken—who can but prophesy?
3: 10 declares **the LORD**, "who hoard plunder and loot in their
3: 11 Therefore this is what **the** Sovereign **LORD** says: "An enemy
3: 12 This is what **the LORD** says: "As a shepherd saves from the
3: 13 house of Jacob," declares the Lord, **the LORD** God Almighty.
3: 15 and the mansions will be demolished," declares **the LORD**.
4: 2 **The** Sovereign **LORD** has sworn by his holiness: "The time will
4: 3 and you will be cast out toward Harmon," declares **the LORD**.
4: 5 for this is what you love to do," declares **the** Sovereign **LORD**.
4: 6 yet you have not returned to me," declares **the LORD**.
4: 8 to drink, yet you have not returned to me," declares **the LORD**.
4: 9 yet you have not returned to me," declares **the LORD**.
4: 10 yet you have not returned to me," declares **the LORD**.
4: 11 the fire, yet you have not returned to me," declares **the LORD**.
4: 13 high places of the earth—**the LORD** God Almighty is his name.
5: 3 This is what **the** Sovereign **LORD** says: "The city that marches
5: 4 This is what **the LORD** says to the house of Israel: "Seek me
5: 6 Seek **the LORD** and live, or he will sweep through the house of
5: 8 them out over the face of the land—**the LORD** is his name—
5: 14 **the LORD** God Almighty will be with you, just as you say he is.
5: 15 Perhaps **the LORD** God Almighty will have mercy on the
5: 16 Therefore this is what the Lord, **the LORD** God Almighty, says:
5: 17 for I will pass through your midst," says **the LORD**.
5: 18 Woe to you who long for the day of **the LORD**! Why do you
5: 18 Why do you long for the day of **the LORD**? That day will be
5: 20 Will not the day of **the LORD** be darkness, not light—pitch-dark,
5: 27 says **the LORD**, whose name is God Almighty.
6: 8 **The** Sovereign **LORD** has sworn by himself—the LORD God
6: 8 has sworn by himself—**the LORD** God Almighty declares:
6: 10 will say, "Hush! We must not mention the name of **the LORD**."
6: 11 For **the LORD** has given the command, and he will smash the
6: 14 For **the LORD** God Almighty declares, "I will stir up a nation
7: 1 This is what **the** Sovereign **LORD** showed me: He was preparing
7: 2 stripped the land clean, I cried out, "Sovereign **LORD**, forgive!
7: 3 So **the LORD** relented. "This will not happen," the LORD said.
7: 3 So the LORD relented. "This will not happen," **the LORD** said.
7: 4 This is what **the** Sovereign **LORD** showed me: The Sovereign
7: 4 **The** Sovereign **LORD** was calling for judgment by fire;
7: 5 I cried out, "Sovereign **LORD**, I beg you, stop! How can Jacob
7: 6 So **the LORD** relented. "This will not happen either,"
7: 6 "This will not happen either," **the** Sovereign **LORD** said.
7: 8 **the LORD** asked me, "What do you see, Amos?" "A plumb
7: 15 But **the LORD** took me from tending the flock and said to me,
7: 15 took me from tending the flock and said to me, **[RPH]** 'Go,
7: 16 Now then, hear the word of **the LORD**. You say, " 'Do not
7: 17 "Therefore this is what **the LORD** says: " 'Your wife will
8: 1 This is what **the** Sovereign **LORD** showed me: a basket of ripe
8: 2 **the LORD** said to me, "The time is ripe for my people Israel;
8: 3 "In that day," declares **the** Sovereign **LORD**, "the songs in the
8: 7 **The LORD** has sworn by the Pride of Jacob: "I will never forget
8: 9 "In that day," declares **the** Sovereign **LORD**, "I will make the
8: 11 "The days are coming," declares **the** Sovereign **LORD**, "when I
8: 11 thirst for water, but a famine of hearing the words of **the LORD**.
8: 12 searching for the word of **the LORD**, but they will not find it.
9: 5 The Lord, **the LORD** Almighty, he who touches the earth
9: 6 pours them out over the face of the land—**the LORD** is his name.
9: 7 declares **the LORD**. "Did I not bring Israel up from Egypt,
9: 8 "Surely the eyes of **the** Sovereign **LORD** are on the sinful
9: 8 I will not totally destroy the house of Jacob," declares **the LORD**.
9: 12 bear my name," declares **the LORD**, who will do these things.
9: 13 "The days are coming," declares **the LORD**, "when the reaper
9: 15 from the land I have given them," says **the LORD** your God.
Ob 1: 1 This is what **the** Sovereign **LORD** says about Edom—We have
1: 1 says about Edom—We have heard a message from **the LORD**:
1: 4 the stars, from there I will bring you down," declares **the LORD**.
1: 8 "In that day," declares **the LORD**, "will I not destroy the wise
1: 15 "The day of **the LORD** is near for all nations. As you have done,
1: 18 be no survivors from the house of Esau." **The LORD** has spoken.
1: 21 of Esau. And the kingdom will be **the LORD's** [+4200].
Jnh 1: 1 The word of **the LORD** came to Jonah son of Amittai:
1: 3 But Jonah ran away from **the LORD** and headed for Tarshish.
1: 3 he went aboard and sailed for Tarshish to flee from **the LORD**.
1: 4 **the LORD** sent a great wind on the sea, and such a violent storm
1: 9 He answered, "I am a Hebrew and I worship **the LORD**,
1: 10 (They knew he was running away from **the LORD**, because he
1: 14 they cried to **the LORD**, "O LORD, please do not let us die for
1: 14 they cried to the LORD, "O **LORD**, please do not let us die for
1: 14 an innocent man, for you, O **LORD**, have done as you pleased."
1: 16 At this the men greatly feared **the LORD**, and they offered a
1: 16 and they offered a sacrifice to **the LORD** and made vows to him.
1: 17 [2:1] **the LORD** provided a great fish to swallow Jonah,
2: 1 [2:2] From inside the fish Jonah prayed to **the LORD** his God.
2: 2 [2:3] "In my distress I called to **the LORD**, and he answered
2: 6 [2:7] you brought my life up from the pit, O **LORD** my God.
2: 7 [2:8] I remembered you, **LORD**, and my prayer rose to you,
2: 9 [2:10] I will make good. Salvation comes from **the LORD**."
2: 10 [2:11] **the LORD** commanded the fish, and it vomited Jonah
3: 1 Then the word of **the LORD** came to Jonah a second time:
3: 3 Jonah obeyed the word of **the LORD** and went to Nineveh.
4: 2 He prayed to **the LORD**, "O LORD, is this not what I said when
4: 2 He prayed to the LORD, "O **LORD**, is this not what I said when
4: 3 Now, O **LORD**, take away my life, for it is better for me to die

Jnh 4: 4 But **the LORD** replied, "Have you any right to be angry?"
4: 6 **the LORD** God provided a vine and made it grow up over Jonah
4: 10 But **the LORD** said, "You have been concerned about this vine,
Mic 1: 1 The word of **the LORD** that came to Micah of Moresheth during
1: 2 who are in it, that **the** Sovereign **LORD** may witness against you,
1: 3 **The LORD** is coming from his dwelling place; he comes down
1: 12 waiting for relief, because disaster has come from **the LORD**,
2: 3 Therefore, **the LORD** says: "I am planning disaster against this
2: 5 Therefore you will have no one in the assembly of **the LORD** to
2: 7 it be said, O house of Jacob: "Is the Spirit of **the LORD** angry?
2: 13 king will pass through before them, **the LORD** at their head."
3: 4 Then they will cry out to **the LORD**, but he will not answer them.
3: 5 This is what **the LORD** says: "As for the prophets who lead my
3: 8 with the Spirit of **the LORD**, and with justice and might,
3: 11 Yet they lean upon **the LORD** and say, "Is not the LORD
3: 11 lean upon the LORD and say, "Is not **the LORD** among us?
4: 1 In the last days the mountain of **the LORD's** temple will be
4: 2 and say, "Come, let us go up to the mountain of **the LORD**,
4: 2 will go out from Zion, the word of **the LORD** from Jerusalem.
4: 4 one will make them afraid, for **the LORD** Almighty has spoken.
4: 5 we will walk in the name of **the LORD** our God for ever
4: 6 "In that day," declares **the LORD**, "I will gather the lame;
4: 7 **The LORD** will rule over them in Mount Zion from that day
4: 10 There **the LORD** will redeem you out of the hand of your
4: 12 they do not know the thoughts of **the LORD**; they do not
4: 13 You will devote their ill-gotten gains to **the LORD**, their wealth
5: 4 [5:3] and shepherd his flock in the strength of **the LORD**,
5: 4 [5:3] in the majesty of the name of **the LORD** his God.
5: 7 [5:6] be in the midst of many peoples like dew from **the LORD**,
5: 10 [5:9] "In that day," declares **the LORD**, "I will destroy your
6: 1 Listen to what **the LORD** says: "Stand up, plead your case before
6: 2 Hear, O mountains, **the LORD's** accusation; listen,
6: 2 For **the LORD** has a case against his people; he is lodging a
6: 5 to Gilgal, that you may know the righteous acts of **the LORD**."
6: 6 With what shall I come before **the LORD** and bow down before
6: 7 Will **the LORD** be pleased with thousands of rams, with ten
6: 8 what does **the LORD** require of you? To act justly and to love
6: 9 **The LORD** is calling to the city—and to fear your name is
7: 7 as for me, I watch in hope for **the LORD**, I wait for God my
7: 8 I will rise. Though I sit in darkness, **the LORD** will be my light.
7: 9 I will bear **the LORD's** wrath, until he pleads my case
7: 10 she who said to me, "Where is **the LORD** your God?"
7: 17 they will turn in fear to **the LORD** our God and will be afraid of
Na 1: 2 **The LORD** is a jealous and avenging God; the LORD takes
1: 2 **the LORD** takes vengeance and is filled with wrath.
1: 2 **The LORD** takes vengeance on his foes and maintains his wrath
1: 3 **The LORD** is slow to anger and great in power; the LORD will
1: 3 great in power; **the LORD** will not leave the guilty unpunished.
1: 7 **The LORD** is good, a refuge in times of trouble. He cares for
1: 9 Whatever they plot against **the LORD** he will bring to an end;
1: 11 Nineveh,⌞ has one come forth who plots evil against **the LORD**
1: 12 This is what **the LORD** says: "Although they have allies
1: 14 **The LORD** has given a command concerning you, ⌞Nineveh⌟:
2: 2 [2:3] **The LORD** will restore the splendor of Jacob like the
2: 13 [2:14] "I am against you," declares **the LORD** Almighty. "I will
3: 5 "I am against you," declares **the LORD** Almighty. "I will lift
Hab 1: 2 How long, O **LORD**, must I call for help, but you do not listen?
1: 12 O **LORD**, are you not from everlasting? My God, my Holy One,
1: 12 O **LORD**, you have appointed them to execute judgment;
2: 2 **the LORD** replied: "Write down the revelation and make it plain
2: 13 Has not **the LORD** Almighty determined that the people's labor
2: 14 earth will be filled with the knowledge of the glory of **the LORD**,
2: 16 The cup from **the LORD's** right hand is coming around to you,
2: 20 **the LORD** is in his holy temple; let all the earth be silent before
3: 2 **LORD**, I have heard of your fame; I stand in awe of your deeds,
3: 2 have heard of your fame; I stand in awe of your deeds, O **LORD**.
3: 8 Were you angry with the rivers, O **LORD**? Was your wrath
3: 18 yet I will rejoice in **the LORD**, I will be joyful in God my Savior.
3: 19 **The** Sovereign **LORD** is my strength; he makes my feet like the
Zep 1: 1 The word of **the LORD** that came to Zephaniah son of Cushi,
1: 2 away everything from the face of the earth," declares **the LORD**.
1: 3 I cut off man from the face of the earth," declares **the LORD**.
1: 5 those who bow down and swear by **the LORD** and who also
1: 6 those who turn back from following **the LORD** and neither seek
1: 6 the LORD and neither seek **the LORD** nor inquire of him.
1: 7 Be silent before **the** Sovereign **LORD**, for the day of the LORD
1: 7 before the Sovereign LORD, for the day of **the LORD** is near.
1: 7 **The LORD** has prepared a sacrifice; he has consecrated those he
1: 8 On the day of **the LORD's** sacrifice I will punish the princes
1: 10 "On that day," declares **the LORD**, "a cry will go up from the
1: 12 who think, '**The LORD** will do nothing, either good or bad.'
1: 14 "The great day of **the LORD** is near—near and coming quickly.
1: 14 The cry on the day of **the LORD** will be bitter, the shouting of
1: 17 like blind men, because they have sinned against **the LORD**.
1: 18 gold will be able to save them on the day of **the LORD's** wrath.
2: 2 like chaff, before the fierce anger of **the LORD** comes upon you,
2: 2 upon you, before the day of **the LORD's** wrath comes upon you.
2: 3 Seek **the LORD**, all you humble of the land, you who do what he
2: 3 perhaps you will be sheltered on the day of **the LORD's** anger.
2: 5 the word of **the LORD** is against you, O Canaan, land of the
2: 7 **The LORD** their God will care for them; he will restore their
2: 9 surely as I live," declares **the LORD** Almighty, the God of Israel,
2: 10 for insulting and mocking the people of **the LORD** Almighty.
2: 11 **The LORD** will be awesome to them when he destroys all the
3: 2 She does not trust in **the LORD**, she does not draw near to her
3: 5 **The LORD** within her is righteous; he does no wrong. Morning
3: 8 Therefore wait for me," declares **the LORD**, "for the day I will
3: 9 that all of them may call on the name of **the LORD** and serve
3: 12 you the meek and humble, who trust in the name of **the LORD**.
3: 15 **The LORD** has taken away your punishment, he has turned back
3: 15 **The LORD**, the King of Israel, is with you; never again will you
3: 17 **The LORD** your God is with you, he is mighty to save. He will
3: 20 I restore your fortunes before your very eyes," says **the LORD**.
Hag 1: 1 the word of **the LORD** came through the prophet Haggai to
1: 2 This is what **the LORD** Almighty says: "These people say,
1: 2 'The time has not yet come for **the LORD's** house to be built.'"
1: 3 Then the word of **the LORD** came through the prophet Haggai:
1: 5 Now this is what **the LORD** Almighty says: "Give careful
1: 7 This is what **the LORD** Almighty says: "Give careful thought to
1: 8 that I may take pleasure in it and be honored," says **the LORD**.
1: 9 I blew away. Why?" declares **the LORD** Almighty.
1: 12 the whole remnant of the people obeyed the voice of **the LORD**
1: 12 the prophet Haggai, because **the LORD** their God had sent him.
1: 12 their God had sent him. And the people feared **the LORD**.
1: 13 Haggai, **the LORD's** messenger, gave this message of the
1: 13 gave this message of **the LORD** to the people:
1: 13 the LORD to the people: "I am with you," declares **the LORD**.
1: 14 So **the LORD** stirred up the spirit of Zerubbabel son of Shealtiel,
1: 14 and began to work on the house of **the LORD** Almighty,
2: 1 the word of **the LORD** came through the prophet Haggai:
2: 4 now be strong, O Zerubbabel,' declares **the LORD**. 'Be strong,
2: 4 all you people of the land,' declares **the LORD**, 'and work.
2: 4 'and work. For I am with you,' declares **the LORD** Almighty.
2: 6 "This is what **the LORD** Almighty says: 'In a little while I will
2: 7 and I will fill this house with glory,' says **the LORD** Almighty.
2: 8 is mine and the gold is mine,' declares **the LORD** Almighty.
2: 9 than the glory of the former house,' says **the LORD** Almighty.
2: 9 in this place I will grant peace,' declares **the LORD** Almighty."
2: 10 of Darius, the word of **the LORD** came to the prophet Haggai:
2: 11 "This is what **the LORD** Almighty says: 'Ask the priests what the
2: 14 with this people and this nation in my sight,' declares **the LORD**.
2: 15 before one stone was laid on another in **the LORD's** temple.
2: 17 and hail, yet you did not turn to me,' declares **the LORD**.
2: 18 to the day when the foundation of **the LORD's** temple was laid.
2: 20 The word of **the LORD** came to Haggai a second time on the
2: 23 " 'On that day,' declares **the LORD** Almighty, 'I will take you,
2: 23 my servant Zerubbabel son of Shealtiel,' declares **the LORD**,
2: 23 for I have chosen you,' declares **the LORD** Almighty."
Zec 1: 1 the word of **the LORD** came to the prophet Zechariah son of
1: 2 "**The LORD** was very angry with your forefathers.
1: 3 This is what **the LORD** Almighty says: 'Return to me,'
1: 3 'Return to me,' declares **the LORD** Almighty, 'and I will return to
1: 3 'and I will return to you,' says **the LORD** Almighty.
1: 4 This is what **the LORD** Almighty says: 'Turn from your evil
1: 4 they would not listen or pay attention to me, declares **the LORD**.
1: 6 '**The LORD** Almighty has done to us what our ways
1: 7 the word of **the LORD** came to the prophet Zechariah son of
1: 10 "They are the ones **the LORD** has sent to go throughout the
1: 11 they reported to the angel of **the LORD**, who was standing
1: 12 the angel of **the LORD** said, "LORD Almighty, how long will
1: 12 the angel of the LORD said, "**LORD** Almighty, how long will
1: 13 So **the LORD** spoke kind and comforting words to the angel who
1: 14 "Proclaim this word: This is what **the LORD** Almighty says:
1: 16 "Therefore, this is what **the LORD** says: 'I will return to
1: 16 be stretched out over Jerusalem,' declares **the LORD** Almighty.
1: 17 "Proclaim further: This is what **the LORD** Almighty says:
1: 17 and **the LORD** will again comfort Zion and choose Jerusalem.'"
1: 20 [2:3] Then **the LORD** showed me four craftsmen.
2: 5 [2:9] declares **the LORD**, 'and I will be its glory within.'
2: 6 [2:10] Flee from the land of the north," declares **the LORD**,
2: 6 [2:10] you to the four winds of heaven," declares **the LORD**.
2: 8 [2:12] For this is what **the LORD** Almighty says: "After he has
2: 9 [2:13] you will know that **the LORD** Almighty has sent me.
2: 10 [2:14] and I will live among you," declares **the LORD**.
2: 11 [2:15] "Many nations will be joined with **the LORD** in that day
2: 11 [2:15] you will know that **the LORD** Almighty has sent me to
2: 12 [2:16] **The LORD** will inherit Judah as his portion in the holy
2: 13 [2:17] Be still before **the LORD**, all mankind, because he has

Zec 3: 1 Joshua the high priest standing before the angel of **the LORD**,
3: 2 **The LORD** said to Satan, "The LORD rebuke you, Satan!
3: 2 The LORD said to Satan, "**The LORD** rebuke you, Satan!
3: 2 Satan! **The LORD**, who has chosen Jerusalem, rebuke you!
3: 5 and clothed him, while the angel of **the LORD** stood by.
3: 6 The angel of **the LORD** gave this charge to Joshua:
3: 7 "This is what **the LORD** Almighty says: 'If you will walk in my
3: 9 and I will engrave an inscription on it,' says **the LORD** Almighty,
3: 10 to sit under his vine and fig tree,' declares **the LORD** Almighty."
4: 6 So he said to me, "This is the word of **the LORD** to Zerubbabel:
4: 6 might nor by power, but by my Spirit,' says **the LORD** Almighty.
4: 8 Then the word of **the LORD** came to me:
4: 9 you will know that **the LORD** Almighty has sent me to you.
4: 10 "(These seven are the eyes of **the LORD**, which range throughout
5: 4 **The LORD** Almighty declares, 'I will send it out, and it will enter
6: 9 The word of **the LORD** came to me:
6: 12 Tell him this is what **the LORD** Almighty says: 'Here is the man
6: 12 will branch out from his place and build the temple of **the LORD**.
6: 13 It is he who will build the temple of **the LORD**, and he will be
6: 14 Hen son of Zephaniah as a memorial in the temple of **the LORD**.
6: 15 far away will come and help to build the temple of **the LORD**,
6: 15 and you will know that **the LORD** Almighty has sent me to you.
6: 15 This will happen if you diligently obey **the LORD** your God."
7: 1 the word of **the LORD** came to Zechariah on the fourth day of
7: 2 together with their men, to entreat **the LORD**
7: 3 by asking the priests of the house of **the LORD** Almighty
7: 4 Then the word of **the LORD** Almighty came to me:
7: 7 Are these not the words **the LORD** proclaimed through the
7: 8 And the word of **the LORD** came again to Zechariah:
7: 9 "This is what **the LORD** Almighty says: 'Administer true justice;
7: 12 or to the words that **the LORD** Almighty had sent by his Spirit
7: 12 the earlier prophets. So **the LORD** Almighty was very angry.
7: 13 when they called, I would not listen,' says **the LORD** Almighty.
8: 1 Again the word of **the LORD** Almighty came to me.
8: 2 This is what **the LORD** Almighty says: "I am very jealous for
8: 3 This is what **the LORD** says: "I will return to Zion and dwell in
8: 3 the mountain of **the LORD** Almighty will be called the Holy
8: 4 This is what **the LORD** Almighty says: "Once again men
8: 6 This is what **the LORD** Almighty says: "It may seem marvelous
8: 6 will it seem marvelous to me?" declares **the LORD** Almighty.
8: 7 This is what **the LORD** Almighty says: "I will save my people
8: 9 This is what **the LORD** Almighty says: "You who now hear
8: 9 the foundation was laid for the house of **the LORD** Almighty,
8: 11 of this people as I did in the past," declares **the LORD** Almighty.
8: 14 This is what **the LORD** Almighty says: "Just as I had determined
8: 14 pity when your fathers angered me," says **the LORD** Almighty,
8: 17 do not love to swear falsely. I hate all this," declares **the LORD**.
8: 18 Again the word of **the LORD** Almighty came to me.
8: 19 This is what **the LORD** Almighty says: "The fasts of the fourth,
8: 20 This is what **the LORD** Almighty says: "Many peoples
8: 21 'Let us go at once to entreat **the LORD** and seek the LORD
8: 21 go at once to entreat the LORD and seek **the LORD** Almighty.
8: 22 powerful nations will come to Jerusalem to seek **the LORD**
8: 22 to Jerusalem to seek the LORD Almighty and to entreat **him**[s]."
8: 23 This is what **the LORD** Almighty says: "In those days ten men
9: 1 An Oracle The word of **the LORD** is against the land of Hadrach
9: 1 for the eyes of men and all the tribes of Israel are on **the LORD**—
9: 14 **the LORD** will appear over them; his arrow will flash like
9: 14 **The** Sovereign **LORD** will sound the trumpet; he will march in
9: 15 and **the LORD** Almighty will shield them. They will destroy
9: 16 **The LORD** their God will save them on that day as the flock of
10: 1 Ask **the LORD** for rain in the springtime; it is the LORD who
10: 1 in the springtime; it is **the LORD** who makes the storm clouds.
10: 3 for **the LORD** Almighty will care for his flock, the house of
10: 5 Because **the LORD** is with them, they will fight and overthrow
10: 6 for I am **the LORD** their God and I will answer them.
10: 7 will see it and be joyful; their hearts will rejoice in **the LORD**.
10: 12 I will strengthen them in **the LORD** and in his name they will
10: 12 the LORD and in his name they will walk," declares **the LORD**.
11: 4 This is what **the LORD** my God says: "Pasture the flock marked
11: 5 Those who sell them say, 'Praise **the LORD**, I am rich!'
11: 6 longer have pity on the people of the land," declares **the LORD**.
11: 11 flock who were watching me knew it was the word of **the LORD**.
11: 13 **the LORD** said to me, "Throw it to the potter"—the handsome
11: 13 and threw them into the house of **the LORD** to the potter.
11: 15 **the LORD** said to me, "Take again the equipment of a foolish
12: 1 An Oracle This is the word of **the LORD** concerning Israel.
12: 1 **The LORD**, who stretches out the heavens, who lays the
12: 4 with panic and its rider with madness," declares **the LORD**.
12: 5 Jerusalem are strong, because **the LORD** Almighty is their God.'
12: 7 "**The LORD** will save the dwellings of Judah first, so that the
12: 8 On that day **the LORD** will shield those who live in Jerusalem,
12: 8 will be like God, like the Angel of **the LORD** going before them.
13: 2 will be remembered no more," declares **the LORD** Almighty.
13: 3 'You must die, because you have told lies in **the LORD's** name.'
13: 7 declares **the LORD** Almighty. "Strike the shepherd,
13: 8 In the whole land," declares **the LORD**, "two-thirds will be
13: 9 are my people,' and they will say, '**The LORD** is our God.' "
14: 1 A day of **the LORD** is coming when your plunder will be divided
14: 3 Then **the LORD** will go out and fight against those nations,
14: 5 **the LORD** my God will come, and all the holy ones with him.
14: 7 without daytime or nighttime—a day known to **the LORD**.
14: 9 **The LORD** will be king over the whole earth. On that day there
14: 9 On that day there will be one **LORD**, and his name the only
14: 12 This is the plague with which **the LORD** will strike all the
14: 13 On that day men will be stricken by **the LORD** with great panic.
14: 16 **the LORD** Almighty, and to celebrate the Feast of Tabernacles.
14: 17 to worship the King, **the LORD** Almighty, they will have no rain.
14: 18 **The LORD** will bring on them the plague he inflicts on the
14: 20 On that day HOLY TO **THE LORD** will be inscribed on the
14: 20 the cooking pots in **the LORD's** house will be like the sacred
14: 21 pot in Jerusalem and Judah will be holy to **the LORD** Almighty,
14: 21 no longer be a Canaanite in the house of **the LORD** Almighty.
Mal 1: 1 An oracle: The word of **the LORD** to Israel through Malachi.
1: 2 "I have loved you," says **the LORD**. "But you ask, 'How have
1: 2 Esau Jacob's brother?" **the LORD** says. "Yet I have loved Jacob,
1: 4 But this is what **the LORD** Almighty says: "They may build,
1: 4 the Wicked Land, a people always under the wrath of **the LORD**.
1: 5 You will see it with your own eyes and say, 'Great is **the LORD**—
1: 6 says **the LORD** Almighty. "It is you, O priests, who show
1: 7 defiled you?' "By saying that **the LORD's** table is contemptible.
1: 8 with you? Would he accept you?" says **the LORD** Almighty.
1: 9 your hands, will he accept you?"—says **the LORD** Almighty.
1: 10 I am not pleased with you," says **the LORD** Almighty, "and I
1: 11 will be great among the nations," says **the LORD** Almighty.
1: 13 and you sniff at it contemptuously," says **the LORD** Almighty.
1: 13 should I accept them from your hands?" says **the LORD**.
1: 14 For I am a great king," says **the LORD** Almighty, "and my name
2: 2 says **the LORD** Almighty, "I will send a curse upon you,
2: 4 covenant with Levi may continue," says **the LORD** Almighty.
2: 7 because he is the messenger of **the LORD** Almighty.
2: 8 have violated the covenant with Levi," says **the LORD** Almighty.
2: 11 Judah has desecrated the sanctuary **the LORD** loves, by marrying
2: 12 he may be, may **the LORD** cut him off from the tents of Jacob—
2: 12 even though he brings offerings to **the LORD** Almighty.
2: 13 You flood **the LORD's** altar with tears. You weep and wail
2: 14 because **the LORD** is acting as the witness between you
2: 16 "I hate divorce," says **the LORD** God of Israel, "and I hate a
2: 16 violence as well as with his garment," says **the LORD** Almighty.
2: 17 You have wearied **the LORD** with your words. "How have we
2: 17 By saying, "All who do evil are good in the eyes of **the LORD**,
3: 1 whom you desire, will come," says **the LORD** Almighty.
3: 3 **the LORD** will have men who will bring offerings in
3: 4 of Judah and Jerusalem will be acceptable to **the LORD**,
3: 5 aliens of justice, but do not fear me," says **the LORD** Almighty.
3: 6 "I **the LORD** do not change. So you, O descendants of Jacob,
3: 7 to me, and I will return to you," says **the LORD** Almighty.
3: 10 Test me in this," says **the LORD** Almighty, "and see if I will not
3: 11 in your fields will not cast their fruit," says **the LORD** Almighty.
3: 12 for yours will be a delightful land," says **the LORD** Almighty.
3: 13 "You have said harsh things against me," says **the LORD**.
3: 14 and going about like mourners before **the LORD** Almighty?
3: 16 Then those who feared **the LORD** talked with each other,
3: 16 talked with each other, and **the LORD** listened and heard.
3: 16 written in his presence concerning those who feared **the LORD**
3: 17 "They will be mine," says **the LORD** Almighty, "in the day when
4: 1 [3:19] coming will set them on fire," says **the LORD** Almighty.
4: 3 [3:21] day when I do these things," says **the LORD** Almighty.
4: 5 [3:23] before that great and dreadful day of **the LORD** comes.

3379 יְהוֹזָבָד *yᵉhôzābād*, n.pr.m. [4] [√ 3378 + 2272]

Jehozabad [4]

2Ki 12: 21 [12:22] Jozabad son of Shimeath and **Jehozabad** son of Shomer.
1Ch 26: 4 **Jehozabad** the second, Joah the third, Sacar the fourth, Nethanel
2Ch 17: 18 next, **Jehozabad**, with 180,000 men armed for battle.
24: 26 and **Jehozabad**, son of Shimrith a Moabite woman.

3380 יְהוֹחָנָן *yᵉhôḥānān*, n.pr.m. [9] [√ 3378 + 2858]

Jehohanan [9]

1Ch 26: 3 Elam the fifth, **Jehohanan** the sixth and Eliehoenai the seventh.
2Ch 17: 15 next, **Jehohanan** the commander, with 280,000;
23: 1 son of Jeroham, Ishmael son of **Jehohanan**, Azariah son of Obed,
28: 12 Azariah son of **Jehohanan**, Berekiah son of Meshillemoth,
Ezr 10: 6 house of God and went to the room of **Jehohanan** son of Eliashib.
10: 28 descendants of Bebai: **Jehohanan**, Hananiah, Zabbai and Athlai.
Ne 6: 18 his son **Jehohanan** had married the daughter of Meshullam son of

Ne 12:13 of Ezra's, Meshullam; of Amariah's, **Jehohanan**;
12:42 Shemaiah, Eleazar, Uzzi, **Jehohanan**, Malkijah, Elam and Ezer.

3381 יְהוֹיָדָע yᵉhôyādāʿ, n.pr.m. [51] [√ 3378 + 3359]

Jehoiada [50], he^s [+2021+3913] [1]

2Sa 8:18 Benaiah son of **Jehoiada** was over the Kerethites and Pelethites;
20:23 Benaiah son of **Jehoiada** was over the Kerethites and Pelethites;
23:20 Benaiah son of **Jehoiada** was a valiant fighter from Kabzeel,
23:22 Such were the exploits of Benaiah son of **Jehoiada**; he too was as
1Ki 1:8 Benaiah son of **Jehoiada**, Nathan the prophet, Shimei and Rei
1:26 your servant, and Zadok the priest, and Benaiah son of **Jehoiada**,
1:32 the priest, Nathan the prophet and Benaiah son of **Jehoiada**."
1:36 Benaiah son of **Jehoiada** answered the king, "Amen!
1:38 Benaiah son of **Jehoiada**, the Kerethites and the Pelethites went
1:44 Benaiah son of **Jehoiada**, the Kerethites and the Pelethites,
2:25 So King Solomon gave orders to Benaiah son of **Jehoiada**,
2:29 Solomon ordered Benaiah son of **Jehoiada**, "Go, strike him
2:34 So Benaiah son of **Jehoiada** went up and struck down Joab
2:35 The king put Benaiah son of **Jehoiada** over the army in Joab's
2:46 Then the king gave the order to Benaiah son of **Jehoiada**,
4:4 Benaiah son of **Jehoiada**—commander in chief; Zadok
2Ki 11:4 In the seventh year **Jehoiada** sent for the commanders of units of a
11:9 The commanders of units of a hundred did just as **Jehoiada** the
11:9 those who were going off duty—and came to **Jehoiada** the priest.
11:15 **Jehoiada** the priest ordered the commanders of units of a hundred,
11:17 **Jehoiada** then made a covenant between the LORD and the king
12:2 [12:3] LORD all the years **Jehoiada** the priest instructed him.
12:7 [12:8] Therefore King Joash summoned **Jehoiada** the priest
12:9 [12:10] **Jehoiada** the priest took a chest and bored a hole in its
1Ch 11:22 Benaiah son of **Jehoiada** was a valiant fighter from Kabzeel,
11:24 Such were the exploits of Benaiah son of **Jehoiada**; he too was as
12:27 [12:28] including **Jehoiada**, leader of the family of Aaron, with
18:17 Benaiah son of **Jehoiada** was over the Kerethites and Pelethites;
27:5 for the third month, was Benaiah son of **Jehoiada** the priest.
27:34 Ahithophel was succeeded by **Jehoiada** son of Benaiah and by
2Ch 22:11 the daughter of King Jehoram and wife of the priest **Jehoiada**,
23:1 In the seventh year **Jehoiada** showed his strength. He made a
23:8 and all the men of Judah did just as **Jehoiada** the priest ordered.
23:8 for **Jehoiada** the priest had not released any of the divisions.
23:9 **he**^s [+2021+3913] gave the commanders of units of a hundred the
23:11 **Jehoiada** and his sons brought out the king's son and put the
23:14 **Jehoiada** the priest sent out the commanders of units of a hundred,
23:16 **Jehoiada** then made a covenant that he and the people and the king
23:18 **Jehoiada** placed the oversight of the temple of the LORD in the
24:2 right in the eyes of the LORD all the years of **Jehoiada** the priest.
24:3 **Jehoiada** chose two wives for him, and he had sons and daughters.
24:6 Therefore the king summoned **Jehoiada** the chief priest and said to
24:12 **Jehoiada** gave it to the men who carried out the work required for
24:14 they brought the rest of the money to the king and **Jehoiada**,
24:14 As long as **Jehoiada** lived, burnt offerings were presented
24:15 Now **Jehoiada** was old and full of years, and he died at the age of
24:17 After the death of **Jehoiada**, the officials of Judah came and paid
24:20 the Spirit of God came upon Zechariah son of **Jehoiada** the priest.
24:22 the kindness Zechariah's father **Jehoiada** had shown him
24:25 against him for murdering the son of **Jehoiada** the priest,
Jer 29:26 'The LORD has appointed you priest in place of **Jehoiada** to be in

3382 יְהוֹיָכִין yᵉhôyākîn, n.pr.m. [10] [→ 3518, 3526, 3527, 4037; cf. 3378 + 3922]

Jehoiachin [10]

2Ki 24:6 with his fathers. And **Jehoiachin** his son succeeded him as king.
24:8 **Jehoiachin** was eighteen years old when he became king,
24:12 **Jehoiachin** king of Judah, his mother, his attendants, his nobles
24:15 Nebuchadnezzar took **Jehoiachin** captive to Babylon. He also took
25:27 In the thirty-seventh year of the exile of **Jehoiachin** king of Judah,
25:27 he released **Jehoiachin** from prison on the twenty-seventh day of
2Ch 36:8 and Judah. And **Jehoiachin** his son succeeded him as king.
36:9 **Jehoiachin** was eighteen years old when he became king,
Jer 52:31 In the thirty-seventh year of the exile of **Jehoiachin** king of Judah,
52:31 he released **Jehoiachin** king of Judah and freed him from prison on

3383 יְהוֹיָקִים yᵉhôyāqîm, n.pr.m. [37 / 36] [√ 3378 + 7756]

Jehoiakim [34], Jehoiakim's [2]

2Ki 23:34 of his father Josiah and changed Eliakim's name to **Jehoiakim**.
23:35 **Jehoiakim** paid Pharaoh Neco the silver and gold he demanded.
23:36 **Jehoiakim** was twenty-five years old when he became king,
24:1 invaded the land, and **Jehoiakim** became his vassal for three years.
24:5 As for the other events of **Jehoiakim's** reign, and all he did,
24:6 **Jehoiakim** rested with his fathers. And Jehoiachin his son
24:19 He did evil in the eyes of the LORD, just as **Jehoiakim** had done.
1Ch 3:15 **Jehoiakim** the second son, Zedekiah the third, Shallum the fourth.
3:16 The successors of **Jehoiakim**: Jehoiachin his son, and Zedekiah.
2Ch 36:4 and Jerusalem and changed Eliakim's name to **Jehoiakim**.
36:5 **Jehoiakim** was twenty-five years old when he became king,
36:8 The other events of **Jehoiakim's** reign, the detestable things he did
Jer 1:3 and through the reign of **Jehoiakim** son of Josiah king of Judah,
22:18 Therefore this is what the LORD says about **Jehoiakim** son of
22:24 "even if you, Jehoiachin son of **Jehoiakim** king of Judah,
24:1 After Jehoiachin son of **Jehoiakim** king of Judah and the officials,
25:1 Judah in the fourth year of **Jehoiakim** son of Josiah king of Judah,
26:1 Early in the reign of **Jehoiakim** son of Josiah king of Judah,
26:21 When King **Jehoiakim** and all his officers and officials heard his
26:22 King **Jehoiakim**, however, sent Elnathan son of Acbor to Egypt,
26:23 They brought Uriah out of Egypt and took him to King **Jehoiakim**,
27:1 Early in the reign of Zedekiah [BHS *Jehoiakim*; NIV 7409]
27:20 of **Jehoiakim** king of Judah into exile from Jerusalem to Babylon,
28:4 I will also bring back to this place Jehoiachin son of **Jehoiakim**
35:1 during the reign of **Jehoiakim** son of Josiah king of Judah:
36:1 In the fourth year of **Jehoiakim** son of Josiah king of Judah,
36:9 In the ninth month of the fifth year of **Jehoiakim** son of Josiah
36:28 were on the first scroll, which **Jehoiakim** king of Judah burned up.
36:29 Also tell **Jehoiakim** king of Judah, 'This is what the LORD says:
36:30 this is what the LORD says about **Jehoiakim** king of Judah:
36:32 Baruch wrote on it all the words of the scroll that **Jehoiakim** king
37:1 of Babylon; he reigned in place of Jehoiachin son of **Jehoiakim**.
45:1 in the fourth year of **Jehoiakim** son of Josiah king of Judah,
46:2 in the fourth year of **Jehoiakim** son of Josiah king of Judah:
52:2 He did evil in the eyes of the LORD, just as **Jehoiakim** had done.
Da 1:1 In the third year of the reign of **Jehoiakim** king of Judah,
1:2 And the Lord delivered **Jehoiakim** king of Judah into his hand,

3384 יְהוֹיָרִיב yᵉhôyārîb, n.pr.m. [2] [√ 3378 + 8189]

Jehoiarib [2]

1Ch 9:10 Of the priests: Jedaiah; **Jehoiarib**; Jakin;
24:7 The first lot fell to **Jehoiarib**, the second to Jedaiah,

3385 יְהוּכַל yᵉhûkal, n.pr.m. [1] [√ 3378 + 3523; cf. 3426]

Jehucal [1]

Jer 37:3 sent **Jehucal** son of Shelemiah with the priest Zephaniah son of

3386 יְהוֹנָדָב yᵉhônādāb, n.pr.m. [8] [√ 3378 + 5605]

Jonadab [5], Jehonadab [3]

2Sa 13:5 "Go to bed and pretend to be ill," **Jonadab** said. "When your
2Ki 10:15 After he left there, he came upon **Jehonadab** son of Recab,
10:15 "I am," **Jehonadab** answered. "If so," said Jehu, "give me your
10:23 and **Jehonadab** son of Recab went into the temple of Baal.
Jer 35:8 We have obeyed everything our forefather **Jonadab** son of Recab
35:14 '**Jonadab** son of Recab ordered his sons not to drink wine
35:16 The descendants of **Jonadab** son of Recab have carried out the
35:18 'You have obeyed the command of your forefather **Jonadab**

3387 יְהוֹנָתָן yᵉhônātān, n.pr.m. [82] [√ 3378 + 5989]

Jonathan [68], *untranslated* [5], he^s [3], Jonathan's [3], Jehonathan [2], me^s [1]

Jdg 18:30 the idols, and **Jonathan** son of Gershom, the son of Moses,
1Sa 14:6 **Jonathan** said to his young armor-bearer, "Come, let's go over to
14:8 **Jonathan** said, "Come, then; we will cross over toward the men
18:1 **Jonathan** became one in spirit with David, and he loved him as
18:1 became one in spirit with David, and **he**^s loved him as himself.
18:3 **Jonathan** made a covenant with David because he loved him as
18:4 **Jonathan** took off the robe he was wearing and gave it to David,
19:1 the attendants to kill David. But **Jonathan** was very fond of David
19:2 **[RPH]** warned him, "My father Saul is looking for a chance to
19:4 **Jonathan** spoke well of David to Saul his father and said to him,
19:6 Saul listened to **Jonathan** and took this oath: "As surely as the
19:7 So **Jonathan** called David and told him the whole conversation.
19:7 called David and **[RPH]** told him the whole conversation.
19:7 **He**^s brought him to Saul, and David was with Saul as before.
20:1 fled from Naioth at Ramah and went to **Jonathan** and asked,
20:3 to himself, '**Jonathan** must not know this or he will be grieved.'
20:4 **Jonathan** said to David, "Whatever you want me to do, I'll do for
20:5 So David said, **[RPH]** "Look, tomorrow is the New Moon
20:9 "Never!" **Jonathan** said. "If I had the least inkling that my father
20:10 **[RPH]** "Who will tell me if your father answers you harshly?"
20:11 "Come," **Jonathan** said, "let's go out into the field." So they went
20:12 Then **Jonathan** said to David: "By the LORD, the God of Israel,
20:13 may the LORD deal with **me**^s, be it ever so severely, if I do not
20:16 So **Jonathan** made a covenant with the house of David, saying,
20:17 And **Jonathan** had David reaffirm his oath out of love for him,
20:18 **Jonathan** said to David: "Tomorrow is the New Moon festival.
20:25 opposite **Jonathan**, and Abner sat next to Saul, but David's place
20:27 Saul said to his son **Jonathan**, "Why hasn't the son of Jesse come

1Sa 20:28 **Jonathan** answered, "David earnestly asked me for permission to
20:30 Saul's anger flared up at **Jonathan** and he said to him, "You son of
20:32 he be put to death? What has he done?" **Jonathan** asked his father.
20:33 Then **Jonathan** knew that his father intended to kill David.
20:34 **Jonathan** got up from the table in fierce anger; on that second day
20:35 In the morning **Jonathan** went out to the field for his meeting with
20:37 When the boy came to the place where **Jonathan's** arrow had
20:37 **Jonathan** called out after him, "Isn't the arrow beyond you?"
20:38 **he**[s] shouted, "Hurry! Go quickly! Don't stop!" The boy picked up
20:38 The boy **[RPH]** picked up the arrow and returned to his master.
20:39 boy knew nothing of all this; only **Jonathan** and David knew.)
20:40 Then **Jonathan** gave his weapons to the boy and said, "Go,
20:42 **Jonathan** said to David, "Go in peace, for we have sworn
20:42 [21:1] Then David left, and **Jonathan** went back to the town.
23:16 Saul's son **Jonathan** went to David at Horesh and helped him find
23:18 Then **Jonathan** went home, but David remained at Horesh.
31: 2 and they killed his sons **Jonathan**, Abinadab and Malki-Shua.
2Sa 1: 4 of them fell and died. And Saul and his son **Jonathan** are dead."
1: 5 "How do you know that Saul and his son **Jonathan** are dead?"
1:12 and wept and fasted till evening for Saul and his son **Jonathan**,
1:17 David took up this lament concerning Saul and his son **Jonathan**,
1:22 the flesh of the mighty, the bow of **Jonathan** did not turn back,
1:23 "Saul and **Jonathan**—in life they were loved and gracious,
1:25 mighty have fallen in battle! **Jonathan** lies slain on your heights.
1:26 I grieve for you, **Jonathan** my brother; you were very dear to me.
4: 4 (**Jonathan** son of Saul had a son who was lame in both feet.
4: 4 old when the news about Saul and **Jonathan** came from Jezreel.
9: 1 house of Saul to whom I can show kindness for **Jonathan's** sake?"
9: 3 Ziba answered the king, "There is still a son of **Jonathan**;
9: 6 When Mephibosheth son of **Jonathan**, the son of Saul, came to
9: 7 surely show you kindness for the sake of your father **Jonathan**.
15:27 in peace, with your son Ahimaaz and **Jonathan** son of Abiathar.
15:36 two sons, Ahimaaz son of Zadok and **Jonathan** son of Abiathar,
17:17 **Jonathan** and Ahimaaz were staying at En Rogel. A servant girl
17:20 at the house, they asked, "Where are Ahimaaz and **Jonathan**?"
21: 7 The king spared Mephibosheth son of **Jonathan**, the son of Saul,
21: 7 oath before the LORD between David and **Jonathan** son of Saul.
21:12 of Saul and his son **Jonathan** from the citizens of Jabesh Gilead.
21:13 David brought the bones of Saul and his son **Jonathan** from there,
21:14 of Saul and his son **Jonathan** in the tomb of Saul's father Kish,
21:21 **Jonathan** son of Shimeah, David's brother, killed him.
23:32 Eliahba the Shaalbonite, the sons of Jashen, **Jonathan**
1Ch 8:33 Saul the father of **Jonathan**, Malki-Shua, Abinadab and Esh-Baal.
8:34 The son of **Jonathan**: Merib-Baal, who was the father of Micah.
9:39 Saul the father of **Jonathan**, Malki-Shua, Abinadab and Esh-Baal.
9:40 The son of **Jonathan**: Merib-Baal, who was the father of Micah.
20: 7 **Jonathan** son of Shimea, David's brother, killed him.
27:25 **Jonathan** son of Uzziah was in charge of the storehouses in the
27:32 **Jonathan**, David's uncle, was a counselor, a man of insight
2Ch 17: 8 **Jehonathan**, Adonijah, Tobijah and Tob-Adonijah—
Ne 12:18 of Bilgah's, Shammua; of Shemaiah's, **Jehonathan**;
Jer 37:15 him beaten and imprisoned in the house of **Jonathan** the secretary,
37:20 Do not send me back to the house of **Jonathan** the secretary,
38:26 'I was pleading with the king not to send me back to **Jonathan's**

3388 יְהוֹסֵף *yᵉhôsēp*, n.pr.m. [1] [cf: 3578]

Joseph [1]

Ps 81: 5 [81:6] He established it as a statute for **Joseph** when he went out

3389 יְהוֹעַדָּה *yᵉhôʿaddâ*, n.pr.m. [2]

Jehoaddah [2]

1Ch 8:36 Ahaz was the father of **Jehoaddah**, Jehoaddah was the father of
8:36 **Jehoaddah** was the father of Alemeth, Azmaveth and Zimri,

3390 יְהוֹעַדִּין *yᵉhôʿaddîn*, n.pr.f. [1]

Jehoaddin [1]

2Ki 14: 2 His mother's name was **Jehoaddin**; [Q 3391] she was from

3391 יְהוֹעַדָּן *yᵉhôʿaddān*, n.pr.f. [1]

Jehoaddin [1]

2Ki 14: 2 [His mother's name was **Jehoaddin**; [Q; see K 3390]]
2Ch 25: 1 His mother's name was **Jehoaddin**; she was from Jerusalem.

3392 יְהוֹצָדָק *yᵉhôṣādāq*, n.pr.m. [8] [√ 3378 + 7405; Ar 10318]

Jehozadak [8]

1Ch 6:14 [5:40] the father of Seraiah, and Seraiah the father of **Jehozadak**.
6:15 [5:41] **Jehozadak** was deported when the LORD sent Judah
Hag 1: 1 of Judah, and to Joshua son of **Jehozadak**, the high priest:
1:12 son of Shealtiel, Joshua son of **Jehozadak**, the high priest,
1:14 and the spirit of Joshua son of **Jehozadak**, the high priest,
2: 2 governor of Judah, to Joshua son of **Jehozadak**, the high priest,
2: 4 'Be strong, O Joshua son of **Jehozadak**, the high priest. Be strong,
Zec 6:11 and set it on the head of the high priest, Joshua son of **Jehozadak**.

3393 יְהוֹרָם *yᵉhôrām*, n.pr.m. [29] [√ 3378 + 8123]

Jehoram [16], Joram [13]

1Ki 22:50 [22:51] of David his father. And **Jehoram** his son succeeded him.
2Ki 1:17 **Joram** succeeded him as king in the second year of Jehoram son of
1:17 Joram succeeded him as king in the second year of **Jehoram** son
3: **Joram** son of Ahab became king of Israel in Samaria in the
3: 6 So at that time King **Joram** set out from Samaria and mobilized all
8:16 **Jehoram** son of Jehoshaphat began his reign as king of Judah.
8:25 of Israel, Ahaziah son of **Jehoram** king of Judah began to reign.
8:29 Ahaziah son of **Jehoram** king of Judah went down to Jezreel to
9:15 King **Joram** had returned to Jezreel to recover from the wounds
9:17 "Get a horseman," **Joram** ordered. "Send him to meet them
9:21 "Hitch up my chariot," **Joram** ordered. And when it was hitched
9:21 **Joram** king of Israel and Ahaziah king of Judah rode out,
9:22 When **Joram** saw Jehu he asked, "Have you come in peace,
9:23 **Joram** turned about and fled, calling out to Ahaziah, "Treachery,
9:24 Then Jehu drew his bow and shot **Joram** between the shoulders.
12:18 [12:19] Jehoshaphat, **Jehoram** and Ahaziah, the kings of Judah—
2Ch 17: 8 and Tob-Adonijah—and the priests Elishama and **Jehoram**.
21: 1 in the City of David. And **Jehoram** his son succeeded him as king.
21: 3 he had given the kingdom to **Jehoram** because he was his firstborn
21: 4 When **Jehoram** established himself firmly over his father's
21: 5 **Jehoram** was thirty-two years old when he became king, and he
21: 9 So **Jehoram** went there with his officers and all his chariots.
21:16 The LORD aroused against **Jehoram** the hostility of the
22: 1 So Ahaziah son of **Jehoram** king of Judah began to reign.
22: 5 He also followed their counsel when he went with **Joram** son of
22: 6 Ahaziah son of **Jehoram** king of Judah went down to Jezreel to
22: 6 king of Judah went down to Jezreel to see **Joram** son of Ahab
22: 7 he went out with **Joram** to meet Jehu son of Nimshi,
22:11 the daughter of King **Jehoram** and wife of the priest Jehoiada,

3394 יְהוֹשֶׁבַע *yᵉhôšebaʿ*, n.pr.f. [1] [√ 3378 + 8682]

Jehosheba [1]

2Ki 11: 2 **Jehosheba**, the daughter of King Jehoram and sister of Ahaziah,

3395 יְהוֹשַׁבְעַת *yᵉhôšabʿat*, n.pr.f. [2] [√ 3378 + 8682]

Jehosheba [2]

2Ch 22:11 **Jehosheba**, the daughter of King Jehoram, took Joash son of
22:11 Because **Jehosheba**, the daughter of King Jehoram and wife of the

3396 יְהוֹשָׁמַע *yᵉhôšāmāʿ*, n.pr.m. Not used in NIV/BHS [√ 3378 + 9052]

3397 יְהוֹשֻׁעַ *yᵉhôšuaʿ*, n.pr.m. [218] [√ 3378 + 8775]

Joshua [203], he[s] [8], *untranslated* [5], him[s] [2]

Ex 17: 9 Moses said to **Joshua**, "Choose some of our men and go out to
17:10 So **Joshua** fought the Amalekites as Moses had ordered, and
17:13 So **Joshua** overcame the Amalekite army with the sword.
17:14 something to be remembered and make sure that **Joshua** hears it,
24:13 Moses set out with **Joshua** his aide, and Moses went up on the
32:17 When **Joshua** heard the noise of the people shouting, he said to
33:11 but his young aide **Joshua** son of Nun did not leave the tent.
Nu 11:28 **Joshua** son of Nun, who had been Moses' aide since youth,
13:16 the land. (Moses gave Hoshea son of Nun the name **Joshua**.)
14: 6 **Joshua** son of Nun and Caleb son of Jephunneh, who were among
14:30 except Caleb son of Jephunneh and **Joshua** son of Nun.
14:38 only **Joshua** son of Nun and Caleb son of Jephunneh survived.
26:65 was left except Caleb son of Jephunneh and **Joshua** son of Nun.
27:18 "Take **Joshua** son of Nun, a man in whom is the spirit, and lay
27:22 He took **Joshua** and had him stand before Eleazar the priest
32:12 Caleb son of Jephunneh the Kenizzite and **Joshua** son of Nun,
32:28 **Joshua** son of Nun and to the family heads of the Israelite tribes.
34:17 you as an inheritance: Eleazar the priest and **Joshua** son of Nun.
Dt 1:38 your assistant, **Joshua** son of Nun, will enter it. Encourage him,
3:21 At that time I commanded **Joshua**: "You have seen with your own
3:28 But commission **Joshua**, and encourage and strengthen him,
31: 3 **Joshua** also will cross over ahead of you, as the LORD said.
31: 7 Moses summoned **Joshua** and said to him in the presence of all
31:14 Call **Joshua** and present yourselves at the Tent of Meeting,
31:14 So Moses and **Joshua** came and presented themselves at the Tent
31:23 The LORD gave this command to **Joshua** son of Nun: "Be strong
34: 9 Now **Joshua** son of Nun was filled with the spirit of wisdom
Jos 1: 1 the LORD, the LORD said to **Joshua** son of Nun, Moses' aide:
1:10 So **Joshua** ordered the officers of the people:

Jos 1:12 the Gadites and the half-tribe of Manasseh, **Joshua** said,
1:16 they answered **Joshua**, "Whatever you have commanded us we
2: 1 Then **Joshua** son of Nun secretly sent two spies from Shittim.
2:23 forded the river and came to **Joshua** son of Nun and told him
2:24 They said to **Joshua**, "The LORD has surely given the whole
3: 1 Early in the morning **Joshua** and all the Israelites set out from
3: 5 **Joshua** told the people, "Consecrate yourselves, for tomorrow the
3: 6 **Joshua** said to the priests, "Take up the ark of the covenant
3: 7 the LORD said to **Joshua**, "Today I will begin to exalt you in the
3: 9 **Joshua** said to the Israelites, "Come here and listen to the words of
3:10 **[RPH]** This is how you will know that the living God is among
4: 1 had finished crossing the Jordan, the LORD said to **Joshua**,
4: 4 So **Joshua** called together the twelve men he had appointed from
4: 5 **[RPH]** "Go over before the ark of the LORD your God into the
4: 8 So the Israelites did as **Joshua** commanded them. They took
4: 8 of the tribes of the Israelites, as the LORD had told **Joshua**;
4: 9 **Joshua** set up the twelve stones that had been in the middle of the
4:10 the LORD had commanded **Joshua** was done by the people,
4:10 Joshua was done by the people, just as Moses had directed **Joshua**.
4:14 That day the LORD exalted **Joshua** in the sight of all Israel;
4:15 Then the LORD said to **Joshua**,
4:17 So **Joshua** commanded the priests, "Come up out of the Jordan."
4:20 **Joshua** set up at Gilgal the twelve stones they had taken out of the
5: 2 At that time the LORD said to **Joshua**, "Make flint knives
5: 3 So **Joshua** made flint knives and circumcised the Israelites at
5: 4 Now this is why **he**[s] did so: All those who came out of Egypt—
5: 7 sons in their place, and these were the ones **Joshua** circumcised.
5: 9 the LORD said to **Joshua**, "Today I have rolled away the
5:13 Now when **Joshua** was near Jericho, he looked up and saw a man
5:13 **Joshua** went up to him and asked, "Are you for us or for our
5:14 **Joshua** fell facedown to the ground in reverence, and asked him,
5:15 **[RPH]** "Take off your sandals, for the place where you are
5:15 for the place where you are standing is holy." And **Joshua** did so.
6: 2 the LORD said to **Joshua**, "See, I have delivered Jericho into
6: 6 So **Joshua** son of Nun called the priests and said to them,
6: 8 When **Joshua** had spoken to the people, the seven priests carrying
6:10 But **Joshua** had commanded the people, "Do not give a war cry,
6:12 **Joshua** got up early the next morning and the priests took up the
6:16 sounded the trumpet blast, **Joshua** commanded the people, "Shout!
6:22 **Joshua** said to the two men who had spied out the land, "Go into
6:25 **Joshua** spared Rahab the prostitute, with her family and all who
6:25 because she hid the men **Joshua** had sent as spies to Jericho—
6:26 At that time **Joshua** pronounced this solemn oath: "Cursed before
6:27 So the LORD was with **Joshua**, and his fame spread throughout
7: 2 Now **Joshua** sent men from Jericho to Ai, which is near Beth Aven
7: 3 When they returned to **Joshua**, they said, "Not all the people will
7: 6 **Joshua** tore his clothes and fell facedown to the ground before the
7: 7 **Joshua** said, "Ah, Sovereign LORD, why did you ever bring this
7:10 The LORD said to **Joshua**, "Stand up! What are you doing down
7:16 Early the next morning **Joshua** had Israel come forward by tribes,
7:19 Then **Joshua** said to Achan, "My son, give glory to the LORD,
7:20 Achan replied, **[RPH]** "It is true! I have sinned against the
7:22 So **Joshua** sent messengers, and they ran to the tent, and there it
7:23 brought them to **Joshua** and all the Israelites and spread them out
7:24 Then **Joshua**, together with all Israel, took Achan son of Zerah,
7:25 **Joshua** said, "Why have you brought this trouble on us?
8: 1 the LORD said to **Joshua**, "Do not be afraid; do not be
8: 3 So **Joshua** and the whole army moved out to attack Ai. He chose
8: 3 **He**[s] chose thirty thousand of his best fighting men and sent them
8: 9 Then **Joshua** sent them off, and they went to the place of ambush
8: 9 to the west of Ai—but **Joshua** spent that night with the people.
8:10 Early the next morning **Joshua** mustered his men, and he
8:13 ambush to the west of it. That night **Joshua** went into the valley.
8:15 **Joshua** and all Israel let themselves be driven back before them,
8:16 and they pursued **Joshua** and were lured away from the city.
8:18 the LORD said to **Joshua**, "Hold out toward Ai the javelin that is
8:18 I will deliver the city." So **Joshua** held out his javelin toward Ai.
8:21 For when **Joshua** and all Israel saw that the ambush had taken the
8:23 But they took the king of Ai alive and brought him to **Joshua**.
8:26 For **Joshua** did not draw back the hand that held out his javelin
8:27 and plunder of this city, as the LORD had instructed **Joshua**.
8:28 So **Joshua** burned Ai and made it a permanent heap of ruins,
8:29 **Joshua** ordered them to take his body from the tree and throw it
8:30 Then **Joshua** built on Mount Ebal an altar to the LORD,
8:35 that **Joshua** did not read to the whole assembly of Israel,
9: 2 they came together to make war against **Joshua** and Israel.
9: 3 when the people of Gibeon heard what **Joshua** had done to Jericho
9: 6 Then they went to **Joshua** in the camp at Gilgal and said to him
9: 8 "We are your servants," they said to **Joshua**. But Joshua asked,
9: 8 But **Joshua** asked, "Who are you and where do you come from?"
9:15 Then **Joshua** made a treaty of peace with them to let them live,
9:22 **Joshua** summoned the Gibeonites and said, "Why did you deceive
9:24 They answered **Joshua**, "Your servants were clearly told how the
9:27 That day **he**[s] made the Gibeonites woodcutters and water carriers
10: 1 Now Adoni-Zedek king of Jerusalem heard that **Joshua** had taken
10: 4 "because it has made peace with **Joshua** and the Israelites."
10: 6 The Gibeonites then sent word to **Joshua** in the camp at Gilgal:
10: 7 So **Joshua** marched up from Gilgal with his entire army, including
10: 8 The LORD said to **Joshua**, "Do not be afraid of them; I have
10: 9 an all-night march from Gilgal, **Joshua** took them by surprise.
10:12 over to Israel, **Joshua** said to the LORD in the presence of Israel:
10:15 Then **Joshua** returned with all Israel to the camp at Gilgal.
10:17 When **Joshua** was told that the five kings had been found hiding in
10:18 **he**[s] said, "Roll large rocks up to the mouth of the cave, and post
10:20 So **Joshua** and the Israelites destroyed them completely—
10:21 then returned safely to **Joshua** in the camp at Makkedah,
10:22 **Joshua** said, "Open the mouth of the cave and bring those five
10:24 When they had brought these kings to **Joshua**, he summoned all
10:24 **he**[s] summoned all the men of Israel and said to the army
10:25 **Joshua** said to them, "Do not be afraid; do not be discouraged.
10:26 **Joshua** struck and killed the kings and hung them on five trees,
10:27 At sunset **Joshua** gave the order and they took them down from
10:28 That day **Joshua** took Makkedah. He put the city and its king to
10:29 **Joshua** and all Israel with him moved on from Makkedah to
10:31 **Joshua** and all Israel with him moved on from Libnah to Lachish;
10:33 come up to help Lachish, but **Joshua** defeated him and his army—
10:34 **Joshua** and all Israel with him moved on from Lachish to Eglon;
10:36 **Joshua** and all Israel with him went up from Eglon to Hebron
10:38 **Joshua** and all Israel with him turned around and attacked Debir.
10:40 So **Joshua** subdued the whole region, including the hill country,
10:41 **Joshua** subdued them from Kadesh Barnea to Gaza and from the
10:42 All these kings and their lands **Joshua** conquered in one campaign,
10:43 Then **Joshua** returned with all Israel to the camp at Gilgal.
11: 6 The LORD said to **Joshua**, "Do not be afraid of them, because by
11: 7 So **Joshua** and his whole army came against them suddenly at the
11: 9 **Joshua** did to them as the LORD had directed: He hamstrung
11:10 At that time **Joshua** turned back and captured Hazor and put its
11:12 **Joshua** took all these royal cities and their kings and put them to
11:13 cities built on their mounds—except Hazor, which **Joshua** burned.
11:15 servant Moses, so Moses commanded **Joshua**, and Joshua did it;
11:15 servant Moses, so Moses commanded Joshua, and **Joshua** did it;
11:16 So **Joshua** took this entire land: the hill country, all the Negev,
11:18 **Joshua** waged war against all these kings for a long time.
11:21 At that time **Joshua** went and destroyed the Anakites from the hill
11:21 country of Israel. **Joshua** totally destroyed them and their towns.
11:23 So **Joshua** took the entire land, just as the LORD had directed
11:23 **he**[s] gave it as an inheritance to Israel according to their tribal
12: 7 These are the kings of the land that **Joshua** and the Israelites
12: 7 which rises toward Seir (their lands **Joshua** gave as an inheritance
13: 1 When **Joshua** was old and well advanced in years, the LORD
14: 1 **Joshua** son of Nun and the heads of the tribal clans of Israel
14: 6 Now the men of Judah approached **Joshua** at Gilgal, and Caleb
14:13 **Joshua** blessed Caleb son of Jephunneh and gave him Hebron as
15:13 **Joshua** gave to Caleb son of Jephunneh a portion in Judah—
17: 4 to Eleazar the priest, **Joshua** son of Nun, and the leaders and said,
17:14 The people of Joseph said to **Joshua**, "Why have you given us
17:15 "If you are so numerous," **Joshua** answered, "and if the hill
17:17 **Joshua** said to the house of Joseph—to Ephraim and Manasseh—
18: 3 So **Joshua** said to the Israelites: "How long will you wait before
18: 8 **Joshua** instructed them, "Go and make a survey of the land
18: 9 in seven parts, and returned to **Joshua** in the camp at Shiloh.
18:10 **Joshua** then cast lots for them in Shiloh in the presence of the
18:10 there **he**[s] distributed the land to the Israelites according to their
19:49 the Israelites gave **Joshua** son of Nun an inheritance among them,
19:51 **Joshua** son of Nun and the heads of the tribal clans of Israel
20: 1 Then the LORD said to **Joshua**:
21: 1 **Joshua** son of Nun, and the heads of the other tribal families of
22: 1 **Joshua** summoned the Reubenites, the Gadites and the half-tribe
22: 6 **Joshua** blessed them and sent them away, and they went to their
22: 7 to the other half of the tribe **Joshua** gave land on the west side of
22: 7 their brothers.) When **Joshua** sent them home, he blessed them,
23: 1 around them, **Joshua**, by then old and well advanced in years,
23: 2 summoned **[RPH]** all Israel—their elders, leaders, judges
24: 1 Then **Joshua** assembled all the tribes of Israel at Shechem.
24: 2 **Joshua** said to all the people, "This is what the LORD, the God
24:19 **Joshua** said to the people, "You are not able to serve the LORD.
24:21 But the people said to **Joshua**, "No! We will serve the LORD."
24:22 **Joshua** said, "You are witnesses against yourselves that you have
24:24 the people said to **Joshua**, "We will serve the LORD our God
24:25 On that day **Joshua** made a covenant for the people, and there at
24:26 And **Joshua** recorded these things in the Book of the Law of God.
24:27 "See!" **he**[s] said to all the people. "This stone will be a witness
24:28 Then **Joshua** sent the people away, each to his own inheritance.
24:29 After these things, **Joshua** son of Nun, the servant of the LORD,
24:31 Israel served the LORD throughout the lifetime of **Joshua**
24:31 the lifetime of Joshua and of the elders who outlived **him**[s]
Jdg 1: 1 After the death of **Joshua**, the Israelites asked the LORD,
2: 6 After **Joshua** had dismissed the Israelites, they went to take

Jdg 2: 7 The people served the LORD throughout the lifetime of **Joshua**
2: 7 the lifetime of Joshua and of the elders who outlived **him**[s]
2: 8 **Joshua** son of Nun, the servant of the LORD, died at the age of a
2: 21 I will no longer drive out before them any of the nations **Joshua**
2: 23 drive them out at once by giving them into the hands of **Joshua**.
1Sa 6: 14 The cart came to the field of **Joshua** of Beth Shemesh, and there it
6: 18 is a witness to this day in the field of **Joshua** of Beth Shemesh.
1Ki 16: 34 in accordance with the word of the LORD spoken by **Joshua** son
2Ki 23: 8 at the entrance to the Gate of **Joshua**, the city governor, which is
1Ch 7: 27 Nun his son and **Joshua** his son.
Hag 1: 1 of Judah, and to **Joshua** son of Jehozadak, the high priest:
1: 12 son of Shealtiel, **Joshua** son of Jehozadak, the high priest,
1: 14 and the spirit of **Joshua** son of Jehozadak, the high priest,
2: 2 governor of Judah, to **Joshua** son of Jehozadak, the high priest,
2: 4 'Be strong, O **Joshua** son of Jehozadak, the high priest. Be strong,
Zec 3: 1 he showed me **Joshua** the high priest standing before the angel of
3: 3 Now **Joshua** was dressed in filthy clothes as he stood before the
3: 6 The angel of the LORD gave this charge to **Joshua**:
3: 8 O high priest **Joshua** and your associates seated before you,
3: 9 See, the stone I have set in front of **Joshua**! There are seven eyes
6: 11 and set it on the head of the high priest, **Joshua** son of Jehozadak.

3398 יְהוֹשָׁפָט¹ *yᵉhôšāpāṭ¹*, n.pr.m. [82] [√ 3378 + 9149]

Jehoshaphat [79], Jehoshaphat's [2], *untranslated* [1]

2Sa 8: 16 was over the army; **Jehoshaphat** son of Ahilud was recorder;
20: 24 charge of forced labor; **Jehoshaphat** son of Ahilud was recorder;
1Ki 4: 3 of Shisha—secretaries; **Jehoshaphat** son of Ahilud—recorder;
4: 17 **Jehoshaphat** son of Paruah—in Issachar;
15: 24 his father David. And **Jehoshaphat** his son succeeded him as king.
22: 2 in the third year **Jehoshaphat** king of Judah went down to see the
22: 4 So he asked **Jehoshaphat**, "Will you go with me to fight against
22: 4 **Jehoshaphat** replied to the king of Israel, "I am as you are,
22: 5 **Jehoshaphat** also said to the king of Israel, "First seek the counsel
22: 7 **Jehoshaphat** asked, "Is there not a prophet of the LORD here
22: 8 The king of Israel answered **Jehoshaphat**, "There is still one man
22: 8 of Imlah." "The king should not say that," **Jehoshaphat** replied.
22: 10 **Jehoshaphat** king of Judah were sitting on their thrones at the
22: 18 The king of Israel said to **Jehoshaphat**, "Didn't I tell you that he
22: 29 and **Jehoshaphat** king of Judah went up to Ramoth Gilead.
22: 30 The king of Israel said to **Jehoshaphat**, "I will enter the battle in
22: 32 When the chariot commanders saw **Jehoshaphat**, they thought,
22: 32 So they turned to attack him, but when **Jehoshaphat** cried out,
22: 41 **Jehoshaphat** son of Asa became king of Judah in the fourth year
22: 42 **Jehoshaphat** was thirty-five years old when he became king,
22: 44 [22:45] **Jehoshaphat** was also at peace with the king of Israel.
22: 45 [22:46] As for the other events of **Jehoshaphat's** reign, the things
22: 48 [22:49] Now **Jehoshaphat** built a fleet of trading ships to go to
22: 49 [22:50] At that time Ahaziah son of Ahab said to **Jehoshaphat**,
22: 49 [22:50] my men sail with your men," but **Jehoshaphat** refused.
22: 50 [22:51] **Jehoshaphat** rested with his fathers and was buried with
22: 51 [22:52] in the seventeenth year of **Jehoshaphat** king of Judah,
2Ki 1: 17 in the second year of Jehoram son of **Jehoshaphat** king of Judah.
3: 1 in Samaria in the eighteenth year of **Jehoshaphat** king of Judah,
3: 7 He also sent this message to **Jehoshaphat** king of Judah:
3: 11 But **Jehoshaphat** asked, "Is there no prophet of the LORD here,
3: 12 **Jehoshaphat** said, "The word of the LORD is with him."
3: 12 So the king of Israel and **Jehoshaphat** and the king of Edom went
3: 14 if I did not have respect for the presence of **Jehoshaphat** king of
8: 16 son of Ahab king of Israel, when **Jehoshaphat** was king of Judah,
8: 16 Jehoram son of **Jehoshaphat** began his reign as king of Judah.
9: 2 get there, look for Jehu son of **Jehoshaphat**, the son of Nimshi.
9: 14 So Jehu son of **Jehoshaphat**, the son of Nimshi, conspired against
12: 18 [12:19] **Jehoshaphat**, Jehoram and Ahaziah, the kings of Judah—
1Ch 3: 10 was Rehoboam, Abijah his son, Asa his son, **Jehoshaphat** his son,
18: 15 was over the army; **Jehoshaphat** son of Ahilud was recorder;
2Ch 17: 1 **Jehoshaphat** his son succeeded him as king and strengthened
17: 3 The LORD was with **Jehoshaphat** because in his early years he
17: 5 all Judah brought gifts to **Jehoshaphat**, so that he had great wealth
17: 10 so that they did not make war with **Jehoshaphat**.
17: 11 Some Philistines brought **Jehoshaphat** gifts and silver as tribute,
17: 12 **Jehoshaphat** became more and more powerful; he built forts
18: 1 Now **Jehoshaphat** had great wealth and honor, and he allied
18: 3 Ahab king of Israel asked **Jehoshaphat** king of Judah, "Will you
18: 4 **Jehoshaphat** also said to the king of Israel, "First seek the counsel
18: 6 **Jehoshaphat** asked, "Is there not a prophet of the LORD here
18: 7 The king of Israel answered **Jehoshaphat**, "There is still one man
18: 7 of Imlah." "The king should not say that," **Jehoshaphat** replied.
18: 9 **Jehoshaphat** king of Judah were sitting on their thrones at the
18: 17 The king of Israel said to **Jehoshaphat**, "Didn't I tell you that he
18: 28 and **Jehoshaphat** king of Judah went up to Ramoth Gilead.
18: 29 The king of Israel said to **Jehoshaphat**, "I will enter the battle in
18: 31 When the chariot commanders saw **Jehoshaphat**, they thought,
18: 31 but **Jehoshaphat** cried out, and the LORD helped him.
19: 1 When **Jehoshaphat** king of Judah returned safely to his palace in
19: 2 **[RPH]** "Should you help the wicked and love those who hate the
19: 4 **Jehoshaphat** lived in Jerusalem, and he went out again among the
19: 8 **Jehoshaphat** appointed some of the Levites, priests and heads of
20: 1 with some of the Meunites came to make war on **Jehoshaphat**.
20: 2 Some men came and told **Jehoshaphat**, "A vast army is coming
20: 3 Alarmed, **Jehoshaphat** resolved to inquire of the LORD,
20: 5 **Jehoshaphat** stood up in the assembly of Judah and Jerusalem at
20: 15 King **Jehoshaphat** and all who live in Judah and Jerusalem!
20: 18 **Jehoshaphat** bowed with his face to the ground, and all the people
20: 20 **Jehoshaphat** stood and said, "Listen to me, Judah and people of
20: 25 So **Jehoshaphat** and his men went to carry off their plunder,
20: 27 Then, led by **Jehoshaphat**, all the men of Judah and Jerusalem
20: 30 the kingdom of **Jehoshaphat** was at peace, for his God had given
20: 31 So **Jehoshaphat** reigned over Judah. He was thirty-five years old
20: 34 The other events of **Jehoshaphat's** reign, from beginning to end,
20: 35 **Jehoshaphat** king of Judah made an alliance with Ahaziah king of
20: 37 son of Dodavahu of Mareshah prophesied against **Jehoshaphat**,
21: 1 **Jehoshaphat** rested with his fathers and was buried with them in
21: 2 the sons of **Jehoshaphat**, were Azariah, Jehiel, Zechariah,
21: 2 and Shephatiah. All these were sons of **Jehoshaphat** king of Israel.
21: 12 'You have not walked in the ways of your father **Jehoshaphat**
22: 9 They buried him, for they said, "He was a son of **Jehoshaphat**,

3399 יְהוֹשָׁפָט² *yᵉhôšāpāṭ²*, n.pr.loc. [2] [√ 3378 + 9149]

Jehoshaphat [2]

Joel 3: 2 [4:2] and bring them down to the Valley of **Jehoshaphat**.
3: 12 [4:12] let them advance into the Valley of **Jehoshaphat**, for there

3400 יָהִיר *yāhîr*, a. [2]

arrogant [2]

Pr 21: 24 The proud and **arrogant** *man*—"Mocker" is his name; he behaves
Hab 2: 5 indeed, wine betrays him; he is **arrogant** and never at rest.

3401 יְהַלֶּלְאֵל *yᵉhallel'ēl*, n.pr.[m.]. [2] [√ 3401 + 446]

Jehallelel [2]

1Ch 4: 16 The sons of **Jehallelel**: Ziph, Ziphah, Tiria and Asarel.
2Ch 29: 12 the Merarites, Kish son of Abdi and Azariah son of **Jehallelel**;

3402 יַהֲלֹם *yāhᵃlōm*, n.[m.]. [3]

emerald [3]

Ex 28: 18 in the second row a turquoise, a sapphire and an **emerald**;
39: 11 in the second row a turquoise, a sapphire and an **emerald**;
Eze 28: 13 ruby, topaz and **emerald**, chrysolite, onyx and jasper, sapphire,

3403 יַהַץ *yahaṣ*, n.pr.loc. [7]

Jahaz [7]

Nu 21: 23 against Israel. When he reached **Jahaz**, he fought with Israel.
Dt 2: 32 and all his army came out to meet us in battle at **Jahaz**,
Jos 13: 18 **Jahaz**, Kedemoth, Mephaath,
21: 36 from the tribe of Reuben, Bezer, **Jahaz**,
Jdg 11: 20 all his men and encamped at **Jahaz** and fought with Israel.
Isa 15: 4 and Elealeh cry out, their voices are heard all the way to **Jahaz**.
Jer 48: 34 "The sound of their cry rises from Heshbon to Elealeh and **Jahaz**,

3404 יַהְצָה *yahṣâ*, n.pr.loc. [2]

Jahzah [2]

1Ch 6: 78 [6:63] east of Jericho they received Bezer in the desert, **Jahzah**,
Jer 48: 21 has come to the plateau—to Holon, **Jahzah** and Mephaath,

3405 יוֹאָב *yô'āb*, n.pr.m. [145] [→ 6502; cf. 3378 + 3]

Joab [132], Joab's [8], he[s] [2], *untranslated* [1], they[s] [+2021+2256+2657+8569] [1], who[s] [1]

1Sa 26: 6 Ahimelech the Hittite and Abishai son of Zeruiah, **Joab's** brother,
2Sa 2: 13 **Joab** son of Zeruiah and David's men went out and met them at
2: 14 Abner said to **Joab**, "Let's have some of the young men get up
2: 14 hand to hand in front of us." "All right, let them do it," **Joab** said.
2: 18 The three sons of Zeruiah were there: **Joab**, Abishai and Asahel.
2: 22 strike you down? How could I look your brother **Joab** in the face?"
2: 24 But **Joab** and Abishai pursued Abner, and as the sun was setting,
2: 26 Abner called out to **Joab**, "Must the sword devour forever?
2: 27 **Joab** answered, "As surely as God lives, if you had not spoken,
2: 28 So **Joab** blew the trumpet, and all the men came to a halt;
2: 30 **Joab** returned from pursuing Abner and assembled all his men.
2: 32 **Joab** and his men marched all night and arrived at Hebron by
3: 22 Just then David's men and **Joab** returned from a raid and brought
3: 23 When **Joab** and all the soldiers with him arrived, he was told that
3: 23 **he**[s] was told that Abner son of Ner had come to the king and that
3: 24 So **Joab** went to the king and said, "What have you done?

2Sa 3:26 **Joab** then left David and sent messengers after Abner, and they
3:27 Abner returned to Hebron, **Joab** took him aside into the gateway,
3:29 May his blood fall upon the head of **Joab** and upon all his father's
3:29 May **Joab's** house never be without someone who has a running
3:30 (**Joab** and his brother Abishai murdered Abner because he had
3:31 David said to **Joab** and all the people with him, "Tear your clothes
8:16 **Joab** son of Zeruiah was over the army; Jehoshaphat son of Ahilud
10:7 David sent **Joab** out with the entire army of fighting men.
10:9 **Joab** saw that there were battle lines in front of him and behind
10:13 **Joab** and the troops with him advanced to fight the Arameans,
10:14 So **Joab** returned from fighting the Ammonites and came to
11:1 David sent **Joab** out with the king's men and the whole Israelite
11:6 So David sent this word to **Joab**: "Send me Uriah the Hittite."
11:6 "Send me Uriah the Hittite." And **Joab** sent him to David.
11:7 David asked him how **Joab** was, how the soldiers were and how
11:11 my master **Joab** and my lord's men are camped in the open fields.
11:14 In the morning David wrote a letter to **Joab** and sent it with Uriah.
11:16 So while **Joab** had the city under siege, he put Uriah at a place
11:17 When the men of the city came out and fought against **Joab**,
11:18 **Joab** sent David a full account of the battle.
11:22 when he arrived he told David everything **Joab** had sent him to
11:25 David told the messenger, "Say this to **Joab**: 'Don't let this upset
12:26 Meanwhile **Joab** fought against Rabbah of the Ammonites
12:27 **Joab** then sent messengers to David, saying, "I have fought against
14:1 **Joab** son of Zeruiah knew that the king's heart longed for
14:2 So **Joab** sent someone to Tekoa and had a wise woman brought
14:3 speak these words to him." And **Joab** put the words in her mouth.
14:19 The king asked, "Isn't the hand of **Joab** with you in all this?"
14:19 it was your servant **Joab** who instructed me to do this and who put
14:20 Your servant **Joab** did this to change the present situation.
14:21 The king said to **Joab**, "Very well, I will do it. Go, bring back the
14:22 **Joab** fell with his face to the ground to pay him honor, and he
14:22 **Joab** said, "Today your servant knows that he has found favor in
14:23 **Joab** went to Geshur and brought Absalom back to Jerusalem.
14:29 Then Absalom sent for **Joab** in order to send him to the king,
14:30 "Look, **Joab's** field is next to mine, and he has barley there.
14:31 Then **Joab** did go to Absalom's house and he said to him,
14:32 Absalom said to **Joab**, "Look, I sent word to you and said,
14:33 So **Joab** went to the king and told him this. Then the king
17:25 Absalom had appointed Amasa over the army in place of **Joab**.
17:25 the daughter of Nahash and sister of Zeruiah the mother of **Joab**.
18:2 a third under the command of **Joab**, a third under Joab's brother
18:2 a third under **Joab's** brother Abishai son of Zeruiah, and a third
18:5 The king commanded **Joab**, Abishai and Ittai, "Be gentle with the
18:10 When one of the men saw this, he told **Joab**, "I just saw Absalom
18:11 **Joab** said to the man who had told him this, "What! You saw him?
18:12 **[RPH]** "Even if a thousand shekels were weighed out into my
18:14 **Joab** said, "I'm not going to wait like this for you." So he took
18:15 And ten of **Joab's** armor-bearers surrounded Absalom, struck him
18:16 **Joab** sounded the trumpet, and the troops stopped pursuing Israel,
18:16 and the troops stopped pursuing Israel, for **Joab** halted them.
18:20 "You are not the one to take the news today," **Joab** told him.
18:21 **Joab** said to a Cushite, "Go, tell the king what you have seen."
18:21 you have seen." The Cushite bowed down before **Joab** and ran off.
18:22 Ahimaaz son of Zadok again said to **Joab**, "Come what may,
18:22 the Cushite." But **Joab** replied, "My son, why do you want to go?
18:29 "I saw great confusion just as **Joab** was about to send the king's
19:1 [19:2] **Joab** was told, "The king is weeping and mourning for
19:5 [19:6] **Joab** went into the house to the king and said, "Today you
19:13 [19:14] are not the commander of my army in place of **Joab**.' "
20:7 So **Joab's** men and the Kerethites and Pelethites and all the mighty
20:8 **Joab** was wearing his military tunic, and strapped over it at his
20:9 **Joab** said to Amasa, "How are you, my brother?" Then Joab took
20:9 **Joab** took Amasa by the beard with his right hand to kiss him.
20:10 Amasa was not on his guard against the dagger in **Joab's** hand,
20:10 Then **Joab** and his brother Abishai pursued Sheba son of Bicri.
20:11 One of **Joab's** men stood beside Amasa and said, "Whoever favors
20:11 Joab's men stood beside Amasa and said, "Whoever favors **Joab**,
20:11 favors Joab, and whoever is for David, let him follow **Joab**!"
20:13 all the men went on with **Joab** to pursue Sheba son of Bicri.
20:15 All the troops with **Joab** came and besieged Sheba in Abel Beth
20:16 "Listen! Listen! Tell **Joab** to come here so I can speak to him."
20:17 He went toward her, and she asked, "Are you **Joab**?" "I am,"
20:20 **Joab** replied, "Far be it from me to swallow up or destroy!
20:21 The woman said to **Joab**, "His head will be thrown to you from the
20:22 they cut off the head of Sheba son of Bicri and threw it to **Joab**.
20:22 to his home. And **Joab** went back to the king in Jerusalem.
20:23 **Joab** was over Israel's entire army; Benaiah son of Jehoiada was
23:18 Abishai the brother of **Joab** son of Zeruiah was chief of the Three.
23:24 Asahel the brother of **Joab**, Elhanan son of Dodo from Bethlehem,
23:37 Naharai the Beerothite, the armor-bearer of **Joab** son of Zeruiah,
24:2 So the king said to **Joab** and the army commanders with him,
24:3 **Joab** replied to the king, "May the LORD your God multiply the
24:4 king's word, however, overruled **Joab** and the army commanders;
24:4 so **they**[s] [+2021+2256+2657+8569] left the presence of the king to
24:9 **Joab** reported the number of the fighting men to the king:
1Ki 1:7 Adonijah conferred with **Joab** son of Zeruiah and with Abiathar
1:19 Abiathar the priest and **Joab** the commander of the army,
1:41 On hearing the sound of the trumpet, **Joab** asked, "What's the
2:5 "Now you yourself know what **Joab** son of Zeruiah did to me—
2:22 for him and for Abiathar the priest and **Joab** son of Zeruiah!"
2:28 When the news reached **Joab**, who had conspired with Adonijah
2:28 **who**[s] had conspired with Adonijah though not with Absalom,
2:28 **he**[s] fled to the tent of the LORD and took hold of the horns of the
2:29 King Solomon was told that **Joab** had fled to the tent of the
2:30 Benaiah reported to the king, "This is how **Joab** answered me."
2:31 my father's house of the guilt of the innocent blood that **Joab** shed.
2:33 May the guilt of their blood rest on the head of **Joab** and his
11:15 **Joab** the commander of the army, who had gone up to bury the
11:16 **Joab** and all the Israelites stayed there for six months, until they
11:21 and that **Joab** the commander of the army was also dead.
1Ch 2:16 and Abigail. Zeruiah's three sons were Abishai, **Joab** and Asahel.
4:14 Seraiah was the father of **Joab**, the father of Ge Harashim.
11:6 **Joab** son of Zeruiah went up first, and so he received the
11:8 to the surrounding wall, while **Joab** restored the rest of the city.
11:20 Abishai the brother of **Joab** was chief of the Three. He raised his
11:26 Asahel the brother of **Joab**, Elhanan son of Dodo from Bethlehem,
11:39 Naharai the Berothite, the armor-bearer of **Joab** son of Zeruiah,
18:15 **Joab** son of Zeruiah was over the army; Jehoshaphat son of Ahilud
19:8 David sent **Joab** out with the entire army of fighting men.
19:10 **Joab** saw that there were battle lines in front of him and behind
19:14 **Joab** and the troops with him advanced to fight the Arameans,
19:15 and went inside the city. So **Joab** went back to Jerusalem.
20:1 the time when kings go off to war, **Joab** led out the armed forces.
20:1 remained in Jerusalem. **Joab** attacked Rabbah and left it in ruins.
21:2 So David said to **Joab** and the commanders of the troops,
21:3 **Joab** replied, "May the LORD multiply his troops a hundred
21:4 The king's word, however, overruled **Joab**; so Joab left and went
21:4 so **Joab** left and went throughout Israel and then came back to
21:5 **Joab** reported the number of the fighting men to David: In all
21:6 But **Joab** did not include Levi and Benjamin in the numbering,
26:28 by Saul son of Kish, Abner son of Ner and **Joab** son of Zeruiah,
27:7 The fourth, for the fourth month, was Asahel the brother of **Joab**;
27:24 **Joab** son of Zeruiah began to count the men but did not finish.
27:34 and by Abiathar. **Joab** was the commander of the royal army.
Ezr 2:6 of Pahath-Moab (through the line of Jeshua and **Joab**) 2,812
8:9 of the descendants of **Joab**, Obadiah son of Jehiel, and with him
Ne 7:11 of Pahath-Moab (through the line of Jeshua and **Joab**) 2,818
Ps 60:T [60:2] when **Joab** returned and struck down twelve thousand

3406 יוֹאָח *yôʾāḥ*, n.pr.m. [11] [√ 3378 + 278]

Joah [11]

2Ki 18:18 and **Joah** son of Asaph the recorder went out to them.
18:26 son of Hilkiah, and Shebna and **Joah** said to the field commander,
18:37 and **Joah** son of Asaph the recorder went to Hezekiah,
1Ch 6:21 [6:6] **Joah** his son, Iddo his son, Zerah his son and Jeatherai his
26:4 the second, **Joah** the third, Sacar the fourth, Nethanel the fifth,
2Ch 29:12 from the Gershonites, **Joah** son of Zimmah and Eden son of Joah;
29:12 from the Gershonites, Joah son of Zimmah and Eden son of **Joah**;
34:8 the ruler of the city, with **Joah** son of Joahaz, the recorder,
Isa 36:3 the secretary, and **Joah** son of Asaph the recorder went out to him.
36:11 Then Eliakim, Shebna and **Joah** said to the field commander,
36:22 and **Joah** son of Asaph the recorder went to Hezekiah,

3407 יוֹאָחָז *yôʾāḥāz*, n.pr.m. [4] [√ 3378 + 296]

Jehoahaz [3], Joahaz [1]

2Ki 14:1 In the second year of Jehoash son of **Jehoahaz** king of Israel,
2Ch 34:8 the ruler of the city, with Joah son of **Joahaz**, the recorder,
36:2 **Jehoahaz** was twenty-three years old when he became king,
36:4 Neco took Eliakim's brother **Jehoahaz** and carried him off to

3408 יוֹאֵל *yôʾēl*, n.pr.m. [19 / 20] [√ 3378 + 446]

Joel [20]

1Sa 8:2 The name of his firstborn was **Joel** and the name of his second was
1Ch 4:35 **Joel**, Jehu son of Joshibiah, the son of Seraiah, the son of Asiel,
5:4 The descendants of **Joel**: Shemaiah his son, Gog his son,
5:8 Bela son of Azaz, the son of Shema, the son of **Joel**. They settled
5:12 **Joel** was the chief, Shapham the second, then Janai and Shaphat,
6:28 [6:13] **Joel** [BHS-] the firstborn and Abijah the second son.
6:33 [6:18] Heman, the musician, the son of **Joel**, the son of Samuel,
6:36 [6:21] the son of Elkanah, the son of **Joel**, the son of Azariah,
7:3 The sons of Izrahiah: Michael, Obadiah, **Joel** and Isshiah.
11:38 **Joel** the brother of Nathan, Mibhar son of Hagri,
15:7 from the descendants of Gershon, **Joel** the leader and 130 relatives;
15:11 Uriel, Asaiah, **Joel**, Shemaiah, Eliel and Amminadab the Levites.

1Ch 15: 17 So the Levites appointed Heman son of **Joel**; from his brothers,
23: 8 The sons of Ladan: Jehiel the first, Zetham and **Joel**—three in all.
26: 22 the sons of Jehieli, Zetham and his brother **Joel**. They were in
27: 20 of Azaziah; over half the tribe of Manasseh: **Joel** son of Pedaiah;
2Ch 29: 12 the Kohathites, Mahath son of Amasai and **Joel** son of Azariah;
Ezr 10: 43 Jeiel, Mattithiah, Zabad, Zebina, Jaddai, **Joel** and Benaiah.
Ne 11: 9 **Joel** son of Zicri was their chief officer, and Judah son of
Joel 1: 1 The word of the LORD that came to **Joel** son of Pethuel.

3409 יוֹאָשׁ *yôʾāš*, n.pr.m. [47] [√ 3378 + 408]

Joash [30], Jehoash [16], him[s] [1]

Jdg 6: 11 sat down under the oak in Ophrah that belonged to **Joash** the
6: 29 they were told, "Gideon son of **Joash** did it."
6: 30 The men of the town demanded of **Joash**, "Bring out your son.
6: 31 **Joash** replied to the hostile crowd around him, "Are you going to
7: 14 "This can be nothing other than the sword of Gideon son of **Joash**,
8: 13 Gideon son of **Joash** then returned from the battle by the Pass of
8: 29 Jerub-Baal son of **Joash** went back home to live.
8: 32 Gideon son of **Joash** died at a good old age and was buried in the
8: 32 was buried in the tomb of his father **Joash** in Ophrah of the
1Ki 22: 26 him back to Amon the ruler of the city and to **Joash** the king's son
2Ki 11: 2 took **Joash** son of Ahaziah and stole him away from among the
12: 19 [12:20] As for the other events of the reign of **Joash**, and all he
12: 20 [12:21] against him and assassinated **him**[s] at Beth Millo,
13: 1 In the twenty-third year of **Joash** son of Ahaziah king of Judah,
13: 9 buried in Samaria. And **Jehoash** his son succeeded him as king.
13: 10 In the thirty-seventh year of **Joash** king of Judah, Jehoash son of
13: 12 As for the other events of the reign of **Jehoash**, all he did and his
13: 13 **Jehoash** rested with his fathers, and Jeroboam succeeded him on
13: 13 the throne. **Jehoash** was buried in Samaria with the kings of Israel.
13: 14 **Jehoash** king of Israel went down to see him and wept over him.
13: 25 Three times **Jehoash** defeated him, and so he recovered the
14: 1 In the second year of **Jehoash** son of Jehoahaz king of Israel,
14: 1 king of Israel, Amaziah son of **Joash** king of Judah began to reign.
14: 3 In everything he followed the example of his father **Joash**.
14: 17 Amaziah son of **Joash** king of Judah lived for fifteen years after
14: 23 In the fifteenth year of Amaziah son of **Joash** king of Judah,
14: 23 Jeroboam son of **Jehoash** king of Israel became king in Samaria,
14: 27 he saved them by the hand of Jeroboam son of **Jehoash**.
1Ch 3: 11 Jehoram his son, Ahaziah his son, **Joash** his son,
4: 22 and **Joash** and Saraph, who ruled in Moab and Jashubi Lehem.
12: 3 Ahiezer their chief and **Joash** the sons of Shemaah the Gibeathite;
2Ch 18: 25 him back to Amon the ruler of the city and to **Joash** the king's son,
22: 11 took **Joash** son of Ahaziah and stole him away from among the
24: 1 **Joash** was seven years old when he became king, and he reigned in
24: 2 **Joash** did what was right in the eyes of the LORD all the years of
24: 4 Some time later **Joash** decided to restore the temple of the
24: 22 King **Joash** did not remember the kindness Zechariah's father
24: 24 the God of their fathers, judgment was executed on **Joash**.
25: 17 he sent this challenge to **Jehoash** son of Jehoahaz, the son of Jehu,
25: 18 But **Jehoash** king of Israel replied to Amaziah king of Judah:
25: 21 So **Jehoash** king of Israel attacked. He and Amaziah king of Judah
25: 23 **Jehoash** king of Israel captured Amaziah king of Judah, the son of
25: 23 of Judah, the son of **Joash**, the son of Ahaziah, at Beth Shemesh.
25: 25 Amaziah son of **Joash** king of Judah lived for fifteen years after
25: 25 years after the death of **Jehoash** son of Jehoahaz king of Israel.
Hos 1: 1 and during the reign of Jeroboam son of **Jehoash** king of Israel:
Am 1: 1 king of Judah and Jeroboam son of **Jehoash** was king of Israel.

3410 יוֹב *yôb*, n.pr.m. [1 / 0]

Ge 46: 13 The sons of Issachar: Tola, Puah, Jashub [BHS *Iob*; NIV 3793]

3411 יוֹבָב[1] *yôbāb*[1], n.pr.m. [2]

Jobab [2]

Ge 10: 29 Ophir, Havilah and **Jobab**. All these were sons of Joktan.
1Ch 1: 23 Ophir, Havilah and **Jobab**. All these were sons of Joktan.

3412 יוֹבָב[2] *yôbāb*[2], n.pr.m. [7] [√ 3291]

Jobab [7]

Ge 36: 33 **Jobab** son of Zerah from Bozrah succeeded him as king.
36: 34 When **Jobab** died, Husham from the land of the Temanites
Jos 11: 1 he sent word to **Jobab** king of Madon, to the kings of Shimron
1Ch 1: 44 **Jobab** son of Zerah from Bozrah succeeded him as king.
1: 45 When **Jobab** died, Husham from the land of the Temanites
8: 9 By his wife Hodesh he had **Jobab**, Zibia, Mesha, Malcam,
8: 18 Ishmerai, Izliah and **Jobab** were the sons of Elpaal.

3413 יוֹבֵל *yôbēl*, n.m. [27] [√ 3301]

jubilee [20], trumpets [+8795] [3], ram's horn [1], rams horns [1], trumpets [+7967] [1], Year of Jubilee [1]

Ex 19: 13 Only when the **ram's horn** sounds a long blast may they go up to
Lev 25: 10 It shall be a **jubilee** for you; each one of you is to return to his
25: 11 The fiftieth year shall be a **jubilee** for you; do not sow and do not
25: 12 For it is a **jubilee** and is to be holy for you; eat only what is taken
25: 13 " 'In this Year of **Jubilee** everyone is to return to his own property.
25: 15 countryman on the basis of the number of years since the **Jubilee**.
25: 28 remain in the possession of the buyer until the Year of **Jubilee**.
25: 28 It will be returned in the **Jubilee**, and he can then go back to his
25: 30 and his descendants. It is not to be returned in the **Jubilee**.
25: 31 They can be redeemed, and they are to be returned in the **Jubilee**.
25: 33 is to be returned in the **Jubilee**, because the houses in the towns of
25: 40 among you; he is to work for you until the Year of **Jubilee**.
25: 50 the time from the year he sold himself up to the Year of **Jubilee**.
25: 52 If only a few years remain until the Year of **Jubilee**, he is to
25: 54 he and his children are to be released in the Year of **Jubilee**,
27: 17 If he dedicates his field during the Year of **Jubilee**, the value that
27: 18 if he dedicates his field after the **Jubilee**, the priest will determine
27: 18 to the number of years that remain until the next Year of **Jubilee**,
27: 21 When the field is released in the **Jubilee**, it will become holy,
27: 23 the priest will determine its value up to the Year of **Jubilee**,
27: 24 In the Year of **Jubilee** the field will revert to the person from
Nu 36: 4 When the **Year of Jubilee** for the Israelites comes, their
Jos 6: 4 Have seven priests carry trumpets of **rams' horns** in front of the
6: 5 When you hear them sound a long blast on the **trumpets** [+7967],
6: 6 and have seven priests carry **trumpets** [+8795] in front of it."
6: 8 the seven priests carrying the seven **trumpets** [+8795] before the
6: 13 The seven priests carrying the seven **trumpets** [+8795] went

3414 יוּבַל[1] *yûbal*[1], n.[m.]. [1] [√ 3297]

stream [1]

Jer 17: 8 a tree planted by the water that sends out its roots by the **stream**.

3415 יוּבָל[2] *yûbāl*[2], n.pr.m. [1]

Jubal [1]

Ge 4: 21 His brother's name was **Jubal**; he was the father of all who play

3416 יוֹזָבָד *yôzābād*, n.pr.m. [11] [√ 3378 + 2272]

Jozabad [11]

2Ki 12: 21 [12:22] The officials who murdered him were **Jozabad** son of
1Ch 12: 4 [12:5] Jahaziel, Johanan, **Jozabad** the Gederathite,
12: 20 [12:21] Adnah, **Jozabad**, Jediael, Michael, Jozabad, Elihu
12: 20 [12:21] Jediael, Michael, **Jozabad**, Elihu and Zillethai,
2Ch 31: 13 Jehiel, Azaziah, Nahath, Asahel, Jerimoth, **Jozabad**, Eliel,
35: 9 and Nethanel, his brothers, and Hashabiah, Jeiel and **Jozabad**,
Ezr 8: 33 so were the Levites **Jozabad** son of Jeshua and Noadiah son of
10: 22 Elioenai, Maaseiah, Ishmael, Nethanel, **Jozabad** and Elasah.
10: 23 **Jozabad**, Shimei, Kelaiah (that is, Kelita), Pethahiah, Judah
Ne 8: 7 Maaseiah, Kelita, Azariah, **Jozabad**, Hanan and Pelaiah—
11: 16 Shabbethai and **Jozabad**, two of the heads of the Levites,

3417 יוֹזָכָר *yôzākār*, n.pr.m. Not used in NIV/BHS

3418 יוֹחָא *yôḥāʾ*, n.pr.m. [2]

Joha [2]

1Ch 8: 16 Michael, Ishpah and **Joha** were the sons of Beriah.
11: 45 Jediael son of Shimri, his brother **Joha** the Tizite,

3419 יוֹחָנָן *yôḥānān*, n.pr.m. [24] [√ 3378 + 2858]

Johanan [24]

2Ki 25: 23 Ishmael son of Nethaniah, **Johanan** son of Kareah, Seraiah son of
1Ch 3: 15 **Johanan** the firstborn, Jehoiakim the second son,
3: 24 Pelaiah, Akkub, **Johanan**, Delaiah and Anani—
6: 9 [5:35] the father of Azariah, Azariah the father of **Johanan**,
6: 10 [5:36] **Johanan** the father of Azariah (it was he who served as
12: 4 [12:5] Jahaziel, **Johanan**, Jozabad the Gederathite,
12: 12 [12:13] **Johanan** the eighth, Elzabad the ninth,
Ezr 8: 12 of Azgad, **Johanan** son of Hakkatan, and with him 110 men;
Ne 12: 22 Joiada, **Johanan** and Jaddua, as well as those of the priests,
12: 23 **Johanan** son of Eliashib were recorded in the book of the annals.
Jer 40: 8 son of Nethaniah, **Johanan** and Jonathan the sons of Kareah,
40: 13 **Johanan** son of Kareah and all the army officers still in the open
40: 15 Then **Johanan** son of Kareah said privately to Gedaliah in Mizpah,
40: 16 But Gedaliah son of Ahikam said to **Johanan** son of Kareah,
41: 11 When **Johanan** son of Kareah and all the army officers who were
41: 13 When all the people Ishmael had with him saw **Johanan** son of
41: 14 captive at Mizpah turned and went over to **Johanan** son of Kareah.

Jer 41:15 eight of his men escaped from **Johanan** and fled to the
41:16 **Johanan** son of Kareah and all the army officers who were with
42: 1 including **Johanan** son of Kareah and Jezaniah son of Hoshaiah,
42: 8 So he called together **Johanan** son of Kareah and all the army
43: 2 Azariah son of Hoshaiah and **Johanan** son of Kareah and all the
43: 4 So **Johanan** son of Kareah and all the army officers and all the
43: 5 **Johanan** son of Kareah and all the army officers led away all the

3420 יוּטָּה ***yûṭṭâ***, n.pr.loc. [2 / 3]

Juttah [3]

Jos 15:55 Maon, Carmel, Ziph, **Juttah**,
21:16 Ain, **Juttah** and Beth Shemesh, together with their pasturelands—
1Ch 6:59 [6:44] Ashan, **Juttah** [BHS-] and Beth Shemesh, together with

3421 יוֹיָדָע ***yôyādā'***, n.pr.m. [5] [√ 3378 + 3359]

Joiada [5]

Ne 3: 6 The Jeshanah Gate was repaired by **Joiada** son of Paseah
12:10 Joiakim the father of Eliashib, Eliashib the father of **Joiada**,
12:11 **Joiada** the father of Jonathan, and Jonathan the father of Jaddua.
12:22 **Joiada**, Johanan and Jaddua, as well as those of the priests,
13:28 One of the sons of **Joiada** son of Eliashib the high priest was

3422 יוֹיָכִין ***yôyākîn***, n.pr.m. [1] [√ 3378 + 3922]

Jehoiachin [1]

Eze 1: 2 the month—it was the fifth year of the exile of King **Jehoiachin**—

3423 יוֹיָקִים ***yôyāqîm***, n.pr.m. [4] [√ 3378 + 7756]

Joiakim [4]

Ne 12:10 Jeshua was the father of **Joiakim**, Joiakim the father of Eliashib,
12:10 **Joiakim** the father of Eliashib, Eliashib the father of Joiada,
12:12 In the days of **Joiakim**, these were the heads of the priestly
12:26 They served in the days of **Joiakim** son of Jeshua, the son of

3424 יוֹיָרִיב ***yôyārîb***, n.pr.m. [5] [√ 3378 + 8189]

Joiarib [4], Joiarib's [1]

Ezr 8:16 and Meshullam, who were leaders, and **Joiarib** and Elnathan,
Ne 11: 5 the son of Hazaiah, the son of Adaiah, the son of **Joiarib**,
11:10 From the priests: Jedaiah; the son of **Joiarib**; Jakin;
12: 6 Shemaiah, **Joiarib**, Jedaiah,
12:19 of **Joiarib's**, Mattenai; of Jedaiah's, Uzzi;

3425 יוֹכֶבֶד ***yôkebed***, n.pr.f. [2] [√ 3378 + 3877]

Jochebed [2]

Ex 6:20 Amram married his father's sister **Jochebed**, who bore him Aaron
Nu 26:59 the name of Amram's wife was **Jochebed**, a descendant of Levi,

3426 יוּכַל ***yûkal***, n.pr.m. [1] [cf. 3385]

Jehucal [1]

Jer 38: 1 of Mattan, Gedaliah son of Pashhur, **Jehucal** son of Shelemiah,

3427 יוֹם ***yôm***[1], n.m. [2302 / 2303] [→ 3429; Ar 10317]

day [950], days [474], today [+2021] [137], time [122], *untranslated* [64], when [+928] [45], today [+2021+2021+2296] [39], annals [+1821] [37], years [21], always [+2021+3972] [18], life [17], now [+2021+2021+2296] [17], reign [17], now [+2021] [14], lived [+2118] [12], times [10], as long as [+3972] [9], lifetime [9], period [9], live long [+799] [8], years [+9102] [8], year [7], daily [+928+3427] [6], reigns [6], as long as [+2021+3972] [5], daily [+3427] [4], day after day [+2021+3972] [4], each day [+928+3427] [4], each year [+2025+3427+4946] [4], first [+2021+3869] [4], for each day [+928+1821+3427] [4], three-day [+8993] [4], annual [3], as long as lived [+3972] [3], day's [3], ever since [+2021+2021+2296+6330] [3], forever [+2021+3972] [3], some time [3], those[s] [3], all day long [+928+2021+2021+2085] [2], always [+3972] [2], annual [+2025+3427+4946] [2], as long as lives [+3972] [2], as usually did [+928+3427+3869] [2], continual [+2021+3972] [2], continually [+2021+3972] [2], daily [+928+1821+3427] [2], daily [+928+2257 +3427] [2], date [2], day by day [+928+1821+2257+3427] [2], day by day [+928+1821+3427] [2], daytime [2], during [2], each day [+2021+2021+3427+4200+4200] [2], each day's [+3427] [2], each day's [+928+2257+3427] [2], each day's [+928+3427] [2], every day [+2256+3427+3972] [2], every day [+928+3427] [2], in the course of time [+3427+4200+4946] [2], lingering [+3427+6584] [2], live [2], never [+2021+3972+4202] [2], now [+465+928+2021+2021] [2], other days [+3427] [2], outlived [+339+799] [2], regularly [+928+3427 +4200] [2], rest [+3972] [2], Sabbath after Sabbath [+928+928+2021 +2021+3427+8701+8701] [2], select a day [+3427+4200+4946] [2], some time later [+4946] [2], still [+2021+2021+2296+6330] [2], that day [+3427] [2], weeks [+8651] [2], when [+928+2021] [2], while [+928] [2], whole [2], after [+928] [1], afternoon [+2021+5742] [1], age [+8044] [1], age [1], ago [+2021] [1], allotted time [1], as long as [+928] [1], as long as endure [+3869] [1], as long as live [+3972] [1], as long as live [+3972+4200+6409] [1], as long as live [+4946] [1], at once [+2021] [1], at once [+928+2021] [1], at once [+928+2021 +2021+2085] [1], at this time [+2021] [1], awhile [+2021+3869] [1], based on the rate paid [+3869] [1], birthday [+906+3528] [1], broad daylight [+240] [1], celebrating [+3202] [1], daily [+2021+4200] [1], daily [+285+4200] [1], day [+919] [1], day after day [1], daylight [1], days as [1], days of life [1], distant future [+8041] [1], during [+928] [1], during that time [1], each day [+2021+4200] [1], each[s] [1], endures [1], enjoy a long life [+799] [1], enjoy long life [+799] [1], enjoyed long life [+8428] [1], ever [+2021+3972] [1], ever [+3972] [1], ever [+4946] [1], ever since [+4946] [1], every day [+2021+4200] [1], every day [1], fate [1], first [+3869] [1], for a while [+285] [1], for life [+2021+3972] [1], forever [+802+4200] [1], from now on [+2021 +3972] [1], full moon [+4057] [1], full years [+9102] [1], full [1], future [+344] [1], future [+4737] [1], how long must wait [+3869+4537] [1], if [+928] [1], immediately [+2021+3869] [1], in lifetime [+3972] [1], in little more than [+6584] [1], in trouble [+7997] [1], it's [+2021] [1], it[s] [1], just [+2021] [1], just now [+2021] [1], lasting [+2021+2021+2296 +6330] [1], later on [+4946] [1], length of days [+9102] [1], life [+889+2118] [1], life span [+5031] [1], lifetime [+2644] [1], light [1], lived [1], lives [+9102] [1], long ago [+4946+7710] [1], many years [+2256+9102] [1], many years [+802] [1], never [+4202+4946] [1], night [1], noon [+2021+4734] [1], old [+2644+9102] [1], old [+4946+7710] [1], older [+2418+4200] [1], older [+3888] [1], one month [+3732] [1], over a year [+196+2296+2296+9102] [1], past [+8037] [1], recently [+2021] [1], regular [+2021+3972] [1], season [1], set time [+4595] [1], seven-day [+8679] [1], seven-day periods [+2021+8679] [1], since [+4200+4946] [1], so long [+802] [1], span of life [1], still [+2021+2021+2296+3869] [1], sun [1], take turns [+2143] [1], then[s] [+928+2021+2021+2085] [1], this[s] [1], today [+2296] [1], today [1], tomorrow [+4737] [1], two[s] [1], used to be [+6409] [1], very old [+928+995+2021+2416] [1], when [+4946] [1], when began [+928] [1], when [1], whenever [+928] [1], while [+3972] [1], while continues [+3972] [1], whole month [+2544] [1], year [+2021+4200] [1], yet [+2021] [1], yet [+2021+2021+2085+6330] [1], yet [+2021+2021+2156+6330] [1], younger [+4200+7582] [1]

Ge 1: 5 God called the light "**day**," and the darkness he called "night."
1: 5 And there was evening, and there was morning—the first **day**.
1: 8 And there was evening, and there was morning—the second **day**.
1:13 And there was evening, and there was morning—the third **day**.
1:14 "Let there be lights in the expanse of the sky to separate the **day**
1:14 and let them serve as signs to mark seasons and **days** and years,
1:16 the greater light to govern the **day** and the lesser light to govern the
1:18 to govern the **day** and the night, and to separate light from
1:19 And there was evening, and there was morning—the fourth **day**.
1:23 And there was evening, and there was morning—the fifth **day**.
1:31 And there was evening, and there was morning—the sixth **day**.
2: 2 By the seventh **day** God had finished the work he had been doing;
2: 2 had been doing; so on the seventh **day** he rested from all his work.
2: 3 God blessed the seventh **day** and made it holy, because on it he
2: 4 **When** [+928] the LORD God made the earth and the heavens—
2:17 and evil, for **when** [+928] you eat of it you will surely die."
3: 5 "For God knows that **when** [+928] you eat of it your eyes will be
3: 8 God as he was walking in the garden in the cool of the **day**,
3:14 crawl on your belly and you will eat dust all the **days** *of* your life.
3:17 through painful toil you will eat of it all the **days** *of* your life.
4: 3 In the course of **time** Cain brought some of the fruits of the soil as
4:14 **Today** [+2021] you are driving me from the land, and I will be
5: 1 **When** [+928] God created man, he made him in the likeness of
5: 2 And **when** [+928] they were created, he called them "man."
5: 4 Adam **lived** [+2118] 800 years and had other sons and daughters.
5: 5 Altogether, Adam lived **[RPH]** 930 years, and then he died.
5: 8 Altogether, Seth **lived** [+2118] 912 years, and then he died.
5:11 Altogether, Enosh **lived** [+2118] 905 years, and then he died.
5:14 Altogether, Kenan **lived** [+2118] 910 years, and then he died.
5:17 Altogether, Mahalalel **lived** [+2118] 895 years, and then he died.
5:20 Altogether, Jared **lived** [+2118] 962 years, and then he died.
5:23 Altogether, Enoch **lived** [+2118] 365 years.
5:27 Altogether, Methuselah **lived** [+2118] 969 years, and then he died.
5:31 Altogether, Lamech **lived** [+2118] 777 years, and then he died.
6: 3 for he is mortal; his **days** will be a hundred and twenty years."
6: 4 The Nephilim were on the earth in those **days**—and also
6: 5 inclination of the thoughts of his heart was only evil all the **time**.
7: 4 Seven **days** from now I will send rain on the earth for forty days
7: 4 Seven days from now I will send rain on the earth for forty **days**
7:10 And after the seven **days** the floodwaters came on the earth.
7:11 year of Noah's life, on the seventeenth **day** of the second month—
7:11 on that **day** all the springs of the great deep burst forth,
7:12 And rain fell on the earth forty **days** and forty nights.

Ge 7:13 On that very **day** Noah and his sons, Shem, Ham and Japheth,
7:17 For forty **days** the flood kept coming on the earth, and as the
7:24 The waters flooded the earth for a hundred and fifty **days**.
8:3 At the end of the hundred and fifty **days** the water had gone down,
8:4 on the seventeenth **day** of the seventh month the ark came to rest
8:6 After forty **days** Noah opened the window he had made in the ark
8:10 He waited seven more **days** and again sent out the dove from the
8:12 He waited seven more **days** and sent the dove out again, but this
8:14 By the twenty-seventh **day** of the second month the earth was
8:22 "As long as the earth **endures**, seedtime and harvest, cold
8:22 and heat, summer and winter, **day** and night will never cease."
9:29 Altogether, Noah **lived** [+2118] 950 years, and then he died.
10:25 One was named Peleg, because in his **time** the earth was divided;
11:32 Terah **lived** [+2118] 205 years, and he died in Haran.
14:1 At *this* **time** Amraphel king of Shinar, Arioch king of Ellasar,
15:18 On that **day** the LORD made a covenant with Abram and said,
17:12 every male among you who is eight **days** old must be circumcised,
17:23 On that very **day** Abraham took his son Ishmael and all those born
17:26 and his son Ishmael were both circumcised on that same **day**.
18:1 he was sitting at the entrance to his tent in the heat of the **day**.
18:11 Abraham and Sarah were already old and well advanced in **years**,
19:37 him Moab; he is the father of the Moabites of **today** [+2021].
19:38 he is the father of the Ammonites of **today** [+2021].
21:4 When his son Isaac was eight **days** old, Abraham circumcised him,
21:8 and on the **day** Isaac was weaned Abraham held a great feast.
21:26 You did not tell me, and I heard about it only **today** [+2021]."
21:34 And Abraham stayed in the land of the Philistines *for* a long **time**.
22:4 On the third **day** Abraham looked up and saw the place in the
22:14 to this **day** it is said, "On the mountain of the LORD it will be
24:1 Abraham was now old and well advanced in **years**,
24:12 God of my master Abraham, give me success **today** [+2021],
24:42 "When I came to the spring **today** [+2021], I said, 'O LORD,
24:55 and her mother replied, "Let the girl remain with us ten **days** or so;
25:7 **[NIE]** Abraham lived a hundred and seventy-five years.
25:24 When the **time** came *for* her to give birth, there were twin boys in
25:31 Jacob replied, "**First** [+2021+3869] sell me your birthright."
25:33 Jacob said, "Swear to me **first** [+3869]." So he swore an oath to
26:1 in the land—besides the earlier famine of Abraham's **time**—
26:8 When Isaac had been there a long **time**, Abimelech king of the
26:15 So all the wells that his father's servants had dug in the **time** *of* his
26:18 Isaac reopened the wells that had been dug in the **time** *of* his father
26:32 That **day** Isaac's servants came and told him about the well they
26:33 and to this **day** the name of the town has been Beersheba.
27:2 "I am now an old man and don't know the **day** *of* my death.
27:41 He said to himself, "The **days** *of* mourning for my father are near;
27:44 Stay with him **for a while** [+285] until your brother's fury
27:45 come back from there. Why should I lose both of you *in* one **day**?"
29:7 "Look," he said, "the **sun** is still high; it is not time for the flocks
29:14 After Jacob had stayed with him for a **whole month** [+2544],
29:20 they seemed like only a few **days** to him because of his love for
29:21 me my wife. My **time** is completed, and I want to lie with her."
30:14 **During** [+928] wheat harvest, Reuben went out into the fields
30:32 Let me go through all your flocks **today** [+2021] and remove from
30:33 And my honesty will testify for me in the **future** [+4737],
30:35 That same **day** he removed all the male goats that were streaked
30:36 Then he put a **three-day** [+8993] journey between himself
31:22 On the third **day** Laban was told that Jacob had fled.
31:23 he pursued Jacob for seven **days** and caught up with him in the hill
31:39 you demanded payment from me for whatever was stolen by **day**
31:40 The heat consumed me in the **daytime** and the cold at night,
31:43 Yet what can I do **today** [+2021] about these daughters of mine,
31:48 "This heap is a witness between you and me **today** [+2021]."
32:32 [32:33] Therefore to this **day** the Israelites do not eat the tendon
33:13 If they are driven hard just one **day**, all the animals will die.
33:16 So that **day** Esau started on his way back to Seir.
34:25 Three **days** later, while all of them were still in pain, two of
35:3 who answered me in the **day** *of* my distress and who has been with
35:20 set up a pillar, and to this **day** that pillar marks Rachel's tomb.
35:28 Isaac **lived** [+2118] a hundred and eighty years.
35:29 and died and was gathered to his people, old and full of **years**.
37:34 his clothes, put on sackcloth and mourned for his son many **days**.
38:12 After a long **time** Judah's wife, the daughter of Shua, died.
39:10 though she spoke to Joseph **day** *after* day, he refused to go to bed
39:10 though she spoke to Joseph day after **day**, he refused to go to bed
39:11 One **day** he went into the house to attend to his duties, and none of
40:4 he attended them. After they had been in custody *for* **some time**,
40:7 in his master's house, "Why are your faces so sad **today** [+2021]?"
40:12 it means," Joseph said to him. "The three branches are three **days**.
40:13 Within three **days** Pharaoh will lift up your head and restore you to
40:18 is what it means," Joseph said. "The three baskets are three **days**.
40:19 Within three **days** Pharaoh will lift off your head and hang you on
40:20 Now the third **day** was Pharaoh's birthday, and he gave a feast for
40:20 Now the third day was Pharaoh's **birthday** [+906+3528],
41:1 When *two* **full years** [+9102] had passed, Pharaoh had a dream:
41:9 the chief cupbearer said to Pharaoh, "**Today** [+2021] I am
42:13 The youngest is **now** [+2021] with our father, and one is no more."
42:17 And he put them all in custody for three **days**.
42:18 On the third **day**, Joseph said to them, "Do this and you will live,
42:32 and the youngest is **now** [+2021] with our father in Canaan.'
43:9 him here before you, I will bear the blame before you all my **life**.
44:32 to you, I will bear the blame before you, my father, all my **life**!'
47:8 Pharaoh asked him, "How **old** [+2644+9102] are you?"
47:9 "The **years of** [+9102] my pilgrimage are a hundred and thirty.
47:9 My **years** [+9102] have been few and difficult, and they do not
47:9 they do not equal the **years** [+9102] of the pilgrimage of my
47:9 they do not equal the years of **[RPH]** the pilgrimage of my
47:23 that I have bought you and your land **today** [+2021] for Pharaoh,
47:26 concerning land in Egypt—still in force **today** [+2021+2021+2296]
47:28 and the **years of** [+9102] his life were a hundred and forty-seven.
47:29 When the **time** drew near *for* Israel to die, he called for his son
48:15 the God who has been my shepherd all my life to this **day**,
48:20 He blessed them that **day** and said, "In your name will Israel
49:1 so I can tell you what will happen to you in **days** to come.
50:3 taking a full forty **days**, for that was the time required for
50:3 a full forty days, for that was the **time** *required for* embalming.
50:3 for embalming. And the Egyptians mourned for him seventy **days**.
50:4 When the **days** *of* mourning had passed, Joseph said to Pharaoh's
50:10 there Joseph observed a **seven-day** [+8679] period of mourning for
50:20 to accomplish what is **now** [+2021+2021+2296] being done,

Ex 2:11 One **day**, after Moses had grown up, he went out to where his own
2:13 The next **day** he went out and saw two Hebrews fighting. He asked
2:18 he asked them, "Why have you returned so early **today** [+2021]?"
2:23 During that long **period**, the king of Egypt died. The Israelites
3:18 Let us take a **three-day** [+8993] journey into the desert to offer
5:3 Now let us take a **three-day** [+8993] journey into the desert to
5:6 That same **day** Pharaoh gave this order to the slave drivers
5:13 the work required of you **for each day** [+928+1821+3427],
5:13 the work required of you **for each day** [+928+1821+3427],
5:14 didn't you meet your quota of bricks yesterday or **today** [+2021],
5:19 bricks required of you **for each day** [+928+1821+3427]."
5:19 bricks required of you **for each day** [+928+1821+3427]."
6:28 Now **when** [+928] the LORD spoke to Moses in Egypt,
7:25 Seven **days** passed after the LORD struck the Nile.
8:22 [8:18] " 'But on that **day** I will deal differently with the land of
8:27 [8:23] We must take a **three-day** [+8993] journey into the desert
9:18 that has ever fallen on Egypt, from the **day** it was founded till now.
10:6 the **day** they settled in this land till now.' " Then Moses turned
10:6 the day they settled in this land till **now** [+2021+2021+2296].' "
10:13 the LORD made an east wind blow across the land all that **day**
10:22 the sky, and total darkness covered all Egypt *for* three **days**.
10:23 No one could see anyone else or leave his place *for* three **days**.
10:28 appear before me again! The **day** you see my face you will die."
12:6 Take care of them until the fourteenth **day** of the month, when all
12:14 "This is a **day** you are to commemorate; for the generations to
12:15 *For* seven **days** you are to eat bread made without yeast. On the
12:15 On the first **day** remove the yeast from your houses, for whoever
12:15 for whoever eats anything with yeast in it from the first **day**
12:15 first day through the seventh **[RPH]** must be cut off from Israel.
12:16 On the first **day** hold a sacred assembly, and another one on the
12:16 day hold a sacred assembly, and another one on the seventh **day**.
12:17 because it was on this very **day** that I brought your divisions out of
12:17 Celebrate this **day** as a lasting ordinance for the generations to
12:18 from the evening of the fourteenth **day** until the evening of the
12:18 of the fourteenth day until the evening of the twenty-first **day**.
12:19 *For* seven **days** no yeast is to be found in your houses. And
12:41 At the end of the 430 years, to the very **day**, all the LORD's
12:51 on that very **day** the LORD brought the Israelites out of Egypt by
13:3 Moses said to the people, "Commemorate this **day**, the day you
13:4 **Today** [+2021], in the month of Abib, you are leaving.
13:6 *For* seven **days** eat bread made without yeast and on the seventh
13:6 without yeast and on the seventh **day** hold a festival to the LORD.
13:7 Eat unleavened bread *during* those seven **days**; nothing with yeast
13:8 On that **day** tell your son, 'I do this because of what the LORD
13:10 You must keep this ordinance at the appointed time **year** after
13:10 must keep this ordinance at the appointed time year after **year**.
14:13 will see the deliverance the LORD will bring you **today** [+2021].
14:13 The Egyptians you see **today** [+2021] you will never see again.
14:30 That **day** the LORD saved Israel from the hands of the Egyptians,
15:22 *For* three **days** they traveled in the desert without finding water.
16:1 on the fifteenth **day** of the second month after they had come out
16:4 are to go out each day and gather enough for **that day** [+3427].
16:4 are to go out each day and gather enough for **that day** [+3427].
16:5 On the sixth **day** they are to prepare what they bring in, and that is
16:5 is to be twice as much as they gather *on* the **other days** [+3427]."
16:5 is to be twice as much as they gather *on* the **other days** [+3427]."
16:22 On the sixth **day**, they gathered twice as much—two omers for
16:25 "Eat it **today** [+2021]," Moses said, "because today is a Sabbath to
16:25 Moses said, "because **today** [+2021] is a Sabbath to the LORD.

Ex 16:25 You will not find any of it on the ground **today** [+2021].
16:26 Six **days** you are to gather it, but on the seventh day, the Sabbath,
16:26 but on the seventh **day**, the Sabbath, there will not be any."
16:27 some of the people went out on the seventh **day** to gather it,
16:29 that is why on the sixth **day** he gives you bread for two days.
16:29 that is why on the sixth day he gives you bread *for two* **days**.
16:29 Everyone is to stay where he is on the seventh **day**; no one is to go
16:30 So the people rested on the seventh **day**.
19: 1 left Egypt—on the very **day**—they came to the Desert of Sinai.
19:10 to the people and consecrate them **today** [+2021] and tomorrow.
19:11 be ready by the third **day**, because on that day the LORD will
19:11 because on that **day** the LORD will come down on Mount Sinai
19:15 Then he said to the people, "Prepare yourselves for the third **day**.
19:16 On the morning of the third **day** there was thunder and lightning,
20: 8 "Remember the Sabbath **day** by keeping it holy.
20: 9 Six **days** you shall labor and do all your work,
20:10 but the seventh **day** is a Sabbath to the LORD your God.
20:11 For *in* six **days** the LORD made the heavens and the earth,
20:11 the sea, and all that is in them, but he rested on the seventh **day**.
20:11 Therefore the LORD blessed the Sabbath **day** and made it holy.
20:12 so that you *may* **live long** [+799] in the land the LORD your God
21:21 but he is not to be punished if the slave gets up after a **day**
21:21 but he is not to be punished if the slave gets up after a day or **two**[s],
22:30 [22:29] Let them stay with their mothers *for* seven **days**, but give
22:30 [22:29] for seven days, but give them to me on the eighth **day**.
23:12 "Six **days** do your work, but on the seventh day do not work,
23:12 on the seventh **day** do not work, so that your ox and your donkey
23:15 *for* seven **days** eat bread made without yeast, as I commanded you.
23:26 or be barren in your land. I will give you a full **life** [+5031] **span**.
24:16 *For* six **days** the cloud covered the mountain, and on the seventh
24:16 on the seventh **day** the LORD called to Moses from within the
24:18 And he stayed on the mountain forty **days** and forty nights.
29:30 Meeting to minister in the Holy Place is to wear them seven **days**.
29:35 I have commanded you, taking seven **days** to ordain them.
29:36 Sacrifice a bull each **day** as a sin offering to make atonement.
29:37 *For* seven **days** make atonement for the altar and consecrate it.
29:38 "This is what you are to offer on the altar regularly each **day**:
31:15 *For* six **days**, work is to be done, but the seventh day is a Sabbath
31:15 work is to be done, but the seventh **day** is a Sabbath of rest,
31:15 Whoever does any work on the Sabbath **day** must be put to death.
31:17 for *in* six **days** the LORD made the heavens and the earth,
31:17 and on the seventh **day** he abstained from work and rested.' "
32:28 and that **day** about three thousand of the people died.
32:29 "You have been set apart to the LORD **today** [+2021],
32:29 your own sons and brothers, and he has blessed you this **day**."
32:34 However, when the **time** comes for me to punish, I will punish
34:11 Obey what I command you **today** [+2021]. I will drive out before
34:18 *For* seven **days** eat bread made without yeast, as I commanded
34:21 "Six **days** you shall labor, but on the seventh day you shall rest;
34:21 "Six days you shall labor, but on the seventh **day** you shall rest;
34:28 Moses was there with the LORD forty **days** and forty nights
35: 2 *For* six **days**, work is to be done, but the seventh day shall be your
35: 2 work is to be done, but the seventh **day** shall be your holy day,
35: 3 Do not light a fire in any of your dwellings on the Sabbath **day**."
40: 2 the Tent of Meeting, on the first **day** *of* the first month.
40:37 if the cloud did not lift, they did not set out—until the **day** it lifted.
Lev 6: 5 [5:24] give it all to the owner on the **day** he presents his guilt
6:20 [6:13] his sons are to bring to the LORD on the **day** he is
7:15 offering of thanksgiving must be eaten on the **day** it is offered;
7:16 freewill offering, the sacrifice shall be eaten on the **day** he offers it,
7:17 Any meat of the sacrifice left over till the third **day** must be burned
7:18 If any meat of the fellowship offering is eaten on the third **day**,
7:35 his sons on the **day** they were presented to serve the LORD as
7:36 On the **day** they were anointed, the LORD commanded that the
7:38 which the LORD gave Moses on Mount Sinai on the **day** he
8:33 Do not leave the entrance to the Tent of Meeting *for* seven **days**,
8:33 until the **days** *of* your ordination are completed, for your ordination
8:33 are completed, **[RPH]** for your ordination will last seven days.
8:33 ordination are completed, for your ordination will last seven **days**.
8:34 What has been done **today** [+2021+2021+2296] was commanded
8:35 and night *for* seven **days** and do what the LORD requires,
9: 1 On the eighth **day** Moses summoned Aaron and his sons and the
9: 4 with oil. For **today** [+2021] the LORD will appear to you.' "
10:19 Aaron replied to Moses, "**Today** [+2021] they sacrificed their sin
10:19 have been pleased if I had eaten the sin offering **today** [+2021]?"
12: 2 gives birth to a son will be ceremonially unclean *for* seven **days**,
12: 2 for seven days, just as she is unclean **during** her monthly period.
12: 3 On the eighth **day** the boy is to be circumcised.
12: 4 the woman must wait thirty-three **days** to be purified from her
12: 4 the woman must wait thirty-three days **[RPH]** to be purified from
12: 4 or go to the sanctuary until the **days** *of* her purification are over.
12: 5 Then she must wait sixty-six **days** to be purified from her bleeding.
12: 5 she must wait sixty-six days **[RPH]** to be purified from her
12: 6 " 'When the **days** *of* her purification for a son or daughter are over,
13: 4 the priest is to put the infected person in isolation *for* seven **days**.
13: 5 On the seventh **day** the priest is to examine him, and if he sees that
13: 5 in the skin, he is to keep him in isolation another seven **days**.
13: 6 On the seventh **day** the priest is to examine him again, and if the
13:14 **whenever** [+928] raw flesh appears on him, he will be unclean.
13:21 has faded, then the priest is to put him in isolation *for* seven **days**.
13:26 has faded, then the priest is to put him in isolation *for* seven **days**.
13:27 On the seventh **day** the priest is to examine him, and if it is
13:31 the priest is to put the infected person in isolation *for* seven **days**.
13:32 On the seventh **day** the priest is to examine the sore, and if the itch
13:33 and the priest is to keep him in isolation another seven **days**.
13:34 On the seventh **day** the priest is to examine the itch, and if it has
13:46 **As long as** [+3972] he has the infection he remains unclean.
13:50 examine the mildew and isolate the affected article *for* seven **days**.
13:51 On the seventh **day** he is to examine it, and if the mildew has
13:54 article be washed. Then he is to isolate it *for* another seven **days**.
14: 2 "These are the regulations for the diseased person at the **time** *of* his
14: 8 into the camp, but he must stay outside his tent *for* seven **days**.
14: 9 On the seventh **day** he must shave off all his hair; he must shave
14:10 "On the eighth **day** he must bring two male lambs and one ewe
14:23 "On the eighth **day** he must bring them for his cleansing to the
14:38 go out the doorway of the house and close it up *for* seven **days**.
14:39 On the seventh **day** the priest shall return to inspect the house.
14:46 "Anyone who goes into the house **while** [+3972] it is closed up
14:57 to determine **when** [+928] something is clean or unclean. These are
14:57 to determine when something is clean or **[RPH]** unclean.
15:13 he is to count off seven **days** for his ceremonial cleansing;
15:14 On the eighth **day** he must take two doves or two young pigeons
15:19 of blood, the impurity of her monthly period will last seven **days**,
15:24 her monthly flow touches him, he will be unclean *for* seven **days**;
15:25 " 'When a woman has a discharge of blood *for* many **days** at a time
15:25 she will be unclean **as long as** [+3972] she has the discharge,
15:25 as long as she has the discharge, just as in the **days** *of* her period.
15:26 Any bed she lies on **while** her discharge **continues** [+3972] will be
15:28 she is cleansed from her discharge, she must count off seven **days**,
15:29 On the eighth **day** she must take two doves or two young pigeons
16:30 because on this **day** atonement will be made for you, to cleanse
19: 6 It shall be eaten on the **day** you sacrifice it or on the next day;
19: 6 next day; anything left over until the third **day** must be burned up.
19: 7 If any of it is eaten on the third **day**, it is impure and will not be
22:27 or a goat is born, it is to remain with its mother *for* seven **days**.
22:27 From the eighth **day** on, it will be acceptable as an offering made
22:28 Do not slaughter a cow or a sheep and its young on the same **day**.
22:30 It must be eaten that same **day**; leave none of it till morning.
23: 3 " 'There are six **days** when you may work, but the seventh day is a
23: 3 but the seventh **day** is a Sabbath of rest, a day of sacred assembly.
23: 6 On the fifteenth **day** of that month the LORD's Feast of
23: 6 *for* seven **days** you must eat bread made without yeast.
23: 7 On the first **day** hold a sacred assembly and do no regular work.
23: 8 *For* seven **days** present an offering made to the LORD by fire.
23: 8 on the seventh **day** hold a sacred assembly and do no regular
23:12 On the **day** you wave the sheaf, you must sacrifice as a burnt
23:14 new grain, until the very **day** you bring this offering to your God.
23:15 the **day** you brought the sheaf of the wave offering, count off seven
23:16 Count off fifty **days** up to the day after the seventh Sabbath,
23:21 On that same **day** you are to proclaim a sacred assembly and do no
23:27 "The tenth day of this seventh month is the **Day** *of* Atonement.
23:28 Do no work on that **day**, because it is the Day of Atonement,
23:28 Do no work on that day, because it is the **Day** *of* Atonement,
23:29 Anyone who does not deny himself on that **day** must be cut off
23:30 from among his people anyone who does any work on that **day**.
23:34 'On the fifteenth **day** of the seventh month the LORD's Feast of
23:34 LORD's Feast of Tabernacles begins, and it lasts *for* seven **days**.
23:35 The first **day** is a sacred assembly; do no regular work.
23:36 *For* seven **days** present offerings made to the LORD by fire,
23:36 on the eighth **day** hold a sacred assembly and present an offering
23:37 sacrifices and drink offerings required for **each day** [+928+3427].
23:37 sacrifices and drink offerings required for **each day** [+928+3427].
23:39 " 'So beginning with the fifteenth **day** of the seventh month,
23:39 of the land, celebrate the festival to the LORD *for* seven **days**;
23:39 the first **day** is a day of rest, and the eighth day also is a day of rest.
23:39 the first day is a day of rest, and the eighth **day** also is a day of rest.
23:40 On the first **day** you are to take choice fruit from the trees,
23:40 and rejoice before the LORD your God *for* seven **days**.
23:41 Celebrate this as a festival to the LORD *for* seven **days** each year.
23:42 Live in booths *for* seven **days**: All native-born Israelites are to
24: 8 This bread is to be set out before the LORD regularly, **Sabbath after Sabbath** [+928+928+2021+2021+3427+8701+8701],
24: 8 This bread is to be set out before the LORD regularly, **Sabbath after Sabbath** [+928+928+2021+2021+3427+8701+8701],
25: 8 so that the seven sabbaths of years amount to a **period** *of*
25: 9 on the **Day** *of* Atonement sound the trumpet throughout your land.
25:29 a full year after its sale. **During that time** he may redeem it.
25:50 **based on the rate paid to** [+3869] a hired man for that number of

Lev 26:34 the land will enjoy its sabbath years all the **time** *that* it lies
26:35 All the **time** that it lies desolate, the land will have the rest it did
27:23 the man must pay its value on that **day** as something holy to the
Nu 3: 1 Moses at the **time** the LORD talked with Moses on Mount Sinai.
3:13 **When** [+928] I struck down all the firstborn in Egypt, I set apart
6: 4 **As long as** [+3972] he is a Nazirite, he must not eat anything that
6: 5 " '*During* the entire **period** *of* his vow of separation no razor may
6: 5 He must be holy until the **period** of his separation to the LORD is
6: 6 Throughout the **period** *of* his separation to the LORD he must not
6: 8 Throughout the **period** *of* his separation he is consecrated to the
6: 9 has dedicated, he must shave his head on the **day** *of* his cleansing—
6: 9 must shave his head on the day of his cleansing—the seventh **day**.
6:10 on the eighth **day** he must bring two doves or two young pigeons
6:11 of the dead body. That same **day** he is to consecrate his head.
6:12 He must dedicate himself to the LORD for the **period** *of* his
6:12 The previous **days** do not count, because he became defiled during
6:13 " 'Now this is the law for the Nazirite **when** [+928] the period of
6:13 " 'Now this is the law for the Nazirite when the **period** *of* his
7: 1 **When** [+928] Moses finished setting up the tabernacle, he anointed
7:10 **When** [+928] the altar was anointed, the leaders brought their
7:11 "**Each day** [+2021+2021+3427+4200+4200] one leader is to bring
7:11 "**Each day** [+2021+2021+3427+4200+4200] one leader is to bring
7:12 The one who brought his offering on the first **day** was Nahshon
7:18 On the second **day** Nethanel son of Zuar, the leader of Issachar,
7:24 On the third **day**, Eliab son of Helon, the leader of the people of
7:30 On the fourth **day** Elizur son of Shedeur, the leader of the people
7:36 On the fifth **day** Shelumiel son of Zurishaddai, the leader of the
7:42 On the sixth **day** Eliasaph son of Deuel, the leader of the people of
7:48 On the seventh **day** Elishama son of Ammihud, the leader of the
7:54 On the eighth **day** Gamaliel son of Pedahzur, the leader of the
7:60 On the ninth **day** Abidan son of Gideoni, the leader of the people
7:66 On the tenth **day** Ahiezer son of Ammishaddai, the leader of the
7:72 On the **[RPH]** eleventh day Pagiel son of Ocran, the leader of the
7:72 On the eleventh **day** Pagiel son of Ocran, the leader of the people
7:78 On the **[RPH]** twelfth day Ahira son of Enan, the leader of the
7:78 On the twelfth **day** Ahira son of Enan, the leader of the people of
7:84 leaders for the dedication of the altar **when** [+928] it was anointed:
8:17 **When** [+928] I struck down all the firstborn in Egypt, I set them
9: 3 at twilight on the fourteenth **day** of this month, in accordance with
9: 5 so in the Desert of Sinai at twilight on the fourteenth **day** of the
9: 6 But some of them could not celebrate the Passover on that **day**
9: 6 of a dead body. So they came to Moses and Aaron that same **day**
9:11 They are to celebrate it on the fourteenth **day** of the second month
9:15 On the **day** the tabernacle, the Tent of the Testimony, was set up,
9:18 **As long as** [+3972] the cloud stayed over the tabernacle,
9:19 When the cloud remained over the tabernacle a long **time**,
9:20 Sometimes the cloud was over the tabernacle only a few **days**;
9:22 Whether the cloud stayed over the tabernacle *for two* **days**
9:22 cloud stayed over the tabernacle for two days or a month or a **year**,
10:10 Also at your **times** *of* rejoicing—your appointed feasts and New
10:33 out from the mountain of the LORD and traveled for three **days**.
10:33 before them *during* those three **days** to find them a place to rest.
11:19 You will not eat it *for* just one **day**, or two days, or five, ten
11:19 not eat it for just one day, or *two* **days**, or five, ten or twenty days,
11:19 it for just one day, or two days, or five, **[RPH]** ten or twenty days,
11:19 it for just one day, or two days, or five, ten **[RPH]** or twenty days,
11:19 not eat it for just one day, or two days, or five, ten or twenty **days**,
11:20 but for a **whole** month—until it comes out of your nostrils
11:21 and you say, 'I will give them meat to eat for a **whole** month!'
11:31 three feet above the ground, as far as a **day's** walk in any direction.
11:31 above the ground, as far as a day's walk in any direction. **[RPH]**
11:32 All that **day** and night and all the next day the people went out
11:32 All that day and night and all the next **day** the people went out
12:14 in her face, would she not have been in disgrace *for* seven **days**?
12:14 Confine her outside the camp *for* seven **days**; after that she can be
12:15 So Miriam was confined outside the camp *for* seven **days**,
13:20 the fruit of the land." (**It**[s] was the season for the first ripe grapes.)
13:20 the fruit of the land." (It was the **season** *for* the first ripe grapes.)
13:25 At the end of forty **days** they returned from exploring the land.
14:34 one year for **each**[s] *of* the forty days you explored the land—
14:34 one year for each of the **[RPH]** forty days you explored the land—
14:34 one year for each of the forty **days** you explored the land—
14:34 one year for each of the forty days **[RPH]** you explored the land—
15:23 from the **day** the LORD gave them and continuing through the
15:32 in the desert, a man was found gathering wood on the Sabbath **day**.
19:11 touches the dead body of anyone will be unclean *for* seven **days**.
19:12 He must purify himself with the water on the third **day** and on the
19:12 himself with the water on the third day and on the seventh **day**;
19:12 if he does not purify himself on the **[RPH]** third and seventh days,
19:12 But if he does not purify himself on the third and seventh **days**,
19:14 the tent and anyone who is in it will be unclean *for* seven **days**,
19:16 touches a human bone or a grave, will be unclean *for* seven **days**.
19:19 sprinkle the unclean person on the third **[RPH]** and seventh days,
19:19 is to sprinkle the unclean person on the third and seventh **days**,
19:19 and seventh days, and on the seventh **day** he is to purify him.
20:15 forefathers went down into Egypt, and we lived there many **years**.
20:29 had died, the entire house of Israel mourned for him thirty **days**.
22:30 I not your own donkey, which you have always ridden, to this **day**?
24:14 let me warn you of what this people will do to your people in **days**
25:18 the woman who was killed **when** [+928] the plague came as a
28: 3 a year old without defect, as a regular burnt offering each **day**.
28: 9 " 'On the Sabbath **day**, make an offering of two lambs a year old
28:16 " 'On the fourteenth **day** of the first month the LORD's Passover
28:17 On the fifteenth **day** of this month there is to be a festival;
28:17 is to be a festival; *for* seven **days** eat bread made without yeast.
28:18 On the first **day** hold a sacred assembly and do no regular work.
28:24 this way prepare the food for the offering made by fire every **day**
28:24 fire every day *for* seven **days** as an aroma pleasing to the LORD;
28:25 On the seventh **day** hold a sacred assembly and do no regular
28:26 " 'On the **day** *of* firstfruits, when you present to the LORD an
29: 1 and do no regular work. It is a **day** for you to sound the trumpets.
29:12 " 'On the fifteenth **day** of the seventh month, hold a sacred
29:12 regular work. Celebrate a festival to the LORD *for* seven **days**.
29:17 " 'On the second **day** prepare twelve young bulls, two rams
29:20 " 'On the third **day** prepare eleven bulls, two rams and fourteen
29:23 " 'On the fourth **day** prepare ten bulls, two rams and fourteen male
29:26 " 'On the fifth **day** prepare nine bulls, two rams and fourteen male
29:29 " 'On the sixth **day** prepare eight bulls, two rams and fourteen male
29:32 " 'On the seventh **day** prepare seven bulls, two rams and fourteen
29:35 " 'On the eighth **day** hold an assembly and do no regular work.
30: 5 [30:6] But if her father forbids her **when** [+928] he hears about it,
30: 7 [30:8] her husband hears about it **[RPH]** but says nothing to her,
30: 8 [30:9] if her husband forbids her **when** [+928] he hears about it,
30:12 [30:13] if her husband nullifies them **when** [+928] he hears about
30:14 [30:15] if her husband says nothing to her about it from **day** to
30:14 [30:15] her husband says nothing to her about it from day to **day**,
30:14 [30:15] He confirms them by saying nothing to her **when** [+928]
31:19 anyone who was killed must stay outside the camp seven **days**.
31:19 On the third and seventh **days** you must purify yourselves
31:19 On the third and seventh days **[RPH]** you must purify yourselves
31:24 On the seventh **day** wash your clothes and you will be clean.
32:10 The LORD's anger was aroused that **day** and he swore this oath:
33: 3 The Israelites set out from Rameses on the fifteenth **day** of the first
33: 8 and when they had traveled *for* three **days** in the Desert of Etham,
Dt 1: 2 (It takes eleven **days** to go from Horeb to Kadesh Barnea by the
1:10 so that **today** [+2021] you are as many as the stars in the sky.
1:39 your children who do not **yet** [+2021] know good from bad—
1:46 so you stayed in Kadesh many **days**—all the time you spent there.
1:46 so you stayed in Kadesh many days—all the **time** you spent there.
2: 1 *For* a long **time** we made our way around the hill country of Seir.
2:14 Thirty-eight years passed from the **time** we left Kadesh Barnea
2:18 "**Today** [+2021] you are to pass by the region of Moab at Ar.
2:22 They drove them out and have lived in their place to this **day**.
2:25 This very **day** I will begin to put the terror and fear of you on all
2:30 give him into your hands, as he has **now** [+2021+2021+2296] done.
3:14 named after him, so that to this **day** Bashan is called Havvoth Jair.)
4: 4 held fast to the LORD your God are still alive **today** [+2021].
4: 8 laws as this body of laws I am setting before you **today** [+2021]?
4: 9 or let them slip from your heart **as long as** [+3972] you live.
4:10 Remember the **day** you stood before the LORD your God at
4:10 so that they may learn to revere me **as long as** [+2021+3972] they
4:15 You saw no form of any kind the **day** the LORD spoke to you at
4:20 the people of his inheritance, as you **now** [+2021+2021+2296] are.
4:26 earth as witnesses against you this **day** that you will quickly perish
4:26 *You will* not **live** there **long** [+799] but will certainly be destroyed.
4:30 then in later **days** you will return to the LORD your God
4:32 Ask now about the former **days**, long before your time, from the
4:32 long before your time, from the **day** God created man on the earth;
4:38 to you for your inheritance, as it is **today** [+2021+2021+2296].
4:39 and take to heart this **day** that the LORD is God in heaven above
4:40 his decrees and commands, which I am giving you **today** [+2021],
4:40 that *you may* **live long** [+799] in the land the LORD your God
4:40 live long in the land the LORD your God gives you *for* all **time**.
5: 1 the decrees and laws I declare in your hearing **today** [+2021].
5: 3 but with us, with all of us who are alive here **today** [+2021].
5:12 "Observe the Sabbath **day** by keeping it holy, as the LORD your
5:13 Six **days** you shall labor and do all your work,
5:14 but the seventh **day** is a Sabbath to the LORD your God.
5:15 your God has commanded you to observe the Sabbath **day**.
5:16 so that you *may* **live long** [+799] and that it may go well with you
5:24 **Today** [+2021+2021+2296] we have seen that a man can live even
5:29 to fear me and keep all my commands **always** [+2021+3972],
5:33 and prolong your **days** in the land that you will possess.
6: 2 your God **as long as** [+3972] you live by keeping all his decrees
6: 2 that I give you, and so that you *may* **enjoy long life** [+799].
6: 6 These commandments that I give you **today** [+2021] are to be
6:24 so that we might **always** [+2021+3972] prosper and be kept alive,
6:24 and be kept alive, as is the case **today** [+2021+2021+2296].

Dt 7:11 follow the commands, decrees and laws I give you **today** [+2021].
8: 1 careful to follow every command I am giving you **today** [+2021],
8:11 his laws and his decrees that I am giving you this **day**.
8:18 he swore to your forefathers, as it is **today** [+2021+2021+2296].
8:19 I testify against you **today** [+2021] that you will surely be
9: 1 You are **now** [+2021] about to cross the Jordan to go in
9: 3 be assured **today** [+2021] that the LORD your God is the one
9: 7 From the **day** you left Egypt until you arrived here, you have been
9: 9 with you, I stayed on the mountain forty **days** and forty nights;
9:10 to you on the mountain out of the fire, on the **day** *of* the assembly.
9:11 At the end of the forty **days** and forty nights, the LORD gave me
9:18 Then once again I fell prostrate before the LORD *for* forty **days**
9:24 You have been rebellious against the LORD **ever since** [+4946] I
9:25 I lay prostrate before the LORD those forty **days** and forty nights
10: 4 to you on the mountain, out of the fire, on the **day** *of* the assembly.
10: 8 blessings in his name, as they still do **today** [+2021+2021+2296].
10:10 Now I had stayed on the mountain forty **days** and nights, as I did
10:10 on the mountain forty days and nights, as I did the first **time**,
10:13 decrees that I am giving you **today** [+2021] for your own good?
10:15 above all the nations, as it is **today** [+2021+2021+2296].
11: 1 his decrees, his laws and his commands **always** [+2021+3972].
11: 2 Remember **today** [+2021] that your children were not the ones
11: 4 how the LORD brought **lasting** [+2021+2021+2296+6330] ruin on
11: 8 therefore all the commands I am giving you **today** [+2021],
11: 9 so that *you may* **live long** [+799] in the land that the LORD
11:13 faithfully obey the commands I am giving you **today** [+2021]—
11:21 so that your **days** and the days of your children may be many in the
11:21 the **days** *of* your children may be many in the land that the LORD
11:21 as many as the **days** that the heavens are above the earth.
11:26 I am setting before you **today** [+2021] a blessing and a curse—
11:27 of the LORD your God that I am giving you **today** [+2021];
11:28 turn from the way that I command you **today** [+2021] by following
11:32 all the decrees and laws I am setting before you **today** [+2021].
12: 1 you to possess—**as long as** [+2021+3972] you live in the land.
12: 8 You are not to do as we do here **today** [+2021], everyone as he
12:19 Be careful not to neglect the Levites **as long as** you **live** [+3972] in
13:18 [13:19] all his commands that I am giving you **today** [+2021]
14:23 may learn to revere the LORD your God **always** [+2021+3972].
15: 5 to follow all these commands I am giving you **today** [+2021].
15:15 That is why I give you this command **today** [+2021].
16: 3 but *for* seven **days** eat unleavened bread, the bread of affliction,
16: 3 so that all the **days** *of* your life you may remember the time of your
16: 3 so that all the days of your life you may remember the **time** *of* your
16: 4 yeast be found in your possession in all your land *for* seven **days**.
16: 4 you sacrifice on the evening of the first **day** remain until morning.
16: 8 *For* six **days** eat unleavened bread and on the seventh day hold an
16: 8 and on the seventh **day** hold an assembly to the LORD your God
16:13 Celebrate the Feast of Tabernacles *for* seven **days** after you have
16:15 *For* seven **days** celebrate the Feast to the LORD your God at the
17: 9 who are Levites, and to the judge who is in office at that **time**.
17:19 he is to read it all the **days** *of* his life so that he may learn to revere
17:20 his descendants will reign a long **time** over his kingdom in Israel.
18: 5 and minister in the LORD's name **always** [+2021+3972].
18:16 your God at Horeb on the **day** *of* the assembly when you said,
19: 9 carefully follow all these laws I command you **today** [+2021]—
19: 9 LORD your God and to walk **always** [+2021+3972] in his ways—
19:17 before the priests and the judges who are in office at the **time**.
20: 3 O Israel, **today** [+2021] you are going into battle against your
20:19 When you lay siege to a city *for* a long **time**, fighting against it to
21:13 in your house and mourned her father and mother for a **full** month,
21:16 **when** [+928] he wills his property to his sons, he must not give the
21:23 Be sure to bury him that same **day**, because anyone who is hung on
22: 7 so that it may go well with you and you may have a long **life**.
22:19 to be his wife; he must not divorce her **as long as** he **lives** [+3972].
22:29 violated her. He can never divorce her **as long as** he **lives** [+3972].
23: 6 [23:7] with them **as long as** you **live** [+3972+4200+6409].
24:15 Pay him his wages each **day** before sunset, because he is poor
25:15 so that you *may* **live long** [+799] in the land the LORD your God
26: 3 say to the priest in office at the **time**, "I declare today to the
26: 3 "I declare **today** [+2021] to the LORD your God that I have come
26:16 The LORD your God commands you this **day** to follow these
26:17 You have declared this **day** that the LORD is your God and that
26:18 And the LORD has declared this **day** that you are his people,
27: 1 "Keep all these commands that I give you **today** [+2021].
27: 2 **When** [+928+2021] you have crossed the Jordan into the land the
27: 4 as I command you **today** [+2021], and coat them with plaster.
27: 9 You have **now** [+2021+2021+2296] become the people of the
27:10 follow his commands and decrees that I give you **today** [+2021]."
27:11 On the same **day** Moses commanded the people:
28: 1 and carefully follow all his commands I give you **today** [+2021],
28:13 to the commands of the LORD your God that I give you this **day**
28:14 turn aside from any of the commands I give you **today** [+2021],
28:15 all his commands and decrees I am giving you **today** [+2021],
28:29 unsuccessful in everything you do; **day** [+2021+3972] **after day**
28:32 out your eyes watching for them **day** [+2021+3972] **after day**,
28:33 and you will have nothing but cruel oppression all your **days**.
29: 4 [29:3] to this **day** the LORD has not given you a mind that
29:10 [29:9] All of you are standing **today** [+2021] in the presence of
29:12 [29:11] a covenant the LORD is making with you this **day**
29:13 [29:12] to confirm you this **day** as his people, that he may be your
29:15 [29:14] who are standing here with us **today** [+2021] in the
29:15 [29:14] but also with those who are not here **today** [+2021].
29:18 [29:17] or tribe among you **today** [+2021] whose heart turns
29:28 [29:27] into another land, as it is **now** [+2021+2021+2296]."
30: 2 your soul according to everything I command you **today** [+2021],
30: 8 and follow all his commands I am giving you **today** [+2021].
30:11 Now what I am commanding you **today** [+2021] is not too difficult
30:15 See, I set before you **today** [+2021] life and prosperity, death
30:16 For I command you **today** [+2021] to love the LORD your God,
30:18 I declare to you this **day** that you will certainly be destroyed.
30:18 *You will* not **live long** [+799] in the land you are crossing the
30:19 This **day** I call heaven and earth as witnesses against you that I
30:20 he will give you **many years** [+802] in the land he swore to give to
31: 2 "I am **now** [+2021] a hundred and twenty years old and I am no
31:13 learn to fear the LORD your God **as long as** [+2021+3972] you
31:14 The LORD said to Moses, "Now the **day** *of* your death is near.
31:17 On that **day** I will become angry with them and forsake them;
31:17 difficulties will come upon them, and on that **day** they will ask,
31:18 I will certainly hide my face on that **day** because of all their
31:21 **[NIE]** even before I bring them into the land I promised them on
31:22 So Moses wrote down this song that **day** and taught it to the
31:27 and with you, **[NIE]** how much more will you rebel after I die!
31:29 In **days** to come, disaster will fall upon you because you will do
32: 7 Remember the **days** of old; consider the generations long past.
32:35 their **day** *of* disaster is near and their doom rushes upon them."
32:46 to heart all the words I have solemnly declared to you this **day**,
32:47 By them *you will* **live long** [+799] in the land you are crossing the
32:48 On that same **day** the LORD told Moses,
33:12 of the LORD rest secure in him, for he shields him all **day** *long*,
33:25 will be iron and bronze, and your strength will equal your **days**.
34: 6 Beth Peor, but to this **day** no one knows where his grave is.
34: 8 The Israelites grieved for Moses in the plains of Moab thirty **days**,
34: 8 thirty days, until the **time** *of* weeping and mourning was over.
Jos 1: 5 No one will be able to stand up against you all the **days** *of* your
1:11 Three **days** from now you will cross the Jordan here to go in
2:16 Hide yourselves there three **days** until they return, and then go on
2:22 they left, they went into the hills and stayed there three **days**,
3: 2 After three **days** the officers went throughout the camp,
3: 7 "**Today** [+2021+2021+2296] I will begin to exalt you in the eyes
3:15 Now the Jordan is at flood stage all **during** harvest. Yet as soon as
4: 9 the ark of the covenant had stood. And they are there to this **day**.
4:14 That **day** the LORD exalted Joshua in the sight of all Israel;
4:14 they revered him all the **days** *of* his life, just as they had revered
4:24 so that you might **always** [+2021+3972] fear the LORD your
5: 9 the LORD said to Joshua, "**Today** [+2021] I have rolled away the
5: 9 Egypt from you." So the place has been called Gilgal to this **day**.
5:10 On the evening of the fourteenth **day** of the month, while camped
5:11 The day after the Passover, that very **day**, they ate some of the
6: 3 around the city once with all the armed men. Do this *for* six **days**.
6: 4 On the seventh **day**, march around the city seven times,
6:10 your voices, do not say a word until the **day** I tell you to shout.
6:14 So on the second **day** they marched around the city once
6:14 the city once and returned to the camp. They did this *for* six **days**.
6:15 On the seventh **day**, they got up at daybreak and marched around
6:15 except that on that **day** they circled the city seven times.
6:25 as spies to Jericho—and she lives among the Israelites to this **day**.
7:25 The LORD will bring trouble on you **today** [+2021+2021+2296]."
7:26 they heaped up a large pile of rocks, which remains to this **day**.
7:26 called the Valley of Achor **ever since** [+2021+2021+2296+6330].
8:25 Twelve thousand men and women fell that **day**—all the people of
8:28 and made it a permanent heap of ruins, a desolate place to this **day**.
8:29 they raised a large pile of rocks over it, which remains to this **day**.
9:12 when we packed it at home on the **day** we left to come to you.
9:16 Three **days** after they made the treaty with the Gibeonites,
9:17 So the Israelites set out and on the third **day** came to their cities:
9:27 That **day** he made the Gibeonites woodcutters and water carriers
9:27 the LORD would choose. And that is what they are to this **day**.
10:12 On the **day** the LORD gave the Amorites over to Israel,
10:13 in the middle of the sky and delayed going down about a full **day**.
10:14 There has never been a **day** like it before or since, a day when the
10:27 of the cave they placed large rocks, which are there to this **day**.
10:28 That **day** Joshua took Makkedah. He put the city and its king to the
10:32 Lachish over to Israel, and Joshua took it on the second **day**.
10:35 They captured it that same **day** and put it to the sword and totally
10:35 destroyed everyone in it, just as they had done to Lachish. **[RPH]**
11:18 Joshua waged war against all these kings *for* a long **time**.
13: 1 When Joshua was old and well advanced in **years**, the LORD said
13: 1 said to him, "You *are* **very old** [+928+995+2021+2416], and there

Jos 13: 13 so they continue to live among the Israelites to this **day**.
14: 9 So on that **day** Moses swore to me, 'The land on which your feet
14: 10 in the desert. So here I am **today** [+2021], eighty-five years old!
14: 11 I am still as strong **today** [+2021] as the day Moses sent me out;
14: 11 I am still as strong today as the **day** Moses sent me out; I'm just as
14: 12 give me this hill country that the LORD promised me that **day**.
14: 12 You yourself heard **then** [+928+2021+2021+2085] that the
14: 14 the Kenizzite **ever since** [+2021+2021+2296+6330],
15: 63 to this **day** the Jebusites live there with the people of Judah.
16: 10 to this **day** the Canaanites live among the people of Ephraim
20: 6 and until the death of the high priest who is serving at that **time**.
22: 3 *For* a long **time** now—to this very day—you have not deserted
22: 3 For a long time now—to this very **day**—you have not deserted
22: 16 **[RPH]** and build yourselves an altar in rebellion against him
22: 16 build yourselves an altar in rebellion against him **now** [+2021]?
22: 17 Up to this very **day** we have not cleansed ourselves from that sin,
22: 18 And are you **now** [+2021] turning away from the LORD?
22: 18 " 'If you rebel against the LORD **today** [+2021], tomorrow he
22: 22 or disobedience to the LORD, do not spare us this **day**.
22: 29 turn away from him **today** [+2021] by building an altar for burnt
22: 31 Manasseh, "**Today** [+2021] we know that the LORD is with us,
23: 1 After a long **time** had passed and the LORD had given Israel rest
23: 1 around them, Joshua, by then old and well advanced in **years**,
23: 2 and said to them: "I am old and well advanced in **years**.
23: 8 to the LORD your God, as you have until **now** [+2021+2021+2296].
23: 9 to this **day** no one has been able to withstand you.
23: 14 "**Now** [+2021] I am about to go the way of all the earth. You know
24: 7 I did to the Egyptians. Then you lived in the desert *for* a long **time**.
24: 15 then choose for yourselves this **day** whom you will serve,
24: 25 On that **day** Joshua made a covenant for the people, and there at
24: 31 Israel served the LORD throughout the **lifetime** *of* Joshua
24: 31 the lifetime of Joshua and **[RPH]** of the elders who outlived him
24: 31 lifetime of Joshua and of the elders who **outlived** [+339+799] him
Jdg 1: 21 to this **day** the Jebusites live there with the Benjamites.
1: 26 he built a city and called it Luz, which is its name to this **day**.
2: 7 The people served the LORD throughout the **lifetime** *of* Joshua
2: 7 the lifetime of Joshua and of **[RPH]** the elders who outlived him
2: 7 lifetime of Joshua and of the elders who **outlived** [+339+799] him
2: 18 them out of the hands of their enemies as long as the judge **lived**;
3: 30 That **day** Moab was made subject to Israel, and the land had peace
4: 14 This is the **day** the LORD has given Sisera into your hands.
4: 23 On that **day** God subdued Jabin, the Canaanite king, before the
5: 1 On that **day** Deborah and Barak son of Abinoam sang this song:
5: 6 "In the **days** *of* Shamgar son of Anath, in the days of Jael,
5: 6 son of Anath, in the **days** *of* Jael, the roads were abandoned;
6: 24 LORD is Peace. To this **day** it stands in Ophrah of the Abiezrites.
6: 32 So that **day** they called Gideon "Jerub-Baal," saying, "Let Baal
8: 28 During Gideon's **lifetime**, the land enjoyed peace forty years.
9: 18 (but **today** [+2021] you have revolted against my father's family,
9: 19 toward Jerub-Baal and his family **today** [+2021+2021+2296],
9: 45 All that **day** Abimelech pressed his attack against the city until he
10: 4 thirty towns in Gilead, which to this **day** are called Havvoth Jair.
10: 15 you think best, but please rescue us **now** [+2021+2021+2296]."
11: 4 **Some time** [+4946] **later**, when the Ammonites made war on
11: 27 decide the dispute this **day** between the Israelites and the
11: 40 that **each year** [+2025+3427+4946] the young women of Israel go
11: 40 that **each year** [+2025+3427+4946] the young women of Israel go
11: 40 that each year the young women of Israel go out *for* four **days** to
12: 3 Now why have you come up **today** [+2021+2021+2296] to fight
13: 7 will be a Nazirite of God from birth until the **day** *of* his death.' "
13: 10 "He's here! The man who appeared to me the other **day**!"
14: 8 **Some time** [+4946] **later**, when he went back to marry her,
14: 12 "If you can give me the answer *within* the seven **days** *of* the feast,
14: 14 something sweet." *For* three **days** they could not give the answer.
14: 15 On the fourth **day**, they said to Samson's wife, "Coax your
14: 17 She cried the whole seven **days** of the feast. So on the seventh day
14: 17 So on the seventh **day** he finally told her, because she continued to
14: 18 Before sunset on the seventh **day** the men of the town said to him,
15: 1 **Later** [+4946] **on**, at the time of wheat harvest, Samson took a
15: 1 Later on, at the **time** *of* wheat harvest, Samson took a young goat
15: 19 En Hakkore, and it is **still** [+2021+2021+2296+6330] there in Lehi.
15: 20 Samson led Israel for twenty years in the **days** *of* the Philistines.
16: 16 With such nagging she prodded him **day** [+2021+3972] **after day**
17: 6 In those **days** Israel had no king; everyone did as he saw fit.
17: 10 and I'll give you ten shekels of silver a **year** [+2021+4200],
18: 1 In those **days** Israel had no king. And in those days the tribe of the
18: 1 in those **days** the tribe of the Danites was seeking a place of their
18: 1 because they had not **yet** [+2021+2021+2085+6330] come into an
18: 12 the place west of Kiriath Jearim is called Mahaneh Dan to this **day**.
18: 30 his sons were priests for the tribe of Dan until the **time** *of* the
18: 31 idols Micah had made, all the **time** the house of God was in Shiloh.
19: 1 In those **days** Israel had no king. Now a Levite who lived in a
19: 2 Judah. After she had been there four months, **[NIE]**
19: 4 so he remained with him three **days**, eating and drinking,
19: 5 On the fourth **day** they got up early and he prepared to leave,
19: 8 On the morning of the fifth **day**, when he rose to go, the girl's
19: 8 father said, "Refresh yourself. Wait till **afternoon** [+2021+5742]!"
19: 9 the girl's father, said, "Now look, **it's** [+2021] almost evening.
19: 9 Spend the night here; the **day** is nearly over. Stay and enjoy
19: 11 When they were near Jebus and the **day** was almost gone,
19: 30 or done, not since the **day** the Israelites came up out of Egypt.
19: 30 of Egypt. **[RPH]** Think about it! Consider it! Tell us what to do!"
20: 15 **At once** [+928+2021+2021+2085] the Benjamites mobilized
20: 21 down twenty-two thousand Israelites on the battlefield that **day**.
20: 22 their positions where they had stationed themselves the first **day**.
20: 24 Then the Israelites drew near to Benjamin the second **day**.
20: 25 This **time**, when the Benjamites came out from Gibeah to oppose
20: 26 They fasted that **day** until evening and presented burnt offerings
20: 27 (In those **days** the ark of the covenant of God was there,
20: 28 **[RPH]** "Shall we go up again to battle with Benjamin our brother,
20: 30 They went up against the Benjamites on the third **day** and took up
20: 35 and on that **day** the Israelites struck down 25,100 Benjamites,
20: 46 On that **day** twenty-five thousand Benjamite swordsmen fell,
21: 3 Why should one tribe be missing from Israel **today** [+2021]?"
21: 6 the Benjamites. "**Today** [+2021] one tribe is cut off from Israel,"
21: 19 there is the **annual** [+2025+3427+4946] festival of the LORD in
21: 19 there is the **annual** [+2025+3427+4946] festival of the LORD in
21: 25 In those **days** Israel had no king; everyone did as he saw fit.
Ru 1: 1 In the **days** *when* the judges ruled, there was a famine in the land,
2: 19 mother-in-law asked her, "Where did you glean **today** [+2021]?
2: 19 "The name of the man I worked with **today** [+2021] is Boaz,"
3: 18 For the man will not rest until the matter is settled **today** [+2021]."
4: 5 "On the **day** you buy the land from Naomi and from Ruth the
4: 9 all the people, "**Today** [+2021] you are witnesses that I have
4: 10 or from the town records. **Today** [+2021] you are witnesses!"
4: 14 who this **day** has not left you without a kinsman-redeemer.
1Sa 1: 3 **Year** after year this man went up from his town to worship
1: 3 Year after **year** this man went up from his town to worship
1: 4 Whenever the **day** came for Elkanah to sacrifice, he would give
1: 11 then I will give him to the LORD *for* all the **days** *of* his life,
1: 20 So in the course of **time** Hannah conceived and gave birth to a son.
1: 21 up with all his family to offer the **annual** sacrifice to the LORD
1: 28 *For* his whole **life** [+889+2118] he will be given over to the
2: 16 "Let the fat be burned up **first** [+2021+3869], and then take
2: 19 **Each year** [+2025+3427+4946] his mother made him a little robe
2: 19 **Each year** [+2025+3427+4946] his mother made him a little robe
2: 19 when she went up with her husband to offer the **annual** sacrifice.
2: 31 The **time** is coming when I will cut short your strength and the
2: 32 family line there will **never** [+2021+3972+4202] be an old man.
2: 34 will be a sign to you—they will both die on the same **day**.
2: 35 he will minister before my anointed one **always** [+2021+3972].
3: 1 In those **days** the word of the LORD was rare; there were not
3: 2 One **night** Eli, whose eyes were becoming so weak that he could
3: 12 At that **time** I will carry out against Eli everything I spoke against
4: 3 "Why did the LORD bring defeat upon us **today** [+2021] before
4: 12 That same **day** a Benjamite ran from the battle line and went to
4: 16 "I have just come from the battle line; I fled from it this very **day**."
5: 5 That is why to this **day** neither the priests of Dagon nor any others
6: 15 On that **day** the people of Beth Shemesh offered burnt offerings
6: 16 Philistines saw all this and then returned that same **day** to Ekron.
6: 18 is a witness to this **day** in the field of Joshua of Beth Shemesh.
7: 2 It was **[RPH]** a long time, twenty years in all, that the ark
7: 2 It was a long **time**, twenty years in all, that the ark remained at
7: 6 On that **day** they fasted and there they confessed, "We have sinned
7: 10 that **day** the LORD thundered with loud thunder against the
7: 13 Throughout Samuel's **lifetime**, the hand of the LORD was against
7: 15 Samuel continued as judge over Israel all the **days** *of* his life.
8: 8 As they have done from the **day** I brought them up out of Egypt
8: 8 done from the day I brought them up out of Egypt until this **day**,
8: 18 When that **day** comes, you will cry out for relief from the king you
8: 18 you have chosen, and the LORD will not answer you in that **day**."
9: 9 because the prophet of **today** [+2021] used to be called a seer.)
9: 12 he has just come to our town **today** [+2021], for the people have a
9: 12 for the people have a sacrifice at the high place. **[RPH]**
9: 13 invited will eat. Go up now; you should find him about this **time**."
9: 15 Now the **day** before Saul came, the LORD had revealed this to
9: 19 for **today** [+2021] you are to eat with me, and in the morning I will
9: 20 As for the donkeys you lost three **days** ago, do not worry about
9: 20 As for the donkeys you lost three days **ago** [+2021], do not worry
9: 24 'I have invited guests.' " And Saul dined with Samuel that **day**.
9: 27 "but you stay here **awhile** [+2021+3869], so that I may give you a
10: 2 When you leave me **today** [+2021], you will meet two men near
10: 8 you must wait seven **days** until I come to you and tell you what
10: 9 changed Saul's heart, and all these signs were fulfilled that **day**.
10: 19 you have **now** [+2021] rejected your God, who saves you out of all
11: 3 "Give us seven **days** so we can send messengers throughout Israel;
11: 11 of the Ammonites and slaughtered them until the heat of the **day**.
11: 13 "No one shall be put to death **today** [+2021+2021+2296], for this

1Sa 11:13 be put to death today, for this **day** the LORD has rescued Israel."
12: 2 with you. I have been your leader from my youth until this **day**.
12: 5 is witness against you, and also his anointed is witness this **day**,
12:17 Is it not wheat harvest **now** [+2021]? I will call upon the LORD
12:18 the LORD, and that same **day** the LORD sent thunder and rain.
13: 8 He waited seven **days**, the time set by Samuel; but Samuel did not
13:11 were scattering, and that you did not come at the **set time** [+4595],
13:22 So on the **day** *of* the battle not a soldier with Saul and Jonathan
14: 1 One **day** Jonathan son of Saul said to the young man bearing his
14:18 "Bring the ark of God." (At that **time** it was with the Israelites.)
14:23 So the LORD rescued Israel that **day**, and the battle moved on
14:24 Now the men of Israel were in distress that **day**, because Saul had
14:28 saying, 'Cursed be any man who eats food **today** [+2021]!'
14:30 **today** [+2021] some of the plunder they took from their enemies.
14:31 That **day**, after the Israelites had struck down the Philistines from
14:33 he said. "Roll a large stone over here **at once** [+2021]."
14:37 them into Israel's hand?" But God did not answer him that **day**.
14:38 and let us find out what sin has been committed **today** [+2021].
14:45 for he did this **today** [+2021+2021+2296] with God's help."
14:52 All the **days** *of* Saul there was bitter war with the Philistines,
15:28 LORD has torn the kingdom of Israel from you **today** [+2021]
15:35 Until the **day** Samuel died, he did not go to see Saul again,
16:13 from that **day** on the Spirit of the LORD came upon David in
17:10 Then the Philistine said, "This **day** I defy the ranks of Israel!
17:12 and in Saul's **time** he was old and well advanced in years.
17:16 *For* forty **days** the Philistine came forward every morning
17:46 This **day** the LORD will hand you over to me, and I'll strike you
17:46 **Today** [+2021+2021+2296] I will give the carcasses of the
18: 2 From that **day** Saul kept David with him and did not let him return
18: 9 And from that **time** on Saul kept a jealous eye on David.
18:10 David was playing the harp, **as** he **usually did** [+928+3427+3869].
18:10 David was playing the harp, **as he usually did** [+928+3427+3869].
18:21 So Saul said to David, "**Now** [+2021] you have a second
18:26 become the king's son-in-law. So before the **allotted time** elapsed,
18:29 afraid of him, and he remained his enemy the rest of his **days**.
19:24 He lay that way all that **day** and night. This is why people say,
20: 6 because an **annual** sacrifice is being made there for his whole
20:19 go to the place where you hid **when** this trouble **began** [+928],
20:26 Saul said nothing that **day**, for he thought, "Something must have
20:27 son of Jesse come to the meal, either yesterday or **today** [+2021]?"
20:31 **As long as** [+2021+3972] the son of Jesse lives on this earth,
20:34 on that second **day** *of* the month he did not eat, because he was
21: 5 [21:6] that are not holy. How much more so **today** [+2021]!"
21: 6 [21:7] and replaced by hot bread on the **day** it was taken away.
21: 7 [21:8] Now one of Saul's servants was there that **day**,
21:10 [21:11] That **day** David fled from Saul and went to Achish king
22: 4 they stayed with him **as long as** [+3972] David was in the
22: 8 lie in wait for me, as he does **today** [+2021+2021+2296]."
22:13 and lies in wait for me, as he does **today** [+2021+2021+2296]?"
22:15 Was that **day** the first time I inquired of God for him? Of course
22:18 That **day** he killed eighty-five men who wore the linen ephod.
22:22 "That **day**, when Doeg the Edomite was there, I knew he would be
23:14 in the hills of the Desert of Ziph. **Day** [+2021+3972] **after day**
24: 4 [24:5] "This is the **day** the LORD spoke of when he said to you,
24:10 [24:11] This **day** you have seen with your own eyes how the
24:10 [24:11] Some urged me to kill you, **[RPH]** but I spared you; I
24:18 [24:19] You have **just now** [+2021] told me of the good you did
24:19 [24:20] the way you treated me **today** [+2021+2021+2296].
25: 7 the whole **time** they were at Carmel nothing of theirs was missing.
25: 8 favorable toward my young men, since we come at a festive **time**.
25:10 Many servants are breaking away from their masters these **days**.
25:15 the whole **time** we were out in the fields near them nothing was
25:16 day they were a wall around us all the **time** we were herding our
25:28 Let no wrongdoing be found in you as long as you **live**.
25:32 who has sent you **today** [+2021+2021+2296] to meet me.
25:33 your good judgment and for keeping me from bloodshed this **day**
25:38 About ten **days** later, the LORD struck Nabal and he died.
26: 8 Abishai said to David, "**Today** [+2021] God has delivered your
26:10 either his **time** will come and he will die, or he will go into battle
26:19 They have **now** [+2021] driven me from my share in the LORD's
26:21 you considered my life precious **today** [+2021+2021+2296],
26:23 The LORD delivered you into my hands **today** [+2021],
26:24 As surely as I valued your life **today** [+2021+2021+2296], so may
27: 1 "One of these **days** I will be destroyed by the hand of Saul.
27: 6 So on that **day** Achish gave him Ziklag, and it has belonged to the
27: 6 to the kings of Judah **ever since** [+2021+2021+2296+6330].
27: 7 **[RPH]** David lived in Philistine territory a year and four months.
27: 7 David lived in Philistine territory a **year** and four months.
27:10 When Achish asked, "Where did you go raiding **today** [+2021]?"
27:11 practice **as long as** [+2021+3972] he lived in Philistine territory.
28: 1 In those **days** the Philistines gathered their forces to fight against
28: 2 I will make you my bodyguard **for life** [+2021+3972]."
28:18 the LORD has done this to you **today** [+2021+2021+2296].
28:20 strength was gone, for he had eaten nothing all that **day** and night.
29: 3 already been with me for **over a year** [+196+2296+2296+9102],
29: 3 from the **day** he left Saul until now, I have found no fault in him."
29: 3 and from the day he left Saul until **now** [+2021+2021+2296],
29: 6 From the **day** you came to me until now, I have found no fault in
29: 6 From the day you came to me until **now** [+2021+2021+2296],
29: 8 "What have you found against your servant from the **day** I came to
29: 8 from the day I came to you until **now** [+2021+2021+2296]?
30: 1 David and his men reached Ziklag on the third **day**.
30:12 eaten any food or drunk any water *for* three **days** and three nights.
30:13 My master abandoned me when I became ill three **days** ago.
30:25 made this a statute and ordinance for Israel from that **day** to this.
30:25 made this a statute and ordinance for Israel from that day to **this**[s].
31: 6 and his armor-bearer and all his men died together that same **day**.
31:13 them under a tamarisk tree at Jabesh, and they fasted seven **days**.
2Sa 1: 1 from defeating the Amalekites and stayed in Ziklag two **days**.
1: 2 On the third **day** a man arrived from Saul's camp, with his clothes
2:11 The length of **time** David was king in Hebron over the house of
2:17 The battle that **day** was very fierce, and Abner and the men of
3: 8 This very **day** I am loyal to the house of your father Saul and to his
3: 8 Yet **now** [+2021] you accuse me of an offense involving this
3:35 all came and urged David to eat something while it was still **day**;
3:37 So on that **day** all the people and all Israel knew that the king had
3:38 realize that a prince and a great man has fallen in Israel this **day**?
3:39 And **today** [+2021], though I am the anointed king, I am weak,
4: 3 Beeroth fled to Gittaim and have lived there as aliens to this **day**.
4: 5 they arrived there in the heat of the **day** while he was taking his
4: 8 This **day** the LORD has avenged my lord the king against Saul
5: 8 On that **day**, David said, "Anyone who conquers the Jebusites will
6: 8 out against Uzzah, and to this **day** that place is called Perez Uzzah.
6: 9 David was afraid of the LORD that **day** and said, "How can the
6:20 "How the king of Israel has distinguished himself **today** [+2021],
6:20 disrobing **[RPH]** in the sight of the slave girls of his servants as
6:23 Michal daughter of Saul had no children to the **day** *of* her death.
7: 6 I have not dwelt in a house from the **day** I brought the Israelites up
7: 6 from the day I brought the Israelites up out of Egypt to this **day**.
7:11 have done ever since the **time** I appointed leaders over my people
7:12 When your **days** are over and you rest with your fathers, I will
11:12 David said to him, "Stay here one more **day**, and tomorrow I will
11:12 you back." So Uriah remained in Jerusalem that **day** and the next.
12:18 On the seventh **day** the child died. David's servants were afraid to
13:23 *Two* **years** [+9102] later, when Absalom's sheepshearers were at
13:32 This has been Absalom's expressed intention ever since the **day**
13:37 king of Geshur. But King David mourned for his son every **day**.
14: 2 Act like a woman who has spent many **days** grieving for the dead.
14:22 Joab said, "**Today** [+2021] your servant knows that he has found
14:26 he used to cut his hair from **time** to time when it became too heavy
14:26 he used to cut his hair from time to **time** when it became too heavy
14:28 Absalom lived *two* **years** [+9102] in Jerusalem without seeing the
15:20 And **today** [+2021] shall I make you wander about with us,
16: 3 because he thinks, '**Today** [+2021] the house of Israel will give
16:12 good for the cursing I am receiving **today** [+2021+2021+2296]."
16:23 Now in those **days** the advice Ahithophel gave was like that of one
18: 7 defeated by David's men, and the casualties that **day** were great—
18: 8 and the forest claimed more lives that **day** than the sword.
18:18 after himself, and it is called Absalom's Monument to this **day**.
18:20 "You are not the one to take the news **today** [+2021+2021+2296],"
18:20 "You may take the news another **time**, but you must not do
18:20 but you must not do so **today** [+2021+2021+2296], because the
18:31 The LORD has delivered you **today** [+2021] from all who rose up
19: 2 [19:3] for the whole army the victory that **day** was turned into
19: 2 [19:3] because on that **day** the troops heard it said, "The king is
19: 3 [19:4] The men stole into the city that **day** as men steal in who are
19: 5 [19:6] said, "**Today** [+2021] you have humiliated all your men,
19: 5 [19:6] who have **just** [+2021] saved your life and the lives of your
19: 6 [19:7] You have made it clear **today** [+2021] that the
19: 6 [19:7] would be pleased if Absalom were alive **today** [+2021]
19: 6 [19:7] were alive today and all of us were dead. **[RPH]**
19:13 [19:14] if **from now on** [+2021+3972] you are not the
19:19 [19:20] Do not remember how your servant did wrong on the **day**
19:20 [19:21] **today** [+2021] I have come here as the first of the whole
19:22 [19:23] of Zeruiah? This **day** you have become my adversaries!
19:22 [19:23] Should anyone be put to death in Israel **today** [+2021]?
19:22 [19:23] Do I not know that **today** [+2021] I am king over Israel?"
19:24 [19:25] or washed his clothes from the **day** the king left until the
19:24 [19:25] from the day the king left until the **day** he returned safely.
19:34 [19:35] the king, "How many more **[NIE]** years will I live,
19:35 [19:36] I am **now** [+2021] eighty years old. Can I tell the
20: 3 They were kept in confinement till the **day** *of* their death, living as
20: 4 "Summon the men of Judah to come to me *within* three **days**,
21: 1 During the **reign** *of* David, there was a famine for three successive
21: 9 they were put to death during the first **days** *of* the harvest,
21:12 where the Philistines had hung them **after** [+928] they struck Saul
22: 1 David sang to the LORD the words of this song **when** [+928] the
22:19 They confronted me in the **day** *of* my disaster, but the LORD was

2Sa 23:10 to the sword. The LORD brought about a great victory that **day**.
23:20 He also went down into a pit on a snowy **day** and killed a lion.
24:8 came back to Jerusalem at the end of nine months and twenty **days**.
24:13 Or three **days** of plague in your land? Now then, think it over
24:18 On that **day** Gad went to David and said to him, "Go up and build
1Ki 1:1 When King David was old and well advanced in **years**, he could
1:6 (His father had **never** [+4202+4946] interfered with him by asking,
1:25 **Today** [+2021] he has gone down and sacrificed great numbers of
1:30 I will surely carry out **today** [+2021+2021+2296] what I swore to
1:48 my eyes to see a successor on my throne **today** [+2021].' "
1:51 'Let King Solomon swear to me **today** [+2021] that he will not put
2:1 When the **time** drew near *for* David to die, he gave a charge to
2:8 who called down bitter curses on me the **day** I went to Mahanaim.
2:11 **[NIE]** He had reigned forty years over Israel—seven years in
2:24 as he promised—Adonijah shall be put to death **today** [+2021]!"
2:26 but I will not put you to death **now** [+2021+2021+2296], because
2:37 The **day** you leave and cross the Kidron Valley, you can be sure
2:38 king has said." And Shimei stayed in Jerusalem *for* a long **time**.
2:42 and warn you, 'On the **day** you leave to go anywhere else,
3:2 because a temple had not **yet** [+2021+2021+2156+6330] been built
3:6 and have given him a son to sit on his throne this very **day**.
3:11 you have asked for this and not for long **life** or wealth for yourself,
3:13 so that **in** your **lifetime** [+3972] you will have no equal among
3:14 commands as David your father did, I will give you a long **life**."
3:18 The third **day** after my child was born, this woman also had a
4:21 [5:1] and were Solomon's subjects all **[NIE]** his life.
4:22 [5:2] Solomon's **daily** [+285+4200] provisions were thirty cors of
4:25 [5:5] During Solomon's **lifetime** Judah and Israel, from Dan to
5:1 [5:15] because he had **always** [+2021+3972] been on friendly
5:7 [5:21] and said, "Praise be to the LORD **today** [+2021],
8:8 the Holy Place; and they are still there **today** [+2021+2021+2296].
8:16 'Since the **day** I brought my people Israel out of Egypt, I have not
8:24 your hand you have fulfilled it—as it is **today** [+2021+2021+2296].
8:28 the prayer that your servant is praying in your presence this **day**.
8:29 May your eyes be open toward this temple night and **day**,
8:40 so that they will fear you all the **time** they live in the land you gave
8:59 the cause of his people Israel according to **each day's** [+3427]
8:59 the cause of his people Israel according to **each day's** [+3427]
8:61 to live by his decrees and obey his commands, as at this **time**."
8:64 On that same **day** the king consecrated the middle part of the
8:65 They celebrated it before the LORD our God for seven **days**
8:65 it before the LORD our God for seven days and seven **days** more,
8:65 our God for seven days and seven days more, fourteen **days** in all.
8:66 On the following **day** he sent the people away. They blessed the
9:3 My eyes and my heart will **always** [+2021+3972] be there.
9:13 he called them the Land of Cabul, a name they have to this **day**.
9:21 Solomon conscripted for his slave labor force, as it is to this **day**.
10:12 much almugwood has never been imported or seen since that **day**.)
10:21 because silver was considered of little value in Solomon's **days**.
11:12 the sake of David your father, I will not do it during your **lifetime**.
11:25 Rezon was Israel's adversary **as long as** Solomon **lived** [+3972],
11:34 I have made him ruler all the **days** *of* his life for the sake of David
11:36 so that David my servant may **always** [+2021+3972] have a lamp
11:39 descendants because of this, but not **forever** [+2021+3972].' "
11:42 **[NIE]** Solomon reigned in Jerusalem over all Israel forty years.
12:5 "Go away for three **days** and then come back to me."
12:7 "If **today** [+2021] you will be a servant to these people and serve
12:7 they will **always** [+2021+3972] be your servants."
12:12 Three **days** later Jeroboam and all the people returned to
12:12 as the king had said, "Come back to me in three **days**."
12:19 Israel has been in rebellion against the house of David to this **day**.
12:32 He instituted a festival on the fifteenth **day** of the eighth month,
12:33 On the fifteenth **day** of the eighth month, a month of his own
13:3 That same **day** the man of God gave a sign: "This is the sign the
13:11 and told him all that the man of God had done there that **day**.
14:14 off the family of Jeroboam. This is the **day**! What? Yes, even now.
14:19 are written in the book of the **annals** [+1821] of the kings of Israel.
14:20 **[NIE]** He reigned for twenty-two years and then rested with his
14:29 are they not written in the book of the **annals** [+1821] of the kings
14:30 There was **continual** [+2021+3972] warfare between Rehoboam
15:5 to keep any of the LORD's commands all the **days** *of* his life—
15:6 and Jeroboam throughout ⌞Abijah's⌟ **lifetime** [+2644].
15:7 are they not written in the book of the **annals** [+1821] of the kings
15:14 Asa's heart was fully committed to the LORD all his **life**.
15:16 between Asa and Baasha king of Israel throughout their **reigns**.
15:23 are they not written in the book of the **annals** [+1821] of the kings
15:31 are they not written in the book of the **annals** [+1821] of the kings
15:32 between Asa and Baasha king of Israel throughout their **reigns**.
16:5 are they not written in the book of the **annals** [+1821] of the kings
16:14 are they not written in the book of the **annals** [+1821] of the kings
16:15 year of Asa king of Judah, Zimri reigned in Tirzah seven **days**.
16:16 of the army, king over Israel that very **day** there in the camp.
16:20 are they not written in the book of the **annals** [+1821] of the kings
16:27 are they not written in the book of the **annals** [+1821] of the kings
16:34 In Ahab's **time**, Hiel of Bethel rebuilt Jericho. He laid its
17:7 **Some time** later the brook dried up because there had been no rain
17:14 the jug of oil will not run dry until the **day** the LORD gives rain
17:15 So there was food **every day** for Elijah and for the woman
18:1 After a long **time**, in the third year, the word of the LORD came
18:15 I serve, I will surely present myself to Ahab **today** [+2021]."
18:36 let it be known **today** [+2021] that you are God in Israel and that I
19:4 while he himself went a **day's** journey into the desert. He came to
19:8 he traveled forty **days** and forty nights until he reached Horeb,
20:13 I will give it into your hand **today** [+2021], and then you will
20:29 *For* seven **days** they camped opposite each other, and on the
20:29 opposite each other, and on the seventh **day** the battle was joined.
20:29 thousand casualties on the Aramean foot soldiers in one **day**.
21:29 he has humbled himself, I will not bring this disaster in his **day**,
21:29 in his day, but I will bring it on his house in the **days** *of* his son."
22:5 Jehoshaphat also said to the king of Israel, "**First** [+2021+3869]
22:25 "You will find out on the **day** you go to hide in an inner room."
22:35 **All day** [+928+2021+2021+2085] **long** the battle raged,
22:39 are they not written in the book of the **annals** [+1821] of the kings
22:45 [22:46] are they not written in the book of the **annals** [+1821] of
22:46 [22:47] who remained there even after the **reign** *of* his father Asa.
2Ki 1:18 are they not written in the book of the **annals** [+1821] of the kings
2:3 the LORD is going to take your master from you **today** [+2021]?"
2:5 the LORD is going to take your master from you **today** [+2021]?"
2:17 sent fifty men, who searched *for* three **days** but did not find him.
2:22 the water has remained wholesome to this **day**, according to the
3:6 So at that **time** King Joram set out from Samaria and mobilized all
3:9 After a roundabout march of seven **days**, the army had no more
4:8 One **day** Elisha went to Shunem. And a well-to-do woman was
4:11 One **day** when Elisha came, he went up to his room and lay down
4:18 The child grew, and one **day** he went out to his father, who was
4:23 "Why go to him **today** [+2021]?" he asked. "It's not the New
6:28 said to me, 'Give up your son so we may eat him **today** [+2021],
6:29 The next **day** I said to her, 'Give up your son so we may eat him,'
6:31 of Elisha son of Shaphat remains on his shoulders **today** [+2021]!"
7:9 This is a **day** *of* good news and we are keeping it to ourselves.
7:9 This is a day of **[RPR]** good news and we are keeping it to
8:6 including all the income from her land from the **day** she left the
8:19 a lamp for David and his descendants **forever** [+2021+3972].
8:20 In the **time** *of* Jehoram, Edom rebelled against Judah and set up its
8:22 To this **day** Edom has been in rebellion against Judah. Libnah
8:23 are they not written in the book of the **annals** [+1821] of the kings
10:27 the temple of Baal, and people have used it for a latrine to this **day**.
10:32 In those **days** the LORD began to reduce the size of Israel.
10:34 are they not written in the book of the **annals** [+1821] of the kings
10:36 The **time** that Jehu reigned over Israel in Samaria was twenty-eight
12:2 [12:3] the LORD all the **years** Jehoiada the priest instructed him.
12:19 [12:20] are they not written in the book of the **annals** [+1821] of
13:3 *for* a long **time** he kept them under the power of Hazael king of
13:8 are they not written in the book of the **annals** [+1821] of the kings
13:12 are they not written in the book of the **annals** [+1821] of the kings
13:22 Hazael king of Aram oppressed Israel throughout the **reign** *of*
14:7 Sela in battle, calling it Joktheel, the name it has to this **day**.
14:15 are they not written in the book of the **annals** [+1821] of the kings
14:18 are they not written in the book of the **annals** [+1821] of the kings
14:28 are they not written in the book of the **annals** [+1821] of the kings
15:5 The LORD afflicted the king with leprosy until the **day** he died,
15:6 are they not written in the book of the **annals** [+1821] of the kings
15:11 are written in the book of the **annals** [+1821] of the kings of Israel.
15:13 king of Judah, and he reigned in Samaria **one month** [+3732].
15:15 are written in the book of the **annals** [+1821] of the kings of Israel.
15:18 *During* his entire **reign** he did not turn away from the sins of
15:21 are they not written in the book of the **annals** [+1821] of the kings
15:26 are written in the book of the **annals** [+1821] of the kings of Israel.
15:29 In the **time** *of* Pekah king of Israel, Tiglath-Pileser king of Assyria
15:31 are they not written in the book of the **annals** [+1821] of the kings
15:36 are they not written in the book of the **annals** [+1821] of the kings
15:37 (In those **days** the LORD began to send Rezin king of Aram
16:6 Edomites then moved into Elath and have lived there to this **day**.
16:19 are they not written in the book of the **annals** [+1821] of the kings
17:23 in Assyria, and they are **still** [+2021+2021+2296+6330] there.
17:34 To this **day** they persist in their former practices. They neither
17:37 You must **always** [+2021+3972] be careful to keep the decrees
17:41 To this **day** their children and grandchildren continue to do as their
18:4 for up to that **time** the Israelites had been burning incense to it.
19:3 This **day** is a day of distress and rebuke and disgrace, as when
19:3 This day is a **day** *of* distress and rebuke and disgrace, as when
19:25 In **days** of old I planned it; now I have brought it to pass, that you
20:1 In those **days** Hezekiah became ill and was at the point of death.
20:5 On the third **day** from now you will go up to the temple of the
20:6 I will add fifteen years to your **life**. And I will deliver you
20:8 that I will go up to the temple of the LORD on the third **day** from
20:17 The **time** will surely come when everything in your palace,
20:17 all that your fathers have stored up until this **day**, will be carried

2Ki 20:19 he thought, "Will there not be peace and security in my **lifetime**?"
20:20 are they not written in the book of the **annals** [+1821] of the kings
21:15 have provoked me to anger from the **day** their forefathers came out
21:15 from the day their forefathers came out of Egypt until this **day**."
21:17 are they not written in the book of the **annals** [+1821] of the kings
21:25 are they not written in the book of the **annals** [+1821] of the kings
23:22 Not since the **days** *of* the judges who led Israel, nor throughout the
23:22 nor throughout the **days** *of* the kings of Israel and the kings of
23:28 are they not written in the book of the **annals** [+1821] of the kings
23:29 **While** [+928] Josiah was king, Pharaoh Neco king of Egypt went
24: 1 During Jehoiakim's **reign**, Nebuchadnezzar king of Babylon
24: 5 are they not written in the book of the **annals** [+1821] of the kings
25:29 and *for* the **rest of** [+3972] his life ate regularly at the king's table.
25:30 **Day** [+928+1821+2257+3427] **by day** the king gave Jehoiachin a
25:30 **Day by day** [+928+1821+2257+3427] the king gave Jehoiachin a
25:30 gave Jehoiachin a regular allowance **as long as** [+3972] he lived.
1Ch 1:19 One was named Peleg, because in his **time** the earth was divided;
4:41 The men whose names were listed came in the **days** *of* Hezekiah
4:41 and completely destroyed them, as is evident to this **day**.
4:43 Amalekites who had escaped, and they have lived there to this **day**.
5:10 During Saul's **reign** they waged war against the Hagrites,
5:17 the genealogical records during the **reigns** *of* Jotham king of Judah
5:17 of Jotham king of Judah and **[RPH]** Jeroboam king of Israel.
5:26 Habor, Hara and the river of Gozan, where they are to this **day**.
7: 2 During the **reign** *of* David, the descendants of Tola listed as
7:22 Their father Ephraim mourned for them many **days**, and his
9:25 and share their duties for **seven-day periods** [+2021+8679].
10:12 bones under the great tree in Jabesh, and they fasted seven **days**.
11:22 He also went down into a pit on a snowy **day** and killed a lion.
12:22 [12:23] **Day** after day men came to help David, until he had a
12:22 [12:23] Day after **day** men came to help David, until he had a
12:39 [12:40] The men spent three **days** there with David, eating
13: 3 back to us, for we did not inquire of it during the **reign** *of* Saul."
13:11 out against Uzzah, and to this **day** that place is called Perez Uzzah.
13:12 David was afraid of God that **day** and asked, "How can I ever
16: 7 That **day** David first committed to Asaph and his associates this
16:23 to the LORD, all the earth; proclaim his salvation **day** after day.
16:23 to the LORD, all the earth; proclaim his salvation day after **day**.
16:37 according to **each day's** [+928+2257+3427] requirements.
16:37 according to **each day's** [+928+2257+3427] requirements.
17: 5 I have not dwelt in a house from the **day** I brought Israel up out of
17: 5 a house from the day I brought Israel up out of Egypt to this **day**.
17:10 have done ever since the **time** I appointed leaders over my people
17:11 When your **days** are over and you go to be with your fathers,
21:12 swords overtaking you, or three **days** of the sword of the LORD—
22: 9 and I will grant Israel peace and quiet during his **reign**.
23: 1 When David was old and full of **years**, he made his son Solomon
26:17 There were six Levites a **day** on the east, four a day on the north,
26:17 four a **day** on the south and two at a time at the storehouse.
27:24 the number was not entered in the book of the **annals** [+1821] of
28: 7 carrying out my commands and laws, as is being done at this **time**.'
29: 5 who is willing to consecrate himself **today** [+2021] to the
29:15 our forefathers. Our **days** on earth are like a shadow, without hope.
29:21 The next **day** they made sacrifices to the LORD and presented
29:22 and drank with great joy in the presence of the LORD that **day**.
29:27 **[NIE]** He ruled over Israel forty years—seven in Hebron
29:28 good old age, having **enjoyed long life** [+8428], wealth and honor.
2Ch 1:11 and since you have not asked for a long **life** but for wisdom
5: 9 the Holy Place; and they are still there **today** [+2021+2021+2296].
6: 5 'Since the **day** I brought my people out of Egypt, I have not chosen
6:15 your hand you have fulfilled it—as it is **today** [+2021+2021+2296].
6:31 walk in your ways all the **time** they live in the land you gave our
7: 8 So Solomon observed the festival at that time *for* seven **days**,
7: 9 On the eighth **day** they held an assembly, for they had celebrated
7: 9 for they had celebrated the dedication of the altar *for* seven **days**
7: 9 of the altar for seven days and the festival *for* seven **days** more.
7:10 On the twenty-third **day** of the seventh month he sent the people to
7:16 My eyes and my heart will **always** [+2021+3972] be there.
8: 8 Solomon conscripted for his slave labor force, as it is to this **day**.
8:13 according to the **daily** [+928+3427] requirement for offerings
8:13 according to the **daily** [+928+3427] requirement for offerings
8:14 to assist the priests according to **each day's** [+928+3427]
8:14 to assist the priests according to **each day's** [+928+3427]
8:16 from the **day** the foundation of the temple of the LORD was laid
9:20 because silver was considered of little value in Solomon's **day**.
10: 5 Rehoboam answered, "Come back to me in three **days**."
10: 7 they will **always** [+2021+3972] be your servants."
10:12 Three **days** later Jeroboam and all the people returned to
10:12 as the king had said, "Come back to me in three **days**."
10:19 Israel has been in rebellion against the house of David to this **day**.
12:15 There was **continual** [+2021+3972] warfare between Rehoboam
13:20 Jeroboam did not regain power during the **time** *of* Abijah.
14: 1 [13:23] and in his **days** the country was at peace for ten years.
15: 3 *For* a long **time** Israel was without the true God, without a priest to
15:11 At that **time** they sacrificed to the LORD seven hundred head of
15:17 Asa's heart was fully committed ⌞to the LORD⌟ all his **life**.
18: 4 Jehoshaphat also said to the king of Israel, "**First** [+2021+3869]
18: 7 never prophesies anything good about me, but **always** [+3972] bad.
18:24 "You will find out on the **day** you go to hide in an inner room."
18:34 **All day** [+928+2021+2021+2085] **long** the battle raged,
20:25 There was so much plunder that it took three **days** to collect it.
20:26 On the fourth **day** they assembled in the Valley of Beracah,
20:26 This is why it is called the Valley of Beracah to this **day**.
21: 7 a lamp for him and his descendants **forever** [+2021+3972].
21: 8 In the **time** *of* Jehoram, Edom rebelled against Judah and set up its
21:10 To this **day** Edom has been in rebellion against Judah. Libnah
21:15 You yourself will be very ill with a **lingering** [+3427+6584]
21:15 You yourself will be very ill with a **lingering** [+3427+6584]
21:19 **In the course** [+3427+4200+4946] **of time**, at the end of the
21:19 **In the course of time** [+3427+4200+4946], at the end of the
21:19 at the end of the second **year**, his bowels came out because of the
24: 2 Joash did what was right in the eyes of the LORD all the **years** *of*
24:11 They did this **regularly** [+928+3427+4200] and collected a great
24:11 They did this **regularly** [+928+3427+4200] and collected a great
24:14 **As long as** Jehoiada **lived** [+3972], burnt offerings were presented
24:15 Now Jehoiada was old and full of **years**, and he died at the age of a
26: 5 He sought God during the **days** *of* Zechariah, who instructed him
26: 5 who instructed him in the fear of God. **As long** [+928] **as** he sought
26:21 King Uzziah had leprosy until the **day** he died. He lived in a
28: 6 In one **day** Pekah son of Remaliah killed a hundred and twenty
29:17 by the eighth **day** of the month they reached the portico of the
29:17 For eight more **days** they consecrated the temple of the LORD
29:17 the LORD itself, finishing on the sixteenth **day** of the first month.
30:21 the Feast of Unleavened Bread *for* seven **days** with great rejoicing,
30:21 and priests sang to the LORD **every day** [+928+3427],
30:21 and priests sang to the LORD **every day** [+928+3427],
30:22 *For* the seven **days** they ate their assigned portion and offered
30:23 then agreed to celebrate the festival seven more **days**;
30:23 more days; so *for* another seven **days** they celebrated joyfully.
30:26 for since the **days** *of* Solomon son of David king of Israel there had
31:16 to perform the **daily** [+928+2257+3427] duties of their various
31:16 to perform the **daily** [+928+2257+3427] duties of their various
32:24 In those **days** Hezekiah became ill and was at the point of death.
32:26 wrath did not come upon them during the **days** *of* Hezekiah.
34:33 **As long as** he **lived** [+3972], they did not fail to follow the
35:16 So at that **time** the entire service of the LORD was carried out for
35:17 and observed the Feast of Unleavened Bread *for* seven **days**.
35:18 observed like this in Israel since the **days** *of* the prophet Samuel;
35:21 It is not you I am attacking **at this time** [+2021], but the house
35:25 to this **day** all the men and women singers commemorate Josiah in
36: 9 and he reigned in Jerusalem three months and ten **days**.
36:21 all the **time** *of* its desolation it rested, until the seventy years were
Ezr 3: 4 number of burnt offerings prescribed for **each day** [+928+3427].
3: 4 number of burnt offerings prescribed for **each day** [+928+3427].
3: 4 number of burnt offerings prescribed for each day. **[RPH]**
3: 4 number of burnt offerings prescribed for each day. **[RPH]**
3: 6 On the first **day** of the seventh month they began to offer burnt
4: 2 have been sacrificing to him since the **time** *of* Esarhaddon king of
4: 5 frustrate their plans during the entire **reign** *of* Cyrus king of Persia
4: 7 And in the **days** *of* Artaxerxes king of Persia, Bishlam, Mithredath,
6:22 *For* seven **days** they celebrated with joy the Feast of Unleavened
8:15 canal that flows toward Ahava, and we camped there three **days**.
8:32 So we arrived in Jerusalem, where we rested three **days**.
8:33 On the fourth **day**, in the house of our God, we weighed out the
9: 7 From the **days** *of* our forefathers until now, our guilt has been
9: 7 From the days of our forefathers until **now** [+2021+2021+2296],
9: 7 at the hand of foreign kings, as it is **today** [+2021+2021+2296].
9:15 God of Israel, you are righteous! We are left this **day** as a remnant.
10: 8 Anyone who failed to appear within three **days** would forfeit all his
10: 9 Within the three **days**, all the men of Judah and Benjamin had
10:13 Besides, this matter cannot be taken care of in a **day** or two,
10:16 On the first **day** of the tenth month they sat down to investigate the
10:17 by the first **day** of the first month they finished dealing with all the
Ne 1: 4 *For some* **days** I mourned and fasted and prayed before the God of
1: 6 to hear the prayer your servant is praying before you **[RPH]** day
1:11 Give your servant success **today** [+2021] by granting him favor in
2:11 I went to Jerusalem, and after staying there three **days**
4: 2 [3:34] Will they offer sacrifices? Will they finish in a **day**?
4:16 [4:10] From that **day** on, half of my men did the work,
4:22 [4:16] can serve us as guards by night and workmen *by* **day**."
5:11 Give back to them **immediately** [+2021+3869] their fields,
5:14 **when** [+4946] I was appointed to be their governor in the land of
5:18 Each **day** one ox, six choice sheep and some poultry were prepared
5:18 and every ten **days** an abundant supply of wine of all kinds.
6:15 wall was completed on the twenty-fifth of Elul, in fifty-two **days**.
6:17 in those **days** the nobles of Judah were sending many letters to
8: 2 So on the first **day** of the seventh month Ezra the priest brought the
8: 3 He read it aloud from daybreak till **noon** [+2021+4734] as he faced

Ne 8: 9 said to them all, "This **day** is sacred to the LORD your God.
8: 10 This **day** is sacred to our Lord. Do not grieve, for the joy of the
8: 11 calmed all the people, saying, "Be still, for this is a sacred **day**.
8: 13 On the second **day** of the month, the heads of all the families,
8: 17 From the **days** *of* Joshua son of Nun until that day, the Israelites
8: 17 From the days of Joshua son of Nun until that **day**, the Israelites
8: 18 **Day** after day, from the first day to the last, Ezra read from the
8: 18 Day after **day**, from the first day to the last, Ezra read from the
8: 18 Day after day, from the first **day** to the last, Ezra read from the
8: 18 Day after day, from the first day to the **[RPH]** last, Ezra read from
8: 18 They celebrated the feast *for* seven **days**, and on the eighth day,
8: 18 on the eighth **day**, in accordance with the regulation, there was an
9: 1 On the twenty-fourth **day** of the same month, the Israelites
9: 3 Book of the Law of the LORD their God *for* a quarter of the **day**,
9: 10 You made a name for yourself, which remains to this **day**.
9: 32 all your people, from the **days** *of* the kings of Assyria until today.
9: 32 the days of the kings of Assyria until **today** [+2021+2021+2296].
9: 36 "But see, we are slaves **today** [+2021], slaves in the land you gave
10: 31 [10:32] bring merchandise or grain to sell on **[RPH]** the Sabbath,
10: 31 [10:32] not buy from them on the Sabbath or on any holy **day**.
11: 23 king's orders, which regulated their **daily** [+928+3427] activity.
11: 23 king's orders, which regulated their **daily** [+928+3427] activity.
12: 7 the leaders of the priests and their associates in the **days** *of* Jeshua.
12: 12 In the **days** *of* Joiakim, these were the heads of the priestly
12: 22 The family heads of the Levites in the **days** *of* Eliashib, Joiada,
12: 23 The family heads among the descendants of Levi up to the **time** *of*
12: 23 son of Eliashib were recorded in the book of the **annals** [+1821].
12: 26 They served in the **days** *of* Joiakim son of Jeshua, the son of
12: 26 and in the **days** *of* Nehemiah the governor and of Ezra the priest
12: 43 on that **day** they offered great sacrifices, rejoicing because God
12: 44 At that **time** men were appointed to be in charge of the storerooms
12: 46 For long ago, in the **days** *of* David and Asaph, there had been
12: 47 So in the **days** *of* Zerubbabel and of Nehemiah, all Israel
12: 47 So in the days of Zerubbabel and **[RPH]** of Nehemiah, all Israel
12: 47 **daily** [+928+1821+3427] portions for the singers and gatekeepers.
12: 47 **daily** [+928+1821+3427] portions for the singers and gatekeepers.
13: 1 On that **day** the Book of Moses was read aloud in the hearing of
13: 6 I had returned to the king. **Some time** later I asked his permission
13: 15 In those **days** I saw men in Judah treading winepresses on the
13: 15 they were bringing all this into Jerusalem on the **[RPH]** Sabbath.
13: 15 Therefore I warned them against selling food on that **day**.
13: 17 is this wicked thing you are doing—desecrating the Sabbath **day**?
13: 19 at the gates so that no load could be brought in on the Sabbath **day**.
13: 22 and guard the gates in order to keep the Sabbath **day** holy.
13: 23 in those **days** I saw men of Judah who had married women from
Est 1: 1 This is what happened during the **time** *of* Xerxes, the Xerxes who
1: 2 At that **time** King Xerxes reigned from his royal throne in the
1: 4 *For* a full 180 **days** he displayed the vast wealth of his kingdom
1: 4 For a full 180 days **[RPH]** he displayed the vast wealth of his
1: 5 When these **days** were over, the king gave a banquet, lasting seven
1: 5 these days were over, the king gave a banquet, lasting seven **days**,
1: 10 On the seventh **day**, when King Xerxes was in high spirits from
1: 18 This very **day** the Persian and Median women of the nobility who
2: 11 **Every day** [+2256+3427+3972] he walked back and forth near the
2: 11 **Every day** [+2256+3427+3972] he walked back and forth near the
2: 12 she had to complete twelve months **[NIE]** of beauty treatments
2: 21 During the **time** Mordecai was sitting at the king's gate, Bigthana
2: 23 All this was recorded in the book of the **annals** [+1821] in the
3: 4 **Day** after day they spoke to him but he refused to comply.
3: 4 Day after **day** they spoke to him but he refused to comply.
3: 7 presence of Haman to **select a day** [+3427+4200+4946] and month.
3: 7 presence of Haman to **select a day** [+3427+4200+4946] and month.
3: 12 on the thirteenth **day** of the first month the royal secretaries were
3: 13 on a single **day**, the thirteenth day of the twelfth month, the month
3: 14 the people of every nationality so they would be ready for that **day**.
4: 11 But thirty **days** have passed since I was called to go to the king."
4: 16 Do not eat or drink *for* three **days**, night or day. I and my maids
4: 16 Do not eat or drink for three days, night or **day**. I and my maids
5: 1 On the third **day** Esther put on her royal robes and stood in the
5: 4 come **today** [+2021] to a banquet I have prepared for him."
5: 9 Haman went out that **day** happy and in high spirits. But when he
6: 1 the record of his **reign**, to be brought in and read to him.
7: 2 as they were drinking wine on that second **day**, the king again
8: 1 That same **day** King Xerxes gave Queen Esther the estate of
8: 12 The **day** appointed for the Jews to do this in all the provinces of
8: 13 so that the Jews would be ready on that **day** to avenge themselves
8: 17 gladness among the Jews, with feasting and **celebrating** [+3202].
9: 1 On the thirteenth **day** of the twelfth month, the month of Adar,
9: 1 On this **day** the enemies of the Jews had hoped to overpower them,
9: 11 slain in the citadel of Susa was reported to the king that same **day**.
9: 13 "give the Jews in Susa permission to carry out this **day's** edict
9: 15 The Jews in Susa came together on the fourteenth **day** of the
9: 17 This happened on the thirteenth **day** of the month of Adar,
9: 17 on the fourteenth they rested and made it a **day** *of* feasting and joy.
9: 18 on the fifteenth they rested and made it a **day** *of* feasting and joy.
9: 19 observe the fourteenth of the month of Adar as a **day** *of* joy
9: 19 a day of joy and feasting, a **day** for giving presents to each other.
9: 21 annually the fourteenth and fifteenth **days** of the month of Adar
9: 21 the fourteenth and fifteenth days **[RPH]** of the month of Adar
9: 22 as the **time** when the Jews got relief from their enemies, and as the
9: 22 was turned into joy and their mourning into a **day** *of* celebration.
9: 22 He wrote them to observe the days as **days** *of* feasting and joy
9: 26 (Therefore these **days** were called Purim, from the word *pur*.)
9: 27 all who join them should without fail observe these two **days** every
9: 28 These **days** should be remembered and observed in every
9: 28 these **days** *of* Purim should never cease to be celebrated by the
9: 31 to establish these **days** *of* Purim at their designated times,
10: 2 are they not written in the book of the **annals** [+1821] of the kings
Job 1: 4 His sons *used to* **take turns** [+2143] holding feasts in their homes,
1: 5 When a **period** *of* feasting had run its course, Job would send
1: 5 in their hearts." This was Job's **regular** [+2021+3972] custom.
1: 6 One **day** the angels came to present themselves before the LORD,
1: 13 One **day** when Job's sons and daughters were feasting
2: 1 On another **day** the angels came to present themselves before the
2: 13 they sat on the ground with him *for* seven **days** and seven nights.
3: 1 After this, Job opened his mouth and cursed the **day** *of* his birth.
3: 3 "May the **day** *of* my birth perish, and the night it was said,
3: 4 That **day**—may it turn to darkness; may God above not care about
3: 5 may a cloud settle over it; may blackness overwhelm its **light**.
3: 6 may it not be included among the **days** *of* the year nor be entered
3: 8 May those who curse **days** curse that day, those who are ready to
7: 1 hard service on earth? Are not his **days** like those of a hired man?
7: 1 hard service on earth? Are not his days like **those**[s] *of* a hired man?
7: 6 "My **days** are swifter than a weaver's shuttle, and they come to an
7: 16 I would not live forever. Let me alone; my **days** have no meaning.
8: 9 and know nothing, and our **days** on earth are but a shadow.
9: 25 "My **days** are swifter than a runner; they fly away without a
10: 5 Are your **days** like those of a mortal or your years like those of a
10: 5 Are your days like **those**[s] *of* a mortal or your years like those of a
10: 5 your days like those of a mortal or your years like **those**[s] *of* a man,
10: 20 Are not my few **days** almost over? Turn away from me so I can
12: 12 found among the aged? Does not long **life** bring understanding?
14: 1 "Man born of woman is of few **days** and full of trouble.
14: 5 Man's **days** are determined; you have decreed the number of his
14: 6 and let him alone, till he has put in his **time** like a hired man.
14: 14 All the **days** *of* my hard service I will wait for my renewal to
15: 10 the aged are on our side, *men even* **older** [+3888] than your father.
15: 20 All his **days** the wicked man suffers torment, the ruthless through
15: 23 food for vultures; he knows the **day** *of* darkness is at hand.
15: 32 Before his **time** he will be paid in full, and his branches will not
17: 1 My spirit is broken, my **days** are cut short, the grave awaits me.
17: 11 My **days** have passed, my plans are shattered, and so are the
17: 12 These men turn night into **day**; in the face of darkness they say,
18: 20 Men of the west are appalled at his **fate**; men of the east are seized
20: 28 will carry off his house, rushing waters on the **day** *of* God's wrath.
21: 13 They spend their **years** in prosperity and go down to the grave in
21: 30 that the evil man is spared from the **day** *of* calamity, that he is
21: 30 the day of calamity, that he is delivered from the **day** *of* wrath?
23: 2 "Even **today** [+2021] my complaint is bitter; his hand is heavy in
24: 1 Why must those who know him look in vain for such **days**?
27: 6 my conscience will not reproach me **as long as I live** [+4946].
29: 2 for the months gone by, for the **days** when God watched over me,
29: 4 Oh, for the **days** when I was in my prime, when God's intimate
29: 18 die in my own house, my **days** as numerous as the grains of sand.
30: 1 "But now they mock me, *men* **younger** [+4200+7582] than I,
30: 16 "And now my life ebbs away; **days** *of* suffering grip me.
30: 25 Have I not wept for *those* **in trouble** [+7997]? Has not my soul
30: 27 The churning inside me never stops; **days** *of* suffering confront me.
32: 4 speaking to Job because they were **older** [+2418+4200] than he.
32: 6 "I am young in **years**, and you are old; that is why I was fearful,
32: 7 I thought, '**Age** should speak; advanced years should teach
33: 25 is renewed like a child's; it is restored as in the **days** *of* his youth.
36: 11 they will spend the rest of their **days** in prosperity and their years
38: 12 "Have you **ever** [+4946] given orders to the morning, or shown the
38: 21 for you were already born! You have lived so many **years**!
38: 23 which I reserve for times of trouble, for **days** *of* war and battle?
42: 17 And so he died, old and full of **years**.
Ps 2: 7 "You are my Son; **today** [+2021] I have become your Father.
7: 11 [7:12] righteous judge, a God who expresses his wrath every **day**.
18: T [18:1] He sang to the LORD the words of this song **when** [+928]
18: 18 [18:19] They confronted me in the **day** *of* my disaster,
19: 2 [19:3] **Day** after day they pour forth speech; night after night they
19: 2 [19:3] Day after **day** they pour forth speech; night after night they
20: 1 [20:2] May the LORD answer you **when** [+928] you are in
20: 9 [20:10] save the king! Answer us **when** [+928] we call!
21: 4 [21:5] and you gave it to him—length of **days**, for ever and ever.
23: 6 Surely goodness and love will follow me all the **days** *of* my life,
23: 6 and I will dwell in the house of the LORD **forever** [+802+4200].

Ps 25: 5 for you are God my Savior, and my hope is in you all **day** *long*.
27: 4 that I may dwell in the house of the LORD all the **days** *of* my life,
27: 5 For in the **day** *of* trouble he will keep me safe in his dwelling;
32: 3 my bones wasted away through my groaning all **day** *long*.
34: 12 [34:13] of you loves life and desires to see *many* good **days**,
35: 28 will speak of your righteousness and of your praises all **day** *long*.
37: 13 the Lord laughs at the wicked, for he knows their **day** is coming.
37: 18 The **days** *of* the blameless are known to the LORD, and their
37: 19 they will not wither; in **days** *of* famine they will enjoy plenty.
37: 26 They are **always** [+2021+3972] generous and lend freely;
38: 6 [38:7] and brought very low; all **day** *long* I go about mourning.
38: 12 [38:13] harm me talk of my ruin; all **day** *long* they plot deception.
39: 4 [39:5] O LORD, my life's end and the number of my **days**;
39: 5 [39:6] You have made my **days** a mere handbreadth; the span of
41: 1 [41:2] for the weak; the LORD delivers him in **times** *of* trouble.
42: 3 [42:4] my food day and night, while men say to me all **day** *long*,
42: 10 [42:11] saying to me all **day** *long*, "Where is your God?"
44: 1 [44:2] our fathers have told us what you did in their **days**, in days
44: 1 [44:2] have told us what you did in their days, in **days** long ago.
44: 8 [44:9] In God we make our boast all **day** *long*, and we will praise
44: 15 [44:16] My disgrace is before me all **day** *long*, and my face is
44: 22 [44:23] Yet for your sake we face death all **day** *long*; we are
49: 5 [49:6] Why should I fear when evil **days** come, when wicked
50: 15 and call upon me in the **day** *of* trouble; I will deliver you,
52: 1 [52:3] Why do you boast all **day** *long*, you who are a disgrace in
55: 23 [55:24] and deceitful men will not live out half their **days**.
56: 1 [56:2] men hotly pursue me; all **day** *long* they press their attack.
56: 2 [56:3] My slanderers pursue me all **day** *long*; many are attacking
56: 3 [56:4] **When** I am afraid, I will trust in you.
56: 5 [56:6] All **day** *long* they twist my words; they are always plotting
56: 9 [56:10] my enemies will turn back **when** [+928] I call for help.
59: 16 [59:17] for you are my fortress, my refuge in **times** *of* trouble.
61: 6 [61:7] Increase **[RPH]** the days of the king's life, his years for
61: 6 [61:7] Increase the **days of** the king's **life**, his years for many
61: 8 [61:9] praise to your name and fulfill my vows **day** *after* day.
61: 8 [61:9] sing praise to your name and fulfill my vows day after **day**.
68: 19 [68:20] to God our Savior, who **daily** [+3427] bears our burdens.
68: 19 [68:20] to God our Savior, who **daily** [+3427] bears our burdens.
71: 8 is filled with your praise, declaring your splendor all **day** *long*.
71: 15 of your salvation all **day** *long*, though I know not its measure.
71: 24 My tongue will tell of your righteous acts all **day** *long*, for those
72: 7 In his **days** the righteous will flourish; prosperity will abound till
72: 15 May people ever pray for him and bless him all **day** *long*.
73: 14 All **day** *long* I have been plagued; I have been punished every
74: 16 The **day** is yours, and yours also the night; you established the sun
74: 22 defend your cause; remember how fools mock you all **day** *long*.
77: 2 [77:3] **When** [+928] I was in distress, I sought the Lord; at night I
77: 5 [77:6] I thought about the former **days**, the years of long ago;
78: 9 though armed with bows, turned back on the **day** *of* battle;
78: 33 So he ended their **days** in futility and their years in terror.
78: 42 his power—the **day** he redeemed them from the oppressor,
81: 3 [81:4] and when the moon is full, on the **day** *of* our Feast;
84: 10 [84:11] Better is *one* **day** in your courts than a thousand
86: 3 Have mercy on me, O Lord, for I call to you all **day** *long*.
86: 7 In the **day** *of* my trouble I will call to you, for you will answer me.
88: 1 [88:2] the God who saves me, **day** and night I cry out before you.
88: 9 [88:10] I call to you, O LORD, every **day**; I spread out my hands
88: 17 [88:18] All **day** *long* they surround me like a flood; they have
89: 16 [89:17] They rejoice in your name all **day** *long*; they exult in your
89: 29 [89:30] his throne **as long** [+3869] **as** the heavens **endure**.
89: 45 [89:46] You have cut short the **days** *of* his youth; you have
90: 4 For a thousand years in your sight are like a **day** [+919] that has
90: 9 All our **days** pass away under your wrath; we finish our years with
90: 10 The **length of** our **days** [+9102] is seventy years—or eighty,
90: 12 Teach us to number our **days** aright, that we may gain a heart of
90: 14 unfailing love, that we may sing for joy and be glad all our **days**.
90: 15 Make us glad *for* as many **days as** you have afflicted us, for as
91: 16 With long **life** will I satisfy him and show him my salvation."
92: T [92:1] A psalm. A song. For the Sabbath **day**.
93: 5 holiness adorns your house for endless **days**, O LORD.
94: 13 you grant him relief from **days** *of* trouble, till a pit is dug for the
95: 7 the flock under his care. **Today** [+2021], if you hear his voice,
95: 8 as you did at Meribah, as you did that **day** *at* Massah in the desert,
96: 2 the LORD, praise his name; proclaim his salvation **day** after day.
96: 2 the LORD, praise his name; proclaim his salvation day after **day**.
102: 2 [102:3] Do not hide your face from me **when** [+928] I am in
102: 2 [102:3] your ear to me; **when** [+928] I call, answer me quickly.
102: 3 [102:4] For my **days** vanish like smoke; my bones burn like
102: 8 [102:9] All **day** *long* my enemies taunt me; those who rail against
102: 11 [102:12] My **days** are like the evening shadow; I wither away like
102: 23 [102:24] of my life he broke my strength; he cut short my **days**.
102: 24 [102:25] not take me away, O my God, in the midst of my **days**;
103: 15 As for man, his **days** are like grass, he flourishes like a flower of
109: 8 May his **days** be few; may another take his place of leadership.
110: 3 Your troops will be willing on your **day** *of* battle. Arrayed in holy
110: 5 is at your right hand; he will crush kings on the **day** *of* his wrath.
116: 2 Because he turned his ear to me, I will call on him as long as I **live**.
118: 24 This is the **day** the LORD has made; let us rejoice and be glad in
119: 84 **How long must** your servant **wait** [+3869+4537]? When will you
119: 91 Your laws endure to this **day**, for all things serve you.
119: 97 Oh, how I love your law! I meditate on it all **day** *long*.
119:164 Seven times a **day** I praise you for your righteous laws.
128: 5 May the LORD bless you from Zion all the **days** *of* your life;
136: 8 the sun to govern the **day**, *His love endures forever.*
137: 7 O LORD, what the Edomites did on the **day** Jerusalem fell.
138: 3 **When** [+928] I called, you answered me; you made me bold
139: 12 the night will shine like the **day**, for darkness is as light to you.
139: 16 All the **days** ordained for me were written in your book before one
140: 2 [140:3] devise evil plans in their hearts and stir up war every **day**.
140: 7 [140:8] who shields my head in the **day** *of* battle—
143: 5 I remember the **days** of long ago; I meditate on all your works
144: 4 Man is like a breath; his **days** are like a fleeting shadow.
145: 2 Every **day** I will praise you and extol your name for ever and ever.
146: 4 return to the ground; on that very **day** their plans come to nothing.
Pr 3: 2 for they will prolong your life **many years** [+2256+9102]
3: 16 Long **life** is in her right hand; in her left hand are riches and honor.
4: 18 first gleam of dawn, shining ever brighter till the full light of **day**.
6: 34 and he will show no mercy **when** [+928] he takes revenge.
7: 9 at twilight, as the **day** was fading, as the dark of night set in.
7: 14 "I have fellowship offerings at home; **today** [+2021] I fulfilled my
7: 20 filled with money and will not be home till **full moon** [+4057]."
8: 30 I was filled with delight **day** *after* day, rejoicing always in his
8: 30 I was filled with delight day after **day**, rejoicing always in his
8: 34 watching **daily** [+3427] at my doors, waiting at my doorway.
8: 34 watching **daily** [+3427] at my doors, waiting at my doorway.
9: 11 For through me your **days** will be many, and years will be added to
10: 27 The fear of the LORD adds length to **life**, but the years of the
11: 4 Wealth is worthless in the **day** *of* wrath, but righteousness delivers
12: 16 A fool shows his annoyance **at once** [+928+2021], but a prudent
15: 15 All the **days** *of* the oppressed are wretched, but the cheerful heart
16: 4 for his own ends—even the wicked for a **day** *of* disaster.
21: 26 All **day** *long* he craves for more, but the righteous give without
21: 31 The horse is made ready for the **day** *of* battle, but victory rests with
22: 19 trust may be in the LORD, I teach you **today** [+2021], even you.
23: 17 but **always** [+2021+3972] be zealous for the fear of the LORD.
24: 10 If you falter in **times** *of* trouble, how small is your strength!
25: 13 Like the coolness of snow at harvest **time** is a trustworthy
25: 19 or a lame foot is reliance on the unfaithful in **times** *of* trouble.
25: 20 Like one who takes away a garment on a cold **day**, or like vinegar
27: 1 Do not boast about **tomorrow** [+4737], for you do not know what
27: 1 about tomorrow, for you do not know what a **day** may bring forth.
27: 10 do not go to your brother's house **when** [+928] disaster strikes
27: 15 A quarrelsome wife is like a constant dripping on a rainy **day**;
28: 16 but he who hates ill-gotten gain *will* **enjoy a long life** [+799].
31: 12 She brings him good, not harm, all the **days** *of* her life.
31: 25 with strength and dignity; she can laugh at the **days** to come.
Ecc 2: 3 for men to do under heaven during the few **days** *of* their lives.
2: 16 not be long remembered; in **days** to come both will be forgotten.
2: 23 All his **days** his work is pain and grief; even at night his mind does
5: 17 [5:16] All his **days** he eats in darkness, with great frustration,
5: 18 [5:17] the sun during the few **days** *of* life God has given him—
5: 20 [5:19] He seldom reflects on the **days** *of* his life, because God
6: 3 yet no matter how long he **lives** [+9102], if he cannot enjoy his
6: 12 the few and meaningless **days** he passes through like a shadow?
7: 1 than fine perfume, and the **day** *of* death better than the day of birth.
7: 1 than fine perfume, and the day of death better than the **day** *of* birth.
7: 10 Do not say, "Why were the old **days** better than these?" For it is
7: 14 When **times** are good, be happy; but when times are bad, consider:
7: 14 When times are good, be happy; but when **times** are bad, consider:
7: 15 In this meaningless **life** *of* mine I have seen both of these:
8: 8 wind to contain it; so no one has power over the **day** *of* his death.
8: 13 go well with them, and their **days** will not lengthen like a shadow.
8: 15 joy will accompany him in his work all the **days** *of* the life God
8: 16 man's labor on earth—his eyes not seeing sleep **day** or night—
9: 9 all the **days** *of* this meaningless life that God has given you under
9: 9 that God has given you under the sun—all your meaningless **days**.
11: 1 bread upon the waters, for after many **days** you will find it again.
11: 8 But let him remember the **days** *of* darkness, for they will be many.
11: 9 and let your heart give you joy in the **days** *of* your youth.
12: 1 Remember your Creator in the **days** *of* your youth, before the days
12: 1 before the **days** *of* trouble come and the years approach when you
12: 3 **when** [+928+2021] the keepers of the house tremble,
SS 2: 17 Until the **day** breaks and the shadows flee, turn, my lover,
3: 11 the crown with which his mother crowned him on the **day** *of* his
3: 11 crowned him on the day of his wedding, the **day** his heart rejoiced.
4: 6 Until the **day** breaks and the shadows flee, I will go to the
8: 8 What shall we do for our sister for the **day** she is spoken for?
Isa 1: 1 Jerusalem that Isaiah son of Amoz saw during the **reigns** *of*

Isa 2: 2 In the last **days** the mountain of the LORD's temple will be
2: 11 of men brought low; the LORD alone will be exalted in that **day**.
2: 12 The LORD Almighty has a **day** in store for all the proud
2: 17 of men humbled; the LORD alone will be exalted in that **day**,
2: 20 In that **day** men will throw away to the rodents and bats their idols
3: 7 But in that **day** he will cry out, "I have no remedy. I have no food
3: 18 In that **day** the Lord will snatch away their finery: the bangles
4: 1 In that **day** seven women will take hold of one man and say,
4: 2 In that **day** the Branch of the LORD will be beautiful
5: 30 In that **day** they will roar over it like the roaring of the sea.
7: 1 **When** [+928] Ahaz son of Jotham, the son of Uzziah, was king of
7: 17 on the house of your father a **time** unlike any since Ephraim broke
7: 17 on the house of your father a time unlike any **since** [+4200+4946]
7: 18 In that **day** the LORD will whistle for flies from the distant
7: 20 In that **day** the Lord will use a razor hired from beyond the River—
7: 21 In that **day**, a man will keep alive a young cow and two goats.
7: 23 In that **day**, in every place where there were a thousand vines
9: 4 [9:3] For as in the **day** *of* Midian's defeat, you have shattered the
9: 14 [9:13] and tail, both palm branch and reed *in* a single **day**;
10: 3 What will you do on the **day** *of* reckoning, when disaster comes
10: 17 in a single **day** it will burn and consume his thorns and his briers.
10: 20 In that **day** the remnant of Israel, the survivors of the house of
10: 27 In that **day** their burden will be lifted from your shoulders,
10: 32 This **day** they will halt at Nob; they will shake their fist at the
11: 10 In that **day** the Root of Jesse will stand as a banner for the peoples;
11: 11 In that **day** the Lord will reach out his hand a second time to
11: 16 as there was for Israel **when** [+928] they came up from Egypt.
12: 1 In that **day** you will say: "I will praise you, O LORD.
12: 4 In that **day** you will say: "Give thanks to the LORD, call on his
13: 6 Wail, for the **day** *of* the LORD is near; it will come like
13: 9 See, the **day** *of* the LORD is coming—a cruel day, with wrath
13: 13 the wrath of the LORD Almighty, in the **day** *of* his burning anger.
13: 22 Her time is at hand, and her **days** will not be prolonged.
14: 3 On the **day** the LORD gives you relief from suffering and turmoil
17: 4 "In that **day** the glory of Jacob will fade; the fat of his body will
17: 7 In that **day** men will look to their Maker and turn their eyes to the
17: 9 In that **day** their strong cities, which they left because of the
17: 11 though on the **day** you set them out, you make them grow,
17: 11 yet the harvest will be as nothing in the **day** *of* disease and
19: 16 In that **day** the Egyptians will be like women. They will shudder
19: 18 In that **day** five cities in Egypt will speak the language of Canaan
19: 19 In that **day** there will be an altar to the LORD in the heart of
19: 21 the Egyptians, and in that **day** they will acknowledge the LORD.
19: 23 In that **day** there will be a highway from Egypt to Assyria.
19: 24 In that **day** Israel will be the third, along with Egypt and Assyria,
20: 6 In that **day** the people who live on this coast will say, 'See what has
22: 5 has a **day** *of* tumult and trampling and terror in the Valley of
22: 8 you looked in that **day** to the weapons in the Palace of the Forest;
22: 12 called you on that **day** to weep and to wail, to tear out your hair
22: 20 "In that **day** I will summon my servant, Eliakim son of Hilkiah.
22: 25 "In that **day**," declares the LORD Almighty, "the peg driven into
23: 7 Is this your city of revelry, the **old** [+4946+7710], old city,
23: 15 At that **time** Tyre will be forgotten for seventy years, the span of a
23: 15 Tyre will be forgotten for seventy years, the **span of** a king's **life**.
24: 21 In that **day** the LORD will punish the powers in the heavens
24: 22 they will be shut up in prison and be punished after many **days**.
25: 9 In that **day** they will say, "Surely this is our God; we trusted in
26: 1 In that **day** this song will be sung in the land of Judah: We have a
27: 1 In that **day**, the LORD will punish with his sword, his fierce,
27: 2 In that **day**—"Sing about a fruitful vineyard:
27: 3 it continually. I guard it **day** and night so that no one may harm it.
27: 8 his fierce blast he drives her out, as on a **day** the east wind blows.
27: 12 In that **day** the LORD will thresh from the flowing Euphrates to
27: 13 in that **day** a great trumpet will sound. Those who were perishing
28: 5 In that **day** the LORD Almighty will be a glorious crown,
28: 19 after morning, by **day** and by night, it will sweep through."
28: 24 plows for planting, does he plow **continually** [+2021+3972]?
29: 18 In that **day** the deaf will hear the words of the scroll, and out of
30: 8 that for the **days** to come it may be an everlasting witness.
30: 23 and plentiful. In that **day** your cattle will graze in broad meadows.
30: 25 In the **day** *of* great slaughter, when the towers fall, streams of
30: 26 will be seven times brighter, like the light of seven *full* **days**,
30: 26 **when** [+928] the LORD binds up the bruises of his people
31: 7 For in that **day** every one of you will reject the idols of silver
32: 10 **In little more than** [+6584] a year you who feel secure will
34: 8 For the LORD has a **day** *of* vengeance, a year of retribution,
37: 3 This **day** is a day of distress and rebuke and disgrace, as when
37: 3 This day is a **day** *of* distress and rebuke and disgrace, as when
37: 26 In **days** of old I planned it; now I have brought it to pass, that you
38: 1 In those **days** Hezekiah became ill and was at the point of death.
38: 5 and seen your tears; I will add fifteen years to your **life**.
38: 10 "In the prime of my **life** must I go through the gates of death
38: 12 cut me off from the loom; **day** and night you made an end of me.
38: 13 lion he broke all my bones; **day** and night you made an end of me.
38: 19 the living—they praise you, as I am doing **today** [+2021];
38: 20 we will sing with stringed instruments all the **days** *of* our lives in
39: 6 The **time** will surely come when everything in your palace,
39: 6 all that your fathers have stored up until this **day**, will be carried
39: 8 For he thought, "There will be peace and security in my **lifetime**."
43: 13 Yes, and from ancient **days** I am he. No one can deliver out of my
47: 9 Both of these will overtake you in a moment, on a single **day**:
48: 7 and not long ago; you have not heard of them before **today**.
49: 8 favor I will answer you, and in the **day** *of* salvation I will help you;
51: 9 of the LORD; awake, as in **days** gone by, as in generations of old.
51: 13 that you live in constant terror every **day** because of the wrath of
52: 5 the LORD. "And all **day** *long* my name is constantly blasphemed.
52: 6 therefore in that **day** they will know that it is I who foretold it.
53: 10 he will see his offspring and prolong his **days**, and the will of the
54: 9 "To me this is like the **days** [BHS 4784] of Noah, when I swore
56: 12 And tomorrow will be like **today** [+2296], or even far better."
58: 2 For **day** *after* day they seek me out; they seem eager to know my
58: 2 For day after **day** they seek me out; they seem eager to know my
58: 3 "Yet on the **day** *of* your fasting, you do as you please and exploit
58: 4 You cannot fast as you do **today** [+2021] and expect your voice to
58: 5 of fast I have chosen, only a **day** *for* a man to humble himself?
58: 5 Is that what you call a fast, a **day** acceptable to the LORD?
58: 13 the Sabbath and from doing as you please on my holy **day**,
60: 20 will be your everlasting light, and your **days** *of* sorrow will end.
61: 2 year of the LORD's favor and the **day** *of* vengeance of our God,
62: 6 on your walls, O Jerusalem; they will never be silent **day** or night.
63: 4 For the **day** *of* vengeance was in my heart, and the year of my
63: 9 he lifted them up and carried them all the **days** of old.
63: 11 Then his people recalled the **days** of old, the days of Moses
65: 2 All **day** *long* I have held out my hands to an obstinate people,
65: 5 people are smoke in my nostrils, a fire that keeps burning all **day**.
65: 20 "Never again will there be in it an infant who lives but a *few* **days**,
65: 20 but a few days, or an old man who does not live out his **years**;
65: 22 For as the **days** *of* a tree, so will be the days of my people;
65: 22 For as the days of a tree, so will be the **days** *of* my people;
66: 8 Can a country be born in a **day** or a nation be brought forth in a
Jer 1: 2 year of the reign of **[RPH]** Josiah son of Amon king of Judah,
1: 3 and through the **reign** *of* Jehoiakim son of Josiah king of Judah,
1: 10 See, **today** [+2021+2021+2296] I appoint you over nations and
1: 18 **Today** [+2021] I have made you a fortified city, an iron pillar
2: 32 Yet my people have forgotten me, **days** without number.
3: 6 During the **reign** *of* King Josiah, the LORD said to me, "Have
3: 16 In those **days**, when your numbers have increased greatly in the
3: 18 In those **days** the house of Judah will join the house of Israel,
3: 25 from our youth till this **day** we have not obeyed the LORD our
4: 9 "In that **day**," declares the LORD, "the king and the officials will
5: 18 "Yet even in those **days**," declares the LORD, "I will not destroy
6: 4 But, alas, the **daylight** is fading, and the shadows of evening grow
6: 11 will be caught in it, and the old, those weighed down with **years**.
7: 22 For **when** [+928] I brought your forefathers out of Egypt and spoke
7: 25 From the **time** your forefathers left Egypt until now, day after day,
7: 25 the time your forefathers left Egypt until **now** [+2021+2021+2296],
7: 25 **day after day**, again and again I sent you my servants the
7: 32 So beware, the **days** are coming, declares the LORD,
9: 25 [9:24] "The **days** are coming," declares the LORD, "when I will
11: 4 the terms I commanded your forefathers **when** [+928] I brought
11: 5 and honey'—the land you possess **today** [+2021+2021+2296]."
11: 7 From the **time** I brought your forefathers up from Egypt until
11: 7 from Egypt until **today** [+2021+2021+2296], I warned them again
12: 3 like sheep to be butchered! Set them apart for the **day** *of* slaughter!
13: 6 Many **days** later the LORD said to me, "Go now to Perath
16: 9 in your **days** I will bring an end to the sounds of joy and gladness
16: 14 "However, the **days** are coming," declares the LORD, "when men
16: 19 my strength and my fortress, my refuge in **time** *of* distress,
17: 11 When his **life** is half gone, they will desert him, and in the end he
17: 16 your shepherd; you know I have not desired the **day** *of* despair.
17: 17 Do not be a terror to me; you are my refuge in the **day** *of* disaster.
17: 18 Bring on them the **day** *of* disaster; destroy them with double
17: 21 Be careful not to carry a load on the Sabbath **day** or bring it
17: 22 a load out of your houses or do any work on **[RPH]** the Sabbath,
17: 22 or do any work on the Sabbath, but keep the Sabbath **day** holy,
17: 24 bring no load through the gates of this city on **[RPH]** the Sabbath,
17: 24 but keep the Sabbath **day** holy by not doing any work on it,
17: 27 if you do not obey me to keep the Sabbath **day** holy by not
17: 27 as you come through the gates of Jerusalem on the Sabbath **day**,
18: 17 show them my back and not my face in the **day** *of* their disaster."
19: 6 So beware, the **days** are coming, declares the LORD,
20: 7 and prevailed. I am ridiculed all **day** *long*; everyone mocks me.
20: 8 of the LORD has brought me insult and reproach all **day** *long*.
20: 14 Cursed be the **day** I was born! May the day my mother bore me not
20: 14 day I was born! May the **day** my mother bore me not be blessed!
20: 18 the womb to see trouble and sorrow and to end my **days** in shame?
22: 30 this man as if childless, a man who will not prosper in his **lifetime**,
23: 5 "The **days** are coming," declares the LORD, "when I will raise up

Jer 23: 6 In his **days** Judah will be saved and Israel will live in safety.
23: 7 "So then, the **days** are coming," declares the LORD,
23: 20 of his heart. In **days** to come you will understand it clearly.
25: 3 year of Josiah son of Amon king of Judah until this very **day**—
25: 18 and scorn and cursing, as they are **today** [+2021+2021+2296];
25: 33 At that **time** those slain by the LORD will be everywhere—
25: 34 For your **time** to be slaughtered has come; you will fall and be
26: 18 "Micah of Moresheth prophesied in the **days** *of* Hezekiah king of
27: 22 and there they will remain until the **day** I come for them,'
28: 3 Within *two* **years** [+9102] I will bring back to this place all the
28: 11 off the neck of all the nations within *two* **years** [+9102].' " At this,
30: 3 The **days** are coming,' declares the LORD, 'when I will bring my
30: 7 How awful that **day** will be! None will be like it. It will be a time
30: 8 " 'In that **day**,' declares the LORD Almighty, 'I will break the
30: 24 the purposes of his heart. In **days** to come you will understand this.
31: 6 There will be a **day** when watchmen cry out on the hills of
31: 27 "The **days** are coming," declares the LORD, "when I will plant
31: 29 "In those **days** people will no longer say, 'The fathers have eaten
31: 31 "The **time** is coming," declares the LORD, "when I will make a
31: 32 **when** [+928] I took them by the hand to lead them out of Egypt,
31: 33 the covenant I will make with the house of Israel after that **time**,"
31: 36 "will the descendants of Israel **ever** [+2021+3972] cease to be a
31: 38 "The **days** are coming," declares the LORD, "when this city will
32: 14 of purchase, and put them in a clay jar so they will last a long **time**.
32: 20 and wonders in Egypt and have continued them to this **day**,
32: 20 gained the renown that is **still** [+2021+2021+2296+3869] yours.
32: 31 From the **day** it was built until now, this city has so aroused my
32: 31 From the day it was built until **now** [+2021+2021+2296], this city
32: 39 so that they will **always** [+2021+3972] fear me for their own good
33: 14 " 'The **days** are coming,' declares the LORD, 'when I will fulfill
33: 15 " 'In those **days** and at that time I will make a righteous Branch
33: 16 In those **days** Judah will be saved and Jerusalem will live in safety.
33: 18 stand before me **continually** [+2021+3972] to offer burnt offerings,
33: 20 'If you can break my covenant with the **day** and my covenant with
34: 13 I made a covenant with your forefathers **when** [+928] I brought
34: 15 **Recently** [+2021] you repented and did what is right in my sight:
35: 1 LORD during the **reign** *of* Jehoiakim son of Josiah king of Judah:
35: 7 have any of these things, but must **always** [+3972] live in tents.
35: 7 Then you will live a long **time** in the land where you are nomads.'
35: 8 wives nor our sons and daughters have **ever** [+3972] drunk wine
35: 14 To this **day** they do not drink wine, because they obey their
35: 19 will **never** [+2021+3972+4202] fail to have a man to serve me.' "
36: 2 all the other nations from the **time** I began speaking to you in the
36: 2 the time I began speaking to you in the **reign** *of* Josiah till now.
36: 2 speaking to you in the reign of Josiah till **now** [+2021+2021+2296].
36: 6 So you go to the house of the LORD on a **day** *of* fasting and read
36: 30 thrown out and exposed to the heat by **day** and the frost by night.
37: 16 into a vaulted cell in a dungeon, where he remained a long **time**.
37: 21 given bread from the street of the bakers **each day** [+2021+4200]
38: 28 Jeremiah remained in the courtyard of the guard until the **day**
39: 10 owned nothing; and at that **time** he gave them vineyards and fields.
39: 16 not prosperity. At that **time** they will be fulfilled before your eyes.
39: 17 I will rescue you on that **day**, declares the LORD; you will not be
40: 4 **today** [+2021] I am freeing you from the chains on your wrists.
41: 4 The **day** after Gedaliah's assassination, before anyone knew about
42: 7 Ten **days** later the word of the LORD came to Jeremiah.
42: 19 'Do not go to Egypt.' Be sure of this: I warn you **today** [+2021]
42: 21 I have told you **today** [+2021], but you still have not obeyed the
44: 2 **Today** [+2021+2021+2296] they lie deserted and in ruins
44: 6 made them the desolate ruins they are **today** [+2021+2021+2296].
44: 10 To this **day** they have not humbled themselves or shown reverence,
44: 22 waste without inhabitants, as it is **today** [+2021+2021+2296].
44: 23 disaster has come upon you, as you **now** [+2021+2021+2296] see."
46: 10 But that **day** belongs to the Lord, the LORD Almighty—
46: 10 a **day** *of* vengeance, for vengeance on his foes.
46: 21 stand their ground, for the **day** *of* disaster is coming upon them,
46: 26 Later, however, Egypt will be inhabited as *in* **times** past,"
47: 4 For the **day** has come to destroy all the Philistines and to cut off all
48: 12 **days** are coming," declares the LORD, "when I will send men
48: 41 In that **day** the hearts of Moab's warriors will be like the heart of a
48: 47 "Yet I will restore the fortunes of Moab in **days** to come,"
49: 2 the **days** are coming," declares the LORD, "when I will sound the
49: 22 In that **day** the hearts of Edom's warriors will be like the heart of a
49: 26 all her soldiers will be silenced in that **day**," declares the LORD
49: 39 "Yet I will restore the fortunes of Elam in **days** to come,"
50: 4 "In those **days**, at that time," declares the LORD, "the people of
50: 20 In those **days**, at that time," declares the LORD, "search will be
50: 27 For their **day** has come, the time for them to be punished.
50: 30 all her soldiers will be silenced in that **day**," declares the LORD.
50: 31 declares the Lord, the LORD Almighty, "for your **day** has come,
51: 2 they will oppose her on every side in the **day** *of* her disaster.
51: 47 For the **time** will surely come when I will punish the idols of
51: 52 "But **days** are coming," declares the LORD, "when I will punish
52: 11 to Babylon, where he put him in prison till the **day** *of* his death.
52: 33 and *for* the **rest of** [+3972] his life ate regularly at the king's table.
52: 34 **Day** [+928+1821+3427] **by day** the king of Babylon gave
52: 34 **Day by day** [+928+1821+3427] the king of Babylon gave
52: 34 gave Jehoiachin a regular allowance **as long as** [+3972] he lived,
52: 34 a regular allowance as long as he lived, till the **day** *of* his death.
La 1: 7 In the **days** *of* her affliction and wandering Jerusalem remembers
1: 7 remembers all the treasures that were hers in **days** of old.
1: 12 that the LORD brought on me in the **day** *of* his fierce anger?
1: 13 and turned me back. He made me desolate, faint all the **day** *long*.
1: 21 May you bring the **day** you have announced so they may become
2: 1 he has not remembered his footstool in the **day** *of* his anger.
2: 7 in the house of the LORD as on the **day** *of* an appointed feast.
2: 16 This is the **day** we have waited for; we have lived to see it."
2: 17 has fulfilled his word, which he decreed **long ago** [+4946+7710].
2: 21 You have slain them in the **day** *of* your anger; you have
2: 22 "As you summon to a feast **day**, so you summoned against me
2: 22 In the **day** *of* the LORD's anger no one escaped or survived;
3: 3 he has turned his hand against me again and again, all **day** *long*.
3: 14 of all my people; they mock me in song all **day** *long*.
3: 57 You came near **when** [+928] I called you, and you said, "Do not
3: 62 what my enemies whisper and mutter against me all **day** *long*.
4: 18 Our end was near, our **days** were numbered, for our end had come.
5: 20 do you always forget us? Why do you forsake us **so long** [+802]?
5: 21 O LORD, that we may return; renew our **days** as of old
Eze 1: 28 Like the appearance of a rainbow in the clouds on a rainy **day**,
2: 3 and their fathers have been in revolt against me to this very **day**.
3: 15 where they were living, I sat among them *for* seven **days**—
3: 16 At the end of seven **days** the word of the LORD came to me:
4: 4 You are to bear their sin *for* the number of **days** you lie on your
4: 5 I have assigned you the same number of **days** as the years of their
4: 5 So *for* 390 **days** you will bear the sin of the house of Israel.
4: 6 house of Judah. I have assigned you 40 **days**, a day for each year.
4: 6 house of Judah. I have assigned you 40 days, a **day** for each year.
4: 6 I have assigned you 40 days, a day for each year. **[RPH]**
4: 8 one side to the other until you have finished the **days** *of* your siege.
4: 9 You are to eat it during the 390 **days** you lie on your side.
4: 9 You are to eat it during the 390 days **[RPH]** you lie on your side.
4: 10 Weigh out twenty shekels of food to eat each **day** and eat it at set
5: 2 When the **days** *of* your siege come to an end, burn a third of the
7: 7 The time has come, the **day** is near; there is panic, not joy,
7: 10 "The **day** is here! It has come! Doom has burst forth, the rod has
7: 12 The time has come, the **day** has arrived. Let not the buyer rejoice
7: 19 gold will not be able to save them in the **day** *of* the LORD's
12: 22 land of Israel: 'The **days** go by and every vision comes to nothing'?
12: 23 Say to them, 'The **days** are near when every vision will be fulfilled.
12: 25 For in your **days**, you rebellious house, I will fulfill whatever I say,
12: 27 of Israel is saying, 'The vision he sees is for many **years** from now,
13: 5 so that it will stand firm in the battle on the **day** *of* the LORD.
16: 4 On the **day** you were born your cord was not cut, nor were you
16: 5 the open field, for on the **day** you were born you were despised.
16: 22 your prostitution you did not remember the **days** *of* your youth,
16: 43 " 'Because you did not remember the **days** *of* your youth
16: 56 You would not even mention your sister Sodom in the **day** *of* your
16: 60 Yet I will remember the covenant I made with you in the **days** *of*
20: 5 On the **day** I chose Israel, I swore with uplifted hand to the
20: 6 On that **day** I swore to them that I would bring them out of Egypt
20: 29 is this high place you go to?' " (It is called Bamah to this **day**.)
20: 31 you continue to defile yourselves with all your idols to this **day**.
21: 25 [21:30] and wicked prince of Israel, whose **day** has come,
21: 29 [21:34] whose **day** has come, whose time of punishment has
22: 4 You have brought your **days** to a close, and the end of your years
22: 14 courage endure or your hands be strong in the **day** I deal with you?
22: 24 are a land that has had no rain or showers in the **day** *of* wrath.'
23: 19 and more promiscuous as she recalled the **days** *of* her youth,
23: 38 At that same **time** they defiled my sanctuary and desecrated my
23: 39 On the very **day** they sacrificed their children to their idols,
24: 2 "Son of man, record this **date**, this very date, because the king of
24: 2 "Son of man, record this date, this very **date**, because the king of
24: 2 the king of Babylon has laid siege to Jerusalem this very **day**.
24: 25 on the **day** I take away their stronghold, their joy and glory,
24: 26 on that **day** a fugitive will come to tell you the news.
24: 27 At that **time** your mouth will be opened; you will speak with him
26: 18 Now the coastlands tremble *on* the **day** *of* your fall; the islands in
27: 27 will sink into the heart of the sea on the **day** *of* your shipwreck.
28: 13 made of gold; on the **day** you were created they were prepared.
28: 15 You were blameless in your ways from the **day** you were created
29: 21 "On that **day** I will make a horn grow for the house of Israel,
30: 2 the Sovereign LORD says: " 'Wail and say, "Alas for that **day**!"
30: 3 For the **day** is near, the day of the LORD is near—a day of
30: 3 For the day is near, the **day** of the LORD is near—a day of
30: 3 LORD is near—a **day** *of* clouds, a time of doom for the nations.
30: 9 " 'On that **day** messengers will go out from me in ships to frighten
30: 9 Anguish will take hold of them on the **day** *of* Egypt's doom,
30: 18 Dark will be the **day** at Tahpanhes when I break the yoke of Egypt;

Eze 31: 15 On the **day** it was brought down to the grave I covered the deep
32: 10 On the **day** *of* your downfall each of them will tremble every
33: 12 of the righteous man will not save him **when** [+928] he disobeys,
33: 12 man will not cause him to fall **when** [+928] he turns from it.
33: 12 The righteous man, **if** [+928] he sins, will not be allowed to live
34: 12 As a shepherd looks after his scattered flock **when** [+928] he is
34: 12 from all the places where they were scattered on a **day** *of* clouds
36: 33 On the **day** I cleanse you from all your sins, I will resettle your
38: 8 After many **days** you will be called to arms. In future years you
38: 10 On that **day** thoughts will come into your mind and you will devise
38: 14 In that **day**, when my people Israel are living in safety, will you not
38: 16 In **days** to come, O Gog, I will bring you against my land,
38: 17 Are you not the one I spoke of in former **days** by my servants the
38: 17 At that **time** they prophesied for years that I would bring you
38: 18 This is what will happen in that **day**: When Gog attacks the land of
38: 18 **When** [+928] Gog attacks the land of Israel, my hot anger will be
38: 19 fiery wrath I declare that at that **time** there shall be a great
39: 8 declares the Sovereign LORD. This is the **day** I have spoken of.
39: 11 " 'On that **day** I will give Gog a burial place in Israel, in the valley
39: 13 and the **day** I am glorified will be a memorable day for them,
39: 22 From that **day** forward the house of Israel will know that I am the
40: 1 on that very **day** the hand of the LORD was upon me and he took
43: 18 and sprinkling blood upon the altar **when** [+928] it is built:
43: 22 "On the second **day** you are to offer a male goat without defect for
43: 25 "*For* seven **days** you are to provide a male goat daily for a sin
43: 25 are to provide a male goat **daily** [+2021+4200] for a sin offering;
43: 26 *For* seven **days** they are to make atonement for the altar
43: 27 At the end of these **days**, from the eighth day on, the priests are to
43: 27 At the end of these days, from the eighth **day** on, the priests are to
44: 26 After he is cleansed, he must wait seven **days**.
44: 27 On the **day** he goes into the inner court of the sanctuary to minister
45: 21 " 'In the first month on the fourteenth **day** you are to observe the
45: 21 a feast lasting seven **days**, during which you shall eat bread made
45: 22 On that **day** the prince is to provide a bull as a sin offering for
45: 23 Every **day** *during* the seven days of the Feast he is to provide
45: 23 Every day during the seven **days** *of* the Feast he is to provide seven
45: 23 offering to the LORD, **[RPH]** and a male goat for a sin offering.
45: 23 offering to the LORD, and a male goat for a sin offering. **[RPH]**
45: 25 " 'During the seven **days** of the Feast, which begins in the seventh
45: 25 the Feast, which begins in the seventh month on the fifteenth **day**,
46: 1 of the inner court facing east is to be shut on the six working **days**,
46: 1 on the Sabbath **day** and on the day of the New Moon it is to be
46: 1 Sabbath day and on the **day** *of* the New Moon it is to be opened.
46: 4 brings to the LORD on the Sabbath **day** is to be six male lambs
46: 6 On the **day** *of* the New Moon he is to offer a young bull, six lambs
46: 12 or his fellowship offerings as he does on the Sabbath **day**.
46: 13 " '**Every day** [+2021+4200] you are to provide a year-old lamb
48: 35 "And the name of the city from that **time** on will be: THE LORD
Da 1: 5 The king assigned them a **daily** [+928+3427] amount of food
1: 5 The king assigned them a **daily** [+928+3427] amount of food
1: 12 "Please test your servants *for* ten **days**: Give us nothing
1: 14 So he agreed to this and tested them *for* ten **days**.
1: 15 At the end of the ten **days** they looked healthier and better
1: 18 At the end of the **time** set by the king to bring them in, the chief
8: 26 but seal up the vision, for it concerns the **distant future** [+8041]."
8: 27 I, Daniel, was exhausted and lay ill *for several* **days**. Then I got up
9: 7 you are righteous, but this **day** we are covered with shame—
9: 15 and who made for yourself a name that endures to this **day**,
10: 2 At that **time** I, Daniel, mourned for three weeks.
10: 2 At that time I, Daniel, mourned *for* three **weeks** [+8651].
10: 3 I used no lotions at all until the three **weeks** [+8651] were over.
10: 4 On the twenty-fourth **day** of the first month, as I was standing on
10: 12 Since the first **day** that you set your mind to gain understanding
10: 13 the prince of the Persian kingdom resisted me twenty-one **days**.
10: 14 to you what will happen to your people in the **future** [+344],
10: 14 people in the future, for the vision concerns a **time** yet to come."
11: 20 In a few **years**, however, he will be destroyed, yet not in anger
11: 33 though *for a* **time** they will fall by the sword or be burned
12: 11 that causes desolation is set up, there will be 1,290 **days**.
12: 12 is the one who waits for and reaches the end of the 1,335 **days**.
12: 13 at the end of the **days** you will rise to receive your allotted
Hos 1: 1 that came to Hosea son of Beeri during the **reigns** *of* Uzziah,
1: 1 and during the **reign** *of* Jeroboam son of Jehoash king of Israel:
1: 5 In that **day** I will break Israel's bow in the Valley of Jezreel."
1: 11 [2:2] come up out of the land, for great will be the **day** *of* Jezreel.
2: 3 [2:5] her naked and make her as bare as on the **day** she was born;
2: 13 [2:15] I will punish her for the **days** she burned incense to the
2: 15 [2:17] There she will sing as in the **days** *of* her youth, as in the
2: 15 [2:17] days of her youth, as in the **day** she came up out of Egypt.
2: 16 [2:18] "In that **day**," declares the LORD, "you will call me 'my
2: 18 [2:20] In that **day** I will make a covenant for them with the beasts
2: 21 [2:23] "In that **day** I will respond," declares the LORD—"I will
3: 3 I told her, "You are to live with me many **days**; you must not be a
3: 4 For the Israelites will live many **days** without king or prince,
3: 5 come trembling to the LORD and to his blessings in the last **days**.
4: 5 You stumble **day** and night, and the prophets stumble with you.
5: 9 Ephraim will be laid waste on the **day** *of* reckoning.
6: 2 After *two* **days** he will revive us; on the third day he will restore
6: 2 on the third **day** he will restore us, that we may live in his
7: 5 On the **day** *of* the festival of our king the princes become inflamed
9: 5 What will you do on the **day** *of* your appointed feasts, on the
9: 5 day of your appointed feasts, on the festival **days** *of* the LORD?
9: 7 The **days** *of* punishment are coming, the days of reckoning are at
9: 7 days of punishment are coming, the **days** *of* reckoning are at hand.
9: 9 They have sunk deep into corruption, as in the **days** *of* Gibeah.
10: 9 "Since the **days** *of* Gibeah, you have sinned, O Israel, and there
10: 14 as Shalman devastated Beth Arbel on the **day** *of* battle,
12: 1 [12:2] he pursues the east wind all **day** and multiplies lies
12: 9 [12:10] live in tents again, as in the **days** *of* your appointed feasts.
Joel 1: 2 Has anything like this ever happened in your **days** or in the days of
1: 2 this ever happened in your days or in the **days** *of* your forefathers?
1: 15 Alas for that **day**! For the day of the LORD is near; it will come
1: 15 For the **day** *of* the LORD is near; it will come like destruction
2: 1 who live in the land tremble, for the **day** *of* the LORD is coming.
2: 2 a **day** *of* darkness and gloom, a day of clouds and blackness.
2: 2 a day of darkness and gloom, a **day** *of* clouds and blackness.
2: 11 The **day** *of* the LORD is great; it is dreadful. Who can endure it?
2: 29 [3:2] and women, I will pour out my Spirit in those **days**.
2: 31 [3:4] the coming of the great and dreadful **day** *of* the LORD.
3: 1 [4:1] "In those **days** and at that time, when I restore the fortunes
3: 14 [4:14] For the **day** *of* the LORD is near in the valley of decision.
3: 18 [4:18] "In that **day** the mountains will drip new wine, and the hills
Am 1: 1 **when** [+928] Uzziah was king of Judah and Jeroboam son of
1: 1 of Judah and **[RPH]** Jeroboam son of Jehoash was king of Israel.
1: 14 will consume her fortresses amid war cries on the **day** *of* battle,
1: 14 war cries on the day of battle, amid violent winds on a stormy **day**.
2: 16 Even the bravest warriors will flee naked on that **day**,"
3: 14 "On the **day** I punish Israel for her sins, I will destroy the altars of
4: 2 "The **time** will surely come when you will be taken away with
4: 4 Bring your sacrifices every morning, your tithes every three **years**.
5: 8 who turns blackness into dawn and darkens **day** into night,
5: 18 Woe to you who long for the **day** *of* the LORD! Why do you long
5: 18 Why do you long for the **day** *of* the LORD? That day will be
5: 20 Will not the **day** *of* the LORD be darkness, not light—pitch-dark,
6: 3 You put off the evil **day** and bring near a reign of terror.
8: 3 "In that **day**," declares the Sovereign LORD, "the songs in the
8: 9 "In that **day**," declares the Sovereign LORD, "I will make the sun
8: 9 go down at noon and darken the earth in **broad daylight** [+240].
8: 10 like mourning for an only son and the end of it like a bitter **day**.
8: 11 "The **days** are coming," declares the Sovereign LORD, "when I
8: 13 "In that **day** "the lovely young women and strong young men will
9: 11 "In that **day** I will restore David's fallen tent. I will repair its
9: 11 restore its ruins, and build it as it **used** [+6409] **to be**,
9: 13 "The **days** are coming," declares the LORD, "when the reaper
Ob 1: 8 "In that **day**," declares the LORD, "will I not destroy the wise
1: 11 On the **day** you stood aloof while strangers carried off his wealth
1: 11 On the day you stood aloof **while** [+928] strangers carried off his
1: 12 You should not look down on **[RPH]** your brother in the day of
1: 12 You should not look down on your brother in the **day** *of* his
1: 12 nor rejoice over the people of Judah in the **day** *of* their destruction,
1: 12 of their destruction, nor boast so much in the **day** *of* their trouble.
1: 13 You should not march through the gates of my people in the **day** *of*
1: 13 nor look down on them in their calamity in the **day** *of* their
1: 13 of their disaster, nor seize their wealth in the **day** *of* their disaster.
1: 14 nor hand over their survivors in the **day** *of* their trouble.
1: 15 "The **day** *of* the LORD is near for all nations. As you have done,
Jnh 1: 17 [2:1] and Jonah was inside the fish three **days** and three nights.
3: 3 Nineveh was a very important city—a visit required three **days**.
3: 4 On the first **day**, Jonah started into the city. He proclaimed:
3: 4 "Forty more **days** and Nineveh will be overturned."
Mic 1: 1 that came to Micah of Moresheth during the **reigns** *of* Jotham,
2: 4 In that **day** men will ridicule you; they will taunt you with this
3: 6 sun will set for the prophets, and the **day** will go dark for them.
4: 1 In the last **days** the mountain of the LORD's temple will be
4: 6 "In that **day**," declares the LORD, "I will gather the lame;
5: 2 [5:1] whose origins are from of old, from ancient **times**."
5: 10 [5:9] "In that **day**," declares the LORD, "I will destroy your
7: 4 The **day** *of* your watchmen has come, the day God visits you.
7: 11 The **day** for building your walls will come, the day for extending
7: 11 your walls will come, the **day** for extending your boundaries.
7: 12 In that **day** people will come to you from Assyria and the cities of
7: 14 Let them feed in Bashan and Gilead as in **days** long ago.
7: 15 "As in the **days** *when* you came out of Egypt, I will show them my
7: 20 as you pledged on oath to our fathers in **days** long ago.
Na 1: 7 The LORD is good, a refuge in **times** *of* trouble. He cares for
2: 3 [2:4] The metal on the chariots flashes on the **day** they are made
3: 17 like swarms of locusts that settle in the walls on a cold **day**—
Hab 1: 5 For I am going to do something in your **days** that you would not

Hab 3: 16 Yet I will wait patiently for the **day** *of* calamity to come on the
Zep 1: 1 during the **reign** *of* Josiah son of Amon king of Judah:
1: 7 before the Sovereign LORD, for the **day** *of* the LORD is near.
1: 8 On the **day** *of* the LORD's sacrifice I will punish the princes
1: 9 On that **day** I will punish all who avoid stepping on the threshold,
1: 10 "On that **day**," declares the LORD, "a cry will go up from the
1: 14 "The great **day** *of* the LORD is near—near and coming quickly.
1: 14 The cry on the **day** *of* the LORD will be bitter, the shouting of the
1: 15 That **day** will be a day of wrath, a day of distress and anguish,
1: 15 That day will be a **day** *of* wrath, a day of distress and anguish,
1: 15 a **day** *of* distress and anguish, a day of trouble and ruin, a day of
1: 15 a day of distress and anguish, a **day** *of* trouble and ruin, a day of
1: 15 a day of trouble and ruin, a **day** *of* darkness and gloom,
1: 15 a day of darkness and gloom, a **day** *of* clouds and blackness,
1: 16 a **day** *of* trumpet and battle cry against the fortified cities
1: 18 gold will be able to save them on the **day** *of* the LORD's wrath.
2: 2 the appointed time arrives and that **day** sweeps on like chaff,
2: 2 upon you, before the **day** *of* the LORD's wrath comes upon you.
2: 3 perhaps you will be sheltered on the **day** *of* the LORD's anger.
3: 8 declares the LORD, "for the **day** I will stand up to testify.
3: 11 On that **day** you will not be put to shame for all the wrongs you
3: 16 On that **day** they will say to Jerusalem, "Do not fear, O Zion;
Hag 1: 1 the second year of King Darius, on the first **day** of the sixth month,
1: 15 on the twenty-fourth **day** of the sixth month in the second year of
2: 15 " 'Now give careful thought to this from this **day** on—consider
2: 18 'From this **day** on, from this twenty-fourth day of the ninth month,
2: 18 'From this day on, from this twenty-fourth **day** of the ninth month,
2: 18 give careful thought to the **day** when the foundation of the
2: 19 tree have not borne fruit. " 'From this **day** on I will bless you.' "
2: 23 " 'On that **day**,' declares the LORD Almighty, 'I will take you,
Zec 1: 7 On the twenty-fourth **day** of the eleventh month, the month of
2: 11 [2:15] "Many nations will be joined with the LORD in that **day**
3: 9 'and I will remove the sin of this land in a single **day**.
3: 10 " 'In that **day** each of you will invite his neighbor to sit under his
4: 10 "Who despises the **day** *of* small things? Men will rejoice when
6: 10 Go the same **day** to the house of Josiah son of Zephaniah.
8: 4 of Jerusalem, each with cane in hand because of his **age** [+8044].
8: 6 "It may seem marvelous to the remnant of this people at that **time**,
8: 9 "You who **now** [+465+928+2021+2021] hear these words spoken
8: 9 **when** [+928] the foundation was laid for the house of the LORD
8: 10 Before that **time** there were no wages for man or beast. No one
8: 11 deal with the remnant of this people as I did in the **past** [+8037],"
8: 15 "so **now** [+465+928+2021+2021] I have determined to do good
8: 23 "In those **days** ten men from all languages and nations will take
9: 12 even **now** [+2021] I announce that I will restore twice as much to
9: 16 The LORD their God will save them on that **day** as the flock of
11: 11 It was revoked on that **day**, and so the afflicted of the flock who
12: 3 On that **day**, when all the nations of the earth are gathered against
12: 4 On that **day** I will strike every horse with panic and its rider with
12: 6 "On that **day** I will make the leaders of Judah like a firepot in a
12: 8 On that **day** the LORD will shield those who live in Jerusalem,
12: 8 like the Angel of the LORD going before them. **[RPH]**
12: 9 On that **day** I will set out to destroy all the nations that attack
12: 11 On that **day** the weeping in Jerusalem will be great,
13: 1 "On that **day** a fountain will be opened to the house of David
13: 2 "On that **day**, I will banish the names of the idols from the land,
13: 4 "On that **day** every prophet will be ashamed of his prophetic
14: 1 A **day** of the LORD is coming when your plunder will be divided
14: 3 fight against those nations, as **[RPH]** he fights in the day of battle.
14: 3 and fight against those nations, as he fights in the **day** *of* battle.
14: 4 On that **day** his feet will stand on the Mount of Olives, east of
14: 5 You will flee as you fled from the earthquake in the **days** *of*
14: 6 On that **day** there will be no light, no cold or frost.
14: 7 It will be a unique **day**, without daytime or nighttime—a day
14: 7 It will be a unique day, without **daytime** or nighttime—a day
14: 8 On that **day** living water will flow out from Jerusalem, half to the
14: 9 On that **day** there will be one LORD, and his name the only
14: 13 On that **day** men will be stricken by the LORD with great panic.
14: 20 On that **day** HOLY TO THE LORD will be inscribed on the bells
14: 21 on that **day** there will no longer be a Canaanite in the house of the
Mal 3: 2 who can endure the **day** *of* his coming? Who can stand when he
3: 4 acceptable to the LORD, as in **days** gone by, as in former years.
3: 7 Ever since the **time** *of* your forefathers you have turned away from
3: 17 "in the **day** when I make up my treasured possession.
4: 1 [3:19] "Surely the **day** is coming; it will burn like a furnace. All
4: 1 [3:19] that **day** that is coming will set them on fire," says the
4: 3 [3:21] they will be ashes under the soles of your feet on the **day**
4: 5 [3:23] before that great and dreadful **day** *of* the LORD comes.

3428 יוֹם² *yôm²*, n.m. Not used in NIV/BHS

3429 יוֹמָם *yômām*, subst. & adv. [51] [√ 3427]

day [23], by day [19], in the daytime [2], by day [+928] [1], constant [1], day after day [+9458] [1], during the day [1], during the daytime [1], every day [1], in daytime [1]

Ex 13: 21 **By day** the LORD went ahead of them in a pillar of cloud to
13: 21 of fire to give them light, so that they could travel **by day** or night.
13: 22 Neither the pillar of cloud **by day** nor the pillar of fire by night left
40: 38 So the cloud of the LORD was over the tabernacle **by day**,
Lev 8: 35 You must stay at the entrance to the Tent of Meeting **day** and night
Nu 9: 21 Whether **by day** or by night, whenever the cloud lifted, they set
10: 34 The cloud of the LORD was over them **by day** when they set out
14: 14 that you go before them in a pillar of cloud **by day** and a pillar of
Dt 1: 33 in fire by night and in a cloud **by day**, to search out places for you
28: 66 filled with dread both night and **day**, never sure of your life.
Jos 1: 8 meditate on it **day** and night, so that you may be careful to do
Jdg 6: 27 the men of the town, he did it at night rather than **in the daytime**.
1Sa 25: 16 **day** they were a wall around us all the time we were herding our
2Sa 21: 10 she did not let the birds of the air touch them **by day** or the wild
1Ki 8: 59 before the LORD, be near to the LORD our God **day** and night,
1Ch 9: 33 because they were responsible for the work **day** and night.
2Ch 6: 20 May your eyes be open toward this temple **day** and night,
Ne 1: 6 open to hear the prayer your servant is praying before you **day**
4: 9 [4:3] we prayed to our God and posted a guard **day** and night to
9: 12 **By day** you led them with a pillar of cloud, and by night with a
9: 19 compassion you did not abandon them in the desert. **By day** [+928]
Job 5: 14 Darkness comes upon them **in the daytime**; at noon they grope as
24: 16 men break into houses, but **by day** they shut themselves in;
Ps 1: 2 the law of the LORD, and on his law he meditates **day** and night.
13: 2 [13:3] with my thoughts and **every day** have sorrow in my heart?
22: 2 [22:3] O my God, I cry out **by day**, but you do not answer, by
32: 4 For **day** and night your hand was heavy upon me; my strength was
42: 3 [42:4] My tears have been my food **day** and night, while men say
42: 8 [42:9] **By day** the LORD directs his love, at night his song is
55: 10 [55:11] **Day** and night they prowl about on its walls; malice
78: 14 He guided them with the cloud **by day** and with light from the fire
91: 5 will not fear the terror of night, nor the arrow that flies **by day**,
121: 6 the sun will not harm you **by day**, nor the moon by night.
Isa 4: 5 and over those who assemble there a cloud of smoke **by day**
4: 6 It will be a shelter and shade from the heat of the **day**, and a refuge
21: 8 And the lookout shouted, "**Day** [+9458] **after day**, my lord,
34: 10 It will not be quenched night and **day**; its smoke will rise forever.
60: 11 gates will always stand open, they will never be shut, **day** or night,
60: 19 The sun will no more be your light **by day**, nor will the brightness
Jer 9: 1 [8:23] I would weep **day** and night for the slain of my people.
14: 17 " 'Let my eyes overflow with tears night and **day** without ceasing;
15: 9 Her sun will set while it is still **day**; she will be disgraced
16: 13 there you will serve other gods **day** and night, for I will show you
31: 35 he who appoints the sun to shine **by day**, who decrees the moon
33: 20 so that **day** and night no longer come at their appointed time,
33: 25 'If I have not established my covenant with **day** and night
La 2: 18 the Daughter of Zion, let your tears flow like a river **day** and night;
Eze 12: 3 son of man, pack your belongings for exile and **in the daytime**,
12: 4 **During the daytime**, while they watch, bring out your belongings
12: 7 **During the day** I brought out my things packed for exile.
30: 16 will be taken by storm; Memphis will be in **constant** distress.

3430 יָוָן *yāwān*, n.pr.g. [11] [→ 3436]

Greece [6], Javan [4], Greeks [1]

Ge 10: 2 Gomer, Magog, Madai, **Javan**, Tubal, Meshech and Tiras.
10: 4 The sons of **Javan**: Elishah, Tarshish, the Kittim and the Rodanim.
1Ch 1: 5 Gomer, Magog, Madai, **Javan**, Tubal, Meshech and Tiras.
1: 7 The sons of **Javan**: Elishah, Tarshish, the Kittim and the Rodanim.
Isa 66: 19 the Libyans and Lydians (famous as archers), to Tubal and **Greece**,
Eze 27: 13 " '**Greece**, Tubal and Meshech traded with you; they exchanged
27: 19 " 'Danites and **Greeks** from Uzal bought your merchandise;
Da 8: 21 The shaggy goat is the king of **Greece**, and the large horn between
10: 20 prince of Persia, and when I go, the prince of **Greece** will come;
11: 2 his wealth, he will stir up everyone against the kingdom of **Greece**.
Zec 9: 13 I will rouse your sons, O Zion, against your sons, O **Greece**,

3431 יָוֵן *yāwēn*, n.[m.]. [2]

mire [1], miry [1]

Ps 40: 2 [40:3] He lifted me out of the slimy pit, out of the mud and **mire**;
69: 2 [69:3] I sink in the **miry** depths, where there is no foothold. I have

3432 יוֹנָדָב *yônādāb*, n.pr.m. [7] [√ 3378 + 5605]

Jonadab [7]

2Sa 13: 3 Now Amnon had a friend named **Jonadab** son of Shimeah,
13: 3 of Shimeah, David's brother. **Jonadab** was a very shrewd man.
13: 32 **Jonadab** son of Shimeah, David's brother, said, "My lord should
13: 35 **Jonadab** said to the king, "See, the king's sons are here; it has

Jer 35: 6 because our forefather **Jonadab** son of Recab gave us this
35: 10 have fully obeyed everything our forefather **Jonadab** commanded
35: 19 '**Jonadab** son of Recab will never fail to have a man to serve

3433 יוֹנָה¹ ***yônâ¹***, n.f. [32] [→ 1807, 3434; cf. 627, 3039]
dove [14], doves [8], pigeons [8], pigeon [2]

Ge 8: 8 he sent out a **dove** to see if the water had receded from the surface
8: 9 the **dove** could find no place to set its feet because there was water
8: 10 waited seven more days and again sent out the **dove** from the ark.
8: 11 When the **dove** returned to him in the evening, there in its beak
8: 12 He waited seven more days and sent the **dove** out again, but this
Lev 1: 14 is a burnt offering of birds, he is to offer a dove or a young **pigeon**.
5: 7 or two young **pigeons** to the LORD as a penalty for his sin—
5: 11 however, he cannot afford two doves or two young **pigeons**,
12: 6 a burnt offering and a young **pigeon** or a dove for a sin offering.
12: 8 she is to bring two doves or two young **pigeons**, one for a burnt
14: 22 and two doves or two young **pigeons**, which he can afford,
14: 30 he shall sacrifice the doves or the young **pigeons**, which the person
15: 14 On the eighth day he must take two doves or two young **pigeons**
15: 29 On the eighth day she must take two doves or two young **pigeons**
Nu 6: 10 or two young **pigeons** to the priest at the entrance to the Tent of
Ps 55: 6 [55:7] I said, "Oh, that I had the wings of a **dove**! I would fly
56: T [56:1] To ˻the tune of˼ "A **Dove** *on* Distant Oaks." Of David.
68: 13 [68:14] the wings of ˻my˼ **dove** are sheathed with silver, its
SS 1: 15 you are, my darling! Oh, how beautiful! Your eyes are **doves**.
2: 14 My **dove** in the clefts of the rock, in the hiding places on the
4: 1 Oh, how beautiful! Your eyes behind your veil are **doves**.
5: 2 "Open to me, my sister, my darling, my **dove**, my flawless one.
5: 12 His eyes are like **doves** by the water streams, washed in milk,
6: 9 my **dove**, my perfect one, is unique, the only daughter of her
Isa 38: 14 I cried like a swift or thrush, I moaned like a mourning **dove**.
59: 11 We all growl like bears; we moan mournfully like **doves**. We look
60: 8 "Who are these that fly along like clouds, like **doves** to their nests?
Jer 48: 28 in Moab. Be like a **dove** that makes its nest at the mouth of a cave.
Eze 7: 16 moaning like **doves** *of* the valleys, each because of his sins.
Hos 7: 11 "Ephraim is like a **dove**, easily deceived and senseless—
11: 11 come trembling like birds from Egypt, like **doves** from Assyria.
Na 2: 7 [2:8] Its slave girls moan like **doves** and beat upon their breasts.

3434 יוֹנָה² ***yônâ²***, n.pr.m. [19] [√ 3433]
Jonah [18], Jonah's [1]

2Ki 14: 25 God of Israel, spoken through his servant **Jonah** son of Amittai,
Jnh 1: 1 The word of the LORD came to **Jonah** son of Amittai:
1: 3 But **Jonah** ran away from the LORD and headed for Tarshish.
1: 5 **Jonah** had gone below deck, where he lay down and fell into a
1: 7 for this calamity." They cast lots and the lot fell on **Jonah**.
1: 15 they took **Jonah** and threw him overboard, and the raging sea grew
1: 17 [2:1] the LORD provided a great fish to swallow **Jonah**,
1: 17 [2:1] and **Jonah** was inside the fish three days and three nights.
2: 1 [2:2] From inside the fish **Jonah** prayed to the LORD his God.
2: 10 [2:11] commanded the fish, and it vomited **Jonah** onto dry land.
3: 1 Then the word of the LORD came to **Jonah** a second time:
3: 3 **Jonah** obeyed the word of the LORD and went to Nineveh.
3: 4 On the first day, **Jonah** started into the city. He proclaimed:
4: 1 But **Jonah** was greatly displeased and became angry.
4: 5 **Jonah** went out and sat down at a place east of the city. There he
4: 6 made it grow up over **Jonah** to give shade for his head to ease his
4: 6 to ease his discomfort, and **Jonah** was very happy about the vine.
4: 8 and the sun blazed on **Jonah's** head so that he grew faint.
4: 9 God said to **Jonah**, "Do you have a right to be angry about the

3435 יוֹנָה³ ***yônâ³***, n.[m.] *or* v.ptcp. Not used in NIV/BHS [cf. 3561]

3436 יְוָנִי ***yᵉwānî***, a.g. [1] [√ 3430]
Greeks [+1201] [1]

Joel 3: 6 [4:6] the people of Judah and Jerusalem to the **Greeks** [+1201],

3437 יוֹנֵק ***yônēq***, n.m. [12] [√ 3567]
infants [6], infant [2], infant's [1], nursed [1], nursing [1], tender shoot [1]

Nu 11: 12 you tell me to carry them in my arms, as a nurse carries an **infant**,
Dt 32: 25 and young women will perish, **infants** and gray-haired men.
1Sa 15: 3 children and **infants**, cattle and sheep, camels and donkeys.' "
22: 19 with its men and women, its children and **infants**, and its cattle,
Ps 8: 2 [8:3] the lips of children and **infants** you have ordained praise
SS 8: 1 to me like a brother, *who* was **nursed** *at* my mother's breasts!
Isa 11: 8 The **infant** will play near the hole of the cobra, and the young child
53: 2 He grew up before him like a **tender shoot**, and like a root out of
Jer 44: 7 the children and **infants**, and so leave yourselves without a
La 2: 11 because children and **infants** faint in the streets of the city.
4: 4 Because of thirst the **infant's** tongue sticks to the roof of its mouth;
Joel 2: 16 the elders, gather the children, *those* **nursing** *at* the breast.

3438 יוֹנֶקֶת ***yôneqet***, n.f. [6] [√ 3567]
shoots [4], new shoots [1], young shoots [1]

Job 8: 16 plant in the sunshine, spreading its **shoots** over the garden;
14: 7 it is cut down, it will sprout again, and its **new shoots** will not fail.
15: 30 a flame will wither his **shoots**, and the breath of God's mouth will
Ps 80: 11 [80:12] out its boughs to the Sea, its **shoots** as far as the River.
Eze 17: 22 I will break off a tender sprig from its topmost **shoots** and plant it
Hos 14: 6 [14:7] his **young shoots** will grow. His splendor will be like an

3439 יוֹנַת אֵלֶם רְחֹקִים ***yônat 'ēlem rᵉḥōqîm***, tt. Not used in NIV/BHS [√ 3433 + 381 + 8178]

3440 יוֹנָתָן ***yônātān***, n.pr.m. [42] [√ 3378 + 5989]
Jonathan [42]

1Sa 13: 2 and a thousand were with **Jonathan** at Gibeah in Benjamin.
13: 3 **Jonathan** attacked the Philistine outpost at Geba,
13: 16 Saul and his son **Jonathan** and the men with them were staying in
13: 22 a soldier with Saul and **Jonathan** had a sword or spear in his hand;
13: 22 or spear in his hand; only Saul and his son **Jonathan** had them.
14: 1 One day **Jonathan** son of Saul said to the young man bearing his
14: 3 priest in Shiloh. No one was aware that **Jonathan** had left.
14: 4 On each side of the pass that **Jonathan** intended to cross to reach
14: 12 The men of the outpost shouted to **Jonathan** and his armor-bearer,
14: 12 So **Jonathan** said to his armor-bearer, "Climb up after me;
14: 13 **Jonathan** climbed up, using his hands and feet, with his
14: 13 The Philistines fell before **Jonathan**, and his armor-bearer
14: 14 In that first attack **Jonathan** and his armor-bearer killed some
14: 17 it was **Jonathan** and his armor-bearer who were not there.
14: 21 went over to the Israelites who were with Saul and **Jonathan**.
14: 27 **Jonathan** had not heard that his father had bound the people with
14: 29 **Jonathan** said, "My father has made trouble for the country.
14: 39 Israel lives, even if it lies with my son **Jonathan**, he must die."
14: 40 stand over there; I and **Jonathan** my son will stand over here."
14: 41 **Jonathan** and Saul were taken by lot, and the men were cleared.
14: 42 Saul said, "Cast the lot between me and **Jonathan** my son."
14: 42 lot between me and Jonathan my son." And **Jonathan** was taken.
14: 43 Then Saul said to **Jonathan**, "Tell me what you have done."
14: 43 So **Jonathan** told him, "I merely tasted a little honey with the end
14: 44 deal with me, be it ever so severely, if you do not die, **Jonathan**."
14: 45 the men said to Saul, "Should **Jonathan** die—he who has brought
14: 45 So the men rescued **Jonathan**, and he was not put to death.
14: 49 Saul's sons were **Jonathan**, Ishvi and Malki-Shua. The name of
19: 1 Saul told his son **Jonathan** and all the attendants to kill David.
1Ki 1: 42 as he was speaking, **Jonathan** son of Abiathar the priest arrived.
1: 43 "Not at all!" **Jonathan** answered. "Our lord King David has made
1Ch 2: 32 The sons of Jada, Shammai's brother: Jether and **Jonathan**.
2: 33 The sons of **Jonathan**: Peleth and Zaza. These were the
10: 2 and they killed his sons **Jonathan**, Abinadab and Malki-Shua.
11: 34 of Hashem the Gizonite, **Jonathan** son of Shagee the Hararite,
Ezr 8: 6 descendants of Adin, Ebed son of **Jonathan**, and with him 50 men;
10: 15 Only **Jonathan** son of Asahel and Jahzeiah son of Tikvah,
Ne 12: 11 Joiada the father of **Jonathan**, and Jonathan the father of Jaddua.
12: 11 Joiada the father of Jonathan, and **Jonathan** the father of Jaddua.
12: 14 of Malluch's, **Jonathan**; of Shecaniah's, Joseph;
12: 35 and also Zechariah son of **Jonathan**, the son of Shemaiah,
Jer 40: 8 son of Nethaniah, Johanan and **Jonathan** the sons of Kareah,

3441 יוֹסֵף ***yôsēp***, n.pr.m. [213] [√ 3578]
Joseph [180], Joseph's [19], he[s] [5], him[s] [4], Joseph [+1201] [2], *untranslated* [1], his[s] [1], they[s] [+1074] [1]

Ge 30: 24 She named him **Joseph**, and said, "May the LORD add to me
30: 25 After Rachel gave birth to **Joseph**, Jacob said to Laban, "Send me
33: 2 Leah and her children next, and Rachel and **Joseph** in the rear.
33: 7 Last of all came **Joseph** and Rachel, and they too bowed down.
35: 24 The sons of Rachel: **Joseph** and Benjamin.
37: 2 **Joseph**, a young man of seventeen, was tending the flocks with his
37: 2 and **he**[s] brought their father a bad report about them.
37: 3 Now Israel loved **Joseph** more than any of his other sons,
37: 5 **Joseph** had a dream, and when he told it to his brothers, they hated
37: 13 Israel said to **Joseph**, "As you know, your brothers are grazing the
37: 17 'Let's go to Dothan.' " So **Joseph** went after his brothers and found
37: 23 So when **Joseph** came to his brothers, they stripped him of his
37: 23 when Joseph came to his brothers, they stripped **him**[s] of his robe—
37: 28 his brothers pulled **Joseph** up out of the cistern and sold him for
37: 28 and sold **him**[s] for twenty shekels of silver to the Ishmaelites,
37: 28 shekels of silver to the Ishmaelites, who took **him**[s] to Egypt.
37: 29 Reuben returned to the cistern and saw that **Joseph** was not there,

Ge 37:31 they got **Joseph's** robe, slaughtered a goat and dipped the robe in
37:33 animal has devoured him. **Joseph** has surely been torn to pieces."
39: 1 Now **Joseph** had been taken down to Egypt. Potiphar, an Egyptian
39: 2 The LORD was with **Joseph** and he prospered, and he lived in the
39: 4 **Joseph** found favor in his eyes and became his attendant. Potiphar
39: 5 LORD blessed the household of the Egyptian because of **Joseph**.
39: 6 So he left in **Joseph's** care everything he had; with Joseph in
39: 6 except the food he ate. Now **Joseph** was well-built and handsome,
39: 7 and after a while his master's wife took notice of **Joseph** and said,
39:10 though she spoke to **Joseph** day after day, he refused to go to bed
39:20 **Joseph's** master took him and put him in prison, the place where
39:21 the LORD was with **him**[s]; he showed him kindness and granted
39:22 So the warden put **Joseph** in charge of all those held in the prison,
40: 3 of the guard, in the same prison where **Joseph** was confined.
40: 4 The captain of the guard assigned them to **Joseph**, and he attended
40: 6 When **Joseph** came to them the next morning, he saw that they
40: 8 Then **Joseph** said to them, "Do not interpretations belong to God?
40: 9 So the chief cupbearer told **Joseph** his dream. He said to him,
40:12 "This is what it means," **Joseph** said to him. "The three branches
40:16 a favorable interpretation, he said to **Joseph**, "I too had a dream:
40:18 "This is what it means," **Joseph** said. "The three baskets are three
40:22 chief baker, just as **Joseph** had said to them in his interpretation.
40:23 The chief cupbearer, however, did not remember **Joseph**;
41:14 So Pharaoh sent for **Joseph**, and he was quickly brought from the
41:15 Pharaoh said to **Joseph**, "I had a dream, and no one can interpret it.
41:16 "I cannot do it," **Joseph** replied to Pharaoh, "but God will give
41:17 Pharaoh said to **Joseph**, "In my dream I was standing on the bank
41:25 Then **Joseph** said to Pharaoh, "The dreams of Pharaoh are one
41:39 Pharaoh said to **Joseph**, "Since God has made all this known to
41:41 So Pharaoh said to **Joseph**, "I hereby put you in charge of the
41:42 took his signet ring from his finger and put it on **Joseph's** finger.
41:44 Pharaoh said to **Joseph**, "I am Pharaoh, but without your word no
41:45 Pharaoh gave **Joseph** the name Zaphenath-Paneah and gave him
41:45 to be his wife. And **Joseph** went throughout the land of Egypt.
41:46 **Joseph** was thirty years old when he entered the service of Pharaoh
41:46 **Joseph** went out from Pharaoh's presence and traveled throughout
41:49 **Joseph** stored up huge quantities of grain, like the sand of the sea;
41:50 two sons were born to **Joseph** by Asenath daughter of Potiphera,
41:51 **Joseph** named his firstborn Manasseh and said, "It is because God
41:54 and the seven years of famine began, just as **Joseph** had said.
41:55 told all the Egyptians, "Go to **Joseph** and do what he tells you."
41:56 **Joseph** opened the storehouses and sold grain to the Egyptians,
41:57 And all the countries came to Egypt to buy grain from **Joseph**,
42: 3 Then ten of **Joseph's** brothers went down to buy grain from Egypt.
42: 4 Jacob did not send Benjamin, **Joseph's** brother, with the others,
42: 6 Now **Joseph** was the governor of the land, the one who sold grain
42: 6 So when **Joseph's** brothers arrived, they bowed down to him with
42: 7 As soon as **Joseph** saw his brothers, he recognized them, but he
42: 8 Although **Joseph** recognized his brothers, they did not recognize
42: 9 Then **he**[s] remembered his dreams about them and said to them,
42:14 **Joseph** said to them, "It is just as I told you: You are spies!
42:18 **Joseph** said to them, "Do this and you will live, for I fear God:
42:23 They did not realize that **Joseph** could understand them, since he
42:25 **Joseph** gave orders to fill their bags with grain, to put each man's
42:36 **Joseph** is no more and Simeon is no more, and now you want to
43:15 They hurried down to Egypt and presented themselves to **Joseph**.
43:16 When **Joseph** saw Benjamin with them, he said to the steward of
43:17 The man did as **Joseph** told him and took the men to Joseph's
43:17 man did as Joseph told him and took the men to **Joseph's** house.
43:18 Now the men were frightened when they were taken to **his**[s] house.
43:19 So they went up to **Joseph's** steward and spoke to him at the
43:24 The steward took the men into **Joseph's** house, gave them water to
43:25 They prepared their gifts for **Joseph's** arrival at noon, because they
43:26 When **Joseph** came home, they presented to him the gifts they had
43:30 of his brother, **Joseph** hurried out and looked for a place to weep.
44: 2 along with the silver for his grain." And he did as **Joseph** said.
44: 4 They had not gone far from the city when **Joseph** said to his
44:14 **Joseph** was still in the house when Judah and his brothers came in,
44:15 **Joseph** said to them, "What is this you have done? Don't you
45: 1 **Joseph** could no longer control himself before all his attendants,
45: 1 So there was no one with **Joseph** when he made himself known to
45: 3 **Joseph** said to his brothers, "I am Joseph! Is my father still
45: 3 Joseph said to his brothers, "I am **Joseph**! Is my father still
45: 4 **Joseph** said to his brothers, "Come close to me." When they had
45: 4 When they had done so, he said, "I am your brother **Joseph**,
45: 9 to my father and say to him, 'This is what your son **Joseph** says:
45:16 When the news reached Pharaoh's palace that **Joseph's** brothers
45:17 Pharaoh said to **Joseph**, "Tell your brothers, 'Do this: Load your
45:21 **Joseph** gave them carts, as Pharaoh had commanded, and he also
45:26 They told him, "**Joseph** is still alive! In fact, he is ruler of all
45:27 But when they told him everything **Joseph** had said to them,
45:27 and when he saw the carts **Joseph** had sent to carry him back,
45:28 My son **Joseph** is still alive. I will go and see him before I die."
46: 4 you back again. And **Joseph's** own hand will close your eyes."
46:19 The sons of Jacob's wife Rachel: **Joseph** and Benjamin.
46:20 Ephraim were born to **Joseph** by Asenath daughter of Potiphera,
46:27 With the two sons who had been born to **Joseph** in Egypt,
46:28 Now Jacob sent Judah ahead of him to **Joseph** to get directions to
46:29 **Joseph** had his chariot made ready and went to Goshen to meet his
46:30 Israel said to **Joseph**, "Now I am ready to die, since I have seen for
46:31 Then **Joseph** said to his brothers and to his father's household,
47: 1 **Joseph** went and told Pharaoh, "My father and brothers, with their
47: 5 Pharaoh said to **Joseph**, "Your father and your brothers have come
47: 7 **Joseph** brought his father Jacob in and presented him before
47:11 So **Joseph** settled his father and his brothers in Egypt and gave
47:12 **Joseph** also provided his father and his brothers and all his father's
47:14 **Joseph** collected all the money that was to be found in Egypt
47:14 the grain they were buying, and **he**[s] brought it to Pharaoh's palace.
47:15 was gone, all Egypt came to **Joseph** and said, "Give us food.
47:16 "Then bring your livestock," said **Joseph**. "I will sell you food in
47:17 So they brought their livestock to **Joseph**, and he gave them food
47:17 and **he**[s] gave them food in exchange for their horses, their sheep
47:20 So **Joseph** bought all the land in Egypt for Pharaoh. The
47:23 **Joseph** said to the people, "Now that I have bought you and your
47:26 So **Joseph** established it as a law concerning land in Egypt—
47:29 he called for his son **Joseph** and said to him, "If I have found favor
48: 1 Some time later **Joseph** was told, "Your father is ill." So he took
48: 2 When Jacob was told, "Your son **Joseph** has come to you,"
48: 3 Jacob said to **Joseph**, "God Almighty appeared to me at Luz in the
48: 8 When Israel saw the sons of **Joseph**, he asked, "Who are these?"
48: 9 are the sons God has given me here," **Joseph** said to his father.
48:11 Israel said to **Joseph**, "I never expected to see your face again,
48:12 **Joseph** removed them from Israel's knees and bowed down with
48:13 **Joseph** took both of them, Ephraim on his right toward Israel's left
48:15 he blessed **Joseph** and said, "May the God before whom my
48:17 When **Joseph** saw his father placing his right hand on Ephraim's
48:18 **Joseph** said to him, "No, my father, this one is the firstborn;
48:21 Israel said to **Joseph**, "I am about to die, but God will be with you
49:22 "**Joseph** is a fruitful vine, a fruitful vine near a spring,
49:26 Let all these rest on the head of **Joseph**, on the brow of the prince
50: 1 **Joseph** threw himself upon his father and wept over him
50: 2 **Joseph** directed the physicians in his service to embalm his father
50: 4 **Joseph** said to Pharaoh's court, "If I have found favor in your
50: 7 So **Joseph** went up to bury his father. All Pharaoh's officials
50: 8 besides all the members of **Joseph's** household and his brothers
50:14 After burying his father, **Joseph** returned to Egypt, together with
50:15 When **Joseph's** brothers saw that their father was dead, they said,
50:15 "What if **Joseph** holds a grudge against us and pays us back for all
50:16 So they sent word to **Joseph**, saying, "Your father left these
50:17 'This is what you are to say to **Joseph**: I ask you to forgive your
50:17 of your father." When their message came to him, **Joseph** wept.
50:19 **Joseph** said to them, "Don't be afraid. Am I in the place of God?
50:22 **Joseph** stayed in Egypt, along with all his father's family.
50:22 with all his father's family. **He**[s] lived a hundred and ten years
50:23 and saw **[RPH]** the third generation of Ephraim's children.
50:23 of Makir son of Manasseh were placed at birth on **Joseph's** knees.
50:24 **Joseph** said to his brothers, "I am about to die. But God will surely
50:25 And **Joseph** made the sons of Israel swear an oath and said,
50:26 So **Joseph** died at the age of a hundred and ten. And after they
Ex 1: 5 of Jacob numbered seventy in all; **Joseph** was already in Egypt.
1: 6 Now **Joseph** and all his brothers and all that generation died,
1: 8 a new king, who did not know about **Joseph**, came to power in
13:19 Moses took the bones of **Joseph** with him because Joseph had
Nu 1:10 from the sons of **Joseph**: from Ephraim, Elishama son of
1:32 From the sons of **Joseph**: From the descendants of Ephraim:
13: 7 from the tribe of Issachar, Igal son of **Joseph**;
13:11 from the tribe of Manasseh (a tribe of **Joseph**), Gaddi son of Susi;
26:28 The descendants of **Joseph** by their clans through Manasseh
26:37 were 32,500. These were the descendants of **Joseph** by their clans.
27: 1 of Manasseh, belonged to the clans of Manasseh son of **Joseph**.
32:33 the half-tribe of Manasseh son of **Joseph** the kingdom of Sihon
34:23 son of Ephod, the leader from the tribe of Manasseh son of **Joseph**;
36: 1 who were from the clans of the descendants of **Joseph**, came
36: 5 "What the tribe of the descendants of **Joseph** is saying is right.
36:12 within the clans of the descendants of Manasseh son of **Joseph**,
Dt 27:12 the people: Simeon, Levi, Judah, Issachar, **Joseph** and Benjamin.
33:13 About **Joseph** he said: "May the LORD bless his land with the
33:16 Let all these rest on the head of **Joseph**, on the brow of the prince
Jos 14: 4 for the sons of **Joseph** had become two tribes—Manasseh
16: 1 The allotment for **Joseph** [+1201] began at the Jordan of Jericho,
16: 4 So Manasseh and Ephraim, the descendants of **Joseph**,
17: 1 This was the allotment for the tribe of Manasseh as **Joseph's**
17: 2 These are the other male descendants of Manasseh son of **Joseph**
17:14 The people of **Joseph** said to Joshua, "Why have you given us only
17:16 The people of **Joseph** replied, "The hill country is not enough for
17:17 Joshua said to the house of **Joseph**—to Ephraim and Manasseh—
18: 5 on the south and the house of **Joseph** in its territory on the north.
18:11 territory lay between the tribes of Judah and **Joseph** [+1201]:

Jos 24:32 **Joseph's** bones, which the Israelites had brought up from Egypt,
24:32 of Shechem. This became the inheritance of **Joseph's** descendants.
Jdg 1:22 Now the house of **Joseph** attacked Bethel, and the LORD was
1:23 When **they**[s] [+1074] sent men to spy out Bethel (formerly called
1:35 but when the power of the house of **Joseph** increased,
2Sa 19:20 [19:21] as the first of the whole house of **Joseph** to come down
1Ki 11:28 put him in charge of the whole labor force of the house of **Joseph**.
1Ch 2:2 Dan, **Joseph**, Benjamin, Naphtali, Gad and Asher.
5:1 his rights as firstborn were given to the sons of **Joseph** son of
5:2 came from him, the rights of the firstborn belonged to **Joseph**)—
7:29 The descendants of **Joseph** son of Israel lived in these towns.
25:2 From the sons of Asaph: Zaccur, **Joseph**, Nethaniah and Asarelah.
25:9 which was for Asaph, fell to **Joseph**, his sons and relatives,
Ezr 10:42 Shallum, Amariah and **Joseph**.
Ne 12:14 of Malluch's, Jonathan; of Shecaniah's, **Joseph**;
Ps 77:15 [77:16] your people, the descendants of Jacob and **Joseph**.
78:67 he rejected the tents of **Joseph**, he did not choose the tribe of
80:1 [80:2] O Shepherd of Israel, you who lead **Joseph** like a flock;
105:17 and he sent a man before them—**Joseph**, sold as a slave.
Eze 37:16 belonging to **Joseph** and all the house of Israel associated with
37:19 I am going to take the stick of **Joseph**—which is in Ephraim's
47:13 among the twelve tribes of Israel, with two portions for **Joseph**.
48:32 the gate of **Joseph**, the gate of Benjamin and the gate of Dan.
Am 5:6 and live, or he will sweep through the house of **Joseph** like a fire;
5:15 LORD God Almighty will have mercy on the remnant of **Joseph**.
6:6 the finest lotions, but you do not grieve over the ruin of **Joseph**.
Ob 1:18 The house of Jacob will be a fire and the house of **Joseph** a flame;
Zec 10:6 "I will strengthen the house of Judah and save the house of **Joseph**.

3442 יוֹסִפְיָה *yôsipyâ*, n.pr.m. [1] [√ 3578 + 3378]

Josiphiah [1]

Ezr 8:10 of Bani, Shelomith son of **Josiphiah**, and with him 160 men;

3443 יוֹעֵאלָה *yô'ē'lâ*, n.pr.m. [1]

Joelah [1]

1Ch 12:7 [12:8] and **Joelah** and Zebadiah the sons of Jeroham from Gedor.

3444 יוֹעֵד *yô'ēd*, n.pr.m. [1] [√ 3378 + 6332]

Joed [1]

Ne 11:7 the son of **Joed**, the son of Pedaiah, the son of Kolaiah, the son of

3445 יוֹעֶזֶר *yô'ezer*, n.pr.m. [1] [√ 3378 + 6469]

Joezer [1]

1Ch 12:6 [12:7] Azarel, **Joezer** and Jashobeam the Korahites;

3446 יוֹעֵץ *yô'ēṣ*, n.m. *or* v.ptcp. [21] [√ 3619]

counselor [7], advisers [6], counselors [5], adviser [1], encouraged [1], one to give counsel [1]

2Sa 15:12 David's **counselor**, to come from Giloh, his hometown.
1Ch 26:14 a wise **counselor**, and the lot for the North Gate fell to him.
27:32 Jonathan, David's uncle, was a **counselor**, a man of insight
27:33 Ahithophel was the king's **counselor**. Hushai the Arkite was the
2Ch 22:3 house of Ahab, for his mother **encouraged** him in doing wrong.
22:4 for after his father's death they became his **advisers**, to his
25:16 king said to him, "Have we appointed you an **adviser** to the king?
Ezr 4:5 They hired **counselors** to work against them and frustrate their
7:28 the king and his **advisers** and all the king's powerful officials.
8:25 his **advisers**, his officials and all Israel present there had donated
Job 3:14 with kings and **counselors** *of* the earth, who built for themselves
12:17 He leads **counselors** away stripped and makes fools of judges.
Pr 11:14 of guidance a nation falls, but many **advisers** make victory sure.
15:22 fail for lack of counsel, but with many **advisers** they succeed.
24:6 for waging war you need guidance, and for victory many **advisers**.
Isa 1:26 your judges as in days of old, your **counselors** as at the beginning.
3:3 the captain of fifty and man of rank, the **counselor**, skilled
9:6 [9:5] And he will be called Wonderful **Counselor**, Mighty God,
19:11 but fools; the wise **counselors** *of* Pharaoh give senseless advice.
41:28 no **one** among them **to give counsel**, no one to give answer when I
Mic 4:9 Has your **counselor** perished, that pain seizes you like that of a

3447 יוֹעָשׁ *yô'āš*, n.pr.m. [2] [√ 3378 + 6429]

Joash [2]

1Ch 7:8 Zemirah, **Joash**, Eliezer, Elioenai, Omri, Jeremoth, Abijah,
27:28 western foothills. **Joash** was in charge of the supplies of olive oil.

3448 יוֹצֵאת *yôṣē't*, n.f. *or* v.ptcp. [1] [√ 3655]

going into captivity [1]

Ps 144:14 of walls, no **going into captivity**, no cry of distress in our streets.

3449 יוֹצָדָק *yôṣādāq*, n.pr.m. [4] [√ 3378 + 7405]

Jozadak [4]

Ezr 3:2 Jeshua son of **Jozadak** and his fellow priests and Zerubbabel son
3:8 Jeshua son of **Jozadak** and the rest of their brothers (the priests
10:18 From the descendants of Jeshua son of **Jozadak**, and his brothers:
Ne 12:26 the son of **Jozadak**, and in the days of Nehemiah the governor

3450 יוֹצֵר *yôṣēr*, n.[m.] *or* v.ptcp. [20] [√ 3670]

potter [11], potter's [4], him[s] [+2021] [1], potters [1], pottery [+3998] [1], pottery [+5574] [1], pottery [1]

2Sa 17:28 brought bedding and bowls and articles of **pottery**. They also
1Ch 4:23 They were the **potters** who lived at Netaim and Gederah;
Ps 2:9 iron scepter; you will dash them to pieces like **pottery** [+3998]."
Isa 29:16 upside down, as if the **potter** were thought to be like the clay!
29:16 make me"? Can the pot say of the **potter**, "He knows nothing"?
30:14 It will break in pieces like **pottery** [+5574], shattered so
41:25 as if they were mortar, as if he were a **potter** treading the clay.
45:9 Does the clay say to the **potter**, 'What are you making?' Does your
64:8 [64:7] We are the clay, you are the **potter**; we are all the work of
Jer 18:2 "Go down to the **potter's** house, and there I will give you my
18:3 So I went down to the **potter's** house, and I saw him working at
18:4 so the **potter** formed it into another pot, shaping it as seemed best
18:4 it into another pot, shaping it as seemed best to **him**[s] [+2021].
18:6 "O house of Israel, can I not do with you as this **potter** does?"
18:6 "Like clay in the hand of the **potter**, so are you in my hand,
19:1 is what the LORD says: "Go and buy a clay jar from a **potter**.
19:11 this city just as this **potter's** jar is smashed and cannot be repaired.
La 4:2 are now considered as pots of clay, the work of a **potter's** hands!
Zec 11:13 the LORD said to me, "Throw it to the **potter**"—the handsome
11:13 and threw them into the house of the LORD to the **potter**.

3451 יוֹקִים *yôqîm*, n.pr.m. [1] [√ 3378? + 7756]

Jokim [1]

1Ch 4:22 **Jokim**, the men of Cozeba, and Joash and Saraph, who ruled in

3452 יוֹרֶה¹ *yôreh¹*, n.[m.] *or* v.ptcp. [2] [√ 3721]

archers [1], they[s] [+2021] [1]

1Ch 10:3 and when the archers overtook him, **they**[s] [+2021] wounded him.
2Ch 35:23 **Archers** shot King Josiah, and he told his officers, "Take me

3453 ²יוֹרֶה *yôreh²*, n.[m.]. [2] [√ 8115]

autumn rains [2]

Dt 11:14 both **autumn** and spring **rains**, so that you may gather in your
Jer 5:24 who gives **autumn** and spring **rains** in season, who assures

3454 יוֹרָה *yôrâ*, n.pr.m. [1]

Jorah [1]

Ezr 2:18 of **Jorah** 112

3455 יוֹרַי *yôray*, n.pr.m. [1]

Jorai [1]

1Ch 5:13 Michael, Meshullam, Sheba, **Jorai**, Jacan, Zia and Eber—

3456 יוֹרָם *yôrām*, n.pr.m. [20] [√ 3378 + 8123]

Joram [14], Jehoram [4], him[s] [1], Jehoram's [1]

2Sa 8:10 he sent his son **Joram** to King David to greet him and congratulate
2Ki 8:16 In the fifth year of **Joram** son of Ahab king of Israel,
8:21 So **Jehoram** went to Zair with all his chariots. The Edomites
8:23 As for the other events of **Jehoram's** reign, and all he did,
8:24 **Jehoram** rested with his fathers and was buried with them in the
8:25 In the twelfth year of **Joram** son of Ahab king of Israel,
8:28 Ahaziah went with **Joram** son of Ahab to war against Hazael king
8:28 king of Aram at Ramoth Gilead. The Arameans wounded **Joram**;
8:29 so King **Joram** returned to Jezreel to recover from the wounds the
8:29 king of Judah went down to Jezreel to see **Joram** son of Ahab,
9:14 son of Jehoshaphat, the son of Nimshi, conspired against **Joram**.
9:14 (Now **Joram** and all Israel had been defending Ramoth Gilead
9:16 because **Joram** was resting there and Ahaziah king of Judah had
9:16 and Ahaziah king of Judah had gone down to see **him**[s].
9:29 (In the eleventh year of **Joram** son of Ahab, Ahaziah had become
11:2 the daughter of King **Jehoram** and sister of Ahaziah,
1Ch 3:11 **Jehoram** his son, Ahaziah his son, Joash his son,
26:25 his son, **Joram** his son, Zicri his son and Shelomith his son.
2Ch 22:5 king of Aram at Ramoth Gilead. The Arameans wounded **Joram**;
22:7 Through Ahaziah's visit to **Joram**, God brought about Ahaziah's

3457 יוּשַׁב חֶסֶד **yûšab ḥesed**, n.pr.m. [1]
Jushab-Hesed [1]
1Ch 3:20 Hashubah, Ohel, Berekiah, Hasadiah and **Jushab-Hesed**.

3458 יוֹשִׁבְיָה **yôšibyâ**, n.pr.m. [1] [√ 3782 + 3378]
Joshibiah [1]
1Ch 4:35 Joel, Jehu son of **Joshibiah**, the son of Seraiah, the son of Asiel,

3459 יוֹשָׁה **yôšâ**, n.pr.m. [1]
Joshah [1]
1Ch 4:34 Meshobab, Jamlech, **Joshah** son of Amaziah,

3460 יוֹשַׁוְיָה **yôšawyâ**, n.pr.m. [1] [√ 3782 + 3378]
Joshaviah [1]
1Ch 11:46 Eliel the Mahavite, Jeribai and **Joshaviah** the sons of Elnaam,

3461 יוֹשָׁפָט **yôšāpāṭ**, n.pr.m. [2] [√ 3378 + 9149]
Joshaphat [2]
1Ch 11:43 Hanan son of Maacah, **Joshaphat** the Mithnite,
15:24 **Joshaphat**, Nethanel, Amasai, Zechariah, Benaiah and Eliezer the

3462 יוֹתָם **yôtām**, n.pr.m. [24] [√ 3378 + 9447]
Jotham [22], Jotham's [2]
Jdg 9: 5 But **Jotham**, the youngest son of Jerub-Baal, escaped by hiding.
9: 7 When **Jotham** was told about this, he climbed up on the top of
9:21 **Jotham** fled, escaping to Beer, and he lived there because he was
9:57 The curse of **Jotham** son of Jerub-Baal came on them.
2Ki 15: 5 **Jotham** the king's son had charge of the palace and governed the
15: 7 in the City of David. And **Jotham** his son succeeded him as king.
15:30 succeeded him as king in the twentieth year of **Jotham** son of
15:32 king of Israel, **Jotham** son of Uzziah king of Judah began to reign.
15:36 As for the other events of **Jotham's** reign, and what he did,
15:38 **Jotham** rested with his fathers and was buried with them in the
16: 1 of Remaliah, Ahaz son of **Jotham** king of Judah began to reign.
1Ch 2:47 sons of Jahdai: Regem, **Jotham**, Geshan, Pelet, Ephah and Shaaph.
3:12 Amaziah his son, Azariah his son, **Jotham** his son,
5:17 the genealogical records during the reigns of **Jotham** king of Judah
2Ch 26:21 **Jotham** his son had charge of the palace and governed the people
26:23 "He had leprosy." And **Jotham** his son succeeded him as king.
27: 1 **Jotham** was twenty-five years old when he became king, and he
27: 6 **Jotham** grew powerful because he walked steadfastly before the
27: 7 The other events in **Jotham's** reign, including all his wars
27: 9 **Jotham** rested with his fathers and was buried in the City of
Isa 1: 1 the reigns of Uzziah, **Jotham**, Ahaz and Hezekiah, kings of Judah.
7: 1 When Ahaz son of **Jotham**, the son of Uzziah, was king of Judah,
Hos 1: 1 **Jotham**, Ahaz and Hezekiah, kings of Judah, and during the reign
Mic 1: 1 that came to Micah of Moresheth during the reigns of **Jotham**,

3463 יוֹתֵר **yôtēr**, n.m. *or* v.ptcp. [10] [√ 3855]
advantage [1], anything in addition [1], benefits [1], but [+2256] [1], gain [1], not only [1], overwise [+2681] [1], profit [1], rest [1], than [+4946] [1]
1Sa 15:15 to the LORD your God, but we totally destroyed the **rest**."
1Ch 18: 4 He hamstrung all **but** [+2256] a hundred of the chariot horses.
Est 6: 6 "Who is there that the king would rather honor **than** [+4946] me?"
Ecc 2:15 What then do I **gain** by being wise?" I said in my heart, "This too
6: 8 What **advantage** has a wise man over a fool? What does a poor
6:11 the words, the less the meaning, and how does that **profit** anyone?
7:11 an inheritance, is a good thing and **benefits** those who see the sun.
7:16 Do not be overrighteous, neither *be* **overwise** [+2681]—why
12: 9 **Not only** was the Teacher wise, but also he imparted knowledge to
12:12 Be warned, my son, of **anything in addition** to them. Of making

3464 יְזוּאֵל **yᵉzûʾēl**, n.pr.m. [0] [cf. 3465]
1Ch 12: 3 [**Jeziel** [K; see Q 3465] and Pelet the sons of Azmaveth;]

3465 יְזִיאֵל **yᵉzîʾēl**, n.pr.m. [1] [cf. 3464, 3466?, 3467?]
Jeziel [1]
1Ch 12: 3 **Jeziel** [K 3464] and Pelet the sons of Azmaveth; Beracah,

3466 יִזִּיָּה **yizziyyâ**, n.pr.m. [1] [cf. 3465?]
Izziah [1]
Ezr 10:25 Ramiah, **Izziah**, Malkijah, Mijamin, Eleazar, Malkijah

3467 יָזִיז **yāzîz**, n.pr.m. [1] [cf. 3465?]
Jaziz [1]
1Ch 27:31 **Jaziz** the Hagrite was in charge of the flocks. All these were the

3468 יִזְלִיאָה **yizlîʾâ**, n.pr.m. [1]
Izliah [1]
1Ch 8:18 Ishmerai, **Izliah** and Jobab were the sons of Elpaal.

3469 יָזַן **yāzan**, v. [1]
lusty [1]
Jer 5: 8 [E] They are well-fed, **lusty** stallions, each neighing for another

3470 יְזַנְיָה **yᵉzanyâ**, n.pr.m. [1]
Jezaniah [1]
Jer 42: 1 including Johanan son of Kareah and **Jezaniah** son of Hoshaiah,

3471 יְזַנְיָהוּ **yᵉzanyāhû**, n.pr.m. [1]
Jaazaniah [1]
Jer 40: 8 and **Jaazaniah** the son of the Maacathite, and their men.

3472 יֶזַע **yezaʿ**, n.[m.]. [1] [→ 2399]
perspire [1]
Eze 44:18 They must not wear anything that makes them **perspire**.

3473 יִזְרָח **yizrāḥ**, a.g. [1]
Izrahite [1]
1Ch 27: 8 for the fifth month, was the commander Shamhuth the **Izrahite**.

3474 יִזְרַחְיָה **yizraḥyâ**, n.pr.m. [3] [√ 2436 + 3378]
Izrahiah [2], Jezrahiah [1]
1Ch 7: 3 The son of Uzzi: **Izrahiah**. The sons of Izrahiah: Michael,
7: 3 Izrahiah. The sons of **Izrahiah**: Michael, Obadiah, Joel
Ne 12:42 and Ezer. The choirs sang under the direction of **Jezrahiah**.

3475 יִזְרְעֶאל¹ **yizrᵉʿeʾl¹**, n.pr.m. [2] [→ 3476, 3477; cf. 2445 + 446]
Jezreel [2]
1Ch 4: 3 These were the sons of Etam: **Jezreel**, Ishma and Idbash. Their
Hos 1: 4 the LORD said to Hosea, "Call him **Jezreel**, because I will soon

3476 יִזְרְעֶאל² **yizrᵉʿeʾl²**, n.pr.loc. [34] [√ 3475]
Jezreel [34]
Jos 15:56 **Jezreel**, Jokdeam, Zanoah,
17:16 Beth Shan and its settlements and those in the Valley of **Jezreel**."
19:18 Their territory included: **Jezreel**, Kesulloth, Shunem,
Jdg 6:33 and crossed over the Jordan and camped in the Valley of **Jezreel**.
1Sa 25:43 David had also married Ahinoam of **Jezreel**, and they both were
29: 1 their forces at Aphek, and Israel camped by the spring in **Jezreel**.
29:11 to the land of the Philistines, and the Philistines went up to **Jezreel**.
2Sa 2: 9 Ashuri and **Jezreel**, and also over Ephraim, Benjamin and all
4: 4 old when the news about Saul and Jonathan came from **Jezreel**.
1Ki 4:12 and in all of Beth Shan next to Zarethan below **Jezreel**,
18:45 the wind rose, a heavy rain came on and Ahab rode off to **Jezreel**.
18:46 his cloak into his belt, he ran ahead of Ahab all the way to **Jezreel**.
21: 1 The vineyard was in **Jezreel**, close to the palace of Ahab king of
21:23 the LORD says: 'Dogs will devour Jezebel by the wall of **Jezreel**.'
2Ki 8:29 so King Joram returned to **Jezreel** to recover from the wounds the
8:29 Ahaziah son of Jehoram king of Judah went down to **Jezreel** to see
9:10 for Jezebel, dogs will devour her on the plot of ground at **Jezreel**,
9:15 King Joram had returned to **Jezreel** to recover from the wounds the
9:15 let anyone slip out of the city to go and tell the news in **Jezreel**."
9:16 he got into his chariot and rode to **Jezreel**, because Joram was
9:17 When the lookout standing on the tower in **Jezreel** saw Jehu's
9:30 Jehu went to **Jezreel**. When Jezebel heard about it, she painted her
9:36 On the plot of ground at **Jezreel** dogs will devour Jezebel's flesh.
9:37 body will be like refuse on the ground in the plot at **Jezreel**,
10: 1 to the officials of **Jezreel**, to the elders and to the guardians of
10: 6 master's sons and come to me in **Jezreel** by this time tomorrow."
10: 7 They put their heads in baskets and sent them to Jehu in **Jezreel**.
10:11 So Jehu killed everyone in **Jezreel** who remained of the house of
2Ch 22: 6 so he returned to **Jezreel** to recover from the wounds they had
22: 6 Ahaziah son of Jehoram king of Judah went down to **Jezreel** to see
Hos 1: 4 I will soon punish the house of Jehu for the massacre at **Jezreel**,
1: 5 In that day I will break Israel's bow in the Valley of **Jezreel**."
1:11 [2:2] come up out of the land, for great will be the day of **Jezreel**.
2:22 [2:24] the new wine and oil, and they will respond to **Jezreel**.

3477 יִזְרְעֵאלִי *yizrᵉʿēʾlî*, a.g. [13] [√ 3475]
Jezreelite [7], of Jezreel [5], *untranslated* [1]

1Sa 27: 3 Ahinoam **of Jezreel** and Abigail of Carmel, the widow of Nabal.
30: 5 Ahinoam **of Jezreel** and Abigail, the widow of Nabal of Carmel.
2Sa 2: 2 Ahinoam **of Jezreel** and Abigail, the widow of Nabal of Carmel.
3: 2 His firstborn was Amnon the son of Ahinoam **of Jezreel**;
1Ki 21: 1 incident involving a vineyard belonging to Naboth the **Jezreelite**.
21: 4 sullen and angry because Naboth the **Jezreelite** had said,
21: 6 He answered her, "Because I said to Naboth the **Jezreelite**,
21: 7 Cheer up. I'll get you the vineyard of Naboth the **Jezreelite**."
21: 15 take possession of the vineyard of Naboth the **Jezreelite** that he
21: 16 and went down to take possession of Naboth's vineyard. **[RPH]**
2Ki 9: 21 at the plot of ground that had belonged to Naboth the **Jezreelite**.
9: 25 and throw him on the field that belonged to Naboth the **Jezreelite**.
1Ch 3: 1 The firstborn was Amnon the son of Ahinoam **of Jezreel**;

3478 יְחֻבָּה *yᵉḥubbâ*, n.pr.m. [0] [√ 2465]

1Ch 7: 34 [The sons of Shomer: Ahi, Rohgah, **Hubbah** [K; see Q 2465] and Aram.]

3479 יָחַד *yāḥad*, v. [3] [→ 3480, 3481, 3495]
join [2], give undivided [1]

Ge 49: 6 [A] Let me not enter their council, *let* me not **join** their assembly,
Ps 86: 11 [D] **give** me an **undivided** heart, that I may fear your name.
Isa 14: 20 [A] *you will* not **join** them in burial, for you have destroyed your

3480 יַחַד *yaḥad*, n.[m.] (used as adv.). [45 / 44] [√ 3479]
together [14], all [8], *untranslated* [4], alike [3], completely [2], each other [2], alone [1], along with [1], also [1], both [1], by no means [+4202] [1], in force [1], regrouped [+665] [1], side by side [1], together in unity [1], unite [+2118+4200+4222+6584] [1], with [1]

Dt 33: 5 the leaders of the people assembled, **along with** the tribes of Israel.
1Sa 11: 11 survived were scattered, so that no two of them were left **together**.
17: 10 the ranks of Israel! Give me a man and let us fight **each other**."
2Sa 10: 15 saw that they had been routed by Israel, *they* **regrouped** [+665].
14: 16 servant from the hand of the man who is trying to cut off **both** me
21: 9 All seven of them fell **together**; they were put to death during the
1Ch 12: 17 [12:18] I *am ready to have* you **unite** [+2118+4200+4222+6584]
Ezr 4: 3 We **alone** will build it for the LORD, the God of Israel, as King
Job 3: 18 Captives **also** enjoy their ease; they no longer hear the slave
6: 2 could be weighed and **all** my misery be placed on the scales!
10: 8 Will you now [BHS ***altogether***; NIV 339] turn and destroy me?
16: 10 they strike my cheek in scorn and unite **together** against me.
17: 16 to the gates of death? Will we descend **together** into the dust?"
19: 12 His troops advance **in force**; they build a siege ramp against me
21: 26 **Side by side** they lie in the dust, and worms cover them both.
24: 4 needy from the path and force **all** the poor of the land into hiding.
31: 38 my land cries out against me and **all** its furrows are wet with tears,
34: 15 all mankind would perish **together** and man would return to the
34: 29 his face, who can see him? Yet he is over man and nation **alike**,
38: 7 while the morning stars sang **together** and all the angels shouted
40: 13 Bury them all in the dust **together**; shroud their faces in the grave.
Ps 2: 2 the rulers gather **together** against the LORD and against his
31: 13 [31:14] they **[NIE]** conspire against me and plot to take my life.
33: 15 he who forms the hearts of **all**, who considers everything they do.
40: 14 [40:15] May **all** who seek to take my life be put to shame
41: 7 [41:8] All my enemies whisper **together** against me; they imagine
49: 2 [49:3] both low and high, rich and poor **alike**:
49: 10 [49:11] the foolish and the senseless **alike** perish and leave their
62: 9 [62:10] they are nothing; **together** they are only a breath.
74: 6 They smashed **all** the carved paneling with their axes and hatchets.
74: 8 They said in their hearts, "We will crush them **completely**!"
88: 17 [88:18] me like a flood; they have **completely** engulfed me.
98: 8 the rivers clap their hands, let the mountains sing **together** for joy;
133: 1 How good and pleasant it is when brothers live **together in unity**!
141: 10 wicked fall into their own nets, **[NIE]** while I pass by in safety.
Isa 22: 3 All your leaders have fled **together**; they have been captured
27: 4 I would march against them in battle; I would set them **all** on fire.
42: 14 like a woman in childbirth, I cry out, I gasp and pant. **[NIE]**
43: 26 Review the past for me, let us argue the matter **together**;
44: 11 they will be brought down to terror and infamy. **[NIE]**
45: 8 open wide, let salvation spring up, let righteousness grow **with** it;
50: 8 Let us face **each other**! Who is my accuser? Let him confront me!
Jer 48: 7 [Chemosh will go into exile, **together with** [K; see Q 3481] his]
Hos 11: 7 call to the Most High, he will **by no means** [+4202] exalt them.
11: 8 My heart is changed within me; **all** my compassion is aroused.
Mic 2: 12 I will bring them **together** like sheep in a pen, like a flock in its

3481 יַחְדָּו *yaḥdāw*, adv. [96] [√ 3479]
together [57], all [7], *untranslated* [6], both [4], alike [3], as well [2], fitted [+9447] [2], together with [2], alone [1], altogether [1], assemble [+5602] [1], assemble [+7695] [1], be reunited [+7695] [1], came together [+7695] [1], each other [1], even [1], joined forces [+665] [1], people[S] [1], two men [+278+408+2256] [1], with one accord [1], with [1]

Ge 13: 6 But the land could not support them while they stayed **together**,
13: 6 possessions were so great that they were not able to stay **together**.
22: 6 carried the fire and the knife. As the two of them went on **together**,
22: 8 burnt offering, my son." And the two of them went on **together**.
22: 19 returned to his servants, and they set off **together** for Beersheba.
36: 7 Their possessions were too great for them to remain **together**;
Ex 19: 8 The people all responded **together**, "We will do everything the
26: 24 bottom all the way to the top, and **fitted** [+9447] into a single ring;
36: 29 bottom all the way to the top and **fitted** [+9447] into a single ring;
Dt 12: 22 or deer. **Both** the ceremonially unclean and the clean may eat.
15: 22 **Both** the ceremonially unclean and the clean may eat it, as if it
22: 10 Do not plow with an ox and a donkey yoked **together**.
22: 11 Do not wear clothes of wool and linen woven **together**.
25: 5 If brothers are living **together** and one of them dies without a son,
25: 11 If **two men** [+278+408+2256] are fighting and the wife of one of
33: 17 them he will gore the nations, **even** those at the ends of the earth.
Jos 9: 2 *they* **came together** [+7695] to make war against Joshua
11: 5 joined forces and made camp **together** at the Waters of Merom,
Jdg 6: 33 Amalekites and other eastern peoples **joined forces** [+665]
19: 6 So the two of them sat down to eat and drink **together**.
1Sa 30: 24 as that of him who went down to the battle. All will share **alike**."
31: 6 and his armor-bearer and all his men died **together** that same day.
2Sa 2: 13 **[NIE]** One group sat down on one side of the pool and one group
2: 16 his dagger into his opponent's side, and they fell down **together**.
12: 3 **[NIE]** It shared his food, drank from his cup and even slept in his
1Ki 3: 18 We were **alone**; there was no one in the house but the two of us.
1Ch 10: 6 So Saul and his three sons died, and all his house died **together**.
Ne 4: 8 [4:2] They all plotted **together** to come and fight against
6: 2 let us meet **together** in one of the villages on the plain of Ono."
6: 7 report will get back to the king; so come, let us confer **together**."
Job 2: 11 and met **together** by agreement to go and sympathize with him
9: 32 I might answer him, that we might confront **each other** in court.
24: 17 For **all** of them, deep darkness is their morning; they make friends
Ps 4: 8 [4:9] and sleep in peace, **[RPH]** for you alone, O LORD,
14: 3 All have turned aside, they have **together** become corrupt;
19: 9 [19:10] of the LORD are sure and **altogether** righteous.
34: 3 [34:4] the LORD with me; let us exalt his name **together**.
35: 26 May **all** who gloat over my distress be put to shame and confusion;
37: 38 **all** sinners will be destroyed; the future of the wicked will be cut
48: 4 [48:5] the kings joined forces, when they advanced **together**,
53: 3 [53:4] has turned away, they have **together** become corrupt;
55: 14 [55:15] **with** whom I once enjoyed sweet fellowship as we
71: 10 speak against me; those who wait to kill me conspire **together**.
83: 5 [83:6] With one mind they plot **together**; they form an alliance
102: 22 [102:23] the kingdoms **assemble** [+7695] to worship the LORD.
122: 3 Jerusalem is built like a city that is closely compacted **together**.
Pr 22: 18 keep them in your heart and have **all** *of them* ready on your lips.
Isa 1: 28 rebels and sinners will **both** be broken, and those who forsake the
1: 31 a spark; both will burn **together**, with no one to quench the fire."
9: 21 [9:20] on Manasseh; **together** they will turn against Judah.
10: 8 'Are not my commanders **all** kings?' he says.
11: 6 down with the goat, the calf and the lion and the yearling **together**;
11: 7 cow will feed with the bear, their young will lie down **together**,
11: 14 to the west; **together** they will plunder the people to the east.
18: 6 They will **all** be left to the mountain birds of prey and to the wild
22: 3 All you who were caught were taken prisoner **together**,
31: 3 will stumble, he who is helped will fall; both will perish **together**.
40: 5 the LORD will be revealed, and all mankind **together** will see it.
41: 1 and speak; let us meet **together** at the place of judgment.
41: 19 I will set pines in the wasteland, the fir and the cypress **together**,
41: 20 so that **people**[S] may see and know, may consider and understand,
41: 23 so that we will be dismayed and filled with fear. **[RPH]**
43: 9 All the nations gather **together** and the peoples assemble.
43: 17 out the chariots and horses, the army and reinforcements **together**,
45: 16 to shame and disgraced; they will go off into disgrace **together**.
45: 20 and come; **assemble, you** [+5602] fugitives from the nations.
45: 21 Declare what is to be, present it—let them take counsel **together**.
46: 2 They stoop and bow down **together**; unable to rescue the burden,
48: 13 out the heavens; when I summon them, they all stand up **together**.
52: 8 Your watchmen lift up their voices; **together** they shout for joy.
52: 9 Burst into songs of joy **together**, you ruins of Jerusalem,
60: 13 the pine, the fir and the cypress **together**, to adorn the place of my
65: 7 **both** your sins and the sins of your fathers," says the LORD.
66: 17 they will meet their end **together**," declares the LORD.
Jer 3: 18 **together** they will come from a northern land to the land I gave
5: 5 **with one accord** they too had broken off the yoke and torn off the
6: 11 the children in the street and on the young men gathered **together**;

Jer 6:12 be turned over to others, **together with** their fields and their wives,
6:21 Fathers and sons **alike** will stumble over them; neighbors
13:14 one against the other, fathers and sons **alike**, declares the LORD.
31: 8 and women in labor; **[NIE]** a great throng will return.
31:13 Then maidens will dance and be glad, young men and old **as well**.
31:24 People will live **together** in Judah and all its towns—farmers
41: 1 son of Ahikam at Mizpah. While they were eating **together** there,
46:12 warrior will stumble over another; both will fall down **together**."
46:21 They too will turn and flee **together**, they will not stand their
48: 7 will go into exile, **together** [K 3480] **with** his priests and officials.
49: 3 will go into exile, together with his priests and **[NIE]** officials.
50: 4 the people of Judah **together** will go in tears to seek the LORD
50:33 people of Israel are oppressed, and the people of Judah **as well**.
51:38 Her people **all** roar like young lions, they growl like lion cubs.
La 2: 8 He made ramparts and walls lament; **together** they wasted away.
Hos 1:11 [2:2] of Judah and the people of Israel *will* **be reunited** [+7695],
Am 1:15 will go into exile, he and his officials **together**," says the LORD.
3: 3 Do two walk **together** unless they have agreed to do so?
Zec 10: 5 [10:4] **Together** they will be like mighty men trampling the

3482 יַחְדּוֹ *yaḥdô*, n.pr.m. [1] [cf. 3483]

Jahdo [1]

1Ch 5:14 of Michael, the son of Jeshishai, the son of **Jahdo**, the son of Buz.

3483 יַחְדַּי *yaḥdōy*, n.pr.m. Not used in NIV/BHS [cf. 3482]

3484 יַחְדִּיאֵל *yaḥdî'ēl*, n.pr.m. [1] [√ 2525 + 446]

Jahdiel [1]

1Ch 5:24 Epher, Ishi, Eliel, Azriel, Jeremiah, Hodaviah and **Jahdiel**.

3485 יֶחְדְּיָהוּ *yeḥdᵉyāhû*, n.pr.m. [2] [√ 2525 + 3378]

Jehdeiah [2]

1Ch 24:20 the sons of Amram: Shubael; from the sons of Shubael: **Jehdeiah**.
27:30 **Jehdeiah** the Meronothite was in charge of the donkeys.

3486 יְחוּאֵל *yᵉḥû'ēl*, n.pr.m. [0] [cf. 3493]

2Ch 29:14 [the descendants of Heman, **Jehiel** [K; see Q 3493] and Shimei;]

3487 יַחֲזִיאֵל *yaḥᵃzî'ēl*, n.pr.m. [6] [√ 2600 + 446]

Jahaziel [6]

1Ch 12: 4 [12:5] **Jahaziel**, Johanan, Jozabad the Gederathite,
16: 6 **Jahaziel** the priests were to blow the trumpets regularly before the
23:19 Amariah the second, **Jahaziel** the third and Jekameam the fourth.
24:23 Amariah the second, **Jahaziel** the third and Jekameam the fourth.
2Ch 20:14 the Spirit of the LORD came upon **Jahaziel** son of Zechariah,
Ezr 8: 5 of Zattu, Shecaniah son of **Jahaziel**, and with him 300 men;

3488 יַחְזְיָה *yaḥzᵉyâ*, n.pr.m. [1] [√ 2600 + 3378]

Jahzeiah [1]

Ezr 10:15 Only Jonathan son of Asahel and **Jahzeiah** son of Tikvah,

3489 יְחֶזְקֵאל *yᵉḥezqē'l*, n.pr.m. [3] [√ 2616 + 446]

Ezekiel [2], Jehezkel [1]

1Ch 24:16 the nineteenth to Pethahiah, the twentieth to **Jehezkel**,
Eze 1: 3 the word of the LORD came to **Ezekiel** the priest, the son of
24:24 **Ezekiel** will be a sign to you; you will do just as he has done.

3490 יְחִזְקִיָּה *yᵉḥizqiyyâ*, n.pr.m. [3] [√ 2616 + 3378]

Hezekiah [3]

Ezr 2:16 of Ater (through **Hezekiah**) 98
Hos 1: 1 Jotham, Ahaz and **Hezekiah**, kings of Judah, and during the reign
Mic 1: 1 during the reigns of Jotham, Ahaz and **Hezekiah**, kings of Judah—

3491 יְחִזְקִיָּהוּ *yᵉḥizqiyyāhû*, n.pr.m. [41] [√ 2616 + 3378]

Hezekiah [37], Hezekiah's [2], he^s [1], Jehizkiah [1]

2Ki 20:10 matter for the shadow to go forward ten steps," said **Hezekiah**.
1Ch 4:41 The men whose names were listed came in the days of **Hezekiah**
2Ch 28:12 **Jehizkiah** son of Shallum, and Amasa son of Hadlai—
28:27 the kings of Israel. And **Hezekiah** his son succeeded him as king.
29: 1 **Hezekiah** was twenty-five years old when he became king,
29:20 Early the next morning King **Hezekiah** gathered the city officials
29:30 King **Hezekiah** and his officials ordered the Levites to praise the
29:31 **Hezekiah** said, "You have now dedicated yourselves to the
29:36 **Hezekiah** and all the people rejoiced at what God had brought
30: 1 **Hezekiah** sent word to all Israel and Judah and also wrote letters to
30:18 But **Hezekiah** prayed for them, saying, "May the LORD,
30:20 And the LORD heard **Hezekiah** and healed the people.
30:22 **Hezekiah** spoke encouragingly to all the Levites, who showed
31: 2 **Hezekiah** assigned the priests and Levites to divisions—each of
31: 8 When **Hezekiah** and his officials came and saw the heaps,
31: 9 **Hezekiah** asked the priests and Levites about the heaps;
31:11 **Hezekiah** gave orders to prepare storerooms in the temple of the
31:13 by appointment of King **Hezekiah** and Azariah the official in
31:20 This is what **Hezekiah** did throughout Judah, doing what was good
32: 2 When **Hezekiah** saw that Sennacherib had come and that he
32: 8 the people gained confidence from what **Hezekiah** the king of
32: 9 he sent his officers to Jerusalem with this message for **Hezekiah**
32:11 When **Hezekiah** says, 'The LORD our God will save us from the
32:12 Did not **Hezekiah** himself remove this god's high places
32:16 further against the LORD God and against his servant **Hezekiah**.
32:17 so the god of **Hezekiah** will not rescue his people from my hand."
32:20 King **Hezekiah** and the prophet Isaiah son of Amoz cried out in
32:22 So the LORD saved **Hezekiah** and the people of Jerusalem from
32:23 for the LORD and valuable gifts for **Hezekiah** king of Judah.
32:24 In those days **Hezekiah** became ill and was at the point of death.
32:25 **Hezekiah's** heart was proud and he did not respond to the kindness
32:26 **Hezekiah** repented of the pride of his heart, as did the people of
32:26 wrath did not come upon them during the days of **Hezekiah**.
32:27 **Hezekiah** had very great riches and honor, and he made treasuries
32:30 It was **Hezekiah** who blocked the upper outlet of the Gihon spring
32:30 of the City of David. **He**^s succeeded in everything he undertook.
32:32 The other events of **Hezekiah's** reign and his acts of devotion are
32:33 **Hezekiah** rested with his fathers and was buried on the hill where
33: 3 He rebuilt the high places his father **Hezekiah** had demolished;
Isa 1: 1 the reigns of Uzziah, Jotham, Ahaz and **Hezekiah**, kings of Judah.
Jer 15: 4 because of what Manasseh son of **Hezekiah** king of Judah did in

3492 יַחְזֵרָה *yaḥzērâ*, n.pr.m. [1] [√ 2614]

Jahzerah [1]

1Ch 9:12 the son of **Jahzerah**, the son of Meshullam, the son of

3493 יְחִיאֵל *yᵉḥî'ēl*, n.pr.m. [14] [→ 3494; cf. 2649 + 446, 3486]

Jehiel [14]

1Ch 15:18 **Jehiel**, Unni, Eliab, Benaiah, Maaseiah, Mattithiah, Eliphelehu,
15:20 **Jehiel**, Unni, Eliab, Maaseiah and Benaiah were to play the lyres
16: 5 **Jehiel**, Mattithiah, Eliab, Benaiah, Obed-Edom and Jeiel.
23: 8 The sons of Ladan: **Jehiel** the first, Zetham and Joel—three in all.
27:32 and a scribe. **Jehiel** son of Hacmoni took care of the king's sons.
29: 8 the temple of the LORD in the custody of **Jehiel** the Gershonite.
2Ch 21: 2 **Jehiel**, Zechariah, Azariahu, Michael and Shephatiah.
29:14 from the descendants of Heman, **Jehiel** [K 3486] and Shimei;
31:13 **Jehiel**, Azaziah, Nahath, Asahel, Jerimoth, Jozabad, Eliel,
35: 8 Hilkiah, Zechariah and **Jehiel**, the administrators of God's temple,
Ezr 8: 9 of Joab, Obadiah son of **Jehiel**, and with him 218 men;
10: 2 Then Shecaniah son of **Jehiel**, one of the descendants of Elam,
10:21 of Harim: Maaseiah, Elijah, Shemaiah, **Jehiel** and Uzziah.
10:26 of Elam: Mattaniah, Zechariah, **Jehiel**, Abdi, Jeremoth and Elijah.

3494 יְחִיאֵלִי *yᵉḥî'ēlî*, n.pr.m. [2] [√ 3493]

Jehieli [2]

1Ch 26:21 heads of families belonging to Ladan the Gershonite, were **Jehieli**,
26:22 the sons of **Jehieli**, Zetham and his brother Joel. They were in

3495 יָחִיד *yāḥîd*, a. & subst. [12] [√ 3479]

only son [5], only child [3], lonely [2], precious life [2]

Ge 22: 2 God said, "Take your son, your **only son**, Isaac, whom you love,
22:12 because you have not withheld from me your son, your **only son**."
22:16 you have done this and have not withheld your son, your **only son**,
Jdg 11:34 dancing to the sound of tambourines! She was an **only child**.
Ps 22:20 [22:21] the sword, my **precious life** from the power of the dogs.
25:16 Turn to me and be gracious to me, for I am **lonely** and afflicted.
35:17 my life from their ravages, my **precious life** from these lions.
68: 6 [68:7] God sets the **lonely** in families, he leads forth the prisoners
Pr 4: 3 in my father's house, still tender, and an **only child** of my mother,
Jer 6:26 mourn with bitter wailing as for an **only son**, for suddenly the
Am 8:10 I will make that time like mourning for an **only son** and the end of
Zec 12:10 and they will mourn for him as one mourns for an **only child**,

3496 יְחִיָּה *yᵉḥiyyâ*, n.pr.m. [1] [√ 2649 + 3378]

Jehiah [1]

1Ch 15:24 Obed-Edom and **Jehiah** were also to be doorkeepers for the ark.

3497 יָחִיל *yāḥîl*, a.vbl. [1] [√ 3498]

wait [1]

La 3:26 it is good to **wait** quietly for the salvation of the LORD.

3498 יָחַל ***yāḥal***, v. [41 / 43] [→ 3497, 3499, 3500, 9347]

put hope [14], hope [7], wait [7], waited [6], expect [1], expectantly [1], given hope [1], hope unfulfilled [1], linger [1], looked [1], looking [1], wait for [1], wait in hope [1]

Ge 8: 10 [D] *He* **waited** [BHS 2655] seven more days and again sent out
8: 12 [C] *He* **waited** seven more days and sent the dove out again,
Jdg 3: 25 [G] *They* **waited** [BHS 2655] to the point of embarrassment,
1Sa 10: 8 [G] *you must* **wait** seven days until I come to you and tell you
13: 8 [G] *He* **waited** seven days, the time set by Samuel; but Samuel
2Sa 18: 14 [G] Joab said, "*I'm* not *going to* **wait** like this for you." So he
2Ki 6: 33 [G] the LORD. Why *should I* **wait** for the LORD any longer?"
Job 6: 11 [D] "What strength do I have, that *I should still* **hope**? What
13: 15 [D] Though he slay me, yet *will I* **hope** in him; I will surely
14: 14 [D] All the days of my hard service *I will* **wait for** my renewal to
29: 21 [D] "Men listened to me **expectantly**, waiting in silence for my
29: 23 [D] *They* **waited** for me as for showers and drank in my words
30: 26 [D] evil came; when *I* **looked** for light, then came darkness.
32: 11 [G] *I* **waited** while you spoke, I listened to your reasoning;
32: 16 [G] *Must I* **wait**, now that they are silent, now that they stand
Ps 31: 24 [31:25] [D] and take heart, all you who **hope** in the LORD.
33: 18 [D] who fear him, on those *whose* **hope** *is* in his unfailing love,
33: 22 [D] rest upon us, O LORD, even as *we* **put** *our* **hope** in you.
38: 15 [38:16] [G] *I* **wait** for you, O LORD; you will answer, O Lord
39: 7 [39:8] [G] Lord, what do I look for? *My* **hope** *is* in you.
42: 5 [42:6] [G] **Put** *your* **hope** in God, for I will yet praise him, my
42: 11 [42:12] [G] **Put** *your* **hope** in God, for I will yet praise him, my
43: 5 [G] **Put** *your* **hope** in God, for I will yet praise him, my Savior
69: 3 [69:4] [D] throat is parched. My eyes fail, **looking** for my God.
71: 14 [D] as for me, *I will* always *have* **hope**; I will praise you more
119: 43 [D] truth from my mouth, for *I have* **put** *my* **hope** in your laws.
119: 49 [D] your word to your servant, for *you have* **given** me **hope**.
119: 74 [D] when they see me, for *I have* **put** *my* **hope** in your word.
119: 81 [D] for your salvation, but *I have* **put** *my* **hope** in your word.
119: 114 [D] my refuge and my shield; *I have* **put** *my* **hope** in your word.
119: 147 [D] and cry for help; *I have* **put** *my* **hope** in your word.
130: 5 [G] the LORD, my soul waits, and in his word *I* **put** *my* **hope**.
130: 7 [D] O Israel, **put** *your* **hope** in the LORD, for with the LORD
131: 3 [D] **put** *your* **hope** in the LORD both now and forevermore.
147: 11 [D] who fear him, who **put** *their* **hope** in his unfailing love.
Isa 42: 4 [G] justice on earth. In his law the islands *will* **put** *their* **hope**."
51: 5 [D] The islands will look to me and **wait in hope** for my arm.
Jer 4: 19 [a] [*I* **writhe** [Q; see K 2655] **in pain**. Oh, the agony of my]
La 3: 21 [G] Yet this I call to mind and therefore *I have* **hope**:
3: 24 [G] "The LORD is my portion; therefore *I will* **wait** for him."
Eze 13: 6 [D] has not sent them; yet *they* **expect** their words to be fulfilled.
19: 5 [C] " 'When she saw *her* **hope unfulfilled**, her expectation gone,
Mic 5: 7 [5:6] [D] which do not wait for man or **linger** for mankind.
7: 7 [G] I watch in hope for the LORD, *I* **wait** for God my Savior;

3499 יַחְלְאֵל ***yaḥleʾēl***, n.pr.m. [2] [→ 3500; cf. 3498 + 446]

Jahleel [2]

Ge 46: 14 The sons of Zebulun: Sered, Elon and **Jahleel**.
Nu 26: 26 through Elon, the Elonite clan; through **Jahleel**, the Jahleelite clan.

3500 יַחְלְאֵלִי ***yaḥleʾēlî***, a.g. [1] [√ 3499; cf. 3498 + 446]

Jahleelite [1]

Nu 26: 26 through Elon, the Elonite clan; through Jahleel, the **Jahleelite** clan.

3501 יָחַם ***yāḥam***, v. [6] [→ 2771, 2779; cf. 2801]

in heat [2], breeding [+2021+7366] [1], conceived [1], mate [1], mated [1]

Ge 30: 38 [A] to drink. When the flocks *were* **in heat** and came to drink,
30: 39 [A] they **mated** in front of the branches. And they bore young
30: 41 [D] Whenever the stronger females *were* **in heat**, Jacob would
30: 41 [D] front of the animals so they *would* **mate** near the branches,
31: 10 [D] "In **breeding** [+2021+7366] season I once had a dream in
Ps 51: 5 [51:7] [D] at birth, sinful from the time my mother **conceived**

3502 יַחְמוּר ***yaḥmûr***, n.[m.]. [2] [√ 2813]

roe deer [1], roebucks [1]

Dt 14: 5 the deer, the gazelle, the **roe deer**, the wild goat, the ibex,
1Ki 4: 23 [5:3] as well as deer, gazelles, **roebucks** and choice fowl.

3503 יַחְמַי ***yaḥmay***, n.pr.m. [1] [√ 2570]

Jahmai [1]

1Ch 7: 2 Uzzi, Rephaiah, Jeriel, **Jahmai**, Ibsam and Samuel—heads of their

3504 יָחֵף ***yāḥēp***, a. [5]

barefoot [4], bare [1]

2Sa 15: 30 weeping as he went; his head was covered and he was **barefoot**.
Isa 20: 2 your feet." And he did so, going around stripped and **barefoot**.
20: 3 my servant Isaiah has gone stripped and **barefoot** for three years,
20: 4 and **barefoot** the Egyptian captives and Cushite exiles,
Jer 2: 25 Do not run until your feet are **bare** and your throat is dry.

3505 יַחְצְאֵל ***yaḥṣeʾēl***, n.pr.m. [2] [→ 3506; cf. 2936 + 446]

Jahzeel [1], Jahziel [1]

Ge 46: 24 The sons of Naphtali: **Jahziel**, Guni, Jezer and Shillem.
Nu 26: 48 through **Jahzeel**, the Jahzeelite clan; through Guni, the Gunite

3506 יַחְצְאֵלִי ***yaḥṣeʾēlî***, a.g. [1] [√ 3505; cf. 2936 + 446]

Jahzeelite [1]

Nu 26: 48 through Jahzeel, the **Jahzeelite** clan; through Guni, the Gunite

3507 יַחֲצִיאֵל ***yaḥaṣîʾēl***, n.pr.m. [1] [√ 2936 + 446]

Jahziel [1]

1Ch 7: 13 **Jahziel**, Guni, Jezer and Shillem—the descendants of Bilhah.

3508 יָחַר ***yāḥar***, v.?. [0] [cf. 336]

2Sa 20: 5 [g] [*he* **took longer** [K; see Q 336] than the time the king had set]

3509 יָחַשׂ ***yāḥaś***, v. [20] [→ 2249, 3510]

family [2], listed in genealogy [2], listed [2], be listed in the genealogical record [1], deal with genealogies [1], enrolled in the genealogical records [1], genealogical record listed [1], kept a genealogical record [1], listed in genealogical records [1], names in the genealogical records [1], registered [1], registration by families [1], was listed in the genealogies [1], were entered in the genealogical records [1], were recorded in the genealogies [1], were registered by genealogy [1], were registered [1]

1Ch 4: 33 [F] were their settlements. And they **kept a genealogical record**.
5: 1 [F] so he *could* not **be listed in the genealogical record** in
5: 7 [F] by clans, **listed** according to their genealogical records:
5: 17 [F] All these **were entered in the genealogical records** during
7: 5 [F] of Issachar, *as* **listed in** their **genealogy**, were 87,000 in all.
7: 7 [F] in all. Their **genealogical record listed** 22,034 fighting men.
7: 9 [F] Their genealogical record **listed** the heads of families and
7: 40 [F] ready for battle, *as* **listed in** their **genealogy**, was 26,000.
9: 1 [F] All Israel **was listed in the genealogies** recorded in the book
9: 22 [F] They **were registered by genealogy** in their villages.
2Ch 12: 15 [F] the prophet and of Iddo the seer *that* **deal with genealogies**?
31: 16 [F] or more whose **names** *were* **in the genealogical records**—
31: 17 [F] priests **enrolled** by their families **in the genealogical records**
31: 18 [F] the whole community **listed in** *these* **genealogical records**.
31: 19 [F] to all *who* **were recorded in the genealogies** of the Levites.
Ezr 2: 62 [F] These searched for their **family** records, but they could not
8: 1 [F] *those* **registered** *with* them who came up with me from
8: 3 [F] Zechariah, and with him **were registered** 150 men;
Ne 7: 5 [F] and the common people for **registration by families**.
7: 64 [F] These searched for their **family** records, but they could not

3510 יַחַשׂ ***yaḥaś***, n.[m.]. [1] [√ 3509]

genealogical [1]

Ne 7: 5 I found the **genealogical** record of those who had been the first to

3511 יַחַת ***yaḥat***, n.pr.m. [8]

Jahath [7], Jehath [1]

1Ch 4: 2 Reaiah son of Shobal was the father of **Jahath**, and Jahath the
4: 2 the father of Jahath, and **Jahath** the father of Ahumai and Lahad.
6: 20 [6:5] Of Gershon: Libni his son, **Jehath** his son, Zimmah his son,
6: 43 [6:28] the son of **Jahath**, the son of Gershon, the son of Levi;
23: 10 the sons of Shimei: **Jahath**, Ziza, Jeush and Beriah. These were
23: 11 **Jahath** was the first and Ziza the second, but Jeush and Beriah did
24: 22 the Izharites: Shelomoth; from the sons of Shelomoth: **Jahath**.
2Ch 34: 12 Over them to direct them were **Jahath** and Obadiah, Levites

3512 יָטַב ***yāṭab***, v. [115] [→ 3513, 3514, 4541, 4774; cf. 3201; Ar 10293, 10320]

go well [14], do good [10], good [10], pleased [+928+6524] [7], reform [4], make prosper [3], well [3], do what is right [2], enjoy [2], really change [+906+906+3512] [2], surely make prosper [+3512+6640] [2], thoroughly [2], treated well [2], adorned [1], appealed to [+928+6524] [1], arranged [1], best [1], better [1], brought success [1], cheer up [+4213] [1], commends [1], correctly

[1], delighted [1], do right [1], do[s] [1], doing good [1], enjoying [1], found favor [1], give joy [1], gives [1], glad [+4213] [1], glad [+928+6524] [1], goes well [1], good do [+906+3208] [1], good done [1], greater [1], ground to powder [+3221] [1], have a right [1], have any right [1], in good spirits [+4213] [1], inclined [1], kind [1], make famous [1], make more prosperous [1], makes cheerful [1], please [1], pleased with [+928+6524] [1], pleased [1], pleases [+928+6524] [1], prosper [1], satisfied [+928+6524] [1], share [1], show kindness [1], skilled [+2006] [1], skilled [1], skillfully [1], stately bearing [1], stately [1], tends [1], thorough [1], to pieces [1], treat well [1], very [1], well provided for [1], wish [+928+6524] [1]

Ge 4: 7 [G] If *you* **do what is right**, will you not be accepted? But if you
4: 7 [G] if *you do* not **do what is right**, sin is crouching at your door;
12: 13 [A] so that I *will be* **treated well** for your sake and my life will
12: 16 [G] *He* **treated** Abram **well** for her sake, and Abram acquired
32: 9 [32:10] [G] and your relatives, and *I will* **make** you **prosper**,'
32: 12 [32:13] [G] '*I will* **surely make** you **prosper** [+3512+6640] and
32: 12 [32:13] [G] '*I will* **surely make** you **prosper** [+3512+6640] and
34: 18 [A] Their proposal seemed **good** *to* Hamor and his son Shechem.
40: 14 [A] when *all* **goes well** with you, remember me and show me
41: 37 [A] The plan seemed **good** to Pharaoh and to all his officials.
45: 16 [A] and all his officials *were* **pleased** [+928+6524].
Ex 1: 20 [G] So God *was* **kind** to the midwives and the people increased
30: 7 [G] incense on the altar every morning when he **tends** the lamps.
Lev 5: 4 [G] thoughtlessly takes an oath to **do** anything, whether **good**
10: 19 [A] *Would* the LORD *have been* **pleased** [+928+6524] if I had
10: 20 [A] When Moses heard this, he *was* **satisfied** [+928+6524].
Nu 10: 29 [G] Come with us and *we will* **treat** you **well**, for the LORD has
10: 32 [G] *we will* **share** with you whatever good things the LORD
10: 32 [G] share with you whatever good things the LORD **gives** us."
Dt 1: 23 [A] The idea seemed **good** to me; so I selected twelve of you,
4: 40 [A] so that *it may* **go well** with you and your children after you
5: 16 [A] that *it may* **go well** with you in the land the LORD your
5: 28 [G] what this people said to you. Everything they said *was* **good**.
5: 29 [A] so that *it might* **go well** with them and their children forever!
6: 3 [A] be careful to obey so that *it may* **go well** with you and that
6: 18 [A] so that *it may* **go well** with you and you may go in and take
8: 16 [G] and to test you so that in the end *it might* **go well** *with* you.
9: 21 [G] I crushed it and **ground** it **to powder** [+3221] as fine as dust
12: 25 [A] so that *it may* **go well** with you and your children after you,
12: 28 [A] so that *it may* always **go well** with you and your children
13: 14 [13:15] [G] must inquire, probe and investigate it **thoroughly**.
17: 4 [G] to your attention, then you must investigate it **thoroughly**.
18: 17 [G] The LORD said to me: "What they say *is* **good**.
19: 18 [G] The judges must make a **thorough** investigation, and if the
22: 7 [A] so that *it may* **go well** with you and you may have a long life.
27: 8 [G] you shall write **very** clearly all the words of this law on these
28: 63 [G] Just as it pleased the LORD to **make you prosper** and
30: 5 [G] *He will* **make** you **more prosperous** and numerous than
Jos 22: 30 [A] and Manasseh had to say, they *were* **pleased** [+928+6524].
22: 33 [A] They *were* **glad** [+928+6524] to hear the report and praised
24: 20 [G] and make an end of you, after *he has been* **good** to you."
Jdg 17: 13 [G] "Now I know that the LORD *will be* **good** to me,
18: 20 [A] the priest *was* **glad** [+4213]. He took the ephod, the other
19: 6 [A] girl's father said, "Please stay tonight and **enjoy** yourself."
19: 9 [A] night here; the day is nearly over. Stay and **enjoy** yourself.
19: 22 [G] *While* they *were* **enjoying** themselves, some of the wicked
Ru 3: 1 [A] find a home for you, where you *will be* **well provided for**?
3: 7 [A] and drinking and *was* **in good** [+4213] **spirits**,
3: 10 [G] "This kindness *is* **greater** than that which you showed
1Sa 2: 32 [G] Although **good** *will be* **done** *to* Israel, in your family line
16: 17 [G] "Find someone who plays **well** and bring him to me."
18: 5 [A] *This* **pleased** [+928+6524] all the people, and Saul's officers
20: 13 [G] if my father *is* **inclined** to harm you, may the LORD deal
24: 4 [24:5] [A] **wish** [+928+6524].' " Then David crept up unnoticed
25: 31 [G] when the LORD *has* **brought** my master **success**,
2Sa 3: 36 [A] All the people took note and *were* **pleased** [+928+6524];
18: 4 [A] The king answered, "I will do whatever seems **best** to you."
1Ki 1: 47 [G] '*May* your God **make** Solomon's name more **famous** than
3: 10 [A] The Lord *was* **pleased** [+928+6524] that Solomon had asked
21: 7 [A] act as king over Israel? Get up and eat! **Cheer** [+4213] **up**.
2Ki 9: 30 [G] her eyes, **arranged** her hair and looked out of a window.
11: 18 [G] They smashed the altars and idols **to pieces** and killed
25: 24 [A] and serve the king of Babylon, and *it will* **go well** with you."
Ne 2: 5 [A] the king and if your servant *has* **found favor** in his sight,
2: 6 [A] get back?" *It* **pleased** the king to send me; so I set a time.
Est 1: 21 [A] and his nobles *were* **pleased** [+928+6524] **with** this advice,
2: 4 [A] let the girl who **pleases** [+928+6524] the king be queen
2: 4 [A] This advice **appealed** [+928+6524] **to** the king, and he
2: 9 [A] The girl **pleased** [+928+6524] him and won his favor.
5: 14 [A] This suggestion **delighted** Haman, and he had the gallows
Job 24: 21 [G] and childless woman, and *to* the widow **show** no **kindness**.
Ps 33: 3 [G] Sing to him a new song; play **skillfully**, and shout for joy.
36: 3 [36:4] [G] he has ceased to be wise and to **do good**.
49: 18 [49:19] [G] and men praise you when *you* **prosper**—
51: 18 [51:20] [G] In your good pleasure **make** Zion **prosper**; build up
69: 31 [69:32] [A] *This will* **please** the LORD more than an ox,
119: 68 [G] You are good, and *what you* **do** *is* **good**; teach me your
125: 4 [G] **Do good**, O LORD, to those who are good, to those who are
Pr 15: 2 [G] The tongue of the wise **commends** knowledge, but the mouth
15: 13 [G] A happy heart **makes** the face **cheerful**, but heartache
17: 22 [G] A cheerful heart *is* **good** medicine, but a crushed spirit dries
30: 29 [G] "There are three things *that are* **stately** *in* their stride, four
30: 29 [G] stately in their stride, four that move *with* **stately bearing**:
Ecc 7: 3 [A] better than laughter, because a sad face *is* **good** *for* the heart.
11: 9 [G] and *let* your heart **give** you **joy** in the days of your youth.
Isa 1: 17 [G] learn *to* **do right**! Seek justice, encourage the oppressed.
23: 16 [G] play the harp **well**, sing many a song, so that you will be
41: 23 [G] **Do** *something*, whether **good** or bad, so that we will be
Jer 1: 12 [G] The LORD said to me, "*You have* seen **correctly**, for I am
2: 33 [G] How **skilled** [+2006] *you are* at pursuing love! Even the
4: 22 [G] are skilled in doing evil; they know not how to **do good**."
7: 3 [G] **Reform** your ways and your actions, and I will let you live in
7: 5 [G] If *you* **really change** [+906+906+3512] your ways and your
7: 5 [G] If *you* **really change** [+906+906+3512] your ways and your
7: 23 [A] in all the ways I command you, that *it may* **go well** with you.
10: 5 [G] fear them; they can do no harm nor *can* they **do** *any* **good**."
13: 23 [G] Neither can you **do good** who are accustomed to doing evil.
18: 10 [G] reconsider the **good** I had intended to **do for** [+906+3208] it.
18: 11 [G] each one of you, and **reform** your ways and your actions.'
26: 13 [G] Now **reform** your ways and your actions and obey the
32: 40 [G] I will never stop **doing good** *to* them, and I will inspire them
35: 15 [G] must turn from your wicked ways and **reform** your actions;
38: 20 [A] Then *it will* **go well** with you, and your life will be spared.
40: 9 [A] and serve the king of Babylon, and *it will* **go well** with you.
42: 6 [A] to whom we are sending you, so that *it will* **go well** with us,
Eze 33: 32 [G] songs with a beautiful voice and plays an instrument **well**,
Hos 10: 1 [G] as his land prospered, *he* **adorned** his sacred stones.
Jnh 4: 4 [G] But the LORD replied, "**Have** you **any right** to be angry?"
4: 9 [G] to Jonah, "*Do* you **have a right** to be angry about the vine?"
4: 9 [G] about the vine?" "I **do**[s]," he said. "I am angry enough to die."
Mic 2: 7 [G] "*Do* not my words **do good** to him whose ways are upright?
7: 3 [G] Both hands *are* **skilled** in doing evil; the ruler demands gifts,
Na 3: 8 [G] *Are you* **better** than Thebes, situated on the Nile, with water
Zep 1: 12 [G] who think, 'The LORD *will do* nothing, either **good** or bad.'
Zec 8: 15 [G] now I have determined to **do good** again to Jerusalem and

3513 יָטְבָה *yoṭbâ*, n.pr.loc. [1] [√ 3512]

Jotbah [1]

2Ki 21: 19 name was Meshullemeth daughter of Haruz; she was from **Jotbah**.

3514 יָטְבָתָה *yoṭbātâ*, n.pr.loc. [3] [√ 3512]

Jotbathah [3]

Nu 33: 33 They left Hor Haggidgad and camped at **Jotbathah**.
33: 34 They left **Jotbathah** and camped at Abronah.
Dt 10: 7 From there they traveled to Gudgodah and on to **Jotbathah**,

3515 יְטוּר *y[e]ṭûr*, n.pr.m. & g. [3] [cf. 3227?]

Jetur [3]

Ge 25: 15 Hadad, Tema, **Jetur**, Naphish and Kedemah.
1Ch 1: 31 **Jetur**, Naphish and Kedemah. These were the sons of Ishmael.
5: 19 They waged war against the Hagrites, **Jetur**, Naphish and Nodab.

3516 יַיִן *yayin*, n.m. [141]

wine [132], grapevine [+1728] [2], wineskins [+5532] [2], banquet [+5492] [1], banquet hall [+1074] [1], old wine [1], sober [+2021+3655+4946] [1], wine offerings [1]

Ge 9: 21 When he drank some of its **wine**, he became drunk and lay
9: 24 When Noah awoke from his **wine** and found out what his youngest
14: 18 Then Melchizedek king of Salem brought out bread and **wine**.
19: 32 Let's get our father to drink **wine** and then lie with him
19: 33 That night they got their father to drink **wine**, and the older
19: 34 Let's get him to drink **wine** again tonight, and you go in and lie
19: 35 So they got their father to drink **wine** that night also,
27: 25 it to him and he ate; and he brought *some* **wine** and he drank.
49: 11 he will wash his garments in **wine**, his robes in the blood of grapes.
49: 12 His eyes will be darker than **wine**, his teeth whiter than milk.
Ex 29: 40 pressed olives, and a quarter of a hin of **wine** as a drink offering.
Lev 10: 9 "You and your sons are not to drink **wine** or other fermented drink
23: 13 and its drink offering of a quarter of a hin of **wine**.
Nu 6: 3 he must abstain from **wine** and other fermented drink and must not
6: 3 other fermented drink and must not drink vinegar made from **wine**
6: 4 he must not eat anything that comes from the **grapevine** [+1728],
6: 20 thigh that was presented. After that, the Nazirite may drink **wine**.

Nu 15: 5 the sacrifice, prepare a quarter of a hin of **wine** as a drink offering.
15: 7 a third of a hin of **wine** as a drink offering. Offer it as an aroma
15: 10 Also bring half a hin of **wine** as a drink offering. It will be an
28: 14 With each bull there is to be a drink offering of half a hin of **wine**;
Dt 14: 26 cattle, sheep, **wine** or other fermented drink, or anything you wish.
28: 39 cultivate them but you will not drink the **wine** or gather the grapes,
29: 6 [29:5] You ate no bread and drank no **wine** or other fermented
32: 33 Their **wine** is the venom of serpents, the deadly poison of cobras.
32: 38 fat of their sacrifices and drank the **wine** *of* their drink offerings?
Jos 9: 4 were loaded with worn-out sacks and old **wineskins** [+5532],
9: 13 these **wineskins** [+5532] that we filled were new, but see how
Jdg 13: 4 Now see to it that you drink no **wine** or other fermented drink
13: 7 drink no **wine** or other fermented drink and do not eat anything
13: 14 She must not eat anything that comes from the **grapevine** [+1728],
13: 14 nor drink any **wine** or other fermented drink nor eat anything
19: 19 for our donkeys and bread and **wine** for ourselves your servants—
1Sa 1: 14 "How long will you keep on getting drunk? Get rid of your **wine**."
1: 15 I have not been drinking **wine** or beer; I was pouring out my soul
1: 24 with a three-year-old bull, an ephah of flour and a skin of **wine**,
10: 3 another three loaves of bread, and another a skin of **wine**.
16: 20 a skin of **wine** and a young goat and sent them with his son David
25: 18 two skins of **wine**, five dressed sheep, five seahs of roasted grain,
25: 37 Then in the morning, when Nabal *was* **sober** [+2021+3655+4946],
2Sa 13: 28 When Amnon is in high spirits from drinking **wine** and I say to
16: 1 cakes of raisins, a hundred cakes of figs and a skin of **wine**.
16: 2 the **wine** is to refresh those who become exhausted in the desert."
1Ch 9: 29 as well as the flour and **wine**, and the oil, incense and spices.
12: 40 [12:41] fig cakes, raisin cakes, **wine**, oil, cattle and sheep,
27: 27 was in charge of the produce of the vineyards for the **wine** vats.
2Ch 2: 10 [2:9] twenty thousand baths of **wine** and twenty thousand baths of
2: 15 [2:14] and barley and the olive oil and **wine** he promised,
11: 11 put commanders in them, with supplies of food, olive oil and **wine**.
Ne 2: 1 when **wine** was brought for him, I took the wine and gave it to the
2: 1 wine was brought for him, I took the **wine** and gave it to the king.
5: 15 took forty shekels of silver from them in addition to food and **wine**.
5: 18 and every ten days an abundant supply of **wine** of all kinds.
13: 15 together with **wine**, grapes, figs and all other kinds of loads.
Est 1: 7 one different from the other, and the royal **wine** was abundant,
1: 10 the seventh day, when King Xerxes was in high spirits from **wine**,
5: 6 As they were drinking **wine**, the king again asked Esther,
7: 2 as they were drinking **wine** on that second day, the king again
7: 7 got up in a rage, left his **wine** and went out into the palace garden.
7: 8 king returned from the palace garden to the **banquet** [+5492] hall,
Job 1: 13 were feasting and drinking **wine** at the oldest brother's house,
1: 18 were feasting and drinking **wine** at the oldest brother's house,
32: 19 inside I am like bottled-up **wine**, like new wineskins ready to burst.
Ps 60: 3 [60:5] you have given us **wine** that makes us stagger.
75: 8 [75:9] In the hand of the LORD is a cup full of foaming **wine**
78: 65 awoke as from sleep, as a man wakes from the stupor of **wine**.
104: 15 **wine** that gladdens the heart of man, oil to make his face shine,
Pr 4: 17 They eat the bread of wickedness and drink the **wine** *of* violence.
9: 2 She has prepared her meat and mixed her **wine**; she has also set her
9: 5 "Come, eat my food and drink the **wine** I have mixed.
20: 1 **Wine** is a mocker and beer a brawler; whoever is led astray by
21: 17 will become poor; whoever loves **wine** and oil will never be rich.
23: 20 Do not join those who drink too much **wine** or gorge themselves
23: 30 Those who linger over **wine**, who go to sample bowls of mixed
23: 31 Do not gaze at **wine** when it is red, when it sparkles in the cup,
31: 4 not for kings to drink **wine**, not for rulers to crave beer,
31: 6 beer to those who are perishing, **wine** to those who are in anguish;
Ecc 2: 3 I tried cheering myself with **wine**, and embracing folly—my mind
9: 7 your food with gladness, and drink your **wine** with a joyful heart,
10: 19 A feast is made for laughter, and **wine** makes life merry,
SS 1: 2 kisses of his mouth—for your love is more delightful than **wine**.
1: 4 and delight in you; we will praise your love more than **wine**.
2: 4 He has taken me to the **banquet hall** [+1074], and his banner over
4: 10 How much more pleasing is your love than **wine**, and the fragrance
5: 1 my honeycomb and my honey; I have drunk my **wine** and my milk.
7: 9 [7:10] your mouth like the best **wine**. May the wine go straight to
8: 2 I would give you spiced **wine** to drink, the nectar of my
Isa 5: 11 who stay up late at night till they are inflamed with **wine**.
5: 12 and lyres at their banquets, tambourines and flutes and **wine**,
5: 22 Woe to those who are heroes at drinking **wine** and champions at
16: 10 no one treads out **wine** at the presses, for I have put an end to the
22: 13 and killing of sheep, eating of meat and drinking of **wine**!
24: 9 No longer do they drink **wine** with a song; the beer is bitter to its
24: 11 In the streets they cry out for **wine**; all joy turns to gloom,
28: 1 of a fertile valley—to that city, the pride of those laid low by **wine**!
28: 7 And these also stagger from **wine** and reel from beer: Priests
28: 7 and prophets stagger from beer and are befuddled with **wine**;
29: 9 be drunk, but not from **wine**, stagger, but not from beer.
51: 21 hear this, you afflicted one, made drunk, but not with **wine**.
55: 1 Come, buy **wine** and milk without money and without cost.
56: 12 "Come," each one cries, "let me get **wine**! Let us drink our fill of
Jer 13: 12 the God of Israel, says: Every wineskin should be filled with **wine**.'
13: 12 'Don't we know that every wineskin should be filled with **wine**?'
23: 9 like a man overcome by **wine**, because of the LORD and his holy
25: 15 "Take from my hand this cup filled with the **wine** of my wrath
35: 2 rooms of the house of the LORD and give them **wine** to drink."
35: 5 I set bowls full of **wine** and some cups before the men of the
35: 5 men of the Recabite family and said to them, "Drink *some* **wine**."
35: 6 they replied, "We do not drink **wine**, because our forefather
35: 6 'Neither you nor your descendants must ever drink **wine**.
35: 8 nor our wives nor our sons and daughters have ever drunk **wine**
35: 14 'Jonadab son of Recab ordered his sons not to drink **wine** and this
40: 10 you are to harvest the **wine**, summer fruit and oil, and put them in
40: 12 And they harvested an abundance of **wine** and summer fruit.
48: 33 I have stopped the flow of **wine** from the presses; no one treads
51: 7 The nations drank her **wine**; therefore they have now gone mad.
La 2: 12 They say to their mothers, "Where is bread and **wine**?" as they
Eze 27: 18 did business with you in **wine** *from* Helbon and wool from Zahar.
44: 21 No priest is to drink **wine** when he enters the inner court.
Da 1: 5 them a daily amount of food and **wine** from the king's table.
1: 8 Daniel resolved not to defile himself with the royal food and **wine**,
1: 16 and the **wine** they were to drink and gave them vegetables instead.
10: 3 I ate no choice food; no meat or **wine** touched my lips; and I used
Hos 4: 11 to prostitution, to **old wine** and new, which take away the
7: 5 of the festival of our king the princes become inflamed with **wine**,
9: 4 They will not pour out **wine offerings** to the LORD, nor will their
14: 7 [14:8] a vine, and his fame will be like the **wine** *from* Lebanon.
Joel 1: 5 Wail, all you drinkers of **wine**; wail because of the new wine,
3: 3 [4:3] for prostitutes; they sold girls for **wine** that they might drink.
Am 2: 8 in pledge. In the house of their god they drink **wine** *taken as* fines.
2: 12 "But you made the Nazirites drink **wine** and commanded the
5: 11 you have planted lush vineyards, you will not drink their **wine**.
6: 6 You drink **wine** by the bowlful and use the finest lotions, but you
9: 14 They will plant vineyards and drink their **wine**; they will make
Mic 2: 11 and says, 'I will prophesy for you plenty of **wine** and beer,'
6: 15 the oil on yourselves, you will crush grapes but not drink the **wine**.
Hab 2: 5 indeed, **wine** betrays him; he is arrogant and never at rest.
Zep 1: 13 not live in them; they will plant vineyards but not drink the **wine**.
Hag 2: 12 that fold touches some bread or stew, some **wine**, oil or other food,
Zec 9: 15 They will drink and roar as with **wine**; they will be full like a bowl
10: 7 like mighty men, and their hearts will be glad as with **wine**.

3517 יָךְ **yak**, var. Not used in NIV/BHS

3518 יְכָנְיָה **yᵉkônᵉyâ**, n.pr.m. Not used in NIV/BHS [√ 3382; cf. 3378 + 3922]

3519 יכח **yākaḥ**, v. [59] [→ 9349, 9350]

rebuke [14], punish [3], rebuked [3], rebukes [3], chosen [2], judge [2], rebuke frankly [+906+3519] [2], settle disputes [2], surely rebuke [+906+3519] [2], accuse [1], accuses [1], arbitrate [1], are vindicated [1], argue case [1], argue [1], arguments [1], be chastened [1], complained [1], convict [1], correct [1], correction [1], corrects [1], decide [1], defend [1], defender [1], disciplines [1], give decisions [1], lodging a charge [1], pleads [1], present case [1], prove [1], proved wrong [1], reason together [1], reproves [1], use[s] [1]

Ge 20: 16 [C] all who are with you; *you* **are** completely **vindicated**."
21: 25 [G] Abraham **complained** *to* Abimelech about a well of water
24: 14 [G] let her be the one *you have* **chosen** for your servant Isaac.
24: 44 [G] let her be the one the LORD *has* **chosen** for my master's
31: 37 [G] and mine, and *let them* **judge** between the two of us.
31: 42 [G] and the toil of my hands, and last night *he* **rebuked** you."
Lev 19: 17 [G] **Rebuke** [+906+3519] your neighbor **frankly** so you will not
19: 17 [G] **Rebuke** your neighbor **frankly** [+906+3519] so you will not
2Sa 7: 14 [G] When he does wrong, *I will* **punish** him with the rod of men,
2Ki 19: 4 [G] that *he will* **rebuke** him for the words the LORD your God
1Ch 12: 17 [12:18] [G] may the God of our fathers see it and **judge** you."
16: 21 [G] no man to oppress them; for their sake *he* **rebuked** kings:
Job 5: 17 [G] "Blessed is the man whom God **corrects**; so do not despise
6: 25 [G] are honest words! But what do your **arguments** prove?
6: 25 [G] are honest words! But what *do* your arguments **prove**?
6: 26 [G] Do you mean to **correct** what I say, and treat the words of a
9: 33 [G] If only there were *someone to* **arbitrate** between us, to lay
13: 3 [G] to speak to the Almighty and *to* **argue** my **case** with God.
13: 10 [G] *He would* **surely rebuke** [+906+3519] you if you secretly
13: 10 [G] *He would* **surely rebuke** [+906+3519] you if you secretly
13: 15 [G] will I hope in him; *I will* surely **defend** my ways to his face.
15: 3 [G] *Would* he **argue** with useless words, with speeches that have
16: 21 [G] on behalf of a man *he* **pleads** with God as a man pleads for
19: 5 [G] yourselves above me and **use**[s] my humiliation against me,
22: 4 [G] "Is it for your piety that *he* **rebukes** you and brings charges
23: 7 [C] There an upright man *could* **present** his **case** before him,
32: 12 [G] not *one* of you *has* **proved** Job **wrong**; none of you has

Job 33:19 [H] Or a man *may* **be chastened** on a bed of pain with constant
40: 2 [G] correct him? Let him *who* **accuses** God answer him!"
Ps 6: 1 [6:2] [G] *do* not **rebuke** me in your anger or discipline me in
38: 1 [38:2] [G] *do* not **rebuke** me in your anger or discipline me in
50: 8 [G] *I do* not **rebuke** you for your sacrifices or your burnt
50:21 [G] like you. But *I will* **rebuke** you and accuse you to your face.
94:10 [G] *Does he* who disciplines nations not **punish**? Does he who
105:14 [G] no one to oppress them; for their sake *he* **rebuked** kings:
141: 5 [G] it is a kindness; *let him* **rebuke** me—it is oil on my head.
Pr 3:12 [G] because the LORD **disciplines** those he loves, as a father
9: 7 [G] invites insult; *whoever* **rebukes** a wicked man incurs abuse.
9: 8 [G] *Do* not **rebuke** a mocker or he will hate you; rebuke a wise
9: 8 [G] or he will hate you; **rebuke** a wise man and he will love you.
15:12 [G] A mocker resents **correction**; he will not consult the wise.
19:25 [G] **rebuke** a discerning man, and he will gain knowledge.
24:25 [G] it will go well with those *who* **convict** the guilty, and rich
25:12 [G] or an ornament of fine gold is a wise man's **rebuke** to a
28:23 [G] *He who* **rebukes** a man will in the end gain more favor than
30: 6 [G] add to his words, or *he will* **rebuke** you and prove you a liar.
Isa 1:18 [C] "Come now, *let us* **reason together**," says the LORD.
2: 4 [G] the nations and *will* **settle disputes** for many peoples.
11: 3 [G] sees with his eyes, or **decide** by what he hears with his ears;
11: 4 [G] with justice *he will* **give decisions** for the poor of the earth.
29:21 [G] who ensnare the **defender** in court and with false testimony
37: 4 [G] that *he will* **rebuke** him for the words the LORD your God
Jer 2:19 [G] will punish you; your backsliding *will* **rebuke** you.
Eze 3:26 [G] so that you will be silent and unable *to* **rebuke** them,
Hos 4: 4 [G] "But let no man bring a charge, *let* no man **accuse** another,
Am 5:10 [G] you hate the *one who* **reproves** in court and despise him who
Mic 4: 3 [G] and *will* **settle disputes** for strong nations far and wide.
6: 2 [F] case against his people; *he is* **lodging a charge** against Israel.
Hab 1:12 [G] O Rock, you have ordained them to **punish**.

3520 יָכִין¹ yākîn¹, n.pr.m. [6] [√ 3922]

Jakin [6]

Ge 46:10 Ohad, **Jakin**, Zohar and Shaul the son of a Canaanite woman.
Ex 6:15 Ohad, **Jakin**, Zohar and Shaul the son of a Canaanite woman.
Nu 26:12 through Jamin, the Jaminite clan; through **Jakin**, the Jakinite clan;
1Ch 9:10 Of the priests: Jedaiah; Jehoiarib; **Jakin**;
24:17 the twenty-first to **Jakin**, the twenty-second to Gamul,
Ne 11:10 From the priests: Jedaiah; the son of Joiarib; **Jakin**;

3521 יָכִין² yākîn², n.pr.m. [2] [→ 3522; cf. 3922]

Jakin [2]

1Ki 7:21 The pillar to the south he named **Jakin** and the one to the north
2Ch 3:17 The one to the south he named **Jakin** and the one to the north

3522 יָכִינִי yākînî, a.g. [1] [√ 3521; cf. 3922]

Jakinite [1]

Nu 26:12 through Jamin, the Jaminite clan; through Jakin, the **Jakinite** clan;

3523 יָכֹל yākōl, v. [193] [→ 3524, 3525; Ar 10321; *also used with compound proper names*]

cannot [+4202] [45], could [38], able [23], can [22], can't [+4202] [7], overcome [5], must [4], *untranslated* [3], overpower [3], prevail [3], succeed [3], allowed [2], bear [2], can [+3523] [2], can certainly do [+3523+4200] [2], can do [2], ever able [+3523] [2], overcame [2], surely triumph [+3523] [2], allowed to [1], attain [1], avail [1], cannot bear [+4202] [1], cannot stand [+4202] [1], could do [1], could risk [1], dare [1], dares [1], endure [1], failed [+4202] [1], gained the victory [1], have time [+4538] [1], incapable [+4202] [1], powerless [+4202] [1], prevailed [1], too heavy a burden to carry [+906+4202+5951] [1], troubled [+4202+9200] [1], unable [+4202] [1], will [1], won [1]

Ge 13: 6 [A] so great that *they were* not **able** to stay together.
13:16 [A] so that if anyone **could** count the dust, then your offspring
15: 5 [A] and count the stars—if indeed *you* **can** count them."
19:19 [A] I **can't** [+4202] flee to the mountains; this disaster will
19:22 [A] because *I* **cannot** [+4202] do anything until you reach it."
24:50 [A] the LORD; *we* **can** say nothing to you one way or the other.
29: 8 [A] "*We* **can't** [+4202]," they replied, "until all the flocks are
30: 8 [A] "I have had a great struggle with my sister, and *I have* **won**."
31:35 [A] my lord, that *I* **cannot** [+4202] stand up in your presence;
32:25 [32:26] [A] When the man saw that *he could* not **overpower**
32:28 [32:29] [A] with God and with men and *have* **overcome**."
34:14 [A] They said to them, "*We* **can't** [+4202] do such a thing;
36: 7 [A] the land where they were staying **could** not support them
37: 4 [A] they hated him and **could** not speak a kind word to him.
43:32 [A] because Egyptians **could** not eat with Hebrews, for that is
44: 1 [A] "Fill the men's sacks with as much food as *they* **can** carry,
44:22 [A] we said to my lord, 'The boy **cannot** [+4202] leave his father;
44:26 [A] we said, '*We* **cannot** [+4202] go down. Only if our youngest
44:26 [A] *We* **cannot** [+4202] see the man's face unless our youngest
45: 1 [A] Joseph **could** no longer control himself before all his
45: 3 [A] his brothers *were* not **able** to answer him, because they were
48:10 [A] were failing because of old age, and *he* **could** hardly see.
Ex 2: 3 [A] when *she* **could** hide him no longer, she got a papyrus basket
7:21 [A] so bad that the Egyptians **could** not drink its water.
7:24 [A] because *they* **could** not drink the water of the river.
8:18 [8:14] [A] to produce gnats by their secret arts, *they* **could** not.
9:11 [A] The magicians **could** not stand before Moses because of the
10: 5 [A] the face of the ground so that it **cannot** [+4202] be seen.
12:39 [A] *did* not **have time** [+4538] to prepare food for themselves.
15:23 [A] *they* **could** not drink its water because it was bitter.
18:18 [A] is too heavy for you; *you* **cannot** [+4202] handle it alone.
18:23 [A] and God so commands, *you will be* **able** to stand the strain,
19:23 [A] "The people **cannot** [+4202] come up Mount Sinai,
33:20 [A] But," he said, "*you* **cannot** [+4202] see my face, for no one
40:35 [A] Moses **could** not enter the Tent of Meeting because the cloud
Nu 9: 6 [A] some of them **could** not celebrate the Passover on that day
11:14 [A] I **cannot** [+4202] carry all these people by myself;
13:30 [A] of the land, for *we* **can** [+3523+4200] **certainly do** it."
13:30 [A] of the land, for *we* **can certainly do** [+3523+4200] it."
13:31 [A] up with him said, "*We* **can't** [+4202] attack those people;
14:16 [A] 'The LORD *was* not **able** to bring these people into the land
22: 6 [A] Perhaps then *I will be* **able** to defeat them and drive them out
22:11 [A] Perhaps then *I will be* **able** to fight them and drive them
22:18 [A] *I* **could** not do anything great or small to go beyond the
22:37 [A] you come to me? *Am I* really not **able** to reward you?"
22:38 [A] Balaam replied. "But **can** [+3523] *I* say just anything?
22:38 [A] Balaam replied. "But **can I** [+3523] say just anything?
24:13 [A] *I* **could** not do anything of my own accord, good or bad,
Dt 1: 9 [A] At that time I said to you, "You *are* **too heavy a burden** for me **to carry** [+906+4202+5951] alone.
7:17 [A] are stronger than we are. How **can** *we* drive them out?"
7:22 [A] *You will* not *be* **allowed to** eliminate them all at once,
9:28 [A] 'Because the LORD *was* not **able** to take them into the land
12:17 [A] *You* **must** not eat in your own towns the tithe of your grain
14:24 [A] the LORD your God and **cannot** [+4202] carry your tithe
16: 5 [A] *You* **must** not sacrifice the Passover in any town the
17:15 [A] **[NIE]** Do not place a foreigner over you, one who is not a
21:16 [A] *he* **must** not give the rights of the firstborn to the son of the
22: 3 [A] or his cloak or anything he loses. Do not ignore it. **[NIE]**
22:19 [A] to be his wife; *he* **must** not divorce her as long as he lives.
22:29 [A] violated her. *He* **can** never divorce her as long as he lives.
24: 4 [A] *is* not **allowed** to marry her again after she has been defiled.
28:27 [A] and the itch, from which *you* **cannot** [+4202] be cured.
28:35 [A] and legs with painful boils that **cannot** [+4202] be cured,
31: 2 [A] and twenty years old and *I am* no longer **able** to lead you.
Jos 7:12 [A] That is why the Israelites **cannot** [+4202] stand against their
7:13 [A] *You* **cannot** [+4202] stand against your enemies until you
9:19 [A] the God of Israel, and *we* **cannot** [+4202] touch them now.
15:63 [A] Judah **could** not dislodge the Jebusites, who were living in
17:12 [A] Yet the Manassites *were* not **able** to occupy these towns,
24:19 [A] said to the people, "*You are* not **able** to serve the LORD.
Jdg 2:14 [A] enemies all around, whom *they were* no longer **able** to resist.
8: 3 [A] What *was I* **able** to do compared to you?" At this, their
11:35 [A] made a vow to the LORD that *I* **cannot** [+4202] break."
14:13 [A] If *you* **can't** [+4202] tell me the answer, you must give me
14:14 [A] For three days *they* **could** not give the answer.
16: 5 [A] how *we can* **overpower** him so we may tie him up
21:18 [A] We **can't** [+4202] give them our daughters as wives,
Ru 4: 6 [A] "Then *I* **cannot** [+4202] redeem it because I might endanger
4: 6 [A] own estate. You redeem it yourself. *I* **cannot** [+4202] do it."
1Sa 3: 2 [A] whose eyes were becoming so weak that *he* **could** barely see,
4:15 [A] years old and whose eyes were set so that *he* **could** not see.
6:20 [A] "Who **can** stand in the presence of the LORD, this holy
17: 9 [A] If *he is* **able** to fight and kill me, we will become your
17: 9 [A] if I **overcome** him and kill him, you will become our subjects
17:33 [A] "*You are* not **able** to go out against this Philistine and fight
17:39 [A] "*I* **cannot** [+4202] go in these," he said to Saul, "because I
26:25 [A] you will do great things and **surely triumph** [+3523]."
26:25 [A] you will do great things and **surely triumph** [+3523]."
2Sa 3:11 [A] Ish-Bosheth *did* not **dare** to say another word to Abner,
12:23 [A] **Can** *I* bring him back again? I will go to him, but he will not
17:17 [A] for *they* **could** not **risk** being seen entering the city.
1Ki 3: 9 [A] For who *is* **able** to govern this great people of yours?"
5: 3 [5:17] [A] *he* **could** not build a temple for the Name of the
8:11 [A] the priests **could** not perform their service because of the
9:21 [A] in the land, whom the Israelites **could** not exterminate—
13: 4 [A] the man shriveled up, so that *he* **could** not pull it back.
13:16 [A] "*I* **cannot** [+4202] turn back and go with you, nor can I eat
14: 4 [A] Now Ahijah **could** not see; his sight was gone because of his
20: 9 [A] this demand *I* **cannot** [+4202] meet.' " They left and took the

1Ki 22:22 [A] " '*You will* **succeed** in enticing him,' said the LORD. 'Go
2Ki 3:26 [A] break through to the king of Edom, but *they* **failed** [+4202].
4:40 [A] of God, there is death in the pot!" And *they* **could** not eat it.
16: 5 [A] and besieged Ahaz, but *they* **could** not overpower him.
18:23 [A] you two thousand horses—if *you* **can** put riders on them!
18:29 [A] deceive you. *He* **cannot** [+4202] deliver you from my hand.
1Ch 21:30 [A] David **could** not go before it to inquire of God, because he
2Ch 5:14 [A] the priests **could** not perform their service because of the
7: 2 [A] The priests **could** not enter the temple of the LORD
7: 7 [A] because the bronze altar he had made **could** not hold the
18:21 [A] " '*You will* **succeed** in enticing him,' said the LORD. 'Go
29:34 [A] however, were too few **[NIE]** to skin all the burnt offerings;
30: 3 [A] *They had* not *been* **able** to celebrate it at the regular time
32:13 [A] *Were* the gods of those nations **ever able** [+3523] to deliver
32:13 [A] *Were* the gods of those nations **ever able** [+3523] to deliver
32:14 [A] fathers destroyed *has been* **able** to save his people from me?
32:14 [A] How then **can** your god deliver you from my hand?
32:15 [A] or kingdom *has been* **able** to deliver his people from my
Ezr 2:59 [A] *they* **could** not show that their families were descended from
Ne 4:10 [4:4] [A] so much rubble that we **cannot** [+4202] rebuild the
6: 3 [A] am carrying on a great project and **cannot** [+4202] go down.
7:61 [A] *they* **could** not show that their families were descended from
Est 6:13 [A] is of Jewish origin, *you* **cannot** [+4202] **stand** against him—
8: 6 [A] For how *can I* **bear** to see disaster fall on my people? How
8: 6 [A] How *can I* **bear** to see the destruction of my family?"
Job 4: 2 [A] will you be impatient? But who **can** keep from speaking?
31:23 [A] and for fear of his splendor *I* **could** not **do** such things.
33: 5 [A] Answer me then, if *you* **can**; prepare yourself and confront
42: 2 [A] "I know that *you* **can do** all things; no plan of yours can be
Ps 13: 4 [13:5] [A] my enemy will say, "*I have* **overcome** him," and my
18:38 [18:39] [A] I crushed them so that *they* **could** not rise; they fell
21:11 [21:12] [A] and devise wicked schemes, *they* cannot **succeed**;
36:12 [36:13] [A] evildoers lie fallen—thrown down, not **able** to rise!
40:12 [40:13] [A] sins have overtaken me, and *I* **cannot** [+4202] see.
78:19 [A] against God, saying, "**Can** God spread a table in the desert?
78:20 [A] streams flowed abundantly. But **can** *he* also give us food?
101: 5 [A] has haughty eyes and a proud heart, him *will I* not **endure**.
129: 2 [A] my youth, but *they have* not **gained the victory** over me.
139: 6 [A] is too wonderful for me, too lofty for *me to* **attain**.
Pr 30:21 [A] the earth trembles, under four *it* **cannot** [+4202] bear up:
Ecc 1: 8 [A] All things are wearisome, more than one **can** say. The eye
1:15 [A] What is twisted **cannot** [+4202] be straightened; what is
1:15 [A] be straightened; what is lacking **cannot** [+4202] be counted.
6:10 [A] no man **can** contend with one who is stronger than he.
7:13 [A] has done: Who **can** straighten what he has made crooked?
8:17 [A] No one **can** comprehend what goes on under the sun.
8:17 [A] claims he knows, *he* **cannot** [+4202] really comprehend it.
SS 8: 7 [A] Many waters **cannot** [+4202] quench love; rivers cannot
Isa 1:13 [A] *I* **cannot bear** [+4202] your evil assemblies.
7: 1 [A] to fight against Jerusalem, but *they* **could** not overpower it.
16:12 [A] when she goes to her shrine to pray, *it is to* no **avail**.
29:11 [A] to him, "Read this, please," he will answer, "*I* **can't** [+4202];
36: 8 [A] you two thousand horses—if *you* **can** put riders on them!
36:14 [A] let Hezekiah deceive you. *He* **cannot** [+4202] deliver you!
46: 2 [A] bow down together; **unable** [+4202] to rescue the burden,
47:11 [A] A calamity will fall upon you that *you* **cannot** [+4202] ward
47:12 [A] Perhaps *you* **will** succeed, perhaps you will cause terror.
56:10 [A] they are all mute dogs, *they* **cannot** [+4202] bark; they lie
57:20 [A] *which* **cannot** [+4202] rest, whose waves cast up mire
59:14 [A] has stumbled in the streets, honesty **cannot** [+4202] enter.
Jer 1:19 [A] They will fight against you but *will* not **overcome** you, for I
3: 5 [A] This is how you talk, but you do all the evil *you* **can**."
5:22 [A] The waves may roll, but they cannot **prevail**; they may roar,
6:10 [A] to me? Their ears are closed so *they* **cannot** [+4202] hear.
11:11 [A] 'I will bring on them a disaster *they* **cannot** [+4202] escape.
13:23 [A] Neither **can** you do good who are accustomed to doing evil.
14: 9 [A] taken by surprise, like a warrior **powerless** [+4202] to save?
15:20 [A] they will fight against you but *will* not **overcome** you, for I
18: 6 [A] house of Israel, **can** *I* not do with you as this potter does?"
19:11 [A] this potter's jar is smashed and **cannot** [+4202] be repaired.
20: 7 [A] and I was deceived; you overpowered me and **prevailed**.
20: 9 [A] I am weary of holding it in; indeed, *I* **cannot** [+4202].
20:10 [A] then *we will* **prevail** over him and take our revenge on him."
20:11 [A] so my persecutors will stumble and not **prevail**.
36: 5 [A] am restricted; *I* **cannot** [+4202] go to the LORD's temple.
38: 5 [A] "The king **can do** nothing to oppose you."
38:22 [A] " 'They misled you and **overcame** you—those trusted friends
44:22 [A] When the LORD **could** no longer endure your wicked
49:10 [A] his hiding places, so that *he* **cannot** [+4202] conceal himself.
49:23 [A] They are disheartened, **troubled** [+4202+9200] like the
La 1:14 [A] He has handed me over to those *I* **cannot** [+4202] withstand.
4:14 [A] so defiled with blood that no *one* **dares** to touch their
Eze 7:19 [A] gold *will* not *be* **able** to save them in the day of the LORD's
33:12 [A] *will* not *be* **allowed** to live because of his former
47: 5 [A] now it was a river that *I* **could** not cross, because the water
Da 10:17 [A] How **can** I, your servant, talk with you, my lord? My
Hos 5:13 [A] But he *is* not **able** to cure you, not able to heal your sores.
8: 5 [A] How long *will they be* **incapable** [+4202] *of* purity?
12: 4 [12:5] [A] He struggled with the angel and **overcame** him;
Am 7:10 [A] heart of Israel. The land **cannot** [+4202] bear all his words.
Ob 1: 7 [A] to the border; your friends will deceive and **overpower** you;
Jnh 1:13 [A] But *they* **could** not, for the sea grew even wilder than before.
Hab 1:13 [A] too pure to look on evil; *you* **cannot** [+4202] tolerate wrong.
Zep 1:18 [A] Neither their silver nor their gold *will be* **able** to save them

3524 יְכָלְיָה *yᵉkolyâ*, n.pr.f. [1] [√ 3523 + 3378]

Jecoliah [1]

2Ch 26: 3 His mother's name was **Jecoliah**; she was from Jerusalem.

3525 יְכָלְיָהוּ *yᵉkolyāhû*, n.pr.f. [1] [√ 3523 + 3378]

Jecoliah [1]

2Ki 15: 2 His mother's name was **Jecoliah**; she was from Jerusalem.

3526 יְכָנְיָה *yᵉkonyâ*, n.pr.m. [6] [√ 3382; cf. 3378 + 3922]

Jehoiachin [6]

1Ch 3:16 The successors of Jehoiakim: **Jehoiachin** his son, and Zedekiah.
3:17 The descendants of **Jehoiachin** the captive: Shealtiel his son,
Est 2: 6 among those taken captive with **Jehoiachin** king of Judah.
Jer 27:20 **Jehoiachin** son of Jehoiakim king of Judah into exile from
28: 4 I will also bring back to this place **Jehoiachin** son of Jehoiakim
29: 2 (This was after King **Jehoiachin** and the queen mother, the court

3527 יְכָנְיָהוּ *yᵉkonyāhû*, n.pr.m. [1] [√ 3382; cf. 3378 + 3922]

Jehoiachin [1]

Jer 24: 1 After **Jehoiachin** son of Jehoiakim king of Judah and the officials,

3528 יָלַד *yālad*, v. [492] [→ 2263, 3529, 3530, 3531, 3533, 3535, 4256, 4580, 4582, 9351?, 9352]

father [147], bore [49], gave birth [46], had [31], born [24], were born [20], give birth [16], borne [13], in labor [12], gives birth [8], *untranslated* [7], have [7], midwives [7], was born [7], is born [5], be born [4], bear children [4], has [4], mother [4], bear [3], bears [3], given birth [3], having children [3], baby [2], been born [2], birth [2], borne children [2], childless [+4202] [2], descendants [2], had a baby [2], had a son [2], had children [2], have children [2], in childbirth [2], midwife [2], was descended [2], arrives [1], be brought forth [1], bear a child [1], bearing children [1], begotten [1], birthday [+906+3427] [1], bore a child [1], bore young [1], bring forth [1], bring to delivery [1], child was born [1], childbirth [1], children born [1], children [1], daughter [1], descendant [1], fathered [1], fathers [1], forefather [1], gave life [1], give delivery [1], giving birth [1], had sons [1], has son [1], have a child [1], have a son [1], help in childbirth [1], indicated ancestry [1], lay [1], making bud [1], menˢ [1], native-born [+824+928+2021] [1], near the time of delivery [1], newborn [1], placed at birth [1], remained childless [+4202] [1], son be born [1], womenˢ [1], yet unborn [1]

Ge 3:16 [A] in childbearing; with pain *you will* **give birth** *to* children.
4: 1 [A] wife Eve, and she became pregnant and **gave birth** *to* Cain.
4: 2 [A] Later *she* **gave birth** *to* his brother Abel. Now Abel kept
4:17 [A] his wife, and she became pregnant and **gave birth** *to* Enoch.
4:18 [C] To Enoch **was born** Irad, and Irad was the father of
4:18 [A] Enoch was born Irad, and Irad *was the* **father** *of* Mehujael,
4:18 [A] of Mehujael, and Mehujael *was the* **father** *of* Methushael,
4:18 [A] of Methushael, and Methushael *was the* **father** *of* Lamech.
4:20 [A] Adah **gave birth** *to* Jabal; he was the father of those who live
4:22 [A] Zillah also **had a son**, Tubal-Cain, who forged all kinds of
4:25 [A] and *she* **gave birth** *to* a son and named him Seth, saying,
4:26 [E] Seth also **had** a son, and he named him Enosh. At that time
5: 3 [G] *he* **had a son** in his own likeness, in his own image;
5: 4 [G] After Seth *was* **born**, Adam lived 800 years and had other
5: 4 [G] Adam lived 800 years and **had** other sons and daughters.
5: 6 [G] Seth had lived 105 years, *he became the* **father** *of* Enosh.
5: 7 [G] after he *became the* **father** *of* Enosh, Seth lived 807 years
5: 7 [G] Seth lived 807 years and **had** other sons and daughters.
5: 9 [G] Enosh had lived 90 years, *he became the* **father** *of* Kenan.
5:10 [G] after he *became the* **father** *of* Kenan, Enosh lived 815 years
5:10 [G] Enosh lived 815 years and **had** other sons and daughters.
5:12 [G] had lived 70 years, *he became the* **father** *of* Mahalalel.
5:13 [G] after he *became the* **father** *of* Mahalalel, Kenan lived 840
5:13 [G] Kenan lived 840 years and **had** other sons and daughters.
5:15 [G] Mahalalel had lived 65 years, *he became the* **father** *of* Jared.
5:16 [G] after he *became the* **father** *of* Jared, Mahalalel lived 830
5:16 [G] Mahalalel lived 830 years and **had** other sons and daughters.
5:18 [G] Jared had lived 162 years, *he became the* **father** *of* Enoch.

Ge 5:19 [G] after he *became the* **father** *of* Enoch, Jared lived 800 years
5:19 [G] Jared lived 800 years and **had** other sons and daughters.
5:21 [G] had lived 65 years, *he became the* **father** *of* Methuselah.
5:22 [G] after he *became the* **father** *of* Methuselah, Enoch walked
5:22 [G] with God 300 years and **had** other sons and daughters.
5:25 [G] had lived 187 years, *he became the* **father** *of* Lamech.
5:26 [G] after he *became the* **father** *of* Lamech, Methuselah lived 782
5:26 [G] lived 782 years and **had** other sons and daughters.
5:28 [G] When Lamech had lived 182 years, *he* **had** a son.
5:30 [G] After Noah *was* **born**, Lamech lived 595 years and had other
5:30 [G] Lamech lived 595 years and **had** other sons and daughters.
5:32 [G] years old, he *became the* **father** *of* Shem, Ham and Japheth.
6:1 [E] in number on the earth and daughters **were born** to them,
6:4 [A] went to the daughters of men and **had children** by them.
6:10 [G] Noah **had** three sons: Shem, Ham and Japheth.
10:1 [C] Noah's sons, who themselves **had** sons after the flood.
10:8 [A] Cush *was the* **father** *of* Nimrod, who grew to be a mighty
10:13 [A] Mizraim *was the* **father** *of* the Ludites, Anamites, Lehabites,
10:15 [A] Canaan *was the* **father** *of* Sidon his firstborn, and *of* the
10:21 [E] *Sons* **were** also **born** to Shem, whose older brother was
10:24 [A] Arphaxad *was the* **father** *of* Shelah, and Shelah the father of
10:24 [A] was the father of Shelah, and Shelah *the* **father** *of* Eber.
10:25 [E] Two sons **were born** to Eber: One was named Peleg,
10:26 [A] Joktan *was the* **father** *of* Almodad, Sheleph, Hazarmaveth,
11:10 [G] Shem was 100 years old, *he became the* **father** *of* Arphaxad.
11:11 [G] after he *became the* **father** *of* Arphaxad, Shem lived 500
11:11 [G] Shem lived 500 years and **had** other sons and daughters.
11:12 [G] had lived 35 years, *he became the* **father** *of* Shelah.
11:13 [G] after he *became the* **father** *of* Shelah, Arphaxad lived 403
11:13 [G] Arphaxad lived 403 years and **had** other sons and daughters.
11:14 [G] Shelah had lived 30 years, *he became the* **father** *of* Eber.
11:15 [G] after he *became the* **father** *of* Eber, Shelah lived 403 years
11:15 [G] Shelah lived 403 years and **had** other sons and daughters.
11:16 [G] Eber had lived 34 years, *he became the* **father** *of* Peleg.
11:17 [G] after he *became the* **father** *of* Peleg, Eber lived 430 years
11:17 [G] Eber lived 430 years and **had** other sons and daughters.
11:18 [G] Peleg had lived 30 years, *he became the* **father** *of* Reu.
11:19 [G] after he *became the* **father** *of* Reu, Peleg lived 209 years
11:19 [G] Peleg lived 209 years and **had** other sons and daughters.
11:20 [G] Reu had lived 32 years, *he became the* **father** *of* Serug.
11:21 [G] after he *became the* **father** *of* Serug, Reu lived 207 years
11:21 [G] Reu lived 207 years and **had** other sons and daughters.
11:22 [G] Serug had lived 30 years, *he became the* **father** *of* Nahor.
11:23 [G] after he *became the* **father** *of* Nahor, Serug lived 200 years
11:23 [G] Serug lived 200 years and **had** other sons and daughters.
11:24 [G] Nahor had lived 29 years, *he became the* **father** *of* Terah.
11:25 [G] after he *became the* **father** *of* Terah, Nahor lived 119 years
11:25 [G] Nahor lived 119 years and **had** other sons and daughters.
11:26 [G] 70 years, *he became the* **father** *of* Abram, Nahor and Haran.
11:27 [G] Terah *became the* **father** *of* Abram, Nahor and Haran.
11:27 [G] and Haran. And Haran *became the* **father** *of* Lot.
16:1 [A] Now Sarai, Abram's wife, *had* **borne** him no **children**.
16:2 [A] to Abram, "The LORD has kept me from **having children**.
16:11 [A] "You are now with child and *you will* **have** a son. You shall
16:15 [A] So Hagar **bore** Abram a son, and Abram gave the name
16:15 [A] and Abram gave the name Ishmael to the son she *had* **borne**.
16:16 [A] Abram was eighty-six years old when Hagar **bore** him
17:17 [C] "*Will* a **son be born** to a man a hundred years old?
17:17 [A] years old? *Will* Sarah **bear a child** at the age of ninety?"
17:19 [A] God said, "Yes, but your wife Sarah *will* **bear** you a son,
17:20 [G] *He will be the* **father** *of* twelve rulers, and I will make him
17:21 [A] whom Sarah *will* **bear** to you by this time next year."
18:13 [A] "Why did Sarah laugh and say, '*Will I* really **have a child**,
19:37 [A] The older daughter **had** a son, and she named him Moab;
19:38 [A] The younger daughter also **had** a son, and she named him
20:17 [A] and his slave girls so *they could* **have children** again,
21:2 [A] became pregnant and **bore** a son to Abraham in his old age,
21:3 [A] Abraham gave the name Isaac to the son Sarah **bore** him.
21:3 [C] gave the name Isaac to the son Sarah bore him. **[RPH]**
21:5 [C] was a hundred years old when his son Isaac **was born** to him.
21:7 [A] nurse children? Yet *I have* **borne** him a son in his old age."
21:9 [A] Sarah saw that the son whom Hagar the Egyptian *had* **borne**
22:20 [A] is also a mother; she *has* **borne** sons to your brother Nahor:
22:23 [A] Bethuel *became the* **father** *of* Rebekah. Milcah bore these
22:23 [A] Milcah **bore** these eight sons to Abraham's brother Nahor.
22:24 [A] also **had sons**: Tebah, Gaham, Tahash and Maacah.
24:15 [E] She *was the* **daughter** of Bethuel son of Milcah, who was
24:24 [A] the daughter of Bethuel, the son that Milcah **bore** to Nahor."
24:36 [A] My master's wife Sarah *has* **borne** him a son in her old age,
24:47 [A] of Bethuel son of Nahor, whom Milcah **bore** to him.'
25:2 [A] *She* **bore** him Zimran, Jokshan, Medan, Midian, Ishbak and
25:3 [A] Jokshan *was the* **father** *of* Sheba and Dedan; the descendants
25:12 [A] Sarah's maidservant, Hagar the Egyptian, **bore** to Abraham.
25:19 [G] Abraham's son Isaac. Abraham *became the* **father** *of* Isaac,
25:24 [A] When the time came for her to **give birth**, there were twin
25:26 [A] Isaac was sixty years old when Rebekah **gave birth** *to* them.
29:32 [A] Leah became pregnant and **gave birth** *to* a son. She named
29:33 [A] conceived again, and when *she* **gave birth** *to* a son she said,
29:34 [A] she conceived, and when *she* **gave birth** *to* a son she said,
29:34 [A] attached to me, because *I have* **borne** him three sons."
29:35 [A] conceived again, and when *she* **gave birth** *to* a son she said,
29:35 [A] So she named him Judah. Then she stopped **having children**.
30:1 [A] Rachel saw that *she was* not **bearing** Jacob any **children**,
30:3 [A] Sleep with her so that *she can* **bear children** for me and that
30:5 [A] and she became pregnant and **bore** him a son.
30:7 [A] servant Bilhah conceived again and **bore** Jacob a second son.
30:9 [A] When Leah saw that she had stopped **having children**, she
30:10 [A] Leah's servant Zilpah **bore** Jacob a son.
30:12 [A] Leah's servant Zilpah **bore** Jacob a second son.
30:17 [A] to Leah, and she became pregnant and **bore** Jacob a fifth son.
30:19 [A] Leah conceived again and **bore** Jacob a sixth son.
30:20 [A] treat me with honor, because *I have* **borne** him six sons."
30:21 [A] Some time later *she* **gave birth** *to* a daughter and named her
30:23 [A] She became pregnant and **gave birth** *to* a son and said,
30:25 [A] After Rachel **gave birth** *to* Joseph, Jacob said to Laban,
30:39 [A] they **bore young** that were streaked or speckled or spotted.
31:8 [A] then all the flocks **gave birth** *to* speckled young;
31:8 [A] will be your wages,' then all the flocks **bore** streaked young.
31:43 [A] daughters of mine, or about the children they *have* **borne**?
34:1 [A] Now Dinah, the daughter Leah *had* **borne** to Jacob, went out
35:16 [A] Rachel *began to* **give birth** and had great difficulty.
35:16 [A] Rachel began to give birth and had great difficulty. **[RPH]**
35:17 [A] as she was having great difficulty in **childbirth**, the midwife
35:17 [D] the **midwife** said to her, "Don't be afraid, for you have
35:26 [E] the sons of Jacob, who **were born** to him in Paddan Aram.
36:4 [A] Adah **bore** Eliphaz to Esau, Basemath bore Reuel,
36:4 [A] Adah bore Eliphaz to Esau, Basemath **bore** Reuel,
36:5 [A] Oholibamah **bore** Jeush, Jalam and Korah. These were the
36:5 [E] were the sons of Esau, who **were born** to him in Canaan.
36:12 [A] also had a concubine named Timna, *who* **bore** him Amalek.
36:14 [A] of Zibeon, whom *she* **bore** to Esau: Jeush, Jalam and Korah.
38:3 [A] she became pregnant and **gave birth** *to* a son, who was
38:4 [A] She conceived again and **gave birth** *to* a son and named him
38:5 [A] *She* **gave birth** *to* still another son and named him Shelah.
38:5 [A] him Shelah. It was at Kezib that she **gave birth** *to* him.
38:27 [A] When the time came for her *to* **give birth**, there were twin
38:28 [A] As she *was* **giving birth**, one of them put out his hand;
38:28 [D] so the **midwife** took a scarlet thread and tied it on his wrist
40:20 [H] Now the third day was Pharaoh's **birthday** [+906+3427],
41:50 [E] two sons **were born** to Joseph by Asenath daughter of
41:50 [A] two sons were born to Joseph **[RPH]** by Asenath daughter
44:27 [A] father said to us, 'You know that my wife **bore** me two sons.
46:15 [A] were the sons Leah **bore** to Jacob in Paddan Aram, besides
46:18 [A] These were the children **born** to Jacob by Zilpah,
46:20 [C] In Egypt, Manasseh and Ephraim **were born** to Joseph by
46:20 [A] Ephraim were born to Joseph **[RPH]** by Asenath daughter
46:22 [E] These were the sons of Rachel who **were born** to Jacob—
46:25 [A] These were the sons **born** to Jacob by Bilhah, whom Laban
46:27 [E] With the two sons who *had* **been born** to Joseph in Egypt,
48:5 [C] your two sons **born** to you in Egypt before I came to you
48:6 [G] Any children **born** *to* you after them will be yours;
50:23 [E] son of Manasseh *were* **placed at birth** on Joseph's knees.
Ex 1:15 [D] The king of Egypt said to the Hebrew **midwives**,
1:16 [D] "When you **help** the Hebrew women **in childbirth** and
1:17 [D] The **midwives**, however, feared God and did not do what the
1:18 [D] the king of Egypt summoned the **midwives** and asked them,
1:19 [D] The **midwives** answered Pharaoh, "Hebrew women are not
1:19 [A] are vigorous and **give birth** before the midwives arrive."
1:19 [D] they are vigorous and give birth before the **midwives** arrive."
1:20 [D] So God was kind to the **midwives** and the people increased
1:21 [D] because the **midwives** feared God, he gave them families of
2:2 [A] she became pregnant and **gave birth** *to* a son. When she saw
2:22 [A] Zipporah **gave birth** *to* a son, and Moses named him
6:20 [A] his father's sister Jochebed, *who* **bore** him Aaron and Moses.
6:23 [A] and *she* **bore** him Nadab and Abihu, Eleazar and Ithamar.
6:25 [A] one of the daughters of Putiel, and *she* **bore** him Phinehas.
21:4 [A] gives him a wife and *she* **bears** him sons or daughters,
Lev 12:2 [A] **gives birth** *to* a son will be ceremonially unclean for seven
12:5 [A] If *she* **gives birth** *to* a daughter, for two weeks the woman
12:7 [A] " 'These are the regulations for the *woman who* **gives birth**
22:27 [C] "When a calf, a lamb or a goat **is born**, it is to remain with its
25:45 [G] among you and members of their clans **born** in your country,
Nu 1:18 [F] The people **indicated** *their* **ancestry** by their clans
11:12 [A] Did I conceive all these people? *Did* I **give** them **birth**?
26:29 [G] the Makirite clan (Makir *was the* **father** *of* Gilead);
26:58 [G] the Korahite clan. (Kohath *was the* **forefather** *of* Amram;
26:59 [A] a descendant of Levi, who *was* **born** to the Levites in Egypt.
26:59 [A] To Amram *she* **bore** Aaron, Moses and their sister Miriam.

Nu 26:60 [C] Aaron *was the* **father** *of* Nadab and Abihu, Eleazar and
Dt 4:25 [G] After *you have* **had** children and grandchildren and have
15:19 [C] LORD your God every firstborn male **[NIE]** of your herds
21:15 [A] both **bear** him sons but the firstborn is the son of the wife he
23: 8 [23:9] [C] The third generation of children **born** to them may
25: 6 [A] The first son *she* **bears** shall carry on the name of the dead
28:41 [G] *You will* **have** sons and daughters but you will not keep
28:57 [A] the afterbirth from her womb and the children *she* **bears**.
32:18 [A] You deserted the Rock, *who* **fathered** you; you forgot the
Jdg 8:31 [A] His concubine, who lived in Shechem, also **bore** him a son,
11: 1 [G] His **father** *was* Gilead; his mother was a prostitute.
11: 2 [A] Gilead's wife also **bore** him sons, and when they were grown
13: 2 [A] had a wife who was sterile and **remained childless** [+4202].
13: 3 [A] to her and said, "You are sterile and **childless** [+4202],
13: 3 [A] and childless, but you are going to conceive and **have** a son.
13: 5 [A] because you will conceive and **give birth** *to* a son. No razor
13: 7 [G] he said to me, 'You will conceive and **give birth** *to* a son.
13: 8 [E] again to teach us how to bring up the boy who *is to* **be born**."
13:24 [A] The woman **gave birth** *to* a boy and named him Samson. He
18:29 [E] it Dan after their forefather Dan, who **was born** to Israel—
Ru 1:12 [A] even if I had a husband tonight and then **gave birth** *to* sons—
4:12 [A] family be like that of Perez, whom Tamar **bore** to Judah."
4:13 [A] enabled her to conceive, and *she* **gave birth** *to* a son.
4:15 [A] who is better to you than seven sons, *has* **given** him **birth**."
4:17 [E] The women living there said, "Naomi **has** a son." And they
4:18 [G] is the family line of Perez: Perez *was the* **father** *of* Hezron,
4:19 [G] Hezron *the* **father** *of* Ram, Ram the father of Amminadab,
4:19 [G] Hezron the father of Ram, Ram *the* **father** *of* Amminadab,
4:20 [G] Amminadab *the* **father** *of* Nahshon, Nahshon the father of
4:20 [G] the father of Nahshon, Nahshon *the* **father** *of* Salmon,
4:21 [G] Salmon *the* **father** *of* Boaz, Boaz the father of Obed,
4:21 [G] Salmon the father of Boaz, Boaz *the* **father** *of* Obed,
4:22 [G] Obed *the* **father** *of* Jesse, and Jesse the father of David.
4:22 [G] Obed the father of Jesse, and Jesse *the* **father** *of* David.
1Sa 1:20 [A] course of time Hannah conceived and **gave birth** *to* a son.
2: 5 [A] She who was barren *has* **borne** seven **children**, but she who
2:21 [A] she conceived and **gave birth** *to* three sons and two
4:19 [A] of Phinehas, was pregnant and **near the time of delivery**.
4:19 [A] her husband were dead, she went into labor and **gave birth**,
4:20 [A] her said, "Don't despair; *you have* **given birth** *to* a son."
2Sa 3: 2 [C] Sons **were born** to David in Hebron: His firstborn was
3: 5 [E] of David's wife Eglah. These **were born** to David in Hebron.
5:13 [C] and more sons and daughters **were born** to him.
11:27 [A] to his house, and she became his wife and **bore** him a son.
12:15 [A] the LORD struck the child that Uriah's wife *had* **borne** to
12:24 [A] *She* **gave birth** *to* a son, and they named him Solomon. The
14:27 [C] Three sons and a daughter **were born** to Absalom. The
21: 8 [A] of Aiah's daughter Rizpah, whom *she had* **borne** to Saul,
21: 8 [A] whom *she had* **borne** to Adriel son of Barzillai the
21:20 [E] twenty-four in all. He also **was descended** from Rapha.
21:22 [E] These four *were* **descendants** of Rapha in Gath, and they fell
1Ki 1: 6 [A] was also very handsome and *was* **born** next after Absalom.)
3:17 [A] the same house. *I* **had a baby** while she was there with me.
3:18 [A] The third day after my **child was born**, this woman also had
3:18 [A] day after my child was born, this woman also **had a baby**.
3:21 [A] the morning light, I saw that it wasn't the son *I had* **borne**."
3:26 [B] said to the king, "Please, my lord, give her the living **baby**!
3:27 [B] "Give the living **baby** to the first woman. Do not kill him;
11:20 [A] The sister of Tahpenes **bore** him a son named Genubath,
13: 2 [C] 'A son named Josiah *will* **be born** to the house of David.
2Ki 4:17 [A] the next year about that same time *she* **gave birth** *to* a son,
20:18 [G] your own flesh and blood, that *will be* **born** *to you*, will be
1Ch 1:10 [A] Cush *was the* **father** *of* Nimrod, who grew to be a mighty
1:11 [A] Mizraim *was the* **father** *of* the Ludites, Anamites, Lehabites,
1:13 [A] Canaan *was the* **father** *of* Sidon his firstborn, and *of* the
1:18 [A] Arphaxad *was the* **father** *of* Shelah, and Shelah the father of
1:18 [A] was the father of Shelah, and Shelah *the* **father** *of* Eber.
1:19 [E] Two sons **were born** to Eber: One was named Peleg,
1:20 [A] Joktan *was the* **father** *of* Almodad, Sheleph, Hazarmaveth,
1:32 [A] The sons **born** *to* Keturah, Abraham's concubine: Zimran,
1:34 [G] Abraham *was the* **father** *of* Isaac. The sons of Isaac: Esau
2: 3 [C] These three **were born** to him by a Canaanite woman,
2: 4 [A] Tamar, Judah's daughter-in-law, **bore** him Perez and Zerah.
2: 9 [C] The sons **born** to Hezron were: Jerahmeel, Ram and Caleb.
2:10 [G] Ram *was the* **father** *of* Amminadab, and Amminadab the
2:10 [G] Amminadab *the* **father** *of* Nahshon, the leader of the people
2:11 [G] Nahshon *was the* **father** *of* Salmon, Salmon the father of
2:11 [G] was the father of Salmon, Salmon *the* **father** *of* Boaz,
2:12 [G] Boaz *the* **father** *of* Obed and Obed the father of Jesse.
2:12 [G] Boaz the father of Obed and Obed *the* **father** *of* Jesse.
2:13 [G] Jesse *was the* **father** *of* Eliab his firstborn; the second son
2:17 [A] Abigail *was the* **mother** *of* Amasa, whose father was Jether
2:18 [G] Caleb son of Hezron **had children** by his wife Azubah
2:19 [A] Azubah died, Caleb married Ephrath, *who* **bore** him Hur.
2:20 [G] Hur *was the* **father** *of* Uri, and Uri the father of Bezalel.
2:20 [G] Hur was the father of Uri, and Uri *the* **father** *of* Bezalel.
2:21 [A] her when he was sixty years old), and *she* **bore** him Segub.
2:22 [G] Segub *was the* **father** *of* Jair, who controlled twenty-three
2:24 [A] Abijah the wife of Hezron **bore** him Ashhur the father of
2:29 [A] wife was named Abihail, *who* **bore** him Ahban and Molid.
2:35 [A] in marriage to his servant Jarha, and *she* **bore** him Attai.
2:36 [G] Attai *was the* **father** *of* Nathan, Nathan the father of Zabad,
2:36 [G] Attai was the father of Nathan, Nathan *the* **father** *of* Zabad,
2:37 [G] Zabad *the* **father** *of* Ephlal, Ephlal the father of Obed,
2:37 [G] Zabad the father of Ephlal, Ephlal *the* **father** *of* Obed,
2:38 [G] Obed *the* **father** *of* Jehu, Jehu the father of Azariah,
2:38 [G] Obed the father of Jehu, Jehu *the* **father** *of* Azariah,
2:39 [G] Azariah *the* **father** *of* Helez, Helez the father of Eleasah,
2:39 [G] Azariah the father of Helez, Helez *the* **father** *of* Eleasah,
2:40 [G] Eleasah *the* **father** *of* Sismai, Sismai the father of Shallum,
2:40 [G] Eleasah the father of Sismai, Sismai *the* **father** *of* Shallum,
2:41 [G] Shallum *the* **father** *of* Jekamiah, and Jekamiah the father of
2:41 [G] the father of Jekamiah, and Jekamiah *the* **father** *of* Elishama.
2:44 [G] Shema *was the* **father** *of* Raham, and Raham the father of
2:44 [G] the father of Jorkeam. Rekem *was the* **father** *of* Shammai.
2:46 [A] concubine Ephah *was the* **mother** *of* Haran, Moza and
2:46 [G] of Haran, Moza and Gazez. Haran *was the* **father** *of* Gazez.
2:48 [A] Caleb's concubine Maacah *was the* **mother** *of* Sheber and
2:49 [A] *She* also **gave birth** *to* Shaaph the father of Madmannah and *to*
3: 1 [C] These were the sons of David **born** to him in Hebron:
3: 4 [C] These six **were born** to David in Hebron, where he reigned
3: 5 [C] and these were *the children* **born** to him there: Shammua,
4: 2 [G] Reaiah son of Shobal *was the* **father** *of* Jahath, and Jahath
4: 2 [G] father of Jahath, and Jahath *the* **father** *of* Ahumai and Lahad.
4: 6 [A] Naarah **bore** him Ahuzzam, Hepher, Temeni and
4: 8 [G] *who was the* **father** *of* Anub and Hazzobebah and of the
4: 9 [A] had named him Jabez, saying, "*I* **gave birth** to him in pain."
4:11 [G] Kelub, Shuhah's brother, *was the* **father** *of* Mehir, who was
4:12 [G] Eshton *was the* **father** *of* Beth Rapha, Paseah and Tehinnah
4:14 [G] Meonothai *was the* **father** *of* Ophrah. Seraiah was the father
4:14 [G] Seraiah *was the* **father** *of* Joab, the father of Ge Harashim.
4:18 [A] **gave birth** *to* Jered the father of Gedor, Heber the father of
6: 4 [5:30] [G] Eleazar *was the* **father** *of* Phinehas,
6: 4 [5:30] [G] father of Phinehas, Phinehas *the* **father** *of* Abishua,
6: 5 [5:31] [G] Abishua *the* **father** *of* Bukki, Bukki the father of
6: 5 [5:31] [G] the father of Bukki, Bukki *the* **father** *of* Uzzi,
6: 6 [5:32] [G] Uzzi *the* **father** *of* Zerahiah, Zerahiah the father of
6: 6 [5:32] [G] father of Zerahiah, Zerahiah *the* **father** *of* Meraioth,
6: 7 [5:33] [G] Meraioth *the* **father** *of* Amariah, Amariah the father
6: 7 [5:33] [G] the father of Amariah, Amariah *the* **father** *of* Ahitub,
6: 8 [5:34] [G] Ahitub *the* **father** *of* Zadok, Zadok the father of
6: 8 [5:34] [G] the father of Zadok, Zadok *the* **father** *of* Ahimaaz,
6: 9 [5:35] [G] Ahimaaz *the* **father** *of* Azariah, Azariah the father of
6: 9 [5:35] [G] the father of Azariah, Azariah *the* **father** *of* Johanan,
6:10 [5:36] [G] Johanan *the* **father** *of* Azariah (it was he who served
6:11 [5:37] [G] Azariah *the* **father** *of* Amariah, Amariah the father
6:11 [5:37] [G] the father of Amariah, Amariah *the* **father** *of* Ahitub,
6:12 [5:38] [G] Ahitub *the* **father** *of* Zadok, Zadok the father of
6:12 [5:38] [G] the father of Zadok, Zadok *the* **father** *of* Shallum,
6:13 [5:39] [G] Shallum *the* **father** *of* Hilkiah, Hilkiah the father of
6:13 [5:39] [G] the father of Hilkiah, Hilkiah *the* **father** *of* Azariah,
6:14 [5:40] [G] Azariah *the* **father** *of* Seraiah, and Seraiah the father
6:14 [5:40] [G] of Seraiah, and Seraiah *the* **father** *of* Jehozadak.
7:14 [A] Asriel *was his* **descendant** *through* his Aramean concubine.
7:14 [A] *She* **gave birth** *to* Makir the father of Gilead.
7:16 [A] Makir's wife Maacah **gave birth** *to* a son and named him
7:18 [A] His sister Hammoleketh **gave birth** *to* Ishhod, Abiezer and
7:21 [C] were killed by the **native-born** [+824+928+2021] men of Gath,
7:23 [A] and she became pregnant and **gave birth** *to* a son.
7:32 [G] Heber *was the* **father** *of* Japhlet, Shomer and Hotham and of
8: 1 [G] Benjamin *was the* **father** *of* Bela his firstborn,
8: 7 [G] deported them and *who was the* **father** *of* Uzza and Ahihud.
8: 8 [G] Sons *were* **born** *to* Shaharaim in Moab after he had divorced
8: 9 [G] By his wife Hodesh *he* **had** Jobab, Zibia, Mesha, Malcam,
8:11 [G] By Hushim *he* **had** Abitub and Elpaal.
8:32 [G] Mikloth, *who was the* **father** *of* Shimeah. They too lived
8:33 [G] Ner *was the* **father** *of* Kish, Kish the father of Saul, and Saul
8:33 [G] Ner was the father of Kish, Kish *the* **father** *of* Saul, and Saul
8:33 [G] Saul *the* **father** *of* Jonathan, Malki-Shua, Abinadab and
8:34 [G] son of Jonathan: Merib-Baal, who *was the* **father** *of* Micah.
8:36 [G] Ahaz *was the* **father** *of* Jehoaddah, Jehoaddah was the father
8:36 [G] Jehoaddah *was the* **father** *of* Alemeth, Azmaveth and Zimri,
8:36 [G] and Zimri, and Zimri *was the* **father** *of* Moza.
8:37 [G] Moza *was the* **father** *of* Binea; Raphah was his son,
9:38 [G] Mikloth *was the* **father** *of* Shimeam. They too lived near
9:39 [G] Ner *was the* **father** *of* Kish, Kish the father of Saul, and Saul
9:39 [G] Ner was the father of Kish, Kish *the* **father** *of* Saul, and Saul
9:39 [G] Saul *the* **father** *of* Jonathan, Malki-Shua, Abinadab and

1Ch 9:40 [G] son of Jonathan: Merib-Baal, who *was the* **father** *of* Micah.
9:42 [G] Ahaz *was the* **father** *of* Jadah, Jadah was the father of
9:42 [G] Jadah *was the* **father** *of* Alemeth, Azmaveth and Zimri,
9:42 [G] and Zimri, and Zimri *was the* **father** *of* Moza.
9:43 [G] Moza *was the* **father** *of* Binea; Rephaiah was his son,
14: 3 [G] and *became the* **father** *of* more sons and daughters.
14: 4 [B] These are the names of the **children born** to him there:
20: 6 [C] twenty-four in all. He also **was descended** from Rapha.
20: 8 [C] These *were* **descendants** of Rapha in Gath, and they fell at
22: 9 [C] But you *will* **have** a son who will be a man of peace and rest,
26: 6 [C] His son Shemaiah also **had** sons, who were leaders in their
2Ch 11:19 [A] *She* **bore** him sons: Jeush, Shemariah and Zaham.
11:20 [A] *who* **bore** him Abijah, Attai, Ziza and Shelomith.
11:21 [G] **[RPH]** twenty-eight sons and sixty daughters.
13:21 [G] and **had** twenty-two sons and sixteen daughters.
24: 3 [G] chose two wives for him, and *he* **had** sons and daughters.
Ezr 10: 3 [C] our God to send away all these women and their **children**,
Ne 12:10 [G] Jeshua *was the* **father** *of* Joiakim, Joiakim the father of
12:10 [G] Joiakim *the* **father** *of* Eliashib, Eliashib the father of Joiada,
12:11 [G] Joiada *the* **father** *of* Jonathan, and Jonathan the father of
12:11 [G] the father of Jonathan, and Jonathan *the* **father** *of* Jaddua.
Job 1: 2 [C] He **had** seven sons and three daughters,
3: 3 [C] "May the day of *my* **birth** perish, and the night it was said,
5: 7 [E] Yet man **is born** to trouble as surely as sparks fly upward.
11:12 [C] become wise than a wild donkey's colt *can* **be born** a man.
14: 1 [B] "Man **born** *of* woman is of few days and full of trouble.
15: 7 [C] "*Are you* the first man ever **born**? Were you brought forth
15:14 [B] "What is man, that he could be pure, or *one* **born** *of* woman,
15:35 [A] They conceive trouble and **give birth** *to* evil; their womb
24:21 [A] They prey on the barren and **childless** [+4202] *woman*,
25: 4 [B] before God? How can *one* **born** *of* woman be pure?
38:21 [C] Surely you know, for *you* **were** already **born**! You have
38:28 [G] Does the rain have a father? Who **fathers** the drops of dew?
38:29 [A] the ice? Who **gives birth** *to* the frost from the heavens
39: 1 [A] "Do you know when the mountain goats **give birth**? Do you
39: 2 [A] months till they bear? Do you know the time they **give birth**?
Ps 2: 7 [A] to me, "You are my Son; today I *have become* your **Father**.
7:14 [7:15] [A] and conceives trouble **gives birth** *to* disillusionment.
22:31 [22:32] [C] proclaim his righteousness to a people **yet unborn**—
48: 6 [48:7] [A] them there, pain like that of a *woman* **in labor**.
78: 6 [C] even the children *yet to* **be born**, and they in turn would tell
87: 4 [E] with Cush—and will say, 'This one **was born** in Zion.' "
87: 5 [E] Zion it will be said, "This one and that one **were born** in her,
87: 6 [E] of the peoples: "This one **was born** in Zion." *Selah*
90: 2 [E] Before the mountains **were born** or you brought forth the
Pr 17:17 [C] friend loves at all times, and a brother **is born** for adversity.
17:21 [A] *To* **have** a fool *for a* **son** brings grief; there is no joy for the
17:25 [A] grief to his father and bitterness to the *one who* **bore** him.
23:22 [A] Listen to your father, who **gave** you **life**, and do not despise
23:24 [A] man has great joy; *he who* **has** a wise **son** delights in him.
23:25 [G] and mother be glad; may *she who* **gave** you **birth** rejoice!
27: 1 [A] for you do not know what a day *may* **bring forth**.
Ecc 3: 2 [A] a time to *be* **born** and a time to die, a time to plant and a time
4:14 [C] or *he may have* **been born** in poverty within his kingdom.
5:14 [5:13] [G] that *when he* **has** a son there is nothing left for him.
6: 3 [G] A man *may* **have** a hundred **children** and live many years;
7: 1 [C] and the day of death better than the day of **birth**.
SS 6: 9 [A] daughter of her mother, the favorite of the *one who* **bore** her.
8: 5 [A] conceived you, there she who was in labor **gave** you **birth**.
Isa 7:14 [A] The virgin will be with child and *will* **give birth** *to* a son,
8: 3 [A] to the prophetess, and she conceived and **gave birth** *to* a son.
9: 6 [9:5] [E] For to us a child **is born**, to us a son is given,
13: 8 [A] will grip them; they will writhe like a *woman* **in labor**.
21: 3 [A] with pain, pangs seize me, like those of a *woman* **in labor**;
23: 4 [A] "I have neither been in labor nor **given birth**; I have neither
26:17 [A] As a woman with child and about to **give birth** writhes
26:18 [A] with child, we writhed in pain, but *we* **gave birth** *to* wind.
33:11 [A] You conceive chaff, *you* **give birth** *to* straw; your breath is a
39: 7 [G] your own flesh and blood who *will be* **born** *to you*, will be
42:14 [A] like a *woman* **in childbirth**, I cry out, I gasp and pant.
45:10 [G] to him who says to his father, 'What *have you* **begotten**?'
49:21 [A] you will say in your heart, 'Who **bore** me these? I was
51:18 [A] Of all the sons *she* **bore** there was none to guide her; of all
54: 1 [A] "Sing, O barren woman, *you who* never **bore a child**;
55:10 [G] it without watering the earth and **making** it **bud** and flourish,
59: 4 [G] and speak lies; they conceive trouble and **give birth** *to* evil.
65:23 [A] will not toil in vain or **bear children** doomed to misfortune;
66: 7 [A] "Before she goes into labor, *she* **gives birth**; before the pains
66: 8 [C] be born in a day or a nation **be brought forth** in a moment?
66: 8 [A] Yet no sooner is Zion in labor than *she* **gives birth** *to* her
66: 9 [G] Do I bring to the moment of birth and not **give delivery**?"
66: 9 [G] "Do I close up the womb when I **bring to delivery**?"
Jer 2:27 [A] 'You are my father,' and to stone, 'You **gave** me **birth**.'
6:24 [A] Anguish has gripped us, pain like that of a *woman* **in labor**.
14: 5 [A] Even the doe in the field deserts *her* **newborn** *fawn*
15: 9 [A] The **mother** *of* seven will grow faint and breathe her last.
15:10 [A] Alas, my mother, that *you* **gave** me **birth**, a man with whom
16: 3 [A] in this land and about the **women**[s] who are their mothers
16: 3 [G] who are their mothers and the **men**[s] who are their fathers:
17:11 [A] Like a partridge that hatches eggs *it did* not **lay** is the man
20:14 [E] Cursed be the day *I was* **born**! May the day my mother bore
20:14 [A] I was born! May the day my mother **bore** me not be blessed!
20:15 [E] who made him very glad, saying, "A child **is born** to you—
22:23 [A] pangs come upon you, pain like that of a *woman* **in labor**!
22:26 [A] and the mother who **gave** you **birth** into another country,
22:26 [E] where neither *of you* **was born**, and there you both will die.
29: 6 [G] Marry and **have** sons and daughters; find wives for your sons
29: 6 [A] in marriage, so that *they* too *may* **have** sons and daughters.
30: 6 [A] Ask and see: *Can* a man **bear children**? Then why do I see
30: 6 [A] man with his hands on his stomach like a *woman* **in labor**,
31: 8 [A] and the lame, expectant mothers and *women* **in labor**;
49:24 [A] and pain have seized her, pain like that of a *woman* **in labor**.
50:12 [A] greatly ashamed; *she who* **gave** you **birth** will be disgraced.
50:43 [A] has gripped him, pain like that of a *woman* **in labor**.
Eze 16: 4 [H] On the day you **were born** your cord was not cut, nor were
16: 5 [H] open field, for on the day you **were born** you were despised.
16:20 [A] you took your sons and daughters whom *you* **bore** to me
18:10 [G] "Suppose *he* **has** a violent son, who sheds blood or does any
18:14 [G] "But suppose this son **has** a son who sees all the sins his
23: 4 [A] They were mine and **gave birth** *to* sons and daughters.
23:37 [A] their children, whom *they* **bore** to me, as food for them.
31: 6 [A] all the beasts of the field **gave birth** under its branches;
47:22 [G] aliens who have settled among you and who **have** children.
Da 11: 6 [A] together with her royal escort and her **father** and the one who
Hos 1: 3 [A] daughter of Diblaim, and she conceived and **bore** him a son.
1: 6 [A] Gomer conceived again and **gave birth** *to* a daughter.
1: 8 [A] After she had weaned Lo-Ruhamah, Gomer **had** another son.
2: 3 [2:5] [C] and make her as bare as on the day she **was born**;
5: 7 [A] to the LORD; *they* **give birth** *to* illegitimate children.
9:16 [A] Even if *they* **bear children**, I will slay their cherished
13:13 [A] Pains as of a *woman* **in childbirth** come to him, but he is a
Mic 4: 9 [A] that pain seizes you like that of a *woman* **in labor**?
4:10 [A] in agony, O Daughter of Zion, like a *woman* **in labor**,
5: 3 [5:2] [A] until the time when *she who is* **in labor** gives birth
5: 3 [5:2] [A] until the time when she who is in labor **gives birth**
Zep 2: 2 [A] before the appointed time **arrives** and that day sweeps on
Zec 13: 3 [A] his father and mother, to whom he *was* **born**, will say to him,
13: 3 [A] When he prophesies, his own parents **[RPH]** will stab him.

3529 יֶלֶד *yeled*, n.m. [89] [√ 3528]

child [21], children [20], young men [11], boy [8], boys [5], baby [4], boy's [3], young [3], sons [2], youth [2], *untranslated* [1], babies [1], baby's [1], brood [1], gives birth prematurely [+3655] [1], little ones [1], pagans [+5799] [1], son [1], young man [1], youths [1]

Ge 4:23 have killed a man for wounding me, a **young man** for injuring me.
21: 8 The **child** grew and was weaned, and on the day Isaac was weaned
21:14 He set them on her shoulders and then sent her off with the **boy**.
21:15 in the skin was gone, she put the **boy** under one of the bushes.
21:16 a bowshot away, for she thought, "I cannot watch the **boy** die."
30:26 Give me my wives and **children**, for whom I have served you,
32:22 [32:23] his two maidservants and his eleven **sons** and crossed the
33: 1 so he divided the **children** among Leah, Rachel and the two
33: 2 He put the maidservants and their **children** in front, Leah
33: 2 Leah and her **children** next, and Rachel and Joseph in the rear.
33: 5 Esau looked up and saw the women and **children**. "Who are these
33: 5 "They are the **children** God has graciously given your servant."
33: 6 the maidservants and their **children** approached and bowed down.
33: 7 Next, Leah and her **children** came and bowed down. Last of all
33:13 "My lord knows that the **children** are tender and that I must care
33:14 slowly at the pace of the droves before me and that of the **children**,
37:30 He went back to his brothers and said, "The **boy** isn't there!
42:22 Reuben replied, "Didn't I tell you not to sin against the **boy**?
44:20 an aged father, and there is a young **son** *born* to him *in* his old age.
Ex 1:17 what the king of Egypt had told them to do; they let the **boys** live.
1:18 "Why have you done this? Why have you let the **boys** live?"
2: 3 she placed the **child** in it and put it among the reeds along the bank
2: 6 She opened it and saw the **baby**. He was crying, and she felt sorry
2: 6 felt sorry for him. "This is one of the Hebrew **babies**," she said.
2: 7 and get one of the Hebrew women to nurse the **baby** for you?"
2: 8 she answered. And the girl went and got the **baby's** mother.
2: 9 "Take this **baby** and nurse him for me, and I will pay you."
2: 9 and I will pay you." So the woman took the **baby** and nursed him.
2:10 When the **child** grew older, she took him to Pharaoh's daughter
21: 4 the woman and her **children** shall belong to her master,
21:22 she **gives birth prematurely** [+3655] but there is no serious
Ru 1: 5 and Naomi was left without her two **sons** and her husband.
4:16 Then Naomi took the **child**, laid him in her lap and cared for him.

1Sa 1: 2 the other Peninnah. Peninnah had **children**, but Hannah had none.
1: 2 Peninnah had children, but Hannah had none. **[RPH]**
2Sa 6: 23 Michal daughter of Saul had no **children** to the day of her death.
12: 15 the LORD struck the **child** that Uriah's wife had borne to David,
12: 18 On the seventh day the **child** died. David's servants were afraid to
12: 18 David's servants were afraid to tell him that the **child** was dead,
12: 18 for they thought, "While the **child** was still living, we spoke to
12: 18 he would not listen to us. How can we tell him the **child** is dead?
12: 19 whispering among themselves and he realized the **child** was dead.
12: 19 "Is the **child** dead?" he asked. "Yes," they replied, "he is dead."
12: 21 While the **child** was alive, you fasted and wept, but now that the
12: 21 you fasted and wept, but now that the **child** is dead, you get up
12: 22 He answered, "While the **child** was still alive, I fasted and wept.
12: 22 The LORD may be gracious to me and let the **child** live.'
1Ki 3: 25 "Cut the living **child** in two and give half to one and half to the
12: 8 and consulted the **young men** who had grown up with him
12: 10 The **young men** who had grown up with him replied, "Tell these
12: 14 he followed the advice of the **young men** and said, "My father
14: 12 go back home. When you set foot in your city, the **boy** will die.
17: 21 he stretched himself out on the **boy** three times and cried to the
17: 21 the LORD, "O LORD my God, let this **boy's** life return to him!"
17: 22 heard Elijah's cry, and the **boy's** life returned to him, and he lived.
17: 23 Elijah picked up the **child** and carried him down from the room
2Ki 2: 24 bears came out of the woods and mauled forty-two of the **youths**.
4: 1 But now his creditor is coming to take my two **boys** as his slaves."
4: 18 The **child** grew, and one day he went out to his father, who was
4: 26 Is your **child** all right?' " "Everything is all right," she said.
4: 34 Then he got on the bed and lay upon the **boy**, mouth to mouth,
4: 34 As he stretched himself out upon him, the **boy's** body grew warm.
2Ch 10: 8 and consulted the **young men** who had grown up with him
10: 10 The **young men** who had grown up with him replied, "Tell the
10: 14 he followed the advice of the **young men** and said, "My father
Ezr 10: 1 of Israelites—men, women and **children**—gathered around him.
Ne 12: 43 had given them great joy. The women and **children** also rejoiced.
Job 21: 11 send forth their children as a flock; their **little ones** dance about.
38: 41 Who provides food for the raven when its **young** cry out to God
39: 3 They crouch down and bring forth their **young**; their labor pains
Ecc 4: 13 Better a poor but wise **youth** than an old but foolish king who no
4: 15 that all who lived and walked under the sun followed the **youth**,
Isa 2: 6 like the Philistines and clasp hands with **pagans** [+5799].
8: 18 Here am I, and the **children** the LORD has given me. We are
9: 6 [9:5] For to us a **child** is born, to us a son is given,
11: 7 cow will feed with the bear, their **young** will lie down together,
29: 23 When they see among them their **children**, the work of my hands,
57: 4 your tongue? Are you not a **brood** *of* rebels, the offspring of liars?
57: 5 you sacrifice your **children** in the ravines and under the
Jer 31: 20 Is not Ephraim my dear son, the **child** *in whom* I delight?
La 4: 10 own hands compassionate women have cooked their own **children**,
Da 1: 4 **young men** without any physical defect, handsome, showing
1: 10 Why should he see you looking worse than the other **young men**
1: 13 compare our appearance with that of the **young men** who eat the
1: 15 better nourished than any of the **young men** who ate the royal
1: 17 To these four **young men** God gave knowledge and understanding
Hos 1: 2 take to yourself an adulterous wife and **children** *of* unfaithfulness,
Joel 3: 3 [4:3] They cast lots for my people and traded **boys** for prostitutes;
Zec 8: 5 The city streets will be filled with **boys** and girls playing there."

3530 יַלְדָּה yaldâ, n.f. [3] [√ 3528]

girls [2], girl [1]

Ge 34: 4 Shechem said to his father Hamor, "Get me this **girl** as my wife."
Joel 3: 3 [4:3] they sold **girls** for wine that they might drink.
Zec 8: 5 The city streets will be filled with boys and **girls** playing there."

3531 יַלְדוּת yaldût, n.f. [3] [√ 3528]

youth [2], young [1]

Ps 110: 3 the womb of the dawn you will receive the dew of your **youth**.
Ecc 11: 9 Be happy, young man, while you are **young**, and let your heart
11: 10 off the troubles of your body, for **youth** and vigor are meaningless.

3532 יָלָה yālah, v. [1] [cf. 4263]

wasted away [1]

Ge 47: 13 [A] both Egypt and Canaan **wasted away** because of the famine.

3533 יִלּוֹד yillôd, a. [5] [√ 3528]

born [4], children born [1]

Ex 1: 22 "Every boy that is **born** you must throw into the Nile, but let every
Jos 5: 5 all the people **born** in the desert during the journey from Egypt had
2Sa 5: 14 These are the names of the **children born** to him there: Shammua,
12: 14 of the LORD show utter contempt, the son **born** to you will die."
Jer 16: 3 daughters **born** in this land and about the women who are their

3534 יָלוֹן yālôn, n.pr.m. [1]

Jalon [1]

1Ch 4: 17 The sons of Ezrah: Jether, Mered, Epher and **Jalon**. One of

3535 יָלִיד yālîd, a. [13] [√ 3528]

descendants [6], born [3], those born [3], slave by birth [+1074] [1]

Ge 14: 14 he called out the 318 trained men **born** *in* his household and went
17: 12 including **those born** *in* your household or bought with money
17: 13 Whether **born** *in* your household or bought with your money,
17: 23 and all **those born** *in* his household or bought with his money,
17: 27 including **those born** *in* his household or bought from a foreigner,
Lev 22: 11 or if a slave is **born** *in* his household, that slave may eat his food.
Nu 13: 22 Sheshai and Talmai, the **descendants** *of* Anak, lived.
13: 28 and very large. We even saw **descendants** *of* Anak there.
Jos 15: 14 Sheshai, Ahiman and Talmai—**descendants** *of* Anak.
2Sa 21: 16 Ishbi-Benob, one of the **descendants** *of* Rapha, whose bronze
21: 18 the Hushathite killed Saph, one of the **descendants** *of* Rapha.
1Ch 20: 4 one of the **descendants** *of* the Rephaites, and the Philistines were
Jer 2: 14 Is Israel a servant, a **slave by birth** [+1074]? Why then has he

3536 יָלַל yālal, v. [30 / 29] [→ 3537, 3538]

wail [26], turn to wailing [1], wails [1], weep [1]

Isa 13: 6 [G] **Wail**, for the day of the LORD is near; it will come like
14: 31 [G] **Wail**, O gate! Howl, O city! Melt away, all you Philistines!
15: 2 [G] its high places to weep; Moab **wails** over Nebo and Medeba.
15: 3 [G] on the roofs and in the public squares they all **wail**,
16: 7 [G] Therefore the Moabites **wail**, they wail together for Moab.
16: 7 [G] Therefore the Moabites wail, they **wail** together for Moab.
23: 1 [G] **Wail**, O ships of Tarshish! For Tyre is destroyed and left
23: 6 [G] Cross over to Tarshish; **wail**, you people of the island.
23: 14 [G] **Wail**, *you* ships of Tarshish; your fortress is destroyed!
52: 5 [d] and those who rule them mock," [BHS ***wail***; NIV 2147]
65: 14 [G] out from anguish of heart and **wail** in brokenness of spirit.
Jer 4: 8 [G] So put on sackcloth, lament and **wail**, for the fierce anger of
25: 34 [G] **Weep** and wail, you shepherds; roll in the dust, you leaders
47: 2 [G] The people will cry out; all who dwell in the land *will* **wail**
48: 20 [G] Moab is disgraced, for she is shattered. **Wail** and cry out!
48: 31 [G] Therefore ***I* wail** over Moab, for all Moab I cry out, I moan
48: 39 [G] "How shattered she is! How *they* **wail**! How Moab turns her
49: 3 [G] "**Wail**, O Heshbon, for Ai is destroyed! Cry out,
51: 8 [G] Babylon will suddenly fall and be broken. **Wail** over her!
Eze 21: 12 [21:17] [G] Cry out and **wail**, son of man, for it is against my
30: 2 [G] Sovereign LORD says: " '**Wail** and say, "Alas for that day!"
Hos 7: 14 [G] not cry out to me from their hearts but **wail** upon their beds.
Joel 1: 5 [G] **Wail**, all you drinkers of wine; wail because of the new wine,
1: 11 [G] Despair, you farmers, **wail**, you vine growers; grieve for the
1: 13 [G] and mourn; **wail**, you who minister before the altar.
Am 8: 3 [G] "the songs in the temple *will* **turn to wailing**.
Mic 1: 8 [G] Because of this I will weep and **wail**; I will go about barefoot
Zep 1: 11 [G] **Wail**, you who live in the market district; all your merchants
Zec 11: 2 [G] **Wail**, O pine tree, for the cedar has fallen; the stately trees
11: 2 [G] **Wail**, oaks of Bashan; the dense forest has been cut down!

3537 יְלֵל yelēl, n.[m.] [1] [√ 3536]

howling [1]

Dt 32: 10 In a desert land he found him, in a barren and **howling** waste.

3538 יְלָלָה yelālâ, n.f. [5] [√ 3536]

wailing [3], lamentation [1], wail [1]

Isa 15: 8 their **wailing** reaches as far as Eglaim, their lamentation as far as
15: 8 reaches as far as Eglaim, their **lamentation** as far as Beer Elim.
Jer 25: 36 the cry of the shepherds, the **wailing** *of* the leaders of the flock,
Zep 1: 10 **wailing** from the New Quarter, and a loud crash from the hills.
Zec 11: 3 Listen to the **wail** *of* the shepherds; their rich pastures are

3539 יַלֶּפֶת yallepet, n.f. [2]

running sores [2]

Lev 21: 20 or who has festering or **running sores** or damaged testicles.
22: 22 the maimed, or anything with warts or festering or **running sores**.

3540 יֶלֶק yeleq, n.m. [9]

grasshoppers [3], locusts [2], young locusts [2], swarm of locusts [1], young locust [1]

Ps 105: 34 He spoke, and the locusts came, **grasshoppers** without number;
Jer 51: 14 I will surely fill you with men, as with a **swarm of locusts**,
51: 27 a commander against her; send up horses like a swarm of **locusts**.
Joel 1: 4 what the great locusts have left the **young locusts** have eaten;
1: 4 what the **young locusts** have left other locusts have eaten.
2: 25 the great locust and the **young locust**, the other locusts

Na 3:15 sword will cut you down and, like **grasshoppers**, consume you.
3:15 consume you. Multiply like **grasshoppers**, multiply like locusts!
3:16 of the sky, but like **locusts** they strip the land and then fly away.

3541 יַלְקוּט *yalqûṭ*, n.[m.]. [1] [√ 4377]

pouch [1]

1Sa 17:40 put them in the **pouch** of his shepherd's bag and, with his sling in

3542 יָם *yām*, n.m. [396 / 394] [cf. 42; Ar 10322]

sea [262], west [37], west [+2025] [28], seas [21], seashore [+8557] [5], seashore [5], western [5], coast [+2572] [4], it[s] [+2021] [4], high seas [+4213] [3], westward [+2025] [3], coast [2], river [2], western [+2025] [2], *untranslated* [1], coast [+8557] [1], distant shores [+362] [1], extend westward [+2025] [1], lake [1], overboard [+448+2021] [1], seafarers [+6296] [1], seamen [+2480] [1], seashore [+2572] [1], shore [+8557] [1], waters [1]

Ge 1:10 the dry ground "land," and the gathered waters he called "**seas**."
1:22 "Be fruitful and increase in number and fill the water in the **seas**,
1:26 and let them rule over the fish of the **sea** and the birds of the air,
1:28 Rule over the fish of the **sea** and the birds of the air and over every
9:2 that moves along the ground, and upon all the fish of the **sea**;
12:8 and pitched his tent, with Bethel on the **west** and Ai on the east.
13:14 where you are and look north and south, east and **west** [+2025].
14:3 latter kings joined forces in the Valley of Siddim (the Salt **Sea**).
22:17 as the stars in the sky and as the sand on the **seashore** [+8557].
28:14 and you will spread out to the **west** and to the east, to the north
32:12 [32:13] and will make your descendants like the sand of the **sea**,
41:49 Joseph stored up huge quantities of grain, like the sand of the **sea**;
49:13 "Zebulun will live by the **seashore** [+2572] and become a haven
Ex 10:19 And the LORD changed the wind to a very strong **west** wind,
10:19 which caught up the locusts and carried them into the Red **Sea**.
13:18 God led the people around by the desert road toward the Red **Sea**.
14:2 and encamp near Pi Hahiroth, between Migdol and the **sea**.
14:2 They are to encamp by the **sea**, directly opposite Baal Zephon.
14:9 and overtook them as they camped by the **sea** near Pi Hahiroth,
14:16 and stretch out your hand over the **sea** to divide the water
14:16 so that the Israelites can go through the **sea** on dry ground.
14:21 Moses stretched out his hand over the **sea**, and all that night the
14:21 all that night the LORD drove the **sea** back with a strong east
14:21 back with a strong east wind and turned **it**[s] [+2021] into dry land.
14:22 the Israelites went through the **sea** on dry ground, with a wall of
14:23 and chariots and horsemen followed them into the **sea**.
14:26 "Stretch out your hand over the **sea** so that the waters may flow
14:27 Moses stretched out his hand over the **sea**, and at daybreak the sea
14:27 hand over the sea, and at daybreak the **sea** went back to its place.
14:27 were fleeing toward it, and the LORD swept them into the **sea**.
14:28 entire army of Pharaoh that had followed the Israelites into the **sea**.
14:29 the Israelites went through the **sea** on dry ground, with a wall of
14:30 and Israel saw the Egyptians lying dead on the **shore** [+8557].
15:1 is highly exalted. The horse and its rider he has hurled into the **sea**.
15:4 Pharaoh's chariots and his army he has hurled into the **sea**.
15:4 The best of Pharaoh's officers are drowned in the Red **Sea**.
15:8 firm like a wall; the deep waters congealed in the heart of the **sea**.
15:10 But you blew with your breath, and the **sea** covered them.
15:19 When Pharaoh's horses, chariots and horsemen went into the **sea**,
15:19 the LORD brought the waters of the **sea** back over them,
15:19 over them, but the Israelites walked through the **sea** on dry ground.
15:21 highly exalted. The horse and its rider he has hurled into the **sea**."
15:22 Moses led Israel from the Red **Sea** and they went into the Desert of
20:11 in six days the LORD made the heavens and the earth, the **sea**,
23:31 "I will establish your borders from the Red **Sea** to the Sea of the
23:31 "I will establish your borders from the Red Sea to the **Sea** *of* the
26:22 for the far end, that is, the **west** [+2025] end of the tabernacle,
26:27 and five for the frames on the **west**, at the far end of the tabernacle.
27:12 "The **west** end of the courtyard shall be fifty cubits wide and have
36:27 for the far end, that is, the **west** [+2025] end *of* the tabernacle,
36:32 and five for the frames on the **west**, at the far end of the tabernacle.
38:12 The **west** end was fifty cubits wide and had curtains, with ten posts
Lev 11:9 " 'Of all the creatures living in the water of the **seas** and the
11:10 But all creatures in the **seas** or streams that do not have fins
Nu 2:18 On the **west** will be the divisions of the camp of Ephraim under
3:23 The Gershonite clans were to camp on the **west**,
11:22 Would they have enough if all the fish in the **sea** were caught for
11:31 a wind went out from the LORD and drove quail in from the **sea**.
13:29 and the Canaanites live near the **sea** and along the Jordan."
14:25 and set out toward the desert along the route to the Red **Sea**."
21:4 They traveled from Mount Hor along the route to the Red **Sea**,
33:8 They left Pi Hahiroth and passed through the **sea** into the desert,
33:10 They left Elim and camped by the Red **Sea**.
33:11 They left the Red **Sea** and camped in the Desert of Sin.
34:3 your southern boundary will start from the end of the Salt **Sea**,
34:5 where it will turn, join the Wadi of Egypt and end at the **Sea**.
34:6 " 'Your **western** boundary will be the coast of the Great Sea.
34:6 " 'Your western boundary will be the coast of the Great **Sea**.
34:6 the coast of the Great Sea. This will be your boundary on the **west**.
34:7 northern boundary, run a line from the Great **Sea** to Mount Hor
34:11 and continue along the slopes east of the **Sea** *of* Kinnereth.
34:12 boundary will go down along the Jordan and end at the Salt **Sea**.
35:5 three thousand on the **west** and three thousand on the north,
Dt 1:7 in the western foothills, in the Negev and along the **coast** [+2572],
1:40 and set out toward the desert along the route to the Red **Sea**."
2:1 and set out toward the desert along the route to the Red **Sea**,
3:17 from Kinnereth to the **Sea** *of* the Arabah (the Salt Sea),
3:17 from Kinnereth to the Sea of the Arabah (the Salt **Sea**),
3:27 top of Pisgah and look **west** [+2025] and north and south and east.
4:49 as far as the **Sea** *of* the Arabah, below the slopes of Pisgah.
11:4 how he overwhelmed them with the waters of the Red **Sea** as they
11:24 to Lebanon, and from the Euphrates River to the western **sea**.
30:13 Nor is it beyond the **sea**, so that you have to ask, "Who will cross
30:13 "Who will cross the **sea** to get it and proclaim it to us so we may
33:19 they will feast on the abundance of the **seas**, on the treasures
33:23 and is full of his blessing; he will inherit southward to the **lake**."
34:2 and Manasseh, all the land of Judah as far as the western **sea**,
Jos 1:4 all the Hittite country—to the Great **Sea** on the west.
2:10 We have heard how the LORD dried up the water of the Red **Sea**
3:16 while the water flowing down to the **Sea** *of* the Arabah (the Salt
3:16 the water flowing down to the Sea of the Arabah (the Salt **Sea**)
4:23 Red **Sea** when he dried it up before us until we had crossed over.
5:1 Now when all the Amorite kings **west** [+2025] *of* the Jordan
5:1 all the Canaanite kings along the **coast** heard how the LORD had
8:9 and lay in wait between Bethel and Ai, to the **west** of Ai—
8:12 set them in ambush between Bethel and Ai, to the **west** of the city.
8:13 the camp to the north of the city and the ambush to the **west** of it.
9:1 along the entire coast of the Great **Sea** as far as Lebanon (the kings
11:2 in the western foothills and in Naphoth Dor on the **west**;
11:3 to the Canaanites in the east and **west**; to the Amorites, Hittites,
11:4 a huge army, as numerous as the sand on the **seashore** [+8557].
12:3 He also ruled over the eastern Arabah from the **Sea** *of* Kinnereth to
12:3 from the Sea of Kinnereth to the **Sea** *of* the Arabah (the Salt Sea),
12:3 from the Sea of Kinnereth to the Sea of the Arabah (the Salt **Sea**),
12:7 and the Israelites conquered on the **west** side of the Jordan,
13:27 of the Jordan, the territory up to the end of the **Sea** *of* Kinnereth).
15:2 boundary started from the bay at the southern end of the Salt **Sea**,
15:4 along to Azmon and joined the Wadi of Egypt, ending at the **sea**.
15:5 The eastern boundary is the Salt **Sea** as far as the mouth of the
15:5 The northern boundary started from the bay of the **sea** at the mouth
15:8 From there it climbed to the top of the hill **west** [+2025] *of* the
15:10 Then it curved **westward** [+2025] from Baalah to Mount Seir,
15:11 Mount Baalah and reached Jabneel. The boundary ended at the **sea**.
15:12 The **western** boundary is the coastline of the Great Sea. These are
15:12 The western boundary is the coastline of the Great **Sea**. These are
15:46 **west** of Ekron, all that were in the vicinity of Ashdod,
15:47 as far as the Wadi of Egypt and the coastline of the Great **Sea**.
16:3 descended **westward** [+2025] to the territory of the Japhletites as
16:3 the region of Lower Beth Horon and on to Gezer, ending at the **sea**.
16:6 continued to the **sea**. From Micmethath on the north it curved
16:8 From Tappuah the border went **west** [+2025] to the Kanah Ravine
16:8 the border went west to the Kanah Ravine and ended at the **sea**.
17:9 Manasseh was the northern side of the ravine and ended at the **sea**.
17:10 The territory of Manasseh reached the **sea** and bordered Asher on
18:12 slope of Jericho and headed **west** [+2025] into the hill country,
18:14 on the south the boundary turned south along the **western** side
18:14 a town of the people of Judah. This was the **western** side.
18:15 southern side began at the outskirts of Kiriath Jearim on the **west**,
18:19 of Beth Hoglah and came out at the northern bay of the Salt **Sea**,
19:11 Going **west** [+2025] it ran to Maralah, touched Dabbesheth,
19:26 On the **west** the boundary touched Carmel and Shihor Libnath.
19:29 toward Hosah and came out at the **sea** in the region of Aczib,
19:34 The boundary ran **west** [+2025] through Aznoth Tabor and came
19:34 on the south, Asher on the **west** and the Jordan on the east.
22:7 to the other half of the tribe Joshua gave land on the **west** [+2025]
23:4 I conquered—between the Jordan and the Great **Sea** in the west.
24:6 When I brought your fathers out of Egypt, you came to the **sea**,
24:6 pursued them with chariots and horsemen as far as the Red **Sea**.
24:7 and the Egyptians; he brought the **sea** over them and covered them.
Jdg 5:17 Asher remained on the **coast** [+2572] and stayed in his coves.
7:12 could no more be counted than the sand on the **seashore** [+8557].
11:16 Israel went through the desert to the Red **Sea** and on to Kadesh.
1Sa 13:5 and soldiers as numerous as the sand on the **seashore** [+8557].
2Sa 17:11 as numerous as the sand on the **seashore**—be gathered to you,
22:16 The valleys of the **sea** were exposed and the foundations of the
1Ki 4:20 of Judah and Israel were as numerous as the sand on the **seashore**;
4:29 [5:9] as measureless as the sand on the **seashore** [+8557].
5:9 [5:23] My men will haul them down from Lebanon to the **sea**,
5:9 [5:23] I will float them in rafts by **sea** to the place you specify.
7:23 He made the **Sea** of cast metal, circular in shape, measuring ten

1Ki 7:24 The gourds were cast in two rows in one piece with the **Sea**.
7:25 three facing **west** [+2025], three facing south and three facing east.
7:25 The **Sea** rested on top of them, and their hindquarters were toward
7:39 He placed the **Sea** on the south side, at the southeast corner of the
7:44 the **Sea** and the twelve bulls under it;
7:44 the Sea and the twelve bulls under **it**ˢ [+2021];
9:26 which is near Elath in Edom, on the shore of the Red **Sea**.
9:27 Hiram sent his men—sailors who knew the **sea**—to serve in the
10:22 The king had a fleet of trading ships at **sea** along with the ships of
18:43 "Go and look toward the **sea**," he told his servant. And he went up
18:44 "A cloud as small as a man's hand is rising from the **sea**."
2Ki 14:25 boundaries of Israel from Lebo Hamath to the **Sea** *of* the Arabah,
16:17 He removed the **Sea** from the bronze bulls that supported it
25:13 and the bronze **Sea** that were at the temple of the LORD
25:16 The bronze from the two pillars, the **Sea** and the movable stands,
1Ch 9:24 were on the four sides: east, **west** [+2025], north and south.
16:32 Let the **sea** resound, and all that is in it; let the fields be jubilant,
18: 8 which Solomon used to make the bronze **Sea**, the pillars
2Ch 2:16 [2:15] you need and will float them in rafts by **sea** down to Joppa.
4: 2 He made the **Sea** of cast metal, circular in shape, measuring ten
4: 3 The bulls were cast in two rows in one piece with the **Sea**.
4: 4 three facing **west** [+2025], three facing south and three facing east.
4: 4 The **Sea** rested on top of them, and their hindquarters were toward
4: 6 were rinsed, but the **Sea** was to be used by the priests for washing.
4:10 He placed the **Sea** on the south side, at the southeast corner.
4:15 the **Sea** and the twelve bulls under it;
8:17 went to Ezion Geber and Elath on the **coast** [+8557] of Edom.
8:18 him ships commanded by his own officers, men who knew the **sea**.
20: 2 is coming against you from Edom, from the other side of the **Sea**.
Ezr 3: 7 so that they would bring cedar logs by **sea** from Lebanon to Joppa,
Ne 9: 6 the earth and all that is on it, the **seas** and all that is in them.
9: 9 of our forefathers in Egypt; you heard their cry at the Red **Sea**.
9:11 You divided the **sea** before them, so that they passed through it on
9:11 so that they passed through **it**ˢ [+2021] on dry ground,
Est 10: 1 tribute throughout the empire, to its **distant shores** [+362].
Job 6: 3 It would surely outweigh the sand of the **seas**—no wonder my
7:12 Am I the **sea**, or the monster of the deep, that you put me under
9: 8 alone stretches out the heavens and treads on the waves of the **sea**.
11: 9 Their measure is longer than the earth and wider than the **sea**.
12: 8 and it will teach you, or let the fish of the **sea** inform you.
14:11 As water disappears from the **sea** or a riverbed becomes parched
26:12 By his power he churned up the **sea**; by his wisdom he cut Rahab
28:14 The deep says, 'It is not in me'; the **sea** says, 'It is not with me.'
36:30 he scatters his lightning about him, bathing the depths of the **sea**.
38: 8 "Who shut up the **sea** behind doors when it burst forth from the
38:16 "Have you journeyed to the springs of the **sea** or walked in the
41:31 [41:23] boiling caldron and stirs up the **sea** like a pot of ointment.
Ps 8: 8 [8:9] the birds of the air, and the fish of the **sea**, all that swim the
8: 8 [8:9] and the fish of the sea, all that swim the paths of the **seas**.
24: 2 for he founded it upon the **seas** and established it upon the waters.
33: 7 He gathers the waters of the **sea** into jars; he puts the deep into
46: 2 [46:3] give way and the mountains fall into the heart of the **sea**,
65: 5 [65:6] the hope of all the ends of the earth and of the farthest **seas**,
65: 7 [65:8] who stilled the roaring of the **seas**, the roaring of their
66: 6 He turned the **sea** into dry land, they passed through the waters on
68:22 [68:23] from Bashan; I will bring them from the depths of the **sea**,
69:34 [69:35] and earth praise him, the **seas** and all that move in them,
72: 8 He will rule from **sea** to sea and from the River to the ends of the
72: 8 He will rule from sea to **sea** and from the River to the ends of the
74:13 It was you who split open the **sea** by your power; you broke the
77:19 [77:20] Your path led through the **sea**, your way through the
78:13 He divided the **sea** and led them through; he made the water stand
78:27 down on them like dust, flying birds like sand on the **seashore**.
78:53 so they were unafraid; but the **sea** engulfed their enemies.
80:11 [80:12] It sent out its boughs to the **Sea**, its shoots as far as the
89: 9 [89:10] You rule over the surging **sea**; when its waves mount up,
89:25 [89:26] I will set his hand over the **sea**, his right hand over the
93: 4 thunder of the great waters, mightier than the breakers of the **sea**—
95: 5 The **sea** is his, for he made it, and his hands formed the dry land.
96:11 let the earth be glad; let the **sea** resound, and all that is in it;
98: 7 Let the **sea** resound, and everything in it, the world, and all who
104:25 There is the **sea**, vast and spacious, teeming with creatures beyond
106: 7 your many kindnesses, and they rebelled by the **sea**, the Red Sea.
106: 7 your many kindnesses, and they rebelled by the sea, the Red **Sea**.
106: 9 He rebuked the Red **Sea**, and it dried up; he led them through the
106:22 miracles in the land of Ham and awesome deeds by the Red **Sea**.
107: 3 from east and west, from north and south. [BHS *the sea*; NIV 3545]
107:23 Others went out on the **sea** in ships; they were merchants on the
114: 3 The **sea** looked and fled, the Jordan turned back;
114: 5 Why was it, O **sea**, that you fled, O Jordan, that you turned back,
135: 6 in the heavens and on the earth, in the **seas** and all their depths.
136:13 to him who divided the Red **Sea** asunder *His love endures*
136:15 swept Pharaoh and his army into the Red **Sea**; *His love*
139: 9 I rise on the wings of the dawn, if I settle on the far side of the **sea**,
146: 6 the Maker of heaven and earth, the **sea**, and everything in them—
Pr 8:29 when he gave the **sea** its boundary so the waters would not
23:34 You will be like one sleeping on the **high seas** [+4213], lying on
30:19 of a snake on a rock, the way of a ship on the **high seas** [+4213],
Ecc 1: 7 All streams flow into the **sea**, yet the sea is never full. To the place
1: 7 All streams flow into the sea, yet the **sea** is never full. To the place
Isa 5:30 In that day they will roar over it like the roaring of the **sea**.
9: 1 [8:23] of the Gentiles, by the way of the **sea**, along the Jordan—
10:22 Though your people, O Israel, be like the sand by the **sea**,
10:26 and he will raise his staff over the **waters**, as he did in Egypt.
11: 9 be full of the knowledge of the LORD as the waters cover the **sea**.
11:11 from Babylonia, from Hamath and from the islands of the **sea**.
11:14 They will swoop down on the slopes of Philistia to the **west**;
11:15 The LORD will dry up the gulf of the Egyptian **sea**; with a
16: 8 the desert. Their shoots spread out and went as far as the **sea**.
17:12 the raging of many nations—they rage like the raging **sea**!
18: 2 which sends envoys by **sea** in papyrus boats over the water.
19: 5 The waters of the **river** will dry up, and the riverbed will be
21: 1 An oracle concerning the Desert by the **Sea**: Like whirlwinds
23: 2 merchants of Sidon, whom the **seafarers** [+6296] have enriched.
23: 4 Be ashamed, O Sidon, and you, O fortress of the **sea**, for the sea
23: 4 O Sidon, and you, O fortress of the sea, for the **sea** has spoken:
23:11 The LORD has stretched out his hand over the **sea** and made its
24:14 shout for joy; from the **west** they acclaim the LORD's majesty.
24:15 name of the LORD, the God of Israel, in the islands of the **sea**.
27: 1 Leviathan the coiling serpent; he will slay the monster of the **sea**.
42:10 you who go down to the **sea**, and all that is in it, you islands,
43:16 he who made a way through the **sea**, a path through the mighty
48:18 have been like a river, your righteousness like the waves of the **sea**.
49:12 some from the north, some from the **west**, some from the region of
50: 2 By a mere rebuke I dry up the **sea**, I turn rivers into a desert;
51:10 Was it not you who dried up the **sea**, the waters of the great deep,
51:10 who made a road in the depths of the **sea** so that the redeemed
51:15 LORD your God, who churns up the **sea** so that its waves roar—
57:20 But the wicked are like the tossing **sea**, which cannot rest,
60: 5 the wealth on the **seas** will be brought to you, to you the riches of
63:11 where is he who brought them through the **sea**, with the shepherd
Jer 5:22 I made the sand a boundary for the **sea**, an everlasting barrier it
6:23 They sound like the roaring **sea** as they ride on their horses;
15: 8 I will make their widows more numerous than the sand of the **sea**.
25:22 kings of Tyre and Sidon; the kings of the coastlands across the **sea**;
27:19 the **Sea**, the movable stands and the other furnishings that are left
31:35 stars to shine by night, who stirs up the **sea** so that its waves roar—
33:22 stars of the sky and as measureless as the sand on the **seashore**.' "
46:18 who is like Tabor among the mountains, like Carmel by the **sea**.
47: 7 when he has ordered it to attack Ashkelon and the **coast** [+2572]?"
48:32 Your branches spread as far as the **sea**; they reached as far as the
48:32 spread as far as the sea; they reached as far as the **sea** *of* Jazer.
49:21 fall the earth will tremble; their cry will resound to the Red **Sea**.
49:23 bad news. They are disheartened, troubled like the restless **sea**.
50:42 They sound like the roaring **sea** as they ride on their horses;
51:36 and avenge you; I will dry up her **sea** and make her springs dry.
51:42 The **sea** will rise over Babylon; its roaring waves will cover her.
52:17 and the bronze **Sea** that were at the temple of the LORD
52:20 the **Sea** and the twelve bronze bulls under it, and the movable
La 2:13 of Zion? Your wound is as deep as the **sea**. Who can heal you?
Eze 25:16 and destroy those remaining along the **coast** [+2572].
26: 3 bring many nations against you, like the **sea** casting up its waves.
26: 5 Out in the **sea** she will become a place to spread fishnets, for I have
26:16 Then all the princes of the **coast** will step down from their thrones
26:17 you are destroyed, O city of renown, peopled by men of the **sea**!
26:17 You were a power on the **seas**, you and your citizens; you put your
26:18 day of your fall; the islands in the **sea** are terrified at your collapse.'
27: 3 Say to Tyre, situated at the gateway to the **sea**, merchant of peoples
27: 4 Your domain was on the **high seas** [+4213]; your builders brought
27: 9 All the ships of the **sea** and their sailors came alongside to trade for
27:25 your wares. You are filled with heavy cargo in the heart of the **sea**.
27:26 But the east wind will break you to pieces in the heart of the **sea**.
27:27 everyone else on board will sink into the heart of the **sea** on the
27:29 the mariners and all the **seamen** [+2480] will stand on the shore.
27:32 "Who was ever silenced like Tyre, surrounded by the **sea**?"
27:33 When your merchandise went out on the **seas**, you satisfied many
27:34 Now you are shattered by the **sea** in the depths of the waters;
28: 2 "I am a god; I sit on the throne of a god in the heart of the **seas**."
28: 8 to the pit, and you will die a violent death in the heart of the **seas**.
32: 2 you are like a monster in the **seas** thrashing about in your streams,
38:20 The fish of the **sea**, the birds of the air, the beasts of the field,
39:11 in Israel, in the valley of those who travel east toward the **Sea**.
41:12 The building facing the temple courtyard on the **west** side was
42:19 he turned to the **west** side and measured; it was five hundred cubits
45: 7 It will **extend westward** [+2025] from the west side and eastward
45: 7 It will extend westward from the **west** side and eastward from the
45: 7 running lengthwise from the **western** to the eastern border parallel
46:19 to the priests, and showed me a place at the **western** [+2025] end.

Eze 47: 8 and goes down into the Arabah, where it enters the **Sea**.
47: 8 When it empties into the **Sea**, the water there becomes fresh.
47: 10 The fish will be of many kinds—like the fish of the Great **Sea**.
47: 15 "On the north side it will run from the Great **Sea** by the Hethlon
47: 17 The boundary will extend from the **sea** to Hazar Enan, along the
47: 18 and the land of Israel, to the eastern **sea** and as far as Tamar.
47: 19 Meribah Kadesh, then along the Wadi ⌊of Egypt⌋ to the Great **Sea**.
47: 20 "On the **west** side, the Great Sea will be the boundary to a point
47: 20 the Great **Sea** will be the boundary to a point opposite Lebo
47: 20 to a point opposite Lebo Hamath. This will be the **west** boundary.
48: 1 will be part of its border from the east side to the **west** *side*.
48: 2 it will border the territory of Dan from east to **west** [+2025].
48: 3 it will border the territory of Asher from east to **west** [+2025].
48: 4 it will border the territory of Naphtali from east to **west** [+2025].
48: 5 it will border the territory of Manasseh from east to **west** [+2025].
48: 6 it will border the territory of Ephraim from east to **west** [+2025].
48: 7 it will border the territory of Reuben from east to **west** [+2025].
48: 8 "Bordering the territory of Judah from east to **west** [+2025] will be
48: 8 its length from east to **west** [+2025] will equal one of the tribal
48: 10 10,000 cubits wide on the **west** *side*, 10,000 cubits wide on the east
48: 16 the east side 4,500 cubits, and the **west** [+2025] side 4,500 cubits.
48: 17 on the south, 250 cubits on the east, and 250 cubits on the **west**.
48: 18 10,000 cubits on the east side and 10,000 cubits on the **west** *side*.
48: 21 **westward** [+2025] from the 25,000 cubits to the western border.
48: 21 westward from the 25,000 cubits to the **western** [+2025] border.
48: 23 it will extend from the east side to the **west** [+2025] side.
48: 24 it will border the territory of Benjamin from east to **west** [+2025].
48: 25 it will border the territory of Simeon from east to **west** [+2025].
48: 26 it will border the territory of Issachar from east to **west** [+2025].
48: 27 it will border the territory of Zebulun from east to **west** [+2025].
48: 28 Meribah Kadesh, then along the Wadi ⌊of Egypt⌋ to the Great **Sea**.
48: 34 "On the **west** side, which is 4,500 cubits long, will be three gates:
Da 8: 4 I watched the ram as he charged toward the **west** and the north
11: 45 He will pitch his royal tents between the **seas** at the beautiful holy
Hos 1: 10 [2:1] "Yet the Israelites will be like the sand on the **seashore**,
4: 3 of the field and the birds of the air and the fish of the **sea** are dying.
11: 10 When he roars, his children will come trembling from the **west**.
Joel 2: 20 with its front columns going into the eastern **sea** and those in the
2: 20 going into the eastern sea and those in the rear into the western **sea**.
Am 5: 8 who calls for the waters of the **sea** and pours them out over the
8: 12 Men will stagger from **sea** to sea and wander from north to east,
8: 12 Men will stagger from sea to **sea** and wander from north to east,
9: 3 Though they hide from me at the bottom of the **sea**, there I will
9: 6 who calls for the waters of the **sea** and pours them out over the
Jnh 1: 4 the LORD sent a great wind on the **sea**, and such a violent storm
1: 4 such a violent storm arose **[RPH]** that the ship threatened to break
1: 5 they threw the cargo into the **sea** to lighten the ship. But Jonah had
1: 9 the LORD, the God of heaven, who made the **sea** and the land."
1: 11 The **sea** was getting rougher and rougher. So they asked him,
1: 11 "What should we do to you to make the **sea** calm down for us?"
1: 12 "Pick me up and throw me into the **sea**," he replied, "and it will
1: 12 me into the sea," he replied, "and **it**[s] [+2021] will become calm.
1: 13 But they could not, for the **sea** grew even wilder than before.
1: 15 Then they took Jonah and threw him **overboard** [+448+2021],
1: 15 and threw him overboard, and the raging **sea** grew calm.
2: 3 [2:4] You hurled me into the deep, into the very heart of the **seas**,
Mic 7: 12 the Euphrates and from **sea** to sea and from mountain to mountain.
7: 12 the Euphrates and from sea to **sea** and from mountain to mountain.
7: 19 sins underfoot and hurl all our iniquities into the depths of the **sea**.
Na 1: 4 He rebukes the **sea** and dries it up; he makes all the rivers run dry.
3: 8 water around her? The **river** was her defense, the waters her wall.
3: 8 river was her defense, the <u>waters</u> [BHS *river*; NIV 4784] her wall.
Hab 1: 14 You have made men like fish in the **sea**, like sea creatures that
2: 14 knowledge of the glory of the LORD, as the waters cover the **sea**.
3: 8 Did you rage against the **sea** when you rode with your horses
3: 15 You trampled the **sea** with your horses, churning the great waters.
Zep 1: 3 I will sweep away the birds of the air and the fish of the **sea**.
2: 5 Woe to you who live by the **sea**, O Kerethite people; the word of
2: 6 The land by the **sea**, where the Kerethites dwell, will be a place for
Hag 2: 6 more shake the heavens and the earth, the **sea** and the dry land.
Zec 9: 4 will take away her possessions and destroy her power on the **sea**,
9: 10 His rule will extend from **sea** to sea and from the River to the ends
9: 10 His rule will extend from sea to **sea** and from the River to the ends
10: 11 They will pass through the **sea** *of* trouble; the surging sea will be
10: 11 the surging **sea** will be subdued and all the depths of the Nile will
14: 4 and the Mount of Olives will be split in two from east to **west**,
14: 8 half to the eastern **sea** and half to the western sea, in summer
14: 8 half to the eastern sea and half to the western **sea**, in summer

3543 יְמוּאֵל *yᵉmû'ēl*, n.pr.m. [2] [cf. 5803]

Jemuel [2]

Ge 46: 10 **Jemuel**, Jamin, Ohad, Jakin, Zohar and Shaul the son of a
Ex 6: 15 The sons of Simeon were **Jemuel**, Jamin, Ohad, Jakin, Zohar

3544 יְמִימָה *yᵉmîmâ*, n.pr.f. [1] [√ 3553?]

Jemimah [1]

Job 42: 14 The first daughter he named **Jemimah**, the second Keziah

3545 יָמִין *yāmîn*[1], n.f. [139 / 140] [→ 1228, 1229, 2124?, 3546, 3547, 3548, 3554, 3556, 9402, 9405]

right [118], south [13], *untranslated* [2], left-handed [+360+3338] [2], south [+4946] [2], hand [1], southward [+448+2021] [1], which way [+196+6584+6584+8520] [1]

Ge 13: 9 I'll go to the right; if you go to the **right**, I'll go to the left."
24: 49 so I may know **which way** [+196+6584+6584+8520] to turn."
48: 13 Ephraim on his **right** toward Israel's left hand and Manasseh on
48: 13 left hand and Manasseh on his left toward Israel's **right** hand,
48: 14 But Israel reached out his **right** hand and put it on Ephraim's head,
48: 17 When Joseph saw his father placing his **right** hand on Ephraim's
48: 18 this one is the firstborn; put your **right** hand on his head."
Ex 14: 22 on dry ground, with a wall of water on their **right** and on their left.
14: 29 on dry ground, with a wall of water on their **right** and on their left.
15: 6 "Your **right** hand, O LORD, was majestic in power. Your right
15: 6 in power. Your **right** hand, O LORD, shattered the enemy.
15: 12 You stretched out your **right** hand and the earth swallowed them.
29: 22 of the liver, both kidneys with the fat on them, and the **right** thigh.
Lev 7: 32 You are to give the **right** thigh of your fellowship offerings to the
7: 33 the fat of the fellowship offering shall have the **right** thigh as his
8: 25 covering of the liver, both kidneys and their fat and the **right** thigh.
8: 26 and a wafer; he put these on the fat portions and on the **right** thigh.
9: 21 and the **right** thigh before the LORD as a wave offering,
Nu 18: 18 as the breast of the wave offering and the **right** thigh are yours.
20: 17 We will travel along the king's highway and not turn to the **right**
22: 26 where there was no room to turn, either to the **right** or to the left.
Dt 2: 27 on the main road; we will not turn aside to the **right** or to the left.
5: 32 has commanded you; do not turn aside to the **right** or to the left.
17: 11 not turn aside from what they tell you, to the **right** or to the left.
17: 20 than his brothers and turn from the law to the **right** or to the left.
28: 14 to the **right** or to the left, following other gods and serving them.
33: 2 He came with myriads of holy ones from the **south**, from his
Jos 1: 7 do not turn from it to the **right** or to the left, that you may be
17: 7 The boundary ran **southward** [+448+2021] from there to include
23: 6 the Law of Moses, without turning aside to the **right** or to the left.
Jdg 3: 15 deliverer—Ehud, a **left-handed** [+360+3338] man, the son of Gera
3: 16 a half long, which he strapped to his **right** thigh under his clothing.
3: 21 drew the sword from his **right** thigh and plunged it into the king's
5: 26 for the tent peg, her **right** hand for the workman's hammer.
7: 20 and holding in their **right** hands the trumpets they were to blow,
16: 29 his **right** hand on the one and his left hand on the other,
20: 16 seven hundred chosen men who were **left-handed** [+360+3338],
1Sa 6: 12 and lowing all the way; they did not turn to the **right** or to the left.
11: 2 on the condition that I gouge out the **right** eye of every one of you
23: 19 at Horesh, on the hill of Hakilah, **south** [+4946] *of* Jeshimon?
23: 24 men were in the Desert of Maon, in the Arabah **south** *of* Jeshimon.
2Sa 2: 19 turning neither to the **right** nor to the left as he pursued him.
2: 21 Then Abner said to him, "Turn aside to the **right** or to the left;
16: 6 all the troops and the special guard were on David's **right** and left.
20: 9 Joab took Amasa by the beard with his **right** hand to kiss him.
24: 5 **south** *of* the town in the gorge, and then went through Gad
1Ki 2: 19 brought for the king's mother, and she sat down at his **right** hand.
7: 39 He placed five of the stands on the **south** [+4946] side of the
7: 49 the lampstands of pure gold (five on the **right** and five on the left,
22: 19 throne with all the host of heaven standing around him on his **right**
2Ki 12: 9 [12:10] on the **right** side as one enters the temple of the LORD.
22: 2 of his father David, not turning aside to the **right** or to the left.
23: 13 that were east of Jerusalem on the **south** of the Hill of Corruption—
1Ch 6: 39 [6:24] Heman's associate Asaph, who served at his **right** hand:
2Ch 3: 17 in the front of the temple, one to the **south** and one to the north.
4: 6 and placed five on the **south** *side* and five on the north.
4: 7 them in the temple, five on the **south** *side* and five on the north.
4: 8 them in the temple, five on the **south** *side* and five on the north.
18: 18 on his throne with all the host of heaven standing on his **right**
34: 2 of his father David, not turning aside to the **right** or to the left.
Ne 8: 4 Beside him on his **right** stood Mattithiah, Shema, Anaiah,
12: 31 One was to proceed on top of the wall to the **right**,
Job 23: 9 not see him; when he turns to the **south**, I catch no glimpse of him.
30: 12 On my **right** the tribe attacks; they lay snares for my feet,
40: 14 I myself will admit to you that your own **right** hand can save you.
Ps 16: 8 before me. Because he is at my **right** hand, I will not be shaken.
16: 11 joy in your presence, with eternal pleasures at your **right** hand.
17: 7 you who save by your **right** hand those who take refuge in you
18: 35 [18:36] your shield of victory, and your **right** hand sustains me;
20: 6 [20:7] his holy heaven with the saving power of his **right** hand.
21: 8 [21:9] on all your enemies; your **right** hand will seize your foes.
26: 10 hands are wicked schemes, whose **right** hands are full of bribes.
44: 3 [44:4] it was your **right** hand, your arm, and the light of your

Ps 45: 4 [45:5] let your **right** hand display awesome deeds.
45: 9 [45:10] at your **right** hand is the royal bride in gold of Ophir.
48: 10 [48:11] of the earth; your **right** hand is filled with righteousness.
60: 5 [60:7] Save us and help us with your **right** hand, that those you
63: 8 [63:9] My soul clings to you; your **right** hand upholds me.
73: 23 Yet I am always with you; you hold me by my **right** hand.
74: 11 Why do you hold back your hand, your **right** hand? Take it from
77: 10 [77:11] the years of the **right** hand *of* the Most High."
78: 54 of his holy land, to the hill country his **right** hand had taken.
80: 15 [80:16] the root your **right** hand has planted, the son you have
80: 17 [80:18] Let your hand rest on the man at your **right** hand, the son
89: 12 [89:13] You created the north and the **south**; Tabor and Hermon
89: 13 [89:14] with power; your hand is strong, your **right** hand exalted.
89: 25 [89:26] set his hand over the sea, his **right** hand over the rivers.
89: 42 [89:43] You have exalted the **right** hand *of* his foes; you have
91: 7 ten thousand at your **right** hand, but it will not come near you.
98: 1 his **right** hand and his holy arm have worked salvation for him.
107: 3 the lands, from east and west, from north and **south**. [BHS 3542]
108: 6 [108:7] Save us and help us with your **right** hand, that those you
109: 6 an evil man to oppose him; let an accuser stand at his **right** hand.
109: 31 For he stands at the **right** hand *of* the needy one, to save his life
110: 1 "Sit at my **right** hand until I make your enemies a footstool for
110: 5 The Lord is at your **right** hand; he will crush kings on the day of
118: 15 the righteous: "The LORD's **right** hand has done mighty things!
118: 16 The LORD's **right** hand is lifted high; the LORD's right hand
118: 16 is lifted high; the LORD's **right** hand has done mighty things!"
121: 5 watches over you—the LORD is your shade at your **right** hand;
137: 5 If I forget you, O Jerusalem, may my **right** hand forget ⌞its skill⌟.
138: 7 against the anger of my foes, with your **right** hand you save me.
139: 10 there your hand will guide me, your **right** hand will hold me fast.
142: 4 [142:5] Look to my **right** and see; no one is concerned for me.
144: 8 whose mouths are full of lies, whose **right** hands are deceitful.
144: 8 mouths are full of lies, whose right hands **[RPH]** are deceitful.
144: 11 whose mouths are full of lies, whose **right** hands are deceitful.
144: 11 mouths are full of lies, whose right hands are **[RPH]** deceitful.
Pr 3: 16 Long life is in her **right** hand; in her left hand are riches and honor.
4: 27 Do not swerve to the **right** or the left; keep your foot from evil.
27: 16 her is like restraining the wind or grasping oil with the **hand**.
Ecc 10: 2 The heart of the wise inclines to the **right**, but the heart of the fool
SS 2: 6 His left arm is under my head, and his **right** arm embraces me.
8: 3 His left arm is under my head and his **right** arm embraces me.
Isa 9: 20 [9:19] On the **right** they will devour, but still be hungry; on the
41: 10 and help you; I will uphold you with my righteous **right** hand.
41: 13 your God, who takes hold of your **right** hand and says to you,
44: 20 save himself, or say, "Is not this thing in my **right** hand a lie?"
45: 1 whose **right** hand I take hold of to subdue nations before him
48: 13 of the earth, and my **right** hand spread out the heavens;
54: 3 For you will spread out to the **right** and to the left; your
62: 8 The LORD has sworn by his **right** hand and by his mighty arm:
63: 12 who sent his glorious arm of power to be at Moses' **right** hand,
Jer 22: 24 were a signet ring on my **right** hand, I would still pull you off.
La 2: 3 He has withdrawn his **right** hand at the approach of the enemy.
2: 4 Like an enemy he has strung his bow; his **right** hand is ready.
Eze 1: 10 on the **right** side each had the face of a lion, and on the left the
10: 3 Now the cherubim were standing on the **south** *side* of the temple
16: 46 who lived to the **south** *of* you with her daughters, was Sodom.
21: 22 [21:27] Into his **right** hand will come the lot for Jerusalem,
39: 3 your left hand and make your arrows drop from your **right** hand.
Da 12: 7 of the river, lifted his **right** hand and his left hand toward heaven,
Jnh 4: 11 twenty thousand people who cannot tell their **right** hand from their
Hab 2: 16 The cup from the LORD's **right** hand is coming around to you,
Zec 3: 1 of the LORD, and Satan standing at his **right** side to accuse him.
4: 3 trees by it, one on the **right** *of* the bowl and the other on its left."
4: 11 "What are these two olive trees on the **right** and the left of the
11: 17 deserts the flock! May the sword strike his arm and his **right** eye!
11: 17 his arm be completely withered, his **right** eye totally blinded!"
12: 6 They will consume **right** and left all the surrounding peoples,

3546 ²יָמִין **yāmîn²**, n.pr.m. [6] [→ 3547; cf. 3545]

Jamin [6]

Ge 46: 10 **Jamin**, Ohad, Jakin, Zohar and Shaul the son of a Canaanite
Ex 6: 15 **Jamin**, Ohad, Jakin, Zohar and Shaul the son of a Canaanite
Nu 26: 12 through **Jamin**, the Jaminite clan; through Jakin, the Jakinite clan;
1Ch 2: 27 sons of Ram the firstborn of Jerahmeel: Maaz, **Jamin** and Eker.
4: 24 descendants of Simeon: Nemuel, **Jamin**, Jarib, Zerah and Shaul;
Ne 8: 7 Jeshua, Bani, Sherebiah, **Jamin**, Akkub, Shabbethai, Hodiah,

3547 יָמִינִי **yāmînî**, a.g. [1] [√ 3546; cf. 3545]

Jaminite [1]

Nu 26: 12 through Jamin, the **Jaminite** clan; through Jakin, the Jakinite clan;

3548 יְמָינִי **yemāynî**, a. [0] [√ 3545]

2Ch 3: 17 [The *one to the* **south** [K; see Q 3556] he named Jakin]
Eze 4: 6 [lie down again, this time on your **right** [K; see Q 3556] side,]

3549 יְמִינִי **yemînî**, a.g. [4] [√ 1228]

Benjamin [+408+1201] [1], Benjamin [1], Benjamite [+408] [1], tribe of Benjamin [+408] [1]

1Sa 9: 1 the son of Becorath, the son of Aphiah of **Benjamin** [+408+1201].
9: 4 he passed through the territory of **Benjamin**, but they did not find
2Sa 20: 1 Sheba son of Bicri, a **Benjamite** [+408], happened to be there.
Est 2: 5 was in the citadel of Susa a Jew of the **tribe of Benjamin** [+408],

3550 יִמְלָא **yimlā'**, n.pr.m. [2] [√ 4848]

Imlah [2]

2Ch 18: 7 good about me, but always bad. He is Micaiah son of **Imlah**."
18: 8 of his officials and said, "Bring Micaiah son of **Imlah** at once."

3551 יִמְלָה **yimlâ**, n.pr.m. [2] [√ 4848]

Imlah [2]

1Ki 22: 8 good about me, but always bad. He is Micaiah son of **Imlah**."
22: 9 of his officials and said, "Bring Micaiah son of **Imlah** at once."

3552 יַמְלֵךְ **yamlēk**, n.pr.m. [1] [√ 4887?]

Jamlech [1]

1Ch 4: 34 Meshobab, **Jamlech**, Joshah son of Amaziah,

3553 יֵמִם **yēmim**, n.[m.]. [1] [√ 3544?]

hot springs [1]

Ge 36: 24 This is the Anah who discovered the **hot springs** in the desert

3554 יָמַן **yāman**, v.den. [5] [√ 3545]

turn to the right [2], go to the right [1], right-handed [1], to the right [1]

Ge 13: 9 [G] If you go to the left, *I'll* **go to the right**; if you go to the
2Sa 14: 19 [G] no one can **turn to the right** or to the left from anything my
1Ch 12: 2 [G] shoot arrows or to sling stones **right-handed** or left-handed;
Isa 30: 21 [G] Whether *you* **turn to the right** or to the left, your ears will
Eze 21: 16 [21:21] [G] O sword, slash **to the right**, then to the left,

3555 יִמְנָה **yimnâ**, n.pr.m. [5] [√ 4948]

Imnah [4], Imnite [1]

Ge 46: 17 The sons of Asher: **Imnah**, Ishvah, Ishvi and Beriah. Their sister
Nu 26: 44 through **Imnah**, the Imnite clan; through Ishvi, the Ishvite clan;
26: 44 through Imnah, the **Imnite** clan; through Ishvi, the Ishvite clan;
1Ch 7: 30 The sons of Asher: **Imnah**, Ishvah, Ishvi and Beriah. Their sister
2Ch 31: 14 Kore son of **Imnah** the Levite, keeper of the East Gate, was in

3556 יְמָנִי **yemānî**, a. [33] [→ 3548; cf. 3545]

right [24], south [9]

Ex 29: 20 and put it on the lobes of the **right** ears of Aaron and his sons,
29: 20 ears of Aaron and his sons, on the thumbs of their **right** hands,
29: 20 thumbs of their right hands, and on the big toes of their **right** feet.
Lev 8: 23 took some of its blood and put it on the lobe of Aaron's **right** ear,
8: 23 on the thumb of his **right** hand and on the big toe of his right foot.
8: 23 on the thumb of his right hand and on the big toe of his **right** foot.
8: 24 and put some of the blood on the lobes of their **right** ears,
8: 24 on the thumbs of their **right** hands and on the big toes of their right
8: 24 thumbs of their right hands and on the big toes of their **right** feet.
14: 14 and put it on the lobe of the **right** ear of the one to be cleansed,
14: 14 on the thumb of his **right** hand and on the big toe of his right foot.
14: 14 on the thumb of his right hand and on the big toe of his **right** foot.
14: 16 dip his **right** forefinger into the oil in his palm, and with his finger
14: 17 in his palm on the lobe of the **right** ear of the one to be cleansed,
14: 17 on the thumb of his **right** hand and on the big toe of his right foot,
14: 17 on the thumb of his right hand and on the big toe of his **right** foot,
14: 25 and put it on the lobe of the **right** ear of the one to be cleansed,
14: 25 on the thumb of his **right** hand and on the big toe of his right foot.
14: 25 on the thumb of his right hand and on the big toe of his **right** foot.
14: 27 with his **right** forefinger sprinkle some of the oil from his palm
14: 28 on the lobe of the **right** ear of the one to be cleansed, on the thumb
14: 28 on the thumb of his **right** hand and on the big toe of his right foot.
14: 28 on the thumb of his right hand and on the big toe of his **right** foot.
1Ki 6: 8 The entrance to the lowest floor was on the **south** side of the
7: 21 The pillar to the **south** he named Jakin and the one to the north
7: 39 He placed the Sea on the **south** side, at the southeast corner of the
2Ki 11: 11 and the temple, from the **south** side to the north side of the temple.
2Ch 3: 17 The *one to the* **south** [K 3548] he named Jakin and the one to the
4: 10 He placed the Sea on the **south** side, at the southeast corner.

2Ch 23:10 and the temple, from the **south** side to the north side of the temple.
Eze 4: 6 finished this, lie down again, this time on your **right** [Q 3548] side,
47: 1 The water was coming down from under the **south** side of the
47: 2 gate facing east, and the water was flowing from the **south** side.

3557 יִמְנָע yimnāʿ, n.pr.m. [1] [√ 4979]

Imna [1]

1Ch 7:35 The sons of his brother Helem: Zophah, **Imna**, Shelesh and Amal.

3558 יָמַר yāmar, v. [1]

changed [1]

Jer 2:11 [G] Has a nation *ever* **changed** its gods? (Yet they are not gods

3559 יִמְרָה yimrâ, n.pr.m. [1] [√ 5286]

Imrah [1]

1Ch 7:36 The sons of Zophah: Suah, Harnepher, Shual, Beri, **Imrah**,

3560 יָמַשׁ yāmaš, v. [0] [cf. 4630, 5491]

Jdg 16:26 [g] ["Put me where I *can* **feel** [K; see Q 4630] the pillars]

3561 יָנָה yānâ, v. [19]

oppress [5], oppressor [3], mistreat [2], oppressors [2], take advantage of [2], crush [1], do wrong [1], driving [1], mistreated [1], oppresses [1]

Ex 22:21 [22:20] [G] "*Do* not **mistreat** an alien or oppress him, for you
Lev 19:33 [G] an alien lives with you in your land, *do* not **mistreat** him.
25:14 [G] or buy any from him, *do* not **take advantage of** each other.
25:17 [G] *Do* not **take advantage of** each other, but fear your God. I
Dt 23:16 [23:17] [G] in whatever town he chooses. *Do* not **oppress** him.
Ps 74: 8 [A] They said in their hearts, "*We will* **crush** them completely!"
123: 4 [a] [much contempt from the **arrogant**. [Q +1450; see K 1456]]
Isa 49:26 [G] I will make your **oppressors** eat their own flesh; they will be
Jer 22: 3 [G] **Do** no **wrong** or violence to the alien, the fatherless
25:38 [A] become desolate because of the sword of the **oppressor** and
46:16 [A] and our native lands, away from the sword of the **oppressor**.'
50:16 [A] Because of the sword of the **oppressor** let everyone return to
Eze 18: 7 [G] *He does* not **oppress** anyone, but returns what he took in
18:12 [G] *He* **oppresses** the poor and needy. He commits robbery. He
18:16 [G] *He does* not **oppress** anyone or require a pledge for a loan.
22: 7 [G] the alien and **mistreated** the fatherless and the widow.
22:29 [G] *they* **oppress** the poor and needy and mistreat the alien,
45: 8 [G] my princes *will* no longer **oppress** my people but will allow
46:18 [G] the inheritance of the people, **driving** them off their property.
Zep 3: 1 [A] Woe to the city of **oppressors**, rebellious and defiled!

3562 יָנוֹחַ yānôaḥ, n.pr.loc. [3] [√ 5663]

Janoah [3]

Jos 16: 6 eastward to Taanath Shiloh, passing by it to **Janoah** on the east.
16: 7 it went down from **Janoah** to Ataroth and Naarah, touched Jericho
2Ki 15:29 and took Ijon, Abel Beth Maacah, **Janoah**, Kedesh and Hazor.

3563 יָנוֹחָה yānôḥâ, n.pr.loc. Not used in NIV/BHS [√ 5663]

3564 יָנוּם yānûm, n.pr.loc. [0] [√ 5670?]

Jos 15:53 [**Janim**, [Q; see K 3565] Beth Tappuah, Aphekah,]

3565 יָנִים yānîm, n.pr.loc. [1] [√ 5670?]

Janim [1]

Jos 15:53 **Janim**, [Q 3564] Beth Tappuah, Aphekah,

3566 יְנִיקָה yᵉnîqâ, n.f. [1] [√ 3567]

shoot [1]

Eze 17: 4 he broke off its topmost **shoot** and carried it away to a land of

3567 יָנַק yānaq, v. [16] [→ 735, 3437, 3438, 3566, 4787; cf. 5682]

nurse [7], nursed [4], drink [1], feast on [1], female [1], nourished [1], suck [1]

Ge 21: 7 [G] "Who would have said to Abraham that Sarah *would* **nurse**
32:15 [32:16] [G] thirty **female** camels with their young, forty cows
Ex 2: 7 [G] get one of the Hebrew women *to* **nurse** the baby for you?"
2: 9 [G] "Take this baby and **nurse** him for me, and I will pay you."
2: 9 [G] will pay you." So the woman took the baby and **nursed** him.
Dt 32:13 [G] *He* **nourished** him *with* honey from the rock, and with oil
33:19 [A] *they will* **feast on** the abundance of the seas, on the treasures
1Sa 1:23 [G] at home and **nursed** her son until she had weaned him.
1Ki 3:21 [G] The next morning, I got up to **nurse** my son—and he was
Job 3:12 [A] knees to receive me and breasts that *I might be* **nursed**?
20:16 [A] *He will* **suck** the poison of serpents; the fangs of an adder
Isa 60:16 [A] *You will* **drink** the milk of nations and be nursed at royal
60:16 [A] will drink the milk of nations and *be* **nursed** *at* royal breasts.
66:11 [A] For *you will* **nurse** and be satisfied at her comforting breasts;
66:12 [A] *you will* **nurse** and be carried on her arm and dandled on her
La 4: 3 [G] Even jackals offer their breasts *to* **nurse** their young, but my

3568 יַנְשׁוּף yanšûp, n.[m.]. [3] [√ 5973]

great owl [3]

Lev 11:17 the little owl, the cormorant, the **great owl**,
Dt 14:16 the little owl, the **great owl**, the white owl,
Isa 34:11 owl will possess it; the **great owl** and the raven will nest there.

3569 יָסַד yāsad¹, v. [40 / 41] [→ 3571, 3572, 3573, 4586, 4587, 4588, 4589, 4996]

laid the foundations [5], the foundation was laid [4], established [3], laid the foundation [3], founded [2], ordained [2], set [2], the foundation laid [2], assigned to positions [1], assigned [1], begun [1], doing^s this [+2021+6894] [1], foundations be laid [1], foundations [1], instructed [1], laid foundations [1], lay foundations [1], lay [1], lays the foundation [1], made a place [1], provide a foundation [1], sets [1], sure [1], the foundation been laid [1], the foundations were laid [1], was founded [1]

Ex 9:18 [C] ever fallen on Egypt, from the day it **was founded** till now.
Jos 6:26 [D] "At the cost of his firstborn son *will he* **lay** its **foundations**;
1Ki 5:17 [5:31] [D] **provide a foundation** *of* dressed stone *for* the
6:37 [E] **The foundation** of the temple of the LORD **was laid** in the
7:10 [E] **The foundations were laid** *with* large stones of good
16:34 [D] *He* **laid** its **foundations** at the cost of his firstborn son
1Ch 9:22 [D] *had been* **assigned to** their **positions** of trust *by* David
2Ch 3: 3 [H] **The foundation** Solomon **laid** for building the temple of
31: 7 [A] They began **doing**^s [+2021+6894] **this** in the third month
Ezr 3: 6 [E] **the foundation** of the LORD's temple *had* not *yet* **been laid**.
3:10 [D] When the builders **laid the foundation** *of* the temple of the
3:11 [H] **the foundation** *of* the house of the LORD **was laid**.
3:12 [A] when they saw **the foundation** *of* this temple *being* **laid**,
7: 9 [D] He *had* **begun** [BHS 3571] his journey from Babylon on the
Est 1: 8 [D] for the king **instructed** all the wine stewards to serve each
Job 38: 4 [A] "Where were you when I **laid** the earth's **foundation**?
Ps 8: 2 [8:3] [D] lips of children and infants *you have* **ordained** praise
24: 2 [A] for he **founded** it upon the seas and established it upon the
78:69 [A] like the heights, like the earth that *he* **established** forever.
89:11 [89:12] [A] the earth; you **founded** the world and all that is in it.
102:25 [102:26] [A] In the beginning *you* **laid the foundations** *of* the
104: 5 [A] *He* **set** the earth on its foundations; it can never be moved.
104: 8 [A] down into the valleys, to the place *you* **assigned** for them.
119:152 [A] Long ago I learned from your statutes that *you* **established**
Pr 3:19 [A] By wisdom the LORD **laid the** earth's **foundations**,
SS 5:15 [E] His legs are pillars of marble **set** on bases of pure gold.
Isa 14:32 [D] "The LORD *has* **established** Zion, and in her his afflicted
23:13 [A] The Assyrians *have* **made** it **a place** for desert creatures;
28:16 [D] "See, I **lay** a stone in Zion, a tested stone, a precious
28:16 [H] a tested stone, a precious cornerstone for a **sure** foundation;
44:28 [C] and of the temple, "*Let its* **foundations be laid**." '
48:13 [A] My own hand **laid the foundations** *of* the earth, and my
51:13 [A] out the heavens and **laid the foundations** *of* the earth,
51:16 [A] *who* **laid the foundations** *of* the earth, and who say to Zion,
54:11 [A] with stones of turquoise, your **foundations** with sapphires.
Am 9: 6 [A] palace in the heavens and **sets** its foundation on the earth,
Hab 1:12 [A] O Rock, *you have* **ordained** them to punish.
Hag 2:18 [E] day when **the foundation** of the LORD's temple **was laid**.
Zec 4: 9 [D] "The hands of Zerubbabel *have* **laid the foundation** *of* this
8: 9 [E] **the foundation was laid** *for* the house of the LORD
12: 1 [A] out the heavens, *who* **lays the foundation** *of* the earth,

3570 ²יָסַד yāsad², v. [2] [cf. 6051]

conspire [1], gather [1]

Ps 2: 2 [C] the rulers **gather** together against the LORD and against his
31:13 [31:14] [C] they **conspire** against me and plot to take my life.

3571 יְסֻד yᵉsud, n.[m.]. [1 / 0] [√ 3569]

Ezr 7: 9 He *had* begun [BHS *beginning*; NIV 3569] his journey from

3572 יְסוֹד yᵉsôd, n.f. & m. [20] [√ 3569]

base [9], foundations [6], foundation [2], foot [1], restoration [1], stand firm [1]

Ex 29:12 with your finger, and pour out the rest of it at the **base** *of* the altar.
Lev 4: 7 The rest of the bull's blood he shall pour out at the **base** *of* the altar
4:18 The rest of the blood he shall pour out at the **base** *of* the altar of

Lev 4:25 and pour out the rest of the blood at the **base** *of* the altar.
4:30 and pour out the rest of the blood at the **base** *of* the altar.
4:34 and pour out the rest of the blood at the **base** *of* the altar.
5: 9 the rest of the blood must be drained out at the **base** *of* the altar.
8:15 He poured out the rest of the blood at the **base** *of* the altar.
9: 9 the rest of the blood he poured out at the **base** *of* the altar.
2Ch 23: 5 third of you at the royal palace and a third at the **Foundation** Gate,
24:27 the record of the **restoration** *of* the temple of God are written in
Job 4:19 whose **foundations** are in the dust, who are crushed more readily
22:16 off before their time, their **foundations** washed away by a flood.
Ps 137: 7 "Tear it down," they cried, "tear it down to its **foundations**!"
Pr 10:25 the wicked are gone, but the righteous **stand firm** forever.
La 4:11 He kindled a fire in Zion that consumed her **foundations**.
Eze 13:14 will level it to the ground so that its **foundation** will be laid bare.
30: 4 her wealth will be carried away and her **foundations** torn down.
Mic 1: 6 I will pour her stones into the valley and lay bare her **foundations**.
Hab 3:13 of the land of wickedness, you stripped him from head to **foot**.

3573 יְסוּדָה *y^esûdâ*, n.f. [1] [√ 3569]

foundation [1]

Ps 87: 1 He has set his **foundation** on the holy mountain;

3574 יִסּוֹר *yissôr*, n.m. [1] [√ 3579]

correct [1]

Job 40: 2 "Will the one who contends with the Almighty **correct** him?

3575 יָסַךְ *yāsak*, v. Not used in NIV/BHS [cf. 5818, 6057]

3576 יִסְכָּה *yiskâ*, n.pr.f. [1]

Iscah [1]

Ge 11:29 was the daughter of Haran, the father of both Milcah and **Iscah**.

3577 יִסְמַכְיָהוּ *yismakyāhû*, n.pr.m. [1] [√ 6164 + 3378]

Ismakiah [1]

2Ch 31:13 Eliel, **Ismakiah**, Mahath and Benaiah were supervisors under

3578 יָסַף *yāsap*, v. [214 / 215] [→ 25, 47, 498, 3441, 3442, 6231; cf. 3388, Ar 10323]

again [26], again [+6388] [22], add [21], severely [12], more [9], longer [8], added [6], more [+6388] [6], *untranslated* [5], longer [+6388] [5], once more [5], anymore [+6388] [4], continued [4], make even heavier [4], anymore [3], do again [3], multiply [3], adding [2], adds [2], all the more [+6388] [2], enlarged [2], far exceeded [2], increased [2], never [+4202] [2], once again [+6388] [2], once again [2], once more [+6388] [2], promote [2], adds length [1], another [+6388] [1], another [1], any longer [+6388] [1], any longer [1], back [+6388] [1], be added [1], bring more and more [1], bring [1], brings [1], by far [1], carried still further [1], continued [+6388] [1], do again [+6388] [1], else [1], ever [1], farther [1], gains [1], gave [1], given even more [+2179+2179+2256+3869+3869+4200] [1], grow stronger [+601] [1], had reaffirm [1], heap [1], heaping [1], increase [+6584] [1], increase [1], join [1], later [1], make again [+6388] [1], make increase [1], making more [1], more [+4200+6388] [1], more [+8041] [1], more and more [+3972+6584] [1], more and more [1], more besides [1], multiplies [1], over [1], persist [1], prolong [1], reach[s] out [1], still another [+6388] [1], still more [1], stirring up more [1], stop [+4202] [1], stopped [+4202+6388] [1], were added [+6388] [1]

Ge 4: 2 [G] **Later** she gave birth to his brother Abel. Now Abel kept
4:12 [G] work the ground, it will no **longer** yield its crops for you.
8:10 [G] seven more days and **again** sent out the dove from the ark.
8:12 [A] dove out again, but this time it did not return **[NIE]** to him.
8:21 [G] "Never **again** [+6388] will I curse the ground because of
8:21 [G] And never **again** [+6388] will I destroy all living creatures,
18:29 [G] **Once again** [+6388] he spoke to him, "What if only forty are
25: 1 [G] Abraham took **another** wife, whose name was Keturah.
30:24 [G] and said, "*May* the LORD **add** to me another son."
37: 5 [G] told it to his brothers, they hated him **all the more** [+6388].
37: 8 [G] they hated him **all the more** [+6388] because of his dream
38: 5 [G] She gave birth to **still another** [+6388] son and named him
38:26 [A] son Shelah." And he did not sleep with her **again** [+6388].
44:23 [G] comes down with you, you will not see my face **again**.'
Ex 1:10 [C] *will* **join** our enemies, fight against us and leave the country."
5: 7 [G] "*You are* no **longer** to supply the people with straw for
8:29 [8:25] [G] **again** by not letting the people go to offer sacrifices
9:28 [G] I will let you go; you don't have to stay **any longer**."
9:34 [G] the rain and hail and thunder had stopped, he sinned **again**:
10:28 [A] of my sight! Make sure you do not appear before me **again**!
10:29 [G] "I will never appear before you **again** [+6388]."
11: 6 [G] worse than there has ever been or *ever will be* **again**.
14:13 [G] Egyptians you see today you will never see **again** [+6388].

Lev 5:16 [G] **add** a fifth of the value to that and give it all to the priest,
6: 5 [5:24] [G] **add** a fifth of the value to it and give it all to the
19:25 [G] In this way your harvest *will be* **increased**. I am the LORD
22:14 [A] to the priest for the offering and **add** a fifth of the value to it.
26:18 [A] listen to me, I will punish you for your sins seven times **over**.
26:21 [A] *I will* **multiply** your afflictions seven times over, as your sins
27:13 [A] wishes to redeem the animal, *he must* **add** a fifth to its value.
27:15 [A] *he must* **add** a fifth to its value, and the house will again
27:19 [A] *he must* **add** a fifth to its value, and the field will again
27:27 [A] buy it back at its set value, **adding** a fifth of the value to it.
27:31 [G] any of his tithe, *he must* **add** a fifth of the value to it.
Nu 5: 7 [A] **add** one fifth to it and give it all to the person he has
11:25 [A] on them, they prophesied, but *they did* not **do** *so* **again**.
22:15 [G] Balak sent **[NIE]** other princes, more numerous and more
22:19 [G] and I will find out what **else** the LORD will tell me."
22:25 [G] crushing Balaam's foot against it. So he beat her **again**.
22:26 [G] the angel of the LORD **[RPH]** moved on ahead and stood
32:14 [A] and **making** the LORD even **more** angry with Israel.
32:15 [A] he *will* **again** [+6388] leave all this people in the desert,
36: 3 [C] and **added** to that of the tribe they marry into.
36: 4 [C] their inheritance *will* **be added** to that of the tribe into which
Dt 1:11 [G] *May* the LORD, the God of your fathers, **increase** [+6584]
3:26 [G] "Do not speak to me **anymore** [+6388] about this matter.
4: 2 [G] *Do* not **add** to what I command you and do not subtract from
5:22 [A] the cloud and the deep darkness; and *he* **added** nothing more.
5:25 [A] hear the voice of the LORD our God **any longer** [+6388].
12:32 [13:1] [A] command you; *do* not **add** to it or take away from it.
13:11 [13:12] [G] no one among you will do such an evil thing **again**.
17:16 [G] told you, "You are not to go back that way **again** [+6388]."
18:16 [G] the LORD our God nor see this great fire **anymore** [+6388],
19: 9 [A] then you are to set aside three **more** [+4200+6388] cities.
19:20 [G] never **again** [+6388] will such an evil thing be done among
20: 8 [A] the officers *shall* **add**, "Is any man afraid or fainthearted?
25: 3 [G] he must not give him **more** *than* forty lashes. If he is flogged
25: 3 [G] If he is flogged **more** [+8041] than that, your brother will be
28:68 [G] on a journey I said you *should* never **make again** [+6388].
32:23 [G] "*I will* **heap** [BHS 6200] calamities upon them and spend
Jos 7:12 [G] I will not be with you **anymore** unless you destroy whatever
23:13 [G] you may be sure that the LORD your God *will* no **longer**
Jdg 2:21 [G] I *will* no **longer** drive out before them any of the nations
3:12 [G] **Once again** the Israelites did evil in the eyes of the LORD,
4: 1 [G] the Israelites **once again** did evil in the eyes of the LORD.
8:28 [A] subdued before the Israelites and did not raise its head **again**.
9:37 [G] Gaal spoke up **again** [+6388]: "Look, people are coming
10: 6 [G] **Again** the Israelites did evil in the eyes of the LORD. They
10:13 [G] and served other gods, so *I will* no **longer** save you.
11:14 [G] Jephthah sent **back** [+6388] messengers to the Ammonite
13: 1 [G] **Again** the Israelites did evil in the eyes of the LORD,
13:21 [A] the LORD *did* not show himself **again** [+6388] to Manoah
20:22 [G] **again** took up their positions where they had stationed
20:23 [G] "*Shall we* go up **again** to battle against the Benjamites,
20:28 [G] "*Shall we* go up **again** [+6388] to battle with Benjamin our
Ru 1:17 [G] *be it* ever so **severely**, if anything but death separates you
1Sa 3: 6 [G] **Again** [+6388] the LORD called, "Samuel!" And Samuel
3: 8 [G] **[RPH]** The LORD called Samuel a third time, and Samuel
3:17 [G] May God deal with you, *be it* ever so **severely**, if you hide
3:21 [G] The LORD **continued** to appear at Shiloh, and there he
7:13 [A] and did not invade Israelite territory **again** [+6388].
9: 8 [G] The servant answered him **again**. "Look," he said, "I have a
12:19 [A] for *we have* **added** to all our other sins the evil of asking for
14:44 [G] with me, *be it* ever so **severely**, if you do not die, Jonathan."
15:35 [A] Until the day Samuel died, he did not go to see Saul **again**,
18:29 [G] Saul *became* still **more** afraid of him, and he remained his
19: 8 [G] **Once more** war broke out, and David went out and fought
19:21 [G] **[NIE]** Saul sent men a third time, and they also prophesied.
20:13 [G] *be it* ever so **severely**, if I do not let you know and send you
20:17 [G] Jonathan **had** David **reaffirm** his oath out of love for him,
23: 4 [G] **Once again** [+6388] David inquired of the LORD,
25:22 [G] May God deal with David, *be it* ever so **severely**, if by
27: 4 [A] had fled to Gath, *he* no **longer** [+6388] searched for him.
2Sa 2:22 [G] **Again** [+6388] Abner warned Asahel, "Stop chasing me!
2:28 [A] longer pursued Israel, nor *did they* fight **anymore** [+6388].
3: 9 [G] May God deal with Abner, *be it* ever so **severely**, if I do not
3:34 [G] wicked men." And all the people wept over him **again**.
3:35 [G] *be it* ever so **severely**, if I taste bread or anything else before
5:22 [G] **Once more** [+6388] the Philistines came up and spread out
7:10 [G] Wicked people will not oppress them **anymore**, as they did
7:20 [G] "What **more** [+6388] can David say to you? For you know
12: 8 [G] And if all this had been too little, *I would have* **given** you **even more** [+2179+2179+2256+3869+3869+4200].
14:10 [G] bring him to me, and he will not bother you **again** [+6388]."
18:22 [G] Ahimaaz son of Zadok **again** [+6388] said to Joab, "Come
19:13 [19:14] [G] May God deal with me, *be it* ever so **severely**, if
24: 1 [G] **Again** the anger of the LORD burned against Israel, and he

2Sa 24: 3 [G] "*May* the LORD your God **multiply** the troops a hundred
1Ki 2: 23 [G] "May God deal with me, *be it* ever so **severely**, if Adonijah
10: 7 [G] and wealth *you have* **far exceeded** the report I heard.
12: 11 [G] father laid on you a heavy yoke; I *will* **make** it **even heavier**.
12: 14 [G] father made your yoke heavy; I *will* **make** it **even heavier**.
16: 33 [G] made an Asherah pole and did **more** to provoke the LORD,
19: 2 [G] to say, "May the gods deal with me, *be it* ever so **severely**,
20: 10 [G] "May the gods deal with me, *be it* ever so **severely**, if
2Ki 6: 23 [A] So the bands from Aram **stopped** [+4202+6388] raiding
6: 31 [G] He said, "May God deal with me, *be it* ever so **severely**, if
19: 30 [A] **Once more** a remnant of the house of Judah will take root
20: 6 [G] *I will* **add** fifteen years to your life. And I will deliver you
21: 8 [G] *I will* not **again** make the feet of the Israelites wander from
24: 7 [G] did not march out from his own country **again** [+6388],
1Ch 14: 13 [G] **Once more** [+6388] the Philistines raided the valley;
17: 9 [G] Wicked people will not oppress them **anymore**, as they did
17: 18 [G] "What **more** [+6388] can David say to you for honoring your
21: 3 [G] "*May* the LORD **multiply** his troops a hundred times over.
22: 14 [G] be weighed, and wood and stone. And *you may* **add** to them.
2Ch 9: 6 [A] was told me; *you have* **far exceeded** the report I heard.
10: 11 [G] father laid on you a heavy yoke; I *will* **make** it **even heavier**.
10: 14 [G] father made your yoke heavy; I *will* **make** it **even heavier**.
28: 13 [G] Do you intend to **add** to our sin and guilt? For our guilt is
28: 22 [G] In his time of trouble King Ahaz *became* even **more**
33: 8 [G] *I will* not **again** make the feet of the Israelites leave the land
Ezr 10: 10 [G] you have married foreign women, **adding** to Israel's guilt.
Ne 13: 18 [G] Now you *are* **stirring up more** wrath against Israel by
Est 8: 3 [G] Esther **again** pleaded with the king, falling at his feet
Job 17: 9 [G] and *those with* clean hands *will* **grow stronger** [+601].
20: 9 [G] The eye that saw him *will* not see him **again**; his place will
27: 1 [G] And Job **continued** his discourse:
29: 1 [G] Job **continued** his discourse:
34: 32 [G] I cannot see; if I have done wrong, *I will* not **do** so **again**.'
34: 37 [G] To his sin *he* **adds** rebellion; scornfully he claps his hands
36: 1 [G] Elihu **continued**:
38: 11 [G] when I said, 'This far you may come and no **farther**; here is
40: 5 [G] but I have no answer—twice, but *I will* say no **more**."
41: 8 [40:32] [G] will remember the struggle and never **do** *it* **again**!
42: 10 [G] and **gave** him twice as much as he had before.
Ps 10: 18 [G] that man, who is of the earth, may terrify no **more** [+6388].
41: 8 [41:9] [G] he will **never** [+4202] get up from the place where he
61: 6 [61:7] [G] **Increase** the days of the king's life, his years for
71: 14 [G] have hope; *I will* praise you **more** [+3972+6584] **and more**.
77: 7 [77:8] [G] Will he never show his favor **again** [+6388]?
78: 17 [G] *they* **continued** [+6388] to sin against him, rebelling in the
115: 14 [G] *May* the LORD **make** you **increase**, both you and your
120: 3 [G] he do to you, and what **more besides**, O deceitful tongue?
Pr 1: 5 [G] let the wise listen and **add** *to* their learning, and let the
3: 2 [G] will prolong your life many years and **bring** you prosperity.
9: 9 [G] teach a righteous man and *he will* **add** *to* his learning.
9: 11 [G] your days will be many, and years *will be* **added** to your life.
10: 22 [G] of the LORD brings wealth, and *he* **adds** no trouble to it.
10: 27 [G] The fear of the LORD **adds length** *to* life, but the years of
11: 24 [C] One man gives freely, yet **gains** even more; another
16: 21 [G] called discerning, and pleasant words **promote** instruction.
16: 23 [G] heart guides his mouth, and his lips **promote** instruction.
19: 4 [G] Wealth **brings** many friends, but a poor man's friend deserts
19: 19 [G] if you rescue him, *you will have to* **do** it **again** [+6388].
23: 28 [G] she lies in wait, and **multiplies** the unfaithful among men.
23: 35 [G] When will I wake up so I can find **another** [+6388] drink?"
30: 6 [G] *Do* not **add** to his words, or he will rebuke you and prove
Ecc 1: 16 [G] **increased** in wisdom more than anyone who has ruled over
1: 18 [G] comes much sorrow; the **more** knowledge, the more grief.
1: 18 [G] comes much sorrow; the more knowledge, the **more** grief.
2: 9 [G] I became greater **by far** than anyone in Jerusalem before me.
3: 14 [G] nothing *can be* **added** to it and nothing taken from it.
Isa 1: 5 [G] Why *do you* **persist** *in* rebellion? Your whole head is
1: 13 [G] **Stop** [+4202] bringing meaningless offerings! Your incense
7: 10 [G] **Again** the LORD spoke to Ahaz,
8: 5 [G] The LORD spoke to me **again** [+6388]:
10: 20 [G] *will* no **longer** [+6388] rely on him who struck them down
11: 11 [G] In that day the Lord *will* **reach**[s] **out** his hand a second time
15: 9 [C] are full of blood, but I will bring **still more** upon Dimon—
23: 12 [G] He said, "No **more** [+6388] *of* your reveling, O Virgin
24: 20 [G] it is the guilt of its rebellion that it falls—never to rise **again**.
26: 15 [A] *You have* **enlarged** the nation, O LORD; you have
26: 15 [A] the nation, O LORD; *you have* **enlarged** the nation.
29: 1 [A] **Add** year to year and let your cycle of festivals go on.
29: 14 [A] Therefore **once more** I will astound these people with
29: 19 [A] **Once more** the humble will rejoice in the LORD; the needy
30: 1 [A] an alliance, but not by my Spirit, **heaping** sin upon sin;
37: 31 [A] **Once more** a remnant of the house of Judah will take root
38: 5 [G] and seen your tears; I *will* **add** fifteen years to your life.
47: 1 [G] No **more** will you be called tender or delicate.
47: 5 [G] no **more** will you be called queen of kingdoms.
51: 22 [G] the goblet of my wrath, you will **never** [+4202] drink again.
52: 1 [G] and defiled will not enter you **again** [+6388].
Jer 7: 21 [A] *Go ahead*, **add** your burnt offerings to your other sacrifices
31: 12 [G] well-watered garden, and *they will* sorrow no **more** [+6388].
36: 32 [C] And many similar words **were added** [+6388] to them.
45: 3 [A] The LORD *has* **added** sorrow to my pain; I am worn out
La 4: 15 [G] among the nations say, "They can stay here no **longer**."
4: 16 [G] himself has scattered them; *he* no **longer** watches over them.
4: 22 [G] your punishment will end; *he will* not **prolong** your exile.
Eze 5: 16 [G] *I will* **bring more and more** famine upon you and cut off
23: 14 [G] "But *she* **carried** her prostitution **still further**. She saw men
36: 12 [G] *you will* never **again** [+6388] deprive them of their children.
Da 10: 18 [G] **Again** the one who looked like a man touched me and gave
Hos 1: 6 [G] for I will no **longer** [+6388] show love to the house of Israel,
9: 15 [G] I will no **longer** love them; all their leaders are rebellious.
13: 2 [G] Now they sin **more and more**; they make idols for
Joel 2: 2 [G] such as never was of old nor **ever** *will be* in ages to come.
Am 5: 2 [G] "Fallen is Virgin Israel, never to rise **again**, deserted in her
7: 8 [G] my people Israel; I will spare them no **longer** [+6388].
7: 13 [G] Don't prophesy **anymore** [+6388] at Bethel, because this is
8: 2 [G] for my people Israel; I will spare them no **longer** [+6388].
Jnh 2: 4 [2:5] [G] yet *I will* look **again** toward your holy temple.'
Na 1: 15 [2:1] [G] No **more** [+6388] will the wicked invade you;
Zep 3: 11 [G] Never **again** [+6388] will you be haughty on my holy hill.

3579 ¹יָסַר ***yāsar*[1]**, v. [42] [→ 3574, 3581, 4592, 5036; cf. 3580]

discipline [10], punish [5], scourged [4], disciplines [3], chastened severely [+3579] [2], instructs [2], scourge [2], take warning [2], accept correction [1], be corrected [1], be warned [1], been disciplined [1], catch [1], correct [1], corrects [1], disciplined [1], instructed [1], taught [1], trained [1], warning [1]

Lev 26: 18 [D] to me, *I will* **punish** you for your sins seven times over.
26: 23 [C] " 'If in spite of these things *you do* not **accept** my **correction**
26: 28 [D] and *I* myself *will* **punish** you for your sins seven times over.
Dt 4: 36 [D] From heaven he made you hear his voice to **discipline** you.
8: 5 [D] Know then in your heart that as a man **disciplines** his son,
8: 5 [D] disciplines his son, so the LORD your God **disciplines** you.
21: 18 [D] and will not listen to them when *they* **discipline** him,
22: 18 [D] and the elders shall take the man and **punish** him.
1Ki 12: 11 [D] My father **scourged** you with whips; I will scourge you with
12: 11 [D] you with whips; I *will* **scourge** you with scorpions.' "
12: 14 [D] My father **scourged** you with whips; I will scourge you with
12: 14 [D] you with whips; I *will* **scourge** you with scorpions."
2Ch 10: 11 [D] My father **scourged** you with whips; I will scourge you with
10: 14 [D] My father **scourged** you with whips; I will scourge you with
Job 4: 3 [D] Think how *you have* **instructed** many, how you have
Ps 2: 10 [C] you kings, be wise; **be warned**, *you* rulers of the earth.
6: 1 [6:2] [D] me in your anger or **discipline** me in your wrath.
16: 7 [D] who counsels me; even at night my heart **instructs** me.
38: 1 [38:2] [D] me in your anger or **discipline** me in your wrath.
39: 11 [39:12] [D] *You* rebuke and **discipline** men for their sin; you
94: 10 [A] Does he *who* **disciplines** nations not punish? Does he who
94: 12 [D] Blessed is the man *you* **discipline**, O LORD, the man you
118: 18 [D] The LORD *has* **chastened** [+3579] me **severely**, but he has
118: 18 [D] The LORD *has* **chastened** me **severely** [+3579], but he has
Pr 9: 7 [A] "*Whoever* **corrects** a mocker invites insult; whoever rebukes
19: 18 [D] **Discipline** your son, for in that there is hope; do not be a
29: 17 [D] **Discipline** your son, and he will give you peace; he will
29: 19 [C] A servant cannot **be corrected** by mere words; though he
31: 1 [D] sayings of King Lemuel—an oracle his mother **taught** him:
Isa 8: 11 [D] upon me, **warning** me not to follow the way of this people.
28: 26 [D] His God **instructs** him and teaches him the right way.
Jer 2: 19 [D] Your wickedness *will* **punish** you; your backsliding will
6: 8 [C] **Take warning**, O Jerusalem, or I will turn away from you
10: 24 [D] **Correct** me, LORD, but only with justice—not in your
30: 11 [D] *I will* **discipline** you but only with justice; I will not let you
31: 18 [D] '*You* **disciplined** me like an unruly calf, and I have been
31: 18 [C] me like an unruly calf, and *I have* **been disciplined**.
46: 28 [D] *I will* **discipline** you but only with justice; I will not let you
Eze 23: 48 [C] that all women *may* **take warning** and not imitate you.
Hos 7: 12 [G] When I hear them flocking together, *I will* **catch** them.
7: 15 [D] I **trained** them and strengthened them, but they plot evil
10: 10 [D] When I please, *I will* **punish** them; nations will be gathered

3580 ²יָסַר ***yāsar*[2]**, v. Not used in NIV/BHS [cf. 3579]

3581 יִסּוֹר ***yāsōr***, n.[m.]. Not used in NIV/BHS [√ 3579]

3582 יָע ***yāʿ***, n.[m.]. [9] [√ 3589]

shovels [9]

Ex 27: 3 and its **shovels**, sprinkling bowls, meat forks and firepans.

Ex 38: 3 its pots, **shovels**, sprinkling bowls, meat forks and firepans.
Nu 4: 14 including the firepans, meat forks, **shovels** and sprinkling bowls.
1Ki 7: 40 He also made the basins and **shovels** and sprinkling bowls.
7: 45 the pots, **shovels** and sprinkling bowls. All these objects that
2Ki 25: 14 **shovels**, wick trimmers, dishes and all the bronze articles used in
2Ch 4: 11 He also made the pots and **shovels** and sprinkling bowls.
4: 16 the pots, **shovels**, meat forks and all related articles. All the objects
Jer 52: 18 **shovels**, wick trimmers, sprinkling bowls, dishes and all the bronze

3583 יַעְבֵּץ ya'bēṣ[1], n.pr.loc. [1] [√ 3584]
Jabez [1]

1Ch 2: 55 and the clans of scribes who lived at **Jabez**: the Tirathites,

3584 יַעְבֵּץ ya'bēṣ[2], n.pr.m. [3] [→ 3583]
Jabez [3]

1Ch 4: 9 **Jabez** was more honorable than his brothers. His mother had
4: 9 His mother had named him **Jabez**, saying, "I gave birth to him in
4: 10 **Jabez** cried out to the God of Israel, "Oh, that you would bless me

3585 יָעַד yā'ad, v. [28] [→ 4595, 4596, 4597, 5676; cf. 6337]
meet [8], banded together [3], assemble [2], challenge [2], gathered [2], joined forces [2], appointed [1], met by agreement [1], ordered [1], placed [1], selected [1], selects [1], set [1], summon [1], turned [1]

Ex 21: 8 [A] If she does not please the master who *has* **selected** her for
21: 9 [A] If *he* **selects** her for his son, he must grant her the rights of a
25: 22 [C] *I will* **meet** with you and give you all my commands for the
29: 42 [C] before the LORD. There *I will* **meet** you and speak to you;
29: 43 [C] there also *I will* **meet** with the Israelites, and the place will be
30: 6 [C] that is over the Testimony—where *I will* **meet** with you.
30: 36 [C] in the Tent of Meeting, where *I will* **meet** with you.
Nu 10: 3 [C] the whole community *is to* **assemble** before you at the
10: 4 [C] the heads of the clans of Israel—*are to* **assemble** before you.
14: 35 [C] wicked community, which *has* **banded together** against me.
16: 11 [C] that you and all your followers *have* **banded together**.
17: 4 [17:19] [C] in front of the Testimony, where *I* **meet** with you.
27: 3 [C] who **banded together** against the LORD, but he died for his
Jos 11: 5 [C] All these kings **joined forces** and made camp together at the
2Sa 20: 5 [A] he took longer than the time the king *had* **set** *for* him.
1Ki 8: 5 [C] the entire assembly of Israel that *had* **gathered** about him
2Ch 5: 6 [C] the entire assembly of Israel that *had* **gathered** about him
Ne 6: 2 [C] *let us* **meet** together in one of the villages on the plain of
6: 10 [C] He said, "*Let us* **meet** in the house of God, inside the temple,
Job 2: 11 [C] **met** together **by agreement** to go and sympathize with him
9: 19 [G] And if it is a matter of justice, who *will* **summon** him?
Ps 48: 4 [48:5] [C] When the kings **joined forces**, when they advanced
Jer 24: 1 [H] the LORD showed me two baskets of figs **placed** in front of
47: 7 [A] when *he has* **ordered** it to attack Ashkelon and the coast?"
49: 19 [G] Who is like me and who *can* **challenge** me? And what
50: 44 [G] Who is like me and who *can* **challenge** me? And what
Eze 21: 16 [21:21] [H] then to the left, wherever your blade *is* **turned**.
Mic 6: 9 [A] is wisdom—"Heed the rod and the One who **appointed** it.

3586 יַעְדָּה ya'dâ, n.pr.m. [0 / 2] [√ 6334? *or* 6335?]
Jadah [2]

1Ch 9: 42 Ahaz was the father of **Jadah**, [BHS 3628] Jadah was the father of
9: 42 **Jadah** [BHS 3628] was the father of Alemeth, Azmaveth

3587 יֶעְדּוֹ yᵉ'dô, n.pr.m. [1] [√ 6335 *or* 6344]
Iddo [1]

2Ch 9: 29 in the visions of **Iddo** [K 3588] the seer concerning Jeroboam son

3588 יֶעְדִּי yᵉ'dî, n.pr.m. [0] [√ 6334? *or* 6335?]

2Ch 9: 29 [in the visions of **Iddo** [K; see Q 3587] the seer concerning]

3589 יָעָה yā'â, v. [1] [→ 3582, 3590?, 3599?]
sweep away [1]

Isa 28: 17 [A] hail *will* **sweep away** your refuge, the lie, and water will

3590 יְעוּאֵל yᵉ'û'ēl, n.pr.m. [1 / 2] [→ 3599; cf. 3589? + 446]
Jeuel [2]

1Ch 9: 6 Of the Zerahites: **Jeuel**. The people from Judah numbered 690.
9: 35 [**Jeiel** [K; see Q 3599] the father of Gibeon lived in Gibeon.]
11: 44 [and **Jeiel** [K; see Q 3599] the sons of Hotham the Aroerite,]
2Ch 26: 11 [their numbers as mustered by **Jeiel** [K; see Q 3599] the secretary]
29: 13 [the descendants of Elizaphan, Shimri and **Jeiel**; [K; see Q 3599]]
Ezr 8: 13 **Jeuel** [BHS 3599] and Shemaiah, and with them 60 men;

3591 יְעוּץ yᵉ'ûṣ, n.pr.m. [1]
Jeuz [1]

1Ch 8: 10 **Jeuz**, Sakia and Mirmah. These were his sons, heads of families.

3592 יָעוּר yā'ûr, n.pr.m. [0] [cf. 3600]

1Ch 20: 5 [Elhanan son of **Jair** [K; see Q 3600] killed Lahmi the brother of]

3593 יְעוּשׁ yᵉ'ûš, n.pr.m. [9] [√ 6429; cf. 3601]
Jeush [9]

Ge 36: 5 and Oholibamah bore **Jeush**, [K 3601] Jalam and Korah.
36: 14 whom she bore to Esau: **Jeush**, [K 3601] Jalam and Korah.
36: 18 sons of Esau's wife Oholibamah: Chiefs **Jeush**, Jalam and Korah.
1Ch 1: 35 The sons of Esau: Eliphaz, Reuel, **Jeush**, Jalam and Korah.
7: 10 **Jeush**, [K 3601] Benjamin, Ehud, Kenaanah, Zethan, Tarshish
8: 39 Ulam his firstborn, **Jeush** the second son and Eliphelet the third.
23: 10 the sons of Shimei: Jahath, Ziza, **Jeush** and Beriah. These were the
23: 11 and Ziza the second, but **Jeush** and Beriah did not have many sons;
2Ch 11: 19 She bore him sons: **Jeush**, Shemariah and Zaham.

3594 יָעַז yā'az, v. [1] [cf. 6451]
arrogant [1]

Isa 33: 19 [C] You will see those **arrogant** people no more, those people of

3595 יַעֲזִיאֵל ya'ᵃzî'ēl, n.pr.m. [1]
Jaaziel [1]

1Ch 15: 18 Zechariah, **Jaaziel**, Shemiramoth, Jehiel, Unni, Eliab, Benaiah,

3596 יַעֲזִיָּהוּ ya'ᵃziyyāhû, n.pr.m. [2]
Jaaziah [2]

1Ch 24: 26 The sons of Merari: Mahli and Mushi. The son of **Jaaziah**: Beno.
24: 27 The sons of Merari: from **Jaaziah**: Beno, Shoham, Zaccur and Ibri.

3597 יַעְזֵיר ya'zēr, n.pr.loc. [13] [√ 6468]
Jazer [13]

Nu 21: 32 After Moses had sent spies to **Jazer**, the Israelites captured its
32: 1 saw that the lands of **Jazer** and Gilead were suitable for livestock.
32: 3 "Ataroth, Dibon, **Jazer**, Nimrah, Heshbon, Elealeh, Sebam,
32: 35 Atroth Shophan, **Jazer**, Jogbehah,
Jos 13: 25 The territory of **Jazer**, all the towns of Gilead and half the
21: 39 Heshbon and **Jazer**, together with their pasturelands—four towns
2Sa 24: 5 the town in the gorge, and then went through Gad and on to **Jazer**.
1Ch 6: 81 [6:66] Heshbon and **Jazer**, together with their pasturelands.
26: 31 capable men among the Hebronites were found at **Jazer** *in* Gilead.
Isa 16: 8 which once reached **Jazer** and spread toward the desert.
16: 9 So I weep, as **Jazer** weeps, for the vines of Sibmah. O Heshbon,
Jer 48: 32 I weep for you, as **Jazer** weeps, O vines of Sibmah. Your branches
48: 32 spread as far as the sea; they reached as far as the sea of **Jazer**.

3598 יָעַט yā'aṭ, v. [1] [cf. 6486]
arrayed [1]

Isa 61: 10 [A] of salvation and **arrayed** me *in* a robe of righteousness,

3599 יְעִיאֵל yᵉ'î'ēl, n.pr.m. [13] [→ 3590; cf. 3589? + 446]
Jeiel [13]

1Ch 5: 7 according to their genealogical records: **Jeiel** the chief, Zechariah,
8: 29 **Jeiel** [BHS-] the father of Gibeon lived in Gibeon. His wife's
9: 35 **Jeiel** [K 3590] the father of Gibeon lived in Gibeon. His wife's
11: 44 Shama and **Jeiel** [K 3590] the sons of Hotham the Aroerite,
15: 18 Eliphelehu, Mikneiah, Obed-Edom and **Jeiel**,
15: 21 Mikneiah, Obed-Edom, **Jeiel** and Azaziah were to play the harps,
16: 5 then **Jeiel**, Shemiramoth, Jehiel, Mattithiah, Eliab, Benaiah,
16: 5 Mattithiah, Eliab, Benaiah, Obed-Edom and **Jeiel**.
2Ch 20: 14 the son of Benaiah, the son of **Jeiel**, the son of Mattaniah,
26: 11 to their numbers as mustered by **Jeiel** [K 3590] the secretary
29: 13 from the descendants of Elizaphan, Shimri and **Jeiel**; [K 3590]
35: 9 and Nethanel, his brothers, and Hashabiah, **Jeiel** and Jozabad,
Ezr 8: 13 <u>Jeuel</u> [BHS *Jeiel*; NIV 3590] and Shemaiah,
10: 43 **Jeiel**, Mattithiah, Zabad, Zebina, Jaddai, Joel and Benaiah.

3600 יָעִיר yā'îr, n.pr.m. [1] [√ 6424; cf. 3592]
Jair [1]

1Ch 20: 5 Elhanan son of **Jair** [K 3592] killed Lahmi the brother of Goliath

3601 יְעִישׁ yᵉ'îš, n.pr.m. [0] [√ 6429; cf. 3593]

Ge 36: 5 [and Oholibamah bore **Jeush**, [K; see Q 3593] Jalam and Korah.]
36: 14 [whom she bore to Esau: **Jeush**, [K; see Q 3593] Jalam and Korah.]

1Ch 7: 10 [**Jeush**, [K; see Q 3593] Benjamin, Ehud, Kenaanah, Zethan,]

3602 יַעְכָּן **yaʿkān**, n.pr.m. [1]

Jacan [1]

1Ch 5: 13 Michael, Meshullam, Sheba, Jorai, **Jacan**, Zia and Eber—

3603 יָעַל **yāʿal**, v. [23] [→ 1175]

gain [3], benefit in the least [+3603+4200] [2], of value [2], succeed [2], worthless idols [+4202] [2], advantage [1], benefit [1], best [1], did good [1], do good [1], have value [1], profit [1], unprofitable [+4202] [1], useless [+4202] [1], worthless [+1153] [1], worthless [+1194] [1], worthless [+4202] [1]

1Sa 12: 21 [G] *They can* **do** you no **good**, nor can they rescue you,
Job 15: 3 [G] argue with useless words, with speeches that **have** no **value**?
21: 15 [G] should serve him? What *would we* **gain** by praying to him?'
30: 13 [G] They break up my road; *they* **succeed** in destroying me—
35: 3 [G] 'What profit is it to me, and what *do I* **gain** by not sinning?'
Pr 10: 2 [G] Ill-gotten treasures *are* **of** no **value**, but righteousness
11: 4 [G] Wealth *is* **worthless** [+4202] in the day of wrath,
Isa 30: 5 [G] be put to shame because of a people **useless** [+4202] to them,
30: 5 [G] who bring neither help nor **advantage**, but only shame and
30: 6 [G] on the humps of camels, to that **unprofitable** [+4202] nation,
44: 9 [G] and the things they treasure *are* **worthless** [+1153].
44: 10 [G] a god and casts an idol, *which can* **profit** him nothing?
47: 12 [G] Perhaps you will **succeed**, perhaps you will cause terror.
48: 17 [G] the LORD your God, who teaches you *what is* **best** for you,
57: 12 [G] and your works, and *they will* not **benefit** you.
Jer 2: 8 [G] prophesied by Baal, following **worthless** [+4202] **idols**.
2: 11 [G] have exchanged their Glory for **worthless** [+4202] **idols**.
7: 8 [G] are trusting in deceptive words *that are* **worthless** [+1194].
12: 13 [G] reap thorns; they will wear themselves out but **gain** nothing.
16: 19 [G] but false gods, worthless idols *that* **did** them no **good**.
23: 32 [G] *They do* not **benefit** [+3603+4200] these people **in the least**,"
23: 32 [G] *They do* not **benefit** these people **in the least** [+3603+4200],"
Hab 2: 18 [G] "**Of** what **value** *is* an idol, since a man has carved it? Or an

3604 יָעֵל¹ **yāʿēl¹**, n.[m.]. [3] [→ 3605, 3606, 3607, 3608]

wild goats [2], goats [1]

1Sa 24: 2 [24:3] for David and his men near the Crags of the **Wild Goats**.
Job 39: 1 "Do you know when the mountain **goats** give birth? Do you watch
Ps 104: 18 The high mountains belong to the **wild goats**; the crags are a

3605 יָעֵל² **yāʿēl²**, n.pr.f. [6] [√ 3604]

Jael [6]

Jdg 4: 17 Sisera, however, fled on foot to the tent of **Jael**, the wife of Heber
4: 18 **Jael** went out to meet Sisera and said to him, "Come, my lord,
4: 21 But **Jael**, Heber's wife, picked up a tent peg and a hammer
4: 22 Barak came by in pursuit of Sisera, and **Jael** went out to meet him.
5: 6 son of Anath, in the days of **Jael**, the roads were abandoned;
5: 24 "Most blessed of women be **Jael**, the wife of Heber the Kenite,

3606 יַעֲלָא **yaʿălāʾ**, n.pr.m. [1] [√ 3607; cf. 3604]

Jaala [1]

Ne 7: 58 **Jaala**, Darkon, Giddel,

3607 יַעֲלָה¹ **yaʿălâ¹**, n.f. [1] [→ 3606, 3608; cf. 3604]

deer [1]

Pr 5: 19 A loving doe, a graceful **deer**—may her breasts satisfy you always,

3608 יַעֲלָה² **yaʿălâ²**, n.pr.m. [1] [√ 3607; cf. 3604]

Jaala [1]

Ezr 2: 56 **Jaala**, Darkon, Giddel,

3609 יַעְלָם **yaʿlām**, n.pr.m. [4] [√ 6596]

Jalam [4]

Ge 36: 5 Oholibamah bore Jeush, **Jalam** and Korah. These were the sons of
36: 14 of Zibeon, whom she bore to Esau: Jeush, **Jalam** and Korah.
36: 18 sons of Esau's wife Oholibamah: Chiefs Jeush, **Jalam** and Korah.
1Ch 1: 35 The sons of Esau: Eliphaz, Reuel, Jeush, **Jalam** and Korah.

3610 יַעַן¹ **yaʿan¹**, subst.pp.c. [99] [√ 6701] See Select Index

because [34], because [+889] [21], *untranslated* [15], because [+3954] [3], because of [3], for [+889] [3], since [+889] [3], because [+928+2256+3610] [2], because [+928+3610] [2], for [2], because [+561+4202] [1], because [+928] [1], but since [1], in [1], since [+3954] [1], since [1], so [+561+4202] [1], so that [+889] [1], therefore [+4027+4200] [1], while [1], why [+4537] [1]

3611 יַעַן² **yaʿan²**, n.pr.loc. Not used in NIV/BHS [→ 1970]

3612 יָעֵן **yāʿēn**, n.[m.]. [1] [cf. 3613]

ostriches [1]

La 4: 3 my people have become heartless like **ostriches** [K 6720] in the

3613 יַעֲנָה **yaʿănâ**, n.f. [8] [cf. 3612, 6720]

owls [+1426] [4], horned owl [+1426] [2], owl [+1426] [2]

Lev 11: 16 the **horned owl** [+1426], the screech owl, the gull, any kind of
Dt 14: 15 the **horned owl** [+1426], the screech owl, the gull, any kind of
Job 30: 29 I have become a brother of jackals, a companion of **owls** [+1426].
Isa 13: 21 there the **owls** [+1426] will dwell, and there the wild goats will
34: 13 She will become a haunt for jackals, a home for **owls** [+1426].
43: 20 The wild animals honor me, the jackals and the **owls** [+1426],
Jer 50: 39 and hyenas will live there, and there the **owl** [+1426] will dwell.
Mic 1: 8 and naked. I will howl like a jackal and moan like an **owl** [+1426].

3614 יַעְנַי **yaʿnay**, n.pr.m. [1] [√ 6699?]

Janai [1]

1Ch 5: 12 the chief, Shapham the second, then **Janai** and Shaphat, in Bashan.

3615 יָעֵף¹ **yāʿēp¹**, v. [8] [→ 3617, 3618; cf. 6545, 6546]

faint [2], tired [2], exhaust [1], fall [1], labor [1], tire [1]

Isa 40: 28 [A] *He will* not *grow* **tired** or weary, and his understanding no
40: 30 [A] Even youths *grow* **tired** and weary, and young men stumble
40: 31 [A] will run and not grow weary, they will walk and not *be* **faint**.
44: 12 [A] and loses his strength; he drinks no water and *grows* **faint**.
Jer 2: 24 [A] Any males that pursue her *need* not **tire** *themselves*;
51: 58 [A] for nothing, the nations' **labor** is only fuel for the flames."
51: 64 [A] And *her people will* **fall**.' " The words of Jeremiah end here.
Hab 2: 13 [A] for the fire, that the nations **exhaust** *themselves* for nothing?

3616 יָעֵף² **yāʿēp²**, v. [1] [→ 3618]

swift flight [+3618] [1]

Da 9: 21 [H] came to me in **swift flight** [+3618] about the time of the

3617 יָעֵף³ **yāʿēp³**, a. [4] [√ 3615]

exhausted [2], weary [2]

Jdg 8: 15 Why should we give bread to your **exhausted** men?' "
2Sa 16: 2 the wine is to refresh those who become **exhausted** in the desert."
Isa 40: 29 He gives strength to the **weary** and increases the power of the
50: 4 me an instructed tongue, to know the word that sustains the **weary**.

3618 יְעָף **yᵉʿāp**, n.[m.]. [1] [√ 3616]

swift flight [+3616] [1]

Da 9: 21 came to me in **swift flight** [+3616] about the time of the evening

3619 יָעַץ **yāʿaṣ**, v. [59] [→ 3446, 4600, 6783; cf. 6418; Ar 10324, 10325]

consulted [5], advice gave [+6783] [3], advise [3], advised [3], planned [3], advice given [+6783] [2], advice [2], counsels [2], determined [2], planned [+6783] [2], plot [2], plotted [2], purposed [2], advice offered [1], advise [+6783] [1], agreed [1], confer [1], conferred [1], conferring [1], conspire [1], consult [1], consulted advisers [1], consulting [1], counsel [1], counseled [1], decided [1], give advice [1], give counsel [1], giving advice [+6783] [1], intend [1], makes plans [1], makes up [1], planning [+6783] [1], plotted [+6783] [1], promote [1], seeking advice [1], take advice [1], take counsel [1], warn [1]

Ex 18: 19 [A] Listen now to me and *I will* **give** you *some* **advice**, and may
Nu 24: 14 [A] *let me* **warn** you of what this people will do to your people
2Sa 16: 23 [A] Now in those days the **advice** [+6783] Ahithophel **gave** was
17: 7 [A] "The **advice** [+6783] Ahithophel *has* **given** is not good this
17: 11 [A] "So *I* **advise** you: Let all Israel, from Dan to Beersheba—as
17: 15 [A] "Ahithophel *has* **advised** Absalom and the elders of Israel to
17: 15 [A] do such and such, but I *have* **advised** them to do so and so.
17: 21 [A] at once; Ahithophel *has* **advised** such and such against you."
1Ki 1: 12 [A] *let me* **advise** [+6783] you how you can save your own life
12: 6 [C] King Rehoboam **consulted** the elders who had served his
12: 6 [C] "How *would* you **advise** me to answer these people?" he
12: 8 [A] Rehoboam rejected the **advice** [+6783] the elders **gave** him
12: 8 [C] and **consulted** the young men who had grown up with him
12: 9 [C] He asked them, "What *is* your **advice**? How should we
12: 13 [A] Rejecting the **advice** [+6783] **given** him by the elders,
12: 28 [C] After **seeking advice**, the king made two golden calves. He
2Ki 6: 8 [C] After **conferring** with his officers, he said, "I will set up my
1Ch 13: 1 [C] David **conferred** with each of his officers, the commanders
2Ch 10: 6 [C] King Rehoboam **consulted** the elders who had served his

2Ch 10: 6 [C] "How *would* you **advise** me to answer these people?"
10: 8 [A] Rehoboam rejected the **advice** [+6783] the elders **gave** him
10: 8 [C] and **consulted** the young men who had grown up with him
10: 9 [C] He asked them, "What *is* your **advice**? How should we
20:21 [C] After **consulting** the people, Jehoshaphat appointed men to
25:16 [A] but said, "I know that God *has* **determined** to destroy you,
25:17 [C] After Amaziah king of Judah **consulted** *his* **advisers**, he sent
30: 2 [C] the whole assembly in Jerusalem **decided** to celebrate the
30:23 [C] then **agreed** to celebrate the festival seven more days;
32: 3 [C] *he* **consulted** with his officials and military staff about
Ne 6: 7 [C] will get back to the king; so come, *let us* **confer** together."
Job 26: 3 [A] What **advice** *you have* **offered** to one without wisdom!
Ps 16: 7 [A] I will praise the LORD, who **counsels** me; even at night my
32: 8 [A] way you should go; *I will* **counsel** you and watch over you.
62: 4 [62:5] [A] *They* fully **intend** to topple him from his lofty place;
71:10 [C] against me; those who wait to kill me **conspire** together.
83: 3 [83:4] [F] your people; *they* **plot** against those you cherish.
83: 5 [83:6] [C] With one mind *they* **plot** together; they form an
Pr 12:20 [A] of those who plot evil, but joy for *those who* **promote** peace.
13:10 [C] but wisdom is found in *those who* **take advice**.
Isa 7: 5 [A] Aram, Ephraim and Remaliah's son *have* **plotted** your ruin,
14:24 [A] so it will be, and as *I have* **purposed**, so it will stand.
14:26 [B] This is the plan **determined** for the whole world; this is the
14:27 [A] For the LORD Almighty *has* **purposed**, and who can
19:12 [A] make known what the LORD Almighty *has* **planned**
19:17 [A] because of what the LORD Almighty *is* **planning** [+6783]
23: 8 [A] Who **planned** this against Tyre, the bestower of crowns,
23: 9 [A] The LORD Almighty **planned** it, to bring low the pride of
32: 7 [A] he **makes up** evil schemes to destroy the poor with lies,
32: 8 [A] the noble man **makes** noble **plans**, and by noble deeds he
40:14 [C] Whom *did* the LORD **consult** to enlighten him, and who
45:21 [C] what is to be, present it—*let them* **take counsel** together.
Jer 38:15 [A] Even if *I did* **give** you **counsel**, you would not listen to me."
49:20 [A] hear what the LORD *has* **planned** [+6783] against Edom,
49:30 [A] "Nebuchadnezzar king of Babylon *has* **plotted** [+6783]
50:45 [A] hear what the LORD *has* **planned** [+6783] against Babylon,
Eze 11: 2 [A] plotting evil and **giving** wicked **advice** [+6783] in this city.
Mic 6: 5 [A] remember what Balak king of Moab **counseled** and what
Na 1:11 [A] who plots evil against the LORD and **counsels** wickedness.
Hab 2:10 [A] *You have* **plotted** the ruin of many peoples, shaming your

3620 יַעֲקֹב ya'aqōb, n.pr.m. & g. [349] [cf. 6811?, 6812?]

Jacob [316], Jacob's [17], he[s] [7], him[s] [5], his[s] [2], Jacob's [+4200] [1], them[s] [+1201] [1]

Ge 25:26 with his hand grasping Esau's heel; so he was named **Jacob**.
25:27 while **Jacob** was a quiet man, staying among the tents.
25:28 had a taste for wild game, loved Esau, but Rebekah loved **Jacob**.
25:29 Once when **Jacob** was cooking some stew, Esau came in from the
25:30 He said to **Jacob**, "Quick, let me have some of that red stew!
25:31 **Jacob** replied, "First sell me your birthright."
25:33 But **Jacob** said, "Swear to me first." So he swore an oath to him,
25:33 So he swore an oath to him, selling his birthright to **Jacob**.
25:34 Then **Jacob** gave Esau some bread and some lentil stew. He ate
27: 6 Rebekah said to her son **Jacob**, "Look, I overheard your father say
27:11 **Jacob** said to Rebekah his mother, "But my brother Esau is a hairy
27:15 she had in the house, and put them on her younger son **Jacob**.
27:17 she handed to her son **Jacob** the tasty food and the bread she had
27:19 **Jacob** said to his father, "I am Esau your firstborn. I have done as
27:21 Then Isaac said to **Jacob**, "Come near so I can touch you,
27:22 **Jacob** went close to his father Isaac, who touched him and said,
27:22 who touched him and said, "The voice is the voice of **Jacob**,
27:30 After Isaac finished blessing **him**[s] and Jacob had scarcely left his
27:30 blessing him and **Jacob** had scarcely left his father's presence,
27:36 Esau said, "Isn't he rightly named **Jacob**? He has deceived me
27:41 Esau held a grudge against **Jacob** because of the blessing his father
27:41 for my father are near; then I will kill my brother **Jacob**."
27:42 Esau had said, she sent for her younger son **Jacob** and said to him,
27:46 If **Jacob** takes a wife from among the women of this land,
28: 1 So Isaac called for **Jacob** and blessed him and commanded him:
28: 5 Then Isaac sent **Jacob** on his way, and he went to Paddan Aram,
28: 5 the brother of Rebekah, who was the mother of **Jacob** and Esau.
28: 6 Now Esau learned that Isaac had blessed **Jacob** and had sent him
28: 7 that **Jacob** had obeyed his father and mother and had gone to
28:10 **Jacob** left Beersheba and set out for Haran.
28:16 When **Jacob** awoke from his sleep, he thought,
28:18 Early the next morning **Jacob** took the stone he had placed under
28:20 Then **Jacob** made a vow, saying, "If God will be with me
29: 1 **Jacob** continued on his journey and came to the land of the eastern
29: 4 **Jacob** asked the shepherds, "My brothers, where are you from?"
29:10 When **Jacob** saw Rachel daughter of Laban, his mother's brother,
29:10 **he**[s] went over and rolled the stone away from the mouth of the
29:11 Then **Jacob** kissed Rachel and began to weep aloud.
29:12 **He**[s] had told Rachel that he was a relative of her father and a son
29:13 As soon as Laban heard the news about **Jacob**, his sister's son,
29:15 Laban said to **him**[s], "Just because you are a relative of mine,
29:18 **Jacob** was in love with Rachel and said, "I'll work for you seven
29:20 So **Jacob** served seven years to get Rachel, but they seemed like
29:21 **Jacob** said to Laban, "Give me my wife. My time is completed,
29:28 **Jacob** did so. He finished the week with Leah, and then Laban
30: 1 When Rachel saw that she was not bearing **Jacob** any children,
30: 1 of her sister. So she said to **Jacob**, "Give me children, or I'll die!"
30: 2 **Jacob** became angry with her and said, "Am I in the place of God,
30: 4 So she gave him her servant Bilhah as a wife. **Jacob** slept with her,
30: 5 and she became pregnant and bore **him**[s] a son.
30: 7 servant Bilhah conceived again and bore **Jacob** a second son.
30: 9 she took her maidservant Zilpah and gave her to **Jacob** as a wife.
30:10 Leah's servant Zilpah bore **Jacob** a son.
30:12 Leah's servant Zilpah bore **Jacob** a second son.
30:16 So when **Jacob** came in from the fields that evening, Leah went
30:17 to Leah, and she became pregnant and bore **Jacob** a fifth son.
30:19 Leah conceived again and bore **Jacob** a sixth son.
30:25 **Jacob** said to Laban, "Send me on my way so I can go back to my
30:31 I give you?" he asked. "Don't give me anything," **Jacob** replied.
30:36 Then he put a three-day journey between himself and **Jacob**,
30:36 while **Jacob** continued to tend the rest of Laban's flocks.
30:37 **Jacob**, however, took fresh-cut branches from poplar, almond
30:40 **Jacob** set apart the young of the flock by themselves, but made the
30:41 **Jacob** would place the branches in the troughs in front of the
30:42 So the weak animals went to Laban and the strong ones to **Jacob**.
31: 1 "**Jacob** has taken everything our father owned and has gained all
31: 2 **Jacob** noticed that Laban's attitude toward him was not what it had
31: 3 the LORD said to **Jacob**, "Go back to the land of your fathers
31: 4 So **Jacob** sent word to Rachel and Leah to come out to the fields
31:11 The angel of God said to me in the dream, '**Jacob**.' I answered,
31:17 Then **Jacob** put his children and his wives on camels,
31:20 **Jacob** deceived Laban the Aramean by not telling him he was
31:22 On the third day Laban was told that **Jacob** had fled.
31:24 "Be careful not to say anything to **Jacob**, either good or bad."
31:25 **Jacob** had pitched his tent in the hill country of Gilead when
31:25 his tent in the hill country of Gilead when Laban overtook **him**[s],
31:26 Laban said to **Jacob**, "What have you done? You've deceived me,
31:29 'Be careful not to say anything to **Jacob**, either good or bad.'
31:31 **Jacob** answered Laban, "I was afraid, because I thought you would
31:32 Now **Jacob** did not know that Rachel had stolen the gods.
31:33 So Laban went into **Jacob's** tent and into Leah's tent and into the
31:36 **Jacob** was angry and took Laban to task. "What is my crime?"
31:36 and took Laban to task. "What is my crime?" **he**[s] asked Laban.
31:43 Laban answered **Jacob**, "The women are my daughters,
31:45 So **Jacob** took a stone and set it up as a pillar.
31:46 **He**[s] said to his relatives, "Gather some stones." So they took
31:47 Laban called it Jegar Sahadutha, and **Jacob** called it Galeed.
31:51 Laban also said to **Jacob**, "Here is this heap, and here is this pillar
31:53 So **Jacob** took an oath in the name of the Fear of his father Isaac.
31:54 **He**[s] offered a sacrifice there in the hill country and invited his
32: 1 [32:2] **Jacob** also went on his way, and the angels of God met
32: 2 [32:3] When **Jacob** saw them, he said, "This is the camp of God!"
32: 3 [32:4] **Jacob** sent messengers ahead of him to his brother Esau in
32: 4 [32:5] 'Your servant **Jacob** says, I have been staying with Laban
32: 6 [32:7] When the messengers returned to **Jacob**, they said,
32: 7 [32:8] distress **Jacob** divided the people who were with him into
32: 9 [32:10] **Jacob** prayed, "O God of my father Abraham, God of my
32:18 [32:19] you are to say, 'They belong to your servant **Jacob**.
32:20 [32:21] 'Your servant **Jacob** is coming behind us.' " For he
32:24 [32:25] So **Jacob** was left alone, and a man wrestled with him till
32:25 [32:26] he touched the socket of **Jacob's** hip so that his hip was
32:27 [32:28] asked him, "What is your name?" "**Jacob**," he answered.
32:28 [32:29] man said, "Your name will no longer be **Jacob**, but Israel,
32:29 [32:30] **Jacob** said, "Please tell me your name." But he replied,
32:30 [32:31] So **Jacob** called the place Peniel, saying, "It is because I
32:32 [32:33] because the socket of **Jacob's** hip was touched near the
33: 1 **Jacob** looked up and there was Esau, coming with his four
33:10 "No, please!" said **Jacob**. "If I have found favor in your eyes,
33:17 **Jacob**, however, went to Succoth, where he built a place for
33:18 After **Jacob** came from Paddan Aram, he arrived safely at the city
34: 1 Now Dinah, the daughter Leah had borne to **Jacob**, went out to
34: 3 His heart was drawn to Dinah daughter of **Jacob**, and he loved the
34: 5 When **Jacob** heard that his daughter Dinah had been defiled,
34: 5 with his livestock; so **he**[s] kept quiet about it until they came home.
34: 6 Then Shechem's father Hamor went out to talk with **Jacob**.
34: 7 Now **Jacob's** sons had come in from the fields as soon as they
34: 7 done a disgraceful thing in Israel by lying with **Jacob's** daughter—
34:13 **Jacob's** sons replied deceitfully as they spoke to Shechem
34:19 what they said, because he was delighted with **Jacob's** daughter.
34:25 two of **Jacob's** sons, Simeon and Levi, Dinah's brothers, took their
34:27 The sons of **Jacob** came upon the dead bodies and looted the city
34:30 **Jacob** said to Simeon and Levi, "You have brought trouble on me
35: 1 Then God said to **Jacob**, "Go up to Bethel and settle there,

Ge 35: 2 So **Jacob** said to his household and to all who were with him,
35: 4 So they gave **Jacob** all the foreign gods they had and the rings in
35: 4 in their ears, and **Jacob** buried them under the oak at Shechem.
35: 5 the towns all around them so that no one pursued **them**[s] [+1201].
35: 6 **Jacob** and all the people with him came to Luz (that is, Bethel)
35: 9 After **Jacob** returned from Paddan Aram, God appeared to him
35: 10 God said to him, "Your name is **Jacob**, but you will no longer be
35: 10 "Your name is Jacob, but you will no longer be called **Jacob**;
35: 14 **Jacob** set up a stone pillar at the place where God had talked with
35: 15 **Jacob** called the place where God had talked with him Bethel.
35: 20 Over her tomb **Jacob** set up a pillar, and to this day that pillar
35: 22 concubine Bilhah, and Israel heard of it. **Jacob** had twelve sons:
35: 23 Reuben the firstborn of **Jacob**, Simeon, Levi, Judah, Issachar
35: 26 These were the sons of **Jacob**, who were born to him in Paddan
35: 27 **Jacob** came home to his father Isaac in Mamre, near Kiriath Arba
35: 29 and full of years. And his sons Esau and **Jacob** buried him.
36: 6 and moved to a land some distance from his brother **Jacob**.
37: 1 **Jacob** lived in the land where his father had stayed, the land of
37: 2 This is the account of **Jacob**. Joseph, a young man of seventeen,
37: 34 **Jacob** tore his clothes, put on sackcloth and mourned for his son
42: 1 When **Jacob** learned that there was grain in Egypt, he said to his
42: 1 **he**[s] said to his sons, "Why do you just keep looking at each other?"
42: 4 **Jacob** did not send Benjamin, Joseph's brother, with the others,
42: 29 When they came to their father **Jacob** in the land of Canaan,
42: 36 Their father **Jacob** said to them, "You have deprived me of my
45: 25 out of Egypt and came to their father **Jacob** in the land of Canaan.
45: 27 had sent to carry him back, the spirit of their father **Jacob** revived.
46: 2 And God spoke to Israel in a vision at night and said, "**Jacob**!
46: 2 God spoke to Israel in a vision at night and said, "Jacob! **Jacob**!"
46: 5 **Jacob** left Beersheba, and Israel's sons took their father Jacob
46: 5 and Israel's sons took their father **Jacob** and their children
46: 6 acquired in Canaan, and **Jacob** and all his offspring went to Egypt.
46: 8 These are the names of the sons of Israel (**Jacob** and his
46: 8 who went to Egypt: Reuben the firstborn of **Jacob**.
46: 15 These were the sons Leah bore to **Jacob** in Paddan Aram,
46: 18 These were the children born to **Jacob** by Zilpah, whom Laban had
46: 19 The sons of **Jacob's** wife Rachel: Joseph and Benjamin.
46: 22 These were the sons of Rachel who were born to **Jacob**—fourteen
46: 25 These were the sons born to **Jacob** by Bilhah, whom Laban had
46: 26 All those who went to Egypt with **Jacob**—those who were his
46: 26 who were his direct descendants, not counting **his**[s] sons' wives—
46: 27 the members of **Jacob's** family, which went to Egypt,
47: 7 Joseph brought his father **Jacob** in and presented him before
47: 7 and presented him before Pharaoh. After **Jacob** blessed Pharaoh,
47: 8 Pharaoh asked **him**[s], "How old are you?"
47: 9 **Jacob** said to Pharaoh, "The years of my pilgrimage are a hundred
47: 10 Then **Jacob** blessed Pharaoh and went out from his presence.
47: 28 **Jacob** lived in Egypt seventeen years, and the years of his life were
47: 28 and the years of **his**[s] life were a hundred and forty-seven.
48: 2 When **Jacob** was told, "Your son Joseph has come to you,"
48: 3 **Jacob** said to Joseph, "God Almighty appeared to me at Luz in the
49: 1 **Jacob** called for his sons and said: "Gather around so I can tell you
49: 2 "Assemble and listen, sons of **Jacob**; listen to your father Israel.
49: 7 so cruel! I will scatter them in **Jacob** and disperse them in Israel.
49: 24 because of the hand of the Mighty One of **Jacob**, because of the
49: 33 When **Jacob** had finished giving instructions to his sons, he drew
50: 24 to the land he promised on oath to Abraham, Isaac and **Jacob**."
Ex 1: 1 are the names of the sons of Israel who went to Egypt with **Jacob**,
1: 5 The descendants of **Jacob** numbered seventy in all; Joseph was
2: 24 his covenant with Abraham, with Isaac and with **Jacob**.
3: 6 the God of Abraham, the God of Isaac and the God of **Jacob**."
3: 15 the God of Abraham, the God of Isaac and the God of **Jacob**—
3: 16 the God of Abraham, Isaac and **Jacob**—appeared to me and said:
4: 5 the God of Abraham, the God of Isaac and the God of **Jacob**—
6: 3 I appeared to Abraham, to Isaac and to **Jacob** as God Almighty,
6: 8 with uplifted hand to give to Abraham, to Isaac and to **Jacob**.
19: 3 "This is what you are to say to the house of **Jacob** and what you
33: 1 Isaac and **Jacob**, saying, 'I will give it to your descendants.'
Lev 26: 42 I will remember my covenant with **Jacob** and my covenant with
Nu 23: 7 'Come,' he said, 'curse **Jacob** for me; come, denounce Israel.'
23: 10 Who can count the dust of **Jacob** or number the fourth part of
23: 21 "No misfortune is seen in **Jacob**, no misery observed in Israel.
23: 23 There is no sorcery against **Jacob**, no divination against Israel.
23: 23 It will now be said of **Jacob** and of Israel, 'See what God has
24: 5 beautiful are your tents, O **Jacob**, your dwelling places, O Israel!
24: 17 A star will come out of **Jacob**; a scepter will rise out of Israel.
24: 19 A ruler will come out of **Jacob** and destroy the survivors of the
32: 11 see the land I promised on oath to Abraham, Isaac and **Jacob**—
Dt 1: 8 to Abraham, Isaac and **Jacob**—and to their descendants after
6: 10 swore to your fathers, to Abraham, Isaac and **Jacob**, to give you—
9: 5 what he swore to your fathers, to Abraham, Isaac and **Jacob**.
9: 27 Remember your servants Abraham, Isaac and **Jacob**. Overlook the
29: 13 [29:12] as he swore to your fathers, Abraham, Isaac and **Jacob**.
30: 20 land he swore to give to your fathers, Abraham, Isaac and **Jacob**.
32: 9 the LORD's portion is his people, **Jacob** his allotted inheritance.
33: 4 law that Moses gave us, the possession of the assembly of **Jacob**.
33: 10 He teaches your precepts to **Jacob** and your law to Israel.
33: 28 **Jacob's** spring is secure in a land of grain and new wine, where the
34: 4 Isaac and **Jacob** when I said, 'I will give it to your descendants.'
Jos 24: 4 to Isaac I gave **Jacob** and Esau. I assigned the hill country of Seir
24: 4 of Seir to Esau, but **Jacob** and his sons went down to Egypt.
24: 32 were buried at Shechem in the tract of land that **Jacob** bought for a
1Sa 12: 8 "After **Jacob** entered Egypt, they cried to the LORD for help,
2Sa 23: 1 the man anointed by the God of **Jacob**, Israel's singer of songs:
1Ki 18: 31 twelve stones, one for each of the tribes descended from **Jacob**,
2Ki 13: 23 for them because of his covenant with Abraham, Isaac and **Jacob**.
17: 34 and commands that the LORD gave the descendants of **Jacob**,
1Ch 16: 13 of Israel his servant, O sons of **Jacob**, his chosen ones.
16: 17 He confirmed it to **Jacob** as a decree, to Israel as an everlasting
Ps 14: 7 the fortunes of his people, let **Jacob** rejoice and Israel be glad!
20: 1 [20:2] in distress; may the name of the God of **Jacob** protect you.
22: 23 [22:24] praise him! All you descendants of **Jacob**, honor him!
24: 6 of those who seek him, who seek your face, O God of **Jacob**.
44: 4 [44:5] are my King and my God, who decrees victories for **Jacob**.
46: 7 [46:8] Almighty is with us; the God of **Jacob** is our fortress.
46: 11 [46:12] Almighty is with us; the God of **Jacob** is our fortress.
47: 4 [47:5] our inheritance for us, the pride of **Jacob**, whom he loved.
53: 6 [53:7] fortunes of his people, let **Jacob** rejoice and Israel be glad!
59: 13 [59:14] known to the ends of the earth that God rules over **Jacob**.
75: 9 [75:10] this forever; I will sing praise to the God of **Jacob**.
76: 6 [76:7] O God of **Jacob**, both horse and chariot lie still.
77: 15 [77:16] your people, the descendants of **Jacob** and Joseph.
78: 5 He decreed statutes for **Jacob** and established the law in Israel,
78: 21 his fire broke out against **Jacob**, and his wrath rose against Israel,
78: 71 the sheep he brought him to be the shepherd of his people **Jacob**,
79: 7 for they have devoured **Jacob** and destroyed his homeland.
81: 1 [81:2] joy to God our strength; shout aloud to the God of **Jacob**!
81: 4 [81:5] is a decree for Israel, an ordinance of the God of **Jacob**.
84: 8 [84:9] O LORD God Almighty; listen to me, O God of **Jacob**.
85: 1 [85:2] your land, O LORD; you restored the fortunes of **Jacob**.
87: 2 loves the gates of Zion more than all the dwellings of **Jacob**.
94: 7 "The LORD does not see; the God of **Jacob** pays no heed."
99: 4 established equity; in **Jacob** you have done what is just and right.
105: 6 of Abraham his servant, O sons of **Jacob**, his chosen ones.
105: 10 He confirmed it to **Jacob** as a decree, to Israel as an everlasting
105: 23 Israel entered Egypt; **Jacob** lived as an alien in the land of Ham.
114: 1 out of Egypt, the house of **Jacob** from a people of foreign tongue,
114: 7 at the presence of the Lord, at the presence of the God of **Jacob**,
132: 2 oath to the LORD and made a vow to the Mighty One of **Jacob**:
132: 5 a place for the LORD, a dwelling for the Mighty One of **Jacob**."
135: 4 For the LORD has chosen **Jacob** to be his own, Israel to be his
146: 5 Blessed is he whose help is the God of **Jacob**, whose hope is in the
147: 19 He has revealed his word to **Jacob**, his laws and decrees to Israel.
Isa 2: 3 to the mountain of the LORD, to the house of the God of **Jacob**.
2: 5 Come, O house of **Jacob**, let us walk in the light of the LORD.
2: 6 You have abandoned your people, the house of **Jacob**. They are
8: 17 for the LORD, who is hiding his face from the house of **Jacob**.
9: 8 [9:7] The Lord has sent a message against **Jacob**; it will fall on
10: 20 that day the remnant of Israel, the survivors of the house of **Jacob**,
10: 21 will return, a remnant of **Jacob** will return to the Mighty God.
14: 1 The LORD will have compassion on **Jacob**; once again he will
14: 1 own land. Aliens will join them and unite with the house of **Jacob**.
17: 4 "In that day the glory of **Jacob** will fade; the fat of his body will
27: 6 In days to come **Jacob** will take root, Israel will bud and blossom
27: 9 By this, then, will **Jacob's** guilt be atoned for, and this will be the
29: 22 the LORD, who redeemed Abraham, says to the house of **Jacob**:
29: 22 "No longer will **Jacob** be ashamed; no longer will their faces grow
29: 23 they will acknowledge the holiness of the Holy One of **Jacob**,
40: 27 Why do you say, O **Jacob**, and complain, O Israel, "My way is
41: 8 "But you, O Israel, my servant, **Jacob**, whom I have chosen,
41: 14 Do not be afraid, O worm **Jacob**, O little Israel, for I myself will
41: 21 says the LORD. "Set forth your arguments," says **Jacob's** King.
42: 24 Who handed **Jacob** over to become loot, and Israel to the
43: 1 he who created you, O **Jacob**, he who formed you, O Israel:
43: 22 "Yet you have not called upon me, O **Jacob**, you have not wearied
43: 28 and I will consign **Jacob** to destruction and Israel to scorn.
44: 1 "But now listen, O **Jacob**, my servant, Israel, whom I have chosen.
44: 2 Do not be afraid, O **Jacob**, my servant, Jeshurun, whom I have
44: 5 to the LORD'; another will call himself by the name of **Jacob**;
44: 21 these things, O **Jacob**, for you are my servant, O Israel.
44: 23 you forests and all your trees, for the LORD has redeemed **Jacob**,
45: 4 For the sake of **Jacob** my servant, of Israel my chosen, I summon
45: 19 I have not said to **Jacob's** descendants, 'Seek me in vain.'
46: 3 "Listen to me, O house of **Jacob**, all you who remain of the house
48: 1 "Listen to this, O house of **Jacob**, you who are called by the name
48: 12 "Listen to me, O **Jacob**, Israel, whom I have called: I am he;
48: 20 of the earth; say, "The LORD has redeemed his servant **Jacob**."
49: 5 he who formed me in the womb to be his servant to bring **Jacob**

Isa 49: 6 small a thing for you to be my servant to restore the tribes of **Jacob**
49: 26 am your Savior, your Redeemer, the Mighty One of **Jacob**."
58: 1 to my people their rebellion and to the house of **Jacob** their sins.
58: 14 of the land and to feast on the inheritance of your father **Jacob**."
59: 20 to those in **Jacob** who repent of their sins," declares the LORD.
60: 16 am your Savior, your Redeemer, the Mighty One of **Jacob**.
65: 9 I will bring forth descendants from **Jacob**, and from Judah those
Jer 2: 4 Hear the word of the LORD, O house of **Jacob**, all you clans of
5: 20 "Announce this to the house of **Jacob** and proclaim it in Judah:
10: 16 He who is the Portion of **Jacob** is not like these, for he is the
10: 25 For they have devoured **Jacob**; they have devoured him
30: 7 It will be a time of trouble for **Jacob**, but he will be saved out of it.
30: 10 " 'So do not fear, O **Jacob** my servant; do not be dismayed,
30: 10 **Jacob** will again have peace and security, and no one will make
30: 18 " 'I will restore the fortunes of **Jacob's** tents and have compassion
31: 7 "Sing with joy for **Jacob**; shout for the foremost of the nations.
31: 11 For the LORD will ransom **Jacob** and redeem them from the
33: 26 then I will reject the descendants of **Jacob** and David my servant
33: 26 his sons to rule over the descendants of Abraham, Isaac and **Jacob**.
46: 27 "Do not fear, O **Jacob** my servant; do not be dismayed, O Israel.
46: 27 **Jacob** will again have peace and security, and no one will make
46: 28 Do not fear, O **Jacob** my servant, for I am with you,"
51: 19 He who is the Portion of **Jacob** is not like these, for he is the
La 1: 17 The LORD has decreed for **Jacob** that his neighbors become his
2: 2 pity the Lord has swallowed up all the dwellings of **Jacob**;
2: 3 He has burned in **Jacob** like a flaming fire that consumes
Eze 20: 5 swore with uplifted hand to the descendants of the house of **Jacob**
28: 25 they will live in their own land, which I gave to my servant **Jacob**.
37: 25 They will live in the land I gave to my servant **Jacob**, the land
39: 25 I will now bring **Jacob** back from captivity and will have
Hos 10: 11 Judah must plow, and **Jacob** must break up the ground.
12: 2 [12:3] he will punish **Jacob** according to his ways and repay him
12: 12 [12:13] **Jacob** fled to the country of Aram; Israel served to get a
Am 3: 13 "Hear this and testify against the house of **Jacob**,"
6: 8 "I abhor the pride of **Jacob** and detest his fortresses; I will deliver
7: 2 forgive! How can **Jacob** survive? He is so small!"
7: 5 "Sovereign LORD, I beg you, stop! How can **Jacob** survive?
8: 7 The LORD has sworn by the Pride of **Jacob**: "I will never forget
9: 8 yet I will not totally destroy the house of **Jacob**,"
Ob 1: 10 Because of the violence against your brother **Jacob**, you will be
1: 17 it will be holy, and the house of **Jacob** will possess its inheritance.
1: 18 The house of **Jacob** will be a fire and the house of Joseph a flame;
Mic 1: 5 All this is because of **Jacob's** transgression, because of the sins of
1: 5 What is **Jacob's** transgression? Is it not Samaria? What is Judah's
2: 7 Should it be said, O house of **Jacob**: "Is the Spirit of the LORD
2: 12 "I will surely gather all of you, O **Jacob**; I will surely bring
3: 1 I said, "Listen, you leaders of **Jacob**, you rulers of the house of
3: 8 and with justice and might, to declare to **Jacob** his transgression,
3: 9 Hear this, you leaders of the house of **Jacob**, you rulers of the
4: 2 to the mountain of the LORD, to the house of the God of **Jacob**.
5: 7 [5:6] The remnant of **Jacob** will be in the midst of many peoples
5: 8 [5:7] The remnant of **Jacob** will be among the nations,
7: 20 You will be true to **Jacob**, and show mercy to Abraham, as you
Na 2: 2 [2:3] The LORD will restore the splendor of **Jacob** like the
Mal 1: 2 "Was not Esau **Jacob's** [+4200] brother?" the LORD says.
1: 2 Esau Jacob's brother?" the LORD says. "Yet I have loved **Jacob**,
2: 12 he may be, may the LORD cut him off from the tents of **Jacob**—
3: 6 do not change. So you, O descendants of **Jacob**, are not destroyed.

3621 יַעֲקֹבָה ya'aqōbâ, n.pr.m. [1]

Jaakobah [1]

1Ch 4: 36 **Jaakobah**, Jeshohaiah, Asaiah, Adiel, Jesimiel, Benaiah,

3622 יַעֲקָן ya'aqān, n.pr.loc. [2 / 1] [→ 942; cf. 6826?]

Jaakanites [+1201] [1]

Dt 10: 6 (The Israelites traveled from the wells of the **Jaakanites** [+1201]
1Ch 1: 42 sons of Ezer: Bilhan, Zaavan and Akan. [BHS *Jaakan*; NIV 6826]

3623 ¹יַעַר ya'ar¹, n.m. [57] [→ 3625, 3627]

forest [38], forests [7], thickets [3], woods [3], finest of forests [+4149] [2], thicket [2], forested [1], groves [1]

Dt 19: 5 a man may go into the **forest** with his neighbor to cut wood,
Jos 17: 15 go up into the **forest** and clear land for yourselves there in the land
17: 18 the **forested** hill country as well. Clear it, and its farthest limits
1Sa 14: 25 The entire army entered the **woods**, and there was honey on the
14: 26 When they went into the **woods**, they saw the honey oozing out,
22: 5 the land of Judah." So David left and went to the **forest** *of* Hereth.
2Sa 18: 6 to fight Israel, and the battle took place in the **forest** *of* Ephraim.
18: 8 and the **forest** claimed more lives that day than the sword.
18: 17 threw him into a big pit in the **forest** and piled up a large heap of
1Ki 7: 2 He built the Palace of the **Forest** *of* Lebanon a hundred cubits
10: 17 The king put them in the Palace of the **Forest** *of* Lebanon.
10: 21 all the household articles in the Palace of the **Forest** *of* Lebanon
2Ki 2: 24 two bears came out of the **woods** and mauled forty-two of the
19: 23 I have reached its remotest parts, the **finest of** its **forests** [+4149].
1Ch 16: 33 the trees of the **forest** will sing, they will sing for joy before the
2Ch 9: 16 The king put them in the Palace of the **Forest** *of* Lebanon.
9: 20 all the household articles in the Palace of the **Forest** *of* Lebanon
Ps 29: 9 The voice of the LORD twists the oaks and strips the **forests** bare.
50: 10 for every animal of the **forest** is mine, and the cattle on a thousand
80: 13 [80:14] Boars from the **forest** ravage it and the creatures of the
83: 14 [83:15] As fire consumes the **forest** or a flame sets the mountains
96: 12 in them. Then all the trees of the **forest** will sing for joy;
104: 20 it becomes night, and all the beasts of the **forest** prowl.
Ecc 2: 6 I made reservoirs to water **groves** *of* flourishing trees.
SS 2: 3 Like an apple tree among the trees of the **forest** is my lover among
Isa 7: 2 were shaken, as the trees of the **forest** are shaken by the wind.
9: 18 [9:17] and thorns, it sets the **forest** thickets ablaze,
10: 18 The splendor of his **forests** and fertile fields it will completely
10: 19 the remaining trees of his **forests** will be so few that a child could
10: 34 He will cut down the **forest** thickets with an ax; Lebanon will fall
21: 13 You caravans of Dedanites, who camp in the **thickets** of Arabia,
22: 8 you looked in that day to the weapons in the Palace of the **Forest**;
29: 17 be turned into a fertile field and the fertile field seem like a **forest**?
32: 15 becomes a fertile field, and the fertile field seems like a **forest**.
32: 19 Though hail flattens the **forest** and the city is leveled completely,
37: 24 have reached its remotest heights, the **finest of** its **forests** [+4149].
44: 14 He let it grow among the trees of the **forest**, or planted a pine,
44: 23 Burst into song, you mountains, you **forests** and all your trees,
56: 9 beasts of the field, come and devour, all you beasts of the **forest**!
Jer 5: 6 Therefore a lion from the **forest** will attack them, a wolf from the
10: 3 they cut a tree out of the **forest**, and a craftsman shapes it with his
12: 8 My inheritance has become to me like a lion in the **forest**.
21: 14 I will kindle a fire in your **forests** that will consume everything
26: 18 heap of rubble, the temple hill a mound overgrown with **thickets**.'
46: 23 They will chop down her **forest**," declares the LORD, "dense
Eze 15: 2 a vine better than that of a branch on any of the trees in the **forest**?
15: 6 As I have given the wood of the vine among the trees of the **forest**
20: 46 [21:2] the south and prophesy against the **forest** *of* the southland.
20: 47 [21:3] Say to the southern **forest**: 'Hear the word of the LORD.
34: 25 so that they may live in the desert and sleep in the **forests** in safety.
39: 10 not need to gather wood from the fields or cut it from the **forests**,
Hos 2: 12 [2:14] I will make them a **thicket**, and wild animals will devour
Am 3: 4 Does a lion roar in the **thicket** when he has no prey? Does he
Mic 3: 12 a heap of rubble, the temple hill a mound overgrown with **thickets**.
5: 8 [5:7] of many peoples, like a lion among the beasts of the **forest**,
7: 14 which lives by itself in a **forest**, in fertile pasturelands.
Zec 11: 2 Wail, oaks of Bashan; the dense **forest** has been cut down!

3624 ²יַעַר ya'ar², n.[m.]. [1] [→ 3626]

honeycomb [1]

SS 5: 1 I have eaten my **honeycomb** and my honey; I have drunk my wine

3625 ³יַעַר ya'ar³, n.pr.m. *or* loc. [1] [√ 3623]

Jaar [1]

Ps 132: 6 We heard it in Ephrathah, we came upon it in the fields of **Jaar**:

3626 ¹יַעְרָה ya'arâ¹, n.f. [1] [√ 3624]

honeycomb [+1831] [1]

1Sa 14: 27 that was in his hand and dipped it into the **honeycomb** [+1831].

3627 ²יַעְרָה ya'arâ², n.m. Not used in NIV/BHS [√ 3623]

3628 יַעְרָה ya'râ, n.pr.m. [2 / 0]

1Ch 9: 42 Ahaz was the father of Jadah, [BHS *Jarah*; NIV 3586]
9: 42 Jadah [BHS *Jarah*; NIV 3586] was the father of Alemeth,

3629 יַעְרֵי אֹרְגִים ya'arê 'ōregîm, n.pr.m. [1] [cf. 762]

Jaare-Oregim [1]

2Sa 21: 19 Elhanan son of **Jaare-Oregim** the Bethlehemite killed Goliath the

3630 יְעָרִים ye'ārîm, n.pr.loc. [1] [→ 7961]

Jearim [1]

Jos 15: 10 ran along the northern slope of Mount **Jearim** (that is, Kesalon),

3631 יַעֲרֶשְׁיָה ya'arešyâ, n.pr.m. [1] [√ 3378]

Jaareshiah [1]

1Ch 8: 27 **Jaareshiah**, Elijah and Zicri were the sons of Jeroham.

3632 יַעֲשׂוּ *ya'ᵃśû*, n.pr.m. [1] [√ 6913]

Jaasu [1]

Ezr 10:37 Mattaniah, Mattenai and **Jaasu**. [Q 3633]

3633 יַעֲשָׂי *ya'ᵃśāy*, n.pr.m. [0] [√ 6913]

Ezr 10:37 [Mattaniah, Mattenai and **Jaasu**. [Q; see K 3632]]

3634 יַעֲשִׂיאֵל *ya'ᵃśî'ēl*, n.pr.m. [2] [√ 6913 + 446]

Jaasiel [2]

1Ch 11:47 Eliel, Obed and **Jaasiel** the Mezobaite.
27:21 Iddo son of Zechariah; over Benjamin: **Jaasiel** son of Abner;

3635 יִפְדְיָה *yipdᵉyâ*, n.pr.m. [1]

Iphdeiah [1]

1Ch 8:25 **Iphdeiah** and Penuel were the sons of Shashak.

3636 יָפָה *yāpâ*, v. [8] [→ 3637, 3638, 3639?, 3642, 3645; cf. 6993]

beautiful [3], adorn yourself [1], adorn [1], delightful [1], majestic [1], most excellent [1]

Ps 45:2 [45:3] [D] *You are the* **most excellent** of men and your lips
SS 4:10 [A] How **delightful** *is* your love, my sister, my bride! How much
7:1 [7:2] [A] How **beautiful** your sandaled feet, O prince's
7:6 [7:7] [A] How **beautiful** *you are* and how pleasing, O love,
Jer 4:30 [F] *You* **adorn yourself** in vain. Your lovers despise you;
10:4 [D] *They* **adorn** it with silver and gold; they fasten it with
Eze 16:13 [A] olive oil. *You became* very **beautiful** and rose to be a queen.
31:7 [A] *It was* **majestic** in beauty, with its spreading boughs, for its

3637 יָפֶה *yāpeh*, a. [42] [√ 3636]

beautiful [23], beautiful [+5260] [3], lovely [3], beautiful [+9307] [2], handsome [+5260] [2], sleek [+5260] [2], fair [1], fine [1], handsome appearance [1], handsome [1], proper [1], sleek [+9307] [1], well-built [+9307] [1]

Ge 12:11 his wife Sarai, "I know what a **beautiful** [+5260] woman you are.
12:14 to Egypt, the Egyptians saw that she was a very **beautiful** woman.
29:17 Leah had weak eyes, but Rachel was **lovely** *in* form, and beautiful.
29:17 weak eyes, but Rachel was lovely in form, and **beautiful** [+5260].
39:6 food he ate. Now Joseph was **well-built** [+9307] and handsome,
39:6 food he ate. Now Joseph was well-built and **handsome** [+5260],
41:2 **sleek** [+5260] and fat, and they grazed among the reeds.
41:4 the cows that were ugly and gaunt ate up the seven **sleek** [+5260],
41:18 fat and **sleek** [+9307], and they grazed among the reeds.
Dt 21:11 if you notice among the captives a **beautiful** [+9307] woman
1Sa 16:12 He was ruddy, with a **fine** appearance and handsome features.
17:42 only a boy, ruddy and **handsome** [+5260], and he despised him.
25:3 She was an intelligent and **beautiful** [+9307] woman, but her
2Sa 13:1 in love with Tamar, the **beautiful** sister of Absalom son of David.
14:25 so highly praised for his **handsome appearance** as Absalom.
14:27 name was Tamar, and she became a **beautiful** [+5260] woman.
1Ki 1:3 they searched throughout Israel for a **beautiful** girl and found
1:4 The girl was very **beautiful**; she took care of the king and waited
Est 2:7 who was also known as Esther, was **lovely** *in* form and features,
Job 42:15 Nowhere in all the land were there found women as **beautiful** as
Ps 48:2 [48:3] It is **beautiful** *in* its loftiness, the joy of the whole earth.
Pr 11:22 Like a gold ring in a pig's snout is a **beautiful** woman who shows
Ecc 3:11 He has made everything **beautiful** in its time. He has also set
5:18 [5:17] that it is good and **proper** for a man to eat and drink,
SS 1:8 If you do not know, *most* **beautiful** of women, follow the tracks of
1:15 How **beautiful** you are, my darling! Oh, how beautiful! Your eyes
1:15 How beautiful you are, my darling! Oh, how **beautiful**! Your eyes
1:16 How **handsome** you are, my lover! Oh, how charming! And our
2:10 lover spoke and said to me, "Arise, my darling, my **beautiful** *one*,
2:13 Arise, come, my darling; my **beautiful** *one*, come with me."
4:1 How **beautiful** you are, my darling! Oh, how beautiful! Your eyes
4:1 How beautiful you are, my darling! Oh, how **beautiful**! Your eyes
4:7 All **beautiful** you are, my darling; there is no flaw in you.
5:9 How is your beloved better than others, *most* **beautiful** of women?
6:1 Where has your lover gone, *most* **beautiful** of women? Which way
6:4 You are **beautiful**, my darling, as Tirzah, lovely as Jerusalem,
6:10 **fair** as the moon, bright as the sun, majestic as the stars in
Jer 11:16 The LORD called you a thriving olive tree with fruit **beautiful** *in*
Eze 31:3 in Lebanon, *with* **beautiful** branches overshadowing the forest;
31:9 I made it **beautiful** with abundant branches, the envy of all the
33:32 nothing more than one who sings love songs with a **beautiful** voice
Am 8:13 "In that day "the **lovely** young women and strong young men will

3638 יְפֵה־פִיָּה *yᵉpēh-piyyâ*, a.f. Not used in NIV/BHS [√ 3636; cf. 3645]

3639 יָפוֹ *yāpô*, n.pr.loc. [4] [√ 3636?]

Joppa [4]

Jos 19:46 Me Jarkon and Rakkon, with the area facing **Joppa**.
2Ch 2:16 [2:15] and will float them in rafts by sea down to **Joppa**.
Ezr 3:7 so that they would bring cedar logs by sea from Lebanon to **Joppa**,
Jnh 1:3 He went down to **Joppa**, where he found a ship bound for that

3640 יָפַח *yāpaḥ*, v. [1] [→ 3641; cf. 7032]

gasping for breath [1]

Jer 4:31 [F] the cry of the Daughter of Zion **gasping for breath**,

3641 יָפֵחַ *yāpēaḥ*, a. [1] [√ 3640]

breathing out [1]

Ps 27:12 for false witnesses rise up against me, **breathing out** violence.

3642 יְפִי *yᵒpî*, n.m. [19] [√ 3636]

beauty [18], beautiful [1]

Est 1:11 in order to display her **beauty** to the people and nobles,
Ps 45:11 [45:12] The king is enthralled by your **beauty**; honor him, for he
50:2 From Zion, perfect in **beauty**, God shines forth.
Pr 6:25 Do not lust in your heart after her **beauty** or let her captivate you
31:30 Charm is deceptive, and **beauty** is fleeting; but a woman who fears
Isa 3:24 instead of fine clothing, sackcloth; instead of **beauty**, branding.
33:17 Your eyes will see the king in his **beauty** and view a land that
La 2:15 "Is this the city that was called the perfection of **beauty**, the joy of
Eze 16:14 your fame spread among the nations on account of your **beauty**,
16:15 " 'But you trusted in your **beauty** and used your fame to become a
16:25 every street you built your lofty shrines and degraded your **beauty**,
27:3 LORD says: " 'You say, O Tyre, "I am perfect in **beauty**."
27:4 on the high seas; your builders brought your **beauty** to perfection.
27:11 shields around your walls; they brought your **beauty** to perfection.
28:7 they will draw their swords against your **beauty** and wisdom
28:12 the model of perfection, full of wisdom and perfect in **beauty**.
28:17 Your heart became proud on account of your **beauty**, and you
31:8 its branches—no tree in the garden of God could match its **beauty**.
Zec 9:17 How attractive and **beautiful** they will be! Grain will make the

3643 יָפִיעַ¹ *yāpîa'¹*, n.pr.loc. [1] [√ 3649]

Japhia [1]

Jos 19:12 of Kisloth Tabor and went on to Daberath and up to **Japhia**.

3644 יָפִיעַ² *yāpîa'²*, n.pr.m. [4] [√ 3649]

Japhia [4]

Jos 10:3 king of Jarmuth, **Japhia** king of Lachish and Debir king of Eglon.
2Sa 5:15 Ibhar, Elishua, Nepheg, **Japhia**,
1Ch 3:7 Nogah, Nepheg, **Japhia**,
14:6 Nogah, Nepheg, **Japhia**,

3645 יְפֵהפִיָּה *yᵉpêpiyyâ*, a.[f.]. [1] [√ 3636; cf. 3638]

beautiful [1]

Jer 46:20 "Egypt is a **beautiful** heifer, but a gadfly is coming against her

3646 יַפְלֵט *yaplēṭ*, n.pr.m. [3] [→ 3647; cf. 7117]

Japhlet [2], Japhlet's [1]

1Ch 7:32 Heber was the father of **Japhlet**, Shomer and Hotham and of their
7:33 The sons of **Japhlet**: Pasach, Bimhal and Ashvath. These were
7:33 Pasach, Bimhal and Ashvath. These were **Japhlet's** sons.

3647 יַפְלֵטִי *yaplēṭî*, a.g. [1] [√ 3646; cf. 7117]

Japhletites [1]

Jos 16:3 descended westward to the territory of the **Japhletites** as far as the

3648 יְפֻנֶּה *yᵉpunneh*, n.pr.m. [16] [√ 7155]

Jephunneh [16]

Nu 13:6 from the tribe of Judah, Caleb son of **Jephunneh**;
14:6 Joshua son of Nun and Caleb son of **Jephunneh**, who were among
14:30 except Caleb son of **Jephunneh** and Joshua son of Nun.
14:38 only Joshua son of Nun and Caleb son of **Jephunneh** survived.
26:65 and not one of them was left except Caleb son of **Jephunneh**
32:12 not one except Caleb son of **Jephunneh** the Kenizzite and Joshua
34:19 are their names: Caleb son of **Jephunneh**, from the tribe of Judah;
Dt 1:36 except Caleb son of **Jephunneh**. He will see it, and I will give him
Jos 14:6 at Gilgal, and Caleb son of **Jephunneh** the Kenizzite said to him,
14:13 Joshua blessed Caleb son of **Jephunneh** and gave him Hebron as
14:14 So Hebron has belonged to Caleb son of **Jephunneh** the Kenizzite
15:13 Joshua gave to Caleb son of **Jephunneh** a portion in Judah—

Jos 21:12 villages around the city they had given to Caleb son of **Jephunneh**
1Ch 4:15 The sons of Caleb son of **Jephunneh**: Iru, Elah and Naam.
6:56 [6:41] around the city were given to Caleb son of **Jephunneh**.
7:38 The sons of Jether: **Jephunneh**, Pispah and Ara.

3649 יָפַע yāpaʻ, v. [8] [→ 3643, 3644, 3650]

shine forth [2], light [1], makes flash [1], shine [1], shines forth [1], shone forth [1], smile [1]

Dt 33:2 [G] over them from Seir; *he* **shone forth** from Mount Paran.
Job 3:4 [G] may God above not care about it; *may* no light **shine** upon it.
10:3 [G] your hands, while *you* **smile** on the schemes of the wicked?
10:22 [G] and disorder, where even the **light** is like darkness."
37:15 [G] how God controls the clouds and **makes** his lightning **flash**?
Ps 50:2 [G] From Zion, perfect in beauty, God **shines forth**.
80:1 [80:2] [G] sit enthroned between the cherubim, **shine forth**
94:1 [G] the God who avenges, O God who avenges, **shine forth**.

3650 יִפְעָה yipʻâ, n.f. [2] [√ 3649]

shining splendor [1], splendor [1]

Eze 28:7 against your beauty and wisdom and pierce your **shining splendor**.
28:17 and you corrupted your wisdom because of your **splendor**.

3651 יֶפֶת yepet, n.pr.m. [11] [√ 7332]

Japheth [11]

Ge 5:32 500 years old, he became the father of Shem, Ham and **Japheth**.
6:10 Noah had three sons: Shem, Ham and **Japheth**.
7:13 On that very day Noah and his sons, Shem, Ham and **Japheth**,
9:18 of Noah who came out of the ark were Shem, Ham and **Japheth**.
9:23 Shem and **Japheth** took a garment and laid it across their
9:27 May God extend the territory of **Japheth**; may Japheth live in the
10:1 This is the account of Shem, Ham and **Japheth**, Noah's sons,
10:2 The sons of **Japheth**: Gomer, Magog, Madai, Javan, Tubal,
10:21 Sons were also born to Shem, whose older brother was **Japheth**;
1Ch 1:4 The sons of Noah: Shem, Ham and **Japheth**.
1:5 The sons of **Japheth**: Gomer, Magog, Madai, Javan, Tubal,

3652 יִפְתָּח yiptāḥ¹, n.pr.loc. [1] [√ 7337]

Iphtah [1]

Jos 15:43 **Iphtah**, Ashnah, Nezib,

3653 ²יִפְתָּח yiptāḥ², n.pr.m. [29] [√ 7337]

Jephthah [22], *untranslated* [2], him[s] [2], he[s] [1], his[s] [1], Jephthah's [1]

Jdg 11:1 **Jephthah** the Gileadite was a mighty warrior. His father was
11:1 **His**[s] father was Gilead; his mother was a prostitute.
11:2 and when they were grown up, they drove **Jephthah** away.
11:3 So **Jephthah** fled from his brothers and settled in the land of Tob,
11:3 where a group of adventurers gathered around **him**[s] and followed
11:5 the elders of Gilead went to get **Jephthah** from the land of Tob.
11:6 "Come," they said, **[RPH]** "be our commander, so we can fight
11:7 **Jephthah** said to them, "Didn't you hate me and drive me from my
11:8 The elders of Gilead said to **him**[s], "Nevertheless, we are turning to
11:9 **Jephthah** answered, "Suppose you take me back to fight the
11:10 The elders of Gilead replied, **[RPH]** "The LORD is our witness;
11:11 So **Jephthah** went with the elders of Gilead, and the people made
11:11 And **he**[s] repeated all his words before the LORD in Mizpah.
11:12 **Jephthah** sent messengers to the Ammonite king with the
11:13 The king of the Ammonites answered **Jephthah's** messengers,
11:14 **Jephthah** sent back messengers to the Ammonite king,
11:15 saying: "This is what **Jephthah** says: Israel did not take the land of
11:28 however, paid no attention to the message **Jephthah** sent him.
11:29 the Spirit of the LORD came upon **Jephthah**. He crossed Gilead
11:30 **Jephthah** made a vow to the LORD: "If you give the Ammonites
11:32 **Jephthah** went over to fight the Ammonites, and the LORD gave
11:34 When **Jephthah** returned to his home in Mizpah, who should come
11:40 four days to commemorate the daughter of **Jephthah** the Gileadite.
12:1 out their forces, crossed over to Zaphon and said to **Jephthah**,
12:2 **Jephthah** answered, "I and my people were engaged in a great
12:4 **Jephthah** then called together the men of Gilead and fought
12:7 **Jephthah** led Israel six years. Then Jephthah the Gileadite died,
12:7 **Jephthah** the Gileadite died, and was buried in a town in Gilead.
1Sa 12:11 Then the LORD sent Jerub-Baal, Barak, **Jephthah** and Samuel,

3654 יִפְתַּח־אֵל yiptaḥ-ʼēl, n.pr.loc. [2] [√ 7337 + 446]

Iphtah El [2]

Jos 19:14 on the north to Hannathon and ended at the Valley of **Iphtah El**.
19:27 touched Zebulun and the Valley of **Iphtah El**, and went north to

3655 יָצָא yāṣāʼ, v. [1069 / 1067] [→ 3448, 3665, 4604, 4605, 4606, 7368, 7556, 9362]

brought out [100], came out [84], went out [82], go out [57], go [40], come out [39], left [38], bring out [35], leave [24], come [21], went [20], serve [14], marched out [12], gone out [11], out [11], set out [10], *untranslated* [9], bring [8], brought [8], coming out [8], came [7], comes [7], get out [7], going out [7], spread [7], goes out [6], take [6], comes out [5], extending [5], took [5], bring forth [4], bringing out [4], brings out [4], coming [4], escape [4], go free [4], gone [4], leaving [4], march out [4], produces [4], released [4], removed [4], returned [4], spreading [4], surrender [4], took out [4], came forward [3], fell [3], free [3], going [3], had brought [3], lead out [3], led out [3], marching out [3], projecting [3], send out [3], sent [3], went on [3], withdrew [3], be brought out [2], began [2], break out [2], bringing [2], brings [2], burst out [2], came out [+3655] [2], come forth [2], come up [2], continued [2], depart [2], departed [2], departure [2], did[s] [2], drive out [2], ever goes outside [+906+3655] [2], experienced soldiers [+7372] [2], exported [2], flesh and blood [+2743+4946] [2], flow out [2], flows [2], forth [2], given [2], goes [2], going off duty [2], gone from [2], has [2], imported [+2256+6590] [2], is [2], led in campaigns [+995+2256+4200+7156] [2], led on military campaigns [+906+995+2256] [2], led [2], left [+907+3655+4946] [2], marches out [2], move out [2], produce [2], promised [+4946+7023] [2], ready for military service [+7372] [2], ready to go out [+7372] [2], remove [2], said [+4946+7023] [2], sank [2], stepped forward [2], surely come out [+3655] [2], surely march out [+3655] [2], surrender [+3655] [2], take out [2], taken out [2], taken [2], took from [2], utter [2], wherever goes [+928+928+995+2256] [2], your own flesh and blood [+3870+4946] [2], accompany [+907] [1], advance [1], advanced [1], advancing [1], announced [1], appearing [1], arise [1], arisen [1], arises [1], avoid [1], away [1], become known [1], been brought out [1], born [+4946+8167] [1], breaks out [1], breathed her last [+5883] [1], bring [+906+2256+4374] [1], bringing forth [1], budded [+7258] [1], burst forth [1], call out [1], carried away [1], carried out [1], carry out duties [+995+2256] [1], carry out [1], carry [1], charges [1], cleared [1], collapse [1], coming forth [1], continue [1], crawling out [1], crossed [1], dart [1], departs [1], descendants [+3751+5883] [1], descended [1], direct descendants [+3751] [1], do[s] [1], draw [1], drawn [1], drew out [1], empties [1], empty [1], encamped [+4722] [1], end [1], escaped [1], escapes [1], exacted [1], extend [1], extended [1], falls [1], fight [+2021+4200+4878] [1], flash [1], flashed out [1], flashed [1], flowed [1], flowing [1], flying [1], follow [+339] [1], follow [1], followed [+339] [1], followed [+6640] [1], followed [1], forges [1], fought in [+4200] [1], fought in [+928] [1], found [1], freed [1], gives birth prematurely [+3529] [1], gives vent to [1], gives [1], go about business [+995+2256] [1], go about [1], go into [1], go off duty [1], go off to war [1], go off [1], go up [1], goes over [1], grows out [1], gushed out [+8041] [1], had difficulty taking possession of [+4946] [1], have leave [1], headed [1], imported [1], issue [1], joined [1], lay [1], lead [+995+2256] [1], lead [+995+2256+4200+7156] [1], leads forth [1], leaves [1], led out [+4200+7156] [1], made come out [1], make shine [1], make spew out [+906+4946+7023] [1], makes come up [1], march on [1], marched into [1], met expenses [1], of [+4946] [1], of his own [+2257+3751] [1], on duty [+995+2256] [1], on the way [1], on way [1], out came [1], out comes [1], out goes [1], paid [1], passing [1], pierced [1], pour out [1], pours [1], prevails [1], produce [+2446+9311] [1], produced [1], promote [1], pursue [+339] [1], put away [1], put out [+906+2021+2575] [1], reached [1], release [1], risen [1], rises [1], rising [1], rode out [1], rush [1], rushed out [1], say [+4946+7023] [1], send away [1], sent out [1], serve [+995+2256] [1], serve in [1], set free [1], sets free [1], shines out [1], slip out [1], sober [+2021+3516+4946] [1], sow [1], speak [1], spoke [1], spreads [1], spring up [1], spring [1], springs up [1], starting [1], stepped out [1], stretch [1], surrendered [1], take back [1], telling [1], took part in [+4200] [1], travel about [+995+2256] [1], turned out [1], undertook [1], unsheathed [+4946+9509] [1], uttered [+4946] [1], venture out [1], vindicated [+906+7407] [1], was brought out [1], went away [1], went outside [1], were [1], whatever[s] [+2021] [1]

Ge 1:12 [G] The land **produced** vegetation: plants bearing seed according
1:24 [G] "*Let* the land **produce** living creatures according to their
2:10 [A] A river watering the garden **flowed** from Eden; from there it
4:16 [A] So Cain **went out** from the LORD's presence and lived in
8:7 [A] *it kept* **flying** back and forth until the water had dried up
8:7 [A] and **forth** until the water had dried up from the earth.
8:16 [A] "**Come out** of the ark, you and your wife and your sons
8:17 [G] **Bring out** every kind of living creature that is with you—
8:18 [A] So Noah **came out**, together with his sons and his wife
8:19 [A] on the earth—**came out** of the ark, one kind after another.
9:10 [A] wild animals, all *those that* **came out** *of* the ark with you—
9:18 [A] The sons of Noah who **came out** of the ark were Shem, Ham
10:11 [A] From that land *he* **went** *to* Assyria, where he built Nineveh,
10:14 [A] Pathrusites, Casluhites (from whom the Philistines **came**)

Ge 11:31 [A] together *they* **set out** from Ur of the Chaldeans to go to
12: 4 [A] Abram was seventy-five years old when he **set out** from
12: 5 [A] *they* **set out** for the land of Canaan, and they arrived there.
14: 8 [A] **marched out** and drew up their battle lines in the Valley of
14:17 [A] the king of Sodom **came out** to meet him in the Valley of
14:18 [G] Melchizedek king of Salem **brought out** bread and wine.
15: 4 [A] but a son **coming** from your own body will be your heir."
15: 5 [G] *He* **took** him outside and said, "Look up at the heavens
15: 7 [G] who **brought** you **out** of Ur of the Chaldeans to give you this
15:14 [A] and afterward *they will* **come out** with great possessions.
17: 6 [A] I will make nations of you, and kings *will* **come** from you.
19: 5 [G] **Bring** them **out** to us so that we can have sex with them."
19: 6 [A] Lot **went** outside to meet them and shut the door behind him
19: 8 [G] *Let me* **bring** them **out** to you, and you can do what you like
19:12 [G] else in the city who belongs to you? **Get** them **out** of here,
19:14 [A] So Lot **went out** and spoke to his sons-in-law, who were
19:14 [A] He said, "Hurry and **get out** of this place,
19:16 [G] and of his two daughters and **led** them safely out of the city,
19:17 [G] As soon as they *had* **brought** them out, one of them said,
19:23 [A] the time Lot reached Zoar, the sun *had* **risen** over the land.
24: 5 [A] then take your son back to the country *you* **came** from?"
24:11 [A] toward evening, the time the women **go out** to draw water.
24:13 [A] the daughters of the townspeople *are* **coming out** to draw
24:15 [A] Rebekah **came out** with her jar on her shoulder.
24:43 [A] if a maiden **comes out** to draw water and I say to her,
24:45 [A] in my heart, Rebekah **came out**, with her jar on her shoulder.
24:50 [A] Laban and Bethuel answered, "This **is** from the LORD;
24:53 [G] the servant **brought out** gold and silver jewelry and articles
24:63 [A] He **went out** to the field one evening to meditate, and as he
25:25 [A] The first *to* **come out** was red, and his whole body was like a
25:26 [A] After this, his brother **came out**, with his hand grasping
27: 3 [A] **go out** *to* the open country to hunt some wild game for me.
27:30 [A] Jacob *had* scarcely **left** [+907+3655+4946] his father's
27:30 [A] Jacob *had* scarcely **left** [+907+3655+4946] his father's
28:10 [A] Jacob **left** Beersheba and set out for Haran.
30:16 [A] in from the fields that evening, Leah **went out** to meet him.
31:13 [A] Now **leave** this land at once and go back to your native
31:33 [A] After *he* **came out** of Leah's tent, he entered Rachel's tent.
34: 1 [A] had borne to Jacob, **went out** to visit the women of the land.
34: 6 [A] Then Shechem's father Hamor **went out** to talk with Jacob.
34:24 [A] All the *men who* **went out** *of* the city gate agreed with
34:24 [A] and every male **[RPH]** in the city was circumcised.
34:26 [A] to the sword and took Dinah from Shechem's house and **left**.
35:11 [A] will come from you, and kings *will* **come** from your body.
35:18 [A] As she **breathed her last** [+5883]—for she was dying—she
38:24 [G] Judah said, "**Bring** her **out** and have her burned to death!"
38:25 [H] *As* she **was** *being* **brought out**, she sent a message to her
38:28 [A] and tied it on his wrist and said, "This one **came out** first."
38:29 [A] he drew back his hand, his brother **came out**, and she said,
38:30 [A] on his wrist, **came out** and he was given the name Zerah.
39:12 [A] But he left his cloak in her hand and ran **out** of the house.
39:15 [A] he left his cloak beside me and ran **out** of the house."
40:14 [G] mention me to Pharaoh and **get** me **out** of this prison.
41:45 [A] be his wife. And Joseph **went** throughout the land of Egypt.
41:46 [A] Joseph **went out** from Pharaoh's presence and traveled
42:15 [A] *you will* not **leave** this place unless your youngest brother
42:28 [A] Their hearts **sank** and they turned to each other trembling
43:23 [G] received your silver." Then *he* **brought** Simeon **out** to them.
43:31 [A] *he* **came out** and, controlling himself, said, "Serve the food."
44: 4 [A] They *had* not **gone** far **from** the city when Joseph said to his
44:28 [A] One of them **went away** from me, and I said, "He has surely
45: 1 [G] and he cried out, "**Have** everyone **leave** my presence!"
46:26 [A] *those who were* his **direct descendants** [+3751], not
47:10 [A] Then Jacob blessed Pharaoh and **went out** from his presence.
48:12 [G] Joseph **removed** them from Israel's knees and bowed down
Ex 1: 5 [A] The **descendants** [+3751+5883] *of* Jacob numbered seventy in
2:11 [A] *he* **went out** to where his own people were and watched them
2:13 [A] The next day *he* **went out** and saw two Hebrews fighting.
3:10 [G] to Pharaoh *to* **bring** my people the Israelites **out** of Egypt."
3:11 [G] should go to Pharaoh and **bring** the Israelites **out** of Egypt?"
3:12 [G] When you *have* **brought** the people **out** of Egypt, you will
4: 6 [G] his cloak, and when *he* **took** it **out**, it was leprous, like snow.
4: 7 [G] when *he* **took** it **out**, it was restored, like the rest of his flesh.
4:14 [A] He *is* already **on** *his* **way** to meet you, and his heart will be
5:10 [A] the slave drivers and the foremen **went out** and said to the
5:20 [A] When they **left** Pharaoh, they found Moses and Aaron
6: 6 [G] *I will* **bring** you **out** from under the yoke of the Egyptians.
6: 7 [G] who **brought** you **out** from under the yoke of the Egyptians.
6:13 [G] and he commanded them to **bring** the Israelites **out** of Egypt.
6:26 [G] "**Bring** the Israelites **out** of Egypt by their divisions."
6:27 [G] king of Egypt about **bringing** the Israelites **out** of Egypt.
7: 4 [G] with mighty acts of judgment *I will* **bring out** my divisions,
7: 5 [G] out my hand against Egypt and **bring** the Israelites **out** of it."
7:15 [A] Go to Pharaoh in the morning *as he* **goes out** to the water.
8:12 [8:8] [A] After Moses and Aaron **left** Pharaoh, Moses cried out
8:18 [8:14] [G] when the magicians tried to **produce** gnats by their
8:20 [8:16] [A] confront Pharaoh *as he* **goes** to the water and say to
8:29 [8:25] [A] Moses answered, "As soon as I **leave** you, I will pray
8:30 [8:26] [A] Then Moses **left** Pharaoh and prayed to the LORD,
9:29 [A] Moses replied, "When I *have* **gone out** *of* the city, I will
9:33 [A] Moses **left** Pharaoh and went out of the city. He spread out
10: 6 [A] in this land till now.' " Then Moses turned and **left** Pharaoh.
10:18 [A] Moses then **left** Pharaoh and prayed to the LORD.
11: 4 [A] LORD says: 'About midnight I *will* **go** throughout Egypt.
11: 8 [A] and saying, '**Go**, you and all the people who follow you!'
11: 8 [A] After that *I will* **leave**." Then Moses, hot with anger,
11: 8 [A] that I will leave." Then Moses, hot with anger, **left** Pharaoh.
12:17 [G] on this very day that *I* **brought** your divisions **out** of Egypt.
12:22 [A] Not one of you *shall* **go out** the door of his house until
12:31 [A] **Leave** my people, you and the Israelites! Go, worship the
12:39 [G] With the dough *they had* **brought** from Egypt, they baked
12:41 [A] to the very day, all the LORD's divisions **left** Egypt.
12:42 [G] Because the LORD kept vigil that night to **bring** them **out**
12:46 [G] inside one house; **take** none of the meat outside the house.
12:51 [G] on that very day the LORD **brought** the Israelites **out** of
13: 3 [A] "Commemorate this day, the day *you* **came out** of Egypt,
13: 3 [G] because the LORD **brought** you **out** of it with a mighty
13: 4 [A] Today, in the month of Abib, you *are* **leaving**.
13: 8 [A] because of what the LORD did for me when I **came out** of
13: 9 [G] For the LORD **brought** you **out** of Egypt with his mighty
13:14 [G] 'With a mighty hand the LORD **brought** us **out** of Egypt,
13:16 [G] a symbol on your forehead that the LORD **brought** us **out**
14: 8 [A] he pursued the Israelites, who *were* **marching out** boldly.
14:11 [G] What have you done to us by **bringing** us **out** of Egypt?
15:20 [A] and all the women **followed** [+339] her, with tambourines
15:22 [A] from the Red Sea and *they* **went** into the Desert of Shur.
16: 1 [A] day of the second month after they *had* **come out** of Egypt.
16: 3 [G] *you have* **brought** us **out** into this desert to starve this entire
16: 4 [A] The people *are to* **go out** each day and gather enough for that
16: 6 [G] know that it was the LORD *who* **brought** you **out** of Egypt,
16:27 [A] some of the people **went out** on the seventh day to gather it,
16:29 [A] to stay where he is on the seventh day; no one *is to* **go out**."
16:32 [G] you to eat in the desert when I **brought** you **out** of Egypt.' "
17: 6 [A] and water *will* **come out** of it for the people to drink."
17: 9 [A] some of our men and **go out** to fight the Amalekites.
18: 1 [G] and how the LORD *had* **brought** Israel **out** of Egypt.
18: 7 [A] So Moses **went out** to meet his father-in-law and bowed
19: 1 [A] In the third month after the Israelites **left** Egypt—on the very
19:17 [G] Moses **led** the people **out** of the camp to meet with God,
20: 2 [G] who **brought** you **out** of Egypt, out of the land of slavery.
21: 2 [A] in the seventh year, *he shall* **go** free, without paying
21: 3 [A] If he comes alone, *he is to* **go free** alone; but if he has a wife
21: 3 [A] but if he has a wife when he comes, she *is to* **go** with him.
21: 4 [A] shall belong to her master, and only the man *shall* **go free**.
21: 5 [A] and my wife and children and *do* not *want to* **go** free,'
21: 7 [A] as a servant, *she is* not *to* **go free** as menservants do.
21: 7 [A] as a servant, she is not to go free as menservants **do**[s].
21:11 [A] *she is to* **go free**, without any payment of money.
21:22 [A] she **gives birth** [+3529] **prematurely** but there is no serious
22: 6 [22:5] [A] "If a fire **breaks out** and spreads into thornbushes
23:15 [A] the month of Abib, for in that month *you* **came out** of Egypt.
23:16 [A] "Celebrate the Feast of Ingathering at the **end** *of* the year,
25:32 [A] Six branches *are to* **extend** from the sides of the lampstand—
25:33 [A] the same for all six branches **extending** from the lampstand.
25:35 [A] One bud shall be under the first pair of branches **extending**
28:35 [A] the Holy Place before the LORD and when he **comes out**,
29:46 [G] who **brought** them **out** of Egypt so that I might dwell among
32:11 [G] whom *you* **brought out** of Egypt with great power and a
32:12 [G] 'It was with evil intent *that he* **brought** them **out**, to kill
32:24 [A] the gold, and I threw it into the fire, and **out came** this calf!"
33: 7 [A] Anyone inquiring of the LORD *would* **go** to the tent of
33: 8 [A] whenever Moses **went out** to the tent, all the people rose
34:18 [A] the month of Abib, for in that month *you* **came out** of Egypt.
34:34 [A] to speak with him, he removed the veil until he **came out**.
34:34 [A] when *he* **came out** and told the Israelites what he had been
35:20 [A] the whole Israelite community **withdrew** from Moses'
37:18 [A] Six branches **extended** from the sides of the lampstand—
37:19 [A] the same for all six branches **extending** from the lampstand.
37:21 [A] One bud was under the first pair of branches **extending** from
Lev 4:12 [G] that is, all the rest of the bull—*he must* **take** outside the
4:21 [G] *he shall* **take** the bull outside the camp and burn it as he
6:11 [6:4] [G] **carry** the ashes outside the camp to a place that is
8:33 [A] *Do* not **leave** the entrance to the Tent of Meeting for seven
9:23 [A] When *they* **came out**, they blessed the people; and the glory
9:24 [A] Fire **came out** from the presence of the LORD
10: 2 [A] So fire **came out** from the presence of the LORD
10: 7 [A] *Do* not **leave** the entrance to the Tent of Meeting or you will
14: 3 [A] The priest *is to* **go** outside the camp and examine him. If the

Lev 14:38 [A] the priest *shall* **go out** the doorway of the house and close it
14:45 [G] the plaster—and **taken out** of the town to an unclean place.
15:16 [A] " 'When a man **has** an emission of semen, he must bathe his
15:32 [A] **[NIE]** for anyone made unclean by an emission of semen,
16:17 [A] make atonement in the Most Holy Place until he **comes out**,
16:18 [A] "Then *he shall* **come out** to the altar that is before the
16:24 [A] *he shall* **come out** and sacrifice the burnt offering for himself
16:27 [G] into the Most Holy Place to make atonement, *must be* **taken**
19:36 [G] I am the LORD your God, who **brought** you **out** of Egypt.
21:12 [A] nor **leave** the sanctuary of his God or desecrate it, because he
22: 4 [A] by a corpse or by anyone who **has** an emission of semen,
22:33 [G] who **brought** you **out** of Egypt to be your God. I am the
23:43 [G] Israelites live in booths when I **brought** them **out** of Egypt.
24:10 [A] and an Egyptian father **went out** among the Israelites,
24:14 [G] "**Take** the blasphemer outside the camp. All those who heard
24:23 [G] *they* **took** the blasphemer outside the camp and stoned him.
25:28 [A] *It will be* **returned** in the Jubilee, and he can then go back to
25:30 [A] and his descendants. *It is* not *to be* **returned** in the Jubilee.
25:31 [A] can be redeemed, and *they are to be* **returned** in the Jubilee.
25:33 [A] *is to be* **returned** in the Jubilee, because the houses in the
25:38 [G] who **brought** you **out** of Egypt to give you the land of
25:41 [A] he and his children *are to be* **released**, and he will go back to
25:42 [G] whom *I* **brought out** of Egypt, they must not be sold as
25:54 [A] and his children *are to be* **released** in the Year of Jubilee,
25:55 [G] They are my servants, whom *I* **brought out** of Egypt. I am
26:10 [G] *you will have to* **move** it **out** to make room for the new.
26:13 [G] who **brought** you **out** of Egypt so that you would no longer
26:45 [G] *I* **brought out** of Egypt in the sight of the nations to be their
27:21 [A] When the field *is* **released** in the Jubilee, it will become holy,
Nu 1: 1 [A] of the second year after the Israelites **came out** of Egypt.
1: 3 [A] twenty years old or more *who are able to* **serve** *in* the army.
1:20 [A] or more *who were able to* **serve** *in* the army were listed by
1:22 [A] or more *who were able to* **serve** *in* the army were counted
1:24 [A] or more *who were able to* **serve** *in* the army were listed by
1:26 [A] or more *who were able to* **serve** *in* the army were listed by
1:28 [A] or more *who were able to* **serve** *in* the army were listed by
1:30 [A] or more *who were able to* **serve** *in* the army were listed by
1:32 [A] or more *who were able to* **serve** *in* the army were listed by
1:34 [A] or more *who were able to* **serve** *in* the army were listed by
1:36 [A] or more *who were able to* **serve** *in* the army were listed by
1:38 [A] or more *who were able to* **serve** *in* the army were listed by
1:40 [A] or more *who were able to* **serve** *in* the army were listed by
1:42 [A] or more *who were able to* **serve** *in* the army were listed by
1:45 [A] or more *who were able to* **serve** *in* Israel's army were
9: 1 [A] first month of the second year after they **came out** of Egypt.
11:20 [A] until *it* **comes out** of your nostrils and you loathe it—
11:20 [A] before him, saying, "Why *did we ever* **leave** Egypt?" ' "
11:24 [A] So Moses **went out** and told the people what the LORD had
11:26 [A] were listed among the elders, but *did* not **go out** to the Tent.
12: 4 [A] Aaron and Miriam, "**Come out** to the Tent of Meeting,
12: 4 [A] of Meeting, all three of you." So the three of them **came out**.
12: 5 [A] and Miriam. When both of them **stepped forward**,
12:12 [A] Do not let her be like a stillborn infant **coming** from its
13:32 [G] *they* **spread** among the Israelites a bad report about the land
14:36 [G] grumble against him by **spreading** a bad report about it—
14:37 [G] these men *responsible for* **spreading** the bad report about
15:36 [G] So the assembly **took** him outside the camp and stoned him
15:41 [G] your God, who **brought** you **out** of Egypt to be your God.
16:27 [A] Dathan and Abiram *had* **come out** and were standing with
16:35 [A] fire **came out** from the LORD and consumed the 250 men
16:46 [17:11] [A] Wrath *has* **come out** from the LORD; the plague
17: 8 [17:23] [G] had not only sprouted but *had* **budded** [+7258],
17: 9 [17:24] [G] Moses **brought out** all the staffs from the LORD's
19: 3 [G] it *is to be* **taken** outside the camp and slaughtered in his
20: 8 [G] *You will* **bring** water **out** of the rock for the community
20:10 [G] you rebels, *must we* **bring** you water **out** of this rock?"
20:11 [A] Water **gushed out** [+8041], and the community and their
20:16 [G] heard our cry and sent an angel and **brought** us **out** of Egypt.
20:18 [A] you try, *we will* **march out** and attack you with the sword."
20:20 [A] Edom **came out** against them with a large and powerful
21:13 [A] which is in the desert **extending** into Amorite territory.
21:23 [A] entire army and **marched out** into the desert against Israel.
21:28 [A] "Fire **went out** from Heshbon, a blaze from the city of Sihon.
21:33 [A] his whole army **marched out** to meet them in battle at Edrei.
22: 5 [A] "A people *has* **come out** of Egypt; they cover the face of the
22:11 [A] 'A people that *has* **come out** of Egypt covers the face of the
22:32 [A] I *have* **come** here to oppose you because your path is a
22:36 [A] *he* **went out** to meet him at the Moabite town on the Arnon
23:22 [G] God **brought** them **out** of Egypt; they have the strength of a
24: 8 [G] "God **brought** them **out** of Egypt; they have the strength of a
26: 2 [A] or more *who are able to* **serve in** the army of Israel."
26: 4 [A] These were the Israelites who **came out** of Egypt:
27:17 [A] *to* **go out** and come in before them, one who will lead them
27:17 [G] before them, *one* who *will* **lead** them **out** and bring them in,
27:21 [A] and the entire community of the Israelites *will* **go out**,
30: 2 [30:3] [A] but must do everything he **said** [+4946+7023].
31:13 [A] all the leaders of the community **went** to meet them outside
31:27 [A] between the soldiers who **took part** [+4200] **in** the battle
31:28 [A] From the soldiers who **fought** [+4200] **in** the battle, set apart
31:36 [A] The half share of those *who* **fought** [+928] **in** the battle was:
32:24 [A] but do what you have **promised** [+4946+7023]."
33: 1 [A] *they* **came out** of Egypt by divisions under the leadership of
33: 3 [A] *They* **marched out** boldly in full view of all the Egyptians,
33:38 [A] of the fortieth year after the Israelites **came out** of Egypt.
33:54 [A] to a smaller group a smaller one. Whatever **falls** to them by
34: 4 [A] Then *it will* **go** *to* Hazar Addar and over to Azmon,
34: 9 [A] **continue** to Ziphron and end at Hazar Enan. This will be
35:26 [A] " 'But if the accused **ever goes outside** [+906+3655] the
35:26 [A] " 'But if the accused **ever goes outside** [+906+3655] the
Dt 1:27 [G] so *he* **brought** us **out** of Egypt to deliver us into the hands of
1:44 [A] The Amorites who lived in those hills **came out** against you;
2:23 [A] the Caphtorites **coming out** from Caphtor destroyed them
2:32 [A] and all his army **came out** to meet us in battle at Jahaz,
3: 1 [A] Og king of Bashan with his whole army **marched out** to
4:20 [G] took you and **brought** you **out** of the iron-smelting furnace,
4:37 [G] *he* **brought** you **out** of Egypt by his Presence and his great
4:45 [A] and laws Moses gave them when they **came out** of Egypt
4:46 [A] by Moses and the Israelites as they **came out** of Egypt.
5: 6 [G] who **brought** you **out** of Egypt, out of the land of slavery.
5:15 [G] that the LORD your God **brought** you **out** of there with a
6:12 [G] who **brought** you **out** of Egypt, out of the land of slavery.
6:21 [G] but the LORD **brought** us **out** of Egypt with a mighty hand.
6:23 [G] *he* **brought** us **out** from there to bring us in and give us the
7: 8 [G] your forefathers that he **brought** you **out** with a mighty hand
7:19 [G] with which the LORD your God **brought** you **out**.
8: 7 [A] pools of water, with springs **flowing** in the valleys and hills;
8:14 [G] who **brought** you **out** of Egypt, out of the land of slavery.
8:15 [G] and scorpions. He **brought** you water **out** of hard rock.
9: 7 [A] From the day *you* **left** Egypt until you arrived here, you have
9:12 [G] because your people whom *you* **brought out** of Egypt have
9:26 [G] great power and **brought out** of Egypt with a mighty hand.
9:28 [G] Otherwise, the country from which *you* **brought** us will say,
9:28 [G] *he* **brought** them **out** to put them to death in the desert.'
9:29 [G] your inheritance that *you* **brought out** by your great power
11:10 [A] from which *you have* **come**, where you planted your seed
13: 5 [13:6] [G] who **brought** you **out** of Egypt and redeemed you
13:10 [13:11] [G] who **brought** you **out** of Egypt, out of the land of
13:13 [13:14] [A] that wicked men *have* **arisen** among you and have
14:22 [A] of all that your fields **produce** [+2446+9311] each year.
14:28 [G] **bring** all the tithes of that year's produce and store it in your
15:16 [A] "*I do* not *want to* **leave** you," because he loves you and your
16: 1 [G] because in the month of Abib he **brought** you **out** of Egypt
16: 3 [A] the bread of affliction, because *you* **left** Egypt in haste—
16: 3 [A] you may remember the time of your **departure** from Egypt.
16: 6 [A] on the anniversary of your **departure** from Egypt.
17: 5 [G] **take** the man or woman who has done this evil deed to your
20: 1 [A] When *you* **go** to war against your enemies and see horses
21: 2 [A] your elders and judges *shall* **go out** and measure the distance
21:10 [A] When *you* **go** to war against your enemies and the LORD
21:19 [G] of him and **bring** him to the elders at the gate of his town.
22:14 [G] slanders her and **gives** her a bad name, saying, "I married this
22:15 [G] the girl's father and mother *shall* **bring** [+906+2256+4374]
22:19 [G] because this man *has* **given** an Israelite virgin a bad name.
22:21 [G] she *shall be* **brought** to the door of her father's house
22:24 [G] *you shall* **take** both of them to the gate of that town
23: 4 [23:5] [A] and water on your way when you **came out** of Egypt,
23: 9 [23:10] [A] When *you are* **encamped** [+4722] against your
23:10 [23:11] [A] *he is to* **go** outside the camp and stay there.
23:12 [23:13] [A] the camp where *you can* **go** to relieve yourself.
24: 2 [A] if after *she* **leaves** his house she becomes the wife of another
24: 5 [A] *he must* not *be* **sent** to war or have any other duty laid on
24: 9 [A] did to Miriam along the way after you **came out** of Egypt.
24:11 [G] the man to whom you are making the loan **bring** the pledge **out**
25:17 [A] did to you along the way when you **came out** of Egypt.
26: 8 [G] So the LORD **brought** us **out** of Egypt with a mighty hand
28: 6 [A] be blessed when you come in and blessed when you **go out**.
28: 7 [A] *They will* **come** at you from one direction but flee from you
28:19 [A] be cursed when you come in and cursed when you **go out**.
28:25 [A] *You will* **come** at them from one direction but flee from them
28:38 [G] *You will* **sow** much seed *in* the field but you will harvest
28:57 [A] the afterbirth **[NIE]** from her womb and the children she
29: 7 [29:6] [A] and Og king of Bashan **came out** to fight against us,
29:25 [29:24] [G] with them when he **brought** them **out** of Egypt.
31: 2 [A] years old and I am no longer able to **lead** [+995+2256] you.
33:18 [A] "Rejoice, Zebulun, in your **going out**, and you, Issachar,
Jos 2: 3 [G] "**Bring out** the men who came to you and entered your
2: 5 [A] At dusk, when it was time to close the city gate, the men **left**.
2: 7 [A] and as soon as the pursuers *had* **gone out**, the gate was shut.

Jos 2:10 [A] water of the Red Sea for you when you **came out** of Egypt,
2:19 [A] If anyone **goes** outside your house into the street, his blood
5: 4 [A] All those who **came out** of Egypt—all the men of military
5: 4 [A] died in the desert on the way after **leaving** Egypt.
5: 5 [A] All the people that **came out** had been circumcised, but all
5: 5 [A] all the people born in the desert during the journey **[RPH]**
5: 6 [A] who were of military age *when* they **left** Egypt had died,
6: 1 [A] of the Israelites. No *one* **went out** and no one came in.
6:10 [A] do not raise your voices, *do* not **say** [+4946+7023] a word
6:22 [G] and **bring** her **out** and all who belong to her,
6:23 [G] **brought out** Rahab, her father and mother and brothers and
6:23 [G] *They* **brought out** her entire family and put them in a place
8: 5 [A] and when the men **come out** against us, as they did before,
8: 6 [A] *They will* **pursue** [+339] us until we have lured them away
8:14 [A] all the men of the city hurried **out** early in the morning to
8:17 [A] a man remained in Ai or Bethel who *did* not **go** after Israel.
8:22 [A] The men of the ambush also **came out** of the city against
9:12 [A] we packed it at home on the day we **left** to come to you.
10:22 [G] the mouth of the cave and **bring** those five kings **out** to me."
10:23 [G] *they* **brought** the five kings **out** of the cave—the kings of
10:24 [G] When they *had* **brought** these kings to Joshua, he
11: 4 [A] They **came out** with all their troops and a large number of
14:11 [A] I'm just as vigorous to **go out** to battle now as I was then.
15: 3 [A] **crossed** south of Scorpion Pass, continued on to Zin
15: 4 [A] then passed along to Azmon and **joined** the Wadi of Egypt,
15: 9 [A] **came out** at the towns of Mount Ephron and went down
15:11 [A] It **went** to the northern slope of Ekron, turned toward
15:11 [A] passed along to Mount Baalah and **reached** Jabneel.
16: 1 [A] The allotment for Joseph **began** at the Jordan of Jericho,
16: 2 [A] *It* **went on** from Bethel (that is, Luz), crossed over to the
16: 6 [A] **continued** to the sea. From Micmethath on the north it
16: 7 [A] and Naarah, touched Jericho and **came out** at the Jordan.
18:11 [A] Their allotted territory **lay** between the tribes of Judah
18:15 [A] The southern side **began** at the outskirts of Kiriath Jearim on
18:15 [A] the boundary **came out** at the spring of the waters of
18:17 [A] It then curved north, **went** *to* En Shemesh, continued to
18:17 [A] curved north, went to En Shemesh, **continued** to Geliloth,
19: 1 [A] The second lot **came out** for the tribe of Simeon, clan by
19:12 [A] of Kisloth Tabor and **went on** to Daberath and up to Japhia.
19:13 [A] Eth Kazin; *it* **came out** at Rimmon and turned toward Neah.
19:17 [A] The fourth lot **came out** for Issachar, clan by clan.
19:24 [A] The fifth lot **came out** for the tribe of Asher, clan by clan.
19:27 [A] north to Beth Emek and Neiel, **passing** Cabul on the left.
19:32 [A] The sixth lot **came out** for Naphtali, clan by clan:
19:34 [A] ran west through Aznoth Tabor and **came out** at Hukkok.
19:40 [A] The seventh lot **came out** for the tribe of Dan, clan by clan.
19:47 [A] **had difficulty taking possession** [+4946] **of** their territory,
21: 4 [A] The first lot **came out** for the Kohathites, clan by clan. The
24: 5 [G] the Egyptians by what I did there, and *I* **brought** you **out**.
24: 6 [G] When *I* **brought** your fathers **out** of Egypt, you came to the
Jdg 1:24 [A] the spies saw a man **coming out** of the city and they said to
2:12 [G] God of their fathers, who *had* **brought** them **out** of Egypt.
2:15 [A] Whenever Israel **went out** to fight, the hand of the LORD
3:10 [A] upon him, so that he became Israel's judge and **went** to war.
3:19 [A] The king said, "Quiet!" And all his attendants **left** him.
3:22 [A] the handle sank in after the blade, *which* **came out** his back.
3:23 [A] Ehud **went out** to the porch; he shut the doors of the upper
3:24 [A] After he *had* **gone**, the servants came and found the doors of
4:14 [A] *Has* not the LORD **gone** ahead of you?" So Barak went
4:18 [A] Jael **went out** to meet Sisera and said to him, "Come,
4:22 [A] came by in pursuit of Sisera, and Jael **went out** to meet him.
5: 4 [A] "O LORD, when you **went out** from Seir, when you
5:31 [A] may they who love you be like the sun *when it* **rises** in its
6: 8 [G] I brought you up out of Egypt, **out** of the land of slavery.
6:18 [G] I come back and **bring** my offering and set it before you."
6:19 [G] *he* **brought** them **out** and offered them to him under the oak.
6:30 [G] men of the town demanded of Joash, "**Bring out** your son.
8:30 [A] He had seventy sons **of his own** [+2257+3751], for he had
9:15 [A] *let* fire **come out** of the thornbush and consume the cedars of
9:20 [A] *let* fire **come out** from Abimelech and consume you,
9:20 [A] of Shechem and Beth Millo, and *let* fire **come out** from you,
9:27 [A] After *they had* **gone out** *into* the fields and gathered the
9:29 [A] I would say to Abimelech, '**Call out** your whole army!' "
9:33 [A] When Gaal and his men **come out** against you, do whatever
9:35 [A] Now Gaal son of Ebed *had* **gone out** and was standing at the
9:38 [A] Aren't these the men you ridiculed? **Go out** and fight them!"
9:39 [A] So Gaal **led out** [+4200+7156] the citizens of Shechem
9:42 [A] The next day the people of Shechem **went out** *to* the fields,
9:43 [A] When he saw the people **coming out** of the city, he rose to
11: 3 [A] adventurers gathered around him and **followed** [+6640] him.
11:31 [A] **whatever**[s] [+2021] comes out of the door of my house to
11:31 [A] whatever **comes out** of the door of my house to meet me
11:34 [A] *who should* **come out** to meet him but his daughter, dancing
11:36 [A] Do to me just as you **promised** [+4946+7023], now
13:14 [A] She must not eat anything that **comes** from the grapevine,
14:14 [A] He replied, "**Out** of the eater, something to eat; out of the
14:14 [A] something to eat; **out** of the strong, something sweet."
15:19 [A] up the hollow place in Lehi, and water **came out** of it.
16:20 [A] and thought, "*I'll* **go out** as before and shake myself free."
19:22 [G] "**Bring out** the man who came to your house so we can have
19:23 [A] The owner of the house **went outside** and said to them, "No,
19:24 [G] *I will* **bring** them **out** to you now, and you can use them
19:25 [G] So the man took his concubine and **sent** her outside to them,
19:27 [A] door of the house and **stepped out** to continue on his way,
20: 1 [A] and from the land of Gilead **came out** as one man
20:14 [A] they came together at Gibeah to **fight** [+2021+4200+4878]
20:20 [A] The men of Israel **went out** to fight the Benjamites and took
20:21 [A] The Benjamites **came out** of Gibeah and cut down
20:25 [A] when the Benjamites **came out** from Gibeah to oppose them,
20:28 [A] "Shall we **go up** again to battle with Benjamin our brother,
20:31 [A] The Benjamites **came out** to meet them and were drawn
21:21 [A] When the girls of Shiloh **come out** to join in the dancing,
21:21 [A] **rush** from the vineyards and each of you seize a wife from
21:24 [A] left that place and **went** home to their tribes and clans,
Ru 1: 7 [A] With her two daughters-in-law *she* **left** the place where she
1:13 [A] because the LORD's hand *has* **gone out** against me!"
2:18 [G] Ruth also **brought out** and gave her what she had left over
2:22 [A] "It will be good for you, my daughter, *to* **go** with his girls,
1Sa 2: 3 [A] so proudly or *let* your mouth **speak** such arrogance,
4: 1 [A] Now the Israelites **went out** to fight against the Philistines.
7:11 [A] The men of Israel **rushed out** of Mizpah and pursued the
8:20 [A] with a king to lead us and *to* **go out** before us and fight our
9:11 [A] they met some girls **coming out** to draw water, and they
9:14 [A] **coming** toward them on his way up to the high place.
9:26 [A] When Saul got ready, he and Samuel **went** outside together.
11: 3 [A] if no one comes to rescue us, *we will* **surrender** to you."
11: 7 [A] done to the oxen of anyone who *does* not **follow** [+339] Saul
11: 7 [A] LORD fell on the people, and *they* **turned out** as one man.
11:10 [A] to the Ammonites, "Tomorrow *we will* **surrender** to you,
12: 8 [G] *who* **brought** your forefathers **out** of Egypt and settled them
13:10 [A] the offering, Samuel arrived, and Saul **went out** to greet him.
13:17 [A] Raiding parties **went out** from the Philistine camp in three
13:23 [A] Now a detachment of Philistines *had* **gone out** to the pass at
14:11 [A] "The Hebrews *are* **crawling out** of the holes they were
14:41 [A] and Saul were taken by lot, and the men *were* **cleared**.
17: 4 [A] who was from Gath, **came out** of the Philistine camp.
17: 8 [A] of Israel, "Why *do you* **come out** and line up for battle?
17:20 [A] He reached the camp as the army *was* **going out** to its battle
17:35 [A] *I* **went** after it, struck it and rescued the sheep from its
17:55 [A] As Saul watched David **going out** to meet the Philistine,
18: 5 [A] David **did**[s] it so successfully that Saul gave him a high rank
18: 6 [A] the women **came out** from all the towns of Israel to meet
18:13 [A] **led** [+995+2256+4200+7156] the troops **in** their **campaigns**.
18:16 [A] he **led** [+995+2256+4200+7156] them **in** their **campaigns**.
18:30 [A] The Philistine commanders *continued to* **go out** to battle,
18:30 [A] continued to go out to battle, and as often as they **did**[s],
19: 3 [A] I *will* **go out** and stand with my father in the field where you
19: 8 [A] broke out, and David **went out** and fought the Philistines.
20:11 [A] "Come," Jonathan said, "*let's* **go out** *into* the field." So they
20:11 [A] "let's go out into the field." So *they* **went** there together.
20:35 [A] In the morning Jonathan **went out** *to* the field for his meeting
21: 5 [21:6] [A] have been kept from us, as usual whenever I **set out**.
22: 3 [A] "*Would you let* my father and mother **come** and stay with
23:13 [A] in number, **left** Keilah and kept moving from place to place.
23:13 [A] told that David had escaped from Keilah, *he did* not **go** there.
23:15 [A] of Ziph, he learned that Saul *had* **come out** to take his life.
24: 8 [24:9] [A] David **went out** of the cave and called out to Saul,
24:13 [24:14] [A] old saying goes, 'From evildoers **come** evil deeds,'
24:14 [24:15] [A] "Against whom *has* the king of Israel **come out**?
25:37 [A] when Nabal *was* **sober** [+2021+3516+4946], his wife told him
26:20 [A] The king of Israel *has* **come out** to look for a flea—as one
28: 1 [A] and your men *will* **accompany** [+907] me in the army."
29: 6 [A] I would be pleased *to have* you **serve** [+995+2256] with me
30:21 [A] *They* **came out** to meet David and the people with him.
2Sa 2:12 [A] Ish-Bosheth son of Saul, **left** Mahanaim and went to Gibeon.
2:13 [A] Joab son of Zeruiah and David's men **went out** and met them
2:23 [A] Asahel's stomach, and the spear **came out** through his back.
3:26 [A] Joab then **left** David and sent messengers after Abner,
5: 2 [G] *who* **led** [+906+995+2256] Israel **on** their **military campaigns**.
5:24 [A] because that will mean the LORD *has* **gone out** in front of
6:20 [A] Michal daughter of Saul **came out** to meet him and said,
7:12 [A] who *will* **come** from your own body, and I will establish his
10: 8 [A] The Ammonites **came out** and drew up in battle formation at
10:16 [G] Hadadezer **had** Arameans **brought** from beyond the River;
11: 1 [A] In the spring, at the time when kings **go off to war**, David
11: 8 [A] So Uriah **left** the palace, and a gift from the king was sent
11: 8 [A] left the palace, and a gift from the king *was* **sent** after him.
11:13 [A] in the evening Uriah **went out** to sleep on his mat among his

2Sa 11:17 [A] When the men of the city **came out** and fought against Joab,
11:23 [A] men overpowered us and **came out** against us in the open,
12:30 [G] *He* **took** a great quantity of plunder **from** the city
12:31 [G] **brought out** the people who were there, consigning them to
13: 9 [G] he refused to eat. "**Send** everyone **out** of here," Amnon said.
13: 9 [A] everyone out of here," Amnon said. So everyone **left** him.
13:18 [G] So his servant **put** her **out** [+906+2021+2575] and bolted the
13:39 [A] the spirit of the king longed to **go** to Absalom, for he was
15:16 [A] The king **set out**, with his entire household following him;
15:17 [A] So the king **set out**, with all the people following him,
16: 5 [A] a man from the same clan as Saul's family **came out** from
16: 5 [A] Shimei son of Gera, and he cursed *as he* **came out** [+3655].
16: 5 [A] Shimei son of Gera, and he cursed *as he* **came out** [+3655].
16: 7 [A] As he cursed, Shimei said, "**Get out**, get out, you man of
16: 7 [A] he cursed, Shimei said, "Get out, **get out**, *you* man of blood,
16:11 [A] all his officials, "My son, who *is* **of** [+4946] my own flesh,
18: 2 [A] "*I* myself *will* **surely march out** [+3655] with you."
18: 2 [A] "*I* myself *will* **surely march out** [+3655] with you."
18: 3 [A] the men said, "*You must* not **go out**; if we are forced to flee,
18: 4 [A] the gate while all the men **marched out** in units of hundreds
18: 6 [A] The army **marched into** the field to fight Israel,
19: 7 [19:8] [A] Now go **out** and encourage your men. I swear by the
19: 7 [19:8] [A] I swear by the LORD that if you don't **go out**, not a
19:19 [19:20] [A] wrong on the day my lord the king **left** Jerusalem.
20: 7 [A] all the mighty warriors **went out** under the command of
20: 7 [A] *They* **marched out** from Jerusalem to pursue Sheba son of
20: 8 [A] As he **stepped forward**, it dropped out of its sheath.
21:17 [A] saying, "Never again *will you* **go out** with us to battle,
22:20 [A] *He* **brought** me **out** into a spacious place; he rescued me
22:49 [G] *who* **sets** me **free** from my enemies. You exalted me above
24: 4 [A] so they **left** the presence of the king to enroll the fighting
24: 7 [A] Finally, *they* **went on** to Beersheba in the Negev of Judah.
24:20 [A] he **went out** and bowed down before the king with his face to
1Ki 2:30 [A] "The king says, '**Come out**!' " But he answered, "No, I will
2:36 [A] in Jerusalem and live there, but *do* not **go** anywhere else.
2:37 [A] The day you **leave** and cross the Kidron Valley, you can be
2:42 [A] and warn you, 'On the day you **leave** to go anywhere else,
2:46 [A] and *he* **went out** and struck Shimei down and killed him.
3: 7 [A] and do not know how *to* **carry** [+995+2256] **out** *my* **duties**.
4:33 [5:13] [A] of Lebanon to the hyssop that **grows out** of walls.
6: 1 [A] and eightieth year after the Israelites *had* **come out** of Egypt,
8: 9 [A] a covenant with the Israelites after they **came out** of Egypt.
8:10 [A] When the priests **withdrew** from the Holy Place, the cloud
8:16 [G] 'Since the day *I* **brought** my people Israel **out** of Egypt,
8:19 [A] your son, who *is* your own **flesh and blood** [+2743+4946]—
8:21 [G] made with our fathers when he **brought** them **out** of Egypt."
8:44 [A] "When your people **go** to war against their enemies,
8:51 [G] and your inheritance, whom *you* **brought out** of Egypt,
8:53 [G] O Sovereign LORD, **brought** our fathers **out** of Egypt."
9: 9 [G] who **brought** their fathers **out** of Egypt, and have embraced
9:12 [A] when Hiram **went** from Tyre to see the towns that Solomon
10:29 [A] *They* **imported** [+2256+6590] a chariot from Egypt for six
10:29 [G] They also **exported** *them* to all the kings of the Hittites
11:29 [A] About that time Jeroboam *was* **going out** of Jerusalem,
12:25 [A] and lived there. From there *he* **went out** and built up Peniel.
15:17 [A] and fortified Ramah to prevent *anyone* from **leaving**
17:13 [G] cake of bread for me from what you have and **bring** it to me,
19:11 [A] "**Go out** and stand on the mountain in the presence of the
19:13 [A] he pulled his cloak over his face and **went out** and stood at
20:16 [A] *They* **set out** at noon while Ben-Hadad and the 32 kings
20:17 [A] The young officers of the provincial commanders **went out**
20:17 [A] who reported, "Men *are* **advancing** from Samaria."
20:18 [A] He said, "If *they have* **come out** for peace, take them alive;
20:18 [A] them alive; if *they have* **come out** for war, take them alive."
20:19 [A] **marched out** of the city with the army behind them
20:21 [A] The king of Israel **advanced** and overpowered the horses
20:31 [A] *Let us* **go** to the king of Israel with sackcloth around our
20:33 [A] When Ben-Hadad **came out**, Ahab had him come up into his
20:39 [A] out to him, "Your servant **went** into the thick of the battle,
21:10 [G] and the king. Then **take** him **out** and stone him to death."
21:13 [G] So *they* **took** him outside the city and stoned him to death.
22:21 [A] Finally, a spirit **came forward**, stood before the LORD
22:22 [A] " '*I will* **go out** and be a lying spirit in the mouths of all his
22:22 [A] will succeed in enticing him,' said the LORD. '**Go** and do it.'
22:34 [G] chariot driver, "Wheel around and **get** me **out** of the fighting.
2Ki 2: 3 [A] The company of the prophets at Bethel **came out** to Elisha
2:21 [A] *he* **went out** to the spring and threw the salt into it, saying,
2:23 [A] some youths **came out** of the town and jeered at him.
2:24 [A] two bears **came out** of the woods and mauled forty-two of
3: 6 [A] So at that time King Joram **set out** from Samaria
4:18 [A] The child grew, and one day *he* **went out** to his father,
4:21 [A] the bed of the man of God, then shut the door and **went out**.
4:37 [A] bowed to the ground. Then she took her son and **went out**.
4:39 [A] One of them **went out** into the fields to gather herbs
5: 2 [A] Now bands from Aram *had* **gone out** and had taken captive a
5:11 [A] "I thought that *he would* **surely come out** [+3655] to me
5:11 [A] "I thought that *he would* **surely come out** [+3655] to me
5:27 [A] Gehazi **went** from Elisha's presence and he was leprous,
6:15 [A] the man of God got up and **went out** early the next morning,
7:12 [A] so *they have* **left** the camp to hide in the countryside,
7:12 [A] '*They will* surely **come out**, and then we will take them alive
7:16 [A] the people **went out** and plundered the camp of the
8: 3 [A] and **went** to the king to beg for her house and land.
9:11 [A] When Jehu **went out** to his fellow officers, one of them
9:15 [A] don't *let* anyone **slip out** of the city to go and tell the news in
9:21 [A] Joram king of Israel and Ahaziah king of Judah **rode out**,
9:21 [A] rode out, each in his own chariot, **[RPH]** to meet Jehu.
9:24 [A] The arrow **pierced** his heart and he slumped down in his
10: 9 [A] The next morning Jehu **went out**. He stood before all the
10:22 [G] of the wardrobe, "**Bring** robes for all the ministers of Baal."
10:22 [G] all the ministers of Baal." So *he* **brought out** robes for them.
10:25 [A] and officers: "Go in and kill them; *let* no one **escape**."
10:26 [G] *They* **brought** the sacred stone **out** *of* the temple of Baal
11: 7 [A] *that* normally **go off** Sabbath **duty** are all to guard the temple
11: 8 [A] close to the king **wherever** he **goes** [+928+928+995+2256]."
11: 9 [A] on duty on the Sabbath and *those who were* **going off duty**—
11:12 [G] Jehoiada **brought out** the king's son and put the crown on
11:15 [G] "**Bring** her **out** between the ranks and put to the sword
12:11 [12:12] [G] *With* it *they* **paid** those who worked on the temple of
12:12 [12:13] [A] **met** all *the other* **expenses** of restoring the temple.
13: 5 [A] for Israel, and *they* **escaped** from the power of Aram.
15:20 [G] Menahem **exacted** this money from Israel. Every wealthy
18: 7 [A] was with him; he was successful in whatever *he* **undertook**.
18:18 [A] and Joah son of Asaph the recorder **went out** to them.
18:31 [A] of Assyria says: Make peace with me and **come out** to me.
19: 9 [A] king ⌞of Egypt⌟, *was* **marching out** to fight against him.
19:27 [A] " 'But I know where you stay and when you come and **go** and
19:31 [A] For out of Jerusalem *will* **come** a remnant, and out of Mount
19:35 [A] That night the angel of the LORD **went out** and put to death
20: 4 [A] Before Isaiah *had* **left** the middle court, the word of the
20:18 [A] your descendants, **your own flesh and blood** [+3870+4946],
21:15 [A] the day their forefathers **came out** of Egypt until this day."
23: 4 [G] the doorkeepers to **remove** from the temple of the LORD
23: 6 [G] *He* **took** the Asherah pole from the temple of the LORD to
24: 7 [A] The king of Egypt *did* not **march out** from his own country
24:12 [A] his nobles and his officials *all* **surrendered** to him.
24:13 [G] Nebuchadnezzar **removed** all the treasures from the temple
1Ch 1:12 [A] Pathrusites, Casluhites (from whom the Philistines **came**)
2:53 [A] From these **descended** the Zorathites and Eshtaolites.
5:18 [A] had 44,760 men **ready for military service** [+7372]—
7:11 [A] There were 17,200 fighting men **ready to go out** [+7372] to
9:28 [G] when they were brought in and *when* they *were* **taken out**.
11: 2 [G] *who* **led** [+906+995+2256] Israel **on** their **military campaigns**.
12:17 [12:18] [A] David **went out** to meet them and said to them,
12:33 [12:34] [A] men of Zebulun, **experienced soldiers** [+7372]
12:36 [12:37] [A] men of Asher, **experienced soldiers** [+7372]
14: 8 [A] for him, but David heard about it and **went out** to meet them.
14:15 [A] marching in the tops of the balsam trees, **move out** to battle,
14:15 [A] because that will mean God *has* **gone out** in front of you to
14:17 [A] So David's fame **spread** throughout every land,
19: 9 [A] The Ammonites **came out** and drew up in battle formation at
19:16 [G] and **had** Arameans **brought** from beyond the River,
20: 1 [A] In the spring, at the time when kings **go off** to war, Joab led
20: 2 [G] *He* **took** a great quantity of plunder **from** the city
20: 3 [G] **brought out** the people who were there, consigning them to
21: 4 [A] so Joab **left** and went throughout Israel and then came back
21:21 [A] *he* **left** the threshing floor and bowed down before David
24: 7 [A] The first lot **fell** to Jehoiarib, the second to Jedaiah,
25: 9 [A] which was for Asaph, **fell** to Joseph, his sons and relatives,
26:14 [A] a wise counselor, and the lot for the North Gate **fell** *to* him.
27: 1 [A] *were* **on duty** [+995+2256] month by month throughout the
2Ch 1:10 [A] that *I may* **lead** [+995+2256+4200+7156] this people, for who
1:17 [G] *They* **imported** [+2256+6590] a chariot from Egypt for six
1:17 [G] They also **exported** them to all the kings of the Hittites
5:10 [A] a covenant with the Israelites after they **came out** of Egypt.
5:11 [A] The priests then **withdrew** from the Holy Place. All the
6: 5 [G] 'Since the day *I* **brought** my people **out** of Egypt, I have not
6: 9 [A] your son, who *is* your own **flesh and blood** [+2743+4946]—
6:34 [A] "When your people **go** to war against their enemies,
7:22 [G] the God of their fathers, who **brought** them **out** of Egypt,
9:28 [G] Solomon's horses *were* **imported** from Egypt and from all
14: 9 [14:8] [A] Zerah the Cushite **marched out** against them with a
14:10 [14:9] [A] Asa **went out** to meet him, and they took up battle
15: 2 [A] *He* **went out** to meet Asa and said to him, "Listen to me, Asa
15: 5 [A] In those days it was not safe to **travel** [+995+2256] **about**,
16: 1 [A] fortified Ramah to prevent *anyone* from **leaving** or entering
16: 2 [G] **took** the silver and gold **out** of the treasuries of the LORD's
18:20 [A] Finally, a spirit **came forward**, stood before the LORD

2Ch 18:21 [A] " '*I will* **go** and be a lying spirit in the mouths of all his
18:21 [A] will succeed in enticing him,' said the LORD. '**Go** and do it.'
18:33 [G] chariot driver, "Wheel around and **get** me **out** of the fighting.
19: 2 [A] the son of Hanani, **went out** to meet him and said to the king,
19: 4 [A] *he* **went out** again among the people from Beersheba to the
20:17 [A] **Go out** to face them tomorrow, and the LORD will be with
20:20 [A] Early in the morning *they* **left** for the Desert of Tekoa. As
20:20 [A] As they **set out**, Jehoshaphat stood and said, "Listen to me,
20:21 [A] praise him for the splendor of his holiness as they **went out**
21:15 [A] until the disease causes your bowels *to* **come out**.' "
21:19 [A] at **[NIE]** the end of the second year, his bowels came out
21:19 [A] his bowels **came out** because of the disease, and he died in
22: 7 [A] *he* **went out** with Joram to meet Jehu son of Nimshi,
23: 7 [A] close to the king **wherever** he **goes** [+928+928+995+2256]."
23: 8 [A] on duty on the Sabbath and *those who were* **going off duty**—
23:11 [G] Jehoiada and his sons **brought out** the king's son and put the
23:14 [G] Jehoiada the priest **sent out** the commanders of units of a
23:14 [G] "**Bring** her **out** *between* the ranks and put to the sword
24: 5 [A] "**Go** to the towns of Judah and collect the money due
25: 5 [A] hundred thousand men **ready for military service** [+7372],
26: 6 [A] *He* **went** to war against the Philistines and broke down the
26:11 [A] **ready to go out** [+7372] by divisions according to their
26:15 [A] His fame **spread** far and wide, for he was greatly helped
26:18 [A] **Leave** the sanctuary, for you have been unfaithful; and you
26:20 [A] Indeed, he himself was eager to **leave**, because the LORD
28: 9 [A] *he* **went out** to meet the army when it returned to Samaria.
29: 5 [G] of your fathers. **Remove** all defilement from the sanctuary.
29:16 [G] *They* **brought out** to the courtyard of the LORD's temple
29:16 [G] The Levites took it and **carried** it **out** to the Kidron Valley.
31: 1 [A] the Israelites who were there **went out** to the towns of Judah,
34:14 [G] While they *were* **bringing out** the money that had been
35:20 [A] the Euphrates, and Josiah **marched out** to meet him in battle.
Ezr 1: 7 [G] King Cyrus **brought out** the articles belonging to the temple
1: 7 [G] which Nebuchadnezzar *had* **carried away** from Jerusalem
1: 8 [G] Cyrus king of Persia **had** them **brought** by Mithredath the
8:17 [g] [*I* **sent** [K; see Q 7422] them to Iddo, the leader in Casiphia.]
10: 3 [G] Now let us make a covenant before our God to **send away** all
10:19 [G] (They all gave their hands in pledge to **put away** their wives,
Ne 2:13 [A] By night *I* **went out** through the Valley Gate toward the
3:25 [A] the tower **projecting** from the upper palace near the court of
3:26 [A] the Water Gate toward the east and the **projecting** tower.
3:27 [A] from the great **projecting** tower to the wall of Ophel.
4:21 [4:15] [A] from the first light of dawn till the stars **came out**.
6:19 [G] to me his good deeds and then **telling** him what I said.
8:15 [A] "**Go out** *into* the hill country and bring back branches from
8:16 [A] So the people **went out** and brought back branches and built
9: 7 [G] chose Abram and **brought** him **out** of Ur of the Chaldeans
9:15 [G] and in their thirst *you* **brought** them water from the rock;
Est 1:17 [A] For the queen's conduct *will* **become known** to all the
1:19 [A] *let* him **issue** a royal decree and let it be written in the laws
3:15 [A] Spurred on by the king's command, the couriers **went out**,
4: 1 [A] put on sackcloth and ashes, and **went out** into the city,
4: 6 [A] So Hathach **went out** to Mordecai in the open square of the
5: 9 [A] Haman **went out** that day happy and in high spirits. But
7: 8 [A] As soon as the word **left** the king's mouth, they covered
8:14 [A] The couriers, riding the royal horses, raced **out**, spurred on
8:15 [A] Mordecai **left** the king's presence wearing royal garments of
Job 1:12 [A] Then Satan **went out** from the presence of the LORD.
1:21 [A] "Naked *I* **came** from my mother's womb, and naked I will
2: 7 [A] So Satan **went out** from the presence of the LORD
3:11 [A] did I not perish at birth, and die *as I* **came** from the womb?
5: 6 [A] For hardship *does* not **spring** from the soil, nor does trouble
8:10 [G] *Will they* not **bring forth** words from their understanding?
8:16 [A] plant in the sunshine, **spreading** its shoots over the garden;
10:18 [G] "Why then *did you* **bring** me **out** of the womb? I wish I had
12:22 [G] things of darkness and **brings** deep shadows into the light.
14: 2 [A] *He* **springs up** like a flower and withers away; like a fleeting
15:13 [G] against God and **pour out** such words from your mouth?
20:25 [A] He pulls it **out** of his back, the gleaming point out of his
23:10 [A] that I take; when he has tested me, *I will* **come forth** as gold.
24: 5 [A] in the desert, the poor **go about** their labor of foraging food;
26: 4 [A] utter these words? And whose spirit **spoke** from your mouth?
28: 5 [A] The earth, from which food **comes**, is transformed below as
28:11 [G] the sources of the rivers and **brings** hidden things *to* light.
29: 7 [A] "When I **went** *to* the gate of the city and took my seat in the
31:34 [A] of the clans that I kept silent and *would* not **go** outside
31:40 [A] *let* briers **come up** instead of wheat and weeds instead of
37: 2 [A] roar of his voice, to the rumbling *that* **comes** from his mouth.
38: 8 [A] "Who shut up the sea behind doors when it burst **forth** from
38:29 [A] From whose womb **comes** the ice? Who gives birth to the
38:32 [G] *Can you* **bring forth** the constellations in their seasons
39: 4 [A] and grow strong in the wilds; *they* **leave** and do not return.
39:21 [A] rejoicing in his strength, and **charges** into the fray.
41:20 [41:12] [A] Smoke **pours** from his nostrils as from a boiling pot
41:21 [41:13] [A] sets coals ablaze, and flames **dart** from his mouth.
Ps 17: 2 [A] *May* my vindication **come** from you; may your eyes see
18:19 [18:20] [G] *He* **brought** me **out** into a spacious place;
19: 4 [19:5] [A] Their voice **goes out** into all the earth, their words to
19: 5 [19:6] [A] which is like a bridegroom **coming forth** from his
25:15 [G] the LORD, for only he *will* **release** my feet from the snare.
25:17 [G] of my heart have multiplied; **free** me from my anguish.
31: 4 [31:5] [G] **Free** me from the trap that is set for me, for you are
37: 6 [G] *He will* **make** your righteousness **shine** like the dawn,
41: 6 [41:7] [A] then *he* **goes out** and spreads it abroad.
44: 9 [44:10] [A] humbled us; *you* no *longer* **go out** with our armies.
60:10 [60:12] have rejected us and no longer **go out** with our armies?
66:12 [G] and water, but *you* **brought** us to a place of abundance.
68: 6 [68:7] [G] in families, he **leads forth** the prisoners with singing;
68: 7 [68:8] [A] When you **went out** before your people, O God,
73: 7 [A] From their callous hearts **comes** iniquity; the evil conceits of
78:16 [G] *he* **brought** streams **out** of a rocky crag and made water flow
81: 5 [81:6] [A] a statute for Joseph when he **went out** against Egypt,
88: 8 [88:9] [A] repulsive to them. *I* am confined and cannot **escape**;
104:14 [G] for man to cultivate—**bringing forth** food from the earth:
104:23 [A] Then man **goes out** to his work, to his labor until evening.
105:37 [G] *He* **brought out** Israel, laden with silver and gold, and from
105:38 [A] Egypt was glad when they **left**, because dread of Israel had
105:43 [G] *He* **brought out** his people with rejoicing, his chosen ones
107:14 [G] *He* **brought** them **out** of darkness and the deepest gloom
107:28 [G] in their trouble, and he **brought** them **out** of their distress.
108:11 [108:12] [A] rejected us and no longer **go out** with our armies?
109: 7 [A] When he is tried, *let him be* **found** guilty, and may his
114: 1 [A] When Israel **came out** of Egypt, the house of Jacob from a
121: 8 [A] over your coming and **going** both now and forevermore.
135: 7 [G] with the rain and **brings out** the wind from his storehouses.
136:11 [A] **brought** Israel **out** from among them *His love*
142: 7 [142:8] [G] **Set** me **free** from my prison, that I may praise your
143:11 [G] my life; in your righteousness, **bring** me **out** of trouble.
146: 4 [A] *When* their spirit **departs**, they return to the ground; on that
Pr 7:15 [A] So *I* **came out** to meet you; I looked for you and have found
10:18 [G] hatred has lying lips, and *whoever* **spreads** slander is a fool.
12:13 [A] by his sinful talk, but a righteous man **escapes** trouble.
22:10 [A] Drive out the mocker, and **out goes** strife; quarrels
25: 4 [A] from the silver, and **out comes** material for the silversmith;
25: 8 [G] *do* not **bring** hastily to court, for what will you do in the end
29:11 [G] A fool **gives** full **vent to** his anger, but a wise man keeps
30:27 [A] locusts have no king, yet they **advance** together in ranks;
30:33 [G] For as churning the milk **produces** butter, and as twisting the
30:33 [G] as twisting the nose **produces** blood, so stirring up anger
30:33 [G] nose produces blood, so stirring up anger **produces** strife."
Ecc 4:14 [A] The youth *may have* **come** from prison to the kingship, or he
5: 2 [5:1] [G] do not be hasty in your heart to **utter** anything before
5:15 [5:14] [A] Naked a *man* **comes** from his mother's womb, and as
7:18 [A] the other. The man who fears God *will* **avoid** all ⌞extremes⌟.
10: 5 [A] seen under the sun, the sort of error that **arises** from a ruler:
SS 1: 8 [A] **follow** the tracks of the sheep and graze your young goats by
3:11 [A] **Come out**, you daughters of Zion, and look at King Solomon
5: 6 [A] lover had left; he was gone. My heart **sank** at his departure.
7:11 [7:12] [A] Come, my lover, *let us* **go** *to* the countryside, let us
8:10 [G] Thus I have become in his eyes like *one* **bringing**
Isa 2: 3 [A] The law *will* **go out** from Zion, the word of the LORD from
7: 3 [A] said to Isaiah, "**Go out**, you and your son Shear-Jashub,
11: 1 [A] A shoot *will* **come up** from the stump of Jesse; from his roots
13:10 [A] The **rising** sun will be darkened and the moon will not give
14:29 [A] from the root of that snake *will* **spring up** a viper, its fruit
26:21 [A] the LORD *is* **coming out** of his dwelling to punish the
28:29 [A] All this also **comes** from the LORD Almighty, wonderful in
30:22 [A] like a menstrual cloth and say to them, "**Away** *with you*!"
36: 3 [A] and Joah son of Asaph the recorder **went out** to him.
36:16 [A] of Assyria says: Make peace with me and **come out** to me.
37: 9 [A] king ⌞of Egypt⌟, *was* **marching out** to fight against him.
37:28 [A] "But I know where you stay and when you come and **go** and
37:32 [A] For out of Jerusalem *will* **come** a remnant, and out of Mount
37:36 [A] the angel of the LORD **went out** and put to death a hundred
39: 7 [A] your descendants, **your own flesh and blood** [+3870+4946]
40:26 [G] He *who* **brings out** the starry host one by one, and calls them
42: 1 [G] put my Spirit on him and *he will* **bring** justice to the nations.
42: 3 [G] will not snuff out. In faithfulness *he will* **bring forth** justice;
42: 7 [G] to **free** captives from prison and to release from the dungeon
42:13 [A] The LORD *will* **march out** like a mighty man, like a
43: 8 [G] **Lead out** those who have eyes but are blind, who have ears
43:17 [G] who **drew out** the chariots and horses, the army
45:23 [A] my mouth *has* **uttered** [+4946] in all integrity a word that
48: 1 [A] called by the name of Israel and **come** from the line of Judah,
48: 3 [A] my mouth **announced** them and I made them known;
48:20 [A] **Leave** Babylon, flee from the Babylonians! Announce this
48:20 [G] **Send** it **out** to the ends of the earth; say, "The LORD has
49: 9 [A] to say to the captives, '**Come out**,' and to those in darkness,

Isa 49:17 [A] hasten back, and those who laid you waste **depart** from you.
51: 4 [A] The law *will* **go out** from me; my justice will become a light
51: 5 [A] draws near speedily, my salvation *is* **on the way**,
52:11 [A] Depart, depart, **go out** from there! Touch no unclean thing!
52:11 [A] **Come out** from it and be pure, you who carry the vessels of
52:12 [A] *you will* not **leave** in haste or go in flight; for the LORD
54:16 [G] fans the coals into flame and **forges** a weapon fit for its work.
55:11 [A] so is my word that **goes out** from my mouth: It will not
55:12 [A] *You will* **go out** in joy and be led forth in peace;
61:11 [G] For as the soil **makes** the sprout **come up** and a garden
62: 1 [A] till her righteousness **shines out** like the dawn, her salvation
65: 9 [G] *I will* **bring forth** descendants from Jacob, and from Judah
66:24 [A] "And *they will* **go out** and look upon the dead bodies of
Jer 1: 5 [A] before *you were* **born** [+4946+8167] I set you apart;
2:37 [A] *You will* also **leave** that place with your hands on your head,
4: 4 [A] or my wrath *will* **break out** and burn like fire because of the
4: 7 [A] has set out. *He has* **left** his place to lay waste your land.
5: 6 [A] wait near their towns to tear to pieces any who **venture out**,
6:25 [A] *Do* not **go out** *to* the fields or walk on the roads,
7:22 [G] For when I **brought** your forefathers **out** of Egypt and spoke
7:25 [A] From the time your forefathers **left** Egypt until now, day after
8: 1 [G] and the bones of the people of Jerusalem *will be* **removed**
9: 3 [9:2] [A] *They* **go** from one sin to another; they do not
10:13 [G] with the rain and **brings out** the wind from his storehouses.
10:20 [A] My sons *are* **gone from** me and are no more; no one is left
11: 4 [G] your forefathers when I **brought** them **out** of Egypt,
11:11 [A] 'I will bring on them a disaster they cannot **escape**. Although
14:18 [A] If *I* **go into** the country, I see those slain by the sword; if I go
15: 1 [A] Send them away from my presence! *Let them* **go**!
15: 2 [A] if they ask you, 'Where *shall we* **go**?' tell them, 'This is what
15:19 [G] if *you* **utter** worthy, not worthless, words, you will be my
17:19 [A] the people, through which the kings of Judah go in and **out**;
17:22 [G] *Do* not **bring** a load **out** of your houses or do any work on
19: 2 [A] **go out** to the Valley of Ben Hinnom, near the entrance of the
20: 3 [G] The next day, when Pashhur **released** him from the stocks,
20:18 [A] Why *did I ever* **come out** of the womb to see trouble
21: 9 [A] whoever **goes out** and surrenders to the Babylonians who are
21:12 [A] or my wrath *will* **break out** and burn like fire because of the
22:11 [A] his father as king of Judah but *has* **gone** from this place:
23:15 [A] of Jerusalem ungodliness *has* **spread** throughout the land."
23:19 [A] See, the storm of the LORD *will* **burst out** in wrath, a
25:32 [A] Disaster *is* **spreading** from nation to nation; a mighty storm
26:23 [G] *They* **brought** Uriah **out** of Egypt and took him to King
29: 2 [A] and the artisans *had* **gone** into exile from Jerusalem.)
29:16 [A] your countrymen who *did* not **go** with you into exile—
30:19 [A] From them *will* **come** songs of thanksgiving and the sound of
30:21 [A] be one of their own; their ruler *will* **arise** from among them.
30:23 [A] See, the storm of the LORD *will* **burst out** *in* wrath,
31: 4 [A] up your tambourines and **go out** to dance with the joyful.
31:32 [G] when I took them by the hand to **lead** them **out** of Egypt,
31:39 [A] The measuring line *will* **stretch** *from* there straight to the hill
32:21 [G] *You* **brought** your people Israel **out** of Egypt with signs
34:13 [G] with your forefathers when *I* **brought** them **out** of Egypt,
37: 4 [A] Now Jeremiah was free to come and **go** among the people,
37: 5 [A] Pharaoh's army *had* **marched out** of Egypt, and when the
37: 7 [A] 'Pharaoh's army, which *has* **marched out** to support you,
37:12 [A] Jeremiah *started to* **leave** the city to go to the territory of
38: 2 [A] but whoever **goes over** to the Babylonians will live.
38: 8 [A] Ebed-Melech **went out** of the palace and said to him,
38:17 [A] 'If *you* **surrender** [+3655] to the officers of the king of
38:17 [A] 'If *you* **surrender** [+3655] to the officers of the king of
38:18 [A] if *you will* not **surrender** to the officers of the king of
38:21 [A] if you refuse to **surrender**, this is what the LORD has
38:22 [H] *will* **be brought out** to the officials of the king of Babylon.
38:23 [G] and children *will be* **brought out** to the Babylonians.
39: 4 [A] *they* **left** the city at night by way of the king's garden,
39: 4 [A] gate between the two walls, and **headed** toward the Arabah.
39:14 [G] the son of Shaphan, to **take** him **back** to his home.
41: 6 [A] Ishmael son of Nethaniah **went out** from Mizpah to meet
43:12 [A] wrap Egypt around himself and **depart** from there unscathed.
44:17 [A] We will certainly do everything we **said** [+4946+7023] we
46: 9 [A] **March on**, O warriors—men of Cush and Put who carry
48: 7 [A] Chemosh *will* **go** into exile, together with his priests
48: 9 [a] for *she will be* laid waste [+3655]; [BHS ***fly away***; NIV 5898]
48: 9 [a] for *she will be* laid waste [+3655]; [BHS ***fly away***; NIV 5898]
48:45 [A] for a fire *has* **gone out** from Heshbon, a blaze from the midst
50: 8 [A] **leave** the land of the Babylonians, and be like the goats that
50:25 [G] his arsenal and **brought out** the weapons of his wrath,
51:10 [G] " 'The LORD *has* **vindicated** [+906+7407] us; come, let us
51:16 [G] with the rain and **brings out** the wind from his storehouses.
51:44 [G] **make** him **spew out** [+906+4946+7023] what he has
51:45 [A] "**Come out** of her, my people! Run for your lives! Run from
52: 7 [A] *They* **left** the city at night through the gate between the two
52:31 [G] **freed** him from prison on the twenty-fifth day of the twelfth
La 1: 6 [A] All the splendor *has* **departed** from the Daughter of Zion.
3: 7 [A] He has walled me in so *I* cannot **escape**; he has weighed me
3:38 [A] of the Most High that both calamities and good things **come**?
Eze 1:13 [A] the creatures; it was bright, and lightning **flashed out** of it.
3:22 [A] he said to me, "Get up and **go out** to the plain, and there I
3:23 [A] So I got up and **went out** to the plain. And the glory of the
3:25 [A] will be bound so that *you* cannot **go out** among the people.
5: 4 [A] A fire *will* **spread** from there to the whole house of Israel.
7:10 [A] Doom *has* **burst forth**, the rod has budded, arrogance has
9: 7 [A] **Go**!" So they went out and began killing throughout the city.
9: 7 [A] Go!" So *they* **went out** and began killing throughout the city.
10: 7 [A] into the hands of the man in linen, who took it and **went out**.
10:18 [A] the glory of the LORD **departed** from over the threshold of
10:19 [A] their wings and rose from the ground, and as they **went**,
11: 7 [G] the meat and this city is the pot, but *I will* **drive** you **out** of it.
11: 9 [G] *I will* **drive** you **out** of the city and hand you over to
12: 4 [G] they watch, **bring out** your belongings packed for exile.
12: 4 [A] while they are watching, **go out** like those who go into exile.
12: 5 [G] dig through the wall and **take** your belongings **out** through it.
12: 6 [G] shoulder as they are watching and **carry** them **out** at dusk.
12: 7 [G] During the day *I* **brought out** my things packed for exile.
12: 7 [G] *I* **took** my belongings **out** at dusk, carrying them on my
12:12 [A] them will put his things on his shoulder at dusk and **leave**,
12:12 [G] and a hole will be dug in the wall for him to **go** through.
14:22 [H] sons and daughters who *will* **be brought out** of it.
14:22 [G] They *will* **come** to you, and when you see their conduct
15: 7 [A] Although *they have* **come out** of the fire, the fire will yet
16:14 [A] your fame **spread** among the nations on account of your
19:14 [A] Fire **spread** from one of its main branches and consumed its
20: 6 [G] On that day I swore to them that *I would* **bring** them **out** of
20: 9 [G] myself to the Israelites by **bringing** them **out** of Egypt.
20:10 [G] Therefore *I* **led** them **out** of Egypt and brought them into the
20:14 [G] eyes of the nations in whose sight *I had* **brought** them **out**.
20:22 [G] eyes of the nations in whose sight *I had* **brought** them **out**.
20:34 [G] *I will* **bring** you from the nations and gather you from the
20:38 [G] Although *I will* **bring** them **out** of the land where they are
20:41 [G] I will accept you as fragrant incense when I **bring** you **out**
21: 3 [21:8] [G] *I will* **draw** my sword from its scabbard and cut off
21: 4 [21:9] [A] my sword *will be* **unsheathed** [+4946+9509] against
21: 5 [21:10] [G] all people will know that I the LORD *have* **drawn**
21:19 [21:24] [A] to take, both **starting** from the same country.
24: 6 [A] to the pot now encrusted, whose deposit *will* not **go** away!
24: 6 [G] **Empty** it piece by piece without casting lots for them.
24:12 [A] its heavy deposit *has* not *been* **removed**, not even by fire.
26:18 [A] your fall; the islands in the sea are terrified at your **collapse**.'
27:33 [A] When your merchandise **went out** on the seas, you satisfied
28:18 [G] So *I* **made** a fire **come out** from you, and it consumed you,
30: 9 [A] " 'On that day messengers *will* **go out** from me in ships to
33:30 [A] and hear the message that *has* **come** from the LORD.'
34:13 [G] *I will* **bring** them **out** from the nations and gather them from
36:20 [A] are the LORD's people, and yet *they had to* **leave** his land.'
37: 1 [G] *he* **brought** me **out** by the Spirit of the LORD and set me in
38: 4 [G] in your jaws and **bring** you **out** with your whole army—
38: 8 [H] They *had* **been brought out** from the nations, and now all of
39: 9 [A] " 'Then those who live in the towns of Israel *will* **go out**
42: 1 [G] the man **led** me northward into the outer court and brought
42:14 [A] *they are* not *to* **go** into the outer court until they leave behind
42:15 [G] *he* **led** me **out** by the east gate and measured the area all
44: 3 [A] way of the portico of the gateway and **go out** the same way."
44:19 [A] When they **go out** into the outer court where the people are,
46: 2 [A] is to worship at the threshold of the gateway and then **go out**,
46: 8 [A] portico of the gateway, and *he is to* **come out** the same way.
46: 9 [A] whoever enters by the north gate to worship *is to* **go out** the
46: 9 [A] whoever enters by the south gate *is to* **go out** the north gate.
46: 9 [A] by which he entered, but *each is to* **go out** the opposite gate.
46:10 [A] going in when they go in and **going out** when they go out.
46:10 [A] going in when they go in and going out when they **go out**.
46:12 [A] *he shall* **go out**, and after he has gone out, the gate will be
46:12 [A] shall go out, and after he *has* **gone out**, the gate will be shut.
46:20 [G] to avoid **bringing** them into the outer court and consecrating
46:21 [G] *He* then **brought** me to the outer court and led me around to
47: 1 [A] I saw water **coming out** from under the threshold of the
47: 2 [G] *He* then **brought** me **out** through the north gate and led me
47: 3 [A] As the man **went** eastward with a measuring line in his hand,
47: 8 [A] "This water **flows** toward the eastern region and goes down
47: 8 [H] *When* it **empties** into the Sea, the water there becomes fresh.
47:12 [A] because the water from the sanctuary **flows** *to* them.
Da 8: 9 [A] Out of one of them **came** another horn, which started small
9:15 [G] who **brought** your people **out** of Egypt with a mighty hand
9:22 [A] *I have* now **come** to give you insight and understanding.
9:23 [A] As soon as you began to pray, an answer *was* **given**, which I
10:20 [A] of Persia, and when I **go**, the prince of Greece will come;
11:11 [A] "Then the king of the South *will* **march out** in a rage and
11:44 [A] *he will* **set out** in a great rage to destroy and annihilate many.

Hos 6: 5 [A] my mouth; my judgments **flashed** like lightning *upon* you.
9: 13 [G] But Ephraim *will* **bring out** their children to the slayer."
Joel 2: 16 [A] *Let* the bridegroom **leave** his room and the bride her
3: 18 [4:18] [A] A fountain *will* **flow out** of the LORD's house
Am 4: 3 [A] *You will* each **go** straight **out** through breaks in the wall,
5: 3 [A] "The city that **marches out** a thousand strong for Israel will
5: 3 [A] the town that **marches out** a hundred strong will have only
6: 10 [G] is to burn the bodies comes to carry them **out** of the house
Jnh 4: 5 [A] Jonah **went out** and sat down at a place east of the city.
Mic 1: 3 [A] The LORD *is* **coming** from his dwelling place; he comes
1: 11 [A] live in Shaphir. Those who live in Zaanan *will* not **come out**.
2: 13 [A] up before them; they will break through the gate and **go out**.
4: 2 [A] The law *will* **go out** from Zion, the word of the LORD from
4: 10 [A] for now *you must* **leave** the city to camp in the open field.
5: 2 [5:1] [A] out of you *will* **come** for me one who will be ruler
7: 9 [G] *He will* **bring** me **out** into the light; I will see his
7: 15 [A] "As in the days when you **came out** of Egypt, I will show
Na 1: 11 [A] ˻O Nineveh,˼ *has one* **come forth** who plots evil against the
Hab 1: 4 [A] Therefore the law is paralyzed, and justice never **prevails**.
1: 4 [A] The wicked hem in the righteous, so that justice **is** perverted.
1: 7 [A] they are a law to themselves and **promote** their own honor.
3: 5 [A] Plague went before him; pestilence **followed** his steps.
3: 13 [A] *You* **came out** to deliver your people, to save your anointed
Hag 1: 11 [G] the oil and whatever the ground **produces**, on men and cattle,
2: 5 [A] 'This is what I covenanted with you when you **came out** of
Zec 2: 3 [2:7] [A] the angel who was speaking to me **left**, and another
2: 3 [2:7] [A] to me left, and another angel **came** to meet him
4: 7 [G] *he will* **bring out** the capstone to shouts of 'God bless it!'
5: 3 [A] "This is the curse that *is* **going out** over the whole land;
5: 4 [G] The LORD Almighty declares, '*I will* **send** it **out**, and it will
5: 5 [A] the angel who was speaking to me **came forward** and said to
5: 5 [A] said to me, "Look up and see what this is that *is* **appearing**."
5: 6 [A] **[RPH]** And he added, "This is the iniquity of the people
5: 9 [A] there before me **were** two women, with the wind in their
6: 1 [A] there before me were four chariots **coming out** from between
6: 5 [A] **going out** from standing in the presence of the Lord of the
6: 6 [A] The one with the black horses *is* **going** toward the north
6: 6 [A] the one with the white horses **[RPH]** toward the west,
6: 6 [A] the one with the dappled horses **[RPH]** toward the south."
6: 7 [A] When the powerful horses **went out**, they were straining to
6: 8 [A] those **going** toward the north country have given my Spirit
8: 10 [A] No one *could* **go** [+995+2256] **about** *his* **business** safely
9: 14 [A] will appear over them; his arrow *will* **flash** like lightning.
10: 4 [A] From Judah *will* **come** the cornerstone, from him the tent
14: 2 [A] Half of the city *will* **go** into exile, but the rest of the people
14: 3 [A] Then the LORD *will* **go out** and fight against those nations,
14: 8 [A] On that day living water *will* **flow out** from Jerusalem,
Mal 4: 2 [3:20] [A] *you will* **go out** and leap like calves released from the

3656 יָצַב *yāṣab*, v. [48 / 49] [cf. 5893, 5895; Ar 10326]

stood [6], stand [5], confront [3], stand up [3], took stand [3], present themselves [2], present yourselves [2], presented themselves [2], serve [2], stay [2], take positions [2], commits himself [1], kept distance [+4946+5584] [1], place [1], present himself [1], sided [1], stand firm [1], stand out [1], stand still [1], standing [1], station myself [1], take a stand [1], take place [1], take stand [1], take up positions [1], took places [1], wait [1], withstand [+6640] [1]

Ex 2: 4 [F] His sister **stood** at a distance to see what would happen to
8: 20 [8:16] [F] **confront** Pharaoh as he goes to the water and say to
9: 13 [F] **confront** Pharaoh and say to him, 'This is what the LORD,
14: 13 [F] **Stand firm** and you will see the deliverance the LORD will
19: 17 [F] to meet with God, and *they* **stood** at the foot of the mountain.
34: 5 [F] the cloud and **stood** there with him and proclaimed his name,
Nu 11: 16 [F] to the Tent of Meeting, that *they may* **stand** there with you.
22: 22 [F] and the angel of the LORD **stood** in the road to oppose him.
23: 3 [F] to Balak, "**Stay** here beside your offering while I go aside.
23: 15 [F] "**Stay** here beside your offering while I meet with him over
Dt 7: 24 [F] No one *will be able to* **stand up** against you; you will
9: 2 [F] heard it said: "Who *can* **stand up** against the Anakites?"
11: 25 [F] No man *will be able to* **stand** against you. The LORD your
31: 14 [F] Call Joshua and **present yourselves** at the Tent of Meeting,
31: 14 [F] and **presented themselves** at the Tent of Meeting.
Jos 1: 5 [F] No one *will be able to* **stand up** against you all the days of
24: 1 [F] of Israel, and *they* **presented themselves** before God.
Jdg 20: 2 [F] Israel **took** *their* **places** in the assembly of the people of God,
1Sa 3: 10 [F] The LORD came and **stood** there, calling as at the other
10: 19 [F] So now **present yourselves** before the LORD by your tribes
10: 23 [F] *as he* **stood** among the people he was a head taller than any
12: 7 [F] Now then, **stand** here, because I am going to confront you
12: 16 [F] **stand still** and see this great thing the LORD is about to do
17: 16 [F] forward every morning and evening and **took** *his* **stand**.
2Sa 18: 13 [F] you *would have* **kept** *your* **distance** [+4946+5584] *from*
18: 30 [F] The king said, "Stand aside and **wait** here." So he stepped
21: 5 [F] have been decimated and *have* no **place** anywhere in Israel,
23: 12 [F] Shammah **took** *his* **stand** in the middle of the field. He
1Ch 11: 14 [F] *they* **took** *their* **stand** in the middle of the field. They
2Ch 11: 13 [F] Levites from all their districts throughout Israel **sided** with
20: 6 [F] are in your hand, and no one *can* **withstand** [+6640] you.
20: 17 [F] **Take up** *your* **positions**; stand firm and see the deliverance
Job 1: 6 [F] One day the angels came to **present themselves** before the
2: 1 [F] On another day the angels came to **present themselves**
2: 1 [F] Satan also came with them to **present himself** before him.
33: 5 [F] me then, if you can; prepare yourself and **confront** me.
38: 14 [F] under a seal; its features **stand out** like those of a garment.
41: 10 [41:2] [F] to rouse him. Who then *is able to* **stand** against me?
Ps 2: 2 [F] The kings of the earth **take** *their* **stand** and the rulers gather
5: 5 [5:6] [F] The arrogant cannot **stand** in your presence; you hate
36: 4 [36:5] [F] *he* **commits himself** to a sinful course and does not
94: 16 [F] the wicked? Who *will* **take a stand** for me against evildoers?
Pr 22: 29 [F] *He will* **serve** before kings; he will not serve before obscure
22: 29 [F] will serve before kings; *he will* not **serve** before obscure men.
Jer 46: 4 [F] mount the steeds! **Take** *your* **positions** with helmets on!
46: 14 [F] '**Take** *your* **positions** and get ready, for the sword devours
Eze 26: 20 [F] or **take** *your* **place** [BHS 5989] in the land of the living.
Hab 2: 1 [F] I will stand at my watch and **station myself** on the ramparts;
Zec 6: 5 [F] going out from **standing** in the presence of the Lord of the

3657 יָצַג *yāṣag*, v. [16] [cf. 3668]

set [4], made [2], placed [2], leave behind [1], leave [1], maintain [1], make bare [1], place [1], presented [1], separate [+906+963+4200] [1], touch [1]

Ge 30: 38 [G] *he* **placed** the peeled branches in all the watering troughs,
33: 15 [G] Esau said, "Then *let me* **leave** some of my men with you."
43: 9 [G] I do not bring him back to you and **set** him here before you,
47: 2 [G] five of his brothers and **presented** them before Pharaoh.
Ex 10: 24 [H] may go with you; only **leave** your flocks and herds **behind**."
Dt 28: 56 [G] gentle that she would not venture *to* **touch** the ground *with*
Jdg 6: 37 [G] look, I *will* **place** a wool fleece on the threshing floor.
7: 5 [G] "**Separate** [+906+963+4200] those who lap the water with
8: 27 [G] the gold into an ephod, which *he* **placed** in Ophrah, his town.
1Sa 5: 2 [G] carried the ark into Dagon's temple and **set** it beside Dagon.
2Sa 6: 17 [G] **set** it in its place inside the tent that David had pitched for it,
1Ch 16: 1 [G] of God and **set** it inside the tent that David had pitched for it,
Job 17: 6 [G] "God *has* **made** me a byword *to* everyone, a man in whose
Jer 51: 34 [G] has thrown us into confusion, *he has* **made** us an empty jar.
Hos 2: 3 [2:5] [G] and **make** her as **bare** as on the day she was born;
Am 5: 15 [G] Hate evil, love good; **maintain** justice in the courts.

3658 [1]יִצְהָר *yiṣhār*[1], n.[m.]. [23] [→ 3659, 3660; cf. 7414]

oil [20], anointed [+1201+2021] [1], olive oil [1], olive trees [+2339] [1]

Nu 18: 12 "I give you all the finest **olive oil** and all the finest new wine
Dt 7: 13 the crops of your land—your grain, new wine and **oil**—
11: 14 so that you may gather in your grain, new wine and **oil**.
12: 17 eat in your own towns the tithe of your grain and new wine and **oil**,
14: 23 Eat the tithe of your grain, new wine and **oil**, and the firstborn of
18: 4 You are to give them the firstfruits of your grain, new wine and **oil**,
28: 51 new wine or **oil**, nor any calves of your herds or lambs of your
2Ki 18: 32 of bread and vineyards, a land of **olive trees** [+2339] and honey.
2Ch 31: 5 new wine, **oil** and honey and all that the fields produced.
32: 28 also made buildings to store the harvest of grain, new wine and **oil**;
Ne 5: 11 the hundredth part of the money, grain, new wine and **oil**."
10: 37 [10:38] of the fruit of all our trees and of our new wine and **oil**.
10: 39 [10:40] **oil** to the storerooms where the articles for the sanctuary
13: 5 new wine and **oil** prescribed for the Levites, singers
13: 12 brought the tithes of grain, new wine and **oil** into the storerooms.
Jer 31: 12 the grain, the new wine and the **oil**, the young of the flocks
Hos 2: 8 [2:10] the new wine and **oil**, who lavished on her the silver
2: 22 [2:24] the new wine and **oil**, and they will respond to Jezreel.
Joel 1: 10 the grain is destroyed, the new wine is dried up, the **oil** fails.
2: 19 "I am sending you grain, new wine and **oil**, enough to satisfy you
2: 24 be filled with grain; the vats will overflow with new wine and **oil**.
Hag 1: 11 the **oil** and whatever the ground produces, on men and cattle,
Zec 4: 14 "These are the two *who are* **anointed** [+1201+2021] to serve the

3659 [2]יִצְהָר *yiṣhār*[2], n.pr.m. [9] [√ 3658; cf. 7414]

Izhar [9]

Ex 6: 18 The sons of Kohath were Amram, **Izhar**, Hebron and Uzziel.
6: 21 The sons of **Izhar** were Korah, Nepheg and Zicri.
Nu 3: 19 The Kohathite clans: Amram, **Izhar**, Hebron and Uzziel.
16: 1 Korah son of **Izhar**, the son of Kohath, the son of Levi, and certain
1Ch 6: 2 [5:28] The sons of Kohath: Amram, **Izhar**, Hebron and Uzziel.
6: 18 [6:3] The sons of Kohath: Amram, **Izhar**, Hebron and Uzziel.
6: 38 [6:23] the son of **Izhar**, the son of Kohath, the son of Levi,
23: 12 sons of Kohath: Amram, **Izhar**, Hebron and Uzziel—four in all.

[F] Hitpael (hitpoel, hitpoal, hitpolel, hitpolal, hitpalel, hitpalal, hitpalpel, hitpalpal, hotpael, hotpaal) [G] Hiphil (hiphtil) [H] Hophal [I] Hishtaphel

1Ch 23:18 The sons of **Izhar**: Shelomith was the first.

3660 יִצְהָרִי *yiṣhārî*, a.g. [4] [√ 3658; cf. 7414]

Izharites [4]

Nu 3:27 the clans of the Amramites, **Izharites**, Hebronites and Uzzielites;
1Ch 24:22 From the **Izharites**: Shelomoth; from the sons of Shelomoth:
26:23 the Amramites, the **Izharites**, the Hebronites and the Uzzielites:
26:29 From the **Izharites**: Kenaniah and his sons were assigned duties

3661 [1]יָצוּעַ *yāṣûa'*[1], n.[m.]. [5] [√ 3667]

bed [2], bed [+6911] [1], couch [1], marriage bed [1]

Ge 49:4 you went up onto your father's bed, onto my **couch** and defiled it.
1Ch 5:1 was the firstborn, but when he defiled his father's **marriage bed**,
Job 17:13 home I hope for is the grave, if I spread out my **bed** in darkness,
Ps 63:6 [63:7] On my **bed** I remember you; I think of you through the
132:3 "I will not enter my house or go to my **bed** [+6911]—

3662 [2]יָצוּעַ *yāṣûa'*[2], n.[m.]. [0]

1Ki 6:5 [he built a **structure** [K; see Q 3666] around the building,]
6:6 [The lowest **floor** [K; see Q 3666] was five cubits wide, the middle]
6:10 [And he built the **side rooms** [K; see Q 3666] all along the temple.]

3663 יִצְחָק *yiṣḥāq*, n.pr.m. [108] [√ 7464; cf. 3773]

Isaac [100], Isaac's [3], he[s] [2], *untranslated* [1], his[s] [1], who[s] [1]

Ge 17:19 your wife Sarah will bear you a son, and you will call him **Isaac**.
17:21 my covenant I will establish with **Isaac**, whom Sarah will bear to
21:3 Abraham gave the name **Isaac** to the son Sarah bore him.
21:4 When his son **Isaac** was eight days old, Abraham circumcised him,
21:5 Abraham was a hundred years old when his son **Isaac** was born to
21:8 and on the day **Isaac** was weaned Abraham held a great feast.
21:10 son will never share in the inheritance with my son **Isaac**."
21:12 because it is through **Isaac** that your offspring will be reckoned.
22:2 God said, "Take your son, your only son, **Isaac**, whom you love,
22:3 He took with him two of his servants and his son **Isaac**.
22:6 took the wood for the burnt offering and placed it on his son **Isaac**,
22:7 **Isaac** spoke up and said to his father Abraham, "Father?"
22:9 He bound his son **Isaac** and laid him on the altar, on top of the
24:4 and my own relatives and get a wife for my son **Isaac**."
24:14 let her be the one you have chosen for your servant **Isaac**.
24:62 Now **Isaac** had come from Beer Lahai Roi, for he was living in the
24:63 **He**[s] went out to the field one evening to meditate, and as he looked
24:64 Rebekah also looked up and saw **Isaac**. She got down from her
24:66 Then the servant told **Isaac** all he had done.
24:67 **Isaac** brought her into the tent of his mother Sarah, and he married
24:67 he loved her; and **Isaac** was comforted after his mother's death.
25:5 Abraham left everything he owned to **Isaac**.
25:6 and sent them away from his son **Isaac** to the land of the east.
25:9 His sons **Isaac** and Ishmael buried him in the cave of Machpelah
25:11 God blessed his son **Isaac**, who then lived near Beer Lahai Roi.
25:11 God blessed his son Isaac, **who**[s] then lived near Beer Lahai Roi.
25:19 This is the account of Abraham's son **Isaac**. Abraham became the
25:19 of Abraham's son Isaac. Abraham became the father of **Isaac**,
25:20 **Isaac** was forty years old when he married Rebekah daughter of
25:21 **Isaac** prayed to the LORD on behalf of his wife, because she was
25:26 **Isaac** was sixty years old when Rebekah gave birth to them.
25:28 **Isaac**, who had a taste for wild game, loved Esau, but Rebekah
26:1 and **Isaac** went to Abimelech king of the Philistines in Gerar.
26:6 So **Isaac** stayed in Gerar.
26:8 down from a window and saw **Isaac** caressing his wife Rebekah.
26:9 So Abimelech summoned **Isaac** and said, "She is really your wife!
26:9 **Isaac** answered him, "Because I thought I might lose my life on
26:12 **Isaac** planted crops in that land and the same year reaped a
26:16 Abimelech said to **Isaac**, "Move away from us; you have become
26:17 So **Isaac** moved away from there and encamped in the Valley of
26:18 **Isaac** reopened the wells that had been dug in the time of his father
26:19 **Isaac's** servants dug in the valley and discovered a well of fresh
26:20 But the herdsmen of Gerar quarreled with **Isaac's** herdsmen
26:25 There he pitched his tent, and there **his**[s] servants dug a well.
26:27 **Isaac** asked them, "Why have you come to me, since you were
26:31 Then **Isaac** sent them on their way, and they left him in peace.
26:32 That day **Isaac's** servants came and told him about the well they
26:35 They were a source of grief to **Isaac** and Rebekah.
27:1 When **Isaac** was old and his eyes were so weak that he could no
27:5 Now Rebekah was listening as **Isaac** spoke to his son Esau.
27:20 **Isaac** asked his son, "How did you find it so quickly, my son?"
27:21 Then **Isaac** said to Jacob, "Come near so I can touch you,
27:22 Jacob went close to his father **Isaac**, who touched him and said,
27:26 his father **Isaac** said to him, "Come here, my son, and kiss me."
27:30 After **Isaac** finished blessing him and Jacob had scarcely left his
27:30 father's presence, **[RPH]** his brother Esau came in from hunting.
27:32 His father **Isaac** asked him, "Who are you?" "I am your son,"
27:33 **Isaac** trembled violently and said, "Who was it, then, that hunted
27:37 **Isaac** answered Esau, "I have made him lord over you and have
27:39 His father **Isaac** answered him, "Your dwelling will be away from
27:46 Rebekah said to **Isaac**, "I'm disgusted with living because of these
28:1 So **Isaac** called for Jacob and blessed him and commanded him:
28:5 Then **Isaac** sent Jacob on his way, and he went to Paddan Aram,
28:6 Now Esau learned that **Isaac** had blessed Jacob and had sent him
28:8 how displeasing the Canaanite women were to his father **Isaac**;
28:13 the God of your father Abraham and the God of **Isaac**.
31:18 in Paddan Aram, to go to his father **Isaac** in the land of Canaan.
31:42 the God of Abraham and the Fear of **Isaac**, had not been with me,
31:53 So Jacob took an oath in the name of the Fear of his father **Isaac**.
32:9 [32:10] God of my father **Isaac**, O LORD, who said to me,
35:12 The land I gave to Abraham and **Isaac** I also give to you, and I will
35:27 Jacob came home to his father **Isaac** in Mamre, near Kiriath Arba
35:27 Arba (that is, Hebron), where Abraham and **Isaac** had stayed.
35:28 **Isaac** lived a hundred and eighty years.
35:29 Then **he**[s] breathed his last and died and was gathered to his people,
46:1 he offered sacrifices to the God of his father **Isaac**.
48:15 the God before whom my fathers Abraham and **Isaac** walked,
48:16 by my name and the names of my fathers Abraham and **Isaac**,
49:31 there **Isaac** and his wife Rebekah were buried, and there I buried
50:24 to the land he promised on oath to Abraham, **Isaac** and Jacob."
Ex 2:24 his covenant with Abraham, with **Isaac** and with Jacob.
3:6 the God of Abraham, the God of **Isaac** and the God of Jacob."
3:15 the God of Abraham, the God of **Isaac** and the God of Jacob—
3:16 the God of Abraham, **Isaac** and Jacob—appeared to me and said:
4:5 the God of Abraham, the God of **Isaac** and the God of Jacob—
6:3 I appeared to Abraham, to **Isaac** and to Jacob as God Almighty,
6:8 with uplifted hand to give to Abraham, to **Isaac** and to Jacob.
32:13 Remember your servants Abraham, **Isaac** and Israel, to whom you
33:1 **Isaac** and Jacob, saying, 'I will give it to your descendants.'
Lev 26:42 and my covenant with **Isaac** and my covenant with Abraham,
Nu 32:11 will see the land I promised on oath to Abraham, **Isaac** and Jacob—
Dt 1:8 to Abraham, **Isaac** and Jacob—and to their descendants after
6:10 swore to your fathers, to Abraham, **Isaac** and Jacob, to give you—
9:5 what he swore to your fathers, to Abraham, **Isaac** and Jacob.
9:27 Remember your servants Abraham, **Isaac** and Jacob. Overlook the
29:13 [29:12] as he swore to your fathers, Abraham, **Isaac** and Jacob.
30:20 land he swore to give to your fathers, Abraham, **Isaac** and Jacob.
34:4 **Isaac** and Jacob when I said, 'I will give it to your descendants.'
Jos 24:3 and gave him many descendants. I gave him **Isaac**,
24:4 to **Isaac** I gave Jacob and Esau. I assigned the hill country of Seir
1Ki 18:36 "O LORD, God of Abraham, **Isaac** and Israel, let it be known
2Ki 13:23 for them because of his covenant with Abraham, **Isaac** and Jacob.
1Ch 1:28 The sons of Abraham: **Isaac** and Ishmael.
1:34 Abraham was the father of **Isaac**. The sons of Isaac: Esau
1:34 was the father of Isaac. The sons of **Isaac**: Esau and Israel.
16:16 the covenant he made with Abraham, the oath he swore to **Isaac**.
29:18 O LORD, God of our fathers Abraham, **Isaac** and Israel,
2Ch 30:6 return to the LORD, the God of Abraham, **Isaac** and Israel,

3664 יִצְחָר *yiṣḥār*, n.pr.m. [0] [cf. 7468]

1Ch 4:7 [The sons of Helah: Zereth, Zohar, [K; see Q 7468] Ethnan,]

3665 יָצִיא *yāṣî'*, a. [1] [√ 3655]

sons [1]

2Ch 32:21 temple of his god, some of his **sons** cut him down with the sword.

3666 יָצִיעַ *yāṣîa'*, n.m. [3] [√ 3667]

floor [1], side rooms [1], structure [1]

1Ki 6:5 inner sanctuary he built a **structure** [K 3662] around the building,
6:6 The lowest **floor** [K 3662] was five cubits wide, the middle floor
6:10 And he built the **side rooms** [K 3662] all along the temple.

3667 יָצַע *yāṣa'*, v. [4] [→ 3661, 3666, 5201]

are spread out [1], lay [1], lying [1], make bed [1]

Est 4:3 [H] and wailing. Many **lay** *in* sackcloth and ashes.
Ps 139:8 [G] you are there; if *I* **make** *my* **bed** *in* the depths, you are there.
Isa 14:11 [H] maggots **are spread out** beneath you and worms cover you.
58:5 [G] one's head like a reed and for **lying** *on* sackcloth and ashes?

3668 יָצַק *yāṣaq*, v. [51] [→ 3669, 4607, 4609, 5187?, 7440?; cf. 3657]

pour [11], cast [10], poured [6], poured out [4], firm [2], hard [2], pouring [2], were cast [2], been anointed [1], beset [1], frozen [1], hard [+2021+4200+4607] [1], is smelted [1], pour out [1], ran [1], serve [1], served [1], set down [1], spread out [1], washed away [1]

Ge 28:18 [A] his head and set it up as a pillar and **poured** oil on top of it.
35:14 [A] he poured out a drink offering on it; *he* also **poured** oil on it.

Ex 25:12 [A] **Cast** four gold rings for it and fasten them to its four feet,
26:37 [A] overlaid with gold. And **cast** five bronze bases for them.
29:7 [A] the anointing oil and anoint him *by* **pouring** it on his head.
36:36 [A] made gold hooks for them and **cast** their four silver bases.
37:3 [A] *He* **cast** four gold rings for it and fastened them to its four
37:13 [A] *They* **cast** four gold rings for the table and fastened them to
38:5 [A] *They* **cast** bronze rings to hold the poles for the four corners
38:27 [A] of silver were used to **cast** the bases for the sanctuary and
Lev 2:1 [A] is to be of fine flour. *He is to* **pour** oil on it, put incense on it
2:6 [A] Crumble it and **pour** oil on it; it is a grain offering.
8:12 [A] *He* **poured** some of the anointing oil on Aaron's head
8:15 [A] *He* **poured out** the rest of the blood at the base of the altar.
9:9 [A] the rest of the blood *he* **poured out** at the base of the altar.
14:15 [A] of the log of oil, **pour** it in the palm of his own left hand,
14:26 [A] The priest *is to* **pour** some of the oil into the palm of his own
21:10 [H] brothers who *has had* the anointing oil **poured** on his head
Nu 5:15 [A] *He must* not **pour** oil on it or put incense on it, because it is
Jos 7:23 [G] all the Israelites and **spread** them **out** before the LORD.
1Sa 10:1 [A] a flask of oil and **poured** it on Saul's head and kissed him,
2Sa 13:9 [A] she took the pan and **served** him the bread, but he refused to
15:24 [G] *They* **set down** the ark of God, and Abiathar offered
1Ki 7:24 [B] The gourds **were cast** in two rows in one piece with the Sea.
7:30 [B] resting on four supports, **cast** *with* wreaths on each side.
7:46 [A] The king *had* them **cast** in clay molds in the plain of the
18:33 [18:34] [A] and **pour** it on the offering and on the wood."
22:35 [A] The blood from his wound **ran** onto the floor of the chariot,
2Ki 3:11 [A] is here. He *used to* **pour** water on the hands of Elijah."
4:4 [A] **Pour** oil into all the jars, and as each is filled, put it to one
4:5 [G] her sons. They brought the jars to her and she *kept* **pouring**.
4:40 [A] The stew *was* **poured out** for the men, but as they began to
4:41 [A] He put it into the pot and said, "**Serve** it to the people to eat."
9:3 [A] Then take the flask and **pour** the oil on his head and declare,
9:6 [A] Then the prophet **poured** the oil on Jehu's head and declared,
2Ch 4:3 [B] The bulls **were cast** in two rows in one piece with the Sea.
4:17 [A] The king *had* them **cast** in clay molds in the plain of the
Job 11:15 [H] face without shame; you will stand **firm** and without fear.
22:16 [H] before their time, their foundations **washed away** *by* a flood.
28:2 [B] Iron is taken from the earth, and copper **is smelted** *from* ore.
29:6 [B] and the rock **poured out** for me streams of olive oil.
37:10 [H] of God produces ice, and the broad waters become **frozen**.
38:38 [A] when the dust *becomes* **hard** [+2021+4200+4607]
41:23 [41:15] [B] are tightly joined; *they are* **firm** and immovable.
41:24 [41:16] [B] His chest *is* **hard** as rock, hard as a lower millstone.
41:24 [41:16] [B] His chest is hard as rock, **hard** as a lower millstone.
Ps 41:8 [41:9] [B] "A vile disease *has* **beset** him; he will never get up
45:2 [45:3] [H] of men and your lips *have* **been anointed** *with* grace,
Isa 44:3 [A] For *I will* **pour** water on the thirsty land, and streams on the
44:3 [A] *I will* **pour out** my Spirit on your offspring, and my blessing
Eze 24:3 [A] " 'Put on the cooking pot; put it on and **pour** water into it.

3669 יְצֻקָה yᵉṣuqâ, n.f. [1] [√ 3668]

one piece with [1]

1Ki 7:24 The gourds were cast in two rows in **one piece with** the Sea.

3670 יָצַר yāṣar, v. [42] [→ 3450, 3671, 3672, 3673, 3674]

formed [15], Maker [4], planned [4], forms [3], made [2], preparing [2], shapes [2], brings on [1], creator [1], fashioned [1], forged [1], form [1], make [1], makes [1], man [1], ordained [1], was formed [1]

Ge 2:7 [A] the LORD God **formed** the man *from* the dust of the
2:8 [A] the east, in Eden; and there he put the man *he had* **formed**.
2:19 [A] *had* **formed** out of the ground all the beasts of the field and
2Ki 19:25 [A] In days of old *I* **planned** it; now I have brought it to pass,
Ps 33:15 [A] he *who* **forms** the hearts of all, who considers everything
74:17 [A] boundaries of the earth; you **made** both summer and winter.
94:9 [A] the ear not hear? Does he *who* **formed** the eye not see?
94:20 [A] allied with you—*one that* **brings on** misery by its decrees?
95:5 [A] sea is his, for he made it, and his hands **formed** the dry land.
104:26 [A] and fro, and the leviathan, which *you* **formed** to frolic there.
139:16 [E] All the days **ordained** for me were written in your book
Isa 22:11 [A] made it, or have regard for the *One who* **planned** it long ago.
27:11 [A] on them, and their **Creator** shows them no favor.
37:26 [A] In days of old *I* **planned** it; now I have brought it to pass,
43:1 [A] he who created you, O Jacob, *he who* **formed** you, O Israel:
43:7 [A] whom I created for my glory, whom *I* **formed** and made."
43:10 [C] Before me no god **was formed**, nor will there be one after
43:21 [A] the people *I* **formed** for myself that they may proclaim my
44:2 [A] he who made you, *who* **formed** you in the womb, and who
44:9 [A] All who **make** idols are nothing, and the things they treasure
44:10 [A] Who **shapes** a god and casts an idol, which can profit him
44:12 [A] *he* **shapes** an idol with hammers, he forges it with the might
44:21 [A] *I have* **made** you, you are my servant; O Israel, I will not
44:24 [A] your Redeemer, *who* **formed** you in the womb:
45:7 [A] I **form** the light and create darkness, I bring prosperity
45:9 [A] "Woe to him who quarrels with his **Maker**, to him who is
45:11 [A] the LORD says—the Holy One of Israel, and its **Maker**:
45:18 [A] is God; *he who* **fashioned** and made the earth, he founded it;
45:18 [A] did not create it to be empty, but **formed** it to be inhabited—
46:11 [A] that will I bring about; what *I have* **planned**, that will I do.
49:5 [A] *he who* **formed** me in the womb to be his servant to bring
54:17 [H] no weapon **forged** against you will prevail, and you will
Jer 1:5 [A] "Before *I* **formed** you in the womb I knew you, before you
10:16 [A] for he *is* the **Maker** *of* all things, including Israel, the tribe of
18:11 [A] I *am* **preparing** a disaster for you and devising a plan against
33:2 [A] the earth, the LORD *who* **formed** it and established it—
51:19 [A] for he *is* the **Maker** *of* all things, including the tribe of his
Am 4:13 [A] *He who* **forms** the mountains, creates the wind, and reveals
7:1 [A] *He was* **preparing** swarms of locusts after the king's share
Hab 2:18 [A] "Of what value is an idol, since a **man** has carved it? Or an
2:18 [A] For *he who* **makes** it trusts in his own creation; he makes
Zec 12:1 [A] and *who* **forms** the spirit of man within him, declares:

3671 יֵצֶר¹ yēṣer[1], n.m. [9] [→ 3672; cf. 3670]

inclination [2], creation [1], desire [+4742] [1], disposed [1], formed [1], mind [1], motive [1], pot [1]

Ge 6:5 that every **inclination** *of* the thoughts of his heart was only evil all
8:21 even though every **inclination** *of* his heart is evil from childhood.
Dt 31:21 I know what they are **disposed** to do, even before I bring them into
1Ch 28:9 every heart and understands every **motive** *behind* the thoughts.
29:18 keep this **desire** [+4742] *in* the hearts of your people forever,
Ps 103:14 for he knows how we are **formed**, he remembers that we are dust.
Isa 26:3 You will keep in perfect peace him whose **mind** is steadfast,
29:16 not make me"? Can the **pot** say of the potter, "He knows nothing"?
Hab 2:18 For he who makes it trusts in his own **creation**; he makes idols that

3672 יֵצֶר² yēṣer[2], n.pr.m. [3] [→ 3673; cf. 3670, 3671]

Jezer [3]

Ge 46:24 The sons of Naphtali: Jahziel, Guni, **Jezer** and Shillem.
Nu 26:49 through **Jezer**, the Jezerite clan; through Shillem, the Shillemite
1Ch 7:13 Jahziel, Guni, **Jezer** and Shillem—the descendants of Bilhah.

3673 יִצְרִי yiṣrî, a.g. & n.pr.m. [2] [√ 3672; cf. 3670]

Izri [1], Jezerite [1]

Nu 26:49 through Jezer, the **Jezerite** clan; through Shillem, the Shillemite
1Ch 25:11 the fourth to **Izri**, his sons and relatives, 12

3674 יְצֻרִים yᵉṣurîm, n.m.pl. [1] [√ 3670]

frame [1]

Job 17:7 eyes have grown dim with grief; my whole **frame** is but a shadow.

3675 יָצַת yāṣat, v. [26] [cf. 7455]

set on fire [+836+906+928+2021] [6], set fire [+836] [4], kindle [3], set on fire [+836+928+2021] [3], been burned [2], are burned [1], burn [1], burns [1], kindled [1], set ablaze [+836+928+2021] [1], set on fire [+836+6584] [1], set on fire [1], sets ablaze [1]

Jos 8:8 [G] you have taken the city, **set** it **on fire** [+836+906+928+2021].
8:19 [G] captured it and quickly **set** it **on fire** [+836+906+928+2021].
Jdg 9:49 [G] the stronghold and **set** it **on fire** [+836+906+928+2021]
2Sa 14:30 [G] he has barley there. Go and **set** it **on fire** [+836+928+2021]."
14:30 [G] servants **set** the field **on fire** [+836+906+928+2021].
14:31 [G] your servants **set** my field **on fire** [+836+906+928+2021]?"
2Ki 22:13 [C] Great is the LORD's anger that **burns** against us
22:17 [C] my anger *will* **burn** against this place and will not be
Ne 1:3 [C] is broken down, and its gates *have* **been burned** with fire."
2:17 [C] lies in ruins, and its gates *have* **been burned** with fire.
Isa 9:18 [9:17] [A] and thorns, *it* **sets** the forest thickets **ablaze**,
33:12 [A] like cut thornbushes *they will be* **set ablaze** [+836+928+2021]."
Jer 2:15 [C] have laid waste his land; his towns **are burned** and deserted.
11:16 [G] the roar of a mighty storm *he will* **set** it **on fire** [+836+6584],
17:27 [G] *I will* **kindle** an unquenchable fire in the gates of Jerusalem
21:14 [G] *I will* **kindle** a fire in your forests that will consume
32:29 [G] will come in and **set** it **on fire** [+836+906+928+2021];
43:12 [G] *He will* **set fire** [+836] to the temples of the gods of Egypt;
49:2 [A] surrounding villages *will be* **set on fire** [+836+928+2021].
49:27 [G] "*I will* **set fire** [+836] to the walls of Damascus; it will
50:32 [G] *I will* **kindle** a fire in her towns that will consume all who are
51:30 [G] Her dwellings *are* **set on fire**; the bars of her gates are
51:58 [A] be leveled and her high gates **set on fire** [+836+928+2021];
La 4:11 [G] *He* **kindled** a fire in Zion that consumed her foundations.
Eze 20:47 [21:3] [G] I *am about to* **set fire** [+836] to you, and it will
Am 1:14 [G] *I will* **set fire** [+836] to the walls of Rabbah that will

3676 יֶקֶב yeqeb, n.m. [16] [cf. 5918]

winepress [7], vats [3], winepresses [3], presses [2], wine vat [1]

Nu 18:27 you as grain from the threshing floor or juice from the **winepress**.
18:30 to you as the product of the threshing floor or the **winepress**.
Dt 15:14 liberally from your flock, your threshing floor and your **winepress**.
16:13 gathered the produce of your threshing floor and your **winepress**.
Jdg 7:25 killed Oreb at the rock of Oreb, and Zeeb at the **winepress** *of* Zeeb.
2Ki 6:27 get help for you? From the threshing floor? From the **winepress**?"
Job 24:11 among the terraces; they tread the **winepresses**, yet suffer thirst.
Pr 3:10 filled to overflowing, and your **vats** will brim over with new wine.
Isa 5:2 He built a watchtower in it and cut out a **winepress** as well.
16:10 no one treads out wine at the **presses**, for I have put an end to the
Jer 48:33 I have stopped the flow of wine from the **presses**; no one treads
Hos 9:2 Threshing floors and **winepresses** will not feed the people;
Joel 2:24 be filled with grain; the **vats** will overflow with new wine and oil.
3:13 [4:13] the grapes, for the winepress is full and the **vats** overflow—
Hag 2:16 When anyone went to a **wine vat** to draw fifty measures, there
Zec 14:10 and from the Tower of Hananel to the royal **winepresses**.

3677 יְקַבְצְאֵל yᵉqabṣᵉʾēl, n.pr.loc. [1] [√ 7695 + 446]

Jekabzeel [1]

Ne 11:25 in Dibon and its settlements, in **Jekabzeel** and its villages,

3678 יָקַד yāqad, v. [8] [→ 3679, 3683, 4611, 4612; Ar 10328, 10329]

be kept burning [3], burn [2], burning [1], burns [1], kindled [1]

Lev 6:9 [6:2] [H] and the fire *must* **be kept burning** on the altar.
6:12 [6:5] [H] The fire on the altar *must* **be kept burning**; it must
6:13 [6:6] [H] The fire *must* **be kept burning** on the altar
Dt 32:22 [A] by my wrath, *one that* **burns** to the realm of death below.
Isa 10:16 [A] under his pomp a fire *will be* **kindled** like a blazing flame.
65:5 [A] are smoke in my nostrils, a fire *that keeps* **burning** all day.
Jer 15:14 [H] for my anger will kindle a fire *that will* **burn** against you."
17:4 [H] for you have kindled my anger, and *it will* **burn** forever."

3679 יְקֹד yᵉqōd, n.[m.]. [2] [√ 3678]

blazing [1], fire [1]

Isa 10:16 under his pomp a **fire** will be kindled like a blazing flame.
10:16 under his pomp a fire will be kindled like a **blazing** flame.

3680 יָקְדְעָם yoqdᵉʿām, n.pr.loc. [1]

Jokdeam [1]

Jos 15:56 Jezreel, **Jokdeam**, Zanoah,

3681 יָקֶה yāqeh, n.pr.m. [1]

Jakeh [1]

Pr 30:1 The sayings of Agur son of **Jakeh**—an oracle: This man declared

3682 יְקָהָה yᵉqāhâ, n.f. [2]

obedience [2]

Ge 49:10 comes to whom it belongs and the **obedience** *of* the nations is his.
Pr 30:17 "The eye that mocks a father, that scorns **obedience** *to* a mother,

3683 יָקוּד yāqûd, n.[m.]. [1] [√ 3678]

hearth [1]

Isa 30:14 pieces not a fragment will be found for taking coals from a **hearth**

3684 יָקוֹט yāqôṭ, a. [1] [cf. 7753]

fragile [1]

Job 8:14 What he trusts in is **fragile**; what he relies on is a spider's web.

3685 יְקוּם yᵉqûm, n.[m.]. [3] [√ 7756]

living thing [2], living creature [1]

Ge 7:4 I will wipe from the face of the earth every **living creature** I have
7:23 Every **living thing** on the face of the earth was wiped out;
Dt 11:6 their tents and every **living thing** that belonged to them.

3686 יָקוֹשׁ yāqôš, n.[m.]. Not used in NIV/BHS [√ 3704]

3687 יָקוּשׁ yāqûš, n.[m.]. [4] [√ 3704]

fowler [1], fowler's [1], men who snare birds [1], snares [+7062] [1]

Ps 91:3 Surely he will save you from the **fowler's** snare and from the
Pr 6:5 the hand of the hunter, like a bird from the snare of the **fowler**.
Jer 5:26 people are wicked men who lie in wait like **men who snare birds**
Hos 9:8 over Ephraim, yet **snares** [+7062] await him on all his paths,

3688 יְקוּתִיאֵל yᵉqûtîʾēl, n.pr.m. [1]

Jekuthiel [1]

1Ch 4:18 Heber the father of Soco, and **Jekuthiel** the father of Zanoah.)

3689 יָקַח yāqaḥ, v. [0 / 1]

insolent [1]

Nu 16:1 [G] and On son of Peleth—*became* **insolent** [BHS 4374]

3690 יָקְטָן yoqṭān, n.pr.m. [6] [√ 3699]

Joktan [6]

Ge 10:25 in his time the earth was divided; his brother was named **Joktan**.
10:26 **Joktan** was the father of Almodad, Sheleph, Hazarmaveth,
10:29 Ophir, Havilah and Jobab. All these were sons of **Joktan**.
1Ch 1:19 in his time the earth was divided; his brother was named **Joktan**.
1:20 **Joktan** was the father of Almodad, Sheleph, Hazarmaveth,
1:23 Ophir, Havilah and Jobab. All these were sons of **Joktan**.

3691 יָקִים yāqîm, n.pr.m. [2] [√ 7756]

Jakim [2]

1Ch 8:19 **Jakim**, Zicri, Zabdi,
24:12 the eleventh to Eliashib, the twelfth to **Jakim**,

3692 יַקִּיר yaqqîr, a. [1] [√ 3700; Ar 10330]

dear [1]

Jer 31:20 Is not Ephraim my **dear** son, the child in whom I delight?

3693 יְקַמְיָה yᵉqamyâ, n.pr.m. [3] [√ 7756 + 3378]

Jekamiah [3]

1Ch 2:41 Shallum the father of **Jekamiah**, and Jekamiah the father of
2:41 the father of Jekamiah, and **Jekamiah** the father of Elishama.
3:18 Shenazzar, **Jekamiah**, Hoshama and Nedabiah.

3694 יְקַמְעָם yᵉqamʿām, n.pr.m. [2] [√ 7756 + 6639]

Jekameam [2]

1Ch 23:19 Amariah the second, Jahaziel the third and **Jekameam** the fourth.
24:23 Amariah the second, Jahaziel the third and **Jekameam** the fourth.

3695 יָקְמְעָם yoqmᵉʿām, n.pr.loc. [2] [√ 3696?]

Jokmeam [2]

1Ki 4:12 from Beth Shan to Abel Meholah across to **Jokmeam**;
1Ch 6:68 [6:53] **Jokmeam**, Beth Horon,

3696 יָקְנְעָם yoqnᵉʿām, n.pr.loc. [3 / 4] [√ 3695?]

Jokneam [4]

Jos 12:22 the king of Kedesh one the king of **Jokneam** in Carmel one
19:11 touched Dabbesheth, and extended to the ravine near **Jokneam**.
21:34 were given: from the tribe of Zebulun, **Jokneam**, Kartah,
1Ch 6:77 [6:62] the tribe of Zebulun they received **Jokneam**, [BHS-]

3697 יָקַע yāqaʿ, v. [8] [cf. 5936]

killed and exposed [2], turned away in disgust [2], been killed and exposed [1], kill and expose [1], turn away [1], wrenched [1]

Ge 32:25 [32:26] [A] so that his hip *was* **wrenched** as he wrestled with
Nu 25:4 [G] **kill** them **and expose** them in broad daylight before the
2Sa 21:6 [G] male descendants be given to us *to be* **killed and exposed**
21:9 [G] *who* **killed and exposed** them on a hill before the LORD.
21:13 [H] the bones of those *who had* **been killed and exposed** were
Jer 6:8 [A] or I *will* **turn away** from you and make your land desolate
Eze 23:17 [A] defiled by them, she **turned away** from them **in disgust**.
23:18 [A] exposed her nakedness, I **turned away** from her **in disgust**,

3698 יְקִפָּאוֹן yᵉqippāʾôn, v. Not used in NIV/BHS [√ 7884]

3699 יָקַץ yāqaṣ, v. [11] [→ 3690; cf. 7810]

awoke [6], woke up [3], awakened [1], wake up [1]

Ge 9:24 [A] When Noah **awoke** from his wine and found out what his
28:16 [A] When Jacob **awoke** from his sleep, he thought,
41:4 [A] ate up the seven sleek, fat cows. Then Pharaoh **woke up**.
41:7 [A] full heads. Then Pharaoh **woke up**; it had been a dream.
41:21 [A] done so; they looked just as ugly as before. Then *I* **woke up**.
Jdg 16:14 [A] *He* **awoke** from his sleep and pulled up the pin and the loom,
16:20 [A] *He* **awoke** from his sleep and thought, "I'll go out as before
1Ki 3:15 [A] Then Solomon **awoke**—and he realized it had been a dream.
18:27 [A] or traveling. Maybe he is sleeping and *must be* **awakened**."
Ps 78:65 [A] the Lord **awoke** as from sleep, as a man wakes from the
Hab 2:7 [A] *Will they* not **wake up** and make you tremble? Then you

3700 יָקַר **yāqar**, v. [11] [→ 3692, 3701, 3702]

precious [4], have respect for [+928+6524] [2], costly [1], make scarcer [1], priced [1], seldom [1], well known [+4394] [1]

1Sa 18: 30 [A] Saul's officers, and his name *became* **well known** [+4394].
26: 21 [A] Because you considered my life **precious** today, I will not try
2Ki 1: 13 [A] "please **have respect** [+928+6524] **for** my life and the lives
1: 14 [A] their men. But now **have respect** [+928+6524] **for** my life!"
Ps 49: 8 [49:9] [A] the ransom for a life *is* **costly**, no payment is ever
72: 14 [A] and violence, for **precious** *is* their blood in his sight.
139: 17 [A] How **precious** to me are your thoughts, O God! How vast is
Pr 25: 17 [G] **Seldom** *set* foot in your neighbor's house—too much of you,
Isa 13: 12 [G] *I will* **make** man **scarcer** than pure gold, more rare than the
43: 4 [A] Since *you are* **precious** and honored in my sight, and
Zec 11: 13 [A] to the potter"—the handsome price at which they **priced** *me*!

3701 יָקָר **yāqār**, a. [35 / 34] [√ 3700]

precious [18], high-grade [2], rare [2], beauty [1], fine [1], good quality [1], honored [1], outweighs [+4946] [1], priceless [1], prizes [1], quality [1], splendor [1], valuable things [+2104] [1], very [1], worthy [1]

1Sa 3: 1 In those days the word of the LORD was **rare**; there were not
2Sa 12: 30 weight was a talent of gold, and it was set with **precious** stones—
1Ki 5: 17 [5:31] **quality** stone to provide a foundation of dressed stone for
7: 9 were made of blocks of **high-grade** stone cut to size and trimmed
7: 10 The foundations were laid with large stones of **good quality**,
7: 11 Above were **high-grade** stones, cut to size, and cedar beams.
10: 2 carrying spices, large quantities of gold, and **precious** stones—
10: 10 120 talents of gold, large quantities of spices, and **precious** stones.
10: 11 they brought great cargoes of almugwood and **precious** stones.
1Ch 20: 2 found to be a talent of gold, and it was set with **precious** stones—
29: 2 stones of various colors, and all kinds of **fine** stone and marble—
2Ch 3: 6 He adorned the temple with **precious** stones. And the gold he used
9: 1 carrying spices, large quantities of gold, and **precious** stones—
9: 9 120 talents of gold, large quantities of spices, and **precious** stones.
9: 10 from Ophir; they also brought algumwood and **precious** stones.
32: 27 made treasuries for his silver and gold and for his **precious** stones,
Job 28: 16 be bought with the gold of Ophir, with **precious** onyx or sapphires.
31: 26 regarded the sun in its radiance or the moon moving *in* **splendor**,
Ps 36: 7 [36:8] How **priceless** is your unfailing love! Both high and low
37: 20 The LORD's enemies will be like the **beauty** *of* the fields,
45: 9 [45:10] Daughters of kings are among your **honored** *women*;
116: 15 **Precious** in the sight of the LORD is the death of his saints.
Pr 1: 13 we will get all sorts of **valuable** [+2104] **things** and fill our houses
3: 15 She is more **precious** than rubies; nothing you desire can compare
6: 26 you to a loaf of bread, and the adulteress preys upon your **very** life.
12: 27 not roast his game, but the diligent man **prizes** his possessions.
17: 27 [man of understanding is **even-tempered** [+8120]. [Q; see K 7922]]
24: 4 through knowledge its rooms are filled with **rare** and beautiful
Ecc 10: 1 a bad smell, so a little folly **outweighs** [+4946] wisdom and honor.
Isa 28: 16 a tested stone, a **precious** cornerstone for a sure foundation;
Jer 15: 19 if you utter **worthy**, not worthless, words, you will be my
La 4: 2 How the **precious** sons of Zion, once worth their weight in gold,
Eze 27: 22 exchanged the finest of all kinds of spices and **precious** stones,
28: 13 in Eden, the garden of God; every **precious** stone adorned you:
Da 11: 38 honor with gold and silver, with **precious** stones and costly gifts.
Zec 14: 6 there will be no light, no cold [BHS *splendor*; NIV 7938] or frost.

3702 יְקָר **yeqār**, n.m. [17] [√ 3700; Ar 10331]

honor [7], riches [2], honor [+6913] [1], precious things [1], price [1], rare [1], respect [+4200+5989] [1], splendor [1], treasures [1], valuables [1]

Est 1: 4 wealth of his kingdom and the **splendor** and glory of his majesty.
1: 20 all the women *will* **respect** [+4200+5989] their husbands,
6: 3 "What **honor** and recognition has Mordecai received for this?"
6: 6 "What should be done for the man the king delights to **honor**?"
6: 6 "Who is there that the king would rather **honor** [+6913] than me?"
6: 7 So he answered the king, "For the man the king delights to **honor**,
6: 9 Let them robe the man the king delights to **honor**, and lead him on
6: 9 'This is what is done for the man the king delights to **honor**!' "
6: 11 "This is what is done for the man the king delights to **honor**!"
8: 16 the Jews it was a time of happiness and joy, gladness and **honor**.
Job 28: 10 He tunnels through the rock; his eyes see all its **treasures**.
Ps 49: 12 [49:13] man, despite his **riches**, does not endure; he is like the
49: 20 [49:21] A man who has **riches** without understanding is like the
Pr 20: 15 in abundance, but lips that speak knowledge are a **rare** jewel.
Jer 20: 5 all its **valuables** and all the treasures of the kings of Judah.
Eze 22: 25 take treasures and **precious things** and make many widows within
Zec 11: 13 it to the potter"—the handsome **price** at which they priced me!

3703 יִקְרָה **yiqrâ**, a. Not used in NIV/BHS [√ 7936]

3704 יָקֹשׁ **yāqaš**, v. [8 / 9] [→ 3686, 3687, 3705, 4613; cf. 5943, 7772]

are ensnared [1], are trapped [1], be ensnared [1], be snared [1], been trapped [1], fowler's [1], laid [1], set a trap [1], snared [1]

Dt 7: 25 [C] do not take it for yourselves, or *you will* **be ensnared** by it,
Ps 9: 16 [9:17] [C] the wicked **are ensnared** [BHS 5943] by the work of
124: 7 [A] We have escaped like a bird out of the **fowler's** snare;
141: 9 [A] Keep me from the snares *they have* **laid** for me, from the
Pr 6: 2 [C] if *you have* **been trapped** by what you said, ensnared by the
Ecc 9: 12 [E] so men **are trapped** by evil times that fall unexpectedly upon
Isa 8: 15 [C] will fall and be broken, *they will* **be snared** and captured."
28: 13 [C] and fall backward, be injured and **snared** and captured.
Jer 50: 24 [A] *I* **set a trap** for you, O Babylon, and you were caught before

3705 יָקְשָׁן **yoqšān**, n.pr.m. [4] [√ 3704]

Jokshan [4]

Ge 25: 2 bore him Zimran, **Jokshan**, Medan, Midian, Ishbak and Shuah.
25: 3 **Jokshan** was the father of Sheba and Dedan; the descendants of
1Ch 1: 32 Zimran, **Jokshan**, Medan, Midian, Ishbak and Shuah. The sons of
1: 32 Ishbak and Shuah. The sons of **Jokshan**: Sheba and Dedan.

3706 יָקְתְאֵל **yoqteʾēl**, n.pr.loc. [2] [√ 446]

Joktheel [2]

Jos 15: 38 Dilean, Mizpah, **Joktheel**,
2Ki 14: 7 Sela in battle, calling it **Joktheel**, the name it has to this day.

3707 יָרֵא **yārēʾ[1]**, v. [330 / 332] [→ 3710, 3711, 4616; cf. 4624]

afraid [118], fear [91], awesome [24], feared [12], revere [11], worship [10], be feared [4], dreadful [4], revered [4], terrified [+4394] [4], awesome wonders [3], fears [3], intimidate [3], stand in awe [3], alarmed [2], frightened [2], have fear [2], have reverence [2], revering [2], worshiped [2], are feared [1], awesome deeds [1], awesome works [1], believer [1], despair [1], dreaded [1], dreadful [+4394] [1], feared [+906+3711] [1], fearfully [1], fearing [1], filled with fear [+4394] [1], frighten [1], held in awe [1], is feared [1], made afraid [1], not daring [1], overawed [1], respect [1], respects [1], reverent [1], shown reverence [1], stood in awe [+906+906+4394] [1], terrified [+1524+3711] [1], terrified [+4394+4394] [1], terrify [1], terror [1]

Ge 3: 10 [A] you in the garden, and *I was* **afraid** because I was naked;
15: 1 [A] "*Do* not *be* **afraid**, Abram. I am your shield, your very great
18: 15 [A] Sarah *was* **afraid**, so she lied and said, "I did not laugh."
19: 30 [A] settled in the mountains, for *he was* **afraid** to stay in Zoar.
20: 8 [A] them all that had happened, they *were* very much **afraid**.
21: 17 [A] *Do* not *be* **afraid**; God has heard the boy crying as he lies
26: 7 [A] my sister," because *he was* **afraid** to say, "She is my wife."
26: 24 [A] *Do* not *be* **afraid**, for I am with you; I will bless you and will
28: 17 [A] *He was* **afraid** and said, "How awesome is this place! This is
28: 17 [C] He was afraid and said, "How **awesome** is this place! This is
31: 31 [A] Jacob answered Laban, "*I was* **afraid**, because I thought you
32: 7 [32:8] [A] *In* great **fear** and distress Jacob divided the people
32: 11 [32:12] [A] for I *am* **afraid** he will come and attack me,
35: 17 [A] the midwife said to her, "Don't *be* **afraid**, for you have
42: 35 [A] their father saw the money pouches, *they were* **frightened**.
43: 18 [A] Now the men *were* **frightened** when they were taken to his
43: 23 [A] "It's all right," he said. "Don't *be* **afraid**. Your God, the God
46: 3 [A] "*Do* not *be* **afraid** to go down to Egypt, for I will make you
50: 19 [A] Joseph said to them, "Don't *be* **afraid**. Am I in the place of
50: 21 [A] So then, don't *be* **afraid**. I will provide for you and your
Ex 1: 17 [A] **feared** God and did not do what the king of Egypt had told
1: 21 [A] because the midwives **feared** God, he gave them families of
2: 14 [A] Moses *was* **afraid** and thought, "What I did must have
3: 6 [A] Moses hid his face, because *he was* **afraid** to look at God.
9: 20 [A] Those officials of Pharaoh who **feared** the word of the
9: 30 [A] and your officials still *do* not **fear** the LORD God."
14: 10 [A] *They were* **terrified** [+4394] and cried out to the LORD.
14: 13 [A] Moses answered the people, "*Do* not *be* **afraid**. Stand firm
14: 31 [A] the people **feared** the LORD and put their trust in him
15: 11 [C] majestic in holiness, **awesome** *in* glory, working wonders?
20: 18 [A] mountain in smoke, they trembled *with* **fear**. [BHS 8011]
20: 20 [A] Moses said to the people, "*Do* not *be* **afraid**. God has come
34: 10 [C] The people you live among will see how **awesome** *is* the
34: 30 [A] his face was radiant, and *they were* **afraid** to come near him.
Lev 19: 3 [A] " 'Each of *you must* **respect** his mother and father, and you
19: 14 [A] a stumbling block in front of the blind, but **fear** your God.
19: 30 [A] my Sabbaths and **have reverence** *for* my sanctuary.
19: 32 [A] the aged, show respect for the elderly and **revere** your God.
25: 17 [A] Do not take advantage of each other, but **fear** your God. I am
25: 36 [A] not take interest of any kind from him, but **fear** your God,
25: 43 [A] Do not rule over them ruthlessly, but **fear** your God.

Lev 26: 2 [A] my Sabbaths and **have reverence** *for* my sanctuary.
Nu 12: 8 [A] *were you* not **afraid** to speak against my servant Moses?"
14: 9 [A] *do* not *be* **afraid** *of* the people of the land, because we will
14: 9 [A] but the LORD is with us. *Do* not *be* **afraid** *of* them."
21:34 [A] The LORD said to Moses, "*Do* not *be* **afraid** *of* him, for I
Dt 1:19 [C] through all that vast and **dreadful** desert that you have seen,
1:21 [A] told you. *Do* not *be* **afraid**; do not be discouraged."
1:29 [A] I said to you, "Do not be terrified; *do* not *be* **afraid** of them.
2: 4 [A] live in Seir. *They will be* **afraid** of you, but be very careful.
3: 2 [A] The LORD said to me, "*Do* not *be* **afraid** *of* him, for I have
3:22 [A] *Do* not *be* **afraid** *of* them; the LORD your God himself will
4:10 [A] so that they may learn to **revere** me as long as they live in
5: 5 [A] because *you were* **afraid** of the fire and did not go up the
5:29 [A] that their hearts would be inclined to **fear** me and keep all
6: 2 [A] their children after them *may* **fear** the LORD your God as
6:13 [A] **Fear** the LORD your God, serve him only and take your
6:24 [A] us to obey all these decrees and to **fear** the LORD our God,
7:18 [A] *do* not *be* **afraid** of them; remember well what the LORD
7:19 [A] your God will do the same to all the peoples you now **fear**.
7:21 [C] your God, who is among you, is a great and **awesome** God.
8: 6 [A] LORD your God, walking in his ways and **revering** him.
8:15 [C] He led you through the vast and **dreadful** desert, that thirsty
10:12 [A] your God ask of you but to **fear** the LORD your God,
10:17 [C] and Lord of lords, the great God, mighty and **awesome**,
10:20 [A] **Fear** the LORD your God and serve him. Hold fast to him
10:21 [C] and **awesome wonders** you saw with your own eyes.
13: 4 [13:5] [A] God you must follow, and him *you must* **revere**.
13:11 [13:12] [A] all Israel will hear and *be* **afraid**, and no one among
14:23 [A] so that you may learn to **revere** the LORD your God
17:13 [A] All the people will hear and *be* **afraid**, and will not be
17:19 [A] of his life so that he may learn to **revere** the LORD his God
19:20 [A] The rest of the people will hear of this and *be* **afraid**,
20: 1 [A] *do* not *be* **afraid** of them, because the LORD your God,
20: 3 [A] Do not be fainthearted or **afraid**; do not be terrified or give
21:21 [A] evil from among you. All Israel will hear of it and *be* **afraid**.
25:18 [A] off all who were lagging behind; *they had* no **fear** *of* God.
28:10 [A] called by the name of the LORD, and *they will* **fear** you.
28:58 [A] and *do* not **revere** this glorious and awesome name—
28:58 [C] and do not revere this glorious and **awesome** name—
31: 6 [A] *Do* not *be* **afraid** or terrified because of them,
31: 8 [A] nor forsake you. *Do* not *be* **afraid**; do not be discouraged."
31:12 [A] so they can listen and learn *to* **fear** the LORD your God
31:13 [A] learn to **fear** the LORD your God as long as you live in the
Jos 4:14 [A] *they* **revered** him all the days of his life, just as they had
4:14 [A] him all the days of his life, just as *they had* **revered** Moses.
4:24 [A] and so that *you might* always **fear** the LORD your God."
8: 1 [A] the LORD said to Joshua, "*Do* not *be* **afraid**; do not be
9:24 [A] So *we* **feared** for our lives because of you, and that is why
10: 2 [A] *He and his people were* very much **alarmed** at this,
10: 8 [A] The LORD said to Joshua, "*Do* not *be* **afraid** of them; I
10:25 [A] Joshua said to them, "*Do* not *be* **afraid**; do not be
11: 6 [A] The LORD said to Joshua, "*Do* not *be* **afraid** of them,
22:25 [A] So your descendants might cause ours to stop **fearing** the
24:14 [A] "Now **fear** the LORD and serve him with all faithfulness.
Jdg 4:18 [A] to him, "Come, my lord, come right in. Don't *be* **afraid**."
6:10 [A] *do* not **worship** the gods of the Amorites, in whose land you
6:23 [A] the LORD said to him, "Peace! *Do* not *be* **afraid**. You are
6:27 [A] because *he was* **afraid** *of* his family and the men of the town,
8:20 [A] draw his sword, because he was only a boy and *was* **afraid**.
13: 6 [C] came to me. He looked like an angel of God, very **awesome**.
Ru 3:11 [A] now, my daughter, don't *be* **afraid**. I will do for you all you
1Sa 3:15 [A] the house of the LORD. He *was* **afraid** to tell Eli the vision,
4: 7 [A] the Philistines *were* **afraid**. "A god has come into the camp,"
4:20 [A] was dying, the women attending her said, "Don't **despair**;
7: 7 [A] heard of it, *they were* **afraid** because of the Philistines.
12:14 [A] If *you* **fear** the LORD and serve and obey him and do not
12:18 [A] people **stood in awe** [+906+906+4394] *of* the LORD and of
12:20 [A] "*Do* not *be* **afraid**," Samuel replied. "You have done all this
12:24 [A] *be sure to* **fear** the LORD and serve him faithfully with all
14:26 [A] one put his hand to his mouth, because they **feared** the oath.
15:24 [A] *I was* **afraid** *of* the people and so I gave in to them.
17:11 [A] and all the Israelites were dismayed and **terrified** [+4394].
17:24 [A] Israelites saw the man, they all ran from him *in* great **fear**.
18:12 [A] Saul *was* **afraid** of David, because the LORD was with
18:29 [A] Saul became still more **afraid** of him, and he remained his
21:12 [21:13] [A] and *was* very much **afraid** of Achish king of Gath.
22:23 [A] Stay with me; don't *be* **afraid**; the man who is seeking your
23:17 [A] "Don't *be* **afraid**," he said. "My father Saul will not lay a
28: 5 [A] When Saul saw the Philistine army, *he was* **afraid**; terror
28:13 [A] The king said to her, "Don't *be* **afraid**. What do you see?"
28:20 [A] **filled with fear** [+4394] because of Samuel's words.
31: 4 [A] his armor-bearer *was* **terrified** [+4394] and would not do it;
2Sa 1:14 [A] "Why *were you* not **afraid** to lift your hand to destroy the
3:11 [A] to say another word to Abner, because he *was* **afraid** *of* him.
6: 9 [A] David *was* **afraid** *of* the LORD that day and said,
7:23 [C] perform great and **awesome wonders** by driving out nations
9: 7 [A] "Don't *be* **afraid**," David said to him, "for I will surely show
10:19 [A] So the Arameans *were* **afraid** to help the Ammonites
12:18 [A] David's servants *were* **afraid** to tell him that the child was
13:28 [A] to you, 'Strike Amnon down,' then kill him. Don't *be* **afraid**.
14:15 [A] my lord the king because the people *have* **made** me **afraid**.
1Ki 1:50 [A] *in* **fear** of Solomon, went and took hold of the horns of the
1:51 [A] "Adonijah *is* **afraid** *of* King Solomon and is clinging to the
3:28 [A] the verdict the king had given, *they* **held** the king **in awe**,
8:40 [A] so that *they will* **fear** you all the time they live in the land
8:43 [A] the peoples of the earth may know your name and **fear** you,
17:13 [A] Elijah said to her, "Don't *be* **afraid**. Go home and do as you
18: 3 [A] of his palace. (Obadiah was a devout **believer** *in* the LORD.
18:12 [A] Yet I your servant *have* **worshiped** the LORD since my
19: 3 [A] Elijah *was* **afraid** [BHS 8011] and ran for his life. When he
2Ki 1:15 [A] said to Elijah, "Go down with him; *do* not *be* **afraid** of him."
4: 1 [A] husband is dead, and you know that he **revered** the LORD.
6:16 [A] "Don't *be* **afraid**," the prophet answered. "Those who are
10: 4 [A] *they were* **terrified** [+4394+4394] and said, "If two kings
17: 7 [A] of Pharaoh king of Egypt. *They* **worshiped** other gods
17:25 [A] they first lived there, *they did* not **worship** the LORD;
17:28 [A] live in Bethel and taught them how *to* **worship** the LORD.
17:35 [A] "*Do* not **worship** any other gods or bow down to them, serve
17:36 [A] and outstretched arm, is the one *you must* **worship**.
17:37 [A] and commands he wrote for you. *Do* not **worship** other gods.
17:38 [A] I have made with you, and *do* not **worship** other gods.
17:39 [A] Rather, **worship** the LORD your God; it is he who will
19: 6 [A] *Do* not *be* **afraid** of what you have heard—those words with
25:24 [A] "*Do* not *be* **afraid** of the Babylonian officials," he said.
25:26 [A] the army officers, fled to Egypt for **fear** of the Babylonians.
1Ch 10: 4 [A] his armor-bearer *was* **terrified** [+4394] and would not do it;
13:12 [A] David *was* **afraid** *of* God that day and asked, "How can I
16:25 [C] and most worthy of praise; he *is to* **be feared** above all gods.
17:21 [C] **awesome wonders** by driving out nations from before your
22:13 [A] Be strong and courageous. *Do* not *be* **afraid** or discouraged.
28:20 [A] *Do* not *be* **afraid** or discouraged, for the LORD God,
2Ch 6:31 [A] so that *they will* **fear** you and walk in your ways all the time
6:33 [A] the peoples of the earth may know your name and **fear** you,
20: 3 [A] **Alarmed**, Jehoshaphat resolved to inquire of the LORD,
20:15 [A] '*Do* not *be* **afraid** or discouraged because of this vast army.
20:17 [A] and Jerusalem. *Do* not *be* **afraid**; do not be discouraged.
32: 7 [A] *Do* not *be* **afraid** or discouraged because of the king of
32:18 [D] to **terrify** them and make them afraid in order to capture the
Ne 1: 5 [C] "O LORD, God of heaven, the great and **awesome** God,
1:11 [A] to the prayer of your servants who delight in **revering** your
2: 2 [A] be nothing but sadness of heart." *I was* very much **afraid**,
4:14 [4:8] [A] and the rest of the people, "Don't *be* **afraid** of them.
4:14 [4:8] [C] Remember the Lord, who is great and **awesome**,
6: 9 [D] They *were* all *trying to* **frighten** us, thinking, "Their hands
6:13 [A] He had been hired to **intimidate** *me* so that I would commit
6:14 [D] the rest of the prophets who have been *trying to* **intimidate**
6:16 [A] all the surrounding nations *were* **afraid** and lost their
6:19 [D] him what I said. And Tobiah sent letters to **intimidate** me.
7: 2 [A] a man of integrity and **feared** God more than most men do.
9:32 [C] O our God, the great, mighty and **awesome** God,
Job 1: 9 [A] "*Does* Job **fear** God for nothing?" Satan replied.
5:21 [A] of the tongue, and *need* not **fear** when destruction comes.
5:22 [A] and famine, and *need* not **fear** the beasts of the earth.
6:21 [A] to be of no help; you see something dreadful and *are* **afraid**.
9:35 [A] I would speak up without **fear** *of* him, but as it now stands
11:15 [A] face without shame; you will stand firm and without **fear**.
32: 6 [A] that is why I was fearful, **not daring** to tell you what I know.
37:22 [C] comes in golden splendor; God comes in **awesome** majesty.
37:24 [A] Therefore, men **revere** him, for does he not have regard for
Ps 3: 6 [3:7] [A] *I will* not **fear** the tens of thousands drawn up against
23: 4 [A] the shadow of death, *I will* **fear** no evil, for you are with me;
27: 1 [A] LORD is my light and my salvation—whom *shall I* **fear**?
27: 3 [A] Though an army besiege me, my heart *will* not **fear**;
33: 8 [A] *Let* all the earth **fear** the LORD; let all the people of the
34: 9 [34:10] [A] **Fear** the LORD, *you* his saints, for those who fear
40: 3 [40:4] [A] will see and **fear** and put their trust in the LORD.
45: 4 [45:5] [C] let your right hand display **awesome** *deeds*.
46: 2 [46:3] [C] Therefore *we will* not **fear**, though the earth give way
47: 2 [47:3] [C] How **awesome** is the LORD Most High, the great
49: 5 [49:6] [A] Why *should I* **fear** when evil days come,
49:16 [49:17] [A] *Do* not *be* **overawed** when a man grows rich,
52: 6 [52:8] [A] The righteous will see and **fear**; they will laugh at
55:19 [55:20] [A] never change their ways and *have* no **fear** *of* God.
56: 3 [56:4] [A] When I *am* **afraid**, I will trust in you.
56: 4 [56:5] [A] word I praise, in God I trust; *I will* not *be* **afraid**.
56:11 [56:12] [A] in God I trust; *I will* not *be* **afraid**. What can man
64: 4 [64:5] [A] they shoot at him suddenly, without **fear**.
64: 9 [64:10] [A] All mankind *will* **fear**; they will proclaim the works

Ps 65: 5 [65:6] [C] You answer us with **awesome deeds** of
65: 8 [65:9] [A] Those living far away **fear** your wonders;
66: 3 [C] Say to God, "How **awesome** are your deeds! So great is your
66: 5 [C] God has done, *how* **awesome** his works in man's behalf!
67: 7 [67:8] [A] bless us, and all the ends of the earth *will* **fear** him.
68: 35 [68:36] [C] *You are* **awesome**, O God, in your sanctuary;
72: 5 [g] *He will* endure [BHS *You will be feared*; NIV 799]
76: 7 [76:8] [C] You alone *are to* **be feared**. Who can stand before
76: 8 [76:9] [A] and the land **feared** and was quiet—
76: 12 [76:13] [C] of rulers; *he* **is feared** by the kings of the earth.
86: 11 [A] give me an undivided heart, that I *may* **fear** your name.
89: 7 [89:8] [C] *he is* more **awesome** than all who surround him.
91: 5 [A] *You will* not **fear** the terror of night, nor the arrow that flies
96: 4 [C] and most worthy of praise; he *is to* **be feared** above all gods.
99: 3 [C] Let them praise your great and **awesome** name—he is holy.
102: 15 [102:16] [A] *will* **fear** the name of the LORD, all the kings of the
106: 22 [C] in the land of Ham and **awesome** *deeds* by the Red Sea.
111: 9 [C] his covenant forever—holy and **awesome** *is* his name.
112: 1 [A] Blessed is the man *who* **fears** the LORD, who finds great
112: 7 [A] *He will* **have** no **fear** of bad news; his heart is steadfast,
112: 8 [A] His heart is secure, *he will* **have** no **fear**; in the end he will
118: 6 [A] The LORD is with me; *I will* not *be* **afraid**. What can man
119: 63 [A] I am a friend to all who **fear** you, to all who follow your
119: 120 [A] flesh trembles in fear of you; *I* **stand in awe** of your laws.
130: 4 [C] But with you there is forgiveness; therefore *you* **are feared**.
139: 14 [C] I praise you because I am **fearfully** and wonderfully made;
145: 6 [C] They will tell of the power of your **awesome works**, and I
Pr 3: 7 [A] not be wise in your own eyes; **fear** the LORD and shun evil.
3: 25 [A] *Have* no **fear** of sudden disaster or of the ruin that overtakes
13: 13 [A] will pay for it, but *he who* **respects** a command is rewarded.
14: 2 [A] He whose walk is upright **fears** the LORD, but he whose
14: 16 [A] A wise man **fears** the LORD and shuns evil, but a fool is
24: 21 [A] **Fear** the LORD and the king, my son, and do not join with
31: 21 [A] When it snows, *she has* no **fear** for her household; for all of
Ecc 3: 14 [A] taken from it. God does it so that *men will* **revere** him.
5: 7 [5:6] [A] are meaningless. Therefore **stand in awe** *of* God.
8: 12 [A] better with God-fearing men, who *are* **reverent** before God.
9: 2 [A] who take oaths, so with *those who are* **afraid** to take them.
12: 5 [A] when *men are* **afraid** of heights and of dangers in the streets;
12: 13 [A] **Fear** God and keep his commandments, for this is the whole
Isa 7: 4 [A] Say to him, 'Be careful, keep calm and don't *be* **afraid**. Do
8: 12 [A] *do* not **fear** what they fear, and do not dread it.
10: 24 [A] *do* not *be* **afraid** of the Assyrians, who beat you with a rod
18: 2 [C] and smooth-skinned, to a people **feared** far and wide,
18: 7 [C] and smooth-skinned, from a people **feared** far and wide,
21: 1 [C] an invader comes from the desert, from a land of **terror**.
25: 3 [A] will honor you; cities of ruthless nations *will* **revere** you.
29: 13 [A] Their **worship** *of* me is made up only of rules taught by men.
35: 4 [A] say to those with fearful hearts, "Be strong, *do* not **fear**; your
37: 6 [A] *Do* not *be* **afraid** of what you have heard—those words with
40: 9 [A] lift up your voice with a shout, lift it up, *do* not *be* **afraid**;
41: 5 [A] The islands have seen it and **fear**; the ends of the earth
41: 10 [A] So *do* not **fear**, for I am with you; do not be dismayed, for I
41: 13 [A] takes hold of your right hand and says to you, *Do* not **fear**;
41: 14 [A] *Do* not *be* **afraid**, O worm Jacob, O little Israel, for I myself
41: 23 [A] so that we will be dismayed and *filled with* **fear**. [Q 8011]
43: 1 [A] "**Fear** not, for I have redeemed you; I have summoned you
43: 5 [A] *Do* not *be* **afraid**, for I am with you; I will bring your
44: 2 [A] *Do* not *be* **afraid**, O Jacob, my servant, Jeshurun, whom I
51: 7 [A] *Do* not **fear** the reproach of men or be terrified by their
51: 12 [A] Who are you that *you* **fear** mortal men, the sons of men,
54: 4 [A] "*Do* not *be* **afraid**; you will not suffer shame. Do not fear
54: 14 [A] Tyranny will be far from you; *you will have* nothing *to* **fear**.
57: 11 [A] so dreaded and **feared** that you have been false to me,
57: 11 [A] because I have long been silent that *you do* not **fear** me?
59: 19 [A] *men will* **fear** the name of the LORD, and from the rising
64: 3 [64:2] [C] For when you did **awesome** *things* that we did not
Jer 1: 8 [A] *Do* not *be* **afraid** of them, for I am with you and will rescue
3: 8 [A] Yet I saw that her unfaithful sister Judah *had* no **fear**; she
5: 22 [A] *Should you* not **fear** me?" declares the LORD. "Should you
5: 24 [A] '*Let us* **fear** the LORD our God, who gives autumn and
10: 5 [A] *Do* not **fear** them; they can do no harm nor can they do any
10: 7 [A] Who *should* not **revere** you, O King of the nations? This is
17: 8 [A] *It does* not **fear** [Q 8011] when heat comes; its leaves are
23: 4 [A] *they will* no longer *be* **afraid** or terrified, nor will any be
26: 19 [A] *Did* not Hezekiah **fear** the LORD and seek his favor? And
26: 21 [A] him to death. But Uriah heard of it and fled *in* **fear** to Egypt.
30: 10 [A] " 'So *do* not **fear**, O Jacob my servant; do not be dismayed,
32: 39 [A] so that they *will* always **fear** me for their own good
40: 9 [A] "*Do* not *be* **afraid** to serve the Babylonians," he said.
41: 18 [A] *They were* **afraid** of them because Ishmael son of Nethaniah
42: 11 [A] *Do* not *be* **afraid** of the king of Babylon, whom you now
42: 11 [A] *Do* not *be* **afraid** of him, declares the LORD, for I am with
44: 10 [A] day they have not humbled themselves or **shown reverence**,
46: 27 [A] "*Do* not **fear**, O Jacob my servant; do not be dismayed,
46: 28 [A] *Do* not **fear**, O Jacob my servant, for I am with you,"
51: 46 [A] lose heart or *be* **afraid** when rumors are heard in the land;
La 3: 57 [A] came near when I called you, and you said, "*Do* not **fear**."
Eze 1: 22 [C] looked like an expanse, sparkling like ice, and **awesome**.
2: 6 [A] son of man, *do* not *be* **afraid** of them or their words.
2: 6 [A] *Do* not *be* **afraid**, though briers and thorns are all around you
2: 6 [A] *Do* not *be* **afraid** of what they say or terrified by them,
3: 9 [A] *Do* not *be* **afraid** *of* them or terrified by them, though they
11: 8 [A] *You* **fear** the sword, and the sword is what I will bring
Da 9: 4 [C] "O Lord, the great and **awesome** God, who keeps his
10: 12 [A] he continued, "*Do* not *be* **afraid**, Daniel. Since the first day
10: 19 [A] "*Do* not *be* **afraid**, O man highly esteemed," he said. "Peace!
Hos 10: 3 [A] "We have no king because *we did* not **revere** the LORD.
Joel 2: 11 [C] The day of the LORD is great; *it is* **dreadful** [+4394]. Who
2: 21 [A] *Be* not **afraid**, O land; be glad and rejoice.
2: 22 [A] *Be* not **afraid**, O wild animals, for the open pastures are
2: 31 [3:4] [C] coming of the great and **dreadful** day of the LORD.
Am 3: 8 [A] The lion has roared—who *will* not **fear**? The Sovereign
Jnh 1: 5 [A] All the sailors *were* **afraid** and each cried out to his own
1: 9 [A] He answered, "I am a Hebrew and I **worship** the LORD,
1: 10 [A] This **terrified** [+1524+3711] them and they asked, "What
1: 16 [A] At this the men greatly **feared** [+906+3711] the LORD,
Mic 6: 9 [A] *to* **fear** [BHS 8011] your name is wisdom—"Heed the rod
7: 17 [A] turn in fear to the LORD our God and *will be* **afraid** of you.
Hab 1: 7 [C] They are a feared and **dreaded** *people*; they are a law to
3: 2 [A] of your fame; *I* **stand in awe** *of* your deeds, O LORD.
Zep 2: 11 [C] The LORD *will be* **awesome** to them when he destroys all
3: 7 [A] to the city, 'Surely *you will* **fear** me and accept correction!'
3: 15 [A] of Israel, is with you; never again *will you* **fear** any harm.
3: 16 [A] On that day they will say to Jerusalem, "*Do* not **fear**, O Zion;
Hag 1: 12 [A] their God had sent him. And the people **feared** the LORD.
2: 5 [A] of Egypt. And my Spirit remains among you. *Do* not **fear**.'
Zec 8: 13 [A] a blessing. *Do* not *be* **afraid**, but let your hands be strong."
8: 15 [A] to do good again to Jerusalem and Judah. *Do* not *be* **afraid**.
9: 5 [A] Ashkelon will see it and **fear**; Gaza will writhe in agony, and
Mal 1: 14 [C] "and my name *is to* **be feared** among the nations.
2: 5 [A] this called for reverence and *he* **revered** me and stood in awe
3: 5 [A] of justice, but *do* not **fear** me," says the LORD Almighty.
4: 5 [3:23] [C] that great and **dreadful** day of the LORD comes.

3708 [2]יָרֵא ***yārē'***[2], v. Not used in NIV/BHS [cf. 3721]

3709 [3]יָרֵא ***yārē'***[3], v. Not used in NIV/BHS [cf. 3722]

3710 [4]יָרֵא ***yārē'***[4], a.vbl. [52] [√ 3707]

fear [32], fears [7], afraid [4], feared [3], worshiped [2], God-fearing [+466+2021] [1], revere [1], worship [1], worshiping [1]

Ge 22: 12 Now I know that you **fear** God, because you have not withheld
42: 18 Joseph said to them, "Do this and you will live, for I **fear** God:
Ex 18: 21 *men who* **fear** God, trustworthy men who hate dishonest gain—
Dt 20: 8 Then the officers shall add, "Is any man **afraid** or fainthearted?
Jdg 7: 3 'Anyone who trembles *with* **fear** may turn back and leave Mount
7: 10 If you are **afraid** to attack, go down to the camp with your servant
1Sa 23: 3 But David's men said to him, "Here in Judah we are **afraid**.
2Ki 17: 32 *They* **worshiped** the LORD, but they also appointed all sorts of
17: 33 *They* **worshiped** the LORD, but they also served their own gods
17: 34 They neither **worship** the LORD nor adhere to the decrees
17: 41 Even while these people were **worshiping** the LORD, they were
Job 1: 1 man was blameless and upright; *he* **feared** God and shunned evil.
1: 8 he is blameless and upright, a man *who* **fears** God and shuns evil."
2: 3 he is blameless and upright, a man *who* **fears** God and shuns evil.
Ps 15: 4 who despises a vile man but honors *those who* **fear** the LORD,
22: 23 [22:24] You *who* **fear** the LORD, praise him! All you
22: 25 [22:26] before *those who* **fear** you will I fulfill my vows.
25: 12 Who, then, is the man *that* **fears** the LORD? He will instruct him
25: 14 The LORD confides in *those who* **fear** him; he makes his
31: 19 [31:20] which you have stored up for *those who* **fear** you,
33: 18 the eyes of the LORD are on *those who* **fear** him, on those whose
34: 7 [34:8] The angel of the LORD encamps around *those who* **fear**
34: 9 [34:10] you his saints, for *those who* **fear** him lack nothing.
60: 4 [60:6] for *those who* **fear** you, you have raised a banner to be
61: 5 [61:6] you have given me the heritage of *those who* **fear** your
66: 16 Come and listen, all you *who* **fear** God; let me tell you what he has
85: 9 [85:10] Surely his salvation is near *those who* **fear** him, that his
103: 11 are above the earth, so great is his love for *those who* **fear** him;
103: 13 so the LORD has compassion on *those who* **fear** him;
103: 17 to everlasting the LORD's love is with *those who* **fear** him,
111: 5 He provides food for *those who* **fear** him; he remembers his
115: 11 You *who* **fear** him, trust in the LORD—he is their help
115: 13 he will bless *those who* **fear** the LORD—small and great alike.
118: 4 Let *those who* **fear** the LORD say: "His love endures forever."
119: 74 May *those who* **fear** you rejoice when they see me, for I have put

Ps 119:79 May *those who* **fear** you turn to me, those who understand your
128: 1 Blessed are all *who* **fear** the LORD, who walk in his ways.
128: 4 Thus is the man blessed *who* **fears** the LORD.
135:20 praise the LORD; you *who* **fear** him, praise the LORD.
145:19 He fulfills the desires of *those who* **fear** him; he hears their cry
147:11 the LORD delights in *those who* **fear** him, who put their hope in
Pr 31:30 is fleeting; but a woman *who* **fears** the LORD is to be praised.
Ecc 7:18 go of the other. The *man who* **fears** God will avoid all ⌞extremes⌟.
8:12 I know that it will go better with **God-fearing** [+466+2021] *men*,
8:13 Yet because the wicked do not **fear** God, it will not go well with
Isa 50:10 Who among you **fears** the LORD and obeys the word of his
Jer 42:11 Do not be afraid of the king of Babylon, whom you now **fear**.
42:16 the sword you **fear** will overtake you there, and the famine you
Da 1:10 but the official told Daniel, "I am **afraid** *of* my lord the king,
Mal 3:16 Then *those who* **feared** the LORD talked with each other,
3:16 written in his presence concerning *those who* **feared** the LORD
4: 2 [3:20] for you *who* **revere** my name, the sun of righteousness will

3711 יִרְאָה yir'â, n.f. [44 / 45] [√ 3707]

fear [34], piety [3], reverence [2], awesome [1], feared [+906+3707] [1], feared [1], fears [1], revere [1], terrified [+1524+3707] [1]

Ge 20:11 "I said to myself, 'There is surely no **fear** *of* God in this place,
Ex 20:20 so that the **fear** *of* God will be with you to keep you from sinning."
Dt 2:25 to put the terror and **fear** *of* you on all the nations under heaven.
2Sa 23: 3 rules over men in righteousness, when he rules in the **fear** *of* God,
2Ch 19: 9 serve faithfully and wholeheartedly in the **fear** *of* the LORD.
26: 5 of Zechariah, who instructed him in the **fear** [BHS 8011] *of* God.
Ne 5: 9 Shouldn't you walk in the **fear** *of* our God to avoid the reproach of
5:15 the people. But out of **reverence** *for* God I did not act like that.
Job 4: 6 Should not your **piety** be your confidence and your blameless ways
6:14 of his friends, even though he forsakes the **fear** *of* the Almighty.
15: 4 But you even undermine **piety** and hinder devotion to God.
22: 4 "Is it for your **piety** that he rebukes you and brings charges against
28:28 And he said to man, 'The **fear** *of* the Lord—that is wisdom,
Ps 2:11 Serve the LORD with **fear** and rejoice with trembling.
5: 7 [5:8] in **reverence** will I bow down toward your holy temple.
19: 9 [19:10] The **fear** *of* the LORD is pure, enduring forever. The
34:11 [34:12] listen to me; I will teach you the **fear** *of* the LORD.
55: 5 [55:6] **Fear** and trembling have beset me; horror has
90:11 your anger? For your wrath is as great as the **fear** *that is due* you.
111:10 The **fear** *of* the LORD is the beginning of wisdom; all who
119:38 Fulfill your promise to your servant, so that you *may be* **feared**.
Pr 1: 7 The **fear** *of* the LORD is the beginning of knowledge, but fools
1:29 they hated knowledge and did not choose to **fear** the LORD,
2: 5 you will understand the **fear** *of* the LORD and find the
8:13 To **fear** the LORD is to hate evil; I hate pride and arrogance,
9:10 "The **fear** *of* the LORD is the beginning of wisdom,
10:27 The **fear** *of* the LORD adds length to life, but the years of the
14:26 *He who* **fears** the LORD has a secure fortress, and for his
14:27 The **fear** *of* the LORD is a fountain of life, turning a man from
15:16 Better a little with the **fear** *of* the LORD than great wealth with
15:33 The **fear** *of* the LORD teaches a man wisdom, and humility
16: 6 is atoned for; through the **fear** *of* the LORD a man avoids evil.
19:23 The **fear** *of* the LORD leads to life: Then one rests content,
22: 4 Humility and the **fear** *of* the LORD bring wealth and honor
23:17 envy sinners, but always be zealous for the **fear** *of* the LORD.
Isa 7:25 you will no longer go there *for* **fear** *of* the briers and thorns;
11: 2 of power, the Spirit of knowledge and of the **fear** *of* the LORD—
11: 3 he will delight in the **fear** *of* the LORD. He will not judge by
33: 6 and knowledge; the **fear** *of* the LORD is the key to this treasure.
63:17 from your ways and harden our hearts so we do not **revere** you?
Jer 32:40 never stop doing good to them, and I will inspire them to **fear** me,
Eze 1:18 Their rims were high and **awesome**, and all four rims were full of
30:13 be a prince in Egypt, and I will spread **fear** throughout the land.
Jnh 1:10 This **terrified** [+1524+3707] them and they asked, "What have
1:16 At this the men greatly **feared** [+906+3707] the LORD, and they

3712 יִרְאוֹן yir'ôn, n.pr.loc. [1]

Iron [1]

Jos 19:38 **Iron**, Migdal El, Horem, Beth Anath and Beth Shemesh. There

3713 יִרְאִיָּיה yir'iyyāyh, n.pr.m. [2] [√ 8011 + 3378]

Irijah [2]

Jer 37:13 whose name was **Irijah** son of Shelemiah, the son of Hananiah,
37:14 But **Irijah** would not listen to him; instead, he arrested Jeremiah

3714 יָרֵב yārēb, n.m. [2] [√ 8045]

great [2]

Hos 5:13 then Ephraim turned to Assyria, and sent to the **great** king for help.
10: 6 It will be carried to Assyria as tribute for the **great** king.

3715 יְרֻבַּעַל yᵉrubba'al, n.pr.m. [14] [√ 8045 + 1251]

Jerub-Baal [11], Jerub-Baal's [3]

Jdg 6:32 So that day they called Gideon "**Jerub-Baal**," saying, "Let Baal
7: 1 Early in the morning, **Jerub-Baal** (that is, Gideon) and all his men
8:29 **Jerub-Baal** son of Joash went back home to live.
8:35 They also failed to show kindness to the family of **Jerub-Baal**
9: 1 Abimelech son of **Jerub-Baal** went to his mother's brothers in
9: 2 to have all seventy of **Jerub-Baal's** sons rule over you, or just one
9: 5 one stone murdered his seventy brothers, the sons of **Jerub-Baal**.
9: 5 But Jotham, the youngest son of **Jerub-Baal**, escaped by hiding.
9:16 if you have been fair to **Jerub-Baal** and his family, and if you have
9:19 and in good faith toward **Jerub-Baal** and his family today,
9:24 God did this in order that the crime against **Jerub-Baal's** seventy
9:28 Isn't he **Jerub-Baal's** son, and isn't Zebul his deputy? Serve the
9:57 The curse of Jotham son of **Jerub-Baal** came on them.
1Sa 12:11 Then the LORD sent **Jerub-Baal**, Barak, Jephthah and Samuel,

3716 יָרָבְעָם yārob'ām, n.pr.m. [104] [√ 8045 + 6639]

Jeroboam [94], Jeroboam's [6], he[s] [4]

1Ki 11:26 Also, **Jeroboam** son of Nebat rebelled against the king. He was
11:28 Now **Jeroboam** was a man of standing, and when Solomon saw
11:29 About that time **Jeroboam** was going out of Jerusalem, and Ahijah
11:31 Then he said to **Jeroboam**, "Take ten pieces for yourself,
11:40 Solomon tried to kill **Jeroboam**, but Jeroboam fled to Egypt,
11:40 to kill Jeroboam, but **Jeroboam** fled to Egypt, to Shishak the king,
12: 2 When **Jeroboam** son of Nebat heard this (he was still in Egypt,
12: 2 where he had fled from King Solomon), **he**[s] returned from Egypt.
12: 3 So they sent for **Jeroboam**, and he and the whole assembly of
12:12 Three days later **Jeroboam** and all the people returned to
12:15 to fulfill the word the LORD had spoken to **Jeroboam** son of
12:20 When all the Israelites heard that **Jeroboam** had returned,
12:25 Then **Jeroboam** fortified Shechem in the hill country of Ephraim
12:26 **Jeroboam** thought to himself, "The kingdom will now likely
12:32 **He**[s] instituted a festival on the fifteenth day of the eighth month,
13: 1 as **Jeroboam** was standing by the altar to make an offering.
13: 4 When King **Jeroboam** heard what the man of God cried out
13:33 Even after this, **Jeroboam** did not change his evil ways, but once
13:34 This was the sin of the house of **Jeroboam** that led to its downfall
14: 1 At that time Abijah son of **Jeroboam** became ill,
14: 2 **Jeroboam** said to his wife, "Go, disguise yourself, so you won't be
14: 2 so you won't be recognized as the wife of **Jeroboam**.
14: 4 So **Jeroboam's** wife did what he said and went to Ahijah's house
14: 5 "**Jeroboam's** wife is coming to ask you about her son, for he is ill,
14: 6 of her footsteps at the door, he said, "Come in, wife of **Jeroboam**.
14: 7 Go, tell **Jeroboam** that this is what the LORD, the God of Israel,
14:10 of this, I am going to bring disaster on the house of **Jeroboam**.
14:10 I will cut off from **Jeroboam** every last male in Israel—slave
14:10 I will burn up the house of **Jeroboam** as one burns dung, until it is
14:11 Dogs will eat those belonging to **Jeroboam** who die in the city,
14:13 He is the only one belonging to **Jeroboam** who will be buried,
14:13 because he is the only one in the house of **Jeroboam** in whom the
14:14 a king over Israel who will cut off the family of **Jeroboam**.
14:16 he will give Israel up because of the sins **Jeroboam** has committed
14:17 Then **Jeroboam's** wife got up and left and went to Tirzah.
14:19 The other events of **Jeroboam's** reign, his wars and how he ruled,
14:20 **He**[s] reigned for twenty-two years and then rested with his fathers.
14:30 There was continual warfare between Rehoboam and **Jeroboam**.
15: 1 In the eighteenth year of the reign of **Jeroboam** son of Nebat,
15: 6 between Rehoboam and **Jeroboam** throughout ⌞Abijah's⌟ lifetime.
15: 7 the kings of Judah? There was war between Abijah and **Jeroboam**.
15: 9 In the twentieth year of **Jeroboam** king of Israel, Asa became king
15:25 Nadab son of **Jeroboam** became king of Israel in the second year
15:29 As soon as he began to reign, he killed **Jeroboam's** whole family.
15:29 He did not leave **Jeroboam** anyone that breathed, but destroyed
15:30 because of the sins **Jeroboam** had committed and had caused
15:34 of the LORD, walking in the ways of **Jeroboam** and in his sin,
16: 2 you walked in the ways of **Jeroboam** and caused my people Israel
16: 3 and I will make your house like that of **Jeroboam** son of Nebat.
16: 7 by the things he did, and becoming like the house of **Jeroboam**—
16:19 walking in the ways of **Jeroboam** and in the sin he had committed
16:26 He walked in all the ways of **Jeroboam** son of Nebat and in his
16:31 He not only considered it trivial to commit the sins of **Jeroboam**
21:22 I will make your house like that of **Jeroboam** son of Nebat
22:52 [22:53] and mother and in the ways of **Jeroboam** son of Nebat,
2Ki 3: 3 Nevertheless he clung to the sins of **Jeroboam** son of Nebat,
9: 9 I will make the house of Ahab like the house of **Jeroboam** son of
10:29 he did not turn away from the sins of **Jeroboam** son of Nebat,
10:31 He did not turn away from the sins of **Jeroboam**, which he had
13: 2 of the LORD by following the sins of **Jeroboam** son of Nebat,
13: 6 they did not turn away from the sins of the house of **Jeroboam**,
13:11 did not turn away from any of the sins of **Jeroboam** son of Nebat,
13:13 with his fathers, and **Jeroboam** succeeded him on the throne.

2Ki 14:16 the kings of Israel. And **Jeroboam** his son succeeded him as king.
14:23 **Jeroboam** son of Jehoash king of Israel became king in Samaria,
14:24 did not turn away from any of the sins of **Jeroboam** son of Nebat,
14:27 he saved them by the hand of **Jeroboam** son of Jehoash.
14:28 As for the other events of **Jeroboam's** reign, all he did, and his
14:29 **Jeroboam** rested with his fathers, the kings of Israel.
15: 1 In the twenty-seventh year of **Jeroboam** king of Israel,
15: 8 Zechariah son of **Jeroboam** became king of Israel in Samaria,
15: 9 He did not turn away from the sins of **Jeroboam** son of Nebat,
15:18 he did not turn away from the sins of **Jeroboam** son of Nebat,
15:24 He did not turn away from the sins of **Jeroboam** son of Nebat,
15:28 He did not turn away from the sins of **Jeroboam** son of Nebat,
17:21 the house of David, they made **Jeroboam** son of Nebat their king.
17:21 **Jeroboam** enticed Israel away from following the LORD
17:22 The Israelites persisted in all the sins of **Jeroboam** and did not
23:15 the altar at Bethel, the high place made by **Jeroboam** son of Nebat,
1Ch 5:17 the reigns of Jotham king of Judah and **Jeroboam** king of Israel.
2Ch 9:29 in the visions of Iddo the seer concerning **Jeroboam** son of Nebat?
10: 2 When **Jeroboam** son of Nebat heard this (he was in Egypt,
10: 2 where he had fled from King Solomon), **he**[s] returned from Egypt.
10: 3 So they sent for **Jeroboam**, and he and all Israel went to
10:12 Three days later **Jeroboam** and all the people returned to
10:15 to fulfill the word the LORD had spoken to **Jeroboam** son of
11: 4 of the LORD and turned back from marching against **Jeroboam**.
11:14 came to Judah and Jerusalem because **Jeroboam** and his sons had
12:15 There was continual warfare between Rehoboam and **Jeroboam**.
13: 1 In the eighteenth year of the reign of **Jeroboam**, Abijah became
13: 2 of Uriel of Gibeah. There was war between Abijah and **Jeroboam**.
13: 3 **Jeroboam** drew up a battle line against him with eight hundred
13: 4 of Ephraim, and said, "**Jeroboam** and all Israel, listen to me!
13: 6 Yet **Jeroboam** son of Nebat, an official of Solomon son of David,
13: 8 have with you the golden calves that **Jeroboam** made to be your
13:13 Now **Jeroboam** had sent troops around to the rear, so that while he
13:15 God routed **Jeroboam** and all Israel before Abijah and Judah.
13:19 Abijah pursued **Jeroboam** and took from him the towns of Bethel,
13:20 **Jeroboam** did not regain power during the time of Abijah.
Hos 1: 1 and during the reign of **Jeroboam** son of Jehoash king of Israel:
Am 1: 1 king of Judah and **Jeroboam** son of Jehoash was king of Israel.
7: 9 with my sword I will rise against the house of **Jeroboam**."
7:10 Amaziah the priest of Bethel sent a message to **Jeroboam** king of
7:11 " '**Jeroboam** will die by the sword, and Israel will surely go into

3717 יְרֻבֶּשֶׁת *yᵉrubbešet*, n.pr.m. [1] [√ 8045 + 1017]

Jerub-Besheth [1]

2Sa 11:21 Who killed Abimelech son of **Jerub-Besheth**? Didn't a woman

3718 יָרַד *yārad*, v. [380 / 381] [→ 3720, 4618]

went down [63], go down [61], come down [28], came down [24], bring down [19], down [13], brought down [8], gone down [8], go [7], take down [7], coming down [6], fall [6], going down [5], took down [4], *untranslated* [3], come [3], comes down [3], descend [3], descended [3], gone [3], leave [+4946] [3], let down [3], lowered [3], overflow [3], be brought down [2], came down [+3718] [2], continued down [2], descending [2], falling [2], fell [2], flowing [2], goes down [2], lead down [2], pull down [2], went [2], abandon [+4946] [1], abandoned [1], are brought down [1], attack [+928] [1], attack [1], been brought down [1], been taken down [1], bowed [1], brings down [1], brought [1], came out [1], came [1], carried down [1], climbed down [1], consign [1], continued [1], cut down [1], descends [1], do[s] so [1], fail [1], fall down [1], fallen [1], falls [1], flattens [1], flow from [1], flow [1], flowed down [1], flowing down [1], goes down [+4200+4752] [1], gone down [+345] [1], got off [+4946+6584] [1], haul down [1], leading down [1], leave [+4946+9348] [1], led down [1], let flow [1], let go down [1], letting run down [1], made flow down [1], march down [1], moved down [1], overflowing [1], poured [1], prostrate [1], pulls down [1], puts [1], ran down [1], removed [1], road down [1], roam [+2143+2256+6584] [1], running down [1], sank down [1], sank [1], send down [1], sends [1], sent down [1], settled [1], sink [1], so[s] [1], step down [1], stepped down [1], subdued [1], take off [+4946+6584] [1], take [1], taken [1], toward evening [+4394] [1], was taken down [1], went aboard [+928] [1], went out [1], will[s] [1]

Ge 11: 5 [A] the LORD **came down** to see the city and the tower that the
11: 7 [A] *let us* **go down** and confuse their language so they will not
12:10 [A] Abram **went down** to Egypt to live there for a while
15:11 [A] birds of prey **came down** on the carcasses, but Abram drove
18:21 [A] that *I will* **go down** and see if what they have done is as bad
24:16 [A] *She* **went down** to the spring, filled her jar and came up
24:18 [G] quickly **lowered** the jar to her hands and gave him a drink.
24:45 [A] *She* **went down** to the spring and drew water, and I said to
24:46 [G] "*She* quickly **lowered** her jar from her shoulder and said,
26: 2 [A] appeared to Isaac and said, "*Do* not **go down** to Egypt;
28:12 [A] and the angels of God were ascending and **descending** on it.
37:25 [G] and they were on their way to **take** them **down** to Egypt.
37:35 [A] "in mourning *will I* **go down** to the grave to my son."
38: 1 [A] and **went down** to stay with a man of Adullam named Hirah.
39: 1 [H] Now Joseph *had* **been taken down** to Egypt. Potiphar,
39: 1 [G] bought him from the Ishmaelites who *had* **taken** him there.
42: 2 [A] **Go down** there and buy some for us, so that we may live
42: 3 [A] ten of Joseph's brothers **went down** to buy grain from Egypt.
42:38 [A] But Jacob said, "My son *will* not **go down** there with you;
42:38 [G] *you will* **bring** my gray head **down** to the grave in sorrow."
43: 4 [A] along with us, *we will* **go down** and buy food for you.
43: 5 [A] send him, *we will* not **go down**, because the man said to us,
43: 7 [G] we to know he would say, '**Bring** your brother **down** here'?"
43:11 [G] land in your bags and **take** them **down** to the man *as* a gift—
43:15 [A] They hurried **down** *to* Egypt and presented themselves to
43:20 [A] "*we* **came down** [+3718] here the first time to buy food.
43:20 [A] "*we* **came down** [+3718] here the first time to buy food.
43:22 [G] *We have* also **brought** additional silver with us to buy food.
44:11 [G] Each of them quickly **lowered** his sack to the ground
44:21 [G] '**Bring** him **down** to me so I can see him for myself.'
44:23 [A] 'Unless your youngest brother **comes down** with you,
44:26 [A] we said, 'We cannot **go down**. Only if our youngest brother is
44:26 [A] go down. Only if our youngest brother is with us *will we* **go**.
44:29 [G] *you will* **bring** my gray head **down** to the grave in misery.'
44:31 [G] Your servants *will* **bring** the gray head of our father **down** to
45: 9 [A] made me lord of all Egypt. **Come down** to me; don't delay.
45:13 [G] you have seen. And **bring** my father **down** here quickly."
46: 3 [A] "Do not be afraid *to* **go down** to Egypt, for I will make you
46: 4 [A] I *will* **go down** to Egypt with you, and I will surely bring you
Ex 2: 5 [A] Then Pharaoh's daughter **went down** to the Nile to bathe,
3: 8 [A] So *I have* **come down** to rescue them from the hand of the
9:19 [A] because the hail *will* **fall** on every man and animal that has
11: 8 [A] All these officials of yours *will* **come** to me, bowing down
15: 5 [A] have covered them; *they* **sank** to the depths like a stone.
19:11 [A] because on that day the LORD *will* **come down** on Mount
19:14 [A] After Moses *had* **gone down** the mountain to the people, he
19:18 [A] with smoke, because the LORD **descended** on it in fire.
19:20 [A] The LORD **descended** to the top of Mount Sinai and called
19:21 [A] "**Go down** and warn the people so they do not force their
19:24 [A] LORD replied, "Go **down** and bring Aaron up with you.
19:25 [A] So Moses **went down** to the people and told them.
32: 1 [A] that Moses was so long in **coming down** from the mountain,
32: 7 [A] the LORD said to Moses, "Go **down**, because your people,
32:15 [A] **went down** the mountain with the two tablets of the
33: 5 [G] Now **take off** [+4946+6584] your ornaments and I will
33: 9 [A] the pillar of cloud *would* **come down** and stay at the
34: 5 [A] the LORD **came down** in the cloud and stood there with
34:29 [A] When Moses **came down** from Mount Sinai with the two
34:29 [A] **[RPH]** he was not aware that his face was radiant
Lev 9:22 [A] burnt offering and the fellowship offering, *he* **stepped down**.
Nu 1:51 [G] the tabernacle is to move, the Levites *are to* **take** it **down**,
4: 5 [G] and his sons are to go in and **take down** the shielding curtain
10:17 [H] Then the tabernacle **was taken down**, and the Gershonites
11: 9 [A] When the dew **settled** on the camp at night, the manna also
11: 9 [A] settled on the camp at night, the manna also **came down**.
11:17 [A] *I will* **come down** and speak with you there, and I will take
11:25 [A] the LORD **came down** in the cloud and spoke with him,
12: 5 [A] the LORD **came down** in a pillar of cloud; he stood at the
14:45 [A] and Canaanites who lived in that hill country **came down**
16:30 [A] that belongs to them, and *they* **go down** alive into the grave,
16:33 [A] They **went down** alive into the grave, with everything they
20:15 [A] Our forefathers **went down** into Egypt, and we lived there
20:28 [A] Then Moses and Eleazar **came down** from the mountain,
34:11 [A] The boundary *will* **go down** from Shepham *to* Riblah on the
34:11 [A] **[RPH]** continue along the slopes east of the Sea of
34:12 [A] the boundary *will* **go down** along the Jordan and end at the
Dt 1:25 [G] fruit of the land, *they* **brought** it **down** to us and reported,
9:12 [A] the LORD told me, "**Go down** from here at once,
9:15 [A] **went down** from the mountain while it was ablaze with fire.
9:21 [A] threw the dust into a stream that **flowed down** the mountain.
10: 5 [A] I came back **down** the mountain and put the tablets in the ark
10:22 [A] Your forefathers *who went* **down** into Egypt were seventy in
20:20 [A] them to build siege works until the city at war with you **falls**.
21: 4 [G] **lead** her **down** to a valley that has not been plowed or
26: 5 [A] *he* **went down** into Egypt with a few people and lived there
28:24 [A] *it will* **come down** from the skies until you are destroyed.
28:43 [A] you higher and higher, but you *will* **sink** lower and lower.
28:52 [A] until the high fortified walls in which you trust **fall down**.
Jos 2:15 [G] So *she* **let** them **down** by a rope through the window,
2:18 [G] scarlet cord in the window through which *you* **let** us **down**,
2:23 [A] *They* **went down** out of the hills, forded the river and came
3:13 [A] its waters **flowing** downstream will be cut off and stand up in
3:16 [A] the water from upstream stopped **flowing**. It piled up in a
3:16 [A] while the water **flowing down** to the Sea of the Arabah (the
8:29 [G] Joshua ordered them *to* **take** his body from the tree

Jos 10:27 [G] gave the order and *they* **took** them **down** from the trees
15:10 [A] **continued down** *to* Beth Shemesh and crossed to Timnah.
16: 3 [A] **descended** westward to the territory of the Japhletites as far
16: 7 [A] *it* **went down** from Janoah to Ataroth and Naarah, touched
17: 9 [A] Then the boundary **continued** south *to* the Kanah Ravine.
18:13 [A] **went down** *to* Ataroth Addar on the hill south of Lower Beth
18:16 [A] The boundary **went down** to the foot of the hill facing the
18:16 [A] *It* **continued down** the Hinnom Valley along the southern
18:16 [A] the southern slope of the Jebusite city and **so**[s] *to* En Rogel.
18:17 [A] and **ran down** *to* the Stone of Bohan son of Reuben.
18:18 [A] northern slope of Beth Arabah and *on* **down** into the Arabah.
24: 4 [A] of Seir to Esau, but Jacob and his sons **went down** *to* Egypt.
Jdg 1: 9 [A] the men of Judah **went down** to fight against the Canaanites
1:34 [A] hill country, not allowing them to **come down** into the plain.
3:27 [A] the Israelites **went down** with him from the hills, with him
3:28 [A] So *they* followed him **down** and, taking possession of the
4:14 [A] So Barak **went down** Mount Tabor, followed by ten
4:15 [A] and Sisera **abandoned** his chariot and fled on foot.
5:11 [A] "Then the people of the LORD **went down** to the city gates.
5:13 [A] "Then the men who were left **came down** to the nobles;
5:13 [A] the people of the LORD **came** to me with the mighty.
5:14 [A] From Makir captains **came down**, from Zebulun those who
7: 4 [G] **Take** them **down** to the water, and I will sift them for you
7: 5 [G] So Gideon **took** the men **down** to the water. There the
7: 9 [A] LORD said to Gideon, "Get up, **go down** against the camp,
7:10 [A] If you are afraid to **attack**, go down to the camp with your
7:10 [A] to attack, **go down** to the camp with your servant Purah
7:11 [A] you will be encouraged *to* **attack** [+928] the camp."
7:11 [A] Purah his servant **went down** to the outposts of the camp.
7:24 [A] "**Come down** against the Midianites and seize the waters of
9:36 [A] people *are* **coming down** from the tops of the mountains!"
9:37 [A] "Look, people *are* **coming down** from the center of the land,
11:37 [A] "Give me two months *to* **roam** [+2143+2256+6584] the hills
14: 1 [A] Samson **went down** to Timnah and saw there a young
14: 5 [A] Samson **went down** to Timnah together with his father
14: 7 [A] *he* **went down** and talked with the woman, and he liked her.
14:10 [A] Now his father **went down** to see the woman. And Samson
14:19 [A] *He* **went down** *to* Ashkelon, struck down thirty of their men,
15: 8 [A] *he* **went down** and stayed in a cave in the rock of Etam.
15:11 [A] three thousand men from Judah **went down** to the cave in the
15:12 [A] "*We've* **come** to tie you up and hand you over to the
16:21 [G] seized him, gouged out his eyes and **took** him **down** to Gaza.
16:31 [A] and his father's whole family **went down** to get him.
19:11 [A] When they were near Jebus and the day *was* almost **gone**,
Ru 3: 3 [A] **go down** *to* the threshing floor, but don't let him know you
3: 6 [A] So *she* **went down** *to* the threshing floor and did everything
1Sa 2: 6 [G] and makes alive; *he* **brings down** *to* the grave and raises up.
6:15 [G] The Levites **took down** the ark of the LORD, together with
6:21 [A] of the LORD. **Come down** and take it up to your place."
9:25 [A] After *they* **came down** from the high place to the town,
9:27 [A] *As* they *were* **going down** to the edge of the town, Samuel
10: 5 [A] you will meet a procession of prophets **coming down** from
10: 8 [A] "**Go down** ahead of me *to* Gilgal. I will surely come down to
10: 8 [A] I *will* surely **come down** to you to sacrifice burnt offerings
13:12 [A] 'Now the Philistines *will* **come down** against me at Gilgal,
13:20 [A] So all Israel **went down** *to* the Philistines to have their
14:36 [A] "*Let us* **go down** after the Philistines by night and plunder
14:37 [A] So Saul asked God, "*Shall I* **go down** after the Philistines?
15: 6 [A] **leave** [+4946+9348] the Amalekites so that I do not destroy
15:12 [A] his own honor and has turned and gone on **down** *to* Gilgal."
17: 8 [A] of Saul? Choose a man and *have him* **come down** to me.
17:28 [A] anger at him and asked, "Why *have you* **come down** here?
17:28 [A] your heart is; *you* **came down** only to watch the battle."
19:12 [G] So Michal **let** David **down** through a window, and he fled
20:19 [A] The day after tomorrow, **toward evening** [+4394], go to the
21:13 [21:14] [G] of the gate and **letting** saliva **run down** his beard.
22: 1 [A] household heard about it, *they* **went down** to him there.
23: 4 [A] and the LORD answered him, "**Go down** *to* Keilah,
23: 6 [A] *had* **brought** the ephod **down** with him when he fled to
23: 8 [A] to **go down** *to* Keilah to besiege David and his men.
23:11 [A] *Will* Saul **come down**, as your servant has heard? O LORD,
23:11 [A] tell your servant." And the LORD said, "*He* **will**[s]."
23:20 [A] Now, O king, **come down** whenever it pleases you to do so,
23:20 [A] Now, O king, come down whenever it pleases you to **do**[s] **so**,
23:25 [A] *he* **went down** *to* the rock and stayed in the Desert of Maon.
25: 1 [A] Then David **moved down** into the Desert of Maon.
25:20 [A] As she came riding her donkey **[RPH]** into a mountain
25:20 [A] there were David and his men **descending** toward her,
25:23 [A] she quickly **got off** [+4946+6584] her donkey and bowed
26: 2 [A] So Saul **went down** to the Desert of Ziph, with his three
26: 6 [A] "Who *will* **go down** into the camp with me to Saul?"
26: 6 [A] the camp with me to Saul?" "I'll **go** with you," said Abishai.
26:10 [A] will come and he will die, or *he will* **go** into battle and perish.
29: 4 [A] *He must* not **go** with us into battle, or he will turn against us
30:15 [G] asked him, "*Can you* **lead** me **down** to this raiding party?"
30:15 [G] me over to my master, and *I will* **take** you **down** to them."
30:16 [G] *He* **led** David **down**, and there they were, scattered over the
30:24 [A] is to be the same as that of him *who* **went down** to the battle.
2Sa 5:17 [A] but David heard about it and **went down** to the stronghold.
11: 8 [A] said to Uriah, "**Go down** to your house and wash your feet."
11: 9 [A] all his master's servants and *did* not **go down** to his house.
11:10 [A] David was told, "Uriah *did* not **go** home," he asked him,
11:10 [A] you just come from a distance? Why didn't *you* **go** home?"
11:13 [A] on his mat among his master's servants; *he did* not **go** home.
17:18 [A] had a well in his courtyard, and *they* **climbed down** *into* it.
19:16 [19:17] [A] hurried **down** with the men of Judah to meet King
19:20 [19:21] [A] the first of the whole house of Joseph to **come down**
19:24 [19:25] [A] Saul's grandson, also **went down** to meet the king.
19:31 [19:32] [A] Barzillai the Gileadite also **came down** from
21:15 [A] David **went down** with his men to fight against the
22:10 [A] He parted the heavens and **came down**; dark clouds were
22:48 [G] is the God who avenges me, *who* **puts** the nations under me,
23:13 [A] three of the thirty chief men came **down** to David at the cave
23:20 [A] He also **went down** into a pit on a snowy day and killed a
23:21 [A] a spear in his hand, Benaiah **went** against him with a club.
1Ki 1:25 [A] Today *he has* **gone down** and sacrificed great numbers of
1:33 [G] my son on my own mule and **take** him **down** to Gihon.
1:38 [A] the Kerethites and the Pelethites **went down** and put
1:53 [G] sent men, and *they* **brought** him **down** from the altar.
2: 6 [G] but *do* not **let** his gray head **go down** *to* the grave in peace.
2: 8 [A] When he **came down** to meet me at the Jordan, I swore to
2: 9 [G] do to him. **Bring** his gray head **down** *to* the grave in blood."
5: 9 [5:23] [G] My men *will* **haul** them **down** from Lebanon to the
17:23 [G] and **carried** him **down** from the room into the house.
18:40 [G] and Elijah *had* them **brought down** to the Kishon Valley
18:44 [A] up your chariot and **go down** before the rain stops you.' "
21:16 [A] and **went down** to take possession of Naboth's vineyard.
21:18 [A] "Go **down** to meet Ahab king of Israel, who rules in Samaria.
21:18 [A] where *he has* **gone** to take possession of it.
22: 2 [A] in the third year Jehoshaphat king of Judah **went down** to see
2Ki 1: 4 [A] '*You will* not **leave** [+4946] the bed you are lying on.
1: 6 [A] Therefore *you will* not **leave** [+4946] the bed you are lying
1: 9 [A] said to him, "Man of God, the king says, '**Come down**!' "
1:10 [A] *may* fire **come down** from heaven and consume you
1:10 [A] fire **fell** from heaven and consumed the captain and his men.
1:11 [A] of God, this is what the king says, '**Come down** at once!' "
1:12 [A] "*may* fire **come down** from heaven and consume you
1:12 [A] the fire of God **fell** from heaven and consumed him and his
1:14 [A] fire *has* **fallen** from heaven and consumed the first two
1:15 [A] The angel of the LORD said to Elijah, "**Go down** with him;
1:15 [A] So Elijah got up and **went down** with him to the king.
1:16 [A] *you will* never **leave** [+4946] the bed you are lying on.
2: 2 [A] you live, I will not leave you." So *they* **went down** *to* Bethel.
3:12 [A] and Jehoshaphat and the king of Edom **went down** to him.
5:14 [A] So *he* **went down** and dipped himself in the Jordan seven
6:18 [A] As the enemy **came down** toward him, Elisha prayed to the
6:33 [A] was still talking to them, the messenger **came down** to him.
7:17 [A] of God had foretold when the king **came down** to his house.
8:29 [A] Ahaziah son of Jehoram king of Judah **went down** to Jezreel
9:16 [A] and Ahaziah king of Judah *had* **gone down** to see him.
10:13 [A] *we have* **come down** to greet the families of the king and of
11:19 [G] *together they* **brought** the king **down** from the temple of the
12:20 [12:21] [A] him at Beth Millo, on the **road down** *to* Silla.
13:14 [A] Jehoash king of Israel **went down** to see him and wept over
16:17 [G] *He* **removed** the Sea from the bronze bulls that supported it
20:11 [A] ten steps *it had* **gone down** [+345] on the stairway of Ahaz.
1Ch 7:21 [A] men of Gath, when *they* **went down** to seize their livestock.
11:15 [A] Three of the thirty chiefs **came down** to David to the rock at
11:22 [A] He also **went down** into a pit on a snowy day and killed a
11:23 [A] rod in his hand, Benaiah **went** against him with a club.
2Ch 7: 1 [A] fire **came down** from heaven and consumed the burnt
7: 3 [A] When all the Israelites saw the fire **coming down**
18: 2 [A] Some years later *he* **went down** to visit Ahab in Samaria.
20:16 [A] Tomorrow **march down** against them. They will be climbing
22: 6 [A] Ahaziah son of Jehoram king of Judah **went down** to Jezreel
23:20 [G] and **brought** the king **down** from the temple of the LORD.
Ne 3:15 [A] as far as the steps **going down** from the City of David.
6: 3 [A] "I am carrying on a great project and cannot **go down**. Why
6: 3 [A] should the work stop while I leave it and **go down** to you?"
9:13 [A] "*You* **came down** on Mount Sinai; you spoke to them from
Job 7: 9 [A] is gone, so *he who* **goes down** *to* the grave does not return.
17:16 [A] *Will it* **go down** *to* the gates of death? Will we descend
33:24 [A] to him and say, 'Spare him from **going down** *to* the pit;
Ps 7:16 [7:17] [A] his violence **comes down** on his own head.
18: 9 [18:10] [A] He parted the heavens and **came down**; dark clouds
22:29 [22:30] [A] all *who* **go down** *to* the dust will kneel before him—
28: 1 [A] I will be like *those who have* **gone down** *to* the pit.
30: 3 [30:4] [A] you spared me from **going down** *into* the pit.

Ps 30: 9 [30:10] [A] in my destruction, in my **going down** into the pit?
49: 17 [49:18] [A] he dies, his splendor *will* not **descend** with him.
55: 15 [55:16] [A] *let them* **go down** alive to the grave, for evil finds
55: 23 [55:24] [G] *will* **bring down** the wicked into the pit of
56: 7 [56:8] [G] in your anger, O God, **bring down** the nations.
59: 11 [59:12] [G] make them wander about, and **bring** them **down**.
72: 6 [A] He will be like rain **falling** on a mown field, like showers
78: 16 [G] out of a rocky crag and **made** water **flow down** like rivers.
88: 4 [88:5] [A] I am counted among *those who* **go down** *to* the pit;
104: 8 [A] flowed over the mountains, *they* **went down** *into* the valleys,
107: 23 [A] *Others* **went out** *on* the sea in ships; they were merchants on
107: 26 [A] mounted up to the heavens and **went down** *to* the depths;
115: 17 [A] dead who praise the LORD, those *who* **go down** *to* silence;
119: 136 [A] Streams of tears **flow** *from* my eyes, for your law is not
133: 2 [A] **running down** on the beard, running down on Aaron's
133: 2 [A] down on Aaron's beard, **down** upon the collar of his robes.
133: 3 [A] It is as if the dew of Hermon *were* **falling** on Mount Zion.
143: 7 [A] face from me or I will be like *those who* **go down** *to* the pit.
144: 5 [A] Part your heavens, O LORD, and **come down**; touch the
Pr 1: 12 [A] like the grave, and whole, like *those who* **go down** *to* the pit;
5: 5 [A] Her feet **go down** *to* death; her steps lead straight to the
7: 27 [A] to the grave, **leading down** to the chambers of death.
18: 8 [A] like choice morsels; they **go down** *to* a man's inmost parts.
21: 22 [G] and **pulls down** the stronghold in which they trust.
26: 22 [A] like choice morsels; they **go down** *to* a man's inmost parts.
30: 4 [A] Who has gone up to heaven and **come down**? Who has
Ecc 3: 21 [A] if the spirit of the animal **goes down** [+4200+4752] into the
SS 6: 2 [A] My lover *has* **gone down** to his garden, to the beds of spices,
6: 11 [A] *I* **went down** to the grove of nut trees to look at the new
Isa 5: 14 [A] into it *will* **descend** their nobles and masses with all their
10: 13 [G] their treasures; like a mighty one *I* **subdued** their kings.
14: 11 [H] All your pomp *has* **been brought down** *to* the grave,
14: 15 [H] *you* **are brought down** to the grave, to the depths of the pit.
14: 19 [A] by the sword, *those who* **descend** to the stones of the pit.
15: 3 [A] in the public squares they all wail, **prostrate** with weeping.
30: 2 [A] who go **down** *to* Egypt without consulting me; who look for
31: 1 [A] Woe to those *who* **go down** *to* Egypt for help, who rely on
31: 4 [A] so the LORD Almighty *will* **come down** to do battle on
32: 19 [A] Though hail **flattens** the forest and the city is leveled
34: 5 [A] see, *it* **descends** in judgment on Edom, the people I have
34: 7 [A] the wild oxen *will* **fall** with them, the bull calves
38: 8 [A] *it has* **gone down** on the stairway of Ahaz.' " So the sunlight
38: 8 [A] So the sunlight went back the ten steps *it had* **gone down**.
38: 18 [A] *those who* **go down** *to* the pit cannot hope for your
42: 10 [A] you *who* **go down** *to* the sea, and all that is in it, you islands,
43: 14 [G] to Babylon and **bring down** as fugitives all the Babylonians,
47: 1 [A] "**Go down**, sit in the dust, Virgin Daughter of Babylon; sit on
52: 4 [A] "At first my people **went down** *to* Egypt to live; lately,
55: 10 [A] As the rain and the snow **come down** from heaven, and do
63: 6 [G] I made them drunk and **poured** their blood on the ground."
63: 14 [A] like cattle *that* **go down** to the plain, they were given rest by
64: 1 [63:19] [A] that you would rend the heavens and **come down**,
64: 3 [64:2] [A] *you* **came down**, and the mountains trembled before
Jer 9: 18 [9:17] [A] and wail over us till our eyes **overflow** *with* tears
13: 17 [A] my eyes will weep bitterly, **overflowing** *with* tears,
13: 18 [A] for your glorious crowns *will* **fall** *from* your heads."
14: 17 [A] " '*Let* my eyes **overflow** *with* tears night and day without
18: 2 [A] "**Go down** *to* the potter's house, and there I will give you my
18: 3 [A] So *I* **went down** *to* the potter's house, and I saw him
22: 1 [A] "**Go down** *to* the palace of the king of Judah and proclaim
36: 12 [A] *he* **went down** to the secretary's room in the royal palace,
48: 15 [A] her finest young men *will* **go down** in the slaughter,"
48: 18 [A] "**Come down** from your glory and sit on the parched ground,
49: 16 [G] from there *I will* **bring** you **down**," declares the LORD.
50: 27 [A] Kill all her young bulls; *let them* **go down** to the slaughter!
51: 40 [G] "*I will* **bring** them **down** like lambs to the slaughter,
La 1: 9 [A] *Her* **fall** was astounding; there was none to comfort her.
1: 13 [G] on high he sent fire, **sent** it **down** [BHS-] into my bones.
1: 16 [A] "This is why I weep and my eyes **overflow** *with* tears. No
2: 10 [G] The young women of Jerusalem *have* **bowed** their heads to
2: 18 [G] of Zion, **let** your tears **flow** like a river day and night;
3: 48 [A] Streams of tears **flow from** my eyes because my people are
Eze 26: 11 [A] the sword, and your strong pillars *will* **fall** to the ground.
26: 16 [A] all the princes of the coast *will* **step down** from their thrones
26: 20 [G] *I will* **bring** you **down** with those who go down to the pit,
26: 20 [A] I will bring you down with *those who* **go down** *to* the pit,
26: 20 [A] as in ancient ruins, with *those who* **go down** *to* the pit, and
27: 29 [A] All who handle the oars *will* **abandon** [+4946] their ships;
28: 8 [G] *They will* **bring** you **down** to the pit, and you will die a
30: 6 [A] allies of Egypt will fall and her proud strength *will* **fail**.
31: 12 [A] All the nations of the earth **came out** from under its shade
31: 14 [A] among mortal men, with *those who* **go down** *to* the pit.
31: 15 [A] On the day it *was* **brought down** to the grave I covered the
31: 16 [G] **brought** it **down** to the grave with those who go down to the
31: 16 [A] it down to the grave with *those who* **go down** *to* the pit.
31: 17 [A] among the nations, *had* also **gone down** to the grave with it,
31: 18 [H] Yet *you*, too, *will* **be brought down** with the trees of Eden to
32: 18 [G] the hordes of Egypt and **consign** to the earth below both her
32: 18 [A] of mighty nations, with *those who* **go down** *to* the pit.
32: 19 [A] than others? **Go down** and be laid among the uncircumcised.'
32: 21 [A] '*They have* **come down** and they lie with the uncircumcised,
32: 24 [A] of the living **went down** uncircumcised to the earth below.
32: 24 [A] They bear their shame with *those who* **go down** *to* the pit.
32: 25 [A] they bear their shame with *those who* **go down** *to* the pit;
32: 27 [A] who **went down** *to* the grave with their weapons of war,
32: 29 [A] with the uncircumcised, with *those who* **go down** *to* the pit.
32: 30 [A] *they* **went down** with the slain in disgrace despite the terror
32: 30 [A] and bear their shame with *those who* **go down** *to* the pit.
34: 26 [G] *I will* **send down** showers in season; there will be showers of
47: 1 [A] The water *was* **coming down** from under the south side of
47: 8 [A] toward the eastern region and **goes down** into the Arabah,
Hos 7: 12 [G] my net over them; *I will* **pull** them **down** like birds of the air.
Joel 2: 23 [G] *He* **sends** you abundant showers, both autumn and spring
3: 2 [4:2] [G] and **bring** them **down** to the Valley of Jehoshaphat.
Am 3: 11 [G] *he will* **pull down** your strongholds and plunder your
6: 2 [A] there to great Hamath, and then **go down** *to* Gath in Philistia.
9: 2 [G] climb up to the heavens, from there *I will* **bring** them **down**.
Ob 1: 3 [G] say to yourself, 'Who *can* **bring** me **down** to the ground?'
1: 4 [G] from there *I will* **bring** you **down**," declares the LORD.
Jnh 1: 3 [A] *He* **went down** *to* Joppa, where he found a ship bound for
1: 3 [A] *he* **went** [+928] **aboard** and sailed for Tarshish to flee from
1: 5 [A] Jonah *had* **gone** below deck, where he lay down and fell into
2: 6 [2:7] [A] To the roots of the mountains *I* **sank down**; the earth
Mic 1: 3 [A] *he* **comes down** and treads the high places of the earth.
1: 12 [A] for relief, because disaster *has* **come** from the LORD,
Hag 2: 22 [A] horses and their riders *will* **fall**, each by the sword of his
Zec 10: 11 [H] Assyria's pride *will* **be brought down** and Egypt's scepter
11: 2 [A] Wail, oaks of Bashan; the dense forest *has been* **cut down**!

3719 יֶרֶד *yered*, n.pr.m. [7]

Jared [6], Jered [1]

Ge 5: 15 When Mahalalel had lived 65 years, he became the father of **Jared**.
5: 16 And after he became the father of **Jared**, Mahalalel lived 830 years
5: 18 When **Jared** had lived 162 years, he became the father of Enoch.
5: 19 of Enoch, **Jared** lived 800 years and had other sons and daughters.
5: 20 Altogether, **Jared** lived 962 years, and then he died.
1Ch 1: 2 Kenan, Mahalalel, **Jared**,
4: 18 (His Judean wife gave birth to **Jered** the father of Gedor, Heber the

3720 יַרְדֵּן *yardēn*, n.pr.loc. [182] [√ 3718]

Jordan [172], *untranslated* [3], Jordan's [3], river [2], its[s] [+2021] [1], there[s] [+928] [1]

Ge 13: 10 and saw that the whole plain of the **Jordan** was well watered,
13: 11 So Lot chose for himself the whole plain of the **Jordan** and set out
32: 10 [32:11] I had only my staff when I crossed this **Jordan**, but now I
50: 10 floor of Atad, near the **Jordan**, they lamented loudly and bitterly;
50: 11 That is why that place near the **Jordan** is called Abel Mizraim.
Nu 13: 29 and the Canaanites live near the sea and along the **Jordan**."
22: 1 plains of Moab and camped along the **Jordan** across from Jericho.
26: 3 So on the plains of Moab by the **Jordan** *across from* Jericho,
26: 63 on the plains of Moab by the **Jordan** *across from* Jericho.
31: 12 camp on the plains of Moab, by the **Jordan** *across from* Jericho.
32: 5 servants as our possession. Do not make us cross the **Jordan**."
32: 19 receive any inheritance with them on the other side of the **Jordan**,
32: 19 our inheritance has come to us on the east side of the **Jordan**."
32: 21 if all of you will go armed over the **Jordan** before the LORD
32: 29 for battle, cross over the **Jordan** with you before the LORD,
32: 32 but the property we inherit will be on this side of the **Jordan**."
33: 48 camped on the plains of Moab by the **Jordan** *across from* Jericho.
33: 49 There on the plains of Moab they camped along the **Jordan** from
33: 50 On the plains of Moab by the **Jordan** *across from* Jericho the
33: 51 and say to them: 'When you cross the **Jordan** into Canaan,
34: 12 the boundary will go down along the **Jordan** and end at the Salt
34: 15 received their inheritance on the east side of the **Jordan** *of* Jericho,
35: 1 On the plains of Moab by the **Jordan** *across from* Jericho,
35: 10 and say to them: 'When you cross the **Jordan** into Canaan,
35: 14 Give three on this side of the **Jordan** and three in Canaan as cities
36: 13 on the plains of Moab by the **Jordan** *across from* Jericho.
Dt 1: 1 words Moses spoke to all Israel in the desert east of the **Jordan**—
1: 5 East of the **Jordan** in the territory of Moab, Moses began to
2: 29 until we cross the **Jordan** into the land the LORD our God is
3: 8 these two kings of the Amorites the territory east of the **Jordan**,
3: 17 Its western border was the **Jordan** in the Arabah, from Kinnereth
3: 20 land that the LORD your God is giving them, across the **Jordan**.
3: 25 Let me go over and see the good land beyond the **Jordan**—
3: 27 with your own eyes, since you are not going to cross this **Jordan**.

Dt 4:21 he solemnly swore that I would not cross the **Jordan** and enter the
4:22 I will die in this land; I will not cross the **Jordan**; but you are
4:26 perish from the land that you are crossing the **Jordan** to possess.
4:41 Then Moses set aside three cities east of the **Jordan**,
4:46 were in the valley near Beth Peor east of the **Jordan**, in the land of
4:47 of Og king of Bashan, the two Amorite kings east of the **Jordan**.
4:49 included all the Arabah east of the **Jordan**, as far as the Sea of the
9: 1 You are now about to cross the **Jordan** to go in and dispossess
11:30 As you know, these mountains are across the **Jordan**, west of the
11:31 You are about to cross the **Jordan** to enter and take possession of
12:10 you will cross the **Jordan** and settle in the land the LORD your
27: 2 When you have crossed the **Jordan** into the land the LORD your
27: 4 when you have crossed the **Jordan**, set up these stones on Mount
27:12 When you have crossed the **Jordan**, these tribes shall stand on
30:18 You will not live long in the land you are crossing the **Jordan** to
31: 2 The LORD has said to me, 'You shall not cross the **Jordan**.'
31:13 as you live in the land you are crossing the **Jordan** to possess."
32:47 By them you will live long in the land you are crossing the **Jordan**
Jos 1: 2 get ready to cross the **Jordan** River into the land I am about to
1:11 Three days from now you will cross the **Jordan** here to go in
1:14 may stay in the land that Moses gave you east of the **Jordan**,
1:15 of the LORD gave you east of the **Jordan** toward the sunrise."
2: 7 of the spies on the road that leads to the fords of the **Jordan**,
2:10 and Og, the two kings of the Amorites east of the **Jordan**,
3: 1 and all the Israelites set out from Shittim and went to the **Jordan**,
3: 8 'When you reach the edge of the **Jordan's** waters, go and stand in
3: 8 reach the edge of the Jordan's waters, go and stand in the **river**.' "
3:11 of the Lord of all the earth will go into the **Jordan** ahead of you.
3:13 set foot in the **Jordan**, its waters flowing downstream will be cut
3:13 set foot in the Jordan, **its**[s] [+2021] waters flowing downstream will
3:14 So when the people broke camp to cross the **Jordan**, the priests
3:15 Now the **Jordan** is at flood stage all during harvest. Yet as soon as
3:15 Yet as soon as the priests who carried the ark reached the **Jordan**
3:17 the LORD stood firm on dry ground in the middle of the **Jordan**,
3:17 whole nation had completed the crossing **[RPH]** on dry ground.
4: 1 When the whole nation had finished crossing the **Jordan**,
4: 3 tell them to take up twelve stones from the middle of the **Jordan**
4: 5 the ark of the LORD your God into the middle of the **Jordan**.
4: 7 tell them that the flow of the **Jordan** was cut off before the ark of
4: 7 When it crossed the **Jordan**, the waters of the Jordan were cut off.
4: 7 When it crossed the Jordan, the waters of the **Jordan** were cut off.
4: 8 They took twelve stones from the middle of the **Jordan**,
4: 9 **Jordan** at the spot where the priests who carried the ark of the
4:10 **Jordan** until everything the LORD had commanded Joshua was
4:16 carrying the ark of the Testimony to come up out of the **Jordan**."
4:17 So Joshua commanded the priests, "Come up out of the **Jordan**."
4:18 the priests came up out of the **river** carrying the ark of the
4:18 dry ground than the waters of the **Jordan** returned to their place
4:19 tenth day of the first month the people went up from the **Jordan**
4:20 set up at Gilgal the twelve stones they had taken out of the **Jordan**.
4:22 tell them, 'Israel crossed the **Jordan** on dry ground.'
4:23 For the LORD your God dried up the **Jordan** before you until
5: 1 Now when all the Amorite kings west of the **Jordan** and all the
5: 1 dried up the **Jordan** before the Israelites until we had crossed over,
7: 7 why did you ever bring this people across the **Jordan** to deliver us
7: 7 only we had been content to stay on the other side of the **Jordan**!
9: 1 Now when all the kings west of the **Jordan** heard about these
9:10 that he did to the two kings of the Amorites east of the **Jordan**—
12: 1 and whose territory they took over east of the **Jordan**,
12: 7 and the Israelites conquered on the west side of the **Jordan**,
13: 8 the inheritance that Moses had given them east of the **Jordan**,
13:23 The boundary of the Reubenites was the bank of the **Jordan**.
13:27 of the realm of Sihon king of Heshbon (the east side of the **Jordan**,
13:27 the territory up to the end of the Sea of Kinnereth). **[RPH]**
13:32 he was in the plains of Moab across the **Jordan** east of Jericho.
14: 3 the two-and-a-half tribes their inheritance east of the **Jordan**
15: 5 eastern boundary is the Salt Sea as far as the mouth of the **Jordan**.
15: 5 started from the bay of the sea at the mouth of the **Jordan**,
16: 1 The allotment for Joseph began at the **Jordan** *of* Jericho, east of
16: 7 and Naarah, touched Jericho and came out at the **Jordan**.
17: 5 of ten tracts of land besides Gilead and Bashan east of the **Jordan**,
18: 7 already received their inheritance on the east side of the **Jordan**.
18:12 On the north side their boundary began at the **Jordan**, passed the
18:19 bay of the Salt Sea, at the mouth of the **Jordan** in the south.
18:20 The **Jordan** formed the boundary on the eastern side. These were
19:22 Shahazumah and Beth Shemesh, and ended at the **Jordan**.
19:33 Adami Nekeb and Jabneel to Lakkum and ending at the **Jordan**.
19:34 on the south, Asher on the west and the **Jordan** on the east.
20: 8 On the east side of the **Jordan** *of* Jericho they designated Bezer in
22: 4 servant of the LORD gave you on the other side of the **Jordan**.
22: 7 gave land on the west side of the **Jordan** with their brothers.)
22:10 When they came to Geliloth near the **Jordan** in the land of
22:10 half-tribe of Manasseh built an imposing altar there by the **Jordan**.
22:11 border of Canaan at Geliloth near the **Jordan** on the Israelite side,
22:25 The LORD has made the **Jordan** a boundary between us
23: 4 I conquered—between the **Jordan** and the Great Sea in the west.
24: 8 you to the land of the Amorites who lived east of the **Jordan**.
24:11 " 'Then you crossed the **Jordan** and came to Jericho. The citizens
Jdg 3:28 taking possession of the fords of the **Jordan** that led to Moab,
5:17 Gilead stayed beyond the **Jordan**. And Dan, why did he linger by
7:24 seize the waters of the **Jordan** ahead of them as far as Beth
7:24 and they took the waters of the **Jordan** as far as Beth Barah.
7:25 the heads of Oreb and Zeeb to Gideon, who was by the **Jordan**.
8: 4 yet keeping up the pursuit, came to the **Jordan** and crossed it.
10: 8 oppressed all the Israelites on the east side of the **Jordan** in Gilead,
10: 9 The Ammonites also crossed the **Jordan** to fight against Judah,
11:13 my land from the Arnon to the Jabbok, all the way to the **Jordan**.
11:22 it from the Arnon to the Jabbok and from the desert to the **Jordan**.
12: 5 The Gileadites captured the fords of the **Jordan** leading to
12: 6 they seized him and killed him at the fords of the **Jordan**.
1Sa 13: 7 Some Hebrews even crossed the **Jordan** to the land of Gad
31: 7 and those across the **Jordan** saw that the Israelite army had fled
2Sa 2:29 They crossed the **Jordan**, continued through the whole Bithron
10:17 he gathered all Israel, crossed the **Jordan** and went to Helam.
17:22 and all the people with him set out and crossed the **Jordan**.
17:22 By daybreak, no one was left who had not crossed the **Jordan**.
17:24 and Absalom crossed the **Jordan** with all the men of Israel.
19:15 [19:16] the king returned and went as far as the **Jordan**.
19:15 [19:16] and meet the king and bring him across the **Jordan**.
19:17 [19:18] They rushed to the **Jordan**, where the king was.
19:18 [19:19] When Shimei son of Gera crossed the **Jordan**, he fell
19:31 [19:32] down from Rogelim to cross the **Jordan** with the king
19:31 [19:32] the king and to send him on his way from **there**[s] [+928].
19:36 [19:37] Your servant will cross over the **Jordan** with the king for
19:39 [19:40] So all the people crossed the **Jordan**, and then the king
19:41 [19:42] and bring him and his household across the **Jordan**,
20: 2 the men of Judah stayed by their king all the way from the **Jordan**
24: 5 After crossing the **Jordan**, they camped near Aroer, south of the
1Ki 2: 8 When he came down to meet me at the **Jordan**, I swore to him by
7:46 The king had them cast in clay molds in the plain of the **Jordan**
17: 3 turn eastward and hide in the Kerith Ravine, east of the **Jordan**.
17: 5 He went to the Kerith Ravine, east of the **Jordan**, and stayed there.
2Ki 2: 6 said to him, "Stay here; the LORD has sent me to the **Jordan**."
2: 7 the place where Elijah and Elisha had stopped at the **Jordan**.
2:13 from Elijah and went back and stood on the bank of the **Jordan**.
5:10 "Go, wash yourself seven times in the **Jordan**, and your flesh will
5:14 So he went down and dipped himself in the **Jordan** seven times,
6: 2 Let us go to the **Jordan**, where each of us can get a pole; and let us
6: 4 with them. They went to the **Jordan** and began to cut down trees.
7:15 They followed them as far as the **Jordan**, and they found the
10:33 east of the **Jordan** in all the land of Gilead (the region of Gad,
1Ch 6:78 [6:63] from the tribe of Reuben across **[RPH]** the Jordan east of
6:78 [6:63] from the tribe of Reuben across the **Jordan** east of Jericho
12:15 [12:16] It was they who crossed the **Jordan** in the first month
12:37 [12:38] from east of the **Jordan**, men of Reuben, Gad
19:17 was told of this, he gathered all Israel and crossed the **Jordan**;
26:30 were responsible in Israel west of the **Jordan** for all the work of
2Ch 4:17 The king had them cast in clay molds in the plain of the **Jordan**
Job 40:23 he is secure, though the **Jordan** should surge against his mouth.
Ps 42: 6 [42:7] therefore I will remember you from the land of the **Jordan**,
114: 3 The sea looked and fled, the **Jordan** turned back;
114: 5 Why was it, O sea, that you fled, O **Jordan**, that you turned back,
Isa 9: 1 [8:23] of the Gentiles, by the way of the sea, along the **Jordan**—
Jer 12: 5 safe country, how will you manage in the thickets by the **Jordan**?
49:19 "Like a lion coming up from **Jordan's** thickets to a rich
50:44 Like a lion coming up from **Jordan's** thickets to a rich
Eze 47:18 along the **Jordan** between Gilead and the land of Israel,
Zec 11: 3 to the roar of the lions; the lush thicket of the **Jordan** is ruined!

3721 יָרָה yārâ[1], v. [25] [→ 3452, 3725, 3748, 3754, 3755, 3756, 4619; cf. 3708]

shoot [10], shot [3], shot with arrows [+3721] [2], cast [1], fallen [1], hurled [1], laid [1], overthrown [1], set up [1], shoot arrows [1], shooting [1], shot arrows [1], throws [1]

Ge 31:51 [A] and here is this pillar *I have* **set up** between you and me.
Ex 15: 4 [A] Pharaoh's chariots and his army *he has* **hurled** into the sea.
19:13 [C] He shall surely be stoned or **shot** [+3721] **with arrows**; not a
19:13 [A] He shall surely be stoned or **shot with arrows** [+3721]; not a
Nu 21:30 [A] "But *we have* **overthrown** them; Heshbon is destroyed all
Jos 18: 6 [A] *I will* **cast** lots for you in the presence of the LORD our
1Sa 20:20 [G] I *will* **shoot** three arrows *to* the side of it, as though I were
20:36 [G] and he said to the boy, "Run and find the arrows I **shoot**."
20:36 [A] I shoot." As the boy ran, he **shot** an arrow beyond him.
20:37 [A] boy came to the place where Jonathan's arrow *had* **fallen**,
2Sa 11:20 [G] Didn't you know *they would* **shoot arrows** from the wall?
11:24 [G] Then the archers **shot arrows** at your servants from the wall,
2Ki 13:17 [A] he said, and he opened it. "**Shoot**!" Elisha said, and he shot.

2Ki 13:17 [G] he said, and he opened it. "Shoot!" Elisha said, and *he* **shot**.
19:32 [G] "He will not enter this city or **shoot** an arrow here. He will
2Ch 26:15 [A] on the corner defenses to **shoot** arrows and hurl large stones.
35:23 [G] Archers **shot** King Josiah, and he told his officers, "Take me
Job 30:19 [G] *He* **throws** me into the mud, and I am reduced to dust
38: 6 [A] On what were its footings set, or who **laid** its cornerstone—
Ps 11: 2 [A] they set their arrows against the strings to **shoot** from the
64: 4 [64:5] [A] They **shoot** from ambush *at* the innocent man;
64: 4 [64:5] [G] *they* **shoot** *at* him suddenly, without fear.
64: 7 [64:8] [G] God *will* **shoot** them with arrows; suddenly they will
Pr 26:18 [A] Like a madman **shooting** firebrands or deadly arrows
Isa 37:33 [G] "He will not enter this city or **shoot** an arrow here. He will

3722 ²יָרָה yārā², v. [3] [→ 4620; cf. 3709]

be refreshed [1], showers [1], water [1]

Pr 11:25 [H] he who refreshes others *will* himself **be refreshed**.
Hos 6: 3 [G] the winter rains, like the spring rains *that* **water** the earth."
10:12 [G] until he comes and **showers** righteousness on you.

3723 ³יָרָה yārā³, v. [46] [→ 4621, 4622, 9368]

teach [25], instruct [3], teaches [3], taught [2], determine [1], direct [1], display [1], get directions [1], give guidance [1], guide [1], instructed [1], instruction [1], instructs [1], motions [1], showed [1], taught [+906+2118] [1], teach [+906+1978] [1]

Ge 46:28 [G] Jacob sent Judah ahead of him to Joseph to **get directions**
Ex 4:12 [G] I will help you speak and *will* **teach** you what to say."
4:15 [G] I will help both of you speak and *will* **teach** you what to do.
15:25 [G] to the LORD, and the LORD **showed** him a piece of wood.
24:12 [G] the law and commands I have written for their **instruction**."
35:34 [G] of Ahisamach, of the tribe of Dan, the ability to **teach** others.
Lev 10:11 [G] you *must* **teach** the Israelites all the decrees the LORD has
14:57 [G] to **determine** when something is clean or unclean. These are
Dt 17:10 [G] Be careful to do everything *they* **direct** you to do.
17:11 [G] Act according to the law *they* **teach** you and the decisions
24: 8 [G] to do exactly as the priests, who are Levites, **instruct** you.
33:10 [G] *He* **teaches** your precepts to Jacob and your law to Israel.
Jdg 13: 8 [G] let the man of God you sent to us come again *to* **teach** us
1Sa 12:23 [G] for you. And *I will* **teach** you the way that is good and right.
1Ki 8:36 [G] **Teach** them the right way to live, and send rain on the land
2Ki 12: 2 [12:3] [G] all the years Jehoiada the priest **instructed** him.
17:27 [G] and **teach** the people what the god of the land requires."
17:28 [G] and **taught** [+906+2118] them how to worship the LORD.
2Ch 6:27 [G] **Teach** them the right way to live, and send rain on the land
15: 3 [G] the true God, without a priest *to* **teach** and without the law.
Job 6:24 [G] "**Teach** me, and I will be quiet; show me where I have been
8:10 [G] *Will* they not **instruct** you and tell you? Will they not bring
12: 7 [G] "But ask the animals, and *they will* **teach** you, or the birds of
12: 8 [G] or speak to the earth, and *it will* **teach** you, or let the fish of
27:11 [G] "*I will* **teach** you about the power of God; the ways of the
34:32 [G] **Teach** me what I cannot see; if I have done wrong, I will not
Ps 25: 8 [G] is the LORD; therefore *he* **instructs** sinners in his ways.
25:12 [G] *He will* **instruct** him in the way chosen for him.
27:11 [G] **Teach** me your way, O LORD; lead me in a straight path
32: 8 [G] I will instruct you and **teach** you in the way you should go;
45: 4 [45:5] [G] *let* your right hand **display** awesome deeds.
86:11 [G] **Teach** me your way, O LORD, and I will walk in your
119:33 [G] **Teach** me, O LORD, to follow your decrees; then I will
119:102 [G] departed from your laws, for *you* yourself *have* **taught** me.
Pr 4: 4 [G] *he* **taught** me and said, "Lay hold of my words with all your
4:11 [G] *I* **guide** you in the way of wisdom and lead you along
6:13 [G] his eye, signals with his feet and **motions** with his fingers,
Isa 2: 3 [G] *He will* **teach** us his ways, so that we may walk in his paths."
9:15 [9:14] [G] are the head, the prophets *who* **teach** lies are the tail.
28: 9 [G] "Who is it *he is trying to* **teach** [+906+1978]? To whom is
28:26 [G] His God instructs him and **teaches** him the right way.
Eze 44:23 [G] *They are to* **teach** my people the difference between the
Mic 3:11 [G] Her leaders judge for a bribe, her priests **teach** for a price,
4: 2 [G] *He will* **teach** us his ways, so that we may walk in his paths."
Hab 2:18 [G] since a man has carved it? Or an image *that* **teaches** lies?
2:19 [G] Or to lifeless stone, 'Wake up!' *Can* it **give guidance**?

3724 יָרָה yārah, v. [1] [cf. 8109]

afraid [1]

Isa 44: 8 [A] Do not tremble, *do* not *be* **afraid**. Did I not proclaim this and

3725 יְרוּאֵל yᵉrû'ēl, n.pr.loc. [1] [√ 3721 + 446]

Jeruel [1]

2Ch 20:16 you will find them at the end of the gorge in the Desert of **Jeruel**.

3726 יָרוֹחַ yārôaḥ, n.pr.m. [1] [√ 3732]

Jaroah [1]

1Ch 5:14 the son of **Jaroah**, the son of Gilead, the son of Michael, the son of

3727 יָרוּם yārûm, a.vbl. Not used in NIV/BHS [→ 3753; cf. 8123]

3728 יָרוֹק yārôq, n.[m.]. [1] [√ 3764]

green thing [1]

Job 39: 8 ranges the hills for his pasture and searches for any **green thing**.

3729 יְרוּשָׁא yᵉrûšā', n.pr.f. [1] [√ 3769]

Jerusha [1]

2Ki 15:33 sixteen years. His mother's name was **Jerusha** daughter of Zadok.

3730 יְרוּשָׁה yᵉrûšā, n.pr.f. [1] [√ 3769]

Jerusha [1]

2Ch 27: 1 sixteen years. His mother's name was **Jerusha** daughter of Zadok.

3731 יְרוּשָׁלַםִ yᵉrûšālaim, n.pr.loc. [643] [→ Ar 10332]

Jerusalem [631], there^s [+928] [6], Jerusalem's [3], *untranslated* [2], the city^s [1]

Jos 10: 1 Now Adoni-Zedek king of **Jerusalem** heard that Joshua had taken
10: 3 So Adoni-Zedek king of **Jerusalem** appealed to Hoham king of
10: 5 the kings of **Jerusalem**, Hebron, Jarmuth, Lachish and Eglon—
10:23 the kings of **Jerusalem**, Hebron, Jarmuth, Lachish and Eglon.
12:10 the king of **Jerusalem** one the king of Hebron one
15: 8 along the southern slope of the Jebusite city (that is, **Jerusalem**).
15:63 could not dislodge the Jebusites, who were living in **Jerusalem**;
15:63 to this day the Jebusites live **there**^s [+928] with the people of
18:28 the Jebusite city (that is, **Jerusalem**), Gibeah and Kiriath—
Jdg 1: 7 I did to them." They brought him to **Jerusalem**, and he died there.
1: 8 The men of Judah attacked **Jerusalem** also and took it. They put
1:21 failed to dislodge the Jebusites, who were living in **Jerusalem**;
1:21 to this day the Jebusites live **there**^s [+928] with the Benjamites.
19:10 **Jerusalem**), with his two saddled donkeys and his concubine.
1Sa 17:54 David took the Philistine's head and brought it to **Jerusalem**,
2Sa 5: 5 in **Jerusalem** he reigned over all Israel and Judah thirty-three
5: 6 and his men marched to **Jerusalem** to attack the Jebusites,
5:13 David took more concubines and wives in **Jerusalem**, and more
5:14 These are the names of the children born to him **there**^s [+928]:
8: 7 to the officers of Hadadezer and brought them to **Jerusalem**.
9:13 Mephibosheth lived in **Jerusalem**, because he always ate at the
10:14 returned from fighting the Ammonites and came to **Jerusalem**.
11: 1 and besieged Rabbah. But David remained in **Jerusalem**.
11:12 you back." So Uriah remained in **Jerusalem** that day and the next.
12:31 Then David and his entire army returned to **Jerusalem**.
14:23 Joab went to Geshur and brought Absalom back to **Jerusalem**.
14:28 Absalom lived two years in **Jerusalem** without seeing the king's
15: 8 'If the LORD takes me back to **Jerusalem**, I will worship the
15:11 Two hundred men from **Jerusalem** had accompanied Absalom.
15:14 David said to all his officials who were with him in **Jerusalem**,
15:29 So Zadok and Abiathar took the ark of God back to **Jerusalem**
15:37 So David's friend Hushai arrived at **Jerusalem** as Absalom was
16: 3 Ziba said to him, "He is staying in **Jerusalem**, because he thinks,
16:15 Meanwhile, Absalom and all the men of Israel came to **Jerusalem**,
17:20 men searched but found no one, so they returned to **Jerusalem**.
19:19 [19:20] did wrong on the day my lord the king left **Jerusalem**.
19:25 [19:26] When he came from **Jerusalem** to meet the king, the king
19:33 [19:34] "Cross over with me and stay with me in **Jerusalem**,
19:34 [19:35] I live, that I should go up to **Jerusalem** with the king?
20: 2 stayed by their king all the way from the Jordan to **Jerusalem**.
20: 3 When David returned to his palace in **Jerusalem**, he took the ten
20: 7 They marched out from **Jerusalem** to pursue Sheba son of Bicri.
20:22 to his home. And Joab went back to the king in **Jerusalem**.
24: 8 they came back to **Jerusalem** at the end of nine months and twenty
24:16 When the angel stretched out his hand to destroy **Jerusalem**,
1Ki 2:11 over Israel—seven years in Hebron and thirty-three in **Jerusalem**.
2:36 said to him, "Build yourself a house in **Jerusalem** and live there,
2:38 king has said." And Shimei stayed in **Jerusalem** for a long time.
2:41 When Solomon was told that Shimei had gone from **Jerusalem** to
3: 1 and the temple of the LORD, and the wall around **Jerusalem**.
3:15 He returned to **Jerusalem**, stood before the ark of the Lord's
8: 1 King Solomon summoned into his presence at **Jerusalem** the
9:15 the wall of **Jerusalem**, and Hazor, Megiddo and Gezer.
9:19 whatever he desired to build in **Jerusalem**, in Lebanon
10: 2 Arriving at **Jerusalem** with a very great caravan—with camels
10:26 which he kept in the chariot cities and also with him in **Jerusalem**.
10:27 The king made silver as common in **Jerusalem** as stones,

1Ki 11: 7 On a hill east of **Jerusalem**, Solomon built a high place for
11: 13 for the sake of David my servant and for the sake of **Jerusalem**,
11: 29 About that time Jeroboam was going out of **Jerusalem**, and Ahijah
11: 32 But for the sake of my servant David and the city of **Jerusalem**,
11: 36 my servant may always have a lamp before me in **Jerusalem**,
11: 42 Solomon reigned in **Jerusalem** over all Israel forty years.
12: 18 however, managed to get into his chariot and escape to **Jerusalem**.
12: 21 When Rehoboam arrived in **Jerusalem**, he mustered the whole
12: 27 go up to offer sacrifices at the temple of the LORD in **Jerusalem**,
12: 28 said to the people, "It is too much for you to go up to **Jerusalem**.
14: 21 he became king, and he reigned seventeen years in **Jerusalem**,
14: 25 of King Rehoboam, Shishak king of Egypt attacked **Jerusalem**.
15: 2 he reigned in **Jerusalem** three years. His mother's name was
15: 4 gave him a lamp in **Jerusalem** by raising up a son to succeed him
15: 4 raising up a son to succeed him and by making **Jerusalem** strong.
15: 10 he reigned in **Jerusalem** forty-one years. His grandmother's name
22: 42 he became king, and he reigned in **Jerusalem** twenty-five years.
2Ki 8: 17 when he became king, and he reigned in **Jerusalem** eight years.
8: 26 old when he became king, and he reigned in **Jerusalem** one year.
9: 28 His servants took him by chariot to **Jerusalem** and buried him with
12: 1 [12:2] became king, and he reigned in **Jerusalem** forty years.
12: 17 [12:18] and captured it. Then he turned to attack **Jerusalem**.
12: 18 [12:19] king of Aram, who then withdrew from **Jerusalem**.
14: 2 he became king, and he reigned in **Jerusalem** twenty-nine years.
14: 2 His mother's name was Jehoaddin; she was from **Jerusalem**.
14: 13 Jehoash went to **Jerusalem** and broke down the wall of Jerusalem
14: 13 broke down the wall of **Jerusalem** from the Ephraim Gate to the
14: 19 They conspired against him in **Jerusalem**, and he fled to Lachish,
14: 20 back by horse and was buried in **Jerusalem** with his fathers,
15: 2 he became king, and he reigned in **Jerusalem** fifty-two years.
15: 2 His mother's name was Jecoliah; she was from **Jerusalem**.
15: 33 when he became king, and he reigned in **Jerusalem** sixteen years.
16: 2 when he became king, and he reigned in **Jerusalem** sixteen years.
16: 5 of Remaliah king of Israel marched up to fight against **Jerusalem**
18: 2 he became king, and he reigned in **Jerusalem** twenty-nine years.
18: 17 with a large army, from Lachish to King Hezekiah at **Jerusalem**.
18: 17 They came up to **Jerusalem** and stopped at the aqueduct of the
18: 22 and altars Hezekiah removed, saying to Judah and **Jerusalem**,
18: 22 "You must worship before this altar in **Jerusalem**"?
18: 35 How then can the LORD deliver **Jerusalem** from my hand?"
19: 10 '**Jerusalem** will not be handed over to the king of Assyria.'
19: 21 The Daughter of **Jerusalem** tosses her head as you flee.
19: 31 For out of **Jerusalem** will come a remnant, and out of Mount Zion
21: 1 he became king, and he reigned in **Jerusalem** fifty-five years.
21: 4 which the LORD had said, "In **Jerusalem** I will put my Name."
21: 7 and to his son Solomon, "In this temple and in **Jerusalem**,
21: 12 I am going to bring such disaster on **Jerusalem** and Judah that the
21: 13 I will stretch out over **Jerusalem** the measuring line used against
21: 13 I will wipe out **Jerusalem** as one wipes a dish, wiping it
21: 16 so much innocent blood that he filled **Jerusalem** from end to end—
21: 19 old when he became king, and he reigned in **Jerusalem** two years.
22: 1 he became king, and he reigned in **Jerusalem** thirty-one years.
22: 14 of the wardrobe. She lived in **Jerusalem**, in the Second District.
23: 1 the king called together all the elders of Judah and **Jerusalem**.
23: 2 of Judah, the people of **Jerusalem**, the priests and the prophets—
23: 4 He burned them outside **Jerusalem** in the fields of the Kidron
23: 5 places of the towns of Judah and on those around **Jerusalem**—
23: 6 the temple of the LORD to the Kidron Valley outside **Jerusalem**
23: 9 high places did not serve at the altar of the LORD in **Jerusalem**,
23: 13 were east of **Jerusalem** on the south of the Hill of Corruption—
23: 20 burned human bones on them. Then he went back to **Jerusalem**.
23: 23 this Passover was celebrated to the LORD in **Jerusalem**.
23: 24 and all the other detestable things seen in Judah and **Jerusalem**.
23: 27 and I will reject **Jerusalem**, the city I chose, and this temple,
23: 30 servants brought his body in a chariot from Megiddo to **Jerusalem**
23: 31 when he became king, and he reigned in **Jerusalem** three months.
23: 33 in the land of Hamath so that he might not reign in **Jerusalem**,
23: 36 when he became king, and he reigned in **Jerusalem** eleven years.
24: 4 For he had filled **Jerusalem** with innocent blood, and the LORD
24: 8 when he became king, and he reigned in **Jerusalem** three months.
24: 8 was Nehushta daughter of Elnathan; she was from **Jerusalem**.
24: 10 of Nebuchadnezzar king of Babylon advanced on **Jerusalem**
24: 14 He carried into exile all **Jerusalem**: all the officers and fighting
24: 15 He also took from **Jerusalem** to Babylon the king's mother,
24: 18 when he became king, and he reigned in **Jerusalem** eleven years.
24: 20 because of the LORD's anger that all this happened to **Jerusalem**
25: 1 Nebuchadnezzar king of Babylon marched against **Jerusalem** with
25: 8 an official of the king of Babylon, came to **Jerusalem**.
25: 9 of the LORD, the royal palace and all the houses of **Jerusalem**.
25: 10 of the imperial guard, broke down the walls around **Jerusalem**.
1Ch 3: 4 and six months. David reigned in **Jerusalem** thirty-three years,
3: 5 and these were the children born to him **there**[s] [+928]: Shammua,
6: 10 [5:36] served as priest in the temple Solomon built in **Jerusalem**),
6: 15 [5:41] and **Jerusalem** into exile by the hand of Nebuchadnezzar.
6: 32 [6:17] Solomon built the temple of the LORD in **Jerusalem**.
8: 28 chiefs as listed in their genealogy, and they lived in **Jerusalem**.
8: 32 of Shimeah. They too lived near their relatives in **Jerusalem**.
9: 3 and from Ephraim and Manasseh who lived in **Jerusalem** were:
9: 34 chiefs as listed in their genealogy, and they lived in **Jerusalem**.
9: 38 of Shimeam. They too lived near their relatives in **Jerusalem**.
11: 4 David and all the Israelites marched to **Jerusalem** (that is,
14: 3 In **Jerusalem** David took more wives and became the father of
14: 4 These are the names of the children born to him **there**[s] [+928]:
15: 3 David assembled all Israel in **Jerusalem** to bring up the ark of the
18: 7 by the officers of Hadadezer and brought them to **Jerusalem**.
19: 15 and went inside the city. So Joab went back to **Jerusalem**.
20: 1 went to Rabbah and besieged it, but David remained in **Jerusalem**.
20: 3 Then David and his entire army returned to **Jerusalem**.
21: 4 and went throughout Israel and then came back to **Jerusalem**.
21: 15 God sent an angel to destroy **Jerusalem**. But as the angel was
21: 16 with a drawn sword in his hand extended over **Jerusalem**.
23: 25 rest to his people and has come to dwell in **Jerusalem** forever,
28: 1 summoned all the officials of Israel to assemble at **Jerusalem**:
29: 27 Israel forty years—seven in Hebron and thirty-three in **Jerusalem**.
2Ch 1: 4 prepared for it, because he had pitched a tent for it in **Jerusalem**.
1: 13 Then Solomon went to **Jerusalem** from the high place at Gibeon,
1: 14 which he kept in the chariot cities and also with him in **Jerusalem**.
1: 15 The king made silver and gold as common in **Jerusalem** as stones,
2: 7 [2:6] to work in Judah and **Jerusalem** with my skilled craftsmen,
2: 16 [2:15] down to Joppa. You can then take them up to **Jerusalem**."
3: 1 Solomon began to build the temple of the LORD in **Jerusalem** on
5: 2 Then Solomon summoned to **Jerusalem** the elders of Israel,
6: 6 But now I have chosen **Jerusalem** for my Name to be there,
8: 6 whatever he desired to build in **Jerusalem**, in Lebanon
9: 1 she came to **Jerusalem** to test him with hard questions.
9: 25 which he kept in the chariot cities and also with him in **Jerusalem**.
9: 27 The king made silver as common in **Jerusalem** as stones,
9: 30 Solomon reigned in **Jerusalem** over all Israel forty years.
10: 18 however, managed to get into his chariot and escape to **Jerusalem**.
11: 1 When Rehoboam arrived in **Jerusalem**, he mustered the house of
11: 5 Rehoboam lived in **Jerusalem** and built up towns for defense in
11: 14 came to Judah and **Jerusalem** because Jeroboam and his sons had
11: 16 followed the Levites to **Jerusalem** to offer sacrifices to the
12: 2 Shishak king of Egypt attacked **Jerusalem** in the fifth year of King
12: 4 captured the fortified cities of Judah and came as far as **Jerusalem**.
12: 5 to the leaders of Judah who had assembled in **Jerusalem** for fear
12: 7 My wrath will not be poured out on **Jerusalem** through Shishak.
12: 9 When Shishak king of Egypt attacked **Jerusalem**, he carried off
12: 13 King Rehoboam established himself firmly in **Jerusalem**
12: 13 he became king, and he reigned seventeen years in **Jerusalem**,
13: 2 he reigned in **Jerusalem** three years. His mother's name was
14: 15 [14:14] and goats and camels. Then they returned to **Jerusalem**.
15: 10 They assembled at **Jerusalem** in the third month of the fifteenth
17: 13 of Judah. He also kept experienced fighting men in **Jerusalem**.
19: 1 king of Judah returned safely to his palace in **Jerusalem**,
19: 4 Jehoshaphat lived in **Jerusalem**, and he went out again among the
19: 8 In **Jerusalem** also, Jehoshaphat appointed some of the Levites,
19: 8 of the LORD and to settle disputes. And they lived in **Jerusalem**.
20: 5 **Jerusalem** at the temple of the LORD in the front of the new
20: 15 King Jehoshaphat and all who live in Judah and **Jerusalem**!
20: 17 the deliverance the LORD will give you, O Judah and **Jerusalem**.
20: 18 of Judah and **Jerusalem** fell down in worship before the LORD.
20: 20 and said, "Listen to me, Judah and people of **Jerusalem**!
20: 27 all the men of Judah and **Jerusalem** returned joyfully to Jerusalem,
20: 27 all the men of Judah and Jerusalem returned joyfully to **Jerusalem**,
20: 28 They entered **Jerusalem** and went to the temple of the LORD
20: 31 king of Judah, and he reigned in **Jerusalem** twenty-five years.
21: 5 when he became king, and he reigned in **Jerusalem** eight years.
21: 11 and had caused the people of **Jerusalem** to prostitute themselves
21: 13 led Judah and the people of **Jerusalem** to prostitute themselves,
21: 20 when he became king, and he reigned in **Jerusalem** eight years.
22: 1 The people of **Jerusalem** made Ahaziah, Jehoram's youngest son,
22: 2 old when he became king, and he reigned in **Jerusalem** one year.
23: 2 families from all the towns. When they came to **Jerusalem**,
24: 1 when he became king, and he reigned in **Jerusalem** forty years.
24: 6 **Jerusalem** the tax imposed by Moses the servant of the LORD
24: 9 **Jerusalem** that they should bring to the LORD the tax that Moses
24: 18 of their guilt, God's anger came upon Judah and **Jerusalem**.
24: 23 it invaded Judah and **Jerusalem** and killed all the leaders of the
25: 1 he became king, and he reigned in **Jerusalem** twenty-nine years.
25: 1 His mother's name was Jehoaddin; she was from **Jerusalem**.
25: 23 Jehoash brought him to **Jerusalem** and broke down the wall of
25: 23 broke down the wall of **Jerusalem** from the Ephraim Gate to the
25: 27 they conspired against him in **Jerusalem** and he fled to Lachish,
26: 3 he became king, and he reigned in **Jerusalem** fifty-two years.
26: 3 His mother's name was Jecoliah; she was from **Jerusalem**.
26: 9 Uzziah built towers in **Jerusalem** at the Corner Gate, at the Valley
26: 15 In **Jerusalem** he made machines designed by skillful men for use

2Ch 27: 1 when he became king, and he reigned in **Jerusalem** sixteen years.
27: 8 when he became king, and he reigned in **Jerusalem** sixteen years.
28: 1 when he became king, and he reigned in **Jerusalem** sixteen years.
28: 10 to make the men and women of Judah and **Jerusalem** your slaves.
28: 24 and set up altars at every street corner in **Jerusalem**.
28: 27 rested with his fathers and was buried in the city of **Jerusalem**,
29: 1 he became king, and he reigned in **Jerusalem** twenty-nine years.
29: 8 the anger of the LORD has fallen on Judah and **Jerusalem**;
30: 1 inviting them to come to the temple of the LORD in **Jerusalem**
30: 2 the whole assembly in **Jerusalem** decided to celebrate the
30: 3 and the people had not assembled in **Jerusalem**.
30: 5 calling the people to come to **Jerusalem** and celebrate the
30: 11 and Zebulun humbled themselves and went to **Jerusalem**.
30: 13 A very large crowd of people assembled in **Jerusalem** to celebrate
30: 14 They removed the altars in **Jerusalem** and cleared away the
30: 21 The Israelites who were present in **Jerusalem** celebrated the Feast
30: 26 There was great joy in **Jerusalem**, for since the days of Solomon
30: 26 David king of Israel there had been nothing like this in **Jerusalem**.
31: 4 He ordered the people living in **Jerusalem** to give the portion due
32: 2 had come and that he intended to make war on **Jerusalem**,
32: 9 he sent his officers to **Jerusalem** with this message for Hezekiah
32: 9 of Judah and for all the people of Judah who were **there**[s] [+928]:
32: 10 your confidence, that you remain in **Jerusalem** under siege?
32: 12 this god's high places and altars, saying to Judah and **Jerusalem**,
32: 18 they called out in Hebrew to the people of **Jerusalem** who were on
32: 19 They spoke about the God of **Jerusalem** as they did about the gods
32: 22 the people of **Jerusalem** from the hand of Sennacherib king of
32: 23 Many brought offerings to **Jerusalem** for the LORD and valuable
32: 25 the LORD's wrath was on him and on Judah and **Jerusalem**.
32: 26 repented of the pride of his heart, as did the people of **Jerusalem**;
32: 33 All Judah and the people of **Jerusalem** honored him when he died.
33: 1 he became king, and he reigned in **Jerusalem** fifty-five years.
33: 4 LORD had said, "My Name will remain in **Jerusalem** forever."
33: 7 and to his son Solomon, "In this temple and in **Jerusalem**,
33: 9 But Manasseh led Judah and the people of **Jerusalem** astray,
33: 13 so he brought him back to **Jerusalem** and to his kingdom.
33: 15 as all the altars he had built on the temple hill and in **Jerusalem**;
33: 21 old when he became king, and he reigned in **Jerusalem** two years.
34: 1 he became king, and he reigned in **Jerusalem** thirty-one years.
34: 3 year he began to purge Judah and **Jerusalem** of high places,
34: 5 the priests on their altars, and so he purged Judah and **Jerusalem**.
34: 7 incense altars throughout Israel. Then he went back to **Jerusalem**.
34: 9 people of Judah and Benjamin and the inhabitants of **Jerusalem**.
34: 22 of the wardrobe. She lived in **Jerusalem**, in the Second District.
34: 29 the king called together all the elders of Judah and **Jerusalem**.
34: 30 of Judah, the people of **Jerusalem**, the priests and the Levites—
34: 32 he had everyone in **Jerusalem** and Benjamin pledge themselves to
34: 32 the people of **Jerusalem** did this in accordance with the covenant
35: 1 Josiah celebrated the Passover to the LORD in **Jerusalem**,
35: 18 all Judah and Israel who were there with the people of **Jerusalem**.
35: 24 put him in the other chariot he had and brought him to **Jerusalem**,
35: 24 of his fathers, and all Judah and **Jerusalem** mourned for him.
36: 1 of Josiah and made him king in **Jerusalem** in place of his father.
36: 2 when he became king, and he reigned in **Jerusalem** three months.
36: 3 The king of Egypt dethroned him in **Jerusalem** and imposed on
36: 4 king over Judah and **Jerusalem** and changed Eliakim's name to
36: 5 when he became king, and he reigned in **Jerusalem** eleven years.
36: 9 and he reigned in **Jerusalem** three months and ten days.
36: 10 Jehoiachin's uncle, Zedekiah, king over Judah and **Jerusalem**.
36: 11 when he became king, and he reigned in **Jerusalem** eleven years.
36: 14 the temple of the LORD, which he had consecrated in **Jerusalem**.
36: 19 set fire to God's temple and broke down the wall of **Jerusalem**;
36: 23 he has appointed me to build a temple for him at **Jerusalem** in
Ezr 1: 2 he has appointed me to build a temple for him at **Jerusalem** in
1: 3 let him go up to **Jerusalem** in Judah and build the temple of the
1: 3 of the LORD, the God of Israel, the God who is in **Jerusalem**.
1: 4 and with freewill offerings for the temple of God in **Jerusalem**.' "
1: 5 prepared to go up and build the house of the LORD in **Jerusalem**.
1: 7 which Nebuchadnezzar had carried away from **Jerusalem**
1: 11 these along when the exiles came up from Babylon to **Jerusalem**.
2: 1 Babylon had taken captive to Babylon (they returned to **Jerusalem**
2: 68 When they arrived at the house of the LORD in **Jerusalem**,
3: 1 in their towns, the people assembled as one man in **Jerusalem**.
3: 8 second year after their arrival at the house of God in **Jerusalem**,
3: 8 and all who had returned from the captivity to **Jerusalem**)
4: 6 lodged an accusation against the people of Judah and **Jerusalem**.
7: 7 also came up to **Jerusalem** in the seventh year of King Artaxerxes.
7: 8 Ezra arrived in **Jerusalem** in the fifth month of the seventh year of
7: 9 and he arrived in **Jerusalem** on the first day of the fifth month,
7: 27 bring honor to the house of the LORD in **Jerusalem** in this way
8: 29 of the house of the LORD in **Jerusalem** before the leading priests
8: 30 weighed out to be taken to the house of our God in **Jerusalem**.
8: 31 first month we set out from the Ahava Canal to go to **Jerusalem**.
8: 32 So we arrived in **Jerusalem**, where we rested three days.
9: 9 and he has given us a wall of protection in Judah and **Jerusalem**.
10: 7 and **Jerusalem** for all the exiles to assemble in Jerusalem.
10: 7 and Jerusalem for all the exiles to assemble in **Jerusalem**.
10: 9 all the men of Judah and Benjamin had gathered in **Jerusalem**.
Ne 1: 2 Jewish remnant that survived the exile, and also about **Jerusalem**.
1: 3 The wall of **Jerusalem** is broken down, and its gates have been
2: 11 I went to **Jerusalem**, and after staying there three days
2: 12 told anyone what my God had put in my heart to do for **Jerusalem**.
2: 13 Jackal Well and the Dung Gate, examining the walls of **Jerusalem**,
2: 17 **Jerusalem** lies in ruins, and its gates have been burned with fire.
2: 17 Come, let us rebuild the wall of **Jerusalem**, and we will no longer
2: 20 you have no share in **Jerusalem** or any claim or historic right to
3: 8 next to that. They restored **Jerusalem** as far as the Broad Wall.
3: 9 Rephaiah son of Hur, ruler of a half-district of **Jerusalem**,
3: 12 Shallum son of Hallohesh, ruler of a half-district of **Jerusalem**,
4: 7 [4:1] the men of Ashdod heard that the repairs to **Jerusalem's**
4: 8 [4:2] and fight against **Jerusalem** and stir up trouble against it.
4: 22 [4:16] every man and his helper stay inside **Jerusalem** at night,
6: 7 prophets to make this proclamation about you in **Jerusalem**:
7: 2 I put in charge of **Jerusalem** my brother Hanani, along with
7: 3 "The gates of **Jerusalem** are not to be opened until the sun is hot.
7: 3 Also appoint residents of **Jerusalem** as guards, some at their posts
7: 6 king of Babylon had taken captive (they returned to **Jerusalem**
8: 15 this word and spread it throughout their towns and in **Jerusalem**:
11: 1 Now the leaders of the people settled in **Jerusalem**, and the rest of
11: 1 people cast lots to bring one out of every ten to live in **Jerusalem**,
11: 2 commended all the men who volunteered to live in **Jerusalem**.
11: 3 These are the provincial leaders who settled in **Jerusalem** (now
11: 4 other people from both Judah and Benjamin lived in **Jerusalem**):
11: 6 The descendants of Perez who lived in **Jerusalem** totaled 468 able
11: 22 The chief officer of the Levites in **Jerusalem** was Uzzi son of
12: 27 At the dedication of the wall of **Jerusalem**, the Levites were
12: 27 were brought to **Jerusalem** to celebrate joyfully the dedication
12: 28 also were brought together from the region around **Jerusalem**—
12: 29 for the singers had built villages for themselves around **Jerusalem**.
12: 43 The sound of rejoicing in **Jerusalem** could be heard far away.
13: 6 while all this was going on, I was not in **Jerusalem**, for in the
13: 7 came back to **Jerusalem**. Here I learned about the evil thing
13: 15 And they were bringing all this into **Jerusalem** on the Sabbath.
13: 16 selling them in **Jerusalem** on the Sabbath to the people of Judah.
13: 19 When evening shadows fell on the gates of **Jerusalem** before the
13: 20 and sellers of all kinds of goods spent the night outside **Jerusalem**.
Est 2: 6 who had been carried into exile from **Jerusalem** by
Ps 51: 18 [51:20] make Zion prosper; build up the walls of **Jerusalem**.
68: 29 [68:30] Because of your temple at **Jerusalem** kings will bring
79: 1 defiled your holy temple, they have reduced **Jerusalem** to rubble.
79: 3 They have poured out blood like water all around **Jerusalem**,
102: 21 [102:22] will be declared in Zion and his praise in **Jerusalem**
116: 19 courts of the house of the LORD—in your midst, O **Jerusalem**.
122: 2 Our feet are standing in your gates, O **Jerusalem**.
122: 3 **Jerusalem** is built like a city that is closely compacted together.
122: 6 Pray for the peace of **Jerusalem**: "May those who love you be
125: 2 As the mountains surround **Jerusalem**, so the LORD surrounds
128: 5 all the days of your life; may you see the prosperity of **Jerusalem**,
135: 21 be to the LORD from Zion, to him who dwells in **Jerusalem**.
137: 5 If I forget you, O **Jerusalem**, may my right hand forget its skill.
137: 6 not remember you, if I do not consider **Jerusalem** my highest joy.
137: 7 O LORD, what the Edomites did on the day **Jerusalem** fell.
147: 2 The LORD builds up **Jerusalem**; he gathers the exiles of Israel.
147: 12 Extol the LORD, O **Jerusalem**; praise your God, O Zion,
Ecc 1: 1 The words of the Teacher, son of David, king in **Jerusalem**:
1: 12 I, the Teacher, was king over Israel in **Jerusalem**.
1: 16 more than anyone who has ruled over **Jerusalem** before me;
2: 7 more herds and flocks than anyone in **Jerusalem** before me.
2: 9 I became greater by far than anyone in **Jerusalem** before me.
SS 1: 5 Dark am I, yet lovely, O daughters of **Jerusalem**, dark like the
2: 7 Daughters of **Jerusalem**, I charge you by the gazelles and by the
3: 5 Daughters of **Jerusalem**, I charge you by the gazelles and by the
3: 10 its interior lovingly inlaid by the daughters of **Jerusalem**.
5: 8 O daughters of **Jerusalem**, I charge you—if you find my lover,
5: 16 This is my lover, this my friend, O daughters of **Jerusalem**.
6: 4 You are beautiful, my darling, as Tirzah, lovely as **Jerusalem**,
8: 4 Daughters of **Jerusalem**, I charge you: Do not arouse or awaken
Isa 1: 1 **Jerusalem** that Isaiah son of Amoz saw during the reigns of
2: 1 is what Isaiah son of Amoz saw concerning Judah and **Jerusalem**:
2: 3 will go out from Zion, the word of the LORD from **Jerusalem**.
3: 1 is about to take from **Jerusalem** and Judah both supply
3: 8 **Jerusalem** staggers, Judah is falling; their words and deeds are
4: 3 who are left in Zion, who remain in **Jerusalem**, will be called holy,
4: 3 called holy, all who are recorded among the living in **Jerusalem**.
4: 4 he will cleanse the bloodstains from **Jerusalem** by a spirit of
5: 3 "Now you dwellers in **Jerusalem** and men of Judah,
7: 1 of Remaliah king of Israel marched up to fight against **Jerusalem**,
8: 14 And for the people of **Jerusalem** he will be a trap and a snare.

Isa 10:10 kingdoms whose images excelled those of **Jerusalem**
10:11 shall I not deal with **Jerusalem** and her images as I dealt with
10:12 Lord has finished all his work against Mount Zion and **Jerusalem**,
10:32 fist at the mount of the Daughter of Zion, at the hill of **Jerusalem**.
22:10 You counted the buildings in **Jerusalem** and tore down houses to
22:21 He will be a father to those who live in **Jerusalem** and to the house
24:23 the LORD Almighty will reign on Mount Zion and in **Jerusalem**,
27:13 and worship the LORD on the holy mountain in **Jerusalem**.
28:14 of the LORD, you scoffers who rule this people in **Jerusalem**.
30:19 O people of Zion, who live in **Jerusalem**, you will weep no more.
31: 5 hovering overhead, the LORD Almighty will shield **Jerusalem**;
31: 9 the LORD, whose fire is in Zion, whose furnace is in **Jerusalem**.
33:20 your eyes will see **Jerusalem**, a peaceful abode, a tent that will not
36: 2 with a large army from Lachish to King Hezekiah at **Jerusalem**.
36: 7 and altars Hezekiah removed, saying to Judah and **Jerusalem**,
36:20 How then can the LORD deliver **Jerusalem** from my hand?"
37:10 '**Jerusalem** will not be handed over to the king of Assyria.'
37:22 The Daughter of **Jerusalem** tosses her head as you flee.
37:32 For out of **Jerusalem** will come a remnant, and out of Mount Zion
40: 2 Speak tenderly to **Jerusalem**, and proclaim to her that her hard
40: 9 You who bring good tidings to **Jerusalem**, lift up your voice with
41:27 here they are!' I gave to **Jerusalem** a messenger of good tidings.
44:26 who says of **Jerusalem**, 'It shall be inhabited,' of the towns of
44:28 he will say of **Jerusalem**, "Let it be rebuilt," and of the temple,
51:17 Rise up, O **Jerusalem**, you who have drunk from the hand of the
52: 1 Put on your garments of splendor, O **Jerusalem**, the holy city.
52: 2 Shake off your dust; rise up, sit enthroned, O **Jerusalem**.
52: 9 Burst into songs of joy together, you ruins of **Jerusalem**,
52: 9 the LORD has comforted his people, he has redeemed **Jerusalem**.
62: 1 I will not keep silent, for **Jerusalem's** sake I will not remain quiet,
62: 6 I have posted watchmen on your walls, O **Jerusalem**; they will
62: 7 give him no rest till he establishes **Jerusalem** and makes her the
64:10 [64:9] a desert; even Zion is a desert, **Jerusalem** a desolation.
65:18 for I will create **Jerusalem** to be a delight and its people a joy.
65:19 I will rejoice over **Jerusalem** and take delight in my people;
66:10 "Rejoice with **Jerusalem** and be glad for her, all you who love her;
66:13 so will I comfort you; and you will be comforted over **Jerusalem**."
66:20 to my holy mountain in **Jerusalem** as an offering to the LORD—
Jer 1: 3 king of Judah, when the people of **Jerusalem** went into exile.
1:15 and set up their thrones in the entrance of the gates of **Jerusalem**;
2: 2 "Go and proclaim in the hearing of **Jerusalem**: " 'I remember the
3:17 At that time they will call **Jerusalem** The Throne of the LORD,
3:17 all nations will gather in **Jerusalem** to honor the name of the
4: 3 is what the LORD says to the men of Judah and to **Jerusalem**:
4: 4 your hearts, you men of Judah and people of **Jerusalem**,
4: 5 "Announce in Judah and proclaim in **Jerusalem** and say: 'Sound
4:10 you have deceived this people and **Jerusalem** by saying,
4:11 At that time this people and **Jerusalem** will be told, "A scorching
4:14 O **Jerusalem**, wash the evil from your heart and be saved.
4:16 "Tell this to the nations, proclaim it to **Jerusalem**: 'A besieging
5: 1 "Go up and down the streets of **Jerusalem**, look around and
6: 1 "Flee for safety, people of Benjamin! Flee from **Jerusalem**!
6: 6 "Cut down the trees and build siege ramps against **Jerusalem**.
6: 8 Take warning, O **Jerusalem**, or I will turn away from you
7:17 are doing in the towns of Judah and in the streets of **Jerusalem**?
7:34 bridegroom in the towns of Judah and the streets of **Jerusalem**,
8: 1 the bones of the people of **Jerusalem** will be removed from their
8: 5 Why does **Jerusalem** always turn away? They cling to deceit;
9:11 [9:10] "I will make **Jerusalem** a heap of ruins, a haunt of jackals;
11: 2 them to the people of Judah and to those who live in **Jerusalem**.
11: 6 these words in the towns of Judah and in the streets of **Jerusalem**:
11: 9 among the people of Judah and those who live in **Jerusalem**.
11:12 The towns of Judah and the people of **Jerusalem** will go and cry
11:13 to that shameful god Baal are as many as the streets of **Jerusalem**.'
13: 9 I will ruin the pride of Judah and the great pride of **Jerusalem**.
13:13 the priests, the prophets and all those living in **Jerusalem**.
13:27 acts on the hills and in the fields. Woe to you, O **Jerusalem**!
14: 2 they wail for the land, and a cry goes up from **Jerusalem**.
14:16 are prophesying to will be thrown out into the streets of **Jerusalem**
15: 4 what Manasseh son of Hezekiah king of Judah did in **Jerusalem**.
15: 5 "Who will have pity on you, O **Jerusalem**? Who will mourn for
17:19 Judah go in and out; stand also at all the other gates of **Jerusalem**.
17:20 and everyone living in **Jerusalem** who come through these gates.
17:21 load on the Sabbath day or bring it through the gates of **Jerusalem**.
17:25 accompanied by the men of Judah and those living in **Jerusalem**,
17:26 come from the towns of Judah and the villages around **Jerusalem**,
17:27 as you come through the gates of **Jerusalem** on the Sabbath day,
17:27 I will kindle an unquenchable fire in the gates of **Jerusalem** that
18:11 therefore say to the people of Judah and those living in **Jerusalem**,
19: 3 word of the LORD, O kings of Judah and people of **Jerusalem**.
19: 7 " 'In this place I will ruin the plans of Judah and **Jerusalem**.
19:13 The houses in **Jerusalem** and those of the kings of Judah will be
22:19 dragged away and thrown outside the gates of **Jerusalem**."
23:14 among the prophets of **Jerusalem** I have seen something horrible:
23:15 because from the prophets of **Jerusalem** ungodliness has spread
24: 1 the artisans of Judah were carried into exile from **Jerusalem** to
24: 8 his officials and the survivors from **Jerusalem**, whether they
25: 2 said to all the people of Judah and to all those living in **Jerusalem**:
25:18 **Jerusalem** and the towns of Judah, its kings and officials,
26:18 be plowed like a field, **Jerusalem** will become a heap of rubble,
27: 3 Sidon through the envoys who have come to **Jerusalem** to
27:18 of the king of Judah and in **Jerusalem** not be taken to Babylon.
27:20 of Jehoiakim king of Judah into exile from **Jerusalem** to Babylon,
27:20 to Babylon, along with all the nobles of Judah and **Jerusalem**—
27:21 and in the palace of the king of Judah and in **Jerusalem**:
29: 1 sent from **Jerusalem** to the surviving elders among the exiles
29: 1 had carried into exile from **Jerusalem** to Babylon.
29: 2 the court officials and the leaders of Judah and **Jerusalem**,
29: 2 and the artisans had gone into exile from **Jerusalem**.)
29: 4 says to all those I carried into exile from **Jerusalem** to Babylon:
29:20 all you exiles whom I have sent away from **Jerusalem** to Babylon.
29:25 You sent letters in your own name to all the people in **Jerusalem**,
32: 2 The army of the king of Babylon was then besieging **Jerusalem**,
32:32 and prophets, the men of Judah and the people of **Jerusalem**.
32:44 in the villages around **Jerusalem**, in the towns of Judah and in the
33:10 the towns of Judah and the streets of **Jerusalem** that are deserted,
33:13 in the villages around **Jerusalem** and in the towns of Judah,
33:16 those days Judah will be saved and **Jerusalem** will live in safety.
34: 1 peoples in the empire he ruled were fighting against **Jerusalem**
34: 6 the prophet told all this to Zedekiah king of Judah, in **Jerusalem**,
34: 7 the army of the king of Babylon was fighting against **Jerusalem**
34: 8 all the people in **Jerusalem** to proclaim freedom for the slaves.
34:19 The leaders of Judah and **Jerusalem**, the court officials, the priests
35:11 we must go to **Jerusalem** to escape the Babylonian and Aramean
35:11 and Aramean armies.' So we have remained in **Jerusalem**."
35:13 Go and tell the men of Judah and the people of **Jerusalem**,
35:17 on everyone living in **Jerusalem** every disaster I pronounced
36: 9 before the LORD was proclaimed for all the people in **Jerusalem**
36: 9 and those who had come from the towns of Judah. **[RPH]**
36:31 I will bring on them and those living in **Jerusalem** and the people
37: 5 when the Babylonians who were besieging **Jerusalem** heard the
37: 5 heard the report about them, they withdrew from **Jerusalem**.
37:11 After the Babylonian army had withdrawn from **Jerusalem**
37:12 Jeremiah started to leave **the city**[s] to go to the territory of
38:28 the courtyard of the guard until the day **Jerusalem** was captured.
38:28 the day Jerusalem was captured. This is how **Jerusalem** was taken:
39: 1 Nebuchadnezzar king of Babylon marched against **Jerusalem** with
39: 8 the houses of the people and broke down the walls of **Jerusalem**.
40: 1 Jeremiah bound in chains among all the captives from **Jerusalem**
42:18 and wrath have been poured out on those who lived in **Jerusalem**,
44: 2 You saw the great disaster I brought on **Jerusalem** and on all the
44: 6 it raged against the towns of Judah and the streets of **Jerusalem**
44: 9 and your wives in the land of Judah and the streets of **Jerusalem**?
44:13 with the sword, famine and plague, as I punished **Jerusalem**.
44:17 officials did in the towns of Judah and in the streets of **Jerusalem**.
44:21 of Judah and the streets of **Jerusalem** by you and your fathers,
51:35 our blood be on those who live in Babylonia," says **Jerusalem**.
51:50 Remember the LORD in a distant land, and think on **Jerusalem**."
52: 1 when he became king, and he reigned in **Jerusalem** eleven years.
52: 3 because of the LORD's anger that all this happened to **Jerusalem**
52: 4 Nebuchadnezzar king of Babylon marched against **Jerusalem** with
52:12 who served the king of Babylon, came to **Jerusalem**.
52:13 of the LORD, the royal palace and all the houses of **Jerusalem**.
52:14 of the imperial guard broke down all the walls around **Jerusalem**.
52:29 in Nebuchadnezzar's eighteenth year, 832 people from **Jerusalem**;
La 1: 7 wandering **Jerusalem** remembers all the treasures that were hers in
1: 8 **Jerusalem** has sinned greatly and so has become unclean.
1:17 his foes; **Jerusalem** has become an unclean thing among them.
2:10 The young women of **Jerusalem** have bowed their heads to the
2:13 With what can I compare you, O Daughter of **Jerusalem**?
2:15 they scoff and shake their heads at the Daughter of **Jerusalem**:
4:12 that enemies and foes could enter the gates of **Jerusalem**.
Eze 4: 1 put it in front of you and draw the city of **Jerusalem** on it.
4: 7 Turn your face toward the siege of **Jerusalem** and with bared arm
4:16 "Son of man, I will cut off the supply of food in **Jerusalem**.
5: 5 This is **Jerusalem**, which I have set in the center of the nations,
8: 3 and heaven and in visions of God he took me to **Jerusalem**,
9: 4 "Go throughout the city of **Jerusalem** and put a mark on the
9: 8 remnant of Israel in this outpouring of your wrath on **Jerusalem**?"
11:15 are those of whom the people of **Jerusalem** have said, 'They are
12:10 This oracle concerns the prince in **Jerusalem** and the whole house
12:19 what the Sovereign LORD says about those living in **Jerusalem**
13:16 those prophets of Israel who prophesied to **Jerusalem** and saw
14:21 How much worse will it be when I send against **Jerusalem** my
14:22 consoled regarding the disaster I have brought upon **Jerusalem**—
15: 6 as fuel for the fire, so will I treat the people living in **Jerusalem**.
16: 2 "Son of man, confront **Jerusalem** with her detestable practices
16: 3 and say, 'This is what the Sovereign LORD says to **Jerusalem**:

Eze 17: 12 'The king of Babylon went to **Jerusalem** and carried off her king
21: 2 [21:7] set your face against **Jerusalem** and preach against the
21: 20 [21:25] and another against Judah and fortified **Jerusalem**.
21: 22 [21:27] Into his right hand will come the lot for **Jerusalem**,
22: 19 you have all become dross, I will gather you into **Jerusalem**.
23: 4 and daughters. Oholah is Samaria, and Oholibah is **Jerusalem**.
24: 2 because the king of Babylon has laid siege to **Jerusalem** this very
26: 2 "Son of man, because Tyre has said of **Jerusalem**, 'Aha! The gate
33: 21 a man who had escaped from **Jerusalem** came to me and said,
36: 38 as numerous as the flocks for offerings at **Jerusalem** during her
Da 1: 1 Nebuchadnezzar king of Babylon came to **Jerusalem** and besieged
9: 2 that the desolation of **Jerusalem** would last seventy years.
9: 7 the men of Judah and people of **Jerusalem** and all Israel, both near
9: 12 nothing has ever been done like what has been done to **Jerusalem**.
9: 16 turn away your anger and your wrath from **Jerusalem**, your city,
9: 16 Our sins and the iniquities of our fathers have made **Jerusalem**
9: 25 decree to restore and rebuild **Jerusalem** until the Anointed One,
Joel 2: 32 [3:5] on Mount Zion and in **Jerusalem** there will be deliverance,
3: 1 [4:1] when I restore the fortunes of Judah and **Jerusalem**,
3: 6 [4:6] You sold the people of Judah and **Jerusalem** to the Greeks,
3: 16 [4:16] LORD will roar from Zion and thunder from **Jerusalem**;
3: 17 [4:17] **Jerusalem** will be holy; never again will foreigners invade
3: 20 [4:20] inhabited forever and **Jerusalem** through all generations.
Am 1: 2 "The LORD roars from Zion and thunders from **Jerusalem**;
2: 5 fire upon Judah that will consume the fortresses of **Jerusalem**."
Ob 1: 11 and foreigners entered his gates and cast lots for **Jerusalem**,
1: 20 the exiles from **Jerusalem** who are in Sepharad will possess the
Mic 1: 1 of Judah—the vision he saw concerning Samaria and **Jerusalem**.
1: 5 Is it not Samaria? What is Judah's high place? Is it not **Jerusalem**?
1: 9 has reached the very gate of my people, even to **Jerusalem** itself.
1: 12 disaster has come from the LORD, even to the gate of **Jerusalem**.
3: 10 who build Zion with bloodshed, and **Jerusalem** with wickedness.
3: 12 be plowed like a field, **Jerusalem** will become a heap of rubble,
4: 2 will go out from Zion, the word of the LORD from **Jerusalem**.
4: 8 to you; kingship will come to the Daughter of **Jerusalem**."
Zep 1: 4 out my hand against Judah and against all who live in **Jerusalem**.
1: 12 At that time I will search **Jerusalem** with lamps and punish those
3: 14 and rejoice with all your heart, O Daughter of **Jerusalem**!
3: 16 On that day they will say to **Jerusalem**, "Do not fear, O Zion;
Zec 1: 12 how long will you withhold mercy from **Jerusalem** and from the
1: 14 LORD Almighty says: 'I am very jealous for **Jerusalem** and Zion,
1: 16 'I will return to **Jerusalem** with mercy, and there my house will be
1: 16 And the measuring line will be stretched out over **Jerusalem**,'
1: 17 and the LORD will again comfort Zion and choose **Jerusalem**.' "
1: 19 [2:2] are the horns that scattered Judah, Israel and **Jerusalem**."
2: 2 [2:6] He answered me, "To measure **Jerusalem**, to find out how
2: 4 [2:8] '**Jerusalem** will be a city without walls because of the great
2: 12 [2:16] portion in the holy land and will again choose **Jerusalem**.
3: 2 Satan! The LORD, who has chosen **Jerusalem**, rebuke you!
7: 7 LORD proclaimed through the earlier prophets when **Jerusalem**
8: 3 the LORD says: "I will return to Zion and dwell in **Jerusalem**.
8: 3 **Jerusalem** will be called the City of Truth, and the mountain of the
8: 4 and women of ripe old age will sit in the streets of **Jerusalem**,
8: 8 I will bring them back to live in **Jerusalem**; they will be my
8: 15 "so now I have determined to do good again to **Jerusalem**
8: 22 powerful nations will come to **Jerusalem** to seek the LORD
9: 9 Shout, Daughter of **Jerusalem**! See, your king comes to you,
9: 10 the chariots from Ephraim and the war-horses from **Jerusalem**,
12: 2 "I am going to make **Jerusalem** a cup that sends all the
12: 2 peoples reeling. Judah will be besieged as well as **Jerusalem**.
12: 3 I will make **Jerusalem** an immovable rock for all the nations.
12: 5 'The people of **Jerusalem** are strong, because the LORD
12: 6 surrounding peoples, but **Jerusalem** will remain intact in her place.
12: 6 but Jerusalem will remain intact in her place. **[RPH]**
12: 7 of **Jerusalem's** inhabitants may not be greater than that of Judah.
12: 8 On that day the LORD will shield those who live in **Jerusalem**,
12: 9 day I will set out to destroy all the nations that attack **Jerusalem**.
12: 10 and the inhabitants of **Jerusalem** a spirit of grace and supplication.
12: 11 On that day the weeping in **Jerusalem** will be great,
13: 1 be opened to the house of David and the inhabitants of **Jerusalem**,
14: 2 I will gather all the nations to **Jerusalem** to fight against it;
14: 4 day his feet will stand on the Mount of Olives, east of **Jerusalem**,
14: 8 On that day living water will flow out from **Jerusalem**, half to the
14: 10 The whole land, from Geba to Rimmon, south of **Jerusalem**,
14: 11 never again will it be destroyed. **Jerusalem** will be secure.
14: 12 LORD will strike all the nations that fought against **Jerusalem**:
14: 14 Judah too will fight at **Jerusalem**. The wealth of all the
14: 16 the survivors from all the nations that have attacked **Jerusalem**
14: 17 If any of the peoples of the earth do not go up to **Jerusalem** to
14: 21 Every pot in **Jerusalem** and Judah will be holy to the LORD
Mal 2: 11 A detestable thing has been committed in Israel and in **Jerusalem**:
3: 4 of Judah and **Jerusalem** will be acceptable to the LORD,

3732 יֶרַח¹ ***yeraḥ¹***, n.m. [12] [→ 3726, 3733, 3734, 3735, 3747; cf. 782; Ar 10333]

month [5], months [5], moon [1], one month [+3427] [1]

Ex 2: 2 she saw that he was a fine child, she hid him *for* three **months**.
Dt 21: 13 in your house and mourned her father and mother *for* a full **month**,
33: 14 the best the sun brings forth and the finest the **moon** can yield;
1Ki 6: 37 of the LORD was laid in the fourth year, in the **month** *of* Ziv.
6: 38 In the eleventh year in the **month** *of* Bul, the eighth month,
8: 2 King Solomon at the time of the festival in the **month** *of* Ethanim,
2Ki 15: 13 king of Judah, and he reigned in Samaria **one month** [+3427].
Job 3: 6 among the days of the year nor be entered in any of the **months**.
7: 3 so I have been allotted **months** *of* futility, and nights of misery
29: 2 "How I long for the **months** gone by, for the days when God
39: 2 Do you count the **months** till they bear? Do you know the time
Zec 11: 8 In one **month** I got rid of the three shepherds. The flock detested

3733 יֶרַח² ***yeraḥ²***, n.pr.m. [2] [√ 3732]

Jerah [2]

Ge 10: 26 Joktan was the father of Almodad, Sheleph, Hazarmaveth, **Jerah**,
1Ch 1: 20 Joktan was the father of Almodad, Sheleph, Hazarmaveth, **Jerah**,

3734 יָרֵחַ ***yārēaḥ***, n.m. [27] [√ 3732]

moon [27]

Ge 37: 9 this time the sun and **moon** and eleven stars were bowing down to
Dt 4: 19 you look up to the sky and see the sun, the **moon** and the stars—
17: 3 bowing down to them or to the sun or the **moon** or the stars of the
Jos 10: 12 "O sun, stand still over Gibeon, O **moon**, over the Valley of
10: 13 So the sun stood still, and the **moon** stopped, till the nation
2Ki 23: 5 to the sun and **moon**, to the constellations and to all the starry
Job 25: 5 If even the **moon** is not bright and the stars are not pure in his eyes,
31: 26 regarded the sun in its radiance or the **moon** moving in splendor,
Ps 8: 3 [8:4] the work of your fingers, the **moon** and the stars, which you
72: 5 as long as the sun, as long as the **moon**, through all generations.
72: 7 will flourish; prosperity will abound till the **moon** is no more.
89: 37 [89:38] it will be established forever like the **moon**, the faithful
104: 19 The **moon** marks off the seasons, and the sun knows when to go
121: 6 the sun will not harm you by day, nor the **moon** by night.
136: 9 the **moon** and stars to govern the night; *His love endures*
148: 3 Praise him, sun and **moon**, praise him, all you shining stars.
Ecc 12: 2 before the sun and the light and the **moon** and the stars grow dark,
Isa 13: 10 rising sun will be darkened and the **moon** will not give its light.
60: 19 light by day, nor will the brightness of the **moon** shine on you,
60: 20 Your sun will never set again, and your **moon** will wane no more;
Jer 8: 2 exposed to the sun and the **moon** and all the stars of the heavens,
31: 35 who decrees the **moon** and stars to shine by night, who stirs up the
Eze 32: 7 cover the sun with a cloud, and the **moon** will not give its light.
Joel 2: 10 the sky trembles, the sun and **moon** are darkened, and the stars no
2: 31 [3:4] the **moon** to blood before the coming of the great
3: 15 [4:15] The sun and **moon** will be darkened, and the stars no
Hab 3: 11 **moon** stood still in the heavens at the glint of your flying arrows,

3735 יְרִחוֹ ***yᵉrîḥô***, n.pr.loc. [57] [√ 3732]

Jericho [56], there[s] [1]

Nu 22: 1 plains of Moab and camped along the Jordan across from **Jericho**.
26: 3 So on the plains of Moab by the Jordan across from **Jericho**,
26: 63 Israelites on the plains of Moab by the Jordan across from **Jericho**.
31: 12 camp on the plains of Moab, by the Jordan across from **Jericho**.
33: 48 camped on the plains of Moab by the Jordan across from **Jericho**.
33: 50 On the plains of Moab by the Jordan across from **Jericho** the
34: 15 received their inheritance on the east side of the Jordan of **Jericho**,
35: 1 On the plains of Moab by the Jordan across from **Jericho**,
36: 13 Israelites on the plains of Moab by the Jordan across from **Jericho**.
Dt 32: 49 to Mount Nebo in Moab, across from **Jericho**, and view Canaan,
34: 1 from the plains of Moab to the top of Pisgah, across from **Jericho**.
34: 3 the Negev and the whole region from the Valley of **Jericho**,
Jos 2: 1 "Go, look over the land," he said, "especially **Jericho**." So they
2: 2 The king of **Jericho** was told, "Look! Some of the Israelites have
2: 3 So the king of **Jericho** sent this message to Rahab: "Bring out the
3: 16 completely cut off. So the people crossed over opposite **Jericho**.
4: 13 crossed over before the LORD to the plains of **Jericho** for war.
4: 19 the Jordan and camped at Gilgal on the eastern border of **Jericho**.
5: 10 while camped at Gilgal on the plains of **Jericho**, the Israelites
5: 13 Now when Joshua was near **Jericho**, he looked up and saw a man
6: 1 Now **Jericho** was tightly shut up because of the Israelites.
6: 2 "See, I have delivered **Jericho** into your hands, along with its king
6: 25 because she hid the men Joshua had sent as spies to **Jericho**—
6: 26 LORD is the man who undertakes to rebuild this city, **Jericho**:
7: 2 Now Joshua sent men from **Jericho** to Ai, which is near Beth Aven
8: 2 You shall do to Ai and its king as you did to **Jericho** and its king,
9: 3 when the people of Gibeon heard what Joshua had done to **Jericho**

Jos 10: 1 doing to Ai and its king as he had done to **Jericho** and its king,
10: 28 did to the king of Makkedah as he had done to the king of **Jericho**.
10: 30 And he did to its king as he had done to the king of **Jericho**.
12: 9 the king of **Jericho** one the king of Ai (near Bethel) one
13: 32 he was in the plains of Moab across the Jordan east of **Jericho**.
16: 1 The allotment for Joseph began at the Jordan of **Jericho**, east of
16: 1 began at the Jordan of Jericho, east of the waters of **Jericho**,
16: 1 went up from **there**[s] through the desert into the hill country of
16: 7 and Naarah, touched **Jericho** and came out at the Jordan.
18: 12 passed the northern slope of **Jericho** and headed west into the hill
18: 21 had the following cities: **Jericho**, Beth Hoglah, Emek Keziz,
20: 8 On the east side of the Jordan of **Jericho** they designated Bezer in
24: 11 " 'Then you crossed the Jordan and came to **Jericho**. The citizens
24: 11 The citizens of **Jericho** fought against you, as did also the
2Sa 10: 5 "Stay at **Jericho** till your beards have grown, and then come back."
1Ki 16: 34 In Ahab's time, Hiel of Bethel rebuilt **Jericho**. He laid its
2Ki 2: 4 to him, "Stay here, Elisha; the LORD has sent me to **Jericho**."
2: 4 and as you live, I will not leave you." So they went to **Jericho**.
2: 5 The company of the prophets at **Jericho** went up to Elisha
2: 15 The company of the prophets from **Jericho**, who were watching,
2: 18 who was staying in **Jericho**, he said to them, "Didn't I tell you not
25: 5 army pursued the king and overtook him in the plains of **Jericho**.
1Ch 6: 78 [6:63] from the tribe of Reuben across the Jordan east of **Jericho**
19: 5 "Stay at **Jericho** till your beards have grown, and then come back."
2Ch 28: 15 So they took them back to their fellow countrymen at **Jericho**,
Ezr 2: 34 of **Jericho** 345
Ne 3: 2 The men of **Jericho** built the adjoining section, and Zaccur son of
7: 36 of **Jericho** 345
Jer 39: 5 pursued them and overtook Zedekiah in the plains of **Jericho**.
52: 8 pursued King Zedekiah and overtook him in the plains of **Jericho**.

3736 יְרֹחָם *y^erōḥām*, n.pr.m. [10] [√ 8163]

Jeroham [10]

1Sa 1: 1 whose name was Elkanah son of **Jeroham**, the son of Elihu,
1Ch 6: 27 [6:12] Eliab his son, **Jeroham** his son, Elkanah his son
6: 34 [6:19] the son of **Jeroham**, the son of Eliel, the son of Toah,
8: 27 Jaareshiah, Elijah and Zicri were the sons of **Jeroham**.
9: 8 Ibneiah son of **Jeroham**; Elah son of Uzzi, the son of Micri;
9: 12 Adaiah son of **Jeroham**, the son of Pashhur, the son of Malkijah;
12: 7 [12:8] and Joelah and Zebadiah the sons of **Jeroham** from Gedor.
27: 22 over Dan: Azarel son of **Jeroham**. These were the officers over the
2Ch 23: 1 Azariah son of **Jeroham**, Ishmael son of Jehohanan, Azariah son
Ne 11: 12 Adaiah son of **Jeroham**, the son of Pelaliah, the son of Amzi,

3737 יְרַחְמְאֵל *y^eraḥm^e'ēl*, n.pr.m. [8] [√ 8163 + 446]

Jerahmeel [8]

1Ch 2: 9 The sons born to Hezron were: **Jerahmeel**, Ram and Caleb.
2: 25 The sons of **Jerahmeel** the firstborn of Hezron: Ram his firstborn,
2: 26 **Jerahmeel** had another wife, whose name was Atarah; she was the
2: 27 The sons of Ram the firstborn of **Jerahmeel**: Maaz, Jamin
2: 33 Peleth and Zaza. These were the descendants of **Jerahmeel**.
2: 42 The sons of Caleb the brother of **Jerahmeel**: Mesha his firstborn,
24: 29 From Kish: the son of Kish: **Jerahmeel**.
Jer 36: 26 Instead, the king commanded **Jerahmeel**, a son of the king,

3738 יְרַחְמְאֵלִי *y^eraḥm^e'ēlî*, a.g. [2] [√ 8163 + 446]

Jerahmeel [1], Jerahmeelites [1]

1Sa 27: 10 the Negev of Judah" or "Against the Negev of **Jerahmeel**"
30: 29 to those in the towns of the **Jerahmeelites** and the Kenites;

3739 יַרְחָע *yarḥā'*, n.pr.m. [2]

Jarha [2]

1Ch 2: 34 only daughters. He had an Egyptian servant named **Jarha**.
2: 35 Sheshan gave his daughter in marriage to his servant **Jarha**,

3740 יָרַט *yāraṭ*, v. [2]

reckless [1], thrown [1]

Nu 22: 32 [A] to oppose you because your path *is a* **reckless** *one* before me.
Job 16: 11 [A] to evil men and **thrown** me into the clutches of the wicked.

3741 יְרִיאֵל *y^erî'ēl*, n.pr.m. [1] [cf. 3746]

Jeriel [1]

1Ch 7: 2 Uzzi, Rephaiah, **Jeriel**, Jahmai, Ibsam and Samuel—heads of their

3742 יָרִיב *yārîb*[1], n.[m.]. [3] [√ 8189]

contend [2], accusers [1]

Ps 35: 1 Contend, O LORD, with *those who* **contend** *with* me;
Isa 49: 25 I will contend with *those who* **contend** *with* you, and your
Jer 18: 19 Listen to me, O LORD; hear what my **accusers** are saying!

3743 [2]יָרִיב *yārîb*[2], n.pr.m. [3]

Jarib [3]

1Ch 4: 24 descendants of Simeon: Nemuel, Jamin, **Jarib**, Zerah and Shaul;
Ezr 8: 16 Elnathan, **Jarib**, Elnathan, Nathan, Zechariah and Meshullam,
10: 18 and his brothers: Maaseiah, Eliezer, **Jarib** and Gedaliah.

3744 יְרִיבַי *y^erîbay*, n.pr.m. [1] [→ 8192?]

Jeribai [1]

1Ch 11: 46 Eliel the Mahavite, **Jeribai** and Joshaviah the sons of Elnaam,

3745 יְרִיָּה *y^eriyyâ*, n.pr.m. [1] [√ 3746]

Jeriah [1]

1Ch 26: 31 **Jeriah** was their chief according to the genealogical records of

3746 יְרִיָּהוּ *y^eriyyāhû*, n.pr.m. [2] [→ 3745; cf. 3741]

Jeriah [2]

1Ch 23: 19 **Jeriah** the first, Amariah the second, Jahaziel the third
24: 23 **Jeriah** the first, Amariah the second, Jahaziel the third

3747 יְרִיחֹה *y^erîḥōh*, n.pr.loc. Not used in NIV/BHS [√ 3732]

3748 יְרִימוֹת *y^erîmôt*, n.pr.m. [7] [√ 3721? + 4637?]

Jerimoth [7]

1Ch 7: 7 Ezbon, Uzzi, Uzziel, **Jerimoth** and Iri, heads of families—
12: 5 [12:6] Eluzai, **Jerimoth**, Bealiah, Shemariah and Shephatiah the
24: 30 the sons of Mushi: Mahli, Eder and **Jerimoth**. These were the
25: 4 Bukkiah, Mattaniah, Uzziel, Shubael and **Jerimoth**; Hananiah,
27: 19 Ishmaiah son of Obadiah; over Naphtali: **Jerimoth** son of Azriel;
2Ch 11: 18 who was the daughter of David's son **Jerimoth** and of Abihail,
31: 13 Jehiel, Azaziah, Nahath, Asahel, **Jerimoth**, Jozabad, Eliel,

3749 יְרִיעָה *y^erî'â*, n.f. [54] [√ 3760]

curtains [18], curtain [14], *untranslated* [10], other[s] [4], tent [3], shelter [2], dwellings [1], shelters [1], tent curtains [1]

Ex 26: 1 "Make the tabernacle with ten **curtains** *of* finely twisted linen
26: 2 All the **curtains** are to be the same size—twenty-eight cubits long
26: 2 same size—twenty-eight cubits long **[RPH]** and four cubits wide.
26: 2 same size—twenty-eight cubits long and four cubits wide. **[RPH]**
26: 3 Join five of the **curtains** together, and do the same with the other
26: 3 five of the curtains together, and do the same with the **other**[s] five.
26: 4 Make loops of blue material along the edge of the end **curtain** in
26: 4 in one set, and do the same with the end **curtain** in the other set.
26: 5 Make fifty loops on one **curtain** and fifty loops on the end curtain
26: 5 on one curtain and fifty loops on the end **curtain** of the other set,
26: 6 make fifty gold clasps and use them to fasten the **curtains** together
26: 7 "Make **curtains** *of* goat hair for the tent over the tabernacle—
26: 7 hair for the tent over the tabernacle—eleven **[RPH]** altogether.
26: 8 All eleven **curtains** are to be the same size—thirty cubits long
26: 8 be the same size—thirty cubits long **[RPH]** and four cubits wide.
26: 8 be the same size—thirty cubits long and four cubits wide. **[RPH]**
26: 9 Join five of the **curtains** together into one set and the other six into
26: 9 curtains together into one set and the **other**[s] six into another set.
26: 9 another set. Fold the sixth **curtain** double at the front of the tent.
26: 10 Make fifty loops along the edge of the end **curtain** in one set
26: 10 and also along the edge of the end **curtain** *in* the other set.
26: 12 As for the additional length of the tent **curtains**, the half curtain
26: 12 the half **curtain** that is left over is to hang down at the rear of the
26: 13 The tent **curtains** will be a cubit longer on both sides; what is left
36: 8 made the tabernacle with ten **curtains** *of* finely twisted linen
36: 9 All the **curtains** were the same size—twenty-eight cubits long
36: 9 All the curtains **[RPH]** were the same size—twenty-eight cubits
36: 9 same size—**[RPH]** twenty-eight cubits long and four cubits wide.
36: 10 They joined five of the **curtains** together and did the same with the
36: 10 five of the curtains together and did the same with the **other**[s] five.
36: 11 they made loops of blue material along the edge of the end **curtain**
36: 11 and the same was done with the end **curtain** in the other set.
36: 12 They also made fifty loops on one **curtain** and fifty loops on the
36: 12 on one curtain and fifty loops on the end **curtain** of the other set,
36: 13 used them to fasten the *two sets of* **curtains** together so that the
36: 14 They made **curtains** *of* goat hair for the tent over the tabernacle—
36: 14 hair for the tent over the tabernacle—eleven altogether. **[RPH]**
36: 15 All eleven **[RPH]** curtains were the same size—thirty cubits long
36: 15 All eleven **curtains** were the same size—thirty cubits long
36: 15 the same size—thirty cubits long and four cubits wide. **[RPH]**
36: 16 They joined five of the **curtains** into one set and the other six into
36: 16 five of the curtains into one set and the **other**[s] six into another set.
36: 17 they made fifty loops along the edge of the end **curtain** in one set
36: 17 and also along the edge of the end **curtain** in the other set.
Nu 4: 25 They are to carry the **curtains** *of* the tabernacle, the Tent of

2Sa 7: 2 living in a palace of cedar, while the ark of God remains in a **tent**."
1Ch 17: 1 while the ark of the covenant of the LORD is under a **tent**."
Ps 104: 2 in light as with a garment; he stretches out the heavens like a **tent**
SS 1: 5 dark like the tents of Kedar, like the **tent curtains** *of* Solomon.
Isa 54: 2 of your tent, stretch your tent **curtains** wide, do not hold back;
Jer 4: 20 In an instant my tents are destroyed, my **shelter** in a moment.
10: 20 no one is left now to pitch my tent or to set up my **shelter**.
49: 29 their **shelters** will be carried off with all their goods and camels.
Hab 3: 7 the tents of Cushan in distress, the **dwellings** *of* Midian in anguish.

3750 יְרִיעוֹת *yᵉrîʿôt*, n.pr.m. [1] [√ 3760]

Jerioth [1]

1Ch 2: 18 son of Hezron had children by his wife Azubah (and by **Jerioth**).

3751 יָרֵךְ *yārēk*, n.f. [34] [→ 3752; Ar 10334]

side [9], thigh [9], hip [5], base [3], breast [2], attacked viciously [+906+5782+6584+8797] [1], descendants [+3655+5883] [1], direct descendants [+3655] [1], leg [1], legs [1], of his own [+2257+3655] [1]

Ge 24: 2 one in charge of all that he had, "Put your hand under my **thigh**.
24: 9 So the servant put his hand under the **thigh** *of* his master Abraham
32: 25 [32:26] he touched the socket of Jacob's **hip** so that his hip was
32: 25 [32:26] so that his **hip** was wrenched as he wrestled with the man.
32: 31 [32:32] he passed Peniel, and he was limping because of his **hip**.
32: 32 [32:33] do not eat the tendon attached to the socket of the **hip**,
32: 32 [32:33] because the socket of Jacob's **hip** was touched near the
46: 26 *those who were* his **direct descendants** [+3655], not counting his
47: 29 put your hand under my **thigh** and promise that you will show me
Ex 1: 5 The **descendants of** [+3655+5883] Jacob numbered seventy in all;
25: 31 "Make a lampstand of pure gold and hammer it out, **base** and shaft;
28: 42 as a covering for the body, reaching from the waist to the **thigh**.
32: 27 the God of Israel, says: 'Each man strap a sword to his **side**.
37: 17 the lampstand of pure gold and hammered it out, **base** and shaft;
40: 22 Moses placed the table in the Tent of Meeting on the north **side** *of*
40: 24 of Meeting opposite the table on the south **side** *of* the tabernacle
Lev 1: 11 He is to slaughter it at the north **side** *of* the altar before the
Nu 3: 29 The Kohathite clans were to camp on the south **side** *of* the
3: 35 of Abihail; they were to camp on the north **side** *of* the tabernacle.
5: 21 and denounce you when he causes your **thigh** to waste away
5: 22 so that your abdomen swells and your **thigh** wastes away."
5: 27 her abdomen will swell and her **thigh** waste away, and she will
8: 4 It was made of hammered gold—from its **base** to its blossoms.
Jdg 3: 16 a half long, which he strapped to his right **thigh** under his clothing.
3: 21 drew the sword from his right **thigh** and plunged it into the king's
8: 30 He had seventy sons **of his own** [+2257+3655], for he had many
15: 8 *He* **attacked** them **viciously** [+906+5782+6584+8797] and
2Ki 16: 14 of the LORD—and put it on the north **side** *of* the new altar.
Ps 45: 3 [45:4] Gird your sword upon your **side**, O mighty one;
SS 3: 8 the sword, all experienced in battle, each with his sword at his **side**,
7: 1 [7:2] Your graceful **legs** are like jewels, the work of a craftsman's
Jer 31: 19 I strayed, I repented; after I came to understand, I beat my **breast**.
Eze 21: 12 [21:17] sword along with my people. Therefore beat your **breast**.
24: 4 the pieces of meat, all the choice pieces—the **leg** and the shoulder.

3752 יְרֵכָה *yᵉrēkâ*, n.[f.]. [28] [√ 3751]

far end [6], ends [4], utmost heights [4], far [3], depths [2], remote area [2], below deck [+2021+6208] [1], border [1], end [1], far back in [+928] [1], rear [1], thereˢ [+928+1074+2021] [1], within [+928] [1]

Ge 49: 13 become a haven for ships; his **border** will extend toward Sidon.
Ex 26: 22 Make six frames for the **far end**, that is, the west end of the
26: 23 and make two frames for the corners at the **far end**.
26: 27 five for the frames on the west, at the **far end** *of* the tabernacle.
36: 27 They made six frames for the **far end**, that is, the west end of the
36: 28 frames were made for the corners of the tabernacle at the **far end**.
36: 32 five for the frames on the west, at the **far end** *of* the tabernacle.
Jdg 19: 1 Now a Levite who lived in a **remote area** *in* the hill country of
19: 18 "We are on our way from Bethlehem in Judah to a **remote area** *in*
1Sa 24: 3 [24:4] and his men were **far** [+928] **back in** the cave.
1Ki 6: 16 He partitioned off twenty cubits at the **rear** *of* the temple with
2Ki 19: 23 the heights of the mountains, the **utmost heights** *of* Lebanon.
Ps 48: 2 [48:3] Like the **utmost heights** *of* Zaphon is Mount Zion, the city
128: 3 Your wife will be like a fruitful vine **within** [+928] your house;
Isa 14: 13 mount of assembly, on the **utmost heights** *of* the sacred mountain.
14: 15 But you are brought down to the grave, to the **depths** *of* the pit.
37: 24 the heights of the mountains, the **utmost heights** *of* Lebanon.
Jer 6: 22 a great nation is being stirred up from the **ends** *of* the earth.
25: 32 to nation; a mighty storm is rising from the **ends** *of* the earth."
31: 8 the land of the north and gather them from the **ends** *of* the earth.
50: 41 and many kings are being stirred up from the **ends** *of* the earth.
Eze 32: 23 Their graves are in the **depths** *of* the pit and her army lies around
38: 6 and Beth Togarmah from the **far** north with all its troops—
38: 15 You will come from your place in the **far** north, you and many
39: 2 I will bring you from the **far** north and send you against the
46: 19 belonged to the priests, and showed me a place at the western **end**.
Am 6: 10 the house and asks anyone still hiding **there**ˢ [+928+1074+2021],
Jnh 1: 5 But Jonah had gone **below** [+2021+6208] **deck**, where he lay down

3753 יָרַם *yāram*, v. Not used in NIV/BHS [√ 3727; cf. 8123]

3754 יַרְמוּת *yarmût*, n.pr.loc. [7] [√ 3721 + 4637?]

Jarmuth [7]

Jos 10: 3 Piram king of **Jarmuth**, Japhia king of Lachish and Debir king of
10: 5 the kings of Jerusalem, Hebron, **Jarmuth**, Lachish and Eglon—
10: 23 the kings of Jerusalem, Hebron, **Jarmuth**, Lachish and Eglon.
12: 11 the king of **Jarmuth** one the king of Lachish one
15: 35 **Jarmuth**, Adullam, Socoh, Azekah,
21: 29 **Jarmuth** and En Gannim, together with their pasturelands—
Ne 11: 29 in En Rimmon, in Zorah, in **Jarmuth**,

3755 יְרָמוֹת *yᵉrāmôt*, n.pr.m. Not used in NIV/BHS [√ 3721]

3756 יְרֵמוֹת *yᵉrēmôt*, n.pr.m. [7] [√ 3721]

Jeremoth [5], Jerimoth [2]

1Ch 7: 8 Zemirah, Joash, Eliezer, Elioenai, Omri, **Jeremoth**, Abijah,
8: 14 Ahio, Shashak, **Jeremoth**,
23: 23 The sons of Mushi: Mahli, Eder and **Jerimoth**—three in all.
25: 22 the fifteenth to **Jerimoth**, his sons and relatives, 12
Ezr 10: 26 Mattaniah, Zechariah, Jehiel, Abdi, **Jeremoth** and Elijah.
10: 27 Elioenai, Eliashib, Mattaniah, **Jeremoth**, Zabad and Aziza.
10: 29 Malluch, Adaiah, Jashub, Sheal and **Jeremoth**. [Q 2256+8238]

3757 יְרֵמַי *yᵉrēmay*, n.pr.m. [1] [cf. 3758?]

Jeremai [1]

Ezr 10: 33 Mattattah, Zabad, Eliphelet, **Jeremai**, Manasseh and Shimei.

3758 יִרְמְיָה *yirmᵉyâ*, n.pr.m. [18] [→ 3759; cf. 3757?, 8227 + 3378]

Jeremiah [16], heˢ [+2021+5566] [1], Jeremiah's [1]

1Ch 5: 24 Epher, Ishi, Eliel, Azriel, **Jeremiah**, Hodaviah and Jahdiel.
12: 4 [12:5] **Jeremiah**, Jahaziel, Johanan, Jozabad the Gederathite,
12: 10 [12:11] Mishmannah the fourth, **Jeremiah** the fifth,
Ezr 1: 1 in order to fulfill the word of the LORD spoken by **Jeremiah**,
Ne 10: 2 [10:3] Seraiah, Azariah, **Jeremiah**,
12: 1 son of Shealtiel and with Jeshua: Seraiah, **Jeremiah**, Ezra,
12: 12 of Seraiah's family, Meraiah; of **Jeremiah's**, Hananiah;
12: 34 Judah, Benjamin, Shemaiah, **Jeremiah**,
Jer 27: 1 king of Judah, this word came to **Jeremiah** from the LORD:
28: 5 the prophet **Jeremiah** replied to the prophet Hananiah before the
28: 6 **He**ˢ [+2021+5566] said, "Amen! May the LORD do so!
28: 10 Hananiah took the yoke off the neck of the prophet **Jeremiah**
28: 11 two years.' " At this, the prophet **Jeremiah** went on his way.
28: 12 had broken the yoke off the neck of the prophet **Jeremiah**,
28: 12 the prophet Jeremiah, the word of the LORD came to **Jeremiah**:
28: 15 Then the prophet **Jeremiah** said to Hananiah the prophet,
29: 1 This is the text of the letter that the prophet **Jeremiah** sent from
Da 9: 2 according to the word of the LORD given to **Jeremiah** the

3759 יִרְמְיָהוּ *yirmᵉyāhû*, n.pr.m. [129] [√ 3758; cf. 8227 + 3378]

Jeremiah [123], heˢ [2], himˢ [2], himˢ [+2021+5566] [1], Jeremiah's [1]

2Ki 23: 31 His mother's name was Hamutal daughter of **Jeremiah**; she was
24: 18 His mother's name was Hamutal daughter of **Jeremiah**; she was
1Ch 12: 13 [12:14] **Jeremiah** the tenth and Macbannai the eleventh.
2Ch 35: 25 **Jeremiah** composed laments for Josiah, and to this day all the men
36: 12 and did not humble himself before **Jeremiah** the prophet,
36: 21 in fulfillment of the word of the LORD spoken by **Jeremiah**.
36: 22 in order to fulfill the word of the LORD spoken by **Jeremiah**,
Jer 1: 1 The words of **Jeremiah** son of Hilkiah, one of the priests at
1: 11 "What do you see, **Jeremiah**?" "I see the branch of an almond
7: 1 This is the word that came to **Jeremiah** from the LORD:
11: 1 This is the word that came to **Jeremiah** from the LORD:
14: 1 This is the word of the LORD to **Jeremiah** concerning the
18: 1 This is the word that came to **Jeremiah** from the LORD:
18: 18 They said, "Come, let's make plans against **Jeremiah**;
19: 14 **Jeremiah** then returned from Topheth, where the LORD had sent
20: 1 temple of the LORD, heard **Jeremiah** prophesying these things,
20: 2 he had **Jeremiah** the prophet beaten and put in the stocks at the
20: 3 The next day, when Pashhur released **him**ˢ from the stocks,
20: 3 when Pashhur released him from the stocks, **Jeremiah** said to him,
21: 1 The word came to **Jeremiah** from the LORD when King

Jer 21: 3 But **Jeremiah** answered them, "Tell Zedekiah,
24: 3 Then the LORD asked me, "What do you see, **Jeremiah**?"
25: 1 The word came to **Jeremiah** concerning all the people of Judah in
25: 2 So **Jeremiah** the prophet said to all the people of Judah and to all
25: 13 in this book and prophesied by **Jeremiah** against all the nations.
26: 7 all the people heard **Jeremiah** speak these words in the house of
26: 8 as soon as **Jeremiah** finished telling all the people everything the
26: 9 all the people crowded around **Jeremiah** in the house of the
26: 12 Then **Jeremiah** said to all the officials and all the people:
26: 20 the same things against this city and this land as **Jeremiah** did.
26: 24 Ahikam son of Shaphan supported **Jeremiah**, and so he was not
29: 27 So why have you not reprimanded **Jeremiah** from Anathoth,
29: 29 the priest, however, read the letter to **Jeremiah** the prophet.
29: 30 Then the word of the LORD came to **Jeremiah**:
30: 1 This is the word that came to **Jeremiah** from the LORD:
32: 1 This is the word that came to **Jeremiah** from the LORD in the
32: 2 **Jeremiah** the prophet was confined in the courtyard of the guard in
32: 6 **Jeremiah** said, "The word of the LORD came to me:
32: 26 Then the word of the LORD came to **Jeremiah**:
33: 1 While **Jeremiah** was still confined in the courtyard of the guard,
33: 19 The word of the LORD came to **Jeremiah**:
33: 23 The word of the LORD came to **Jeremiah**:
34: 1 surrounding towns, this word came to **Jeremiah** from the LORD:
34: 6 Then **Jeremiah** the prophet told all this to Zedekiah king of Judah,
34: 8 The word came to **Jeremiah** from the LORD after King Zedekiah
34: 12 Then the word of the LORD came to **Jeremiah**:
35: 1 This is the word that came to **Jeremiah** from the LORD during
35: 3 So I went to get Jaazaniah son of **Jeremiah**, the son of
35: 12 Then the word of the LORD came to **Jeremiah**, saying:
35: 18 **Jeremiah** said to the family of the Recabites, "This is what the
36: 1 king of Judah, this word came to **Jeremiah** from the LORD:
36: 4 So **Jeremiah** called Baruch son of Neriah, and while Jeremiah
36: 4 while **Jeremiah** dictated all the words the LORD had spoken to
36: 5 **Jeremiah** told Baruch, "I am restricted; I cannot go to the
36: 8 Baruch son of Neriah did everything **Jeremiah** the prophet told
36: 10 at the LORD's temple the words of **Jeremiah** from the scroll.
36: 19 the officials said to Baruch, "You and **Jeremiah**, go and hide.
36: 26 of Abdeel to arrest Baruch the scribe and **Jeremiah** the prophet.
36: 27 the words that Baruch had written at **Jeremiah's** dictation,
36: 27 at Jeremiah's dictation, the word of the LORD came to **Jeremiah**:
36: 32 So **Jeremiah** took another scroll and gave it to the scribe Baruch
36: 32 it to the scribe Baruch son of Neriah, and as **Jeremiah** dictated,
37: 2 the words the LORD had spoken through **Jeremiah** the prophet.
37: 3 son of Maaseiah to **Jeremiah** the prophet with this message:
37: 4 Now **Jeremiah** was free to come and go among the people,
37: 6 Then the word of the LORD came to **Jeremiah** the prophet:
37: 12 **Jeremiah** started to leave the city to go to the territory of
37: 13 the son of Hananiah, arrested **him**[s] [+2021+5566] and said,
37: 14 "That's not true!" **Jeremiah** said. "I am not deserting to the
37: 14 instead, he arrested **Jeremiah** and brought him to the officials.
37: 15 They were angry with **Jeremiah** and had him beaten and
37: 16 **Jeremiah** was put into a vaulted cell in a dungeon, where he
37: 16 into a vaulted cell in a dungeon, where **he**[s] remained a long time.
37: 17 "Yes," **Jeremiah** replied, "you will be handed over to the king of
37: 18 **Jeremiah** said to King Zedekiah, "What crime have I committed
37: 21 gave orders for **Jeremiah** to be placed in the courtyard of the
37: 21 was gone. So **Jeremiah** remained in the courtyard of the guard.
38: 1 Pashhur son of Malkijah heard what **Jeremiah** was telling all the
38: 6 So they took **Jeremiah** and put him into the cistern of Malkijah,
38: 6 They lowered **Jeremiah** by ropes into the cistern; it had no water
38: 6 no water in it, only mud, and **Jeremiah** sank down into the mud.
38: 7 the royal palace, heard that they had put **Jeremiah** into the cistern.
38: 9 these men have acted wickedly in all they have done to **Jeremiah**
38: 10 and lift **Jeremiah** the prophet out of the cistern before he dies."
38: 11 and let them down with ropes to **Jeremiah** in the cistern.
38: 12 Ebed-Melech the Cushite said to **Jeremiah**, "Put these old rags
38: 12 clothes under your arms to pad the ropes." **Jeremiah** did so,
38: 13 they pulled **him**[s] up with the ropes and lifted him out of the
38: 13 the cistern. And **Jeremiah** remained in the courtyard of the guard.
38: 14 King Zedekiah sent for **Jeremiah** the prophet and had him brought
38: 14 "I am going to ask you something," the king said to **Jeremiah**.
38: 15 **Jeremiah** said to Zedekiah, "If I give you an answer, will you not
38: 16 King Zedekiah swore this oath secretly to **Jeremiah**: "As surely as
38: 17 **Jeremiah** said to Zedekiah, "This is what the LORD God
38: 19 King Zedekiah said to **Jeremiah**, "I am afraid of the Jews who
38: 20 "They will not hand you over," **Jeremiah** replied. "Obey the
38: 24 Zedekiah said to **Jeremiah**, "Do not let anyone know about this
38: 27 All the officials did come to **Jeremiah** and question him, and he
38: 28 **Jeremiah** remained in the courtyard of the guard until the day
39: 11 **Jeremiah** through Nebuzaradan commander of the imperial guard:
39: 14 and had **Jeremiah** taken out of the courtyard of the guard.
39: 15 While **Jeremiah** had been confined in the courtyard of the guard,
40: 1 The word came to **Jeremiah** from the LORD after Nebuzaradan
40: 2 When the commander of the guard found **Jeremiah**, he said to
40: 6 So **Jeremiah** went to Gedaliah son of Ahikam at Mizpah
42: 2 **Jeremiah** the prophet and said to him, "Please hear our petition
42: 4 "I have heard you," replied **Jeremiah** the prophet. "I will certainly
42: 5 they said to **Jeremiah**, "May the LORD be a true and faithful
42: 7 Ten days later the word of the LORD came to **Jeremiah**.
43: 1 When **Jeremiah** finished telling the people all the words of the
43: 2 Johanan son of Kareah and all the arrogant men said to **Jeremiah**,
43: 6 of Shaphan, and **Jeremiah** the prophet and Baruch son of Neriah.
43: 8 In Tahpanhes the word of the LORD came to **Jeremiah**:
44: 1 This word came to **Jeremiah** concerning all the Jews living in
44: 15 all the people living in Lower and Upper Egypt, said to **Jeremiah**,
44: 20 Then **Jeremiah** said to all the people, both men and women,
44: 24 Then **Jeremiah** said to all the people, including the women,
45: 1 This is what **Jeremiah** the prophet told Baruch son of Neriah in
45: 1 after Baruch had written on a scroll the words **Jeremiah** was
46: 1 This is the word of the LORD that came to **Jeremiah** the prophet
46: 13 This is the message the LORD spoke to **Jeremiah** the prophet
47: 1 This is the word of the LORD that came to **Jeremiah** the prophet
49: 34 This is the word of the LORD that came to **Jeremiah** the prophet
50: 1 This is the word the LORD spoke through **Jeremiah** the prophet
51: 59 This is the message **Jeremiah** gave to the staff officer Seraiah son
51: 60 **Jeremiah** had written on a scroll about all the disasters that would
51: 61 **He**[s] said to Seraiah, "When you get to Babylon, see that you read
51: 64 And her people will fall.' " The words of **Jeremiah** end here.
52: 1 His mother's name was Hamutal daughter of **Jeremiah**; she was

3760 יָרַע *yāra'*, v. [1] [→ 3749, 3750]

faint [1]

Isa 15: 4 [A] the armed men of Moab cry out, and their hearts *are* **faint**.

3761 יִרְפְּאֵל *yirp^{e}'ēl*, n.pr.loc. [1] [√ 8324 + 446]

Irpeel [1]

Jos 18: 27 Rekem, **Irpeel**, Taralah,

3762 יָרַק *yāraq*, v. [3] [→ 3765?; cf. 8394]

spit [+3762] [2], spit [1]

Nu 12: 14 [A] replied to Moses, "If her father *had* **spit** [+3762] in her face,
12: 14 [A] replied to Moses, "If her father *had* **spit** [+3762] in her face,
Dt 25: 9 [A] take off one of his sandals, **spit** in his face and say,

3763 יָרָק *yārāq*, n.[m.]. [3] [√ 3764]

vegetable [2], vegetables [1]

Dt 11: 10 planted your seed and irrigated it by foot as in a **vegetable** garden.
1Ki 21: 2 "Let me have your vineyard to use for a **vegetable** garden,
Pr 15: 17 Better a meal of **vegetables** where there is love than a fattened calf

3764 יֶרֶק *yereq*, n.m. [8] [→ 3728, 3763, 3765?, 3766, 3768]

green [4], tender shoots [2], grass [1], plants [1]

Ge 1: 30 that has the breath of life in it—I give every **green** plant for food."
9: 3 Just as I gave you the **green** plants, I now give you everything.
Ex 10: 15 Nothing **green** remained on tree or plant in all the land of Egypt.
Nu 22: 4 up everything around us, as an ox licks up the **grass** *of* the field."
2Ki 19: 26 like **tender** green **shoots**, like grass sprouting on the roof,
Ps 37: 2 they will soon wither, like green **plants** they will soon die away.
Isa 15: 6 grass is withered; the vegetation is gone and nothing **green** is left.
37: 27 like **tender** green **shoots**, like grass sprouting on the roof,

3765 יַרְקוֹן *yarqôn*, n.pr.loc. Not used in NIV/BHS [√ 3762? 3764?]

3766 יֵרָקוֹן *yērāqôn*, n.m. [6] [√ 3764]

mildew [5], deathly pale [1]

Dt 28: 22 with scorching heat and drought, with blight and **mildew**,
1Ki 8: 37 comes to the land, or blight or **mildew**, locusts or grasshoppers,
2Ch 6: 28 comes to the land, or blight or **mildew**, locusts or grasshoppers,
Jer 30: 6 stomach like a woman in labor, every face turned **deathly pale**?
Am 4: 9 your gardens and vineyards, I struck them with blight and **mildew**.
Hag 2: 17 **mildew** and hail, yet you did not turn to me,' declares the LORD.

3767 יָרְקְעָם *yorq^{o}'ām*, n.pr.m. [1] [√ 8392]

Jorkeam [1]

1Ch 2: 44 was the father of Raham, and Raham the father of **Jorkeam**.

3768 יְרַקְרַק *y^{e}raqraq*, a. [3] [√ 3764]

greenish [2], shining [1]

Lev 13: 49 or knitted material, or any leather article, is **greenish** or reddish,
14: 37 if it has **greenish** or reddish depressions that appear to be deeper

Ps 68: 13 [68:14] are sheathed with silver, its feathers with **shining** gold."

3769 יָרַשׁ **yāraš[1]**, v. [231] [→ 3729, 3730, 3771, 3772, 4625, 4627, 8397, 8407, 9408; cf. 3770, 8133]

possess [48], take possession [31], drive out [24], driven out [11], inherit [11], drove out [9], took possession [9], take over [6], took over [6], dispossess [5], taken over [5], heir [4], occupy [4], taken possession [4], dislodge [3], certainly drive out [+906+906+906+906+906+3769] [2], destroy [2], drive out completely [+3769] [2], drove out completely [+3769] [2], possessed [2], take [2], *untranslated* [1], become poor [1], belonged [1], capturing [1], conquer [1], conqueror [1], destitute [1], displaces [1], dispossessing [1], drive from [1], drove [1], fell heir [1], gain possession [1], gave as an inheritance [1], give [1], given [1], gives [1], grow poor [1], heirs [1], inheritance [1], inherited [1], inherits [1], leave as an inheritance [1], make inherit [1], make vomit up [1], new owners [1], occupied [1], own [1], poor [1], prosperous [+6807] [1], push out [1], rob [1], seize [1], seized property [1], sends poverty [1], share in the inheritance [1], take away possessions [1], this[s] [+2257+4202] [1], won [1]

Ge 15: 3 [A] no children; so a servant in my household *will be* my **heir**."
15: 4 [A] "This man *will* not *be* your **heir**, but a son coming from your
15: 4 [A] but a son coming from your own body *will be* your **heir**."
15: 7 [A] the Chaldeans to give you this land to **take possession** *of* it."
15: 8 [A] how can I know that *I will* **gain possession** *of* it?"
21: 10 [A] son *will* never **share in the inheritance** with my son Isaac."
22: 17 [A] Your descendants *will* **take possession** *of* the cities of their
24: 60 [A] *may* your offspring **possess** the gates of their enemies."
28: 4 [A] so that you *may* **take possession** *of* the land where you now
45: 11 [C] and all who belong to you *will become* **destitute**.'
Ex 15: 9 [G] I will draw my sword and my hand *will* **destroy** them.'
34: 24 [G] *I will* **drive out** nations before you and enlarge your
Lev 20: 24 [A] I said to you, "You *will* **possess** their land; I will give it to
20: 24 [A] I will give it to you as an **inheritance**, a land flowing with
25: 46 [A] You can will them to your children as **inherited** property
Nu 13: 30 [A] and said, "We should go up and **take possession** *of* the land,
14: 12 [G] I will strike them down with a plague and **destroy** them, but I
14: 24 [G] into the land he went to, and his descendants *will* **inherit** it.
21: 24 [A] and **took over** his land from the Arnon to the Jabbok,
21: 32 [G] and **drove out** the Amorites who were there.
21: 35 [A] them no survivors. And *they* **took possession** *of* his land.
27: 11 [A] to the nearest relative in his clan, that *he may* **possess** it.
32: 21 [G] the LORD until he *has* **driven** his enemies **out** before him—
32: 39 [G] captured it and **drove out** the Amorites who were there.
33: 52 [G] **drive out** all the inhabitants of the land before you. Destroy
33: 53 [G] **Take possession** *of* the land and settle in it, for I have given
33: 53 [A] and settle in it, for I have given you the land to **possess**.
33: 55 [G] " 'But if *you do* not **drive out** the inhabitants of the land,
36: 8 [A] Every daughter *who* **inherits** land in any Israelite tribe must
36: 8 [A] so that every Israelite *will* **possess** the inheritance of his
Dt 1: 8 [A] **take possession** *of* the land that the LORD swore he would
1: 21 [A] Go up and **take possession** *of* it as the LORD, the God of
1: 39 [A] I will give it to them and they *will* **take possession** *of* it.
2: 12 [A] to live in Seir, but the descendants of Esau **drove** them **out**.
2: 21 [A] *who* **drove** them **out** and settled in their place.
2: 22 [A] *They* **drove** them **out** and have lived in their place to this
2: 24 [A] Begin *to* **take possession** *of* it and engage him in battle.
2: 31 [A] over to you. Now begin *to* **conquer** and possess his land."
2: 31 [A] over to you. Now begin to conquer and **possess** his land."
3: 12 [A] Of the land that *we* **took over** at that time, I gave the
3: 18 [A] your God has given you this land to **take possession** *of* it.
3: 20 [A] they too *have* **taken over** the land that the LORD your God
4: 1 [A] may go in and **take possession** *of* the land that the LORD,
4: 5 [A] them in the land you are entering to **take possession** *of* it.
4: 14 [A] follow in the land that you are crossing the Jordan to **possess**.
4: 22 [A] about to cross over and **take possession** *of* that good land.
4: 26 [A] from the land that you are crossing the Jordan to **possess**.
4: 38 [G] to **drive out** before you nations greater and stronger than you
4: 47 [A] *They* **took possession** *of* his land and the land of Og king of
5: 31 [A] them to follow in the land I am giving them to **possess**."
5: 33 [A] and prolong your days in the land that *you will* **possess**.
6: 1 [A] in the land that you are crossing the Jordan to **possess**,
6: 18 [A] **take over** the good land that the LORD promised on oath to
7: 1 [A] your God brings you into the land you are entering to **possess**
7: 17 [G] are stronger than we are. How can we **drive** them **out**?"
8: 1 [A] **possess** the land that the LORD promised on oath to your
9: 1 [A] to go in and **dispossess** nations greater and stronger than you,
9: 3 [G] And *you will* **drive** them **out** and annihilate them quickly,
9: 4 [A] "The LORD has brought me here to **take possession** *of* this
9: 4 [G] that the LORD *is going to* **drive** them **out** before you.
9: 5 [A] or your integrity that you are going in to **take possession** *of*
9: 5 [G] the LORD your God *will* **drive** them **out** before you, to
9: 6 [A] LORD your God is giving you this good land to **possess**,
9: 23 [A] "Go up and **take possession** *of* the land I have given you."
10: 11 [A] **possess** the land that I swore to their fathers to give them."
11: 8 [A] **take over** the land that you are crossing the Jordan to
11: 8 [A] take over the land that you are crossing the Jordan to **possess**,
11: 10 [A] The land you are entering to **take over** is not like the land of
11: 11 [A] the land you are crossing the Jordan to **take possession** *of* is
11: 23 [G] then the LORD *will* **drive out** all these nations before you,
11: 23 [A] and *you will* **dispossess** nations larger and stronger than you.
11: 29 [A] has brought you into the land you are entering to **possess**,
11: 31 [A] **take possession** *of* the land the LORD your God is giving
11: 31 [A] When *you have* **taken** it **over** and are living there,
12: 1 [A] the God of your fathers, has given you to **possess**—
12: 2 [A] where the nations you *are* **dispossessing** worship their gods.
12: 29 [A] you the nations you are about to invade and **dispossess**.
12: 29 [A] when *you have* **driven** them **out** and settled in their land,
15: 4 [A] for in the land the LORD your God is giving you to **possess**
16: 20 [A] and **possess** the land the LORD your God is giving you.
17: 14 [A] giving you and *have* **taken possession** *of* it and settled in it,
18: 12 [G] LORD your God *will* **drive out** those nations before you.
18: 14 [A] The nations you *will* **dispossess** listen to those who practice
19: 1 [A] when *you have* **driven** them **out** and settled in their towns
19: 2 [A] in the land the LORD your God is giving you to **possess**.
19: 14 [A] in the land the LORD your God is giving you to **possess**.
21: 1 [A] in the land the LORD your God is giving you to **possess**,
23: 20 [23:21] [A] your hand to in the land you are entering to **possess**.
25: 19 [A] you in the land he is giving you to **possess** as an inheritance,
26: 1 [A] and *have* **taken possession** *of* it and settled in it,
28: 21 [A] has destroyed you from the land you are entering to **possess**.
28: 42 [D] Swarms of locusts *will* **take over** all your trees and the crops
28: 63 [A] will be uprooted from the land you are entering to **possess**.
30: 5 [A] He will bring you to the land that **belonged** *to* your fathers,
30: 5 [A] belonged to your fathers, and *you will* **take possession** *of* it.
30: 16 [A] God will bless you in the land you are entering to **possess**.
30: 18 [A] in the land you are crossing the Jordan to enter and **possess**.
31: 3 [A] before you, and *you will* **take possession** *of* their land.
31: 13 [A] you live in the land you are crossing the Jordan to **possess**."
32: 47 [A] live long in the land you are crossing the Jordan to **possess**."
33: 23 [A] is full of his blessing; *he will* **inherit** southward to the lake."
Jos 1: 11 [A] **take possession** *of* the land the LORD your God is giving
1: 11 [A] the land the LORD your God is giving you for your **own**.' "
1: 15 [A] until they too *have* **taken possession** *of* the land that the
1: 15 [A] After that, you may go back and **occupy** your own land,
3: 10 [G] *he will* **certainly drive** [+906+906+906+906+906+3769] **out**
3: 10 [G] *he will* **certainly drive out** [+906+906+906+906+906+3769]
8: 7 [G] you are to rise up from ambush and **take** the city. The
12: 1 [A] and whose territory *they* **took over** east of the Jordan,
13: 1 [A] and there are still very large areas of land to *be* **taken over**.
13: 6 [G] *I* myself *will* **drive** them **out** before the Israelites.
13: 12 [G] Moses had defeated them and **taken over** their land.
13: 13 [G] the Israelites *did* not **drive out** the people of Geshur and
14: 12 [G] LORD helping me, *I will* **drive** them **out** just as he said."
15: 14 [G] Caleb **drove out** the three Anakites—Sheshai, Ahiman and
15: 63 [G] Judah could not **dislodge** the Jebusites, who were living in
16: 10 [G] *They did* not **dislodge** the Canaanites living in Gezer; to this
17: 12 [G] Yet the Manassites were not able to **occupy** these towns,
17: 13 [G] forced labor but *did* not **drive** [+3769] them **out completely**.
17: 13 [G] forced labor but *did* not **drive** them **out completely** [+3769].
17: 18 [G] and though they are strong, *you can* **drive** them **out**."
18: 3 [A] you begin to **take possession** *of* the land that the LORD,
19: 47 [A] attacked Leshem, took it, put it to the sword and **occupied** it.
21: 43 [A] and *they* **took possession** *of* it and settled there.
23: 5 [G] *He will* **push** them **out** before you, and you will take
23: 5 [A] out before you, and *you will* **take possession** *of* their land,
23: 9 [G] "The LORD *has* **driven out** before you great and powerful
23: 13 [G] your God will no longer **drive out** these nations before you.
24: 4 [A] to Esau, **[NIE]** but Jacob and his sons went down to Egypt.
24: 8 [A] them from before you, and *you* **took possession** *of* their land.
Jdg 1: 19 [G] *They* **took possession** *of* the hill country, but they were
1: 19 [G] but *they were* unable to **drive** the people **from** the plains,
1: 20 [G] given to Caleb, *who* **drove** from it the three sons of Anak.
1: 21 [G] The Benjamites, however, failed *to* **dislodge** the Jebusites,
1: 27 [G] *did* not **drive out** the people of Beth Shan or Taanach or Dor
1: 28 [G] forced labor but never **drove** [+3769] them **out completely**.
1: 28 [G] forced labor but never **drove** them **out completely** [+3769].
1: 29 [G] Nor *did* Ephraim **drive out** the Canaanites living in Gezer,
1: 30 [G] *did* Zebulun **drive out** the Canaanites living in Kitron or
1: 31 [G] Nor *did* Asher **drive out** those living in Acco or Sidon or
1: 32 [G] because of **this**[s] [+2257+4202] the people of Asher lived
1: 33 [G] Neither *did* Naphtali **drive out** those living in Beth Shemesh
2: 6 [A] they went to **take possession** *of* the land, each to his own
2: 21 [G] I will no longer **drive out** before them any of the nations
2: 23 [G] *he did* not **drive** them **out** at once by giving them into the
3: 13 [A] and *they* **took possession** *of* the City of Palms.
11: 21 [A] Israel **took over** all the land of the Amorites who lived in

Jdg 11:22 [A] **capturing** all of it from the Arnon to the Jabbok and from
11:23 [G] *has* **driven** the Amorites **out** before his people Israel,
11:23 [A] before his people Israel, what right have you *to* **take** it **over**?
11:24 [A] *Will you* not **take** what your god Chemosh gives you?
11:24 [G] Will you not take what your god Chemosh **gives** you?
11:24 [G] Likewise, whatever the LORD our God *has* **given** us,
11:24 [A] whatever the LORD our God has given us, *we will* **possess**.
14:15 [D] household to death. Did you invite us here to **rob** us?"
18: 7 [A] their land lacked nothing, *they were* **prosperous** [+6807].
18: 9 [A] to do something? Don't hesitate to go there and **take** it **over**.
1Sa 2: 7 [G] The LORD **sends poverty** and wealth; he humbles and he
2Sa 14: 7 [A] whom he killed; then we will get rid of the **heir** as well.'
1Ki 14:24 [G] the nations the LORD *had* **driven out** before the Israelites.
21:15 [A] **take possession** *of* the vineyard of Naboth the Jezreelite that
21:16 [A] and went down to **take possession** *of* Naboth's vineyard.
21:18 [A] where he has gone to **take possession** *of* it.
21:19 [A] Have you not murdered a man and **seized** his **property**?'
21:26 [G] like the Amorites the LORD **drove out** before Israel.)
2Ki 16: 3 [G] the nations the LORD *had* **driven out** before the Israelites.
17: 8 [G] of the nations the LORD *had* **driven out** before them,
17:24 [A] the Israelites. *They* **took over** Samaria and lived in its towns.
21: 2 [G] the nations the LORD *had* **driven out** before the Israelites.
1Ch 28: 8 [A] that *you may* **possess** this good land and pass it on as an
2Ch 20: 7 [G] *did* you not **drive out** the inhabitants of this land before your
20:11 [G] us out of the possession *you* **gave** us **as an inheritance**.
28: 3 [G] the nations the LORD *had* **driven out** before the Israelites.
33: 2 [G] the nations the LORD *had* **driven out** before the Israelites.
Ezr 9:11 [A] 'The land you are entering to **possess** is a land polluted by the
9:12 [G] and **leave** it to your children **as an** everlasting **inheritance**.'
Ne 9:15 [A] **take possession** *of* the land you had sworn with uplifted
9:22 [A] *They* **took over** the country of Sihon king of Heshbon and
9:23 [A] into the land that you told their fathers to enter and **possess**.
9:24 [A] Their sons went in and **took possession** *of* the land. You
9:25 [A] *they* **took possession** *of* houses filled with all kinds of good
Job 13:26 [G] things against me and **make** me **inherit** the sins of my youth.
20:15 [G] he swallowed; God *will* **make** his stomach **vomit** them **up**.
Ps 25:13 [A] days in prosperity, and his descendants *will* **inherit** the land.
37: 9 [A] but those who hope in the LORD *will* **inherit** the land.
37:11 [A] But the meek *will* **inherit** the land and enjoy great peace.
37:22 [A] those the LORD blesses *will* **inherit** the land, but those he
37:29 [A] the righteous *will* **inherit** the land and dwell in it forever.
37:34 [A] He will exalt you to **inherit** the land; when the wicked are
44: 2 [44:3] [G] *With* your hand you **drove out** the nations
44: 3 [44:4] [A] It was not by their sword that *they* **won** the land, nor
69:35 [69:36] [A] Then people will settle there and **possess** it;
83:12 [83:13] [A] "*Let us* **take possession** *of* the pasturelands of
105:44 [A] the nations, and *they* **fell heir** *to* what others had toiled for—
Pr 20:13 [C] Do not love sleep or *you will* **grow poor**; stay awake and
23:21 [C] for drunkards and gluttons *become* **poor**, and drowsiness
30: 9 [C] Or *I may* **become poor** and steal, and so dishonor the name
30:23 [A] is married, and a maidservant *who* **displaces** her mistress.
Isa 14:21 [A] they are not to rise *to* **inherit** the land and cover the earth
34:11 [A] The desert owl and screech owl *will* **possess** it; the great owl
34:17 [A] *They will* **possess** it forever and dwell there from generation
54: 3 [A] your descendants *will* **dispossess** nations and settle in their
57:13 [A] refuge will inherit the land and **possess** my holy mountain."
60:21 [A] people be righteous and *they will* **possess** the land forever.
61: 7 [A] so *they will* **inherit** a double portion in their land,
63:18 [A] For a little while your people **possessed** your holy place,
65: 9 [A] and from Judah *those who will* **possess** my mountains;
65: 9 [A] my chosen people *will* **inherit** them, and there will my
Jer 8:10 [A] give their wives to other men and their fields to **new owners**.
30: 3 [A] restore them to the land I gave their forefathers *to* **possess**,'
32:23 [A] They came in and **took possession** *of* it, but they did not
49: 1 [A] Has she no **heirs**? Why then has Molech taken possession of
49: 1 [A] no heirs? Why then *has* Molech **taken possession** *of* Gad?
49: 2 [A] Israel *will* **drive out** those who drove her out,"
49: 2 [A] Israel will drive out *those who* **drove** her **out**,"
Eze 7:24 [A] wicked of the nations *to* **take possession** *of* their houses;
33:24 [A] 'Abraham was only one man, yet *he* **possessed** the land.
33:25 [A] your idols and shed blood, *should you* then **possess** the land?
33:26 [A] his neighbor's wife. *Should you* then **possess** the land?'
35:10 [A] countries will be ours and *we will* **take possession** *of* them,"
36:12 [A] *They will* **possess** you, and you will be their inheritance; you
Hos 9: 6 [A] Their treasures of silver *will be* **taken over** *by* briers, and
Am 2:10 [A] I led you forty years in the desert to **give** you the land of the
9:12 [A] so that *they may* **possess** the remnant of Edom and all the
Ob 1:17 [A] be holy, and the house of Jacob *will* **possess** its inheritance.
1:19 [A] *will* **occupy** the mountains of Esau, and people from the
1:19 [A] *They will* **occupy** the fields of Ephraim and Samaria,
1:20 [A] the exiles from Jerusalem who are in Sepharad *will* **possess**
Mic 1:15 [A] I will bring a **conqueror** against you who live in Mareshah.
Hab 1: 6 [A] who sweep across the whole earth to **seize** dwelling places
Zec 9: 4 [G] the Lord *will* **take away** her **possessions** and destroy her

3770 יָרַשׁ² ***yāraš²***, n.m. Not used in NIV/BHS [cf. 3769]

3771 יְרֵשָׁה ***yᵉrēšâ***, n.f. [2] [√ 3769]

conquered [2]

Nu 24:18 Edom will be **conquered**; Seir, his enemy, will be conquered,
24:18 Seir, his enemy, will be **conquered**, but Israel will grow strong.

3772 יְרֻשָּׁה ***yᵉruššâ***, n.f. [14] [√ 3769]

possession [7], own [2], heirs [1], heritage [1], inheritance [1], part [1], possess [1]

Dt 2: 5 your foot on. I have given Esau the hill country of Seir as his **own**.
2: 9 provoke them to war, for I will not give you any **part** of their land.
2: 9 I have given Ar to the descendants of Lot as a **possession**."
2:12 as Israel did in the land the LORD gave them as their **possession**.)
2:19 for I will not give you **possession** of any land belonging to the
2:19 I have given it as a **possession** to the descendants of Lot."
3:20 each of you may go back to the **possession** I have given you."
Jos 1:15 After that, you may go back and occupy your **own** land, which
12: 6 the Gadites and the half-tribe of Manasseh to be their **possession**.
12: 7 which rises toward Seir (their lands Joshua gave as an **inheritance**
Jdg 21:17 The Benjamite survivors must have **heirs**," they said, "so that a
2Ch 20:11 to drive us out of the **possession** you gave us as an inheritance.
Ps 61: 5 [61:6] you have given me the **heritage** *of* those who fear your
Jer 32: 8 Since it is your right to redeem it and **possess** it, buy it for

3773 יִשְׂחָק ***yiśḥāq***, n.pr.m. [4] [√ 8471; cf. 3663]

Isaac [4]

Ps 105: 9 the covenant he made with Abraham, the oath he swore to **Isaac**.
Jer 33:26 his sons to rule over the descendants of Abraham, **Isaac** and Jacob.
Am 7: 9 "The high places of **Isaac** will be destroyed and the sanctuaries of
7:16 against Israel, and stop preaching against the house of **Isaac**.'

3774 יְשִׂימִאֵל ***yᵉśîmi'ēl***, n.pr.m. [1] [√ 8492 + 446]

Jesimiel [1]

1Ch 4:36 Jaakobah, Jeshohaiah, Asaiah, Adiel, **Jesimiel**, Benaiah,

3775 יָשַׂם ***yāśam***, v. Not used in NIV/BHS [cf. 8492]

3776 יִשְׂרָאֵל ***yiśrā'ēl***, n.pr.m. & g. [2505] [→ 449, 3778; cf. 8575; Ar 10335]

Israel [1712], Israelites [+1201] [485], Israelites [72], Israelite [+1201] [50], Israel's [35], Israel [+1201] [21], *untranslated* [17], Israelite [16], Israelites [+408] [14], them[s] [+1201] [12], they[s] [+1201] [9], Israel [+824] [7], them[s] [7], Israelite [+408+1074+4946] [6], Israel [+1074] [5], Israelite [+408] [5], Israel's [+4200] [3], Israelite [+408+1201+4946] [2], Israelites [+1201+4946] [2], their[s] [2], them[s] [+3972+7736] [2], her[s] [+141] [1], her[s] [1], Israel [+408] [1], Israel [+6639] [1], Israel's [+928] [1], Israelite [+1074] [1], Israelite [+1201+4200] [1], Israelite [+1201+4946] [1], Israelite [+4946] [1], Israelite [+928] [1], Israelite [+928+1201] [1], Israelites [+1074] [1], Israelites [+1201+6639] [1], Israelites [+4946] [1], Israelites [+906+1201] [1], the whole land[s] [1], their [+3276+6639] [1], their[s] [+6584] [1], them[s] [+3972] [1], they[s] [+3972] [1], who[s] [+1201] [1]

Ge 32:28 [32:29] man said, "Your name will no longer be Jacob, but **Israel**,
32:32 [32:33] Therefore to this day the **Israelites** [+1201] do not eat the
34: 7 because Shechem had done a disgraceful thing in **Israel** by lying
35:10 but you will no longer be called Jacob; your name will be **Israel**."
35:10 called Jacob; your name will be Israel." So he named him **Israel**.
35:21 **Israel** moved on again and pitched his tent beyond Migdal Eder.
35:22 While **Israel** was living in that region, Reuben went in and slept
35:22 and slept with his father's concubine Bilhah, and **Israel** heard of it.
36:31 who reigned in Edom before any **Israelite** [+1201] king reigned:
37: 3 Now **Israel** loved Joseph more than any of his other sons,
37:13 **Israel** said to Joseph, "As you know, your brothers are grazing the
42: 5 So **Israel's** sons were among those who went to buy grain,
43: 6 **Israel** asked, "Why did you bring this trouble on me by telling the
43: 8 Then Judah said to **Israel** his father, "Send the boy along with me
43:11 Then their father **Israel** said to them, "If it must be, then do this:
45:21 So the sons of **Israel** did this. Joseph gave them carts, as Pharaoh
45:28 And **Israel** said, "I'm convinced! My son Joseph is still alive.
46: 1 So **Israel** set out with all that was his, and when he reached
46: 2 And God spoke to **Israel** in a vision at night and said, "Jacob!
46: 5 and **Israel's** sons took their father Jacob and their children
46: 8 These are the names of the sons of **Israel** (Jacob and his
46:29 chariot made ready and went to Goshen to meet his father **Israel**.
46:30 **Israel** said to Joseph, "Now I am ready to die, since I have seen for
47:27 Now the **Israelites** settled in Egypt in the region of Goshen.
47:29 When the time drew near for **Israel** to die, he called for his son
47:31 to him, and **Israel** worshiped as he leaned on the top of his staff.

Ge 48: 2 has come to you," **Israel** rallied his strength and sat up on the bed.
48: 8 When **Israel** saw the sons of Joseph, he asked, "Who are these?"
48: 10 Now **Israel's** eyes were failing because of old age, and he could
48: 11 **Israel** said to Joseph, "I never expected to see your face again,
48: 13 Ephraim on his right toward **Israel's** left hand and Manasseh on
48: 13 left hand and Manasseh on his left toward **Israel's** right hand,
48: 14 But **Israel** reached out his right hand and put it on Ephraim's head,
48: 20 and said, "In your name will **Israel** pronounce this blessing:
48: 21 **Israel** said to Joseph, "I am about to die, but God will be with you
49: 2 "Assemble and listen, sons of Jacob; listen to your father **Israel**.
49: 7 so cruel! I will scatter them in Jacob and disperse them in **Israel**.
49: 16 will provide justice for his people as one of the tribes of **Israel**.
49: 24 Mighty One of Jacob, because of the Shepherd, the Rock of **Israel**,
49: 28 All these are the twelve tribes of **Israel**, and this is what their
50: 2 directed the physicians in his service to embalm his father **Israel**.
50: 25 And Joseph made the sons of **Israel** swear an oath and said,
Ex 1: 1 These are the names of the sons of **Israel** who went to Egypt with
1: 7 but the **Israelites** [+1201] were fruitful and multiplied greatly
1: 9 "the **Israelites** [+1201+6639] have become much too numerous for
1: 12 and spread; so the Egyptians came to dread the **Israelites** [+1201]
1: 13 and worked **them**[s] [+1201] ruthlessly.
2: 23 The **Israelites** [+1201] groaned in their slavery and cried out,
2: 25 So God looked on the **Israelites** [+1201] and was concerned about
3: 9 And now the cry of the **Israelites** [+1201] has reached me,
3: 10 Pharaoh to bring my people the **Israelites** [+1201] out of Egypt."
3: 11 go to Pharaoh and bring the **Israelites** [+1201] out of Egypt?"
3: 13 to God, "Suppose I go to the **Israelites** [+1201] and say to them,
3: 14 WHO I AM. This is what you are to say to the **Israelites** [+1201]:
3: 15 also said to Moses, "Say to the **Israelites** [+1201], 'The LORD,
3: 16 "Go, assemble the elders of **Israel** and say to them, 'The LORD,
3: 18 "The elders of **Israel** will listen to you. Then you and the elders are
4: 22 'This is what the LORD says: **Israel** is my firstborn son,
4: 29 and Aaron brought together all the elders of the **Israelites** [+1201],
4: 31 they heard that the LORD was concerned about **them**[s] [+1201]
5: 1 and said, "This is what the LORD, the God of **Israel**, says:
5: 2 "Who is the LORD, that I should obey him and let **Israel** go?
5: 2 Israel go? I do not know the LORD and I will not let **Israel** go."
5: 14 The **Israelite** [+1201] foremen appointed by Pharaoh's slave
5: 15 Then the **Israelite** [+1201] foremen went and appealed to Pharaoh:
5: 19 The **Israelite** [+1201] foremen realized they were in trouble when
6: 5 Moreover, I have heard the groaning of the **Israelites** [+1201],
6: 6 "Therefore, say to the **Israelites** [+1201]: 'I am the LORD,
6: 9 Moses reported this to the **Israelites** [+1201], but they did not
6: 11 tell Pharaoh king of Egypt to let the **Israelites** [+1201] go out of
6: 12 said to the LORD, "If the **Israelites** [+1201] will not listen to me,
6: 13 and Aaron about the **Israelites** [+1201] and Pharaoh king of Egypt,
6: 13 he commanded them to bring the **Israelites** [+1201] out of Egypt.
6: 14 The sons of Reuben the firstborn son of **Israel** were Hanoch
6: 26 "Bring the **Israelites** [+1201] out of Egypt by their divisions."
6: 27 king of Egypt about bringing the **Israelites** [+1201] out of Egypt.
7: 2 your brother Aaron is to tell Pharaoh to let the **Israelites** [+1201]
7: 4 I will bring out my divisions, my people the **Israelites** [+1201].
7: 5 my hand against Egypt and bring the **Israelites** [+1201] out of it."
9: 4 the LORD will make a distinction between the livestock of **Israel**
9: 4 so that no animal belonging to the **Israelites** [+1201] will die.' "
9: 6 but not one animal belonging to the **Israelites** [+1201] died.
9: 7 found that not even one of the animals of the **Israelites** had died.
9: 26 hail was the land of Goshen, where the **Israelites** [+1201] were.
9: 35 heart was hard and he would not let the **Israelites** [+1201] go,
10: 20 Pharaoh's heart, and he would not let the **Israelites** [+1201] go.
10: 23 Yet all the **Israelites** [+1201] had light in the places where they
11: 7 But among the **Israelites** [+1201] not a dog will bark at any man
11: 7 that the LORD makes a distinction between Egypt and **Israel**.
11: 10 and he would not let the **Israelites** [+1201] go out of his country.
12: 3 Tell the whole community of **Israel** that on the tenth day of this
12: 6 when all the people of the community of **Israel** must slaughter
12: 15 from the first day through the seventh must be cut off from **Israel**.
12: 19 with yeast in it must be cut off from the community of **Israel**,
12: 21 Then Moses summoned all the elders of **Israel** and said to them,
12: 27 who passed over the houses of the **Israelites** [+1201] in Egypt
12: 28 The **Israelites** [+1201] did just what the LORD commanded
12: 31 Leave my people, you and the **Israelites** [+1201]! Go, worship the
12: 35 The **Israelites** [+1201] did as Moses instructed and asked the
12: 37 The **Israelites** [+1201] journeyed from Rameses to Succoth.
12: 40 Now the length of time the **Israelite** [+1201] *people* lived in Egypt
12: 42 on this night all the **Israelites** [+1201] are to keep vigil to honor
12: 47 The whole community of **Israel** must celebrate it.
12: 50 All the **Israelites** [+1201] did just what the LORD had
12: 51 on that very day the LORD brought the **Israelites** [+1201] out of
13: 2 The first offspring of every womb among the **Israelites** [+1201]
13: 18 The **Israelites** [+1201] went up out of Egypt armed for battle.
13: 19 because Joseph had made the sons of **Israel** swear an oath.
14: 2 "Tell the **Israelites** [+1201] to turn back and encamp near Pi
14: 3 'The **Israelites** [+1201] are wandering around the land in
14: 5 We have let the **Israelites** go and have lost their services!"
14: 8 so that he pursued the **Israelites** [+1201], who were marching out
14: 8 so that he pursued the Israelites, **who**[s] [+1201] were marching out
14: 10 As Pharaoh approached, the **Israelites** [+1201] looked up,
14: 10 They were terrified and cried out **[RPH]** to the LORD.
14: 15 are you crying out to me? Tell the **Israelites** [+1201] to move on.
14: 16 so that the **Israelites** [+1201] can go through the sea on dry
14: 19 who had been traveling in front of **Israel's** army, withdrew
14: 20 coming between the armies of Egypt and **Israel**. Throughout the
14: 22 and the **Israelites** [+1201] went through the sea on dry ground,
14: 25 And the Egyptians said, "Let's get away from the **Israelites**!
14: 29 But the **Israelites** [+1201] went through the sea on dry ground,
14: 30 That day the LORD saved **Israel** from the hands of the Egyptians,
14: 30 and **Israel** saw the Egyptians lying dead on the shore.
14: 31 when the **Israelites** saw the great power the LORD displayed
15: 1 and the **Israelites** [+1201] sang this song to the LORD:
15: 19 but the **Israelites** [+1201] walked through the sea on dry ground.
15: 22 Moses led **Israel** from the Red Sea and they went into the Desert
16: 1 The whole **Israelite** [+1201] community set out from Elim
16: 2 In the desert the whole community **[RPH]** grumbled against
16: 3 The **Israelites** [+1201] said to them, "If only we had died by the
16: 6 So Moses and Aaron said to all the **Israelites** [+1201],
16: 9 Moses told Aaron, "Say to the entire **Israelite** [+1201] community,
16: 10 While Aaron was speaking to the whole **Israelite** [+1201]
16: 12 "I have heard the grumbling of the **Israelites** [+1201]. Tell them,
16: 15 When the **Israelites** [+1201] saw it, they said to each other,
16: 17 The **Israelites** [+1201] did as they were told; some gathered much,
16: 31 The people of **Israel** called the bread manna. It was white like
16: 35 The **Israelites** [+1201] ate manna forty years, until they came to a
17: 1 The whole **Israelite** [+1201] community set out from the Desert of
17: 5 Take with you some of the elders of **Israel** and take in your hand
17: 6 to drink." So Moses did this in the sight of the elders of **Israel**.
17: 7 and Meribah because the **Israelites** [+1201] quarreled and
17: 8 The Amalekites came and attacked the **Israelites** at Rephidim.
17: 11 the **Israelites** were winning, but whenever he lowered his hands,
18: 1 of everything God had done for Moses and for his people **Israel**,
18: 1 and how the LORD had brought **Israel** out of Egypt.
18: 8 the Egyptians for **Israel's** sake and about all the hardships they had
18: 9 done for **Israel** in rescuing them from the hand of the Egyptians.
18: 12 Aaron came with all the elders of **Israel** to eat bread with Moses'
18: 25 He chose capable men from all **Israel** and made them leaders of
19: 1 In the third month after the **Israelites** [+1201] left Egypt—
19: 2 and **Israel** camped there in the desert in front of the mountain.
19: 3 to the house of Jacob and what you are to tell the people of **Israel**:
19: 6 These are the words you are to speak to the **Israelites** [+1201]."
20: 22 Then the LORD said to Moses, "Tell the **Israelites** [+1201] this:
24: 1 and Aaron, Nadab and Abihu, and seventy of the elders of **Israel**.
24: 4 set up twelve stone pillars representing the twelve tribes of **Israel**.
24: 5 he sent young **Israelite** [+1201] men, and they offered burnt
24: 9 Nadab and Abihu, and the seventy elders of **Israel** went up
24: 10 saw the God of **Israel**. Under his feet was something like a
24: 11 not raise his hand against these leaders of the **Israelites** [+1201];
24: 17 To the **Israelites** [+1201] the glory of the LORD looked like a
25: 2 "Tell the **Israelites** [+1201] to bring me an offering. You are to
25: 22 and give you all my commands for the **Israelites** [+1201].
27: 20 "Command the **Israelites** [+1201] to bring you clear oil of pressed
27: 21 This is to be a lasting ordinance among the **Israelites** [+1201] for
28: 1 your brother brought to you from among the **Israelites** [+1201],
28: 9 onyx stones and engrave on them the names of the sons of **Israel**
28: 11 Engrave the names of the sons of **Israel** on the two stones the way
28: 12 pieces of the ephod as memorial stones for the sons of **Israel**.
28: 21 be twelve stones, one for each of the names of the sons of **Israel**,
28: 29 he will bear the names of the sons of **Israel** over his heart on the
28: 30 for the **Israelites** [+1201] over his heart before the LORD.
28: 38 guilt involved in the sacred gifts the **Israelites** [+1201] consecrate,
29: 28 This is always to be the regular share from the **Israelites** [+1201]
29: 28 It is the contribution the **Israelites** [+1201] are to make to the
29: 43 there also I will meet with the **Israelites** [+1201], and the place
29: 45 Then I will dwell among the **Israelites** [+1201] and be their God.
30: 12 "When you take a census of the **Israelites** [+1201] to count them,
30: 16 Receive the atonement money from the **Israelites** [+1201]
30: 16 It will be a memorial for the **Israelites** [+1201] before the LORD,
30: 31 Say to the **Israelites** [+1201], 'This is to be my sacred anointing oil
31: 13 "Say to the **Israelites** [+1201], 'You must observe my Sabbaths.
31: 16 The **Israelites** [+1201] are to observe the Sabbath, celebrating it
31: 17 It will be a sign between me and the **Israelites** [+1201] forever,
32: 4 they said, "These are your gods, O **Israel**, who brought you up out
32: 8 and sacrificed to it and have said, 'These are your gods, O **Israel**,
32: 13 Remember your servants Abraham, Isaac and **Israel**, to whom you
32: 20 scattered it on the water and made the **Israelites** [+1201] drink it.
32: 27 he said to them, "This is what the LORD, the God of **Israel**, says:
33: 5 "Tell the **Israelites** [+1201], 'You are a stiff-necked people.
33: 6 So the **Israelites** [+1201] stripped off their ornaments at Mount
34: 23 men are to appear before the Sovereign LORD, the God of **Israel**.

Ex 34:27 these words I have made a covenant with you and with **Israel**."
34:30 When Aaron and all the **Israelites** [+1201] saw Moses, his face
34:32 Afterward all the **Israelites** [+1201] came near him, and he gave
34:34 and told the **Israelites** [+1201] what he had been commanded,
34:35 **they**[s] [+1201] saw that his face was radiant. Then Moses would
35: 1 Moses assembled the whole **Israelite** [+1201] community
35: 4 Moses said to the whole **Israelite** [+1201] community, "This is
35:20 the whole **Israelite** [+1201] community withdrew from Moses'
35:29 All the **Israelite** [+1201] men and women who were willing
35:30 Moses said to the **Israelites** [+1201], "See, the LORD has chosen
36: 3 They received from Moses all the offerings the **Israelites** [+1201]
39: 6 and engraved them like a seal with the names of the sons of **Israel**.
39: 7 pieces of the ephod as memorial stones for the sons of **Israel**,
39:14 were twelve stones, one for each of the names of the sons of **Israel**,
39:32 The **Israelites** [+1201] did everything just as the LORD
39:42 The **Israelites** [+1201] had done all the work just as the LORD
40:36 In all the travels of the **Israelites** [+1201], whenever the cloud
40:38 in the sight of all the house of **Israel** during all their travels.
Lev 1: 2 "Speak to the **Israelites** [+1201] and say to them: 'When any of
4: 2 "Say to the **Israelites** [+1201]: 'When anyone sins unintentionally
4:13 " 'If the whole **Israelite** community sins unintentionally and does
7:23 "Say to the **Israelites** [+1201]: 'Do not eat any of the fat of cattle,
7:29 "Say to the **Israelites** [+1201]: 'Anyone who brings a fellowship
7:34 From the fellowship offerings of the **Israelites** [+1201], I have
7:34 and his sons as their regular share from the **Israelites** [+1201].' "
7:36 the LORD commanded that the **Israelites** [+1201] give this to
7:38 the **Israelites** [+1201] to bring their offerings to the LORD,
9: 1 day Moses summoned Aaron and his sons and the elders of **Israel**.
9: 3 say to the **Israelites** [+1201]: 'Take a male goat for a sin offering,
10: 6 your relatives, all the house of **Israel**, may mourn for those the
10:11 you must teach the **Israelites** [+1201] all the decrees the LORD
10:14 your children as your share of the **Israelites** [+1201]' fellowship
11: 2 "Say to the **Israelites** [+1201]: 'Of all the animals that live on land,
12: 2 "Say to the **Israelites** [+1201]: 'A woman who becomes pregnant
15: 2 "Speak to the **Israelites** [+1201] and say to them: 'When any man
15:31 " 'You must keep the **Israelites** [+1201] separate from things that
16: 5 From the **Israelite** [+1201] community he is to take two male goats
16:16 because of the uncleanness and rebellion of the **Israelites** [+1201],
16:17 for himself, his household and the whole community of **Israel**.
16:19 and to consecrate it from the uncleanness of the **Israelites** [+1201].
16:21 over it all the wickedness and rebellion of the **Israelites** [+1201]—
16:34 is to be made once a year for all the sins of the **Israelites** [+1201]."
17: 2 and his sons and to all the **Israelites** [+1201] and say to them:
17: 3 Any **Israelite** [+408+1074+4946] who sacrifices an ox, a lamb or a
17: 5 so the **Israelites** [+1201] will bring to the LORD the sacrifices
17: 8 "Say to them: 'Any **Israelite** [+408+1074+4946] or any alien
17:10 " 'Any **Israelite** [+408+1074+4946] or any alien living among
17:12 Therefore I say to the **Israelites** [+1201], "None of you may eat
17:13 " 'Any **Israelite** [+408+1201+4946] or any alien living among you
17:14 That is why I have said to the **Israelites** [+1201], "You must not
18: 2 "Speak to the **Israelites** [+1201] and say to them: 'I am the LORD
19: 2 "Speak to the entire assembly of **Israel** [+1201] and say to them:
20: 2 "Say to the **Israelites** [+1201]: 'Any Israelite or any alien living in
20: 2 'Any **Israelite** [+408+1201+4946] or any alien living in Israel who
20: 2 or any alien living in **Israel** who gives any of his children to
21:24 told this to Aaron and his sons and to all the **Israelites** [+1201].
22: 2 the sacred offerings the **Israelites** [+1201] consecrate to me,
22: 3 yet comes near the sacred offerings that the **Israelites** [+1201]
22:15 the sacred offerings the **Israelites** [+1201] present to the LORD
22:18 and his sons and to all the **Israelites** [+1201] and say to them:
22:18 'If any of you—either an **Israelite** [+408+1074+4946] or an alien
22:18 'If any of you—either an Israelite or an alien living in **Israel**—
22:32 I must be acknowledged as holy by the **Israelites** [+1201].
23: 2 "Speak to the **Israelites** [+1201] and say to them: 'These are my
23:10 "Speak to the **Israelites** [+1201] and say to them: 'When you enter
23:24 "Say to the **Israelites** [+1201]: 'On the first day of the seventh
23:34 "Say to the **Israelites** [+1201]: 'On the fifteenth day of the seventh
23:42 for seven days: All native-born **Israelites** are to live in booths
23:43 so your descendants will know that I had the **Israelites** [+1201]
23:44 So Moses announced to the **Israelites** [+1201] the appointed feasts
24: 2 "Command the **Israelites** [+1201] to bring you clear oil of pressed
24: 8 on behalf of the **Israelites** [+1201], as a lasting covenant.
24:10 and an Egyptian father went out among the **Israelites** [+1201],
24:15 Say to the **Israelites** [+1201]: 'If anyone curses his God, he will be
24:23 Moses spoke to the **Israelites** [+1201], and they took the
24:23 The **Israelites** [+1201] did as the LORD commanded Moses.
25: 2 "Speak to the **Israelites** [+1201] and say to them: 'When you enter
25:33 of the Levites are their property among the **Israelites** [+1201].
25:46 you must not rule over your fellow **Israelites** [+1201] ruthlessly.
25:55 for the **Israelites** [+1201] belong to me as servants. They are my
26:46 Sinai between himself and the **Israelites** [+1201] through Moses.
27: 2 "Speak to the **Israelites** [+1201] and say to them: 'If anyone makes
27:34 the LORD gave Moses on Mount Sinai for the **Israelites** [+1201].
Nu 1: 2 "Take a census of the whole **Israelite** [+1201] community by their
1: 3 Aaron are to number by their divisions all the men in **Israel** twenty
1:16 of their ancestral tribes. They were the heads of the clans of **Israel**.
1:20 From the descendants of Reuben the firstborn son of **Israel**:
1:44 men counted by Moses and Aaron and the twelve leaders of **Israel**,
1:45 All the **Israelites** [+1201] twenty years old or more who were able
1:45 or more who were able to serve in **Israel's** [+928] army were
1:49 or include them in the census of the other **Israelites** [+1201].
1:52 The **Israelites** [+1201] are to set up their tents by divisions,
1:53 so that wrath will not fall on the **Israelite** [+1201] community.
1:54 The **Israelites** [+1201] did all this just as the LORD commanded
2: 2 "The **Israelites** [+1201] are to camp around the Tent of Meeting
2:32 These are the **Israelites** [+1201], counted according to their
2:33 were not counted along with the other **Israelites** [+1201],
2:34 So the **Israelites** [+1201] did everything the LORD commanded
3: 8 fulfilling the obligations of the **Israelites** [+1201] by doing the
3: 9 they are the **Israelites** [+1201] who are to be given wholly to him.
3:12 "I have taken the Levites from among the **Israelites** [+1201] in
3:12 place of the first male offspring of every **Israelite** [+1201] woman.
3:13 I set apart for myself every firstborn in **Israel**, whether man
3:38 for the care of the sanctuary on behalf of the **Israelites** [+1201].
3:40 "Count all the firstborn **Israelite** [+1201] males who are a month
3:41 for me in place of all the firstborn of the **Israelites** [+1201],
3:41 place of all the firstborn of the livestock of the **Israelites** [+1201].
3:42 So Moses counted all the firstborn of the **Israelites** [+1201],
3:45 "Take the Levites in place of all the firstborn of **Israel** [+1201],
3:46 To redeem the 273 firstborn **Israelites** [+1201] who exceed the
3:50 From the firstborn of the **Israelites** [+1201] he collected silver
4:46 and the leaders of **Israel** counted all the Levites by their clans
5: 2 "Command the **Israelites** [+1201] to send away from the camp
5: 4 The **Israelites** [+1201] did this; they sent them outside the camp.
5: 4 they sent them outside the camp. **They**[s] [+1201] did just as the
5: 6 "Say to the **Israelites** [+1201]: 'When a man or woman wrongs
5: 9 All the sacred contributions the **Israelites** [+1201] bring to a priest
5:12 "Speak to the **Israelites** [+1201] and say to them: 'If a man's wife
6: 2 "Speak to the **Israelites** [+1201] and say to them: 'If a man
6:23 and his sons, 'This is how you are to bless the **Israelites** [+1201].
6:27 "So they will put my name on the **Israelites** [+1201], and I will
7: 2 the leaders of **Israel**, the heads of families who were the tribal
7:84 These were the offerings of the **Israelite** leaders for the dedication
8: 6 "Take the Levites from among the other **Israelites** [+1201]
8: 9 of Meeting and assemble the whole **Israelite** [+1201] community.
8:10 and the **Israelites** [+906+1201] are to lay their hands on them.
8:11 before the LORD as a wave offering from the **Israelites** [+1201],
8:14 you are to set the Levites apart from the other **Israelites** [+1201],
8:16 They are the **Israelites** [+1201] who are to be given wholly to me.
8:16 the first male offspring from every **Israelite** [+1201] woman.
8:17 Every firstborn male in **Israel** [+1201], whether man or animal,
8:18 the Levites in place of all the firstborn sons in **Israel** [+1201].
8:19 Of all the **Israelites** [+1201], I have given the Levites as gifts to
8:19 the work at the Tent of Meeting on behalf of the **Israelites** [+1201]
8:19 to make atonement for **them**[s] [+1201] so that no plague will strike
8:19 so that no plague will strike the **Israelites** [+1201] when they go
8:19 so that no plague will strike the Israelites when **they**[s] [+1201] go
8:20 the whole **Israelite** [+1201] community did with the Levites just as
8:20 with the Levites just as the LORD commanded Moses. **[RPH]**
9: 2 "Have the **Israelites** [+1201] celebrate the Passover at the
9: 4 So Moses told the **Israelites** [+1201] to celebrate the Passover,
9: 5 The **Israelites** [+1201] did everything just as the LORD
9: 7 offering with the other **Israelites** [+1201] at the appointed time?"
9:10 "Tell the **Israelites** [+1201]: 'When any of you or your descendants
9:17 the cloud lifted from above the Tent, the **Israelites** [+1201] set out;
9:17 wherever the cloud settled, the **Israelites** [+1201] encamped.
9:18 At the LORD's command the **Israelites** [+1201] set out,
9:19 the **Israelites** [+1201] obeyed the LORD's order and did not set
9:22 the **Israelites** [+1201] would remain in camp and not set out;
10: 4 only one is sounded, the leaders—the heads of the clans of **Israel**—
10:12 Then the **Israelites** [+1201] set out from the Desert of Sinai
10:28 This was the order of march for the **Israelite** [+1201] divisions as
10:29 treat you well, for the LORD has promised good things to **Israel**."
10:36 "Return, O LORD, to the countless thousands of **Israel**."
11: 4 again the **Israelites** [+1201] started wailing and said, "If only we
11:16 "Bring me seventy of **Israel's** elders who are known to you as
11:30 Then Moses and the elders of **Israel** returned to the camp.
13: 2 the land of Canaan, which I am giving to the **Israelites** [+1201].
13: 3 Desert of Paran. All of them were leaders of the **Israelites** [+1201].
13:24 because of the cluster of grapes the **Israelites** [+1201] cut off
13:26 the whole **Israelite** [+1201] community at Kadesh in the Desert of
13:32 they spread among the **Israelites** [+1201] a bad report about the
14: 2 All the **Israelites** [+1201] grumbled against Moses and Aaron,
14: 5 Aaron fell facedown in front of the whole **Israelite** [+1201]
14: 7 said to the entire **Israelite** [+1201] assembly, "The land we passed
14:10 appeared at the Tent of Meeting to all the **Israelites** [+1201].
14:27 I have heard the complaints of these grumbling **Israelites** [+1201].
14:39 When Moses reported this to all the **Israelites** [+1201], they

Nu 15: 2 "Speak to the **Israelites** [+1201] and say to them: 'After you enter
15:18 "Speak to the **Israelites** [+1201] and say to them: 'When you enter
15:25 The priest is to make atonement for the whole **Israelite** [+1201]
15:26 The whole **Israelite** [+1201] community and the aliens living
15:29 whether he is a native-born **Israelite** [+928+1201] or an alien.
15:32 While the **Israelites** [+1201] were in the desert, a man was found
15:38 "Speak to the **Israelites** [+1201] and say to them: 'Throughout the
16: 2 With them were 250 **Israelite** [+1201] men, well-known
16: 9 Isn't it enough for you that the God of **Israel** has separated you
16: 9 Israel has separated you from the rest of the **Israelite** community
16:25 went to Dathan and Abiram, and the elders of **Israel** followed him.
16:34 At their cries, all the **Israelites** around them fled, shouting,
16:38 [17:3] become holy. Let them be a sign to the **Israelites** [+1201]."
16:40 [17:5] This was to remind the **Israelites** [+1201] that no one
16:41 [17:6] The next day the whole **Israelite** [+1201] community
17: 2 [17:17] "Speak to the **Israelites** [+1201] and get twelve staffs
17: 5 [17:20] grumbling against you by the **Israelites** [+1201]."
17: 6 [17:21] So Moses spoke to the **Israelites** [+1201], and their
17: 9 [17:24] from the LORD's presence to all the **Israelites** [+1201].
17:12 [17:27] The **Israelites** [+1201] said to Moses, "We will die!
18: 5 so that wrath will not fall on the **Israelites** [+1201] again.
18: 6 fellow Levites from among the **Israelites** [+1201] as a gift to you,
18: 8 all the holy offerings the **Israelites** [+1201] give me I give to you
18:11 from the gifts of all the wave offerings of the **Israelites** [+1201].
18:14 "Everything in **Israel** that is devoted to the LORD is yours.
18:19 is set aside from the holy offerings the **Israelites** [+1201]
18:20 I am your share and your inheritance among the **Israelites** [+1201].
18:21 "I give to the Levites all the tithes in **Israel** as their inheritance in
18:22 From now on the **Israelites** [+1201] must not go near the Tent of
18:23 They will receive no inheritance among the **Israelites** [+1201].
18:24 that the **Israelites** [+1201] present as an offering to the LORD.
18:24 'They will have no inheritance among the **Israelites** [+1201].' "
18:26 'When you receive from the **Israelites** [+1201] the tithe I give you
18:28 LORD from all the tithes you receive from the **Israelites** [+1201].
18:32 you will not defile the holy offerings of the **Israelites** [+1201],
19: 2 Tell the **Israelites** [+1201] to bring you a red heifer without defect
19: 9 They shall be kept by the **Israelite** [+1201] community for use in
19:10 This will be a lasting ordinance both for the **Israelites** [+1201]
19:13 the LORD's tabernacle. That person must be cut off from **Israel**.
20: 1 In the first month the whole **Israelite** [+1201] community arrived
20:12 enough to honor me as holy in the sight of the **Israelites** [+1201],
20:13 where the **Israelites** [+1201] quarreled with the LORD and where
20:14 the king of Edom, saying: "This is what your brother **Israel** says:
20:19 The **Israelites** [+1201] replied: "We will go along the main road,
20:21 Since Edom refused to let **them**[s] go through their territory,
20:21 let them go through their territory, **Israel** turned away from them.
20:22 The whole **Israelite** [+1201] community set out from Kadesh
20:24 He will not enter the land I give the **Israelites** [+1201],
20:29 had died, the entire house of **Israel** mourned for him thirty days.
21: 1 heard that **Israel** was coming along the road to Atharim,
21: 1 to Atharim, he attacked the **Israelites** and captured some of them.
21: 2 **Israel** made this vow to the LORD: "If you will deliver these
21: 3 The LORD listened to **Israel's** plea and gave the Canaanites over
21: 6 among them; they bit the people and many **Israelites** [+4946] died.
21:10 The **Israelites** [+1201] moved on and camped at Oboth.
21:17 Then **Israel** sang this song: "Spring up, O well! Sing about it,
21:21 **Israel** sent messengers to say to Sihon king of the Amorites:
21:23 Sihon would not let **Israel** pass through his territory. He mustered
21:23 his entire army and marched out into the desert against **Israel**.
21:23 against Israel. When he reached Jahaz, he fought with **Israel**.
21:24 **Israel**, however, put him to the sword and took over his land from
21:25 **Israel** captured all the cities of the Amorites and occupied them,
21:25 captured all the cities of the Amorites and occupied **[RPH]** them,
21:31 So **Israel** settled in the land of the Amorites.
22: 1 Then the **Israelites** [+1201] traveled to the plains of Moab
22: 2 Now Balak son of Zippor saw all that **Israel** had done to the
22: 3 Moab was filled with dread because of the **Israelites** [+1201].
23: 7 'Come,' he said, 'curse Jacob for me; come, denounce **Israel**.'
23:10 can count the dust of Jacob or number the fourth part of **Israel**?
23:21 "No misfortune is seen in Jacob, no misery observed in **Israel**.
23:23 There is no sorcery against Jacob, no divination against **Israel**.
23:23 It will now be said of Jacob and of **Israel**, 'See what God has
24: 1 Now when Balaam saw that it pleased the LORD to bless **Israel**,
24: 2 When Balaam looked out and saw **Israel** encamped tribe by tribe,
24: 5 beautiful are your tents, O Jacob, your dwelling places, O **Israel**!
24:17 A star will come out of Jacob; a scepter will rise out of **Israel**.
24:18 his enemy, will be conquered, but **Israel** will grow strong.
25: 1 While **Israel** was staying in Shittim, the men began to indulge in
25: 3 So **Israel** joined in worshiping the Baal of Peor. And the LORD's
25: 3 the Baal of Peor. And the LORD's anger burned against **them**[s].
25: 4 so that the LORD's fierce anger may turn away from **Israel**."
25: 5 So Moses said to **Israel's** judges, "Each of you must put to death
25: 6 an **Israelite** [+1201+4946] man brought to his family a Midianite
25: 6 the whole assembly of **Israel** [+1201] while they were weeping at
25: 8 followed the **Israelite** [+408] into the tent. He drove the spear
25: 8 of them—through the **Israelite** [+408] and into the woman's body.
25: 8 Then the plague against the **Israelites** [+1201] was stopped;
25:11 the priest, has turned my anger away from the **Israelites** [+1201];
25:11 so that in my zeal I did not put an end to **them**[s] [+1201].
25:13 honor of his God and made atonement for the **Israelites** [+1201]."
25:14 The name of the **Israelite** [+408] who was killed with the
26: 2 "Take a census of the whole **Israelite** [+1201] community by
26: 2 years old or more who are able to serve in the army of **Israel**."
26: 4 These were the **Israelites** [+1201] who came out of Egypt:
26: 5 The descendants of Reuben, the firstborn son of **Israel**, were:
26:51 The total number of the men of **Israel** was 601,730.
26:62 They were not counted along with the other **Israelites** [+1201]
26:62 because they received no inheritance among **them**[s] [+1201].
26:63 Eleazar the priest when they counted the **Israelites** [+1201] on the
26:64 Aaron the priest when they counted the **Israelites** [+1201] in the
27: 8 "Say to the **Israelites** [+1201], 'If a man dies and leaves no son,
27:11 This is to be a legal requirement for the **Israelites** [+1201],
27:12 Abarim range and see the land I have given the **Israelites** [+1201].
27:20 so the whole **Israelite** [+1201] community will obey him.
27:21 and the entire community of the **Israelites** [+1201] will go out,
28: 2 "Give this command to the **Israelites** [+1201] and say to them:
29:40 [30:1] Moses told the **Israelites** [+1201] all that the LORD
30: 1 [30:2] Moses said to the heads of the tribes of **Israel** [+1201]:
31: 2 "Take vengeance on the Midianites for the **Israelites** [+1201].
31: 4 Send into battle a thousand men from each of the tribes of **Israel**."
31: 5 a thousand from each tribe, were supplied from the clans of **Israel**.
31: 9 The **Israelites** [+1201] captured the Midianite women and children
31:12 the **Israelite** [+1201] assembly at their camp on the plains of
31:16 were the means of turning the **Israelites** [+1201] away from the
31:30 From the **Israelites** [+1201]' half, select one out of every fifty,
31:42 The half belonging to the **Israelites** [+1201], which Moses set
31:47 From the **Israelites** [+1201]' half, Moses selected one out of every
31:54 as a memorial for the **Israelites** [+1201] before the LORD.
32: 4 the land the LORD subdued before the people of **Israel**—
32: 7 Why do you discourage the **Israelites** [+1201] from going over
32: 9 they discouraged the **Israelites** [+1201] from entering the land the
32:13 The LORD's anger burned against **Israel** and he made them
32:14 your fathers and making the LORD even more angry with **Israel**.
32:17 go ahead of the **Israelites** [+1201] until we have brought them to
32:18 We will not return to our homes until every **Israelite** [+1201] has
32:22 and be free from your obligation to the LORD and to **Israel**.
32:28 son of Nun and to the family heads of the **Israelite** [+1201] tribes.
33: 1 Here are the stages in the journey of the **Israelites** [+1201] when
33: 3 The **Israelites** [+1201] set out from Rameses on the fifteenth day
33: 5 The **Israelites** [+1201] left Rameses and camped at Succoth.
33:38 of the fortieth year after the **Israelites** [+1201] came out of Egypt.
33:40 Negev of Canaan, heard that the **Israelites** [+1201] were coming.
33:51 "Speak to the **Israelites** [+1201] and say to them: 'When you cross
34: 2 "Command the **Israelites** [+1201] and say to them: 'When you
34:13 Moses commanded the **Israelites** [+1201]: "Assign this land by lot
34:29 the inheritance to the **Israelites** [+1201] in the land of Canaan.
35: 2 "Command the **Israelites** [+1201] to give the Levites towns to live
35: 8 towns you give the Levites from the land the **Israelites** [+1201]
35:10 "Speak to the **Israelites** [+1201] and say to them: 'When you cross
35:15 These six towns will be a place of refuge for **Israelites** [+1201],
35:34 for I, the LORD, dwell among the **Israelites** [+1201].' "
36: 1 and the leaders, the heads of the **Israelite** [+1201] families.
36: 2 to give the land as an inheritance to the **Israelites** [+1201] by lot,
36: 3 Now suppose they marry men from other **Israelite** [+1201] tribes;
36: 4 When the Year of Jubilee for the **Israelites** [+1201] comes,
36: 5 command Moses gave this order to the **Israelites** [+1201]:
36: 7 No inheritance in **Israel** [+1201] is to pass from tribe to tribe,
36: 7 for every **Israelite** [+1201] shall keep the tribal land inherited from
36: 8 Every daughter who inherits land in any **Israelite** [+1201] tribe
36: 8 so that every **Israelite** [+1201] will possess the inheritance of his
36: 9 for each **Israelite** [+1201] tribe is to keep the land it inherits."
36:13 **Israelites** [+1201] on the plains of Moab by the Jordan across from

Dt 1: 1 These are the words Moses spoke to all **Israel** in the desert east of
1: 3 Moses proclaimed to the **Israelites** [+1201] all that the LORD
1:38 enter it. Encourage him, because he will lead **Israel** to inherit it.
2:12 just as **Israel** did in the land the LORD gave them as their
3:18 must cross over ahead of your brother **Israelites** [+1201].
4: 1 Hear now, O **Israel**, the decrees and laws I am about to teach you.
4:44 This is the law Moses set before the **Israelites** [+1201].
4:45 laws Moses gave **them**[s] [+1201] when they came out of Egypt
4:46 by Moses and the **Israelites** [+1201] as they came out of Egypt.
5: 1 Moses summoned all **Israel** and said: Hear, O Israel, the decrees
5: 1 Hear, O **Israel**, the decrees and laws I declare in your hearing
6: 3 Hear, O **Israel**, and be careful to obey so that it may go well with
6: 4 Hear, O **Israel**: The LORD our God, the LORD is one.
9: 1 Hear, O **Israel**. You are now about to cross the Jordan to go in
10: 6 (The **Israelites** [+1201] traveled from the wells of the Jaakanites to
10:12 And now, O **Israel**, what does the LORD your God ask of you

Dt 11: 6 when the earth opened its mouth right in the middle of all **Israel**
13: 11 [13:12] all **Israel** will hear and be afraid, and no one among you
17: 4 has been proved that this detestable thing has been done in **Israel**,
17: 12 God must be put to death. You must purge the evil from **Israel**.
17: 20 his descendants will reign a long time over his kingdom in **Israel**.
18: 1 tribe of Levi—are to have no allotment or inheritance with **Israel**.
18: 6 If a Levite moves from one of your towns anywhere in **Israel**
19: 13 You must purge from **Israel** the guilt of shedding innocent blood,
20: 3 "Hear, O **Israel**, today you are going into battle against your
21: 8 Accept this atonement for your people **Israel**, whom you have
21: 8 do not hold your people **[RPH]** guilty of the blood of an innocent
21: 21 the evil from among you. All **Israel** will hear of it and be afraid.
22: 19 because this man has given an **Israelite** virgin a bad name.
22: 21 She has done a disgraceful thing in **Israel** by being promiscuous
22: 22 and the woman must die. You must purge the evil from **Israel**.
23: 17 [23:18] No **Israelite** [+4946] man or woman is to become a shrine
23: 17 [23:18] or woman **[RPH]** is to become a shrine prostitute.
24: 7 is caught kidnapping one of his brother **Israelites** [+1201+4946]
25: 6 dead brother so that his name will not be blotted out from **Israel**.
25: 7 husband's brother refuses to carry on his brother's name in **Israel**.
25: 10 That man's line shall be known in **Israel** as The Family of the
26: 15 bless your people **Israel** and the land you have given us as you
27: 1 Moses and the elders of **Israel** commanded the people: "Keep all
27: 9 who are Levites, said to all **Israel**, "Be silent, O Israel, and listen!
27: 9 who are Levites, said to all Israel, "Be silent, O **Israel**, and listen!
27: 14 The Levites shall recite to all the people of **Israel** in a loud voice:
29: 1 [28:69] Moses to make with the **Israelites** [+1201] in Moab,
29: 2 [29:1] Moses summoned all the **Israelites** and said to them: Your
29: 10 [29:9] your elders and officials, and all the other men of **Israel**,
29: 21 [29:20] single him out from all the tribes of **Israel** for disaster,
31: 1 Then Moses went out and spoke these words to all **Israel**:
31: 7 summoned Joshua and said to him in the presence of all **Israel**,
31: 9 ark of the covenant of the LORD, and to all the elders of **Israel**.
31: 11 when all **Israel** comes to appear before the LORD your God at
31: 11 you shall read this law before **them**[s] [+3972] in their hearing.
31: 19 and teach it to the **Israelites** [+1201] and have them sing it,
31: 19 so that it may be a witness for me against **them**[s] [+1201].
31: 22 down this song that day and taught it to the **Israelites** [+1201].
31: 23 for you will bring the **Israelites** [+1201] into the land I promised
31: 30 beginning to end in the hearing of the whole assembly of **Israel**:
32: 8 for the peoples according to the number of the sons of **Israel**.
32: 45 When Moses finished reciting all these words to all **Israel**,
32: 49 the land I am giving the **Israelites** [+1201] as their own
32: 51 **Israelites** [+1201] at the waters of Meribah Kadesh in the Desert
32: 51 you did not uphold my holiness among the **Israelites** [+1201].
32: 52 you will not enter the land I am giving to the people of **Israel**."
33: 1 man of God pronounced on the **Israelites** [+1201] before his death.
33: 5 the leaders of the people assembled, along with the tribes of **Israel**.
33: 10 He teaches your precepts to Jacob and your law to **Israel**.
33: 21 LORD's righteous will, and his judgments concerning **Israel**."
33: 28 So **Israel** will live in safety alone; Jacob's spring is secure in a
33: 29 Blessed are you, O **Israel**! Who is like you, a people saved by the
34: 8 The **Israelites** [+1201] grieved for Moses in the plains of Moab
34: 9 So the **Israelites** [+1201] listened to him and did what the LORD
34: 10 Since then, no prophet has risen in **Israel** like Moses,
34: 12 the awesome deeds that Moses did in the sight of all **Israel**.
Jos 1: 2 into the land I am about to give to them—to the **Israelites** [+1201].
2: 2 Some of the **Israelites** [+1201] have come here tonight to spy out
3: 1 all the **Israelites** [+1201] set out from Shittim and went to the
3: 7 to Joshua, "Today I will begin to exalt you in the eyes of all **Israel**,
3: 9 Joshua said to the **Israelites** [+1201], "Come here and listen to the
3: 12 Now then, choose twelve men from the tribes of **Israel**, one from
3: 17 while all **Israel** passed by until the whole nation had completed the
4: 4 the twelve men he had appointed from the **Israelites** [+1201],
4: 5 according to the number of the tribes of the **Israelites** [+1201],
4: 7 These stones are to be a memorial to the people of **Israel** forever."
4: 8 So the **Israelites** [+1201] did as Joshua commanded them.
4: 8 according to the number of the tribes of the **Israelites** [+1201],
4: 12 armed, in front of the **Israelites** [+1201], as Moses had directed
4: 14 That day the LORD exalted Joshua in the sight of all **Israel**;
4: 21 He said to the **Israelites** [+1201], "In the future when your
4: 22 tell them, '**Israel** crossed the Jordan on dry ground.'
5: 1 the Jordan before the **Israelites** [+1201] until we had crossed over,
5: 1 and they no longer had the courage to face the **Israelites** [+1201].
5: 2 "Make flint knives and circumcise the **Israelites** [+1201] again."
5: 3 and circumcised the **Israelites** [+1201] at Gibeath Haaraloth.
5: 6 The **Israelites** [+1201] had moved about in the desert forty years
5: 10 camped at Gilgal on the plains of Jericho, the **Israelites** [+1201]
5: 12 there was no longer any manna for the **Israelites** [+1201],
6: 1 Now Jericho was tightly shut up because of the **Israelites** [+1201].
6: 18 Otherwise you will make the camp of **Israel** liable to destruction
6: 23 entire family and put them in a place outside the camp of **Israel**.
6: 25 as spies to Jericho—and she lives among the **Israelites** to this day.
7: 1 the **Israelites** [+1201] acted unfaithfully in regard to the devoted
7: 1 of them. So the LORD's anger burned against **Israel** [+1201].
7: 6 The elders of **Israel** did the same, and sprinkled dust on their
7: 8 what can I say, now that **Israel** has been routed by its enemies?
7: 11 **Israel** has sinned; they have violated my covenant, which I
7: 12 That is why the **Israelites** [+1201] cannot stand against their
7: 13 for tomorrow; for this is what the LORD, the God of **Israel**, says:
7: 13 God of Israel, says: That which is devoted is among you, O **Israel**.
7: 15 of the LORD and has done a disgraceful thing in **Israel**!' "
7: 16 Early the next morning Joshua had **Israel** come forward by tribes,
7: 19 glory to the LORD, the God of **Israel**, and give him the praise.
7: 20 "It is true! I have sinned against the LORD, the God of **Israel**.
7: 23 brought them to Joshua and all the **Israelites** [+1201] and spread
7: 24 Then Joshua, together with all **Israel**, took Achan son of Zerah,
7: 25 Then all **Israel** stoned him, and after they had stoned the rest,
8: 10 and he and the leaders of **Israel** marched before them to Ai.
8: 14 to meet **Israel** in battle at a certain place overlooking the Arabah.
8: 15 Joshua and all **Israel** let themselves be driven back before them,
8: 17 Not a man remained in Ai or Bethel who did not go after **Israel**.
8: 17 after Israel. They left the city open and went in pursuit of **Israel**.
8: 21 when Joshua and all **Israel** saw that the ambush had taken the city
8: 22 that they were caught in the middle, with **Israelites** on both sides.
8: 24 When **Israel** had finished killing all the men of Ai in the fields
8: 24 all the **Israelites** returned to Ai and killed those who were in it.
8: 27 **Israel** did carry off for themselves the livestock and plunder of this
8: 30 built on Mount Ebal an altar to the LORD, the God of **Israel**,
8: 31 the servant of the LORD had commanded the **Israelites** [+1201].
8: 32 There, in the presence of the **Israelites** [+1201], Joshua copied on
8: 33 All **Israel**, aliens and citizens alike, with their elders, officials
8: 33 when he gave instructions to bless the people of **Israel**.
8: 35 that Joshua did not read to the whole assembly of **Israel**,
9: 2 they came together to make war against Joshua and **Israel**.
9: 6 Joshua in the camp at Gilgal and said to him and the men of **Israel**,
9: 7 The men of **Israel** said to the Hivites, "But perhaps you live near
9: 17 So the **Israelites** [+1201] set out and on the third day came to their
9: 18 the **Israelites** [+1201] did not attack them, because the leaders of
9: 18 had sworn an oath to them by the LORD, the God of **Israel**.
9: 19 by the LORD, the God of **Israel**, and we cannot touch them now.
9: 26 So Joshua saved them from the **Israelites** [+1201], and they did
10: 1 that the people of Gibeon had made a treaty of peace with **Israel**
10: 4 it has made peace with Joshua and the **Israelites** [+1201]."
10: 10 The LORD threw them into confusion before **Israel**, who
10: 11 As they fled before **Israel** on the road down from Beth Horon to
10: 11 hailstones than were killed by the swords of the **Israelites** [+1201].
10: 12 On the day the LORD gave the Amorites over to **Israel** [+1201],
10: 12 over to Israel, Joshua said to the LORD in the presence of **Israel**:
10: 14 listened to a man. Surely the LORD was fighting for **Israel**!
10: 15 Then Joshua returned with all **Israel** to the camp at Gilgal.
10: 20 So Joshua and the **Israelites** [+1201] destroyed them completely—
10: 21 and no one uttered a word against the **Israelites** [+1201].
10: 24 he summoned all the men of **Israel** and said to the army
10: 29 and all **Israel** with him moved on from Makkedah to Libnah
10: 30 The LORD also gave that city and its king into **Israel's** hand.
10: 31 and all **Israel** with him moved on from Libnah to Lachish;
10: 32 The LORD handed Lachish over to **Israel**, and Joshua took it on
10: 34 and all **Israel** with him moved on from Lachish to Eglon;
10: 36 and all **Israel** with him went up from Eglon to Hebron
10: 38 Joshua and all **Israel** with him turned around and attacked Debir.
10: 40 just as the LORD, the God of **Israel**, had commanded.
10: 42 because the LORD, the God of **Israel**, fought for Israel.
10: 42 because the LORD, the God of Israel, fought for **Israel**.
10: 43 Then Joshua returned with all **Israel** to the camp at Gilgal.
11: 5 camp together at the Waters of Merom, to fight against **Israel**.
11: 6 by this time tomorrow I will hand all of them over to **Israel**,
11: 8 the LORD gave them into the hand of **Israel**. They defeated them
11: 13 Yet **Israel** did not burn any of the cities built on their mounds—
11: 14 The **Israelites** [+1201] carried off for themselves all the plunder
11: 16 the Arabah and the mountains of **Israel** with their foothills,
11: 19 not one city made a treaty of peace with the **Israelites** [+1201],
11: 20 himself who hardened their hearts to wage war against **Israel**,
11: 21 all the hill country of Judah, and from all the hill country of **Israel**.
11: 22 No Anakites were left in **Israelite** [+1201] territory; only in Gaza,
11: 23 he gave it as an inheritance to **Israel** according to their tribal
12: 1 These are the kings of the land whom the **Israelites** [+1201] had
12: 6 servant of the LORD, and the **Israelites** [+1201] conquered them.
12: 7 the **Israelites** [+1201] conquered on the west side of the Jordan,
12: 7 to the tribes of **Israel** according to their tribal divisions—
13: 6 I myself will drive them out before the **Israelites** [+1201].
13: 6 Be sure to allocate this land to **Israel** for an inheritance, as I have
13: 13 But the **Israelites** [+1201] did not drive out the people of Geshur
13: 13 so they continue to live among the **Israelites** to this day.
13: 14 the God of **Israel**, are their inheritance, as he promised them.
13: 22 the **Israelites** [+1201] had put to the sword Balaam son of Beor,
13: 33 the LORD, the God of **Israel**, is their inheritance, as he promised
14: 1 Now these are the areas the **Israelites** [+1201] received as an

Jos 14: 1 and the heads of the tribal clans of **Israel** [+1201] allotted to them.
14: 5 So the **Israelites** [+1201] divided the land, just as the LORD had
14: 10 time he said this to Moses, while **Israel** moved about in the desert.
14: 14 he followed the LORD, the God of **Israel**, wholeheartedly.
17: 13 However, when the **Israelites** [+1201] grew stronger, they
18: 1 The whole assembly of the **Israelites** [+1201] gathered at Shiloh
18: 2 there were still seven **Israelite** [+1201] tribes who had not yet
18: 3 So Joshua said to the **Israelites** [+1201]: "How long will you wait
18: 10 there he distributed the land to the **Israelites** [+1201] according to
19: 49 the **Israelites** [+1201] gave Joshua son of Nun an inheritance
19: 51 the heads of the tribal clans of **Israel** [+1201] assigned by lot at
20: 2 "Tell the **Israelites** [+1201] to designate the cities of refuge,
20: 9 Any of the **Israelites** [+1201] or any alien living among them who
21: 1 and the heads of the other tribal families of **Israel** [+1201]
21: 3 the **Israelites** [+1201] gave the Levites the following towns
21: 8 So the **Israelites** [+1201] allotted to the Levites these towns
21: 41 the territory held by the **Israelites** [+1201] were forty-eight in all,
21: 43 So the LORD gave **Israel** all the land he had sworn to give their
21: 45 Not one of all the LORD's good promises to the house of **Israel**
22: 9 the half-tribe of Manasseh left the **Israelites** [+1201] at Shiloh in
22: 11 when the **Israelites** [+1201] heard that they had built the altar on
22: 11 of Canaan at Geliloth near the Jordan on the **Israelite** [+1201] side,
22: 12 the whole assembly of **Israel** [+1201] gathered at Shiloh to go to
22: 12 the whole assembly of Israel gathered **[RPH]** at Shiloh to go to
22: 13 So the **Israelites** [+1201] sent Phinehas son of Eleazar, the priest,
22: 14 they sent ten of the chief men, one for each of the tribes of **Israel**,
22: 14 each the head of a family division among the **Israelite** clans.
22: 16 'How could you break faith with the God of **Israel** like this?
22: 18 tomorrow he will be angry with the whole community of **Israel**.
22: 20 did not wrath come upon the whole community of **Israel**?
22: 21 half-tribe of Manasseh replied to the heads of the clans of **Israel**:
22: 22 Mighty One, God, the LORD! He knows! And let **Israel** know!
22: 24 'What do you have to do with the LORD, the God of **Israel**?
22: 30 the heads of the clans of the **Israelites**—heard what Reuben,
22: 31 Now you have rescued the **Israelites** [+1201] from the LORD's
22: 32 and Gadites in Gilead and reported to the **Israelites** [+1201].
22: 33 **They**[s] [+1201] were glad to hear the report and praised God.
22: 33 **[RPH]** And they talked no more about going to war against them
23: 1 the LORD had given **Israel** rest from all their enemies around
23: 2 summoned all **Israel**—their elders, leaders, judges and officials—
24: 1 Then Joshua assembled all the tribes of **Israel** at Shechem.
24: 1 He summoned the elders, leaders, judges and officials of **Israel**,
24: 2 all the people, "This is what the LORD, the God of **Israel**, says:
24: 9 son of Zippor, the king of Moab, prepared to fight against **Israel**,
24: 23 and yield your hearts to the LORD, the God of **Israel**."
24: 31 **Israel** served the LORD throughout the lifetime of Joshua
24: 31 who had experienced everything the LORD had done for **Israel**.
24: 32 which the **Israelites** [+1201] had brought up from Egypt,
Jdg 1: 1 the death of Joshua, the **Israelites** [+1201] asked the LORD,
1: 28 When **Israel** became strong, they pressed the Canaanites into
2: 4 the LORD had spoken these things to all the **Israelites** [+1201],
2: 6 After Joshua had dismissed the **Israelites** [+1201], they went to
2: 7 who had seen all the great things the LORD had done for **Israel**.
2: 10 who knew neither the LORD nor what he had done for **Israel**.
2: 11 Then the **Israelites** [+1201] did evil in the eyes of the LORD
2: 14 In his anger against **Israel** the LORD handed them over to raiders
2: 20 Therefore the LORD was very angry with **Israel** and said,
2: 22 I will use them to test **Israel** and see whether they will keep the
3: 1 These are the nations the LORD left to test all those **Israelites**
3: 2 **Israelites** [+1201] who had not had previous battle experience):
3: 4 They were left to test the **Israelites** to see whether they would
3: 5 The **Israelites** [+1201] lived among the Canaanites, Hittites,
3: 7 The **Israelites** [+1201] did evil in the eyes of the LORD;
3: 8 The anger of the LORD burned against **Israel** so that he sold
3: 8 to whom the **Israelites** [+1201] were subject for eight years.
3: 9 when **they**[s] [+1201] cried out to the LORD, he raised up for them
3: 9 he raised up for **them**[s] [+1201] a deliverer, Othniel son of Kenaz,
3: 10 came upon him, so that he became **Israel's** judge and went to war.
3: 12 Once again the **Israelites** [+1201] did evil in the eyes of the
3: 12 this evil the LORD gave Eglon king of Moab power over **Israel**.
3: 13 and Amalekites to join him, Eglon came and attacked **Israel**,
3: 14 The **Israelites** [+1201] were subject to Eglon king of Moab for
3: 15 Again the **Israelites** [+1201] cried out to the LORD, and he gave
3: 15 The **Israelites** [+1201] sent him with tribute to Eglon king of
3: 27 and the **Israelites** [+1201] went down with him from the hills,
3: 30 That day Moab was made subject to **Israel**, and the land had peace
3: 31 down six hundred Philistines with an oxgoad. He too saved **Israel**.
4: 1 the **Israelites** [+1201] once again did evil in the eyes of the
4: 3 and had cruelly oppressed the **Israelites** [+1201] for twenty years,
4: 3 had cruelly oppressed the Israelites for twenty years, **they**[s] [+1201]
4: 4 the wife of Lappidoth, was leading **Israel** at that time.
4: 5 the **Israelites** [+1201] came to her to have their disputes decided.
4: 6 and said to him, "The LORD, the God of **Israel**, commands you:
4: 23 subdued Jabin, the Canaanite king, before the **Israelites** [+1201].
4: 24 the hand of the **Israelites** [+1201] grew stronger and stronger
5: 2 "When the princes in **Israel** take the lead, when the people
5: 3 I will sing; I will make music to the LORD, the God of **Israel**.
5: 5 the One of Sinai, before the LORD, the God of **Israel**.
5: 7 Village life in **Israel** ceased, ceased until I, Deborah, arose,
5: 7 ceased until I, Deborah, arose, arose a mother in **Israel**.
5: 8 and not a shield or spear was seen among forty thousand in **Israel**.
5: 9 My heart is with **Israel's** princes, with the willing volunteers
5: 11 acts of the LORD, the righteous acts of his warriors in **Israel**.
6: 1 Again the **Israelites** [+1201] did evil in the eyes of the LORD,
6: 2 **[RPH]** the Israelites prepared shelters for themselves in mountain
6: 2 the **Israelites** [+1201] prepared shelters for themselves in
6: 3 Whenever the **Israelites** planted their crops, the Midianites,
6: 4 all the way to Gaza and did not spare a living thing for **Israel**,
6: 6 so impoverished the **Israelites** that they cried out to the LORD
6: 6 so impoverished the Israelites that **they**[s] [+1201] cried out to the
6: 7 When the **Israelites** [+1201] cried to the LORD because of
6: 8 he sent **them**[s] [+1201] a prophet, who said, "This is what the
6: 8 who said, "This is what the LORD, the God of **Israel**, says:
6: 14 "Go in the strength you have and save **Israel** out of Midian's hand.
6: 15 "But Lord," Gideon asked, "how can I save **Israel**? My clan is the
6: 36 "If you will save **Israel** by my hand as you have promised—
6: 37 I will know that you will save **Israel** by my hand, as you said."
7: 2 In order that **Israel** may not boast against me that her own strength
7: 8 So Gideon sent the rest of the **Israelites** [+408] to their tents
7: 14 other than the sword of Gideon son of Joash, the **Israelite** [+408].
7: 15 He returned to the camp of **Israel** and called out, "Get up!
7: 23 **Israelites** [+408] from Naphtali, Asher and all Manasseh were
8: 22 The **Israelites** [+408] said to Gideon, "Rule over us—you,
8: 27 All **Israel** prostituted themselves by worshiping it there, and it
8: 28 Thus Midian was subdued before the **Israelites** [+1201] and did
8: 33 No sooner had Gideon died than the **Israelites** [+1201] again
8: 34 did not remember **[RPH]** the LORD their God, who had rescued
8: 35 (that is, Gideon) for all the good things he had done for **them**[s].
9: 22 After Abimelech had governed **Israel** three years,
9: 55 When the **Israelites** [+408] saw that Abimelech was dead,
10: 1 of Issachar, Tola son of Puah, the son of Dodo, rose to save **Israel**.
10: 2 He led **Israel** twenty-three years; then he died, and was buried in
10: 3 was followed by Jair of Gilead, who led **Israel** twenty-two years.
10: 6 Again the **Israelites** [+1201] did evil in the eyes of the LORD.
10: 7 he became angry with **them**[s]. He sold them into the hands of the
10: 8 who that year shattered and crushed **them**[s] [+1201]. For eighteen
10: 8 For eighteen years they oppressed all the **Israelites** [+1201] on the
10: 9 and the house of Ephraim; and **Israel** was in great distress.
10: 10 the **Israelites** [+1201] cried out to the LORD, "We have sinned
10: 11 **[RPH]** "When the Egyptians, the Amorites, the Ammonites,
10: 15 But the **Israelites** [+1201] said to the LORD, "We have sinned.
10: 16 served the LORD. And he could bear **Israel's** misery no longer.
10: 17 in Gilead, the **Israelites** [+1201] assembled and camped at Mizpah.
11: 4 Some time later, when the Ammonites made war on **Israel**,
11: 5 the **[RPH]** elders of Gilead went to get Jephthah from the land of
11: 13 "When **Israel** came up out of Egypt, they took away my land from
11: 15 **Israel** did not take the land of Moab or the land of the Ammonites.
11: 16 **Israel** went through the desert to the Red Sea and on to Kadesh.
11: 17 Then **Israel** sent messengers to the king of Edom, saying,
11: 17 to the king of Moab, and he refused. So **Israel** stayed at Kadesh.
11: 19 "Then **Israel** sent messengers to Sihon king of the Amorites,
11: 19 **[RPH]** 'Let us pass through your country to our own place.'
11: 20 however, did not trust **Israel** to pass through his territory.
11: 20 all his men and encamped at Jahaz and fought with **Israel**.
11: 21 the God of **Israel**, gave Sihon and all his men into Israel's hands,
11: 21 the God of Israel, gave Sihon and all his men into **Israel's** hands,
11: 21 **Israel** took over all the land of the Amorites who lived in that
11: 23 "Now since the LORD, the God of **Israel**, has driven the
11: 23 God of Israel, has driven the Amorites out before his people **Israel**,
11: 25 king of Moab? Did he ever quarrel with **Israel** or fight with them?
11: 26 For three hundred years **Israel** occupied Heshbon, Aroer, the
11: 27 decide the dispute this day between the **Israelites** [+1201]
11: 33 as far as Abel Keramim. Thus **Israel** [+1201] subdued Ammon.
11: 39 she was a virgin. From this comes the **Israelite** [+928] custom
11: 40 that each year the young women of **Israel** go out for four days to
12: 7 Jephthah led **Israel** six years. Then Jephthah the Gileadite died,
12: 8 After him, Ibzan of Bethlehem led **Israel**.
12: 9 as wives from outside his clan. Ibzan led **Israel** seven years.
12: 11 After him, Elon the Zebulunite led **Israel** ten years.
12: 11 After him, Elon the Zebulunite led Israel **[RPH]** ten years.
12: 13 After him, Abdon son of Hillel, from Pirathon, led **Israel**.
12: 14 who rode on seventy donkeys. He led **Israel** eight years.
13: 1 Again the **Israelites** [+1201] did evil in the eyes of the LORD,
13: 5 he will begin the deliverance of **Israel** from the hands of the
14: 4 the Philistines; for at that time they were ruling over **Israel**.)
15: 20 Samson led **Israel** for twenty years in the days of the Philistines.
16: 31 in the tomb of Manoah his father. He had led **Israel** twenty years.
17: 6 In those days **Israel** had no king; everyone did as he saw fit.

[F] Hitpael (hitpoel, hitpoal, hitpolel, hitpolal, hitpalel, hitpalal, hitpalpel, hitpalpal, hotpael, hotpaal) [G] Hiphil (hiphtil) [H] Hophal [I] Hishtaphel

Jdg 18: 1 In those days **Israel** had no king. And in those days the tribe of the
18: 1 had not yet come into an inheritance among the tribes of **Israel**.
18: 19 and clan in **Israel** as priest rather than just one man's household?"
18: 29 named it Dan after their forefather Dan, who was born to **Israel**—
19: 1 In those days **Israel** had no king. Now a Levite who lived in a
19: 12 into an alien city, whose people are not **Israelites** [+1201+4946].
19: 29 into twelve parts and sent them into all the areas of **Israel**.
19: 30 not since the day the **Israelites** [+1201] came up out of Egypt.
20: 1 all the **Israelites** [+1201] from Dan to Beersheba and from the land
20: 2 The leaders of all the people of the tribes of **Israel** took their places
20: 3 (The Benjamites heard that the **Israelites** [+1201] had gone up to
20: 3 the **Israelites** [+1201] said, "Tell us how this awful thing
20: 6 and sent one piece to each region of **Israel's** inheritance,
20: 6 because they committed this lewd and disgraceful act in **Israel**.
20: 7 Now, all you **Israelites** [+1201], speak up and give your verdict."
20: 10 take ten men out of every hundred from all the tribes of **Israel**,
20: 10 give them what they deserve for all this vileness done in **Israel**."
20: 11 So all the men of **Israel** got together and united as one man against
20: 12 The tribes of **Israel** sent men throughout the tribe of Benjamin,
20: 13 so that we may put them to death and purge the evil from **Israel**."
20: 13 the Benjamites would not listen to their fellow **Israelites** [+1201].
20: 14 came together at Gibeah to fight against the **Israelites** [+1201].
20: 17 **Israel** [+408], apart from Benjamin, mustered four hundred
20: 18 The **Israelites** [+1201] went up to Bethel and inquired of God.
20: 19 The next morning the **Israelites** [+1201] got up and pitched camp
20: 20 The men of **Israel** went out to fight the Benjamites and took up
20: 20 and **[RPH]** took up battle positions against them at Gibeah.
20: 21 cut down twenty-two thousand **Israelites** on the battlefield that
20: 22 the men of **Israel** encouraged one another and again took up their
20: 23 The **Israelites** [+1201] went up and wept before the LORD until
20: 24 Then the **Israelites** [+1201] drew near to Benjamin the second day.
20: 25 they cut down another eighteen thousand **Israelites** [+1201],
20: 26 Then the **Israelites** [+1201], all the people, went up to Bethel,
20: 27 the **Israelites** [+1201] inquired of the LORD. (In those days the
20: 29 Then **Israel** set an ambush around Gibeah.
20: 30 **They**[s] [+1201] went up against the Benjamites on the third day
20: 31 so that about thirty men **[RPH]** fell in the open field and on the
20: 32 the **Israelites** [+1201] were saying, "Let's retreat and draw them
20: 33 All the men of **Israel** moved from their places and took up
20: 33 the **Israelite** ambush charged out of its place on the west of
20: 34 ten thousand of **Israel's** finest men made a frontal attack on
20: 35 The LORD defeated Benjamin before **Israel**, and on that day the
20: 35 on that day the **Israelites** [+1201] struck down 25,100 Benjamites,
20: 36 Now the men of **Israel** had given way before Benjamin,
20: 38 The men of **Israel** had arranged with the ambush that they should
20: 39 then the men of **Israel** would turn in the battle. The Benjamites had
20: 39 The Benjamites had begun to inflict casualties on the men of **Israel**
20: 41 the men of **Israel** turned on them, and the men of Benjamin were
20: 42 So they fled before the **Israelites** [+408] in the direction of the
20: 48 The men of **Israel** went back to Benjamin and put all the towns to
21: 1 The men of **Israel** had taken an oath at Mizpah: "Not one of us
21: 3 "O LORD, the God of **Israel**," they cried, "why has this
21: 3 the God of Israel," they cried, "why has this happened to **Israel**?
21: 3 to Israel? Why should one tribe be missing from **Israel** today?"
21: 5 the **Israelites** [+1201] asked, "Who from all the tribes of Israel has
21: 5 "Who from all the tribes of **Israel** has failed to assemble before the
21: 6 Now the **Israelites** [+1201] grieved for their brothers,
21: 6 the Benjamites. "Today one tribe is cut off from **Israel**," they said.
21: 8 "Which one of the tribes of **Israel** failed to assemble before the
21: 15 because the LORD had made a gap in the tribes of **Israel**.
21: 17 they said, "so that a tribe of **Israel** will not be wiped out.
21: 18 as wives, since we **Israelites** [+1201] have taken this oath:
21: 24 At that time the **Israelites** [+1201] left that place and went home to
21: 25 In those days **Israel** had no king; everyone did as he saw fit.
Ru 2: 12 May you be richly rewarded by the LORD, the God of **Israel**,
4: 7 (Now in earlier times in **Israel**, for the redemption and transfer of
4: 7 the other. This was the method of legalizing transactions in **Israel**.)
4: 11 like Rachel and Leah, who together built up the house of **Israel**.
4: 14 a kinsman-redeemer. May he become famous throughout **Israel**!
1Sa 1: 17 and may the God of **Israel** grant you what you have asked of him."
2: 14 This is how they treated all the **Israelites** who came to Shiloh.
2: 22 heard about everything his sons were doing to all **Israel** and how
2: 28 I chose your father out of all the tribes of **Israel** to be my priest,
2: 28 house all the offerings made with fire by the **Israelites** [+1201].
2: 29 on the choice parts of every offering made by my people **Israel**?'
2: 30 "Therefore the LORD, the God of **Israel**, declares: 'I promised
2: 32 Although good will be done to **Israel**, in your family line there will
3: 11 I am about to do something in **Israel** that will make the ears of
3: 20 all **Israel** from Dan to Beersheba recognized that Samuel was
4: 1 Samuel's word came to all **Israel**. Now the Israelites went out to
4: 1 Now the **Israelites** went out to fight against the Philistines.
4: 2 The Philistines deployed their forces to meet **Israel**, and as the
4: 2 and as the battle spread, **Israel** was defeated by the Philistines,
4: 3 When the soldiers returned to camp, the elders of **Israel** asked,
4: 5 all **Israel** raised such a great shout that the ground shook.
4: 10 and the **Israelites** were defeated and every man fled to his tent.
4: 10 slaughter was very great; **Israel** lost thirty thousand foot soldiers.
4: 17 "**Israel** fled before the Philistines, and the army has suffered heavy
4: 18 for he was an old man and heavy. He had led **Israel** forty years.
4: 21 the boy Ichabod, saying, "The glory has departed from **Israel**"—
4: 22 She said, "The glory has departed from **Israel**, for the ark of God
5: 7 they said, "The ark of the god of **Israel** must not stay here with us,
5: 8 asked them, "What shall we do with the ark of the god of **Israel**?"
5: 8 "Have the ark of the god of **Israel** moved to Gath."
5: 8 Israel moved to Gath." So they moved the ark of the God of **Israel**.
5: 10 "They have brought the ark of the god of **Israel** around to us to kill
5: 11 of the Philistines and said, "Send the ark of the god of **Israel** away;
6: 3 They answered, "If you return the ark of the god of **Israel**,
6: 5 rats that are destroying the country, and pay honor to **Israel's** god.
7: 2 and all the people of **Israel** mourned and sought after the LORD.
7: 3 Samuel said to the whole house of **Israel**, "If you are returning to
7: 4 So the **Israelites** [+1201] put away their Baals and Ashtoreths,
7: 5 "Assemble all **Israel** at Mizpah and I will intercede with the
7: 6 the LORD." And Samuel was leader of **Israel** [+1201] at Mizpah.
7: 7 When the Philistines heard that **Israel** [+1201] had assembled at
7: 7 at Mizpah, the rulers of the Philistines came up to attack **them**[s].
7: 7 And when the **Israelites** [+1201] heard of it, they were afraid
7: 8 **They**[s] [+1201] said to Samuel, "Do not stop crying out to the
7: 9 He cried out to the LORD on **Israel's** behalf, and the LORD
7: 10 burnt offering, the Philistines drew near to engage **Israel** in battle.
7: 10 them into such a panic that they were routed before the **Israelites**.
7: 11 The men of **Israel** rushed out of Mizpah and pursued the
7: 13 were subdued and did not invade **Israelite** territory again.
7: 14 that the Philistines had captured from **Israel** were restored to her,
7: 14 that the Philistines had captured from Israel were restored to **her**[s],
7: 14 **Israel** delivered the neighboring territory from the power of the
7: 14 And there was peace between **Israel** and the Amorites.
7: 15 Samuel continued as judge over **Israel** all the days of his life.
7: 16 from Bethel to Gilgal to Mizpah, judging **Israel** in all those places.
7: 17 to Ramah, where his home was, and there he also judged **Israel**.
8: 1 When Samuel grew old, he appointed his sons as judges for **Israel**.
8: 4 So all the elders of **Israel** gathered together and came to Samuel at
8: 22 Samuel said to the men of **Israel**, "Everyone go back to his town."
9: 2 young man without equal among the **Israelites** [+1201]—
9: 9 (Formerly in **Israel**, if a man went to inquire of God, he would say,
9: 16 Anoint him leader over my people **Israel**; he will deliver my
9: 20 And to whom is all the desire of **Israel** turned, if not to you
9: 21 "But am I not a Benjamite, from the smallest tribe of **Israel**,
10: 18 said to **them**[s] [+1201], "This is what the LORD, the God of
10: 18 said to them, "This is what the LORD, the God of **Israel**, says:
10: 18 'I brought **Israel** up out of Egypt, and I delivered you from the
10: 20 When Samuel brought all the tribes of **Israel** near, the tribe of
11: 2 right eye of every one of you and so bring disgrace on all **Israel**."
11: 3 "Give us seven days so we can send messengers throughout **Israel**;
11: 7 and sent the pieces by messengers throughout **Israel**, proclaiming,
11: 8 the men of **Israel** numbered three hundred thousand and the men
11: 13 be put to death today, for this day the LORD has rescued **Israel**."
11: 15 and Saul and all the **Israelites** [+408] held a great celebration.
12: 1 Samuel said to all **Israel**, "I have listened to everything you said to
13: 1 he became king, and he reigned over **Israel** ⌞forty-⌟two years.
13: 2 Saul chose three thousand men from **Israel**; two thousand were
13: 4 So all **Israel** heard the news: "Saul has attacked the Philistine
13: 4 and now **Israel** has become a stench to the Philistines."
13: 5 The Philistines assembled to fight **Israel**, with three thousand
13: 6 When the men of **Israel** saw that their situation was critical
13: 13 he would have established your kingdom over **Israel** for all time.
13: 19 Not a blacksmith could be found in the whole land of **Israel**,
13: 20 So all **Israel** went down to the Philistines to have their plowshares,
14: 12 up after me; the LORD has given them into the hand of **Israel**."
14: 18 the ark of God." (At that time it was with the **Israelites** [+1201].)
14: 21 had gone up with them to their camp went over to the **Israelites**
14: 22 When all the **Israelites** [+408] who had hidden in the hill country
14: 23 So the LORD rescued **Israel** that day, and the battle moved on
14: 24 Now the men of **Israel** were in distress that day, because Saul had
14: 37 Will you give them into **Israel's** hand?" But God did not answer
14: 39 As surely as the LORD who rescues **Israel** lives, even if it lies
14: 40 Saul then said to all the **Israelites**, "You stand over there;
14: 41 to the LORD, the God of **Israel**, "Give me the right answer."
14: 45 he who has brought about this great deliverance in **Israel**?
14: 47 After Saul had assumed rule over **Israel**, he fought against their
14: 48 delivering **Israel** from the hands of those who had plundered them.
15: 1 the one the LORD sent to anoint you king over his people **Israel**;
15: 2 'I will punish the Amalekites for what they did to **Israel** when they
15: 6 for you showed kindness to all the **Israelites** [+1201] when they
15: 17 own eyes, did you not become the head of the tribes of **Israel**?
15: 17 of the tribes of Israel? The LORD anointed you king over **Israel**.
15: 26 the LORD, and the LORD has rejected you as king over **Israel**!"
15: 28 "The LORD has torn the kingdom of **Israel** from you today

1Sa 15:29 He who is the Glory of **Israel** does not lie or change his mind;
15:30 please honor me before the elders of my people and before **Israel**;
15:35 the LORD was grieved that he had made Saul king over **Israel**.
16: 1 you mourn for Saul, since I have rejected him as king over **Israel**?
17: 2 Saul and the **Israelites** [+408] assembled and camped in the Valley
17: 3 The Philistines occupied one hill and the **Israelites** another,
17: 8 Goliath stood and shouted to the ranks of **Israel**, "Why do you
17:10 Then the Philistine said, "This day I defy the ranks of **Israel**!
17:11 Saul and all the **Israelites** were dismayed and terrified.
17:19 They are with Saul and all the men of **Israel** in the Valley of Elah,
17:21 **Israel** and the Philistines were drawing up their lines facing each
17:24 When the **Israelites** [+408] saw the man, they all ran from him in
17:25 Now the **Israelites** [+408] had been saying, "Do you see how this
17:25 see how this man keeps coming out? He comes out to defy **Israel**.
17:25 and will exempt his father's family from taxes in **Israel**."
17:26 who kills this Philistine and removes this disgrace from **Israel**?
17:45 the God of the armies of **Israel**, whom you have defied.
17:46 and the whole world will know that there is a God in **Israel**.
17:52 Then the men of **Israel** and Judah surged forward with a shout
17:53 When the **Israelites** [+1201] returned from chasing the Philistines,
18: 6 the women came out from all the towns of **Israel** to meet King
18:16 all **Israel** and Judah loved David, because he led them in their
18:18 "Who am I, and what is my family or my father's clan in **Israel**,
19: 5 The LORD won a great victory for all **Israel**, and you saw it
20:12 "By the LORD, the God of **Israel**, I will surely sound out my
23:10 David said, "O LORD, God of **Israel**, your servant has heard
23:11 O LORD, God of **Israel**, tell your servant." And the LORD said,
23:17 You will be king over **Israel**, and I will be second to you.
24: 2 [24:3] So Saul took three thousand chosen men from all **Israel**
24:14 [24:15] "Against whom has the king of **Israel** come out?
24:20 [24:21] that the kingdom of **Israel** will be established in your
25: 1 Now Samuel died, and all **Israel** assembled and mourned for him;
25:30 concerning him and has appointed him leader over **Israel**,
25:32 David said to Abigail, "Praise be to the LORD, the God of **Israel**,
25:34 Otherwise, as surely as the LORD, the God of **Israel**, lives,
26: 2 with his three thousand chosen men of **Israel**, to search there for
26:15 "You're a man, aren't you? And who is like you in **Israel**?
26:20 The king of **Israel** has come out to look for a flea—as one hunts a
27: 1 Then Saul will give up searching for me anywhere in **Israel**,
27:12 to himself, "He has become so odious to his people, the **Israelites**,
28: 1 days the Philistines gathered their forces to fight against **Israel**.
28: 3 all **Israel** had mourned for him and buried him in his own town of
28: 4 while Saul gathered all the **Israelites** and set up camp at Gilboa.
28:19 The LORD will hand over both **Israel** and you to the Philistines,
28:19 The LORD will also hand over the army of **Israel** to the
29: 1 their forces at Aphek, and **Israel** camped by the spring in Jezreel.
29: 3 "Is this not David, who was an officer of Saul king of **Israel**?
30:25 made this a statute and ordinance for **Israel** from that day to this.
31: 1 Now the Philistines fought against **Israel**; the Israelites fled before
31: 1 the **Israelites** [+408] fled before them, and many fell slain on
31: 7 When the **Israelites** [+408] along the valley and those across the
31: 7 and those across the Jordan saw that the **Israelite** army had fled
2Sa 1: 3 He answered, "I have escaped from the **Israelite** camp."
1:12 and for the army of the LORD and the house of **Israel**,
1:19 "Your glory, O **Israel**, lies slain on your heights. How the mighty
1:24 "O daughters of **Israel**, weep for Saul, who clothed you in scarlet
2: 9 and Jezreel, and also over Ephraim, Benjamin and all **Israel**.
2:10 son of Saul was forty years old when he became king over **Israel**,
2:17 and Abner and the men of **Israel** were defeated by David's men.
2:28 they no longer pursued **Israel**, nor did they fight anymore.
3:10 establish David's throne over **Israel** and Judah from Dan to
3:12 with me, and I will help you bring all **Israel** over to you."
3:17 Abner conferred with the elders of **Israel** and said, "For some time
3:18 'By my servant David I will rescue my people **Israel** from the hand
3:19 Then he went to Hebron to tell David everything that **Israel**
3:21 "Let me go at once and assemble all **Israel** for my lord the king,
3:37 all **Israel** knew that the king had no part in the murder of Abner
3:38 realize that a prince and a great man has fallen in **Israel** this day?
4: 1 died in Hebron, he lost courage, and all **Israel** became alarmed.
5: 1 All the tribes of **Israel** came to David at Hebron and said,
5: 2 you were the one who led **Israel** on their military campaigns.
5: 2 And the LORD said to you, 'You will shepherd my people **Israel**,
5: 2 my people Israel, and you will become **their**[s] [+6584] ruler.' "
5: 3 When all the elders of **Israel** had come to King David at Hebron,
5: 3 before the LORD, and they anointed David king over **Israel**.
5: 5 in Jerusalem he reigned over all **Israel** and Judah thirty-three
5:12 knew that the LORD had established him as king over **Israel**
5:12 and had exalted his kingdom for the sake of his people **Israel**.
5:17 Philistines heard that David had been anointed king over **Israel**,
6: 1 David again brought together out of **Israel** chosen men,
6: 5 the whole house of **Israel** were celebrating with all their might
6:15 the entire house of **Israel** brought up the ark of the LORD with
6:19 a cake of raisins to each person in the whole crowd of **Israelites**,
6:20 and said, "How the king of **Israel** has distinguished himself today,
6:21 when he appointed me ruler over the LORD's people **Israel**—
7: 6 day I brought the **Israelites** [+1201] up out of Egypt to this day.
7: 7 Wherever I have moved with all the **Israelites** [+1201], did I ever
7: 7 did I ever say to any of **their**[s] rulers whom I commanded to
7: 7 of their rulers whom I commanded to shepherd my people **Israel**,
7: 8 and from following the flock to be ruler over my people **Israel**.
7:10 And I will provide a place for my people **Israel** and will plant them
7:11 done ever since the time I appointed leaders over my people **Israel**.
7:23 who is like your people **Israel**—the one nation on earth that God
7:24 You have established your people **Israel** as your very own forever,
7:26 Then men will say, 'The LORD Almighty is God over **Israel**!'
7:27 "O LORD Almighty, God of **Israel**, you have revealed this to
8:15 David reigned over all **Israel**, doing what was just and right for all
10: 9 so he selected some of the best troops in **Israel** and deployed them
10:15 After the Arameans saw that they had been routed by **Israel**,
10:17 he gathered all **Israel**, crossed the Jordan and went to Helam.
10:18 they fled before **Israel**, and David killed seven hundred of their
10:19 vassals of Hadadezer saw that they had been defeated by **Israel**,
10:19 they made peace with the **Israelites** and became subject to them.
11: 1 sent Joab out with the king's men and the whole **Israelite** army.
11:11 "The ark and **Israel** and Judah are staying in tents, and my master
12: 7 are the man! This is what the LORD, the God of **Israel**, says:
12: 7 'I anointed you king over **Israel**, and I delivered you from the hand
12: 8 I gave you the house of **Israel** and Judah. And if all this had been
12:12 but I will do this thing in broad daylight before all **Israel**.' "
13:12 "Don't force me. Such a thing should not be done in **Israel**!
13:13 about you? You would be like one of the wicked fools in **Israel**.
14:25 In all **Israel** there was not a man so highly praised for his
15: 2 would answer, "Your servant is from one of the tribes of **Israel**."
15: 6 Absalom behaved in this way toward all the **Israelites** who came
15: 6 asking for justice, and so he stole the hearts of the men of **Israel**.
15:10 Absalom sent secret messengers throughout the tribes of **Israel** to
15:13 told David, "The hearts of the men of **Israel** are with Absalom."
16: 3 'Today the house of **Israel** will give me back my grandfather's
16:15 Meanwhile, Absalom and all the men of **Israel** came to Jerusalem,
16:18 by the LORD, by these people, and by all the men of **Israel**—
16:21 all **Israel** will hear that you have made yourself a stench in your
16:22 and he lay with his father's concubines in the sight of all **Israel**.
17: 4 This plan seemed good to Absalom and to all the elders of **Israel**.
17:10 for all **Israel** knows that your father is a fighter and that those with
17:11 Let all **Israel**, from Dan to Beersheba—as numerous as the sand on
17:13 withdraws into a city, then all **Israel** will bring ropes to that city,
17:14 Absalom and all the men of **Israel** said, "The advice of Hushai the
17:15 has advised Absalom and the elders of **Israel** to do such and such,
17:24 and Absalom crossed the Jordan with all the men of **Israel**.
17:26 The **Israelites** and Absalom camped in the land of Gilead.
18: 6 The army marched into the field to fight **Israel**, and the battle took
18: 7 There the army of **Israel** was defeated by David's men,
18:16 and the troops stopped pursuing **Israel**, for Joab halted them.
18:17 rocks over him. Meanwhile, all the **Israelites** fled to their homes.
19: 8 [19:9] Meanwhile, the **Israelites** had fled to their homes.
19: 9 [19:10] Throughout the tribes of **Israel**, the people were all
19:11 [19:12] since what is being said throughout **Israel** has reached the
19:22 [19:23] Should anyone be put to death in **Israel** today?
19:22 [19:23] Do I not know that today I am king over **Israel**?"
19:40 [19:41] and half the troops of **Israel** had taken the king over.
19:41 [19:42] Soon all the men of **Israel** were coming to the king
19:42 [19:43] All the men of Judah answered the men of **Israel**,
19:43 [19:44] the men of **Israel** answered the men of Judah, "We have
19:43 [19:44] responded even more harshly than the men of **Israel**.
20: 1 in David, no part in Jesse's son! Every man to his tent, O **Israel**!"
20: 2 So all the men of **Israel** deserted David to follow Sheba son of
20:14 Sheba passed through all the tribes of **Israel** to Abel Beth Maacah
20:19 We are the peaceful and faithful in **Israel**. You are trying to
20:19 in Israel. You are trying to destroy a city that is a mother in **Israel**.
20:23 Joab was over **Israel's** entire army; Benaiah son of Jehoiada was
21: 2 (Now the Gibeonites were not a part of **Israel** [+1201] but were
21: 2 the **Israelites** [+1201] had sworn to ⌞spare⌟ them, but Saul in his
21: 2 Saul in his zeal for **Israel** [+1201] and Judah had tried to annihilate
21: 4 nor do we have the right to put anyone in **Israel** to death."
21: 5 we have been decimated and have no place anywhere in **Israel**,
21:15 Once again there was a battle between the Philistines and **Israel**.
21:17 us to battle, so that the lamp of **Israel** will not be extinguished."
21:21 When he taunted **Israel**, Jonathan son of Shimeah, David's
23: 1 the man anointed by the God of Jacob, **Israel's** singer of songs:
23: 3 The God of **Israel** spoke, the Rock of Israel said to me: 'When one
23: 3 The God of Israel spoke, the Rock of **Israel** said to me: 'When one
23: 9 ⌞at Pas Dammim⌟ for battle. Then the men of **Israel** retreated,
24: 1 Again the anger of the LORD burned against **Israel**, and he
24: 1 against them, saying, "Go and take a census of **Israel** and Judah."
24: 2 "Go throughout the tribes of **Israel** from Dan to Beersheba
24: 4 left the presence of the king to enroll the fighting men of **Israel**.
24: 9 In **Israel** there were eight hundred thousand able-bodied men who
24:15 So the LORD sent a plague on **Israel** from that morning until the

2Sa 24:25 prayer in behalf of the land, and the plague on **Israel** was stopped.
1Ki 1: 3 they searched throughout **Israel** for a beautiful girl and found
1:20 My lord the king, the eyes of all **Israel** are on you, to learn from
1:30 out today what I swore to you by the LORD, the God of **Israel**:
1:34 the priest and Nathan the prophet anoint him king over **Israel**.
1:35 in my place. I have appointed him ruler over **Israel** and Judah."
1:48 said, 'Praise be to the LORD, the God of **Israel**, who has allowed
2: 4 and soul, you will never fail to have a man on the throne of **Israel**.'
2: 5 what he did to the two commanders of **Israel's** armies, Abner son
2:11 He had reigned forty years over **Israel**—seven years in Hebron
2:15 All **Israel** looked to me as their king. But things changed,
2:32 Abner son of Ner, commander of **Israel's** army, and Amasa son of
3:28 When all **Israel** heard the verdict the king had given, they held the
4: 1 So King Solomon ruled over all **Israel**.
4: 7 Solomon also had twelve district governors over all **Israel**,
4:20 of Judah and **Israel** were as numerous as the sand on the seashore;
4:25 [5:5] During Solomon's lifetime Judah and **Israel**, from Dan to
5:13 [5:27] King Solomon conscripted laborers from all **Israel**—thirty
6: 1 eightieth year after the **Israelites** [+1201] had come out of Egypt,
6: 1 in the fourth year of Solomon's reign over **Israel**, in the month of
6:13 I will live among the **Israelites** [+1201] and will not abandon my
6:13 live among the Israelites and will not abandon my people **Israel**."
8: 1 summoned into his presence at Jerusalem the elders of **Israel**,
8: 1 heads of the tribes and the chiefs of the **Israelite** [+1201] families,
8: 2 All the men of **Israel** came together to King Solomon at the time
8: 3 When all the elders of **Israel** had arrived, the priests took up the
8: 5 the entire assembly of **Israel** that had gathered about him were
8: 9 where the LORD made a covenant with the **Israelites** [+1201]
8:14 While the whole assembly of **Israel** was standing there, the king
8:14 the king turned around and blessed **them**[s] [+3972+7736].
8:15 "Praise be to the LORD, the God of **Israel**, who with his own
8:16 'Since the day I brought my people **Israel** out of Egypt, I have not
8:16 I have not chosen a city in any tribe of **Israel** to have a temple built
8:16 to be there, but I have chosen David to rule my people **Israel**.'
8:17 to build a temple for the Name of the LORD, the God of **Israel**.
8:20 succeeded David my father and now I sit on the throne of **Israel**,
8:20 built the temple for the Name of the LORD, the God of **Israel**.
8:22 the altar of the LORD in front of the whole assembly of **Israel**,
8:23 "O LORD, God of **Israel**, there is no God like you in heaven
8:25 "Now LORD, God of **Israel**, keep for your servant David my
8:25 never fail to have a man to sit before me on the throne of **Israel**,
8:26 now, O God of **Israel**, let your word that you promised your
8:30 and of your people **Israel** when they pray toward this place.
8:33 "When your people **Israel** have been defeated by an enemy
8:34 then hear from heaven and forgive the sin of your people **Israel**
8:36 and forgive the sin of your servants, your people **Israel**.
8:38 and when a prayer or plea is made by any of your people **Israel**—
8:41 "As for the foreigner who does not belong to your people **Israel**
8:43 may know your name and fear you, as do your own people **Israel**,
8:52 open to your servant's plea and to the plea of your people **Israel**,
8:55 He stood and blessed the whole assembly of **Israel** in a loud voice,
8:56 who has given rest to his people **Israel** just as he promised.
8:59 and the cause of his people **Israel** according to each day's need,
8:62 and all **Israel** with him offered sacrifices before the LORD.
8:63 and all the **Israelites** [+1201] dedicated the temple of the LORD.
8:65 observed the festival at that time, and all **Israel** with him—
8:66 the LORD had done for his servant David and his people **Israel**.
9: 5 I will establish your royal throne over **Israel** forever, as I promised
9: 5 'You shall never fail to have a man on the throne of **Israel**.'
9: 7 I will cut off **Israel** from the land I have given them and will reject
9: 7 **Israel** will then become a byword and an object of ridicule among
9:20 and Jebusites (these peoples were not **Israelites** [+1201]),
9:21 in the land, whom the **Israelites** [+1201] could not exterminate—
9:22 But Solomon did not make slaves of any of the **Israelites** [+1201];
10: 9 who has delighted in you and placed you on the throne of **Israel**.
10: 9 Because of the LORD's eternal love for **Israel**, he has made you
11: 2 nations about which the LORD had told the **Israelites** [+1201],
11: 9 the LORD, the God of **Israel**, who had appeared to him twice.
11:16 Joab and all the **Israelites** stayed there for six months, until they
11:25 Rezon was **Israel's** [+4200] adversary as long as Solomon lived,
11:25 by Hadad. So Rezon ruled in Aram and was hostile toward **Israel**.
11:31 for yourself, for this is what the LORD, the God of **Israel**, says:
11:32 which I have chosen out of all the tribes of **Israel**, he will have one
11:37 rule over all that your heart desires; you will be king over **Israel**.
11:38 as enduring as the one I built for David and will give **Israel** to you.
11:42 Solomon reigned in Jerusalem over all **Israel** forty years.
12: 1 to Shechem, for all the **Israelites** had gone there to make him king.
12: 3 and he and the whole assembly of **Israel** went to Rehoboam
12:16 When all **Israel** saw that the king refused to listen to them,
12:16 have in David, what part in Jesse's son? To your tents, O **Israel**!
12:16 after your own house, O David!" So the **Israelites** went home.
12:17 as for the **Israelites** [+1201] who were living in the towns of
12:18 was in charge of forced labor, but all **Israel** stoned him to death.
12:19 So **Israel** has been in rebellion against the house of David to this
12:20 When all the **Israelites** heard that Jeroboam had returned,
12:20 and called him to the assembly and made him king over all **Israel**.
12:21 to make war against the house of **Israel** and to regain the kingdom
12:24 Do not go up to fight against your brothers, the **Israelites** [+1201].
12:28 Here are your gods, O **Israel**, who brought you up out of Egypt."
12:33 So he instituted the festival for the **Israelites** [+1201] and went up
14: 7 tell Jeroboam that this is what the LORD, the God of **Israel**, says:
14: 7 among the people and made you a leader over my people **Israel**.
14:10 I will cut off from Jeroboam every last male in **Israel**—slave
14:13 All **Israel** will mourn for him and bury him. He is the only one
14:13 in whom the LORD, the God of **Israel**, has found anything good.
14:14 "The LORD will raise up for himself a king over **Israel** who will
14:15 the LORD will strike **Israel**, so that it will be like a reed swaying
14:15 He will uproot **Israel** from this good land that he gave to their
14:16 he will give **Israel** up because of the sins Jeroboam has committed
14:16 sins Jeroboam has committed and has caused **Israel** to commit."
14:18 They buried him, and all **Israel** mourned for him, as the LORD
14:19 are written in the book of the annals of the kings of **Israel**.
14:21 the city the LORD had chosen out of all the tribes of **Israel** in
14:24 nations the LORD had driven out before the **Israelites** [+1201].
15: 9 In the twentieth year of Jeroboam king of **Israel**, Asa became king
15:16 between Asa and Baasha king of **Israel** throughout their reigns.
15:17 Baasha king of **Israel** went up against Judah and fortified Ramah
15:19 Now break your treaty with Baasha king of **Israel** so he will
15:20 and sent the commanders of his forces against the towns of **Israel**.
15:25 Nadab son of Jeroboam became king of **Israel** in the second year
15:25 year of Asa king of Judah, and he reigned over **Israel** two years.
15:26 of his father and in his sin, which he had caused **Israel** to commit.
15:27 a Philistine town, while Nadab and all **Israel** were besieging it.
15:30 the sins Jeroboam had committed and had caused **Israel** to commit,
15:30 because he provoked the LORD, the God of **Israel**, to anger.
15:31 they not written in the book of the annals of the kings of **Israel**?
15:32 between Asa and Baasha king of **Israel** throughout their reigns.
15:33 Baasha son of Ahijah became king of all **Israel** in Tirzah,
15:34 of Jeroboam and in his sin, which he had caused **Israel** to commit.
16: 2 you up from the dust and made you leader of my people **Israel**,
16: 2 in the ways of Jeroboam and caused my people **Israel** to sin
16: 5 they not written in the book of the annals of the kings of **Israel**?
16: 8 Elah son of Baasha became king of **Israel**, and he reigned in
16:13 and his son Elah had committed and had caused **Israel** to commit,
16:13 the LORD, the God of **Israel**, to anger by their worthless idols.
16:14 they not written in the book of the annals of the kings of **Israel**?
16:16 the king and murdered him, **they**[s] [+3972] proclaimed Omri,
16:16 of the army, king over **Israel** that very day there in the camp.
16:17 and all the **Israelites** with him withdrew from Gibbethon
16:19 and in the sin he had committed and had caused **Israel** to commit.
16:20 they not written in the book of the annals of the kings of **Israel**?
16:21 the people of **Israel** were split into two factions; half supported
16:23 Omri became king of **Israel**, and he reigned twelve years,
16:26 son of Nebat and in his sin, which he had caused **Israel** to commit,
16:26 the LORD, the God of **Israel**, to anger by their worthless idols.
16:27 they not written in the book of the annals of the kings of **Israel**?
16:29 of Asa king of Judah, Ahab son of Omri became king of **Israel**,
16:29 of Israel, and he reigned in Samaria over **Israel** twenty-two years.
16:33 and did more to provoke the LORD, the God of **Israel**,
16:33 God of Israel, to anger than did all the kings of **Israel** before him.
17: 1 to Ahab, "As the LORD, the God of **Israel**, lives, whom I serve,
17:14 For this is what the LORD, the God of **Israel**, says: 'The jar of
18:17 he saw Elijah, he said to him, "Is that you, you troubler of **Israel**?"
18:18 "I have not made trouble for **Israel**," Elijah replied. "But you
18:19 Now summon the people from all over **Israel** to meet me on
18:20 So Ahab sent word throughout all **Israel** [+1201] and assembled
18:31 of the LORD had come, saying, "Your name shall be **Israel**."
18:36 "O LORD, God of Abraham, Isaac and **Israel**, let it be known
18:36 let it be known today that you are God in **Israel** and that I am your
19:10 The **Israelites** [+1201] have rejected your covenant, broken down
19:14 The **Israelites** [+1201] have rejected your covenant, broken down
19:16 Also, anoint Jehu son of Nimshi king over **Israel**, and anoint
19:18 Yet I reserve seven thousand in **Israel**—all whose knees have not
20: 2 He sent messengers into the city to Ahab king of **Israel**, saying,
20: 4 The king of **Israel** answered, "Just as you say, my lord the king.
20: 7 The king of **Israel** summoned all the elders of the land and said to
20:11 The king of **Israel** answered, "Tell him: 'One who puts on his
20:13 Meanwhile a prophet came to Ahab king of **Israel** and announced,
20:15 Then he assembled the rest of the **Israelites** [+1201], 7,000 in all.
20:20 At that, the Arameans fled, with the **Israelites** in pursuit.
20:21 The king of **Israel** advanced and overpowered the horses
20:22 Afterward, the prophet came to the king of **Israel** and said,
20:26 the Arameans and went up to Aphek to fight against **Israel**.
20:27 When the **Israelites** [+1201] were also mustered and given
20:27 The **Israelites** [+1201] camped opposite them like two small flocks
20:28 The man of God came up and told the king of **Israel**, "This is what
20:29 The **Israelites** [+1201] inflicted a hundred thousand casualties on
20:31 we have heard that the kings of the house of **Israel** are merciful.

1Ki 20:31 Let us go to the king of **Israel** with sackcloth around our waists
20:32 ropes around their heads, they went to the king of **Israel** and said,
20:40 man disappeared." "That is your sentence," the king of **Israel** said.
20:41 and the king of **Israel** recognized him as one of the prophets.
20:43 and angry, the king of **Israel** went to his palace in Samaria.
21: 7 Jezebel his wife said, "Is this how you act as king over **Israel**?
21:18 "Go down to meet Ahab king of **Israel**, who rules in Samaria.
21:21 your descendants and cut off from Ahab every last male in **Israel**—
21:22 you have provoked me to anger and have caused **Israel** to sin.'
21:26 like the Amorites the LORD drove out before **Israel** [+1201].)
22: 1 For three years there was no war between Aram and **Israel**.
22: 2 Jehoshaphat king of Judah went down to see the king of **Israel**.
22: 3 The king of **Israel** had said to his officials, "Don't you know that
22: 4 Jehoshaphat replied to the king of **Israel**, "I am as you are,
22: 5 Jehoshaphat also said to the king of **Israel**, "First seek the counsel
22: 6 So the king of **Israel** brought together the prophets—about four
22: 8 The king of **Israel** answered Jehoshaphat, "There is still one man
22: 9 So the king of **Israel** called one of his officials and said,
22:10 the king of **Israel** and Jehoshaphat king of Judah were sitting on
22:17 "I saw all **Israel** scattered on the hills like sheep without a
22:18 The king of **Israel** said to Jehoshaphat, "Didn't I tell you that he
22:26 The king of **Israel** then ordered, "Take Micaiah and send him back
22:29 So the king of **Israel** and Jehoshaphat king of Judah went up to
22:30 The king of **Israel** said to Jehoshaphat, "I will enter the battle in
22:30 So the king of **Israel** disguised himself and went into battle.
22:31 not fight with anyone, small or great, except the king of **Israel**."
22:32 saw Jehoshaphat, they thought, "Surely this is the king of **Israel**."
22:33 the chariot commanders saw that he was not the king of **Israel**
22:34 and hit the king of **Israel** between the sections of his armor.
22:39 they not written in the book of the annals of the kings of **Israel**?
22:41 became king of Judah in the fourth year of Ahab king of **Israel**.
22:44 [22:45] Jehoshaphat was also at peace with the king of **Israel**.
22:51 [22:52] Ahaziah son of Ahab became king of **Israel** in Samaria in
22:51 [22:52] king of Judah, and he reigned over **Israel** two years.
22:52 [22:53] ways of Jeroboam son of Nebat, who caused **Israel** to sin.
22:53 [22:54] the God of **Israel**, to anger, just as his father had done.
2Ki 1: 1 After Ahab's death, Moab rebelled against **Israel**.
1: 3 because there is no God in **Israel** that you are going off to consult
1: 6 because there is no God in **Israel** that you are sending men to
1:16 because there is no God in **Israel** for you to consult that you have
1:18 they not written in the book of the annals of the kings of **Israel**?
2:12 "My father! My father! The chariots and horsemen of **Israel**!"
3: 1 Joram son of Ahab became king of **Israel** in Samaria in the
3: 3 of Jeroboam son of Nebat, which he had caused **Israel** to commit;
3: 4 he had to supply the king of **Israel** with a hundred thousand lambs
3: 5 Ahab died, the king of Moab rebelled against the king of **Israel**.
3: 6 time King Joram set out from Samaria and mobilized all **Israel**.
3: 9 So the king of **Israel** set out with the king of Judah and the king of
3:10 "What!" exclaimed the king of **Israel**. "Has the LORD called us
3:11 An officer of the king of **Israel** answered, "Elisha son of Shaphat
3:12 So the king of **Israel** and Jehoshaphat and the king of Edom went
3:13 Elisha said to the king of **Israel**, "What do we have to do with each
3:13 "No," the king of **Israel** answered, "because it was the LORD
3:24 when the Moabites came to the camp of **Israel**, the Israelites rose
3:24 of Israel, the **Israelites** rose up and fought them until they fled.
3:27 The fury against **Israel** was great; they withdrew and returned to
5: 2 gone out and had taken captive a young girl from **Israel** [+824],
5: 4 his master and told him what the girl from **Israel** [+824] had said.
5: 5 "I will send a letter to the king of **Israel**." So Naaman left,
5: 6 The letter that he took to the king of **Israel** read: "With this letter I
5: 7 As soon as the king of **Israel** read the letter, he tore his robes
5: 8 When Elisha the man of God heard that the king of **Israel** had torn
5: 8 come to me and he will know that there is a prophet in **Israel**."
5:12 the rivers of Damascus, better than any of the waters of **Israel**?
5:15 "Now I know that there is no God in all the world except in **Israel**.
6: 8 Now the king of Aram was at war with **Israel**. After conferring
6: 9 The man of God sent word to the king of **Israel**: "Beware of
6:10 So the king of **Israel** checked on the place indicated by the man of
6:11 you not tell me which of us is on the side of the king of **Israel**?"
6:12 said one of his officers, "but Elisha, the prophet who is in **Israel**,
6:12 tells the king of **Israel** the very words you speak in your bedroom."
6:21 When the king of **Israel** saw them, he asked Elisha, "Shall I kill
6:23 So the bands from Aram stopped raiding **Israel's** territory.
6:26 As the king of **Israel** was passing by on the wall, a woman cried to
7: 6 the king of **Israel** has hired the Hittite and Egyptian kings to attack
7:13 Their plight will be like that of all the **Israelites** left here—
7:13 they will only be like all these **Israelites** who are doomed.
8:12 "Because I know the harm you will do to the **Israelites** [+1201],"
8:16 In the fifth year of Joram son of Ahab king of **Israel**,
8:18 He walked in the ways of the kings of **Israel**, as the house of Ahab
8:25 In the twelfth year of Joram son of Ahab king of **Israel**,
8:26 name was Athaliah, a granddaughter of Omri king of **Israel**.
9: 3 I anoint you king over **Israel**.' Then open the door and run;
9: 6 and declared, "This is what the LORD, the God of **Israel**, says:
9: 6 of Israel, says: 'I anoint you king over the LORD's people **Israel**.
9: 8 I will cut off from Ahab every last male in **Israel**—slave or free.
9:12 'This is what the LORD says: I anoint you king over **Israel**.' "
9:14 all **Israel** had been defending Ramoth Gilead against Hazael king
9:21 Joram king of **Israel** and Ahaziah king of Judah rode out,
10:21 he sent word throughout **Israel**, and all the ministers of Baal came;
10:28 So Jehu destroyed Baal worship in **Israel**.
10:29 of Jeroboam son of Nebat, which he had caused **Israel** to commit—
10:30 your descendants will sit on the throne of **Israel** to the fourth
10:31 to keep the law of the LORD, the God of **Israel**, with all his heart.
10:31 from the sins of Jeroboam, which he had caused **Israel** to commit.
10:32 In those days the LORD began to reduce the size of **Israel**.
10:32 Hazael overpowered the **Israelites** throughout their territory
10:34 they not written in the book of the annals of the kings of **Israel**?
10:36 The time that Jehu reigned over **Israel** in Samaria was
13: 1 Jehoahaz son of Jehu became king of **Israel** in Samaria, and he
13: 2 which he had caused **Israel** to commit, and he did not turn away
13: 3 So the LORD's anger burned against **Israel**, and for a long time
13: 4 for he saw how severely the king of Aram was oppressing **Israel**.
13: 5 The LORD provided a deliverer for **Israel**, and they escaped from
13: 5 So the **Israelites** [+1201] lived in their own homes as they had
13: 6 of the house of Jeroboam, which he had caused **Israel** to commit;
13: 8 they not written in the book of the annals of the kings of **Israel**?
13:10 Jehoash son of Jehoahaz became king of **Israel** in Samaria,
13:11 of Jeroboam son of Nebat, which he had caused **Israel** to commit;
13:12 they not written in the book of the annals of the kings of **Israel**?
13:13 the throne. Jehoash was buried in Samaria with the kings of **Israel**.
13:14 Jehoash king of **Israel** went down to see him and wept over him.
13:14 My father!" he cried. "The chariots and horsemen of **Israel**!"
13:16 "Take the bow in your hands," he said to the king of **Israel**.
13:18 Then he said, "Take the arrows," and the king **[RPH]** took them.
13:22 Hazael king of Aram oppressed **Israel** throughout the reign of
13:25 Jehoash defeated him, and so he recovered the **Israelite** towns.
14: 1 In the second year of Jehoash son of Jehoahaz king of **Israel**,
14: 8 of Jehoahaz, the son of Jehu, king of **Israel**, with the challenge:
14: 9 But Jehoash king of **Israel** replied to Amaziah king of Judah:
14:11 however, would not listen, so Jehoash king of **Israel** attacked.
14:12 Judah was routed by **Israel**, and every man fled to his home.
14:13 Jehoash king of **Israel** captured Amaziah king of Judah, the son of
14:15 they not written in the book of the annals of the kings of **Israel**?
14:16 with his fathers and was buried in Samaria with the kings of **Israel**.
14:17 years after the death of Jehoash son of Jehoahaz king of **Israel**.
14:23 Jeroboam son of Jehoash king of **Israel** became king in Samaria,
14:24 of Jeroboam son of Nebat, which he had caused **Israel** to commit.
14:25 He was the one who restored the boundaries of **Israel** from Lebo
14:25 in accordance with the word of the LORD, the God of **Israel**,
14:26 The LORD had seen how bitterly everyone in **Israel**, whether
14:26 or free, was suffering; there was no one to help **them**[s].
14:27 since the LORD had not said he would blot out the name of **Israel**
14:28 including how he recovered for **Israel** both Damascus and Hamath,
14:28 they not written in the book of the annals of the kings of **Israel**?
14:29 Jeroboam rested with his fathers, the kings of **Israel**.
15: 1 In the twenty-seventh year of Jeroboam king of **Israel**, Azariah son
15: 8 Zechariah son of Jeroboam became king of **Israel** in Samaria,
15: 9 of Jeroboam son of Nebat, which he had caused **Israel** to commit.
15:11 reign are written in the book of the annals of the kings of **Israel**.
15:12 "Your descendants will sit on the throne of **Israel** to the fourth
15:15 are written in the book of the annals of the kings of **Israel**.
15:17 Menahem son of Gadi became king of **Israel**, and he reigned in
15:18 of Jeroboam son of Nebat, which he had caused **Israel** to commit.
15:20 Menahem exacted this money from **Israel**. Every wealthy man had
15:21 they not written in the book of the annals of the kings of **Israel**?
15:23 Pekahiah son of Menahem became king of **Israel** in Samaria,
15:24 of Jeroboam son of Nebat, which he had caused **Israel** to commit.
15:26 are written in the book of the annals of the kings of **Israel**.
15:27 Pekah son of Remaliah became king of **Israel** in Samaria,
15:28 of Jeroboam son of Nebat, which he had caused **Israel** to commit.
15:29 In the time of Pekah king of **Israel**, Tiglath-Pileser king of Assyria
15:31 they not written in the book of the annals of the kings of **Israel**?
15:32 In the second year of Pekah son of Remaliah king of **Israel**,
16: 3 He walked in the ways of the kings of **Israel** and even sacrificed
16: 3 nations the LORD had driven out before the **Israelites** [+1201].
16: 5 Pekah son of Remaliah king of **Israel** marched up to fight against
16: 7 me out of the hand of the king of Aram and of the king of **Israel**,
17: 1 Hoshea son of Elah became king of **Israel** in Samaria, and he
17: 2 of the LORD, but not like the kings of **Israel** who preceded him.
17: 6 of Assyria captured Samaria and deported the **Israelites** to Assyria.
17: 7 because the **Israelites** [+1201] had sinned against the LORD their
17: 8 of the nations the LORD had driven out before **them**[s] [+1201],
17: 8 as well as the practices that the kings of **Israel** had introduced.
17: 9 The **Israelites** [+1201] secretly did things against the LORD their
17:13 The LORD warned **Israel** and Judah through all his prophets
17:18 So the LORD was very angry with **Israel** and removed them from
17:19 their God. They followed the practices **Israel** had introduced.

2Ki 17:20 Therefore the LORD rejected all the people of **Israel**; he afflicted
17:21 When he tore **Israel** away from the house of David, they made
17:21 Jeroboam enticed **Israel** away from following the LORD
17:22 The **Israelites** [+1201] persisted in all the sins of Jeroboam
17:23 until the LORD removed **them**[s] from his presence, as he had
17:23 So the people of **Israel** were taken from their homeland into exile
17:24 them in the towns of Samaria to replace the **Israelites** [+1201].
17:34 LORD gave the descendants of Jacob, whom he named **Israel**.
18: 1 In the third year of Hoshea son of Elah king of **Israel**,
18: 4 for up to that time the **Israelites** [+1201] had been burning incense
18: 5 Hezekiah trusted in the LORD, the God of **Israel**. There was no
18: 9 which was the seventh year of Hoshea son of Elah king of **Israel**,
18:10 sixth year, which was the ninth year of Hoshea king of **Israel**.
18:11 The king of Assyria deported **Israel** to Assyria and settled them in
19:15 "O LORD, God of **Israel**, enthroned between the cherubim,
19:20 to Hezekiah: "This is what the LORD, the God of **Israel**, says:
19:22 and lifted your eyes in pride? Against the Holy One of **Israel**!
21: 2 nations the LORD had driven out before the **Israelites** [+1201].
21: 3 and made an Asherah pole, as Ahab king of **Israel** had done.
21: 7 in Jerusalem, which I have chosen out of all the tribes of **Israel**,
21: 8 I will not again make the feet of the **Israelites** wander from the
21: 9 nations the LORD had destroyed before the **Israelites** [+1201].
21:12 Therefore this is what the LORD, the God of **Israel**, says:
22:15 said to them, "This is what the LORD, the God of **Israel**, says:
22:18 'This is what the LORD, the God of **Israel**, says concerning the
23:13 the ones Solomon king of **Israel** had built for Ashtoreth the vile
23:15 made by Jeroboam son of Nebat, who had caused **Israel** to sin—
23:19 defiled all the shrines at the high places that the kings of **Israel** had
23:22 Not since the days of the judges who led **Israel**, nor throughout the
23:22 nor throughout the days of the kings of **Israel** and the kings of
23:27 "I will remove Judah also from my presence as I removed **Israel**,
24:13 took away all the gold articles that Solomon king of **Israel** had
1Ch 1:34 was the father of Isaac. The sons of Isaac: Esau and **Israel**.
1:43 reigned in Edom before any **Israelite** [+1201+4200] king reigned:
2: 1 These were the sons of **Israel**: Reuben, Simeon, Levi, Judah,
2: 7 who brought trouble on **Israel** by violating the ban on taking
4:10 Jabez cried out to the God of **Israel**, "Oh, that you would bless me
5: 1 The sons of Reuben the firstborn of **Israel** (he was the firstborn,
5: 1 rights as firstborn were given to the sons of Joseph son of **Israel**;
5: 3 the sons of Reuben the firstborn of **Israel**: Hanoch, Pallu,
5:17 the reigns of Jotham king of Judah and Jeroboam king of **Israel**.
5:26 So the God of **Israel** stirred up the spirit of Pul king of Assyria
6:38 [6:23] the son of Kohath, the son of Levi, the son of **Israel**;
6:49 [6:34] making atonement for **Israel**, in accordance with all that
6:64 [6:49] So the **Israelites** [+1201] gave the Levites these towns
7:29 The descendants of Joseph son of **Israel** lived in these towns.
9: 1 All **Israel** was listed in the genealogies recorded in the book of the
9: 1 in the genealogies recorded in the book of the kings of **Israel**.
9: 2 on their own property in their own towns were *some* **Israelites**,
10: 1 Now the Philistines fought against **Israel**; the Israelites fled before
10: 1 the **Israelites** [+408] fled before them, and many fell slain on
10: 7 When all the **Israelites** [+408] in the valley saw that the army had
11: 1 All **Israel** came together to David at Hebron and said, "We are
11: 2 you were the one who led **Israel** on their military campaigns.
11: 2 'You will shepherd my people **Israel**, and you will become their
11: 2 people Israel, and you will become **their**[s] [+3276+6639] ruler.' "
11: 3 When all the elders of **Israel** had come to King David at Hebron,
11: 3 they anointed David king over **Israel**, as the LORD had promised
11: 4 David and all the **Israelites** marched to Jerusalem (that is,
11:10 they, together with all **Israel**, gave his kingship strong support to
11:10 gave his kingship strong support to extend it over **the whole land**[s],
12:32 [12:33] understood the times and knew what **Israel** should do—
12:38 [12:39] fully determined to make David king over all **Israel**.
12:38 [12:39] All the rest of the **Israelites** were also of one mind to
12:40 [12:41] oil, cattle and sheep, for there was joy in **Israel**.
13: 2 He then said to the whole assembly of **Israel**, "If it seems good to
13: 2 wide to the rest of our brothers throughout the territories of **Israel**,
13: 5 So David assembled all the **Israelites**, from the Shihor River in
13: 6 all the **Israelites** with him went to Baalah of Judah (Kiriath Jearim)
13: 8 all the **Israelites** were celebrating with all their might before God,
14: 2 knew that the LORD had established him as king over **Israel**
14: 2 kingdom had been highly exalted for the sake of his people **Israel**.
14: 8 Philistines heard that David had been anointed king over all **Israel**,
15: 3 David assembled all **Israel** in Jerusalem to bring up the ark of the
15:12 the LORD, the God of **Israel**, to the place I have prepared for it.
15:14 in order to bring up the ark of the LORD, the God of **Israel**.
15:25 So David and the elders of **Israel** and the commanders of units of a
15:28 So all **Israel** brought up the ark of the covenant of the LORD
16: 3 and a cake of raisins to each **Israelite** [+408] man and woman.
16: 4 to give thanks, and to praise the LORD, the God of **Israel**:
16:13 O descendants of **Israel** his servant, O sons of Jacob, his chosen
16:17 it to Jacob as a decree, to **Israel** as an everlasting covenant:
16:36 Praise be to the LORD, the God of **Israel**, from everlasting to
16:40 written in the Law of the LORD, which he had given **Israel**.
17: 5 I have not dwelt in a house from the day I brought **Israel** up out of
17: 6 Wherever I have moved with all the **Israelites**, did I ever say to
17: 6 did I ever say to any of **their**[s] leaders whom I commanded to
17: 7 and from following the flock, to be ruler over my people **Israel**.
17: 9 And I will provide a place for my people **Israel** and will plant them
17:10 done ever since the time I appointed leaders over my people **Israel**.
17:21 who is like your people **Israel**—the one nation on earth whose God
17:22 You made your people **Israel** your very own forever, and you,
17:24 'The LORD Almighty, the God over **Israel**, is Israel's God!'
17:24 LORD Almighty, the God over Israel, is **Israel's** [+4200] God!'
18:14 David reigned over all **Israel**, doing what was just and right for all
19:10 so he selected some of the best troops in **Israel** and deployed them
19:16 After the Arameans saw that they had been routed by **Israel**,
19:17 was told of this, he gathered all **Israel** and crossed the Jordan;
19:18 they fled before **Israel**, and David killed seven thousand of their
19:19 vassals of Hadadezer saw that they had been defeated by **Israel**,
20: 7 When he taunted **Israel**, Jonathan son of Shimea, David's brother,
21: 1 Satan rose up against **Israel** and incited David to take a census of
21: 1 rose up against Israel and incited David to take a census of **Israel**.
21: 2 of the troops, "Go and count the **Israelites** from Beersheba to Dan.
21: 3 my lord want to do this? Why should he bring guilt on **Israel**?"
21: 4 so Joab left and went throughout **Israel** and then came back to
21: 5 In all **Israel** there were one million one hundred thousand men
21: 7 command was also evil in the sight of God; so he punished **Israel**.
21:12 with the angel of the LORD ravaging every part of **Israel**.'
21:14 So the LORD sent a plague on **Israel**, and seventy thousand men
21:14 a plague on Israel, and seventy thousand men of **Israel** fell dead.
22: 1 God is to be here, and also the altar of burnt offering for **Israel**."
22: 2 David gave orders to assemble the aliens living in **Israel** [+824],
22: 6 charged him to build a house for the LORD, the God of **Israel**.
22: 9 and I will grant **Israel** peace and quiet during his reign.
22:10 And I will establish the throne of his kingdom over **Israel** forever.'
22:12 and understanding when he puts you in command over **Israel**,
22:13 the decrees and laws that the LORD gave Moses for **Israel**.
22:17 David ordered all the leaders of **Israel** to help his son Solomon.
23: 1 and full of years, he made his son Solomon king over **Israel**.
23: 2 He also gathered together all the leaders of **Israel**, as well as the
23:25 For David had said, "Since the LORD, the God of **Israel**,
24:19 as the LORD, the God of **Israel**, had commanded him.
26:29 duties away from the temple, as officials and judges over **Israel**.
26:30 were responsible in **Israel** west of the Jordan for all the work of the
27: 1 This is the list of the **Israelites** [+1201]—heads of families,
27:16 The officers over the tribes of **Israel**: over the Reubenites:
27:22 son of Jeroham. These were the officers over the tribes of **Israel**.
27:23 because the LORD had promised to make **Israel** as numerous as
27:24 Wrath came on **Israel** on account of this numbering,
28: 1 David summoned all the officials of **Israel** to assemble at
28: 4 "Yet the LORD, the God of **Israel**, chose me from my whole
28: 4 chose me from my whole family to be king over **Israel** forever.
28: 4 my father's sons he was pleased to make me king over all **Israel**.
28: 5 to sit on the throne of the kingdom of the LORD over **Israel**.
28: 8 "So now I charge you in the sight of all **Israel** and of the assembly
29: 6 Then the leaders of families, the officers of the tribes of **Israel**,
29:10 saying, "Praise be to you, O LORD, God of our father **Israel**,
29:18 O LORD, God of our fathers Abraham, Isaac and **Israel**,
29:21 drink offerings, and other sacrifices in abundance for all **Israel**.
29:23 place of his father David. He prospered and all **Israel** obeyed him.
29:25 The LORD highly exalted Solomon in the sight of all **Israel**
29:25 bestowed on him royal splendor such as no king over **Israel** ever
29:26 David son of Jesse was king over all **Israel**.
29:27 He ruled over **Israel** forty years—seven in Hebron and thirty-three
29:30 surrounded him and **Israel** and the kingdoms of all the other lands.
2Ch 1: 2 Solomon spoke to all **Israel**—to the commanders of thousands
1: 2 to the judges and to all the leaders in **Israel**, the heads of families—
1:13 from before the Tent of Meeting. And he reigned over **Israel**.
2: 4 [2:3] the LORD our God. This is a lasting ordinance for **Israel**.
2:12 [2:11] the God of **Israel**, who made heaven and earth!
2:17 [2:16] took a census of all the aliens who were in **Israel** [+824],
5: 2 Then Solomon summoned to Jerusalem the elders of **Israel**,
5: 2 heads of the tribes and the chiefs of the **Israelite** [+1201] families,
5: 3 all the men of **Israel** came together to the king at the time of the
5: 4 When all the elders of **Israel** had arrived, the Levites took up the
5: 6 the entire assembly of **Israel** that had gathered about him were
5:10 where the LORD made a covenant with the **Israelites** [+1201]
6: 3 While the whole assembly of **Israel** was standing there, the king
6: 3 the king turned around and blessed **them**[s] [+3972+7736].
6: 4 "Praise be to the LORD, the God of **Israel**, who with his hands
6: 5 I have not chosen a city in any tribe of **Israel** to have a temple built
6: 5 nor have I chosen anyone to be the leader over my people **Israel**.
6: 6 to be there, and I have chosen David to rule my people **Israel**.'
6: 7 to build a temple for the Name of the LORD, the God of **Israel**.
6:10 succeeded David my father and now I sit on the throne of **Israel**,
6:10 built the temple for the Name of the LORD, the God of **Israel**.
6:11 covenant of the LORD that he made with the people of **Israel**."

2Ch 6:12 the altar of the LORD in front of the whole assembly of **Israel**
6:13 and then knelt down before the whole assembly of **Israel**
6:14 "O LORD, God of **Israel**, there is no God like you in heaven
6:16 "Now LORD, God of **Israel**, keep for your servant David my
6:16 never fail to have a man to sit before me on the throne of **Israel**,
6:17 now, O LORD, God of **Israel**, let your word that you promised
6:21 and of your people **Israel** when they pray toward this place.
6:24 "When your people **Israel** have been defeated by an enemy
6:25 then hear from heaven and forgive the sin of your people **Israel**
6:27 and forgive the sin of your servants, your people **Israel**.
6:29 and when a prayer or plea is made by any of your people **Israel**—
6:32 "As for the foreigner who does not belong to your people **Israel**
6:33 may know your name and fear you, as do your own people **Israel**,
7:3 When all the **Israelites** [+1201] saw the fire coming down
7:6 the priests blew their trumpets, and all the **Israelites** were standing.
7:8 the festival at that time for seven days, and all **Israel** with him—
7:10 had done for David and Solomon and for his people **Israel**.
7:18 when I said, 'You shall never fail to have a man to rule over **Israel**.'
8:2 that Hiram had given him, and settled **Israelites** [+1201] in them.
8:7 and Jebusites (these peoples were not **Israelites**),
8:8 in the land, whom the **Israelites** [+1201] had not destroyed—
8:9 Solomon did not make slaves of the **Israelites** [+1201] for his
8:11 "My wife must not live in the palace of David king of **Israel**,
9:8 Because of the love of your God for **Israel** and his desire to uphold
9:30 Solomon reigned in Jerusalem over all **Israel** forty years.
10:1 to Shechem, for all the **Israelites** had gone there to make him king.
10:3 and he and all **Israel** went to Rehoboam and said to him:
10:16 When all **Israel** saw that the king refused to listen to them,
10:16 have in David, what part in Jesse's son? To your tents, O **Israel**!
10:16 after your own house, O David!" So all the **Israelites** went home.
10:17 as for the **Israelites** [+1201] who were living in the towns of
10:18 of forced labor, but the **Israelites** [+1201] stoned him to death.
10:19 So **Israel** has been in rebellion against the house of David to this
11:1 to make war against **Israel** and to regain the kingdom for
11:3 king of Judah and to all the **Israelites** in Judah and Benjamin,
11:13 Levites from all their districts throughout **Israel** sided with him.
11:16 Those from every tribe of **Israel** who set their hearts on seeking
11:16 the God of **Israel**, followed the Levites to Jerusalem to offer
12:1 and all **Israel** with him abandoned the law of the LORD.
12:6 The leaders of **Israel** and the king humbled themselves and said,
12:13 the city the LORD had chosen out of all the tribes of **Israel** in
13:4 of Ephraim, and said, "Jeroboam and all **Israel**, listen to me!
13:5 Don't you know that the LORD, the God of **Israel**, has given the
13:5 has given the kingship of **Israel** to David and his descendants
13:12 Men of **Israel**, do not fight against the LORD, the God of your
13:15 God routed Jeroboam and all **Israel** before Abijah and Judah.
13:16 The **Israelites** [+1201] fled before Judah, and God delivered them
13:17 so that there were five hundred thousand casualties among **Israel's**
13:18 The men of **Israel** were subdued on that occasion, and the men of
15:3 For a long time **Israel** was without the true God, without a priest to
15:4 the God of **Israel**, and sought him, and he was found by them.
15:9 for large numbers had come over to him from **Israel** when they
15:13 the God of **Israel**, were to be put to death, whether small or great,
15:17 Although he did not remove the high places from **Israel**,
16:1 In the thirty-sixth year of Asa's reign Baasha king of **Israel** went
16:3 Now break your treaty with Baasha king of **Israel** so he will
16:4 and sent the commanders of his forces against the towns of **Israel**.
16:11 to end, are written in the book of the kings of Judah and **Israel**.
17:1 son succeeded him as king and strengthened himself against **Israel**.
17:4 and followed his commands rather than the practices of **Israel**.
18:3 Ahab king of **Israel** asked Jehoshaphat king of Judah, "Will you
18:4 Jehoshaphat also said to the king of **Israel**, "First seek the counsel
18:5 So the king of **Israel** brought together the prophets—four hundred
18:7 The king of **Israel** answered Jehoshaphat, "There is still one man
18:8 So the king of **Israel** called one of his officials and said,
18:9 the king of **Israel** and Jehoshaphat king of Judah were sitting on
18:16 "I saw all **Israel** scattered on the hills like sheep without a
18:17 The king of **Israel** said to Jehoshaphat, "Didn't I tell you that he
18:19 'Who will entice Ahab king of **Israel** into attacking Ramoth Gilead
18:25 The king of **Israel** then ordered, "Take Micaiah and send him back
18:28 So the king of **Israel** and Jehoshaphat king of Judah went up to
18:29 The king of **Israel** said to Jehoshaphat, "I will enter the battle in
18:29 So the king of **Israel** disguised himself and went into battle.
18:30 not fight with anyone, small or great, except the king of **Israel**."
18:31 saw Jehoshaphat, they thought, "This is the king of **Israel**."
18:32 the chariot commanders saw that he was not the king of **Israel**,
18:33 and hit the king of **Israel** between the sections of his armor.
18:34 the king of **Israel** propped himself up in his chariot facing the
19:8 and heads of **Israelite** families to administer the law of the LORD
20:7 not drive out the inhabitants of this land before your people **Israel**
20:10 whose territory you would not allow **Israel** to invade when they
20:19 and praised the LORD, the God of **Israel**, with very loud voice.
20:29 heard how the LORD had fought against the enemies of **Israel**.
20:34 of Hanani, which are recorded in the book of the kings of **Israel**.
20:35 king of Judah made an alliance with Ahaziah king of **Israel**,
21:2 and Shephatiah. All these were sons of Jehoshaphat king of **Israel**.
21:4 his brothers to the sword along with some of the princes of **Israel**.
21:6 He walked in the ways of the kings of **Israel**, as the house of Ahab
21:13 you have walked in the ways of the kings of **Israel**, and you have
22:5 of **Israel** to war against Hazael king of Aram at Ramoth Gilead.
23:2 the Levites and the heads of **Israelite** families from all the towns.
24:5 towns of Judah and collect the money due annually from all **Israel**,
24:6 and by the assembly of **Israel** for the Tent of the Testimony?"
24:9 that Moses the servant of God had required of **Israel** in the desert.
24:16 because of the good he had done in **Israel** for God and his temple.
25:6 He also hired a hundred thousand fighting men from **Israel** for a
25:7 "O king, these troops from **Israel** must not march with you,
25:7 Israel must not march with you, for the LORD is not with **Israel**—
25:9 "But what about the hundred talents I paid for these **Israelite**
25:17 to Jehoash son of Jehoahaz, the son of Jehu, king of **Israel**:
25:18 But Jehoash king of **Israel** replied to Amaziah king of Judah:
25:21 So Jehoash king of **Israel** attacked. He and Amaziah king of Judah
25:22 Judah was routed by **Israel**, and every man fled to his home.
25:23 Jehoash king of **Israel** captured Amaziah king of Judah, the son of
25:25 years after the death of Jehoash son of Jehoahaz king of **Israel**.
25:26 are they not written in the book of the kings of Judah and **Israel**?
27:7 he did, are written in the book of the kings of **Israel** and Judah.
28:2 He walked in the ways of the kings of **Israel** and also made cast
28:3 nations the LORD had driven out before the **Israelites** [+1201].
28:5 He was also given into the hands of the king of **Israel**, who
28:8 The **Israelites** [+1201] took captive from their kinsmen two
28:13 For our guilt is already great, and his fierce anger rests on **Israel**."
28:19 The LORD had humbled Judah because of Ahaz king of **Israel**,
28:23 But they were his downfall and the downfall of all **Israel**.
28:26 to end, are written in the book of the kings of Judah and **Israel**.
28:27 but he was not placed in the tombs of the kings of **Israel**.
29:7 or present any burnt offerings at the sanctuary to the God of **Israel**.
29:10 the God of **Israel**, so that his fierce anger will turn away from us.
29:24 their blood on the altar for a sin offering to atone for all **Israel**,
29:24 had ordered the burnt offering and the sin offering for all **Israel**.
29:27 by trumpets and the instruments of David king of **Israel**.
30:1 Hezekiah sent word to all **Israel** and Judah and also wrote letters to
30:1 and celebrate the Passover to the LORD, the God of **Israel**.
30:5 They decided to send a proclamation throughout **Israel**,
30:5 and celebrate the Passover to the LORD, the God of **Israel**.
30:6 couriers went throughout **Israel** and Judah with letters from the
30:6 "People of **Israel**, return to the LORD, the God of Abraham,
30:6 return to the LORD, the God of Abraham, Isaac and **Israel**,
30:21 The **Israelites** [+1201] who were present in Jerusalem celebrated
30:25 the priests and Levites and all who had assembled from **Israel**,
30:25 including the aliens who had come from **Israel** [+824] and those
30:26 for since the days of Solomon son of David king of **Israel** there
31:1 the **Israelites** who were there went out to the towns of Judah,
31:1 the **Israelites** [+1201] returned to their own towns and to their own
31:5 the **Israelites** [+1201] generously gave the firstfruits of their grain,
31:6 The men of **Israel** and Judah who lived in the towns of Judah also
31:8 the heaps, they praised the LORD and blessed his people **Israel**.
32:17 the LORD, the God of **Israel**, and saying this against him:
32:32 Isaiah son of Amoz in the book of the kings of Judah and **Israel**.
33:2 nations the LORD had driven out before the **Israelites** [+1201].
33:7 in Jerusalem, which I have chosen out of all the tribes of **Israel**,
33:8 I will not again make the feet of the **Israelites** leave the land I
33:9 nations the LORD had destroyed before the **Israelites** [+1201].
33:16 on it, and told Judah to serve the LORD, the God of **Israel**.
33:18 the God of **Israel**, are written in the annals of the kings of Israel.
33:18 the God of Israel, are written in the annals of the kings of **Israel**.
34:7 and cut to pieces all the incense altars throughout **Israel** [+824].
34:9 Ephraim and the entire remnant of **Israel** and from all the people
34:21 and inquire of the LORD for me and for the remnant in **Israel**
34:23 said to them, "This is what the LORD, the God of **Israel**, says:
34:26 'This is what the LORD, the God of **Israel**, says concerning the
34:33 idols from all the territory belonging to the **Israelites** [+1201],
34:33 he had all who were present in **Israel** serve the LORD their God.
35:3 who instructed all **Israel** and who had been consecrated to the
35:3 ark in the temple that Solomon son of David king of **Israel** built.
35:3 Now serve the LORD your God and his people **Israel**.
35:4 according to the directions written by David king of **Israel**
35:17 The **Israelites** [+1201] who were present celebrated the Passover
35:18 The Passover had not been observed like this in **Israel** since the
35:18 none of the kings of **Israel** had ever celebrated such a Passover as
35:18 all Judah and **Israel** who were there with the people of Jerusalem.
35:25 These became a tradition in **Israel** and are written in the Laments.
35:27 to end, are written in the book of the kings of **Israel** and Judah.
36:8 are written in the book of the kings of **Israel** and Judah.
36:13 his heart and would not turn to the LORD, the God of **Israel**.
Ezr 1:3 of the LORD, the God of **Israel**, the God who is in Jerusalem.
2:2 Rehum and Baanah): The list of the men of the people of **Israel**:
2:59 could not show that their families were descended from **Israel**:

Ezr 2:70 other people, and the rest of the **Israelites** settled in their towns.
3: 1 month came and the **Israelites** [+1201] had settled in their towns,
3: 2 his associates began to build the altar of the God of **Israel** to
3:10 places to praise the LORD, as prescribed by David king of **Israel**.
3:11 to the LORD: "He is good; his love to **Israel** endures forever."
4: 1 exiles were building a temple for the LORD, the God of **Israel**,
4: 3 and the rest of the heads of the families of **Israel** answered,
4: 3 the God of **Israel**, as King Cyrus, the king of Persia,
6:21 So the **Israelites** [+1201] who had returned from the exile ate it,
6:21 Gentile neighbors in order to seek the LORD, the God of **Israel**.
6:22 assisted them in the work on the house of God, the God of **Israel**.
7: 6 Law of Moses, which the LORD, the God of **Israel**, had given.
7: 7 Some of the **Israelites** [+1201], including priests, Levites,
7:10 Law of the LORD, and to teaching its decrees and laws in **Israel**.
7:11 concerning the commands and decrees of the LORD for **Israel**:
7:28 and gathered leading men from **Israel** to go up with me.
8:18 the son of **Israel**, and Sherebiah's sons and brothers, 18 men;
8:25 and all **Israel** present there had donated for the house of our God.
8:29 the leading priests and the Levites and the family heads of **Israel**."
8:35 from captivity sacrificed burnt offerings to the God of **Israel**:
8:35 twelve bulls for all **Israel**, ninety-six rams, seventy-seven male
9: 1 the leaders came to me and said, "The people of **Israel**,
9: 4 everyone who trembled at the words of the God of **Israel** gathered
9:15 O LORD, God of **Israel**, you are righteous! We are left this day
10: 1 down before the house of God, a large crowd of **Israelites**—
10: 2 peoples around us. But in spite of this, there is still hope for **Israel**.
10: 5 and all **Israel** under oath to do what had been suggested.
10:10 you have married foreign women, adding to **Israel's** guilt.
10:25 And among the other **Israelites**: From the descendants of Parosh:
Ne 1: 6 before you day and night for your servants, the people of **Israel**.
1: 6 I confess the sins we **Israelites** [+1201], including myself
2:10 had come to promote the welfare of the **Israelites** [+1201].
7: 7 Nehum and Baanah): The list of the men of **Israel** [+6639]:
7:61 could not show that their families were descended from **Israel**:
7:73 [7:72] with certain of the people and the rest of the **Israelites**,
7:73 [7:72] and the **Israelites** [+1201] had settled in their towns,
8: 1 the Law of Moses, which the LORD had commanded for **Israel**.
8:14 that the **Israelites** [+1201] were to live in booths during the feast
8:17 until that day, the **Israelites** [+1201] had not celebrated it like this.
9: 1 the **Israelites** [+1201] gathered together, fasting and wearing
9: 2 Those of **Israelite** descent had separated themselves from all
10:33 [10:34] for sin offerings to make atonement for **Israel**;
10:39 [10:40] The people of **Israel**, including the Levites, are to bring
11: 3 provincial leaders who settled in Jerusalem (now *some* **Israelites**,
11:20 The rest of the **Israelites**, with the priests and Levites, were in all
12:47 all **Israel** contributed the daily portions for the singers and
13: 2 because they had not met the **Israelites** [+1201] with food
13: 3 they excluded from **Israel** all who were of foreign descent.
13:18 Now you are stirring up more wrath against **Israel** by desecrating
13:26 because of marriages like these that Solomon king of **Israel**
13:26 He was loved by his God, and God made him king over all **Israel**,
Ps 14: 7 Oh, that salvation for **Israel** would come out of Zion!
14: 7 the fortunes of his people, let Jacob rejoice and **Israel** be glad!
22: 3 [22:4] are enthroned as the Holy One; you are the praise of **Israel**.
22:23 [22:24] honor him! Revere him, all you descendants of **Israel**!
25:22 Redeem **Israel**, O God, from all their troubles!
41:13 [41:14] Praise be to the LORD, the God of **Israel**,
50: 7 "Hear, O my people, and I will speak, O **Israel**, and I will testify
53: 6 [53:7] Oh, that salvation for **Israel** would come out of Zion!
53: 6 [53:7] fortunes of his people, let Jacob rejoice and **Israel** be glad!
59: 5 [59:6] O LORD God Almighty, the God of **Israel**,
68: 8 [68:9] the One of Sinai, before God, the God of **Israel**.
68:26 [68:27] praise the LORD in the assembly of **Israel**.
68:34 [68:35] Proclaim the power of God, whose majesty is over **Israel**,
68:35 [68:36] the God of **Israel** gives power and strength to his people.
69: 6 [69:7] you not be put to shame because of me, O God of **Israel**.
71:22 I will sing praise to you with the lyre, O Holy One of **Israel**.
72:18 Praise be to the LORD God, the God of **Israel**, who alone does
73: 1 Surely God is good to **Israel**, to those who are pure in heart.
76: 1 [76:2] In Judah God is known; his name is great in **Israel**.
78: 5 He decreed statutes for Jacob and established the law in **Israel**,
78:21 his fire broke out against Jacob, and his wrath rose against **Israel**,
78:31 the sturdiest among them, cutting down the young men of **Israel**.
78:41 again they put God to the test; they vexed the Holy One of **Israel**.
78:55 as an inheritance; he settled the tribes of **Israel** in their homes.
78:59 God heard them, he was very angry; he rejected **Israel** completely.
78:71 to be the shepherd of his people Jacob, of **Israel** his inheritance.
80: 1 [80:2] Hear us, O Shepherd of **Israel**, you who lead Joseph like a
81: 4 [81:5] this is a decree for **Israel**, an ordinance of the God of
81: 8 [81:9] I will warn you—if you would but listen to me, O **Israel**!
81:11 [81:12] would not listen to me; **Israel** would not submit to me.
81:13 [81:14] but listen to me, if **Israel** would follow my ways,
83: 4 [83:5] a nation, that the name of **Israel** be remembered no more."
89:18 [89:19] to the LORD, our king to the Holy One of **Israel**.
98: 3 remembered his love and his faithfulness to the house of **Israel**;
103: 7 made known his ways to Moses, his deeds to the people of **Israel**:
105:10 it to Jacob as a decree, to **Israel** as an everlasting covenant:
105:23 **Israel** entered Egypt; Jacob lived as an alien in the land of Ham.
106:48 Praise be to the LORD, the God of **Israel**, from everlasting to
114: 1 When **Israel** came out of Egypt, the house of Jacob from a people
114: 2 Judah became God's sanctuary, **Israel** his dominion.
115: 9 O house of **Israel**, trust in the LORD—he is their help and shield.
115:12 He will bless the house of **Israel**, he will bless the house of Aaron,
118: 2 Let **Israel** say: "His love endures forever."
121: 4 he who watches over **Israel** will neither slumber nor sleep.
122: 4 the name of the LORD according to the statute given to **Israel**.
124: 1 If the LORD had not been on our side—let **Israel** say—
125: 5 the LORD will banish with the evildoers. Peace be upon **Israel**.
128: 6 may you live to see your children's children. Peace be upon **Israel**.
129: 1 They have greatly oppressed me from my youth—let **Israel** say—
130: 7 O **Israel**, put your hope in the LORD, for with the LORD is
130: 8 He himself will redeem **Israel** from all their sins.
131: 3 O **Israel**, put your hope in the LORD both now and forevermore.
135: 4 chosen Jacob to be his own, **Israel** to be his treasured possession.
135:12 their land as an inheritance, an inheritance to his people **Israel**.
135:19 O house of **Israel**, praise the LORD; O house of Aaron, praise the
136:11 brought **Israel** out from among them *His love endures*
136:14 brought **Israel** through the midst of it, *His love endures*
136:22 an inheritance to his servant **Israel**; *His love endures*
147: 2 The LORD builds up Jerusalem; he gathers the exiles of **Israel**.
147:19 He has revealed his word to Jacob, his laws and decrees to **Israel**.
148:14 the praise of all his saints, of **Israel** [+1201], the people close to his
149: 2 Let **Israel** rejoice in their Maker; let the people of Zion be glad in
Pr 1: 1 The proverbs of Solomon son of David, king of **Israel**:
Ecc 1:12 I, the Teacher, was king over **Israel** in Jerusalem.
SS 3: 7 escorted by sixty warriors, the noblest of **Israel**,
Isa 1: 3 but **Israel** does not know, my people do not understand."
1: 4 they have spurned the Holy One of **Israel** and turned their backs
1:24 the LORD Almighty, the Mighty One of **Israel**, declares:
4: 2 of the land will be the pride and glory of the survivors in **Israel**.
5: 7 The vineyard of the LORD Almighty is the house of **Israel**,
5:19 Let it approach, let the plan of the Holy One of **Israel** come,
5:24 LORD Almighty and spurned the word of the Holy One of **Israel**.
7: 1 Pekah son of Remaliah king of **Israel** marched up to fight against
8:14 for both houses of **Israel** he will be a stone that causes men to
8:18 We are signs and symbols in **Israel** from the LORD Almighty,
9: 8 [9:7] Lord has sent a message against Jacob; it will fall on **Israel**.
9:12 [9:11] Philistines from the west have devoured **Israel** with open
9:14 [9:13] So the LORD will cut off from **Israel** both head and tail,
10:17 The Light of **Israel** will become a fire, their Holy One a flame;
10:20 In that day the remnant of **Israel**, the survivors of the house of
10:20 but will truly rely on the LORD, the Holy One of **Israel**.
10:22 Though your people, O **Israel**, be like the sand by the sea,
11:12 will raise a banner for the nations and gather the exiles of **Israel**;
11:16 as there was for **Israel** when they came up from Egypt.
12: 6 people of Zion, for great is the Holy One of **Israel** among you."
14: 1 once again he will choose **Israel** and will settle them in their own
14: 2 And the house of **Israel** will possess the nations as menservants
17: 3 remnant of Aram will be like the glory of the **Israelites** [+1201],"
17: 6 on the fruitful boughs," declares the LORD, the God of **Israel**.
17: 7 look to their Maker and turn their eyes to the Holy One of **Israel**.
17: 9 strong cities, which they left because of the **Israelites** [+1201],
19:24 In that day **Israel** will be the third, along with Egypt and Assyria,
19:25 my people, Assyria my handiwork, and **Israel** my inheritance."
21:10 I have heard from the LORD Almighty, from the God of **Israel**.
21:17 will be few." The LORD, the God of **Israel**, has spoken.
24:15 name of the LORD, the God of **Israel**, in the islands of the sea.
27: 6 **Israel** will bud and blossom and fill all the world with fruit.
27:12 and you, O **Israelites** [+1201], will be gathered up one by one.
29:19 in the LORD; the needy will rejoice in the Holy One of **Israel**.
29:23 the Holy One of Jacob, and will stand in awe of the God of **Israel**.
30:11 off this path, and stop confronting us with the Holy One of **Israel**!"
30:12 Therefore, this is what the Holy One of **Israel** says: "Because you
30:15 This is what the Sovereign LORD, the Holy One of **Israel**, says:
30:29 with flutes to the mountain of the LORD, to the Rock of **Israel**.
31: 1 do not look to the Holy One of **Israel**, or seek help from the
31: 6 to him you have so greatly revolted against, O **Israelites** [+1201].
37:16 "O LORD Almighty, God of **Israel**, enthroned between the
37:21 to Hezekiah: "This is what the LORD, the God of **Israel**, says:
37:23 and lifted your eyes in pride? Against the Holy One of **Israel**!
40:27 Why do you say, O Jacob, and complain, O **Israel**, "My way is
41: 8 "But you, O **Israel**, my servant, Jacob, whom I have chosen,
41:14 Do not be afraid, O worm Jacob, O little **Israel**, for I myself will
41:14 declares the LORD, your Redeemer, the Holy One of **Israel**.
41:16 you will rejoice in the LORD and glory in the Holy One of **Israel**.
41:17 will answer them; I, the God of **Israel**, will not forsake them.
41:20 LORD has done this, that the Holy One of **Israel** has created it.
42:24 handed Jacob over to become loot, and **Israel** to the plunderers?

Isa 43: 1 he who created you, O Jacob, he who formed you, O **Israel**:
43: 3 I am the LORD, your God, the Holy One of **Israel**, your Savior;
43: 14 is what the LORD says—your Redeemer, the Holy One of **Israel**:
43: 15 I am the LORD, your Holy One, **Israel's** Creator, your King."
43: 22 O Jacob, you have not wearied yourselves for me, O **Israel**.
43: 28 and I will consign Jacob to destruction and **Israel** to scorn.
44: 1 "But now listen, O Jacob, my servant, **Israel**, whom I have chosen.
44: 5 write on his hand, 'The LORD's,' and will take the name **Israel**.
44: 6 **Israel's** King and Redeemer, the LORD Almighty:
44: 21 these things, O Jacob, for you are my servant, O **Israel**.
44: 21 have made you, you are my servant; O **Israel**, I will not forget you.
44: 23 the LORD has redeemed Jacob, he displays his glory in **Israel**.
45: 3 I am the LORD, the God of **Israel**, who summons you by name.
45: 4 of **Israel** my chosen, I summon you by name and bestow on you a
45: 11 is what the LORD says—the Holy One of **Israel**, and its Maker:
45: 15 you are a God who hides himself, O God and Savior of **Israel**.
45: 17 **Israel** will be saved by the LORD with an everlasting salvation;
45: 25 in the LORD all the descendants of **Israel** will be found righteous
46: 3 O house of Jacob, all you who remain of the house of **Israel**,
46: 13 be delayed. I will grant salvation to Zion, my splendor to **Israel**.
47: 4 the LORD Almighty is his name—is the Holy One of **Israel**.
48: 1 you who are called by the name of **Israel** and come from the line
48: 1 oaths in the name of the LORD and invoke the God of **Israel**—
48: 2 yourselves citizens of the holy city and rely on the God of **Israel**—
48: 12 "Listen to me, O Jacob, **Israel**, whom I have called: I am he;
48: 17 is what the LORD says—your Redeemer, the Holy One of **Israel**:
49: 3 He said to me, "You are my servant, **Israel**, in whom I will display
49: 5 his servant to bring Jacob back to him and gather **Israel** to himself,
49: 6 the tribes of Jacob and bring back those of **Israel** I have kept.
49: 7 the Redeemer and Holy One of **Israel**—to him who was despised
49: 7 who is faithful, the Holy One of **Israel**, who has chosen you."
52: 12 will go before you, the God of **Israel** will be your rear guard.
54: 5 the Holy One of **Israel** is your Redeemer; he is called the God of
55: 5 because of the LORD your God, the Holy One of **Israel**,
56: 8 Sovereign LORD declares—he who gathers the exiles of **Israel**:
60: 9 to the honor of the LORD your God, the Holy One of **Israel**,
60: 14 call you the City of the LORD, Zion of the Holy One of **Israel**.
63: 7 the many good things he has done for the house of **Israel**,
63: 16 though Abraham does not know us or **Israel** acknowledge us;
66: 20 bring them, as the **Israelites** [+1201] bring their grain offerings,
Jer 2: 3 **Israel** was holy to the LORD, the firstfruits of his harvest;
2: 4 the LORD, O house of Jacob, all you clans of the house of **Israel**.
2: 14 Is **Israel** a servant, a slave by birth? Why then has he become
2: 26 disgraced when he is caught, so the house of **Israel** is disgraced—
2: 31 "Have I been a desert to **Israel** or a land of great darkness?
3: 6 said to me, "Have you seen what faithless **Israel** has done?
3: 8 I gave faithless **Israel** her certificate of divorce and sent her away
3: 11 to me, "Faithless **Israel** is more righteous than unfaithful Judah.
3: 12 " 'Return, faithless **Israel**,' declares the LORD, 'I will frown on
3: 18 In those days the house of Judah will join the house of **Israel**,
3: 20 been unfaithful to me, O house of **Israel**," declares the LORD.
3: 21 barren heights, the weeping and pleading of the people of **Israel**,
3: 23 surely in the LORD our God is the salvation of **Israel**.
4: 1 "If you will return, O **Israel**, return to me," declares the LORD.
5: 11 The house of **Israel** and the house of Judah have been utterly
5: 15 O house of **Israel**," declares the LORD, "I am bringing a distant
6: 9 "Let them glean the remnant of **Israel** as thoroughly as a vine;
7: 3 This is what the LORD Almighty, the God of **Israel**, says:
7: 12 see what I did to it because of the wickedness of my people **Israel**.
7: 21 " 'This is what the LORD Almighty, the God of **Israel**, says:
9: 15 [9:14] this is what the LORD Almighty, the God of **Israel**, says:
9: 26 [9:25] even the whole house of **Israel** is uncircumcised in heart."
10: 1 Hear what the LORD says to you, O house of **Israel**.
10: 16 Maker of all things, including **Israel**, the tribe of his inheritance—
11: 3 Tell them that this is what the LORD, the God of **Israel**, says:
11: 10 Both the house of **Israel** and the house of Judah have broken the
11: 17 because the house of **Israel** and the house of Judah have done evil
12: 14 neighbors who seize the inheritance I gave my people **Israel**,
13: 11 so I bound the whole house of **Israel** and the whole house of Judah
13: 12 "Say to them: 'This is what the LORD, the God of **Israel**, says:
14: 8 O Hope of **Israel**, its Savior in times of distress, why are you like a
16: 9 For this is what the LORD Almighty, the God of **Israel**, says:
16: 14 LORD lives, who brought the **Israelites** [+1201] up out of Egypt,'
16: 15 who brought the **Israelites** [+1201] up out of the land of the north
17: 13 O LORD, the hope of **Israel**, all who forsake you will be put to
18: 6 "O house of **Israel**, can I not do with you as this potter does?"
18: 6 in the hand of the potter, so are you in my hand, O house of **Israel**.
18: 13 like this? A most horrible thing has been done by Virgin **Israel**.
19: 3 This is what the LORD Almighty, the God of **Israel**, says:
19: 15 "This is what the LORD Almighty, the God of **Israel**, says:
21: 4 'This is what the LORD, the God of **Israel**, says: I am about to
23: 2 Therefore this is what the LORD, the God of **Israel**, says to the
23: 6 In his days Judah will be saved and **Israel** will live in safety.
23: 7 LORD lives, who brought the **Israelites** [+1201] up out of Egypt,'
23: 8 who brought the descendants of **Israel** [+1074] up out of the land
23: 13 They prophesied by Baal and led my people **Israel** astray.
24: 5 "This is what the LORD, the God of **Israel**, says: 'Like these
25: 15 This is what the LORD, the God of **Israel**, said to me:
25: 27 'This is what the LORD Almighty, the God of **Israel**, says:
27: 4 'This is what the LORD Almighty, the God of **Israel**, says:
27: 21 yes, this is what the LORD Almighty, the God of **Israel**,
28: 2 "This is what the LORD Almighty, the God of **Israel**, says:
28: 14 This is what the LORD Almighty, the God of **Israel**, says:
29: 4 This is what the LORD Almighty, the God of **Israel**, says to all
29: 8 this is what the LORD Almighty, the God of **Israel**, says:
29: 21 the God of **Israel**, says about Ahab son of Kolaiah and Zedekiah
29: 23 For they have done outrageous things in **Israel**; they have
29: 25 "This is what the LORD Almighty, the God of **Israel**, says:
30: 2 "This is what the LORD, the God of **Israel**, says: 'Write in a book
30: 3 'when I will bring my people **Israel** and Judah back from captivity
30: 4 These are the words the LORD spoke concerning **Israel**
30: 10 my servant; do not be dismayed, O **Israel**,' declares the LORD.
31: 1 declares the LORD, "I will be the God of all the clans of **Israel**,
31: 2 will find favor in the desert; I will come to give rest to **Israel**."
31: 4 I will build you up again and you will be rebuilt, O Virgin **Israel**.
31: 7 and say, 'O LORD, save your people, the remnant of **Israel**.'
31: 9 because I am **Israel's** [+4200] father, and Ephraim is my firstborn
31: 10 'He who scattered **Israel** will gather them and will watch over his
31: 21 road that you take. Return, O Virgin **Israel**, return to your towns.
31: 23 This is what the LORD Almighty, the God of **Israel**, says:
31: 27 "when I will plant the house of **Israel** and the house of Judah with
31: 31 "when I will make a new covenant with the house of **Israel**
31: 33 "This is the covenant I will make with the house of **Israel** after that
31: 36 "will the descendants of **Israel** ever cease to be a nation before
31: 37 below be searched out will I reject all the descendants of **Israel**
32: 14 'This is what the LORD Almighty, the God of **Israel**, says:
32: 15 For this is what the LORD Almighty, the God of **Israel**, says:
32: 20 continued them to this day, both in **Israel** and among all mankind,
32: 21 You brought your people **Israel** out of Egypt with signs
32: 30 "The people of **Israel** and Judah have done nothing but evil in my
32: 30 the people of **Israel** have done nothing but provoke me with what
32: 32 The people of **Israel** and Judah have provoked me by all the evil
32: 36 of Babylon'; but this is what the LORD, the God of **Israel**, says:
33: 4 For this is what the LORD, the God of **Israel**, says about the
33: 7 I will bring Judah and **Israel** back from captivity and will rebuild
33: 14 I will fulfill the gracious promise I made to the house of **Israel**
33: 17 never fail to have a man to sit on the throne of the house of **Israel**,
34: 2 "This is what the LORD, the God of **Israel**, says: Go to Zedekiah
34: 13 "This is what the LORD, the God of **Israel**, says: I made a
35: 13 "This is what the LORD Almighty, the God of **Israel**, says:
35: 17 this is what the LORD God Almighty, the God of **Israel**, says:
35: 18 "This is what the LORD Almighty, the God of **Israel**, says:
35: 19 this is what the LORD Almighty, the God of **Israel**, says:
36: 2 write on it all the words I have spoken to you concerning **Israel**,
37: 7 "This is what the LORD, the God of **Israel**, says: Tell the king of
38: 17 "This is what the LORD God Almighty, the God of **Israel**, says:
39: 16 'This is what the LORD Almighty, the God of **Israel**, says:
41: 9 Asa had made as part of his defense against Baasha king of **Israel**.
42: 9 He said to them, "This is what the LORD, the God of **Israel**,
42: 15 This is what the LORD Almighty, the God of **Israel**, says:
42: 18 This is what the LORD Almighty, the God of **Israel**, says:
43: 10 'This is what the LORD Almighty, the God of **Israel**, says:
44: 2 "This is what the LORD Almighty, the God of **Israel**, says:
44: 7 this is what the LORD God Almighty, the God of **Israel**, says:
44: 11 this is what the LORD Almighty, the God of **Israel**, says:
44: 25 This is what the LORD Almighty, the God of **Israel**, says:
45: 2 "This is what the LORD, the God of **Israel**, says to you, Baruch:
46: 25 The LORD Almighty, the God of **Israel**, says: "I am about to
46: 27 "Do not fear, O Jacob my servant; do not be dismayed, O **Israel**.
48: 1 This is what the LORD Almighty, the God of **Israel**, says:
48: 13 as the house of **Israel** was ashamed when they trusted in Bethel.
48: 27 Was not **Israel** the object of your ridicule? Was she caught among
49: 1 "Has **Israel** no sons? Has she no heirs? Why then has Molech
49: 2 **Israel** will drive out those who drove her out," says the LORD.
50: 4 "the people of **Israel** and the people of Judah together will go in
50: 17 "**Israel** is a scattered flock that lions have chased away. The first to
50: 18 this is what the LORD Almighty, the God of **Israel**, says:
50: 19 I will bring **Israel** back to his own pasture and he will graze on
50: 20 declares the LORD, "search will be made for **Israel's** guilt,
50: 29 has done. For she has defied the LORD, the Holy One of **Israel**.
50: 33 "The people of **Israel** are oppressed, and the people of Judah as
51: 5 For **Israel** and Judah have not been forsaken by their God,
51: 5 though their land is full of guilt before the Holy One of **Israel**.
51: 33 This is what the LORD Almighty, the God of **Israel**, says:
51: 49 "Babylon must fall because of **Israel's** slain, just as the slain in all
La 2: 1 He has hurled down the splendor of **Israel** from heaven to earth;
2: 3 In fierce anger he has cut off every horn of **Israel**. He has
2: 5 The Lord is like an enemy; he has swallowed up **Israel**. He has

Eze 2: 3 "Son of man, I am sending you to the **Israelites** [+1201], to a
3: 1 eat this scroll; then go and speak to the house of **Israel**."
3: 4 go now to the house of **Israel** and speak my words to them.
3: 5 obscure speech and difficult language, but to the house of **Israel**—
3: 7 the house of **Israel** is not willing to listen to you because they are
3: 7 to me, for the whole house of **Israel** is hardened and obstinate.
3: 17 "Son of man, I have made you a watchman for the house of **Israel**;
4: 3 and you shall besiege it. This will be a sign to the house of **Israel**.
4: 4 your left side and put the sin of the house of **Israel** upon yourself.
4: 5 So for 390 days you will bear the sin of the house of **Israel**.
4: 13 "In this way the people of **Israel** will eat defiled food among the
5: 4 A fire will spread from there to the whole house of **Israel**.
6: 2 "Son of man, set your face against the mountains of **Israel**;
6: 3 'O mountains of **Israel**, hear the word of the Sovereign LORD.
6: 5 I will lay the dead bodies of the **Israelites** [+1201] in front of their
6: 11 of all the wicked and detestable practices of the house of **Israel**,
7: 2 this is what the Sovereign LORD says to the land of **Israel**:
8: 4 there before me was the glory of the God of **Israel**, as in the vision
8: 6 the utterly detestable things the house of **Israel** is doing here,
8: 10 and detestable animals and all the idols of the house of **Israel**.
8: 11 In front of them stood seventy elders of the house of **Israel**,
8: 12 have you seen what the elders of the house of **Israel** are doing in
9: 3 Now the glory of the God of **Israel** went up from above the
9: 8 Are you going to destroy the entire remnant of **Israel** in this
9: 9 "The sin of the house of **Israel** and Judah is exceedingly great;
10: 19 and the glory of the God of **Israel** was above them.
10: 20 creatures I had seen beneath the God of **Israel** by the Kebar River,
11: 5 That is what you are saying, O house of **Israel**, but I know what is
11: 10 and I will execute judgment on you at the borders of **Israel**.
11: 11 meat in it; I will execute judgment on you at the borders of **Israel**.
11: 13 Will you completely destroy the remnant of **Israel**?"
11: 15 who are your blood relatives and the whole house of **Israel**—
11: 17 been scattered, and I will give you back the land of **Israel** again.'
11: 22 their wings, and the glory of the God of **Israel** was above them.
12: 6 see the land, for I have made you a sign to the house of **Israel**."
12: 9 "Son of man, did not that rebellious house of **Israel** ask you,
12: 10 prince in Jerusalem and the whole house of **Israel** who are there.'
12: 19 says about those living in Jerusalem and in the land of **Israel**:
12: 22 "Son of man, what is this proverb you have in the land of **Israel**:
12: 23 an end to this proverb, and they will no longer quote it in **Israel**.'
12: 24 false visions or flattering divinations among the people of **Israel**.
12: 27 "Son of man, the house of **Israel** is saying, 'The vision he sees is
13: 2 prophesy against the prophets of **Israel** who are now prophesying.
13: 4 Your prophets, O **Israel**, are like jackals among ruins.
13: 5 gone up to the breaks in the wall to repair it for the house of **Israel**
13: 9 of my people or be listed in the records of the house of **Israel**,
13: 9 records of the house of Israel, nor will they enter the land of **Israel**.
13: 16 those prophets of **Israel** who prophesied to Jerusalem and saw
14: 1 Some of the elders of **Israel** came to me and sat down in front of
14: 4 When any **Israelite** [+408+1074+4946] sets up idols in his heart
14: 5 I will do this to recapture the hearts of the people of **Israel**,
14: 6 "Therefore say to the house of **Israel**, 'This is what the Sovereign
14: 7 " 'When any **Israelite** [+408+1074+4946] or any alien living in
14: 7 any Israelite or any alien living in **Israel** separates himself from me
14: 9 hand against him and destroy him from among my people **Israel**.
14: 11 the people of **Israel** will no longer stray from me, nor will they
17: 2 set forth an allegory and tell the house of **Israel** a parable.
17: 23 On the mountain heights of **Israel** I will plant it; it will produce
18: 2 you people mean by quoting this proverb about the land of **Israel**:
18: 3 Sovereign LORD, you will no longer quote this proverb in **Israel**.
18: 6 at the mountain shrines or look to the idols of the house of **Israel**.
18: 15 at the mountain shrines or look to the idols of the house of **Israel**.
18: 25 of the Lord is not just.' Hear, O house of **Israel**: Is my way unjust?
18: 29 Yet the house of **Israel** says, 'The way of the Lord is not just.'
18: 29 of the Lord is not just.' Are my ways unjust, O house of **Israel**?
18: 30 "Therefore, O house of **Israel**, I will judge you, each one
18: 31 a new heart and a new spirit. Why will you die, O house of **Israel**?
19: 1 "Take up a lament concerning the princes of **Israel**
19: 9 so his roar was heard no longer on the mountains of **Israel**.
20: 1 some of the elders of **Israel** came to inquire of the LORD,
20: 3 "Son of man, speak to the elders of **Israel** and say to them,
20: 5 On the day I chose **Israel**, I swore with uplifted hand to the
20: 13 " 'Yet the people of **Israel** rebelled against me in the desert.
20: 27 son of man, speak to the people of **Israel** and say to them,
20: 30 "Therefore say to the house of **Israel**: 'This is what the Sovereign
20: 31 Am I to let you inquire of me, O house of **Israel**? As surely as I
20: 38 where they are living, yet they will not enter the land of **Israel**.
20: 39 " 'As for you, O house of **Israel**, this is what the Sovereign
20: 40 For on my holy mountain, the high mountain of **Israel**,
20: 40 there in the land the entire house of **Israel** will serve me, and there
20: 42 that I am the LORD, when I bring you into the land of **Israel**,
20: 44 to your evil ways and your corrupt practices, O house of **Israel**,
21: 2 [21:7] against the sanctuary. Prophesy against the land of **Israel**
21: 3 [21:8] say to **her**[s] [+141]: 'This is what the LORD says: I am
21: 12 [21:17] is against my people; it is against all the princes of **Israel**.
21: 25 [21:30] " 'O profane and wicked prince of **Israel**, whose day has
22: 6 " 'See how each of the princes of **Israel** who are in you uses his
22: 18 "Son of man, the house of **Israel** has become dross to me;
24: 21 Say to the house of **Israel**, 'This is what the Sovereign LORD
25: 3 was desecrated and over the land of **Israel** when it was laid waste
25: 6 with all the malice of your heart against the land of **Israel**,
25: 14 I will take vengeance on Edom by the hand of my people **Israel**,
27: 17 " 'Judah and **Israel** [+824] traded with you; they exchanged wheat
28: 24 " 'No longer will the people of **Israel** have malicious neighbors
28: 25 When I gather the people of **Israel** from the nations where they
29: 6 " 'You have been a staff of reed for the house of **Israel**.
29: 16 will no longer be a source of confidence for the people of **Israel**
29: 21 "On that day I will make a horn grow for the house of **Israel**,
33: 7 "Son of man, I have made you a watchman for the house of **Israel**;
33: 10 "Son of man, say to the house of **Israel**, 'This is what you are
33: 11 Turn from your evil ways! Why will you die, O house of **Israel**?'
33: 20 Yet, O house of **Israel**, you say, 'The way of the Lord is not just.'
33: 24 the people living in those ruins in the land of **Israel** are saying,
33: 28 the mountains of **Israel** will become desolate so that no one will
34: 2 "Son of man, prophesy against the shepherds of **Israel**; prophesy
34: 2 Woe to the shepherds of **Israel** who only take care of themselves!
34: 13 I will pasture them on the mountains of **Israel**, in the ravines
34: 14 and the mountain heights of **Israel** will be their grazing land.
34: 14 there they will feed in a rich pasture on the mountains of **Israel**.
34: 30 am with them and that they, the house of **Israel**, are my people,
35: 5 delivered the **Israelites** [+1201] over to the sword at the time of
35: 12 contemptible things you have said against the mountains of **Israel**.
35: 15 Because you rejoiced when the inheritance of the house of **Israel**
36: 1 "Son of man, prophesy to the mountains of **Israel** and say,
36: 1 to the mountains of Israel and say, 'O mountains of **Israel**,
36: 4 therefore, O mountains of **Israel**, hear the word of the Sovereign
36: 6 Therefore prophesy concerning the land of **Israel** and say to the
36: 8 " 'But you, O mountains of **Israel**, will produce branches and fruit
36: 8 of Israel, will produce branches and fruit for my people **Israel**,
36: 10 the number of people upon you, even the whole house of **Israel**.
36: 12 I will cause people, my people **Israel**, to walk upon you. They will
36: 17 of man, when the people of **Israel** were living in their own land,
36: 21 which the house of **Israel** profaned among the nations where they
36: 22 "Therefore say to the house of **Israel**, 'This is what the Sovereign
36: 22 It is not for your sake, O house of **Israel**, that I am going to do
36: 32 Be ashamed and disgraced for your conduct, O house of **Israel**!
36: 37 Once again I will yield to the plea of the house of **Israel** and do
37: 11 "Son of man, these bones are the whole house of **Israel**. They say,
37: 12 bring you up from them; I will bring you back to the land of **Israel**.
37: 16 to Judah and the **Israelites** [+1201] associated with him.'
37: 16 to Joseph and all the house of **Israel** associated with him.'
37: 19 of the **Israelite** tribes associated with him, and join it to Judah's
37: 21 I will take the **Israelites** [+1201] out of the nations where they
37: 22 will make them one nation in the land, on the mountains of **Israel**.
37: 28 Then the nations will know that I the LORD make **Israel** holy,
38: 8 were gathered from many nations to the mountains of **Israel**,
38: 14 In that day, when my people **Israel** are living in safety, will you
38: 16 You will advance against my people **Israel** like a cloud that covers
38: 17 I spoke of in former days by my servants the prophets of **Israel**?
38: 18 When Gog attacks the land of **Israel**, my hot anger will be aroused,
38: 19 at that time there shall be a great earthquake in the land of **Israel**.
39: 2 from the far north and send you against the mountains of **Israel**.
39: 4 On the mountains of **Israel** you will fall, you and all your troops
39: 7 " 'I will make known my holy name among my people **Israel**.
39: 7 the nations will know that I the LORD am the Holy One in **Israel**.
39: 9 " 'Then those who live in the towns of **Israel** will go out and use
39: 11 " 'On that day I will give Gog a burial place in **Israel**, in the valley
39: 12 " 'For seven months the house of **Israel** will be burying them in
39: 17 preparing for you, the great sacrifice on the mountains of **Israel**.
39: 22 From that day forward the house of **Israel** will know that I am the
39: 23 the nations will know that the people of **Israel** went into exile for
39: 25 and will have compassion on all the people of **Israel**,
39: 29 for I will pour out my Spirit on the house of **Israel**,
40: 2 In visions of God he took me to the land of **Israel** and set me on a
40: 4 been brought here. Tell the house of **Israel** everything you see."
43: 2 and I saw the glory of the God of **Israel** coming from the east.
43: 7 This is where I will live among the **Israelites** [+1201] forever.
43: 7 The house of **Israel** will never again defile my holy name—
43: 10 "Son of man, describe the temple to the people of **Israel**, that they
44: 2 It is to remain shut because the LORD, the God of **Israel**,
44: 6 Say to the rebellious house of **Israel**, 'This is what the Sovereign
44: 6 Enough of your detestable practices, O house of **Israel**!
44: 9 not even the foreigners who live among the **Israelites** [+1201].
44: 10 " 'The Levites who went far from me when **Israel** went astray
44: 12 presence of their idols and made the house of **Israel** fall into sin,
44: 15 of my sanctuary when the **Israelites** [+1201] went astray from me,
44: 22 they may marry only virgins of **Israelite** [+1074] descent
44: 28 You are to give them no possession in **Israel**; I will be their

Eze 44:29 everything in **Israel** devoted to the LORD will belong to them.
45: 6 the sacred portion; it will belong to the whole house of **Israel**.
45: 8 This land will be his possession in **Israel**. And my princes will no
45: 8 will allow the house of **Israel** to possess the land according to their
45: 9 You have gone far enough, O princes of **Israel**! Give up your
45:15 flock of two hundred from the well-watered pastures of **Israel**.
45:16 participate in this special gift for the use of the prince in **Israel**.
45:17 the Sabbaths—at all the appointed feasts of the house of **Israel**.
45:17 fellowship offerings to make atonement for the house of **Israel**.
47:13 the land for an inheritance among the twelve tribes of **Israel**,
47:18 along the Jordan between Gilead and the land of **Israel**,
47:21 this land among yourselves according to the tribes of **Israel**.
47:22 You are to consider them as native-born **Israelites** [+1201];
47:22 they are to be allotted an inheritance among the tribes of **Israel**.
48:11 did not go astray as the Levites did when the **Israelites** [+1201]
48:19 from the city who farm it will come from all the tribes of **Israel**.
48:29 is the land you are to allot as an inheritance to the tribes of **Israel**,
48:31 the gates of the city will be named after the tribes of **Israel**.
Da 1: 3 to bring in some of the **Israelites** [+1201] from the royal family
9: 7 the men of Judah and people of Jerusalem and all **Israel**, both near
9:11 All **Israel** has transgressed your law and turned away, refusing to
9:20 confessing my sin and the sin of my people **Israel** and making my
Hos 1: 1 and during the reign of Jeroboam son of Jehoash king of **Israel**:
1: 4 at Jezreel, and I will put an end to the kingdom of **Israel** [+1074].
1: 5 In that day I will break **Israel's** bow in the Valley of Jezreel."
1: 6 for I will no longer show love to the house of **Israel**,
1:10 [2:1] "Yet the **Israelites** [+1201] will be like the sand on the
1:11 [2:2] people of Judah and the people of **Israel** will be reunited,
3: 1 Love her as the LORD loves the **Israelites** [+1201], though they
3: 4 For the **Israelites** [+1201] will live many days without king
3: 5 Afterward the **Israelites** [+1201] will return and seek the LORD
4: 1 Hear the word of the LORD, you **Israelites** [+1201],
4:15 you commit adultery, O **Israel**, let not Judah become guilty.
4:16 The **Israelites** are stubborn, like a stubborn heifer. How then can
5: 1 Pay attention, you **Israelites** [+1074]! Listen, O royal house!
5: 3 I know all about Ephraim; **Israel** is not hidden from me. Ephraim,
5: 3 Ephraim, you have now turned to prostitution; **Israel** is corrupt.
5: 5 **Israel's** arrogance testifies against them; the Israelites,
5: 5 the **Israelites**, even Ephraim, stumble in their sin; Judah also
5: 9 of reckoning. Among the tribes of **Israel** I proclaim what is certain.
6:10 I have seen a horrible thing in the house of **Israel**. There Ephraim
6:10 There Ephraim is given to prostitution and **Israel** is defiled.
7: 1 whenever I would heal **Israel**, the sins of Ephraim are exposed
7:10 **Israel's** arrogance testifies against him, but despite all this he does
8: 2 **Israel** cries out to me, 'O our God, we acknowledge you!'
8: 3 But **Israel** has rejected what is good; an enemy will pursue him.
8: 6 They are from **Israel**! This calf—a craftsman has made it;
8: 8 **Israel** is swallowed up; now she is among the nations like a
8:14 **Israel** has forgotten his Maker and built palaces; Judah has
9: 1 Do not rejoice, O **Israel**; do not be jubilant like the other nations.
9: 7 Let **Israel** know this. Because your sins are so many and your
9:10 "When I found **Israel**, it was like finding grapes in the desert;
10: 1 **Israel** was a spreading vine; he brought forth fruit for himself.
10: 6 will be disgraced; **Israel** will be ashamed of its wooden idols.
10: 8 high places of wickedness will be destroyed—it is the sin of **Israel**.
10: 9 "Since the days of Gibeah, you have sinned, O **Israel**, and there
10:15 that day dawns, the king of **Israel** will be completely destroyed.
11: 1 "When **Israel** was a child, I loved him, and out of Egypt I called
11: 8 can I give you up, Ephraim? How can I hand you over, **Israel**?
11:12 [12:1] surrounded me with lies, the house of **Israel** with deceit.
12:12 [12:13] **Israel** served to get a wife, and to pay for her he tended
12:13 [12:14] The LORD used a prophet to bring **Israel** up from
13: 1 When Ephraim spoke, men trembled; he was exalted in **Israel**.
13: 9 "You are destroyed, O **Israel**, because you are against me,
14: 1 [14:2] Return, O **Israel**, to the LORD your God. Your sins have
14: 5 [14:6] I will be like the dew to **Israel**; he will blossom like a lily.
Joel 2:27 you will know that I am in **Israel**, that I am the LORD your God,
3: 2 [4:2] my people **Israel**, for they scattered my people among the
3:16 [4:16] refuge for his people, a stronghold for the people of **Israel**.
Am 1: 1 what he saw concerning **Israel** two years before the earthquake,
1: 1 king of Judah and Jeroboam son of Jehoash was king of **Israel**.
2: 6 "For three sins of **Israel**, even for four, I will not turn back ⌊my
2:11 Is this not true, people of **Israel**?" declares the LORD.
3: 1 this word the LORD has spoken against you, O people of **Israel**—
3:12 or a piece of an ear, so will the **Israelites** [+1201] be saved,
3:14 "On the day I punish **Israel** for her sins, I will destroy the altars of
4: 5 boast about them, you **Israelites** [+1201], for this is what you love
4:12 **Israel**, and because I will do this to you, prepare to meet your God,
4:12 because I will do this to you, prepare to meet your God, O **Israel**."
5: 1 Hear this word, O house of **Israel**, this lament I take up concerning
5: 2 "Fallen is Virgin **Israel**, never to rise again, deserted in her own
5: 3 "The city that marches out a thousand strong for **Israel** [+1074]
5: 4 This is what the LORD says to the house of **Israel**: "Seek me
5:25 and offerings forty years in the desert, O house of **Israel**?
6: 1 men of the foremost nation, to whom the people of **Israel** come!
6:14 "I will stir up a nation against you, O house of **Israel**,
7: 8 "Look, I am setting a plumb line among my people **Israel**;
7: 9 Isaac will be destroyed and the sanctuaries of **Israel** will be ruined;
7:10 the priest of Bethel sent a message to Jeroboam king of **Israel**:
7:10 a conspiracy against you in the very heart of **Israel** [+1074].
7:11 and **Israel** will surely go into exile, away from their native land.' "
7:15 the flock and said to me, 'Go, prophesy to my people **Israel**.'
7:16 You say, " 'Do not prophesy against **Israel**, and stop preaching
7:17 **Israel** will certainly go into exile, away from their native land.' "
8: 2 the LORD said to me, "The time is ripe for my people **Israel**;
9: 7 "Are not you **Israelites** [+1201] the same to me as the Cushites?"
9: 7 "Did I not bring **Israel** up from Egypt, the Philistines from Caphtor
9: 9 I will shake the house of **Israel** among all the nations as grain is
9:14 I will bring back my exiled people **Israel**; they will rebuild the
Ob 1:20 This company of **Israelite** [+1201] exiles who are in Canaan will
Mic 1: 5 of Jacob's transgression, because of the sins of the house of **Israel**.
1:13 of Zion, for the transgressions of **Israel** were found in you.
1:14 The town of Aczib will prove deceptive to the kings of **Israel**.
1:15 in Mareshah. He who is the glory of **Israel** will come to Adullam.
2:12 O Jacob; I will surely bring together the remnant of **Israel**.
3: 1 "Listen, you leaders of Jacob, you rulers of the house of **Israel**.
3: 8 and might, to declare to Jacob his transgression, to **Israel** his sin.
3: 9 you rulers of the house of **Israel**, who despise justice and distort all
5: 1 [4:14] They will strike **Israel's** ruler on the cheek with a rod.
5: 2 [5:1] of you will come for me one who will be ruler over **Israel**,
5: 3 [5:2] the rest of his brothers return to join the **Israelites** [+1201].
6: 2 has a case against his people; he is lodging a charge against **Israel**.
Na 2: 2 [2:3] will restore the splendor of Jacob like the splendor of **Israel**,
Zep 2: 9 surely as I live," declares the LORD Almighty, the God of **Israel**,
3:13 The remnant of **Israel** will do no wrong; they will speak no lies,
3:14 Sing, O Daughter of Zion; shout aloud, O **Israel**! Be glad
3:15 The LORD, the King of **Israel**, is with you; never again will you
Zec 1:19 [2:2] are the horns that scattered Judah, **Israel** and Jerusalem."
8:13 O Judah and **Israel** [+1074], so will I save you, and you will be a
9: 1 for the eyes of men and all the tribes of **Israel** are on the LORD—
11:14 called Union, breaking the brotherhood between Judah and **Israel**.
12: 1 An Oracle This is the word of the LORD concerning **Israel**.
Mal 1: 1 An oracle: The word of the LORD to **Israel** through Malachi.
1: 5 'Great is the LORD—even beyond the borders of **Israel**!'
2:11 A detestable thing has been committed in **Israel** and in Jerusalem:
2:16 "I hate divorce," says the LORD God of **Israel**, "and I hate a
4: 4 [3:22] the decrees and laws I gave him at Horeb for all **Israel**.

3777 יְשַׂרְאֵלָה *yᵉśar'ēlâ*, n.pr.m. [1] [cf. 833]

Jesarelah [1]

1Ch 25:14 the seventh to **Jesarelah**, his sons and relatives, 12

3778 יִשְׂרְאֵלִי *yiśrᵉ'ēlî*, a.g. [5] [√ 3776]

Israelite [3], him [+1201+2021] [1], Israelite [+408+2021] [1]

Lev 24:10 Now the son of an **Israelite** mother and an Egyptian father went
24:10 and a fight broke out in the camp between **him**[s] [+1201+2021]
24:10 broke out in the camp between him and an **Israelite** [+408+2021].
24:11 The son of the **Israelite** woman blasphemed the Name with a
2Sa 17:25 an **Israelite** who had married Abigail, the daughter of Nahash

3779 יִשָּׂשכָר *yiśśāśkār*, n.pr.m. [43] [√ 408 + 8510]

Issachar [38], Issachar [+1201] [4], *untranslated* [1]

Ge 30:18 my maidservant to my husband." So she named him **Issachar**.
35:23 the firstborn of Jacob, Simeon, Levi, Judah, **Issachar** and Zebulun.
46:13 The sons of **Issachar**: Tola, Puah, Jashub and Shimron.
49:14 "**Issachar** is a rawboned donkey lying down between two
Ex 1: 3 **Issachar**, Zebulun and Benjamin;
Nu 1: 8 from **Issachar**, Nethanel son of Zuar;
1:28 From the descendants of **Issachar**: All the men twenty years old
1:29 The number from the tribe of **Issachar** was 54,400.
2: 5 The tribe of **Issachar** will camp next to them. The leader of the
2: 5 The leader of the people of **Issachar** is Nethanel son of Zuar.
7:18 Nethanel son of Zuar, the leader of **Issachar**, brought his offering.
10:15 son of Zuar was over the division of the tribe of **Issachar** [+1201],
13: 7 from the tribe of **Issachar**, Igal son of Joseph;
26:23 The descendants of **Issachar** by their clans were: through Tola,
26:25 These were the clans of **Issachar**; those numbered were 64,300.
34:26 Paltiel son of Azzan, the leader from the tribe of **Issachar** [+1201];
Dt 27:12 the people: Simeon, Levi, Judah, **Issachar**, Joseph and Benjamin.
33:18 Zebulun, in your going out, and you, **Issachar**, in your tents.
Jos 17:10 and bordered Asher on the north and **Issachar** on the east.
17:11 Within **Issachar** and Asher, Manasseh also had Beth Shan,
19:17 The fourth lot came out for **Issachar** [+1201], clan by clan.
19:17 The fourth lot came out for Issachar, **[RPH]** clan by clan.
19:23 their villages were the inheritance of the tribe of **Issachar** [+1201],

Jos 21: 6 allotted thirteen towns from the clans of the tribes of **Issachar**,
21: 28 from the tribe of **Issachar**, Kishion, Daberath,
Jdg 5: 15 The princes of **Issachar** were with Deborah; yes, Issachar was with
5: 15 yes, **Issachar** was with Barak, rushing after him into the valley.
10: 1 After the time of Abimelech a man of **Issachar**, Tola son of Puah,
1Ki 4: 17 Jehoshaphat son of Paruah—in **Issachar**;
15: 27 Baasha son of Ahijah of the house of **Issachar** plotted against him,
1Ch 2: 1 sons of Israel: Reuben, Simeon, Levi, Judah, **Issachar**, Zebulun,
6: 62 [6:47] were allotted thirteen towns from the tribes of **Issachar**,
6: 72 [6:57] from the tribe of **Issachar** they received Kedesh, Daberath,
7: 1 The sons of **Issachar**: Tola, Puah, Jashub and Shimron—four in
7: 5 who were fighting men belonging to all the clans of **Issachar**,
12: 32 [12:33] men of **Issachar**, who understood the times and knew
12: 40 [12:41] Also, their neighbors from as far away as **Issachar**,
26: 5 Ammiel the sixth, **Issachar** the seventh and Peullethai the eighth.
27: 18 over Judah: Elihu, a brother of David; over **Issachar**: Omri son of
2Ch 30: 18 Manasseh, **Issachar** and Zebulun had not purified themselves,
Eze 48: 25 "**Issachar** will have one portion; it will border the territory of
48: 26 it will border the territory of **Issachar** from east to west.
48: 33 the gate of Simeon, the gate of **Issachar** and the gate of Zebulun.

3780 יֵשׁ yēš, subst. [138] [→ 409, 838, 3807?, 3808?; cf. 9370; Ar 10029] See Select Index

there is [27], *untranslated* [25], have [+4200] [12], is [11], is there [8], be [5], are [4], have [4], will [4], am [3], has [+928] [3], there are [3], there was [3], has [2], have [+907] [2], owned [+4200] [2], sometimes [+889] [2], are there [1], continue [1], do [1], had [+4200] [1], had [1], have [+3338+9393] [1], have [+928] [1], have on hand [+3338+9393] [1], it is [1], lies [1], owns [+4200] [1], so[s] [1], there were [1], there will be [1], this is [1], wealth [1], were [1], yes [1]

3781 יִשְׁאָל yiš'āl, n.pr.m. Not used in NIV/BHS [√ 8626]

3782 יָשַׁב yāšab, v. [1084 / 1086] [→ 4632, 8699, 8859?, 9369; Ar 10338; *also used with compound proper names*]

live [141], lived [91], people [73], live in [68], sit [59], settled [43], stay [40], living [39], sitting [39], living in [33], stayed [32], sat [31], inhabitants [30], sat down [22], *untranslated* [18], remained [18], dwell [14], inhabited [13], lived in [12], settle [12], enthroned [11], sits [11], dwelling [10], lives [10], remain [9], seated [9], dwell in [8], occupied [8], reigned [8], staying [8], wait [6], married [5], settle down [5], sit enthroned [5], men [4], sits enthroned [4], be [3], inhabitant [3], left [3], lived at [3], sit down [3], at rest [2], be inhabited [2], dwells [2], dwelt [2], everyone [+3972] [2], king [2], lies [2], make dwell [2], marrying [2], occupy [2], reign [2], resettle [2], resettled [2], residents [2], ruling [2], seat [2], seats [2], situated [2], stand [2], stays [2], supposed to dine [+430+3782] [2], took seat [2], took up residence [2], were [2], avoid [+4946] [1], brought to live [1], citizens [1], continually [1], crouching [1], deserted [+1172+4946] [1], deserted [+401+4946] [1], deserted [+401+928] [1], deserted [+4202] [1], did[s] so [1], dwellers [1], dwellings [1], endures [1], enthrones [+2021+4058+4200] [1], give [1], go [1], had live [1], have a home [1], held court [1], hide in [1], hold out [1], intact [1], kings [1], lay in wait [1], left behind [1], let live [1], lie [1], live securely [1], living at [1], lounging [1], made dwell [1], make live [1], makes dwell [1], meet [1], meeting [1], mounted like jewels [+4859+6584] [1], occupants [1], peopled [1], reigns [1], relieve yourself [+2575] [1], remains [1], rest [1], rested [1], restore [1], rule [1], sat up [1], sat waiting [1], securely [1], set up [1], sets [1], settle in [1], settle on [1], settles [1], sit as judge [1], spent [1], stay [+3782] [1], stay [+8740] [1], stay in [1], stay up [1], stayed at home [1], stayed night [+2256+4328] [1], stopping [1], succeeded [1], successor [1], taken seat [1], takes [+6584] [1], takes seat [1], throne [1], thrones [1], took place [1], took places [1], took seats [1], was [1], withdrew [1]

Ge 4: 16 [A] out from the LORD's presence and **lived** in the land of Nod,
4: 20 [A] he was the father of *those who* **live in** tents and raise
11: 2 [A] they found a plain in Shinar and **settled** there.
11: 31 [A] to Canaan. But when they came to Haran, *they* **settled** there.
13: 6 [A] the land could not support them while they **stayed** together,
13: 6 [A] so great that they were not able to **stay** together.
13: 7 [A] and Perizzites *were* also **living** in the land at that time.
13: 12 [A] Abram **lived** in the land of Canaan, while Lot lived among
13: 12 [A] while Lot **lived** among the cities of the plain and pitched his
13: 18 [A] and went *to* **live** near the great trees of Mamre at Hebron,
14: 7 [A] as well as the Amorites who *were* **living** in Hazazon Tamar.
14: 12 [A] and his possessions, since he *was* **living** in Sodom.
16: 3 [A] So after Abram *had been* **living** in Canaan ten years,
18: 1 [A] *was* **sitting** *at* the entrance to his tent in the heat of the day.
19: 1 [A] in the evening, and Lot *was* **sitting** in the gateway of the city.
19: 25 [A] and the entire plain, including all *those* **living in** the cities—
19: 29 [A] the catastrophe that overthrew the cities where Lot *had* **lived**.
19: 30 [A] and his two daughters left Zoar and **settled** in the mountains,
19: 30 [A] settled in the mountains, for he was afraid to **stay** in Zoar.
19: 30 [A] to stay in Zoar. He and his two daughters **lived** in a cave.
20: 1 [A] the region of the Negev and **lived** between Kadesh and Shur.
20: 15 [A] "My land is before you; **live** wherever you like."
21: 16 [A] she went off and **sat down** nearby, about a bowshot away,
21: 16 [A] the boy die." And *as she* **sat** there nearby, she began to sob.
21: 20 [A] as he grew up. *He* **lived** in the desert and became an archer.
21: 21 [A] While *he was* **living** in the Desert of Paran, his mother got a
22: 5 [A] "**Stay** here with the donkey while I and the boy go over
22: 19 [A] together for Beersheba. And Abraham **stayed** in Beersheba.
23: 10 [A] Ephron the Hittite *was* **sitting** among his people and he
24: 3 [A] the daughters of the Canaanites, among whom I *am* **living**,
24: 37 [A] from the daughters of the Canaanites, in whose land I **live**,
24: 55 [A] mother replied, "*Let* the girl **remain** with us ten days or so;
24: 62 [A] come from Beer Lahai Roi, for he *was* **living** in the Negev.
25: 11 [A] blessed his son Isaac, who then **lived** near Beer Lahai Roi.
25: 27 [A] while Jacob was a quiet man, **staying** *among* the tents.
26: 6 [A] So Isaac **stayed** in Gerar.
26: 17 [A] and encamped in the Valley of Gerar and **settled** there.
27: 19 [A] Please **sit** up and eat some of my game so that you may give
27: 44 [A] **Stay** with him for a while until your brother's fury subsides.
29: 14 [A] After Jacob *had* **stayed** with him *for* a whole month,
29: 19 [A] give her to you than to some other man. **Stay** *here* with me."
31: 34 [A] put them inside her camel's saddle and *was* **sitting** on them.
34: 10 [A] *You can* **settle** among us; the land is open to you. Live in it,
34: 10 [A] open to you. **Live in** it, trade in it, and acquire property in it."
34: 16 [A] *We'll* **settle** among you and become one people with you.
34: 21 [A] "*Let them* **live** in our land and trade in it; the land has plenty
34: 22 [A] the men will consent to **live** with us as one people only on the
34: 23 [A] us give our consent to them, and *they will* **settle** among us."
34: 30 [A] the Canaanites and Perizzites, the *people* **living in** this land.
35: 1 [A] Then God said to Jacob, "Go up to Bethel and **settle** there,
36: 7 [A] Their possessions were too great for them *to* **remain**
36: 8 [A] So Esau (that is, Edom) **settled** in the hill country of Seir.
36: 20 [A] the sons of Seir the Horite, *who were* **living in** the region:
37: 1 [A] Jacob **lived** in the land where his father had stayed, the land
37: 25 [A] As *they* **sat down** to eat their meal, they looked up and saw a
38: 11 [A] "**Live** as a widow **in** your father's house until my son Shelah
38: 11 [A] his brothers." So Tamar went *to* **live in** her father's house.
38: 14 [A] then **sat down** at the entrance to Enaim, which is on the road
43: 33 [A] The men *had been* **seated** before him in the order of their
44: 33 [A] please *let* your servant **remain** here as my lord's slave in
45: 10 [A] *You shall* **live** in the region of Goshen and be near me—you,
46: 34 [A] Then *you will be allowed to* **settle** in the region of Goshen,
47: 4 [A] So now, please *let* your servants **settle** in Goshen."
47: 6 [G] **settle** your father and your brothers in the best part of the
47: 6 [A] brothers in the best part of the land. *Let them* **live** in Goshen.
47: 11 [G] So Joseph **settled** his father and his brothers in Egypt
47: 27 [A] Now the Israelites **settled** in Egypt in the region of Goshen.
48: 2 [A] to you," Israel rallied his strength and **sat up** on the bed.
49: 24 [A] But his bow **remained** steady, his strong arms stayed limber,
50: 11 [A] When the Canaanites *who* **lived** there saw the mourning at
50: 22 [A] Joseph **stayed** in Egypt, along with all his father's family.
Ex 2: 15 [A] but Moses fled from Pharaoh and went *to* **live** in Midian,
2: 15 [A] and went to live in Midian, where *he* **sat down** by a well.
2: 21 [A] Moses agreed to **stay** with the man, who gave his daughter
11: 5 [A] from the firstborn son of Pharaoh, who **sits** on the throne,
12: 29 [A] from the firstborn of Pharaoh, who **sat** on the throne,
12: 40 [A] Now the length of time the Israelite people **lived** in Egypt
15: 14 [A] and tremble; anguish will grip the **people** *of* Philistia.
15: 15 [A] seized with trembling, the **people** *of* Canaan will melt away;
15: 17 [A] the place, O LORD, you made for your **dwelling**,
16: 3 [A] There we **sat** around pots of meat and ate all the food we
16: 29 [A] Everyone *is to* **stay** where he is on the seventh day; no one is
16: 35 [C] manna forty years, until they came to a land *that was* **settled**;
17: 12 [A] they took a stone and put it under him and *he* **sat** on it.
18: 13 [A] The next day Moses **took** *his* **seat** to serve as judge for the
18: 14 [A] Why *do* you alone **sit as judge**, while all these people stand
23: 31 [A] I will hand over to you the *people who* **live in** the land
23: 33 [A] *Do* not *let them* **live** in your land, or they will cause you to
24: 14 [A] to the elders, "**Wait** here for us until we come back to you.
32: 6 [A] Afterward *they* **sat down** to eat and drink and got up to
34: 12 [A] Be careful not to make a treaty with *those who* **live in** the
34: 15 [A] "Be careful not to make a treaty with *those who* **live in** the
Lev 8: 35 [A] *You must* **stay** at the entrance to the Tent of Meeting day
12: 4 [A] the woman *must* **wait** thirty-three days to be purified from
12: 5 [A] *she must* **wait** sixty-six days to be purified from her
13: 46 [A] *He must* **live** alone; he must live outside the camp.
14: 8 [A] the camp, but *he must* **stay** outside his tent for seven days.
15: 4 [A] on will be unclean, and anything *he* **sits** on will be unclean.
15: 6 [A] Whoever **sits** on anything that the man with a discharge sat
15: 6 [A] Whoever sits on anything that the man with a discharge **sat**
15: 20 [A] will be unclean, and anything *she* **sits** on will be unclean.
15: 22 [A] Whoever touches anything *she* **sits** on must wash his clothes

Lev 15:23 [A] Whether it is the bed or anything she *was* **sitting** on, when
15:26 [A] anything *she* **sits** on will be unclean, as during her period.
18: 3 [A] You must not do as they do in Egypt, where *you used to* **live**,
18:25 [A] it for its sin, and the land vomited out its **inhabitants**.
20:22 [A] so that the land where I am bringing you to **live** may not
23:42 [A] **Live** in booths for seven days: All native-born Israelites are
23:42 [A] seven days: All native-born Israelites *are to* **live** in booths
23:43 [G] so your descendants will know that *I* **had** the Israelites **live** in
25:10 [A] proclaim liberty throughout the land to all its **inhabitants**.
25:18 [A] careful to obey my laws, and *you will* **live** safely in the land.
25:19 [A] its fruit, and you will eat your fill and **live** there in safety.
26: 5 [A] will eat all the food you want and **live** in safety in your land.
26:32 [A] so that your enemies who **live** there will be appalled.
26:35 [A] the rest it did not have during the sabbaths you **lived** in it.
Nu 13:18 [A] and whether the people who **live** there are strong or weak,
13:19 [A] What kind of land *do* they **live** in? Is it good or bad? What
13:19 [A] Is it good or bad? What kind of towns *do* they **live** in? Are
13:28 [A] the people who **live** there are powerful, and the cities are
13:29 [A] The Amalekites **live** in the Negev; the Hittites, Jebusites
13:29 [A] the Hittites, Jebusites and Amorites **live** in the hill country;
13:29 [A] and the Canaanites **live** near the sea and along the Jordan."
13:32 [A] They said, "The land we explored devours *those* **living** in it.
14:14 [A] they will tell the **inhabitants** *of* this land about it. They have
14:25 [A] the Amalekites and Canaanites *are* **living** in the valleys,
14:45 [A] Canaanites who **lived** in that hill country came down
20: 1 [A] arrived at the Desert of Zin, and they **stayed** at Kadesh.
20:15 [A] went down into Egypt, and *we* **lived** there many years.
21: 1 [A] When the Canaanite king of Arad, *who* **lived in** the Negev,
21:25 [A] **occupied** them, including Heshbon and all its surrounding
21:31 [A] So Israel **settled** in the land of the Amorites.
21:34 [A] did to Sihon king of the Amorites, who **reigned** in Heshbon."
22: 5 [A] they cover the face of the land and *have* **settled** next to me.
22: 8 [A] LORD gives me." So the Moabite princes **stayed** with him.
22:19 [A] Now **stay** here tonight as the others did, and I will find out
25: 1 [A] While Israel *was* **staying** in Shittim, the men began to
32: 6 [A] "Shall your countrymen go to war while you **sit** here?
32:17 [A] our women and children *will* **live** in fortified cities,
32:17 [A] for protection from the **inhabitants** *of* the land.
32:40 [A] the descendants of Manasseh, and *they* **settled** there.
33:40 [A] Canaanite king of Arad, who **lived** in the Negev of Canaan,
33:52 [A] drive out all the **inhabitants** *of* the land before you. Destroy
33:53 [A] Take possession of the land and **settle** in it, for I have given
33:55 [A] " 'But if you do not drive out the **inhabitants** *of* the land,
33:55 [A] They will give you trouble in the land where you *will* **live**.
35: 2 [A] "Command the Israelites to give the Levites towns to **live in**
35: 3 [A] they will have towns to **live in** and pasturelands for their
35:25 [A] *He must* **stay** there until the death of the high priest,
35:28 [A] The accused *must* **stay** in his city of refuge until the death of
35:32 [A] and **live** on his own land before the death of the high priest.
35:34 [A] Do not defile the land where you **live** and where I dwell, for
Dt 1: 4 [A] who **reigned** in Heshbon, and at Edrei had defeated Og king
1: 4 [A] had defeated Og king of Bashan, who **reigned** in Ashtaroth.
1: 6 [A] us at Horeb, "You *have* **stayed** long enough at this mountain.
1:44 [A] The Amorites who **lived** in those hills came out against you;
1:46 [A] so *you* **stayed** in Kadesh many days—all the time you spent
1:46 [A] stayed in Kadesh many days—all the time *you* **spent** there.
2: 4 [A] of your brothers the descendants of Esau, who **live** in Seir.
2: 8 [A] past our brothers the descendants of Esau, who **live** in Seir.
2:10 [A] (The Emites used to **live** there—a people strong
2:12 [A] Horites used to **live** in Seir, but the descendants of Esau
2:12 [A] the Horites from before them and **settled** in their place,
2:20 [A] considered a land of the Rephaites, who used to **live** there;
2:21 [A] who drove them out and **settled** in their place.
2:22 [A] who **lived** in Seir, when he destroyed the Horites from before
2:22 [A] drove them out and *have* **lived** in their place to this day.
2:23 [A] And as for the Avvites who **lived** in villages as far as Gaza,
2:23 [A] out from Caphtor destroyed them and **settled** in their place.)
2:29 [A] who **live** in Seir, and the Moabites, who live in Ar, did for
2:29 [A] live in Seir, and the Moabites, who **live** in Ar, did for us—
3: 2 [A] did to Sihon king of the Amorites, who **reigned** in Heshbon."
3:19 [A] much livestock) *may* **stay** in the towns I have given you,
3:29 [A] So *we* **stayed** in the valley near Beth Peor.
4:46 [A] who **reigned** in Heshbon and was defeated by Moses
6: 7 [A] Talk about them when you **sit** at home and when you walk
8:12 [A] are satisfied, when you build fine houses and **settle down**,
9: 9 [A] *I* **stayed** on the mountain forty days and forty nights;
11:19 [A] talking about them when you **sit** at home and when you walk
11:30 [A] in the territory of those Canaanites **living** in the Arabah in the
11:31 [A] When you have taken it over and *are* **living** there,
12:10 [A] **settle** in the land the LORD your God is giving you as an
12:10 [A] all your enemies around you so that *you will* **live** in safety.
12:29 [A] But when you have driven them out and **settled** in their land,
13:12 [13:13] [A] towns the LORD your God is giving you to **live in**
13:13 [13:14] [A] and have led the **people** *of* their town astray,
13:15 [13:16] [A] you must certainly put to the sword all *who* **live in**
17:14 [A] is giving you and have taken possession of it and **settled** in it,
17:18 [A] When he **takes** [+6584] the throne of his kingdom, he is to
19: 1 [A] have driven them out and **settled** in their towns and houses,
21:13 [A] After *she has* **lived** in your house and mourned her father
23:13 [23:14] [A] when you **relieve** [+2575] **yourself**, dig a hole and
23:16 [23:17] [A] *Let him* **live** among you wherever he likes and in
25: 5 [A] If brothers *are* **living** together and one of them dies without a
26: 1 [A] and have taken possession of it and **settled** in it,
28:30 [A] ravish her. You will build a house, but *you will* not **live** in it.
29:16 [29:15] [A] You yourselves know how *we* **lived** in Egypt
30:20 [A] he *will* **give** you many years in the land he swore to give to
Jos 1:14 [A] your livestock *may* **stay** in the land that Moses gave you east
2: 9 [A] so that all *who* **live in** this country are melting in fear
2:15 [A] for the house she **lived in** was part of the city wall.
2:22 [A] they left, they went into the hills and **stayed** there three days,
2:24 [A] our hands; all the **people** are melting in fear because of us."
5: 8 [A] *they* **remained** where they were in camp until they were
6:25 [A] to Jericho—and *she* **lives** among the Israelites to this day.
7: 7 [A] If only we had been content *to* **stay** on the other side of the
7: 9 [A] and the other **people** *of* the country will hear about this
8: 9 [A] the place of ambush and **lay in wait** between Bethel and Ai,
8:24 [A] When Israel had finished killing all the **men** *of* Ai in the
8:26 [A] out his javelin until he had destroyed all *who* **lived in** Ai.
9: 3 [A] when the **people** *of* Gibeon heard what Joshua had done to
9: 7 [A] of Israel said to the Hivites, "But perhaps you **live** near us.
9:11 [A] And our elders and all *those* **living in** our country said to us,
9:16 [A] Israelites heard that they were neighbors, **living** near them.
9:22 [A] 'We **live** a long way from you,' while actually you live near
9:24 [A] and to wipe out all its **inhabitants** from before you.
10: 1 [A] that the **people** *of* Gibeon had made a treaty of peace with
10: 6 [A] because all the Amorite kings from the hill country **[NIE]**
11:19 [A] Except for the Hivites **living in** Gibeon, not one city made a
12: 2 [A] Sihon king of the Amorites, who **reigned** in Heshbon.
12: 4 [A] last of the Rephaites, who **reigned** in Ashtaroth and Edrei.
13: 6 [A] "As for all the **inhabitants** *of* the mountain regions from
13:13 [A] so they *continue to* **live** among the Israelites to this day.
13:21 [A] princes allied with Sihon—*who* **lived in** that country.
14: 4 [A] received no share of the land but only towns to **live in**,
15:15 [A] From there he marched against the *people* **living in** Debir
15:63 [A] not dislodge the Jebusites, *who were* **living in** Jerusalem;
15:63 [A] to this day the Jebusites **live** there with the people of Judah.
16:10 [A] They did not dislodge the Canaanites **living** in Gezer; to this
16:10 [A] to this day the Canaanites **live** among the people of Ephraim
17: 7 [A] from there to include the *people* **living at** En Tappuah.
17:11 [A] Ibleam and the **people** *of* Dor, Endor, Taanach and Megiddo,
17:11 [A] the people of Dor, **[RPH]** Endor, Taanach and Megiddo,
17:11 [A] the people of Dor, Endor, **[RPH]** Taanach and Megiddo,
17:11 [A] the people of Dor, Endor, Taanach and **[RPH]** Megiddo,
17:12 [A] for the Canaanites were determined to **live** in that region.
17:16 [A] all the Canaanites who **live** in the plain have iron chariots,
19:47 [A] *They* **settled** in Leshem and named it Dan after their
19:50 [A] of Ephraim. And he built up the town and **settled** there.
20: 4 [A] him into their city and give him a place *to* **live** with them.
20: 6 [A] *He is to* **stay** in that city until he has stood trial before the
21: 2 [A] commanded through Moses that you give us towns to **live in**,
21:43 [A] and they took possession of it and **settled** there.
22:33 [A] the country where the Reubenites and the Gadites **lived**.
24: 2 [A] and Nahor, **lived** beyond the River and worshiped other gods.
24: 7 [A] the Egyptians. Then *you* **lived** in the desert for a long time.
24: 8 [A] " 'I brought you to the land of the Amorites who **lived** east of
24:13 [A] *you* **live** in them and eat from vineyards and olive groves that
24:15 [A] or the gods of the Amorites, in whose land you *are* **living**.
24:18 [A] all the nations, including the Amorites, *who* **lived in** the land.
Jdg 1: 9 [A] to fight against the Canaanites **living in** the hill country,
1:10 [A] They advanced against the Canaanites **living** in Hebron
1:11 [A] From there they advanced against the *people* **living in** Debir
1:16 [A] went up from the City of Palms with the men of Judah *to* **live**
1:17 [A] their brothers and attacked the Canaanites **living in** Zephath,
1:19 [A] they were unable to drive the **people** from the plains,
1:21 [A] to dislodge the Jebusites, *who were* **living in** Jerusalem;
1:21 [A] to this day the Jebusites **live** there with the Benjamites.
1:27 [A] Manasseh did not drive out *the* **people** *of* Beth Shan or
1:27 [A] or Taanach or Dor or **[RPH]** Ibleam or Megiddo and their
1:27 or Taanach or Dor or Ibleam or **[RPH]** Megiddo and their
1:27 [A] for the Canaanites were determined to **live** in that land.
1:29 [A] Nor did Ephraim drive out the Canaanites **living** in Gezer,
1:29 [A] but the Canaanites *continued to* **live** there among them.
1:30 [A] Neither did Zebulun drive out the Canaanites **living in** Kitron
1:30 [A] drive out the Canaanites living in Kitron or **[RPH]** Nahalol,
1:30 [A] living in Kitron or Nahalol, *who* **remained** among them;
1:31 [A] Nor did Asher drive out *those* **living in** Acco or Sidon
1:31 [A] or **[RPH]** Sidon or Ahlab or Aczib or Helbah or Aphek
1:32 [A] because of this the people of Asher **lived** among the

Jdg 1:32 [A] of Asher lived among the Canaanite **inhabitants** *of* the land.
1:33 [A] did Naphtali drive out *those* **living in** Beth Shemesh or
1:33 [A] out those living in Beth Shemesh or **[RPH]** Beth Anath;
1:33 [A] the Naphtalites too **lived** among the Canaanite inhabitants of
1:33 [A] the Naphtalites too lived among the Canaanite **inhabitants** *of*
1:33 [A] *those* **living in** Beth Shemesh and Beth Anath became forced
1:35 [A] the Amorites were determined also to **hold out** in Mount
2:2 [A] you shall not make a covenant with the **people** *of* this land,
3:3 [A] the Hivites **living in** the Lebanon mountains from Mount
3:5 [A] The Israelites **lived** among the Canaanites, Hittites,
3:20 [A] approached him while he *was* **sitting** alone in the upper room
4:2 [A] of his army was Sisera, who **lived** in Harosheth Haggoyim.
4:5 [A] She **held court** under the Palm of Deborah between Ramah
5:10 [A] who ride on white donkeys, **sitting** on your saddle blankets,
5:16 [A] Why *did you* **stay** among the campfires to hear the whistling
5:17 [A] Asher **remained** on the coast and stayed in his coves.
5:23 [A] 'Curse its **people** bitterly, because they did not come to help
6:10 [A] worship the gods of the Amorites, in whose land you **live**.'
6:11 [A] **sat down** under the oak in Ophrah that belonged to Joash the
6:18 [A] And the LORD said, "I *will* **wait** until you return."
8:29 [A] Jerub-Baal son of Joash went back home *to* **live**.
9:21 [A] *he* **lived** there because he was afraid of his brother
9:41 [A] Abimelech **stayed** in Arumah, and Zebul drove Gaal and his
9:41 [A] Zebul drove Gaal and his brothers out of **[NIE]** Shechem.
10:1 [A] He **lived** in Shamir, in the hill country of Ephraim.
10:18 [A] Ammonites will be the head of all *those* **living in** Gilead."
11:3 [A] fled from his brothers and **settled** in the land of Tob,
11:8 [A] and you will be our head over all *who* **live in** Gilead."
11:17 [A] king of Moab, and he refused. So Israel **stayed** at Kadesh.
11:21 [A] Israel took over all the land of the Amorites *who* **lived in** that
11:26 [A] For three hundred years Israel **occupied** Heshbon, Aroer, the
13:9 [A] the angel of God came again to the woman while she **was** out
15:8 [A] Then he went down and **stayed** in a cave in the rock of Etam.
16:9 [A] With men hidden **[NIE]** in the room, she called to him,
16:12 [A] Then, with men hidden **[NIE]** in the room, she called to
17:10 [A] said to him, "**Live** with me and be my father and priest,
17:11 [A] So the Levite agreed to **live** with him, and the young man
18:1 [A] was seeking a place of their own where they *might* **settle**,
18:7 [A] where they saw that the people *were* **living** in safety, like the
18:28 [A] Beth Rehob. The Danites rebuilt the city and **settled** there.
19:4 [A] so *he* **remained** with him three days, eating and drinking,
19:6 [A] So the two of them **sat down** to eat and drink together.
19:7 [A] persuaded him, so *he* **stayed** [+2256+4328] there *that* **night**.
19:15 [A] They went and **sat** in the city square, but no one took them
20:15 [A] addition to seven hundred chosen men from *those* **living in**
20:26 [A] up to Bethel, and there *they* **sat** weeping before the LORD.
20:47 [A] to the rock of Rimmon, where *they* **stayed** four months.
21:2 [A] where *they* **sat** before God until evening, raising their voices
21:9 [A] they found that none of the **people** *of* Jabesh Gilead were
21:10 [A] go to Jabesh Gilead and put to the sword *those* **living** there,
21:12 [A] They found among the *people* **living in** Jabesh Gilead four
21:23 [A] to their inheritance and rebuilt the towns and **settled** in them.
Ru 1:4 [A] the other Ruth. After *they had* **lived** there about ten years,
2:7 [A] from morning till now, except for a short **rest** in the shelter."
2:14 [A] When *she* **sat down** with the harvesters, he offered her some
2:23 [A] were finished. And *she* **lived** with her mother-in-law.
3:18 [A] Naomi said, "**Wait**, my daughter, until you find out what
4:1 [A] Meanwhile Boaz went up to the town gate and **sat** there.
4:1 [A] Boaz said, "Come over here, my friend, and **sit down**."
4:1 [A] my friend, and sit down." So he went over and **sat down**.
4:2 [A] Boaz took ten of the elders of the town and said, "**Sit** here,"
4:2 [A] the elders of the town and said, "Sit here," and *they* **did**[s] **so**.
4:4 [A] suggest that you buy it in the presence of these **seated** here
1Sa 1:9 [A] Now Eli the priest *was* **sitting** on a chair by the doorpost of
1:22 [A] him before the LORD, and *he will* **live** there always."
1:23 [A] "**Stay** here until you have weaned him; only may the LORD
1:23 [A] So the woman **stayed at home** and nursed her son until she
2:8 [G] *he* **seats** them with princes and has them inherit a throne of
4:4 [A] LORD Almighty, *who is* **enthroned** *between* the cherubim.
4:13 [A] there was Eli **sitting** on his chair by the side of the road,
5:7 [A] "The ark of the god of Israel *must* not **stay** here with us,
6:21 [A] Then they sent messengers to the **people** *of* Kiriath Jearim,
7:2 [A] twenty years in all, that the ark **remained** at Kiriath Jearim,
12:8 [G] your forefathers out of Egypt and **settled** them in this place.
12:11 [A] of your enemies on every side, so that *you* **lived** securely.
13:16 [A] and the men with them *were* **staying** in Gibeah in Benjamin,
14:2 [A] Saul *was* **staying** on the outskirts of Gibeah under a
19:2 [A] your guard tomorrow morning; **go** into hiding and stay there.
19:9 [A] Saul as he *was* **sitting** in his house with his spear in his hand.
19:18 [A] to him. Then he and Samuel went to Naioth and **stayed** there.
20:5 [A] and I *am* **supposed to dine** [+430+3782] with the king;
20:5 [A] and I *am* **supposed to dine** [+430+3782] with the king;
20:19 [A] you hid when this trouble began, and **wait** by the stone Ezel.
20:24 [A] when the New Moon festival came, the king **sat down** to eat.
20:25 [A] He **sat** in his customary place by the wall, opposite Jonathan,
20:25 [A] opposite Jonathan, and Abner **sat** next to Saul, but David's
22:4 [A] *they* **stayed** with him as long as David was in the stronghold.
22:5 [A] prophet Gad said to David, "*Do* not **stay** in the stronghold.
22:6 [A] *was* **seated** under the tamarisk tree on the hill at Gibeah,
22:23 [A] **Stay** with me; don't be afraid; the man who is seeking your
23:5 [A] losses on the Philistines and saved the **people** *of* Keilah.
23:14 [A] David **stayed** in the desert strongholds and in the hills of the
23:14 [A] and **[RPH]** in the hills of the Desert of Ziph.
23:18 [A] Then Jonathan went home, but David **remained** at Horesh.
23:25 [A] he went down to the rock and **stayed** in the Desert of Maon.
23:29 [24:1] [A] from there and **lived** in the strongholds of En Gedi.
24:3 [24:4] [A] and his men **were** far back in the cave.
25:13 [A] up with David, while two hundred **stayed** with the supplies.
26:3 [A] of Hakilah facing Jeshimon, but David **stayed** in the desert.
27:3 [A] David and his men **settled** in Gath with Achish. Each man
27:5 [A] to me in one of the country towns, that *I may* **live** there.
27:5 [A] Why *should* your servant **live** in the royal city with you?"
27:7 [A] David **lived** in Philistine territory a year and four months.
27:8 [A] (From ancient times these peoples *had* **lived in** the land
27:11 [A] was his practice as long as *he* **lived** in Philistine territory.
28:23 [A] to them. He got up from the ground and **sat** on the couch.
30:21 [G] to follow him and who *were* **left behind** at the Besor Ravine.
30:24 [A] The share of the *man who* **stayed** with the supplies is to be
31:7 [A] and fled. And the Philistines came and **occupied** them.
31:11 [A] When the **people** *of* Jabesh Gilead heard of what the
2Sa 1:1 [A] defeating the Amalekites and **stayed** in Ziklag two days.
2:3 [A] with his family, and *they* **settled** in Hebron and its towns.
2:13 [A] One group **sat down** on one side of the pool and one group
5:6 [A] to Jerusalem to attack the Jebusites, *who* **lived** there.
5:9 [A] David then **took up residence** in the fortress and called it the
6:2 [A] *who is* **enthroned** *between* the cherubim that are on the ark.
6:11 [A] The ark of the LORD **remained** *in* the house of
7:1 [A] After the king *was* **settled** in his palace and the LORD had
7:2 [A] Nathan the prophet, "Here I am, **living** in a palace of cedar,
7:2 [A] in a palace of cedar, while the ark of God **remains** in a tent."
7:5 [A] Are you the one to build me a house to **dwell in**?
7:6 [A] *I have* not **dwelt** in a house from the day I brought the
7:18 [A] King David went in and **sat** before the LORD, and he said:
9:13 [A] Mephibosheth **lived** in Jerusalem, because he always ate at
10:5 [A] "**Stay** at Jericho till your beards have grown, and then come
11:1 [A] and besieged Rabbah. But David **remained** in Jerusalem.
11:11 [A] "The ark and Israel and Judah *are* **staying** in tents, and my
11:12 [A] David said to him, "**Stay** here one more day, and tomorrow I
11:12 [A] So Uriah **remained** in Jerusalem that day and the next.
13:20 [A] Tamar **lived in** her brother Absalom's house, a desolate
14:28 [A] Absalom **lived** two years in Jerusalem without seeing the
15:8 [A] While your servant *was* **living** at Geshur in Aram, I made
15:19 [A] Go back and **stay** with King Absalom. You are a foreigner,
15:29 [A] took the ark of God back to Jerusalem and **stayed** there.
16:3 [A] Ziba said to him, "*He is* **staying** in Jerusalem, because he
16:18 [A] the men of Israel—his I will be, and *I will* **remain** with him.
18:24 [A] While David *was* **sitting** between the inner and outer gates,
19:8 [19:9] [A] So the king got up and **took** *his* **seat** in the gateway.
19:8 [19:9] [A] men were told, "The king *is* **sitting** in the gateway,"
1Ki 1:13 [A] son shall be king after me, and he *will* **sit** on my throne"?
1:17 [A] your son shall be king after me, and he *will* **sit** on my throne.'
1:20 [A] to learn from you who *will* **sit** on the throne of my lord the
1:24 [A] shall be king after you, and that he *will* **sit** on your throne?
1:27 [A] who *should* **sit** on the throne of my lord the king after him?"
1:30 [A] be king after me, and he *will* **sit** on my throne in my place."
1:35 [A] and he is to come and **sit** on my throne and reign in my place.
1:46 [A] Moreover, Solomon *has* **taken** *his* **seat** on the royal throne.
1:48 [A] who has allowed my eyes to see a **successor** on my throne
2:12 [A] So Solomon **sat** on the throne of his father David, and his
2:19 [A] to meet her, bowed down to her and **sat down** on his throne.
2:19 [A] for the king's mother, and *she* **sat down** at his right hand.
2:24 [G] he who has established me **securely** on the throne of my
2:36 [A] to him, "Build yourself a house in Jerusalem and **live** there,
2:38 [A] has said." And Shimei **stayed** in Jerusalem for a long time.
3:6 [A] and have given him a son *to* **sit** on his throne this very day.
3:17 [A] "My lord, this woman and I **live** in the same house.
4:25 [5:5] [A] and Israel, from Dan to Beersheba, **lived** in safety,
7:8 [A] the palace in which *he was to* **live**, set farther back, was
8:13 [A] temple for you, a place for you to **dwell** forever."
8:20 [A] David my father and now *I* **sit** on the throne of Israel,
8:25 [A] 'You shall never fail to have a man *to* **sit** before me on the
8:27 [A] "But *will* God really **dwell** on earth? The heavens,
8:30 [A] Hear from heaven, your **dwelling** place, and when you hear,
8:39 [A] then hear from heaven, your **dwelling** place. Forgive and act;
8:43 [A] hear from heaven, your **dwelling** place, and do whatever the
8:49 [A] your **dwelling** place, hear their prayer and their plea,
9:16 [A] He killed its Canaanite **inhabitants** and then gave it as a
11:16 [A] Joab and all the Israelites **stayed** there for six months,

1Ki 11:24 [A] went to Damascus, where *they* **settled** and took control.
12: 2 [a] he returned [BHS ***remained in***; NIV 8740] from Egypt.
12:17 [A] as for the Israelites who *were* **living** in the towns of Judah,
12:25 [A] Shechem in the hill country of Ephraim and **lived** there.
13:11 [A] Now *there was* a certain old prophet **living** in Bethel, whose
13:14 [A] He found him **sitting** under an oak tree and asked, "Are you
13:20 [A] While they were **sitting** at the table, the word of the LORD
13:25 [A] and reported it in the city where the old prophet **lived**.
15:18 [A] of Hezion, the king of Aram, who *was* **ruling** in Damascus.
15:21 [A] he stopped building Ramah and **withdrew** to Tirzah.
16:11 [A] As soon as he began to reign and *was* **seated** on the throne,
17: 5 [A] to the Kerith Ravine, east of the Jordan, and **stayed** there.
17: 9 [A] "Go at once to Zarephath of Sidon and **stay** there. I have
17:19 [A] carried him to the upper room where he *was* **staying**,
19: 4 [A] a broom tree, **sat down** under it and prayed that he might die.
21: 8 [A] to the elders and nobles who **lived** in Naboth's city with him.
21: 9 [G] and **seat** Naboth in a prominent place among the people.
21:10 [G] **seat** two scoundrels opposite him and have them testify that
21:11 [A] nobles who **lived** in Naboth's city did as Jezebel directed in
21:12 [G] and **seated** Naboth in a prominent place among the people.
21:13 [A] two scoundrels came and **sat** opposite him and brought
22: 1 [A] **[NIE]** For three years there was no war between Aram
22:10 [A] Jehoshaphat king of Judah *were* **sitting** on their thrones at
22:19 [A] I saw the LORD **sitting** on his throne with all the host of
2Ki 1: 9 [A] *who was* **sitting** on the top of a hill, and said to him, "Man of
2: 2 [A] Elijah said to Elisha, "**Stay** here; the LORD has sent me to
2: 4 [A] Elijah said to him, "**Stay** here, Elisha; the LORD has sent
2: 6 [A] Elijah said to him, "**Stay** here; the LORD has sent me to the
2:18 [A] who *was* **staying** in Jericho, he said to them, "Didn't I tell
4:13 [A] She replied, "I **have a home** among my own people."
4:20 [A] the boy **sat** on her lap until noon, and then he died.
4:38 [A] While the company of the prophets *was* **meeting** with him,
6: 1 [A] "Look, the place where we **meet** with you is too small for us.
6: 2 [A] us can get a pole; and let us build a place there for us to **live**."
6:32 [A] Now Elisha *was* **sitting** in his house, and the elders were
6:32 [A] was sitting in his house, and the elders *were* **sitting** with him.
7: 3 [A] They said to each other, "Why **stay** here until we die?
7: 4 [A] is there, and we will die. And if *we* **stay** here, we will die.
9: 5 [A] When he arrived, he found the army officers **sitting** together.
10:30 [A] your descendants *will* **sit** on the throne of Israel to the fourth
11:19 [A] the guards. The king then **took** *his* **place** on the royal throne,
13: 5 [A] So the Israelites **lived** in their own homes as they had before.
13:13 [A] with his fathers, and Jeroboam **succeeded** him on the throne.
14:10 [A] Glory in your victory, but **stay** at home! Why ask for trouble
15: 5 [A] until the day he died, and *he* **lived** in a separate house.
15:12 [A] "Your descendants *will* **sit** on the throne of Israel to the
16: 6 [A] then moved into Elath and *have* **lived** there to this day.
17: 6 [G] *He* **settled** them in Halah, in Gozan on the Habor River
17:24 [G] **settled** them in the towns of Samaria to replace the Israelites.
17:24 [A] the Israelites. They took over Samaria and **lived** in its towns.
17:25 [A] When they first **lived** there, they did not worship the
17:26 [G] **resettled** in the towns of Samaria do not know what the god
17:27 [A] priests you took captive from Samaria go back *to* **live** there
17:28 [A] who had been exiled from Samaria came *to* **live** in Bethel
17:29 [A] made its own gods in the several towns where they **settled**,
18:27 [A] to say these things, and not to the men **sitting** on the wall—
19:15 [A] God of Israel, **enthroned** *between* the cherubim,
19:26 [A] Their **people**, drained of power, are dismayed and put to
19:27 [A] " 'But I know *where* you **stay** and when you come and go
19:36 [A] and withdrew. He returned to Nineveh and **stayed** there.
22:14 [A] the wardrobe. She **lived** in Jerusalem, in the Second District.
22:16 [A] I am going to bring disaster on this place and its **people**,
22:19 [A] heard what I have spoken against this place and its **people**,
23: 2 [A] the **people** *of* Jerusalem, the priests and the prophets—
25:24 [A] "**Settle down** in the land and serve the king of Babylon,
1Ch 2:55 [A] and the clans of scribes *who* **lived at** Jabez: the Tirathites,
4:23 [A] They were the potters *who* **lived at** Netaim and Gederah;
4:23 [A] and Gederah; *they* **stayed** there and worked for the king.
4:28 [A] *They* **lived** in Beersheba, Moladah, Hazar Shual,
4:40 [A] peaceful and quiet. Some Hamites *had* **lived** there formerly.
4:41 [A] *they* **settled** in their place, because there was pasture for their
4:43 [A] who had escaped, and *they have* **lived** there to this day.
5: 8 [A] They **settled** in the area from Aroer to Nebo and Baal Meon.
5: 9 [A] To the east *they* **occupied** the land up to the edge of the
5:10 [A] *they* **occupied** the dwellings of the Hagrites throughout the
5:11 [A] The Gadites **lived** next to them in Bashan, as far as Salecah:
5:16 [A] The Gadites **lived** in Gilead, in Bashan and its outlying
5:22 [A] battle was God's. And *they* **occupied** the land until the exile.
5:23 [A] *they* **settled** in the land from Bashan to Baal Hermon, that is,
7:29 [A] The descendants of Joseph son of Israel **lived** in these towns.
8: 6 [A] who were heads of families of *those* **living in** Geba and were
8:13 [A] who were heads of families of *those* **living in** Aijalon
8:13 [A] living in Aijalon and who drove out the **inhabitants** *of* Gath.
8:28 [A] as listed in their genealogy, and they **lived** in Jerusalem.
8:29 [A] Jeiel the father of Gibeon **lived** in Gibeon. His wife's name
8:32 [A] of Shimeah. They too **lived** near their relatives in Jerusalem.
9: 2 [A] Now the first *to* **resettle** on their own property in their own
9: 3 [A] from Benjamin, and from Ephraim and Manasseh *who* **lived**
9:16 [A] of Elkanah, who **lived** in the villages of the Netophathites.
9:34 [A] as listed in their genealogy, and they **lived** in Jerusalem.
9:35 [A] Jeiel the father of Gibeon **lived** in Gibeon. His wife's name
9:38 [A] of Shimeam. They too **lived** near their relatives in Jerusalem.
10: 7 [A] and fled. And the Philistines came and **occupied** them.
11: 4 [A] to Jerusalem (that is, Jebus). The Jebusites *who* **lived** there
11: 5 [A] **[RPH]** said to David, "You will not get in here."
11: 7 [A] David then **took up residence** in the fortress, and so it was
13: 6 [A] God the LORD, *who is* **enthroned** *between* the cherubim—
13:14 [A] The ark of God **remained** with the family of Obed-Edom in
17: 1 [A] After David *was* **settled** in his palace, he said to Nathan the
17: 1 [A] Nathan the prophet, "Here I am, **living** in a palace of cedar,
17: 4 [A] You are not the one to build me a house to **dwell in**.
17: 5 [A] *I have* not **dwelt** in a house from the day I brought Israel up
17:16 [A] King David went in and **sat** before the LORD, and he said:
19: 5 [A] "**Stay** at Jericho till your beards have grown, and then come
20: 1 [A] to Rabbah and besieged it, but David **remained** in Jerusalem.
22:18 [A] For he has handed the **inhabitants** *of* the land over to me,
28: 5 [A] he has chosen my son Solomon to **sit** on the throne of the
29:23 [A] So Solomon **sat** on the throne of the LORD as king in place
2Ch 2: 3 [2:2] [A] when you sent him cedar to build a palace to **live** in.
6: 2 [A] temple for you, a place for you to **dwell** forever."
6:10 [A] David my father and now *I* **sit** on the throne of Israel,
6:16 [A] 'You shall never fail to have a man *to* **sit** before me on the
6:18 [A] "But *will* God really **dwell** on earth with men? The heavens,
6:21 [A] Hear from heaven, your **dwelling** place; and when you hear,
6:30 [A] hear from heaven, your **dwelling** place. Forgive, and deal
6:33 [A] hear from heaven, your **dwelling** place, and do whatever the
6:39 [A] your **dwelling** place, hear their prayer and their pleas,
8: 2 [G] that Hiram had given him, and **settled** Israelites in them.
8:11 [A] "My wife *must* not **live** in the palace of David king of Israel,
10:17 [A] as for the Israelites who *were* **living** in the towns of Judah,
11: 5 [A] Rehoboam **lived** in Jerusalem and built up towns for defense
15: 5 [A] for all the **inhabitants** *of* the lands were in great turmoil.
16: 2 [A] it to Ben-Hadad king of Aram, who *was* **ruling** in Damascus.
18: 9 [A] Jehoshaphat king of Judah *were* **sitting** on their thrones at
18: 9 [A] **[RPH]** at the threshing floor by the entrance to the gate of
18:18 [A] I saw the LORD **sitting** on his throne with all the host of
19: 4 [A] Jehoshaphat **lived** in Jerusalem, and he went out again
19: 8 [A] to settle disputes. And *they* **lived** [BHS 8740] **in** Jerusalem.
19:10 [A] you from your fellow countrymen who **live** in the cities—
20: 7 [A] did you not drive out the **inhabitants** *of* this land before your
20: 8 [A] *They have* **lived** in it and have built in it a sanctuary for your
20:15 [A] King Jehoshaphat and all *who* **live in** Judah and Jerusalem!
20:18 [A] all the **people** *of* Judah and Jerusalem fell down in worship
20:20 [A] and said, "Listen to me, Judah and **people** *of* Jerusalem!
20:23 [A] Moab rose up against the **men** *from* Mount Seir to destroy
20:23 [A] After they finished slaughtering the **men** *from* Seir,
21:11 [A] had caused the **people** *of* Jerusalem to prostitute themselves
21:13 [A] and the **people** *of* Jerusalem to prostitute themselves,
22: 1 [A] The **people** *of* Jerusalem made Ahaziah, Jehoram's youngest
23:20 [G] the Upper Gate and **seated** the king on the royal throne,
25:19 [A] and now you are arrogant and proud. But **stay** at home!
26: 7 [A] against the Arabs who **lived** in Gur Baal and against the
26:21 [A] *He* **lived in** a separate house—leprous, and excluded from
28:18 [A] They captured and **occupied** Beth Shemesh, Aijalon
30:25 [A] who had come from Israel and those *who* **lived** in Judah.
31: 4 [A] He ordered the people **living in** Jerusalem to give the portion
31: 6 [A] Judah who **lived** in the towns of Judah also brought a tithe of
32:10 [A] your confidence, that you **remain** in Jerusalem under siege?
32:22 [A] the **people** *of* Jerusalem from the hand of Sennacherib king
32:26 [A] of the pride of his heart, as did the **people** *of* Jerusalem;
32:33 [A] and the **people** *of* Jerusalem honored him when he died.
33: 9 [A] But Manasseh led Judah and the **people** *of* Jerusalem astray,
34: 9 [A] and Benjamin and the **inhabitants** [Q 8740] *of* Jerusalem.
34:22 [A] the wardrobe. She **lived** in Jerusalem, in the Second District.
34:24 [A] I am going to bring disaster on this place and its **people**—
34:27 [A] you heard what he spoke against this place and its **people**,
34:28 [A] on *those who* **live** here.' " So they took her answer back to
34:30 [A] the **people** *of* Jerusalem, the priests and the Levites—
34:32 [A] the **people** *of* Jerusalem did this in accordance with the
35:18 [A] and Israel who were there with the **people** *of* Jerusalem.
Ezr 2:70 [A] and the temple servants **settled** in their own towns,
4: 6 [A] they lodged an accusation against the **people** *of* Judah
8:32 [A] So we arrived in Jerusalem, where *we* **rested** three days.
9: 3 [A] pulled hair from my head and beard and **sat down** appalled.
9: 4 [A] And I **sat** there appalled until the evening sacrifice.
10: 2 [G] "We have been unfaithful to our God *by* **marrying** foreign
10: 9 [A] all the people *were* **sitting** in the square before the house of
10:10 [G] *you have* **married** foreign women, adding to Israel's guilt.

Ezr 10: 14 [G] let everyone in our towns who *has* **married** a foreign woman
10: 16 [A] On the first day of the tenth month *they* **sat down** to
10: 17 [G] dealing with all the men who *had* **married** foreign women.
10: 18 [G] of the priests, the following *had* **married** foreign women:
Ne 1: 4 [A] When I heard these things, *I* **sat down** and wept. For some
2: 6 [A] Then the king, with the queen **sitting** beside him, asked me,
3: 13 [A] Gate was repaired by Hanun and the **residents** *of* Zanoah.
3: 26 [A] the temple servants **living** on the hill of Ophel made repairs
4: 12 [4:6] [A] the Jews who **lived** near them came and told us ten
7: 3 [A] Also appoint **residents** *of* Jerusalem as guards, some at their
7: 73 [7:72] [A] the rest of the Israelites, **settled** in their own towns.
8: 14 [A] that the Israelites *were to* **live** in booths during the feast of
8: 17 [A] that had returned from exile built booths and **lived** in them.
9: 24 [A] subdued before them the Canaanites, *who* **lived in** the land;
11: 1 [A] Now the leaders of the people **settled** in Jerusalem,
11: 1 [A] cast lots to bring one out of every ten to **live** in Jerusalem,
11: 2 [A] The people commended all the men who volunteered to **live**
11: 3 [A] These are the provincial leaders who **settled** in Jerusalem
11: 3 [A] descendants of Solomon's servants **lived** in the towns of
11: 4 [A] people from both Judah and Benjamin **lived** in Jerusalem):
11: 6 [A] The descendants of Perez who **lived** in Jerusalem totaled 468
11: 21 [A] The temple servants **lived** on the hill of Ophel, and Ziha
11: 25 [A] some of the people of Judah **lived** in Kiriath Arba and its
13: 16 [A] Men from Tyre *who* **lived** in Jerusalem were bringing in fish
13: 23 [G] in those days I saw men of Judah *who had* **married** women
13: 27 [G] are being unfaithful to our God by **marrying** foreign
Est 1: 2 [A] At that time King Xerxes **reigned** from his royal throne in
1: 14 [A] special access to the king and **were** highest in the kingdom.
2: 19 [A] a second time, Mordecai *was* **sitting** at the king's gate.
2: 21 [A] During the time Mordecai *was* **sitting** at the king's gate,
3: 15 [A] The king and Haman **sat down** to drink, but the city of Susa
5: 1 [A] The king *was* **sitting** on his royal throne in the hall, facing
5: 13 [A] as long as I see that Jew Mordecai **sitting** at the king's gate."
6: 10 [A] suggested for Mordecai the Jew, who **sits** at the king's gate.
9: 19 [A] That is why rural Jews—those **living** in villages—observe
Job 2: 8 [A] and scraped himself with it as he **sat** among the ashes.
2: 13 [A] *they* **sat** on the ground with him for seven days and seven
15: 28 [A] he will inhabit ruined towns and houses where no *one* **lives**,
22: 8 [A] a powerful man, owning land—an honored man, **living** on it.
24: 13 [A] the light, who do not know its ways or **stay** in its paths.
29: 25 [A] I chose the way for them and **sat** as their chief; I dwelt as a
36: 7 [G] *he* **enthrones** [+2021+4058+4200] them with kings and exalts
38: 40 [A] when they crouch in their dens or **lie** in wait in a thicket?
Ps 1: 1 [A] or stand in the way of sinners or **sit** in the seat of mockers.
2: 4 [A] The *One* **enthroned** in heaven laughs; the Lord scoffs at
4: 8 [4:9] [G] for you alone, O LORD, **make** me **dwell** in safety.
7: 7 [7:8] [A] **Rule** [BHS 8740] over them from on high;
9: 4 [9:5] [A] *you have* **sat** on your throne, judging righteously.
9: 7 [9:8] [A] The LORD **reigns** forever; he has established his
9: 11 [9:12] [A] Sing praises to the LORD, **enthroned** *in* Zion;
10: 8 [A] *He* **lies** in wait near the villages; from ambush he murders the
17: 12 [A] a lion hungry for prey, like a great lion **crouching** in cover.
22: 3 [22:4] [A] Yet you *are* **enthroned** as the Holy One; you are the
23: 6 [A] my life, and *I will* **dwell** in the house of the LORD forever.
24: 1 [A] and everything in it, the world, and *all who* **live** in it;
26: 4 [A] *I do* not **sit** with deceitful men, nor do I consort with
26: 5 [A] the assembly of evildoers and refuse *to* **sit** with the wicked.
27: 4 [A] that I *may* **dwell** in the house of the LORD all the days of
29: 10 [A] The LORD **sits enthroned** over the flood; the LORD is
29: 10 [A] over the flood; the LORD *is* **enthroned** as King forever.
33: 8 [A] fear the LORD; let all the **people** *of* the world revere him.
33: 14 [A] from his **dwelling** place he watches all who live on earth—
33: 14 [A] from his dwelling place he watches all *who* **live** *on* earth—
47: 8 [47:9] [A] over the nations; God *is* **seated** on his holy throne.
49: 1 [49:2] [A] all you peoples; listen, all *who* **live in** this world,
50: 20 [A] You speak **continually** against your brother and slander your
55: 19 [55:20] [A] God, *who is* **enthroned** forever, will hear them
61: 7 [61:8] [A] *May he be* **enthroned** in God's presence forever;
65: 8 [65:9] [A] *Those* **living** far away fear your wonders;
68: 6 [68:7] [G] God **sets** the lonely in families, he leads forth the
68: 10 [68:11] [A] Your people **settled** in it, and from your bounty,
68: 16 [68:17] [A] at the mountain where God chooses to **reign**,
69: 12 [69:13] [A] *Those who* **sit** *at* the gate mock me, and I am the
69: 25 [69:26] [A] let there be no *one to* **dwell** in their tents.
69: 35 [69:36] [A] Then *people will* **settle** there and possess it;
75: 3 [75:4] [A] When the earth and all its **people** quake, it is I who
80: 1 [80:2] [A] you *who* **sit enthroned** *between* the cherubim,
83: 7 [83:8] [A] and Amalek, Philistia, with the **people** *of* Tyre.
84: 4 [84:5] [A] Blessed are *those who* **dwell in** your house; they are
91: 1 [A] *He who* **dwells** in the shelter of the Most High will rest in the
98: 7 [A] and everything in it, the world, and *all who* **live** in it.
99: 1 [A] *he* **sits enthroned** *between* the cherubim, let the earth shake.
101: 6 [A] be on the faithful in the land, that they *may* **dwell** with me;
101: 7 [A] No one who practices deceit *will* **dwell** in my house; no one
102: 12 [102:13] [A] you, O LORD, **sit enthroned** forever; your
107: 10 [A] *Some* **sat** *in* darkness and the deepest gloom,
107: 34 [A] because of the wickedness of *those who* **lived** there.
107: 36 [G] there *he* **brought** the hungry **to live**, and they founded a city
110: 1 [A] "**Sit** at my right hand until I make your enemies a footstool
113: 5 [A] the LORD our God, the One who **sits enthroned** on high,
113: 8 [G] he **seats** them with princes, with the princes of their people.
113: 9 [G] *He* **settles** the barren woman in her home as a happy mother
119: 23 [A] Though rulers **sit** *together* and slander me, your servant will
122: 5 [A] There the thrones for judgment **stand**, the thrones of the
123: 1 [A] I lift up my eyes to you, to you *whose* **throne** is in heaven.
125: 1 [A] Mount Zion, which cannot be shaken but **endures** forever.
127: 2 [A] In vain you rise early and **stay up** late, toiling for food to
132: 12 [A] then their sons *will* **sit** on your throne for ever and ever."
132: 14 [A] and ever; here *I will* **sit enthroned**, for I have desired it—
133: 1 [A] and pleasant it is *when* brothers **live** together in unity!
137: 1 [A] By the rivers of Babylon *we* **sat** and wept when we
139: 2 [A] You know *when* I **sit** and when I rise; you perceive my
140: 13 [140:14] [A] your name and the upright *will* **live** before you.
143: 3 [G] *he* **makes** me **dwell** in darkness like those long dead.
Pr 3: 29 [A] harm against your neighbor, who **lives** trustfully near you.
9: 14 [A] *She* **sits** at the door of her house, on a seat at the highest
20: 3 [A] It is to a man's honor *to* **avoid** [+4946] strife, but every fool
20: 8 [A] *When* a king **sits** on his throne to judge, he winnows out all
21: 9 [A] Better to **live** on a corner of the roof than share a house with
21: 19 [A] Better *to* **live** in a desert than with a quarrelsome and
23: 1 [A] When *you* **sit** to dine with a ruler, note well what is before
25: 24 [A] Better *to* **live** on a corner of the roof than share a house with
31: 23 [A] where he **takes** his **seat** among the elders of the land.
Ecc 10: 6 [A] in many high positions, while the rich **occupy** the low ones.
SS 2: 3 [A] I delight *to* **sit** in his shade, and his fruit is sweet to my taste.
5: 12 [A] washed in milk, **mounted** [+4859+6584] **like jewels**.
8: 13 [A] You who **dwell** in the gardens with friends in attendance,
Isa 3: 26 [A] will lament and mourn; destitute, *she will* **sit** on the ground.
5: 3 [A] "Now you **dwellers** *in* Jerusalem and men of Judah,
5: 8 [H] to field till no space is left and *you* **live** alone in the land.
5: 9 [A] become desolate, the fine mansions left without **occupants**.
6: 1 [A] I saw the Lord **seated** on a throne, high and exalted,
6: 5 [A] of unclean lips, and I **live** among a people of unclean lips,
6: 11 [A] "Until the cities lie ruined and without **inhabitant**,
8: 14 [A] And for the **people** *of* Jerusalem he will be a trap and a snare.
9: 2 [9:1] [A] on *those* **living** in the land of the shadow of death a
9: 9 [9:8] [A] Ephraim and the **inhabitants** *of* Samaria—who say
10: 13 [A] their treasures; like a mighty one I subdued their **kings**.
10: 24 [A] "O my people *who* **live in** Zion, do not be afraid of the
10: 31 [A] Madmenah is in flight; the **people** *of* Gebim take cover.
12: 6 [A] Shout aloud and sing for joy, **people** *of* Zion, for great is the
13: 20 [A] *She will* never *be* **inhabited** or lived in through all
14: 13 [A] *I will* **sit enthroned** on the mount of assembly, on the utmost
16: 5 [A] in faithfulness *a man will* **sit** on it—one from the house of
18: 3 [A] All you **people** *of* the world, you who live on the earth,
20: 6 [A] In that day the *people who* **live** *on* this coast will say,
21: 14 [A] you *who* **live in** Tema, bring food for the fugitives.
22: 21 [A] He will be a father to *those who* **live in** Jerusalem and to the
23: 2 [A] you **people** *of* the island and you merchants of Sidon,
23: 6 [A] Cross over to Tarshish; wail, you **people** *of* the island.
23: 18 [A] Her profits will go to those *who* **live** before the LORD,
24: 1 [A] devastate it; he will ruin its face and scatter its **inhabitants**—
24: 5 [A] The earth is defiled by its **people**; they have disobeyed the
24: 6 [A] a curse consumes the earth; its **people** must bear their guilt.
24: 6 [A] Therefore earth's **inhabitants** are burned up, and very few
24: 17 [A] Terror and pit and snare await you, O **people** *of* the earth.
26: 5 [A] He humbles *those who* **dwell** on high, he lays the lofty city
26: 9 [A] upon the earth, the **people** *of* the world learn righteousness.
26: 18 [A] to the earth; we have not given birth to **people** *of* the world.
26: 21 [A] his dwelling to punish the **people** *of* the earth for their sins.
28: 6 [A] He will be a spirit of justice to him *who* **sits** in judgment, a
30: 19 [A] O people of Zion, *who* **live** in Jerusalem, you will weep no
32: 16 [A] dwell in the desert and righteousness **live** in the fertile field.
32: 18 [A] My people *will* **live** in peaceful dwelling places, in secure
33: 24 [A] and the sins of those who **dwell** there will be forgiven.
36: 12 [A] to say these things, and not to the men **sitting** on the wall—
37: 16 [A] God of Israel, **enthroned** *between* the cherubim,
37: 27 [A] Their **people**, drained of power, are dismayed and put to
37: 28 [A] "But I know *where* you **stay** and when you come and go and
37: 37 [A] and withdrew. He returned to Nineveh and **stayed** there.
38: 11 [A] on mankind, or be with *those who now* **dwell in** this world.
40: 22 [A] He **sits enthroned** above the circle of the earth, and its
40: 22 [A] the circle of the earth, and its **people** are like grasshoppers.
40: 22 [A] like a canopy, and spreads them out like a tent to **live in**.
42: 7 [A] and to release from the dungeon *those who* **sit** *in* darkness.
42: 10 [A] and all that is in it, you islands, and *all who* **live in** them.
42: 11 [A] their voices; let the settlements where Kedar **lives** rejoice.
42: 11 [A] Let the **people** *of* Sela sing for joy; let them shout from the

Isa 44:13 [A] of man, of man in all his glory, that it *may* **dwell in** a shrine.
44:26 [H] '*It shall* **be inhabited**,' of the towns of Judah, 'They shall be
45:18 [A] did not create it to be empty, but formed it to *be* **inhabited**—
47: 1 [A] "Go down, **sit** in the dust, Virgin Daughter of Babylon; sit on
47: 1 [A] **sit** on the ground without a throne, Daughter of the
47: 5 [A] "**Sit** in silence, go into darkness, Daughter of the
47: 8 [A] **lounging** in your security and saying to yourself, 'I am,
47: 8 [A] *I will* never **be** a widow or suffer the loss of children.'
47:14 [A] Here are no coals to warm anyone; here is no fire to **sit** by.
49:19 [A] land laid waste, now you will be too small for your **people**,
49:20 [A] 'This place is too small for us; give us more space *to* **live in**.'
51: 6 [A] will wear out like a garment and its **inhabitants** die like flies.
52: 2 [A] Shake off your dust; rise up, **sit enthroned**, O Jerusalem.
54: 3 [G] will dispossess nations and **settle in** their desolate cities.
58:12 [A] of Broken Walls, Restorer of Streets with **Dwellings**.
65: 4 [A] who **sit** among the graves and spend their nights keeping
65:21 [A] They will build houses and **dwell in** them; they will plant
65:22 [A] No longer will they build houses and others **live in** them,
Jer 1:14 [A] "From the north disaster will be poured out on all *who* **live in**
2: 6 [A] and darkness, a land where no one travels and no one **lives**?'
2:15 [A] his land; his towns are burned and **deserted** [+1172+4946].
3: 2 [A] By the roadside *you* **sat waiting** for lovers, sat like a nomad
4: 4 [A] your hearts, you men of Judah and **people** *of* Jerusalem,
4: 7 [A] your land. Your towns will lie in ruins without **inhabitant**.
4:29 [A] the rocks. All the towns are deserted; no one **lives** in them.
6: 8 [C] and make your land desolate so no *one can* **live in** *it*."
6:12 [A] when I stretch out my hand against *those who* **live in** the
8: 1 [A] the bones of the **people** *of* Jerusalem will be removed from
8:14 [A] "Why *are* we **sitting** here? Gather together! Let us flee to the
8:16 [A] the land and everything in it, the city and *all who* **live** there."
9: 6 [9:5] [A] You **live** in the midst of deception; in their deceit they
9:11 [9:10] [A] waste the towns of Judah so no *one can* **live** there."
9:26 [9:25] [A] and all who **live** in the desert in distant places.
10:17 [A] your belongings to leave the land, you *who* **live** under siege.
10:18 [A] "At this time I will hurl out *those who* **live in** this land; I will
11: 2 [A] to the people of Judah and to *those who* **live in** Jerusalem.
11: 9 [A] among the people of Judah and *those who* **live in** Jerusalem.
11:12 [A] The towns of Judah and the **people** *of* Jerusalem will go
12: 4 [A] Because *those who* **live** in it are wicked, the animals
13:13 [A] I am going to fill with drunkenness all *who* **live in** this land,
13:13 [A] including the kings who **sit** on David's throne, the priests,
13:13 [A] the priests, the prophets and all *those* **living in** Jerusalem.
13:18 [A] and to the queen mother, "Come down from *your* **thrones**,
15:17 [A] *I* never **sat** in the company of revelers, never made merry
15:17 [A] *I* **sat** alone because your hand was on me and you had filled
16: 8 [A] a house where there is feasting and **sit down** to eat and drink.
17: 6 [A] places of the desert, in a salt land where no *one* **lives**.
17:20 [A] everyone **living in** Jerusalem who come through these gates.
17:25 [A] kings *who* **sit** on David's throne will come through the gates
17:25 [A] by the men of Judah and *those* **living in** Jerusalem,
17:25 [A] living in Jerusalem, and this city *will be* **inhabited** forever.
18:11 [A] say to the people of Judah and *those* **living in** Jerusalem,
19: 3 [A] of the LORD, O kings of Judah and **people** *of* Jerusalem.
19:12 [A] is what I will do to this place and to *those who* **live** here,
20: 6 [A] and all *who* **live in** your house will go into exile to Babylon.
21: 6 [A] I will strike down *those who* **live in** this city—both men
21: 9 [A] Whoever **stays** in this city will die by the sword, famine
21:13 [A] ⌞Jerusalem,⌟ you *who* **live** *above* this valley *on* the rocky
22: 2 [A] O king of Judah, you who **sit** on David's throne—
22: 4 [A] kings *who* **sit** on David's throne will come through the gates
22: 6 [C] will surely make you like a desert, like towns not **inhabited**.
22:23 [A] You *who* **live** in 'Lebanon,' who are nestled in cedar
22:30 [A] none *will* **sit** on the throne of David or rule anymore in
23: 8 [A] had banished them.' Then *they will* **live** in their own land."
23:14 [A] Sodom to me; the **people** *of* Jerusalem are like Gomorrah."
24: 8 [A] whether they remain in this land or **live** in Egypt.
25: 2 [A] all the people of Judah and to all *those* **living in** Jerusalem:
25: 5 [A] *you can* **stay** in the land the LORD gave to you and your
25: 9 [A] "and I will bring them against this land and its **inhabitants**
25:29 [A] for I am calling down a sword upon all *who* **live** *on* the earth,
25:30 [A] who tread the grapes, shout against all *who* **live** *on* the earth.
26: 9 [A] and this city will be desolate and **deserted** [+401+4946]?"
26:10 [A] **took** *their* **places** at the entrance of the New Gate of the
26:15 [A] on yourselves and on this city and on *those who* **live in** it,
27:11 [A] that nation remain in its own land to till it and *to* **live** there,
29: 5 [A] "Build houses and **settle down**; plant gardens and eat what
29:16 [A] this is what the LORD says about the king who **sits** on
29:16 [A] on David's throne and all the people who **remain** in this city,
29:28 [A] Therefore build houses and **settle down**; plant gardens
29:32 [A] He will have no one **left** among this people, nor will he see
30:18 [A] on her ruins, and the palace *will* **stand** in its proper place.
31:24 [A] *People will* **live** together in Judah and all its towns—farmers
32:12 [A] and of all the Jews **sitting** in the courtyard of the guard.
32:32 [A] and prophets, the men of Judah and the **people** *of* Jerusalem.
32:37 [G] will bring them back to this place and **let** them **live** in safety.
33:10 [A] **inhabited** *by* neither men nor animals, there will be heard
33:17 [A] 'David will never fail to have a man *to* **sit** on the throne of
34:22 [A] I will lay waste the towns of Judah so no *one can* **live** there."
35: 7 [A] never have any of these things, but *must* always **live** in tents.
35: 9 [A] or built houses to **live in** or had vineyards, fields or crops.
35:10 [A] *We have* **lived** in tents and have fully obeyed everything our
35:11 [A] and Aramean armies.' So *we have* **remained** in Jerusalem."
35:13 [A] Go and tell the men of Judah and the **people** *of* Jerusalem,
35:15 [A] *you will* **live** in the land I have given to you and your
35:17 [A] on everyone **living in** Jerusalem every disaster I pronounced
36:12 [A] room in the royal palace, where all the officials *were* **sitting**:
36:15 [A] They said to him, "**Sit down**, please, and read it to us."
36:22 [A] ninth month and the king *was* **sitting** in the winter apartment,
36:30 [A] He will have no *one to* **sit** on the throne of David; his body
36:31 [A] I will bring on them and *those* **living in** Jerusalem and the
37:16 [A] a vaulted cell in a dungeon, where he **remained** a long time.
37:21 [A] So Jeremiah **remained** in the courtyard of the guard.
38: 2 [A] 'Whoever **stays** in this city will die by the sword, famine
38: 7 [A] the cistern. While the king *was* **sitting** in the Benjamin Gate,
38:13 [A] And Jeremiah **remained** in the courtyard of the guard.
38:28 [A] Jeremiah **remained** in the courtyard of the guard until the
39: 3 [A] the king of Babylon came and **took seats** in the Middle Gate:
39:14 [A] back to his home. So *he* **remained** among his own people.
40: 5 [A] **live** with him among the people, or go anywhere else you
40: 6 [A] **stayed** with him among the people who were left behind in
40: 9 [A] "**Settle down** in the land and serve the king of Babylon,
40:10 [A] *I* myself *will* **stay** at Mizpah to represent you before the
40:10 [A] your storage jars, and **live** in the towns you have taken over."
41:17 [A] **stopping** at Geruth Kimham near Bethlehem on their way to
42:10 [A] 'If *you* **stay** [+3782] in this land, I will build you up and not
42:10 [A] 'If *you* **stay** [+3782] [BHS 8740] in this land, I will build you
42:13 [A] '*We will* not **stay** in this land,' and so disobey the LORD
42:14 [A] if you say, 'No, we will go and **live in** Egypt, where we will
42:18 [A] wrath have been poured out on *those who* **lived in**
43: 4 [A] all the people disobeyed the LORD's command to **stay** in
44: 1 [A] This word came to Jeremiah concerning all the Jews **living** in
44: 1 [A] **[RPH]** in Migdol, Tahpanhes and Memphis—and in Upper
44: 2 [A] of Judah. Today they *lie* **deserted** [+401+928] and in ruins
44:13 [A] I will punish those *who* **live** in Egypt with the sword, famine
44:14 [A] to the land of Judah, to which they long to return and **live**;
44:15 [A] all the people **living** in Lower and Upper Egypt, said to
44:22 [A] object of cursing and a desolate waste without **inhabitants**,
44:26 [A] But hear the word of the LORD, all Jews **living** in Egypt:
46: 8 [A] and cover the earth; I will destroy cities and their **people**.'
46:19 [A] you *who* **live in** Egypt, for Memphis will be laid waste
46:19 [A] will be laid waste and lie in ruins without **inhabitant**.
47: 2 [A] and everything in it, the towns and *those who* **live** in them.
47: 2 [A] The people will cry out; all *who* **dwell in** the land will wail
48: 9 [A] her towns will become desolate, with no *one to* **live** in them.
48:18 [A] "Come down from your glory and **sit** on the parched ground,
48:18 [A] the parched ground, O **inhabitants** *of* the Daughter of Dibon,
48:19 [A] Stand by the road and watch, *you who* **live in** Aroer.
48:28 [A] and dwell among the rocks, you *who* **live in** Moab.
48:43 [A] Terror and pit and snare await you, O **people** *of* Moab,"
49: 1 [A] possession of Gad? Why *do* his people **live** in its towns?
49: 8 [A] Turn and flee, **hide in** deep caves, you who live in Dedan,
49: 8 [A] Turn and flee, hide in deep caves, you *who* **live in** Dedan,
49:18 [A] says the LORD, "so no one *will* **live** there;
49:20 [A] what he has purposed against *those who* **live in** Teman:
49:30 [A] **Stay in** deep caves, you who live in Hazor,"
49:30 [A] Stay in deep caves, you *who* **live in** Hazor,"
49:31 [A] at ease, *which* **lives** in confidence," declares the LORD,
49:33 [A] No one *will* **live** there; no man will dwell in it."
50: 3 [A] No *one will* **live** in it; both men and animals will flee away.
50:13 [A] Because of the LORD's anger *she will* not *be* **inhabited**
50:21 [A] "Attack the land of Merathaim and *those who* **live in** Pekod.
50:34 [A] rest to their land, but unrest to *those who* **live in** Babylon.
50:35 [A] "against *those who* **live in** Babylon and against her officials
50:39 [A] "So desert creatures and hyenas *will* **live** there, and there the
50:39 [A] and hyenas will live there, and there the owl *will* **dwell**.
50:39 [A] *It will* never again *be* **inhabited** or lived in from generation
50:40 [A] declares the LORD, "so no one *will* **live** there;
51: 1 [A] of a destroyer against Babylon and the **people** *of* Leb Kamai.
51:12 [A] out his purpose, his decree against the **people** *of* Babylon.
51:24 [A] all *who* **live in** Babylonia for all the wrong they have done in
51:29 [A] lay waste the land of Babylon so that no *one will* **live** there.
51:30 [A] have stopped fighting; *they* **remain** in their strongholds.
51:35 [A] to our flesh be upon Babylon," say the **inhabitants** *of* Zion.
51:35 [A] "May our blood be on *those who* **live in** Babylonia,"
51:37 [A] an object of horror and scorn, a place where no *one* **lives**.
51:43 [A] be desolate, a dry and desert land, a land where no one **lives**,
51:62 [A] this place, so that neither man nor animal *will* **live** in it;
La 1: 1 [A] How deserted **lies** the city, once so full of people! How like a

La 1: 3 [A] She **dwells** among the nations; she finds no resting place.
2: 10 [A] The elders of the Daughter of Zion **sit** on the ground in
3: 6 [G] *He has* **made** me **dwell** in darkness like those long dead.
3: 28 [A] *Let him* **sit** alone in silence, for the LORD has laid it on
3: 63 [A] at them! **Sitting** or standing, they mock me in their songs.
4: 12 [A] nor did any of the world's **people**, that enemies and foes
4: 21 [A] O Daughter of Edom, you *who* **live** in the land of Uz.
5: 19 [A] You, O LORD, **reign** forever; your throne endures from
Eze 2: 6 [A] and thorns are all around you and you **live** among scorpions.
3: 15 [A] I came to the exiles who **lived at** Tel Abib near the Kebar
3: 15 [A] there, where they *were* **living**, I sat among them for seven
3: 15 [A] they were living, *I* **sat** [K 889] among them for seven days—
3: 15 [A] they were living, I sat **[RPH]** among them for seven days—
7: 7 [A] Doom has come upon you—you *who* **dwell in** the land.
8: 1 [A] *while* I *was* **sitting** in my house and the elders of Judah were
8: 1 [A] in my house and the elders of Judah *were* **sitting** before me,
8: 14 [A] and I saw women **sitting** there, mourning for Tammuz.
11: 15 [A] are those of whom the **people** *of* Jerusalem have said,
12: 2 [A] "Son of man, you *are* **living** among a rebellious people. They
12: 19 [A] the Sovereign LORD says about *those* **living in** Jerusalem
12: 19 [A] everything in it because of the violence of all who **live** there.
12: 20 [C] The **inhabited** towns will be laid waste and the land will be
14: 1 [A] the elders of Israel came to me and **sat down** in front of me.
15: 6 [A] fuel for the fire, so will I treat the *people* **living in** Jerusalem.
16: 46 [A] who **lived** to the north of you with her daughters;
16: 46 [A] who **lived** to the south of you with her daughters,
20: 1 [A] to inquire of the LORD, and *they* **sat down** in front of me.
23: 41 [A] *You* **sat** on an elegant couch, with a table spread before it on
25: 4 [D] *They will* **set up** their camps and pitch their tents among
26: 16 [A] Clothed with terror, *they will* **sit** on the ground, trembling
26: 17 [C] are destroyed, O city of renown, **peopled** *by men* of the sea!
26: 17 [A] You were a power on the seas, you and your **citizens**; you
26: 17 [A] and your citizens; you put your terror on all *who* **lived** there.
26: 19 [C] I make you a desolate city, like cities no longer **inhabited**,
26: 20 [G] *I will* **make** you **dwell** in the earth below, as in ancient ruins,
26: 20 [a] and *you will* not return [BHS ***remain***; NIV 8740]
27: 3 [A] Say to Tyre, **situated** at the gateway to the sea, merchant of
27: 8 [A] **Men** *of* Sidon and Arvad were your oarsmen; your skilled
27: 35 [A] All *who* **live in** the coastlands are appalled at you; their kings
28: 2 [A] a god; *I* **sit** *on* the throne of a god in the heart of the seas."
28: 25 [A] *they will* **live** in their own land, which I gave to my servant
28: 26 [A] *They will* **live** there in safety and will build houses and plant
28: 26 [A] *they will* **live** in safety when I inflict punishment on all their
29: 6 [A] Then all *who* **live in** Egypt will know that I am the LORD.
29: 11 [A] will pass through it; no *one will* **live** there for forty years.
31: 6 [A] under its branches; all the great nations **lived** in its shade.
31: 17 [A] Those *who* **lived** in its shade, its allies among the nations,
32: 15 [A] of everything in it, when I strike down all *who* **live** there,
33: 24 [A] the *people* **living in** those ruins in the land of Israel are
33: 31 [A] as they usually do, and **sit** before you to listen to your words,
34: 25 [A] rid the land of wild beasts so that *they may* **live** in the desert
34: 28 [A] *They will* **live** in safety, and no one will make them afraid.
35: 9 [A] desolate forever; your towns *will* not *be* **inhabited**. [Q 8740]
36: 10 [C] of Israel. The towns *will* **be inhabited** and the ruins rebuilt.
36: 11 [G] *I will* **settle** *people* **on** you as in the past and will make you
36: 17 [A] *when* the people of Israel *were* **living** in their own land,
36: 28 [A] *You will* **live** in the land I gave your forefathers; you will be
36: 33 [G] *I will* **resettle** your towns, and the ruins will be rebuilt.
36: 35 [A] desolate and destroyed, *are now* fortified and **inhabited**."
37: 25 [A] *They will* **live** in the land I gave to my servant Jacob,
37: 25 [A] I gave to my servant Jacob, the land where your fathers **lived**.
37: 25 [A] and their children's children *will* **live** there forever,
38: 8 [A] out from the nations, and now all of them **live** in safety.
38: 11 [A] I will attack a peaceful and unsuspecting **people**—all of them
38: 11 [A] all of them **living** without walls and without gates and bars.
38: 12 [C] and loot and turn my hand against the **resettled** ruins
38: 12 [A] rich in livestock and goods, **living** at the center of the land."
38: 14 [A] In that day, when my people Israel *are* **living** in safety, will
39: 6 [A] on Magog and on *those who* **live** in safety **in** the coastlands,
39: 9 [A] " 'Then *those who* **live in** the towns of Israel will go out
39: 26 [A] the unfaithfulness they showed toward me when they **lived**
44: 3 [A] The prince himself is the only one *who may* **sit** inside the
45: 5 [A] as their possession for towns to **live** [BHS 4384] **in**.
Da 9: 7 [A] the men of Judah and **people** *of* Jerusalem and all Israel,
Hos 3: 3 [A] I told her, "*You are to* **live** with me many days; you must not
3: 4 [A] For the Israelites *will* **live** many days without king or prince,
4: 1 [A] has a charge to bring against *you who* **live in** the land:
4: 3 [A] of this the land mourns, and all *who* **live** in it waste away;
9: 3 [A] *They will* not **remain** in the LORD's land; Ephraim will
11: 11 [G] *I will* **settle** them in their homes," declares the LORD.
12: 9 [12:10] [G] *I will* **make** you **live** in tents again, as in the days of
14: 7 [14:8] [A] *Men will* **dwell** again in his shade. He will flourish
Joel 1: 2 [A] Hear this, you elders; listen, all *who* **live in** the land. Has
1: 14 [A] all *who* **live in** the land to the house of the LORD your
2: 1 [A] Let all *who* **live in** the land tremble, for the day of the
3: 12 [4:12] [A] there *I will* **sit** to judge all the nations on every side.
3: 20 [4:20] [A] Judah *will be* **inhabited** forever and Jerusalem
Am 1: 5 [A] I will destroy the **king** *who is* in the Valley of Aven
1: 8 [A] I will destroy the **king** of Ashdod and the one who holds the
3: 12 [A] those *who* **sit** in Samaria on the edge of their beds and in
5: 11 [A] you have built stone mansions, *you will* not **live** in them;
8: 8 [A] not the land tremble for this, and all *who* **live** in it mourn?
9: 5 [A] touches the earth and it melts, and all *who* **live** in it mourn—
9: 14 [A] they will rebuild the ruined cities and **live in** them.
Jnh 3: 6 [A] covered himself with sackcloth and **sat down** in the dust.
4: 5 [A] Jonah went out and **sat down** at a place east of the city.
4: 5 [A] **sat** in its shade and waited to see what would happen to the
Mic 1: 11 [A] Pass on in nakedness and shame, *you who* **live in** Shaphir.
1: 11 [A] live in Shaphir. *Those who* **live in** Zaanan will not come out.
1: 12 [A] *Those who* **live in** Maroth writhe in pain, waiting for relief,
1: 13 [A] *You who* **live in** Lachish, harness the team to the chariot.
1: 15 [A] I will bring a conqueror against you *who* **live in** Mareshah.
4: 4 [A] Every man *will* **sit** under his own vine and under his own fig
5: 4 [5:3] [A] *they will* **live securely**, for then his greatness will
6: 12 [A] her **people** are liars and their tongues speak deceitfully.
6: 16 [A] I will give you over to ruin and your **people** to derision;
7: 8 [A] Though *I* **sit** in darkness, the LORD will be my light.
7: 13 [A] The earth will become desolate because of its **inhabitants**,
Na 1: 5 [A] trembles at his presence, the world and all *who* **live** in it.
3: 8 [A] than Thebes, **situated** on the Nile, with water around her?
Hab 2: 8 [A] destroyed lands and cities and **everyone** [+3972] in them.
2: 17 [A] destroyed lands and cities and **everyone** [+3972] in them.
Zep 1: 4 [A] my hand against Judah and against all *who* **live in** Jerusalem.
1: 11 [A] Wail, *you who* **live in** the market district; all your merchants
1: 13 [A] They will build houses but not **live in** them; they will plant
1: 18 [A] for he will make a sudden end of all *who* **live in** the earth."
2: 5 [A] Woe to *you who* **live** by the sea, O Kerethite people;
2: 5 [A] of the Philistines. "I will destroy you, and none *will be* **left**."
2: 15 [A] This is the carefree city that **lived** in safety. She said to
3: 6 [A] Their cities are destroyed; no *one will be* **left**—no one at all.
Hag 1: 4 [A] "Is it a time for you yourselves to *be* **living** in your paneled
Zec 1: 11 [A] the earth and found the whole world **at rest** and in peace."
2: 4 [2:8] [A] 'Jerusalem *will* **be** a city without walls because of the
2: 7 [2:11] [A] Escape, *you who* **live in** the Daughter of Babylon!"
3: 8 [A] O high priest Joshua and your associates **seated** before you,
5: 7 [A] of lead was raised, and there in the basket **sat** a woman!
6: 13 [A] be clothed with majesty and *will* **sit** and rule on his throne.
7: 7 [A] and its surrounding towns were **at rest** and prosperous,
7: 7 [A] and the Negev and the western foothills *were* **settled**?' "
8: 4 [A] and women of ripe old age *will* **sit** in the streets of Jerusalem,
8: 20 [A] and the **inhabitants** *of* many cities will yet come,
8: 21 [A] and the **inhabitants** *of* one city will go to another and say,
9: 5 [A] will lose her king and Ashkelon *will be* **deserted** [+4202].
9: 6 [A] Foreigners *will* **occupy** Ashdod, and I will cut off the pride
10: 6 [G] *I will* **restore** them because I have compassion on them.
11: 6 [A] For I will no longer have pity on the **people** *of* the land,"
12: 5 [A] 'The **people** *of* Jerusalem are strong, because the LORD
12: 6 [A] but Jerusalem *will* remain **intact** in her place.
12: 7 [A] of Jerusalem's **inhabitants** may not be greater than that of
12: 8 [A] On that day the LORD will shield *those who* **live in**
12: 10 [A] the **inhabitants** *of* Jerusalem a spirit of grace
13: 1 [A] to the house of David and the **inhabitants** *of* Jerusalem,
14: 10 [A] Jerusalem will be raised up and **remain** in its place, from the
14: 11 [A] It *will be* **inhabited**; never again will it be destroyed.
14: 11 [A] never again will it be destroyed. Jerusalem *will* **be** secure.
Mal 3: 3 [A] *He will* **sit** as a refiner and purifier of silver; he will purify

3783 יֹשֵׁב בַּשֶּׁבֶת *yōšēb baššebet*, n.pr.m. [1] [cf. 1416]

Josheb-Basshebeth [1]

2Sa 23: 8 **Josheb-Basshebeth**, a Tahkemonite, was chief of the Three;

3784 יֶשֶׁבְאָב *yešeb'āb*, n.pr.m. [1] [√ 8740 + 3]

Jeshebeab [1]

1Ch 24: 13 the thirteenth to Huppah, the fourteenth to **Jeshebeab**,

3785 יִשְׁבּוֹ בְּנֹב *yišbô benōb*, n.pr.m. [0] [cf. 1216]

2Sa 21: 16 [**Ishbi-Benob**, [K; see Q 3787] one of the descendants of Rapha,]

3786 יִשְׁבָּח *yišbāḥ*, n.pr.m. [1] [√ 8655]

Ishbah [1]

1Ch 4: 17 birth to Miriam, Shammai and **Ishbah** the father of Eshtemoa.

3787 יִשְׁבִּי בְּנֹב ***yišbî bᵉnōb***, n.pr.m. [1] [cf. 1216]

Ishbi-Benob [1]

2Sa 21:16 And **Ishbi-Benob**, [K 3785] one of the descendants of Rapha,

3788 יָשֻׁבִי לֶחֶם ***yāšubî leḥem***, n.pr.m. [1] [√ 3794 + 4312]

Jashubi Lehem [1]

1Ch 4:22 and Joash and Saraph, who ruled in Moab and **Jashubi Lehem**.

3789 יִשְׁבַּעַל ***yišbaʿal***, n.pr.m. Not used in NIV/BHS [√ 408 + 1251]

3790 יָשָׁבְעָם ***yāšobʿām***, n.pr.m. [3]

Jashobeam [3]

1Ch 11:11 **Jashobeam**, a Hacmonite, was chief of the officers; he raised his
12: 6 [12:7] Azarel, Joezer and **Jashobeam** the Korahites;
27: 2 first division, for the first month, was **Jashobeam** son of Zabdiel.

3791 יִשְׁבָּק ***yišbāq***, n.pr.m. [2] [→ 8749]

Ishbak [2]

Ge 25: 2 bore him Zimran, Jokshan, Medan, Midian, **Ishbak** and Shuah.
1Ch 1:32 Zimran, Jokshan, Medan, Midian, **Ishbak** and Shuah. The sons of

3792 יָשְׁבְּקָשָׁה ***yošbᵉqāšâ***, n.pr.m. [2]

Joshbekashah [2]

1Ch 25: 4 **Joshbekashah**, Mallothi, Hothir and Mahazioth.
25:24 the seventeenth to **Joshbekashah**, his sons and relatives, 12

3793 יָשׁוּב ***yāšûb¹***, n.pr.m. [3 / 4] [→ 3795; cf. 3806, 8740]

Jashub [4]

Ge 46:13 sons of Issachar: Tola, Puah, **Jashub** [BHS 3410] and Shimron.
Nu 26:24 through **Jashub**, the Jashubite clan; through Shimron,
1Ch 7: 1 Tola, Puah, **Jashub** [K 3806] and Shimron—four in all.
Ezr 10:29 Meshullam, Malluch, Adaiah, **Jashub**, Sheal and Jeremoth.

3794 ²יָשׁוּב ***yāšûb²***, n.loc. Not used in NIV/BHS [→ 3788]

3795 יָשׁוּבִי ***yāšûbî***, a.g. [1] [√ 3793; cf. 8740]

Jashubite [1]

Nu 26:24 through Jashub, the **Jashubite** clan; through Shimron,

3796 יִשְׁוָה ***yišwâ***, n.pr.m. [2] [√ 8750]

Ishvah [2]

Ge 46:17 The sons of Asher: Imnah, **Ishvah**, Ishvi and Beriah. Their sister
1Ch 7:30 The sons of Asher: Imnah, **Ishvah**, Ishvi and Beriah. Their sister

3797 יְשׁוֹחָיָה ***yᵉšôḥāyâ***, n.pr.m. [1] [√ 3378 + 8820?]

Jeshohaiah [1]

1Ch 4:36 Jaakobah, **Jeshohaiah**, Asaiah, Adiel, Jesimiel, Benaiah,

3798 ¹יִשְׁוִי ***yišwî¹***, n.pr.m. [4] [√ 8750]

Ishvi [4]

Ge 46:17 The sons of Asher: Imnah, Ishvah, **Ishvi** and Beriah. Their sister
Nu 26:44 through **Ishvi**, the Ishvite clan; through Beriah, the Beriite clan;
1Sa 14:49 Saul's sons were Jonathan, **Ishvi** and Malki-Shua. The name of his
1Ch 7:30 The sons of Asher: Imnah, Ishvah, **Ishvi** and Beriah. Their sister

3799 ²יִשְׁוִי ***yišwî²***, a.g. [1] [√ 8750]

Ishvite [1]

Nu 26:44 through Ishvi, the **Ishvite** clan; through Beriah, the Beriite clan;

3800 ¹יֵשׁוּעַ ***yēšûaʿ¹***, n.pr.m. [28] [√ 3801; cf. 3828; Ar 10336]

Jeshua [27], Joshua [1]

1Ch 24:11 the ninth to **Jeshua**, the tenth to Shecaniah,
2Ch 31:15 **Jeshua**, Shemaiah, Amariah and Shecaniah assisted him faithfully
Ezr 2: 2 **Jeshua**, Nehemiah, Seraiah, Reelaiah, Mordecai, Bilshan,
2: 6 of Pahath-Moab (through the line of **Jeshua** and Joab) 2,812
2:36 the descendants of Jedaiah (through the family of **Jeshua**)
2:40 the descendants of **Jeshua** and Kadmiel (through the line of
3: 2 **Jeshua** son of Jozadak and his fellow priests and Zerubbabel son
3: 8 **Jeshua** son of Jozadak and the rest of their brothers (the priests
3: 9 **Jeshua** and his sons and brothers and Kadmiel and his sons
4: 3 **Jeshua** and the rest of the heads of the families of Israel answered,
8:33 so were the Levites Jozabad son of **Jeshua** and Noadiah son of
10:18 From the descendants of **Jeshua** son of Jozadak, and his brothers:
Ne 3:19 Next to him, Ezer son of **Jeshua**, ruler of Mizpah, repaired another
7: 7 **Jeshua**, Nehemiah, Azariah, Raamiah, Nahamani, Mordecai,
7:11 of Pahath-Moab (through the line of **Jeshua** and Joab) 2,818
7:39 the descendants of Jedaiah (through the family of **Jeshua**)
7:43 the descendants of **Jeshua** (through Kadmiel through the line of
8: 7 **Jeshua**, Bani, Sherebiah, Jamin, Akkub, Shabbethai, Hodiah,
8:17 From the days of **Joshua** son of Nun until that day, the Israelites
9: 4 **Jeshua**, Bani, Kadmiel, Shebaniah, Bunni, Sherebiah, Bani
9: 5 **Jeshua**, Kadmiel, Bani, Hashabneiah, Sherebiah, Hodiah,
10: 9 [10:10] **Jeshua** son of Azaniah, Binnui of the sons of Henadad,
12: 1 who returned with Zerubbabel son of Shealtiel and with **Jeshua**:
12: 7 the leaders of the priests and their associates in the days of **Jeshua**.
12: 8 The Levites were **Jeshua**, Binnui, Kadmiel, Sherebiah, Judah,
12:10 **Jeshua** was the father of Joiakim, Joiakim the father of Eliashib,
12:24 Sherebiah, **Jeshua** son of Kadmiel, and their associates, who stood
12:26 They served in the days of Joiakim son of **Jeshua**, the son of

3801 ²יֵשׁוּעַ ***yēšûaʿ²***, n.pr.loc. [1] [√ 3800; cf. 3828]

Jeshua [1]

Ne 11:26 in **Jeshua**, in Moladah, in Beth Pelet,

3802 יְשׁוּעָה ***yᵉšûʿâ***, n.f. [78] [√ 3828]

salvation [47], deliverance [9], Savior [6], victories [5], save [2], victorious [2], deliver [1], deliverer [1], rescue [1], safety [1], saves [1], saving [1], victory [1]

Ge 49:18 "I look for your **deliverance**, O LORD.
Ex 14:13 and you will see the **deliverance** the LORD will bring you today.
15: 2 LORD is my strength and my song; he has become my **salvation**.
Dt 32:15 the God who made him and rejected the Rock his **Savior**.
1Sa 2: 1 mouth boasts over my enemies, for I delight in your **deliverance**.
14:45 he who has brought about this great **deliverance** in Israel?
2Sa 10:11 are too strong for me, then you are to come to my **rescue**;
22:51 He gives his king great **victories**; he shows unfailing kindness to
1Ch 16:23 to the LORD, all the earth; proclaim his **salvation** day after day.
2Ch 20:17 stand firm and see the **deliverance** the LORD will give you,
Job 13:16 Indeed, this will turn out for my **deliverance**, for no godless man
30:15 is driven away as by the wind, my **safety** vanishes like a cloud.
Ps 3: 2 [3:3] Many are saying of me, "God *will* not **deliver** him."
3: 8 [3:9] From the LORD comes **deliverance**. May your blessing be
9:14 [9:15] of the Daughter of Zion and there rejoice in your **salvation**.
13: 5 [13:6] in your unfailing love; my heart rejoices in your **salvation**.
14: 7 Oh, that **salvation** *for* Israel would come out of Zion!
18:50 [18:51] He gives his king great **victories**; he shows unfailing
20: 5 [20:6] We will shout for joy when you are **victorious** and will lift
21: 1 [21:2] How great is his joy in the **victories** you give!
21: 5 [21:6] Through the **victories** you gave, his glory is great;
22: 1 [22:2] Why are you so far from **saving** me, so far from the words
28: 8 strength of his people, a fortress of **salvation** *for* his anointed one.
35: 3 those who pursue me. Say to my soul, "I am your **salvation**."
35: 9 my soul will rejoice in the LORD and delight in his **salvation**.
42: 5 [42:6] your hope in God, for I will yet praise him, my **Savior** and
42:11 [42:12] in God, for I will yet praise him, my **Savior** and my God.
43: 5 hope in God, for I will yet praise him, my **Savior** and my God.
44: 4 [44:5] are my King and my God, who decrees **victories** *for* Jacob.
53: 6 [53:7] Oh, that **salvation** *for* Israel would come out of Zion!
62: 1 [62:2] finds rest in God alone; my **salvation** comes from him.
62: 2 [62:3] He alone is my rock and my **salvation**; he is my fortress,
62: 6 [62:7] He alone is my rock and my **salvation**; he is my fortress,
67: 2 [67:3] may be known on earth, your **salvation** among all nations.
68:19 [68:20] Praise be to the Lord, to God our **Savior**, who daily bears
69:29 [69:30] and distress; may your **salvation**, O God, protect me.
70: 4 [70:5] may those who love your **salvation** always say, "Let God
74:12 are my king from of old; you bring **salvation** upon the earth.
78:22 for they did not believe in God or trust in his **deliverance**.
80: 2 [80:3] and Manasseh. Awaken your might; come and **save** us.
88: 1 [88:2] the God who **saves** me, day and night I cry out before you.
89:26 [89:27] to me, 'You are my Father, my God, the Rock my **Savior**.'
91:16 With long life will I satisfy him and show him my **salvation**."
96: 2 the LORD, praise his name; proclaim his **salvation** day after day.
98: 2 The LORD has made his **salvation** known and revealed his
98: 3 all the ends of the earth have seen the **salvation** *of* our God.
106: 4 show favor to your people, come to my aid when you **save** them,
116:13 I will lift up the cup of **salvation** and call on the name of the
118:14 LORD is my strength and my song; he has become my **salvation**.
118:15 Shouts of joy and **victory** resound in the tents of the righteous:
118:21 you thanks, for you answered me; you have become my **salvation**.
119:123 My eyes fail, looking for your **salvation**, looking for your
119:155 **Salvation** is far from the wicked, for they do not seek out your
119:166 I wait for your **salvation**, O LORD, and I follow your commands.
119:174 I long for your **salvation**, LORD, O LORD, and your law is my delight.
140: 7 [140:8] O Sovereign LORD, my strong **deliverer**, who shields
149: 4 takes delight in his people; he crowns the humble with **salvation**.

Isa 12: 2 Surely God is my **salvation**; I will trust and not be afraid.
12: 2 is my strength and my song; he has become my **salvation**."
12: 3 With joy you will draw water from the wells of **salvation**.
25: 9 we trusted in him; let us rejoice and be glad in his **salvation**."
26: 1 have a strong city; God makes **salvation** its walls and ramparts.
26: 18 We have not brought **salvation** to the earth; we have not given
33: 2 Be our strength every morning, our **salvation** in time of distress.
33: 6 your times, a rich store of **salvation** and wisdom and knowledge;
49: 6 that you may bring my **salvation** to the ends of the earth."
49: 8 favor I will answer you, and in the day of **salvation** I will help you;
51: 6 my **salvation** will last forever, my righteousness will never fail.
51: 8 will last forever, my **salvation** through all generations."
52: 7 who proclaim **salvation**, who say to Zion, "Your God reigns!"
52: 10 and all the ends of the earth will see the **salvation** *of* our God.
56: 1 for my **salvation** is close at hand and my righteousness will soon
59: 11 look for justice, but find none; for **deliverance**, but it is far away.
59: 17 as his breastplate, and the helmet of **salvation** on his head;
60: 18 but you will call your walls **Salvation** and your gates Praise.
62: 1 shines out like the dawn, her **salvation** like a blazing torch.
Jnh 2: 9 [2:10] I will make good. **Salvation** comes from the LORD."
Hab 3: 8 sea when you rode with your horses and your **victorious** chariots?

3803 יֶשַׁח yešaḥ, n.[m.]. [1]

empty [1]

Mic 6: 14 You will eat but not be satisfied; your stomach will still be **empty**.

3804 יָשַׁט yāšaṭ, v. [3]

extend [1], extended [1], held out [1]

Est 4: 11 [G] The only exception to this is for the king *to* **extend** the gold
5: 2 [G] and **held out** to her the gold scepter that was in his hand.
8: 4 [G] the king **extended** the gold scepter to Esther and she arose

3805 יִשַׁי yišay, n.pr.m. [41] [→ 414]

Jesse [34], Jesse's [5], *untranslated* [1], him[s] [1]

Ru 4: 17 named him Obed. He was the father of **Jesse**, the father of David.
4: 22 Obed the father of **Jesse**, and Jesse the father of David.
4: 22 Obed the father of Jesse, and **Jesse** the father of David.
1Sa 16: 1 and be on your way; I am sending you to **Jesse** of Bethlehem.
16: 3 Invite **Jesse** to the sacrifice, and I will show you what to do.
16: 5 he consecrated **Jesse** and his sons and invited them to the sacrifice.
16: 8 Then **Jesse** called Abinadab and had him pass in front of Samuel.
16: 9 **Jesse** then had Shammah pass by, but Samuel said, "Nor has the
16: 10 **Jesse** had seven of his sons pass before Samuel, but Samuel said to
16: 10 but Samuel said to **him**[s], "The LORD has not chosen these."
16: 11 So he asked **Jesse**, "Are these all the sons you have?" "There is
16: 11 Samuel said, **[RPH]** "Send for him; we will not sit down until he
16: 18 "I have seen a son of **Jesse** of Bethlehem who knows how to play
16: 19 Saul sent messengers to **Jesse** and said, "Send me your son David,
16: 20 So **Jesse** took a donkey loaded with bread, a skin of wine and a
16: 22 Saul sent word to **Jesse**, saying, "Allow David to remain in my
17: 12 Now David was the son of an Ephrathite named **Jesse**, who was
17: 13 **Jesse's** three oldest sons had followed Saul to the war: The
17: 17 Now **Jesse** said to his son David, "Take this ephah of roasted grain
17: 20 flock with a shepherd, loaded up and set out, as **Jesse** had directed.
17: 58 David said, "I am the son of your servant **Jesse** of Bethlehem."
20: 27 "Why hasn't the son of **Jesse** come to the meal, either yesterday
20: 30 Don't I know that you have sided with the son of **Jesse** to your
20: 31 As long as the son of **Jesse** lives on this earth, neither you nor your
22: 7 Will the son of **Jesse** give all of you fields and vineyards?
22: 8 one tells me when my son makes a covenant with the son of **Jesse**.
22: 9 "I saw the son of **Jesse** come to Ahimelech son of Ahitub at Nob.
22: 13 you and the son of **Jesse**, giving him bread and a sword
25: 10 David's servants, "Who is this David? Who is this son of **Jesse**?
2Sa 20: 1 and shouted, "We have no share in David, no part in **Jesse's** son!
23: 1 "The oracle of David son of **Jesse**, the oracle of the man exalted by
1Ki 12: 16 "What share do we have in David, what part in **Jesse's** son?
1Ch 2: 12 Boaz the father of Obed and Obed the father of **Jesse**.
10: 14 him to death and turned the kingdom over to David son of **Jesse**.
12: 18 [12:19] We are with you, O son of **Jesse**! Success, success to you,
29: 26 David son of **Jesse** was king over all Israel.
2Ch 10: 16 "What share do we have in David, what part in **Jesse's** son?
11: 18 son Jerimoth and of Abihail, the daughter of **Jesse's** son Eliab.
Ps 72: 20 This concludes the prayers of David son of **Jesse**.
Isa 11: 1 A shoot will come up from the stump of **Jesse**; from his roots a
11: 10 In that day the Root of **Jesse** will stand as a banner for the peoples;

3806 יָשִׁיב yāšîb, n.pr.m. [0] [cf. 3793]

1Ch 7: 1 [Tola, Puah, **Jashub** [K; see Q 3793] and Shimron—four in all.]

3807 יִשִּׁיָּה yiššiyyâ, n.pr.m. [6] [√ 3780? + 3378]

Isshiah [5], Ishijah [1]

1Ch 7: 3 The sons of Izrahiah: Michael, Obadiah, Joel and **Isshiah**.
23: 20 The sons of Uzziel: Micah the first and **Isshiah** the second.
24: 21 As for Rehabiah, from his sons: **Isshiah** was the first.
24: 25 brother of Micah: **Isshiah**; from the sons of Isshiah: Zechariah.
24: 25 brother of Micah: Isshiah; from the sons of **Isshiah**: Zechariah.
Ezr 10: 31 of Harim: Eliezer, **Ishijah**, Malkijah, Shemaiah, Shimeon,

3808 יִשִּׁיָּהוּ yiššiyyāhû, n.pr.m. [1] [√ 3780? + 3378]

Isshiah [1]

1Ch 12: 6 [12:7] **Isshiah**, Azarel, Joezer and Jashobeam the Korahites;

3809 יְשִׁימָה y^e^šîmâ, n.f. Not used in NIV/BHS [√ 3815]

3810 יְשִׁימוֹן y^e^šîmôn, n.m. [13] [√ 3815]

wasteland [7], Jeshimon [4], waste [1], wastelands [1]

Nu 21: 20 valley in Moab where the top of Pisgah overlooks the **wasteland**.
23: 28 Balak took Balaam to the top of Peor, overlooking the **wasteland**.
Dt 32: 10 In a desert land he found him, in a barren and howling **waste**.
1Sa 23: 19 strongholds at Horesh, on the hill of Hakilah, south of **Jeshimon**?
23: 24 men were in the Desert of Maon, in the Arabah south of **Jeshimon**.
26: 1 not David hiding on the hill of Hakilah, which faces **Jeshimon**?"
26: 3 his camp beside the road on the hill of Hakilah facing **Jeshimon**,
Ps 68: 7 [68:8] O God, when you marched through the **wasteland**,
78: 40 against him in the desert and grieved him in the **wasteland**!
106: 14 gave in to their craving; in the **wasteland** they put God to the test.
107: 4 Some wandered in desert **wastelands**, finding no way to a city
Isa 43: 19 I am making a way in the desert and streams in the **wasteland**.
43: 20 because I provide water in the desert and streams in the **wasteland**,

3811 יְשִׁימוֹת y^e^šîmôt, n.pr.loc. Not used in NIV/BHS [→ 1093, 2127]

3812 יַשִּׁימָוֶת yaššîmāwet, n.f. [0] [√ 3815]

Ps 55: 15 [55:16] [Let **death** [K; see Q 4638] take my enemies by surprise;]

3813 יָשִׁישׁ yāšîš, a. [4] [→ 3814?; cf. 3844]

aged [2], old men [1], old [1]

Job 12: 12 Is not wisdom found among the **aged**? Does not long life bring
15: 10 The gray-haired and the **aged** are on our side, men even older than
29: 8 men saw me and stepped aside and the **old men** rose to their feet;
32: 6 "I am young in years, and you are **old**; that is why I was fearful,

3814 יְשִׁישַׁי y^e^šîšay, n.pr.m. [1] [√ 3813?]

Jeshishai [1]

1Ch 5: 14 of Michael, the son of **Jeshishai**, the son of Jahdo, the son of Buz.

3815 יָשַׁם yāšam, v. Not used in NIV/BHS [→ 3809, 3810, 3812; cf. 9037]

3816 יִשְׁמָא yišmā', n.pr.m. [1] [√ 3817]

Ishma [1]

1Ch 4: 3 These were the sons of Etam: Jezreel, **Ishma** and Idbash. Their

3817 יִשְׁמָעֵאל yišmā'ē'l, n.pr.m. [48] [→ 3816, 3818; cf. 9048 + 446]

Ishmael [47], he[s] [1]

Ge 16: 11 You shall name him **Ishmael**, for the LORD has heard of your
16: 15 and Abram gave the name **Ishmael** to the son she had borne.
16: 16 Abram was eighty-six years old when Hagar bore him **Ishmael**.
17: 18 said to God, "If only **Ishmael** might live under your blessing!"
17: 20 And as for **Ishmael**, I have heard you: I will surely bless him;
17: 23 On that very day Abraham took his son **Ishmael** and all those born
17: 25 and his son **Ishmael** was thirteen;
17: 26 and his son **Ishmael** were both circumcised on that same day.
25: 9 and **Ishmael** buried him in the cave of Machpelah near Mamre,
25: 12 This is the account of Abraham's son **Ishmael**, whom Sarah's
25: 13 These are the names of the sons of **Ishmael**, listed in the order of
25: 13 Nebaioth the firstborn of **Ishmael**, Kedar, Adbeel, Mibsam,
25: 16 These were the sons of **Ishmael**, and these are the names of the
25: 17 Altogether, **Ishmael** lived a hundred and thirty-seven years.
28: 9 so he went to **Ishmael** and married Mahalath, the sister of
28: 9 the sister of Nebaioth and daughter of **Ishmael** son of Abraham,
36: 3 also Basemath daughter of **Ishmael** and sister of Nebaioth.
2Ki 25: 23 **Ishmael** son of Nethaniah, Johanan son of Kareah, Seraiah son of
25: 25 however, **Ishmael** son of Nethaniah, the son of Elishama,

1Ch 1:28 The sons of Abraham: Isaac and **Ishmael**.
1:29 Nebaioth the firstborn of **Ishmael**, Kedar, Adbeel, Mibsam,
1:31 Jetur, Naphish and Kedemah. These were the sons of **Ishmael**.
8:38 Azrikam, Bokeru, **Ishmael**, Sheariah, Obadiah and Hanan.
9:44 Azrikam, Bokeru, **Ishmael**, Sheariah, Obadiah and Hanan.
2Ch 19:11 and Zebadiah son of **Ishmael**, the leader of the tribe of Judah,
23:1 son of Jeroham, **Ishmael** son of Jehohanan, Azariah son of Obed,
Ezr 10:22 Elioenai, Maaseiah, **Ishmael**, Nethanel, Jozabad and Elasah.
Jer 40:8 **Ishmael** son of Nethaniah, Johanan and Jonathan the sons of
40:14 Ammonites has sent **Ishmael** son of Nethaniah to take your life?"
40:15 "Let me go and kill **Ishmael** son of Nethaniah, and no one will
40:16 do such a thing! What you are saying about **Ishmael** is not true."
41:1 In the seventh month **Ishmael** son of Nethaniah, the son of
41:2 **Ishmael** son of Nethaniah and the ten men who were with him got
41:3 **Ishmael** also killed all the Jews who were with Gedaliah at
41:6 **Ishmael** son of Nethaniah went out from Mizpah to meet them,
41:7 **Ishmael** son of Nethaniah and the men who were with him
41:8 But ten of them said to **Ishmael**, "Don't kill us! We have wheat
41:9 Now the cistern where **he**[s] threw all the bodies of the men he had
41:9 king of Israel. **Ishmael** son of Nethaniah filled it with the dead.
41:10 **Ishmael** made captives of all the rest of the people who were in
41:10 **Ishmael** son of Nethaniah took them captive and set out to cross
41:11 about all the crimes **Ishmael** son of Nethaniah had committed,
41:12 took all their men and went to fight **Ishmael** son of Nethaniah.
41:13 When all the people **Ishmael** had with him saw Johanan son of
41:14 All the people **Ishmael** had taken captive at Mizpah turned
41:15 **Ishmael** son of Nethaniah and eight of his men escaped from
41:16 **Ishmael** son of Nethaniah after he had assassinated Gedaliah son
41:18 because **Ishmael** son of Nethaniah had killed Gedaliah son of

3818 יִשְׁמְעֵאלִי ***yišmᵉʿēʾlî***, a.g. [8] [√ 3817]

Ishmaelites [6], Ishmaelite [2]

Ge 37:25 looked up and saw a caravan of **Ishmaelites** coming from Gilead.
37:27 let's sell him to the **Ishmaelites** and not lay our hands on him;
37:28 and sold him for twenty shekels of silver to the **Ishmaelites**,
39:1 bought him from the **Ishmaelites** who had taken him there.
Jdg 8:24 (It was the custom of the **Ishmaelites** to wear gold earrings.)
1Ch 2:17 was the mother of Amasa, whose father was Jether the **Ishmaelite**.
27:30 Obil the **Ishmaelite** was in charge of the camels. Jehdeiah the
Ps 83:6 [83:7] the tents of Edom and the **Ishmaelites**, of Moab

3819 יִשְׁמַעְיָה ***yišmaʿyâ***, n.pr.m. [1] [→ 3820, 3821?; cf. 9048 + 3378]

Ishmaiah [1]

1Ch 12:4 and **Ishmaiah** the Gibeonite, a mighty man among the Thirty,

3820 יִשְׁמַעְיָהוּ ***yišmaʿyāhû***, n.pr.m. [1] [√ 3819; cf. 9048 + 3378]

Ishmaiah [1]

1Ch 27:19 over Zebulun: **Ishmaiah** son of Obadiah; over Naphtali:

3821 יִשְׁמְרַי ***yišmᵉray***, n.pr.m. [1] [√ 3819?; cf. 9048 + 3378]

Ishmerai [1]

1Ch 8:18 **Ishmerai**, Izliah and Jobab were the sons of Elpaal.

3822 יָשֵׁן[1] ***yāšēn***[1], v. [17 / 18] [→ 3823?, 3825, 3826?, 9104, 9097]

sleep [8], fell asleep [2], sleep [+9104] [2], sleeping [2], asleep [1], put to sleep [1], sleeps [1], smolders [1]

Ge 2:21 [A] while *he was* **sleeping**, he took one of the man's ribs
41:5 [A] *He* **fell asleep** again and had a second dream: Seven heads of
Jdg 16:13 [A] So *while he was* **sleeping**, [BHS-] Delilah took the seven
16:19 [D] *Having* **put** him **to sleep** on her lap, she called a man to
1Ki 19:5 [A] he lay down under the tree and **fell asleep**. All at once an
Job 3:13 [A] would be lying down in peace; *I would be* **asleep** and at rest
Ps 3:5 [3:6] [A] I lie down and **sleep**; I wake again,
4:8 [4:9] [A] I will lie down and **sleep** in peace, for you alone,
13:3 [13:4] [A] Give light to my eyes, or *I will* **sleep** *in* death;
44:23 [44:24] [A] Awake, O Lord! Why *do you* **sleep**?
121:4 [A] he who watches over Israel will neither slumber nor **sleep**.
Pr 4:16 [A] For *they* cannot **sleep** till they do evil; they are robbed of
Ecc 5:12 [5:11] [A] the abundance of a rich man permits him no **sleep**.
Isa 5:27 [A] of them grows tired or stumbles, not one slumbers or **sleeps**;
Jer 51:39 [A] **sleep** [+9104] forever and not awake," declares the LORD.
51:57 [A] *they will* **sleep** [+9104] forever and not awake,"
Eze 34:25 [A] they may live in the desert and **sleep** in the forests in safety.
Hos 7:6 [A] Their passion **smolders** all night; in the morning it blazes

3823 יָשֵׁן[2] ***yāšēn***[2], v. [3] [→ 3824; cf. 3822?]

chronic [1], last year's harvest [+3824] [1], lived a long time [1]

Lev 13:11 [C] it is a **chronic** skin disease and the priest shall pronounce him
26:10 [C] You will still be eating **last year's harvest** [+3824] when
Dt 4:25 [C] and grandchildren and *have* **lived** in the land **a long time**—

3824 יָשָׁן ***yāšān***, a. [6] [→ 3827?; cf. 3823]

old [3], it[s] [2], last year's harvest [+3823] [1]

Lev 25:22 you will eat from the **old** crop and will continue to eat from it until
25:22 will continue to eat from **it**[s] until the harvest of the ninth year
26:10 You will still be eating **last** [+3823] **year's harvest** when you will
26:10 when you will have to move **it**[s] out to make room for the new.
SS 7:13 [7:14] both new and **old**, that I have stored up for you, my lover.
Isa 22:11 a reservoir between the two walls for the water of the **Old** Pool,

3825 יָשֵׁן[3] ***yāšēn***[3], a. [8 / 7] [√ 3822]

asleep [2], sleep [2], sleeping [2], slept [1]

1Sa 26:7 lying **asleep** inside the camp with his spear stuck in the ground
26:12 They *were* all **sleeping**, because the LORD had put them into a
1Ki 3:20 and took my son from my side while I your servant was **asleep**.
18:27 or traveling. Maybe he is **sleeping** and must be awakened."
Ps 78:65 the Lord awoke as from **sleep**, as a man wakes from the stupor of
SS 5:2 I **slept** but my heart was awake. Listen! My lover is knocking:
7:9 [7:10] gently over lips and teeth. [BHS *of sleepers*; NIV 9094]
Da 12:2 Multitudes *who* **sleep** *in* the dust of the earth will awake: some to

3826 יָשֵׁן[4] ***yāšēn***[4], n.pr.m. [1] [√ 3822?]

Jashen [1]

2Sa 23:32 Eliahba the Shaalbonite, the sons of **Jashen**, Jonathan

3827 יְשָׁנָה ***yᵉšānâ***, n.pr.loc. [3] [√ 3824?]

Jeshanah [3]

2Ch 13:19 of Bethel, **Jeshanah** and Ephron, with their surrounding villages.
Ne 3:6 The **Jeshanah** Gate was repaired by Joiada son of Paseah
12:39 the **Jeshanah** Gate, the Fish Gate, the Tower of Hananel

3828 יָשַׁע ***yāšaʿ***, v. [184] [→ 3802, 3829, 3830, 4635, 4636, 4795, 4796, 9591; *also used with compound proper names*]

save [86], saved [22], be saved [11], saves [10], rescue [8], help [7], deliver [5], gave victory [4], rescued [3], worked salvation [3], am saved [2], avenging [2], bring victory [2], give victory [2], help at all [+3828+4200] [2], *untranslated* [1], are saved [1], avenged [1], be delivered [1], brought about victory [+9591] [1], came to rescue [1], deliverance [1], get help for [1], having salvation [1], is saved [1], kept safe [1], preserve [1], salvation [1], saving [1], spare [1]

Ex 2:17 [G] Moses got up and **came to** their **rescue** and watered their
14:30 [G] That day the LORD **saved** Israel from the hands of the
Nu 10:9 [C] by the LORD your God and **rescued** from your enemies.
Dt 20:4 [G] to fight for you against your enemies to **give** you **victory**."
28:31 [G] will be given to your enemies, and no *one will* **rescue** them.
33:29 [C] O Israel! Who is like you, a people **saved** by the LORD?
Jos 10:6 [G] Come up to us quickly and **save** us! Help us, because all the
22:22 [G] or disobedience to the LORD, *do* not **spare** us this day.
Jdg 2:16 [G] up judges, *who* **saved** them out of the hands of these raiders.
2:18 [G] **saved** them out of the hands of their enemies as long as the
3:9 [G] son of Kenaz, Caleb's younger brother, *who* **saved** them.
3:31 [G] six hundred Philistines with an oxgoad. He too **saved** Israel.
6:14 [G] the strength you have and **save** Israel out of Midian's hand.
6:15 [G] "But Lord," Gideon asked, "how *can I* **save** Israel? My clan
6:31 [G] going to plead Baal's cause? *Are* you *trying to* **save** him?
6:36 [G] "If you will **save** Israel by my hand as you have promised—
6:37 [G] I will know that *you will* **save** Israel by my hand, as you
7:2 [G] not boast against me that her own strength *has* **saved** her,
7:7 [G] "With the three hundred men that lapped *I will* **save** you
8:22 [G] because *you have* **saved** us out of the hand of Midian."
10:1 [G] Tola son of Puah, the son of Dodo, rose to **save** Israel.
10:12 [G] cried to me for help, *did I* not **save** you from their hands?
10:13 [G] and served other gods, so I will no longer **save** you.
10:14 [G] have chosen. *Let* them **save** you when you are in trouble!"
12:2 [G] and although I called, *you* didn't **save** me out of their hands.
12:3 [G] When I saw that you wouldn't **help**, I took my life in my
13:5 [G] he will begin the **deliverance** *of* Israel from the hands of the
1Sa 4:3 [G] it may go with us and **save** us from the hand of our enemies."
7:8 [G] that *he may* **rescue** us from the hand of the Philistines."
9:16 [G] *he will* **deliver** my people from the hand of the Philistines.
10:19 [G] who **saves** you out of all your calamities and distresses.
10:27 [G] some troublemakers said, "How *can* this fellow **save** us?"
14:6 [G] Nothing can hinder the LORD from **saving**, whether by

1Sa 14:23 [G] So the LORD **rescued** Israel that day, and the battle moved
17:47 [G] know that it is not by sword or spear that the LORD **saves**;
23: 2 [G] answered him, "Go, attack the Philistines and **save** Keilah."
23: 5 [G] losses on the Philistines and **saved** the people of Keilah.
25:26 [G] and from **avenging** yourself with your own hands,
25:31 [G] burden of needless bloodshed or of *having* **avenged** himself.
25:33 [G] this day and from **avenging** myself with my own hands.
2Sa 3:18 [G] 'By my servant David I *will* **rescue** my people Israel from the
8: 6 [G] The LORD **gave** David **victory** wherever he went.
8:14 [G] The LORD **gave** David **victory** wherever he went.
10:11 [G] are too strong for you, then I will come to **rescue** you.
10:19 [G] So the Arameans were afraid to **help** the Ammonites
14: 4 [G] ground to pay him honor, and she said, "**Help** me, O king!"
22: 3 [G] my refuge and my savior—from violent men *you* **save** me.
22: 4 [C] who is worthy of praise, and *I* **am saved** from my enemies.
22:28 [G] *You* **save** the humble, but your eyes are on the haughty to
2Ki 6:26 [G] a woman cried to him, "**Help** me, my lord the king!"
6:27 [G] The king replied, "If the LORD *does* not **help** you, where
6:27 [G] the LORD does not help you, where *can I* **get help for** you?
14:27 [G] *he* **saved** them by the hand of Jeroboam son of Jehoash.
16: 7 [G] Come up and **save** me out of the hand of the king of Aram
19:19 [G] Now, O LORD our God, **deliver** us from his hand, so that
19:34 [G] I will defend this city and **save** it, for my sake and for the
1Ch 11:14 [G] and the LORD **brought about** a great **victory** [+9591].
16:35 [G] Cry out, "**Save** us, O God our Savior; gather us and deliver
18: 6 [G] The LORD **gave** David **victory** everywhere he went.
18:13 [G] The LORD **gave** David **victory** everywhere he went.
19:12 [G] the Ammonites are too strong for you, then *I will* **rescue** you.
19:19 [G] So the Arameans were not willing to **help** the Ammonites
2Ch 20: 9 [G] out to you in our distress, and you will hear us and **save** us.'
32:22 [G] So the LORD **saved** Hezekiah and the people of Jerusalem
Ne 9:27 [G] *who* **rescued** them from the hand of their enemies.
Job 5:15 [G] *He* **saves** the needy from the sword in their mouth; he saves
22:29 [G] and you say, 'Lift them up!' then *he will* **save** the downcast.
26: 2 [G] the powerless! How *you have* **saved** the arm that is feeble!
40:14 [G] I myself will admit to you that your own right hand *can* **save**
Ps 3: 7 [3:8] [G] Arise, O LORD! **Deliver** me, O my God! Strike all
6: 4 [6:5] [G] deliver me; **save** me because of your unfailing love.
7: 1 [7:2] [G] in you; **save** and deliver me from all who pursue me,
7:10 [7:11] [G] is God Most High, *who* **saves** the upright in heart.
12: 1 [12:2] [G] **Help**, LORD, for the godly are no more; the faithful
17: 7 [G] you *who* **save** by your right hand those who take refuge in
18: 3 [18:4] [C] worthy of praise, and *I* **am saved** from my enemies.
18:27 [18:28] [G] You **save** the humble but bring low those whose
18:41 [18:42] [G] They cried for help, but there was no *one to* **save**
20: 6 [20:7] [G] Now I know that the LORD **saves** his anointed;
20: 9 [20:10] [G] O LORD, **save** the king! Answer us when we call!
22:21 [22:22] [G] **Rescue** me from the mouth of the lions; save me
28: 9 [G] **Save** your people and bless your inheritance; be their
31: 2 [31:3] [G] be my rock of refuge, a strong fortress to **save** me.
31:16 [31:17] [G] on your servant; **save** me in your unfailing love.
33:16 [C] No king **is saved** by the size of his army; no warrior escapes
34: 6 [34:7] [G] heard him; *he* **saved** him out of all his troubles.
34:18 [34:19] [G] and **saves** those who are crushed in spirit.
36: 6 [36:7] [G] O LORD, *you* **preserve** both man and beast.
37:40 [G] he delivers them from the wicked and **saves** them,
44: 3 [44:4] [G] won the land, nor *did* their arm **bring** them **victory**;
44: 6 [44:7] [G] in my bow, my sword *does* not **bring** me **victory**;
44: 7 [44:8] [G] *you* **give** us **victory** over our enemies, you put our
54: 1 [54:3] [G] **Save** me, O God, by your name; vindicate me by
55:16 [55:17] [G] But I call to God, and the LORD **saves** me.
57: 3 [57:4] [G] He sends from heaven and **saves** me, rebuking those
59: 2 [59:3] [G] from evildoers and **save** me from bloodthirsty men.
60: 5 [60:7] [G] **Save** us and help us with your right hand, that those
69: 1 [69:2] [G] **Save** me, O God, for the waters have come up to my
69:35 [69:36] [G] for God *will* **save** Zion and rebuild the cities of
71: 2 [G] me in your righteousness; turn your ear to me and **save** me.
71: 3 [G] give the command to **save** me, for you are my rock and my
72: 4 [G] among the people and **save** the children of the needy;
72:13 [G] on the weak and the needy and **save** the needy *from* death.
76: 9 [76:10] [G] rose up to judge, to **save** all the afflicted of the land.
80: 3 [80:4] [C] make your face shine upon us, that *we may* **be saved**.
80: 7 [80:8] [C] make your face shine upon us, that *we may* **be saved**.
80:19 [80:20] [C] your face shine upon us, that *we may* **be saved**.
86: 2 [G] You are my God; **save** your servant who trusts in you.
86:16 [G] to your servant and **save** the son of your maidservant.
98: 1 [G] right hand and his holy arm *have* **worked salvation** for him.
106: 8 [G] Yet *he* **saved** them for his name's sake, to make his mighty
106:10 [G] *He* **saved** them from the hand of the foe; from the hand of
106:21 [G] They forgot the God *who* **saved** them, who had done great
106:47 [G] **Save** us, O LORD our God, and gather us from the nations,
107:13 [G] in their trouble, and *he* **saved** them from their distress.
107:19 [G] in their trouble, and *he* **saved** them from their distress.
108: 6 [108:7] [G] **Save** us and help us *with* your right hand, that those
109:26 [G] O LORD my God; **save** me in accordance with your love.
109:31 [G] the needy one, to **save** his life from those who condemn him.
116: 6 [G] the simplehearted; when I was in great need, *he* **saved** me.
118:25 [G] O LORD, **save** us; O LORD, grant us success.
119:94 [G] **Save** me, for I am yours; I have sought out your precepts.
119:117 [C] Uphold me, and *I will* **be delivered**; I will always have
119:146 [G] I call out to you; **save** me and I will keep your statutes.
138: 7 [G] the anger of my foes, *with* your right hand *you* **save** me.
145:19 [G] of those who fear him; he hears their cry and **saves** them.
Pr 20:22 [G] this wrong!" Wait for the LORD, and *he will* **deliver** you.
28:18 [C] He whose walk is blameless *is* **kept safe**, but he whose ways
Isa 25: 9 [G] "Surely this is our God; we trusted in him, and *he* **saved** us.
30:15 [C] "In repentance and rest *is your* **salvation**, in quietness
33:22 [G] the LORD is our king; it is he *who will* **save** us.
35: 4 [G] with divine retribution he will come *to* **save** you."
37:20 [G] Now, O LORD our God, **deliver** us from his hand, so that
37:35 [G] "I will defend this city and **save** it, for my sake and for the
38:20 [G] The LORD *will* **save** me, and we will sing with stringed
43:12 [G] I have revealed and **saved** and proclaimed—I, and not some
45:17 [C] Israel *will* **be saved** by the LORD with an everlasting
45:20 [G] about idols of wood, who pray to gods *that* cannot **save**.
45:22 [C] "Turn to me and **be saved**, all *you* ends of the earth; for I am
46: 7 [G] to it, it does not answer; *it* cannot **save** him from his troubles.
47:13 [G] by month, *let them* **save** you from what is coming upon you.
47:15 [G] them goes on in his error; there is not *one that can* **save** you.
49:25 [G] those who contend with you, and your children I *will* **save**.
59: 1 [G] Surely the arm of the LORD is not too short *to* **save**, nor his
59:16 [G] so his own arm **worked salvation** for him, and his own
63: 1 [G] "It is I, speaking in righteousness, mighty to **save**."
63: 5 [G] so my own arm **worked salvation** for me, and my own wrath
63: 9 [G] too was distressed, and the angel of his presence **saved** them.
64: 5 [64:4] [C] you were angry. How then *can we* **be saved**?
Jer 2:27 [G] yet when they are in trouble, they say, 'Come and **save** us!'
2:28 [G] Let them come if *they can* **save** you when you are in trouble!
4:14 [C] O Jerusalem, wash the evil from your heart and **be saved**.
8:20 [C] is past, the summer has ended, and we **are** not **saved**."
11:12 [G] *they will* not **help** [+3828+4200] them **at all** when disaster
11:12 [G] *they will* not **help** them **at all** [+3828+4200] when disaster
14: 9 [G] a man taken by surprise, like a warrior powerless to **save**?
15:20 [G] for I am with you to **rescue** and save you,"
17:14 [G] **save** me and I will be saved, for you are the one I praise.
17:14 [C] save me and *I will* **be saved**, for you are the one I praise.
23: 6 [C] In his days Judah *will* **be saved** and Israel will live in safety.
30: 7 [C] be a time of trouble for Jacob, but *he will* **be saved** out of it.
30:10 [G] 'I *will* surely **save** you out of a distant place, your
30:11 [G] I am with you and *will* **save** you,' declares the LORD.
31: 7 [G] and say, 'O LORD, **save** your people, the remnant of Israel.'
33:16 [C] In those days Judah *will* **be saved** and Jerusalem will live in
42:11 [G] for I am with you and *will* **save** you and deliver you from his
46:27 [G] I *will* surely **save** you out of a distant place, your descendants
La 4:17 [G] from our towers we watched for a nation *that could* not **save**
Eze 34:22 [G] *I will* **save** my flock, and they will no longer be plundered.
36:29 [G] *I will* **save** you from all your uncleanness. I will call for the
37:23 [G] for *I will* **save** them from all their sinful backsliding, and I
Hos 1: 7 [G] *I will* **save** them—not by bow, sword or battle, or by horses
1: 7 [G] not **[RPH]** by bow, sword or battle, or by horses
13:10 [G] Where is your king, that *he may* **save** you? Where are your
14: 3 [14:4] [G] Assyria cannot **save** us; we will not mount
Hab 1: 2 [G] Or cry out to you, "Violence!" but *you do* not **save**?
Zep 3:17 [G] The LORD your God is with you, *he is* mighty *to* **save**.
3:19 [G] *I will* **rescue** the lame and gather those who have been
Zec 8: 7 [G] "I *will* **save** my people from the countries of the east and the
8:13 [G] O Judah and Israel, so *will I* **save** you, and you will be a
9: 9 [C] righteous and **having salvation**, gentle and riding on a
9:16 [G] The LORD their God *will* **save** them on that day as the
10: 6 [G] strengthen the house of Judah and **save** the house of Joseph.
12: 7 [G] "The LORD *will* **save** the dwellings of Judah first, so that

3829 יֵשַׁע ***yēša'***, n.m. [36] [→ 3801; cf. 3828; *also used with compound proper names*]

salvation [15], Savior [13], safety [2], victory [2], deliver [1], protect [+928+8883] [1], save [1], saving [1]

2Sa 22: 3 in whom I take refuge, my shield and the horn of my **salvation**.
22:36 You give me your shield of **victory**; you stoop down to make me
22:47 Praise be to my Rock! Exalted be God, the Rock, my **Savior**!
23: 5 Will he not bring to fruition my **salvation** and grant me my every
1Ch 16:35 Cry out, "Save us, O God our **Savior**; gather us and deliver us
Job 5: 4 His children are far from **safety**, crushed in court without a
5:11 lowly he sets on high, and those who mourn are lifted to **safety**.
Ps 12: 5 [12:6] says the LORD. "*I will* **protect** [+928+8883] them *from*
18: 2 [18:3] He is my shield and the horn of my **salvation**,
18:35 [18:36] You give me your shield of **victory**, and your right hand
18:46 [18:47] Praise be to my Rock! Exalted be God my **Savior**!

Ps 20: 6 [20:7] he answers him from his holy heaven with the **saving**
24: 5 blessing from the LORD and vindication from God his **Savior**.
25: 5 guide me in your truth and teach me, for you are God my **Savior**,
27: 1 The LORD is my light and my **salvation**—whom shall I fear?
27: 9 my helper. Do not reject me or forsake me, O God my **Savior**.
50: 23 he prepares the way so that I may show him the **salvation** *of* God."
51: 12 [51:14] Restore to me the joy of your **salvation** and grant me a
62: 7 [62:8] My **salvation** and my honor depend on God; he is my
65: 5 [65:6] O God our **Savior**, the hope of all the ends of the earth
69: 13 [69:14] great love, O God, answer me with your sure **salvation**.
79: 9 Help us, O God our **Savior**, for the glory of your name; deliver us
85: 4 [85:5] Restore us again, O God our **Savior**, and put away your
85: 7 [85:8] unfailing love, O LORD, and grant us your **salvation**.
85: 9 [85:10] Surely his **salvation** is near those who fear him, that his
95: 1 joy to the LORD; let us shout aloud to the Rock of our **salvation**.
132: 16 I will clothe her priests with **salvation**, and her saints will ever sing
Isa 17: 10 You have forgotten God your **Savior**; you have not remembered
45: 8 Let the earth open wide, let **salvation** spring up, let righteousness
51: 5 My righteousness draws near speedily, my **salvation** is on the way,
61: 10 For he has clothed me with garments of **salvation** and arrayed me
62: 11 "Say to the Daughter of Zion, 'See, your **Savior** comes! See,
Mic 7: 7 I watch in hope for the LORD, I wait for God my **Savior**;
Hab 3: 13 You came out to **deliver** your people, to save your anointed one.
3: 13 You came out to deliver your people, to **save** your anointed one.
3: 18 yet I will rejoice in the LORD, I will be joyful in God my **Savior**.

3830 יֹשַׁע *yōša'*, n.[m.] Not used in NIV/BHS [√ 3828]

3831 יִשְׁעִי *yiš'î*, n.pr.m. [5] [√ 3828? + 3378?]

Ishi [4], who[s] [1]

1Ch 2: 31 The son of Appaim: **Ishi**, who was the father of Sheshan. Sheshan
2: 31 The son of Appaim: Ishi, **who**[s] was the father of Sheshan.
4: 20 and Tilon. The descendants of **Ishi**: Zoheth and Ben-Zoheth.
4: 42 led by Pelatiah, Neariah, Rephaiah and Uzziel, the sons of **Ishi**,
5: 24 Epher, **Ishi**, Eliel, Azriel, Jeremiah, Hodaviah and Jahdiel.

3832 יְשַׁעְיָה *yeša'yâ*, n.pr.m. [4] [√ 3828 + 3378]

Jeshaiah [4]

1Ch 3: 21 Pelatiah and **Jeshaiah**, and the sons of Rephaiah, of Arnan,
Ezr 8: 7 of Elam, **Jeshaiah** son of Athaliah, and with him 70 men;
8: 19 together with **Jeshaiah** from the descendants of Merari,
Ne 11: 7 the son of Maaseiah, the son of Ithiel, the son of **Jeshaiah**,

3833 יְשַׁעְיָהוּ *yeša'yāhû*, n.pr.m. [35] [√ 3828 + 3378]

Isaiah [30], Jeshaiah [3], *untranslated* [2]

2Ki 19: 2 all wearing sackcloth, to the prophet **Isaiah** son of Amoz.
19: 5 When King Hezekiah's officials came to **Isaiah**,
19: 6 **Isaiah** said to them, "Tell your master, 'This is what the LORD
19: 20 **Isaiah** son of Amoz sent a message to Hezekiah: "This is what the
20: 1 The prophet **Isaiah** son of Amoz went to him and said, "This is
20: 4 Before **Isaiah** had left the middle court, the word of the LORD
20: 7 Then **Isaiah** said, "Prepare a poultice of figs." They did so
20: 8 Hezekiah had asked **Isaiah**, "What will be the sign that the
20: 9 **Isaiah** answered, "This is the LORD's sign to you that the
20: 11 the prophet **Isaiah** called upon the LORD, and the LORD made
20: 14 Then **Isaiah** the prophet went to King Hezekiah and asked,
20: 16 Then **Isaiah** said to Hezekiah, "Hear the word of the LORD:
20: 19 **[RPH]** For he thought, "Will there not be peace and security in
1Ch 25: 3 Gedaliah, Zeri, **Jeshaiah**, Shimei, Hashabiah and Mattithiah,
25: 15 the eighth to **Jeshaiah**, his sons and relatives, 12
26: 25 **Jeshaiah** his son, Joram his son, Zicri his son and Shelomith his
2Ch 26: 22 beginning to end, are recorded by the prophet **Isaiah** son of Amoz.
32: 20 the prophet **Isaiah** son of Amoz cried out in prayer to heaven about
32: 32 his acts of devotion are written in the vision of the prophet **Isaiah**
Isa 1: 1 Jerusalem that **Isaiah** son of Amoz saw during the reigns of
2: 1 This is what **Isaiah** son of Amoz saw concerning Judah
7: 3 the LORD said to **Isaiah**, "Go out, you and your son
13: 1 An oracle concerning Babylon that **Isaiah** son of Amoz saw:
20: 2 at that time the LORD spoke through **Isaiah** son of Amoz.
20: 3 "Just as my servant **Isaiah** has gone stripped and barefoot for three
37: 2 all wearing sackcloth, to the prophet **Isaiah** son of Amoz.
37: 5 When King Hezekiah's officials came to **Isaiah**,
37: 6 **Isaiah** said to them, "Tell your master, 'This is what the LORD
37: 21 **Isaiah** son of Amoz sent a message to Hezekiah: "This is what the
38: 1 The prophet **Isaiah** son of Amoz went to him and said, "This is
38: 4 Then the word of the LORD came to **Isaiah**:
38: 21 **Isaiah** had said, "Prepare a poultice of figs and apply it to the boil,
39: 3 Then **Isaiah** the prophet went to King Hezekiah and asked,
39: 5 **Isaiah** said to Hezekiah, "Hear the word of the LORD Almighty:
39: 8 **[RPH]** For he thought, "There will be peace and security in my

3834 יִשְׁפָּה *yišpâ*, n.pr.m. [1] [√ 9142]

Ishpah [1]

1Ch 8: 16 Michael, **Ishpah** and Joha were the sons of Beriah.

3835 יָשְׁפֵה *yāšepēh*, n.[m.]. [3]

jasper [3]

Ex 28: 20 in the fourth row a chrysolite, an onyx and a **jasper**. Mount them
39: 13 in the fourth row a chrysolite, an onyx and a **jasper**. They were
Eze 28: 13 chrysolite, onyx and **jasper**, sapphire, turquoise and beryl.

3836 יִשְׁפָּן *yišpān*, n.pr.m. [1] [√ 9142?]

Ishpan [1]

1Ch 8: 22 **Ishpan**, Eber, Eliel,

3837 יָשַׁר *yāšar*, v. [25] [→ 3838, 3839, 3840, 3841, 3842, 3843, 4793, 4797, 9227, 9228]

make straight [4], right [3], please [+928+6524] [2], pleased [+928+6524] [2], best [1], channeled [1], consider right [1], fix directly [1], go straight [1], good [1], hammered evenly [1], keeps straight [1], level [1], liked [+928+6524] [1], makes straight [1], pleased with [+928+6524] [1], upright [1], went straight [1]

Nu 23: 27 [A] Perhaps *it will* **please** [+928+6524] God to let you curse
Jdg 14: 3 [A] to his father, "Get her for me. She's the **right** *one* for me."
14: 7 [A] and talked with the woman, and he **liked** [+928+6524] her.
1Sa 6: 12 [D] the cows **went straight** *up* toward Beth Shemesh, keeping
18: 20 [A] when they told Saul about it, he *was* **pleased** [+928+6524].
18: 26 [A] he *was* **pleased** [+928+6524] to become the king's
2Sa 17: 4 [A] This plan seemed **good** to Absalom and to all the elders of
1Ki 6: 35 [E] overlaid them with gold **hammered evenly** over the carvings.
9: 12 [A] had given him, he *was* not **pleased** [+928+6524] **with** them.
1Ch 13: 4 [A] agreed to do this, because it seemed **right** to all the people.
2Ch 30: 4 [A] The plan seemed **right** both to the king and to the whole
32: 30 [D] **channeled** the water down to the west side of the City of
Ps 5: 8 [5:9] [G] of my enemies—**make straight** your way before me.
119: 128 [D] because *I* **consider** all your precepts **right**, I hate every
Pr 3: 6 [D] acknowledge him, and he *will* **make** your paths **straight**.
4: 25 [G] eyes look straight ahead, **fix** your gaze **directly** before you.
9: 15 [D] out to those who pass by, who **go straight** *on* their way.
11: 5 [D] The righteousness of the blameless **makes** *a* **straight** way for
15: 21 [D] but a man of understanding **keeps** a **straight** course.
Isa 40: 3 [D] **make straight** in the wilderness a highway for our God.
45: 2 [D] I will go before you and *will* **level** the mountains; I will break
45: 13 [D] *I will* **make** all his ways **straight**. He will rebuild my city
Jer 18: 4 [A] formed it into another pot, shaping it as seemed **best** to him.
27: 5 [A] that are on it, and I give it to anyone I **please** [+928+6524].
Hab 2: 4 [A] "See, he is puffed up; his desires *are* not **upright**—but the

3838 יָשָׁר *yāšār*[1], a. [117] [√ 3837]

upright [48], right [44], fit [3], just [2], straight [2], alliance [1], conscientious [+4222] [1], faultless [1], in accord with [+4222] [1], innocent [1], level [1], please [+928+2256+3202+6524] [1], please [+928+6524] [1], pleased [+928+6524] [1], reliable [1], right and true [1], righteous [1], safe [1], stretched out [1], truth [1], upright [+2006] [1], uprightness [1], worthy [1]

Ex 15: 26 the voice of the LORD your God and do what is **right** in his eyes,
Nu 23: 10 Let me die the death of the **righteous**, and may my end be like
Dt 6: 18 Do what is **right** and good in the LORD's sight, so that it may go
12: 8 You are not to do as we do here today, everyone as he sees **fit**,
12: 25 because you will be doing what is **right** in the eyes of the LORD.
12: 28 doing what is good and **right** in the eyes of the LORD your God.
13: 18 [13:19] I am giving you today and doing what is **right** in his eyes.
21: 9 since you have done what is **right** in the eyes of the LORD.
32: 4 A faithful God who does no wrong, upright and **just** is he.
Jos 9: 25 in your hands. Do to us whatever seems good and **right** to you."
Jdg 17: 6 In those days Israel had no king; everyone did as he saw **fit**.
21: 25 In those days Israel had no king; everyone did as he saw **fit**.
1Sa 12: 23 pray for you. And I will teach you the way that is good and **right**.
29: 6 to him, "As surely as the LORD lives, you have been **reliable**,
2Sa 19: 6 [19:7] I see that you would be **pleased** [+928+6524] if Absalom
1Ki 11: 33 nor done what is **right** in my eyes, nor kept my statutes and laws as
11: 38 do what is **right** in my eyes by keeping my statutes and commands,
14: 8 me with all his heart, doing only what was **right** in my eyes.
15: 5 For David had done what was **right** in the eyes of the LORD
15: 11 Asa did what was **right** in the eyes of the LORD, as his father
22: 43 stray from them; he did what was **right** in the eyes of the LORD.
2Ki 10: 3 choose the best and most **worthy** of your master's sons and set him
10: 15 Jehu greeted him and said, "Are you **in accord** [+4222] **with** me,
10: 30 "Because you have done well in accomplishing what is **right** in my
12: 2 [12:3] Joash did what was **right** in the eyes of the LORD all the
14: 3 He did what was **right** in the eyes of the LORD, but not as his

[F] Hitpael (hitpoel, hitpoal, hitpolel, hitpolal, hitpalel, hitpalal, hitpalpel, hitpalpal, hotpael, hotpaal) [G] Hiphil (hiphtil) [H] Hophal [I] Hishtaphel

2Ki 15: 3 He did what was **right** in the eyes of the LORD, just as his father
15:34 He did what was **right** in the eyes of the LORD, just as his father
16: 2 he did not do what was **right** in the eyes of the LORD his God.
18: 3 He did what was **right** in the eyes of the LORD, just as his father
22: 2 He did what was **right** in the eyes of the LORD and walked in all
2Ch 14: 2 [14:1] was good and **right** in the eyes of the LORD his God.
20:32 stray from them; he did what was **right** in the eyes of the LORD.
24: 2 Joash did what was **right** in the eyes of the LORD all the years of
25: 2 He did what was **right** in the eyes of the LORD, but not
26: 4 He did what was **right** in the eyes of the LORD, just as his father
27: 2 He did what was **right** in the eyes of the LORD, just as his father
28: 1 his father, he did not do what was **right** in the eyes of the LORD.
29: 2 He did what was **right** in the eyes of the LORD, just as his father
29:34 for the Levites had been more **conscientious** [+4222] in
31:20 doing what was good and **right** and faithful before the LORD his
34: 2 He did what was **right** in the eyes of the LORD and walked in the
Ezr 8:21 our God and ask him for a **safe** journey for us and our children,
Ne 9:13 You gave them regulations and laws that are **just** and right,
Job 1: 1 This man was blameless and **upright**; he feared God and shunned
1: 8 he is blameless and **upright**, a man who fears God and shuns evil."
2: 3 he is blameless and **upright**, a man who fears God and shuns evil.
4: 7 has ever perished? Where were the **upright** ever destroyed?
8: 6 if you are pure and **upright**, even now he will rouse himself on
17: 8 **Upright** *men* are appalled at this; the innocent are aroused against
23: 7 There an **upright** *man* could present his case before him,
33:27 he comes to men and says, 'I sinned, and perverted *what* was **right**,
Ps 7:10 [7:11] shield is God Most High, who saves the **upright** *in* heart.
11: 2 the strings to shoot from the shadows at the **upright** *in* heart.
11: 7 is righteous, he loves justice; **upright** *men* will see his face.
19: 8 [19:9] The precepts of the LORD are **right**, giving joy to the
25: 8 Good and **upright** is the LORD; therefore he instructs sinners in
32:11 and be glad, you righteous; sing, all you *who* are **upright** *in* heart!
33: 1 you righteous; it is fitting for the **upright** to praise him.
33: 4 For the word of the LORD is **right and true**; he is faithful in all
36:10 [36:11] know you, your righteousness to the **upright** *in* heart.
37:14 down the poor and needy, to slay *those* whose ways are **upright**.
37:37 Consider the blameless, observe the **upright**; there is a future for
49:14 [49:15] The **upright** will rule over them in the morning; their
64:10 [64:11] take refuge in him; let all the **upright** *in* heart praise him!
92:15 [92:16] proclaiming, "The LORD is **upright**; he is my Rock,
94:15 on righteousness, and all the **upright** *in* heart will follow it.
97:11 Light is shed upon the righteous and joy on the **upright** *in* heart.
107: 7 He led them by a **straight** way to a city where they could settle.
107:42 The **upright** see and rejoice, but all the wicked shut their mouths.
111: 1 extol the LORD with all my heart in the council of the **upright**
111: 8 steadfast for ever and ever, done in faithfulness and **uprightness**.
112: 2 mighty in the land; the generation of the **upright** will be blessed.
112: 4 Even in darkness light dawns for the **upright**, for the gracious
119:137 Righteous are you, O LORD, and your laws are **right**.
125: 4 to those who are good, to *those who* are **upright** in heart.
140:13 [140:14] praise your name and the **upright** will live before you.
Pr 2: 7 He holds victory in store for the **upright**, he is a shield to those
2:21 For the **upright** will live in the land, and the blameless will remain
3:32 detests a perverse man but takes the **upright** into his confidence.
8: 9 of them are right; they are **faultless** to those who have knowledge.
11: 3 The integrity of the **upright** guides them, but the unfaithful are
11: 6 The righteousness of the **upright** delivers them, but the unfaithful
11:11 Through the blessing of the **upright** a city is exalted, but by the
12: 6 lie in wait for blood, but the speech of the **upright** rescues them.
12:15 The way of a fool seems **right** to him, but a wise man listens to
14: 9 making amends for sin, but goodwill is found among the **upright**.
14:11 wicked will be destroyed, but the tent of the **upright** will flourish.
14:12 There is a way that seems **right** to a man, but in the end it leads to
15: 8 sacrifice of the wicked, but the prayer of the **upright** pleases him.
15:19 is blocked with thorns, but the path of the **upright** is a highway.
16:13 pleasure in honest lips; they value a man who speaks the **truth**.
16:17 The highway of the **upright** avoids evil; he who guards his way
16:25 There is a way that seems **right** to a man, but in the end it leads to
20:11 is known by his actions, by whether his conduct is pure and **right**.
21: 2 All a man's ways seem **right** to him, but the LORD weighs the
21: 8 of the guilty is devious, but the conduct of the **innocent** is upright.
21:18 a ransom for the righteous, and the unfaithful for the **upright**.
21:29 up a bold front, but an **upright** *man* gives thought to his ways.
28:10 He who leads the **upright** along an evil path will fall into his own
29:10 men hate a man of integrity and seek to kill the **upright**.
29:27 detest the dishonest; the wicked detest the **upright** [+2006].
Ecc 7:29 God made mankind **upright**, but men have gone in search of many
Isa 26: 7 O **upright** *One*, you make the way of the righteous smooth.
Jer 26:14 in your hands; do with me whatever you think is good and **right**.
31: 9 I will lead them beside streams of water on a **level** path where they
34:15 Recently you repented and did *what* is **right** in my sight: Each of
40: 4 go wherever you **please** [+928+2256+3202+6524]."
40: 5 among the people, or go anywhere else you **please** [+928+6524]."
Eze 1: 7 Their legs were **straight**; their feet were like those of a calf
1:23 Under the expanse their wings were **stretched out** one toward the
Da 11:17 and will make an **alliance** with the king of the South.
Hos 14: 9 [14:10] The ways of the LORD are **right**; the righteous walk in
Mic 2: 7 "Do not my words do good to him whose ways are **upright**?
3: 9 the house of Israel, who despise justice and distort all that is **right**;
7: 2 have been swept from the land; not one **upright** man remains.
7: 4 of them is like a brier, the most **upright** worse than a thorn hedge.

3839 ²יָשָׁר *yāšār²*, n.pr.m. [2] [√ 3837]

Jashar [2]

Jos 10:13 itself on its enemies, as it is written in the Book of **Jashar**.
2Sa 1:18 taught this lament of the bow (it is written in the Book of **Jashar**):

3840 יֵשֶׁר *yēšer*, n.pr.m. [1] [√ 3837]

Jesher [1]

1Ch 2:18 (and by Jerioth). These were her sons: **Jesher**, Shobab and Ardon.

3841 יֹשֶׁר *yōšer*, n.m. [14] [√ 3837]

upright [4], honest [2], straight [2], uprightness [2], integrity [+4222] [1], integrity [1], right [1], unduly [+4946] [1]

Dt 9: 5 or your **integrity** [+4222] that you are going in to take possession
1Ki 9: 4 if you walk before me in integrity of heart and **uprightness**,
1Ch 29:17 All these things have I given willingly and with **honest** intent.
Job 6:25 How painful are **honest** words! But what do your arguments
33: 3 My words come from an **upright** heart; my lips sincerely speak
33:23 one out of a thousand, to tell a man *what* is **right** *for* him,
Ps 25:21 May integrity and **uprightness** protect me, because my hope is in
119: 7 I will praise you with an **upright** heart as I learn your righteous
Pr 2:13 who leave the **straight** paths to walk in dark ways,
4:11 guide you in the way of wisdom and lead you along **straight** paths.
11:24 another withholds **unduly** [+4946], but comes to poverty.
14: 2 He whose walk is **upright** fears the LORD, but he whose ways
17:26 to punish an innocent man, or to flog officials for their **integrity**.
Ecc 12:10 find just the right words, and what he wrote was **upright** and true.

3842 יִשְׁרָה *yišrâ*, n.f. [1] [√ 3837]

upright [1]

1Ki 3: 6 because he was faithful to you and righteous and **upright** *in* heart.

3843 יְשֻׁרוּן *yᵉšurûn*, n.pr.m. [4] [√ 3837]

Jeshurun [4]

Dt 32:15 **Jeshurun** grew fat and kicked; filled with food, he became heavy
33: 5 He was king over **Jeshurun** when the leaders of the people
33:26 "There is no one like the God of **Jeshurun**, who rides on the
Isa 44: 2 Do not be afraid, O Jacob, my servant, **Jeshurun**, whom I have

3844 יָשֵׁשׁ *yāšēš*, a. [1] [→ 3813]

aged [1]

2Ch 36:17 and spared neither young man nor young woman, old man or **aged**.

3845 יָתֵד *yātēd*, n.f. [24 / 25]

tent pegs [7], peg [4], pin [3], tent peg [3], stakes [2], those[s] [2], *untranslated* [1], firm place [1], pegs [1], something to dig with [1]

Ex 27:19 including all the **tent pegs** *for* it and those for the courtyard,
27:19 including all the tent pegs for it and **those**[s] *for* the courtyard,
35:18 the **tent pegs** *for* the tabernacle and for the courtyard, and their
35:18 the tent pegs for the tabernacle and **[RPH]** for the courtyard,
38:20 All the **tent pegs** of the tabernacle and of the surrounding
38:31 and those for its entrance and all the **tent pegs** *for* the tabernacle
38:31 pegs for the tabernacle and **those**[s] *for* the surrounding courtyard.
39:40 the ropes and **tent pegs** *for* the courtyard; all the furnishings for
Nu 3:37 of the surrounding courtyard with their bases, **tent pegs** and ropes.
4:32 **tent pegs**, ropes, all their equipment and everything related to their
Dt 23:13 [23:14] As part of your equipment have **something to dig with**,
Jdg 4:21 picked up a tent **peg** and a hammer and went quietly to him while
4:21 She drove the **peg** through his temple into the ground, and he died.
4:22 and there lay Sisera with the **tent peg** through his temple—
5:26 Her hand reached for the **tent peg**, her right hand for the
16:13 into the fabric ˛on the loom˛ and tighten it with the **pin**, [BHS-]
16:14 and tightened it with the **pin**. Again she called to him, "Samson,
16:14 He awoke from his sleep and pulled up the **pin** and the loom,
Ezr 9: 8 leaving us a remnant and giving us a **firm place** in his sanctuary,
Isa 22:23 I will drive him like a **peg** into a firm place; he will be a seat of
22:25 "the **peg** driven into the firm place will give way;
33:20 its **stakes** will never be pulled up, nor any of its ropes broken.
54: 2 do not hold back; lengthen your cords, strengthen your **stakes**.
Eze 15: 3 anything useful? Do they make **pegs** from it to hang things on?
Zec 10: 4 from him the **tent peg**, from him the battle bow, from him every

3846 יָתוֹם ***yātôm***, n.[m.]. [42]

fatherless [36], orphans [2], fatherless child [1], fatherless children [1], orphan [1], orphan's [1]

Ex 22:22 [22:21] "Do not take advantage of a widow or an **orphan**.
22:24 [22:23] wives will become widows and your children **fatherless**.
Dt 10:18 He defends the cause of the **fatherless** and the widow, and loves
14:29 the **fatherless** and the widows who live in your towns may come
16:11 and the aliens, the **fatherless** and the widows living among you.
16:14 the aliens, the **fatherless** and the widows who live in your towns.
24:17 Do not deprive the alien or the **fatherless** of justice, or take the
24:19 Leave it for the alien, the **fatherless** and the widow, so that the
24:20 Leave what remains for the alien, the **fatherless** and the widow.
24:21 Leave what remains for the alien, the **fatherless** and the widow.
26:12 shall give it to the Levite, the alien, the **fatherless** and the widow,
26:13 have given it to the Levite, the alien, the **fatherless** and the widow,
27:19 who withholds justice from the alien, the **fatherless** or the widow."
Job 6:27 You would even cast lots for the **fatherless** and barter away your
22:9 away empty-handed and broke the strength of the **fatherless**.
24:3 They drive away the **orphan's** donkey and take the widow's ox in
24:9 The **fatherless child** is snatched from the breast; the infant of the
29:12 who cried for help, and the **fatherless** who had none to assist him.
31:17 I have kept my bread to myself, not sharing it with the **fatherless**—
31:21 if I have raised my hand against the **fatherless**, knowing that I had
Ps 10:14 commits himself to you; you are the helper of the **fatherless**.
10:18 defending the **fatherless** and the oppressed, in order that man,
68:5 [68:6] A father to the **fatherless**, a defender of widows, is God in
82:3 Defend the cause of the weak and **fatherless**; maintain the rights of
94:6 They slay the widow and the alien; they murder the **fatherless**.
109:9 May his children be **fatherless** and his wife a widow.
109:12 one extend kindness to him or take pity on his **fatherless children**.
146:9 watches over the alien and sustains the **fatherless** and the widow,
Pr 23:10 ancient boundary stone or encroach on the fields of the **fatherless**,
Isa 1:17 Defend the cause of the **fatherless**, plead the case of the widow.
1:23 They do not defend the cause of the **fatherless**; the widow's case
9:17 [9:16] nor will he pity the **fatherless** and widows, for everyone is
10:2 my people, making widows their prey and robbing the **fatherless**.
Jer 5:28 they do not plead the case of the **fatherless** to win it, they do not
7:6 the **fatherless** or the widow and do not shed innocent blood in this
22:3 Do no wrong or violence to the alien, the **fatherless** or the widow,
49:11 Leave your **orphans**; I will protect their lives. Your widows too
La 5:3 We have become **orphans** and fatherless, our mothers like
Eze 22:7 oppressed the alien and mistreated the **fatherless** and the widow.
Hos 14:3 [14:4] have made, for in you the **fatherless** find compassion."
Zec 7:10 Do not oppress the widow or the **fatherless**, the alien or the poor.
Mal 3:5 who oppress the widows and the **fatherless**, and deprive aliens of

3847 יְתוּר ***yᵉtûr***, var. Not used in NIV/BHS [cf. 9365]

3848 יַתִּיר ***yattîr***, n.pr.loc. [4] [√ 3855]

Jattir [4]

Jos 15:48 In the hill country: Shamir, **Jattir**, Socoh,
21:14 **Jattir**, Eshtemoa,
1Sa 30:27 He sent it to those who were in Bethel, Ramoth Negev and **Jattir**;
1Ch 6:57 [6:42] Hebron (a city of refuge), and Libnah, **Jattir**, Eshtemoa,

3849 יִתְלָה ***yitlâ***, n.pr.loc. [1] [√ 9434; cf. 9002]

Ithlah [1]

Jos 19:42 Shaalabbin, Aijalon, **Ithlah**,

3850 יִתְמָה ***yitmâ***, n.pr.m. [1]

Ithmah [1]

1Ch 11:46 Jeribai and Joshaviah the sons of Elnaam, **Ithmah** the Moabite,

3851 יָתַן ***yātan¹***, v. Not used in NIV/BHS [→ 419, 923, 3853, 3854]

3852 ²יָתַן ***yātan²***, v. Not used in NIV/BHS [cf. 5989]

3853 יַתְנִיאֵל ***yatnîʾēl***, n.pr.m. [1] [√ 3851 + 446]

Jathniel [1]

1Ch 26:2 Jediael the second, Zebadiah the third, **Jathniel** the fourth,

3854 יִתְנָן ***yitnān***, n.pr.loc. [1] [√ 3851]

Ithnan [1]

Jos 15:23 Kedesh, Hazor, **Ithnan**,

3855 יָתַר ***yātar***, v. [105] [→ 2110, 3463, 3848?, 3856, 3858, 3859, 3860, 3861, 3862, 3863, 3864, 3866, 4639, 4798; Ar 10339; *also used with compound proper names*]

left [24], rest [20], remaining [7], left over [6], remain [5], be left [3], leave [3], spare [3], *untranslated* [2], had left over [2], remains [2], some [2], allow to remain [1], are left [1], be left alive [1], been left alive [1], escaped [1], excel [1], grant abundant [1], had some left over [1], have left over [1], holding out [1], it[s] [+2021] [1], keep [1], kept [1], leaving [1], more [1], most [1], preserve [1], remained [1], sparing [1], still [1], stopped [+928+4202] [1], survived [1], surviving [+889+3856] [1], survivors [1], was detained [1], was left [1]

Ge 30:36 [C] while Jacob continued to tend the **rest** *of* Laban's flocks.
32:24 [32:25] [C] So Jacob *was* **left** alone, and a man wrestled with
44:20 [C] is dead, and he *is* the only one of his mother's sons **left**,
49:4 [G] Turbulent as the waters, *you will* no longer **excel**, for you
Ex 10:15 [G] They devoured all that *was* **left** after the hail—
10:15 [C] Nothing green **remained** on tree or plant in all the land of
12:10 [G] *Do* not **leave** any of it till morning; if some is left till
12:10 [C] it till morning; if some *is* **left** till morning, you must burn it.
16:19 [G] said to them, "No one *is to* **keep** any of it until morning."
16:20 [G] *they* **kept** part of it until morning, but it was full of maggots
28:10 [C] six names on one stone and the **remaining** six on the other.
29:34 [C] of the ordination ram or any bread *is* **left over** till morning,
29:34 [C] or any bread is left over till morning, burn **it**[s] [+2021] up.
36:7 [G] because what they already had *was* **more** *than* enough to do
Lev 2:3 [C] The **rest** of the grain offering belongs to Aaron and his sons;
2:10 [C] The **rest** of the grain offering belongs to Aaron and his sons;
6:16 [6:9] [C] Aaron and his sons shall eat the **rest** of it, but it is to
7:16 [C] offers it, but anything **left over** may be eaten on the next day.
7:17 [C] Any meat of the sacrifice **left over** till the third day must be
8:32 [C] Then burn up the **rest** of the meat and the bread.
10:12 [C] Moses said to Aaron and his **remaining** sons, Eleazar
10:12 [C] "Take the grain offering **left over** from the offerings made to
10:16 [C] and Ithamar, Aaron's **remaining** sons, and asked,
14:18 [C] The **rest** of the oil in his palm the priest shall put on the head
14:29 [C] The **rest** of the oil in his palm the priest shall put on the head
19:6 [C] anything **left over** until the third day must be burned up.
22:30 [G] It must be eaten that same day; **leave** none of it till morning.
27:18 [C] number of years that **remain** until the next Year of Jubilee,
Nu 26:65 [C] and not one of them *was* **left** except Caleb son of Jephunneh
33:55 [G] out the inhabitants of the land, those *you* **allow to remain**
Dt 28:11 [G] The LORD *will* **grant** you **abundant** prosperity—
28:54 [G] or the wife he loves or his **surviving** [+889+3856] children,
30:9 [G] the LORD your God *will make* you **most** prosperous in all
Jos 11:11 [C] totally destroyed them, not **sparing** anything that breathed,
11:22 [C] No Anakites *were* **left** in Israelite territory; only in Gaza,
17:2 [C] So this allotment was for the **rest** of the people of
17:6 [C] The land of Gilead belonged to the **rest** of the descendants of
18:2 [C] *there were* **still** seven Israelite tribes who had not yet
21:5 [C] The **rest** of Kohath's descendants were allotted ten towns
21:20 [C] The **rest** of the Kohathite clans of the Levites were allotted
21:26 [C] their pasturelands were given to the **rest** of the Kohathite
21:34 [C] The Merarite clans (the **rest** of the Levites) were given:
21:40 [C] who *were the* **rest** of the Levites, were twelve.
Jdg 8:10 [C] all that *were* **left** of the armies of the eastern peoples;
9:5 [C] the youngest son of Jerub-Baal, **escaped** by hiding.
21:7 [C] "How can we provide wives for those who *are* **left**, since we
21:16 [C] how shall we provide wives for the *men who are* **left**?
Ru 2:14 [G] roasted grain. She ate all she wanted and **had some left over**.
2:18 [G] gave her what *she* **had left over** after she had eaten enough.
1Sa 2:36 [C] everyone **left** in your family line will come and bow down
25:34 [C] not one male belonging to Nabal *would have* **been left alive**
30:9 [C] him came to the Besor Ravine, where **some** stayed behind,
2Sa 8:4 [G] He hamstrung all but **[NIE]** a hundred of the chariot horses.
9:1 [C] "Is there anyone still **left** of the house of Saul to whom I can
13:30 [C] has struck down all the king's sons; not one of them *is* **left**."
17:12 [C] the ground. Neither he nor any of his men *will* **be left alive**.
1Ki 9:20 [C] All the people **left** from the Amorites, Hittites, Perizzites,
9:21 [C] that is, their descendants **remaining** in the land,
15:18 [C] gold that *was* **left** in the treasuries of the LORD's temple
17:17 [C] and worse, and finally **stopped** [+928+4202] breathing.
18:22 [C] to them, "I *am* the only one *of* the LORD's prophets **left**,
19:10 [C] I *am* the only one **left**, and now they are trying to kill me
19:14 [C] I *am* the only one **left**, and now they are trying to kill me
20:30 [C] The **rest** of them escaped to the city of Aphek, where the
20:30 [C] **[RPH]** And Ben-Hadad fled to the city and hid in an inner
2Ki 4:7 [C] pay your debts. You and your sons can live on what *is* **left**."
4:43 [G] the LORD says: 'They will eat and **have** *some* **left over**.' "
4:44 [G] he set it before them, and they ate and **had** *some* **left over**,
20:17 [C] carried off to Babylon. Nothing *will* **be left**, says the LORD.
1Ch 6:61 [6:46] [C] The **rest** of Kohath's descendants were allotted ten
6:70 [6:55] [C] their pasturelands, to the **rest** of the Kohathite clans.

1Ch 6:77 [6:62] [C] The Merarites (the **rest** of the Levites)
24:20 [C] As for the **rest** of the descendants of Levi: from the sons of
2Ch 8: 7 [C] All the people **left** from the Hittites, Amorites, Perizzites,
8: 8 [C] that is, their descendants **remaining** in the land,
31:10 [G] we have had enough to eat and plenty *to* **spare**, because the
31:10 [C] has blessed his people, and this great amount *is* **left over**."
Ne 6: 1 [C] that I had rebuilt the wall and not a gap **was left** in it—
Ps 79:11 [G] by the strength of your arm **preserve** those condemned to
106:11 [C] waters covered their adversaries; not one of them **survived**.
Pr 2:21 [C] will live in the land, and the blameless *will* **remain** in it;
Isa 1: 8 [C] The Daughter of Zion *is* **left** like a shelter in a vineyard,
1: 9 [G] Unless the LORD Almighty *had* **left** us some survivors,
4: 3 [C] left in Zion, who **remain** in Jerusalem, will be called holy,
7:22 [C] to eat. All who **remain** in the land will eat curds and honey.
30:17 [C] till *you are* **left** like a flagstaff on a mountaintop, like a
39: 6 [C] carried off to Babylon. Nothing *will* **be left**, says the LORD.
Jer 27:18 [C] that the furnishings **remaining** in the house of the LORD
27:19 [C] and the other furnishings that *are* **left** in this city,
27:21 [C] says about the things that *are* **left** in the house of the LORD
34: 7 [C] and the other cities of Judah that *were still* **holding out**—
44: 7 [G] and infants, and so **leave** yourselves without a remnant?
Eze 6: 8 [G] " 'But *I will* **spare** some, for some of you will escape the
12:16 [G] *I will* **spare** a few of them from the sword, famine
14:22 [C] Yet *there will be* **some** survivors—sons and daughters who
34:18 [C] clear water? Must you also muddy the **rest** with your feet?
39:14 [C] to them, others will bury those *that* **remain** on the ground.
39:28 [G] I will gather them to their own land, not **leaving** any behind.
48:15 [C] "The **remaining** *area*, 5,000 cubits wide and 25,000 cubits
48:18 [C] What **remains** of the area, bordering on the sacred portion
48:21 [C] "What **remains** on both sides of the area formed by the
Da 10:13 [C] because I **was detained** there with the king of Persia.
Am 6: 9 [C] If ten men **are left** in one house, they too will die.
Zec 13: 8 [C] will be struck down and perish; yet one-third *will* **be left** in it.
14:16 [C] the **survivors** from all the nations that have attacked

3856 יֶתֶר¹ *yeter*¹, n.m. [95] [→ 3658; cf. 3855]

other [45], rest [21], left [5], *untranslated* [3], survivors [3], excelling [2], last [2], remaining [2], wealth [2], arrogant [1], even far [+4394] [1], full [1], leave [1], little left [+7129+8636] [1], others [1], power [1], remnant [1], surviving [+889+3855] [1], surviving [1]

Ge 49: 3 first sign of my strength, **excelling** *in* honor, excelling in power.
49: 3 first sign of my strength, excelling in honor, **excelling** *in* power.
Ex 10: 5 They will devour what **little** you have **left** [+7129+8636] after the
23:11 get food from it, and the wild animals may eat *what* they **leave**.
Lev 14:17 The priest is to put some of the oil **remaining** in his palm on the
Nu 31:32 The plunder **remaining** *from* the spoils that the soldiers took was
Dt 3:11 (Only Og king of Bashan was left of the **remnant** *of* the Rephaites.
3:13 The **rest** *of* Gilead and also all of Bashan, the kingdom of Og,
28:54 or the wife he loves or his **surviving** [+889+3855] children,
Jos 12: 4 one of the **last** *of* the Rephaites, who reigned in Ashtaroth
13:12 and Edrei and had survived as one of the **last** *of* the Rephaites.
13:27 Zaphon with the **rest** *of* the realm of Sihon king of Heshbon (the
23:12 ally yourselves with the **survivors** *of* these nations that remain
Jdg 7: 6 to their mouths. All the **rest** got down on their knees to drink.
1Sa 13: 2 in Benjamin. The **rest** *of* the men he sent back to their homes.
2Sa 10:10 He put the **rest** *of* the men under the command of Abishai his
12:28 Now muster the **rest** *of* the troops and besiege the city and capture
21: 2 were not a part of Israel but were **survivors** of the Amorites;
1Ki 11:41 As for the **other** events of Solomon's reign—all he did
12:23 whole house of Judah and Benjamin, and to the **rest** *of* the people,
14:19 The **other** events of Jeroboam's reign, his wars and how he ruled,
14:29 As for the **other** events of Rehoboam's reign, and all he did,
15: 7 As for the **other** events of Abijah's reign, and all he did, are they
15:23 As for all the **other** events of Asa's reign, all his achievements,
15:31 As for the **other** events of Nadab's reign, and all he did, are they
16: 5 As for the **other** events of Baasha's reign, what he did and his
16:14 As for the **other** events of Elah's reign, and all he did, are they not
16:20 As for the **other** events of Zimri's reign, and the rebellion he
16:27 As for the **other** events of Omri's reign, what he did and the things
22:39 As for the **other** events of Ahab's reign, including all he did,
22:45 [22:46] As for the **other** events of Jehoshaphat's reign, the things
22:46 [22:47] He rid the land of the **rest** *of* the male shrine prostitutes
2Ki 1:18 As for *all* the **other** events of Ahaziah's reign, and what he did,
8:23 As for the **other** events of Jehoram's reign, and all he did,
10:34 As for the **other** events of Jehu's reign, all he did, and all his
12:19 [12:20] As for the **other** events of the reign of Joash, and all he
13: 8 As for the **other** events of the reign of Jehoahaz, all he did
13:12 As for the **other** events of the reign of Jehoash, all he did and his
14:15 As for the **other** events of the reign of Jehoash, what he did
14:18 As for the **other** events of Amaziah's reign, are they not written in
14:28 As for the **other** events of Jeroboam's reign, all he did, and his
15: 6 As for the **other** events of Azariah's reign, and all he did,
15:11 The **other** events of Zechariah's reign are written in the book of
15:15 The **other** events of Shallum's reign, and the conspiracy he led,
15:21 As for the **other** events of Menahem's reign, and all he did,
15:26 The **other** events of Pekahiah's reign, and all he did, are written in
15:31 As for the **other** events of Pekah's reign, and all he did, are they
15:36 As for the **other** events of Jotham's reign, and what he did,
16:19 As for the **other** events of the reign of Ahaz, and what he did,
20:20 As for the **other** events of Hezekiah's reign, all his achievements
21:17 As for the **other** events of Manasseh's reign, and all he did,
21:25 As for the **other** events of Amon's reign, and what he did,
23:28 As for the **other** events of Josiah's reign, and all he did, are they
24: 5 As for the **other** events of Jehoiakim's reign, and all he did,
25:11 **[NIE]** along with the rest of the populace and those who had gone
25:11 along with the **rest** *of* the populace and those who had gone over to
1Ch 19:11 He put the **rest** *of* the men under the command of Abishai his
2Ch 13:22 The **other** events of Abijah's reign, what he did and what he said,
20:34 The **other** events of Jehoshaphat's reign, from beginning to end,
25:26 As for the **other** events of Amaziah's reign, from beginning to end,
26:22 The **other** events of Uzziah's reign, from beginning to end,
27: 7 The **other** events in Jotham's reign, including all his wars
28:26 The **other** events of his reign and all his ways, from beginning to
32:32 The **other** events of Hezekiah's reign and his acts of devotion are
33:18 The **other** events of Manasseh's reign, including his prayer to his
35:26 The **other** events of Josiah's reign and his acts of devotion,
36: 8 The **other** events of Jehoiakim's reign, the detestable things he did
Ne 2:16 or nobles or officials or *any* **others** who would be doing the work.
4:14 [4:8] said to the nobles, the officials and the **rest** *of* the people,
4:19 [4:13] the officials and the **rest** *of* the people, "The work is
6: 1 the Arab and the **rest** *of* our enemies that I had rebuilt the wall
6:14 and the **rest** *of* the prophets who have been trying to intimidate me.
Job 22:20 'Surely our foes are destroyed, and fire devours their **wealth**.'
Ps 17:14 their sons have plenty, and they store up **wealth** for their children.
31:23 [31:24] preserves the faithful, but the proud he pays back in **full**.
Pr 17: 7 **Arrogant** lips are unsuited to a fool—how much worse lying lips
Isa 38:10 through the gates of death and be robbed of the **rest** *of* my years?"
44:19 and I ate. Shall I make a detestable thing from *what* is **left**?
56:12 And tomorrow will be like today, or **even far** [+4394] better."
Jer 27:19 movable stands and the **other** furnishings that are left in this city,
29: 1 sent from Jerusalem to the **surviving** elders among the exiles
39: 9 into exile to Babylon **[NIE]** the people who remained in the city,
39: 9 with those who had gone over to him, and the **rest** *of* the people.
52:15 **[RPH]** Nebuzaradan the commander of the guard carried into
52:15 along with the **rest** *of* the craftsmen and those who had gone over
Eze 34:18 Must you also trample the **rest** *of* your pasture with your feet?
48:23 "As for the **rest** *of* the tribes: Benjamin will have one portion;
Da 8: 9 which started small but grew in **power** to the south and to the east
Joel 1: 4 *What* the locust swarm has **left** the great locusts have eaten;
1: 4 *what* the great locusts have **left** the young locusts have eaten;
1: 4 *what* the young locusts have **left** other locusts have eaten.
Mic 5: 3 [5:2] and the **rest** *of* his brothers return to join the Israelites.
Hab 2: 8 plundered many nations, the peoples who are **left** will plunder you.
Zep 2: 9 plunder them; the **survivors** *of* my nation will inherit their land."
Zec 14: 2 into exile, but the **rest** *of* the people will not be taken from the city.

3857 יֶתֶר² *yeter*², n.m. [6] [→ 4798]

thongs [3], bow [1], cords of tent [1], strings [1]

Jdg 16: 7 "If anyone ties me with seven fresh **thongs** that have not been
16: 8 the rulers of the Philistines brought her seven fresh **thongs** that had
16: 9 he snapped the **thongs** as easily as a piece of string snaps when it
Job 4:21 Are not the **cords of** their **tent** pulled up, so that they die without
30:11 Now that God has unstrung my **bow** and afflicted me, they throw
Ps 11: 2 they set their arrows against the **strings** to shoot from the shadows

3858 יֶתֶר³ *yeter*³, n.pr.m. [9] [→ 3863; cf. 3855, 3856]

Jether [8], Jethro [1]

Ex 4:18 Then Moses went back to **Jethro** his father-in-law and said to him,
Jdg 8:20 Turning to **Jether**, his oldest son, he said, "Kill them!" But Jether
1Ki 2: 5 of Israel's armies, Abner son of Ner and Amasa son of **Jether**.
2:32 son of Ner, commander of Israel's army, and Amasa son of **Jether**,
1Ch 2:17 was the mother of Amasa, whose father was **Jether** the Ishmaelite.
2:32 The sons of Jada, Shammai's brother: **Jether** and Jonathan.
2:32 Jether and Jonathan. **Jether** died without children.
4:17 The sons of Ezrah: **Jether**, Mered, Epher and Jalon. One of
7:38 The sons of **Jether**: Jephunneh, Pispah and Ara.

3859 יִתְרָא *yitrā'*, n.pr.m. [1] [√ 3855]

Jether [1]

2Sa 17:25 Amasa was the son of a man named **Jether**, an Israelite who had

3860 יִתְרָה *yitrâ*, n.f. [2] [√ 3855]

wealth [2]

Isa 15: 7 So the **wealth** they have acquired and stored up they carry away

Jer 48:36 for the men of Kir Hareseth. The **wealth** they acquired is gone.

3861 יִתְרוֹ *yitrô*, n.pr.m. [9] [√ 3855]

Jethro [8], he[s] [1]

Ex 3: 1 Now Moses was tending the flock of **Jethro** his father-in-law,
4:18 any of them are still alive." **Jethro** said, "Go, and I wish you well."
18: 1 Now **Jethro**, the priest of Midian and father-in-law of Moses,
18: 2 sent away his wife Zipporah, his father-in-law **Jethro** received her
18: 5 **Jethro**, Moses' father-in-law, together with Moses' sons and wife,
18: 6 Jethro had sent word to him, "I, your father-in-law **Jethro**,
18: 9 **Jethro** was delighted to hear about all the good things the LORD
18:10 **He**[s] said, "Praise be to the LORD, who rescued you from the
18:12 Then **Jethro**, Moses' father-in-law, brought a burnt offering

3862 יִתְרוֹן *yitrôn*, n.[m.]. [10] [√ 3855]

gain [3], better [2], advantage [1], gained [1], increase [1], profit [1], success [1]

Ecc 1: 3 What does man **gain** from all his labor at which he toils under the
2:11 a chasing after the wind; nothing was **gained** under the sun.
2:13 I saw that wisdom is **better** than folly, just as light is better than
2:13 wisdom is better than folly, just as light is **better** than darkness.
3: 9 What does the worker **gain** from his toil?
5: 9 [5:8] The **increase** *from* the land is taken by all; the king himself
5:16 [5:15] As a man comes, so he departs, and what does he **gain**,
7:12 as money is a shelter, but the **advantage** *of* knowledge is this:
10:10 more strength is needed but skill will bring **success**.
10:11 snake bites before it is charmed, there is no **profit** for the charmer.

3863 יִתְרִי *yitrî*, a.g. [5] [√ 3858; cf. 3855]

Ithrite [4], Ithrites [1]

2Sa 23:38 Ira the **Ithrite**, Gareb the Ithrite
23:38 Ira the Ithrite, Gareb the **Ithrite**
1Ch 2:53 Kiriath Jearim: the **Ithrites**, Puthites, Shumathites and Mishraites.
11:40 Ira the **Ithrite**, Gareb the Ithrite,
11:40 Ira the Ithrite, Gareb the **Ithrite**,

3864 יִתְרָן *yitrān*, n.pr.m. [3] [√ 3855]

Ithran [3]

Ge 36:26 The sons of Dishon: Hemdan, Eshban, **Ithran** and Keran.
1Ch 1:41 The sons of Dishon: Hemdan, Eshban, **Ithran** and Keran.
7:37 Bezer, Hod, Shamma, Shilshah, **Ithran** and Beera.

3865 יִתְרְעָם *yitrᵉʿām*, n.pr.m. [2] [√ 3856 + 6639]

Ithream [2]

2Sa 3: 5 the sixth, **Ithream** the son of David's wife Eglah. These were born
1Ch 3: 3 the son of Abital; and the sixth, **Ithream**, by his wife Eglah.

3866 יֹתֶרֶת *yōteret*, n.f. [11] [√ 3855]

covering [11]

Ex 29:13 the **covering** of the liver, and both kidneys with the fat on them,
29:22 the fat tail, the fat around the inner parts, the **covering** *of* the liver,
Lev 3: 4 the **covering** of the liver, which he will remove with the kidneys.
3:10 the **covering** of the liver, which he will remove with the kidneys.
3:15 the **covering** of the liver, which he will remove with the kidneys.
4: 9 the **covering** of the liver, which he will remove with the kidneys—
7: 4 the **covering** of the liver, which is to be removed with the kidneys.
8:16 the **covering** *of* the liver, and both kidneys and their fat,
8:25 the **covering** of the liver, both kidneys and their fat and the right
9:10 the kidneys and the **covering** of the liver from the sin offering,
9:19 the layer of fat, the kidneys and the **covering** *of* the liver—

3867 יְתֵת *yᵉtēt*, n.pr.m. [2]

Jetheth [2]

Ge 36:40 according to their clans and regions: Timna, Alvah, **Jetheth**,
1Ch 1:51 also died. The chiefs of Edom were: Timna, Alvah, **Jetheth**,

כ, k

3868 כ *k*, letter. Not used in NIV/BHS [→ Ar 10340]

3869 -כְּ *kᵉ-*, subst.pref. [2904 / 2908] [→ 3876, 3904, 4015, 4017; Ar 10341] Not indexed

like [899], as [425], as [+889] [271], *untranslated* [258], when [112], according to [86], just as [+889] [58], about [41], when [+889] [38], in accordance with [30], in [30], as soon as [24], just as [+889+3972] [24], what [21], for [20], what [+889] [18], just as [+889+4027] [17], just as [16], same [16], such [15], after [+889] [14], at [13], after [12], as [+889+4027] [12], like [+889] [12], to [12], as if [11], same as [11], while [9], as though [8], by [8], such as [8], with [8], whatever [+889] [7], because [6], like [+5126] [6], similar [6], because [+889] [5], following [5], whatever [+889+3972] [5], alike [4], as [+889+3972] [4], first [+2021+3427] [4], in keeping with [4], unlike [+4202] [4], whenever [4], as common as [3], how [+4537] [3], if [+889] [3], into [3], like [+5260] [3], so [3], soon [+5071] [3], such [+2296] [3], whatever [3], according to [+6584] [2], agree [+285+2118] [2], almost [+5071] [2], as before [+928+7193+7193] [2], as much as [+889] [2], as soon as [+889] [2], at once [+8092] [2], because of [2], but [2], compared to [2], conformed to [+6913] [2], equal [2], even as [+889] [2], exactly as [+889+4027] [2], follow [+6913] [2], followed [2], given even more [+2179+2179+2256 +3578+3869+4200] [2], had [2], here is what [+2256+2296+2296+3869] [2], how many [+4537+6330] [2], how often [+4537] [2], imitate [+6913] [2], in the order of [2], in way [2], indeed [2], just the way [+889] [2], just what [+889+4027] [2], now [+2021+6961] [2], numbered [+285] [2], out of [2], so [+2296] [2], way [2], what [+2256+2296+2296+3869] [2], what [+2256+2296+2297+3869] [2], what [+889+4027] [2], what deserve [+5126] [2], whatever [+3972] [2], whatever [+889+4027] [2], according to [+7023] [1], according to [+889] [1], according to the rules [1], accordingly [+7023] [1], adhere to [+6913] [1], after [+9005] [1], against [+4202] [1], age of childbearing [+784+851+2021] [1], all around [+1885+2021] [1], all together [+285+408] [1], all [1], among [1], and [1], appear [+928+2118+6524] [1], appropriate [1], as [+2021] [1], as [+4027] [1], as [+6961] [1], as deserve [1], as done before [+928+7193+7193] [1], as easily as [+889] [1], as far as possible [+1896] [1], as far as [1], as for [1], as good as [1], as in the case of [1], as in times past [+3972] [1], as is the case [1], as long as [+889] [1], as long as endure [+3427] [1], as many as [1], as many [1], as measureless as [1], as much as [+7023] [1], as much as [1], as soon as [+4027] [1], as surely as [1], as though [+889] [1], as usual [+8997+9453] [1], as usually did [+928+3427+3427] [1], as usually [1], as well as [+2256] [1], as well as [1], as with [1], at [+6590] [1], awhile [+2021+3427] [1], based on the rate paid [+3427] [1], because [+889+7023] [1], because of [+889] [1], both alike [1], both and [1], by the time [1], callous [+2021+2693] [1], closest friend [+889+3870+5883+8276] [1], compare with [+2118] [1], compare with [1], contrary to [+4202] [1], contrary to [+928+4202] [1], customary [+928+7193+7193] [1], deserves [+1896] [1], desire [1], equal to [1], equally [+278+408+2257] [1], equally [+285] [1], equally among them [+278+408+2257] [1], equally [1], even for [1], even [1], exactly as [+889+3972] [1], exactly like [+4027] [1], exactly like [+889+3972+4027] [1], fared like [1], few [+5071] [1], first [+3427] [1], follow [1], followed the example [+6913+6913] [1], from [1], fulfill [+4027+6913+7023] [1], ghostlike [+200] [1], heart and soul [+4222] [1], how long [+4537] [1], how long must wait [+3427+4537] [1], how many [+4537] [1], how many more [+4537] [1], how quickly [+5071] [1], how [1], if only [+889] [1], if [1], immediately [+2021+3427] [1], in a moment [+5071] [1], in accordance with [+4027] [1], in accordance with [+889] [1], in proportion to [+7023] [1], in proportion to [+889+5002] [1], in proportion to [1], in the way [1], in unison [+285] [1], joined together [+285+6641] [1], just as [+3972] [1], just as [+4027] [1], just as [+889+3972+4027] [1], just like [+4027] [1], just like [+7023] [1], just like [1], just what [+889] [1], kind [+889] [1], kind [1], large enough [1], like [+1952] [1], like [+5477] [1], like [+6524] [1], like [+6886] [1], like [+889+3972] [1], like [+889+4027] [1], might well have [+5071] [1], mistake for [+906+8011] [1], more [+889] [1], more [1], natural [+132+2021+3972] [1], nearly [+401] [1], no end [+1896] [1], no sooner than [+889] [1], no sooner than [1], not[s] [1], nothing but [1], nothing more than [1], now that [+889] [1], obeyed [+7756] [1], of little value [+5071] [1], of [1], once again [+2021+8037] [1], one for each [+5031] [1], only [1], or [1], outcome different [+4202] [1], persisted in [+6913] [1], prescribed [+5477] [1], previously [+919+8997] [1], quotas [+5477] [1], remains [1], same [+889] [1], scarcely [+5071] [1], share [+889+4200] [1], similar [+2021+5260] [1], so [+6584] [1], so [+889] [1], so many [+4537] [1], so that [+7023] [1], so with [+889] [1], so with [1], some [+5071] [1], some [1], soon [+5071+7775] [1], sort [1], spokesman [+7023] [1], standing [1], still [+2021+2021+2296+3427] [1], such [+2297] [1], suddenly [+8092] [1], sufficient means [+1896] [1], suitable [+5584] [1], suitable for [+5584] [1], than [1], the same as [1], then [+889] [1], this is how [+465+1821+2021+2021] [1], this is how [+889] [1], thoroughly purge away [+1342+2021+7671] [1], though [1], through [+1821] [1], together [+285] [1], too [1], treated as [1], usual [1], very things [+889+4027] [1], what deserve for [1], what deserve [1], what deserves [1], whatever [+889+3972+4027] [1], whenever [+889] [1], whether [1], while [+889] [1], without [+1172] [1], yet [1]

3870 ךָ- -kā, ךְ- -āk, כֵה- -kēh, p.m.s.suf. [7067] [→ 3871, 4013, 4032] Not indexed

your [3459], you [2610], *untranslated* [563], the[s] [85], your own [65], yourself [43], your [+4200] [36], yours [+4200] [24], you [+5883] [21], yours [19], him [10], a[s] [8], he[s] [+466+3378] [7], yourselves [7], his [6], its [4], my [4], your own [+4200] [4], yourself [+4222] [4], yourself [+5883] [4], him[s] [+466+3378] [3], their[s] [+1201] [3], toward [+995+2025] [3], what are you doing [+4200+4537] [3], an[s] [2], he[s] [+278] [2], he[s] [+3] [2], him[s] [+1201] [2], his[s] [+466+3378] [2], their [2], this [2], us [+2256+3276] [2], you [+3338] [2], your own flesh and blood [+3655+4946] [2], your very own [+4200] [2], yourself [+4213] [2], yourselves [+4222] [2], yourselves [+5883] [2], all the way to [+995+6330] [1], any[s] [1], boast so much [+1540+7023] [1], both of you [+2084+2256] [1], closest friend [+889+3869+5883+8276] [1], each other[s] [1], he[s] [+6269] [1], her[s] [+563] [1], her [1], here[s] [+6584] [1], him[s] [+278] [1], him[s] [+6269] [1], his[s] [+8276] [1], I[s] [+6269] [1], Israelite[s] [1], it[s] [+3338] [1], its[s] [1], keep away [+448+7928] [1], lead on [+339] [1], me[s] [+563] [1], me[s] [+6269] [1], me [1], one[s] [1], their[s] [+2446] [1], their[s] [+367] [1], them[s] [+1821] [1], them[s] [+3] [1], them[s] [+4621] [1], them[s] [+906+2446] [1], they[s] [+1821] [1], to the vicinity of [+995+6330] [1], toward [+995] [1], very own brother [+278+562+1201] [1], what right have you [+4200+4537] [1], whose [1], you [+1414] [1], you [+4213] [1], you [+561] [1], you [+8120] [1], you yourself [+7156] [1], you[s] [1], your [+907] [1], your [+928] [1], your own self [1]

3871 ךְ- -k, כִי- -kî, p.f.s.suf. [1272 / 1270] [√ 3870] Not indexed

your [615], you [487], *untranslated* [115], the[s] [13], your [+4200] [10], you [+5883] [4], her [2], their [2], whose [2], you [+7156] [2], your own [2], yours [2], yourself [2], yourselves [2], her[s] [+3304] [1], these [1], this city[s] [1], what is the matter [+4200+4537] [1], whom [1], your [+4946] [1], your [+6584] [1], yours [+4200] [1], yourself [+4213] [1], yourself [+4222] [1]

3872 כָּאַב kā'ab, v. [8] [→ 3873, 4799]

in pain [2], ache [1], brought grief [1], feels pain [1], ruin [1], sharp [1], wounds [1]

Ge 34:25 [A] Three days later, while all of them were *still* **in pain**, two of
2Ki 3:19 [G] up all the springs, and **ruin** every good field with stones."
Job 5:18 [G] For he **wounds**, but he also binds up; he injures, but his
14:22 [A] *He* **feels** but *the* **pain** of his own body and mourns only for
Ps 69:29 [69:30] [A] I *am* **in pain** and distress; may your salvation,
Pr 14:13 [A] Even in laughter the heart *may* **ache**, and joy may end in
Eze 13:22 [G] when I *had* **brought** them no **grief**, and because you
28:24 [G] malicious neighbors who are painful briers and **sharp** thorns.

3873 כְּאֵב kᵉ'ēb, n.m. [6] [√ 3872]

pain [3], anguish [2], suffering [1]

Job 2:13 said a word to him, because they saw how great his **suffering** was.
16:6 "Yet if I speak, my **pain** is not relieved; and if I refrain, it does not
Ps 39:2 [39:3] not even saying anything good, my **anguish** increased.
Isa 17:11 harvest will be as nothing in the day of disease and incurable **pain**.
65:14 you will cry out from **anguish** *of* heart and wail in brokenness of
Jer 15:18 Why is my **pain** unending and my wound grievous and incurable?

3874 כָּאָה kā'â, v. [3] [→ 3875; cf. 3909]

brokenhearted [+4222] [1], disheartened [+4213] [1], lose heart [1]

Ps 109:16 [C] the poor and the needy and the **brokenhearted** [+4222].
Eze 13:22 [G] Because you **disheartened** [+4213] the righteous with your
Da 11:30 [C] western coastlands will oppose him, and *he will* **lose heart**.

3875 כָּאֶה kā'eh, a. [0] [√ 3874]

Ps 10:10 [His **victims** [Q +2657; see K 2724] are crushed, they collapse;]

3876 כַּאֲשֶׁר ka'ašer, c. Not used in NIV/BHS [√ 3869 + 889]

3877 כָּבֵד kābēd[1], v. [114] [→ 3878, 3879, 3880, 3881, 3883, 3884, 3885]

honor [19], heavy [8], honored [6], hardened [4], honors [4], be honored [3], gain glory [3], honorable [3], glorify [2], glorious [2], highly respected [2], honoring [2], made heavy [2], multiply [2], nobles [2], put heavy [2], renowned [2], reward handsomely [+3877] [2], reward handsomely [+3877+4394] [2], was held in honor [2], abounding [1], am glorified [1], am honored [1], be held in honor [1], bring glory [1], bring honor [1], burden [1], did[s] [+906+4213+4392] [1], distinguished himself [1], distinguished [1], dull [1], failing [1], fierce [1], gain glory for myself [1], gained glory for yourself [1], give glory [1], glorified [1], glory [1], grew fierce [1], grievous [1], harden [1], harder [1], heavy [+3878] [1], heavy [+4394] [1], held in honor [1], increased [1], is honored [1], laid heavy [1], make dull [1], makes wealthy [1], outweigh [+4946] [1], placed a heavy burden [1], pretend to be somebody [1], proud [1], reward [1], stopped up [+4946+9048] [1], unyielding [1], was honored [1], wealthy [1], weighed down [1]

Ge 13:2 [A] Abram *had become* very **wealthy** in livestock and in silver
18:20 [A] and Gomorrah is so great and their sin so **grievous**
34:19 [C] who *was* the most **honored** of all his father's household,
48:10 [A] Now Israel's eyes *were* **failing** because of old age, and he
Ex 5:9 [A] *Make* the work **harder** for the men so that they keep
8:15 [8:11] [G] *he* **hardened** his heart and would not listen to Moses
8:32 [8:28] [G] this time also Pharaoh **hardened** his heart and would
9:7 [A] Yet his heart *was* **unyielding** and he would not let the people
9:34 [G] he sinned again: He and his officials **hardened** their hearts.
10:1 [G] for I *have* **hardened** his heart and the hearts of his officials
14:4 [C] *I will* **gain glory for myself** through Pharaoh and all his
14:17 [C] *I will* **gain glory** through Pharaoh and all his army,
14:18 [C] that I am the LORD when I **gain glory** through Pharaoh,
20:12 [D] "**Honor** your father and your mother, so that you may live
Lev 10:3 [C] in the sight of all the people *I will* **be honored**.' " Aaron
Nu 22:15 [C] more numerous and more **distinguished** than the first.
22:17 [D] because *I will* **reward** [+3877+4394] you **handsomely** and
22:17 [D] because *I will* **reward** you **handsomely** [+3877+4394] and do
22:37 [D] you come to me? Am I really not able *to* **reward** you?"
24:11 [D] I said *I would* **reward** [+3877] you **handsomely**, but the
24:11 [D] I said *I would* **reward** you **handsomely** [+3877], but the
Dt 5:16 [D] "**Honor** your father and your mother, as the LORD your
28:58 [C] and do not revere this **glorious** and awesome name—
Jdg 1:35 [A] but when the power of the house of Joseph **increased**,
9:9 [D] I give up my oil, by which both gods and men *are* **honored**,
13:17 [D] so that *we may* **honor** you when your word comes true?"
20:34 [A] The fighting *was so* **heavy** that the Benjamites did not realize
1Sa 2:29 [D] Why *do you* **honor** your sons more than me by fattening
2:30 [D] *Those who* **honor** me I will honor, but those who despise me
2:30 [D] Those who honor me *I will* **honor**, but those who despise me
5:6 [A] The LORD's hand *was* **heavy** upon the people of Ashdod
5:11 [A] the city with panic; God's hand *was* very **heavy** *upon* it.
6:6 [D] Why *do you* **harden** your hearts as the Egyptians
6:6 [D] as the Egyptians and Pharaoh **did**[s] [+906+4213+4392]?
9:6 [C] he *is* **highly respected**, and everything he says comes true.
15:30 [D] please **honor** me before the elders of my people and before
22:14 [C] of your bodyguard and **highly respected** in your household?
31:3 [A] The fighting *grew* **fierce** around Saul, and when the archers
2Sa 6:20 [C] "How the king of Israel *has* **distinguished himself** today,
6:22 [C] by these slave girls you spoke of, *I will* **be held in honor**."
10:3 [D] "Do you think David *is* **honoring** your father by sending
13:25 [C] of us should not go; *we would* only *be a* **burden** to you."
23:19 [C] *Was he* not **held in** greater **honor** than the Three? He
23:23 [C] *He* **was held in** greater **honor** than any of the Thirty, but he
1Ki 12:10 [G] 'Your father **put** *a* **heavy** yoke on us, but make our yoke
12:14 [G] the young men and said, "My father **made** your yoke **heavy**;
2Ki 14:10 [C] **Glory** in your victory, but stay at home! Why ask for trouble
1Ch 4:9 [C] Jabez was more **honorable** than his brothers. His mother had
10:3 [A] The fighting **grew fierce** around Saul, and when the archers
11:21 [C] *He* **was** doubly **honored** above the Three and became their
11:25 [C] He **was held in** greater **honor** than any of the Thirty, but he
19:3 [D] "Do you think David *is* **honoring** your father by sending
2Ch 10:10 [G] 'Your father **put** *a* **heavy** yoke on us, but make our yoke
10:14 [G] the young men and said, "My father **made** your yoke **heavy**;
25:19 [G] have defeated Edom, and now you are arrogant and **proud**.
Ne 5:15 [G] **placed a heavy burden** on the people and took forty shekels
5:18 [A] because the demands *were* **heavy** on these people.
Job 6:3 [A] *It would* surely **outweigh** [+4946] the sand of the seas—no
14:21 [A] If his sons *are* **honored**, he does not know it; if they are
23:2 [A] complaint is bitter; his hand *is* **heavy** in spite of my groaning.
33:7 [A] should alarm you, nor *should* my hand *be* **heavy** upon you.
Ps 15:4 [D] despises a vile man but **honors** those who fear the LORD,
22:23 [22:24] [D] All *you* descendants of Jacob, **honor** him!
32:4 [A] For day and night your hand *was* **heavy** upon me;
38:4 [38:5] [A] me like a burden too **heavy** [+3878] to bear.
50:15 [D] day of trouble; I will deliver you, and *you will* **honor** me."
50:23 [D] He who sacrifices thank offerings **honors** me, and he
86:9 [D] before you, O Lord; *they will* **bring glory** to your name.
86:12 [D] my God, with all my heart; *I will* **glorify** your name forever.
87:3 [C] **Glorious** *things* are said of you, O city of God: *Selah*
91:15 [D] be with him in trouble, I will deliver him and **honor** him.
149:8 [C] their kings with fetters, their **nobles** with shackles of iron,
Pr 3:9 [D] **Honor** the LORD with your wealth, with the firstfruits of
4:8 [D] and she will exalt you; embrace her, and *she will* **honor** you.
8:24 [C] when there were no springs **abounding** *with* water;
12:9 [F] yet have a servant than **pretend to be somebody** and have no
13:18 [E] and shame, but whoever heeds correction **is honored**.
14:31 [D] their Maker, but whoever is kind to the needy **honors** God.

Pr 27:18 [E] its fruit, and he who looks after his master *will* **be honored**.
Isa 3:5 [C] will rise up against the old, the base against the **honorable**.
6:10 [G] people calloused; **make** their ears **dull** and close their eyes.
9:1 [8:23] [G] in the future *he will* **honor** Galilee of the Gentiles,
23:8 [C] are princes, whose traders *are* **renowned** *in* the earth?
23:9 [C] all glory and to humble all *who are* **renowned** *on* the earth.
24:15 [D] Therefore in the east **give glory** *to* the LORD;
24:20 [A] *so* **heavy** upon it *is* the guilt of its rebellion that it falls—
25:3 [D] Therefore strong peoples *will* **honor** you; cities of ruthless
26:15 [C] *You have* **gained glory for yourself**; you have extended all
29:13 [D] near to me with their mouth and **honor** me with their lips,
43:4 [C] Since you are precious and **honored** in my sight, and
43:20 [D] The wild animals **honor** me, the jackals and the owls,
43:23 [D] for burnt offerings, nor **honored** me *with* your sacrifices.
47:6 [G] no mercy. Even on the aged *you* **laid** a very **heavy** yoke.
49:5 [C] for *I* **am honored** in the eyes of the LORD and my God has
58:13 [E] the Sabbath a delight and the LORD's holy day **honorable**,
58:13 [D] if *you* **honor** it by not going your own way and not doing as
59:1 [A] LORD is not too short to save, nor his ear too **dull** to hear.
60:13 [D] of my sanctuary; and *I will* **glorify** the place of my feet.
66:5 [A] of my name, have said, '*Let* the LORD *be* **glorified**,
Jer 30:19 [G] *I will* **bring** them **honor**, and they will not be disdained.
La 1:8 [D] All *who* **honored** her despise her, for they have seen her
3:7 [G] so I cannot escape; *he has* **weighed** me **down** *with* chains.
Eze 27:25 [A] You are filled with **heavy** [+4394] *cargo* in the heart of the
28:22 [C] am against you, O Sidon, and *I will* **gain glory** within you.
39:13 [C] and the day I **am glorified** will be a memorable day for them,
Da 11:38 [D] Instead of them, *he will* **honor** a god of fortresses; a god
11:38 [D] a god unknown to his fathers *he will* **honor** with gold
Na 3:10 [C] Lots were cast for her **nobles**, and all her great men were put
3:15 [F] **Multiply** like grasshoppers, multiply like locusts!
3:15 [F] Multiply like grasshoppers, **multiply** like locusts!
Hab 2:6 [G] up stolen goods and **makes** himself **wealthy** by extortion!
Hag 1:8 [C] so that I may take pleasure in it and **be honored**," says the
Zec 7:11 [G] turned their backs and **stopped** [+4946+9048] **up** their ears.
Mal 1:6 [D] "A son **honors** his father, and a servant his master. If I am a

3878 כָּבֵד² ***kābēd²***, a. [40] [√ 3877]

heavy [8], great [4], large [4], severe [4], difficult [2], worst [+4394] [2], *untranslated* [1], bitterly [+4394] [1], dense [1], great numbers [+4394] [1], heavier [1], heavy [+3877] [1], large [+4394] [1], loaded [1], severe [+4394] [1], slow [1], solemn [1], strong [1], terrible [+4394] [1], thick [1], tired [1], unyielding [1]

Ge 12:10 to Egypt to live there for a while because the famine was **severe**.
41:31 because the famine that follows it will be so **severe**.
43:1 Now the famine was still **severe** in the land.
47:4 because the famine is **severe** in Canaan and your servants' flocks
47:13 in the whole region because the famine was **severe** [+4394];
50:9 and horsemen also went up with him. It was a very **large** company.
50:10 near the Jordan, they lamented loudly and **bitterly** [+4394];
50:11 "The Egyptians are holding a **solemn** ceremony of mourning."
Ex 4:10 you have spoken to your servant. I am **slow** *of* speech and tongue."
4:10 spoken to your servant. I am slow of speech and **[RPH]** tongue."
7:14 Then the LORD said to Moses, "Pharaoh's heart is **unyielding**;
8:24 [8:20] **Dense** swarms of flies poured into Pharaoh's palace
9:3 the hand of the LORD will bring a **terrible** [+4394] plague on
9:18 at this time tomorrow I will send the **worst** [+4394] hailstorm that
9:24 It was the **worst** [+4394] storm in all the land of Egypt since it had
10:14 down in every area of the country *in* **great numbers** [+4394].
12:38 as well as **large** [+4394] droves of livestock, both flocks and herds.
17:12 When Moses' hands grew **tired**, they took a stone and put it under
18:18 The work is too **heavy** for you; you cannot handle it alone.
19:16 was thunder and lightning, with a **thick** cloud over the mountain,
Nu 11:14 carry all these people by myself; the burden is too **heavy** for me.
20:20 Edom came out against them with a **large** and powerful army.
1Sa 4:18 neck was broken and he died, for he was an old man and **heavy**.
2Sa 14:26 he used to cut his hair from time to time when it became too **heavy**
1Ki 3:9 and wrong. For who is able to govern this **great** people of yours?"
10:2 Arriving at Jerusalem with a very **great** caravan—with camels
12:4 but now lighten the harsh labor and the **heavy** yoke he put on us,
12:11 My father laid on you a **heavy** yoke; I will make it even heavier.
2Ki 6:14 Then he sent horses and chariots and a **strong** force there.
18:17 his chief officer and his field commander with a **large** army,
2Ch 9:1 Arriving with a very **great** caravan—with camels carrying spices,
10:4 but now lighten the harsh labor and the **heavy** yoke he put on us,
10:11 My father laid on you a **heavy** yoke; I will make it even heavier.
Ps 38:4 [38:5] overwhelmed me like a burden too **heavy** [+3877] to bear.
Pr 27:3 and sand a burden, but provocation by a fool is **heavier** than both.
Isa 1:4 Ah, sinful nation, a people **loaded** *with* guilt, a brood of evildoers,
32:2 water in the desert and the shadow of a **great** rock in a thirsty land.
36:2 the king of Assyria sent his field commander with a **large** army
Eze 3:5 being sent to a people of obscure speech and **difficult** language,
3:6 not to many peoples of obscure speech and **difficult** language,

3879 כָּבֵד³ ***kābēd³***, n.m. [14] [√ 3877]

liver [13], heart [1]

Ex 29:13 the covering of the **liver**, and both kidneys with the fat on them,
29:22 the fat tail, the fat around the inner parts, the covering of the **liver**,
Lev 3:4 the covering of the **liver**, which he will remove with the kidneys.
3:10 the covering of the **liver**, which he will remove with the kidneys.
3:15 the covering of the **liver**, which he will remove with the kidneys.
4:9 the covering of the **liver**, which he will remove with the kidneys—
7:4 the covering of the **liver**, which is to be removed with the kidneys.
8:16 the covering of the **liver**, and both kidneys and their fat,
8:25 the covering of the **liver**, both kidneys and their fat and the right
9:10 the kidneys and the covering of the **liver** from the sin offering,
9:19 the layer of fat, the kidneys and the covering of the **liver**—
Pr 7:23 till an arrow pierces his **liver**, like a bird darting into a snare,
La 2:11 my **heart** is poured out on the ground because my people are
Eze 21:21 [21:26] he will consult his idols, he will examine the **liver**.

3880 כֹּבֶד ***kōbed***, n.[m.]. [4] [√ 3877]

dense [1], heat [1], heavy [1], piles [1]

Pr 27:3 Stone is **heavy** and sand a burden, but provocation by a fool is
Isa 21:15 the drawn sword, from the bent bow and from the **heat** *of* battle.
30:27 comes from afar, with burning anger and **dense** clouds of smoke;
Na 3:3 Many casualties, **piles** *of* dead, bodies without number, people

3881 כְּבֵדֻת ***kᵉbēdut***, n.f. [1] [√ 3877]

difficulty [1]

Ex 14:25 of their chariots come off so that they had **difficulty** driving.

3882 כָּבָה ***kābâ***, v. [24]

quenched [7], quench [4], go out [3], put out [2], snuff out [2], extinguished [1], goes out [1], gone out [1], quench fire [1], snuffed out [1], unquenchable [+4202] [1]

Lev 6:12 [6:5] [A] on the altar must be kept burning; *it must* not **go out**.
6:13 [6:6] [A] burning on the altar continuously; *it must* not **go out**.
1Sa 3:3 [A] The lamp of God *had* not yet **gone out**, and Samuel was
2Sa 14:7 [D] *They would* **put out** the only burning coal I have left,
21:17 [D] to battle, so that the lamp of Israel *will* not *be* **extinguished**."
2Ki 22:17 [A] anger will burn against this place and *will* not *be* **quenched**.'
2Ch 29:7 [D] also shut the doors of the portico and **put out** the lamps.
34:25 [A] will be poured out on this place and *will* not *be* **quenched**.'
Pr 26:20 [A] Without wood a fire **goes out**; without gossip a quarrel dies
31:18 [A] trading is profitable, and her lamp *does* not **go out** at night.
SS 8:7 [D] Many waters cannot **quench** love; rivers cannot wash it
Isa 1:31 [D] both will burn together, with no *one to* **quench** *the* **fire**."
34:10 [A] *It will* not *be* **quenched** night and day; its smoke will rise
42:3 [D] will not break, and a smoldering wick *he will* not **snuff out**.
43:17 [A] never to rise again, extinguished, **snuffed out** like a wick:
66:24 [A] their worm will not die, nor will their fire *be* **quenched**,
Jer 4:4 [D] of the evil you have done—burn with no *one to* **quench** it.
7:20 [A] the fruit of the ground, and it will burn and not *be* **quenched**.
17:27 [A] I will kindle an **unquenchable** [+4202] fire in the gates of
21:12 [D] of the evil you have done—burn with no *one to* **quench** it.
Eze 20:47 [21:3] [A] The blazing flame *will* not *be* **quenched**, and every
20:48 [21:4] [A] LORD have kindled it; *it will* not *be* **quenched**.' "
32:7 [D] When I **snuff** you **out**, I will cover the heavens and darken
Am 5:6 [D] it will devour, and Bethel will have no *one to* **quench** it.

3883 כָּבוֹד¹ ***kābôd¹***, n.m. [200] [→ 376; cf. 3877]

glory [120], honor [33], glorious [10], splendor [6], pomp [3], wealth [3], dignity [2], honored [2], me [+3276] [2], riches [2], soul [2], vast [2], abundance [1], gloriously [1], heart [1], honor [+4200+5989] [1], honorable [1], honored [+4200+6913] [1], honoring [1], lie in state [+928+8886] [1], men of rank [1], respect [1], rewarded [1], splendid [1], tongue [1]

Ge 31:1 and has gained all this **wealth** from what belonged to our father."
45:13 Tell my father about all the **honor** *accorded* me in Egypt
49:6 me not enter their council, let **me** [+3276] not join their assembly,
Ex 16:7 in the morning you will see the **glory** *of* the LORD, because he
16:10 and there was the **glory** *of* the LORD appearing in the cloud.
24:16 the **glory** *of* the LORD settled on Mount Sinai. For six days the
24:17 To the Israelites the **glory** *of* the LORD looked like a consuming
28:2 garments for your brother Aaron, to give him **dignity** and honor.
28:40 and headbands for Aaron's sons, to give them **dignity** and honor.
29:43 with the Israelites, and the place will be consecrated by my **glory**.
33:18 Then Moses said, "Now show me your **glory**."
33:22 When my **glory** passes by, I will put you in a cleft in the rock
40:34 Tent of Meeting, and the **glory** *of* the LORD filled the tabernacle.
40:35 settled upon it, and the **glory** *of* the LORD filled the tabernacle.
Lev 9:6 you to do, so that the **glory** *of* the LORD may appear to you."
9:23 the people; and the **glory** *of* the LORD appeared to all the people.

Nu 14:10 the **glory** *of* the LORD appeared at the Tent of Meeting to all the
14:21 and as surely as the **glory** *of* the LORD fills the whole earth,
14:22 not one of the men who saw my **glory** and the miraculous signs I
16:19 the **glory** *of* the LORD appeared to the entire assembly.
16:42 [17:7] the cloud covered it and the **glory** *of* the LORD appeared.
20: 6 and fell facedown, and the **glory** *of* the LORD appeared to them.
24:11 but the LORD has kept you from being **rewarded**."
Dt 5:24 "The LORD our God has shown us his **glory** and his majesty,
Jos 7:19 "My son, give **glory** to the LORD, the God of Israel, and give
1Sa 2: 8 he seats them with princes and has them inherit a throne of **honor**.
4:21 the boy Ichabod, saying, "The **glory** has departed from Israel"—
4:22 She said, "The **glory** has departed from Israel, for the ark of God
6: 5 rats that are destroying the country, and pay **honor** to Israel's god.
1Ki 3:13 give you what you have not asked for—both riches and **honor**—
8:11 because of the cloud, for the **glory** *of* the LORD filled his temple.
1Ch 16:24 Declare his **glory** among the nations, his marvelous deeds among
16:28 O families of nations, ascribe to the LORD **glory** and strength,
16:29 ascribe to the LORD the **glory** *due* his name. Bring an offering
17:18 "What more can David say to you for **honoring** your servant?
29:12 Wealth and **honor** come from you; you are the ruler of all things.
29:28 died at a good old age, having enjoyed long life, wealth and **honor**.
2Ch 1:11 for wealth, riches or **honor**, nor for the death of your enemies,
1:12 I will also give you wealth, riches and **honor**, such as no king who
5:14 of the cloud, for the **glory** *of* the LORD filled the temple of God.
7: 1 and the sacrifices, and the **glory** *of* the LORD filled the temple.
7: 2 the temple of the LORD because the **glory** *of* the LORD filled it.
7: 3 fire coming down and the **glory** *of* the LORD above the temple,
17: 5 gifts to Jehoshaphat, so that he had great wealth and **honor**.
18: 1 Now Jehoshaphat had great wealth and **honor**, and he allied
26:18 been unfaithful; and you will not be **honored** by the LORD God."
32:27 Hezekiah had very great riches and **honor**, and he made treasuries
32:33 the people of Jerusalem **honored** [+4200+6913] him when he died.
Ne 9: 5 "Blessed be your **glorious** name, and may it be exalted above all
Est 1: 4 For a full 180 days he displayed the **vast** wealth of his kingdom
5:11 Haman boasted to them about his **vast** wealth, his many sons,
Job 19: 9 He has stripped me of my **honor** and removed the crown from my
29:20 My **glory** will remain fresh in me, the bow ever new in my hand.'
Ps 3: 3 [3:4] O LORD; you bestow **glory** *on* me and lift up my head.
4: 2 [4:3] How long, O men, will you turn my **glory** into shame?
7: 5 [7:6] life to the ground and make **me** [+3276] sleep in the dust.
8: 5 [8:6] the heavenly beings and crowned him with **glory** and honor.
16: 9 Therefore my heart is glad and my **tongue** rejoices; my body also
19: 1 [19:2] The heavens declare the **glory** *of* God; the skies proclaim
21: 5 [21:6] Through the victories you gave, his **glory** is great;
24: 7 lifted up, you ancient doors, that the King of **glory** may come in.
24: 8 Who is this King of **glory**? The LORD strong and mighty,
24: 9 them up, you ancient doors, that the King of **glory** may come in.
24:10 Who is he, this King of **glory**? The LORD Almighty—he is the
24:10 The LORD Almighty—he is the King of **glory**. *Selah*
26: 8 where you live, O LORD, the place where your **glory** dwells.
29: 1 O mighty ones, ascribe to the LORD **glory** and strength.
29: 2 Ascribe to the LORD the **glory** *due* his name; worship the
29: 3 the God of **glory** thunders, the LORD thunders over the mighty
29: 9 and strips the forests bare. And in his temple all cry, "**Glory**!"
30:12 [30:13] that my **heart** may sing to you and not be silent.
49:16 [49:17] grows rich, when the **splendor** *of* his house increases;
49:17 [49:18] when he dies, his **splendor** will not descend with him.
57: 5 [57:6] above the heavens; let your **glory** be over all the earth.
57: 8 [57:9] Awake, my **soul**! Awake, harp and lyre! I will awaken the
57:11 [57:12] above the heavens; let your **glory** be over all the earth.
62: 7 [62:8] My salvation and my **honor** depend on God; he is my
63: 2 [63:3] in the sanctuary and beheld your power and your **glory**.
66: 2 Sing the **glory** *of* his name; make his praise glorious!
66: 2 Sing the glory of his name; make his praise **glorious**!
72:19 Praise be to his **glorious** name forever; may the whole earth be
72:19 name forever; may the whole earth be filled with his **glory**.
73:24 me with your counsel, and afterward you will take me into **glory**.
79: 9 Help us, O God our Savior, for the **glory** *of* your name; deliver us
84:11 [84:12] is a sun and shield; the LORD bestows favor and **honor**;
85: 9 [85:10] those who fear him, that his **glory** may dwell in our land.
96: 3 Declare his **glory** among the nations, his marvelous deeds among
96: 7 O families of nations, ascribe to the LORD **glory** and strength.
96: 8 Ascribe to the LORD the **glory** *due* his name; bring an offering
97: 6 proclaim his righteousness, and all the peoples see his **glory**.
102:15 [102:16] all the kings of the earth will revere your **glory**.
102:16 [102:17] the LORD will rebuild Zion and appear in his **glory**.
104:31 May the **glory** *of* the LORD endure forever; may the LORD
106:20 They exchanged their **Glory** for an image of a bull, which eats
108: 1 [108:2] O God; I will sing and make music with all my **soul**.
108: 5 [108:6] the heavens, and let your **glory** be over all the earth.
112: 9 endures forever; his horn will be lifted high in **honor**.
113: 4 is exalted over all the nations, his **glory** above the heavens.
115: 1 Not to us, O LORD, not to us but to your name be the **glory**,
138: 5 of the ways of the LORD, for the **glory** *of* the LORD is great.
145: 5 They will speak of the **glorious** splendor of your majesty,
145:11 They will tell of the **glory** *of* your kingdom and speak of your
145:12 of your mighty acts and the **glorious** splendor of your kingdom.
149: 5 Let the saints rejoice in this **honor** and sing for joy on their beds.
Pr 3:16 Long life is in her right hand; in her left hand are riches and **honor**.
3:35 The wise inherit **honor**, but fools he holds up to shame.
8:18 With me are riches and **honor**, enduring wealth and prosperity.
11:16 A kindhearted woman gains **respect**, but ruthless men gain only
15:33 LORD teaches a man wisdom, and humility comes before **honor**.
18:12 downfall a man's heart is proud, but humility comes before **honor**.
20: 3 It is to a man's **honor** to avoid strife, but every fool is quick to
21:21 pursues righteousness and love finds life, prosperity and **honor**.
22: 4 and the fear of the LORD bring wealth and **honor** and life.
25: 2 It is the **glory** *of* God to conceal a matter; to search out a matter is
25: 2 to conceal a matter; to search out a matter is the **glory** *of* kings.
25:27 eat too much honey, nor is it **honorable** to seek one's own honor.
25:27 eat too much honey, nor is it honorable to seek one's own **honor**.
26: 1 snow in summer or rain in harvest, **honor** is not fitting for a fool.
26: 8 Like tying a stone in a sling is the giving of **honor** to a fool.
29:23 man's pride brings him low, but a man of lowly spirit gains **honor**.
Ecc 6: 2 God gives a man wealth, possessions and **honor**, so that he lacks
10: 1 perfume a bad smell, so a little folly outweighs wisdom and **honor**.
Isa 3: 8 and deeds are against the LORD, defying his **glorious** presence.
4: 2 that day the Branch of the LORD will be beautiful and **glorious**,
4: 5 a glow of flaming fire by night; over all the **glory** will be a canopy.
5:13 their **men of rank** will die of hunger and their masses will be
6: 3 holy is the LORD Almighty; the whole earth is full of his **glory**."
8: 7 floodwaters of the River—the king of Assyria with all his **pomp**.
10: 3 To whom will you run for help? Where will you leave your **riches**?
10:16 under his **pomp** a fire will be kindled like a blazing flame.
10:18 The **splendor** *of* his forests and fertile fields it will completely
11:10 the nations will rally to him, and his place of rest will be **glorious**.
14:18 All the kings of the nations **lie in state** [+928+8886], each in his
16:14 Moab's **splendor** and all her many people will be despised,
17: 3 the remnant of Aram will be like the **glory** *of* the Israelites,"
17: 4 "In that day the **glory** *of* Jacob will fade; the fat of his body will
21:16 would count it, all the **pomp** *of* Kedar will come to an end.
22:18 There you will die and there your **splendid** chariots will remain—
22:23 a firm place; he will be a seat of **honor** for the house of his father.
22:24 All the **glory** *of* his family will hang on him: its offspring
24:23 on Mount Zion and in Jerusalem, and before its elders, **gloriously**.
35: 2 The **glory** *of* Lebanon will be given to it, the splendor of Carmel
35: 2 they will see the **glory** *of* the LORD, the splendor of our God.
40: 5 the **glory** *of* the LORD will be revealed, and all mankind together
42: 8 my name! I will not give my **glory** to another or my praise to idols.
42:12 Let them give **glory** to the LORD and proclaim his praise in the
43: 7 whom I created for my **glory**, whom I formed and made."
48:11 can I let myself be defamed? I will not yield my **glory** to another.
58: 8 before you, and the **glory** *of* the LORD will be your rear guard.
59:19 and from the rising of the sun, they will revere his **glory**.
60: 1 your light has come, and the **glory** *of* the LORD rises upon you.
60: 2 but the LORD rises upon you and his **glory** appears over you.
60:13 "The **glory** *of* Lebanon will come to you, the pine, the fir
61: 6 feed on the wealth of nations, and in their **riches** you will boast.
62: 2 The nations will see your righteousness, and all kings your **glory**;
66:11 you will drink deeply and delight in her overflowing **abundance**."
66:12 to her like a river, and the **wealth** *of* nations like a flooding stream;
66:18 all nations and tongues, and they will come and see my **glory**.
66:19 distant islands that have not heard of my fame or seen my **glory**.
66:19 or seen my glory. They will proclaim my **glory** among the nations.
Jer 2:11 But my people have exchanged their **Glory** for worthless idols.
13:16 Give **glory** to the LORD your God before he brings the darkness,
14:21 your name do not despise us; do not dishonor your **glorious** throne.
17:12 A **glorious** throne, exalted from the beginning, is the place of our
48:18 "Come down from your **glory** and sit on the parched ground,
Eze 1:28 This was the appearance of the likeness of the **glory** *of* the
3:12 May the **glory** *of* the LORD be praised in his dwelling place!—
3:23 the **glory** *of* the LORD was standing there, like the glory I had
3:23 like the **glory** I had seen by the Kebar River, and I fell facedown.
8: 4 there before me was the **glory** *of* the God of Israel, as in the vision
9: 3 Now the **glory** *of* the God of Israel went up from above the
10: 4 Then the **glory** *of* the LORD rose from above the cherubim
10: 4 and the court was full of the radiance of the **glory** *of* the LORD.
10:18 the **glory** *of* the LORD departed from over the threshold of the
10:19 and the **glory** *of* the God of Israel was above them.
11:22 their wings, and the **glory** *of* the God of Israel was above them.
11:23 The **glory** *of* the LORD went up from within the city and stopped
31:18 of the trees of Eden can be compared with you in **splendor**
39:21 "I will display my **glory** among the nations, and all the nations will
43: 2 and I saw the **glory** *of* the God of Israel coming from the east.
43: 2 the roar of rushing waters, and the land was radiant with his **glory**.
43: 4 The **glory** *of* the LORD entered the temple through the gate
43: 5 into the inner court, and the **glory** *of* the LORD filled the temple.
44: 4 and saw the **glory** *of* the LORD filling the temple of the LORD,

Da 11:39 a foreign god and will greatly **honor** those who acknowledge him.
Hos 4:7 against me; they exchanged their **Glory** for something disgraceful.
9:11 Ephraim's **glory** will fly away like a bird—no birth, no pregnancy,
10:5 its idolatrous priests, those who had rejoiced over its **splendor**,
Mic 1:15 in Mareshah. He who is the **glory** *of* Israel will come to Adullam.
Na 2:9 [2:10] The supply is endless, the **wealth** from all its treasures!
Hab 2:14 For the earth will be filled with the knowledge of the **glory** *of* the
2:16 You will be filled with shame instead of **glory**. Now it is your turn!
2:16 hand is coming around to you, and disgrace will cover your **glory**.
Hag 2:3 'Who of you is left who saw this house in its former **glory**?
2:7 and I will fill this house with **glory**,' says the LORD Almighty.
2:9 'The **glory** *of* this present house will be greater than the glory of
Zec 2:5 [2:9] declares the LORD, 'and I will be its **glory** within.'
2:8 [2:12] "After he has **honored** me and has sent me against the
Mal 1:6 If I am a father, where is the **honor** *due* me? If I am a master,
2:2 and if you do not set your heart to **honor** [+4200+5989] my name,"

3884 ²כָּבוֹד *kābôd²*, a. [2] [√ 3877]

elegant [1], glorious [1]

Ps 45:13 [45:14] All **glorious** is the princess within ⌊her chamber⌋;
Eze 23:41 You sat on an **elegant** couch, with a table spread before it on

3885 כְּבוּדָּה *kᵉbûddâ*, n.f. [1] [√ 3877]

possessions [1]

Jdg 18:21 their livestock and their **possessions** in front of them, they turned

3886 כָּבוּל *kābûl*, n.pr.loc. [2] [√ 3890]

Cabul [2]

Jos 19:27 and went north to Beth Emek and Neiel, passing **Cabul** on the left.
1Ki 9:13 he called them the Land of **Cabul**, a name they have to this day.

3887 כַּבּוֹן *kabbôn*, n.pr.loc. [1]

Cabbon [1]

Jos 15:40 **Cabbon**, Lahmas, Kitlish,

3888 כַּבִּיר *kabbîr*, a. [10] [√ 3892]

mighty [4], blustering [1], feeble [+4202] [1], flooding downpour [+8851] [1], fortune [1], great [1], older [+3427] [1]

Job 8:2 long will you say such things? Your words are a **blustering** wind.
15:10 the aged are on our side, *men even* **older** [+3427] than your father.
31:25 rejoiced over my great wealth, the **fortune** my hands had gained,
34:17 hates justice govern? Will you condemn the just and **mighty** *One*?
34:24 Without inquiry he shatters the **mighty** and sets up others in their
36:5 "God is **mighty**, but does not despise men; he is mighty, and firm
36:5 but does not despise men; he is **mighty**, and firm in his purpose.
Isa 16:14 and her survivors will be very few and **feeble** [+4202]."
17:12 uproar of the peoples—they roar like the roaring of **great** waters!
28:2 like a driving rain and a **flooding downpour** [+8851],

3889 כָּבִיר *kābîr*, n.[m.]. [2] [√ 3892]

goats hair [+6436] [2]

1Sa 19:13 it with a garment and putting some **goats' hair** [+6436] at the head.
19:16 the idol in the bed, and at the head was some **goats' hair** [+6436].

3890 כֶּבֶל *kebel*, n.[m.]. [2] [→ 3886]

shackles [2]

Ps 105:18 They bruised his feet with **shackles**, his neck was put in irons,
149:8 to bind their kings with fetters, their nobles with **shackles** *of* iron,

3891 כָּבַס *kābas*, v. [51] [cf. 3899]

wash [36], washed [5], washerman's [3], be washed [2], been washed [2], *untranslated* [1], launderer's [1], wash away [1]

Ge 49:11 [D] *he will* **wash** his garments in wine, his robes in the blood of
Ex 19:10 [D] them today and tomorrow. *Have them* **wash** their clothes
19:14 [D] he consecrated them, and *they* **washed** their clothes.
Lev 6:27 [6:20] [D] on a garment, *you must* **wash** it in a holy place.
11:25 [D] Whoever picks up one of their carcasses *must* **wash** his
11:28 [D] Anyone who picks up their carcasses *must* **wash** his clothes,
11:40 [D] Anyone who eats some of the carcass *must* **wash** his clothes,
11:40 [D] Anyone who picks up the carcass *must* **wash** his clothes,
13:6 [D] a rash. The man *must* **wash** his clothes, and he will be clean.
13:34 [D] him clean. *He must* **wash** his clothes, and he will be clean.
13:54 [D] he shall order that the contaminated article *be* **washed**. Then
13:55 [F] After the affected article *has* **been washed**, the priest is to
13:56 [F] the mildew has faded after the article *has* **been washed**,
13:58 [D] or any leather article that *has been* **washed** and is rid of the
13:58 [E] of the mildew, *must* **be washed** again, and it will be clean."
14:8 [D] "The person to be cleansed *must* **wash** his clothes, shave off
14:9 [D] *He must* **wash** his clothes and bathe himself with water,
14:47 [D] **[RPH]** or eats in the house must wash his clothes.
14:47 [D] who sleeps or eats in the house *must* **wash** his clothes.
15:5 [D] Anyone who touches his bed *must* **wash** his clothes
15:6 [D] that the man with a discharge sat on *must* **wash** his clothes
15:7 [D] " 'Whoever touches the man who has a discharge *must* **wash**
15:8 [D] that person *must* **wash** his clothes and bathe with water,
15:10 [D] whoever picks up those things *must* **wash** his clothes
15:11 [D] without rinsing his hands with water *must* **wash** his clothes
15:13 [D] *he must* **wash** his clothes and bathe himself with fresh water,
15:17 [E] or leather that has semen on it *must* **be washed** with water,
15:21 [D] Whoever touches her bed *must* **wash** his clothes and bathe
15:22 [D] Whoever touches anything she sits on *must* **wash** his clothes
15:27 [D] *he must* **wash** his clothes and bathe with water, and he will
16:26 [D] "The man who releases the goat as a scapegoat *must* **wash**
16:28 [D] The man who burns them *must* **wash** his clothes and bathe
17:15 [D] or torn by wild animals *must* **wash** his clothes and bathe
17:16 [D] if *he does* not **wash** his clothes and bathe himself, he will be
Nu 8:7 [D] have them shave their whole bodies and **wash** their clothes,
8:21 [D] The Levites purified themselves and **washed** their clothes.
19:7 [D] the priest *must* **wash** his clothes and bathe himself with
19:8 [D] The man who burns it *must* also **wash** his clothes and bathe
19:10 [D] gathers up the ashes of the heifer *must* also **wash** his clothes,
19:19 [D] The person being cleansed *must* **wash** his clothes and bathe
19:21 [D] sprinkles the water of cleansing *must* also **wash** his clothes,
31:24 [D] On the seventh day **wash** your clothes and you will be clean.
2Sa 19:24 [19:25] [D] or **washed** his clothes from the day the king left
2Ki 18:17 [A] of the Upper Pool, on the road to the **Washerman's** Field.
Ps 51:2 [51:4] [D] **Wash away** all my iniquity and cleanse me from my
51:7 [51:9] [D] be clean; **wash** me, and I will be whiter than snow.
Isa 7:3 [A] of the Upper Pool, on the road to the **Washerman's** Field.
36:2 [A] of the Upper Pool, on the road to the **Washerman's** Field,
Jer 2:22 [D] Although *you* **wash** *yourself* with soda and use an
4:14 [D] O Jerusalem, **wash** the evil from your heart and be saved.
Mal 3:2 [D] For he will be like a refiner's fire or a **launderer's** soap.

3892 כָּבַר *kābar*, v. [2] [→ 3888, 3889, 3893, 3894, 3895, 3896, 4802]

abundance [1], multiplies [1]

Job 35:16 [G] with empty talk; without knowledge *he* **multiplies** words."
36:31 [G] way he governs the nations and provides food in **abundance**.

3893 ¹כְּבָר *kᵉbār¹*, adv. [9] [√ 3892]

already [5], *untranslated* [1], before [1], long since [1], now [1]

Ecc 1:10 It was here **already**, long ago; it was here before our time.
2:12 What more can the king's successor do than what has **already** been
2:16 long remembered; in **[NIE]** days to come both will be forgotten.
3:15 Whatever is has **already** been, and what will be has been before;
3:15 Whatever is has already been, and what will be has been **before**;
4:2 who had **already** died, are happier than the living, who are still
6:10 Whatever exists has **already** been named, and what man is has
9:6 Their love, their hate and their jealousy have **long since** vanished;
9:7 wine with a joyful heart, for it is **now** that God favors what you do.

3894 ²כְּבָר *kᵉbār²*, n.pr.loc. [8] [√ 3892]

Kebar [8]

Eze 1:1 while I was among the exiles by the **Kebar** River, the heavens
1:3 the son of Buzi, by the **Kebar** River in the land of the Babylonians.
3:15 I came to the exiles who lived at Tel Abib near the **Kebar** River.
3:23 like the glory I had seen by the **Kebar** River, and I fell facedown.
10:15 These were the living creatures I had seen by the **Kebar** River.
10:20 creatures I had seen beneath the God of Israel by the **Kebar** River,
10:22 had the same appearance as those I had seen by the **Kebar** River.
43:3 destroy the city and like the visions I had seen by the **Kebar** River,

3895 ¹כְּבָרָה *kᵉbārâ¹*, n.f. [1] [√ 3892]

sieve [1]

Am 9:9 house of Israel among all the nations as grain is shaken in a **sieve**,

3896 ²כְּבָרָה *kᵉbārâ²*, n.f. [3] [√ 3892]

little distance [+824] [1], some distance [+824] [1], some distance [+824+2021] [1]

Ge 35:16 While they were still **some distance** [+824+2021] from Ephrath,
48:7 we were still on the way, a **little distance** [+824] from Ephrath.
2Ki 5:19 Elisha said. After Naaman had traveled **some distance** [+824],

3897 כֶּבֶשׂ kebeś, n.m. [107] [→ 3898; cf. 4166]
male lambs [35], lambs [25], lamb [19], male lamb [15], *untranslated* [8], sheep [3], lamb [+928+2021+8445] [1], sheep [+7366] [1]

Ex 12: 5 and you may take them from the **sheep** or the goats.
29: 38 are to offer on the altar regularly each day: two **lambs** a year old.
29: 39 Offer one **[RPH]** in the morning and the other at twilight.
29: 39 Offer one in the morning and the other **[RPH]** at twilight.
29: 40 With the first **lamb** offer a tenth of an ephah of fine flour mixed
29: 41 Sacrifice the other **lamb** at twilight with the same grain offering
Lev 4: 32 " 'If he brings a **lamb** as his sin offering, he is to bring a female
9: 3 'Take a male goat for a sin offering, a calf and a **lamb**—both a year
12: 6 to the Tent of Meeting a year-old **lamb** for a burnt offering
14: 10 "On the eighth day he must bring two **male lambs** and one ewe
14: 12 "Then the priest is to take one of the **male lambs** and offer it as a
14: 13 He is to slaughter the **lamb** in the holy place where the sin offering
14: 21 he must take one **male lamb** as a guilt offering to be waved to
14: 24 The priest is to take the **lamb** *for* the guilt offering, together with
14: 25 He shall slaughter the **lamb** *for* the guilt offering and take some of
23: 12 you must sacrifice as a burnt offering to the LORD a **lamb** a year
23: 18 Present with this bread seven **male lambs**, each a year old
23: 19 Then sacrifice one male goat for a sin offering and two **lambs**,
23: 20 The priest is to wave the two **lambs** before the LORD as a wave
Nu 6: 12 and must bring a year-old **male lamb** as a guilt offering.
6: 14 a year-old **male lamb** without defect for a burnt offering, a
7: 15 one young bull, one ram and one **male lamb** a year old, for a burnt
7: 17 five rams, five male goats and five **male lambs** a year old,
7: 21 one young bull, one ram and one **male lamb** a year old, for a burnt
7: 23 five rams, five male goats and five **male lambs** a year old,
7: 27 one young bull, one ram and one **male lamb** a year old, for a burnt
7: 29 five rams, five male goats and five **male lambs** a year old,
7: 33 one young bull, one ram and one **male lamb** a year old, for a burnt
7: 35 five rams, five male goats and five **male lambs** a year old,
7: 39 one young bull, one ram and one **male lamb** a year old, for a burnt
7: 41 five rams, five male goats and five **male lambs** a year old,
7: 45 one young bull, one ram and one **male lamb** a year old, for a burnt
7: 47 five rams, five male goats and five **male lambs** a year old,
7: 51 one young bull, one ram and one **male lamb** a year old, for a burnt
7: 53 five rams, five male goats and five **male lambs** a year old,
7: 57 one young bull, one ram and one **male lamb** a year old, for a burnt
7: 59 five rams, five male goats and five **male lambs** a year old,
7: 63 one young bull, one ram and one **male lamb** a year old, for a burnt
7: 65 five rams, five male goats and five **male lambs** a year old,
7: 69 one young bull, one ram and one **male lamb** a year old, for a burnt
7: 71 five rams, five male goats and five **male lambs** a year old,
7: 75 one young bull, one ram and one **male lamb** a year old, for a burnt
7: 77 five rams, five male goats and five **male lambs** a year old,
7: 81 one young bull, one ram and one **male lamb** a year old, for a burnt
7: 83 five rams, five male goats and five **male lambs** a year old,
7: 87 twelve rams and twelve **male lambs** a year old, together with their
7: 88 sixty rams, sixty male goats and sixty **male lambs** a year old.
15: 5 With each **lamb** for the burnt offering or the sacrifice, prepare a
15: 11 Each bull or ram, each **lamb** [+928+2021+8445] or young goat,
28: 3 two **lambs** a year old without defect, as a regular burnt offering
28: 4 Prepare one **lamb** in the morning and the other at twilight,
28: 4 Prepare one lamb in the morning and the other **[RPH]** at twilight,
28: 7 is to be a quarter of a hin of fermented drink with each **lamb**.
28: 8 Prepare the second **lamb** at twilight, along with the same kind of
28: 9 make an offering of two **lambs** a year old without defect,
28: 11 one ram and seven **male lambs** a year old, all without defect.
28: 13 with each **lamb**, a grain offering of a tenth of an ephah of fine flour
28: 14 the ram, a third of a hin; and with each **lamb**, a quarter of a hin.
28: 19 one ram and seven **male lambs** a year old, all without defect.
28: 21 and with each of the seven **lambs**, one-tenth.
28: 21 and with each of the seven lambs, one-tenth. **[RPH]**
28: 27 seven **male lambs** a year old as an aroma pleasing to the LORD.
28: 29 and with each of the seven **lambs**, one-tenth.
28: 29 and with each of the seven lambs, **[RPH]** one-tenth.
29: 2 one ram and seven **male lambs** a year old, all without defect.
29: 4 and with each of the seven **lambs**, one-tenth.
29: 4 and with each of the seven lambs, one-tenth. **[RPH]**
29: 8 one ram and seven **male lambs** a year old, all without defect.
29: 10 and with each of the seven **lambs**, one-tenth.
29: 10 and with each of the seven lambs, **[RPH]** one-tenth.
29: 13 two rams and fourteen **male lambs** a year old, all without defect.
29: 15 and with each of the fourteen **lambs**, one-tenth.
29: 15 and with each of the fourteen lambs, **[RPH]** one-tenth.
29: 17 two rams and fourteen **male lambs** a year old, all without defect.
29: 18 With the bulls, rams and **lambs**, prepare their grain offerings
29: 20 two rams and fourteen **male lambs** a year old, all without defect.
29: 21 With the bulls, rams and **lambs**, prepare their grain offerings
29: 23 two rams and fourteen **male lambs** a year old, all without defect.
29: 24 With the bulls, rams and **lambs**, prepare their grain offerings
29: 26 two rams and fourteen **male lambs** a year old, all without defect.
29: 27 With the bulls, rams and **lambs**, prepare their grain offerings
29: 29 two rams and fourteen **male lambs** a year old, all without defect.
29: 30 With the bulls, rams and **lambs**, prepare their grain offerings
29: 32 two rams and fourteen **male lambs** a year old, all without defect.
29: 33 With the bulls, rams and **lambs**, prepare their grain offerings
29: 36 one ram and seven **male lambs** a year old, all without defect.
29: 37 With the bull, the ram and the **lambs**, prepare their grain offerings
1Ch 29: 21 a thousand bulls, a thousand rams and a thousand **male lambs**,
2Ch 29: 21 seven **male lambs** and seven male goats as a sin offering for the
29: 22 they slaughtered the **lambs** and sprinkled their blood on the altar.
29: 32 was seventy bulls, a hundred rams and two hundred **male lambs**—
35: 7 lay people who were there a total of thirty thousand **sheep** [+7366]
Ezr 8: 35 ninety-six rams, seventy-seven **male lambs** and, as a sin offering,
Job 31: 20 did not bless me for warming him with the fleece from my **sheep**,
Pr 27: 26 the **lambs** will provide you with clothing, and the goats with the
Isa 1: 11 I have no pleasure in the blood of bulls and **lambs** and goats.
5: 17 **sheep** will graze as in their own pasture; lambs will feed among
11: 6 The wolf will live with the **lamb**, the leopard will lie down with
Jer 11: 19 I had been like a gentle **lamb** led to the slaughter; I did not realize
Eze 46: 4 brings to the LORD on the Sabbath day is to be six **male lambs**
46: 5 the grain offering with the **lambs** is to be as much as he pleases,
46: 6 he is to offer a young bull, six **lambs** and a ram, all without defect.
46: 7 with the ram, and with the **lambs** as much as he wants to give,
46: 11 an ephah with a ram, and with the **lambs** as much as one pleases,
46: 13 " 'Every day you are to provide a year-old **lamb** without defect for
46: 15 So the **lamb** and the grain offering and the oil shall be provided
Hos 4: 16 then can the LORD pasture them like **lambs** in a meadow?

3898 כִּבְשָׂה kibśâ, n.f. [8] [√ 3897]
ewe lamb [4], ewe lambs [2], lamb [1], lambs [1]

Ge 21: 28 Abraham set apart seven **ewe lambs** *from* the flock,
21: 29 "What is the meaning of these seven **ewe lambs** you have set apart
21: 30 "Accept these seven **lambs** from my hand as a witness that I dug
Lev 14: 10 day he must bring two male lambs and one **ewe lamb** a year old,
Nu 6: 14 a year-old **ewe lamb** without defect for a sin offering, a ram
2Sa 12: 3 the poor man had nothing except one little **ewe lamb** he had
12: 4 he took the **ewe lamb** *that belonged to* the poor man and prepared
12: 6 He must pay for that **lamb** four times over, because he did such a

3899 כָּבַשׁ kābaš, v. [14] [→ 3900, 3901; cf. 3891, 4115]
is subdued [2], been enslaved [1], enslaved [+2256+4200+4200+6269+9148] [1], forced [1], is subject [1], make men slaves [+4200+4200+6269] [1], molest [1], overcome [1], subdue [1], subdued [1], subject [1], tread underfoot [1], was brought under control [1]

Ge 1: 28 [A] and increase in number; fill the earth and **subdue** it.
Nu 32: 22 [C] when the land **is subdued** before the LORD, you may return
32: 29 [C] when the land **is subdued** before you, give them the land of
Jos 18: 1 [C] The country **was brought under** their **control**,
2Sa 8: 11 [D] the silver and gold from all the nations *he had* **subdued**:
1Ch 22: 18 [C] and the land **is subject** to the LORD and to his people.
2Ch 28: 10 [A] now you intend to **make** the **men** and women of Judah and Jerusalem your **slaves** [+4200+4200+6269].
Ne 5: 5 [A] yet we *have to* **subject** our sons and daughters to slavery.
5: 5 [C] Some of our daughters *have already* **been enslaved**, but we
Est 7: 8 [A] "*Will* he even **molest** the queen while she is with me in the
Jer 34: 11 [A] and **enslaved** [+2256+4200+4200+6269+9148] them again.
34: 16 [A] *You have* **forced** them to become your slaves again.
Mic 7: 19 [A] *you will* **tread** our sins **underfoot** and hurl all our iniquities
Zec 9: 15 [A] They will destroy and **overcome** *with* slingstones. They will

3900 כֶּבֶשׁ kebeš, n.[m.]. [1] [√ 3899]
footstool [1]

2Ch 9: 18 The throne had six steps, and a **footstool** of gold was attached to it.

3901 כִּבְשָׁן kibšān, n.m. [4] [√ 3899]
furnace [4]

Ge 19: 28 saw dense smoke rising from the land, like smoke from a **furnace**.
Ex 9: 8 "Take handfuls of soot from a **furnace** and have Moses toss it into
9: 10 So they took soot from a **furnace** and stood before Pharaoh.
19: 18 The smoke billowed up from it like smoke from a **furnace**,

3902 כַּד kad, n.f. [18]
jar [12], jars [3], *untranslated* [1], large jars [1], pitcher [1]

Ge 24: 14 'Please let down your **jar** that I may have a drink,' and she says,
24: 15 finished praying, Rebekah came out with her **jar** on her shoulder.
24: 16 She went down to the spring, filled her **jar** and came up again.
24: 17 to meet her and said, "Please give me a little water from your **jar**."
24: 18 and quickly lowered the **jar** to her hands and gave him a drink.
24: 20 So she quickly emptied her **jar** into the trough, ran back to the well

Ge 24:43 and I say to her, "Please let me drink a little water from your **jar**,"
24:45 in my heart, Rebekah came out, with her **jar** on her shoulder.
24:46 "She quickly lowered her **jar** from her shoulder and said, 'Drink,
Jdg 7:16 he placed trumpets and empty **jars** in the hands of all of them,
7:16 empty jars in the hands of all of them, with torches inside. **[RPH]**
7:19 blew their trumpets and broke the **jars** that were in their hands.
7:20 The three companies blew the trumpets and smashed the **jars**.
1Ki 17:12 any bread—only a handful of flour in a **jar** and a little oil in a jug.
17:14 'The **jar** *of* flour will not be used up and the jug of oil will not run
17:16 For the **jar** *of* flour was not used up and the jug of oil did not run
18:33 [18:34] "Fill four **large jars** with water and pour it on the offering
Ecc 12: 6 before the **pitcher** is shattered at the spring, or the wheel broken at

3903 כַּדּוּר **kaddûr**, n.[m.]. Not used in NIV/BHS [√ 3960]

3904 כְּדֵי **kᵉdê**, subst. Not used in NIV/BHS [√ 3869 + 1896]

3905 כַּדְכֹּד **kadkōd**, n.[m.]. [2]

rubies [2]

Isa 54:12 I will make your battlements of **rubies**, your gates of sparkling
Eze 27:16 fine linen, coral and **rubies** for your merchandise.

3906 כְּדָרְלָעֹמֶר כְּדָר־לָעֹמֶר **kᵉdorlāʿōmer**, **kᵉdor-lāʿōmer**, n.pr.m. [5]

Kedorlaomer [5]

Ge 14: 1 of Ellasar, **Kedorlaomer** king of Elam and Tidal king of Goiim
14: 4 For twelve years they had been subject to **Kedorlaomer**, but in the
14: 5 **Kedorlaomer** and the kings allied with him went out and defeated
14: 9 against **Kedorlaomer** king of Elam, Tidal king of Goiim,
14:17 After Abram returned from defeating **Kedorlaomer** and the kings

3907 כֹּה **kōh**, adv.demo. [576] [→ 3970; Ar 10345] See Select Index

this is what [471], *untranslated* [48], this [16], ever so [12], here [4], so [3], if [+561] [2], in any direction [+2256+3907] [2], meanwhile [+2256+3907+6330+6330] [2], this is how [2], abundantly [+889+6330+6330] [1], like this [1], now [1], over there [1], same [1], such [1], that [+928] [1], that is what [1], that [1], there [1], this [+928] [1], this way [1], what happened [1], what [1]

3908 כָּהָה **kāhâ¹**, v. [9] [→ 3910, 3911; cf. 3909]

faded [2], totally blinded [+3908] [2], weak [2], faint [1], falter [1], grown dim [1]

Ge 27: 1 [A] and his eyes *were so* **weak** that he could no longer see,
Lev 13: 6 [D] if the sore *has* **faded** and has not spread in the skin, the priest
13:56 [D] the mildew *has* **faded** after the article has been washed,
Dt 34: 7 [A] he died, yet his eyes *were* not **weak** nor his strength gone.
Job 17: 7 [A] My eyes *have* **grown dim** with grief; my whole frame is
Isa 42: 4 [A] *he will* not **falter** or be discouraged till he establishes justice
Eze 21: 7 [21:12] [D] every spirit *will become* **faint** and every knee
Zec 11:17 [A] completely withered, his right eye **totally blinded** [+3908]!"
11:17 [A] completely withered, his right eye **totally blinded** [+3908]!"

3909 ²כָּהָה **kāhâ²**, v. [1] [cf. 3908, 3874]

restrain [1]

1Sa 3:13 [D] themselves contemptible, and *he* failed *to* **restrain** them.

3910 כֵּהֶה **kēheh**, a. [7] [√ 3908]

faded [3], despair [1], dull [1], smoldering [1], weak [1]

Lev 13:21 no white hair in it and it is not more than skin deep and has **faded**,
13:26 hair in the spot and if it is not more than skin deep and has **faded**,
13:28 the spot is unchanged and has not spread in the skin but has **faded**,
13:39 the priest is to examine them, and if the spots are **dull** white,
1Sa 3: 2 whose eyes were becoming *so* **weak** that he could barely see,
Isa 42: 3 he will not break, and a **smoldering** wick he will not snuff out.
61: 3 of mourning, and a garment of praise instead of a spirit of **despair**.

3911 כֵּהָה **kēhâ**, n.f. [1] [√ 3908]

heal [1]

Na 3:19 Nothing can **heal** your wound; your injury is fatal. Everyone who

3912 כָּהַן **kāhan**, v.den. [23] [√ 3913]

serve as priests [12], priest [2], priests [2], serve as priest [2], served as priests [2], high priest [1], served as priest [1], serving as priests [1]

Ex 28: 1 [D] Eleazar and Ithamar, so they *may* **serve** me **as priests**.
28: 3 [D] for his consecration, so he *may* **serve** me **as priest**.
28: 4 [D] brother Aaron and his sons, so they *may* **serve** me **as priests**.
28:41 [D] Consecrate them so *they may* **serve** me **as priests**.
29: 1 [D] to do to consecrate them, so *they may* **serve** me **as priests**:
29:44 [D] will consecrate Aaron and his sons to **serve** me **as priests**.
30:30 [D] and consecrate them so they *may* **serve** me **as priests**.
31:10 [D] and the garments for his sons when *they* **serve as priests**,
35:19 [D] and the garments for his sons when *they* **serve as priests**."
39:41 [D] and the garments for his sons when **serving as priests**.
40:13 [D] and consecrate him so *he may* **serve** me **as priest**.
40:15 [D] you anointed their father, so *they may* **serve** me **as priests**.
Lev 7:35 [D] the day they were presented to **serve** the LORD **as priests**.
16:32 [D] ordained to succeed his father as **high priest** is to make
Nu 3: 3 [D] the anointed priests, who were ordained to **serve as priests**.
3: 4 [D] Ithamar **served as priests** during the lifetime of their father
Dt 10: 6 [D] and was buried, and Eleazar his son succeeded him *as* **priest**.
1Ch 6:10 [5:36] [D] **served as priest** in the temple Solomon built in
24: 2 [D] had no sons; so Eleazar and Ithamar **served as** *the* **priests**.
2Ch 11:14 [D] and his sons had rejected them as **priests** of the LORD.
Isa 61:10 [D] as a bridegroom adorns his head *like a* **priest**,
Eze 44:13 [D] They are not to come near to **serve** me **as priests** or come
Hos 4: 6 [D] you have rejected knowledge, I also reject you as my **priests**;

3913 כֹּהֵן **kōhēn**, n.m. [750] [→ 3912, 3914; Ar 10347]

priest [390], priests [301], *untranslated* [19], he^s [+2021] [16], priest's [5], who^s [+2021] [4], them^s [+2021] [3], his^s own [+2021] [2], priestly [2], they^s [+2021] [2], he^s [+2021+3381] [1], he^s himself [+2021] [1], idolatrous priests [1], priesthood [1], royal advisers [1], their^s [+2021] [1]

Ge 14:18 brought out bread and wine. He was **priest** of God Most High,
41:45 him Asenath daughter of Potiphera, **priest** *of* On, to be his wife.
41:50 born to Joseph by Asenath daughter of Potiphera, **priest** *of* On.
46:20 born to Joseph by Asenath daughter of Potiphera, **priest** *of* On.
47:22 However, he did not buy the land of the **priests**, because they
47:22 because **they**^s [+2021] received a regular allotment from Pharaoh
47:26 It was only the land of the **priests** that did not become Pharaoh's.
Ex 2:16 Now a **priest** *of* Midian had seven daughters, and they came to
3: 1 the **priest** *of* Midian, and he led the flock to the far side of the
18: 1 Now Jethro, the **priest** *of* Midian and father-in-law of Moses,
19: 6 you will be for me a kingdom of **priests** and a holy nation.'
19:22 Even the **priests**, who approach the LORD, must consecrate
19:24 the **priests** and the people must not force their way through to
29:30 The son who succeeds him as **priest** and comes to the Tent of
31:10 both the sacred garments for Aaron the **priest** and the garments for
35:19 both the sacred garments for Aaron the **priest** and the garments for
38:21 the Levites under the direction of Ithamar son of Aaron, the **priest**.
39:41 both the sacred garments for Aaron the **priest** and the garments for
Lev 1: 5 then Aaron's sons the **priests** shall bring the blood and sprinkle it
1: 7 The sons of Aaron the **priest** are to put fire on the altar and arrange
1: 8 Aaron's sons the **priests** shall arrange the pieces, including the
1: 9 the legs with water, and the **priest** is to burn all of it on the altar.
1:11 Aaron's sons the **priests** shall sprinkle its blood against the altar on
1:12 and the **priest** shall arrange them, including the head and the fat,
1:13 and the **priest** is to bring all of it and burn it on the altar.
1:15 The **priest** shall bring it to the altar, wring off the head and burn it
1:17 the **priest** shall burn it on the wood that is on the fire on the altar.
2: 2 take it to Aaron's sons the **priests**. The priest shall take a handful
2: 2 The **priest** shall take a handful of the fine flour and oil, together
2: 8 to the LORD; present it to the **priest**, who shall take it to the altar.
2: 9 **He**^s [+2021] shall take out the memorial portion from the grain
2:16 The **priest** shall burn the memorial portion of the crushed grain
3: 2 Aaron's sons the **priests** shall sprinkle the blood against the altar
3:11 The **priest** shall burn them on the altar as food, an offering made to
3:16 The **priest** shall burn them on the altar as food, an offering made
4: 3 "'If the anointed **priest** sins, bringing guilt on the people,
4: 5 Then the anointed **priest** shall take some of the bull's blood
4: 6 **He**^s [+2021] is to dip his finger into the blood and sprinkle some of
4: 7 The **priest** shall then put some of the blood on the horns of the
4:10 Then the **priest** shall burn them on the altar of burnt offering.
4:16 the anointed **priest** is to take some of the bull's blood into the Tent
4:17 **He**^s [+2021] shall dip his finger into the blood and sprinkle it
4:20 In this way the **priest** will make atonement for them, and they will
4:25 the **priest** shall take some of the blood of the sin offering with his
4:26 In this way the **priest** will make atonement for the man's sin,
4:30 Then the **priest** is to take some of the blood with his finger
4:31 the **priest** shall burn it on the altar as an aroma pleasing to the
4:31 In this way the **priest** will make atonement for him, and he will be
4:34 the **priest** shall take some of the blood of the sin offering with his
4:35 the **priest** shall burn it on the altar on top of the offerings made to
4:35 In this way the **priest** will make atonement for him for the sin he
5: 6 and the **priest** shall make atonement for him for his sin.
5: 8 He is to bring them to the **priest**, who shall first offer the one for
5:10 The **priest** shall then offer the other as a burnt offering in the
5:12 He is to bring it to the **priest**, who shall take a handful of it as a
5:12 He is to bring it to the priest, **who**^s [+2021] shall take a handful of
5:13 In this way the **priest** will make atonement for him for any of these

Lev 5:13 The rest of the offering will belong to the **priest**, as in the case of
5:16 add a fifth of the value to that and give it all to the **priest**,
5:16 give it all to the priest, **who**[s] [+2021] will make atonement for him
5:18 He is to bring to the **priest** as a guilt offering a ram from the flock,
5:18 In this way the **priest** will make atonement for him for the wrong
6: 6 [5:25] as a penalty he must bring to the **priest**, that is, to the
6: 7 [5:26] In this way the **priest** will make atonement for him before
6:10 [6:3] The **priest** shall then put on his linen clothes, with linen
6:12 [6:5] Every morning the **priest** is to add firewood and arrange the
6:22 [6:15] The son who is to succeed him as anointed **priest** shall
6:23 [6:16] Every grain offering of a **priest** shall be burned
6:26 [6:19] The **priest** who offers it shall eat it; it is to be eaten in a
6:29 [6:22] Any male in a **priest's** family may eat it; it is most holy.
7: 5 The **priest** shall burn them on the altar as an offering made to the
7: 6 Any male in a **priest's** family may eat it, but it must be eaten in a
7: 7 They belong to the **priest** who makes atonement with them.
7: 8 The **priest** who offers a burnt offering for anyone may keep its
7: 8 a burnt offering for anyone may keep its hide for himself. **[RPH]**
7: 9 cooked in a pan or on a griddle belongs to the **priest** who offers it,
7:14 it belongs to the **priest** who sprinkles the blood of the fellowship
7:31 The **priest** shall burn the fat on the altar, but the breast belongs to
7:32 thigh of your fellowship offerings to the **priest** as a contribution.
7:34 the thigh that is presented and have given them to Aaron the **priest**
12: 6 she is to bring to the **priest** at the entrance to the Tent of Meeting a
12: 8 In this way the **priest** will make atonement for her, and she will be
13: 2 he must be brought to Aaron the **priest** or to one of his sons who is
13: 2 be brought to Aaron the priest or to one of his sons who is a **priest**.
13: 3 The **priest** is to examine the sore on his skin, and if the hair in the
13: 3 When the **priest** examines him, he shall pronounce him
13: 4 the **priest** is to put the infected person in isolation for seven days.
13: 5 On the seventh day the **priest** is to examine him, and if he sees that
13: 5 has not spread in the skin, **he**[s] [+2021] is to keep him in isolation
13: 6 On the seventh day the **priest** is to examine him again, and if the
13: 6 has not spread in the skin, the **priest** shall pronounce him clean;
13: 7 after he has shown himself to the **priest** to be pronounced clean,
13: 7 to be pronounced clean, he must appear before the **priest** again.
13: 8 The **priest** is to examine him, and if the rash has spread in the skin,
13: 8 if the rash has spread in the skin, **he**[s] [+2021] shall pronounce him
13: 9 has an infectious skin disease, he must be brought to the **priest**.
13:10 The **priest** is to examine him, and if there is a white swelling in the
13:11 a chronic skin disease and the **priest** shall pronounce him unclean.
13:12 disease breaks out all over his skin and, so far as the **priest** can see,
13:13 the **priest** is to examine him, and if the disease has covered his
13:15 When the **priest** sees the raw flesh, he shall pronounce him
13:16 the raw flesh change and turn white, he must go to the **priest**.
13:17 The **priest** is to examine him, and if the sores have turned white,
13:17 turned white, the **priest** shall pronounce the infected person clean;
13:19 reddish-white spot appears, he must present himself to the **priest**.
13:20 The **priest** is to examine it, and if it appears to be more than skin
13:20 hair in it has turned white, the **priest** shall pronounce him unclean.
13:21 But if, when the **priest** examines it, there is no white hair in it
13:21 has faded, then the **priest** is to put him in isolation for seven days.
13:22 it is spreading in the skin, the **priest** shall pronounce him unclean;
13:23 only a scar from the boil, and the **priest** shall pronounce him clean.
13:25 the **priest** is to examine the spot, and if the hair in it has turned
13:25 The **priest** shall pronounce him unclean; it is an infectious skin
13:26 But if the **priest** examines it and there is no white hair in the spot
13:26 has faded, then the **priest** is to put him in isolation for seven days.
13:27 On the seventh day the **priest** is to examine him, and if it is
13:27 it is spreading in the skin, the **priest** shall pronounce him unclean;
13:28 a swelling from the burn, and the **priest** shall pronounce him clean;
13:30 the **priest** is to examine the sore, and if it appears to be more than
13:30 is yellow and thin, the **priest** shall pronounce that person unclean;
13:31 if, when the **priest** examines this kind of sore, it does not seem to
13:31 the **priest** is to put the infected person in isolation for seven days.
13:32 On the seventh day the **priest** is to examine the sore, and if the itch
13:33 and the **priest** is to keep him in isolation another seven days.
13:34 On the seventh day the **priest** is to examine the itch, and if it has
13:34 to be no more than skin deep, the **priest** shall pronounce him clean.
13:36 the **priest** is to examine him, and if the itch has spread in the skin,
13:36 spread in the skin, the **priest** does not need to look for yellow hair;
13:37 is healed. He is clean, and the **priest** shall pronounce him clean.
13:39 the **priest** is to examine them, and if the spots are dull white,
13:43 The **priest** is to examine him, and if the swollen sore on his head
13:44 The **priest** shall pronounce him unclean because of the sore on his
13:49 it is a spreading mildew and must be shown to the **priest**.
13:50 The **priest** is to examine the mildew and isolate the affected article
13:53 "But if, when the **priest** examines it, the mildew has not spread in
13:54 **he**[s] [+2021] shall order that the contaminated article be washed.
13:55 the affected article has been washed, the **priest** is to examine it,
13:56 If, when the **priest** examines it, the mildew has faded after the
14: 2 time of his ceremonial cleansing, when he is brought to the **priest**:
14: 3 The **priest** is to go outside the camp and examine him. If the
14: 3 **[RPH]** If the person has been healed of his infectious skin
14: 4 the **priest** shall order that two live clean birds and some cedar
14: 5 the **priest** shall order that one of the birds be killed over fresh
14:11 The **priest** who pronounces him clean shall present both the one to
14:12 "Then the **priest** is to take one of the male lambs and offer it as a
14:13 Like the sin offering, the guilt offering belongs to the **priest**;
14:14 The **priest** is to take some of the blood of the guilt offering
14:14 put **[RPH]** it on the lobe of the right ear of the one to be cleansed,
14:15 The **priest** shall then take some of the log of oil, pour it in the palm
14:15 of the log of oil, pour it in the palm of **his**[s] [+2021] **own** left hand,
14:16 dip **[RPH]** his right forefinger into the oil in his palm, and with
14:17 The **priest** is to put some of the oil remaining in his palm on the
14:18 The rest of the oil in his palm the **priest** shall put on the head of
14:18 and make atonement for him **[RPH]** before the LORD.
14:19 "Then the **priest** is to sacrifice the sin offering and make
14:20 and offer it **[RPH]** on the altar, together with the grain offering,
14:20 and make atonement for him, **[RPH]** and he will be clean.
14:23 his cleansing to the **priest** at the entrance to the Tent of Meeting,
14:24 The **priest** is to take the lamb for the guilt offering, together with
14:24 and wave them **[RPH]** before the LORD as a wave offering.
14:25 the lamb for the guilt offering and take **[RPH]** some of its blood
14:26 The **priest** is to pour some of the oil into the palm of his own left
14:26 pour some of the oil into the palm of **his**[s] [+2021] **own** left hand,
14:27 with his right forefinger sprinkle **[RPH]** some of the oil from his
14:28 Some of the oil in his palm **he**[s] [+2021] is to put on the same
14:29 The rest of the oil in his palm the **priest** shall put on the head of
14:31 In this way the **priest** will make atonement before the LORD on
14:35 the owner of the house must go and tell the **priest**, 'I have seen
14:36 The **priest** is to order the house to be emptied before he goes in to
14:36 The priest is to order the house to be emptied before **he**[s] [+2021]
14:36 After this the **priest** is to go in and inspect the house.
14:38 the **priest** shall go out the doorway of the house and close it up for
14:39 On the seventh day the **priest** shall return to inspect the house.
14:40 **he**[s] [+2021] is to order that the contaminated stones be torn out
14:44 the **priest** is to go and examine it and, if the mildew has spread in
14:48 "But if the **priest** comes to examine it and the mildew has not
14:48 has not spread after the house has been plastered, **he**[s] [+2021]
15:14 to the entrance to the Tent of Meeting and give them to the **priest**.
15:15 The **priest** is to sacrifice them, the one for a sin offering
15:15 In this way **he**[s] [+2021] will make atonement before the LORD
15:29 and bring them to the **priest** at the entrance to the Tent of Meeting.
15:30 The **priest** is to sacrifice one for a sin offering and the other for a
15:30 In this way **he**[s] [+2021] will make atonement for her before the
16:32 The **priest** who is anointed and ordained to succeed his father as
16:33 the altar, and for the **priests** and all the people of the community.
17: 5 They must bring them to the **priest**, that is, to the LORD,
17: 6 The **priest** is to sprinkle the blood against the altar of the LORD
19:22 With the ram of the guilt offering the **priest** is to make atonement
21: 1 "Speak to the **priests**, the sons of Aaron, and say to them:
21: 9 " 'If a **priest's** daughter defiles herself by becoming a prostitute,
21:10 " 'The high **priest**, the one among his brothers who has had the
21:21 No descendant of Aaron the **priest** who has any defect is to come
22:10 nor may the guest of a **priest** or his hired worker eat it.
22:11 if a **priest** buys a slave with money, or if a slave is born in his
22:12 If a **priest's** daughter marries anyone other than a priest, she may
22:13 But if a **priest's** daughter becomes a widow or is divorced,
22:14 he must make restitution to the **priest** for the offering and add a
23:10 its harvest, bring to the **priest** a sheaf of the first grain you harvest.
23:11 your behalf; the **priest** is to wave it on the day after the Sabbath.
23:20 The **priest** is to wave the two lambs before the LORD as a wave
23:20 They are a sacred offering to the LORD for the **priest**.
27: 8 pay the specified amount, he is to present the person to the **priest**,
27: 8 he is to present the person to the priest, **who**[s] [+2021] will set the
27: 8 according to what the man making the vow can afford. **[RPH]**
27:11 to the LORD—the animal must be presented to the **priest**,
27:12 **who**[s] [+2021] will judge its quality as good or bad.
27:12 Whatever value the **priest** then sets, that is what it will be.
27:14 holy to the LORD, the **priest** will judge its quality as good or bad.
27:14 or bad. Whatever value the **priest** then sets, so it will remain.
27:18 the **priest** will determine the value according to the number of
27:21 devoted to the LORD; it will become the property of the **priests**.
27:23 the **priest** will determine its value up to the Year of Jubilee,

Nu 3: 3 the anointed **priests**, who were ordained to serve as priests.
3: 6 the tribe of Levi and present them to Aaron the **priest** to assist him.
3:32 chief leader of the Levites was Eleazar son of Aaron, the **priest**.
4:16 "Eleazar son of Aaron, the **priest**, is to have charge of the oil for
4:28 are to be under the direction of Ithamar son of Aaron, the **priest**.
4:33 Meeting under the direction of Ithamar son of Aaron, the **priest**."
5: 8 restitution belongs to the LORD and must be given to the **priest**,
5: 9 All the sacred contributions the Israelites bring to a **priest** will
5:10 but what he gives to the **priest** will belong to the priest.' "
5:15 he is to take his wife to the **priest**. He must also take an offering of
5:16 " 'The **priest** shall bring her and have her stand before the LORD.
5:17 Then **he**[s] [+2021] shall take some holy water in a clay jar
5:17 and put **[RPH]** some dust from the tabernacle floor into the water.

Nu 5:18 After the **priest** has had the woman stand before the LORD,
5:18 while **he**[s] [+2021] **himself** holds the bitter water that brings a
5:19 Then the **priest** shall put the woman under oath and say to her,
5:21 here the **priest** is to put the woman under this curse of the oath—
5:21 **[RPH]** "may the LORD cause your people to curse
5:23 " 'The **priest** is to write these curses on a scroll and then wash
5:25 The **priest** is to take from her hands the grain offering for jealousy,
5:26 The **priest** is then to take a handful of the grain offering as a
5:30 The **priest** is to have her stand before the LORD and is to apply
6:10 or two young pigeons to the **priest** at the entrance to the Tent of
6:11 The **priest** is to offer one as a sin offering and the other as a burnt
6:16 " 'The **priest** is to present them before the LORD and make the
6:17 **He**[s] [+2021] is to present the basket of unleavened bread and is to
6:19 the **priest** is to place in his hands a boiled shoulder of the ram,
6:20 The **priest** shall then wave them before the LORD as a wave
6:20 they are holy and belong to the **priest**, together with the breast that
7:8 were all under the direction of Ithamar son of Aaron, the **priest**.
10:8 "The sons of Aaron, the **priests**, are to blow the trumpets.
15:25 The **priest** is to make atonement for the whole Israelite
15:28 The **priest** is to make atonement before the LORD for the one
16:37 [17:2] "Tell Eleazar son of Aaron, the **priest**, to take the censers
16:39 [17:4] So Eleazar the **priest** collected the bronze censers brought
18:28 tithes you must give the LORD's portion to Aaron the **priest**.
19:3 Give it to Eleazar the **priest**; it is to be taken outside the camp
19:4 Then Eleazar the **priest** is to take some of its blood on his finger
19:6 The **priest** is to take some cedar wood, hyssop and scarlet wool
19:7 the **priest** must wash his clothes and bathe himself with water.
19:7 but **he**[s] [+2021] will be ceremonially unclean till evening.
25:7 the son of Aaron, the **priest**, saw this, he left the assembly,
25:11 "Phinehas son of Eleazar, the son of Aaron, the **priest**, has turned
26:1 the LORD said to Moses and Eleazar son of Aaron, the **priest**,
26:3 Moses and Eleazar the **priest** spoke with them and said,
26:63 Eleazar the **priest** when they counted the Israelites on the plains of
26:64 Aaron the **priest** when they counted the Israelites in the Desert of
27:2 Eleazar the **priest**, the leaders and the whole assembly, and said,
27:19 Have him stand before Eleazar the **priest** and the entire assembly
27:21 He is to stand before Eleazar the **priest**, who will obtain decisions
27:22 He took Joshua and had him stand before Eleazar the **priest**
31:6 from each tribe, along with Phinehas son of Eleazar, the **priest**,
31:12 spoils and plunder to Moses and Eleazar the **priest** and the Israelite
31:13 Eleazar the **priest** and all the leaders of the community went to
31:21 Eleazar the **priest** said to the soldiers who had gone into battle,
31:26 "You and Eleazar the **priest** and the family heads of the
31:29 half share and give it to Eleazar the **priest** as the LORD's part.
31:31 and Eleazar the **priest** did as the LORD commanded Moses.
31:41 Moses gave the tribute to Eleazar the **priest** as the LORD's part,
31:51 Moses and Eleazar the **priest** accepted from them the gold—
31:54 Eleazar the **priest** accepted the gold from the commanders of
32:2 So they came to Moses and Eleazar the **priest** and to the leaders of
32:28 Moses gave orders about them to Eleazar the **priest** and Joshua son
33:38 At the LORD's command Aaron the **priest** went up Mount Hor,
34:17 you as an inheritance: Eleazar the **priest** and Joshua son of Nun.
35:25 He must stay there until the death of the high **priest**, who was
35:28 must stay in his city of refuge until the death of the high **priest**;
35:28 only after the death of the high **priest** may he return to his own
35:32 and live on his own land before the death of the high **priest**.
Dt 17:9 Go to the **priests**, who are Levites, and to the judge who is in
17:12 or for the **priest** who stands ministering there to the LORD your
17:18 a copy of this law, taken from that of the **priests**, who are Levites.
18:1 The **priests**, who are Levites—indeed the whole tribe of Levi—
18:3 This is the share due the **priests** from the people who sacrifice a
18:3 or a sheep: **[RPH]** the shoulder, the jowls and the inner parts.
19:17 must stand in the presence of the LORD before the **priests**
20:2 go into battle, the **priest** shall come forward and address the army.
21:5 The **priests**, the sons of Levi, shall step forward, for the LORD
24:8 of leprous diseases be very careful to do exactly as the **priests**,
26:3 say to the **priest** in office at the time, "I declare today to the
26:4 The **priest** shall take the basket from your hands and set it down in
27:9 Then Moses and the **priests**, who are Levites, said to all Israel,
31:9 So Moses wrote down this law and gave it to the **priests**, the sons
Jos 3:3 the **priests**, who are Levites, carrying it, you are to move out from
3:6 Joshua said to the **priests**, "Take up the ark of the covenant
3:8 Tell the **priests** who carry the ark of the covenant: 'When you
3:13 And as soon as the **priests** who carry the ark of the LORD—
3:14 the **priests** carrying the ark of the covenant went ahead of them.
3:15 Yet as soon as the **priests** who carried the ark reached the Jordan
3:17 The **priests** who carried the ark of the covenant of the LORD
4:3 from the middle of the Jordan from right where the **priests** stood
4:9 where the **priests** who carried the ark of the covenant had stood.
4:10 Now the **priests** who carried the ark remained standing in the
4:11 and the **priests** came to the other side while the people watched.
4:16 "Command the **priests** carrying the ark of the Testimony to come
4:17 So Joshua commanded the **priests**, "Come up out of the Jordan."
4:18 the **priests** came up out of the river carrying the ark of the
4:18 No sooner had **they**[s] [+2021] set their feet on the dry ground than
6:4 Have seven **priests** carry trumpets of rams' horns in front of the
6:4 around the city seven times, with the **priests** blowing the trumpets.
6:6 So Joshua son of Nun called the **priests** and said to them,
6:6 the LORD and have seven **priests** carry trumpets in front of it."
6:8 the seven **priests** carrying the seven trumpets before the LORD
6:9 The armed guard marched ahead of the **priests** who blew the
6:12 the next morning and the **priests** took up the ark of the LORD.
6:13 The seven **priests** carrying the seven trumpets went forward,
6:16 seventh time around, when the **priests** sounded the trumpet blast,
8:33 facing those who carried it—the **priests**, who were Levites.
14:1 which Eleazar the **priest**, Joshua son of Nun and the heads of the
17:4 They went to Eleazar the **priest**, Joshua son of Nun, and the
19:51 These are the territories that Eleazar the **priest**, Joshua son of Nun
20:6 and until the death of the high **priest** who is serving at that time.
21:1 the family heads of the Levites approached Eleazar the **priest**,
21:4 The Levites who were descendants of Aaron the **priest** were
21:13 So to the descendants of Aaron the **priest** they gave Hebron (a city
21:19 All the towns for the **priests**, the descendants of Aaron,
22:13 sent Phinehas son of Eleazar, the **priest**, to the land of Gilead—
22:30 When Phinehas the **priest** and the leaders of the community—
22:31 son of Eleazar, the **priest**, said to Reuben, Gad and Manasseh,
22:32 Phinehas son of Eleazar, the **priest**, and the leaders returned to
Jdg 17:5 and some idols and installed one of his sons as his **priest**.
17:10 Micah said to him, "Live with me and be my father and **priest**,
17:12 and the young man became his **priest** and lived in his house.
17:13 will be good to me, since this Levite has become my **priest**."
18:4 had done for him, and said, "He has hired me and I am his **priest**."
18:6 The **priest** answered them, "Go in peace. Your journey has the
18:17 the other household gods and the cast idol while the **priest**
18:18 the other household gods and the cast idol, the **priest** said to them,
18:19 Don't say a word. Come with us, and be our father and **priest**.
18:19 and clan in Israel as **priest** rather than just one man's household?"
18:19 in Israel as priest rather than just one man's household?" **[RPH]**
18:20 the **priest** was glad. He took the ephod, the other household gods
18:24 "You took the gods I made, and my **priest**, and went away.
18:27 his **priest**, and went on to Laish, against a peaceful
18:30 his sons were **priests** for the tribe of Dan until the time of the
1Sa 1:3 and Phinehas, the two sons of Eli, were **priests** of the LORD.
1:9 Now Eli the **priest** was sitting on a chair by the doorpost of the
2:11 but the boy ministered before the LORD under Eli the **priest**.
2:13 Now it was the practice of the **priests** with the people that
2:13 the servant of the **priest** would come with a three-pronged fork in
2:14 the **priest** would take for himself whatever the fork brought up.
2:15 the servant of the **priest** would come and say to the man who was
2:15 the man who was sacrificing, "Give the **priest** some meat to roast;
2:28 I chose your father out of all the tribes of Israel to be my **priest**,
2:35 I will raise up for myself a faithful **priest**, who will do according to
5:5 That is why to this day neither the **priests** *of* Dagon nor any others
6:2 the Philistines called for the **priests** and the diviners and said,
14:3 son of Phinehas, the son of Eli, the LORD's **priest** in Shiloh.
14:19 While Saul was talking to the **priest**, the tumult in the Philistine
14:19 and more. So Saul said to the **priest**, "Withdraw your hand."
14:36 they replied. But the **priest** said, "Let us inquire of God here."
21:1 [21:2] David went to Nob, to Ahimelech the **priest**. Ahimelech
21:2 [21:3] David answered Ahimelech the **priest**, "The king charged
21:4 [21:5] the **priest** answered David, "I don't have any ordinary
21:5 [21:6] **[RPH]** "Indeed women have been kept from us,
21:6 [21:7] So the **priest** gave him the consecrated bread, since there
21:9 [21:10] The **priest** replied, "The sword of Goliath the Philistine,
22:11 Then the king sent for the **priest** Ahimelech son of Ahitub
22:11 who were the **priests** at Nob, and they all came to the king.
22:17 "Turn and kill the **priests** *of* the LORD, because they too have
22:17 were not willing to raise a hand to strike the **priests** *of* the LORD.
22:18 then ordered Doeg, "You turn and strike down the **priests**."
22:18 So Doeg the Edomite turned and struck **them**[s] [+2021] down.
22:19 the town of the **priests**, with its men and women, its children
22:21 He told David that Saul had killed the **priests** *of* the LORD.
23:9 against him, he said to Abiathar the **priest**, "Bring the ephod."
30:7 Then David said to Abiathar the **priest**, the son of Ahimelech,
2Sa 8:17 Zadok son of Ahitub and Ahimelech son of Abiathar were **priests**;
8:18 and Pelethites; and David's sons were **royal advisers**.
15:27 The king also said to Zadok the **priest**, "Aren't you a seer?
15:35 Won't the **priests** Zadok and Abiathar be there with you?
15:35 Tell them **[RPH]** anything you hear in the king's palace.
17:15 Hushai told Zadok and Abiathar, the **priests**, "Ahithophel has
19:11 [19:12] sent this message to Zadok and Abiathar, the **priests**:
20:25 Sheva was secretary; Zadok and Abiathar were **priests**;
20:26 and Ira the Jairite was David's **priest**.
1Ki 1:7 conferred with Joab son of Zeruiah and with Abiathar the **priest**,
1:8 Zadok the **priest**, Benaiah son of Jehoiada, Nathan the prophet,
1:19 Abiathar the **priest** and Joab the commander of the army,
1:25 king's sons, the commanders of the army and Abiathar the **priest**.
1:26 me your servant, and Zadok the **priest**, and Benaiah son of

1Ki 1:32 King David said, "Call in Zadok the **priest**, Nathan the prophet
1:34 There have Zadok the **priest** and Nathan the prophet anoint him
1:38 So Zadok the **priest**, Nathan the prophet, Benaiah son of Jehoiada,
1:39 Zadok the **priest** took the horn of oil from the sacred tent
1:42 as he was speaking, Jonathan son of Abiathar the **priest** arrived.
1:44 The king has sent with him Zadok the **priest**, Nathan the prophet,
1:45 Zadok the **priest** and Nathan the prophet have anointed him king at
2:22 for him and for Abiathar the **priest** and Joab son of Zeruiah!"
2:26 To Abiathar the **priest** the king said, "Go back to your fields in
2:27 So Solomon removed Abiathar from the **priesthood** of the
2:35 in Joab's position and replaced Abiathar with Zadok the **priest**.
4: 2 these were his chief officials: Azariah son of Zadok—the **priest**;
4: 4 of Jehoiada—commander in chief; Zadok and Abiathar—**priests**;
4: 5 Zabud son of Nathan—a **priest** and personal adviser to the king;
8: 3 all the elders of Israel had arrived, the **priests** took up the ark,
8: 4 sacred furnishings in it. The **priests** and Levites carried them up,
8: 6 The **priests** then brought the ark of the LORD's covenant to its
8:10 When the **priests** withdrew from the Holy Place, the cloud filled
8:11 the **priests** could not perform their service because of the cloud,
12:31 on high places and appointed **priests** from all sorts of people,
12:32 at Bethel he also installed **priests** *at* the high places he had made.
13: 2 On you he will sacrifice the **priests** *of* the high places who now
13:33 once more appointed **priests** *for* the high places from all sorts of
13:33 Anyone who wanted to become a **priest** he consecrated *for* the
2Ki 10:11 his close friends and his **priests**, leaving him no survivor.
10:19 all the prophets of Baal, all his ministers and all his **priests**.
11: 9 of units of a hundred did just as Jehoiada the **priest** ordered.
11: 9 those who were going off duty—and came to Jehoiada the **priest**.
11:10 **he**[s] [+2021] gave the commanders the spears and shields that had
11:15 Jehoiada the **priest** ordered the commanders of units of a hundred,
11:15 For the **priest** had said, "She must not be put to death in the temple
11:18 to pieces and killed Mattan the **priest** *of* Baal in front of the altars.
11:18 Jehoiada the **priest** posted guards at the temple of the LORD.
12: 2 [12:3] LORD all the years Jehoiada the **priest** instructed him.
12: 4 [12:5] Joash said to the **priests**, "Collect all the money that is
12: 5 [12:6] Let every **priest** receive the money from one of the
12: 6 [12:7] by the twenty-third year of King Joash the **priests** still had
12: 7 [12:8] Therefore King Joash summoned Jehoiada the **priest**
12: 7 [12:8] Jehoiada the priest and the other **priests** and asked them,
12: 8 [12:9] The **priests** agreed that they would not collect any more
12: 9 [12:10] Jehoiada the **priest** took a chest and bored a hole in its lid.
12: 9 [12:10] The **priests** who guarded the entrance put into the chest
12:10 [12:11] the royal secretary and the high **priest** came, counted the
12:16 [12:17] into the temple of the LORD; it belonged to the **priests**.
16:10 altar in Damascus and sent to Uriah the **priest** a sketch of the altar,
16:11 So Uriah the **priest** built an altar in accordance with all the plans
16:11 from Damascus and finished it **[RPH]** before King Ahaz returned.
16:15 King Ahaz then gave these orders to Uriah the **priest**: "On the
16:16 And Uriah the **priest** did just as King Ahaz had ordered.
17:27 "Have one of the **priests** you took captive from Samaria go back to
17:28 So one of the **priests** who had been exiled from Samaria came to
17:32 to officiate for them as **priests** in the shrines at the high places.
19: 2 Shebna the secretary and the leading **priests**, all wearing sackcloth,
22: 4 "Go up to Hilkiah the high **priest** and have him get ready the
22: 8 Hilkiah the high **priest** said to Shaphan the secretary, "I have
22:10 informed the king, "Hilkiah the **priest** has given me a book."
22:12 He gave these orders to Hilkiah the **priest**, Ahikam son of
22:14 Hilkiah the **priest**, Ahikam, Acbor, Shaphan and Asaiah went to
23: 2 of Judah, the people of Jerusalem, the **priests** and the prophets—
23: 4 The king ordered Hilkiah the high **priest**, the priests next in rank
23: 4 the **priests** next in rank and the doorkeepers to remove from the
23: 8 Josiah brought all the **priests** from the towns of Judah
23: 8 from Geba to Beersheba, where the **priests** had burned incense.
23: 9 Although the **priests** *of* the high places did not serve at the altar of
23:20 Josiah slaughtered all the **priests** *of* those high places on the altars
23:24 that Hilkiah the **priest** had discovered in the temple of the LORD.
25:18 commander of the guard took as prisoners Seraiah the chief **priest**,
25:18 Zephaniah the **priest** next in rank and the three doorkeepers.
1Ch 9: 2 towns were some Israelites, **priests**, Levites and temple servants.
9:10 Of the **priests**: Jedaiah; Jehoiarib; Jakin;
9:30 But some of the **priests** took care of mixing the spices.
13: 2 also to the **priests** and Levites who are with them in their towns
15:11 Then David summoned Zadok and Abiathar the **priests**, and Uriel,
15:14 So the **priests** and Levites consecrated themselves in order to bring
15:24 Eliezer the **priests** were to blow trumpets before the ark of God.
16: 6 Jahaziel the **priests** were to blow the trumpets regularly before the
16:39 David left Zadok the **priest** and his fellow priests before the
16:39 his fellow **priests** before the tabernacle of the LORD at the high
18:16 Zadok son of Ahitub and Ahimelech son of Abiathar were **priests**;
23: 2 together all the leaders of Israel, as well as the **priests** and Levites.
24: 6 Zadok the **priest**, Ahimelech son of Abiathar and the heads of
24: 6 and the heads of families of the **priests** and of the Levites—
24:31 and the heads of families of the **priests** and of the Levites.
27: 5 for the third month, was Benaiah son of Jehoiada the **priest**.
28:13 He gave him instructions for the divisions of the **priests**
28:21 The divisions of the **priests** and Levites are ready for all the work
29:22 him before the LORD to be ruler and Zadok to be **priest**.
2Ch 4: 6 were rinsed, but the Sea was to be used by the **priests** for washing.
4: 9 He made the courtyard of the **priests**, and the large court
5: 5 furnishings in it. The **priests**, who were Levites, carried them up;
5: 7 The **priests** then brought the ark of the LORD's covenant to its
5:11 The **priests** then withdrew from the Holy Place. All the priests
5:11 All the **priests** who were there had consecrated themselves,
5:12 They were accompanied by 120 **priests** sounding trumpets.
5:14 the **priests** could not perform their service because of the cloud,
6:41 May your **priests**, O LORD God, be clothed with salvation,
7: 2 The **priests** could not enter the temple of the LORD
7: 6 The **priests** took their positions, as did the Levites with the
7: 6 Opposite the Levites, the **priests** blew their trumpets, and all the
8:14 he appointed the divisions of the **priests** for their duties,
8:14 and to assist the **priests** according to each day's requirement.
8:15 They did not deviate from the king's commands to the **priests**
11:13 The **priests** and Levites from all their districts throughout Israel
11:15 he appointed his own **priests** for the high places and for the goat
13: 9 didn't you drive out the **priests** *of* the LORD, the sons of Aaron,
13: 9 and make **priests** of your own as the peoples of other lands do?
13: 9 and seven rams may become a **priest** of what are not gods.
13:10 The **priests** who serve the LORD are sons of Aaron,
13:12 His **priests** with their trumpets will sound the battle cry against
13:14 they cried out to the LORD. The **priests** blew their trumpets
15: 3 the true God, without a **priest** to teach and without the law.
17: 8 and Tob-Adonijah—and the **priests** Elishama and Jehoram.
19: 8 **priests** and heads of Israelite families to administer the law of the
19:11 "Amariah the chief **priest** will be over you in any matter
22:11 the daughter of King Jehoram and wife of the **priest** Jehoiada,
23: 4 A third of you **priests** and Levites who are going on duty on the
23: 6 No one is to enter the temple of the LORD except the **priests**
23: 8 and all the men of Judah did just as Jehoiada the **priest** ordered.
23: 8 for Jehoiada the **priest** had not released any of the divisions.
23: 9 **he**[s] [+2021+3381] gave the commanders of units of a hundred the
23:14 Jehoiada the **priest** sent out the commanders of units of a hundred,
23:14 For the **priest** had said, "Do not put her to death at the temple of
23:17 and idols and killed Mattan the **priest** *of* Baal in front of the altars.
23:18 oversight of the temple of the LORD in the hands of the **priests**,
24: 2 right in the eyes of the LORD all the years of Jehoiada the **priest**.
24: 5 He called together the **priests** and Levites and said to them,
24:11 the royal secretary and the officer of the chief **priest** would come
24:20 the Spirit of God came upon Zechariah son of Jehoiada the **priest**.
24:25 conspired against him for murdering the son of Jehoiada the **priest**,
26:17 Azariah the **priest** with eighty other courageous priests of the
26:17 Azariah the priest with eighty other courageous **priests** of the
26:18 That is for the **priests**, the descendants of Aaron, who have been
26:19 While he was raging at the **priests** in their presence before the
26:19 While he was raging at the priests in **their**[s] [+2021] presence
26:20 When Azariah the chief **priest** and all the other priests looked at
26:20 Azariah the chief priest and all the other **priests** looked at him,
29: 4 He brought in the **priests** and the Levites, assembled them in the
29:16 The **priests** went into the sanctuary of the LORD to purify it.
29:21 The king commanded the **priests**, the descendants of Aaron,
29:22 and the **priests** took the blood and sprinkled it on the altar;
29:24 The **priests** then slaughtered the goats and presented their blood on
29:26 with David's instruments, and the **priests** with their trumpets.
29:34 The **priests**, however, were too few to skin all the burnt offerings;
29:34 the task was finished and until other **priests** had been consecrated,
29:34 in consecrating themselves than the **priests** had been.
30: 3 because not enough **priests** had consecrated themselves
30:15 The **priests** and the Levites were ashamed and consecrated
30:16 The **priests** sprinkled the blood handed to them by the Levites.
30:21 while the Levites and **priests** sang to the LORD every day,
30:24 and goats. A great number of **priests** consecrated themselves.
30:25 along with the **priests** and Levites and all who had assembled from
30:27 The **priests** and the Levites stood to bless the people, and God
31: 2 Hezekiah assigned the **priests** and Levites to divisions—each of
31: 2 each of them according to their duties as **priests** or Levites—
31: 4 the people living in Jerusalem to give the portion due the **priests**
31: 9 Hezekiah asked the **priests** and Levites about the heaps;
31:10 and Azariah the chief **priest**, from the family of Zadok, answered,
31:15 and Shecaniah assisted him faithfully in the towns of the **priests**,
31:17 they distributed to the **priests** enrolled by their families in the
31:19 As for the **priests**, the descendants of Aaron, who lived on the
31:19 by name to distribute portions to every male among **them**[s] [+2021]
34: 5 He burned the bones of the **priests** on their altars, and so he purged
34: 9 They went to Hilkiah the high **priest** and gave him the money that
34:14 Hilkiah the **priest** found the Book of the Law of the LORD that
34:18 informed the king, "Hilkiah the **priest** has given me a book."
34:30 of Judah, the people of Jerusalem, the **priests** and the Levites—
35: 2 He appointed the **priests** to their duties and encouraged them in the
35: 8 contributed voluntarily to the people and the **priests** and Levites.

2Ch 35: 8 gave the **priests** twenty-six hundred Passover offerings and three
35: 10 the **priests** stood in their places with the Levites in their divisions
35: 11 and the **priests** sprinkled the blood handed to them,
35: 14 they made preparations for themselves and for the **priests**,
35: 14 preparations for themselves and for the priests, because the **priests**,
35: 14 made preparations for themselves and for the Aaronic **priests**.
35: 18 with the **priests**, the Levites and all Judah and Israel who were
36: 14 all the leaders of the **priests** and the people became more and more
Ezr 1: 5 family heads of Judah and Benjamin, and the **priests** and Levites—
2: 36 The **priests**: the descendants of Jedaiah (through the family of
2: 61 And from among the **priests**: The descendants of Hobaiah,
2: 63 most sacred food until there was a **priest** ministering with the Urim
2: 69 drachmas of gold, 5,000 minas of silver and 100 **priestly** garments.
2: 70 The **priests**, the Levites, the singers, the gatekeepers
3: 2 Jeshua son of Jozadak and his fellow **priests** and Zerubbabel son
3: 8 and the rest of their brothers (the **priests** and the Levites
3: 10 the **priests** in their vestments and with trumpets, and the Levites
3: 12 But many of the older **priests** and Levites and family heads,
6: 20 The **priests** and Levites had purified themselves and were all
6: 20 for all the exiles, for their brothers the **priests** and for themselves.
7: 5 of Phinehas, the son of Eleazar, the son of Aaron the chief **priest**—
7: 7 including **priests**, Levites, singers, gatekeepers and temple
7: 11 is a copy of the letter King Artaxerxes had given to Ezra the **priest**
8: 15 When I checked among the people and the **priests**, I found no
8: 24 I set apart twelve of the leading **priests**, together with Sherebiah,
8: 29 of the house of the LORD in Jerusalem before the leading **priests**
8: 30 the **priests** and Levites received the silver and gold and sacred
8: 33 sacred articles into the hands of Meremoth son of Uriah, the **priest**.
9: 1 "The people of Israel, including the **priests** and the Levites,
9: 7 and our **priests** have been subjected to the sword and captivity,
10: 5 So Ezra rose up and put the leading **priests** and Levites and all
10: 10 Ezra the **priest** stood up and said to them, "You have been
10: 16 Ezra the **priest** selected men who were family heads, one from
10: 18 Among the descendants of the **priests**, the following had married
Ne 2: 16 or the **priests** or nobles or officials or any others who would be
3: 1 Eliashib the high **priest** and his fellow priests went to work
3: 1 Eliashib the high priest and his fellow **priests** went to work
3: 20 the angle to the entrance of the house of Eliashib the high **priest**.
3: 22 The repairs next to him were made by the **priests** *from* the
3: 28 Above the Horse Gate, the **priests** made repairs, each in front of
5: 12 I summoned the **priests** and made the nobles and officials take an
7: 39 The **priests**: the descendants of Jedaiah (through the family of
7: 63 And from among the **priests**: the descendants of Hobaiah,
7: 65 food until there should be a **priest** ministering with the Urim
7: 70 [7:69] drachmas of gold, 50 bowls and 530 garments for **priests**.
7: 72 [7:71] of gold, 2,000 minas of silver and 67 garments for **priests**.
7: 73 [7:72] The **priests**, the Levites, the gatekeepers, the singers and
8: 2 So on the first day of the seventh month Ezra the **priest** brought
8: 9 Nehemiah the governor, Ezra the **priest** and scribe, and the Levites
8: 13 the heads of all the families, along with the **priests** and the Levites,
9: 32 upon our kings and leaders, upon our **priests** and prophets,
9: 34 our leaders, our **priests** and our fathers did not follow your law;
9: 38 [10:1] our Levites and our **priests** are affixing their seals to it."
10: 8 [10:9] Maaziah, Bilgai and Shemaiah. These were the **priests**.
10: 28 [10:29] **priests**, Levites, gatekeepers, singers, temple servants
10: 34 [10:35] "We—the **priests**, the Levites and the people—have cast
10: 36 [10:37] to the house of our God, to the **priests** ministering there.
10: 37 [10:38] to the **priests**, the first of our ground meal, of our ⌞grain⌟
10: 38 [10:39] A **priest** descended from Aaron is to accompany the
10: 39 [10:40] the sanctuary are kept and where the ministering **priests**,
11: 3 **priests**, Levites, temple servants and descendants of Solomon's
11: 10 From the **priests**: Jedaiah; the son of Joiarib; Jakin;
11: 20 The rest of the Israelites, with the **priests** and Levites, were in all
12: 1 These were the **priests** and Levites who returned with Zerubbabel
12: 7 These were the leaders of the **priests** and their associates in the
12: 12 the days of Joiakim, these were the heads of the **priestly** families:
12: 22 Joiada, Johanan and Jaddua, as well as those of the **priests**,
12: 26 days of Nehemiah the governor and of Ezra the **priest** and scribe.
12: 30 When the **priests** and Levites had purified themselves
12: 35 as well as some **priests** with trumpets, and also Zechariah son of
12: 41 as well as the **priests**—Eliakim, Maaseiah, Miniamin, Micaiah,
12: 44 into the storerooms the portions required by the Law for the **priests**
12: 44 for Judah was pleased with the ministering **priests** and Levites.
13: 4 Eliashib the **priest** had been put in charge of the storerooms of the
13: 5 and gatekeepers, as well as the contributions for the **priests**.
13: 13 I put Shelemiah the **priest**, Zadok the scribe, and a Levite named
13: 28 One of the sons of Joiada son of Eliashib the high **priest** was
13: 30 So I purified the **priests** and the Levites of everything foreign,
Job 12: 19 He leads **priests** away stripped and overthrows men long
Ps 78: 64 their **priests** were put to the sword, and their widows could not
99: 6 Moses and Aaron were among his **priests**, Samuel was among
110: 4 his mind: "You are a **priest** forever, in the order of Melchizedek."
132: 9 May your **priests** be clothed with righteousness; may your saints
132: 16 I will clothe her **priests** with salvation, and her saints will ever sing
Isa 8: 2 I will call in Uriah the **priest** and Zechariah son of Jeberekiah as
24: 2 it will be the same for **priest** as for people, for master as for
28: 7 **Priests** and prophets stagger from beer and are befuddled with
37: 2 Shebna the secretary, and the leading **priests**, all wearing
61: 6 you will be called **priests** *of* the LORD, you will be named
66: 21 And I will select some of them also to be **priests** and Levites,"
Jer 1: 1 one of the **priests** at Anathoth in the territory of Benjamin.
1: 18 kings of Judah, its officials, its **priests** and the people of the land.
2: 8 The **priests** did not ask, 'Where is the LORD?' Those who deal
2: 26 their kings and their officials, their **priests** and their prophets.
4: 9 and the officials will lose heart, the **priests** will be horrified,
5: 31 The prophets prophesy lies, the **priests** rule by their own authority,
6: 13 are greedy for gain; prophets and **priests** alike, all practice deceit.
8: 1 and officials of Judah, the bones of the **priests** and prophets,
8: 10 are greedy for gain; prophets and **priests** alike, all practice deceit.
13: 13 the **priests**, the prophets and all those living in Jerusalem.
14: 18 Both prophet and **priest** have gone to a land they know not.' "
18: 18 for the teaching of the law by the **priest** will not be lost, nor will
19: 1 Take along some of the elders of the people and of the **priests**
20: 1 When the **priest** Pashhur son of Immer, the chief officer in the
21: 1 son of Malkijah and the **priest** Zephaniah son of Maaseiah.
23: 11 "Both prophet and **priest** are godless; even in my temple I find
23: 33 "When these people, or a prophet or a **priest**, ask you, 'What is the
23: 34 If a prophet or a **priest** or anyone else claims, 'This is the oracle of
26: 7 The **priests**, the prophets and all the people heard Jeremiah speak
26: 8 the **priests**, the prophets and all the people seized him and said,
26: 11 the **priests** and the prophets said to the officials and all the people,
26: 16 the officials and all the people said to the **priests** and the prophets,
27: 16 I said to the **priests** and all these people, "This is what the LORD
28: 1 to me in the house of the LORD in the presence of the **priests**
28: 5 Jeremiah replied to the prophet Hananiah before the **priests**
29: 1 to the surviving elders among the exiles and to the **priests**,
29: 25 to Zephaniah son of Maaseiah the **priest**, and to all the other
29: 25 Zephaniah son of Maaseiah the priest, and to all the other **priests**.
29: 26 'The LORD has appointed you **priest** in place of Jehoiada to be in
29: 26 'The LORD has appointed you priest in place of Jehoiada **[RPH]**
29: 29 Zephaniah the **priest**, however, read the letter to Jeremiah the
31: 14 I will satisfy the **priests** with abundance, and my people will be
32: 32 they, their kings and officials, their **priests** and prophets, the men
33: 18 nor will the **priests**, who are Levites, ever fail to have a man to
33: 21 my covenant with the Levites who are **priests** ministering before
34: 19 the **priests** and all the people of the land who walked between the
37: 3 sent Jehucal son of Shelemiah with the **priest** Zephaniah son of
48: 7 Chemosh will go into exile, together with his **priests** and officials.
49: 3 Molech will go into exile, together with his **priests** and officials.
52: 24 commander of the guard took as prisoners Seraiah the chief **priest**,
52: 24 Zephaniah the **priest** next in rank and the three doorkeepers.
La 1: 4 her **priests** groan, her maidens grieve, and she is in bitter anguish.
1: 19 My **priests** and my elders perished in the city while they searched
2: 6 in his fierce anger he has spurned both king and **priest**.
2: 20 Should **priest** and prophet be killed in the sanctuary of the Lord?
4: 13 because of the sins of her prophets and the iniquities of her **priests**,
4: 16 over them. The **priests** are shown no honor, the elders no favor.
Eze 1: 3 the word of the LORD came to Ezekiel the **priest**, the son of
7: 26 the teaching of the law by the **priest** will be lost, as will the
22: 26 Her **priests** do violence to my law and profane my holy things;
40: 45 "The room facing south is for the **priests** who have charge of the
40: 46 the room facing north is for the **priests** who have charge of the
42: 13 where the **priests** who approach the LORD will eat the most holy
42: 14 Once the **priests** enter the holy precincts, they are not to go into
43: 19 You are to give a young bull as a sin offering to the **priests**,
43: 24 the **priests** are to sprinkle salt on them and sacrifice them as a
43: 27 the **priests** are to present your burnt offerings and fellowship
44: 15 " 'But the **priests**, who are Levites and descendants of Zadok
44: 21 No **priest** is to drink wine when he enters the inner court.
44: 22 may marry only virgins of Israelite descent or widows of **priests**.
44: 30 the firstfruits and of all your special gifts will belong to the **priests**.
44: 30 You are to give **them**[s] [+2021] the first portion of your ground
44: 31 The **priests** must not eat anything, bird or animal, found dead
45: 4 It will be the sacred portion of the land for the **priests**,
45: 19 The **priest** is to take some of the blood of the sin offering
46: 2 The **priests** are to sacrifice his burnt offering and his fellowship
46: 19 which belonged to the **priests**, and showed me a place at the
46: 20 "This is the place where the **priests** will cook the guilt offering
48: 10 This will be the sacred portion for the **priests**. It will be 25,000
48: 11 This will be for the consecrated **priests**, the Zadokites, who were
48: 13 "Alongside the territory of the **priests**, the Levites will have an
Hos 4: 4 for your people are like those who bring charges against a **priest**.
4: 9 it will be: Like people, like **priests**. I will punish both of them for
5: 1 "Hear this, you **priests**! Pay attention, you Israelites! Listen,
6: 9 As marauders lie in ambush for a man, so do bands of **priests**;
Joel 1: 9 The **priests** are in mourning, those who minister before the
1: 13 Put on sackcloth, O **priests**, and mourn; wail, you who minister
2: 17 Let the **priests**, who minister before the LORD, weep between

Am 7:10 Amaziah the **priest** *of* Bethel sent a message to Jeroboam king of
Mic 3:11 Her leaders judge for a bribe, her **priests** teach for a price,
Zep 1: 4 of Baal, the names of the pagan and the **idolatrous priests**—
3: 4 Her **priests** profane the sanctuary and do violence to the law.
Hag 1: 1 of Judah, and to Joshua son of Jehozadak, the high **priest**:
1:12 son of Shealtiel, Joshua son of Jehozadak, the high **priest**,
1:14 and the spirit of Joshua son of Jehozadak, the high **priest**,
2: 2 governor of Judah, to Joshua son of Jehozadak, the high **priest**,
2: 4 'Be strong, O Joshua son of Jehozadak, the high **priest**. Be strong,
2:11 the LORD Almighty says: 'Ask the **priests** what the law says:
2:12 does it become consecrated?' " The **priests** answered, "No."
2:13 become defiled?" "Yes," the **priests** replied, "it becomes defiled."
Zec 3: 1 he showed me Joshua the high **priest** standing before the angel of
3: 8 O high **priest** Joshua and your associates seated before you,
6:11 and make a crown, and set it on the head of the high **priest**,
6:13 and rule on his throne. And he will be a **priest** on his throne.
7: 3 by asking the **priests** of the house of the LORD Almighty
7: 5 "Ask all the people of the land and the **priests**, 'When you fasted
Mal 1: 6 "It is you, O **priests**, who show contempt for my name. "But you
2: 1 "And now this admonition is for you, O **priests**.
2: 7 "For the lips of a **priest** ought to preserve knowledge, and from his

3914 כְּהֻנָּה **kᵉhunnâ**, n.f. [14] [√ 3913]

priesthood [9], priestly office [2], priests [2], priestly service [1]

Ex 29: 9 and his sons. The **priesthood** is theirs by a lasting ordinance.
40:15 Their anointing will be to a **priesthood** that will continue for all
Nu 3:10 Appoint Aaron and his sons to serve as **priests**; anyone else who
16:10 near himself, but now you are trying to get the **priesthood** too.
18: 1 are to bear the responsibility for offenses against the **priesthood**.
18: 7 your sons may serve as **priests** in connection with everything at the
18: 7 the curtain. I am giving you the service of the **priesthood** as a gift.
25:13 and his descendants will have a covenant of a lasting **priesthood**,
Jos 18: 7 because the **priestly service** *of* the LORD is their inheritance.
1Sa 2:36 "Appoint me to some **priestly office** so I can have food to eat." '"
Ezr 2:62 find them and so were excluded from the **priesthood** as unclean.
Ne 7:64 find them and so were excluded from the **priesthood** as unclean.
13:29 because they defiled the **priestly office** and the covenant of the
13:29 and the covenant of the **priesthood** and of the Levites.

3915 כּוּב **kûb**, n.pr.g. [1 / 0]

Eze 30: 5 Libya [BHS *Cub*; NIV 4275] and the people of the covenant land

3916 כּוֹבַע **kôbaʿ**, n.m. [6] [cf. 7746]

helmets [4], helmet [2]

1Sa 17: 5 He had a bronze **helmet** on his head and wore a coat of scale armor
2Ch 26:14 spears, **helmets**, coats of armor, bows and slingstones for the entire
Isa 59:17 as his breastplate, and the **helmet** *of* salvation on his head;
Jer 46: 4 the horses, mount the steeds! Take your positions with **helmets** on!
Eze 27:10 They hung their shields and **helmets** on your walls, bringing you
38: 5 Cush and Put will be with them, all with shields and **helmets**,

3917 כָּוָה **kāwâ**, v. [2] [→ 3918, 3953, 4805]

be burned [1], being scorched [1]

Pr 6:28 [C] a man walk on hot coals without his feet **being scorched**?
Isa 43: 2 [C] When you walk through the fire, *you will* not **be burned**;

3918 כְּוִיָּה **kᵉwiyyâ**, n.f. [2] [√ 3817]

burn [2]

Ex 21:25 **burn** for burn, wound for wound, bruise for bruise.
21:25 burn for **burn**, wound for wound, bruise for bruise.

3919 כּוֹכָב **kôkāb**, n.m. [37]

stars [33], star [2], stargazers [+928+2600] [1], starry [1]

Ge 1:16 and the lesser light to govern the night. He also made the **stars**.
15: 5 and said, "Look up at the heavens and count the **stars**—
22:17 and make your descendants as numerous as the **stars** *in* the sky
26: 4 I will make your descendants as numerous as the **stars** *in* the sky
37: 9 the sun and moon and eleven **stars** were bowing down to me."
Ex 32:13 'I will make your descendants as numerous as the **stars** *in* the sky
Nu 24:17 A **star** will come out of Jacob; a scepter will rise out of Israel.
Dt 1:10 your numbers so that today you are as many as the **stars** *in* the sky.
4:19 you look up to the sky and see the sun, the moon and the **stars**—
10:22 your God has made you as numerous as the **stars** *in* the sky.
28:62 You who were as numerous as the **stars** *in* the sky will be left
Jdg 5:20 From the heavens the **stars** fought, from their courses they fought
1Ch 27:23 had promised to make Israel as numerous as the **stars** *in* the sky.
Ne 4:21 [4:15] from the first light of dawn till the **stars** came out.
9:23 You made their sons as numerous as the **stars** *in* the sky, and you
Job 3: 9 May its morning **stars** become dark; may it wait for daylight in
9: 7 to the sun and it does not shine; he seals off the light of the **stars**.
22:12 in the heights of heaven? And see how lofty are the highest **stars**!
25: 5 even the moon is not bright and the **stars** are not pure in his eyes,
38: 7 while the morning **stars** sang together and all the angels shouted
Ps 8: 3 [8:4] the work of your fingers, the moon and the **stars**, which you
136: 9 the moon and **stars** to govern the night; *His love endures*
147: 4 He determines the number of the **stars** and calls them each by
148: 3 Praise him, sun and moon, praise him, all you shining **stars**.
Ecc 12: 2 before the sun and the light and the moon and the **stars** grow dark,
Isa 13:10 The **stars** *of* heaven and their constellations will not show their
14:13 ascend to heaven; I will raise my throne above the **stars** *of* God;
47:13 those **stargazers** [+928+2600] who make predictions month by
Jer 31:35 who decrees the moon and **stars** to shine by night, who stirs up the
Eze 32: 7 I snuff you out, I will cover the heavens and darken their **stars**;
Da 8:10 it threw some of the **starry** host down to the earth and trampled on
12: 3 who lead many to righteousness, like the **stars** for ever and ever.
Joel 2:10 the sun and moon are darkened, and the **stars** no longer shine.
3:15 [4:15] and moon will be darkened, and the **stars** no longer shine.
Am 5:26 of your king, the pedestal of your idols, the **star** *of* your god—
Ob 1: 4 you soar like the eagle and make your nest among the **stars**,
Na 3:16 of your merchants till they are more than the **stars** *of* the sky,

3920 כּוּל **kûl**, v. [38] [cf. 4005?]

contain [3], endure [3], held [3], hold [3], provide [3], provided [3], feed [2], supplied provisions [2], supplied [2], sustain [2], bear [1], conducts [1], consume [1], given provisions [1], hold in [1], holding in [1], holding [1], holds [1], provide supplies [1], supply with food [1], sustained [1], sustains [1]

Ge 45:11 [D] *I will* **provide** *for* you there, because five years of famine are
47:12 [D] **provided** his father and his brothers and all his father's
50:21 [D] don't be afraid. I *will* **provide** *for* you and your children."
Ru 4:15 [D] He will renew your life and **sustain** you *in* your old age.
2Sa 19:32 [19:33] [D] He *had* **provided** *for* the king during his stay in
19:33 [19:34] [D] with me in Jerusalem, and *I will* **provide** *for* you."
20: 3 [D] *He* **provided** *for* them, but did not lie with them.
1Ki 4: 7 [D] *who* **supplied provisions** *for* the king and the royal
4: 7 [D] Each one had to **provide supplies** *for* one month in the year.
4:27 [5:7] [D] **supplied provisions** *for* King Solomon and all who
7:26 [G] rim of a cup, like a lily blossom. *It* **held** two thousand baths.
7:38 [G] each **holding** forty baths and measuring four cubits across,
8:27 [D] The heavens, even the highest heaven, cannot **contain** you.
8:64 [G] too small *to* **hold** the burnt offerings, the grain offerings and
17: 4 [D] the brook, and I have ordered the ravens to **feed** you there."
17: 9 [D] commanded a widow in that place to **supply** you **with food**."
18: 4 [D] fifty in each, and *had* **supplied** them *with* food and water.)
18:13 [D] fifty in each, and **supplied** them *with* food and water.
20:27 [E] When the Israelites were also mustered and **given provisions**,
2Ch 2: 6 [2:5] [D] even the highest heavens, cannot **contain** him?
4: 5 [G] of a cup, like a lily blossom. *It* **held** three thousand baths.
6:18 [D] The heavens, even the highest heavens, cannot **contain** you.
7: 7 [G] could not **hold** the burnt offerings, the grain offerings and
Ne 9:21 [D] For forty years *you* **sustained** them in the desert; they lacked
Ps 55:22 [55:23] [D] Cast your cares on the LORD and he *will* **sustain**
112: 5 [D] and lends freely, *who* **conducts** his affairs with justice.
Pr 18:14 [D] A man's spirit **sustains** him in sickness, but a crushed spirit
Isa 40:12 [A] *Who has* **held** the dust of the earth in a basket, or weighed
Jer 2:13 [G] their own cisterns, broken cisterns that cannot **hold** water.
6:11 [G] I am full of the wrath of the LORD, and I cannot **hold** it **in**.
10:10 [G] the earth trembles; the nations cannot **endure** his wrath.
20: 9 [D] in my bones. I am weary of **holding** it **in**; indeed, I cannot.
Eze 21:28 [21:33] [G] polished to **consume** and to flash like lightning!
23:32 [G] it will bring scorn and derision, for it **holds** so much.
Joel 2:11 [G] of the LORD is great; it is dreadful. Who *can* **endure** it?
Am 7:10 [G] the very heart of Israel. The land cannot **bear** all his words.
Zec 11:16 [D] or seek the young, or heal the injured, or **feed** the healthy,
Mal 3: 2 [D] who *can* **endure** the day of his coming? Who can stand when

3921 כּוּמָז **kûmāz**, n.[m.]. [2]

necklaces [1], ornaments [1]

Ex 35:22 gold jewelry of all kinds: brooches, earrings, rings and **ornaments**.
Nu 31:50 armlets, bracelets, signet rings, earrings and **necklaces**—to make

3922 כּוּן **kûn**[1], v. [216] [→ 3382, 3422, 3520, 3521, 3925, 4026, 4042, 4806, 4807, 4828, 5788, 5789, 9414; cf. 4029]

established [22], prepared [14], be established [10], establish [10], prepare [10], provided [9], steadfast [6], ready [5], founded [4], get ready [4], made preparations [4], formed [3], is firmly established [3], provide [3], right [3], set in place [3], set [3], been proved [2], direct [2], establishes [2], firm [2], is established [2], loyal [2], turn [2], was carried out [2], was established [2], *untranslated* [1], about to [1], aim [1], appear [+4604] [1], appointed [1], are prepared [1], be restored [1], be secure [1], be set [1], be trusted [1], been firmly decided [1], been made ready [1], bent on [1], brought about [1], build [1], built [1], commit [1], confirmed [1], could [1], definite information [1], definitely [+448] [1], determines [1], devote [1], devoted [1], done[s] [1], encourage [+4213] [1], endure [1], erected [1], establishing [1], fashions [1], find out [1], finish [1], form [1], full [1], gave a firm [1], have ready [1], is made ready [1], is [1], keep loyal [1], lays up [1], made plans [1], made ready [1], make preparation [1], make preparations [1], make secure [1], make [1], makes firm [1], makes secure [1], on the alert [1], ordained [1], piles [1], prepare [+2118] [1], preparing [1], provides [1], put in place [1], refreshed [1], secure [1], set in order [1], set on [1], set up [1], sets [1], spread [1], stand [1], steadfastly [1], stood [+5163+8079] [1], stood [1], store up [1], stores [1], string [1], succeed [1], supplied provisions [1], supplies [1], supply [1], support [1], sustain [1], took [1], was arranged [1], was firmly established [1], was reestablished [1], were attached [1], were formed [1], were prepared [1]

Ge 41:32 [C] forms is that the matter *has* **been firmly decided** by God,
43:16 [G] men to my house, slaughter an animal and **prepare** dinner;
43:25 [G] *They* **prepared** their gifts for Joseph's arrival at noon,
Ex 8:26 [8:22] [C] Moses said, "That *would* not *be* **right**. The sacrifices
15:17 [D] the sanctuary, O Lord, your hands **established**.
16:5 [G] On the sixth day *they are to* **prepare** what they bring in,
19:11 [C] be **ready** by the third day, because on that day the LORD
19:15 [C] he said to the people, "**Prepare** [+2118] *yourselves* for the
23:20 [G] along the way and to bring you to the place *I have* **prepared**.
34:2 [C] Be **ready** in the morning, and then come up on Mount Sinai.
Nu 21:27 [F] to Heshbon and let it be rebuilt; *let* Sihon's city **be restored**.
23:1 [G] altars here, and **prepare** seven bulls and seven rams for me."
23:29 [G] altars here, and **prepare** seven bulls and seven rams for me."
Dt 13:14 [13:15] [C] *it has* **been proved** that this detestable thing has
17:4 [C] *it has* **been proved** that this detestable thing has been done in
19:3 [G] **Build** roads to them and divide into three parts the land the
32:6 [D] your Father, your Creator, who made you and **formed** you?
Jos 1:11 [G] the camp and tell the people, '**Get** your supplies **ready**.
3:17 [G] stood **firm** on dry ground in the middle of the Jordan,
4:3 [G] the Jordan from right where the priests **stood** [+5163+8079]
4:4 [G] So Joshua called together the twelve men *he had* **appointed**
8:4 [C] the city. Don't go very far from it. All of you be **on the alert**.
Jdg 12:6 [G] because he **could** not pronounce the word correctly,
16:26 [C] "Put me where I can feel the pillars that **support** the temple,
16:29 [C] toward the two central pillars on which the temple **stood**.
1Sa 7:3 [G] and the Ashtoreths and **commit** yourselves to the LORD
13:13 [G] he *would have* **established** your kingdom over Israel for all
20:31 [C] this earth, neither you nor your kingdom *will* **be established**.
23:22 [G] Go and **make** further **preparation**. Find out where David
23:23 [C] he uses and come back to me with **definite information**.
26:4 [C] and learned that Saul had **definitely** [+448] arrived.
2Sa 5:12 [G] David knew that the LORD *had* **established** him as king
7:12 [G] come from your own body, and *I will* **establish** his kingdom.
7:13 [D] and *I will* **establish** the throne of his kingdom forever.
7:16 [C] before me; your throne will be **established** forever.' "
7:24 [D] *You have* **established** your people Israel as your very own
7:26 [C] the house of your servant David will be **established** before
1Ki 2:12 [C] of his father David, and his rule **was** firmly **established**.
2:24 [G] *he* who *has* **established** me securely on the throne of my
2:45 [C] David's throne will remain **secure** before the LORD
2:46 [C] The kingdom **was** now **firmly established** in Solomon's
5:18 [5:32] [G] and the men of Gebal cut and **prepared** the timber
6:19 [G] *He* **prepared** the inner sanctuary within the temple to set the
1Ch 9:32 [G] of their Kohathite brothers were in charge of **preparing**
12:39 [12:40] [G] for their families *had* **supplied provisions** for them.
14:2 [G] David knew that the LORD *had* **established** him as king
15:1 [G] *he* **prepared** a place for the ark of God and pitched a tent for
15:3 [G] up the ark of the LORD to the place *he had* **prepared** for it.
15:12 [G] the God of Israel, to the place *I have* **prepared** for it.
16:30 [C] The world **is firmly established**; it cannot be moved.
17:11 [G] one of your own sons, and *I will* **establish** his kingdom.
17:12 [D] build a house for me, and *I will* **establish** his throne forever.
17:14 [C] kingdom forever; his throne will be **established** forever.' "
17:24 [C] the house of your servant David *will* **be established** before
22:3 [G] He **provided** a large amount of iron to make nails for the
22:5 [G] all the nations. Therefore *I will* **make preparations** for it."
22:5 [G] So David **made** extensive **preparations** before his death.
22:10 [G] *I will* **establish** the throne of his kingdom over Israel
22:14 [G] "I have taken great pains *to* **provide** for the temple of the
22:14 [G] and wood and stone. **[RPH]** And you may add to them.
28:2 [G] for the footstool of our God, and *I* **made plans** to build it.
28:7 [G] *I will* **establish** his kingdom forever if he is unswerving in
29:2 [G] With all my resources *I have* **provided** for the temple of my
29:3 [G] and above everything *I have* **provided** for this holy temple:
29:16 [G] as for all this abundance that *we have* **provided** for building
29:18 [G] of your people forever, and **keep** their hearts **loyal** to you.
29:19 [G] to build the palatial structure for which *I have* **provided**."
2Ch 1:4 [G] God from Kiriath Jearim to the place he *had* **prepared** for it,
2:7 [2:6] [G] skilled craftsmen, whom my father David **provided**.
2:9 [2:8] [G] to **provide** me *with* plenty of lumber,
3:1 [G] floor of Araunah the Jebusite, the place **provided** *by* David.
8:16 [C] All Solomon's work **was carried out**, from the day the
12:1 [G] After Rehoboam's position as king *was* **established** and he
12:14 [G] because *he had* not **set** his heart on seeking the LORD.
17:5 [G] The LORD **established** the kingdom under his control;
19:3 [G] the Asherah poles and *have* **set** your heart **on** seeking God."
20:33 [G] the people still *had* not **set** their hearts on the God of their
26:14 [G] **provided** shields, spears, helmets, coats of armor, bows and
27:6 [G] because he walked **steadfastly** before the LORD his God.
29:19 [G] *We have* **prepared** and consecrated all the articles that King
29:35 [C] the service of the temple of the LORD **was reestablished**.
29:36 [G] all the people rejoiced at what God *had* **brought about** for
30:19 [G] *who* **sets** his heart on seeking God—the LORD, the God of
31:11 [G] Hezekiah gave orders to **prepare** storerooms in the temple of
31:11 [G] storerooms in the temple of the LORD, and *this was* **done**[s].
33:16 [g] [*he* **restored** [K; see Q 1215] the altar of the LORD]
35:4 [G] **Prepare** *yourselves* by families in your divisions,
35:6 [G] and **prepare** ⌞the lambs⌟ for your fellow countrymen,
35:10 [C] The service **was arranged** and the priests stood in their
35:14 [G] *they* **made preparations** for themselves and for the priests,
35:14 [G] So the Levites **made preparations** for themselves and for
35:15 [G] because their fellow Levites **made** *the* **preparations** for
35:16 [C] LORD **was carried out** for the celebration of the Passover
35:20 [G] After all this, when Josiah *had* **set** the temple **in order**, Neco
Ezr 3:3 [G] *they* **built** the altar on its foundation and sacrificed burnt
7:10 [G] For Ezra *had* **devoted** himself to the study and observance of
Ne 8:10 [C] and send some to those *who have* nothing **prepared**.
Est 6:4 [G] hanging Mordecai on the gallows *he had* **erected** for him.
7:10 [G] So they hanged Haman on the gallows *he had* **prepared** for
Job 8:8 [D] former generations and **find out** what their fathers learned,
11:13 [G] "Yet if you **devote** your heart to him and stretch out your
15:23 [C] food for vultures; he knows the day of darkness **is** at hand.
15:35 [G] and give birth to evil; their womb **fashions** deceit."
18:12 [C] is hungry for him; disaster *is* **ready** for him when he falls.
21:8 [C] They see their children **established** around them, their
27:16 [G] he heaps up silver like dust and clothes like **piles** of clay,
27:17 [G] what *he* **lays up** the righteous will wear, and the innocent
28:27 [G] at wisdom and appraised it; *he* **confirmed** it and tested it.
29:7 [G] to the gate of the city and **took** my seat in the public square,
31:15 [A] *Did* not the same one **form** us both within our mothers?
38:41 [G] Who **provides** food for the raven when its young cry out to
42:7 [C] because you have not spoken of me *what is* **right**,
42:8 [C] You have not spoken of me *what is* **right**, as my servant Job
Ps 5:9 [5:10] [C] Not a *word* from their mouth *can* **be trusted**;
7:9 [7:10] [D] of the wicked and **make** the righteous **secure**.
7:12 [7:13] [D] sharpen his sword; he will bend and **string** his bow.
7:13 [7:14] [G] *He has* **prepared** his deadly weapons; he makes
8:3 [8:4] [D] the moon and the stars, which *you have* **set in place**,
9:7 [9:8] [D] *he has* **established** his throne for judgment.
10:17 [G] *you* **encourage** [+4213] them, and you listen to their cry,
11:2 [D] *they* **set** their arrows against the strings to shoot from the
21:12 [21:13] [D] their backs when *you* **aim** at them with drawn bow.
24:2 [D] founded it upon the seas and **established** it upon the waters.
37:23 [E] LORD delights in a man's way, he **makes** his steps **firm**;
38:17 [38:18] [C] For I *am* **about to** fall, and my pain is ever with me.
40:2 [40:3] [D] my feet on a rock and **gave** me **a firm** place to stand.
48:8 [48:9] [D] of our God: God **makes** her **secure** forever. *Selah*
51:10 [51:12] [C] O God, and renew a **steadfast** spirit within me.
57:6 [57:7] [G] *They* **spread** a net for my feet—I was bowed down
57:7 [57:8] [C] My heart *is* **steadfast**, O God, my heart is steadfast;
57:7 [57:8] [C] My heart is steadfast, O God, my heart *is* **steadfast**;
59:4 [59:5] [F] I have done no wrong, yet *they are* **ready** to attack
65:6 [65:7] [G] *who* **formed** the mountains by your power,
65:9 [65:10] [G] filled with water *to* **provide** the people *with* grain,
65:9 [65:10] [G] the people with grain, for so *you have* **ordained** it.
68:9 [68:10] [D] O God; you **refreshed** your weary inheritance.
68:10 [68:11] [G] your bounty, O God, *you* **provided** for the poor.
74:16 [G] and yours also the night; you **established** the sun and moon.
78:8 [G] rebellious generation, whose hearts *were* not **loyal** to God,
78:20 [G] he also give us food? *Can he* **supply** meat for his people?"
78:37 [C] their hearts *were* not **loyal** to him, they were not faithful to
87:5 [D] born in her, and the Most High himself *will* **establish** her."
89:2 [89:3] [G] *you* **established** your faithfulness in heaven itself.
89:4 [89:5] [G] '*I will* **establish** your line forever and make your
89:21 [89:22] [C] My hand *will* **sustain** him; surely my arm will
89:37 [89:38] [C] *it will* **be established** forever like the moon,
90:17 [D] **establish** the work of our hands for us—yes, establish the
90:17 [D] of our hands for us—yes, **establish** the work of our hands.
93:1 [C] The world **is firmly established**; it cannot be moved.
93:2 [C] Your throne **was established** long ago; you are from all
96:10 [C] The world **is firmly established**, it cannot be moved; he will

Ps 99: 4 [D] is mighty, he loves justice—you *have* **established** equity;
101: 7 [C] no one who speaks falsely *will* **stand** in my presence.
102:28 [102:29] [C] their descendants *will* **be established** before you."
103:19 [G] The LORD *has* **established** his throne in heaven, and his
107:36 [D] to live, and *they* **founded** a city where they could settle.
108: 1 [108:2] [C] My heart *is* **steadfast**, O God; I will sing and make
112: 7 [C] of bad news; his heart *is* **steadfast**, trusting in the LORD.
119: 5 [C] Oh, that my ways *were* **steadfast** in obeying your decrees!
119:73 [D] Your hands made me and **formed** me; give me understanding
119:90 [D] all generations; *you* **established** the earth, and it endures.
119:133 [G] **Direct** my footsteps according to your word; let no sin rule
140:11 [140:12] [C] *Let* slanderers not **be established** in the land;
141: 2 [C] *May* my prayer **be set** before you like incense;
147: 8 [G] he **supplies** the earth *with* rain and makes grass grow on the
Pr 3:19 [D] by understanding *he* **set** the heavens **in place**;
4:18 [C] gleam of dawn, shining ever brighter till the **full** light of day.
4:26 [C] level paths for your feet and take only ways *that are* **firm**.
6: 8 [G] yet *it* **stores** its provisions in summer and gathers its food at
8:27 [G] I was there when he **set** the heavens **in place**, when he
12: 3 [C] A man cannot **be established** through wickedness,
12:19 [C] Truthful lips **endure** forever, but a lying tongue lasts only a
16: 3 [C] to the LORD whatever you do, and your plans *will* **succeed**.
16: 9 [G] a man plans his course, but the LORD **determines** his steps.
16:12 [C] for a throne **is established** through righteousness.
19:29 [C] Penalties **are prepared** for mockers, and beatings for the
20:18 [C] **Make** plans by seeking advice; if you wage war,
21:29 [g] [but an upright man **gives thought** [K; see Q 1067] *to* his ways.]
21:31 [H] The horse **is made ready** for the day of battle, but victory
22:18 [C] them in your heart and **have** all of them **ready** on your lips.
24: 3 [F] a house is built, and through understanding *it* **is established**;
24:27 [G] **Finish** your outdoor work and get your fields ready; after
25: 5 [C] and his throne *will* **be established** through righteousness.
29:14 [C] the poor with fairness, his throne *will* always **be secure**.
30:25 [G] of little strength, yet *they* **store up** their food in the summer;
Isa 2: 2 [C] temple will be **established** as chief among the mountains;
9: 7 [9:6] [G] **establishing** and upholding it with justice
14:21 [G] **Prepare** a place to slaughter his sons for the sins of their
16: 5 [H] In love a throne *will* **be established**; in faithfulness a man
30:33 [H] long been prepared; it *has* **been made ready** for the king.
40:20 [G] He looks for a skilled craftsman to **set up** an idol that will not
45:18 [D] is God; he who fashioned and made the earth, he **founded** it;
51:13 [D] of the wrath of the oppressor, who *is* **bent on** destruction?
54:14 [F] In righteousness *you will* **be established**: Tyranny will be far
62: 7 [D] give him no rest till *he* **establishes** Jerusalem and makes her
Jer 10:12 [G] *he* **founded** the world by his wisdom and stretched out the
10:23 [G] man's life is not his own; it is not for man *to* **direct** his steps.
30:20 [C] of old, and their community *will* **be established** before me;
33: 2 [G] the earth, the LORD who formed it and **established** it—
46:14 [G] 'Take your positions and **get ready**, for the sword devours
51:12 [G] the guard, station the watchmen, **prepare** an ambush!
51:15 [G] *he* **founded** the world by his wisdom and stretched out the
Eze 4: 3 [G] wall between you and the city and **turn** your face toward it.
4: 7 [G] **Turn** your face toward the siege of Jerusalem and with bared
7:14 [G] Though they blow the trumpet and **get** everything **ready**, no
16: 7 [C] Your breasts **were formed** and your hair grew, you who were
28:13 [E] of gold; on the day you were created *they* **were prepared**.
38: 7 [C] " '**Get ready**; be prepared, you and all the hordes gathered
38: 7 [G] *be* **prepared**, you and all the hordes gathered about you,
40:43 [H] a handbreadth long, **were attached** to the wall all around.
Hos 6: 3 [C] As surely as the sun rises, he *will* **appear** [+4604]; he will
Am 4:12 [C] I will do this to you, **prepare** to meet your God, O Israel."
Mic 4: 1 [C] temple will be **established** as chief among the mountains;
Na 2: 3 [2:4] [G] the chariots flashes on the day they *are* **made ready**;
2: 5 [2:6] [H] to the city wall; the protective shield *is* **put in place**.
Hab 2:12 [D] a city with bloodshed and **establishes** a town by crime!
Zep 1: 7 [G] The LORD *has* **prepared** a sacrifice; he has consecrated
Zec 5:11 [H] When *it is* **ready**, the basket will be set there in its place."

3923 ²כּוּן kûn², n.pr.loc. [1]

Cun [1]

1Ch 18: 8 From Tebah and **Cun**, towns that belonged to Hadadezer,

3924 כַּוָּן kawwān, n.[m.]. [2]

cakes of bread [1], cakes [1]

Jer 7:18 the dough and make **cakes of bread** for the Queen of Heaven.
44:19 did not our husbands know that we were making **cakes** like her

3925 כּוֹנַנְיָהוּ kônanyāhû, n.pr.m. [0] [√ 3922 + 3378]

2Ch 31:12 [**Conaniah**, [K; see Q 4042] a Levite, was in charge of these things]
31:13 [under **Conaniah** [K; see Q 4042] and Shimei his brother]
35: 9 [**Conaniah** [K; see Q 4042] along with Shemaiah and Nethanel,]

3926 ¹כּוֹס kôs¹, n.f. [31]

cup [26], goblet [+7694] [2], cups [1], give a drink [+906+9197] [1], lot [+4987] [1]

Ge 40:11 Pharaoh's **cup** was in my hand, and I took the grapes, squeezed
40:11 squeezed them into Pharaoh's **cup** and put the cup in his hand."
40:11 squeezed them into Pharaoh's cup and put the **cup** in his hand."
40:13 you to your position, and you will put Pharaoh's **cup** in his hand,
40:21 his position, so that he once again put the **cup** into Pharaoh's hand,
2Sa 12: 3 It shared his food, drank from his **cup** and even slept in his arms.
1Ki 7:26 and its rim was like the rim of a **cup**, like a lily blossom.
2Ch 4: 5 and its rim was like the rim of a **cup**, like a lily blossom.
Ps 11: 6 and burning sulfur; a scorching wind will be their **lot** [+4987].
16: 5 LORD, you have assigned me my portion and my **cup**; you have
23: 5 of my enemies. You anoint my head with oil; my **cup** overflows.
75: 8 [75:9] In the hand of the LORD is a **cup** full of foaming wine
116:13 I will lift up the **cup** *of* salvation and call on the name of the
Pr 23:31 when it sparkles in the **cup**, [K 3967] when it goes down
Isa 51:17 you who have drunk from the hand of the LORD the **cup** *of* his
51:17 you who have drained to its dregs the **goblet** [+7694] that makes
51:22 I have taken out of your hand the **cup** that made you stagger;
51:22 from that cup, the **goblet of** [+7694] my wrath, you will never
Jer 16: 7 nor *will anyone* **give** them **a drink** [+906+9197] to console them.
25:15 "Take from my hand this **cup** *filled with* the wine of my wrath
25:17 So I took the **cup** from the LORD's hand and made all the nations
25:28 But if they refuse to take the **cup** from your hand and drink,
35: 5 *some* **cups** before the men of the Recabite family and said to them,
49:12 "If those who do not deserve to drink the **cup** must drink it,
51: 7 Babylon was a gold **cup** in the LORD's hand; she made the
La 4:21 to you also the **cup** will be passed; you will be drunk and stripped
Eze 23:31 gone the way of your sister; so I will put her **cup** into your hand.
23:32 "You will drink your sister's **cup**, a cup large and deep; it will
23:33 filled with drunkenness and sorrow, the **cup** *of* ruin and desolation,
23:33 the cup of ruin and desolation, the **cup** *of* your sister Samaria.
Hab 2:16 The **cup** *from* the LORD's right hand is coming around to you,

3927 ²כּוֹס kôs², n.[m.]. [3]

little owl [2], owl [1]

Lev 11:17 the **little owl**, the cormorant, the great owl,
Dt 14:16 the **little owl**, the great owl, the white owl,
Ps 102: 6 [102:7] I am like a desert owl, like an **owl** *among* the ruins.

3928 ¹כּוּר kûr¹, v. Not used in NIV/BHS [cf. 4839]

3929 ²כּוּר kûr², n.[m.]. [9] [cf. 3968]

furnace [9]

Dt 4:20 took you and brought you out of the iron-smelting **furnace**,
1Ki 8:51 whom you brought out of Egypt, out of that iron-smelting **furnace**.
Pr 17: 3 The crucible for silver and the **furnace** for gold, but the LORD
27:21 The crucible for silver and the **furnace** for gold, but man is tested
Isa 48:10 though not as silver; I have tested you in the **furnace** *of* affliction.
Jer 11: 4 I brought them out of Egypt, out of the iron-smelting **furnace**.'
Eze 22:18 all of them are the copper, tin, iron and lead left inside a **furnace**.
22:20 iron, lead and tin into a **furnace** to melt it with a fiery blast,
22:22 As silver is melted in a **furnace**, so you will be melted inside her,

3930 כּוֹר עָשָׁן kôr ʿāšān, n.pr.loc. Not used in NIV/BHS [cf. 1014, 1016]

3931 כּוֹרֶשׁ kôreš, n.pr.m. [15] [→ Ar 10350]

Cyrus [15]

2Ch 36:22 In the first year of **Cyrus** king of Persia, in order to fulfill the word
36:22 the LORD moved the heart of **Cyrus** king of Persia to make a
36:23 "This is what **Cyrus** king of Persia says: " 'The LORD, the God
Ezr 1: 1 In the first year of **Cyrus** king of Persia, in order to fulfill the word
1: 1 the LORD moved the heart of **Cyrus** king of Persia to make a
1: 2 "This is what **Cyrus** king of Persia says: " 'The LORD, the God
1: 7 King **Cyrus** brought out the articles belonging to the temple of the
1: 8 **Cyrus** king of Persia had them brought by Mithredath the
3: 7 sea from Lebanon to Joppa, as authorized by **Cyrus** king of Persia.
4: 3 the God of Israel, as King **Cyrus**, the king of Persia,
4: 5 frustrate their plans during the entire reign of **Cyrus** king of Persia
Isa 44:28 who says of **Cyrus**, 'He is my shepherd and will accomplish all
45: 1 "This is what the LORD says to his anointed, to **Cyrus**,
Da 1:21 And Daniel remained there until the first year of King **Cyrus**.
10: 1 In the third year of **Cyrus** king of Persia, a revelation was given to

3932 ¹כּוּשׁ kûš¹, n.pr.loc. [29] [→ 3934, 3935]

Cush [26], Cushite [3]

Ge 2:13 second river is the Gihon; it winds through the entire land of **Cush**.

[A] Qal [B] Qal passive [C] Niphal [D] Piel (poel, polel, pilel, pilal, pealal, pilpel) [E] Pual (poal, polal, poalal, pulal, pualal)

Ge 10: 6 The sons of Ham: **Cush**, Mizraim, Put and Canaan.
10: 7 The sons of **Cush**: Seba, Havilah, Sabtah, Raamah and Sabteca.
10: 8 **Cush** was the father of Nimrod, who grew to be a mighty warrior
2Ki 19: 9 the **Cushite** king ˻of Egypt˼, was marching out to fight against
1Ch 1: 8 The sons of Ham: **Cush**, Mizraim, Put and Canaan.
1: 9 The sons of **Cush**: Seba, Havilah, Sabta, Raamah and Sabteca.
1: 10 **Cush** was the father of Nimrod, who grew to be a mighty warrior
Est 1: 1 who ruled over 127 provinces stretching from India to **Cush**:
8: 9 and nobles of the 127 provinces stretching from India to **Cush**.
Job 28: 19 The topaz of **Cush** cannot compare with it; it cannot be bought
Ps 68: 31 [68:32] will come from Egypt; **Cush** will submit herself to God.
87: 4 Philistia too, and Tyre, along with **Cush**—and will say, 'This one
Isa 11: 11 from **Cush**, from Elam, from Babylonia, from Hamath and from
18: 1 Woe to the land of whirring wings along the rivers of **Cush**,
20: 3 for three years, as a sign and portent against Egypt and **Cush**,
20: 4 and barefoot the Egyptian captives and **Cushite** exiles,
20: 5 Those who trusted in **Cush** and boasted in Egypt will be afraid
37: 9 the **Cushite** king ˻of Egypt˼, was marching out to fight against
43: 3 I give Egypt for your ransom, **Cush** and Seba in your stead.
45: 14 "The products of Egypt and the merchandise of **Cush**, and those
Jer 46: 9 men of **Cush** and Put who carry shields, men of Lydia who draw
Eze 29: 10 waste from Migdol to Aswan, as far as the border of **Cush**.
30: 4 sword will come against Egypt, and anguish will come upon **Cush**.
30: 5 **Cush** and Put, Lydia and all Arabia, Libya and the people of the
30: 9 go out from me in ships to frighten **Cush** out of her complacency.
38: 5 Persia, **Cush** and Put will be with them, all with shields
Na 3: 9 **Cush** and Egypt were her boundless strength; Put and Libya were
Zep 3: 10 From beyond the rivers of **Cush** my worshipers, my scattered

3933 ²כּוּשׁ *kûš²*, n.pr.m. [1]

Cush [1]

Ps 7: T [7:1] which he sang to the LORD concerning **Cush**,

3934 ¹כּוּשִׁי *kûšî¹*, a.g. [25] [√ 3932]

Cushite [14], Cushites [7], *untranslated* [1], Cushites [+1201] [1], Ethiopian [1], Nubians [1]

Nu 12: 1 Aaron began to talk against Moses because of his **Cushite** wife,
12: 1 because of his Cushite wife, for he had married a **Cushite**.
2Sa 18: 21 Joab said to a **Cushite**, "Go, tell the king what you have seen."
18: 21 you have seen." The **Cushite** bowed down before Joab and ran off.
18: 22 to Joab, "Come what may, please let me run behind the **Cushite**."
18: 23 Then Ahimaaz ran by way of the plain and outran the **Cushite**.
18: 31 the **Cushite** arrived and said, "My lord the king, hear the good
18: 31 Then the Cushite arrived and said, **[RPH]** "My lord the king,
18: 32 The king asked the **Cushite**, "Is the young man Absalom safe?"
18: 32 The **Cushite** replied, "May the enemies of my lord the king
2Ch 12: 3 of Libyans, Sukkites and **Cushites** that came with him from Egypt,
14: 9 [14:8] Zerah the **Cushite** marched out against them with a vast
14: 12 [14:11] The LORD struck down the **Cushites** before Asa
14: 12 [14:11] the Cushites before Asa and Judah. The **Cushites** fled,
14: 13 [14:12] Such a great number of **Cushites** fell that they could not
16: 8 Were not the **Cushites** and Libyans a mighty army with great
21: 16 of the Philistines and of the Arabs who lived near the **Cushites**.
Jer 13: 23 Can the **Ethiopian** change his skin or the leopard its spots?
38: 7 But Ebed-Melech, a **Cushite**, an official in the royal palace,
38: 10 the king commanded Ebed-Melech the **Cushite**, "Take thirty men
38: 12 Ebed-Melech the **Cushite** said to Jeremiah, "Put these old rags
39: 16 "Go and tell Ebed-Melech the **Cushite**, 'This is what the LORD
Da 11: 43 the riches of Egypt, with the Libyans and **Nubians** in submission.
Am 9: 7 "Are not you Israelites the same to me as the **Cushites** [+1201]?"
Zep 2: 12 "You too, O **Cushites**, will be slain by my sword."

3935 ²כּוּשִׁי *kûšî²*, n.pr.m. [2] [√ 3932]

Cushi [2]

Jer 36: 14 the son of Shelemiah, the son of **Cushi**, to say to Baruch,
Zep 1: 1 The word of the LORD that came to Zephaniah son of **Cushi**,

3936 כּוּשָׁן *kûšān*, n.pr.loc. [1]

Cushan [1]

Hab 3: 7 I saw the tents of **Cushan** in distress, the dwellings of Midian in

3937 כּוּשַׁן רִשְׁעָתַיִם *kûšan riš'ātayim*, n.pr.m. [4] [cf. 8403]

Cushan-Rishathaim [2], him[s] [1], whom[s] [1]

Jdg 3: 8 so that he sold them into the hands of **Cushan-Rishathaim** king of
3: 8 to **whom**[s] the Israelites were subject for eight years.
3: 10 The LORD gave **Cushan-Rishathaim** king of Aram into the
3: 10 king of Aram into the hands of Othniel, who overpowered **him**[s].

3938 כּוֹשָׁרָה *kôšārâ*, n.f. [1] [cf. 8876]

singing [1]

Ps 68: 6 [68:7] in families, he leads forth the prisoners with **singing**;

3939 כּוּת *kût*, n.pr.loc. [1] [→ 3940]

Cuthah [1]

2Ki 17: 30 the men from **Cuthah** made Nergal, and the men from Hamath

3940 כּוּתָה *kûtâ*, n.pr.loc. [1] [√ 3939]

Cuthah [1]

2Ki 17: 24 **Cuthah**, Avva, Hamath and Sepharvaim and settled them in the

3941 כָּזַב *kāzab*, v. [16] [→ 423, 424?, 3942, 3943, 3945]

lie [3], false [2], lying [2], prove false [2], considered a liar [1], deceive [1], fail [1], liar [+8120] [1], liars [1], mislead [1], prove a liar [1]

Nu 23: 19 [D] God is not a man, that *he should* **lie**, nor a son of man,
2Ki 4: 16 [D] she objected. "Don't **mislead** your servant, O man of God!"
Job 6: 28 [D] now be so kind as to look at me. *Would I* **lie** to your face?
24: 25 [G] who *can* **prove** me **false** and reduce my words to nothing?"
34: 6 [D] Although I am right, *I am* **considered a liar**; although I am
41: 9 [41:1] [C] Any hope of subduing him *is* **false**; the mere sight of
Ps 78: 36 [D] flatter him with their mouths, **lying** to him with their tongues;
89: 35 [89:36] [D] sworn by my holiness—and *I will* not **lie** to David—
116: 11 [A] And in my dismay I said, "All men *are* **liars**."
Pr 14: 5 [D] A truthful witness *does* not **deceive**, but a false witness pours
30: 6 [C] add to his words, or he will rebuke you and **prove** *you* **a liar**.
Isa 57: 11 [D] so dreaded and feared that *you have been* **false** to me,
58: 11 [D] a well-watered garden, like a spring whose waters never **fail**.
Eze 13: 19 [D] By **lying** to my people, who listen to lies, you have killed
Mic 2: 11 [D] If a **liar** [+8120] and deceiver comes and says, 'I will
Hab 2: 3 [D] appointed time; it speaks of the end and *will* not **prove false**.

3942 כָּזָב *kāzāb*, n.m. [31] [√ 3941; Ar 10343, 10344]

lies [11], lying [5], lie [4], false gods [3], false [2], deceptive [1], liar [+408] [1], lie [+1819] [1], lied [+1819] [1], lies [+1821] [1], lying [+1819] [1]

Jdg 16: 10 to Samson, "You have made a fool of me; *you* **lied** [+1819] to me.
16: 13 you have been making a fool of me and **lying** [+1819] to me.
Ps 4: 2 [4:3] How long will you love delusions and seek **false gods**?
5: 6 [5:7] You destroy those who tell **lies**; bloodthirsty and deceitful
40: 4 [40:5] not look to the proud, to those who turn aside to **false gods**.
58: 3 [58:4] go astray; from the womb they are wayward and speak **lies**.
62: 4 [62:5] to topple him from his lofty place; they take delight in **lies**.
62: 9 [62:10] Lowborn men are but a breath, the highborn are but a **lie**;
Pr 6: 19 a false witness who pours out **lies** and a man who stirs up
14: 5 truthful witness does not deceive, but a false witness pours out **lies**.
14: 25 A truthful witness saves lives, but a **false** witness is deceitful.
19: 5 will not go unpunished, and he who pours out **lies** will not go free.
19: 9 will not go unpunished, and he who pours out **lies** will perish.
19: 22 a man desires is unfailing love; better to be poor than a **liar** [+408].
21: 28 A **false** witness will perish, and whoever listens to him will be
23: 3 Do not crave his delicacies, for that food is **deceptive**.
30: 8 Keep falsehood and **lies** [+1821] far from me; give me neither
Isa 28: 15 for we have made a **lie** our refuge and falsehood our hiding place."
28: 17 hail will sweep away your refuge, the **lie**, and water will overflow
Eze 13: 6 Their visions are false and their divinations a **lie**. They say,
13: 7 not seen false visions and uttered **lying** divinations when you say,
13: 8 Because of your false words and **lying** visions, I am against you,
13: 9 the prophets who see false visions and utter **lying** divinations.
13: 19 By lying to my people, who listen to **lies**, you have killed those
21: 29 [21:34] visions concerning you and **lying** divinations about you,
22: 28 these deeds for them by false visions and **lying** divinations.
Da 11: 27 will sit at the same table and **lie** [+1819] *to each other*, but to no
Hos 7: 13 against me! I long to redeem them but they speak **lies** against me.
12: 1 [12:2] the east wind all day and multiplies **lies** and violence.
Am 2: 4 kept his decrees, because they have been led astray by **false gods**,
Zep 3: 13 they will speak no **lies**, nor will deceit be found in their mouths.

3943 כֹּזֵבָא *kōzēbā'*, n.pr.loc. [1] [√ 3941]

Cozeba [1]

1Ch 4: 22 Jokim, the men of **Cozeba**, and Joash and Saraph, who ruled in

3944 כָּזְבִּי *kozbî*, n.pr.f. [2]

Cozbi [2]

Nu 25: 15 the name of the Midianite woman who was put to death was **Cozbi**
25: 18 when they deceived you in the affair of Peor and their sister **Cozbi**,

3945 כְּזִיב kᵉzîb, n.pr.loc. [1] [√ 3941]

Kezib [1]

Ge 38: 5 and named him Shelah. It was at **Kezib** that she gave birth to him.

3946 כֹּחַ¹ kōaḥ¹, n.m. [125]

strength [56], power [31], might [4], powerful [4], *untranslated* [2], ability [2], able [+6806] [2], helpless [+4202+6806] [2], wealth [2], cannot [+401] [1], crops [1], firm [1], great [1], helpless [+4946] [1], mighty [+1475] [1], mighty [1], power [+2432] [1], powerless [+401] [1], powerless [+4202] [1], powerless [+928+4202] [1], qualified [1], resources [1], shout [1], strengthened [1], very strong [+6793] [1], vigorous [1], weakness [+4202] [1], weary [+3329] [1], yield [1]

Ge 4: 12 you work the ground, it will no longer yield its **crops** for you.
31: 6 You know that I've worked for your father with all my **strength**,
49: 3 "Reuben, you are my firstborn, my **might**, the first sign of my
Ex 9: 16 that I might show you my **power** and that my name might be
15: 6 "Your right hand, O LORD, was majestic in **power**. Your right
32: 11 whom you brought out of Egypt with great **power** and a mighty
Lev 26: 20 Your **strength** will be spent in vain, because your soil will not
Nu 14: 13 By your **power** you brought these people up from among them.
14: 17 "Now may the Lord's **strength** be displayed, just as you have
Dt 4: 37 brought you out of Egypt by his Presence and his great **strength**,
8: 17 "My **power** and the strength of my hands have produced this
8: 18 for it is he who gives you the **ability** to produce wealth, and
9: 29 your inheritance that you brought out by your great **power**
Jos 14: 11 I'm just as **vigorous** to go out to battle now as I was then.
14: 11 I'm just as vigorous to go out to battle now as I was then. **[RPH]**
17: 17 and Manasseh—"You are numerous and very **powerful**.
Jdg 6: 14 "Go in the **strength** you have and save Israel out of Midian's hand.
16: 5 you can lure him into showing you the secret of his great **strength**
16: 6 "Tell me the secret of your great **strength** and how you can be tied
16: 9 close to a flame. So the secret of his **strength** was not discovered.
16: 15 fool of me and haven't told me the secret of your great **strength**."
16: 17 If my head were shaved, my **strength** would leave me, and I would
16: 19 of his hair, and so began to subdue him. And his **strength** left him.
16: 30 he pushed with all his **might**, and down came the temple on the
1Sa 2: 9 be silenced in darkness. "It is not by **strength** that one prevails;
28: 20 His **strength** was gone, for he had eaten nothing all that day
28: 22 so you may eat and have the **strength** to go on your way."
30: 4 and his men wept aloud until they had no **strength** left to weep.
1Ki 19: 8 **Strengthened** by that food, he traveled forty days and forty nights
2Ki 17: 36 who brought you up out of Egypt with mighty **power**
19: 3 come to the point of birth and there is no **strength** to deliver them.
1Ch 26: 8 their relatives were capable men with the **strength** to do the
29: 2 With all my **resources** I have provided for the temple of my God—
29: 12 In your hands are **strength** and power to exalt and give strength to
29: 14 that *we should be* **able** [+6806] to give as generously as this?
2Ch 2: 6 [2:5] who *is* **able** [+6806] to build a temple for him,
13: 20 Jeroboam did not regain **power** during the time of Abijah.
14: 11 [14:10] there is no one like you to help the **powerless** [+401]
20: 6 **Power** and might are in your hand, and no one can withstand you.
20: 12 For we have no **power** to face this vast army that is attacking us.
22: 9 So there was no one in the house of Ahaziah **powerful** *enough* to
25: 8 before the enemy, for God has the **power** to help or to overthrow."
26: 13 for war, a **powerful** force to support the king against his enemies.
Ezr 2: 69 According to their **ability** they gave to the treasury for this work
10: 13 and it is the rainy season; so we **cannot** [+401] stand outside.
Ne 1: 10 whom you redeemed by your great **strength** and your mighty
4: 10 [4:4] "The **strength** *of* the laborers is giving out, and there is
Job 3: 17 cease from turmoil, and there the **weary** [+3329] are at rest.
6: 11 "What **strength** do I have, that I should still hope? What prospects,
6: 12 Do **[RPH]** I have the strength of stone? Is my flesh bronze?
6: 12 Do I have the **strength** *of* stone? Is my flesh bronze?
6: 22 something on my behalf, pay a ransom for me from your **wealth**,
9: 4 His wisdom is profound, his **power** is vast. Who has resisted him
9: 19 If it is a matter of **strength**, he is mighty! And if it is a matter of
23: 6 Would he oppose me with great **power**? No, he would not press
24: 22 God drags away the mighty by his **power**; though they become
26: 2 "How you have helped the **powerless** [+4202]! How you have
26: 12 By his **power** he churned up the sea; by his wisdom he cut Rahab
30: 2 Of what use was the **strength** *of* their hands to me, since their
30: 18 In his great **power** ⌞God⌟ becomes like clothing to me; he binds me
31: 39 if I have devoured its **yield** without payment or broken the spirit of
36: 5 but does not despise men; he is mighty, and **firm** *in* his purpose.
36: 19 Would your wealth or even all your **mighty** efforts sustain you
36: 22 "God is exalted in his **power**. Who is a teacher like him?
37: 23 The Almighty is beyond our reach and exalted in **power**; in his
39: 11 Will you rely on him for his great **strength**? Will you leave your
39: 21 He paws fiercely, rejoicing in his **strength**, and charges into the
40: 16 What **strength** he has in his loins, what power in the muscles of
Ps 22: 15 [22:16] My **strength** is dried up like a potsherd, and my tongue
29: 4 The voice of the LORD is **powerful**; the voice of the LORD is
31: 10 [31:11] my **strength** fails because of my affliction, and my bones
33: 16 by the size of his army; no warrior escapes by his great **strength**.
38: 10 [38:11] My heart pounds, my **strength** fails me; even the light has
65: 6 [65:7] who formed the mountains by your **power**, having armed
71: 9 away when I am old; do not forsake me when my **strength** is gone.
102: 23 [102:24] In the course of my life he broke my **strength**; he cut
103: 20 you his angels, you **mighty ones** [+1475] who do his bidding,
111: 6 He has shown his people the **power** *of* his works, giving them the
147: 5 Great is our Lord and mighty in **power**; his understanding has no
Pr 5: 10 lest strangers feast on your **wealth** and your toil enrich another
14: 4 but from the **strength** *of* an ox comes an abundant harvest.
20: 29 The glory of young men is their **strength**, gray hair the splendor of
24: 5 man has great power, and a man of knowledge increases **strength**;
24: 10 If you falter in times of trouble, how small is your **strength**!
Ecc 4: 1 **power** was on the side of their oppressors—and they have no
9: 10 do it with all your **might**, for in the grave, where you are going,
Isa 10: 13 " 'By the **strength** *of* my hand I have done this, and by my
37: 3 come to the point of birth and there is no **strength** to deliver them.
40: 9 lift up your voice with a **shout**, lift it up, do not be afraid;
40: 26 Because of his great power and mighty **strength**, not one of them
40: 29 He gives **strength** to the weary and increases the power of the
40: 31 but those who hope in the LORD will renew their **strength**.
41: 1 silent before me, you islands! Let the nations renew their **strength**!
44: 12 an idol with hammers, he forges it with the **might** *of* his arm.
44: 12 He gets hungry and loses his **strength**; he drinks no water
49: 4 to no purpose; I have spent my **strength** in vain and for nothing.
50: 2 Do I lack the **strength** to rescue you? By a mere rebuke I dry up
63: 1 in splendor, striding forward in the greatness of his **strength**?
Jer 10: 12 God made the earth by his **power**; he founded the world by his
27: 5 With my great **power** and outstretched arm I made the earth
32: 17 and the earth by your great **power** and outstretched arm.
48: 45 "In the shadow of Heshbon the fugitives stand **helpless** [+4946],
51: 15 "He made the earth by his **power**; he founded the world by his
La 1: 6 no pasture; in **weakness** [+4202] they have fled before the pursuer.
1: 14 have come upon my neck and the Lord has sapped my **strength**.
Da 1: 4 quick to understand, and **qualified** to serve in the king's palace.
8: 6 seen standing beside the canal and charged at him in **great** rage.
8: 7 The ram was **powerless** [+928+4202] to stand against him;
8: 22 that will emerge from his nation but will not have the same **power**.
8: 24 *He will become* **very strong** [+6793], but not by his own power.
8: 24 He will become very strong, but not by his own **power**. He will
10: 8 I had no **strength** left, my face turned deathly pale and I was
10: 8 my face turned deathly pale and *I was* **helpless** [+4202+6806].
10: 16 because of the vision, my lord, and *I am* **helpless** [+4202+6806].
10: 17 with you, my lord? My **strength** is gone and I can hardly breathe."
11: 6 she will not retain her **power** [+2432], and he and his power will
11: 15 to resist; even their best troops will not have the **strength** to stand.
11: 25 "With a large army he will stir up his **strength** and courage against
Hos 7: 9 Foreigners sap his **strength**, but he does not realize it. His hair is
Am 2: 14 The swift will not escape, the strong will not muster their **strength**,
Mic 3: 8 as for me, I am filled with **power**, with the Spirit of the LORD,
Na 1: 3 The LORD is slow to anger and great in **power**; the LORD will
2: 1 [2:2] watch the road, brace yourselves, marshal all your **strength**!
Hab 1: 11 and go on—guilty men, whose own **strength** is their god."
Zec 4: 6 'Not by might nor by **power**, but by my Spirit,' says the LORD

3947 ²כֹּחַ kōaḥ², n.[m.]. [1]

monitor lizard [1]

Lev 11: 30 the gecko, the **monitor lizard**, the wall lizard, the skink

3948 כָּחַד kāḥad, v. [32]

hide [8], hidden [3], conceal [2], hiding [2], annihilated [1], are destroyed [1], denied [1], destroy [1], got rid of [1], hides [1], keep back [1], keep [1], led to downfall [1], lost [1], perish [1], perishing [1], ruined [1], was hidden [1], were destroyed [1], wipe out [1], wiped [1]

Ge 47: 18 [D] "*We* cannot **hide** from our lord the fact that since our money
Ex 9: 15 [C] your people with a plague *that would have* **wiped** *you* off
23: 23 [G] Canaanites, Hivites and Jebusites, and *I will* **wipe** them **out**.
Jos 7: 19 [D] Tell me what you have done; *do* not **hide** it from me."
1Sa 3: 17 [D] Eli asked. "*Do* not **hide** it from me. May God deal with you,
3: 17 [D] so severely, if *you* **hide** from me anything he told you."
3: 18 [D] So Samuel told him everything, **hiding** nothing from him.
2Sa 14: 18 [D] "*Do* not **keep** from me the answer to what I am going to ask
18: 13 [C] my life in jeopardy—and nothing *is* **hidden** from the king—
1Ki 13: 34 [G] was the sin of the house of Jeroboam that **led to** its **downfall**
2Ch 32: 21 [G] *who* **annihilated** all the fighting men and the leaders
Job 4: 7 [C] has ever perished? Where **were** the upright *ever* **destroyed**?
6: 10 [D] that *I had* not **denied** the words of the Holy One.
15: 18 [D] have declared, **hiding** nothing received from their fathers
15: 28 [C] he will inhabit **ruined** towns and houses where no one lives,
20: 12 [G] evil is sweet in his mouth and *he* **hides** it under his tongue,
22: 20 [C] 'Surely our foes **are destroyed**, and fire devours their

Job 27:11 [D] power of God; the ways of the Almighty *I will* not **conceal**.
Ps 40:10 [40:11] [D] *I do* not **conceal** your love and your truth from the
69: 5 [69:6] [C] my folly, O God; my guilt *is* not **hidden** from you.
78: 4 [D] *We will* not **hide** them from their children; we will tell the
83: 4 [83:5] [G] "Come," they say, "*let us* **destroy** them as a nation,
139:15 [C] My frame **was** not **hidden** from you when I was made in the
Isa 3: 9 [D] they parade their sin like Sodom; *they do* not **hide** it.
Jer 38:14 [D] the king said to Jeremiah. "*Do* not **hide** anything from me."
38:25 [D] king said to you; *do* not **hide** it from us or we will kill you,'
50: 2 [D] **keep** nothing **back**, but say, 'Babylon will be captured;
Hos 5: 3 [C] I know all about Ephraim; Israel *is* not **hidden** from me.
Zec 11: 8 [G] In one month *I* **got rid of** the three shepherds. The flock
11: 9 [C] your shepherd. Let the dying die, and the **perishing** perish.
11: 9 [C] be your shepherd. Let the dying die, and the perishing **perish**.
11:16 [C] up a shepherd over the land who will not care for the **lost**,

3949 כָּחַל kāḥal, v. [1]

painted [1]

Eze 23:40 [A] for them, **painted** your eyes and put on your jewelry.

3950 כָּחַשׁ kāḥaš, v. [22] [→ 3951, 3952]

cringe [3], lied [3], lying [2], come cringing [1], cower [1], deceive [1], deceiving [1], disown [1], disowns [1], fail [1], fails [1], lie [1], lies [1], thin [1], treachery [1], unfaithful [1], untrue [1]

Ge 18:15 [D] Sarah was afraid, so *she* **lied** and said, "I did not laugh."
Lev 6: 2 [5:21] [D] is unfaithful to the LORD *by* **deceiving** his
6: 3 [5:22] [D] or if he finds lost property and **lies** about it, or if he
19:11 [D] " 'Do not steal. " '*Do* not **lie**. " 'Do not deceive one another.
Dt 33:29 [C] Your enemies *will* **cower** before you, and you will trample
Jos 7:11 [D] they have stolen, *they have* **lied**, they have put them with
24:27 [D] It will be a witness against you if *you are* **untrue** to your
2Sa 22:45 [F] and foreigners **come cringing** to me; as soon as they hear me,
1Ki 13:18 [D] may eat bread and drink water.' " (But *he was* **lying** to him.)
Job 8:18 [D] its spot, that place **disowns** it and says, 'I never saw you.'
31:28 [D] be judged, for *I would have been* **unfaithful** to God on high.
Ps 18:44 [18:45] [D] they obey me; foreigners **cringe** before me.
66: 3 [D] So great is your power that your enemies **cringe** before you.
81:15 [81:16] [D] Those who hate the LORD *would* **cringe** before
109:24 [A] My knees give way from fasting; my body *is* **thin** and gaunt.
Pr 30: 9 [D] Otherwise, I may have too much and **disown** you and say,
Isa 59:13 [D] rebellion and **treachery** against the LORD, turning our
Jer 5:12 [D] *They have* **lied** about the LORD; they said, "He will do
Hos 4: 2 [D] is only cursing, **lying** and murder, stealing and adultery;
9: 2 [D] will not feed the people; the new wine *will* **fail** them.
Hab 3:17 [D] though the olive crop **fails** and the fields produce no food,
Zec 13: 4 [D] not put on a prophet's garment of hair in order to **deceive**.

3951 כַּחַשׁ kaḥaš, n.m. [6] [√ 3950]

lies [4], deception [1], gauntness [1]

Job 16: 8 become a witness; my **gauntness** rises up and testifies against me.
Ps 59:12 [59:13] be caught in their pride. For the curses and **lies** they utter,
Hos 7: 3 delight the king with their wickedness, the princes with their **lies**.
10:13 you have reaped evil, you have eaten the fruit of **deception**.
11:12 [12:1] Ephraim has surrounded me with **lies**, the house of Israel
Na 3: 1 the city of blood, full of **lies**, full of plunder, never without victims!

3952 כֶּחָשׁ keḥāš, a. [1] [√ 3950]

deceitful [1]

Isa 30: 9 These are rebellious people, **deceitful** children, children unwilling

3953 כִּי¹ kî¹, n.[m.]. [1] [√ 3917]

branding [1]

Isa 3:24 instead of fine clothing, sackcloth; instead of beauty, **branding**.

3954 כִּי² kî², c. [4484 / 4483] [→ 3955, 3956] See Select Index

untranslated [1229], for [1059], that [564], because [531], when [221], if [149], but [108], though [54], since [46], surely [43], but [+561] [39], how [39], except [+561] [24], and [20], yet [19], even [14], so [14], although [12], only [12], only [+561] [11], if [+561] [10], as [8], now [8], why [8], because [+6584] [6], because of [6], by [6], even though [6], how much less [+677] [6], unless [+561] [6], indeed [5], whenever [5], yes [5], after [4], how much more [+677] [4], however [4], if not [+4295] [4], then [4], because [+3610] [3], even if [3], how much worse [+677] [3], however [+561] [3], if not [3], instead [3], just [3], now that [3], or [3], therefore [3], until [+6330] [3], while [3], after all [2], as for [2], because [+6813] [2], but [+700] [2], but only [+561] [2], but only [2], certainly [2], even [+1685] [2], for [+4027+6584] [2], how much more so [+677] [2], in fact [2], instead [+561] [2], nevertheless [2], no [2], or [+2256] [2], other than [+561] [2], out of [2], perhaps [2], so that [2], still [2], suppose [2], surely [+561] [2], than [+561] [2], though [+561] [2], too [2], what [2], whether [2], without [+561] [2], all [1], although [+1685] [1], although [+561] [1], as well [1], at all [1], at least [1], at [1], because [+4027+6584] [1], because [+4200+4537] [1], because [+9393] [1], because of [+4946+7156] [1], because that will mean [1], before [+401] [1], but [+421] [1], clearly [+8011] [1], despite [1], even [+561] [1], even [+677+2256] [1], even when [1], ever [1], for [+1237] [1], for otherwise [1], for surely [1], greater [1], how much better [+677] [1], how much less [+677+4202] [1], how much more [+677+2256] [1], how well [1], however [+700] [1], if anything but [1], if so [+6964] [1], in doing this [1], in order to [1], indeed [+561] [1], indeed [+677+2256] [1], is that why [1], it was the custom of [1], just because [1], moreover [+1685] [1], moreover [1], not [+561] [1], not only [1], now [+2296] [1], on the contrary [1], once [1], or [+1685] [1], other than [1], rather [+4202] [1], rather [+561] [1], rather [1], really [+677] [1], really [1], rightly [1], since [+3610] [1], since [+4027+6584] [1], since [+9393] [1], so [+4394] [1], surely [+2180] [1], surely [+6964] [1], that if [1], that really [1], this [1], till [+6330] [1], truly [1], unless [+561+4200+7156] [1], unless [+561+4202] [1], until [+561] [1], very well then [1], well [1], what more [+4537] [1], when [+4200+7023] [1], whenever [+1896+4946] [1], where [1], with [1], won't until [+561] [1], yes [+4202] [1], yet [+561] [1], yet [+700] [1]

3955 כִּי־אִם kî-'im, c. *or* pt. Not used in NIV/BHS [√ 3954 + 561]

3956 כִּי עַל כֵּן kî 'al kēn, c.+pp.+adv. Not used in NIV/BHS [√ 3954 + 6586]

3957 כִּיד kîd, n.[m.]. [1]

destruction [1]

Job 21:20 Let his own eyes see his **destruction**; let him drink of the wrath of

3958 כִּידוֹד kîdôd, n.m. [1]

sparks [1]

Job 41:19 [41:11] stream from his mouth; **sparks** *of* fire shoot out.

3959 כִּידוֹן kîdôn, n.[m.]. [9] [→ 3961?]

javelin [5], lance [2], spear [1], spears [1]

Jos 8:18 to Joshua, "Hold out toward Ai the **javelin** that is in your hand,
8:18 I will deliver the city." So Joshua held out his **javelin** toward Ai.
8:26 For Joshua did not draw back the hand that held out his **javelin**
1Sa 17: 6 wore bronze greaves, and a bronze **javelin** was slung on his back.
17:45 "You come against me with sword and spear and **javelin**,
Job 39:23 rattles against his side, along with the flashing spear and **lance**.
41:29 [41:21] but a piece of straw; he laughs at the rattling of the **lance**.
Jer 6:23 They are armed with bow and **spear**; they are cruel and show no
50:42 They are armed with bows and **spears**; they are cruel and without

3960 כִּידוֹר kîdôr, n.[m.]. [1] [→ 3903]

attack [1]

Job 15:24 him with terror; they overwhelm him, like a king poised to **attack**,

3961 כִּידֹן kîdōn, n.pr.m. [1] [√ 3959?]

Kidon [1]

1Ch 13: 9 When they came to the threshing floor of **Kidon**, Uzzah reached

3962 כִּיּוּן kiyyûn, n.m. [1]

pedestal [1]

Am 5:26 of your king, the **pedestal** *of* your idols, the star of your god—

3963 כִּיּוֹר kiyyôr, n.m. [23]

basin [12], basins [6], *untranslated* [2], firepot [+836] [1], pan [1], platform [1]

Ex 30:18 "Make a bronze **basin**, with its bronze stand, for washing.
30:28 of burnt offering and all its utensils, and the **basin** with its stand.
31: 9 altar of burnt offering and all its utensils, the **basin** with its stand—
35:16 its poles and all its utensils; the bronze **basin** with its stand;
38: 8 They made the bronze **basin** and its bronze stand from the mirrors
39:39 its poles and all its utensils; the **basin** with its stand;
40: 7 place the **basin** between the Tent of Meeting and the altar
40:11 Anoint the **basin** and its stand and consecrate them.
40:30 He placed the **basin** between the Tent of Meeting and the altar
Lev 8:11 anointing the altar and all its utensils and the **basin** with its stand,
1Sa 2:14 He would plunge it into the **pan** or kettle or caldron or pot,
1Ki 7:30 each had a **basin** resting on four supports, cast with wreaths on
7:38 He then made ten bronze **basins**, each holding forty baths
7:38 each **[RPH]** holding forty baths and measuring four cubits across,
7:38 cubits across, **[RPH]** one basin to go on each of the ten stands.

1Ki 7:38 four cubits across, one **basin** to go on each of the ten stands.
7:40 He also made the **basins** and shovels and sprinkling bowls.
7:43 the ten stands with their ten **basins**;
2Ki 16:17 the side panels and removed the **basins** from the movable stands.
2Ch 4: 6 He then made ten **basins** for washing and placed five on the south
4:14 the stands with their **basins**;
6:13 Now he had made a bronze **platform**, five cubits long, five cubits
Zec 12: 6 "On that day I will make the leaders of Judah like a **firepot** [+836]

3964 כִּילַי ***kîlay***, n.m. [2] [√ 5792?]

scoundrel [1], scoundrel's [1]

Isa 32: 5 No longer will the fool be called noble nor the **scoundrel** be highly
32: 7 The **scoundrel's** methods are wicked, he makes up evil schemes to

3965 כֵּילַפּוֹת ***kêlappôt***, n.[f.]. [1] [√ 3990?]

hatchets [1]

Ps 74: 6 They smashed all the carved paneling with their axes and **hatchets**.

3966 כִּימָה ***kîmâ***, n.f. [3]

Pleiades [3]

Job 9: 9 and Orion, the **Pleiades** and the constellations of the south.
38:31 "Can you bind the beautiful **Pleiades**? Can you loose the cords of
Am 5: 8 (he who made the **Pleiades** and Orion, who turns blackness into

3967 כִּיס ***kîs***, n.m. [5]

bag [3], bags [1], purse [1]

Dt 25:13 Do not have two differing weights in your **bag**—one heavy,
Pr 1:14 throw in your lot with us, and we will share a common **purse**"—
16:11 are from the LORD; all the weights in the **bag** are of his making.
23:31 [when it sparkles in the **cup**, [K; see Q 3926] when it goes down]
Isa 46: 6 Some pour out gold from their **bags** and weigh out silver on the
Mic 6:11 I acquit a man with dishonest scales, with a **bag** *of* false weights?

3968 כִּיר ***kîr***, n.[m.]. [1] [cf. 3929]

cooking pot [1]

Lev 11:35 on becomes unclean; an oven or **cooking pot** must be broken up.

3969 כִּישׁוֹר ***kîšôr***, n.[m.]. [1]

distaff [1]

Pr 31:19 In her hand she holds the **distaff** and grasps the spindle with her

3970 כָּכָה ***kākâ***, adv. [37] [√ 3907]

so [5], *untranslated* [4], this is how [4], this is what [4], this [4], in this way [3], in the same way [2], such a thing [2], as [1], because of [+6584] [1], in this manner [1], like this [1], such and such [1], such [1], that [1], thus [1], true [1]

Ex 12:11 **This is how** you are to eat it: with your cloak tucked into your belt,
29:35 for Aaron and his sons **[NIE]** everything I have commanded you,
Nu 8:26 **This**, then, **is how** you are to assign the responsibilities of the
11:15 If **this is how** you are going to treat me, put me to death right
15:11 each lamb or young goat, is to be prepared **in this manner**.
15:12 Do **this** for each one, for as many as you prepare.
15:13 " 'Everyone who is native-born must do these things **in this way**
Dt 25: 9 "**This is what** is done to the man who will not build up his
29:24 [29:23] "Why has the LORD done **this** to this land? Why this
Jos 10:25 **This is what** the LORD will do to all the enemies you are going
1Sa 2:14 **This is how** they treated all the Israelites who came to Shiloh.
19:17 "Why did you deceive me **like this** and send my enemy away
2Sa 13: 4 do you, the king's son, look **so** haggard morning after morning?
17:21 river at once; Ahithophel has advised **such and such** against you."
1Ki 1: 6 interfered with him by asking, "Why do you behave **as** you do?"
1:48 and **[NIE]** said, 'Praise be to the LORD, the God of Israel,
9: 8 'Why has the LORD done **such** *a thing* to this land and to this
2Ch 7:21 'Why has the LORD done **such a thing** to this land and to this
18:19 going to his death there?' "One suggested **this**, and another that.
18:19 going to his death there?' "One suggested this, and another **that**.
Ne 5:13 "**In this way** may God shake out of his house and possessions
5:13 **So** may such a man be shaken out and emptied!" At this the whole
Est 6: 9 '**This is what** is done for the man the king delights to honor!' "
6:11 "**This is what** is done for the man the king delights to honor!"
9:26 **because of** [+6584] what they had seen and what had happened to
Job 1: 5 and cursed God in their hearts." **This** was Job's regular custom.
Ps 144:15 Blessed are the people of whom *this* is **true**; blessed are the people
Ecc 11: 5 **so** you cannot understand the work of God, the Maker of all things.
SS 5: 9 How is your beloved better than others, that you charge us **so**?
Jer 13: 9 '**In the same way** I will ruin the pride of Judah and the great pride
19:11 **[NIE]** I will smash this nation and this city just as this potter's jar
22: 8 'Why has the LORD done **such a thing** to this great city?'
28:11 '**In the same way** will I break the yoke of Nebuchadnezzar king of
51:64 '**So** will Babylon sink to rise no more because of the disaster I will
Eze 4:13 "**In this way** the people of Israel will eat defiled food among the
31:18 " 'Which of the trees of Eden can be compared with you **[NIE]** in
Hos 10:15 **Thus** will it happen to you, O Bethel, because your wickedness is

3971 כִּכָּר ***kikkār***, n.f. [68] [√ 4159; Ar 10352]

talents [38], plain [10], talent [9], bread [+4312] [2], loaf [2], cover [1], crust [1], loaf [+4312] [1], loaves [1], region [1], surrounding region [1], whole region [1]

Ge 13:10 and saw that the whole **plain** *of* the Jordan was well watered,
13:11 So Lot chose for himself the whole **plain** *of* the Jordan and set out
13:12 while Lot lived among the cities of the **plain** and pitched his tents
19:17 your lives! Don't look back, and don't stop anywhere in the **plain**!
19:25 Thus he overthrew those cities and the entire **plain**, including all
19:28 toward Sodom and Gomorrah, toward all the land of the **plain**,
19:29 So when God destroyed the cities of the **plain**, he remembered
Ex 25:39 A **talent** *of* pure gold is to be used for the lampstand and all these
29:23 take a **loaf** [+4312], and a cake made with oil, and a wafer.
37:24 the lampstand and all its accessories from *one* **talent** *of* pure gold.
38:24 offering used for all the work on the sanctuary was 29 **talents**
38:25 of the community who were counted in the census was 100 **talents**
38:27 The 100 **talents** *of* silver were used to cast the bases for the
38:27 100 bases from the 100 **talents**, one talent for each base.
38:27 100 bases from the 100 talents, one **talent** for each base.
38:29 The bronze from the wave offering was 70 **talents** and 2,400
Dt 34: 3 the Negev and the **whole region** *from* the Valley of Jericho,
Jdg 8: 5 said to the men of Succoth, "Give my troops *some* **bread** [+4312];
1Sa 2:36 before him for a piece of silver and a **crust** *of* bread and plead,
10: 3 another three **loaves** *of* bread, and another a skin of wine.
2Sa 12:30 its weight was a **talent** *of* gold, and it was set with precious
18:23 Then Ahimaaz ran by way of the **plain** and outran the Cushite.
1Ki 7:46 The king had them cast in clay molds in the **plain** *of* the Jordan
9:14 Now Hiram had sent to the king 120 **talents** *of* gold.
9:28 They sailed to Ophir and brought back 420 **talents** of gold,
10:10 she gave the king 120 **talents** *of* gold, large quantities of spices,
10:14 weight of the gold that Solomon received yearly was 666 **talents**,
16:24 He bought the hill of Samaria from Shemer for *two* **talents** *of*
20:39 it will be your life for his life, or you must pay a **talent** *of* silver.'
2Ki 5: 5 So Naaman left, taking with him ten **talents** *of* silver, six thousand
5:22 Please give them a **talent** *of* silver and two sets of clothing.' "
5:23 "By all means, take *two* **talents**," said Naaman. He urged Gehazi
5:23 then tied up the *two* **talents** of silver in two bags, with two sets of
15:19 Menahem gave him a thousand **talents** *of* silver to gain his support
18:14 from Hezekiah king of Judah three hundred **talents** *of* silver
18:14 of Judah three hundred talents of silver and thirty **talents** *of* gold.
23:33 and he imposed on Judah a levy of a hundred **talents** *of* silver
23:33 on Judah a levy of a hundred talents of silver and a **talent** *of* gold.
1Ch 16: 3 he gave a **loaf** *of* bread, a cake of dates and a cake of raisins to
19: 6 the Ammonites sent a thousand **talents** *of* silver to hire chariots
20: 2 its weight was found to be a **talent** *of* gold, and it was set with
22:14 for the temple of the LORD a hundred thousand **talents** *of* gold,
22:14 a million **talents** of silver, quantities of bronze and iron too great to
29: 4 three thousand **talents** *of* gold (gold of Ophir) and seven thousand
29: 4 seven thousand **talents** *of* refined silver, for the overlaying of the
29: 7 gave toward the work on the temple of God five thousand **talents**
29: 7 and ten thousand darics of gold, ten thousand **talents** of silver,
29: 7 eighteen thousand **talents** of bronze and a hundred thousand talents
29: 7 thousand talents of bronze and a hundred thousand **talents** of iron.
2Ch 3: 8 He overlaid the inside with six hundred **talents** of fine gold.
4:17 The king had them cast in clay molds in the **plain** *of* the Jordan
8:18 to Ophir and brought back four hundred and fifty **talents** *of* gold,
9: 9 she gave the king 120 **talents** *of* gold, large quantities of spices,
9:13 weight of the gold that Solomon received yearly was 666 **talents**,
25: 6 thousand fighting men from Israel for a hundred **talents** *of* silver.
25: 9 "But what about the hundred **talents** I paid for these Israelite
27: 5 That year the Ammonites paid him a hundred **talents** *of* silver,
36: 3 and imposed on Judah a levy of a hundred **talents** *of* silver
36: 3 on Judah a levy of a hundred talents of silver and a **talent** *of* gold.
Ezr 8:26 I weighed out to them 650 **talents** of silver, silver articles weighing
8:26 of silver, silver articles weighing 100 **talents**, 100 talents of gold,
8:26 of silver, silver articles weighing 100 talents, 100 **talents** of gold,
Ne 3:22 to him were made by the priests from the **surrounding region**.
12:28 The singers also were brought together from the **region** around
Est 3: 9 I will put ten thousand **talents** *of* silver into the royal treasury for
Pr 6:26 for the prostitute reduces you to a **loaf** *of* bread, and the adulteress
Jer 37:21 given **bread** [+4312] from the street of the bakers each day until
Zec 5: 7 the **cover** *of* lead was raised, and there in the basket sat a woman!

3972 כֹּל ***kōl***, n.m. [5413 / 5414] [→ 3997; cf. 4005; Ar 10353, 10354]

all [3246], every [311], *untranslated* [307], whole [265], everything [189], any [155], entire [82], everyone [49], throughout [+928] [47], anyone [38], anything [37], no [+4202] [31], whatever [+889] [30], each [26], just as [+889+3869] [24], whoever [22], always [+2021+3427] [18], whatever [17], a [16], altogether [14], none [+4202] [14], throughout [14], one [13], rest [13], everything [+1821+2021] [11], nothing [+4202] [11], total [11], wherever [+889+928] [10], wherever [+928] [10], as long as [+3427] [9], other[s] [9], those[s] [9], anything [+1821] [7], anywhere [7], everyone [+2021+5883] [7], full [7], everyone [+408] [6], always [+928+6961] [5], as [+889+3869] [5], as long as [+2021+3427] [5], completely [5], everything [+1821] [5], whatever [+889+3869] [5], both [4], day after day [+2021+3427] [4], everything [+5126] [4], in all [4], much [4], some [+4946] [4], any [+285] [3], as long as lived [+3427] [3], at all [3], everything [+4213] [3], everywhere [3], forever [+2021+3427] [3], fully [3], nothing [+401] [3], throughout [+4200] [3], throughout [+928+1473] [3], whenever [+928] [3], wherever [+448+889] [3], all [+2162] [2], always [+3427] [2], an [2], anyone [+2021+5883] [2], anyone [+408] [2], anyone [+5883] [2], anything [+2021+3998] [2], anything [+4399] [2], anywhere [+928+5226] [2], as long as [+6388] [2], as long as lives [+3427] [2], completely [+2021+4200] [2], continual [+2021+3427] [2], continually [+2021+3427] [2], during [2], even [2], ever [2], everyone [+1414] [2], everyone [+2021+6639] [2], everyone [+3782] [2], everyone [+5883] [2], everything [+3998] [2], everywhere [+5226] [2], everywhere [+928] [2], great [+8044] [2], great [2], in full force [2], it[s] [2], never [+2021+3427+4202] [2], no [+4202+4946] [2], nothing [+1821+4202] [2], rest [+3427] [2], something [2], them[s] [+2021+6639] [2], them[s] [+3776+7736] [2], this[s] [2], together [2], totaled [2], various [2], what[s] [2], whatever [+3869] [2], wherever [+889+928+2021+5226] [2], wholeheartedly [+928+4213] [2], wholeheartedly [+928+4222] [2], your[s] [2], abundant [1], all kinds [+4946] [1], all over [1], all-night [+2021+4326] [1], although [+889+928] [1], always [1], among [+4200] [1], an[s] [1], annually [+928+2256+9102+9102] [1], any [+408] [1], anyone [+132] [1], anyone [+408+2021] [1], anything [+1821+1821+2021+4946] [1], anything [+1821+2021] [1], anything [+1821+4946] [1], anything [+3998] [1], anything [+889] [1], anywhere [+1473] [1], anywhere in [+928+1473] [1], around [1], as [+6645+8611] [1], as [+889+928] [1], as in times past [+3869] [1], as long as [+928+6961] [1], as long as live [+3427] [1], as long as live [+3427+4200+6409] [1], as long as [1], as [1], at flood stage [+1536+4848+6584] [1], at flood stage [+1536+6584] [1], at random [1], at wits end [+1182+2683] [1], body [1], constantly [+928+6961] [1], covered with [1], crowd [+889+6641] [1], depth [1], detailed [1], details [1], dire [1], eagerly [+928+8356] [1], ever [+2021+3427] [1], ever [+3427] [1], everlasting [+6409] [1], every day [+2256+3427+3427] [1], every way [1], everyone [+132] [1], everyone [+132+2021] [1], everyone [+408+2021] [1], everyone else [+7736] [1], everyone's [1], everything [+2021] [1], everything [+2021+4856] [1], everything [+465+1821+2021+2021] [1], everything [+5626] [1], everything [+8214] [1], everywhere [+2021+5226] [1], everywhere [+928+5226] [1], exactly as [+889+3869] [1], exactly like [+889+3869+4027] [1], farthest recesses [+9417] [1], filled [+928+2118] [1], for life [+2021+3427] [1], four[s] [1], from now on [+2021+3427] [1], full force [1], gave the message [+465+1819+1821+2021+2021] [1], had nothing [+2893] [1], in accordance with [+889] [1], in lifetime [+3427] [1], just as [+3869] [1], just as [+889+3869+4027] [1], just as [+889+4200] [1], like [+889+3869] [1], long [1], men[s] [1], more and more [+3578+6584] [1], more [1], natural [+132+2021+3869] [1], no yet [+3270] [1], none [+4202+4946] [1], none [+4202+5883] [1], nothing [+2021+4202] [1], nothing [+561+4946] [1], nothing [+889+4202] [1], nothing but [1], nothing whatever [+401+1821] [1], numbered [1], one[s] [+1414] [1], only [1], open [1], people[s] [+889+928] [1], prosperity [+8044] [1], regular [+2021+3427] [1], rest[s] [1], shrub [+8489] [1], so far as [+4200] [1], solid [1], something [+3998] [1], sound [1], still [+6388] [1], such [+4946] [1], such [1], that[s] [1], the storehouses[s] [+889+928+2157] [1], them[s] [+3776] [1], them[s] [+6551] [1], there is no [+401] [1], there is nothing [+401] [1], these[s] things [1], these[s] [1], they[s] [+1251+4463+8901] [1], they[s] [+2021+6639] [1], they[s] [+3776] [1], things [+3998] [1], this is how [+465+928] [1], throng [1], through [1], throughout [+4946] [1], throughout [+6584+7156] [1], total [+4200+5031] [1], total [+7212] [1], transfer of property [+1821+9455] [1], utter [1], vast [1], we [+5646] [1], whatever [+889+3869+4027] [1], whatever [+889+928] [1], whenever [+4200] [1], whenever [+889+928] [1], whenever [+928+6961] [1], whenever [1], wherever [+2021+4946+5226] [1], wherever [+889+2021+5226+6584] [1], wherever [+889+6584] [1], wherever [+889+9004] [1], wherever [+928+2021+5226] [1], while [+3427] [1], while continues [+3427] [1], who[s] [1], whoever [+132+2021] [1], whoever [+408+889] [1]

Ge 1:21 So God created the great creatures of the sea and **every** living
1:21 to their kinds, and **every** winged bird according to its kind.
1:25 **all** the creatures that move along the ground according to their
1:26 and the birds of the air, over the livestock, over **all** the earth,
1:26 the earth, and over **all** the creatures that move along the ground."
1:28 and over **every** living creature that moves on the ground."
1:29 "I give you **every** seed-bearing plant on the face of the whole earth
1:29 "I give you every seed-bearing plant on the face of the **whole** earth
1:29 face of the whole earth and **every** tree that has fruit with seed in it.
1:30 And to **all** the beasts of the earth and all the birds of the air
1:30 And to all the beasts of the earth and **all** the birds of the air
1:30 the birds of the air and **all** the creatures that move on the ground—
1:30 that has the breath of life in it—I give **every** green plant for food."
1:31 God saw **all** that he had made, and it was very good. And there was
2: 1 the heavens and the earth were completed in **all** their vast array.
2: 2 had been doing; so on the seventh day he rested from **all** his work.
2: 3 because on it he rested from **all** the work of creating that he had
2: 5 and no **shrub of** [+8489] the field had yet appeared on the earth
2: 5 on the earth and **no** plant of the field had **yet** [+3270] sprung up,
2: 6 up from the earth and watered the **whole** surface of the ground—
2: 9 the LORD God made **all** *kinds of* trees grow out of the ground—
2:11 it winds through the **entire** land of Havilah, where there is gold.
2:13 second river is the Gihon; it winds through the **entire** land of Cush.
2:16 the man, "You are free to eat from **any** tree in the garden;
2:19 Now the LORD God had formed out of the ground **all** the beasts
2:19 of the ground all the beasts of the field and **all** the birds of the air.
2:19 and **whatever** [+889] the man called each living creature,
2:20 So the man gave names to **all** the livestock, the birds of the air
2:20 all the livestock, the birds of the air and **all** the beasts of the field.
3: 1 Now the serpent was more crafty than **any** *of* the wild animals the
3: 1 God really say, 'You must not eat from **any** tree in the garden'?"
3:14 "Cursed are you above **all** the livestock and all the wild animals!
3:14 "Cursed are you above all the livestock and **all** the wild animals!
3:14 crawl on your belly and you will eat dust **all** the days of your life.
3:17 through painful toil you will eat of it **all** the days of your life.
3:20 wife Eve, because she would become the mother of **all** the living.
4:14 restless wanderer on the earth, and **whoever** finds me will kill me."
4:15 if **anyone** kills Cain, he will suffer vengeance seven times over."
4:15 put a mark on Cain so that no **one** who found him would kill him.
4:21 was Jubal; he was the father of **all** who play the harp and flute.
4:22 Tubal-Cain, who forged **all** *kinds of* tools out of bronze and iron.
5: 5 **Altogether**, Adam lived 930 years, and then he died.
5: 8 **Altogether**, Seth lived 912 years, and then he died.
5:11 **Altogether**, Enosh lived 905 years, and then he died.
5:14 **Altogether**, Kenan lived 910 years, and then he died.
5:17 **Altogether**, Mahalalel lived 895 years, and then he died.
5:20 **Altogether**, Jared lived 962 years, and then he died.
5:23 **Altogether**, Enoch lived 365 years.
5:27 **Altogether**, Methuselah lived 969 years, and then he died.
5:31 **Altogether**, Lamech lived 777 years, and then he died.
6: 2 of men were beautiful, and they married **any** of them they chose.
6: 5 that **every** inclination of the thoughts of his heart was only evil all
6: 5 that every inclination of the thoughts of his heart was only evil **all**
6:12 had become, for **all** the people on earth had corrupted their ways.
6:13 So God said to Noah, "I am going to put an end to **all** people,
6:17 I am going to bring floodwaters on the earth to destroy **all** life
6:17 that has the breath of life in it. **Everything** on earth will perish.
6:19 You are to bring into the ark two of **all** living creatures, male
6:19 You are to bring into the ark two of all living **[RPH]** creatures,
6:19 **[RPH]** male and female, to keep them alive with you.
6:20 of **every** kind of creature that moves along the ground will come to
6:20 of every kind of creature that moves along the ground **[RPH]** will
6:21 You are to take **every** *kind of* food that is to be eaten and store it
6:22 Noah did **everything** just as God commanded him.
7: 1 then said to Noah, "Go into the ark, you and your **whole** family,
7: 2 Take with you seven of **every** *kind of* clean animal, a male
7: 3 keep their various kinds alive **throughout** [+6584+7156] the earth.
7: 4 I will wipe from the face of the earth **every** living creature I have
7: 5 And Noah did **all** that the LORD commanded him.
7: 8 of birds and of **all** creatures that move along the ground,
7:11 on that day **all** the springs of the great deep burst forth,
7:14 They had with them **every** wild animal according to its kind,
7:14 animal according to its kind, **all** livestock according to their kinds,
7:14 **every** creature that moves along the ground according to its kind
7:14 ground according to its kind and **every** bird according to its kind,
7:14 every bird according to its kind, **[RPH]** everything with wings.
7:14 and every bird according to its kind, **everything** *with* wings.
7:15 Pairs of **all** creatures that have the breath of life in them came to
7:16 The animals going in were male and female of **every** living thing,
7:19 and **all** the high mountains under the entire heavens were covered.
7:19 and all the high mountains under the **entire** heavens were covered.
7:21 **Every** living thing that moved on the earth perished—birds,
7:21 livestock, wild animals, **all** the creatures that swarm over the earth,
7:21 all the creatures that swarm over the earth, and **all** mankind.
7:22 **Everything** on dry land that had the breath of life in its nostrils
7:22 Everything on dry land **[RPH]** that had the breath of life in its
7:23 **Every** living thing on the face of the earth was wiped out;
8: 1 God remembered Noah and **all** the wild animals and the livestock
8: 1 and **[RPH]** the livestock that were with him in the ark,

Ge 8: 9 set its feet because there was water over **all** the surface of the earth;
8: 17 Bring out **every** *kind of* living creature that is with you—the birds,
8: 17 Bring out every kind of living **[RPH]** creature that is with you—
8: 17 the animals, and **all** the creatures that move along the ground—
8: 19 **All** the animals and all the creatures that move along the ground
8: 19 All the animals and **all** the creatures that move along the ground
8: 19 and all the creatures that move along the ground and **all** the birds—
8: 19 the ground and all the birds—**everything** that moves on the earth—
8: 20 taking some of **all** the clean animals and clean birds, he sacrificed
8: 20 taking some of all the clean animals and **[RPH]** clean birds,
8: 21 And never again will I destroy **all** living creatures, as I have done.
8: 22 "**As long as** [+6388] the earth endures, seedtime and harvest,
9: 2 The fear and dread of you will fall upon **all** the beasts of the earth
9: 2 will fall upon all the beasts of the earth and **all** the birds of the air,
9: 2 birds of the air, upon **every** creature that moves along the ground,
9: 2 that moves along the ground, and upon **all** the fish of the sea;
9: 3 **Everything** that lives and moves will be food for you. Just as I
9: 3 Just as I gave you the green plants, I now give you **everything**.
9: 5 I will demand an accounting from **every** animal. And from each
9: 10 and with **every** living creature that was with you—the birds,
9: 10 the birds, the livestock and **all** the wild animals, all those that came
9: 10 all the wild animals, **all** those that came out of the ark with you—
9: 10 that came out of the ark with you—**every** living creature on earth.
9: 11 Never again will **all** life be cut off by the waters of a flood;
9: 12 making between me and you and **every** living creature with you,
9: 15 between me and you and **all** living creatures of every kind.
9: 15 between me and you and all living creatures of **every** kind.
9: 15 Never again will the waters become a flood to destroy **all** life.
9: 16 between God and **all** living creatures of every kind on the earth."
9: 16 between God and all living creatures of **every** kind on the earth."
9: 17 covenant I have established between me and **all** life on the earth."
9: 19 from them came the people who were scattered over **[NIE]** the
9: 29 **Altogether**, Noah lived 950 years, and then he died.
10: 21 brother was Japheth; Shem was the ancestor of **all** the sons of Eber.
10: 29 Ophir, Havilah and Jobab. **All** these were sons of Joktan.
11: 1 Now the **whole** world had one language and a common speech.
11: 4 and not be scattered over the face of the **whole** earth."
11: 6 "If as one people speaking the same language **[NIE]** they have
11: 6 then **nothing** [+4202] they plan to do will be impossible for them.
11: 8 So the LORD scattered them from there over **all** the earth,
11: 9 because there the LORD confused the language of the **whole**
11: 9 From there the LORD scattered them over the face of the **whole**
12: 3 I will curse; and **all** peoples on earth will be blessed through you."
12: 5 **all** the possessions they had accumulated and the people they had
12: 20 and they sent him on his way, with his wife and **everything** he had.
13: 1 with his wife and **everything** he had, and Lot went with him.
13: 9 Is not the **whole** land before you? Let's part company. If you go to
13: 10 and saw that the **whole** plain of the Jordan was well watered,
13: 10 **[RPH]** like the garden of the LORD, like the land of Egypt,
13: 11 So Lot chose for himself the **whole** plain of the Jordan and set out
13: 15 **All** the land that you see I will give to you and your offspring
14: 3 **All** these latter kings joined forces in the Valley of Siddim (the Salt
14: 7 and they conquered the **whole** territory of the Amalekites,
14: 11 The four kings seized **all** the goods of Sodom and Gomorrah
14: 11 seized all the goods of Sodom and Gomorrah and **all** their food;
14: 16 He recovered **all** the goods and brought back his relative Lot
14: 20 into your hand." Then Abram gave him a tenth of **everything**.
14: 23 that I will accept **nothing** [+561+4946] belonging to you,
15: 10 Abram brought **all** these to him, cut them in two and arranged the
16: 12 his hand will be against **everyone** and everyone's hand against
16: 12 hand will be against everyone and **everyone's** hand against him,
16: 12 against him, and he will live in hostility toward **all** his brothers."
17: 8 The **whole** land of Canaan, where you are now an alien, I will give
17: 10 you are to keep: **Every** male among you shall be circumcised.
17: 12 For the generations to come **every** male among you who is eight
17: 12 born in your household or bought with money from **a** foreigner—
17: 23 and **all** those born in his household or bought with his money,
17: 23 all those born in his household or **[RPH]** bought with his money,
17: 23 **every** male in his household, and circumcised them, as God told
17: 27 **every** male in Abraham's household, including those born in his
18: 18 and **all** nations on earth will be blessed through him.
18: 25 Far be it from you! Will not the Judge of **all** the earth do right?"
18: 26 in the city of Sodom, I will spare the **whole** place for their sake."
18: 28 Will you destroy the **whole** city because of five people?" "If I find
19: 4 gone to bed, **all** the men from every part of the city of Sodom—
19: 12 or daughters, or **anyone** else in the city who belongs to you?
19: 17 your lives! Don't look back, and don't stop **anywhere** in the plain!
19: 25 Thus he overthrew those cities and the **entire** plain, including all
19: 25 and the entire plain, including **all** those living in the cities—
19: 28 toward Sodom and Gomorrah, toward **all** the land of the plain,
19: 31 man around here to lie with us, as is the custom **all** *over* the earth.
20: 7 do not return her, you may be sure that you and **all** yours will die."
20: 8 Early the next morning Abimelech summoned **all** his officials,
20: 8 when he told them **all** that had happened, they were very much
20: 13 **Everywhere** [+2021+5226] we go, say of me, "He is my brother."
20: 16 This is to cover the offense against you before **all** who are with
20: 16 you before all who are with you; you are **completely** vindicated."
20: 18 for the LORD had closed up **every** womb in Abimelech's
21: 6 and **everyone** who hears about this will laugh with me."
21: 12 Listen to **whatever** [+889] Sarah tells you, because it is through
21: 22 forces said to Abraham, "God is with you in **everything** you do.
22: 18 and through your offspring **all** nations on earth will be blessed,
23: 10 he replied to Abraham in the hearing of **all** the Hittites who had
23: 17 and the cave in it, and **all** the trees within the borders of the field—
23: 17 cave in it, and all the trees within **[NIE]** the borders of the field—
23: 18 to Abraham as his property in the presence of **all** the Hittites who
24: 1 advanced in years, and the LORD had blessed him in **every way**.
24: 2 the one in charge of **all** that he had, "Put your hand under my
24: 10 taking with him **all** *kinds of* good things from his master.
24: 20 the well to draw more water, and drew enough for **all** his camels.
24: 36 a son in her old age, and he has given him **everything** he owns.
24: 66 Then the servant told Isaac **all** he had done.
25: 4 Abida and Eldaah. **All** these were descendants of Keturah.
25: 5 Abraham left **everything** he owned to Isaac.
25: 18 And they lived in hostility toward **all** their brothers.
25: 25 to come out was red, and his **whole** *body* was like a hairy garment;
26: 3 For to you and your descendants I will give **all** these lands
26: 4 numerous as the stars in the sky and will give them **all** these lands,
26: 4 and through your offspring **all** nations on earth will be blessed,
26: 11 So Abimelech gave orders to **all** the people: "Anyone who molests
26: 15 So **all** the wells that his father's servants had dug in the time of his
27: 33 I ate **it**[s] just before you came and I blessed him—and indeed he
27: 37 him lord over you and have made **all** his relatives his servants,
28: 14 **All** peoples on earth will be blessed through you and your
28: 15 with you and will watch over you **wherever** [+889+928] you go,
28: 22 God's house, and of **all** that you give me I will give you a tenth."
29: 3 When **all** the flocks were gathered there, the shepherds would roll
29: 8 "until **all** the flocks are gathered and the stone has been rolled
29: 13 brought him to his home, and there Jacob told him **all** these things.
29: 22 So Laban brought together **all** the people of the place and gave a
30: 32 Let me go through **all** your flocks today and remove from them
30: 32 and remove from them **every** speckled or spotted sheep,
30: 32 **every** dark-colored lamb and every spotted or speckled goat.
30: 33 **Any** goat in my possession that is not speckled or spotted,
30: 35 **all** the speckled or spotted female goats (all that had white on
30: 35 the speckled or spotted female goats (**all** that had white on them)
30: 35 **all** the dark-colored lambs, and he placed them in the care of his
30: 40 and **[NIE]** dark-colored animals that belonged to Laban.
30: 41 **Whenever** [+928] the stronger females were in heat, Jacob would
31: 1 "Jacob has taken **everything** our father owned and has gained all
31: 1 and has gained **all** this wealth from what belonged to our father."
31: 6 You know that I've worked for your father with **all** my strength,
31: 8 be your wages,' then **all** the flocks gave birth to speckled young;
31: 8 ones will be your wages,' then **all** the flocks bore streaked young.
31: 12 and see that **all** the male goats mating with the flock are streaked,
31: 12 or spotted, for I have seen **all** that Laban has been doing to you.
31: 16 Surely **all** the wealth that God took away from our father belongs
31: 16 and our children. So do **whatever** [+889] God has told you."
31: 18 he drove **all** his livestock ahead of him, along with all the goods he
31: 18 along with **all** the goods he had accumulated in Paddan Aram,
31: 21 So he fled with **all** he had, and crossing the River, he headed for
31: 34 Laban searched through **everything** *in* the tent but found nothing.
31: 37 Now that you have searched through **all** my goods, what have you
31: 37 what have you found that belongs to **[RPH]** your household?
31: 43 are my children, and the flocks are my flocks. **All** you see is mine.
32: 10 [32:11] I am unworthy of **all** the kindness and faithfulness you
32: 10 [32:11] and **[RPH]** faithfulness you have shown your servant.
32: 19 [32:20] the third and **all** the others who followed the herds:
33: 8 Esau asked, "What do you mean by **all** these droves I met?"
33: 11 to you, for God has been gracious to me and I have **all** I *need*."
33: 13 If they are driven hard just one day, **all** the animals will die.
34: 15 that you become like us by circumcising **all** your males.
34: 19 who was the most honored of **all** his father's household,
34: 22 only on the condition that our **[RPH]** males be circumcised,
34: 23 their property and **all** their other animals become ours?
34: 24 **All** the men who went out of the city gate agreed with Hamor
34: 24 and his son Shechem, and **every** male in the city was circumcised.
34: 24 son Shechem, and every male **[RPH]** in the city was circumcised.
34: 25 their swords and attacked the unsuspecting city, killing **every** male.
34: 29 They carried off **all** their wealth and all their women and children,
34: 29 They carried off all their wealth and **all** their women and children,
34: 29 and children, taking as plunder **everything** in the houses.
35: 2 So Jacob said to his household and to **all** who were with him,
35: 4 So they gave Jacob **all** the foreign gods they had and the rings in
35: 6 Jacob and **all** the people with him came to Luz (that is, Bethel)
36: 6 and sons and daughters and **all** the members of his household,
36: 6 as well as his livestock and **all** his other animals and all the goods
36: 6 all his other animals and **all** the goods he had acquired in Canaan,

Ge 37: 3 Now Israel loved Joseph more than **any** *of* his other sons,
37: 4 When his brothers saw that their father loved him more than **any** *of*
37:35 **All** his sons and daughters came to comfort him, but he refused to
37:35 All his sons and **[RPH]** daughters came to comfort him, but he
39: 3 and that the LORD gave him success in **everything** he did,
39: 4 his household, and he entrusted to his care **everything** he owned.
39: 5 he put him in charge of his household and of **all** that he owned,
39: 5 The blessing of the LORD was on **everything** Potiphar had,
39: 6 So he left in Joseph's care **everything** he had; with Joseph in
39: 8 in the house; **everything** he owns he has entrusted to my care.
39:22 So the warden put Joseph in charge of **all** those held in the prison,
39:22 and he was made responsible for **all** that was done there.
39:23 The warden paid no attention to **anything** [+4399] under Joseph's
40:17 In the top basket were **all** [+4946] **kinds** *of* baked goods for
40:20 was Pharaoh's birthday, and he gave a feast for **all** his officials.
41: 8 so he sent for **all** the magicians and wise men of Egypt.
41: 8 so he sent for all the magicians and **[RPH]** wise men of Egypt.
41:19 and lean. I had never seen such ugly cows in **all** the land of Egypt.
41:29 Seven years of great abundance are coming **throughout** [+928] the
41:30 **all** the abundance in Egypt will be forgotten, and the famine will
41:35 They should collect **all** the food of these good years that are
41:37 The plan seemed good to Pharaoh and to **all** his officials.
41:39 "Since God has made **all** this known to you, there is no one
41:40 of my palace, and **all** my people are to submit to your orders.
41:41 to Joseph, "I hereby put you in charge of the **whole** land of Egypt."
41:43 Thus he put him in charge of the **whole** land of Egypt.
41:44 but without your word no one will lift hand or foot in **all** Egypt."
41:46 from Pharaoh's presence and traveled **throughout** [+928] Egypt.
41:48 Joseph collected **all** the food produced in those seven years of
41:51 "It is because God has made me forget **all** my trouble and all my
41:51 has made me forget all my trouble and **all** my father's household."
41:54 There was famine in **all** the other lands, but in the whole land of
41:54 all the other lands, but in the **whole** land of Egypt there was food.
41:55 When **all** Egypt began to feel the famine, the people cried to
41:55 Pharaoh told **all** the Egyptians, "Go to Joseph and do what he tells
41:56 When the famine had spread over the **whole** country, Joseph
41:56 Joseph opened **the storehouses**° [+889+928+2157] and sold grain
41:57 And **all** the countries came to Egypt to buy grain from Joseph,
41:57 grain from Joseph, because the famine was severe in **all** the world.
42: 6 the governor of the land, the one who sold grain to **all** its people.
42:11 We are **all** the sons of one man. Your servants are honest men,
42:29 in the land of Canaan, they told him **all** that had happened to them.
42:36 you want to take Benjamin. **Everything** [+5626] is against me!"
43: 9 him here before you, I will bear the blame before you **all** my life.
43:34 Benjamin's portion was five times as much as **anyone** else's.
44:32 to you, I will bear the blame before you, my father, **all** my life!'
45: 1 Joseph could no longer control himself before **all** his attendants,
45: 1 and he cried out, "Have **everyone** [+408] leave my presence!"
45: 8 to Pharaoh, lord of his **entire** household and ruler of all Egypt.
45: 8 to Pharaoh, lord of his entire household and ruler of **all** Egypt.
45: 9 God has made me lord of **all** Egypt. Come down to me;
45:10 and grandchildren, your flocks and herds, and **all** you have.
45:11 your household and **all** who belong to you will become destitute.'
45:13 Tell my father about **all** the honor accorded me in Egypt and about
45:13 honor accorded me in Egypt and about **everything** you have seen.
45:15 he kissed **all** his brothers and wept over them. Afterward his
45:20 your belongings, because the best of **all** Egypt will be yours.' "
45:22 To **each** *of* them he gave new clothing, but to Benjamin he gave
45:26 In fact, he is ruler of **all** Egypt." Jacob was stunned; he did not
45:27 when they told him **everything** [+1821] Joseph had said to them,
46: 1 So Israel set out with **all** that was his, and when he reached
46: 6 acquired in Canaan, and Jacob and **all** his offspring went to Egypt.
46: 7 and his daughters and granddaughters—**all** his offspring.
46:15 These sons and daughters of his were thirty-three *in* **all**.
46:22 were the sons of Rachel who were born to Jacob—fourteen *in* **all**.
46:25 whom Laban had given to his daughter Rachel—seven *in* **all**.
46:26 **All** those who went to Egypt with Jacob—those who were his
46:26 not counting his sons' wives—**numbered** sixty-six persons.
46:27 of Jacob's family, which went to Egypt, were seventy *in* **all**.
46:32 brought along their flocks and herds and **everything** they own.'
46:34 of Goshen, for **all** shepherds are detestable to the Egyptians."
47: 1 and brothers, with their flocks and herds and **everything** they own,
47:12 his father and his brothers and **all** his father's household with food,
47:13 however, in the **whole** region because the famine was severe;
47:14 Joseph collected **all** the money that was to be found in Egypt
47:15 was gone, **all** Egypt came to Joseph and said, "Give us food.
47:17 he brought them through that year with food in exchange for **all**
47:20 So Joseph bought **all** the land in Egypt for Pharaoh. The Egyptians,
48:16 the Angel who has delivered me from **all** harm—may he bless
49:28 **All** these are the twelve tribes of Israel, and this is what their father
50: 7 **All** Pharaoh's officials accompanied him—the dignitaries of his
50: 7 the dignitaries of his court and **all** the dignitaries of Egypt—
50: 8 besides **all** *the members of* Joseph's household and his brothers
50:14 and **all** the others who had gone with him to bury his father.
50:15 against us and pays us back for **all** the wrongs we did to him?"
Ex 1: 5 The descendants of Jacob numbered seventy *in* **all**; Joseph was
1: 6 Now Joseph and **all** his brothers and all that generation died,
1: 6 Now Joseph and all his brothers and **all** that generation died,
1:14 labor in brick and mortar and with **all** *kinds of* work in the fields;
1:14 in **all** their hard labor the Egyptians used them ruthlessly.
1:22 Pharaoh gave this order to **all** his people: "Every boy that is born
1:22 "**Every** boy that is born you must throw into the Nile, but let every
1:22 that is born you must throw into the Nile, but let **every** girl live."
3:20 strike the Egyptians with **all** the wonders that I will perform among
4:19 back to Egypt, for **all** the men who wanted to kill you are dead."
4:21 see that you perform before Pharaoh **all** the wonders I have given
4:28 Moses told Aaron **everything** the LORD had sent him to say,
4:28 also about **all** the miraculous signs he had commanded him to
4:29 and Aaron brought together **all** the elders of the Israelites,
4:30 Aaron told them **everything** [+1821] the LORD had said to
5:12 So the people scattered **all** over Egypt to gather stubble to use for
6:29 am the LORD. Tell Pharaoh king of Egypt **everything** I tell you."
7: 2 You are to say **everything** I command you, and your brother
7:19 the streams and canals, over the ponds and **all** the reservoirs'—
7:19 Blood will be **everywhere** in Egypt, even in the wooden buckets
7:20 the water of the Nile, and **all** the water was changed into blood.
7:21 could not drink its water. Blood was **everywhere** in Egypt.
7:24 And **all** the Egyptians dug along the Nile to get drinking water,
8: 2 [7:27] to let them go, I will plague your **whole** country with frogs.
8: 4 [7:29] will go up on you and your people and **all** your officials.' "
8:16 [8:12] **throughout** [+928] the land of Egypt the dust will become
8:17 [8:13] **All** the dust throughout the land of Egypt became gnats.
8:17 [8:13] All the dust **throughout** [+928] the land of Egypt became
8:24 [8:20] **throughout** [+928] Egypt the land was ruined by the flies.
9: 4 so that **no** [+4202+4946] animal belonging to the Israelites will
9: 6 **All** the livestock of the Egyptians died, but not one animal
9: 9 It will become fine dust over the **whole** land of Egypt,
9: 9 will break out on men and animals **throughout** [+928] the land."
9:11 because of the boils that were on them and on **all** the Egyptians.
9:14 or this time I will send the **full force** *of* my plagues against you
9:14 so you may know that there is no one like me in **all** the earth.
9:16 my power and that my name might be proclaimed in **all** the earth.
9:19 and **everything** you have in the field to a place of shelter,
9:19 because the hail will fall on **every** man and animal that has not
9:22 out your hand toward the sky so that hail will fall **all** over Egypt—
9:22 and animals and on **everything** growing in the fields of Egypt."
9:24 It was the worst storm in **all** the land of Egypt since it had become
9:25 **Throughout** [+928] Egypt hail struck everything in the fields—
9:25 Throughout Egypt hail struck **everything** in the fields—both men
9:25 it beat down **everything** growing in the fields and stripped every
9:25 beat down everything growing in the fields and stripped **every** tree.
10: 5 after the hail, including **every** tree that is growing in your fields.
10: 6 your houses and those of **all** your officials and all the Egyptians—
10: 6 your houses and those of all your officials and **all** the Egyptians—
10:12 swarm over the land and devour **everything** growing in the fields,
10:12 everything growing in the fields, **everything** left by the hail."
10:13 the LORD made an east wind blow across the land **all** that day
10:13 an east wind blow across the land all that day and **all** that night.
10:14 they invaded **all** Egypt and settled down in every area of the
10:14 and settled down in **every** area of the country in great numbers.
10:15 They covered **all** the ground until it was black. They devoured all
10:15 They devoured **all** that was left after the hail—everything growing
10:15 **everything** growing in the fields and the fruit on the trees.
10:15 **Nothing** [+4202] green remained on tree or plant in all the land of
10:15 Nothing green remained on tree or plant in **all** the land of Egypt.
10:19 them into the Red Sea. Not a locust was left **anywhere** in Egypt.
10:22 toward the sky, and total darkness covered **all** Egypt for three days.
10:23 Yet **all** the Israelites had light in the places where they lived.
11: 5 **Every** firstborn son in Egypt will die, from the firstborn son of
11: 5 who is at her hand mill, and **all** the firstborn of the cattle as well.
11: 6 There will be loud wailing **throughout** [+928] Egypt—worse than
11: 7 But **among** [+4200] the Israelites not a dog will bark at any man
11: 8 **All** these officials of yours will come to me, bowing down before
11: 8 before me and saying, 'Go, you and **all** the people who follow you!'
11:10 Moses and Aaron performed **all** these wonders before Pharaoh,
12: 3 Tell the **whole** community of Israel that on the tenth day of this
12: 6 when **all** the people of the community of Israel must slaughter
12:12 night I will pass through Egypt and strike down **every** firstborn—
12:12 and animals—and I will bring judgment on **all** the gods of Egypt.
12:15 for **whoever** eats anything with yeast in it from the first day
12:16 Do no work **at all** on these days, except to prepare food for
12:16 on these days, except to prepare food for **everyone** [+5883] to eat—
12:19 **whoever** eats anything with yeast in it must be cut off from the
12:20 Eat **nothing** [+4202] made with yeast. Wherever you live,
12:20 **Wherever** [+928] you live, you must eat unleavened bread."
12:21 Then Moses summoned **all** the elders of Israel and said to them,
12:29 At midnight the LORD struck down **all** the firstborn in Egypt,
12:29 was in the dungeon, and the firstborn of **all** the livestock as well.

Ex 12:30 Pharaoh and **all** his officials and all the Egyptians got up during the
12:30 and all his officials and **all** the Egyptians got up during the night,
12:33 leave the country. "For otherwise," they said, "we will **all** die!"
12:41 430 years, to the very day, **all** the LORD's divisions left Egypt.
12:42 on this night **all** the Israelites are to keep vigil to honor the LORD
12:43 "These are the regulations for the Passover: "**No** [+4202] foreigner
12:44 **Any** slave you have bought may eat of it after you have
12:47 The **whole** community of Israel must celebrate it.
12:48 Passover must have **all** the males in his household circumcised;
12:48 he may take part like one born in the land. **No** [+4202]
12:50 **All** the Israelites did just what the LORD had commanded Moses
13: 2 "Consecrate to me **every** firstborn male. The first offspring of
13: 2 The first offspring of **every** womb among the Israelites belongs to
13: 7 nor shall any yeast be seen **anywhere** within your borders.
13:12 you are to give over to the LORD the first offspring of **every**
13:12 **All** the firstborn males of your livestock belong to the LORD.
13:13 Redeem with a lamb **every** firstborn donkey, but if you do not
13:13 break its neck. Redeem **every** firstborn among your sons.
13:15 the LORD killed **every** firstborn in Egypt, both man and animal.
13:15 I sacrifice to the LORD the first male offspring of **every** womb
13:15 offspring of every womb and redeem **each** *of* my firstborn sons.'
14: 4 But I will gain glory for myself through Pharaoh and **all** his army,
14: 7 along with **all** the other chariots of Egypt, with officers over all of
14: 7 with all the other chariots of Egypt, with officers over **all** *of* them.
14: 9 **all** Pharaoh's horses and chariots, horsemen and troops—
14:17 I will gain glory through Pharaoh and **all** his army, through his
14:20 light to the other side; so neither went near the other **all** night *long*.
14:21 **all** that night the LORD drove the sea back with a strong east
14:23 **all** Pharaoh's horses and chariots and horsemen followed them into
14:28 the **entire** army of Pharaoh that had followed the Israelites into the
15:15 with trembling, **[NIE]** the people of Canaan will melt away;
15:20 and **all** the women followed her, with tambourines and dancing.
15:26 if you pay attention to his commands and keep **all** his decrees,
15:26 I will not bring on you **any** *of* the diseases I brought on the
16: 1 The **whole** Israelite community set out from Elim and came to the
16: 2 In the desert the **whole** community grumbled against Moses
16: 3 you have brought us out into this desert to starve this **entire**
16: 6 So Moses and Aaron said to **all** the Israelites, "In the evening you
16: 9 Then Moses told Aaron, "Say to the **entire** Israelite community,
16:10 While Aaron was speaking to the **whole** Israelite community,
16:22 **[NIE]** the leaders of the community came and reported this to
16:23 want to boil. Save **whatever** is left and keep it until morning.' "
17: 1 The **whole** Israelite community set out from the Desert of Sin,
18: 1 heard of **everything** God had done for Moses and for his people
18: 8 Moses told his father-in-law about **everything** the LORD had
18: 8 and about **all** the hardships they had met along the way
18: 9 Jethro was delighted to hear about **all** the good things the LORD
18:11 Now I know that the LORD is greater than **all** other gods,
18:12 Aaron came with **all** the elders of Israel to eat bread with Moses'
18:14 When his father-in-law saw **all** that Moses was doing for the
18:14 while **all** these people stand around you from morning till
18:21 But select capable men from **all** the people—men who fear God,
18:22 Have them serve as judges for the people at **all** times, but have
18:22 people at all times, but have them bring **every** difficult case to you;
18:22 case to you; **[RPH]** the simple cases they can decide themselves.
18:23 to stand the strain, and **all** these people will go home satisfied."
18:24 Moses listened to his father-in-law and did **everything** he said.
18:25 He chose capable men from **all** Israel and made them leaders of the
18:26 They served as judges for the people at **all** times. The difficult
18:26 to Moses, but **[RPH]** the simple ones they decided themselves.
19: 5 then out of **all** nations you will be my treasured possession.
19: 5 will be my treasured possession. Although the **whole** earth is mine,
19: 7 set before them **all** the words the LORD had commanded him to
19: 8 The people **all** responded together, "We will do everything the
19: 8 responded together, "We will do **everything** the LORD has said."
19:11 will come down on Mount Sinai in the sight of **all** the people.
19:12 **Whoever** touches the mountain shall surely be put to death.
19:16 **Everyone** [+2021+6639] in the camp trembled.
19:18 with smoke, **[NIE]** because the LORD descended on it in fire.
19:18 like smoke from a furnace, the **whole** mountain trembled violently,
20: 1 And God spoke **all** these words:
20: 4 "You shall not make for yourself an idol in the form *of* **anything** in
20: 9 Six days you shall labor and do **all** your work,
20:10 On it you shall not do **any** work, neither you, nor your son
20:11 made the heavens and the earth, the sea, and **all** that is in them,
20:17 his ox or donkey, or **anything** that belongs to your neighbor."
20:18 When **[NIE]** the people saw the thunder and lightning and heard
20:24 **Wherever** [+889+928+2021+5226] I cause my name to be
21:30 he may redeem his life by paying **whatever** [+889+3869] is
22: 9 [22:8] In **all** cases of illegal possession of an ox, a donkey, a
22: 9 [22:8] or **any** *other* lost property about which somebody says,
22:10 [22:9] or **any** *other* animal to his neighbor for safekeeping
22:19 [22:18] "**Anyone** who has sexual relations with an animal must be
22:22 [22:21] "Do not take advantage of **a** widow or an orphan.
23:13 "Be careful to do **everything** I have said to you. Do not invoke the
23:17 "Three times a year **all** the men are to appear before the Sovereign
23:22 If you listen carefully to what he says and do **all** that I say,
23:27 ahead of you and throw into confusion **every** nation you encounter.
23:27 I will make **all** your enemies turn their backs and run.
24: 3 Moses went and told the people **all** the LORD's words and laws,
24: 3 and told the people all the LORD's words and **[RPH]** laws,
24: 3 LORD's words and laws, **[RPH]** they responded with one voice,
24: 3 "**Everything** [+1821+2021] the LORD has said we will do."
24: 4 Moses then wrote down **everything** the LORD had said.
24: 7 They responded, "We will do **everything** the LORD has said;
24: 8 LORD has made with you in accordance with **all** these words."
25: 2 You are to receive the offering for me from **each** man whose heart
25: 9 and **all** its furnishings exactly like the pattern I will show you.
25: 9 all its furnishings **exactly like** [+889+3869+4027] the pattern I will
25:22 meet with you and give you **all** my commands for the Israelites.
25:36 and branches shall **all** be of one piece with the lampstand,
25:39 pure gold is to be used for the lampstand and **all** these accessories.
26: 2 **All** the curtains are to be the same size—twenty-eight cubits long
26:17 to each other. Make **all** the frames of the tabernacle in this way.
27: 3 Make **all** its utensils of bronze—its pots to remove the ashes,
27:17 **All** the posts around the courtyard are to have silver bands
27:19 **All** the other articles used in the service of the tabernacle,
27:19 **whatever** their function, including all the tent pegs for it and those
27:19 including **all** the tent pegs for it and those for the courtyard,
27:19 all the tent pegs for it and **[RPH]** those for the courtyard,
28: 3 Tell **all** the skilled men to whom I have given wisdom in such
28:38 sacred gifts the Israelites consecrate, **whatever** their gifts may be.
29:12 with your finger, and pour out the **rest** *of* it at the base of the altar.
29:13 take **all** the fat around the inner parts, the covering of the liver,
29:18 burn the **entire** ram on the altar. It is a burnt offering to the
29:24 Put **all** these in the hands of Aaron and his sons and wave them
29:35 "Do for Aaron and his sons **everything** I have commanded you,
29:37 the altar will be most holy, and **whatever** touches it will be holy.
30:13 **Each** one who crosses over to those already counted is to give a
30:14 **All** who cross over, those twenty years old or more, are to give an
30:27 the table and **all** its articles, the lampstand and its accessories,
30:28 the altar of burnt offering and **all** its utensils, and the basin with its
30:29 they will be most holy, and **whatever** touches them will be holy.
31: 3 of God, with skill, ability and knowledge in **all** *kinds of* crafts—
31: 5 to work in wood, and to engage in **all** *kinds of* craftsmanship.
31: 6 Also I have given skill to **all** the craftsmen to make everything I
31: 6 Also I have given skill to all the craftsmen to make **everything** I
31: 7 the atonement cover on it, and **all** the other furnishings of the tent—
31: 8 and its articles, the pure gold lampstand and **all** its accessories,
31: 9 the altar of burnt offering and **all** its utensils, the basin with its
31:11 They are to make them **just as** [+889+3869] I commanded you."
31:14 **whoever** does any work on that day must be cut off from his
31:15 **Whoever** does any work on the Sabbath day must be put to death.
32: 3 So **all** the people took off their earrings and brought them to
32:13 and I will give your descendants **all** this land I promised them,
32:26 is for the LORD, come to me." And **all** the Levites rallied to him.
33: 7 **Anyone** inquiring of the LORD would go to the tent of meeting
33: 8 **all** the people rose and stood at the entrances to their tents,
33:10 Whenever **[RPH]** the people saw the pillar of cloud standing at
33:10 they **all** stood and worshiped, each at the entrance to his tent.
33:16 and your people from **all** the other people on the face of the earth?"
33:19 LORD said, "I will cause **all** my goodness to pass in front of you,
34: 3 No one is to come with you or be seen **anywhere** on the mountain;
34:10 Before **all** your people I will do wonders never before done in any
34:10 Before all your people I will do wonders never before done in **any**
34:10 I will do wonders never before done in any nation in **all** the world.
34:10 **[RPH]** The people you live among will see how awesome is the
34:19 "The first offspring of **every** womb belongs to me, including all
34:19 including **all** the firstborn males of your livestock, whether from
34:20 do not redeem it, break its neck. Redeem **all** your firstborn sons.
34:23 Three times a year **all** your men are to appear before the Sovereign
34:30 When Aaron and **all** the Israelites saw Moses, his face was radiant,
34:31 so Aaron and **all** the leaders of the community came back to him,
34:32 Afterward **all** the Israelites came near him, and he gave them all
34:32 he gave them **all** the commands the LORD had given him on
35: 1 Moses assembled the **whole** Israelite community and said to them,
35: 2 to the LORD. **Whoever** does any work on it must be put to death.
35: 3 Do not light a fire in **any** *of* your dwellings on the Sabbath day."
35: 4 Moses said to the **whole** Israelite community, "This is what the
35: 5 **Everyone** *who* is willing is to bring to the LORD an offering of
35:10 "**All** who are skilled among you are to come and make everything
35:10 are to come and make **everything** the LORD has commanded:
35:13 the table with its poles and **all** its articles and the bread of the
35:16 burnt offering with its bronze grating, its poles and **all** its utensils;
35:20 the **whole** Israelite community withdrew from Moses' presence,
35:21 **everyone** [+408] who was willing and whose heart moved him
35:21 everyone **[RPH]** who was willing and whose heart moved him
35:21 the Tent of Meeting, for **all** its service, and for the sacred garments.

Ex 35:22 **All** *who* were willing, men and women alike, came and brought
35:22 and women alike, came and brought gold jewelry of **all** *kinds*:
35:22 They **all** presented their gold as a wave offering to the LORD.
35:23 **Everyone** [+408] who had blue, purple or scarlet yarn or fine
35:24 **Those**[s] presenting an offering of silver or bronze brought it as an
35:24 **everyone** who had acacia wood for any part of the work brought it.
35:24 everyone who had acacia wood for **any** part of the work brought it.
35:25 **Every** skilled woman spun with her hands and brought what she
35:26 **all** the women who were willing and had the skill spun the goat
35:29 **All** the Israelite men and women who were willing brought to the
35:29 **all** the work the LORD through Moses had commanded them to
35:31 of God, with skill, ability and knowledge in **all** *kinds of* crafts—
35:33 work in wood and to engage in **all** kinds of artistic craftsmanship.
35:35 He has filled them with skill to do **all** *kinds of* work as craftsmen,
35:35 and weavers—**all** *of* them master craftsmen and designers.
36: 1 and **every** skilled person to whom the LORD has given skill
36: 1 ability to know how to carry out **all** the work of constructing the
36: 1 to do the work **just as** [+889+4200] the LORD has commanded."
36: 2 and **every** skilled person to whom the LORD had given ability
36: 2 and **[RPH]** who was willing to come and do the work.
36: 3 They received from Moses **all** the offerings the Israelites had
36: 4 So **all** the skilled craftsmen who were doing all the work on the
36: 4 So all the skilled craftsmen who were doing **all** the work on the
36: 7 because what they already had was more than enough to do **all** the
36: 8 **All** the skilled men among the workmen made the tabernacle with
36: 9 same size—**[RPH]** twenty-eight cubits long and four cubits wide.
36:22 each other. They made **all** the frames of the tabernacle in this way.
37:22 and the branches were **all** of one piece with the lampstand,
37:24 the lampstand and **all** its accessories from one talent of pure gold.
38: 3 They made **all** its utensils of bronze—its pots, shovels, sprinkling
38: 3 shovels, sprinkling bowls, meat forks and firepans. **[RPH]**
38:16 **All** the curtains around the courtyard were of finely twisted linen.
38:17 with silver; so **all** the posts of the courtyard had silver bands.
38:20 **All** the tent pegs of the tabernacle and of the surrounding courtyard
38:22 tribe of Judah, made **everything** the LORD commanded Moses;
38:24 The **total** *amount of* the gold from the wave offering used for all
38:24 The total amount of the gold from the wave offering used for **all**
38:26 from **everyone** who had crossed over to those counted,
38:30 the bronze altar with its bronze grating and **all** its utensils,
38:31 and those for its entrance and **all** the tent pegs for the tabernacle
38:31 for the tabernacle and **[RPH]** those for the surrounding courtyard.
39:32 So **all** the work on the tabernacle, the Tent of Meeting,
39:32 The Israelites did **everything** just as the LORD commanded
39:33 the tent and **all** its furnishings, its clasps, frames, crossbars,
39:36 the table with **all** its articles and the bread of the Presence;
39:37 pure gold lampstand with its row of lamps and **all** its accessories,
39:39 bronze altar with its bronze grating, its poles and **all** its utensils;
39:40 **all** the furnishings for the tabernacle, the Tent of Meeting;
39:42 The Israelites had done **all** the work just as the LORD had
39:42 The Israelites had done all the work just as **[RPH]** the LORD
39:43 Moses inspected **[RPH]** the work and saw that they had done it
40: 9 the anointing oil and anoint the tabernacle and **everything** in it;
40: 9 in it; consecrate it and **all** its furnishings, and it will be holy.
40:10 Then anoint the altar of burnt offering and **all** its utensils;
40:16 Moses did **everything** just as the LORD commanded him.
40:36 In **all** the travels of the Israelites, whenever the cloud lifted from
40:38 in the sight of **all** the house of Israel during all their travels.
40:38 in the sight of all the house of Israel during **all** their travels.
Lev 1: 9 the legs with water, and the priest is to burn **all** *of* it on the altar.
1:13 and the priest is to bring **all** *of* it and burn it on the altar.
2: 2 a handful of the fine flour and oil, together with **all** the incense,
2:11 " '**Every** grain offering you bring to the LORD must be made
2:11 for you are not to burn **any** yeast or honey in an offering made to
2:11 or **[RPH]** honey in an offering made to the LORD by fire.
2:13 Season **all** your grain offerings with salt. Do not leave the salt of
2:13 your God out of your grain offerings; add salt to **all** your offerings.
2:16 of the crushed grain and the oil, together with **all** the incense,
3: 3 **all** the fat that covers the inner parts or is connected to them,
3: 9 **all** the fat that covers the inner parts or is connected to them,
3:14 **all** the fat that covers the inner parts or is connected to them,
3:16 made by fire, a pleasing aroma. **All** the fat is the LORD's.
3:17 ordinance for the generations to come, **wherever** [+928] you live:
3:17 wherever you live: You must not eat **any** fat or any blood.' "
3:17 wherever you live: You must not eat any fat or **any** blood.' "
4: 2 and does what is forbidden in **any** *of* the LORD's commands—
4: 7 The **rest** *of* the bull's blood he shall pour out at the base of the altar
4: 8 He shall remove **all** the fat from the bull of the sin offering—
4: 8 the fat that covers the inner parts or **[RPH]** is connected to them,
4:11 But the hide of the bull and **all** its flesh, as well as the head
4:12 that is, **all** *the rest of* the bull—he must take outside the camp to a
4:13 " 'If the **whole** Israelite community sins unintentionally and does
4:13 does what is forbidden in **any** [+285] *of* the LORD's commands,
4:18 The **rest** *of* the blood he shall pour out at the base of the altar of
4:19 He shall remove **all** the fat from it and burn it on the altar,
4:22 does what is forbidden in **any** [+285] *of* the commands of the
4:26 He shall burn **all** the fat on the altar as he burned the fat of the
4:30 and pour out the **rest** *of* the blood at the base of the altar.
4:31 He shall remove **all** the fat, just as the fat is removed from the
4:34 and pour out the **rest** *of* the blood at the base of the altar.
4:35 He shall remove **all** the fat, just as the fat is removed from the lamb
5: 2 " 'Or if a person touches **anything** [+1821] ceremonially unclean—
5: 3 **anything** that would make him unclean—even though he is
5: 4 or evil—in **any** matter one might carelessly swear about—
5:17 does what is forbidden in **any** [+285] *of* the LORD's commands,
6: 3 [5:22] or if he commits **any** such sin that people may do—
6: 5 [5:24] or **whatever** [+889] it was he swore falsely about. He must
6: 7 [5:26] he will be forgiven for any of **these**[s] **things** he did that
6: 9 [6:2] is to remain on the altar hearth **throughout** the night,
6:15 [6:8] and oil, together with **all** the incense on the grain offering,
6:18 [6:11] **Any** male descendant of Aaron may eat it. It is his regular
6:18 [6:11] **Whatever** [+889] touches them will become holy.' "
6:23 [6:16] **Every** grain offering of a priest shall be burned
6:27 [6:20] **Whatever** [+889] touches any of the flesh will become
6:29 [6:22] **Any** male in a priest's family may eat it; it is most holy.
6:30 [6:23] **any** sin offering whose blood is brought into the Tent of
7: 3 **All** its fat shall be offered: the fat tail and the fat that covers the
7: 6 **Any** male in a priest's family may eat it, but it must be eaten in a
7: 9 **Every** grain offering baked in an oven or cooked in a pan
7: 9 Every grain offering baked in an oven or **[RPH]** cooked in a pan
7:10 **every** grain offering, whether mixed with oil or dry,
7:10 mixed with oil or dry, belongs equally to **all** the sons of Aaron.
7:14 He is to bring one of **each** *kind* as an offering, a contribution to the
7:19 " 'Meat that touches **anything** ceremonially unclean must not be
7:19 As for other meat, **anyone** ceremonially clean may eat it.
7:21 If anyone touches **something** unclean—whether human
7:21 whether human uncleanness or an unclean animal or **any** unclean,
7:23 to the Israelites: 'Do not eat **any** *of* the fat of cattle, sheep or goats.
7:24 or torn by wild animals may be used for **any** other purpose,
7:25 **Anyone** who eats the fat of an animal from which an offering by
7:26 **wherever** [+928] you live, you must not eat the blood of any bird
7:26 you live, you must not eat the blood of **any** bird or animal.
7:27 If **anyone** [+5883] eats blood, that person must be cut off from his
7:27 If anyone eats **[RPH]** blood, that person must be cut off from his
8: 3 gather the **entire** assembly at the entrance to the Tent of Meeting."
8:10 the anointing oil and anointed the tabernacle and **everything** in it,
8:11 anointing the altar and **all** its utensils and the basin with its stand,
8:16 Moses also took **all** the fat around the inner parts, the covering of
8:21 and burned the **whole** ram on the altar as a burnt offering,
8:25 He took the fat, the fat tail, **all** the fat around the inner parts,
8:27 He put **all** these in the hands of Aaron and his sons and waved
8:36 So Aaron and his sons did **everything** [+1821+2021] the LORD
9: 5 and the **entire** assembly came near and stood before the LORD.
9:23 the people; and the glory of the LORD appeared to **all** the people.
9:24 when **all** the people saw it, they shouted for joy and fell facedown.
10: 3 in the sight of **all** the people I will be honored.' " Aaron remained
10: 6 and the LORD will be angry with the **whole** community.
10: 6 your relatives, **all** the house of Israel, may mourn for those the
10:11 you must teach the Israelites **all** the decrees the LORD has given
11: 2 'Of **all** the animals that live on land, these are the ones you may
11: 3 You may eat **any** animal that has a split hoof completely divided
11: 9 " 'Of **all** the creatures living in the water of the seas and the
11: 9 and the streams, you may eat **any** that have fins and scales.
11:10 But **all** creatures in the seas or streams that do not have fins
11:10 whether among **all** the swarming things or among all the other
11:10 or among **all** the other living creatures in the water—
11:12 **Anything** living in the water that does not have fins and scales is
11:15 **any** kind of raven,
11:20 " '**All** flying insects that walk on all fours are to be detestable to
11:21 **some** [+4946] winged creatures that walk on all fours that you may
11:23 But **all** other winged creatures that have four legs you are to detest.
11:24 **whoever** touches their carcasses will be unclean till evening.
11:25 **Whoever** picks up one of their carcasses must wash his clothes,
11:26 " '**Every** animal that has a split hoof not completely divided
11:26 **whoever** touches ⌞the carcass of⌟ any of them will be unclean.
11:27 Of **all** the animals that walk on all fours, those that walk on their
11:27 on all fours, **those**[s] that walk on their paws are unclean for you;
11:27 **whoever** touches their carcasses will be unclean till evening.
11:31 Of **all** those that move along the ground, these are unclean for you.
11:31 **Whoever** touches them when they are dead will be unclean till
11:32 When **one** of them dies and falls on something, that article,
11:32 falls on something, **that**[s] article, whatever its use, will be unclean,
11:32 **[RPH]** whether it is made of wood, cloth, hide or sackcloth.
11:33 If one of them falls into **a** clay pot, everything in it will be unclean,
11:33 **everything** in it will be unclean, and you must break the pot.
11:34 **Any** food that could be eaten but has water on it from such a pot is
11:34 that could be eaten but has water on it from **such** a pot is unclean,
11:34 is unclean, and **any** liquid that could be drunk from it is unclean.
11:35 **Anything** that one of their carcasses falls on becomes unclean;

Lev 11:37 If a carcass falls on **any** seeds that are to be planted, they remain
11:41 " '**Every** creature that moves about on the ground is detestable;
11:42 You are not to eat **any** creature that moves about on the ground,
11:42 **[RPH]** whether it moves on its belly or walks on all fours
11:42 it moves on its belly or **[RPH]** walks on all fours or on many feet;
11:42 it moves on its belly or walks on all fours or **[RPH]** on many feet;
11:43 Do not defile yourselves by **any** *of* these creatures. Do not make
11:44 Do not make yourselves unclean by **any** creature that moves about
11:46 **every** living thing that moves in the water and every creature that
11:46 in the water and **every** creature that moves about on the ground.
12: 4 She must not touch **anything** sacred or go to the sanctuary until the
13:12 "If the disease breaks out all over his skin and, **so far** [+4200] **as**
13:12 it covers **all** the skin of the infected person from head to foot,
13:13 is to examine him, and if the disease has covered his **whole** body,
13:13 that person clean. Since it has **all** turned white, he is clean.
13:46 **As long** [+3427] **as** he has the infection he remains unclean.
13:48 of linen or wool, any leather or **anything** made of leather—
13:49 or knitted material, or **any** leather article, is greenish or reddish,
13:51 or knitted material, or the leather, **whatever** [+889] its use,
13:52 or linen, or **any** leather article that has the contamination in it,
13:53 or the woven or knitted material, or the **[RPH]** leather article,
13:57 or knitted material, or in the **[RPH]** leather article, it is spreading,
13:58 or **any** leather article that has been washed and is rid of the
13:59 or linen clothing, woven or knitted material, or **any** leather article,
14: 8 must wash his clothes, shave off **all** his hair and bathe with water;
14: 9 On the seventh day he must shave off **all** his hair; he must shave
14: 9 shave his head, his beard, his eyebrows and the **rest** *of* his hair.
14:36 so that **nothing** [+4202] in the house will be pronounced unclean.
14:45 It must be torn down—its stones, timbers and **all** the plaster—
14:46 "Anyone who goes into the house **while** [+3427] it is closed up
14:54 These are the regulations for **any** infectious skin disease, for an
15: 4 " '**Any** bed the man with a discharge lies on will be unclean,
15: 4 be unclean, and **anything** [+2021+3998] he sits on will be unclean.
15: 9 " '**Everything** the man sits on when riding will be unclean,
15:10 **whoever** touches any of the things that were under him will be
15:10 whoever touches **any** *of the things* that were under him will be
15:11 " '**Anyone** the man with a discharge touches without rinsing his
15:12 must be broken, and **any** wooden article is to be rinsed with water.
15:16 he must bathe his **whole** body with water, and he will be unclean
15:17 **Any** clothing or leather that has semen on it must be washed with
15:17 or **[RPH]** leather that has semen on it must be washed with water,
15:19 and **anyone** who touches her will be unclean till evening.
15:20 " '**Anything** she lies on during her period will be unclean,
15:20 period will be unclean, and **anything** she sits on will be unclean.
15:21 **Whoever** touches her bed must wash his clothes and bathe with
15:22 **Whoever** touches anything she sits on must wash his clothes
15:22 Whoever touches **anything** [+3998] she sits on must wash his
15:24 will be unclean for seven days; **any** bed he lies on will be unclean.
15:25 she will be unclean **as long** [+3427] **as** she has the discharge,
15:26 **Any** bed she lies on while her discharge continues will be unclean,
15:26 Any bed she lies on **while** [+3427] her discharge **continues** will be
15:26 **anything** [+2021+3998] she sits on will be unclean, as during her
15:27 **Whoever** touches them will be unclean; he must wash his clothes
16: 2 "Tell your brother Aaron not to come **whenever** [+928+6961] he
16:16 and rebellion of the Israelites, **whatever** their sins have been.
16:17 **No** [+4202] one is to be in the Tent of Meeting from the time
16:17 for himself, his household and the **whole** community of Israel.
16:21 confess over it **all** the wickedness and rebellion of the Israelites—
16:21 over it all the wickedness and **[RPH]** rebellion of the Israelites—
16:21 it all the wickedness and rebellion of the Israelites—**all** their sins—
16:22 The goat will carry on itself **all** their sins to a solitary place;
16:29 seventh month you must deny yourselves and not do **any** work—
16:30 Then, before the LORD, you will be clean from **all** your sins.
16:33 the altar, and for the priests and **all** the people of the community.
16:34 Atonement is to be made once a year for **all** the sins of the
17: 2 to Aaron and his sons and to **all** the Israelites and say to them:
17:10 or any alien living among them who eats **any** blood—
17:12 Therefore I say to the Israelites, "**None** [+4202+5883] of you may
17:14 because the life of **every** creature is its blood. That is why I have
17:14 said to the Israelites, "You must not eat the blood of **any** creature,
17:14 of any creature, because the life of **every** creature is its blood;
17:14 of every creature is its blood; **anyone** who eats it must be cut off."
17:15 " '**Anyone** [+5883], whether native-born or alien, who eats
18: 6 " 'No one is to approach **any** close relative to have sexual relations.
18:23 " 'Do not have sexual relations with **an** animal and defile yourself
18:24 " 'Do not defile yourselves in **any** *of* these ways, because this is
18:24 because **this is how** [+465+928] the nations that I am going to
18:26 the aliens living among you must not do **any** of these detestable
18:27 for **all** these things were done by the people who lived in the land
18:29 " '**Everyone** who does any of these detestable things—such
18:29 " 'Everyone who does **any** of these detestable things—such
19: 2 "Speak to the **entire** assembly of Israel and say to them: 'Be holy
19:23 " 'When you enter the land and plant **any** *kind of* fruit tree,
19:24 In the fourth year **all** its fruit will be holy, an offering of praise to
19:37 " 'Keep **all** my decrees and all my laws and follow them. I am the
19:37 " 'Keep all my decrees and **all** my laws and follow them. I am the
20: 5 and **all** who follow him in prostituting themselves to Molech.
20:16 " 'If a woman approaches **an** animal to have sexual relations with
20:22 " 'Keep **all** my decrees and laws and follow them, so that the land
20:22 " 'Keep all my decrees and **[RPH]** laws and follow them,
20:23 out before you. Because they did **all** these things, I abhorred them.
20:25 by any animal or bird or **anything** that moves along the ground—
21:11 He must not enter a place where there is **a** dead body. He must not
21:18 **No** [+4202] man who has any defect may come near: no man who
21:21 **No** [+4202] descendant of Aaron the priest who has any defect is
21:24 So Moses told this to Aaron and his sons and to **all** the Israelites.
22: 3 if **any** [+408] of your descendants is ceremonially unclean
22: 3 if any of **[RPH]** your descendants is ceremonially unclean
22: 4 He will also be unclean if he touches **something** defiled by a
22: 5 or if he touches **any** crawling thing that makes him unclean,
22: 5 person who makes him unclean, **whatever** the uncleanness may be.
22:10 " 'No **one** outside a priest's family may eat the sacred offering,
22:13 **No** [+4202] unauthorized person, however, may eat any of it.
22:18 to Aaron and his sons and to **all** the Israelites and say to them:
22:18 to the LORD, either to fulfill **a** vow or as a freewill offering,
22:18 to the LORD, either to fulfill a vow or as **a** freewill offering,
22:20 Do not bring **anything** with a defect, because it will not be
22:21 it must be without defect or **[NIE]** blemish to be acceptable.
22:25 you must not accept **such** [+4946] animals from the hand of a
23: 3 You are not to do **any** work; wherever you live, it is a Sabbath to
23: 3 **wherever** [+928] you live, it is a Sabbath to the LORD.
23: 7 first day hold a sacred assembly and do **no** [+4202] regular work.
23: 8 day hold a sacred assembly and do **no** [+4202] regular work.' "
23:14 ordinance for the generations to come, **wherever** [+928] you live.
23:21 are to proclaim a sacred assembly and do **no** [+4202] regular work.
23:21 ordinance for the generations to come, **wherever** [+928] you live.
23:25 Do **no** [+4202] regular work, but present an offering made to the
23:28 Do **no** [+4202] work on that day, because it is the Day of
23:29 **Anyone** [+2021+5883] who does not deny himself on that day
23:30 I will destroy from among his people **anyone** [+2021+5883] who
23:30 I will destroy from among his people anyone who does **any** work
23:31 You shall do no work **at all**. This is to be a lasting ordinance for
23:31 ordinance for the generations to come, **wherever** [+928] you live.
23:35 The first day is a sacred assembly; do **no** [+4202] regular work.
23:36 by fire. It is the closing assembly; do **no** [+4202] regular work.
23:38 and in addition to your gifts and **whatever** you have vowed
23:38 have vowed and **all** the freewill offerings you give to the LORD.)
23:42 for seven days: **All** native-born Israelites are to live in booths
24:14 **All** those who heard him are to lay their hands on his head,
24:14 their hands on his head, and the **entire** assembly is to stone him.
24:16 The **entire** assembly must stone him. Whether an alien
24:17 " 'If anyone takes the life of **a** human being, he must be put to
25: 7 animals in your land. **Whatever** the land produces may be eaten.
25: 9 on the Day of Atonement sound the trumpet **throughout** [+928]
25:10 and proclaim liberty throughout the land to **all** its inhabitants.
25:24 **Throughout** [+928] the country that you hold as a possession,
26:14 if you will not listen to me and carry out **all** these commands,
26:15 and abhor my laws and fail to carry out **all** my commands and
26:34 the land will enjoy its sabbath years **all** the time that it lies desolate
26:35 **All** the time that it lies desolate, the land will have the rest it did
27: 9 the LORD, such **an**ˢ animal given to the LORD becomes holy.
27:11 If what he vowed is **a** ceremonially unclean animal—one that is
27:25 **Every** value is to be set according to the sanctuary shekel,
27:28 " 'But **nothing** [+4202] that a man owns and devotes to the
27:28 " 'But nothing that a man **[RPH]** owns and devotes to the
27:28 or redeemed; **everything** so devoted is most holy to the LORD.
27:29 " '**No** [+4202] person devoted to destruction may be ransomed;
27:30 " 'A tithe of **everything** *from* the land, whether grain from the soil
27:32 The **entire** tithe of the herd and flock—every tenth animal that
27:32 **every** tenth animal that passes under the shepherd's rod—
Nu 1: 2 "Take a census of the **whole** Israelite community by their clans
1: 2 by their clans and families, listing **every** man by name, one by one.
1: 3 Aaron are to number by their divisions **all** the men in Israel twenty
1:18 they called the **whole** community together on the first day of the
1:20 **All** the men twenty years old or more who were able to serve in the
1:20 according to the records of their clans and families. **[RPH]**
1:22 **All** the men twenty years old or more who were able to serve in the
1:22 according to the records of their clans and families. **[RPH]**
1:24 **All** the men twenty years old or more who were able to serve in the
1:26 or more **[NIE]** who were able to serve in the army were listed by
1:28 **All** the men twenty years old or more who were able to serve in the
1:30 **All** the men twenty years old or more who were able to serve in the
1:32 **All** the men twenty years old or more who were able to serve in the
1:34 **All** the men twenty years old or more who were able to serve in the
1:36 **All** the men twenty years old or more who were able to serve in the
1:38 **All** the men twenty years old or more who were able to serve in the
1:40 **All** the men twenty years old or more who were able to serve in the
1:42 **All** the men twenty years old or more who were able to serve in the

Nu 1:45 **All** the Israelites twenty years old or more who were able to serve
1:45 or more **[RPH]** who were able to serve in Israel's army were
1:46 The **total** number was 603,550.
1:50 over **all** its furnishings and everything belonging to it.
1:50 over all its furnishings and **everything** belonging to it.
1:50 They are to carry the tabernacle and **all** its furnishings; they are to
1:54 The Israelites did **all** this just as the LORD commanded Moses.
2: 9 **All** the men assigned to the camp of Judah, according to their
2:16 **All** the men assigned to the camp of Reuben, according to their
2:24 **All** the men assigned to the camp of Ephraim, according to their
2:31 **All** the men assigned to the camp of Dan number 157,600.
2:32 **All** *those in* the camps, by their divisions, number 603,550.
2:34 So the Israelites did **everything** the LORD commanded Moses;
3: 7 for the **whole** community at the Tent of Meeting by doing the work
3: 8 They are to take care of **all** the furnishings of the Tent of Meeting,
3:12 in place of the first male offspring of **every** Israelite woman.
3:13 for **all** the firstborn are mine. When I struck down all the firstborn
3:13 When I struck down **all** the firstborn in Egypt, I set apart for
3:13 I set apart for myself **every** firstborn in Israel, whether man
3:15 their families and clans. Count **every** male a month old or more."
3:22 The number of **all** the males a month old or more who were
3:26 and altar, and the ropes—and **everything** related to their use.
3:28 The number of **all** the males a month old or more was 8,600.
3:31 in ministering, the curtain, and **everything** *related to* their use.
3:34 The number of **all** the males a month old or more who were
3:36 its crossbars, posts, bases, **all** its equipment, and everything related
3:36 bases, all its equipment, and **everything** *related to* their use,
3:39 The **total** number of Levites counted at the LORD's command by
3:39 their clans, including **every** male a month old or more, was 22,000.
3:40 "Count **all** the firstborn Israelite males who are a month old
3:41 Take the Levites for me in place of **all** the firstborn of the
3:41 the livestock of the Levites in place of **all** the firstborn of the
3:42 So Moses counted **all** the firstborn of the Israelites, as the LORD
3:43 The **total** number of firstborn males a month old or more,
3:45 "Take the Levites in place of **all** the firstborn of Israel, and the
4: 3 Count **all** the men from thirty to fifty years of age who come to
4: 9 and trays, and **all** its jars for the oil used to supply it.
4:10 to wrap it and **all** its accessories in a covering of hides of sea cows
4:12 "They are to take **all** the articles used for ministering in the
4:14 they are to place on it **all** the utensils used for ministering at the
4:14 **[RPH]** Over it they are to spread a covering of hides of sea cows
4:15 finished covering the holy furnishings and **all** the holy articles,
4:16 He is to be in charge of the **entire** tabernacle and everything in it,
4:16 He is to be in charge of the entire tabernacle and **everything** in it,
4:23 Count **all** the men from thirty to fifty years of age who come to
4:26 for the entrance, the ropes and **all** the equipment used in its service.
4:26 The Gershonites are to do **all** that needs to be done with these
4:27 **All** their service, whether carrying or doing other work, is to be
4:27 All their service, whether **[RPH]** carrying or doing other work,
4:27 All their service, whether carrying or doing **other**[s] work, is to be
4:27 You shall assign to them as their responsibility **all** they are to
4:30 Count **all** the men from thirty to fifty years of age who come to
4:31 This is their duty as **[RPH]** they perform service at the Tent of
4:32 ropes, **all** their equipment and everything related to their use.
4:32 ropes, all their equipment and **everything** related to their use.
4:33 This is the service of the Merarite clans as **[NIE]** they work at the
4:35 **All** the men from thirty to fifty years of age who came to serve in
4:37 This was the total of **all** *those in* the Kohathite clans who served in
4:39 **All** the men from thirty to fifty years of age who came to serve in
4:41 This was the **total** [+7212] *of those in* the Gershonite clans who
4:43 **All** the men from thirty to fifty years of age who came to serve in
4:46 and the leaders of Israel counted **all** the Levites by their clans
4:47 **All** the men from thirty to fifty years of age who came to do the
5: 2 "Command the Israelites to send away from the camp **anyone** who
5: 2 who has an infectious skin disease or a discharge *of* **any** *kind*,
5: 2 any kind, or **who**[s] is ceremonially unclean because of a dead body.
5: 6 'When a man or woman wrongs another in **any** *way* and so is
5: 9 **All** the sacred contributions the Israelites bring to a priest will
5: 9 All **[RPH]** the sacred contributions the Israelites bring to a priest
5:30 her stand before the LORD and is to apply this **entire** law to her.
6: 3 He must not drink **[NIE]** grape juice or eat grapes or raisins.
6: 4 **As long** [+3427] **as** he is a Nazirite, he must not eat anything that
6: 4 he must not eat **anything** that comes from the grapevine, not even
6: 5 " 'During the **entire** period of his vow of separation no razor may
6: 6 **Throughout** the period of his separation to the LORD he must
6: 8 **Throughout** the period of his separation he is consecrated to the
7: 1 he anointed it and consecrated it and **all** its furnishings.
7: 1 He also anointed and consecrated the altar and **all** its utensils.
7:85 **Altogether**, the silver dishes weighed two thousand four hundred
7:86 **Altogether**, the gold dishes weighed a hundred and twenty shekels.
7:87 The **total** *number of* animals for the burnt offering came to twelve
7:88 The **total** *number of* animals for the sacrifice of the fellowship
8: 7 then have them shave their **whole** bodies and wash their clothes,
8: 9 the Tent of Meeting and assemble the **whole** Israelite community.
8:16 the first male offspring from **[RPH]** every Israelite woman.
8:16 the firstborn, the first male offspring from **every** Israelite woman.
8:17 **Every** firstborn male in Israel, whether man or animal, is mine.
8:17 When I struck down **all** the firstborn in Egypt, I set them apart for
8:18 I have taken the Levites in place of **all** the firstborn sons in Israel.
8:20 the **whole** Israelite community did with the Levites just as the
8:20 **just as** [+889+3869+4027] the LORD commanded Moses.
9: 3 day of this month, in accordance with **all** its rules and regulations."
9: 3 in accordance with all its rules and **[RPH]** regulations."
9: 5 The Israelites did **everything** just as the LORD commanded
9:12 they celebrate the Passover, they must follow **all** the regulations.
9:18 **As long** [+3427] **as** the cloud stayed over the tabernacle,
10: 3 the **whole** community is to assemble before you at the entrance to
10:25 Finally, as the rear guard for **all** the units, the divisions of the camp
11: 6 we have lost our appetite; we never see **anything** but this manna!"
11:11 What have I done to displease you that you put the burden of **all**
11:12 Did I conceive **all** these people? Did I give them birth? Why do
11:13 Where can I get meat for **all** these people? They keep wailing to
11:14 I cannot carry **all** these people by myself; the burden is too heavy
11:22 Would they have enough if **all** the fish in the sea were caught for
11:29 I wish that **all** the LORD's people were prophets and that the
11:32 **All** that day and night and all the next day the people went out
11:32 All that day and **[RPH]** night and all the next day the people went
11:32 All that day and night and **all** the next day the people went out
12: 3 more humble than **anyone** else on the face of the earth.)
12: 7 this is not true of my servant Moses; he is faithful in **all** my house.
13: 2 to the Israelites. From **each** ancestral tribe send one of its leaders."
13: 3 from the Desert of Paran. **All** *of* them were leaders of the Israelites.
13:26 the **whole** Israelite community at Kadesh in the Desert of Paran.
13:26 There they reported to them and to the **whole** assembly
13:32 those living in it. **All** the people we saw there are of great size.
14: 1 That night **all** the people *of* the community raised their voices
14: 2 **All** the Israelites grumbled against Moses and Aaron,
14: 2 against Moses and Aaron, and the **whole** assembly said to them,
14: 5 Aaron fell facedown in front of the **whole** Israelite assembly
14: 7 said to the **entire** Israelite assembly, "The land we passed through
14:10 the **whole** assembly talked about stoning them. Then the glory of
14:10 the glory of the LORD appeared at the Tent of Meeting to **all** the
14:11 in spite of **all** the miraculous signs I have performed among them?
14:21 and as surely as the glory of the LORD fills the **whole** earth,
14:22 not **one** *of* the men who saw my glory and the miraculous signs I
14:23 No **one** who has treated me with contempt will ever see it.
14:29 **every** *one of* you twenty years old or more who was counted in the
14:29 twenty years old or more who was counted in **[RPH]** the census
14:35 and I will surely do these things to this **whole** wicked community,
14:36 made the **whole** community grumble against him by spreading a
14:39 When Moses reported this to **all** the Israelites, they mourned
15:13 " '**Everyone** who is native-born must do these things in this way
15:22 " 'Now if you unintentionally fail to keep **any** *of* these commands
15:23 **any** *of* the LORD's commands to you through him, from the day
15:24 the **whole** community is to offer a young bull for a burnt offering
15:25 The priest is to make atonement for the **whole** Israelite community,
15:26 The **whole** Israelite community and the aliens living among them
15:26 because **all** the people were involved in the unintentional wrong.
15:33 wood brought him to Moses and Aaron and the **whole** assembly,
15:35 must die. The **whole** assembly must stone him outside the camp."
15:36 So the **[RPH]** assembly took him outside the camp and stoned
15:39 and so you will remember **all** the commands of the LORD,
15:40 you will remember to obey **all** my commands and will be
16: 3 The **whole** community is holy, every one of them, and the LORD
16: 3 is holy, **every** *one of* them, and the LORD is with them.
16: 5 he said to Korah and **all** his followers: "In the morning the LORD
16: 6 You, Korah, and **all** your followers are to do this: Take censers
16:10 He has brought you and **all** your fellow Levites near himself,
16:11 the LORD that you and **all** your followers have banded together.
16:16 and **all** your followers are to appear before the LORD tomorrow—
16:19 When Korah had gathered **all** his followers in opposition to them at
16:19 the glory of the LORD appeared to the **entire** assembly.
16:22 and cried out, "O God, God of the spirits of **all** mankind,
16:22 will you be angry with the **entire** assembly when only one man
16:26 Do not touch **anything** belonging to them, or you will be swept
16:26 to them, or you will be swept away because of **all** their sins."
16:28 "This is how you will know that the LORD has sent me to do **all**
16:29 If these men die a **natural** [+132+2021+3869] death and
16:29 and experience only what usually happens to **[RPH]** men,
16:30 and swallows them, with **everything** that belongs to them,
16:31 As soon as he finished saying **all** this, the ground under them split
16:32 with their households and **all** Korah's men and all their
16:32 their households and all Korah's men and **all** their possessions.
16:33 They went down alive into the grave, with **everything** they owned;
16:34 At their cries, **all** the Israelites around them fled, shouting,
16:41 [17:6] The next day the **whole** Israelite community grumbled
17: 2 [17:17] one from the leader of **each** of their ancestral tribes.
17: 6 [17:21] and **[RPH]** their leaders gave him twelve staffs,

Nu 17: 9 [17:24] Moses brought out **all** the staffs from the LORD's
17: 9 [17:24] the staffs from the LORD's presence to **all** the Israelites.
17: 12 [17:27] said to Moses, "We will die! We are lost, we are **all** lost!
17: 13 [17:28] **Anyone** who even comes near the tabernacle of the
18: 3 be responsible to you and are to perform **all** the duties of the Tent,
18: 4 **all** the work at the Tent—and no one else may come near where
18: 7 serve as priests in connection with **everything** [+1821] *at* the altar
18: 8 **all** the holy offerings the Israelites give me I give to you and your
18: 9 From **all** the gifts they bring me as most holy offerings,
18: 9 whether **[RPH]** grain or sin or guilt offerings, that part belongs to
18: 9 whether grain or **[RPH]** sin or guilt offerings, that part belongs to
18: 9 whether grain or sin or **[RPH]** guilt offerings, that part belongs to
18: 10 Eat it as something most holy; **every** male shall eat it. You must
18: 11 whatever is set aside from the gifts of **all** the wave offerings of the
18: 11 **Everyone** in your household *who* is ceremonially clean may eat it.
18: 12 "I give you **all** the finest olive oil and all the finest new wine
18: 12 "I give you all the finest olive oil and **all** the finest new wine
18: 13 **All** the land's firstfruits that they bring to the LORD will be
18: 13 **Everyone** in your household *who* is ceremonially clean may eat it.
18: 14 "**Everything** in Israel that is devoted to the LORD is yours.
18: 15 The first offspring of **every** womb, both man and animal, that is
18: 15 The first offspring of every womb, **[RPH]** both man and animal,
18: 19 **Whatever** is set aside from the holy offerings the Israelites present
18: 21 "I give to the Levites **all** the tithes in Israel as their inheritance in
18: 28 this way you also will present an offering to the LORD from **all**
18: 29 You must present as **[RPH]** the LORD's portion the best
18: 29 You must present as the LORD's portion **[RPH]** the best
18: 29 portion the best and holiest part of **everything** given to you.'
18: 31 and your households may eat the rest of it **anywhere** [+928+5226],
19: 11 "Whoever touches the dead body of **anyone** [+132] will be unclean
19: 13 **Whoever** touches the dead body of anyone and fails to purify
19: 14 **Anyone** who enters the tent and anyone who is in it will be unclean
19: 14 the tent and **anyone** who is in it will be unclean for seven days,
19: 15 **every** open container without a lid fastened on it will be unclean.
19: 16 "**Anyone** out in the open who touches someone who has been
19: 18 dip it in the water and sprinkle the tent and **all** the furnishings
19: 22 **Anything** that an unclean person touches becomes unclean,
20: 1 In the first month the **whole** Israelite community arrived at the
20: 14 You know about **all** the hardships that have come upon us.
20: 22 The **whole** Israelite community set out from Kadesh and came to
20: 27 They went up Mount Hor in the sight of the **whole** community.
20: 29 and when the **whole** community learned that Aaron had died,
20: 29 had died, the **entire** house of Israel mourned for him thirty days.
21: 8 put it up on a pole; **anyone** who is bitten can look at it and live."
21: 23 He mustered his **entire** army and marched out into the desert
21: 25 Israel captured **all** the cities of the Amorites and occupied them,
21: 25 captured all the cities of the Amorites and occupied **[RPH]** them,
21: 25 including Heshbon and **all** its surrounding settlements.
21: 26 of Moab and had taken from him **all** his land as far as the Arnon.
21: 33 and his **whole** army marched out to meet them in battle at Edrei.
21: 34 I have handed him over to you, with his **whole** army and his land.
21: 35 they struck him down, together with his sons and his **whole** army,
22: 2 Now Balak son of Zippor saw **all** that Israel had done to the
22: 4 "This horde is going to lick up **everything** around us, as an ox
22: 17 I will reward you handsomely and do **whatever** [+889] you say.
23: 6 him standing beside his offering, with **all** the princes of Moab.
23: 13 you can see them; you will see only a part but not **all** *of* them.
23: 26 "Did I not tell you I must do **whatever** [+889] the LORD says?"
24: 17 crush the foreheads of Moab, the skulls of **all** the sons of Sheth.
25: 4 "Take **all** the leaders of these people, kill them and expose them in
25: 6 the **whole** assembly of Israel while they were weeping at the
26: 2 "Take a census of the **whole** Israelite community by families—
26: 2 **all** *those* twenty years old or more who are able to serve in the
26: 43 **All** *of* them were Shuhamite clans; and those numbered were
26: 62 **All** the male Levites a month old or more numbered 23,000.
27: 2 Eleazar the priest, the leaders and the **whole** assembly, and said,
27: 16 "May the LORD, the God of the spirits of **all** mankind, appoint a
27: 19 and the **entire** assembly and commission him in their presence.
27: 20 of your authority so the **whole** Israelite community will obey him.
27: 21 and the **entire** community of the Israelites will go out,
27: 21 will go out, and at his command they will come in." **[RPH]**
27: 22 had him stand before Eleazar the priest and the **whole** assembly.
28: 18 first day hold a sacred assembly and do **no** [+4202] regular work.
28: 25 day hold a sacred assembly and do **no** [+4202] regular work.
28: 26 of Weeks, hold a sacred assembly and do **no** [+4202] regular work.
29: 1 month hold a sacred assembly and do **no** [+4202] regular work.
29: 7 You must deny yourselves and do **no** [+4202] work.
29: 12 hold a sacred assembly and do **no** [+4202] regular work.
29: 35 the eighth day hold an assembly and do **no** [+4202] regular work.
29: 40 [30:1] Moses told the Israelites **all** that the LORD commanded
30: 2 [30:3] must not break his word but must do **everything** he said.
30: 4 [30:5] **all** her vows and every pledge by which she obligated
30: 4 [30:5] and **every** pledge by which she obligated herself will stand.
30: 5 [30:6] **none of** [+4202] her vows or the pledges by which she
30: 9 [30:10] "**Any** vow or obligation taken by a widow or divorced
30: 11 [30:12] **all** her vows or the pledges by which she obligated herself
30: 11 [30:12] or **[RPH]** the pledges by which she obligated herself will
30: 12 [30:13] **none** [+4202] of the vows or pledges that came from her
30: 13 [30:14] Her husband may confirm or nullify **any** vow she makes
30: 13 [30:14] any vow she makes or **any** sworn pledge to deny herself.
30: 14 [30:15] he confirms **all** her vows or the pledges binding on her.
30: 14 [30:15] all her vows or **[RPH]** the pledges binding on her.
31: 4 Send into battle a thousand men from **each** *of* the tribes of Israel."
31: 7 as the LORD commanded Moses, and killed **every** man.
31: 9 Midianite women and children and took **all** the Midianite herds,
31: 9 took all the Midianite herds, **[RPH]** flocks and goods as plunder.
31: 9 took all the Midianite herds, flocks and **[RPH]** goods as plunder.
31: 10 They burned **all** the towns where the Midianites had settled,
31: 10 towns where the Midianites had settled, as well as **all** their camps.
31: 11 They took **all** the plunder and spoils, including the people
31: 11 They took all the plunder and **[RPH]** spoils, including the people
31: 13 **all** the leaders of the community went to meet them outside the
31: 15 "Have you allowed **all** the women to live?" he asked them.
31: 17 Now kill **all** the boys. And kill every woman who has slept with a
31: 17 kill all the boys. And kill **every** woman who has slept with a man,
31: 18 but save for yourselves **every** girl who has never slept with a man.
31: 19 "**All** *of* you who have killed anyone or touched anyone who was
31: 19 or **[RPH]** touched anyone who was killed must stay outside the
31: 20 Purify **every** garment as well as everything made of leather,
31: 20 Purify every garment as well as **everything** [+3998] made of
31: 20 as well as everything made of leather, **[RPH]** goat hair or wood."
31: 20 as well as everything made of leather, goat hair or **[RPH]** wood."
31: 23 **anything** [+1821] else that can withstand fire must be put through
31: 23 **whatever** [+889] cannot withstand fire must be put through that
31: 27 soldiers who took part in the battle and the **rest** *of* the community.
31: 30 whether persons, cattle, donkeys, sheep, goats or **other**[s] animals.
31: 35 and 32,000 women who had never slept with **a** man.
31: 51 the priest accepted from them the gold—**all** the crafted articles.
31: 52 **All** the gold from the commanders of thousands and commanders
32: 13 until the **whole** generation of those who had done evil in his sight
32: 15 following him, he will again leave **all** this people in the desert,
32: 21 if **all** of you will go armed over the Jordan before the LORD until
32: 26 and **[NIE]** herds will remain here in the cities of Gilead.
32: 27 your servants, **every** man armed for battle, will cross over to fight
32: 29 "If the Gadites and Reubenites, **every** man armed for battle,
33: 3 They marched out boldly in full view of **all** the Egyptians,
33: 4 who were burying **all** their firstborn, whom the LORD had struck
33: 52 drive out **all** the inhabitants of the land before you. Destroy all
33: 52 Destroy **all** their carved images and their cast idols, and demolish
33: 52 Destroy all their carved images and **[RPH]** their cast idols,
33: 52 and their cast idols, and demolish **all** their high places.
35: 3 pasturelands for their cattle, flocks and **all** their other livestock.
35: 7 *In* **all** you must give the Levites forty-eight towns, together with
35: 15 so that **anyone** who has killed another accidentally can flee there.
35: 22 or throws **something** [+3998] at him unintentionally
35: 23 seeing him, drops **a** stone on him that could kill him, and he dies,
35: 29 throughout the generations to come, **wherever** [+928] you live.
35: 30 " '**Anyone** who kills a person is to be put to death as a murderer
36: 8 **Every** daughter who inherits land in any Israelite tribe must marry
Dt 1: 1 These are the words Moses spoke to **all** Israel in the desert east of
1: 3 Moses proclaimed to the Israelites **all** that the LORD had
1: 7 go to **all** the neighboring peoples in the Arabah, in the mountains,
1: 18 at that time I told you **everything** [+1821+2021] you were to do.
1: 19 went toward the hill country of the Amorites through **all** that vast
1: 22 **all** *of* you came to me and said, "Let us send men ahead to spy out
1: 30 will fight for you, **as** [+889+3869] he did for you in Egypt,
1: 31 carries his son, **all** the way you went until you reached this place."
1: 41 and fight, **as** [+889+3869] the LORD our God commanded us."
2: 7 The LORD your God has blessed you in **all** the work of your
2: 14 that **entire** generation of fighting men had perished from the camp,
2: 16 Now when the last of **[NIE]** these fighting men among the people
2: 25 to put the terror and fear of you on **all** the nations under heaven.
2: 32 and **all** his army came out to meet us in battle at Jahaz,
2: 33 we struck him down, together with his sons and his **whole** army.
2: 34 At that time we took **all** his towns and completely destroyed
2: 34 we took all his towns and completely destroyed **them**[s] [+6551]—
2: 36 was too strong for us. The LORD our God gave us **all** of them.
2: 37 **in accordance with** [+889] the command of the LORD our God,
2: 37 you did not encroach on **any** *of* the land of the Ammonites,
3: 1 Og king of Bashan with his **whole** army marched out to meet us in
3: 2 for I have handed him over to you with his **whole** army and his
3: 3 God also gave into our hands Og king of Bashan and **all** his army.
3: 4 At that time we took **all** his cities. There was not one of the sixty
3: 4 from them—the **whole** region of Argob, Og's kingdom in Bashan.
3: 5 **All** these cities were fortified with high walls and with gates
3: 6 we had done with Sihon king of Heshbon, destroying **every** city—
3: 7 **all** the livestock and the plunder from their cities we carried off for
3: 10 We took **all** the towns on the plateau, and all Gilead, and all

Dt 3:10 and **all** Gilead, and all Bashan as far as Salecah and Edrei,
3:10 and all Gilead, and **all** Bashan as far as Salecah and Edrei,
3:13 The rest of Gilead and also **all** *of* Bashan, the kingdom of Og,
3:13 (The **whole** region of Argob in Bashan used to be known as a land
3:13 (The whole region of Argob in **[RPH]** Bashan used to be known
3:14 took the **whole** region of Argob as far as the border of the
3:18 **all** your able-bodied men, armed for battle, must cross over ahead
3:21 "You have seen with your own eyes **all** that the LORD your God
3:21 The LORD will do the same to **all** the kingdoms over there where
4:3 among you **everyone** [+408+2021] who followed the Baal of Peor,
4:4 **all** *of* you who held fast to the LORD your God are still alive
4:6 to the nations, who will hear about **all** these decrees and say,
4:7 the LORD our God is near us **whenever** [+928] we pray to him?
4:8 and laws as this **body** *of* laws I am setting before you today?
4:9 or let them slip from your heart **as long** [+3427] **as** you live.
4:10 so that they may learn to revere me **as long** [+2021+3427] **as** they
4:15 You saw no form *of* **any** *kind* the day the LORD spoke to you at
4:16 an image of **any** shape, whether formed like a man or a woman,
4:17 or like **any** animal on earth or any bird that flies in the air,
4:17 or like any animal on earth or **any** bird that flies in the air,
4:18 or like **any** creature that moves along the ground or any fish in the
4:18 that moves along the ground or **any** fish in the waters below.
4:19 and see the sun, the moon and the stars—**all** the heavenly array—
4:19 worshiping things the LORD your God has apportioned to **all** the
4:19 your God has apportioned to all the nations under **[RPH]** heaven.
4:23 do not make for yourselves an idol in the form of **anything** the
4:25 if you then become corrupt and make **any** kind of idol, doing evil
4:29 you will find him if you look for him with **all** your heart and with
4:29 him if you look for him with all your heart and with **all** your soul.
4:30 you are in distress and **all** these things have happened to you,
4:34 like **all** the things the LORD your God did for you in Egypt
4:40 live long in the land the LORD your God gives you for **all** time.
4:49 included **all** the Arabah east of the Jordan, as far as the Sea of the
5:1 Moses summoned **all** Israel and said: Hear, O Israel, the decrees
5:3 this covenant, but with us, with **all** *of* us who are alive here today.
5:8 "You shall not make for yourself an idol in the form of **anything** in
5:13 Six days you shall labor and do **all** your work,
5:14 On it you shall not do **any** work, neither you, nor your son
5:14 or maidservant, nor your ox, your donkey or **any** *of* your animals,
5:21 his ox or donkey, or **anything** that belongs to your neighbor."
5:22 to your **whole** assembly there on the mountain from out of the fire,
5:23 **all** the leading men of your tribes and your elders came to me.
5:26 For what mortal man has **ever** heard the voice of the living God
5:27 Go near and listen to **all** that the LORD our God says. Then tell
5:27 Then tell us **whatever** [+889] the LORD our God tells you.
5:28 what this people said to you. **Everything** they said was good.
5:29 would be inclined to fear me and keep **all** my commands always,
5:29 to fear me and keep all my commands **always** [+2021+3427],
5:31 you stay here with me so that I may give you **all** the commands,
5:33 Walk in **all** the way that the LORD your God has commanded
6:2 your God **as long** [+3427] **as** you live by keeping all his decrees
6:2 LORD your God as long as you live by keeping **all** his decrees
6:5 Love the LORD your God with **all** your heart and with all your
6:5 all your heart and with **all** your soul and with all your strength.
6:5 all your heart and with all your soul and with **all** your strength.
6:11 houses filled with **all** *kinds of* good things you did not provide,
6:19 thrusting out **all** your enemies before you, as the LORD said.
6:22 and terrible—upon Egypt and Pharaoh and his **whole** household.
6:24 The LORD commanded us to obey **all** these decrees and to fear
6:24 so that we might **always** [+2021+3427] prosper and be kept alive,
6:25 if we are careful to obey **all** this law before the LORD our God,
7:6 The LORD your God has chosen you out of **all** the peoples on the
7:7 choose you because you were more numerous than **other**[s] peoples,
7:7 than other peoples, for you were the fewest of **all** peoples.
7:14 You will be blessed more than **any** other people; none of your men
7:15 The LORD will keep you free from **every** disease. He will not
7:15 He will not inflict on you **[RPH]** the horrible diseases you knew
7:15 you knew in Egypt, but he will inflict them on **all** who hate you.
7:16 You must destroy **all** the peoples the LORD your God gives over
7:18 well what the LORD your God did to Pharaoh and to **all** Egypt.
7:19 The LORD your God will do the same to **all** the peoples you now
8:1 Be careful to follow **every** command I am giving you today,
8:2 Remember how the LORD your God led you **all** the way in the
8:3 but on **every** word that comes from the mouth of the LORD.
8:9 where bread will not be scarce and you will lack **nothing** [+4202];
8:13 and your silver and gold increase and **all** you have is multiplied,
9:10 On them were **all** the commandments the LORD proclaimed to
9:18 and drank no water, because of **all** the sin you had committed,
10:12 to fear the LORD your God, to walk in **all** his ways, to love him,
10:12 to serve the LORD your God with **all** your heart and with all your
10:12 the LORD your God with all your heart and with **all** your soul,
10:14 even the highest heavens, the earth and **everything** in it.
10:15 chose you, their descendants, above **all** the nations, as it is today.
11:1 his decrees, his laws and his commands **always** [+2021+3427].
11:3 of Egypt, both to Pharaoh king of Egypt and to his **whole** country;
11:6 when the earth opened its mouth right in the middle of **all** Israel
11:6 their tents and **every** living thing that belonged to them.
11:7 it was your own eyes that saw **all** these great things the LORD
11:8 Observe therefore **all** the commands I am giving you today,
11:13 and to serve him with **all** your heart and with all your soul—
11:13 and to serve him with all your heart and with **all** your soul—
11:22 If you carefully observe **all** these commands I am giving you to
11:22 LORD your God, to walk in **all** his ways and to hold fast to him—
11:23 then the LORD will drive out **all** these nations before you,
11:24 **Every** place where you set your foot will be yours: Your territory
11:25 will put the terror and fear of you on the **whole** land, wherever you
11:32 be sure that you obey **all** the decrees and laws I am setting before
12:1 you to possess—**as long** [+2021+3427] **as** you live in the land.
12:2 Destroy completely **all** the places on the high mountains and on the
12:2 under **every** spreading tree where the nations you are dispossessing
12:5 from among **all** your tribes to put his Name there for his dwelling.
12:7 and shall rejoice in **everything** you have put your hand to,
12:8 You are not to do **as** [+889+3869] we do here today, everyone as
12:8 You are not to do as we do here today, everyone **as** he sees fit,
12:10 and he will give you rest from **all** your enemies around you
12:11 for his Name—there you are to bring **everything** I command you:
12:11 and **all** the choice possessions you have vowed to the LORD.
12:13 sacrifice your burnt offerings **anywhere** [+928+5226] you please.
12:14 one of your tribes, and there observe **everything** I command you.
12:15 you may slaughter your animals in **any** *of* your towns and eat as
12:15 in any of your towns and eat as **much** *of* the meat as you want,
12:17 of your herds and flocks, or **whatever** you have vowed to give,
12:18 you are to rejoice before the LORD your God in **everything** you
12:19 Be careful not to neglect the Levites **as long** [+3427] **as** you **live** in
12:20 like some meat," then you may eat as **much** *of* it as you want.
12:21 and in your own towns you may eat as **much** *of* them as you want.
12:28 Be careful to obey **all** these regulations I am giving you, so that it
12:31 their gods, they do **all** *kinds of* detestable things the LORD hates.
12:32 [13:1] See that you do **all** I command you; do not add to it or take
13:3 [13:4] you to find out whether you love him with **all** your heart
13:3 [13:4] you love him with all your heart and with **all** your soul.
13:9 [13:10] putting him to death, and then the hands of **all** the people.
13:11 [13:12] **all** Israel will hear and be afraid, and no one among you
13:15 [13:16] both its **people**[s] [+889+928] and its livestock.
13:16 [13:17] Gather **all** the plunder of the town into the middle of the
13:16 [13:17] **all** its plunder as a whole burnt offering to the LORD
13:18 [13:19] keeping **all** his commands that I am giving you today
14:2 Out of **all** the peoples on the face of the earth, the LORD has
14:3 Do not eat **any** detestable thing.
14:6 You may eat **any** animal that has a split hoof divided in two
14:9 Of **all** the creatures living in the water, you may eat any that has
14:9 living in the water, you may eat **any** that has fins and scales.
14:10 But **anything** that does not have fins and scales you may not eat;
14:11 You may eat **any** clean bird.
14:14 **any** kind of raven,
14:19 **All** flying insects that swarm are unclean to you; do not eat them.
14:20 But **any** winged creature that is clean you may eat.
14:21 Do not eat **anything** you find already dead. You may give it to an
14:22 Be sure to set aside a tenth of **all** that your fields produce each
14:23 may learn to revere the LORD your God **always** [+2021+3427].
14:26 Use the silver to buy **whatever** [+889] you like: cattle, sheep,
14:26 sheep, wine or other fermented drink, or **anything** you wish.
14:28 bring **all** the tithes of that year's produce and store it in your towns,
14:29 so that the LORD your God may bless you in **all** the work of your
15:2 **Every** creditor shall cancel the loan he has made to his fellow
15:5 are careful to follow **all** these commands I am giving you today.
15:10 because of this the LORD your God will bless you in **all** your
15:10 bless you in all your work and in **everything** you put your hand to.
15:18 And the LORD your God will bless you in **everything** you do.
15:19 Set apart for the LORD your God **every** firstborn male of your
15:21 If an animal has a defect, is lame or blind, or has **any** serious flaw,
16:3 so that **all** the days of your life you may remember the time of your
16:4 Let no yeast be found in your possession in **all** your land for seven
16:15 For the LORD your God will bless you in **all** your harvest
16:15 will bless you in all your harvest and in **all** the work of your hands,
16:16 Three times a year **all** your men must appear before the LORD
16:18 officials for each of your tribes in **every** town the LORD your
16:21 Do not set up **any** wooden Asherah pole beside the altar you build
17:1 your God an ox or a sheep that has **any** defect or flaw in it,
17:3 to them or to the sun or the moon or **[NIE]** the stars of the sky,
17:7 first in putting him to death, and then the hands of **all** the people.
17:10 will choose. Be careful to do **everything** they direct you to do.
17:13 **All** the people will hear and be afraid, and will not be
17:14 you say, "Let us set a king over us like **all** the nations around us,"
17:19 he is to read it **all** the days of his life so that he may learn to revere
17:19 and follow carefully **all** the words of this law and these decrees
18:1 The priests, who are Levites—indeed the **whole** tribe of Levi—
18:5 chosen them and their descendants out of **all** your tribes to stand

Dt 18: 5 and minister in the LORD's name **always** [+2021+3427].
18: 6 If a Levite moves from one of your towns **anywhere** in Israel
18: 6 and comes in **all** earnestness to the place the LORD will choose,
18: 7 he may minister in the name of the LORD his God like **all** his
18: 12 **Anyone** who does these things is detestable to the LORD,
18: 16 For **this**[s] is what you asked of the LORD your God at Horeb on
18: 18 in his mouth, and he will tell them **everything** I command him.
19: 3 as an inheritance, so that **anyone** who kills a man may flee there.
19: 8 your forefathers, and gives you the **whole** land he promised them,
19: 9 because you carefully follow **all** these laws I command you today—
19: 9 LORD your God and to walk **always** [+2021+3427] in his ways—
19: 15 One witness is not enough to convict a man accused of **any** crime
19: 15 accused of any crime or **[RPH]** offense he may have committed.
19: 15 accused of any crime or offense **[RPH]** he may have committed.
20: 11 **all** the people in it shall be subject to forced labor and shall work
20: 13 God delivers it into your hand, put to the sword **all** the men in it.
20: 14 the children, the livestock and **everything** else in the city,
20: 14 else in the city, you may take **these**[s] as plunder for yourselves.
20: 15 This is how you are to treat **all** the cities that are at a distance from
20: 16 you as an inheritance, do not leave alive **anything** that breathes.
20: 18 they will teach you to follow **all** the detestable things they do in
21: 5 name of the LORD and to decide **all** cases of dispute and assault.
21: 5 the LORD and to decide all cases of dispute and **[RPH]** assault.
21: 6 **all** the elders of the town nearest the body shall wash their hands
21: 17 wife as the firstborn by giving him a double share of **all** he has.
21: 21 **all** the men of his town shall stone him to death. You must purge
21: 21 the evil from among you. **All** Israel will hear of it and be afraid.
22: 3 you find your brother's donkey or his cloak or **anything** he loses.
22: 5 for the LORD your God detests **anyone** who does this.
22: 6 either in **a** tree or on the ground, and the mother is sitting on the
22: 19 to be his wife; he must not divorce her **as long** [+3427] **as** he **lives**.
22: 29 violated her. He can never divorce her **as long** [+3427] **as** he **lives**.
23: 6 [23:7] with them **as long** [+3427+4200+6409] **as** you **live**.
23: 9 [23:10] keep away from **everything** [+1821] impure.
23: 18 [23:19] into the house of the LORD your God to pay **any** vow,
23: 19 [23:20] or food or **anything** [+1821] else that may earn interest.
23: 20 [23:21] that the LORD your God may bless you in **everything**
24: 5 he must not be sent to war or have **any** other duty laid on him.
24: 8 diseases be very careful to do **exactly as** [+889+3869] the priests,
24: 19 so that the LORD your God may bless you in **all** the work of your
25: 16 For the LORD your God detests **anyone** who does these things,
25: 16 anyone who does these things, **anyone** who deals dishonestly.
25: 18 met you on your journey and cut off **all** who were lagging behind;
25: 19 When the LORD your God gives you rest from **all** the enemies
26: 2 take some of the firstfruits of **all** that you produce from the soil of
26: 11 the aliens among you shall rejoice in **all** the good things the
26: 12 When you have finished setting aside a tenth of **all** your produce in
26: 13 the fatherless and the widow, according to **all** you commanded.
26: 14 the LORD my God; I have done **everything** you commanded me.
26: 16 carefully observe them with **all** your heart and with all your soul.
26: 16 carefully observe them with all your heart and with **all** your soul.
26: 18 as he promised, and that you are to keep **all** his commands.
26: 19 fame and honor high above **all** the nations he has made and that
27: 1 the people: "Keep **all** these commands that I give you today.
27: 3 Write on them **all** the words of this law when you have crossed
27: 8 you shall write very clearly **all** the words of this law on these
27: 9 who are Levites, said to **all** Israel, "Be silent, O Israel, and listen!
27: 14 The Levites shall recite to **all** the people of Israel in a loud voice:
27: 15 and sets it up in secret." Then **all** the people shall say, "Amen!"
27: 16 his father or his mother." Then **all** the people shall say, "Amen!"
27: 17 boundary stone." Then **all** the people shall say, "Amen!"
27: 18 blind astray on the road." Then **all** the people shall say, "Amen!"
27: 19 or the widow." Then **all** the people shall say, "Amen!"
27: 20 dishonors his father's bed." Then **all** the people shall say, "Amen!"
27: 21 "Cursed is the man who has sexual relations with **any** animal."
27: 21 relations with any animal." Then **all** the people shall say, "Amen!"
27: 22 daughter of his mother." Then **all** the people shall say, "Amen!"
27: 23 with his mother-in-law." Then **all** the people shall say, "Amen!"
27: 24 kills his neighbor secretly." Then **all** the people shall say, "Amen!"
27: 25 to kill an innocent person." Then **all** the people shall say, "Amen!"
27: 26 law by carrying them out." Then **all** the people shall say, "Amen!"
28: 1 your God and carefully follow **all** his commands I give you today,
28: 1 the LORD your God will set you high above **all** the nations on
28: 2 **All** these blessings will come upon you and accompany you if you
28: 8 a blessing on your barns and on **everything** you put your hand to.
28: 10 **all** the peoples on earth will see that you are called by the name of
28: 12 rain on your land in season and to bless **all** the work of your hands.
28: 14 Do not turn aside from **any** *of* the commands I give you today,
28: 15 do not carefully follow **all** his commands and decrees I am giving
28: 15 you today, **all** these curses will come upon you and overtake you:
28: 20 confusion and rebuke in **everything** you put your hand to,
28: 25 and you will become a thing of horror to **all** the kingdoms on earth.
28: 26 Your carcasses will be food for **all** the birds of the air and the
28: 29 unsuccessful in everything you do; **day after day** [+2021+3427]
28: 32 out your eyes watching for them **day after day** [+2021+3427],
28: 33 do not know will eat what your land and **[NIE]** labor produce,
28: 33 and you will have nothing but cruel oppression **all** your days.
28: 37 and ridicule to **all** the nations where the LORD will drive you.
28: 40 You will have olive trees **throughout** [+928] your country
28: 42 Swarms of locusts will take over **all** your trees and the crops of
28: 45 **All** these curses will come upon you. They will pursue you
28: 47 your God joyfully and gladly in the time of **prosperity** [+8044],
28: 48 therefore in hunger and thirst, in nakedness and **dire** poverty,
28: 52 They will lay siege to **all** the cities throughout your land until the
28: 52 They will lay siege to all the cities **throughout** [+928] your land
28: 52 They will besiege **all** the cities throughout the land the LORD
28: 52 They will besiege all the cities **throughout** [+928] the land the
28: 55 It will be **all** he has left because of the suffering your enemy will
28: 55 your enemy will inflict on you during the siege of **all** your cities.
28: 57 For she intends to eat them secretly **[RPH]** during the siege
28: 58 If you do not carefully follow **all** the words of this law, which are
28: 60 He will bring upon you **all** the diseases of Egypt that you dreaded,
28: 61 The LORD will also bring on you **every** *kind of* sickness
28: 61 and **[RPH]** disaster not recorded in this Book of the Law,
28: 64 the LORD will scatter you among **all** nations, from one end of the
29: 2 [29:1] Moses summoned **all** the Israelites and said to them: Your
29: 2 [29:1] Your eyes have seen **all** that the LORD did in Egypt to
29: 2 [29:1] in Egypt to Pharaoh, to **all** his officials and to all his land.
29: 2 [29:1] in Egypt to Pharaoh, to all his officials and to **all** his land.
29: 9 [29:8] so that you may prosper in **everything** you do.
29: 10 [29:9] **All** *of* you are standing today in the presence of the
29: 10 [29:9] your elders and officials, and **all** the other men of Israel,
29: 20 [29:19] **All** the curses written in this book will fall upon him,
29: 21 [29:20] The LORD will single him out from **all** the tribes of
29: 21 [29:20] according to **all** the curses of the covenant written in this
29: 23 [29:22] The **whole** land will be a burning waste of salt
29: 23 [29:22] nothing sprouting, **no** [+4202] vegetation growing on it.
29: 24 [29:23] **All** the nations will ask: "Why has the LORD done this
29: 27 [29:26] so that he brought on it **all** the curses written in this book.
29: 29 [29:28] that we may follow **all** the words of this law.
30: 1 When **all** these blessings and curses I have set before you come
30: 1 the LORD your God disperses you among **[NIE]** the nations,
30: 2 return to the LORD your God and obey him with **all** your heart
30: 2 with **all** your soul according to everything I command you today,
30: 2 with all your soul according to **everything** I command you today,
30: 3 and gather you again from **all** the nations where he scattered you.
30: 6 so that you may love him with **all** your heart and with all your soul,
30: 6 so that you may love him with all your heart and with **all** your soul,
30: 7 The LORD your God will put **all** these curses on your enemies
30: 8 the LORD and follow **all** his commands I am giving you today.
30: 9 the LORD your God will make you most prosperous in **all** the
30: 10 turn to the LORD your God with **all** your heart and with all your
30: 10 to the LORD your God with all your heart and with **all** your soul.
31: 1 Then Moses went out and spoke these words to **all** Israel:
31: 5 to you, and you must do to them **all** that I have commanded you.
31: 7 summoned Joshua and said to him in the presence of **all** Israel,
31: 9 ark of the covenant of the LORD, and to **all** the elders of Israel.
31: 11 when **all** Israel comes to appear before the LORD your God at the
31: 11 you shall read this law before **them**[s] [+3776] in their hearing.
31: 12 LORD your God and follow carefully **all** the words of this law.
31: 13 learn to fear the LORD your God **as long** [+2021+3427] **as** you
31: 18 that day because of **all** their wickedness in turning to other gods.
31: 28 Assemble before me **all** the elders of your tribes and all your
31: 30 beginning to end in the hearing of the **whole** assembly of Israel:
32: 4 He is the Rock, his works are perfect, and **all** his ways are just.
32: 27 'Our hand has triumphed; the LORD has not done **all** this.' "
32: 44 and spoke **all** the words of this song in the hearing of the people.
32: 45 When Moses finished reciting **all** these words to all Israel,
32: 45 When Moses finished reciting all these words to **all** Israel,
32: 46 "Take to heart **all** the words I have solemnly declared to you this
32: 46 so that you may command your children to obey carefully **all** the
33: 3 it is you who love the people; **all** the holy ones are in your hand.
33: 12 of the LORD rest secure in him, for he shields him **all** day long,
34: 1 There the LORD showed him the **whole** land—from Gilead to
34: 2 **all** *of* Naphtali, the territory of Ephraim and Manasseh, all the land
34: 2 and Manasseh, **all** the land of Judah as far as the western sea,
34: 11 who did **all** those miraculous signs and wonders the LORD sent
34: 11 in Egypt—to Pharaoh and to **all** his officials and to his whole land.
34: 11 in Egypt—to Pharaoh and to all his officials and to his **whole** land.
34: 12 For no one has ever shown **[RPH]** the mighty power or performed
34: 12 or **[RPH]** performed the awesome deeds that Moses did in the
34: 12 or performed the awesome deeds that Moses did in the sight of **all**
Jos 1: 2 Now then, you and **all** these people, get ready to cross the Jordan
1: 3 I will give you **every** place where you set your foot, as I promised
1: 4 and from the great river, the Euphrates—**all** the Hittite country—
1: 5 No one will be able to stand up against you **all** the days of your
1: 7 Be careful to obey **all** the law my servant Moses gave you;
1: 7 that you may be successful **wherever** [+889+928] you go.

Jos 1: 8 so that you may be careful to do **everything** written in it.
1: 9 for the LORD your God will be with you **wherever** [+889+928]
1: 14 **all** your fighting men, fully armed, must cross over ahead of your
1: 16 "**Whatever** [+889] you have commanded us we will do,
1: 16 us we will do, and **wherever** [+448+889] you send us we will go.
1: 17 Just as we **fully** obeyed Moses, so we will obey you. Only may the
1: 18 **Whoever** [+408+889] rebels against your word and does not obey
1: 18 **whatever** [+889] you may command them, will be put to death.
2: 3 your house, because they have come to spy out the **whole** land."
2: 9 so that **all** who live in this country are melting in fear because of
2: 13 and mother, my brothers and sisters, and **all** who belong to them,
2: 18 and mother, your brothers and **all** your family into your house.
2: 19 If **anyone** goes outside your house into the street, his blood will be
2: 19 As for **anyone** who is in the house with you, his blood will be on
2: 22 until the pursuers had searched **all** along the road and returned
2: 23 son of Nun and told him **everything** that had happened to them.
2: 24 "The LORD has surely given the **whole** land into our hands;
2: 24 into our hands; **all** the people are melting in fear because of us."
3: 1 and **all** the Israelites set out from Shittim and went to the Jordan,
3: 7 to Joshua, "Today I will begin to exalt you in the eyes of **all** Israel,
3: 11 the ark of the covenant of the Lord of **all** the earth will go into the
3: 13 the Lord of **all** the earth—set foot in the Jordan, its waters flowing
3: 15 Now the Jordan *is* **at flood stage** [+1536+4848+6584] all during
3: 15 Now the Jordan is at flood stage **all** during harvest.
3: 17 while **all** Israel passed by until the whole nation had completed the
3: 17 while all Israel passed by until the **whole** nation had completed the
4: 1 When the **whole** nation had finished crossing the Jordan,
4: 10 in the middle of the Jordan until **everything** [+1821+2021]
4: 10 by the people, **just as** [+889+3869] Moses had directed Joshua.
4: 11 and as soon as **all** *of* them had crossed, the ark of the LORD
4: 14 That day the LORD exalted Joshua in the sight of **all** Israel;
4: 14 they revered him **all** the days of his life, just as they had revered
4: 18 to their place and ran **at flood** [+1536+6584] **stage** as before.
4: 24 so that **all** the peoples of the earth might know that the hand of the
4: 24 so that you might **always** [+2021+3427] fear the LORD your
5: 1 Now when **all** the Amorite kings west of the Jordan and all the
5: 1 **all** the Canaanite kings along the coast heard how the LORD had
5: 4 **All** those who came out of Egypt—all the men of military age—
5: 4 All those who came out of Egypt—**all** the men of military age—
5: 5 **All** the people that came out had been circumcised, but all the
5: 5 **all** the people born in the desert during the journey from Egypt had
5: 6 The Israelites had moved about in the desert forty years until **all**
5: 8 after the **whole** nation had been circumcised, they remained where
6: 3 March around the city once with **all** the armed men. Do this for six
6: 5 a long blast on the trumpets, have **all** the people give a loud shout;
6: 17 The city and **all** that is in it are to be devoted to the LORD.
6: 17 the prostitute and **all** who are with her in her house shall be spared,
6: 19 **All** the silver and gold and the articles of bronze and iron are
6: 21 the LORD and destroyed with the sword **every** living thing in it—
6: 22 the prostitute's house and bring her out and **all** who belong to her,
6: 23 her father and mother and brothers and **all** who belonged to her.
6: 23 They brought out her **entire** family and put them in a place outside
6: 24 they burned the whole city and **everything** in it, but they put the
6: 25 Rahab the prostitute, with her family and **all** who belonged to her,
6: 27 was with Joshua, and his fame spread **throughout** [+928] the land.
7: 3 they said, "Not **all** the people will have to go up against Ai.
7: 3 or three thousand men to take it and do not weary **all** the people,
7: 9 and the **other**[s] people of the country will hear about this
7: 15 shall be destroyed by fire, along with **all** that belongs to him.
7: 23 brought them to Joshua and **all** the Israelites and spread them out
7: 24 Then Joshua, together with **all** Israel, took Achan son of Zerah,
7: 24 his cattle, donkeys and sheep, his tent and **all** that he had,
7: 25 Then **all** Israel stoned him, and after they had stoned the rest,
8: 1 Take the **whole** army with you, and go up and attack Ai.
8: 3 So Joshua and the **whole** army moved out to attack Ai. He chose
8: 4 the city. Don't go very far from it. **All** *of* you be on the alert.
8: 5 I and **all** those with me will advance on the city, and when the men
8: 11 The **entire** force that was with him marched up and approached the
8: 13 **all** *those in* the camp to the north of the city and the ambush to the
8: 14 **all** the men of the city hurried out early in the morning to meet
8: 15 Joshua and **all** Israel let themselves be driven back before them,
8: 16 **All** the men of Ai were called to pursue them, and they pursued
8: 21 when Joshua and **all** Israel saw that the ambush had taken the city
8: 24 When Israel had finished killing **all** the men of Ai in the fields
8: 24 when **every** *one of* them had been put to the sword, all the
8: 24 **all** the Israelites returned to Ai and killed those who were in it.
8: 25 Twelve thousand men and women **[RPH]** fell that day—
8: 25 thousand men and women fell that day—**all** the people of Ai.
8: 26 that held out his javelin until he had destroyed **all** who lived in Ai.
8: 33 **All** Israel, aliens and citizens alike, with their elders, officials
8: 34 Afterward, Joshua read **all** the words of the law—the blessings
8: 34 and the curses—just as **it**[s] is written in the Book of the Law.
8: 35 There was not a word of **all** that Moses had commanded that
8: 35 that Joshua did not read to the **whole** assembly of Israel,
9: 1 Now when **all** the kings west of the Jordan heard about these
9: 1 along the **entire** coast of the Great Sea as far as Lebanon (the kings
9: 5 old clothes. **All** the bread of their food supply was dry and moldy.
9: 9 For we have heard reports of him: **all** that he did in Egypt,
9: 10 **all** that he did to the two kings of the Amorites east of the Jordan—
9: 11 And our elders and **all** those living in our country said to us,
9: 18 God of Israel. The **whole** assembly grumbled against the leaders,
9: 19 **all** the leaders answered, "We have given them our oath by the
9: 19 **[RPH]** "We have given them our oath by the LORD, the God of
9: 21 them be woodcutters and water carriers for the **entire** community."
9: 24 God had commanded his servant Moses to give you the **whole** land
9: 24 the whole land and to wipe out **all** its inhabitants from before you.
10: 2 it was larger than Ai, and **all** its men were good fighters.
10: 5 They moved up with **all** their troops and took up positions against
10: 6 because **all** the Amorite kings from the hill country have joined
10: 7 So Joshua marched up from Gilgal with his **entire** army, including
10: 7 Gilgal with his entire army, including **all** the best fighting men.
10: 9 After an **all-night** [+2021+4326] march from Gilgal, Joshua took
10: 15 Then Joshua returned with **all** Israel to the camp at Gilgal.
10: 21 The **whole** army then returned safely to Joshua in the camp at
10: 24 he summoned **all** the men of Israel and said to the army
10: 25 This is what the LORD will do to **all** the enemies you are going to
10: 28 to the sword and totally destroyed **everyone** [+2021+5883] in it.
10: 29 and **all** Israel with him moved on from Makkedah to Libnah
10: 30 and **everyone** [+2021+5883] in it Joshua put to the sword.
10: 31 and **all** Israel with him moved on from Libnah to Lachish;
10: 32 The city and **everyone** [+2021+5883] in it he put to the sword,
10: 32 it he put to the sword, **just as** [+889+3869] he had done to Libnah.
10: 34 and **all** Israel with him moved on from Lachish to Eglon;
10: 35 it to the sword and totally destroyed **everyone** [+2021+5883] in it,
10: 35 everyone in it, **just as** [+889+3869] they had done to Lachish.
10: 36 Then Joshua and **all** Israel with him went up from Eglon to Hebron
10: 37 together with its king, **[RPH]** its villages and everyone in it.
10: 37 with its king, its villages and **everyone** [+2021+5883] in it.
10: 37 **Just as** [+889+3869] at Eglon, they totally destroyed it
10: 37 they totally destroyed it and **everyone** [+2021+5883] in it.
10: 38 Joshua and **all** Israel with him turned around and attacked Debir.
10: 39 They took the city, its king and **[NIE]** its villages, and put them to
10: 39 **Everyone** [+5883] in it they totally destroyed. They left no
10: 40 So Joshua subdued the **whole** region, including the hill country,
10: 40 and the mountain slopes, together with **all** their kings.
10: 40 He totally destroyed **all** who breathed, just as the LORD,
10: 41 Barnea to Gaza and from the **whole** region of Goshen to Gibeon.
10: 42 **All** these kings and their lands Joshua conquered in one campaign,
10: 43 Then Joshua returned with **all** Israel to the camp at Gilgal.
11: 4 They came out with **all** their troops and a large number of horses
11: 5 **All** these kings joined forces and made camp together at the Waters
11: 6 because by this time tomorrow I will hand **all** *of* them over to
11: 7 his **whole** army came against them suddenly at the Waters of
11: 10 to the sword. (Hazor had been the head of **all** these kingdoms.)
11: 11 **Everyone** [+2021+5883] in it they put to the sword.
11: 11 They totally destroyed them, not sparing **anything** that breathed,
11: 12 Joshua took **all** these royal cities and their kings and put them to
11: 12 royal cities and **[RPH]** their kings and put them to the sword.
11: 13 Yet Israel did not burn **any** *of* the cities built on their mounds—
11: 14 The Israelites carried off for themselves **all** the plunder
11: 14 **all** the people they put to the sword until they completely destroyed
11: 14 they completely destroyed them, not sparing **anyone** that breathed.
11: 15 he left nothing undone of **all** that the LORD commanded Moses.
11: 16 So Joshua took this **entire** land: the hill country, all the Negev,
11: 16 the hill country, **all** the Negev, the whole region of Goshen,
11: 16 the hill country, all the Negev, the **whole** region of Goshen,
11: 17 He captured **all** their kings and struck them down, putting them to
11: 18 Joshua waged war against **all** these kings for a long time.
11: 19 a treaty of peace with the Israelites, who took them **all** in battle.
11: 21 from Hebron, Debir and Anab, from **all** the hill country of Judah,
11: 21 all the hill country of Judah, and from **all** the hill country of Israel.
11: 23 So Joshua took the **entire** land, just as the LORD had directed
11: 23 entire land, **just as** [+889+3869] the LORD had directed Moses,
12: 1 to Mount Hermon, including **all** the eastern side of the Arabah:
12: 5 **all** *of* Bashan to the border of the people of Geshur and Maacah,
12: 24 the king of Tirzah one thirty-one kings **in all**.
13: 2 land that remains: **all** the regions of the Philistines and Geshurites:
13: 2 all the regions of the Philistines and **[RPH]** Geshurites:
13: 4 from the south, **all** the land of the Canaanites, from Arah of the
13: 5 **all** Lebanon to the east, from Baal Gad below Mount Hermon to
13: 6 "As for **all** the inhabitants of the mountain regions from Lebanon
13: 6 that is, **all** the Sidonians, I myself will drive them out before the
13: 9 and included the **whole** plateau of Medeba as far as Dibon,
13: 10 **all** the towns of Sihon king of the Amorites, who ruled in Heshbon,
13: 11 **all** *of* Mount Hermon and all Bashan as far as Salecah—
13: 11 all of Mount Hermon and **all** Bashan as far as Salecah—
13: 12 that is, the **whole** kingdom of Og in Bashan, who had reigned in
13: 16 in the middle of the gorge, and the **whole** plateau past Medeba

Jos 13:17 to Heshbon and **all** its towns on the plateau, including Dibon,
13:21 —**all** the towns on the plateau and the entire realm of Sihon king of
13:21 on the plateau and the **entire** realm of Sihon king of the Amorites,
13:25 **all** the towns of Gilead and half the Ammonite country as far as
13:30 territory extending from Mahanaim and including **all** *of* Bashan,
13:30 including all of Bashan, the **entire** realm of Og king of Bashan—
13:30 king of Bashan—**all** the settlements of Jair in Bashan, sixty towns,
15:32 and Rimmon—a **total** *of* twenty-nine towns and their villages.
15:46 west of Ekron, **all** that were in the vicinity of Ashdod,
16: 9 It also included **all** the towns and their villages that were set aside
17:16 and **all** the Canaanites who live in the plain have iron chariots,
18: 1 The **whole** assembly of the Israelites gathered at Shiloh and set up
19: 8 **all** the villages around these towns as far as Baalath Beer (Ramah
20: 9 **Any** *of* the Israelites or any alien living among them who killed
20: 9 or **any** alien living among them who killed someone accidentally
21:19 **All** the towns for the priests, the descendants of Aaron,
21:26 **All** these ten towns and their pasturelands were given to the rest of
21:33 **All** the towns of the Gershonite clans were thirteen, together with
21:39 and Jazer, together with their pasturelands—four towns *in* **all**.
21:40 **All** the towns allotted to the Merarite clans, who were the rest of
21:41 Levites in the territory held by the Israelites were forty-eight *in* **all**,
21:42 had pasturelands surrounding it; this was true for **all** these towns.
21:43 So the LORD gave Israel **all** the land he had sworn to give their
21:44 every side, **just as** [+889+3869] he had sworn to their forefathers.
21:44 Not one of **[NIE]** their enemies withstood them; the LORD
21:44 withstood them; the LORD handed **all** their enemies over to them.
21:45 Not one of **all** the LORD's good promises to the house of Israel
21:45 promises to the house of Israel failed; **every** *one* was fulfilled.
22: 2 "You have done **all** that Moses the servant of the LORD
22: 2 and you have obeyed me in **everything** I commanded.
22: 5 to walk in **all** his ways, to obey his commands, to hold fast to him
22: 5 to hold fast to him and to serve him with **all** your heart and all your
22: 5 fast to him and to serve him with all your heart and **all** your soul."
22:12 the **whole** assembly of Israel gathered at Shiloh to go to war
22:14 they sent ten of the chief men, one for **each** *of* the tribes of Israel,
22:16 "The **whole** assembly of the LORD says: 'How could you break
22:18 tomorrow he will be angry with the **whole** community of Israel.
22:20 did not wrath come upon the **whole** community of Israel?
23: 1 the LORD had given Israel rest from **all** their enemies around
23: 2 summoned **all** Israel—their elders, leaders, judges and officials—
23: 3 You yourselves have seen **everything** the LORD your God has
23: 3 the LORD your God has done to **all** these nations for your sake;
23: 4 Remember how I have allotted as an inheritance for your tribes **all**
23: 6 be careful to obey **all** that is written in the Book of the Law of
23:14 "Now I am about to go the way of **all** the earth. You know with all
23:14 You know with **all** your heart and soul that not one of all the good
23:14 **[RPH]** soul that not one of all the good promises the LORD
23:14 soul that not one of **all** the good promises the LORD your God
23:14 has failed. **Every** promise has been fulfilled; not one has failed.
23:15 just as **every** good promise of the LORD your God has come true,
23:15 so the LORD will bring on you **all** the evil he has threatened,
24: 1 Then Joshua assembled **all** the tribes of Israel at Shechem.
24: 2 Joshua said to **all** the people, "This is what the LORD, the God of
24: 3 led him **throughout** [+928] Canaan and gave him many
24:17 He protected us on our **entire** journey and among all the nations
24:17 and among **all** the nations through which we traveled.
24:18 the LORD drove out before us **all** the nations, including the
24:27 "See!" he said to **all** the people. "This stone will be a witness
24:27 against us. It has heard **all** the words the LORD has said to us.
24:31 Israel served the LORD **throughout** the lifetime of Joshua
24:31 the lifetime of Joshua and **[RPH]** of the elders who outlived him
24:31 who had experienced **everything** [+5126] the LORD had done for
Jdg 1:25 put the city to the sword but spared the man and his **whole** family.
2: 4 When the angel of the LORD had spoken these things to **all** the
2: 7 The people served the LORD **throughout** the lifetime of Joshua
2: 7 the lifetime of Joshua and **[RPH]** of the elders who outlived him
2: 7 who had seen **all** the great things the LORD had done for Israel.
2:10 After that **whole** generation had been gathered to their fathers,
2:15 **Whenever** [+889+928] Israel went out to fight, the hand of the
2:18 saved them out of the hands of their enemies **as long as** the judge
3: 1 These are the nations the LORD left to test **all** *those* Israelites
3: 1 Israelites who had not experienced **any** *of* the wars in Canaan
3: 3 the five rulers of the Philistines, **all** the Canaanites, the Sidonians,
3:19 O king." The king said, "Quiet!" And **all** his attendants left him.
3:29 struck down about ten thousand Moabites, **all** vigorous and strong;
3:29 all vigorous and strong; **[RPH]** not a man escaped.
4:13 Sisera gathered together **[RPH]** his nine hundred iron chariots
4:13 together his nine hundred iron chariots and **all** the men with him,
4:15 LORD routed Sisera and **all** his chariots and army by the sword,
4:15 routed Sisera and all his chariots and **[RPH]** army by the sword,
4:16 **All** the troops of Sisera fell by the sword; not a man was left.
5:31 "So may **all** your enemies perish, O LORD! But may they who
6: 9 from the power of Egypt and from the hand of **all** your oppressors.
6:13 "if the LORD is with us, why has **all** this happened to us?
6:13 Where are **all** his wonders that our fathers told us about when they
6:31 But Joash replied to the hostile **crowd** [+889+6641] around him,
6:33 Now **all** the Midianites, Amalekites and other eastern peoples
6:35 He sent messengers **throughout** [+928] Manasseh, calling them to
6:37 If there is dew only on the fleece and **all** the ground is dry,
6:39 make the fleece dry and the ground covered with **[RPH]** dew."
6:40 Only the fleece was dry; **all** the ground was covered with dew.
7: 1 (that is, Gideon) and **all** his men camped at the spring of Harod.
7: 4 **[NIE]** if I say, 'This one shall not go with you,' he shall not go."
7: 5 "Separate **those**[s] who lap the water with their tongues like a dog
7: 5 their tongues like a dog from **those**[s] who kneel down to drink."
7: 6 to their mouths. **All** the rest got down on their knees to drink.
7: 7 into your hands. Let **all** the other men go, each to his own place."
7: 8 So Gideon sent the **rest**[s] *of* the Israelites to their tents but kept the
7:12 and **all** the other eastern peoples had settled in the valley,
7:14 God has given the Midianites and the **whole** camp into his hands."
7:16 he placed trumpets and empty jars in the hands of **all** *of* them,
7:18 When I and **all** who are with me blow our trumpets, then from all
7:18 from **all** around the camp blow yours and shout, 'For the LORD
7:21 around the camp, **all** the Midianites ran, crying out as they fled.
7:22 the LORD caused the men **throughout** [+928] the camp to turn
7:23 Israelites from Naphtali, Asher and **all** Manasseh were called out,
7:24 Gideon sent messengers **throughout** [+928] the hill country of
7:24 So **all** the men of Ephraim were called out and they took the waters
8:10 **all** that were left of the armies of the eastern peoples;
8:10 all that were left of **[RPH]** the armies of the eastern peoples;
8:12 but he pursued them and captured them, routing their **entire** army.
8:27 **All** Israel prostituted themselves by worshiping it there, and it
8:34 who had rescued them from the hands of **all** their enemies on every
8:35 (that is, Gideon) for **all** the good things he had done for them.
9: 1 brothers in Shechem and said to them and to **all** his mother's clan,
9: 2 "Ask **all** the citizens of Shechem, 'Which is better for you:
9: 2 to have **all** seventy of Jerub-Baal's sons rule over you, or just one
9: 3 When the brothers repeated **all** this to the citizens of Shechem,
9: 3 When the brothers repeated all this to **[NIE]** the citizens of
9: 6 **all** the citizens of Shechem and Beth Millo gathered beside the
9: 6 **[RPH]** Beth Millo gathered beside the great tree at the pillar in
9:14 "Finally **all** the trees said to the thornbush, 'Come and be our king.'
9:25 men on the hilltops to ambush and rob **everyone** who passed by,
9:34 So Abimelech and **all** his troops set out by night and took up
9:44 two companies rushed upon **those**[s] in the fields and struck them
9:45 **All** that day Abimelech pressed his attack against the city until he
9:46 **[NIE]** the citizens in the tower of Shechem went into the
9:47 Abimelech heard that **they**[s] [+1251+4463+8901] had assembled
9:48 he and **all** his men went up Mount Zalmon. He took an ax
9:49 So **all** the men cut branches and followed Abimelech. They piled
9:49 So **all** the people in the tower of Shechem, about a thousand men
9:51 however, was a strong tower, to which **all** the men and women—
9:51 to which all the men and women—**all** the people of the city—fled.
9:57 God also made the men of Shechem pay for **all** their wickedness.
10: 8 For eighteen years they oppressed **all** the Israelites on the east side
10:15 Do with us **whatever** [+3869] you think best, but please rescue us
10:18 the Ammonites will be the head of **all** those living in Gilead."
11: 8 and you will be our head over **all** who live in Gilead."
11:11 And he repeated **all** his words before the LORD in Mizpah.
11:20 He mustered **all** his men and encamped at Jahaz and fought with
11:21 the God of Israel, gave Sihon and **all** his men into Israel's hands,
11:21 Israel took over **all** the land of the Amorites who lived in that
11:22 capturing **all** *of* it from the Arnon to the Jabbok and from the desert
11:24 Likewise, **whatever** [+889] the LORD our God has given us,
11:26 the surrounding settlements and **all** the towns along the Arnon.
12: 4 Jephthah then called together **[RPH]** the men of Gilead
13: 4 or other fermented drink and that you do not eat **anything** unclean,
13: 7 or other fermented drink and do not eat **anything** unclean,
13:13 the LORD answered, "Your wife must do **all** that I have told her.
13:14 She must not eat **anything** that comes from the grapevine,
13:14 drink any wine or other fermented drink nor eat **anything** unclean.
13:14 She must do **everything** I have commanded her."
13:23 from our hands, nor shown us **all** these things or now told us this."
14: 3 acceptable woman among your relatives or among **all** our people?
16: 2 the place and lay in wait for him **all** night at the city gate.
16: 2 They made no move **during** the night, saying, "At dawn we'll kill
16:16 With such nagging she prodded him **day after day** [+2021+3427]
16:17 So he told her **everything** [+4213]. "No razor has ever been used
16:17 would leave me, and I would become as weak as **any** other man."
16:18 When Delilah saw that he had told her **everything** [+4213],
16:18 "Come back once more; he has told me **everything** [+4213]."
16:27 **all** the rulers of the Philistines were there, and on the roof were
16:30 and down came the temple on the rulers and **all** the people in it.
16:31 his brothers and his father's **whole** family went down to get him.
18:10 into your hands, a land that lacks **nothing whatever** [+401+1821]."
18:31 idols Micah had made, **all** the time the house of God was in Shiloh.
19:19 and the young man with us. We don't need **anything** [+1821]."
19:20 my house," the old man said. "Let me supply **whatever** you need.

Jdg 19:25 they raped her and abused her **throughout** the night, and at dawn
19:29 into twelve parts and sent them into **all** the areas of Israel.
19:30 **Everyone** who saw it said, "Such a thing has never been seen
20: 1 **all** the Israelites from Dan to Beersheba and from the land of
20: 2 The leaders of **all** the people of the tribes of Israel took their places
20: 2 The leaders of all the people of **[RPH]** the tribes of Israel took
20: 6 and sent one piece to **each** region of Israel's inheritance,
20: 7 Now, **all** you Israelites, speak up and give your verdict."
20: 8 **All** the people rose as one man, saying, "None of us will go home.
20:10 We'll take ten men out of every hundred from **all** the tribes of
20:10 it can give them what they deserve for **all** this vileness done in
20:11 So **all** the men of Israel got together and united as one man against
20:12 The tribes of Israel sent men **throughout** [+928] the tribe of
20:16 Among **all** these soldiers there were seven hundred chosen men
20:16 **each** *of* whom could sling a stone at a hair and not miss.
20:17 four hundred thousand swordsmen, **all** *of* them fighting men.
20:25 eighteen thousand Israelites, **all** *of* them armed with swords.
20:26 Then **[RPH]** the Israelites, all the people, went up to Bethel,
20:26 the Israelites, **all** the people, went up to Bethel, and there they sat
20:33 **All** the men of Israel moved from their places and took up
20:34 ten thousand of **[NIE]** Israel's finest men made a frontal attack on
20:35 Israelites struck down 25,100 Benjamites, **all** armed with swords.
20:37 dash into Gibeah, spread out and put the **whole** city to the sword.
20:44 Eighteen thousand Benjamites fell, **all** *of* them valiant fighters.
20:46 On that day twenty-five thousand Benjamite swordsmen **[RPH]**
20:46 thousand Benjamite swordsmen fell, **all** *of* them valiant fighters.
20:48 the sword, including the animals and **everything** else they found.
20:48 else they found. **All** the towns they came across they set on fire.
21: 5 "Who from **all** the tribes of Israel has failed to assemble before the
21:11 they said. "Kill **every** male and every woman who is not a virgin."
21:11 they said. "Kill every male and **every** woman who is not a virgin."
21:13 the **whole** assembly sent an offer of peace to the Benjamites at the
Ru 1:19 the **whole** town was stirred because of them, and the women
2:11 "I've been told **all** about what you have done for your
2:21 'Stay with my workers until they finish harvesting **all** my grain.' "
3: 5 "I will do **whatever** [+889] you say," Ruth answered.
3: 6 and did **everything** her mother-in-law told her to do.
3:11 my daughter, don't be afraid. I will do for you **all** you ask.
3:11 **All** my fellow townsmen know that you are a woman of noble
3:16 Then she told her **everything** Boaz had done for her
4: 7 and **transfer of property** [+1821+9455] to become final,
4: 9 Boaz announced to the elders and **all** the people, "Today you are
4: 9 "Today you are witnesses that I have bought from Naomi **all** the
4: 9 Naomi all the property of Elimelech, **[RPH]** Kilion and Mahlon.
4:11 Then the elders and **all** those at the gate said, "We are witnesses.
1Sa 1: 4 of the meat to his wife Peninnah and to **all** her sons and daughters.
1:11 then I will give him to the LORD for **all** the days of his life,
1:21 When the man Elkanah went up with **all** his family to offer the
1:28 For his **whole** life he will be given over to the LORD."
2:13 with the people that whenever **anyone** [+408] offered a sacrifice
2:14 the priest would take for himself **whatever** [+889] the fork brought
2:14 This is how they treated **all** the Israelites who came to Shiloh.
2:22 heard about **everything** his sons were doing to all Israel and how
2:22 heard about everything his sons were doing to **all** Israel and how
2:23 I hear from **all** the people about these wicked deeds of yours.
2:28 I chose your father out of **all** the tribes of Israel to be my priest,
2:28 I also gave your father's house **all** the offerings made with fire by
2:29 on the choice parts of **every** offering made by my people Israel?'
2:32 **Although** [+889+928] good will be done to Israel, in your family
2:32 family line there will **never** [+2021+3427+4202] be an old man.
2:33 your heart, and **all** your descendants will die in the prime of life.
2:35 he will minister before my anointed one **always** [+2021+3427].
2:36 **everyone** left in your family line will come and bow down before
3:11 in Israel that will make the ears of **everyone** who hears of it tingle.
3:12 At that time I will carry out against Eli **everything** I spoke against
3:17 if you hide from me **anything** [+1821+1821+2021+4946] he told
3:18 So Samuel told him **everything** [+1821+2021], hiding nothing
3:19 grew up, and he let **none** [+4202] of his words fall to the ground.
3:20 **all** Israel from Dan to Beersheba recognized that Samuel was
4: 1 Samuel's word came to **all** Israel. Now the Israelites went out to
4: 5 the camp, **all** Israel raised such a great shout that the ground shook.
4: 8 They are the gods who struck the Egyptians with **all** *kinds of*
4:13 and told what had happened, the **whole** town sent up a cry.
5: 5 That is why to this day neither the priests of Dagon nor **any** others
5: 8 So they called together **all** the rulers of the Philistines and asked
5:11 So they called together **all** the rulers of the Philistines and said,
5:11 For death *had* **filled** the city **with** [+928+2118] panic; God's hand
6: 4 because the same plague has struck both **[NIE]** you and your
6:18 the number of the gold rats was according to the number of **[NIE]**
7: 2 and **all** the people of Israel mourned and sought after the LORD.
7: 3 Samuel said to the **whole** house of Israel, "If you are returning to
7: 3 "If you are returning to the LORD with **all** your hearts, then rid
7: 5 "Assemble **all** Israel at Mizpah and I will intercede with the
7:13 **Throughout** Samuel's lifetime, the hand of the LORD was
7:15 Samuel continued as judge over Israel **all** the days of his life.
7:16 from Bethel to Gilgal to Mizpah, judging Israel in **all** those places.
8: 4 So **all** the elders of Israel gathered together and came to Samuel at
8: 5 now appoint a king to lead us, such as **all** the other nations have."
8: 7 "Listen to **all** that the people are saying to you; it is not you they
8: 8 As **[NIE]** they have done from the day I brought them up out of
8:10 Samuel told **all** the words of the LORD to the people who were
8:20 Then we will be like **all** the other nations, with a king to lead us
8:21 When Samuel heard **all** that the people said, he repeated it before
9: 2 equal among the Israelites—a head taller than **any** *of* the others.
9: 6 he is highly respected, and **everything** he says comes true.
9:19 morning I will let you go and will tell you **all** that is in your heart.
9:20 And to whom is **all** the desire of Israel turned, if not to you
9:20 desire of Israel turned, if not to you and **all** your father's family?"
9:21 is not my clan the least of **all** the clans of the tribe of Benjamin?
10: 9 changed Saul's heart, and **all** these signs were fulfilled that day.
10:11 When **all** those who had formerly known him saw him
10:18 from the power of Egypt and **all** the kingdoms that oppressed you.'
10:19 your God, who saves you out of **all** your calamities and distresses.
10:20 When Samuel brought **all** the tribes of Israel near, the tribe of
10:23 as he stood among the people he was a head taller than **any** *of* the
10:24 Samuel said to **all** the people, "Do you see the man the LORD has
10:24 There is no one like him among **all** the people." Then the people
10:24 Then **[RPH]** the people shouted, "Long live the king!"
10:25 Then Samuel dismissed **[RPH]** the people, each to his own home.
11: 1 And **all** the men of Jabesh said to him, "Make a treaty with us,
11: 2 on the condition that I gouge out the right eye of **every** *one of* you
11: 2 right eye of every one of you and so bring disgrace on **all** Israel."
11: 3 so we can send messengers **throughout** [+928+1473] Israel;
11: 4 and reported these terms to the people, they **all** wept aloud.
11: 7 and sent the pieces by messengers **throughout** [+928+1473] Israel,
11:10 and you can do to us **whatever** [+3869] seems good to you."
11:15 So **all** the people went to Gilgal and confirmed Saul as king in the
11:15 the LORD, and Saul and **all** the Israelites held a great celebration.
12: 1 Samuel said to **all** Israel, "I have listened to everything you said to
12: 1 "I have listened to **everything** you said to me and have set a king
12: 7 as to **all** the righteous acts performed by the LORD for you
12:18 So **all** the people stood in awe of the LORD and of Samuel.
12:19 The people **all** said to Samuel, "Pray to the LORD your God for
12:19 for we have added to **all** our other sins the evil of asking for a
12:20 "You have done **all** this evil; yet do not turn away from the
12:20 away from the LORD, but serve the LORD with **all** your heart.
12:24 to fear the LORD and serve him faithfully with **all** your heart;
13: 3 Then Saul had the trumpet blown **throughout** [+928] the land
13: 4 So **all** Israel heard the news: "Saul has attacked the Philistine
13: 7 at Gilgal, and **all** the troops with him were quaking with fear.
13:19 Not a blacksmith could be found in the **whole** land of Israel,
13:20 So **all** Israel went down to the Philistines to have their plowshares,
13:22 So on the day of the battle not **a** soldier with Saul and Jonathan had
14: 7 "Do **all** that you have in mind," his armor-bearer said. "Go ahead;
14:15 Then panic struck the **whole** army—those in the camp and field,
14:20 Then Saul and **all** his men assembled and went to the battle.
14:22 When **all** the Israelites who had hidden in the hill country of
14:24 on my enemies!" So **none of** [+4202] the troops tasted food.
14:25 The **entire** army entered the woods, and there was honey on the
14:34 still in it.' " So **everyone** [+2021+6639] brought his ox that night
14:36 "Do **whatever** seems best to you," they replied. But the priest said,
14:38 therefore said, "Come here, **all** you who are leaders of the army,
14:39 son Jonathan, he must die." But not **one** of the men said a word.
14:40 Saul then said to **all** the Israelites, "You stand over there; I
14:47 over Israel, he fought against **[NIE]** their enemies on every side:
14:47 **Wherever** [+889+928] he turned, he inflicted punishment on them.
14:52 **All** the days of Saul there was bitter war with the Philistines,
14:52 whenever Saul saw **a** mighty or brave man, he took him into his
14:52 whenever Saul saw a mighty or **[RPH]** brave man, he took him
15: 3 and totally destroy **everything** that belongs to them.
15: 6 for you showed kindness to **all** the Israelites when they came up
15: 8 and **all** his people he totally destroyed with the sword.
15: 9 and cattle, the fat calves and lambs—**everything** that was good.
15: 9 but **everything** [+2021+4856] that was despised and weak they
15:11 Samuel was troubled, and he cried out to the LORD **all** that night.
17:11 Saul and **all** the Israelites were dismayed and terrified.
17:19 They are with Saul and **all** the men of Israel in the Valley of Elah,
17:24 the Israelites saw the man, they **all** ran from him in great fear.
17:46 and the **whole** world will know that there is a God in Israel.
17:47 **All** those gathered here will know that it is not by sword or spear
18: 5 **Whatever** [+889+928] Saul sent him to do, David did it
18: 5 the army. This pleased **all** the people, and Saul's officers as well.
18: 6 the women came out from **all** the towns of Israel to meet King Saul
18:14 In **everything** he did he had great success, because the LORD
18:16 **all** Israel and Judah loved David, because he led them in their
18:22 the king is pleased with you, and his attendants **all** like you;
18:29 afraid of him, and he remained his enemy the **rest** *of* his days.
18:30 David met with more success than the **rest** *of* Saul's officers,

1Sa 19: 1 Saul told his son Jonathan and **all** the attendants to kill David.
19: 5 The LORD won a great victory for **all** Israel, and you saw it
19: 7 So Jonathan called David and told him the **whole** conversation.
19:18 to Samuel at Ramah and told him **all** that Saul had done to him.
19:24 He lay that way **all** that day and night. This is why people say,
19:24 He lay that way all that day and **[RPH]** night. This is why people
20: 6 because an annual sacrifice is being made there for his **whole** clan.'
20:31 **As long** [+2021+3427] **as** the son of Jesse lives on this earth,
22: 1 his brothers and **[NIE]** his father's household heard about it,
22: 2 **All** those who were in distress or in debt or discontented gathered
22: 2 All those who were in distress or **[RPH]** in debt or discontented
22: 2 in distress or in debt or **[RPH]** discontented gathered around him,
22: 4 they stayed with him **as long** [+3427] **as** David was in the
22: 6 on the hill at Gibeah, with **all** his officials standing around him.
22: 7 Will the son of Jesse give **all** *of* you fields and vineyards?
22: 7 Will he make **all** *of* you commanders of thousands
22: 8 Is that why you have **all** conspired against me? No one tells me
22:11 the priest Ahimelech son of Ahitub and his father's **whole** family,
22:11 who were the priests at Nob, and they **all** came to the king.
22:14 "Who of **all** your servants is as loyal as David, the king's
22:15 Let not the king accuse your servant or **any** *of* his father's family,
22:15 for your servant knows nothing at all about this **whole** affair."
22:16 will surely die, Ahimelech, you and your father's **whole** family."
22:22 I am responsible for the death of your father's **whole** family.
23: 8 Saul called up **all** his forces for battle, to go down to Keilah to
23:14 in the hills of the Desert of Ziph. **Day after day** [+2021+3427]
23:20 Now, O king, come down **whenever** it pleases you to do so,
23:23 Find out about **all** the hiding places he uses and come back to me
23:23 is in the area, I will track him down among **all** the clans of Judah."
24: 2 [24:3] So Saul took three thousand chosen men from **all** Israel
25: 1 Now Samuel died, and **all** Israel assembled and mourned for him;
25: 6 to you and your household! And good health to **all** that is yours!
25: 7 the **whole** time they were at Carmel nothing of theirs was missing.
25: 9 they gave Nabal **[NIE]** this message in David's name.
25:12 and went back. When they arrived, they reported **every** word.
25:15 the **whole** time we were out in the fields near them nothing was
25:16 day they were a wall around us **all** the time we were herding our
25:17 disaster is hanging over our master and his **whole** household.
25:21 **all** my watching over this fellow's property in the desert so that
25:21 property in the desert so that nothing of **[RPH]** his was missing.
25:22 if by morning I leave alive one male of **all** who belong to him!"
25:30 When the LORD has done for my master **every** good thing he
26:12 They were **all** sleeping, because the LORD had put them into a
26:24 so may the LORD value my life and deliver me from **all** trouble."
27: 1 Saul will give up searching for me **anywhere** [+1473] in Israel,
27:11 practice **as long** [+2021+3427] **as** he lived in Philistine territory.
28: 2 I will make you my bodyguard **for life** [+2021+3427]."
28: 3 **all** Israel had mourned for him and buried him in his own town of
28: 4 while Saul gathered **all** the Israelites and set up camp at Gilboa.
28:20 strength was gone, for he had eaten nothing **all** that day and night.
28:20 was gone, for he had eaten nothing all that day and **[RPH]** night.
29: 1 The Philistines gathered **all** their forces at Aphek, and Israel
30: 6 **each** one was bitter in spirit because of his sons and daughters.
30:16 scattered over **[NIE]** the countryside, eating, drinking
30:16 because of **[NIE]** the great amount of plunder they had taken from
30:18 David recovered **everything** the Amalekites had taken,
30:19 or old, boy or girl, plunder or **anything** *else* they had taken.
30:19 else they had taken. David brought **everything** [+2021] back.
30:20 He took **all** the flocks and herds, and his men drove them ahead of
30:22 **all** the evil men and troublemakers among David's followers said,
30:31 to those in **all** the other places where David and his men had
31: 6 and his armor-bearer and **all** his men died together that same day.
31:12 **all** their valiant men journeyed through the night to Beth Shan.
31:12 all their valiant men journeyed **through** the night to Beth Shan.
2Sa 1: 9 and kill me! I am in the throes of death, but I'm **still** [+6388] alive.'
1:11 Then David and **all** the men with him took hold of their clothes
2: 9 and Jezreel, and also over Ephraim, Benjamin and **all** Israel.
2:23 **every** *man* stopped when he came to the place where Asahel had
2:28 So Joab blew the trumpet, and **all** the men came to a halt; they no
2:29 **All** that night Abner and his men marched through the Arabah.
2:29 continued through the **whole** Bithron and came to Mahanaim.
2:30 Joab returned from pursuing Abner and assembled **all** his men.
2:32 Joab and his men marched **all** night and arrived at Hebron by
3:12 with me, and I will help you bring **all** Israel over to you."
3:18 hand of the Philistines and from the hand of **all** their enemies.' "
3:19 Then he went to Hebron to tell David **everything** that Israel
3:19 that Israel and the **whole** house of Benjamin wanted to do.
3:21 "Let me go at once and assemble **all** Israel for my lord the king,
3:21 with you, and that you may rule over **all** that your heart desires."
3:23 When Joab and **all** the soldiers with him arrived, he was told that
3:25 observe your movements and find out **everything** you are doing."
3:29 blood fall upon the head of Joab and upon **all** his father's house!
3:31 David said to Joab and **all** the people with him, "Tear your clothes
3:32 and the king wept aloud at Abner's tomb. **All** the people wept also.
3:34 falls before wicked men." And **all** the people wept over him again.
3:35 they **all** came and urged David to eat something while it was still
3:35 if I taste bread or **anything** [+4399] *else* before the sun sets!"
3:36 **All** the people took note and were pleased; indeed, everything the
3:36 and were pleased; indeed, **everything** the king did pleased them.
3:36 indeed, everything the king did pleased **them**[s] [+2021+6639].
3:37 So on that day **all** the people and all Israel knew that the king had
3:37 **all** Israel knew that the king had no part in the murder of Abner
4: 1 had died in Hebron, he lost courage, and **all** Israel became alarmed.
4: 7 Taking it with them, they traveled **all** night by way of the Arabah.
4: 9 as the LORD lives, who has delivered me out of **all** trouble,
5: 1 **All** the tribes of Israel came to David at Hebron and said, "We are
5: 3 When **all** the elders of Israel had come to King David at Hebron,
5: 5 in Jerusalem he reigned over **all** Israel and Judah thirty-three years.
5: 8 "**Anyone** who conquers the Jebusites will have to use the water
5:17 they went up **in full force** to search for him, but David heard about
6: 1 brought together out of Israel chosen men, thirty thousand **in all**.
6: 2 **all** his men set out from Baalah of Judah to bring up from there the
6: 5 the **whole** house of Israel were celebrating with all their might
6: 5 the whole house of Israel were celebrating with **all** their might
6:11 and the LORD blessed him and his **entire** household.
6:12 has blessed the household of Obed-Edom and **everything** he has,
6:14 a linen ephod, danced before the LORD with **all** his might,
6:15 the **entire** house of Israel brought up the ark of the LORD with
6:19 a cake of raisins to **each** person in the whole crowd of Israelites,
6:19 a cake of raisins to each person in the **whole** crowd of Israelites,
6:19 both men and women. And **all** the people went to their homes.
6:21 or **anyone** *from* his house when he appointed me ruler over the
7: 1 the LORD had given him rest from **all** his enemies around him,
7: 3 the king, "**Whatever** [+889] you have in mind, go ahead and do it,
7: 7 **Wherever** [+889+928] I have moved with all the Israelites,
7: 7 Wherever I have moved with **all** the Israelites, did I ever say to any
7: 9 I have been with you **wherever** [+889+928] you have gone,
7: 9 have gone, and I have cut off **all** your enemies from before you.
7:11 my people Israel. I will also give you rest from **all** your enemies.
7:17 Nathan reported to David **all** the words of this entire revelation.
7:17 Nathan reported to David all the words of this **entire** revelation.
7:21 you have done **[NIE]** this great thing and made it known to your
7:22 is no God but you, as **[NIE]** we have heard with our own ears.
8: 4 foot soldiers. He hamstrung **all** but a hundred of the chariot horses.
8: 6 The LORD gave David victory **wherever** [+889+928] he went.
8: 9 heard that David had defeated the **entire** army of Hadadezer,
8:11 done with the silver and gold from **all** the nations he had subdued:
8:14 He put garrisons **throughout** [+928] Edom, and all the Edomites
8:14 throughout Edom, and **all** the Edomites became subject to David.
8:14 The LORD gave David victory **wherever** [+889+928] he went.
8:15 David reigned over **all** Israel, doing what was just and right for all
8:15 over all Israel, doing what was just and right for **all** his people.
9: 7 I will restore to you **all** the land that belonged to your grandfather
9: 9 "I have given your master's grandson **everything** that belonged to
9: 9 grandson everything that belonged to Saul and **[RPH]** his family.
9:11 "Your servant will do **whatever** [+889+3869+4027] my lord the
9:12 **all** the members of Ziba's household were servants of
10: 7 David sent Joab out with the **entire** army of fighting men.
10: 9 so he selected **some** [+4946] *of* the best troops in Israel and
10:17 he gathered **all** Israel, crossed the Jordan and went to Helam.
10:19 When **all** the kings who were vassals of Hadadezer saw that they
11: 1 sent Joab out with the king's men and the **whole** Israelite army.
11: 9 Uriah slept at the entrance to the palace with **all** his master's
11:18 Joab sent David a **full** account of the battle.
11:19 "When you have finished giving the king **this**[s] account of the
11:22 when he arrived he told David **everything** Joab had sent him to
12: 3 the poor man had **nothing** [+401] except one little ewe lamb he
12:12 but I will do this thing in broad daylight before **all** Israel.' "
12:29 So David mustered the **entire** army and went to Rabbah,
12:31 He did this to **all** the Ammonite towns. Then David and his entire
12:31 Then David and his **entire** army returned to Jerusalem.
13: 9 refused to eat. "Send **everyone** [+408] out of here," Amnon said.
13: 9 everyone out of here," Amnon said. So **everyone** [+408] left him.
13:21 When King David heard **all** this, he was furious.
13:23 the border of Ephraim, he invited **all** the king's sons to come there.
13:25 "**All** *of* us should not go; we would only be a burden to you."
13:27 so he sent with him Amnon and the **rest** *of* the king's sons.
13:29 Then **all** the king's sons got up, mounted their mules and fled.
13:30 "Absalom has struck down **all** the king's sons; not one of them is
13:31 on the ground; and **all** his servants stood by with their clothes torn.
13:32 said, "My lord should not think that they killed **all** the princes;
13:33 My lord the king should not be concerned about the report that **all**
13:36 The king, too, and **all** his servants wept very bitterly.
13:37 king of Geshur. But King David mourned for his son **every** day.
14: 7 Now the **whole** clan has risen up against your servant; they say,
14:19 The king asked, "Isn't the hand of Joab with you in **all** this?"
14:19 turn to the right or to the left from **anything** my lord the king says.
14:19 and who put **all** these words into the mouth of your servant.

2Sa 14:20 an angel of God—he knows **everything** that happens in the land."
14:25 In **all** Israel there was not a man so highly praised for his
15: 2 Whenever **anyone** [+408+2021] came with a complaint to be
15: 4 **everyone** [+408] who has a complaint or case could come to me
15: 6 Absalom behaved in this way toward **all** the Israelites who came to
15:10 Absalom sent secret messengers **throughout** [+928] the tribes of
15:11 went quite innocently, knowing **nothing** [+4202] about the matter.
15:14 David said to **all** his officials who were with him in Jerusalem,
15:15 "Your servants are ready to do **whatever** [+889+3869] our lord the
15:16 The king set out, with his **entire** household following him;
15:17 So the king set out, with **all** the people following him, and they
15:18 **All** his men marched past him, along with all the Kerethites
15:18 marched past him, along with **all** the Kerethites and Pelethites;
15:18 past him, along with all the Kerethites and **[RPH]** Pelethites;
15:18 **all** the six hundred Gittites who had accompanied him from Gath
15:22 So Ittai the Gittite marched on with **all** his men and the families
15:22 on with all his men and **[NIE]** the families that were with him.
15:23 The **whole** countryside wept aloud as all the people passed by.
15:23 The whole countryside wept aloud as **all** the people passed by.
15:23 the Kidron Valley, and **all** the people moved on toward the desert.
15:24 **all** the Levites who were with him were carrying the ark of the
15:24 Abiathar offered sacrifices until **all** the people had finished leaving
15:30 **All** the people with him covered their heads too and were weeping
15:35 Tell them **anything** [+1821+2021] you hear in the king's palace.
15:36 with them. Send them to me with **anything** [+1821] you hear."
16: 4 said to Ziba, "**All** that belonged to Mephibosheth is now yours."
16: 6 He pelted David and **all** the king's officials with stones, though all
16: 6 though **all** the troops and the special guard were on David's right
16: 6 and **[RPH]** the special guard were on David's right and left.
16: 8 The LORD has repaid you for **all** the blood you shed in the
16:11 David then said to Abishai and **all** his officials, "My son, who is of
16:14 and **all** the people with him arrived at their destination exhausted.
16:15 Meanwhile, Absalom and **all** the men of Israel came to Jerusalem,
16:18 by the LORD, by these people, and by **all** the men of Israel—
16:21 **all** Israel will hear that you have made yourself a stench in your
16:21 and the hands of **everyone** with you will be strengthened."
16:22 and he lay with his father's concubines in the sight of **all** Israel.
16:23 how both David and Absalom regarded **all** *of* Ahithophel's advice.
17: 2 strike him with terror, and then **all** the people with him will flee.
17: 3 bring **all** the people back to you. The death of the man you seek
17: 3 The death of the man you seek will mean the return of **all**;
17: 3 seek will mean the return of all; **all** the people will be unharmed."
17: 4 This plan seemed good to Absalom and to **all** the elders of Israel.
17:10 for **all** Israel knows that your father is a fighter and that those with
17:11 Let **all** Israel, from Dan to Beersheba—as numerous as the sand on
17:12 on the ground. Neither he nor **any** *of* his men will be left alive.
17:13 he withdraws into a city, then **all** Israel will bring ropes to that city,
17:14 Absalom and **all** the men of Israel said, "The advice of Hushai the
17:16 or the king and **all** the people with him will be swallowed up.' "
17:22 So David and **all** the people with him set out and crossed the
17:24 and Absalom crossed the Jordan with **all** the men of Israel.
18: 4 So the king stood beside the gate while **all** the men marched out in
18: 5 **all** the troops heard the king giving orders concerning Absalom to
18: 5 giving orders concerning Absalom to **each** *of* the commanders.
18: 8 The battle spread out over the **whole** countryside, and the forest
18:13 in jeopardy—and **nothing** [+1821+4202] is hidden from the king—
18:17 of rocks over him. Meanwhile, **all** the Israelites fled to their homes.
18:31 The LORD has delivered you today from **all** who rose up against
18:32 the king and **all** who rise up to harm you be like that young man."
19: 2 [19:3] for the **whole** army the victory that day was turned into
19: 5 [19:6] and said, "Today you have humiliated **all** your men,
19: 6 [19:7] if Absalom were alive today and **all** *of* us were dead.
19: 7 [19:8] This will be worse for you than **all** the calamities that have
19: 8 [19:9] When **[NIE]** the men were told, "The king is sitting in the
19: 8 [19:9] king is sitting in the gateway," they **all** came before him.
19: 9 [19:10] **Throughout** [+928] the tribes of Israel, the people were
19: 9 [19:10] the people were **all** arguing with each other, saying,
19:11 [19:12] since what is being said **throughout** Israel has reached
19:13 [19:14] if **from now on** [+2021+3427] you are not the
19:14 [19:15] He won over the hearts of **all** the men of Judah as though
19:14 [19:15] sent word to the king, "Return, you and **all** your men."
19:20 [19:21] today I have come here as the first of the **whole** house of
19:28 [19:29] **All** my grandfather's descendants deserved nothing
19:30 [19:31] Mephibosheth said to the king, "Let him take **everything**,
19:38 [19:39] And **anything** you desire from me I will do for you."
19:39 [19:40] So **all** the people crossed the Jordan, and then the king
19:40 [19:41] **All** the troops of Judah and half the troops of Israel had
19:41 [19:42] Soon **all** the men of Israel were coming to the king
19:41 [19:42] household across the Jordan, together with **all** his men?"
19:42 [19:43] **All** the men of Judah answered the men of Israel, "We did
20: 2 So **all** the men of Israel deserted David to follow Sheba son of
20: 7 **all** the mighty warriors went out under the command of Abishai.
20:12 the road, and the man saw that **all** the troops came to a halt there.
20:12 When he realized that **everyone** who came up to Amasa stopped,
20:13 **all** the men went on with Joab to pursue Sheba son of Bicri.
20:14 Sheba passed through **all** the tribes of Israel to Abel Beth Maacah
20:14 to Abel Beth Maacah and through the **entire** *region of* the Berites,
20:15 **All** the troops with Joab came and besieged Sheba in Abel Beth
20:22 Then the woman went to **all** the people with her wise advice,
20:23 Joab was over Israel's **entire** army; Benaiah son of Jehoiada was
21: 5 and have no place **anywhere in** [+928+1473] Israel,
21:14 at Zela in Benjamin, and did **everything** the king commanded.
22: 1 when the LORD delivered him from the hand of **all** his enemies
22:23 **All** his laws are before me; I have not turned away from his
22:31 LORD is flawless. He is a shield for **all** who take refuge in him.
23: 5 me an everlasting covenant, arranged and secured in **every** *part*?
23: 5 Will he not bring to fruition **[RPH]** my salvation and grant me my
23: 5 not bring to fruition my salvation and grant me my **every** desire?
23: 6 evil men are **all** to be cast aside like thorns, which are not gathered
23:39 and Uriah the Hittite. There were thirty-seven **in all**.
24: 2 "Go **throughout** [+928] the tribes of Israel from Dan to Beersheba
24: 7 fortress of Tyre and **all** the towns of the Hivites and Canaanites.
24: 8 After they had gone through the **entire** land, they came back to
24:23 O king, Araunah gives **all** this to the king." Araunah also said to
1Ki 1: 3 they searched **throughout** [+928+1473] Israel for a beautiful girl
1: 9 He invited **all** his brothers, the king's sons, and all the men of
1: 9 the king's sons, and **all** the men of Judah who were royal officials,
1:19 fattened calves, and sheep, and has invited **all** the king's sons,
1:20 My lord the king, the eyes of **all** Israel are on you, to learn from
1:25 He has invited **all** the king's sons, the commanders of the army
1:29 as the LORD lives, who has delivered me out of **every** trouble,
1:39 Then they sounded the trumpet and **all** the people shouted,
1:40 **all** the people went up after him, playing flutes and rejoicing
1:41 **all** the guests who were with him heard it as they were finishing
1:49 At this, **all** Adonijah's guests rose in alarm and dispersed.
2: 2 "I am about to go the way of **all** the earth," he said. "So be strong,
2: 3 so that you may prosper in **all** you do and wherever you go,
2: 3 you may prosper in all you do and **wherever** [+889+9004] you go,
2: 4 and if they walk faithfully before me with **all** their heart and soul,
2: 4 walk faithfully before me with all their heart and **[RPH]** soul,
2:15 **All** Israel looked to me as their king. But things changed,
2:26 before my father David and shared **all** my father's hardships."
2:44 "You know in your heart **all** the wrong you did to my father David.
3:13 so that **in your lifetime** [+3427] you will have no equal among
3:15 and fellowship offerings. Then he gave a feast for **all** his court.
3:28 When **all** Israel heard the verdict the king had given, they held the
4: 1 So King Solomon ruled over **all** Israel.
4: 7 Solomon also had twelve district governors over **all** Israel,
4:10 in Arubboth (Socoh and **all** the land of Hepher were his);
4:11 in **[RPH]** Naphoth Dor (he was married to Taphath daughter of
4:12 and in **all** *of* Beth Shan next to Zarethan below Jezreel,
4:21 [5:1] Solomon ruled over **all** the kingdoms from the River to the
4:21 [5:1] brought tribute and were Solomon's subjects **all** his life.
4:24 [5:4] For he ruled over **all** the kingdoms west of the River,
4:24 [5:4] from Tiphsah to Gaza, **[RPH]** and had peace on all sides.
4:24 [5:4] the River, from Tiphsah to Gaza, and had peace on **all** sides.
4:25 [5:5] **During** Solomon's lifetime Judah and Israel, from Dan to
4:27 [5:7] for King Solomon and **all** who came to the king's table.
4:30 [5:10] Solomon's wisdom was greater than the wisdom of **all** the
4:30 [5:10] men of the East, and greater than **all** the wisdom of Egypt.
4:31 [5:11] He was wiser than **any** other man, including Ethan the
4:31 [5:11] And his fame spread to **all** the surrounding nations.
4:34 [5:14] Men of **all** nations came to listen to Solomon's wisdom,
4:34 [5:14] sent by **all** the kings of the world, who had heard of his
5: 1 [5:15] because he had **always** [+2021+3427] been on friendly
5: 6 [5:20] I will pay you for your men **whatever** [+889+3869] wages
5: 8 [5:22] will do **all** you want in providing the cedar and pine logs.
5:10 [5:24] In this way Hiram kept Solomon supplied with **all** the
5:13 [5:27] King Solomon conscripted laborers from **all** Israel—thirty
6: 7 or **any** other iron tool was heard at the temple site while it was
6:10 he built the side rooms **all** along the temple. The height of each
6:12 out my regulations and keep **all** my commands and obey them,
6:18 and open flowers. **Everything** was cedar; no stone was to be seen.
6:22 So he overlaid the **whole** interior with gold. He also overlaid with
6:22 **[RPH]** He also overlaid with gold the altar that belonged to the
6:22 He also overlaid with gold **[RPH]** the altar that belonged to the
6:29 On the walls **all** around the temple, in both the inner and outer
6:38 the temple was finished in **all** its details according to its
6:38 the temple was finished in all its details according to **[RPH]** its
7: 1 however, to complete **[NIE]** the construction of his palace.
7: 5 **All** the doorways had rectangular frames; they were in the front
7: 9 **All** these structures, from the outside to the great courtyard
7:14 was highly skilled and experienced in **all** *kinds of* bronze work.
7:14 He came to King Solomon and did **all** the work assigned to him.
7:25 top of them, and **[NIE]** their hindquarters were toward the center.
7:33 the axles, rims, spokes and hubs were **all** *of* cast metal.
7:37 They were **all** cast in the same molds and were identical in size
7:40 So Huram finished **all** the work he had undertaken for King

1Ki 7:45 **All** these objects that Huram made for King Solomon for the
7:47 Solomon left **all** these things unweighed, because there were
7:48 Solomon also made **all** the furnishings that were in the LORD's
7:51 When **all** the work King Solomon had done for the temple of the
8: 1 **all** the heads of the tribes and the chiefs of the Israelite families,
8: 2 **All** the men of Israel came together to King Solomon at the time of
8: 3 When **all** the elders of Israel had arrived, the priests took up the
8: 4 and the Tent of Meeting and **all** the sacred furnishings in it.
8: 5 the **entire** assembly of Israel that had gathered about him were
8:14 While the **whole** assembly of Israel was standing there, the king
8:14 the king turned around and blessed **them**[s] [+3776+7736].
8:16 I have not chosen a city in **any** tribe of Israel to have a temple built
8:22 Solomon stood before the altar of the LORD in front of the **whole**
8:23 servants who continue **wholeheartedly** [+928+4213] in your way.
8:37 them in any of their cities, **whatever** disaster or disease may come,
8:37 any of their cities, whatever disaster or **[RPH]** disease may come,
8:38 and when **a** prayer or plea is made by any of your people Israel—
8:38 a prayer or **[RPH]** plea is made by any of your people Israel—
8:38 and when a prayer or plea is made by **any** of your people Israel—
8:38 a prayer or plea is made by any of **[RPH]** your people Israel—
8:39 deal with each man according to **all** he does, since you know his
8:39 since you know his heart (for you alone know the hearts of **all**
8:40 so that they will fear you **all** the time they live in the land you gave
8:43 and do **whatever** [+889+3869] the foreigner asks of you,
8:43 so that **all** the peoples of the earth may know your name and fear
8:48 if they turn back to you with **all** their heart and soul in the land of
8:48 **[RPH]** soul in the land of their enemies who took them captive,
8:50 forgive **all** the offenses they have committed against you,
8:52 and may you listen to them **whenever** [+928] they cry out to you.
8:53 For you singled them out from **all** the nations of the world to be
8:54 When Solomon had finished **all** these prayers and supplications to
8:55 He stood and blessed the **whole** assembly of Israel in a loud voice,
8:56 who has given rest to his people Israel **just as** [+889+3869] he
8:56 Not one word has failed of **all** the good promises he gave through
8:58 to walk in **all** his ways and to keep the commands, decrees
8:60 so that **all** the peoples of the earth may know that the LORD is
8:62 and **all** Israel with him offered sacrifices before the LORD.
8:63 the king and **all** the Israelites dedicated the temple of the LORD.
8:65 observed the festival at that time, and **all** Israel with him—
8:66 glad in heart for **all** the good things the LORD had done for his
9: 1 and the royal palace, and had achieved **all** he had desired to do,
9: 3 My eyes and my heart will **always** [+2021+3427] be there.
9: 4 father did, and do **all** I command and observe my decrees and laws,
9: 7 then become a byword and an object of ridicule among **all** peoples.
9: 8 **all** who pass by will be appalled and will scoff and say,
9: 9 that is why the LORD brought **all** this disaster on them.' "
9:11 because Hiram had supplied him with **all** the cedar and pine
9:19 as well as **all** his store cities and the towns for his chariots
9:19 in Jerusalem, in Lebanon and throughout **all** the territory he ruled.
9:20 **All** the people left from the Amorites, Hittites, Perizzites, Hivites
10: 2 to Solomon and talked with him about **all** that she had on her mind.
10: 3 Solomon answered **all** her questions; nothing was too hard for the
10: 4 When the queen of Sheba saw **all** the wisdom of Solomon
10:13 King Solomon gave the queen of Sheba **all** she desired and asked
10:15 traders and from **all** the Arabian kings and the governors of the
10:20 Nothing like it had ever been made for **any** other kingdom.
10:21 **All** King Solomon's goblets were gold, and all the household
10:21 **all** the household articles in the Palace of the Forest of Lebanon
10:23 greater in riches and wisdom than **all** the other kings of the earth.
10:24 The **whole** world sought audience with Solomon to hear the
10:29 They also exported them to **all** the kings of the Hittites and of the
11: 8 He did the same for **all** his foreign wives, who burned incense
11:13 Yet I will not tear the **whole** kingdom from him, but will give him
11:15 gone up to bury the dead, had struck down **all** the men in Edom.
11:16 Joab and **all** the Israelites stayed there for six months, until they
11:16 there for six months, until they had destroyed **all** the men in Edom.
11:25 Rezon was Israel's adversary **as long** [+3427] **as** Solomon **lived**,
11:28 he put him in charge of the **whole** labor force of the house of
11:32 which I have chosen out of **all** the tribes of Israel, he will have one
11:34 " 'But I will not take the **whole** kingdom out of Solomon's hand;
11:34 I have made him ruler **all** the days of his life for the sake of David
11:36 so that David my servant may **always** [+2021+3427] have a lamp
11:37 I will take you, and you will rule over **all** that your heart desires;
11:38 If you do **whatever** [+889] I command you and walk in my ways
11:39 descendants because of this, but not **forever** [+2021+3427].' "
11:41 of Solomon's reign—**all** he did and the wisdom he displayed—
11:42 Solomon reigned in Jerusalem over **all** Israel forty years.
12: 1 to Shechem, for **all** the Israelites had gone there to make him king.
12: 3 and he and the **whole** assembly of Israel went to Rehoboam
12: 7 they will **always** [+2021+3427] be your servants."
12:12 days later Jeroboam and **all** the people returned to Rehoboam,
12:16 When **all** Israel saw that the king refused to listen to them,
12:18 was in charge of forced labor, but **all** Israel stoned him to death.
12:20 When **all** the Israelites heard that Jeroboam had returned, they sent
12:20 and called him to the assembly and made him king over **all** Israel.
12:21 he mustered the **whole** house of Judah and the tribe of Benjamin—
12:23 to the **whole** house of Judah and Benjamin, and to the rest of the
13:11 and told him **all** that the man of God had done there that day.
13:32 against **all** the shrines on the high places in the towns of Samaria
14: 8 who kept my commands and followed me with **all** his heart,
14: 9 You have done more evil than **all** who lived before you. You have
14:13 **All** Israel will mourn for him and bury him. He is the only one
14:18 They buried him, and **all** Israel mourned for him, as the LORD
14:21 the city the LORD had chosen out of **all** the tribes of Israel in
14:22 up his jealous anger more than **[NIE]** their fathers had done.
14:23 sacred stones and Asherah poles on **every** high hill and under
14:23 Asherah poles on every high hill and under **every** spreading tree.
14:24 the people engaged in **all** the detestable practices of the nations the
14:26 He took **everything**, including all the gold shields Solomon had
14:26 took everything, including **all** the gold shields Solomon had made.
14:29 As for the other events of Rehoboam's reign, and **all** he did,
14:30 There was **continual** [+2021+3427] warfare between Rehoboam
15: 3 He committed **all** the sins his father had done before him;
15: 5 had not failed to keep **any** *of* the LORD's commands all the days
15: 5 had not failed to keep any of the LORD's commands **all** the days
15: 6 between Rehoboam and Jeroboam **throughout** ⌊Abijah's⌋ lifetime.
15: 7 As for the other events of Abijah's reign, and **all** he did, are they
15:12 from the land and got rid of **all** the idols his fathers had made.
15:14 Asa's heart was fully committed to the LORD **all** his life.
15:16 between Asa and Baasha king of Israel **throughout** their reigns.
15:18 Asa then took **all** the silver and gold that was left in the treasuries
15:20 Abel Beth Maacah and **all** Kinnereth in addition to Naphtali.
15:20 Beth Maacah and all Kinnereth in addition to **[RPH]** Naphtali.
15:22 Then King Asa issued an order to **all** Judah—no one was exempt—
15:23 As for **all** the other events of Asa's reign, all his achievements,
15:23 Asa's reign, **all** his achievements, all he did and the cities he built,
15:23 Asa's reign, all his achievements, **all** he did and the cities he built,
15:27 a Philistine town, while Nadab and **all** Israel were besieging it.
15:29 As soon as he began to reign, he killed Jeroboam's **whole** family.
15:29 He did not leave Jeroboam **anyone** that breathed, but destroyed
15:31 As for the other events of Nadab's reign, and **all** he did, are they
15:32 between Asa and Baasha king of Israel **throughout** their reigns.
15:33 Baasha son of Ahijah became king of **all** Israel in Tirzah, and he
16: 7 because of **all** the evil he had done in the eyes of the LORD,
16:11 and was seated on the throne, he killed off Baasha's **whole** family.
16:12 So Zimri destroyed the **whole** family of Baasha, in accordance
16:13 because of **all** the sins Baasha and his son Elah had committed
16:14 As for the other events of Elah's reign, and **all** he did, are they not
16:16 the king and murdered him, **they**[s] [+3776] proclaimed Omri,
16:17 and **all** the Israelites with him withdrew from Gibbethon
16:25 the eyes of the LORD and sinned more than **all** those before him.
16:26 He walked in **all** the ways of Jeroboam son of Nebat and in his sin,
16:30 more evil in the eyes of the LORD than **any** *of* those before him.
16:33 God of Israel, to anger than did **all** the kings of Israel before him.
18: 5 to Obadiah, "Go through the land to **all** the springs and valleys.
18: 5 "Go through the land to all the springs and **[RPH]** valleys.
18:19 Now summon the people from **all over** Israel to meet me on Mount
18:20 So Ahab sent word throughout **all** Israel and assembled the
18:21 Elijah went before **[RPH]** the people and said, "How long will
18:24 he is God." Then **all** the people said, "What you say is good."
18:30 Elijah said to **all** the people, "Come here to me." They came to
18:30 the people, "Come here to me." **They**[s] [+2021+6639] came to him,
18:36 I am your servant and have done **all** these things at your command.
18:39 When **all** the people saw this, they fell prostrate and cried,
19: 1 Now Ahab told Jezebel **everything** Elijah had done and how he
19: 1 and **[RPH]** how he had killed all the prophets with the sword.
19: 1 had done and how he had killed **all** the prophets with the sword.
19:18 **all** whose knees have not bowed down to Baal and all whose
19:18 bowed down to Baal and **all** whose mouths have not kissed him."
20: 1 Now Ben-Hadad king of Aram mustered his **entire** army.
20: 4 "Just as you say, my lord the king. I and **all** I have are yours."
20: 6 They will seize **everything** you value and carry it away.' "
20: 7 The king of Israel summoned **all** the elders of the land and said to
20: 8 **[RPH]** The elders and the people all answered, "Don't listen to
20: 8 The elders and the people **all** answered, "Don't listen to him
20: 9 the king, 'Your servant will do **all** you demanded the first time,
20:10 if enough dust remains in Samaria to give **each** *of* my men a
20:13 "This is what the LORD says: 'Do you see **[NIE]** this vast army?
20:15 232 men. Then he assembled the **rest** *of* the Israelites, 7,000 in all.
20:15 232 men. Then he assembled the rest of the Israelites, 7,000 **in all**.
20:28 your hands, and you will know **[NIE]** that I am the LORD.' "
21:26 **like** [+889+3869] the Amorites the LORD drove out before
22:10 the gate of Samaria, with **all** the prophets prophesying before them.
22:12 **All** the other prophets were prophesying the same thing. "Attack
22:17 "I saw **all** Israel scattered on the hills like sheep without a
22:19 I saw the LORD sitting on his throne with **all** the host of heaven
22:22 will go out and be a lying spirit in the mouths of **all** his prophets,'
22:23 "So now the LORD has put a lying spirit in the mouths of **all**

1Ki 22:28 through me." Then he added, "Mark my words, **all** you people!"
22:39 including **all** he did, the palace he built and inlaid with ivory,
22:39 he built and inlaid with ivory, and **[RPH]** the cities he fortified,
22:43 In **everything** he walked in the ways of his father Asa and did not
22:53 [22:54] to anger, **just as** [+889+3869] his father had done.
2Ki 3: 6 time King Joram set out from Samaria and mobilized **all** Israel.
3:19 You will overthrow **every** fortified city and every major town.
3:19 You will overthrow every fortified city and **every** major town.
3:19 You will cut down **every** good tree, stop up all the springs,
3:19 You will cut down every good tree, stop up **all** the springs,
3:19 stop up all the springs, and ruin **every** good field with stones."
3:21 Now **all** the Moabites had heard that the kings had come to fight
3:21 so **every** *man, young* and old, who could bear arms was called up
3:25 each man threw a stone on **every** good field until it was covered.
3:25 They stopped up **all** the springs and cut down every good tree.
3:25 They stopped up all the springs and cut down **every** good tree.
4: 2 "Your servant has nothing there **at all**," she said, "except a little
4: 3 Elisha said, "Go around and ask **all** your neighbors for empty jars.
4: 4 Pour oil into **all** the jars, and as each is filled, put it to one side."
4:13 said to him, "Tell her, 'You have gone to **all** this trouble for us.
5:12 the rivers of Damascus, better than **any** *of* the waters of Israel?
5:15 Then Naaman and **all** his attendants went back to the man of God.
5:15 "Now I know that there is no God in **all** the world except in Israel.
6:24 Ben-Hadad king of Aram mobilized his **entire** army and marched
7:13 Their plight will be like that of **all** [+2162] the Israelites left here—
7:13 they will only be like **all** [+2162] these Israelites who are doomed.
7:15 they found the **whole** road strewn with the clothing and equipment
8: 4 and had said, "Tell me about **all** the great things Elisha has done."
8: 6 and said to him, "Give back **everything** that belonged to her,
8: 6 including **all** the income from her land from the day she left the
8: 9 taking with him as a gift forty camel-loads of **all** the finest wares of
8:19 a lamp for David and his descendants **forever** [+2021+3427].
8:21 So Jehoram went to Zair with **all** his chariots. The Edomites
8:23 As for the other events of Jehoram's reign, and **all** he did,
9: 5 message for you, commander," he said. "For which of **[NIE]** us?"
9: 7 and the blood of **all** the LORD's servants shed by Jezebel.
9: 8 The **whole** house of Ahab will perish. I will cut off from Ahab
9:14 **all** Israel had been defending Ramoth Gilead against Hazael king
10: 5 "We are your servants and we will do **anything** you say. We will
10: 9 He stood before **all** the people and said, "You are innocent.
10: 9 against my master and killed him, but who killed **all** these?
10:11 So Jehu killed **everyone** in Jezreel who remained of the house of
10:11 as well as **all** his chief men, his close friends and his priests,
10:17 to Samaria, he killed **all** who were left there of Ahab's family;
10:18 Then Jehu brought **all** the people together and said to them,
10:19 Now summon **all** the prophets of Baal, all his ministers and all his
10:19 all the prophets of Baal, **all** his ministers and all his priests.
10:19 all the prophets of Baal, all his ministers and **all** his priests.
10:19 sacrifice for Baal. **Anyone** who fails to come will no longer live."
10:21 he sent word **throughout** [+928] Israel, and all the ministers of
10:21 he sent word throughout Israel, and **all** the ministers of Baal came;
10:22 keeper of the wardrobe, "Bring robes for **all** the ministers of Baal."
10:30 and have done to the house of Ahab **all** I had in mind to do,
10:31 to keep the law of the LORD, the God of Israel, with **all** his heart.
10:32 Hazael overpowered the Israelites **throughout** [+928] their
10:33 east of the Jordan in **all** the land of Gilead (the region of Gad,
10:34 other events of Jehu's reign, **all** he did, and all his achievements,
10:34 other events of Jehu's reign, all he did, and **all** his achievements,
11: 1 her son was dead, she proceeded to destroy the **whole** royal family.
11: 7 go off Sabbath duty are **all** to guard the temple for the king.
11: 9 The commanders of units of a hundred did **just as** [+889+3869]
11:14 and **all** the people of the land were rejoicing and blowing trumpets.
11:18 **All** the people of the land went to the temple of Baal and tore it
11:19 of hundreds, the Carites, the guards and **all** the people of the land,
11:20 and **all** the people of the land rejoiced. And the city was quiet,
12: 2 [12:3] Joash did what was right in the eyes of the LORD **all** the
12: 4 [12:5] "Collect **all** the money that is brought as sacred offerings to
12: 4 [12:5] and **[NIE]** the money brought voluntarily to the temple.
12: 5 [12:6] let it be used to repair **whatever** [+889] damage is found in
12: 9 [12:10] The priests who guarded the entrance put into the chest **all**
12:12 [12:13] and met **all** the other expenses of restoring the temple.
12:13 [12:14] trumpets or **any** other articles of gold or silver for the
12:18 [12:19] Joash king of Judah took **all** the sacred objects dedicated
12:18 [12:19] **all** the gold found in the treasuries of the temple of the
12:19 [12:20] for the other events of the reign of Joash, and **all** he did,
13: 3 for a **long** time he kept them under the power of Hazael king of
13: 8 events of the reign of Jehoahaz, **all** he did and his achievements,
13:11 did not turn away from **any** *of* the sins of Jeroboam son of Nebat,
13:12 events of the reign of Jehoash, **all** he did and his achievements,
13:22 Hazael king of Aram oppressed Israel **throughout** the reign of
14: 3 *In* **everything** he followed the example of his father Joash.
14:14 He took **all** the gold and silver and all the articles found in the
14:14 and silver and **all** the articles found in the temple of the LORD
14:21 **all** the people of Judah took Azariah, who was sixteen years old,
14:24 did not turn away from **any** *of* the sins of Jeroboam son of Nebat,
14:28 of Jeroboam's reign, **all** he did, and his military achievements,
15: 3 of the LORD, **just as** [+889+3869] his father Amaziah had done.
15: 6 As for the other events of Azariah's reign, and **all** he did, are they
15:16 attacked Tiphsah and **everyone** in the city and its vicinity,
15:16 He sacked Tiphsah and ripped open **all** the pregnant women.
15:18 During his **entire** reign he did not turn away from the sins of
15:20 **Every** wealthy man had to contribute fifty shekels of silver to be
15:21 As for the other events of Menahem's reign, and **all** he did,
15:26 The other events of Pekahiah's reign, and **all** he did, are written in
15:29 He took Gilead and Galilee, including **all** the land of Naphtali,
15:31 As for the other events of Pekah's reign, and **all** he did, are they
15:34 of the LORD, **just as** [+889+3869] his father Uzziah had done.
16: 4 at the high places, on the hilltops and under **every** spreading tree.
16:10 priest a sketch of the altar, with **detailed** plans for its construction.
16:11 So Uriah the priest built an altar in accordance with **all** the plans
16:15 grain offering, and the burnt offering of **all** the people of the land,
16:15 Sprinkle on the altar **all** the blood of the burnt offerings
16:15 the altar all the blood of the burnt offerings and **[RPH]** sacrifices.
16:16 Uriah the priest did **just as** [+889+3869] King Ahaz had ordered.
17: 5 The king of Assyria invaded the **entire** land, marched against
17: 9 to fortified city they built themselves high places in **all** their towns.
17:10 They set up sacred stones and Asherah poles on **every** high hill
17:10 Asherah poles on every high hill and under **every** spreading tree.
17:11 At **every** high place they burned incense, as the nations whom the
17:13 warned Israel and Judah through **all** his prophets and seers:
17:13 and Judah through all his prophets and **[RPH]** seers:
17:13 in accordance with the **entire** Law that I commanded your fathers
17:16 They forsook **all** the commands of the LORD their God and made
17:16 They bowed down to **all** the starry hosts, and they worshiped Baal.
17:20 Therefore the LORD rejected **all** the people of Israel; he afflicted
17:22 The Israelites persisted in **all** the sins of Jeroboam and did not turn
17:23 as he had warned through **all** his servants the prophets.
17:37 You must **always** [+2021+3427] be careful to keep the decrees
17:39 it is he who will deliver you from the hand of **all** your enemies."
18: 3 of the LORD, **just as** [+889+3869] his father David had done.
18: 5 There was no one like him among **all** the kings of Judah,
18: 7 was with him; he was successful in **whatever** [+889] he undertook.
18:12 **all** that Moses the servant of the LORD commanded.
18:13 Sennacherib king of Assyria attacked **all** the fortified cities of
18:15 So Hezekiah gave him **all** the silver that was found in the temple of
18:21 on it! Such is Pharaoh king of Egypt to **all** who depend on him.
18:35 Who of **all** the gods of these countries has been able to save his
19: 4 It may be that the LORD your God will hear **all** the words of the
19:11 Surely you have heard what the kings of Assyria have done to **all**
19:15 you alone are God over **all** the kingdoms of the earth.
19:19 so that **all** kingdoms on earth may know that you alone, O LORD,
19:24 With the soles of my feet I have dried up **all** the streams of Egypt."
19:35 people got up the next morning—there were **all** the dead bodies!
20:13 the messengers and showed them **all** that was *in* his storehouses—
20:13 fine oil—his armory and **everything** found among his treasures.
20:13 his palace or in **all** his kingdom that Hezekiah did not show them.
20:15 "They saw **everything** in my palace," Hezekiah said.
20:17 The time will surely come when **everything** in your palace,
20:20 **all** his achievements and how he made the pool and the tunnel by
21: 3 He bowed down to **all** the starry hosts and worshiped them.
21: 5 of the temple of the LORD, he built altars to **all** the starry hosts.
21: 7 in Jerusalem, which I have chosen out of **all** the tribes of Israel,
21: 8 if only they will be careful to do **everything** I commanded them
21: 8 and will keep the **whole** Law that my servant Moses gave them."
21:11 He has done **more** evil than the Amorites who preceded him
21:12 and Judah that the ears of **everyone** who hears of it will tingle.
21:14 their enemies. They will be looted and plundered by **all** their foes,
21:17 Manasseh's reign, and **all** he did, including the sin he committed,
21:21 He walked in **all** the ways of his father; he worshiped the idols his
21:24 the people of the land killed **all** who had plotted against King
22: 2 eyes of the LORD and walked in **all** the ways of his father David,
22:13 for **all** Judah about what is written in this book that has been found.
22:13 they have not acted in accordance with **all** that is written there
22:16 according to **everything** written in the book the king of Judah has
22:17 and provoked me to anger by **all** the idols their hands have made,
22:20 Your eyes will not see **all** the disaster I am going to bring on this
23: 1 Then the king called together **all** the elders of Judah and Jerusalem.
23: 2 He went up to the temple of the LORD with **[RPH]** the men of
23: 2 **[RPH]** the people of Jerusalem, the priests and the prophets—
23: 2 and the prophets—**all** the people from the least to the greatest.
23: 2 He read in their hearing **all** the words of the Book of the Covenant,
23: 3 and decrees with **all** his heart and all his soul,
23: 3 and decrees with all his heart and **all** his soul,
23: 3 this book. Then **all** the people pledged themselves to the covenant.
23: 4 the doorkeepers to remove from the temple of the LORD **all** the
23: 4 all the articles made for Baal and Asherah and **all** the starry hosts.
23: 5 and moon, to the constellations and to **all** the starry hosts.
23: 8 Josiah brought **all** the priests from the towns of Judah

2Ki 23:19 **Just as** [+3869] he had done at Bethel, Josiah removed and defiled
23:19 defiled **all** the shrines at the high places that the kings of Israel had
23:20 Josiah slaughtered **all** the priests of those high places on the altars
23:21 The king gave this order to **all** the people: "Celebrate the Passover
23:22 nor **throughout** the days of the kings of Israel and the kings of
23:24 the idols and **all** the other detestable things seen in Judah
23:25 with **all** his heart and with all his soul and with all his strength,
23:25 with all his heart and with **all** his soul and with all his strength,
23:25 with all his heart and with all his soul and with **all** his strength,
23:25 and with all his strength, in accordance with **all** the Law of Moses.
23:26 because of **all** that Manasseh had done to provoke him to anger.
23:28 As for the other events of Josiah's reign, and **all** he did, are they
23:32 the eyes of the LORD, **just as** [+889+3869] his fathers had done.
23:37 the eyes of the LORD, **just as** [+889+3869] his fathers had done.
24: 3 his presence because of the sins of Manasseh and **all** he had done,
24: 5 As for the other events of Jehoiakim's reign, and **all** he did,
24: 7 because the king of Babylon had taken **all** his territory, from the
24: 9 the eyes of the LORD, **just as** [+889+3869] his father had done.
24:13 Nebuchadnezzar removed **all** the treasures from the temple of the
24:13 took away **all** the gold articles that Solomon king of Israel had
24:14 He carried into exile **all** Jerusalem: all the officers and fighting
24:14 **all** the officers and fighting men, and all the craftsmen
24:14 all the officers and **[RPH]** fighting men, and all the craftsmen
24:14 the officers and fighting men, and **all** the craftsmen and artisans—
24:16 The king of Babylon also deported to Babylon the **entire** *force of*
24:16 **[RPH]** strong and fit for war, and a thousand craftsmen
24:19 the eyes of the LORD, **just as** [+889+3869] Jehoiakim had done.
25: 1 king of Babylon marched against Jerusalem with his **whole** army.
25: 4 the **whole** army fled at night through the gate between the two
25: 5 of Jericho. **All** his soldiers were separated from him and scattered,
25: 9 of the LORD, the royal palace and **all** the houses of Jerusalem.
25: 9 houses of Jerusalem. **Every** important building he burned down.
25:10 The **whole** Babylonian army, under the commander of the imperial
25:14 dishes and **all** the bronze articles used in the temple service.
25:16 temple of the LORD, was more than could be weighed. **[NIE]**
25:17 decorated with a network and pomegranates of bronze **all** around.
25:23 When **all** the army officers and their men heard that the king of
25:26 At this, **all** the people from the least to the greatest, together with
25:29 and *for* the **rest** [+3427] *of* his life ate regularly at the king's table.
25:30 gave Jehoiachin a regular allowance **as long** [+3427] **as** he lived.
1Ch 1:23 Ophir, Havilah and Jobab. **All** these were sons of Joktan.
1:33 Abida and Eldaah. **All** these were descendants of Keturah.
2: 4 bore him Perez and Zerah. Judah had five sons *in* **all**.
2: 6 of Zerah: Zimri, Ethan, Heman, Calcol and Darda—five *in* **all**.
2:23 **All** these were descendants of Makir the father of Gilead.
3: 9 **All** *these* were the sons of David, besides his sons by his
4:27 so their **entire** clan did not become as numerous as the people of
4:33 **all** the villages around these towns as far as Baalath. These were
5:10 they occupied the dwellings of the Hagrites throughout the **entire**
5:16 and on **all** the pasturelands of Sharon as far as they extended.
5:17 **All** these were entered in the genealogical records during the reigns
5:20 and God handed the Hagrites and **all** their allies over to them,
6:48 [6:33] Their fellow Levites were assigned to **all** the other duties of
6:49 [6:34] on the altar of incense in connection with **all** that was done
6:49 [6:34] in accordance with **all** that Moses the servant of God had
6:60 [6:45] distributed among the Kohathite clans, were thirteen *in* **all**.
7: 3 Michael, Obadiah, Joel and Isshiah. **All** five *of* them were chiefs.
7: 5 The relatives who were fighting men belonging to **all** the clans of
7: 5 clans of Issachar, as listed in their genealogy, were 87,000 in **all**.
7: 8 Abijah, Anathoth and Alemeth. **All** these were the sons of Beker.
7:11 **All** these sons of Jediael were heads of families. There were 17,200
7:40 **All** these were descendants of Asher—heads of families, choice
8:38 Sheariah, Obadiah and Hanan. **All** these were the sons of Azel.
8:40 150 in all. **All** these were the descendants of Benjamin.
9: 1 **All** Israel was listed in the genealogies recorded in the book of the
9: 9 numbered 956. **All** these men were heads of their families.
9:22 **Altogether**, those chosen to be gatekeepers at the thresholds
9:29 care of the furnishings and **all** the other articles of the sanctuary,
10: 6 So Saul and his three sons died, and **all** his house died together.
10: 7 When **all** the Israelites in the valley saw that the army had fled
10:11 When **all** the inhabitants of Jabesh Gilead heard of everything the
10:11 When all the inhabitants of Jabesh Gilead heard of **everything** the
10:12 **all** their valiant men went and took the bodies of Saul and his sons
11: 1 **All** Israel came together to David at Hebron and said, "We are your
11: 3 When **all** the elders of Israel had come to King David at Hebron,
11: 4 David and **all** the Israelites marched to Jerusalem (that is,
11: 6 "**Whoever** leads the attack on the Jebusites will become
11:10 they, together with **all** Israel, gave his kingship strong support to
12:15 [12:16] in the first month when it was overflowing **all** its banks,
12:15 [12:16] they put to flight **everyone** *living in* the valleys,
12:21 [12:22] for **all** *of* them were brave warriors, and they were
12:32 [12:33] 200 chiefs, with **all** their relatives under their command;
12:33 [12:34] soldiers prepared for battle with **every** *type of* weapon,
12:37 [12:38] of Manasseh, armed with **every** *type of* weapon—
12:38 [12:39] **All** these were fighting men who volunteered to serve in
12:38 [12:39] fully determined to make David king over **all** Israel.
12:38 [12:39] **All** the rest of the Israelites were also of one mind to
13: 1 David conferred with **each** *of* his officers, the commanders of
13: 2 He then said to the **whole** assembly of Israel, "If it seems good to
13: 2 wide to the rest of our brothers **throughout** [+928] the territories
13: 4 The **whole** assembly agreed to do this, because it seemed right to
13: 4 agreed to do this, because it seemed right to **all** the people.
13: 5 So David assembled **all** the Israelites, from the Shihor River in
13: 6 **all** the Israelites with him went to Baalah of Judah (Kiriath Jearim)
13: 8 **all** the Israelites were celebrating with all their might before God,
13: 8 all the Israelites were celebrating with **all** their might before God,
13:14 and the LORD blessed his household and **everything** he had.
14: 8 Philistines heard that David had been anointed king over **all** Israel,
14: 8 they went up **in full force** to search for him, but David heard about
14:17 So David's fame spread throughout **every** land, and the LORD
14:17 every land, and the LORD made **all** the nations fear him.
15: 3 David assembled **all** Israel in Jerusalem to bring up the ark of the
15:27 as were **all** the Levites who were carrying the ark, and as were the
15:28 So **all** Israel brought up the ark of the covenant of the LORD with
16: 3 of dates and a cake of raisins to **each** Israelite man and woman.
16: 9 Sing to him, sing praise to him; tell of **all** his wonderful acts.
16:14 He is the LORD our God; his judgments are in **all** the earth.
16:23 Sing to the LORD, **all** the earth; proclaim his salvation day after
16:24 glory among the nations, his marvelous deeds among **all** peoples.
16:25 and most worthy of praise; he is to be feared above **all** gods.
16:26 For **all** the gods of the nations are idols, but the LORD made the
16:30 Tremble before him, **all** the earth! The world is firmly established;
16:32 all that is in it; let the fields be jubilant, and **everything** in them!
16:36 Then **all** the people said "Amen" and "Praise the LORD."
16:40 in accordance with **everything** written in the Law of the LORD,
16:43 **all** the people left, each for his own home, and David returned
17: 2 "**Whatever** [+889] you have in mind, do it, for God is with you."
17: 6 **Wherever** [+889+928] I have moved with all the Israelites,
17: 6 Wherever I have moved with **all** the Israelites, did I ever say to any
17: 8 I have been with you **wherever** [+889+928] you have gone,
17: 8 have gone, and I have cut off **all** your enemies from before you.
17:10 I will also subdue **all** your enemies. " 'I declare to you that the
17:15 Nathan reported to David **all** the words of this entire revelation.
17:15 Nathan reported to David all the words of this **entire** revelation.
17:19 you have done **[RPH]** this great thing and made known all these
17:19 done this great thing and made known **all** these great promises.
17:20 but you, **as** [+889+928] we have heard with our own ears.
18: 4 foot soldiers. He hamstrung **all** but a hundred of the chariot horses.
18: 6 The LORD gave David victory **everywhere** [+928] he went.
18: 9 David had defeated the **entire** army of Hadadezer king of Zobah,
18:10 Hadoram brought **all** *kinds of* articles of gold and silver
18:11 done with the silver and gold he had taken from **all** these nations:
18:13 garrisons in Edom, and **all** the Edomites became subject to David.
18:13 The LORD gave David victory **everywhere** [+928] he went.
18:14 David reigned over **all** Israel, doing what was just and right for all
18:14 over all Israel, doing what was just and right for **all** his people.
19: 8 David sent Joab out with the **entire** army of fighting men.
19:10 so he selected **some** [+4946] *of* the best troops in Israel
19:17 was told of this, he gathered **all** Israel and crossed the Jordan;
20: 3 iron picks and axes. David did this to **all** the Ammonite towns.
20: 3 Then David and his **entire** army returned to Jerusalem.
21: 3 My lord the king, are they not **all** my lord's subjects? Why does
21: 4 so Joab left and went **throughout** [+928] Israel and then came
21: 5 In **all** Israel there were one million one hundred thousand men who
21:12 with the angel of the LORD ravaging **every** part of Israel.'
21:23 the wood, and the wheat for the grain offering. I will give **all** this."
22: 5 and fame and splendor in the sight of **all** the nations.
22: 9 and I will give him rest from **all** his enemies on every side.
22:15 and carpenters, as well as **men**[s] skilled in every kind of work
22:15 and carpenters, as well as men skilled in **every** *kind of* work
22:17 David ordered **all** the leaders of Israel to help his son Solomon.
23: 2 He also gathered together **all** the leaders of Israel, as well as the
23:26 to carry the tabernacle or **any** *of* the articles used in its service."
23:28 the purification of **all** sacred things and the performance of other
23:29 and the mixing, and **all** measurements of quantity and size.
23:31 **whenever** [+4200] burnt offerings were presented to the LORD
25: 5 **All** these were sons of Heman the king's seer. They were given
25: 6 **All** these men were under the supervision of their fathers for the
25: 7 **all** *of* them trained and skilled in music for the LORD—
26: 8 **All** these were descendants of Obed-Edom; they and their sons
26:11 the fourth. The sons and relatives of Hosah were 13 *in* **all**.
26:26 his relatives were in charge of **all** the treasuries for the things
26:28 **everything** dedicated by Samuel the seer and by Saul son of Kish,
26:28 and **all** the other dedicated things were in the care of Shelomith
26:30 were responsible in Israel west of the Jordan for **all** the work of the
26:32 and the half-tribe of Manasseh for **every** matter pertaining to God
27: 1 who served the king in **all** that concerned the army divisions that
27: 1 that were on duty month by month **throughout** [+4200] the year.

1Ch 27: 3 of Perez and chief of **all** the army officers for the first month.
27: 31 **All** these were the officials in charge of King David's property.
28: 1 David summoned **all** the officials of Israel to assemble at
28: 1 the officials in charge of **all** the property and livestock belonging to
28: 1 the palace officials, the mighty men and **all** the brave warriors.
28: 4 chose me from my **whole** family to be king over Israel forever.
28: 4 from my father's sons he was pleased to make me king over **all**
28: 5 Of **all** my sons—and the LORD has given me many—he has
28: 8 "So now I charge you in the sight of **all** Israel and of the assembly
28: 8 Be careful to follow **all** the commands of the LORD your God,
28: 9 for the LORD searches **every** heart and understands every motive
28: 9 every heart and understands **every** motive behind the thoughts.
28: 12 He gave him the plans of **all** that the Spirit had put in his mind for
28: 12 courts of the temple of the LORD and **all** the surrounding rooms,
28: 13 and for **all** the work of serving in the temple of the LORD,
28: 13 the LORD, as well as for **all** the articles to be used in its service.
28: 14 He designated the weight of gold for **all** the gold articles to be used
28: 14 the weight of silver for **all** the silver articles to be used in various
28: 14 the weight of silver for all the silver articles to be used in **[RPH]**
28: 19 "**All** this," David said, "I have in writing from the hand of the
28: 19 and he gave me understanding in **all** the details of the plan."
28: 20 or forsake you until **all** the work for the service of the temple of the
28: 21 and Levites are ready for **all** the work on the temple of God,
28: 21 **every** willing man skilled in any craft will help you in all the work.
28: 21 every willing man skilled in **any** craft will help you in all the work.
28: 21 every willing man skilled in any craft will help you in **all** the work.
28: 21 The officials and **all** the people will obey your every command."
28: 21 The officials and all the people will obey your **every** command."
29: 1 Then King David said to the **whole** assembly: "My son Solomon,
29: 2 With **all** my resources I have provided for the temple of my God—
29: 2 stones of various colors, and **all** *kinds of* fine stone and marble—
29: 3 and above **everything** I have provided for this holy temple:
29: 5 the silver work, and for **all** the work to be done by the craftsmen.
29: 10 David praised the LORD in the presence of the **whole** assembly,
29: 11 and the splendor, for **everything** in heaven and earth is yours.
29: 11 O LORD, is the kingdom; you are exalted as head over **all**.
29: 12 and honor come from you; you are the ruler of **all** *things*.
29: 12 your hands are strength and power to exalt and give strength to **all**.
29: 14 **Everything** comes from you, and we have given you only what
29: 15 are aliens and strangers in your sight, as were **all** our forefathers.
29: 16 as for **all** this abundance that we have provided for building you a
29: 16 Holy Name, it comes from your hand, and **all** of it belongs to you.
29: 17 **All** these things have I given willingly and with honest intent.
29: 19 to do **everything** to build the palatial structure for which I have
29: 20 David said to the **whole** assembly, "Praise the LORD your God."
29: 20 So they **all** praised the LORD, the God of their fathers; they
29: 21 drink offerings, and other sacrifices in abundance for **all** Israel.
29: 23 place of his father David. He prospered and **all** Israel obeyed him.
29: 24 **All** the officers and mighty men, as well as all of King David's
29: 24 the officers and mighty men, as well as **all** *of* King David's sons,
29: 25 The LORD highly exalted Solomon in the sight of **all** Israel
29: 25 bestowed on him royal splendor such as no king over Israel **ever**
29: 26 David son of Jesse was king over **all** Israel.
29: 30 together with the **details** *of* his reign and power, and the
29: 30 surrounded him and Israel and the kingdoms of **all** the other lands.
2Ch 1: 2 Solomon spoke to **all** Israel—to the commanders of thousands
1: 2 to the judges and to **all** the leaders in Israel, the heads of families—
1: 2 to the judges and to all the leaders in **[RPH]** Israel, the heads of
1: 3 and the **whole** assembly went to the high place at Gibeon,
1: 17 They also exported them to **all** the kings of the Hittites and of the
2: 5 [2:4] will be great, because our God is greater than **all** other gods.
2: 14 [2:13] He is experienced in **all** *kinds of* engraving and can
2: 14 [2:13] of engraving and can execute **any** design given to him.
2: 16 [2:15] we will cut **all** the logs from Lebanon that you need
2: 17 [2:16] Solomon took a census of **all** the aliens who were in Israel,
4: 4 top of them, and **[NIE]** their hindquarters were toward the center.
4: 16 the pots, shovels, meat forks and **all** related articles. All the objects
4: 18 **All** these things that Solomon made amounted to so much that the
4: 19 Solomon also made **all** the furnishings that were in God's temple:
5: 1 When **all** the work Solomon had done for the temple of the
5: 1 the silver and gold and **all** the furnishings—and he placed them in
5: 2 **all** the heads of the tribes and the chiefs of the Israelite families,
5: 3 **all** the men of Israel came together to the king at the time of the
5: 4 When **all** the elders of Israel had arrived, the Levites took up the
5: 5 and the Tent of Meeting and **all** the sacred furnishings in it.
5: 6 the **entire** assembly of Israel that had gathered about him were
5: 11 **All** the priests who were there had consecrated themselves,
5: 12 **All** the Levites who were musicians—Asaph, Heman, Jeduthun
6: 3 While the **whole** assembly of Israel was standing there, the king
6: 3 the king turned around and blessed **them**[s] [+3776+7736].
6: 5 I have not chosen a city in **any** tribe of Israel to have a temple built
6: 12 Solomon stood before the altar of the LORD in front of the **whole**
6: 13 and then knelt down before the **whole** assembly of Israel
6: 14 servants who continue **wholeheartedly** [+928+4213] in your way.
6: 28 them in any of their cities, **whatever** disaster or disease may come,
6: 28 any of their cities, whatever disaster or **[RPH]** disease may come,
6: 29 and when **a** prayer or plea is made by any of your people Israel—
6: 29 a prayer or **[RPH]** plea is made by any of your people Israel—
6: 29 and when a prayer or plea is made by **any** *of* your people Israel—
6: 29 a prayer or plea is made by any of **[RPH]** your people Israel—
6: 30 Forgive, and deal with each man according to **all** he does,
6: 31 walk in your ways **all** the time they live in the land you gave our
6: 33 and do **whatever** [+889+3869] the foreigner asks of you,
6: 33 so that **all** the peoples of the earth may know your name and fear
6: 38 if they turn back to you with **all** their heart and soul in the land of
6: 38 **[RPH]** soul in the land of their captivity where they were taken,
7: 3 When **all** the Israelites saw the fire coming down and the glory of
7: 4 the king and **all** the people offered sacrifices before the LORD.
7: 5 So the king and **all** the people dedicated the temple of God.
7: 6 the priests blew their trumpets, and **all** the Israelites were standing.
7: 8 the festival at that time for seven days, and **all** Israel with him—
7: 11 had succeeded in carrying out **all** he had in mind to do in the
7: 16 My eyes and my heart will **always** [+2021+3427] be there.
7: 17 and do **all** I command, and observe my decrees and laws,
7: 20 will make it a byword and an object of ridicule among **all** peoples.
7: 21 is now so imposing, **all** who pass by will be appalled and say,
7: 22 serving them—that is why he brought **all** this disaster on them.' "
8: 4 Tadmor in the desert and **all** the store cities he had built in Hamath.
8: 6 as well as Baalath and **all** his store cities, and all the cities for his
8: 6 store cities, and **all** the cities for his chariots and for his horses—
8: 6 **whatever** he desired to build in Jerusalem, in Lebanon
8: 6 in Jerusalem, in Lebanon and throughout **all** the territory he ruled.
8: 7 **All** the people left from the Hittites, Amorites, Perizzites, Hivites
8: 15 the king's commands to the priests or to the Levites in **any** matter,
8: 16 **All** Solomon's work was carried out, from the day the foundation
9: 1 to Solomon and talked with him about **all** she had on her mind.
9: 2 Solomon answered **all** her questions; nothing was too hard for him
9: 12 King Solomon gave the queen of Sheba **all** she desired and asked
9: 14 Also **all** the kings of Arabia and the governors of the land brought
9: 19 Nothing like it had ever been made for **any** other kingdom.
9: 20 **All** King Solomon's goblets were gold, and all the household
9: 20 **all** the household articles in the Palace of the Forest of Lebanon
9: 22 greater in riches and wisdom than **all** the other kings of the earth.
9: 23 **All** the kings of the earth sought audience with Solomon to hear
9: 26 He ruled over **all** the kings from the River to the land of the
9: 28 horses were imported from Egypt and from **all** other countries.
9: 30 Solomon reigned in Jerusalem over **all** Israel forty years.
10: 1 to Shechem, for **all** the Israelites had gone there to make him king.
10: 3 and he and **all** Israel went to Rehoboam and said to him:
10: 7 they will **always** [+2021+3427] be your servants."
10: 12 days later Jeroboam and **all** the people returned to Rehoboam,
10: 16 When **all** Israel saw that the king refused to listen to them,
10: 16 after your own house, O David!" So **all** the Israelites went home.
11: 3 king of Judah and to **all** the Israelites in Judah and Benjamin,
11: 12 He put shields and spears in **all** the cities, and made them very
11: 13 Levites from **all** their districts throughout Israel sided with him.
11: 13 Levites from all their districts **throughout** [+928] Israel sided with
11: 16 Those from **every** tribe of Israel who set their hearts on seeking the
11: 21 Rehoboam loved Maacah daughter of Absalom more than **any** *of*
11: 23 dispersing **some of** [+4946] his sons throughout the districts of
11: 23 dispersing some of his sons **throughout** [+4200] the districts of
11: 23 the districts of Judah and Benjamin, and to **all** the fortified cities.
12: 1 and **all** Israel with him abandoned the law of the LORD.
12: 9 He took **everything**, including the gold shields Solomon had made.
12: 13 the city the LORD had chosen out of **all** the tribes of Israel in
12: 15 There was **continual** [+2021+3427] warfare between Rehoboam
13: 4 of Ephraim, and said, "Jeroboam and **all** Israel, listen to me!
13: 9 **Whoever** comes to consecrate himself with a young bull and seven
13: 15 God routed Jeroboam and **all** Israel before Abijah and Judah.
14: 5 [14:4] the high places and incense altars in **every** town in Judah,
14: 8 [14:7] and with bows. **All** these were brave fighting men.
14: 14 [14:13] They destroyed **all** the villages around Gerar,
14: 14 [14:13] They plundered **all** these villages, since there was much
15: 2 and said to him, "Listen to me, Asa and **all** Judah and Benjamin.
15: 5 for **all** the inhabitants of the lands were in great turmoil.
15: 6 because God was troubling them with **every** *kind of* distress.
15: 8 He removed the detestable idols from the **whole** land of Judah
15: 9 he assembled **all** Judah and Benjamin and the people from
15: 12 the LORD, the God of their fathers, with **all** their heart and soul.
15: 12 the God of their fathers, with all their heart and **[RPH]** soul.
15: 13 **All** who would not seek the LORD, the God of Israel, were to be
15: 15 **All** Judah rejoiced about the oath because they had sworn it
15: 15 oath because they had sworn it **wholeheartedly** [+928+4222].
15: 15 They sought God **eagerly** [+928+8356], and he was found by
15: 17 Asa's heart was fully committed ⌞to the LORD⌟ **all** his life.
16: 4 Dan, Abel Maim and **all** the store cities of Naphtali.
16: 6 King Asa brought **all** the men of Judah, and they carried away
16: 9 For the eyes of the LORD range **throughout** [+928] the earth to

2Ch 17: 2 He stationed troops in **all** the fortified cities of Judah and put
17: 5 **all** Judah brought gifts to Jehoshaphat, so that he had great wealth
17: 9 they went around to **all** the towns of Judah and taught the people.
17:10 The fear of the LORD fell on **all** the kingdoms of the lands
17:19 besides those he stationed in the fortified cities **throughout** [+928]
18: 7 never prophesies anything good about me, but **always** [+3427] bad.
18: 9 the gate of Samaria, with **all** the prophets prophesying before them.
18:11 **All** the other prophets were prophesying the same thing. "Attack
18:16 "I saw **all** Israel scattered on the hills like sheep without a
18:18 I saw the LORD sitting on his throne with **all** the host of heaven
18:21 " 'I will go and be a lying spirit in the mouths of **all** his prophets,'
18:27 through me." Then he added, "Mark my words, **all** you people!"
19: 5 judges in the land, in **each** *of* the fortified cities of Judah.
19:10 *In* **every** case that comes before you from your fellow countrymen
19:11 "Amariah the chief priest will be over you in **any** matter
19:11 tribe of Judah, will be over you in **any** matter concerning the king,
20: 3 to inquire of the LORD, and he proclaimed a fast for **all** Judah.
20: 4 indeed, they came from **every** town in Judah to seek him.
20: 6 You rule over **all** the kingdoms of the nations. Power and might are
20:13 **All** the men of Judah, with their wives and children and little ones,
20:15 King Jehoshaphat and **all** who live in Judah and Jerusalem!
20:18 **all** the people of Judah and Jerusalem fell down in worship before
20:27 **all** the men of Judah and Jerusalem returned joyfully to Jerusalem,
20:29 The fear of God came upon **all** the kingdoms of the countries when
21: 2 and Shephatiah. **All** these were sons of Jehoshaphat king of Israel.
21: 4 he put **all** his brothers to the sword along with some of the princes
21: 7 a lamp for him and his descendants **forever** [+2021+3427].
21: 9 So Jehoram went there with his officers and **all** his chariots.
21:14 your sons, your wives and **everything** [+8214] *that* is yours,
21:17 invaded it and carried off **all** the goods found in the king's palace,
21:18 After **all** this, the LORD afflicted Jehoram with an incurable
22: 1 came with the Arabs into the camp, had killed **all** the older sons.
22: 9 a son of Jehoshaphat, who sought the LORD with **all** his heart."
22:10 she proceeded to destroy the **whole** royal family of the house of
23: 2 the Levites and the heads of Israelite families from **all** the towns.
23: 3 the **whole** assembly made a covenant with the king at the temple of
23: 5 **all** the other men are to be in the courtyards of the temple of the
23: 6 **all** the other men are to guard what the LORD has assigned to
23: 8 and **all** the men of Judah did just as Jehoiada the priest ordered.
23: 8 all the men of Judah did **just as** [+889+3869] Jehoiada the priest
23:10 He stationed **all** the men, each with his weapon in his hand,
23:13 and **all** the people of the land were rejoicing and blowing trumpets,
23:16 Jehoiada then made a covenant that he and **[NIE]** the people
23:17 **All** the people went to the temple of Baal and tore it down.
23:19 so that no one who was in **any** way unclean might enter.
23:20 the rulers of the people and **all** the people of the land and brought
23:21 and **all** the people of the land rejoiced. And the city was quiet,
24: 2 Joash did what was right in the eyes of the LORD **all** the years of
24: 5 towns of Judah and collect the money due annually from **all** Israel,
24: 7 and had used even **[NIE]** its sacred objects for the Baals.
24:10 **All** the officials and all the people brought their contributions
24:10 the officials and **all** the people brought their contributions gladly,
24:14 **As long** [+3427] **as** Jehoiada **lived**, burnt offerings were presented
24:23 and Jerusalem and killed **all** the leaders of the people.
24:23 of the people. They sent **all** the plunder to their king in Damascus.
25: 5 and commanders of hundreds for **all** Judah and Benjamin.
25: 7 LORD is not with Israel—not with **any** *of* the people of Ephraim.
25:12 of a cliff and threw them down so that **all** were dashed to pieces.
25:24 He took **all** the gold and silver and all the articles found in the
25:24 **all** the articles found in the temple of God that had been in the care
26: 1 **all** the people of Judah took Uzziah, who was sixteen years old,
26: 4 of the LORD, **just as** [+889+3869] his father Amaziah had done.
26:12 The **total** number of family leaders over the fighting men was
26:14 helmets, coats of armor, bows and slingstones for the **entire** army.
26:20 Azariah the chief priest and **all** the other priests looked at him,
27: 2 of the LORD, **just as** [+889+3869] his father Uzziah had done,
27: 7 Jotham's reign, including **all** his wars and the other things he did,
28: 4 at the high places, on the hilltops and under **every** spreading tree.
28: 6 **[NIE]** because Judah had forsaken the LORD, the God of their
28:14 and plunder in the presence of the officials and **all** the assembly.
28:15 and from the plunder they clothed **all** who were naked.
28:15 and healing balm. **All** those who were weak they put on donkeys.
28:23 But they were his downfall and the downfall of **all** Israel.
28:24 and set up altars at **every** street corner in Jerusalem.
28:25 In **every** town in Judah he built high places to burn sacrifices to
28:26 The other events of his reign and **all** his ways, from beginning to
29: 2 of the LORD, **just as** [+889+3869] his father David had done.
29:16 **everything** unclean that they found in the temple of the LORD.
29:18 "We have purified the **entire** temple of the LORD, the altar of
29:18 the altar of burnt offering with **all** its utensils, and the table for
29:18 the table for setting out the consecrated bread, with **all** its articles.
29:19 consecrated **all** the articles that King Ahaz removed in his
29:24 presented their blood on the altar for a sin offering to atone for **all**
29:24 had ordered the burnt offering and the sin offering for **all** Israel.
29:28 The **whole** assembly bowed in worship, while the singers sang
29:28 **All** this continued until the sacrifice of the burnt offering was
29:29 the king and **everyone** present with him knelt down
29:31 and **all** *whose* hearts were willing brought burnt offerings.
29:32 male lambs—**all** *of* them for burnt offerings to the LORD.
29:34 The priests, however, were too few to skin **all** the burnt offerings;
29:36 **all** the people rejoiced at what God had brought about for his
30: 1 Hezekiah sent word to **all** Israel and Judah and also wrote letters to
30: 2 the **whole** assembly in Jerusalem decided to celebrate the Passover
30: 4 The plan seemed right both to the king and to the **whole** assembly.
30: 5 They decided to send a proclamation **throughout** [+928] Israel,
30: 6 couriers went **throughout** [+928] Israel and Judah with letters
30:14 the altars in Jerusalem and cleared away **[NIE]** the incense altars
30:17 the Levites had to kill the Passover lambs for **all** those who were
30:18 [30:19] saying, "May the LORD, who is good, pardon **everyone**
30:22 Hezekiah spoke encouragingly to **all** the Levites, who showed
30:23 The **whole** assembly then agreed to celebrate the festival seven
30:25 The **entire** assembly of Judah rejoiced, along with the priests
30:25 with the priests and Levites and **all** who had assembled from Israel,
31: 1 When **all** this had ended, the Israelites who were there went out to
31: 1 **[RPH]** the Israelites who were there went out to the towns of
31: 1 the altars **throughout** [+4946] Judah and Benjamin and in Ephraim
31: 1 **[RPH]** the Israelites returned to their own towns and to their own
31: 5 new wine, oil and honey and **all** that the fields produced.
31: 5 They brought a great amount, a tithe of **everything**.
31:16 **all** who would enter the temple of the LORD to perform the daily
31:18 They included **all** the little ones, the wives, and the sons
31:18 daughters of the **whole** community listed in these genealogical
31:19 lived on the farm lands around their towns or in **any** *other* towns,
31:19 men were designated by name to distribute portions to **every** male
31:19 and to **all** who were recorded in the genealogies of the Levites.
31:20 This is what Hezekiah did **throughout** [+928] Judah, doing what
31:21 In **everything** [+5126] that he undertook in the service of God's
31:21 he sought his God and worked **wholeheartedly** [+928+4222].
32: 4 they blocked **all** the springs and the stream that flowed through the
32: 5 Then he worked hard repairing **all** the broken sections of the wall
32: 7 because of the king of Assyria and the **vast** army with him,
32: 9 king of Assyria and **all** his forces were laying siege to Lachish,
32: 9 king of Judah and for **all** the people of Judah who were there:
32:13 and my fathers have done to **all** the peoples of the other lands?
32:14 Who of **all** the gods of these nations that my fathers destroyed has
32:15 for **no** [+4202] god of any nation or kingdom has been able to
32:15 for no god of **any** nation or kingdom has been able to deliver his
32:21 who annihilated **all** the fighting men and the leaders and officers in
32:22 of Sennacherib king of Assyria and from the hand of **all** others.
32:23 of Judah. From then on he was highly regarded by **all** the nations.
32:27 for his precious stones, spices, shields and **all** kinds of valuables.
32:28 he made stalls for **various** kinds of cattle, and pens for the flocks.
32:30 of the City of David. He succeeded in **everything** he undertook.
32:31 left him to test him and to know **everything** that was in his heart.
32:33 **All** Judah and the people of Jerusalem honored him when he died.
33: 3 He bowed down to **all** the starry hosts and worshiped them.
33: 5 of the temple of the LORD, he built altars to **all** the starry hosts.
33: 7 in Jerusalem, which I have chosen out of **all** the tribes of Israel,
33: 8 if only they will be careful to do **everything** I commanded them
33: 8 to do everything I commanded them concerning **all** the laws,
33:14 He stationed military commanders in **all** the fortified cities in
33:15 as well as **all** the altars he had built on the temple hill and in
33:19 as well as **all** his sins and unfaithfulness, and the sites where he
33:22 and offered sacrifices to **all** the idols Manasseh had made.
33:25 the people of the land killed **all** who had plotted against King
34: 7 to powder and cut to pieces **all** the incense altars throughout Israel.
34: 7 and cut to pieces all the incense altars **throughout** [+928] Israel.
34: 9 Ephraim and the **entire** remnant of Israel and from all the people
34: 9 remnant of Israel and from **all** the people of Judah and Benjamin
34:12 **all** who were skilled in playing musical instruments—
34:13 of the laborers and supervised **all** the workers from job to job.
34:16 "Your officials are doing **everything** that has been committed to
34:21 they have not acted in accordance with **all** that is written in this
34:24 **all** the curses written in the book that has been read in the presence
34:25 and provoked me to anger by **all** that their hands have made,
34:28 Your eyes will not see **all** the disaster I am going to bring on this
34:29 Then the king called together **all** the elders of Judah and Jerusalem.
34:30 He went up to the temple of the LORD with **[RPH]** the men of
34:30 and the Levites—**all** the people from the least to the greatest.
34:30 He read in their hearing **all** the words of the Book of the Covenant,
34:31 and decrees with **all** his heart and all his soul,
34:31 and decrees with all his heart and **all** his soul,
34:32 he had **everyone** in Jerusalem and Benjamin pledge themselves to
34:33 Josiah removed **all** the detestable idols from all the territory
34:33 Josiah removed all the detestable idols from **all** the territory
34:33 he had **all** who were present in Israel serve the LORD their God.
34:33 **As long** [+3427] **as** he **lived**, they did not fail to follow the
35: 3 who instructed **all** Israel and who had been consecrated to the

2Ch 35: 7 Josiah provided for **all** the lay people who were there a total of
35: 7 who were there a **total** [+4200+5031] of thirty thousand sheep
35: 13 caldrons and pans and served them quickly to **all** the people.
35: 16 So at that time the **entire** service of the LORD was carried out for
35: 18 **none of** [+4202] the kings of Israel had ever celebrated such a
35: 18 the Levites and **all** Judah and Israel who were there with the people
35: 20 After **all** this, when Josiah had set the temple in order, Neco king
35: 24 tombs of his fathers, and **all** Judah and Jerusalem mourned for him.
35: 25 to this day **all** the men and women singers commemorate Josiah in
36: 14 **all** the leaders of the priests and the people became more and more
36: 14 following **all** the detestable practices of the nations and defiling the
36: 17 or aged. God handed **all** of them over to Nebuchadnezzar.
36: 18 He carried to Babylon **all** the articles from the temple of God,
36: 18 and the treasures of the king and his officials. **[RPH]**
36: 19 they burned **all** the palaces and destroyed everything of value
36: 19 all the palaces and destroyed **everything** [+3998] *of* value there.
36: 21 **all** the time of its desolation it rested, until the seventy years were
36: 22 of Persia to make a proclamation **throughout** [+928] his realm
36: 23 has given me **all** the kingdoms of the earth and he has appointed
36: 23 Anyone of **[NIE]** his people among you—may the LORD his
Ezr 1: 1 of Persia to make a proclamation **throughout** [+928] his realm
1: 2 has given me **all** the kingdoms of the earth and he has appointed
1: 3 Anyone of **[NIE]** his people among you—may his God be with
1: 4 the people of **any** place where survivors may now be living are to
1: 4 the people of any place where **[RPH]** survivors may now be
1: 5 the priests and Levites—**everyone** whose heart God had moved—
1: 6 **All** their neighbors assisted them with articles of silver and gold,
1: 6 and with valuable gifts, in addition to **all** the freewill offerings.
1: 11 *In* **all**, there were 5,400 articles of gold and of silver.
1: 11 Sheshbazzar brought **all** these along when the exiles came up from
2: 42 of Shallum, Ater, Talmon, Akkub, Hatita and Shobai **[NIE]** 139
2: 58 **[NIE]** The temple servants and the descendants of the servants of
2: 64 The **whole** company numbered 42,360,
2: 70 the other people, and the **rest** *of* the Israelites settled in their towns.
3: 5 and the sacrifices for **all** the appointed sacred feasts of the LORD,
3: 5 as well as **those**[s] brought as freewill offerings to the LORD.
3: 8 and **all** who had returned from the captivity to Jerusalem)
3: 11 And **all** the people gave a great shout of praise to the LORD,
4: 5 frustrate their plans during the **entire** reign of Cyrus king of Persia
6: 20 Levites had purified themselves and were **all** ceremonially clean.
6: 20 The Levites slaughtered the Passover lamb for **all** the exiles,
6: 21 together with **all** who had separated themselves from the unclean
7: 6 The king had granted him **everything** he asked, for the hand of the
7: 28 the king and his advisers and **all** the king's powerful officials.
8: 20 had established to assist the Levites. **All** were registered by name.
8: 21 for a safe journey for us and our children, with **all** our possessions.
8: 22 "The gracious hand of our God is on **everyone** who looks to him,
8: 22 looks to him, but his great anger is against **all** who forsake him."
8: 25 and **all** Israel present there had donated for the house of our God.
8: 34 **Everything** was accounted for by number and weight,
8: 34 and weight, and the **entire** weight was recorded at that time.
8: 35 twelve bulls for **all** Israel, ninety-six rams, seventy-seven male
8: 35 twelve male goats. **All** this was a burnt offering to the LORD.
9: 4 **everyone** who trembled at the words of the God of Israel gathered
9: 13 "**What**[s] has happened to us is a result of our evil deeds and our
10: 3 Now let us make a covenant before our God to send away **all** these
10: 5 and **all** Israel under oath to do what had been suggested.
10: 7 and Jerusalem for **all** the exiles to assemble in Jerusalem.
10: 8 **Anyone** who failed to appear within three days would forfeit all his
10: 8 Anyone who failed to appear within three days would forfeit **all** his
10: 9 **all** the men of Judah and Benjamin had gathered in Jerusalem.
10: 9 **all** the people were sitting in the square before the house of God,
10: 12 The **whole** assembly responded with a loud voice: "You are right!
10: 14 Let our officials act for the **whole** assembly. Then let everyone in
10: 14 let **everyone** in our towns who has married a foreign woman come
10: 16 from each family division, and **all** *of* them designated by name.
10: 17 by the first day of the first month they finished dealing with **all** the
10: 44 **All** these had married foreign women, and some of them had
Ne 4: 6 [3:38] So we rebuilt the wall till **all** *of* it reached half its height,
4: 8 [4:2] They **all** plotted together to come and fight against
4: 12 [4:6] "**Wherever** [+2021+4946+5226] you turn, they will attack
4: 15 [4:9] we **all** returned to the wall, each to his own work.
4: 16 [4:10] The officers posted themselves behind **all** the people of
5: 13 and possessions **every** man who does not keep this promise.
5: 13 At this the **whole** assembly said, "Amen," and praised the LORD.
5: 16 **All** my men were assembled there for the work; we did not acquire
5: 18 and every ten days an abundant supply of wine of **all** *kinds*.
5: 19 me with favor, O my God, for **all** I have done for these people.
6: 9 They were **all** trying to frighten us, thinking, "Their hands will get
6: 16 When **all** our enemies heard about this, all the surrounding nations
6: 16 **all** the surrounding nations were afraid and lost their
7: 60 **[NIE]** The temple servants and the descendants of the servants of
7: 66 The **whole** company numbered 42,360,
7: 73 [7:72] with certain of the people and the **rest** *of* the Israelites,
8: 1 **all** the people assembled as one man in the square before the Water
8: 2 made up of men and women and **all** who were able to understand.
8: 3 And **all** the people listened attentively to the Book of the Law.
8: 5 **All** the people could see him because he was standing above them;
8: 5 see him because he was standing above **them**[s] [+2021+6639];
8: 5 standing above them; and as he opened it, the people **all** stood up.
8: 6 and **all** the people lifted their hands and responded, "Amen!
8: 9 and the Levites who were instructing the people said to them **all**,
8: 9 For **all** the people had been weeping as they listened to the words
8: 11 The Levites calmed **all** the people, saying, "Be still, for this is a
8: 12 **all** the people went away to eat and drink, to send portions of food
8: 13 the heads of **all** the families, along with the priests and the Levites,
8: 15 and spread it **throughout** [+928] their towns and in Jerusalem:
8: 17 The **whole** company that had returned from exile built booths
9: 2 Those of Israelite descent had separated themselves from **all**
9: 5 glorious name, and may it be exalted above **all** blessing and praise.
9: 6 and **all** their starry host, the earth and all that is on it, the seas
9: 6 the earth and **all** that is on it, the seas and all that is in them.
9: 6 the earth and all that is on it, the seas and **all** that is in them.
9: 6 You give life to **everything**, and the multitudes of heaven worship
9: 10 against **all** his officials and all the people of his land,
9: 10 against all his officials and **all** the people of his land,
9: 25 they took possession of houses filled with **all** *kinds of* good things,
9: 32 of love, do not let **all** this hardship seem trifling in your eyes—
9: 32 our priests and prophets, upon our fathers and **all** your people,
9: 33 In **all** that has happened to us, you have been just; you have acted
9: 38 [10:1] "In view of **all** this, we are making a binding agreement,
10: 28 [10:29] **all** who separated themselves from the neighboring
10: 28 [10:29] together with their wives and **all** their sons and daughters
10: 29 [10:30] servant of God and to obey carefully **all** the commands,
10: 31 [10:32] bring merchandise or **[NIE]** grain to sell on the Sabbath,
10: 31 [10:32] we will forgo working the land and will cancel **all** debts.
10: 33 [10:34] for Israel; and for **all** the duties of the house of our God.
10: 35 [10:36] year the firstfruits of our crops and of **every** fruit tree.
10: 35 [10:36] the firstfruits of our crops and of every fruit **[RPH]** tree.
10: 37 [10:38] of the fruit of **all** our trees and of our new wine and oil.
10: 37 [10:38] for it is the Levites who collect the tithes in **all** the towns
11: 2 The people commended **all** the men who volunteered to live in
11: 6 The descendants of Perez who lived in Jerusalem **totaled** 468 able
11: 18 The Levites in the holy city **totaled** 284.
11: 20 with the priests and Levites, were in **all** the towns of Judah,
11: 24 of Judah, was the king's agent in **all** affairs relating to the people.
12: 27 the Levites were sought out from **[NIE]** where they lived
12: 47 **all** Israel contributed the daily portions for the singers and
13: 3 they excluded from Israel **all** who were of foreign descent.
13: 6 while **all** this was going on, I was not in Jerusalem, for in the
13: 8 and threw **all** Tobiah's household goods out of the room.
13: 12 **All** Judah brought the tithes of grain, new wine and oil into the
13: 15 together with wine, grapes, figs and **all** *other kinds of* loads.
13: 16 in Jerusalem were bringing in fish and **all** *kinds of* merchandise
13: 18 so that our God brought **all** this calamity upon us and upon this
13: 20 and sellers of **all** *kinds of* goods spent the night outside Jerusalem.
13: 26 He was loved by his God, and God made him king over **all** Israel,
13: 27 Must we hear now that you too are doing **all** this terrible
13: 30 So I purified the priests and the Levites of **everything** foreign,
Est 1: 3 in the third year of his reign he gave a banquet for **all** his nobles
1: 5 for **all** the people from the least to the greatest, who were in the
1: 8 for the king instructed **all** the wine stewards to serve each man
1: 13 Since it was customary for the king to consult **[NIE]** experts in
1: 16 not only against the king but also against **all** the nobles and the
1: 16 and **[RPH]** the peoples of all the provinces of King Xerxes.
1: 16 all the nobles and the peoples of **all** the provinces of King Xerxes.
1: 17 For the queen's conduct will become known to **all** the women,
1: 18 conduct will respond to **all** the king's nobles in the same way.
1: 20 when the king's edict is proclaimed throughout **all** his vast realm,
1: 20 **all** the women will respect their husbands, from the least to the
1: 22 He sent dispatches to **all** parts of the kingdom, to each province in
1: 22 proclaiming in each people's tongue that **every** man should be
2: 3 Let the king appoint commissioners in **every** province of his realm
2: 3 bring **all** these beautiful girls into the harem at the citadel of Susa.
2: 11 **Every day** [+2256+3427+3427] he walked back and forth near the
2: 13 **Anything** [+889] she wanted was given her to take with her from
2: 15 suggested. And Esther won the favor of **everyone** who saw her.
2: 17 Now the king was attracted to Esther more than to **any** *of* the other
2: 17 she won his favor and approval more than **any** *of* the other virgins.
2: 18 a great banquet, Esther's banquet, for **all** his nobles and officials.
3: 1 giving him a seat of honor higher than that of **all** the other nobles.
3: 2 **All** the royal officials at the king's gate knelt down and paid honor
3: 6 Instead Haman looked for a way to destroy **all** Mordecai's people,
3: 6 the Jews, throughout the **whole** kingdom of Xerxes.
3: 8 scattered among the peoples in **all** the provinces of your kingdom
3: 8 whose customs are different from those of **all** other people
3: 12 in the language of each people **all** Haman's orders to the king's
3: 13 Dispatches were sent by couriers to **all** the king's provinces with

Est 3:13 with the order to destroy, kill and annihilate **all** the Jews—
3:14 A copy of the text of the edict was to be issued as law in **every**
3:14 made known to the people of **every** nationality so they would be
4:1 When Mordecai learned of **all** that had been done, he tore his
4:3 In **every** province to which the edict and order of the king came,
4:7 Mordecai told him **everything** that had happened to him,
4:11 "**All** the king's officials and the people of the royal provinces know
4:11 and the people of the royal provinces know that for **any** man
4:13 because you are in the king's house you alone of **all** the Jews will
4:16 "Go, gather together **all** the Jews who are in Susa, and fast for me.
4:17 So Mordecai went away and carried out **all** *of* Esther's instructions.
5:11 **all** the ways the king had honored him and how he had elevated
5:13 **all** this gives me no satisfaction as long as I see that Jew Mordecai
5:13 all this gives me no satisfaction **as long** [+928+6961] **as** I see that
5:14 His wife Zeresh and **all** his friends said to him, "Have a gallows
6:10 Do not neglect **anything** [+1821+4946] you have recommended."
6:13 his wife and **all** his friends everything that had happened to him.
6:13 his wife and all his friends **everything** that had happened to him.
8:5 devised and wrote to destroy the Jews in **all** the king's provinces.
8:9 They wrote out **all** Mordecai's orders to the Jews, and to the
8:11 The king's edict granted the Jews in **every** city the right to
8:11 kill and annihilate **any** armed force of any nationality or province
8:12 The day appointed for the Jews to do this in **all** the provinces of
8:13 A copy of the text of the edict was to be issued as law in **every**
8:13 every province and made known to the people of **every** nationality
8:17 In **every** province and in every city, wherever the edict of the king
8:17 In every province and in **every** city, wherever the edict of the king
9:2 The Jews assembled in their cities in **all** the provinces of King
9:2 because the people of **all** the other nationalities were afraid of
9:3 And **all** the nobles of the provinces, the satraps, the governors
9:4 his reputation spread **throughout** [+928] the provinces, and he
9:5 The Jews struck down **all** their enemies with the sword, killing
9:20 he sent letters to **all** the Jews throughout the provinces of King
9:20 he sent letters to all the Jews **throughout** [+928] the provinces of
9:21 to have them celebrate **annually** [+928+2256+9102+9102] the
9:24 son of Hammedatha, the Agagite, the enemy of **all** the Jews,
9:26 Because of **everything** written in this letter and because of what
9:27 **all** who join them should without fail observe these two days every
9:27 all who join them should without fail observe these two days **every**
9:28 be remembered and observed in **every** generation by every family,
9:29 wrote with **full** authority to confirm this second letter concerning
9:30 Mordecai sent letters to **all** the Jews in the 127 provinces of the
10:2 **all** his acts of power and might, together with a full account of the
10:3 the good of his people and spoke up for the welfare of **all** the Jews.
Job 1:3 He was the greatest man among **all** the people of the East.
1:5 the morning he would sacrifice a burnt offering for **each** *of* them,
1:5 in their hearts." This was Job's **regular** [+2021+3427] custom.
1:10 put a hedge around him and his household and **everything** he has?
1:11 stretch out your hand and strike **everything** he has, and he will
1:12 said to Satan, "Very well, then, **everything** he has is in your hands,
1:22 In **all** this, Job did not sin by charging God with wrongdoing.
2:4 Satan replied. "A man will give **all** he has for his own life.
2:10 and not trouble?" In **all** this, Job did not sin in what he said.
2:11 heard about **all** the troubles that had come upon him,
8:12 and uncut, they wither more quickly than **[NIE]** grass.
8:13 Such is the destiny of **all** who forget God; so perishes the hope of
9:28 I still dread **all** my sufferings, for I know you will not hold me
12:9 Which of **all** these does not know that the hand of the LORD has
12:10 In his hand is the life of **every** creature and the breath of all
12:10 his hand is the life of every creature and the breath of **all** mankind.
13:1 "My eyes have seen **all** *this*, my ears have heard and understood it.
13:4 smear me with lies; you are worthless physicians, **all** *of* you!
13:27 you keep close watch on **all** my paths by putting marks on the soles
14:14 **All** the days of my hard service I will wait for my renewal to come.
15:20 **All** his days the wicked man suffers torment, the ruthless through
16:2 heard many things like these; miserable comforters are you **all**!
16:7 you have worn me out; you have devastated my **entire** household.
17:7 eyes have grown dim with grief; my **whole** frame is but a shadow.
17:10 "But come on, **all** *of* you, try again! I will not find a wise man
19:19 **All** my intimate friends detest me; those I love have turned against
20:22 will overtake him; the **full** force of misery will come upon him.
20:26 **total** darkness lies in wait for his treasures. A fire unfanned will
21:23 One man dies in full vigor, **completely** secure and at ease,
21:33 **all** men follow after him, and a countless throng goes before him.
24:24 are gone; they are brought low and gathered up like **all** *others*;
27:3 **as long as** [+6388] I have life within me, the breath of God in my
27:10 find delight in the Almighty? Will he call upon God at **all** times?
27:12 You have **all** seen this yourselves. Why then this meaningless talk?
28:3 he searches the **farthest recesses** [+9417] for ore in the blackest
28:10 He tunnels through the rock; his eyes see **all** its treasures.
28:21 It is hidden from the eyes of **every** living thing, concealed even
28:24 views the ends of the earth and sees **everything** under the heavens.
30:23 bring me down to death, to the place appointed for **all** the living.
31:4 Does he not see my ways and count my **every** step?
31:12 burns to Destruction; it would have uprooted **[NIE]** my harvest.
33:1 Job, listen to my words; pay attention to **everything** I say.
33:11 fastens my feet in shackles; he keeps close watch on **all** my paths.'
33:13 Why do you complain to him that he answers **none of** [+4202]
33:29 "God does **all** these things to a man—twice, even three times—
34:13 him over the earth? Who put him in charge of the **whole** world?
34:15 **all** mankind would perish together and man would return to the
34:19 favor the rich over the poor, for they are **all** the work of his hands?
34:21 "His eyes are on the ways of men; he sees their **every** step.
34:27 turned from following him and had no regard for **any** *of* his ways.
36:19 Would your wealth or even **all** your mighty efforts sustain you
36:25 **All** mankind has seen it; men gaze on it from afar.
37:3 He unleashes his lightning beneath the **whole** heaven and sends it
37:7 So that **all** men he has made may know his work, he stops every
37:7 has made may know his work, he stops **every** man from his labor.
37:12 face of the whole earth to do **whatever** [+889] he commands them.
37:24 revere him, for does he not have regard for **all** the wise in heart?"
38:7 the morning stars sang together and **all** the angels shouted for joy?
38:18 the vast expanses of the earth? Tell me, if you know **all** this.
39:8 He ranges the hills for his pasture and searches for **any** green thing.
40:11 fury of your wrath, look at **every** proud man and bring him low,
40:12 look at **every** proud man and humble him, crush the wicked where
40:20 hills bring him their produce, and **all** the wild animals play nearby.
41:11 [41:3] that I must pay? **Everything** under heaven belongs to me.
41:34 [41:26] He looks down on **all** that are haughty; he is king over all
41:34 [41:26] on all that are haughty; he is king over **all** that are proud."
42:2 "I know that you can do **all** *things*; no plan of yours can be
42:10 prosperous again and gave him twice as **much** as he had before.
42:11 **All** his brothers and sisters and everyone who had known him
42:11 All his brothers and **[RPH]** sisters and everyone who had known
42:11 and sisters and **everyone** who had known him before came
42:11 consoled him over **all** the trouble the LORD had brought upon
42:15 Nowhere in **all** the land were there found women as beautiful as
Ps 1:3 whose leaf does not wither. **Whatever** [+889] he does prospers.
2:12 can flare up in a moment. Blessed are **all** who take refuge in him.
3:7 [3:8] Strike **all** my enemies on the jaw; break the teeth of the
5:5 [5:6] cannot stand in your presence; you hate **all** who do wrong.
5:11 [5:12] let **all** who take refuge in you be glad; let them ever sing
6:6 [6:7] **all** night *long* I flood my bed with weeping and drench my
6:7 [6:8] grow weak with sorrow; they fail because of **all** my foes.
6:8 [6:9] Away from me, **all** you who do evil, for the LORD has
6:10 [6:11] **All** my enemies will be ashamed and dismayed; they will
7:1 [7:2] refuge in you; save and deliver me from **all** who pursue me,
7:11 [7:12] righteous judge, a God who expresses his wrath **every** day.
8:1 [8:2] our Lord, how majestic is your name in **all** the earth!
8:6 [8:7] the works of your hands; you put **everything** under his feet:
8:7 [8:8] **all** flocks and herds, and the beasts of the field,
8:9 [8:10] our Lord, how majestic is your name in **all** the earth!
9:1 [9:2] I will praise you, O LORD, with **all** my heart; I will tell of
9:1 [9:2] O LORD, with all my heart; I will tell of **all** your wonders.
9:14 [9:15] that I may declare **[NIE]** your praises in the gates of the
9:17 [9:18] wicked return to the grave, **all** the nations that forget God.
10:4 does not seek him; in **all** his thoughts there is no room for God.
10:5 His ways are **always** [+928+6961] prosperous; he is haughty
10:5 and your laws are far from him; he sneers at **all** his enemies.
12:3 [12:4] May the LORD cut off **all** flattering lips and every
14:3 **All** have turned aside, they have together become corrupt;
14:4 **[NIE]** Will evildoers never learn—those who devour my people
16:3 in the land, they are the glorious ones in whom is **all** my delight.
18:T [18:1] the LORD delivered him from the hand of **all** his enemies
18:22 [18:23] **All** his laws are before me; I have not turned away from
18:30 [18:31] is flawless. He is a shield for **all** who take refuge in him.
19:4 [19:5] Their voice goes out into **all** the earth, their words to the
20:3 [20:4] May he remember **all** your sacrifices and accept your burnt
20:4 [20:5] the desire of your heart and make **all** your plans succeed.
20:5 [20:6] name of our God. May the LORD grant **all** your requests.
21:8 [21:9] Your hand will lay hold on **all** your enemies; your right
22:7 [22:8] **All** who see me mock me; they hurl insults, shaking their
22:14 [22:15] poured out like water, and **all** my bones are out of joint.
22:17 [22:18] I can count **all** my bones; people stare and gloat over me.
22:23 [22:24] praise him! **All** you descendants of Jacob, honor him!
22:23 [22:24] honor him! Revere him, **all** you descendants of Israel!
22:27 [22:28] **All** the ends of the earth will remember and turn to the
22:27 [22:28] **all** the families of the nations will bow down before him,
22:29 [22:30] **All** the rich of the earth will feast and worship; all who go
22:29 [22:30] **all** who go down to the dust will kneel before him—
23:6 Surely goodness and love will follow me **all** the days of my life,
25:3 No **one** whose hope is in you will ever be put to shame, but they
25:5 for you are God my Savior, and my hope is in you **all** day long.
25:10 **All** the ways of the LORD are loving and faithful for those who
25:18 upon my affliction and my distress and take away **all** my sins.
25:22 Redeem Israel, O God, from **all** their troubles!
26:7 aloud your praise and telling of **all** your wonderful deeds.
27:4 that I may dwell in the house of the LORD **all** the days of my life,

Ps 29: 9 and strips the forests bare. And in his temple **all** cry, "Glory!"
31: 11 [31:12] Because of **all** my enemies, I am the utter contempt of my
31: 23 [31:24] Love the LORD, **all** his saints! The LORD preserves
31: 24 [31:25] and take heart, **all** you who hope in the LORD.
32: 3 my bones wasted away through my groaning **all** day long.
32: 6 Therefore let **everyone** who is godly pray to you while you may be
32: 11 and be glad, you righteous; sing, **all** you who are upright in heart!
33: 4 word of the LORD is right and true; he is faithful in **all** he does.
33: 6 heavens made, **[NIE]** their starry host by the breath of his mouth.
33: 8 Let **all** the earth fear the LORD; let all the people of the world
33: 8 earth fear the LORD; let **all** the people of the world revere him.
33: 13 From heaven the LORD looks down and sees **all** mankind;
33: 14 from his dwelling place he watches **all** who live on earth—
33: 15 he who forms the hearts of all, who considers **everything** they do.
34: 1 [34:2] I will extol the LORD at **all** times; his praise will always
34: 4 [34:5] and he answered me; he delivered me from **all** my fears.
34: 6 [34:7] the LORD heard him; he saved him out of **all** his troubles.
34: 10 [34:11] those who seek the LORD lack **no** [+4202] good thing.
34: 17 [34:18] hears them; he delivers them from **all** their troubles.
34: 19 [34:20] but the LORD delivers him from them **all**;
34: 20 [34:21] he protects **all** his bones, not one of them will be broken.
34: 22 [34:23] no **one** will be condemned who takes refuge in him.
35: 10 My **whole** being will exclaim, "Who is like you, O LORD?
35: 28 will speak of your righteousness and of your praises **all** day long.
37: 26 They are **always** [+2021+3427] generous and lend freely;
38: 6 [38:7] and brought very low; **all** day long I go about mourning.
38: 9 [38:10] **All** my longings lie open before you, O Lord; my sighing
38: 12 [38:13] harm me talk of my ruin; **all** day long they plot deception.
39: 5 [39:6] before you. **Each** man's life is but a breath. *Selah*
39: 5 [39:6] before you. Each man's life is but **a** breath. *Selah*
39: 8 [39:9] Save me from **all** my transgressions; do not make me the
39: 11 [39:12] their wealth like a moth—**each** man is but a breath.
39: 12 [39:13] with you as an alien, a stranger, as **all** my fathers were.
40: 16 [40:17] may **all** who seek you rejoice and be glad in you;
41: 3 [41:4] his sickbed and restore him from **[NIE]** his bed of illness.
41: 7 [41:8] **All** my enemies whisper together against me; they imagine
42: 3 [42:4] my food day and night, while men say to me **all** day long,
42: 7 [42:8] **all** your waves and breakers have swept over me.
42: 10 [42:11] saying to me **all** day long, "Where is your God?"
44: 8 [44:9] In God we make our boast **all** day long, and we will praise
44: 15 [44:16] My disgrace is before me **all** day long, and my face is
44: 17 [44:18] **All** this happened to us, though we had not forgotten you
44: 22 [44:23] Yet for your sake we face death **all** day long; we are
45: 8 [45:9] **All** your robes are fragrant with myrrh and aloes
45: 13 [45:14] **All** glorious is the princess within ⌞her chamber⌟;
45: 16 [45:17] you will make them princes **throughout** [+928] the land.
45: 17 [45:18] I will perpetuate your memory through **all** generations;
47: 1 [47:2] Clap your hands, **all** you nations; shout to God with cries
47: 2 [47:3] is the LORD Most High, the great King over **all** the earth!
47: 7 [47:8] For God is the King of **all** the earth; sing to him a psalm of
48: 2 [48:3] It is beautiful in its loftiness, the joy of the **whole** earth.
49: 1 [49:2] Hear this, **all** you peoples; listen, all who live in this world,
49: 1 [49:2] Hear this, all you peoples; listen, **all** who live in this world,
49: 17 [49:18] for he will take **nothing** [+2021+4202] with him when he
50: 10 for **every** animal of the forest is mine, and the cattle on a thousand
50: 11 I know **every** bird in the mountains, and the creatures of the field
51: 9 [51:11] Hide your face from my sins and blot out **all** my iniquity.
52: 1 [52:3] Why do you boast **all** day long, you who are a disgrace in
52: 4 [52:6] You love **every** harmful word, O you deceitful tongue!
53: 3 [53:4] **Everyone** has turned away, they have together become
54: 7 [54:9] For he has delivered me from **all** my troubles, and my eyes
56: 1 [56:2] men hotly pursue me; **all** day long they press their attack.
56: 2 [56:3] My slanderers pursue me **all** day long; many are attacking
56: 5 [56:6] **All** day long they twist my words; they are always plotting
56: 5 [56:6] they twist my words; they are **always** plotting to harm me.
57: 5 [57:6] above the heavens; let your glory be over **all** the earth.
57: 11 [57:12] above the heavens; let your glory be over **all** the earth.
59: 5 [59:6] the God of Israel, rouse yourself to punish **all** the nations;
59: 5 [59:6] all the nations; show no mercy to **[RPH]** wicked traitors.
59: 8 [59:9] O LORD, laugh at them; you scoff at **all** those nations.
62: 3 [62:4] Would **all** *of* you throw him down—this leaning wall,
62: 8 [62:9] Trust in him at **all** times, O people; pour out your hearts to
63: 11 [63:12] **all** who swear by God's name will praise him,
64: 8 [64:9] to ruin; **all** who see them will shake their heads in scorn.
64: 9 [64:10] **All** mankind will fear; they will proclaim the works of
64: 10 [64:11] take refuge in him; let **all** the upright in heart praise him!
65: 2 [65:3] O you who hear prayer, to you **all** men will come.
65: 5 [65:6] the hope of **all** the ends of the earth and of the farthest seas,
66: 1 Shout with joy to God, **all** the earth!
66: 4 **All** the earth bows down to you; they sing praise to you, they sing
66: 16 Come and listen, **all** you who fear God; let me tell you what he has
67: 2 [67:3] may be known on earth, your salvation among **all** nations.
67: 3 [67:4] peoples praise you, O God; may **all** the peoples praise you.
67: 5 [67:6] peoples praise you, O God; may **all** the peoples praise you.
67: 7 [67:8] will bless us, and **all** the ends of the earth will fear him.
69: 19 [69:20] and shamed; **all** my enemies are before you.
69: 34 [69:35] and earth praise him, the seas and **all** that move in them,
70: 4 [70:5] may **all** who seek you rejoice and be glad in you; may
71: 8 is filled with your praise, declaring your splendor **all** day long.
71: 14 have hope; *I will* praise you **more and more** [+3578+6584].
71: 15 of your salvation **all** day long, though I know not its measure.
71: 18 power to the next generation, your might to **all** who are to come.
71: 24 My tongue will tell of your righteous acts **all** day long, for those
72: 11 **All** kings will bow down to him and all nations will serve him.
72: 11 All kings will bow down to him and **all** nations will serve him.
72: 15 May people ever pray for him and bless him **all** day long.
72: 17 **All** nations will be blessed through him, and they will call him
72: 19 name forever; may the **whole** earth be filled with his glory.
73: 14 **All** day long I have been plagued; I have been punished every
73: 27 far from you will perish; you destroy **all** who are unfaithful to you.
73: 28 the Sovereign LORD my refuge; I will tell of **all** your deeds.
74: 3 **all** this destruction the enemy has brought on the sanctuary.
74: 8 They burned **every** place where God was worshiped in the land.
74: 17 It was you who set **all** the boundaries of the earth; you made both
74: 22 defend your cause; remember how fools mock you **all** day long.
75: 3 [75:4] When the earth and **all** its people quake, it is I who hold its
75: 8 [75:9] **all** the wicked of the earth drink it down to its very dregs.
75: 10 [75:11] I will cut off the horns of **all** the wicked, but the horns of
76: 5 [76:6] their last sleep; not **one** *of* the warriors can lift his hands.
76: 9 [76:10] rose up to judge, to save **all** the afflicted of the land.
76: 11 [76:12] let **all** the neighboring lands bring gifts to the One to be
77: 12 [77:13] I will meditate on **all** your works and consider all your
78: 14 them with the cloud by day and with light from the fire **all** night.
78: 32 In spite of **all** this, they kept on sinning; in spite of his wonders,
78: 38 after time he restrained his anger and did not stir up his **full** wrath.
78: 51 He struck down **all** the firstborn of Egypt, the firstfruits of
80: 12 [80:13] down its walls so that **all** who pass by pick its grapes?
82: 5 walk about in darkness; **all** the foundations of the earth are shaken.
82: 6 "I said, 'You are "gods"; you are **all** sons of the Most High.'
82: 8 O God, judge the earth, for **all** the nations are your inheritance.
83: 11 [83:12] and Zeeb, **all** their princes like Zebah and Zalmunna,
83: 18 [83:19] that you alone are the Most High over **all** the earth.
85: 2 [85:3] the iniquity of your people and covered **all** their sins.
85: 3 [85:4] You set aside **all** your wrath and turned from your fierce
86: 3 Have mercy on me, O Lord, for I call to you **all** day long.
86: 5 and good, O Lord, abounding in love to **all** who call to you.
86: 9 **All** the nations you have made will come and worship before you,
86: 12 I will praise you, O Lord my God, with **all** my heart; I will glorify
87: 2 the LORD loves the gates of Zion more than **all** the dwellings of
87: 7 As they make music they will sing, "**All** my fountains are in you."
88: 7 [88:8] upon me; you have overwhelmed me with **all** your waves.
88: 9 [88:10] I call to you, O LORD, **every** day; I spread out my hands
88: 17 [88:18] **All** day long they surround me like a flood; they have
89: 7 [89:8] he is more awesome than **all** who surround him.
89: 16 [89:17] They rejoice in your name **all** day long; they exult in your
89: 40 [89:41] You have broken through **all** his walls and reduced his
89: 41 [89:42] **All** who pass by have plundered him; he has become the
89: 42 [89:43] hand of his foes; you have made **all** his enemies rejoice.
89: 47 [89:48] is my life. For what futility you have created **all** men!
89: 50 [89:51] how I bear in my heart the taunts of **all** the nations,
90: 9 **All** our days pass away under your wrath; we finish our years with
90: 14 unfailing love, that we may sing for joy and be glad **all** our days.
91: 11 For he will command his angels concerning you to guard you in **all**
92: 7 [92:8] the wicked spring up like grass and **all** evildoers flourish,
92: 9 [92:10] your enemies will perish; **all** evildoers will be scattered.
94: 4 They pour out arrogant words; **all** the evildoers are full of boasting.
94: 15 on righteousness, and **all** the upright in heart will follow it.
95: 3 For the LORD is the great God, the great King above **all** gods.
96: 1 Sing to the LORD a new song; sing to the LORD, **all** the earth.
96: 3 glory among the nations, his marvelous deeds among **all** peoples.
96: 4 and most worthy of praise; he is to be feared above **all** gods.
96: 5 For **all** the gods of the nations are idols, but the LORD made the
96: 9 in the splendor of his holiness; tremble before him, **all** the earth.
96: 12 let the fields be jubilant, and **everything** in them. Then all the trees
96: 12 in them. Then **all** the trees of the forest will sing for joy;
97: 5 melt like wax before the LORD, before the Lord of **all** the earth.
97: 6 proclaim his righteousness, and **all** the peoples see his glory.
97: 7 **All** who worship images are put to shame, those who boast in
97: 7 to shame, those who boast in idols—worship him, **all** you gods!
97: 9 For you, O LORD, are the Most High over **all** the earth; you are
97: 9 Most High over all the earth; you are exalted far above **all** gods.
98: 3 **all** the ends of the earth have seen the salvation of our God.
98: 4 Shout for joy to the LORD, **all** the earth, burst into jubilant song
99: 2 Great is the LORD in Zion; he is exalted over **all** the nations.
100: 1 Shout for joy to the LORD, **all** the earth.
101: 8 Every morning I will put to silence **all** the wicked in the land;
101: 8 the land; I will cut off **every** evildoer from the city of the LORD.
102: 8 [102:9] **All** day long my enemies taunt me; those who rail against

Ps 102:15 [102:16] **all** the kings of the earth will revere your glory.
102:26 [102:27] but you remain; they will **all** wear out like a garment.
103: 1 the LORD, O my soul; **all** my inmost being, praise his holy name.
103: 2 Praise the LORD, O my soul, and forget not **all** his benefits—
103: 3 who forgives **all** your sins and heals all your diseases,
103: 3 who forgives all your sins and heals **all** your diseases,
103: 6 The LORD works righteousness and justice for **all** the oppressed.
103:19 established his throne in heaven, and his kingdom rules over **all**.
103:21 Praise the LORD, **all** his heavenly hosts, you his servants who do
103:22 Praise the LORD, **all** his works everywhere in his dominion.
103:22 the LORD, all his works **everywhere** [+5226] in his dominion.
104:11 They give water to **all** the beasts of the field; the wild donkeys
104:20 it becomes night, and **all** the beasts of the forest prowl.
104:24 In wisdom you made them **all**; the earth is full of your creatures.
104:27 These **all** look to you to give them their food at the proper time.
105: 2 Sing to him, sing praise to him; tell of **all** his wonderful acts.
105: 7 He is the LORD our God; his judgments are in **all** the earth.
105:16 down famine on the land and destroyed **all** their supplies of food;
105:21 He made him master of his household, ruler over **all** he possessed,
105:31 came swarms of flies, and gnats **throughout** [+928] their country.
105:35 they ate up **every** green thing in their land, ate up the produce of
105:36 he struck down **all** the firstborn in their land, the firstfruits of all
105:36 all the firstborn in their land, the firstfruits of **all** their manhood.
106: 2 proclaim the mighty acts of the LORD or **fully** declare his praise?
106: 3 maintain justice, who **constantly** [+928+6961] do what is right.
106:46 He caused them to be pitied by **all** who held them captive.
106:48 to everlasting. Let **all** the people say, "Amen!" Praise the LORD.
107:18 They loathed **all** food and drew near the gates of death.
107:27 like drunken men; they *were* **at** their **wits' end** [+1182+2683].
107:42 The upright see and rejoice, but **all** the wicked shut their mouths.
108: 5 [108:6] the heavens, and let your glory be over **all** the earth.
109:11 May a creditor seize **all** he has; may strangers plunder the fruits of
111: 1 I will extol the LORD with **all** my heart in the council of the
111: 2 of the LORD; they are pondered by **all** who delight in them.
111: 7 of his hands are faithful and just; **all** his precepts are trustworthy.
111:10 of wisdom; **all** who follow his precepts have good understanding.
113: 4 The LORD is exalted over **all** the nations, his glory above the
115: 3 Our God is in heaven; he does **whatever** [+889] pleases him.
115: 8 make them will be like them, and so will **all** who trust in them.
115:17 the dead who praise the LORD, **those**' who go down to silence;
116:11 And in my dismay I said, "**All** men are liars."
116:12 How can I repay the LORD for **all** his goodness to me?
116:14 I will fulfill my vows to the LORD in the presence of **all** his
116:18 I will fulfill my vows to the LORD in the presence of **all** his
117: 1 Praise the LORD, **all** you nations; extol him, all you peoples.
117: 1 Praise the LORD, all you nations; extol him, **all** you peoples.
118:10 **All** the nations surrounded me, but in the name of the LORD I cut
119: 2 are they who keep his statutes and seek him with **all** their heart.
119: 6 I would not be put to shame when I consider **all** your commands.
119:10 I seek you with **all** my heart; do not let me stray from your
119:13 With my lips I recount **all** the laws that come from your mouth.
119:14 I rejoice in following your statutes as one rejoices in **great** riches.
119:20 My soul is consumed with longing for your laws at **all** times.
119:34 and I will keep your law and obey it with **all** my heart.
119:58 I have sought your face with **all** my heart; be gracious to me
119:63 I am a friend to **all** who fear you, to all who follow your precepts.
119:69 have smeared me with lies, I keep your precepts with **all** my heart.
119:86 **All** your commands are trustworthy; help me, for men persecute
119:91 Your laws endure to this day, for **all** *things* serve you.
119:96 To **all** perfection I see a limit; but your commands are boundless.
119:97 Oh, how I love your law! I meditate on it **all** day long.
119:99 I have more insight than **all** my teachers, for I meditate on your
119:101 I have kept my feet from **every** evil path so that I might obey your
119:104 from your precepts; therefore I hate **every** wrong path.
119:118 You reject **all** who stray from your decrees, for their deceitfulness
119:119 **All** the wicked of the earth you discard like dross; therefore I love
119:128 because I consider **all** your precepts right, I hate every wrong path.
119:128 I consider all your precepts right, **[RPH]** I hate every wrong path.
119:128 because I consider all your precepts right, I hate **every** wrong path.
119:133 footsteps according to your word; let no sin rule over me. **[NIE]**
119:145 I call with **all** my heart; answer me, O LORD, and I will obey
119:151 Yet you are near, O LORD, and **all** your commands are true.
119:160 All your words are true; **all** your righteous laws are eternal.
119:168 your precepts and your statutes, for **all** my ways are known to you.
119:172 my tongue sing of your word, for **all** your commands are righteous.
121: 7 The LORD will keep you from **all** harm—he will watch over your
128: 1 Blessed are **all** who fear the LORD, who walk in his ways.
128: 5 May the LORD bless you from Zion **all** the days of your life;
129: 5 May **all** who hate Zion be turned back in shame.
130: 8 He himself will redeem Israel from **all** their sins.
132: 1 O LORD, remember David and **all** the hardships he endured.
134: 1 **all** you servants of the LORD who minister by night in the house
135: 5 that the LORD is great, that our Lord is greater than **all** gods.
135: 6 The LORD does **whatever** [+889] pleases him, in the heavens
135: 6 in the heavens and on the earth, in the seas and **all** their depths.
135: 9 into your midst, O Egypt, against Pharaoh and **all** his servants.
135:11 of the Amorites, Og king of Bashan and **all** the kings of Canaan—
135:18 make them will be like them, and so will **all** who trust in them.
136:25 who gives food to **every** creature. *His love endures*
138: 1 I will praise you, O LORD, with **all** my heart; before the "gods" I
138: 2 for you have exalted above **all** *things* your name and your word.
138: 4 May **all** the kings of the earth praise you, O LORD, when they
139: 3 going out and my lying down; you are familiar with **all** my ways.
139: 4 Before a word is on my tongue you know it **completely**,
139:16 **All** the days ordained for me were written in your book before one
140: 2 [140:3] devise evil plans in their hearts and stir up war **every** day.
143: 2 servant into judgment, for no **one** living is righteous before you.
143: 5 I meditate on **all** your works and consider what your hands have
143:12 silence my enemies; destroy **all** my foes, for I am your servant.
145: 2 **Every** day I will praise you and extol your name for ever and ever.
145: 9 The LORD is good to **all**; he has compassion on all he has made.
145: 9 The LORD is good to all; he has compassion on **all** he has made.
145:10 **All** you have made will praise you, O LORD; your saints will
145:13 Your kingdom is an **everlasting** [+6409] kingdom, and your
145:13 and your dominion endures through **all** generations.
145:13 The LORD is faithful to **all** [BHS-] his promises and loving
145:13 to all his promises and loving toward **all** [BHS-] he has made.
145:14 The LORD upholds **all** those who fall and lifts up all who are
145:14 upholds all those who fall and lifts up **all** who are bowed down.
145:15 The eyes of **all** look to you, and you give them their food at the
145:16 You open your hand and satisfy the desires of **every** living thing.
145:17 The LORD is righteous in **all** his ways and loving toward all he
145:17 is righteous in all his ways and loving toward **all** he has made.
145:18 The LORD is near to **all** who call on him, to all who call on him
145:18 is near to all who call on him, to **all** who call on him in truth.
145:20 The LORD watches over **all** who love him, but all the wicked he
145:20 watches over all who love him, but **all** the wicked he will destroy.
145:21 Let **every** creature praise his holy name for ever and ever.
146: 6 the Maker of heaven and earth, the sea, and **everything** in them—
147: 4 determines the number of the stars and calls them **each** by name.
147:20 He has done this for no **other**' nation; they do not know his laws.
148: 2 Praise him, **all** his angels, praise him, all his heavenly hosts.
148: 2 Praise him, all his angels, praise him, **all** his heavenly hosts.
148: 3 Praise him, sun and moon, praise him, **all** you shining stars.
148: 7 from the earth, you great sea creatures and **all** ocean depths,
148: 9 you mountains and **all** hills, fruit trees and all cedars,
148: 9 you mountains and all hills, fruit trees and **all** cedars,
148:10 wild animals and **all** cattle, small creatures and flying birds,
148:11 kings of the earth and **all** nations, you princes and all rulers on
148:11 of the earth and all nations, you princes and **all** rulers on earth,
148:14 the praise of **all** his saints, of Israel, the people close to his heart.
149: 9 against them. This is the glory of **all** his saints. Praise the LORD.
150: 6 Let **everything** that has breath praise the LORD.
Pr 1:13 we will get **all** *sorts of* valuable things and fill our houses with
1:14 in your lot with us, and **we** [+5646] will share a common purse"—
1:17 How useless to spread a net in full view of **all** the birds!
1:19 Such is the end of **all** who go after ill-gotten gain; it takes away the
1:25 since you ignored **all** my advice and would not accept my rebuke,
1:30 they would not accept my advice and spurned **[NIE]** my rebuke,
2: 9 will understand what is right and just and fair—**every** good path.
2:19 **None** [+4202] who go to her return or attain the paths of life.
3: 5 Trust in the LORD with **all** your heart and lean not on your own
3: 6 in **all** your ways acknowledge him, and he will make your paths
3: 9 the LORD with your wealth, with the firstfruits of **all** your crops;
3:15 than rubies; **nothing** [+4202] you desire can compare with her.
3:17 Her ways are pleasant ways, and **all** her paths are peace.
3:31 Do not envy a violent man or choose **any** *of* his ways,
4: 7 get wisdom. Though it cost **all** you have, get understanding.
4:22 are life to those who find them and health to a man's **whole** body.
4:23 Above **all** else, guard your heart, for it is the wellspring of life.
4:26 Make level paths for your feet and take **only** ways that are firm.
5:14 I have come to the brink of **utter** ruin in the midst of the whole
5:19 may her breasts satisfy you **always** [+928+6961], may you ever be
5:21 ways are in full view of the LORD, and he examines **all** his paths.
6:14 deceit in his heart—he **always** [+928+6961] stirs up dissension.
6:29 another man's wife; no **one** who touches her will go unpunished.
6:31 must pay sevenfold, though it costs him **all** the wealth of his house.
6:35 He will not accept **any** compensation; he will refuse the bribe,
7:12 now in the street, now in the squares, at **every** corner she lurks.)
7:26 the victims she has brought down; her slain are a mighty **throng**.
8: 8 **All** the words of my mouth are just; none of them is crooked
8: 9 To the discerning **all** *of* them are right; they are faultless to those
8:11 than rubies, and **nothing** [+4202] you desire can compare with her.
8:16 by me princes govern, and **all** nobles who rule on earth.
8:30 day after day, rejoicing **always** [+928+6961] in his presence,
8:36 fails to find me harms himself; **all** who hate me love death."
10:12 Hatred stirs up dissension, but love covers over **all** wrongs.
12:21 **No** [+4202] harm befalls the righteous, but the wicked have their

Pr 13: 7 One man pretends to be rich, yet *has* **nothing** [+401]; another
13: 16 **Every** prudent man acts out of knowledge, but a fool exposes his
14: 15 A simple man believes **anything** [+1821], but a prudent man gives
14: 23 **All** hard work brings a profit, but mere talk leads only to poverty.
15: 3 The eyes of the LORD are **everywhere** [+928+5226], keeping
15: 15 **All** the days of the oppressed are wretched, but the cheerful heart
16: 2 **All** a man's ways seem innocent to him, but motives are weighed
16: 4 The LORD works out **everything** for his own ends—even the
16: 5 The LORD detests **all** the proud of heart. Be sure of this:
16: 11 are from the LORD; **all** the weights in the bag are of his making.
16: 33 lot is cast into the lap, but its **every** decision is from the LORD.
17: 8 the one who gives it; **wherever** [+448+889] he turns, he succeeds.
17: 17 A friend loves at **all** times, and a brother is born for adversity.
18: 1 unfriendly man pursues selfish ends; he defies **all** sound judgment.
19: 6 with a ruler, and **everyone** is the friend of a man who gives gifts.
19: 7 A poor man is shunned by **all** his relatives—how much more do
20: 1 and beer a brawler; **whoever** is led astray by them is not wise.
20: 3 to a man's honor to avoid strife, but **every** fool is quick to quarrel.
20: 8 sits on his throne to judge, he winnows out **all** evil with his eyes.
20: 27 the spirit of a man; it searches out **[NIE]** his inmost being.
21: 1 he directs it like a watercourse **wherever** [+889+6584] he pleases.
21: 2 **All** a man's ways seem right to him, but the LORD weighs the
21: 5 The plans of the diligent lead to profit as surely as **[NIE]** haste
21: 26 **All** day long he craves for more, but the righteous give without
22: 2 poor have this in common: The LORD is the Maker of them **all**.
23: 17 but **always** [+2021+3427] be zealous for the fear of the LORD.
24: 4 through knowledge its rooms are filled with **[NIE]** rare
24: 31 thorns had come up **everywhere**, the ground was covered with
26: 10 Like an archer who wounds **at random** is he who hires a fool
27: 7 loathes honey, but to the hungry **even** what is bitter tastes sweet.
28: 5 but those who seek the LORD understand it **fully**.
29: 11 A fool gives **full** vent to his anger, but a wise man keeps himself
29: 12 If a ruler listens to lies, **all** his officials become wicked.
30: 4 Who has established **all** the ends of the earth? What is his name,
30: 5 "**Every** word of God is flawless; he is a shield to those who take
30: 27 locusts have no king, yet they advance **together** in ranks;
30: 30 mighty among beasts, who retreats before **nothing** [+4202];
31: 5 what the law decrees, and deprive **all** the oppressed of their rights.
31: 8 cannot speak for themselves, for the rights of **all** who are destitute.
31: 12 She brings him good, not harm, **all** the days of her life.
31: 21 has no fear for her household; for **all** *of* them are clothed in scarlet.
31: 29 "Many women do noble things, but you surpass them **all**."
Ecc 1: 2 the Teacher. "Utterly meaningless! **Everything** is meaningless."
1: 3 What does man gain from **all** his labor at which he toils under the
1: 7 **All** streams flow into the sea, yet the sea is never full. To the place
1: 8 **All** things are wearisome, more than one can say. The eye never
1: 9 will be done again; **there is nothing** [+401] new under the sun.
1: 13 to study and to explore by wisdom **all** that is done under heaven.
1: 14 I have seen **all** the things that are done under the sun; all of them
1: 14 the sun; **all** of them are meaningless, a chasing after the wind.
1: 16 increased in wisdom more than **anyone** who has ruled over
2: 5 and parks and planted **all** *kinds of* fruit trees in them.
2: 7 owned more herds and flocks than **anyone** in Jerusalem before me.
2: 9 I became greater by far than **anyone** in Jerusalem before me.
2: 10 I denied myself **nothing** [+4202] my eyes desired; I refused my
2: 10 my eyes desired; I refused my heart **no** [+4202+4946] pleasure.
2: 10 My heart took delight in **all** my work, and this was the reward for
2: 10 delight in all my work, and this was the reward for **all** my labor.
2: 11 Yet when I surveyed **all** that my hands had done and what I had
2: 11 to achieve, **everything** was meaningless, a chasing after the wind;
2: 14 but I came to realize that the same fate overtakes them **both**.
2: 16 not be long remembered; in days to come **both** will be forgotten.
2: 17 grievous to me. **All** of it is meaningless, a chasing after the wind.
2: 18 I hated **all** the things I had toiled for under the sun, because I must
2: 19 Yet he will have control over **all** the work into which I have poured
2: 20 So my heart began to despair over **all** my toilsome labor under the
2: 22 What does a man get for **all** the toil and anxious striving with
2: 23 **All** his days his work is pain and grief; even at night his mind does
3: 1 There is a time for **everything**, and a season for every activity
3: 1 time for everything, and a season for **every** activity under heaven:
3: 11 He has made **everything** beautiful in its time. He has also set
3: 13 That **everyone** [+132+2021] may eat and drink, and find
3: 13 everyone may eat and drink, and find satisfaction in **all** his toil—
3: 14 I know that **everything** God does will endure forever; nothing can
3: 17 and the wicked, for there will be a time for **every** activity,
3: 17 for there will be a time for every activity, a time for **every** deed."
3: 19 **All** have the same breath; man has no advantage over the animal.
3: 19 man has no advantage over the animal. **Everything** is meaningless.
3: 20 **All** go to the same place; all come from dust, and to dust all return.
3: 20 All go to the same place; **all** come from dust, and to dust all return.
3: 20 All go to the same place; all come from dust, and to dust **all** return.
4: 1 and saw **all** the oppression that was taking place under the sun:
4: 4 I saw that **all** labor and all achievement spring from man's envy of
4: 4 and **all** achievement spring from man's envy of his neighbor.
4: 8 There was no end to **[NIE]** his toil, yet his eyes were not content
4: 15 I saw that **all** who lived and walked under the sun followed the
4: 16 There was no end to **all** the people who were before them.
4: 16 There was no end to all the people **[RPH]** who were before them.
5: 9 [5:8] The increase from the land is taken by **all**; the king himself
5: 16 [5:15] This too is a grievous evil: **As** [+6645+8611] a man comes,
5: 17 [5:16] **All** his days he eats in darkness, with great frustration,
5: 18 [5:17] to find satisfaction in **[NIE]** his toilsome labor under the
5: 19 [5:18] when God gives **any** man wealth and possessions,
6: 2 and honor, so that he lacks **nothing** [+401] his heart desires,
6: 6 but fails to enjoy his prosperity. Do not **all** go to the same place?
6: 7 **All** man's efforts are for his mouth, yet his appetite is never
7: 2 to go to a house of feasting, for death is the destiny of **every** man;
7: 15 In this meaningless life of mine I have seen **both** of these:
7: 18 go of the other. The man who fears God will avoid **all** ⌊extremes⌋.
7: 21 Do not pay attention to **every** word people say, or you may hear
7: 23 **All** this I tested by wisdom and I said, "I am determined to be
7: 28 among a thousand, but not one ⌊upright⌋ woman among them **all**.
8: 3 up for a bad cause, for he will do **whatever** [+889] he pleases.
8: 6 For there is a proper time and procedure for **every** matter,
8: 9 **All** this I saw, as I applied my mind to everything done under the
8: 9 as I applied my mind to **everything** [+5126] done under the sun.
8: 17 I saw **all** that God has done. No one can comprehend what goes on
9: 1 So I reflected on **all** this and concluded that the righteous
9: 1 on all this and concluded **[RPH]** that the righteous and the wise
9: 1 but no man knows whether love or hate **[RPH]** awaits him.
9: 2 **All** share a common destiny—the righteous and the wicked,
9: 2 All share **[RPH]** a common destiny—the righteous and the
9: 3 This is the evil in **everything** that happens under the sun: The
9: 3 The same destiny overtakes **all**. The hearts of men, moreover,
9: 4 Anyone who is among **[NIE]** the living has hope—even a live
9: 6 never again will they have a part in **anything** that happens under
9: 8 **Always** [+928+6961] be clothed in white, and always anoint your
9: 9 **all** the days of this meaningless life that God has given you under
9: 9 that God has given you under the sun—**all** your meaningless days.
9: 10 **Whatever** [+889] your hand finds to do, do it with all your might,
9: 11 or favor to the learned; but time and chance happen to them **all**.
10: 3 the fool lacks sense and shows **everyone** how stupid he is.
10: 19 wine makes life merry, but money is the answer for **everything**.
11: 5 you cannot understand the work of God, the Maker of **all** *things*.
11: 8 However many years a man may live, let him enjoy them **all**.
11: 8 for they will be many. **Everything** to come is meaningless.
11: 9 but know that for **all** these things God will bring you to judgment.
12: 4 men rise up at the sound of birds, but **all** their songs grow faint;
12: 8 Meaningless!" says the Teacher. "**Everything** is meaningless!"
12: 13 Now **all** has been heard; here is the conclusion of the matter:
12: 13 and keep his commandments, for this is the **whole** ⌊duty⌋ *of* man.
12: 14 For God will bring **every** deed into judgment, including every
12: 14 including **every** hidden thing, whether it is good or evil.
SS 3: 6 with myrrh and incense made from **all** the spices of the merchant?
3: 8 **all** *of* them wearing the sword, all experienced in battle, each with
4: 2 up from the washing. **Each** has its twin; not one of them is alone.
4: 4 on it hang a thousand shields, **all** *of* them shields of warriors.
4: 7 **All** beautiful you are, my darling; there is no flaw in you.
4: 10 love than wine, and the fragrance of your perfume than **any** spice!
4: 14 with **every** *kind of* incense tree, with myrrh and aloes and all the
4: 14 kind of incense tree, with myrrh and aloes and **all** the finest spices.
5: 16 His mouth is sweetness itself; he is **altogether** lovely. This is my
6: 6 up from the washing. **Each** has its twin, not one of them is alone.
7: 13 [7:14] at our door is **every** delicacy, both new and old, that I have
8: 7 If one were to give **all** the wealth of his house for love, it would be
Isa 1: 5 Your **whole** head is injured, your whole heart afflicted.
1: 5 Your whole head is injured, your **whole** heart afflicted.
1: 23 companions of thieves; they **all** love bribes and chase after gifts.
1: 25 thoroughly purge away your dross and remove **all** your impurities.
2: 2 it will be raised above the hills, and **all** nations will stream to it.
2: 12 The LORD Almighty has a day in store for **all** the proud
2: 12 and lofty, for **all** that is exalted (and they will be humbled),
2: 13 for **all** the cedars of Lebanon, tall and lofty, and all the oaks of
2: 13 the cedars of Lebanon, tall and lofty, and **all** the oaks of Bashan,
2: 14 for **all** the towering mountains and all the high hills,
2: 14 for all the towering mountains and **all** the high hills,
2: 15 for **every** lofty tower and every fortified wall,
2: 15 for every lofty tower and **every** fortified wall,
2: 16 for **every** trading ship and every stately vessel.
2: 16 for every trading ship and **every** stately vessel.
3: 1 and support: **all** supplies of food and all supplies of water,
3: 1 and support: all supplies of food and **all** supplies of water,
4: 3 be called holy, **all** who are recorded among the living in Jerusalem.
4: 5 the LORD will create over **all** *of* Mount Zion and over those who
4: 5 a glow of flaming fire by night; over **all** the glory will be a canopy.
5: 25 Yet for **all** this, his anger is not turned away, his hand is still
5: 28 Their arrows are sharp, **all** their bows are strung; their horses'
6: 3 holy is the LORD Almighty; the **whole** earth is full of his glory."

Isa 7: 19 They will **all** come and settle in the steep ravines and in the
7: 19 in the rocks, on **all** the thornbushes and at all the water holes.
7: 19 in the rocks, on all the thornbushes and at **all** the water holes.
7: 22 curds to eat. **All** who remain in the land will eat curds and honey.
7: 23 in **every** place where there were a thousand vines worth a thousand
7: 24 and arrow, for the land will be **covered with** briers and thorns.
7: 25 As for **all** the hills once cultivated by the hoe, you will no longer
8: 7 floodwaters of the River—the king of Assyria with **all** his pomp.
8: 7 his pomp. It will overflow **all** its channels, run over all its banks
8: 7 his pomp. It will overflow all its channels, run over **all** its banks
8: 9 you nations, and be shattered! Listen, **all** you distant lands.
8: 12 "Do not call conspiracy **everything** that these people call
9: 5 [9:4] **Every** warrior's boot used in battle and every garment rolled
9: 9 [9:8] **All** the people will know it—Ephraim and the inhabitants of
9: 12 [9:11] Philistines from the west have devoured Israel with **open**
9: 12 [9:11] Yet for **all** this, his anger is not turned away, his hand is
9: 17 [9:16] and widows, for **everyone** is ungodly and wicked,
9: 17 [9:16] is ungodly and wicked, **every** mouth speaks vileness.
9: 17 [9:16] Yet for **all** this, his anger is not turned away, his hand is
9: 21 [9:20] Yet for **all** this, his anger is not turned away, his hand is
10: 4 Yet for **all** this, his anger is not turned away, his hand is still
10: 12 When the Lord has finished **all** his work against Mount Zion
10: 14 as men gather abandoned eggs, so I gathered **all** the countries;
10: 23 will carry out the destruction decreed upon the **whole** land.
11: 9 They will neither harm nor destroy on **all** my holy mountain,
12: 5 for he has done glorious things; let this be known to **all** the world.
13: 5 and the weapons of his wrath—to destroy the **whole** country.
13: 7 Because of this, **all** hands will go limp, every man's heart will
13: 7 of this, all hands will go limp, **every** man's heart will melt.
13: 15 **Whoever** is captured will be thrust through; all who are caught
13: 15 will be thrust through; **all** who are caught will fall by the sword.
14: 7 **All** the lands are at rest and at peace; they break into singing.
14: 9 **all** those who were leaders in the world; it makes them rise from
14: 9 rise from their thrones—**all** those who were kings over the nations.
14: 10 They will **all** respond, they will say to you, "You also have become
14: 18 **All** the kings of the nations lie in state, each in his own tomb.
14: 18 the kings of the nations lie in state, **[RPH]** each in his own tomb.
14: 26 This is the plan determined for the **whole** world; this is the hand
14: 26 for the whole world; this is the hand stretched out over **all** nations.
14: 29 Do not rejoice, **all** you Philistines, that the rod that struck you is
14: 31 Wail, O gate! Howl, O city! Melt away, **all** you Philistines!
15: 2 and Medeba. **Every** head is shaved and every beard cut off.
15: 2 and Medeba. Every head is shaved and **every** beard cut off.
15: 3 on the roofs and in the public squares they **all** wail, prostrate with
16: 7 Therefore the Moabites wail, they wail **together** for Moab.
16: 14 Moab's splendor and **all** her many people will be despised,
18: 3 **All** you people of the world, you who live on the earth, when a
18: 6 will feed on them all summer, **[NIE]** the wild animals all winter.
19: 7 **Every** sown field along the Nile will become parched, will blow
19: 8 fishermen will groan and lament, **all** who cast hooks into the Nile;
19: 10 will be dejected, and **all** the wage earners will be sick at heart.
19: 14 they make Egypt stagger in **all** that she does, as a drunkard
19: 17 **everyone** to whom Judah is mentioned will be terrified, because of
21: 2 lay siege! I will bring to an end **all** the groaning she caused.
21: 8 my lord, I stand on the watchtower; **every** night I stay at my post.
21: 9 **All** the images of its gods lie shattered on the ground!' "
21: 16 contract would count it, **all** the pomp of Kedar will come to an end.
22: 1 What troubles you now, that you have **all** gone up on the roofs,
22: 3 **All** your leaders have fled together; they have been captured
22: 3 **All** you who were caught were taken prisoner together, having fled
22: 24 **All** the glory of his family will hang on him: its offspring
22: 24 and offshoots—**all** its lesser vessels, from the bowls to all the jars.
22: 24 and offshoots—all its lesser vessels, from the bowls to **all** the jars.
23: 9 to bring low the pride of **all** glory and to humble all who are
23: 9 pride of all glory and to humble **all** who are renowned on the earth.
23: 17 will ply her trade with **all** the kingdoms on the face of the earth.
24: 7 new wine dries up and the vine withers; **all** the merrymakers groan.
24: 10 The ruined city lies desolate; the entrance to **every** house is barred.
24: 11 **all** joy turns to gloom, all gaiety is banished from the earth.
25: 6 LORD Almighty will prepare a feast of rich food for **all** peoples,
25: 7 On this mountain he will destroy the shroud that enfolds **all**
25: 7 shroud that enfolds all peoples, the sheet that covers **all** nations;
25: 8 The Sovereign LORD will wipe away the tears from **all** faces;
25: 8 he will remove the disgrace of his people from **all** the earth.
26: 12 peace for us; **all** that we have accomplished you have done for us.
26: 14 and brought them to ruin; you wiped out **all** memory of them.
26: 15 glory for yourself; you have extended **all** the borders of the land.
27: 9 and this will be the **full** fruitage of the removal of his sin:
27: 9 When he makes **all** the altar stones to be like chalk stones crushed
28: 8 **All** the tables are covered with vomit and there is not a spot
28: 22 has told me of the destruction decreed against the **whole** land.
28: 24 plows for planting, does he plow **continually** [+2021+3427]?
29: 7 the hordes of **all** the nations that fight against Ariel, that attack her
29: 7 **[RPH]** that attack her and her fortress and besiege her, will be as
29: 8 So will it be with the hordes of **all** the nations that fight against
29: 11 For you this **whole** vision is nothing but words sealed in a scroll.
29: 20 will disappear, and **all** who have an eye for evil will be cut down—
30: 5 **everyone** will be put to shame because of a people useless to them,
30: 18 the LORD is a God of justice. Blessed are **all** who wait for him!
30: 25 streams of water will flow on **every** high mountain and every lofty
30: 25 of water will flow on every high mountain and **every** lofty hill.
30: 32 **Every** stroke the LORD lays on them with his punishing rod will
31: 3 will stumble, he who is helped will fall; **both** will perish together.
32: 13 mourn for **all** houses of merriment and for this city of revelry.
32: 20 sowing your seed by **every** stream, and letting your cattle
33: 20 its stakes will never be pulled up, nor **any** *of* its ropes broken.
34: 1 and all that is in it, the world, and **all** that comes out of it!
34: 2 The LORD is angry with **all** nations; his wrath is upon all their
34: 2 LORD is angry with all nations; his wrath is upon **all** their armies.
34: 4 **All** the stars of the heavens will be dissolved and the sky rolled up
34: 4 **all** the starry host will fall like withered leaves from the vine,
34: 12 there to be called a kingdom, **all** her princes will vanish away.
36: 1 Sennacherib king of Assyria attacked **all** the fortified cities of
36: 6 on it! Such is Pharaoh king of Egypt to **all** who depend on him.
36: 20 Who of **all** the gods of these countries has been able to save his
37: 11 Surely you have heard what the kings of Assyria have done to **all**
37: 16 you alone are God over **all** the kingdoms of the earth.
37: 17 listen to **all** the words Sennacherib has sent to insult the living
37: 18 that the Assyrian kings have laid waste **all** these peoples and their
37: 20 so that **all** kingdoms on earth may know that you alone, O LORD,
37: 25 With the soles of my feet I have dried up **all** the streams of Egypt.'
37: 36 people got up the next morning—there were **all** the dead bodies!
38: 13 I waited patiently till dawn, but like a lion he broke **all** my bones;
38: 15 I will walk humbly **all** my years because of this anguish of my
38: 16 such things men live; and my spirit finds life in **[NIE]** them too.
38: 17 the pit of destruction; you have put **all** my sins behind your back.
38: 20 we will sing with stringed instruments **all** the days of our lives in
39: 2 his **entire** armory and everything found among his treasures.
39: 2 his entire armory and **everything** found among his treasures.
39: 2 his palace or in **all** his kingdom that Hezekiah did not show them.
39: 4 "They saw **everything** in my palace," Hezekiah said.
39: 6 The time will surely come when **everything** in your palace,
40: 2 that she has received from the LORD's hand double for **all** her
40: 4 **Every** valley shall be raised up, every mountain and hill made low;
40: 4 Every valley shall be raised up, **every** mountain and hill made low;
40: 5 the LORD will be revealed, and **all** mankind together will see it.
40: 6 "**All** men are like grass, and all their glory is like the flowers of the
40: 6 are like grass, and **all** their glory is like the flowers of the field.
40: 17 Before him **all** the nations are as nothing; they are regarded by him
40: 26 brings out the starry host one by one, and calls them **each** by name.
41: 11 "**All** who rage against you will surely be ashamed and disgraced;
41: 29 See, they are **all** false! Their deeds amount to nothing; their images
42: 15 lay waste the mountains and hills and dry up **all** their vegetation;
42: 22 and looted, **all** *of* them trapped in pits or hidden away in prisons.
43: 7 **everyone** who is called by my name, whom I created for my glory,
43: 9 **All** the nations gather together and the peoples assemble. Which of
43: 14 send to Babylon and bring down as fugitives **all** the Babylonians,
44: 9 **All** who make idols are nothing, and the things they treasure are
44: 11 kind will be put to shame; **[NIE]** craftsmen are nothing but men.
44: 11 Let them **all** come together and take their stand; they will be
44: 23 Burst into song, you mountains, you forests and **all** your trees,
44: 24 I am the LORD, who has made **all** *things*, who alone stretched
44: 28 of Cyrus, 'He is my shepherd and will accomplish **all** that I please;
45: 7 and create disaster; I, the LORD, do **all** these things.
45: 12 stretched out the heavens; I marshaled their **[NIE]** starry hosts.
45: 13 I will make **all** his ways straight. He will rebuild my city and set
45: 16 **All** the makers of idols will be put to shame and disgraced;
45: 22 "Turn to me and be saved, **all** you ends of the earth; for I am God,
45: 23 Before me **every** knee will bow; by me every tongue will swear.
45: 23 Before me every knee will bow; by me **every** tongue will swear.
45: 24 and strength.' " **All** who have raged against him will come to him
45: 25 in the LORD **all** the descendants of Israel will be found righteous
46: 3 O house of Jacob, **all** you who remain of the house of Israel,
46: 10 I say: My purpose will stand, and I will do **all** that I please.
48: 6 You have heard these things; look at them **all**. Will you not admit
48: 14 "Come together, **all** *of* you, and listen: Which of ⌞the idols⌟ has
49: 9 will feed beside the roads and find pasture on **every** barren hill.
49: 11 I will turn **all** my mountains into roads, and my highways will be
49: 18 your eyes and look around; **all** your sons gather and come to you.
49: 18 declares the LORD, "you will wear them **all** as ornaments;
49: 26 Then **all** mankind will know that I, the LORD, am your Savior,
50: 9 They will **all** wear out like a garment; the moths will eat them up.
50: 11 **all** you who light fires and provide yourselves with flaming
51: 3 comfort Zion and will look with compassion on **all** her ruins;
51: 13 that you live in constant terror **every** day because of the wrath of
51: 18 Of **all** the sons she bore there was none to guide her; of all the sons
51: 18 of **all** the sons she reared there was none to take her by the hand.
51: 20 they lie at the head of **every** street, like antelope caught in a net.

Isa 52: 5 the LORD. "And **all** day long my name is constantly blasphemed.
52: 10 The LORD will lay bare his holy arm in the sight of **all** the
52: 10 and **all** the ends of the earth will see the salvation of our God.
53: 6 We **all**, like sheep, have gone astray, each of us has turned to his
53: 6 his own way; and the LORD has laid on him the iniquity of us **all**.
54: 5 of Israel is your Redeemer; he is called the God of **all** the earth.
54: 12 gates of sparkling jewels, and **all** your walls of precious stones.
54: 13 **All** your sons will be taught by the LORD, and great will be your
54: 17 **no** [+4202] weapon forged against you will prevail, and you will
54: 17 you will prevail, and you will refute **every** tongue that accuses you.
55: 1 "Come, **all** you who are thirsty, come to the waters; and you who
55: 12 song before you, and **all** the trees of the field will clap their hands.
56: 2 without desecrating it, and keeps his hand from doing **any** evil."
56: 6 **all** who keep the Sabbath without desecrating it and who hold fast
56: 7 for my house will be called a house of prayer for **all** nations."
56: 9 Come, **all** you beasts of the field, come and devour, all you beasts
56: 9 beasts of the field, come and devour, **all** you beasts of the forest!
56: 10 Israel's watchmen are blind, they **all** lack knowledge; they are all
56: 10 they are **all** mute dogs, they cannot bark; they lie around
56: 11 they **all** turn to their own way, each seeks his own gain.
57: 5 You burn with lust among the oaks and under **every** spreading tree;
57: 13 The wind will carry **all** *of* them off, a mere breath will blow them
58: 3 of your fasting, you do as you please and exploit **all** your workers.
58: 6 cords of the yoke, to set the oppressed free and break **every** yoke?
59: 8 into crooked roads; no **one** who walks in them will know peace.
59: 11 We **all** growl like bears; we moan mournfully like doves. We look
60: 4 **All** assemble and come to you; your sons come from afar,
60: 6 **all** from Sheba will come, bearing gold and incense
60: 7 **All** Kedar's flocks will be gathered to you, the rams of Nebaioth
60: 14 **all** who despise you will bow down at your feet and will call you
60: 21 will **all** your people be righteous and they will possess the land
61: 2 and the day of vengeance of our God, to comfort **all** who mourn,
61: 9 **All** who see them will acknowledge that they are a people the
61: 11 will make righteousness and praise spring up before **all** nations.
62: 2 The nations will see your righteousness, and **all** kings your glory;
62: 6 O Jerusalem; they will never be silent **[NIE]** day or night.
62: 6 O Jerusalem; they will never be silent day or **[NIE]** night.
63: 3 their blood spattered my garments, and I stained **all** my clothing.
63: 7 he is to be praised, according to **all** the LORD has done for us—
63: 9 In **all** their distress he too was distressed, and the angel of his
63: 9 he lifted them up and carried them **all** the days of old.
64: 6 [64:5] **All** *of* us have become like one who is unclean, and all our
64: 6 [64:5] is unclean, and **all** our righteous acts are like filthy rags;
64: 6 [64:5] we **all** shrivel up like a leaf, and like the wind our sins
64: 8 [64:7] you are the potter; we are **all** the work of your hand.
64: 9 [64:8] look upon us, we pray, for we are **all** your people.
64: 11 [64:10] burned with fire, and **all** that we treasured lies in ruins.
65: 2 **All** day long I have held out my hands to an obstinate people,
65: 5 people are smoke in my nostrils, a fire that keeps burning **all** day.
65: 8 so will I do in behalf of my servants; I will not destroy them **all**.
65: 12 you for the sword, and you will **all** bend down for the slaughter;
65: 25 They will neither harm nor destroy on **all** my holy mountain,"
66: 2 Has not my hand made **all** these things, and so they came into
66: 2 hand made all these things, and so **[RPH]** they came into being?"
66: 10 "Rejoice with Jerusalem and be glad for her, **all** you who love her;
66: 10 who love her; rejoice greatly with her, **all** you who mourn over her.
66: 16 with his sword the LORD will execute judgment upon **all** men,
66: 18 am about to come and gather **all** nations and tongues, and they will
66: 20 And they will bring **all** your brothers, from all the nations,
66: 20 And they will bring all your brothers, from **all** the nations,
66: 23 **all** mankind will come and bow down before me,"
66: 24 their fire be quenched, and they will be loathsome to **all** mankind."
Jer 1: 7 You must go to **everyone** I send you to and say whatever I
1: 7 everyone I send you to and say **whatever** [+889] I command you.
1: 14 "From the north disaster will be poured out on **all** who live in the
1: 15 I am about to summon **all** the peoples of the northern kingdoms,"
1: 15 they will come against **all** her surrounding walls and against all the
1: 15 all her surrounding walls and against **all** the towns of Judah.
1: 16 on my people because of **[NIE]** their wickedness in forsaking me,
1: 17 Stand up and say to them **whatever** [+889] I command you.
1: 18 an iron pillar and a bronze wall to stand against the **whole** land—
2: 3 **all** who devoured her were held guilty, and disaster overtook
2: 4 the LORD, O house of Jacob, **all** you clans of the house of Israel.
2: 20 on **every** high hill and under every spreading tree you lay down as
2: 20 and under **every** spreading tree you lay down as a prostitute.
2: 21 I had planted you like a choice vine of **sound** and reliable stock.
2: 24 **Any** males that pursue her need not tire themselves; at mating time
2: 29 You have **all** rebelled against me," declares the LORD.
2: 34 though you did not catch them breaking in. Yet in spite of **all** this
3: 6 She has gone up on **every** high hill and under every spreading tree
3: 6 and under **every** spreading tree and has committed adultery there.
3: 7 I thought that after she had done **all** this she would return to me
3: 8 of divorce and sent her away because of **all** her adulteries.
3: 10 In spite of **all** this, her unfaithful sister Judah did not return to me
3: 10 her unfaithful sister Judah did not return to me with **all** her heart,
3: 13 you have scattered your favors to foreign gods under **every**
3: 17 **all** nations will gather in Jerusalem to honor the name of the
4: 20 Disaster follows disaster; the **whole** land lies in ruins. In an instant
4: 24 the mountains, and they were quaking; **all** the hills were swaying.
4: 25 and there were no people; **every** bird in the sky had flown away.
4: 26 **all** its towns lay in ruins before the LORD, before his fierce
4: 27 "The **whole** land will be ruined, though I will not destroy it
4: 29 At the sound of horsemen and archers **every** town takes to flight.
4: 29 among the rocks. **All** the towns are deserted; no one lives in them.
5: 6 a leopard will lie in wait near their towns to tear to pieces **any** who
5: 16 quivers are like an open grave; **all** *of* them are mighty warriors.
5: 19 the people ask, 'Why has the LORD our God done **all** this to us?'
6: 6 This city must be punished; it is filled with **[NIE]** oppression.
6: 13 "From the least to the greatest, **all** are greedy for gain; prophets
6: 13 are greedy for gain; prophets and priests alike, **all** practice deceit.
6: 28 They are **all** hardened rebels, going about to slander. They are
6: 28 about to slander. They are bronze and iron; they **all** act corruptly.
7: 2 **all** you people of Judah who come through these gates to worship
7: 10 and say, "We are safe"—safe to do **all** these detestable things?
7: 13 While you were doing **all** these things, declares the LORD,
7: 15 my presence, just as I did **all** your brothers, the people of Ephraim.'
7: 15 just as I did all your brothers, **[NIE]** the people of Ephraim.'
7: 23 Walk in **all** the ways I command you, that it may go well with you.
7: 25 again and again I sent you **[NIE]** my servants the prophets.
7: 27 "When you tell them **all** this, they will not listen to you; when you
8: 2 exposed to the sun and the moon and **all** the stars of the heavens,
8: 3 **Wherever** [+928+2021+5226] I banish them, all the survivors
8: 3 **all** the survivors of this evil nation will prefer death to life,
8: 6 **Each** pursues his own course like a horse charging into battle.
8: 10 From the least to the greatest, **all** are greedy for gain; prophets
8: 10 are greedy for gain; prophets and priests alike, **all** practice deceit.
8: 16 at the neighing of their stallions the **whole** land trembles.
9: 2 [9:1] for they are **all** adulterers, a crowd of unfaithful people.
9: 4 [9:3] "Beware of your friends; do not trust **your**[s] brothers.
9: 4 [9:3] For **every** brother is a deceiver, and every friend a slanderer.
9: 4 [9:3] For every brother is a deceiver, and **every** friend a slanderer.
9: 25 [9:24] "when I will punish **all** who are circumcised only in the
9: 26 [9:25] and **all** who live in the desert in distant places.
9: 26 [9:25] For **all** these nations are really uncircumcised, and even the
9: 26 [9:25] even the **whole** house of Israel is uncircumcised in heart."
10: 7 Among **all** the wise men of the nations and in all their kingdoms,
10: 7 Among all the wise men of the nations and in **all** their kingdoms,
10: 9 then dressed in blue and purple—**all** made by skilled workers.
10: 14 **Everyone** [+132] is senseless and without knowledge;
10: 14 and without knowledge; **every** goldsmith is shamed by his idols.
10: 16 for he is the Maker of **all** *things*, including Israel, the tribe of his
10: 20 My tent is destroyed; **all** its ropes are snapped. My sons are gone
10: 21 the LORD; so they do not prosper and **all** their flock is scattered.
11: 4 I said, 'Obey me and do **everything** I command you, and you will
11: 6 "Proclaim **all** these words in the towns of Judah and in the streets
11: 8 So I brought on them **all** the curses of the covenant I had
12: 1 way of the wicked prosper? Why do **all** the faithless live at ease?
12: 4 will the land lie parched and the grass in **every** field be withered?
12: 9 Go and gather **all** the wild beasts; bring them to devour.
12: 11 the **whole** land will be laid waste because there is no one who
12: 12 Over **all** the barren heights in the desert destroyers will swarm,
12: 12 from one end of the land to the other; no **one**[s] [+1414] will be safe.
12: 14 "As for **all** my wicked neighbors who seize the inheritance I gave
13: 7 but now it was ruined and **completely** [+2021+4200] useless.
13: 10 will be like this belt—**completely** [+2021+4200] useless!
13: 11 so I bound the **whole** house of Israel and the whole house of Judah
13: 11 the whole house of Israel and the **whole** house of Judah to me,'
13: 12 the God of Israel, says: **Every** wineskin should be filled with wine.'
13: 12 'Don't we know that **every** wineskin should be filled with wine?'
13: 13 I am going to fill with drunkenness **all** who live in this land,
13: 13 the priests, the prophets and **all** those living in Jerusalem.
13: 19 **All** Judah will be carried into exile, carried completely away.
14: 22 Therefore our hope is in you, for you are the one who does **all** this.
15: 4 I will make them abhorrent to **all** the kingdoms of the earth
15: 10 me birth, a man with whom the **whole** land strives and contends!
15: 10 I have neither lent nor borrowed, yet **everyone** curses me.
15: 13 without charge, because of **all** your sins throughout your country.
15: 13 because of all your sins **throughout** [+928] your country.
16: 10 "When you tell these people **all** this and they ask you, 'Why has the
16: 10 'Why has the LORD decreed **[NIE]** such a great disaster against
16: 15 the north and out of **all** the countries where he had banished them.'
16: 16 and they will hunt them down on **every** mountain and hill
16: 16 and **[RPH]** hill and from the crevices of the rocks.
16: 17 My eyes are on **all** their ways; they are not hidden from me,
17: 3 and your wealth and **all** your treasures I will give away as plunder,
17: 3 your high places, because of sin **throughout** [+928] your country.
17: 9 The heart is deceitful above **all** *things* and beyond cure. Who can
17: 13 the hope of Israel, **all** who forsake you will be put to shame.

Jer 17:19 Judah go in and out; stand also at **all** the other gates of Jerusalem.
17:20 O kings of Judah and **all** people of Judah and everyone living in
17:20 and **everyone** living in Jerusalem who come through these gates.
17:22 not bring a load out of your houses or do **any** work on the Sabbath,
17:24 but keep the Sabbath day holy by not doing **any** work on it,
18:16 **all** who pass by will be appalled and will shake their heads.
18:18 him with our tongues and pay no attention to **anything** he says."
18:23 you know, O LORD, **all** their plots to kill me. Do not forgive
19: 3 place that will make the ears of **everyone** who hears of it tingle.
19: 8 **all** who pass by will be appalled and will scoff because of all its
19: 8 pass by will be appalled and will scoff because of **all** its wounds.
19:13 **all** the houses where they burned incense on the roofs to all the
19:13 all the houses where they burned incense on the roofs to **all** the
19:14 in the court of the LORD's temple and said to **all** the people,
19:15 the villages **around** it every disaster I pronounced against them,
19:15 the villages around it **every** disaster I pronounced against them,
20: 4 'I will make you a terror to yourself and to **all** your friends;
20: 4 I will hand **all** Judah over to the king of Babylon, who will carry
20: 5 I will hand over to their enemies **all** the wealth of this city—
20: 5 **all** its products, all its valuables and all the treasures of the kings of
20: 5 **all** its valuables and all the treasures of the kings of Judah.
20: 5 all its valuables and **all** the treasures of the kings of Judah.
20: 6 and **all** who live in your house will go into exile to Babylon.
20: 6 and **all** your friends to whom you have prophesied lies.' "
20: 7 and prevailed. I am ridiculed **all** day long; everyone mocks me.
20: 7 and prevailed. I am ridiculed all day long; **everyone** mocks me.
20: 8 of the LORD has brought me insult and reproach **all** day long.
20:10 **All** my friends are waiting for me to slip, saying, "Perhaps he will
21: 2 the LORD will perform wonders for us **as in times past** [+3869]
21:14 I will kindle a fire in your forests that will consume **everything**
22:20 in Bashan, cry out from Abarim, for **all** your allies are crushed.
22:22 The wind will drive **all** your shepherds away, and your allies will
22:22 you will be ashamed and disgraced because of **all** your wickedness.
23: 3 "I myself will gather the remnant of my flock out of **all** the
23: 8 the north and out of **all** the countries where he had banished them.'
23: 9 My heart is broken within me; **all** my bones tremble. I am like a
23:14 They are **all** like Sodom to me; the people of Jerusalem are like
23:15 Jerusalem ungodliness has spread **throughout** [+4200] the land."
23:17 And to **all** who follow the stubbornness of their hearts they say,
24: 7 I will be their God, for they will return to me with **all** their heart.
24: 9 them abhorrent and an offense to **all** the kingdoms of the earth,
24: 9 and cursing, **wherever** [+889+928+2021+5226] I banish them.
25: 1 The word came to Jeremiah concerning **all** the people of Judah in
25: 2 So Jeremiah the prophet said to **all** the people of Judah and to all
25: 2 said to all the people of Judah and to **all** those living in Jerusalem:
25: 4 though the LORD has sent **all** his servants the prophets to you
25: 9 I will summon **all** the peoples of the north and my servant
25: 9 and its inhabitants and against **all** the surrounding nations.
25:11 This **whole** country will become a desolate wasteland, and these
25:13 I will bring upon that land **all** the things I have spoken against it,
25:13 **all** that are written in this book and prophesied by Jeremiah against
25:13 in this book and prophesied by Jeremiah against **all** the nations.
25:15 of my wrath and make **all** the nations to whom I send you drink it.
25:17 and made **all** the nations to whom he sent me drink it:
25:19 king of Egypt, his attendants, his officials and **all** his people,
25:20 **all** the foreign people there; all the kings of Uz; all the kings of the
25:20 all the foreign people there; **all** the kings of Uz; all the kings of the
25:20 **all** the kings of the Philistines (those of Ashkelon, Gaza, Ekron,
25:22 **all** the kings of Tyre and Sidon; the kings of the coastlands across
25:22 all the kings of Tyre and **[RPH]** Sidon; the kings of the coastlands
25:23 Dedan, Tema, Buz and **all** who are in distant places;
25:24 **all** the kings of Arabia and all the kings of the foreign people who
25:24 and **all** the kings of the foreign people who live in the desert;
25:25 **all** the kings of Zimri, Elam and Media;
25:25 all the kings of Zimri, **[RPH]** Elam and Media;
25:25 all the kings of Zimri, Elam and **[RPH]** Media;
25:26 and **all** the kings of the north, near and far, one after the other—
25:26 one after the other—**all** the kingdoms on the face of the earth.
25:29 for I am calling down a sword upon **all** who live on the earth,
25:30 "Now prophesy **all** these words against them and say to them:
25:30 those who tread the grapes, shout against **all** who live on the earth.
25:31 he will bring judgment on **all** mankind and put the wicked to the
26: 2 speak to **all** the people of the towns of Judah who come to worship
26: 2 Tell them **everything** [+1821+2021] I command you; do not omit
26: 6 this city an object of cursing among **all** the nations of the earth.' "
26: 7 **all** the people heard Jeremiah speak these words in the house of the
26: 8 as soon as Jeremiah finished telling **all** the people everything the
26: 8 as soon as Jeremiah finished telling all the people **everything** the
26: 8 the priests, the prophets and **all** the people seized him and said,
26: 9 **all** the people crowded around Jeremiah in the house of the
26:11 the priests and the prophets said to the officials and **all** the people,
26:12 Jeremiah said to **all** the officials and all the people: "The LORD
26:12 Jeremiah said to all the officials and **all** the people: "The LORD
26:12 against this house and this city **all** the things you have heard.
26:15 for in truth the LORD has sent me to you to speak **all** these words
26:16 the officials and **all** the people said to the priests and the prophets,
26:17 the land stepped forward and said to the **entire** assembly of people,
26:18 He told **all** the people of Judah, 'This is what the LORD Almighty
26:19 Hezekiah king of Judah or **anyone** *else in* Judah put him to death?
26:20 he prophesied the **[NIE]** same things against this city and this
26:21 When King Jehoiakim and **all** his officers and officials heard his
26:21 and all his officers and **[RPH]** officials heard his words,
27: 6 Now I will hand **all** your countries over to my servant
27: 7 **All** nations will serve him and his son and his grandson until the
27:12 *I* **gave the** same **message** [+465+1819+1821+2021+2021] to
27:16 I said to the priests and **all** these people, "This is what the LORD
27:20 to Babylon, along with **all** the nobles of Judah and Jerusalem—
28: 1 of the LORD in the presence of the priests and **all** the people:
28: 3 Within two years I will bring back to this place **all** the articles of
28: 4 and **all** the other exiles from Judah who went to Babylon,'
28: 5 and **all** the people who were standing in the house of the LORD.
28: 6 LORD's house and **all** the exiles back to this place from Babylon.
28: 7 I have to say in your hearing and in the hearing of **all** the people:
28:11 and he said before **all** the people, "This is what the LORD says:
28:11 Babylon off the neck of **all** the nations within two years.' " At this,
28:14 I will put an iron yoke on the necks of **all** these nations to make
29: 1 **all** the other people Nebuchadnezzar had carried into exile from
29: 4 says to **all** those I carried into exile from Jerusalem to Babylon:
29:13 will seek me and find me when you seek me with **all** your heart.
29:14 I will gather you from **all** the nations and places where I have
29:14 all the nations and **[RPH]** places where I have banished you,"
29:16 sits on David's throne and **all** the people who remain in this city,
29:18 and will make them abhorrent to **all** the kingdoms of the earth
29:18 of scorn and reproach, among **all** the nations where I drive them.
29:20 **all** you exiles whom I have sent away from Jerusalem to Babylon.
29:22 **all** the exiles from Judah who are in Babylon will use this curse:
29:25 You sent letters in your own name to **all** the people in Jerusalem,
29:25 Zephaniah son of Maaseiah the priest, and to **all** the other priests.
29:26 you should put **any** madman who acts like a prophet into the stocks
29:31 "Send this message to **all** the exiles: 'This is what the LORD says
30: 2 of Israel, says: 'Write in a book **all** the words I have spoken to you.
30: 6 why do I see **every** strong man with his hands on his stomach like
30: 6 his stomach like a woman in labor, **every** face turned deathly pale?
30:11 'Though I completely destroy **all** the nations among which I scatter
30:14 **All** your allies have forgotten you; they care nothing for you.
30:16 " 'But **all** who devour you will be devoured; all your enemies will
30:16 devour you will be devoured; **all** your enemies will go into exile.
30:16 you will be devoured; all your enemies **[RPH]** will go into exile.
30:16 you will be plundered; **all** who make spoil of you I will despoil.
30:20 will be established before me; I will punish **all** who oppress them.
31: 1 declares the LORD, "I will be the God of **all** the clans of Israel,
31:24 People will live together in Judah and **all** its towns—farmers
31:25 I will refresh the weary and satisfy **[NIE]** the faint."
31:30 **whoever** [+132+2021] eats sour grapes—his own teeth will be set
31:34 saying, 'Know the LORD,' because they will **all** know me,
31:36 "will the descendants of Israel **ever** [+2021+3427] cease to be a
31:37 the foundations of the earth below be searched out will I reject **all**
31:37 I reject all the descendants of Israel because of **all** they have done,"
31:40 The **whole** valley where dead bodies and ashes are thrown,
31:40 **all** the terraces out to the Kidron Valley on the east as far as the
32:12 the deed and of **all** the Jews sitting in the courtyard of the guard.
32:17 and outstretched arm. **Nothing** [+1821+4202] is too hard for you.
32:19 Your eyes are open to **all** the ways of men; you reward everyone
32:23 your law; they did not do **what**[s] you commanded them to do.
32:23 them to do. So you brought **all** this disaster upon them.
32:27 "I am the LORD, the God of **all** mankind. Is anything too hard for
32:27 the God of all mankind. Is **anything** [+1821] too hard for me?
32:32 and Judah have provoked me by **all** the evil they have done—
32:37 I will surely gather them from **all** the lands where I banish them in
32:39 so that they will **always** [+2021+3427] fear me for their own good
32:41 and will assuredly plant them in this land with **all** my heart
32:41 plant them in this land with all my heart and **[RPH]** soul.
32:42 As I have brought **all** this great calamity on this people, so I will
32:42 so I will give them **all** the prosperity I have promised them.
33: 5 I will hide my face from this city because of **all** its wickedness.
33: 8 I will cleanse them from **all** the sin they have committed against
33: 8 against me and will forgive **all** their sins of rebellion against me.
33: 9 honor before **all** nations on earth that hear of all the good things I
33: 9 honor before all nations on earth that hear of **all** the good things I
33: 9 they will be in awe and will tremble at the **abundant** prosperity
33: 9 at the abundant prosperity and **[RPH]** peace I provide for it.'
33:12 in **all** its towns there will again be pastures for shepherds to rest
33:18 stand before me **continually** [+2021+3427] to offer burnt offerings,
34: 1 king of Babylon and **all** his army and all the kingdoms
34: 1 king of Babylon and all his army and **all** the kingdoms
34: 1 peoples in the **[RPH]** empire he ruled were fighting against
34: 1 were fighting against Jerusalem and **all** its surrounding towns,
34: 6 Then Jeremiah the prophet told **all** this to Zedekiah king of Judah,

Jer 34: 7 and the **other**ˢ cities of Judah that were still holding out—
34: 8 with **all** the people in Jerusalem to proclaim freedom for the slaves.
34: 10 So **all** the officials and people who entered into this covenant
34: 10 **[RPH]** people who entered into this covenant agreed that they
34: 17 I will make you abhorrent to **all** the kingdoms of the earth.
34: 19 **all** the people of the land who walked between the pieces of the
35: 3 the son of Habazziniah, and his brothers and **all** his sons—
35: 3 his brothers and all his sons—the **whole** family of the Recabites.
35: 7 have any of these things, but must **always** [+3427] live in tents.
35: 8 We have obeyed **everything** our forefather Jonadab son of Recab
35: 8 wives nor our sons and daughters have **ever** [+3427] drunk wine
35: 10 have fully obeyed **everything** our forefather Jonadab commanded
35: 15 Again and again I sent **all** my servants the prophets to you.
35: 17 on **everyone** living in Jerusalem every disaster I pronounced
35: 17 on everyone living in Jerusalem **every** disaster I pronounced
35: 18 have followed **all** his instructions and have done everything he
35: 18 followed all his instructions and have done **everything** he ordered.'
35: 19 will **never** [+2021+3427+4202] fail to have a man to serve me.' "
36: 2 write on it **all** the words I have spoken to you concerning Israel,
36: 2 **all** the other nations from the time I began speaking to you in the
36: 3 Perhaps when the people of Judah hear about **every** disaster I plan
36: 4 while Jeremiah dictated **all** the words the LORD had spoken to
36: 6 Read them to **all** *the people of* Judah who come in from their
36: 8 Baruch son of Neriah did **everything** Jeremiah the prophet told
36: 9 a time of fasting before the LORD was proclaimed for **all** the
36: 9 and **[RPH]** those who had come from the towns of Judah.
36: 10 Baruch read to **all** the people at the LORD's temple the words of
36: 11 son of Shaphan, heard **all** the words of the LORD from the scroll,
36: 12 room in the royal palace, where **all** the officials were sitting:
36: 12 of Shaphan, Zedekiah son of Hananiah, and **all** the other officials.
36: 13 After Micaiah told them **everything** [+1821+2021] he had heard
36: 14 **all** the officials sent Jehudi son of Nethaniah, the son of Shelemiah,
36: 16 When they heard **all** these words, they looked at each other in fear
36: 16 and said to Baruch, "We must report **all** these words to the king."
36: 17 they asked Baruch, "Tell us, how did you come to write **all** this?
36: 18 "Yes," Baruch replied, "he dictated **all** these words to me,
36: 20 in the courtyard and reported **everything** [+1821+2021] to him.
36: 21 and read it to the king and **all** the officials standing beside him.
36: 23 them into the firepot, until the **entire** scroll was burned in the fire.
36: 24 and **all** his attendants who heard all these words showed no fear,
36: 24 and all his attendants who heard **all** these words showed no fear,
36: 28 and write on it **all** the words that were on the first scroll,
36: 31 and the people of Judah **every** disaster I pronounced against them,
36: 32 Baruch wrote on it **all** the words of the scroll that Jehoiakim king
37: 10 Even if you were to defeat the **entire** Babylonian army that is
37: 21 given bread from the street of the bakers each day until **all** the
38: 1 Pashhur son of Malkijah heard what Jeremiah was telling **all** the
38: 4 as well as **all** the people, by the things he is saying to them.
38: 9 these men have acted wickedly *in* **all** they have done to Jeremiah
38: 22 **All** the women left in the palace of the king of Judah will be
38: 23 "**All** your wives and children will be brought out to the
38: 27 **All** the officials did come to Jeremiah and question him, and he
38: 27 and he told them **everything** the king had ordered him to say.
39: 1 king of Babylon marched against Jerusalem with his **whole** army
39: 3 **all** the officials of the king of Babylon came and took seats in the
39: 3 a high official and **all** the other officials of the king of Babylon.
39: 4 When Zedekiah king of Judah and **all** the soldiers saw them,
39: 6 of Zedekiah before his eyes and also killed **all** the nobles of Judah.
39: 13 a high official and **all** the other officers of the king of Babylon
40: 1 He had found Jeremiah bound in chains among **all** the captives
40: 4 Look, the **whole** country lies before you; go wherever you please."
40: 5 live with him among the people, or go **anywhere** *else* you please."
40: 7 When **all** the army officers and their men who were still in the
40: 11 When **all** the Jews in Moab, Ammon, Edom and all the other
40: 11 **all** the other countries heard that the king of Babylon had left a
40: 12 they **all** came back to the land of Judah, to Gedaliah at Mizpah,
40: 12 at Mizpah, from **all** the countries where they had been scattered.
40: 13 **all** the army officers still in the open country came to Gedaliah at
40: 15 and cause **all** the Jews who are gathered around you to be scattered
41: 3 Ishmael also killed **all** the Jews who were with Gedaliah at
41: 9 Now the cistern where he threw **all** the bodies of the men he had
41: 10 Ishmael made captives of **all** the rest of the people who were in
41: 10 the king's daughters along with **all** the others who were left there,
41: 11 **all** the army officers who were with him heard about all the crimes
41: 11 all the army officers who were with him heard about **all** the crimes
41: 12 they took **all** their men and went to fight Ishmael son of Nethaniah.
41: 13 When **all** the people Ishmael had with him saw Johanan son of
41: 13 son of Kareah and **[RPH]** the army officers who were with him,
41: 14 **All** the people Ishmael had taken captive at Mizpah turned
41: 16 **all** the army officers who were with him led away all the survivors
41: 16 all the army officers who were with him led away **all** the survivors
42: 1 Then **all** the army officers, including Johanan son of Kareah
42: 1 and **all** the people from the least to the greatest approached
42: 2 and pray to the LORD your God for this **entire** remnant.
42: 4 I will tell you **everything** [+1821+2021] the LORD says and will
42: 5 if we do not act in accordance with **everything** [+1821+2021] the
42: 8 son of Kareah and **all** the army officers who were with him
42: 8 who were with him and **all** the people from the least to the greatest.
42: 17 **all** who are determined to go to Egypt to settle there will die by the
42: 20 our God for us; tell us **everything** he says and we will do it.'
42: 21 you still have not obeyed the LORD your God in **all** he sent me to
43: 1 When Jeremiah finished telling **[RPH]** the people all the words of
43: 1 When Jeremiah finished telling the people **all** the words of the
43: 1 **everything** [+465+1821+2021+2021] the LORD had sent him to
43: 2 Johanan son of Kareah and **all** the arrogant men said to Jeremiah,
43: 4 So Johanan son of Kareah and **all** the army officers and all the
43: 4 **all** the people disobeyed the LORD's command to stay in the land
43: 5 **all** the army officers led away all the remnant of Judah who had
43: 5 all the army officers led away **all** the remnant of Judah who had
43: 5 land of Judah from **all** the nations where they had been scattered.
43: 6 They also led away **all** the men, women and children
44: 1 This word came to Jeremiah concerning **all** the Jews living in
44: 2 You saw the **great** disaster I brought on Jerusalem and on all the
44: 2 great disaster I brought on Jerusalem and on **all** the towns of Judah.
44: 4 Again and again I sent **[NIE]** my servants the prophets, who said,
44: 8 an object of cursing and reproach among **all** the nations on earth.
44: 11 I am determined to bring disaster on you and to destroy **all** Judah.
44: 12 They will **all** perish in Egypt; they will fall by the sword or die
44: 15 **all** the men who knew that their wives were burning incense to
44: 15 to other gods, along with **all** the women who were present—
44: 15 **all** the people living in Lower and Upper Egypt, said to Jeremiah,
44: 17 We will certainly do **everything** [+1821+2021] we said we would:
44: 18 *we have* **had nothing** [+2893] and have been perishing by sword
44: 20 Then Jeremiah said to **all** the people, both men and women,
44: 20 both men and women, **[RPH]** who were answering him,
44: 24 Then Jeremiah said to **all** the people, including the women,
44: 24 including **[RPH]** the women, "Hear the word of the LORD,
44: 24 "Hear the word of the LORD, **all** you people of Judah in Egypt.
44: 26 But hear the word of the LORD, **all** Jews living in Egypt:
44: 26 'that no **[NIE]** one from Judah living anywhere in Egypt will ever
44: 26 'that no one from Judah living **anywhere** in Egypt will ever again
44: 27 Egypt will perish by sword and famine until they are **all** destroyed.
44: 28 the **whole** remnant of Judah who came to live in Egypt will know
45: 4 I have built and uproot what I have planted, **throughout** the land.
45: 5 For I will bring disaster on **all** people, declares the LORD,
45: 5 but **wherever** [+889+2021+5226+6584] you go I will let you
46: 28 "Though I completely destroy **all** the nations among which I
47: 2 The people will cry out; **all** who dwell in the land will wail
47: 4 For the day has come to destroy **all** the Philistines and to cut off all
47: 4 and to cut off **all** survivors who could help Tyre and Sidon.
48: 8 The destroyer will come against **every** town, and not a town will
48: 17 Mourn for her, **all** who live around her, all who know her fame;
48: 17 Mourn for her, all who live around her, **all** who know her fame;
48: 24 to Kerioth and Bozrah—to **all** the towns of Moab, far and near.
48: 31 Therefore I wail over Moab, for **all** Moab I cry out, I moan for the
48: 37 **Every** head is shaved and every beard cut off; every hand is
48: 37 Every head is shaved and **every** beard cut off; every hand is
48: 37 **every** hand is slashed and every waist is covered with sackcloth.
48: 38 On **all** the roofs in Moab and in the public squares there is nothing
48: 38 in Moab and in the public squares there is **nothing but** mourning,
48: 39 an object of ridicule, an object of horror to **all** those around her."
49: 5 I will bring terror on you from **all** those around you,"
49: 13 and of cursing; and **all** its towns will be in ruins forever."
49: 17 **all** who pass by will be appalled and will scoff because of all its
49: 17 pass by will be appalled and will scoff because of **all** its wounds.
49: 26 **all** her soldiers will be silenced in that day," declares the LORD
49: 29 their shelters will be carried off with **all** their goods and camels.
49: 32 I will scatter to **[NIE]** the winds those who are in distant places
49: 32 in distant places and will bring disaster on them from **every** side,"
49: 36 I will scatter them to the **four**ˢ winds, and there will not be a nation
50: 7 **Whoever** found them devoured them; their enemies said, 'We are
50: 10 **all** who plunder her will have their fill," declares the LORD.
50: 13 anger she will not be inhabited but will be **completely** desolate.
50: 13 **All** who pass Babylon will be horrified and scoff because of all her
50: 13 pass Babylon will be horrified and scoff because of **all** her wounds.
50: 14 up your positions around Babylon, **all** you who draw the bow.
50: 21 declares the LORD. "Do **everything** I have commanded you.
50: 23 How broken and shattered is the hammer of the **whole** earth!
50: 27 Kill **all** her young bulls; let them go down to the slaughter!
50: 29 "Summon archers against Babylon, **all** those who draw the bow.
50: 29 Repay her for her deeds; do to her **as** [+889+3869] she has done.
50: 30 **all** her soldiers will be silenced in that day," declares the LORD.
50: 32 I will kindle a fire in her towns that will consume **all** who are
50: 33 as well. **All** their captors hold them fast, refusing to let them go.
50: 37 against her horses and chariots and **all** the foreigners in her ranks!
51: 3 Do not spare her young men; completely destroy **[NIE]** her army.
51: 7 a gold cup in the LORD's hand; she made the **whole** earth drunk.
51: 17 "**Every** man is senseless and without knowledge; every goldsmith

Jer 51:17 and without knowledge; **every** goldsmith is shamed by his idols.
51:19 for he is the Maker of **all** *things*, including the tribe of his
51:24 **all** who live in Babylonia for all the wrong they have done in
51:24 all who live in Babylonia for **all** the wrong they have done in
51:25 you who destroy the **whole** earth," declares the LORD.
51:28 the kings of the Medes, their governors and **all** their officials,
51:28 and all their officials, and **all** the countries they rule.
51:41 Sheshach will be captured, the boast of the **whole** earth seized!
51:43 a dry and desert land, a land where **no** [+4202] one lives,
51:47 her **whole** land will be disgraced and her slain will all lie fallen
51:47 land will be disgraced and her slain will **all** lie fallen within her.
51:48 and earth and **all** that is in them will shout for joy over Babylon,
51:49 just as the slain in **all** the earth have fallen because of Babylon.
51:52 her idols, and **throughout** [+928] her land the wounded will groan.
51:60 Jeremiah had written on a scroll about **all** the disasters that would
51:60 upon Babylon—**all** that had been recorded concerning Babylon.
51:61 "When you get to Babylon, see that you read **all** these words aloud.
52: 2 the eyes of the LORD, **just as** [+889+3869] Jehoiakim had done.
52: 4 king of Babylon marched against Jerusalem with his **whole** army.
52: 7 Then the city wall was broken through, and the **whole** army fled.
52: 8 of Jericho. **All** his soldiers were separated from him and scattered,
52:10 Zedekiah before his eyes; he also killed **all** the officials of Judah.
52:13 of the LORD, the royal palace and **all** the houses of Jerusalem.
52:13 houses of Jerusalem. **Every** important building he burned down.
52:14 The **whole** Babylonian army under the commander of the imperial
52:14 of the imperial guard broke down **all** the walls around Jerusalem.
52:17 temple of the LORD and they carried **all** the bronze to Babylon.
52:18 dishes and **all** the bronze articles used in the temple service.
52:20 temple of the LORD, was more than could be weighed. **[NIE]**
52:22 decorated with a network and pomegranates of bronze **all** around.
52:23 the **total** *number* of pomegranates above the surrounding network
52:30 commander of the imperial guard. There were 4,600 people *in* **all**.
52:33 and *for* the **rest** [+3427] *of* his life ate regularly at the king's table.
52:34 gave Jehoiachin a regular allowance **as long** [+3427] **as** he lived,
La 1: 2 her cheeks. Among **all** her lovers there is none to comfort her.
1: 2 **All** her friends have betrayed her; they have become her enemies.
1: 3 **All** who pursue her have overtaken her in the midst of her distress.
1: 4 **All** her gateways are desolate, her priests groan, her maidens
1: 6 **All** the splendor has departed from the Daughter of Zion.
1: 7 wandering Jerusalem remembers **all** the treasures that were hers in
1: 8 **All** who honored her despise her, for they have seen her nakedness;
1:10 The enemy laid hands on **all** her treasures; she saw pagan nations
1:11 **All** her people groan as they search for bread; they barter their
1:12 "Is it nothing to you, **all** you who pass by? Look around and see.
1:13 and turned me back. He made me desolate, faint **all** the day long.
1:15 "The Lord has rejected **all** the warriors in my midst; he has
1:18 Listen, **all** you peoples; look upon my suffering. My young men
1:21 **All** my enemies have heard of my distress; they rejoice at what you
1:22 "Let **all** their wickedness come before you; deal with them as you
1:22 deal with them as you have dealt with me because of **all** my sins.
2: 2 Without pity the Lord has swallowed up **all** the dwellings of Jacob;
2: 3 In fierce anger he has cut off **every** horn of Israel. He has
2: 4 Like a foe he has slain **all** who were pleasing to the eye; he has
2: 5 He has swallowed up **all** her palaces and destroyed her
2:15 **All** who pass your way clap their hands at you; they scoff
2:15 was called the perfection of beauty, the joy of the **whole** earth?"
2:16 **All** your enemies open their mouths wide against you; they scoff
2:19 of your children, who faint from hunger at the head of **every** street.
3: 3 he has turned his hand against me again and again, **all** day long.
3:14 I became the laughingstock of **all** my people; they mock me in
3:14 laughingstock of all my people; they mock me in song **all** day long.
3:34 To crush underfoot **all** prisoners in the land,
3:46 "**All** our enemies have opened their mouths wide against us.
3:51 I see brings grief to my soul because of **all** the women of my city.
3:60 You have seen the **depth** *of* their vengeance, all their plots against
3:60 have seen the depth of their vengeance, **all** their plots against me.
3:61 O LORD, you have heard their insults, **all** their plots against me—
3:62 what my enemies whisper and mutter against me **all** day long.
4: 1 The sacred gems are scattered at the head of **every** street.
4:12 nor did **any** *of* the world's people, that enemies and foes could
Eze 3: 7 to me, for the **whole** house of Israel is hardened and obstinate.
3:10 listen carefully and take to heart **all** the words I speak to you.
5: 4 A fire will spread from there to the **whole** house of Israel.
5: 9 Because of **all** your detestable idols, I will do to you what I have
5:10 punishment on you and will scatter **all** your survivors to the winds.
5:10 on you and will scatter all your survivors to **[RPH]** the winds.
5:11 because you have defiled my sanctuary with **all** your vile images
5:11 with all your vile images and **[RPH]** detestable practices,
5:12 a third I will scatter to **[NIE]** the winds and pursue with drawn
5:14 among the nations around you, in the sight of **all** who pass by.
6: 6 **Wherever** [+928] you live, the towns will be laid waste
6: 9 for the evil they have done and for **all** their detestable practices.
6:11 because of **all** the wicked and detestable practices of the house of
6:13 on **every** high hill and on all the mountaintops, under every
6:13 on every high hill and on **all** the mountaintops, under every
6:13 the mountaintops, under **every** spreading tree and every leafy oak—
6:13 the mountaintops, under every spreading tree and **every** leafy oak—
6:13 places where they offered fragrant incense to **all** their idols.
6:14 waste from the desert to Diblah—**wherever** [+928] they live.
7: 3 to your conduct and repay you for **all** your detestable practices.
7: 8 to your conduct and repay you for **all** your detestable practices.
7:12 rejoice nor the seller grieve, for wrath is upon the **whole** crowd.
7:13 for the vision concerning the **whole** crowd will not be reversed.
7:14 Though they blow the trumpet and get **everything** ready, no one
7:14 no one will go into battle, for my wrath is upon the **whole** crowd.
7:16 **All** who survive and escape will be in the mountains, moaning like
7:17 **Every** hand will go limp, and every knee will become as weak as
7:17 hand will go limp, and **every** knee will become as weak as water.
7:18 Their **[NIE]** faces will be covered with shame and their heads will
7:18 will be covered with shame and **[NIE]** their heads will be shaved.
8:10 and I saw portrayed all over the walls **all** kinds of crawling things
8:10 and detestable animals and **all** the idols of the house of Israel.
9: 4 and lament over **all** the detestable things that are done in it."
9: 6 and children, but do not touch **anyone** [+408] who has the mark.
9: 8 Are you going to destroy the **entire** remnant of Israel in this
9:11 saying, "I have done **as** [+889+3869] you commanded."
10:12 Their **entire** bodies, including their backs, their hands and their
11:15 who are your blood relatives and the **whole** house of Israel—
11:15 **[RPH]** are those of whom the people of Jerusalem have said,
11:18 will return to it and remove **all** its vile images and detestable idols.
11:18 and remove all its vile images and **[RPH]** detestable idols.
11:25 I told the exiles **everything** [+1821] the LORD had shown me.
12:10 prince in Jerusalem and the **whole** house of Israel who are there.'
12:14 I will scatter to **[RPH]** the winds all those around him—his staff
12:14 I will scatter to the winds **all** those around him—his staff and all
12:14 his staff and **all** his troops—and I will pursue them with drawn
12:16 so that in the nations where they go they may acknowledge **all**
12:19 of everything in it because of the violence of **all** who live there.
12:22 land of Israel: 'The days go by and **every** vision comes to nothing'?
12:23 Say to them, 'The days are near when **every** vision will be fulfilled.
12:24 For there will be no more **[RPH]** false visions or flattering
12:28 **None of** [+4202] my words will be delayed any longer; whatever I
13:18 Woe to the women who sew magic charms on **all** their wrists
13:18 make veils of **various** lengths for their heads in order to ensnare
14: 5 of the people of Israel, who have **all** deserted me for their idols.'
14: 6 Turn from your idols and renounce **all** your detestable practices!
14:11 nor will they defile themselves anymore with **all** their sins.
14:22 brought upon Jerusalem—**every** disaster I have brought upon it.
14:23 for you will know that I have done **nothing** [+889+4202] in it
15: 2 how is the wood of a vine better than that of a branch on **any** of the
15: 3 Do they make pegs from it to hang **things** [+3998] on?
16:15 You lavished your favors on **anyone** who passed by and your
16:22 In **all** your detestable practices and your prostitution you did not
16:23 the Sovereign LORD. In addition to **all** your other wickedness,
16:24 mound for yourself and made a lofty shrine in **every** public square.
16:25 At the head of **every** street you built your lofty shrines
16:25 offering your body with increasing promiscuity to **anyone** who
16:30 when you do **all** these things, acting like a brazen prostitute!
16:31 When you built your mounds at the head of **every** street and made
16:31 of every street and made your lofty shrines in **every** public square,
16:33 **Every** prostitute receives a fee, but you give gifts to all your
16:33 Every prostitute receives a fee, but you give gifts to **all** your lovers,
16:36 because of **all** your detestable idols, and because you gave them
16:37 therefore I am going to gather **all** your lovers, with whom you
16:37 you found pleasure, **those**[s] you loved as well as those you hated.
16:37 you found pleasure, those you loved as well as **those**[s] you hated.
16:37 strip you in front of them, and they will see **all** your nakedness.
16:43 the days of your youth but enraged me with **all** these things,
16:43 Did you not add lewdness to **all** your other detestable practices?
16:44 " '**Everyone** who quotes proverbs will quote this proverb about
16:47 but in **all** your ways you soon became more depraved than they.
16:51 have made your sisters seem righteous by **all** these things you have
16:54 and be ashamed of **all** you have done in giving them comfort.
16:57 and **all** her neighbors and the daughters of the Philistines—
16:63 Then, when I make atonement for you for **all** you have done,
17: 9 of its fruit so that it withers? **All** its new growth will wither.
17:18 he had given his hand in pledge and yet did **all** these things,
17:21 **All** his fleeing troops will fall by the sword, and the survivors will
17:21 All his fleeing **[RPH]** troops will fall by the sword,
17:21 the sword, and the survivors will be scattered to **[RPH]** the winds.
17:23 Birds **[RPH]** of every kind will nest in it; they will find shelter in
17:23 Birds *of* **every** *kind* will nest in it; they will find shelter in the
17:24 **All** the trees of the field will know that I the LORD bring down
18: 4 For **every** living soul belongs to me, the father as well as the son—
18:11 (though the father has done **none of** [+4202] them): "He eats at the
18:13 Because he has done **all** these detestable things, he will surely be
18:14 "But suppose this son has a son who sees **all** the sins his father
18:19 what is just and right and has been careful to keep **all** my decrees,

Eze 18: 21 "But if a wicked man turns away from **all** the sins he has
18: 21 and keeps **all** my decrees and does what is just and right,
18: 22 **None of** [+4202] the offenses he has committed will be
18: 24 and does the same **[NIE]** detestable things the wicked man does,
18: 24 **None of** [+4202] the righteous things he has done will be
18: 28 Because he considers **all** the offenses he has committed and turns
18: 30 Turn away from **all** your offenses; then sin will not be your
18: 31 Rid yourselves of **all** the offenses you have committed, and get a
20: 6 a land flowing with milk and honey, the most beautiful of **all** lands.
20: 15 a land flowing with milk and honey, most beautiful of **all** lands—
20: 26 the sacrifice of **every** firstborn—that I might fill them with horror
20: 28 sworn to give them and they saw **any** high hill or any leafy tree,
20: 28 sworn to give them and they saw any high hill or **any** leafy tree,
20: 31 you continue to defile yourselves with **all** your idols to this day.
20: 40 there in the land the **entire** house of Israel will serve me, and there
20: 40 there in the land the entire house of Israel **[RPH]** will serve me,
20: 40 and your choice gifts, along with **all** your holy sacrifices.
20: 43 and **all** the actions by which you have defiled yourselves,
20: 43 and you will loathe yourselves for **all** the evil you have done.
20: 47 [21:3] and it will consume **all** your trees, both green and dry.
20: 47 [21:3] it will consume all your trees, both green and **[RPH]** dry.
20: 47 [21:3] and **every** face from south to north will be scorched by it.
20: 48 [21:4] **Everyone** [+1414] will see that I the LORD have kindled
21: 4 [21:9] my sword will be unsheathed against **everyone** [+1414]
21: 5 [21:10] **all** people will know that I the LORD have drawn my
21: 7 [21:12] **Every** heart will melt and every hand go limp; every spirit
21: 7 [21:12] Every heart will melt and **every** hand go limp; every spirit
21: 7 [21:12] **every** spirit will become faint and every knee become as
21: 7 [21:12] become faint and **every** knee become as weak as water.'
21: 10 [21:15] of my son ⌞Judah⌟? The sword despises **every** such stick.
21: 12 [21:17] is against my people; it is against **all** the princes of Israel.
21: 15 [21:20] I have stationed the sword for slaughter at **all** their gates.
21: 24 [21:29] open rebellion, revealing your sins in **all** that you do—
22: 2 of bloodshed? Then confront her with **all** her detestable practices
22: 4 of scorn to the nations and a laughingstock to **all** the countries.
22: 18 **all** *of* them are the copper, tin, iron and lead left inside a furnace.
22: 19 'Because you have **all** become dross, I will gather you into
23: 6 governors and commanders, **all** *of* them handsome young men,
23: 7 She gave herself as a prostitute to **all** the elite of the Assyrians
23: 7 and defiled herself with **all** the idols of everyone she lusted after.
23: 7 and defiled herself with all the idols of **everyone** she lusted after.
23: 12 in full dress, mounted horsemen, **all** handsome young men.
23: 15 **all** *of* them looked like Babylonian chariot officers, natives of
23: 23 the Babylonians and **all** the Chaldeans, the men of Pekod and Shoa
23: 23 men of Pekod and Shoa and Koa, and **all** the Assyrians with them,
23: 23 **all** *of* them governors and commanders, chariot officers and men of
23: 23 chariot officers and men of high rank, **all** mounted on horses.
23: 29 with you in hatred and take away **everything** you have worked for.
23: 48 in the land, that **all** women may take warning and not imitate you.
24: 4 Put into it the pieces of meat, **all** the choice pieces—the leg
24: 24 will be a sign to you; you will do **just as** [+889+3869] he has done.
25: 6 rejoicing with **all** the malice of your heart against the land of Israel,
25: 8 the house of Judah has become like **all** the other nations,"
26: 11 The hoofs of his horses will trample **all** your streets; he will kill
26: 16 Then **all** the princes of the coast will step down from their thrones
26: 17 and your citizens; you put your terror on **all** who lived there.
27: 5 They made **all** your timbers of pine trees from Senir; they took a
27: 9 **All** the ships of the sea and their sailors came alongside to trade for
27: 12 business with you because of your **great** [+8044] wealth of goods;
27: 18 because of your many products and **great** [+8044] wealth of goods,
27: 21 " 'Arabia and **all** the princes of Kedar were your customers;
27: 22 for your merchandise they exchanged the finest of **all** *kinds of*
27: 22 the finest of all kinds of spices and **[RPH]** precious stones,
27: 27 seamen and shipwrights, your merchants and **all** your soldiers,
27: 27 **everyone** [+7736] **else** on board will sink into the heart of the sea
27: 29 **All** who handle the oars will abandon their ships; the mariners
27: 29 their ships; the mariners and **all** the seamen will stand on the shore.
27: 34 your wares and **all** your company have gone down with you.
27: 35 **All** who live in the coastlands are appalled at you; their kings
28: 3 Are you wiser than Daniel? Is no secret hidden from **[NIE]** you?
28: 13 in Eden, the garden of God; **every** precious stone adorned you:
28: 18 I reduced you to ashes on the ground in the sight of **all** who were
28: 19 **All** the nations who knew you are appalled at you; you have come
28: 24 " 'No longer will the people of Israel have malicious **[NIE]**
28: 26 they will live in safety when I inflict punishment on **all** their
29: 2 king of Egypt and prophesy against him and against **all** Egypt.
29: 4 from among your streams, with **all** the fish sticking to your scales.
29: 5 I will leave you in the desert, you and **all** the fish of your streams.
29: 6 Then **all** who live in Egypt will know that I am the LORD.
29: 7 you splintered and you tore open their **[NIE]** shoulders;
29: 7 leaned on you, you broke and **[NIE]** their backs were wrenched.
29: 18 **every** head was rubbed bare and every shoulder made raw.
29: 18 every head was rubbed bare and **every** shoulder made raw.
30: 5 Lydia and **all** Arabia, Libya and the people of the covenant land
30: 8 when I set fire to Egypt and **all** her helpers are crushed.
31: 4 around its base and sent their channels to **all** the trees of the field.
31: 5 So it towered higher than **all** the trees of the field; its boughs
31: 6 **All** the birds of the air nested in its boughs, all the beasts of the
31: 6 its boughs, **all** the beasts of the field gave birth under its branches;
31: 6 birth under its branches; **all** the great nations lived in its shade.
31: 8 **no** [+4202] tree in the garden of God could match its beauty.
31: 9 the envy of **all** the trees of Eden in the garden of God.
31: 12 Its boughs fell on the mountains and in **all** the valleys; its branches
31: 12 the valleys; its branches lay broken in **all** the ravines of the land.
31: 12 **All** the nations of the earth came out from under its shade
31: 13 **All** the birds of the air settled on the fallen tree, and all the beasts
31: 13 fallen tree, and **all** the beasts of the field were among its branches.
31: 14 Therefore no **other**[s] trees by the waters are ever to tower proudly
31: 14 No **other**[s] trees so well-watered are ever to reach such a height;
31: 14 they are **all** destined for death, for the earth below, among mortal
31: 15 Lebanon with gloom, and **all** the trees of the field withered away.
31: 16 Then **all** the trees of Eden, the choicest and best of Lebanon,
31: 16 and best of Lebanon, **all** the trees that were well-watered,
31: 18 " 'This is Pharaoh and **all** his hordes, declares the Sovereign
32: 4 I will let **all** the birds of the air settle on you and all the beasts of
32: 4 on you and **all** the beasts of the earth gorge themselves on you.
32: 8 **All** the shining lights in the heavens I will darken over you;
32: 12 fall by the swords of mighty men—the most ruthless of **all** nations.
32: 12 shatter the pride of Egypt, and **all** her hordes will be overthrown.
32: 13 I will destroy **all** her cattle from beside abundant waters no longer
32: 15 the land of everything in it, when I strike down **all** who live there,
32: 16 for Egypt and **all** her hordes they will chant it,
32: 20 The sword is drawn; let her be dragged off with **all** her hordes.
32: 22 "Assyria is there with her **whole** army; she is surrounded by the
32: 22 she is surrounded by the graves of **all** her slain, all who have fallen
32: 23 **All** who had spread terror in the land of the living are slain,
32: 24 "Elam is there, with **all** her hordes around her grave. All of them
32: 24 hordes around her grave. **All** *of* them are slain, fallen by the sword.
32: 25 made for her among the slain, with **all** her hordes around her grave.
32: 25 her grave. **All** *of* them are uncircumcised, killed by the sword.
32: 26 and Tubal are there, with **all** their hordes around their graves.
32: 26 **All** *of* them are uncircumcised, killed by the sword because they
32: 29 "Edom is there, her kings and **all** her princes; despite their power,
32: 30 "**All** the princes of the north and all the Sidonians are there;
32: 30 "All the princes of the north and **all** the Sidonians are there;
32: 31 "Pharaoh—he and **all** his army—will see them and he will be
32: 31 he will be consoled for **all** his hordes that were killed by the sword,
32: 32 Pharaoh and **all** his hordes will be laid among the uncircumcised,
33: 13 **none of** [+4202] the righteous things he has done will be
33: 16 **None of** [+4202] the sins he has committed will be remembered
33: 29 desolate waste because of **all** the detestable things they have done.'
34: 5 when they were scattered they became food for **all** the wild
34: 6 My sheep wandered over **all** the mountains and on every high hill.
34: 6 My sheep wandered over all the mountains and on **every** high hill.
34: 6 They were scattered over the **whole** earth, and no one searched
34: 8 has been plundered and has become food for **all** the wild animals,
34: 12 I will rescue them from **all** the places where they were scattered on
34: 13 of Israel, in the ravines and in **all** the settlements in the land.
34: 21 butting **all** the weak sheep with your horns until you have driven
35: 8 will fall on your hills and in your valleys and in **all** your ravines.
35: 12 you will know that I the LORD have heard **all** the contemptible
35: 14 While the **whole** earth rejoices, I will make you desolate.
35: 15 You will be desolate, O Mount Seir, you and **all** *of* Edom.
35: 15 of Edom. **[RPH]** Then they will know that I am the LORD.' "
36: 5 against **all** Edom, for with glee and with malice in their hearts they
36: 5 with malice in their **[NIE]** hearts they made my land their own
36: 10 the number of people upon you, even the **whole** house of Israel.
36: 10 **[RPH]** The towns will be inhabited and the ruins rebuilt.
36: 24 I will gather you from **all** the countries and bring you back into
36: 25 I will cleanse you from **all** your impurities and from all your idols.
36: 25 I will cleanse you from all your impurities and from **all** your idols.
36: 29 I will save you from **all** your uncleanness. I will call for the grain
36: 33 On the day I cleanse you from **all** your sins, I will resettle your
36: 34 instead of lying desolate in the sight of **all** who pass through it.
37: 11 "Son of man, these bones are the **whole** house of Israel. They say,
37: 16 to Joseph and **all** the house of Israel associated with him.'
37: 22 There will be one king over **all** *of* them and they will never again
37: 23 with their idols and vile images or with **any** *of* their offenses,
37: 23 for I will save them from **all** their sinful backsliding, and I will
37: 24 David will be king over them, and they will **all** have one shepherd.
38: 4 put hooks in your jaws and bring you out with your **whole** army—
38: 4 **[RPH]** and a great horde with large and small shields,
38: 4 with large and small shields, **all** *of* them brandishing their swords.
38: 5 Cush and Put will be with them, **all** with shields and helmets,
38: 6 also Gomer with **all** its troops, and Beth Togarmah from the far
38: 6 and Beth Togarmah from the far north with **all** its troops—
38: 7 be prepared, you and **all** the hordes gathered about you, and take
38: 8 brought out from the nations, and now **all** *of* them live in safety.

Eze 38: 9 You and **all** your troops and the many nations with you will go up,
38: 11 **all** *of* them living without walls and without gates and bars.
38: 13 and the merchants of Tarshish and **all** her villages will say to you,
38: 15 **all** *of* them riding on horses, a great horde, a mighty army.
38: 20 the beasts of the field, **every** creature that moves along the ground,
38: 20 **all** the people on the face of the earth will tremble at my presence.
38: 20 the cliffs will crumble and **every** wall will fall to the ground.
38: 21 I will summon a sword against Gog on **all** my mountains,
39: 4 you will fall, you and **all** your troops and the nations with you.
39: 4 I will give you as food to **all** kinds of carrion birds and to the wild
39: 11 of travelers, because Gog and **all** his hordes will be buried there.
39: 13 **All** the people of the land will bury them, and the day I am
39: 17 Call out to **every** kind of bird and all the wild animals: 'Assemble
39: 17 Call out to every kind of bird and **all** the wild animals: 'Assemble
39: 18 goats and bulls—**all** *of* them fattened animals from Bashan.
39: 20 fill of horses and riders, mighty men and soldiers of **every** *kind*,'
39: 21 **all** the nations will see the punishment I inflict and the hand I lay
39: 23 handed them over to their enemies, and they **all** fell by the sword.
39: 25 and will have compassion on **all** the people of Israel,
39: 26 **all** the unfaithfulness they showed toward me when they lived in
40: 4 your ears and pay attention to **everything** I am going to show you,
40: 4 been brought here. Tell the house of Israel **everything** you see."
41: 17 and on **[NIE]** the walls at regular intervals all around the inner
41: 19 tree on the other. They were carved all around the **whole** temple.
42: 11 same length and width, with **[NIE]** similar exits and dimensions.
43: 11 if they are ashamed of **all** they have done, make known to them the
43: 11 and entrances—its **whole** design and all its regulations and laws.
43: 11 and entrances—its whole design and **all** its regulations and laws.
43: 11 and all its regulations and [BHS+ its ***whole*** design] laws.
43: 11 its whole design and all its regulations and **[RPH]** laws.
43: 11 so that they may be faithful to **[RPH]** its design and follow all its
43: 11 that they may be faithful to its design and follow **all** its regulations.
43: 12 **All** the surrounding area on top of the mountain will be most holy.
44: 5 give attention to **everything** I tell you concerning all the
44: 5 give attention to everything I tell you concerning **all** the
44: 5 **[RPH]** Give attention to the entrance of the temple and all the
44: 5 to the entrance of the temple and **all** the exits of the sanctuary.
44: 6 Enough of **[RPH]** your detestable practices, O house of Israel!
44: 7 In addition to **all** your other detestable practices, you brought
44: 9 This is what the Sovereign LORD says: **No** [+4202] foreigner
44: 9 not **even** the foreigners who live among the Israelites.
44: 13 or come near **any** *of* my holy things or my most holy offerings;
44: 14 of the duties of the temple and **all** the work that is to be done in it.
44: 14 of the temple and all the work **[RPH]** that is to be done in it.
44: 21 **No** [+4202] priest is to drink wine when he enters the inner court.
44: 24 are to keep my laws and my decrees for **all** my appointed feasts,
44: 29 **everything** in Israel devoted to the LORD will belong to them.
44: 30 The best of **all** the firstfruits and of all your special gifts will
44: 30 **[RPH]** and of all your special gifts will belong to the priests.
44: 30 the firstfruits and of **all** your special gifts will belong to the priests.
44: 30 and of all your special gifts **[RPH]** will belong to the priests.
44: 30 and of all your special gifts **[RPH]** will belong to the priests.
44: 31 The priests must not eat **anything**, bird or animal, found dead
45: 1 cubits long and 20,000 cubits wide; the **entire** area will be holy.
45: 6 the sacred portion; it will belong to the **whole** house of Israel.
45: 16 **All** the people of the land will participate in this special gift for the
45: 17 and the Sabbaths—at **all** the appointed feasts of the house of Israel.
45: 22 bull as a sin offering for himself and for **all** the people of the land.
47: 9 Swarms of **[RPH]** living creatures will live wherever the river
47: 9 Swarms of living creatures will live **wherever** [+448+889] the
47: 9 the salt water fresh; so where the river flows **everything** will live.
47: 12 Fruit trees of **all** *kinds* will grow on both banks of the river.
48: 13 Its **total** length will be 25,000 cubits and its width 10,000 cubits.
48: 19 The workers from the city who farm it will come from **all** the tribes
48: 20 The **entire** portion will be a square, 25,000 cubits on each side.
Da 1: 4 young men without **any** physical defect, handsome, showing
1: 4 handsome, showing aptitude for **every** *kind of* learning, well
1: 15 better nourished than **any** *of* the young men who ate the royal food.
1: 17 and understanding of **all** *kinds of* literature and learning.
1: 17 And Daniel could understand visions and dreams of **all** *kinds*.
1: 19 and he found **none** [+4202+4946] equal to Daniel, Hananiah,
1: 20 In **every** matter of wisdom and understanding about which the king
1: 20 he found them ten times better than **all** the magicians
1: 20 better than all the magicians and enchanters in his **whole** kingdom.
8: 4 and the south. **No** [+4202] animal could stand against him,
8: 5 the west, crossing the **whole** earth without touching the ground.
9: 6 our princes and our fathers, and to **all** the people of the land.
9: 7 the men of Judah and people of Jerusalem and **all** Israel, both near
9: 7 in **all** the countries where you have scattered us because of our
9: 11 **All** Israel has transgressed your law and turned away, refusing to
9: 12 Under the **whole** heaven nothing has ever been done like what has
9: 13 is written in the Law of Moses, **all** this disaster has come upon us,
9: 14 for the LORD our God is righteous in **everything** [+5126] he
9: 16 O Lord, in keeping with **all** your righteous acts, turn away your
9: 16 and your people an object of scorn to **all** those around us.
11: 2 and then a fourth, who will be far richer than **all** *the others*.
11: 2 his wealth, he will stir up **everyone** against the kingdom of Greece.
11: 17 He will determine to come with the might of his **entire** kingdom
11: 36 He will exalt and magnify himself above **every** god and will say
11: 37 or for the one desired by women, nor will he regard **any** god,
11: 37 nor will he regard any god, but will exalt himself above *them* **all**.
11: 43 of the treasures of gold and silver and **all** the riches of Egypt,
12: 1 **everyone** whose name is found written in the book—will be
12: 7 people has been finally broken, **all** these things will be completed."
12: 10 **None of** [+4202] the wicked will understand, but those who are
Hos 2: 11 [2:13] I will stop **all** her celebrations: her yearly festivals,
2: 11 [2:13] New Moons, her Sabbath days—**all** her appointed feasts.
4: 3 Because of this the land mourns, and **all** who live in it waste away;
5: 2 The rebels are deep in slaughter. I will discipline **all** *of* them.
7: 2 but they do not realize that I remember **all** their evil deeds.
7: 4 They are **all** adulterers, burning like an oven whose fire the baker
7: 6 Their passion smolders **all** night; in the morning it blazes like a
7: 7 **All** *of* them are hot as an oven; they devour their rulers. All their
7: 7 their rulers. **All** their kings fall, and none of them calls on me.
7: 10 but despite **all** this he does not return to the LORD his God
9: 1 you love the wages of a prostitute at **every** threshing floor.
9: 4 them like the bread of mourners; **all** who eat them will be unclean.
9: 8 the watchman over Ephraim, yet snares await him on **all** his paths,
9: 15 "Because of **all** their wickedness in Gilgal, I hated them there.
9: 15 I will no longer love them; **all** their leaders are rebellious.
10: 14 against your people, so that **all** your fortresses will be devastated—
12: 1 [12:2] he pursues the east wind **all** day and multiplies lies
12: 8 [12:9] With **all** my wealth they will not find in me any iniquity
13: 2 cleverly fashioned images, **all** *of* them the work of craftsmen.
13: 10 Where are your rulers in **all** your towns, of whom you said,
13: 15 well dry up. His storehouse will be plundered of **all** its treasures.
14: 2 [14:3] "Forgive **all** our sins and receive us graciously, that we
Joel 1: 2 Hear this, you elders; listen, **all** who live in the land. Has anything
1: 5 Wail, **all** you drinkers of wine; wail because of the new wine,
1: 12 and the apple tree—**all** the trees of the field—are dried up.
1: 14 and **all** who live in the land to the house of the LORD your God,
1: 19 open pastures and flames have burned up **all** the trees of the field.
2: 1 Let **all** who live in the land tremble, for the day of the LORD is
2: 6 At the sight of them, nations are in anguish; **every** face turns pale.
2: 12 "return to me with **all** your heart, with fasting and weeping
2: 28 [3:1] "And afterward, I will pour out my Spirit on **all** people.
2: 32 [3:5] **everyone** who calls on the name of the LORD will be
3: 2 [4:2] I will gather **all** nations and bring them down to the Valley
3: 4 [4:4] O Tyre and Sidon and **all** you regions of Philistia?
3: 9 [4:9] the warriors! Let **all** the fighting men draw near and attack.
3: 11 [4:11] Come quickly, **all** you nations from every side,
3: 12 [4:12] for there I will sit to judge **all** the nations on every side.
3: 18 [4:18] with milk; **all** the ravines of Judah will run with water.
Am 2: 3 I will destroy her ruler and kill **all** her officials with him,"
2: 8 They lie down beside **every** altar on garments taken in pledge.
3: 1 of Israel—against the **whole** family I brought up out of Egypt:
3: 2 "You only have I chosen of **all** the families of the earth; therefore I
3: 2 families of the earth; therefore I will punish you for **all** your sins."
4: 6 "I gave you empty stomachs in **every** city and lack of bread in
4: 6 you empty stomachs in every city and lack of bread in **every** town,
5: 16 "There will be wailing in **all** the streets and cries of anguish in
5: 16 in all the streets and cries of anguish in **every** public square.
5: 17 There will be wailing in **all** the vineyards, for I will pass through
7: 10 you in the very heart of Israel. The land cannot bear **all** his words.
8: 3 Many, many bodies—flung **everywhere** [+5226]! Silence!"
8: 7 the Pride of Jacob: "I will never forget **anything** they have done.
8: 8 "Will not the land tremble for this, and **all** who live in it mourn?
8: 8 The **whole** land will rise like the Nile; it will be stirred up
8: 10 religious feasts into mourning and **all** your singing into weeping.
8: 10 I will make **all** *of* you wear sackcloth and shave your heads.
8: 10 I will make all of you wear sackcloth and shave **your**[s] heads.
9: 1 Bring them down on the heads of **all** the people; those who are left
9: 5 who touches the earth and it melts, and **all** who live in it mourn—
9: 5 the **whole** land rises like the Nile, then sinks like the river of
9: 9 I will shake the house of Israel among **all** the nations as grain is
9: 10 **All** the sinners among my people will die by the sword, all those
9: 12 the remnant of Edom and **all** the nations that bear my name,"
9: 13 New wine will drip from the mountains and flow from **all** the hills.
Ob 1: 7 **All** your allies will force you to the border; your friends will
1: 15 "The day of the LORD is near for **all** nations. As you have done,
1: 16 you drank on my holy hill, so **all** the nations will drink continually;
Jnh 2: 3 [2:4] about me; **all** your waves and breakers swept over me.
Mic 1: 2 O peoples, **all** *of* you, listen, O earth and all who are in it,
1: 5 **All** this is because of Jacob's transgression, because of the sins of
1: 7 **All** her idols will be broken to pieces; all her temple gifts will be
1: 7 **all** her temple gifts will be burned with fire; I will destroy all her
1: 7 temple gifts will be burned with fire; I will destroy **all** her images.
2: 12 "I will surely gather **all** *of* you, O Jacob; I will surely bring

Mic 3: 7 They will **all** cover their faces because there is no answer from
3: 9 the house of Israel, who despise justice and distort **all** that is right;
4: 5 **All** the nations may walk in the name of their gods; we will walk in
4: 13 gains to the LORD, their wealth to the Lord of **all** the earth.
5: 9 [5:8] over your enemies, and **all** your foes will be destroyed.
5: 11 [5:10] the cities of your land and tear down **all** your strongholds.
6: 16 the statutes of Omri and **all** the practices of Ahab's house,
7: 2 **All** men lie in wait to shed blood; each hunts his brother with a net.
7: 16 Nations will see and be ashamed, deprived of **all** their power.
7: 19 sins underfoot and hurl **all** our iniquities into the depths of the sea.
Na 1: 4 He rebukes the sea and dries it up; he makes **all** the rivers run dry.
1: 5 The earth trembles at his presence, the world and **all** who live in it.
1: 15 [2:1] the wicked invade you; they will be **completely** destroyed.
2: 9 [2:10] The supply is endless, the wealth from **all** its treasures!
2: 10 [2:11] Hearts melt, knees give way, **[RPH]** bodies tremble,
2: 10 [2:11] knees give way, bodies tremble, **every** face grows pale.
3: 1 city of blood, **full** *of* lies, full of plunder, never without victims!
3: 7 **All** who see you will flee from you and say, 'Nineveh is in ruins—
3: 10 Her infants were dashed to pieces at the head of **every** street.
3: 10 were cast for her nobles, and **all** her great men were put in chains.
3: 12 **All** your fortresses are like fig trees with their first ripe fruit;
3: 19 **Everyone** who hears the news about you claps his hands at your
Hab 1: 9 they **all** come bent on violence. Their hordes advance like a desert
1: 10 They laugh at **all** fortified cities; they build earthen ramps
1: 15 The wicked foe pulls **all** *of* them up with hooks, he catches them in
2: 5 he gathers to himself **all** the nations and takes captive all the
2: 5 gathers to himself all the nations and takes captive **all** the peoples.
2: 6 "Will not **all** *of* them taunt him with ridicule and scorn, saying,
2: 8 many nations, **[NIE]** the peoples who are left will plunder you.
2: 8 you have destroyed lands and cities and **everyone** [+3782] in them.
2: 17 you have destroyed lands and cities and **everyone** [+3782] in them.
2: 19 It is covered with gold and silver; **there is no** [+401] breath in it.
2: 20 is in his holy temple; let **all** the earth be silent before him."
Zep 1: 2 "I will sweep away **everything** from the face of the earth,"
1: 4 out my hand against Judah and against **all** who live in Jerusalem.
1: 8 and the king's sons and **all** those clad in foreign clothes.
1: 9 On that day I will punish **all** who avoid stepping on the threshold,
1: 11 **all** your merchants will be wiped out, all who trade with silver will
1: 11 will be wiped out, **all** who trade with silver will be ruined.
1: 18 In the fire of his jealousy the **whole** world will be consumed,
1: 18 for he will make a sudden end of **all** who live in the earth."
2: 3 Seek the LORD, **all** you humble of the land, you who do what he
2: 11 The LORD will be awesome to them when he destroys **all** the
2: 11 The nations on **every** shore will worship him, every one in its own
2: 14 Flocks and herds will lie down there, creatures of **every** kind.
2: 15 lair for wild beasts! **All** who pass by her scoff and shake their fists.
3: 7 would not be cut off, nor **all** my punishments come upon her.
3: 7 upon her. But they were still eager to act corruptly in **all** they did.
3: 8 and to pour out my wrath on them—**all** my fierce anger.
3: 8 The **whole** world will be consumed by the fire of my jealous anger.
3: 9 that **all** *of* them may call on the name of the LORD and serve him
3: 11 On that day you will not be put to shame for **all** the wrongs you
3: 14 Be glad and rejoice with **all** your heart, O Daughter of Jerusalem!
3: 19 At that time I will deal with **all** who oppressed you; I will rescue
3: 19 them praise and honor in **every** land where they were put to shame.
3: 20 praise among **all** the peoples of the earth when I restore your
Hag 1: 11 on men and cattle, and on the **[NIE]** labor of your hands."
1: 12 the **whole** remnant of the people obeyed the voice of the LORD
1: 14 the high priest, and the spirit of the **whole** remnant of the people.
2: 4 Be strong, **all** you people of the land,' declares the LORD,
2: 7 I will shake **all** nations, and the desired of all nations will come,
2: 7 I will shake all nations, and the desired of **all** nations will come,
2: 12 fold touches some bread or stew, some wine, oil or **other**[s] food,
2: 13 "If a person defiled by contact with a dead body touches **one** *of*
2: 14 '**Whatever** they do and whatever they offer there is defiled.
2: 17 I struck **all** the work of your hands with blight, mildew and hail,
Zec 1: 11 the earth and found the **whole** world at rest and in peace."
2: 13 [2:17] Be still before the LORD, **all** mankind, because he has
4: 2 "I see a **solid** gold lampstand with a bowl at the top and seven
4: 10 eyes of the LORD, which range **throughout** [+928] the earth.)"
4: 14 "These are the two who are anointed to serve the Lord of **all** the
5: 3 said to me, "This is the curse that is going out over the **whole** land;
5: 3 according to what it says on one side, **every** thief will be banished,
5: 3 it says on the other, **everyone** who swears falsely will be banished.
5: 6 "This is the iniquity of the people **throughout** [+928] the land."
6: 5 going out from standing in the presence of the Lord of the **whole**
7: 5 "Ask **all** the people of the land and the priests, 'When you fasted
7: 14 'I scattered them with a whirlwind among **all** the nations,
8: 10 of his enemy, for I had turned **every** man against his neighbor.
8: 12 I will give **all** these things as an inheritance to the remnant of this
8: 17 do not love to swear falsely. I hate **all** this," declares the LORD.
8: 23 "In those days ten men from **all** languages and nations will take
9: 1 for the eyes of men and **all** the tribes of Israel are on the LORD—
10: 4 him the tent peg, from him the battle bow, from him **every** ruler.
10: 11 sea will be subdued and **all** the depths of the Nile will dry up.
11: 10 broke it, revoking the covenant I had made with **all** the nations.
12: 2 "I am going to make Jerusalem a cup that sends **all** the surrounding
12: 3 that day, when **all** the nations of the earth are gathered against her,
12: 3 I will make Jerusalem an immovable rock for **all** the nations.
12: 3 for all the nations. **All** who try to move it will injure themselves.
12: 4 On that day I will strike **every** horse with panic and its rider with
12: 4 the house of Judah, but I will blind **all** the horses of the nations.
12: 6 They will consume right and left **all** the surrounding peoples,
12: 9 On that day I will set out to destroy **all** the nations that attack
12: 14 and **all** the rest of the clans and their wives.
13: 8 In the **whole** land," declares the LORD, "two-thirds will be struck
14: 2 I will gather **all** the nations to Jerusalem to fight against it;
14: 5 the LORD my God will come, and **all** the holy ones with him.
14: 9 The LORD will be king over the **whole** earth. On that day there
14: 10 The **whole** land, from Geba to Rimmon, south of Jerusalem,
14: 12 This is the plague with which the LORD will strike **all** the nations
14: 14 The wealth of **all** the surrounding nations will be collected—
14: 15 the camels and donkeys, and **all** the animals in those camps.
14: 16 **[RPH]** the survivors from all the nations that have attacked
14: 16 the survivors from **all** the nations that have attacked Jerusalem will
14: 19 the punishment of **all** the nations that do not go up to celebrate the
14: 21 **Every** pot in Jerusalem and Judah will be holy to the LORD
14: 21 **all** who come to sacrifice will take some of the pots and cook in
Mal 1: 11 In **every** place incense and pure offerings will be brought to my
2: 9 caused you to be despised and humiliated before **all** the people,
2: 10 Have we not **all** one Father? Did not one God create us? Why do
2: 17 By saying, "**All** who do evil are good in the eyes of the LORD,
3: 9 You are under a curse—the **whole** nation *of* you—because you are
3: 10 Bring the **whole** tithe into the storehouse, that there may be food in
3: 12 "Then **all** the nations will call you blessed, for yours will be a
4: 1 [3:19] **All** the arrogant and every evildoer will be stubble, and that
4: 1 [3:19] All the arrogant and **every** evildoer will be stubble,
4: 4 [3:22] the decrees and laws I gave him at Horeb for **all** Israel.

3973 ¹כָּלָא ***kālā'¹***, v. [17] [→ 3975, 3989, 4813; cf. 3974, 3983, 3984; 3998]

were restrained [2], *untranslated* [1], am confined [1], confined [1], contain [1], hold back [1], imprisoned [1], keeping [1], kept [1], penned up [+906+928+1074+2021] [1], refuse [1], seal [1], stop [1], stopped falling [1], withheld [1], withhold [1]

Ge 8: 2 [C] been closed, and the rain *had* **stopped falling** from the sky.
23: 6 [A] None of us *will* **refuse** you his tomb for burying your dead."
Ex 36: 6 [C] And so the people **were restrained** from bringing more,
Nu 11: 28 [A] spoke up and said, "Moses, my lord, **stop** them!"
1Sa 6: 10 [A] and **penned up** [+906+928+1074+2021] their calves.
25: 33 [A] good judgment and for **keeping** me from bloodshed this day
Ps 40: 9 [40:10] [A] *I do* not **seal** my lips, as you know, O LORD.
40: 11 [40:12] [A] *Do* not **withhold** your mercy from me, O LORD;
88: 8 [88:9] [B] repulsive to them. **I am confined** and cannot escape;
119: 101 [A] *I have* **kept** my feet from every evil path so that I might obey
Ecc 8: 8 [A] No man has power over the wind to **contain** it; so no one has
Isa 43: 6 [A] 'Give them up!' and to the south, '*Do* not **hold** them **back**.'
Jer 32: 2 [B] Jeremiah the prophet was **confined** in the courtyard of the
32: 3 [A] Now Zedekiah king of Judah *had* **imprisoned** him there,
Eze 31: 15 [C] back its streams, and its abundant waters **were restrained**.
Hag 1: 10 [A] because of you the heavens *have* **withheld** their dew
1: 10 [A] have withheld their dew and the earth **[RPH]** its crops.

3974 ²כָּלָא ***kālā'²***, v. [1] [cf. 3973, 3998]

finish [1]

Da 9: 24 [D] for your people and your holy city to **finish** transgression,

3975 כֶּלֶא ***kele'***, n.[m.]. [10] [√ 3973; cf. 3999]

prison [+1074+2021] [4], prison [+1074] [2], prison [2], dungeon [+1074] [1], prisons [+1074] [1]

1Ki 22: 27 Put this fellow in **prison** [+1074+2021] and give him nothing
2Ki 17: 4 Therefore Shalmaneser seized him and put him in **prison** [+1074].
25: 27 he released Jehoiachin from **prison** [+1074] on the twenty-seventh
25: 29 So Jehoiachin put aside his **prison** clothes and for the rest of his
2Ch 18: 26 Put this fellow in **prison** [+1074+2021] and give him nothing
Isa 42: 7 to release from the **dungeon** [+1074] those who sit in darkness.
42: 22 all of them trapped in pits or hidden away in **prisons** [+1074].
Jer 37: 15 the secretary, which they had made into a **prison** [+1074+2021].
37: 18 or this people, that you have put me in **prison** [+1074+2021]?
52: 33 So Jehoiachin put aside his **prison** clothes and for the rest of his

3976 כִּלְאָב ***kil'āb***, n.pr.m. [1]

Kileab [1]

2Sa 3: 3 **Kileab** the son of Abigail the widow of Nabal of Carmel;

3977 כִּלְאַיִם *kil'ayim*, n.[m.]. [4]
two kinds [3], different kinds [1]

Lev 19: 19 " 'Keep my decrees. " 'Do not mate **different kinds** *of* animals.
19: 19 kinds of animals. " 'Do not plant your field with **two kinds** *of* seed.
19: 19 of seed. " 'Do not wear clothing woven of **two kinds** of material.
Dt 22: 9 Do not plant **two kinds** of seed in your vineyard; if you do,

3978 כֶּלֶב *keleb*, n.m. [32] [→ 3979; cf. 3990]
dogs [19], dog [10], dog's [2], male prostitute [1]

Ex 11: 7 But among the Israelites not a **dog** will bark at any man or animal.'
22: 31 [22:30] of an animal torn by wild beasts; throw it to the **dogs**.
Dt 23: 18 [23:19] or of a **male prostitute** into the house of the LORD your
Jdg 7: 5 "Separate those who lap the water with their tongues like a **dog**
1Sa 17: 43 He said to David, "Am I a **dog**, that you come at me with sticks?"
24: 14 [24:15] come out? Whom are you pursuing? A dead **dog**? A flea?
2Sa 3: 8 of what Ish-Bosheth said and he answered, "Am I a **dog's** head—
9: 8 "What is your servant, that you should notice a dead **dog** like me?"
16: 9 to the king, "Why should this dead **dog** curse my lord the king?
1Ki 14: 11 **Dogs** will eat those belonging to Jeroboam who die in the city,
16: 4 **Dogs** will eat those belonging to Baasha who die in the city,
21: 19 In the place where **dogs** licked up Naboth's blood, dogs will lick
21: 19 dogs licked up Naboth's blood, **dogs** will lick up your blood—
21: 23 the LORD says: '**Dogs** will devour Jezebel by the wall of Jezreel.'
21: 24 "**Dogs** will eat those belonging to Ahab who die in the city,
22: 38 the **dogs** licked up his blood, as the word of the LORD had
2Ki 8: 13 "How could your servant, a mere **dog**, accomplish such a feat?"
9: 10 for Jezebel, **dogs** will devour her on the plot of ground at Jezreel,
9: 36 On the plot of ground at Jezreel **dogs** will devour Jezebel's flesh.
Job 30: 1 whose fathers I would have disdained to put with my sheep **dogs**.
Ps 22: 16 [22:17] **Dogs** have surrounded me; a band of evil men has
22: 20 [22:21] the sword, my precious life from the power of the **dogs**.
59: 6 [59:7] They return at evening, snarling like **dogs**, and prowl about
59: 14 [59:15] They return at evening, snarling like **dogs**, and prowl
68: 23 [68:24] while the tongues of your **dogs** have their share."
Pr 26: 11 As a **dog** returns to its vomit, so a fool repeats his folly.
26: 17 Like one who seizes a **dog** by the ears is a passer-by who meddles
Ecc 9: 4 the living has hope—even a live **dog** is better off than a dead lion!
Isa 56: 10 they are all mute **dogs**, they cannot bark; they lie around
56: 11 They are **dogs** *with* mighty appetites; they never have enough.
66: 3 and whoever offers a lamb, like one who breaks a **dog's** neck;
Jer 15: 3 "the sword to kill and the **dogs** to drag away and the birds of the air

3979 כָּלֵב *kālēb*, n.pr.m. [35] [→ 3980, 3981, 3982, 3990, 3992; cf. 3978]
Caleb [29], Caleb's [6]

Nu 13: 6 from the tribe of Judah, **Caleb** son of Jephunneh;
13: 30 **Caleb** silenced the people before Moses and said, "We should go
14: 6 Joshua son of Nun and **Caleb** son of Jephunneh, who were among
14: 24 because my servant **Caleb** has a different spirit and follows me
14: 30 your home, except **Caleb** son of Jephunneh and Joshua son of Nun.
14: 38 only Joshua son of Nun and **Caleb** son of Jephunneh survived.
26: 65 and not one of them was left except **Caleb** son of Jephunneh
32: 12 not one except **Caleb** son of Jephunneh the Kenizzite and Joshua
34: 19 are their names: **Caleb** son of Jephunneh, from the tribe of Judah;
Dt 1: 36 except **Caleb** son of Jephunneh. He will see it, and I will give him
Jos 14: 6 at Gilgal, and **Caleb** son of Jephunneh the Kenizzite said to him,
14: 13 Joshua blessed **Caleb** son of Jephunneh and gave him Hebron as
14: 14 So Hebron has belonged to **Caleb** son of Jephunneh the Kenizzite
15: 13 Joshua gave to **Caleb** son of Jephunneh a portion in Judah—
15: 14 From Hebron **Caleb** drove out the three Anakites—Sheshai,
15: 16 **Caleb** said, "I will give my daughter Acsah in marriage to the man
15: 17 Othniel son of Kenaz, **Caleb's** brother, took it; so Caleb gave his
15: 18 she got off her donkey, **Caleb** asked her, "What can I do for you?"
21: 12 villages around the city they had given to **Caleb** son of Jephunneh
Jdg 1: 12 **Caleb** said, "I will give my daughter Acsah in marriage to the man
1: 13 Othniel son of Kenaz, **Caleb's** younger brother, took it; so Caleb
1: 14 she got off her donkey, **Caleb** asked her, "What can I do for you?"
1: 15 of water." Then **Caleb** gave her the upper and lower springs.
1: 20 As Moses had promised, Hebron was given to **Caleb**, who drove
3: 9 Othniel son of Kenaz, **Caleb's** younger brother, who saved them.
1Sa 30: 14 and the territory belonging to Judah and the Negev of **Caleb**.
1Ch 2: 18 **Caleb** son of Hezron had children by his wife Azubah (and by
2: 19 When Azubah died, **Caleb** married Ephrath, who bore him Hur.
2: 42 The sons of **Caleb** the brother of Jerahmeel: Mesha his firstborn,
2: 46 **Caleb's** concubine Ephah was the mother of Haran, Moza
2: 48 **Caleb's** concubine Maacah was the mother of Sheber
2: 49 the father of Macbenah and Gibea. **Caleb's** daughter was Acsah.
2: 50 These were the descendants of **Caleb**. The sons of Hur the
4: 15 The sons of **Caleb** son of Jephunneh: Iru, Elah and Naam.
6: 56 [6:41] villages around the city were given to **Caleb** son of

3980 כָּלֵב אֶפְרָתָה *kālēb 'eprātâ*, n.pr.loc. [1] [√ 3979 + 716]
Caleb Ephrathah [1]

1Ch 2: 24 After Hezron died in **Caleb Ephrathah**, Abijah the wife of Hezron

3981 כָּלִבּוֹ *kālibbiw*, a.g. Not used in NIV/BHS [√ 3979]

3982 כָּלִבִּי *kālibbî*, a.g. [1] [√ 3979]
Calebite [1]

1Sa 25: 3 but her husband, a **Calebite**, was surly and mean in his dealings.

3983 כָּלָה *kālâ*[1], v. [204 / 205] [→ 432, 3985, 3986, 4001, 4002, 4816, 9416, 9417; cf. 3973, 3974, 3998, 4005, 5801]
finished [55], destroyed [14], destroy [11], fail [9], spend [8], completed [6], finish [6], perish [6], end [4], put an end [4], consume [3], ended [3], gone [3], spent [3], vanish [3], *untranslated* [2], cease [2], come to an end [2], complete [2], completely [2], consumed [2], determined [2], fails [2], finishing [2], fulfill [2], used up [2], very [2], after [+561] [1], after [1], all [1], bent on [1], blind [1], came to an end [1], completely [+6330] [1], completely destroyed [+6330] [1], completion [1], concludes [1], crushed [1], decided [1], destroy completely [1], destroys [1], disappear [1], done [1], eliminate [1], ending [1], failed [1], faints with longing [1], faints [1], finally [1], full [1], given full vent [1], grow weary [1], hanging [1], intended [1], longed [1], made an end [1], make an end [1], meet [1], overcome [1], ravage [1], settled [1], stopped [1], strip bare [1], vanishes [1], wastes away [1], were completed [1], wipe [1], wiped out [1], wiped [1], yearns [1]

Ge 2: 1 [E] and the earth **were completed** in all their vast array.
2: 2 [D] By the seventh day God *had* **finished** the work he had been
6: 16 [D] a roof for it and **finish** the ark to within 18 inches of the top.
17: 22 [D] When *he had* **finished** speaking with Abraham, God went up
18: 33 [D] When the LORD *had* **finished** speaking with Abraham, he
21: 15 [A] When the water in the skin *was* **gone**, she put the boy under
24: 15 [D] Before he *had* **finished** praying, Rebekah came out with her
24: 19 [D] **After** she had given him a drink, she said, "I'll draw water
24: 19 [D] for your camels too, until *they have* **finished** drinking."
24: 22 [D] When the camels *had* **finished** drinking, the man took out a
24: 45 [D] "Before I **finished** praying in my heart, Rebekah came out,
27: 30 [D] After Isaac **finished** blessing him and Jacob had scarcely left
41: 30 [D] Egypt will be forgotten, and the famine *will* **ravage** the land.
41: 53 [A] The seven years of abundance in Egypt **came to an end**,
43: 2 [D] So when they had eaten **all** the grain they had brought from
44: 12 [D] beginning with the oldest and **ending** with the youngest.
49: 33 [D] When Jacob *had* **finished** giving instructions to his sons, he
Ex 5: 13 [D] saying, "**Complete** the work required of you for each day,
5: 14 [D] "Why didn't *you* **meet** your quota of bricks yesterday
31: 18 [D] When the LORD **finished** speaking to Moses on Mount
32: 10 [D] anger may burn against them and that *I may* **destroy** them.
32: 12 [D] in the mountains and to **wipe** them off the face of the earth'?
33: 3 [D] a stiff-necked people and *I might* **destroy** you on the way."
33: 5 [D] to go with you even for a moment, *I might* **destroy** you.
34: 33 [D] When Moses **finished** speaking to them, he put a veil over
39: 32 [A] work on the tabernacle, the Tent of Meeting, *was* **completed**.
40: 33 [D] entrance to the courtyard. And so Moses **finished** the work.
Lev 16: 20 [D] "When Aaron *has* **finished** making atonement for the Most
19: 9 [D] do not reap to the **very** edges of your field or gather the
23: 22 [D] do not reap to the **very** edges of your field or gather the
26: 16 [D] wasting diseases and fever *that will* **destroy** your sight
26: 44 [D] reject them or abhor them so as to **destroy** them **completely**,
Nu 4: 15 [D] and his sons *have* **finished** covering the holy furnishings
7: 1 [D] When Moses **finished** setting up the tabernacle, he anointed
16: 21 [D] from this assembly so *I can* **put an end** *to* them at once."
16: 31 [D] As soon as he **finished** saying all this, the ground under
16: 45 [17:10] [D] this assembly so *I can* **put an end** *to* them at once."
17: 10 [17:25] [D] *This will* **put an end** *to* their grumbling against me,
25: 11 [D] so that in my zeal *I did* not **put an end** *to* them.
Dt 7: 22 [D] You will not be allowed to **eliminate** them all at once,
20: 9 [D] When the officers *have* **finished** speaking to the army, they
26: 12 [D] When *you have* **finished** setting aside a tenth of all your
28: 21 [D] *has* **destroyed** you from the land you are entering to possess.
31: 24 [D] After Moses **finished** writing in a book the words of this law
32: 23 [D] calamities upon them and **spend** my arrows against them.
32: 45 [D] When Moses **finished** reciting all these words to all Israel,
Jos 8: 24 [D] When Israel *had* **finished** killing all the men of Ai in the
10: 20 [D] So Joshua and the Israelites destroyed them **completely**—
19: 49 [D] When *they had* **finished** dividing the land into its allotted
19: 51 [D] the Tent of Meeting. And so *they* **finished** dividing the land.
24: 20 [D] will turn and bring disaster on you and **make an end** *of* you,
Jdg 3: 18 [D] After Ehud **[NIE]** had presented the tribute, he sent on their
15: 17 [D] When he **finished** speaking, he threw away the jawbone; and

Ru 2:21 [D] 'Stay with my workers until *they* **finish** harvesting all my
2:23 [A] to glean until the barley and wheat harvests *were* **finished**.
3: 3 [D] don't let him know you are there until he *has* **finished** eating
3:18 [D] For the man will not rest until the matter *is* **settled** today."
1Sa 2:33 [D] my altar will be spared only to **blind** your eyes with tears
3:12 [D] I spoke against his family—from beginning to **end**.
10:13 [D] After Saul **stopped** prophesying, he went to the high place.
13:10 [D] Just as he **finished** making the offering, Samuel arrived,
15:18 [D] make war on them until you *have* **wiped** them **out**.'
18: 1 [D] After David *had* **finished** talking with Saul, Jonathan
20: 7 [A] you can be sure that he *is* **determined** *to* harm me.
20: 9 [A] "If I had the least inkling that my father *was* **determined** to
20:33 [A] Then Jonathan knew that his father **intended** to kill David.
24:16 [24:17] [D] When David **finished** saying this, Saul asked, "Is
25:17 [A] because disaster *is* **hanging** over our master and his whole
2Sa 6:18 [D] After he *had* **finished** sacrificing the burnt offerings
11:19 [D] "When you *have* **finished** giving the king this account of the
13:36 [D] As he **finished** speaking, the king's sons came in, wailing
13:39 [A] And the spirit of the king **longed** [BHS-] to go to Absalom,
21: 5 [D] "As for the man who **destroyed** us and plotted against us
22:38 [D] crushed them; I did not turn back till they *were* **destroyed**.
1Ki 1:41 [D] were with him heard it as they *were* **finishing** their feast.
3: 1 [D] He brought her to the City of David until he **finished**
6: 9 [D] So he built the temple and **completed** it, roofing it with
6:14 [D] So Solomon built the temple and **completed** it.
6:38 [A] the temple *was* **finished** in all its details according to its
7: 1 [D] however, *to* **complete** the construction of his palace.
7:40 [D] So Huram **finished** all the work he had undertaken for King
8:54 [D] When Solomon *had* **finished** all these prayers
9: 1 [D] When Solomon *had* **finished** building the temple of the
17:14 [A] 'The jar of flour *will* not *be* **used up** and the jug of oil will
17:16 [A] For the jar of flour *was* not **used up** and the jug of oil did not
22:11 [D] you will gore the Arameans until they *are* **destroyed**.' "
2Ki 10:25 [D] As soon as Jehu *had* **finished** making the burnt offering, he
13:17 [D] Elisha declared. "You will **completely** [+6330] destroy the
13:19 [D] have defeated Aram and **completely destroyed** [+6330] it.
1Ch 16: 2 [D] After David *had* **finished** sacrificing the burnt offerings
27:24 [D] son of Zeruiah began to count the men but *did* not **finish**.
28:20 [A] work for the service of the temple of the LORD *is* **finished**.
2Ch 4:11 [D] So Huram **finished** the work he had undertaken for King
7: 1 [D] When Solomon **finished** praying, fire came down from
7:11 [D] *had* **finished** the temple of the LORD and the royal palace, and
8: 8 [D] in the land, whom the Israelites *had* not **destroyed**—
8:16 [A] of the temple of the LORD was laid until its **completion**.
18:10 [D] you will gore the Arameans until they *are* **destroyed**.' "
20:23 [D] After they **finished** slaughtering the men from Seir,
24:10 [D] dropping them into the chest until it *was* **full**.
24:14 [D] When they *had* **finished**, they brought the rest of the money
29:17 [D] **finishing** on the sixteenth day of the first month.
29:28 [A] until the sacrifice of the burnt offering *was* **completed**.
29:29 [D] When the offerings *were* **finished**, the king and everyone
29:34 [A] kinsmen the Levites helped them until the task *was* **finished**
31: 1 [D] When all this *had* **ended**, the Israelites who were there went
31: 1 [D] After they *had* **destroyed** all of them, the Israelites returned
31: 7 [D] this in the third month and **finished** in the seventh month.
36:22 [A] in order to **fulfill** the word of the LORD spoken by
Ezr 1: 1 [A] in order to **fulfill** the word of the LORD spoken by
9: 1 [D] After these things *had been* **done**, the leaders came to me
9:14 [D] you not be angry enough with us *to* **destroy** us, leaving us
10:17 [D] by the first day of the first month *they* **finished** dealing with
Ne 4: 2 [3:34] [D] Will they offer sacrifices? *Will they* **finish** in a day?
Est 7: 7 [A] realizing that the king *had already* **decided** his fate,
Job 4: 9 [A] God they are destroyed; at the blast of his anger *they* **perish**.
7: 6 [A] a weaver's shuttle, and *they* **come to an end** without hope.
7: 9 [A] As a cloud **vanishes** and is gone, so he who goes down to the
9:22 [D] why I say, 'He **destroys** both the blameless and the wicked.'
11:20 [A] the eyes of the wicked *will* **fail**, and escape will elude them;
17: 5 [A] his friends for reward, the eyes of his children *will* **fail**.
19:27 [A] I, and not another. How my heart **yearns** within me!
21:13 [D] *They* **spend** [K 1162] their years in prosperity and go down
31:16 [D] desires of the poor or *let* the eyes of the widow **grow weary**,
33:21 [A] His flesh **wastes away** to nothing, and his bones, once
36:11 [D] *they will* **spend** the rest of their days in prosperity and their
Ps 18:37 [18:38] [D] I did not turn back till they *were* **destroyed**.
31:10 [31:11] [A] My life *is* **consumed** by anguish and my years by
37:20 [A] will be like the beauty of the fields, *they will* **vanish**—
37:20 [A] the beauty of the fields, they will vanish—**vanish** like smoke.
39:10 [39:11] [A] from me; I *am* **overcome** by the blow of your hand.
59:13 [59:14] [D] **consume** them in wrath, consume them till they are
59:13 [59:14] [D] them in wrath, **consume** them till they are no more.
69: 3 [69:4] [A] throat is parched. My eyes **fail**, looking for my God.
71: 9 [A] when I am old; do not forsake me when my strength *is* **gone**.
71:13 [A] *May* my accusers **perish** in shame; may those who want to
72:20 [E] *This* **concludes** the prayers of David son of Jesse.
73:26 [A] My flesh and my heart *may* **fail**, but God is the strength of
74:11 [D] Take it from the folds of your garment and **destroy** them!
78:33 [D] So *he* **ended** their days in futility and their years in terror.
84: 2 [84:3] [A] My soul yearns, even **faints**, for the courts of the
90: 7 [A] *We are* **consumed** by your anger and terrified by your
90: 9 [D] away under your wrath; *we* **finish** our years with a moan.
102: 3 [102:4] [A] For my days **vanish** like smoke; my bones burn like
119:81 [A] My soul **faints with longing** for your salvation, but I have
119:82 [A] My eyes **fail**, looking for your promise; I say, "When will
119:87 [D] *They* almost **wiped** me from the earth, but I have not
119:123 [A] My eyes **fail**, looking for your salvation, looking for your
143: 7 [A] Answer me quickly, O LORD; my spirit **fails**. Do not hide
Pr 5:11 [A] life you will groan, when your flesh and body *are* **spent**.
16:30 [D] is plotting perversity; he who purses his lips *is* **bent on** evil.
22: 8 [A] reaps trouble, and the rod of his fury *will be* **destroyed**.
Isa 1:28 [A] be broken, and those who forsake the LORD *will* **perish**.
10:18 [D] of his forests and fertile fields *it will* completely **destroy**,
10:25 [A] Very soon my anger against you *will* **end** and my wrath will
15: 6 [A] is withered; the vegetation *is* **gone** and nothing green is left.
16: 4 [A] oppressor will come to an end, and destruction *will* **cease**;
21:16 [A] would count it, all the pomp of Kedar *will* **come to an end**.
24:13 [A] or as when gleanings are left **after** [+561] the grape harvest.
27:10 [D] there they lie down; *they* **strip** its branches **bare**.
29:20 [A] The ruthless will vanish, the mockers *will* **disappear**, and all
31: 3 [A] he who is helped will fall; both *will* **perish** together.
32:10 [A] the grape harvest *will* **fail**, and the harvest of fruit will not
49: 4 [D] *I have* **spent** my strength in vain and for nothing.
Jer 5: 3 [D] felt no pain; *you* **crushed** them, but they refused correction.
8:20 [A] "The harvest is past, the summer *has* **ended**, and we are not
9:16 [9:15] [D] them with the sword until *I have* **destroyed** them."
10:25 [D] they have devoured him **completely** and destroyed his
14: 6 [A] and pant like jackals; their eyesight **fails** for lack of pasture."
14:12 [D] I *will* **destroy** them with the sword, famine and plague."
16: 4 [A] *They will* **perish** by sword and famine, and their dead bodies
20:18 [A] to see trouble and sorrow and *to* **end** my days in shame?
26: 8 [D] as soon as Jeremiah **finished** telling all the people everything
43: 1 [D] When Jeremiah **finished** telling the people all the words of
44:27 [A] will perish by sword and famine until they *are* all **destroyed**.
49:37 [D] them with the sword until I *have* **made an end** *of* them.
51:63 [D] When you **finish** reading this scroll, tie a stone to it
La 2:11 [A] My eyes **fail** from weeping, I am in torment within, my heart
2:22 [D] those I cared for and reared, my enemy *has* **destroyed**."
3:22 [A] love we are not consumed, for his compassions never **fail**.
4:11 [D] The LORD *has* **given full vent** *to* his wrath; he has poured
4:17 [A] Moreover, our eyes **failed**, looking in vain for help; from our
Eze 4: 6 [D] "After *you have* **finished** this, lie down again, this time on
4: 8 [D] to the other until you *have* **finished** the days of your siege.
5:12 [A] people will die of the plague or **perish** by famine inside you;
5:13 [A] "Then my anger *will* **cease** and my wrath against them will
5:13 [D] when I *have* **spent** my wrath upon them, they will know that
6:12 [D] will die of famine. So *will I* **spend** my wrath upon them.
7: 8 [D] pour out my wrath on you and **spend** my anger against you;
13:14 [A] When it falls, *you will be* **destroyed** in it; and you will know
13:15 [D] So *I will* **spend** my wrath against the wall and against those
20: 8 [D] wrath on them and **spend** my anger against them in Egypt.
20:13 [D] pour out my wrath on them and **destroy** them in the desert.
20:21 [D] on them and **spend** my anger against them in the desert.
22:31 [D] my wrath on them and **consume** them with my fiery anger,
42:15 [D] When *he had* **finished** measuring what was inside the temple
43:23 [D] When you *have* **finished** purifying it, you are to offer a
43:27 [D] *At the* **end** *of* these days, from the eighth day on, the priests
Da 11:36 [A] He will be successful until the time of wrath *is* **completed**,
12: 7 [D] When the power of the holy people has been **finally** broken,
12: 7 [A] has been finally broken, all these things *will be* **completed**."
Hos 11: 6 [D] *will* **destroy** the bars of their gates and put an end to their
Am 7: 2 [D] When [NIE] they had stripped the land clean, I cried out,
Zec 5: 4 [D] in his house and **destroy** it, both its timbers and its stones.' "
Mal 3: 6 [A] So you, O descendants of Jacob, *are* not **destroyed**.

3984 ²כָּלָה kālâ², v. Not used in NIV/BHS [cf. 3973]

3985 כָּלֶה kāleh, a. [1] [√ 3983]

wear out [1]

Dt 28:32 and you will **wear out** your eyes watching for them day after day,

3986 ³כָּלָה kālâ³, n.f. [21] [√ 3983]

end [6], completely destroy [+906+6913] [3], completely destroy [+928+6913] [2], destroy completely [+6913] [2], destruction [2], bad [1], completely [1], destroy completely [+907+6913] [1], destructive [1], power to destroy [1], totally [1]

Ge 18:21 see if what they have done is as **bad** as the outcry that has reached
Ex 11: 1 go from here, and when he does, he will drive you out **completely**.

2Ch 12:12 anger turned from him, and he was not **totally** destroyed.
Ne 9:31 in your great mercy you did not put an **end** to them or abandon
Isa 10:23 will carry out the **destruction** decreed upon the whole land.
28:22 has told me of the **destruction** decreed against the whole land.
Jer 4:27 will be ruined, though *I will* not **destroy** it **completely** [+6913].
5:10 and ravage them, but *do* not **destroy** them **completely** [+6913].
5:18 the LORD, "*I will* not **destroy** you **completely** [+907+6913].
30:11 'Though *I* **completely** [+928+6913] **destroy** all the nations among
30:11 I scatter you, *I will* not **completely** [+906+6913] **destroy** you.
46:28 "Though *I* **completely** [+928+6913] **destroy** all the nations among
46:28 I scatter you, *I will* not **completely** [+906+6913] **destroy** you.
Eze 11:13 *Will* you **completely** [+906+6913] **destroy** the remnant of Israel?"
13:13 anger hailstones and torrents of rain will fall with **destructive** fury.
20:17 and did not destroy them or put an **end** to them in the desert.
Da 9:27 until the **end** that is decreed is poured out on him."
11:16 in the Beautiful Land and will have the **power to destroy** it.
Na 1:8 but with an overwhelming flood he will make an **end** of ⌞Nineveh⌟;
1:9 Whatever they plot against the LORD he will bring to an **end**;
Zep 1:18 for he will make a sudden **end** of all who live in the earth."

3987 כַּלָּה *kallâ*, n.f. [34] [→ 3994]

bride [15], daughter-in-law [14], daughters-in-law [5]

Ge 11:31 and his **daughter-in-law** Sarai, the wife of his son Abram,
38:11 Judah then said to his **daughter-in-law** Tamar, "Live as a widow
38:16 Not realizing that she was his **daughter-in-law**, he went over to
38:24 "Your **daughter-in-law** Tamar is guilty of prostitution, and as a
Lev 18:15 " 'Do not have sexual relations with your **daughter-in-law**.
20:12 " 'If a man sleeps with his **daughter-in-law**, both of them must be
Ru 1:6 and her **daughters-in-law** prepared to return home from there.
1:7 With her two **daughters-in-law** she left the place where she had
1:8 Then Naomi said to her two **daughters-in-law**, "Go back,
1:22 her **daughter-in-law**, arriving in Bethlehem as the barley harvest
2:20 "The LORD bless him!" Naomi said to her **daughter-in-law**.
2:22 Naomi said to Ruth her **daughter-in-law**, "It will be good for you,
4:15 For your **daughter-in-law**, who loves you and who is better to you
1Sa 4:19 His **daughter-in-law**, the wife of Phinehas, was pregnant
1Ch 2:4 Tamar, Judah's **daughter-in-law**, bore him Perez and Zerah.
SS 4:8 with me from Lebanon, my **bride**, come with me from Lebanon.
4:9 You have stolen my heart, my sister, my **bride**; you have stolen
4:10 How delightful is your love, my sister, my **bride**! How much more
4:11 Your lips drop sweetness as the honeycomb, my **bride**; milk
4:12 You are a garden locked up, my sister, my **bride**; you are a spring
5:1 I have come into my garden, my sister, my **bride**; I have gathered
Isa 49:18 wear them all as ornaments; you will put them on, like a **bride**.
61:10 his head like a priest, and as a **bride** adorns herself with her jewels.
62:5 as a bridegroom rejoices over his **bride**, so will your God rejoice
Jer 2:32 Does a maiden forget her jewelry, a **bride** her wedding ornaments?
7:34 gladness and to the voices of **bride** and bridegroom in the towns of
16:9 gladness and to the voices of **bride** and bridegroom in this place.
25:10 sounds of joy and gladness, the voices of **bride** and bridegroom,
33:11 sounds of joy and gladness, the voices of **bride** and bridegroom,
Eze 22:11 another shamefully defiles his **daughter-in-law**, and another
Hos 4:13 turn to prostitution and your **daughters-in-law** to adultery.
4:14 nor your **daughters-in-law** when they commit adultery,
Joel 2:16 Let the bridegroom leave his room and the **bride** her chamber.
Mic 7:6 against her mother, a **daughter-in-law** against her mother-in-law—

3988 כְּלֻהַי *k^{e}luhî*, n.pr.m. [1] [cf. 3993]

Keluhi [1]

Ezr 10:35 Benaiah, Bedeiah, **Keluhi**, [Q 3993]

3989 כְּלוּא *k^{e}lû'* n.[m.] [2] [√ 3973]

prison [+1074+2021] [2]

Jer 37:4 for he had not yet been put in **prison** [+1074+2021; K 3999].
52:31 freed him from **prison** [+1074+2021; K 3999] on the twenty-fifth

3990 [1]כְּלוּב *k^{e}lûb[1]*, n.m. [3] [→ 3965?, 3978, 3979, 3990, 3991?]

basket [2], cages [1]

Jer 5:27 Like **cages** full of birds, their houses are full of deceit; they have
Am 8:1 is what the Sovereign LORD showed me: a **basket** *of* ripe fruit.
8:2 do you see, Amos?" he asked. "A **basket** *of* ripe fruit," I answered.

3991 [2]כְּלוּב *k^{e}lûb[2]*, n.pr.m. [2] [√ 3990?]

Kelub [2]

1Ch 4:11 **Kelub**, Shuhah's brother, was the father of Mehir, who was the
27:26 Ezri son of **Kelub** was in charge of the field workers who farmed

3992 כְּלוּבָי *k^{e}lûbāy*, n.pr.m. [1] [√ 3979]

Caleb [1]

1Ch 2:9 The sons born to Hezron were: Jerahmeel, Ram and **Caleb**.

3993 כְּלוּהוּ *k^{e}lûhû*, n.pr.m. [0] [cf. 3988]

Ezr 10:35 [Benaiah, Bedeiah, **Keluhi**, [Q; see K 3988]]

3994 כְּלוּלֹת *k^{e}lûlōt*, n.f. [1] [√ 3987]

bride [1]

Jer 2:2 how as a **bride** you loved me and followed me through the desert,

3995 [1]כֶּלַח *kelaḥ[1]*, n.m. [2]

full vigor [1], vigor [1]

Job 5:26 You will come to the grave in **full vigor**, like sheaves gathered in
30:2 of their hands to me, since their **vigor** had gone from them?

3996 [2]כֶּלַח *kelaḥ[2]*, n.pr.loc. [2]

Calah [2]

Ge 10:11 he went to Assyria, where he built Nineveh, Rehoboth Ir, **Calah**
10:12 Resen, which is between Nineveh and **Calah**; that is the great city.

3997 כָּל־חֹזֶה *kol-ḥōzeh*, n.pr.m. [2] [√ 3972 + 2602]

Col-Hozeh [2]

Ne 3:15 The Fountain Gate was repaired by Shallun son of **Col-Hozeh**,
11:5 the son of **Col-Hozeh**, the son of Hazaiah, the son of Adaiah,

3998 כְּלִי *k^{e}lî*, n.m. [325] [cf. 3973?, 3974?, 3983?]

articles [67], *untranslated* [23], furnishings [21], armor-bearer [+5951] [18], weapons [14], utensils [13], instruments [11], jar [9], pot [9], article [8], equipment [8], accessories [7], jars [7], weapon [7], things [6], armor [5], jewelry [5], belongings [4], goods [4], objects [4], supplies [4], armed [+2520] [3], object [3], vessels [3], anything [+2021+3972] [2], anything [2], armor-bearers [+5951] [2], armory [+1074] [2], bag [2], bags [2], everything [+3972] [2], goblets [+5482] [2], household articles [2], jewels [2], one[s] [2], packed [2], pottery [2], treasures [+2775] [2], another[s] [1], anything [+3972] [1], baggage [1], basket [1], boats [1], cargo [+641+889+928+2021] [1], clothing [1], container [1], dishes [1], goblets [1], instruments [+8877] [1], it[s] [1], jewel [1], kinds [1], material [1], methods [1], other[s] [1], possessions [1], pots [1], pottery [+3450] [1], sacks [1], something [+3972] [1], specific things [+5466] [1], storage jar [1], storage jars [1], them[s] [+466+1074+2021] [1], thing [1], things [+3972] [1], tool [1], weapon [+4878] [1], weapon [+4878+7372] [1], weapon [+5424] [1], weapons [+4878] [1], yokes [1]

Ge 24:53 Then the servant brought out **[RPH]** gold and silver jewelry
24:53 silver **jewelry** and articles of clothing and gave them to Rebekah;
27:3 Now then, get your **weapons**—your quiver and bow—and go out
31:37 Now that you have searched through all my **goods**, what have you
31:37 what have you found that belongs to **[RPH]** your household?
42:25 Joseph gave orders to fill their **bags** with grain, to put each man's
43:11 Put some of the best products of the land in your **bags** and take
45:20 Never mind about your **belongings**, because the best of all Egypt
49:5 and Levi are brothers—their swords are **weapons** *of* violence.
Ex 3:22 and any woman living in her house for **articles** *of* silver and gold
3:22 her house for articles of silver and **[RPH]** gold and for clothing,
11:2 and women alike are to ask their neighbors for **articles** *of* silver
11:2 are to ask their neighbors for articles of silver and **[RPH]** gold."
12:35 asked the Egyptians for **articles** *of* silver and gold and for clothing.
12:35 Egyptians for articles of silver and **[RPH]** gold and for clothing.
22:7 [22:6] a man gives his neighbor silver or **goods** for safekeeping
25:9 and all its **furnishings** exactly like the pattern I will show you.
25:39 pure gold is to be used for the lampstand and all these **accessories**.
27:3 Make all its **utensils** of bronze—its pots to remove the ashes,
27:19 All the other **articles** *used* in the service of the tabernacle,
30:27 the table and all its **articles**, the lampstand and its accessories,
30:27 the table and all its articles, the lampstand and its **accessories**,
30:28 the altar of burnt offering and all its **utensils**, and the basin with its
31:7 atonement cover on it, and all the other **furnishings** *of* the tent—
31:8 the table and its **articles**, the pure gold lampstand and all its
31:8 and its articles, the pure gold lampstand and all its **accessories**,
31:9 the altar of burnt offering and all its **utensils**, the basin with its
35:13 the table with its poles and all its **articles** and the bread of the
35:14 the lampstand that is for light with its **accessories**, lamps and oil
35:16 burnt offering with its bronze grating, its poles and all its **utensils**;
35:22 and women alike, came and brought gold **jewelry** *of* all kinds:
37:16 And they made from pure gold the **articles** for the table—
37:24 the lampstand and all its **accessories** from one talent of pure gold.
38:3 They made all its **utensils** *of* bronze—its pots, shovels, sprinkling
38:3 shovels, sprinkling bowls, meat forks and firepans. **[RPH]**

Ex 38:30 the bronze altar with its bronze grating and all its **utensils**,
39:33 the tent and all its **furnishings**, its clasps, frames, crossbars,
39:36 the table with all its **articles** and the bread of the Presence;
39:37 pure gold lampstand with its row of lamps and all its **accessories**,
39:39 bronze altar with its bronze grating, its poles and all its **utensils**;
39:40 all the **furnishings** *for* the tabernacle, the Tent of Meeting;
40: 9 in it; consecrate it and all its **furnishings**, and it will be holy.
40:10 Then anoint the altar of burnt offering and all its **utensils**;
Lev 6:28 [6:21] The clay **pot** the meat is cooked in must be broken; but if it
6:28 [6:21] but if it is cooked in a bronze **pot**, the pot is to be scoured
8:11 anointing the altar and all its **utensils** and the basin with its stand,
11:32 falls on something, that **article**, whatever its use, will be unclean,
11:32 be unclean, whether **it**[s] is made of wood, cloth, hide or sackcloth.
11:33 If one of them falls into a clay **pot**, everything in it will be unclean,
11:34 that could be eaten but has water on it from such a **pot** is unclean,
13:49 or knitted material, or any leather **article**, is greenish or reddish,
13:52 or linen, or any leather **article** that has the contamination in it,
13:53 or the woven or knitted material, or the leather **article**,
13:57 or knitted material, or in the leather **article**, it is spreading,
13:58 or any leather **article** that has been washed and is rid of the
13:59 or linen clothing, woven or knitted material, or any leather **article**,
14: 5 order that one of the birds be killed over fresh water in a clay **pot**.
14:50 He shall kill one of the birds over fresh water in a clay **pot**.
15: 4 be unclean, and **anything** [+2021+3972] he sits on will be unclean.
15: 6 Whoever sits on **anything** that the man with a discharge sat on
15:12 " 'A clay **pot** that the man touches must be broken, and any
15:12 must be broken, and any wooden **article** is to be rinsed with water.
15:22 Whoever touches **anything** [+3972] she sits on must wash his
15:23 Whether it is the bed or **anything** she was sitting on, when anyone
15:26 **anything** [+2021+3972] she sits on will be unclean, as during her
Nu 1:50 over all its **furnishings** and everything belonging to it.
1:50 They are to carry the tabernacle and all its **furnishings**; they are to
3: 8 They are to take care of all the **furnishings** *of* the Tent of Meeting,
3:31 the altars, the **articles** *of* the sanctuary used in ministering,
3:36 its crossbars, posts, bases, all its **equipment**, and everything
4: 9 and trays, and all its **jars** *for* the oil used to supply it.
4:10 to wrap it and all its **accessories** in a covering of hides of sea cows
4:12 "They are to take all the **articles** used for ministering in the
4:14 they are to place on it all the **utensils** used for ministering at the
4:14 **[RPH]** Over it they are to spread a covering of hides of sea cows
4:15 finished covering the holy furnishings and all the holy **articles**,
4:16 and everything in it, including its holy furnishings and **articles**."
4:26 the entrance, the ropes and all the **equipment** *used in* its service.
4:32 ropes, all their **equipment** and everything related to their use.
4:32 Assign to each man the **specific things** [+5466] he is to carry.
5:17 he shall take some holy water in a clay **jar** and put some dust from
7: 1 he anointed it and consecrated it and all its **furnishings**.
7: 1 He also anointed and consecrated the altar and all its **utensils**.
7:85 the silver **dishes** weighed two thousand four hundred shekels,
18: 3 but they must not go near the **furnishings** *of* the sanctuary
19:15 every open **container** without a lid fastened on it will be unclean.
19:17 put some ashes from the burned purification offering into a **jar**
19:18 dip it in the water and sprinkle the tent and all the **furnishings**
31: 6 who took with him **articles** *from* the sanctuary and the trumpets
31:20 Purify every garment as well as **everything** [+3972] made of
31:20 as well as everything made of leather, goat hair or **[RPH]** wood."
31:50 So we have brought as an offering to the LORD the gold **articles**
31:51 the priest accepted from them the gold—all the crafted **articles**.
35:16 " 'If a man strikes someone with an iron **object** so that he dies,
35:18 Or if anyone has a wooden **object** *in* his hand that could kill,
35:22 or throws **something** [+3972] at him unintentionally
Dt 1:41 So every one of you put on his **weapons** [+4878], thinking it easy
22: 5 A woman must not wear men's **clothing**, nor a man wear women's
23:24 [23:25] the grapes you want, but do not put any in your **basket**.
Jos 6:19 All the silver and gold and the **articles** *of* bronze and iron are
6:24 but they put the silver and gold and the **articles** *of* bronze
7:11 they have lied, they have put them with their own **possessions**.
Jdg 9:54 Hurriedly he called to his **armor-bearer** [+5951], "Draw your
18:11 **armed for** [+2520] battle, set out from Zorah and Eshtaol.
18:16 The six hundred Danites, **armed for** [+2520] battle, stood at the
18:17 the six hundred **armed** [+2520] men stood at the entrance to the
Ru 2: 9 go and get a drink from the water **jars** the men have filled."
1Sa 6: 8 in a chest beside it put the gold **objects** you are sending back to
6:15 together with the chest containing the gold **objects**, and placed
8:12 still others to make **weapons** *of* war and equipment for his
8:12 others to make weapons of war and **equipment** *for* his chariots.
9: 7 what can we give the man? The food in our **sacks** is gone.
10:22 LORD said, "Yes, he has hidden himself among the **baggage**."
14: 1 day Jonathan son of Saul said to the young man bearing his **armor**,
14: 6 Jonathan said to his young **armor-bearer** [+5951], "Come,
14: 7 "Do all that you have in mind," his **armor-bearer** [+5951] said.
14:12 of the outpost shouted to Jonathan and his **armor-bearer** [+5951],
14:12 So Jonathan said to his **armor-bearer** [+5951], "Climb up after
14:13 and feet, with his **armor-bearer** [+5951] right behind him.
14:13 and his **armor-bearer** [+5951] followed and killed behind him.
14:14 his **armor-bearer** [+5951] killed some twenty men in an area of
14:17 was Jonathan and his **armor-bearer** [+5951] who were not there.
16:21 very much, and David became one of his **armor-bearers** [+5951].
17:22 David left his **things** with the keeper of supplies, ran to the battle
17:22 David left his things with the keeper of **supplies**, ran to the battle
17:40 put them in the pouch of his shepherd's **bag** and, with his sling in
17:49 Reaching into his **bag** and taking out a stone, he slung it and struck
17:54 to Jerusalem, and he put the Philistine's **weapons** in his own tent.
20:40 Then Jonathan gave his **weapons** to the boy and said, "Go,
21: 5 [21:6] The men's **things** are holy even on missions that are not
21: 5 [21:6] that are not holy. How much more so today!" **[RPH]**
21: 8 [21:9] I haven't brought my sword or any *other* **weapon**, because
25:13 went up with David, while two hundred stayed with the **supplies**.
30:24 The share of the man who stayed with the **supplies** is to be the
31: 4 Saul said to his **armor-bearer** [+5951], "Draw your sword
31: 4 But his **armor-bearer** [+5951] was terrified and would not do it;
31: 5 When the **armor-bearer** [+5951] saw that Saul was dead,
31: 6 So Saul and his three sons and his **armor-bearer** [+5951]
31: 9 They cut off his head and stripped off his **armor**, and they sent
31:10 They put his **armor** in the temple of the Ashtoreths and fastened
2Sa 1:27 the mighty have fallen! The **weapons** *of* war have perished!"
8:10 Joram brought with him **articles** *of* silver and gold and bronze.
8:10 brought with him articles of silver and **[RPH]** gold and bronze.
8:10 brought with him articles of silver and gold and **[RPH]** bronze.
17:28 brought bedding and bowls and **articles** *of* pottery. They also
18:15 And ten of Joab's **armor-bearers** [+5951] surrounded Absalom,
23:37 the Beerothite, the **armor-bearer of** [+5951] Joab son of Zeruiah,
24:22 and here are threshing sledges and ox **yokes** for the wood.
1Ki 6: 7 or any other iron **tool** was heard at the temple site while it was
7:45 All these **objects** that Huram made for King Solomon for the
7:47 Solomon left all these **things** unweighed, because there were
7:48 Solomon also made all the **furnishings** that were in the LORD's
7:51 David had dedicated—the silver and gold and the **furnishings**—
8: 4 and the Tent of Meeting and all the sacred **furnishings** in it.
10:21 All King Solomon's **goblets** [+5482] were gold, and all the
10:21 all the **household articles** *in* the Palace of the Forest of Lebanon
10:25 **articles** *of* silver and gold, robes, weapons and spices, and horses
10:25 articles of silver and **[RPH]** gold, robes, weapons and spices,
15:15 and gold and the **articles** that he and his father had dedicated.
17:10 "Would you bring me a little water in a **jar** so I may have a drink?"
19:21 He burned the plowing **equipment** to cook the meat and gave it to
2Ki 4: 3 Elisha said, "Go around and ask all your neighbors for empty **jars**.
4: 3 all your neighbors for empty jars. **[RPH]** Don't ask for just a few.
4: 4 Pour oil into all the **jars**, and as each is filled, put it to one side."
4: 6 When all the **jars** were full, she said to her son, "Bring me another
4: 6 all the jars were full, she said to her son, "Bring me another **one**[s]."
4: 6 "Bring me another one." But he replied, "There is not a **jar** left."
7:15 **equipment** the Arameans had thrown away in their headlong
11: 8 yourselves around the king, each man with his **weapon** in his hand.
11:11 The guards, each with his **weapon** in his hand,
12:13 [12:14] trumpets or any other **articles** *of* gold or silver for the
12:13 [12:14] of gold or **[RPH]** silver for the temple of the LORD;
14:14 and silver and all the **articles** found in the temple of the LORD
20:13 his **armory** [+1074] and everything found among his treasures.
23: 4 from the temple of the LORD all the **articles** made for Baal
24:13 took away all the gold **articles** that Solomon king of Israel had
25:14 dishes and all the bronze **articles** used in the temple service.
25:16 temple of the LORD, was more than could be weighed. **[RPH]**
1Ch 9:28 Some of them were in charge of the **articles** *used in* the temple
9:29 Others were assigned to take care of the **furnishings** and all the
9:29 care of the furnishings and all the other **articles** *of* the sanctuary,
10: 4 Saul said to his **armor-bearer** [+5951], "Draw your sword
10: 4 But his **armor-bearer** [+5951] was terrified and would not do it;
10: 5 When the **armor-bearer** [+5951] saw that Saul was dead,
10: 9 They stripped him and took his head and his **armor**, and sent
10:10 They put his **armor** *in* the temple of their gods and hung up his
11:39 the Berothite, the **armor-bearer of** [+5951] Joab son of Zeruiah,
12:33 [12:34] prepared for battle with every type of **weapon** [+4878],
12:37 [12:38] armed with every type of **weapon** [+4878+7372]—
15:16 singers to sing joyful songs, accompanied by musical **instruments**:
16: 5 They were to play the **[NIE]** lyres and harps, Asaph was to sound
16:42 and for the playing of the other **instruments** *for* sacred song.
18: 8 to make the bronze Sea, the pillars and various bronze **articles**.
18:10 Hadoram brought all kinds of **articles** *of* gold and silver
22:19 the sacred **articles** *belonging to* God into the temple that will be
23: 5 with the *musical* **instruments** I have provided for that purpose."
23:26 to carry the tabernacle or any of the **articles** used in its service."
28:13 the LORD, as well as for all the **articles** *to be used in* its service.
28:14 gold for all the gold **articles** *to be used in* various kinds of service,
28:14 the weight of silver for all the silver **articles** *to be used in* various
28:14 the weight of silver for all the silver articles to be used in **[RPH]**
2Ch 4:16 the pots, shovels, meat forks and all related **articles**. All the objects
4:18 All these **things** that Solomon made amounted to so much that the

2Ch 4:19 Solomon also made all the **furnishings** that were in God's temple:
5: 1 the silver and gold and all the **furnishings**—and he placed them in
5: 5 and the Tent of Meeting and all the sacred **furnishings** in it.
5:13 by trumpets, cymbals and other **instruments** [+8877],
7: 6 as did the Levites with the LORD's musical **instruments**,
9:20 All King Solomon's **goblets** [+5482] were gold, and all the
9:20 all the **household articles** *in* the Palace of the Forest of Lebanon
9:24 **articles** *of* silver and gold, and robes, weapons and spices,
9:24 articles of silver and **[RPH]** gold, and robes, weapons and spices,
15:18 and gold and the **articles** that he and his father had dedicated.
20:25 amount of equipment and clothing and also **articles** *of* value—
23: 7 around the king, each man with his **weapons** in his hand.
23:13 and singers with musical **instruments** were leading the praises.
24:14 and with it were made **articles** for the LORD's temple:
24:14 **articles** *for* the service and for the burnt offerings, and also dishes
24:14 and also dishes and other **objects** *of* gold and silver.
25:24 all the **articles** found in the temple of God that had been in the care
28:24 Ahaz gathered together the **furnishings** *from* the temple of God
28:24 from the temple of God and took **them**ˢ [+466+1074+2021] away.
29:18 the altar of burnt offering with all its **utensils**, and the table for
29:18 the table for setting out the consecrated bread, with all its **articles**.
29:19 consecrated all the **articles** that King Ahaz removed in his
29:26 So the Levites stood ready with David's **instruments**,
29:27 by trumpets and the **instruments** *of* David king of Israel.
30:21 every day, accompanied by the LORD's **instruments** *of* praise.
32:27 for his precious stones, spices, shields and all **kinds** *of* valuables.
34:12 all who were skilled in playing musical **instruments**—
36: 7 Nebuchadnezzar also took to Babylon **articles** *from* the temple of
36:10 together with **articles** *of* value from the temple of the LORD,
36:18 He carried to Babylon all the **articles** *from* the temple of God,
36:19 all the palaces and destroyed **everything of** [+3972] value there.
Ezr 1: 6 All their neighbors assisted them with **articles** *of* silver and gold,
1: 7 King Cyrus brought out the **articles** *belonging to* the temple of the
1:10 gold bowls 30 matching silver bowls 410 other **articles** 1,000
1:11 In all, there were 5,400 **articles** of gold and of silver.
8:25 them the offering of silver and gold and the **articles** that the king,
8:26 of silver, silver **articles** weighing 100 talents, 100 talents of gold,
8:27 and two fine **articles** *of* polished bronze, as precious as gold.
8:28 "You as well as these **articles** are consecrated to the LORD.
8:30 sacred **articles** that had been weighed out to be taken to the house
8:33 and the sacred **articles** into the hands of Meremoth son of Uriah,
Ne 10:39 [10:40] oil to the storerooms where the **articles** *for* the sanctuary
12:36 with musical **instruments** ⌞prescribed by⌟ David the man of God.
13: 5 used to store the grain offerings and incense and temple **articles**,
13: 8 and threw all Tobiah's household **goods** out of the room.
13: 9 then I put back into them the **equipment** *of* the house of God,
Est 1: 7 Wine was served in **goblets** *of* gold, each one different from the
1: 7 *each* **one**ˢ different from the other, and the royal wine was
1: 7 each one different from the **other**ˢ, and the royal wine was
Job 28:17 crystal can compare with it, nor can it be had for **jewels** *of* gold.
Ps 2: 9 iron scepter; you will dash them to pieces like **pottery** [+3450]."
7:13 [7:14] He has prepared his deadly **weapons**; he makes ready his
31:12 [31:13] though I were dead; I have become like broken **pottery**.
71:22 I will praise you with the **[NIE]** harp for your faithfulness,
Pr 20:15 in abundance, but lips that speak knowledge are a rare **jewel**.
25: 4 dross from the silver, and out comes **material** for the silversmith;
Ecc 9:18 Wisdom is better than **weapons** *of* war, but one sinner destroys
Isa 10:28 they pass through Migron; they store **supplies** at Micmash.
13: 5 the LORD and the **weapons** *of* his wrath—to destroy the whole
18: 2 which sends envoys by sea in papyrus **boats** over the water.
22:24 and offshoots—all its lesser **vessels**, from the bowls to all the jars.
22:24 all its lesser vessels, from **[RPH]** the bowls to all the jars.
22:24 all its lesser vessels, from the bowls to all **[RPH]** the jars.
32: 7 The scoundrel's **methods** are wicked, he makes up evil schemes to
39: 2 his entire **armory** [+1074] and everything found among his
52:11 out from it and be pure, you who carry the **vessels** *of* the LORD.
54:16 who fans the coals into flame and forges a **weapon** fit for its work.
54:17 no **weapon** forged against you will prevail, and you will refute
61:10 his head like a priest, and as a bride adorns herself with her **jewels**.
65: 4 eat the flesh of pigs, and whose **pots** hold broth of unclean meat;
66:20 to the temple of the LORD in ceremonially clean **vessels**.
Jer 14: 3 They return with their **jars** unfilled; dismayed and despairing,
18: 4 But the **pot** he was shaping from the clay was marred in his hands;
18: 4 so the potter formed it into another **pot**, shaping it as seemed best
19:11 this city just as this potter's **jar** is smashed and cannot be repaired.
21: 4 I am about to turn against you the **weapons** *of* war that are in your
22: 7 I will send destroyers against you, each man with his **weapons**,
22:28 man Jehoiachin a despised, broken pot, an **object** no one wants?
25:34 has come; you will fall and be shattered like fine **pottery**.
27:16 'Very soon now the **articles** *from* the LORD's house will be
27:18 let them plead with the LORD Almighty that the **furnishings**
27:19 movable stands and the other **furnishings** that are left in this city,
27:21 says about the **things** that are left in the house of the LORD
28: 3 Within two years I will bring back to this place all the **articles** *of*
28: 6 have prophesied by bringing the **articles** *of* the LORD's house
32:14 and put them in a clay **jar** so they will last a long time.
40:10 the wine, summer fruit and oil, and put them in your **storage jars**,
46:19 Pack your **belongings** *for* exile, you who live in Egypt,
48:11 like wine left on its dregs, not poured from *one* **jar** to another—
48:11 like wine left on its dregs, not poured from one jar to **another**ˢ—
48:12 will pour her out; they will empty her **jars** and smash her jugs.
48:38 for I have broken Moab like a **jar** that no one wants,"
49:29 their shelters will be carried off with all their **goods** and camels.
50:25 has opened his arsenal and brought out the **weapons** *of* his wrath,
51:20 "You are my war club, my **weapon** *for* battle—with you I shatter
51:34 he has thrown us into confusion, he has made us an empty **jar**.
52:18 dishes and all the bronze **articles** used in the temple service.
52:20 temple of the LORD, was more than could be weighed. **[NIE]**
Eze 4: 9 put them in a **storage jar** and use them to make bread for yourself.
9: 1 guards of the city here, each with a **weapon** [+5424] in his hand."
9: 2 which faces north, each with a deadly **weapon** in his hand.
12: 3 son of man, pack your **belongings** *for* exile and in the daytime,
12: 4 while they watch, bring out your **belongings** packed for exile.
12: 4 while they watch, bring out your belongings **packed** *for* exile.
12: 7 During the day I brought out my **things** packed for exile.
12: 7 During the day I brought out my things **packed** *for* exile.
15: 3 Do they make pegs from it to hang **things** [+3972] on?
16:17 You also took the fine **jewelry** I gave you, the jewelry made of my
16:39 and take your fine **jewelry** and leave you naked and bare.
23:26 They will also strip you of your clothes and take your fine **jewelry**.
27:13 they exchanged slaves and **articles** *of* bronze for your wares.
32:27 who went down to the grave with their **weapons** *of* war, whose
40:42 On them were placed the **utensils** for slaughtering the burnt
Da 1: 2 his hand, along with some of the **articles** *from* the temple of God.
1: 2 god in Babylonia and put **[RPH]** in the treasure house of his god.
11: 8 their metal images and their valuable **articles** *of* silver and gold
Hos 8: 8 now she is among the nations like a worthless **thing**.
13:15 His storehouse will be plundered of all its **treasures** [+2775].
Am 6: 5 on your harps like David and improvise on musical **instruments**.
Jnh 1: 5 And they threw the **cargo** [+641+889+928+2021] into the sea to
Na 2: 9 [2:10] is endless, the wealth from all its **treasures** [+2775]!
Zec 11:15 said to me, "Take again the **equipment** *of* a foolish shepherd.

3999 כְּלִיא kᵉlî', n.[m.]. [0] [cf. 3975]

Jer 37: 4 [he had not yet been put in **prison** [K +1074+2021].; see Q 3989]
52:31 [freed him from **prison** [K +1074+2021; see Q 3989] on the]

4000 כִּלְיָה kilyâ, n.f. [31]

kidneys [18], heart [4], mind [3], inmost being [2], hearts [1], kernels [1], minds [1], spirit [1]

Ex 29:13 the covering of the liver, and both **kidneys** with the fat on them,
29:22 of the liver, both **kidneys** with the fat on them, and the right thigh.
Lev 3: 4 both **kidneys** with the fat on them near the loins, and the covering
3: 4 the covering of the liver, which he will remove with the **kidneys**.
3:10 both **kidneys** with the fat on them near the loins, and the covering
3:10 the covering of the liver, which he will remove with the **kidneys**.
3:15 both **kidneys** with the fat on them near the loins, and the covering
3:15 the covering of the liver, which he will remove with the **kidneys**.
4: 9 both **kidneys** with the fat on them near the loins, and the covering
4: 9 the covering of the liver, which he will remove with the **kidneys**—
7: 4 both **kidneys** with the fat on them near the loins, and the covering
7: 4 the covering of the liver, which is to be removed with the **kidneys**.
8:16 the covering of the liver, and both **kidneys** and their fat,
8:25 covering of the liver, both **kidneys** and their fat and the right thigh.
9:10 the **kidneys** and the covering of the liver from the sin offering,
9:19 the layer of fat, the **kidneys** and the covering of the liver—
Dt 32:14 with choice rams of Bashan and the finest **kernels** *of* wheat.
Job 16:13 he pierces my **kidneys** and spills my gall on the ground.
19:27 own eyes—I, and not another. How my **heart** yearns within me!
Ps 7: 9 [7:10] O righteous God, who searches **minds** and hearts, bring to
16: 7 who counsels me; even at night my **heart** instructs me.
26: 2 Test me, O LORD, and try me, examine my **heart** and my mind;
73:21 When my heart was grieved and my **spirit** embittered,
139:13 For you created my **inmost being**; you knit me together in my
Pr 23:16 my **inmost being** will rejoice when your lips speak what is right.
Isa 34: 6 the blood of lambs and goats, fat from the **kidneys** *of* rams.
Jer 11:20 you who judge righteously and test the heart and **mind**,
12: 2 bear fruit. You are always on their lips but far from their **hearts**.
17:10 "I the LORD search the heart and examine the **mind**, to reward a
20:12 you who examine the righteous and probe the heart and **mind**,
La 3:13 He pierced my **heart** with arrows from his quiver.

4001 כִּלָּיוֹן killāyôn, n.m. [2] [√ 3983]

destruction [1], weary with longing [1]

Dt 28:65 an anxious mind, eyes **weary with longing**, and a despairing heart.
Isa 10:22 **Destruction** has been decreed, overwhelming and righteous.

4002 כִּלְיוֹן *kilyôn*, n.pr.m. [3] [√ 3983]

Kilion [3]

Ru 1: 2 and the names of his two sons were Mahlon and **Kilion**.
1: 5 both Mahlon and **Kilion** also died, and Naomi was left without her
4: 9 from Naomi all the property of Elimelech, **Kilion** and Mahlon.

4003 כָּלִיל *kālîl*, a. & subst. [15] [√ 4005]

perfect [3], whole [3], completely [2], entirely [2], perfection [1], solid [1], totally [1], whole burnt offering [1], whole burnt offerings [1]

Ex 28: 31 "Make the robe of the ephod **entirely** *of* blue cloth,
39: 22 They made the robe of the ephod **entirely** *of* blue cloth—the work
Lev 6: 22 [6:15] the LORD's regular share and is to be burned **completely**.
6: 23 [6:16] grain offering of a priest shall be burned **completely**;
Nu 4: 6 spread a cloth of **solid** blue over that and put the poles in place.
Dt 13: 16 [13:17] all its plunder as a **whole burnt offering** to the LORD
33: 10 offers incense before you and **whole burnt offerings** on your altar.
Jdg 20: 40 and saw the smoke of the **whole** city going up into the sky.
1Sa 7: 9 and offered it up as a **whole** burnt offering to the LORD.
Ps 51: 19 [51:21] righteous sacrifices, **whole** burnt offerings to delight you;
Isa 2: 18 and the idols will **totally** disappear.
La 2: 15 "Is this the city that was called the **perfection** *of* beauty, the joy of
Eze 16: 14 because the splendor I had given you made your beauty **perfect**,
27: 3 LORD says: " 'You say, O Tyre, "I am **perfect** *in* beauty."
28: 12 the model of perfection, full of wisdom and **perfect** *in* beauty.

4004 כַּלְכֹּל *kalkōl*, n.pr.m. [2] [√ 4005?]

Calcol [2]

1Ki 4: 31 [5:11] wiser than Heman, **Calcol** and Darda, the sons of Mahol.
1Ch 2: 6 of Zerah: Zimri, Ethan, Heman, **Calcol** and Darda—five in all.

4005 כָּלַל *kālal*, v. [2] [→ 3972, 3997, 4003, 4004?, 4006, 4814, 4815, 4817; cf. 3920?, 3983; Ar 10353, 10354]

brought to perfection [2]

Eze 27: 4 [A] high seas; your builders **brought** your beauty **to perfection**.
27: 11 [A] around your walls; they **brought** your beauty **to perfection**.

4006 כְּלָל *kᵉlāl*, n.pr.m. [1] [√ 4005]

Kelal [1]

Ezr 10: 30 Adna, **Kelal**, Benaiah, Maaseiah, Mattaniah, Bezalel, Binnui

4007 כָּלַם *kālam*, v. [38] [→ 4009, 4010]

ashamed [6], disgraced [6], humiliated [3], blush [2], disgrace [2], mistreat [2], be disgraced [1], be put to shame [1], been in disgrace [1], blush with shame [1], despairing [1], disgraces [1], embarrass [1], fear disgrace [1], humbled [1], in disgrace [1], lacked [1], put to shame [1], puts to shame [1], rebuke [1], reproached [1], shameful treatment [1], were shocked [1]

Nu 12: 14 [C] *would she* not *have* **been in disgrace** for seven days?
Jdg 18: 7 [G] And since their land **lacked** nothing, they were prosperous.
Ru 2: 15 [G] if she gathers among the sheaves, don't **embarrass** her.
1Sa 20: 34 [G] he was grieved at his father's **shameful treatment** *of*
25: 7 [G] your shepherds were with us, *we did* not **mistreat** them,
25: 15 [H] They *did* not **mistreat** *us*, and the whole time we were out in
2Sa 10: 5 [C] to meet the men, for they were greatly **humiliated**.
19: 3 [19:4] [C] steal in who *are* **ashamed** when they flee from battle.
1Ch 19: 5 [C] messengers to meet them, for they were greatly **humiliated**.
2Ch 30: 15 [C] The priests and the Levites *were* **ashamed** and consecrated
Ezr 9: 6 [C] I am too ashamed and **disgraced** to lift up my face to you,
Job 11: 3 [G] men to silence? *Will* no *one* **rebuke** you when you mock?
19: 3 [G] Ten times now *you have* **reproached** me; shamelessly you
Ps 35: 4 [C] May those who seek my life be disgraced and **put to shame**;
40: 14 [40:15] [C] all who desire my ruin be turned back *in* **disgrace**.
44: 9 [44:10] [G] now you have rejected and **humbled** us; you no
69: 6 [69:7] [C] *may* those who seek you not **be put to shame**
70: 2 [70:3] [C] all who desire my ruin be turned back **in disgrace**.
74: 21 [C] Do not let the oppressed retreat *in* **disgrace**; may the poor
Pr 25: 8 [G] will you do in the end if your neighbor **puts** you **to shame**?
28: 7 [G] but a companion of gluttons **disgraces** his father.
Isa 41: 11 [C] who rage against you will surely be ashamed and **disgraced**;
45: 16 [C] All the makers of idols will be put to shame and **disgraced**;
45: 17 [C] you will never be put to shame or **disgraced**, to ages
50: 7 [C] the Sovereign LORD helps me, *I will* not **be disgraced**.
54: 4 [C] *Do* not **fear disgrace**; you will not be humiliated.
Jer 3: 3 [C] brazen look of a prostitute; you refuse *to* **blush with shame**.
6: 15 [G] have no shame at all; they do not even know how *to* **blush**.
8: 12 [C] have no shame at all; they do not even know how *to* **blush**.
14: 3 [H] dismayed and **despairing**, they cover their heads.
22: 22 [C] you will be ashamed and **disgraced** because of all your
31: 19 [C] I was ashamed and **humiliated** because I bore the disgrace of
Eze 16: 27 [C] of the Philistines, who **were shocked** by your lewd conduct.
16: 54 [C] *be* **ashamed** of all you have done in giving them comfort.
16: 61 [C] your ways and *be* **ashamed** when you receive your sisters,
36: 32 [C] Be ashamed and **disgraced** for your conduct, O house of
43: 10 [C] the people of Israel, that *they may be* **ashamed** of their sins.
43: 11 [C] if *they are* **ashamed** of all they have done, make known to

4008 כִּלְמַד *kilmad*, n.pr.loc. [1]

Kilmad [1]

Eze 27: 23 and merchants of Sheba, Asshur and **Kilmad** traded with you.

4009 כְּלִמָּה *kᵉlimmâ*, n.f. [30] [√ 4007]

disgrace [12], shame [9], scorn [3], dishonor [1], dishonors [1], humiliation [1], mocking [1], shamed [1], taunts [1]

Job 20: 3 I hear a rebuke that **dishonors** me, and my understanding inspires
Ps 4: 2 [4:3] How long, O men, will you turn my glory into **shame**?
35: 26 exalt themselves over me be clothed with shame and **disgrace**.
44: 15 [44:16] My **disgrace** is before me all day long, and my face is
69: 7 [69:8] I endure scorn for your sake, and **shame** covers my face.
69: 19 [69:20] You know how I am scorned, disgraced and **shamed**; all
71: 13 those who want to harm me be covered with scorn and **disgrace**.
109: 29 My accusers will be clothed with **disgrace** and wrapped in shame
Pr 18: 13 He who answers before listening—that is his folly and his **shame**.
Isa 30: 3 will be to your shame, Egypt's shade will bring you **disgrace**.
45: 16 put to shame and disgraced; they will go off into **disgrace** together.
50: 6 out my beard; I did not hide my face from **mocking** and spitting.
61: 7 and instead of **disgrace** they will rejoice in their inheritance;
Jer 3: 25 Let us lie down in our shame, and let our **disgrace** cover us.
20: 11 be thoroughly disgraced; their **dishonor** will never be forgotten.
51: 51 for we have been insulted and **shame** covers our faces,
Eze 16: 52 Bear your **disgrace**, for you have furnished some justification for
16: 52 So then, be ashamed and bear your **disgrace**, for you have made
16: 54 so that you may bear your **disgrace** and be ashamed of all you
16: 63 and never again open your mouth because of your **humiliation**,
32: 24 They bear their **shame** with those who go down to the pit.
32: 25 they bear their **shame** with those who go down to the pit;
32: 30 the sword and bear their **shame** with those who go down to the pit.
34: 29 be victims of famine in the land or bear the **scorn** *of* the nations.
36: 6 jealous wrath because you have suffered the **scorn** *of* the nations.
36: 7 uplifted hand that the nations around you will also suffer **scorn**.
36: 15 No longer will I make you hear the **taunts** *of* the nations, and no
39: 26 They will forget their **shame** and all the unfaithfulness they
44: 13 they must bear the **shame** *of* their detestable practices.
Mic 2: 6 not prophesy about these things; **disgrace** will not overtake us."

4010 כְּלִמּוּת *kᵉlimmût*, n.f. [1] [√ 4007]

shame [1]

Jer 23: 40 everlasting **shame** that will not be forgotten."

4011 כַּלְנֵה *kalnēh*, n.pr.loc. [2] [cf. 4012]

Calneh [2]

Ge 10: 10 his kingdom were Babylon, Erech, Akkad and **Calneh**, in Shinar.
Am 6: 2 Go to **Calneh** and look at it; go from there to great Hamath,

4012 כַּלְנוֹ *kalnô*, n.pr.loc. [1] [cf. 4011]

Calno [1]

Isa 10: 9 'Has not **Calno** fared like Carchemish? Is not Hamath like Arpad,

4013 כֶם- *-kem*, p.m.pl.suf. [2652 / 2651] [√ 3870] Not indexed

you [1268], your [940], *untranslated* [235], the[s] [52], your [+4200] [48], yourselves [36], your own [18], yourselves [+5883] [12], their [4], yours [+4200] [4], your own [+4200] [3], yours [3], them[s] [+7700] [2], you [+5883] [2], yourselves [+7156] [2], a[s] [1], an[s] [1], every[s] [1], him[s] [+466+3378] [1], see for yourselves [+6524+8011] [1], the people[s] [1], the [1], their [+4200] [1], them[s] [+1201] [1], them[s] [+3] [1], them [1], they[s] [+3] [1], think [+4200+8492] [1], us [+2256+3276] [1], what do you mean [+4200+4537] [1], you [+6795] [1], you [+7156] [1], you're [1], your [+4946] [1], your [+6584] [1], yourselves [+4222] [1], yourselves [+7418] [1]

4014 כָּמַה *kāmah*, v. [1] [→ 4016]

longs for [1]

Ps 63: 1 [63:2] [A] my body **longs for** you, in a dry and weary land

4015 כַּמָּה *kammâ*, pp.+p.inter. Not used in NIV/BHS [√ 3869 + 4537; Ar 10356]

4016 כִּמְהָם ***kimhām***, n.pr.m. [3] [→ 1745; cf. 4014, 4018]
Kimham [3]

2Sa 19:37 [19:38] my father and mother. But here is your servant **Kimham**.
19:38 [19:39] The king said, "**Kimham** shall cross over with me, and I
19:40 [19:41] king crossed over to Gilgal, **Kimham** crossed with him.

4017 כְּמוֹ ***kᵉmô***, adv. & c. [141] [√ 3869 + 4537] See Select Index

like [80], as [25], *untranslated* [11], according to [2], with [2], all [1], as though [1], as well as [1], but [1], deepest night [+694+6547] [1], equal to [1], equal [1], even so [1], for [1], in a moment [+8092] [1], kind [1], or [1], same [1], seem [+928+6524] [1], such [+4027] [1], such as [1], thus [1], what [+889] [1], whether [1], worse [+4202] [1], worth [1]

4018 כִּמְוהָם ***kimwhām***, n.pr.m. [0] [cf. 4016]

Jer 41:17 [stopping at **Geruth Kimham** [K; see Q 1745] near Bethlehem]

4019 כְּמוֹשׁ ***kᵉmôš***, n.pr. [8] [cf. 4020]
Chemosh [8]

Nu 21:29 Woe to you, O Moab! You are destroyed, O people of **Chemosh**!
Jdg 11:24 Will you not take what your god **Chemosh** gives you? Likewise,
1Ki 11: 7 Solomon built a high place for **Chemosh** the detestable god of
11:33 **Chemosh** the god of the Moabites, and Molech the god of the
2Ki 23:13 for **Chemosh** the vile god of Moab, and for Molech the detestable
Jer 48: 7 **Chemosh** will go into exile, together with his priests and officials.
48:13 Moab will be ashamed of **Chemosh**, as the house of Israel was
48:46 The people of **Chemosh** are destroyed; your sons are taken into

4020 כְּמִישׁ ***kᵉmîš***, var. Not used in NIV/BHS [cf. 4019]

4021 כַּמֹּן ***kammōn***, n.m. [3]
cummin [3]

Isa 28:25 leveled the surface, does he not sow caraway and scatter **cummin**?
28:27 not threshed with a sledge, nor is a cartwheel rolled over **cummin**;
28:27 caraway is beaten out with a rod, and **cummin** with a stick.

4022 כָּמַס ***kāmas***, v. [1] [→ 4820, 4825]
kept in reserve [1]

Dt 32:34 [B] "*Have* I not **kept** this **in reserve** and sealed it in my vaults?

4023 כָּמַר ***kāmar***, v. [4] [→ 4024]
aroused [1], deeply moved [+8171] [1], filled with [1], hot [1]

Ge 43:30 [C] **Deeply moved** [+8171] at the sight of his brother,
1Ki 3:26 [C] The woman whose son was alive *was* **filled with** compassion
La 5:10 [C] Our skin *is* **hot** as an oven, feverish from hunger.
Hos 11: 8 [C] heart is changed within me; all my compassion *is* **aroused**.

4024 כֹּמֶר ***kōmer***, n.m. [3] [√ 4023]
idolatrous priests [1], pagan priests [1], pagan [1]

2Ki 23: 5 He did away with the **pagan priests** appointed by the kings of
Hos 10: 5 Its people will mourn over it, and so will its **idolatrous priests**,
Zep 1: 4 of Baal, the names of the **pagan** and the idolatrous priests—

4025 כַּמְרִיר ***kamrîr***, n.m. [1]
blackness [1]

Job 3: 5 may a cloud settle over it; may **blackness** overwhelm its light.

4026 כֵּן ***kēn¹***, a. [19] [→ 4027; cf. 3922]
right [7], honest [5], agreed [1], aright [1], correctly [1], order [1], truly [1], unjustly [+4202] [1], yes [1]

Ge 42:11 all the sons of one man. Your servants are **honest** *men*, not spies."
42:19 If you are **honest** *men*, let one of your brothers stay here in prison,
42:31 But we said to him, 'We are **honest** *men*; we are not spies.
42:33 said to us, 'This is how I will know whether you are **honest** *men*:
42:34 brother to me so I will know that you are not spies but **honest** *men*.
Nu 27: 7 "What Zelophehad's daughters are saying is **right**. You must
36: 5 "What the tribe of the descendants of Joseph is saying is **right**.
Jos 2: 4 She said, "**Yes**, the men came to me, but I did not know where they
2:21 "**Agreed**," she replied. "Let it be as you say." So she sent them
Jdg 12: 6 "Sibboleth," because he could not pronounce the word **correctly**,
2Sa 23: 5 "Is not my house **right** with God? Has he not made with me an
2Ki 7: 9 they said to each other, "We're not doing **right**. This is a day of
17: 9 did things against the LORD their God that were not **right**.
Ezr 10:12 with a loud voice: "You are **right**! We must do as you say.
Ps 90:12 Teach us to number our days **aright**, that we may gain a heart of
Pr 11:19 The **truly** righteous man attains life, but he who pursues evil goes
28: 2 but a man of understanding and knowledge maintains **order**.
Jer 8: 6 I have listened attentively, but they do not say *what* is **right**.
23:10 follow an evil course and use their power **unjustly** [+4202].

4027 כֵּן ***kēn²***, adv. [753] [→ 4026, 4338, 6586; Ar 10357]
See Select Index

therefore [+4200] [146], so [88], *untranslated* [85], therefore [+6584] [52], that is why [+6584] [34], this [32], so [+6584] [25], same [23], that [20], just as [+889+3869] [17], afterward [+339] [15], as [+889+3869] [12], so [+4200] [10], in the course of time [+339] [8], such [7], as [6], because [+6584] [5], but [+4200] [5], this is why [+6584] [5], after [+339] [4], true [4], what [4], in this way [3], it[s] [3], later [+339] [3], some time later [+339] [3], that is what [3], then [+4200] [3], this is what [3], and [2], because [+3954+6584] [2], exactly as [+889+3869] [2], exactly [2], for [+3954+6584] [2], for [+4200] [2], in way [2], just what [+889+3869] [2], like that [2], like this [2], like [2], more [2], no [+4202] [2], no wonder [+6584] [2], so that [+6584] [2], surely [+4200] [2], that is how [2], that is the way [2], then [+339] [2], this is how [2], very well [+4200] [2], what [+889+3869] [2], whatever [+889+3869] [2], accordingly [1], alike [1], also sweet[s] [1], also [1], and [+4200] [1], and [+6584] [1], and so [+6584] [1], as [+3869] [1], as soon as [+3869] [1], as well [1], because [+4200] [1], because of [+6584] [1], because of this [+4200] [1], because of this [+6584] [1], custom [+6913] [1], customary [+1821] [1], empty [+4202] [1], enough [1], exactly like [+3869] [1], exactly like [+889+3869+3972] [1], follow [+6913] [1], follow lead [+6913] [1], followed [+6913] [1], follows [+339] [1], for [1], from then on [+339+4946] [1], fulfill [+3869+6913+7023] [1], fulfilled [+2118] [1], further [1], futile [+4202] [1], greatly [1], happening[s] [1], how [+6584] [1], however [+4200] [1], in accordance with [+3869] [1], in the course of time [+339+4946] [1], in the same order [1], in the same way [1], it must be [1], just as [+3869] [1], just as [+889+3869+3972] [1], just as [1], just for that [+4200] [1], just like [+3869] [1], later [+339+4946] [1], let it be [+2085] [1], like [+889+3869] [1], nevertheless [+4200] [1], not [1], nothing [+4202] [1], particularly [+4200] [1], similar [1], since [+3954+6584] [1], since [+6584] [1], so much [1], so then [+4200] [1], still [+4200] [1], such [+4017] [1], that [+6584] [1], that was how [1], that's why [+6584] [1], then [+6584] [1], then [1], therefore [+3610+4200] [1], this reason [1], this was the kind [1], this was what [1], this way [1], thus [1], too [1], tried [+6913] [1], unlike [+4202+6913] [1], very things [+889+3869] [1], very well [1], whatever [+889+3869+3972] [1], why [+561+4200+4537] [1], yes [1], yet [+4200] [1], yet [1]

4028 כֵּן ***kēn³***, pt.rel. Not used in NIV/BHS

4029 כֵּן ***kēn⁴***, n.m. [10] [→ 4030, 4039, 4040, 4041; cf. 3922]
stand [8], basework [+5126] [1], mast [+9568] [1]

Ex 30:18 "Make a bronze basin, with its bronze **stand**, for washing.
30:28 of burnt offering and all its utensils, and the basin with its **stand**.
31: 9 altar of burnt offering and all its utensils, the basin with its **stand**—
35:16 its poles and all its utensils; the bronze basin with its **stand**;
38: 8 its bronze **stand** from the mirrors of the women who served at the
39:39 its poles and all its utensils; the basin with its **stand**;
40:11 Anoint the basin and its **stand** and consecrate them.
Lev 8:11 anointing the altar and all its utensils and the basin with its **stand**,
1Ki 7:31 and with its **basework** [+5126] it measured a cubit and a half.
Isa 33:23 The **mast** [+9568] is not held secure, the sail is not spread.

4030 כֵּן ***kēn⁵***, n.m. [6] [√ 4029]
position [2], instead of [+6584] [1], place [1], succeeded [+6584+6641] [1], successor [+6584+6641] [1]

Ge 40:13 Pharaoh will lift up your head and restore you to your **position**,
41:13 I was restored to my **position**, and the other man was hanged."
Da 11: 7 "One from her family line will arise to take her **place**. He will
11:20 "His **successor** [+6584+6641] will send out a tax collector to
11:21 "He *will be* **succeeded by** [+6584+6641] a contemptible person
11:38 **Instead of** [+6584] them, he will honor a god of fortresses;

4031 כֵּן ***kēn⁶***, n.[m.] [5] [→ 4038]
gnats [4], flies [1]

Ex 8:16 [8:12] throughout the land of Egypt the dust will become **gnats**."
8:17 [8:13] All the dust throughout the land of Egypt became **gnats**.
8:18 [8:14] when the magicians tried to produce **gnats** by their secret
Ps 105:31 there came swarms of flies, and **gnats** throughout their country.
Isa 51: 6 earth will wear out like a garment and its inhabitants die like **flies**.

4032 כֶן- **-ken**, כֶנָה- **-kenâ**, p.f.pl.suf. [19] [√ 3870] Not indexed

your [13], you [5], your own [1]

4033 כָּנָה **kānâ**, v. [4]

bestow a title of honor [1], flatter [1], flattery [1], take [1]

Job 32:21 [D] I will show partiality to no one, nor *will I* **flatter** any man;
32:22 [D] for if I were skilled in **flattery**, my Maker would soon take
Isa 44: 5 [D] on his hand, 'The LORD's,' and *will* **take** the name Israel.
45: 4 [D] I summon you by name and **bestow** *on* you **a title of honor**,

4034 כַּנֵּה **kannēh**, n.pr.loc. [1]

Canneh [1]

Eze 27:23 **Canneh** and Eden and merchants of Sheba, Asshur and Kilmad

4035 כַּנָּה **kannâ**, n.f. [1]

root [1]

Ps 80:15 [80:16] the **root** your right hand has planted, the son you have

4036 כִּנּוֹר **kinnôr**, n.m. [42]

harp [21], harps [19], lutes [1], lyre [1]

Ge 4:21 was Jubal; he was the father of all who play the **harp** and flute.
31:27 away with joy and singing to the music of tambourines and **harps**?
1Sa 10: 5 tambourines, flutes and **harps** being played before them, and they
16:16 his servants here to search for someone who can play the **harp**.
16:23 from God came upon Saul, David would take his **harp** and play.
2Sa 6: 5 with songs and with **harps**, lyres, tambourines, sistrums
1Ki 10:12 the royal palace, and to make **harps** and lyres for the musicians.
1Ch 13: 8 with songs and with **harps**, lyres, tambourines, cymbals
15:16 accompanied by musical instruments: lyres, **harps** and cymbals.
15:21 Mikneiah, Obed-Edom, Jeiel and Azaziah were to play the **harps**,
15:28 and trumpets, and of cymbals, and the playing of lyres and **harps**.
16: 5 They were to play the lyres and **harps**, Asaph was to sound the
25: 1 of prophesying, accompanied by **harps**, lyres and cymbals.
25: 3 using the **harp** in thanking and praising the LORD.
25: 6 with cymbals, lyres and **harps**, for the ministry at the house of
2Ch 5:12 dressed in fine linen and playing cymbals, **harps** and lyres.
9:11 the royal palace, and to make **harps** and lyres for the musicians.
20:28 to the temple of the LORD with harps and **lutes** and trumpets.
29:25 **harps** and lyres in the way prescribed by David and Gad the king's
Ne 12:27 of thanksgiving and with the music of cymbals, **harps** and lyres.
Job 21:12 They sing to the music of tambourine and **harp**; they make merry
30:31 My **harp** is tuned to mourning, and my flute to the sound of
Ps 33: 2 Praise the LORD with the **harp**; make music to him on the
43: 4 and my delight. I will praise you with the **harp**, O God, my God.
49: 4 [49:5] ear to a proverb; with the **harp** I will expound my riddle:
57: 8 [57:9] Awake, my soul! Awake, **harp** and lyre! I will awaken the
71:22 I will sing praise to you with the **lyre**, O Holy One of Israel.
81: 2 [81:3] strike the tambourine, play the melodious **harp** and lyre.
92: 3 [92:4] music of the ten-stringed lyre and the melody of the **harp**.
98: 5 make music to the LORD with the **harp**, with the harp
98: 5 the LORD with the harp, with the **harp** and the sound of singing,
108: 2 [108:3] Awake, **harp** and lyre! I will awaken the dawn.
137: 2 There on the poplars we hung our **harps**,
147: 7 LORD with thanksgiving; make music to our God on the **harp**.
149: 3 with dancing and make music to him with tambourine and **harp**.
150: 3 the sounding of the trumpet, praise him with the **harp** and lyre,
Isa 5:12 They have **harps** and lyres at their banquets, tambourines
16:11 My heart laments for Moab like a **harp**, my inmost being for Kir
23:16 "Take up a **harp**, walk through the city, O prostitute forgotten;
24: 8 the noise of the revelers has stopped, the joyful **harp** is silent.
30:32 his punishing rod will be to the music of tambourines and **harps**,
Eze 26:13 noisy songs, and the music of your **harps** will be heard no more.

4037 כָּנְיָהוּ **konyāhû**, n.pr.m. [3] [√ 3382; cf. 3378 + 3922]

Jehoiachin [3]

Jer 22:24 "even if you, **Jehoiachin** son of Jehoiakim king of Judah,
22:28 Is this man **Jehoiachin** a despised, broken pot, an object no one
37: 1 of Babylon; he reigned in place of **Jehoiachin** son of Jehoiakim.

4038 כִּנָּם **kinnām**, n.[m.]. [2] [√ 4031]

gnats [2]

Ex 8:17 [8:13] the dust of the ground, **gnats** came upon men and animals.
8:18 [8:14] they could not. And the **gnats** were on men and animals.

4039 כְּנָנִי **k^enānî**, n.pr.m. [1] [→ 4040; cf. 4029 + 3378]

Kenani [1]

Ne 9: 4 Kadmiel, Shebaniah, Bunni, Sherebiah, Bani and **Kenani**—

4040 כְּנַנְיָה **k^enanyâ**, n.pr.m. [1] [√ 4039; cf. 4029 + 3378]

Kenaniah [1]

1Ch 15:27 as were the singers, and **Kenaniah**, who was in charge of the

4041 כְּנַנְיָהוּ **k^enanyāhû**, n.pr.m. [2] [√ 4039; cf. 4029 + 3378]

Kenaniah [2]

1Ch 15:22 **Kenaniah** the head Levite was in charge of the singing; that was
26:29 **Kenaniah** and his sons were assigned duties away from the

4042 כָּנַנְיָהוּ **kānanyāhû**, n.pr.m. [3] [√ 3378 + 3922]

Conaniah [3]

2Ch 31:12 **Conaniah**, [K 3925] a Levite, was in charge of these things,
31:13 and Benaiah were supervisors under **Conaniah** [K 3925]
35: 9 Also **Conaniah** [K 3925] along with Shemaiah and Nethanel,

4043 כָּנַס **kānas**, v. [11] [→ 4829; Ar 10359]

gather [3], gathers [2], amassed [1], assemble [1], bring [1], gather together [1], storing up wealth [1], wrap around [1]

1Ch 22: 2 [A] So David gave orders to **assemble** the aliens living in Israel,
Ne 12:44 [A] From the fields around the towns they were to **bring** into the
Est 4:16 [A] "Go, **gather together** all the Jews who are in Susa, and fast
Ps 33: 7 [A] *He* **gathers** the waters of the sea into jars; he puts the deep
147: 2 [D] LORD builds up Jerusalem; *he* **gathers** the exiles of Israel.
Ecc 2: 8 [A] *I* **amassed** silver and gold for myself, and the treasure of
2:26 [A] **storing up wealth** to hand it over to the one who pleases
3: 5 [A] a time to scatter stones and a time *to* **gather** them, a time to
Isa 28:20 [F] stretch out on, the blanket too narrow *to* **wrap around** *you*.
Eze 22:21 [D] *I will* **gather** you and I will blow on you with my fiery
39:28 [D] *I will* **gather** them to their own land, not leaving any behind.

4044 כָּנַע **kāna'**, v. [36] [→ 4045]

humbled himself [5], subdued [5], humbled themselves [4], humbled yourself [3], subdue [3], humble himself [2], subjected [2], were subdued [2], *untranslated* [1], are humbled [1], humble themselves [1], humble [1], humbled [1], made subject to [+3338+9393] [1], repented [1], silence [1], was subdued [1], were subjugated [1]

Lev 26:41 [C] when their uncircumcised hearts **are humbled** and they pay
Dt 9: 3 [G] He will destroy them; he *will* **subdue** them before you.
Jdg 3:30 [C] That day Moab *was* **made subject** [+3338+9393] **to** Israel,
4:23 [G] On that day God **subdued** Jabin, the Canaanite king, before
8:28 [C] Thus Midian **was subdued** before the Israelites and did not
11:33 [C] as far as Abel Keramim. Thus Israel **subdued** Ammon.
1Sa 7:13 [C] So the Philistines **were subdued** and did not invade Israelite
2Sa 8: 1 [G] of time, David defeated the Philistines and **subdued** them,
1Ki 21:29 [C] "Have you noticed how Ahab *has* **humbled himself** before
21:29 [C] Because *he has* **humbled himself**, I will not bring this
2Ki 22:19 [C] *you* **humbled yourself** before the LORD when you heard
1Ch 17:10 [G] *I will* also **subdue** all your enemies. " 'I declare to you that
18: 1 [G] David defeated the Philistines and **subdued** them, and he
20: 4 [C] of the Rephaites, and the Philistines **were subjugated**.
2Ch 7:14 [C] *will* **humble themselves** and pray and seek my face and turn
12: 6 [C] leaders of Israel and the king **humbled themselves** and said,
12: 7 [C] When the LORD saw that *they* **humbled themselves**,
12: 7 [C] "Since *they have* **humbled themselves**, I will not destroy
12:12 [C] Because Rehoboam **humbled himself**, the LORD's anger
13:18 [C] The men of Israel **were subdued** on that occasion,
28:19 [G] The LORD *had* **humbled** Judah because of Ahaz king of
30:11 [C] Manasseh and Zebulun **humbled themselves** and went to
32:26 [C] Hezekiah **repented** of the pride of his heart, as did the people
33:12 [C] and **humbled himself** greatly before the God of his fathers.
33:19 [C] set up Asherah poles and idols before he **humbled himself**—
33:23 [C] unlike **[RPH]** his father Manasseh, he did not humble
33:23 [C] *he did* not **humble himself** before the LORD;
34:27 [C] *you* **humbled yourself** before God when you heard what he
34:27 [C] because *you* **humbled yourself** before me and tore your
36:12 [C] and *did* not **humble himself** before Jeremiah the prophet,
Ne 9:24 [G] *You* **subdued** before them the Canaanites, who lived in the
Job 40:12 [G] look at every proud man and **humble** him, crush the wicked
Ps 81:14 [81:15] [G] how quickly *would I* **subdue** their enemies and turn
106:42 [C] enemies oppressed them and **subjected** *them* to their power.
107:12 [G] So *he* **subjected** them to bitter labor; they stumbled,
Isa 25: 5 [G] *You* **silence** the uproar of foreigners; as heat is reduced by

4045 כִּנְעָה **kin'â**, n.f. [1] [√ 4044]

belongings [1]

Jer 10:17 Gather up your **belongings** to leave the land, you who live under

4046 כְּנַעַן ***k[e]na'an[1]***, n.pr.m. & loc. [89] [→ 4049?, 4050]

Canaan [51], Canaan [+824] [29], Canaanite [5], *untranslated* [1], him[s] [+3296+4889] [1], Phoenicia [1], there[s] [+824+2025] [1]

Ge 9: 18 were Shem, Ham and Japheth. (Ham was the father of **Canaan**.)
9: 22 Ham, the father of **Canaan**, saw his father's nakedness and told his
9: 25 he said, "Cursed be **Canaan**! The lowest of slaves will he be to his
9: 26 the LORD, the God of Shem! May **Canaan** be the slave of Shem.
9: 27 Japheth live in the tents of Shem, and may **Canaan** be his slave."
10: 6 The sons of Ham: Cush, Mizraim, Put and **Canaan**.
10: 15 **Canaan** was the father of Sidon his firstborn, and of the Hittites,
11: 31 they set out from Ur of the Chaldeans to go to **Canaan** [+824].
12: 5 and they set out for the land of **Canaan**, and they arrived there.
12: 5 out for the land of Canaan, and they arrived **there**[s] [+824+2025].
13: 12 Abram lived in the land of **Canaan**, while Lot lived among the
16: 3 So after Abram had been living in **Canaan** [+824] ten years,
17: 8 The whole land of **Canaan**, where you are now an alien, I will give
23: 2 in the land of **Canaan**, and Abraham went to mourn for Sarah
23: 19 near Mamre (which is at Hebron) in the land of **Canaan**.
28: 1 and commanded him: "Do not marry a **Canaanite** woman.
28: 6 him he commanded him, "Do not marry a **Canaanite** woman,"
28: 8 realized how displeasing the **Canaanite** women were to his father
31: 18 in Paddan Aram, to go to his father Isaac in the land of **Canaan**.
33: 18 he arrived safely at the city of Shechem in **Canaan** [+824]
35: 6 with him came to Luz (that is, Bethel) in the land of **Canaan**.
36: 2 Esau took his wives from the women of **Canaan**: Adah daughter of
36: 5 were the sons of Esau, who were born to him in **Canaan** [+824].
36: 6 other animals and all the goods he had acquired in **Canaan** [+824],
37: 1 lived in the land where his father had stayed, the land of **Canaan**.
42: 5 went to buy grain, for the famine was in the land of **Canaan** also.
42: 7 he asked. "From the land of **Canaan**," they replied, "to buy food."
42: 13 the sons of one man, who lives in the land of **Canaan**.
42: 29 When they came to their father Jacob in the land of **Canaan**,
42: 32 and the youngest is now with our father in **Canaan** [+824].'
44: 8 We even brought back to you from the land of **Canaan** the silver
45: 17 'Do this: Load your animals and return to the land of **Canaan**,
45: 25 out of Egypt and came to their father Jacob in the land of **Canaan**.
46: 6 and the possessions they had acquired in **Canaan** [+824],
46: 12 and Zerah (but Er and Onan had died in the land of **Canaan**).
46: 31 who were living in the land of **Canaan**, have come to me.
47: 1 have come from the land of **Canaan** and are now in Goshen."
47: 4 because the famine is severe in **Canaan** [+824] and your servants'
47: 13 both Egypt and **Canaan** [+824] wasted away because of the
47: 14 and **Canaan** [+824] in payment for the grain they were buying,
47: 15 the money of the people of Egypt and **Canaan** [+824] was gone,
48: 3 "God Almighty appeared to me at Luz in the land of **Canaan**,
48: 7 to my sorrow Rachel died in the land of **Canaan** while we were
49: 30 the cave in the field of Machpelah, near Mamre in **Canaan** [+824],
50: 5 bury me in the tomb I dug for myself in the land of **Canaan**."
50: 13 They carried him to the land of **Canaan** and buried him in the cave
Ex 6: 4 my covenant with them to give them the land of **Canaan**,
15: 15 be seized with trembling, the people of **Canaan** will melt away;
16: 35 they ate manna until they reached the border of **Canaan** [+824].
Lev 14: 34 "When you enter the land of **Canaan**, which I am giving you as
18: 3 used to live, and you must not do as they do in the land of **Canaan**,
25: 38 who brought you out of Egypt to give you the land of **Canaan**
Nu 13: 2 "Send some men to explore the land of **Canaan**, which I am giving
13: 17 When Moses sent them to explore **Canaan** [+824], he said,
26: 19 and Onan were sons of Judah, but they died in **Canaan** [+824].
32: 30 they must accept their possession with you in **Canaan** [+824]."
32: 32 We will cross over before the LORD into **Canaan** [+824] armed,
33: 40 king of Arad, who lived in the Negev of **Canaan** [+824],
33: 51 and say to them: 'When you cross the Jordan into **Canaan** [+824],
34: 2 'When you enter **Canaan** [+824], the land that will be allotted to
34: 2 to you as an inheritance will have these boundaries: **[RPH]**
34: 29 to assign the inheritance to the Israelites in the land of **Canaan**.
35: 10 and say to them: 'When you cross the Jordan into **Canaan** [+824],
35: 14 side of the Jordan and three in **Canaan** [+824] as cities of refuge.
Dt 32: 49 to Mount Nebo in Moab, across from Jericho, and view **Canaan**,
Jos 5: 12 but that year they ate of the produce of **Canaan** [+824].
14: 1 the Israelites received as an inheritance in the land of **Canaan**,
21: 2 at Shiloh in **Canaan** [+824] and said to them, "The LORD
22: 9 left the Israelites at Shiloh in **Canaan** [+824] to return to Gilead,
22: 10 When they came to Geliloth near the Jordan in the land of **Canaan**,
22: 11 of **Canaan** [+824] at Geliloth near the Jordan on the Israelite side,
22: 32 the leaders returned to **Canaan** [+824] from their meeting with the
24: 3 led him throughout **Canaan** [+824] and gave him many
Jdg 3: 1 Israelites who had not experienced any of the wars in **Canaan**
4: 2 into the hands of Jabin, a king of **Canaan**, who reigned in Hazor.
4: 23 day God subdued Jabin, the **Canaanite** king, before the Israelites.
4: 24 against Jabin, the **Canaanite** king, until they destroyed him.
4: 24 the Canaanite king, until they destroyed **him**[s] [+3296+4889].
5: 19 the kings of **Canaan** fought at Taanach by the waters of Megiddo,
21: 12 and they took them to the camp at Shiloh in **Canaan** [+824].
1Ch 1: 8 The sons of Ham: Cush, Mizraim, Put and **Canaan**.
1: 13 **Canaan** was the father of Sidon his firstborn, and of the Hittites,
16: 18 "To you I will give the land of **Canaan** as the portion you will
Ps 105: 11 "To you I will give the land of **Canaan** as the portion you will
106: 38 and daughters, whom they sacrificed to the idols of **Canaan**,
135: 11 of the Amorites, Og king of Bashan and all the kings of **Canaan**—
Isa 19: 18 In that day five cities in Egypt will speak the language of **Canaan**
23: 11 He has given an order concerning **Phoenicia** that her fortresses be
Zep 2: 5 of the LORD is against you, O **Canaan**, land of the Philistines.

4047 [2]כְּנַעַן ***k[e]na'an[2]***, n.[m.]. [4] [→ 4048, 4051]

merchants [2], merchant [1], merchants [+6639] [1]

Eze 16: 29 a land of **merchants**, but even with this you were not satisfied.
17: 4 off its topmost shoot and carried it away to a land of **merchants**,
Hos 12: 7 [12:8] The **merchant** uses dishonest scales; he loves to defraud.
Zep 1: 11 all your **merchants** [+6639] will be wiped out, all who trade with

4048 כִּנְעָן ***kin'ān***, n.m. [1] [√ 4047]

traders [1]

Isa 23: 8 merchants are princes, whose **traders** are renowned in the earth?

4049 כְּנַעֲנָה ***k[e]na'anâ***, n.pr.m. [5] [√ 4046?]

Kenaanah [5]

1Ki 22: 11 Now Zedekiah son of **Kenaanah** had made iron horns and he
22: 24 Zedekiah son of **Kenaanah** went up and slapped Micaiah in the
1Ch 7: 10 Benjamin, Ehud, **Kenaanah**, Zethan, Tarshish and Ahishahar.
2Ch 18: 10 Now Zedekiah son of **Kenaanah** had made iron horns, and he
18: 23 Zedekiah son of **Kenaanah** went up and slapped Micaiah in the

4050 כְּנַעֲנִי ***k[e]na'anî[1]***, a.g. [71] [√ 4046]

Canaanites [56], Canaanite [13], Canaan [1], in Canaan [1]

Ge 10: 18 Zemarites and Hamathites. Later the **Canaanite** clans scattered
10: 19 the borders of **Canaan** reached from Sidon toward Gerar as far as
12: 6 Moreh at Shechem. At that time the **Canaanites** were in the land.
13: 7 The **Canaanites** and Perizzites were also living in the land at that
15: 21 Amorites, **Canaanites**, Girgashites and Jebusites."
24: 3 not get a wife for my son from the daughters of the **Canaanites**,
24: 37 not get a wife for my son from the daughters of the **Canaanites**,
34: 30 brought trouble on me by making me a stench to the **Canaanites**
38: 2 There Judah met the daughter of a **Canaanite** man named Shua.
46: 10 Ohad, Jakin, Zohar and Shaul the son of a **Canaanite** *woman*.
50: 11 When the **Canaanites** who lived there saw the mourning at the
Ex 3: 8 the home of the **Canaanites**, Hittites, Amorites, Perizzites,
3: 17 up out of your misery in Egypt into the land of the **Canaanites**,
6: 15 Ohad, Jakin, Zohar and Shaul the son of a **Canaanite** *woman*.
13: 5 When the LORD brings you into the land of the **Canaanites**,
13: 11 "After the LORD brings you into the land of the **Canaanites**
23: 23 Hittites, Perizzites, **Canaanites**, Hivites and Jebusites, and I will
23: 28 you to drive the Hivites, **Canaanites** and Hittites out of your way.
33: 2 I will send an angel before you and drive out the **Canaanites**,
34: 11 **Canaanites**, Hittites, Perizzites, Hivites and Jebusites.
Nu 13: 29 and the **Canaanites** live near the sea and along the Jordan."
14: 25 Since the Amalekites and **Canaanites** are living in the valleys,
14: 43 for the Amalekites and **Canaanites** will face you there.
14: 45 and **Canaanites** who lived in that hill country came down
21: 1 When the **Canaanite** king of Arad, who lived in the Negev,
21: 3 listened to Israel's plea and gave the **Canaanites** over to them.
33: 40 The **Canaanite** king of Arad, who lived in the Negev of Canaan,
Dt 1: 7 and along the coast, to the land of the **Canaanites** and to Lebanon,
7: 1 **Canaanites**, Perizzites, Hivites and Jebusites,
11: 30 in the territory of those **Canaanites** living in the Arabah in the
20: 17 Amorites, **Canaanites**, Perizzites, Hivites and Jebusites—
Jos 3: 10 and that he will certainly drive out before you the **Canaanites**,
5: 1 all the **Canaanite** kings along the coast heard how the LORD had
7: 9 The **Canaanites** and the other people of the country will hear
9: 1 Amorites, **Canaanites**, Perizzites, Hivites and Jebusites)—
11: 3 to the **Canaanites** in the east and west; to the Amorites, Hittites,
12: 8 Amorites, **Canaanites**, Perizzites, Hivites and Jebusites):
13: 3 all of it counted as **Canaanite** (the territory of the five Philistine
13: 4 from the south, all the land of the **Canaanites**, from Arah of the
16: 10 They did not dislodge the **Canaanites** living in Gezer; to this day
16: 10 to this day the **Canaanites** live among the people of Ephraim
17: 12 for the **Canaanites** were determined to live in that region.
17: 13 they subjected the **Canaanites** to forced labor but did not drive
17: 16 and all the **Canaanites** who live in the plain have iron chariots,
17: 18 though the **Canaanites** have iron chariots and though they are
24: 11 Perizzites, **Canaanites**, Hittites, Girgashites, Hivites and Jebusites,
Jdg 1: 1 will be the first to go up and fight for us against the **Canaanites**?"
1: 3 us into the territory allotted to us, to fight against the **Canaanites**.
1: 4 the LORD gave the **Canaanites** and Perizzites into their hands
1: 5 fought against him, putting to rout the **Canaanites** and Perizzites.

Jdg 1: 9 the men of Judah went down to fight against the **Canaanites** living
1: 10 They advanced against the **Canaanites** living in Hebron (formerly
1: 17 their brothers and attacked the **Canaanites** living in Zephath,
1: 27 for the **Canaanites** were determined to live in that land.
1: 28 they pressed the **Canaanites** into forced labor but never drove
1: 29 Nor did Ephraim drive out the **Canaanites** living in Gezer,
1: 29 in Gezer, but the **Canaanites** continued to live there among them.
1: 30 Neither did Zebulun drive out the **Canaanites** living in Kitron
1: 32 because of this the people of Asher lived among the **Canaanite**
1: 33 the Naphtalites too lived among the **Canaanite** inhabitants of the
3: 3 the five rulers of the Philistines, all the **Canaanites**, the Sidonians,
3: 5 The Israelites lived among the **Canaanites**, Hittites, Amorites,
2Sa 24: 7 fortress of Tyre and all the towns of the Hivites and **Canaanites**.
1Ki 9: 16 He killed its **Canaanite** inhabitants and then gave it as a wedding
1Ch 2: 3 These three were born to him by a **Canaanite** *woman*,
Ezr 9: 1 like those of the **Canaanites**, Hittites, Perizzites, Jebusites,
Ne 9: 8 with him to give to his descendants the land of the **Canaanites**,
9: 24 You subdued before them the **Canaanites**, who lived in the land;
Eze 16: 3 Your ancestry and birth were in the land of the **Canaanites**;
Ob 1: 20 This company of Israelite exiles who are **in Canaan** will possess
Zec 14: 21 on that day there will no longer be a **Canaanite** in the house of the

4051 כְּנַעֲנִי² **k^{e}naʿ^{a}nî^2**, n.m. [2] [√ 4047]

merchants [2]

Job 41: 6 [40:30] for him? Will they divide him up among the **merchants**?
Pr 31: 24 and sells them, and supplies the **merchants** with sashes.

4052 כָּנַף **kānap**, v.den. [1] [√ 4053]

hidden [1]

Isa 30: 20 [C] the water of affliction, your teachers *will be* **hidden** no more;

4053 כָּנָף **kānāp**, n.f. [109] [→ 4052]

wings [56], wing [14], corner [3], corners [3], *untranslated* [2], corner of garment [2], ends [2], flying [2], fold [2], them^s [+2157] [2], bird [+7606] [1], bird on the wing [+1251] [1], birds [+1251] [1], birds [+7606] [1], clothes [1], dishonor bed [+1655] [1], dishonors bed [+1655] [1], each^s [1], edges [1], folds of garment [1], hem of robe [1], hem [1], kind^s [1], kinds^s [1], other^s [1], piece [1], quarters [1], sweep away [+906+928+7674] [1], those^s [1], total wingspan [+802] [1], winged [1]

Ge 1: 21 to their kinds, and every **winged** bird according to its kind.
7: 14 and every bird according to its kind, everything with **wings**.
Ex 19: 4 and how I carried you on eagles' **wings** and brought you to myself.
25: 20 The cherubim are to have their **wings** spread upward,
25: 20 spread upward, overshadowing the cover with **them**^{s} [+2157].
37: 9 The cherubim had their **wings** spread upward, overshadowing the
37: 9 spread upward, overshadowing the cover with **them**^{s} [+2157].
Lev 1: 17 He shall tear it open by the **wings**, not severing it completely,
Nu 15: 38 to come you are to make tassels on the **corners** *of* your garments,
15: 38 corners of your garments, with a blue cord on each tassel. **[RPH]**
Dt 4: 17 or like any animal on earth or any **bird** [+7606] that flies in the air,
22: 12 Make tassels on the four **corners** *of* the cloak you wear.
22: 30 [23:1] *he must* not **dishonor** his father's **bed** [+1655].
27: 20 with his father's wife, for *he* **dishonors** his father's **bed** [+1655]."
32: 11 that spreads its **wings** to catch them and carries them on its pinions.
Ru 2: 12 God of Israel, under whose **wings** you have come to take refuge."
3: 9 "Spread the **corner of** your **garment** over me, since you are a
1Sa 15: 27 to leave, Saul caught hold of the **hem** *of* his robe, and it tore.
24: 4 [24:5] crept up unnoticed and cut off a **corner** *of* Saul's robe.
24: 5 [24:6] conscience-stricken for having cut off a **corner** *of* his robe.
24: 11 [24:12] my father, look at this **piece** *of* your robe in my hand!
24: 11 [24:12] I cut off the **corner** *of* your robe but did not kill you.
2Sa 22: 11 the cherubim and flew; he soared on the **wings** *of* the wind.
1Ki 6: 24 One **wing** *of* the first cherub was five cubits long, and the other
6: 24 first cherub was five cubits long, and the other **wing** five cubits—
6: 24 the other wing five cubits—ten cubits from **wing** tip to wing tip.
6: 24 the other wing five cubits—ten cubits from wing tip to **wing** tip.
6: 27 the innermost room of the temple, with their **wings** spread out.
6: 27 The **wing** *of* one cherub touched one wall, while the wing of the
6: 27 one wall, while the **wing** *of* the other touched the other wall,
6: 27 and their **wings** touched each other in the middle of the room.
6: 27 and their wings touched **each**^{s} other in the middle of the room.
6: 27 and their wings touched each **other**^{s} in the middle of the room.
8: 6 the Most Holy Place, and put it beneath the **wings** *of* the cherubim.
8: 7 The cherubim spread their **wings** over the place of the ark
2Ch 3: 11 The **total wingspan** [+802] *of* the cherubim was twenty cubits.
3: 11 One **wing** *of* the first cherub was five cubits long and touched the
3: 11 touched the temple wall, while its other **wing**, also five cubits long,
3: 11 also five cubits long, touched the **wing** *of* the other cherub.
3: 12 Similarly one **wing** *of* the second cherub was five cubits long
3: 12 the other temple wall, and its other **wing**, also five cubits long,
3: 12 also five cubits long, touched the **wing** *of* the first cherub.
3: 13 The **wings** *of* these cherubim extended twenty cubits. They stood
5: 7 the Most Holy Place, and put it beneath the **wings** *of* the cherubim.
5: 8 The cherubim spread their **wings** over the place of the ark
Job 37: 3 beneath the whole heaven and sends it to the **ends** *of* the earth.
38: 13 that it might take the earth by the **edges** and shake the wicked out
39: 13 "The **wings** *of* the ostrich flap joyfully, but they cannot compare
39: 26 take flight by your wisdom and spread his **wings** toward the south?
Ps 17: 8 me as the apple of your eye; hide me in the shadow of your **wings**
18: 10 [18:11] and flew; he soared on the **wings** *of* the wind.
36: 7 [36:8] low among men find refuge in the shadow of your **wings**.
57: 1 [57:2] I will take refuge in the shadow of your **wings** until the
61: 4 [61:5] tent forever and take refuge in the shelter of your **wings**.
63: 7 [63:8] you are my help, I sing in the shadow of your **wings**.
68: 13 [68:14] the **wings** *of* ⌞my⌟ dove are sheathed with silver, its
78: 27 down on them like dust, **flying** birds like sand on the seashore.
91: 4 you with his feathers, and under his **wings** you will find refuge;
104: 3 makes the clouds his chariot and rides on the **wings** *of* the wind.
139: 9 If I rise on the **wings** *of* the dawn, if I settle on the far side of the
148: 10 wild animals and all cattle, small creatures and **flying** birds,
Pr 1: 17 How useless to spread a net in full view of all the **birds** [+1251]!
23: 5 for they will surely sprout **wings** and fly off to the sky like an
Ecc 10: 20 and a **bird on the wing** [+1251] may report what you say.
Isa 6: 2 Above him were seraphs, each with six **wings**: With two wings
6: 2 **[RPH]** With two wings they covered their faces, with two they
8: 8 Its outspread **wings** will cover the breadth of your land,
10: 14 not one flapped a **wing**, or opened its mouth to chirp.' "
11: 12 the scattered people of Judah from the four **quarters** *of* the earth.
18: 1 Woe to the land of whirring **wings** along the rivers of Cush,
24: 16 From the **ends** *of* the earth we hear singing: "Glory to the
Jer 2: 34 On your **clothes** men find the lifeblood of the innocent poor,
48: 40 An eagle is swooping down, spreading its **wings** over Moab.
49: 22 eagle will soar and swoop down, spreading its **wings** over Bozrah.
Eze 1: 6 but each of them had four faces and four **wings**.
1: 8 Under their **wings** on their four sides they had the hands of a man.
1: 8 they had the hands of a man. All four of them had faces and **wings**,
1: 9 their **wings** touched one another. Each one went straight ahead;
1: 11 Their **wings** were spread out upward; each had two wings,
1: 23 Under the expanse their **wings** were stretched out one toward the
1: 24 When the creatures moved, I heard the sound of their **wings**,
1: 24 tumult of an army. When they stood still, they lowered their **wings**.
1: 25 the expanse over their heads as they stood with lowered **wings**.
3: 13 the sound of the **wings** *of* the living creatures brushing against each
5: 3 strands of hair and tuck them away in the **folds of** your **garment**.
7: 2 The end! The end has come upon the four **corners** *of* the land.
10: 5 The sound of the **wings** *of* the cherubim could be heard as far away
10: 8 (Under the **wings** of the cherubim could be seen what looked like
10: 12 entire bodies, including their backs, their hands and their **wings**,
10: 16 and when the cherubim spread their **wings** to rise from the ground,
10: 19 the cherubim spread their **wings** and rose from the ground,
10: 21 Each had four faces and four **wings**, and under their wings was
10: 21 and under their **wings** was what looked like the hands of a man.
11: 22 the cherubim, with the wheels beside them, spread their **wings**,
16: 8 I spread the **corner of** my **garment** over you and covered your
17: 3 A great eagle with powerful **wings**, long feathers and full plumage
17: 7 " 'But there was another great eagle with powerful **wings** and full
17: 23 **Birds** [+7606] of every kind will nest in it; they will find shelter in
39: 4 I will give you as food to all **kinds**^{s} *of* carrion birds and to the wild
39: 17 Call out to every **kind**^{s} *of* bird and all the wild animals: 'Assemble
Da 9: 27 on a **wing** ⌞*of* the temple⌟ he will set up an abomination that causes
Hos 4: 19 A whirlwind *will* **sweep** them **away** [+906+928+7674], and their
Hag 2: 12 If a person carries consecrated meat in the **fold** *of* his garment,
2: 12 that **fold** touches some bread or stew, some wine, oil or other food,
Zec 5: 9 there before me were two women, with the wind in their **wings**!
5: 9 They had **wings** like those of a stork, and they lifted up the basket
5: 9 They had wings like **those**^{s} *of* a stork, and they lifted up the basket
8: 23 and nations will take firm hold of one Jew by the **hem of** his **robe**
Mal 4: 2 [3:20] the sun of righteousness will rise with healing in its **wings**.

4054 כנרות **kinrôt**, כִּנֲרוֹת **kin^{a}rôt**, n.pr.loc. [3] [→ 4055]

Kinnereth [3]

Jos 11: 2 in the Arabah south of **Kinnereth**, in the western foothills
12: 3 He also ruled over the eastern Arabah from the Sea of **Kinnereth**
1Ki 15: 20 Abel Beth Maacah and all **Kinnereth** in addition to Naphtali.

4055 כִּנֶּרֶת **kinneret**, n.pr.loc. [4] [√ 4054]

Kinnereth [4]

Nu 34: 11 and continue along the slopes east of the Sea of **Kinnereth**.
Dt 3: 17 from **Kinnereth** to the Sea of the Arabah (the Salt Sea),
Jos 13: 27 of the Jordan, the territory up to the end of the Sea of **Kinnereth**).
19: 35 fortified cities were Ziddim, Zer, Hammath, Rakkath, **Kinnereth**,

4056 כְּנָת kᵉnāt, n.f. [1] [→ Ar 10360]

associates [1]

Ezr 4: 7 Tabeel and the rest of his **associates** wrote a letter to Artaxerxes.

4057 כֶּסֶא kese', n.[m.]. [2 / 3] [→ 4060, 4061]

full moon [+3427] [1], full moon [1], moon full [1]

Job 26: 9 He covers the face of the **full moon**, [BHS 4061] spreading his
Ps 81: 3 [81:4] and when the **moon** is **full**, on the day of our Feast;
Pr 7: 20 filled with money and will not be home till **full moon** [+3427]."

4058 כִּסֵּא kissē', n.m. [135] [→ 4066; Ar 10372]

throne [110], thrones [8], chair [4], seat of honor [3], seat [3], those[s] [2], *untranslated* [1], authority [1], enthrones [+2021+3782+4200] [1], it[s] [+2021] [1], its[s] [+2021+4200] [1]

Ge 41: 40 Only with respect to the **throne** will I be greater than you."
Ex 11: 5 from the firstborn son of Pharaoh, who sits on the **throne**,
12: 29 from the firstborn of Pharaoh, who sat on the **throne**,
17: 16 He said, "For hands were lifted up to the **throne** *of* the LORD.
Dt 17: 18 When he takes the **throne** *of* his kingdom, he is to write for
Jdg 3: 20 have a message from God for you." As the king rose from his **seat**,
1Sa 1: 9 Now Eli the priest was sitting on a **chair** by the doorpost of the
2: 8 he seats them with princes and has them inherit a **throne** *of* honor.
4: 13 there was Eli sitting on his **chair** *by* the side of the road, watching,
4: 18 ark of God, Eli fell backward off his **chair** by the side of the gate.
2Sa 3: 10 establish David's **throne** over Israel and Judah from Dan to
7: 13 my Name, and I will establish the **throne** *of* his kingdom forever.
7: 16 forever before me; your **throne** will be established forever.' "
14: 9 father's family, and let the king and his **throne** be without guilt."
1Ki 1: 13 your son shall be king after me, and he will sit on my **throne**"?
1: 17 your son shall be king after me, and he will sit on my **throne**.'
1: 20 to learn from you who will sit on the **throne** *of* my lord the king
1: 24 shall be king after you, and that he will sit on your **throne**?
1: 27 know who should sit on the **throne** *of* my lord the king after him?"
1: 30 shall be king after me, and he will sit on my **throne** in my place."
1: 35 and he is to come and sit on my **throne** and reign in my place.
1: 37 so may he be with Solomon to make his **throne** even greater than
1: 37 his throne even greater than the **throne** *of* my lord King David!"
1: 46 Moreover, Solomon has taken his seat on the royal **throne**.
1: 47 name more famous than yours and his **throne** greater than yours!'
1: 47 than yours!' **[RPH]** And the king bowed in worship on his bed
1: 48 who has allowed my eyes to see a successor on my **throne**
2: 4 and soul, you will never fail to have a man on the **throne** *of* Israel.'
2: 12 So Solomon sat on the **throne** *of* his father David, and his rule was
2: 19 up to meet her, bowed down to her and sat down on his **throne**.
2: 19 He had a **throne** brought for the king's mother, and she sat down
2: 24 he who has established me securely on the **throne** *of* my father
2: 33 But on David and his descendants, his house and his **throne**,
2: 45 David's **throne** will remain secure before the LORD forever."
3: 6 and have given him a son to sit on his **throne** this very day.
5: 5 [5:19] 'Your son whom I will put on the **throne** in your place will
7: 7 He built the **throne** hall, the Hall of Justice, where he was to judge,
8: 20 succeeded David my father and now I sit on the **throne** *of* Israel,
8: 25 never fail to have a man to sit before me on the **throne** *of* Israel,
9: 5 I will establish your royal **throne** over Israel forever, as I promised
9: 5 'You shall never fail to have a man on the **throne** *of* Israel.'
10: 9 who has delighted in you and placed you on the **throne** *of* Israel.
10: 18 the king made a great **throne** *inlaid with* ivory and overlaid with
10: 19 The **throne** had six steps, and its back had a rounded top. On both
10: 19 had six steps, and **its**[s] [+2021+4200] back had a rounded top.
16: 11 As soon as he began to reign and was seated on the **throne**,
22: 10 Jehoshaphat king of Judah were sitting on their **thrones** at the
22: 19 I saw the LORD sitting on his **throne** with all the host of heaven
2Ki 4: 10 and put in it a bed and a table, a **chair** and a lamp for him.
10: 3 worthy of your master's sons and set him on his father's **throne**.
10: 30 your descendants will sit on the **throne** *of* Israel to the fourth
11: 19 of the guards. The king then took his place on the royal **throne**,
13: 13 with his fathers, and Jeroboam succeeded him on the **throne**.
15: 12 "Your descendants will sit on the **throne** *of* Israel to the fourth
25: 28 gave him a **seat of honor** higher than those of the other kings who
25: 28 gave him a seat of honor higher than **those**[s] *of* the other kings who
1Ch 17: 12 will build a house for me, and I will establish his **throne** forever.
17: 14 and my kingdom forever; his **throne** will be established forever.' "
22: 10 And I will establish the **throne** *of* his kingdom over Israel forever.'
28: 5 he has chosen my son Solomon to sit on the **throne** *of* the kingdom
29: 23 So Solomon sat on the **throne** *of* the LORD as king in place of
2Ch 6: 10 succeeded David my father and now I sit on the **throne** *of* Israel,
6: 16 never fail to have a man to sit before me on the **throne** *of* Israel,
7: 18 I will establish your royal **throne**, as I covenanted with David your
9: 8 placed you on his **throne** as king to rule for the LORD your God.
9: 17 the king made a great **throne** *inlaid with* ivory and overlaid with
9: 18 The **throne** had six steps, and a footstool of gold was attached to it.
9: 18 had six steps, and a footstool of gold was attached to **it**[s] [+2021].
18: 9 Jehoshaphat king of Judah were sitting on their **thrones** at the
18: 18 I saw the LORD sitting on his **throne** with all the host of heaven
23: 20 through the Upper Gate and seated the king on the royal **throne**,
Ne 3: 7 places under the **authority** *of* the governor of Trans-Euphrates.
Est 1: 2 At that time King Xerxes reigned from his royal **throne** in the
3: 1 giving him a **seat of honor** higher than that of all the other nobles.
5: 1 The king was sitting on his royal **throne** in the hall, facing the
Job 36: 7 He does not take his eyes off the righteous; *he* **enthrones** [+2021+3782+4200] them with kings and exalts them forever.
Ps 9: 4 [9:5] my cause; you have sat on your **throne**, judging righteously.
9: 7 [9:8] reigns forever; he has established his **throne** for judgment.
11: 4 is in his holy temple; the LORD is on his heavenly **throne**.
45: 6 [45:7] Your **throne**, O God, will last for ever and ever; a scepter
47: 8 [47:9] reigns over the nations; God is seated on his holy **throne**.
89: 4 [89:5] make your **throne** firm through all generations.' " *Selah*
89: 14 [89:15] and justice are the foundation of your **throne**;
89: 29 [89:30] his line forever, his **throne** as long as the heavens endure.
89: 36 [89:37] and his **throne** endure before me like the sun;
89: 44 [89:45] an end to his splendor and cast his **throne** to the ground.
93: 2 Your **throne** was established long ago; you are from all eternity.
94: 20 Can a corrupt **throne** be allied with you—one that brings on
97: 2 righteousness and justice are the foundation of his **throne**.
103: 19 The LORD has established his **throne** in heaven, and his
122: 5 There the **thrones** for judgment stand, the thrones of the house of
122: 5 the thrones for judgment stand, the **thrones** of the house of David.
132: 11 "One of your own descendants I will place on your **throne**—
132: 12 then their sons will sit on your **throne** for ever and ever."
Pr 9: 14 at the door of her house, on a **seat** *at* the highest point of the city,
16: 12 for a **throne** is established through righteousness.
20: 8 When a king sits on his **throne** to judge, he winnows out all evil
20: 28 keep a king safe; through love his **throne** is made secure.
25: 5 and his **throne** will be established through righteousness.
29: 14 judges the poor with fairness, his **throne** will always be secure.
Isa 6: 1 Uzziah died, I saw the Lord seated on a **throne**, high and exalted,
9: 7 [9:6] He will reign on David's **throne** and over his kingdom,
14: 9 were leaders in the world; it makes them rise from their **thrones**—
14: 13 ascend to heaven; I will raise my **throne** above the stars of God;
16: 5 In love a **throne** will be established; in faithfulness a man will sit
22: 23 a firm place; he will be a **seat** *of* honor for the house of his father.
47: 1 sit on the ground without a **throne**, Daughter of the Babylonians.
66: 1 LORD says: "Heaven is my **throne**, and the earth is my footstool.
Jer 1: 15 and set up their **thrones** in the entrance of the gates of Jerusalem;
3: 17 At that time they will call Jerusalem The **Throne** *of* the LORD,
13: 13 including the kings who sit on David's **throne**, the priests,
14: 21 name do not despise us; do not dishonor your glorious **throne**.
17: 12 A glorious **throne**, exalted from the beginning, is the place of our
17: 25 kings who sit on David's **throne** will come through the gates of
22: 2 of the LORD, O king of Judah, you who sit on David's **throne**—
22: 4 kings who sit on David's **throne** will come through the gates of
22: 30 none will sit on the **throne** *of* David or rule anymore in Judah."
29: 16 what the LORD says about the king who sits on David's **throne**
33: 17 'David will never fail to have a man to sit on the **throne** *of* the
33: 21 and David will no longer have a descendant to reign on his **throne**.
36: 30 He will have no one to sit on the **throne** *of* David; his body will be
43: 10 and I will set his **throne** over these stones I have buried here;
49: 38 I will set my **throne** in Elam and destroy her king and officials,"
52: 32 gave him a **seat of honor** higher than those of the other kings who
52: 32 gave him a seat of honor higher than **those**[s] *of* the other kings who
La 5: 19 reign forever; your **throne** endures from generation to generation.
Eze 1: 26 Above the expanse over their heads was what looked like a **throne**
1: 26 and high above on the **throne** was a figure like that of a man.
10: 1 I saw the likeness of a **throne** of sapphire above the expanse that
26: 16 Then all the princes of the coast will step down from their **thrones**
43: 7 this is the place of my **throne** and the place for the soles of my
Jnh 3: 6 he rose from his **throne**, took off his royal robes, covered himself
Hag 2: 22 I will overturn royal **thrones** and shatter the power of the foreign
Zec 6: 13 he will be clothed with majesty and will sit and rule on his **throne**.
6: 13 and rule on his throne. And he will be a priest on his **throne**.

4059 כָּסָה kāsâ, v. [152] [→ 4062, 4064, 4832, 4833]

covered [37], cover [26], covers [15], covering [7], decorating [4], be covered [3], cover [+906+4832] [3], cover up [3], hide [3], put on [3], wearing [3], were covered [3], around [2], clothed [2], conceal [2], concealed [2], conceals [2], keeps [2], overwhelms [2], provides [2], put over [2], *untranslated* [1], are covered [1], bathing [1], blindfolds [+7156] [1], buried [1], closed [1], clothe [1], cover themselves [1], cover up [+906+2256+8740] [1], covered herself [1], covered up [1], covers over [1], decorate [1], engulfed [1], fills [1], flood [1], is shrouded [1], keep [1], overlooks [1], overwhelm [1], overwhelmed [1], shield [1], was covered [1], wear [1]

Ge 7: 19 [E] the high mountains under the entire heavens **were covered**.
7: 20 [E] **covered** the mountains to a depth of more than twenty feet.

[A] Qal [B] Qal passive [C] Niphal [D] Piel (poel, polel, pilel, pilal, pealal, pilpel) [E] Pual (poal, polal, poaal, pulal, pualal)

Ge 9:23 [D] walked in backward and **covered** their father's nakedness.
18:17 [D] "*Shall* I **hide** from Abraham what I am about to do?
24:65 [F] servant answered. So she took her veil and **covered herself**.
37:26 [D] will we gain if we kill our brother and **cover up** his blood?
38:14 [D] **covered** *herself* with a veil to disguise herself, and then sat
38:15 [D] thought she was a prostitute, for *she had* **covered** her face.
Ex 8:6 [8:2] [D] of Egypt, and the frogs came up and **covered** the land.
10:5 [D] *They will* **cover** the face of the ground so that it cannot be
10:15 [D] *They* **covered** all the ground until it was black. They
14:28 [D] water flowed back and **covered** the chariots and horsemen—
15:5 [D] The deep waters *have* **covered** them; they sank to the depths
15:10 [D] But you blew with your breath, and the sea **covered** them.
16:13 [D] That evening quail came and **covered** the camp, and in the
21:33 [D] or digs one and fails *to* **cover** it and an ox or a donkey falls
24:15 [D] When Moses went up on the mountain, the cloud **covered** it,
24:16 [D] For six days the cloud **covered** the mountain, and on the
26:13 [D] will hang over the sides of the tabernacle so as to **cover** it.
28:42 [D] "Make linen undergarments as a **covering** *for* the body,
29:13 [D] take all the fat **around** the inner parts, the covering of the
29:22 [D] the fat tail, the fat **around** the inner parts, the covering of the
40:34 [D] the cloud **covered** the Tent of Meeting, and the glory of the
Lev 3:3 [D] all the fat that **covers** the inner parts or is connected to them,
3:9 [D] all the fat that **covers** the inner parts or is connected to them,
3:14 [D] all the fat that **covers** the inner parts or is connected to them,
4:8 [D] the fat that **covers** the inner parts or is connected to them,
7:3 [D] be offered: the fat tail and the fat that **covers** the inner parts,
13:12 [D] it **covers** all the skin of the infected person from head to foot,
13:13 [D] examine him, and if the disease *has* **covered** his whole body,
16:13 [D] the smoke of the incense *will* **conceal** the atonement cover
17:13 [D] be eaten must drain out the blood and **cover** it with earth,
Nu 4:5 [D] shielding curtain and **cover** the ark of the Testimony with it.
4:8 [D] **cover** [+906+4832] that with hides of sea cows and put its
4:9 [D] **cover** the lampstand that is for light, together with its lamps,
4:11 [D] **cover** [+906+4832] that with hides of sea cows and put its
4:12 [D] **cover** [+906+4832] that with hides of sea cows and put them
4:15 [D] his sons have finished **covering** the holy furnishings and all
9:15 [D] the Tent of the Testimony, was set up, the cloud **covered** it.
9:16 [D] to be; the cloud **covered** it, and at night it looked like fire.
16:33 [D] the earth **closed** over them, and they perished and were gone
16:42 [17:7] [D] suddenly the cloud **covered** it and the glory of the
22:5 [D] *they* **cover** the face of the land and have settled next to me.
22:11 [D] 'A people that has come out of Egypt **covers** the face of the
Dt 13:8 [13:9] [D] Show him no pity. Do not spare him or **shield** him.
22:12 [D] Make tassels on the four corners of the cloak *you* **wear**.
23:13 [23:14] [D] and **cover** [+906+2256+8740] **up** your excrement.
Jos 24:7 [D] he brought the sea over them and **covered** them.
Jdg 4:18 [D] So he entered her tent, and *she* **put** a covering **over** him.
4:19 [D] a skin of milk, gave him a drink, and **covered** him **up**.
1Sa 19:13 [D] **covering** it with a garment and putting some goats' hair at the
1Ki 1:1 [D] he could not keep warm even when *they* **put** covers **over**
7:18 [D] each network to **decorate** the capitals on top of the pillars.
7:41 [D] the two sets of network **decorating** the two bowl-shaped
7:42 [D] **decorating** the bowl-shaped capitals on top of the pillars);
11:29 [F] prophet of Shiloh met him on the way, **wearing** a new cloak.
2Ki 19:1 [F] he tore his clothes and **put on** sackcloth and went into the
19:2 [F] the secretary and the leading priests, *all* **wearing** sackcloth,
1Ch 21:16 [E] and the elders, **clothed** in sackcloth, fell facedown.
2Ch 4:12 [D] the two sets of network **decorating** the two bowl-shaped
4:13 [D] **decorating** the bowl-shaped capitals on top of the pillars);
5:8 [D] place of the ark and **covered** the ark and its carrying poles.
Ne 4:5 [3:37] [D] *Do* not **cover up** their guilt or blot out their sins from
Job 9:24 [D] the hands of the wicked, *he* **blindfolds** [+7156] its judges.
15:27 [D] "Though his face *is* **covered** with fat and his waist bulges
16:18 [D] "O earth, *do* not **cover** my blood; may my cry never be laid
21:26 [D] Side by side they lie in the dust, and worms **cover** them both.
22:11 [D] so dark you cannot see, and why a flood of water **covers** you.
23:17 [D] by the darkness, by the thick darkness *that* **covers** my face.
31:33 [D] if *I have* **concealed** my sin as men do, by hiding my guilt in
33:17 [D] to turn man from wrongdoing and **keep** him from pride,
36:30 [D] his lightning about him, **bathing** the depths of the sea.
36:32 [D] *He* **fills** his hands *with* lightning and commands it to strike
38:34 [D] voice to the clouds and **cover** yourself *with* a flood of water?
Ps 32:1 [B] whose transgressions are forgiven, *whose* sins **are covered**.
32:5 [D] my sin to you and *did* not **cover up** my iniquity.
40:10 [40:11] [D] *I do* not **hide** your righteousness in my heart;
44:15 [44:16] [D] all day long, and my face *is* **covered** *with* shame
44:19 [44:20] [D] for jackals and **covered** us over with deep darkness.
55:5 [55:6] [D] have beset me; horror *has* **overwhelmed** me.
69:7 [69:8] [D] scorn for your sake, and shame **covers** my face.
78:53 [D] so they were unafraid; but the sea **engulfed** their enemies.
80:10 [80:11] [E] The mountains **were covered** *with* its shade,
85:2 [85:3] [D] the iniquity of your people and **covered** all their sins.
104:6 [D] *You* **covered** it *with* the deep as with a garment; the waters
104:9 [D] they cannot cross; never again *will they* **cover** the earth.
106:11 [D] The waters **covered** their adversaries; not one of them
106:17 [D] and swallowed Dathan; *it* **buried** the company of Abiram.
140:9 [140:10] [D] *Let* the heads of those who surround me *be* **covered**
143:9 [D] me from my enemies, O LORD, for *I* **hide** *myself* in you.
147:8 [D] He **covers** the sky with clouds; he supplies the earth with rain
Pr 10:6 [D] but violence **overwhelms** the mouth of the wicked.
10:11 [D] of life, but violence **overwhelms** the mouth of the wicked.
10:12 [D] Hatred stirs up dissension, but love **covers** over all wrongs.
10:18 [D] *He who* **conceals** his hatred has lying lips, and whoever
11:13 [D] betrays a confidence, but a trustworthy man **keeps** a secret.
12:16 [A] annoyance at once, but a prudent man **overlooks** an insult.
12:23 [A] A prudent man **keeps** his knowledge *to himself*, but the heart
17:9 [D] *He who* **covers over** an offense promotes love, but whoever
24:31 [E] the ground **was covered** *with* weeds, and the stone wall was
26:26 [F] His malice *may be* **concealed** by deception, but his
28:13 [D] *He who* **conceals** his sins does not prosper, but whoever
Ecc 6:4 [E] it departs in darkness, and in darkness its name **is shrouded**.
Isa 6:2 [D] With two wings *they* **covered** their faces, with two they
6:2 [D] with two *they* **covered** their feet, and with two they were
11:9 [D] of the knowledge of the LORD as the waters **cover** the sea.
26:21 [D] blood shed upon her; *she will* **conceal** her slain no longer.
29:10 [D] eyes (the prophets); *he has* **covered** your heads (the seers).
37:1 [F] he tore his clothes and **put on** sackcloth and went into the
37:2 [F] the secretary, and the leading priests, *all* **wearing** sackcloth,
51:16 [D] your mouth and **covered** you with the shadow of my hand—
58:7 [D] when you see the naked, *to* **clothe** him, and not to turn away
59:6 [F] *they* cannot **cover themselves** with what they make.
60:2 [D] darkness **covers** the earth and thick darkness is over the
60:6 [D] Herds of camels *will* **cover** your land, young camels of
Jer 3:25 [D] Let us lie down in our shame, and *let* our disgrace **cover** us.
46:8 [D] She says, 'I will rise and **cover** the earth; I will destroy cities
51:42 [C] sea will rise over Babylon; its roaring waves *will* **cover** *her*.
51:51 [D] for we have been insulted and shame **covers** our faces,
Eze 1:11 [D] creature on either side, and two wings **covering** its body.
1:23 [D] toward the other, and each had two wings **covering** its body.
1:23 [D] and each had two wings covering its body. **[RPH]**
7:18 [D] They will put on sackcloth and *be* **clothed** *with* terror. Their
12:6 [D] **Cover** your face so that you cannot see the land, for I have
12:12 [D] *He will* **cover** his face so that he cannot see the land.
16:8 [D] corner of my garment over you and **covered** your nakedness.
16:10 [D] you in fine linen and **covered** you *with* costly garments.
16:18 [D] you took your embroidered clothes *to* **put on** them, and you
18:7 [D] his food to the hungry and **provides** clothing *for* the naked.
18:16 [D] his food to the hungry and **provides** clothing *for* the naked.
24:7 [D] did not pour it on the ground, where the dust *would* **cover** it.
24:8 [C] her blood on the bare rock, so that it *would* not **be covered**.
26:10 [D] horses will be so many that *they will* **cover** you *with* dust.
26:19 [D] the ocean depths over you and its vast waters **cover** you,
30:18 [D] She *will be* **covered** *with* clouds, and her villages will go
31:15 [D] On the day it was brought down to the grave *I* **covered** the
32:7 [D] snuff you out, *I will* **cover** the heavens and darken their stars;
32:7 [D] *I will* **cover** the sun with a cloud, and the moon will not give
38:9 [D] like a storm; you will be like a cloud **covering** the land.
38:16 [D] against my people Israel like a cloud *that* **covers** the land.
41:16 [E] the wall up to the windows, and the windows **were covered**.
Hos 2:9 [2:11] [D] and my linen, intended to **cover** her nakedness.
10:8 [D] they will say to the mountains, "**Cover** us!" and to the hills,
Ob 1:10 [D] against your brother Jacob, you *will be* **covered** *with* shame;
Jnh 3:6 [D] **covered** *himself* with sackcloth and sat down in the dust.
3:8 [F] *let* man and beast **be covered** with sackcloth. Let everyone
Mic 7:10 [D] Then my enemy will see it and *will* **be covered** *with* shame,
Hab 2:14 [D] of the glory of the LORD, as the waters **cover** the sea.
2:17 [D] The violence you have done to Lebanon *will* **overwhelm**
3:3 [D] *Selah* His glory **covered** the heavens and his praise filled
Mal 2:13 [D] *You* **flood** the LORD's altar *with* tears. You weep and wail
2:16 [D] "and I hate a *man's* **covering** *himself* *with* violence as well

4060 כֶּסֶה kēseh, n.[m.]. Not used in NIV/BHS [√ 4057]

4061 כִּסֵּה kissēh, n.m. [1 / 0] [√ 4058]

Job 26:9 He covers the face of the full moon, [BHS *his throne*; NIV 4057]

4062 כָּסוּי kāsûy, n.[m.]. [2] [√ 4059]

cover [+5989+6584] [1], covering [1]

Nu 4:6 Then *they are to* **cover** [+5989+6584] this *with* hides of sea cows,
4:14 Over it they are to spread a **covering** *of* hides of sea cows

4063 כְּסוּלוֹת kᵉsûlôt, n.pr.loc. [1] [√ 4071]

Kesulloth [1]

Jos 19:18 Their territory included: Jezreel, **Kesulloth**, Shunem,

4064 כְּסוּת kᵉsût, n.f. [8] [√ 4059]
covering [2], cloak [1], clothing [1], cover the offense [+6524] [1], cover [1], garment [1], uncovered [+401] [1]

Ge 20: 16 This is to **cover** [+6524] **the offense** against you before all who are
Ex 21: 10 not deprive the first one of her food, **clothing** and marital rights.
22: 27 [22:26] because his cloak is the only **covering** he has for his
Dt 22: 12 Make tassels on the four corners of the **cloak** you wear.
Job 24: 7 the night naked; they have nothing to **cover** themselves in the cold.
26: 6 Death is naked before God; Destruction lies **uncovered** [+401].
31: 19 perishing for lack of clothing, or a needy man without a **garment**,
Isa 50: 3 I clothe the sky with darkness and make sackcloth its **covering**."

4065 כָּסַח kāsaḥ, v. [2]
cut [1], is cut down [1]

Ps 80: 16 [80:17] [B] Your vine **is cut down**, it is burned with fire; at your
Isa 33: 12 [B] as if to lime; like **cut** thornbushes they will be set ablaze."

4066 כֵּסְיָה kēsyāh, n.m. Not used in NIV/BHS [√ 4058]

4067 ¹כְּסִיל kᵉsîl¹ n.m. [70] [→ 4068; cf. 4071]
fool [36], fools [21], foolish [9], fool's [4]

Ps 49: 10 [49:11] the **foolish** and the senseless alike perish and leave their
92: 6 [92:7] The senseless man does not know, **fools** do not understand,
94: 8 ones among the people; you **fools**, when will you become wise?
Pr 1: 22 long will mockers delight in mockery and **fools** hate knowledge?
1: 32 will kill them, and the complacency of **fools** will destroy them;
3: 35 The wise inherit honor, but **fools** he holds up to shame.
8: 5 gain prudence; you who are **foolish**, gain understanding.
10: 1 son brings joy to his father, but a **foolish** son grief to his mother.
10: 18 his hatred has lying lips, and whoever spreads slander is a **fool**.
10: 23 A **fool** finds pleasure in evil conduct, but a man of understanding
12: 23 his knowledge to himself, but the heart of **fools** blurts out folly.
13: 16 prudent man acts out of knowledge, but a **fool** exposes his folly.
13: 19 fulfilled is sweet to the soul, but **fools** detest turning from evil.
13: 20 with the wise grows wise, but a companion of **fools** suffers harm.
14: 7 Stay away from a **foolish** man, for you will not find knowledge on
14: 8 is to give thought to their ways, but the folly of **fools** is deception.
14: 16 the LORD and shuns evil, but a **fool** is hotheaded and reckless.
14: 24 wealth of the wise is their crown, but the folly of **fools** yields folly.
14: 33 of the discerning and even among **fools** she lets herself be known.
15: 2 wise commends knowledge, but the mouth of the **fool** gushes folly.
15: 7 The lips of the wise spread knowledge; not so the hearts of **fools**.
15: 14 heart seeks knowledge, but the mouth of a **fool** feeds on folly.
15: 20 son brings joy to his father, but a **foolish** man despises his mother.
17: 10 impresses a man of discernment more than a hundred lashes a **fool**.
17: 12 Better to meet a bear robbed of her cubs than a **fool** in his folly.
17: 16 Of what use is money in the hand of a **fool**, since he has no desire
17: 21 To have a **fool** for a son brings grief; there is no joy for the father
17: 24 wisdom in view, but a **fool's** eyes wander to the ends of the earth.
17: 25 A **foolish** son brings grief to his father and bitterness to the one
18: 2 A **fool** finds no pleasure in understanding but delights in airing his
18: 6 A **fool's** lips bring him strife, and his mouth invites a beating.
18: 7 A **fool's** mouth is his undoing, and his lips are a snare to his soul.
19: 1 Better a poor man whose walk is blameless than a **fool** whose lips
19: 10 It is not fitting for a **fool** to live in luxury—how much worse for a
19: 13 A **foolish** son is his father's ruin, and a quarrelsome wife is like a
19: 29 are prepared for mockers, and beatings for the backs of **fools**.
21: 20 stores of choice food and oil, but a **foolish** man devours all he has.
23: 9 Do not speak to a **fool**, for he will scorn the wisdom of your words.
26: 1 snow in summer or rain in harvest, honor is not fitting for a **fool**.
26: 3 the horse, a halter for the donkey, and a rod for the backs of **fools**!
26: 4 Do not answer a **fool** according to his folly, or you will be like him
26: 5 Answer a **fool** according to his folly, or he will be wise in his own
26: 6 drinking violence is the sending of a message by the hand of a **fool**.
26: 7 lame man's legs that hang limp is a proverb in the mouth of a **fool**.
26: 8 Like tying a stone in a sling is the giving of honor to a **fool**.
26: 9 thornbush in a drunkard's hand is a proverb in the mouth of a **fool**.
26: 10 Like an archer who wounds at random is he who hires a **fool**
26: 11 As a dog returns to its vomit, so a **fool** repeats his folly.
26: 12 wise in his own eyes? There is more hope for a **fool** than for him.
28: 26 He who trusts in himself is a **fool**, but he who walks in wisdom is
29: 11 A **fool** gives full vent to his anger, but a wise man keeps himself
29: 20 who speaks in haste? There is more hope for a **fool** than for him.
Ecc 2: 14 man has eyes in his head, while the **fool** walks in the darkness;
2: 15 I thought in my heart, "The fate of the **fool** will overtake me also.
2: 16 For the wise man, like the **fool**, will not be long remembered;
2: 16 both will be forgotten. Like the **fool**, the wise man too must die!
4: 5 The **fool** folds his hands and ruins himself.
4: 13 but **foolish** king who no longer knows how to take warning.
5: 1 [4:17] Go near to listen rather than to offer the sacrifice of **fools**,
5: 3 [5:2] so the speech of a **fool** when there are many words.
5: 4 [5:3] in fulfilling it. He has no pleasure in **fools**; fulfill your vow.
6: 8 What advantage has a wise man over a **fool**? What does a poor
7: 4 of mourning, but the heart of **fools** is in the house of pleasure.
7: 5 to heed a wise man's rebuke than to listen to the song of **fools**.
7: 6 the crackling of thorns under the pot, so is the laughter of **fools**.
7: 9 provoked in your spirit, for anger resides in the lap of **fools**.
9: 17 the wise are more to be heeded than the shouts of a ruler of **fools**.
10: 2 of the wise inclines to the right, but the heart of the **fool** to the left.
10: 12 man's mouth are gracious, but a **fool** is consumed by his own lips.
10: 15 A **fool's** work wearies him; he does not know the way to town.

4068 ²כְּסִיל kᵉsîl², n.m. [4] [√ 4067; cf. 4071]
Orion [3], constellations [1]

Job 9: 9 He is the Maker of the Bear and **Orion**, the Pleiades
38: 31 you bind the beautiful Pleiades? Can you loose the cords of **Orion**?
Isa 13: 10 stars of heaven and their **constellations** will not show their light.
Am 5: 8 (he who made the Pleiades and **Orion**, who turns blackness into

4069 ³כְּסִיל kᵉsîl³, n.pr.loc. [1]
Kesil [1]

Jos 15: 30 Eltolad, **Kesil**, Hormah,

4070 כְּסִילוּת kᵉsîlût, n.f. [1] [√ 4071]
Folly [1]

Pr 9: 13 The woman **Folly** is loud; she is undisciplined and without

4071 כָּסַל kāsal, v. [1] [→ 4063, 4067, 4068, 4070, 4072?, 4073, 4074, 4076, 4077]
foolish [1]

Jer 10: 8 [A] They are all senseless and **foolish**; they are taught by

4072 ¹כֶּסֶל kesel¹, n.m. [7] [→ 4079?; cf. 4071]
loins [5], back [1], waist [1]

Lev 3: 4 both kidneys with the fat on them near the **loins**, and the covering
3: 10 both kidneys with the fat on them near the **loins**, and the covering
3: 15 both kidneys with the fat on them near the **loins**, and the covering
4: 9 both kidneys with the fat on them near the **loins**, and the covering
7: 4 both kidneys with the fat on them near the **loins**, and the covering
Job 15: 27 his face is covered with fat and his **waist** bulges with flesh,
Ps 38: 7 [38:8] My **back** is filled with searing pain; there is no health in

4073 ²כֶּסֶל kesel², n.m. [6] [√ 4071]
trust [3], confidence [1], stupidity [1], trusts in [1]

Job 8: 14 What he **trusts in** is fragile; what he relies on is a spider's web.
31: 24 "If I have put my **trust** in gold or said to pure gold, 'You are my
Ps 49: 13 [49:14] This is the fate of those who **trust** in themselves, and of
78: 7 they would put their **trust** in God and would not forget his deeds
Pr 3: 26 for the LORD will be your **confidence** and will keep your foot
Ecc 7: 25 scheme of things and to understand the **stupidity** of wickedness

4074 כִּסְלָה kislâ, n.f. [2] [√ 4071]
confidence [1], folly [1]

Job 4: 6 Should not your piety be your **confidence** and your blameless
Ps 85: 8 [85:9] to his people, his saints—but let them not return to **folly**.

4075 כִּסְלֵו kislēw, n.pr.[m.]. [2]
Kislev [2]

Ne 1: 1 In the month of **Kislev** in the twentieth year, while I was in the
Zec 7: 1 on the fourth day of the ninth month, the month of **Kislev**.

4076 כְּסָלוֹן kᵉsālôn, n.pr.loc. [1] [√ 4071]
Kesalon [1]

Jos 15: 10 **Kesalon**), continued down to Beth Shemesh and crossed to

4077 כִּסְלוֹן kislôn, n.pr.m. [1] [√ 4071]
Kislon [1]

Nu 34: 21 Elidad son of **Kislon**, from the tribe of Benjamin;

4078 כַּסְלֻחִים kasluḥîm, n.pr.g. [2]
Casluhites [2]

Ge 10: 14 Pathrusites, **Casluhites** (from whom the Philistines came)
1Ch 1: 12 Pathrusites, **Casluhites** (from whom the Philistines came)

4079 כִּסְלֹת תָּבוֹר *kislōt tābôr*, n.pr.loc. [1] [√ 4072? + 9314]

Kisloth Tabor [1]

Jos 19:12 from Sarid toward the sunrise to the territory of **Kisloth Tabor**

4080 כָּסַם *kāsam*, v. [2] [→ 4081; cf. 1612, 4155]

keep hair trimmed [+906+4080] [2]

Eze 44:20 [A] *they are to* **keep** *the* **hair** of their heads **trimmed** [+906+4080].
44:20 [A] *they are to* **keep** *the* **hair** of their heads **trimmed** [+906+4080].

4081 כֻּסֶּמֶת *kussemet*, n.f. [3] [√ 4080]

spelt [3]

Ex 9:32 The wheat and **spelt**, however, were not destroyed, because they
Isa 28:25 not plant wheat in its place, barley in its plot, and **spelt** in its field?
Eze 4:9 "Take wheat and barley, beans and lentils, millet and **spelt**;

4082 כָּסַס *kāsas*, v. [1] [→ 4830, 4831]

determine amount needed [1]

Ex 12:4 [A] *You are to* **determine** the **amount** *of* lamb **needed** in

4083 כָּסַף *kāsap*, v. [6] [→ 4084]

longed [+4083] [2], hungry [1], long for [1], shameful [+4202] [1], yearns [1]

Ge 31:30 [C] because *you* **longed** [+4083] *to return* to your father's
31:30 [C] because *you* **longed** *to* **return** [+4083] to your father's
Job 14:15 [A] *you will* **long for** the creature your hands have made.
Ps 17:12 [A] They are like a lion **hungry** for prey, like a great lion
84:2 [84:3] [C] My soul **yearns**, even faints, for the courts of the
Zep 2:1 [C] Gather together, gather together, O **shameful** [+4202] nation,

4084 כֶּסֶף *kesep*, n.m. [403 / 402] [√ 4083; Ar 10362]

silver [303], money [61], *untranslated* [8], price [7], silver [+4084] [4], bought [+5239] [2], shekels [2], value [+6886] [2], bought [+928+2021+7864] [1], buy [+928] [1], it[s] [+2021] [1], must sell [+928+2021+4835+4835] [1], pay [+4200+5989] [1], pay [+4200+8740] [1], pay [+9202] [1], payment [1], property [1], sell [+906+928+4200+5989] [1], sell [+928+4200+5989] [1], value [1], what paid [1]

Ge 13:2 had become very wealthy in livestock and in **silver** and gold.
17:12 born in your household or bought with **money** from a foreigner—
17:13 Whether born in your household or bought with your **money**,
17:23 and all those born in his household or bought with his **money**,
17:27 those born in his household or **bought** [+5239] from a foreigner,
20:16 he said, "I am giving your brother a thousand shekels of **silver**.
23:9 Ask him to sell it to me for the full **price** as a burial site among
23:13 "Listen to me, if you will. I will pay the **price** *of* the field.
23:15 the land is worth four hundred shekels of **silver**, but what is that
23:16 weighed out for him the **price** he had named in the hearing of the
23:16 four hundred shekels of **silver**, according to the weight current
24:35 He has given him sheep and cattle, **silver** and gold, menservants
24:53 **silver** jewelry and articles of clothing and gave them to Rebekah;
31:15 Not only has he sold us, but he has used up **what** was **paid** *for* us.
37:28 and sold him for twenty shekels of **silver** to the Ishmaelites,
42:25 to put each man's **silver** back in his sack, and to give them
42:27 feed for his donkey, and he saw his **silver** in the mouth of his sack.
42:28 "My **silver** has been returned," he said to his brothers. "Here it is
42:35 their sacks, there in each man's sack was his pouch of **silver**!
42:35 When they and their father saw the **money** pouches, they were
43:12 Take double the amount of **silver** with you, for you must return the
43:12 for you must return the **silver** that was put back into the mouths of
43:15 So the men took the gifts and double the amount of **silver**,
43:18 because of the **silver** that was put back into our sacks the first time.
43:21 for the night we opened our sacks and each of us found his **silver**—
43:21 his silver—**[RPH]** the exact weight—in the mouth of his sack.
43:22 We have also brought additional **silver** with us to buy food.
43:22 us to buy food. We don't know who put our **silver** in our sacks."
43:23 has given you treasure in your sacks; I received your **silver**."
44:1 they can carry, and put each man's **silver** in the mouth of his sack.
44:2 put my cup, the **silver** one, in the mouth of the youngest one's
44:2 of the youngest one's sack, along with the **silver** *for* his grain."
44:8 We even brought back to you from the land of Canaan the **silver**
44:8 So why would we steal **silver** or gold from your master's house?
45:22 to Benjamin he gave three hundred shekels of **silver** and five sets
47:14 Joseph collected all the **money** that was to be found in Egypt
47:14 they were buying, and he brought **it**[s] [+2021] to Pharaoh's palace.
47:15 When the **money** of the people of Egypt and Canaan was gone,
47:15 Why should we die before your eyes? Our **money** is used up."
47:16 food in exchange for your livestock, since your **money** is gone."
47:18 "We cannot hide from our lord the fact that since our **money** is
Ex 3:22 and any woman living in her house for articles of **silver** and gold
11:2 and women alike are to ask their neighbors for articles of **silver**
12:35 asked the Egyptians for articles of **silver** and gold and for clothing.
12:44 Any slave you have **bought** [+5239] may eat of it after you have
20:23 do not make for yourselves gods of **silver** or gods of gold.
21:11 three things, she is to go free, without any payment *of* **money**.
21:21 the slave gets up after a day or two, since the slave is his **property**.
21:32 the owner must pay thirty shekels of **silver** to the master of the
21:34 owner of the pit must pay for the loss; *he must* **pay** [+4200+8740]
21:35 they are to sell the live one and divide both the **money** and the
22:7 [22:6] "If a man gives his neighbor **silver** or goods for
22:17 [22:16] *he must still* **pay** [+9202] the bride-price for virgins.
22:25 [22:24] "If you lend **money** to one of my people among you who
25:3 the offerings you are to receive from them: gold, **silver** and bronze;
26:19 make forty **silver** bases to go under them—two bases for each
26:21 and forty **silver** bases—two under each frame.
26:25 So there will be eight frames and sixteen **silver** bases—two under
26:32 acacia wood overlaid with gold and standing on four **silver** bases.
27:10 twenty bronze bases and with **silver** hooks and bands on the posts.
27:11 twenty bronze bases and with **silver** hooks and bands on the posts.
27:17 All the posts around the courtyard are to have **silver** bands
27:17 are to have silver bands and hooks, **[RPH]** and bronze bases.
30:16 Receive the atonement **money** from the Israelites and use it for the
31:4 to make artistic designs for work in gold, **silver** and bronze,
35:5 is to bring to the LORD an offering of gold, **silver** and bronze;
35:24 Those presenting an offering of **silver** or bronze brought it as an
35:32 to make artistic designs for work in gold, **silver** and bronze,
36:24 made forty **silver** bases to go under them—two bases for each
36:26 and forty **silver** bases—two under each frame.
36:30 So there were eight frames and sixteen **silver** bases—two under
36:36 They made gold hooks for them and cast their four **silver** bases.
38:10 twenty bronze bases, and with **silver** hooks and bands on the posts.
38:11 and twenty bronze bases, with **silver** hooks and bands on the posts.
38:12 ten posts and ten bases, with **silver** hooks and bands on the posts.
38:17 The hooks and bands on the posts were **silver**, and their tops were
38:17 on the posts were silver, and their tops were overlaid with **silver**;
38:17 with silver; so all the posts of the courtyard had **silver** bands.
38:19 Their hooks and bands were **silver**, and their tops were overlaid
38:19 and bands were silver, and their tops were overlaid with **silver**.
38:25 The **silver** *obtained from* those of the community who were
38:27 The 100 talents of **silver** were used to cast the bases for the
Lev 5:15 one without defect and of the proper value in **silver**, according to
22:11 if a priest buys a slave with **money**, or if a slave is born in his
25:37 You must not lend him **money** at interest or sell him food at a
25:50 The **price** *for* his release is to be based on the rate paid to a hired
25:51 he must pay for his redemption a larger share of the **price** paid for
27:3 male between the ages of twenty and sixty at fifty shekels of **silver**,
27:6 set the value of a male at five shekels of **silver** and that of a female
27:6 five shekels of silver and that of a female at three shekels of **silver**.
27:15 he must add a fifth to its **value** [+6886], and the house will again
27:16 required for it—fifty shekels of **silver** to a homer of barley seed.
27:18 the priest will determine the **value** according to the number of
27:19 he must add a fifth to its **value** [+6886], and the field will again
Nu 3:48 Give the **money** for the redemption of the additional Israelites to
3:49 So Moses collected the redemption **money** from those who
3:50 From the firstborn of the Israelites he collected **silver** weighing
3:51 Moses gave the redemption **money** to Aaron and his sons,
7:13 His offering was one **silver** plate weighing a hundred and thirty
7:13 and one **silver** sprinkling bowl weighing seventy shekels,
7:19 The offering he brought was one **silver** plate weighing a hundred
7:19 and one **silver** sprinkling bowl weighing seventy shekels,
7:25 His offering was one **silver** plate weighing a hundred and thirty
7:25 and one **silver** sprinkling bowl weighing seventy shekels,
7:31 His offering was one **silver** plate weighing a hundred and thirty
7:31 and one **silver** sprinkling bowl weighing seventy shekels,
7:37 His offering was one **silver** plate weighing a hundred and thirty
7:37 and one **silver** sprinkling bowl weighing seventy shekels,
7:43 His offering was one **silver** plate weighing a hundred and thirty
7:43 and one **silver** sprinkling bowl weighing seventy shekels,
7:49 His offering was one **silver** plate weighing a hundred and thirty
7:49 and one **silver** sprinkling bowl weighing seventy shekels,
7:55 His offering was one **silver** plate weighing a hundred and thirty
7:55 and one **silver** sprinkling bowl weighing seventy shekels,
7:61 His offering was one **silver** plate weighing a hundred and thirty
7:61 and one **silver** sprinkling bowl weighing seventy shekels,
7:67 His offering was one **silver** plate weighing a hundred and thirty
7:67 and one **silver** sprinkling bowl weighing seventy shekels,
7:73 His offering was one **silver** plate weighing a hundred and thirty
7:73 and one **silver** sprinkling bowl weighing seventy shekels,
7:79 His offering was one **silver** plate weighing a hundred and thirty
7:79 and one **silver** sprinkling bowl weighing seventy shekels,
7:84 twelve **silver** plates, twelve silver sprinkling bowls and twelve
7:84 twelve **silver** sprinkling bowls and twelve gold dishes.
7:85 Each **silver** plate weighed a hundred and thirty shekels, and each

Nu 7:85 the **silver** dishes weighed two thousand four hundred shekels,
10: 2 "Make two trumpets of hammered **silver**, and use them for calling
18:16 redeem them at the redemption price set at five shekels of **silver**,
22:18 "Even if Balak gave me his palace filled with **silver** and gold,
24:13 'Even if Balak gave me his palace filled with **silver** and gold,
31:22 Gold, **silver**, bronze, iron, tin, lead
Dt 2: 6 You are to pay them in **silver** for the food you eat and the water
2: 6 in silver for the food you eat and the water **[RPH]** you drink.' "
2:28 **[RPH]** Sell us food to eat and water to drink for their price in
2:28 Sell us food to eat and water to drink for their price in **silver**.
7:25 Do not covet the **silver** and gold on them, and do not take it for
8:13 your herds and flocks grow large and your **silver** and gold increase
14:25 then exchange your tithe for **silver**, and take the silver with you
14:25 take the **silver** with you and go to the place the LORD your God
14:26 Use the **silver** to buy whatever you like: cattle, sheep, wine
17:17 He must not accumulate large amounts of **silver** and gold.
21:14 *You* **must** not **sell** [+928+2021+4835+4835] her or treat her as a
22:19 They shall fine him a hundred shekels of **silver** and give them to
22:29 he shall pay the girl's father fifty shekels of **silver**. He must marry
23:19 [23:20] whether on **money** or food or anything else that may earn
29:17 [29:16] and idols of wood and stone, of **silver** and gold.
Jos 6:19 All the **silver** and gold and the articles of bronze and iron are
6:24 they put the **silver** and gold and the articles of bronze and iron into
7:21 two hundred shekels of **silver** and a wedge of gold weighing fifty
7:21 hidden in the ground inside my tent, with the **silver** underneath."
7:22 and there it was, hidden in his tent, with the **silver** underneath.
7:24 the **silver**, the robe, the gold wedge, his sons and daughters,
22: 8 with large herds of livestock, with **silver**, gold, bronze and iron,
Jdg 5:19 the waters of Megiddo, but they carried off no **silver**, no plunder.
9: 4 They gave him seventy shekels of **silver** from the temple of
16: 5 Each one of us will give you eleven hundred shekels of **silver**."
16:18 So the rulers of the Philistines returned with the **silver** in their
17: 2 "The eleven hundred shekels of **silver** that were taken from you
17: 2 I heard you utter a curse—I have that **silver** with me; I took it."
17: 3 When he returned the eleven hundred shekels of **silver** to his
17: 3 "I solemnly consecrate my **silver** to the LORD for my son to
17: 4 So he returned the **silver** to his mother, and she took two hundred
17: 4 she took two hundred shekels of **silver** and gave them to a
17:10 my father and priest, and I'll give you ten shekels of **silver** a year,
1Sa 2:36 and bow down before him for a piece of **silver** and a crust of bread
9: 8 "Look," he said, "I have a quarter of a shekel of **silver**. I will give
2Sa 8:10 Joram brought with him articles of **silver** and gold and bronze.
8:11 as he had done with the **silver** and gold from all the nations he had
18:11 I would have had to give you ten shekels of **silver** and a warrior's
18:12 "Even if a thousand **shekels** were weighed out into my hands,
21: 4 "We have no right to demand **silver** or gold from Saul or his
24:24 and the oxen and paid fifty shekels of **silver** for them.
1Ki 7:51 David had dedicated—the **silver** and gold and the furnishings—
10:21 Nothing was made of **silver**, because silver was considered of little
10:22 it returned, carrying gold, **silver** and ivory, and apes and baboons.
10:25 articles of **silver** and gold, robes, weapons and spices, and horses
10:27 The king made **silver** as common in Jerusalem as stones, and cedar
10:29 imported a chariot from Egypt for six hundred shekels of **silver**,
15:15 He brought into the temple of the LORD the **silver** and gold
15:18 Asa then took all the **silver** and gold that was left in the treasuries
15:19 and your father. See, I am sending you a gift of **silver** and gold.
16:24 bought the hill of Samaria from Shemer for two talents of **silver**
20: 3 'Your **silver** and gold are mine, and the best of your wives
20: 5 'I sent to demand your **silver** and gold, your wives and your
20: 7 he sent for my wives and my children, my **silver** and my gold,
20:39 it will be your life for his life, or you must pay a talent of **silver**.'
21: 2 if you prefer, *I will* **pay** [+4200+5989] you whatever it is worth."
21: 6 the Jezreelite, '**Sell** [+906+928+4200+5989] me your vineyard;
21:15 the Jezreelite that he refused to **sell** [+928+4200+5989] you.
2Ki 5: 5 So Naaman left, taking with him ten talents of **silver**, six thousand
5:22 Please give them a talent of **silver** and two sets of clothing.' "
5:23 then tied up the two talents of **silver** in two bags, with two sets of
5:26 Is this the time to take **money**, or to accept clothes, olive groves,
6:25 so long that a donkey's head sold for eighty shekels of **silver**,
6:25 of silver, and a quarter of a cab of seed pods for five **shekels**.
7: 8 They ate and drank, and carried away **silver**, gold and clothes,
12: 4 [12:5] "Collect all the **money** that is brought as sacred offerings
12: 4 [12:5] the **money** *collected in* the census, the money received
12: 4 [12:5] the **money** *received from* personal vows and the money
12: 4 [12:5] and the **money** brought voluntarily to the temple.
12: 7 [12:8] Take no more **money** from your treasurers, but hand it over
12: 8 [12:9] they would not collect any more **money** from the people
12: 9 [12:10] the **money** that was brought to the temple of the LORD.
12:10 [12:11] saw that there was a large amount of **money** in the chest,
12:10 [12:11] counted the **money** that had been brought into the temple
12:11 [12:12] they gave the **money** to the men appointed to supervise
12:13 [12:14] The **money** brought into the temple was not spent for
12:13 [12:14] into the temple was not spent for making **silver** basins,
12:13 [12:14] articles of gold or **silver** for the temple of the LORD;
12:15 [12:16] those to whom they gave the **money** to pay the workers,
12:16 [12:17] The **money** *from* the guilt offerings and sin offerings was
12:16 [12:17] **[RPH]** sin offerings was not brought into the temple of
14:14 He took all the gold and **silver** and all the articles found in the
15:19 Menahem gave him a thousand talents of **silver** to gain his support
15:20 Menahem exacted this **money** from Israel. Every wealthy man had
15:20 Every wealthy man had to contribute fifty shekels of **silver** to be
16: 8 Ahaz took the **silver** and gold found in the temple of the LORD
18:14 from Hezekiah king of Judah three hundred talents of **silver**
18:15 So Hezekiah gave him all the **silver** that was found in the temple of
20:13 the **silver**, the gold, the spices and the fine oil—his armory
22: 4 have him get ready the **money** that has been brought into the
22: 7 But they need not account for the **money** entrusted to them,
22: 9 "Your officials have paid out the **money** that was in the temple of
23:33 and he imposed on Judah a levy of a hundred talents of **silver**
23:35 Jehoiakim paid Pharaoh Neco the **silver** and gold he demanded.
23:35 **[RPH]** he taxed the land and exacted the silver and gold from the
23:35 he taxed the land and exacted the **silver** and gold from the people
25:15 all that were made of pure gold or **silver** [+4084].
25:15 all that were made of pure gold or **silver** [+4084].
1Ch 18:10 brought all kinds of articles of gold and **silver** and bronze.
18:11 as he had done with the **silver** and gold he had taken from all these
19: 6 and the Ammonites sent a thousand talents of **silver** to hire chariots
21:22 on the people may be stopped. Sell it to me at the full **price**."
21:24 David replied to Araunah, "No, I insist on paying the full **price**.
22:14 a million talents of **silver**, quantities of bronze and iron too great to
22:16 in gold and **silver**, bronze and iron—craftsmen beyond number.
28:14 the weight of silver for all the **silver** articles to be used in various
28:15 and the weight of **silver** for each silver lampstand and its lamps,
28:16 for consecrated bread; the weight of **silver** for the silver tables;
28:16 for consecrated bread; the weight of silver for the **silver** tables;
28:17 of gold for each gold dish; the weight of **silver** for each silver dish;
29: 2 **silver** for the silver, bronze for the bronze, iron for the iron
29: 2 silver for the **silver**, bronze for the bronze, iron for the iron
29: 3 my personal treasures of gold and **silver** for the temple of my God,
29: 4 seven thousand talents of refined **silver**, for the overlaying of the
29: 5 for the gold work and the **silver** *work*, and for all the work to be
29: 5 **[RPH]** and for all the work to be done by the craftsmen.
29: 7 and ten thousand darics of gold, ten thousand talents of **silver**,
2Ch 1:15 The king made **silver** and gold as common in Jerusalem as stones,
1:17 imported a chariot from Egypt for six hundred shekels of **silver**,
2: 7 [2:6] a man skilled to work in gold and **silver**, bronze and iron,
2:14 [2:13] He is trained to work in gold and **silver**, bronze and iron,
5: 1 the **silver** and gold and all the furnishings—and he placed them in
9:14 and the governors of the land brought gold and **silver** to Solomon.
9:20 Nothing was made of **silver**, because silver was considered of little
9:21 it returned, carrying gold, **silver** and ivory, and apes and baboons.
9:24 articles of **silver** and gold, and robes, weapons and spices,
9:27 The king made **silver** as common in Jerusalem as stones, and cedar
15:18 He brought into the temple of God the **silver** and gold
16: 2 Asa then took the **silver** and gold out of the treasuries of the
16: 3 my father and your father. See, I am sending you **silver** and gold.
17:11 Some Philistines brought Jehoshaphat gifts and **silver** as tribute,
21: 3 Their father had given them many gifts of **silver** and gold
24: 5 towns of Judah and collect the **money** due annually from all Israel,
24:11 and they saw that there was a large amount of **money**,
24:11 They did this regularly and collected a great amount of **money**.
24:14 they brought the rest of the **money** to the king and Jehoiada,
24:14 and also dishes and other objects of gold and **silver**.
25: 6 thousand fighting men from Israel for a hundred talents of **silver**.
25:24 He took all the gold and **silver** and all the articles found in the
27: 5 That year the Ammonites paid him a hundred talents of **silver**,
32:27 he made treasuries for his **silver** and gold and for his precious
34: 9 gave him the **money** that had been brought into the temple of God,
34:14 While they were bringing out the **money** that had been taken into
34:17 They have paid out the **money** that was in the temple of the
36: 3 and imposed on Judah a levy of a hundred talents of **silver**
Ezr 1: 4 where survivors may now be living are to provide him with **silver**
1: 6 All their neighbors assisted them with articles of **silver** and gold,
1: 9 the inventory: gold dishes 30 **silver** dishes 1,000 silver pans 29
1:10 gold bowls 30 matching **silver** bowls 410 other articles 1,000
1:11 In all, there were 5,400 articles of gold and of **silver**.
2:69 drachmas of gold, 5,000 minas of **silver** and 100 priestly garments.
3: 7 they gave **money** to the masons and carpenters, and gave food
8:25 I weighed out to them the offering of **silver** and gold and the
8:26 I weighed out to them 650 talents of **silver**, silver articles weighing
8:26 of silver, **silver** articles weighing 100 talents, 100 talents of gold,
8:28 The **silver** and gold are a freewill offering to the LORD,
8:30 the priests and Levites received the **silver** and gold and sacred
8:33 we weighed out the **silver** and gold and the sacred articles into the
Ne 5: 4 "We have had to borrow **money** to pay the king's tax on our fields
5:10 and my men are also lending the people **money** and grain.
5:11 the hundredth part of the **money**, grain, new wine and oil."
5:15 and took forty shekels of **silver** from them in addition to food

Ne 7:71 [7:70] work 20,000 drachmas of gold and 2,200 minas of **silver**.
7:72 [7:71] of gold, 2,000 minas of **silver** and 67 garments for priests.
Est 1: 6 of white linen and purple material to **silver** rings on marble pillars.
1: 6 couches of gold and **silver** on a mosaic pavement of porphyry,
3: 9 I will put ten thousand talents of **silver** into the royal treasury for
3:11 "Keep the **money**," the king said to Haman, "and do with the
4: 7 including the exact amount of **money** Haman had promised to pay
Job 3:15 with rulers who had gold, who filled their houses with **silver**.
22:25 then the Almighty will be your gold, the choicest **silver** for you.
27:16 Though he heaps up **silver** like dust and clothes like piles of clay,
27:17 up the righteous will wear, and the innocent will divide his **silver**.
28: 1 "There is a mine for **silver** and a place where gold is refined.
28:15 bought with the finest gold, nor can its price be weighed in **silver**.
31:39 if I have devoured its yield without **payment** or broken the spirit of
Ps 12: 6 [12:7] like **silver** refined in a furnace of clay, purified seven
15: 5 who lends his **money** without usury and does not accept a bribe
66:10 For you, O God, tested us; you refined us like **silver**.
68:13 [68:14] the wings of ⌞my⌟ dove are sheathed with **silver**, its
68:30 [68:31] Humbled, may it bring bars of **silver**. Scatter the nations
105:37 He brought out Israel, laden with **silver** and gold, and from among
115: 4 But their idols are **silver** and gold, made by the hands of men.
119:72 mouth is more precious to me than thousands of pieces of **silver**
135:15 The idols of the nations are **silver** and gold, made by the hands of
Pr 2: 4 if you look for it as for **silver** and search for it as for hidden
3:14 for she is more profitable than **silver** and yields better returns than
7:20 He took his purse filled with **money** and will not be home till full
8:10 Choose my instruction instead of **silver**, knowledge rather than
8:19 fruit is better than fine gold; what I yield surpasses choice **silver**.
10:20 The tongue of the righteous is choice **silver**, but the heart of the
16:16 get wisdom than gold, to choose understanding rather than **silver**!
17: 3 The crucible for **silver** and the furnace for gold, but the LORD
22: 1 than great riches; to be esteemed is better than **silver** or gold.
25: 4 Remove the dross from the **silver**, and out comes material for the
25:11 A word aptly spoken is like apples of gold in settings of **silver**.
26:23 <u>Like</u> [BHS *silver*; NIV 3869] a coating of glaze over earthenware
27:21 The crucible for **silver** and the furnace for gold, but man is tested
Ecc 2: 8 I amassed **silver** and gold for myself, and the treasure of kings
5:10 [5:9] Whoever loves **money** never has money enough; whoever
5:10 [5:9] Whoever loves money never has **money** enough; whoever
7:12 Wisdom is a shelter as **money** is a shelter, but the advantage of
10:19 wine makes life merry, but **money** is the answer for everything.
12: 6 before the **silver** cord is severed, or the golden bowl is broken;
SS 1:11 We will make you earrings of gold, studded with **silver**.
3:10 Its posts he made of **silver**, its base of gold. Its seat was
8: 9 If she is a wall, we will build towers of **silver** on her. If she is a
8:11 Each was to bring for its fruit a thousand shekels of **silver**.
Isa 1:22 Your **silver** has become dross, your choice wine is diluted with
2: 7 Their land is full of **silver** and gold; there is no end to their
2:20 away to the rodents and bats their idols of **silver** and idols of gold,
7:23 where there were a thousand vines worth a thousand **silver** shekels,
13:17 the Medes, who do not care for **silver** and have no delight in gold.
30:22 you will defile your idols overlaid with **silver** and your images
31: 7 For in that day every one of you will reject the idols of **silver**
39: 2 the **silver**, the gold, the spices, the fine oil, his entire armory
40:19 a goldsmith overlays it with gold and fashions **silver** chains for it.
43:24 *You have* not **bought** [+928+2021+7864] any fragrant calamus for
46: 6 pour out gold from their bags and weigh out **silver** on the scales;
48:10 See, I have refined you, though not as **silver**; I have tested you in
52: 3 were sold for nothing, and without **money** you will be redeemed."
55: 1 to the waters; and you who have no **money**, come, buy and eat!
55: 1 Come, buy wine and milk without **money** and without cost.
55: 2 Why spend **money** on what is not bread, and your labor on what
60: 9 bringing your sons from afar, with their **silver** and gold,
60:17 Instead of bronze I will bring you gold, and **silver** in place of iron.
Jer 6:30 They are called rejected **silver**, because the LORD has rejected
10: 4 They adorn it with **silver** and gold; they fasten it with hammer
10: 9 Hammered **silver** is brought from Tarshish and gold from Uphaz.
32: 9 and weighed out for him **[RPH]** seventeen shekels of silver.
32: 9 and weighed out for him seventeen shekels of **silver**.
32:10 had it witnessed, and weighed out the **silver** on the scales.
32:25 'Buy the field with **silver** and have the transaction witnessed.' "
32:44 Fields will be bought for **silver**, and deeds will be signed,
52:19 drink offerings—all that were made of pure gold or **silver** [+4084].
52:19 drink offerings—all that were made of pure gold or **silver** [+4084].
La 5: 4 We must **buy** [+928] the water we drink; our wood can be had only
Eze 7:19 They will throw their **silver** into the streets, and their gold will be
7:19 Their **silver** and gold will not be able to save them in the day of the
16:13 So you were adorned with gold and **silver**; your clothes were of
16:17 the jewelry made of my gold and **silver**, and you made for yourself
22:18 and lead left inside a furnace. They are but the dross of **silver**.
22:20 As men gather **silver**, copper, iron, lead and tin into a furnace to
22:22 As **silver** is melted in a furnace, so you will be melted inside her,
27:12 they exchanged **silver**, iron, tin and lead for your merchandise.
28: 4 wealth for yourself and amassed gold and **silver** in your treasuries.
38:13 to carry off **silver** and gold, to take away livestock and goods
Da 11: 8 their metal images and their valuable articles of **silver** and gold
11:38 a god unknown to his fathers he will honor with gold and **silver**,
11:43 of the treasures of gold and **silver** and all the riches of Egypt,
Hos 2: 8 [2:10] and oil, who lavished on her the **silver** and gold—
3: 2 So I bought her for fifteen shekels of **silver** and about a homer
8: 4 With their **silver** and gold they make idols for themselves to their
9: 6 Their treasures of **silver** will be taken over by briers, and thorns
13: 2 they make idols for themselves from their **silver**, cleverly
Joel 3: 5 [4:5] For you took my **silver** and my gold and carried off my
Am 2: 6 They sell the righteous for **silver**, and the needy for a pair of
8: 6 buying the poor with **silver** and the needy for a pair of sandals,
Mic 3:11 priests teach for a price, and her prophets tell fortunes for **money**.
Na 2: 9 [2:10] Plunder the **silver**! Plunder the gold! The supply is endless,
Hab 2:19 It is covered with gold and **silver**; there is no breath in it.
Zep 1:11 will be wiped out, all who trade with **silver** will be ruined.
1:18 Neither their **silver** nor their gold will be able to save them on the
Hag 2: 8 'The **silver** is mine and the gold is mine,' declares the LORD
Zec 6:11 Take the **silver** and gold and make a crown, and set it on the head
9: 3 she has heaped up **silver** like dust, and gold like the dirt of the
11:12 but if not, keep it." So they paid me thirty pieces of **silver**.
11:13 So I took the thirty pieces of **silver** and threw them into the house
13: 9 into the fire; I will refine them like **silver** and test them like gold.
14:14 will be collected—great quantities of gold and **silver** and clothing.
Mal 3: 3 He will sit as a refiner and purifier of **silver**; he will purify the
3: 3 he will purify the Levites and refine them like gold and **silver**.

4085 כָּסִפְיָא ***kāsipyā'***, n.pr.loc. [2]

Casiphia [2]

Ezr 8:17 I sent them to Iddo, the leader in **Casiphia**. I told them what to say
8:17 to say to Iddo and his kinsmen, the temple servants in **Casiphia**,

4086 כֶּסֶת ***keset***, n.f. [2]

magic charms [2]

Eze 13:18 Woe to the women who sew **magic charms** on all their wrists
13:20 I am against your **magic charms** with which you ensnare people

4087 כָּעַס ***kā'as***, v. [54] [→ 4088; cf. 4089]

provoked to anger [19], provoke to anger [7], provoking to anger [6], provoked [4], angered [3], angry [2], provoke [2], frustration [1], incensed [1], kept provoking [+1685+4088] [1], make angry [1], provoke to anger [+4088] [1], provoked to anger [+4088] [1], provoked to anger [+906+4088] [1], provoking [1], thrown insults [1], trouble [1], vexed [1]

Dt 4:25 [G] eyes of the LORD your God and **provoking** him **to anger**,
9:18 [G] evil in the LORD's sight and so **provoking** him **to anger**.
31:29 [G] and **provoke** him **to anger** by what your hands have made."
32:16 [G] foreign gods and **angered** him with their detestable idols.
32:21 [D] by what is no god and **angered** me with their worthless idols.
32:21 [G] *I will* **make** them **angry** by a nation that has no
Jdg 2:12 [G] peoples around them. *They* **provoked** the LORD **to anger**
1Sa 1: 6 [D] her rival **kept provoking** [+1685+4088] her in order to irritate
1: 7 [G] her rival **provoked** her till she wept and would not eat.
1Ki 14: 9 [G] you *have* **provoked** me **to anger** and thrust me behind your
14:15 [G] because *they* **provoked** the LORD **to anger** by making
15:30 [G] **provoked** [+906+4088] the LORD, the God of Israel, **to anger**.
16: 2 [G] people Israel to sin and to **provoke** me **to anger** by their sins.
16: 7 [G] **provoking** him **to anger** by the things he did, and becoming
16:13 [G] that *they* **provoked** the LORD, the God of Israel, **to anger**
16:26 [G] that *they* **provoked** the LORD, the God of Israel, **to anger**
16:33 [G] did more to **provoke** the LORD, the God of Israel, **to anger**
21:22 [G] because *you have* **provoked** [+4088] me **to anger** and have
22:53 [22:54] [G] **provoked** the LORD, the God of Israel, **to anger**,
2Ki 17:11 [G] They did wicked things that **provoked** the LORD **to anger**.
17:17 [G] do evil in the eyes of the LORD, **provoking** him **to anger**.
21: 6 [G] evil in the eyes of the LORD, **provoking** him **to anger**.
21:15 [G] have **provoked** me **to anger** from the day their forefathers
22:17 [G] **provoked** me **to anger** by all the idols their hands have
23:19 [G] towns of Samaria that *had* **provoked** the LORD **to anger**.
23:26 [G] that Manasseh *had done to* **provoke** [+4088] him **to anger**.
2Ch 16:10 [A] Asa *was* **angry** with the seer because of this; he was
28:25 [G] and **provoked** the LORD, the God of his fathers, **to anger**.
33: 6 [G] evil in the eyes of the LORD, **provoking** him **to anger**.
34:25 [G] **provoked** me **to anger** by all that their hands have made,
Ne 4: 1 [3:33] [A] the wall, he became angry and *was* greatly **incensed**.
4: 5 [3:37] [G] *they have* **thrown insults** in the face of the builders.
Ps 78:58 [G] *They* **angered** him with their high places; they aroused his
106:29 [G] *they* **provoked** the LORD **to anger** by their wicked deeds,
112:10 [A] The wicked man will see and *be* **vexed**, he will gnash his
Ecc 5:17 [5:16] [A] with great **frustration**, affliction and anger.
7: 9 [A] *Do* not *be* quickly **provoked** in your spirit, for anger resides

Isa 65: 3 [G] a people who continually **provoke** me to my very face,
Jer 7: 18 [G] out drink offerings to other gods to **provoke** me **to anger**.
7: 19 [G] But am I the one they *are* **provoking**? declares the LORD.
8: 19 [G] "Why *have they* **provoked** me **to anger** with their images,
11: 17 [G] and **provoked** me **to anger** by burning incense to Baal.
25: 6 [G] *do* not **provoke** me **to anger** with what your hands have
25: 7 [G] "and *you have* **provoked** me with what your hands have
32: 29 [G] *the people* **provoked** me **to anger** by burning incense on the
32: 30 [G] but **provoke** me with what their hands have made,
32: 32 [G] Judah *have* **provoked** me by all the evil they have done—
44: 3 [G] They **provoked** me **to anger** by burning incense and by
44: 8 [G] Why **provoke** me **to anger** with what your hands have made,
Eze 8: 17 [G] land with violence and continually **provoke** me **to anger**?
16: 26 [G] **provoked** me **to anger** with your increasing promiscuity.
16: 42 [A] will turn away from you; I will be calm and no longer **angry**.
32: 9 [G] *I will* **trouble** the hearts of many peoples when I bring about
Hos 12: 14 [12:15] [G] Ephraim *has* bitterly **provoked** him **to anger**; his

4088 כַּעַס ka'as, n.m. [21] [√ 4087]

grief [4], sorrow [4], anger [1], angered [1], annoyance [1], anxiety [1], displeasure [1], ill-tempered [1], kept provoking [+1685+4087] [1], provocation [1], provoke to anger [+4087] [1], provoked to anger [+4087] [1], provoked to anger [+906+4087] [1], provoked to anger [1], taunt [1]

Dt 32: 19 rejected them because he was **angered** *by* his sons and daughters.
32: 27 I dreaded the **taunt** *of* the enemy, lest the adversary misunderstand
1Sa 1: 6 her rival **kept provoking** [+1685+4087] her in order to irritate her.
1: 16 I have been praying here out of my great anguish and **grief**."
1Ki 15: 30 **provoked** the LORD, the God of Israel, **to anger** [+906+4087].
21: 22 because *you have* **provoked** me **to anger** [+4087] and have
2Ki 23: 26 of all that Manasseh *had done to* **provoke** him **to anger** [+4087].
Ps 6: 7 [6:8] My eyes grow weak with **sorrow**; they fail because of all
10: 14 you, O God, do see trouble and **grief**; you consider it to take it in
31: 9 [31:10] my eyes grow weak with **sorrow**, my soul and my body
85: 4 [85:5] God our Savior, and put away your **displeasure** toward us.
Pr 12: 16 A fool shows his **annoyance** at once, but a prudent man overlooks
17: 25 A foolish son brings **grief** to his father and bitterness to the one
21: 19 to live in a desert than with a quarrelsome and **ill-tempered** wife.
27: 3 and sand a burden, but **provocation** *by* a fool is heavier than both.
Ecc 1: 18 For with much wisdom comes much **sorrow**; the more knowledge,
2: 23 All his days his work is pain and **grief**; even at night his mind does
7: 3 **Sorrow** is better than laughter, because a sad face is good for the
7: 9 provoked in your spirit, for **anger** resides in the lap of fools.
11: 10 banish **anxiety** from your heart and cast off the troubles of your
Eze 20: 28 made offerings that **provoked** me **to anger**, presented their

4089 כַּעַשׂ ka'aś, n.m. [4] [√ 4088; cf. 4087]

anger [1], anguish [1], grief [1], resentment [1]

Job 5: 2 **Resentment** kills a fool, and envy slays the simple.
6: 2 "If only my **anguish** could be weighed and all my misery be
10: 17 new witnesses against me and increase your **anger** toward me;
17: 7 My eyes have grown dim with **grief**; my whole frame is but a

4090 כַּף kap, n.f. [192] [√ 4104]

hands [76], hand [32], dish [12], dishes [12], palm [6], soles [6], feet [+8079] [5], *untranslated* [4], foot [+8079] [4], hands together [+448+4090] [4], sole [4], hands [+3338] [3], socket [3], grasp [2], handful [+4850] [2], palm of hand [2], arms [1], be taken captive [+928+2021+9530] [1], clutches [1], each[s] [+2021] [1], earnings [+7262] [1], fingers [1], from [+4946] [1], fruit of labor [+3330] [1], handles [1], palms of hands [1], paws [1], pocket [1], their[s] [+928+2157] [1], those[s] [+8079] [1], took a handful [+4848] [1]

Ge 8: 9 the dove could find no place to set its **feet** [+8079] because there
20: 5 I have done this with a clear conscience and clean **hands**."
31: 42 God has seen my hardship and the toil of my **hands**, and last night
32: 25 [32:26] he touched the **socket** *of* Jacob's hip so that his hip was
32: 25 [32:26] so that his **[RPH]** hip was wrenched as he wrestled with
32: 32 [32:33] do not eat the tendon attached to the **socket** *of* the hip,
32: 32 [32:33] because the **socket** *of* Jacob's hip was touched near the
40: 11 squeezed them into Pharaoh's cup and put the cup in his **hand**."
40: 21 his position, so that he once again put the cup into Pharaoh's **hand**,
Ex 4: 4 took hold of the snake and it turned back into a staff in his **hand**.
9: 29 out of the city, I will spread out my **hands** in prayer to the LORD.
9: 33 He spread out his **hands** toward the LORD; the thunder and hail
25: 29 And make its plates and **dishes** of pure gold, as well as its pitchers
29: 24 Put all these in the **hands** *of* Aaron and his sons and wave them
29: 24 Put all these in the hands of Aaron and **[RPH]** his sons and wave
33: 22 in the rock and cover you with my **hand** until I have passed by.
33: 23 I will remove my **hand** and you will see my back; but my face
37: 16 its plates and **dishes** and bowls and its pitchers for the pouring out
Lev 8: 27 He put all these in the **hands** *of* Aaron and his sons and waved
8: 27 He put all these in the hands of Aaron and **[RPH]** his sons
8: 28 Moses took them from their **hands** and burned them on the altar on
9: 17 He also brought the grain offering, **took a handful** [+4848] of it
11: 27 on all fours, those that walk on their **paws** are unclean for you;
14: 15 some of the log of oil, pour it in the **palm of** his own left **hand**,
14: 16 dip his right forefinger into the oil in his **palm**, and with his finger
14: 17 The priest is to put some of the oil remaining in his **palm** on the
14: 18 The rest of the oil in his **palm** the priest shall put on the head of the
14: 26 priest is to pour some of the oil into the **palm of** his own left **hand**,
14: 27 with his right forefinger sprinkle some of the oil from his **palm**
14: 28 Some of the oil in his **palm** he is to put on the same places he put
14: 29 The rest of the oil in his **palm** the priest shall put on the head of the
Nu 4: 7 to spread a blue cloth and put on it the plates, **dishes** and bowls,
5: 18 shall loosen her hair and place in her **hands** the reminder offering,
6: 19 the priest is to place in his **hands** a boiled shoulder of the ram,
7: 14 one gold **dish** weighing ten shekels, filled with incense;
7: 20 one gold **dish** weighing ten shekels, filled with incense;
7: 26 one gold **dish** weighing ten shekels, filled with incense;
7: 32 one gold **dish** weighing ten shekels, filled with incense;
7: 38 one gold **dish** weighing ten shekels, filled with incense;
7: 44 one gold **dish** weighing ten shekels, filled with incense;
7: 50 one gold **dish** weighing ten shekels, filled with incense;
7: 56 one gold **dish** weighing ten shekels, filled with incense;
7: 62 one gold **dish** weighing ten shekels, filled with incense;
7: 68 one gold **dish** weighing ten shekels, filled with incense;
7: 74 one gold **dish** weighing ten shekels, filled with incense;
7: 80 one gold **dish** weighing ten shekels, filled with incense;
7: 84 twelve silver sprinkling bowls and twelve gold **dishes**.
7: 86 The twelve gold **dishes** filled with incense weighed ten shekels
7: 86 gold dishes filled with incense weighed ten shekels **each**[s] [+2021],
7: 86 Altogether, the gold **dishes** weighed a hundred and twenty shekels.
24: 10 He struck his **hands** together and said to him, "I summoned you to
Dt 2: 5 you any of their land, not even enough to put your **foot** [+8079] on.
11: 24 Every place where you set your **foot** [+8079] will be yours:
25: 12 you shall cut off her **hand**. Show her no pity.
28: 35 spreading from the **soles** *of* your feet to the top of your head.
28: 56 would not venture to touch the ground with the **sole** *of* her foot—
28: 65 you will find no repose, no resting place for the **sole** *of* your foot.
Jos 1: 3 I will give you every place where you set your **foot** [+8079],
3: 13 set **foot** [+8079] in the Jordan, its waters flowing downstream will
4: 18 No sooner had they set their **feet** [+8079] on the dry ground than
Jdg 6: 13 the LORD has abandoned us and put us into the **hand** *of* Midian."
6: 14 "Go in the strength you have and save Israel out of Midian's **hand**.
8: 6 "Do you already have the **hands** *of* Zebah and Zalmunna in your
8: 15 'Do you already have the **hands** *of* Zebah and Zalmunna in your
12: 3 I took my life in my **hands** and crossed over to fight the
14: 9 which he scooped out with his **hands** and ate as he went along.
1Sa 4: 3 that it may go with us and save us from the **hand** *of* our enemies."
5: 4 His head and **hands** [+3338] had been broken off and were lying
19: 5 He took his life in his **hands** when he killed the Philistine.
25: 29 the lives of your enemies he will hurl away as from the **pocket** *of* a
28: 21 I took my life in my **hands** and did what you told me to do.
2Sa 14: 16 Perhaps the king will agree to deliver his servant from the **hand** *of*
14: 25 From the top of his head to the **sole** *of* his foot there was no
18: 12 "Even if a thousand shekels were weighed out into my **hands**,
18: 14 So he took three javelins in his **hand** and plunged them into
19: 9 [19:10] "The king delivered us from the **hand** *of* our enemies;
19: 9 [19:10] he is the one who rescued us from the **hand** *of* the
22: 1 when the LORD delivered him from the **hand** *of* all his enemies
22: 1 him from the hand of all his enemies and from the **hand** *of* Saul.
1Ki 5: 3 [5:17] until the LORD put his enemies under his **feet** [+8079].
7: 50 gold basins, wick trimmers, sprinkling bowls, **dishes** and censers;
8: 22 the whole assembly of Israel, spread out his **hands** toward heaven
8: 38 of his own heart, and spreading out his **hands** toward this temple—
8: 54 where he had been kneeling with his **hands** spread out toward
17: 12 only a **handful** [+4850] *of* flour in a jar and a little oil in a jug.
18: 44 "A cloud as small as a man's **hand** is rising from the sea."
2Ki 4: 34 lay upon the boy, mouth to mouth, eyes to eyes, **hands** to hands.
4: 34 lay upon the boy, mouth to mouth, eyes to eyes, hands to **hands**.
9: 35 found nothing except her skull, her feet and her **hands** [+3338].
11: 12 anointed him, and the people clapped their **hands** and shouted,
16: 7 Come up and save me out of the **hand** *of* the king of Aram
16: 7 of the hand of the king of Aram and of **[RPH]** the king of Israel,
18: 21 which pierces a man's **hand** and wounds him if he leans on it!
19: 24 With the **soles** *of* my feet I have dried up all the streams of Egypt."
20: 6 will deliver you and this city from the **hand** *of* the king of Assyria.
25: 14 **dishes** and all the bronze articles used in the temple service.
1Ch 12: 17 [12:18] to my enemies when my **hands** are free from violence,
2Ch 4: 22 the pure gold wick trimmers, sprinkling bowls, **dishes** and censers;
6: 12 in front of the whole assembly of Israel and spread out his **hands**.
6: 13 whole assembly of Israel and spread out his **hands** toward heaven.
6: 29 and pains, and spreading out his **hands** toward this temple—
24: 14 and also **dishes** and other objects of gold and silver.
30: 6 are left, who have escaped from the **hand** *of* the kings of Assyria.

2Ch 32: 11 'The LORD our God will save us from the **hand** *of* the king of
Ezr 8: 31 he protected us **from** [+4946] enemies and bandits along the way.
9: 5 fell on my knees with my **hands** spread out to the LORD my
Job 2: 7 afflicted Job with painful sores from the **soles** *of* his feet to the top
9: 30 if I washed myself with soap and my **hands** with washing soda,
10: 3 Does it please you to oppress me, to spurn the work of your **hands**,
11: 13 if you devote your heart to him and stretch out your **hands** to him,
13: 14 Why do I put myself in jeopardy and take my life in my **hands**?
13: 21 Withdraw your **hand** far from me, and stop frightening me with
16: 17 yet my **hands** have been free of violence and my prayer is pure.
22: 30 who will be delivered through the cleanness of your **hands**."
27: 23 It claps its **hands** in derision and hisses him out of his place.
29: 9 from speaking and covered their mouths with their **hands**;
31: 7 heart has been led by my eyes, or if my **hands** have been defiled,
36: 32 He fills his **hands** with lightning and commands it to strike its
41: 8 [40:32] If you lay a **hand** on him, you will remember the struggle
Ps 7: 3 [7:4] my God, if I have done this and there is guilt on my **hands**—
9: 16 [9:17] the wicked are ensnared by the work of their **hands**.
18: T [18:1] the LORD delivered him from the **hand** *of* all his enemies
24: 4 He who has clean **hands** and a pure heart, who does not lift up his
26: 6 I wash my **hands** in innocence, and go about your altar, O LORD,
44: 20 [44:21] of our God or spread out our **hands** to a foreign god,
47: 1 [47:2] Clap your **hands**, all you nations; shout to God with cries
63: 4 [63:5] as long as I live, and in your name I will lift up my **hands**.
71: 4 from the hand of the wicked, from the **grasp** *of* evil and cruel men.
73: 13 kept my heart pure; in vain have I washed my **hands** in innocence.
78: 72 them with integrity of heart; with skillful **hands** he led them.
81: 6 [81:7] their shoulders; their **hands** were set free from the basket.
88: 9 [88:10] O LORD, every day; I spread out my **hands** to you.
91: 12 they will lift you up in their **hands**, so that you will not strike your
98: 8 Let the rivers clap their **hands**, let the mountains sing together for
119: 48 I lift up my **hands** to your commands, which I love, and I meditate
119: 109 Though I constantly take my life in my **hands**, I will not forget
128: 2 You will eat the **fruit of** your **labor** [+3330]; blessings and
129: 7 with it the reaper cannot fill his **hands**, nor the one who gathers fill
139: 5 hem me in—behind and before; you have laid your **hand** upon me.
141: 2 may the lifting up of my **hands** be like the evening sacrifice.
Pr 6: 1 for your neighbor, if you have struck **hands** in pledge for another,
6: 3 to free yourself, since you have fallen into your neighbor's **hands**:
10: 4 Lazy **hands** make a man poor, but diligent hands bring wealth.
17: 18 A man lacking in judgment strikes **hands** in pledge and puts up
22: 26 Do not be a man who strikes **hands** in pledge or puts up security
31: 13 She selects wool and flax and works with eager **hands**.
31: 16 and buys it; out of her **earnings** [+7262] she plants a vineyard.
31: 19 hand she holds the distaff and grasps the spindle with her **fingers**.
31: 20 She opens her **arms** to the poor and extends her hands to the
Ecc 4: 6 Better *one* **handful** [+4850] with tranquillity than two handfuls
SS 5: 5 my fingers with flowing myrrh, on the **handles** *of* the lock.
Isa 1: 6 From the **sole** *of* your foot to the top of your head there is no
1: 15 When you spread out your **hands** in prayer, I will hide my eyes
28: 4 as soon as someone sees it and takes it in his **hand**, he swallows it.
33: 15 gain from extortion and keeps his **hand** from accepting bribes,
36: 6 which pierces a man's **hand** and wounds him if he leans on it!
37: 25 With the **soles** *of* my feet I have dried up all the streams of Egypt.'
38: 6 will deliver you and this city from the **hand** *of* the king of Assyria.
49: 16 See, I have engraved you on the **palms of** my **hands**; your walls
55: 12 song before you, and all the trees of the field will clap their **hands**.
59: 3 For your **hands** are stained with blood, your fingers with guilt.
59: 6 Their deeds are evil deeds, and acts of violence are in their **hands**.
60: 14 all who despise you will bow down at your **feet** [+8079] and will
62: 3 in the LORD's hand, a royal diadem in the **hand** *of* your God.
Jer 4: 31 gasping for breath, stretching out her **hands** and saying, "Alas!
12: 7 I will give the one I love into the **hands** *of* her enemies.
15: 21 hands of the wicked and redeem you from the **grasp** *of* the cruel."
52: 18 **dishes** and all the bronze articles used in the temple service.
52: 19 pots, lampstands, **dishes** and bowls used for drink offerings—
La 2: 15 All who pass your way clap their **hands** at you; they scoff
2: 19 Lift up your **hands** to him for the lives of your children, who faint
3: 41 Let us lift up our hearts and our **hands** to God in heaven, and say:
Eze 1: 7 their **feet** [+8079] were like those of a calf and gleamed like
1: 7 their feet were like **those**[s] **of** [+8079] a calf and gleamed like
6: 11 Strike your **hands** together and stamp your feet and cry out "Alas!"
21: 11 [21:16] is appointed to be polished, to be grasped with the **hand**;
21: 14 [21:19] prophesy and strike your **hands** [+448+4090] **together**.
21: 14 [21:19] prophesy and strike your **hands together** [+448+4090].
21: 17 [21:22] I too will strike my **hands** [+448+4090] **together**, and my
21: 17 [21:22] I too will strike my **hands together** [+448+4090], and my
21: 24 [21:29] done this, *you will* **be taken captive** [+928+2021+9530].
22: 13 " 'I will surely strike my **hands** together at the unjust gain you
29: 7 When they grasped you with their **hands**, you splintered and you
43: 7 this is the place of my throne and the place for the **soles** *of* my feet.
Da 10: 10 touched me and set me trembling on my **hands** [+3338] and knees.
Jnh 3: 8 Let them give up their evil ways and **their**[s] [+928+2157] violence.
Mic 4: 10 There the LORD will redeem you out of the **hand** *of* your
7: 3 *Both* **hands** are skilled in doing evil; the ruler demands gifts,
Na 3: 19 Everyone who hears the news about you claps his **hands** at your
Hab 2: 9 unjust gain to set his nest on high, to escape the **clutches** *of* ruin!
Hag 1: 11 on men and cattle, and on the labor of your **hands**."
Mal 4: 3 [3:21] they will be ashes under the **soles** *of* your feet on the day

4091 כֵּף kēp, n.[m.]. [2]

rocks [2]

Job 30: 6 in the dry stream beds, among the **rocks** and in holes in the ground.
Jer 4: 29 Some go into the thickets; some climb up among the **rocks**.

4092 כָּפָה kāpâ, v. [1]

soothes [1]

Pr 21: 14 [A] A gift given in secret **soothes** anger, and a bribe concealed in

4093 כִּפָּה kippâ, n.f. [4] [√ 4104]

palm branch [2], branches [1], fronds [1]

Lev 23: 40 palm **fronds**, leafy branches and poplars, and rejoice before the
Job 15: 32 his time he will be paid in full, and his **branches** will not flourish.
Isa 9: 14 [9:13] and tail, both **palm branch** and reed in a single day;
19: 15 There is nothing Egypt can do—head or tail, **palm branch** or reed.

4094 כְּפוֹר¹ k^{e}pôr[1], n.m. [9]

each dish [+2256+4094] [4], bowls [3], *untranslated* [2]

1Ch 28: 17 and pitchers; the weight of gold for **each** gold **dish** [+2256+4094];
28: 17 and pitchers; the weight of gold for **each** gold **dish** [+2256+4094];
28: 17 each gold dish; **[RPH]** the weight of silver for each silver dish;
28: 17 gold dish; the weight of silver for **each** silver **dish** [+2256+4094];
28: 17 gold dish; the weight of silver for **each** silver **dish** [+2256+4094];
28: 17 each gold dish; the weight of silver for each silver dish; **[RPH]**
Ezr 1: 10 gold **bowls** 30 matching silver bowls 410 other articles 1,000
1: 10 gold bowls 30 matching silver **bowls** 410 other articles 1,000
8: 27 20 **bowls** *of* gold valued at 1,000 darics, and two fine articles of

4095 כְּפוֹר² k^{e}pôr[2], n.m. [3] [√ 4105]

frost [3]

Ex 16: 14 thin flakes like **frost** on the ground appeared on the desert floor.
Job 38: 29 comes the ice? Who gives birth to the **frost** *from* the heavens
Ps 147: 16 He spreads the snow like wool and scatters the **frost** like ashes.

4096 כָּפִיס kāpîs, n.m. [1]

beams [1]

Hab 2: 11 the wall will cry out, and the **beams** of the woodwork will echo it.

4097 כְּפִיר k^{e}pîr, n.m. [30] [√ 4105]

lion [7], lions [7], great lion [4], young lions [4], strong lion [3], great lions [1], he[s] [1], young lion [+787] [1], young lion [1], young [1]

Jdg 14: 5 suddenly a **young lion** [+787] came roaring toward him.
Job 4: 10 may roar and growl, yet the teeth of the **great lions** are broken.
38: 39 hunt the prey for the lioness and satisfy the hunger of the **lions**
Ps 17: 12 are like a lion hungry for prey, like a **great lion** crouching in cover.
34: 10 [34:11] The **lions** may grow weak and hungry, but those who seek
35: 17 my life from their ravages, my precious life from these **lions**.
58: 6 [58:7] O God; tear out, O LORD, the fangs of the **lions**!
91: 13 and the cobra; you will trample the **great lion** and the serpent.
104: 21 The **lions** roar for their prey and seek their food from God.
Pr 19: 12 A king's rage is like the roar of a **lion**, but his favor is like dew on
20: 2 A king's wrath is like the roar of a **lion**; he who angers him forfeits
28: 1 flees though no one pursues, but the righteous are as bold as a **lion**.
Isa 5: 29 Their roar is like that of the lion, they roar like **young lions**;
11: 6 down with the goat, the calf and the **lion** and the yearling together;
31: 4 "As a lion growls, a **great lion** over his prey—and though a whole
Jer 2: 15 **Lions** have roared; they have growled at him. They have laid waste
25: 38 Like a **lion** he will leave his lair, and their land will become
51: 38 Her people all roar like **young lions**, they growl like lion cubs.
Eze 19: 2 She lay down among the **young lions** and reared her cubs.
19: 3 She brought up one of her cubs, and he became a **strong lion**.
19: 5 she took another of her cubs and made him a **strong lion**.
19: 6 He prowled among the lions, for he was now a **strong lion**.
32: 2 " 'You are like a **lion** *among* the nations; you are like a monster in
41: 19 one side and the face of a **lion** toward the palm tree on the other.
Hos 5: 14 For I will be like a lion to Ephraim, like a **great lion** to Judah.
Am 3: 4 no prey? Does **he**[s] growl in his den when he has caught nothing?
Mic 5: 8 [5:7] like a **young lion** among flocks of sheep, which mauls
Na 2: 11 [2:12] the place where they fed their **young**, where the lion
2: 13 [2:14] in smoke, and the sword will devour your **young lions**.
Zec 11: 3 Listen to the roar of the **lions**; the lush thicket of the Jordan is

[F] Hitpael (hitpoel, hitpoal, hitpolel, hitpolal, hitpalel, hitpalal, hitpalpel, hitpalpal, hotpael, hotpaal) [G] Hiphil (hiphtil) [H] Hophal [I] Hishtaphel

4098 כְּפִירָה kᵉpîrâ, n.pr.loc. [4] [√ 4107]
Kephirah [4]

Jos 9:17 to their cities: Gibeon, **Kephirah**, Beeroth and Kiriath Jearim.
18:26 Mizpah, **Kephirah**, Mozah,
Ezr 2:25 of Kiriath Jearim, **Kephirah** and Beeroth 743
Ne 7:29 of Kiriath Jearim, **Kephirah** and Beeroth 743

4099 כְּפִירִים kᵉpîrîm, n.m.[loc.?]. [2] [√ 4107]
villages [2]

Ne 6:2 let us meet together in one of the **villages** on the plain of Ono."
Eze 38:13 and the merchants of Tarshish and all her **villages** will say to you,

4100 כָּפַל kāpal, v. [5] [→ 4101, 4834]
folded double [2], *untranslated* [1], fold double [1], strike twice [1]

Ex 26:9 [A] **Fold** the sixth curtain **double** at the front of the tent.
28:16 [B] a span long and a span wide—and **folded double**.
39:9 [B] a span long and a span wide—and **folded double**.
39:9 [B] a span long and a span wide—and folded double. **[RPH]**
Eze 21:14 [21:19] [C] *Let* the sword **strike twice**, even three times. It is a

4101 כֶּפֶל kepel, n.[m.]. [3] [√ 4100]
bridle [+8270] [1], double [1], two sides [1]

Job 11:6 to you the secrets of wisdom, for true wisdom has **two sides**.
41:13 [41:5] Who would approach him with a **bridle** [+8270]?
Isa 40:2 that she has received from the LORD's hand **double** for all her

4102 כָּפַן kāpan, v. [1] [→ 4103]
sent out [1]

Eze 17:7 [A] The vine now **sent out** its roots toward him from the plot

4103 כָּפָן kāpān, n.[m.]. [2] [√ 4102]
famine [1], hunger [1]

Job 5:22 You will laugh at destruction and **famine**, and need not fear the
30:3 Haggard from want and **hunger**, they roamed the parched land in

4104 כָּפַף kāpap, v. [5] [→ 4090, 4093]
are bowed down [2], bow down [1], bowed down in distress [1], bowing [1]

Ps 57:6 [57:7] [A] a net for my feet—I *was* **bowed down in distress**.
145:14 [B] all those who fall and lifts up all who **are bowed down**.
146:8 [B] the LORD lifts up *those who* **are bowed down**, the LORD
Isa 58:5 [A] Is it only for **bowing** one's head like a reed and for lying on
Mic 6:6 [C] before the LORD and **bow down** before the exalted God?

4105 כָּפַר¹ kāpar¹, v. [101] [→ 4095, 4097, 4106, 4109, 4111, 4113, 4114; cf. 4106, 4109]
make atonement [58], making atonement [6], atonement made [5], made atonement [4], atone [3], be atoned for [3], *untranslated* [2], forgave [2], forgive [2], makes atonement [2], accept atonement [1], appease [1], atoned for [1], atonement be made [1], atonement made [+4113] [1], atonement was made [1], atonement [1], be annulled [1], be atoned [1], is atoned for [1], make amends [1], pacify [+7156] [1], pardon [1], ward off with a ransom [1]

Ge 32:20 [32:21] [D] "*I will* **pacify** [+7156] him with these gifts I am
Ex 29:33 [E] offerings by which **atonement was made** for their ordination
29:36 [D] Purify the altar by **making atonement** for it, and anoint it to
29:37 [D] For seven days **make atonement** for the altar and consecrate
30:10 [D] Once a year Aaron *shall* **make atonement** on its horns.
30:10 [D] This annual **atonement** *must be* **made** with the blood of the
30:15 [D] you make the offering to the LORD to **atone** for your lives.
30:16 [D] before the LORD, **making atonement** for your lives."
32:30 [D] to the LORD; perhaps *I can* **make atonement** for your sin."
Lev 1:4 [D] it will be accepted on his behalf to **make atonement** for him.
4:20 [D] In this way the priest *will* **make atonement** for them,
4:26 [D] In this way the priest *will* **make atonement** for the man's
4:31 [D] In this way the priest *will* **make atonement** for him, and he
4:35 [D] In this way the priest *will* **make atonement** for him for the
5:6 [D] and the priest *shall* **make atonement** for him for his sin.
5:10 [D] and **make atonement** for him for the sin he has committed,
5:13 [D] In this way the priest *will* **make atonement** for him for any
5:16 [D] who *will* **make atonement** for him with the ram as a guilt
5:18 [D] In this way the priest *will* **make atonement** for him for the
6:7 [5:26] [D] In this way the priest *will* **make atonement** for him
6:30 [6:23] [D] **make atonement** in the Holy Place must not be
7:7 [D] They belong to the priest who **makes atonement** with them.
8:15 [D] of the altar. So he consecrated it to **make atonement** for it.
8:34 [D] was commanded by the LORD to make **atonement** for you.
9:7 [D] and **make atonement** for yourself and the people;
9:7 [D] offering that is for the people and **make atonement** for them,
10:17 [D] by **making atonement** for them before the LORD.
12:7 [D] He shall offer them before the LORD *to* **make atonement**
12:8 [D] In this way the priest *will* **make atonement** for her, and she
14:18 [D] and **make atonement** for him before the LORD.
14:19 [D] **make atonement** for the one to be cleansed from his
14:20 [D] and **make atonement** for him, and he will be clean.
14:21 [D] as a guilt offering to be waved to **make atonement** for him,
14:29 [D] be cleansed, to **make atonement** for him before the LORD.
14:31 [D] In this way the priest *will* **make atonement** before the
14:53 [D] In this way *he will* **make atonement** for the house, and it
15:15 [D] In this way he *will* **make atonement** before the LORD for
15:30 [D] In this way he *will* **make atonement** for her before the
16:6 [D] bull for his own sin offering *to* **make atonement** for himself
16:10 [D] **making atonement** by sending it into the desert as a
16:11 [D] bull for his own sin offering *to* **make atonement** for himself
16:16 [D] In this way *he will* **make atonement** for the Most Holy Place
16:17 [D] **make atonement** in the Most Holy Place until he comes out,
16:17 [D] *having* **made atonement** for himself, his household and the
16:18 [D] altar that is before the LORD and **make atonement** for it.
16:20 [D] **making atonement** *for* the Most Holy Place, the Tent of
16:24 [D] *to* **make atonement** for himself and for the people.
16:27 [D] was brought into the Most Holy Place to **make atonement**,
16:30 [D] because on this day **atonement** *will be* **made** for you,
16:32 [D] to succeed his father as high priest *is to* **make atonement**.
16:33 [D] **make atonement** *for* the Most Holy Place, for the Tent of
16:33 [D] **[RPH]** for the priests and all the people of the community.
16:33 [D] for the priests and all the people of the community. **[RPH]**
16:34 [D] **Atonement** *is to be* **made** once a year for all the sins of the
17:11 [D] I have given it to you to **make atonement** for yourselves on
17:11 [D] the altar; it is the blood *that* **makes atonement** for one's life.
19:22 [D] *is to* **make atonement** for him before the LORD for the sin
23:28 [D] when **atonement** *is* **made** for you before the LORD your
Nu 5:8 [D] along with the ram with which **atonement** [+4113] *is* **made**
6:11 [D] and the other as a burnt offering *to* **make atonement** for him
8:12 [D] for a burnt offering, to **make atonement** for the Levites.
8:19 [D] to **make atonement** for them so that no plague will strike the
8:21 [D] the LORD and **made atonement** for them to purify them.
15:25 [D] The priest is *to* **make atonement** for the whole Israelite
15:28 [D] The priest *is to* **make atonement** before the LORD for the
15:28 [D] when **atonement** *has been* **made** for him, he will be
16:46 [17:11] [D] hurry to the assembly *to* **make atonement** for them.
16:47 [17:12] [D] offered the incense and **made atonement** for them.
25:13 [D] honor of his God and **made atonement** for the Israelites."
28:22 [D] Include one male goat as a sin offering to **make atonement**
28:30 [D] Include one male goat to **make atonement** for you.
29:5 [D] Include one male goat as a sin offering to **make atonement**
31:50 [D] to **make atonement** for ourselves before the LORD."
35:33 [E] **atonement** cannot **be made** for the land on which blood has
Dt 21:8 [D] **Accept** *this* **atonement** for your people Israel, whom you
21:8 [C] of an innocent man." And the bloodshed *will* **be atoned** for.
32:43 [D] his enemies and **make atonement** *for* his land and people.
1Sa 3:14 [F] 'The guilt of Eli's house *will* never **be atoned for** by sacrifice
2Sa 21:3 [D] How *shall I* **make amends** so that you will bless the
1Ch 6:49 [6:34] [D] **making atonement** for Israel, in accordance with all
2Ch 29:24 [D] presented their blood on the altar for a sin offering to **atone**
30:18 [D] saying, "*May* the LORD, who is good, **pardon** everyone
Ne 10:33 [10:34] [D] for sin offerings to **make atonement** for Israel;
Ps 65:3 [65:4] [D] by sins, you **forgave** our transgressions.
78:38 [D] *he* **forgave** their iniquities and did not destroy them.
79:9 [D] deliver us and **forgive** our sins for your name's sake.
Pr 16:6 [E] Through love and faithfulness sin **is atoned for**; through the
16:14 [D] is a messenger of death, but a wise man *will* **appease** it.
Isa 6:7 [E] your lips; your guilt is taken away and your sin **atoned for**."
22:14 [E] "Till your dying day this sin *will* not **be atoned for**," says the
27:9 [E] By this, then, *will* Jacob's guilt **be atoned for**, and this will
28:18 [E] Your covenant with death *will* **be annulled**; your agreement
47:11 [D] will fall upon you that you cannot **ward off with a ransom**;
Jer 18:23 [D] *Do* not **forgive** their crimes or blot out their sins from your
Eze 16:63 [D] when I **make atonement** for you for all you have done,
43:20 [D] the rim, and so purify the altar and **make atonement** *for* it.
43:26 [D] For seven days *they are to* **make atonement** *for* the altar
45:15 [D] and fellowship offerings to **make atonement** for the people,
45:17 [D] fellowship offerings to **make atonement** for the house of
45:20 [D] so *you are to* **make atonement** *for* the temple.
Da 9:24 [D] to put an end to sin, to **atone** *for* wickedness, to bring in

4106 ²כָּפַר kāpar², v.den. [1] [√ 4109; cf. 4105]
coat [1]

Ge 6:14 [A] make rooms in it and **coat** it with pitch inside and out.

4107 כָּפָר kāpār, n.m. [2] [→ 4098, 4099, 4108, 4112]
villages [2]

1Ch 27:25 outlying districts, in the towns, the **villages** and the watchtowers.
SS 7:11 [7:12] go to the countryside, let us spend the night in the **villages**.

4108 ¹כֹּפֶר kōper[1], n.[m.]. [1] [√ 4107]
villages [1]

1Sa 6:18 to the five rulers—the fortified towns with their country **villages**.

4109 ²כֹּפֶר kōper[2], n.m. [1] [→ 4106; cf. 4105]
pitch [1]

Ge 6:14 make rooms in it and coat it with **pitch** inside and out.

4110 ³כֹּפֶר kōper[3], n.m. [2]
henna blossoms [1], henna [1]

SS 1:14 My lover is to me a cluster of **henna blossoms** from the vineyards
4:13 orchard of pomegranates with choice fruits, with **henna** and nard,

4111 ⁴כֹּפֶר kōper[4], n.m. [13] [√ 4105]
ransom [8], bribe [2], bribes [1], compensation [1], payment [1]

Ex 21:30 However, if **payment** is demanded of him, he may redeem his life
30:12 each one must pay the LORD a **ransom** *for* his life at the time he
Nu 35:31 " 'Do not accept a **ransom** for the life of a murderer, who deserves
35:32 " 'Do not accept a **ransom** *for* anyone who has fled to a city of
1Sa 12:3 From whose hand have I accepted a **bribe** to make me shut my
Job 33:24 him from going down to the pit; I have found a **ransom** for him'—
36:18 one entices you by riches; do not let a large **bribe** turn you aside.
Ps 49:7 [49:8] the life of another or give to God a **ransom** *for* him—
Pr 6:35 He will not accept any **compensation**; he will refuse the bribe,
13:8 A man's riches may **ransom** his life, but a poor man hears no
21:18 The wicked become a **ransom** for the righteous, and the unfaithful
Isa 43:3 I give Egypt for your **ransom**, Cush and Seba in your stead.
Am 5:12 You oppress the righteous and take **bribes** and you deprive the

4112 כְּפַר הָעַמֹּנִי kᵉpar hā'ammōnî, n.pr.loc. [1] [√ 4107 + 2194; cf. 6671]
Kephar Ammoni [1]

Jos 18:24 **Kephar Ammoni**, [Q 2024+6671] Ophni and Geba—twelve towns

4113 כִּפֻּרִים kippurîm, n.pl.abst. [8] [√ 4105]
atonement [6], atonement made [+4105] [1], atoning [1]

Ex 29:36 Sacrifice a bull each day as a sin offering to make **atonement**.
30:10 This annual atonement must be made with the blood of the **atoning**
30:16 Receive the **atonement** money from the Israelites and use it for the
Lev 23:27 "The tenth day of this seventh month is the Day of **Atonement**.
23:28 Do no work on that day, because it is the Day of **Atonement**,
25:9 on the Day of **Atonement** sound the trumpet throughout your land.
Nu 5:8 along with the ram with which **atonement** *is* **made** [+4105] for
29:11 in addition to the sin offering for **atonement** and the regular burnt

4114 כַּפֹּרֶת kappōret, n. [27] [√ 4105]
atonement cover [15], cover [10], atonement [1], it [+2021] [1]

Ex 25:17 "Make an **atonement cover** *of* pure gold—two and a half cubits
25:18 make two cherubim out of hammered gold at the ends of the **cover**.
25:19 make the cherubim of one piece with the **cover**, at the two ends.
25:20 their wings spread upward, overshadowing the **cover** with them.
25:20 The cherubim are to face each other, looking toward the **cover**.
25:21 Place the **cover** on top of the ark and put in the ark the Testimony,
25:22 above the **cover** between the two cherubim that are over the ark of
26:34 Put the **atonement cover** on the ark of the Testimony in the Most
30:6 before the **atonement cover** that is over the Testimony—where I
31:7 the ark of the Testimony with the **atonement cover** on it,
35:12 the ark with its poles and the **atonement cover** and the curtain that
37:6 He made the **atonement cover** of pure gold—two and a half cubits
37:7 made two cherubim out of hammered gold at the ends of the **cover**.
37:8 at the two ends he made them of one piece with the **cover**.
37:9 their wings spread upward, overshadowing the **cover** with them.
37:9 The cherubim faced each other, looking toward the **cover**.
39:35 the ark of the Testimony with its poles and the **atonement cover**;
40:20 attached the poles to the ark and put the **atonement cover** over it.
Lev 16:2 behind the curtain in front of the **atonement cover** on the ark,
16:2 will die, because I appear in the cloud over the **atonement cover**.
16:13 the smoke of the incense will conceal the **atonement cover** above
16:14 and with his finger sprinkle it on the front of the **atonement cover**;
16:14 some of it with his finger seven times before the **atonement cover**.
16:15 He shall sprinkle it on the **atonement cover** and in front of it.
16:15 shall sprinkle it on the atonement cover and in front of **it** [+2021].
Nu 7:89 cherubim above the **atonement cover** on the ark of the Testimony.
1Ch 28:11 its upper parts, its inner rooms and the place of **atonement**.

4115 כָּפַשׁ kāpaš, v. [1] [cf. 3899]
trampled [1]

La 3:16 [G] my teeth with gravel; *he has* **trampled** me in the dust.

4116 ¹כַּפְתּוֹר kaptôr[1], n.pr.loc. [3] [→ 4118]
Caphtor [3]

Dt 2:23 the Caphtorites coming out from **Caphtor** destroyed them
Jer 47:4 to destroy the Philistines, the remnant from the coasts of **Caphtor**.
Am 9:7 the Philistines from **Caphtor** and the Arameans from Kir?

4117 ²כַּפְתּוֹר kaptôr[2], n.m. [18]
buds [8], bud [6], *untranslated* [2], columns [1], tops of the pillars [1]

Ex 25:31 flowerlike cups, **buds** and blossoms shall be of one piece with it.
25:33 Three cups shaped like almond flowers with **buds** and blossoms
25:33 **[RPH]** and the same for all six branches extending from the
25:34 there are to be four cups shaped like almond flowers with **buds**
25:35 One **bud** shall be under the first pair of branches extending from
25:35 a second **bud** under the second pair, and a third bud under the third
25:35 bud under the second pair, and a third **bud** under the third pair—
25:36 The **buds** and branches shall all be of one piece with the
37:17 its flowerlike cups, **buds** and blossoms were of one piece with it.
37:19 Three cups shaped like almond flowers with **buds** and blossoms
37:19 three **[RPH]** on the next branch and the same for all six branches
37:20 lampstand were four cups shaped like almond flowers with **buds**
37:21 One **bud** was under the first pair of branches extending from the
37:21 a second **bud** under the second pair, and a third bud under the third
37:21 bud under the second pair, and a third **bud** under the third pair—
37:22 The **buds** and the branches were all of one piece with the
Am 9:1 "Strike the **tops of the pillars** so that the thresholds shake.
Zep 2:14 The desert owl and the screech owl will roost on her **columns**.

4118 כַּפְתֹּרִי kaptōrî, a.g. [3] [√ 4116]
Caphtorites [3]

Ge 10:14 Casluhites (from whom the Philistines came) and **Caphtorites**.
Dt 2:23 the **Caphtorites** coming out from Caphtor destroyed them
1Ch 1:12 Casluhites (from whom the Philistines came) and **Caphtorites**.

4119 ¹כַּר kar[1], n.[m.]. [12] [√ 4159]
lambs [8], battering rams [3], choice lambs [+4946+7366] [1]

Dt 32:14 and milk from herd and flock and with fattened **lambs** and goats,
1Sa 15:9 and the best of the sheep and cattle, the fat calves and **lambs**—
2Ki 3:4 he had to supply the king of Israel with a hundred thousand **lambs**
Isa 16:1 Send **lambs** as tribute to the ruler of the land, from Sela,
34:6 the blood of **lambs** and goats, fat from the kidneys of rams.
Jer 51:40 "I will bring them down like **lambs** to the slaughter, like rams
Eze 4:2 up to it, set up camps against it and put **battering rams** around it.
21:22 [21:27] where he is to set up **battering rams**, to give the
21:22 [21:27] to set **battering rams** against the gates, to build a ramp
27:21 they did business with you in **lambs**, rams and goats.
39:18 blood of the princes of the earth as if they were rams and **lambs**,
Am 6:4 You dine on **choice lambs** [+4946+7366] and fattened calves.

4120 ²כַּר kar[2], n.m. [3]
meadows [2], fields [1]

Ps 37:20 The LORD's enemies will be like the beauty of the **fields**,
65:13 [65:14] The **meadows** are covered with flocks and the valleys are
Isa 30:23 and plentiful. In that day your cattle will graze in broad **meadows**.
Zep 2:6 by the sea, where the **Kerethites** [BHS *pastures*; NIV 4165] dwell,

4121 ³כַּר kar[3], n.[m.]. [1]
saddle [1]

Ge 31:34 and put them inside her camel's **saddle** and was sitting on them.

4122 כָּר kār, n.pr.loc. Not used in NIV/BHS [→ 1105]

4123 כֹּר kōr, n.[m.]. [8 / 7] [→ Ar 10367]
cors [6], cor [1]

1Ki 4:22 [5:2] Solomon's daily provisions were thirty **cors** *of* fine flour
4:22 [5:2] were thirty cors of fine flour and sixty **cors** *of* meal,
5:11 [5:25] Solomon gave Hiram twenty thousand **cors** *of* wheat as
5:11 [5:25] addition to twenty thousand baths [BHS *cors*; NIV 1427] *of*
2Ch 2:10 [2:9] twenty thousand **cors** of ground wheat, twenty thousand
2:10 [2:9] twenty thousand **cors** of barley, twenty thousand baths of
27:5 ten thousand **cors** of wheat and ten thousand cors of barley.
Eze 45:14 is a tenth of a bath from each **cor** (which consists of ten baths

[F] Hitpael (hitpoel, hitpoal, hitpolel, hitpolal, hitpalel, hitpalal, hitpalpel, hitpalpal, hotpael, hotpaal) [G] Hiphil (hiphtil) [H] Hophal [I] Hishtaphel

4124 כִּרְבֵּל *kirbēl*, v.den. [1] [→ Ar 10368]
was clothed [1]
1Ch 15:27 [E] Now David **was clothed** in a robe of fine linen, as were all

4125 ¹כָּרָה *kārâ¹*, v. [14 / 15] [→ 4129, 4808, 4838]
dug [5], digs [3], pierced [2], cut out [1], dig [1], is dug [1], plots [1], sank [1]
Ge 26:25 [A] There he pitched his tent, and there his servants **dug** a well.
50: 5 [A] bury me in the tomb *I* **dug** for myself in the land of Canaan."
Ex 21:33 [A] or **digs** one and fails to cover it and an ox or a donkey falls
Nu 21:18 [A] well that the princes dug, that the nobles of the people **sank**—
2Ch 16:14 [A] They buried him in the tomb that *he had* **cut out** for himself
Ps 7:15 [7:16] [A] *He who* **digs** a hole and scoops it out falls into the pit
22:16 [22:17] [A] *they have* **pierced** [BHS 3869] my hands and my
40: 6 [40:7] [A] you did not desire, but my ears *you have* **pierced**;
57: 6 [57:7] [A] *They* **dug** a pit in my path—but they have fallen into
94:13 [C] relief from days of trouble, till a pit **is dug** for the wicked.
119:85 [A] The arrogant **dig** pitfalls for me, contrary to your law.
Pr 16:27 [A] A scoundrel **plots** evil, and his speech is like a scorching fire.
26:27 [A] If a *man* **digs** a pit, he will fall into it; if a man rolls a stone,
Jer 18:20 [A] good be repaid with evil? Yet *they have* **dug** a pit for me.
18:22 [A] for *they have* **dug** a pit to capture me and have hidden snares

4126 ²כָּרָה *kārâ²*, v. [4]
untranslated [1], barter away [1], barter [1], bought [1]
Dt 2: 6 [A] for the food you eat and the water **[RPH]** you drink.' "
Job 6:27 [A] even cast lots for the fatherless and **barter away** your friend.
41: 6 [40:30] [A] *Will* traders **barter** for him? Will they divide him
Hos 3: 2 [A] So *I* **bought** her for fifteen shekels of silver and about a

4127 ³כָּרָה *kārâ³*, v. [1] [√ 4130]
prepared a feast [+4130] [1]
2Ki 6:23 [A] So *he* **prepared a** great **feast** [+4130] for them, and after

4128 ⁴כָּרָה *kārâ⁴*, v. Not used in NIV/BHS

4129 ⁵כָּרָה *kārâ⁵*, n.f. Not used in NIV/BHS [√ 4125]

4130 כֵּרָה *kērâ*, n.f. [1] [→ 4127]
prepared a feast [+4127] [1]
2Ki 6:23 So *he* **prepared a** great **feast** [+4127] for them, and after they had

4131 ¹כְּרוּב *kᵉrûb¹*, n.m. [91]
cherubim [66], cherub [15], *untranslated* [6], them[s] [+2021] [2], one[s] [+2021] [1], their[s] [+2021] [1]
Ge 3:24 he placed on the east side of the Garden of Eden **cherubim**
Ex 25:18 make two **cherubim** out of hammered gold at the ends of the
25:19 Make one **cherub** on one end and the second cherub on the other;
25:19 Make one cherub on one end and the second **cherub** on the other;
25:19 make the **cherubim** of one piece with the cover, at the two ends.
25:20 The **cherubim** are to have their wings spread upward,
25:20 The **cherubim** are to face each other, looking toward the cover.
25:22 above the cover between the two **cherubim** that are over the ark of
26: 1 with **cherubim** worked into them by a skilled craftsman.
26:31 twisted linen, with **cherubim** worked into it by a skilled craftsman.
36: 8 with **cherubim** worked into them by a skilled craftsman.
36:35 twisted linen, with **cherubim** worked into it by a skilled craftsman.
37: 7 he made two **cherubim** out of hammered gold at the ends of the
37: 8 He made one **cherub** on one end and the second cherub on the
37: 8 made one cherub on one end and the second **cherub** on the other;
37: 8 at the two ends he made **them**[s] [+2021] of one piece with the
37: 9 The **cherubim** had their wings spread upward, overshadowing the
37: 9 The **cherubim** faced each other, looking toward the cover.
Nu 7:89 heard the voice speaking to him from between the two **cherubim**
1Sa 4: 4 of the LORD Almighty, who is enthroned between the **cherubim**.
2Sa 6: 2 who is enthroned between the **cherubim** that are on the ark.
22:11 He mounted the **cherubim** and flew; he soared on the wings of the
1Ki 6:23 In the inner sanctuary he made a pair of **cherubim** of olive wood,
6:24 One wing of the first **cherub** was five cubits long, and the other
6:24 was five cubits long, and the other wing **[RPH]** five cubits—
6:25 The second **cherub** also measured ten cubits, for the two cherubim
6:25 ten cubits, for the two **cherubim** were identical in size and shape.
6:26 The height of each **cherub** was ten cubits.
6:26 The height of each cherub was ten cubits. **[RPH]**
6:27 He placed the **cherubim** inside the innermost room of the temple,
6:27 room of the temple, with **their**[s] [+2021] wings spread out.
6:27 The wing of one **cherub** touched one wall, while the wing of the
6:28 He overlaid the **cherubim** with gold.
6:29 outer rooms, he carved **cherubim**, palm trees and open flowers.
6:32 And on the two olive wood doors he carved **cherubim**, palm trees
6:32 and overlaid the **cherubim** and palm trees with beaten gold.
6:35 He carved **cherubim**, palm trees and open flowers on them
7:29 the panels between the uprights were lions, bulls and **cherubim**—
7:36 He engraved **cherubim**, lions and palm trees on the surfaces of the
8: 6 Most Holy Place, and put it beneath the wings of the **cherubim**.
8: 7 The **cherubim** spread their wings over the place of the ark
8: 7 and **[RPH]** overshadowed the ark and its carrying poles.
2Ki 19:15 "O LORD, God of Israel, enthroned between the **cherubim**,
1Ch 13: 6 ark of God the LORD, who is enthroned between the **cherubim**—
28:18 the **cherubim** of gold that spread their wings and shelter the ark of
2Ch 3: 7 of the temple with gold, and he carved **cherubim** on the walls.
3:10 In the Most Holy Place he made a pair of sculptured **cherubim**
3:11 The total wingspan of the **cherubim** was twenty cubits. One wing
3:11 also five cubits long, touched the wing of the other **cherub**.
3:12 Similarly one wing of the second **cherub** was five cubits long
3:12 also five cubits long, touched the wing of the first **cherub**.
3:13 The wings of these **cherubim** extended twenty cubits. They stood
3:14 and crimson yarn and fine linen, with **cherubim** worked into it.
5: 7 Most Holy Place, and put it beneath the wings of the **cherubim**.
5: 8 The **cherubim** spread their wings over the place of the ark
5: 8 place of the ark and covered **[RPH]** the ark and its carrying poles.
Ps 18:10 [18:11] He mounted the **cherubim** and flew; he soared on the
80: 1 [80:2] you who sit enthroned between the **cherubim**, shine forth
99: 1 he sits enthroned between the **cherubim**, let the earth shake.
Isa 37:16 God of Israel, enthroned between the **cherubim**,
Eze 9: 3 the glory of the God of Israel went up from above the **cherubim**,
10: 1 above the expanse that was over the heads of the **cherubim**.
10: 2 clothed in linen, "Go in among the wheels beneath the **cherubim**.
10: 2 Fill your hands with burning coals from among the **cherubim**
10: 3 Now the **cherubim** were standing on the south side of the temple
10: 4 Then the glory of the LORD rose from above the **cherubim**
10: 5 The sound of the wings of the **cherubim** could be heard as far
10: 6 from among the **cherubim**," the man went in and stood beside a
10: 7 **one**[s] [+2021] of the cherubim reached out his hand to the fire that
10: 7 one of the **cherubim** reached out his hand to the fire that was
10: 7 reached out his hand to the fire that was among **them**[s] [+2021].
10: 8 (Under the wings of the **cherubim** could be seen what looked like
10: 9 I looked, and I saw beside the **cherubim** four wheels, one beside
10: 9 beside the cherubim four wheels, one beside each of the **cherubim**;
10: 9 each of the cherubim; **[RPH]** the wheels sparkled like chrysolite.
10:14 One face was that of a **cherub**, the second the face of a man,
10:15 the **cherubim** rose upward. These were the living creatures I had
10:16 When the **cherubim** moved, the wheels beside them moved;
10:16 and when the **cherubim** spread their wings to rise from the ground,
10:18 over the threshold of the temple and stopped above the **cherubim**.
10:19 the **cherubim** spread their wings and rose from the ground,
10:20 Israel by the Kebar River, and I realized that they were **cherubim**.
11:22 the **cherubim**, with the wheels beside them, spread their wings,
28:14 You were anointed as a guardian **cherub**, for so I ordained you.
28:16 I expelled you, O guardian **cherub**, from among the fiery stones.
41:18 were carved **cherubim** and palm trees. Palm trees alternated with
41:18 and palm trees. Palm trees alternated with **cherubim**.
41:18 alternated with cherubim. **[RPH]** Each cherub had two faces:
41:18 Palm trees alternated with cherubim. Each **cherub** had two faces:
41:20 **cherubim** and palm trees were carved on the wall of the outer
41:25 And on the doors of the outer sanctuary were carved **cherubim**

4132 ²כְּרוּב *kᵉrûb²*, n.pr.loc. [2]
Kerub [2]
Ezr 2:59 the towns of Tel Melah, Tel Harsha, **Kerub**, Addon and Immer,
Ne 7:61 the towns of Tel Melah, Tel Harsha, **Kerub**, Addon and Immer,

4133 כָּרִי *kārî*, a.g. [2]
Carites [2]
2Sa 20:23 [Benaiah son of Jehoiada was over the **Kerethites** [K; see Q 4165]]
2Ki 11: 4 the **Carites** and the guards and had them brought to him at the
11:19 of hundreds, the **Carites**, the guards and all the people of the land,

4134 כְּרִית *kᵉrît*, n.pr.loc. [2] [√ 4162]
Kerith [2]
1Ki 17: 3 "Leave here, turn eastward and hide in the **Kerith** Ravine,
17: 5 He went to the **Kerith** Ravine, east of the Jordan, and stayed there.

4135 כְּרִיתוּת *kᵉrîtût*, n.f. [4] [√ 4162]
divorce [4]
Dt 24: 1 he writes her a certificate of **divorce**, gives it to her and sends her
24: 3 second husband dislikes her and writes her a certificate of **divorce**,
Isa 50: 1 "Where is your mother's certificate of **divorce** with which I sent
Jer 3: 8 I gave faithless Israel her certificate of **divorce** and sent her away

4136 כַּרְכֹּב *karkōb*, n.[m.]. [2]

ledge [2]

Ex 27: 5 Put it under the **ledge** *of* the altar so that it is halfway up the altar.
38: 4 a bronze network, to be under its **ledge**, halfway up the altar.

4137 כַּרְכֹּם *karkōm*, n.[m.]. [1]

saffron [1]

SS 4: 14 nard and **saffron**, calamus and cinnamon, with every kind of

4138 כַּרְכְּמִישׁ *karkᵉmîš*, n.pr.loc. [3]

Carchemish [3]

2Ch 35: 20 Neco king of Egypt went up to fight at **Carchemish** on the
Isa 10: 9 'Has not Calno fared like **Carchemish**? Is not Hamath like Arpad,
Jer 46: 2 which was defeated at **Carchemish** on the Euphrates River by

4139 כַּרְכַּס *karkas*, n.pr.m. [1]

Carcas [1]

Est 1: 10 Mehuman, Biztha, Harbona, Bigtha, Abagtha, Zethar and **Carcas**—

4140 כִּרְכָּרָה *kirkārâ*, n.f. [1] [√ 4159]

camels [1]

Isa 66: 20 on horses, in chariots and wagons, and on mules and **camels**,"

4141 כָּרַם *kāram*, v. Not used in NIV/BHS [√ 4142]

4142 כֶּרֶם[1] *kerem*[1], n.m. [92 / 93] [→ 4141, 4143, 4144, 4145?, 4146?, 4149]

vineyards [49], vineyard [41], *untranslated* [1], grapes [1], vintage [1]

Ge 9: 20 Noah, a man of the soil, proceeded to plant a **vineyard**.
Ex 22: 5 [22:4] or **vineyard** and lets them stray and they graze in another
22: 5 [22:4] restitution from the best of his own field or **vineyard**.
23: 11 they leave. Do the same with your **vineyard** and your olive grove.
Lev 19: 10 Do not go over your **vineyard** a second time or pick up the grapes
19: 10 **[RPH]** Leave them for the poor and the alien. I am the LORD
25: 3 and for six years prune your **vineyards** and gather their crops.
25: 4 to the LORD. Do not sow your fields or prune your **vineyards**.
Nu 16: 14 and honey or given us an inheritance of fields and **vineyards**.
20: 17 We will not go through any field or **vineyard**, or drink water from
21: 22 We will not turn aside into any field or **vineyard**, or drink water
22: 24 of the LORD stood in a narrow path between two **vineyards**,
Dt 6: 11 did not dig, and **vineyards** and olive groves you did not plant—
20: 6 Has anyone planted a **vineyard** and not begun to enjoy it?
22: 9 Do not plant two kinds of seed in your **vineyard**; if you do,
22: 9 crops you plant but also the fruit of the **vineyard** will be defiled.
23: 24 [23:25] If you enter your neighbor's **vineyard**, you may eat all
24: 21 When you harvest the grapes in your **vineyard**, do not go over the
28: 30 You will plant a **vineyard**, but you will not even begin to enjoy its
28: 39 You will plant **vineyards** and cultivate them but you will not drink
Jos 24: 13 you live in them and eat from **vineyards** and olive groves that you
Jdg 9: 27 gone out into the fields and gathered the **grapes** and trodden them,
14: 5 As they approached the **vineyards** *of* Timnah, suddenly a young
15: 5 and standing grain, together with the **vineyards** and olive groves.
21: 20 instructed the Benjamites, saying, "Go and hide in the **vineyards**
21: 21 rush from the **vineyards** and each of you seize a wife from the
1Sa 8: 14 and **vineyards** and olive groves and give them to his attendants.
8: 15 and of your **vintage** and give it to his officials and attendants.
22: 7 Will the son of Jesse give all of you fields and **vineyards**?
1Ki 21: 1 Some time later there was an incident involving a **vineyard**
21: 2 "Let me have your **vineyard** to use for a vegetable garden,
21: 2 In exchange I will give you a better **vineyard** or, if you prefer,
21: 6 "Because I said to Naboth the Jezreelite, 'Sell me your **vineyard**;
21: 6 or if you prefer, I will give you another **vineyard** in its place.'
21: 6 in its place.' But he said, 'I will not give you my **vineyard**.' "
21: 7 Cheer up. I'll get you the **vineyard** *of* Naboth the Jezreelite."
21: 15 take possession of the **vineyard** *of* Naboth the Jezreelite that he
21: 16 he got up and went down to take possession of Naboth's **vineyard**.
21: 18 He is now in Naboth's **vineyard**, where he has gone to take
2Ki 5: 26 olive groves, **vineyards**, flocks, herds, or menservants
18: 32 a land of grain and new wine, a land of bread and **vineyards**,
19: 29 in the third year sow and reap, plant **vineyards** and eat their fruit.
1Ch 27: 27 Shimei the Ramathite was in charge of the **vineyards**. Zabdi the
27: 27 Zabdi the Shiphmite was in charge of the produce of the **vineyards**
Ne 5: 3 our **vineyards** and our homes to get grain during the famine."
5: 4 to borrow money to pay the king's tax on our fields and **vineyards**.
5: 5 because our fields and our **vineyards** belong to others."
5: 11 **vineyards**, olive groves and houses, and also the usury you are
9: 25 already dug, **vineyards**, olive groves and fruit trees in abundance.
Job 24: 6 fodder in the fields and glean in the **vineyards** *of* the wicked.
24: 18 portion of the land is cursed, so that no one goes to the **vineyards**.
Ps 107: 37 sowed fields and planted **vineyards** that yielded a fruitful harvest;
Pr 24: 30 of the sluggard, past the **vineyard** *of* the man who lacks judgment;
31: 16 a field and buys it; out of her earnings she plants a **vineyard**.
Ecc 2: 4 great projects: I built houses for myself and planted **vineyards**.
SS 1: 6 sons were angry with me and made me take care of the **vineyards**;
1: 6 me take care of the vineyards; my own **vineyard** I have neglected.
1: 14 to me a cluster of henna blossoms from the **vineyards** *of* En Gedi.
2: 15 Catch for us the foxes, the little foxes that ruin the **vineyards**,
2: 15 little foxes that ruin the vineyards, our **vineyards** that are in bloom.
7: 12 [7:13] Let us go early to the **vineyards** to see if the vines have
8: 11 Solomon had a **vineyard** in Baal Hamon; he let out his vineyard to
8: 11 had a vineyard in Baal Hamon; he let out his **vineyard** to tenants.
8: 12 my own **vineyard** is mine to give; the thousand shekels are for
Isa 1: 8 The Daughter of Zion is left like a shelter in a **vineyard**, like a hut
3: 14 "It is you who have ruined my **vineyard**; the plunder from the poor
5: 1 I will sing for the one I love a song about his **vineyard**: My loved
5: 1 his vineyard: My loved one had a **vineyard** on a fertile hillside.
5: 3 and men of Judah, judge between me and my **vineyard**.
5: 4 What more could have been done for my **vineyard** than I have
5: 5 Now I will tell you what I am going to do to my **vineyard**:
5: 7 The **vineyard** *of* the LORD Almighty is the house of Israel,
5: 10 A ten-acre **vineyard** will produce only a bath of wine, a homer of
16: 10 no one sings or shouts in the **vineyards**; no one treads out wine at
27: 2 In that day—"Sing about a fruitful **vineyard**:
36: 17 a land of grain and new wine, a land of bread and **vineyards**.
37: 30 in the third year sow and reap, plant **vineyards** and eat their fruit.
65: 21 and dwell in them; they will plant **vineyards** and eat their fruit.
Jer 12: 10 Many shepherds will ruin my **vineyard** and trample down my
31: 5 Again you will plant **vineyards** on the hills of Samaria; the farmers
32: 15 Houses, fields and **vineyards** will again be bought in this land.'
35: 7 Also you must never build houses, sow seed or plant **vineyards**;
35: 9 or built houses to live in or had **vineyards**, fields or crops.
39: 10 and at that time he gave them **vineyards** and fields.
Eze 19: 10 " 'Your mother was like a vine in your **vineyard** [BHS 1947]
28: 26 will live there in safety and will build houses and plant **vineyards**;
Hos 2: 15 [2:17] There I will give her back her **vineyards**, and will make
Am 4: 9 "Many times I struck your gardens and **vineyards**, I struck them
5: 11 though you have planted lush **vineyards**, you will not drink their
5: 17 There will be wailing in all the **vineyards**, for I will pass through
9: 14 They will plant **vineyards** and drink their wine; they will make
Mic 1: 6 make Samaria a heap of rubble, a place for planting **vineyards**.
Zep 1: 13 not live in them; they will plant **vineyards** but not drink the wine.

4143 כֶּרֶם[2] *kerem*[2], n.pr.loc. Not used in NIV/BHS [√ 4142]

4144 כֹּרֵם *kōrēm*, n.[m.] *or* v.ptcp. [5] [√ 4142]

work vineyards [2], vine growers [1], vineyards [1], working fields and vineyards [1]

2Ki 25: 12 some of the poorest people of the land to **work** *the* **vineyards**
2Ch 26: 10 He had people **working** his **fields and vineyards** in the hills
Isa 61: 5 your flocks; foreigners will work your fields and **vineyards**.
Jer 52: 16 the rest of the poorest people of the land to **work** the **vineyards**
Joel 1: 11 Despair, you farmers, wail, you **vine growers**; grieve for the wheat

4145 כַּרְמִי[1] *karmî*[1], n.pr.m. [8] [→ 4146; cf. 4142?]

Carmi [8]

Ge 46: 9 The sons of Reuben: Hanoch, Pallu, Hezron and **Carmi**.
Ex 6: 14 firstborn son of Israel were Hanoch and Pallu, Hezron and **Carmi**.
Nu 26: 6 the Hezronite clan; through **Carmi**, the Carmite clan.
Jos 7: 1 Achan son of **Carmi**, the son of Zimri, the son of Zerah,
7: 18 and Achan son of **Carmi**, the son of Zimri, the son of Zerah,
1Ch 2: 7 The son of **Carmi**: Achar, who brought trouble on Israel by
4: 1 The descendants of Judah: Perez, Hezron, **Carmi**, Hur and Shobal.
5: 3 Reuben the firstborn of Israel: Hanoch, Pallu, Hezron and **Carmi**.

4146 כַּרְמִי[2] *karmî*[2], a.g. [1] [√ 4145; cf. 4142?]

Carmite [1]

Nu 26: 6 the Hezronite clan; through Carmi, the **Carmite** clan.

4147 כַּרְמִיל *karmîl*, n.[m.]. [3]

crimson [3]

2Ch 2: 7 [2:6] and iron, and in purple, **crimson** and blue yarn,
2: 14 [2:13] and with purple and blue and **crimson** yarn and fine linen.
3: 14 made the curtain of blue, purple and **crimson** yarn and fine linen,

4148 כְּרָמִים *kᵉrāmîm*, n.pr.loc. Not used in NIV/BHS [→ 70]

4149 ¹כַּרְמֶל **karmel¹**, n.m. [14] [→ 4150, 4151, 4153; cf. 4142]
fertile field [5], finest of forests [+3623] [2], orchards [2], fertile fields [1], fertile lands [1], fertile pasturelands [1], fertile [1], fruitful land [1]

2Ki 19:23 I have reached its remotest parts, the **finest of** its **forests** [+3623].
2Ch 26:10 his fields and vineyards in the hills and in the **fertile lands**,
Isa 10:18 splendor of his forests and **fertile fields** it will completely destroy,
16:10 Joy and gladness are taken away from the **orchards**; no one sings
29:17 will not Lebanon be turned into a **fertile field** and the fertile field
29:17 be turned into a fertile field and the **fertile field** seem like a forest?
32:15 the desert becomes a **fertile field**, and the fertile field seems like a
32:15 becomes a fertile field, and the **fertile field** seems like a forest.
32:16 will dwell in the desert and righteousness live in the **fertile field**.
37:24 have reached its remotest heights, the **finest of** its **forests** [+3623].
Jer 2:7 I brought you into a **fertile** land to eat its fruit and rich produce.
4:26 I looked, and the **fruitful land** was a desert; all its towns lay in
48:33 Joy and gladness are gone from the **orchards** and fields of Moab.
Mic 7:14 which lives by itself in a forest, in **fertile pasturelands**.

4150 ²כַּרְמֶל **karmel²**, n.pr.loc. [7] [→ 4153; cf. 4149]
Carmel [7]

Jos 15:55 Maon, **Carmel**, Ziph, Juttah,
1Sa 15:12 and went to meet Saul, but he was told, "Saul has gone to **Carmel**.
25:2 in Maon, who had property there at **Carmel**, was very wealthy.
25:2 and three thousand sheep, which he was shearing in **Carmel**.
25:5 to them, "Go up to Nabal at **Carmel** and greet him in my name.
25:7 the whole time they were at **Carmel** nothing of theirs was missing.
25:40 His servants went to **Carmel** and said to Abigail, "David has sent

4151 ³כַּרְמֶל **karmel³**, n.pr.loc. [15] [√ 4149]
Carmel [15]

Jos 12:22 the king of Kedesh one the king of Jokneam in **Carmel** one
19:26 On the west the boundary touched **Carmel** and Shihor Libnath.
1Ki 18:19 the people from all over Israel to meet me on Mount **Carmel**.
18:20 all Israel and assembled the prophets on Mount **Carmel**.
18:42 went off to eat and drink, but Elijah climbed to the top of **Carmel**,
2Ki 2:25 he went on to Mount **Carmel** and from there returned to Samaria.
4:25 So she set out and came to the man of God at Mount **Carmel**.
SS 7:5 [7:6] Your head crowns you like Mount **Carmel**. Your hair is like
Isa 33:9 is like the Arabah, and Bashan and **Carmel** drop their leaves.
35:2 of Lebanon will be given to it, the splendor of **Carmel** and Sharon;
Jer 46:18 who is like Tabor among the mountains, like **Carmel** by the sea.
50:19 back to his own pasture and he will graze on **Carmel** and Bashan;
Am 1:2 pastures of the shepherds dry up, and the top of **Carmel** withers."
9:3 Though they hide themselves on the top of **Carmel**, there I will
Na 1:4 Bashan and **Carmel** wither and the blossoms of Lebanon fade.

4152 ⁴כַּרְמֶל **karmel⁴**, n.m. [3]
new grain [2], heads of new grain [1]

Lev 2:14 the LORD, offer crushed heads of **new grain** roasted in the fire.
23:14 You must not eat any bread, or roasted or **new grain**, until the very
2Ki 4:42 from the first ripe grain, along with *some* **heads of new grain**.

4153 כַּרְמְלִי **karmᵉlî**, a.g. [7] [√ 4150; cf. 4149]
of Carmel [5], Carmelite [2]

1Sa 27:3 Ahinoam of Jezreel and Abigail **of Carmel**, the widow of Nabal.
30:5 Ahinoam of Jezreel and Abigail, the widow of Nabal **of Carmel**.
2Sa 2:2 Ahinoam of Jezreel and Abigail, the widow of Nabal **of Carmel**.
3:3 Kileab the son of Abigail the widow of Nabal **of Carmel**;
23:35 Hezro the **Carmelite**, Paarai the Arbite,
1Ch 3:1 of Jezreel; the second, Daniel the son of Abigail **of Carmel**;
11:37 Hezro the **Carmelite**, Naarai son of Ezbai,

4154 כְּרָן **kᵉrān**, n.pr.m. [2]
Keran [2]

Ge 36:26 The sons of Dishon: Hemdan, Eshban, Ithran and **Keran**.
1Ch 1:41 Dishon. The sons of Dishon: Hemdan, Eshban, Ithran and **Keran**.

4155 כִּרְסֵם **kirsēm**, v. [1] [cf. 4080]
ravage [1]

Ps 80:13 [80:14] [D] Boars from the forest **ravage** it and the creatures of

4156 כָּרַע **kāra'**, v. [36] [√ 4157]
sank [3], bow down [2], bow [2], fell [2], kneel down [2], knelt down [2], made bow [2], made miserable [+4156] [2], bend down [1], bowed down [1], bows down [1], bring down [1], brought to knees [1], cringe [1], crouch down [1], crouch [1], crouches [1], cutting down [1], down [1], faltering [1], got down [1], kneel [1], kneeling [+1386+6584] [1], knelt [1], sleep with [+6584] [1], slumped down [1], went into labor [1]

Ge 49:9 [A] Like a lion *he* **crouches** and lies down, like a lioness—
Nu 24:9 [A] Like a lion *they* **crouch** and lie down, like a lioness—
Jdg 5:27 [A] At her feet *he* **sank**, he fell; there he lay. At her feet he sank,
5:27 [A] At her feet *he* **sank**, he fell; where he sank, there he fell—
5:27 [A] her feet he sank, he fell; where *he* **sank**, there he fell—dead.
7:5 [A] tongues like a dog from those who kneel **down** to drink."
7:6 [A] to their mouths. All the rest **got down** on their knees to drink.
11:35 [G] You *have* **made** me **miserable** [+4156] and wretched,
11:35 [G] You *have* **made** me **miserable** [+4156] and wretched,
1Sa 4:19 [A] her husband were dead, *she* **went into labor** and gave birth,
2Sa 22:40 [G] strength for battle; *you* **made** my adversaries **bow** at my feet.
1Ki 8:54 [A] where *he had been* **kneeling** [+1386+6584] with his hands
19:18 [A] all whose knees *have* not **bowed down** to Baal and all whose
2Ki 1:13 [A] This third captain went up and **fell** on his knees before Elijah.
9:24 [A] arrow pierced his heart and *he* **slumped down** in his chariot.
2Ch 7:3 [A] *they* **knelt** on the pavement with their faces to the ground,
29:29 [A] the king and everyone present with him **knelt down**
Ezr 9:5 [A] **fell** on my knees with my hands spread out to the LORD
Est 3:2 [A] All the royal officials at the king's gate **knelt down** and paid
3:2 [A] But Mordecai *would* not **kneel down** or pay him honor.
3:5 [A] When Haman saw that Mordecai *would* not **kneel down**
Job 4:4 [A] those who stumbled; you have strengthened **faltering** knees.
31:10 [A] man's grain, and *may* other men **sleep** [+6584] **with** her.
39:3 [A] *They* **crouch down** and bring forth their young; their labor
Ps 17:13 [G] Rise up, O LORD, confront them, **bring** them **down**;
18:39 [18:40] [G] *you* **made** my adversaries **bow** at my feet.
20:8 [20:9] [A] They *are* **brought to** *their* **knees** and fall, but we
22:29 [22:30] [A] all who go down to the dust *will* **kneel** before him—
72:9 [A] The desert tribes *will* **bow** before him and his enemies will
78:31 [G] sturdiest among them, **cutting down** the young men of Israel.
95:6 [A] Come, *let us* **bow down** in worship, let us kneel before the
Isa 10:4 [A] Nothing will remain but *to* **cringe** among the captives or fall
45:23 [A] Before me every knee *will* **bow**; by me every tongue will
46:1 [A] Bel **bows down**, Nebo stoops low; their idols are borne by
46:2 [A] They stoop and **bow down** together; unable to rescue the
65:12 [A] for the sword, and you *will* all **bend down** for the slaughter;

4157 כֶּרַע **kera'**, n.[f.]. [9] [→ 4156]
legs [8], leg bones [1]

Ex 12:9 in water, but roast it over the fire—head, **legs** and inner parts.
29:17 Cut the ram into pieces and wash the inner parts and the **legs**,
Lev 1:9 He is to wash the inner parts and the **legs** with water, and the priest
1:13 He is to wash the inner parts and the **legs** with water, and the priest
4:11 all its flesh, as well as the head and **legs**, the inner parts and offal—
8:21 He washed the inner parts and the **legs** with water and burned the
9:14 He washed the inner parts and the **legs** and burned them on top of
11:21 may eat: those that have jointed **legs** for hopping on the ground.
Am 3:12 "As a shepherd saves from the lion's mouth only two **leg bones**

4158 כַּרְפַּס **karpas**, n.m. [1]
hangings of linen [1]

Est 1:6 The garden had **hangings of** white and blue **linen**, fastened with

4159 כָּרַר **kārar**, v. [2] [→ 3929?, 3971, 4119, 4140]
danced [1], dancing [1]

2Sa 6:14 [D] a linen ephod, **danced** before the LORD with all his might,
6:16 [D] she saw King David leaping and **dancing** before the LORD,

4160 כָּרֵשׂ **kārēś**, n.[m.]. [1]
stomach [1]

Jer 51:34 he has swallowed us and filled his **stomach** with our delicacies,

4161 כַּרְשְׁנָא **karšᵉnā'**, n.pr.m. [1]
Carshena [1]

Est 1:14 **Carshena**, Shethar, Admatha, Tarshish, Meres, Marsena

4162 כָּרַת **kārat**, v. [288] [→ 4134?, 4135, 4164]
cut off [56], made [45], be cut off [37], make [27], cut down [20], destroy [14], fail to have [+4200] [8], cut [7], kill [6], be destroyed [4], destroyed [4], making [4], be cut down [3], made a covenant [3], be ruined [2], covenanted [2], must surely be cut off [+4162] [2], put an end [2], renewed [2], was cut off [2], are cut off [1], banish [1], be broken [1], be consumed [1], be cut out [1], be rid of [1], be struck down [1], be taken [1], be without [+4946] [1], been broken off [1], been cut off [1], been snatched [1], cease [1], chop down [1], conquered [1], cut up [1], cutting [+9163] [1], cutting off [1], cutting [1], destruction [1], disappear [1], entered [1], fell [1], felling [1], form

[1], is cut down [1], killing off [1], killing [1], leave no [1], made a pact [1], make a treaty [1], makes a covenant [1], makes [1], take away [1], vanished [1], was cut [1], were cut off [1], wipe out [1]

Ge 9:11 [C] Never again *will* all life **be cut off** by the waters of a flood;
15:18 [A] On that day the LORD **made** a covenant with Abram
17:14 [C] circumcised in the flesh, *will* **be cut off** from his people;
21:27 [A] and gave them to Abimelech, and the two men **made** a treaty.
21:32 [A] After the treaty *had been* **made** at Beersheba, Abimelech
26:28 [A] between us and you. *Let us* **make** a treaty with you
31:44 [A] Come now, *let's* **make** a covenant, you and I, and let it serve
41:36 [C] so that the country *may* not **be ruined** by the famine."
Ex 4:25 [A] **cut off** her son's foreskin and touched ⌊Moses'⌋ feet with it.
8: 9 [8:5] [G] your people that you and your houses *may* **be rid of**
12:15 [C] the first day through the seventh *must* **be cut off** from Israel.
12:19 [C] whoever eats anything with yeast in it *must* **be cut off** from
23:32 [A] *Do* not **make** a covenant with them or with their gods.
24: 8 [A] "This is the blood of the covenant that the LORD *has* **made**
30:33 [C] other than a priest *must* **be cut off** from his people.' "
30:38 [C] it to enjoy its fragrance *must* **be cut off** from his people."
31:14 [C] whoever does any work on that day *must* **be cut off** from his
34:10 [A] Then the LORD said: "I *am* **making** a covenant with you.
34:12 [A] Be careful not *to* **make** a treaty with those who live in the
34:13 [A] smash their sacred stones and **cut down** their Asherah poles.
34:15 [A] "Be careful not *to* **make** a treaty with those who live in the
34:27 [A] for in accordance with these words *I have* **made** a covenant
Lev 7:20 [C] to the LORD, that person *must* **be cut off** from his people.
7:21 [C] the LORD, that person *must* **be cut off** from his people.' "
7:25 [C] may be made to the LORD *must* **be cut off** from his people.
7:27 [C] eats blood, that person *must* **be cut off** from his people.' "
17: 4 [C] he has shed blood and *must* **be cut off** from his people.
17: 9 [C] it to the LORD—that man *must* **be cut off** from his people.
17:10 [G] person who eats blood and *will* **cut** him **off** from his people.
17:14 [C] creature is its blood; anyone who eats it *must* **be cut off**."
18:29 [C] such persons *must* **be cut off** from their people.
19: 8 [C] to the LORD; that person *must* **be cut off** from his people.
20: 3 [G] face against that man and *I will* **cut** him **off** from his people;
20: 5 [G] *will* **cut off** from their people both him and all who follow
20: 6 [G] by following them, and *I will* **cut** him **off** from his people.
20:17 [C] *They must* **be cut off** before the eyes of their people.
20:18 [C] Both of them *must* **be cut off** from their people.
22: 3 [C] the LORD, that person *must* **be cut off** from my presence.
22:24 [B] an animal whose testicles are bruised, crushed, torn or **cut**.
23:29 [C] deny himself on that day *must* **be cut off** from his people.
26:22 [G] **destroy** your cattle and make you so few in number that your
26:30 [G] **cut down** your incense altars and pile your dead bodies on
Nu 4:18 [G] "*See that* the Kohathite tribal clans *are* not **cut off** from the
9:13 [C] that person *must* **be cut off** from his people because he did
11:33 [C] still between their teeth and before *it could* **be consumed**,
13:23 [A] *they* **cut off** a branch bearing a single cluster of grapes.
13:24 [A] because of the cluster of grapes the Israelites **cut off** there.
15:30 [C] the LORD, and that person *must* **be cut off** from his people.
15:31 [C] his commands, that person **must surely be cut** [+4162] **off**;
15:31 [C] his commands, that person **must surely be cut off** [+4162];
19:13 [C] That person *must* **be cut off** from Israel.
19:20 [C] he *must* **be cut off** from the community, because he has
Dt 4:23 [A] covenant of the LORD your God that *he* **made** with you;
5: 2 [A] The LORD our God **made** a covenant with us at Horeb.
5: 3 [A] It was not with our fathers that the LORD **made** this
7: 2 [A] **Make** no treaty with them, and show them no mercy.
9: 9 [A] the tablets of the covenant that the LORD *had* **made** with
12:29 [G] The LORD your God *will* **cut off** before you the nations
19: 1 [G] When the LORD your God *has* **destroyed** the nations
19: 5 [A] and as he swings his ax to **fell** a tree, the head may fly off
20:19 [A] because you can eat their fruit. *Do* not **cut** them **down**.
20:20 [A] *you may* **cut down** trees that you know are not fruit trees
23: 1 [23:2] [B] or **cutting** [+9163] may enter the assembly of the
29: 1 [28:69] [A] Moses to **make** with the Israelites in Moab,
29: 1 [28:69] [A] in addition to the covenant *he had* **made** with them
29:12 [29:11] [A] a covenant the LORD *is* **making** with you this day
29:14 [29:13] [A] I *am* **making** this covenant, with its oath, not only
29:25 [29:24] [A] the covenant *he* **made** with them when he brought
31:16 [A] will forsake me and break the covenant *I* **made** with them.
Jos 3:13 [C] its waters flowing downstream *will* **be cut off** and stand up in
3:16 [C] the Sea of the Arabah (the Salt Sea) **was** completely **cut off**.
4: 7 [C] tell them that the flow of the Jordan **was cut off** before the
4: 7 [C] it crossed the Jordan, the waters of the Jordan **were cut off**.
7: 9 [G] they will surround us and **wipe out** our name from the earth.
9: 6 [A] have come from a distant country; **make** a treaty with us."
9: 7 [A] you live near us. How then *can we* **make** a treaty with you?"
9:11 [A] say to them, "We are your servants; **make** a treaty with us." '
9:15 [A] Joshua **made** a treaty of peace with them to let them live,
9:16 [A] Three days after *they* **made** the treaty with the Gibeonites,
9:23 [C] *will* never **cease** to serve as woodcutters and water carriers
11:21 [G] and **destroyed** the Anakites from the hill country:
23: 4 [G] the nations *I* **conquered**—between the Jordan and the Great
24:25 [A] On that day Joshua **made** a covenant for the people,
Jdg 2: 2 [A] you *shall* not **make** a covenant with the people of this land,
4:24 [G] against Jabin, the Canaanite king, until *they* **destroyed** him.
6:25 [A] altar to Baal and **cut down** the Asherah pole beside it.
6:26 [A] Using the wood of the Asherah pole that *you* **cut down**, offer
6:28 [E] with the Asherah pole beside it **cut down** and the second bull
6:30 [A] down Baal's altar and **cut down** the Asherah pole beside it."
9:48 [A] He took an ax and **cut off** some branches, which he lifted to
9:49 [A] So all the men **cut** branches and followed Abimelech. They
Ru 4:10 [C] so that his name *will* not **disappear** from among his family
1Sa 2:33 [G] Every one of you that *I do* not **cut off** from my altar will be
5: 4 [B] His head and hands *had* **been broken off** and were lying on
11: 1 [A] "**Make** a treaty with us, and we will be subject to you."
11: 2 [A] "*I will* **make a treaty** with you only on the condition that I
17:51 [A] After he killed him, *he* **cut off** his head with the sword.
18: 3 [A] Jonathan **made** a covenant with David because he loved him
20:15 [G] *do* not ever **cut off** your kindness from my family—not even
20:15 [G] not even when the LORD *has* **cut off** every one of David's
20:16 [A] So Jonathan **made a covenant** with the house of David,
22: 8 [A] No one tells me when my son **makes a covenant** with the
23:18 [A] The two of them **made** a covenant before the LORD.
24: 4 [24:5] [A] up unnoticed and **cut off** a corner of Saul's robe.
24: 5 [24:6] [A] David was conscience-stricken for *having* **cut off** a
24:11 [24:12] [A] I **cut off** the corner of your robe but did not kill you.
24:21 [24:22] [G] LORD that *you will* not **cut off** my descendants
28: 9 [G] *He has* **cut off** the mediums and spiritists from the land.
31: 9 [A] *They* **cut off** his head and stripped off his armor, and they
2Sa 3:12 [A] **Make** an agreement with me, and I will help you bring all
3:13 [A] "Good," said David. "I *will* **make** an agreement with you.
3:21 [A] lord the king, so that *they may* **make** a compact with you,
3:29 [C] *May* Joab's house never **be without** [+4946] someone who
5: 3 [A] the king **made** a compact with them at Hebron before the
7: 9 [G] and *I have* **cut off** all your enemies from before you.
10: 4 [A] **cut off** their garments in the middle at the buttocks, and sent
20:22 [A] *they* **cut off** the head of Sheba son of Bicri and threw it to
1Ki 2: 4 [C] you *will* never **fail** [+4200] **to have** a man on the throne of
5: 6 [5:20] [A] "So give orders that cedars of Lebanon *be* **cut** for
5: 6 [5:20] [A] no one so skilled in **felling** timber as the Sidonians."
5:12 [5:26] [A] and Solomon, and the two of them **made** a treaty.
8: 9 [A] where the LORD **made a covenant** with the Israelites after
8:21 [A] in which is the covenant of the LORD that *he* **made** with
8:25 [C] 'You *shall* never **fail** [+4200] **to have** a man to sit before me
9: 5 [C] '*You shall* never **fail** [+4200] **to have** a man on the throne of
9: 7 [G] *I will* **cut off** Israel from the land I have given them and will
11:16 [G] six months, until *they had* **destroyed** all the men in Edom.
14:10 [G] *I will* **cut off** from Jeroboam every last male in Israel—slave
14:14 [G] a king over Israel who *will* **cut off** the family of Jeroboam.
15:13 [A] Asa **cut** the pole **down** and burned it in the Kidron Valley.
18: 4 [G] While Jezebel *was* **killing off** the LORD's prophets,
18: 5 [G] mules alive so *we will* not *have to* **kill** any of our animals."
20:34 [A] set you free." So *he* **made** a treaty with him, and let him go.
21:21 [G] and **cut off** from Ahab every last male in Israel—
2Ki 9: 8 [G] *I will* **cut off** from Ahab every last male in Israel—slave
11: 4 [A] *He* **made** a covenant with them and put them under oath at
11:17 [A] Jehoiada then **made** a covenant between the LORD and the
17:15 [A] his decrees and the covenant *he had* **made** with their fathers
17:35 [A] When the LORD **made** a covenant with the Israelites, he
17:38 [A] Do not forget the covenant *I have* **made** with you, and do not
18: 4 [A] smashed the sacred stones and **cut down** the Asherah poles.
19:23 [A] *I have* **cut down** its tallest cedars, the choicest of its pines.
23: 3 [A] and **renewed** the covenant in the presence of the LORD—
23:14 [A] smashed the sacred stones and **cut down** the Asherah poles
1Ch 11: 3 [A] *he* **made** a compact with them at Hebron before the LORD,
16:16 [A] the covenant *he* **made** with Abraham, the oath he swore to
17: 8 [G] and *I have* **cut off** all your enemies from before you.
19: 4 [A] **cut off** their garments in the middle at the buttocks,
2Ch 2: 8 [2:7] [A] for I know that your men are skilled in **cutting** timber
2:10 [2:9] [A] give your servants, the woodsmen *who* **cut** the timber,
2:16 [2:15] [C] we *will* **cut** all the logs from Lebanon that you need
5:10 [A] where the LORD **made a covenant** with the Israelites after
6:11 [A] in which is the covenant of the LORD that *he* **made** with
6:16 [C] 'You *shall* never **fail** [+4200] **to have** a man to sit before me
7:18 [A] as *I* **covenanted** with David your father when I said,
7:18 [C] 'You *shall* never **fail** [+4200] **to have** a man to rule over
15:16 [A] Asa **cut** the pole **down**, broke it up and burned it in the
21: 7 [A] because of the covenant the LORD *had* **made** with David,
22: 7 [G] whom the LORD had anointed to **destroy** the house of
23: 3 [A] the whole assembly **made** a covenant with the king at the
23:16 [A] Jehoiada then **made** a covenant that he and the people
29:10 [A] Now I intend to **make** a covenant with the LORD, the God
34:31 [A] and **renewed** the covenant in the presence of the LORD—
Ezr 10: 3 [A] Now *let us* **make** a covenant before our God to send away all

Ne 9: 8 [A] you **made** a covenant with him to give to his descendants the
9:38 [10:1] [A] "In view of all this, we *are* **making** a binding
Job 14: 7 [C] If *it* **is cut down**, it will sprout again, and its new shoots will
31: 1 [A] "*I* **made** a covenant with my eyes not to look lustfully at a
41: 4 [40:28] [A] *Will he* **make** an agreement with you for you to
Ps 12: 3 [12:4] [G] *May* the LORD **cut off** all flattering lips and every
34:16 [34:17] [G] to **cut off** the memory of them from the earth.
37: 9 [C] For evil men *will* **be cut off**, but those who hope in the
37:22 [C] will inherit the land, but those he curses *will* **be cut off**.
37:28 [C] but the offspring of the wicked *will* **be cut off**;
37:34 [C] inherit the land; when the wicked **are cut off**, you will see it.
37:38 [C] will be destroyed; the future of the wicked *will* **be cut off**.
50: 5 [A] *who* **made** a covenant with me by sacrifice."
83: 5 [83:6] [A] plot together; *they* **form** an alliance against you—
89: 3 [89:4] [A] You said, "*I have* **made** a covenant with my chosen
101: 8 [G] I *will* **cut off** every evildoer from the city of the LORD.
105: 9 [A] the covenant *he* **made** with Abraham, the oath he swore to
109:13 [G] May his descendants be **cut off**, their names blotted out from
109:15 [G] that *he may* **cut off** the memory of them from the earth.
Pr 2:22 [C] the wicked *will* **be cut off** from the land, and the unfaithful
10:31 [C] brings forth wisdom, but a perverse tongue *will* **be cut out**.
23:18 [C] a future hope for you, and your hope *will* not **be cut off**.
24:14 [C] is a future hope for you, and your hope *will* not **be cut off**.
Isa 9:14 [9:13] [G] So the LORD *will* **cut off** from Israel both head
10: 7 [G] his purpose is to destroy, to **put an end** *to* many nations.
11:13 [C] jealousy will vanish, and Judah's enemies *will* **be cut off**;
14: 8 [A] have been laid low, no *woodsman* comes *to* **cut** us **down**."
14:22 [G] "*I will* **cut off** from Babylon her name and survivors, her
18: 5 [A] *he will* **cut off** the shoots with pruning knives, and cut down
22:25 [C] and will fall, and the load hanging on it *will* **be cut down**."
28:15 [A] You boast, "*We have* **entered** *into* a covenant with death,
29:20 [C] and all who have an eye for evil *will* **be cut down**—
37:24 [A] *I have* **cut down** its tallest cedars, the choicest of its pines.
44:14 [A] He **cut down** cedars, or perhaps took a cypress or oak. He let
48: 9 [G] of my praise I hold it back from you, so as not *to* **cut** you **off**.
48:19 [C] their name *would* never **be cut off** nor destroyed from before
55: 3 [A] *I will* **make** an everlasting covenant with you, my faithful
55:13 [C] for an everlasting sign, *which will* not **be destroyed**."
56: 5 [C] I will give them an everlasting name that *will* not **be cut off**.
57: 8 [A] *you* **made a pact** with those whose beds you love, and you
61: 8 [A] reward them and **make** an everlasting covenant with them.
Jer 6: 6 [A] "**Cut down** the trees and build siege ramps against
7:28 [C] Truth has perished; *it has* **vanished** from their lips.
9:21 [9:20] [G] *it has* **cut off** the children from the streets
10: 3 [A] *they* **cut** a tree out of the forest, and a craftsman shapes it
11:10 [A] the house of Judah have broken the covenant *I* **made** with
11:19 [A] *let us* **cut** him **off** from the land of the living, that his name
22: 7 [A] *they will* **cut up** your fine cedar beams and throw them into
31:31 [A] "when *I will* **make** a new covenant with the house of Israel
31:32 [A] It will not be like the covenant *I* **made** with their forefathers
31:33 [A] "This is the covenant *I will* **make** with the house of Israel
32:40 [A] *I will* **make** an everlasting covenant with them: I will never
33:17 [C] 'David *will* never **fail** [+4200] **to have** a man to sit on the
33:18 [C] *will* the priests, who are Levites, *ever* **fail** [+4200] **to have**
34: 8 [A] *had* **made** a covenant with all the people in Jerusalem to
34:13 [A] I **made** a covenant with your forefathers when I brought
34:15 [A] *You* even **made** a covenant before me in the house that bears
34:18 [A] have not fulfilled the terms of the covenant *they* **made**
34:18 [A] I will treat like the calf *they* **cut** in two and then walked
35:19 [C] 'Jonadab son of Recab *will* never **fail** [+4200] **to have** a man
44: 7 [G] Why bring such great disaster on yourselves by **cutting off**
44: 8 [G] You *will* **destroy** yourselves and make yourselves an object
44:11 [G] determined to bring disaster on you and to **destroy** all Judah.
46:23 [A] *They will* **chop down** her forest," declares the LORD,
47: 4 [G] and to **cut off** all survivors who could help Tyre and Sidon.
48: 2 [G] 'Come, *let us* **put an end** to that nation.' You too,
50:16 [A] **Cut off** from Babylon the sower, and the reaper with his
51:62 [G] 'O LORD, you have said you *will* **destroy** this place,
Eze 14: 8 [G] an example and a byword. *I will* **cut** him **off** from my people.
14:13 [G] and send famine upon it and **kill** its men and their animals,
14:17 [G] throughout the land,' and *I* **kill** its men and their animals,
14:19 [G] upon it through bloodshed, **killing** its men and their animals,
14:21 [A] wild beasts and plague—to **kill** its men and their animals!
16: 4 [E] On the day you were born your cord **was** not **cut**, nor were
17:13 [A] a member of the royal family and **made** a treaty with him,
17:17 [G] are built and siege works erected to **destroy** many lives.
21: 3 [21:8] [G] **cut off** from you both the righteous and the wicked.
21: 4 [21:9] [G] Because *I am going to* **cut off** the righteous
25: 7 [G] *I will* **cut** you **off** from the nations and exterminate you from
25:13 [G] out my hand against Edom and **kill** its men and their animals.
25:16 [G] *I will* **cut off** the Kerethites and destroy those remaining
29: 8 [G] a sword against you and **kill** your men and their animals.
30:15 [G] the stronghold of Egypt, and **cut off** the hordes of Thebes.
31:12 [A] the most ruthless of foreign nations **cut** it **down** and left it.
34:25 [A] " '*I will* **make** a covenant of peace with them and rid the land
35: 7 [G] a desolate waste and **cut off** from it all who come and go.
37:26 [A] *I will* **make** a covenant of peace with them; it will be an
Da 9:26 [C] the Anointed One *will* **be cut off** and will have nothing.
Hos 2:18 [2:20] [A] In that day *I will* **make** a covenant for them with the
8: 4 [C] they make idols for themselves to *their own* **destruction**.
10: 4 [A] make many promises, take false oaths and **make** agreements;
12: 1 [12:2] [A] *He* **makes** a treaty with Assyria and sends olive oil to
Joel 1: 5 [C] of the new wine, for *it has* **been snatched** from your lips.
1: 9 [H] drink offerings *are* **cut off** from the house of the LORD.
1:16 [C] *Has* not the food **been cut off** before our very eyes—joy
Am 1: 5 [G] *I will* **destroy** the king who is in the Valley of Aven
1: 8 [G] *I will* **destroy** the king of Ashdod and the one who holds the
2: 3 [G] *I will* **destroy** her ruler and kill all her officials with him,"
Ob 1: 9 [C] everyone in Esau's mountains *will* **be cut down** in the
1:10 [C] will be covered with shame; *you will* **be destroyed** forever.
1:14 [G] You should not wait at the crossroads to **cut down** their
Mic 5: 9 [5:8] [C] your enemies, and all your foes *will* **be destroyed**.
5:10 [5:9] [G] "*I will* **destroy** your horses from among you
5:11 [5:10] [G] *I will* **destroy** the cities of your land and tear down
5:12 [5:11] [G] *I will* **destroy** your witchcraft and you will no longer
5:13 [5:12] [G] *I will* **destroy** your carved images and your sacred
Na 1:14 [G] *I will* **destroy** the carved images and cast idols that are in the
1:15 [2:1] [C] invade you; they *will* **be** completely **destroyed**.
2:13 [2:14] [G] young lions. *I will* **leave** you **no** prey on the earth.
3:15 [G] the sword *will* **cut** you **down** and, like grasshoppers,
Zep 1: 3 [G] The wicked will have only heaps of rubble when *I* **cut off**
1: 4 [G] *I will* **cut off** from this place every remnant of Baal,
1:11 [C] will be wiped out, all who trade with silver *will* **be ruined**.
3: 6 [G] "*I have* **cut off** nations; their strongholds are demolished.
3: 7 [C] her dwelling *would* not **be cut off**, nor all my punishments
Hag 2: 5 [A] 'This is what *I* **covenanted** with you when you came out of
Zec 9: 6 [G] occupy Ashdod, and *I will* **cut off** the pride of the Philistines.
9:10 [G] *I will* **take away** the chariots from Ephraim
9:10 [C] from Jerusalem, and the battle bow *will* **be broken**.
11:10 [A] revoking the covenant *I had* **made** with all the nations.
13: 2 [G] that day, *I will* **banish** the names of the idols from the land,
13: 8 [C] the LORD, "two-thirds *will* **be struck down** and perish;
14: 2 [C] but the rest of the people *will* not **be taken** from the city.
Mal 2:12 [G] *may* the LORD **cut** him **off** from the tents of Jacob—

4163 כְּרֹת k^erōt, var. Not used in NIV/BHS [cf. 4165]

4164 כְּרֻתוֹת k^erutôt, n.[f.pl.]. [3] [√ 4162]

trimmed beams [3]

1Ki 6:36 courses of dressed stone and one course of **trimmed** cedar **beams**.
7: 2 four rows of cedar columns supporting **trimmed** cedar **beams**.
7:12 courses of dressed stone and one course of **trimmed** cedar **beams**,

4165 כְּרֵתִי k^erētî, a.g. [10 / 11] [cf. 7152?]

Kerethites [10], Kerethite [1]

1Sa 30:14 We raided the Negev of the **Kerethites** and the territory belonging
2Sa 8:18 Benaiah son of Jehoiada was over the **Kerethites** and Pelethites;
15:18 marched past him, along with all the **Kerethites** and Pelethites;
20: 7 So Joab's men and the **Kerethites** and Pelethites and all the mighty
20:23 Benaiah son of Jehoiada was over the **Kerethites** [K 4133]
1Ki 1:38 the **Kerethites** and the Pelethites went down and put Solomon on
1:44 Benaiah son of Jehoiada, the **Kerethites** and the Pelethites,
1Ch 18:17 Benaiah son of Jehoiada was over the **Kerethites** and Pelethites;
Eze 25:16 I will cut off the **Kerethites** and destroy those remaining along the
Zep 2: 5 Woe to you who live by the sea, O **Kerethite** people; the word of
2: 6 The land by the sea, where the **Kerethites** [BHS 4120] dwell,

4166 כֶּשֶׂב keśeb, n.[m.]. [13] [→ 4167; cf. 3897]

lamb [5], sheep [4], lamb [+928+2021+8445] [1], lambs [1], sheep [+8445] [1], young of the flock [1]

Ge 30:32 every dark-colored **lamb** [+928+2021+8445] and every spotted or
30:33 is not speckled or spotted, or any **lamb** that is not dark-colored,
30:35 all the dark-colored **lambs**, and he placed them in the care of his
30:40 Jacob set apart the **young of the flock** by themselves, but made the
Lev 1:10 from either the **sheep** or the goats, he is to offer a male without
3: 7 If he offers a **lamb**, he is to present it before the LORD.
4:35 just as the fat is removed from the **lamb** *of* the fellowship offering,
7:23 to the Israelites: 'Do not eat any of the fat of cattle, **sheep** or goats.
17: 3 who sacrifices an ox, a **lamb** or a goat in the camp or outside of it
22:19 **sheep** or goats in order that it may be accepted on your behalf.
22:27 "When a calf, a **lamb** or a goat is born, it is to remain with its
Nu 18:17 "But you must not redeem the firstborn of an ox, a **sheep** or a goat;
Dt 14: 4 are the animals you may eat: the ox, the **sheep** [+8445], the goat,

4167 כִּשְׂבָּה kiśbâ, n.f. [1] [√ 4166]

lamb [1]

Lev 5: 6 he must bring to the LORD a female **lamb** or goat from the flock

4168 כֶּשֶׂד keśed, n.pr.m. [1] [√ 4169]

Kesed [1]

Ge 22:22 **Kesed**, Hazo, Pildash, Jidlaph and Bethuel."

4169 כַּשְׂדִּים kaśdîm, n.pr.g. [80] [→ 4168; cf. 951; Ar 10361, 10373]

Babylonians [50], Babylonian [12], Chaldeans [8], Babylonia [5], astrologers [2], Chaldea [2], Babylon [+824] [1]

Ge 11:28 Haran died in Ur of the **Chaldeans**, in the land of his birth.
11:31 together they set out from Ur of the **Chaldeans** to go to Canaan.
15: 7 who brought you out of Ur of the **Chaldeans** to give you this land
2Ki 24: 2 The LORD sent **Babylonian**, Aramean, Moabite and Ammonite
25: 4 king's garden, though the **Babylonians** were surrounding the city.
25: 5 the **Babylonian** army pursued the king and overtook him in the
25:10 The whole **Babylonian** army, under the commander of the
25:13 The **Babylonians** broke up the bronze pillars, the movable stands
25:24 their men. "Do not be afraid of the **Babylonian** officials," he said.
25:25 men of Judah and the **Babylonians** who were with him at Mizpah.
25:26 with the army officers, fled to Egypt for fear of the **Babylonians**.
2Ch 36:17 He brought up against them the king of the **Babylonians**, who
Ne 9: 7 who chose Abram and brought him out of Ur of the **Chaldeans**
Job 1:17 "The **Chaldeans** formed three raiding parties and swept down on
Isa 13:19 the jewel of kingdoms, the glory of the **Babylonians**' pride,
23:13 Look at the land of the **Babylonians**, this people that is now of no
43:14 send to Babylon and bring down as fugitives all the **Babylonians**,
47: 1 sit on the ground without a throne, Daughter of the **Babylonians**.
47: 5 "Sit in silence, go into darkness, Daughter of the **Babylonians**;
48:14 purpose against Babylon; his arm will be against the **Babylonians**.
48:20 Leave Babylon, flee from the **Babylonians**! Announce this with
Jer 21: 4 and the **Babylonians** who are outside the wall besieging you.
21: 9 and surrenders to the **Babylonians** who are besieging you will live;
22:25 to Nebuchadnezzar king of Babylon and to the **Babylonians**.
24: 5 whom I sent away from this place to the land of the **Babylonians**.
25:12 the king of Babylon and his nation, the land of the **Babylonians**,
32: 4 king of Judah will not escape out of the hands of the **Babylonians**
32: 5 If you fight against the **Babylonians**, you will not succeed.' "
32:24 the city will be handed over to the **Babylonians** who are attacking
32:25 And though the city will be handed over to the **Babylonians**,
32:28 I am about to hand this city over to the **Babylonians** and to
32:29 The **Babylonians** who are attacking this city will come in
32:43 or animals, for it has been handed over to the **Babylonians**.'
33: 5 in the fight with the **Babylonians**: 'They will be filled with the
35:11 we must go to Jerusalem to escape the **Babylonian** and Aramean
37: 5 when the **Babylonians** who were besieging Jerusalem heard the
37: 8 the **Babylonians** will return and attack this city; they will capture it
37: 9 thinking, 'The **Babylonians** will surely leave us.'
37:10 Even if you were to defeat the entire **Babylonian** army that is
37:11 After the **Babylonian** army had withdrawn from Jerusalem
37:13 arrested him and said, "You are deserting to the **Babylonians**!"
37:14 not true!" Jeremiah said. "I am not deserting to the **Babylonians**."
38: 2 or plague, but whoever goes over to the **Babylonians** will live.
38:18 this city will be handed over to the **Babylonians** and they will burn
38:19 "I am afraid of the Jews who have gone over to the **Babylonians**,
38:23 your wives and children will be brought out to the **Babylonians**.
39: 5 the **Babylonian** army pursued them and overtook Zedekiah in the
39: 8 The **Babylonians** set fire to the royal palace and the houses of the
40: 9 their men. "Do not be afraid to serve the **Babylonians**," he said.
40:10 Mizpah to represent you before the **Babylonians** who come to us,
41: 3 at Mizpah, as well as the **Babylonian** soldiers who were there.
41:18 to escape the **Babylonians**. They were afraid of them
43: 3 is inciting you against us to hand us over to the **Babylonians**,
50: 1 the prophet concerning Babylon and the land of the **Babylonians**:
50: 8 leave the land of the **Babylonians**, and be like the goats that lead
50:10 So **Babylonia** will be plundered; all who plunder her will have
50:25 LORD Almighty has work to do in the land of the **Babylonians**.
50:35 "A sword against the **Babylonians**!" declares the LORD—
50:45 what he has purposed against the land of the **Babylonians**:
51: 4 They will fall down slain in **Babylon** [+824], fatally wounded in
51:24 all who live in **Babylonia** for all the wrong they have done in
51:35 "May our blood be on those who live in **Babylonia**,"
51:54 the sound of great destruction from the land of the **Babylonians**.
52: 7 king's garden, though the **Babylonians** were surrounding the city.
52: 8 the **Babylonian** army pursued King Zedekiah and overtook him in
52:14 The whole **Babylonian** army under the commander of the imperial
52:17 The **Babylonians** broke up the bronze pillars, the movable stands
Eze 1: 3 the son of Buzi, by the Kebar River in the land of the **Babylonians**.
11:24 brought me to the exiles in **Babylonia** in the vision given by the
12:13 the land of the **Chaldeans**, but he will not see it, and there he will
16:29 Then you increased your promiscuity to include **Babylonia**,
23:14 men portrayed on a wall, figures of **Chaldeans** portrayed in red,
23:15 them looked like Babylonian chariot officers, natives of **Chaldea**.
23:16 she lusted after them and sent messengers to them in **Chaldea**.
23:23 the Babylonians and all the **Chaldeans**, the men of Pekod
Da 1: 4 was to teach them the language and literature of the **Babylonians**.
2: 2 sorcerers and **astrologers** to tell him what he had dreamed.
2: 4 Then the **astrologers** answered the king in Aramaic, "O king,
9: 1 by descent), who was made ruler over the **Babylonian** kingdom—
Hab 1: 6 I am raising up the **Babylonians**, that ruthless and impetuous

4170 כָּשָׂה kāśâ, v. [1]

sleek [1]

Dt 32:15 [A] and kicked; filled with food, he became heavy and **sleek**.

4171 כָּשַׁח kāšaḥ, v. Not used in NIV/BHS

4172 כַּשִּׁיל kaššîl, n.[m.]. [1] [√ 4173]

axes [1]

Ps 74: 6 They smashed all the carved paneling with their **axes** and hatchets.

4173 כָּשַׁל kāšal, v. [62] [→ 4172, 4174, 4842, 4843]

stumble [23], fall [5], stumbled [4], stumbles [3], be brought down [2], downfall [2], give way [2], overthrow [2], stumble and fall [+4173] [2], are brought down [1], bring to ruin [1], cause to fall [1], caused to stumble [1], fails [1], faltered [1], feeblest [1], giving out [1], made stumble [1], make fall [1], overthrown [1], sapped [1], stagger [1], staggers [1], stumbling [1], weak [1], without success [1]

Lev 26:37 [A] *They will* **stumble** over one another as though fleeing from
1Sa 2: 4 [C] are broken, but *those who* **stumbled** are armed with strength.
2Ch 25: 8 [G] God *will* **overthrow** you before the enemy, for God has the
25: 8 [G] the enemy, for God has the power to help or to **overthrow**."
28:15 [A] All *those who were* **weak** they put on donkeys.
28:23 [G] But they were his **downfall** and the downfall of all Israel.
Ne 4:10 [4:4] [A] "The strength of the laborers *is* **giving out**, and there is
Job 4: 4 [A] Your words have supported *those who* **stumbled**; you have
Ps 9: 3 [9:4] [C] turn back; *they* **stumble** and perish before you.
27: 2 [A] and my foes attack me, they *will* **stumble** and fall.
31:10 [31:11] [A] my strength **fails** because of my affliction, and my
64: 8 [64:9] [G] own tongues against them and **bring** them **to ruin**;
105:37 [A] and gold, and from among their tribes no *one* **faltered**.
107:12 [A] to bitter labor; *they* **stumbled**, and there was no one to help.
109:24 [A] My knees **give way** from fasting; my body is thin and gaunt.
Pr 4:12 [C] will not be hampered; when you run, *you will* not **stumble**.
4:16 [G] they are robbed of slumber till *they* **make** someone **fall**.
4:19 [C] deep darkness; they do not know what *makes them* **stumble**.
24:16 [C] rises again, but the wicked **are brought down** by calamity.
24:17 [A] enemy falls; when he **stumbles**, do not let your heart rejoice,
Isa 3: 8 [A] Jerusalem **staggers**, Judah is falling; their words and deeds
5:27 [A] Not one of them grows tired or **stumbles**, not one slumbers
8:15 [A] Many of them *will* **stumble**; they will fall and be broken,
28:13 [A] so that they will go and **fall** backward, be injured and snared
31: 3 [A] he who helps *will* **stumble**, he who is helped will fall;
35: 3 [A] Strengthen the feeble hands, steady the knees *that* **give way**;
40:30 [C] and weary, and young men **stumble** [+4173] **and fall**;
40:30 [A] and weary, and young men **stumble and fall** [+4173];
59:10 [A] At midday *we* **stumble** as if it were twilight;
59:14 [A] truth *has* **stumbled** in the streets, honesty cannot enter.
63:13 [C] Like a horse in open country, *they did* not **stumble**;
Jer 6:15 [C] *they will* **be brought down** when I punish them,"
6:21 [A] Fathers and sons alike *will* **stumble** over them; neighbors
8:12 [C] *they will* **be brought down** when they are punished,
18:15 [G] *which* **made** them **stumble** in their ways and in the ancient
18:23 [H] Let them be **overthrown** before you; deal with them in the
20:11 [C] so my persecutors *will* **stumble** and not prevail.
31: 9 [C] streams of water on a level path where *they will* not **stumble**,
46: 6 [A] In the north by the River Euphrates *they* **stumble** and fall.
46:12 [A] One warrior *will* **stumble** over another; both will fall down
46:16 [A] They will **stumble** repeatedly; they will fall over each other.
50:32 [A] The arrogant one *will* **stumble** and fall and no one will help
La 1:14 [G] come upon my neck and the Lord *has* **sapped** my strength.
5:13 [A] men toil at the millstones; boys **stagger** under loads of wood.
Eze 33:12 [C] the wickedness of the wicked man *will* not *cause him to* **fall**
36:14 [d] [devour men or **make** your nation **childless**, [K; see Q 8897]]
36:15 [G] suffer the scorn of the peoples or **cause** your nation **to fall**,
Da 11:14 [C] will rebel in fulfillment of the vision, but **without success**.
11:19 [C] the fortresses of his own country but *will* **stumble** and fall,
11:33 [C] though for a time *they will* **fall** by the sword or be burned
11:34 [C] When they **fall**, they will receive a little help, and many who
11:35 [C] Some of the wise *will* **stumble**, so that they may be refined,

Da 11:41 [C] Many countries *will* **fall**, but Edom, Moab and the leaders of
Hos 4: 5 [A] *You* **stumble** day and night, and the prophets stumble with
4: 5 [A] stumble day and night, and the prophets **stumble** with you.
5: 5 [C] the Israelites, even Ephraim, **stumble** in their sin; Judah also
5: 5 [A] stumble in their sin; Judah also **stumbles** with them.
14: 1 [14:2] [A] your God. Your sins *have been your* **downfall**!
14: 9 [14:10] [C] walk in them, but the rebellious **stumble** in them.
Na 2: 5 [2:6] [C] his picked troops, yet *they* **stumble** on their way.
3: 3 [A] bodies without number, *people* **stumbling** over the corpses—
Zec 12: 8 [C] so that the **feeblest** among them will be like David,
Mal 2: 8 [G] the way and by your teaching *have* **caused** many **to stumble**;

4174 כִּשָּׁלוֹן *kiššālôn*, n.[m.]. [1] [√ 4173]

fall [1]

Pr 16:18 Pride goes before destruction, a haughty spirit before a **fall**.

4175 כָּשַׁף *kāšap*, v.den. [6] [→ 439, 4176, 4177]

sorcerers [3], engages in witchcraft [1], sorceress [1], witchcraft [1]

Ex 7:11 [D] Pharaoh then summoned wise men and **sorcerers**,
22:18 [22:17] [D] "Do not allow a **sorceress** to live.
Dt 18:10 [D] or sorcery, interprets omens, **engages in witchcraft**,
2Ch 33: 6 [D] practiced sorcery, divination and **witchcraft**, and consulted
Da 2: 2 [D] **sorcerers** and astrologers to tell him what he had dreamed.
Mal 3: 5 [D] I will be quick to testify against **sorcerers**, adulterers

4176 כֶּשֶׁף *kešep*, n.m. [6] [√ 4175]

sorceries [3], witchcraft [3]

2Ki 9:22 as all the idolatry and **witchcraft** *of* your mother Jezebel abound?"
Isa 47: 9 in spite of your many **sorceries** and all your potent spells.
47:12 then, with your magic spells and with your many **sorceries**,
Mic 5:12 [5:11] I will destroy your **witchcraft** and you will no longer cast
Na 3: 4 of the wanton lust of a harlot, alluring, the mistress of **sorceries**,
3: 4 enslaved nations by her prostitution and peoples by her **witchcraft**.

4177 כַּשָּׁף *kaššāp*, n.m. [1] [√ 4175]

sorcerers [1]

Jer 27: 9 of dreams, your mediums or your **sorcerers** who tell you,

4178 כָּשֵׁר *kāšēr*, v. [3] [→ 4179]

bring [1], succeed [1], thinks right [1]

Est 8: 5 [A] he regards me with favor and **thinks** *it* the **right** thing to do,
Ecc 10:10 [G] more strength is needed but skill *will* **bring** success.
11: 6 [A] for you do not know which *will* **succeed**, whether this or that,

4179 כִּשְׁרוֹן *kišrôn*, n.[m.]. [3] [√ 4178]

achievement [+5126] [1], benefit [1], skill [1]

Ecc 2:21 knowledge and **skill**, and then he must leave all he owns to
4: 4 all **achievement** [+5126] spring from man's envy of his neighbor.
5:11 [5:10] what **benefit** are they to the owner except to feast his eyes

4180 כָּתַב *kātab*, v. [223] [→ 4181, 4182, 4844; Ar 10374]

written [107], write [25], wrote [23], recorded [9], write down [6], wrote down [5], be written [3], inscribed [3], signed [3], were recorded [3], be listed [2], engraved [2], issue decrees [+4180] [2], was recorded [2], were written [2], write a description [2], writes [2], wrote out [2], *untranslated* [1], been recorded [1], copied [+906+5467] [1], decree be issued [1], listed [1], lodged [1], map out [1], order be written [1], put in writing [1], putting in writing [1], record [+906+906+4200+9005] [1], record [1], register [1], was written down [1], was written [1], were listed [1], words [1], writing [1], written descriptions [1], wrote description [1]

Ex 17:14 [A] "**Write** this on a scroll as something to be remembered
24: 4 [A] Moses then **wrote down** everything the LORD had said.
24:12 [A] the law and commands *I have* **written** for their instruction."
31:18 [B] the tablets of stone **inscribed** by the finger of God.
32:15 [B] They *were* **inscribed** on both sides, front and back.
32:15 [B] They were inscribed on both sides, front and back. **[RPH]**
32:32 [A] but if not, then blot me out of the book *you have* **written**."
34: 1 [A] *I will* **write** on them the words that were on the first tablets,
34:27 [A] Then the LORD said to Moses, "**Write down** these words,
34:28 [A] *he* **wrote** on the tablets the words of the covenant—the Ten
39:30 [A] the sacred diadem, out of pure gold and **engraved** on it,
Nu 5:23 [A] " 'The priest *is to* **write** these curses on a scroll and
11:26 [B] They **were listed** among the elders, but did not go out to the
17: 2 [17:17] [A] **Write** the name of each man on his staff.
17: 3 [17:18] [A] On the staff of Levi **write** Aaron's name, for there
33: 2 [A] At the LORD's command Moses **recorded** the stages in
Dt 4:13 [A] you to follow and then **wrote** them on two stone tablets.
5:22 [A] *he* **wrote** them on two stone tablets and gave them to me.
6: 9 [A] **Write** them on the doorframes of your houses and on your
9:10 [B] The LORD gave me two stone tablets **inscribed** by the
10: 2 [A] *I will* **write** on the tablets the words that were on the first
10: 4 [A] The LORD **wrote** on these tablets what he had written
11:20 [A] **Write** them on the doorframes of your houses and on your
17:18 [A] *he is to* **write** for himself on a scroll a copy of this law,
24: 1 [A] *he* **writes** her a certificate of divorce, gives it to her
24: 3 [A] husband dislikes her and **writes** her a certificate of divorce,
27: 3 [A] **Write** on them all the words of this law when you have
27: 8 [A] *you shall* **write** very clearly all the words of this law on
28:58 [B] which *are* **written** in this book, and do not revere this
28:61 [B] and disaster not **recorded** in this Book of the Law,
29:20 [29:19] [B] All the curses **written** in this book will fall upon
29:21 [29:20] [B] according to all the curses of the covenant **written**
29:27 [29:26] [B] so that he brought on it all the curses **written** in this
30:10 [B] and decrees that *are* **written** in this Book of the Law
31: 9 [A] So Moses **wrote down** this law and gave it to the priests,
31:19 [A] "Now **write down** for yourselves this song and teach it to the
31:22 [A] So Moses **wrote down** this song that day and taught it to the
31:24 [A] After Moses finished **writing** in a book the words of this law
Jos 1: 8 [B] so that you may be careful to do everything **written** in it.
8:31 [B] He built it according to what *is* **written** in the Book of the
8:32 [A] Joshua **copied** [+906+5467] on stones the law of Moses,
8:32 [A] copied on stones the law of Moses, which *he had* **written**.
8:34 [B] and the curses—just as it *is* **written** in the Book of the Law.
10:13 [B] itself on its enemies, as it *is* **written** in the Book of Jashar.
18: 4 [A] to make a survey of the land and *to* **write a description** *of* it,
18: 6 [A] After you *have* **written descriptions** *of* the seven parts of
18: 8 [A] As the men started on their way to **map out** the land, Joshua
18: 8 [A] and make a survey of the land and **write a description** *of* it.
18: 9 [A] *They* **wrote** its **description** on a scroll, town by town,
23: 6 [B] be careful to obey all that *is* **written** in the Book of the Law
24:26 [A] Joshua **recorded** these things in the Book of the Law of God.
Jdg 8:14 [A] the young man **wrote down** for him the names of the
1Sa 10:25 [A] *He* **wrote** them **down** on a scroll and deposited it before the
2Sa 1:18 [B] this lament of the bow (*it is* **written** in the Book of Jashar):
11:14 [A] In the morning David **wrote** a letter to Joab and sent it with
11:15 [A] In it *he* **wrote**, "Put Uriah in the front line where the fighting
1Ki 2: 3 [B] his laws and requirements, as **written** in the Law of Moses,
11:41 [B] *are* they not **written** in the book of the annals of Solomon?
14:19 [B] *are* **written** in the book of the annals of the kings of Israel.
14:29 [B] *are* they not **written** in the book of the annals of the kings of
15: 7 [B] *are* they not **written** in the book of the annals of the kings of
15:23 [B] *are* they not **written** in the book of the annals of the kings of
15:31 [B] *are* they not **written** in the book of the annals of the kings of
16: 5 [B] *are* they not **written** in the book of the annals of the kings of
16:14 [B] *are* they not **written** in the book of the annals of the kings of
16:20 [B] *are* they not **written** in the book of the annals of the kings of
16:27 [B] *are* they not **written** in the book of the annals of the kings of
21: 8 [A] So *she* **wrote** letters in Ahab's name, placed his seal on
21: 9 [A] In those letters *she* **wrote**: "Proclaim a day of fasting
21:11 [B] did as Jezebel directed in the letters she *had* **written** to them.
22:39 [B] *are* they not **written** in the book of the annals of the kings of
22:45 [22:46] [B] *are* they not **written** in the book of the annals of the
2Ki 1:18 [B] *are* they not **written** in the book of the annals of the kings of
8:23 [B] *are* they not **written** in the book of the annals of the kings of
10: 1 [A] So Jehu **wrote** letters and sent them to Samaria:
10: 6 [A] Jehu **wrote** them a second letter, saying, "If you are on my
10:34 [B] *are* they not **written** in the book of the annals of the kings of
12:19 [12:20] [B] *are* they not **written** in the book of the annals of the
13: 8 [B] *are* they not **written** in the book of the annals of the kings of
13:12 [B] *are* they not **written** in the book of the annals of the kings of
14: 6 [B] in accordance with what *is* **written** in the Book of the Law of
14:15 [B] *are* they not **written** in the book of the annals of the kings of
14:18 [B] *are* they not **written** in the book of the annals of the kings of
14:28 [B] *are* they not **written** in the book of the annals of the kings of
15: 6 [B] *are* they not **written** in the book of the annals of the kings of
15:11 [B] The other events of Zechariah's reign *are* **written** in the
15:15 [B] *are* **written** in the book of the annals of the kings of Israel.
15:21 [B] *are* they not **written** in the book of the annals of the kings of
15:26 [B] *are* **written** in the book of the annals of the kings of Israel.
15:31 [B] *are* they not **written** in the book of the annals of the kings of
15:36 [B] *are* they not **written** in the book of the annals of the kings of
16:19 [B] *are* they not **written** in the book of the annals of the kings of
17:37 [A] and ordinances, the laws and commands *he* **wrote** for you.
20:20 [B] *are* they not **written** in the book of the annals of the kings of
21:17 [B] *are* they not **written** in the book of the annals of the kings of
21:25 [B] *are* they not **written** in the book of the annals of the kings of
22:13 [B] they have not acted in accordance with all that *is* **written**
23: 3 [B] thus confirming the words of the covenant **written** in this
23:21 [B] your God, as *it is* **written** in this Book of the Covenant."
23:24 [B] This he did to fulfill the requirements of the law **written** in
23:28 [B] *are* they not **written** in the book of the annals of the kings of
24: 5 [B] *are* they not **written** in the book of the annals of the kings of

1Ch 4:41 [B] The men whose names *were* **listed** came in the days of
9: 1 [B] All Israel was listed in the genealogies **recorded** in the book
16:40 [B] in accordance with everything **written** in the Law of the
24: 6 [A] **recorded** their names in the presence of the king and of the
29:29 [B] to end, they *are* **written** in the records of Samuel the seer,
2Ch 9:29 [B] *are* they not **written** in the records of Nathan the prophet,
12:15 [B] *are* they not **written** in the records of Shemaiah the prophet
13:22 [B] he said, *are* **written** in the annotations of the prophet Iddo.
16:11 [B] *are* **written** in the book of the kings of Judah and Israel.
20:34 [B] to end, *are* **written** in the annals of Jehu son of Hanani,
23:18 [B] to present the burnt offerings of the LORD as **written** in the
24:27 [B] the record of the restoration of the temple of God *are* **written**
25: 4 [B] acted in accordance with what *is* **written** in the Law,
25:26 [B] *are* they not **written** in the book of the kings of Judah
26:22 [A] to end, *are* **recorded** *by* the prophet Isaiah son of Amoz.
27: 7 [B] *are* **written** in the book of the kings of Israel and Judah.
28:26 [B] *are* **written** in the book of the kings of Judah and Israel.
30: 1 [A] and Judah and also **wrote** letters to Ephraim and Manasseh,
30: 5 [B] celebrated in large numbers according to what *was* **written**.
30:18 [B] yet they ate the Passover, contrary to what *was* **written**.
31: 3 [B] and appointed feasts as **written** in the Law of the LORD.
32:17 [A] The king also **wrote** letters insulting the LORD, the God of
32:32 [B] his acts of devotion *are* **written** in the vision of the prophet
33:19 [B] humbled himself—all *are* **written** in the records of the seers.
34:21 [B] they have not acted in accordance with all that *is* **written** in
34:24 [B] all the curses **written** in the book that has been read in the
34:31 [B] and to obey the words of the covenant **written** in this book.
35:12 [B] to offer to the LORD, as *is* **written** in the Book of Moses.
35:25 [B] became a tradition in Israel and *are* **written** in the Laments.
35:26 [B] according to what *is* **written** in the Law of the LORD—
35:27 [B] *are* **written** in the book of the kings of Israel and Judah.
36: 8 [B] *are* **written** in the book of the kings of Israel and Judah.
Ezr 3: 2 [B] in accordance with what *is* **written** in the Law of Moses the
3: 4 [B] in accordance with what *is* **written**, they celebrated the Feast
4: 6 [A] *they* **lodged** an accusation against the people of Judah
4: 7 [A] and the rest of his associates **wrote** a letter to Artaxerxes.
4: 7 [B] The letter *was* **written** in Aramaic script and in the Aramaic
8:34 [C] and weight, and the entire weight **was recorded** at that time.
Ne 6: 6 [B] in which *was* **written**: "It is reported among the nations—
7: 5 [B] been the first to return. This is what I found **written** there:
8:14 [B] They found **written** in the Law, which the LORD had
8:15 [B] and shade trees, to make booths"—as it *is* **written**.
9:38 [10:1] [A] **putting** it **in writing**, and our leaders, our Levites
10:34 [10:35] [B] of the LORD our God, as it *is* **written** in the Law.
10:36 [10:37] [B] "As it *is* also **written** in the Law, we will bring the
12:22 [B] the priests, **were recorded** in the reign of Darius the Persian.
12:23 [B] son of Eliashib **were recorded** in the book of the annals.
13: 1 [B] there it was found **written** that no Ammonite or Moabite
Est 1:19 [C] and *let it* **be written** in the laws of Persia and Media,
2:23 [C] *All this* **was recorded** in the book of the annals in the
3: 9 [C] If it pleases the king, *let a* **decree be issued** to destroy them,
3:12 [C] *They* **wrote out** in the script of each province and in the
3:12 [C] *These* **were written** in the name of King Xerxes himself
6: 2 [B] It was found **recorded** there that Mordecai had exposed
8: 5 [C] *let an* **order be written** overruling the dispatches that
8: 5 [A] and **wrote** to destroy the Jews in all the king's provinces.
8: 8 [A] Now **write** another decree in the king's name in behalf of the
8: 8 [C] for no document **written** in the king's name and sealed with
8: 9 [C] *They* **wrote out** all Mordecai's orders to the Jews, and to the
8:10 [A] Mordecai **wrote** in the name of King Xerxes, sealed the
9:20 [A] Mordecai **recorded** these events, and he sent letters to all the
9:23 [A] they had begun, doing what Mordecai *had* **written** to them.
9:29 [A] **wrote** with full authority to confirm this second letter
9:32 [C] about Purim, and *it* **was written down** in the records.
10: 2 [B] *are* they not **written** in the book of the annals of the kings of
Job 13:26 [A] For *you* **write down** bitter things against me and make me
19:23 [C] "Oh, that my words **were recorded**, that they were written
31:35 [A] answer me; *let* my accuser **put** *his* indictment **in writing**.
Ps 40: 7 [40:8] [B] I have come—*it is* **written** about me in the scroll.
69:28 [69:29] [C] the book of life and not **be listed** with the righteous.
87: 6 [A] The LORD will write in the **register** *of* the peoples:
102:18 [102:19] [C] *Let* this **be written** for a future generation, that a
139:16 [C] All the days ordained for me **were written** in your book
149: 9 [B] to carry out the sentence **written** against them. This is the
Pr 3: 3 [A] around your neck, **write** them on the tablet of your heart.
7: 3 [A] them on your fingers; **write** them on the tablet of your heart.
22:20 [A] *Have I* not **written** thirty sayings for you, sayings of counsel
Ecc 12:10 [B] just the right words, and what *he* **wrote** was upright and true.
Isa 4: 3 [B] all who *are* **recorded** among the living in Jerusalem.
8: 1 [A] "Take a large scroll and **write** on it with an ordinary pen:
10: 1 [D] unjust laws, to *those who* **issue** oppressive **decrees** [+4180],
10: 1 [D] unjust laws, to *those who* **issue** oppressive **decrees** [+4180],
10:19 [A] forests will be so few that a child *could* **write** them **down**.
30: 8 [A] Go now, **write** it on a tablet for them, inscribe it on a scroll,
44: 5 [A] still another *will* **write** *on* his hand, 'The LORD's,' and will
65: 6 [B] "See, *it stands* **written** before me: I will not keep silent but
Jer 17: 1 [B] "Judah's sin *is* **engraved** with an iron tool, inscribed with a
17:13 [C] Those who turn away from you *will* **be written** in the dust
22:30 [A] "**Record** this man as if childless, a man who will not prosper
25:13 [B] all that *are* **written** in this book and prophesied by Jeremiah
30: 2 [A] says: '**Write** in a book all the words I have spoken to you.
31:33 [A] "I will put my law in their minds and **write** it on their hearts.
32:10 [A] *I* **signed** and sealed the deed, had it witnessed, and weighed
32:12 [A] and of the witnesses who *had* **signed** the deed
32:44 [A] deeds *will be* **signed**, sealed and witnessed in the territory of
36: 2 [A] **write** on it all the words I have spoken to you concerning
36: 4 [A] LORD had spoken to him, Baruch **wrote** them on the scroll.
36: 6 [A] scroll the words of the LORD that *you* **wrote** as I dictated.
36:17 [A] asked Baruch, "Tell us, how *did you come to* **write** all this?
36:18 [A] all these words to me, and I **wrote** them in ink on the scroll."
36:27 [A] the words that Baruch *had* **written** at Jeremiah's dictation,
36:28 [A] and **write** on it all the words that were on the first scroll,
36:29 [A] "Why *did you* **write** on it that the king of Babylon would
36:32 [A] Baruch **wrote** on it all the words of the scroll that Jehoiakim
45: 1 [A] after Baruch *had* **written** on a scroll the words Jeremiah was
51:60 [A] Jeremiah *had* **written** on a scroll *about* all the disasters that
51:60 [B] all that *had* **been recorded** concerning Babylon.
Eze 2:10 [B] On both sides of it *were* **written** words of lament
2:10 [B] On both sides of it were written **words** *of* lament
13: 9 [C] my people or **be listed** in the records of the house of Israel,
24: 2 [A] "Son of man, **record** [+906+906+4200+9005] this date,
37:16 [A] "Son of man, take a stick of wood and **write** on it,
37:16 [A] **write** on it, 'Ephraim's stick, belonging to Joseph and all the
37:20 [A] Hold before their eyes the sticks *you have* **written** on
43:11 [A] **Write** these **down** before them so that they may be faithful to
Da 9:11 [B] and sworn judgments **written** in the Law of Moses,
9:13 [B] Just as *it is* **written** in the Law of Moses, all this disaster has
12: 1 [B] everyone whose name is found **written** in the book—will be
Hos 8:12 [A] *I* **wrote** for them the many things of my law, but they
Hab 2: 2 [A] "**Write down** the revelation and make it plain on tablets so
Mal 3:16 [C] A scroll of remembrance **was written** in his presence

4181 כְּתָב *kᵉtāb*, n.m. [17] [√ 4180; Ar 10375]

script [5], records [3], text [3], book [1], directions written [1], document [1], letter [1], prescribed [1], writing [1]

1Ch 28:19 "I have in **writing** from the hand of the LORD upon me,
2Ch 2:11 [2:10] Hiram king of Tyre replied by **letter** to Solomon:
35: 4 according to the **directions written** *by* David king of Israel
Ezr 2:62 These searched for their family **records**, but they could not find
4: 7 The letter was written in Aramaic **script** and in the Aramaic
Ne 7:64 These searched for their family **records**, but they could not find
Est 1:22 to each province in its own **script** and to each people in its own
3:12 They wrote out in the **script** *of* each province and in the language
3:14 A copy of the **text** of the edict was to be issued as law in every
4: 8 He also gave him a copy of the **text** *of* the edict for their
8: 8 for no **document** written in the king's name and sealed with his
8: 9 These orders were written in the **script** *of* each province and the
8: 9 each people and also to the Jews in their own **script** and language.
8:13 A copy of the **text** of the edict was to be issued as law in every
9:27 days every year, in the way **prescribed** and at the time appointed.
Eze 13: 9 of my people or be listed in the **records** *of* the house of Israel,
Da 10:21 but first I will tell you what is written in the **Book** *of* Truth.

4182 כְּתֹבֶת *kᵉtōbet*, n.f. [1] [√ 4180]

marks [1]

Lev 19:28 not cut your bodies for the dead or put tattoo **marks** on yourselves.

4183 כִּתִּיִּים *kittiyyîm*, a. & n.g. [8]

Kittim [4], Cyprus [3], western coastlands [1]

Ge 10: 4 The sons of Javan: Elishah, Tarshish, the **Kittim** and the Rodanim.
Nu 24:24 Ships will come from the shores of **Kittim**; they will subdue
1Ch 1: 7 The sons of Javan: Elishah, Tarshish, the **Kittim** and the Rodanim.
Isa 23: 1 or harbor. From the land of **Cyprus** word has come to them.
23:12 "Up, cross over to **Cyprus**; even there you will find no rest."
Jer 2:10 Cross over to the coasts of **Kittim** and look, send to Kedar
Eze 27: 6 of cypress wood from the coasts of **Cyprus** they made your deck,
Da 11:30 Ships of the **western coastlands** will oppose him, and he will lose

4184 כָּתִית *kātît*, a. [5] [√ 4198]

pressed olives [2], pressed [2], pressed olive [1]

Ex 27:20 "Command the Israelites to bring you clear oil of **pressed** olives
29:40 fine flour mixed with a quarter of a hin of oil from **pressed olives**,
Lev 24: 2 "Command the Israelites to bring you clear oil of **pressed** olives
Nu 28: 5 fine flour mixed with a quarter of a hin of oil from **pressed olives**.
1Ki 5:11 [5:25] in addition to twenty thousand baths of **pressed olive** oil.

4185 כֹּתֶל kōtel, n.[m.]. [1] [→ Ar 10376]

wall [1]

SS 2: 9 There he stands behind our **wall**, gazing through the windows,

4186 כִּתְלִישׁ kitlîš, n.pr.loc. [1]

Kitlish [1]

Jos 15: 40 Cabbon, Lahmas, **Kitlish**,

4187 כָּתַם kātam, v. [1]

stain [1]

Jer 2: 22 [C] abundance of soap, the **stain** of your guilt *is still* before me,"

4188 כֶּתֶם ketem, n.m. [9] [cf. 4846?]

gold [5], fine gold [1], finest gold [+233] [1], pure gold [1], purest gold [+7058] [1]

Job 28: 16 It cannot be bought with the **gold** *of* Ophir, with precious onyx
28: 19 Cush cannot compare with it; it cannot be bought with pure **gold**.
31: 24 "If I have put my trust in gold or said to **pure gold**, 'You are my
Ps 45: 9 [45:10] at your right hand is the royal bride in **gold** *of* Ophir.
Pr 25: 12 or an ornament of **fine gold** is a wise man's rebuke to a listening
SS 5: 11 His head is **purest gold** [+7058]; his hair is wavy and black as a
Isa 13: 12 man scarcer than pure gold, more rare than the **gold** *of* Ophir.
La 4: 1 How the gold has lost its luster, the fine **gold** become dull!
Da 10: 5 in linen, with a belt of the **finest gold** [+233] around his waist.

4189 כֻּתֹּנֶת kuttōnet, n.f. [29]

robe [13], tunics [6], tunic [5], garments [4], garment [1]

Ge 3: 21 The LORD God made **garments** *of* skin for Adam and his wife
37: 3 him in his old age; and he made a richly ornamented **robe** for him.
37: 23 when Joseph came to his brothers, they stripped him of his **robe**—
37: 23 him of his robe—the richly ornamented **robe** he was wearing—
37: 31 they got Joseph's **robe**, slaughtered a goat and dipped the robe in
37: 31 Joseph's robe, slaughtered a goat and dipped the **robe** in the blood.
37: 32 They took the ornamented **robe** back to their father and said,
37: 32 "We found this. Examine it to see whether it is your son's **robe**."
37: 33 He recognized it and said, "It is my son's **robe**! Some ferocious
Ex 28: 4 a breastpiece, an ephod, a robe, a woven **tunic**, a turban and a sash.
28: 39 "Weave the **tunic** *of* fine linen and make the turban of fine linen.
28: 40 Make **tunics**, sashes and headbands for Aaron's sons, to give them
29: 5 Take the garments and dress Aaron with the **tunic**, the robe of the
29: 8 Bring his sons and dress them in **tunics**
39: 27 For Aaron and his sons, they made **tunics** *of* fine linen—the work
40: 14 Bring his sons and dress them in **tunics**.
Lev 8: 7 He put the **tunic** on Aaron, tied the sash around him, clothed him
8: 13 put **tunics** on them, tied sashes around them and put headbands on
10: 5 So they came and carried them, still in their **tunics**, outside the
16: 4 He is to put on the sacred linen **tunic**, with linen undergarments
2Sa 13: 18 She was wearing a richly ornamented **robe**, for this was the kind of
13: 19 ashes on her head and tore the ornamented **robe** she was wearing.
15: 32 Arkite was there to meet him, his **robe** torn and dust on his head.
Ezr 2: 69 of gold, 5,000 minas of silver and 100 priestly **garments**.
Ne 7: 70 [7:69] drachmas of gold, 50 bowls and 530 **garments** *for* priests.
7: 72 [7:71] of gold, 2,000 minas of silver and 67 **garments** *for* priests.
Job 30: 18 like clothing to me; he binds me like the neck of my **garment**.
SS 5: 3 I have taken off my **robe**—must I put it on again? I have washed
Isa 22: 21 I will clothe him with your **robe** and fasten your sash around him

4190 כָּתֵף kātēp, n.f. [67 / 68]

side [18], shoulders [10], shoulder pieces [8], slope [8], shoulder [5], *untranslated* [3], backs [3], projecting walls [2], slopes [2], arm [1], flank [1], handles [1], one[s] [1], sides [1], sidewalls [1], slung on back [+1068] [1], supports [+7193] [1], wall [1]

Ex 27: 14 Curtains fifteen cubits long are to be on one **side** of the entrance,
27: 15 and curtains fifteen cubits long are to be on the other **side**,
28: 7 It is to have two **shoulder pieces** attached to two of its corners,
28: 12 fasten them on the **shoulder pieces** *of* the ephod as memorial
28: 12 Aaron is to bear the names on his **shoulders** as a memorial before
28: 25 attaching them to the **shoulder pieces** *of* the ephod at the front.
28: 27 attach them to the bottom of the **shoulder pieces** on the front of the
38: 14 Curtains fifteen cubits long were on one **side** of the entrance,
38: 15 curtains fifteen cubits long were on the other **side** of the entrance
39: 4 They made **shoulder pieces** for the ephod, which were attached to
39: 7 they fastened them on the **shoulder pieces** *of* the ephod as
39: 18 attaching them to the **shoulder pieces** *of* the ephod at the front.
39: 20 attached them to the bottom of the **shoulder pieces** on the front of
Nu 7: 9 because they were to carry on their **shoulders** the holy things,
34: 11 and continue along the **slopes** east *of* the Sea of Kinnereth.
Dt 33: 12 and the one the LORD loves rests between his **shoulders**."
Jos 15: 8 it ran up the Valley of Ben Hinnom along the southern **slope** *of* the
15: 10 ran along the northern **slope** *of* Mount Jearim (that is, Kesalon),
15: 11 It went to the northern **slope** *of* Ekron, turned toward Shikkeron,
18: 12 passed the northern **slope** *of* Jericho and headed west into the hill
18: 13 From there it crossed to the south **slope** *of* Luz (that is, Bethel)
18: 16 It continued down the Hinnom Valley along the southern **slope** *of*
18: 18 It continued to the northern **slope** *of* Beth Arabah and on down into
18: 19 It then went to the northern **slope** *of* Beth Hoglah and came out at
Jdg 16: 3 He lifted them to his **shoulders** and carried them to the top of the
1Sa 17: 6 and a bronze javelin was **slung on** his **back** [+1068].
1Ki 6: 8 The entrance to the lowest floor was on the south **side** *of* the
7: 30 each had a basin resting on four **supports** [+7193], cast with
7: 30 resting on four supports, **[RPH]** cast with wreaths on each side.
7: 34 Each stand had four **handles**, one on each corner, projecting from
7: 34 had four handles, **one**[s] on each corner, projecting from the stand.
7: 39 He placed five of the stands on the south **side** *of* the temple
7: 39 on the south side of the temple and five on **[RPH]** the north.
7: 39 He placed the Sea on the south **side**, at the southeast corner of the
2Ki 11: 11 and the temple, from the south **side** to the north side of the temple.
11: 11 and the temple, from the south side to the north **side** *of* the temple.
1Ch 15: 15 Levites carried the ark of God with the poles on their **shoulders**,
2Ch 4: 10 He placed the Sea on the south **side**, at the southeast corner.
23: 10 and the temple, from the south **side** to the north side of the temple.
23: 10 and the temple, from the south side to the north **side** *of* the temple.
35: 3 It is not to be carried about on your **shoulders**. Now serve the
Ne 9: 29 Stubbornly they turned their **backs** on you, became stiff-necked
Job 31: 22 let my **arm** fall from the shoulder, let it be broken off at the joint.
Isa 11: 14 They will swoop down on the **slopes** *of* Philistia to the west;
30: 6 darting snakes, the envoys carry their riches on donkeys' **backs**,
46: 7 They lift it to their **shoulders** and carry it; they set it up in its
49: 22 sons in their arms and carry your daughters on their **shoulders**.
Eze 12: 6 Put them on your **shoulder** as they are watching and carry them
12: 7 out at dusk, carrying them on my **shoulders** while they watched.
12: 12 "The prince among them will put his things on his **shoulder** at
24: 4 the pieces of meat, all the choice pieces—the leg and the **shoulder**.
25: 9 therefore I will expose the **flank** *of* Moab, beginning at its frontier
29: 7 with their hands, you splintered and you tore open their **shoulders**;
29: 18 every head was rubbed bare and every **shoulder** made raw.
34: 21 Because you shove with flank and **shoulder**, butting all the weak
40: 18 It abutted the **sides** *of* the gateways and was as wide as they were
40: 40 By the outside **wall** of the portico of the gateway, near the steps at
40: 40 were two tables, and on the other **side** of the steps were two tables.
40: 41 So there were four tables on one side of **[RPH]** the gateway
40: 44 were two rooms, one at the **side** *of* the north gate and facing south,
40: 44 and another at the **side** *of* the south gate and facing north.
40: 48 its **projecting walls** [BHS-] were three cubits wide on either side.
41: 2 and the **projecting walls** on each side *of* it were five cubits wide.
41: 26 On the **sidewalls** *of* the portico were narrow windows with palm
46: 19 the man brought me through the entrance at the **side** *of* the gate to
47: 1 The water was coming down from under the south **side** *of* the
47: 2 gate facing east, and the water was flowing from the south **side**.
Zec 7: 11 stubbornly they turned their **backs** and stopped up their ears.

4191 כְּתֹף k[e]tōp, var. Not used in NIV/BHS [√ 9512]

4192 כָּתַר¹ kātar[1], v. [1] [→ 4194; cf. 4193, 4194]

bear [1]

Job 36: 2 [D] "**Bear** with me a little longer and I will show you that there is

4193 כָּתַר² kātar[2], v. [4] [√ 4195?, 4196?; cf. 4192, 4194]

encircle [1], gather about [1], hem in [1], surrounded [1]

Jdg 20: 43 [D] *They* **surrounded** the Benjamites, chased them and easily
Ps 22: 12 [22:13] [D] surround me; strong bulls of Bashan **encircle** me.
142: 7 [142:8] [G] the righteous *will* **gather about** me because of your
Hab 1: 4 [G] The wicked **hem in** the righteous, so that justice is perverted.

4194 כָּתַר³ kātar[3], v. [1] [√ 4195?, 4196?; cf. 4192, 4193]

crowned [1]

Pr 14: 18 [G] inherit folly, but the prudent *are* **crowned** *with* knowledge.

4195 כֶּתֶר keter, n.m. [3] [√ 4194 *or* 4193]

crown [2], crest [1]

Est 1: 11 to bring before him Queen Vashti, wearing her royal **crown**,
2: 17 So he set a royal **crown** on her head and made her queen instead of
6: 8 horse the king has ridden, one with a royal **crest** placed on its head.

4196 כֹּתֶרֶת kōteret, n.f. [24] [√ 4194 *or* 4193]

capitals [11], *untranslated* [7], capital [5], circular frame [1]

1Ki 7: 16 He also made two **capitals** of cast bronze to set on the tops of the
7: 16 to set on the tops of the pillars; each **capital** was five cubits high.
7: 16 the tops of the pillars; each capital was five cubits high. **[RPH]**

1Ki 7: 17 A network of interwoven chains festooned the **capitals** on top of
7: 17 festooned the capitals on top of the pillars, seven for each **capital**.
7: 17 the capitals on top of the pillars, seven for each capital. **[RPH]**
7: 18 each network to decorate the **capitals** on top of the pillars.
7: 18 the capitals on top of the pillars. He did the same for each **capital**.
7: 19 The **capitals** on top of the pillars in the portico were in the shape
7: 20 On the **capitals** of both pillars, above the bowl-shaped part next to
7: 20 were the two hundred pomegranates in rows all around. **[RPH]**
7: 31 there was an opening that had a **circular frame** one cubit deep.
7: 41 the two pillars; the two bowl-shaped **capitals** on top of the pillars;
7: 41 the two sets of network decorating the two bowl-shaped **capitals**
7: 42 decorating the bowl-shaped **capitals** on top of the pillars);
2Ki 25: 17 The bronze **capital** on top of one pillar was four and a half feet
25: 17 and a half feet high **[RPH]** and was decorated with a network
25: 17 all around. **[RPH]** The other pillar, with its network, was similar.
2Ch 4: 12 the two pillars; the two bowl-shaped **capitals** on top of the pillars;
4: 12 the two sets of network decorating the two bowl-shaped **capitals**
4: 13 decorating the bowl-shaped **capitals** on top of the pillars);
Jer 52: 22 The bronze **capital** on top of the one pillar was five cubits high
52: 22 The bronze capital on top of the one pillar **[RPH]** was five cubits
52: 22 was decorated with **[RPH]** a network and pomegranates of bronze

4197 כָּתַשׁ ***kātaš***, v. [1] [→ 4847]

grind [1]

Pr 27: 22 [A] Though *you* **grind** a fool in a mortar, grinding him like grain

4198 כָּתַת ***kātat***, v. [17] [→ 4184, 4185]

beat [3], crushed [3], beat down [2], are broken to pieces [1], are defeated [1], battered to pieces [+8625] [1], be broken to pieces [1], broke into pieces [1], crush [1], oppress [1], shattered [1], was crushed [1]

Lev 22: 24 [B] an animal whose testicles are bruised, **crushed**, torn or cut.
Nu 14: 45 [G] attacked them and **beat** them **down** all the way to Hormah.
Dt 1: 44 [G] of bees and **beat** you **down** from Seir all the way to Hormah.
9: 21 [A] *I* **crushed** it and ground it to powder as fine as dust
2Ki 18: 4 [D] *He* **broke into pieces** the bronze snake Moses had made,
2Ch 15: 6 [E] One nation **was** *being* **crushed** by another and one city by
34: 7 [D] and the Asherah poles and **crushed** the idols to powder
Job 4: 20 [H] Between dawn and dusk *they* **are broken to pieces**;
Ps 89: 23 [89:24] [A] *I will* **crush** his foes before him and strike down his
Isa 2: 4 [D] *They will* **beat** their swords into plowshares and their spears
24: 12 [H] city is left in ruins, its gate *is* **battered** [+8625] **to pieces**.
30: 14 [B] **shattered** so mercilessly that among its pieces not a fragment
Jer 46: 5 [H] are terrified, they are retreating, their warriors **are defeated**.
Joel 3: 10 [4:10] [A] **Beat** your plowshares into swords and your pruning
Mic 1: 7 [H] All her idols *will* **be broken to pieces**; all her temple gifts
4: 3 [D] *They will* **beat** their swords into plowshares and their spears
Zec 11: 6 [D] *They will* **oppress** the land, and I will not rescue them from

ל, *l*

4199 ל ***l***, letter. Not used in NIV/BHS [→ Ar 10377]

4200 ¹-לְ ***lᵉ-1***, pp.pref. [20702 / 20705] [→ 2131, 3189?, 4210, 4240, 4307, 4338, 4342, 4344, 4345, 4346, 4348, 4359, 4367, 4368; cf. 4201?; Ar 10378] Not indexed

untranslated [7358], to [4730], for [1684], of [756], before [+7156] [542], in [365], with [219], as [210], by [209], why [+4537] [165], from [157], therefore [+4027] [146], on [137], forever [+6409] [136], into [110], at [102], have [94], against [91], had [90], his [+2257] [79], through [79], so that [+5100] [78], my [+3276] [77], that [74], before [71], in front of [+7156] [66], according to [61], so that [60], had [+2118] [50], has [50], to [+7156] [50], your [+4013] [48], have [+2118] [47], ahead [+7156] [45], about [42], alone [+963] [40], over [40], to [+5100] [36], your [+3870] [36], their [+2157] [35], mine [+3276] [33], belongs to [28], the LORD's [+3378] [27], so [26], belong to [25], belonging to [25], to [+7023] [25], upon [25], when [25], before [+4946+7156] [24], that [+5100] [24], yours [+3870] [24], for sake [+5100] [22], for the sake of [+5100] [22], our [+5646] [22], by [+7156] [21], in order to [21], among [20], like [19], presence [+7156] [19], and [18], every [18], forever [+5905] [18], in addition to [+963+4946] [18], because of [+5100] [17], so [+5100] [17], toward [17], belonged to [16], concerning [16], only [+963] [16], against [+7156] [13], before [+5584] [13], as for [12], forever [+6329] [12], have [+3780] [12], after [11], belong to [+2118] [11], from [+4946+7156] [11], for [+7156] [10], so [+4027] [10], then [+5100] [10], under [10], your [+3871] [10], besides [+963+4946] [9], to [+7754] [9], David's [+1858] [8], fail to have [+4162] [8], from [+7156] [8], his own [+2257] [8], never [+4202+6409] [8], only one [+963] [8], and [+5100] [7], formerly [+7156] [7], meet [+7156] [7], on behalf [7], Solomon's [+8976] [7], with [+7156] [7], because of [6], near [+7156] [6], near [6], serve [+6641+7156] [6], their [+4564] [6], upward [+2025+5087] [6], before [+6524] [5], belonged to [+2118] [5], but [+4027] [5], close to [+6645] [5], consider [+2118] [5], destined for [5], ever [+6409] [5], for [+5100] [5], for sake [5], give in marriage [+851+906+5989] [5], has [+2118] [5], have to do with [5], her [+2023] [5], in order to [+5100] [5], on side [5], sent for [+2256+7924 +8938] [5], their own [+2157] [5], used to [+7156] [5], what [+4537] [5], while [5], with [+7023] [5], above [+2025+4946+5087] [4], always [+5905] [4], belongs to [+2118] [4], by themselves [+963+4392] [4], concerns [4], escape with [+8965] [4], falsely [+2021+9214] [4], father's [+3] [4], gave in marriage [+851+906+5989] [4], given to [4], great [+8044] [4], greet [+4200+8626+8934] [4], greeted [+4200+8626+8934] [4], in honor [4], in vain [+2021+8736] [4], in vain [+8198] [4], its [+2257] [4], king's [+4889] [4], lord's [+123] [4], my own [+3276] [4], one by one [+1653+4392] [4], owned [4], owns [4], plentiful [+8044] [4], received [4], Saul's [+8620] [4], their [+2257] [4], therefore [+5100] [4], throughout [4], till [4], to belong [4], within [4], your own [+3870] [4], yours [+4013] [4], above [+2025+5087] [3], along [3], apart [+963] [3], as if [3], as soon as [3], attack [+995] [3], awaits [3], become [3], below [+4752] [3], between [3], bring [+2118] [3], by [+7023] [3], down [+4752] [3], entered [+995] [3], eternal [+6409] [3], face [+7156] [3], faced [3], get [3], great amount [+8044] [3], greatly [+8044] [3], in abundance [+8044] [3], in behalf of [3], Israel's [+3776] [3], keep [+2118] [3], large numbers [+8044] [3], leading [+7156] [3], leads to [3], marry [+851+2118+4200] [3], mean by [3], never [+4202+5905] [3], opposite [+7156] [3], over [+2025+4946+5087] [3], related to [3], sight [+7156] [3], theirs [+2157] [3], then [+4027] [3], throughout [+3972] [3], to belonged [3], until [3], watch [+6524] [3], watched [+6524] [3], what are you doing [+3870+4537] [3], whose [+2257] [3], whose [+4769] [3], without [+4202] [3], your own [+4013] [3], a matter of [2], accompanies [+7156] [2], according to [+7023] [2], across [2], after [+7891] [2], along with [+6645] [2], always [+6409] [2], any [2], applies to [2], as [+6645] [2], as long as [+7156] [2], as much as [+7023] [2], as well as [+963+4946] [2], assigned to [2], at [+7156] [2], at each successive level [+2025+2025+4200+5087+5087] [2], at random [+9448] [2], at table[s] [+7156] [2], at the point of [2], be sure of this [+3338+3338] [2], bent on [2], beside [+6645] [2], beside [+7156] [2], bind [+2118+3213] [2], bloodshed [+1947+1947] [2], bottom [+4752+4946] [2], bring [+2118+4200] [2], brings [2], cause [2], clan by clan [+5476] [2], completely [+2021+3972] [2], covered with [+7156] [2], do for [2], during [2], each day [+2021+2021+3427 +3427+4200] [2], each morning [+1332+1332+2021+2021+4200] [2], each [2], enslaved [+2256+3899+4200+6269+9148] [2], entered service [+6641+7156] [2], entering [+995] [2], eternal [+6329] [2], ever [+6329] [2], extensive [+8044] [2], for [+4027] [2], forever [+6330+6409] [2], from [+4974] [2], gently [+351] [2], give [2], given [2], have in common [2], have to do with [+2256+4200] [2], highly [+2025+5087] [2], his [+4564] [2], his[s] [+8976] [2], holding [2], in [+5584] [2], in [+6961] [2], in accordance with [2], in addition to [+963] [2], in ascending stages [+2025+2025+4200+5087+5087] [2], in behalf [2], in connection with [2], in front of [+5584] [2], in order that [2], in presence [+5584+6524] [2], in such a way that [2], in way [+7156] [2], inside [+7156] [2], its [+2023] [2], just as [+6645] [2], large quantities [+8044] [2], leader [+2143+7156] [2], led in campaigns [+995+2256+3655+7156] [2], let inquire of [+2011] [2], liable to [2], long ago [+4946+8158] [2], man's [+132] [2], many [+8044] [2], married [+851+2118+4200] [2], married [+851+906 +2257+4200+4374] [2], married [+851+906+4200+4374] [2], marry [+851+2118] [2], marry [+851+4200+4374] [2], mean to [2], misuse [+906+2021+5951+8736] [2], misuses [+906+2021+5951+8736] [2], much [+8044] [2], never [+1153+5905] [2], never [+1153+6409] [2], never [+440+6409] [2], never again [+4202+6409] [2], not counting [+963+4946] [2], not including [+963+4946] [2], of [+4946+7156] [2], of [+7156] [2], on account of [2], on behalf of [2], opposite [+5584] [2], ours [+5646] [2], own [2], owned [+3780] [2], owner [+2257] [2], parallel to [+6645] [2], Pharaoh's [+7281] [2], plenty [+8044] [2], preceded [+2118+7156] [2], preceded [+7156] [2], receive [+2118] [2], regard [+5584+8492] [2], regard as [+2118] [2], remain unmarried [+408+1194+2118+4200+6328] [2], representing [2], resist [+6641+7156] [2], safely [+1055] [2], see [+7156] [2], seems to [+7156] [2], served [+6641+7156] [2], serving [+6641+7156] [2], some [2], surely [+4027] [2], their [+2177] [2], their own [+2257] [2], to [+6524] [2], to belongs [2], top [+2025+4946+5087] [2], turned into [+2118] [2], under [+7156] [2], up [+2025+5087] [2], use [+2118] [2], used to [+2021+8037] [2], very [+2025+5087] [2], very well [+4027] [2], watching [+6524] [2], what do I care about [+2296+3276 +4200+4537] [2], when [+6961] [2], when [+7023] [2], without [+1172] [2], withstand [+6641+7156] [2], won [+5951+7156] [2], your very own [+3870] [2], Aaron's [+195] [1], above [+4946+4946 +5087+6645] [1], above [1], abroad [+2021+2575] [1], Absalom's

[+94] [1], abundant [+8044] [1], accompanied [1], accompany [+2143+5584] [1], accused of [1], accuses [+907+2021+5477+7756] [1], acquired [+2118] [1], adjoining [+6645] [1], Adonijah's [+154] [1], adopted [+1426+4200+4374] [1], adorned [+906+7596+9514] [1], affects [1], again [+6409] [1], agent [+3338] [1], agreed with [+7754+9048] [1], ahead [+4946+7156] [1], ahead [1], alike [+6645] [1], all [+963] [1], all alone [+963] [1], all by myself [+963+3276] [1], allotted [1], allowed [1], alone [+970] [1], along [+3338] [1], along with [+963+4946] [1], along with [1], alongside [+6645] [1], alongside of [+6645] [1], also [+963] [1], always [+1887+1887+2256] [1], always [+6329] [1], among [+3972] [1], and [+4027] [1], anyone [+963] [1], apart [+970] [1], around [1], as [+6961] [1], as a result [1], as in [1], as long as live [+3427+3972+6409] [1], as well as [+6645] [1], asked how they were [+4200+8626+8934] [1], assaults [+5596+5596] [1], assigned [1], assistant [+6641+7156] [1], at [+6645] [1], at [+7023] [1], at advance [+7156] [1], at hand [+995+7940] [1], at sanctuary[s] [+7156] [1], at the head of [+7156] [1], attack [+6913] [1], attack [1], attains [1], attend [+6641+7156] [1], attend [+7156] [1], attended by [+2143+8079] [1], attending [+7156] [1], attention [+7156] [1], avoid [+4202+6843] [1], awaits [+7156] [1], backward [+294] [1], bake thoroughly [+8596+8599] [1], banded together [+665+2021+2653] [1], be given in marriage [+851+906+5989] [1], be kept from [+1194+1757] [1], became [1], because [+3954+4537] [1], because [+4027] [1], because of this [+4027] [1], because [1], become [+2118] [1], become wife [+851+4374] [1], befalls [+628] [1], before [+5584+6524] [1], before [+678] [1], before eyes [+7156] [1], before time [+4946+7156] [1], beforehand [+4946+7156] [1], belonging to [+2118] [1], bent on [+5100] [1], beside [+3338] [1], besides [+963] [1], besides [1], beyond [+2134+4946] [1], bodyguard [+8031+9068] [1], bordering [+6645] [1], borne by [1], bravely [+1201+2657] [1], bring [1], bringing [1], brings to ruin [+2021+6156+8273] [1], brought [1], but why [+4537] [1], but [1], by [+4946] [1], by [+6524] [1], by himself [+963+2257] [1], by itself [+963] [1], by itself [+963+2257] [1], by itself [+970] [1], by myself [+963+3276] [1], call in honor of [+7727] [1], check [+995+7156] [1], children's [+1201] [1], choose [1], come across [+7156+7925] [1], committed [1], condemn [+2118+2631] [1], consult [+7156] [1], contains [1], continually [+6329] [1], continually [+8092] [1], controlled [+2118] [1], controlled [1], corresponding to [1], count [+2118+4200] [1], covered [+8492] [1], crown [1], crowns [+8031] [1], cry out [+606+5951] [1], daily [+2021+3427] [1], daily [+285+3427] [1], Danite [+1968+4751] [1], depth [+2025+5087] [1], despite [+928+8611] [1], despoil [+1020+5989] [1], directed to [1], directly in front of [+5790] [1], directly opposite [+5790+7156] [1], dispersed [+2006+2143] [1], done this[s] [+1215+3378+4640] [1], doomed to [1], downcast [+2118] [1], downstream [+2025+4946+5087] [1], droves [+8044] [1], each[s] [+5031] [1], each day [+2021+3427] [1], endless [+5905] [1], endure [+2118+4200] [1], enough [+1896+4537] [1], enter [+995] [1], enter service [+6641+7156] [1], entered the service [+6641+7156] [1], enters [+995] [1], enthrones [+2021+3782+4058] [1], even though [+963] [1], ever [+7156] [1], ever again [+5905+5905] [1], ever since [+4946] [1], everlasting [+5905] [1], everlasting [+6409] [1], every day [+2021+3427] [1], exceedingly [+2025+5087] [1], extends to [+4946] [1], faced [+7156] [1], far and wide [+4946+6330+8158] [1], far away [+4946+6330+8158] [1], fault [+928+8611] [1], fell facedown [+678+2556] [1], fight [+2021+3655+4878] [1], find [1], finds [1], firstborn belongs to [+1144] [1], fit for [1], fleet of trading ships [+641+2143+9576] [1], fluent [+1819+4554] [1], for life [+6409] [1], for relief from [+4946+7156] [1], for the sake of [1], for the use of [1], for then [+5100] [1], forced to [1], forever [+6518] [1], forever [+802+3427] [1], forward [+7156] [1], fought in [+3655] [1], found [+906+7156+8011] [1], from [+1068] [1], from [+4946] [1], from among [1], from place to place [+5023] [1], gain [1], gave in marriage [+851+906+4200+5989] [1], gave permission [1], girl's [+5853] [1], give [+2118+4200] [1], give [+7156] [1], give [+851+4200+5989] [1], give in marriage [+408+906+5989] [1], give in marriage [+851+5989] [1], given over to [1], God's [+466] [1], goes down [+3718+4752] [1], going [1], got [+2118] [1], great number [+8044] [1], great numbers [+8044] [1], great quantities [+4394+8044] [1], had [+3780] [1], had [+5162] [1], had been [+7156] [1], harbored [+2118] [1], hard [+2021+3668+4607] [1], has [+2118+4200] [1], has [+5162] [1], has to do with [1], have [+2118+4200] [1], have [+5989] [1], have [+889] [1], have part [1], have regard for [+5564] [1], have right [1], have sexual relations [+2446+5989+8888] [1], have the right [1], having [+2118] [1], having [1], hear [+5877+7156] [1], heights [+2025+5087] [1], help [+2118] [1], help [+3338] [1], help [+6913] [1], help [1], her [+3276] [1], here [+7156] [1], hers [+2023] [1], Hezekiah's [+2624] [1], Hezekiah's [+2625] [1], high above [+2025+4946+5087] [1], higher than [+2025+5087+8049] [1], his [+4202] [1], his[s] [+4889+5213] [1], his[s] [+5557] [1], his[s] [+8620] [1], his[s] [+90] [1], his [1], hold [1], how was [+8934] [1], how was going [+8934] [1], how were [+8934] [1], however [+4027] [1], huge [+1524+4394+6330] [1], hunt down [+4511+7421] [1], imposing [+1524+5260] [1], in [+7156] [1], in accordance with [+7023] [1], in addition [+963] [1], in addition [+963+4946] [1], in behalf of [+5100] [1], in broad daylight [+2021+2021+2296+6524+9087] [1], in charge of [1], in debt [+5957] [1], in earlier times [+7156] [1], in eyes [+7156] [1], in front of [+6524] [1], in fulfillment of [1], in large numbers [+8044] [1], in opposition to [1], in order to [+906+5100] [1], in path [+7156] [1], in possession [1], in preparation for [1], in service [+7156] [1], in the course of time [+3427+3427+4946] [1], in the eyes of [+7156] [1], in the face of [+5584] [1], in the sight of [1], in this way [+5100] [1], in this way [1], inclines to [1], individually [+1653] [1], inner [+7156] [1], inner [+7163] [1], inquire of [+2011] [1], inside [+1074+4946] [1], inside [+7163] [1], instead of [+1194] [1], instead of [+7156] [1], instead of [1], intimate with [1], into [+7163] [1], into another set [+963] [1], into marry [+2118] [1], into one set [+963] [1], invaded [+2143] [1], invading [+995] [1], involved in [1], Israelite [+1201+3776] [1], it means [1], its[s] [+2021+4058] [1], Jacob's [+3620] [1], jointed [+4946+5087+8079] [1], just as [+889+3972] [1], just for that [+4027] [1], keep [1], keeps company [+782+2495] [1], kept [1], killed [+906+2995+5782+7023] [1], Korah's [+7946] [1], lack [+401] [1], large amount [+8044] [1], larger [+8044] [1], lasting [+6409] [1], later [+7891] [1], later [1], lawsuits [+1907+1907] [1], lead [+2143+7156] [1], lead [+7156] [1], lead [+995+2256+3655+7156] [1], lead across [+6296+7156] [1], lead to [1], leading into [+7023] [1], leading into [1], leading to [1], learned [+906+5583] [1], leaves [1], led [+7156] [1], led out [+3655+7156] [1], led to [1], left [+2118] [1], length [+6645] [1], let inquire of at all [+2011+2011] [1], lets happen [+628+3338] [1], life will not be worth living [+2644+4537] [1], like [+6645] [1], likes [+928+2021+3202] [1], long [+6409] [1], long ago [+6409] [1], long life [+2021+2644] [1], lover's [+1856] [1], made fall [+2118+4200+4842] [1], make serve [+8492] [1], make sport of [+2118+4200+5442] [1], married [+851+2118] [1], married [+851+4200+4200+4374] [1], married [+851+906+4374] [1], married to [+851+2118+4200] [1], marries [+2118] [1], marries [+408+2118] [1], marries [+408+2118+2118] [1], marry [+408+2118] [1], marry [+851+4374] [1], marry [+851+906+4200+4374] [1], marry into [+2118] [1], match for [1], mighty [+8044] [1], mine [+3276+8611] [1], misuse [+2021+5951+8736] [1], more [+2025+5087] [1], more [+401] [1], more [+8044] [1], more and more powerful [+1541+2025+2143+2256+5087+6330] [1], more for [1], more quickly than [+7156] [1], more readily than [+7156] [1], more than [+401] [1], more than [+963+4946] [1], Moses [+5407] [1], my [+3276+7156] [1], my own [+3276+8611] [1], Nebuchadnezzar's [+5557] [1], never [+401+6409] [1], never [+4202+7156] [1], never [+561+5905] [1], nevertheless [+4027] [1], next to [+5584] [1], next to [+6298] [1], next to [1], not circumcised [+2257+6889] [1], numerous [+8044] [1], obey [+7754+9048] [1], obey [1], of [+4946+8611] [1], of what use [+2296+4537] [1], of what use [+4537] [1], offered a kiss of homage [+5975+7023] [1], older [+2418+3427] [1], on behalf of [+5466] [1], on behalf of [+5790] [1], on high [+2021+5294] [1], once for all [+5905] [1], one kind after another [+2157+5476] [1], one[s] [+2157] [1], only [+963+2314] [1], only exception [+963] [1], only one [+963+2257] [1], open [+7156] [1], opposite [+6645] [1], other than [+963+1194] [1], other than [+963+4946] [1], otherwise [+889+4202+5100] [1], ours [+3276] [1], ours [+5646+7156] [1], out of way [+4946+7156] [1], out [1], outer [+2021+2575] [1], outer [+2025+4946+5087] [1], over [+4946+6584] [1], over [+7156] [1], over and above [+2025+5087] [1], over here [+285+6298] [1], over there [+285+6298] [1], overlooking [+7156] [1], overtake [1], overtakes [1], overturned [+2025+2200+5087] [1], own [+2118] [1], owning [1], owns [+3780] [1], paid any attention [+265+906+5742+9048] [1], particularly [+4027] [1], pay [1], people's [+6639] [1], per [1], perjurers [+2021+8678+9214] [1], perjury [+2021+8678+9214] [1], permanently [+2021+7552] [1], permanently [+7552] [1], piece by piece [+5984] [1], plentifully [+7859] [1], powerless [+401+445] [1], powerless [+401+445+3338] [1], preceding [+7156] [1], predecessor [+889+2118+7156] [1], present [+5877+7156] [1], present [+7156] [1], previous [+7156] [1], project upward [+2025+5087] [1], property[s] [+889+2118] [1], provide with [1], provided for [+430+2118+2256+4312] [1], provides for [1], punished less [+3104+4752] [1], put [+995+7156] [1], put [+995+9202] [1], put up security [+3338+9546] [1], quantities [+8044] [1], quarrel between [1], quite innocently [+9448] [1], reached [+995] [1], ready for battle [+408+2021+4878+7372] [1], ready for [1], realize [+606+4222] [1], receive [1], received [+2118] [1], received [+995] [1], receives [+5989] [1], reduced to servitude [+906+906+6296+6551] [1], referring to [1], reflects a face [+2021+2021+7156+7156] [1], reflects the man [+132+2021] [1], regard [+2118+7156] [1], regarded in the sight of [+7156] [1], regarded [1], regardless [+401+9068] [1], regards [+5162+7156] [1], regularly [+928+3427+3427] [1], relating to [1], relation to [1], renowned [+9005] [1], represent [1], represented [1], resisted [+5584+6641] [1], resort to [+2143+7925] [1], responding to [+6645] [1], responsible for [+5584] [1], responsible for [+889+928] [1], responsible for [+928+8611] [1], responsible for [1], rests with [1], retains [+2118] [1], reward [1], right before [+5584] [1], right before

[1], right for [1], risked [+3070+4637] [1], ruined [+7914] [1], ruthlessly [+425] [1], safely [+2021+8934] [1], safely [+8934] [1], same as [1], saying [+606] [1], see [+6524] [1], see [+906+2021 +6524+8011] [1], see to it [+6524] [1], seeks [1], select a day [+3427+3427+4946] [1], self-control [+5110+8120] [1], sent for [+906+906+7924+8938] [1], separate [+906+963+3657] [1], separate [+963] [1], servants [+6269] [1], serve [+2118] [1], serve [+2118+7156] [1], serve [+7156] [1], served [+2118+7156] [1], service of [1], setting the time [+5503] [1], severe [+2025+5087] [1], Shalmaneser's[s] [+2257] [1], share [+2118] [1], share [+889+3869] [1], Shimei's [+9059] [1], show [+2118] [1], show [+7156] [1], shows to be [+2118] [1], sided with [+1047] [1], since [+3427+4946] [1], sing songs [+928+7754+8123+9048] [1], slaughter [+2222+5422] [1], slept with [+2351+3359+5435] [1], slept with [+408+3359+5435] [1], slow down [+6806+8206] [1], slowly [+351] [1], so as to [1], so as [1], so far as [+3972] [1], so many [+8044] [1], so then [+4027] [1], Solomon's [+8611+8976] [1], some years later [+7891+9102] [1], started [+6991] [1], stationed at [1], still [+4027] [1], stole into [+995+1704] [1], stolen goods [+2257+4202] [1], storerooms [+238+5969] [1], straight ahead [+5790] [1], straight to [1], struck [1], subject to [1], succeed against [+5584] [1], such as [1], suffered [+2118] [1], summoned [+4200+4200+7924+8938] [1], supply [+2118] [1], take [+2118] [1], take care of [+2118+4200+5466] [1], take command [+2118+5464] [1], take for [+906+5989+7156] [1], taken from [+4946+7156] [1], taken [1], testify [+6332+6699] [1], than [1], that[s] [+8079] [1], that is why [+5100] [1], their[s] [+2021+2498] [1], their [+2179] [1], their [+4013] [1], theirs [+2257] [1], therefore [+3610+4027] [1], think [+4013+8492] [1], this [+5100] [1], this fellow's[s] [+2296] [1], this one [+963] [1], thoughtlessly [+928+1051 +8557] [1], thus [+5100] [1], thus [1], till [+5100] [1], to [+4946] [1], to [+6584+7156] [1], to [+928+6288] [1], to fulfill [1], to honor [1], to the point of [1], to the very end [+6409+6813] [1], to turned [1], together with [1], told [+448+606+8938] [1], took in marriage [+851+906+4200 +4374] [1], took part in [+3655] [1], top [+2025+5087] [1], top of [+2025+4946+5087] [1], tore apart [+7973+7974+9109] [1], total [+3972+5031] [1], total [1], treated the same as [+6645] [1], troubles [1], trustfully [+1055] [1], tuned to [1], turn against [+2118+4200 +8477] [1], turn into [1], under [+1074] [1], under blessing [+7156] [1], under direction [+7156] [1], under supervision [+7156] [1], unintentionally [+8705] [1], unite [+2118+3480+4222+6584] [1], unless [+561+3954+7156] [1], unmarried [+408+2118+4202] [1], unsuspecting [+1055] [1], unto [1], upstream [+2025+5087] [1], upward [+2025+4946+5087] [1], used as [1], used by [1], used for [1], used in [1], useless [+2021+9214] [1], uses [1], valued at [1], very [+2025+5087+6330] [1], very [+466] [1], wage war [+1741+2021 +4878] [1], walled [+2570] [1], want [1], wanted to make [+906+1335] [1], was given in marriage [+851+5989] [1], watched [+7156] [1], wear [1], were fettered [+5602+5733] [1], what do you mean [+4013+4537] [1], what is doing [+4537] [1], what is the matter [+3871+4537] [1], what right have you [+3870+4537] [1], when [+3954+7023] [1], whenever [+3972] [1], whenever [+7023] [1], where[s] [+4564] [1], where[s] [+7156] [1], wherever [+8079] [1], wherever [1], whether [1], while [+6961] [1], whose [+889] [1], why [+361 +2296] [1], why [+4537+8611] [1], why [+561+4027+4537] [1], wielding [+995+2025+5087] [1], wish well [+8934] [1], with [+3338] [1], with [+6645] [1], without [+401] [1], worship [+7156] [1], year [+2021+3427] [1], yet [+4027] [1], younger [+3427+7582] [1], yours [+3871] [1], Zedekiah's [+7409] [1]

4201 ²-לְ ***lᵉ-²***, pt.pref. Not used in NIV/BHS [cf. 4200?]

4202 לֹא ***lō'***, adv. [5173 / 5172] [→ 218?, 4203, 4204, 4205, 4257, 4274; Ar 10379, 10384; *also used with compound proper names*] See Select Index

not [2963], no [613], *untranslated* [312], never [155], nor [+2256] [109], cannot [101], nothing [68], without [67], cannot [+3523] [45], neither [42], don't [33], no [+3972] [31], didn't [30], none [29], nothing [+1821] [18], isn't [14], none [+3972] [14], or [+2256] [14], or [14], surely [+561] [14], won't [13], before [12], haven't [11], nor [11], nothing [+3972] [11], refused [+14] [11], without [+928] [9], failed [8], never [+4200+6409] [8], can't [+3523] [7], nothing [+4399] [7], refused [7], unwilling [+14] [7], aren't [5], forbidden [+6913] [5], hasn't [5], never [+6388] [5], none [+408] [5], refuse [5], little [4], neither [+1685] [4], unjust [+9419] [4], unless [+561] [4], unlike [+3869] [4], wouldn't [4], before [+889+6330] [3], before [+928] [3], beyond [3], fail [3], fails [3], injustice [+5477] [3], instead of [3], more than [3], neither [+2256] [3], never [+4200+5905] [3], nor [+1685] [3], unclean [+3196] [3], unknown [+3359] [3], without [+4200] [3], as you know [+2022] [2], before [+928+3270] [2], but [+561] [2], can't [2], childless [+3528] [2], disobeyed [+928+7754+9048] [2], displeases [+2911] [2], doesn't [2], free from [2], from [2], hardly [2], helpless [+3946+6806] [2], ignorant [+3359] [2], lack [2], never [+2021+3427 +3972] [2], never [+3578] [2], never [+6330+6409] [2], never again [+4200+6409] [2], no [+3972+4946] [2], no [+4027] [2], nothing [+1821+3972] [2], nowhere [2], overwhelmed [+928+2118+6388 +8120] [2], rather than [+2256] [2], rather than [2], refuse [+14] [2], shouldn't [2], that [+561] [2], till [+561] [2], time and again [+285+2256+4202+9109] [2], trackless [+2006] [2], unable [2], unaware [+3359] [2], useless [+7503] [2], whether [+561] [2], worthless idols [+3603] [2], against [+3869] [1], agreed [1], always be [+2532] [1], anything[s] [1], as[s] [1], avoid [+4200+6843] [1], barely [1], because [+2256] [1], because [+561+3610] [1], before [+6330] [1], before [+6388] [1], before elapsed [+4848] [1], better than [1], bottled-up [+7337] [1], but [1], by no means [+3480] [1], by surprise [+3359] [1], can hardly breathe [+928+5972+8636] [1], cannot bear [+3523] [1], cannot read [+3359+6219] [1], cannot stand [+3523] [1], certainly [+561] [1], cloudless [+6265] [1], contrary to [+3869] [1], contrary to [+928+3869] [1], contrary to [1], contrary [1], couldn't [1], delayed [+237] [1], dense [+2983] [1], denying [1], deserted [+3782] [1], despairs [+586] [1], die [+2649] [1], disobedience [+928+7754 +9048] [1], disobey [+448+9048] [1], disobeyed [+4200+9048] [1], disobeyed [+928+9048] [1], disorder [+6043] [1], displease [+928+2834+5162+6524] [1], displeasing [+928+2834+5162+6524] [1], disregarding [+2349] [1], either [1], else [1], empty [+4027] [1], ever [1], except [+889] [1], except for [+2256] [1], fail [+8505] [1], failed [+3523] [1], failed [+6388+7756] [1], fails [+586] [1], feeble [+3888] [1], feeble [+6437] [1], forbidden [+6584+7422] [1], forbidden [+7422] [1], free from [+928] [1], free of [1], futile [+4027] [1], gives way [+6641] [1], go unanswered [+6699] [1], gone [+928+2118] [1], gone [+928+6641] [1], hidden [+8011] [1], how much less [+677+3954] [1], if [1], ignored [+448+4213+8492] [1], in vain [1], incapable [+3523] [1], keeps [+4614] [1], lack [+928] [1], lest [+889] [1], little value [+4399] [1], make countless [+889+906 +906+6218+8049] [1], many [+5071] [1], measureless [+4499] [1], mercilessly [+2798] [1], neglected [+5757] [1], neither [+2296] [1], never [+3427+4946] [1], never [+4200+7156] [1], never [+5905+6330] [1], never [+6409] [1], never [+8041] [1], never [+9458] [1], nobody [+132] [1], none [+285] [1], none [+3972+4946] [1], none [+3972+5883] [1], none [+4399] [1], nor [+1685+2256] [1], nothing [+1524+1821+2256+7785] [1], nothing [+2021+3972] [1], nothing [+4027] [1], nothing [+4312] [1], nothing [+5126] [1], nothing [+889+3972] [1], nothing [+906+1821] [1], of no account [1], only [+1194] [1], only [+2022] [1], only [+2314] [1], only [+8370] [1], only[s] [1], or [+889] [1], other than [1], otherwise [+2256] [1], otherwise [+889+4200+5100] [1], outcome different [+3869] [1], past [1], pittance [+2104] [1], powerless [+3523] [1], powerless [+3946] [1], powerless [+928+3946] [1], powerless [1], precious [+5877] [1], rather [+3954] [1], refused [+448+9048] [1], remained childless [+3528] [1], resents [+170] [1], scarcely [1], seldom [+2221] [1], shameful [+4083] [1], shamelessly [+1017] [1], silent [+1819] [1], since [1], sinful [+3202] [1], so [+561+3610] [1], stay [+448+995] [1], stayed away [+995] [1], still to come [+6913] [1], stolen goods [+2257+4200] [1], stop [+3578] [1], stop [1], stopped [+3578+6388] [1], stopped [+928+3855] [1], stops [1], stranger [+3359] [1], strangers [+3359] [1], surely [1], than [+2256] [1], this[s] [+2257+3769] [1], till [1], too heavy a burden to carry [+906+3523+5951] [1], too [1], troubled [+3523+9200] [1], turned a deaf ear [+263] [1], unable [+3523] [1], unafraid [+7064] [1], unceasingly [+1949] [1], unchanged [+4614] [1], unclean [+3197] [1], uncut [+7786] [1], undivided loyalty [+2256+4213+4213] [1], uneaten [+1180] [1], unfaithful [+574] [1], unfamiliar [+3359] [1], unfanned [+5870] [1], ungodly [+2883] [1], unintentionally [+928+7402] [1], unjust [+5477] [1], unjustly [+4026] [1], unless [+2022] [1], unless [+561+3954] [1], unless [1], unlike [+4027+6913] [1], unlike [1], unmarried [+408+2118+4200] [1], unprofitable [+3603] [1], unpunished [+870] [1], unquenchable [+3882] [1], unrelenting [+2798] [1], unrighteousness [+7406] [1], unruly [+4340] [1], unsharpened [+7837] [1], unsuccessful [+906+7503] [1], unsuited [+5534] [1], unthinkable [+597] [1], untiring [+7028] [1], unwise [+2682] [1], useless [+3603] [1], useless [+6122] [1], useless [1], virgin [+408+3359] [1], wasn't [+2118] [1], weakness [+3946] [1], what about [+2022] [1], whether [+561+2022] [1], who[s] [1], wicked [+3202] [1], withheld[s] [+4763] [1], withhold [1], worse [+4017] [1], worthless [+3603] [1], wrong [+3202] [1], yes [+3954] [1]

4203 לֹא דָבָר ***lō' dābār***, לֹא דְבַר ***lō' dᵉbār***, n.pr.loc. [2] [√ 4202 + 1818]

Lo Debar [2]

2Sa 17:27 Makir son of Ammiel from **Lo Debar**, and Barzillai the Gileadite
Am 6:13 you who rejoice in the conquest of **Lo Debar** and say, "Did we not

4204 לֹא עַמִּי ***lō' 'ammî***, n.pr.m. [1] [√ 4202 + 6652]

Lo-Ammi [1]

Hos 1:9 the LORD said, "Call him **Lo-Ammi**, for you are not my people,

4205 לֹא רֻחָמָה ***lō' ruḥāmâ***, n.pr.f. [2] [√ 4202 + 8170]

Lo-Ruhamah [2]

Hos 1: 6 Then the LORD said to Hosea, "Call her **Lo-Ruhamah**,
1: 8 After she had weaned **Lo-Ruhamah**, Gomer had another son.

4206 לָאָה ***lā'â***, v. [19] [→ 9430; cf. 4264]

weary [3], worn out [3], try patience [2], burdened [1], can no longer [1], cannot [1], could not [1], discouraged [1], frustrated [1], impatient [1], lazy [1], not be able [1], wears herself out [1], weary themselves [1]

Ge 19: 11 [A] and old, with blindness so that *they* **could not** find the door.
Ex 7: 18 [C] the Egyptians *will* **not be able** to drink its water.' "
Job 4: 2 [A] someone ventures a word with you, *will you be* **impatient**?
4: 5 [A] But now trouble comes to you, and *you are* **discouraged**;
16: 7 [G] Surely, O God, *you have* **worn** me **out**; you have devastated
Ps 68: 9 [68:10] [C] O God; you refreshed your **weary** inheritance.
Pr 26: 15 [C] hand in the dish; *he is too* **lazy** to bring it back to his mouth.
Isa 1: 14 [C] have become a burden to me; *I am* **weary** *of* bearing them.
7: 13 [G] house of David! Is it not enough *to* **try** *the* **patience** *of* men?
7: 13 [G] patience of men? *Will you* **try** *the* **patience** *of* my God also?
16: 12 [C] Moab appears at her high place, *she* only **wears herself out**;
47: 13 [C] All the counsel you have received *has only* **worn** *you* **out**!
Jer 6: 11 [C] I am full of the wrath of the LORD, and *I* **cannot** hold it in.
9: 5 [9:4] [C] tongues to lie; *they* **weary themselves** *with* sinning.
12: 5 [G] have raced with men on foot and *they have* **worn** you **out**,
15: 6 [C] on you and destroy you; *I* **can no longer** show compassion.
20: 9 [C] in my bones. *I am* **weary** *of* holding it in; indeed, I cannot.
Eze 24: 12 [G] *It has* **frustrated** all efforts; its heavy deposit has not been
Mic 6: 3 [G] have I done to you? How *have I* **burdened** you? Answer me.

4207 לֵאָה ***lē'â***, n.pr.f. [34]

Leah [28], Leah's [5], *untranslated* [1]

Ge 29: 16 the name of the older was **Leah**, and the name of the younger was
29: 17 **Leah** *had* weak eyes, but Rachel was lovely in form, and beautiful.
29: 23 he took his daughter **Leah** and gave her to Jacob, and Jacob lay
29: 24 Laban gave his servant girl Zilpah to his daughter **[RPH]** as her
29: 25 When morning came, there was **Leah**! So Jacob said to Laban,
29: 30 Jacob lay with Rachel also, and he loved Rachel more than **Leah**.
29: 31 When the LORD saw that **Leah** was not loved, he opened her
29: 32 **Leah** became pregnant and gave birth to a son. She named him
30: 9 When **Leah** saw that she had stopped having children, she took her
30: 10 **Leah's** servant Zilpah bore Jacob a son.
30: 11 Then **Leah** said, "What good fortune!" So she named him Gad.
30: 12 **Leah's** servant Zilpah bore Jacob a second son.
30: 13 **Leah** said, "How happy I am! The women will call me happy."
30: 14 some mandrake plants, which he brought to his mother **Leah**.
30: 14 Rachel said to **Leah**, "Please give me some of your son's
30: 16 came in from the fields that evening, **Leah** went out to meet him.
30: 17 God listened to **Leah**, and she became pregnant and bore Jacob a
30: 18 **Leah** said, "God has rewarded me for giving my maidservant to
30: 19 **Leah** conceived again and bore Jacob a sixth son.
30: 20 Then **Leah** said, "God has presented me with a precious gift.
31: 4 and **Leah** to come out to the fields where his flocks were.
31: 14 Rachel and **Leah** replied, "Do we still have any share in the
31: 33 So Laban went into Jacob's tent and into **Leah's** tent and into the
31: 33 After he came out of **Leah's** tent, he entered Rachel's tent.
33: 1 so he divided the children among **Leah**, Rachel and the two
33: 2 **Leah** and her children next, and Rachel and Joseph in the rear.
33: 7 Next, **Leah** and her children came and bowed down. Last of all
34: 1 Now Dinah, the daughter **Leah** had borne to Jacob, went out to
35: 23 The sons of **Leah**: Reuben the firstborn of Jacob, Simeon,
35: 26 The sons of **Leah's** maidservant Zilpah: Gad and Asher.
46: 15 These were the sons **Leah** bore to Jacob in Paddan Aram,
46: 18 to Jacob by Zilpah, whom Laban had given to his daughter **Leah**—
49: 31 and his wife Rebekah were buried, and there I buried **Leah**.
Ru 4: 11 the woman who is coming into your home like Rachel and **Leah**,

4208 לָאז ***lā'z***, adv.?. Not used in NIV/BHS [√ 2296; cf. 2137]

4209 לָאט ***lā'aṭ***, v. [1 / 0] [cf. 4286]

2Sa 19: 4 [19:5] [a] The king covered [BHS *covered* ?; NIV 4286] his face

4210 לָאֵל ***lā'ēl***, n.pr.m. [1] [√ 4200 + 446]

Lael [1]

Nu 3: 24 leader of the families of the Gershonites was Eliasaph son of **Lael**.

4211 לְאֹם ***le'ōm***, n.m. [31 / 35]

peoples [18], nations [9], people [4], nation [1], other[s] [1], others[s] [1], subjects [1]

Ge 25: 23 in your womb, and two **peoples** from within you will be separated;
25: 23 *one* **people** will be stronger than the other, and the older will serve
25: 23 one people will be stronger than the **other**[s], and the older will
27: 29 May nations serve you and **peoples** bow down to you. Be lord over
Ps 2: 1 Why do the nations conspire and the **peoples** plot in vain?
7: 7 [7:8] Let the assembled **peoples** gather around you. Rule over
9: 8 [9:9] in righteousness; he will govern the **peoples** with justice.
44: 2 [44:3] you crushed the **peoples** and made our fathers flourish.
44: 14 [44:15] the **peoples** [BHS 569] shake their heads at us.
47: 3 [47:4] He subdued nations under us, **peoples** under our feet.
57: 9 [57:10] I will sing of you among the **peoples**. [BHS 569]
65: 7 [65:8] the roaring of their waves, and the turmoil of the **nations**.
67: 4 [67:5] May the **nations** be glad and sing for joy, for you rule the
67: 4 [67:5] rule the peoples justly and guide the **nations** of the earth.
105: 44 of the nations, and they fell heir to what **others**[s] had toiled for—
108: 3 [108:4] I will sing of you among the **peoples**. [BHS 569]
148: 11 kings of the earth and all **nations**, you princes and all rulers on
149: 7 on the nations and punishment on the **peoples**, [BHS 569]
Pr 11: 26 **People** curse the man who hoards grain, but blessing crowns him
14: 28 is a king's glory, but without **subjects** a prince is ruined.
14: 34 Righteousness exalts a nation, but sin is a disgrace to any **people**.
24: 24 are innocent"—peoples will curse him and **nations** denounce him.
Isa 17: 12 Oh, the uproar of the **peoples**—they roar like the roaring of great
17: 13 Although the **peoples** roar like the roar of surging waters,
34: 1 Come near, you nations, and listen; pay attention, you **peoples**!
41: 1 silent before me, you islands! Let the **nations** renew their strength!
43: 4 men in exchange for you, and **people** in exchange for your life.
43: 9 All the nations gather together and the **peoples** assemble. Which of
49: 1 Listen to me, you islands; hear this, you distant **nations**: Before I
51: 4 "Listen to me, my people; hear me, my **nation**: The law will go out
55: 4 See, I have made him a witness to the **peoples**, a leader
55: 4 a witness to the peoples, a leader and commander of the **peoples**.
60: 2 darkness covers the earth and thick darkness is over the **peoples**,
Jer 51: 58 for nothing, the **nations**' labor is only fuel for the flames."
Hab 2: 13 fuel for the fire, that the **nations** exhaust themselves for nothing?

4212 לְאֻמִּים ***le'ummîm***, n.pr.g. [1]

Leummites [1]

Ge 25: 3 of Dedan were the Asshurites, the Letushites and the **Leummites**.

4213 לֵב ***lēb***, n.m. [600] [→ 4214, 4221, 4222, 4223; Ar 10380]

heart [310], hearts [74], mind [21], judgment [11], himself [+2257] [10], attention [7], minds [7], skilled [+2682] [6], in high spirits [+3201] [5], understanding [5], *untranslated* [3], brokenhearted [+8689] [3], everything [+3972] [3], high seas [+3542] [3], myself [+3276] [3], tenderly [+6584] [3], arrogant [+5951] [2], conscience-stricken [+906+5782] [2], courage [2], deception [+2256+4213] [2], imagination [2], senseless [+401] [2], thoughts [2], undivided loyalty [+2256+4202+4213] [2], wholehearted devotion [+8969] [2], wholeheartedly [+928+3972] [2], will [2], willing [+5618] [2], wise [2], yourself [+3870] [2], ability [+928+2683] [1], ability [1], accord [1], again give allegiance [+8740] [1], am forgotten [+4946+8894] [1], anxious striving [+8301] [1], attitude [1], bravest [+579] [1], call to mind [+448+8740] [1], care [+448+8492] [1], care about [+448+8492] [1], careful attention [1], cares [+6584+8492] [1], cheer up [+3512] [1], chest [1], concerned about [+448+8492] [1], confide in [+907] [1], conscience [1], consider [+6584+8492] [1], consider [+8492] [1], consider well [+4200+8883] [1], considered [+448+8492] [1], considered [+6584+8492] [1], craftsmen [+2682] [1], dared [+4848] [1], deceived [+906+1704] [1], decided [+2118+6640] [1], desire [1], did[s] [+906+3877+4392] [1], discourage [+906+5648] [1], discouraged [+906+5648] [1], disheartened [+3874] [1], encourage [+1819+6584] [1], encourage [+3922] [1], encouragingly [+6584] [1], enraged [+6192+6584] [1], faithless [+6047] [1], glad [+3512] [1], has full confidence [+1053] [1], head [1], heartache [+6780] [1], his own [+2257+4946] [1], I [+3276] [1], idea [+4946] [1], ignored [+448+4202+8492] [1], in [+928] [1], in good spirits [+3512] [1], inclined [+5742] [1], intent [1], intention [+448+8492] [1], it[s] [+3276] [1], kindly [1], led astray [+906+5742] [1], merrymakers [+8524] [1], obstinate [+7997] [1], opinions [1], persist in own way [+9244] [1], persuade [+1819+6584] [1], pride [+1467] [1], proud [+8123] [1], purpose [1], reason [1], reflected on [+448+906+5989] [1], refreshed [+6184] [1], resolved [+6584+8492] [1], rip open [+6033+7973] [1], sense [1], skill [+2683] [1], spirit [1], spoken kindly [+1819+6584] [1], stops to think [+448+8740] [1], stubborn [+2617] [1], stubborn-hearted [+52] [1], stunned [+7028] [1], take heart [+599] [1], take note [+8883] [1], them [+4392] [1], themselves [+4392] [1], think [+5989] [1], think [+606+928] [1], think about [+6584+6590] [1], to [+928] [1], tried [+928+9365] [1], valiant men [+52] [1], very [1], voluntarily [+408+6584+6590] [1], wholeheartedly [+928+8969] [1], willful [1], willing [+5951] [1], willing [+906+5605] [1], willing [+906+5951] [1], willingly [+4946] [1], wisdom [1], wise [+2682] [1], worry [+906+8492] [1], you [+3870] [1], yourself [+2257] [1], yourself [+3871] [1]

Ge 6: 5 that every inclination of the thoughts of his **heart** was only evil all
6: 6 he had made man on the earth, and his **heart** was filled with pain.
8:21 The LORD smelled the pleasing aroma and said in his **heart**:
8:21 even though every inclination of his **heart** is evil from childhood.
17:17 he laughed and said to **himself** [+2257], "Will a son be born to a
18: 5 so you *can be* **refreshed** [+6184] and then go on your way—
24:45 "Before I finished praying in my **heart**, Rebekah came out,
27:41 He said to **himself** [+2257], "The days of mourning for my father
31:20 Jacob **deceived** [+906+1704] Laban the Aramean by not telling
34: 3 of Jacob, and he loved the girl and spoke **tenderly** [+6584] *to* her.
42:28 Their **hearts** sank and they turned to each other trembling
45:26 all Egypt." Jacob *was* **stunned** [+7028]; he did not believe them.
50:21 your children." And he reassured them and spoke **kindly** to them.
Ex 4:14 his way to meet you, and his **heart** will be glad when he sees you.
4:21 But I will harden his **heart** so that he will not let the people go.
7: 3 I will harden Pharaoh's **heart**, and though I multiply my
7:13 Yet Pharaoh's **heart** became hard and he would not listen to them,
7:14 Then the LORD said to Moses, "Pharaoh's **heart** is unyielding;
7:22 same things by their secret arts, and Pharaoh's **heart** became hard;
7:23 and went into his palace, and did not take even this to **heart**.
8:15 [8:11] he hardened his **heart** and would not listen to Moses
8:19 [8:15] Pharaoh's **heart** was hard and he would not listen, just as
8:32 [8:28] this time also Pharaoh hardened his **heart** and would not
9: 7 Yet his **heart** was unyielding and he would not let the people go.
9:12 the LORD hardened Pharaoh's **heart** and he would not listen to
9:14 time I will send the full force of my plagues against **you** [+3870]
9:21 But those who **ignored** [+448+4202+8492] the word of the LORD
9:34 he sinned again: He and his officials hardened their **hearts**.
9:35 So Pharaoh's **heart** was hard and he would not let the Israelites go,
10: 1 for I have hardened his **heart** and the hearts of his officials
10: 1 for I have hardened his heart and the **hearts** *of* his officials
10:20 the LORD hardened Pharaoh's **heart**, and he would not let the
10:27 the LORD hardened Pharaoh's **heart**, and he was not willing to
11:10 the LORD hardened Pharaoh's **heart**, and he would not let the
14: 4 And I will harden Pharaoh's **heart**, and he will pursue them.
14: 8 The LORD hardened the **heart** *of* Pharaoh king of Egypt,
14:17 I will harden the **hearts** *of* the Egyptians so that they will go in
15: 8 firm like a wall; the deep waters congealed in the **heart** *of* the sea.
25: 2 You are to receive the offering for me from each man whose **heart**
28: 3 Tell all the **skilled men** [+2682] to whom I have given wisdom in
28:29 he will bear the names of the sons of Israel over his **heart** on the
28:30 so they may be over Aaron's **heart** whenever he enters the
28:30 decisions for the Israelites over his **heart** before the LORD.
31: 6 Also I have given skill **to** [+928] all the craftsmen to make
31: 6 Also I have given skill to all the **craftsmen** [+2682] to make
35: 5 Everyone who is **willing** [+5618] is to bring to the LORD an
35:10 "All *who* are **skilled** [+2682] among you are to come and make
35:21 and everyone who was willing and whose **heart** moved him came
35:22 All who were **willing** [+5618], men and women alike, came
35:25 Every **skilled** [+2682] woman spun with her hands and brought
35:26 all the women who *were* **willing** [+906+5951] and had the skill
35:29 women who *were* **willing** [+906+5605] brought to the LORD
35:34 son of Ahisamach, of the tribe of Dan, the **ability** to teach others.
35:35 He has filled them with **skill** [+2683] to do all kinds of work as
36: 1 every **skilled** [+2682] person to whom the LORD has given skill
36: 2 every **skilled** [+2682] person to whom the LORD had given
36: 2 skilled person to whom the LORD had given **ability** [+928+2683]
36: 2 and who *was* **willing** [+5951] to come and do the work.
36: 8 All the **skilled men** [+2682] among the workmen made the
Nu 16:28 sent me to do all these things and that it was not my **idea** [+4946]:
24:13 and gold, I could not do anything of my own **accord**, good or bad,
32: 7 Why *do you* **discourage** [+906+5648] the Israelites from going
32: 9 *they* **discouraged** [+906+5648] the Israelites from entering the
Dt 4:11 foot of the mountain while it blazed with fire to the **very** heavens,
28:65 There the LORD will give you an anxious **mind**, eyes weary with
29: 4 [29:3] to this day the LORD has not given you a **mind** that
29:19 [29:18] even though I **persist** in going my **own way** [+9244]."
Jos 11:20 For it was the LORD himself who hardened their **hearts** to wage
14: 8 my brothers who went up with me made the **hearts** *of* the people
Jdg 5: 9 My **heart** is with Israel's princes, with the willing volunteers
5:15 In the districts of Reuben there was much searching of **heart**.
5:16 In the districts of Reuben there was much searching of **heart**.
9: 3 they *were* **inclined** [+5742] to follow Abimelech, for they said,
16:15 can you say, 'I love you,' when you won't **confide** [+907] **in** me?
16:17 So he told her **everything** [+3972]. "No razor has ever been used
16:18 When Delilah saw that he had told her **everything** [+3972],
16:18 "Come back once more; he has told me **everything** [+3972]."
16:25 While they *were* **in high spirits** [+3201], they shouted, "Bring out
18:20 the priest *was* **glad** [+3512]. He took the ephod, the other
19: 3 her husband went to her to **persuade** [+1819+6584] her to return.
19: 5 his son-in-law, "Refresh **yourself** [+3870] with something to eat;
19: 6 girl's father said, "Please stay tonight and enjoy **yourself** [+3870]."
19:22 While they were enjoying **themselves** [+4392], some of the wicked
Ru 2:13 and *have* **spoken kindly to** [+1819+6584] your servant—
3: 7 had finished eating and drinking and *was* **in good spirits** [+3512],
1Sa 1:13 Hannah was praying in her **heart**, and her lips were moving
2: 1 "My **heart** rejoices in the LORD; in the LORD my horn is lifted
4:13 of the road, watching, because his **heart** feared for the ark of God.
4:20 birth to a son." But she did not respond or pay *any* **attention**.
6: 6 your hearts as the Egyptians and Pharaoh **did** [+906+3877+4392]?
9:20 you lost three days ago, *do* not **worry** [+906+8492] about them;
10: 9 As Saul turned to leave Samuel, God changed Saul's **heart**,
10:26 accompanied by valiant men whose **hearts** God had touched.
17:32 said to Saul, "Let no one lose **heart** on account of this Philistine;
24: 5 [24:6] Afterward, David *was* **conscience-stricken** [+906+5782] for
25:25 May my lord pay no **attention** to that wicked man Nabal.
25:31 my master will not have on his **conscience** the staggering burden
25:36 He *was* **in high spirits** [+3201] and very drunk. So she told him
25:37 these things, and his **heart** failed him and he became like a stone.
27: 1 David thought to **himself** [+2257], "One of these days I will be
28: 5 Saul saw the Philistine army, he was afraid; terror filled his **heart**.
2Sa 6:16 and dancing before the LORD, she despised him in her **heart**.
7:21 For the sake of your word and according to your **will**, you have
7:27 So your servant has found **courage** to offer you this prayer.
13:20 my sister; he is your brother. Don't take this thing to **heart**."
13:28 When Amnon *is* **in high spirits** [+3201] from drinking wine
13:33 My lord the king *should* not *be* **concerned about** [+448+8492] the
14: 1 Joab son of Zeruiah knew that the king's **heart** longed for
15: 6 asking for justice, and so he stole the **hearts** *of* the men of Israel.
15:13 told David, "The **hearts** *of* the men of Israel are with Absalom."
17:10 whose **heart** is like the heart of a lion, will melt with fear,
17:10 whose heart is like the **heart** *of* a lion, will melt with fear,
18: 3 if we are forced to flee, *they* won't **care** [+448+8492] **about** us.
18: 3 Even if half of us die, *they* won't **care** [+448+8492]; but you are
18:14 plunged them into Absalom's **heart** while Absalom was still alive
18:14 heart while Absalom was still alive **in** [+928] the oak tree.
19: 7 [19:8] Now go out and **encourage** [+1819+6584] your men.
19:19 [19:20] king left Jerusalem. May the king put it out of his **mind**.
24:10 David *was* **conscience-stricken** [+906+5782] after he had counted
1Ki 3: 9 So give your servant a discerning **heart** to govern your people
3:12 I will give you a wise and discerning **heart**, so that there will never
4:29 [5:9] a breadth of **understanding** as measureless as the sand on
8:23 servants who continue **wholeheartedly** [+928+3972] in your way.
8:47 if they have a change of **heart** in the land where they are held
8:66 glad in **heart** for all the good things the LORD had done for his
9: 3 Name there forever. My eyes and my **heart** will always be there.
10:24 with Solomon to hear the wisdom God had put in his **heart**.
11: 3 hundred concubines, and his wives **led** him **astray** [+906+5742].
12:26 Jeroboam thought to **himself** [+2257], "The kingdom will now
12:27 they *will* **again give** their **allegiance** [+8740] to their lord,
12:33 of the eighth month, a month of **his own** [+2257+4946] choosing,
18:37 are God, and that you are turning their **hearts** back again."
21: 7 you act as king over Israel? Get up and eat! **Cheer up** [+3512].
2Ki 5:26 "Was not my **spirit** with you when the man got down from his
6:11 This **enraged** [+6192+6584] the king of Aram. He summoned his
9:24 The arrow pierced his **heart** and he slumped down in his chariot.
12: 4 [12:5] brought **voluntarily** [+408+6584+6590] to the temple.
14:10 have indeed defeated Edom and now you *are* **arrogant** [+5951].
23: 3 regulations and decrees with all his **heart** and all his soul,
1Ch 12:33 [12:34] help David with **undivided loyalty** [+2256+4202+4213]—
12:33 [12:34] help David with **undivided loyalty** [+2256+4202+4213]—
12:38 [12:39] All the rest of the Israelites were also of one **mind** to
15:29 David dancing and celebrating, she despised him in her **heart**.
16:10 holy name; let the **hearts** *of* those who seek the LORD rejoice.
17:19 For the sake of your servant and according to your **will**, you have
28: 9 serve him with **wholehearted** [+8969] **devotion** and with a willing
29: 9 had given freely and **wholeheartedly** [+928+8969] to the LORD.
2Ch 6:14 servants who continue **wholeheartedly** [+928+3972] in your way.
6:38 if they turn back to you with all their **heart** and soul in the land of
7:10 glad in **heart** for the good things the LORD had done for David
7:11 had succeeded in carrying out all he had in **mind** to do in the
7:16 may be there forever. My eyes and my **heart** will always be there.
9:23 with Solomon to hear the wisdom God had put in his **heart**.
12:14 did evil because he had not set his **heart** on seeking the LORD.
17: 6 His **heart** was devoted to the ways of the LORD; furthermore,
24: 4 Some time later Joash **decided** [+2118+6640] to restore the temple
25:19 defeated Edom, and now you *are* **arrogant** [+5951] and proud.
26:16 Uzziah became powerful, his **pride** [+1467] led to his downfall.
29:31 and all whose **hearts** were willing brought burnt offerings.
30:12 the people to give them unity of **mind** to carry out what the king
30:22 Hezekiah spoke **encouragingly** [+6584] to all the Levites,
32:25 Hezekiah's **heart** was proud and he did not respond to the kindness
32:26 Hezekiah repented of the pride of his **heart**, as did the people of
Ezr 6:22 them with joy by changing the **attitude** *of* the king of Assyria,
7:27 who has put it into the king's **heart** to bring honor to the house of

Ne 2: 2 This can be nothing but sadness of **heart**." I was very much afraid,
2: 12 I had not told anyone what my God had put in my **heart** to do for
4: 6 [3:38] half its height, for the people worked *with all* their **heart**.
5: 7 I pondered them in my **mind** and then accused the nobles
6: 8 saying is happening; you are just making it up out of your **head**."
7: 5 So my God put it into my **heart** to assemble the nobles, the
Est 1: 10 when King Xerxes *was* **in high spirits** [+3201] from wine,
5: 9 Haman went out that day happy and **in high spirits** [+3201].
6: 6 Now Haman thought to **himself** [+2257], "Who is there that the
7: 5 Where is the man who *has* **dared** [+4848] to do such a thing?"
Job 1: 8 to Satan, "*Have you* **considered** [+6584+8492] my servant Job?
2: 3 to Satan, "*Have you* **considered** [+448+8492] my servant Job?
7: 17 you make so much of him, that you give him so much **attention**,
8: 10 Will they not bring forth words from their **understanding**?
11: 13 "Yet if you devote your **heart** to him and stretch out your hands to
12: 24 He deprives the leaders of the earth of their **reason**; he sends them
15: 12 Why has your **heart** carried you away, and why do your eyes flash,
17: 4 You have closed their **minds** to understanding; therefore you will
23: 16 God has made my **heart** faint; the Almighty has terrified me.
29: 13 man who was dying blessed me; I made the widow's **heart** sing.
31: 7 if my **heart** has been led by my eyes, or if my hands have been
31: 9 "If my **heart** has been enticed by a woman, or if I have lurked at
31: 27 so that my **heart** was secretly enticed and my hand offered them a
33: 3 My words come from an upright **heart**; my lips sincerely speak
34: 14 If it *were* his **intention** [+448+8492] and he withdrew his spirit
36: 5 but does not despise men; he is mighty, and firm in his **purpose**.
36: 13 "The godless in **heart** harbor resentment; even when he fetters
37: 1 "At this my **heart** pounds and leaps from its place.
37: 24 revere him, for does he not have regard for all the wise in **heart**?"
41: 24 [41:16] His **chest** is hard as rock, hard as a lower millstone.
Ps 4: 7 [4:8] You have filled my **heart** with greater joy than when their
7: 9 [7:10] O righteous God, who searches minds and **hearts**, bring to
7: 10 [7:11] shield is God Most High, who saves the upright in **heart**.
9: 1 [9:2] I will praise you, O LORD, with all my **heart**; I will tell of
10: 6 He says to **himself** [+2257], "Nothing will shake me; I'll always be
10: 11 He says to **himself** [+2257], "God has forgotten; he covers his face
10: 13 Why does he say to **himself** [+2257], "He won't call me to
10: 17 *you* **encourage** [+3922] them, and you listen to their cry,
11: 2 the strings to shoot from the shadows at the upright in **heart**.
12: 2 [12:3] their flattering lips speak with **deception** [+2256+4213].
12: 2 [12:3] their flattering lips speak with **deception** [+2256+4213].
13: 5 [13:6] in your unfailing love; my **heart** rejoices in your salvation.
14: 1 The fool says in his **heart**, "There is no God." They are corrupt,
16: 9 Therefore my **heart** is glad and my tongue rejoices; my body also
17: 3 Though you probe my **heart** and examine me at night, though you
19: 8 [19:9] precepts of the LORD are right, giving joy to the **heart**.
19: 14 [19:15] and the meditation of my **heart** be pleasing in your sight,
21: 2 [21:3] You have granted him the desire of his **heart** and have not
22: 14 [22:15] My **heart** has turned to wax; it has melted away within
26: 2 Test me, O LORD, and try me, examine my heart and my **mind**;
27: 3 Though an army besiege me, my **heart** will not fear; though war
27: 8 My **heart** says of you, "Seek his face!" Your face, LORD,
27: 14 be strong and **take heart** [+599] and wait for the LORD.
28: 7 and my shield; my **heart** trusts in him, and I am helped.
28: 7 My **heart** leaps for joy and I will give thanks to him in song.
31: 12 [31:13] *I* **am forgotten** [+4946+8894] by them as though I were
32: 11 and be glad, you righteous; sing, all you who are upright in **heart**!
33: 11 firm forever, the purposes of his **heart** through all generations.
33: 15 he who forms the **hearts** *of* all, who considers everything they do.
33: 21 In him our **hearts** rejoice, for we trust in his holy name.
34: 18 [34:19] The LORD is close to the **brokenhearted** [+8689] and
35: 25 *Do* not *let them* **think** [+606+928], "Aha, just what we wanted!"
36: 1 [36:2] An oracle is within my **heart** concerning the sinfulness of
36: 10 [36:11] know you, your righteousness to the upright in **heart**.
37: 4 in the LORD and he will give you the desires of your **heart**.
37: 15 their swords will pierce their own **hearts**, and their bows will be
37: 31 The law of his God is in his **heart**; his feet do not slip.
38: 8 [38:9] am feeble and utterly crushed; I groan in anguish of **heart**.
38: 10 [38:11] My **heart** pounds, my strength fails me; even the light has
39: 3 [39:4] My **heart** grew hot within me, and as I meditated, the fire
40: 10 [40:11] I do not hide your righteousness in my **heart**; I speak of
40: 12 [40:13] than the hairs of my head, and my **heart** fails within me.
41: 6 [41:7] see me, he speaks falsely, while his **heart** gathers slander;
44: 18 [44:19] Our **hearts** had not turned back; our feet had not strayed
44: 21 [44:22] discovered it, since he knows the secrets of the **heart**?
45: 1 [45:2] My **heart** is stirred by a noble theme as I recite my verses
45: 5 [45:6] Let your sharp arrows pierce the **hearts** *of* the king's
46: 2 [46:3] give way and the mountains fall into the **heart** *of* the sea,
48: 13 [48:14] **consider well** [+4200+8883] her ramparts, view her
49: 3 [49:4] the utterance from my **heart** will give understanding.
51: 10 [51:12] Create in me a pure **heart**, O God, and renew a steadfast
51: 17 [51:19] a broken and contrite **heart**, O God, you will not despise.
53: 1 [53:2] The fool says in his **heart**, "There is no God." They are
55: 4 [55:5] My **heart** is in anguish within me; the terrors of death
55: 21 [55:22] His speech is smooth as butter, yet war is in his **heart**;
57: 7 [57:8] My **heart** is steadfast, O God, my heart is steadfast; I will
57: 7 [57:8] My heart is steadfast, O God, my **heart** is steadfast; I will
58: 2 [58:3] No, in your **heart** you devise injustice, and your hands
61: 2 [61:3] of the earth I call to you, I call as my **heart** grows faint;
62: 10 [62:11] your riches increase, do not set your **heart** on them.
64: 6 [64:7] Surely the mind and **heart** of man are cunning.
64: 10 [64:11] take refuge in him; let all the upright in **heart** praise him!
66: 18 If I had cherished sin in my **heart**, the Lord would not have
69: 20 [69:21] Scorn has broken my **heart** and has left me helpless; I
74: 8 They said in their **hearts**, "We will crush them completely!"
76: 5 [76:6] **Valiant men** [+52] lie plundered, they sleep their last
78: 8 and rebellious generation, whose **hearts** were not loyal to God,
78: 37 their **hearts** were not loyal to him, they were not faithful to his
81: 12 [81:13] So I gave them over to their stubborn **hearts** to follow
83: 5 [83:6] *With one* **mind** they plot together; they form an alliance
84: 2 [84:3] my **heart** and my flesh cry out for the living God.
94: 15 on righteousness, and all the upright in **heart** will follow it.
97: 11 Light is shed upon the righteous and joy on the upright in **heart**.
102: 4 [102:5] My **heart** is blighted and withered like grass; I forget to
105: 3 holy name; let the **hearts** *of* those who seek the LORD rejoice.
105: 25 whose **hearts** he turned to hate his people, to conspire against his
107: 12 So he subjected **them** [+4392] to bitter labor; they stumbled,
108: 1 [108:2] My **heart** is steadfast, O God; I will sing and make music
109: 22 For I am poor and needy, and my **heart** is wounded within me.
112: 7 no fear of bad news; his **heart** is steadfast, trusting in the LORD.
112: 8 His **heart** is secure, he will have no fear; in the end he will look in
119: 2 are they who keep his statutes and seek him with all their **heart**.
119: 10 I seek you with all my **heart**; do not let me stray from your
119: 11 I have hidden your word in my **heart** that I might not sin against
119: 32 run in the path of your commands, for you have set my **heart** free.
119: 34 and I will keep your law and obey it with all my **heart**.
119: 36 Turn my **heart** toward your statutes and not toward selfish gain.
119: 58 I have sought your face with all my **heart**; be gracious to me
119: 69 have smeared me with lies, I keep your precepts with all my **heart**.
119: 70 Their **hearts** are callous and unfeeling, but I delight in your law.
119: 80 May my **heart** be blameless toward your decrees, that I may not be
119:111 Your statutes are my heritage forever; they are the joy of my **heart**.
119:112 My **heart** is set on keeping your decrees to the very end.
119:145 I call with all my **heart**; answer me, O LORD, and I will obey
119:161 persecute me without cause, but my **heart** trembles at your word.
125: 4 to those who are good, to those who are upright in **heart**.
131: 1 My **heart** is not proud, O LORD, my eyes are not haughty;
138: 1 I will praise you, O LORD, with all my **heart**; before the "gods" I
140: 2 [140:3] who devise evil plans in their **hearts** and stir up war every
141: 4 Let not my **heart** be drawn to what is evil, to take part in wicked
143: 4 my spirit grows faint within me; my **heart** within me is dismayed.
147: 3 He heals the **brokenhearted** [+8689] and binds up their wounds.
Pr 2: 2 your ear to wisdom and applying your **heart** to understanding,
2: 10 For wisdom will enter your **heart**, and knowledge will be pleasant
3: 1 do not forget my teaching, but keep my commands in your **heart**,
3: 3 them around your neck, write them on the tablet of your **heart**.
3: 5 Trust in the LORD with all your **heart** and lean not on your own
4: 4 he taught me and said, "Lay hold of my words with all your **heart**;
4: 23 Above all else, guard your **heart**, for it is the wellspring of life.
5: 12 "How I hated discipline! How my **heart** spurned correction!
6: 14 who plots evil with deceit in his **heart**—he always stirs up
6: 18 a **heart** that devises wicked schemes, feet that are quick to rush
6: 21 Bind them upon your **heart** forever; fasten them around your neck.
6: 32 But a man who commits adultery lacks **judgment**; whoever does
7: 3 Bind them on your fingers; write them on the tablet of your **heart**.
7: 7 I noticed among the young men, a youth who lacked **judgment**.
7: 10 to meet him, dressed like a prostitute and with crafty **intent**.
7: 25 Do not let your **heart** turn to her ways or stray into her paths.
8: 5 gain prudence; you who are foolish, gain **understanding**.
9: 4 are simple come in here!" she says to those who lack **judgment**.
9: 16 are simple come in here!" she says to those who lack **judgment**.
10: 8 The wise in **heart** accept commands, but a chattering fool comes to
10: 13 but a rod is for the back of him who lacks **judgment**.
10: 20 is choice silver, but the **heart** *of* the wicked is of little value.
10: 21 of the righteous nourish many, but fools die for lack of **judgment**.
11: 12 A man who lacks **judgment** derides his neighbor, but a man of
11: 20 The LORD detests men of perverse **heart** but he delights in those
11: 29 inherit only wind, and the fool will be servant to the **wise** [+2682].
12: 8 to his wisdom, but men with warped **minds** are despised.
12: 11 have abundant food, but he who chases fantasies lacks **judgment**.
12: 20 There is deceit in the **hearts** *of* those who plot evil, but joy for
12: 23 his knowledge to himself, but the **heart** *of* fools blurts out folly.
12: 25 An anxious **heart** weighs a man down, but a kind word cheers him
13: 12 Hope deferred makes the **heart** sick, but a longing fulfilled is a tree
14: 10 *Each* **heart** knows its own bitterness, and no one else can share its
14: 13 Even in laughter the **heart** may ache, and joy may end in grief.
14: 14 The **faithless** [+6047] will be fully repaid for their ways,
14: 30 A **heart** at peace gives life to the body, but envy rots the bones.

Pr 14:33 Wisdom reposes in the **heart** *of* the discerning and even among
15: 7 The lips of the wise spread knowledge; not so the **hearts** *of* fools.
15:11 lie open before the LORD—how much more the **hearts** *of* men!
15:13 A happy **heart** makes the face cheerful, but heartache crushes the
15:13 makes the face cheerful, but **heartache** [+6780] crushes the spirit.
15:14 The discerning **heart** seeks knowledge, but the mouth of a fool
15:15 are wretched, but the cheerful **heart** has a continual feast.
15:21 Folly delights a man who lacks **judgment**, but a man of
15:28 The **heart** *of* the righteous weighs its answers, but the mouth of the
15:30 A cheerful look brings joy to the **heart**, and good news gives
15:32 but whoever heeds correction gains **understanding**.
16: 1 To man belong the plans of the **heart**, but from the LORD comes
16: 5 The LORD detests all the proud of **heart**. Be sure of this:
16: 9 In his **heart** a man plans his course, but the LORD determines his
16:21 The wise in **heart** are called discerning, and pleasant words
16:23 A wise man's **heart** guides his mouth, and his lips promote
17: 3 for silver and the furnace for gold, but the LORD tests the **heart**.
17:16 money in the hand of a fool, since he has no **desire** to get wisdom?
17:18 A man lacking in **judgment** strikes hands in pledge and puts up
17:20 A man of perverse **heart** does not prosper; he whose tongue is
17:22 A cheerful **heart** is good medicine, but a crushed spirit dries up the
18: 2 pleasure in understanding but delights in airing his own **opinions**.
18:12 Before his downfall a man's **heart** is proud, but humility comes
18:15 The **heart** *of* the discerning acquires knowledge; the ears of the
19: 3 own folly ruins his life, yet his **heart** rages against the LORD.
19: 8 He who gets **wisdom** loves his own soul; he who cherishes
19:21 Many are the plans in a man's **heart**, but it is the LORD's
20: 5 The purposes of a man's **heart** are deep waters, but a man of
20: 9 Who can say, "I have kept my **heart** pure; I am clean and without
21: 1 The king's **heart** is in the hand of the LORD; he directs it like a
21: 2 a man's ways seem right to him, but the LORD weighs the **heart**.
21: 4 Haughty eyes and a proud **heart**, the lamp of the wicked, are sin!
22:11 He who loves a pure **heart** and whose speech is gracious will have
22:15 Folly is bound up in the **heart** *of* a child, but the rod of discipline
22:17 listen to the sayings of the wise; apply your **heart** to what I teach,
23: 7 "Eat and drink," he says to you, but his **heart** is not with you.
23:12 Apply your **heart** to instruction and your ears to words of
23:15 My son, if your **heart** is wise, then my heart will be glad;
23:15 My son, if your heart is wise, then my **heart** will be glad;
23:17 Do not let your **heart** envy sinners, but always be zealous for the
23:19 my son, and be wise, and keep your **heart** on the right path.
23:26 My son, give me your **heart** and let your eyes keep to my ways,
23:33 will see strange sights and your **mind** imagine confusing things.
23:34 You will be like one sleeping on the **high seas** [+3542], lying on
24: 2 for their **hearts** plot violence, and their lips talk about making
24:12 nothing about this," does not he who weighs the **heart** perceive it?
24:17 your enemy falls; when he stumbles, do not let your **heart** rejoice,
24:30 of the sluggard, past the vineyard of the man who lacks **judgment**;
24:32 I applied my **heart** to what I observed and learned a lesson from
25: 3 and the earth is deep, so the **hearts** *of* kings are unsearchable.
25:20 vinegar poured on soda, is one who sings songs to a heavy **heart**.
26:23 of glaze over earthenware are fervent lips with an evil **heart**.
26:25 do not believe him, for seven abominations fill his **heart**.
27: 9 Perfume and incense bring joy to the **heart**, and the pleasantness of
27:11 Be wise, my son, and bring joy to my **heart**; then I can answer
27:19 As water reflects a face, so a man's **heart** reflects the man.
27:23 the condition of your flocks, give **careful attention** to your herds;
28:14 fears the LORD, but he who hardens his **heart** falls into trouble.
28:26 He who trusts in **himself** [+2257] is a fool, but he who walks in
30:19 of a snake on a rock, the way of a ship on the **high seas** [+3542],
31:11 Her husband **has full confidence** [+1053] in her and lacks nothing
Ecc 1:13 I devoted **myself** [+3276] to study and to explore by wisdom all
1:16 I thought to **myself** [+3276], "Look, I have grown and increased in
1:16 than anyone who has ruled over Jerusalem before me; **I** [+3276]
1:17 Then I applied **myself** [+3276] to the understanding of wisdom,
2: 1 I thought in my **heart**, "Come now, I will test you with pleasure to
2: 3 ***I* tried** [+928+9365] cheering myself with wine, and embracing
2: 3 and embracing folly—my **mind** still guiding me with wisdom.
2:10 myself nothing my eyes desired; I refused my **heart** no pleasure.
2:10 My **heart** took delight in all my work, and this was the reward for
2:15 I thought in my **heart**, "The fate of the fool will overtake me also.
2:15 gain by being wise?" I said in my **heart**, "This too is meaningless."
2:20 So my **heart** began to despair over all my toilsome labor under the
2:22 and **anxious striving** [+8301] with which he labors under the sun?
2:23 his work is pain and grief; even at night his **mind** does not rest.
3:11 He has also set eternity in the **hearts** *of* men; yet they cannot
3:17 I thought in my **heart**, "God will bring to judgment both the
3:18 I also thought, **[RPH]** "As for men, God tests them so that they
5: 2 [5:1] do not be hasty in your **heart** to utter anything before God.
5:20 [5:19] because God keeps him occupied with gladness of **heart**.
7: 2 is the destiny of every man; the living should take this to **heart**.
7: 3 is better than laughter, because a sad face is good for the **heart**.
7: 4 The **heart** *of* the wise is in the house of mourning, but the heart of
7: 4 of mourning, but the **heart** *of* fools is in the house of pleasure.
7: 7 turns a wise man into a fool, and a bribe corrupts the **heart**.
7:21 *Do* not pay **attention** to every word people say, or you may hear
7:22 for you know in your **heart** that many times you yourself have
7:25 So I turned my **mind** to understand, to investigate and to search out
7:26 who is a snare, whose **heart** is a trap and whose hands are chains.
8: 5 and the wise **heart** will know the proper time and procedure.
8: 9 this I saw, as I applied my **mind** to everything done under the sun.
8:11 the **hearts** *of* the people are filled with schemes to do wrong.
8:16 When I applied my **mind** to know wisdom and to observe man's
9: 1 So ***I* reflected on** [+448+906+5989] all this and concluded that the
9: 3 The **hearts** *of* men, moreover, are full of evil and there is madness
9: 7 your food with gladness, and drink your wine with a joyful **heart**,
10: 2 The **heart** *of* the wise inclines to the right, but the heart of the fool
10: 2 of the wise inclines to the right, but the **heart** *of* the fool to the left.
10: 3 the fool lacks **sense** and shows everyone how stupid he is.
11: 9 and let your **heart** give you joy in the days of your youth.
11: 9 Follow the ways of your **heart** and whatever your eyes see,
11:10 banish anxiety from your **heart** and cast off the troubles of your
SS 3:11 crowned him on the day of his wedding, the day his **heart** rejoiced.
5: 2 I slept but my **heart** was awake. Listen! My lover is knocking:
8: 6 Place me like a seal over your **heart**, like a seal on your arm;
Isa 6:10 Make the **heart** *of* this people calloused; make their ears dull
15: 5 My **heart** cries out over Moab; her fugitives flee as far as Zoar,
24: 7 and the vine withers; all the **merrymakers** [+8524] groan.
29:13 and honor me with their lips, but their **hearts** are far from me.
32: 6 For the fool speaks folly, his **mind** is busy with evil: He practices
33:18 In your **thoughts** you will ponder the former terror: "Where is that
35: 4 say to those with fearful **hearts**, "Be strong, do not fear; your God
38: 3 before you faithfully and with **wholehearted** [+8969] **devotion**
40: 2 Speak **tenderly** [+6584] to Jerusalem, and proclaim to her that her
41:22 so that we *may* **consider** [+8492] them and know their final
42:25 not understand; it consumed them, but they did not take it to **heart**.
44:18 they cannot see, and their **minds** closed so they cannot understand.
44:19 No one **stops to think** [+448+8740], no one has the knowledge
44:20 He feeds on ashes, a deluded **heart** misleads him; he cannot save
46: 8 "Remember this, fix it in mind, take it to **heart**, you rebels.
46:12 you **stubborn-hearted** [+52], you who are far from righteousness.
47: 7 *you did* not **consider** [+6584+8492] these things or reflect on what
47:10 and knowledge mislead you when you say to **yourself** [+3871],
51: 7 know what is right, you people who have my law in your **hearts**:
57: 1 The righteous perish, and no one ponders it in his **heart**; devout
57:11 have neither remembered me nor pondered this in your **hearts**?
57:15 revive the spirit of the lowly and to revive the **heart** *of* the contrite.
57:17 and hid my face in anger, yet he kept on in his **willful** ways.
59:13 and revolt, uttering lies our **hearts** have conceived.
61: 1 He has sent me to bind up the **brokenhearted** [+8689], to proclaim
63: 4 For the day of vengeance was in my **heart**, and the year of my
63:17 from your ways and harden our **hearts** so we do not revere you?
65:14 My servants will sing out of the joy of their **hearts**, but you will
65:14 you will cry out from anguish of **heart** and wail in brokenness of
65:17 former things will not be remembered, nor will they come to **mind**.
66:14 see this, your **heart** will rejoice and you will flourish like grass;
Jer 3:10 her unfaithful sister Judah did not return to me with all her **heart**,
3:15 I will give you shepherds after my own **heart**, who will lead you
3:16 It will never enter their **minds** or be remembered; it will not be
3:17 No longer will they follow the stubbornness of their evil **hearts**.
4: 9 declares the LORD, "the king and the officials will lose **heart**,
4: 9 the officials will lose heart, **[RPH]** the priests will be horrified,
4:14 O Jerusalem, wash the evil from your **heart** and be saved.
4:18 is your punishment. How bitter it is! How it pierces to the **heart**!"
4:19 my anguish! I writhe in pain. Oh, the agony of my **heart**!
4:19 of my heart! My **heart** pounds within me, I cannot keep silent.
5:21 Hear this, you foolish and **senseless** [+401] people, who have eyes
5:23 these people have stubborn and rebellious **hearts**; they have turned
7:24 they followed the stubborn inclinations of their evil **hearts**.
7:31 the fire—something I did not command, nor did it enter my **mind**.
8:18 O my Comforter in sorrow, my **heart** is faint within me.
9:14 [9:13] they have followed the stubbornness of their **hearts**;
9:26 [9:25] even the whole house of Israel is uncircumcised in **heart**."
11: 8 instead, they followed the stubbornness of their evil **hearts**.
11:20 you who judge righteously and test the **heart** and mind,
12: 3 know me, O LORD; you see me and test my **thoughts** about you.
12:11 be laid waste because there is no one *who* **cares** [+6584+8492].
13:10 who follow the stubbornness of their **hearts** and go after other
14:14 divinations, idolatries and the delusions of their own **minds**.
16:12 how each of you is following the stubbornness of his evil **heart**
17: 1 on the tablets of their **hearts** and on the horns of their altars.
17: 5 for his strength and whose **heart** turns away from the LORD.
17: 9 The **heart** is deceitful above all things and beyond cure. Who can
17:10 "I the LORD search the **heart** and examine the mind, to reward a
18:12 each of us will follow the stubbornness of his evil **heart**.' "
19: 5 I did not command or mention, nor did it enter my **mind**.
20: 9 his word is in my **heart** like a fire, a fire shut up in my bones.
20:12 you who examine the righteous and probe the **heart** and mind,

Jer 22:17 "But your eyes and your **heart** are set only on dishonest gain,
23: 9 My **heart** is broken within me; all my bones tremble. I am like a
23:16 They speak visions from their own **minds**, not from the mouth of
23:17 And to all who follow the stubbornness of their **hearts** they say,
23:20 not turn back until he fully accomplishes the purposes of his **heart**.
23:26 How long will this continue in the **hearts** *of* these lying prophets,
23:26 lying prophets, who prophesy the delusions of their own **minds**?
24: 7 I will give them a **heart** to know me, that I am the LORD.
24: 7 I will be their God, for they will return to me with all their **heart**.
30:21 for who is he who will devote **himself** [+2257] to be close to me?'
30:24 not turn back until he fully accomplishes the purposes of his **heart**.
31:21 **Take note** [+8883] of the highway, the road that you take.
31:33 "I will put my law in their minds and write it on their **hearts**.
32:35 to Molech, though I never commanded, nor did it enter my **mind**,
32:39 I will give them singleness of **heart** and action, so that they will
32:41 and will assuredly plant them in this land with all my **heart**
44:21 **think** [+6584+6590] **about** the incense burned in the towns of
48:29 her pride and arrogance and the haughtiness of her **heart**.
48:36 "So my **heart** laments for Moab like a flute; it laments like a flute
48:36 **it**[s] [+3276] laments like a flute for the men of Kir Hareseth.
48:41 In that day the **hearts** *of* Moab's warriors will be like the heart of a
48:41 In that day the hearts of Moab's warriors will be like the **heart** *of* a
49:16 terror you inspire and the pride of your **heart** have deceived you,
49:22 In that day the **hearts** *of* Edom's warriors will be like the heart of a
49:22 In that day the hearts of Edom's warriors will be like the **heart** *of* a
La 1:20 I am in torment within, and in my **heart** I am disturbed, for I have
1:22 because of all my sins. My groans are many and my **heart** is faint."
2:18 The **hearts** *of* the people cry out to the Lord. O wall of the
2:19 pour out your **heart** like water in the presence of the Lord.
3:21 Yet this I **call to mind** [+448+8740] and therefore I have hope:
3:33 For he does not **willingly** [+4946] bring affliction or grief to the
3:65 Put a veil over their **hearts**, and may your curse be on them!
5:15 Joy is gone from our **hearts**; our dancing has turned to mourning.
5:17 Because of this our **hearts** are faint, because of these things our
Eze 2: 4 to whom I am sending you are obstinate and **stubborn** [+2617].
3: 7 for the whole house of Israel is hardened and **obstinate** [+7997].
6: 9 how I have been grieved by their adulterous **hearts**, which have
11:19 I will give them an undivided **heart** and put a new spirit in them;
11:19 I will remove from them their **heart** *of* stone and give them a heart
11:19 from them their heart of stone and give them a **heart** *of* flesh.
11:21 But as for those whose **hearts** are devoted to their vile images
11:21 as for those whose hearts **[RPH]** are devoted to their vile images
13: 2 Say to those who prophesy out of their own **imagination**:
13:17 of your people who prophesy out of their own **imagination**.
13:22 Because you **disheartened** [+3874] the righteous with your lies,
14: 3 these men have set up idols in their **hearts** and put wicked
14: 4 When any Israelite sets up idols in his **heart** and puts a wicked
14: 5 I will do this to recapture the **hearts** *of* the people of Israel,
14: 7 sets up idols in his **heart** and puts a wicked stumbling block before
18:31 you have committed, and get a new **heart** and a new spirit.
20:16 my Sabbaths. For their **hearts** were devoted to their idols.
21: 7 [21:12] Every **heart** will melt and every hand go limp; every
21:15 [21:20] So that **hearts** may melt and the fallen be many, I have
22:14 Will your **courage** endure or your hands be strong in the day I deal
27: 4 Your domain was on the **high seas** [+3542]; your builders brought
27:25 your wares. You are filled with heavy cargo in the **heart** *of* the sea.
27:26 But the east wind will break you to pieces in the **heart** *of* the sea.
27:27 everyone else on board will sink into the **heart** *of* the sea on the
28: 2 " 'In the pride of your **heart** you say, "I am a god; I sit on the
28: 2 "I am a god; I sit on the throne of a god in the **heart** *of* the seas."
28: 2 and not a god, though *you* **think** [+5989] you are as wise as a god.
28: 2 a man and not a god, though you think you are as **wise** as a god.
28: 6 LORD says: " 'Because you think you are wise, as **wise** as a god,
28: 8 to the pit, and you will die a violent death in the **heart** *of* the seas.
28:17 Your **heart** became proud on account of your beauty, and you
32: 9 I will trouble the **hearts** *of* many peoples when I bring about your
33:31 they express devotion, but their **hearts** are greedy for unjust gain.
36:26 I will give you a new **heart** and put a new spirit in you; I will
36:26 I will remove from you your **heart** *of* stone and give you a heart of
36:26 remove from you your heart of stone and give you a **heart** *of* flesh.
40: 4 your ears and pay **attention** to everything I am going to show you,
44: 5 give **attention** to everything I tell you concerning all the
44: 5 Give **attention** to the entrance of the temple and all the exits of the
44: 7 you brought foreigners uncircumcised in **heart** and flesh into my
44: 9 No foreigner uncircumcised in **heart** and flesh is to enter my
Da 1: 8 Daniel **resolved** [+6584+8492] not to defile himself with the royal
10:12 Since the first day that you set your **mind** to gain understanding
Hos 2:14 [2:16] lead her into the desert and speak **tenderly** [+6584] to her.
4:11 to old wine and new, which take away the **understanding**
7: 6 Their **hearts** are like an oven; they approach him with intrigue.
7:11 "Ephraim is like a dove, easily deceived and **senseless** [+401]—
7:14 They do not cry out to me from their **hearts** but wail upon their
10: 2 Their **heart** is deceitful, and now they must bear their guilt.
11: 8 My **heart** is changed within me; all my compassion is aroused.
13: 6 when they were satisfied, they *became* **proud** [+8123];
13: 8 of her cubs, I will attack them and **rip** them **open** [+6033+7973].
Am 2:16 Even the **bravest** [+579] warriors will flee naked on that day,"
Ob 1: 3 The pride of your **heart** has deceived you, you who live in the
1: 3 make your home on the heights, you who say to **yourself** [+2257],
Na 2:10 [2:11] **Hearts** melt, knees give way, bodies tremble, every face
Zep 3:14 Be glad and rejoice with all your **heart**, O Daughter of Jerusalem!
Zec 7:12 They made their **hearts** as hard as flint and would not listen to the
10: 7 like mighty men, and their **hearts** will be glad as with wine.
10: 7 will see it and be joyful; their **hearts** will rejoice in the LORD.
12: 5 the leaders of Judah will say in their **hearts**, 'The people of
Mal 2: 2 do not listen, and if you do not set your **heart** to honor my name,"
2: 2 cursed them, because you have not set your **heart** to honor me.
4: 6 [3:24] He will turn the **hearts** *of* the fathers to their children,
4: 6 [3:24] and the **hearts** *of* the children to their fathers;

4214 לֵב קָמָי ***lēb qāmāy***, n.pr.loc. [1] [√ 4213 + 7856]

Leb Kamai [1]

Jer 51: 1 spirit of a destroyer against Babylon and the people of **Leb Kamai**.

4215 לָבֹא ***lābō'***, n.pr.loc. Not used in NIV/BHS [→ 4217]

4216 לָבֶא ***lebe'***, n.m. [1] [→ 1106, 4218, 4219, 4232, 4233, 4234]

lions [1]

Ps 57: 4 [57:5] I am in the midst of **lions**; I lie among ravenous beasts—

4217 לְבֹא חֲמָת ***l**e**bō' ḥ**a**māt***, n.pr.loc. [12] [√ 4215 + 2828]

Lebo Hamath [12]

Nu 13:21 from the Desert of Zin as far as Rehob, toward **Lebo Hamath**.
34: 8 from Mount Hor to **Lebo Hamath**. Then the boundary will go to
Jos 13: 5 the east, from Baal Gad below Mount Hermon to **Lebo Hamath**.
Jdg 3: 3 Lebanon mountains from Mount Baal Hermon to **Lebo Hamath**.
1Ki 8:65 a vast assembly, people from **Lebo Hamath** to the Wadi of Egypt.
2Ki 14:25 boundaries of Israel from **Lebo Hamath** to the Sea of the Arabah,
1Ch 13: 5 all the Israelites, from the Shihor River in Egypt to **Lebo Hamath**,
2Ch 7: 8 a vast assembly, people from **Lebo Hamath** to the Wadi of Egypt.
Eze 47:15 the Great Sea by the Hethlon road past **Lebo Hamath** to Zedad,
47:20 Great Sea will be the boundary to a point opposite **Lebo Hamath**.
48: 1 it will follow the Hethlon road to **Lebo Hamath**; Hazar Enan
Am 6:14 that will oppress you all the way from **Lebo Hamath** to the valley

4218 לְבִאָה ***lib'â***, n.f. [1] [√ 4216]

mate [1]

Na 2:12 [2:13] enough for his cubs and strangled the prey for his **mate**,

4219 לְבָאוֹת ***l**e**bā'ôt***, n.pr.loc. [1] [→ 1106; cf. 4216]

Lebaoth [1]

Jos 15:32 **Lebaoth**, Shilhim, Ain and Rimmon—a total of twenty-nine towns

4220 לָבַב¹ ***lābab¹***, v.den. [3] [→ 4226]

stolen heart [2], become wise [1]

Job 11:12 [C] a witless man *can* no more **become wise** than a wild
SS 4: 9 [D] *You have* **stolen** my **heart**, my sister, my bride; you have
4: 9 [D] *you have* **stolen** my **heart** with one glance of your eyes,

4221 לָבַב² ***lābab²***, v.den. [2] [√ 4223; cf. 4213]

made bread [1], make special bread [+4223] [1]

2Sa 13: 6 [D] to come and **make** some **special bread** [+4223] in my sight,
13: 8 [D] kneaded it, **made** *the* **bread** in his sight and baked it.

4222 לֵבָב ***lēbāb***, n.m. & f. [252] [√ 4213; Ar 10381]

heart [120], hearts [46], mind [10], give careful thought [+8492] [5], *untranslated* [4], yourself [+3870] [4], conscience [3], heart's [2], minds [2], understanding [2], wholehearted devotion [+8969] [2], wholeheartedly [+928+3972] [2], wholeheartedly [+928+8969] [2], yourselves [+3870] [2], breasts [1], brokenhearted [+3874] [1], conscientious [+3838] [1], consider [+928] [1], consider better [+8123] [1], convictions [+6640] [1], courage [1], deceived [+906+1704] [1], disheartened [+906+5022] [1], downhearted [+8317] [1], encouraged [+1819+6584] [1], enticed [+7331] [1], fainthearted [+8205] [1], fainthearted [+8216] [1], filled with pride [+8123] [1], fully determined [+928+8969] [1], gladly [+928+3206] [1], harbor [+2118+6640] [1], hardhearted [+599+906] [1], has in mind [+3108] [1], heart and soul [+3869] [1], herself [+2023] [1], himself [+2257] [1], in a rage [+2801] [1], in accord with [+3838] [1], indecisive [+8205] [1], inspire [+906+928+5989] [1], integrity [+3841] [1], intend [+6640] [1], intent [1], plot against [+906+928+3108] [1], profound [1], proud [+8123] [1], purpose [1], realize [+606+4200] [1], take heart [+599] [1], themselves [+4392] [1], think [+606+928] [1], think [+6584+6590] [1], think [+906+5989] [1], thinks [+606+928] [1], unite [+2118+3480+4200+6584] [1], willfully [+928] [1], yourself [+2023] [1], yourself [+3871] [1], yourselves [+4013] [1]

Ge 20: 5 I have done this with a clear **conscience** and clean hands."
20: 6 I know you did this with a clear **conscience**, and so I have kept you
31: 26 *You've* **deceived** [+906+1704] me, and you've carried off my
Ex 14: 5 Pharaoh and his officials changed their **minds** about them
Lev 19: 17 " 'Do not hate your brother in your **heart**. Rebuke your neighbor
26: 36 I will make their **hearts** so fearful in the lands of their enemies that
26: 41 when their uncircumcised **hearts** are humbled and they pay for
Nu 15: 39 prostitute yourselves by going after the lusts of your own **hearts**
Dt 1: 28 Our brothers have made us lose **heart**. They say, 'The people are
2: 30 and his **heart** obstinate in order to give him into your hands,
4: 9 eyes have seen or let them slip from your **heart** as long as you live.
4: 29 you will find him if you look for him with all your **heart** and with
4: 39 and take to **heart** this day that the LORD is God in heaven above
5: 29 that their **hearts** would be inclined to fear me and keep all my
6: 5 Love the LORD your God with all your **heart** and with all your
6: 6 commandments that I give you today are to be upon your **hearts**.
7: 17 You may say to **yourselves** [+3870], "These nations are stronger
8: 2 and to test you in order to know what was in your **heart**,
8: 5 Know then in your **heart** that as a man disciplines his son,
8: 14 your **heart** will become proud and you will forget the LORD your
8: 17 You may say to **yourself** [+3870], "My power and the strength of
9: 4 has driven them out before you, do not say to **yourself** [+3870],
9: 5 or your **integrity** [+3841] that you are going in to take possession
10: 12 to serve the LORD your God with all your **heart** and with all
10: 16 Circumcise your **hearts**, therefore, and do not be stiff-necked any
11: 13 and to serve him with all your **heart** and with all your soul—
11: 16 or you *will be* **enticed** [+7331] to turn away and worship other
11: 18 Fix these words of mine in your **hearts** and minds; tie them as
13: 3 [13:4] you to find out whether you love him with all your **heart**
15: 7 *do* not *be* **hardhearted** [+599+906] or tightfisted toward your poor
15: 9 Be careful not *to* **harbor** [+2118+6640] this wicked thought:
15: 10 Give generously to him and do so without a grudging **heart**;
17: 17 He must not take many wives, or his **heart** will be led astray.
17: 20 and not **consider** himself **better** [+8123] than his brothers
18: 21 You may say to **yourselves** [+3870], "How can we know when a
19: 6 the avenger of blood might pursue him **in a rage** [+2801],
20: 3 *Do* not *be* **fainthearted** [+8216] or afraid; do not be terrified
20: 8 the officers shall add, "Is any man afraid or **fainthearted** [+8205]?
20: 8 that his brothers *will* not *become* **disheartened** [+906+5022] too."
20: 8 so that his brothers will not become disheartened too." **[RPH]**
26: 16 carefully observe them with all your **heart** and with all your soul.
28: 28 will afflict you with madness, blindness and confusion of **mind**.
28: 47 God joyfully and **gladly** [+928+3206] in the time of prosperity,
28: 67 because of the terror that will fill your **hearts** and the sights that
29: 18 [29:17] or tribe among you today whose **heart** turns away from
29: 19 [29:18] a blessing on himself and therefore **thinks** [+606+928],
30: 1 you take them to **heart** wherever the LORD your God disperses
30: 2 return to the LORD your God and obey him with all your **heart**
30: 6 The LORD your God will circumcise your **hearts** and the hearts
30: 6 will circumcise your hearts and the **hearts** *of* your descendants,
30: 6 so that you may love him with all your **heart** and with all your
30: 10 turn to the LORD your God with all your **heart** and with all your
30: 14 near you; it is in your mouth and in your **heart** so you may obey it.
30: 17 if your **heart** turns away and you are not obedient, and if you are
32: 46 "Take to **heart** all the words I have solemnly declared to you this
Jos 2: 11 our **hearts** melted and everyone's courage failed because of you,
5: 1 their **hearts** melted and they no longer had the courage to face the
7: 5 At this the **hearts** *of* the people melted and became like water.
14: 7 I brought him back a report according to my **convictions** [+6640],
22: 5 to hold fast to him and to serve him with all your **heart** and all
23: 14 You know with all your **heart** and soul that not one of all the good
24: 23 gods that are among you and yield your **hearts** to the LORD,
Jdg 19: 8 he rose to go, the girl's father said, "Refresh **yourself** [+3870].
19: 9 night here; the day is nearly over. Stay and enjoy **yourself** [+3870].
1Sa 1: 8 Why don't you eat? Why *are* you **downhearted** [+8317]?
2: 35 who will do according to what is in my **heart** and mind.
6: 6 Why do you harden your **hearts** as the Egyptians and Pharaoh did?
7: 3 "If you are returning to the LORD with all your **hearts**, then rid
7: 3 and the Ashtoreths and commit **yourselves** [+4013] to the LORD
9: 19 morning I will let you go and will tell you all that is in your **heart**.
12: 20 away from the LORD, but serve the LORD with all your **heart**.
12: 24 to fear the LORD and serve him faithfully with all your **heart**;
13: 14 the LORD has sought out a man after his own **heart**
14: 7 "Do all that you have in **mind**," his armor-bearer said. "Go ahead;
14: 7 "Go ahead; I am with you **heart** [+3869] **and soul**."
16: 7 at the outward appearance, but the LORD looks at the **heart**."
17: 28 I know how conceited you are and how wicked your **heart** is;
21: 12 [21:13] David took these words to **heart** and was very much

2Sa 7: 3 to the king, "Whatever you have in **mind**, go ahead and do it,
19: 14 [19:15] He won over the **hearts** *of* all the men of Judah as though
1Ki 2: 4 and if they walk faithfully before me with all their **heart** and soul,
2: 44 "You know in your **heart** all the wrong you did to my father
3: 6 because he was faithful to you and righteous and upright in **heart**.
8: 17 "My father David had it in his **heart** to build a temple for the
8: 18 'Because it was in your **heart** to build a temple for my Name,
8: 18 a temple for my Name, you did well to have this in your **heart**.
8: 38 each one aware of the afflictions of his own **heart**, and spreading
8: 39 since you know his **heart** (for you alone know the hearts of all
8: 39 since you know his heart (for you alone know the **hearts** *of* all
8: 48 if they turn back to you with all their **heart** and soul in the land of
8: 58 May he turn our **hearts** to him, to walk in all his ways and to keep
8: 61 But your **hearts** must be fully committed to the LORD our God,
9: 4 if you walk before me in integrity of **heart** and uprightness,
10: 2 and talked with him about all that she had on her **mind**.
11: 2 because they will surely turn your **hearts** after their gods."
11: 4 As Solomon grew old, his wives turned his **heart** after other gods,
11: 4 and his **heart** was not fully devoted to the LORD his God,
11: 4 to the LORD his God, as the **heart** *of* David his father had been.
11: 9 because his **heart** had turned away from the LORD,
14: 8 who kept my commands and followed me with all his **heart**,
15: 3 his **heart** was not fully devoted to the LORD his God, as the heart
15: 3 the LORD his God, as the **heart** *of* David his forefather had been.
15: 14 Asa's **heart** was fully committed to the LORD all his life.
2Ki 10: 15 Jehu greeted him and said, "Are you **in accord with** [+3838] me,
10: 15 and said, "Are you in accord with me, as **[RPH]** I am with you?"
10: 15 and said, "Are you in accord with me, as I am with **[RPH]** you?"
10: 30 and have done to the house of Ahab all I had in **mind** to do,
10: 31 keep the law of the LORD, the God of Israel, with all his **heart**.
20: 3 before you faithfully and with **wholehearted** [+8969] **devotion**
22: 19 Because your **heart** was responsive and you humbled yourself
23: 25 with all his **heart** and with all his soul and with all his strength,
1Ch 12: 17 [12:18] I *am ready to have* you **unite** [+2118+3480+4200+6584]
12: 38 [12:39] They came to Hebron **fully determined** [+928+8969] to
17: 2 "Whatever you have in **mind**, do it, for God is with you."
22: 7 I had it in my **heart** to build a house for the Name of the LORD
22: 19 Now devote your **heart** and soul to seeking the LORD your God.
28: 2 I had it in my **heart** to build a house as a place of rest for the ark of
28: 9 for the LORD searches every **heart** and understands every motive
29: 17 my God, that you test the **heart** and are pleased with integrity.
29: 17 All these things have I given willingly and with honest **intent**.
29: 18 and Israel, keep this desire in the **hearts** *of* your people forever,
29: 18 hearts of your people forever, and keep their **hearts** loyal to you.
29: 19 give my son Solomon the **wholehearted** [+8969] **devotion** to keep
2Ch 1: 11 "Since this is your **heart's** desire and you have not asked for
6: 7 "My father David had it in his **heart** to build a temple for the
6: 8 'Because it was in your **heart** to build a temple for my Name,
6: 8 a temple for my Name, you did well to have this in your **heart**.
6: 30 since you know his **heart** (for you alone know the hearts of men),
6: 30 since you know his heart (for you alone know the **hearts** *of* men),
6: 37 if they have a change of **heart** in the land where they are held
9: 1 to Solomon and talked with him about all she had on her **mind**.
11: 16 Those from every tribe of Israel who set their **hearts** on seeking
13: 7 and **indecisive** [+8205] and not strong enough to resist them.
15: 12 the LORD, the God of their fathers, with all their **heart** and soul.
15: 15 the oath because they had sworn it **wholeheartedly** [+928+3972].
15: 17 Asa's **heart** was fully committed ⌞to the LORD⌟ all his life.
16: 9 earth to strengthen those whose **hearts** are fully committed to him.
19: 3 of the Asherah poles and have set your **heart** on seeking God."
19: 9 "You must serve faithfully and **wholeheartedly** [+928+8969] in
20: 33 the people still had not set their **hearts** on the God of their fathers.
22: 9 a son of Jehoshaphat, who sought the LORD with all his **heart**."
25: 2 in the eyes of the LORD, but not **wholeheartedly** [+928+8969].
29: 10 Now I **intend** [+6640] to make a covenant with the LORD,
29: 34 for the Levites had been more **conscientious** [+3838] in
30: 19 who sets his **heart** on seeking God—the LORD, the God of his
31: 21 he sought his God and worked **wholeheartedly** [+928+3972].
32: 6 city gate and **encouraged** [+1819+6584] them with these words:
32: 31 left him to test him and to know everything that was in his **heart**.
34: 27 Because your **heart** was responsive and you humbled yourself
34: 31 regulations and decrees with all his **heart** and all his soul,
36: 13 He became stiff-necked and hardened his **heart** and would not turn
Ezr 7: 10 For Ezra had devoted **himself** [+2257] to the study and observance
Ne 9: 8 You found his **heart** faithful to you, and you made a covenant with
Job 1: 5 "Perhaps my children have sinned and cursed God in their **hearts**."
9: 4 His wisdom is **profound**, his power is vast. Who has resisted him
10: 13 "But this is what you concealed in your **heart**, and I know that this
12: 3 But I have a **mind** as well as you; I am not inferior to you.
17: 11 my plans are shattered, and so are the desires of my **heart**.
22: 22 instruction from his mouth and lay up his words in your **heart**.
27: 6 let go of it; my **conscience** will not reproach me as long as I live.
34: 10 "So listen to me, you men of **understanding**. Far be it from God to
34: 34 "Men of **understanding** declare, wise men who hear me say to me,

Ps 4: 4 [4:5] you are on your beds, search your **hearts** and be silent.
13: 2 [13:3] with my thoughts and every day have sorrow in my **heart**?
15: 2 who does what is righteous, who speaks the truth from his **heart**
20: 4 [20:5] May he give you the desire of your **heart** and make all
22:26 [22:27] LORD will praise him—may your **hearts** live forever!
24: 4 He who has clean hands and a pure **heart**, who does not lift up his
25:17 The troubles of my **heart** have multiplied; free me from my
28: 3 cordially with their neighbors but harbor malice in their **hearts**.
31:24 [31:25] Be strong and **take heart** [+599], all you who hope in the
62: 8 [62:9] pour out your **hearts** to him, for God is our refuge.
69:32 [69:33] and be glad—you who seek God, may your **hearts** live!
73: 1 Surely God is good to Israel, to those who are pure in **heart**.
73: 7 comes iniquity; the evil conceits of their **minds** know no limits.
73:13 Surely in vain have I kept my **heart** pure; in vain have I washed
73:21 When my **heart** was grieved and my spirit embittered,
73:26 My flesh and my **heart** may fail, but God is the strength of my
73:26 but God is the strength of my **heart** and my portion forever.
77: 6 [77:7] songs in the night. My **heart** mused and my spirit inquired:
78:18 They **willfully** [+928] put God to the test by demanding the food
78:72 David shepherded them with integrity of **heart**; with skillful hands
84: 5 [84:6] strength is in you, who have set their **hearts** on pilgrimage.
86:11 your truth; give me an undivided **heart**, that I may fear your name.
86:12 I will praise you, O Lord my God, with all my **heart**; I will glorify
90:12 us to number our days aright, that we may gain a **heart** *of* wisdom.
95: 8 do not harden your **hearts** as you did at Meribah, as you did that
95:10 I said, "They are a people whose **hearts** go astray, and they have
101: 2 you come to me? I will walk in my house with blameless **heart**.
101: 4 Men of perverse **heart** shall be far from me; I will have nothing to
101: 5 whoever has haughty eyes and a proud **heart**, him will I not
104:15 wine that gladdens the **heart** *of* man, oil to make his face shine,
104:15 oil to make his face shine, and bread that sustains his **heart**.
109:16 to death the poor and the needy and the **brokenhearted** [+3874].
111: 1 I will extol the LORD with all my **heart** in the council of the
119: 7 I will praise you with an upright **heart** as I learn your righteous
139:23 Search me, O God, and know my **heart**; test me and know my
Pr 4:21 Do not let them out of your sight, keep them within your **heart**;
6:25 Do not lust in your **heart** after her beauty or let her captivate you
Ecc 9: 3 are full of evil and there is madness in their **hearts** while they live,
Isa 1: 5 Your whole head is injured, your whole **heart** afflicted.
6:10 their ears, understand with their **hearts**, and turn and be healed."
7: 2 so the **hearts** *of* Ahaz and his people were shaken, as the trees of
7: 2 so the hearts of Ahaz and **[RPH]** his people were shaken,
7: 4 Do not lose **heart** because of these two smoldering stubs of
9: 9 [9:8] of Samaria—who say with pride and arrogance of **heart**,
10: 7 is not what he intends, this is not what he **has in mind** [+3108];
10: 7 in mind; his **purpose** is to destroy, to put an end to many nations.
10:12 "I will punish the king of Assyria for the willful pride of his **heart**
13: 7 of this, all hands will go limp, every man's **heart** will melt.
14:13 You said in your **heart**, "I will ascend to heaven; I will raise my
19: 1 before him, and the **hearts** *of* the Egyptians melt within them.
21: 4 My **heart** falters, fear makes me tremble; the twilight I longed for
30:29 your **hearts** will rejoice as when people go up with flutes to the
32: 4 The **mind** *of* the rash will know and understand,
47: 8 lounging in your security and saying to **yourself** [+2023],
49:21 you will say in your **heart**, 'Who bore me these? I was bereaved
60: 5 will look and be radiant, your **heart** will throb and swell with joy;
Jer 4: 4 circumcise your **hearts**, you men of Judah and people of
5:24 They do not say to **themselves** [+4392], 'Let us fear the LORD
13:22 if you ask **yourself** [+3871], "Why has this happened to me?"—
15:16 they were my joy and my **heart's** delight, for I bear your name,
29:13 will seek me and find me when you seek me with all your **heart**.
32:40 and *I will* **inspire** [+906+928+5989] them to fear me, so that they
51:46 Do not lose **heart** or be afraid when rumors are heard in the land;
51:50 LORD in a distant land, and **think** [+6584+6590] *on* Jerusalem."
La 3:41 Let us lift up our **hearts** and our hands to God in heaven, and say:
Eze 3:10 listen carefully and take to **heart** all the words I speak to you.
28: 5 and because of your wealth your **heart** has grown proud.
28: 6 " 'Because you **think** [+906+5989] you are wise, as wise as a god,
31:10 the thick foliage, and because *it was* **proud** [+8123] of its height,
36: 5 with malice in their **hearts** they made my land their own
38:10 On that day thoughts will come into your **mind** and you will devise
Da 8:25 deceit to prosper, and he will **consider** [+928] himself superior.
11:12 the king of the South *will be* **filled with pride** [+8123] and will
11:25 will stir up his strength and **courage** against the king of the South.
11:27 The two kings, with their **hearts** bent on evil, will sit at the same
11:28 great wealth, but his **heart** will be set against the holy covenant.
Hos 7: 2 they *do* not **realize** [+606+4200] that I remember all their evil
Joel 2:12 "return to me with all your **heart**, with fasting and weeping
2:13 Rend your **heart** and not your garments. Return to the LORD
Jnh 2: 3 [2:4] You hurled me into the deep, into the very **heart** *of* the seas,
Na 2: 7 [2:8] Its slave girls moan like doves and beat upon their **breasts**.
Zep 1:12 who **think** [+606+928], 'The LORD will do nothing, either good
2:15 She said to **herself** [+2023], "I am, and there is none besides me."
Hag 1: 5 what the LORD Almighty says: "**Give careful thought** [+8492]
1: 7 what the LORD Almighty says: "**Give careful thought** [+8492]
2:15 " 'Now **give careful thought** [+8492] to this from this day on—
2:18 day of the ninth month, **give careful thought** [+8492]
2:18 of the LORD's temple was laid. **Give careful thought** [+8492]:
Zec 7:10 or the poor. In your **hearts** do not think evil of each other.'
8:17 *do* not **plot** evil **against** [+906+928+3108] your neighbor,

4223 לְבִבָה lᵉbibâ, n.f. [3] [→ 4221; cf. 4213]

bread [1], it[s] [+2021] [1], make special bread [+4221] [1]

2Sa 13: 6 to come and **make** some **special bread** [+4221] in my sight,
13: 8 kneaded it, made the bread in his sight and baked **it**[s] [+2021].
13:10 Tamar took the **bread** she had prepared and brought it to her

4224 לָבַד lᵉbad, n.m. Not used in NIV/BHS [√ 969]

4225 לַבָּה labbâ, n.f. [1] [cf. 4259]

flames [1]

Ex 3: 2 There the angel of the LORD appeared to him in **flames** *of* fire

4226 לִבָּה libbâ, n.[f.]. [1] [√ 4220]

weak-willed [+581] [1]

Eze 16:30 " 'How **weak-willed** [+581] you are, declares the Sovereign

4227 ¹לְבוֹנָה lᵉbônâ[1], n.f. Not used in NIV/BHS [→ 4228; cf. 4237]

4228 ²לְבוֹנָה lᵉbônâ[2], n.pr.loc. [1] [√ 4227]

Lebonah [1]

Jdg 21:19 that goes from Bethel to Shechem, and to the south of **Lebonah**."

4229 לָבוּשׁ lābûš, n.m. [15] [√ 4252]

clothed [7], in [3], armed [1], covered [1], dress [1], dressed [1], wore [1]

1Sa 17: 5 **wore** a coat of scale armor of bronze weighing five thousand
Pr 31:21 has no fear for her household; for all of them are **clothed** *in* scarlet.
Isa 14:19 you are **covered** *with* the slain, with those pierced by the sword,
Eze 9: 2 With them was a man **clothed** *in* linen who had a writing kit at his
9: 3 the LORD called to the man **clothed** *in* linen who had the writing
9:11 the man **in** linen with the writing kit at his side brought back word,
10: 2 The LORD said to the man **clothed** *in* linen, "Go in among the
10: 6 When the LORD commanded the man **in** linen, "Take fire from
10: 7 He took up some of it and put it into the hands of the man **in** linen,
23: 6 **clothed** *in* blue, governors and commanders, all of them handsome
23:12 governors and commanders, warriors *in* full **dress**,
38: 4 your horses, your horsemen fully **armed**, and a great horde with
Da 10: 5 I looked up and there before me was a man **dressed** *in* linen,
12: 6 One of them said to the man **clothed** *in* linen, who was above the
12: 7 The man **clothed** *in* linen, who was above the waters of the river,

4230 לְבוּשׁ lᵉbûš, n.m. [31] [√ 4252; Ar 10382]

clothing [5], garments [5], garment [4], robe [4], clothed [3], clothes [2], coat [1], dressed [1], gown [1], military tunic [+4496] [1], put on [+5989] [1], put on [1], robed [1], robes [1]

Ge 49:11 he will wash his **garments** in wine, his robes in the blood of
2Sa 1:24 and finery, who adorned your **garments** with ornaments of gold.
20: 8 Joab was wearing his **military tunic** [+4496], and strapped over it
2Ki 10:22 keeper of the wardrobe, "Bring **robes** for all the ministers of Baal."
Est 4: 2 because no *one* **clothed** in sackcloth was allowed to enter it.
6: 8 have them bring a royal **robe** the king has worn and a horse the
6: 9 let the **robe** and horse be entrusted to one of the king's most noble
6:10 "Get the **robe** and the horse and do just as you have suggested for
6:11 So Haman got the **robe** and the horse. He robed Mordecai,
8:15 Mordecai left the king's presence wearing royal **garments** *of* blue
Job 24: 7 Lacking **clothes**, they spend the night naked; they have nothing to
24:10 Lacking **clothes**, they go about naked; they carry the sheaves,
30:18 In his great power ⌞God⌟ becomes like **clothing** *to* me; he binds me
31:19 if I have seen anyone perishing for lack of **clothing**, or a needy
38: 9 when I made the clouds its **garment** and wrapped it in thick
38:14 clay under a seal; its features stand out like those of a **garment**.
41:13 [41:5] Who can strip off his outer **coat**? Who would approach him
Ps 22:18 [22:19] my garments among them and cast lots for my **clothing**.
35:13 they were ill, **I put on** sackcloth and humbled myself with fasting.
45:13 [45:14] within ⌞her chamber⌟; her **gown** is interwoven with gold.
69:11 [69:12] when *I* **put on** [+5989] sackcloth, people make sport of
102:26 [102:27] Like **clothing** you will change them and they will be
104: 6 You covered it with the deep as with a **garment**; the waters stood
Pr 27:26 the lambs will provide you with **clothing**, and the goats with the
31:22 coverings for her bed; she is **clothed** in fine linen and purple.
31:25 She is **clothed** *with* strength and dignity; she can laugh at the days

Isa 63: 1 Who is this, **robed** in splendor, striding forward in the greatness of
63: 2 Why are your **garments** red, like those of one treading the
Jer 10: 9 and goldsmith have made is then **dressed** *in* blue and purple—
La 4: 14 so defiled with blood that no one dares to touch their **garments**.
Mal 2: 16 covering himself with violence as well as with his **garment**,"

4231 לָבַט **lābaṭ**, v. [3]

comes to ruin [2], come to ruin [1]

Pr 10: 8 [C] heart accept commands, but a chattering fool **comes to ruin**.
10: 10 [C] maliciously causes grief, and a chattering fool **comes to ruin**.
Hos 4: 14 [C] a people without understanding *will* **come to ruin**!

4232 לְבִי **lᵉbî**, n.[m. & f.]. Not used in NIV/BHS [√ 4216]

4233 לָבִיא **lābî'**, n.m. & f. [11] [√ 4216]

lioness [7], lion [3], lionesses [1]

Ge 49: 9 Like a lion he crouches and lies down, like a **lioness**—who dares to
Nu 23: 24 The people rise like a **lioness**; they rouse themselves like a lion
24: 9 Like a lion they crouch and lie down, like a **lioness**—who dares to
Dt 33: 20 Gad's domain! Gad lives there like a **lion**, tearing at arm or head.
Job 4: 11 perishes for lack of prey, and the cubs of the **lioness** are scattered.
38: 39 "Do you hunt the prey for the **lioness** and satisfy the hunger of the
Isa 5: 29 Their roar is like that of the **lion**, they roar like young lions;
30: 6 and distress, of lions and **lionesses**, of adders and darting snakes,
Hos 13: 8 Like a **lion** I will devour them; a wild animal will tear them apart.
Joel 1: 6 without number; it has the teeth of a lion, the fangs of a **lioness**.
Na 2: 11 [2:12] where the lion and **lioness** went, and the cubs, with nothing

4234 לְבִיָּא **lᵉbiyyā'**, n.f. [1] [√ 4216]

lioness [1]

Eze 19: 2 and say: " 'What a **lioness** was your mother among the lions!

4235 ¹לָבַן **lāban¹**, v. [5] [→ 4227, 4228, 4237, 4238, 4239, 4242, 4243?, 4244, 4245, 4247, 4248]

made spotless [2], leaving white [1], white [1], whiter [1]

Ps 51: 7 [51:9] [G] be clean; wash me, and *I will be* **whiter** than snow.
Isa 1: 18 [G] your sins are like scarlet, *they shall be* as **white** as snow;
Da 11: 35 [G] purified and **made spotless** until the time of the end,
12: 10 [F] Many will be purified, **made spotless** and refined,
Joel 1: 7 [G] their bark and thrown it away, **leaving** their branches **white**.

4236 ²לָבַן **lāban²**, v.den. [3] [√ 4246]

bricks [1], make bricks [+4246] [1], making bricks [+4246] [1]

Ge 11: 3 [A] *let's* **make bricks** [+4246] and bake them thoroughly."
Ex 5: 7 [A] to supply the people with straw for **making bricks** [+4246];
5: 14 [A] "Why didn't you meet your quota of **bricks** yesterday

4237 ¹לָבָן **lābān¹**, a. [29] [→ 4227, 4238, 4239?, 4244, 4247; cf. 4235]

white [24], reddish-white [+140] [4], whiter [1]

Ge 30: 35 the speckled or spotted female goats (all that had **white** on them)
30: 37 and plane trees and made **white** stripes on them by peeling the bark
30: 37 the bark and exposing the **white** inner *wood* of the branches.
49: 12 His eyes will be darker than wine, his teeth **whiter** than milk.
Ex 16: 31 It was **white** like coriander seed and tasted like wafers made with
Lev 13: 3 if the hair in the sore has turned **white** and the sore appears to be
13: 4 If the spot on his skin is **white** but does not appear to be more than
13: 4 to be more than skin deep and the hair in it has not turned **white**,
13: 10 if there is a **white** swelling in the skin that has turned the hair white
13: 10 if there is a white swelling in the skin that has turned the hair **white**
13: 13 that person clean. Since it has all turned **white**, he is clean.
13: 16 Should the raw flesh change and turn **white**, he must go to the
13: 17 The priest is to examine him, and if the sores have turned **white**,
13: 19 where the boil was, a **white** swelling or reddish-white spot appears,
13: 19 boil was, a white swelling or **reddish-white** [+140] spot appears,
13: 20 to be more than skin deep and the hair in it has turned **white**,
13: 21 there is no **white** hair in it and it is not more than skin deep
13: 24 someone has a burn on his skin and a **reddish-white** [+140]
13: 24 a reddish-white or **white** spot appears in the raw flesh of the burn,
13: 25 priest is to examine the spot, and if the hair in it has turned **white**,
13: 26 But if the priest examines it and there is no **white** hair in the spot
13: 38 "When a man or woman has **white** spots on the skin,
13: 39 the priest is to examine them, and if the spots are dull **white**,
13: 42 But if he has a **reddish-white** [+140] sore on his bald head
13: 43 or forehead is **reddish-white** [+140] like an infectious skin
Ecc 9: 8 Always be clothed in **white**, and always anoint your head with oil.
Zec 1: 8 trees in a ravine. Behind him were red, brown and **white** horses.
6: 3 the third **white**, and the fourth dappled—all of them powerful.
6: 6 the one with the **white** horses toward the west, and the one with the

4238 ²לָבָן **lābān²**, n.pr.m. [54] [√ 4237]

Laban [45], Laban's [5], he[s] [2], *untranslated* [1], him[s] [1]

Ge 24: 29 Now Rebekah had a brother named **Laban**, and he hurried out to
24: 29 brother named Laban, and **he**[s] hurried out to the man at the spring.
24: 50 **Laban** and Bethuel answered, "This is from the LORD; we can
25: 20 the Aramean from Paddan Aram and sister of **Laban** the Aramean.
27: 43 do what I say: Flee at once to my brother **Laban** in Haran.
28: 2 from among the daughters of **Laban**, your mother's brother.
28: 5 to **Laban** son of Bethuel the Aramean, the brother of Rebekah,
29: 5 He said to them, "Do you know **Laban**, Nahor's grandson?"
29: 10 When Jacob saw Rachel daughter of **Laban**, his mother's brother,
29: 10 **Laban's** sheep, he went over and rolled the stone away from the
29: 10 from the mouth of the well and watered his uncle's **[RPH]** sheep.
29: 13 As soon as **Laban** heard the news about Jacob, his sister's son,
29: 13 him to his home, and there Jacob told **him**[s] all these things.
29: 14 Then **Laban** said to him, "You are my own flesh and blood."
29: 15 **Laban** said to him, "Just because you are a relative of mine,
29: 16 Now **Laban** had two daughters; the name of the older was Leah,
29: 19 **Laban** said, "It's better that I give her to you than to some other
29: 21 Jacob said to **Laban**, "Give me my wife. My time is completed,
29: 22 So **Laban** brought together all the people of the place and gave a
29: 24 **Laban** gave his servant girl Zilpah to his daughter as her
29: 25 So Jacob said to **Laban**, "What is this you have done to me?
29: 26 **Laban** replied, "It is not our custom here to give the younger
29: 29 **Laban** gave his servant girl Bilhah to his daughter Rachel as her
30: 25 Jacob said to **Laban**, "Send me on my way so I can go back to my
30: 27 But **Laban** said to him, "If I have found favor in your eyes,
30: 34 "Agreed," said **Laban**. "Let it be as you have said."
30: 36 while Jacob continued to tend the rest of **Laban's** flocks.
30: 40 the streaked and dark-colored animals that belonged to **Laban**.
30: 40 flocks for himself and did not put them with **Laban's** animals.
30: 42 So the weak animals went to **Laban** and the strong ones to Jacob.
31: 1 Jacob heard that **Laban's** sons were saying, "Jacob has taken
31: 2 Jacob noticed that **Laban's** attitude toward him was not what it
31: 12 or spotted, for I have seen all that **Laban** has been doing to you.
31: 19 When **Laban** had gone to shear his sheep, Rachel stole her father's
31: 20 Jacob deceived **Laban** the Aramean by not telling him he was
31: 22 On the third day **Laban** was told that Jacob had fled.
31: 24 Then God came to **Laban** the Aramean in a dream at night
31: 25 had pitched his tent in the hill country of Gilead when **Laban**
31: 25 overtook him, and **Laban** and his relatives camped there too.
31: 26 **Laban** said to Jacob, "What have you done? You've deceived me,
31: 31 Jacob answered **Laban**, "I was afraid, because I thought you
31: 33 So **Laban** went into Jacob's tent and into Leah's tent and into the
31: 34 **Laban** searched through everything in the tent but found nothing.
31: 36 Jacob was angry and took **Laban** to task. "What is my crime?"
31: 36 and took Laban to task. "What is my crime?" he asked **Laban**.
31: 43 **Laban** answered Jacob, "The women are my daughters,
31: 47 **Laban** called it Jegar Sahadutha, and Jacob called it Galeed.
31: 48 **Laban** said, "This heap is a witness between you and me today."
31: 51 **Laban** also said to Jacob, "Here is this heap, and here is this pillar
31: 55 [32:1] Early the next morning **Laban** kissed his grandchildren
31: 55 [32:1] and blessed them. Then **he**[s] left and returned home.
32: 4 [32:5] I have been staying with **Laban** and have remained there
46: 18 to Jacob by Zilpah, whom **Laban** had given to his daughter Leah—
46: 25 Jacob by Bilhah, whom **Laban** had given to his daughter Rachel—

4239 ³לָבָן **lābān³**, n.pr.loc. [1] [√ 4237?]

Laban [1]

Dt 1: 1 between Paran and Tophel, **Laban**, Hazeroth and Dizahab.

4240 לַבֵּן **labbēn**, tt. Not used in NIV/BHS [√ 4200 + 2021 + 1201]

4241 לְבָנָהא **lᵉbānāh'**, var. Not used in NIV/BHS [√ 4244]

4242 לִבְנֶה **libneh**, n.[m.]. [2] [√ 4235]

poplar [2]

Ge 30: 37 took fresh-cut branches from **poplar**, almond and plane trees
Hos 4: 13 under oak, **poplar** and terebinth, where the shade is pleasant.

4243 לִבְנָה **libnâ**, n.pr.loc. [18] [√ 4235?]

Libnah [17], it[s] [1]

Nu 33: 20 They left Rimmon Perez and camped at **Libnah**.
33: 21 They left **Libnah** and camped at Rissah.
Jos 10: 29 and all Israel with him moved on from Makkedah to **Libnah**
10: 29 with him moved on from Makkedah to Libnah and attacked **it**[s].
10: 31 and all Israel with him moved on from **Libnah** to Lachish;
10: 32 everyone in it he put to the sword, just as he had done to **Libnah**.
10: 39 its king as they had done to **Libnah** and its king and to Hebron.

Jos 12: 15 the king of **Libnah** one the king of Adullam one
15: 42 **Libnah**, Ether, Ashan,
21: 13 gave Hebron (a city of refuge for one accused of murder), **Libnah**,
2Ki 8: 22 been in rebellion against Judah. **Libnah** revolted at the same time.
19: 8 he withdrew and found the king fighting against **Libnah**.
23: 31 name was Hamutal daughter of Jeremiah; she was from **Libnah**.
24: 18 name was Hamutal daughter of Jeremiah; she was from **Libnah**.
1Ch 6: 57 [6:42] Hebron (a city of refuge), and **Libnah**, Jattir, Eshtemoa,
2Ch 21: 10 **Libnah** revolted at the same time, because Jehoram had forsaken
Isa 37: 8 he withdrew and found the king fighting against **Libnah**.
Jer 52: 1 name was Hamutal daughter of Jeremiah; she was from **Libnah**.

4244 לְבָנָה[1] *lᵉbānâ[1]*, n.f. [3] [→ 4241, 4245; cf. 4237]

moon [3]

SS 6: 10 fair as the **moon**, bright as the sun, majestic as the stars in
Isa 24: 23 The **moon** will be abashed, the sun ashamed; for the LORD
30: 26 The **moon** will shine like the sun, and the sunlight will be seven

4245 לְבָנָה[2] *lᵉbānâ[2]*, n.pr.loc. [2] [√ 4244; cf. 4241]

Lebana [1], Lebanah [1]

Ezr 2: 45 **Lebanah**, Hagabah, Akkub,
Ne 7: 48 **Lebana**, Hagaba, Shalmai,

4246 לְבֵנָה *lᵉbēnâ*, n.f. [12] [→ 4236, 4861]

bricks [5], brick [2], altars of brick [1], clay tablet [1], make bricks [+4236] [1], making bricks [+4236] [1], pavement [1]

Ge 11: 3 "Come, *let's* **make bricks** [+4236] and bake them thoroughly."
11: 3 They used **brick** instead of stone, and tar for mortar.
Ex 1: 14 They made their lives bitter with hard labor in **brick** and mortar
5: 7 longer to supply the people with straw for **making bricks** [+4236];
5: 8 But require them to make the same number of **bricks** as before;
5: 16 Your servants are given no straw, yet we are told, 'Make **bricks**!'
5: 18 given any straw, yet you must produce your full quota of **bricks**."
5: 19 "You are not to reduce the number of **bricks** *required of* you for
24: 10 Under his feet was something like a **pavement** made of sapphire,
Isa 9: 10 [9:9] "The **bricks** have fallen down, but we will rebuild with
65: 3 sacrifices in gardens and burning incense on **altars of brick**;
Eze 4: 1 "Now, son of man, take a **clay tablet**, put it in front of you

4247 לְבֹנָה *lᵉbōnâ*, n.f. [21] [√ 4237]

incense [20], frankincense [1]

Ex 30: 34 and galbanum—and pure **frankincense**, all in equal amounts,
Lev 2: 1 is to be of fine flour. He is to pour oil on it, put **incense** on it
2: 2 a handful of the fine flour and oil, together with all the **incense**,
2: 15 Put oil and **incense** on it; it is a grain offering.
2: 16 of the crushed grain and the oil, together with all the **incense**,
5: 11 He must not put oil or **incense** on it, because it is a sin offering.
6: 15 [6:8] and oil, together with all the **incense** on the grain offering,
24: 7 Along each row put *some* pure **incense** as a memorial portion to
Nu 5: 15 He must not pour oil on it or put **incense** on it, because it is a grain
1Ch 9: 29 as well as the flour and wine, and the oil, **incense** and spices.
Ne 13: 5 used to store the grain offerings and **incense** and temple articles,
13: 9 of the house of God, with the grain offerings and the **incense**.
SS 3: 6 with myrrh and **incense** made from all the spices of the merchant?
4: 6 I will go to the mountain of myrrh and to the hill of **incense**.
4: 14 with every kind of **incense** tree, with myrrh and aloes and all the
Isa 43: 23 with grain offerings nor wearied you with demands for **incense**.
60: 6 bearing gold and **incense** and proclaiming the praise of the
66: 3 whoever burns memorial **incense**, like one who worships an idol.
Jer 6: 20 What do I care about **incense** from Sheba or sweet calamus from a
17: 26 **incense** and thank offerings to the house of the LORD.
41: 5 grain offerings and **incense** with them to the house of the LORD.

4248 לְבָנוֹן *lᵉbānôn*, n.pr.loc. [71] [√ 4235]

Lebanon [68], cedar of Lebanon [2], there[s] [1]

Dt 1: 7 and along the coast, to the land of the Canaanites and to **Lebanon**,
3: 25 land beyond the Jordan—that fine hill country and **Lebanon**."
11: 24 Your territory will extend from the desert to **Lebanon**, and from
Jos 1: 4 Your territory will extend from the desert to **Lebanon**, and from
9: 1 along the entire coast of the Great Sea as far as **Lebanon** (the kings
11: 17 to Baal Gad in the Valley of **Lebanon** below Mount Hermon.
12: 7 from Baal Gad in the Valley of **Lebanon** to Mount Halak,
13: 5 all **Lebanon** to the east, from Baal Gad below Mount Hermon to
13: 6 "As for all the inhabitants of the mountain regions from **Lebanon**
Jdg 3: 3 the Hivites living in the **Lebanon** mountains from Mount Baal
9: 15 come out of the thornbush and consume the cedars of **Lebanon**!'
1Ki 4: 33 [5:13] from the cedar of **Lebanon** to the hyssop that grows out of
5: 6 [5:20] "So give orders that cedars of **Lebanon** be cut for me. My
5: 9 [5:23] My men will haul them down from **Lebanon** to the sea,
5: 14 [5:28] He sent them off to **Lebanon** in shifts of ten thousand a
5: 14 [5:28] so that they spent one month in **Lebanon** and two months
7: 2 He built the Palace of the Forest of **Lebanon** a hundred cubits
9: 19 in Jerusalem, in **Lebanon** and throughout all the territory he ruled.
10: 17 The king put them in the Palace of the Forest of **Lebanon**.
10: 21 all the household articles in the Palace of the Forest of **Lebanon**
2Ki 14: 9 "A thistle in **Lebanon** sent a message to a cedar in Lebanon,
14: 9 "A thistle in Lebanon sent a message to a cedar in **Lebanon**,
14: 9 a wild beast in **Lebanon** came along and trampled the thistle
19: 23 the heights of the mountains, the utmost heights of **Lebanon**.
2Ch 2: 8 [2:7] "Send me also cedar, pine and algum logs from **Lebanon**,
2: 8 [2:7] I know that your men are skilled in cutting timber **there**[s].
2: 16 [2:15] we will cut all the logs from **Lebanon** that you need
8: 6 in Jerusalem, in **Lebanon** and throughout all the territory he ruled.
9: 16 The king put them in the Palace of the Forest of **Lebanon**.
9: 20 all the household articles in the Palace of the Forest of **Lebanon**
25: 18 "A thistle in **Lebanon** sent a message to a cedar in Lebanon,
25: 18 "A thistle in Lebanon sent a message to a cedar in **Lebanon**,
25: 18 a wild beast in **Lebanon** came along and trampled the thistle
Ezr 3: 7 so that they would bring cedar logs by sea from **Lebanon** to Joppa,
Ps 29: 5 the cedars; the LORD breaks in pieces the cedars of **Lebanon**.
29: 6 He makes **Lebanon** skip like a calf, Sirion like a young wild ox.
72: 16 Let its fruit flourish like **Lebanon**; let it thrive like the grass of the
92: 12 [92:13] like a palm tree, they will grow like a cedar of **Lebanon**;
104: 16 LORD are well watered, the cedars of **Lebanon** that he planted.
SS 3: 9 made for himself the carriage; he made it of wood from **Lebanon**.
4: 8 Come with me from **Lebanon**, my bride, come with me from
4: 8 with me from Lebanon, my bride, come with me from **Lebanon**.
4: 11 The fragrance of your garments is like that of **Lebanon**.
4: 15 a well of flowing water streaming down from **Lebanon**.
5: 15 of pure gold. His appearance is like **Lebanon**, choice as its cedars.
7: 4 [7:5] Your nose is like the tower of **Lebanon** looking toward
Isa 2: 13 for all the cedars of **Lebanon**, tall and lofty, and all the oaks of
10: 34 thickets with an ax; **Lebanon** will fall before the Mighty One.
14: 8 the pine trees and the cedars of **Lebanon** exult over you and say,
29: 17 will not **Lebanon** be turned into a fertile field and the fertile field
33: 9 land mourns and wastes away, **Lebanon** is ashamed and withers;
35: 2 The glory of **Lebanon** will be given to it, the splendor of Carmel
37: 24 the heights of the mountains, the utmost heights of **Lebanon**.
40: 16 **Lebanon** is not sufficient for altar fires, nor its animals enough for
60: 13 "The glory of **Lebanon** will come to you, the pine, the fir
Jer 18: 14 Does the snow of **Lebanon** ever vanish from its rocky slopes?
22: 6 "Though you are like Gilead to me, like the summit of **Lebanon**,
22: 20 "Go up to **Lebanon** and cry out, let your voice be heard in Bashan,
22: 23 You who live in '**Lebanon**,' who are nestled in cedar buildings,
Eze 17: 3 long feathers and full plumage of varied colors came to **Lebanon**.
27: 5 they took a cedar from **Lebanon** to make a mast for you.
31: 3 Consider Assyria, once a cedar in **Lebanon**, with beautiful
31: 15 Because of it I clothed **Lebanon** with gloom, and all the trees of
31: 16 Then all the trees of Eden, the choicest and best of **Lebanon**,
Hos 14: 5 [14:6] Like a **cedar of Lebanon** he will send down his roots;
14: 6 [14:7] like an olive tree, his fragrance like a **cedar of Lebanon**.
14: 7 [14:8] a vine, and his fame will be like the wine from **Lebanon**.
Na 1: 4 Bashan and Carmel wither and the blossoms of **Lebanon** fade.
Hab 2: 17 The violence you have done to **Lebanon** will overwhelm you,
Zec 10: 10 I will bring them to Gilead and **Lebanon**, and there will not be
11: 1 Open your doors, O **Lebanon**, so that fire may devour your cedars!

4249 לִבְנִי[1] *libnî[1]*, n.pr.m. [5] [→ 4250]

Libni [5]

Ex 6: 17 The sons of Gershon, by clans, were **Libni** and Shimei.
Nu 3: 18 These were the names of the Gershonite clans: **Libni** and Shimei.
1Ch 6: 17 [6:2] are the names of the sons of Gershon: **Libni** and Shimei.
6: 20 [6:5] Of Gershon: **Libni** his son, Jehath his son, Zimmah his son,
6: 29 [6:14] Mahli, **Libni** his son, Shimei his son, Uzzah his son,

4250 לִבְנִי[2] *libnî[2]*, a.g. [2] [√ 4249]

Libnite [1], Libnites [1]

Nu 3: 21 To Gershon belonged the clans of the **Libnites** and Shimeites;
26: 58 the **Libnite** clan, the Hebronite clan, the Mahlite clan, the Mushite

4251 לִבְנָת *libnāt*, n.pr.loc. Not used in NIV/BHS [→ 8866]

4252 לָבַשׁ *lābaš*, v. [97] [→ 4229, 4230, 4860, 9432; Ar 10383]

put on [23], clothed [15], clothe [10], wear [9], dress [5], came upon [3], dressed in [3], dressed [3], robed [3], *untranslated* [2], covered [2], wore [2], clad [1], clothed [+955] [1], clothes [1], dress in [1], provide [1], provided with clothes [1], put clothes on [1], put on [+9432] [1], put on as clothing [1], put on clothes [1], put on robes [1], puts on [1], putting on [1], robe [1], vestments [1], wear clothes [1], worn [1]

Ge 3: 21 [G] garments of skin for Adam and his wife and **clothed** them.
27: 15 [G] had in the house, and **put** them **on** her younger son Jacob.

[A] Qal [B] Qal passive [C] Niphal [D] Piel (poel, polel, pilel, pilal, pealal, pilpel) [E] Pual (poal, polal, poalal, pulal, pualal)

Ge 27:16 [G] *She* also **covered** his hands and the smooth part of his neck *with*
28:20 [A] I am taking and will give me food to eat and clothes to **wear**
38:19 [A] she took off her veil and **put on** her widow's clothes again.
41:42 [G] *He* **dressed** him *in* robes of fine linen and put a gold chain
Ex 28:41 [G] After *you* **put** these **clothes on** your brother Aaron and his
29: 5 [G] **dress** Aaron *with* the tunic, the robe of the ephod, the ephod
29: 8 [G] Bring his sons and **dress** them *in* tunics
29:30 [A] to minister in the Holy Place *is to* **wear** them seven days.
40:13 [G] **dress** Aaron *in* the sacred garments, anoint him
40:14 [G] Bring his sons and **dress** them *in* tunics.
Lev 6:10 [6:3] [A] The priest *shall* then **put on** his linen clothes,
6:10 [6:3] [A] **[RPH]** and shall remove the ashes of the burnt
6:11 [6:4] [A] he is to take off these clothes and **put on** others, and
8: 7 [G] **clothed** him *with* the robe and put the ephod on him.
8:13 [G] **put** tunics **on** them, tied sashes around them and put
16: 4 [A] *He is to* **put on** the sacred linen tunic, with linen
16: 4 [A] so he must bathe himself with water before *he* **puts** them **on**.
16:23 [A] take off the linen garments *he* **put on** before he entered the
16:24 [A] with water in a holy place and **put on** his regular garments.
16:32 [A] make atonement. *He is to* **put on** the sacred linen garments
21:10 [A] and who has been ordained to **wear** the priestly garments,
Nu 20:26 [G] Remove Aaron's garments and **put** them **on** his son Eleazar,
20:28 [G] removed Aaron's garments and **put** them **on** his son Eleazar.
Dt 22: 5 [A] not wear men's clothing, nor a man **wear** women's clothing,
22:11 [A] *Do* not **wear clothes** of wool and linen woven together.
Jdg 6:34 [A] the Spirit of the LORD **came upon** Gideon, and he blew a
1Sa 17:38 [G] Saul **dressed** David *in* his own tunic. He put a coat of armor
17:38 [G] *He* **put** a coat of armor **on** him and a bronze helmet on his
28: 8 [A] **putting on** other clothes, and at night he and two men went
2Sa 1:24 [G] weep for Saul, who **clothed** you *in* scarlet and finery,
13:18 [A] the kind of garment the virgin daughters of the king **wore**.
14: 2 [A] **Dress in** mourning clothes, and don't use any cosmetic
1Ki 22:10 [E] **Dressed in** their royal robes, the king of Israel
22:30 [A] enter the battle in disguise, but you **wear** your royal robes."
1Ch 12:18 [12:19] [A] the Spirit **came upon** Amasai, chief of the Thirty,
2Ch 5:12 [E] **dressed** *in* fine linen and playing cymbals, harps and lyres.
6:41 [A] *May* your priests, O LORD God, *be* **clothed** *with* salvation,
18: 9 [E] **Dressed in** their royal robes, the king of Israel
18:29 [A] enter the battle in disguise, but you **wear** your royal robes."
24:20 [A] the Spirit of God **came upon** Zechariah son of Jehoiada the
28:15 [G] and from the plunder *they* **clothed** all who were naked.
28:15 [G] *They* **provided** them **with clothes** and sandals, food and
Ezr 3:10 [E] the priests *in their* **vestments** and with trumpets,
Est 4: 1 [A] he tore his clothes, **put on** sackcloth and ashes, and went out
4: 4 [G] She sent clothes for him to **put on** instead of his sackcloth,
5: 1 [A] On the third day Esther **put on** *her* royal **robes** and stood in
6: 8 [A] have them bring a royal robe the king *has* **worn** and a horse
6: 9 [G] *Let them* **robe** the man the king delights to honor, and lead
6:11 [G] *He* **robed** Mordecai, and led him on horseback through the
Job 7: 5 [A] My body *is* **clothed** *with* worms and scabs, my skin is
8:22 [A] Your enemies *will be* **clothed** *in* shame, and the tents of the
10:11 [G] **clothe** me *with* skin and flesh and knit me together with
27:17 [A] what he lays up the righteous *will* **wear**, and the innocent
29:14 [A] *I* **put on** righteousness **as** *my* **clothing**; justice was my robe
29:14 [A] as my clothing; justice **[RPH]** was my robe and my turban.
39:19 [G] horse his strength or **clothe** his neck *with* a flowing mane?
40:10 [A] and splendor, and **clothe** *yourself in* honor and majesty.
Ps 35:26 [A] *may* all who exalt themselves over me *be* **clothed** *with*
65:13 [65:14] [A] The meadows *are* **covered** *with* flocks
93: 1 [A] The LORD reigns, *he is* **robed** *in* majesty; the LORD is
93: 1 [A] the LORD *is* **robed** *in* majesty and is armed with strength.
104: 1 [A] are very great; *you are* **clothed** *with* splendor and majesty.
109:18 [A] *He* **wore** cursing as his garment; it entered into his body like
109:29 [A] My accusers *will be* **clothed** *with* disgrace and wrapped in
132: 9 [A] *May* your priests *be* **clothed** *with* righteousness; may your
132:16 [G] *I will* **clothe** her priests *with* salvation, and her saints will
132:18 [G] *I will* **clothe** his enemies *with* shame, but the crown on his
Pr 23:21 [G] gluttons become poor, and drowsiness **clothes** them *in* rags.
SS 5: 3 [A] I have taken off my robe—*must I* **put** it **on** again? I have
Isa 4: 1 [A] "We will eat our own food and **provide** our own clothes;
22:21 [G] *I will* **clothe** him *with* your robe and fasten your sash around
49:18 [A] declares the LORD, "*you will* **wear** them all as ornaments;
50: 3 [G] *I* **clothe** the sky *with* darkness and make sackcloth its
51: 9 [A] **Clothe** *yourself with* strength, O arm of the LORD; awake,
52: 1 [A] Awake, awake, O Zion, **clothe** *yourself with* strength. Put on
52: 1 [A] **Put on** your garments of splendor, O Jerusalem, the holy
59:17 [A] *He* **put on** righteousness as his breastplate, and the helmet of
59:17 [A] *he* **put** [+9432] **on** the garments of vengeance and wrapped
61:10 [G] For *he has* **clothed** me *with* garments of salvation
Jer 4:30 [A] Why **dress** *yourself in* scarlet and put on jewels of gold?
46: 4 [A] with helmets on! Polish your spears, **put on** your armor!
Eze 7:27 [A] The king will mourn, the prince *will be* **clothed** *with* despair,
16:10 [G] *I* **clothed** you *with* an embroidered dress and put leather
26:16 [A] **Clothed** *with* terror, they will sit on the ground, trembling
34: 3 [A] **clothe** *yourselves with* the wool and slaughter the choice
42:14 [A] *They are to* **put on** other clothes before they go near the
44:17 [A] the gates of the inner court, *they are to* **wear** linen clothes;
44:19 [A] to leave them in the sacred rooms, and **put on** other clothes,
Jnh 3: 5 [A] all of them, from the greatest to the least, **put on** sackcloth.
Zep 1: 8 [A] and the king's sons and all those **clad** *in* foreign clothes.
Hag 1: 6 [A] *You* **put on clothes**, but are not warm. You earn wages, only
Zec 3: 3 [B] Now Joshua was **dressed in** filthy clothes as he stood before
3: 4 [G] taken away your sin, and *I will* **put** rich garments **on** you."
3: 5 [G] they put a clean turban on his head and **clothed** [+955] him,
13: 4 [A] *He will* not **put on** a prophet's garment of hair in order to

4253 לֹג *lōg*, n.m. [5]

log [5]

Lev 14:10 of fine flour mixed with oil for a grain offering, and one **log** *of* oil.
14:12 male lambs and offer it as a guilt offering, along with the **log** *of* oil;
14:15 The priest shall then take some of the **log** *of* oil, pour it in the palm
14:21 ephah of fine flour mixed with oil for a grain offering, a **log** *of* oil,
14:24 to take the lamb for the guilt offering, together with the **log** *of* oil,

4254 לֹד *lōd*, n.pr.loc. [4]

Lod [4]

1Ch 8:12 Shemed (who built Ono and **Lod** with its surrounding villages),
Ezr 2:33 of **Lod**, Hadid and Ono 725
Ne 7:37 of **Lod**, Hadid and Ono 721
11:35 in **Lod** and Ono, and in the Valley of the Craftsmen.

4255 לִדְבִר *lidbir*, n.pr.loc. Not used in NIV/BHS

4256 לֵדָה *lēdâ*, n.[f.] *or* v.inf. [4] [√ 3528]

deliver [2], birth [1], in labor [1]

2Ki 19: 3 come to the point of birth and there is no strength to **deliver** them.
Isa 37: 3 come to the point of birth and there is no strength to **deliver** them.
Jer 13:21 Will not pain grip you like that of a woman **in labor**?
Hos 9:11 will fly away like a bird—no **birth**, no pregnancy, no conception.

4257 לֹה *lōh*, adv. [1] [√ 4202]

untranslated [1]

Dt 3:11 and six feet wide. **[NIE]** It is still in Rabbah of the Ammonites.)

4258 לַהַב *lahab*, n.m. [12] [→ 4259, 8927]

flames [3], fire [+836] [2], flame [2], flashing [2], aflame [1], blade [1], it[s] [+2021] [1]

Jdg 3:22 Even the handle sank in after the **blade**, which came out his back.
3:22 did not pull the sword out, and the fat closed in over **it**[s] [+2021].
13:20 As the **flame** blazed up from the altar toward heaven, the angel of
13:20 toward heaven, the angel of the LORD ascended in the **flame**.
Job 39:23 rattles against his side, along with the **flashing** spear and lance.
41:21 [41:13] breath sets coals ablaze, and **flames** dart from his mouth.
Isa 13: 8 in labor. They will look aghast at each other, their faces **aflame**.
29: 6 with windstorm and tempest and **flames** *of* a devouring fire.
30:30 arm coming down with raging anger and consuming **fire** [+836],
66:15 bring down his anger with fury, and his rebuke with **flames** *of* fire.
Joel 2: 5 like a crackling **fire** [+836] consuming stubble, like a mighty army
Na 3: 3 Charging cavalry, **flashing** swords and glittering spears! Many

4259 לֶהָבָה *lehābâ*, n.f. [19] [√ 4258; cf. 4225]

flame [6], flames [3], flaming [3], blaze [2], blazing [1], burned [1], flashes [1], lightning [+836] [1], point [1]

Nu 21:28 "Fire went out from Heshbon, a **blaze** from the city of Sihon.
1Sa 17: 7 a weaver's rod, and its iron **point** weighed six hundred shekels.
Ps 29: 7 The voice of the LORD strikes with **flashes** *of* lightning.
83:14 [83:15] consumes the forest or a **flame** sets the mountains ablaze,
105:32 their rain into hail, with **lightning** [+836] throughout their land;
106:18 Fire blazed among their followers; a **flame** consumed the wicked.
Isa 4: 5 there a cloud of smoke by day and a glow of **flaming** fire by night;
5:24 of fire lick up straw and as dry grass sinks down in the **flames**,
10:17 The Light of Israel will become a fire, their Holy One a **flame**;
43: 2 you will not be burned; the **flames** will not set you ablaze.
47:14 They cannot even save themselves from the power of the **flame**.
Jer 48:45 a fire has gone out from Heshbon, a **blaze** from the midst of Sihon;
La 2: 3 He has burned in Jacob like a **flaming** fire that consumes
Eze 20:47 [21:3] The **blazing** flame will not be quenched, and every face
Da 11:33 they will fall by the sword or be **burned** or captured or plundered.
Hos 7: 6 smolders all night; in the morning it blazes like a **flaming** fire.
Joel 1:19 open pastures and **flames** have burned up all the trees of the field.
2: 3 Before them fire devours, behind them a **flame** blazes. Before
Ob 1:18 The house of Jacob will be a fire and the house of Joseph a **flame**;

4260 לְהָבִים *l**e**hābîm*, n.pr.g. [2]

Lehabites [2]

Ge 10:13 was the father of the Ludites, Anamites, **Lehabites**, Naphtuhites,
1Ch 1:11 was the father of the Ludites, Anamites, **Lehabites**, Naphtuhites,

4261 לַהַג *lahag*, n.m. [1]

study [1]

Ecc 12:12 many books there is no end, and much **study** wearies the body.

4262 לַהַד *lāhad*, n.pr.m. [1]

Lahad [1]

1Ch 4: 2 the father of Jahath, and Jahath the father of Ahumai and **Lahad**.

4263 לָהַהּ *lāhah*, v. [1] [cf. 3532, 4271]

madman [1]

Pr 26:18 [F] Like a **madman** shooting firebrands or deadly arrows

4264 לָהָה *lāhâ*, v. Not used in NIV/BHS [cf. 4206]

4265 לָהַט *lāhaṭ*[1], v. [10] [→ 4266, 4267; cf. 4358]

sets ablaze [2], blazes [1], burned up [1], consumed [1], consumes [1], flames [1], in flames [1], set afire [1], set on fire [1]

Dt 32:22 [D] its harvests and **set afire** the foundations of the mountains.
Job 41:21 [41:13] [D] His breath **sets** coals **ablaze**, and flames dart from
Ps 83:14 [83:15] [D] the forest or a flame **sets** the mountains **ablaze**,
97: 3 [D] Fire goes before him and **consumes** his foes on every side.
104: 4 [A] He makes winds his messengers, **flames** *of* fire his servants.
106:18 [D] blazed among their followers; a flame **consumed** the wicked.
Isa 42:25 [D] *It* enveloped them **in flames**, yet they did not understand;
Joel 1:19 [D] and flames *have* **burned up** all the trees of the field.
2: 3 [D] Before them fire devours, behind them a flame **blazes**.
Mal 4: 1 [3:19] [D] that day that is coming *will* **set** them **on fire**," says

4266 לָהַט *lāhaṭ*[2], v. [1] [√ 4265]

ravenous beasts [1]

Ps 57: 4 [57:5] [A] in the midst of lions; I lie among **ravenous beasts**—

4267 לַהַט *lahaṭ*, n.[m.]. [1] [√ 4265]

flaming [1]

Ge 3:24 a **flaming** sword flashing back and forth to guard the way to the

4268 לְהָטִים *l**e**hāṭîm*, n.m.pl. [1] [cf. 4286]

secret arts [1]

Ex 7:11 Egyptian magicians also did the same things by their **secret arts**:

4269 לָהַם *lāham*, v. [2]

choice morsels [2]

Pr 18: 8 [F] The words of a gossip are like **choice morsels**; they go down
26:22 [F] The words of a gossip are like **choice morsels**; they go down

4270 לָהֵן *lāhēn*, c. Not used in NIV/BHS [→ Ar 10385]

4271 לִהְלֵהַּ *lihlēah*, v. Not used in NIV/BHS [cf. 4263]

4272 לַהֲקָה *lah**a**qâ*, n.f. [1]

group [1]

1Sa 19:20 when they saw a **group** *of* prophets prophesying, with Samuel

4273 לוּ *lû*, c. [22 / 25] [→ 467, 4295]

if [12], if only [8], *untranslated* [1], let [1], oh [1], what if [1], will [1]

Ge 17:18 said to God, "**If only** Ishmael might live under your blessing!"
23:13 and he said to Ephron in their hearing, "Listen to me, if you **will**.
30:34 "Agreed," said Laban. "**Let** it be as you have said."
50:15 "**What if** Joseph holds a grudge against us and pays us back for all
Nu 14: 2 the whole assembly said to them, "**If only** we had died in Egypt!
14: 2 to them, "If only we had died in Egypt! Or in this desert! **[RPH]**
20: 3 "**If only** we had died when our brothers fell dead before the
22:29 of me! **If** I had a sword in my hand, I would kill you right now."
Dt 32:29 **If only** they were wise and would understand this and discern what
Jos 7: 7 **If only** we had been content to stay on the other side of the Jordan!
Jdg 8:19 LORD lives, **if** you had spared their lives, I would not kill you."
13:23 But his wife answered, "**If** the LORD had meant to kill us,
1Sa 14:30 How much better it would have been **if** the men had eaten today
2Sa 18:12 "Even **if** [K 4202] a thousand shekels were weighed out into my
19: 6 [19:7] I see that you would be pleased **if** [K 4202] Absalom were
Job 6: 2 "**If only** my anguish could be weighed and all my misery be placed
9:33 **If** [BHS 4202] **only** there were someone to arbitrate between us,
16: 4 I also could speak like you, **if** you were in my place; I could make
Ps 55:12 [55:13] **If** [BHS 4202] an enemy were insulting me, I could
55:12 [55:13] **if** [BHS 4202] a foe were raising himself against me, I
81:13 [81:14] "**If** my people would but listen to me, if Israel would
Isa 48:18 **If only** you had paid attention to my commands, your peace would
64: 1 [63:19] **Oh**, that you would rend the heavens and come down,
Eze 14:15 "Or **if** I send wild beasts through that country and they leave it
Mic 2:11 **If** a liar and deceiver comes and says, 'I will prophesy for you

4274 לֹו דְבַר *lô d**e**bār*, n.pr.loc. [2] [√ 4202 + 1818]

Lo Debar [2]

2Sa 9: 4 "He is at the house of Makir son of Ammiel in **Lo Debar**."
9: 5 So King David had him brought from **Lo Debar**, from the house of

4275 לוּב *lûb*, n.g.pl. [4 / 5]

Libyans [3], Libya [2]

2Ch 12: 3 sixty thousand horsemen and the innumerable troops of **Libyans**,
16: 8 and **Libyans** a mighty army with great numbers of chariots
Eze 30: 5 **Libya** [BHS 3915] and the people of the covenant land will fall by
Da 11:43 the riches of Egypt, with the **Libyans** and Nubians in submission.
Na 3: 9 were her boundless strength; Put and **Libya** were among her allies.

4276 לוּד *lûd*, n.pr.m. & g. [8]

Lud [2], Ludites [2], Lydia [2], Lydians [1], men of Lydia [1]

Ge 10:13 Mizraim was the father of the **Ludites**, Anamites, Lehabites,
10:22 The sons of Shem: Elam, Asshur, Arphaxad, **Lud** and Aram.
1Ch 1:11 Mizraim was the father of the **Ludites**, Anamites, Lehabites,
1:17 Elam, Asshur, Arphaxad, **Lud** and Aram. The sons of Aram:
Isa 66:19 to the Libyans and **Lydians** (famous as archers), to Tubal
Jer 46: 9 and Put who carry shields, **men of Lydia** who draw the bow.
Eze 27:10 " 'Men of Persia, **Lydia** and Put served as soldiers in your army.
30: 5 **Lydia** and all Arabia, Libya and the people of the covenant land

4277 לָוָה *lāwâ*[1], v. [12] [→ 4290, 4291, 4292, 4293; cf. 4339]

join [5], bind themselves [2], accompany [1], attached [1], be joined [1], bound himself [1], joined [1]

Ge 29:34 [C] "Now at last my husband *will become* **attached** to me,
Nu 18: 2 [C] Bring your fellow Levites from your ancestral tribe *to* **join**
18: 4 [C] *They are to* **join** you and be responsible for the care of the
Est 9:27 [C] all who **join** them should without fail observe these two days
Ps 83: 8 [83:9] [C] Even Assyria *has* **joined** them to lend strength to the
Ecc 8:15 [A] joy *will* **accompany** him in his work all the days of the life
Isa 14: 1 [C] Aliens *will* **join** them and unite with the house of Jacob.
56: 3 [C] Let no foreigner who *has* **bound himself** to the LORD say,
56: 6 [C] foreigners who **bind themselves** to the LORD to serve him,
Jer 50: 5 [C] **bind themselves** to the LORD in an everlasting covenant
Da 11:34 [C] a little help, and many who are not sincere *will* **join** them.
Zec 2:11 [2:15] [C] "Many nations *will* **be joined** with the LORD in

4278 לָוָה *lāwâ*[2], v. [14]

lend [4], borrow [3], borrower [2], lender [2], lend freely [1], lends freely [1], lends [1]

Ex 22:25 [22:24] [G] "If *you* **lend** money *to* one of my people among you
Dt 28:12 [G] *You will* **lend** *to* many nations but will borrow from none.
28:12 [A] You will lend to many nations but *will* **borrow** *from* none.
28:44 [G] He *will* **lend** *to* you, but you will not lend to him. He will be
28:44 [G] He will lend to you, but you *will* not **lend** *to* him. He will be
Ne 5: 4 [A] "*We have had to* **borrow** money to pay the king's tax on
Ps 37:21 [A] The wicked **borrow** and do not repay, but the righteous give
37:26 [G] They are always generous and **lend freely**; their children will
112: 5 [G] Good will come to him who is generous and **lends freely**,
Pr 19:17 [G] He who is kind to the poor **lends** *to* the LORD, and he will
22: 7 [A] rule over the poor, and the **borrower** is servant to the lender.
22: 7 [G] rule over the poor, and the borrower is servant to the **lender**.
Isa 24: 2 [A] for maid, for seller as for buyer, for **borrower** as for lender,
24: 2 [G] for maid, for seller as for buyer, for borrower as for **lender**,

4279 לוּז *lûz*[1], v. [6] [→ 4299]

devious [2], let out [2], deceit [1], perverse [1]

Pr 2:15 [C] whose paths are crooked and *who are* **devious** in their ways.
3:21 [A] and discernment, *do* not **let** *them* **out** of your sight;
3:32 [C] for the LORD detests a **perverse** *man* but takes the upright
4:21 [G] *Do* not **let** *them* **out** of your sight, keep them within your
14: 2 [C] the LORD, but *he* whose ways *are* **devious** despises him.
Isa 30:12 [C] this message, relied on oppression and depended on **deceit**,

4280 ²לוּז **lûz²**, n.[m.]. [1] [→ 4281]

almond [1]

Ge 30:37 **almond** and plane trees and made white stripes on them by peeling

4281 ³לוּז **lûz³**, n.pr.loc. [8] [→ 4282; cf. 4280]

Luz [7], *untranslated* [1]

Ge 28:19 He called that place Bethel, though the city used to be called **Luz**.
35: 6 Jacob and all the people with him came to **Luz** (that is, Bethel)
48: 3 "God Almighty appeared to me at **Luz** in the land of Canaan,
Jos 16: 2 It went on from Bethel (that is, **Luz**), crossed over to the territory
18:13 From there it crossed to the south slope of **Luz** (that is, Bethel)
18:13 From there it crossed to the south slope of Luz **[RPH]** (that is,
Jdg 1:23 When they sent men to spy out Bethel (formerly called **Luz**),
1:26 where he built a city and called it **Luz**, which is its name to this

4282 לוּזָה **lûzâ**, n.pr.loc. Not used in NIV/BHS [√ 4281 + 2025]

4283 לוּחַ **lûaḥ**, n.m. [43] [→ 4284; cf. 4300]

tablets [33], tablet [3], boards [2], panels [1], surfaces [1], them[s] [+2021] [1], they[s] [1], timbers [1]

Ex 24:12 I will give you the **tablets** *of* stone, with the law and commands I
27: 8 Make the altar hollow, out of **boards**. It is to be made just as you
31:18 he gave him the two **tablets** *of* the Testimony, the tablets of stone
31:18 the Testimony, the **tablets** *of* stone inscribed by the finger of God.
32:15 went down the mountain with the two **tablets** *of* the Testimony in
32:15 in his hands. **They**[s] were inscribed on both sides, front and back.
32:16 The **tablets** were the work of God; the writing was the writing of
32:16 the writing was the writing of God, engraved on the **tablets**.
32:19 his anger burned and he threw the **tablets** out of his hands,
34: 1 said to Moses, "Chisel out two stone **tablets** like the first ones,
34: 1 I will write on **them**[s] [+2021] the words that were on the first
34: 1 and I will write on them the words that were on the first **tablets**,
34: 4 So Moses chiseled out two stone **tablets** like the first ones
34: 4 commanded him; and he carried the two stone **tablets** in his hands.
34:28 he wrote on the **tablets** the words of the covenant—the Ten
34:29 When Moses came down from Mount Sinai with the two **tablets** *of*
38: 7 of the altar for carrying it. They made it hollow, out of **boards**.
Dt 4:13 you to follow and then wrote them on two stone **tablets**.
5:22 Then he wrote them on two stone **tablets** and gave them to me.
9: 9 When I went up on the mountain to receive the **tablets** *of* stone,
9: 9 the **tablets** *of* the covenant that the LORD had made with you,
9:10 The LORD gave me two stone **tablets** inscribed by the finger of
9:11 and forty nights, the LORD gave me the two stone **tablets**,
9:11 LORD gave me the two stone tablets, the **tablets** *of* the covenant.
9:15 with fire. And the two **tablets** *of* the covenant were in my hands.
9:17 So I took the two **tablets** and threw them out of my hands,
10: 1 "Chisel out two stone **tablets** like the first ones and come up to me
10: 2 I will write on the **tablets** the words that were on the first tablets,
10: 2 I will write on the tablets the words that were on the first **tablets**,
10: 3 acacia wood and chiseled out two stone **tablets** like the first ones,
10: 3 and I went up on the mountain with the two **tablets** in my hands.
10: 4 The LORD wrote on these **tablets** what he had written before,
10: 5 back down the mountain and put the **tablets** in the ark I had made,
1Ki 7:36 lions and palm trees on the **surfaces** of the supports and on the
8: 9 There was nothing in the ark except the two stone **tablets** that
2Ch 5:10 There was nothing in the ark except the two **tablets** that Moses had
Pr 3: 3 them around your neck, write them on the **tablet** *of* your heart.
7: 3 Bind them on your fingers; write them on the **tablet** *of* your heart.
SS 8: 9 on her. If she is a door, we will enclose her with **panels** *of* cedar.
Isa 30: 8 Go now, write it on a **tablet** for them, inscribe it on a scroll,
Jer 17: 1 on the **tablets** *of* their hearts and on the horns of their altars.
Eze 27: 5 They made all your **timbers** of pine trees from Senir; they took a
Hab 2: 2 "Write down the revelation and make it plain on **tablets** so that a

4284 לוּחִית **lûḥît**, n.pr.loc. [2] [√ 4283; cf. 4300, 4304]

Luhith [2]

Isa 15: 5 They go up the way to **Luhith**, weeping as they go; on the road to
Jer 48: 5 They go up the way to **Luhith**, [K 4304] weeping bitterly as they

4285 לוֹחֵשׁ **lôḥēš**, n.pr.m. Not used in NIV/BHS [√ 4317]

4286 לוּט **lûṭ**, v. [3 / 4] [→ 4287, 4319, 4320; cf. 4209, 4268]

covered [1], enfolds [1], pulled over [1], wrapped [1]

1Sa 21: 9 [21:10] [B] is here; it *is* **wrapped** in a cloth behind the ephod.
2Sa 19: 4 [19:5] [A] The king **covered** [BHS 4209] his face and cried
1Ki 19:13 [G] *he* **pulled** his cloak **over** his face and went out and stood at
Isa 25: 7 [A] On this mountain he will destroy the shroud that **enfolds** all

4287 ¹לוֹט **lôṭ¹**, n.m. [1] [√ 4286]

shroud [1]

Isa 25: 7 On this mountain he will destroy the **shroud** that enfolds all

4288 ²לוֹט **lôṭ²**, n.pr.m. [33] [→ 4289]

Lot [30], *untranslated* [1], he[s] [1], Lot's [1]

Ge 11:27 of Abram, Nahor and Haran. And Haran became the father of **Lot**.
11:31 Terah took his son Abram, his grandson **Lot** son of Haran,
12: 4 Abram left, as the LORD had told him; and **Lot** went with him.
12: 5 He took his wife Sarai, his nephew **Lot**, all the possessions they
13: 1 with his wife and everything he had, and **Lot** went with him.
13: 5 Now **Lot**, who was moving about with Abram, also had flocks
13: 7 arose between Abram's herdsmen and the herdsmen of **Lot**.
13: 8 So Abram said to **Lot**, "Let's not have any quarreling between you
13:10 **Lot** looked up and saw that the whole plain of the Jordan was well
13:11 So **Lot** chose for himself the whole plain of the Jordan and set out
13:11 the whole plain of the Jordan and set out **[RPH]** toward the east.
13:12 while **Lot** lived among the cities of the plain and pitched his tents
13:14 The LORD said to Abram after **Lot** had parted from him,
14:12 They also carried off Abram's nephew **Lot** and his possessions,
14:16 all the goods and brought back his relative **Lot** and his possessions,
19: 1 in the evening, and **Lot** was sitting in the gateway of the city.
19: 1 When **he**[s] saw them, he got up to meet them and bowed down with
19: 5 They called to **Lot**, "Where are the men who came to you tonight?
19: 6 **Lot** went outside to meet them and shut the door behind him
19: 9 They kept bringing pressure on **Lot** and moved forward to break
19:10 reached out and pulled **Lot** back into the house and shut the door.
19:12 The two men said to **Lot**, "Do you have anyone else here—
19:14 So **Lot** went out and spoke to his sons-in-law, who were pledged to
19:15 With the coming of dawn, the angels urged **Lot**, saying, "Hurry!
19:18 But **Lot** said to them, "No, my lords, please!
19:23 By the time **Lot** reached Zoar, the sun had risen over the land.
19:29 he brought **Lot** out of the catastrophe that overthrew the cities
19:29 of the catastrophe that overthrew the cities where **Lot** had lived.
19:30 **Lot** and his two daughters left Zoar and settled in the mountains,
19:36 So both of **Lot's** daughters became pregnant by their father.
Dt 2: 9 I have given Ar to the descendants of **Lot** as a possession."
2:19 I have given it as a possession to the descendants of **Lot**."
Ps 83: 8 [83:9] has joined them to lend strength to the descendants of **Lot**.

4289 לוֹטָן **lôṭān**, n.pr.m. [7] [√ 4288]

Lotan [5], Lotan's [2]

Ge 36:20 who were living in the region: **Lotan**, Shobal, Zibeon, Anah,
36:22 The sons of **Lotan**: Hori and Homam. Timna was Lotan's sister.
36:22 The sons of Lotan: Hori and Homam. Timna was **Lotan's** sister.
36:29 These were the Horite chiefs: **Lotan**, Shobal, Zibeon, Anah,
1Ch 1:38 of Seir: **Lotan**, Shobal, Zibeon, Anah, Dishon, Ezer and Dishan.
1:39 The sons of **Lotan**: Hori and Homam. Timna was Lotan's sister.
1:39 The sons of Lotan: Hori and Homam. Timna was **Lotan's** sister.

4290 ¹לֵוִי **lēwî¹**, n.pr.m. [62] [√ 4277; Ar 10387]

Levi [42], Levites [+1201] [15], Levite [2], Levites [2], Levites [+4751] [1]

Ge 29:34 because I have borne him three sons." So he was named **Levi**.
34:25 Simeon and **Levi**, Dinah's brothers, took their swords and attacked
34:30 Jacob said to Simeon and **Levi**, "You have brought trouble on me
35:23 the firstborn of Jacob, Simeon, **Levi**, Judah, Issachar and Zebulun.
46:11 The sons of **Levi**: Gershon, Kohath and Merari.
49: 5 "Simeon and **Levi** are brothers—their swords are weapons of
Ex 1: 2 Reuben, Simeon, **Levi** and Judah;
2: 1 Now a man of the house of **Levi** married a Levite woman,
2: 1 Now a man of the house of Levi married a **Levite** woman,
6:16 These were the names of the sons of **Levi** according to their
6:16 their records: Gershon, Kohath and Merari. **Levi** lived 137 years.
6:19 These were the clans of **Levi** according to their records.
32:26 come to me." And all the **Levites** [+1201] rallied to him.
32:28 The **Levites** [+1201] did as Moses commanded, and that day about
Nu 1:49 "You must not count the tribe of **Levi** or include them in the
3: 6 "Bring the tribe of **Levi** and present them to Aaron the priest to
3:15 "Count the **Levites** [+1201] by their families and clans. Count
3:17 These were the names of the sons of **Levi**: Gershon, Kohath
4: 2 "Take a census of the Kohathite branch of the **Levites** [+1201] by
16: 1 Korah son of Izhar, the son of Kohath, the son of **Levi**, and certain
16: 7 be the one who is holy. You **Levites** [+1201] have gone too far!"
16: 8 Moses also said to Korah, "Now listen, you **Levites** [+1201]!
16:10 has brought you and all your fellow **Levites** [+1201] near himself,
17: 3 [17:18] On the staff of **Levi** write Aaron's name, for there must
17: 8 [17:23] which represented the house of **Levi**, had not only
18: 2 Bring your fellow **Levites** [+4751] from your ancestral tribe to join
18:21 "I give to the **Levites** [+1201] all the tithes in Israel as their
26:58 These also were **Levite** clans: the Libnite clan, the Hebronite clan,

Nu 26:59 a descendant of **Levi**, who was born to the Levites in Egypt.
26:59 a descendant of Levi, who was born to the **Levites** in Egypt.
Dt 10: 8 At that time the LORD set apart the tribe of **Levi** to carry the ark
10: 9 That is why the **Levites** have no share or inheritance among their
18: 1 The priests, who are Levites—indeed the whole tribe of **Levi**—
21: 5 The priests, the sons of **Levi**, shall step forward, for the LORD
27:12 the people: Simeon, **Levi**, Judah, Issachar, Joseph and Benjamin.
31: 9 wrote down this law and gave it to the priests, the sons of **Levi**,
33: 8 About **Levi** he said: "Your Thummim and Urim belong to the man
Jos 21:10 Aaron who were from the Kohathite clans of the **Levites** [+1201],
1Ki 12:31 all sorts of people, even though they were not **Levites** [+1201].
1Ch 2: 1 the sons of Israel: Reuben, Simeon, **Levi**, Judah, Issachar, Zebulun,
6: 1 [5:27] The sons of **Levi**: Gershon, Kohath and Merari.
6:16 [6:1] The sons of **Levi**: Gershon, Kohath and Merari.
6:38 [6:23] the son of Kohath, the son of **Levi**, the son of Israel;
6:43 [6:28] the son of Jahath, the son of Gershon, the son of **Levi**;
6:47 [6:32] the son of Mushi, the son of Merari, the son of **Levi**.
9:18 the gatekeepers belonging to the camp of the **Levites** [+1201].
21: 6 But Joab did not include **Levi** and Benjamin in the numbering,
23: 6 divided the Levites into groups corresponding to the sons of **Levi**:
23:14 of Moses the man of God were counted as part of the tribe of **Levi**.
23:24 These were the descendants of **Levi** by their families—the heads of
23:27 the **Levites** [+1201] were counted from those twenty years old
24:20 As for the rest of the descendants of **Levi**: from the sons of
24:30 These were the **Levites** [+1201], according to their families.
27:17 over **Levi**: Hashabiah son of Kemuel; over Aaron: Zadok;
Ne 12:23 The family heads among the descendants of **Levi** up to the time of
Ps 135:20 O house of **Levi**, praise the LORD; you who fear him, praise the
Eze 40:46 who are the only **Levites** [+1201] who may draw near to the
48:31 will be the gate of Reuben, the gate of Judah and the gate of **Levi**.
Zec 12:13 the clan of the house of **Levi** and their wives, the clan of Shimei
Mal 2: 4 you this admonition so that my covenant with **Levi** may continue,"
2: 8 you have violated the covenant with **Levi**," says the LORD
3: 3 he will purify the **Levites** [+1201] and refine them like gold

4291 [2]לֵוִי *lēwî[2]*, a.g. [288] [√ 4277; Ar 10387]

Levites [245], Levite [26], Levi [5], *untranslated* [3], Levites [+1201] [3], Levitical [2], them[s] [+2021] [2], Levites [+5476] [1], they[s] [+2021] [1]

Ex 4:14 and he said, "What about your brother, Aaron the **Levite**?
6:25 These were the heads of the **Levite** families, clan by clan.
38:21 which were recorded at Moses' command by the **Levites** under the
Lev 25:32 " 'The **Levites** always have the right to redeem their houses in the
25:32 have the right to redeem their houses in the **Levitical** towns,
25:33 So the property of the **Levites** is redeemable—that is, a house sold
25:33 because the houses in the towns of the **Levites** are their property
Nu 1:47 The families of the tribe of **Levi**, however, were not counted along
1:50 appoint the **Levites** to be in charge of the tabernacle of the
1:51 the tabernacle is to move, the **Levites** are to take it down,
1:51 and whenever the tabernacle is to be set up, the **Levites** shall do it.
1:53 The **Levites**, however, are to set up their tents around the
1:53 The **Levites** are to be responsible for the care of the tabernacle of
2:17 and the camp of the **Levites** will set out in the middle of the camps.
2:33 The **Levites**, however, were not counted along with the other
3: 9 Give the **Levites** to Aaron and his sons; they are the Israelites who
3:12 "I have taken the **Levites** from among the Israelites in place of the
3:12 male offspring of every Israelite woman. The **Levites** are mine,
3:20 These were the **Levite** clans, according to their families.
3:32 The chief leader of the **Levites** was Eleazar son of Aaron,
3:39 The total number of **Levites** counted at the LORD's command by
3:41 Take the **Levites** for me in place of all the firstborn of the
3:41 the livestock of the **Levites** in place of all the firstborn of the
3:45 "Take the **Levites** in place of all the firstborn of Israel, and the
3:45 and the livestock of the **Levites** in place of their livestock.
3:45 of their livestock. The **Levites** are to be mine. I am the LORD.
3:46 the 273 firstborn Israelites who exceed the number of the **Levites**,
3:49 from those who exceeded the number redeemed by the **Levites**.
4:18 that the Kohathite tribal clans are not cut off from the **Levites**.
4:46 and the leaders of Israel counted all the **Levites** by their clans
7: 5 Give them to the **Levites** as each man's work requires."
7: 6 So Moses took the carts and oxen and gave them to the **Levites**.
8: 6 "Take the **Levites** from among the other Israelites and make them
8: 9 Bring the **Levites** to the front of the Tent of Meeting and assemble
8:10 You are to bring the **Levites** before the LORD, and the Israelites
8:10 and the Israelites are to lay their hands on **them**[s] [+2021].
8:11 Aaron is to present the **Levites** before the LORD as a wave
8:12 "After the **Levites** lay their hands on the heads of the bulls,
8:12 the other for a burnt offering, to make atonement for the **Levites**.
8:13 Have the **Levites** stand in front of Aaron and his sons and
8:14 In this way you are to set the **Levites** apart from the other
8:14 apart from the other Israelites, and the **Levites** will be mine.
8:15 "After you have purified the **Levites** and presented them as a wave
8:18 I have taken the **Levites** in place of all the firstborn sons in Israel.
8:19 I have given the **Levites** as gifts to Aaron and his sons to do the
8:20 the whole Israelite community did with the **Levites** just as the
8:20 with the Levites just as the LORD commanded Moses. **[RPH]**
8:21 The **Levites** purified themselves and washed their clothes.
8:22 the **Levites** came to do their work at the Tent of Meeting under the
8:22 They did with the **Levites** just as the LORD commanded Moses.
8:24 "This applies to the **Levites**: Men twenty-five years old or more
8:26 is how you are to assign the responsibilities of the **Levites**."
18: 6 I myself have selected your fellow **Levites** from among the
18:23 It is the **Levites** who are to do the work at the Tent of Meeting
18:24 I give to the **Levites** as their inheritance the tithes that the Israelites
18:26 "Speak to the **Levites** and say to them: 'When you receive from the
18:30 "Say to the **Levites**: 'When you present the best part, it will be
26:57 These were the **Levites** who were counted by their clans:
31:30 Give them to the **Levites**, who are responsible for the care of the
31:47 as the LORD commanded him, and gave them to the **Levites**,
35: 2 "Command the Israelites to give the **Levites** towns to live in from
35: 2 And give **them**[s] [+2021] pasturelands around the towns.
35: 4 "The pasturelands around the towns that you give the **Levites** will
35: 6 "Six of the towns you give the **Levites** will be cities of refuge,
35: 7 In all you must give the **Levites** forty-eight towns, together with
35: 8 The towns you give the **Levites** from the land the Israelites possess
Dt 12:12 and maidservants, and the **Levites** from your towns,
12:18 and maidservants, and the **Levites** from your towns—
12:19 Be careful not to neglect the **Levites** as long as you live in your
14:27 do not neglect the **Levites** living in your towns, for they have no
14:29 so that the **Levites** (who have no allotment or inheritance of their
16:11 the **Levites** in your towns, and the aliens, the fatherless
16:14 the **Levites**, the aliens, the fatherless and the widows who live in
17: 9 Go to the priests, who are **Levites**, and to the judge who is in office
17:18 a copy of this law, taken from that of the priests, who are **Levites**.
18: 1 The priests, who are **Levites**—indeed the whole tribe of Levi—
18: 6 If a **Levite** moves from one of your towns anywhere in Israel
18: 7 his fellow **Levites** who serve there in the presence of the LORD.
24: 8 careful to do exactly as the priests, who are **Levites**, instruct you.
26:11 you and the **Levites** and the aliens among you shall rejoice in all
26:12 you shall give it to the **Levite**, the alien, the fatherless and the
26:13 from my house the sacred portion and have given it to the **Levite**,
27: 9 Then Moses and the priests, who are **Levites**, said to all Israel,
27:14 The **Levites** shall recite to all the people of Israel in a loud voice:
31:25 he gave this command to the **Levites** who carried the ark of the
Jos 3: 3 the priests, who are **Levites**, carrying it, you are to move out from
8:33 facing those who carried it—the priests, who were **Levites**.
13:14 to the tribe of **Levi** he gave no inheritance, since the offerings
13:33 to the tribe of **Levi**, Moses had given no inheritance; the LORD,
14: 3 but had not granted the **Levites** an inheritance among the rest,
14: 4 The **Levites** received no share of the land but only towns to live in,
18: 7 The **Levites**, however, do not get a portion among you,
21: 1 Now the family heads of the **Levites** approached Eleazar the priest,
21: 3 the Israelites gave the **Levites** the following towns
21: 4 The **Levites** who were descendants of Aaron the priest were
21: 8 So the Israelites allotted to the **Levites** these towns and their
21:20 The rest of the Kohathite clans of the **Levites** were allotted towns
21:27 The **Levite** clans of the Gershonites were given: from the half-tribe
21:34 The Merarite clans (the rest of the **Levites**) were given: from the
21:40 who were the rest of the **Levites** [+5476], were twelve.
21:41 The towns of the **Levites** in the territory held by the Israelites were
Jdg 17: 7 A young **Levite** from Bethlehem in Judah, who had been living
17: 9 "I'm a **Levite** from Bethlehem in Judah," he said, "and I'm looking
17:10 ten shekels of silver a year, your clothes and your food." **[RPH]**
17:11 So the **Levite** agreed to live with him, and the young man was to
17:12 Micah installed the **Levite**, and the young man became his priest
17:13 will be good to me, since this **Levite** has become my priest."
18: 3 Micah's house, they recognized the voice of the young **Levite**;
18:15 and went to the house of the young **Levite** *at* Micah's place
19: 1 Now a **Levite** who lived in a remote area in the hill country of
20: 4 So the **Levite**, the husband of the murdered woman, said, "I
1Sa 6:15 The **Levites** took down the ark of the LORD, together with the
2Sa 15:24 all the **Levites** who were with him were carrying the ark of the
1Ki 8: 4 sacred furnishings in it. The priests and **Levites** carried them up,
1Ch 6:19 [6:4] These are the clans of the **Levites** listed according to their
6:48 [6:33] Their fellow **Levites** were assigned to all the other duties
6:64 [6:49] So the Israelites gave the **Levites** these towns and their
9: 2 towns were some Israelites, priests, **Levites** and temple servants.
9:14 Of the **Levites**: Shemaiah son of Hasshub, the son of Azrikam,
9:26 the four principal gatekeepers, who were **Levites**, were entrusted
9:31 A **Levite** named Mattithiah, the firstborn son of Shallum the
9:33 Those who were musicians, heads of **Levite** families, stayed in the
9:34 All these were heads of **Levite** families, chiefs as listed in their
12:26 [12:27] men of **Levi**—4,600,
13: 2 and **Levites** who are with them in their towns and pasturelands,
15: 2 David said, "No one but the **Levites** may carry the ark of God,
15: 4 He called together the descendants of Aaron and the **Levites**:
15:11 Asaiah, Joel, Shemaiah, Eliel and Amminadab the **Levites**.
15:12 He said to them, "You are the heads of the **Levitical** families;

1Ch 15:14 **Levites** consecrated themselves in order to bring up the ark of the
15:15 the **Levites** [+1201] carried the ark of God with the poles on their
15:16 David told the leaders of the **Levites** to appoint their brothers as
15:17 So the **Levites** appointed Heman son of Joel; from his brothers,
15:22 Kenaniah the head **Levite** was in charge of the singing; that was
15:26 Because God had helped the **Levites** who were carrying the ark of
15:27 as were all the **Levites** who were carrying the ark, and as were the
16: 4 He appointed some of the **Levites** to minister before the ark of the
23: 2 together all the leaders of Israel, as well as the priests and **Levites**.
23: 3 The **Levites** thirty years old or more were counted, and the total
23:26 the **Levites** no longer need to carry the tabernacle or any of the
24: 6 The scribe Shemaiah son of Nethanel, a **Levite**, recorded their
24: 6 and the heads of families of the priests and of the **Levites**—
24:31 and the heads of families of the priests and of the **Levites**.
26:17 There were six **Levites** a day on the east, four a day on the north,
26:20 Their fellow **Levites** were in charge of the treasuries of the house
28:13 gave him instructions for the divisions of the priests and **Levites**,
28:21 and **Levites** are ready for all the work on the temple of God,
2Ch 5: 4 all the elders of Israel had arrived, the **Levites** took up the ark,
5: 5 furnishings in it. The priests, who were **Levites**, carried them up;
5:12 All the **Levites** who were musicians—Asaph, Heman, Jeduthun
7: 6 as did the **Levites** with the LORD's musical instruments,
8:14 the **Levites** to lead the praise and to assist the priests according to
8:15 the king's commands to the priests or to the **Levites** in any matter,
11:13 **Levites** from all their districts throughout Israel sided with him.
11:14 The **Levites** even abandoned their pasturelands and property,
13: 9 out the priests of the LORD, the sons of Aaron, and the **Levites**,
13:10 serve the LORD are sons of Aaron, and the **Levites** assist them.
17: 8 With them were certain **Levites**—Shemaiah, Nethaniah, Zebadiah,
17: 8 **[RPH]** and the priests Elishama and Jehoram.
19: 8 Jehoshaphat appointed some of the **Levites**, priests and heads of
19:11 the king, and the **Levites** will serve as officials before you.
20:14 of Jeiel, the son of Mattaniah, a **Levite** and descendant of Asaph,
20:19 Then some **Levites** from the Kohathites and Korahites stood up
23: 2 They went throughout Judah and gathered the **Levites**
23: 4 **Levites** who are going on duty on the Sabbath are to keep watch at
23: 6 the temple of the LORD except the priests and **Levites** on duty;
23: 7 The **Levites** are to station themselves around the king, each man
23: 8 The **Levites** and all the men of Judah did just as Jehoiada the priest
23:18 who were **Levites**, to whom David had made assignments in the
24: 5 He called together the priests and **Levites** and said to them,
24: 5 of your God. Do it now." But the **Levites** did not act at once.
24: 6 "Why haven't you required the **Levites** to bring in from Judah
24:11 Whenever the chest was brought in by the **Levites** to the king's
29: 4 He brought in the priests and the **Levites**, assembled them in the
29: 5 and said: "Listen to me, **Levites**! Consecrate yourselves now
29:12 these **Levites** set to work: from the Kohathites, Mahath son of
29:16 The **Levites** took it and carried it out to the Kidron Valley.
29:25 He stationed the **Levites** in the temple of the LORD with
29:26 So the **Levites** stood ready with David's instruments,
29:30 his officials ordered the **Levites** to praise the LORD with the
29:34 so their kinsmen the **Levites** helped them until the task was
29:34 for the **Levites** had been more conscientious in consecrating
30:15 The priests and the **Levites** were ashamed and consecrated
30:16 The priests sprinkled the blood handed to them by the **Levites**.
30:17 the **Levites** had to kill the Passover lambs for all those who were
30:21 while the **Levites** and priests sang to the LORD every day,
30:22 Hezekiah spoke encouragingly to all the **Levites**, who showed
30:25 along with the priests and **Levites** and all who had assembled from
30:27 The priests and the **Levites** stood to bless the people, and God
31: 2 Hezekiah assigned the priests and **Levites** to divisions—each of
31: 2 each of them according to their duties as priests or **Levites**—
31: 4 **Levites** so they could devote themselves to the Law of the
31: 9 Hezekiah asked the priests and **Levites** about the heaps;
31:12 Conaniah, a **Levite**, was in charge of these things, and his brother
31:14 Kore son of Imnah the **Levite**, keeper of the East Gate, was in
31:17 and likewise to the **Levites** twenty years old or more,
31:19 and to all who were recorded in the genealogies of the **Levites**.
34: 9 which the **Levites** who were the doorkeepers had collected from
34:12 them were Jahath and Obadiah, **Levites** descended from Merari,
34:12 The **Levites**—all who were skilled in playing musical
34:13 Some of the **Levites** were secretaries, scribes and doorkeepers.
34:30 of Judah, the people of Jerusalem, the priests and the **Levites**—
35: 3 He said to the **Levites**, who instructed all Israel and who had been
35: 5 "Stand in the holy place with a group of **Levites** for each
35: 8 contributed voluntarily to the people and the priests and **Levites**.
35: 9 and Hashabiah, Jeiel and Jozabad, the leaders of the **Levites**,
35: 9 Passover offerings and five hundred head of cattle for the **Levites**.
35:10 the priests stood in their places with the **Levites** in their divisions
35:11 the blood handed to them, while the **Levites** skinned the animals.
35:14 So the **Levites** made preparations for themselves and for the
35:15 because their fellow **Levites** made the preparations for them.
35:18 the **Levites** and all Judah and Israel who were there with the
Ezr 1: 5 family heads of Judah and Benjamin, and the priests and **Levites**—
2:40 The **Levites**: the descendants of Jeshua and Kadmiel (through the
2:70 The priests, the **Levites**, the singers, the gatekeepers
3: 8 of Jozadak and the rest of their brothers (the priests and the **Levites**
3: 8 appointing **Levites** twenty years of age and older to supervise the
3: 9 and the sons of Henadad and their sons and brothers—all **Levites**—
3:10 and with trumpets, and the **Levites** (the sons of Asaph)
3:12 But many of the older priests and **Levites** and family heads,
6:20 The priests and **Levites** had purified themselves and were all
7: 7 **Levites**, singers, gatekeepers and temple servants,
8:15 the people and the priests, I found no **Levites** [+1201] there.
8:18 a capable man, from the descendants of Mahli son of **Levi**,
8:20 that David and the officials had established to assist the **Levites**.
8:29 the leading priests and the **Levites** and the family heads of Israel."
8:30 the priests and **Levites** received the silver and gold and sacred
8:33 so were the **Levites** Jozabad son of Jeshua and Noadiah son of
9: 1 "The people of Israel, including the priests and the **Levites**,
10: 5 So Ezra rose up and put the leading priests and **Levites** and all
10:15 supported by Meshullam and Shabbethai the **Levite**, opposed this.
10:23 Among the **Levites**: Jozabad, Shimei, Kelaiah (that is, Kelita),
Ne 3:17 the repairs were made by the **Levites** under Rehum son of Bani.
7: 1 the gatekeepers and the singers and the **Levites** were appointed.
7:43 The **Levites**: the descendants of Jeshua (through Kadmiel through
7:73 [7:72] The priests, the **Levites**, the gatekeepers, the singers and
8: 7 The **Levites**—Jeshua, Bani, Sherebiah, Jamin, Akkub, Shabbethai,
8: 9 and the **Levites** who were instructing the people said to them all,
8:11 The **Levites** calmed all the people, saying, "Be still, for this is a
8:13 the heads of all the families, along with the priests and the **Levites**,
9: 4 Standing on the stairs were the **Levites**—Jeshua, Bani, Kadmiel,
9: 5 And the **Levites**—Jeshua, Kadmiel, Bani, Hashabneiah, Sherebiah,
9:38 [10:1] our **Levites** and our priests are affixing their seals to it."
10: 9 [10:10] The **Levites**: Jeshua son of Azaniah, Binnui of the sons of
10:28 [10:29] priests, **Levites**, gatekeepers, singers, temple servants
10:34 [10:35] "We—the priests, the **Levites** and the people—have cast
10:37 [10:38] we will bring a tithe of our crops to the **Levites**, for it is
10:37 [10:38] for it is the **Levites** who collect the tithes in all the towns
10:38 [10:39] is to accompany the **Levites** when they receive the tithes,
10:38 [10:39] the Levites when **they**[s] [+2021] receive the tithes,
10:38 [10:39] the **Levites** are to bring a tenth of the tithes up to the
10:39 [10:40] The people of Israel, including the **Levites** [+1201], are to
11: 3 priests, **Levites**, temple servants and descendants of Solomon's
11:15 From the **Levites**: Shemaiah son of Hasshub, the son of Azrikam,
11:16 Shabbethai and Jozabad, two of the heads of the **Levites**, who had
11:18 The **Levites** in the holy city totaled 284.
11:20 The rest of the Israelites, with the priests and **Levites**, were in all
11:22 The chief officer of the **Levites** in Jerusalem was Uzzi son of Bani,
11:36 Some of the divisions of the **Levites** *of* Judah settled in Benjamin.
12: 1 and **Levites** who returned with Zerubbabel son of Shealtiel
12: 8 The **Levites** were Jeshua, Binnui, Kadmiel, Sherebiah, Judah,
12:22 The family heads of the **Levites** in the days of Eliashib, Joiada,
12:24 And the leaders of the **Levites** were Hashabiah, Sherebiah,
12:27 the **Levites** were sought out from where they lived and were
12:30 the priests and **Levites** had purified themselves ceremonially,
12:44 the portions required by the Law for the priests and the **Levites**,
12:44 for Judah was pleased with the ministering priests and **Levites**.
12:47 They also set aside the portion for the other **Levites**,
12:47 and the **Levites** set aside the portion for the descendants of Aaron.
13: 5 new wine and oil prescribed for the **Levites**, singers
13:10 I also learned that the portions assigned to the **Levites** had not been
13:10 that all the **Levites** and singers responsible for the service had gone
13:13 a **Levite** named Pedaiah in charge of the storerooms and made
13:22 Then I commanded the **Levites** to purify themselves and go
13:29 and the covenant of the priesthood and of the **Levites**.
13:30 So I purified the priests and the **Levites** of everything foreign,
Isa 66:21 And I will select some of them also to be priests and **Levites**,"
Jer 33:18 nor will the priests, who are **Levites**, ever fail to have a man to
33:21 my covenant with the **Levites** who are priests ministering before
33:22 the **Levites** who minister before me as countless as the stars of the
Eze 43:19 who are **Levites**, of the family of Zadok, who come near to
44:10 " 'The **Levites** who went far from me when Israel went astray
44:15 who are **Levites** and descendants of Zadok and who faithfully
45: 5 cubits long and 10,000 cubits wide will belong to the **Levites**,
48:11 did not go astray as the **Levites** did when the Israelites went astray.
48:12 a most holy portion, bordering the territory of the **Levites**.
48:13 the **Levites** will have an allotment 25,000 cubits long and 10,000
48:22 So the property of the **Levites** and the property of the city will lie

4292 לִוְיָה *liwyâ*, n.f. [2] [√ 4277]

garland [2]

Pr 1: 9 They will be a **garland** to grace your head and a chain to adorn
4: 9 She will set a **garland** *of* grace on your head and present you with

4293 לִוְיָתָן ***liwyātān***, n.m. [6] [√ 4277]

leviathan [6]

Job 3: 8 curse days curse that day, those who are ready to rouse **Leviathan**.
41: 1 [40:25] "Can you pull in the **leviathan** with a fishhook or tie
Ps 74: 14 It was you who crushed the heads of **Leviathan** and gave him as
104: 26 There the ships go to and fro, and the **leviathan**, which you formed
Isa 27: 1 great and powerful sword, **Leviathan** the gliding serpent,
27: 1 Leviathan the gliding serpent, **Leviathan** the coiling serpent;

4294 לוּל ***lûl***, n.[m.]. [1]

stairway [1]

1Ki 6: 8 a **stairway** led up to the middle level and from there to the third.

4295 לוּלֵא ***lûlēʾ***, c. [14] [√ 4273]

if not [5], if not [+3954] [4], unless [2], but [1], not [1], still [1]

Ge 31: 42 **If** the God of my father, … had **not** been with me,
43: 10 As it is, **if** [+3954] we had **not** delayed, we could have gone
Dt 32: 27 **but** I dreaded the taunt of the enemy, lest the adversary
Jdg 14: 18 Samson said to them, "**If** you had **not** plowed with my heifer,
1Sa 25: 34 who has kept me from harming you, **if** [+3954] you had **not** come
2Sa 2: 27 "As surely as God lives, **if** [+3954] you had **not** spoken,
2Ki 3: 14 whom I serve, **if** [+3954] I did **not** have respect for the presence of
Ps 27: 13 I am **still** confident of this: I will see the goodness of the LORD
94: 17 **Unless** the LORD had given me help, I would soon have dwelt in
106: 23 had **not** Moses, his chosen one, stood in the breach before him to
119: 92 **If** your law had **not** been my delight, I would have perished in my
124: 1 **If** the LORD had **not** been on our side—let Israel say—
124: 2 **if** the LORD had **not** been on our side when men attacked us,
Isa 1: 9 **Unless** the LORD Almighty had left us some survivors, we would

4296 לוּן ***lûn***, v. [15] [→ 9442]

grumbled [7], grumble [3], constant grumbling [+9442] [1], grumbling [+9442] [1], grumbling [1], howl [1], made grumble [1]

Ex 15: 24 [C] So the people **grumbled** against Moses, saying, "What are
16: 2 [C] In the desert the whole community **grumbled** against Moses
16: 7 [G] Who are we, that *you should* **grumble** against us?"
16: 8 [G] because he has heard your **grumbling** [+9442] against him.
17: 3 [G] thirsty for water there, and they **grumbled** against Moses.
Nu 14: 2 [C] All the Israelites **grumbled** against Moses and Aaron,
14: 27 [G] "How long *will* this wicked community **grumble** against
14: 27 [G] I have heard the complaints of these **grumbling** Israelites.
14: 29 [G] counted in the census and who *has* **grumbled** against me.
14: 36 [G] **made** the whole community **grumble** against him by
16: 11 [C] Who is Aaron that *you should* **grumble** against him?"
16: 41 [17:6] [C] whole Israelite community **grumbled** against Moses
17: 5 [17:20] [G] **constant grumbling** against you **by** [+9442] the
Jos 9: 18 [C] of Israel. The whole assembly **grumbled** against the leaders,
Ps 59: 15 [59:16] [G] wander about for food and **howl** if not satisfied.

4297 לוּשׁ ***lûš***, v. [5]

knead [2], kneaded [2], kneading [1]

Ge 18: 6 [A] three seahs of fine flour and **knead** it and bake some bread."
1Sa 28: 24 [A] took some flour, **kneaded** it and baked bread without yeast.
2Sa 13: 8 [A] She took some dough, **kneaded** it, made the bread in his
Jer 7: 18 [A] the women **knead** the dough and make cakes of bread for the
Hos 7: 4 [A] need not stir from the **kneading** *of* the dough till it rises.

4298 לָוִשׁ ***lāwiš***, n.pr.m. [0] [√ 4330]

2Sa 3: 15 [away from her husband Paltiel son of **Laish**. [K; see Q 4331]]

4299 לָזוּת ***lāzût***, n.f. [1] [√ 4279]

corrupt talk [1]

Pr 4: 24 perversity from your mouth; keep **corrupt talk** far from your lips.

4300 לַח ***laḥ***, a. [6] [→ 4283, 4284, 4301]

fresh [2], green [2], fresh-cut [1], grapes or raisins [+2256+3313+6694] [1]

Ge 30: 37 took **fresh-cut** branches from poplar, almond and plane trees
Nu 6: 3 not drink grape juice or eat **grapes or raisins** [+2256+3313+6694].
Jdg 16: 7 "If anyone ties me with seven **fresh** thongs that have not been
16: 8 the rulers of the Philistines brought her seven **fresh** thongs that had
Eze 17: 24 I dry up the **green** tree and make the dry tree flourish.
20: 47 [21:3] and it will consume all your trees, both **green** and dry.

4301 לֵחַ ***lēaḥ***, n.m. [1] [√ 4300]

strength [1]

Dt 34: 7 when he died, yet his eyes were not weak nor his **strength** gone.

4302 ¹לְחוּם ***lᵉḥûm[1]***, n.[m.]. [1]

entrails [1]

Zep 1: 17 blood will be poured out like dust and their **entrails** like filth.

4303 ²לְחוּם ***lᵉḥûm[2]***, n.[m.]. [1] [√ 4309]

blows [1]

Job 20: 23 his burning anger against him and rain down his **blows** upon him.

4304 לֻחוֹת ***luḥôt***, n.pr.loc. [0] [cf. 4284]

Jer 48: 5 [They go up the way to **Luhith**, [K; see Q 4284] weeping bitterly]

4305 ¹לְחִי ***lᵉḥî[1]***, n.m. [20] [→ 4306?, 8257?]

cheeks [4], jawbone [4], cheek [3], jaws [3], face [2], jaw [2], jowls [1], neck [1]

Dt 18: 3 a bull or a sheep: the shoulder, the **jowls** and the inner parts.
Jdg 15: 15 Finding a fresh **jawbone** *of* a donkey, he grabbed it and struck
15: 16 "With a donkey's **jawbone** I have made donkeys of them.
15: 16 of them. With a donkey's **jawbone** I have killed a thousand men."
15: 17 When he finished speaking, he threw away the **jawbone**; and the
1Ki 22: 24 son of Kenaanah went up and slapped Micaiah in the **face**.
2Ch 18: 23 son of Kenaanah went up and slapped Micaiah in the **face**.
Job 16: 10 they strike my **cheek** in scorn and unite together against me.
41: 2 [40:26] put a cord through his nose or pierce his **jaw** with a hook?
Ps 3: 7 [3:8] Strike all my enemies on the **jaw**; break the teeth of the
SS 1: 10 Your **cheeks** are beautiful with earrings, your neck with strings of
5: 13 His **cheeks** are like beds of spice yielding perfume. His lips are
Isa 30: 28 he places in the **jaws** *of* the peoples a bit that leads them astray.
50: 6 those who beat me, my **cheeks** to those who pulled out my beard;
La 1: 2 Bitterly she weeps at night, tears are upon her **cheeks**. Among all
3: 30 Let him offer his **cheek** to one who would strike him, and let him
Eze 29: 4 I will put hooks in your **jaws** and make the fish of your streams
38: 4 put hooks in your **jaws** and bring you out with your whole army—
Hos 11: 4 I lifted the yoke from their **neck** and bent down to feed them.
Mic 5: 1 [4:14] They will strike Israel's ruler on the **cheek** with a rod.

4306 ²לְחִי ***lᵉḥî[2]***, n.pr.loc. [4] [√ 4305?]

Lehi [4]

Jdg 15: 9 Philistines went up and camped in Judah, spreading out near **Lehi**.
15: 14 As he approached **Lehi**, the Philistines came toward him shouting.
15: 19 God opened up the hollow place in **Lehi**, and water came out of it.
15: 19 So the spring was called En Hakkore, and it is still there in **Lehi**.

4307 לַחַי רֹאִי ***laḥay rōʾî***, n.pr.loc. Not used in NIV/BHS [√ 4200 + 2649 + 8022]

4308 לָחַךְ ***lāḥak***, v. [6]

lick [3], lick up [1], licked up [1], licks up [1]

Nu 22: 4 [D] "This horde *is* going to **lick up** everything around us, as an
22: 4 [A] around us, as an ox **licks up** the grass of the field."
1Ki 18: 38 [D] and the soil, and also **licked up** the water in the trench.
Ps 72: 9 [D] tribes will bow before him and his enemies *will* **lick** the dust.
Isa 49: 23 [D] their faces to the ground; *they will* **lick** the dust at your feet.
Mic 7: 17 [D] *They will* **lick** dust like a snake, like creatures that crawl on

4309 ¹לָחַם ***lāḥam[1]***, v. [171] [→ 4303, 4311, 4878]

fight [70], fought [30], attacked [15], fighting [11], attack [7], attacking [5], battle [5], make war [5], fights [4], war [3], fight [+4309] [2], made war [2], *untranslated* [1], at war [1], engage in battle [1], fight battle [1], military exploits [1], military [1], overpower [+6584] [1], overpower [1], pressed attack [1], stormed [1], waging war [1], wars [1]

Ex 1: 10 [C] will join our enemies, **fight** against us and leave the country."
14: 14 [C] The LORD *will* **fight** for you; you need only to be still."
14: 25 [C] The LORD *is* **fighting** for them against Egypt."
17: 8 [C] Amalekites came and **attacked** the Israelites at Rephidim.
17: 9 [C] some of our men and go out *to* **fight** the Amalekites.
17: 10 [C] So Joshua **fought** the Amalekites as Moses had ordered, and
Nu 21: 1 [C] *he* **attacked** the Israelites and captured some of them.
21: 23 [C] against Israel. When he reached Jahaz, *he* **fought** with Israel.
21: 26 [C] who *had* **fought** against the former king of Moab and had
22: 11 [C] Perhaps then I will be able to **fight** them and drive them
Dt 1: 30 [C] your God, who is going before you, *will* **fight** for you,
1: 41 [C] We will go up and **fight**, as the LORD our God commanded
1: 42 [C] the LORD said to me, "Tell them, 'Do not go up and **fight**,
3: 22 [C] of them; the LORD your God himself *will* **fight** for you."
20: 4 [C] to **fight** for you against your enemies to give you victory."
20: 10 [C] When you march up to **attack** a city, make its people an offer
20: 19 [C] siege to a city for a long time, **fighting** against it to capture it,
Jos 9: 2 [C] they came together to **make war** against Joshua and Israel.

Jos 10: 5 [C] and took up positions against Gibeon and **attacked** it.
10: 14 [C] listened to a man. Surely the LORD *was* **fighting** for Israel!
10: 25 [C] LORD will do to all the enemies you *are going to* **fight**."
10: 29 [C] him moved on from Makkedah to Libnah and **attacked** it.
10: 31 [C] to Lachish; he took up positions against it and **attacked** it.
10: 34 [C] to Eglon; they took up positions against it and **attacked** it.
10: 36 [C] with him went up from Eglon to Hebron and **attacked** it.
10: 38 [C] and all Israel with him turned around and **attacked** Debir.
10: 42 [C] because the LORD, the God of Israel, **fought** for Israel.
11: 5 [C] together at the Waters of Merom, to **fight** against Israel.
19: 47 [C] so they went up and **attacked** Leshem, took it, put it to the
23: 3 [C] your sake; it was the LORD your God who **fought** for you.
23: 10 [C] because the LORD your God **fights** for you, just as he
24: 8 [C] *They* **fought** against you, but I gave them into your hands.
24: 9 [C] of Zippor, the king of Moab, prepared *to* **fight** against Israel,
24: 11 [C] The citizens of Jericho **fought** against you, as did also the
Jdg 1: 1 [C] be the first to go up and **fight** for us against the Canaanites?"
1: 3 [C] the territory allotted to us, *to* **fight** against the Canaanites.
1: 5 [C] there that they found Adoni-Bezek and **fought** against him,
1: 8 [C] The men of Judah **attacked** Jerusalem also and took it. They
1: 9 [C] the men of Judah went down to **fight** against the Canaanites
5: 19 [C] "Kings came, *they* **fought**; the kings of Canaan fought at
5: 19 [C] the kings of Canaan **fought** at Taanach by the waters of
5: 20 [C] From the heavens the stars **fought**, from their courses they
5: 20 [C] stars fought, from their courses *they* **fought** against Sisera.
8: 1 [C] Why didn't you call us when you went to **fight** Midian?"
9: 17 [C] to think that my father **fought** for you, risked his life to
9: 38 [C] Aren't these the men you ridiculed? Go out and **fight** them!"
9: 39 [C] Gaal led out the citizens of Shechem and **fought** Abimelech.
9: 45 [C] All that day Abimelech **pressed** *his* **attack** against the city
9: 52 [C] Abimelech went to the tower and **stormed** it. But as he
10: 9 [C] The Ammonites also crossed the Jordan to **fight** against
10: 18 [C] "Whoever will launch *the* **attack** against the Ammonites will
11: 4 [C] Some time later, when the Ammonites **made war** on Israel,
11: 5 [C] the **[RPH]** elders of Gilead went to get Jephthah from the
11: 6 [C] "be our commander, so *we can* **fight** the Ammonites."
11: 8 [C] come with us *to* **fight** the Ammonites, and you will be our
11: 9 [C] "Suppose you take me back to **fight** the Ammonites
11: 12 [C] "What do you have against us that *you have* **attacked** our
11: 20 [C] all his men and encamped at Jahaz and **fought** with Israel.
11: 25 [C] Did he ever quarrel with Israel or **fight** [+4309] with them?
11: 25 [C] Did he ever quarrel with Israel or **fight** [+4309] with them?
11: 27 [C] but you are doing me wrong by **waging war** against me.
11: 32 [C] Jephthah went over to **fight** the Ammonites, and the LORD
12: 1 [C] "Why did you go to **fight** the Ammonites without calling us
12: 3 [C] over them. Now why have you come up today to **fight** me?"
12: 4 [C] together the men of Gilead and **fought** against Ephraim.
1Sa 4: 9 [C] the Hebrews, as they have been to you. Be men, and **fight**!"
4: 10 [C] So the Philistines **fought**, and the Israelites were defeated
8: 20 [C] king to lead us and to go out before us and **fight** our battles."
12: 9 [C] and the king of Moab, *who* **fought** against them.
13: 5 [C] The Philistines assembled to **fight** Israel, with three thousand
14: 47 [C] over Israel, *he* **fought** against their enemies on every side:
15: 18 [C] **make war** on them until you have wiped them out.'
17: 9 [C] If he is able to **fight** and kill me, we will become your
17: 10 [C] ranks of Israel! Give me a man and *let us* **fight** each other."
17: 19 [C] Israel in the Valley of Elah, **fighting** against the Philistines."
17: 32 [C] of this Philistine; your servant will go and **fight** him."
17: 33 [C] are not able to go out against this Philistine and **fight** him;
18: 17 [C] only serve me bravely and **fight** the battles of the LORD."
19: 8 [C] broke out, and David went out and **fought** the Philistines.
23: 1 [C] the Philistines *are* **fighting** against Keilah and are looting the
23: 5 [C] **fought** the Philistines and carried off their livestock.
25: 28 [C] for my master, because he **fights** the LORD's battles.
28: 1 [C] In those days the Philistines gathered their forces to **fight**
28: 15 [C] "The Philistines *are* **fighting** against me, and God has turned
29: 8 [C] can't I go and **fight** against the enemies of my lord the king?"
31: 1 [C] Now the Philistines **fought** against Israel; the Israelites fled
2Sa 2: 28 [C] they no longer pursued Israel, nor did they **fight** anymore.
8: 10 [C] congratulate him on his victory *in* **battle** over Hadadezer,
10: 17 [C] their battle lines to meet David and **fought** against him.
11: 17 [C] When the men of the city came out and **fought** against Joab,
11: 20 [C] may ask you, 'Why did you get so close to the city to **fight**?
12: 26 [C] Meanwhile Joab **fought** against Rabbah of the Ammonites
12: 27 [C] "*I have* **fought** against Rabbah and taken its water supply.
12: 29 [C] and went to Rabbah, and **attacked** and captured it.
21: 15 [C] David went down with his men *to* **fight** *against* the
1Ki 12: 21 [C] to **make war** against the house of Israel and to regain the
12: 24 [C] Do not go up *to* **fight** against your brothers, the Israelites.
14: 19 [C] other events of Jeroboam's reign, *his* **wars** and how he ruled,
20: 1 [C] he went up and besieged Samaria and **attacked** it.
20: 23 [C] if *we* **fight** them on the plains, surely we will be stronger than
20: 25 [C] and chariot for chariot—so *we can* **fight** Israel on the plains.
22: 31 [C] "*Do* not **fight** *with* anyone, small or great, except the king of
22: 32 [C] So they turned to **attack** him, but when Jehoshaphat cried
22: 45 [22:46] [C] the things he achieved and *his* **military exploits**,
2Ki 3: 21 [C] had heard that the kings had come to **fight** against them;
6: 8 [C] Now the king of Aram was **at war** with Israel.
8: 29 [C] on him at Ramoth in his **battle** with Hazael king of Aram.
9: 15 [C] had inflicted on him in the **battle** with Hazael king of Aram.)
10: 3 [C] on his father's throne. Then **fight** for your master's house."
12: 17 [12:18] [C] of Aram went up and **attacked** Gath and captured it.
13: 12 [C] including *his* **war** against Amaziah king of Judah,
14: 15 [C] including *his* **war** against Amaziah king of Judah,
14: 28 [C] Jeroboam's reign, all he did, and his **military** achievements,
16: 5 [C] and besieged Ahaz, but they could not **overpower** him.
19: 8 [C] he withdrew and found the king **fighting** against Libnah.
19: 9 [C] king ⌊of Egypt⌋, was marching out to **fight** against him.
1Ch 10: 1 [C] Now the Philistines **fought** against Israel; the Israelites fled
18: 10 [C] congratulate him on his victory *in* **battle** over Hadadezer,
19: 17 [C] to meet the Arameans in battle, and *they* **fought** against him.
2Ch 11: 1 [C] to **make war** against Israel and to regain the kingdom for
11: 4 [C] Do not go up *to* **fight** against your brothers. Go home,
13: 12 [C] Men of Israel, *do* not **fight** against the LORD, the God of
17: 10 [C] so that *they did* not **make war** with Jehoshaphat.
18: 30 [C] "*Do* not **fight** *with* anyone, small or great, except the king of
18: 31 [C] So they turned to **attack** him, but Jehoshaphat cried out,
20: 17 [C] You *will* not *have* to **fight** this **battle**. Take up your
20: 29 [C] how the LORD *had* **fought** against the enemies of Israel.
22: 6 [C] on him at Ramoth in his **battle** with Hazael king of Aram.
26: 6 [C] He went *to* **war** against the Philistines and broke down the
27: 5 [C] Jotham **made war** on the king of the Ammonites
32: 8 [C] us is the LORD our God to help us and to **fight** our battles."
35: 20 [C] Neco king of Egypt went up to **fight** at Carchemish on the
35: 22 [C] from him, but disguised himself to **engage** him **in battle**.
35: 22 [C] but went to **fight** him on the plain of Megiddo.
Ne 4: 8 [4:2] [C] **fight** against Jerusalem and stir up trouble against it.
4: 14 [4:8] [C] **fight** for your brothers, your sons and your daughters,
4: 20 [4:14] [C] the trumpet, join us there. Our God *will* **fight** for us!"
Ps 35: 1 [A] contend with me; **fight** against those who fight against me.
35: 1 [A] contend with me; fight against *those who* **fight** *against* me.
56: 1 [56:2] [A] hotly pursue me; all day long they press *their* **attack**.
56: 2 [56:3] [A] all day long; many *are* **attacking** me in their pride.
109: 3 [C] of hatred they surround me; *they* **attack** me without cause.
Isa 7: 1 [C] against Jerusalem, but they could not **overpower** [+6584] it.
19: 2 [C] brother *will* **fight** against brother, neighbor against neighbor,
20: 1 [C] of Assyria, came to Ashdod and **attacked** and captured it—
30: 32 [C] *as he* **fights** them in battle *with* the blows of his arm.
37: 8 [C] he withdrew and found the king **fighting** against Libnah.
37: 9 [C] king ⌊of Egypt⌋, was marching out to **fight** against him.
63: 10 [C] and became their enemy and *he* himself **fought** against them.
Jer 1: 19 [C] *They will* **fight** against you but will not overcome you, for I
15: 20 [C] *they will* **fight** against you but will not overcome you, for I
21: 2 [C] because Nebuchadnezzar king of Babylon *is* **attacking** us.
21: 4 [C] which you *are* using *to* **fight** the king of Babylon and the
21: 5 [C] *I* myself *will* **fight** against you with an outstretched hand
32: 5 [C] If *you* **fight** against the Babylonians, you will not succeed.' "
32: 24 [C] will be handed over to the Babylonians who *are* **attacking** it.
32: 29 [C] The Babylonians who *are* **attacking** this city will come in
33: 5 [C] *in the* **fight** with the Babylonians: 'They will be filled with
34: 1 [C] peoples in the empire he ruled *were* **fighting** against
34: 7 [C] while the army of the king of Babylon *was* **fighting** against
34: 22 [C] this city. *They will* **fight** against it, take it and burn it down.
37: 8 [C] the Babylonians will return and **attack** this city; they will
37: 10 [C] to defeat the entire Babylonian army that *is* **attacking** you
41: 12 [C] all their men and went to **fight** Ishmael son of Nethaniah.
51: 30 [C] Babylon's warriors have stopped **fighting**; they remain in
Da 10: 20 [C] Soon I will return to **fight** against the prince of Persia,
11: 11 [C] march out in a rage and **fight** against the king of the North,
Zec 10: 5 [C] is with them, *they will* **fight** and overthrow the horsemen.
14: 3 [C] Then the LORD will go out and **fight** against those nations,
14: 3 [C] fight against those nations, as he **fights** in the day of battle.
14: 14 [C] Judah too *will* **fight** at Jerusalem. The wealth of all the

4310 ²לָחַם *lāḥam*², v. [6] [√ 4312]

eat [4], consuming [1], dine [1]

Dt 32: 24 [B] against them, **consuming** pestilence and deadly plague;
Ps 141: 4 [A] men who are evildoers; *let me* not **eat** of their delicacies.
Pr 4: 17 [A] *They* **eat** the bread of wickedness and drink the wine of
9: 5 [A] "Come, **eat** my food and drink the wine I have mixed.
23: 1 [A] When you sit to **dine** with a ruler, note well what is before
23: 6 [A] *Do* not **eat** the food of a stingy man, do not crave his

4311 לָחֶם *lāḥem*, n.[m.]. [1] [√ 4309]

war [1]

Jdg 5: 8 **war** came to the city gates, and not a shield or spear was seen

4312 לֶחֶם leḥem, n.m. & f. [298] [→ 1107, 3788, 4310; Ar 10389]

food [124], bread [116], *untranslated* [24], loaves of bread [6], something[s] [3], bread [+3971] [2], meal [2], provisions [2], something to eat [+7326] [2], baked [1], cake [+2705] [1], crops [1], daily bread [+2976] [1], eat [1], feast [1], feed [1], food [+7326] [1], fruit [1], loaf [+3971] [1], loaves [1], meal [+430] [1], nothing [+4202] [1], overfed [+8430] [1], provided for [+430+2118+2256+4200] [1], stay for a meal [+430] [1], swallow up [1]

Ge 3:19 By the sweat of your brow you will eat your **food** until you return
14:18 Then Melchizedek king of Salem brought out **bread** and wine.
18: 5 Let me get you **something to eat** [+7326], so you can be refreshed
21:14 Early the next morning Abraham took *some* **food** and a skin of
25:34 Then Jacob gave Esau *some* **bread** and some lentil stew. He ate
27:17 to her son Jacob the tasty food and the **bread** she had made.
28:20 I am taking and will give me **food** to eat and clothes to wear
31:54 there in the hill country and invited his relatives to a **meal** [+430].
31:54 to a meal. After they had eaten, **[NIE]** they spent the night there.
37:25 As they sat down to eat their **meal**, they looked up and saw a
39: 6 he did not concern himself with anything except the **food** he ate.
41:54 all the other lands, but in the whole land of Egypt there was **food**.
41:55 began to feel the famine, the people cried to Pharaoh for **food**.
43:25 because they had heard that they were to eat there. **[NIE]**
43:31 he came out and, controlling himself, said, "Serve the **food**."
43:32 not eat with Hebrews, **[NIE]** for that is detestable to Egyptians.
45:23 loaded with grain and **bread** and other provisions for his journey.
47:12 his father and his brothers and all his father's household with **food**,
47:13 There was no **food**, however, in the whole region
47:15 was gone, all Egypt came to Joseph and said, "Give us **food**.
47:17 and he gave them **food** in exchange for their horses, their sheep
47:17 he brought them through that year with **food** in exchange for all
47:19 Buy us and our land in exchange for **food**, and we with our land
49:20 "Asher's **food** will be rich; he will provide delicacies fit for a king.
Ex 2:20 "Why did you leave him? Invite him to have **something**[s] to eat."
16: 3 There we sat around pots of meat and ate all the **food** we wanted,
16: 4 said to Moses, "I will rain down **bread** from heaven for you.
16: 8 to eat in the evening and all the **bread** you want in the morning,
16:12 will eat meat, and in the morning you will be filled with **bread**.
16:15 said to them, "It is the **bread** the LORD has given you to eat.
16:22 gathered twice as much—**[RPH]** two omers for each person—
16:29 that is why on the sixth day he gives you **bread** for two days.
16:32 so they can see the **bread** I gave you to eat in the desert when I
18:12 Aaron came with all the elders of Israel to eat **bread** with Moses'
23:25 your God, and his blessing will be on your **food** and water.
25:30 Put the **bread** *of* the Presence on this table to be before me at all
29: 2 without yeast, make **bread**, and cakes mixed with oil, and wafers
29:23 take a **loaf** [+3971], and a cake made with oil, and a wafer.
29:23 take a loaf, and a **cake** *made* **with** [+2705] oil, and a wafer.
29:32 are to eat the meat of the ram and the **bread** that is in the basket.
29:34 meat of the ordination ram or any **bread** is left over till morning,
34:28 forty days and forty nights without eating **bread** or drinking water.
35:13 with its poles and all its articles and the **bread** *of* the Presence;
39:36 the table with all its articles and the **bread** *of* the Presence;
40:23 set out the **bread** on it before the LORD, as the LORD
Lev 3:11 The priest shall burn them on the altar as **food**, an offering made to
3:16 The priest shall burn them on the altar as **food**, an offering made
7:13 he is to present an offering with cakes of **bread** made with yeast.
8:26 took a cake of bread, and **[RPH]** one made with oil, and a wafer;
8:31 eat it there with the **bread** from the basket of ordination offerings,
8:32 Then burn up the rest of the meat and the **bread**.
21: 6 to the LORD by fire, the **food** *of* their God, they are to be holy.
21: 8 Regard them as holy, because they offer up the **food** *of* your God.
21:17 who has a defect may come near to offer the **food** *of* his God.
21:21 has a defect; he must not come near to offer the **food** *of* his God.
21:22 He may eat the most holy **food** *of* his God, as well as the holy
22: 7 and after that he may eat the sacred offerings, for they are his **food**.
22:11 or if a slave is born in his household, that slave may eat his **food**.
22:13 her father's house as in her youth, she may eat of her father's **food**.
22:25 the hand of a foreigner and offer them as the **food** *of* your God.
23:14 You must not eat any **bread**, or roasted or new grain, until the very
23:17 bring two **loaves** made of two-tenths of an ephah of fine flour,
23:18 Present with this **bread** seven male lambs, each a year old
23:20 as a wave offering, together with the **bread** *of* the firstfruits.
24: 7 some pure incense as a memorial portion to represent the **bread**
26: 5 you will eat all the **food** you want and live in safety in your land.
26:26 When I cut off your supply of **bread**, ten women will be able to
26:26 of bread, ten women will be able to bake your **bread** in one oven,
26:26 bread in one oven, and they will dole out the **bread** by weight.
Nu 4: 7 the **bread** that is continually there is to remain on it.
14: 9 afraid of the people of the land, because we will **swallow** them **up**.
15:19 you eat the **food** *of* the land, present a portion as an offering to the
21: 5 There is no **bread**! There is no water! And we detest this miserable
21: 5 is no bread! There is no water! And we detest this miserable **food**!"
28: 2 'See that you present to me at the appointed time the **food** for my
28:24 In this way prepare the **food** *for* the offering made by fire every
Dt 8: 3 to teach you that man does not live on **bread** alone but on every
8: 9 a land where **bread** will not be scarce and you will lack nothing;
9: 9 forty days and forty nights; I ate no **bread** and drank no water.
9:18 I ate no **bread** and drank no water, because of all the sin you had
10:18 and the widow, and loves the alien, giving him **food** and clothing.
16: 3 the **bread** *of* affliction, because you left Egypt in haste—
23: 4 [23:5] For they did not come to meet you with **bread** and water
29: 6 [29:5] You ate no **bread** and drank no wine or other fermented
Jos 9: 5 old clothes. All the **bread** *of* their food supply was dry and moldy.
9:12 This **bread** *of* ours was warm when we packed it at home on the
Jdg 7:13 "A round loaf of barley **bread** came tumbling into the Midianite
8: 5 said to the men of Succoth, "Give my troops *some* **bread** [+3971];
8: 6 in your possession? Why should we give **bread** to your troops?"
8:15 Why should we give **bread** to your exhausted men?' "
13:16 "Even though you detain me, I will not eat any of your **food**.
19: 5 his son-in-law, "Refresh yourself with **something to eat** [+7326];
19:19 We have both straw and fodder for our donkeys and **bread**
Ru 1: 6 had come to the aid of his people by providing **food** for them,
2:14 over here. Have some **bread** and dip it in the wine vinegar."
1Sa 2: 5 Those who were full hire themselves out for **food**, but those who
2:36 before him for a piece of silver and a crust of **bread** and plead,
2:36 me to some priestly office so I can have **food** [+7326] to eat." '"
9: 7 what can we give the man? The **food** in our sacks is gone.
10: 3 another three loaves of **bread**, and another a skin of wine.
10: 4 They will greet you and offer you two loaves of **bread**, which you
14:24 "Cursed be any man who eats **food** before evening comes,
14:24 myself on my enemies!" So none of the troops tasted **food**.
14:28 a strict oath, saying, 'Cursed be any man who eats **food** today!'
16:20 So Jesse took a donkey loaded with **bread**, a skin of wine
17:17 these ten **loaves of bread** for your brothers and hurry to their
20:24 the New Moon festival came, the king sat down **[NIE]** to eat.
20:27 "Why hasn't the son of Jesse come to the **meal**, either yesterday
20:34 **[RPH]** because he was grieved at his father's shameful treatment
21: 3 [21:4] Give me five **loaves of bread**, or whatever you can find."
21: 4 [21:5] "I don't have any ordinary **bread** on hand;
21: 4 [21:5] on hand; however, there is *some* consecrated **bread** here—
21: 6 [21:7] since there was no **bread** there except the bread of the
21: 6 [21:7] since there was no bread there except the **bread** *of* the
21: 6 [21:7] and replaced by hot **bread** on the day it was taken away.
22:13 giving him **bread** and a sword and inquiring of God for him,
25:11 Why should I take my **bread** and water, and the meat I have
25:18 She took two hundred **loaves of bread**, two skins of wine,
28:20 was gone, for he had eaten **nothing** [+4202] all that day and night.
28:22 to your servant and let me give you some **food** so you may eat
30:11 him to David. They gave him water to drink and **food** to eat—
30:12 for he had not eaten *any* **food** or drunk any water for three days
2Sa 3:29 leans on a crutch or who falls by the sword or who lacks **food**."
3:35 all came and urged David to eat **something**[s] while it was still day;
3:35 so severely, if I taste **bread** or anything else before the sun sets!"
6:19 he gave a loaf of **bread**, a cake of dates and a cake of raisins to
9: 7 grandfather Saul, and you will always eat **[NIE]** at my table."
9:10 master's grandson *may be* **provided for** [+430+2118+2256+4200].
9:10 grandson of your master, will always eat **[NIE]** at my table."
12:17 but he refused, and he would not eat any **food** with them.
12:20 his own house, and at his request they served him **food**, and he ate.
12:21 but now that the child is dead, you get up and eat!" **[NIE]**
13: 5 like my sister Tamar to come and give me **something**[s] to eat.
16: 1 of donkeys saddled and loaded with two hundred **loaves of bread**,
16: 2 household to ride on, the **bread** and fruit are for the men to eat,
1Ki 4:22 [5:2] Solomon's daily **provisions** were thirty cors of fine flour
5: 9 [5:23] you are to grant my wish by providing **food** for my royal
7:48 the golden table on which was the **bread** *of* the Presence;
11:18 who gave Hadad a house and land and provided him with **food**.
13: 8 would not go with you, nor would I eat **bread** or drink water here.
13: 9 'You must not eat **bread** or drink water or return by the way you
13:15 the prophet said to him, "Come home with me and eat." **[RPH]**
13:16 with you, nor can I eat **bread** or drink water with you in this place.
13:17 'You must not eat **bread** or drink water there or return by the way
13:18 'Bring him back with you to your house so that he may eat **bread**
13:19 of God returned with him and ate **[RPH]** and drank in his house.
13:22 You came back and ate **bread** and drank water in the place where
13:22 water in the place where he told you not to eat **[RPH]** or drink.
13:23 When the man of God had finished eating **[RPH]** and drinking,
14: 3 Take ten **loaves of bread** with you, some cakes and a jar of honey,
17: 6 The ravens brought him **bread** and meat in the morning and bread
17: 6 and meat in the morning and **bread** and meat in the evening,
17:11 going to get it, he called, "And bring me, please, a piece of **bread**."
18: 4 fifty in each, and had supplied them with **food** and water.)
18:13 in two caves, fifty in each, and supplied them with **food** and water.
21: 4 my fathers." He lay on his bed sulking and refused to eat. **[NIE]**
21: 5 asked him, "Why are you so sullen? Why won't you eat?" **[NIE]**

1Ki 21: 7 how you act as king over Israel? Get up and eat! **[NIE]** Cheer up.
22:27 Put this fellow in prison and give him nothing but **bread**
2Ki 4: 8 woman was there, who urged him to **stay for a meal** [+430].
4: 8 So whenever he came by, he stopped there to eat. **[RPH]**
4:42 bringing the man of God twenty **loaves of** barley **bread** baked
4:42 God twenty loaves of barley bread **baked** *from* the first ripe grain,
6:22 Set **food** and water before them so that they may eat and drink
18:32 a land of grain and new wine, a land of **bread** and vineyards,
25: 3 had become so severe that there was no **food** for the people to eat.
25:29 and for the rest of his life ate **[NIE]** regularly at the king's table.
1Ch 9:32 of preparing for every Sabbath the **bread** set out on the table.
12:40 [12:41] Zebulun and Naphtali came bringing **food** on donkeys,
16: 3 he gave a loaf of **bread**, a cake of dates and a cake of raisins to
23:29 They were in charge of the **bread** set out on the table, the flour for
2Ch 4:19 golden altar; the tables on which was the **bread** *of* the Presence;
13:11 They set out the **bread** on the ceremonially clean table and light
18:26 Put this fellow in prison and give him nothing but **bread**
Ezr 10: 6 While he was there, he ate no **food** and drank no water, because he
Ne 5:14 neither I nor my brothers ate the **food** *allotted to* the governor.
5:15 and took forty shekels of silver from them in addition to **food**
5:18 of all this, I never demanded the **food** *allotted to* the governor,
9:15 In their hunger you gave them **bread** from heaven and in their
10:33 [10:34] for the **bread** set out on the table; for the regular grain
13: 2 because they had not met the Israelites with **food** and water
Job 3:24 For sighing comes to me instead of **food**; my groans pour out like
6: 7 I refuse to touch it; such **food** makes me ill.
15:23 He wanders about—**food** for vultures; he knows the day of
20:14 yet his **food** will turn sour in his stomach; it will become the
22: 7 no water to the weary and you withheld **food** from the hungry,
24: 5 of foraging food; the wasteland provides **food** for their children.
27:14 their fate is the sword; his offspring will never have enough to **eat**.
28: 5 The earth, from which **food** comes, is transformed below as by
30: 4 gathered salt herbs, and their **food** was the root of the broom tree.
33:20 so that his very being finds **food** repulsive and his soul loathes the
42:11 had known him before came and ate **[NIE]** with him in his house.
Ps 14: 4 those who devour my people as men eat **bread** and who do not call
37:25 never seen the righteous forsaken or their children begging **bread**.
41: 9 [41:10] close friend, whom I trusted, he who shared my **bread**,
42: 3 [42:4] My tears have been my **food** day and night, while men say
53: 4 [53:5] those who devour my people as men eat **bread** and who do
78:20 and streams flowed abundantly. But can he also give us **food**?
78:25 Men ate the **bread** *of* angels; he sent them all the food they could
80: 5 [80:6] You have fed them with the **bread** *of* tears; you have made
102: 4 [102:5] and withered like grass; I forget to eat my **food**.
102: 9 [102:10] For I eat ashes as my **food** and mingle my drink with
104:14 plants for man to cultivate—bringing forth **food** from the earth:
104:15 oil to make his face shine, and **bread** that sustains his heart.
105:16 down famine on the land and destroyed all their supplies of **food**;
105:40 he brought them quail and satisfied them with the **bread** *of* heaven.
127: 2 In vain you rise early and stay up late, toiling for **food** to eat—
132:15 her with abundant provisions; her poor will I satisfy with **food**.
136:25 who gives **food** to every creature.
146: 7 upholds the cause of the oppressed and gives **food** to the hungry.
147: 9 He provides **food** for the cattle and for the young ravens when they
Pr 4:17 They eat the **bread** *of* wickedness and drink the wine of violence.
6: 8 yet it stores its **provisions** in summer and gathers its food at
6:26 for the prostitute reduces you to a loaf of **bread**, and the adulteress
9: 5 "Come, eat my **food** and drink the wine I have mixed.
9:17 "Stolen water is sweet; **food** eaten in secret is delicious!"
12: 9 yet have a servant than pretend to be somebody and have no **food**.
12:11 He who works his land will have abundant **food**, but he who chases
20:13 or you will grow poor; stay awake and you will have **food** to spare.
20:17 **Food** *gained by* fraud tastes sweet to a man, but he ends up with a
22: 9 man will himself be blessed, for he shares his **food** with the poor.
23: 3 Do not crave his delicacies, for that **food** is deceptive.
23: 6 Do not eat the **food** *of* a stingy man, do not crave his delicacies;
25:21 If your enemy is hungry, give him **food** to eat; if he is thirsty,
27:27 You will have plenty of goats' milk to **feed** you and your family
27:27 and **[RPH]** your family and to nourish your servant girls.
28: 3 who oppresses the poor is like a driving rain that leaves no **crops**.
28:19 He who works his land will have abundant **food**, but the one who
28:21 is not good—yet a man will do wrong for a piece of **bread**.
30: 8 poverty nor riches, but give me only my **daily bread** [+2976].
30:22 a servant who becomes king, a fool who is full of **food**,
30:25 of little strength, yet they store up their **food** in the summer;
31:14 She is like the merchant ships, bringing her **food** from afar.
31:27 the affairs of her household and does not eat the **bread** *of* idleness.
Ecc 9: 7 Go, eat your **food** with gladness, and drink your wine with a joyful
9:11 nor does **food** come to the wise or wealth to the brilliant or favor to
10:19 A **feast** is made for laughter, and wine makes life merry,
11: 1 Cast your **bread** upon the waters, for after many days you will find
Isa 3: 1 and support: all supplies of **food** and all supplies of water,
3: 7 I have no **food** or clothing in my house; do not make me the leader
4: 1 and say, "We will eat our own **food** and provide our own clothes;
21:14 for the thirsty; you who live in Tema, bring **food** *for* the fugitives.
28:28 Grain must be ground to make **bread**; so one does not go on
30:20 Although the Lord gives you the **bread** *of* adversity and the water
30:23 and the **food** that comes from the land will be rich and plentiful.
33:16 His **bread** will be supplied, and water will not fail him.
36:17 a land of grain and new wine, a land of **bread** and vineyards.
44:15 it he takes and warms himself, he kindles a fire and bakes **bread**.
44:19 I even baked **bread** over its coals, I roasted meat and I ate.
51:14 they will not die in their dungeon, nor will they lack **bread**.
55: 2 Why spend money on *what* is not **bread**, and your labor on what
55:10 so that it yields seed for the sower and **bread** for the eater,
58: 7 Is it not to share your **food** with the hungry and to provide the poor
65:25 lion will eat straw like the ox, but dust will be the serpent's **food**.
Jer 5:17 They will devour your harvests and **food**, devour your sons
11:19 plotted against me, saying, "Let us destroy the tree and its **fruit**;
37:21 given **bread** [+3971] from the street of the bakers each day until
37:21 of the bakers each day until all the **bread** in the city was gone.
38: 9 where he will starve to death when there is no longer any **bread** in
41: 1 Ahikam at Mizpah. While they were eating **[NIE]** together there,
42:14 we will not see war or hear the trumpet or be hungry for **bread**,'
44:17 At that time we had plenty of **food** and were well off and suffered
52: 6 had become so severe that there was no **food** for the people to eat.
52:33 and for the rest of his life ate **[NIE]** regularly at the king's table.
La 1:11 All her people groan as they search for **bread**; they barter their
4: 4 its mouth; the children beg for **bread**, but no one gives it to them.
5: 6 We submitted to Egypt and Assyria to get enough **bread**.
5: 9 We get our **bread** at the risk of our lives because of the sword in
Eze 4: 9 put them in a storage jar and use them to make **bread** for yourself.
4:13 "In this way the people of Israel will eat defiled **food** among the
4:15 "I will let you bake your **bread** over cow manure instead of human
4:16 "Son of man, I will cut off the supply of **food** in Jerusalem.
4:16 The people will eat rationed **food** in anxiety and drink rationed
4:17 for **food** and water will be scarce. They will be appalled at the
5:16 and more famine upon you and cut off your supply of **food**.
12:18 "Son of man, tremble as you eat your **food**, and shudder in fear as
12:19 They will eat their **food** in anxiety and drink their water in despair,
13:19 my people for a few handfuls of barley and scraps of **bread**.
14:13 and I stretch out my hand against it to cut off its **food** supply
16:19 Also the **food** I provided for you—the fine flour, olive oil
16:49 her daughters were arrogant, **overfed** [+8430] and unconcerned;
18: 7 He does not commit robbery but gives his **food** to the hungry
18:16 He does not commit robbery but gives his **food** to the hungry
24:17 lower part of your face or eat the customary **food** ⌞*of* mourners⌟."
24:22 lower part of your face or eat the customary **food** ⌞*of* mourners⌟.
44: 3 sit inside the gateway to eat **[NIE]** in the presence of the LORD.
44: 7 desecrating my temple while you offered me **food**, fat and blood,
48:18 west side. Its produce will supply **food** for the workers of the city.
Da 10: 3 I ate no choice **food**; no meat or wine touched my lips; and I used
Hos 2: 5 [2:7] who give me my **food** and my water, my wool and my linen,
9: 4 Such sacrifices will be to them like the **bread** *of* mourners;
9: 4 This **food** will be for themselves; it will not come into the temple
Am 4: 6 you empty stomachs in every city and lack of **bread** in every town,
7:12 of Judah. Earn your **bread** there and do your prophesying there.
8:11 not a famine of **food** or a thirst for water, but a famine of hearing
Ob 1: 7 those who eat your **bread** will set a trap for you, but you will not
Hag 2:12 and that fold touches some **bread** or stew, some wine, oil
Mal 1: 7 "You place defiled **food** on my altar. "But you ask, 'How have we

4313 לַחְמִי *laḥmî*, n.pr.m. [1]

Lahmi [1]

1Ch 20: 5 Elhanan son of Jair killed **Lahmi** the brother of Goliath the Gittite,

4314 לַחְמָס *laḥmās*, n.pr.loc. [1]

Lahmas [1]

Jos 15:40 Cabbon, **Lahmas**, Kitlish,

4315 לָחַץ *lāḥaṣ*, v. [19] [→ 4316; cf. 5722]

oppressed [6], oppress [4], oppressors [2], confined [1], crushing [1], hold shut [1], oppressing [1], press [1], pressed close [1], severely oppressing [+906+4316] [1]

Ex 3: 9 [A] and I have seen the way the Egyptians *are* **oppressing** them.
22:21 [22:20] [A] "Do not mistreat an alien or **oppress** him, for you
23: 9 [A] "*Do* not **oppress** an alien; you yourselves know how it feels
Nu 22:25 [C] *she* **pressed close** to the wall, crushing Balaam's foot against
22:25 [A] pressed close to the wall, **crushing** Balaam's foot against it.
Jdg 1:34 [A] The Amorites **confined** the Danites to the hill country, not
2:18 [A] on them as they groaned under *those who* **oppressed**
4: 3 [A] and *had* cruelly **oppressed** the Israelites for twenty years,
6: 9 [A] power of Egypt and from the hand of all your **oppressors**.
10:12 [A] the Amalekites and the Maonites **oppressed** you and you
1Sa 10:18 [A] power of Egypt and all the kingdoms that **oppressed** you.'

2Ki 6:32 [A] shut the door and **hold** it **shut** *against* him.
13: 4 [A] how **severely** the king of Aram *was* **oppressing** [+906+4316]
13:22 [A] Hazael king of Aram **oppressed** Israel throughout the reign
Ps 56: 1 [56:2] [A] hotly pursue me; all day long *they* **press** their attack.
106:42 [A] Their enemies **oppressed** them and subjected them to their
Isa 19:20 [A] they cry out to the LORD because of their **oppressors**,
Jer 30:20 [A] established before me; I will punish all *who* **oppress** them.
Am 6:14 [A] *that will* **oppress** you all the way from Lebo Hamath to the

4316 לַחַץ *laḥaṣ*, n.m. [12] [√ 4315]

untranslated [2], affliction [2], nothing but [2], oppressed [2], oppression [2], severely oppressing [+906+4315] [1], way[s] [1]

Ex 3: 9 and I have seen the **way**[s] the Egyptians are oppressing them.
Dt 26: 7 LORD heard our voice and saw our misery, toil and **oppression**.
1Ki 22:27 Put this fellow in prison and give him **nothing but** bread
22:27 him nothing but bread and water **[RPH]** until I return safely.' "
2Ki 13: 4 how **severely** the king of Aram *was* **oppressing** [+906+4315]
2Ch 18:26 Put this fellow in prison and give him **nothing but** bread
18:26 him nothing but bread and **[RPH]** water until I return safely.' "
Job 36:15 he delivers in their suffering; he speaks to them in their **affliction**.
Ps 42: 9 [42:10] must I go about mourning, **oppressed** by the enemy?"
43: 2 Why must I go about mourning, **oppressed** by the enemy?
44:24 [44:25] you hide your face and forget our misery and **oppression**?
Isa 30:20 Lord gives you the bread of adversity and the water of **affliction**,

4317 לָחַשׁ *lāḥaš*, v. [3] [→ 2135, 4285, 4318; cf. 5727]

charmer [1], whisper [1], whispering among themselves [1]

2Sa 12:19 [F] that his servants *were* **whispering among themselves**
Ps 41: 7 [41:8] [F] All my enemies **whisper** together against me;
58: 5 [58:6] [D] that will not heed the tune of the **charmer**,

4318 לַחַשׁ *laḥaš*, n.[m.]. [5] [√ 4317]

charmed [2], barely whisper a prayer [+7440] [1], charms [1], enchanter [1]

Ecc 10:11 If a snake bites before it is **charmed**, there is no profit for the
Isa 3: 3 of rank, the counselor, skilled craftsman and clever **enchanter**.
3:20 and ankle chains and sashes, the perfume bottles and **charms**,
26:16 disciplined them, *they could* **barely whisper** [+7440] **a prayer**.
Jer 8:17 vipers that cannot be **charmed**, and they will bite you,"

4319 לָט *lāṭ*, n.[m.]. [7] [√ 4286]

secret arts [3], quietly [+928+2021] [2], privately [+928+2021] [1], unnoticed [+928+2021] [1]

Ex 7:22 the Egyptian magicians did the same things by their **secret arts**,
8: 7 [8:3] But the magicians did the same things by their **secret arts**;
8:18 [8:14] the magicians tried to produce gnats by their **secret arts**,
Jdg 4:21 and went **quietly** [+928+2021] to him while he lay fast asleep,
Ru 3: 7 Ruth approached **quietly** [+928+2021], uncovered his feet
1Sa 18:22 "Speak to David **privately** [+928+2021] and say, 'Look, the king is
24: 4 [24:5] you wish.' " Then David crept up **unnoticed** [+928+2021]

4320 לֹט *lōṭ*, n.[m.]. [2] [√ 4286]

myrrh [2]

Ge 37:25 Their camels were loaded with spices, balm and **myrrh**, and they
43:11 a little balm and a little honey, some spices and **myrrh**,

4321 לְטָאָה *lᵉṭā'â*, n.f. [1]

wall lizard [1]

Lev 11:30 the monitor lizard, the **wall lizard**, the skink and the chameleon.

4322 לְטוּשִׁים *lᵉṭûšîm*, n.pr.g. [1] [√ 4323]

Letushites [1]

Ge 25: 3 of Dedan were the Asshurites, the **Letushites** and the Leummites.

4323 לָטַשׁ *lāṭaš*, v. [5] [→ 4322]

sharpened [2], fastens piercing [1], forged [1], sharpen [1]

Ge 4:22 [A] *who* **forged** all kinds of tools *out of* bronze and iron.
1Sa 13:20 [A] *have* their plowshares, mattocks, axes and sickles **sharpened**.
Job 16: 9 [A] teeth at me; my opponent **fastens** on me his **piercing** eyes.
Ps 7:12 [7:13] [A] If he does not relent, *he will* **sharpen** his sword;
52: 2 [52:4] [E] it is like a **sharpened** razor, you who practice deceit.

4324 לֹיָה *lōyā*, n.f. [3] [cf. 4339]

wreaths [3]

1Ki 7:29 and below the lions and bulls were **wreaths** *of* hammered work.
7:30 a basin resting on four supports, cast with **wreaths** on each side.
7:36 on the panels, in every available space, with **wreaths** all around.

4325 לַיִל *layil*, n.m. [6] [→ 4326, 4327; cf. 4328; Ar 10391]

night [6]

Ex 12:42 Because the LORD kept vigil that **night** to bring them out of
Pr 31:18 [and her lamp does not go out at **night**. [K; see Q 4326]]
Isa 15: 1 Ar in Moab is ruined, destroyed in a **night**! Kir in Moab is ruined,
15: 1 destroyed in a night! Kir in Moab is ruined, destroyed in a **night**!
16: 3 render a decision. Make your shadow like **night**—at high noon.
21:11 what is left of the night? Watchman, what is left of the **night**?"
30:29 And you will sing as on the **night** you celebrate a holy festival;
La 2:19 [Arise, cry out in the **night**, [K; see Q 4326] as the watches]

4326 לַיְלָה *laylâ*, n.m. [227] [√ 4325; cf. 4328; Ar 10391]

night [189], nights [14], tonight [+2021] [10], midnight [+2940] [2], overnight [+1201] [2], *untranslated* [1], all night long [+928+2021] [1], all-night [+2021+3972] [1], dark [1], last night [+2021] [1], midnight [+2021+2942] [1], nightfall [+2021] [1], nightfall [1], nighttime [1], nocturnal [1]

Ge 1: 5 God called the light "day," and the darkness he called "**night**."
1:14 lights in the expanse of the sky to separate the day from the **night**,
1:16 light to govern the day and the lesser light to govern the **night**.
1:18 to govern the day and the **night**, and to separate light from
7: 4 now I will send rain on the earth for forty days and forty **nights**,
7:12 And rain fell on the earth forty days and forty **nights**.
8:22 and heat, summer and winter, day and **night** will never cease."
14:15 *During the* **night** Abram divided his men to attack them and he
19: 5 to Lot, "Where are the men who came to you **tonight** [+2021]?
19:33 That **night** they got their father to drink wine, and the older
19:34 Let's get him to drink wine again **tonight** [+2021], and you go in
19:35 So they got their father to drink wine that **night** also,
20: 3 But God came to Abimelech in a dream one **night** and said to him,
26:24 That **night** the LORD appeared to him and said, "I am the God of
30:15 "he can sleep with you **tonight** [+2021] in return for your son's
30:16 you with my son's mandrakes." So he slept with her that **night**.
31:24 Then God came to Laban the Aramean in a dream at **night**
31:39 payment from me for whatever was stolen by day or **night**.
31:40 The heat consumed me in the daytime and the cold at **night**,
32:13 [32:14] He spent the **night** there, and from what he had with him
32:21 [32:22] ahead of him, but he himself spent the **night** in the camp.
32:22 [32:23] That **night** Jacob got up and took his two wives, his two
40: 5 had a dream the same **night**, and each dream had a meaning of its
41:11 Each of us had a dream the same **night**, and each dream had a
46: 2 And God spoke to Israel in a vision at **night** and said, "Jacob!
Ex 10:13 an east wind blow across the land all that day and all that **night**.
11: 4 'About **midnight** [+2940] I will go throughout Egypt.
12: 8 That same **night** they are to eat the meat roasted over the fire,
12:12 "On that same **night** I will pass through Egypt and strike down
12:29 At **midnight** [+2021+2942] the LORD struck down all the
12:30 and all his officials and all the Egyptians got up *during* the **night**,
12:31 *During* the **night** Pharaoh summoned Moses and Aaron and said,
12:42 on this **night** all the Israelites are to keep vigil to honor the LORD
13:21 on their way and *by* **night** in a pillar of fire to give them light,
13:21 of fire to give them light, so that they could travel by day or **night**.
13:22 Neither the pillar of cloud by day nor the pillar of fire *by* **night** left
14:20 *Throughout* the **night** the cloud brought darkness to the one side
14:20 light to the other side; so neither went near the other all **night** long.
14:21 all that **night** the LORD drove the sea back with a strong east
24:18 And he stayed on the mountain forty days and forty **nights**.
34:28 forty days and forty **nights** without eating bread or drinking water.
40:38 fire was in the cloud *by* **night**, in the sight of all the house of Israel
Lev 6: 9 [6:2] is to remain on the altar hearth throughout the **night**,
8:35 and **night** for seven days and do what the LORD requires,
Nu 9:16 to be; the cloud covered it, and *at* **night** it looked like fire.
9:21 Whether by day or *by* **night**, whenever the cloud lifted, they set
11: 9 When the dew settled on the camp *at* **night**, the manna also came
11:32 All that day and **night** and all the next day the people went out
14: 1 That **night** all the people of the community raised their voices
14:14 before them in a pillar of cloud by day and a pillar of fire *by* **night**.
22: 8 "Spend the **night** here," Balaam said to them, "and I will bring you
22:19 Now stay here **tonight** [+2021] as the others did, and I will find
22:20 That **night** God came to Balaam and said, "Since these men have
Dt 1:33 in fire *by* **night** and in a cloud by day, to search out places for you
9: 9 with you, I stayed on the mountain forty days and forty **nights**;
9:11 At the end of the forty days and forty **nights**, the LORD gave me
9:18 I fell prostrate before the LORD for forty days and forty **nights**;
9:25 I lay prostrate before the LORD those forty days and forty **nights**
10:10 Now I had stayed on the mountain forty days and **nights**, as I did
16: 1 in the month of Abib he brought you out of Egypt *by* **night**.
23:10 [23:11] of your men is unclean because of a **nocturnal** emission,
28:66 filled with dread both **night** and day, never sure of your life.
Jos 1: 8 meditate on it day and **night**, so that you may be careful to do
2: 2 Some of the Israelites have come here **tonight** [+2021] to spy out
4: 3 and put them down at the place where you stay **tonight** [+2021]."

Jos 8: 3 thirty thousand of his best fighting men and sent them out *at* **night**
8: 9 to the west of Ai—but Joshua spent that **night** with the people.
8: 13 ambush to the west of it. That **night** Joshua went into the valley.
10: 9 After an **all-night** [+2021+3972] march from Gilgal, Joshua took
Jdg 6: 25 That same **night** the LORD said to him, "Take the second bull
6: 27 the men of the town, he did it *at* **night** rather than in the daytime.
6: 40 That **night** God did so. Only the fleece was dry; all the ground was
7: 9 During that **night** the LORD said to Gideon, "Get up, go down
9: 32 *during* the **night** you and your men should come and lie in wait in
9: 34 So Abimelech and all his troops set out *by* **night** and took up
16: 2 the place and lay in wait for him all **night** at the city gate.
16: 2 They made no move during the **night**, saying, "At dawn we'll kill
16: 3 Samson lay there only until the middle of the **night**. Then he got
16: 3 Then he got up **[RPH]** and took hold of the doors of the city gate,
19: 25 they raped her and abused her throughout the **night**, and at dawn
20: 5 *During* the **night** the men of Gibeah came after me and surrounded
Ru 1: 12 even if I had a husband **tonight** [+2021] and then gave birth to
3: 2 a kinsman of ours? **Tonight** [+2021] he will be winnowing barley
3: 8 In the middle of the **night** something startled the man, and he
3: 13 Stay here *for* the **night**, and in the morning if he wants to redeem,
1Sa 14: 34 meat with blood still in it.' " So everyone brought his ox that **night**
14: 36 "Let us go down after the Philistines *by* **night** and plunder them till
15: 11 Samuel was troubled, and he cried out to the LORD all that **night**.
15: 16 "Let me tell you what the LORD said to me **last night** [+2021]."
19: 10 the spear into the wall. That **night** David made good his escape.
19: 11 warned him, "If you don't run for your life **tonight** [+2021],
19: 24 He lay that way all that day and **night**. This is why people say,
25: 16 **Night** and day they were a wall around us all the time we were
26: 7 So David and Abishai went to the army *by* **night**, and there was
28: 8 on other clothes, and *at* **night** he and two men went to the woman.
28: 20 strength was gone, for he had eaten nothing all that day and **night**.
28: 25 and his men, and they ate. That same **night** they got up and left.
30: 12 eaten any food or drunk any water for three days and three **nights**.
31: 12 all their valiant men journeyed through the **night** to Beth Shan.
2Sa 2: 29 All that **night** Abner and his men marched through the Arabah.
2: 32 Joab and his men marched all **night** and arrived at Hebron by
4: 7 Taking it with them, they traveled all **night** by way of the Arabah.
7: 4 That **night** the word of the LORD came to Nathan, saying:
17: 1 thousand men and set out **tonight** [+2021] in pursuit of David.
17: 16 and tell David, 'Do not spend the **night** at the fords in the desert;
19: 7 [19:8] not a man will be left with you *by* **nightfall** [+2021].
21: 10 the birds of the air touch them by day or the wild animals *by* **night**.
1Ki 3: 5 At Gibeon the LORD appeared to Solomon *during* the **night** in a
3: 19 "*During* the **night** this woman's son died because she lay on him.
3: 20 So she got up in the middle of the **night** and took my son from my
8: 29 May your eyes be open toward this temple **night** and day,
8: 59 before the LORD, be near to the LORD our God day and **night**,
19: 8 he traveled forty days and forty **nights** until he reached Horeb,
2Ki 6: 14 a strong force there. They went *by* **night** and surrounded the city.
7: 12 The king got up *in* the **night** and said to his officers, "I will tell
8: 21 chariot commanders, but he rose up and broke through *by* **night**;
19: 35 That **night** the angel of the LORD went out and put to death a
25: 4 the whole army fled *at* **night** through the gate between the two
1Ch 9: 33 because they were responsible for the work day and **night**.
17: 3 That **night** the word of God came to Nathan, saying:
2Ch 1: 7 That **night** God appeared to Solomon and said to him, "Ask for
6: 20 May your eyes be open toward this temple day and **night**,
7: 12 the LORD appeared to him at **night** and said: "I have heard your
21: 9 chariot commanders, but he rose up and broke through *by* **night**.
35: 14 sacrificing the burnt offerings and the fat portions until **nightfall**.
Ne 1: 6 your servant is praying before you day and **night** for your servants,
2: 12 I set out *during* the **night** with a few men. I had not told anyone
2: 13 *By* **night** I went out through the Valley Gate toward the Jackal
2: 15 so I went up the valley *by* **night**, examining the wall. Finally,
4: 9 [4:3] and posted a guard day and **night** to meet this threat.
4: 22 [4:16] so they can serve us as guards *by* **night** and workmen by
6: 10 are coming to kill you—*by* **night** they are coming to kill you."
9: 12 *by* **night** with a pillar of fire to give them light on the way they
9: 19 nor the pillar of fire by **night** to shine on the way they were to take.
Est 4: 16 Do not eat or drink for three days, **night** or day. I and my maids
6: 1 That **night** the king could not sleep; so he ordered the book of the
Job 2: 13 they sat on the ground with him for seven days and seven **nights**.
3: 3 day of my birth perish, and the **night** it was said, 'A boy is born!'
3: 6 That **night**—may thick darkness seize it; may it not be included
3: 7 May that **night** be barren; may no shout of joy be heard in it.
4: 13 Amid disquieting dreams in the **night**, when deep sleep falls on
5: 14 upon them in the daytime; at noon they grope as *in* the **night**.
7: 3 months of futility, and **nights** *of* misery have been assigned to me.
17: 12 These men turn **night** into day; in the face of darkness they say,
20: 8 no more to be found, banished like a vision of the **night**.
24: 14 kills the poor and needy; in the **night** he steals forth like a thief.
27: 20 him like a flood; a tempest snatches him away *in* the **night**.
30: 17 **Night** pierces my bones; my gnawing pains never rest.
33: 15 In a dream, in a vision of the **night**, when deep sleep falls on men
34: 20 They die in an instant, in the middle of the **night**; the people are
34: 25 their deeds, he overthrows them *in* the **night** and they are crushed.
35: 10 one says, 'Where is God my Maker, who gives songs in the **night**,
36: 20 Do not long for the **night**, to drag people away from their homes.
Ps 1: 2 the law of the LORD, and on his law he meditates day and **night**.
6: 6 [6:7] all **night** long I flood my bed with weeping and drench my
16: 7 who counsels me; even *at* **night** my heart instructs me.
17: 3 Though you probe my heart and examine me *at* **night**, though you
19: 2 [19:3] forth speech; **night** after night they display knowledge.
19: 2 [19:3] forth speech; night after **night** they display knowledge.
22: 2 [22:3] by day, but you do not answer, *by* **night**, and am not silent.
32: 4 For day and **night** your hand was heavy upon me; my strength was
42: 3 [42:4] My tears have been my food day and **night**, while men say
42: 8 [42:9] the LORD directs his love, at **night** his song is with me—
55: 10 [55:11] Day and **night** they prowl about on its walls; malice
74: 16 The day is yours, and yours also the **night**; you established the sun
77: 2 [77:3] *at* **night** I stretched out untiring hands and my soul refused
77: 6 [77:7] I remembered my songs in the **night**. My heart mused
78: 14 them with the cloud by day and with light from the fire all **night**.
88: 1 [88:2] the God who saves me, day and **night** I cry out before you.
90: 4 are like a day that has just gone by, or like a watch in the **night**.
91: 5 You will not fear the terror of **night**, nor the arrow that flies by
92: 2 [92:3] your love in the morning and your faithfulness at **night**,
104: 20 You bring darkness, it becomes **night**, and all the beasts of the
105: 39 spread out a cloud as a covering, and a fire to give light at **night**.
119: 55 In the **night** I remember your name, O LORD, and I will keep
119: 62 *At* **midnight** [+2940] I rise to give you thanks for your righteous
121: 6 the sun will not harm you by day, nor the moon by **night**.
134: 1 all you servants of the LORD who minister by **night** in the house
136: 9 the moon and stars to govern the **night**; *His love endures*
139: 11 the darkness will hide me and the light become **night** around me,"
139: 12 the **night** will shine like the day, for darkness is as light to you.
Pr 7: 9 at twilight, as the day was fading, as the dark of **night** set in.
31: 15 She gets up while it is still **dark**; she provides food for her family
31: 18 is profitable, and her lamp does not go out at **night**. [K 4325]
Ecc 2: 23 his work is pain and grief; even at **night** his mind does not rest.
8: 16 man's labor on earth—his eyes not seeing sleep day or **night**—
SS 3: 1 **All night** [+928+2021] **long** on my bed I looked for the one my
3: 8 with his sword at his side, prepared for the terrors of the **night**.
5: 2 is drenched with dew, my hair with the dampness of the **night**."
Isa 4: 5 there a cloud of smoke by day and a glow of flaming fire *by* **night**;
21: 8 my lord, I stand on the watchtower; every **night** I stay at my post.
21: 11 calls to me from Seir, "Watchman, what is left of the **night**?
21: 12 The watchman replies, "Morning is coming, but also the **night**.
26: 9 My soul yearns for you in the **night**; in the morning my spirit longs
27: 3 it continually. I guard it day and **night** so that no one may harm it.
28: 19 after morning, by day and by **night**, it will sweep through."
29: 7 will be as it is with a dream, with a vision in the **night**—
34: 10 It will not be quenched **night** and day; its smoke will rise forever.
38: 12 cut me off from the loom; day and **night** you made an end of me.
38: 13 lion he broke all my bones; day and **night** you made an end of me.
60: 11 gates will always stand open, they will never be shut, day or **night**,
62: 6 on your walls, O Jerusalem; they will never be silent day or **night**.
Jer 6: 5 So arise, let us attack at **night** and destroy her fortresses!"
9: 1 [8:23] I would weep day and **night** for the slain of my people.
14: 17 " 'Let my eyes overflow with tears **night** and day without ceasing;
16: 13 there you will serve other gods day and **night**, for I will show you
31: 35 who decrees the moon and stars to shine *by* **night**, who stirs up the
33: 20 break my covenant with the day and my covenant with the **night**,
33: 20 so that day and **night** no longer come at their appointed time,
33: 25 with day and **night** and the fixed laws of heaven and earth,
36: 30 thrown out and exposed to the heat by day and the frost by **night**.
39: 4 they left the city *at* **night** by way of the king's garden,
49: 9 If thieves came during the **night**, would they not steal only as
52: 7 They left the city *at* **night** through the gate between the two walls
La 1: 2 Bitterly she weeps at **night**, tears are upon her cheeks. Among all
2: 18 the Daughter of Zion, let your tears flow like a river day and **night**;
2: 19 Arise, cry out in the **night**, [K 4325] as the watches of the night
Hos 4: 5 You stumble day and **night**, and the prophets stumble with you.
7: 6 Their passion smolders all **night**; in the morning it blazes like a
Am 5: 8 who turns blackness into dawn and darkens day into **night**,
Ob 1: 5 "If thieves came to you, if robbers in the **night**—Oh, what a
Jnh 1: 17 [2:1] and Jonah was inside the fish three days and three **nights**.
4: 10 make it grow. It sprang up **overnight** [+1201] and died overnight.
4: 10 make it grow. It sprang up overnight and died **overnight** [+1201].
Mic 3: 6 Therefore **night** will come over you, without visions, and darkness,
Zec 1: 8 During the **night** I had a vision—and there before me was a man
14: 7 It will be a unique day, without daytime or **nighttime**—a day

4327 לִילִית *lîlît*, n.f. [1] [√ 4325; cf. 4328]

night creatures [1]

Isa 34: 14 there the **night creatures** will also repose and find for themselves

[F] Hitpael (hitpoel, hitpoal, hitpolel, hitpolal, hitpalel, hitpalal, hitpalpel, hitpalpal, hotpael, hotpaal) [G] Hiphil (hiphtil) [H] Hophal [I] Hishtaphel

4328 לִין *lîn*, v. [69] [→ 4349, 4869, 4870; cf. 4325, 4326, 4327]

spend the night [17], spent the night [6], stay [6], remain [4], spent [3], dwell [2], spend [2], stay at night [2], at home [1], camp [1], camped [1], endure [1], for the night [1], harbor [+928+7931] [1], hold back overnight [+907+1332+6330] [1], kept [1], leave overnight [1], left [1], lie all night [1], remains [1], resides [1], rest [1], resting [1], rests [1], roost [1], sleeping [1], spend days [1], spend nights [1], spent the nights [1], stay night [1], stay tonight [1], stayed night [+2256+3782] [1], stays at night [1], stays only a night [+5742] [1], stopped for the night [1]

Ge 19: 2 [A] You can wash your feet and **spend the night** and then go on
19: 2 [A] they answered, "*we will* **spend the night** in the square."
24: 23 [A] there room in your father's house for us to **spend the night**?"
24: 25 [A] and fodder, as well as room for you to **spend the night**."
24: 54 [A] who were with him ate and drank and **spent the night** there.
28: 11 [A] *he* **stopped for the night** because the sun had set.
31: 54 [A] to a meal. After they had eaten, *they* **spent the night** there.
32: 13 [32:14] [A] *He* **spent** the night there, and from what he had with
32: 21 [32:22] [A] of him, but *he* himself **spent** the night in the camp.
Ex 23: 18 [A] "The fat of my festival offerings *must* not *be* **kept** until
34: 25 [A] *do* not *let* any of the sacrifice from the Passover Feast **remain**
Lev 19: 13 [G] " '*Do* not **hold back** the wages of a hired man **overnight** [+907+1332+6330].
Nu 22: 8 [A] "**Spend** the night here," Balaam said to them, "and I will
Dt 16: 4 [A] *Do* not *let* any of the meat you sacrifice on the evening of the first day **remain**
21: 23 [G] *you must* not **leave** his body on the tree **overnight**. Be sure
Jos 3: 1 [A] went to the Jordan, where *they* **camped** before crossing over.
4: 3 [A] and put them down at the place where *you* **stay** tonight."
6: 11 [A] Then the people returned to camp and **spent the night** there.
8: 9 [A] the west of Ai—but Joshua **spent** that night with the people.
Jdg 18: 2 [A] and came to the house of Micah, where *they* **spent the night**.
19: 4 [A] with him three days, eating and drinking, and **sleeping** there.
19: 6 [A] girl's father said, "Please **stay tonight** and enjoy yourself."
19: 7 [A] persuaded him, so *he* **stayed** there *that* **night** [+2256+3782].
19: 9 [A] **Spend the night** here; the day is nearly over. Stay and enjoy
19: 9 [A] night here; the day is nearly over. **Stay** and enjoy yourself.
19: 10 [A] But, unwilling to **stay** another **night**, the man left and went
19: 11 [A] let's stop at this city of the Jebusites and **spend the night**."
19: 13 [A] or Ramah and **spend the night** in one of those places."
19: 15 [A] There they stopped to **spend the night**. They went and sat in
19: 15 [A] but no one took them into his home **for the night**.
19: 20 [A] you need. Only don't **spend the night** in the square."
20: 4 [A] concubine came to Gibeah in Benjamin to **spend the night**.
Ru 1: 16 [A] Where you go I will go, and where *you* **stay** I will stay.
1: 16 [A] Where you go I will go, and where you stay *I will* **stay**.
3: 13 [A] **Stay** here for the night, and in the morning if he wants to
2Sa 12: 16 [A] into his house and **spent the nights** lying on the ground.
17: 8 [A] *he will* not **spend the night** with the troops.
17: 16 [A] tell David, '*Do* not **spend** the night at the fords in the desert;
19: 7 [19:8] [A] go out, not a man *will be* **left** with you by nightfall.
1Ki 19: 9 [A] There he went into a cave and **spent the night**. And the word
1Ch 9: 27 [A] *They would* **spend the night** stationed around the house of
Ne 4: 22 [4:16] [A] every man and his helper **stay** inside Jerusalem **at night**,
13: 20 [A] sellers of all kinds of goods **spent the night** outside
13: 21 [A] and said, "Why *do* you **spend the night** by the wall?
Job 17: 2 [A] mockers surround me; my eyes *must* **dwell** *on* their hostility.
19: 4 [A] that I have gone astray, my error **remains** my concern alone.
24: 7 [A] Lacking clothes, *they* **spend the night** naked; they have
29: 19 [A] to the water, and the dew *will* **lie all night** on my branches.
31: 32 [A] no stranger *had to* **spend the night** in the street, for my door
39: 9 [A] consent to serve you? *Will he* **stay** by your manger **at night**?
39: 28 [F] He dwells on a cliff and **stays** there **at night**; a rocky crag is
41: 22 [41:14] [A] Strength **resides** in his neck; dismay goes before
Ps 25: 13 [A] He *will* **spend** *his* **days** in prosperity, and his descendants
30: 5 [30:6] [A] weeping *may* **remain** for a night, but rejoicing
49: 12 [49:13] [A] man, despite his riches, *does* not **endure**; he is like
55: 7 [55:8] [A] I would flee far away and **stay** in the desert; *Selah*
91: 1 [F] He who dwells in the shelter of the Most High *will* **rest** in the
Pr 15: 31 [A] He who listens to a life-giving rebuke *will be* **at home**
19: 23 [A] leads to life: Then *one* **rests** content, untouched by trouble.
SS 1: 13 [A] My lover is to me a sachet of myrrh **resting** between my
7: 11 [7:12] [A] *let us* **spend the night** in the villages.
Isa 1: 21 [A] righteousness *used to* **dwell** in her—but now murderers!
21: 13 [A] caravans of Dedanites, *who* **camp** in the thickets of Arabia,
65: 4 [A] the graves and **spend** *their* **nights** keeping secret vigil;
Jer 4: 14 [G] How long *will you* **harbor** [+928+7931] wicked thoughts?
14: 8 [A] in the land, like a traveler *who* **stays** [+5742] **only a night**?
Joel 1: 13 [A] Come, **spend the night** in sackcloth, you who minister
Zep 2: 14 [A] desert owl and the screech owl *will* **roost** on her columns.
Zec 5: 4 [A] *It will* **remain** in his house and destroy it, both its timbers

4329 לִיץ *lîṣ*, v. [6] [→ 4370, 4371, 4372, 4885, 4886]

mock [2], mocks [2], mocker [1], mocking [1]

Ps 119: 51 [G] The arrogant **mock** me without restraint, but I do not turn
Pr 3: 34 [G] He **mocks** proud mockers but gives grace to the humble.
9: 12 [A] will reward you; if *you are a* **mocker**, you alone will suffer."
14: 9 [G] Fools **mock** *at* making amends for sin, but goodwill is found
19: 28 [G] A corrupt witness **mocks** *at* justice, and the mouth of the
Isa 28: 22 [F] Now stop *your* **mocking**, or your chains will become

4330 לַיִשׁ *layiš*[1], n.m. [3] [→ 4298, 4331, 4332, 4333]

lion [2], lions [1]

Job 4: 11 The **lion** perishes for lack of prey, and the cubs of the lioness are
Pr 30: 30 a **lion**, mighty among beasts, who retreats before nothing;
Isa 30: 6 and distress, of **lions** and lionesses, of adders and darting snakes,

4331 לַיִשׁ *layiš*[2], n.pr.m. [2] [√ 4330]

Laish [2]

1Sa 25: 44 David's wife, to Paltiel son of **Laish**, who was from Gallim.
2Sa 3: 15 her taken away from her husband Paltiel son of **Laish**. [K 4298]

4332 לַיִשׁ *layiš*[3], n.pr.loc. [4] [√ 4330; cf. 4386]

Laish [4]

Jdg 18: 7 So the five men left and came to **Laish**, where they saw that the
18: 14 the five men who had spied out the land of **Laish** said to their
18: 27 his priest, and went on to **Laish**, against a peaceful
18: 29 who was born to Israel—though the city used to be called **Laish**.

4333 לַיְשָׁה *layᵉšâ*, n.pr.loc. [1] [√ 4330]

Laishah [1]

Isa 10: 30 O Daughter of Gallim! Listen, O **Laishah**! Poor Anathoth!

4334 לָכַד *lākad*, v. [121] [→ 4335, 4892]

captured [33], took [17], capture [9], be captured [6], was taken [6], be caught [4], take [4], takes [4], caught [3], taken [3], was chosen [3], captures [2], catch [+4334] [2], ensnare [2], was captured [2], are caught [1], are trapped [1], assumed [1], be taken captive [1], catch [1], catches [1], cling together [1], conquered [1], ensnared [1], entangle [1], frozen [1], held fast [1], is captured [1], is caught [1], seize [1], taking possession [1], took prisoner [1], trapped [1], was caught [1], were caught [1], were taken [1]

Nu 21: 32 [A] the Israelites **captured** its surrounding settlements and drove
32: 39 [A] **captured** it and drove out the Amorites who were there.
32: 41 [A] **captured** their settlements and called them Havvoth Jair.
32: 42 [A] And Nobah **captured** Kenath and its surrounding settlements
Dt 2: 34 [A] At that time *we* **took** all his towns and completely destroyed
2: 35 [A] the plunder from the towns *we had* **captured** we carried off
3: 4 [A] At that time *we* **took** all his cities. There was not one of the
Jos 6: 20 [A] so every man charged straight in, and *they* **took** the city.
7: 14 [A] The tribe that the LORD **takes** shall come forward clan by
7: 14 [A] the clan that the LORD **takes** shall come forward family by
7: 14 [A] the family that the LORD **takes** shall come forward man by
7: 15 [C] *He* who **is caught** with the devoted things shall be destroyed
7: 16 [C] had Israel come forward by tribes, and Judah **was taken**.
7: 17 [A] The clans of Judah came forward, and *he* **took** the Zerahites.
7: 17 [C] Zerahites come forward by families, and Zimri **was taken**.
7: 18 [C] of Zimri, the son of Zerah, of the tribe of Judah, **was taken**.
8: 19 [A] They entered the city and **captured** it and quickly set it on
8: 21 [A] and all Israel saw that the ambush *had* **taken** the city
10: 1 [A] king of Jerusalem heard that Joshua *had* **taken** Ai
10: 28 [A] That day Joshua **took** Makkedah. He put the city and its king
10: 32 [A] Lachish over to Israel, and Joshua **took** it on the second day.
10: 35 [A] *They* **captured** it that same day and put it to the sword
10: 37 [A] *They* **took** the city and put it to the sword, together with its
10: 39 [A] *They* **took** the city, its king and its villages, and put them to
10: 42 [A] All these kings and their lands Joshua **conquered** in one
11: 10 [A] and **captured** Hazor and put its king to the sword.
11: 12 [A] Joshua **took** all these royal cities and their kings and put
11: 17 [A] *He* **captured** all their kings and struck them down, putting
15: 16 [A] to the man who attacks and **captures** Kiriath Sepher."
15: 17 [A] Othniel son of Kenaz, Caleb's brother, **took** it; so Caleb gave
19: 47 [A] attacked Leshem, **took** it, put it to the sword and occupied it.
Jdg 1: 8 [A] The men of Judah attacked Jerusalem also and **took** it. They
1: 12 [A] to the man who attacks and **captures** Kiriath Sepher."
1: 13 [A] Othniel son of Kenaz, Caleb's younger brother, **took** it;
1: 18 [A] The men of Judah also **took** Gaza, Ashkelon and Ekron—
3: 28 [A] **taking possession** *of* the fords of the Jordan that led to
7: 24 [A] **seize** the waters of the Jordan ahead of them as far as Beth

Jdg 7:24 [A] and *they* **took** the waters of the Jordan as far as Beth Barah.
7:25 [A] *They* also **captured** two of the Midianite leaders, Oreb and
8:12 [A] of Midian, fled, but he pursued them and **captured** them,
8:14 [A] *He* **caught** a young man of Succoth and questioned him,
9:45 [A] pressed his attack against the city until *he had* **captured** it
9:50 [A] Abimelech went to Thebez and besieged it and **captured** it.
12:5 [A] The Gileadites **captured** the fords of the Jordan leading to
15:4 [A] So he went out and **caught** three hundred foxes and tied them
1Sa 10:20 [C] all the tribes of Israel near, the tribe of Benjamin **was chosen**.
10:21 [C] tribe of Benjamin, clan by clan, and Matri's clan **was chosen**.
10:21 [C] clan was chosen. Finally Saul son of Kish **was chosen**.
14:41 [C] Jonathan and Saul **were taken** by lot, and the men were
14:42 [C] between me and Jonathan my son." And Jonathan **was taken**.
14:47 [A] After Saul *had* **assumed** rule over Israel, he fought against
2Sa 5:7 [A] Nevertheless, David **captured** the fortress of Zion, the City
8:4 [A] David **captured** a thousand of his chariots, seven thousand
12:26 [A] Rabbah of the Ammonites and **captured** the royal citadel.
12:27 [A] "I have fought against Rabbah and **taken** its water supply.
12:28 [A] the rest of the troops and besiege the city and **capture** it.
12:28 [A] Otherwise I *will* **take** the city, and it will be named after
12:29 [A] and went to Rabbah, and attacked and **captured** it.
1Ki 9:16 [A] (Pharaoh king of Egypt had attacked and **captured** Gezer.
16:18 [C] When Zimri saw that the city **was taken**, he went into the
2Ki 12:17 [12:18] [A] Aram went up and attacked Gath and **captured** it.
17:6 [A] the king of Assyria **captured** Samaria and deported the
18:10 [A] At the end of three years the Assyrians **took** it. So Samaria
18:10 [C] So Samaria **was captured** in Hezekiah's sixth year,
1Ch 11:5 [A] Nevertheless, David **captured** the fortress of Zion, the City
18:4 [A] David **captured** a thousand of his chariots, seven thousand
2Ch 12:4 [A] *he* **captured** the fortified cities of Judah and came as far as
13:19 [A] pursued Jeroboam and **took** from him the towns of Bethel,
15:8 [A] and from the towns *he had* **captured** in the hills of Ephraim.
17:2 [A] in the towns of Ephraim that his father Asa *had* **captured**.
22:9 [A] and *his men* **captured** him while he was hiding in Samaria.
28:18 [A] *They* **captured** and occupied Beth Shemesh, Aijalon and
32:18 [A] and make them afraid in order to **capture** the city.
33:11 [A] *who* **took** Manasseh **prisoner**, put a hook in his nose, bound
Ne 9:25 [A] *They* **captured** fortified cities and fertile land; they took
Job 5:13 [A] *He* **catches** the wise in their craftiness, and the schemes of
36:8 [C] if men are bound in chains, **held fast** by cords of affliction,
38:30 [F] hard as stone, when the surface of the deep *is* **frozen**?
41:17 [41:9] [F] *they* **cling together** and cannot be parted.
Ps 9:15 [9:16] [C] their feet **are caught** in the net they have hidden.
35:8 [A] *may* the net they hid **entangle** them, may they fall into the
59:12 [59:13] [C] of their lips, *let them* **be caught** in their pride.
Pr 5:22 [A] The evil deeds of a wicked man **ensnare** him; the cords of
6:2 [C] by what you said, **ensnared** by the words of your mouth,
11:6 [C] delivers them, but the unfaithful **are trapped** by evil desires.
16:32 [A] a man who controls his temper than *one who* **takes** a city.
Ecc 7:26 [C] pleases God will escape her, but the sinner she *will* **ensnare**.
Isa 8:15 [C] will fall and be broken, they will be snared and **captured**."
20:1 [A] of Assyria, came to Ashdod and attacked and **captured** it—
24:18 [C] a pit; whoever climbs out of the pit *will* **be caught** in a snare.
28:13 [C] and fall backward, be injured and snared and **captured**.
Jer 5:26 [A] who snare birds and like those who set traps *to* **catch** men.
6:11 [C] both husband and wife *will* **be caught** in it, and the old,
8:9 [C] will be put to shame; they will be dismayed and **trapped**.
18:22 [A] for they have dug a pit to **capture** me and have hidden snares
32:3 [A] this city over to the king of Babylon, and *he will* **capture** it.
32:24 [A] "See how the siege ramps are built up to **take** the city.
32:28 [A] to Nebuchadnezzar king of Babylon, *who will* **capture** it.
34:22 [A] this city. They will fight against it, **take** it and burn it down.
37:8 [A] and attack this city; *they will* **capture** it and burn it down.'
38:3 [A] to the army of the king of Babylon, *who will* **capture** it.' "
38:28 [C] courtyard of the guard until the day Jerusalem **was captured**.
38:28 [C] Jerusalem was captured. This is how Jerusalem **was taken**:
48:1 [C] Kiriathaim will be disgraced and **captured**; the stronghold
48:7 [C] trust in your deeds and riches, you too *will* **be taken captive**,
48:41 [C] Kerioth *will* **be captured** and the strongholds taken. In that
48:44 [C] a pit, whoever climbs out of the pit *will* **be caught** in a snare;
50:2 [C] keep nothing back, but say, 'Babylon *will* **be captured**;
50:9 [C] against her, and from the north *she will* **be captured**.
50:24 [C] O Babylon, and *you* **were caught** before you knew it;
51:31 [C] to the king of Babylon that his entire city **is captured**,
51:41 [C] "How Sheshach *will* **be captured**, the boast of the whole
51:56 [C] her warriors *will* **be captured**, and their bows will be broken.
La 4:20 [C] our very life breath, **was caught** in their traps.
Da 11:15 [A] and build up siege ramps and *will* **capture** a fortified city.
11:18 [A] his attention to the coastlands and *will* **take** many of them,
Am 3:4 [A] Does he growl in his den when *he has* **caught** nothing?
3:5 [A] up from the earth when there is nothing *to* **catch** [+4334]?
3:5 [A] up from the earth when there is nothing *to* **catch** [+4334]?
Hab 1:10 [A] fortified cities; they build earthen ramps and **capture** them.
Zec 14:2 [C] the city *will* **be captured**, the houses ransacked,

4335 לֶכֶד *leked*, n.[m.]. [1] [√ 4334]

snared [1]

Pr 3:26 be your confidence and will keep your foot from being **snared**.

4336 לֵכָה *lēkâ*, n.pr.loc. [1]

Lecah [1]

1Ch 4:21 Er the father of **Lecah**, Laadah the father of Mareshah

4337 לָכִישׁ *lākîš*, n.pr.loc. [24]

Lachish [24]

Jos 10:3 king of Jarmuth, Japhia king of **Lachish** and Debir king of Eglon.
10:5 the kings of Jerusalem, Hebron, Jarmuth, **Lachish** and Eglon—
10:23 the kings of Jerusalem, Hebron, Jarmuth, **Lachish** and Eglon.
10:31 and all Israel with him moved on from Libnah to **Lachish**;
10:32 The LORD handed **Lachish** over to Israel, and Joshua took it on
10:33 Meanwhile, Horam king of Gezer had come up to help **Lachish**,
10:34 and all Israel with him moved on from **Lachish** to Eglon;
10:35 totally destroyed everyone in it, just as they had done to **Lachish**.
12:11 the king of Jarmuth one the king of **Lachish** one
15:39 **Lachish**, Bozkath, Eglon,
2Ki 14:19 and he fled to **Lachish**, but they sent men after him to Lachish
14:19 but they sent men after him to **Lachish** and killed him there.
18:14 king of Judah sent this message to the king of Assyria at **Lachish**:
18:17 with a large army, from **Lachish** to King Hezekiah at Jerusalem.
19:8 field commander heard that the king of Assyria had left **Lachish**,
2Ch 11:9 Adoraim, **Lachish**, Azekah,
25:27 they conspired against him in Jerusalem and he fled to **Lachish**,
25:27 but they sent men after him to **Lachish** and killed him there.
32:9 king of Assyria and all his forces were laying siege to **Lachish**,
Ne 11:30 in **Lachish** and its fields, and in Azekah and its settlements.
Isa 36:2 with a large army from **Lachish** to King Hezekiah at Jerusalem.
37:8 field commander heard that the king of Assyria had left **Lachish**,
Jer 34:7 cities of Judah that were still holding out—**Lachish** and Azekah.
Mic 1:13 You who live in **Lachish**, harness the team to the chariot.

4338 לָכֵן *lākēn*, adv. & pp. Not used in NIV/BHS [√ 4200 + 4027]

4339 לֻלָאוֹת *lulā'ôt*, n.f. [13] [cf. 4277, 4324]

loops [11], *untranslated* [2]

Ex 26:4 Make **loops** *of* blue material along the edge of the end curtain in
26:5 Make fifty **loops** on one curtain and fifty loops on the end curtain
26:5 on one curtain and fifty **loops** on the end curtain of the other set,
26:5 the end curtain of the other set, with the **loops** opposite each other.
26:10 Make fifty **loops** along the edge of the end curtain in one set
26:10 and also **[RPH]** along the edge of the end curtain in the other set.
26:11 and put them in the **loops** to fasten the tent together as a unit.
36:11 they made **loops** *of* blue material along the edge of the end curtain
36:12 They also made fifty **loops** on one curtain and fifty loops on the
36:12 on one curtain and fifty **loops** on the end curtain of the other set,
36:12 the end curtain of the other set, with the **loops** opposite each other.
36:17 they made fifty **loops** along the edge of the end curtain in one set
36:17 and also **[RPH]** along the edge of the end curtain in the other set.

4340 לָמַד *lāmad*, v. [86] [→ 4341, 4913, 9441]

teach [30], learn [15], taught [14], learned [3], teaches [3], trains [3], learn well [+906+4340] [2], teaching [2], train [2], trained [2], *untranslated* [1], accept [1], adopted [1], cultivated [1], experienced [1], imparted [1], instructors [1], teachers [1], unruly [+4202] [1], were trained [1]

Dt 4:1 [D] O Israel, the decrees and laws I *am about to* **teach** you.
4:5 [D] *I have* **taught** you decrees and laws as the LORD my God
4:10 [A] so that *they may* **learn** to revere me as long as they live in
4:10 [D] they live in the land and *may* **teach** them *to* their children."
4:14 [D] the LORD directed me at that time to **teach** you the decrees
5:1 [A] your hearing today. **Learn** them and be sure to follow them.
5:31 [D] laws *you are to* **teach** them to follow in the land I am giving
6:1 [D] laws the LORD your God directed me to **teach** you to
11:19 [D] **Teach** them *to* your children, talking about them when you
14:23 [A] so that *you may* **learn** to revere the LORD your God
17:19 [A] of his life so that *he may* **learn** to revere the LORD his God
18:9 [A] *do* not **learn** to imitate the detestable ways of the nations
20:18 [D] *they will* **teach** you to follow all the detestable things they do
31:12 [A] so they can listen and **learn** to fear the LORD your God
31:13 [A] **learn** to fear the LORD your God as long as you live in the
31:19 [D] this song and **teach** it *to* the Israelites and have them sing it,
31:22 [D] wrote down this song that day and **taught** it *to* the Israelites.
Jdg 3:2 [D] (he did this only to **teach** warfare *to* the descendants of the
2Sa 1:18 [D] ordered that the men of Judah *be* **taught** this lament of the
22:35 [D] *He* **trains** my hands for battle; my arms can bend a bow of

1Ch 5:18 [B] who could use a bow, and *who* **were trained** *for* battle.
25: 7 [E] all of *them* **trained** and skilled *in* music for the LORD—
2Ch 17: 7 [D] and Micaiah to **teach** in the towns of Judah.
17: 9 [D] *They* **taught** throughout Judah, taking with them the Book of
17: 9 [D] went around to all the towns of Judah and **taught** the people.
Ezr 7:10 [D] of the LORD, and to **teaching** its decrees and laws in Israel.
Job 21:22 [D] "*Can anyone* **teach** knowledge to God, since he judges even
Ps 18:34 [18:35] [D] *He* **trains** my hands for battle; my arms can bend a
25: 4 [D] Show me your ways, O LORD, **teach** me your paths;
25: 5 [D] guide me in your truth and **teach** me, for you are God my
25: 9 [D] guides the humble in what is right and **teaches** them his way.
34:11 [34:12] [D] to me; *I will* **teach** you the fear of the LORD.
51:13 [51:15] [D] *I will* **teach** transgressors your ways, and sinners
60: T [60:1] [D] A *miktam* of David. For **teaching**. When he fought
71:17 [D] Since my youth, O God, *you have* **taught** me, and to this day
94:10 [D] not punish? Does *he who* **teaches** man lack knowledge?
94:12 [D] you discipline, O LORD, the man *you* **teach** from your law;
106:35 [A] but they mingled with the nations and **adopted** their customs.
119: 7 [A] I will praise you with an upright heart as I **learn** your
119:12 [D] Praise be to you, O LORD; **teach** me your decrees.
119:26 [D] my ways and you answered me; **teach** me your decrees.
119:64 [D] is filled with your love, O LORD; **teach** me your decrees.
119:66 [D] **Teach** me knowledge and good judgment, for I believe in
119:68 [D] are good, and what you do is good; **teach** me your decrees.
119:71 [A] for me to be afflicted so that *I might* **learn** your decrees.
119:73 [A] formed me; give me understanding *to* **learn** your commands.
119:99 [D] I have more insight than all my **teachers**, for I meditate on
119:108 [D] the willing praise of my mouth, and **teach** me your laws.
119:124 [D] servant according to your love and **teach** me your decrees.
119:135 [D] face shine upon your servant and **teach** me your decrees.
119:171 [D] my lips overflow with praise, for *you* **teach** me your decrees.
132:12 [D] if your sons keep my covenant and the statutes *I* **teach** them,
143:10 [D] **Teach** me to do your will, for you are my God; may your
144: 1 [D] who **trains** my hands for war, my fingers for battle.
Pr 5:13 [D] I would not obey my teachers or listen to my **instructors**.
30: 3 [A] *I have* not **learned** wisdom, nor have I knowledge of the
Ecc 12: 9 [D] Teacher wise, but also *he* **imparted** knowledge to the people.
SS 3: 8 [E] all of them wearing the sword, all **experienced** *in* battle,
8: 2 [D] bring you to my mother's house—*she who has* **taught** me.
Isa 1:17 [A] **learn** to do right! Seek justice, encourage the oppressed.
2: 4 [A] sword against nation, nor *will they* **train** *for* war anymore.
26: 9 [A] upon the earth, the people of the world **learn** righteousness.
26:10 [A] is shown to the wicked, *they do* not **learn** righteousness;
29:13 [E] Their worship of me is made up only of rules **taught** *by* men.
29:24 [A] those who complain *will* **accept** instruction."
40:14 [D] consult to enlighten him, and *who* **taught** him the right way?
40:14 [D] *Who* was it that **taught** him knowledge or showed him the
48:17 [D] the LORD your God, *who* **teaches** you what is best for you,
Jer 2:33 [D] Even the worst of women *can* **learn** *from* your ways.
9: 5 [9:4] [D] *They have* **taught** their tongues to lie; they weary
9:14 [9:13] [D] followed the Baals, as their fathers **taught** them."
9:20 [9:19] [D] **Teach** your daughters how to wail; teach one another
10: 2 [A] "*Do* not **learn** the ways of the nations or be terrified by signs
12:16 [A] And if *they* **learn** [+906+4340] **well** the ways of my people
12:16 [A] And if *they* **learn well** [+906+4340] the ways of my people
12:16 [D] even as *they once* **taught** my people to swear by Baal—
13:21 [D] sets over you those you **cultivated** as your special allies?
31:18 [E] 'You disciplined me like an **unruly** [+4202] calf, and I have
31:34 [D] No longer *will* a man **teach** his neighbor, or a man his
32:33 [D] though I **taught** them again and again, they would not listen
32:33 [D] **[RPH]** they would not listen or respond to discipline.
Eze 19: 3 [A] *He* **learned** to tear the prey and he devoured men.
19: 6 [A] *He* **learned** to tear the prey and he devoured men.
Da 1: 4 [D] He was to **teach** them the language and literature of the
Hos 10:11 [E] Ephraim *is* a **trained** heifer that loves to thresh; so I will put
Mic 4: 3 [A] sword against nation, nor *will they* **train** *for* war anymore.

4341 לִמֻּד ***limmud***, a. [6] [√ 4340]

accustomed to [2], disciples [1], instructed [1], one taught [1], taught [1]

Isa 8:16 Bind up the testimony and seal up the law among my **disciples**.
50: 4 The Sovereign LORD has given me an **instructed** tongue,
50: 4 by morning, wakens my ear to listen like **one** being **taught**.
54:13 All your sons will be **taught** *by* the LORD, and great will be your
Jer 2:24 a wild donkey **accustomed to** the desert, sniffing the wind in her
13:23 Neither can you do good *who* are **accustomed to** doing evil.

4342 לָמָּה ***lāmmâ***, p.inter. & indef. Not used in NIV/BHS [√ 4200 + 4537]

4343 לָמוֹ ***lāmô***, pp.+p.suf. Not used in NIV/BHS [√ 4200 + 4564]

4344 לְמוֹ ***lᵉmô***, pp. [4] [√ 4200]

untranslated [1], for [1], in [1], over [1]

Job 27:14 However many his children, their **[RPH]** fate is the sword;
29:21 listened to me expectantly, waiting in silence **for** my counsel.
38:40 when they crouch in their dens or lie **in** wait in a thicket?
40: 4 how can I reply to you? I put my hand **over** my mouth.

4345 לְמוּאֵל ***lᵉmû'ēl***, n.pr.m. [2] [√ 4200 + 446]

Lemuel [2]

Pr 31: 1 The sayings of King **Lemuel**—an oracle his mother taught him:
31: 4 "It is not for kings, O **Lemuel**—not for kings to drink wine,

4346 לְמוֹאֵל ***lᵉmô'ēl***, n.pr.m. Not used in NIV/BHS [√ 4200 + 4578]

4347 לֶמֶךְ ***lemek***, n.pr.m. [11]

Lamech [11]

Ge 4:18 father of Methushael, and Methushael was the father of **Lamech**.
4:19 **Lamech** married two women, one named Adah and the other
4:23 **Lamech** said to his wives, "Adah and Zillah, listen to me;
4:23 and Zillah, listen to me; wives of **Lamech**, hear my words.
4:24 Cain is avenged seven times, then **Lamech** seventy-seven times."
5:25 Methuselah had lived 187 years, he became the father of **Lamech**.
5:26 after he became the father of **Lamech**, Methuselah lived 782 years
5:28 When **Lamech** had lived 182 years, he had a son.
5:30 **Lamech** lived 595 years and had other sons and daughters.
5:31 Altogether, **Lamech** lived 777 years, and then he died.
1Ch 1: 3 Enoch, Methuselah, **Lamech**, Noah.

4348 לְמַעַן ***lᵉma'an***, pr.+subst. Not used in NIV/BHS [√ 4200 + 6701]

4349 לֵן ***lēn***, n.[m.] *or* v.ptcp. Not used in NIV/BHS [√ 4328]

4350 לֹעַ ***lōa'***, n.[m.]. [1] [√ 4363]

throat [1]

Pr 23: 2 and put a knife to your **throat** if you are given to gluttony.

4351 לָעַב ***lā'ab***, v. [1]

mocked [1]

2Ch 36:16 [G] *they* **mocked** God's messengers, despised his words

4352 לָעַג ***lā'ag***, v. [18 / 19] [→ 4353, 4354; cf. 6589]

mock [6], mocks [6], ridiculed [2], maliciously mocked [+4352] [1], mocked [1], scoff [1], scoffs [1], strange [1]

2Ki 19:21 [A] " 'The Virgin Daughter of Zion despises you and **mocks** you.
2Ch 30:10 [G] as far as Zebulun, but the people scorned and **ridiculed** them.
Ne 2:19 [G] the Arab heard about it, *they* **mocked** and ridiculed us.
4: 1 [3:33] [G] and was greatly incensed. *He* **ridiculed** the Jews,
Job 9:23 [A] brings sudden death, *he* **mocks** the despair of the innocent.
11: 3 [A] men to silence? Will no one rebuke you when *you* **mock**?
21: 3 [G] with me while I speak, and after I have spoken, **mock** *on*.
22:19 [A] see their ruin and rejoice; the innocent **mock** them, saying,
Ps 2: 4 [A] One enthroned in heaven laughs; the Lord **scoffs** at them.
22: 7 [22:8] [G] All who see me **mock** me; they hurl insults,
35:16 [A] the ungodly *they* **maliciously mocked** [+4353]; [BHS 4353]
59: 8 [59:9] [A] laugh at them; *you* **scoff** at all those nations.
80: 6 [80:7] [A] to our neighbors, and our enemies **mock** us.
Pr 1:26 [A] at your disaster; *I will* **mock** when calamity overtakes you—
17: 5 [A] *He who* **mocks** the poor shows contempt for their Maker;
30:17 [A] "The eye *that* **mocks** a father, that scorns obedience to a
Isa 33:19 [C] obscure speech, with their **strange**, incomprehensible tongue.
37:22 [A] "The Virgin Daughter of Zion despises and **mocks** you.
Jer 20: 7 [A] I am ridiculed all day long; everyone **mocks** me.

4353 לַעַג ***la'ag***, n.[m.]. [9] [√ 4352]

scorn [3], ridiculed [2], derision [1], foreign [1], maliciously mocked [+4352] [1], ridicule [1]

Job 34: 7 What man is like Job, who drinks **scorn** like water?
Ps 35:16 *they* maliciously mocked; [BHS *mockers of a feast*; NIV 4352]
35:16 Like the ungodly *they* **maliciously mocked** [+4352]; they gnashed
44:13 [44:14] our neighbors, the **scorn** and derision of those around us.
79: 4 to our neighbors, of **scorn** and derision to those around us.
123: 4 We have endured much **ridicule** from the proud, much contempt
Isa 28:11 with **foreign** lips and strange tongues God will speak to this
Eze 23:32 and deep; it will bring scorn and **derision**, for it holds so much.
36: 4 and **ridiculed** by the rest of the nations around you—

Hos 7:16 insolent words. For this they *will be* **ridiculed** in the land of Egypt.

4354 לָעֵג ***lā'ēg***, a. Not used in NIV/BHS [√ 4352]

4355 לַעְדָּה ***la'dâ***, n.pr.m. [1] [→ 4356]

Laadah [1]

1Ch 4:21 **Laadah** the father of Mareshah and the clans of the linen workers

4356 לַעְדָּן ***la'dān***, n.pr.m. [7] [√ 4355]

Ladan [7]

1Ch 7:26 **Ladan** his son, Ammihud his son, Elishama his son,
23: 7 Belonging to the Gershonites: **Ladan** and Shimei.
23: 8 The sons of **Ladan**: Jehiel the first, Zetham and Joel—three in all.
23: 9 three in all. These were the heads of the families of **Ladan**.
26:21 The descendants of **Ladan**, who were Gershonites through Ladan
26:21 who were Gershonites through **Ladan** and who were heads of
26:21 who were heads of families belonging to **Ladan** the Gershonite,

4357 לָעַז ***lā'az***, v. [1]

foreign tongue [1]

Ps 114: 1 [A] the house of Jacob from a people of **foreign tongue**,

4358 לָעַט ***lā'aṭ***, v. [1] [cf. 4265]

let have [1]

Ge 25:30 [G] He said to Jacob, "Quick, **let** me **have** some of that red stew!

4359 לָעִיר ***lā'îr***, n.[pr.loc.?]. Not used in NIV/BHS [√ 4200 + 6551]

4360 לַעֲנָה ***la'ᵃnâ***, n.f. [8]

bitter [3], gall [3], bitterness [2]

Dt 29:18 [29:17] is no root among you that produces such **bitter** poison.
Pr 5: 4 but in the end she is bitter as **gall**, sharp as a double-edged sword.
Jer 9:15 [9:14] I will make this people eat **bitter** food and drink poisoned
23:15 "I will make them eat **bitter** food and drink poisoned water,
La 3:15 He has filled me with bitter herbs and sated me with **gall**.
3:19 my affliction and my wandering, the bitterness and the **gall**.
Am 5: 7 You who turn justice into **bitterness** and cast righteousness to the
6:12 justice into poison and the fruit of righteousness into **bitterness**—

4361 לְעַנּוֹת ***lᵉ'annôt***, n.[pl.] *or* v.ptcp. [1] [√ 6700?]

leannoth [1]

Ps 88: T [88:1] director of music. According to *mahalath* **leannoth**.

4362 לָעַע ***lā'a'[1]***, v. [2]

impetuous [1], rashly [1]

Job 6: 3 [A] of the seas—no wonder my words *have been* **impetuous**.
Pr 20:25 [A] It is a trap for a man *to* dedicate something **rashly** and only

4363 2לָעַע ***lā'a'[2]***, v. [1] [→ 4350; cf. 6633]

drink [1]

Ob 1:16 [A] they will drink and **drink** and be as if they had never been.

4364 לְעַפְרָה ***lᵉ'aprâ***, n.pr.loc. Not used in NIV/BHS [→ 1108; cf. 6765]

4365 לַפִּיד ***lappîd***, n.m. [13] [→ 4366?]

torches [5], torch [4], *untranslated* [1], firebrands [1], flaming torches [1], lightning [1]

Ge 15:17 a smoking firepot with a blazing **torch** appeared and passed
Ex 20:18 **lightning** and heard the trumpet and saw the mountain in smoke,
Jdg 7:16 and empty jars in the hands of all of them, with **torches** inside.
7:20 Grasping the **torches** in their left hands and holding in their right
15: 4 three hundred foxes and **[RPH]** tied them tail to tail in pairs.
15: 4 tail to tail in pairs. He then fastened a **torch** to every pair of tails,
15: 5 lit the **torches** and let the foxes loose in the standing grain of the
Job 41:19 [41:11] **Firebrands** stream from his mouth; sparks of fire shoot
Isa 62: 1 shines out like the dawn, her salvation like a blazing **torch**.
Eze 1:13 the living creatures was like burning coals of fire or like **torches**.
Da 10: 6 his eyes like flaming **torches**, his arms and legs like the gleam of
Na 2: 4 [2:5] They look like **flaming torches**; they dart about like
Zec 12: 6 like a firepot in a woodpile, like a flaming **torch** among sheaves.

4366 לַפִּידוֹת ***lappîdôt***, n.pr.m. [1] [√ 4365?]

Lappidoth [1]

Jdg 4: 4 Deborah, a prophetess, the wife of **Lappidoth**, was leading Israel

4367 לִפְנֵי ***lipnê***, pp.+n.m. Not used in NIV/BHS [√ 4200 + 7155]

4368 לִפְנָי ***lipnāy***, pp.+n. Not used in NIV/BHS [√ 4200 + 7155]

4369 לָפַת ***lāpat***, v. [3]

reached toward [1], turn aside [1], turned [1]

Jdg 16:29 [A] Samson **reached toward** the two central pillars on which the
Ru 3: 8 [C] and *he* **turned** and discovered a woman lying at his feet.
Job 6:18 [C] Caravans **turn aside** *from* their routes; they go up into the

4370 לֵץ ***lēṣ***, n.[m.] *or* v.ptcp. [16] [√ 4329]

mocker [11], mockers [4], proud mockers [1]

Ps 1: 1 or stand in the way of sinners or sit in the seat of **mockers**.
Pr 1:22 How long will **mockers** delight in mockery and fools hate
3:34 He mocks **proud mockers** but gives grace to the humble.
9: 7 "Whoever corrects a **mocker** invites insult; whoever rebukes a
9: 8 Do not rebuke a **mocker** or he will hate you; rebuke a wise man
13: 1 his father's instruction, but a **mocker** does not listen to rebuke.
14: 6 The **mocker** seeks wisdom and finds none, but knowledge comes
15:12 A **mocker** resents correction; he will not consult the wise.
19:25 Flog a **mocker**, and the simple will learn prudence; rebuke a
19:29 Penalties are prepared for **mockers**, and beatings for the backs of
20: 1 Wine is a **mocker** and beer a brawler; whoever is led astray by
21:11 When a **mocker** is punished, the simple gain wisdom; when a wise
21:24 The proud and arrogant man—"**Mocker**" is his name; he behaves
22:10 Drive out the **mocker**, and out goes strife; quarrels and insults are
24: 9 The schemes of folly are sin, and men detest a **mocker**.
Isa 29:20 The ruthless will vanish, the **mockers** will disappear, and all who

4371 לָצוֹן ***lāṣôn***, n.[m.]. [3] [√ 4329]

mockers [+408] [1], mockery [1], scoffers [+408] [1]

Pr 1:22 How long will mockers delight in **mockery** and fools hate
29: 8 **Mockers** [+408] stir up a city, but wise men turn away anger.
Isa 28:14 you **scoffers** [+408] who rule this people in Jerusalem.

4372 לָצַץ ***lāṣaṣ***, n.[m.] *or* v.ptcp. [1] [√ 4329]

mockers [1]

Hos 7: 5 [A] inflamed with wine, and he joins hands with the **mockers**.

4373 לַקּוּם ***laqqûm***, n.pr.loc. [1]

Lakkum [1]

Jos 19:33 passing Adami Nekeb and Jabneel to **Lakkum** and ending at the

4374 לָקַח ***lāqaḥ***, v. [966 / 965] [→ 4375, 4376, 4917, 4918?, 4920, 5228, 5229]

take [238], took [238], get [46], taken [32], accept [23], *untranslated* [21], bring [20], brought [20], married [16], taking [14], take away [12], receive [11], received [11], took away [10], marry [8], accepted [7], choose [7], accepts [6], carried off [6], got [6], selected [6], takes [6], capture [5], captured [5], marries [5], bring back [4], put [4], seize [4], seized [4], taken away [4], was taken [4], be taken [3], been captured [3], carried away [3], carried [3], collected [3], married [+851+906+4200+4200] [3], marry [+851] [3], respond to [3], select [3], took hold [3], use [3], am taken [2], carry away [2], collect [2], found [2], is taken [2], keep [2], kill [+5883] [2], led away [2], married [+851] [2], married [+851+4200] [2], married [+851+4946] [2], married [+851+906+4200] [2], marry [+851+4200] [2], marry [+851+4200+4200] [2], picked up [2], purchased [+928+4697] [2], takes away [2], took as prisoners [2], was taken away [2], were taken [2], accepting [1], acquiring [1], adopted [+1426+4200+4200] [1], appoint [1], are gathered [1], are taken [1], arrest [1], be brought [1], be taken away [1], become wife [+851+4200] [1], been taken away [1], been taken [1], being led away [1], blow away [1], bring [+906+2256+3655] [1], buy [1], buys [1], captivate [1], carried [+906+906+928+3338] [1], catch [1], caught [1], choose as wives [1], chose [1], come back [1], did[s] so [+448+2256+2932+8008] [1], did[s] so [1], did[s] [1], disgraced [+1423] [1], drew [1], find [1], flashed back and forth [+928+9348] [1], flashing [1], force to give [1], get back [1], gets [1], given [1], grabbed [1], had brought [+2256+8938] [1], had brought [1], had removed [+906+2256+8938] [1], have come [1], have [1], invites [1], kept [1], learn [1], learned [1], loaded [1], made

[+906+906+928+4200+4200+4200] [1], make [1], married [+851+4200+4200+4200] [1], married [+851+906] [1], married [+851+906+2257+4200+4200] [1], married [+851+906+906] [1], marries [+1249+2256] [1], marry [+851+906+4200+4200] [1], need [1], open to [1], pledged to marry [1], prefer [1], prepare [1], recaptured [+906+2256+8740] [1], receives [1], removed [1], responded to [1], retake [1], sampled [1], send for [+2256+8938] [1], send for [+906+2256+8938] [1], sent for [+906+2256+4200+4200 +8938] [1], sent for [1], share [1], snatched [1], strip of [1], stripped [1], suffer [1], summon [+448+906+2256+8938] [1], take up [1], takes life [1], taking hold [1], took down [1], took in marriage [+851+906 +4200+4200] [1], took out [1], took over [1], took prisoner [1], use as [1], wag [1], want [1], was captured [1], wins [1]

Ge 2: 15 [A] The LORD God **took** the man and put him in the Garden of
2: 21 [A] *he* **took** one of the man's ribs and closed up the place with
2: 22 [A] the LORD God made a woman from the rib *he had* **taken**
2: 23 [E] she shall be called 'woman,' for she **was taken** out of man."
3: 6 [A] also desirable for gaining wisdom, *she* **took** some and ate it.
3: 19 [E] until you return to the ground, since from it *you* **were taken**;
3: 22 [A] reach out his hand and **take** also from the tree of life and eat,
3: 23 [E] of Eden to work the ground from which *he had* **been taken**.
4: 11 [A] which opened its mouth to **receive** your brother's blood from
4: 19 [A] Lamech **married** two women, one named Adah and the other
5: 24 [A] then he was no more, because God **took** him **away**.
6: 2 [A] and *they* **married** [+851+4200] any of them they chose.
6: 21 [A] You *are to* **take** every kind of food that is to be eaten
7: 2 [A] **Take** with you seven of every kind of clean animal, a male
8: 9 [A] He reached out his hand and **took** the dove and brought it
8: 20 [A] **taking** some of all the clean animals and clean birds, he
9: 23 [A] Shem and Japheth **took** a garment and laid it across their
11: 29 [A] Abram and Nahor both **married** [+851+4200]. The name of
11: 31 [A] **took** his son Abram, his grandson Lot son of Haran, and
12: 5 [A] **took** his wife Sarai, his nephew Lot, all the possessions they
12: 15 [E] praised her to Pharaoh, and she **was taken** *into* his palace.
12: 19 [A] you say, 'She is my sister,' so that *I* **took** her to be my wife?
12: 19 [A] be my wife? Now then, here is your wife. **Take** her and go!"
14: 11 [A] four kings **seized** all the goods of Sodom and Gomorrah and
14: 12 [A] *They* also **carried** off Abram's nephew Lot and his
14: 21 [A] "Give me the people and **keep** the goods for yourself."
14: 23 [A] that *I will* **accept** nothing belonging to you, not even a thread
14: 24 [A] to Aner, Eshcol and Mamre. *Let* them **have** their share."
15: 9 [A] "**Bring** me a heifer, a goat and a ram, each three years old,
15: 10 [A] Abram **brought** all these to him, cut them in two
16: 3 [A] Sarai his wife **took** her Egyptian maidservant Hagar and gave
17: 23 [A] **took** his son Ishmael and all those born in his household or
18: 4 [E] *Let* a little water **be brought**, and then you may all wash
18: 5 [A] *Let me* **get** you something to eat, so you can be refreshed
18: 7 [A] he ran to the herd and **selected** a choice, tender calf and gave
18: 8 [A] *He* then **brought** some curds and milk and the calf that had
19: 14 [A] his sons-in-law, *who were* **pledged to marry** his daughters.
19: 15 [A] **Take** your wife and your two daughters who are here, or you
20: 2 [A] Then Abimelech king of Gerar sent for Sarah and **took** her.
20: 3 [A] are as good as dead because of the woman *you have* **taken**;
20: 14 [A] Abimelech **brought** sheep and cattle and male and female
21: 14 [A] Early the next morning Abraham **took** some food and a skin
21: 21 [A] Desert of Paran, his mother **got** a wife for him from Egypt.
21: 27 [A] So Abraham **brought** sheep and cattle and gave them to
21: 30 [A] "**Accept** these seven lambs from my hand as a witness that I
22: 2 [A] God said, "**Take** your son, your only son, Isaac, whom you
22: 3 [A] *He* **took** with him two of his servants and his son Isaac.
22: 6 [A] Abraham **took** the wood for the burnt offering and placed it
22: 6 [A] and *he* himself **carried** [+906+906+928+3338] the fire and the
22: 10 [A] he reached out his hand and **took** the knife to slay his son.
22: 13 [A] He went over and **took** the ram and sacrificed it as a burnt
23: 13 [A] of the field. **Accept** it from me so I can bury my dead there."
24: 3 [A] that *you will* not **get** a wife for my son from the daughters of
24: 4 [A] and my own relatives and **get** a wife for my son Isaac."
24: 7 [A] who **brought** me out of my father's household and my native
24: 7 [A] before you so that *you can* **get** a wife for my son from there.
24: 10 [A] the servant **took** ten of his master's camels and left, taking
24: 22 [A] the man **took out** a gold nose ring weighing a beka and two
24: 37 [A] '*You must* not **get** a wife for my son from the daughters of
24: 38 [A] and to my own clan, and **get** a wife for my son.'
24: 40 [A] so that *you can* **get** a wife for my son from my own clan
24: 48 [A] who had led me on the right road to **get** the granddaughter of
24: 51 [A] **take** her and go, and let her become the wife of your master's
24: 61 [A] back with the man. So the servant **took** Rebekah and left.
24: 65 [A] servant answered. So *she* **took** her veil and covered herself.
24: 67 [A] into the tent of his mother Sarah, and *he* **married** Rebekah.
25: 1 [A] Abraham **took** another wife, whose name was Keturah.
25: 20 [A] when he **married** [+851+906+2257+4200+4200] Rebekah
26: 34 [A] *he* **married** [+851+906+906] Judith daughter of Beeri the
27: 9 [A] Go out to the flock and **bring** me two choice young goats,
27: 13 [A] curse fall on me. Just do what I say; go and **get** them for me."
27: 14 [A] So he went and **got** them and brought them to his mother,
27: 15 [A] Then Rebekah **took** the best clothes of Esau her older son,
27: 35 [A] "Your brother came deceitfully and **took** your blessing."
27: 36 [A] *He* **took** my birthright, and now he's taken my blessing!"
27: 36 [A] He took my birthright, and now *he's* **taken** my blessing!"
27: 45 [A] did to him, I'll send word for you *to* **come back** from there.
27: 46 [A] If Jacob **takes** a wife from among the women of this land,
28: 1 [A] "*Do* not **marry** [+851] a Canaanite woman.
28: 2 [A] **Take** a wife for yourself there, from among the daughters of
28: 6 [A] and had sent him to Paddan Aram to **take** a wife from there,
28: 6 [A] "*Do* not **marry** [+851] a Canaanite woman,"
28: 9 [A] and **married** [+851+906+4200+4200] Mahalath, the sister of
28: 11 [A] **Taking** one of the stones there, he put it under his head
28: 18 [A] Early the next morning Jacob **took** the stone he had placed
29: 23 [A] *he* **took** his daughter Leah and gave her to Jacob, and Jacob
30: 9 [A] *she* **took** her maidservant Zilpah and gave her to Jacob as a
30: 15 [A] to her, "Wasn't it enough that you **took away** my husband?
30: 15 [A] *Will you* **take** my son's mandrakes too?" "Very well,"
30: 37 [A] **took** fresh-cut branches from poplar, almond and plane trees
31: 1 [A] "Jacob *has* **taken** everything our father owned and has
31: 23 [A] **Taking** his relatives with him, he pursued Jacob for seven
31: 32 [A] there is anything of yours here with me; and if so, **take** it."
31: 34 [A] Now Rachel *had* **taken** the household gods and put them
31: 45 [A] So Jacob **took** a stone and set it up as a pillar.
31: 46 [A] So *they* **took** stones and piled them in a heap, and they ate
31: 50 [A] my daughters or if *you* **take** any wives besides my daughters,
32: 13 [32:14] [A] from what he had with him *he* **selected** a gift for his
32: 22 [32:23] [A] **took** his two wives, his two maidservants and his
32: 23 [32:24] [A] After **[RPH]** he had sent them across the stream,
33: 10 [A] "If I have found favor in your eyes, **accept** this gift from me.
33: 11 [A] Please **accept** the present that was brought to you, for God
33: 11 [A] all I need." And because Jacob insisted, Esau **accepted** it.
34: 2 [A] the ruler of that area, saw her, *he* **took** her and violated her.
34: 4 [A] said to his father Hamor, "**Get** me this girl as my wife."
34: 9 [A] us your daughters and **take** our daughters for yourselves.
34: 16 [A] you our daughters and **take** your daughters for ourselves.
34: 17 [A] not agree to be circumcised, *we'll* **take** our sister and go."
34: 21 [A] We *can* **marry** [+851+906+4200+4200] their daughters and
34: 25 [A] **took** their swords and attacked the unsuspecting city,
34: 26 [A] to the sword and **took** Dinah from Shechem's house and left.
34: 28 [A] *They* **seized** their flocks and herds and donkeys and everything
36: 2 [A] Esau **took** his wives from the women of Canaan: Adah
36: 6 [A] **took** his wives and sons and daughters and all the members of
37: 24 [A] *they* **took** him and threw him into the cistern.
37: 31 [A] *they* **got** Joseph's robe, slaughtered a goat and dipped the
38: 2 [A] man named Shua. *He* **married** her and lay with her;
38: 6 [A] Judah **got** a wife for Er, his firstborn, and her name was
38: 20 [A] Adullamite in order to **get** his pledge **back** from the woman,
38: 23 [A] Judah said, "*Let her* **keep** what she has, or we will become a
38: 28 [A] so the midwife **took** a scarlet thread and tied it on his wrist
39: 20 [A] Joseph's master **took** him and put him in prison, the place
40: 11 [A] Pharaoh's cup was in my hand, and *I* **took** the grapes,
42: 16 [A] Send one of your number *to* **get** your brother; the rest of you
42: 24 [A] *He had* Simeon **taken** from them and bound before their
42: 33 [A] with me, and **take** food *for* your starving households and go.
42: 36 [A] Simeon is no more, and now *you want to* **take** Benjamin.
43: 11 [A] **Put** some of the best products of the land in your bags
43: 12 [A] **Take** double the amount of silver with you, for you must
43: 13 [A] **Take** your brother also and go back to the man at once.
43: 15 [A] So the men **took** the gifts and double the amount of silver,
43: 15 [A] and double the amount of silver, **[RPH]** and Benjamin also.
43: 18 [A] overpower us and **seize** us as slaves and take our donkeys."
44: 29 [A] If *you* **take** this one from me too and harm comes to him,
45: 18 [A] **bring** your father and your families back to me. I will give
45: 19 [A] **Take** some carts from Egypt for your children and your
46: 6 [A] *They* also **took** with them their livestock and the possessions
47: 2 [A] *He* **chose** five of his brothers and presented them before
48: 1 [A] So *he* **took** his two sons Manasseh and Ephraim along with
48: 9 [A] Then Israel said, "**Bring** them to me so I may bless them."
48: 13 [A] **took** both of them, Ephraim on his right toward Israel's left
48: 22 [A] I give the ridge of land *I* **took** from the Amorites with my
Ex 2: 1 [A] Now a man of the house of Levi **married** a Levite woman,
2: 3 [A] *she* **got** a papyrus basket for him and coated it with tar
2: 5 [A] the basket among the reeds and sent her slave girl *to* **get** it.
2: 9 [A] will pay you." So the woman **took** the baby and nursed him.
4: 9 [A] **take** some water from the Nile and pour it on the dry ground.
4: 9 [A] The water *you* **take** from the river will become blood on the
4: 17 [A] **take** this staff in your hand so you can perform miraculous
4: 20 [A] So Moses **took** his wife and sons, put them on a donkey
4: 20 [A] back to Egypt. And he **took** the staff of God in his hand.
4: 25 [A] Zipporah **took** a flint knife, cut off her son's foreskin
5: 11 [A] Go and **get** your own straw wherever you can find it,
6: 7 [A] *I will* **take** you as my own people, and I will be your God.

Ex 6:20 [A] Amram **married** [+851+906+4200+4200] his father's sister
6:23 [A] Aaron **married** [+851+906+4200+4200] Elisheba, daughter of
6:25 [A] Eleazar son of Aaron **married** [+851+4200+4200+4200] one
7: 9 [A] '**Take** your staff and throw it down before Pharaoh,'
7:15 [A] **take** in your hand the staff that was changed into a snake.
7:19 [A] '**Take** your staff and stretch out your hand over the waters of
9: 8 [A] "**Take** handfuls of soot from a furnace and have Moses toss
9:10 [A] So *they* **took** soot from a furnace and stood before Pharaoh.
9:24 [F] hail fell and lightning **flashed** [+928+9348] **back and forth.**
10:26 [A] *We have to* **use** some of them in worshiping the LORD our
12: 3 [A] day of this month each man *is to* **take** a lamb for his family,
12: 4 [A] they *must* **share** one with their nearest neighbor,
12: 5 [A] and *you may* **take** them from the sheep or the goats.
12: 7 [A] *they are to* **take** some of the blood and put it on the sides
12:21 [A] "Go at once and **select** the animals for your families
12:22 [A] **Take** a bunch of hyssop, dip it into the blood in the basin
12:32 [A] **Take** your flocks and herds, as you have said, and go.
13:19 [A] Moses **took** the bones of Joseph with him because Joseph
14: 6 [A] he had his chariot made ready and **took** his army with him.
14: 7 [A] *He* **took** six hundred of the best chariots, along with all the
14:11 [A] because there were no graves in Egypt *that you* **brought** us
15:20 [A] Aaron's sister, **took** a tambourine in her hand,
16:16 [A] **Take** an omer for each person you have in your tent.' "
16:33 [A] said to Aaron, "**Take** a jar and put an omer of manna in it.
17: 5 [A] **Take** with you some of the elders of Israel and take in your
17: 5 [A] **take** in your hand the staff with which you struck the Nile,
17:12 [A] *they* **took** a stone and put it under him and he sat on it.
18: 2 [A] his wife Zipporah, his father-in-law Jethro **received** her
18:12 [A] **brought** a burnt offering and other sacrifices to God,
21:10 [A] If *he* **marries** another woman, he must not deprive the first
21:14 [A] **take** him away from my altar and put him to death.
22:11 [22:10] [A] The owner *is to* **accept** this, and no restitution is
23: 8 [A] "*Do* not **accept** a bribe, for a bribe blinds those who see
24: 6 [A] Moses **took** half of the blood and put it in bowls,
24: 7 [A] *he* **took** the Book of the Covenant and read it to the people.
24: 8 [A] Moses then **took** the blood, sprinkled it on the people
25: 2 [A] "Tell the Israelites *to* **bring** me an offering. You are to
25: 2 [A] *You are to* **receive** the offering for me from each man whose
25: 3 [A] These are the offerings *you are to* **receive** from them: gold,
27:20 [A] "Command the Israelites *to* **bring** you clear oil of pressed
28: 5 [A] *Have* them **use** gold, and blue, purple and scarlet yarn, and
28: 9 [A] "**Take** two onyx stones and engrave on them the names of
29: 1 [A] as priests: **Take** a young bull and two rams without defect.
29: 5 [A] **Take** the garments and dress Aaron with the tunic, the robe
29: 7 [A] **Take** the anointing oil and anoint him by pouring it on his
29:12 [A] **Take** some of the bull's blood and put it on the horns of the
29:13 [A] **take** all the fat around the inner parts, the covering of the liver,
29:15 [A] "**Take** one of the rams, and Aaron and his sons shall lay their
29:16 [A] Slaughter it and **take** the blood and sprinkle it against the
29:19 [A] "**Take** the other ram, and Aaron and his sons shall lay their
29:20 [A] **take** some of its blood and put it on the lobes of the right ears
29:21 [A] **take** some of the blood on the altar and some of the anointing
29:22 [A] "**Take** from this ram the fat, the fat tail, the fat around the inner
29:25 [A] **take** them from their hands and burn them on the altar along
29:26 [A] After *you* **take** the breast of the ram for Aaron's ordination,
29:31 [A] "**Take** the ram for the ordination and cook the meat in a
30:16 [A] **Receive** the atonement money from the Israelites and use it
30:23 [A] "**Take** the following fine spices: 500 shekels of liquid myrrh,
30:34 [A] the LORD said to Moses, "**Take** fragrant spices—
32: 4 [A] *He* **took** what they handed him and made it into an idol cast
32:20 [A] And *he* **took** the calf they had made and burned it in the fire;
33: 7 [A] Now Moses *used to* **take** a tent and pitch it outside the camp
34: 4 [A] and *he* **carried** the two stone tablets in his hands.
34:16 [A] when *you* **choose** some of their daughters **as wives** for your
35: 5 [A] From what you have, **take** an offering for the LORD.
36: 3 [A] *They* **received** from Moses all the offerings the Israelites had
40: 9 [A] "**Take** the anointing oil and anoint the tabernacle
40:20 [A] *He* **took** the Testimony and placed it in the ark, attached the
Lev 4: 5 [A] Then the anointed priest *shall* **take** some of the bull's blood
4:25 [A] the priest *shall* **take** some of the blood of the sin offering
4:30 [A] Then the priest *is to* **take** some of the blood with his finger
4:34 [A] the priest *shall* **take** some of the blood of the sin offering
7:34 [A] *I have* **taken** the breast that is waved and the thigh that is
8: 2 [A] "**Bring** Aaron and his sons, their garments, the anointing oil,
8:10 [A] Moses **took** the anointing oil and anointed the tabernacle
8:15 [A] Moses slaughtered the bull and **took** some of the blood,
8:16 [A] **took** all the fat around the inner parts, the covering of the liver,
8:23 [A] Moses slaughtered the ram and **took** some of its blood
8:25 [A] *He* **took** the fat, the fat tail, all the fat around the inner parts,
8:26 [A] *he* **took** a cake of bread, and one made with oil, and a wafer;
8:28 [A] Moses **took** them from their hands and burned them on the
8:29 [A] He also **took** the breast—Moses' share of the ordination
8:30 [A] Moses **took** some of the anointing oil and some of the blood
9: 2 [A] "**Take** a bull calf for your sin offering and a ram for your
9: 3 [A] '**Take** a male goat for a sin offering, a calf and a lamb—
9: 5 [A] *They* **took** the things Moses commanded to the front of the
9:15 [A] *He* **took** the goat for the people's sin offering
10: 1 [A] Aaron's sons Nadab and Abihu **took** their censers, put fire in
10:12 [A] "**Take** the grain offering left over from the offerings made to
12: 8 [A] *she is to* **bring** two doves or two young pigeons, one for a
14: 4 [A] and hyssop *be* **brought** for the one to be cleansed.
14: 6 [A] *He is* then *to* **take** the live bird and dip it, together with the
14:10 [A] "On the eighth day *he must* **bring** two male lambs and one
14:12 [A] "Then the priest *is to* **take** one of the male lambs and offer it
14:14 [A] The priest *is to* **take** some of the blood of the guilt offering
14:15 [A] The priest *shall* then **take** some of the log of oil, pour it in
14:21 [A] *he must* **take** one male lamb as a guilt offering to be waved
14:24 [A] priest *is to* **take** the lamb for the guilt offering, together with
14:25 [A] the lamb for the guilt offering and **take** some of its blood
14:42 [A] *they are to* **take** other stones to replace these and take new
14:42 [A] to replace these and **take** new clay and plaster the house.
14:49 [A] To purify the house *he is to* **take** two birds and some cedar
14:51 [A] *he is to* **take** the cedar wood, the hyssop, the scarlet yarn and
15:14 [A] On the eighth day *he must* **take** two doves or two young
15:29 [A] On the eighth day *she must* **take** two doves or two young
16: 5 [A] From the Israelite community *he is to* **take** two male goats
16: 7 [A] *he is to* **take** the two goats and present them before the
16:12 [A] *He is to* **take** a censer full of burning coals from the altar
16:14 [A] *He is to* **take** some of the bull's blood and with his finger
16:18 [A] *He shall* **take** some of the bull's blood and some of the
18:17 [A] **[NIE]** Do not have sexual relations with either her son's
18:18 [A] " '*Do* not **take** your wife's sister as a rival wife and have
20:14 [A] " 'If a man **marries** both a woman and her mother, it is
20:17 [A] " 'If a man **marries** his sister, the daughter of either his father
20:21 [A] " 'If a man **marries** his brother's wife, it is an act of
21: 7 [A] " '*They must* not **marry** women defiled by prostitution
21: 7 [A] their husbands, **[RPH]** because priests are holy to their God.
21:13 [A] " 'The woman he **marries** must be a virgin.
21:14 [A] *He must* not **marry** a widow, a divorced woman, or a
21:14 [A] but only a virgin from his own people, **[RPH]**
23:40 [A] On the first day *you are to* **take** choice fruit from the trees,
24: 2 [A] "Command the Israelites *to* **bring** you clear oil of pressed
24: 5 [A] "**Take** fine flour and bake twelve loaves of bread,
25:36 [A] *Do* not **take** interest of any kind from him, but fear your
Nu 1:17 [A] and Aaron **took** these men whose names had been given,
3:12 [A] "I *have* **taken** the Levites from among the Israelites in place
3:41 [A] **Take** the Levites for me in place of all the firstborn of the
3:45 [A] "**Take** the Levites in place of all the firstborn of Israel, and
3:47 [A] **collect** five shekels for each one, according to the sanctuary
3:47 [A] the sanctuary shekel, **[RPH]** which weighs twenty gerahs.
3:49 [A] So Moses **collected** the redemption money from those who
3:50 [A] From the firstborn of the Israelites *he* **collected** silver
4: 9 [A] "*They are to* **take** a blue cloth and cover the lampstand that
4:12 [A] "*They are to* **take** all the articles used for ministering in the
5:17 [A] he *shall* **take** some holy water in a clay jar and put some dust
5:17 [A] **[RPH]** put some dust from the tabernacle floor into the
5:25 [A] The priest *is to* **take** from her hands the grain offering for
6:18 [A] *He is to* **take** the hair and put it in the fire that is under the
6:19 [A] the priest **[NIE]** is to place in his hands a boiled shoulder of
7: 5 [A] "**Accept** these from them, that they may be used in the work
7: 6 [A] So Moses **took** the carts and oxen and gave them to the
8: 6 [A] "**Take** the Levites from among the other Israelites and make
8: 8 [A] *Have them* **take** a young bull with its grain offering of fine
8: 8 [A] then *you are to* **take** a second young bull for a sin offering.
8:16 [A] *I have* **taken** them as my own in place of the firstborn,
8:18 [A] *I have* **taken** the Levites in place of all the firstborn sons in
11:16 [A] **Have** them **come** to the Tent of Meeting, that they may stand
12: 1 [A] of his Cushite wife, **[RPH]** for he had married a Cushite.
12: 1 [A] of his Cushite wife, for *he had* **married** [+851] a Cushite.
13:20 [A] Do your best *to* **bring back** some of the fruit of the land."
16: 1 [g] On son of Peleth—*became* insolent [BHS ***took*** *men*; NIV 3689]
16: 6 [A] Korah, and all your followers are to do this: **Take** censers
16:17 [A] Each man *is to* **take** his censer and put incense in it—
16:18 [A] So each man **took** his censer, put fire and incense in it, and
16:39 [17:4] [A] So Eleazar the priest **collected** the bronze censers
16:46 [17:11] [A] to Aaron, "**Take** your censer and put incense in it,
16:47 [17:12] [A] So Aaron **did**[s] as Moses said, and ran into the midst
17: 2 [17:17] [A] "Speak to the Israelites and **get** twelve staffs from
17: 9 [17:24] [A] looked at them, and each man **took** his own staff.
18: 6 [A] *I* myself *have* **selected** your fellow Levites from among the
18:26 [A] 'When *you* **receive** from the Israelites the tithe I give you as
18:28 [A] LORD from all the tithes *you* **receive** from the Israelites.
19: 2 [A] Tell the Israelites *to* **bring** you a red heifer without defect
19: 4 [A] Eleazar the priest *is to* **take** some of its blood on his finger
19: 6 [A] The priest *is to* **take** some cedar wood, hyssop and scarlet
19:17 [A] **put** some ashes from the burned purification offering into a
19:18 [A] a man who is ceremonially clean *is to* **take** some hyssop,
20: 8 [A] "**Take** the staff, and you and your brother Aaron gather the

Nu 20: 9 [A] So Moses **took** the staff from the LORD's presence, just as
20: 25 [A] **Get** Aaron and his son Eleazar and take them up Mount Hor.
21: 25 [A] Israel **captured** all the cities of the Amorites and occupied
21: 26 [A] and *had* **taken** from him all his land as far as the Arnon.
22: 41 [A] The next morning Balak **took** Balaam up to Bamoth Baal,
23: 11 [A] *I* **brought** you to curse my enemies, but you have done
23: 14 [A] So *he* **took** him *to* the field of Zophim on the top of Pisgah,
23: 20 [A] *I have* **received** a command to bless; he has blessed, and I
23: 27 [A] said to Balaam, "Come, *let me* **take** you to another place.
23: 28 [A] Balak **took** Balaam *to* the top of Peor, overlooking the
25: 4 [A] "**Take** all the leaders of these people, kill them and expose
25: 7 [A] saw this, he left the assembly, **took** a spear in his hand
27: 18 [A] "**Take** Joshua son of Nun, a man in whom is the spirit,
27: 22 [A] *He* **took** Joshua and had him stand before Eleazar the priest
31: 11 [A] *They* **took** all the plunder and spoils, including the people
31: 29 [A] **Take** this tribute from their half share and give it to Eleazar
31: 30 [A] **select** one out of every fifty, whether persons, cattle,
31: 47 [A] Moses **selected** one out of every fifty persons and animals,
31: 51 [A] Moses and Eleazar the priest **accepted** from them the gold—
31: 54 [A] Eleazar the priest **accepted** the gold from the commanders of
34: 14 [A] the half-tribe of Manasseh **[RPH]** have received their
34: 14 [A] the half-tribe of Manasseh *have* **received** their inheritance.
34: 15 [A] a half tribes *have* **received** their inheritance on the east side
34: 18 [A] **appoint** one leader from each tribe to help assign the land.
35: 31 [A] " '*Do* not **accept** a ransom for the life of a murderer,
35: 32 [A] " '*Do* not **accept** a ransom for anyone who has fled to a city
Dt 1: 15 [A] So *I* **took** the leading men of your tribes, wise and respected
1: 23 [A] to me; so *I* **selected** twelve of you, one man from each tribe.
1: 25 [A] **Taking** with them some of the fruit of the land, they brought
3: 4 [A] There was not one of the sixty cities that *we did* not **take**
3: 8 [A] So at that time *we* **took** from these two kings of the Amorites
3: 14 [A] **took** the whole region of Argob as far as the border of the
4: 20 [A] the LORD **took** you and brought you out of the
4: 34 [A] Has any god ever tried to **take** for himself one nation out of
7: 3 [A] daughters to their sons or **take** their daughters for your sons,
7: 25 [A] and gold on them, and *do* not **take** it for yourselves,
9: 9 [A] When I went up on the mountain to **receive** the tablets of
9: 21 [A] Also *I* **took** that sinful thing of yours, the calf you had made,
10: 17 [A] who shows no partiality and **accepts** no bribes.
15: 17 [A] **take** an awl and push it through his ear lobe into the door,
16: 19 [A] *Do* not **accept** a bribe, for a bribe blinds the eyes of the wise
19: 12 [A] of his town shall send for him, **bring** him **back** from the city,
20: 7 [A] anyone become pledged to a woman and not **married** her?
20: 7 [A] or he may die in battle and someone else **marry** her."
21: 3 [A] the elders of the town nearest the body *shall* **take** a heifer
21: 11 [A] and are attracted to her, *you may* **take** her as your wife.
22: 6 [A] or on the eggs, *do* not **take** the mother with the young.
22: 7 [A] *You may* **take** the young, but be sure to let the mother go,
22: 13 [A] If a man **takes** a wife and, after lying with her, dislikes her
22: 14 [A] and gives her a bad name, saying, "*I* **married** this woman,
22: 15 [A] girl's father and mother *shall* **bring** [+906+2256+3655] proof
22: 18 [A] and the elders *shall* **take** the man and punish him.
22: 30 [23:1] [A] A man *is* not *to* **marry** his father's wife; he must not
24: 1 [A] If a man **marries** [+1249+2256] a woman who becomes
24: 3 [A] it to her and sends her from his house, or if he dies, **[RPH]**
24: 4 [A] is not allowed to **marry** [+851+4200] her again after she has
24: 5 [A] If a man *has* recently **married** [+851], he must not be sent to
24: 5 [A] at home and bring happiness to the wife *he has* **married**.
24: 19 [A] your field and you overlook a sheaf, do not go back to **get** it.
25: 5 [A] shall take her and **marry** [+851+4200+4200] her and fulfill the
25: 7 [A] if a man does not want to **marry** his brother's wife,
25: 8 [A] to him. If he persists in saying, "I do not want to **marry** her,"
26: 2 [A] **take** some of the firstfruits of all that you produce from the
26: 4 [A] The priest *shall* **take** the basket from your hands and set it
27: 25 [A] "Cursed is the man *who* **accepts** a bribe to kill an innocent
29: 8 [29:7] [A] *We* **took** their land and gave it as an inheritance to
30: 4 [A] the LORD your God will gather you and **bring** you **back**.
30: 12 [A] "Who will ascend into heaven *to* **get** it and proclaim it to us
30: 13 [A] "Who will cross the sea *to* **get** it and proclaim it to us so we
31: 26 [A] "**Take** this Book of the Law and place it beside the ark of the
32: 11 [A] that spreads its wings *to* **catch** them and carries them on its
Jos 2: 4 [A] the woman *had* **taken** the two men and hidden them. She
3: 12 [A] Now then, **choose** twelve men from the tribes of Israel, one
4: 2 [A] "**Choose** twelve men from among the people, one from each
4: 20 [A] Joshua set up at Gilgal the twelve stones *they had* **taken** out
6: 18 [A] not bring about your own destruction *by* **taking** any of them.
7: 1 [A] the son of Zerah, of the tribe of Judah, **took** some of them.
7: 11 [A] *They have* **taken** some of the devoted things; they have
7: 21 [A] gold weighing fifty shekels, I coveted them and **took** them.
7: 23 [A] *They* **took** the things from the tent, brought them to Joshua
7: 24 [A] **took** Achan son of Zerah, the silver, the robe, the gold wedge,
8: 1 [A] **Take** the whole army with you, and go up and attack Ai.
8: 12 [A] Joshua *had* **taken** about five thousand men and set them in
9: 4 [A] They went as a delegation whose donkeys *were* **loaded** *with*
9: 11 [A] in our country said to us, '**Take** provisions for your journey;
9: 14 [A] The men of Israel **sampled** their provisions but did not
11: 16 [A] So Joshua **took** this entire land: the hill country, all the
11: 19 [A] of peace with the Israelites, *who* **took** them all in battle.
11: 23 [A] So Joshua **took** the entire land, just as the LORD had
13: 8 [A] the Gadites *had* **received** the inheritance that Moses had
18: 7 [A] the half-tribe of Manasseh *have already* **received** their
24: 3 [A] *I* **took** your father Abraham from the land beyond the River
24: 26 [A] *he* **took** a large stone and set it up there under the oak near
Jdg 3: 6 [A] **took** [+851+906+4200+4200] their daughters **in marriage** and
3: 21 [A] **drew** the sword from his right thigh and plunged it into the
3: 25 [A] the doors of the room, *they* **took** a key and unlocked them.
4: 6 [A] **take** with you ten thousand men of Naphtali and Zebulun
4: 21 [A] **picked up** a tent peg and a hammer and went quietly to him
5: 19 [A] of Megiddo, but *they* **carried off** no silver, no plunder.
6: 20 [A] "**Take** the meat and the unleavened bread, place them on this
6: 25 [A] "**Take** the second bull from your father's herd, the one seven
6: 26 [A] cut down, **[NIE]** offer the second bull as a burnt offering."
6: 27 [A] So Gideon **took** ten of his servants and did as the LORD
7: 8 [A] *who* **took over** the provisions and trumpets of the others.
8: 16 [A] *He* **took** the elders of the town and taught the men of Succoth a
8: 21 [A] killed them, and **took** the ornaments off their camels' necks.
9: 43 [A] So *he* **took** his men, divided them into three companies
9: 48 [A] He **took** an ax and cut off some branches, which he lifted to
11: 5 [A] the elders of Gilead went to **get** Jephthah from the land of
11: 13 [A] they **took away** my land from the Arnon to the Jabbok, all
11: 15 [A] Israel *did* not **take** the land of Moab or the land of the
13: 19 [A] Manoah **took** a young goat, together with the grain offering,
13: 23 [A] *he would* not *have* **accepted** a burnt offering and grain
14: 2 [A] woman in Timnah; now **get** her for me as my wife."
14: 3 [A] Must you go to the uncircumcised Philistines to **get** a wife?"
14: 3 [A] Samson said to his father, "**Get** her for me. She's the right
14: 8 [A] Some time later, when he went back to **marry** her, he turned
14: 11 [A] When he appeared, he *was* **given** thirty companions.
14: 19 [A] **stripped** them *of* their belongings and gave their clothes to
15: 4 [A] three hundred foxes and **[NIE]** tied them tail to tail in pairs.
15: 6 [A] because **[NIE]** his wife was given to his friend."
15: 15 [A] of a donkey, *he* **grabbed** it and struck down a thousand men.
16: 12 [A] So Delilah **took** new ropes and tied him with them. Then,
17: 2 [E] "The eleven hundred shekels of silver that **were taken** from
17: 2 [A] you utter a curse—I have that silver with me; *I* **took** it."
17: 4 [A] she **took** two hundred shekels of silver and gave them to a
18: 17 [A] **took** the carved image, the ephod, the other household gods and
18: 18 [A] **took** the carved image, the ephod, the other household gods and
18: 20 [A] *He* **took** the ephod, the other household gods and the carved
18: 24 [A] He replied, "*You* **took** the gods I made, and my priest,
18: 27 [A] they **took** what Micah had made, and his priest, and went on
19: 1 [A] of Ephraim **took** a concubine from Bethlehem in Judah.
19: 28 [A] Then the man **put** her on his donkey and set out for home.
19: 29 [A] *he* **took** a knife and cut up his concubine, limb by limb, into
20: 10 [A] *We'll* **take** ten men out of every hundred from all the tribes
20: 10 [A] a thousand from ten thousand, to **get** provisions for the army.
21: 22 [A] because *we did* not **get** wives for them during the war,
Ru 4: 2 [A] Boaz **took** ten of the elders of the town and said, "Sit here,"
4: 13 [A] So Boaz **took** Ruth and she became his wife. Then he went to
4: 16 [A] Naomi **took** the child, laid him in her lap and cared for him.
1Sa 2: 14 [A] the priest *would* **take** for himself whatever the fork brought
2: 15 [A] *he* won't **accept** boiled meat from you, but only raw."
2: 16 [A] then **take** whatever you want," the servant would
2: 16 [A] "No, hand it over now; if you don't, *I'll* **take** it by force."
4: 3 [A] *Let us* **bring** the ark of the LORD's covenant from Shiloh,
4: 11 [C] The ark of God **was captured**, and Eli's two sons, Hophni
4: 17 [C] are dead, and the ark of God *has* **been captured**."
4: 19 [C] she heard the news that the ark of God *had* **been captured**
4: 21 [C] because of the **capture** *of* the ark of God and the deaths of
4: 22 [C] departed from Israel, for the ark of God *has* **been captured**."
5: 1 [A] After the Philistines *had* **captured** the ark of God, they took
5: 2 [A] they **carried** the ark *into* Dagon's temple and set it beside
5: 3 [A] *They* **took** Dagon and put him back in his place.
6: 7 [A] "Now then, **get** a new cart ready, with two cows that have
6: 8 [A] **Take** the ark of the LORD and put it on the cart, and in a
6: 10 [A] *They* **took** two such cows and hitched them to the cart
7: 9 [A] Samuel **took** a suckling lamb and offered it up as a whole
7: 12 [A] Samuel **took** a stone and set it up between Mizpah and Shen.
7: 14 [A] Philistines *had* **captured** from Israel were restored to her,
8: 3 [A] dishonest gain and **accepted** bribes and perverted justice.
8: 11 [A] *He will* **take** your sons and make them serve with his
8: 13 [A] *He will* **take** your daughters to be perfumers and cooks
8: 14 [A] *He will* **take** the best of your fields and vineyards and olive
8: 16 [A] and the best of your cattle and donkeys *he will* **take**
9: 3 [A] "**Take** one of the servants with you and go and look for the
9: 22 [A] Samuel **[NIE]** brought Saul and his servant into the hall
10: 1 [A] Then Samuel **took** a flask of oil and poured it on Saul's head
10: 4 [A] you two loaves of bread, which *you will* **accept** from them.

1Sa 10:23 [A] They ran and **brought** him out, and as he stood among the
11: 7 [A] *He* **took** a pair of oxen, cut them into pieces, and sent the
12: 3 [A] of the LORD and his anointed. Whose ox *have I* **taken**?
12: 3 [A] Whose donkey *have I* **taken**? Whom have I cheated?
12: 3 [A] From whose hand *have I* **accepted** a bribe to make me shut
12: 4 [A] "*You have* not **taken** anything from anyone's hand."
14:32 [A] pounced on the plunder and, **taking** sheep, cattle and calves,
15:21 [A] The soldiers **took** sheep and cattle from the plunder, the best
16: 2 [A] The LORD said, "**Take** a heifer with you and say, 'I have
16:11 [A] Samuel said, "**Send for** [+2256+8938] him; we will not sit
16:13 [A] So Samuel **took** the horn of oil and anointed him in the
16:20 [A] So Jesse **took** a donkey loaded with bread, a skin of wine
16:23 [A] God came upon Saul, David *would* **take** his harp and play.
17:17 [A] "**Take** this ephah of roasted grain and these ten loaves of
17:18 [A] your brothers are and **bring back** some assurance from them.
17:31 [A] was overheard and reported to Saul, and Saul **sent for** him.
17:40 [A] *he* **took** his staff in his hand, chose five smooth stones from
17:49 [A] Reaching into his bag and **taking** out a stone, he slung it
17:51 [A] *He* **took hold** *of* the Philistine's sword and drew it from the
17:54 [A] David **took** the Philistine's head and brought it to Jerusalem,
17:57 [A] Abner **took** him and brought him before Saul, with David
18: 2 [A] From that day Saul **kept** David with him and did not let him
19:13 [A] Michal **took** an idol and laid it on the bed, covering it with a
19:14 [A] When Saul sent the men to **capture** David, Michal said,
19:20 [A] so he sent men to **capture** him. But when they saw a group
20:21 [A] **bring** them here,' then come, because, as surely as the
20:31 [A] Now send and **bring** him to me, for he must die!"
21: 6 [21:7] [C] replaced by hot bread on the day it **was taken away**.
21: 8 [21:9] [A] *I* haven't **brought** my sword or any other weapon,
21: 9 [21:10] [A] If *you* **want** it, take it; there is no sword here but
21: 9 [21:10] [A] If you want it, **take** it; there is no sword here but
24: 2 [24:3] [A] So Saul **took** three thousand chosen men from all
24:11 [24:12] [A] but you are hunting me down to **take** my life.
25:11 [A] Why *should I* **take** my bread and water, and the meat I have
25:18 [A] *She* **took** two hundred loaves of bread, two skins of wine,
25:35 [A] David **accepted** from her hand what she had brought him
25:39 [A] word to Abigail, asking her to **become** his **wife** [+851+4200].
25:40 [A] "David has sent us to you to **take** you to become his wife."
25:43 [A] David *had* also **married** Ahinoam of Jezreel, and they both
26:11 [A] Now **get** the spear and water jug that are near his head, and
26:12 [A] So David **took** the spear and water jug near Saul's head,
26:22 [A] "Let one of your young men come over and **get** it.
27: 9 [A] but **took** sheep and cattle, donkeys and camels, and clothes.
28:24 [A] *She* **took** some flour, kneaded it and baked bread without
30:11 [A] They found an Egyptian in a field and **brought** him to David.
30:16 [A] because of the great amount of plunder *they had* **taken** from
30:18 [A] David recovered everything the Amalekites *had* **taken**,
30:19 [A] or old, boy or girl, plunder or anything else *they had* **taken**.
30:20 [A] He **took** all the flocks and herds, and his men drove them
31: 4 [A] would not do it; so Saul **took** his own sword and fell on it.
31:12 [A] *They* **took down** the bodies of Saul and his sons from the
31:13 [A] *they* **took** their bones and buried them under a tamarisk tree
2Sa 1:10 [A] *I* **took** the crown that was on his head and the band on his
2: 8 [A] *had* **taken** Ish-Bosheth son of Saul and brought him over to
2:21 [A] take on one of the young men and **strip** him **of** his weapons."
3:15 [A] *had* her **taken away** from her husband Paltiel son of Laish.
4: 6 [A] They went into the inner part of the house as if *to* **get** some
4: 7 [A] **Taking** it with them, they traveled all night by way of the
4:12 [A] *they* **took** the head of Ish-Bosheth and buried it in Abner's
5:13 [A] David **took** more concubines and wives in Jerusalem,
7: 8 [A] I **took** you from the pasture and from following the flock to
8: 1 [A] he **took** Metheg Ammah from the control of the Philistines.
8: 7 [A] David **took** the gold shields that belonged to the officers of
8: 8 [A] to Hadadezer, King David **took** a great quantity of bronze.
9: 5 [A] So King David **had** him **brought** [+2256+8938] from Lo
10: 4 [A] So Hanun **seized** David's men, shaved off half of each man's
11: 4 [A] Then David sent messengers *to* **get** her. She came to him,
12: 4 [A] but the rich man refrained from **taking** one of his own sheep
12: 4 [A] *he* **took** the ewe lamb that belonged to the poor man
12: 9 [A] the Hittite with the sword and **took** his wife to be your own.
12:10 [A] and **took** the wife of Uriah the Hittite to be your own.'
12:11 [A] Before your very eyes *I will* **take** your wives and give them
12:30 [A] *He* **took** the crown from the head of their king—its weight
13: 8 [A] *She* **took** some dough, kneaded it, made the bread in his sight
13: 9 [A] *she* **took** the pan and served him the bread, but he refused to
13:10 [A] Tamar **took** the bread she had prepared and brought it to her
13:19 [A] Tamar **put** ashes on her head and tore the ornamented robe
14: 2 [A] to Tekoa and **had** a wise woman **brought** from there.
17:19 [A] His wife **took** a covering and spread it out over the opening
18:14 [A] So *he* **took** three javelins in his hand and plunged them into
18:17 [A] *They* **took** Absalom, threw him into a big pit in the forest
18:18 [A] During his lifetime Absalom *had* **taken** a pillar and erected it
19:30 [19:31] [A] said to the king, "*Let him* **take** everything,
20: 3 [A] he **took** the ten concubines he had left to take care of the
20: 6 [A] **Take** your master's men and pursue him, or he will find
21: 8 [A] **took** Armoni and Mephibosheth, the two sons of Aiah's
21:10 [A] Rizpah daughter of Aiah **took** sackcloth and spread it out for
21:12 [A] **took** the bones of Saul and his son Jonathan from the citizens
22:17 [A] "He reached down from on high and **took hold** *of* me;
23: 6 [A] cast aside like thorns, *which* **are** not **gathered** with the hand.
24:22 [A] "*Let* my lord the king **take** whatever pleases him and offer it
1Ki 1:33 [A] "**Take** your lord's servants with you and set Solomon my son
1:39 [A] Zadok the priest **took** the horn of oil from the sacred tent
3: 1 [A] with Pharaoh king of Egypt and **married** his daughter.
3:20 [A] **took** my son from my side while I your servant was asleep.
3:24 [A] the king said, "**Bring** me a sword." So they brought a sword
4:15 [A] (he *had* **married** [+851+906+4200] Basemath daughter of
7: 8 [A] like this hall for Pharaoh's daughter, whom *he had* **married**.
7:13 [A] King Solomon sent to Tyre and **brought** Huram,
9:28 [A] They sailed to Ophir and **brought** back 420 talents of gold,
10:28 [A] the royal merchants **purchased** [+928+4697] them from
11:18 [A] Then **taking** men from Paran with them, they went to Egypt,
11:31 [A] he said to Jeroboam, "**Take** ten pieces for yourself, for this is
11:34 [A] " 'But *I will* not **take** the whole kingdom out of Solomon's
11:35 [A] *I will* **take** the kingdom from his son's hands and give you
11:37 [A] However, as for you, *I will* **take** you, and you will rule over
14: 3 [A] **Take** ten loaves of bread with you, some cakes and a jar of
14:26 [A] *He* **carried off** the treasures of the temple of the LORD and
14:26 [A] *He* **took** everything, including all the gold shields Solomon
14:26 [A] including **[RPH]** all the gold shields Solomon had made.
15:18 [A] Asa then **took** all the silver and gold that was left in the
16:31 [A] *he* also **married** [+851+906] Jezebel daughter of Ethbaal
17:10 [A] "*Would you* **bring** me a little water in a jar so I may have a
17:11 [A] As she was going to **get** it, he called, "And bring me, please,
17:11 [A] to get it, he called, "And **bring** me, please, a piece of bread."
17:19 [A] *He* **took** him from her arms, carried him to the upper room
17:23 [A] Elijah **picked up** the child and carried him down from the
18: 4 [A] Obadiah *had* **taken** a hundred prophets and hidden them in
18:26 [A] So *they* **took** the bull given them and prepared it. Then they
18:31 [A] Elijah **took** twelve stones, one for each of the tribes
19: 4 [A] he said. "**Take** my life; I am no better than my ancestors."
19:10 [A] one left, and now they are trying to **kill** [+5883] me too."
19:14 [A] one left, and now they are trying to **kill** [+5883] me too."
19:21 [A] went back. *He* **took** his yoke of oxen and slaughtered them.
20: 6 [A] They will seize everything you value and **carry** it **away**.' "
20:33 [A] they said. "Go and **get** him," the king said.
20:34 [A] "I will return the cities my father **took** from your father,"
22: 3 [A] yet we are doing nothing *to* **retake** it from the king of
22:26 [A] "**Take** Micaiah and send him back to Amon the ruler of the
2Ki 2: 3 [A] "Do you know that the LORD *is going to* **take** your master
2: 5 [A] "Do you know that the LORD *is going to* **take** your master
2: 8 [A] Elijah **took** his cloak, rolled it up and struck the water with it.
2: 9 [C] what can I do for you before *I* **am taken** from you?"
2:10 [E] Elijah said, "yet if you see me when I **am taken** from you,
2:14 [A] *he* **took** the cloak that had fallen from him and struck the
2:20 [A] "**Bring** me a new bowl," he said, "and put salt in it." So they
2:20 [A] he said, "and put salt in it." So *they* **brought** it to him.
3:15 [A] But now **bring** me a harpist." While the harpist was playing,
3:26 [A] *he* **took** with him seven hundred swordsmen to break through
3:27 [A] *he* **took** his firstborn son, who was to succeed him as king,
4: 1 [A] now his creditor is coming to **take** my two boys as his
4:29 [A] your cloak into your belt, **take** my staff in your hand and run.
4:41 [A] Elisha said, "**Get** some flour." He put it into the pot and said,
5: 5 [A] So Naaman left, **taking** with him ten talents of silver, six
5:15 [A] except in Israel. Please **accept** now a gift from your servant."
5:16 [A] the LORD lives, whom I serve, *I will* not **accept** a thing."
5:16 [A] And even though Naaman urged him, **[RPH]** he refused.
5:20 [A] this Aramean, by not **accepting** from him what he brought.
5:20 [A] I will run after him and **get** something from him."
5:23 [A] "By all means, **take** two talents," said Naaman. He urged
5:24 [A] *he* **took** the things from the servants and put them away in
5:26 [A] Is this the time to **take** money, or to accept clothes, olive
5:26 [A] or to **accept** clothes, olive groves, vineyards, flocks, herds,
6: 2 [A] Let us go to the Jordan, where each of *us can* **get** a pole;
6: 7 [A] he said. Then the man reached out his hand and **took** it.
6:13 [A] the king ordered, "so I can send men and **capture** him."
7:13 [A] "*Have some men* **take** five of the horses that are left in the
7:14 [A] So *they* **selected** two chariots with their horses, and the king
8: 8 [A] "**Take** a gift with you and go to meet the man of God.
8: 9 [A] **taking** with him as a gift forty camel-loads of all the finest
8:15 [A] the next day *he* **took** a thick cloth, soaked it in water
9: 1 [A] **take** this flask of oil with you and go to Ramoth Gilead.
9: 3 [A] Then **take** the flask and pour the oil on his head and declare,
9:13 [A] They hurried and **took** their cloaks and spread them under
9:17 [A] "**Get** a horseman," Joram ordered. "Send him to meet them
10: 6 [A] **take** the heads of your master's sons and come to me in
10: 7 [A] these men **took** the princes and slaughtered all seventy of
11: 2 [A] **took** Joash son of Ahaziah and stole him away from among

2Ki 11: 4 [A] Jehoiada **sent for** [+906+2256+4200+4200+8938] the
11: 9 [A] Each one **took** his men—those who were going on duty on
11: 19 [A] *He* **took** with him the commanders of hundreds, the Carites,
12: 5 [12:6] [A] *Let* every priest **receive** the money from one of the
12: 7 [12:8] [A] **Take** no more money from your treasurers, but hand
12: 8 [12:9] [A] The priests agreed that *they would* not **collect** any
12: 9 [12:10] [A] Jehoiada the priest **took** a chest and bored a hole in
12: 18 [12:19] [A] **took** all the sacred objects dedicated by his fathers—
13: 15 [A] Elisha said, "**Get** a bow and some arrows," and he did so.
13: 15 [A] and some arrows," and *he* **did**[s] [+448+2256+2932+8008] **so**.
13: 18 [A] Then he said, "**Take** the arrows," and the king took them.
13: 18 [A] Then he said, "Take the arrows," and the king **took** them.
13: 25 [A] Jehoash son of Jehoahaz **recaptured** [+906+2256+8740] from
13: 25 [A] the towns *he had* **taken** in battle from his father Jehoahaz.
14: 14 [A] *He* **took** all the gold and silver and all the articles found in
14: 21 [A] all the people of Judah **took** Azariah, who was sixteen years
15: 29 [A] king of Assyria came and **took** Ijon, Abel Beth Maacah,
16: 8 [A] Ahaz **took** the silver and gold found in the temple of the
18: 32 [A] until I come and **take** you to a land like your own, a land of
19: 14 [A] Hezekiah **received** the letter from the messengers and read it.
20: 7 [A] Then Isaiah said, "**Prepare** a poultice of figs." They did so
20: 7 [A] *They* **did**[s] **so** and applied it to the boil, and he recovered.
20: 18 [A] and blood, that will be born to you, *will be* **taken away**,
23: 16 [A] *he* **had** the bones **removed** [+906+2256+8938] from them and
23: 30 [A] the people of the land **took** Jehoahaz son of Josiah
23: 34 [A] *he* **took** Jehoahaz and carried him off to Egypt, and there he
24: 7 [A] because the king of Babylon *had* **taken** all his territory, from
24: 12 [A] reign of the king of Babylon, *he* **took** Jehoiachin **prisoner**.
25: 14 [A] *They* also **took away** the pots, shovels, wick trimmers,
25: 15 [A] commander of the imperial guard **took away** the censers and
25: 18 [A] **took as prisoners** Seraiah the chief priest, Zephaniah the priest
25: 19 [A] *he* **took** the officer in charge of the fighting men and five
25: 20 [A] Nebuzaradan the commander **took** them all and brought them
1Ch 2: 19 [A] Azubah died, Caleb **married** Ephrath, who bore him Hur.
2: 21 [A] of Gilead (he *had* **married** her when he was sixty years old),
2: 23 [A] Aram **captured** Havvoth Jair, as well as Kenath with its
4: 18 [A] of Pharaoh's daughter Bithiah, whom Mered *had* **married**.
7: 15 [A] Makir **took** a wife from among the Huppites and Shuppites.
7: 21 [A] men of Gath, when they went down to **seize** their livestock.
10: 4 [A] would not do it; so Saul **took** his own sword and fell on it.
14: 3 [A] In Jerusalem David **took** more wives and became the father
17: 7 [A] I **took** you from the pasture and from following the flock,
18: 1 [A] *he* **took** Gath and its surrounding villages from the control of
18: 7 [A] David **took** the gold shields carried by the officers of
18: 8 [A] to Hadadezer, David **took** a great quantity of bronze,
19: 4 [A] So Hanun **seized** David's men, shaved them, cut off their
20: 2 [A] David **took** the crown from the head of their king—its
21: 23 [A] Araunah said to David, "**Take** it! Let my lord the king do
2Ch 1: 16 [A] the royal merchants **purchased** [+928+4697] them from
8: 18 [A] sailed to Ophir and **brought** back four hundred and fifty
11: 18 [A] Rehoboam **married** [+851+906+4200] Mahalath, who was the
11: 20 [A] *he* **married** Maacah daughter of Absalom, who bore him
12: 9 [A] *he* **carried off** the treasures of the temple of the LORD and
12: 9 [A] *He* **took** everything, including the gold shields Solomon had
12: 9 [A] including **[RPH]** the gold shields Solomon had made.
16: 6 [A] King Asa **brought** all the men of Judah, and they carried
18: 25 [A] "**Take** Micaiah and send him back to Amon the ruler of the
22: 11 [A] **took** Joash son of Ahaziah and stole him away from among
23: 1 [A] *He* **made** [+906+906+906+928+4200+4200+4200] a covenant
23: 8 [A] Each one **took** his men—those who were going on duty on
23: 20 [A] *He* **took** with him the commanders of hundreds, the nobles,
26: 1 [A] all the people of Judah **took** Uzziah, who was sixteen years
36: 1 [A] the people of the land **took** Jehoahaz son of Josiah and made
36: 4 [A] Neco **took** Eliakim's brother Jehoahaz and carried him off to
Ezr 2: 61 [A] Barzillai (a man who *had* **married** [+851+4946] a daughter
Ne 5: 2 [A] in order for us to eat and stay alive, *we must* **get** grain."
5: 3 [A] our vineyards and our homes *to* **get** grain during the famine."
5: 15 [A] and **took** forty shekels of silver from them in addition to food
6: 18 [A] his son Jehohanan *had* **married** the daughter of Meshullam
7: 63 [A] Barzillai (a man who *had* **married** [+851+4946] a daughter
10: 30 [10:31] [A] around us or **take** their daughters for our sons.
10: 31 [10:32] [A] *we will* not **buy** from them on the Sabbath or on any
Est 2: 7 [A] Mordecai *had* **taken** her as his own daughter when her father
2: 8 [C] Esther also **was taken** to the king's palace and entrusted to
2: 15 [A] Esther (the girl Mordecai *had* **adopted** [+1426+4200+4200],
2: 16 [C] She **was taken** to King Xerxes in the royal residence in the
6: 10 [A] "**Get** the robe and the horse and do just as you have
6: 11 [A] So Haman **got** the robe and the horse. He robed Mordecai,
Job 1: 15 [A] the Sabeans attacked and **carried** them **off**. They put the
1: 17 [A] and swept down on your camels and **carried** them **off**.
1: 21 [A] The LORD gave and the LORD *has* **taken away**;
2: 8 [A] Job **took** a piece of broken pottery and scraped himself with
3: 6 [A] That night—*may* thick darkness **seize** it; may it not be
4: 12 [A] was secretly brought to me, my ears **caught** a whisper of it.
5: 5 [A] consume his harvest, **taking** it even from among thorns,
12: 20 [A] of trusted advisers and **takes away** the discernment of elders.
15: 12 [A] Why *has* your heart **carried** you **away**, and why do your
22: 22 [A] **Accept** instruction from his mouth and lay up his words in
27: 13 [A] the heritage a ruthless man **receives** from the Almighty:
28: 2 [E] Iron **is taken** from the earth, and copper is smelted from ore.
35: 7 [A] do you give to him, or what *does he* **receive** from your hand?
38: 20 [A] *Can you* **take** them to their places? Do you know the paths
40: 24 [A] *Can anyone* **capture** him by the eyes, or trap him and pierce
41: 4 [40:28] [A] with you for *you to* **take** him as your slave for life?
42: 8 [A] So now **take** seven bulls and seven rams and go to my
Ps 6: 9 [6:10] [A] my cry for mercy; the LORD **accepts** my prayer.
15: 5 [A] and *does* not **accept** a bribe against the innocent.
18: 16 [18:17] [A] He reached down from on high and **took hold** *of*
31: 13 [31:14] [A] they conspire against me and plot to **take** my life.
49: 15 [49:16] [A] from the grave; *he will* surely **take** me to himself.
49: 17 [49:18] [A] for *he will* **take** nothing with him when he dies,
50: 9 [A] *I have* no **need** *of* a bull from your stall or of goats from
51: 11 [51:13] [A] your presence or **take** your Holy Spirit from me.
68: 18 [68:19] [A] *you* **received** gifts from men, even from the
73: 24 [A] your counsel, and afterward *you will* **take** me *into* glory.
75: 2 [75:3] [A] You say, "*I* **choose** the appointed time; it is I who
78: 70 [A] chose David his servant and **took** him from the sheep pens;
109: 8 [A] his days be few; *may* another **take** his place of leadership.
Pr 1: 3 [A] for **acquiring** a disciplined and prudent life, doing what is
1: 19 [A] ill-gotten gain; *it* **takes away** the lives of those who get it.
2: 1 [A] if *you* **accept** my words and store up my commands within
4: 10 [A] Listen, my son, **accept** what I say, and the years of your life
6: 25 [A] heart after her beauty or *let her* **captivate** you with her eyes,
7: 20 [A] *He* **took** his purse filled with money and will not be home till
8: 10 [A] **Choose** my instruction instead of silver, knowledge rather
9: 7 [A] "Whoever corrects a mocker **invites** insult; whoever rebukes
10: 8 [A] The wise in heart **accept** commands, but a chattering fool
11: 30 [A] the righteous is a tree of life, and *he who* **wins** souls is wise.
17: 23 [A] A wicked man **accepts** a bribe in secret to pervert the course
20: 16 [A] **Take** the garment of one who puts up security for a stranger;
21: 11 [A] when a wise man is instructed, *he* **gets** knowledge.
22: 25 [A] or you may learn his ways and **get** yourself ensnared.
22: 27 [A] to pay, your very bed *will be* **snatched** from under you.
24: 11 [B] Rescue *those* **being led away** to death; hold back those
24: 32 [A] to what I observed and **learned** a lesson from what I saw:
27: 13 [A] **Take** the garment of one who puts up security for a stranger;
31: 16 [A] She considers a field and **buys** it; out of her earnings she
Isa 6: 6 [A] in his hand, which *he had* **taken** with tongs from the altar.
8: 1 [A] "**Take** a large scroll and write on it with an ordinary pen:
14: 2 [A] Nations *will* **take** them and bring them to their own place.
23: 16 [A] "**Take up** a harp, walk through the city, O prostitute
28: 19 [A] As often as it comes *it will* **carry** you **away**; morning after
36: 17 [A] until I come and **take** you to a land like your own—a land of
37: 14 [A] Hezekiah **received** the letter from the messengers and read it.
39: 7 [A] and blood who will be born to you, *will be* **taken away**,
40: 2 [A] that *she has* **received** from the LORD's hand double for all
44: 14 [A] He cut down cedars, or perhaps **took** a cypress or oak. He let
44: 15 [A] some of it *he* **takes** and warms himself, he kindles a fire
47: 2 [A] **Take** millstones and grind flour; take off your veil. Lift up
47: 3 [A] *I will* **take** vengeance; I will spare no one."
49: 24 [E] *Can* plunder **be taken** from warriors, or captives rescued
49: 25 [E] "Yes, captives *will* **be taken** *from* warriors, and plunder
51: 22 [A] *I have* **taken** out of your hand the cup that made you stagger;
52: 5 [E] "For my people *have* **been taken away** for nothing,
53: 8 [E] By oppression and judgment *he* **was taken away**. And who
56: 12 [A] "Come," each one cries, "*let me* **get** wine! Let us drink our
57: 13 [A] carry all of them off, a mere breath *will* **blow** them **away**.
66: 21 [A] *I will* **select** some of them also to be priests and Levites,"
Jer 2: 30 [A] I punished your people; *they did* not **respond to** correction.
3: 14 [A] *I will* **choose** you—one from a town and two from a clan—
5: 3 [A] you crushed them, but they refused **[NIE]** correction.
7: 28 [A] not obeyed the LORD its God or **responded to** correction.
9: 20 [9:19] [A] **open** your ears **to** the words of his mouth.
13: 4 [A] "**Take** the belt you bought and are wearing around your
13: 6 [A] "Go now to Perath and **get** the belt I told you to hide there."
13: 7 [A] up the belt and **took** it from the place where I had hidden it,
15: 15 [A] You are long-suffering—*do* not **take** me **away**; think of how
16: 2 [A] "*You must* not **marry** [+851+4200] and have sons
17: 23 [A] and would not listen or **respond to** discipline.
20: 5 [A] *They will* **take** it **away** as plunder and carry it off to
20: 10 [A] then we will prevail over him and **take** our revenge on him."
23: 31 [A] "I am against the prophets who **wag** their own tongues
25: 9 [A] I *will* **summon** [+448+906+2256+8938] all the peoples of the
25: 15 [A] "**Take** from my hand this cup filled with the wine of my
25: 17 [A] So *I* **took** the cup from the LORD's hand and made all the
25: 28 [A] But if they refuse to **take** the cup from your hand and drink,
27: 20 [A] which Nebuchadnezzar king of Babylon *did* not **take away**
28: 3 [A] that Nebuchadnezzar king of Babylon **removed** from here

Jer 28:10 [A] the prophet Hananiah **took** the yoke off the neck of the
29: 6 [A] **Marry** [+851] and have sons and daughters; find wives for
29: 6 [A] **find** wives for your sons and give your daughters in
29:22 [E] all the exiles from Judah who are in Babylon *will* **use** this
32:11 [A] *I* **took** the deed of purchase—the sealed copy containing the
32:14 [A] **Take** these documents, both the sealed and unsealed copies
32:33 [A] and again, they would not listen or **respond to** discipline.
33:26 [A] *will* not **choose** one of his sons to rule over the descendants
35: 3 [A] *I went to* **get** Jaazaniah son of Jeremiah, the son of Habazziniah
35:13 [A] '*Will you* not **learn** a lesson and obey my words?'
36: 2 [A] "**Take** a scroll and write on it all the words I have spoken to
36:14 [A] "**Bring** the scroll from which you have read to the people
36:14 [A] So Baruch son of Neriah went to them with **[RPH]** the
36:21 [A] The king sent Jehudi to **get** the scroll, and Jehudi brought it
36:21 [A] Jehudi **brought** it from the room of Elishama the secretary
36:26 [A] Shelemiah son of Abdeel to **arrest** Baruch the scribe and
36:28 [A] "**Take** another scroll and write on it all the words that were
36:32 [A] So Jeremiah **took** another scroll and gave it to the scribe
37:17 [A] Zedekiah sent for him and *had* him **brought** to the palace,
38: 6 [A] So *they* **took** Jeremiah and put him into the cistern of
38:10 [A] "**Take** thirty men from here with you and lift Jeremiah the
38:11 [A] So Ebed-Melech **took** the men with him and went to a room
38:11 [A] *He* **took** some old rags and worn-out clothes from there
38:14 [A] *had* him **brought** to the third entrance to the temple of the
39: 5 [A] *They* **captured** him and took him to Nebuchadnezzar king of
39:12 [A] "**Take** him and look after him; don't harm him but do for
39:14 [A] and *had* Jeremiah **taken** out of the courtyard of the guard.
40: 1 [A] He *had* **found** Jeremiah bound in chains among all the
40: 2 [A] When the commander of the guard **found** Jeremiah, he said
41:12 [A] *they* **took** all their men and went to fight Ishmael son of
41:16 [A] all the army officers who were with him **led away** all the
43: 5 [A] all the army officers **led away** all the remnant of Judah who
43: 9 [A] **take** some large stones with you and bury them in clay in the
43:10 [A] I *will* **send for** [+906+2256+8938] my servant
44:12 [A] *I will* **take away** the remnant of Judah who were determined
46:11 [A] "Go up to Gilead and **get** balm, O Virgin Daughter of Egypt.
48:46 [E] your sons **are taken** into exile and your daughters into
49:29 [A] Their tents and their flocks *will be* **taken**; their shelters will
51: 8 [A] over her! **Get** balm for her pain; perhaps she can be healed.
51:26 [A] No rock *will* **be taken** from you for a cornerstone, nor any
52:18 [A] *They* also **took away** the pots, shovels, wick trimmers,
52:19 [A] **took away** the basins, censers, sprinkling bowls, pots,
52:24 [A] of the guard **took as prisoners** Seraiah the chief priest,
52:25 [A] in the city, *he* **took** the officer in charge of the fighting men,
52:26 [A] Nebuzaradan the commander **took** them all and brought them
Eze 1: 4 [F] an immense cloud with **flashing** lightning and surrounded by
3:10 [A] listen carefully and **take** to heart all the words I speak to you.
3:14 [A] The Spirit then lifted me up and **took** me **away**, and I went in
4: 1 [A] "Now, son of man, **take** a clay tablet, put it in front of you
4: 3 [A] Then **take** an iron pan, place it as an iron wall between you
4: 9 [A] "**Take** wheat and barley, beans and lentils, millet and spelt;
5: 1 [A] **take** a sharp sword and use it as a barber's razor to shave
5: 1 [A] **use** it **as** a barber's razor to shave your head and your beard.
5: 1 [A] your beard. Then **take** a set of scales and divide up the hair.
5: 2 [A] **Take** a third and strike it with the sword all around the city.
5: 3 [A] **take** a few strands of hair and tuck them away in the folds of
5: 4 [A] **take** a few of these and throw them into the fire and burn
8: 3 [A] what looked like a hand and **took** me by the hair of my head.
10: 6 [A] "**Take** fire from among the wheels, from among the
10: 7 [A] into the hands of the man in linen, *who* **took** it and went out.
15: 3 [E] **Is** wood *ever* **taken** from it to make anything useful? Do they
15: 3 [A] *Do they* **make** pegs from it to hang things on?
16:16 [A] *You* **took** some of your garments to make gaudy high places,
16:17 [A] *You* also **took** the fine jewelry I gave you, the jewelry made
16:18 [A] *you* **took** your embroidered clothes to put on them, and you
16:20 [A] " 'And *you* **took** your sons and daughters whom you bore to
16:32 [A] adulterous wife! *You* **prefer** strangers to your own husband!
16:39 [A] and **take** your fine jewelry and leave you naked and bare.
16:61 [A] your ways and be ashamed when you **receive** your sisters,
17: 3 [A] colors came to Lebanon. **Taking hold** *of* the top of a cedar,
17: 5 [A] " '*He* **took** some of the seed of your land and put it in fertile
17: 5 [A] He planted it like a willow by abundant water, **[RPH]**
17:12 [A] went to Jerusalem and **carried off** her king and her nobles,
17:13 [A] *he* **took** a member of the royal family and made a treaty with
17:13 [A] *He* also **carried away** the leading men of the land,
17:22 [A] *I* myself *will* **take** a shoot from the very top of a cedar
18: 8 [A] He does not lend at usury or **take** excessive interest.
18:13 [A] He lends at usury and **takes** excessive interest. Will such a
18:17 [A] his hand from sin and **takes** no usury or excessive interest.
19: 5 [A] *she* **took** another of her cubs and made him a strong lion.
22:12 [A] In you *men* **accept** bribes to shed blood; you take usury
22:12 [A] *you* **take** usury and excessive interest and make unjust gain
22:25 [A] **take** treasures and precious things and make many widows
23:10 [A] **took away** her sons and daughters and killed her with the
23:25 [A] They *will* **take away** your sons and daughters, and those of
23:26 [A] will also strip you of your clothes and **take** your fine jewelry.
23:29 [A] in hatred and **take away** everything you have worked for.
24: 5 [A] **take** the pick of the flock. Pile wood beneath it for the bones;
24:16 [A] with one blow I *am about to* **take away** from you the delight
24:25 [A] on the day I **take away** their stronghold, their joy and glory,
27: 5 [A] *they* **took** a cedar from Lebanon to make a mast for you.
30: 4 [A] her wealth *will be* **carried away** and her foundations torn
33: 2 [A] the people of the land **choose** one of their men and make him
33: 4 [A] not take warning and the sword comes and **takes** his **life**,
33: 6 [A] and the sword comes and **takes** the life of one of them,
33: 6 [C] one of them, that man *will* **be taken away** because of his sin,
36:24 [A] " 'For *I will* **take** you out of the nations; I will gather you
36:30 [A] so that *you will* no longer **suffer** disgrace among the nations
37:16 [A] "Son of man, **take** a stick of wood and write on it,
37:16 [A] **take** another stick of wood, and write on it, 'Ephraim's stick,
37:19 [A] I *am going to* **take** the stick of Joseph—which is in
37:21 [A] I *will* **take** the Israelites out of the nations where they have
38:13 [A] to **take away** livestock and goods and to seize much
43:20 [A] *You are to* **take** some of its blood and put it on the four
43:21 [A] *You are to* **take** the bull for the sin offering and burn it in
44:22 [A] *They must* not **marry** [+851+4200+4200] widows or divorced
44:22 [A] *they may* **marry** only virgins of Israelite descent or widows
45:18 [A] In the first month on the first day *you are to* **take** a young
45:19 [A] The priest *is to* **take** some of the blood of the sin offering
46:18 [A] The prince *must* not **take** any of the inheritance of the
Hos 1: 2 [A] **take** to yourself an adulterous wife and children of
1: 3 [A] So *he* **married** Gomer daughter of Diblaim, and she
2: 9 [2:11] [A] "Therefore *I will* **take away** my grain when it ripens,
4:11 [A] to old wine and new, *which* **take away** the understanding
10: 6 [A] Ephraim *will be* **disgraced** [+1423]; Israel will be ashamed
11: 3 [A] was I who taught Ephraim to walk, **taking** them by the arms;
13:11 [A] anger I gave you a king, and in my wrath *I* **took** him **away**.
14: 2 [14:3] [A] **Take** words with you and return to the LORD.
14: 2 [14:3] [A] "Forgive all our sins and **receive** us graciously,
Joel 3: 5 [4:5] [A] For *you* **took** my silver and my gold and carried off
Am 5:11 [A] You trample on the poor and **force** him **to give** you grain.
5:12 [A] You oppress the righteous and **take** bribes and you deprive
6:13 [A] and say, "*Did we* not **take** Karnaim by our own strength?"
7:15 [A] the LORD **took** me from tending the flock and said to me,
9: 2 [A] the depths of the grave, from there my hand *will* **take** them.
9: 3 [A] top of Carmel, there I will hunt them down and **seize** them.
Jnh 4: 3 [A] Now, O LORD, **take** away my life, for it is better for me to
Mic 1:11 [A] Beth Ezel is in mourning; its protection *is* **taken** from you.
2: 9 [A] *You* **take away** my blessing from their children forever.
Zep 3: 2 [A] She obeys no one, *she* **accepts** no correction. She does not
3: 7 [A] to the city, 'Surely you will fear me and **accept** correction!'
Hag 2:23 [A] that day,' declares the LORD Almighty, '*I will* **take** you,
Zec 6:10 [A] "**Take** ⌞silver and gold⌟ from the exiles Heldai, Tobijah
6:11 [A] **Take** the silver and gold and make a crown, and set it on the
11: 7 [A] *I* **took** two staffs and called one Favor and the other Union,
11:10 [A] *I* **took** my staff called Favor and broke it, revoking the
11:13 [A] So *I* **took** the thirty pieces of silver and threw them into the
11:15 [A] said to me, "**Take** again the equipment of a foolish shepherd.
14:21 [A] all who come to sacrifice *will* **take** some of the pots and cook
Mal 2:13 [A] or **accepts** them with pleasure from your hands.

4375 לֶקַח *leqaḥ*, n.m. [9] [√ 4374]

instruction [3], learning [3], beliefs [1], persuasive words [1], teaching [1]

Dt 32: 2 Let my **teaching** fall like rain and my words descend like dew,
Job 11: 4 say to God, 'My **beliefs** are flawless and I am pure in your sight.'
Pr 1: 5 let the wise listen and add to their **learning**, and let the discerning
4: 2 I give you sound **learning**, so do not forsake my teaching.
7:21 With **persuasive words** she led him astray; she seduced him with
9: 9 wiser still; teach a righteous man and he will add to his **learning**.
16:21 are called discerning, and pleasant words promote **instruction**.
16:23 man's heart guides his mouth, and his lips promote **instruction**.
Isa 29:24 gain understanding; those who complain will accept **instruction**."

4376 לִקְחִי *liqḥî*, n.pr.m. [1] [√ 4374]

Likhi [1]

1Ch 7:19 The sons of Shemida were: Ahian, Shechem, **Likhi** and Aniam.

4377 לָקַט *lāqaṭ*, v. [37] [→ 3541, 4378]

gather [11], gathered [8], glean [6], pick up [3], be gathered up [1], collected [1], gather up [1], gathering [1], gathers [1], gleaned [1], gleans [1], picked up scraps [1], picked up [1]

Ge 31:46 [A] He said to his relatives, "**Gather** some stones." So they took
47:14 [D] Joseph **collected** all the money that was to be found in Egypt
Ex 16: 4 [A] are to go out each day and **gather** enough for that day.
16: 5 [A] that is to be twice as much as *they* **gather** on the other days."

[F] Hitpael (hitpoel, hitpoal, hitpolel, hitpolal, hitpalel, hitpalal, hitpalpel, hitpalpal, hotpael, hotpaal) [G] Hiphil (hiphtil) [H] Hophal [I] Hishtaphel

Ex 16: 16 [A] has commanded: 'Each one *is to* **gather** as much as he needs.
16: 17 [A] did as they were told; *some* **gathered** much, some little.
16: 18 [A] not have too little. Each one **gathered** as much as he needed.
16: 21 [A] Each morning everyone **gathered** as much as he needed,
16: 22 [A] On the sixth day, *they* **gathered** twice as much—two omers
16: 26 [A] Six days *you are to* **gather** it, but on the seventh day,
16: 27 [A] some of the people went out on the seventh day to **gather** it,
Lev 19: 9 [D] edges of your field or **gather** the gleanings of your harvest.
19: 10 [D] a second time or **pick up** the grapes that have fallen.
23: 22 [D] edges of your field or **gather** the gleanings of your harvest.
Nu 11: 8 [A] The people went around **gathering** it, and then ground it in a
Jdg 1: 7 [D] and big toes cut off *have* **picked up scraps** under my table.
11: 3 [F] where a group of adventurers **gathered** around him
Ru 2: 2 [D] **pick up** the leftover grain behind anyone in whose eyes I
2: 3 [D] and *began to* **glean** in the fields behind the harvesters.
2: 7 [D] 'Please *let me* **glean** and gather among the sheaves behind
2: 8 [A] Don't go and **glean** in another field and don't go away from
2: 15 [D] As she got up to **glean**, Boaz gave orders to his men, "Even
2: 15 [D] "Even if *she* **gathers** among the sheaves, don't embarrass
2: 16 [D] for her from the bundles and leave them for *her to* **pick up**,
2: 17 [D] So Ruth **gleaned** in the field until evening. Then she threshed
2: 17 [D] she threshed the barley *she had* **gathered**, and it amounted to
2: 18 [D] and her mother-in-law saw how much *she had* **gathered**.
2: 19 [D] Her mother-in-law asked her, "Where *did you* **glean** today?
2: 23 [D] So Ruth stayed close to the servant girls of Boaz to **glean**
1Sa 20: 38 [D] The boy **picked up** the arrow and returned to his master.
2Ki 4: 39 [D] One of them went out into the fields to **gather** herbs
4: 39 [D] *He* **gathered** some of its gourds and filled the fold of his
Ps 104: 28 [A] When you give it to them, *they* **gather** it **up**; when you open
SS 6: 2 [A] beds of spices, to browse in the gardens and to **gather** lilies.
Isa 17: 5 [D] as *when a man* **gleans** heads of grain in the Valley of
27: 12 [E] and you, O Israelites, *will* **be gathered up** one by one.
Jer 7: 18 [D] The children **gather** wood, the fathers light the fire,

4378 לֶקֶט *leqeṭ*, n.[m.]. [2] [√ 4377]

gleanings [2]

Lev 19: 9 very edges of your field or gather the **gleanings** *of* your harvest.
23: 22 very edges of your field or gather the **gleanings** *of* your harvest.

4379 לָקַק *lāqaq*, v. [7]

lapped [2], licked up [2], *untranslated* [1], lap [1], lick up [1]

Jdg 7: 5 [A] "Separate those who **lap** the water with their tongues like a
7: 5 [A] like **[RPH]** a dog from those who kneel down to drink."
7: 6 [D] Three hundred men **lapped** with their hands to their mouths.
7: 7 [D] "With the three hundred men that **lapped** I will save you
1Ki 21: 19 [A] In the place where dogs **licked up** Naboth's blood, dogs will
21: 19 [A] licked up Naboth's blood, dogs *will* **lick up** your blood—
22: 38 [A] the dogs **licked up** his blood, as the word of the LORD had

4380 לָקַשׁ *lāqaš*, v.den. [1] [→ 4381, 4919]

glean [1]

Job 24: 6 [D] fodder in the fields and **glean** *in* the vineyards of the wicked.

4381 לֶקֶשׁ *leqeš*, n.[m.]. [2] [√ 4380]

untranslated [1], second crop [1]

Am 7: 1 had been harvested and just as the **second crop** was coming up.
7: 1 been harvested and just as the second crop **[RPH]** was coming up.

4382 לָשָׁד *lāšād*, n.m. [2]

something made [1], strength [1]

Nu 11: 8 it into cakes. And it tasted like **something made** *with* olive oil.
Ps 32: 4 heavy upon me; my **strength** was sapped as in the heat of summer.

4383 לָשׁוֹן *lāšôn*, n.m. [117] [→ 4387; Ar 10392]

tongue [62], tongues [23], language [11], bay [3], languages [3], wedge [2], words [2], bark [+3076] [1], charmer [+1251] [1], deceit [+9567] [1], fangs [1], gulf [1], lips [1], object of malicious talk [+6584+6590+8557] [1], on the tip of tongue [+928+2674] [1], slanderers [+408] [1], speech [1], uttered a word [+906+3076] [1]

Ge 10: 5 by their clans within their nations, each with its own **language**.)
10: 20 These are the sons of Ham by their clans and **languages**, in their
10: 31 These are the sons of Shem by their clans and **languages**,
Ex 4: 10 you have spoken to your servant. I am slow of speech and **tongue**."
11: 7 But among the Israelites not a dog *will* **bark** [+3076] at any man
Dt 28: 49 swooping down, a nation whose **language** you will not understand,
Jos 7: 21 shekels of silver and a **wedge** *of* gold weighing fifty shekels,
7: 24 the robe, the gold **wedge**, his sons and daughters, his cattle,
10: 21 and no one **uttered a word** [+906+3076] against the Israelites.
15: 2 Their southern boundary started from the **bay** at the southern end
15: 5 The northern boundary started from the **bay** *of* the sea at the mouth
18: 19 of Beth Hoglah and came out at the northern **bay** *of* the Salt Sea,
Jdg 7: 5 "Separate those who lap the water with their **tongues** like a dog
2Sa 23: 2 of the LORD spoke through me; his word was on my **tongue**.
Ne 13: 24 language of Ashdod or the **language** *of* one of the other peoples,
Est 1: 22 province in its own script and to each people in its own **language**,
1: 22 proclaiming in each people's **tongue** that every man should be
3: 12 in the **language** *of* each people all Haman's orders to the king's
8: 9 the **language** *of* each people and also to the Jews in their own
8: 9 each people and also to the Jews in their own script and **language**.
Job 5: 21 You will be protected from the lash of the **tongue**, and need not
6: 30 Is there any wickedness on my **lips**? Can my mouth not discern
15: 5 Your sin prompts your mouth; you adopt the **tongue** *of* the crafty.
20: 12 evil is sweet in his mouth and he hides it under his **tongue**,
20: 16 suck the poison of serpents; the **fangs** *of* an adder will kill him.
27: 4 lips will not speak wickedness, and my **tongue** will utter no deceit.
29: 10 were hushed, and their **tongues** stuck to the roof of their mouths.
33: 2 my mouth; my words are **on the tip of** my **tongue** [+928+2674].
41: 1 [40:25] with a fishhook or tie down his **tongue** with a rope?
Ps 5: 9 [5:10] is an open grave; with their **tongue** they speak deceit.
10: 7 and lies and threats; trouble and evil are under his **tongue**.
12: 3 [12:4] cut off all flattering lips and every boastful **tongue**
12: 4 [12:5] that says, "We will triumph with our **tongues**; we own our
15: 3 and has no slander on his **tongue**, who does his neighbor no wrong
22: 15 [22:16] a potsherd, and my **tongue** sticks to the roof of my mouth;
31: 20 [31:21] your dwelling you keep them safe from accusing **tongues**.
34: 13 [34:14] keep your **tongue** from evil and your lips from speaking
35: 28 My **tongue** will speak of your righteousness and of your praises all
37: 30 righteous man utters wisdom, and his **tongue** speaks what is just.
39: 1 [39:2] "I will watch my ways and keep my **tongue** from sin;
39: 3 [39:4] I meditated, the fire burned; then I spoke with my **tongue**:
45: 1 [45:2] for the king; my **tongue** is the pen of a skillful writer.
50: 19 You use your mouth for evil and harness your **tongue** to deceit.
51: 14 [51:16] saves me, and my **tongue** will sing of your righteousness.
52: 2 [52:4] Your **tongue** plots destruction; it is like a sharpened razor,
52: 4 [52:6] You love every harmful word, O you deceitful **tongue**!
55: 9 [55:10] O Lord, confound their **speech**, for I see violence
57: 4 [57:5] are spears and arrows, whose **tongues** are sharp swords.
64: 3 [64:4] They sharpen their **tongues** like swords and aim their
64: 8 [64:9] He will turn their own **tongues** against them and bring
66: 17 I cried out to him with my mouth; his praise was on my **tongue**.
68: 23 [68:24] while the **tongues** *of* your dogs have their share."
71: 24 My **tongue** will tell of your righteous acts all day long, for those
73: 9 lay claim to heaven, and their **tongues** take possession of the earth.
78: 36 flatter him with their mouths, lying to him with their **tongues**;
109: 2 against me; they have spoken against me with lying **tongues**.
119:172 May my **tongue** sing of your word, for all your commands are
120: 2 Save me, O LORD, from lying lips and from deceitful **tongues**.
120: 3 will he do to you, and what more besides, O deceitful **tongue**?
126: 2 mouths were filled with laughter, our **tongues** with songs of joy.
137: 6 May my **tongue** cling to the roof of my mouth if I do not
139: 4 Before a word is on my **tongue** you know it completely,
140: 3 [140:4] They make their **tongues** as sharp as a serpent's;
140: 11 [140:12] Let **slanderers** [+408] not be established in the land;
Pr 6: 17 haughty eyes, a lying **tongue**, hands that shed innocent blood,
6: 24 immoral woman, from the smooth **tongue** *of* the wayward wife.
10: 20 The **tongue** *of* the righteous is choice silver, but the heart of the
10: 31 brings forth wisdom, but a perverse **tongue** will be cut out.
12: 18 pierce like a sword, but the **tongue** *of* the wise brings healing.
12: 19 lips endure forever, but a lying **tongue** lasts only a moment.
15: 2 The **tongue** *of* the wise commends knowledge, but the mouth of
15: 4 The **tongue** that brings healing is a tree of life, but a deceitful
16: 1 of the heart, but from the LORD comes the reply of the **tongue**.
17: 4 man listens to evil lips; a liar pays attention to a malicious **tongue**.
17: 20 does not prosper; he whose **tongue** is deceitful falls into trouble.
18: 21 The **tongue** has the power of life and death, and those who love it
21: 6 A fortune made by a lying **tongue** is a fleeting vapor and a deadly
21: 23 who guards his mouth and his **tongue** keeps himself from calamity.
25: 15 a ruler can be persuaded, and a gentle **tongue** can break a bone.
25: 23 As a north wind brings rain, so a sly **tongue** brings angry looks.
26: 28 A lying **tongue** hates those it hurts, and a flattering mouth works
28: 23 in the end gain more favor than he who has a flattering **tongue**.
31: 26 She speaks with wisdom, and faithful instruction is on her **tongue**.
Ecc 10: 11 before it is charmed, there is no profit for the **charmer** [+1251].
SS 4: 11 the honeycomb, my bride; milk and honey are under your **tongue**.
Isa 3: 8 their **words** and deeds are against the LORD, defying his glorious
5: 24 as **tongues** *of* fire lick up straw and as dry grass sinks down in the
11: 15 The LORD will dry up the **gulf** *of* the Egyptian sea; with a
28: 11 foreign lips and strange **tongues** God will speak to this people,
30: 27 his lips are full of wrath, and his **tongue** is a consuming fire.
32: 4 and the stammering **tongue** will be fluent and clear.
33: 19 of an obscure speech, with their strange, incomprehensible **tongue**.
35: 6 will the lame leap like a deer, and the mute **tongue** shout for joy.
41: 17 for water, but there is none; their **tongues** are parched with thirst.

Isa 45:23 Before me every knee will bow; by me every **tongue** will swear.
50: 4 The Sovereign LORD has given me an instructed **tongue**,
54:17 will prevail, and you will refute every **tongue** that accuses you.
57: 4 you mocking? At whom do you sneer and stick out your **tongue**?
59: 3 lips have spoken lies, and your **tongue** mutters wicked things.
66:18 am about to come and gather all nations and **tongues**, and they will
Jer 5:15 and enduring nation, a people whose **language** you do not know,
9: 3 [9:2] "They make ready their **tongue** like a bow, to shoot lies; it is
9: 5 [9:4] They have taught their **tongues** to lie; they weary
9: 8 [9:7] Their **tongue** is a deadly arrow; it speaks with deceit.
18:18 let's attack him with our **tongues** and pay no attention to anything
23:31 "I am against the prophets who wag their own **tongues** and yet
La 4: 4 Because of thirst the infant's **tongue** sticks to the roof of its mouth;
Eze 3: 5 being sent to a people of obscure speech and difficult **language**,
3: 6 not to many peoples of obscure speech and difficult **language**,
3:26 I will make your **tongue** stick to the roof of your mouth so that you
36: 3 and *the* **object of** people's **malicious talk** [+6584+6590+8557] and
Da 1: 4 He was to teach them the **language** and literature of the
Hos 7:16 leaders will fall by the sword because of their insolent **words**.
Mic 6:12 are violent; her people are liars and their **tongues** speak deceitfully.
Zep 3:13 speak no lies, nor will **deceit** [+9567] be found in their mouths.
Zec 8:23 "In those days ten men from all **languages** and nations will take
14:12 will rot in their sockets, and their **tongues** will rot in their mouths.

4384 לִשְׁכָּה *liškâ*, n.f. [47 / 46] [cf. 5969]

rooms [21], room [13], storerooms [5], side rooms [2], *untranslated* [1], chambers [1], hall [1], priests rooms [+7731] [1], that[s] [1]

1Sa 9:22 Samuel brought Saul and his servant into the **hall** and seated them
2Ki 23:11 They were in the court near the **room** *of* an official named
1Ch 9:26 were entrusted with the responsibility for the **rooms** and treasuries
9:33 stayed in the **rooms** of the temple and were exempt from other
23:28 to be in charge of the courtyards, the **side rooms**, the purification
28:12 courts of the temple of the LORD and all the surrounding **rooms**,
2Ch 31:11 Hezekiah gave orders to prepare **storerooms** in the temple of the
Ezr 8:29 Guard them carefully until you weigh them out in the **chambers** *of*
10: 6 house of God and went to the **room** *of* Jehohanan son of Eliashib.
Ne 10:37 [10:38] we will bring to the **storerooms** *of* the house of our God,
10:38 [10:39] the house of our God, to the **storerooms** of the treasury.
10:39 [10:40] oil to the **storerooms** where the articles for the sanctuary
13: 4 Eliashib the priest had been put in charge of the **storerooms** *of* the
13: 5 he had provided him with a large **room** formerly used to store the
13: 8 and threw all Tobiah's household goods out of the **room**.
13: 9 I gave orders to purify the **rooms**, and then I put back into them the
Jer 35: 2 invite them to come to one of the **side rooms** of the house of the
35: 4 into the **room** *of* the sons of Hanan son of Igdaliah the man of
35: 4 It was next to the **room** *of* the officials, which was over that of
35: 4 which was over **that**[s] *of* Maaseiah son of Shallum the doorkeeper.
36:10 From the **room** *of* Gemariah son of Shaphan the secretary,
36:12 he went down to the secretary's **room** in the royal palace,
36:20 After they put the scroll in the **room** *of* Elishama the secretary,
36:21 and Jehudi brought it from the **room** *of* Elishama the secretary
Eze 40:17 There I saw *some* **rooms** and a pavement that had been constructed
40:17 all around the court; there were thirty **rooms** along the pavement.
40:38 A **room** with a doorway was by the portico in each of the inner
40:44 Outside the inner gate, within the inner court, were two **rooms**,
40:45 "The **room** facing south is for the priests who have charge of the
40:46 the **room** facing north is for the priests who have charge of the
41:10 the ⌊priests'⌋ **rooms** was twenty cubits wide all around the temple.
42: 1 and brought me to the **rooms** opposite the temple courtyard
42: 4 In front of the **rooms** was an inner passageway ten cubits wide
42: 5 Now the upper **rooms** were narrower, for the galleries took more
42: 7 There was an outer wall parallel to the **rooms** and the outer court;
42: 7 the outer court; it extended in front of the **rooms** for fifty cubits.
42: 8 While the row of **rooms** on the side next to the outer court was
42: 9 The lower **rooms** had an entrance on the east side as one enters
42:10 the temple courtyard and opposite the outer wall, were **rooms**
42:11 These were like the **rooms** on the north; they had the same length
42:12 were the doorways of the **rooms** on the south. There was a
42:13 and south **rooms** facing the temple courtyard are the priests' rooms,
42:13 south rooms **[RPH]** facing the temple courtyard are the priests'
42:13 rooms facing the temple courtyard are the **priests' rooms** [+7731],
44:19 been ministering in and are to leave them in the sacred **rooms**,
45: 5 as their possession for towns to <u>live in</u>. [BHS ***rooms***; NIV 3782]
46:19 entrance at the side of the gate to the sacred **rooms** facing north,

4385 לֶשֶׁם¹ *lešem¹*, n.[m.]. [2]

jacinth [2]

Ex 28:19 in the third row a **jacinth**, an agate and an amethyst;
39:12 in the third row a **jacinth**, an agate and an amethyst;

4386 ²לֶשֶׁם *lešem²*, n.pr.loc. [2] [cf. 4332]

Leshem [2]

Jos 19:47 so they went up and attacked **Leshem**, took it, put it to the sword
19:47 They settled in **Leshem** and named it Dan after their forefather.)

4387 לָשַׁן *lāšan*, v.den. [2] [√ 4383]

slander [1], slanders [1]

Ps 101: 5 [D] *Whoever* **slanders** his neighbor in secret, him will I put to
Pr 30:10 [G] "*Do* not **slander** a servant to his master, or he will curse you,

4388 לֶשַׁע *leša'*, n.pr.loc. [1]

Lasha [1]

Ge 10:19 toward Sodom, Gomorrah, Admah and Zeboiim, as far as **Lasha**.

4389 לַשָּׁרוֹן *laššārôn*, n.pr.loc. [1] [cf. 9227]

Lasharon [1]

Jos 12:18 the king of Aphek one the king of **Lasharon** one

4390 לֶתֶךְ *lētek*, n.[m.]. [1]

lethek [1]

Hos 3: 2 fifteen shekels of silver and about a homer and a **lethek** *of* barley.

מ, m

4391 מ *m*, letter. Not used in NIV/BHS [→ Ar 10393]

4392 ם- *-ām*, ם- *-m*, p.m.pl.suf. [3933 / 3937] [→ 307?, 2023] Not indexed

them [1550], their [1012], *untranslated* [621], they [252], the[s] [124], their own [43], it [31], whose [15], a[s] [14], these [12], those [12], you [11], its [10], the people[s] [9], themselves [+5883] [9], his [7], which[s] [7], Israel[s] [6], men[s] [6], themselves [6], who [6], the Israelites[s] [5], them [+5883] [5], by themselves [+963+4200] [4], he [4], one by one [+1653+4200] [4], the creatures[s] [4], they [+5883] [4], this [4], us [4], all[s] [3], each [3], her [3], him [3], our [3], she [3], that[s] [3], the cherubim[s] [3], the Levites[s] [3], the men[s] [3], the rest[s] [3], which [3], your [3], courts[s] [2], gods[s] [2], Judah[s] [2], my people[s] [2], our fathers[s] [2], that [2], the enemies[s] [2], the shields[s] [2], the wicked[s] [2], these articles[s] [2], things[s] [2], whom [2], almost to a man [+6330+9462] [1], an[s] [1], anyone [1], Babylon[s] [1], battle[s] [1], did [+906+3877+4213] [1], each[s] [1], Egypt[s] [1], else's [1], extremes[s] [1], his enemies[s] [1], his offerings[s] [1], his own [1], his sons[s] [1], its people[s] [1], keep themselves alive [+906+5883+8740] [1], man's[s] [1], man[s] [1], men [1], Moses[s] and Aaron [1], one's own [1], priests[s] [1], prophets[s] [1], that[s] [+2388] [1], that person[s] [1], the Arameans[s] [1], the army[s] [1], the Canaanites[s] [1], the case[s] [1], the censers[s] [1], the days[s] [1], the enemies [1], the flock[s] [+5883] [1], the forces[s] [1], the Gibeonites[s] [1], the goats[s] [1], the gods[s] [1], the hair[s] [1], the Horites[s] [1], the kings[s] [1], the Midianite[s] [1], the Midianites[s] [1], the nations[s] [1], the nobles[s] and officials [1], the others[s] [1], the people [1], the priests[s] [1], the procession[s] [1], the ropes[s] [1], the servants[s] [1], the stones[s] [1], the things[s] [1], the water[s] [1], their enemies[s] [1], their gods[s] [1], their leaders[s] [1], their sons[s] [1], their temples[s] [1], theirs [1], them [+1414] [1], them [+2652] [1], them [+4213] [1], them [+74+928+2021] [1], themselves [+4213] [1], themselves [+4222] [1], there[s] [+928+9348] [1], these offerings[s] [1], they [+9307] [1], this is the way [+928] [1], those nations[s] [1], your brothers[s] [1], your lovers[s] [1], your sons[s] [1]

4393 מַאֲבוּס *maᵃbûs*, n.[m.]. [1] [√ 80]

granaries [1]

Jer 50:26 Break open her **granaries**; pile her up like heaps of grain.

4394 מְאֹד *mᵉʾōd*, n.m. (used as adv.). [300]

very [71], greatly [22], great [18], so [7], large [6], most [6], very [+6330] [6], exceedingly [+4394] [4], exceedingly [+928+4394] [4], great quantity [+2221] [4], greatly [+928+4394] [4], terrified [+3707] [4], very [+928+4394] [4], very much [4], *untranslated* [3], beyond measure [+6330] [3], how [3], all [2], burned [+3013] [2], closely [2], deep [2], desperate [2], fully [2], great [+1524] [2], greatly [+4394] [2], large [+8041] [2], much [2], overweening [2], so [+4394] [2], strength [2], terrified [+3707+4394] [2], thoroughly [2], utterly [+6330] [2], utterly [2], vast [+1524+4394] [2], worst [+3878] [2], abundance [+2221] [1], abundantly [1], accumulate large amounts [+4200+8049] [1], aged [+2416] [1], almost [1], at a distance [+8158] [1], badly [1], behaved in the vilest manner [+9493] [1], beyond number [+8041] [1], bitterly [+3878] [1], bitterly [1], boundless [+8146] [1], come quickly [+4554] [1], coming quickly [+4554] [1], completely [1], critically [1], crushing [+2703] [1], destroyed [+1524+4804+5782] [1], devastated [+1524+4804+5782] [1], devout [1], dismayed [+987] [1], dreadful [+3707] [1], enough [1], even far [+3856] [1], even more [1], ever-present [+5162] [1], exceedingly [1], exhausted [+6545] [1], far [1], filled with fear [+3707] [1], firmly [1], full well [1], furious [+3013+4200] [1], furious [+678+3013] [1], furious [+7911] [1], fury [+3013+4200] [1], great [+1540] [1], great [+2221] [1], great numbers [+2221] [1], great numbers [+3878] [1], great quantities [+4200+8044] [1], greatly [+2221] [1], grew louder and louder [+2143+2256+2618] [1], grew worse and worse [+2118+2617+2716] [1], heavy [+3877] [1], highly regarded [+1524] [1], highly [1], huge [+1524+4200+6330] [1], huge [1], in anguish [+987] [1], intense [+1524] [1], kept bringing pressure [+7210] [1], large [+1524] [1], large [+3878] [1], large amount [+2221] [1], least [1], long way [+8158] [1], lost self-confidence [+928+5877+6524] [1], loud [+1524+6330] [1], make as great as you like [+6584+8049] [1], many [+8041] [1], more than [1], more [1], much [+6330] [1], quickly [1], reward handsomely [+3877+3877] [1], severe [+3878] [1], severe [+8041] [1], so [+3954] [1], so highly [1], so much [1], stand firm [+586] [1], stood in awe [+906+906+3707] [1], strongly [1], tempest rages [+8548] [1], terrible [+3878] [1], terror filled [+3006] [1], too [1], total [+1524] [1], toward evening [+3718] [1], trembled violently [+1524+3006+3010+6330] [1], utter [1], vast [+1524] [1], very [+2221] [1], very [+6786] [1], violently [1], well known [+3700] [1], without restraint [+6330] [1], writhe in agony [+2655] [1]

Ge 1:31 God saw all that he had made, and it was **very** good. And there
4:5 with favor. So Cain was **very** angry, and his face was downcast.
7:18 The waters rose and increased **greatly** on the earth, and the ark
7:19 They rose **greatly** [+4394] on the earth, and all the high mountains
7:19 They rose **greatly** [+4394] on the earth, and all the high mountains
12:14 to Egypt, the Egyptians saw that she was a **very** beautiful woman.
13:2 Abram had become **very** wealthy in livestock and in silver
13:13 Sodom were wicked and were sinning **greatly** against the LORD.
15:1 not be afraid, Abram. I am your shield, your **very** great reward."
17:2 and you and will **greatly** [+928+4394] increase your numbers."
17:2 and you and will **greatly** [+928+4394] increase your numbers."
17:6 I will make you **very** [+928+4394] fruitful; I will make nations of
17:6 I will make you **very** [+928+4394] fruitful; I will make nations of
17:20 him fruitful and will **greatly** [+928+4394] increase his numbers.
17:20 him fruitful and will **greatly** [+928+4394] increase his numbers.
18:20 and Gomorrah is so great and their sin **so** [+3954] grievous
19:3 he insisted *so* **strongly** that they did go with him and entered his
19:9 *They* **kept bringing pressure** [+7210] on Lot and moved forward
20:8 he told them all that had happened, they were **very much** afraid.
21:11 The matter distressed Abraham **greatly** because it concerned his
24:16 The girl was **very** beautiful, a virgin; no man had ever lain with
24:35 The LORD has blessed my master **abundantly**, and he has
26:13 and his wealth continued to grow until he became **very** wealthy.
26:16 "Move away from us; you have become **too** powerful for us."
27:33 Isaac **trembled violently** [+1524+3006+3010+6330] and said,
27:34 he burst out with a **loud** [+1524+6330] and bitter cry and said to
30:43 In this way the man grew **exceedingly** [+4394] prosperous
30:43 In this way the man grew **exceedingly** [+4394] prosperous
32:7 [32:8] In **great** fear and distress Jacob divided the people who
34:7 They were filled with grief and **fury** [+3013+4200], because
34:12 **Make** the price for the bride … **as great as you like** [+6584+8049],
41:19 seven other cows came up—scrawny and **very** ugly and lean.
41:31 because the famine that follows it will be **so** severe.
41:49 Joseph stored up **huge** quantities of grain, like the sand of the sea;
47:13 in the whole region because the famine was **severe** [+3878];
47:27 property there and were fruitful and increased **greatly** in number.
50:9 and horsemen also went up with him. It was a **very** large company.
50:10 near the Jordan, they lamented loudly and **bitterly** [+3878];
Ex 1:7 and became **exceedingly** [+928+4394] numerous, so that the land
1:7 and became **exceedingly** [+928+4394] numerous, so that the land
1:20 and the people increased and became **even more** numerous.
9:3 the hand of the LORD will bring a **terrible** [+3878] plague on
9:18 at this time tomorrow I will send the **worst** [+3878] hailstorm that
9:24 It was the **worst** [+3878] storm in all the land of Egypt since it had
10:14 down in every area of the country *in* **great numbers** [+3878].
10:19 And the LORD changed the wind to a **very** strong west wind,
11:3 Moses himself was **highly regarded** [+1524] in Egypt by
12:38 as well as **large** [+3878] droves of livestock, both flocks and herds.
14:10 *They were* **terrified** [+3707] and cried out to the LORD.
19:16 a thick cloud over the mountain, and a **very** loud trumpet blast.
19:18 like smoke from a furnace, the whole mountain trembled **violently**,
19:19 the trumpet **grew louder and louder** [+2143+2256+2618].
Nu 11:10 The LORD became **exceedingly** angry, and Moses was troubled.
11:33 the people, and he struck them with a **severe** [+8041] plague.
12:3 (Now Moses was a **very** humble man, more humble than anyone
13:28 live there are powerful, and the cities are fortified and **very** large.
14:7 land we passed through and explored is **exceedingly** [+4394] good.
14:7 land we passed through and explored is **exceedingly** [+4394] good.
14:39 Moses reported this to all the Israelites, they mourned **bitterly**.
16:15 Moses became **very** angry and said to the LORD, "Do not accept
22:3 and Moab was terrified because there were **so** many people.
22:17 because *I will* **reward** you **handsomely** [+3877+3877] and do
32:1 and Gadites, who had **very** [+6786] large herds and flocks,
Dt 2:4 who live in Seir. They will be afraid of you, but be **very** careful.
3:5 and bars, and there were also a **great** many unwalled villages.
4:9 watch yourselves **closely** so that you do not forget the things your
4:15 at Horeb out of the fire. Therefore watch yourselves **very** carefully,
6:3 and that you may increase **greatly** in a land flowing with milk
6:5 all your heart and with all your soul and with all your **strength**.
9:20 And the LORD was angry **enough** with Aaron to destroy him,
17:17 *He must* not **accumulate large amounts of** [+4200+8049] silver
20:15 are to treat all the cities that are **at a distance** [+8158] from you
24:8 In cases of leprous diseases be **very** careful to do exactly as the
28:54 Even the **most** gentle and sensitive man among you will have no
30:14 No, the word is **very** near you; it is in your mouth and in your heart
Jos 1:7 Be strong and **very** courageous. Be careful to obey all the law my
3:16 It piled up in a heap a **great** distance away, at a town called Adam
8:4 the city. Don't go **very** far from it. All of you be on the alert.
9:9 "Your servants have come from a **very** distant country because of
9:13 our clothes and sandals are worn out by the **very** long journey."
9:22 'We live a **long way** [+8158] from you,' while actually you live
9:24 So we feared **[NIE]** for our lives because of you, and that is why
10:2 He and his people were **very much** alarmed at this,
10:20 So Joshua and the Israelites **destroyed** [+1524+4804+5782] them
11:4 with all their troops and a **large** number of horses and chariots—
13:1 and there are still **very** large areas of land to be taken over.
22:5 be **very** careful to keep the commandment and the law that Moses
22:8 with **large** [+8041] herds of livestock, with silver, gold, bronze
22:8 bronze and iron, and a **great quantity of** [+2221] clothing—
23:6 "Be **very** strong; be careful to obey all that is written in the Book
23:11 So be **very** careful to love the LORD your God.
Jdg 2:15 just as he had sworn to them. They were in **great** distress.
3:17 the tribute to Eglon king of Moab, who was a **very** fat man.
6:6 **so** impoverished the Israelites that they cried out to the LORD for
10:9 and the house of Ephraim; and Israel was in **great** distress.
11:33 *He* **devastated** [+1524+4804+5782] twenty towns from Aroer to
12:2 my people were engaged in a **great** struggle with the Ammonites,
13:6 God came to me. He looked like an angel of God, **very** awesome.
15:18 Because he was **very** thirsty, he cried out to the LORD, "You
18:9 let's attack them! We have seen that the land is **very** good.
19:11 When they were near Jebus and the day was **almost** gone,
Ru 1:13 It is **more** bitter for me than for you, because the LORD's hand
1:20 "Call me Mara, because the Almighty has made my life **very** bitter.
1Sa 2:17 This sin of the young men was **very** great in the LORD's sight,
2:22 Now Eli, who was **very** old, heard about everything his sons were
4:10 The slaughter was **very** great; Israel lost thirty thousand foot
5:9 hand was against that city, throwing it into a **great** [+1524] panic.
5:11 had filled the city with panic; God's hand was **very** heavy upon it.
11:6 God came upon him in power, and he **burned** [+3013] with anger.
11:15 the LORD, and Saul and all the Israelites held a **great** celebration.
12:18 the people **stood in awe of** [+906+906+3707] the LORD and of
14:20 They found the Philistines in **total** [+1524] confusion,
14:31 from Micmash to Aijalon, *they were* **exhausted** [+6545].
16:21 Saul liked him **very much**, and David became one of his
17:11 and all the Israelites were dismayed and **terrified** [+3707].
17:24 the Israelites saw the man, they all ran from him in **great** fear.
18:8 Saul was **very** angry; this refrain galled him. "They have credited
18:15 When Saul saw **how** successful he was, he was afraid of him.
18:30 rest of Saul's officers, and his name *became* **well known** [+3700].
19:1 the attendants to kill David. But Jonathan was **very** fond of David
19:4 not wronged you, and what he has done has benefited you **greatly**.
20:19 The day after tomorrow, **toward evening** [+3718], go to the place
21:12 [21:13] and was **very much** afraid of Achish king of Gath.
25:2 in Maon, who had property there at Carmel, was **very** wealthy.
25:15 Yet these men were **very** good to us. They did not mistreat us,
25:36 He was in high spirits and **very** [+6330] drunk. So she told him
26:21 Surely I have acted like a fool and have erred **greatly** [+2221]."
28:5 the Philistine army, he was afraid; **terror filled** [+3006] his heart.
28:15 "I am in **great** distress," Saul said. "The Philistines are fighting
28:20 the ground, **filled with fear** [+3707] because of Samuel's words.
28:21 the woman came to Saul and saw that he was **greatly** shaken,
30:6 David was **greatly** distressed because the men were talking of
31:3 and when the archers overtook him, they wounded him **critically**.
31:4 But his armor-bearer *was* **terrified** [+3707] and would not do it;
2Sa 1:26 I grieve for you, Jonathan my brother; you were **very** dear to me.
2:17 The battle that day was **very** [+6330] fierce, and Abner
3:8 Abner was **very** angry because of what Ish-Bosheth said and he
8:8 King David took a **great quantity** [+2221] of bronze.
10:5 sent messengers to meet the men, for they were **greatly** humiliated.
11:2 the roof he saw a woman bathing. The woman was **very** beautiful,

2Sa 12: 2 The rich man had a **very** large number of sheep and cattle,
12: 5 David **burned with** [+3013] anger against the man and said to
12:30 He took a **great quantity of** [+2221] plunder from the city
13: 3 son of Shimeah, David's brother. Jonadab was a **very** shrewd man.
13:15 Then Amnon hated her with **intense** [+1524] hatred. In fact,
13:21 When King David heard all this, he *was* **furious** [+3013+4200].
13:36 The king, too, and all his servants wept **very** bitterly.
14:25 **so highly** praised for his handsome appearance as Absalom.
18:17 in the forest and piled up a **large** [+1524] heap of rocks over him.
19:32 [19:33] Now Barzillai was a **very** old man, eighty years of age.
19:32 [19:33] his stay in Mahanaim, for he was a **very** wealthy man.
24:10 he said to the LORD, "I have sinned **greatly** in what I have done.
24:10 away the guilt of your servant. I have done a **very** foolish thing."
24:14 David said to Gad, "I am in **deep** distress. Let us fall into the hands
1Ki 1: 4 The girl was **very** [+6330] beautiful; she took care of the king
1: 6 He was also **very** handsome and was born next after Absalom.)
1:15 So Bathsheba went to see the **aged** [+2416] king in his room,
2:12 the throne of his father David, and his rule was **firmly** established.
4:29 [5:9] God gave Solomon wisdom and **very** great insight, and a
5: 7 [5:21] he was **greatly** pleased and said, "Praise be to the LORD
7:47 all these things unweighed, because there were **so** [+4394] many;
7:47 all these things unweighed, because there were **so** [+4394] many;
10: 2 Arriving at Jerusalem with a **very** great caravan—with camels
10: 2 carrying spices, **large** quantities of gold, and precious stones—
10:10 120 talents of gold, **large** quantities of spices, and precious stones.
10:11 and from there they brought **great** *cargoes* **of** [+2221] almugwood
11:19 **so** pleased with Hadad that he gave him a sister of his own wife,
17:17 He **grew worse and worse** [+2118+2617+2716], and finally
18: 3 of his palace. (Obadiah was a **devout** believer in the LORD.
21:26 *He* **behaved in the vilest manner** [+9493] by going after idols,
2Ki 10: 4 *they were* **terrified** [+3707+4394] and said, "If two kings could
10: 4 *they were* **terrified** [+3707+4394] and said, "If two kings could
14:26 The LORD had seen **how** bitterly everyone in Israel, whether
17:18 So the LORD was **very** angry with Israel and removed them from
21:16 **so** much innocent blood that he filled Jerusalem from end to end—
23:25 with all his heart and with all his soul and with all his **strength**,
1Ch 10: 4 But his armor-bearer *was* **terrified** [+3707] and would not do it;
16:25 For great is the LORD and **most** worthy of praise; he is to be
18: 8 that belonged to Hadadezer, David took a **great** quantity of bronze,
19: 5 he sent messengers to meet them, for they were **greatly** humiliated.
20: 2 He took a **great quantity of** [+2221] plunder from the city
21: 8 Then David said to God, "I have sinned **greatly** by doing this.
21: 8 away the guilt of your servant. I have done a **very** foolish thing."
21:13 David said to Gad, "I am in **deep** distress. Let me fall into the
21:13 me fall into the hands of the LORD, for his mercy is **very** great;
2Ch 4:18 **so** much that the weight of the bronze was not determined.
7: 8 a **vast** [+1524] assembly, people from Lebo Hamath to the Wadi of
9: 1 Arriving with a **very** great caravan—with camels carrying spices,
9: 9 120 talents of gold, **large** quantities of spices, and precious stones.
11:12 and spears in all the cities, and made them **very** [+2221] strong.
14:13 [14:12] The men of Judah carried off a **large amount** [+2221] of
16: 8 Libyans a mighty army with **great numbers** [+2221] of chariots
16:14 and they made a **huge** [+1524+4200+6330] fire in his honor.
24:24 the LORD delivered into their hands a **much** larger army.
25:10 They *were* **furious** [+678+3013] with Judah and left for home in a
30:13 A **very** large crowd of people assembled in Jerusalem to celebrate
32:27 Hezekiah had **very** great riches and honor, and he made treasuries
32:29 of flocks and herds, for God had given him **very** great riches.
33:12 and humbled himself **greatly** before the God of his fathers.
33:14 and encircling the hill of Ophel; he also made it **much** higher.
35:23 and he told his officers, "Take me away; I am **badly** wounded."
Ezr 10: 1 before the house of God, a **large** [+8041] crowd of Israelites—
Ne 2: 2 This can be nothing but sadness of heart." I was **very** much afraid,
4: 7 [4:1] and that the gaps were being closed, they were **very** angry.
5: 6 When I heard their outcry and these charges, I was **very** angry.
6:16 were afraid and **lost** their **self-confidence** [+928+5877+6524],
8:17 had not celebrated it like this. And their joy was **very** great.
13: 8 I was **greatly** displeased and threw all Tobiah's household goods
Est 1:12 Then the king *became* **furious** [+7911] and burned with anger.
4: 4 and told her about Mordecai, she was in **great** distress.
Job 1: 3 and five hundred donkeys, and had a **large** number of servants.
2:13 to him, because they saw how **great** his suffering **was** [+1540].
8: 7 beginnings will seem humble, **so** prosperous will your future be.
35:15 never punishes and he does not take the **least** notice of wickedness.
Ps 6: 3 [6:4] My soul *is* **in anguish** [+987]. How long, O LORD,
6:10 [6:11] All my enemies will be ashamed and **dismayed** [+987];
21: 1 [21:2] How **great** is his joy in the victories you give!
31:11 [31:12] all my enemies, I am the **utter** contempt of my neighbors;
38: 6 [38:7] I am bowed down and brought **very** [+6330] low; all day
38: 8 [38:9] I am feeble and **utterly** [+6330] crushed; I groan in
46: 1 [46:2] and strength, an **ever-present** [+5162] help in trouble.
47: 9 [47:10] kings of the earth belong to God; he is **greatly** exalted.
48: 1 [48:2] Great is the LORD, and **most** worthy of praise, in the city
50: 3 fire devours before him, and around him a **tempest rages** [+8548].
78:29 They ate till they had **more than** enough, for he had given them
78:59 God heard them, he was very angry; he rejected Israel **completely**.
79: 8 your mercy come quickly to meet us, for we are in **desperate** need.
92: 5 [92:6] are your works, O LORD, **how** profound your thoughts!
93: 5 Your statutes **stand firm** [+586]; holiness adorns your house for
96: 4 For great is the LORD and **most** worthy of praise; he is to be
97: 9 Most High over all the earth; you are exalted **far** above all gods.
104: 1 O LORD my God, you are **very** great; you are clothed with
105:24 The LORD made his people **very** fruitful; he made them too
107:38 he blessed them, and their numbers **greatly** increased, and he did
109:30 With my mouth I will **greatly** extol the LORD; in the great
112: 1 who fears the LORD, who finds **great** delight in his commands.
116:10 I believed; therefore I said, "I am **greatly** afflicted."
119: 4 You have laid down precepts that are to be **fully** obeyed.
119: 8 I will obey your decrees; do not **utterly** [+6330] forsake me.
119:43 truth from my mouth, **[NIE]** for I have put my hope in your laws.
119:51 The arrogant mock me **without restraint** [+6330], but I do not
119:96 I see a limit; but your commands are **boundless** [+8146].
119:107 I have suffered **much** [+6330]; preserve my life, O LORD,
119:138 you have laid down are righteous; they are **fully** trustworthy.
119:140 Your promises have been **thoroughly** tested, and your servant
119:167 I obey your statutes, for I love them **greatly**.
139:14 your works are wonderful, I know that **full well**.
142: 6 [142:7] Listen to my cry, for I am in **desperate** need; rescue me
145: 3 Great is the LORD and **most** worthy of praise; his greatness no
Isa 16: 6 her **overweening** pride and conceit, her pride and her insolence—
31: 1 of their chariots and in the **great** strength of their horsemen,
47: 6 them no mercy. Even on the aged you laid a **very** heavy yoke.
47: 9 in spite of your many sorceries and **all** your potent spells.
52:13 will act wisely; he will be raised and lifted up and **highly** exalted.
56:12 And tomorrow will be like today, or **even far** [+3856] better."
64: 9 [64:8] Do not be angry **beyond measure** [+6330], O LORD; do
64:12 [64:11] you keep silent and punish us **beyond measure** [+6330]?
Jer 2:10 the coasts of Kittim and look, send to Kedar and observe **closely**;
2:12 Be appalled at this, O heavens, and shudder with **great** horror,"
2:36 Why do you go about **so much**, changing your ways? You will be
9:19 [9:18] 'How ruined we are! How **great** is our shame! We must
14:17 has suffered a grievous wound, a **crushing** [+2703] blow.
18:13 like this? A **most** horrible thing has been done by Virgin Israel.
20:11 They will fail and be **thoroughly** disgraced; their dishonor will
24: 2 One basket had **very** good figs, like those that ripen early;
24: 2 the other basket had **very** poor figs, so bad they could not be eaten.
24: 3 "The good ones are **very** good, but the poor ones are so bad they
24: 3 but the poor ones **[RPH]** are so bad they cannot be eaten."
40:12 they harvested an **abundance** [+2221] of wine and summer fruit.
48:16 fall of Moab is at hand; her calamity *will* **come quickly** [+4554].
48:29 her **overweening** pride and conceit, her pride and arrogance
49:30 "Flee **quickly** away! Stay in deep caves, you who live in Hazor,"
50:12 your mother will be **greatly** ashamed; she who gave you birth will
La 5:22 utterly rejected us and are angry with us **beyond measure** [+6330].
Eze 9: 9 of the house of Israel and Judah is **exceedingly** [+928+4394] great;
9: 9 of the house of Israel and Judah is **exceedingly** [+928+4394] great;
16:13 honey and olive oil. You became **very** [+928+4394] beautiful
16:13 honey and olive oil. You became **very** [+928+4394] beautiful
20:13 them will live by them—and they **utterly** desecrated my Sabbaths.
27:25 You are filled with **heavy cargo** [+3877] in the heart of the sea.
37: 2 and I saw a **great** many bones on the floor of the valley,
37: 2 many bones on the floor of the valley, bones that were **very** dry.
37:10 to life and stood up on their feet—a **vast** [+1524+4394] army.
37:10 to life and stood up on their feet—a **vast** [+1524+4394] army.
40: 2 took me to the land of Israel and set me on a **very** high mountain,
47: 7 I saw a **great** number of trees on each side of the river.
47: 9 There will be **large** numbers of fish, because this water flows there
47:10 The fish will be of **many** [+8041] kinds—like the fish of the Great
Da 8: 8 The goat became **very** [+6330] great, but at the height of his power
11:25 South will wage war with a large and **very** [+6330] powerful army,
Joel 2:11 his forces are **beyond number** [+8041], and mighty are those who
2:11 The day of the LORD is great; *it is* **dreadful** [+3707]. Who can
Ob 1: 2 make you small among the nations; you will be **utterly** despised.
Na 2: 1 [2:2] watch the road, brace yourselves, marshal **all** your strength!
Zep 1:14 day of the LORD is near—near and **coming quickly** [+4554].
Zec 9: 2 on it, and upon Tyre and Sidon, though they are **very** skillful.
9: 5 Gaza *will* **writhe in agony** [+2655], and Ekron too, for her hope
9: 9 Rejoice **greatly**, O Daughter of Zion! Shout, Daughter of
14: 4 forming a **great** [+1524] valley, with half of the mountain moving
14:14 nations will be collected—**great quantities of** [+4200+8044]

4395 מֵאָה¹ *mē'â¹*, n.f. [579 / 580] [→ 4396?, 4405; Ar 10395]

hundred [233], hundreds [18], 250 [+2256+2822] [10], 100 [8], 4,500 [+547+752+2256+2822] [8], 603,550 [+547+547+2256+2256+2256 +2822+2822+4395+8993+9252] [6], units of a hundred [6], 120 [+2256+6929] [5], 200 [5], 500 [+2822] [5], 1,254 [+547+752+2256 +2822] [4], 128 [+2256+6929+9046] [4], 127 [+2256+2256+6929

+8679] [3], 40,500 [+547+752+2256+2822] [3], 430 [+752+2256 +8993] [3], 53,400 [+547+752+2256+2256+2822+8993] [3], eleven hundred [+547+2256] [3], 1,247 [+547+752+2256+8679] [2], 1,775 [+547+2256+2256+2256+2822+8679+8679] [2], 108,100 [+547+547 +2256+2256+4395+9046] [2], 112 [+2256+6925+9109] [2], 123 [+2256+6929+8993] [2], 130 [+2256+8993] [2], 137 [+2256+2256 +8679+8993] [2], 150 [+2256+2822] [2], 151,450 [+285+547+547 +752+2256+2256+2256+2256+2822+2822+4395] [2], 153,600 [+547+547+2256+2256+2256+2822+4395+8993+9252] [2], 157,600 [+547+547+2256+2256+2256+2822+4395+8679+9252] [2], 186,400 [+547+547+547+752+2256+2256+2256+4395+9046+9252] [2], 200,000 [+547] [2], 220 [+2256+6929] [2], 223 [+2256+6929+8993] [2], 245 [+752+2256+2822] [2], 30,500 [+547+2256+2822+8993] [2], 300 [+8993] [2], 307,500 [+547+547+2256+2256+2822+4395+8679 +8993] [2], 32,200 [+547+2256+2256+8993+9109] [2], 320 [+2256+6929+8993] [2], 337,500 [+547+547+547+2256+2256+2256 +2822+4395+8679+8993+8993] [2], 337,500 [+547+547+547+2256 +2256+2822+4395+8679+8993+8993] [2], 345 [+752+2256+2822 +8993] [2], 35,400 [+547+752+2256+2256+2822+8993] [2], 372 [+2256+8679+8993+9109] [2], 390 [+2256+8993+9596] [2], 392 [+2256+8993+9109+9596] [2], 4,600 [+547+752+2256+9252] [2], 403 [+752+2256+8993] [2], 41,500 [+285+547+752+2256 +2256+2822] [2], 435 [+752+2256+2822+8993] [2], 45,650 [+547+752+2256+2256+2256+2822+2822+9252] [2], 46,500 [+547+752+2256+2256+2822+9252] [2], 54,400 [+547+752+752 +2256+2256+2822] [2], 57,400 [+547+752+2256+2256+2822+8679] [2], 59,300 [+547+2256+2256+2822+8993+9596] [2], 6,720 [+547+2256+6929+8679+9252] [2], 601,730 [+547+547+2256+2256 +4395+8679+8993+9252] [2], 62,700 [+547+2256+2256+8679 +9109+9252] [2], 621 [+285+2256+6929+9252] [2], 652 [+2256+2822+9109+9252] [2], 666 [+2256+9252+9252+9252] [2], 7,337 [+547+2256+8679+8679+8993+8993] [2], 74,600 [+547+752 +2256+2256+8679+9252] [2], 736 [+2256+8679+8993+9252] [2], 760 [+2256+8679+9252] [2], 800 [+9046] [2], 973 [+2256+8679 +8993+9596] [2], *untranslated* [2], about six hundred feet [+564+752] [2], fourteen hundred [+547+752+2256] [2], hundredth [2], seventeen hundred [+547+2256+8679] [2], units of hundreds [2], 1,222 [+547+2256+6929+9109] [1], 1,290 [+547+2256+9596] [1], 1,335 [+547+2256+2822+8993+8993] [1], 1,365 [+547+2256+2256+2256 +2822+8993+9252] [1], 1,760 [+547+2256+2256+8679+9252] [1], 105 [+2256+2822] [1], 110 [+2256+6927] [1], 112 [+6925+9109] [1], 119 [+2256+6926+9596] [1], 120,000 [+547+2256+6929] [1], 122 [+2256+2256+6929+9109] [1], 122 [+2256+6929+9109] [1], 133 [+2256+2256+8993+8993] [1], 138 [+2256+8993+9046] [1], 139 [+2256+8993+9596] [1], 14,700 [+547+752+2256+6925+8679] [1], 148 [+752+2256+9046] [1], 156 [+2256+2822+9252] [1], 16,750 [+547+2256+2822+6925+8679+9252] [1], 160 [+2256+9252] [1], 162 [+2256+2256+9109+9252] [2], 17,200 [+547+2256+6925+8679] [1], 172 [+2256+8679+9109] [1], 180 [+2256+9046] [1], 180,000 [+547+2256+9046] [1], 182 [+2256+2256+9046+9109] [1], 187 [+2256+2256+8679+9046] [1], 188 [+2256+9046+9046] [1], 2,172 [+547+2256+2256+8679+9109] [1], 2,172 [+547+2256+8679+9109] [1], 2,200 [+547+2256] [1], 2,300 [+547+2256+8993] [1], 2,322 [+547+2256+6929+8993+9109] [1], 2,400 [+547+752+2256] [1], 2,600 [+547+2256+9252] [1], 2,630 [+547+2256+2256+8993+9252] [1], 2,750 [+547+2256+2822+8679] [1], 2,812 [+547+2256+6925 +9046+9109] [1], 2,818 [+547+2256+6925+9046+9046] [1], 20,200 [+547+2256+6929] [1], 20,800 [+547+2256+6929+9046] [1], 205 [+2256+2822] [1], 207 [+2256+8679] [1], 209 [+2256+9596] [1], 212 [+2256+6925+9109] [1], 218 [+2256+6925+9046] [1], 22,200 [+547+2256+2256+6929+9109] [1], 22,273 [+547+2256+2256+2256 +6929+8679+8993+9109] [1], 22,600 [+547+2256+2256+6929 +9109+9252] [1], 232 [+2256+8993+9109] [1], 242 [+752+2256 +9109] [1], 245 [+752+2256+2256+2822] [1], 25,100 [+547+2256 +2256+2822+6929] [1], 273 [+2256+2256+8679+8993] [1], 28,600 [+547+2256+2256+6929+9046+9252] [1], 280,000 [+547+2256 +9046] [1], 284 [+752+2256+9046] [1], 288 [+2256+9046+9046] [1], 3,200 [+547+2256+8993] [1], 3,600 [+547+2256+8993+9252] [1], 3,630 [+547+2256+2256+8993+8993+9252] [1], 3,700 [+547+2256 +8679+8993] [1], 3,930 [+547+2256+8993+8993+9596] [1], 300,000 [+547+8993] [1], 318 [+2256+6925+8993+9046] [1], 32,500 [+547+2256+2256+2822+8993+9109] [1], 323 [+2256+6929+8993 +8993] [1], 324 [+752+2256+6929+8993] [1], 328 [+2256+6929 +8993+9046] [1], 350 [+2256+2822+8993] [1], 365 [+2256+2256 +2822+8993+9252] [1], 410 [+752+2256+6927] [1], 42,360 [+547+752+2256+8052+8993+9252] [1], 42,360 [+547+752+8052 +8993+9252] [1], 420 [+752+2256+6929] [1], 43,730 [+547+752 +2256+2256+2256+8679+8993+8993] [1], 44,760 [+547+752+752 +2256+2256+2256+8679+9252] [1], 45,400 [+547+752+752+2256 +2256+2822] [1], 45,600 [+547+752+2256+2256+2822+9252] [1], 450 feet [+564+8993] [1], 454 [+752+752+2256+2822] [1], 468 [+752+2256+9046+9252] [1], 5,400 [+547+752+2256+2822] [1], 52,700 [+547+2256+2256+2822+8679+9109] [1], 530 [+2256+2822 +8993] [1], 550 [+2256+2822+2822] [1], 595 [+2256+2256+2822 +2822+9596] [1], 6,200 [+547+2256+9252] [1], 6,800 [+547+2256 +9046+9252] [1], 60,500 [+547+2256+2822+9252] [1], 623 [+2256+6929+8993+9252] [1], 628 [+2256+6929+9046+9252] [1], 64,300 [+547+752+2256+2256+8993+9252] [1], 64,400 [+547+752 +752+2256+2256+9252] [1], 642 [+752+2256+2256+9109+9252] [1], 642 [+752+2256+9109+9252] [1], 648 [+752+2256+9046+9252] [1], 650 [+2256+2822+9252] [1], 655 [+2256+2822+2822+9252] [1], 666 [+2256+2256+9252+9252+9252] [1], 667 [+2256+8679+9252 +9252] [1], 675 [+2256+2822+8679+9252] [1], 675,000 [+547+547 +547+2256+2256+2822+8679+9252] [1], 690 [+2256+9252+9596] [1], 7,100 [+547+2256+8679] [1], 7,500 [+547+2256+2822+8679] [1], 721 [+285+2256+2256+6929+8679] [1], 725 [+2256+2822 +6929+8679] [1], 730 [+2256+8679+8993] [1], 743 [+752+2256 +2256+8679+8993] [1], 743 [+752+2256+8679+8993] [1], 745 [+752+2256+2822+8679] [1], 76,500 [+547+2256+2256+2822 +8679+9252] [1], 775 [+2256+2822+8679+8679] [1], 777 [+2256 +2256+8679+8679+8679] [1], 782 [+2256+2256+8679+9046+9109] [1], 8,580 [+547+2256+2256+2822+9046+9046] [1], 8,600 [+547+2256+9046+9252] [1], 807 [+2256+8679+9046] [1], 815 [+2256+2822+6926+9046] [1], 822 [+2256+6929+9046+9109] [1], 830 [+2256+8993+9046] [1], 832 [+2256+8993+9046+9109] [1], 840 [+752+2256+9046] [1], 845 [+752+2256+2822+9046] [1], 895 [+2256+2256+2822+9046+9596] [1], 905 [+2256+2822+9596] [1], 910 [+2256+6924+9596] [1], 912 [+2256+6926+9109+9596] [1], 928 [+2256+6929+9046+9596] [1], 930 [+2256+8993+9596] [1], 945 [+752+2256+2256+2822+9596] [1], 950 [+2256+2822+9596] [1], 956 [+2256+2256+2822+9252+9596] [1], 962 [+2256+2256+9109 +9252+9596] [1], 969 [+2256+2256+9252+9596+9596] [1], hundredfold [+9134] [1], thirty-six hundred [+547+2256+8993+9252] [1], thirty-three hundred [+547+2256+8993+8993] [1], twelve hundred [+547+2256] [1], twenty-seven hundred [+547+2256+8679] [1], twenty-six hundred [+547+2256+9252] [1], two hundred [1]

Ge 5: 3 When Adam had lived **130** [+2256+8993] years, he had a son in
5: 4 Adam lived **800** [+9046] years and had other sons and daughters.
5: 5 Adam lived **930** [+2256+8993+9596] years, and then he died.
5: 6 When Seth had lived **105** [+2256+2822] years, he became the
5: 7 Seth lived **807** [+2256+8679+9046] years and had other sons and
5: 8 Seth lived **912** [+2256+6926+9109+9596] years, and then he died.
5: 10 Enosh lived **815** [+2256+2822+6926+9046] years and had other
5: 11 Enosh lived **905** [+2256+2822+9596] years, and then he died.
5: 13 Kenan lived **840** [+752+2256+9046] years and had other sons
5: 14 Kenan lived **910** [+2256+6924+9596] years, and then he died.
5: 16 Mahalalel lived **830** [+2256+8993+9046] years and had other sons
5: 17 Mahalalel lived **895** [+2256+2256+2822+9046+9596] years, and
5: 18 When Jared had lived **162** [+2256+2256+9109+9252] years, he
5: 19 Jared lived **800** [+9046] years and had other sons and daughters.
5: 20 Jared lived **962** [+2256+2256+9109+9252+9596] years, and then
5: 22 Enoch walked with God **300** [+8993] years and had other sons
5: 23 Enoch lived **365** [+2256+2256+2822+8993+9252] years.
5: 25 When Methuselah had lived **187** [+2256+2256+8679+9046] years,
5: 26 Methuselah lived **782** [+2256+2256+8679+9046+9109] years and
5: 27 Methuselah lived **969** [+2256+2256+9252+9596+9596] years, and
5: 28 When Lamech had lived **182** [+2256+2256+9046+9109] years, he
5: 30 Lamech lived **595** [+2256+2256+2822+2822+9596] years and had
5: 31 Lamech lived **777** [+2256+2256+8679+8679+8679] years, and
5: 32 After Noah was **500** [+2822] years old, he became the father of
6: 3 for he is mortal; his days will be a **hundred** and twenty years."
6: 15 The ark is to be **450 feet** [+564+8993] long, 75 feet wide and 45
7: 6 Noah was six **hundred** years old when the floodwaters came on
7: 11 In the six **hundredth** year of Noah's life, on the seventeenth day of
7: 24 The waters flooded the earth for a **hundred** and fifty days.
8: 3 At the end of the **hundred** and fifty days the water had gone down,
8: 13 By the first day of the first month of Noah's six **hundred** and first
9: 28 After the flood Noah lived **350** [+2256+2822+8993] years.
9: 29 Noah lived **950** [+2256+2822+9596] years, and then he died.
11: 10 Two years after the flood, when Shem was **100** years old,
11: 11 Shem lived **500** [+2822] years and had other sons and daughters.
11: 13 Arphaxad lived **403** [+752+2256+8993] years and had other sons
11: 15 Shelah lived **403** [+752+2256+8993] years and had other sons
11: 17 Eber lived **430** [+752+2256+8993] years and had other sons
11: 19 Peleg lived **209** [+2256+9596] years and had other sons
11: 21 Reu lived **207** [+2256+8679] years and had other sons
11: 23 of Nahor, Serug lived **200** years and had other sons and daughters.
11: 25 Nahor lived **119** [+2256+6926+9596] years and had other sons and
11: 32 Terah lived **205** [+2256+2822] years, and he died in Haran.
14: 14 he called out the **318** [+2256+6925+8993+9046] trained men born
15: 13 and they will be enslaved and mistreated four **hundred** years.
17: 17 said to himself, "Will a son be born to a man a **hundred** years old?
21: 5 Abraham was a **hundred** years old when his son Isaac was born to
23: 1 Sarah lived to be a **hundred** and twenty-seven years old.
23: 15 the land is worth four **hundred** shekels of silver, but what is that
23: 16 four **hundred** shekels of silver, according to the weight current
25: 7 Altogether, Abraham lived a **hundred** and seventy-five years.

Ge 25:17 Altogether, Ishmael lived a **hundred** and thirty-seven years.
26:12 in that land and the same year reaped a **hundredfold** [+9134],
32: 6 [32:7] coming to meet you, and four **hundred** men are with him."
32:14 [32:15] *two* **hundred** female goats and twenty male goats,
32:14 [32:15] twenty male goats, *two* **hundred** ewes and twenty rams,
33: 1 looked up and there was Esau, coming with his four **hundred** men;
33:19 For a **hundred** pieces of silver, he bought from the sons of Hamor,
35:28 Isaac lived a **hundred** and eighty years.
45:22 to Benjamin he gave three **hundred** shekels of silver and five sets
47: 9 to Pharaoh, "The years of my pilgrimage are a **hundred** and thirty.
47:28 and the years of his life were a **hundred** and forty-seven.
50:22 with all his father's family. He lived a **hundred** and ten years
50:26 So Joseph died at the age of a **hundred** and ten. And after they
Ex 6:16 Levi lived **137** [+2256+2256+8679+8993] years.
6:18 Kohath lived **133** [+2256+2256+8993+8993] years.
6:20 Amram lived **137** [+2256+2256+8679+8993] years.
12:37 There were about six **hundred** thousand men on foot, besides
12:40 Israelite people lived in Egypt was **430** [+752+2256+8993] years.
12:41 At the end of the **430** [+752+2256+8993] years, to the very day,
14: 7 He took six **hundred** *of* the best chariots, along with all the other
18:21 them as officials over thousands, **hundreds**, fifties and tens.
18:25 of the people, officials over thousands, **hundreds**, fifties and tens.
27: 9 The south side shall be a **hundred** cubits long and is to have
27:11 The north side shall also be a **hundred** cubits long and is to have
27:18 The courtyard shall be a **hundred** cubits long and fifty cubits wide,
30:23 **500** [+2822] shekels of liquid myrrh, half as much (that is,
30:23 of liquid myrrh, half as much (that is, **250** [+2256+2822] shekels)
30:23 of fragrant cinnamon, **250** [+2256+2822] shekels of fragrant cane,
30:24 **500** [+2822] shekels of cassia—all according to the sanctuary
38: 9 The south side was a **hundred** cubits long and had curtains of
38:11 The north side was also a **hundred** cubits long and had twenty
38:24 the sanctuary was 29 talents and **730** [+2256+8679+8993] shekels,
38:25 of the community who were counted in the census was **100** talents
38:25 and **1,775** [+547+2256+2256+2256+2822+8679+8679] shekels,
38:26 twenty years old or more, a total of **603,550** [+547+547+2256 +2256+2256+2822+2822+4395+8993+9252] men.
38:26 twenty years old or more, a total of **603,550** [+547+547+2256 +2256+2256+2822+2822+4395+8993+9252] men.
38:27 The **100** talents of silver were used to cast the bases for the
38:27 **100** bases from the 100 talents, one talent for each base.
38:27 100 bases from the **100** talents, one talent for each base.
38:28 the **1,775** [+547+2256+2256+2256+2822+8679+8679] shekels to
38:29 wave offering was 70 talents and **2,400** [+547+752+2256] shekels.
Lev 26: 8 Five of you will chase a **hundred**, and a hundred of you will chase
26: 8 chase a hundred, and a **hundred** of you will chase ten thousand,
Nu 1:21 tribe of Reuben was **46,500** [+547+752+2256+2256+2822+9252].
1:23 tribe of Simeon was **59,300** [+547+2256+2256+2822+8993+9596].
1:25 Gad was **45,650** [+547+752+2256+2256+2256+2822+2822+9252].
1:27 tribe of Judah was **74,600** [+547+752+2256+2256+8679+9252].
1:29 tribe of Issachar was **54,400** [+547+752+752+2256+2256+2822].
1:31 tribe of Zebulun was **57,400** [+547+752+2256+2256+2822+8679].
1:33 from the tribe of Ephraim was **40,500** [+547+752+2256+2822].
1:35 the tribe of Manasseh was **32,200** [+547+2256+2256+8993+9109].
1:37 of Benjamin was **35,400** [+547+752+2256+2256+2822+8993].
1:39 tribe of Dan was **62,700** [+547+2256+2256+8679+9109+9252].
1:41 tribe of Asher was **41,500** [+285+547+752+2256+2256+2822].
1:43 tribe of Naphtali was **53,400** [+547+752+2256+2256+2822+8993].
1:46 The total number was **603,550** [+547+547+2256+2256+2256 +2822+2822+4395+8993+9252].
1:46 The total number was **603,550** [+547+547+2256+2256+2256 +2822+2822+4395+8993+9252].
2: 4 His division numbers **74,600** [+547+752+2256+2256+8679+9252].
2: 6 His division numbers **54,400** [+547+752+752+2256+2256+2822].
2: 8 His division numbers **57,400** [+547+752+2256+2256+2822+8679].
2: 9 to the camp of Judah, according to their divisions, number **186,400** [+547+547+547+752+2256+2256+2256+4395+9046+9252].
2: 9 to the camp of Judah, according to their divisions, number **186,400** [+547+547+547+752+2256+2256+2256+4395+9046+9252].
2:11 His division numbers **46,500** [+547+752+2256+2256+2822+9252].
2:13 division numbers **59,300** [+547+2256+2256+2822+8993+9596].
2:15 numbers **45,650** [+547+752+2256+2256+2256+2822+2822+9252].
2:16 the camp of Reuben, according to their divisions, number **151,450** [+285+547+547+752+2256+2256+2256+2256+2822+2822+4395].
2:16 the camp of Reuben, according to their divisions, number **151,450** [+285+547+547+752+2256+2256+2256+2256+2822+2822+4395].
2:19 His division numbers **40,500** [+547+752+2256+2822].
2:21 His division numbers **32,200** [+547+2256+2256+8993+9109].
2:23 His division numbers **35,400** [+547+752+2256+2256+2822+8993].
2:24 divisions, number **108,100** [+547+547+2256+2256+4395+9046].
2:24 divisions, number **108,100** [+547+547+2256+2256+4395+9046].
2:26 division numbers **62,700** [+547+2256+2256+8679+9109+9252].
2:28 His division numbers **41,500** [+285+547+752+2256+2256+2822].
2:30 His division numbers **53,400** [+547+752+2256+2256+2822+8993].
2:31 **157,600** [+547+547+2256+2256+2256+2822+4395+8679+9252].
2:31 **157,600** [+547+547+2256+2256+2256+2822+4395+8679+9252].
2:32 All those in the camps, by their divisions, number **603,550** [+547+547+2256+2256+2256+2822+2822+4395+8993+9252].
2:32 All those in the camps, by their divisions, number **603,550** [+547+547+2256+2256+2256+2822+2822+4395+8993+9252].
3:22 who were counted was **7,500** [+547+2256+2822+8679].
3:28 males a month old or more was **8,600** [+547+2256+9046+9252].
3:34 or more who were counted was **6,200** [+547+2256+9252].
3:43 was **22,273** [+547+2256+2256+2256+6929+8679+8993+9109].
3:46 To redeem the **273** [+2256+2256+8679+8993] firstborn Israelites
3:50 **1,365** [+547+2256+2256+2256+2822+8993+9252] shekels,
4:36 counted by clans, were **2,750** [+547+2256+2822+8679].
4:40 clans and families, were **2,630** [+547+2256+2256+8993+9252].
4:44 counted by their clans, were **3,200** [+547+2256+8993].
4:48 numbered **8,580** [+547+2256+2256+2822+9046+9046].
7:13 His offering was one silver plate weighing a **hundred** and thirty
7:19 The offering he brought was one silver plate weighing a **hundred**
7:25 His offering was one silver plate weighing a **hundred** and thirty
7:31 His offering was one silver plate weighing a **hundred** and thirty
7:37 His offering was one silver plate weighing a **hundred** and thirty
7:43 His offering was one silver plate weighing a **hundred** and thirty
7:49 His offering was one silver plate weighing a **hundred** and thirty
7:55 His offering was one silver plate weighing a **hundred** and thirty
7:61 His offering was one silver plate weighing a **hundred** and thirty
7:67 His offering was one silver plate weighing a **hundred** and thirty
7:73 His offering was one silver plate weighing a **hundred** and thirty
7:79 His offering was one silver plate weighing a **hundred** and thirty
7:85 Each silver plate weighed a **hundred** and thirty shekels, and each
7:85 the silver dishes weighed two thousand four **hundred** shekels,
7:86 the gold dishes weighed a **hundred** and twenty shekels.
11:21 "Here I am among six **hundred** thousand men on foot, and you
16: 2 With them were **250** [+2256+2822] Israelite men, well-known
16:17 his censer and put incense in it—**250** [+2256+2822] censers in all—
16:35 consumed the **250** [+2256+2822] men who were offering the
16:49 [17:14] But **14,700** [+547+752+2256+6925+8679] people died
26: 7 were **43,730** [+547+752+2256+2256+2256+8679+8993+8993].
26:10 followers died when the fire devoured the **250** [+2256+2822] men.
26:14 Simeon; there were **22,200** [+547+2256+2256+6929+9109] men.
26:18 of Gad; those numbered were **40,500** [+547+752+2256+2822].
26:22 numbered were **76,500** [+547+2256+2256+2822+8679+9252].
26:25 numbered were **64,300** [+547+752+2256+2256+8993+9252].
26:27 Zebulun; those numbered were **60,500** [+547+2256+2822+9252].
26:34 numbered were **52,700** [+547+2256+2256+2822+8679+9109].
26:37 numbered were **32,500** [+547+2256+2256+2822+8993+9109].
26:41 numbered were **45,600** [+547+752+2256+2256+2822+9252].
26:43 numbered were **64,400** [+547+752+752+2256+2256+9252].
26:47 numbered were **53,400** [+547+752+2256+2256+2822+8993].
26:50 numbered were **45,400** [+547+752+752+2256+2256+2822].
26:51 **601,730** [+547+547+2256+2256+4395+8679+8993+9252].
26:51 **601,730** [+547+547+2256+2256+4395+8679+8993+9252].
31:14 the commanders of thousands and commanders of **hundreds**—
31:28 set apart as tribute for the LORD one out of every five **hundred**,
31:32 **675,000** [+547+547+547+2256+2256+2822+8679+9252] sheep,
31:36 share of those who fought in the battle was: **337,500** [+547+547 +547+2256+2256+2256+2822+4395+8679+8993+8993] sheep,
31:36 share of those who fought in the battle was: **337,500** [+547+547 +547+2256+2256+2256+2822+4395+8679+8993+8993] sheep,
31:37 the tribute for the LORD was **675** [+2256+2822+8679+9252];
31:39 **30,500** [+547+2256+2822+8993] donkeys, of which the tribute for
31:43 the community's half—was **337,500** [+547+547+547+2256+2256 +2822+4395+8679+8993+8993] sheep,
31:43 the community's half—was **337,500** [+547+547+547+2256+2256 +2822+4395+8679+8993+8993] sheep,
31:45 **30,500** [+547+2256+2822+8993] donkeys
31:48 the commanders of thousands and commanders of **hundreds**—
31:52 of thousands and commanders of **hundreds** that Moses
31:52 weighed **16,750** [+547+2256+2822+6925+8679+9252] shekels.
31:54 from the commanders of thousands and commanders of **hundreds**
33:39 Aaron was a **hundred** and twenty-three years old when he died on
Dt 1:15 of **hundreds**, of fifties and of tens and as tribal officials.
22:19 They shall fine him a **hundred** shekels of silver and give them to
31: 2 "I am now a **hundred** and twenty years old and I am no longer
34: 7 Moses was a **hundred** and twenty years old when he died,
Jos 7:21 *two* **hundred** shekels of silver and a wedge of gold weighing fifty
24:29 the servant of the LORD, died at the age of a **hundred** and ten.
24:32 bought for a **hundred** pieces of silver from the sons of Hamor,
Jdg 2: 8 the servant of the LORD, died at the age of a **hundred** and ten.
3:31 who struck down six **hundred** Philistines with an oxgoad.
4: 3 Because he had nine **hundred** iron chariots and had cruelly
4:13 Sisera gathered together his nine **hundred** iron chariots and all the
7: 6 Three **hundred** men lapped with their hands to their mouths.
7: 7 "With the three **hundred** men that lapped I will save you and give
7: 8 the rest of the Israelites to their tents but kept the three **hundred**,
7:16 Dividing the three **hundred** men into three companies, he placed

Jdg 7:19 the **hundred** men with him reached the edge of the camp at the
7:22 When the three **hundred** trumpets sounded, the LORD caused the
8:4 Gideon and his three **hundred** men, exhausted yet keeping up the
8:10 a **hundred** and twenty thousand swordsmen had fallen.
8:26 came to **seventeen hundred** [+547+2256+8679] shekels,
11:26 For three **hundred** years Israel occupied Heshbon, Aroer,
15:4 So he went out and caught three **hundred** foxes and tied them tail
16:5 Each one of us will give you **eleven hundred** [+547+2256] shekels
17:2 "The **eleven hundred** [+547+2256] shekels of silver that were
17:3 When he returned the **eleven hundred** [+547+2256] shekels of
17:4 she took *two* **hundred** shekels of silver and gave them to a
18:11 six **hundred** men from the clan of the Danites, armed for battle,
18:16 The six **hundred** Danites, armed for battle, stood at the entrance to
18:17 and the six **hundred** armed men stood at the entrance to the gate.
20:2 of God, four **hundred** thousand soldiers armed with swords.
20:10 We'll take ten men out of every **hundred** from all the tribes of
20:10 a **hundred** from a thousand, and a thousand from ten thousand,
20:15 in addition to seven **hundred** chosen men from those living in
20:16 Among all these soldiers there were seven **hundred** chosen men
20:17 from Benjamin, mustered four **hundred** thousand swordsmen,
20:35 Israelites struck down **25,100** [+547+2256+2256+2822+6929]
20:47 six **hundred** men turned and fled into the desert to the rock of
21:12 found among the people living in Jabesh Gilead four **hundred**
1Sa 11:8 the men of Israel numbered three **hundred** thousand and the men
13:15 the men who were with him. They numbered about six **hundred**.
14:2 tree in Migron. With him were about six **hundred** men,
15:4 *two* **hundred** thousand foot soldiers and ten thousand men from
17:7 a weaver's rod, and its iron point weighed six **hundred** shekels.
18:25 'The king wants no other price for the bride than a **hundred**
18:27 and his men went out and killed *two* **hundred** Philistines.
22:2 he became their leader. About four **hundred** men were with him.
22:7 of you commanders of thousands and commanders of **hundreds**?
23:13 about six **hundred** in number, left Keilah and kept moving from
25:13 About four **hundred** men went up with David, while two hundred
25:13 went up with David, while *two* **hundred** stayed with the supplies.
25:18 She took *two* **hundred** loaves of bread, two skins of wine,
25:18 a **hundred** cakes of raisins and two hundred cakes of pressed figs,
25:18 a hundred cakes of raisins and *two* **hundred** cakes of pressed figs,
27:2 So David and the six **hundred** men with him left and went over to
29:2 As the Philistine rulers marched with their **units of hundreds**
30:9 and the six **hundred** men with him came to the Besor Ravine,
30:10 for *two* **hundred** men were too exhausted to cross the ravine.
30:10 But David and four **hundred** men continued the pursuit.
30:17 except four **hundred** young men who rode off on camels and fled.
30:21 David came to the *two* **hundred** men who had been too exhausted
2Sa 2:31 David's men had killed three **hundred** and sixty Benjamites who
3:14 whom I betrothed to myself for the price of a **hundred** Philistine
8:4 seven thousand [BHS *seventeen hundred*; NIV 547] charioteers
8:4 He hamstrung all but a **hundred** of the chariot horses.
10:18 David killed seven **hundred** of their charioteers and forty thousand
14:26 and its weight was *two* **hundred** shekels by the royal standard.
15:11 *Two* **hundred** men from Jerusalem had accompanied Absalom.
15:18 all the six **hundred** Gittites who had accompanied him from Gath
16:1 of donkeys saddled and loaded with *two* **hundred** loaves of bread,
16:1 a **hundred** cakes of raisins, a hundred cakes of figs and a skin of
16:1 cakes of raisins, a **hundred** cakes of figs and a skin of wine.
18:1 them commanders of thousands and commanders of **hundreds**.
18:4 the gate while all the men marched out in **units of hundreds**
21:16 whose bronze spearhead weighed three **hundred** shekels and who
23:8 he raised his spear against eight **hundred** men, whom he killed in
23:18 He raised his spear against three **hundred** men, whom he killed,
24:3 "May the LORD your God multiply the troops a **hundred** times
24:9 In Israel there were eight **hundred** thousand able-bodied men who
24:9 who could handle a sword, and in Judah five **hundred** thousand.
1Ki 4:23 [5:3] twenty of pasture-fed cattle and a **hundred** sheep and goats,
5:16 [5:30] as well as **thirty-three hundred** [+547+2256+8993+8993]
6:1 In the four **hundred** and eightieth year after the Israelites had
7:2 He built the Palace of the Forest of Lebanon a **hundred** cubits
7:20 were the *two* **hundred** pomegranates in rows all around.
7:42 the four **hundred** pomegranates for the two sets of network (two
8:63 and a **hundred** and twenty thousand sheep and goats.
9:14 Now Hiram had sent to the king **120** [+2256+6929] talents of gold.
9:23 of Solomon's projects—**550** [+2256+2822+2822] officials
9:28 and brought back **420** [+752+2256+6929] talents of gold,
10:10 she gave the king **120** [+2256+6929] talents of gold, large
10:14 received yearly was **666** [+2256+9252+9252+9252] talents,
10:16 King Solomon made *two* **hundred** large shields of hammered
10:16 hammered gold; six **hundred** bekas of gold went into each shield.
10:17 He also made three **hundred** small shields of hammered gold,
10:26 he had **fourteen hundred** [+547+752+2256] chariots and twelve
10:29 They imported a chariot from Egypt for six **hundred** shekels of
10:29 six hundred shekels of silver, and a horse for a **hundred** and fifty.
11:3 He had seven **hundred** wives of royal birth and three hundred
11:3 seven hundred wives of royal birth and three **hundred** concubines,
12:21 tribe of Benjamin—a **hundred** and eighty thousand fighting men—
18:4 Obadiah had taken a **hundred** prophets and hidden them in two
18:13 I hid a **hundred** of the LORD's prophets in two caves, fifty in
18:19 bring the four **hundred** and fifty prophets of Baal and the four
18:19 fifty prophets of Baal and the four **hundred** prophets of Asherah,
18:22 prophets left, but Baal has four **hundred** and fifty prophets.
20:15 the provincial commanders, **232** [+2256+8993+9109] men.
20:29 The Israelites inflicted a **hundred** thousand casualties on the
22:6 about four **hundred** men—and asked them, "Shall I go to war
2Ki 3:4 he had to supply the king of Israel with a **hundred** thousand lambs
3:4 thousand lambs and with the wool of a **hundred** thousand rams.
3:26 he took with him seven **hundred** swordsmen to break through to
4:43 "How can I set this before a **hundred** men?" his servant asked.
11:4 year Jehoiada sent for the commanders of **units of a hundred**,
11:9 The commanders of **units of a hundred** did just as Jehoiada the
11:10 he gave the commanders **[RPH]** the spears and shields that had
11:15 Jehoiada the priest ordered the commanders of **units of a hundred**,
11:19 He took with him the commanders of **hundreds**, the Carites,
14:13 Corner Gate—a section **about six hundred feet** [+564+752] long.
18:14 from Hezekiah king of Judah three **hundred** talents of silver
19:35 night the angel of the LORD went out and put to death a **hundred**
23:33 and he imposed on Judah a levy of a **hundred** talents of silver
1Ch 4:42 And five **hundred** of these Simeonites, led by Pelatiah, Neariah,
5:18 had **44,760** [+547+752+752+2256+2256+2256+8679+9252] men
5:21 *two* **hundred** fifty thousand sheep and two thousand donkeys.
5:21 They also took *one* **hundred** thousand people captive,
7:2 numbered **22,600** [+547+2256+2256+6929+9109+9252].
7:9 the heads of families and **20,200** [+547+2256+6929] fighting men.
7:11 There were **17,200** [+547+2256+6925+8679] fighting men ready to
8:40 They had many sons and grandsons—**150** [+2256+2822] in all.
9:6 The people from Judah numbered **690** [+2256+9252+9596].
9:9 their genealogy, numbered **956** [+2256+2256+2822+9252+9596].
9:13 of families, numbered **1,760** [+547+2256+2256+8679+9252].
9:22 gatekeepers at the thresholds numbered **212** [+2256+6925+9109].
11:11 he raised his spear against three **hundred** men, whom he killed in
11:20 He raised his spear against three **hundred** men, whom he killed,
12:14 [12:15] the least was a match for a **hundred**, and the greatest for
12:24 [12:25] **6,800** [+547+2256+9046+9252] armed for battle;
12:25 [12:26] warriors ready for battle—**7,100** [+547+2256+8679];
12:26 [12:27] men of Levi—**4,600** [+547+752+2256+9252],
12:27 [12:28] with **3,700** [+547+2256+8679+8993] men,
12:30 [12:31] in their own clans—**20,800** [+547+2256+6929+9046];
12:32 [12:33] **200** chiefs, with all their relatives under their command;
12:35 [12:36] for battle—**28,600** [+547+2256+2256+6929+9046+9252];
12:37 [12:38] with every type of weapon—**120,000** [+547+2256+6929].
13:1 the commanders of thousands and commanders of **hundreds**.
15:5 of Kohath, Uriel the leader and **120** [+2256+6929] relatives;
15:6 of Merari, Asaiah the leader and **220** [+2256+6929] relatives;
15:7 of Gershon, Joel the leader and **130** [+2256+8993] relatives;
15:8 descendants of Elizaphan, Shemaiah the leader and **200** relatives;
15:10 Amminadab the leader and **112** [+2256+6925+9109] relatives.
18:4 He hamstrung all but a **hundred** of the chariot horses.
21:3 "May the LORD multiply his troops a **hundred** times over.
21:5 In all Israel there were one million *one* **hundred** thousand men
21:5 a sword, including four **hundred** and seventy thousand in Judah.
21:25 So David paid Araunah six **hundred** shekels of gold for the site.
22:14 for the temple of the LORD a **hundred** thousand talents of gold,
25:7 for the LORD—they numbered **288** [+2256+9046+9046].
26:26 were the commanders of thousands and commanders of **hundreds**,
26:30 **seventeen hundred** [+547+2256+8679] able men—
26:32 Jeriah had **twenty-seven hundred** [+547+2256+8679] relatives,
27:1 commanders of thousands and commanders of **hundreds**,
28:1 the commanders of thousands and commanders of **hundreds**,
29:6 the commanders of thousands and commanders of **hundreds**,
29:7 thousand talents of bronze and a **hundred** thousand talents of iron.
2Ch 1:2 to the commanders of thousands and commanders of **hundreds**,
1:14 he had **fourteen hundred** [+547+752+2256] chariots and twelve
1:17 They imported a chariot from Egypt for six **hundred** shekels of
1:17 six hundred shekels of silver, and a horse for a **hundred** and fifty.
2:2 [2:1] and **thirty-six hundred** [+547+2256+8993+9252] as foremen
2:17 [2:16] his father David had taken; and they were found to be
153,600 [+547+547+2256+2256+2256+2822+4395+8993+9252].
2:17 [2:16] his father David had taken; and they were found to be
153,600 [+547+547+2256+2256+2256+2822+4395+8993+9252].
2:18 [2:17] with **3,600** [+547+2256+8993+9252] foremen over them to
3:4 and twenty cubits [BHS ***hundred and twenty***; NIV 564] high.
3:8 He overlaid the inside with six **hundred** talents of fine gold.
3:16 He also made a **hundred** pomegranates and attached them to the
4:8 five on the north. He also made a **hundred** gold sprinkling bowls.
4:13 the four **hundred** pomegranates for the two sets of network (two
5:12 They were accompanied by **120** [+2256+6929] priests sounding
7:5 of cattle and a **hundred** and twenty thousand sheep and goats.
8:10 **two hundred** and fifty officials supervising the men.
8:18 sailed to Ophir and brought back four **hundred** and fifty talents of

2Ch 9: 9 Then she gave the king **120** [+2256+6929] talents of gold,
9: 13 received yearly was **666** [+2256+2256+9252+9252+9252] talents,
9: 15 King Solomon made *two* **hundred** large shields of hammered
9: 15 six **hundred** bekas of hammered gold went into each shield.
9: 16 He also made three **hundred** small shields of hammered gold,
9: 16 hammered gold, with three **hundred** bekas of gold in each shield.
11: 1 and Benjamin—a **hundred** and eighty thousand fighting men—
12: 3 With **twelve hundred** [+547+2256] chariots and sixty thousand
13: 3 Abijah went into battle with a force of four **hundred** thousand able
13: 3 Jeroboam drew up a battle line against him with eight **hundred**
13: 17 so that there were five **hundred** thousand casualties among Israel's
14: 8 [14:7] Asa had an army of three **hundred** thousand men from
14: 8 [14:7] and *two* **hundred** and eighty thousand from Benjamin,
14: 9 [14:8] against them with a vast army and three **hundred** chariots,
15: 11 At that time they sacrificed to the LORD seven **hundred** head of
17: 11 seven thousand seven **hundred** rams and seven thousand seven
17: 11 seven hundred rams and seven thousand seven **hundred** goats.
17: 14 Adnah the commander, with **300,000** [+547+8993] fighting men;
17: 15 next, Jehohanan the commander, with **280,000** [+547+2256+9046];
17: 16 himself for the service of the LORD, with **200,000** [+547].
17: 17 with **200,000** [+547] men armed with bows and shields;
17: 18 Jehozabad, with **180,000** [+547+2256+9046] men armed for battle.
18: 5 four **hundred** men—and asked them, "Shall we go to war against
23: 1 He made a covenant with the commanders of **units of a hundred**:
23: 9 Then he gave the commanders of **units of a hundred** the spears
23: 14 the priest sent out the commanders of **units of a hundred**,
23: 20 He took with him the commanders of **hundreds**, the nobles,
24: 15 and full of years, and he died at the age of a **hundred** and thirty.
25: 5 and commanders of **hundreds** for all Judah and Benjamin.
25: 5 found that there were three **hundred** thousand men ready for
25: 6 He also hired a **hundred** thousand fighting men from Israel for a
25: 6 thousand fighting men from Israel for a **hundred** talents of silver.
25: 9 "But what about the **hundred** talents I paid for these Israelite
25: 23 Corner Gate—a section **about six hundred feet** [+564+752] long.
26: 12 family leaders over the fighting men was **2,600** [+547+2256+9252].
26: 13 of **307,500** [+547+547+2256+2256+2822+4395+8679+8993] men
26: 13 of **307,500** [+547+547+2256+2256+2822+4395+8679+8993] men
27: 5 That year the Ammonites paid him a **hundred** talents of silver,
28: 6 In one day Pekah son of Remaliah killed a **hundred** and twenty
28: 8 The Israelites took captive from their kinsmen *two* **hundred**
29: 32 was seventy bulls, a **hundred** rams and two hundred male lambs—
29: 32 was seventy bulls, a hundred rams and *two* **hundred** male lambs—
29: 33 The animals consecrated as sacrifices amounted to six **hundred**
35: 8 gave the priests **twenty-six hundred** [+547+2256+9252] Passover
35: 8 twenty-six hundred Passover offerings and three **hundred** cattle.
35: 9 Passover offerings and five **hundred** head of cattle for the Levites.
36: 3 and imposed on Judah a levy of a **hundred** talents of silver
Ezr 1: 10 gold bowls 30 matching silver bowls **410** [+752+2256+6927]
1: 11 In all, there were **5,400** [+547+752+2256+2822] articles of gold
2: 3 the descendants of Parosh **2,172** [+547+2256+8679+9109]
2: 4 of Shephatiah **372** [+2256+8679+8993+9109]
2: 5 of Arah **775** [+2256+2822+8679+8679]
2: 6 of Jeshua and Joab) **2,812** [+547+2256+6925+9046+9109]
2: 7 of Elam **1,254** [+547+752+2256+2822]
2: 8 of Zattu **945** [+752+2256+2256+2822+9596]
2: 9 of Zaccai **760** [+2256+8679+9252]
2: 10 of Bani **642** [+752+2256+9109+9252]
2: 11 of Bebai **623** [+2256+6929+8993+9252]
2: 12 of Azgad **1,222** [+547+2256+6929+9109]
2: 13 of Adonikam **666** [+2256+9252+9252+9252]
2: 15 of Adin **454** [+752+752+2256+2822]
2: 17 of Bezai **323** [+2256+6929+8993+8993]
2: 18 of Jorah **112** [+2256+6925+9109]
2: 19 of Hashum **223** [+2256+6929+8993]
2: 21 the men of Bethlehem **123** [+2256+6929+8993]
2: 23 of Anathoth **128** [+2256+6929+9046]
2: 25 Kephirah and Beeroth **743** [+752+2256+2256+8679+8993]
2: 26 of Ramah and Geba **621** [+285+2256+6929+9252]
2: 27 of Micmash **122** [+2256+6929+9109]
2: 28 of Bethel and Ai **223** [+2256+6929+8993]
2: 30 of Magbish **156** [+2256+2822+9252]
2: 31 of the other Elam **1,254** [+547+752+2256+2822]
2: 32 of Harim **320** [+2256+6929+8993]
2: 33 of Lod, Hadid and Ono **725** [+2256+2822+6929+8679]
2: 34 of Jericho **345** [+752+2256+2822+8993]
2: 35 of Senaah **3,630** [+547+2256+2256+8993+8993+9252]
2: 36 (through the family of Jeshua) **973** [+2256+8679+8993+9596]
2: 38 of Pashhur **1,247** [+547+752+2256+8679]
2: 41 The singers: the descendants of Asaph **128** [+2256+6929+9046]
2: 42 Ater, Talmon, Akkub, Hatita and Shobai **139** [+2256+8993+9596]
2: 58 of the servants of Solomon **392** [+2256+8993+9109+9596]
2: 60 Delaiah, Tobiah and Nekoda **652** [+2256+2822+9109+9252]
2: 64 whole company numbered **42,360** [+547+752+8052+8993+9252],
2: 65 their **7,337** [+547+2256+8679+8679+8993+8993] menservants
2: 65 and maidservants; and they also had **200** men and women singers.
2: 66 They had **736** [+2256+8679+8993+9252] horses, 245 mules,
2: 66 They had 736 horses, **245** [+752+2256+2822] mules,
2: 67 **435** [+752+2256+2822+8993] camels and 6,720 donkeys.
2: 67 435 camels and **6,720** [+547+2256+6929+8679+9252] donkeys.
2: 69 drachmas of gold, 5,000 minas of silver and **100** priestly garments.
8: 3 Zechariah, and with him were registered **150** [+2256+2822] men;
8: 4 Eliehoenai son of Zerahiah, and with him **200** men;
8: 5 Shecaniah son of Jahaziel, and with him **300** [+8993] men;
8: 9 Obadiah son of Jehiel, and with him **218** [+2256+6925+9046] men;
8: 10 Shelomith son of Josiphiah, and with him **160** [+2256+9252] men;
8: 12 Johanan son of Hakkatan, and with him **110** [+2256+6927] men;
8: 20 They also brought **220** [+2256+6929] of the temple servants—
8: 26 I weighed out to them **650** [+2256+2822+9252] talents of silver,
8: 26 of silver, silver articles weighing **100** talents, 100 talents of gold,
8: 26 of silver, silver articles weighing 100 talents, **100** talents of gold,
Ne 5: 11 the **hundredth** *part of* the money, grain, new wine and oil."
5: 17 a **hundred** and fifty Jews and officials ate at my table,
7: 8 the descendants of Parosh **2,172** [+547+2256+2256+8679+9109]
7: 9 of Shephatiah **372** [+2256+8679+8993+9109]
7: 10 of Arah **652** [+2256+2822+9109+9252]
7: 11 of Jeshua and Joab) **2,818** [+547+2256+6925+9046+9046]
7: 12 of Elam **1,254** [+547+752+2256+2822]
7: 13 of Zattu **845** [+752+2256+2822+9046]
7: 14 of Zaccai **760** [+2256+8679+9252]
7: 15 of Binnui **648** [+752+2256+9046+9252]
7: 16 of Bebai **628** [+2256+6929+9046+9252]
7: 17 of Azgad **2,322** [+547+2256+6929+8993+9109]
7: 18 of Adonikam **667** [+2256+8679+9252+9252]
7: 20 of Adin **655** [+2256+2822+2822+9252]
7: 22 of Hashum **328** [+2256+6929+8993+9046]
7: 23 of Bezai **324** [+752+2256+6929+8993]
7: 24 of Hariph **112** [+6925+9109]
7: 26 the men of Bethlehem and Netophah **188** [+2256+9046+9046]
7: 27 of Anathoth **128** [+2256+6929+9046]
7: 29 Kephirah and Beeroth **743** [+752+2256+8679+8993]
7: 30 of Ramah and Geba **621** [+285+2256+6929+9252]
7: 31 of Micmash **122** [+2256+2256+6929+9109]
7: 32 of Bethel and Ai **123** [+2256+6929+8993]
7: 34 of the other Elam **1,254** [+547+752+2256+2822]
7: 35 of Harim **320** [+2256+6929+8993]
7: 36 of Jericho **345** [+752+2256+2822+8993]
7: 37 of Lod, Hadid and Ono **721** [+285+2256+2256+6929+8679]
7: 38 of Senaah **3,930** [+547+2256+8993+8993+9596]
7: 39 (through the family of Jeshua) **973** [+2256+8679+8993+9596]
7: 41 of Pashhur **1,247** [+547+752+2256+8679]
7: 44 The singers: the descendants of Asaph **148** [+752+2256+9046]
7: 45 Ater, Talmon, Akkub, Hatita and Shobai **138** [+2256+8993+9046]
7: 60 of the servants of Solomon **392** [+2256+8993+9109+9596]
7: 62 Tobiah and Nekoda **642** [+752+2256+2256+9109+9252]
7: 66 company numbered **42,360** [+547+752+2256+8052+8993+9252],
7: 67 their **7,337** [+547+2256+8679+8679+8993+8993] menservants
7: 67 had **245** [+752+2256+2256+2822] men and women singers.
7: 68 [7:67] There were **736** [+2256+8679+8993+9252] [BHS-] horses,
7: 68 [7:67] 736 horses, **245** [+752+2256+2822] [BHS-] mules,
7: 69 [7:68] **435** [+752+2256+2822+8993] camels and 6,720 donkeys.
7: 69 [7:68] camels and **6,720** [+547+2256+6929+8679+9252] donkeys.
7: 70 [7:69] and **530** [+2256+2822+8993] garments for priests.
7: 71 [7:70] drachmas of gold and **2,200** [+547+2256] minas of silver.
11: 6 in Jerusalem totaled **468** [+752+2256+9046+9252] able men.
11: 8 Gabbai and Sallai—**928** [+2256+6929+9046+9596] men.
11: 12 **822** [+2256+6929+9046+9109] men; Adaiah son of Jeroham,
11: 13 **242** [+752+2256+9109] men; Amashsai son of Azarel, the son of
11: 14 and his associates, who were able men—**128** [+2256+6929+9046].
11: 18 The Levites in the holy city totaled **284** [+752+2256+9046].
11: 19 who kept watch at the gates—**172** [+2256+8679+9109] men.
Est 1: 1 Xerxes who ruled over **127** [+2256+2256+6929+8679] provinces
1: 4 For a full **180** [+2256+9046] days he displayed the vast wealth of
8: 9 and nobles of the **127** [+2256+2256+6929+8679] provinces
9: 6 citadel of Susa, the Jews killed and destroyed five **hundred** men.
9: 12 "The Jews have killed and destroyed five **hundred** men and the ten
9: 15 they put to death in Susa three **hundred** men, but they did not lay
9: 30 to all the Jews in the **127** [+2256+2256+6929+8679] provinces of
Job 1: 3 five **hundred** yoke of oxen and five hundred donkeys,
1: 3 five hundred yoke of oxen and five **hundred** donkeys,
42: 16 After this, Job lived a **hundred** and forty years; he saw his children
Pr 17: 10 A rebuke impresses a man of discernment more than a **hundred**
Ecc 6: 3 A man may have a **hundred** children and live many years;
8: 12 Although a wicked man commits a **hundred** crimes and still lives
SS 8: 12 O Solomon, and *two* **hundred** are for those who tend its fruit.
Isa 37: 36 Then the angel of the LORD went out and put to death a **hundred**
65: 20 his years; he who dies at a **hundred** will be thought a mere youth;
65: 20 he who fails to reach a **hundred** will be considered accursed.
Jer 52: 23 of pomegranates above the surrounding network was a **hundred**.

Jer 52:29 year, **832** [+2256+8993+9046+9109] people from Jerusalem;
52:30 in his twenty-third year, **745** [+752+2256+2822+8679] Jews taken
52:30 There were **4,600** [+547+752+2256+9252] people in all.
Eze 4: 5 So for **390** [+2256+8993+9596] days you will bear the sin of the
4: 9 eat it during the **390** [+2256+8993+9596] days you lie on your side.
40:19 it was a **hundred** cubits on the east side as well as on the north.
40:23 from one gate to the opposite one; it was a **hundred** cubits.
40:27 gate to the outer gate on the south side; it was a **hundred** cubits.
40:47 It was square—a **hundred** cubits long and a hundred cubits wide.
40:47 It was square—a hundred cubits long and a **hundred** cubits wide.
41:13 it was a **hundred** cubits long, and the temple courtyard
41:13 and the building with its walls were also a **hundred** cubits long.
41:14 the east, including the front of the temple, was a **hundred** cubits.
41:15 including its galleries on each side; it was a **hundred** cubits.
42: 2 The building whose door faced north was a **hundred** cubits long
42: 4 ten cubits wide and a **hundred** [BHS 285] cubits long.
42: 8 the row on the side nearest the sanctuary was a **hundred** cubits
42:16 side with the measuring rod; it was five **hundred** [K 564] cubits.
42:17 the north side; it was five **hundred** cubits by the measuring rod.
42:18 the south side; it was five **hundred** cubits by the measuring rod.
42:19 and measured; it was five **hundred** cubits by the measuring rod.
42:20 around it, five **hundred** cubits long and five hundred cubits wide,
42:20 around it, five hundred cubits long and five **hundred** cubits wide,
45: 2 a section **500** [+2822] cubits square is to be for the sanctuary,
45: 2 for the sanctuary, **[RPH]** with 50 cubits around it for open land.
45:15 Also one sheep is to be taken from every flock of *two* **hundred**
48:16 the north side **4,500** [+547+752+2256+2822] cubits, the south side
48:16 the south side **4,500** [+547+752+2256+2822] cubits, the east side
48:16 the east side **4,500** [+547+752+2256+2822] cubits, and the west
48:16 and the west side **4,500** [+547+752+2256+2822] cubits.
48:17 The pastureland for the city will be **250** [+2256+2822] cubits on
48:17 **250** [+2256+2822] cubits on the south, 250 cubits on the east,
48:17 250 cubits on the south, **250** [+2256+2822] cubits on the east,
48:17 250 cubits on the east, and **250** [+2256+2822] cubits on the west.
48:30 the north side, which is **4,500** [+547+752+2256+2822] cubits long,
48:32 "On the east side, which is **4,500** [+547+752+2256+2822] cubits
48:33 south side, which measures **4,500** [+547+752+2256+2822] cubits,
48:34 the west side, which is **4,500** [+547+752+2256+2822] cubits long,
Da 8:14 "It will take **2,300** [+547+2256+8993] evenings and mornings;
12:11 desolation is set up, there will be **1,290** [+547+2256+9596] days.
12:12 reaches the end of the **1,335** [+547+2256+2822+8993+8993] days.
Am 5: 3 out a thousand strong for Israel will have only a **hundred** left;
5: 3 the town that marches out a **hundred** strong will have only ten

4396 ²מֵאָה mē'â², n.pr.loc. [2] [√ 4395?; Ar 10395]

Hundred [2]

Ne 3: 1 building as far as the Tower of the **Hundred**, which they
12:39 Fish Gate, the Tower of Hananel and the Tower of the **Hundred**,

4397 מַאֲוַיִּים ma'ᵃwiyyîm, n.[m.pl.]. [1] [√ 203]

desires [1]

Ps 140: 8 [140:9] do not grant the wicked their **desires**, O LORD; do not

4398 מְאוּם mᵉ'ûm, n.m. [0] [→ 4399; cf. 4583]

Da 1: 4 [young men without any **physical defect**, [K; see Q 4583]]

4399 מְאוּמָה mᵉ'ûmâ, p.indef. [32] [√ 4398]

anything [10], nothing [+4202] [7], anything [+3972] [2], nothing [+401] [2], there is nothing [+401] [2], *untranslated* [1], all [1], any kind [1], bare [+401+928] [1], fault [1], little value [+4202] [1], little value [1], none [+4202] [1], something [1]

Ge 22:12 not lay a hand on the boy," he said. "Do not do **anything** to him.
30:31 I give you?" he asked. "Don't give me **anything**," Jacob replied.
39: 6 he did not concern himself with **anything** except the food he ate.
39: 9 My master has withheld **nothing** [+4202] from me except you,
39:23 The warden paid no attention to **anything** [+3972] under Joseph's
40:15 even here I have done **nothing** [+4202] to deserve being put in a
Nu 22:38 come to you now," Balaam replied. "But can I say just **anything**?
Dt 13:17 [13:18] **None** [+4202] of those condemned things shall be found
24:10 When you make a loan of **any kind** to your neighbor, do not go
Jdg 14: 6 so that he tore the lion apart with his **bare** [+401+928] hands as he
1Sa 12: 4 they replied. "You have not taken **anything** from anyone's hand."
12: 5 is witness this day, that you have not found **anything** in my hand."
20:26 Saul said **nothing** [+4202] that day, for he thought,
20:39 (The boy knew nothing of **all** this; only Jonathan and David knew.)
21: 2 [21:3] 'No one is to know **anything** about your mission and your
25: 7 the whole time they were at Carmel **nothing** [+4202] of theirs was
25:15 we were out in the fields near them **nothing** [+4202] was missing.
25:21 property in the desert so that **nothing** [+4202] of his was missing.
29: 3 from the day he left Saul until now, I have found no **fault** in him."
2Sa 3:35 if I taste bread or **anything else** [+3972] before the sun sets!"
13: 2 a virgin, and it seemed impossible for him to do **anything** to her.
1Ki 10:21 because silver was considered of **little** [+4202] **value** in Solomon's
18:43 he went up and looked. "**There is nothing** [+401] there," he said.
2Ki 5:20 LORD lives, I will run after him and get **something** from him."
2Ch 9:20 because silver was considered of **little value** in Solomon's day.
Ecc 5:14 [5:13] so that when he has a son **there is nothing** [+401] left for
5:15 [5:14] He takes **nothing** [+4202] from his labor that he can carry
7:14 Therefore, a man cannot discover **anything** about his future.
9: 5 living know that they will die, but the dead know **nothing** [+401];
Jer 39:10 of Judah some of the poor people, who owned **nothing** [+401];
39:12 don't harm him **[NIE]** but do for him whatever he asks."
Jnh 3: 7 Do not let any man or beast, herd or flock, taste **anything**;

4400 מָאוֹס mā'ôs, n.[m.]. [1] [√ 4415]

refuse [1]

La 3:45 You have made us scum and **refuse** among the nations.

4401 מָאוֹר mā'ôr, n.m. [19] [√ 239]

light [13], lights [4], cheerful [1], moon [1]

Ge 1:14 "Let there be **lights** in the expanse of the sky to separate the day
1:15 let them be **lights** in the expanse of the sky to give light on the
1:16 God made two great **lights**—the greater light to govern the day
1:16 the greater **light** to govern the day and the lesser light to govern the
1:16 light to govern the day and the lesser **light** to govern the night.
Ex 25: 6 olive oil for the **light**; spices for the anointing oil and for the
27:20 the Israelites to bring you clear oil of pressed olives for the **light**
35: 8 olive oil for the **light**; spices for the anointing oil and for the
35:14 the lampstand that is for **light** with its accessories, lamps and oil
35:14 that is for light with its accessories, lamps and oil for the **light**;
35:28 brought spices and olive oil for the **light** and for the anointing oil
39:37 its row of lamps and all its accessories, and the oil for the **light**;
Lev 24: 2 the Israelites to bring you clear oil of pressed olives for the **light**
Nu 4: 9 are to take a blue cloth and cover the lampstand that is for **light**,
4:16 the priest, is to have charge of the oil for the **light**, the fragrant
Ps 74:16 and yours also the night; you established the sun and **moon**.
90: 8 iniquities before you, our secret sins in the **light** *of* your presence.
Pr 15:30 A **cheerful** look brings joy to the heart, and good news gives
Eze 32: 8 All the shining **lights** in the heavens I will darken over you;

4402 מְאוּרָה mᵉ'ûrâ, n.f. [1] [√ 239?]

nest [1]

Isa 11: 8 of the cobra, and the young child put his hand into the viper's **nest**.

4403 מֵאָז mē'āz, pp. & adv. Not used in NIV/BHS [√ 4946 + 255]

4404 מֹאזְנַיִם mō'znayim, n.[m.]du. [15] [→ Ar 10396]

scales [12], balance [2], set of scales [+5486] [1]

Lev 19:36 Use honest **scales** and honest weights, an honest ephah and an
Job 6: 2 could be weighed and all my misery be placed on the **scales**!
31: 6 let God weigh me in honest **scales** and he will know that I am
Ps 62: 9 [62:10] but a lie; if weighed on a **balance**, they are nothing;
Pr 11: 1 The LORD abhors dishonest **scales**, but accurate weights are his
16:11 Honest **scales** and balances are from the LORD; all the weights in
20:23 detests differing weights, and dishonest **scales** do not please him.
Isa 40:12 or weighed the mountains on the scales and the hills in a **balance**?
40:15 are like a drop in a bucket; they are regarded as dust on the **scales**;
Jer 32:10 had it witnessed, and weighed out the silver on the **scales**.
Eze 5: 1 Then take a **set of scales** [+5486] and divide up the hair.
45:10 You are to use accurate **scales**, an accurate ephah and an accurate
Hos 12: 7 [12:8] The merchant uses dishonest **scales**; he loves to defraud.
Am 8: 5 the measure, boosting the price and cheating with dishonest **scales**,
Mic 6:11 Shall I acquit a man with dishonest **scales**, with a bag of false

4405 מְאָיוֹת mᵉ'āyôt, var. Not used in NIV/BHS [√ 4395]

4406 מֵאַיִן mē'ayin, adv. Not used in NIV/BHS [√ 4946 + 402]

4407 מַאֲכָל ma'ᵃkāl, n.m. & f. [30] [√ 430]

food [21], fruit [4], baked goods [+685+5126] [1], devoured [1], meal [1], something to eat [1], supplies [1]

Ge 2: 9 the ground—trees that were pleasing to the eye and good for **food**.
3: 6 When the woman saw that the fruit of the tree was good for **food**
6:21 You are to take every kind of **food** that is to be eaten and store it
40:17 In the top basket were all kinds of **baked goods for** [+685+5126]
Lev 19:23 " 'When you enter the land and plant any kind of **fruit** tree,
Dt 20:20 you may cut down trees that you know are not **fruit** trees and use
28:26 Your carcasses will be **food** for all the birds of the air and the
Jdg 14:14 He replied, "Out of the eater, **something to eat**; out of the strong,

1Ki 10: 5 the **food** *on* his table, the seating of his officials, the attending
1Ch 12: 40 [12:41] There were plentiful **supplies** of flour, fig cakes, raisin
2Ch 9: 4 the **food** *on* his table, the seating of his officials, the attending
11: 11 put commanders in them, with supplies of **food**, olive oil and wine.
Ezr 3: 7 and gave **food** and drink and oil to the people of Sidon and Tyre,
Ne 9: 25 already dug, vineyards, olive groves and **fruit** trees in abundance.
Job 33: 20 being finds food repulsive and his soul loathes the choicest **meal**.
Ps 44: 11 [44:12] You gave us up to be **devoured** like sheep and have
74: 14 of Leviathan and gave him as **food** to the creatures of the desert.
79: 2 They have given the dead bodies of your servants as **food** to the
Pr 6: 8 it stores its provisions in summer and gathers its **food** at harvest.
Isa 62: 8 "Never again will I give your grain as **food** for your enemies,
Jer 7: 33 the carcasses of this people will become **food** for the birds of the
16: 4 and their dead bodies will become **food** for the birds of the air
19: 7 and I will give their carcasses as **food** to the birds of the air
34: 20 Their dead bodies will become **food** for the birds of the air
Eze 4: 10 Weigh out twenty shekels of **food** to eat each day and eat it at set
47: 12 **Fruit** trees of all kinds will grow on both banks of the river.
47: 12 Their fruit will serve for **food** and their leaves for healing."
Da 1: 10 afraid of my lord the king, who has assigned your **food** and drink.
Hab 1: 16 for by his net he lives in luxury and enjoys the choicest **food**.
Hag 2: 12 that fold touches some bread or stew, some wine, oil or other **food**,

4408 מַאֲכֶלֶת ma'akelet, n.f. [4] [√ 430]

knife [3], knives [1]

Ge 22: 6 it on his son Isaac, and he himself carried the fire and the **knife**.
22: 10 Then he reached out his hand and took the **knife** to slay his son.
Jdg 19: 29 he took a **knife** and cut up his concubine, limb by limb, into twelve
Pr 30: 14 whose jaws are set with **knives** to devour the poor from the earth,

4409 מַאֲכֹלֶת ma'akōlet, n.f. [2] [√ 430]

fuel [2]

Isa 9: 5 [9:4] blood will be destined for burning, will be **fuel** *for* the fire.
9: 19 [9:18] will be scorched and the people will be **fuel** *for* the fire;

4410 מַאֲמָץ ma'amāṣ, n.[m.]. [1] [√ 599]

efforts [1]

Job 36: 19 Would your wealth or even all your mighty **efforts** sustain you

4411 מַאֲמַר ma'amār, n.m. [3] [√ 606; Ar 10397]

command [1], decree [1], instructions [1]

Est 1: 15 "She has not obeyed the **command** *of* King Xerxes that the
2: 20 for she continued to follow Mordecai's **instructions** as she had
9: 32 Esther's **decree** confirmed these regulations about Purim,

4412 מָאֵן mā'an, v. [46] [→ 4413, 4414]

refused [22], refuse [15], absolutely refuses [+4412] [2], refuses [2], refusing [2], incurable [+8324] [1], rejected [1], resist [1]

Ge 37: 35 [D] came to comfort him, but *he* **refused** to be comforted.
39: 8 [D] *he* **refused**. "With me in charge," he told her, "my master
48: 19 [D] But his father **refused** and said, "I know, my son, I know.
Ex 4: 23 [D] *you* **refused** to let him go; so I will kill your firstborn son.' "
7: 14 [D] heart is unyielding; *he* **refuses** to let the people go.
8: 2 [7:27] [D] If you **refuse** to let them go, I will plague your whole
9: 2 [D] If you **refuse** to let them go and continue to hold them back,
10: 3 [D] 'How long *will you* **refuse** to humble yourself before me?
10: 4 [D] If you **refuse** to let them go, I will bring locusts into your
16: 28 [D] "How long *will you* **refuse** to keep my commands and my
22: 17 [22:16] [D] If her father **absolutely refuses** [+4412] to give her
22: 17 [22:16] [D] If her father **absolutely refuses** [+4412] to give her
Nu 20: 21 [D] Since Edom **refused** to let them go through their territory,
22: 13 [D] for the LORD *has* **refused** to let me go with you."
22: 14 [D] to Balak and said, "Balaam **refused** to come with us."
Dt 25: 7 [D] "My husband's brother **refuses** to carry on his brother's
1Sa 8: 19 [D] But the people **refused** to listen to Samuel. "No!" they said.
28: 23 [D] *He* **refused** and said, "I will not eat." But his men joined the
2Sa 2: 23 [D] Asahel **refused** to give up the pursuit; so Abner thrust the
13: 9 [D] took the pan and served him the bread, but *he* **refused** to eat.
1Ki 20: 35 [D] "Strike me with your weapon," but the man **refused**.
21: 15 [D] vineyard of Naboth the Jezreelite that *he* **refused** to sell you.
2Ki 5: 16 [D] a thing." And even though Naaman urged him, *he* **refused**.
Ne 9: 17 [D] *They* **refused** to listen and failed to remember the miracles
Est 1: 12 [D] the king's command, Queen Vashti **refused** to come.
Job 6: 7 [D] I **refuse** to touch it; such food makes me ill.
Ps 77: 2 [77:3] [D] untiring hands and my soul **refused** to be comforted.
78: 10 [D] did not keep God's covenant and **refused** to live by his law.
Pr 1: 24 [D] since *you* **rejected** me when I called and no one gave heed
21: 7 [D] will drag them away, for *they* **refuse** to do what is right.
21: 25 [D] will be the death of him, because his hands **refuse** to work.
Isa 1: 20 [D] if *you* **resist** and rebel, you will be devoured by the sword."
Jer 3: 3 [D] brazen look of a prostitute; *you* **refuse** to blush with shame.
5: 3 [D] felt no pain; you crushed them, but *they* **refused** correction.
5: 3 [D] made their faces harder than stone and **refused** to repent.
8: 5 [D] turn away? They cling to deceit; *they* **refuse** to return.
9: 6 [9:5] [D] in their deceit *they* **refuse** to acknowledge me,"
11: 10 [D] sins of their forefathers, who **refused** to listen to my words.
13: 10 [D] These wicked people, who **refuse** to listen to my words,
15: 18 [D] and my wound grievous and **incurable** [+8324]?
25: 28 [D] But if *they* **refuse** to take the cup from your hand and drink,
31: 15 [D] weeping for her children and **refusing** to be comforted,
38: 21 [D] if you **refuse** to surrender, this is what the LORD has
50: 33 [D] All their captors hold them fast, **refusing** to let them go.
Hos 11: 5 [D] not Assyria rule over them because *they* **refuse** to repent?
Zec 7: 11 [D] "But *they* **refused** to pay attention; stubbornly they turned

4413 מָאֵן mā'ēn, a.v. Not used in NIV/BHS [√ 4412]

4414 מֵאֵן mē'ēn, a. Not used in NIV/BHS [√ 4412]

4415 מָאַס mā'as[1], v. [74] [→ 4400]

rejected [34], reject [12], despise [8], despised [3], despises [3], rejected completely [+906+4415] [2], utterly rejected [+4415] [2], be rejected [1], denied [1], disdained [1], refuse [1], rejects [1], ridiculed [1], scorn [1], spurn [1], spurned [1], vile [1]

Lev 26: 15 [A] if you **reject** my decrees and abhor my laws and fail to carry
26: 43 [A] because they **rejected** my laws and abhorred my decrees.
26: 44 [A] *I will* not **reject** them or abhor them so as to destroy them
Nu 11: 20 [A] because *you have* **rejected** the LORD, who is among you,
14: 31 [A] I will bring them in to enjoy the land *you have* **rejected**.
Jdg 9: 38 [A] Aren't these the men *you* **ridiculed**? Go out and fight them!"
1Sa 8: 7 [A] it is not you *they have* **rejected**, but they have rejected me as
8: 7 [A] they have rejected, but *they have* **rejected** me as their king.
10: 19 [A] you *have* now **rejected** your God, who saves you out of all
15: 23 [A] Because *you have* **rejected** the word of the LORD, he has
15: 23 [A] the word of the LORD, *he has* **rejected** you as king."
15: 26 [A] *You have* **rejected** the word of the LORD, and the LORD
15: 26 [A] and the LORD *has* **rejected** you as king over Israel!"
16: 1 [A] for Saul, since I *have* **rejected** him as king over Israel?
16: 7 [A] his appearance or his height, for *I have* **rejected** him.
2Ki 17: 15 [A] *They* **rejected** his decrees and the covenant he had made
17: 20 [A] Therefore the LORD **rejected** all the people of Israel; he
23: 27 [A] and *I will* **reject** Jerusalem, the city I chose, and this temple,
Job 5: 17 [A] so *do* not **despise** the discipline of the Almighty.
7: 16 [A] *I* **despise** my life; I would not live forever. Let me alone; my
8: 20 [A] "Surely God *does* not **reject** a blameless man or strengthen
9: 21 [A] I have no concern for myself; *I* **despise** my own life.
10: 3 [A] please you to oppress me, *to* **spurn** the work of your hands,
19: 18 [A] Even the little boys **scorn** me; when I appear, they ridicule
30: 1 [A] whose fathers *I would have* **disdained** to put with my sheep
31: 13 [A] "If *I have* **denied** justice *to* my menservants
34: 33 [A] then reward you on your terms, when *you* **refuse** to repent?
36: 5 [A] "God is mighty, but *does* not **despise** men; he is mighty,
42: 6 [A] Therefore *I* **despise** *myself* and repent in dust and ashes."
Ps 15: 4 [C] who despises a **vile** *man* but honors those who fear the
36: 4 [36:5] [A] to a sinful course and *does* not **reject** what is wrong.
53: 5 [53:6] [A] you put them to shame, for God **despised** them.
78: 59 [A] he was very angry; *he* **rejected** Israel completely.
78: 67 [A] *he* **rejected** the tents of Joseph, he did not choose the tribe of
89: 38 [89:39] [A] you have rejected, *you have* **spurned**, you have
106: 24 [A] *they* **despised** the pleasant land; they did not believe his
118: 22 [A] The stone the builders **rejected** has become the capstone;
Pr 3: 11 [A] *do* not **despise** the LORD's discipline and do not resent his
15: 32 [A] He who ignores discipline **despises** himself, but whoever
Isa 5: 24 [A] for *they have* **rejected** the law of the LORD Almighty
7: 15 [A] and honey when he knows enough *to* **reject** the wrong
7: 16 [A] before the boy knows enough *to* **reject** the wrong and choose
8: 6 [A] "Because this people *has* **rejected** the gently flowing waters
30: 12 [A] "Because you *have* **rejected** this message, relied on
31: 7 [A] For in that day every one of *you will* **reject** the idols of silver
33: 8 [A] is broken, its witnesses *are* **despised**, no one is respected.
33: 15 [A] *who* **rejects** gain from extortion and keeps his hand from
41: 9 [A] my servant'; I have chosen you and *have* not **rejected** you.
54: 6 [C] who married young, only *to* **be rejected**," says your God.
Jer 2: 37 [A] on your head, for the LORD *has* **rejected** those you trust;
4: 30 [A] in vain. Your lovers **despise** you; they seek your life.
6: 19 [A] have not listened to my words and *have* **rejected** my law.
6: 30 [C] They are called **rejected** silver, because the LORD has
6: 30 [A] rejected silver, because the LORD *has* **rejected** them."
7: 29 [A] for the LORD *has* **rejected** and abandoned this generation
8: 9 [A] Since *they have* **rejected** the word of the LORD, what kind
14: 19 [A] *Have you* **rejected** [+906+4415] Judah **completely**? Do you
14: 19 [A] *Have you* **rejected** Judah **completely** [+906+4415]?
31: 37 [A] be searched out *will* I **reject** all the descendants of Israel

Jer 33:24 [A] 'The LORD *has* **rejected** the two kingdoms he chose'?
33:26 [A] *I will* **reject** the descendants of Jacob and David my servant
La 5:22 [A] unless *you have* **utterly rejected** [+4415] us and are angry
5:22 [A] unless *you have* **utterly rejected** [+4415] us and are angry
Eze 5: 6 [A] *She has* **rejected** my laws and has not followed my decrees.
20:13 [A] They did not follow my decrees but **rejected** my laws—
20:16 [A] because *they* **rejected** my laws and did not follow my
20:24 [A] but *had* **rejected** my decrees and desecrated my Sabbaths,
21:10 [21:15] [A] son ⌞Judah⌟? The sword **despises** every such stick.
21:13 [21:18] [A] which the sword **despises**, does not continue?
Hos 4: 6 [A] "Because you *have* **rejected** knowledge, I also reject you as
4: 6 [A] you have rejected knowledge, *I* also **reject** you as my priests;
9:17 [A] My God *will* **reject** them because they have not obeyed him;
Am 2: 4 [A] Because they *have* **rejected** the law of the LORD and have
5:21 [A] "I hate, *I* **despise** your religious feasts; I cannot stand your

4416 ²מָאַס *mā'as²*, v. [2] [cf. 4998, 5022]

festering [1], vanish [1]

Job 7: 5 [C] with worms and scabs, my skin is broken and **festering**.
Ps 58: 7 [58:8] [C] *Let them* **vanish** like water that flows away; when

4417 מְאַסֵּף *mᵉ'assēp*, v.ptcp. Not used in NIV/BHS [√ 665]

4418 מַאֲפֶה *ma'ᵃpeh*, n.[m.]. [1] [√ 684]

baked [1]

Lev 2: 4 [D] " 'If you bring a grain offering **baked** *in* an oven, it is to

4419 מַאֲפֵל *ma'ᵃpēl*, n.[m.]. [1] [√ 694?]

darkness [1]

Jos 24: 7 for help, and he put **darkness** between you and the Egyptians;

4420 מַאְפֵּלְיָה *ma'pēlyâ*, n.f. [1] [√ 694?]

great darkness [1]

Jer 2:31 "Have I been a desert to Israel or a land of **great darkness**?

4421 מָאַר *mā'ar*, v. [4]

destructive [3], painful [1]

Lev 13:51 [G] or the leather, whatever its use, it is a **destructive** mildew;
13:52 [G] the contamination in it, because the mildew *is* **destructive**;
14:44 [G] mildew has spread in the house, it *is* a **destructive** mildew;
Eze 28:24 [G] of Israel have malicious neighbors *who are* **painful** briers

4422 מַאֲרָב *ma'ᵃrāb*, n.m. [5] [√ 741]

ambush [1], hiding place [1], place of ambush [1], troops [1], wait [1]

Jos 8: 9 they went to the **place of ambush** and lay in wait between Bethel
Jdg 9:35 as Abimelech and his soldiers came out from their **hiding place**.
2Ch 13:13 Now Jeroboam had sent **troops** around to the rear, so that while he
13:13 so that while he was in front of Judah the **ambush** was behind
Ps 10: 8 He lies in **wait** *near* the villages; from ambush he murders the

4423 מְאֵרָה *mᵉ'ērâ*, n.f. [5] [√ 826]

curse [2], curses [2], curse [+826] [1]

Dt 28:20 The LORD will send on you **curses**, confusion and rebuke in
Pr 3:33 The LORD's **curse** is on the house of the wicked, but he blesses
28:27 but he who closes his eyes to them receives many **curses**.
Mal 2: 2 says the LORD Almighty, "I will send a **curse** upon you,
3: 9 You *are* under a **curse** [+826]—the whole nation of you—

4424 מֵאֲשֶׁר *mē'ᵃšer*, adv. & c. Not used in NIV/BHS [√ 4946 + 889]

4425 מֵאֵת *mē'ēt*, pp.+pp. Not used in NIV/BHS [√ 4946 + 907]

4426 מִבְדָּלוֹת *mibdālôt*, n.f. [1] [√ 976]

set aside [1]

Jos 16: 9 their villages that were **set aside** for the Ephraimites within the

4427 מָבוֹא *mābô'*, n.m. [24 / 25] [→ 4569; cf. 995]

entrance [7], enter [2], place where sets [2], setting [2], west [+9087] [2], *untranslated* [1], do[s] [1], entrances [+7339] [1], entryway [1], gateway [1], go down [1], harbor [1], how to get into [1], on the west [+2021+9087] [1], outskirts [1]

Dt 11:30 west of the road, toward the **setting** sun, near the great trees of
Jos 1: 4 the Hittite country—to the Great Sea **on the west** [+2021+9087].
23: 4 between the Jordan and the Great Sea in the **west** [+9087].
Jdg 1:24 "Show us **how to get into** the city and we will see that you are
1:25 **[RPH]** and they put the city to the sword but spared the man
2Ki 11:16 So they seized her as she reached the place where the horses **enter**
16:18 removed the royal **entryway** outside the temple of the LORD,
1Ch 4:39 they went to the **outskirts** *of* Gedor to the east of the valley in
9:19 for guarding the **entrance** to the dwelling of the LORD.
2Ch 23:13 and there was the king, standing by his pillar at the **entrance**.
23:15 So they seized her as she reached the **entrance** *of* the Horse Gate
Ps 50: 1 the earth from the rising of the sun to the **place where** it **sets**.
104:19 moon marks off the seasons, and the sun knows when to **go down**.
113: 3 From the rising of the sun to the **place where** it **sets**, the name of
Pr 8: 3 leading into the city, at the **entrances** [+7339], she cries aloud:
Isa 23: 1 Tyre is destroyed and left without house or **harbor**. [BHS 995]
Jer 38:14 had him brought to the third **entrance** to the temple of the LORD.
Eze 26:10 chariots when he enters your gates as *men* **enter** a city whose
27: 3 Say to Tyre, situated at the **gateway** *to* the sea, merchant of
33:31 My people come to you, as they usually **do**[s], and sit before you to
42: 9 The lower rooms had an **entrance** [Q 995] on the east side as one
44: 5 Give attention to the **entrance** *of* the temple and all the exits of the
46:19 the man brought me through the **entrance** at the side of the gate to
Zec 8: 7 my people from the countries of the east and the **west** [+9087].
Mal 1:11 great among the nations, from the rising to the **setting** *of* the sun.

4428 מְבוּכָה *mᵉbûkâ*, n.f. [2] [√ 1003]

confusion [1], terror [1]

Isa 22: 5 a day of tumult and trampling and **terror** in the Valley of Vision,
Mic 7: 4 the day God visits you. Now is the time of their **confusion**.

4429 מַבּוּל *mabbûl*, n.m. [13] [√ 5574]

flood [10], floodwaters [+4784] [3]

Ge 6:17 I am going to bring **floodwaters** [+4784] on the earth to destroy all
7: 6 Noah was six hundred years old when the **floodwaters** [+4784]
7: 7 his sons' wives entered the ark to escape the waters of the **flood**.
7:10 after the seven days the **floodwaters** [+4784] came on the earth.
7:17 For forty days the **flood** kept coming on the earth, and as the
9:11 Never again will all life be cut off by the waters of a **flood**;
9:11 of a flood; never again will there be a **flood** to destroy the earth."
9:15 Never again will the waters become a **flood** to destroy all life.
9:28 After the **flood** Noah lived 350 years.
10: 1 and Japheth, Noah's sons, who themselves had sons after the **flood**.
10:32 From these the nations spread out over the earth after the **flood**.
11:10 Two years after the **flood**, when Shem was 100 years old,
Ps 29:10 The LORD sits enthroned over the **flood**; the LORD is

4430 מְבוֹנִים *mᵉbônîm*, var. Not used in NIV/BHS

4431 מְבוּסָה *mᵉbûsâ*, n.f. [3] [√ 1008]

aggressive [2], trampling [1]

Isa 18: 2 people feared far and wide, an **aggressive** nation of strange speech,
18: 7 people feared far and wide, an **aggressive** nation of strange speech,
22: 5 has a day of tumult and **trampling** and terror in the Valley of

4432 מַבּוּעַ *mabbûa'*, n.[m.]. [3] [√ 5580]

bubbling springs [+4784] [1], spring [1], springs [1]

Ecc 12: 6 before the pitcher is shattered at the **spring**, or the wheel broken at
Isa 35: 7 will become a pool, the thirsty ground **bubbling springs** [+4784].
49:10 on them will guide them and lead them beside **springs** *of* water.

4433 מְבוּקָה *mᵉbûqâ*, n.f. [1] [√ 1011]

plundered [1]

Na 2:10 [2:11] She is pillaged, **plundered**, stripped! Hearts melt, knees

4434 מְבוּשִׁים *mᵉbûšîm*, n.[m.]. [1] [√ 1017]

private parts [1]

Dt 25:11 and she reaches out and seizes him by his **private parts**,

4435 מִבְחוֹר *mibḥôr*, n.[m.]. [2] [√ 1047]

choicest [1], major [1]

2Ki 3:19 You will overthrow every fortified city and every **major** town.
19:23 I have cut down its tallest cedars, the **choicest** *of* its pines.

4436 ¹מִבְחָר *mibḥār¹*, n.[m.] & f. [12] [→ 4437; cf. 1047]

choicest [4], best [3], choice possessions [1], elite [1], fine [1], finest [1], pick [1]

Ge 23: 6 prince among us. Bury your dead in the **choicest** *of* our tombs.
Ex 15: 4 The **best** *of* Pharaoh's officers are drowned in the Red Sea.
Dt 12:11 and all the **choice possessions** you have vowed to the LORD.
Isa 22: 7 Your **choicest** valleys are full of chariots, and horsemen are posted

Isa 37:24 I have cut down its tallest cedars, the **choicest** *of* its pines.
Jer 22: 7 they will cut up your **fine** cedar beams and throw them into the
48:15 her **finest** young men will go down in the slaughter,"
Eze 23: 7 She gave herself as a prostitute to all the **elite** *of* the Assyrians
24: 4 the leg and the shoulder. Fill it with the **best** *of* these bones;
24: 5 take the **pick** *of* the flock. Pile wood beneath it for the bones;
31:16 Then all the trees of Eden, the **choicest** and best of Lebanon,
Da 11:15 to resist; even their **best** troops will not have the strength to stand.

4437 ²מִבְחָר **mibḥār²**, n.pr.m. [1] [√ 4436; cf. 1047]

Mibhar [1]

1Ch 11:38 Joel the brother of Nathan, **Mibhar** son of Hagri,

4438 מַבָּט **mabbāṭ**, n.m. [3] [√ 5564]

hope [1], relied on [1], trusted in [1]

Isa 20: 5 Those who **trusted in** Cush and boasted in Egypt will be afraid
20: 6 'See what has happened to *those* we **relied on**, those we fled to for
Zec 9: 5 Gaza will writhe in agony, and Ekron too, for her **hope** will wither.

4439 מִבְטָא **mibṭā'**, n.[m.]. [2] [√ 1051]

rash promise [2]

Nu 30: 6 [30:7] or after her lips utter a **rash promise** by which she
30: 8 [30:9] or the **rash promise** by which she obligates herself,

4440 מִבְטָח **mibṭāḥ**, n.[m.]. [15] [√ 1053]

trust [4], confidence [2], secure [2], security [2], hope [1], reliance [1], source of confidence [1], trusted [1], what relies on [1]

Job 8:14 What he trusts in is fragile; **what** he **relies on** is a spider's web.
18:14 He is torn from the **security** *of* his tent and marched off to the king
31:24 put my trust in gold or said to pure gold, 'You are my **security**,'
Ps 40: 4 [40:5] Blessed is the man who makes the LORD his **trust**, who
65: 5 [65:6] the **hope** *of* all the ends of the earth and of the farthest seas,
71: 5 my hope, O Sovereign LORD, my **confidence** since my youth.
Pr 14:26 He who fears the LORD has a **secure** fortress, and for his
21:22 of the mighty and pulls down the stronghold in which they **trust**.
22:19 So that your **trust** may be in the LORD, I teach you today,
25:19 or a lame foot is **reliance** *on* the unfaithful in times of trouble.
Isa 32:18 dwelling places, in **secure** homes, in undisturbed places of rest.
Jer 2:37 hands on your head, for the LORD has rejected *those* you **trust**;
17: 7 is the man who trusts in the LORD, whose **confidence** is in him.
48:13 as the house of Israel was ashamed when they **trusted** in Bethel.
Eze 29:16 Egypt will no longer be a **source of confidence** for the people of

4441 מַבָּךְ **mabbāk**, n.m. [0 / 1] [√ 1134]

sources [1]

Job 28:11 He searches the **sources** [BHS 4946] *of* the rivers and brings

4442 מַבֵּל **mabbēl**, n.[m.]. [0 / 1] [√ 1162]

fire [1]

Job 18:15 **Fire** [BHS 4946] resides in his tent; burning sulfur is scattered

4443 מַבְלִיגִית **mablîgît**, n.f. [1] [√ 1564]

Comforter [1]

Jer 8:18 O my **Comforter** in sorrow, my heart is faint within me.

4444 מְבֻלָּקָה **mᵉbulāqâ**, n.[f.] *or* v.ptcp. Not used in NIV/BHS [√ 1191]

4445 מִבְנֶה **mibneh**, n.m. [1] [√ 1215]

buildings [1]

Eze 40: 2 on whose south side were *some* **buildings** that looked like a city.

4446 מְבֻנַּי **mᵉbunnay**, n.pr.m. [1]

Mebunnai [1]

2Sa 23:27 Abiezer from Anathoth, **Mebunnai** the Hushathite,

4447 מַבְנִית **mabnît**, n.f. Not used in NIV/BHS [√ 1067]

4448 ¹מִבְצָר **mibṣār¹**, n.m. [36] [→ 4449; cf. 1307]

fortified [21], strongholds [5], fortresses [3], fortified cities [2], defenses [1], fortified city [1], fortified places [1], fortress [1], mightiest fortresses [+5057] [1]

Nu 13:19 kind of towns do they live in? Are they unwalled or **fortified**?
32:17 Meanwhile our women and children will live in **fortified** cities,
32:36 Beth Nimrah and Beth Haran as **fortified** cities, and built pens for
Jos 10:20 to a man—but the few who were left reached their **fortified** cities.
19:29 turned back toward Ramah and went to the **fortified** city of Tyre,
19:35 The **fortified** cities were Ziddim, Zer, Hammath, Rakkath,
1Sa 6:18 to the five rulers—the **fortified** towns with their country villages.
2Sa 24: 7 they went toward the **fortress** *of* Tyre and all the towns of the
2Ki 3:19 You will overthrow every **fortified** city and every major town.
8:12 "You will set fire to their **fortified places**, kill their young men
10: 2 and you have chariots and horses, a **fortified** city and weapons,
17: 9 From watchtower to **fortified** city they built themselves high
18: 8 From watchtower to **fortified** city, he defeated the Philistines,
2Ch 17:19 besides those he stationed in the **fortified** cities throughout Judah.
Ps 89:40 [89:41] all his walls and reduced his **strongholds** to ruins.
108:10 [108:11] Who will bring me to the **fortified** city? Who will lead
Isa 17: 3 The **fortified** city will disappear from Ephraim, and royal power
25:12 He will bring down your high **fortified** walls and lay them low;
34:13 will overrun her citadels, nettles and brambles her **strongholds**.
Jer 1:18 Today I have made you a **fortified** city, an iron pillar and a bronze
4: 5 and say: 'Gather together! Let us flee to the **fortified** cities!'
5:17 With the sword they will destroy the **fortified** cities in which you
8:14 Gather together! Let us flee to the **fortified** cities and perish there!
34: 7 and Azekah. These were the only **fortified** cities left in Judah.
48:18 Moab will come up against you and ruin your **fortified cities**.
La 2: 2 in his wrath he has torn down the **strongholds** *of* the Daughter of
2: 5 has swallowed up all her palaces and destroyed her **strongholds**.
Da 11:15 and build up siege ramps and will capture a **fortified** city.
11:24 He will plot the overthrow of **fortresses**—but only for a time.
11:39 He will attack the **mightiest fortresses** [+5057] with the help of a
Hos 10:14 against your people, so that all your **fortresses** will be devastated—
Am 5: 9 destruction on the stronghold and brings the **fortified city** to ruin),
Mic 5:11 [5:10] the cities of your land and tear down all your **strongholds**.
Na 3:12 All your **fortresses** are like fig trees with their first ripe fruit;
3:14 Draw water for the siege, strengthen your **defenses**! Work the clay,
Hab 1:10 They laugh at all **fortified cities**; they build earthen ramps

4449 ²מִבְצָר **mibṣār²**, n.pr.m. [2] [√ 4448; cf. 1307]

Mibzar [2]

Ge 36:42 Kenaz, Teman, **Mibzar**,
1Ch 1:53 Kenaz, Teman, **Mibzar**,

4450 ³מִבְצָר **mibṣār³**, n.m. [1] [√ 1308]

ore [1]

Jer 6:27 "I have made you a tester of metals and my people the **ore**,

4451 מִבְרָח **mibrāḥ**, n.m. [1] [√ 1368]

fleeing [1]

Eze 17:21 All his **fleeing** troops will fall by the sword, and the survivors will

4452 מִבְשָׂם **mibśām**, n.pr.m. [3]

Mibsam [3]

Ge 25:13 Nebaioth the firstborn of Ishmael, Kedar, Adbeel, **Mibsam**,
1Ch 1:29 Nebaioth the firstborn of Ishmael, Kedar, Adbeel, **Mibsam**,
4:25 Shallum was Shaul's son, **Mibsam** his son and Mishma his son.

4453 מְבַשְּׁלוֹת **mᵉbaššᵉlôt**, n.f.pl. [1] [√ 1418]

places for fire [1]

Eze 46:23 of stone, with **places for fire** built all around under the ledge.

4454 מָג **māg**, n.m. [2] [→ 8059]

official [2]

Jer 39: 3 Nergal-Sharezer a high **official** and all the other officials of the
39:13 Nergal-Sharezer a high **official** and all the other officers of the

4455 מַגְבִּישׁ **magbîš**, n.pr.m. [1]

Magbish [1]

Ezr 2:30 of **Magbish** 156

4456 מִגְבָּלוֹת **migbālôt**, n.f.pl. [1] [√ 1491]

braided [1]

Ex 28:14 two **braided** chains of pure gold, like a rope, and attach the chains

4457 מִגְבָּעָה **migbā'â**, n.f.pl. [4] [√ 1483?]

headbands [3], headbands [+6996] [1]

Ex 28:40 Make tunics, sashes and **headbands** for Aaron's sons, to give them
29: 9 put **headbands** on them. Then tie sashes on Aaron and his sons.
39:28 the linen **headbands** [+6996] and the undergarments of finely
Lev 8:13 on them, tied sashes around them and put **headbands** on them,

4458 מֶגֶד *meged*, n.m. [12] [→ 4459, 4461, 4462, 4469]
best [2], choice [2], valuable gifts [2], articles of value [1], costly gifts [1], delicacy [1], finest [1], fruitfulness [1], precious [1]

Ge 24:53 he also gave **costly gifts** to her brother and to her mother.
Dt 33:13 "May the LORD bless his land with the **precious** dew from
33:14 with the **best** the sun brings forth and the finest the moon can
33:14 the best the sun brings forth and the **finest** the moon can yield;
33:15 the ancient mountains and the **fruitfulness** *of* the everlasting hills;
33:16 with the **best** gifts *of* the earth and its fullness and the favor of him
2Ch 21: 3 had given them many gifts of silver and gold and **articles of value**,
32:23 for the LORD and **valuable gifts** for Hezekiah king of Judah.
Ezr 1: 6 and gold, with goods and livestock, and with **valuable gifts**,
SS 4:13 Your plants are an orchard of pomegranates with **choice** fruits,
4:16 Let my lover come into his garden and taste its **choice** fruits.
7:13 [7:14] at our door is every **delicacy**, both new and old, that I have

4459 מְגִדּוֹ *m^{e}giddô*, n.pr.loc. [11] [→ 4461; cf. 4458]
Megiddo [11]

Jos 12:21 the king of Taanach one the king of **Megiddo** one
17:11 Ibleam and the people of Dor, Endor, Taanach and **Megiddo**,
Jdg 1:27 or Taanach or Dor or Ibleam or **Megiddo** and their surrounding
5:19 the kings of Canaan fought at Taanach by the waters of **Megiddo**,
1Ki 4:12 in Taanach and **Megiddo**, and in all of Beth Shan next to Zarethan
9:15 the wall of Jerusalem, and Hazor, **Megiddo** and Gezer.
2Ki 9:27 up to Gur near Ibleam, but he escaped to **Megiddo** and died there.
23:29 meet him in battle, but Neco faced him and killed him at **Megiddo**.
23:30 Josiah's servants brought his body in a chariot from **Megiddo** to
1Ch 7:29 Taanach, **Megiddo** and Dor, together with their villages.
2Ch 35:22 at God's command but went to fight him on the plain of **Megiddo**.

4460 מִגְדּוֹל *migdôl*, n.m. [0] [√ 1540]

2Sa 22:51 [*He* **gives** his king **great** [Q; see K 1540] victories;]

4461 מְגִדּוֹן *m^{e}giddôn*, n.pr.loc. [1] [√ 4459; cf. 4458]
Megiddo [1]

Zec 12:11 like the weeping of Hadad Rimmon in the plain of **Megiddo**.

4462 מַגְדִּיאֵל *magdî'ēl*, n.pr.m. [2] [√ 4458 + 446]
Magdiel [2]

Ge 36:43 **Magdiel** and Iram. These were the chiefs of Edom, according to
1Ch 1:54 **Magdiel** and Iram. These were the chiefs of Edom.

4463 מִגְדָּל[1] *migdāl[1]*, n.m. [49 / 48] [→ 4464, 4465, 4466, 4467, 4468; cf. 1540]
tower [28], towers [13], watchtower [+5915] [2], watchtower [2], high platform [1], they[s] [+1251+3972+8901] [1], watchtowers [1]

Ge 11: 4 us build ourselves a city, with a **tower** that reaches to the heavens,
11: 5 down to see the city and the **tower** that the men were building.
Jdg 8: 9 of Peniel, "When I return in triumph, I will tear down this **tower**."
8:17 He also pulled down the **tower** *of* Peniel and killed the men of the
9:46 the citizens in the **tower** *of* Shechem went into the stronghold of
9:47 Abimelech heard that **they**[s] [+1251+3972+8901] had assembled
9:49 So all the people in the **tower** *of* Shechem, about a thousand men
9:51 Inside the city, however, was a strong **tower**, to which all the men
9:51 They locked themselves in and climbed up on the **tower** roof.
9:52 Abimelech went to the **tower** and stormed it. But as he approached
9:52 But as he approached the entrance to the **tower** to set it on fire,
2Ki 9:17 When the lookout standing on the **tower** in Jezreel saw Jehu's
17: 9 From **watchtower** [+5915] to fortified city they built themselves
18: 8 From **watchtower** [+5915] to fortified city, he defeated the
1Ch 27:25 outlying districts, in the towns, the villages and the **watchtowers**.
2Ch 14: 7 [14:6] "and put walls around them, with **towers**, gates and bars.
26: 9 Uzziah built **towers** in Jerusalem at the Corner Gate, at the Valley
26:10 He also built **towers** in the desert and dug many cisterns,
26:15 he made machines designed by skillful men for use on the **towers**
27: 4 towns in the Judean hills and forts and **towers** in the wooded areas.
32: 5 all the broken sections of the wall and building **towers** on it.
Ne 3: 1 building as far as the **Tower** *of* the Hundred, which they dedicated,
3: 1 which they dedicated, and as far as the **Tower** *of* Hananel.
3:11 repaired another section and the **Tower** *of* the Ovens.
3:25 the **tower** projecting from the upper palace near the court of the
3:26 opposite the Water Gate toward the east and the projecting **tower**.
3:27 from the great projecting **tower** to the wall of Ophel.
8: 4 Ezra the scribe stood on a **high** wooden **platform** built for the
12:38 half the people—past the **Tower** *of* the Ovens to the Broad Wall,
12:39 Fish Gate, the **Tower** *of* Hananel and the Tower of the Hundred,
12:39 Fish Gate, the Tower of Hananel and the **Tower** *of* the Hundred,
Ps 48:12 [48:13] Walk about Zion, go around her, count her **towers**,
61: 3 [61:4] you have been my refuge, a strong **tower** against the foe.
Pr 18:10 The name of the LORD is a strong **tower**; the righteous run to it
SS 4: 4 Your neck is like the **tower** *of* David, built with elegance;
5:13 like beds of spice <u>yielding</u> [BHS *towers of*; NIV 1540] perfume.
7: 4 [7:5] Your neck is like an ivory **tower**. Your eyes are the pools of
7: 4 [7:5] Your nose is like the **tower** *of* Lebanon looking toward
8:10 I am a wall, and my breasts are like **towers**. Thus I have become in
Isa 2:15 for every lofty **tower** and every fortified wall,
5: 2 He built a **watchtower** in it and cut out a winepress as well.
30:25 In the day of great slaughter, when the **towers** fall, streams of
33:18 took the revenue? Where is the officer in charge of the **towers**?"
Jer 31:38 "when this city will be rebuilt for me from the **Tower** *of* Hananel
Eze 26: 4 They will destroy the walls of Tyre and pull down her **towers**;
26: 9 against your walls and demolish your **towers** with his weapons.
27:11 your walls on every side; men of Gammad were in your **towers**.
Mic 4: 8 As for you, O **watchtower** *of* the flock, O stronghold of the
Zec 14:10 and from the **Tower** *of* Hananel to the royal winepresses.

4464 מִגְדָּל[2] *migdāl[2]*, n.pr.loc. Not used in NIV/BHS [√ 4463; cf. 1540]

4465 מִגְדֹּל *migdōl*, n.pr.loc. [6] [√ 4463; cf. 1540]
Migdol [6]

Ex 14: 2 and encamp near Pi Hahiroth, between **Migdol** and the sea.
Nu 33: 7 Pi Hahiroth, to the east of Baal Zephon, and camped near **Migdol**.
Jer 44: 1 in **Migdol**, Tahpanhes and Memphis—and in Upper Egypt:
46:14 "Announce this in Egypt, and proclaim it in **Migdol**; proclaim it
Eze 29:10 land of Egypt a ruin and a desolate waste from **Migdol** to Aswan,
30: 6 From **Migdol** to Aswan they will fall by the sword within her,

4466 מִגְדַּל־אֵל *migdal-'ēl*, n.pr.loc. [1] [√ 4463 + 446; cf. 1540]
Migdal El [1]

Jos 19:38 Iron, **Migdal El**, Horem, Beth Anath and Beth Shemesh. There

4467 מִגְדַּל־גָּד *migdal-gad*, n.pr.loc. [1] [√ 4463 + 1514; cf. 1540]
Migdal Gad [1]

Jos 15:37 Zenan, Hadashah, **Migdal Gad**,

4468 מִגְדַּל־עֵדֶר *migdal-'ēder*, n.pr.loc. [1] [√ 4463 + 6374]
Migdal Eder [1]

Ge 35:21 Israel moved on again and pitched his tent beyond **Migdal Eder**.

4469 מִגְדָּנוֹת *migdānôt*, n.f.[pl.]. Not used in NIV/BHS [√ 4458]

4470 מָגוֹג *māgôg*, n.pr.loc. [4] [√ 1573]
Magog [4]

Ge 10: 2 Gomer, **Magog**, Madai, Javan, Tubal, Meshech and Tiras.
1Ch 1: 5 Gomer, **Magog**, Madai, Javan, Tubal, Meshech and Tiras.
Eze 38: 2 "Son of man, set your face against Gog, of the land of **Magog**,
39: 6 I will send fire on **Magog** and on those who live in safety in the

4471 מָגוֹר[1] *māgôr[1]*, n.m. [8] [→ 4475; cf. 1593]
terror [7], terrors [1]

Ps 31:13 [31:14] there is **terror** on every side; they conspire against me
Isa 31: 9 Their stronghold will fall because of **terror**; at sight of the battle
Jer 6:25 for the enemy has a sword, and there is **terror** on every side.
20: 4 'I will make you a **terror** to yourself and to all your friends;
20:10 I hear many whispering, "**Terror** on every side! Report him!
46: 5 and there is **terror** on every side," declares the LORD.
49:29 and camels. Men will shout to them, '**Terror** on every side!'
La 2:22 to a feast day, so you summoned *against* me **terrors** on every side.

4472 מָגוֹר[2] *māgôr[2]*, n.[m.]. [11] [√ 1591]
pilgrimage [2], alien [1], live as an alien [1], lived [1], living [1], lodge [+1074] [1], lodging [1], stayed [1], staying [1], where lived [1]

Ge 17: 8 The whole land of Canaan, where you are now an **alien**, I will give
28: 4 may take possession of the land where you now **live as an alien**,
36: 7 the land where they were **staying** could not support them both
37: 1 Jacob lived in the land where his father *had* **stayed**, the land of
47: 9 to Pharaoh, "The years of my **pilgrimage** are a hundred and thirty.
47: 9 and they do not equal the years of the **pilgrimage** *of* my fathers."
Ex 6: 4 them to give them the land of Canaan, **where** they **lived** as aliens.
Job 18:19 or descendants among his people, no survivor where once he **lived**.
Ps 55:15 [55:16] alive to the grave, for evil finds **lodging** among them.
119:54 Your decrees are the theme of my song wherever I **lodge** [+1074].

Eze 20:38 Although I will bring them out of the land where they are **living**,

4473 ³מָגוֹר **māgôr³**, n.[m.]. Not used in NIV/BHS [→ 4476, 4923]

4474 מָגוֹר מִסָּבִיב **māgôr missābîb**, n.pr.m. [1] [√ 1593 + 4992]

Magor-Missabib [1]

Jer 20: 3 LORD's name for you is not Pashhur, but **Magor-Missabib**.

4475 מְגוֹרָה **m**^e**gôrâ**, n.f. [3] [√ 4471; cf. 1593]

dread [1], dreads [1], fears [1]

Ps 34: 4 [34:5] and he answered me; he delivered me from all my **fears**.
Pr 10:24 *What* the wicked **dreads** will overtake him; what the righteous
Isa 66: 4 treatment for them and will bring upon them *what* they **dread**.

4476 מְגוּרָה **m**^e**gûrâ**, n.f. [1] [√ 4473]

barn [1]

Hag 2:19 Is there yet any seed left in the **barn**? Until now, the vine

4477 מַגְזֵרָה **magzērâ**, n.f. [1] [√ 1615]

axes [1]

2Sa 12:31 consigning them to labor with saws and with iron picks and **axes**,

4478 מַגָּל **maggāl**, n.[m.]. [2] [cf. 1670?]

sickle [2]

Jer 50:16 from Babylon the sower, and the reaper with his **sickle** at harvest.
Joel 3:13 [4:13] Swing the **sickle**, for the harvest is ripe. Come,

4479 מְגִלָּה **m**^e**gillâ**, n.f. [21] [√ 1670; Ar 10399]

scroll [17], scroll [+6219] [4]

Ps 40: 7 [40:8] I have come—it is written about me in the **scroll** [+6219].
Jer 36: 2 "Take a **scroll** [+6219] and write on it all the words I have spoken
36: 4 had spoken to him, Baruch wrote them on the **scroll** [+6219].
36: 6 read to the people from the **scroll** the words of the LORD that
36:14 "Bring the **scroll** from which you have read to the people
36:14 So Baruch son of Neriah went to them with the **scroll** in his hand.
36:20 After they put the **scroll** in the room of Elishama the secretary,
36:21 The king sent Jehudi to get the **scroll**, and Jehudi brought it from
36:23 them into the firepot, until the entire **scroll** was burned in the fire.
36:25 Delaiah and Gemariah urged the king not to burn the **scroll**,
36:27 After the king burned the **scroll** containing the words that Baruch
36:28 "Take another **scroll** and write on it all the words that were on the
36:28 and write on it all the words that were on the first **scroll**,
36:29 You burned that **scroll** and said, "Why did you write on it that the
36:32 So Jeremiah took another **scroll** and gave it to the scribe Baruch
Eze 2: 9 and I saw a hand stretched out to me. In it was a **scroll** [+6219],
3: 1 he said to me, "Son of man, eat what is before you, eat this **scroll**;
3: 2 So I opened my mouth, and he gave me the **scroll** to eat.
3: 3 eat this **scroll** I am giving you and fill your stomach with it."
Zec 5: 1 I looked again—and there before me was a flying **scroll**!
5: 2 I answered, "I see a flying **scroll**, thirty feet long and fifteen feet

4480 מְגַמָּה **m**^e**gammâ**, n.f. [1] [cf. 1685]

hordes [1]

Hab 1: 9 Their **hordes** advance like a desert wind and gather prisoners like

4481 מָגַן **māgan**, v. [3] [→ 4484]

delivered [1], hand over [1], present [1]

Ge 14:20 [D] Most High, who **delivered** your enemies into your hand."
Pr 4: 9 [D] on your head and **present** you *with* a crown of splendor."
Hos 11: 8 [D] I give you up, Ephraim? How *can I* **hand** you **over**, Israel?

4482 ¹מָגֵן **māgēn¹**, n.m. [63] [√ 1713]

shield [34], shields [17], small shields [6], armed [2], kings [1], large shields [1], rulers [1], shields small [1]

Ge 15: 1 not be afraid, Abram. I am your **shield**, your very great reward."
Dt 33:29 the LORD? He is your **shield** and helper and your glorious sword.
Jdg 5: 8 and not a **shield** or spear was seen among forty thousand in Israel.
2Sa 1:21 For there the **shield** *of* the mighty was defiled, the shield of Saul—
1:21 For there the shield of the mighty was defiled, the **shield** *of* Saul—
22: 3 in whom I take refuge, my **shield** and the horn of my salvation.
22:31 LORD is flawless. He is a **shield** for all who take refuge in him.
22:36 You give me your **shield** *of* victory; you stoop down to make me
1Ki 10:17 He also made three hundred **small shields** of hammered gold,
10:17 shields of hammered gold, with three minas of gold in each **shield**.
14:26 took everything, including all the gold **shields** Solomon had made.
14:27 So King Rehoboam made bronze **shields** to replace them
2Ki 19:32 He will not come before it *with* **shield** or build a siege ramp
1Ch 5:18 able-bodied men who could handle **shield** and sword, who could
2Ch 9:16 He also made three hundred **small shields** of hammered gold,
9:16 hammered gold, with three hundred bekas of gold in each **shield**.
12: 9 He took everything, including the gold **shields** Solomon had made.
12:10 So King Rehoboam made bronze **shields** to replace them
14: 8 [14:7] from Benjamin, armed with **small shields** and with bows.
17:17 a valiant soldier, with 200,000 men armed with bows and **shields**;
23: 9 and the **large** and small **shields** that had belonged to King David
26:14 Uzziah provided **shields**, spears, helmets, coats of armor, bows
32: 5 of David. He also made large numbers of weapons and **shields**.
32:27 for his precious stones, spices, **shields** and all kinds of valuables.
Ne 4:16 [4:10] half were equipped with spears, **shields**, bows and armor.
Job 15:26 defiantly charging against him with a thick, strong **shield**.
41:15 [41:7] His back has rows of **shields** tightly sealed together;
Ps 3: 3 [3:4] you are a **shield** around me, O LORD; you bestow glory on
7:10 [7:11] My **shield** is God Most High, who saves the upright in
18: 2 [18:3] He is my **shield** and the horn of my salvation,
18:30 [18:31] is flawless. He is a **shield** for all who take refuge in him.
18:35 [18:36] You give me your **shield** *of* victory, and your right hand
28: 7 The LORD is my strength and my **shield**; my heart trusts in him,
33:20 We wait in hope for the LORD; he is our help and our **shield**.
35: 2 Take up **shield** and buckler; arise and come to my aid.
47: 9 [47:10] of Abraham, for the **kings** *of* the earth belong to God;
59:11 [59:12] do not kill them, O Lord our **shield**, or my people will
76: 3 [76:4] the **shields** and the swords, the weapons of war.
84: 9 [84:10] Look upon our **shield**, O God; look with favor on your
84:11 [84:12] For the LORD God is a sun and **shield**; the LORD
89:18 [89:19] Indeed, our **shield** belongs to the LORD, our king to the
115: 9 O house of Israel, trust in the LORD—he is their help and **shield**.
115:10 O house of Aaron, trust in the LORD—he is their help and **shield**.
115:11 who fear him, trust in the LORD—he is their help and **shield**.
119:114 You are my refuge and my **shield**; I have put my hope in your
144: 2 and my fortress, my stronghold and my deliverer, my **shield**,
Pr 2: 7 for the upright, he is a **shield** to those whose walk is blameless,
6:11 will come on you like a bandit and scarcity like an **armed** man.
24:34 will come on you like a bandit and scarcity like an **armed** man.
30: 5 of God is flawless; he is a **shield** to those who take refuge in him.
SS 4: 4 on it hang a thousand **shields**, all of them shields of warriors.
Isa 21: 5 the rugs, they eat, they drink! Get up, you officers, oil the **shields**!
22: 6 with her charioteers and horses; Kir uncovers the **shield**.
37:33 He will not come before it *with* **shield** or build a siege ramp
Jer 46: 3 "Prepare your **shields**, both large and **small**, and march out for
46: 9 men of Cush and Put who carry **shields**, men of Lydia who draw
Eze 23:24 you on every side with large and **small shields** and with helmets.
27:10 They hung their **shields** and helmets on your walls, bringing you
38: 4 fully armed, and a great horde with large and **small shields**,
38: 5 Cush and Put will be with them, all with **shields** and helmets,
39: 9 the **small** and large **shields**, the bows and arrows, the war clubs
Hos 4:18 continue their prostitution; their **rulers** dearly love shameful ways.
Na 2: 3 [2:4] The **shields** *of* his soldiers are red; the warriors are clad in

4483 ²מָגֵן **māgēn²**, n.m. *or* a. Not used in NIV/BHS [→ 4485]

4484 מֶגֶן **megen**, n.m. & f. Not used in NIV/BHS [√ 4481]

4485 מְגִנָּה **m**^e**ginnâ**, n.f. [1] [√ 4483]

veil [1]

La 3:65 Put a **veil** *over* their hearts, and may your curse be on them!

4486 מִגְעֶרֶת **mig'eret**, n.f. [1] [√ 1721]

rebuke [1]

Dt 28:20 confusion and **rebuke** in everything you put your hand to,

4487 מַגֵּפָה **maggēpâ**, n.f. [26] [√ 5597]

plague [19], blow [2], *untranslated* [1], casualties [1], losses [1], plagues [1], slaughter [1]

Ex 9:14 or this time I will send the full force of my **plagues** against you
Nu 14:37 land were struck down and died of a **plague** before the LORD.
16:48 [17:13] between the living and the dead, and the **plague** stopped.
16:49 [17:14] 14,700 people died from the **plague**, in addition to those
16:50 [17:15] to the Tent of Meeting, for the **plague** had stopped.
25: 8 woman's body. Then the **plague** against the Israelites was stopped;
25: 9 but those who died in the **plague** numbered 24,000.
25:18 the woman who was killed when the **plague** came as a result of
26: 1 [25:19] After the **plague** the LORD said to Moses and Eleazar
31:16 happened at Peor, so that a **plague** struck the LORD's people.
1Sa 4:17 fled before the Philistines, and the army has suffered heavy **losses**.
6: 4 because the same **plague** has struck both you and your rulers.

2Sa 17: 9 'There has been a **slaughter** among the troops who follow
18: 7 defeated by David's men, and the **casualties** that day were great—
24: 21 to the LORD, that the **plague** on the people may be stopped."
24: 25 prayer in behalf of the land, and the **plague** on Israel was stopped.
1Ch 21: 17 and my family, but do not let this **plague** remain on your people."
21: 22 altar to the LORD, that the **plague** on the people may be stopped.
2Ch 21: 14 your wives and everything that is yours, with a heavy **blow**.
Ps 106: 29 anger by their wicked deeds, and a **plague** broke out among them.
106: 30 Phinehas stood up and intervened, and the **plague** was checked.
Eze 24: 16 with *one* **blow** I am about to take away from you the delight of
Zec 14: 12 This is the **plague** with which the LORD will strike all the
14: 15 A similar **plague** will strike the horses and mules, the camels
14: 15 and donkeys, and all the animals in those camps. **[RPH]**
14: 18 The LORD will bring on them the **plague** he inflicts on the

4488 מַגְפִּיעָשׁ *magpî'āš*, n.pr.m. [1]

Magpiash [1]

Ne 10: 20 [10:21] **Magpiash**, Meshullam, Hezir,

4489 מָגַר *māgar*, v. [2] [→ Ar 10400]

cast [1], thrown [1]

Ps 89: 44 [89:45] [D] to his splendor and **cast** his throne to the ground.
Eze 21: 12 [21:17] [B] They are **thrown** to the sword along with my

4490 מְגֵרָה *m^e^gērâ*, n.f. [4] [√ 1760]

saws [2], axes [1], saw [1]

2Sa 12: 31 consigning them to labor with **saws** and with iron picks and axes,
1Ki 7: 9 cut to size and trimmed with a **saw** on their inner and outer faces.
1Ch 20: 3 consigning them to labor with **saws** and with iron picks and axes.
20: 3 consigning them to labor with saws and with iron picks and **axes**.

4491 מִגְרוֹן *migrôn*, n.pr.loc. [2]

Migron [2]

1Sa 14: 2 on the outskirts of Gibeah under a pomegranate tree in **Migron**.
Isa 10: 28 They enter Aiath; they pass through **Migron**; they store supplies at

4492 מִגְרָעוֹת *migrā'ôt*, n.f. [1] [√ 1757]

offset ledges [1]

1Ki 6: 6 He made **offset ledges** around the outside of the temple so that

4493 מֶגְרָפָה *megrāpâ*, n.f. [1] [√ 1759]

clods [1]

Joel 1: 17 The seeds are shriveled beneath the **clods**. The storehouses are in

4494 מִגְרָשׁ *migrāš*, n.m. [115 / 119] [√ 1763]

untranslated [69], pasturelands [41], pastureland [5], farm [1], open land [1], pastureland [+8441] [1], shorelands [1]

Lev 25: 34 the **pastureland** [+8441] *belonging to* their towns must not be
Nu 35: 2 will possess. And give them **pasturelands** around the towns.
35: 3 they will have towns to live in and **pasturelands** for their cattle,
35: 4 "The **pasturelands** around the towns that you give the Levites will
35: 5 the center. They will have this area as **pastureland** *for* the towns.
35: 7 the Levites forty-eight towns, together with their **pasturelands**.
Jos 14: 4 only towns to live in, with **pasturelands** for their flocks and herds.
21: 2 you give us towns to live in, with **pasturelands** for our livestock."
21: 3 following towns and **pasturelands** out of their own inheritance:
21: 8 allotted to the Levites these towns and their **pasturelands**,
21: 11 Hebron), with its surrounding **pastureland**, in the hill country of
21: 13 (a city of refuge for one accused of murder), **[RPH]** Libnah,
21: 13 (a city of refuge for one accused of murder), Libnah, **[RPH]**
21: 14 Jattir, **[RPH]** Eshtemoa,
21: 14 Jattir, Eshtemoa, **[RPH]**
21: 15 Holon, **[RPH]** Debir,
21: 15 Holon, Debir, **[RPH]**
21: 16 Ain, **[RPH]** Juttah and Beth Shemesh, together with their
21: 16 Ain, Juttah **[RPH]** and Beth Shemesh, together with their
21: 16 Juttah and Beth Shemesh, together with their **pasturelands**—
21: 17 from the tribe of Benjamin they gave them Gibeon, **[RPH]** Geba,
21: 17 from the tribe of Benjamin they gave them Gibeon, Geba, **[RPH]**
21: 18 Anathoth **[RPH]** and Almon, together with their pasturelands—
21: 18 Anathoth and Almon, together with their **pasturelands**—
21: 19 of Aaron, were thirteen, together with their **pasturelands**.
21: 21 (a city of refuge for one accused of murder) **[RPH]** and Gezer,
21: 21 (a city of refuge for one accused of murder) and Gezer, **[RPH]**
21: 22 Kibzaim **[RPH]** and Beth Horon, together with their
21: 22 Kibzaim and Beth Horon, together with their **pasturelands**—
21: 23 from the tribe of Dan they received Eltekeh, **[RPH]** Gibbethon,
21: 23 from the tribe of Dan they received Eltekeh, Gibbethon, **[RPH]**
21: 24 Aijalon **[RPH]** and Gath Rimmon, together with their
21: 24 Aijalon and Gath Rimmon, together with their **pasturelands**—
21: 25 of Manasseh they received Taanach **[RPH]** and Gath Rimmon,
21: 25 and Gath Rimmon, together with their **pasturelands**—
21: 26 their **pasturelands** were given to the rest of the Kohathite clans.
21: 27 **[RPH]** and Be Eshtarah, together with their pasturelands—
21: 27 and Be Eshtarah, together with their **pasturelands**—two towns;
21: 28 from the tribe of Issachar, Kishion, **[RPH]** Daberath,
21: 28 from the tribe of Issachar, Kishion, Daberath, **[RPH]**
21: 29 Jarmuth **[RPH]** and En Gannim, together with their
21: 29 Jarmuth and En Gannim, together with their **pasturelands**—
21: 30 from the tribe of Asher, Mishal, **[RPH]** Abdon,
21: 30 from the tribe of Asher, Mishal, Abdon, **[RPH]**
21: 31 Helkath **[RPH]** and Rehob, together with their pasturelands—
21: 31 Helkath and Rehob, together with their **pasturelands**—four towns;
21: 32 **[RPH]** Hammoth Dor and Kartan, together with their
21: 32 Hammoth Dor **[RPH]** and Kartan, together with their
21: 32 Hammoth Dor and Kartan, together with their **pasturelands**—
21: 33 Gershonite clans were thirteen, together with their **pasturelands**.
21: 34 were given: from the tribe of Zebulun, Jokneam, **[RPH]** Kartah,
21: 34 were given: from the tribe of Zebulun, Jokneam, Kartah, **[RPH]**
21: 35 Dimnah and **[RPH]** Nahalal, together with their pasturelands—
21: 35 Dimnah and Nahalal, together with their **pasturelands**—
21: 36 from the tribe of Reuben, Bezer, **[RPH]** Jahaz,
21: 36 from the tribe of Reuben, Bezer, Jahaz, **[RPH]**
21: 37 Kedemoth **[RPH]** and Mephaath, together with their
21: 37 Kedemoth and Mephaath, together with their **pasturelands**—
21: 38 (a city of refuge for one accused of murder), **[RPH]** Mahanaim,
21: 38 (a city of refuge for one accused of murder), Mahanaim, **[RPH]**
21: 39 Heshbon **[RPH]** and Jazer, together with their pasturelands—
21: 39 Heshbon and Jazer, together with their **pasturelands**—four towns
21: 41 Israelites were forty-eight in all, together with their **pasturelands**.
21: 42 Each of these towns had **pasturelands** surrounding it; this was true
1Ch 5: 16 and on all the **pasturelands** *of* Sharon as far as they extended.
6: 55 [6:40] given Hebron in Judah with its surrounding **pasturelands**.
6: 57 [6:42] (a city of refuge), and Libnah, **[RPH]** Jattir, Eshtemoa,
6: 57 [6:42] (a city of refuge), and Libnah, Jattir, Eshtemoa, **[RPH]**
6: 58 [6:43] Hilen, **[RPH]** Debir,
6: 58 [6:43] Hilen, Debir, **[RPH]**
6: 59 [6:44] Ashan, **[RPH]** Juttah and Beth Shemesh, together with
6: 59 [6:44] Ashan, Juttah **[RPH]** [BHS-] and Beth Shemesh,
6: 59 [6:44] and Beth Shemesh, together with their **pasturelands**.
6: 60 [6:45] **[RPH]** [BHS-] Geba, Alemeth and Anathoth,
6: 60 [6:45] Geba, **[RPH]** Alemeth and Anathoth, together with their
6: 60 [6:45] Geba, Alemeth **[RPH]** and Anathoth, together with their
6: 60 [6:45] Alemeth and Anathoth, together with their **pasturelands**.
6: 64 [6:49] gave the Levites these towns and their **pasturelands**.
6: 67 [6:52] were given Shechem (a city of refuge), **[RPH]** and Gezer,
6: 67 [6:52] were given Shechem (a city of refuge), and Gezer, **[RPH]**
6: 68 [6:53] Jokmeam, **[RPH]** Beth Horon,
6: 68 [6:53] Jokmeam, Beth Horon, **[RPH]**
6: 69 [6:54] Aijalon and **[RPH]** Gath Rimmon, together with their
6: 69 [6:54] and Gath Rimmon, together with their **pasturelands**.
6: 70 [6:55] of Manasseh the Israelites gave Aner **[RPH]** and Bileam,
6: 70 [6:55] gave Aner and Bileam, together with their **pasturelands**,
6: 71 [6:56] they received Golan in Bashan **[RPH]** and also Ashtaroth,
6: 71 [6:56] and also Ashtaroth, together with their **pasturelands**;
6: 72 [6:57] tribe of Issachar they received Kedesh, **[RPH]** Daberath,
6: 72 [6:57] tribe of Issachar they received Kedesh, Daberath, **[RPH]**
6: 73 [6:58] Ramoth and **[RPH]** Anem, together with their
6: 73 [6:58] Ramoth and Anem, together with their **pasturelands**;
6: 74 [6:59] the tribe of Asher they received Mashal, **[RPH]** Abdon,
6: 74 [6:59] the tribe of Asher they received Mashal, Abdon, **[RPH]**
6: 75 [6:60] Hukok **[RPH]** and Rehob, together with their
6: 75 [6:60] Hukok and Rehob, together with their **pasturelands**;
6: 76 [6:61] **[RPH]** Hammon and Kiriathaim, together with their
6: 76 [6:61] Hammon **[RPH]** and Kiriathaim, together with their
6: 76 [6:61] Hammon and Kiriathaim, together with their **pasturelands**.
6: 77 [6:62] **[RPH]** [BHS-] Kartah, Rimmono and Tabor,
6: 77 [6:62] Kartah, **[RPH]** [BHS-] Rimmono and Tabor,
6: 77 [6:62] Kartah, Rimmono **[RPH]** and Tabor, together with their
6: 77 [6:62] and Tabor, together with their **pasturelands**;
6: 78 [6:63] Jericho they received Bezer in the desert, **[RPH]** Jahzah,
6: 78 [6:63] Jericho they received Bezer in the desert, Jahzah, **[RPH]**
6: 79 [6:64] Kedemoth **[RPH]** and Mephaath, together with their
6: 79 [6:64] and Mephaath, together with their **pasturelands**;
6: 80 [6:65] Gad they received Ramoth in Gilead, **[RPH]** Mahanaim,
6: 80 [6:65] Gad they received Ramoth in Gilead, Mahanaim, **[RPH]**
6: 81 [6:66] Heshbon **[RPH]** and Jazer, together with their
6: 81 [6:66] Heshbon and Jazer, together with their **pasturelands**.
13: 2 and Levites who are with them in their towns and **pasturelands**,
2Ch 11: 14 The Levites even abandoned their **pasturelands** and property,
31: 19 who lived on the **farm** lands *around* their towns or in any other
Eze 27: 28 The **shorelands** will quake when your seamen cry out.
36: 5 their own possession so that they might plunder its **pastureland**.'

Eze 45: 2 is to be for the sanctuary, with 50 cubits around it for **open land**.
48: 15 be for the common use of the city, for houses and for **pastureland**.
48: 17 The **pastureland** for the city will be 250 cubits on the north,

4495 מִגְרְשׁוֹת migr^{e}šôt, var. Not used in NIV/BHS [√ 1763]

4496 מַד mad, n.m. [11] [√ 4499; cf. 4503]

tunic [3], clothes [2], clothing [1], decreed [1], garment [1], military tunic [+4230] [1], robes [1], saddle blankets [1]

Lev 6: 10 [6:3] The priest shall then put on his linen **clothes**, with linen
Jdg 3: 16 a half long, which he strapped to his right thigh under his **clothing**.
5: 10 "You who ride on white donkeys, sitting on your **saddle blankets**,
1Sa 4: 12 and went to Shiloh, his **clothes** torn and dust on his head.
17: 38 Saul dressed David in his own **tunic**. He put a coat of armor on
17: 39 David fastened on his sword over the **tunic** and tried walking
18: 4 along with his **tunic**, and even his sword, his bow and his belt.
2Sa 20: 8 Joab was wearing his **military tunic** [+4230], and strapped over it
Ps 109: 18 He wore cursing as his **garment**; it entered into his body like
133: 2 down on Aaron's beard, down upon the collar of his **robes**.
Jer 13: 25 This is your lot, the portion I have **decreed** *for* you," declares the

4497 מִדְבָּרִי midbār[1], n.m. [270] [√ 1818]

desert [256], open [3], wasteland [2], wilderness [2], barren wilderness [1], desert [+824] [1], deserts [1], here[s] [+928+2021] [1], open country [1], there[s] [+2334] [1], there[s] [1]

Ge 14: 6 in the hill country of Seir, as far as El Paran near the **desert**.
16: 7 The angel of the LORD found Hagar near a spring in the **desert**;
21: 14 She went on her way and wandered in the **desert** *of* Beersheba.
21: 20 boy as he grew up. He lived in the **desert** and became an archer.
21: 21 While he was living in the **Desert** *of* Paran, his mother got a wife
36: 24 This is the Anah who discovered the hot springs in the **desert**
37: 22 Throw him into this cistern here in the **desert**, but don't lay a hand
Ex 3: 1 he led the flock to the far side of the **desert** and came to Horeb,
3: 18 Let us take a three-day journey into the **desert** to offer sacrifices to
4: 27 The LORD said to Aaron, "Go into the **desert** to meet Moses."
5: 1 people go, so that they may hold a festival to me in the **desert**.' "
5: 3 Now let us take a three-day journey into the **desert** to offer
7: 16 Let my people go, so that they may worship me in the **desert**.
8: 27 [8:23] We must take a three-day journey into the **desert** to offer
8: 28 [8:24] go to offer sacrifices to the LORD your God in the **desert**,
13: 18 So God led the people around by the **desert** road toward the Red
13: 20 leaving Succoth they camped at Etham on the edge of the **desert**.
14: 3 wandering around the land in confusion, hemmed in by the **desert**.'
14: 11 were no graves in Egypt that you brought us to the **desert** to die?
14: 12 been better for us to serve the Egyptians than to die in the **desert**!"
15: 22 led Israel from the Red Sea and they went into the **Desert** *of* Shur.
15: 22 For three days they traveled in the **desert** without finding water.
16: 1 community set out from Elim and came to the **Desert** *of* Sin,
16: 2 In the **desert** the whole community grumbled against Moses
16: 3 you have brought us out into this **desert** to starve this entire
16: 10 to the whole Israelite community, they looked toward the **desert**,
16: 14 thin flakes like frost on the ground appeared on the **desert** floor.
16: 32 so they can see the bread I gave you to eat in the **desert** when I
17: 1 The whole Israelite community set out from the **Desert** *of* Sin,
18: 5 together with Moses' sons and wife, came to him in the **desert**,
19: 1 left Egypt—on the very day—they came to the **Desert** *of* Sinai.
19: 2 After they set out from Rephidim, they entered the **Desert** *of* Sinai,
19: 2 and Israel camped there in the **desert** in front of the mountain.
23: 31 Sea to the Sea of the Philistines, and from the **desert** to the River.
Lev 7: 38 to bring their offerings to the LORD, in the **Desert** *of* Sinai.
16: 10 for making atonement by sending it into the **desert** as a scapegoat.
16: 21 He shall send the goat away into the **desert** in the care of a man
16: 22 sins to a solitary place; and the man shall release it in the **desert**.
Nu 1: 1 LORD spoke to Moses in the Tent of Meeting in the **Desert** *of*
1: 19 And so he counted them in the **Desert** *of* Sinai:
3: 4 offering with unauthorized fire before him in the **Desert** *of* Sinai.
3: 14 The LORD said to Moses in the **Desert** *of* Sinai,
9: 1 The LORD spoke to Moses in the **Desert** *of* Sinai in the first
9: 5 so in the **Desert** *of* Sinai at twilight on the fourteenth day of the
10: 12 the Israelites set out from the **Desert** *of* Sinai and traveled from
10: 12 place to place until the cloud came to rest in the **Desert** *of* Paran.
10: 31 You know where we should camp in the **desert**, and you can be
12: 16 the people left Hazeroth and encamped in the **Desert** *of* Paran.
13: 3 command Moses sent them out from the **Desert** *of* Paran.
13: 21 and explored the land from the **Desert** *of* Zin as far as Rehob,
13: 26 the whole Israelite community at Kadesh in the **Desert** *of* Paran.
14: 2 said to them, "If only we had died in Egypt! Or in this **desert**!
14: 16 he promised them on oath; so he slaughtered them in the **desert**.'
14: 22 and in the **desert** but who disobeyed me and tested me ten times—
14: 25 and set out toward the **desert** along the route to the Red Sea."
14: 29 In this **desert** your bodies will fall—every one of you twenty years
14: 32 But you—your bodies will fall in this **desert**.
14: 33 Your children will be shepherds **here**[s] [+928+2021] for forty
14: 33 your unfaithfulness, until the last of your bodies lies in the **desert**.
14: 35 They will meet their end in this **desert**; here they will die."
15: 32 While the Israelites were in the **desert**, a man was found gathering
16: 13 out of a land flowing with milk and honey to kill us in the **desert**?
20: 1 month the whole Israelite community arrived at the **Desert** *of* Zin,
20: 4 Why did you bring the LORD's community into this **desert**,
21: 5 "Why have you brought us up out of Egypt to die in the **desert**?
21: 11 in Iye Abarim, in the **desert** that faces Moab toward the sunrise.
21: 13 the Arnon, which is in the **desert** extending into Amorite territory.
21: 18 and staffs." Then they went from the **desert** to Mattanah,
21: 23 his entire army and marched out into the **desert** against Israel.
24: 1 to sorcery as at other times, but turned his face toward the **desert**.
26: 64 Aaron the priest when they counted the Israelites in the **Desert** *of*
26: 65 had told those Israelites they would surely die in the **desert**,
27: 3 "Our father died in the **desert**. He was not among Korah's
27: 14 for when the community rebelled at the waters in the **Desert** *of*
27: 14 (These were the waters of Meribah Kadesh, in the **Desert** *of* Zin.)
32: 13 against Israel and he made them wander in the **desert** forty years,
32: 15 following him, he will again leave all this people in the **desert**,
33: 6 They left Succoth and camped at Etham, on the edge of the **desert**.
33: 8 They left Pi Hahiroth and passed through the sea into the **desert**,
33: 8 and when they had traveled for three days in the **Desert** *of* Etham,
33: 11 They left the Red Sea and camped in the **Desert** *of* Sin.
33: 12 They left the **Desert** *of* Sin and camped at Dophkah.
33: 15 They left Rephidim and camped in the **Desert** *of* Sinai.
33: 16 They left the **Desert** *of* Sinai and camped at Kibroth Hattaavah.
33: 36 They left Ezion Geber and camped at Kadesh, in the **Desert** *of* Zin.
34: 3 " 'Your southern side will include some of the **Desert** *of* Zin along
Dt 1: 1 These are the words Moses spoke to all Israel in the **desert** east of
1: 19 through all that vast and dreadful **desert** that you have seen,
1: 31 in the **desert**. There you saw how the LORD your God carried
1: 40 and set out toward the **desert** along the route to the Red Sea."
2: 1 and set out toward the **desert** along the route to the Red Sea,
2: 7 He has watched over your journey through this vast **desert**.
2: 8 and Ezion Geber, and traveled along the **desert** road of Moab.
2: 26 From the **desert** *of* Kedemoth I sent messengers to Sihon king of
4: 43 Bezer in the **desert** plateau, for the Reubenites; Ramoth in Gilead,
8: 2 your God led you all the way in the **desert** these forty years,
8: 15 He led you through the vast and dreadful **desert**, that thirsty
8: 16 He gave you manna to eat in the **desert**, something your fathers
9: 7 how you provoked the LORD your God to anger in the **desert**.
9: 28 hated them, he brought them out to put them to death in the **desert**.'
11: 5 It was not your children who saw what he did for you in the **desert**
11: 24 Your territory will extend from the **desert** to Lebanon, and from
29: 5 [29:4] During the forty years that I led you through the **desert**,
32: 10 In a **desert** land he found him, in a barren and howling waste.
32: 51 the Israelites at the waters of Meribah Kadesh in the **Desert** *of* Zin
Jos 1: 4 Your territory will extend from the **desert** to Lebanon, and from
5: 4 of military age—died in the **desert** on the way after leaving Egypt.
5: 5 all the people born in the **desert** during the journey from Egypt had
5: 6 The Israelites had moved about in the **desert** forty years until all
8: 15 be driven back before them, and they fled toward the **desert**.
8: 20 for the Israelites who had been fleeing toward the **desert** had
8: 24 of Ai in the fields and in the **desert** where they had chased them,
12: 8 the Arabah, the mountain slopes, the **desert** and the Negev—
14: 10 time he said this to Moses, while Israel moved about in the **desert**.
15: 1 to the territory of Edom, to the **Desert** *of* Zin in the extreme south.
15: 61 In the **desert**: Beth Arabah, Middin, Secacah,
16: 1 went up from there through the **desert** into the hill country of
18: 12 west into the hill country, coming out at the **desert** *of* Beth Aven.
20: 8 Bezer in the **desert** on the plateau in the tribe of Reuben,
24: 7 I did to the Egyptians. Then you lived in the **desert** for a long time.
Jdg 1: 16 among the people of the **Desert** *of* Judah in the Negev near Arad.
8: 7 into my hand, I will tear your flesh with **desert** thorns and briers."
8: 16 taught the men of Succoth a lesson by punishing them with **desert**
11: 16 Israel went through the **desert** to the Red Sea and on to Kadesh.
11: 18 "Next they traveled through the **desert**, skirted the lands of Edom
11: 22 it from the Arnon to the Jabbok and from the **desert** to the Jordan.
20: 42 So they fled before the Israelites in the direction of the **desert**,
20: 45 As they turned and fled toward the **desert** to the rock of Rimmon,
20: 47 men turned and fled into the **desert** to the rock of Rimmon,
1Sa 4: 8 who struck the Egyptians with all kinds of plagues in the **desert**.
13: 18 borderland overlooking the Valley of Zeboim facing the **desert**.
17: 28 And with whom did you leave those few sheep in the **desert**?
23: 14 David stayed in the **desert** strongholds and in the hills of the
23: 14 in the desert strongholds and in the hills of the **Desert** *of* Ziph.
23: 15 While David was at Horesh in the **Desert** *of* Ziph, he learned that
23: 24 Now David and his men were in the **Desert** *of* Maon,
23: 25 he went down to the rock and stayed in the **Desert** *of* Maon.
23: 25 heard this, he went into the **Desert** *of* Maon in pursuit of David.
24: 1 [24:2] he was told, "David is in the **Desert** *of* En Gedi."
25: 1 in Ramah. Then David moved down into the **Desert** *of* Maon.
25: 4 While David was in the **desert**, he heard that Nabal was shearing

1Sa 25:14 "David sent messengers from the **desert** to give our master his
25:21 all my watching over this fellow's property in the **desert** so that
26: 2 So Saul went down to the **Desert** *of* Ziph, with his three thousand
26: 2 thousand chosen men of Israel, to search **there**ˢ [+2334] for David.
26: 3 the hill of Hakilah facing Jeshimon, but David stayed in the **desert**.
26: 3 in the desert. When he saw that Saul had followed him **there**ˢ,
2Sa 2:24 hill of Ammah, near Giah on the way to the **wasteland** *of* Gibeon.
15:23 the Kidron Valley, and all the people moved on toward the **desert**.
15:28 I will wait at the fords in the **desert** until word comes from you to
16: 2 the wine is to refresh those who become exhausted in the **desert**."
17:16 and tell David, 'Do not spend the night at the fords in the **desert**;
17:29 people have become hungry and tired and thirsty in the **desert**."
1Ki 2:34 and killed him, and he was buried on his own land in the **desert**.
9:18 Baalath, and Tadmor in the **desert**, within his land,
19: 4 while he himself went a day's journey into the **desert**. He came to
19:15 "Go back the way you came, and go to the **Desert** *of* Damascus.
2Ki 3: 8 he asked. "Through the **Desert** *of* Edom," he answered.
1Ch 5: 9 To the east they occupied the land up to the edge of the **desert** that
6:78 [6:63] Jordan east of Jericho they received Bezer in the **desert**,
12: 8 [12:9] Gadites defected to David at his stronghold in the **desert**.
21:29 tabernacle of the LORD, which Moses had made in the **desert**,
2Ch 1: 3 which Moses the LORD's servant had made in the **desert**.
8: 4 He also built up Tadmor in the **desert** and all the store cities he had
20:16 you will find them at the end of the gorge in the **Desert** *of* Jeruel.
20:20 Early in the morning they left for the **Desert** *of* Tekoa. As they set
20:24 When the men of Judah came to the place that overlooks the **desert**
24: 9 that Moses the servant of God had required of Israel in the **desert**.
26:10 He also built towers in the **desert** and dug many cisterns,
Ne 9:19 of your great compassion you did not abandon them in the **desert**.
9:21 For forty years you sustained them in the **desert**; they lacked
Job 1:19 when suddenly a mighty wind swept in from the **desert** and struck
24: 5 Like wild donkeys in the **desert**, the poor go about their labor of
38:26 to water a land where no man lives, a **desert** with no one in it,
Ps 29: 8 The voice of the LORD shakes the **desert**; the LORD shakes the
29: 8 shakes the desert; the LORD shakes the **Desert** *of* Kadesh.
55: 7 [55:8] I would flee far away and stay in the **desert**; *Selah*
63: T [63:1] A psalm of David. When he was in the **Desert** *of* Judah.
65:12 [65:13] The grasslands of the **desert** overflow; the hills are
75: 6 [75:7] the east or the west or from the **desert** can exalt a man.
78:15 He split the rocks in the **desert** and gave them water as abundant as
78:19 spoke against God, saying, "Can God spread a table in the **desert**?
78:40 How often they rebelled against him in the **desert** and grieved him
78:52 people out like a flock; he led them like sheep through the **desert**.
95: 8 as you did at Meribah, as you did that day at Massah in the **desert**,
102: 6 [102:7] I am like a **desert** owl, like an owl among the ruins.
106: 9 and it dried up; he led them through the depths as through a **desert**.
106:14 In the **desert** they gave in to their craving; in the wasteland they
106:26 with uplifted hand that he would make them fall in the **desert**,
107: 4 Some wandered in **desert** wastelands, finding no way to a city
107:33 He turned rivers into a **desert**, flowing springs into thirsty ground,
107:35 He turned the **desert** into pools of water and the parched ground
136:16 to him who led his people through the **desert**, *His love*
Pr 21:19 Better to live in a **desert** [+824] than with a quarrelsome and
SS 3: 6 Who is this coming up from the **desert** like a column of smoke,
8: 5 Who is this coming up from the **desert** leaning on her lover?
Isa 14:17 the man who made the world a **desert**, who overthrew its cities
16: 1 from Sela, across the **desert**, to the mount of the Daughter of Zion.
16: 8 which once reached Jazer and spread toward the **desert**.
21: 1 An oracle concerning the **Desert** *by* the Sea: Like whirlwinds
21: 1 an invader comes from the **desert**, from a land of terror.
27:10 stands desolate, an abandoned settlement, forsaken like the **desert**;
32:15 the **desert** becomes a fertile field, and the fertile field seems like a
32:16 Justice will dwell in the **desert** and righteousness live in the fertile
35: 1 The **desert** and the parched land will be glad; the wilderness will
35: 6 Water will gush forth in the **wilderness** and streams in the desert.
40: 3 "In the **desert** prepare the way for the LORD; make straight in
41:18 I will turn the **desert** into pools of water, and the parched ground
41:19 I will put in the **desert** the cedar and the acacia, the myrtle
42:11 Let the **desert** and its towns raise their voices; let the settlements
43:19 I am making a way in the **desert** and streams in the wasteland.
43:20 because I provide water in the **desert** and streams in the wasteland,
50: 2 By a mere rebuke I dry up the sea, I turn rivers into a **desert**;
51: 3 he will make her **deserts** like Eden, her wastelands like the garden
63:13 the depths? Like a horse in **open country**, they did not stumble;
64:10 [64:9] Your sacred cities have become a **desert**; even Zion is a
64:10 [64:9] a desert; even Zion is a **desert**, Jerusalem a desolation.
Jer 2: 2 how as a bride you loved me and followed me through the **desert**,
2: 6 us up out of Egypt and led us through the **barren wilderness**,
2:24 a wild donkey accustomed to the **desert**, sniffing the wind in her
2:31 "Have I been a **desert** to Israel or a land of great darkness?
3: 2 roadside you sat waiting for lovers, sat like a nomad in the **desert**.
4:11 "A scorching wind from the barren heights in the **desert** blows
4:26 I looked, and the fruitful land was a **desert**; all its towns lay in
9: 2 [9:1] Oh, that I had in the **desert** a lodging place for travelers,
9:10 [9:9] and take up a lament concerning the **desert** pastures.
9:12 [9:11] and laid waste like a **desert** that no one can cross?
9:26 [9:25] and all who live in the **desert** in distant places.
12:10 they will turn my pleasant field into a desolate **wasteland**.
12:12 Over all the barren heights in the **desert** destroyers will swarm,
13:24 "I will scatter you like chaff driven by the **desert** wind.
17: 6 He will dwell in the parched places of the **desert**, in a salt land
22: 6 I will surely make you like a **desert**, like towns not inhabited.
23:10 the land lies parched and the pastures in the **desert** are withered.
25:24 and all the kings of the foreign people who live in the **desert**;
31: 2 "The people who survive the sword will find favor in the **desert**;
48: 6 Flee! Run for your lives; become like a bush in the **desert**.
50:12 will be the least of the nations—a **wilderness**, a dry land, a desert.
La 4: 3 but my people have become heartless like ostriches in the **desert**.
4:19 chased us over the mountains and lay in wait for us in the **desert**.
5: 9 bread at the risk of our lives because of the sword in the **desert**.
Eze 6:14 and make the land a desolate waste from the **desert** to Diblah—
19:13 Now it is planted in the **desert**, in a dry and thirsty land.
20:10 I led them out of Egypt and brought them into the **desert**.
20:13 " 'Yet the people of Israel rebelled against me in the **desert**.
20:13 I would pour out my wrath on them and destroy them in the **desert**.
20:15 Also with uplifted hand I swore to them in the **desert** that I would
20:17 and did not destroy them or put an end to them in the **desert**.
20:18 I said to their children in the **desert**, "Do not follow the statutes of
20:21 my wrath on them and spend my anger against them in the **desert**.
20:23 Also with uplifted hand I swore to them in the **desert** that I would
20:35 I will bring you into the **desert** *of* the nations and there, face to
20:36 As I judged your fathers in the **desert** *of* the land of Egypt,
23:42 Sabeans were brought from the **desert** along with men from the
29: 5 I will leave you in the **desert**, you and all the fish of your streams.
34:25 and rid the land of wild beasts so that they may live in the **desert**
Hos 2: 3 [2:5] I will make her like a **desert**, turn her into a parched land,
2:14 [2:16] I will lead her into the **desert** and speak tenderly to her.
9:10 "When I found Israel, it was like finding grapes in the **desert**;
13: 5 I cared for you in the **desert**, in the land of burning heat.
13:15 east wind from the LORD will come, blowing in from the **desert**;
Joel 1:19 for fire has devoured the **open** pastures and flames have burned up
1:20 of water have dried up and fire has devoured the **open** pastures.
2: 3 the land is like the garden of Eden, behind them, a **desert** waste—
2:22 O wild animals, for the **open** pastures are becoming green.
3:19 [4:19] Egypt will be desolate, Edom a **desert** waste, because of
Am 2:10 I led you forty years in the **desert** to give you the land of the
5:25 you bring me sacrifices and offerings forty years in the **desert**,
Zep 2:13 leaving Nineveh utterly desolate and dry as the **desert**.
Mal 1: 3 into a wasteland and left his inheritance to the **desert** jackals."

4498 ²מִדְבָּר midbār², n.m. [1] [√ 1819]

mouth [1]

SS 4: 3 Your lips are like a scarlet ribbon; your **mouth** is lovely.

4499 מָדַד mādad, v. [52 / 50] [→ 4496, 4500, 4924]

measured [30], measured off [5], measure off [3], be measured [2], measure [2], *untranslated* [1], consider [1], drags on [1], measure distance [1], measure the full payment [1], measureless [+4202] [1], poured into measures [1], stretched himself out [1]

Ex 16:18 [A] when *they* **measured** it by the omer, he who gathered much
Nu 35: 5 [A] **measure** three thousand feet on the east side, three thousand on the south side, three thousand on the west and
Dt 21: 2 [A] **measure** *the* **distance** from the body to the neighboring
Ru 3:15 [A] *he* **poured into** it six **measures** of barley and put it on her.
2Sa 8: 2 [D] on the ground and **measured** them **off** with a length of cord.
8: 2 [D] **[RPH]** Every two lengths of them were put to death,
1Ki 17:21 [F] *he* **stretched himself out** on the boy three times and cried to
Job 7: 4 [D] before I get up?' The night **drags on**, and I toss till dawn.
Ps 60: 6 [60:8] [D] out Shechem and **measure off** the Valley of Succoth.
108: 7 [108:8] [D] and **measure off** the Valley of Succoth.
Isa 40:12 [A] Who *has* **measured** the waters in the hollow of his hand,
65: 7 [A] *I will* **measure** into their laps **the full payment** *for* their
Jer 31:37 [C] "Only if the heavens above *can* **be measured**
33:22 [C] and as **measureless** [+4202] as the sand on the seashore.' "
Eze 40: 5 [A] *He* **measured** the wall; it was one measuring rod thick
40: 6 [A] He climbed its steps and **measured** the threshold of the gate;
40: 8 [A] Then *he* **measured** the portico of the gateway;
40: 9 [a] [BHS+ *Then he **measured** the portico*] it was eight cubits deep
40:11 [A] Then *he* **measured** the width of the entrance to the gateway;
40:13 [A] *he* **measured** the gateway from the top of the rear wall of
40:19 [A] *he* **measured** the distance from the inside of the lower
40:20 [A] *he* **measured** the length and width of the gate facing north,
40:23 [A] *He* **measured** from one gate to the opposite one; it was a
40:24 [A] *He* **measured** its jambs and its portico, and they had the
40:27 [A] *he* **measured** from this gate to the outer gate on the south
40:28 [A] through the south gate, and *he* **measured** the south gate;

Eze 40:32 [A] inner court on the east side, and *he* **measured** the gateway;
40:35 [A] he brought me to the north gate and **measured** it. It had the
40:47 [A] *he* **measured** the court: It was square—a hundred cubits long
40:48 [A] portico of the temple and **measured** the jambs of the portico;
41: 1 [A] brought me to the outer sanctuary and **measured** the jambs;
41: 2 [A] *He* also **measured** the outer sanctuary; it was forty cubits
41: 3 [A] the inner sanctuary and **measured** the jambs of the entrance;
41: 4 [A] *he* **measured** the length of the inner sanctuary; it was twenty
41: 5 [A] *he* **measured** the wall of the temple; it was six cubits thick,
41:13 [A] Then *he* **measured** the temple; it was a hundred cubits long,
41:15 [A] *he* **measured** the length of the building facing the courtyard
42:15 [A] me out by the east gate and **measured** the area all around:
42:16 [A] *He* **measured** the east side with the measuring rod; it was
42:17 [A] *He* **measured** the north side; it was five hundred cubits by
42:18 [A] *He* **measured** the south side; it was five hundred cubits by
42:19 [A] he turned to the west side and **measured**; it was five hundred
42:20 [A] So *he* **measured** the area on all four sides. It had a wall
43:10 [A] may be ashamed of their sins. *Let them* **consider** the plan,
45: 3 [A] **measure off** a section 25,000 cubits long and 10,000 cubits
47: 3 [A] *he* **measured off** a thousand cubits and then led me through
47: 4 [A] *He* **measured off** another thousand cubits and led me
47: 4 [A] *He* **measured off** another thousand and led me through water
47: 5 [A] *He* **measured off** another thousand, but now it was a river
47:18 [a] sea and as far as Tamar. [BHS *you will measure*; NIV 9471]
Hos 1:10 [2:1] [C] the seashore, which cannot **be measured** or counted.
Zec 2: 2 [2:6] [A] He answered me, "To **measure** Jerusalem, to find out

4500 ¹מִדָּה **middâ¹**, n.f. [54 / 55] [√ 4499; cf. 4515]

measurements [12], size [10], measuring [9], section [7], *untranslated* [2], huge [2], at regular intervals [1], district [1], great size [1], great [1], length [1], long [1], measure [1], measured out [+928+9419] [1], measures [1], number [1], standard [1], tall [+408] [1], tall [1]

Ex 26: 2 All the curtains are to be the same **size**—twenty-eight cubits long
26: 8 All eleven curtains are to be the same **size**—thirty cubits long
36: 9 All the curtains were the same **size**—twenty-eight cubits long
36:15 All eleven curtains were the same **size**—thirty cubits long
Lev 19:35 " 'Do not use dishonest standards when measuring **length**,
Nu 13:32 those living in it. All the people we saw there are of **great size**.
Jos 3: 4 **[NIE]** Then you will know which way to go, since you have never
2Sa 21:20 there was a **huge** [BHS 4515] man with six fingers on each hand
1Ki 6:25 ten cubits, for the two cherubim were identical in **size** and shape.
7: 9 were made of blocks of high-grade stone cut to **size** and trimmed
7:11 Above were high-grade stones, cut to **size**, and cedar beams.
7:37 all cast in the same molds and were identical in **size** and shape.
1Ch 11:23 he struck down an Egyptian who was seven and a half feet **tall**.
20: 6 there was a **huge** man with six fingers on each hand and six toes on
23:29 and the mixing, and all measurements of quantity and **size**.
2Ch 3: 3 and twenty cubits wide (using the cubit of the old **standard**).
Ne 3:11 and Hasshub son of Pahath-Moab repaired another **section**
3:19 Ezer son of Jeshua, ruler of Mizpah, repaired another **section**,
3:20 to him, Baruch son of Zabbai zealously repaired another **section**,
3:21 son of Uriah, the son of Hakkoz, repaired another **section**,
3:24 Next to him, Binnui son of Henadad repaired another **section**,
3:27 Next to them, the men of Tekoa repaired another **section**, from the
3:30 and Hanun, the sixth son of Zalaph, repaired another **section**.
Job 11: 9 Their **measure** is longer than the earth and wider than the sea.
28:25 the force of the wind and **measured** [+928+9419] **out** the waters,
Ps 39: 4 [39:5] O LORD, my life's end and the **number** *of* my days;
Isa 45:14 and the merchandise of Cush, and those **tall** [+408] Sabeans—
Jer 22:14 'I will build myself a **great** palace with spacious upper rooms.'
31:39 The **measuring** line will stretch from there straight to the hill of
Eze 40: 3 in the gateway with a linen cord and a **measuring** rod in his hand.
40: 5 The length of the **measuring** rod in the man's hand was six long
40:10 the three had the same **measurements**, and the faces of the
40:10 of the projecting walls on each side had the same **measurements**.
40:21 its portico had the same **measurements** as those of the first
40:22 its palm tree decorations had the same **measurements** as those of
40:24 and its portico, and they had the same **measurements** as the others.
40:28 the south gate; it had the same **measurements** as the others.
40:29 and its portico had the same **measurements** as the others.
40:32 the gateway; it had the same **measurements** as the others.
40:33 and its portico had the same **measurements** as the others.
40:35 and measured it. It had the same **measurements** as the others,
41:17 and on the walls **at regular intervals** all around the inner
42:15 When he had finished **measuring** what was inside the temple area,
42:16 He measured the east side with the **measuring** rod; it was five
42:16 side with the measuring rod; it was five hundred cubits. **[RPH]**
42:17 the north side; it was five hundred cubits by the **measuring** rod.
42:18 the south side; it was five hundred cubits by the **measuring** rod.
42:19 and measured; it was five hundred cubits by the **measuring** rod.
43:13 "These are the **measurements** *of* the altar in long cubits, that cubit
45: 3 In the sacred **district**, measure off a section 25,000 cubits long
46:22 each of the courts in the four corners was the same **size**.
48:16 and will have these **measurements**: the north side 4,500 cubits,
48:30 of the city: Beginning on the north side, which is 4,500 cubits **long**,
48:33 the south side, which **measures** 4,500 cubits, will be three gates:
Zec 2: 1 [2:5] there before me was a man with a **measuring** line in his

4501 ²מִדָּה **middâ²**, n.f. [1] [cf. 5989; Ar 10402, 10429]

tax [1]

Ne 5: 4 "We have had to borrow money to pay the king's **tax** on our fields

4502 מַדְהֵבָה **madhēbâ**, n.f. [1 / 0] [cf. 5290, 8104]

Isa 14: 4 How his fury [BHS *the golden one* ?; NIV 5290] has ended!

4503 מַדּוּ **mādû**, ¹מַדְוֶה **madweh¹**, n.m. [2] [cf. 4496]

garments [2]

2Sa 10: 4 cut off their **garments** in the middle at the buttocks, and sent them
1Ch 19: 4 shaved them, cut off their **garments** in the middle at the buttocks,

4504 ²מַדְוֶה **madweh²**, n.m. [2] [√ 1864]

diseases [2]

Dt 7:15 He will not inflict on you the horrible **diseases** you knew *in* Egypt,
28:60 He will bring upon you all the **diseases** *of* Egypt that you dreaded,

4505 מַדּוּחִים **maddûḥîm**, n.[m.]. [1] [√ 5615]

misleading [1]

La 2:14 The oracles they gave you were false and **misleading**.

4506 ¹מָדוֹן **mādôn¹**, n.m. [22] [→ 4517; cf. 1906, 4515]

dissension [7], quarrelsome [6], disputes [2], quarrel [2], strife [2], conflict [1], contends [1], source of contention [1]

Ps 80: 6 [80:7] You have made us a **source of contention** to our
Pr 6:14 plots evil with deceit in his heart—he always stirs up **dissension**.
6:19 pours out lies and a man who stirs up **dissension** among brothers.
10:12 Hatred stirs up **dissension**, but love covers over all wrongs.
15:18 A hot-tempered man stirs up **dissension**, but a patient man calms a
16:28 A perverse man stirs up **dissension**, and a gossip separates close
17:14 Starting a **quarrel** is like breaching a dam; so drop the matter
18:18 Casting the lot settles **disputes** and keeps strong opponents apart.
18:19 a fortified city, and **disputes** are like the barred gates of a citadel.
19:13 father's ruin, and a **quarrelsome** wife is like a constant dripping.
21: 9 a corner of the roof than share a house with a **quarrelsome** wife.
21:19 Better to live in a desert than with a **quarrelsome** and ill-tempered
22:10 Drive out the mocker, and out goes **strife**; quarrels and insults are
23:29 Who has woe? Who has sorrow? Who has **strife**? Who has
25:24 a corner of the roof than share a house with a **quarrelsome** wife.
26:20 Without wood a fire goes out; without gossip a **quarrel** dies down.
26:21 and as wood to fire, so is a **quarrelsome** man for kindling strife.
27:15 A **quarrelsome** wife is like a constant dripping on a rainy day;
28:25 A greedy man stirs up **dissension**, but he who trusts in the LORD
29:22 An angry man stirs up **dissension**, and a hot-tempered one
Jer 15:10 me birth, a man with whom the whole land strives and **contends**!
Hab 1: 3 and violence are before me; there is strife, and **conflict** abounds.

4507 ²מָדוֹן **mādôn²**, n.pr.loc. [2] [√ 1906]

Madon [2]

Jos 11: 1 he sent word to Jobab king of **Madon**, to the kings of Shimron
12:19 the king of **Madon** one the king of Hazor one

4508 מַדּוּעַ **maddûa'**, adv. [72]

why [70], what [1], what's the meaning of [1]

Ge 26:27 Isaac asked them, "**Why** have you come to me, since you were
40: 7 him in his master's house, "**Why** are your faces so sad today?"
Ex 1:18 the midwives and asked them, "**Why** have you done this?
2:18 he asked them, "**Why** have you returned so early today?"
3: 3 and see this strange sight—**why** the bush does not burn up."
5:14 "**Why** didn't you meet your quota of bricks yesterday or today,
18:14 **Why** do you alone sit as judge, while all these people stand around
Lev 10:17 "**Why** didn't you eat the sin offering in the sanctuary area?
Nu 12: 8 **Why** then were you not afraid to speak against my servant
16: 3 **Why** then do you set yourselves above the LORD's assembly?"
Jos 17:14 "**Why** have you given us only one allotment and one portion for an
Jdg 5:28 the lattice she cried out, '**Why** is his chariot so long in coming?
5:28 so long in coming? **Why** is the clatter of his chariots delayed?'
9:28 of Hamor, Shechem's father! **Why** should we serve Abimelech?
11: 7 **Why** do you come to me now, when you're in trouble?"
11:26 along the Arnon. **Why** didn't you retake them during that time?
12: 1 "**Why** did you go to fight the Ammonites without calling us to go
Ru 2:10 "**Why** have I found such favor in your eyes that you notice me—
1Sa 20: 2 confiding in me. **Why** would he hide this from me? It's not so!"

1Sa 20:27 "Why hasn't the son of Jesse come to the meal, either yesterday
21: 1 [21:2] when he met him, and asked, "Why are you alone?
2Sa 3: 7 said to Abner, "Why did you sleep with my father's concubine?"
11:10 you just come from a distance? Why didn't you go home?"
11:20 and he may ask you, 'Why did you get so close to the city to fight?
12: 9 Why did you despise the word of the LORD by doing what is evil
13: 4 "Why do you, the king's son, look so haggard morning after
16:10 said to him, 'Curse David,' who can ask, 'Why do you do this?' "
18:11 saw him? Why didn't you strike him to the ground right there?
19:41 [19:42] saying to him, "Why did our brothers, the men of Judah,
19:43 [19:44] than you have. So why do you treat us with contempt?
24:21 Araunah said, "Why has my lord the king come to his servant?"
1Ki 1: 6 interfered with him by asking, "Why do you behave as you do?"
1:13 he will sit on my throne"? Why then has Adonijah become king?'
1:41 Joab asked, "What's the meaning of all the noise in the city?"
2:43 Why then did you not keep your oath to the LORD and obey the
2Ki 4:23 "Why go to him today?" he asked. "It's not the New Moon
8:12 "Why is my lord weeping?" asked Hazael. "Because I know the
9:11 Why did this madman come to you?" "You know the man
12: 7 [12:8] "Why aren't you repairing the damage done to the temple?
2Ch 24: 6 "Why haven't you required the Levites to bring in from Judah
Ne 2: 2 asked me, "Why does your face look so sad when you are not ill?
2: 3 Why should my face not look sad when the city where my fathers
13:11 and asked them, "Why is the house of God neglected?"
13:21 I warned them and said, "Why do you spend the night by the wall?
Est 3: 3 gate asked Mordecai, "Why do you disobey the king's command?"
Job 3:12 Why were there knees to receive me and breasts that I might be
18: 3 Why are we regarded as cattle and considered stupid in your sight?
21: 4 "Is my complaint directed to man? Why should I not be impatient?
21: 7 Why do the wicked live on, growing old and increasing in power?
24: 1 "Why does the Almighty not set times for judgment? Why must
33:13 Why do you complain to him that he answers none of man's
Isa 5: 4 When I looked for good grapes, why did it yield only bad?
50: 2 When I came, why was there no one? When I called, why was
63: 2 Why are your garments red, like those of one treading the
Jer 2:14 a servant, a slave by birth? Why then has he become plunder?
2:31 Why do my people say, 'We are free to roam; we will come to you
8: 5 Why then have these people turned away? Why does Jerusalem
8:19 "Why have they provoked me to anger with their images,
8:22 Why then is there no healing for the wound of my people?
12: 1 Why does the way of the wicked prosper? Why do all the faithless
13:22 And if you ask yourself, "Why has this happened to me?"—
14:19 Why have you afflicted us so that we cannot be healed? We hoped
22:28 Why will he and his children be hurled out, cast into a land they do
26: 9 Why do you prophesy in the LORD's name that this house will
30: 6 why do I see every strong man with his hands on his stomach like
32: 3 imprisoned him there, saying, "Why do you prophesy as you do?
36:29 "Why did you write on it that the king of Babylon would certainly
46: 5 What do I see? They are terrified, they are retreating, their
46:15 Why will your warriors be laid low? They cannot stand,
49: 1 Has she no heirs? Why then has Molech taken possession of Gad?
Eze 18:19 "Yet you ask, 'Why does the son not share the guilt of his father?'
Mal 2:10 Why do we profane the covenant of our fathers by breaking faith

4509 מְדוּרָה mᵉdûrâ, n.f. [2] [√ 1883]

fire pit [1], wood [1]

Isa 30:33 Its **fire pit** has been made deep and wide, with an abundance of
Eze 24: 9 " 'Woe to the city of bloodshed! I, too, will pile the **wood** high.

4510 מִדְחֶה midḥeh, n.m. [1] [√ 1890]

ruin [1]

Pr 26:28 tongue hates those it hurts, and a flattering mouth works **ruin**.

4511 מַדְחֵפָה madḥēpâ, n.f. [1] [√ 1894]

hunt down [+4200+7421] [1]

Ps 140:11 [140:12] *may* disaster **hunt down** [+4200+7421] men of

4512 מָדַי māday, n.pr.g. & loc. [16] [→ 4513; Ar 10404, 10405]

Media [7], Medes [5], Madai [2], Mede [1], Median [1]

Ge 10: 2 Gomer, Magog, **Madai**, Javan, Tubal, Meshech and Tiras.
2Ki 17: 6 in Gozan on the Habor River and in the towns of the **Medes**.
18:11 in Halah, in Gozan on the Habor River and in towns of the **Medes**.
1Ch 1: 5 Gomer, Magog, **Madai**, Javan, Tubal, Meshech and Tiras.
Est 1: 3 The military leaders of Persia and **Media**, the princes,
1:14 nobles of Persia and **Media** who had special access to the king
1:18 **Median** women of the nobility who have heard about the queen's
1:19 a royal decree and let it be written in the laws of Persia and **Media**,
10: 2 are they not written in the book of the annals of the kings of **Media**
Isa 13:17 See, I will stir up against them the **Medes**, who do not care for
21: 2 the looter takes loot. Elam, attack! **Media**, lay siege!
Jer 25:25 all the kings of Zimri, Elam and **Media**;
51:11 The LORD has stirred up the kings of the **Medes**, because his
51:28 the kings of the **Medes**, their governors and all their officials,
Da 8:20 The two-horned ram that you saw represents the kings of **Media**
9: 1 In the first year of Darius son of Xerxes (a **Mede** by descent),

4513 מָדִי mādî, a.g. [1] [√ 4512]

Mede [1]

Da 11: 1 in the first year of Darius the **Mede**, I took my stand to support

4514 מַדַּי madday, pp.+subst. Not used in NIV/BHS [√ 1896 + 4537 *or* 4946]

4515 מָדִין mādîn, n.m. [1 / 0] [√ 4506 *or* 4500]

2Sa 21:20 was a huge [BHS ***contentious***; NIV 4500] man with six fingers

4516 מִדִּין middîn, n.pr.loc. [1]

Middin [1]

Jos 15:61 In the desert: Beth Arabah, **Middin**, Secacah,

4517 מִדְיָן midyān[1], n.m. Not used in NIV/BHS [→ 4506, 4518, 4520; cf. 1906]

4518 ²מִדְיָן midyān[2], n.pr.m. & loc. [59] [→ 4520; cf. 1906, 4517]

Midian [32], Midianites [12], Midianite [8], *untranslated* [2], Midian [+824] [2], Midian's [2], them[s] [1]

Ge 25: 2 She bore him Zimran, Jokshan, Medan, **Midian**, Ishbak and Shuah.
25: 4 The sons of **Midian** were Ephah, Epher, Hanoch, Abida
36:35 son of Bedad, who defeated **Midian** in the country of Moab,
Ex 2:15 but Moses fled from Pharaoh and went to live in **Midian** [+824],
2:16 Now a priest of **Midian** had seven daughters, and they came to
3: 1 the priest of **Midian**, and he led the flock to the far side of the
4:19 Now the LORD had said to Moses in **Midian**, "Go back to Egypt,
18: 1 Now Jethro, the priest of **Midian** and father-in-law of Moses,
Nu 22: 4 The Moabites said to the elders of **Midian**, "This horde is going to
22: 7 The elders of Moab and **Midian** left, taking with them the fee for
25:15 was Cozbi daughter of Zur, a tribal chief of a **Midianite** family.
25:18 and their sister Cozbi, the daughter of a **Midianite** leader,
31: 3 "Arm some of your men to go to war against the **Midianites**
31: 3 the Midianites and to carry out the LORD's vengeance on **them**[s].
31: 7 They fought against **Midian**, as the LORD commanded Moses,
31: 8 Among their **[RPH]** victims were Evi, Rekem, Zur, Hur
31: 8 were Evi, Rekem, Zur, Hur and Reba—the five kings of **Midian**.
31: 9 The Israelites captured the **Midianite** women and children
Jos 13:21 Moses had defeated him and the **Midianite** chiefs, Evi, Rekem,
Jdg 6: 1 and for seven years he gave them into the hands of the **Midianites**.
6: 2 Because the power of **Midian** was so oppressive, the Israelites
6: 2 **[RPH]** the Israelites prepared shelters for themselves in mountain
6: 3 the **Midianites**, Amalekites and other eastern peoples invaded the
6: 6 **Midian** so impoverished the Israelites that they cried out to the
6: 7 When the Israelites cried to the LORD because of **Midian**,
6:11 was threshing wheat in a winepress to keep it from the **Midianites**.
6:13 the LORD has abandoned us and put us into the hand of **Midian**."
6:14 "Go in the strength you have and save Israel out of **Midian's** hand.
6:16 be with you, and you will strike down all the **Midianites** together."
6:33 Now all the **Midianites**, Amalekites and other eastern peoples
7: 1 The camp of **Midian** was north of them in the valley near the hill
7: 2 "You have too many men for me to deliver **Midian** into their
7: 7 lapped I will save you and give the **Midianites** into your hands.
7: 8 the others. Now the camp of **Midian** lay below him in the valley.
7:12 The **Midianites**, the Amalekites and all the other eastern peoples
7:13 "A round loaf of barley bread came tumbling into the **Midianite**
7:14 God has given the **Midianites** and the whole camp into his hands."
7:15 The LORD has given the **Midianite** camp into your hands."
7:23 all Manasseh were called out, and they pursued the **Midianites**.
7:24 "Come down against the **Midianites** and seize the waters of the
7:25 They also captured two of the **Midianite** leaders, Oreb and Zeeb.
7:25 They pursued the **Midianites** and brought the heads of Oreb
8: 1 Why didn't you call us when you went to fight **Midian**?" And they
8: 3 God gave Oreb and Zeeb, the **Midianite** leaders, into your hands.
8: 5 and I am still pursuing Zebah and Zalmunna, the kings of **Midian**."
8:12 Zebah and Zalmunna, the two kings of **Midian**, fled, but he
8:22 because you have saved us out of the hand of **Midian**."
8:26 the pendants and the purple garments worn by the kings of **Midian**
8:28 Thus **Midian** was subdued before the Israelites and did not raise its
9:17 for you, risked his life to rescue you from the hand of **Midian**
1Ki 11:18 They set out from **Midian** and went to Paran. Then taking men
1Ch 1:32 Zimran, Jokshan, Medan, **Midian**, Ishbak and Shuah. The sons of

1Ch 1:33 The sons of **Midian**: Ephah, Epher, Hanoch, Abida and Eldaah.
1:46 son of Bedad, who defeated **Midian** in the country of Moab,
Ps 83: 9 [83:10] Do to them as you did to **Midian**, as you did to Sisera
Isa 9: 4 [9:3] For as in the day of **Midian's** defeat, you have shattered the
10:26 with a whip, as when he struck down **Midian** at the rock of Oreb;
60: 6 camels will cover your land, young camels of **Midian** and Ephah.
Hab 3: 7 of Cushan in distress, the dwellings of **Midian** [+824] in anguish.

4519 מְדִינָה m*e*dînâ, n.f. [53] [√ 1906; Ar 10406]

provinces [20], province [10], each province [+2256+4519] [6], *untranslated* [5], provincial [5], every province [+2256+4519] [2], various provinces [+2256+4519] [2], district [1], parts [1], regions [1]

1Ki 20:14 'The young officers of the **provincial** commanders will do it.' "
20:15 So Ahab summoned the young officers of the **provincial**
20:17 The young officers of the **provincial** commanders went out first.
20:19 The young officers of the **provincial** commanders marched out of
Ezr 2: 1 Now these are the people of the **province** who came up from the
Ne 1: 3 and are back in the **province** are in great trouble and disgrace.
7: 6 These are the people of the **province** who came up from the
11: 3 These are the **provincial** leaders who settled in Jerusalem (now
Est 1: 1 the Xerxes who ruled over 127 **provinces** stretching from India to
1: 3 the princes, and the nobles of the **provinces** were present.
1:16 all the nobles and the peoples of all the **provinces** *of* King Xerxes.
1:22 He sent dispatches to all **parts** *of* the kingdom, to each province in
1:22 to **each province** [+2256+4519] in its own script and to each
1:22 to **each province** [+2256+4519] in its own script and to each
2: 3 Let the king appoint commissioners in every **province** *of* his realm
2:18 He proclaimed a holiday throughout the **provinces** and distributed
3: 8 scattered among the peoples in all the **provinces** *of* your kingdom
3:12 They wrote out in the script of **each province** [+2256+4519]
3:12 They wrote out in the script of **each province** [+2256+4519]
3:12 the governors of the **various provinces** [+2256+4519] and the
3:12 the governors of the **various provinces** [+2256+4519] and the
3:13 Dispatches were sent by couriers to all the king's **provinces** with
3:14 of the text of the edict was to be issued as law in every **province**
3:14 **[RPH]** and made known to the people of every nationality
4: 3 In every **province** to which the edict and order of the king came,
4: 3 In every province **[NIE]** to which the edict and order of the king
4:11 and the people of the royal **provinces** know that for any man
8: 5 devised and wrote to destroy the Jews in all the king's **provinces**.
8: 9 and nobles of the 127 **provinces** stretching from India to Cush.
8: 9 nobles of the 127 provinces **[RPH]** stretching from India to Cush.
8: 9 orders were written in the script of **each province** [+2256+4519]
8: 9 orders were written in the script of **each province** [+2256+4519]
8:11 or **province** that might attack them and their women and children;
8:12 The day appointed for the Jews to do this in all the **provinces** *of*
8:13 of the text of the edict was to be issued as law in every **province**
8:13 **[RPH]** and made known to the people of every nationality
8:17 In every **province** and in every city, wherever the edict of the king
8:17 In every province **[RPH]** and in every city, wherever the edict of
9: 2 The Jews assembled in their cities in all the **provinces** *of* King
9: 3 And all the nobles of the **provinces**, the satraps, the governors
9: 4 his reputation spread throughout the **provinces**, and he became
9:12 What have they done in all the rest of the king's **provinces**?
9:16 the remainder of the Jews who were in the king's **provinces** also
9:20 he sent letters to all the Jews throughout the **provinces** *of* King
9:28 and in **every province** [+2256+4519] and in every city.
9:28 and in **every province** [+2256+4519] and in every city.
9:30 Mordecai sent letters to all the Jews in the 127 **provinces** of the
Ecc 2: 8 and gold for myself, and the treasure of kings and **provinces**.
5: 8 [5:7] If you see the poor oppressed in a **district**, and justice
La 1: 1 She who was queen among the **provinces** has now become a slave.
Eze 19: 8 the nations came against him, those from **regions** round about.
Da 8: 2 In my vision I saw myself in the citadel of Susa in the **province** *of*
11:24 When the richest **provinces** feel secure, he will invade them

4520 מִדְיָנִי midyānî, a.g. [7 / 8] [√ 4518; cf. 1906, 4517]

Midianite [5], Midianites [3]

Ge 37:28 So when the **Midianite** merchants came by, his brothers pulled
37:36 the **Midianites** [BHS 4527] sold Joseph in Egypt to Potiphar,
Nu 10:29 Now Moses said to Hobab son of Reuel the **Midianite**,
25: 6 an Israelite man brought to his family a **Midianite** *woman* right
25:14 who was killed with the **Midianite** *woman* was Zimri son of Salu,
25:15 the name of the **Midianite** woman who was put to death was Cozbi
25:17 "Treat the **Midianites** as enemies and kill them,
31: 2 "Take vengeance on the **Midianites** for the Israelites. After that,

4521 מְדֹכָה m*e*dōkâ, n.f. [1] [√ 1870]

mortar [1]

Nu 11: 8 and then ground it in a handmill or crushed it in a **mortar**.

4522 מַדְמֵן madmēn, n.pr.loc. [1] [→ 4524, 4526]

Madmen [1]

Jer 48: 2 You too, O **Madmen**, will be silenced; the sword will pursue you.

4523 [1]מַדְמֵנָה madmēnâ[1], n.f. [1] [√ 1961]

manure [1]

Isa 25:10 be trampled under him as straw is trampled down in the **manure**.

4524 [2]מַדְמֵנָה madmēnâ[2], n.pr.loc. [1] [√ 4522]

Madmenah [1]

Isa 10:31 **Madmenah** is in flight; the people of Gebim take cover.

4525 [1]מַדְמַנָּה madmannâ[1], n.pr.m. [1]

Madmannah [1]

1Ch 2:49 She also gave birth to Shaaph the father of **Madmannah** and to

4526 [2]מַדְמַנָּה madmannâ[2], n.pr.loc. [1] [√ 4522]

Madmannah [1]

Jos 15:31 Ziklag, **Madmannah**, Sansannah,

4527 [1]מְדָן m*e*dān[1], n.pr.m. [3 / 2] [√ 1972]

Medan [2]

Ge 25: 2 She bore him Zimran, Jokshan, **Medan**, Midian, Ishbak and Shuah.
37:36 the Midianites [BHS *Medanites*; NIV 4520] sold Joseph
1Ch 1:32 Zimran, Jokshan, **Medan**, Midian, Ishbak and Shuah. The sons of

4528 [2]מְדָן m*e*dān[2], n.m. Not used in NIV/BHS [√ 1906]

4529 מַדָּע maddāʿ, n.m. [6] [√ 3359; Ar 10430]

knowledge [4], quick to understand [+1067] [1], thoughts [1]

2Ch 1:10 Give me wisdom and **knowledge**, that I may lead this people,
1:11 **knowledge** to govern my people over whom I have made you king,
1:12 therefore wisdom and **knowledge** will be given you. And I will
Ecc 10:20 Do not revile the king even in your **thoughts**, or curse the rich in
Da 1: 4 well informed, **quick to understand** [+1067], and qualified to
1:17 To these four young men God gave **knowledge** and understanding

4530 מֹדַע mōdāʿ, n.m. [2] [→ 4531; cf. 3359]

kinsman [1], relative [1]

Ru 2: 1 Now Naomi had a **relative** [K 3359] on her husband's side,
Pr 7: 4 "You are my sister," and call understanding your **kinsman**;

4531 מֹדַעַת mōdaʿat, n.f. [1] [√ 4530; cf. 3359]

kinsman [1]

Ru 3: 2 with whose servant girls you have been, a **kinsman** *of* ours?

4532 מַדְקֵרָה madqērâ, n.f. [1] [√ 1991]

pierce [1]

Pr 12:18 Reckless words **pierce** like a sword, but the tongue of the wise

4533 מַדְרֵגָה madrēgâ, n.f. [2]

cliffs [1], mountainside [1]

SS 2:14 in the hiding places on the **mountainside**, show me your face,
Eze 38:20 the **cliffs** will crumble and every wall will fall to the ground.

4534 מִדְרָךְ midrāk, n.[m.]. [1] [√ 2005]

put on [1]

Dt 2: 5 give you any of their land, not even enough to **put** your foot **on**.

4535 מִדְרָשׁ midrāš, n.[m.]. [2] [√ 2011]

annotations [2]

2Ch 13:22 what he said, are written in the **annotations** *of* the prophet Iddo.
24:27 of God are written in the **annotations** *on* the book of the kings.

4536 מְדֻשָׁה m*e*dušâ, n.f. [1] [√ 1889]

crushed [1]

Isa 21:10 O my people, **crushed** *on* the threshing floor, I tell you what I have

4537 מָה **mâ**, p.inter. & indef. [752] [→ 1174, 4015, 4017, 4342, 4548, 4643, 4943, 5505, 8975; cf. 4768, 4942; Ar 10394, 10408] See Select Index

what [343], why [+4200] [165], how [69], why [33], how [+928] [16], why [+6584] [13], *untranslated* [12], whatever [7], what [+4200] [5], how long [+6330] [4], what mean [4], who [4], how [+3869] [3], O [3], secret [+928] [3], what are you doing [+3870+4200] [3], what's the matter [3], by what means [+928] [2], come what may [+2118] [2], how many [+3869+6330] [2], how often [+3869] [2], not [2], what [+928] [2], anything [1], because [+3954+4200] [1], but why [+4200] [1], enough [+1896+4200] [1], ever so [1], future [+2118+8611] [1], how [+2296] [1], how [+686+928] [1], how find things [1], how long [+3869] [1], how long must wait [+3427+3869] [1], how many [+3869] [1], how many more [+3869] [1], how much [1], if [+196] [1], life will not be worth living [+2644+4200] [1], not[s] [1], nothing [+1172] [1], of what use [+2296+4200] [1], of what use [+4200] [1], so many [+3869] [1], speech [+1819] [1], that [1], this is how [1], what [+6584] [1], what about [1], what do I care about [+2296+3276+4200+4200] [1], what do you mean [+4013+4200] [1], what is doing [+4200] [1], what is the matter [+3871+4200] [1], what is the meaning [+2179] [1], what is the meaning of [1], what is the meaning [1], what is troubling [1], what is wrong [1], what kind [1], what like [1], what more [+3954] [1], what right have you [+3870+4200] [1], what's [1], whatever [+1821] [1], when [+6330] [1], where [1], whether [1], which [1], why [+3610] [1], why [+4200+8611] [1], why [+561+4027+4200] [1], why [+928] [1], why [+9393] [1]

4538 מָהַהּ **māhah**, v. [8]

wait [2], delay [1], delayed [1], have time [+3523] [1], hesitated [1], linger [1], waited [1]

Ge 19:16 [F] When *he* **hesitated**, the men grasped his hand and the hands
43:10 [F] As it is, if *we had* not **delayed**, we could have gone
Ex 12:39 [F] *did* not **have time** [+3523] to prepare food for themselves.
Jdg 3:26 [F] While they **waited**, Ehud got away. He passed by the idols
19: 8 [F] the girl's father said, "Refresh yourself. **Wait** till afternoon!"
2Sa 15:28 [F] I *will* **wait** at the fords in the desert until word comes from
Ps 119:60 [F] I will hasten and not **delay** to obey your commands.
Hab 2: 3 [F] Though *it* **linger**, wait for it; it will certainly come and will

4539 מְהוּמָה **mᵉhûmâ**, n.f. [12] [√ 2101]

panic [4], turmoil [3], confusion [2], throwing into confusion [+2169] [1], tumult [1], unrest [1]

Dt 7:23 **throwing** them **into** great **confusion** [+2169] until they are
28:20 **confusion** and rebuke in everything you put your hand to,
1Sa 5: 9 LORD's hand was against that city, throwing it into a great **panic**.
5:11 For death had filled the city with **panic**; God's hand was very
14:20 They found the Philistines in total **confusion**, striking each other
2Ch 15: 5 for all the inhabitants of the lands were in great **turmoil**.
Pr 15:16 a little with the fear of the LORD than great wealth with **turmoil**.
Isa 22: 5 has a day of **tumult** and trampling and terror in the Valley of
Eze 7: 7 the day is near; there is **panic**, not joy, upon the mountains.
22: 5 who are far away will mock you, O infamous city, full of **turmoil**.
Am 3: 9 see the great **unrest** within her and the oppression among her
Zec 14:13 On that day men will be stricken by the LORD with great **panic**.

4540 מְהוּמָן **mᵉhûmān**, n.pr.m. [1]

Mehuman [1]

Est 1:10 **Mehuman**, Biztha, Harbona, Bigtha, Abagtha, Zethar and Carcas—

4541 מְהֵיטַבְאֵל **mᵉhêṭab'ēl**, n.pr.m. & f. [3] [√ 3512 + 446]

Mehetabel [3]

Ge 36:39 and his wife's name was **Mehetabel** daughter of Matred,
1Ch 1:50 and his wife's name was **Mehetabel** daughter of Matred,
Ne 6:10 of Delaiah, the son of **Mehetabel**, who was shut in at his home.

4542 מָהִיר **māhîr**, a. [4] [√ 4554]

skilled [1], skillful [1], speeds [1], well versed [1]

Ezr 7: 6 He was a teacher **well versed** in the Law of Moses,
Ps 45: 1 [45:2] for the king; my tongue is the pen of a **skillful** writer.
Pr 22:29 Do you see a man **skilled** in his work? He will serve before kings;
Isa 16: 5 who in judging seeks justice and **speeds** the cause of righteousness.

4543 מָהַל **māhal**, v. [1] [→ 1197; cf. 4576]

diluted [1]

Isa 1:22 [B] has become dross, your choice wine *is* **diluted** with water.

4544 מַהֲלָךְ **mahᵃlāk**, n.m. [5] [√ 2143]

untranslated [1], journey [1], passageway [1], place [1], visit [1]

Ne 2: 6 asked me, "How long will your **journey** take, and when will you
Eze 42: 4 In front of the rooms was an inner **passageway** ten cubits wide
Jnh 3: 3 Nineveh was a very important city—a **visit** required three days.
3: 4 On the **[NIE]** first day, Jonah started into the city. He proclaimed:
Zec 3: 7 my courts, and I will give you a **place** among these standing here.

4545 מַהֲלָל **mahᵃlāl**, n.[m.]. [1] [→ 4546; cf. 2146]

praise [1]

Pr 27:21 the furnace for gold, but man is tested by the **praise** he *receives*.

4546 מַהֲלַלְאֵל **mahᵃlal'ēl**, n.pr.m. [7] [√ 4545 + 446]

Mahalalel [7]

Ge 5:12 Kenan had lived 70 years, he became the father of **Mahalalel**.
5:13 after he became the father of **Mahalalel**, Kenan lived 840 years
5:15 When **Mahalalel** had lived 65 years, he became the father of Jared.
5:16 **Mahalalel** lived 830 years and had other sons and daughters.
5:17 Altogether, **Mahalalel** lived 895 years, and then he died.
1Ch 1: 2 Kenan, **Mahalalel**, Jared,
Ne 11: 4 the son of Amariah, the son of Shephatiah, the son of **Mahalalel**,

4547 מַהֲלֻמוֹת **mahᵃlumôt**, n.f.pl. [2] [√ 2150]

beating [1], beatings [1]

Pr 18: 6 A fool's lips bring him strife, and his mouth invites a **beating**.
19:29 are prepared for mockers, and **beatings** for the backs of fools.

4548 מָהֵם **māhēm**, var. Not used in NIV/BHS [√ 4537 + 2157]

4549 מַהֲמֹרוֹת **mahᵃmōrôt**, n.f.[pl.]. [1]

miry pits [1]

Ps 140:10 [140:11] they be thrown into the fire, into **miry pits**, never to rise.

4550 מַהְפֵּכָה **mahpēkâ**, n.f. [6] [√ 2200]

overthrown [3], overthrew [2], destruction [1]

Dt 29:23 [29:22] It will be like the **destruction** *of* Sodom and Gomorrah,
Isa 1: 7 right before you, laid waste as when **overthrown** *by* strangers.
13:19 will be **overthrown** *by* God like Sodom and Gomorrah.
Jer 49:18 As Sodom and Gomorrah were **overthrown**, along with their
50:40 As God **overthrew** Sodom and Gomorrah along with their
Am 4:11 "I overthrew some of you as I **overthrew** Sodom and Gomorrah.

4551 מַהְפֶּכֶת **mahpeket**, n.f. [4] [√ 2200]

stocks [3], prison [+1074+2021] [1]

2Ch 16:10 he was so enraged that he put him in **prison** [+1074+2021].
Jer 20: 2 put in the **stocks** at the Upper Gate of Benjamin at the LORD's
20: 3 The next day, when Pashhur released him from the **stocks**,
29:26 you should put any madman who acts like a prophet into the **stocks**

4552 מְהוֹלָה **mᵉhôlâ**, n.pr.loc. Not used in NIV/BHS [→ 71]

4553 מְהֻקְצָעוֹת **mᵉhuqṣā'ôt**, n.[pl.] *or* v.ptcp. Not used in NIV/BHS [√ 7910]

4554 מָהַר **māhar[1]**, v. [82] [→ 4542, 4556, 4557, 4559, 4561]

quickly [26], hurried [9], quick [6], at once [4], hurry [4], bring at once [3], soon [3], swift [3], immediately [2], act at once [1], all at once [1], are swept away [1], come quickly [+4394] [1], come quickly [1], coming quickly [+4394] [1], darting [1], dash [1], do now [1], early [1], fearful [1], fluent [+1819+4200] [1], go at once [1], hasten [1], hastily [1], hasty [1], impetuous [1], lost no time [1], move quickly [1], rash [1], run [1], sudden [1]

Ge 18: 6 [D] So Abraham **hurried** into the tent to Sarah. "Quick," he said,
18: 6 [D] "**Quick**," he said, "get three seahs of fine flour and knead it
18: 7 [D] and gave it to a servant, *who* **hurried** to prepare it.
19:22 [D] flee there **quickly**, because I cannot do anything until you
24:18 [D] **quickly** lowered the jar to her hands and gave him a drink.
24:20 [D] So *she* **quickly** emptied her jar into the trough, ran back to
24:46 [D] "She **quickly** lowered her jar from her shoulder and said,
27:20 [D] asked his son, "How did you find it *so* **quickly**, my son?"
41:32 [D] has been firmly decided by God, and God will do it **soon**.
43:30 [D] Joseph **hurried** *out* and looked for a place to weep.
44:11 [D] Each of them **quickly** lowered his sack to the ground
45: 9 [D] Now **hurry** back to my father and say to him, 'This is what
45:13 [D] you have seen. And bring my father down here **quickly**."
Ex 2:18 [D] he asked them, "Why have you returned *so* **early** today?"
10:16 [D] Pharaoh **quickly** summoned Moses and Aaron and said,

Ex 12:33 [D] The Egyptians urged the people to **hurry** and leave the
32: 8 [D] *They have been* **quick** to turn away from what I commanded
34: 8 [D] Moses bowed to the ground **at once** and worshiped.
Dt 4:26 [D] earth as witnesses against you this day that you will **quickly**
7: 4 [D] anger will burn against you and will **quickly** destroy you.
7:22 [D] You will not be allowed to eliminate them **all at once**,
9: 3 [D] And you will drive them out and annihilate them **quickly**,
9:12 [D] the LORD told me, "Go down from here **at once**,
9:12 [D] They have turned away **quickly** from what I commanded
9:16 [D] You had turned aside **quickly** from the way that the LORD
28:20 [D] until you are destroyed and come to **sudden** ruin because of
Jos 2: 5 [D] Go after them **quickly**. You may catch up with them."
4:10 [D] just as Moses had directed Joshua. The people **hurried** over,
8:14 [D] all the men of the city **hurried** out early in the morning to
8:19 [D] entered the city and captured it and **quickly** set it on fire.
Jdg 2:17 [D] they **quickly** turned from the way in which their fathers had
2:23 [D] he did not drive them out **at once** by giving them into the
9:48 [D] to his shoulders. He ordered the men with him, "**Quick**!
13:10 [D] The woman **hurried** to tell her husband, "He's here!
1Sa 4:14 [D] is the meaning of this uproar?" The man **hurried** over to Eli,
9:12 [D] **Hurry** now; he has just come to our town today,
17:48 [D] David ran **quickly** toward the battle line to meet him.
23:27 [D] a messenger came to Saul, saying, "Come **quickly**! The
25:18 [D] Abigail **lost no time**. She took two hundred loaves of bread,
25:23 [D] *she* **quickly** got off her donkey and bowed down before
25:34 [D] from harming you, if you had not come **quickly** to meet me,
25:42 [D] Abigail **quickly** got on a donkey and, attended by her five
28:20 [D] **Immediately** Saul fell full length on the ground, filled with
28:24 [D] had a fattened calf at the house, which she butchered **at once**.
2Sa 15:14 [D] *We must* leave **immediately**, or he will move quickly to
15:14 [D] or *he will* **move quickly** to overtake us and bring ruin upon
19:16 [19:17] [D] **hurried** down with the men of Judah to meet King
1Ki 20:33 [D] took this as a good sign and *were* **quick** to pick up his word.
20:41 [D] the prophet **quickly** removed the headband from his eyes,
22: 9 [D] his officials and said, "**Bring** Micaiah son of Imlah **at once**."
2Ki 9:13 [D] *They* **hurried** and took their cloaks and spread them under
1Ch 12: 8 [12:9] [D] and they were as **swift** as gazelles in the mountains.
2Ch 18: 8 [D] his officials and said, "**Bring** Micaiah son of Imlah **at once**."
24: 5 [D] from all Israel, to repair the temple of your God. **Do it now**."
24: 5 [D] of your God. Do it now." But the Levites *did* not **act at once**.
Est 5: 5 [D] "**Bring** Haman **at once**," the king said, "so that we may do
6:10 [D] "**Go at once**," the king commanded Haman. "Get the robe
Job 5:13 [C] their craftiness, and the schemes of the wily **are swept away**.
Ps 16: 4 [D] The sorrows of those will increase *who* **run** *after* other gods.
69:17 [69:18] [D] answer me **quickly**, for I am in trouble.
79: 8 [D] may your mercy come **quickly** to meet us, for we are in
102: 2 [102:3] [D] your ear to me; when I call, answer me **quickly**.
106:13 [D] they **soon** forgot what he had done and did not wait for his
143: 7 [D] Answer me **quickly**, O LORD; my spirit fails. Do not hide
Pr 1:16 [D] for their feet rush into sin, *they are* **swift** to shed blood.
6:18 [D] wicked schemes, feet *that are* **quick** to rush into evil,
7:23 [D] till an arrow pierces his liver, like a bird **darting** into a snare,
25: 8 [D] do not bring **hastily** to court, for what will you do in the end
Ecc 5: 2 [5:1] [D] *do* not *be* **hasty** in your heart to utter anything before
Isa 5:19 [D] to those who say, "*Let* God **hurry**, let him hasten his work
32: 4 [C] The mind of the **rash** will know and understand,
32: 4 [D] the stammering tongue *will be* **fluent** [+1819+4200] and
35: 4 [C] say to *those with* **fearful** hearts, "Be strong, do not fear; your
49:17 [D] Your sons **hasten** back, and those who laid you waste depart
51:14 [D] The cowering prisoners will **soon** be set free; they will not
59: 7 [D] feet rush into sin; *they are* **swift** to shed innocent blood.
Jer 9:18 [9:17] [D] *Let them* **come quickly** and wail over us till our eyes
48:16 [D] of Moab is at hand; her calamity *will* **come quickly** [+4394].
Na 2: 5 [2:6] [D] *They* **dash** to the city wall; the protective shield is put
Hab 1: 6 [C] up the Babylonians, that ruthless and **impetuous** people,
Zep 1:14 [D] of the LORD is near—near and **coming quickly** [+4394].
Mal 3: 5 [D] I will be **quick** to testify against sorcerers, adulterers

4555 ²מָהַר ***māhar²***, v.den. [2] [√ 4558]

must pay bride-price [+4555] [2]

Ex 22:16 [22:15] [A] with her, *he* **must pay** the **bride-price** [+4555],
22:16 [22:15] [A] with her, *he* **must pay** the **bride-price** [+4555],

4556 ¹מָהִר ***mahēr¹***, a. Not used in NIV/BHS [√ 4554]

4557 ²מַהֵר ***mahēr²***, adv. Not used in NIV/BHS [√ 4554]

4558 מֹהַר ***mōhar***, n.m. [3] [→ 4555, 4560]

bride-price [1], price for bride [1], price for the bride [1]

Ge 34:12 Make the **price for the bride** and the gift I am to bring as great as
Ex 22:17 [22:16] her to him, he must still pay the **bride-price** *for* virgins.
1Sa 18:25 'The king wants no other **price for** *the* **bride** than a hundred

4559 מְהֵרָה ***mᵉhērâ***, n.f. [20] [√ 4554]

quickly [7], at once [2], soon [2], hurriedly [1], hurry [+2143] [1], hurry [1], immediately [1], quickly [+928] [1], speedily [1], swiftly [+6330] [1], swiftly [1], very soon [1]

Nu 16:46 [17:11] **hurry** [+2143] to the assembly to make atonement for
Dt 11:17 you will **soon** perish from the good land the LORD is giving you.
Jos 8:19 the men in the ambush rose **quickly** from their position and rushed
10: 6 Come up to us **quickly** and save us! Help us, because all the
23:16 and you will **quickly** perish from the good land he has given you."
Jdg 9:54 **Hurriedly** he called to his armor-bearer, "Draw your sword
1Sa 20:38 he shouted, "**Hurry**! Go quickly! Don't stop!" The boy picked up
2Sa 17:16 Now send a message **immediately** and tell David, 'Do not spend
17:18 So the two of them left **quickly** and went to the house of a man in
17:21 They said to him, "Set out and cross the river **at once**; Ahithophel
2Ki 1:11 "Man of God, this is what the king says, 'Come down **at once**!' "
Ps 31: 2 [31:3] Turn your ear to me, come **quickly** to my rescue; be my
37: 2 for like the grass they will **soon** wither, like green plants they will
147:15 He sends his command to the earth; his word runs **swiftly** [+6330].
Ecc 4:12 A cord of three strands is not **quickly** [+928] broken.
8:11 When the sentence for a crime is not **quickly** carried out, the hearts
Isa 5:26 at the ends of the earth. Here they come, **swiftly** and speedily!
58: 8 break forth like the dawn, and your healing will **quickly** appear;
Jer 27:16 '**Very soon** now the articles from the LORD's house will be
Joel 3: 4 [4:4] and **speedily** return on your own heads what you have done.

4560 מַהֲרַי ***mahᵃray***, n.pr.m. [3] [√ 4558]

Maharai [3]

2Sa 23:28 Zalmon the Ahohite, **Maharai** the Netophathite,
1Ch 11:30 **Maharai** the Netophathite, Heled son of Baanah the Netophathite,
27:13 for the tenth month, was **Maharai** the Netophathite, a Zerahite.

4561 מַהֵר שָׁלָל חָשׁ בַּז ***mahēr šālāl ḥāš baz***, n.pr.m. [2] [√ 4554 + 8965 + 2590 + 1020]

Maher-Shalal-Hash-Baz [2]

Isa 8: 1 and write on it with an ordinary pen: **Maher-Shalal-Hash-Baz**.
8: 3 And the LORD said to me, "Name him **Maher-Shalal-Hash-Baz**.

4562 מַהֲתַלָּה ***mahᵃtallâ***, n.f. [1] [√ 9438]

illusions [1]

Isa 30:10 visions of what is right! Tell us pleasant things, prophesy **illusions**.

4563 מוֹ ***mô***, n.?. Not used in NIV/BHS

4564 -מוֹ, -מוּ ***-mô, -mû***, p.suf. [117 / 118] [√ 2023] Not indexed

them [47], their [23], *untranslated* [11], their [+4200] [6], themselves [5], him [3], they [3], us [3], his [+4200] [2], it [2], the[s] [2], each other[s] [1], he [1], his people[s] [1], his [1], its [1], my enemies[s] [1], Shem[s] [1], those [1], water[s] [1], where[s] [+4200] [1], who [1]

4565 ¹מוֹאָב ***môʼāb¹***, n.pr.m. [2] [→ 4566, 4567, 7075]

Moab [2]

Ge 19:37 The older daughter had a son, and she named him **Moab**; he is the
36:35 Hadad son of Bedad, who defeated Midian in the country of **Moab**,

4566 ²מוֹאָב ***môʼāb²***, n.pr.m. & loc. [179] [√ 4565]

Moab [136], Moabites [12], Moab [+8441] [7], Moab's [7], Moabite [7], Moab [+824] [5], its[s] [1], Moabites [+1201] [1], Moabites [+408] [1], there[s] [+8441] [1], they[s] [1]

Ge 19:37 she named him Moab; he is the father of the **Moabites** of today.
Ex 15:15 will be terrified, the leaders of **Moab** will be seized with trembling,
Nu 21:11 in Iye Abarim, in the desert that faces **Moab** toward the sunrise.
21:13 The Arnon is the border of **Moab**, between Moab and the
21:13 Arnon is the border of Moab, between **Moab** and the Amorites.
21:15 that lead to the site of Ar and lie along the border of **Moab**."
21:20 from Bamoth to the valley in **Moab** [+8441] where the top of
21:26 who had fought against the former king of **Moab** and had taken
21:28 It consumed Ar of **Moab**, the citizens of Arnon's heights.
21:29 Woe to you, O **Moab**! You are destroyed, O people of Chemosh!
22: 1 the Israelites traveled to the plains of **Moab** and camped along the
22: 3 and **Moab** was terrified because there were so many people.
22: 3 Indeed, **Moab** was filled with dread because of the Israelites.
22: 4 The **Moabites** said to the elders of Midian, "This horde is going to
22: 4 So Balak son of Zippor, who was king of **Moab** at that time,
22: 7 The elders of **Moab** and Midian left, taking with them the fee for
22: 8 the LORD gives me." So the **Moabite** princes stayed with him.
22:10 "Balak son of Zippor, king of **Moab**, sent me this message:
22:14 So the **Moabite** princes returned to Balak and said,

Nu 22:21 saddled his donkey and went with the princes of **Moab**.
22:36 he went out to meet him at the **Moabite** town on the Arnon border,
23: 6 him standing beside his offering, with all the princes of **Moab**.
23: 7 me from Aram, the king of **Moab** from the eastern mountains.
23:17 found him standing beside his offering, with the princes of **Moab**.
24:17 He will crush the foreheads of **Moab**, the skulls of all the sons of
25: 1 the men began to indulge in sexual immorality with **Moabite**
26: 3 So on the plains of **Moab** by the Jordan across from Jericho,
26:63 Israelites on the plains of **Moab** by the Jordan across from Jericho.
31:12 and the Israelite assembly at their camp on the plains of **Moab**,
33:44 left Oboth and camped at Iye Abarim, on the border of **Moab**.
33:48 camped on the plains of **Moab** by the Jordan across from Jericho.
33:49 There on the plains of **Moab** they camped along the Jordan from
33:50 On the plains of **Moab** by the Jordan across from Jericho the
35: 1 On the plains of **Moab** by the Jordan across from Jericho,
36:13 Israelites on the plains of **Moab** by the Jordan across from Jericho.
Dt 1: 5 East of the Jordan in the territory of **Moab**, Moses began to
2: 8 and Ezion Geber, and traveled along the desert road of **Moab**.
2: 9 said to me, "Do not harass the **Moabites** or provoke them to war,
2:18 "Today you are to pass by the region of **Moab** at Ar.
29: 1 [28:69] Moses to make with the Israelites in **Moab** [+824],
32:49 "Go up into the Abarim Range to Mount Nebo in **Moab** [+824],
34: 1 Moses climbed Mount Nebo from the plains of **Moab** to the top of
34: 5 And Moses the servant of the LORD died there in **Moab** [+824],
34: 6 He buried him in **Moab** [+824], in the valley opposite Beth Peor,
34: 8 The Israelites grieved for Moses in the plains of **Moab** thirty days,
Jos 13:32 he was in the plains of **Moab** across the Jordan east of Jericho.
24: 9 When Balak son of Zippor, the king of **Moab**, prepared to fight
Jdg 3:12 because they did this evil the LORD gave Eglon king of **Moab**
3:14 The Israelites were subject to Eglon king of **Moab** for eighteen
3:15 The Israelites sent him with tribute to Eglon king of **Moab**.
3:17 He presented the tribute to Eglon king of **Moab**, who was a very
3:28 he ordered, "for the LORD has given **Moab**, your enemy,
3:28 taking possession of the fords of the Jordan that led to **Moab**,
3:29 that time they struck down about ten thousand **Moabites** [+408],
3:30 That day **Moab** was made subject to Israel, and the land had peace
10: 6 and the gods of Aram, the gods of Sidon, the gods of **Moab**,
11:15 Israel did not take the land of **Moab** or the land of the Ammonites.
11:17 They sent also to the king of **Moab**, and he refused. So Israel
11:18 traveled through the desert, skirted the lands of Edom and **Moab**,
11:18 and Moab, passed along the eastern side of the country of **Moab**,
11:18 They did not enter the territory of **Moab**, for the Arnon was its
11:18 did not enter the territory of Moab, for the Arnon was **its**[s] border.
11:25 Are you better than Balak son of Zippor, king of **Moab**? Did he
Ru 1: 1 and two sons, went to live for a while in the country of **Moab**.
1: 2 And they went to **Moab** [+8441] and lived there.
1: 6 When she heard in **Moab** [+8441] that the LORD had come to the
1: 6 her daughters-in-law prepared to return home from **there**[s] [+8441].
1:22 So Naomi returned from **Moab** [+8441] accompanied by Ruth the
2: 6 "She is the Moabitess who came back from **Moab** [+8441] with
4: 3 "Naomi, who has come back from **Moab** [+8441],
1Sa 12: 9 and into the hands of the Philistines and the king of **Moab**,
14:47 **Moab**, the Ammonites, Edom, the kings of Zobah, and the
22: 3 From there David went to Mizpah in **Moab** and said to the king of
22: 3 there David went to Mizpah in Moab and said to the king of **Moab**,
22: 4 So he left them with the king of **Moab**, and they stayed with him
2Sa 8: 2 David also defeated the **Moabites**. He made them lie down on the
8: 2 So the **Moabites** became subject to David and brought tribute.
8:12 Edom and **Moab**, the Ammonites and the Philistines, and Amalek.
23:20 great exploits. He struck down two of **Moab's** best men.
1Ki 11: 7 built a high place for Chemosh the detestable god of **Moab**,
11:33 Chemosh the god of the **Moabites**, and Molech the god of the
2Ki 1: 1 After Ahab's death, **Moab** rebelled against Israel.
3: 4 Now Mesha king of **Moab** raised sheep, and he had to supply the
3: 5 Ahab died, the king of **Moab** rebelled against the king of Israel.
3: 7 "The king of **Moab** has rebelled against me. Will you go with me
3: 7 Will you go with me to fight against **Moab**?" "I will go with you,"
3:10 called us three kings together only to hand us over to **Moab**?"
3:13 who called us three kings together to hand us over to **Moab**."
3:18 in the eyes of the LORD; he will also hand **Moab** over to you.
3:21 Now all the **Moabites** had heard that the kings had come to fight
3:22 To the **Moabites** across the way, the water looked red—like blood.
3:23 and slaughtered each other. Now to the plunder, **Moab**!"
3:24 when the **Moabites** came to the camp of Israel, the Israelites rose
3:24 And the Israelites invaded the land and slaughtered the **Moabites**.
3:26 When the king of **Moab** saw that the battle had gone against him,
13:20 Now **Moabite** raiders used to enter the country every spring.
23:13 for Chemosh the vile god of **Moab**, and for Molech the detestable
24: 2 **Moabite** and Ammonite raiders against him.
1Ch 1:46 Hadad son of Bedad, who defeated Midian in the country of **Moab**,
4:22 and Joash and Saraph, who ruled in **Moab** and Jashubi Lehem.
8: 8 Sons were born to Shaharaim in **Moab** [+8441] after he had
11:22 great exploits. He struck down two of **Moab's** best men.
18: 2 David also defeated the **Moabites**, and they became subject to him
18: 2 the Moabites, and **they**[s] became subject to him and brought tribute.
18:11 Edom and **Moab**, the Ammonites and the Philistines, and Amalek.
2Ch 20: 1 the **Moabites** [+1201] and Ammonites with some of the Meunites
20:10 "But now here are men from Ammon, **Moab** and Mount Seir,
20:22 of Ammon and **Moab** and Mount Seir who were invading Judah,
20:23 and **Moab** rose up against the men from Mount Seir to destroy
Ps 60: 8 [60:10] **Moab** is my washbasin, upon Edom I toss my sandal;
83: 6 [83:7] of Edom and the Ishmaelites, of **Moab** and the Hagrites,
108: 9 [108:10] **Moab** is my washbasin, upon Edom I toss my sandal;
Isa 11:14 They will lay hands on Edom and **Moab**, and the Ammonites will
15: 1 An oracle concerning **Moab**: Ar in Moab is ruined, destroyed in a
15: 1 Ar in **Moab** is ruined, destroyed in a night! Kir in Moab is ruined,
15: 1 destroyed in a night! Kir in **Moab** is ruined, destroyed in a night!
15: 2 to its high places to weep; **Moab** wails over Nebo and Medeba.
15: 4 Therefore the armed men of **Moab** cry out, and their hearts are
15: 5 My heart cries out over **Moab**; her fugitives flee as far as Zoar,
15: 8 Their outcry echoes along the border of **Moab**; their wailing
15: 9 a lion upon the fugitives of **Moab** and upon those who remain in
16: 2 from the nest, so are the women of **Moab** at the fords of the Arnon.
16: 4 Let the **Moabite** fugitives stay with you; be their shelter from the
16: 6 We have heard of **Moab's** pride—her overweening pride
16: 7 Therefore the **Moabites** wail, they wail together for Moab.
16: 7 Therefore the Moabites wail, they wail together for **Moab**.
16:11 My heart laments for **Moab** like a harp, my inmost being for Kir
16:12 When **Moab** appears at her high place, she only wears herself out;
16:13 This is the word the LORD has already spoken concerning **Moab**.
16:14 **Moab's** splendor and all her many people will be despised,
25:10 **Moab** will be trampled under him as straw is trampled down in the
Jer 9:26 [9:25] **Moab** and all who live in the desert in distant places.
25:21 Edom, **Moab** and Ammon;
27: 3 **Moab**, Ammon, Tyre and Sidon through the envoys who have
40:11 When all the Jews in **Moab**, Ammon, Edom and all the other
48: 1 Concerning **Moab**: This is what the LORD Almighty, the God of
48: 2 **Moab** will be praised no more; in Heshbon men will plot her
48: 4 **Moab** will be broken; her little ones will cry out.
48: 9 Put salt on **Moab**, for she will be laid waste; her towns will
48:11 "**Moab** has been at rest from youth, like wine left on its dregs,
48:13 **Moab** will be ashamed of Chemosh, as the house of Israel was
48:15 **Moab** will be destroyed and her towns invaded; her finest young
48:16 "The fall of **Moab** is at hand; her calamity will come quickly.
48:18 for he who destroys **Moab** will come up against you and ruin your
48:20 **Moab** is disgraced, for she is shattered. Wail and cry out!
48:20 and cry out! Announce by the Arnon that **Moab** is destroyed.
48:24 and Bozrah—to all the towns of **Moab** [+824], far and near.
48:25 **Moab's** horn is cut off; her arm is broken," declares the LORD.
48:26 Let **Moab** wallow in her vomit; let her be an object of ridicule.
48:28 your towns and dwell among the rocks, you who live in **Moab**.
48:29 "We have heard of **Moab's** pride—her overweening pride
48:31 Therefore I wail over **Moab**, for all Moab I cry out, I moan for the
48:31 Therefore I wail over Moab, for all **Moab** I cry out, I moan for the
48:33 and gladness are gone from the orchards and fields of **Moab**.
48:35 In **Moab** I will put an end to those who make offerings on the high
48:36 "So my heart laments for **Moab** like a flute; it laments like a flute
48:38 On all the roofs in **Moab** and in the public squares there is nothing
48:38 for I have broken **Moab** like a jar that no one wants,"
48:39 she is! How they wail! How **Moab** turns her back in shame!
48:39 **Moab** has become an object of ridicule, an object of horror to all
48:40 An eagle is swooping down, spreading its wings over **Moab**.
48:41 In that day the hearts of **Moab's** warriors will be like the heart of a
48:42 **Moab** will be destroyed as a nation because she defied the
48:43 Terror and pit and snare await you, O people of **Moab**,"
48:44 for I will bring upon **Moab** the year of her punishment,"
48:45 it burns the foreheads of **Moab**, the skulls of the noisy boasters.
48:46 Woe to you, O **Moab**! The people of Chemosh are destroyed;
48:47 "Yet I will restore the fortunes of **Moab** in days to come,"
48:47 to come," declares the LORD. Here ends the judgment on **Moab**.
Eze 25: 8 'Because **Moab** and Seir said, "Look, the house of Judah has
25: 9 therefore I will expose the flank of **Moab**, beginning at its frontier
25:11 I will inflict punishment on **Moab**. Then they will know that I am
Da 11:41 **Moab** and the leaders of Ammon will be delivered from his hand.
Am 2: 1 "For three sins of **Moab**, even for four, I will not turn back ⌊my
2: 2 I will send fire upon **Moab** that will consume the fortresses of
2: 2 **Moab** will go down in great tumult amid war cries and the blast of
Mic 6: 5 remember what Balak king of **Moab** counseled and what Balaam
Zep 2: 8 "I have heard the insults of **Moab** and the taunts of the
2: 9 the God of Israel, "surely **Moab** will become like Sodom,

4567 מוֹאָבִי *mô'ābî*, a.g. [16] [√ 4565]

Moabitess [6], Moabite [5], Moabites [4], Moab [1]

Dt 2:11 were considered Rephaites, but the **Moabites** called them Emites.
2:29 who live in Seir, and the **Moabites**, who live in Ar, did for us—
23: 3 [23:4] No Ammonite or **Moabite** or any of his descendants may
Ru 1: 4 They married **Moabite** *women*, one named Orpah and the other

Ru 1:22 Naomi returned from Moab accompanied by Ruth the **Moabitess**,
2: 2 And Ruth the **Moabitess** said to Naomi, "Let me go to the fields
2: 6 "She is the **Moabitess** who came back from Moab with Naomi.
2:21 Ruth the **Moabitess** said, "He even said to me, 'Stay with my
4: 5 day you buy the land from Naomi and from Ruth the **Moabitess**,
4:10 I have also acquired Ruth the **Moabitess**, Mahlon's widow,
1Ki 11: 1 **Moabites**, Ammonites, Edomites, Sidonians and Hittites.
1Ch 11:46 Jeribai and Joshaviah the sons of Elnaam, Ithmah the **Moabite**,
2Ch 24:26 and Jehozabad, son of Shimrith a **Moabite** *woman*.
Ezr 9: 1 Jebusites, Ammonites, **Moabites**, Egyptians and Amorites.
Ne 13: 1 or **Moabite** should ever be admitted into the assembly of God,
13:23 Judah who had married women from Ashdod, Ammon and **Moab**.

4568 מוֹאל *mô'l*, subst. & pp. Not used in NIV/BHS [cf. 4578]

4569 מוֹבָא *môbā'*, n.[m.]. [2] [√ 4427; cf. 995]

entrances [1], movements [+2256+4604] [1]

2Sa 3:25 came to deceive you and observe your **movements** [+2256+4604]
Eze 43:11 its arrangement, its exits and **entrances**—its whole design

4570 מוּג *mûg*, v. [17]

melt away [3], melting in fear [2], melts [2], collapses [1], disheartened [1], flow [1], made waste away [1], melt [1], melted away [1], melting away [+2143+2256] [1], quake [1], soften [1], toss about [1]

Ex 15:15 [C] seized with trembling, the people of Canaan *will* **melt away**;
Jos 2: 9 [C] so that all who live in this country *are* **melting in fear**
2:24 [C] our hands; all the people *are* **melting in fear** because of us."
1Sa 14:16 [C] saw the army **melting** [+2143+2256] **away** in all directions.
Job 30:22 [D] drive me before the wind; *you* **toss** me **about** in the storm.
Ps 46: 6 [46:7] [A] kingdoms fall; he lifts his voice, the earth **melts**.
65:10 [65:11] [D] *you* **soften** it with showers and bless its crops.
75: 3 [75:4] [C] *When* the earth and all its people **quake**, it is I who
107:26 [F] down to the depths; in their peril their courage **melted away**.
Isa 14:31 [C] Wail, O gate! Howl, O city! **Melt away**, all you Philistines!
64: 7 [64:6] [A] and **made** us **waste away** because of our sins.
Jer 49:23 [C] *They are* **disheartened**, troubled like the restless sea.
Eze 21:15 [21:20] [A] So that hearts *may* **melt** and the fallen be many,
Am 9: 5 [A] the LORD Almighty, he who touches the earth and *it* **melts**,
9:13 [F] wine will drip from the mountains and **flow** *from* all the hills.
Na 1: 5 [F] The mountains quake before him and the hills **melt away**.
2: 6 [2:7] [C] river gates are thrown open and the palace **collapses**.

4571 מוֹד *môd*, v. [1]

shook [1]

Hab 3: 6 [D] He stood, and **shook** the earth; he looked, and made the

4572 מוֹט¹ *môṭ¹*, v. [40] [→ 4573, 4574]

be shaken [8], fall [5], be moved [4], is thoroughly shaken [+4572] [2], removed [2], slip [2], slipping [2], topple [2], are shaken [1], be uprooted [+9247] [1], be uprooted [1], bring down [1], gives way [1], immovable [+1153] [1], let fall [1], quaking [1], shake [1], slipped [1], slips [1], staggering [1], unable to support [+3338] [1]

Lev 25:35 [A] and *is* **unable to support** [+3338] himself among you,
Dt 32:35 [A] In due time their foot *will* **slip**; their day of disaster is near
1Ch 16:30 [C] The world is firmly established; *it* cannot **be moved**.
Job 41:23 [41:15] [C] they are firm and **immovable** [+1153].
Ps 10: 6 [C] He says to himself, "Nothing *will* **shake** *me*; I'll always be
13: 4 [13:5] [C] overcome him," and my foes will rejoice when *I* **fall**.
15: 5 [C] the innocent. He who does these things *will* never **be shaken**.
16: 8 [C] Because he is at my right hand, *I will* not **be shaken**.
17: 5 [C] My steps have held to your paths; my feet *have* not **slipped**.
21: 7 [21:8] [C] love of the Most High *he will* not **be shaken**.
30: 6 [30:7] [C] When I felt secure, I said, "*I will* never **be shaken**."
38:16 [38:17] [A] or exalt themselves over me when my foot **slips**."
46: 2 [46:3] [A] and the mountains **fall** into the heart of the sea,
46: 5 [46:6] [C] God is within her, *she will* not **fall**; God will help her
46: 6 [46:7] [A] Nations are in uproar, kingdoms **fall**; he lifts his
55: 3 [55:4] [G] for *they* **bring down** suffering upon me and revile
55:22 [55:23] [A] will sustain you; he will never let the righteous **fall**.
60: 2 [60:4] [A] and torn it open; mend its fractures, for *it is* **quaking**.
62: 2 [62:3] [C] he is my fortress, *I will* never **be shaken**.
62: 6 [62:7] [C] my salvation; he is my fortress, *I will* not **be shaken**.
66: 9 [A] he has preserved our lives and kept our feet from **slipping**.
82: 5 [C] in darkness; all the foundations of the earth **are shaken**.
93: 1 [C] The world is firmly established; *it* cannot **be moved**.
94:18 [A] When I said, "My foot *is* **slipping**," your love, O LORD,
96:10 [C] The world is firmly established, *it* cannot **be moved**; he will
104: 5 [C] He set the earth on its foundations; *it can* never **be moved**.
112: 6 [C] Surely *he will* never **be shaken**; a righteous man will be
121: 3 [A] He will not let your foot **slip**—he who watches over you will
125: 1 [C] Mount Zion, *which* cannot **be shaken** but endures forever.
140:10 [140:11] [G] **Let** burning coals **fall** upon them; may they be
Pr 10:30 [C] The righteous *will* never **be uprooted**, but the wicked will
12: 3 [C] but the righteous cannot **be uprooted** [+9247].
24:11 [A] away to death; hold back *those* **staggering** toward slaughter.
25:26 [A] or a polluted well is a righteous man *who* **gives way** to the
Isa 24:19 [F] is split asunder, the earth **is thoroughly shaken** [+4572].
24:19 [A] is split asunder, the earth **is thoroughly shaken** [+4572].
40:20 [C] for a skilled craftsman to set up an idol *that will* not **topple**.
41: 7 [C] "It is good." He nails down the idol so *it will* not **topple**.
54:10 [A] Though the mountains be shaken and the hills *be* **removed**,
54:10 [A] will not be shaken nor my covenant of peace *be* **removed**,"

4573 מוֹט² *môṭ²*, n.[m.]. [4] [√ 4572]

carrying frame [2], pole [1], yoke [1]

Nu 4:10 in a covering of hides of sea cows and put it on a **carrying frame**.
4:12 that with hides of sea cows and put them on a **carrying frame**.
13:23 Two of them carried it on a **pole** between them, along with some
Na 1:13 Now I will break their **yoke** from your neck and tear your shackles

4574 מוֹטָה *môṭâ*, n.f. [12] [√ 4572]

yoke [8], bars [2], crossbars [1], poles [1]

Lev 26:13 I broke the **bars** *of* your yoke and enabled you to walk with heads
1Ch 15:15 the Levites carried the ark of God with the **poles** on their
Isa 58: 6 to loose the chains of injustice and untie the cords of the **yoke**,
58: 6 cords of the yoke, to set the oppressed free and break every **yoke**?
58: 9 "If you do away with the **yoke** of oppression, with the pointing
Jer 27: 2 "Make a yoke out of straps and **crossbars** and put it on your neck.
28:10 the prophet Hananiah took the **yoke** off the neck of the prophet
28:12 Shortly after the prophet Hananiah had broken the **yoke** off the
28:13 You have broken a wooden **yoke**, but in its place you will get a
28:13 broken a wooden yoke, but in its place you will get a **yoke** *of* iron.
Eze 30:18 Dark will be the day at Tahpanhes when I break the **yoke** *of* Egypt;
34:27 when I break the **bars** *of* their yoke and rescue them from the

4575 מוּךְ *mûk*, v. [5] [cf. 4812]

poor [4], poor to pay [1]

Lev 25:25 [A] " 'If one of your countrymen *becomes* **poor** and sells some
25:35 [A] " 'If one of your countrymen *becomes* **poor** and is unable to
25:39 [A] " 'If one of your countrymen *becomes* **poor** among you
25:47 [A] one of your countrymen *becomes* **poor** and sells himself to
27: 8 [A] If anyone making the vow *is* too **poor to pay** the specified

4576 מוּל¹ *mûl¹*, v. [31] [→ 4581; cf. 4543, 4909]

circumcised [7], be circumcised [4], been circumcised [2], must be circumcised [+4576] [2], was circumcised [2], *untranslated* [1], are[s] [1], be circumcised [+1414+6889] [1], been circumcised [+906+6889] [1], circumcise [+906+6889] [1], circumcise yourselves [1], circumcise [1], circumcised [+906+1414+6889] [1], circumcising [1], did[s] so [1], had[s] [1], undergo circumcision [+906+1414+6889] [1], was circumcised [+1414+6889] [1], were circumcised [1]

Ge 17:10 [C] are to keep: Every male among you *shall* **be circumcised**.
17:11 [C] You *are to* **undergo circumcision** [+906+1414+6889], and it
17:12 [C] male among you who is eight days old *must* **be circumcised**,
17:13 [C] with your money, *they* **must be circumcised** [+4576].
17:13 [C] with your money, *they* **must be circumcised** [+4576].
17:14 [C] who *has* not **been circumcised** [+906+6889] *in* the flesh,
17:23 [A] and **circumcised** [+906+1414+6889] them, as God told him.
17:24 [C] ninety-nine years old when he **was circumcised** [+1414+6889],
17:25 [C] and his son Ishmael was thirteen; **[RPH]**
17:26 [C] his son Ishmael **were** *both* **circumcised** on that same day.
17:27 [C] or bought from a foreigner, **was circumcised** with him.
21: 4 [A] Abraham **circumcised** him, as God commanded him.
34:15 [C] that you become like us by **circumcising** all your males.
34:17 [C] if you will not agree to **be circumcised**, we'll take our sister
34:22 [C] people only on the condition that our males **be circumcised**,
34:22 [C] that our males be circumcised, as they *themselves* **are**[s].
34:24 [C] son Shechem, and every male in the city **was circumcised**.
Ex 12:44 [A] have bought may eat of it after *you have* **circumcised** him,
12:48 [C] *must have* all the males in his household **circumcised**;
Lev 12: 3 [C] On the eighth day the boy *is to* **be circumcised** [+1414+6889].
Dt 10:16 [A] **Circumcise** [+906+6889] your hearts, therefore, and do not be
30: 6 [A] The LORD your God *will* **circumcise** your hearts and the
Jos 5: 3 [A] and **circumcised** the Israelites at Gibeath Haaraloth.
5: 4 [A] Now this is why he **did**[s] so: All those who came out of
5: 5 [B] All the people that came out *had* **been circumcised**, but all
5: 5 [A] born in the desert during the journey from Egypt **had**[s] not.
5: 7 [A] in their place, and these were the ones Joshua **circumcised**.
5: 7 [A] because they *had* not *been* **circumcised** on the way.
5: 8 [C] after the whole nation *had* **been circumcised**, they remained
Jer 4: 4 [C] **Circumcise yourselves** to the LORD, circumcise your
9:25 [9:24] [B] "when I will punish all *who are* **circumcised** only in

4577 ²מוּל mûl², v. [3]

cut off [3]

Ps 118: 10 [G] but in the name of the LORD *I* **cut** them **off**.
118: 11 [G] on every side, but in the name of the LORD *I* **cut** them **off**.
118: 12 [G] as burning thorns; in the name of the LORD *I* **cut** them **off**.

4578 ³מוּל mûl³, subst. & pp. [36 / 35] [cf. 3283, 4568]

at [+448] [3], in front of [+448] [3], corner [2], in front of [+4946] [2], near [2], on [+448] [2], on [+4946] [2], opposite [2], toward [2], as far as [+448] [1], before [1], border [1], faced forward [+448+7156] [1], facing [1], from [+4946] [1], in front of [+448+7156] [1], in the front line [+448+7156] [1], in the front part [1], in the vicinity of [1], next to [+4946] [1], off [+4946] [1], opposite direction [1], to [+448] [1], to [1]

Ex 18: 19 You must be the people's representative **before** God and bring
26: 9 Fold the sixth curtain double **at** [+448] the front of the tent.
28: 25 attaching them to the shoulder pieces of the ephod **at** [+448] the
28: 27 attach them to the bottom of the shoulder pieces **on** [+4946] the
28: 37 attach it to the turban; it is to be **on** [+448] the front of the turban.
34: 3 the flocks and herds may graze **in front** [+448] **of** the mountain."
39: 18 attaching them to the shoulder pieces of the ephod **at** [+448] the
39: 20 attached them to the bottom of the shoulder pieces **on** [+4946] the
Lev 5: 8 He is to wring its head **from** [+4946] its neck, not severing it
8: 9 and set the gold plate, the sacred diadem, **on** [+448] the front of it,
Nu 8: 2 they are to light the area **in front of** [+448+7156] the
8: 3 so that they **faced forward on** [+448+7156] the lampstand,
22: 5 cover the face of the land and have settled **next** [+4946] **to** me.
Dt 1: 1 **opposite** Suph, between Paran and Tophel, Laban, Hazeroth
2: 19 When you come **to** the Ammonites, do not harass them or provoke
3: 29 So we stayed in the valley **near** Beth Peor.
4: 46 were in the valley **near** Beth Peor east of the Jordan, in the land of
11: 30 of those Canaanites living in the Arabah **in the vicinity of** Gilgal.
34: 6 He buried him in Moab, in the valley **opposite** Beth Peor,
Jos 8: 33 Half of the people stood **in front** [+448] **of** Mount Gerizim
8: 33 of Mount Gerizim and half of them **in front** [+448] **of** Mount Ebal,
9: 1 along the entire coast of the Great Sea **as far as** [+448] Lebanon
18: 18 slope of Beth Arabah [BHS ***in front of*** *the Arabah*; NIV 1098]
19: 46 Me Jarkon and Rakkon, with the area **facing** Joppa.
22: 11 the Israelites heard that they had built the altar on the **border** *of*
1Sa 14: 5 One cliff stood to the north **toward** Micmash, the other to the
14: 5 to the north toward Micmash, the other to the south **toward** Geba.
17: 30 He then turned away **to** [+448] someone else and brought up the
2Sa 5: 23 behind them and attack them **in front** [+4946] **of** the balsam trees.
11: 15 "Put Uriah **in the front line** [+448+7156] where the fighting is
1Ki 7: 5 they were **in the front part** in sets of three, facing each other.
7: 39 the Sea on the south side, at the southeast **corner** of the temple.
1Ch 14: 14 around them and attack them **in front** [+4946] **of** the balsam trees.
2Ch 4: 10 He placed the Sea on the south side, at the southeast **corner**.
Ne 12: 38 The second choir proceeded in the **opposite direction**. I followed
Mic 2: 8 You strip **off** [+4946] the rich robe from those who pass by without

4579 מוֹלָדָה môlādâ, n.pr.loc. [4]

Moladah [4]

Jos 15: 26 Amam, Shema, **Moladah**,
19: 2 It included: Beersheba (or Sheba), **Moladah**,
1Ch 4: 28 They lived in Beersheba, **Moladah**, Hazar Shual,
Ne 11: 26 in Jeshua, in **Moladah**, in Beth Pelet,

4580 מוֹלֶדֶת môledet, n.f. [22] [√ 3528]

native [4], relatives [3], *untranslated* [2], birth [2], family background [2], family [2], people [2], born in the same home [+1074] [1], born [1], children [1], homeland [+824] [1], natives [1]

Ge 11: 28 Haran died in Ur of the Chaldeans, in the land of his **birth**.
12: 1 your **people** and your father's household and go to the land I will
24: 4 will go to my country and my own **relatives** and get a wife for my
24: 7 my **native** land and who spoke to me and promised me on oath,
31: 3 "Go back to the land of your fathers and to your **relatives**,
31: 13 Now leave this land at once and go back to your **native** land.' "
32: 9 [32:10] said to me, 'Go back to your country and your **relatives**,
43: 7 "The man questioned us closely about ourselves and our **family**.
48: 6 Any **children** born to you after them will be yours; in the territory
Lev 18: 9 whether she was **born** [+1074] **in the same home** or elsewhere.
18: 9 whether she was born in the same home or **[RPH]** elsewhere.
18: 11 with the daughter of your father's wife, **born** *to* your father;
Nu 10: 30 will not go; I am going back to my own land and my own **people**."
Ru 2: 11 how you left your father and mother and your **homeland** [+824]
Est 2: 10 Esther had not revealed her nationality and **family background**,
2: 20 Esther had kept secret her **family background** and nationality just
8: 6 my people? How can I bear to see the destruction of my **family**?"
Jer 22: 10 because he will never return nor see his **native** land again.
46: 16 'Get up, let us go back to our own people and our **native** lands,
Eze 16: 3 Your ancestry and **birth** were in the land of the Canaanites;
16: 4 **[RPH]** On the day you were born your cord was not cut,
23: 15 them looked like Babylonian chariot officers, **natives** *of* Chaldea.

4581 מוּלָה mûlâ, n.f. [1] [√ 4576]

circumcision [1]

Ex 4: 26 time she said "bridegroom of blood," referring to **circumcision**.)

4582 מוֹלִיד môlîd, n.pr.m. [1] [√ 3528]

Molid [1]

1Ch 2: 29 wife was named Abihail, who bore him Ahban and **Molid**.

4583 מוּם mûm, n.m. [21] [cf. 4398]

defect [8], blemish [3], flaw [2], shame [2], abuse [1], defects [1], defiled [+928+1815] [1], injured [+928+5989] [1], injures [+928+5989] [1], physical defect [1]

Lev 21: 17 who has a **defect** may come near to offer the food of his God.
21: 18 No man who has any **defect** may come near: no man who is blind
21: 21 No descendant of Aaron the priest who has any **defect** is to come
21: 21 He has a **defect**; he must not come near to offer the food of his
21: 23 yet because of his **defect**, he must not go near the curtain
22: 20 Do not bring anything with a **defect**, because it will not be
22: 21 it must be without defect or **blemish** to be acceptable.
22: 25 on your behalf, because they are deformed and have **defects**.' "
24: 19 If anyone **injures** [+928+5989] his neighbor, whatever he has done
24: 20 As *he has* **injured** [+928+5989] the other, so he is to be injured.
Nu 19: 2 without defect or **blemish** and that has never been under a yoke.
Dt 15: 21 If an animal has a **defect**, is lame or blind, or has any serious flaw,
15: 21 If an animal has a defect, is lame or blind, or has any serious **flaw**,
17: 1 your God an ox or a sheep that has any **defect** or flaw in it,
32: 5 to their **shame** they are no longer his children, but a warped
2Sa 14: 25 top of his head to the sole of his foot there was no **blemish** in him.
Job 11: 15 then you will lift up your face without **shame**; you will stand firm
31: 7 led by my eyes, or if my hands *have been* **defiled** [+928+1815],
Pr 9: 7 invites insult; whoever rebukes a wicked man incurs **abuse**.
SS 4: 7 All beautiful you are, my darling; there is no **flaw** in you.
Da 1: 4 young men without any **physical defect**, [K 4398] handsome,

4584 מְמוּכָן mᵉwmukān, n.pr.m. [0] [√ 4925]

Est 1: 16 **[Memucan** [K; see Q 4925] replied in the presence of the king]

4585 מוּסָב mûsāb, n.m. Not used in NIV/BHS [√ 6015]

4586 מוּסָד mûsād, n.m. [2] [→ 4588; cf. 3569]

foundation laid [1], foundation [1]

2Ch 8: 16 from the day the **foundation** *of* the temple of the LORD was **laid**
Isa 28: 16 a tested stone, a precious cornerstone for a sure **foundation**;

4587 מוֹסָד môsād, n.m. [8] [→ 4589; cf. 3569]

foundations [8]

Dt 32: 22 and its harvests and set afire the **foundations** *of* the mountains.
Ps 18: 7 [18:8] and quaked, and the **foundations** *of* the mountains shook;
82: 5 about in darkness; all the **foundations** *of* the earth are shaken.
Pr 8: 29 and when he marked out the **foundations** *of* the earth.
Isa 24: 18 of the heavens are opened, the **foundations** *of* the earth shake.
58: 12 rebuild the ancient ruins and will raise up the age-old **foundations**;
Jer 31: 37 the **foundations** *of* the earth below be searched out will I reject all
Mic 6: 2 listen, you everlasting **foundations** *of* the earth.

4588 מוּסָדָה mûsādâ, n.f. [2 / 1] [√ 4586; cf. 3569]

foundation [1]

Isa 30: 32 with his punishing [BHS ***foundation***; NIV 4592] rod
Eze 41: 8 raised base all around it, forming the **foundation** *of* the side rooms.

4589 מוֹסָדָה môsādâ, n.m. [5] [√ 4587; cf. 3569]

foundations [3], foundation [1], founded [1]

2Sa 22: 8 earth trembled and quaked, the **foundations** *of* the heavens shook;
22: 16 the **foundations** *of* the earth laid bare at the rebuke of the LORD,
Ps 18: 15 [18:16] and the **foundations** *of* the earth laid bare at your rebuke,
Isa 40: 21 Have you not understood since the earth was **founded**?
Jer 51: 26 nor any stone for a **foundation**, for you will be desolate forever,"

4590 מוּסָךְ mûsāk, n.m. [1] [√ 6114; cf. 4788]

canopy [1]

2Ki 16: 18 He took away the Sabbath **canopy** [K 4788] that had been built at

4591 מוֹסֵר ***môsēr***, n.m. [3 / 5] [→ 4593, 5035; cf. 673]
chains [3], noose [1], shackles [1]

Job 12:18 He takes off the **shackles** [BHS 4592] *put on by* kings
Ps 116:16 the son of your maidservant; you have freed me from my **chains**.
Pr 7:22 to the slaughter, like a deer stepping into a **noose** [BHS 4592]
Isa 28:22 Now stop your mocking, or your **chains** will become heavier;
52:2 Free yourself from the **chains** *on* your neck, O captive Daughter of

4592 מוּסָר ***mûsār***, n.m. [51 / 50] [→ 5036; cf. 3579]
discipline [21], instruction [10], correction [6], disciplined [2], lesson [2], punishment [2], punished [1], punishing [1], rebuke [1], taught [1], teaches [1], warning [1], warnings [1]

Dt 11:2 who saw and experienced the **discipline** *of* the LORD your God:
Job 5:17 God corrects; so do not despise the **discipline** *of* the Almighty.
12:18 takes off the shackles [BHS ***discipline***; NIV 4591] *put on by* kings
20:3 I hear a **rebuke** *that* dishonors me, and my understanding inspires
33:16 he may speak in their ears and terrify them with **warnings**,
36:10 He makes them listen to **correction** and commands them to repent
Ps 50:17 You hate my **instruction** and cast my words behind you.
Pr 1:2 for attaining wisdom and **discipline**; for understanding words of
1:3 for acquiring a **disciplined** and prudent life, doing what is right
1:7 beginning of knowledge, but fools despise wisdom and **discipline**.
1:8 to your father's **instruction** and do not forsake your mother's
3:11 do not despise the LORD's **discipline** and do not resent his
4:1 Listen, my sons, to a father's **instruction**; pay attention and gain
4:13 Hold on to **instruction**, do not let it go; guard it well, for it is your
5:12 You will say, "How I hated **discipline**! How my heart spurned
5:23 He will die for lack of **discipline**, led astray by his own great folly.
6:23 is a light, and the corrections of **discipline** are the way to life,
7:22 like a deer stepping into a noose [BHS ***discipline***; NIV 4591]
8:10 Choose my **instruction** instead of silver, knowledge rather than
8:33 Listen to my **instruction** and be wise; do not ignore it.
10:17 He who heeds **discipline** shows the way to life, but whoever
12:1 Whoever loves **discipline** loves knowledge, but he who hates
13:1 A wise son heeds his father's **instruction**, but a mocker does not
13:18 He who ignores **discipline** comes to poverty and shame,
13:24 hates his son, but he who loves him is careful to **discipline** him.
15:5 A fool spurns his father's **discipline**, but whoever heeds correction
15:10 Stern **discipline** awaits him who leaves the path; he who hates
15:32 He who ignores **discipline** despises himself, but whoever heeds
15:33 The fear of the LORD **teaches** a man wisdom, and humility
16:22 of life to those who have it, but folly brings **punishment** *to* fools.
19:20 Listen to advice and accept **instruction**, and in the end you will be
19:27 Stop listening to **instruction**, my son, and you will stray from the
22:15 heart of a child, but the rod of **discipline** will drive it far from him.
23:12 Apply your heart to **instruction** and your ears to words of
23:13 Do not withhold **discipline** from a child; if you punish him with
23:23 and do not sell it; get wisdom, **discipline** and understanding.
24:32 my heart to what I observed and learned a **lesson** from what I saw:
Isa 26:16 when you **disciplined** them, they could barely whisper a prayer.
30:32 his **punishing** [BHS 4588] rod will be to the music of tambourines
53:5 the **punishment** *that brought* us peace was upon him, and by his
Jer 2:30 vain I punished your people; they did not respond to **correction**.
5:3 they felt no pain; you crushed them, but they refused **correction**.
7:28 has not obeyed the LORD its God or responded to **correction**.
10:8 and foolish; they are **taught** *by* worthless wooden idols.
17:23 were stiff-necked and would not listen or respond to **discipline**.
30:14 you as an enemy would and **punished** you as would the cruel,
32:33 and again, they would not listen or respond to **discipline**.
35:13 of Jerusalem, 'Will you not learn a **lesson** and obey my words?'
Eze 5:15 a **warning** and an object of horror to the nations around you when
Hos 5:2 The rebels are deep in slaughter. I will **discipline** all of them.
Zep 3:2 She obeys no one, she accepts no **correction**. She does not trust in
3:7 I said to the city, 'Surely you will fear me and accept **correction**!'

4593 מוֹסֵרָה¹ ***môsērâ¹***, n.m. [8] [√ 4591; cf. 673]
bonds [3], chains [2], ropes [1], shackles [1], yoke of straps [1]

Job 39:5 "Who let the wild donkey go free? Who untied his **ropes**?
Ps 2:3 "Let us break their **chains**," they say, "and throw off their fetters."
107:14 of darkness and the deepest gloom and broke away their **chains**.
Jer 2:20 "Long ago you broke off your yoke and tore off your **bonds**;
5:5 accord they too had broken off the yoke and torn off the **bonds**.
27:2 "Make a **yoke** *out* **of straps** and crossbars and put it on your neck.
30:8 'I will break the yoke off their necks and will tear off their **bonds**;
Na 1:13 break their yoke from your neck and tear your **shackles** away."

4594 מוֹסֵרָה² ***môsērâ²***, n.pr.loc. [1] [√ 673?; cf. 5035]
Moserah [1]

Dt 10:6 Israelites traveled from the wells of the Jaakanites to **Moserah**.

4595 מוֹעֵד ***mô'ēd***, n.m. [223] [√ 3585]
meeting [147], appointed feasts [24], appointed time [15], time [7], appointed [2], festivals [2], seasons [2], anniversary [1], appointed feast [1], appointed seasons [1], appointed times [1], army [1], arranged [+2118+4200] [1], assembly [1], assigned portion [1], certain place [1], council [1], designated [1], feast [1], feasts [1], festival offerings [1], in [+928] [1], occasion [1], opportunity [1], place of meeting [1], place where met [1], place where worshiped [1], ready [1], set time [+3427] [1], time set [1], times [1]

Ge 1:14 and let them serve as signs to mark **seasons** and days and years,
17:21 with Isaac, whom Sarah will bear to you by this **time** next year."
18:14 I will return to you at the **appointed** time next year and Sarah will
21:2 to Abraham in his old age, at the very **time** God had promised him.
Ex 9:5 The LORD set a **time** and said, "Tomorrow the LORD will do
13:10 You must keep this ordinance at the **appointed time** year after
23:15 Do this at the **appointed time** in the month of Abib, for in that
27:21 In the Tent of **Meeting**, outside the curtain that is in front of the
28:43 his sons must wear them whenever they enter the Tent of **Meeting**
29:4 bring Aaron and his sons to the entrance to the Tent of **Meeting**
29:10 "Bring the bull to the front of the Tent of **Meeting**, and Aaron
29:11 it in the LORD's presence at the entrance to the Tent of **Meeting**.
29:30 comes to the Tent of **Meeting** to minister in the Holy Place is to
29:32 At the entrance to the Tent of **Meeting**, Aaron and his sons are to
29:42 at the entrance to the Tent of **Meeting** before the LORD.
29:44 "So I will consecrate the Tent of **Meeting** and the altar and will
30:16 the Israelites and use it for the service of the Tent of **Meeting**.
30:18 Place it between the Tent of **Meeting** and the altar, and put water
30:20 Whenever they enter the Tent of **Meeting**, they shall wash with
30:26 use it to anoint the Tent of **Meeting**, the ark of the Testimony,
30:36 and place it in front of the Testimony in the Tent of **Meeting**,
31:7 the Tent of **Meeting**, the ark of the Testimony with the atonement
33:7 the camp some distance away, calling it the "tent of **meeting**."
33:7 Anyone inquiring of the LORD would go to the tent of **meeting**
34:18 Do this at the **appointed time** *in* the month of Abib, for in that
35:21 an offering to the LORD for the work on the Tent of **Meeting**,
38:8 of the women who served at the entrance to the Tent of **Meeting**.
38:30 used it to make the bases for the entrance to the Tent of **Meeting**,
39:32 the work on the tabernacle, the Tent of **Meeting**, was completed.
39:40 all the furnishings for the tabernacle, the Tent of **Meeting**;
40:2 "Set up the tabernacle, the Tent of **Meeting**, on the first day of the
40:6 in front of the entrance to the tabernacle, the Tent of **Meeting**;
40:7 place the basin between the Tent of **Meeting** and the altar
40:12 "Bring Aaron and his sons to the entrance to the Tent of **Meeting**
40:22 Moses placed the table in the Tent of **Meeting** on the north side of
40:24 He placed the lampstand in the Tent of **Meeting** opposite the table
40:26 Moses placed the gold altar in the Tent of **Meeting** in front of the
40:29 the Tent of **Meeting**, and offered on it burnt offerings and grain
40:30 He placed the basin between the Tent of **Meeting** and the altar
40:32 They washed whenever they entered the Tent of **Meeting**
40:34 the cloud covered the Tent of **Meeting**, and the glory of the
40:35 Moses could not enter the Tent of **Meeting** because the cloud had
Lev 1:1 called to Moses and spoke to him from the Tent of **Meeting**.
1:3 He must present it at the entrance to the Tent of **Meeting** so that it
1:5 against the altar on all sides at the entrance to the Tent of **Meeting**.
3:2 his offering and slaughter it at the entrance to the Tent of **Meeting**.
3:8 of his offering and slaughter it in front of the Tent of **Meeting**.
3:13 hand on its head and slaughter it in front of the Tent of **Meeting**.
4:4 He is to present the bull at the entrance to the Tent of **Meeting**
4:5 take some of the bull's blood and carry it into the Tent of **Meeting**.
4:7 fragrant incense that is before the LORD in the Tent of **Meeting**.
4:7 of the altar of burnt offering at the entrance to the Tent of **Meeting**.
4:14 bull as a sin offering and present it before the Tent of **Meeting**.
4:16 priest is to take some of the bull's blood into the Tent of **Meeting**.
4:18 horns of the altar that is before the LORD in the Tent of **Meeting**.
4:18 of the altar of burnt offering at the entrance to the Tent of **Meeting**.
6:16 [6:9] they are to eat it in the courtyard of the Tent of **Meeting**.
6:26 [6:19] in a holy place, in the courtyard of the Tent of **Meeting**.
6:30 [6:23] **Meeting** to make atonement in the Holy Place must not be
8:3 gather the entire assembly at the entrance to the Tent of **Meeting**."
8:4 and the assembly gathered at the entrance to the Tent of **Meeting**.
8:31 "Cook the meat at the entrance to the Tent of **Meeting** and eat it
8:33 Do not leave the entrance to the Tent of **Meeting** for seven days,
8:35 You must stay at the entrance to the Tent of **Meeting** day and night
9:5 the things Moses commanded to the front of the Tent of **Meeting**,
9:23 Moses and Aaron then went into the Tent of **Meeting**. When they
10:7 Do not leave the entrance to the Tent of **Meeting** or you will die,
10:9 other fermented drink whenever you go into the Tent of **Meeting**,
12:6 she is to bring to the priest at the entrance to the Tent of **Meeting** a
14:11 before the LORD at the entrance to the Tent of **Meeting**.
14:23 his cleansing to the priest at the entrance to the Tent of **Meeting**,
15:14 come before the LORD to the entrance to the Tent of **Meeting**
15:29 and bring them to the priest at the entrance to the Tent of **Meeting**.
16:7 them before the LORD at the entrance to the Tent of **Meeting**.

Lev 16: 16 He is to do the same for the Tent of **Meeting**, which is among them
16: 17 No one is to be in the Tent of **Meeting** from the time Aaron goes in
16: 20 the Tent of **Meeting** and the altar, he shall bring forward the live
16: 23 "Then Aaron is to go into the Tent of **Meeting** and take off the
16: 33 for the Tent of **Meeting** and the altar, and for the priests and all the
17: 4 instead of bringing it to the entrance to the Tent of **Meeting** to
17: 5 at the entrance to the Tent of **Meeting** and sacrifice them as
17: 6 the altar of the LORD at the entrance to the Tent of **Meeting**
17: 9 does not bring it to the entrance to the Tent of **Meeting** to sacrifice
19: 21 must bring a ram to the entrance to the Tent of **Meeting** for a guilt
23: 2 'These are my **appointed feasts**, the appointed feasts of the
23: 2 are my appointed feasts, the **appointed feasts** *of* the LORD,
23: 4 " 'These are the LORD's **appointed feasts**, the sacred assemblies
23: 4 sacred assemblies you are to proclaim at their **appointed times**:
23: 37 (" 'These are the LORD's **appointed feasts**, which you are to
23: 44 So Moses announced to the Israelites the **appointed feasts** *of* the
24: 3 Outside the curtain of the Testimony in the Tent of **Meeting**,
Nu 1: 1 The LORD spoke to Moses in the Tent of **Meeting** in the Desert
2: 2 "The Israelites are to camp around the Tent of **Meeting** some
2: 17 the Tent of **Meeting** and the camp of the Levites will set out in the
3: 7 for the whole community at the Tent of **Meeting** by doing the
3: 8 They are to take care of all the furnishings of the Tent of **Meeting**,
3: 25 At the Tent of **Meeting** the Gershonites were responsible for the
3: 25 its coverings, the curtain at the entrance to the Tent of **Meeting**,
3: 38 the tabernacle, toward the sunrise, in front of the Tent of **Meeting**.
4: 3 of age who come to serve in the work in the Tent of **Meeting**.
4: 4 "This is the work of the Kohathites in the Tent of **Meeting**:
4: 15 are to carry those things that are in the Tent of **Meeting**.
4: 23 years of age who come to serve in the work at the Tent of **Meeting**.
4: 25 the Tent of **Meeting**, its covering and the outer covering of hides
4: 25 of sea cows, the curtains for the entrance to the Tent of **Meeting**,
4: 28 This is the service of the Gershonite clans at the Tent of **Meeting**.
4: 30 years of age who come to serve in the work at the Tent of **Meeting**.
4: 31 This is their duty as they perform service at the Tent of **Meeting**:
4: 33 the Tent of **Meeting** under the direction of Ithamar son of Aaron,
4: 35 years of age who came to serve in the work in the Tent of **Meeting**,
4: 37 all those in the Kohathite clans who served in the Tent of **Meeting**.
4: 39 years of age who came to serve in the work at the Tent of **Meeting**,
4: 41 those in the Gershonite clans who served at the Tent of **Meeting**.
4: 43 years of age who came to serve in the work at the Tent of **Meeting**,
4: 47 came to do the work of serving and carrying the Tent of **Meeting**
6: 10 young pigeons to the priest at the entrance to the Tent of **Meeting**.
6: 13 He is to be brought to the entrance to the Tent of **Meeting**.
6: 18 " 'Then at the entrance to the Tent of **Meeting**, the Nazirite must
7: 5 that they may be used in the work at the Tent of **Meeting**.
7: 89 When Moses entered the Tent of **Meeting** to speak with the
8: 9 Bring the Levites to the front of the Tent of **Meeting** and assemble
8: 15 they are to come to do their work at the Tent of **Meeting**.
8: 19 his sons to do the work at the Tent of **Meeting** on behalf of the
8: 22 the Levites came to do their work at the Tent of **Meeting** under the
8: 24 or more shall come to take part in the work at the Tent of **Meeting**,
8: 26 their brothers in performing their duties at the Tent of **Meeting**,
9: 2 "Have the Israelites celebrate the Passover at the **appointed time**.
9: 3 Celebrate it at the **appointed time**, at twilight on the fourteenth
9: 7 offering with the other Israelites at the **appointed time**?"
9: 13 he did not present the LORD's offering at the **appointed time**.
10: 3 is to assemble before you at the entrance to the Tent of **Meeting**.
10: 10 of rejoicing—your **appointed feasts** and New Moon festivals—
11: 16 Have them come to the Tent of **Meeting**, that they may stand there
12: 4 Aaron and Miriam, "Come out to the Tent of **Meeting**, all three of
14: 10 the glory of the LORD appeared at the Tent of **Meeting** to all the
15: 3 for special vows or freewill offerings or **festival offerings**—
16: 2 leaders who had been appointed members of the **council**.
16: 18 with Moses and Aaron at the entrance to the Tent of **Meeting**.
16: 19 in opposition to them at the entrance to the Tent of **Meeting**,
16: 42 [17:7] and Aaron and turned toward the Tent of **Meeting**,
16: 43 [17:8] and Aaron went to the front of the Tent of **Meeting**,
16: 50 [17:15] returned to Moses at the entrance to the Tent of **Meeting**,
17: 4 [17:19] Place them in the Tent of **Meeting** in front of the
18: 4 join you and be responsible for the care of the Tent of **Meeting**—
18: 6 dedicated to the LORD to do the work at the Tent of **Meeting**.
18: 21 return for the work they do while serving at the Tent of **Meeting**.
18: 22 From now on the Israelites must not go near the Tent of **Meeting**,
18: 23 It is the Levites who are to do the work at the Tent of **Meeting**
18: 31 for it is your wages for your work at the Tent of **Meeting**.
19: 4 sprinkle it seven times toward the front of the Tent of **Meeting**.
20: 6 went from the assembly to the entrance to the Tent of **Meeting**
25: 6 while they were weeping at the entrance to the Tent of **Meeting**.
27: 2 the entrance to the Tent of **Meeting** and stood before Moses,
28: 2 'See that you present to me at the **appointed time** the food for my
29: 39 prepare these for the LORD at your **appointed feasts**:
31: 54 brought it into the Tent of **Meeting** as a memorial for the Israelites
Dt 16: 6 sun goes down, on the **anniversary** *of* your departure from Egypt.
31: 10 **in** [+928] the year for canceling debts, during the Feast of
31: 14 Call Joshua and present yourselves at the Tent of **Meeting**,
31: 14 and Joshua came and presented themselves at the Tent of **Meeting**.
Jos 8: 14 to meet Israel in battle at a **certain place** overlooking the Arabah.
18: 1 Israelites gathered at Shiloh and set up the Tent of **Meeting** there.
19: 51 the presence of the LORD at the entrance to the Tent of **Meeting**.
Jdg 20: 38 The men of Israel *had* **arranged** [+2118+4200] with the ambush
1Sa 2: 22 with the women who served at the entrance to the Tent of **Meeting**.
9: 24 Eat, because it was set aside for you for this **occasion**,
13: 8 He waited seven days, the **time set** by Samuel; but Samuel did not
13: 11 were scattering, and that you did not come at the **set time** [+3427],
20: 35 In the morning Jonathan went out to the field for his **meeting** *with*
2Sa 20: 5 he took longer than the **time** the king had set for him.
24: 15 on Israel from that morning until the end of the time **designated**,
1Ki 8: 4 and the Tent of **Meeting** and all the sacred furnishings in it.
2Ki 4: 16 "About this **time** next year," Elisha said, "you will hold a son in
4: 17 and the next year about that same **time** she gave birth to a son,
1Ch 6: 32 [6:17] with music before the tabernacle, the Tent of **Meeting**,
9: 21 was the gatekeeper at the entrance to the Tent of **Meeting**.
23: 31 on Sabbaths and at New Moon festivals and at **appointed feasts**.
23: 32 Levites carried out their responsibilities for the Tent of **Meeting**,
2Ch 1: 3 to the high place at Gibeon, for God's Tent of **Meeting** was there,
1: 6 up to the bronze altar before the LORD in the Tent of **Meeting**
1: 13 from the high place at Gibeon, from before the Tent of **Meeting**.
2: 4 [2:3] and at the **appointed feasts** *of* the LORD our God.
5: 5 they brought up the ark and the Tent of **Meeting** and all the sacred
8: 13 by Moses for Sabbaths, New Moons and the three annual **feasts**—
30: 22 For the seven days they ate their **assigned portion** and offered
31: 3 and **appointed feasts** as written in the Law of the LORD.
Ezr 3: 5 the sacrifices for all the **appointed** sacred **feasts** *of* the LORD,
Ne 10: 33 [10:34] the Sabbaths, New Moon festivals and **appointed feasts**;
Job 30: 23 bring me down to death, to the place **appointed** for all the living.
Ps 74: 4 Your foes roared in the **place where** you **met** with us; they set up
74: 8 They burned every **place where** God was **worshiped** in the land.
75: 2 [75:3] You say, "I choose the **appointed time**; it is I who judge
102: 13 [102:14] time to show favor to her; the **appointed time** has come.
104: 19 The moon marks off the **seasons**, and the sun knows when to go
Isa 1: 14 New Moon festivals and your **appointed feasts** my soul hates.
14: 13 I will sit enthroned on the mount of **assembly**, on the utmost
33: 20 Look upon Zion, the city of our **festivals**; your eyes will see
Jer 8: 7 Even the stork in the sky knows her **appointed seasons**,
46: 17 king of Egypt is only a loud noise; he has missed his **opportunity**.'
La 1: 4 roads to Zion mourn, for no one comes to her **appointed feasts**.
1: 15 he has summoned an **army** against me to crush my young men.
2: 6 his dwelling like a garden; he has destroyed his **place of meeting**.
2: 6 The LORD has made Zion forget her **appointed feasts** and her
2: 7 in the house of the LORD as on the day of an **appointed feast**.
2: 22 "As you summon to a **feast** day, so you summoned against me
Eze 36: 38 the flocks for offerings at Jerusalem during her **appointed feasts**.
44: 24 are to keep my laws and my decrees for all my **appointed feasts**,
45: 17 the Sabbaths—at all the **appointed feasts** *of* the house of Israel.
46: 9 of the land come before the LORD at the **appointed feasts**,
46: 11 " 'At the festivals and the **appointed feasts**, the grain offering is to
Da 8: 19 because the vision concerns the **appointed time** *of* the end.
11: 27 to no avail, because an end will still come at the **appointed time**.
11: 29 "At the **appointed time** he will invade the South again, but this
11: 35 the time of the end, for it will still come at the **appointed time**.
12: 7 lives forever, saying, "It will be for a **time**, times and half a time.
12: 7 lives forever, saying, "It will be for a time, **times** and half a time.
Hos 2: 9 [2:11] grain when it ripens, and my new wine when it is **ready**.
2: 11 [2:13] New Moons, her Sabbath days—all her **appointed feasts**.
9: 5 What will you do on the day of your **appointed feasts**, on the
12: 9 [12:10] in tents again, as in the days of your **appointed feasts**.
Hab 2: 3 For the revelation awaits an **appointed time**; it speaks of the end
Zep 3: 18 "The sorrows for the **appointed feasts** I will remove from you;
Zec 8: 19 become joyful and glad occasions and happy **festivals** for Judah.

4596 מוֹעָד ***mô'ād***, n.[m.]. [1] [√ 3585]

ranks [1]
Isa 14: 31 comes from the north, and there is not a straggler in its **ranks**.

4597 מוּעָדָה ***mû'ādâ***, n.f. [1] [√ 3585]

designated [1]
Jos 20: 9 killed someone accidentally could flee to these **designated** cities

4598 מוֹעַדְיָה ***mô'adyâ***, n.pr.m. [1] [√ 5048 + 3378; cf. 5049]

Moadiah's [1]
Ne 12: 17 of Abijah's, Zicri; of Miniamin's and of **Moadiah's**, Piltai;

4599 מוּעָף ***mû'āp***, n.[m.]. [1] [√ 6415]

gloom [1]
Isa 9: 1 [8:23] there will be no more **gloom** for those who were in distress.

4600 מוֹעֵצָה *mô'ēṣâ*, n.f. [7] [√ 3619]

counsel [1], devices [1], inclinations [1], intrigues [1], plans [1], schemes [1], traditions [1]

Ps 5:10 [5:11] them guilty, O God! Let their **intrigues** be their downfall.
81:12 [81:13] over to their stubborn hearts to follow their own **devices**.
Pr 1:31 the fruit of their ways and be filled with the fruit of their **schemes**.
22:20 written thirty sayings for you, sayings of **counsel** and knowledge,
Jer 7:24 they followed the stubborn **inclinations** *of* their evil hearts.
Hos 11: 6 will destroy the bars of their gates and put an end to their **plans**.
Mic 6:16 practices of Ahab's house, and you have followed their **traditions**.

4601 מוּעָקָה *mû'āqâ*, n.f. [1] [√ 6421?]

burdens [1]

Ps 66:11 You brought us into prison and laid **burdens** on our backs.

4602 מוֹפַעַת *môpa'at*, n.pr.loc. [0] [cf. 4789]

Jer 48:21 [to Holon, Jahzah and **Mephaath**, [K; see Q 4789]]

4603 מוֹפֵת *môpēt*, n.m. [36]

wonders [17], sign [7], wonder [3], miracles [2], miraculous sign [2], portent [2], miracle [1], symbolic of things to come [1], symbols [1]

Ex 4:21 see that you perform before Pharaoh all the **wonders** I have given
7: 3 and though I multiply my miraculous signs and **wonders** in Egypt,
7: 9 'Perform a **miracle**,' then say to Aaron, 'Take your staff and throw
11: 9 to listen to you—so that my **wonders** may be multiplied in Egypt."
11:10 Moses and Aaron performed all these **wonders** before Pharaoh,
Dt 4:34 by testings, by miraculous signs and **wonders**, by war, by a mighty
6:22 Before our eyes the LORD sent miraculous signs and **wonders**—
7:19 the miraculous signs and **wonders**, the mighty hand
13: 1 [13:2] and announces to you a miraculous sign or **wonder**,
13: 2 [13:3] if the sign or **wonder** of which he has spoken takes place,
26: 8 with great terror and with miraculous signs and **wonders**.
28:46 They will be a sign and a **wonder** to you and your descendants
29: 3 [29:2] great trials, those miraculous signs and great **wonders**.
34:11 and **wonders** the LORD sent him to do in Egypt—
1Ki 13: 3 That same day the man of God gave a **sign**: "This is the sign the
13: 3 "This is the **sign** the LORD has declared: The altar will be split
13: 5 its ashes poured out according to the **sign** given by the man of God
1Ch 16:12 he has done, his **miracles**, and the judgments he pronounced,
2Ch 32:24 the LORD, who answered him and gave him a **miraculous sign**.
32:31 to ask him about the **miraculous sign** that had occurred in the land,
Ne 9:10 You sent miraculous signs and **wonders** against Pharaoh,
Ps 71: 7 I have become like a **portent** to many, but you are my strong
78:43 his miraculous signs in Egypt, his **wonders** in the region of Zoan.
105: 5 he has done, his **miracles**, and the judgments he pronounced,
105:27 his miraculous signs among them, his **wonders** in the land of Ham.
135: 9 He sent his signs and **wonders** into your midst, O Egypt,
Isa 8:18 We are signs and **symbols** in Israel from the LORD Almighty,
20: 3 for three years, as a sign and **portent** against Egypt and Cush,
Jer 32:20 You performed miraculous signs and **wonders** in Egypt and have
32:21 brought your people Israel out of Egypt with signs and **wonders**,
Eze 12: 6 see the land, for I have made you a **sign** to the house of Israel."
12:11 Say to them, 'I am a **sign** *to* you.' "As I have done, so it will be
24:24 Ezekiel will be a **sign** to you; you will do just as he has done.
24:27 So you will be a **sign** to them, and they will know that I am the
Joel 2:30 [3:3] I will show **wonders** in the heavens and on the earth, blood
Zec 3: 8 seated before you, who are men **symbolic of things to come**:

4604 מוֹצָא¹ *môṣā'¹*, n.m. [27] [√ 3655]

exits [3], flowing springs [+4784] [2], imported [2], spring [+4784] [2], stages [2], appear [+3922] [1], came from [1], east [1], go [1], grass [+2013] [1], issuing [1], mine [1], movements [+2256+4569] [1], outlet [1], rises [1], springs [+4784] [1], utter [1], what passes [1], what uttered [1], where dawns [1], word that comes from [1]

Nu 30:12 [30:13] of the vows or pledges that **came from** her lips will stand.
33: 2 At the LORD's command Moses recorded the **stages** in their
33: 2 recorded the stages in their journey. This is their journey by **stages**:
Dt 8: 3 but on every **word that comes from** the mouth of the LORD.
23:23 [23:24] Whatever your lips **utter** you must be sure to do,
2Sa 3:25 came to deceive you and observe your **movements** [+2256+4569]
1Ki 10:28 Solomon's horses were **imported** from Egypt and from Kue—
2Ki 2:21 Then he went out to the **spring** [+4784] and threw the salt into it,
2Ch 1:16 Solomon's horses were **imported** from Egypt and from Kue—
32:30 It was Hezekiah who blocked the upper **outlet** *of* the Gihon spring
Job 28: 1 "There is a **mine** for silver and a place where gold is refined.
38:27 a desolate wasteland and make it sprout with **grass** [+2013]?
Ps 19: 6 [19:7] It **rises** at one end of the heavens and makes its circuit to
65: 8 [65:9] **where** morning **dawns** and evening fades you call forth
75: 6 [75:7] No one from the **east** or the west or from the desert can
89:34 [89:35] violate my covenant or alter **what** my lips have **uttered**.
107:33 rivers into a desert, **flowing springs** [+4784] into thirsty ground,
107:35 of water and the parched ground into **flowing springs** [+4784];
Isa 41:18 into pools of water, and the parched ground into **springs** [+4784].
58:11 like a **spring** [+4784] whose waters never fail.
Jer 17:16 the day of despair. **What passes** my lips is open before you.
Eze 12: 4 while they are watching, go out like *those who* **go** *into* exile.
42:11 had the same length and width, with similar **exits** and dimensions.
43:11 its arrangement, its **exits** and entrances—its whole design
44: 5 to the entrance of the temple and all the **exits** *of* the sanctuary.
Da 9:25 From the **issuing** *of* the decree to restore and rebuild Jerusalem
Hos 6: 3 As surely as the sun rises, he *will* **appear** [+3922]; he will come to

4605 מוֹצָא² *môṣā'²*, n.pr.m. [5] [√ 3655]

Moza [5]

1Ch 2:46 concubine Ephah was the mother of Haran, **Moza** and Gazez.
8:36 Azmaveth and Zimri, and Zimri was the father of **Moza**.
8:37 **Moza** was the father of Binea; Raphah was his son, Eleasah his son
9:42 Azmaveth and Zimri, and Zimri was the father of **Moza**.
9:43 **Moza** was the father of Binea; Rephaiah was his son, Eleasah his

4606 מוֹצָאָה *môṣā'â*, n.f. [1] [√ 3655]

origins [1]

2Ki 10:27 [and people have used it for a **latrine** [Q; see K 4738] to this day.]
Mic 5: 2 [5:1] whose **origins** are from of old, from ancient times."

4607 מוּצָק¹ *mûṣāq¹*, n.m. [7] [→ 4609; cf. 3668]

cast metal [3], cast bronze [1], cast in molds [1], cast [1], hard [+2021+3668+4200] [1]

1Ki 7:16 He also made two capitals of **cast** bronze to set on the tops of the
7:23 He made the Sea of **cast metal**, circular in shape, measuring ten
7:33 the axles, rims, spokes and hubs were all of **cast metal**.
7:37 They were all **cast in** the same **molds** and were identical in size
2Ch 4: 2 He made the Sea of **cast metal**, circular in shape, measuring ten
Job 37:18 him in spreading out the skies, hard as a mirror of **cast bronze**?
38:38 when the dust *becomes* **hard** [+2021+3668+4200] and the clods of

4608 מוּצָק² *mûṣāq²*, n.[m.]. [2] [√ 7439]

distress [1], restriction [1]

Job 36:16 from the jaws of distress to a spacious place free from **restriction**,
Isa 9: 1 [8:23] will be no more gloom for those who were *in* **distress**.

4609 מוּצָקָה *mûṣāqâ*, n.f. [2] [√ 4607; cf. 3668]

channels [1], one piece with [1]

2Ch 4: 3 The bulls were cast in two rows in **one piece with** the Sea.
Zec 4: 2 at the top and seven lights on it, with seven **channels** to the lights.

4610 מוּק *mûq*, v. [1]

scoff [1]

Ps 73: 8 [G] *They* **scoff**, and speak with malice; in their arrogance they

4611 מוֹקֵד *môqēd*, n.[m.]. [2] [→ 4612; cf. 3678]

burning [1], glowing embers [1]

Ps 102: 3 [102:4] vanish like smoke; my bones burn like **glowing embers**.
Isa 33:14 consuming fire? Who of us can dwell with everlasting **burning**?"

4612 מוֹקְדָה *môqᵉdâ*, n.f. [1] [√ 4611; cf. 3678]

hearth [1]

Lev 6: 9 [6:2] The burnt offering is to remain on the altar **hearth**

4613 מוֹקֵשׁ *môqēš*, n.m. [27] [√ 3704]

snare [12], snares [6], trap [3], traps [3], ensnared [1], snared [1], trapped [1]

Ex 10: 7 officials said to him, "How long will this man be a **snare** to us?
23:33 because the worship of their gods will certainly be a **snare** to you."
34:12 the land where you are going, or they will be a **snare** among you.
Dt 7:16 and do not serve their gods, for that will be a **snare** to you.
Jos 23:13 Instead, they will become snares and **traps** for you, whips on your
Jdg 2: 3 be ⌊thorns⌋ in your sides and their gods will be a **snare** to you."
8:27 it there, and it became a **snare** to Gideon and his family.
1Sa 18:21 "so that she may be a **snare** to him and so that the hand of the
2Sa 22: 6 of the grave coiled around me; the **snares** *of* death confronted me.
Job 34:30 keep a godless man from ruling, from laying **snares** *for* the people.
40:24 anyone capture him by the eyes, or **trap** him and pierce his nose?
Ps 18: 5 [18:6] coiled around me; the **snares** *of* death confronted me.
64: 5 [64:6] each other in evil plans, they talk about hiding their **snares**;
69:22 [69:23] become a snare; may it become retribution and a **trap**.
106:36 They worshiped their idols, which became a **snare** to them.

Ps 140: 5 [140:6] of their net and have set **traps** for me along my path.
141: 9 the snares they have laid for me, from the **traps** *set by* evildoers.
Pr 12: 13 An evil man is **trapped** by his sinful talk, but a righteous man
13: 14 wise is a fountain of life, turning a man from the **snares** *of* death.
14: 27 is a fountain of life, turning a man from the **snares** *of* death.
18: 7 A fool's mouth is his undoing, and his lips are a **snare** *to* his soul.
20: 25 It is a **trap** *for* a man to dedicate something rashly and only later to
22: 25 or you may learn his ways and get yourself **ensnared**.
29: 6 An evil man is **snared** by his own sin, but a righteous one can sing
29: 25 Fear of man will prove to be a **snare**, but whoever trusts in the
Isa 8: 14 And for the people of Jerusalem he will be a trap and a **snare**.
Am 3: 5 Does a bird fall into a trap on the ground where no **snare** has been

4614 ¹מוּר **mûr¹**, v. [14] [→ 9455; cf. 4615]

exchanged [3], make a substitution [+4614] [2], substitute [+4614] [2], divided up [1], exchange [1], give way [1], keeps [+4202] [1], make substitution [1], substitute [1], unchanged [+4202] [1]

Lev 27: 10 [G] must not exchange it or **substitute** a good one for a bad one,
27: 10 [G] if *he should* **substitute** [+4614] one animal for another,
27: 10 [G] if *he should* **substitute** [+4614] one animal for another,
27: 33 [G] pick out the good from the bad or **make** any **substitution**.
27: 33 [G] If *he does* **make a substitution** [+4614], both the animal
27: 33 [G] If *he does* **make a substitution** [+4614], both the animal
Ps 15: 4 [G] honors those who fear the LORD, *who* **keeps** [+4202] his
46: 2 [46:3] [G] though the earth **give way** and the mountains fall into
106: 20 [G] *They* **exchanged** their Glory for an image of a bull,
Jer 2: 11 [G] my people *have* **exchanged** their Glory for worthless idols.
48: 11 [C] she tastes as she did, and her aroma *is* **unchanged** [+4202].
Eze 48: 14 [G] They must not sell or **exchange** any of it. This is the best of
Hos 4: 7 [G] *they* **exchanged** their Glory for something disgraceful.
Mic 2: 4 [G] 'We are utterly ruined; my people's possession *is* **divided up**.

4615 ²מוּר **mûr²**, v. Not used in NIV/BHS [cf. 4614]

4616 מוֹרָא **môrā'**, n.m. [11 / 12] [√ 3707; cf. 4624]

fear [4], terror [3], awesome deeds [1], awesome [1], feared [1], respect [1], reverence [1]

Ge 9: 2 The **fear** and dread of you will fall upon all the beasts of the earth
Dt 4: 34 and an outstretched arm, or by great and **awesome deeds**,
11: 25 will put the terror and **fear** *of* you on the whole land, wherever you
26: 8 with great **terror** and with miraculous signs and wonders.
34: 12 or performed the **awesome** deeds that Moses did in the sight of all
Ps 9: 20 [9:21] Strike them with **terror**, [BHS 4624] O LORD;
76: 11 [76:12] the neighboring lands bring gifts to the *One* to be **feared**.
Isa 8: 12 call conspiracy; do not fear *what* they **fear**, and do not dread it.
8: 13 he is the one you are to **fear**, he is the one you are to dread,
Jer 32: 21 by a mighty hand and an outstretched arm and with great **terror**.
Mal 1: 6 If I am a master, where is the **respect** *due* me?" says the LORD
2: 5 this called for **reverence** and he revered me and stood in awe of

4617 מוֹרָג **môrag**, n.m. [3]

threshing sledges [2], threshing sledge [1]

2Sa 24: 22 and here are **threshing sledges** and ox yokes for the wood.
1Ch 21: 23 the **threshing sledges** for the wood, and the wheat for the grain
Isa 41: 15 "See, I will make you into a **threshing sledge**, new and sharp,

4618 מוֹרָד **môrād**, n.[m.]. [5] [√ 3718]

road down [2], hammered [1], slope [1], slopes [1]

Jos 7: 5 as far as the stone quarries and struck them down on the **slopes**.
10: 11 As they fled before Israel on the **road down** *from* Beth Horon to
1Ki 7: 29 and below the lions and bulls were wreaths of **hammered** work.
Jer 48: 5 on the **road down** *to* Horonaim anguished cries over the
Mic 1: 4 like wax before the fire, like water rushing down a **slope**.

4619 ¹מוֹרֶה **môreh¹**, n.[m.] *or* v.ptcp. [4] [√ 3721]

archers [+408+928+2021+8008] [1], archers [+928+2021+8008] [1], archers [1], they[s] [+2021] [1]

1Sa 31: 3 Saul, and when the **archers** [+408+928+2021+8008] overtook him,
31: 3 when the archers overtook him, **they**[s] [+2021] wounded him
2Sa 11: 24 Then the **archers** shot arrows at your servants from the wall,
1Ch 10: 3 Saul, and when the **archers** [+928+2021+8008] overtook him,

4620 ²מוֹרֶה **môreh²**, n.m. [3] [√ 3722]

autumn rains [3]

Ps 84: 6 [84:7] of springs; the **autumn rains** also cover it with pools.
Joel 2: 23 your God, for he has given you the **autumn rains** in righteousness.
2: 23 you abundant showers, both **autumn** and spring **rains**, as before.

4621 ³מוֹרֶה **môreh³**, n.m. [4] [√ 3723]

teachers [2], teacher [1], them[s] [+3870] [1]

Job 36: 22 "God is exalted in his power. Who is a **teacher** like him?
Pr 5: 13 I would not obey my **teachers** or listen to my instructors.
Isa 30: 20 and the water of affliction, your **teachers** will be hidden no more;
30: 20 hidden no more; with your own eyes you will see **them**[s] [+3870].

4622 ⁴מוֹרֶה **môreh⁴**, n.pr.[loc.?]. [3] [√ 3723]

Moreh [3]

Ge 12: 6 the land as far as the site of the great tree of **Moreh** at Shechem.
Dt 11: 30 of the road, toward the setting sun, near the great trees of **Moreh**,
Jdg 7: 1 of Midian was north of them in the valley near the hill of **Moreh**.

4623 ¹מוֹרָה **môrâ¹**, n.m. [3] [√ 6867]

razor [3]

Jdg 13: 5 No **razor** may be used on his head, because the boy is to be a
16: 17 "No **razor** has ever been used on my head," he said, "because I
1Sa 1: 11 all the days of his life, and no **razor** will ever be used on his head."

4624 ²מוֹרָה **môrâ²**, n.[m.]. [1 / 0] [cf. 3707]

Ps 9: 20 [9:21] Strike them with terror, [BHS *terror* ?; NIV 4616] O LORD;

4625 ¹מוֹרָשׁ **môrāš¹**, n.[m.]. [2] [→ 4627; cf. 3769]

inheritance [1], place [1]

Isa 14: 23 "I will turn her into a **place** *for* owls and into swampland;
Ob 1: 17 it will be holy, and the house of Jacob will possess its **inheritance**.

4626 ²מוֹרָשׁ **môrāš²**, n.[m.]. [1] [√ 830]

desires [1]

Job 17: 11 my plans are shattered, and so are the **desires** *of* my heart.

4627 מוֹרָשָׁה **môrāšâ**, n.f. [9] [√ 4625; cf. 3769]

possession [9]

Ex 6: 8 to Isaac and to Jacob. I will give it to you as a **possession**.
Dt 33: 4 law that Moses gave us, the **possession** *of* the assembly of Jacob.
Eze 11: 15 from the LORD; this land was given to us as our **possession**.'
25: 4 I am going to give you to the people of the East as a **possession**.
25: 10 with the Ammonites to the people of the East as a **possession**,
33: 24 are many; surely the land has been given to us as our **possession**.'
36: 2 "Aha! The ancient heights have become our **possession**." '
36: 3 so that you became the **possession** of the rest of the nations
36: 5 with malice in their hearts they made my land their own **possession**

4628 מוֹרֶשֶׁת גַּת **môrešet gat**, n.pr.loc. [1] [→ 4629]

Moresheth Gath [1]

Mic 1: 14 Therefore you will give parting gifts to **Moresheth Gath**.

4629 מוֹרַשְׁתִּי **môraštî**, a.g. [2] [√ 4628]

of Moresheth [2]

Jer 26: 18 "Micah **of Moresheth** prophesied in the days of Hezekiah king of
Mic 1: 1 The word of the LORD that came to Micah **of Moresheth** during

4630 ¹מוּשׁ **mûš¹**, v. [3] [cf. 3560, 5491]

feel [2], touch [1]

Ge 27: 21 [A] Isaac said to Jacob, "Come near so *I can* **touch** you, my son,
Jdg 16: 26 [G] "Put me where I *can* **feel** [K 3560] the pillars that support
Ps 115: 7 [G] they have hands, but cannot **feel**, feet, but they cannot walk;

4631 ²מוּשׁ **mûš²**, v. [20]

leave [3], depart [2], shaken [2], departed [1], fails [1], give way [1], go away [1], left place [1], move [1], moved [1], moving [1], remove [1], save [1], takes [1], vanish [1], without [1]

Ex 13: 22 [A] the pillar of fire by night **left** *its* **place** in front of the people.
33: 11 [A] but his young aide Joshua son of Nun *did* not **leave** the tent.
Nu 14: 44 [A] nor the ark of the LORD's covenant **moved** from the camp.
Jos 1: 8 [A] *Do* not *let* this Book of the Law **depart** from your mouth;
Jdg 6: 18 [A] Please *do* not **go away** until I come back and bring my
Job 23: 12 [A] *I have* not **departed** *from* the commands of his lips; I have
Ps 55: 11 [55:12] [A] in the city; threats and lies never **leave** its streets.
Pr 17: 13 [A] man pays back evil for good, evil *will* never **leave** his house.
Isa 22: 25 [A] "the peg driven into the firm place *will* **give way**;
46: 7 [A] its place, and there it stands. From that spot *it* cannot **move**.
54: 10 [A] Though the mountains *be* **shaken** and the hills be removed,
54: 10 [A] yet my unfailing love for you *will* not *be* **shaken** nor my
59: 21 [A] my words that I have put in your mouth *will* not **depart** from
Jer 17: 8 [A] no worries in a year of drought and never **fails** to bear fruit."

Jer 31:36 [A] "Only if these decrees **vanish** from my sight,"
Mic 2: 3 [G] against this people, from which *you* cannot **save** yourselves.
2: 4 [A] *He* **takes** it from me! He assigns our fields to traitors.' "
Na 3: 1 [A] of blood, full of lies, full of plunder, never **without** victims!
Zec 3: 9 [A] 'and *I will* **remove** the sin of this land in a single day.
14: 4 [A] with half of the mountain **moving** north and half moving

4632 מוֹשָׁב *môšāb*, n.m. [44 / 43] [√ 3782]

live [12], settlements [5], seat [3], where settle [3], dwelling [2], seating [2], *untranslated* [1], council [1], dwelling place [1], dwellings [1], home [1], house [+1074] [1], houses [1], length of time [1], members [1], place [1], places where lived [1], region where lived [1], settled [1], situated [1], stood [1], throne [1]

Ge 10:30 The **region where** they **lived** stretched from Mesha toward Sephar,
27:39 "Your **dwelling** will be away from the earth's richness,
36:43 of Edom, according to their **settlements** in the land they occupied.
Ex 10:23 Yet all the Israelites had light in the **places where** they **lived**.
12:20 with yeast. Wherever you **live**, you must eat unleavened bread."
12:40 Now the **length of time** the Israelite people lived in Egypt was 430
35: 3 Do not light a fire in any of your **dwellings** on the Sabbath day."
Lev 3:17 a lasting ordinance for the generations to come, wherever you **live**:
7:26 And wherever you **live**, you must not eat the blood of any bird
13:46 He must live alone; he must **live** outside the camp.
23: 3 to do any work; wherever you **live**, it is a Sabbath to the LORD.
23:14 a lasting ordinance for the generations to come, wherever you **live**.
23:17 From *wherever* you **live**, bring two loaves made of two-tenths of
23:21 a lasting ordinance for the generations to come, wherever you **live**.
23:31 a lasting ordinance for the generations to come, wherever you **live**.
25:29 " 'If a man sells a **house in** [+1074] a walled city, he retains the
Nu 15: 2 say to them: 'After you enter the land I am giving you as a **home**
24:21 "Your **dwelling place** is secure, your nest is set in a rock;
31:10 They burned all the towns where the Midianites had **settled**,
35:29 for you throughout the generations to come, wherever you **live**.
1Sa 20:18 You will be missed, because your **seat** will be empty.
20:25 He sat in his customary **place** by the wall, opposite Jonathan,
20:25 He sat in his customary place by **[RPH]** the wall, opposite
2Sa 9:12 all the **members** *of* Ziba's household were servants of
1Ki 10: 5 the food on his table, the **seating** *of* his officials, the attending
2Ki 2:19 "Look, our lord, this town is well **situated**, as you can see,
1Ch 4:33 These were their **settlements**. And they kept a genealogical record.
6:54 [6:39] These were the locations of their **settlements** allotted as
7:28 Their lands and **settlements** included Bethel and its surrounding
2Ch 9: 4 the food on his table, the **seating** *of* his officials, the attending
Job 29: 7 I went to the gate of the city and took my **seat** in the public square,
Ps 1: 1 or stand in the way of sinners or sit in the **seat** *of* mockers.
107: 4 finding no way to a city **where** they could **settle**.
107: 7 He led them by a straight way to a city **where** they could **settle**.
107:32 assembly of the people and praise him in the **council** *of* the elders.
107:36 the hungry to live, and they founded a city **where** they could **settle**.
132:13 For the LORD has chosen Zion, he has desired it for his **dwelling**:
Eze 6: 6 Wherever you **live**, the towns will be laid waste and the high places
6:14 a desolate waste from the desert to Diblah—wherever they **live**.
8: 3 of the inner court, where the idol that provokes to jealousy **stood**.
28: 2 "I am a god; I sit on the **throne** *of* a god in the heart of the seas."
34:13 of Israel, in the ravines and in all the **settlements** *in* the land.
37:23 from all their sinful backsliding, [BHS ***dwelling places***; NIV 5412]
48:15 be for the common use of the city, for **houses** and for pastureland.

4633 מוּשִׁי *mûšî*[1], n.pr.m. [8] [→ 4634]

Mushi [8]

Ex 6:19 The sons of Merari were Mahli and **Mushi**. These were the clans
Nu 3:20 The Merarite clans: Mahli and **Mushi**. These were the Levite
1Ch 6:19 [6:4] The sons of Merari: Mahli and **Mushi**. These are the clans
6:47 [6:32] the son of Mahli, the son of **Mushi**, the son of Merari,
23:21 of Merari: Mahli and **Mushi**. The sons of Mahli: Eleazar and Kish.
23:23 The sons of **Mushi**: Mahli, Eder and Jerimoth—three in all.
24:26 The sons of Merari: Mahli and **Mushi**. The son of Jaaziah: Beno.
24:30 the sons of **Mushi**: Mahli, Eder and Jerimoth. These were the

4634 מוּשִׁי *mûšî*[2], a.g. [2] [√ 4633]

Mushite [1], Mushites [1]

Nu 3:33 To Merari belonged the clans of the Mahlites and the **Mushites**;
26:58 the Mahlite clan, the **Mushite** clan, the Korahite clan,

4635 מוֹשִׁיעַ *môšîa'*, n.[m.] *or* v.ptcp. [21] [√ 3828]

savior [11], deliverer [3], rescue [3], deliverers [2], rescues [1], save [1]

Dt 22:27 the betrothed girl screamed, there was no *one to* **rescue** her.
28:29 day you will be oppressed and robbed, with no *one to* **rescue** you.
Jdg 3: 9 he raised up for them a **deliverer**, Othniel son of Kenaz,
3:15 Israelites cried out to the LORD, and he gave them a **deliverer**—
1Sa 11: 3 if no *one* comes *to* **rescue** us, we will surrender to you."
14:39 As surely as the LORD who **rescues** Israel lives, even if it lies
2Sa 22: 3 He is my stronghold, my refuge and my **savior**—from violent men
22:42 They cried for help, but there was no *one to* **save** them—
2Ki 13: 5 The LORD provided a **deliverer** for Israel, and they escaped from
Ne 9:27 and in your great compassion you gave them **deliverers**,
Isa 19:20 he will send them a **savior** and defender, and he will rescue them.
43: 3 I am the LORD, your God, the Holy One of Israel, your **Savior**;
43:11 even I, am the LORD, and apart from me there is no **savior**.
45:15 you are a God who hides himself, O God and **Savior** of Israel.
45:21 And there is no God apart from me, a righteous God and a **Savior**;
49:26 the LORD, am your **Savior**, your Redeemer, the Mighty One of
60:16 the LORD, am your **Savior**, your Redeemer, the Mighty One of
63: 8 sons who will not be false to me"; and so he became their **Savior**.
Jer 14: 8 O Hope of Israel, its **Savior** in times of distress, why are you like a
Hos 13: 4 You shall acknowledge no God but me, no **Savior** except me.
Ob 1:21 **Deliverers** will go up on Mount Zion to govern the mountains of

4636 מוֹשָׁעָה *môšā'â*, n.f. [1] [√ 3828]

saves [1]

Ps 68:20 [68:21] Our God is a God who **saves**; from the Sovereign LORD

4637 מוּת *mût*, v. [844 / 847] [→ 4638, 4926, 9456; *also used with compound proper names*]

die [200], died [162], dead [103], put to death [43], kill [36], must be put to death [+4637] [36], killed [31], death [30], be put to death [26], dies [25], surely die [+4637] [14], die [+4637] [10], kill [+4637] [8], must die [+4637] [8], shall be put to death [+4637] [8], surely be put to death [+4637] [8], *untranslated* [7], certainly die [+4637] [6], assassinated [5], dying [5], slay [4], putting to death [3], be murdered [2], brings death [2], causing to die [2], certainly be put to death [+4637] [2], destroy [2], died a natural death [2], doomed to die [+4637] [2], in fact die [+4637] [2], killing [2], kills [2], must put to death [+4637] [2], perish [2], put to death [+4637] [2], put[s] [2], slain [2], anyone[s] [+2021] [1], as good as dead [1], assassinated [+906+906+906+2256+5782] [1], assassination [1], be killed [1], body [1], bring about death [1], die out [1], end [1], executed [+906+2256+5782] [1], failed [1], fell dead [1], go down [1], had executed [+906+2256+5782] [1], his[s] [+2021] [1], is put to death [1], killed [+5782] [1], killing off [1], kills [+2256+5782+5883] [1], lifeless [1], lives [1], lose life [1], make die [1], man[s] [1], messengers of death [1], mortal [1], murder [1], must be put to death [1], put death [1], ready to die [1], risked [+3070+4200] [1], slays [1], someone[s] [1], stillborn infant [1], struck down and died [1], was killed [1], was put to death [1], were put to death [1], widow [+851] [1]

Ge 2:17 [A] and evil, for when you eat of it *you will* **surely die** [+4637]."
2:17 [A] and evil, for when you eat of it *you will* **surely die** [+4637]."
3: 3 [A] of the garden, and you must not touch it, or *you will die*.' "
3: 4 [A] "*You will* not **surely die** [+4637]," the serpent said to the
3: 4 [A] "*You will* not **surely die** [+4637]," the serpent said to the
5: 5 [A] Altogether, Adam lived 930 years, and then *he* **died**.
5: 8 [A] Altogether, Seth lived 912 years, and then *he* **died**.
5:11 [A] Altogether, Enosh lived 905 years, and then *he* **died**.
5:14 [A] Altogether, Kenan lived 910 years, and then *he* **died**.
5:17 [A] Altogether, Mahalalel lived 895 years, and then *he* **died**.
5:20 [A] Altogether, Jared lived 962 years, and then *he* **died**.
5:27 [A] Altogether, Methuselah lived 969 years, and then *he* **died**.
5:31 [A] Altogether, Lamech lived 777 years, and then *he* **died**.
7:22 [A] on dry land that had the breath of life in its nostrils **died**.
9:29 [A] Altogether, Noah lived 950 years, and then *he* **died**.
11:28 [A] Haran **died** in Ur of the Chaldeans, in the land of his birth.
11:32 [A] Terah lived 205 years, and he **died** in Haran.
18:25 [G] to **kill** the righteous with the wicked, treating the righteous
19:19 [A] to the mountains; this disaster will overtake me, and *I'll* **die**.
20: 3 [A] "You *are* **as good as dead** because of the woman you have
20: 7 [A] you may be sure that you and all yours *will* **die** [+4637]."
20: 7 [A] you may be sure that you and all yours *will* **die** [+4637]."
23: 2 [A] She **died** at Kiriath Arba (that is, Hebron) in the land of
23: 3 [A] Abraham rose from beside his **dead** *wife* and spoke to the
23: 4 [A] some property for a burial site here so I can bury my **dead**."
23: 6 [A] among us. Bury your **dead** in the choicest of our tombs.
23: 6 [A] None of us will refuse you his tomb for burying your **dead**."
23: 8 [A] He said to them, "If you are willing to let me bury my **dead**,
23:11 [A] give it to you in the presence of my people. Bury your **dead**."
23:13 [A] of the field. Accept it from me so I can bury my **dead** there."
23:15 [A] but what is that between me and you? Bury your **dead**."
25: 8 [A] Then Abraham breathed his last and **died** at a good old age,
25:17 [A] He breathed his last and **died**, and he was gathered to his
25:32 [A] "Look, I am about to **die**," Esau said. "What good is the
26: 9 [A] "Because I thought *I* might **lose** *my* **life** on account of her."
26:11 [H] this man or his wife *shall* **surely be put to death** [+4637]."
26:11 [A] this man or his wife *shall* **surely be put to death** [+4637]."
27: 4 [A] me to eat, so that I may give you my blessing before *I* **die**."

Ge 30: 1 [A] So she said to Jacob, "Give me children, or I'll **die**!"
33: 13 [A] If they are driven hard just one day, all the animals *will* **die**.
35: 8 [A] **died** and was buried under the oak below Bethel.
35: 18 [A] As she breathed her last—for *she was* **dying**—she named her
35: 19 [A] So Rachel **died** and was buried on the way to Ephrath (that
35: 29 [A] he breathed his last and **died** and was gathered to his people,
36: 33 [A] When Bela **died**, Jobab son of Zerah from Bozrah succeeded
36: 34 [A] When Jobab **died**, Husham from the land of the Temanites
36: 35 [A] When Husham **died**, Hadad son of Bedad, who defeated
36: 36 [A] When Hadad **died**, Samlah from Masrekah succeeded him as
36: 37 [A] When Samlah **died**, Shaul from Rehoboth on the river
36: 38 [A] When Shaul **died**, Baal-Hanan son of Acbor succeeded him
36: 39 [A] When Baal-Hanan son of Acbor **died**, Hadad succeeded him
37: 18 [G] and before he reached them, they plotted to **kill** him.
38: 7 [G] in the LORD's sight; so the LORD **put** him **to death**.
38: 10 [G] wicked in the LORD's sight; so *he* **put** him **to death** also.
38: 11 [A] For he thought, "He may **die** too, just like his brothers."
38: 12 [A] After a long time Judah's wife, the daughter of Shua, **died**.
42: 2 [A] and buy some for us, so that we may live and not **die**."
42: 20 [A] that your words may be verified and that *you may* not **die**."
42: 37 [G] "*You may* **put** both of my sons **to death** if I do not bring
42: 38 [A] there with you; his brother *is* **dead** and he is the only one left.
43: 8 [A] so that we and you and our children may live and not **die**.
44: 9 [A] If any of your servants is found to have it, *he will* **die**; and
44: 20 [A] His brother *is* **dead**, and he is the only one of his mother's
44: 22 [A] cannot leave his father; if he leaves him, his father *will* **die**.'
44: 31 [A] sees that the boy isn't there, *he will* **die**. Your servants will
45: 28 [A] son Joseph is still alive. I will go and see him before *I* **die**."
46: 12 [A] and Zerah (but Er and Onan *had* **died** in the land of Canaan).
46: 30 [A] Israel said to Joseph, "Now *I am* **ready to die**, since I have
47: 15 [A] "Give us food. Why *should we* **die** before your eyes?
47: 19 [A] Why *should we* **perish** before your eyes—we and our land
47: 19 [A] Give us seed so that we may live and not **die**, and that the
47: 29 [A] When the time drew near for Israel to **die**, he called for his
48: 7 [A] to my sorrow Rachel **died** in the land of Canaan while we
48: 21 [A] "I *am about to* **die**, but God will be with you and take you
50: 5 [A] father made me swear an oath and said, "I *am about to* **die**;
50: 15 [A] When Joseph's brothers saw that their father *was* **dead**, they
50: 24 [A] Joseph said to his brothers, "I *am about to* **die**. But God will
50: 26 [A] So Joseph **died** at the age of a hundred and ten. And after
Ex 1: 6 [A] Now Joseph and all his brothers and all that generation **died**,
1: 16 [G] observe them on the delivery stool, if it is a boy, **kill** him;
2: 23 [A] During that long period, the king of Egypt **died**. The
4: 19 [A] to Egypt, for all the men who wanted to kill you *are* **dead**."
4: 24 [G] the way, the LORD met ⌊Moses⌋ and was about to **kill** him.
7: 18 [A] The fish in the Nile *will* **die**, and the river will stink;
7: 21 [A] The fish in the Nile **died**, and the river smelled so bad that
8: 13 [8:9] [A] The frogs **died** in the houses, in the courtyards and in
9: 4 [A] so that no animal belonging to the Israelites *will* **die**.' "
9: 6 [A] All the livestock of the Egyptians **died**, but not one animal
9: 6 [A] but not one animal belonging to the Israelites **died**.
9: 7 [A] that not even one of the animals of the Israelites *had* **died**.
9: 19 [A] brought in and is still out in the field, and *they will* **die**.' "
10: 28 [A] before me again! The day you see my face *you will* **die**."
11: 5 [A] Every firstborn son in Egypt *will* **die**, from the firstborn son
12: 30 [A] in Egypt, for there was not a house without *someone* **dead**.
12: 33 [A] the country. "For otherwise," they said, "we *will* all **die**!"
14: 11 [A] no graves in Egypt that you brought us to the desert to **die**?
14: 12 [A] better for us to serve the Egyptians than *to* **die** in the desert!"
14: 30 [A] and Israel saw the Egyptians *lying* **dead** on the shore.
16: 3 [A] "If only we *had* **died** by the LORD's hand in Egypt!
16: 3 [G] out into this desert to starve this entire assembly *to* **death**."
17: 3 [G] out of Egypt to **make** us and our children and livestock **die**
19: 12 [H] touches the mountain *shall* **surely be put to death** [+4637].
19: 12 [A] touches the mountain *shall* **surely be put to death** [+4637].
20: 19 [A] will listen. But do not have God speak to us or *we will* **die**."
21: 12 [A] who strikes a man and **kills** him shall surely be put to death.
21: 12 [H] a man and kills him *shall* **surely be put to death** [+4637].
21: 12 [A] a man and kills him *shall* **surely be put to death** [+4637].
21: 14 [A] take him away from my altar and *put* him *to* **death**.
21: 15 [H] his father or his mother **must be put to death** [+4637].
21: 15 [A] his father or his mother **must be put to death** [+4637].
21: 16 [H] has him when he is caught **must be put to death** [+4637].
21: 16 [A] has him when he is caught **must be put to death** [+4637].
21: 17 [H] curses his father or mother **must be put to death** [+4637].
21: 17 [A] curses his father or mother **must be put to death** [+4637].
21: 18 [A] or with his fist and *he does* not **die** but is confined to bed,
21: 20 [A] female slave with a rod and the slave **dies** as a direct result,
21: 28 [A] "If a bull gores a man or a woman *to* **death**, the bull must be
21: 29 [G] but has not kept it penned up and *it* **kills** a man or woman,
21: 29 [H] must be stoned and the owner also *must* **be put to death**.
21: 34 [A] he must pay its owner, and the **dead** *animal* will be his.
21: 35 [A] "If a man's bull injures the bull of another and *it* **dies**, they
21: 35 [A] and divide both the money and the **dead** *animal* equally.
21: 36 [A] animal for animal, and the **dead** *animal* will be his.
22: 2 [22:1] [A] is caught breaking in and is struck so that *he* **dies**,
22: 10 [22:9] [A] *it* **dies** or is injured or is taken away while no one is
22: 14 [22:13] [A] it is injured or **dies** while the owner is not present,
22: 19 [22:18] [H] with an animal **must be put to death** [+4637].
22: 19 [22:18] [A] with an animal **must be put to death** [+4637].
28: 35 [A] the LORD and when he comes out, so that *he will* not **die**.
28: 43 [A] in the Holy Place, so that they will not incur guilt and **die**.
30: 20 [A] they shall wash with water so that *they will* not **die**.
30: 21 [A] they shall wash their hands and feet so that *they will* not **die**.
31: 14 [H] Anyone who desecrates it **must be put to death** [+4637];
31: 14 [A] Anyone who desecrates it **must be put to death** [+4637];
31: 15 [H] any work on the Sabbath day **must be put to death** [+4637].
31: 15 [A] any work on the Sabbath day **must be put to death** [+4637].
35: 2 [H] Whoever does any work on it *must* **be put to death**.
Lev 8: 35 [A] and do what the LORD requires, so *you will* not **die**;
10: 2 [A] and consumed them, and *they* **died** before the LORD.
10: 6 [A] or *you will* **die** and the LORD will be angry with the whole
10: 7 [A] not leave the entrance to the Tent of Meeting or *you will* **die**,
10: 9 [A] whenever you go into the Tent of Meeting, or *you will* **die**.
11: 31 [A] Whoever touches them when they *are* **dead** will be unclean
11: 32 [A] When one of them **dies** and falls on something, that article,
11: 39 [A] " 'If an animal that you are allowed to eat **dies**, anyone who
15: 31 [A] so *they will* not **die** in their uncleanness for defiling my
16: 1 [A] sons of Aaron *who* **died** when they approached the LORD.
16: 2 [A] or else *he will* **die**, because I appear in the cloud over the
16: 13 [A] cover above the Testimony, so that *he will* not **die**.
19: 20 [H] Yet *they are* not *to* **be put to death**, because she had not
20: 2 [H] any of his children to Molech **must be put to death** [+4637].
20: 2 [A] any of his children to Molech **must be put to death** [+4637].
20: 4 [G] of his children to Molech and they fail to **put** him **to death**,
20: 9 [H] his father or mother, *he* **must be put to death** [+4637].
20: 9 [A] his father or mother, *he* **must be put to death** [+4637].
20: 10 [H] and the adulteress **must be put to death** [+4637].
20: 10 [A] and the adulteress **must be put to death** [+4637].
20: 11 [H] Both the man and the woman **must** *be* **put to death** [+4637];
20: 11 [A] Both the man and the woman **must** *be* **put to death** [+4637];
20: 12 [H] both of them **must be put to death** [+4637].
20: 12 [A] both of them **must be put to death** [+4637].
20: 13 [H] *They* **must be put to death** [+4637]; their blood will be on
20: 13 [A] *They* **must be put to death** [+4637]; their blood will be on
20: 15 [H] *he* **must be put to death** [+4637], and you must kill the
20: 15 [A] *he* **must be put to death** [+4637], and you must kill the
20: 16 [H] *They* **must be put to death** [+4637]; their blood will be on
20: 16 [A] *They* **must be put to death** [+4637]; their blood will be on
20: 20 [A] They will be held responsible; *they will* **die** childless.
20: 27 [H] or spiritist among you **must be put to death** [+4637].
20: 27 [A] or spiritist among you **must be put to death** [+4637].
21: 11 [A] He must not enter a place where there is a **dead** body.
22: 9 [A] not become guilty and **die** for treating them with contempt.
24: 16 [H] the name of the LORD **must be put to death** [+4637].
24: 16 [A] the name of the LORD **must be put to death** [+4637].
24: 16 [H] when he blasphemes the Name, *he* **must be put to death**.
24: 17 [H] the life of a human being, *he* **must be put to death** [+4637].
24: 17 [A] the life of a human being, *he* **must be put to death** [+4637].
24: 21 [H] but whoever kills a man *must* **be put to death**.
27: 29 [H] may be ransomed; *he* **must be put to death** [+4637].
27: 29 [A] may be ransomed; *he* **must be put to death** [+4637].
Nu 1: 51 [H] do it. Anyone else who goes near it *shall* **be put to death**.
3: 4 [A] **fell dead** before the LORD when they made an offering
3: 10 [H] else who approaches the sanctuary *must* **be put to death**."
3: 38 [H] else who approached the sanctuary *was to* **be put to death**.
4: 15 [A] But they must not touch the holy things or *they will* **die**.
4: 19 [A] and not **die** when they come near the most holy things,
4: 20 [A] look at the holy things, even for a moment, or *they will* **die**."
6: 6 [A] separation to the LORD he must not go near a **dead** body.
6: 7 [A] Even if his own father or mother or brother or sister **dies**, he
6: 9 [A] " 'If **someone**[s] dies suddenly in his presence, thus defiling
6: 9 [A] " 'If someone **dies** suddenly in his presence, thus defiling the
12: 12 [A] Do not let her be like a **stillborn infant** coming from its
14: 2 [A] whole assembly said to them, "If only *we had* **died** in Egypt!
14: 2 [A] "If only we had died in Egypt! Or in this desert! **[RPH]**
14: 15 [G] If *you* **put** these people **to death** all at one time, the nations
14: 35 [A] They will meet their end in this desert; here *they will* **die**."
14: 37 [A] the bad report about the land *were* **struck down and died**
15: 35 [H] the LORD said to Moses, "The man **must die** [+4637].
15: 35 [A] the LORD said to Moses, "The man **must die** [+4637].
15: 36 [A] took him outside the camp and stoned him *to* **death**,
16: 13 [G] a land flowing with milk and honey to **kill** us in the desert?
16: 29 [A] If these men **die** a natural death and experience only what
16: 41 [17:6] [G] "You *have* **killed** the LORD's people," they said.
16: 48 [17:13] [A] He stood between the living and the **dead**,
16: 49 [17:14] [A] 14,700 *people* **died** from the plague, in addition to
16: 49 [17:14] [A] addition to those *who had* **died** because of Korah.

Nu 17:10 [17:25] [A] grumbling against me, so that *they will* not **die**."
17:13 [17:28] [A] comes near the tabernacle of the LORD *will* **die**.
18: 3 [A] of the sanctuary or the altar, or both they and you *will* **die**.
18: 7 [H] else who comes near the sanctuary *must* **be put to death**."
18:22 [A] or they will bear the consequences of their sin and *will* **die**.
18:32 [A] the holy offerings of the Israelites, and *you will* not **die**.' "
19:11 [A] "Whoever touches the **dead** body of anyone will be unclean
19:13 [A] Whoever touches the **dead** body of anyone and fails to purify
19:13 [A] **[RPH]** and fails to purify himself defiles the LORD's
19:14 [A] "This is the law that applies when a person **dies** in a tent:
19:16 [A] with a sword or *someone who has* **died a natural death**,
19:18 [A] has been killed or someone *who has* **died a natural death**.
20: 1 [A] they stayed at Kadesh. There Miriam **died** and was buried.
20: 4 [A] into this desert, that we and our livestock *should* **die** here?
20:26 [A] for Aaron will be gathered to his people; *he will* **die** there."
20:28 [A] And Aaron **died** there on top of the mountain. Then Moses
21: 5 [A] "Why have you brought us up out of Egypt to **die** in the
21: 6 [A] among them; they bit the people and many Israelites **died**.
23:10 [A] *Let* me **die** the death of the righteous, and may my end be
25: 9 [A] but those *who* **died** in the plague numbered 24,000.
26:10 [A] whose followers **died** when the fire devoured the 250 men.
26:11 [A] The line of Korah, however, *did* not **die out**.
26:19 [A] Er and Onan were sons of Judah, but *they* **died** in Canaan.
26:61 [A] Abihu **died** when they made an offering before the LORD
26:65 [A] those Israelites *they would* **surely die** [+4637] in the desert,
26:65 [A] those Israelites *they would* **surely die** [+4637] in the desert,
27: 3 [A] "Our father **died** in the desert. He was not among Korah's
27: 3 [A] the LORD, but *he* **died** for his own sin and left no sons.
27: 8 [A] "Say to the Israelites, 'If a man **dies** and leaves no son, turn
33:38 [A] where *he* **died** on the first day of the fifth month of the
33:39 [A] and twenty-three years old when he **died** on Mount Hor.
35:12 [A] so that a person accused of murder *may* not **die** before he
35:16 [A] a man strikes someone with an iron object so that *he* **dies**,
35:16 [H] is a murderer; the murderer **shall be put to death** [+4637].
35:16 [A] is a murderer; the murderer **shall be put to death** [+4637].
35:17 [A] Or if anyone has a stone in his hand that *could* **kill**, and he
35:17 [A] and he strikes someone so that *he* **dies**, he is a murderer;
35:17 [H] is a murderer; the murderer **shall be put to death** [+4637].
35:17 [A] is a murderer; the murderer **shall be put to death** [+4637].
35:18 [A] Or if anyone has a wooden object in his hand that *could* **kill**,
35:18 [A] and he hits someone so that *he* **dies**, he is a murderer;
35:18 [H] is a murderer; the murderer **shall be put to death** [+4637].
35:18 [A] is a murderer; the murderer **shall be put to death** [+4637].
35:19 [G] The avenger of blood *shall* **put** the murderer **to death**; when
35:19 [G] to death; when he meets him, he *shall* **put** him **to death**.
35:20 [A] or throws something at him intentionally so that *he* **dies**
35:21 [A] or if in hostility he hits him with his fist so that *he* **dies**,
35:21 [H] so that he dies, that person **shall be put to death** [+4637];
35:21 [A] so that he dies, that person **shall be put to death** [+4637];
35:21 [G] The avenger of blood *shall* **put** the murderer **to death** when
35:23 [A] drops a stone on him that *could* **kill** him, and he dies,
35:23 [A] *he* **dies**, then since he was not his enemy and he did not
35:25 [A] He must stay there until the **death** *of* the high priest,
35:30 [A] no one *is to be* **put to death** on the testimony of only one
35:31 [A] a ransom for the life of a murderer, who deserves to **die**.
35:31 [H] deserves to die. *He* **must** surely **be put to death** [+4637].
35:31 [A] deserves to die. *He* **must** surely **be put to death** [+4637].
Dt 2:16 [A] the last of these fighting men among the people *had* **died**,
4:22 [A] I *will* **die** in this land; I will not cross the Jordan; but you are
5:25 [A] now, why *should we* **die**? This great fire will consume us,
5:25 [A] *we will* **die** if we hear the voice of the LORD our God any
9:28 [G] he brought them out to **put** them **to death** in the desert.'
10: 6 [A] There Aaron **died** and was buried, and Eleazar his son
13: 5 [13:6] [H] That prophet or dreamer *must* **be put to death**,
13: 9 [13:10] [G] hand must be the first in **putting** him **to death**,
13:10 [13:11] [A] Stone him *to* **death**, because he tried to turn you
14: 1 [A] cut yourselves or shave the front of your heads for the **dead**,
17: 5 [A] evil deed to your city gate and stone that person *to* **death**.
17: 6 [A] of two or three witnesses a **man**[s] shall be put to death,
17: 6 [H] of two or three witnesses a man *shall* **be put to death**,
17: 6 [H] no *one shall* **be put to death** on the testimony of only one
17: 7 [G] of the witnesses must be the first in **putting** him **to death**,
17:12 [A] there to the LORD your God *must be* **put to death**.
18:11 [A] or who is a medium or spiritist or who consults the **dead**.
18:16 [A] our God nor see this great fire anymore, or *we will* **die**."
18:20 [A] speaks in the name of other gods, *must be* **put to death**."
19: 5 [A] a tree, the head may fly off and hit his neighbor and **kill** him.
19:11 [A] in wait for him, assaults and **kills** [+2256+5782+5883] him,
19:12 [A] the city, and hand him over to the avenger of blood *to* **die**.
20: 5 [A] or *he may* **die** in battle and someone else may dedicate it.
20: 6 [A] go home, or *he may* **die** in battle and someone else enjoy it.
20: 7 [A] or *he may* **die** in battle and someone else marry her."
21:21 [A] all the men of his town shall stone him *to* **death**. You must
21:22 [H] If a man guilty of a capital offense **is put to death** and his
22:21 [A] and there the men of her town shall stone her *to* **death**.
22:22 [A] both the man who slept with her and the woman *must* **die**.
22:24 [A] of them to the gate of that town and stone them *to* **death**—
22:25 [A] and rapes her, only the man who has done this *shall* **die**.
24: 3 [A] gives it to her and sends her from his house, or if he **dies**,
24: 7 [A] treats him as a slave or sells him, the kidnapper *must* **die**.
24:16 [H] Fathers *shall* not **be put to death** for their children, nor
24:16 [H] for their children, nor children **put to death** for their fathers;
24:16 [H] put to death for their fathers; each *is to* **die** for his own sin.
25: 5 [A] are living together and one of them **dies** without a son,
25: 5 [A] a son, his **widow** [+851] must not marry outside the family.
25: 6 [A] The first son she bears shall carry on the name of the **dead**
26:14 [A] while I was unclean, nor have I offered any of it to the **dead**.
31:14 [A] LORD said to Moses, "Now the day of your **death** is near.
32:39 [G] I **put to death** and I bring to life, I have wounded and I will
32:50 [A] There on the mountain that you have climbed *you will* **die**
32:50 [A] just as your brother Aaron **died** on Mount Hor and was
33: 6 [A] "Let Reuben live and not **die**, nor his men be few."
34: 5 [A] And Moses the servant of the LORD **died** there in Moab,
34: 7 [A] Moses was a hundred and twenty years old when he **died**,
Jos 1: 2 [A] "Moses my servant *is* **dead**. Now then, you and all these
1:18 [H] whatever you may command them, *will* **be put to death**.
2:14 [A] "Our lives for your lives!" **[NIE]** the men assured her.
5: 4 [A] **died** in the desert on the way after leaving Egypt.
10:11 [A] more of them **died** from the hailstones than were killed by
10:11 [A] more of them died **[RPH]** from the hailstones than were
10:26 [G] Joshua struck and **killed** the kings and hung them on five
11:17 [G] all their kings and struck them down, **putting** them **to death**.
20: 9 [A] not *be* **killed** by the avenger of blood prior to standing trial
24:29 [A] servant of the LORD, **died** at the age of a hundred and ten.
24:33 [A] And Eleazar son of Aaron **died** and was buried at Gibeah,
Jdg 1: 7 [A] to them." They brought him to Jerusalem, and *he* **died** there.
2: 8 [A] servant of the LORD, **died** at the age of a hundred and ten.
2:21 [A] out before them any of the nations Joshua left when *he* **died**.
3:11 [A] had peace for forty years, until Othniel son of Kenaz **died**.
3:25 [A] There they saw their lord fallen to the floor, **dead**.
4: 1 [A] After Ehud **died**, the Israelites once again did evil in the eyes
4:21 [A] the peg through his temple into the ground, and *he* **died**.
4:22 [A] there lay Sisera with the tent peg through his temple—**dead**.
5:18 [A] The people of Zebulun **risked** [+3070+4200] their very lives;
6:23 [A] to him, "Peace! Do not be afraid. *You are* not *going to* **die**."
6:30 [A] *He must* **die**, because he has broken down Baal's altar and
6:31 [H] Whoever fights for him *shall* **be put to death** by morning!
8:32 [A] Gideon son of Joash **died** at a good old age and was buried in
8:33 [A] No sooner *had* Gideon **died** than the Israelites again
9:49 [A] of Shechem, about a thousand men and women, also **died**.
9:54 [D] "Draw your sword and **kill** me, so that they can't say,
9:54 [A] killed him.' " So his servant ran him through, and *he* **died**.
9:55 [A] When the Israelites saw that Abimelech *was* **dead**, they went
10: 2 [A] twenty-three years; then *he* **died**, and was buried in Shamir.
10: 5 [A] When Jair **died**, he was buried in Kamon.
12: 7 [A] Jephthah the Gileadite **died**, and was buried in a town in
12:10 [A] Then Ibzan **died**, and was buried in Bethlehem.
12:12 [A] Elon **died**, and was buried in Aijalon in the land of Zebulun.
12:15 [A] Abdon son of Hillel **died**, and was buried at Pirathon in
13:22 [A] "*We are* **doomed to die** [+4637]!" he said to his wife. "We
13:22 [A] "*We are* **doomed to die** [+4637]!" he said to his wife. "We
13:23 [G] But his wife answered, "If the LORD had meant to **kill** us,
15:13 [G] and hand you over to them. *We will* not **kill** [+4637] you."
15:13 [G] and hand you over to them. *We will* not **kill** [+4637] you."
15:18 [A] *Must I* now **die** of thirst and fall into the hands of the
16:16 [A] she prodded him day after day until he was tired to **death**.
16:30 [A] Samson said, "*Let* me **die** with the Philistines!" Then he
16:30 [G] Thus *he* **killed** many more when he died than while he lived.
16:30 [A] Thus he killed **[RPH]** many more when he died than while
16:30 [G] Thus he killed many more when he died than **[RPH]** while
20: 5 [A] intending to kill me. They raped my concubine, and *she* **died**.
20:13 [G] so that *we may* **put** them **to death** and purge the evil from
21: 5 [H] at Mizpah *should* **certainly be put to death** [+4637].
21: 5 [A] at Mizpah *should* **certainly be put to death** [+4637].
Ru 1: 3 [A] Now Elimelech, Naomi's husband, **died**, and she was left
1: 5 [A] both Mahlon and Kilion also **died**, and Naomi was left
1: 8 [A] kindness to you, as you have shown to your **dead** and to me.
1:17 [A] Where *you* **die** I will die, and there I will be buried. May the
1:17 [A] Where you die *I will* **die**, and there I will be buried. May the
2:20 [A] not stopped showing his kindness to the living and the **dead**."
4: 5 [A] Ruth the Moabitess, you acquire the **dead** *man's* widow,
4: 5 [A] in order to maintain the name of the **dead** with his property."
4:10 [A] in order to maintain the name of the **dead** with his property,
4:10 [A] so that **his**[s] [+2021] name will not disappear from among his
1Sa 2: 6 [G] "The LORD **brings death** and makes alive; he brings down
2:25 [G] for it was the LORD's will to **put** them **to death**.
2:33 [A] and all your descendants *will* **die** in the prime of life.
2:34 [A] will be a sign to you—they *will* both **die** on the same day.

1Sa 4: 11 [A] and Eli's two sons, Hophni and Phinehas, **died**.
4: 17 [A] Also your two sons, Hophni and Phinehas, *are* **dead**,
4: 18 [A] His neck was broken and *he* **died**, for he was an old man
4: 19 [A] and that her father-in-law and her husband *were* **dead**,
4: 20 [A] As she *was* **dying**, the women attending her said,
5: 10 [G] brought the ark of the god of Israel around to us to **kill** us and
5: 11 [G] it go back to its own place, or *it will* **kill** us and our people."
5: 12 [A] Those who *did* not **die** were afflicted with tumors, and the
11: 12 [G] Bring these men to us and *we will* **put** them **to death**."
11: 13 [H] Saul said, "No one *shall* **be put to death** today, for this day
12: 19 [A] LORD your God for your servants so that *we will* not **die**,
14: 13 [D] and his armor-bearer followed and **killed** behind him.
14: 39 [A] even if it lies with my son Jonathan, *he* **must die** [+4637]."
14: 39 [A] even if it lies with my son Jonathan, *he* **must die** [+4637]."
14: 43 [A] a little honey with the end of my staff. And now *must* I **die**?"
14: 44 [A] be it ever so severely, if *you do* not **die** [+4637], Jonathan."
14: 44 [A] be it ever so severely, if *you do* not **die** [+4637], Jonathan."
14: 45 [A] the men said to Saul, "*Should* Jonathan **die**—he who has
14: 45 [A] So the men rescued Jonathan, and *he was* not **put to death**.
15: 3 [G] **put to death** men and women, children and infants, cattle
17: 35 [G] it turned on me, I seized it by its hair, struck it and **killed** it.
17: 50 [G] in his hand he struck down the Philistine and **killed** him.
17: 51 [D] After *he* **killed** him, he cut off his head with the sword.
17: 51 [A] When the Philistines saw that their hero *was* **dead**, they
19: 1 [G] told his son Jonathan and all the attendants to **kill** David.
19: 2 [G] "My father Saul is looking for a chance to **kill** you.
19: 5 [G] to an innocent man like David by **killing** him for no reason?"
19: 6 [H] surely as the LORD lives, David *will* not **be put to death**."
19: 11 [G] to David's house to watch it and to **kill** him in the morning.
19: 11 [H] don't run for your life tonight, tomorrow you'll **be killed**."
19: 15 [G] "Bring him up to me in his bed so that I *may* **kill** him."
19: 17 [G] "He said to me, 'Let me get away. Why *should I* **kill** you?' "
20: 2 [A] "*You are* not *going to* **die**! Look, my father doesn't do
20: 8 [G] If I am guilty, then **kill** me yourself! Why hand me over to
20: 14 [A] of the LORD as long as I live, so that *I may* not *be* **killed**,
20: 32 [H] "Why *should he* **be put to death**? What has he done?"
20: 33 [G] Then Jonathan knew that his father intended to **kill** David.
22: 16 [A] "*You will* **surely die** [+4637], Ahimelech, you and your
22: 16 [A] "*You will* **surely die** [+4637], Ahimelech, you and your
22: 17 [G] "Turn and **kill** the priests of the LORD, because they too
22: 18 [G] That day *he* **killed** eighty-five men who wore the linen
24: 14 [24:15] [A] Whom are you pursuing? A **dead** dog? A flea?
25: 1 [A] Now Samuel **died**, and all Israel assembled and mourned for
25: 37 [A] and his heart **failed** him and he became like a stone.
25: 38 [A] About ten days later, the LORD struck Nabal and *he* **died**.
25: 39 [A] When David heard that Nabal *was* **dead**, he said, "Praise be
26: 10 [A] either his time will come and *he will* **die**, or he will go into
28: 3 [A] Now Samuel *was* **dead**, and all Israel had mourned for him
28: 9 [G] have you set a trap for my life to **bring about** my **death**?"
30: 2 [G] *They* **killed** none of them, but carried them off as they went
30: 15 [G] "Swear to me before God that *you will* not **kill** me or hand
31: 5 [A] When the armor-bearer saw that Saul *was* **dead**, he too fell
31: 5 [A] Saul was dead, he too fell on his sword and **died** with him.
31: 6 [A] his armor-bearer and all his men **died** together that same day.
31: 7 [A] Israelite army had fled and that Saul and his sons *had* **died**,
2Sa 1: 4 [A] Many of them fell and **died**. And Saul and his son Jonathan
1: 4 [A] them fell and died. And Saul and his son Jonathan *are* **dead**."
1: 5 [A] do you know that Saul and his son Jonathan *are* **dead**?"
1: 9 [D] "Then he said to me, 'Stand over me and **kill** me! I am in the
1: 10 [D] "So I stood over him and **killed** him, because I knew that
1: 15 [A] "Go, strike him down!" So he struck him down, and *he* **died**.
1: 16 [D] you when you said, 'I **killed** the LORD's anointed.' "
2: 7 [A] Now then, be strong and brave, for Saul your master *is* **dead**,
2: 23 [A] out through his back. He fell there and **died** on the spot.
2: 23 [A] when he came to the place where Asahel had fallen and **died**.
2: 31 [A] David's men *had* **killed** [+5782] three hundred and sixty
3: 27 [A] Joab stabbed him in the stomach, and *he* **died**.
3: 30 [G] because *he had* **killed** their brother Asahel in the battle at
3: 33 [A] for Abner: "*Should* Abner *have* **died** as the lawless die?
3: 37 [G] all Israel knew that the king had no part in *the* **murder** *of*
4: 1 [A] When Ish-Bosheth son of Saul heard that Abner *had* **died** in
4: 7 [G] After they stabbed and **killed** him, they cut off his head.
4: 10 [A] when a man told me, 'Saul *is* **dead**,' and thought he was
6: 7 [A] struck him down and *he* **died** there beside the ark of God.
8: 2 [G] Every two lengths of them *were* **put to death**, and the third
9: 8 [A] is your servant, that you should notice a **dead** dog like me?"
10: 1 [A] In the course of time, the king of the Ammonites **died**,
10: 18 [A] Shobach the commander of their army, and *he* **died** there.
11: 15 [A] Then withdraw from him so he will be struck down and **die**."
11: 17 [A] men in David's army fell; moreover, Uriah the Hittite **died**.
11: 21 [A] millstone on him from the wall, so that *he* **died** in Thebez?
11: 21 [A] say to him, 'Also, your servant Uriah the Hittite *is* **dead**.' "
11: 24 [A] servants from the wall, and some of the king's men **died**.
11: 24 [A] men died. Moreover, your servant Uriah the Hittite *is* **dead**."
11: 26 [A] When Uriah's wife heard that her husband *was* **dead**, she
12: 13 [A] LORD has taken away your sin. *You are* not *going to* **die**.
12: 14 [A] show utter contempt, the son born to you *will* **die** [+4637]."
12: 14 [A] show utter contempt, the son born to you *will* **die** [+4637]."
12: 18 [A] On the seventh day the child **died**. David's servants were
12: 18 [A] servants were afraid to tell him that the child *was* **dead**,
12: 18 [A] not listen to us. How can we tell him the child *is* **dead**?
12: 19 [A] among themselves and he realized the child *was* **dead**.
12: 19 [A] "*Is* the child **dead**?" he asked. "Yes," they replied, "he is
12: 19 [A] the child dead?" he asked. "Yes," they replied, "*he is* **dead**."
12: 21 [A] you fasted and wept, but now that the child *is* **dead**, you get
12: 23 [A] now that *he is* **dead**, why should I fast? Can I bring him back
13: 28 [G] and I say to you, 'Strike Amnon down,' then **kill** him.
13: 32 [G] "My lord should not think that *they* **killed** all the princes;
13: 32 [A] think that they killed all the princes; only Amnon *is* **dead**.
13: 33 [A] concerned about the report that all the king's sons *are* **dead**.
13: 33 [A] that all the king's sons are dead. Only Amnon *is* **dead**."
13: 39 [A] to Absalom, for he was consoled concerning Amnon's **death**.
14: 2 [A] a woman who has spent many days grieving for the **dead**.
14: 5 [A] She said, "I am indeed a widow; my husband *is* **dead**.
14: 6 [G] there to separate them. One struck the other and **killed** him.
14: 7 [G] so that *we may* **put** him **to death** for the life of his brother
14: 14 [A] which cannot be recovered, so *we* **must die** [+4637].
14: 14 [A] which cannot be recovered, so *we* **must die** [+4637].
14: 32 [G] and if I am guilty of anything, *let him* **put** me **to death**."
16: 9 [A] the king, "Why should this **dead** dog curse my lord the king?
17: 23 [A] So *he* **died** and was buried in his father's tomb.
18: 3 [A] Even if half of us **die**, they won't care; but you are worth ten
18: 15 [G] surrounded Absalom, struck him and **killed** him.
18: 20 [A] you must not do so today, because the king's son *is* **dead**."
18: 33 [19:1] [A] If only I *had* **died** instead of you—O Absalom,
19: 6 [19:7] [A] if Absalom were alive today and all of us *were* **dead**.
19: 10 [19:11] [A] we anointed to rule over us, *has* **died** in battle.
19: 21 [19:22] [H] "Shouldn't Shimei **be put to death** for this?
19: 22 [19:23] [H] *Should* anyone **be put to death** in Israel today?
19: 23 [19:24] [A] So the king said to Shimei, "*You shall* not **die**."
19: 37 [19:38] [A] that *I may* **die** in my own town near the tomb of my
20: 3 [A] They were kept in confinement till the day of their **death**,
20: 10 [A] Without being stabbed again, Amasa **died**. Then Joab and his
20: 19 [G] You are trying to **destroy** a city that is a mother in Israel.
21: 1 [G] it is because *he* **put** the Gibeonites **to death**."
21: 4 [G] nor do we have the right to **put** anyone in Israel *to* **death**."
21: 9 [H] they **were put to death** during the first days of the harvest,
21: 17 [G] David's rescue; he struck the Philistine down and **killed** him.
24: 15 [A] seventy thousand of the people from Dan to Beersheba **died**.
1Ki 1: 51 [G] that *he will* not **put** his servant **to death** with the sword.' "
1: 52 [A] fall to the ground; but if evil is found in him, *he will* **die**."
2: 1 [A] When the time drew near for David to **die**, he gave a charge
2: 8 [G] by the LORD: '*I will* not **put** you **to death** by the sword.'
2: 24 [H] me as he promised—Adonijah *shall* **be put to death** today!"
2: 25 [A] son of Jehoiada, and he struck down Adonijah and *he* **died**.
2: 26 [G] You deserve to die, but *I will* not **put** you **to death** now,
2: 30 [A] 'Come out!' " But he answered, "No, *I will* **die** here."
2: 34 [G] of Jehoiada went up and struck down Joab and **killed** him,
2: 37 [A] the Kidron Valley, you can be sure *you will* **die** [+4637];
2: 37 [A] the Kidron Valley, you can be sure *you will* **die** [+4637];
2: 42 [A] to go anywhere else, you can be sure *you will* **die** [+4637]'?
2: 42 [A] to go anywhere else, you can be sure *you will* **die** [+4637]'?
2: 46 [A] and he went out and struck Shimei down and **killed** him.
3: 19 [A] "During the night this woman's son **died** because she lay on
3: 20 [A] She put him by her breast and put her **dead** son by my breast.
3: 21 [A] next morning, I got up to nurse my son—and *he was* **dead**!
3: 22 [A] "No! The living one is my son; the **dead** *one* is yours."
3: 22 [A] The **dead** *one* is yours; the living one is mine." And so they
3: 23 [A] "This one says, 'My son is alive and your son *is* **dead**,'
3: 23 [A] that one says, 'No! Your son *is* **dead** and mine is alive.' "
3: 26 [G] Don't **kill** [+4637] him!" But the other said, "Neither I nor
3: 26 [G] Don't **kill** [+4637] him!" But the other said, "Neither I nor
3: 27 [G] the first woman. *Do* not **kill** [+4637] him; she is his mother."
3: 27 [G] the first woman. *Do* not **kill** [+4637] him; she is his mother."
11: 21 [A] and that Joab the commander of the army *was* also **dead**.
11: 40 [G] Solomon tried to **kill** Jeroboam, but Jeroboam fled to Egypt,
12: 18 [A] in charge of forced labor, but all Israel stoned him *to* **death**.
13: 24 [G] went on his way, a lion met him on the road and **killed** him,
13: 26 [G] him over to the lion, which has mauled him and **killed** him,
14: 11 [A] Dogs will eat those belonging to Jeroboam *who* **die** in the
14: 11 [A] the birds of the air will feed on those *who* **die** in the country.
14: 12 [A] back home. When you set foot in your city, the boy *will* **die**.
14: 17 [A] as she stepped over the threshold of the house, the boy **died**.
15: 28 [G] Baasha **killed** Nadab in the third year of Asa king of Judah
16: 4 [A] Dogs will eat those belonging to Baasha *who* **die** in the city,
16: 4 [A] the birds of the air will feed on those *who* **die** in the
16: 10 [G] **killed** him in the twenty-seventh year of Asa king of Judah.
16: 18 [A] and set the palace on fire around him. So *he* **died**,

1Ki 16:22 [A] of Tibni son of Ginath. So Tibni **died** and Omri became king.
17:12 [A] a meal for myself and my son, that we may eat it—and **die**."
17:18 [G] Did you come to remind me of my sin and **kill** my son?"
17:20 [G] this widow I am staying with, by **causing** her son **to die**?"
18: 9 [G] are handing your servant over to Ahab to *be* **put to death**?
19: 4 [A] a broom tree, sat down under it and prayed that he *might* **die**.
19:17 [G] Jehu *will* **put to death** any who escape the sword of Hazael,
19:17 [G] Elisha *will* **put to death** any who escape the sword of Jehu.
21:10 [A] and the king. Then take him out and stone him *to* **death**."
21:13 [A] So they took him outside the city and stoned him *to* **death**.
21:14 [A] sent word to Jezebel: "Naboth has been stoned and *is* **dead**."
21:15 [A] soon as Jezebel heard that Naboth had been stoned *to* **death**,
21:15 [A] that he refused to sell you. He is no longer alive, but **dead**."
21:16 [A] When Ahab heard that Naboth *was* **dead**, he got up and went
21:24 [A] "Dogs will eat those belonging to Ahab *who* **die** in the city,
21:24 [A] the birds of the air will feed on those *who* **die** in the
22:35 [A] ran onto the floor of the chariot, and that evening *he* **died**.
22:37 [A] So the king **died** and was brought to Samaria, and they
2Ki 1: 4 [A] lying on. *You will* **certainly die** [+4637]!' " So Elijah went.
1: 4 [A] lying on. *You will* **certainly die** [+4637]!' " So Elijah went.
1: 6 [A] bed you are lying on. *You will* **certainly die** [+4637]!" ' "
1: 6 [A] bed you are lying on. *You will* **certainly die** [+4637]!" ' "
1:16 [A] the bed you are lying on. *You will* **certainly die** [+4637]!"
1:16 [A] the bed you are lying on. *You will* **certainly die** [+4637]!"
1:17 [A] So *he* **died**, according to the word of the LORD that Elijah
4: 1 [A] "Your servant my husband *is* **dead**, and you know that he
4:20 [A] the boy sat on her lap until noon, and then *he* **died**.
4:32 [A] the house, there was the boy lying **dead** on his couch.
5: 7 [G] and said, "Am I God? *Can I* **kill** and bring back to life?
7: 3 [A] They said to each other, "Why stay here until we **die**?
7: 4 [A] 'We'll go into the city'—the famine is there, and *we will* **die**.
7: 4 [A] is there, and we will die. And if we stay here, *we will* **die**.
7: 4 [G] If they spare us, we live; if *they* **kill** us, then we die."
7: 4 [A] If they spare us, we live; if they kill us, then *we* **die**."
7:17 [A] and the people trampled him in the gateway, and *he* **died**,
7:20 [A] for the people trampled him in the gateway, and *he* **died**.
8: 5 [A] was telling the king how Elisha had restored the **dead** to life,
8:10 [A] LORD has revealed to me that *he will* **in fact die** [+4637]."
8:10 [A] LORD has revealed to me that *he will* **in fact die** [+4637]."
8:15 [A] it in water and spread it over the king's face, so that *he* **died**.
9:27 [A] Gur near Ibleam, but he escaped to Megiddo and **died** there.
11: 1 [A] Athaliah the mother of Ahaziah saw that her son *was* **dead**,
11: 2 [H] among the royal princes, who *were about to* **be murdered**.
11: 2 [H] a bedroom to hide him from Athaliah; so *he* **was** not **killed**.
11: 8 [H] Anyone who approaches your ranks *must* **be put to death**.
11:15 [G] the ranks and **put**[s] to the sword anyone who follows her."
11:15 [H] "*She must* not **be put to death** in the temple of the
11:16 [H] enter the palace grounds, and there *she* **was put to death**.
11:20 [G] because Athaliah *had been* **slain** with the sword at the
12:21 [12:22] [A] *He* **died** and was buried with his fathers in the City
13:14 [A] Elisha was suffering from the illness from which *he* **died**.
13:20 [A] Elisha **died** and was buried. Now Moabite raiders used to
13:24 [A] Hazael king of Aram **died**, and Ben-Hadad his son succeeded
14: 6 [G] Yet *he did* not **put** the sons of the assassins **to death**, in
14: 6 [H] "Fathers *shall* not **be put to death** for their children, nor
14: 6 [H] for their children, nor children **put to death** for their fathers;
14: 6 [A] put to death for their fathers; each *is to* **die** for his own sins."
14:19 [G] but they sent men after him to Lachish and **killed** him there.
15: 5 [A] LORD afflicted the king with leprosy until the day he **died**,
15:10 [G] of the people, **assassinated** him and succeeded him as king.
15:14 [G] in Samaria, **assassinated** him and succeeded him as king.
15:25 [G] So Pekah **killed** Pekahiah and succeeded him as king.
15:30 [G] He attacked and **assassinated** him, and then succeeded him
16: 9 [G] He deported its inhabitants to Kir and **put** Rezin **to death**.
17:26 [G] He has sent lions among them, which *are* **killing** them **off**,
18:32 [A] a land of olive trees and honey. Choose life and not **death**!
19:35 [A] got up the next morning—there were all the **dead** bodies!
20: 1 [A] days Hezekiah became ill and was at the point of **death**.
20: 1 [A] Put your house in order, because you *are going to* **die**; you
21:23 [G] against him and **assassinated** the king in his palace.
23:29 [G] him in battle, but Neco faced him and **killed** him at Megiddo.
23:30 [A] Josiah's servants brought *his* **body** in a chariot from
23:34 [A] and carried him off to Egypt, and there *he* **died**.
25:21 [G] of Hamath, the king *had* them **executed** [+906+2256+5782].
25:25 [A] **assassinated** [+906+906+906+2256+5782] Gedaliah and also
1Ch 1:44 [A] When Bela **died**, Jobab son of Zerah from Bozrah succeeded
1:45 [A] When Jobab **died**, Husham from the land of the Temanites
1:46 [A] When Husham **died**, Hadad son of Bedad, who defeated
1:47 [A] When Hadad **died**, Samlah from Masrekah succeeded him as
1:48 [A] When Samlah **died**, Shaul from Rehoboth on the river
1:49 [A] When Shaul **died**, Baal-Hanan son of Acbor succeeded him
1:50 [A] When Baal-Hanan **died**, Hadad succeeded him as king. His
1:51 [A] Hadad also **died**. The chiefs of Edom were: Timna, Alvah,
2: 3 [G] in the LORD's sight; so the LORD **put** him **to death**.
2:19 [A] When Azubah **died**, Caleb married Ephrath, who bore him
2:30 [A] of Nadab: Seled and Appaim. Seled **died** without children.
2:32 [A] Jether and Jonathan. Jether **died** without children.
10: 5 [A] When the armor-bearer saw that Saul *was* **dead**, he too fell
10: 5 [A] saw that Saul was dead, he too fell on his sword and **died**.
10: 6 [A] So Saul and his three sons **died**, and all his house died
10: 6 [A] and his three sons died, and all his house **died** together.
10: 7 [A] that the army had fled and that Saul and his sons *had* **died**,
10:13 [A] Saul **died** because he was unfaithful to the LORD; he did
10:14 [G] So the LORD **put** him **to death** and turned the kingdom
13:10 [A] he had put his hand on the ark. So *he* **died** there before God.
19: 1 [A] In the course of time, Nahash king of the Ammonites **died**,
19:18 [G] *He* also **killed** Shophach the commander of their army.
23:22 [A] Eleazar **died** without having sons: he had only daughters.
24: 2 [A] Nadab and Abihu **died** before their father did, and they had
29:28 [A] *He* **died** at a good old age, having enjoyed long life, wealth
2Ch 10:18 [A] charge of forced labor, but the Israelites stoned him *to* **death**.
13:20 [A] of Abijah. And the LORD struck him down and *he* **died**.
15:13 [H] *were to* **be put to death**, whether small or great, man or
16:13 [A] in the forty-first year of his reign Asa **died** and rested with
18:34 [A] facing the Arameans until evening. Then at sunset *he* **died**.
21:19 [A] came out because of the disease, and *he* **died** in great pain.
22: 9 [G] He was brought to Jehu and **put to death**. They buried him,
22:10 [A] Athaliah the mother of Ahaziah saw that her son *was* **dead**,
22:11 [H] among the royal princes who *were about to* **be murdered**
22:11 [G] she hid the child from Athaliah so *she could* not **kill** him.
23: 7 [H] Anyone who enters the temple *must* **be put to death**.
23:14 [H] the ranks and **put**[s] to the sword anyone who follows her."
23:14 [G] "*Do* not **put** her **to death** *at* the temple of the LORD."
23:15 [G] Gate on the palace grounds, and there *they* **put** her **to death**.
23:21 [G] was quiet, because Athaliah *had been* **slain** with the sword.
24:15 [A] full of years, and *he* **died** at the age of a hundred and thirty.
24:25 [A] So *he* **died** and was buried in the City of David, but not in
25: 4 [G] Yet *he did* not **put** their sons **to death**, but acted in
25: 4 [A] "Fathers *shall* not *be put to* **death** for their children, nor
25: 4 [A] for their children, nor children *put to* **death** for their fathers;
25: 4 [A] put to death for their fathers; each *is to* **die** for his own sins."
25:27 [G] but they sent men after him to Lachish and **killed** him there.
32:11 [A] he is misleading you, to let you **die** of hunger and thirst.
32:24 [A] days Hezekiah became ill and was at the point of **death**.
32:33 [A] and the people of Jerusalem honored him when he **died**.
33:24 [G] conspired against him and **assassinated** him in his palace.
35:24 [A] chariot he had and brought him to Jerusalem, where *he* **died**.
Est 4:11 [G] summoned the king has but one law: that he *be* **put to death**.
Job 1:19 [A] It collapsed on them and *they are* **dead**, and I am the only
2: 9 [A] you still holding on to your integrity? Curse God and **die**!"
3:11 [A] "Why *did I* not **perish** at birth, and die as I came from the
4:21 [A] of their tent pulled up, so that *they* **die** without wisdom?'
5: 2 [G] Resentment kills a fool, and envy **slays** the simple.
9:23 [G] When a scourge **brings** sudden **death**, he mocks the despair
12: 2 [A] you are the people, and wisdom *will* **die** with you!
14: 8 [A] may grow old in the ground and its stump **die** in the soil,
14:10 [A] man **dies** and is laid low; he breathes his last and is no more.
14:14 [A] If a man **dies**, will he live again? All the days of my hard
21:23 [A] One man **dies** in full vigor, completely secure and at ease,
21:25 [A] Another man **dies** in bitterness of soul, never having enjoyed
24:12 [a] The groans of the **dying** [BHS 5493] rise from the city,
33:22 [G] draws near to the pit, and his life to the **messengers of death**.
34:20 [A] *They* **die** in an instant, in the middle of the night; the people
36:14 [A] They **die** in their youth, among male prostitutes of the
42:17 [A] And so he **died**, old and full of years.
Ps 9: T [9:1] [a] "The **Death** [BHS 6629] of the Son."
31:12 [31:13] [A] I am forgotten by them as though I *were* **dead**; I
34:21 [34:22] [D] Evil *will* **slay** the wicked; the foes of the righteous
37:32 [G] wicked lie in wait for the righteous, seeking their very **lives**;
41: 5 [41:6] [A] in malice, "When *will he* **die** and his name perish?"
48:14 [48:15] [A] and ever; he will be our guide even to the **end**.
49:10 [49:11] [A] For all can see that wise men **die**; the foolish
59: T [59:1] [G] sent men to watch David's house in order to **kill** him.
82: 7 [A] *you will* **die** like mere men; you will fall like every other
88: 5 [88:6] [A] I am set apart with the **dead**, like the slain who lie in
88:10 [88:11] [A] Do you show your wonders to the **dead**? Do those
105:29 [G] He turned their waters into blood, **causing** their fish **to die**.
106:28 [A] to the Baal of Peor and ate sacrifices offered to **lifeless** gods;
109:16 [D] hounded to **death** the poor and the needy
115:17 [A] It is not the **dead** who praise the LORD, those who go down
118:17 [A] *I will* not **die** but live, and will proclaim what the LORD
143: 3 [A] he makes me dwell in darkness like *those* long **dead**.
Pr 5:23 [A] He *will* **die** for lack of discipline, led astray by his own great
10:21 [A] righteous nourish many, but fools **die** for lack of judgment.
15:10 [A] him who leaves the path; he who hates correction *will* **die**.
19:16 [A] his life, but he who is contemptuous of his ways *will* **die**.
19:18 [G] in that there is hope; do not be a willing party to his **death**.
21:25 [G] The sluggard's craving *will be the* **death** *of* him, because his

Pr 23: 13 [A] from a child; if you punish him with the rod, *he will* not **die**.
30: 7 [A] things I ask of you, O LORD; do not refuse me before *I* **die**:
Ecc 2: 16 [A] will be forgotten. Like the fool, the wise man too *must* **die**!
3: 2 [A] a time to be born and a time to **die**, a time to plant and a time
4: 2 [A] I declared that the **dead**, who had already died, are happier
4: 2 [A] who *had* already **died**, are happier than the living, who are
7: 17 [A] and do not be a fool—why **die** before your time?
9: 3 [A] their hearts while they live, and afterward they join the **dead**.
9: 4 [A] has hope—even a live dog is better off than a **dead** lion!
9: 5 [A] For the living know that *they will* **die**, but the dead know
9: 5 [A] living know that they will die, but the **dead** know nothing;
Isa 5: 13 [a] their men of rank *will* **die** [BHS 5493] *of* hunger and their
8: 19 [A] of their God? Why consult the **dead** on behalf of the living?
11: 4 [G] his mouth; with the breath of his lips *he will* **slay** the wicked.
14: 30 [G] your root *I will* **destroy** by famine; it will slay your
22: 2 [A] slain were not killed by the sword, nor *did they* **die** *in* battle.
22: 13 [A] "Let us eat and drink," you say, "for tomorrow *we* **die**!"
22: 14 [A] "Till *your* **dying** day this sin will not be atoned for," says the
22: 18 [A] There *you will* **die** and there your splendid chariots will
26: 14 [A] *They are now* **dead**, they live no more; those departed spirits
26: 19 [A] your **dead** will live; their bodies will rise. You who dwell in
37: 36 [A] got up the next morning—there were all the **dead** bodies!
38: 1 [A] days Hezekiah became ill and was at the point of **death**.
38: 1 [A] Put your house in order, because you *are going to* **die**; you
50: 2 [A] into a desert; their fish rot for lack of water and **die** of thirst.
51: 6 [A] will wear out like a garment and its inhabitants **die** like flies.
51: 12 [A] Who are you that you fear **mortal** men, the sons of men,
51: 14 [A] *they will* not **die** in their dungeon, nor will they lack bread.
59: 5 [A] Whoever eats their eggs *will* **die**, and when one is broken,
59: 10 [A] as if it were twilight; among the strong, we *are* like the **dead**.
65: 15 [G] the Sovereign LORD *will* **put** you **to death**, but to his
65: 20 [A] *he who* **dies** at a hundred will be thought a mere youth;
66: 24 [A] their worm *will* not **die**, nor will their fire be quenched,
Jer 11: 21 [A] in the name of the LORD or *you will* **die** by our hands'—
11: 22 [A] Their young men *will* **die** by the sword, their sons
11: 22 [A] by the sword, their sons and daughters **[RPH]** by famine.
16: 4 [A] "*They will* **die** *of* deadly diseases. They will not be mourned
16: 6 [A] "Both high and low *will* **die** in this land. They will not be
16: 7 [A] will offer food to comfort those who mourn for the **dead**—
20: 6 [A] There *you will* **die** and be buried, you and all your friends to
20: 17 [D] For *he did* not **kill** me in the womb, with my mother as my
21: 6 [A] and animals—and *they will* **die** of a terrible plague.
21: 9 [A] Whoever stays in this city *will* **die** by the sword, famine
22: 10 [A] Do not weep for the **dead** ˻king˼ or mourn his loss; rather,
22: 12 [A] *He will* **die** in the place where they have led him captive; he
22: 26 [A] where neither of you was born, and there *you both will* **die**.
26: 8 [A] all the people seized him and said, "*You* **must die** [+4637]!
26: 8 [A] all the people seized him and said, "*You* **must die** [+4637]!
26: 15 [G] Be assured, however, that if you **put** me **to death**, you will
26: 19 [G] of Judah or anyone else in Judah **put** him **to death** [+4637]?
26: 19 [G] of Judah or anyone else in Judah **put** him **to death** [+4637]?
26: 21 [G] heard his words, the king sought to **put** him **to death**.
26: 24 [G] so he was not handed over to the people to *be* **put to death**.
27: 13 [A] Why *will* you and your people **die** by the sword, famine
28: 16 [A] This very year you *are going to* **die**, because you have
28: 17 [A] seventh month of that same year, Hananiah the prophet **died**.
31: 30 [A] Instead, everyone *will* **die** for his own sin; whoever eats sour
34: 4 [A] LORD says concerning you: *You will* not **die** by the sword;
34: 5 [A] *you will* **die** peacefully. As people made a funeral fire in
37: 20 [A] to the house of Jonathan the secretary, or *I will* **die** there."
38: 2 [A] 'Whoever stays in this city *will* **die** by the sword, famine
38: 4 [H] officials said to the king, "This man *should* **be put to death**.
38: 9 [A] where *he will* starve *to* **death** when there is no longer any
38: 10 [A] lift Jeremiah the prophet out of the cistern before *he* **dies**."
38: 15 [G] "If I give you an answer, *will you* not **kill** [+4637] me?
38: 15 [G] "If I give you an answer, *will you* not **kill** [+4637] me?
38: 16 [G] *I will* neither **kill** you nor hand you over to those who are
38: 24 [A] not let anyone know about this conversation, or *you may* **die**.
38: 25 [G] king said to you; do not hide it from us or *we will* **kill** you,'
38: 26 [A] king not to send me back to Jonathan's house to **die** there.' "
41: 2 [G] **killing** the one whom the king of Babylon had appointed as
41: 4 [G] The day after Gedaliah's **assassination**, before anyone knew
41: 8 [G] ten of them said to Ishmael, "Don't **kill** us! We have wheat
41: 8 [G] So he let them alone and *did* not **kill** them with the others.
42: 16 [A] you dread will follow you into Egypt, and there *you will* **die**.
42: 17 [A] all who are determined to go to Egypt to settle there *will* **die**
42: 22 [A] *You will* **die** by the sword, famine and plague in the place
43: 3 [G] so they *may* **kill** us or carry us into exile to Babylon."
44: 12 [A] the least to the greatest, *they will* **die** by sword or famine.
52: 27 [G] of Hamath, the king **had** them **executed** [+906+2256+5782].
La 3: 6 [A] He has made me dwell in darkness like *those* long **dead**.
Eze 3: 18 [A] '*You will* **surely die** [+4637],' and you do not warn him
3: 18 [A] '*You will* **surely die** [+4637],' and you do not warn him
3: 18 [A] that wicked man *will* **die** for his sin, and I will hold you
3: 19 [A] his wickedness or from his evil ways, he *will* **die** for his sin;
3: 20 [A] does evil, and I put a stumbling block before him, he *will* **die**.
3: 20 [A] will die. Since you did not warn him, *he will* **die** for his sin.
5: 12 [A] A third of your people *will* **die** of the plague or perish by
6: 12 [A] He that is far away *will* **die** of the plague, and he that is near
6: 12 [A] and he that survives and is spared *will* **die** of famine.
7: 15 [A] those in the country *will* **die** by the sword, and those in the
11: 13 [A] Now as I was prophesying, Pelatiah son of Benaiah **died**.
12: 13 [A] of the Chaldeans, but he will not see it, and there *he will* **die**.
13: 19 [G] you *have* **killed** those who should not have died and have
13: 19 [A] you have killed those who *should* not *have* **died** and have
17: 16 [A] declares the Sovereign LORD, *he shall* **die** in Babylon,
18: 4 [A] belong to me. The soul who sins is the one *who will* **die**.
18: 13 [H] *he will* **surely be put to death** [+4637] and his blood will be
18: 13 [A] *he will* **surely be put to death** [+4637] and his blood will be
18: 17 [A] He *will* not **die** for his father's sin; he will surely live.
18: 18 [A] his father *will* **die** for his own sin, because he practiced
18: 20 [A] The soul who sins is the one *who will* **die**. The son will not
18: 21 [A] what is just and right, he will surely live; *he will* not **die**.
18: 24 [A] and because of the sins he has committed, *he will* **die**.
18: 26 [A] from his righteousness and commits sin, *he will* **die** for it;
18: 26 [A] die for it; because of the sin he has committed *he will* **die**.
18: 28 [A] turns away from them, he will surely live; *he will* not **die**.
18: 31 [A] and a new spirit. Why *will you* **die**, O house of Israel?
18: 32 [A] For I take no pleasure in the death of **anyone**[s] [+2021],
24: 17 [A] Groan quietly; do not mourn for the **dead**. Keep your turban
24: 18 [A] the people in the morning, and in the evening my wife **died**.
28: 8 [A] and *you will* **die** a violent death in the heart of the seas.
28: 10 [A] *You will* **die** the death of the uncircumcised at the hands of
33: 8 [A] to the wicked, 'O wicked man, *you will* **surely die** [+4637],'
33: 8 [A] to the wicked, 'O wicked man, *you will* **surely die** [+4637],'
33: 8 [A] that wicked man *will* **die** for his sin, and I will hold you
33: 9 [A] from his ways and he does not do so, he *will* **die** for his sin,
33: 11 [A] from your evil ways! Why *will you* **die**, O house of Israel?'
33: 13 [A] will be remembered; *he will* **die** for the evil he has done.
33: 14 [A] '*You will* **surely die** [+4637],' but he then turns away from
33: 14 [A] '*You will* **surely die** [+4637],' but he then turns away from
33: 15 [A] give life, and does no evil, he will surely live; *he will* not **die**.
33: 18 [A] turns from his righteousness and does evil, *he will* **die** for it.
33: 27 [A] and those in strongholds and caves *will* **die** of a plague.
44: 25 [A] " 'A priest must not defile himself by going near a **dead**
Hos 2: 3 [2:5] [G] turn her into a parched land, and **slay** her with thirst.
9: 16 [G] if they bear children, *I will* **slay** their cherished offspring."
13: 1 [A] in Israel. But he became guilty of Baal worship and **died**.
Am 2: 2 [A] Moab *will* **go down** in great tumult amid war cries and the
6: 9 [A] If ten men are left in one house, *they* too *will* **die**.
7: 11 [A] " 'Jeroboam *will* **die** by the sword, and Israel will surely go
7: 17 [A] and divided up, and *you* yourself *will* **die** in a pagan country.
9: 10 [A] All the sinners among my people *will* **die** by the sword,
Jnh 4: 8 [A] He wanted to **die**, and said, "It would be better for me to die
Hab 1: 12 [A] My God, my Holy One, *we will* not **die**. O LORD, you have
Zec 11: 9 [A] be your shepherd. Let the **dying** die, and the perishing perish.
11: 9 [A] be your shepherd. *Let* the dying **die**, and the perishing perish.

4638 מָוֶת *māwet*, n.m. [152 / 151] [→ 2975; cf. 4637; Ar 10409]

death [109], die [11], died [11], dies [5], deadly [3], dead [2], *untranslated* [1], capital offense [+5477] [1], deadly plague [1], death's [1], dying [1], immortality [+440] [1], kill [1], must die [+1201] [1], plague [1], put to death [+2222] [1]

Ge 21: 16 a bowshot away, for she thought, "I cannot watch the boy **die**."
25: 11 After Abraham's **death**, God blessed his son Isaac, who then lived
26: 18 which the Philistines had stopped up after Abraham **died**,
27: 2 "I am now an old man and don't know the day of my **death**.
27: 7 give you my blessing in the presence of the LORD before I **die**.'
27: 10 father to eat, so that he may give you his blessing before he **dies**."
50: 16 saying, "Your father left these instructions before he **died**:
Ex 10: 17 pray to the LORD your God to take this **deadly plague** away
Lev 16: 1 The LORD spoke to Moses after the **death** *of* the two sons of
Nu 16: 29 If these men die a natural **death** and experience only what usually
23: 10 Let me die the **death** *of* the righteous, and may my end be like
35: 28 The accused must stay in his city of refuge until the **death** *of* the
35: 28 only after the **death** *of* the high priest may he return to his own
35: 32 and live on his own land before the **death** *of* the high priest.
Dt 19: 6 is too great, and kill him even though he is not deserving of **death**,
21: 22 If a man guilty of a **capital** [+5477] **offense** is put to death
22: 26 Do nothing to the girl; she has committed no sin deserving **death**.
30: 15 I set before you today life and prosperity, **death** and destruction.
30: 19 as witnesses against you that I have set before you life and **death**,
31: 27 still alive and with you, how much more will you rebel after I **die**!
31: 29 For I know that after my **death** you are sure to become utterly
33: 1 the man of God pronounced on the Israelites before his **death**.
Jos 1: 1 After the **death** *of* Moses the servant of the LORD, the LORD

Jos 2:13 and all who belong to them, and that you will save us from **death**."
20: 6 and until the **death** *of* the high priest who is serving at that time.
Jdg 1: 1 After the **death** *of* Joshua, the Israelites asked the LORD,
2:19 when the judge **died**, the people returned to ways even more
13: 7 will be a Nazirite of God from birth until the day of his **death**.' "
16:30 Thus he killed many more when he **died** than while he lived.
Ru 1:17 so severely, if anything but **death** separates you and me."
2:11 done for your mother-in-law since the **death** *of* your husband—
1Sa 5:11 For **death** had filled the city with panic; God's hand was very
15:32 him confidently, thinking, "Surely the bitterness of **death** is past."
15:35 Until the day Samuel **died**, he did not go to see Saul again,
20: 3 and as you live, there is only a step between me and **death**."
20:31 Now send and bring him to me, for he **must die** [+1201]!"
26:16 As surely as the LORD lives, you and your men deserve to **die**,
2Sa 1: 1 After the **death** *of* Saul, David returned from defeating the
1:23 they were loved and gracious, and in **death** they were not parted.
3:33 this lament for Abner: "Should Abner have died as the lawless **die**?
6:23 Michal daughter of Saul had no children to the day of her **death**.
12: 5 surely as the LORD lives, the man who did this deserves to **die**!
15:21 whether it means life or **death**, there will your servant be."
19:28 [19:29] deserved nothing but **death** from my lord the king,
22: 5 "The waves of **death** swirled about me; the torrents of destruction
22: 6 of the grave coiled around me; the snares of **death** confronted me.
1Ki 2:26 You deserve to **die**, but I will not put you to death now, because
11:40 to Shishak the king, and stayed there until Solomon's **death**.
13:31 After burying him, he said to his sons, "When I **die**, bury me in the
2Ki 1: 1 After Ahab's **death**, Moab rebelled against Israel.
2:21 Never again will it cause **death** or make the land unproductive.' "
3: 5 after Ahab **died**, the king of Moab rebelled against the king of
4:40 they cried out, "O man of God, there is **death** in the pot!"
14:17 years after the **death** *of* Jehoash son of Jehoahaz king of Israel.
1Ch 2:24 After Hezron **died** in Caleb Ephrathah, Abijah the wife of Hezron
22: 5 for it." So David made extensive preparations before his **death**.
2Ch 22: 4 for after his father's **death** they became his advisers, to his
24:15 of years, and he died at the age of a hundred and thirty. **[RPH]**
24:17 After the **death** *of* Jehoiada, the officials of Judah came and paid
24:22 had shown him but killed his son, who said as he lay **dying**,
25:25 years after the **death** *of* Jehoash son of Jehoahaz king of Israel.
26:21 King Uzziah had leprosy until the day he **died**. He lived in a
Est 2: 7 taken her as his own daughter when her father and mother **died**.
Job 3:21 to those who long for **death** that does not come, who search for it
5:20 In famine he will ransom you from **death**, and in battle from the
7:15 so that I prefer strangling and **death**, rather than this body of mine.
18:13 It eats away parts of his skin; **death's** firstborn devours his limbs.
27:15 The **plague** will bury those who survive him, and their widows
28:22 Destruction and **Death** say, 'Only a rumor of it has reached our
30:23 I know you will bring me down to **death**, to the place appointed
38:17 Have the gates of **death** been shown to you? Have you seen the
Ps 6: 5 [6:6] No one remembers you when he is **dead**. Who praises you
7:13 [7:14] He has prepared his **deadly** weapons; he makes ready his
9:13 [9:14] Have mercy and lift me up from the gates of **death**,
13: 3 [13:4] my God. Give light to my eyes, or I will sleep in **death**;
18: 4 [18:5] The cords of **death** entangled me; the torrents of
18: 5 [18:6] coiled around me; the snares of **death** confronted me.
22:15 [22:16] to the roof of my mouth; you lay me in the dust of **death**.
33:19 to deliver them from **death** and keep them alive in famine.
49:14 [49:15] are destined for the grave, and **death** will feed on them.
49:17 [49:18] for he will take nothing with him when he **dies**,
55: 4 [55:5] is in anguish within me; the terrors of **death** assail me.
55:15 [55:16] Let **death** [K 3812] take my enemies by surprise; let
56:13 [56:14] For you have delivered me from **death** and my feet from
68:20 [68:21] from the Sovereign LORD comes escape from **death**.
73: 4 They [BHS *At their death*; NIV 4564] have no struggles;
78:50 he did not spare them from **death** but gave them over to the
89:48 [89:49] What man can live and not see **death**, or save himself
107:18 They loathed all food and drew near the gates of **death**.
116: 3 The cords of **death** entangled me, the anguish of the grave came
116: 8 For you, O LORD, have delivered my soul from **death**, my eyes
116:15 Precious in the sight of the LORD is the **death** of his saints.
118:18 has chastened me severely, but he has not given me over to **death**.
Pr 2:18 For her house leads down to **death** and her paths to the spirits of
5: 5 Her feet go down to **death**; her steps lead straight to the grave.
7:27 is a highway to the grave, leading down to the chambers of **death**.
8:36 fails to find me harms himself; all who hate me love **death**."
10: 2 treasures are of no value, but righteousness delivers from **death**.
11: 4 in the day of wrath, but righteousness delivers from **death**.
11: 7 When a wicked man **dies**, his hope perishes; all he expected from
11:19 man attains life, but he who pursues evil goes to his **death**.
12:28 righteousness there is life; along that path is **immortality** [+440].
13:14 wise is a fountain of life, turning a man from the snares of **death**.
14:12 is a way that seems right to a man, but in the end it leads to **death**.
14:27 is a fountain of life, turning a man from the snares of **death**.
14:32 are brought down, but even in **death** the righteous have a refuge.
16:14 A king's wrath is a messenger of **death**, but a wise man will
16:25 is a way that seems right to a man, but in the end it leads to **death**.
18:21 The tongue has the power of life and **death**, and those who love it
21: 6 made by a lying tongue is a fleeting vapor and a **deadly** snare.
24:11 Rescue those being led away to **death**; hold back those staggering
26:18 Like a madman shooting firebrands or **deadly** arrows
Ecc 3:19 As one **dies**, so dies the other. All have the same breath; man has
3:19 As one dies, so **dies** the other. All have the same breath; man has
7: 1 fine perfume, and the day of **death** better than the day of birth.
7:26 I find more bitter than **death** the woman who is a snare, whose
8: 8 wind to contain it; so no one has power over the day of his **death**.
10: 1 As **dead** flies give perfume a bad smell, so a little folly outweighs
SS 8: 6 for love is as strong as **death**, its jealousy unyielding as the grave.
Isa 6: 1 In the year that King Uzziah **died**, I saw the Lord seated on a
14:28 This oracle came in the year King Ahaz **died**:
25: 8 he will swallow up **death** forever. The Sovereign LORD will
28:15 You boast, "We have entered into a covenant with **death**,
28:18 Your covenant with **death** will be annulled; your agreement with
38:18 For the grave cannot praise you, **death** cannot sing your praise;
53: 9 and with the rich in his **death**, though he had done no violence,
53:12 because he poured out his life unto **death**, and was numbered with
Jer 8: 3 all the survivors of this evil nation will prefer **death** to life,
9:21 [9:20] **Death** has climbed in through our windows and has
15: 2 " 'Those destined for **death**, to death; those for the sword,
15: 2 " 'Those destined for death, to **death**; those for the sword,
18:21 let their men be **put to death** [+2222], their young men slain by
18:23 you know, O LORD, all their plots to **kill** me. Do not forgive
21: 8 I am setting before you the way of life and the way of **death**.
26:11 "This man should be sentenced to **death** because he has prophesied
26:16 and the prophets, "This man should not be sentenced to **death**!
43:11 and attack Egypt, bringing **death** to those destined for death,
43:11 and attack Egypt, bringing death to those destined for **death**,
52:11 to Babylon, where he put him in prison till the day of his **death**.
52:34 a regular allowance as long as he lived, till the day of his **death**.
La 1:20 Outside, the sword bereaves; inside, there is only **death**.
Eze 18:23 Do I take any pleasure in the **death** *of* the wicked?
18:32 For I take no pleasure in the **death** *of* anyone,
28:10 You will die the **death** *of* the uncircumcised at the hands of
31:14 they are all destined for **death**, for the earth below, among mortal
33:11 Sovereign LORD, I take no pleasure in the **death** *of* the wicked,
Hos 13:14 them from the power of the grave; I will redeem them from **death**.
13:14 Where, O **death**, are your plagues? Where, O grave, is your
Jnh 4: 3 take away my life, for it is better for me to **die** than to live."
4: 8 to die, and said, "It would be better for me to **die** than to live."
4: 9 angry about the vine?" "I do," he said. "I am angry enough to **die**."
Hab 2: 5 he is as greedy as the grave and like **death** is never satisfied,

4639 מוֹתָר *môtār*, n.m. [3] [√ 3855]

profit [2], advantage [1]

Pr 14:23 All hard work brings a **profit**, but mere talk leads only to poverty.
21: 5 The plans of the diligent lead to **profit** as surely as haste leads to
Ecc 3:19 All have the same breath; man has no **advantage** over the animal.

4640 מִזְבֵּחַ *mizbēaḥ*, n.m. [401] [√ 2284; Ar 10401]

altar [337], altars [50], it[s] [+2021] [6], *untranslated* [4], its[s] [+2021] [3], done this[s] [+1215+3378+4200] [1]

Ge 8:20 Noah built an **altar** to the LORD and, taking some of all the clean
8:20 and clean birds, he sacrificed burnt offerings on **it**[s] [+2021].
12: 7 So he built an **altar** there to the LORD, who had appeared to him.
12: 8 There he built an **altar** to the LORD and called on the name of
13: 4 where he had first built an **altar**. There Abram called on the name
13:18 trees of Mamre at Hebron, where he built an **altar** to the LORD.
22: 9 Abraham built an **altar** there and arranged the wood on it.
22: 9 He bound his son Isaac and laid him on the **altar**, on top of the
26:25 Isaac built an **altar** there and called on the name of the LORD.
33:20 There he set up an **altar** and called it El Elohe Israel.
35: 1 "Go up to Bethel and settle there, and build an **altar** there to God,
35: 3 let us go up to Bethel, where I will build an **altar** to God,
35: 7 There he built an **altar**, and he called the place El Bethel, because
Ex 17:15 Moses built an **altar** and called it The LORD is my Banner.
20:24 " 'Make an **altar** *of* earth for me and sacrifice on it your burnt
20:25 If you make an **altar** *of* stones for me, do not build it with dressed
20:26 do not go up to my **altar** on steps, lest your nakedness be exposed
21:14 take him away from my **altar** and put him to death.
24: 4 the next morning and built an **altar** at the foot of the mountain
24: 6 and put it in bowls, and the other half he sprinkled on the **altar**.
27: 1 "Build an **altar** *of* acacia wood, three cubits high; it is to be square,
27: 1 three cubits high; **it**[s] [+2021] is to be square, five cubits long
27: 5 Put it under the ledge of the **altar** so that it is halfway up the altar.
27: 5 Put it under the ledge of the altar so that it is halfway up the **altar**.
27: 6 Make poles of acacia wood for the **altar** and overlay them with
27: 7 so they will be on two sides of the **altar** when it is carried.
28:43 of Meeting or approach the **altar** to minister in the Holy Place,

[F] Hitpael (hitpoel, hitpoal, hitpolel, hitpolal, hitpalel, hitpalal, hitpalpel, hitpalpal, hotpael, hotpaal) [G] Hiphil (hiphtil) [H] Hophal [I] Hishtaphel

Ex 29:12 bull's blood and put it on the horns of the **altar** with your finger,
29:12 with your finger, and pour out the rest of it at the base of the **altar**.
29:13 and both kidneys with the fat on them, and burn them on the **altar**.
29:16 and take the blood and sprinkle it against the **altar** on all sides.
29:18 burn the entire ram on the **altar**. It is a burnt offering to the
29:20 their right feet. Then sprinkle blood against the **altar** on all sides.
29:21 take some of the blood on the **altar** and some of the anointing oil
29:25 burn them on the **altar** along with the burnt offering for a pleasing
29:36 Purify the **altar** by making atonement for it, and anoint it to
29:37 For seven days make atonement for the **altar** and consecrate it.
29:37 the **altar** will be most holy, and whatever touches it will be holy.
29:37 will be most holy, and whatever touches **it**[s] [+2021] will be holy.
29:38 "This is what you are to offer on the **altar** regularly each day:
29:44 the **altar** and will consecrate Aaron and his sons to serve me as
30: 1 "Make an **altar** *of* acacia wood *for* burning incense.
30:18 Place it between the Tent of Meeting and the **altar**, and put water
30:20 when they approach the **altar** to minister by presenting an offering
30:27 its articles, the lampstand and its accessories, the **altar** *of* incense,
30:28 the **altar** *of* burnt offering and all its utensils, and the basin with its
31: 8 pure gold lampstand and all its accessories, the **altar** *of* incense,
31: 9 the **altar** *of* burnt offering and all its utensils, the basin with its
32: 5 saw this, he built an **altar** in front of the calf and announced,
34:13 Break down their **altars**, smash their sacred stones and cut down
35:15 the **altar** *of* incense with its poles, the anointing oil and the
35:16 the **altar** *of* burnt offering with its bronze grating, its poles
37:25 They made the **altar** *of* incense out of acacia wood. It was square,
38: 1 They built the **altar** *of* burnt offering of acacia wood, three cubits
38: 3 They made all **its**[s] [+2021] utensils of bronze—its pots, shovels,
38: 4 They made a grating for the **altar**, a bronze network, to be under
38: 7 the rings so they would be on the sides of the **altar** for carrying it.
38:30 the bronze **altar** with its bronze grating and all its utensils,
38:30 bronze altar with its bronze grating and all **its**[s] [+2021] utensils,
39:38 the gold **altar**, the anointing oil, the fragrant incense, and the
39:39 the bronze **altar** with its bronze grating, its poles and all its
40: 5 Place the gold **altar** of incense in front of the ark of the Testimony
40: 6 "Place the **altar** *of* burnt offering in front of the entrance to the
40: 7 between the Tent of Meeting and the **altar** and put water in it.
40:10 Then anoint the **altar** *of* burnt offering and all its utensils;
40:10 and all its utensils; consecrate the **altar**, and it will be most holy.
40:10 its utensils; consecrate the altar, and **it**[s] [+2021] will be most holy.
40:26 Moses placed the gold **altar** in the Tent of Meeting in front of the
40:29 He set the **altar** *of* burnt offering near the entrance to the
40:30 the Tent of Meeting and the **altar** and put water in it for washing,
40:32 they entered the Tent of Meeting or approached the **altar**,
40:33 and **altar** and put up the curtain at the entrance to the courtyard.
Lev 1: 5 sprinkle it against the **altar** on all sides at the entrance to the Tent
1: 7 The sons of Aaron the priest are to put fire on the **altar** and arrange
1: 8 the head and the fat, on the burning wood that is on the **altar**.
1: 9 the legs with water, and the priest is to burn all of it on the **altar**.
1:11 He is to slaughter it at the north side of the **altar** before the
1:11 Aaron's sons the priests shall sprinkle its blood against the **altar** on
1:12 the head and the fat, on the burning wood that is on the **altar**.
1:13 and the priest is to bring all of it and burn it on the **altar**.
1:15 The priest shall bring it to the **altar**, wring off the head and burn it
1:15 bring it to the altar, wring off the head and burn it on the **altar**;
1:15 on the altar; its blood shall be drained out on the side of the **altar**.
1:16 the crop with its contents and throw it to the east side of the **altar**,
1:17 the priest shall burn it on the wood that is on the fire on the **altar**.
2: 2 burn this as a memorial portion on the **altar**, an offering made by
2: 8 the LORD; present it to the priest, who shall take it to the **altar**.
2: 9 grain offering and burn it on the **altar** as an offering made by fire,
2:12 but they are not to be offered on the **altar** as a pleasing aroma.
3: 2 Aaron's sons the priests shall sprinkle the blood against the **altar**
3: 5 Aaron's sons are to burn it on the **altar** on top of the burnt offering
3: 8 Aaron's sons shall sprinkle its blood against the **altar** on all sides.
3:11 The priest shall burn them on the **altar** as food, an offering made
3:13 Aaron's sons shall sprinkle its blood against the **altar** on all sides.
3:16 The priest shall burn them on the **altar** as food, an offering made
4: 7 put some of the blood on the horns of the **altar** *of* fragrant incense
4: 7 the **altar** *of* burnt offering at the entrance to the Tent of Meeting.
4:10 Then the priest shall burn them on the **altar** *of* burnt offering.
4:18 He is to put some of the blood on the horns of the **altar** that is
4:18 The rest of the blood he shall pour out at the base of the **altar** *of*
4:19 He shall remove all the fat from it and burn it on the **altar**,
4:25 put it on the horns of the **altar** *of* burnt offering and pour out the
4:25 and pour out the rest of the blood at the base of the **altar**.
4:26 He shall burn all the fat on the **altar** as he burned the fat of the
4:30 put it on the horns of the **altar** *of* burnt offering and pour out the
4:30 and pour out the rest of the blood at the base of the **altar**.
4:31 the priest shall burn it on the **altar** as an aroma pleasing to the
4:34 put it on the horns of the **altar** *of* burnt offering and pour out the
4:34 and pour out the rest of the blood at the base of the **altar**.
4:35 the priest shall burn it on the **altar** on top of the offerings made to
5: 9 some of the blood of the sin offering against the side of the **altar**;
5: 9 the rest of the blood must be drained out at the base of the **altar**.
5:12 burn it on the **altar** on top of the offerings made to the LORD by
6: 9 [6:2] The burnt offering is to remain on the **altar** hearth
6: 9 [6:2] till morning, and the fire must be kept burning on the **altar**.
6:10 [6:3] of the burnt offering that the fire has consumed on the **altar**
6:10 [6:3] has consumed on the altar and place them beside the **altar**.
6:12 [6:5] The fire on the **altar** must be kept burning; it must not go
6:13 [6:6] The fire must be kept burning on the **altar** continuously;
6:14 [6:7] sons are to bring it before the LORD, in front of the **altar**.
6:15 [6:8] burn the memorial portion on the **altar** as an aroma pleasing
7: 2 and its blood is to be sprinkled against the **altar** on all sides.
7: 5 The priest shall burn them on the **altar** as an offering made to the
7:31 The priest shall burn the fat on the **altar**, but the breast belongs to
8:11 He sprinkled some of the oil on the **altar** seven times, anointing
8:11 anointing the **altar** and all its utensils and the basin with its stand,
8:15 with his finger he put it on all the horns of the **altar** to purify the
8:15 his finger he put it on all the horns of the altar to purify the **altar**.
8:15 He poured out the rest of the blood at the base of the **altar**.
8:16 the liver, and both kidneys and their fat, and burned it on the **altar**.
8:19 the ram and sprinkled the blood against the **altar** on all sides.
8:21 and burned the whole ram on the **altar** as a burnt offering,
8:24 right feet. Then he sprinkled blood against the **altar** on all sides.
8:28 burned them on the **altar** on top of the burnt offering as an
8:30 and some of the blood from the **altar** and sprinkled them on Aaron
9: 7 "Come to the **altar** and sacrifice your sin offering and your burnt
9: 8 So Aaron came to the **altar** and slaughtered the calf as a sin
9: 9 dipped his finger into the blood and put it on the horns of the **altar**;
9: 9 the rest of the blood he poured out at the base of the **altar**.
9:10 On the **altar** he burned the fat, the kidneys and the covering of the
9:12 him the blood, and he sprinkled it against the **altar** on all sides.
9:13 by piece, including the head, and he burned them on the **altar**.
9:14 and burned them on top of the burnt offering on the **altar**.
9:17 burned it on the **altar** in addition to the morning's burnt offering.
9:18 him the blood, and he sprinkled it against the **altar** on all sides.
9:20 they laid on the breasts, and then Aaron burned the fat on the **altar**.
9:24 and consumed the burnt offering and the fat portions on the **altar**.
10:12 LORD by fire and eat it prepared without yeast beside the **altar**,
14:20 offer it on the **altar**, together with the grain offering, and make
16:12 He is to take a censer full of burning coals from the **altar** before
16:18 "Then he shall come out to the **altar** that is before the LORD
16:18 some of the goat's blood and put it on all the horns of the **altar**.
16:20 the Tent of Meeting and the **altar**, he shall bring forward the live
16:25 He shall also burn the fat of the sin offering on the **altar**.
16:33 for the Tent of Meeting and the **altar**, and for the priests and all the
17: 6 The priest is to sprinkle the blood against the **altar** *of* the LORD
17:11 given it to you to make atonement for yourselves on the **altar**;
21:23 he must not go near the curtain or approach the **altar**, and
22:22 Do not place any of these on the **altar** as an offering made to the
Nu 3:26 the entrance to the courtyard surrounding the tabernacle and **altar**,
3:31 for the care of the ark, the table, the lampstand, the **altars**,
4:11 "Over the gold **altar** they are to spread a blue cloth and cover that
4:13 "They are to remove the ashes from the bronze **altar** and spread a
4:14 **[RPH]** Over it they are to spread a covering of hides of sea cows
4:26 the curtains of the courtyard surrounding the tabernacle and **altar**,
5:25 for jealousy, wave it before the LORD and bring it to the **altar**.
5:26 the grain offering as a memorial offering and burn it on the **altar**;
7: 1 He also anointed and consecrated the **altar** and all its utensils.
7:10 When the **altar** was anointed, the leaders brought their offerings
7:10 offerings for its dedication and presented them before the **altar**.
7:11 one leader is to bring his offering for the dedication of the **altar**."
7:84 leaders for the dedication of the **altar** when it was anointed:
7:88 These were the offerings for the dedication of the **altar** after it was
16:38 [17:3] Hammer the censers into sheets to overlay the **altar**,
16:39 [17:4] and he had them hammered out to overlay the **altar**,
16:46 [17:11] and put incense in it, along with fire from the **altar**,
18: 3 they must not go near the furnishings of the sanctuary or the **altar**,
18: 5 are to be responsible for the care of the sanctuary and the **altar**,
18: 7 sons may serve as priests in connection with everything at the **altar**
18:17 Sprinkle their blood on the **altar** and burn their fat as an offering
23: 1 Balaam said, "Build me seven **altars** here, and prepare seven bulls
23: 2 and the two of them offered a bull and a ram on each **altar**.
23: 4 met with him, and Balaam said, "I have prepared seven **altars**,
23: 4 seven altars, and on each **altar** I have offered a bull and a ram."
23:14 there he built seven **altars** and offered a bull and a ram on each
23:14 he built seven altars and offered a bull and a ram on each **altar**.
23:29 Balaam said, "Build me seven **altars** here, and prepare seven bulls
23:30 did as Balaam had said, and offered a bull and a ram on each **altar**.
Dt 7: 5 Break down their **altars**, smash their sacred stones, cut down their
12: 3 Break down their **altars**, smash their sacred stones and burn their
12:27 Present your burnt offerings on the **altar** *of* the LORD your God,
12:27 The blood of your sacrifices must be poured beside the **altar** *of* the
16:21 Do not set up any wooden Asherah pole beside the **altar** you build
26: 4 and set it down in front of the **altar** *of* the LORD your God.
27: 5 Build there an **altar** to the LORD your God, an altar of stones.

Dt 27: 5 Build there an altar to the LORD your God, an **altar** *of* stones.
27: 6 Build the **altar** *of* the LORD your God with fieldstones and offer
33: 10 offers incense before you and whole burnt offerings on your **altar**.
Jos 8: 30 Then Joshua built on Mount Ebal an **altar** to the LORD,
8: 31 an **altar** *of* uncut stones, on which no iron tool had been used.
9: 27 for the **altar** *of* the LORD at the place the LORD would choose.
22: 10 the half-tribe of Manasseh built an imposing **altar** there by the
22: 10 the half-tribe of Manasseh built an imposing altar **[RPH]** there by
22: 11 when the Israelites heard that they had built the **altar** on the border
22: 16 and build yourselves an **altar** in rebellion against him now?
22: 19 the LORD or against us by building an **altar** for yourselves,
22: 19 altar for yourselves, other than the **altar** *of* the LORD our God.
22: 23 If we have built our own **altar** to turn away from the LORD
22: 26 "That is why we said, 'Let us get ready and build an **altar**—
22: 28 Look at the replica of the LORD's **altar**, which our fathers built,
22: 29 turn away from him today by building an **altar** for burnt offerings,
22: 29 other than the **altar** *of* the LORD our God that stands before his
22: 34 And the Reubenites and the Gadites gave the **altar** this name:
Jdg 2: 2 with the people of this land, but you shall break down their **altars**.'
6: 24 So Gideon built an **altar** to the LORD there and called it The
6: 25 Tear down your father's **altar** *to* Baal and cut down the Asherah
6: 26 build a proper kind of **altar** to the LORD your God on the top of
6: 28 there was Baal's **altar**, demolished, with the Asherah pole beside it
6: 28 it cut down and the second bull sacrificed on the newly built **altar**!
6: 30 because he has broken down Baal's **altar** and cut down the
6: 31 he can defend himself when someone breaks down his **altar**."
6: 32 "Let Baal contend with him," because he broke down Baal's **altar**.
13: 20 As the flame blazed up from the **altar** toward heaven, the angel of
13: 20 **[RPH]** Seeing this, Manoah and his wife fell with their faces to
21: 4 Early the next day the people built an **altar** and presented burnt
1Sa 2: 28 to go up to my **altar**, to burn incense, and to wear an ephod in my
2: 33 Every one of you that I do not cut off from my **altar** will be spared
7: 17 he also judged Israel. And he built an **altar** there to the LORD.
14: 35 Saul built an **altar** to the LORD; it was the first time he had done
14: 35 it was the first time *he had* **done**[s] **this** [+1215+3378+4200].
2Sa 24: 18 build an **altar** to the LORD on the threshing floor of Araunah the
24: 21 David answered, "so I can build an **altar** to the LORD,
24: 25 David built an **altar** to the LORD there and sacrificed burnt
1Ki 1: 50 in fear of Solomon, went and took hold of the horns of the **altar**.
1: 51 is afraid of King Solomon and is clinging to the horns of the **altar**.
1: 53 Solomon sent men, and they brought him down from the **altar**.
2: 28 to the tent of the LORD and took hold of the horns of the **altar**.
2: 29 Joab had fled to the tent of the LORD and was beside the **altar**.
3: 4 and Solomon offered a thousand burnt offerings on that **altar**.
6: 20 the inside with pure gold, and he also overlaid the **altar** *of* cedar.
6: 22 He also overlaid with gold the **altar** that belonged to the inner
7: 48 the golden **altar**; the golden table on which was the bread of the
8: 22 Solomon stood before the **altar** *of* the LORD in front of the
8: 31 and he comes and swears the oath before your **altar** in this temple,
8: 54 to the LORD, he rose from before the **altar** *of* the LORD,
8: 64 because the bronze **altar** before the LORD was too small to hold
9: 25 and fellowship offerings on the **altar** he had built for the LORD,
12: 32 like the festival held in Judah, and offered sacrifices on the **altar**.
12: 33 he offered sacrifices on the **altar** he had built at Bethel.
12: 33 for the Israelites and went up to the **altar** to make offerings.
13: 1 as Jeroboam was standing by the **altar** to make an offering.
13: 2 He cried out against the **altar** by the word of the LORD:
13: 2 "O **altar**, altar! This is what the LORD says: 'A son named Josiah
13: 2 "O altar, **altar**! This is what the LORD says: 'A son named Josiah
13: 3 The **altar** will be split apart and the ashes on it will be poured out."
13: 4 heard what the man of God cried out against the **altar** at Bethel,
13: 4 he stretched out his hand from the **altar** and said, "Seize him!"
13: 5 the **altar** was split apart and its ashes poured out according to the
13: 5 **its**[s] [+2021] ashes poured out according to the sign given by the
13: 32 he declared by the word of the LORD against the **altar** in Bethel
16: 32 He set up an **altar** for Baal in the temple of Baal that he built in
18: 26 one answered. And they danced around the **altar** they had made.
18: 30 They came to him, and he repaired the **altar** *of* the LORD,
18: 32 With the stones he built an **altar** in the name of the LORD,
18: 32 he dug a trench around **it**[s] [+2021] large enough to hold two seahs
18: 35 The water ran down around the **altar** and even filled the trench.
19: 10 Israelites have rejected your covenant, broken down your **altars**,
19: 14 Israelites have rejected your covenant, broken down your **altars**,
2Ki 11: 11 near the **altar** and the temple, from the south side to the north side
11: 18 They smashed the **altars** and idols to pieces and killed Mattan the
11: 18 to pieces and killed Mattan the priest of Baal in front of the **altars**.
12: 9 [12:10] He placed it beside the **altar**, on the right side as one
16: 10 He saw an **altar** in Damascus and sent to Uriah the priest a sketch
16: 10 altar in Damascus and sent to Uriah the priest a sketch of the **altar**,
16: 11 So Uriah the priest built an **altar** in accordance with all the plans
16: 12 When the king came back from Damascus and saw the **altar**,
16: 12 the altar, he approached **it**[s] [+2021] and presented offerings on it.
16: 13 and sprinkled the blood of his fellowship offerings on the **altar**.
16: 14 The bronze **altar** that stood before the LORD he brought from the
16: 14 from between the new **altar** and the temple of the LORD—
16: 14 of the LORD—and put it on the north side of the new **altar**.
16: 15 "On the large new **altar**, offer the morning burnt offering
16: 15 But I will use the bronze **altar** for seeking guidance."
18: 22 isn't he the one whose high places and **altars** Hezekiah removed,
18: 22 and Jerusalem, "You must worship before this **altar** in Jerusalem"?
21: 3 he also erected **altars** to Baal and made an Asherah pole, as Ahab
21: 4 He built **altars** in the temple of the LORD, of which the LORD
21: 5 of the temple of the LORD, he built **altars** to all the starry hosts.
23: 9 Although the priests of the high places did not serve at the **altar** *of*
23: 12 He pulled down the **altars** the kings of Judah had erected on the
23: 12 the **altars** Manasseh had built in the two courts of the temple of the
23: 15 Even the **altar** at Bethel, the high place made by Jeroboam son of
23: 15 caused Israel to sin—even that **altar** and high place he demolished.
23: 16 the bones removed from them and burned on the **altar** to defile it,
23: 17 pronounced against the **altar** *of* Bethel the very things you have
23: 20 Josiah slaughtered all the priests of those high places on the **altars**
1Ch 6: 49 [6:34] ones who presented offerings on the **altar** *of* burnt offering
6: 49 [6:34] on the **altar** *of* incense in connection with all that was done
16: 40 to present burnt offerings to the LORD on the **altar** *of* burnt
21: 18 build an **altar** to the LORD on the threshing floor of Araunah the
21: 22 site of your threshing floor so I can build an **altar** to the LORD,
21: 26 David built an **altar** to the LORD there and sacrificed burnt
21: 26 the LORD answered him with fire from heaven on the **altar** *of*
21: 29 the **altar** *of* burnt offering were at that time on the high place at
22: 1 God is to be here, and also the **altar** of burnt offering for Israel."
28: 18 and the weight of the refined gold for the **altar** *of* incense.
2Ch 1: 5 But the bronze **altar** that Bezalel son of Uri, the son of Hur,
1: 6 Solomon went up to the bronze **altar** before the LORD in the
4: 1 He made a bronze **altar** twenty cubits long, twenty cubits wide
4: 19 the golden **altar**; the tables on which was the bread of the
5: 12 stood on the east side of the **altar**, dressed in fine linen and playing
6: 12 Solomon stood before the **altar** *of* the LORD in front of the
6: 22 and he comes and swears the oath before your **altar** in this temple,
7: 7 because the bronze **altar** he had made could not hold the burnt
7: 9 for they had celebrated the dedication of the **altar** for seven days
8: 12 On the **altar** *of* the LORD that he had built in front of the portico,
14: 3 [14:2] He removed the foreign **altars** and the high places,
15: 8 He repaired the **altar** *of* the LORD that was in front of the portico
23: 10 near the **altar** and the temple, from the south side to the north side
23: 17 They smashed the **altars** and idols and killed Mattan the priest of
23: 17 and idols and killed Mattan the priest of Baal in front of the **altars**.
26: 16 entered the temple of the LORD to burn incense on the **altar** *of*
26: 19 in their presence before the incense **altar** in the LORD's temple,
28: 24 and set up **altars** at every street corner in Jerusalem.
29: 18 the **altar** *of* burnt offering with all its utensils, and the table for
29: 19 while he was king. They are now in front of the LORD's **altar**."
29: 21 descendants of Aaron, to offer these on the **altar** *of* the LORD.
29: 22 and the priests took the blood and sprinkled it on the **altar**;
29: 22 they slaughtered the rams and sprinkled their blood on the **altar**;
29: 22 they slaughtered the lambs and sprinkled their blood on the **altar**.
29: 24 presented their blood on the **altar** for a sin offering to atone for all
29: 27 Hezekiah gave the order to sacrifice the burnt offering on the **altar**.
30: 14 They removed the **altars** in Jerusalem and cleared away the
31: 1 and the **altars** throughout Judah and Benjamin and in Ephraim
32: 12 not Hezekiah himself remove this god's high places and **altars**,
32: 12 'You must worship before one **altar** and burn sacrifices on it'?
33: 3 he also erected **altars** to the Baals and made Asherah poles.
33: 4 He built **altars** in the temple of the LORD, of which the LORD
33: 5 of the temple of the LORD, he built **altars** to all the starry hosts.
33: 15 as well as all the **altars** he had built on the temple hill and in
33: 16 he restored the **altar** *of* the LORD and sacrificed fellowship
34: 4 Under his direction the **altars** *of* the Baals were torn down;
34: 5 He burned the bones of the priests on their **altars**, and so he purged
34: 7 he tore down the **altars** and the Asherah poles and crushed the
35: 16 and the offering of burnt offerings on the **altar** *of* the LORD,
Ezr 3: 2 his associates began to build the **altar** *of* the God of Israel to
3: 3 they built the **altar** on its foundation and sacrificed burnt offerings
Ne 10: 34 [10:35] of wood to burn on the **altar** *of* the LORD our God,
Ps 26: 6 wash my hands in innocence, and go about your **altar**, O LORD,
43: 4 Then will I go to the **altar** *of* God, to God, my joy and my delight.
51: 19 [51:21] to delight you; then bulls will be offered on your **altar**.
84: 3 [84:4] a place near your **altar**, O LORD Almighty, my King
118: 27 in hand, join in the festal procession up to the horns of the **altar**.
Isa 6: 6 live coal in his hand, which he had taken with tongs from the **altar**.
17: 8 They will not look to the **altars**, the work of their hands, and they
19: 19 In that day there will be an **altar** to the LORD in the heart of
27: 9 When he makes all the **altar** stones to be like chalk stones crushed
36: 7 isn't he the one whose high places and **altars** Hezekiah removed,
36: 7 to Judah and Jerusalem, "You must worship before this **altar**"?
56: 7 Their burnt offerings and sacrifices will be accepted on my **altar**;
60: 7 they will be accepted as offerings on my **altar**, and I will adorn my
Jer 11: 13 the **altars** you have set up to burn incense to that shameful god
11: 13 god **[RPH]** Baal are as many as the streets of Jerusalem.'

Jer 17: 1 on the tablets of their hearts and on the horns of their **altars**.
17: 2 Even their children remember their **altars** and Asherah poles
La 2: 7 The Lord has rejected his **altar** and abandoned his sanctuary.
Eze 6: 4 Your **altars** will be demolished and your incense altars will be
6: 5 of their idols, and I will scatter your bones around your **altars**.
6: 6 so that your **altars** will be laid waste and devastated, your idols
6: 13 when their people lie slain among their idols around their **altars**,
8: 5 in the entrance north of the gate of the **altar** I saw this idol of
8: 16 between the portico and the **altar**, were about twenty-five men.
9: 2 kit at his side. They came in and stood beside the bronze **altar**.
40: 46 room facing north is for the priests who have charge of the **altar**.
40: 47 a hundred cubits wide. And the **altar** was in front of the temple.
41: 22 There was a wooden **altar** three cubits high and two cubits square;
43: 13 "These are the measurements of the **altar** in long cubits, that cubit
43: 13 of one span around the edge. And this is the height of the **altar**:
43: 18 burnt offerings and sprinkling blood upon the **altar** when it is built:
43: 22 and the **altar** is to be purified as it was purified with the bull.
43: 26 For seven days they are to make atonement for the **altar**
43: 27 present your burnt offerings and fellowship offerings on the **altar**.
45: 19 on the four corners of the upper ledge of the **altar** and on the
47: 1 down from under the south side of the temple, south of the **altar**.
Hos 8: 11 "Though Ephraim built many **altars** for sin offerings, these have
8: 11 many altars for sin offerings, these have become **altars** for sinning.
10: 1 As his fruit increased, he built more **altars**; as his land prospered,
10: 2 The LORD will demolish their **altars** and destroy their sacred
10: 8 of Israel. Thorns and thistles will grow up and cover their **altars**.
12: 11 [12:12] Their **altars** will be like piles of stones on a plowed field.
Joel 1: 13 O priests, and mourn; wail, you who minister before the **altar**.
2: 17 before the LORD, weep between the temple porch and the **altar**.
Am 2: 8 They lie down beside every **altar** on garments taken in pledge.
3: 14 day I punish Israel for her sins, I will destroy the **altars** *of* Bethel;
3: 14 the horns of the **altar** will be cut off and fall to the ground.
9: 1 I saw the Lord standing by the **altar**, and he said: "Strike the tops
Zec 9: 15 will be full like a bowl used for sprinkling the corners of the **altar**.
14: 20 LORD's house will be like the sacred bowls in front of the **altar**.
Mal 1: 7 "You place defiled food on my **altar**. "But you ask, 'How have we
1: 10 temple doors, so that you would not light useless fires on my **altar**!
2: 13 You flood the LORD's **altar** with tears. You weep and wail

4641 מֶזֶג ***mezeg***, n.m. [1]
blended wine [1]

SS 7: 2 [7:3] navel is a rounded goblet that never lacks **blended wine**.

4642 מָזֶה ***māzeh***, a. [1]
wasting [1]

Dt 32: 24 I will send **wasting** famine against them, consuming pestilence

4643 מַזֶּה ***mazzeh***, var. Not used in NIV/BHS [√ 4537 + 2296]

4644 מִזֶּה ***mizzeh***, var. Not used in NIV/BHS [√ 4946 + 2296]

4645 מִזָּה ***mizzâ***, n.pr.m. [3]
Mizzah [3]

Ge 36: 13 The sons of Reuel: Nahath, Zerah, Shammah and **Mizzah**.
36: 17 of Esau's son Reuel: Chiefs Nahath, Zerah, Shammah and **Mizzah**.
1Ch 1: 37 The sons of Reuel: Nahath, Zerah, Shammah and **Mizzah**.

4646 מָזוּ ***māzû***, n.m. [1] [cf. 2312]
barns [1]

Ps 144: 13 Our **barns** will be filled with every kind of provision. Our sheep

4647 מְזוּזָה ***m***^e^***zûzâ***, n.f. [19]
doorposts [4], doorframe [3], doorframes [3], doorpost [2], doorway [+7339] [1], doorways [+7339] [1], gatepost [+9133] [1], gateposts [+9133] [1], jambs [+382] [1], jambs [1], posts [1]

Ex 12: 7 tops of the **doorframes** of the houses where they eat the lambs.
12: 22 some of the blood on the top and on both sides of the **doorframe**.
12: 23 he will see the blood on the top and sides of the **doorframe**
21: 6 He shall take him to the door or the **doorpost** and pierce his ear
Dt 6: 9 Write them on the **doorframes** *of* your houses and on your gates.
11: 20 Write them on the **doorframes** *of* your houses and on your gates,
Jdg 16: 3 together with the two **posts**, and tore them loose, bar and all.
1Sa 1: 9 Now Eli the priest was sitting on a chair by the **doorpost** *of* the
1Ki 6: 31 he made doors of olive wood with five-sided **jambs** [+382].
6: 33 In the same way he made four-sided **jambs** *of* olive wood for the
7: 5 All the **doorways** [+7339] had rectangular frames; they were in the
Pr 8: 34 watching daily at my doors, waiting at my **doorway** [+7339].
Isa 57: 8 your doors and your **doorposts** you have put your pagan symbols.
Eze 41: 21 The outer sanctuary had a rectangular **doorframe**, and the one at
43: 8 next to my threshold and their **doorposts** beside my doorposts,
43: 8 next to my threshold and their doorposts beside my **doorposts**,
45: 19 blood of the sin offering and put it on the **doorposts** *of* the temple,
45: 19 ledge of the altar and on the **gateposts** [+9133] *of* the inner court.
46: 2 the portico of the gateway and stand by the **gatepost** [+9133].

4648 מָזוֹן ***māzôn***, n.m. [2] [√ 2315]
provisions [2]

Ge 45: 23 loaded with grain and bread and *other* **provisions** for his journey.
2Ch 11: 23 He gave them abundant **provisions** and took many wives for them.

4649 ¹מָזוֹר ***māzôr***[1], n.[m.]. [3]
sores [2], sore [1]

Jer 30: 13 to plead your cause, no remedy for your **sore**, no healing for you.
Hos 5: 13 his sickness, and Judah his **sores**, then Ephraim turned to Assyria,
5: 13 But he is not able to cure you, not able to heal your **sores**.

4650 ²מָזוֹר ***māzôr***[2], n.m. [1]
trap [1]

Ob 1: 7 those who eat your bread will set a **trap** for you, but you will not

4651 ¹מֵזַח ***mēzaḥ***[1], n.m. [1] [→ 4685]
harbor [1]

Isa 23: 10 O Daughter of Tarshish, for you no longer have a **harbor**.

4652 ²מֵזַח ***mēzaḥ***[2], n.m. [1] [→ 4653]
belt [1]

Ps 109: 19 a cloak wrapped about him, like a **belt** tied forever around him.

4653 מָזִיחַ ***māzîaḥ***, n.m. [1] [√ 4652]
disarms [+8332] [1]

Job 12: 21 He pours contempt on nobles and **disarms** [+8332] the mighty.

4654 מַזְכִּיר ***mazkîr***, n.m. *or* v.ptcp. [9] [√ 2349]
recorder [9]

2Sa 8: 16 was over the army; Jehoshaphat son of Ahilud *was* **recorder**;
20: 24 charge of forced labor; Jehoshaphat son of Ahilud was **recorder**;
1Ki 4: 3 of Shisha—secretaries; Jehoshaphat son of Ahilud—**recorder**;
2Ki 18: 18 and Joah son of Asaph the **recorder** went out to them.
18: 37 and Joah son of Asaph the **recorder** went to Hezekiah,
1Ch 18: 15 was over the army; Jehoshaphat son of Ahilud was **recorder**;
2Ch 34: 8 the ruler of the city, with Joah son of Joahaz, the **recorder**,
Isa 36: 3 the secretary, and Joah son of Asaph the **recorder** went out to him.
36: 22 and Joah son of Asaph the **recorder** went to Hezekiah,

4655 מַזָּל ***mazzāl***, n.[f.]pl. [1] [cf. 4666]
constellations [1]

2Ki 23: 5 and moon, to the **constellations** and to all the starry hosts.

4656 מִזְלָג ***mizlāg***, n.m. & f. Not used in NIV/BHS [→ 4657, 4658]

4657 מַזְלֵג ***mazlēg***, n.m. [7] [√ 4656]
meat forks [4], fork [2], forks [1]

Ex 27: 3 and its shovels, sprinkling bowls, **meat forks** and firepans.
38: 3 its pots, shovels, sprinkling bowls, **meat forks** and firepans.
Nu 4: 14 including the firepans, **meat forks**, shovels and sprinkling bowls.
1Sa 2: 13 the servant of the priest would come with a three-pronged **fork** in
2: 14 the priest would take for himself whatever the **fork** brought up.
1Ch 28: 17 the weight of pure gold for the **forks**, sprinkling bowls
2Ch 4: 16 the pots, shovels, **meat forks** and all related articles.

4658 מִזְלָגָה ***mizlāgâ***, n.[f.]. Not used in NIV/BHS [√ 4656]

4659 מְזִמָּה ***m***^e^***zimmâ***, n.f. [19] [√ 2372]
discretion [4], crafty [2], purposes [2], schemes [2], wicked schemes [2], discernment [1], evil intent [1], evil schemes [1], plan [1], purpose [1], schemer [+1251] [1], thoughts [1]

Job 21: 27 you are thinking, the **schemes** by which you would wrong me.
42: 2 know that you can do all things; no **plan** of yours can be thwarted.
Ps 10: 2 hunts down the weak, who are caught in the **schemes** he devises.
10: 4 does not seek him; in all his **thoughts** there is no room for God.
21: 11 [21:12] they plot evil against you and devise **wicked schemes**,
37: 7 succeed in their ways, when they carry out their **wicked schemes**.
139: 20 They speak of you with **evil intent**; your adversaries misuse your
Pr 1: 4 prudence to the simple, knowledge and **discretion** to the young—
2: 11 **Discretion** will protect you, and understanding will guard you.

Pr 3:21 My son, preserve sound judgment and **discernment**, do not let
5: 2 that you may maintain **discretion** and your lips may preserve
8:12 dwell together with prudence; I possess knowledge and **discretion**.
12: 2 favor from the LORD, but the LORD condemns a **crafty** man.
14:17 man does foolish things, and a **crafty** man is hated.
24: 8 He who plots evil will be known as a **schemer** [+1251].
Jer 11:15 doing in my temple as she works out her **evil schemes** with many?
23:20 not turn back until he fully accomplishes the **purposes** *of* his heart.
30:24 not turn back until he fully accomplishes the **purposes** *of* his heart.
51:11 the kings of the Medes, because his **purpose** is to destroy Babylon.

4660 מִזְמוֹר **mizmôr**, n.[m.]. [57] [√ 2376]

psalm [57]

Ps 3: T [3:1] A **psalm** of David. When he fled from his son Absalom.
4: T [4:1] of music. With stringed instruments. A **psalm** of David.
5: T [5:1] For the director of music. For flutes. A **psalm** of David.
6: T [6:1] According to *sheminith*. A **psalm** of David.
8: T [8:1] director of music. According to *gittith*. A **psalm** of David.
9: T [9:1] To ⸤the tune of⸥ "The Death of the Son." A **psalm** of David.
12: T [12:1] of music. According to *sheminith*. A **psalm** of David.
13: T [13:1] For the director of music. A **psalm** of David.
15: T [15:1] A **psalm** of David.
19: T [19:1] For the director of music. A **psalm** of David.
20: T [20:1] For the director of music. A **psalm** of David.
21: T [21:1] For the director of music. A **psalm** of David.
22: T [22:1] tune of⸥ "The Doe of the Morning." A **psalm** of David.
23: T [23:1] A **psalm** of David.
24: T [24:1] Of David. A **psalm**.
29: T [29:1] A **psalm** of David.
30: T [30:1] A **psalm**. A song. For the dedication of the temple.
31: T [31:1] For the director of music. A **psalm** of David.
38: T [38:1] A **psalm** of David. A petition.
39: T [39:1] For the director of music. For Jeduthun. A **psalm** of David.
40: T [40:1] For the director of music. Of David. A **psalm**.
41: T [41:1] For the director of music. A **psalm** of David.
47: T [47:1] For the director of music. Of the Sons of Korah. A **psalm**.
48: T [48:1] A song. A **psalm** of the Sons of Korah.
49: T [49:1] For the director of music. Of the Sons of Korah. A **psalm**.
50: T [50:1] A **psalm** of Asaph.
51: T [51:1] For the director of music. A **psalm** of David.
62: T [62:1] For the director of music. For Jeduthun. A **psalm** of David.
63: T [63:1] A **psalm** of David. When he was in the Desert of Judah.
64: T [64:1] For the director of music. A **psalm** of David.
65: T [65:1] For the director of music. A **psalm** of David. A song.
66: T [66:1] For the director of music. A song. A **psalm**.
67: T [67:1] of music. With stringed instruments. A **psalm**. A song.
68: T [68:1] For the director of music. Of David. A **psalm**. A song.
73: T [73:1] A **psalm** of Asaph.
75: T [75:1] the tune of⸥ "Do Not Destroy." A **psalm** of Asaph. A song.
76: T [76:1] With stringed instruments. A **psalm** of Asaph. A song.
77: T [77:1] the director of music. For Jeduthun. Of Asaph. A **psalm**.
79: T [79:1] A **psalm** of Asaph.
80: T [80:1] tune of⸥ "The Lilies of the Covenant." Of Asaph. A **psalm**.
82: T [82:1] A **psalm** of Asaph.
83: T [83:1] A song. A **psalm** of Asaph.
84: T [84:1] According to *gittith*. Of the Sons of Korah. A **psalm**.
85: T [85:1] For the director of music. Of the Sons of Korah. A **psalm**.
87: T [87:1] Of the Sons of Korah. A **psalm**. A song.
88: T [88:1] A song. A **psalm** of the Sons of Korah. For the director of
92: T [92:1] A **psalm**. A song. For the Sabbath day.
98: T [98:1] A **psalm**.
100: T [100:1] A **psalm**. For giving thanks.
101: T [101:1] Of David. A **psalm**.
108: T [108:1] A song. A **psalm** of David.
109: T [109:1] For the director of music. Of David. A **psalm**.
110: T [110:1] Of David. A **psalm**.
139: T [139:1] For the director of music. Of David. A **psalm**.
140: T [140:1] For the director of music. A **psalm** of David.
141: T [141:1] A **psalm** of David.
143: T [143:1] A **psalm** of David.

4661 מַזְמֵרָה **mazmērâ**, n.f. [4] [√ 2377]

pruning hooks [3], pruning knives [1]

Isa 2: 4 their swords into plowshares and their spears into **pruning hooks**.
18: 5 he will cut off the shoots with **pruning knives**, and cut down
Joel 3:10 [4:10] into swords and your **pruning hooks** into spears.
Mic 4: 3 their swords into plowshares and their spears into **pruning hooks**.

4662 מְזַמֶּרֶת **m^ezammeret**, n.f. [5] [√ 2377]

wick trimmers [5]

1Ki 7:50 gold basins, **wick trimmers**, sprinkling bowls, dishes and censers;
2Ki 12:13 [12:14] **wick trimmers**, sprinkling bowls, trumpets or any other
25:14 **wick trimmers**, dishes and all the bronze articles used in the
2Ch 4:22 the pure gold **wick trimmers**, sprinkling bowls, dishes
Jer 52:18 shovels, **wick trimmers**, sprinkling bowls, dishes and all the

4663 מִזְעָר **miz'ār**, n.[m.]. [4] [√ 2402]

in a very short time [+5071+6388] [1], very few [+5071] [1], very few [+632] [1], very soon [+5071+6388] [1]

Isa 10:25 **Very soon** [+5071+6388] my anger against you will end and my
16:14 and her survivors will be **very few** [+5071] and feeble."
24: 6 earth's inhabitants are burned up, and **very few** [+632] are left.
29:17 **In a very short time** [+5071+6388], will not Lebanon be turned

4664 מָזַר **māzar**, v. Not used in NIV/BHS [cf. 2430]

4665 מִזְרֶה **mizreh**, n.[m.]. [2] [√ 2430]

shovel [1], winnowing fork [1]

Isa 30:24 the soil will eat fodder and mash, spread out with fork and **shovel**.
Jer 15: 7 I will winnow them with a **winnowing fork** at the city gates of the

4666 מַזָּרוֹת **mazzārôt**, n.[f.]pl. [1] [cf. 4655]

constellations [1]

Job 38:32 Can you bring forth the **constellations** in their seasons or lead out

4667 מִזְרָח **mizrāḥ**, n.[m.]. [74] [√ 2436]

east [34], east [+2025] [7], rising [6], sunrise [5], east [+2021+9087] [3], sunrise [+9087] [3], east [+2021+2025+9087] [2], east [+9087] [2], eastern [+2025] [2], *untranslated* [1], east [+2025+6298] [1], east [+928+2025+6298] [1], east [+928+2025+6298+9087] [1], east [+928+6298+9087] [1], eastern [+9087] [1], eastern [1], eastward [+2025] [1], eastward [+2025+2025+7711] [1], western[s] [+2025] [1]

Ex 27:13 On the east end, toward the **sunrise**, the courtyard shall also be
38:13 The east end, toward the **sunrise**, was also fifty cubits wide.
Nu 2: 3 On the east, toward the **sunrise**, the divisions of the camp of Judah
3:38 the tabernacle, toward the **sunrise**, in front of the Tent of Meeting.
21:11 in the desert that faces Moab toward the **sunrise** [+9087].
32:19 because our inheritance has come to us on the **east** side of the
34:15 on the east side of the Jordan of Jericho, toward the **sunrise**."
Dt 3:17 Its **western**[s] [+2025] border was the Jordan in the Arabah,
3:27 top of Pisgah and look west and north and south and **east** [+2025].
4:41 set aside three cities **east** [+928+2025+6298+9087] *of* the Jordan,
4:47 the two Amorite kings **east** [+928+6298+9087] *of* the Jordan.
4:49 and included all the Arabah **east** [+2025+6298] *of* the Jordan,
Jos 1:15 LORD gave you east of the Jordan toward the **sunrise** [+9087]."
4:19 the Jordan and camped at Gilgal on the **eastern** border of Jericho.
11: 3 to the Canaanites in the **east** and west; to the Amorites, Hittites,
11: 8 to Misrephoth Maim, and to the Valley of Mizpah on the **east**,
12: 1 territory they took over **east** [+2021+2025+9087] *of* the Jordan,
12: 1 including all the **eastern** [+2025] *side of* the Arabah:
12: 3 He also ruled over the **eastern** [+2025] Arabah from the Sea of
12: 3 **[RPH]** to Beth Jeshimoth, and then southward below the slopes of
13: 5 all Lebanon to the **east** [+2021+9087], from Baal Gad below
13: 8 that Moses had given them **east** [+928+2025+6298] of the Jordan,
13:27 of the realm of Sihon king of Heshbon (the **east** side of the Jordan,
13:32 in the plains of Moab across the Jordan **east** [+2025] *of* Jericho.
16: 1 at the Jordan of Jericho, **east** [+2025] of the waters of Jericho,
16: 5 went from Ataroth Addar in the **east** to Upper Beth Horon
16: 6 From Micmethath on the north it curved **eastward** [+2025] to
16: 6 eastward to Taanath Shiloh, passing by it to Janoah on the **east**.
17:10 and bordered Asher on the north and Issachar on the **east**.
18: 7 already received their inheritance on the **east** side of the Jordan.
19:12 It turned east from Sarid *toward* the **sunrise** [+9087] to the
19:13 Then it continued **eastward** [+2025+2025+7711] to Gath Hepher
19:27 It then turned **east** [+2021+9087] toward Beth Dagon, touched
19:34 on the south, Asher on the west and the Jordan on the **east** [+9087].
20: 8 On the **east** [+2025] side of the Jordan of Jericho they designated
Jdg 11:18 passed along the **eastern** [+9087] side of the country of Moab,
20:43 easily overran them in the vicinity of Gibeah on the **east** [+9087].
21:19 and **east** [+2021+2025+9087] of the road that goes from Bethel to
1Ki 7:25 three facing west, three facing south and three facing **east** [+2025].
2Ki 10:33 **east** [+2021+9087] of the Jordan in all the land of Gilead (the
1Ch 4:39 they went to the outskirts of Gedor to the **east** *of* the valley in
5: 9 To the **east** they occupied the land up to the edge of the desert that
5:10 of the Hagrites throughout the entire region **east** of Gilead.
6:78 [6:63] from the tribe of Reuben across the Jordan **east** *of* Jericho
7:28 Naaran to the **east**, Gezer and its villages to the west, and Shechem
9:18 being stationed at the King's Gate on the **east**, up to the present
9:24 gatekeepers were on the four sides: **east**, west, north and south.
12:15 [12:16] everyone living in the valleys, to the **east** and to the west.
26:14 The lot for the **East** Gate fell to Shelemiah. Then lots were cast for
26:17 There were six Levites a day on the **east**, four a day on the north,

2Ch 4: 4 three facing west, three facing south and three facing **east** [+2025].
5: 12 stood on the **east** *side* of the altar, dressed in fine linen and playing
29: 4 and the Levites, assembled them in the square on the **east** *side*
31: 14 Kore son of Imnah the Levite, keeper of the **East** [+2025] Gate,
Ne 3: 26 made repairs up to a point opposite the Water Gate toward the **east**
3: 29 son of Shecaniah, the guard at the **East** Gate, made repairs.
12: 37 passed above the house of David to the Water Gate *on* the **east**.
Ps 50: 1 summons the earth from the **rising** *of* the sun to the place where it
103: 12 as far as the **east** is from the west, so far has he removed our
107: 3 gathered from the lands, from **east** and west, from north and south.
113: 3 From the **rising** *of* the sun to the place where it sets, the name of
Isa 41: 2 "Who has stirred up one from the **east**, calling him in
41: 25 and he comes—one from the **rising** sun who calls on my name.
43: 5 I will bring your children from the **east** and gather you from the
45: 6 so that from the **rising** *of* the sun to the place of its setting men
46: 11 From the **east** I summon a bird of prey; from a far-off land,
59: 19 and from the **rising** *of* the sun, they will revere his glory.
Jer 31: 40 all the terraces out to the Kidron Valley on the **east** as far as the
Da 8: 9 which started small but grew in power to the south and to the **east**
11: 44 reports from the **east** and the north will alarm him, and he will set
Am 8: 12 Men will stagger from sea to sea and wander from north to **east**,
Zec 8: 7 "I will save my people from the countries of the **east** and the west.
14: 4 and the Mount of Olives will be split in two from **east** to west,
Mal 1: 11 great among the nations, from the **rising** to the setting of the sun.

4668 מְזָרִים **mᵉzārîm**, n.m. *or* v.ptcp. [1] [√ 2430]

driving winds [1]

Job 37: 9 comes out from its chamber, the cold from the **driving winds**.

4669 מִזְרָע **mizrā'**, n.[m.]. [1] [√ 2445]

sown field [1]

Isa 19: 7 Every **sown field** *along* the Nile will become parched, will blow

4670 מִזְרָק **mizrāq**, n.m. [32] [√ 2450]

sprinkling bowls [15], sprinkling bowl [13], bowl used for sprinkling [1], bowlful [1], bowls [1], sacred bowls [1]

Ex 27: 3 and its shovels, **sprinkling bowls**, meat forks and firepans.
38: 3 its pots, shovels, **sprinkling bowls**, meat forks and firepans.
Nu 4: 14 including the firepans, meat forks, shovels and **sprinkling bowls**.
7: 13 and one silver **sprinkling bowl** weighing seventy shekels,
7: 19 and one silver **sprinkling bowl** weighing seventy shekels,
7: 25 and one silver **sprinkling bowl** weighing seventy shekels,
7: 31 and one silver **sprinkling bowl** weighing seventy shekels,
7: 37 and one silver **sprinkling bowl** weighing seventy shekels,
7: 43 and one silver **sprinkling bowl** weighing seventy shekels,
7: 49 and one silver **sprinkling bowl** weighing seventy shekels,
7: 55 and one silver **sprinkling bowl** weighing seventy shekels,
7: 61 and one silver **sprinkling bowl** weighing seventy shekels,
7: 67 and one silver **sprinkling bowl** weighing seventy shekels,
7: 73 and one silver **sprinkling bowl** weighing seventy shekels,
7: 79 and one silver **sprinkling bowl** weighing seventy shekels,
7: 84 twelve silver **sprinkling bowls** and twelve gold dishes.
7: 85 and thirty shekels, and each **sprinkling bowl** seventy shekels.
1Ki 7: 40 He also made the basins and shovels and **sprinkling bowls**.
7: 45 the pots, shovels and **sprinkling bowls**. All these objects that
7: 50 gold basins, wick trimmers, **sprinkling bowls**, dishes and censers;
2Ki 12: 13 [12:14] **sprinkling bowls**, trumpets or any other articles of gold
25: 15 the imperial guard took away the censers and **sprinkling bowls**—
1Ch 28: 17 weight of pure gold for the forks, **sprinkling bowls** and pitchers;
2Ch 4: 8 five on the north. He also made a hundred gold **sprinkling bowls**.
4: 11 He also made the pots and shovels and **sprinkling bowls**.
4: 22 pure gold wick trimmers, **sprinkling bowls**, dishes and censers;
Ne 7: 70 [7:69] drachmas of gold, 50 **bowls** and 530 garments for priests.
Jer 52: 18 **sprinkling bowls**, dishes and all the bronze articles used in the
52: 19 censers, **sprinkling bowls**, pots, lampstands, dishes and bowls
Am 6: 6 You drink wine by the **bowlful** and use the finest lotions, but you
Zec 9: 15 they will be full like a **bowl used for sprinkling** the corners of the
14: 20 LORD's house will be like the **sacred bowls** in front of the altar.

4671 מֵחַ **mēaḥ**, n.[m.]. [2] [→ 4672; cf. 4683]

fat animals [1], rich [1]

Ps 66: 15 I will sacrifice **fat animals** to you and an offering of rams;
Isa 5: 17 in their own pasture; lambs will feed among the ruins of the **rich**.

4672 מֹחַ **mōaḥ**, n.m. [1] [√ 4671; cf. 4683]

marrow [1]

Job 21: 24 his body well nourished, his bones rich with **marrow**.

4673 מָחָא **māḥā'**[1], v. [3] [→ 4686; cf. 4682; Ar 10411]

clap [2], clapped [1]

Ps 98: 8 [A] *Let* the rivers **clap** their hands, let the mountains sing
Isa 55: 12 [A] before you, and all the trees of the field *will* **clap** their hands.
Eze 25: 6 [A] Because you *have* **clapped** your hands and stamped your

4674 מָחָא **māḥā'**[2], v.den. Not used in NIV/BHS [cf. 4683]

4675 מַחֲבֵא **maḥᵃbē'**, n.[m.]. [1] [√ 2461]

shelter [1]

Isa 32: 2 Each man will be like a **shelter** *from* the wind and a refuge from

4676 מַחֲבֹא **maḥᵃbō'**, n.[m.]. [1] [√ 2461]

hiding places [1]

1Sa 23: 23 Find out about all the **hiding places** he uses and come back to me

4677 מְחַבְּרוֹת **mᵉḥabbᵉrôt**, n.f. [2] [√ 2489]

fittings [1], joists [1]

1Ch 22: 3 to make nails for the doors of the gateways and for the **fittings**,
2Ch 34: 11 timber for **joists** and beams for the buildings that the kings of

4678 מַחְבֶּרֶת **maḥberet**, n.f. [8] [√ 2489]

set [6], seam [2]

Ex 26: 4 in one set, and do the same with the end curtain in the other **set**.
26: 5 on one curtain and fifty loops on the end curtain of the other **set**,
28: 27 the ephod, close to the **seam** just above the waistband of the ephod.
36: 11 loops of blue material along the edge of the end curtain in one **set**,
36: 11 and the same was done with the end curtain in the other **set**.
36: 12 on one curtain and fifty loops on the end curtain of the other **set**,
36: 17 they made fifty loops along the edge of the end curtain in one **set**
39: 20 the ephod, close to the **seam** just above the waistband of the ephod.

4679 מַחֲבַת **maḥᵃbat**, n.f. [5] [√ 2503]

griddle [3], baking [1], pan [1]

Lev 2: 5 If your grain offering is prepared on a **griddle**, it is to be made of
6: 21 [6:14] Prepare it with oil on a **griddle**; bring it well-mixed
7: 9 cooked in a pan or on a **griddle** belongs to the priest who offers it,
1Ch 23: 29 grain offerings, the unleavened wafers, the **baking** and the mixing,
Eze 4: 3 Then take an iron **pan**, place it as an iron wall between you

4680 מַחֲגֹרֶת **maḥᵃgōret**, n.f. [1] [√ 2520]

sackcloth [+8566] [1]

Isa 3: 24 baldness; instead of fine clothing, **sackcloth** [+8566];

4681 מָחָה **māḥā**[1], v. [34] [→ 9457?]

blot out [11], be blotted out [3], blotted out [2], completely blot out [+906+4681] [2], wipe [2], wiped out [2], wipes [2], be wiped away [1], be wiped out [1], blots out [1], ruin [1], swept away [1], wash off [1], were wiped [1], wipe away [1], wipe out [1], wiping [1]

Ge 6: 7 [A] So the LORD said, "*I will* **wipe** mankind, whom I have
7: 4 [A] *I will* **wipe** from the face of the earth every living creature I
7: 23 [A] Every living thing on the face of the earth *was* **wiped out**;
7: 23 [C] and the birds of the air **were wiped** from the earth.
Ex 17: 14 [A] because *I will* **completely blot** [+906+4681] **out** the memory
17: 14 [A] because *I will* **completely blot out** [+906+4681] the memory
32: 32 [A] but if not, then **blot** me **out** of the book you have written."
32: 33 [A] "Whoever has sinned against me *I will* **blot out** of my book.
Nu 5: 23 [A] on a scroll and then **wash** them **off** into the bitter water.
Dt 9: 14 [A] destroy them and **blot out** their name from under heaven.
25: 6 [C] so that his name *will* not **be blotted out** from Israel.
25: 19 [A] *you shall* **blot out** the memory of Amalek from under
29: 20 [29:19] [A] the LORD *will* **blot out** his name from under
Jdg 21: 17 [C] they said, "so that a tribe of Israel *will* not **be wiped out**.
2Ki 14: 27 [A] since the LORD had not said he *would* **blot out** the name of
21: 13 [A] *I will* **wipe out** Jerusalem as one wipes a dish, wiping it
21: 13 [A] I will wipe out Jerusalem as *one* **wipes** a dish, wiping it
21: 13 [A] as one wipes a dish, **wiping** it and turning it upside down.
Ne 4: 5 [3:37] [C] up their guilt or **blot out** their sins from your sight,
13: 14 [G] *do* not **blot out** what I have so faithfully done for the house
Ps 9: 5 [9:6] [A] *you have* **blotted out** their name for ever and ever.
51: 1 [51:3] [A] according to your great compassion **blot out** my
51: 9 [51:11] [A] your face from my sins and **blot out** all my iniquity.
69: 28 [69:29] [C] *May they* **be blotted out** of the book of life and not
109: 13 [C] be cut off, their names **blotted out** from the next generation.
109: 14 [C] the LORD; *may* the sin of his mother never **be blotted out**.
Pr 6: 33 [C] are his lot, and his shame *will* never **be wiped away**;
30: 20 [A] She eats and **wipes** her mouth and says, 'I've done nothing
31: 3 [A] strength on women, your vigor on *those who* **ruin** kings.

Isa 25: 8 [A] The Sovereign LORD *will* **wipe away** the tears from all
43:25 [A] "I, even I, am he *who* **blots out** your transgressions, for my
44:22 [A] *I have* **swept away** your offenses like a cloud, your sins like
Jer 18:23 [G] not forgive their crimes or **blot out** their sins from your sight.
Eze 6: 6 [C] altars broken down, and what you have made **wiped out**.

4682 ²מָחָה **$māḥā^2$**, v. [1] [√ 4693; cf. 4673; Ar 10411]

continue [1]

Nu 34:11 [A] and **continue** along the slopes east of the Sea of Kinnereth.

4683 ³מָחָה **$māḥā^3$**, v.den. [1] [cf. 4674, 4671, 4672]

meats [1]

Isa 25: 6 [E] of aged wine—the best of **meats** and the finest of wines.

4684 מְחוּגָה **$m^eḥûgâ$**, n.f. [1] [√ 2552]

compasses [1]

Isa 44:13 he roughs it out with chisels and marks it with **compasses**.

4685 מָחוֹז **$māḥôz$**, n.[m.]. [1] [√ 4651]

haven [1]

Ps 107:30 when it grew calm, and he guided them to their desired **haven**.

4686 מְחוּיָאֵל **$m^eḥûyā'ēl$**, n.pr.m. [2] [√ 4673 + 446; cf. 4696]

Mehujael [2]

Ge 4:18 To Enoch was born Irad, and Irad was the father of **Mehujael**,
4:18 father of Mehujael, and **Mehujael** was the father of Methushael,

4687 מַחֲוִים **$maḥ^awîm$**, a.g. [1]

Mahavite [1]

1Ch 11:46 Eliel the **Mahavite**, Jeribai and Joshaviah the sons of Elnaam,

4688 ¹מָחוֹל **$māḥôl^1$**, n.m. [6] [→ 4689, 4703; cf. 2565]

dancing [4], dance [2]

Ps 30:11 [30:12] You turned my wailing into **dancing**; you removed my
149: 3 Let them praise his name with **dancing** and make music to him
150: 4 praise him with tambourine and **dancing**, praise him with the
Jer 31: 4 will take up your tambourines and go out to **dance** *with* the joyful.
31:13 Then maidens will **dance** and be glad, young men and old as well.
La 5:15 Joy is gone from our hearts; our **dancing** has turned to mourning.

4689 ²מָחוֹל **$māḥôl^2$**, n.pr.m. [1] [√ 4688; cf. 2565]

Mahol [1]

1Ki 4:31 [5:11] wiser than Heman, Calcol and Darda, the sons of **Mahol**.

4690 מַחֲזֶה **$maḥ^azeh$**, n.[m.]. [4] [√ 2600]

vision [3], visions [1]

Ge 15: 1 After this, the word of the LORD came to Abram in a **vision**:
Nu 24: 4 who sees a **vision** *from* the Almighty, who falls prostrate,
24:16 who sees a **vision** *from* the Almighty, who falls prostrate,
Eze 13: 7 Have you not seen false **visions** and uttered lying divinations when

4691 מֶחֱזָה **$meḥ^ezâ$**, n.f. [4] [√ 2600]

facing each other [+448+4691] [4]

1Ki 7: 4 were placed high in sets of three, **facing** [+448+4691] **each other**.
7: 4 were placed high in sets of three, **facing each other** [+448+4691].
7: 5 in the front part in sets of three, **facing** [+448+4691] **each other**.
7: 5 in the front part in sets of three, **facing each other** [+448+4691].

4692 מַחֲזִיאוֹת **$maḥ^azî'ôt$**, n.pr.m. [2] [√ 2600]

Mahazioth [2]

1Ch 25: 4 Joshbekashah, Mallothi, Hothir and **Mahazioth**.
25:30 the twenty-third to **Mahazioth**, his sons and relatives, 12

4693 מְחִי **$m^eḥî$**, n.[m.]. [1] [√ 4682]

blows [1]

Eze 26: 9 He will direct the **blows** *of* his battering rams against your walls

4694 מְחִידָא **$m^eḥîdā'$**, n.pr.m. [2]

Mehida [2]

Ezr 2:52 Bazluth, **Mehida**, Harsha,
Ne 7:54 Bazluth, **Mehida**, Harsha,

4695 מִחְיָה **$miḥyâ$**, n.f. [8] [√ 2649]

food [1], living thing [1], new life [1], raw [+2645] [1], raw flesh [1], recover [1], relief [1], save lives [1]

Ge 45: 5 because it was to **save lives** that God sent me ahead of you.
Lev 13:10 the hair white and if there is **raw** [+2645] flesh in the swelling,
13:24 a reddish-white or white spot appears in the **raw flesh** *of* the burn,
Jdg 6: 4 all the way to Gaza and did not spare a **living thing** for Israel,
17:10 give you ten shekels of silver a year, your clothes and your **food**."
2Ch 14:13 [14:12] great number of Cushites fell that they could not **recover**;
Ezr 9: 8 so our God gives light to our eyes and a little **relief** in our bondage.
9: 9 He has granted us **new life** to rebuild the house of our God

4696 מְחִיָּיאֵל **$m^eḥiyyāy'ēl$**, n.pr.m. Not used in NIV/BHS [cf. 4686]

4697 ¹מְחִיר **$m^eḥîr^1$**, n.m. [15] [→ 4698]

price [6], purchased [+928+4374] [2], *untranslated* [1], charge [1], cost [1], insist on paying for [+907+928+4946+7864+7864] [1], money [1], sale [1], worth [1]

Dt 23:18 [23:19] or **[RPH]** of a male prostitute into the house of the
2Sa 24:24 "No, *I* **insist on paying** you **for** [+907+928+4946+7864+7864] it.
1Ki 10:28 the royal merchants **purchased** [+928+4374] them from Kue.
21: 2 vineyard or, if you prefer, I will pay you *whatever* it is **worth**."
2Ch 1:16 the royal merchants **purchased** [+928+4374] them from Kue.
Job 28:15 bought with the finest gold, nor can its **price** be weighed in silver.
Ps 44:12 [44:13] people for a pittance, gaining nothing from their **sale**.
Pr 17:16 Of what use is **money** in the hand of a fool, since he has no desire
27:26 provide you with clothing, and the goats with the **price** *of* a field.
Isa 45:13 my city and set my exiles free, but not for a **price** or reward,
55: 1 Come, buy wine and milk without money and without **cost**.
Jer 15:13 and your treasures I will give as plunder, without **charge**,
La 5: 4 must buy the water we drink; our wood can be had only at a **price**.
Da 11:39 rulers over many people and will distribute the land at a **price**.
Mic 3:11 Her leaders judge for a bribe, her priests teach for a **price**,

4698 ²מְחִיר **$m^eḥîr^2$**, n.pr.m. [1] [√ 4697]

Mehir [1]

1Ch 4:11 Kelub, Shuhah's brother, was the father of **Mehir**, who was the

4699 מַחֲלֵב **$maḥ^alēb$**, n.pr.loc. Not used in NIV/BHS

4700 מַחֲלֶה **$maḥ^aleh$**, n.[m.]. [2] [→ 4701; cf. 2703]

disease [1], sickness [1]

2Ch 21:15 You yourself will be very ill with a lingering **disease** *of* the
Pr 18:14 A man's spirit sustains him in **sickness**, but a crushed spirit who

4701 מַחֲלָה **$maḥ^alâ$**, n.f. [4] [√ 4700; cf. 2703]

disease [2], diseases [1], sickness [1]

Ex 15:26 I will not bring on you any of the **diseases** I brought on the
23:25 your food and water. I will take away **sickness** from among you,
1Ki 8:37 them in any of their cities, whatever disaster or **disease** may come,
2Ch 6:28 them in any of their cities, whatever disaster or **disease** may come,

4702 מַחְלָה **$maḥlâ$**, n.pr.f. [& m.?]. [5]

Mahlah [5]

Nu 26:33 whose names were **Mahlah**, Noah, Hoglah, Milcah and Tirzah.)
27: 1 The names of the daughters were **Mahlah**, Noah, Hoglah,
36:11 **Mahlah**, Tirzah, Hoglah, Milcah and Noah—
Jos 17: 3 whose names were **Mahlah**, Noah, Hoglah, Milcah and Tirzah.
1Ch 7:18 sister Hammoleketh gave birth to Ishhod, Abiezer and **Mahlah**.

4703 מְחֹלָה **$m^eḥōlâ$**, n.f. [8] [√ 4688; cf. 71, 2565]

dancing [5], dances [2], dance [1]

Ex 15:20 and all the women followed her, with tambourines and **dancing**.
32:19 Moses approached the camp and saw the calf and the **dancing**,
Jdg 11:34 meet him but his daughter, **dancing** to the sound of tambourines!
21:21 When the girls of Shiloh come out to join in the **dancing**,
1Sa 18: 6 all the towns of Israel to meet King Saul with singing and **dancing**,
21:11 [21:12] the land? Isn't he the one they sing about in their **dances**:
29: 5 Isn't this the David they sang about in their **dances**: " 'Saul has
SS 6:13 [7:1] Why would you gaze on the Shulammite as on the **dance** *of*

4704 מְחִלָּה **$m^eḥillâ$**, n.f. [1] [√ 2726]

holes [1]

Isa 2:19 to **holes** *in* the ground from dread of the LORD and the splendor

4705 מַחְלוֹן mahlôn, n.pr.m. [4] [√ 2703?]

Mahlon [3], Mahlon's [1]

Ru 1: 2 and the names of his two sons were **Mahlon** and Kilion.
1: 5 both **Mahlon** and Kilion also died, and Naomi was left without her
4: 9 from Naomi all the property of Elimelech, Kilion and **Mahlon**.
4: 10 also acquired Ruth the Moabitess, **Mahlon's** widow, as my wife,

4706 מַחְלִי mahlî[1], n.pr.m. [12] [√ 2703?]

Mahli [12]

Ex 6: 19 The sons of Merari were **Mahli** and Mushi. These were the clans
Nu 3: 20 The Merarite clans: **Mahli** and Mushi. These were the Levite
1Ch 6: 19 [6:4] The sons of Merari: **Mahli** and Mushi. These are the clans
6: 29 [6:14] **Mahli**, Libni his son, Shimei his son, Uzzah his son,
6: 47 [6:32] the son of **Mahli**, the son of Mushi, the son of Merari,
23: 21 of Merari: **Mahli** and Mushi. The sons of Mahli: Eleazar and Kish.
23: 21 of Merari: Mahli and Mushi. The sons of **Mahli**: Eleazar and Kish.
23: 23 The sons of Mushi: **Mahli**, Eder and Jerimoth—three in all.
24: 26 The sons of Merari: **Mahli** and Mushi. The son of Jaaziah: Beno.
24: 28 From **Mahli**: Eleazar, who had no sons.
24: 30 the sons of Mushi: **Mahli**, Eder and Jerimoth. These were the
Ezr 8: 18 a capable man, from the descendants of **Mahli** son of Levi,

4707 מַחְלִי mahlî[2], a.g. [2] [√ 2703?]

Mahlite [1], Mahlites [1]

Nu 3: 33 To Merari belonged the clans of the **Mahlites** and the Mushites;
26: 58 the **Mahlite** clan, the Mushite clan, the Korahite clan.

4708 מַחֲלֻיִים mahaluyîm, n.m. [1] [√ 2703]

wounded [1]

2Ch 24: 25 When the Arameans withdrew, they left Joash severely **wounded**.

4709 מַחְלָף mahalāp, n.m. [1] [√ 2736?]

pans [1]

Ezr 1: 9 the inventory: gold dishes 30 silver dishes 1,000 silver **pans** 29

4710 מַחְלָפָה mahalāpâ, n.f. [2 / 3] [√ 2736]

braids [3]

Jdg 16: 13 "If you weave the seven **braids** *of* my head into the fabric ⌞on the
16: 13 was sleeping, Delilah took the seven **braids** [BHS-] *of* his head,
16: 19 she called a man to shave off the seven **braids** *of* his hair,

4711 מַחֲלָצוֹת mahalāṣôt, n.f.[pl.]. [2] [√ 2740]

fine robes [1], rich garments [1]

Isa 3: 22 the **fine robes** and the capes and cloaks, the purses
Zec 3: 4 I have taken away your sin, and I will put **rich garments** on you."

4712 מַחְלְקוֹת mahleqôt, n.f.pl. Not used in NIV/BHS [√ 2744; cf. 2165, 6154]

4713 מַחֲלֹקֶת mahalōqet, n.f. [42] [√ 2745; Ar 10412]

divisions [19], division [17], tribal divisions [2], *untranslated* [1], army divisions [1], groups [1], portions [1]

Jos 11: 23 it as an inheritance to Israel according to their tribal **divisions**.
12: 7 to the tribes of Israel according to their **tribal divisions**—
18: 10 the land to the Israelites according to their **tribal divisions**.
1Ch 23: 6 David divided the Levites into **groups** corresponding to the sons of
24: 1 These were the **divisions** of the sons of Aaron: The sons of Aaron
26: 1 The **divisions** of the gatekeepers: From the Korahites:
26: 12 These **divisions** *of* the gatekeepers, through their chief men,
26: 19 These were the **divisions** *of* the gatekeepers who were descendants
27: 1 who served the king in all that concerned the **army divisions** that
27: 1 month throughout the year. Each **division** consisted of 24,000 men.
27: 2 In charge of the first **division**, for the first month, was Jashobeam
27: 2 Jashobeam son of Zabdiel. There were 24,000 men in his **division**.
27: 4 In charge of the **division** *for* the second month was Dodai the
27: 4 was Dodai the Ahohite; Mikloth was the leader of his **division**.
27: 4 the leader of his division. There were 24,000 men in his **division**.
27: 5 the priest. He was chief and there were 24,000 men in his **division**.
27: 6 over the Thirty. His son Ammizabad was in charge of his **division**.
27: 7 was his successor. There were 24,000 men in his **division**.
27: 8 Shamhuth the Izrahite. There were 24,000 men in his **division**.
27: 9 son of Ikkesh the Tekoite. There were 24,000 men in his **division**.
27: 10 an Ephraimite. There were 24,000 men in his **division**.
27: 11 the Hushathite, a Zerahite. There were 24,000 men in his **division**.
27: 12 a Benjamite. There were 24,000 men in his **division**.
27: 13 a Zerahite. There were 24,000 men in his **division**.
27: 14 an Ephraimite. There were 24,000 men in his **division**.
27: 15 from the family of Othniel. There were 24,000 men in his **division**.
28: 1 the commanders of the **divisions** in the service of the king,
28: 13 He gave him instructions for the **divisions** *of* the priests
28: 21 The **divisions** *of* the priests and Levites are ready for all the work
2Ch 5: 11 there had consecrated themselves, regardless of their **divisions**.
8: 14 he appointed the **divisions** *of* the priests for their duties,
8: 14 He also appointed the gatekeepers by **divisions** for the various
23: 8 for Jehoiada the priest had not released any of the **divisions**.
31: 2 Hezekiah assigned the priests and Levites to **divisions**—each of
31: 2 **[RPH]** each of them according to their duties as priests
31: 15 distributing to their fellow priests according to their **divisions**,
31: 16 according to their responsibilities and their **divisions**.
31: 17 or more, according to their responsibilities and their **divisions**.
35: 4 Prepare yourselves by families in your **divisions**, according to the
35: 10 the priests stood in their places with the Levites in their **divisions**
Ne 11: 36 Some of the **divisions** *of* the Levites of Judah settled in Benjamin.
Eze 48: 29 and these will be their **portions**," declares the Sovereign LORD.

4714 מַחֲלַת mahalat[1], n.f. [2] [√ 2565? *or* 2704?]

mahalath [2]

Ps 53: T [53:1] of music. According to ***mahalath***. A *maskil* of David.
88: T [88:1] director of music. According to ***mahalath*** *leannoth*.

4715 מַחֲלַת mahalat[2], n.pr.f. [2]

Mahalath [2]

Ge 28: 9 so he went to Ishmael and married **Mahalath**, the sister of
2Ch 11: 18 Rehoboam married **Mahalath**, who was the daughter of David's

4716 מְחֹלָתִי mehōlātî, a.g. [2] [cf. 71?]

Meholathite [1], of Meholah [1]

1Sa 18: 19 given to David, she was given in marriage to Adriel **of Meholah**.
2Sa 21: 8 whom she had borne to Adriel son of Barzillai the **Meholathite**.

4717 מַחְמָאֹת mahmā'ōt, n.f.pl. [1] [cf. 2772]

butter [1]

Ps 55: 21 [55:22] His speech is smooth as **butter**, yet war is in his heart;

4718 מַחְמָד mahmād, n.m. [13] [√ 2773]

treasures [4], delight [3], cherished [1], lovely [1], pleasing [1], treasured [1], value [+6524] [1], value [1]

1Ki 20: 6 They will seize everything you **value** [+6524] and carry it away.' "
2Ch 36: 19 burned all the palaces and destroyed everything of **value** there.
SS 5: 16 His mouth is sweetness itself; he is altogether **lovely**. This is my
Isa 64: 11 [64:10] burned with fire, and all *that* we **treasured** lies in ruins.
La 1: 10 The enemy laid hands on all her **treasures**; she saw pagan nations
1: 11 they barter their **treasures** [K 4719] for food to keep themselves
2: 4 Like a foe he has slain all *who* were **pleasing** *to* the eye; he has
Eze 24: 16 with one blow I am about to take away from you the **delight** *of*
24: 21 take pride, the **delight** *of* your eyes, the object of your affection.
24: 25 their joy and glory, the **delight** *of* their eyes, their heart's desire,
Hos 9: 6 Their **treasures** of silver will be taken over by briers, and thorns
9: 16 Even if they bear children, I will slay their **cherished** offspring."
Joel 3: 5 [4:5] my gold and carried off my finest **treasures** to your temples.

4719 מַחְמֹד mahmōd, n.[m.]. [1] [√ 2773]

treasures [1]

La 1: 7 wandering Jerusalem remembers all the **treasures** that were hers in
1: 11 [they barter their **treasures** [K; see Q 4718] for food]

4720 מַחְמָל mahmāl, n.[m.]. [1] [√ 2798?]

object [1]

Eze 24: 21 take pride, the delight of your eyes, the **object** *of* your affection.

4721 מַחְמֶצֶת mahmeṣet, n.f. [2] [√ 2806]

anything with yeast in it [1], made with yeast [1]

Ex 12: 19 whoever eats **anything with yeast in it** must be cut off from the
12: 20 Eat nothing **made with yeast**. Wherever you live, you must eat

4722 מַחֲנֶה mahaneh, n.m. & f. [214] [→ 4724; cf. 2837]

camp [144], army [23], camps [8], *untranslated* [6], forces [5], troops [3], armies [2], dwelling [2], fighting [2], group [2], groups [2], lines [2], attendants [1], band [1], company [1], droves [1], encamped [+3655] [1], force [1], it[s] [+2021] [1], it[s] [+5213] [1], Midianites[s] [1], there[s] [+928+2021] [1], tribes [1], units [1], unwalled [1]

Ge 32: 2 [32:3] When Jacob saw them, he said, "This is the **camp** *of* God!"
32: 7 [32:8] divided the people who were with him into two **groups**,
32: 8 [32:9] He thought, "If Esau comes and attacks one **group**,

Ge 32: 8 [32:9] and attacks one group, the **group** that is left may escape."
32: 10 [32:11] I crossed this Jordan, but now I have become two **groups**.
32: 21 [32:22] ahead of him, but he himself spent the night in the **camp**.
33: 8 Esau asked, "What do you mean by all these **droves** I met?"
50: 9 and horsemen also went up with him. It was a very large **company**.
Ex 14: 19 who had been traveling in front of Israel's **army**, withdrew
14: 20 coming between the **armies** *of* Egypt and Israel. Throughout the
14: 20 coming between the armies of Egypt and **[RPH]** Israel.
14: 24 and cloud at the Egyptian **army** and threw it into confusion.
14: 24 cloud at the Egyptian army and threw **it**[s] [+5213] into confusion.
16: 13 That evening quail came and covered the **camp**, and in the
16: 13 and in the morning there was a layer of dew around the **camp**.
19: 16 and a very loud trumpet blast. Everyone in the **camp** trembled.
19: 17 Then Moses led the people out of the **camp** to meet with God,
29: 14 burn the bull's flesh and its hide and its offal outside the **camp**.
32: 17 he said to Moses, "There is the sound of war in the **camp**."
32: 19 When Moses approached the **camp** and saw the calf
32: 26 So he stood at the entrance to the **camp** and said, "Whoever is for
32: 27 Go back and forth through the **camp** from one end to the other,
33: 7 to take a tent and pitch it outside the **camp** some distance away,
33: 7 camp some distance away, **[RPH]** calling it the "tent of meeting."
33: 7 of the LORD would go to the tent of meeting outside the **camp**.
33: 11 Moses would return to the **camp**, but his young aide Joshua son of
36: 6 Moses gave an order and they sent this word throughout the **camp**:
Lev 4: 12 he must take outside the **camp** to a place ceremonially clean,
4: 21 he shall take the bull outside the **camp** and burn it as he burned the
6: 11 [6:4] carry the ashes outside the **camp** to a place that is
8: 17 its hide and its flesh and its offal he burned up outside the **camp**,
9: 11 the flesh and the hide he burned up outside the **camp**.
10: 4 carry your cousins outside the **camp**, away from the front of the
10: 5 still in their tunics, outside the **camp**, as Moses ordered.
13: 46 He must live alone; he must live outside the **camp**.
14: 3 The priest is to go outside the **camp** and examine him. If the
14: 8 After this he may come into the **camp**, but he must stay outside his
16: 26 bathe himself with water; afterward he may come into the **camp**.
16: 27 Holy Place to make atonement, must be taken outside the **camp**;
16: 28 bathe himself with water; afterward he may come into the **camp**.
17: 3 who sacrifices an ox, a lamb or a goat in the **camp** or outside of it
17: 3 an ox, a lamb or a goat in the camp or outside of **it**[s] [+2021]
24: 10 and a fight broke out in the **camp** between him and an Israelite.
24: 14 "Take the blasphemer outside the **camp**. All those who heard him
24: 23 and they took the blasphemer outside the **camp** and stoned him.
Nu 1: 52 by divisions, each man in his own **camp** under his own standard.
2: 3 the divisions of the **camp** *of* Judah are to encamp under their
2: 9 All the men assigned to the **camp** *of* Judah, according to their
2: 10 On the south will be the divisions of the **camp** *of* Reuben under
2: 16 All the men assigned to the **camp** *of* Reuben, according to their
2: 17 the **camp** *of* the Levites will set out in the middle of the camps.
2: 17 the camp of the Levites will set out in the middle of the **camps**.
2: 18 On the west will be the divisions of the **camp** *of* Ephraim under
2: 24 All the men assigned to the **camp** *of* Ephraim, according to their
2: 25 On the north will be the divisions of the **camp** *of* Dan, under their
2: 31 All the men assigned to the **camp** *of* Dan number 157,600.
2: 32 All those in the **camps**, by their divisions, number 603,550.
4: 5 When the **camp** is to move, Aaron and his sons are to go in
4: 15 and all the holy articles, and when the **camp** is ready to move,
5: 2 "Command the Israelites to send away from the **camp** anyone who
5: 3 send them outside the **camp** so they will not defile their camp,
5: 3 send them outside the camp so they will not defile their **camp**,
5: 4 The Israelites did this; they sent them outside the **camp**. They did
10: 2 calling the community together and for having the **camps** set out.
10: 5 blast is sounded, the **tribes** camping on the east are to set out.
10: 6 sounding of a second blast, the **camps** on the south are to set out.
10: 14 The divisions of the **camp** *of* Judah went first, under their standard.
10: 18 The divisions of the **camp** *of* Reuben went next, under their
10: 22 The divisions of the **camp** *of* Ephraim went next, under their
10: 25 Finally, as the rear guard for all the **units**, the divisions of the camp
10: 25 the divisions of the **camp** *of* Dan set out, under their standard.
10: 34 LORD was over them by day when they set out from the **camp**.
11: 1 among them and consumed some of the outskirts of the **camp**.
11: 9 When the dew settled on the **camp** at night, the manna also came
11: 26 whose names were Eldad and Medad, had remained in the **camp**.
11: 26 the Spirit also rested on them, and they prophesied in the **camp**.
11: 27 and told Moses, "Eldad and Medad are prophesying in the **camp**."
11: 30 Then Moses and the elders of Israel returned to the **camp**.
11: 31 It brought them down all around the **camp** to about three feet
11: 31 It brought them down all around the camp to **[RPH]** about three
11: 32 than ten homers. Then they spread them out all around the **camp**.
12: 14 Confine her outside the **camp** for seven days; after that she can be
12: 15 So Miriam was confined outside the **camp** for seven days,
13: 19 kind of towns do they live in? Are they **unwalled** or fortified?
14: 44 nor the ark of the LORD's covenant moved from the **camp**.
15: 35 must die. The whole assembly must stone him outside the **camp**."
15: 36 So the assembly took him outside the **camp** and stoned him to
19: 3 it is to be taken outside the **camp** and slaughtered in his presence.
19: 7 He may then come into the **camp**, but he will be ceremonially
19: 9 and put them in a ceremonially clean place outside the **camp**.
31: 12 and the Israelite assembly at their **camp** on the plains of Moab,
31: 13 the leaders of the community went to meet them outside the **camp**.
31: 19 or touched anyone who was killed must stay outside the **camp**
31: 24 and you will be clean. Then you may come into the **camp**."
Dt 2: 14 that entire generation of fighting men had perished from the **camp**,
2: 15 them until he had completely eliminated them from the **camp**.
23: 9 [23:10] When *you are* **encamped** [+3655] against your enemies,
23: 10 [23:11] he is to go outside the **camp** and stay there.
23: 10 [23:11] he is to go outside the camp and stay **[RPH]** there.
23: 11 [23:12] to wash himself, and at sunset he may return to the **camp**.
23: 12 [23:13] Designate a place outside the **camp** where you can go to
23: 14 [23:15] For the LORD your God moves about in your **camp** to
23: 14 [23:15] Your **camp** must be holy, so that he will not see among
29: 11 [29:10] the aliens living in your **camps** who chop your wood
Jos 1: 11 "Go through the **camp** and tell the people, 'Get your supplies
3: 2 After three days the officers went throughout the **camp**,
5: 8 they remained where they were in **camp** until they were healed.
6: 11 Then the people returned to **camp** and spent the night there.
6: 11 people returned to camp and spent the night **there**[s] [+928+2021].
6: 14 day they marched around the city once and returned to the **camp**.
6: 18 Otherwise you will make the **camp** *of* Israel liable to destruction
6: 23 entire family and put them in a place outside the **camp** *of* Israel.
8: 13 all those in the **camp** to the north of the city and the ambush to the
9: 6 Then they went to Joshua in the **camp** at Gilgal and said to him
10: 5 They moved up with all their **troops** and took up positions against
10: 6 The Gibeonites then sent word to Joshua in the **camp** at Gilgal:
10: 15 Then Joshua returned with all Israel to the **camp** at Gilgal.
10: 21 then returned safely to Joshua in the **camp** at Makkedah,
10: 43 Then Joshua returned with all Israel to the **camp** at Gilgal.
11: 4 They came out with all their **troops** and a large number of horses
18: 9 in seven parts, and returned to Joshua in the **camp** at Shiloh.
Jdg 4: 15 LORD routed Sisera and all his chariots and **army** by the sword,
4: 16 pursued the chariots and **army** as far as Harosheth Haggoyim.
4: 16 All the **troops** *of* Sisera fell by the sword; not a man was left.
7: 1 The **camp** *of* Midian was north of them in the valley near the hill
7: 8 the others. Now the **camp** *of* Midian lay below him in the valley.
7: 9 the LORD said to Gideon, "Get up, go down against the **camp**,
7: 10 are afraid to attack, go down to the **camp** with your servant Purah
7: 11 Afterward, you will be encouraged to attack the **camp**." So he
7: 11 and Purah his servant went down to the outposts of the **camp**.
7: 13 round loaf of barley bread came tumbling into the Midianite **camp**.
7: 14 God has given the Midianites and the whole **camp** into his hands."
7: 15 He returned to the **camp** *of* Israel and called out, "Get up!
7: 15 The LORD has given the Midianite **camp** into your hands."
7: 17 my lead. When I get to the edge of the **camp**, do exactly as I do.
7: 18 from all around the **camp** blow yours and shout, 'For the LORD
7: 19 the hundred men with him reached the edge of the **camp** at the
7: 21 While each man held his position around the **camp**, all the
7: 21 around the camp, all the **Midianites**[s] ran, crying out as they fled.
7: 22 the LORD caused the men throughout the **camp** to turn on each
7: 22 The **army** fled to Beth Shittah toward Zererah as far as the border
8: 10 Zalmunna were in Karkor with a **force** of about fifteen thousand
8: 10 all that were left of the **armies** *of* the eastern peoples;
8: 11 east of Nobah and Jogbehah and fell upon the unsuspecting **army**.
8: 11 and Jogbehah and fell upon the unsuspecting army. **[RPH]**
8: 12 but he pursued them and captured them, routing their entire **army**.
21: 8 no one from Jabesh Gilead had come to the **camp** for the assembly.
21: 12 with a man, and they took them to the **camp** *at* Shiloh in Canaan.
1Sa 4: 3 When the soldiers returned to **camp**, the elders of Israel asked,
4: 5 When the ark of the LORD's covenant came into the **camp**,
4: 6 Philistines asked, "What's all this shouting in the Hebrew **camp**?"
4: 6 they learned that the ark of the LORD had come into the **camp**,
4: 7 "A god has come into the **camp**," they said. "We're in trouble!
11: 11 during the last watch of the night they broke into the **camp** of the
13: 17 Raiding parties went out from the Philistine **camp** in three
14: 15 those in the **camp** and field, and those in the outposts and raiding
14: 19 the tumult in the Philistine **camp** increased more and more.
14: 21 had gone up with them to their **camp** went over to the Israelites
17: 1 Now the Philistines gathered their **forces** for war and assembled at
17: 4 who was from Gath, came out of the Philistine **camp**.
17: 17 these ten loaves of bread for your brothers and hurry to their **camp**.
17: 46 Today I will give the carcasses of the Philistine **army** to the birds
17: 53 returned from chasing the Philistines, they plundered their **camp**.
26: 6 "Who will go down into the **camp** with me to Saul?"
28: 1 In those days the Philistines gathered their **forces** to fight against
28: 1 that you and your men will accompany me in the **army**."
28: 5 When Saul saw the Philistine **army**, he was afraid; terror filled his
28: 19 The LORD will also hand over the **army** *of* Israel to the
29: 1 The Philistines gathered all their **forces** at Aphek, and Israel
29: 6 and I would be pleased to have you serve with me in the **army**.
2Sa 1: 2 On the third day a man arrived from Saul's **camp**, with his clothes

2Sa 1: 3 asked him. He answered, "I have escaped from the Israelite **camp**."
5: 24 LORD has gone out in front of you to strike the Philistine **army**."
23: 16 So the three mighty men broke through the Philistine **lines**,
1Ki 16: 16 of the army, king over Israel that very day there in the **camp**.
22: 34 his chariot driver, "Wheel around and get me out of the **fighting**.
22: 36 As the sun was setting, a cry spread through the **army**: "Every man
2Ki 3: 9 the **army** had no more water for themselves or for the animals with
3: 24 when the Moabites came to the **camp** *of* Israel, the Israelites rose
5: 15 Then Naaman and all his **attendants** went back to the man of God.
6: 24 Ben-Hadad king of Aram mobilized his entire **army** and marched
7: 4 So let's go over to the **camp** *of* the Arameans and surrender.
7: 5 At dusk they got up and went to the **camp** *of* the Arameans.
7: 5 When they reached the edge of the **camp**, not a man was there,
7: 6 for the Lord had caused the Arameans to hear **[RPH]** the sound of
7: 7 and donkeys. They left the **camp** as it was and ran for their lives.
7: 8 The men who had leprosy reached the edge of the **camp**
7: 10 "We went into the Aramean **camp** and not a man was there—
7: 12 so they have left the **camp** to hide in the countryside, thinking,
7: 14 with their horses, and the king sent them after the Aramean **army**.
7: 16 the people went out and plundered the **camp** *of* the Arameans.
19: 35 a hundred and eighty-five thousand men in the Assyrian **camp**.
1Ch 9: 18 These were the gatekeepers belonging to the **camp** *of* the Levites.
9: 19 for guarding the entrance to the **dwelling** *of* the LORD.
11: 15 while a **band** *of* Philistines was encamped in the Valley of
11: 18 So the Three broke through the Philistine **lines**, drew water from
12: 22 [12:23] until he had a great **army**, like the army of God.
12: 22 [12:23] until he had a great army, like the **army** *of* God.
14: 15 God has gone out in front of you to strike the Philistine **army**."
14: 16 they struck down the Philistine **army**, all the way from Gibeon to
2Ch 14: 13 [14:12] they were crushed before the LORD and his **forces**.
18: 33 the chariot driver, "Wheel around and get me out of the **fighting**.
22: 1 since the raiders, who came with the Arabs into the **camp**,
31: 2 and to sing praises at the gates of the LORD's **dwelling**.
32: 21 and the leaders and officers in the **camp** *of* the Assyrian king.
Ps 27: 3 Though an **army** besiege me, my heart will not fear; though war
78: 28 He made them come down inside their **camp**, all around their tents.
106: 16 In the **camp** they grew envious of Moses and of Aaron, who was
Isa 37: 36 a hundred and eighty-five thousand men in the Assyrian **camp**.
Eze 1: 24 like the voice of the Almighty, like the tumult of an **army**.
4: 2 up to it, set up **camps** against it and put battering rams around it.
Joel 2: 11 his **forces** are beyond number, and mighty are those who obey his
Am 4: 10 I filled your nostrils with the stench of your **camps**, yet you have
Zec 14: 15 the camels and donkeys, and all the animals in those **camps**.

4723 מַחֲנֵה־דָן *maḥ^{a}nēh-dān*, n.pr.loc. [2]
Mahaneh Dan [2]
Jdg 13: 25 of the LORD began to stir him while he was in **Mahaneh Dan**,
18: 12 is why the place west of Kiriath Jearim is called **Mahaneh Dan**

4724 מַחֲנַיִם *maḥ^{a}nayim*, n.pr.loc. [14] [√ 4722; cf. 2837]
Mahanaim [14]
Ge 32: 2 [32:3] is the camp of God!" So he named that place **Mahanaim**.
Jos 13: 26 and Betonim, and from **Mahanaim** to the territory of Debir;
13: 30 The territory extending from **Mahanaim** and including all of
21: 38 in Gilead (a city of refuge for one accused of murder), **Mahanaim**,
2Sa 2: 8 Ish-Bosheth son of Saul and brought him over to **Mahanaim**.
2: 12 of Ish-Bosheth son of Saul, left **Mahanaim** and went to Gibeon.
2: 29 continued through the whole Bithron and came to **Mahanaim**.
17: 24 David went to **Mahanaim**, and Absalom crossed the Jordan with
17: 27 When David came to **Mahanaim**, Shobi son of Nahash from
19: 32 [19:33] had provided for the king during his stay in **Mahanaim**,
1Ki 2: 8 who called down bitter curses on me the day I went to **Mahanaim**.
4: 14 Ahinadab son of Iddo—in **Mahanaim**;
1Ch 6: 80 [6:65] tribe of Gad they received Ramoth in Gilead, **Mahanaim**,
SS 6: 13 [7:1] you gaze on the Shulammite as on the dance of **Mahanaim**?

4725 מַחֲנָק *maḥ^{a}nāq*, n.[m.]. [1] [√ 2871]
strangling [1]
Job 7: 15 so that I prefer **strangling** and death, rather than this body of mine.

4726 מַחְסֶה *maḥseh*, n.m. [20] [→ 4729; cf. 2879]
refuge [18], shelter [2]
Job 24: 8 drenched by mountain rains and hug the rocks for lack of **shelter**.
Ps 14: 6 frustrate the plans of the poor, but the LORD is their **refuge**.
46: 1 [46:2] God is our **refuge** and strength, an ever-present help in
61: 3 [61:4] For you have been my **refuge**, a strong tower against the
62: 7 [62:8] honor depend on God; he is my mighty rock, my **refuge**.
62: 8 [62:9] pour out your hearts to him, for God is our **refuge**.
71: 7 have become like a portent to many, but you are my strong **refuge**.
73: 28 I have made the Sovereign LORD my **refuge**; I will tell of all
91: 2 "He is my **refuge** and my fortress, my God, in whom I trust."
91: 9 Most High your dwelling—even the LORD, who is my **refuge**—
94: 22 become my fortress, and my God the rock in whom I take **refuge**.
104: 18 belong to the wild goats; the crags are a **refuge** for the coneys.
142: 5 [142:6] I say, "You are my **refuge**, my portion in the land of the
Pr 14: 26 has a secure fortress, and for his children it will be a **refuge**.
Isa 4: 6 of the day, and a **refuge** and hiding place from the storm and rain.
25: 4 in his distress, a **shelter** from the storm and a shade from the heat.
28: 15 for we have made a lie our **refuge** and falsehood our hiding place."
28: 17 hail will sweep away your **refuge**, the lie, and water will overflow
Jer 17: 17 Do not be a terror to me; you are my **refuge** in the day of disaster.
Joel 3: 16 [4:16] the LORD will be a **refuge** for his people, a stronghold

4727 מַחְסוֹם *maḥsôm*, n.m. [1] [√ 2888]
muzzle [1]
Ps 39: 1 [39:2] I will put a **muzzle** on my mouth as long as the wicked are

4728 מַחְסֹר *maḥsôr*, n.[m.]. [13] [√ 2893]
poverty [4], lack [2], need [2], scarcity [2], lacks [1], needs [+2893] [1], poor [1]
Dt 15: 8 be openhanded and freely lend him whatever he **needs** [+2893].
Jdg 18: 10 God has put into your hands, a land that **lacks** nothing whatever."
19: 19 and the young man with us. We don't **need** anything."
19: 20 my house," the old man said. "Let me supply whatever you **need**.
Ps 34: 9 [34:10] you his saints, for those who fear him **lack** nothing.
Pr 6: 11 will come on you like a bandit and **scarcity** like an armed man.
11: 24 gains even more; another withholds unduly, but comes to **poverty**.
14: 23 All hard work brings a profit, but mere talk leads only to **poverty**.
21: 5 of the diligent lead to profit as surely as haste leads to **poverty**.
21: 17 He who loves pleasure will become **poor**; whoever loves wine
22: 16 and he who gives gifts to the rich—both come to **poverty**.
24: 34 will come on you like a bandit and **scarcity** like an armed man.
28: 27 He who gives to the poor will **lack** nothing, but he who closes his

4729 מַחְסֵיָה *maḥsēyâ*, n.pr.m. [2] [√ 4726 + 3378]
Mahseiah [2]
Jer 32: 12 the son of **Mahseiah**, in the presence of my cousin Hanamel
51: 59 to the staff officer Seraiah son of Neriah, the son of **Mahseiah**,

4730 מָחַץ *māḥaṣ*, v. [14 / 13] [→ 4731; Ar 10411]
crush [3], crushed [2], crushed completely [+430+2256] [1], crushing [1], cut to pieces [1], injures [1], pierce [1], shattered [1], smite [1], wounded [1]
Nu 24: 8 [A] their bones in pieces; with their arrows *they* **pierce** them.
24: 17 [A] *He will* **crush** the foreheads of Moab, the skulls of all the
Dt 32: 39 [A] to death and I bring to life, *I have* **wounded** and I will heal,
33: 11 [A] **Smite** the loins of those who rise up against him; strike his
Jdg 5: 26 [A] she crushed his head, *she* **shattered** and pierced his temple.
2Sa 22: 39 [A] *I* **crushed** [+430+2256] them **completely**, and they could not
Job 5: 18 [A] but he also binds up; *he* **injures**, but his hands also heal.
26: 12 [A] churned up the sea; by his wisdom *he* **cut** Rahab **to pieces**.
Ps 18: 38 [18:39] [A] *I* **crushed** them so that they could not rise; they fell
68: 21 [68:22] [A] Surely God *will* **crush** the heads of his enemies,
68: 23 [68:24] [a] *you may* <u>plunge</u> [BHS ***crush** them with*; NIV 8175]
110: 5 [A] your right hand; *he will* **crush** kings on the day of his wrath.
110: 6 [A] up the dead and **crushing** the rulers of the whole earth.
Hab 3: 13 [A] *You* **crushed** the leader of the land of wickedness,

4731 מַחַץ *maḥaṣ*, n.[m.]. [1] [√ 4730]
wounds [1]
Isa 30: 26 up the bruises of his people and heals the **wounds** he inflicted.

4732 מַחְצֵב *maḥṣēb*, n.[m.]. [3] [√ 2933]
dressed [3]
2Ki 12: 12 [12:13] **dressed** stone for the repair of the temple of the LORD,
22: 6 have them purchase timber and **dressed** stone to repair the temple.
2Ch 34: 11 money to the carpenters and builders to purchase **dressed** stone,

4733 מֶחֱצָה *meḥ^{e}ṣâ*, n.f. [2] [√ 2936]
half [2]
Nu 31: 36 The **half** share of those who fought in the battle was:
31: 43 the community's **half**—was 337,500 sheep,

4734 מַחֲצִית *maḥ^{a}ṣît*, n.f. [16] [√ 2936]
half [13], half as much [1], half share [1], noon [+2021+3427] [1]
Ex 30: 13 who crosses over to those already counted is to give a **half** shekel,
30: 13 twenty gerahs. This **half** shekel is an offering to the LORD.
30: 15 The rich are not to give more than a **half** shekel and the poor are
30: 23 500 shekels of liquid myrrh, **half as much** (that is, 250 shekels)

[A] Qal [B] Qal passive [C] Niphal [D] Piel (poel, polel, pilel, pilal, pealal, pilpel) [E] Pual (poal, polal, poalal, pulal, pualal)

Ex 38:26 one beka per person, that is, **half** a shekel, according to the
Lev 6:20 [6:13] **half** *of* it in the morning and half in the evening.
6:20 [6:13] half of it in the morning and **half** in the evening.
Nu 31:29 Take this tribute from their **half share** and give it to Eleazar the
31:30 From the Israelites' **half**, select one out of every fifty,
31:42 The **half** *belonging to* the Israelites, which Moses set apart from
31:47 From the Israelites' **half**, Moses selected one out of every fifty
Jos 21:25 From **half** the tribe of Manasseh they received Taanach and Gath
1Ki 16:9 one of his officials, who had command of **half** his chariots,
1Ch 6:61 [6:46] ten towns from the clans of **half** the tribe of Manasseh.
6:70 [6:55] from **half** the tribe of Manasseh the Israelites gave Aner
Ne 8:3 He read it aloud from daybreak till **noon** [+2021+3427] as he faced

4735 מָחַק **māḥaq**, v. [1]

crushed [1]

Jdg 5:26 [A] *she* **crushed** his head, she shattered and pierced his temple.

4736 מֶחְקָר **meḥqār**, n.m. [1] [√ 2983]

depths [1]

Ps 95:4 In his hand are the **depths** *of* the earth, and the mountain peaks

4737 מָחָר **māḥār**, n.m. (used as adv.). [52] [→ 4740; cf. 336]

tomorrow [43], in the future [4], days to come [1], ever [1], future [+3427] [1], some day [1], tomorrow [+3427] [1]

Ge 30:33 And my honesty will testify for me in the **future** [+3427],
Ex 8:10 [8:6] "**Tomorrow**," Pharaoh said. Moses replied, "It will be as
8:23 [8:19] your people. This miraculous sign will occur **tomorrow**.' "
8:29 [8:25] and **tomorrow** the flies will leave Pharaoh and his officials
9:5 and said, "**Tomorrow** the LORD will do this in the land."
9:18 at this time **tomorrow** I will send the worst hailstorm that has ever
10:4 to let them go, I will bring locusts into your country **tomorrow**.
13:14 "*In* **days to come**, when your son asks you, 'What does this mean?'
16:23 '**Tomorrow** is to be a day of rest, a holy Sabbath to the LORD.
17:9 **Tomorrow** I will stand on top of the hill with the staff of God in
19:10 "Go to the people and consecrate them today and **tomorrow**.
32:5 "**Tomorrow** there will be a festival to the LORD."
Nu 11:18 'Consecrate yourselves in preparation for **tomorrow**, when you
14:25 turn back **tomorrow** and set out toward the desert along the route
16:7 and **tomorrow** put fire and incense in them before the LORD.
16:16 all your followers are to appear before the LORD **tomorrow**—
Dt 6:20 **In the future**, when your son asks you, "What is the meaning of
Jos 3:5 for **tomorrow** the LORD will do amazing things among you."
4:6 **In the future**, when your children ask you, 'What do these stones
4:21 "**In the future** when your descendants ask their fathers,
7:13 Tell them, 'Consecrate yourselves in preparation for **tomorrow**;
11:6 because by this time **tomorrow** I will hand all of them over to
22:18 **tomorrow** he will be angry with the whole community of Israel.
22:24 We did it for fear that **some day** your descendants might say to
22:27 **in the future** your descendants will not be able to say to ours,
22:28 "And we said, 'If they **ever** say this to us, or to our descendants,
Jdg 19:9 Early **tomorrow** morning you can get up and be on your way
20:28 "Go, for **tomorrow** I will give them into your hands."
1Sa 9:16 "About this time **tomorrow** I will send you a man from the land of
11:9 to the men of Jabesh Gilead, 'By the time the sun is hot **tomorrow**,
11:10 said to the Ammonites, "**Tomorrow** we will surrender to you,
19:11 "If you don't run for your life tonight, **tomorrow** you'll be killed."
20:5 So David said, "Look, **tomorrow** is the New Moon festival,
20:12 surely sound out my father by this time the day after **tomorrow**!
20:18 "**Tomorrow** is the New Moon festival. You will be missed,
28:19 the Philistines, and **tomorrow** you and your sons will be with me.
2Sa 11:12 "Stay here one more day, and **tomorrow** I will send you back."
1Ki 19:2 if by this time **tomorrow** I do not make your life like that of one of
20:6 about this time **tomorrow** I am going to send my officials to
2Ki 6:28 so we may eat him today, and **tomorrow** we'll eat my son.'
7:1 About this time **tomorrow**, a seah of flour will sell for a shekel
7:18 "About this time **tomorrow**, a seah of flour will sell for a shekel
10:6 master's sons and come to me in Jezreel by this time **tomorrow**."
2Ch 20:16 **Tomorrow** march down against them. They will be climbing up by
20:17 Go out to face them **tomorrow**, and the LORD will be with
Est 5:8 and Haman come **tomorrow** to the banquet I will prepare for them.
5:12 she gave. And she has invited me along with the king **tomorrow**.
9:13 in Susa permission to carry out this day's edict **tomorrow** also,
Pr 3:28 say to your neighbor, "Come back later; I'll give it **tomorrow**"—
27:1 Do not boast about **tomorrow** [+3427], for you do not know what
Isa 22:13 of wine! "Let us eat and drink," you say, "for **tomorrow** we die!"
56:12 fill of beer! And **tomorrow** will be like today, or even far better."

4738 מַחֲרָאָה **maḥᵃrā'â**, n.f. [1] [√ 2989]

latrine [1]

2Ki 10:27 and people have used it for a **latrine** [Q 4606] to this day.

4739 מַחֲרֵשָׁה **maḥᵃrēšâ**, n.f. [3 / 2] [√ 3086]

plowshares [2]

1Sa 13:20 So all Israel went down to the Philistines to have their **plowshares**,
13:20 axes and sickles [BHS ***plowshares***; NIV 3058] sharpened.
13:21 The price was two thirds of a shekel for sharpening **plowshares**

4740 מָחֳרָת **moḥºrāt**, n.f. [32] [√ 4737; cf. 336]

next day [22], day after [6], next [3], following [1]

Ge 19:34 The **next day** the older daughter said to the younger, "Last night I
Ex 9:6 the **next day** the LORD did it: All the livestock of the Egyptians
18:13 The **next day** Moses took his seat to serve as judge for the people,
32:6 So the **next day** the people rose early and sacrificed burnt offerings
32:30 The **next day** Moses said to the people, "You have committed a
Lev 7:16 he offers it, but anything left over may be eaten on the **next day**.
19:6 It shall be eaten on the day you sacrifice it or on the **next day**;
23:11 your behalf; the priest is to wave it on the **day after** the Sabbath.
23:15 " 'From the **day after** the Sabbath, the day you brought the sheaf of
23:16 Count off fifty days up to the **day after** the seventh Sabbath,
Nu 11:32 All that day and night and all the **next** day the people went out
16:41 [17:6] The **next day** the whole Israelite community grumbled
17:8 [17:23] The **next day** Moses entered the Tent of the Testimony
33:3 on the fifteenth day of the first month, the **day after** the Passover.
Jos 5:11 The **day after** the Passover, that very day, they ate some of the
5:12 The manna stopped the **day after** they ate this food from the land;
Jdg 6:38 Gideon rose early the **next day**; he squeezed the fleece and wrung
9:42 The **next day** the people of Shechem went out to the fields,
21:4 Early the **next day** the people built an altar and presented burnt
1Sa 5:3 When the people of Ashdod rose early the **next day**, there was
5:4 But the **following** morning when they rose, there was Dagon,
11:11 The **next day** Saul separated his men into three divisions;
18:10 The **next day** an evil spirit from God came forcefully upon Saul.
20:27 the **next day**, the second day of the month, David's place was
30:17 David fought them from dusk until the evening of the **next day**,
31:8 The **next day**, when the Philistines came to strip the dead,
2Sa 11:12 you back." So Uriah remained in Jerusalem that day and the **next**.
2Ki 8:15 the **next day** he took a thick cloth, soaked it in water and spread it
1Ch 10:8 The **next day**, when the Philistines came to strip the dead,
29:21 The **next** day they made sacrifices to the LORD and presented
Jer 20:3 The **next day**, when Pashhur released him from the stocks,
Jnh 4:7 at dawn the **next day** God provided a worm, which chewed the

4741 מַחְשֹׂף **maḥśōp**, n.m. [1] [√ 3106]

exposing [1]

Ge 30:37 the bark and **exposing** the white inner wood of the branches.

4742 מַחֲשָׁבָה **maḥᵃšābâ**, n.f. [56] [√ 3108]

thoughts [14], plans [9], plan [3], plots [3], purposes [3], artistic designs [2], imaginations [2], purposed [+3108] [2], scheme [2], schemes [2], artistic craftsmanship [1], design [1], designed [1], designers [+3110] [1], desire [+3671] [1], devised [1], make plans [+3108] [1], overthrow [1], plans have [+3108] [1], plotted [+3108] [1], plotting [1], things planned [1], ways [1], what thinking [1]

Ge 6:5 that every inclination of the **thoughts** *of* his heart was only evil all
Ex 31:4 to make **artistic designs** for work in gold, silver and bronze,
35:32 to make **artistic designs** for work in gold, silver and bronze,
35:33 work in wood and to engage in all kinds of **artistic craftsmanship**.
35:35 all of them master craftsmen and **designers** [+3110].
2Sa 14:14 he devises **ways** so that a banished person may not remain
1Ch 28:9 every heart and understands every motive behind the **thoughts**.
29:18 keep this **desire in** [+3671] the hearts of your people forever,
2Ch 2:14 [2:13] of engraving and can execute any **design** given to him.
26:15 In Jerusalem he made machines **designed** *by* skillful men for use
Est 8:3 She begged him to put an end to the evil **plan** *of* Haman the
8:5 **devised** and wrote to destroy the Jews in all the king's provinces.
9:25 he issued written orders that the evil **scheme** Haman had devised
Job 5:12 He thwarts the **plans** *of* the crafty, so that their hands achieve no
21:27 "I know full well **what** you are **thinking**, the schemes by which
Ps 33:10 the plans of the nations; he thwarts the **purposes** *of* the peoples.
33:11 firm forever, the **purposes** *of* his heart through all generations.
40:5 [40:6] The **things** you **planned** for us no one can recount to you;
56:5 [56:6] they twist my words; they are always **plotting** to harm me.
92:5 [92:6] are your works, O LORD, how profound your **thoughts**!
94:11 The LORD knows the **thoughts** *of* man; he knows that they are
Pr 6:18 a heart that devises wicked **schemes**, feet that are quick to rush into
12:5 The **plans** *of* the righteous are just, but the advice of the wicked is
15:22 **Plans** fail for lack of counsel, but with many advisers they
15:26 The LORD detests the **thoughts** *of* the wicked, but those of the
16:3 to the LORD whatever you do, and your **plans** will succeed.
19:21 Many are the **plans** in a man's heart, but it is the LORD's
20:18 Make **plans** by seeking advice; if you wage war, obtain guidance.
21:5 The **plans** *of* the diligent lead to profit as surely as haste leads to

Isa 55: 7 Let the wicked forsake his way and the evil man his **thoughts**.
55: 8 "For my **thoughts** are not your thoughts, neither are your ways my
55: 8 "For my thoughts are not your **thoughts**, neither are your ways my
55: 9 ways higher than your ways and my **thoughts** than your thoughts.
55: 9 ways higher than your ways and my thoughts than your **thoughts**.
59: 7 Their **thoughts** are evil thoughts; ruin and destruction mark their
59: 7 Their thoughts are evil **thoughts**; ruin and destruction mark their
65: 2 who walk in ways not good, pursuing their own **imaginations**—
66: 18 "And I, because of their actions and their **imaginations**, am about
Jer 4: 14 and be saved. How long will you harbor wicked **thoughts**?
6: 19 I am bringing disaster on this people, the fruit of their **schemes**,
11: 19 I did not realize that *they had* **plotted** [+3108] against me,
18: 11 I am preparing a disaster for you and devising a **plan** against you.
18: 12 We will continue with our own **plans**; each of us will follow the
18: 18 They said, "Come, *let's* **make plans** [+3108] against Jeremiah;
29: 11 For I know the **plans** I **have** [+3108] for you,"
29: 11 declares the LORD, "**plans** to prosper you and not to harm you,
49: 20 what *he has* **purposed** [+3108] against those who live in Teman:
49: 30 has plotted against you; he has devised a **plan** against you.
50: 45 what *he has* **purposed** [+3108] against the land of the
51: 29 and writhes, for the LORD's **purposes** against Babylon stand—
La 3: 60 have seen the depth of their vengeance, all their **plots** against me.
3: 61 O LORD, you have heard their insults, all their **plots** against me—
Eze 38: 10 will come into your mind and you will devise an evil **scheme**.
Da 11: 24 He will plot the **overthrow** *of* fortresses—but only for a time.
11: 25 will not be able to stand because of the **plots** devised against him.
Mic 4: 12 they do not know the **thoughts** *of* the LORD; they do not

4743 מַחְשָׁךְ *maḥšāk*, n.m. [7] [√ 3124]

darkness [5], dark places [1], darkest [1]

Ps 74: 20 because haunts of violence fill the **dark places** *of* the land.
88: 6 [88:7] You have put me in the lowest pit, in the **darkest** depths.
88: 18 [88:19] loved ones from me; the **darkness** is my closest friend.
143: 3 the ground; he makes me dwell in **darkness** like those long dead.
Isa 29: 15 who do their work in **darkness** and think, "Who sees us?
42: 16 I will turn the **darkness** into light before them and make the rough
La 3: 6 He has made me dwell in **darkness** like those long dead.

4744 מַחַת *maḥat*, n.pr.m. [3] [√ 3169?]

Mahath [3]

1Ch 6: 35 [6:20] the son of Elkanah, the son of **Mahath**, the son of Amasai,
2Ch 29: 12 the Kohathites, **Mahath** son of Amasai and Joel son of Azariah;
31: 13 **Mahath** and Benaiah were supervisors under Conaniah and Shimei

4745 מְחִתָּה *m[e]ḥittâ*, n.f. [11] [√ 3169]

ruin [4], terror [3], object of horror [1], ruined [1], ruins [1], undoing [1]

Ps 89: 40 [89:41] through all his walls and reduced his strongholds to **ruins**.
Pr 10: 14 men store up knowledge, but the mouth of a fool invites **ruin**.
10: 15 of the rich is their fortified city, but poverty is the **ruin** *of* the poor.
10: 29 is a refuge for the righteous, but it is the **ruin** of those who do evil.
13: 3 his lips guards his life, but he who speaks rashly will come to **ruin**.
14: 28 is a king's glory, but without subjects a prince is **ruined**.
18: 7 A fool's mouth is his **undoing**, and his lips are a snare to his soul.
21: 15 is done, it brings joy to the righteous but **terror** to evildoers.
Isa 54: 14 to fear. **Terror** will be far removed; it will not come near you.
Jer 17: 17 Do not be a **terror** to me; you are my refuge in the day of disaster.
48: 39 an object of ridicule, an **object of horror** to all those around her."

4746 מַחְתָּה *maḥtâ*, n.f. [22] [√ 3149]

censers [11], censer [4], firepans [3], trays [3], it[s] [1]

Ex 25: 38 Its wick trimmers and **trays** are to be of pure gold.
27: 3 and its shovels, sprinkling bowls, meat forks and **firepans**.
37: 23 seven lamps, as well as its wick trimmers and **trays**, of pure gold.
38: 3 its pots, shovels, sprinkling bowls, meat forks and **firepans**.
Lev 10: 1 Aaron's sons Nadab and Abihu took their **censers**, put fire in them
16: 12 He is to take a **censer** full of burning coals from the altar before
Nu 4: 9 is for light, together with its lamps, its wick trimmers and **trays**,
4: 14 including the **firepans**, meat forks, shovels and sprinkling bowls.
16: 6 Korah, and all your followers are to do this: Take **censers**
16: 17 Each man is to take his **censer** and put incense in it—250 censers
16: 17 man is to take his censer and put incense in it—250 **censers** in all—
16: 17 in it—250 censers in all—and present **it**[s] before the LORD.
16: 17 the LORD. You and Aaron are to present your **censers** also."
16: 18 So each man took his **censer**, put fire and incense in it, and stood
16: 37 [17:2] to take the **censers** out of the smoldering remains
16: 38 [17:3] the **censers** *of* the men who sinned at the cost of their lives.
16: 39 [17:4] So Eleazar the priest collected the bronze **censers** brought
16: 46 [17:11] said to Aaron, "Take your **censer** and put incense in it,
1Ki 7: 50 gold basins, wick trimmers, sprinkling bowls, dishes and **censers**;
2Ki 25: 15 The commander of the imperial guard took away the **censers**
2Ch 4: 22 the pure gold wick trimmers, sprinkling bowls, dishes and **censers**;
Jer 52: 19 **censers**, sprinkling bowls, pots, lampstands, dishes and bowls used

4747 מַחְתֶּרֶת *maḥteret*, n.m. [2] [√ 3168]

breaking in [2]

Ex 22: 2 [22:1] "If a thief is caught **breaking in** and is struck so that he
Jer 2: 34 of the innocent poor, though you did not catch them **breaking in**.

4748 מַטְאֲטֵא *maṭ'[a]ṭē'*, n.[m.]. [1] [√ 3173; cf. 3226]

broom [1]

Isa 14: 23 I will sweep her with the **broom** *of* destruction,"

4749 מַטְבֵּחַ *maṭbēaḥ*, n.[m.]. [1] [√ 3180]

place to slaughter [1]

Isa 14: 21 Prepare a **place to slaughter** his sons for the sins of their

4750 מָטֶה *māṭeh*, n.m. Not used in NIV/BHS [√ 5742; Ar 10413]

4751 מַטֶּה *maṭṭeh*, n.m. [& f.?]. [252 / 253] [√ 5742]

tribe [124], staff [37], *untranslated* [25], tribes [21], tribal [8], rod [6], half-tribe [+2942] [5], staffs [5], supply [4], club [3], branches [2], scepter [2], arrows [1], bar [1], branch [1], Danite [+1968+4200] [1], family [1], Levites [+4290] [1], main branches [+964] [1], one[s] [1], spear [1], supplies [1], them[s] [1]

Ge 38: 18 "Your seal and its cord, and the **staff** in your hand," she answered.
38: 25 "See if you recognize whose seal and cord and **staff** these are."
47: 31 Israel worshiped as he leaned on the top of his **staff**. [BHS 4753]
Ex 4: 2 said to him, "What is that in your hand?" "A **staff**," he replied.
4: 4 took hold of the snake and it turned back into a **staff** in his hand.
4: 17 take this **staff** in your hand so you can perform miraculous signs
4: 20 started back to Egypt. And he took the **staff** *of* God in his hand.
7: 9 say to Aaron, 'Take your **staff** and throw it down before Pharaoh,'
7: 10 Aaron threw his **staff** down in front of Pharaoh and his officials,
7: 12 Each one threw down his **staff** and it became a snake. But Aaron's
7: 12 and it became a snake. But Aaron's **staff** swallowed up their staffs.
7: 12 and it became a snake. But Aaron's staff swallowed up their **staffs**.
7: 15 and take in your hand the **staff** that was changed into a snake.
7: 17 With the **staff** that is in my hand I will strike the water of the Nile,
7: 19 'Take your **staff** and stretch out your hand over the waters of
7: 20 He raised his **staff** in the presence of Pharaoh and his officials
8: 5 [8:1] 'Stretch out your hand with your **staff** over the streams
8: 16 [8:12] 'Stretch out your **staff** and strike the dust of the ground,'
8: 17 [8:13] when Aaron stretched out his hand with the **staff**
9: 23 When Moses stretched out his **staff** toward the sky, the LORD
10: 13 So Moses stretched out his **staff** over Egypt, and the LORD made
14: 16 Raise your **staff** and stretch out your hand over the sea to divide
17: 5 and take in your hand the **staff** with which you struck the Nile,
17: 9 Tomorrow I will stand on top of the hill with the **staff** *of* God in
31: 2 chosen Bezalel son of Uri, the son of Hur, of the **tribe** *of* Judah,
31: 6 Oholiab son of Ahisamach, of the **tribe** *of* Dan, to help him.
35: 30 chosen Bezalel son of Uri, the son of Hur, of the **tribe** *of* Judah,
35: 34 son of Ahisamach, of the **tribe** *of* Dan, the ability to teach others.
38: 22 (Bezalel son of Uri, the son of Hur, of the **tribe** *of* Judah,
38: 23 with him was Oholiab son of Ahisamach, of the **tribe** *of* Dan—
Lev 24: 11 was Shelomith, the daughter of Dibri the **Danite** [+1968+4200].)
26: 26 When I cut off your **supply** *of* bread, ten women will be able to
Nu 1: 4 One man from each **tribe**, each the head of his family, is to help
1: 16 from the community, the leaders of their ancestral **tribes**.
1: 21 The number from the **tribe** *of* Reuben was 46,500.
1: 23 The number from the **tribe** *of* Simeon was 59,300.
1: 25 The number from the **tribe** *of* Gad was 45,650.
1: 27 The number from the **tribe** *of* Judah was 74,600.
1: 29 The number from the **tribe** *of* Issachar was 54,400.
1: 31 The number from the **tribe** *of* Zebulun was 57,400.
1: 33 The number from the **tribe** *of* Ephraim was 40,500.
1: 35 The number from the **tribe** *of* Manasseh was 32,200.
1: 37 The number from the **tribe** *of* Benjamin was 35,400.
1: 39 The number from the **tribe** *of* Dan was 62,700.
1: 41 The number from the **tribe** *of* Asher was 41,500.
1: 43 The number from the **tribe** *of* Naphtali was 53,400.
1: 47 The families of the **tribe** *of* Levi, however, were not counted along
1: 49 "You must not count the **tribe** *of* Levi or include them in the
2: 5 The **tribe** *of* Issachar will camp next to them. The leader of the
2: 7 The **tribe** *of* Zebulun will be next. The leader of the people of
2: 12 The **tribe** *of* Simeon will camp next to them. The leader of the
2: 14 The **tribe** *of* Gad will be next. The leader of the people of Gad is
2: 20 The **tribe** *of* Manasseh will be next to them. The leader of the
2: 22 The **tribe** *of* Benjamin will be next. The leader of the people of
2: 27 The **tribe** *of* Asher will camp next to them. The leader of the
2: 29 The **tribe** *of* Naphtali will be next. The leader of the people of
3: 6 "Bring the **tribe** *of* Levi and present them to Aaron the priest to
7: 2 the heads of families who were the **tribal** leaders in charge of

Nu 7:12 first day was Nahshon son of Amminadab of the **tribe** *of* Judah.
10:15 Nethanel son of Zuar was over the division of the **tribe** *of* Issachar,
10:16 Eliab son of Helon was over the division of the **tribe** *of* Zebulun.
10:19 Shelumiel son of Zurishaddai was over the division of the **tribe** *of*
10:20 Eliasaph son of Deuel was over the division of the **tribe** *of* Gad.
10:23 Gamaliel son of Pedahzur was over the division of the **tribe** *of*
10:24 Abidan son of Gideoni was over the division of the **tribe** *of*
10:26 Pagiel son of Ocran was over the division of the **tribe** *of* Asher,
10:27 Ahira son of Enan was over the division of the **tribe** *of* Naphtali.
13: 2 to the Israelites. From each ancestral **tribe** send one of its leaders."
13: 4 their names: from the **tribe** *of* Reuben, Shammua son of Zaccur;
13: 5 from the **tribe** *of* Simeon, Shaphat son of Hori;
13: 6 from the **tribe** *of* Judah, Caleb son of Jephunneh;
13: 7 from the **tribe** *of* Issachar, Igal son of Joseph;
13: 8 from the **tribe** *of* Ephraim, Hoshea son of Nun;
13: 9 from the **tribe** *of* Benjamin, Palti son of Raphu;
13:10 from the **tribe** *of* Zebulun, Gaddiel son of Sodi;
13:11 from the **tribe** *of* Manasseh (a tribe of Joseph), Gaddi son of Susi;
13:11 from the tribe of Manasseh (a **tribe** *of* Joseph), Gaddi son of Susi;
13:12 from the **tribe** *of* Dan, Ammiel son of Gemalli;
13:13 from the **tribe** *of* Asher, Sethur son of Michael;
13:14 from the **tribe** *of* Naphtali, Nahbi son of Vophsi;
13:15 from the **tribe** *of* Gad, Geuel son of Maki.
17: 2 [17:17] "Speak to the Israelites and get twelve **staffs** from them,
17: 2 [17:17] **one**[s] from the leader of each of their ancestral tribes.
17: 2 [17:17] one **[RPH]** from the leader of each of their ancestral
17: 2 [17:17] ancestral tribes. Write the name of each man on his **staff**.
17: 3 [17:18] On the **staff** *of* Levi write Aaron's name, for there must
17: 3 [17:18] for there must be one **staff** for the head of each ancestral
17: 5 [17:20] The **staff** *belonging to* the man I choose will sprout, and I
17: 6 [17:21] to the Israelites, and their leaders gave him twelve **staffs**,
17: 6 [17:21] one **[RPH]** for the leader of each of their ancestral tribes,
17: 6 [17:21] their ancestral tribes, and Aaron's **staff** was among them.
17: 6 [17:21] and Aaron's staff **[RPH]** was among them.
17: 6 [17:21] their ancestral tribes, and Aaron's staff was among **them**[s].
17: 7 [17:22] Moses placed the **staffs** before the LORD in the Tent of
17: 8 [17:23] the Tent of the Testimony and saw that Aaron's **staff**,
17: 9 [17:24] Moses brought out all the **staffs** from the LORD's
17: 9 [17:24] They looked at them, and each man took his own **staff**.
17:10 [17:25] "Put back Aaron's **staff** in front of the Testimony,
18: 2 Bring your fellow **Levites** [+4290] from your ancestral tribe to join
20: 8 "Take the **staff**, and you and your brother Aaron gather the
20: 9 So Moses took the **staff** from the LORD's presence, just as he
20:11 Then Moses raised his arm and struck the rock twice with his **staff**.
26:55 inherits will be according to the names for its ancestral **tribe**.
30: 1 [30:2] Moses said to the heads of the **tribes** of Israel: "This is
31: 4 Send into battle a thousand men from each of the **tribes** *of* Israel."
31: 4 battle a thousand men from each of the tribes of Israel." **[RPH]**
31: 4 battle a thousand men from each of the tribes of Israel." **[RPH]**
31: 5 a thousand from each **tribe**, were supplied from the clans of Israel.
31: 6 Moses sent them into battle, a thousand from each **tribe**,
32:28 Joshua son of Nun and to the family heads of the Israelite **tribes**.
33:54 lot will be theirs. Distribute it according to your ancestral **tribes**.
34:13 LORD has ordered that it be given to the nine and a half **tribes**,
34:13 has ordered that it be given to the nine and a half tribes, **[RPH]**
34:14 because the families of the **tribe** *of* Reuben, the tribe of Gad
34:14 the **tribe** *of* Gad and the half-tribe of Manasseh have received their
34:14 the **half-tribe of** [+2942] Manasseh have received their
34:15 **[RPH]** and a half tribes have received their inheritance on the east
34:15 a half **tribes** have received their inheritance on the east side of the
34:18 And appoint one leader from each **tribe** to help assign the land.
34:19 are their names: Caleb son of Jephunneh, from the **tribe** *of* Judah;
34:20 Shemuel son of Ammihud, from the **tribe** *of* Simeon;
34:21 Elidad son of Kislon, from the **tribe** *of* Benjamin;
34:22 Bukki son of Jogli, the leader from the **tribe** *of* Dan;
34:23 son of Ephod, the leader from the **tribe** *of* Manasseh son of Joseph;
34:24 of Shiphtan, the leader from the **tribe** *of* Ephraim son of Joseph;
34:25 Elizaphan son of Parnach, the leader from the **tribe** *of* Zebulun;
34:26 Paltiel son of Azzan, the leader from the **tribe** *of* Issachar;
34:27 Ahihud son of Shelomi, the leader from the **tribe** *of* Asher;
34:28 Pedahel son of Ammihud, the leader from the **tribe** *of* Naphtali."
36: 3 ancestral inheritance and added to that of the **tribe** they marry into.
36: 4 their inheritance will be added to that of the **tribe** into which they
36: 4 their property will be taken from the **tribal** inheritance of our
36: 5 "What the **tribe** *of* the descendants of Joseph is saying is right.
36: 6 please as long as they marry within the **tribal** clan of their father.
36: 7 No inheritance in Israel is to pass from **tribe** to tribe, for every
36: 7 No inheritance in Israel is to pass from tribe to **tribe**, for every
36: 7 for every Israelite shall keep the **tribal** land inherited from his
36: 8 Every daughter who inherits land in any Israelite **tribe** must marry
36: 8 any Israelite tribe must marry someone in her father's **tribal** clan,
36: 9 No inheritance may pass from **tribe** to tribe, for each Israelite tribe
36: 9 No inheritance may pass from tribe to **tribe**, for each Israelite tribe
36: 9 tribe to tribe, for each Israelite **tribe** is to keep the land it inherits."
36:12 and their inheritance remained in their father's clan and **tribe**.
Jos 7: 1 the son of Zimri, the son of Zerah, of the **tribe** *of* Judah, took some
7:18 the son of Zimri, the son of Zerah, of the **tribe** *of* Judah, was taken.
13:15 This is what Moses had given to the **tribe** *of* Reuben, clan by clan:
13:24 This is what Moses had given to the **tribe** *of* Gad, clan by clan:
13:29 that is, to half the **family** *of* the descendants of Manasseh,
14: 1 and the heads of the **tribal** clans of Israel allotted to them.
14: 2 inheritances were assigned by lot to the nine-and-a-half **tribes**,
14: 2 **[RPH]** as the LORD had commanded through Moses.
14: 3 Moses had granted the two-and-a-half **tribes** their inheritance east
14: 3 Moses had granted the two-and-a-half tribes **[RPH]** their
14: 4 for the sons of Joseph had become two **tribes**—Manasseh
15: 1 The allotment for the **tribe** *of* Judah, clan by clan, extended down
15:20 This is the inheritance of the **tribe** *of* Judah, clan by clan:
15:21 The southernmost towns of the **tribe** *of* Judah in the Negev toward
16: 8 This was the inheritance of the **tribe** *of* the Ephraimites, clan by
17: 1 This was the allotment for the **tribe** *of* Manasseh as Joseph's
18:11 The lot came up for the **tribe** *of* Benjamin, clan by clan. Their
18:21 The **tribe** *of* Benjamin, clan by clan, had the following cities:
19: 1 The second lot came out for the **tribe** *of* Simeon, clan by clan.
19: 8 This was the inheritance of the **tribe** *of* the Simeonites, clan by
19:23 and their villages were the inheritance of the **tribe** *of* Issachar,
19:24 The fifth lot came out for the **tribe** *of* Asher, clan by clan.
19:31 and their villages were the inheritance of the **tribe** *of* Asher,
19:39 and their villages were the inheritance of the **tribe** *of* Naphtali,
19:40 The seventh lot came out for the **tribe** *of* Dan, clan by clan.
19:48 and their villages were the inheritance of the **tribe** *of* Dan,
19:51 the heads of the **tribal** clans of Israel assigned by lot at Shiloh in
20: 8 Bezer in the desert on the plateau in the **tribe** *of* Reuben,
20: 8 Ramoth in Gilead in the **tribe** *of* Gad, and Golan in Bashan in the
20: 8 in the tribe of Gad, and Golan in Bashan in the **tribe** *of* Manasseh.
21: 1 son of Nun, and the heads of the other **tribal** families of Israel
21: 4 the priest were allotted thirteen towns from the **tribes** *of* Judah,
21: 4 towns from the tribes of Judah, **[RPH]** Simeon and Benjamin.
21: 4 towns from the tribes of Judah, Simeon and **[RPH]** Benjamin.
21: 5 were allotted ten towns from the clans of the **tribes** *of* Ephraim,
21: 5 clans of the tribes of Ephraim, **[RPH]** Dan and half of Manasseh.
21: 5 clans of the tribes of Ephraim, Dan and half of **[RPH]** Manasseh.
21: 6 allotted thirteen towns from the clans of the **tribes** *of* Issachar,
21: 6 **[RPH]** Asher, Naphtali and the half-tribe of Manasseh in Bashan.
21: 6 **[RPH]** Naphtali and the half-tribe of Manasseh in Bashan.
21: 6 Naphtali and the **half-tribe of** [+2942] Manasseh in Bashan.
21: 7 received twelve towns from the **tribes** *of* Reuben, Gad
21: 7 twelve towns from the tribes of Reuben, **[RPH]** Gad and Zebulun.
21: 7 twelve towns from the tribes of Reuben, Gad and **[RPH]** Zebulun.
21: 9 From the **tribes** *of* Judah and Simeon they allotted the following
21: 9 and **[RPH]** Simeon they allotted the following towns by name
21:17 And from the **tribe** *of* Benjamin they gave them Gibeon, Geba,
21:20 clans of the Levites were allotted towns from the **tribe** *of* Ephraim:
21:23 Also from the **tribe** *of* Dan they received Eltekeh, Gibbethon,
21:25 From half the **tribe** *of* Manasseh they received Taanach and Gath
21:27 from the **half-tribe of** [+2942] Manasseh, Golan in Bashan (a city
21:28 from the **tribe** *of* Issachar, Kishion, Daberath,
21:30 from the **tribe** *of* Asher, Mishal, Abdon,
21:32 from the **tribe** *of* Naphtali, Kedesh in Galilee (a city of refuge for
21:34 were given: from the **tribe** *of* Zebulun, Jokneam, Kartah,
21:36 from the **tribe** *of* Reuben, Bezer, Jahaz,
21:38 from the **tribe** *of* Gad, Ramoth in Gilead (a city of refuge for one
22: 1 the Gadites and the **half-tribe of** [+2942] Manasseh
22:14 they sent ten of the chief men, one for each of the **tribes** *of* Israel,
1Sa 14:27 so he reached out the end of the **staff** that was in his hand
14:43 told him, "I merely tasted a little honey with the end of my **staff**.
1Ki 7:14 whose mother was a widow from the **tribe** *of* Naphtali and whose
8: 1 all the heads of the **tribes** and the chiefs of the Israelite families,
1Ch 6:60 [6:45] And from the **tribe** *of* Benjamin they were given Gibeon,
6:61 [6:46] towns from the clans of **[RPH]** half the tribe of Manasseh.
6:61 [6:46] ten towns from the clans of half the **tribe** *of* Manasseh.
6:62 [6:47] were allotted thirteen towns from the **tribes** *of* Issachar,
6:62 [6:47] from the tribes of Issachar, **[RPH]** Asher and Naphtali,
6:62 [6:47] from the tribes of Issachar, Asher and **[RPH]** Naphtali,
6:62 [6:47] from the part of the **tribe** *of* Manasseh that is in Bashan.
6:63 [6:48] were allotted twelve towns from the **tribes** *of* Reuben, Gad
6:63 [6:48] from the tribes of Reuben, **[RPH]** Gad and Zebulun.
6:63 [6:48] from the tribes of Reuben, Gad and **[RPH]** Zebulun.
6:65 [6:50] From the **tribes** *of* Judah, Simeon and Benjamin they
6:65 [6:50] **[RPH]** Simeon and Benjamin they allotted the previously
6:65 [6:50] **[RPH]** Benjamin they allotted the previously named
6:66 [6:51] given as their territory towns from the **tribe** *of* Ephraim.
6:70 [6:55] from half the **tribe** *of* Manasseh the Israelites gave Aner
6:71 [6:56] From the clan of the **half-tribe of** [+2942] Manasseh they
6:72 [6:57] from the **tribe** *of* Issachar they received Kedesh, Daberath,
6:74 [6:59] from the **tribe** *of* Asher they received Mashal, Abdon,
6:76 [6:61] from the **tribe** *of* Naphtali they received Kedesh in Galilee,
6:77 [6:62] From the **tribe** *of* Zebulun they received Jokneam, Kartah,

1Ch 6:78 [6:63] from the **tribe** *of* Reuben across the Jordan east of Jericho
6:80 [6:65] and from the **tribe** *of* Gad they received Ramoth in Gilead,
12:31 [12:32] men of half the **tribe** *of* Manasseh, designated by name to
2Ch 5:2 all the heads of the **tribes** and the chiefs of the Israelite families,
Ps 105:16 down famine on the land and destroyed all their **supplies** *of* food;
110:2 The LORD will extend your mighty **scepter** from Zion; you will
Isa 9:4 [9:3] the **bar** *across* their shoulders, the rod of their oppressor.
10:5 the rod of my anger, in whose hand is the **club** of my wrath!
10:15 wield him who lifts it up, or a **club** brandish him who is not wood!
10:24 who beat you with a rod and lift up a **club** against you, as Egypt
10:26 and he will raise his **staff** over the waters, as he did in Egypt.
14:5 The LORD has broken the **rod** *of* the wicked, the scepter of the
28:27 caraway is beaten out with a **rod**, and cummin with a stick.
30:32 Every stroke the LORD lays on them with his punishing **rod** will
Jer 48:17 say, 'How broken is the mighty **scepter**, how broken the glorious
Eze 4:16 "Son of man, I will cut off the **supply** *of* food in Jerusalem.
5:16 and more famine upon you and cut off your **supply** *of* food.
7:10 Doom has burst forth, the **rod** has budded, arrogance has
7:11 Violence has grown into a **rod** *to punish* wickedness; none of the
14:13 and I stretch out my hand against it to cut off its food **supply**
19:11 Its **branches** were strong, fit for a ruler's scepter. It towered high
19:12 of its fruit; its strong **branches** withered and fire consumed them.
19:14 Fire spread from one of its **main branches** [+964] and consumed
19:14 No strong **branch** is left on it fit for a ruler's scepter.' This is a
Mic 6:9 name is wisdom—"Heed the **rod** and the One who appointed it.
Hab 3:9 You uncovered your bow, you called for many **arrows**.
3:14 With his own **spear** you pierced his head when his warriors

4752 מַטָּה maṭṭâ, adv. [19] [√ 5742]

below [+4200] [3], bottom [3], down [+4200] [3], *untranslated* [2], bottom [+4200+4946] [2], lower [2], goes down [+3718+4200] [1], going down to [1], less [1], punished less [+3104+4200] [1]

Ex 26:24 At these two corners they must be double from the **bottom** all the
27:5 under the ledge of the altar **[NIE]** so that it is halfway up the altar.
28:27 attach them to the **bottom** [+4200+4946] *of* the shoulder pieces on
36:29 At these two corners the frames were double from the **bottom** all
38:4 bronze network, to be under its ledge, **[NIE]** halfway up the altar.
39:20 attached them to the **bottom** [+4200+4946] *of* the shoulder pieces
Dt 28:13 follow them, you will always be at the top, never at the **bottom**.
28:43 above you higher and higher, but you will sink **lower** and lower.
28:43 above you higher and higher, but you will sink lower and **lower**.
2Ki 19:30 more a remnant of the house of Judah will take root **below** [+4200]
1Ch 27:23 David did not take the number of the men twenty years old or **less**,
2Ch 32:30 channeled the water **down** [+4200] to the west side of the City of
Ezr 9:13 you *have* **punished** us **less** [+3104+4200] than our sins have
Pr 15:24 upward for the wise to keep him from **going down to** the grave.
Ecc 3:21 if the spirit of the animal **goes down** [+3718+4200] into the earth?"
Isa 37:31 more a remnant of the house of Judah will take root **below** [+4200]
Jer 31:37 the foundations of the earth **below** [+4200] be searched out will I
Eze 1:27 if full of fire, and that from there **down** [+4200] he looked like fire;
8:2 From what appeared to be his waist **down** [+4200] he was like fire,

4753 מִטָּה miṭṭâ, n.f. [29 / 28] [√ 5742]

bed [17], couch [4], bedroom [+2540] [2], beds [2], bier [1], carriage [1], couches [1]

Ge 47:31 as he leaned on the top of his staff. [BHS *bed*; NIV 4751]
48:2 has come to you," Israel rallied his strength and sat up on the **bed**.
49:33 he drew his feet up into the **bed**, breathed his last and was gathered
Ex 8:3 [7:28] up into your palace and your bedroom and onto your **bed**,
1Sa 19:13 Michal took an idol and laid it on the **bed**, covering it with a
19:15 told them, "Bring him up to me in his **bed** so that I may kill him."
19:16 when the men entered, there was the idol in the **bed**, and at the
28:23 listened to them. He got up from the ground and sat on the **couch**.
2Sa 3:31 in front of Abner." King David himself walked behind the **bier**.
4:7 They had gone into the house while he was lying on the **bed** in his
1Ki 17:19 to the upper room where he was staying, and laid him on his **bed**.
21:4 of my fathers." He lay on his **bed** sulking and refused to eat.
2Ki 1:4 the LORD says: 'You will not leave the **bed** you are lying on.
1:6 of Ekron? Therefore you will not leave the **bed** you are lying on.
1:16 you have done this, you will never leave the **bed** you are lying on.
4:10 Let's make a small room on the roof and put in it a **bed** and a table,
4:21 She went up and laid him on the **bed** *of* the man of God, then shut
4:32 reached the house, there was the boy lying dead on his **couch**.
11:2 and his nurse in a **bedroom** [+2540] to hide him from Athaliah;
2Ch 22:11 to be murdered and put him and his nurse in a **bedroom** [+2540].
24:25 the son of Jehoiada the priest, and they killed him in his **bed**.
Est 1:6 There were **couches** *of* gold and silver on a mosaic pavement of
7:8 Haman was falling on the **couch** where Esther was reclining.
Ps 6:6 [6:7] all night long I flood my **bed** with weeping and drench my
Pr 26:14 As a door turns on its hinges, so a sluggard turns on his **bed**.
SS 3:7 It is Solomon's **carriage**, escorted by sixty warriors, the noblest of
Eze 23:41 You sat on an elegant **couch**, with a table spread before it on which
Am 3:12 those who sit in Samaria on the edge of their **beds** and in
6:4 You lie on **beds** *inlaid with* ivory and lounge on your couches.

4754 מֻטֶּה muṭṭeh, n.[m.]. [1] [√ 5742]

injustice [1]

Eze 9:9 the land is full of bloodshed and the city is full of **injustice**.

4755 מֻטָּה muṭṭâ, n.f. Not used in NIV/BHS [√ 5742]

4756 מִטְהָר miṭhār, n.[m.]. Not used in NIV/BHS [√ 3197]

4757 מַטְוֶה maṭweh, n.[m.]. [1] [√ 3211]

what spun [1]

Ex 35:25 woman spun with her hands and brought **what** she had **spun**—

4758 מָטִיל māṭîl, n.m. [1]

rods [1]

Job 40:18 His bones are tubes of bronze, his limbs like **rods** *of* iron.

4759 מַטְמוֹן maṭmôn, n.m. [5] [√ 3243]

hidden treasure [2], hidden [1], riches [1], treasure [1]

Ge 43:23 the God of your father, has given you **treasure** in your sacks;
Job 3:21 does not come, who search for it more than for **hidden treasure**,
Pr 2:4 look for it as for silver and search for it as for **hidden treasure**,
Isa 45:3 give you the treasures of darkness, **riches** *stored in* secret places,
Jer 41:8 We have wheat and barley, oil and honey, **hidden** in a field."

4760 מַטָּע maṭṭā', n.m. [6] [√ 5749]

planted [2], planting [2], base [1], land for crops [1]

Isa 60:21 They are the shoot I have **planted**, the work of my hands,
61:3 a **planting** *of* the LORD for the display of his splendor.
Eze 17:7 sent out its roots toward him from the plot where it was **planted**
31:4 all their streams flowed all around its **base** and sent their channels to
34:29 I will provide for them a **land** renowned **for** its **crops**, and they
Mic 1:6 make Samaria a heap of rubble, a place for **planting** vineyards.

4761 מַטְעָם maṭ'ām, n.m. [8] [√ 3247]

tasty food [6], delicacies [2]

Ge 27:4 Prepare me the kind of **tasty food** I like and bring it to me to eat,
27:7 'Bring me some game and prepare me *some* **tasty food** to eat,
27:9 so I can prepare *some* **tasty food** for your father, just the way he
27:14 and she prepared *some* **tasty food**, just the way his father liked it.
27:17 she handed to her son Jacob the **tasty food** and the bread she had
27:31 He too prepared *some* **tasty food** and brought it to his father.
Pr 23:3 Do not crave his **delicacies**, for that food is deceptive.
23:6 Do not eat the food of a stingy man, do not crave his **delicacies**;

4762 מִטְפַּחַת miṭpaḥat, n.f. [2] [√ 3254]

cloaks [1], shawl [1]

Ru 3:15 also said, "Bring me the **shawl** you are wearing and hold it out."
Isa 3:22 the fine robes and the capes and **cloaks**, the purses

4763 מָטַר māṭar, v.den. [17 / 18] [√ 4764]

rained down [3], had rain [2], rain down [2], sent rain [2], had[s] [1], pour down [1], rain [+4764] [1], rain [1], rained [1], send rain [1], send [1], water [1], withheld[s] [+4202] [1]

Ge 2:5 [G] for the LORD God *had* not **sent rain** on the earth and there
7:4 [G] Seven days from now I *will* **send rain** on the earth for forty
19:24 [G] the LORD **rained down** burning sulfur on Sodom
Ex 9:18 [G] at this time tomorrow I *will* **send** the worst hailstorm that has
9:23 [G] the ground. So the LORD **rained** hail on the land of Egypt;
16:4 [G] said to Moses, "I *will* **rain down** bread from heaven for you.
Job 20:23 [G] anger against him and **rain down** his blows upon him.
38:26 [G] to **water** a land where no man lives, a desert with no one in
Ps 11:6 [G] On the wicked *he will* **rain** fiery coals and burning sulfur;
78:24 [G] *he* **rained down** manna for the people to eat, he gave them
78:27 [G] *He* **rained** meat **down** on them like dust, flying birds like
Isa 5:6 [G] I will command the clouds not *to* **rain** [+4764] on it."
Eze 22:24 [h] 'You are a land that *has* **had** no **rain** [BHS 3197] or showers
38:22 [G] *I will* **pour down** torrents of rain, hailstones and burning
Am 4:7 [G] *I* **sent rain** on one town, but withheld it from another. One
4:7 [G] rain on one town, but **withheld**[s] [+4202] it from another.
4:7 [C] One field **had rain**; another had none and dried up.
4:7 [G] One field had rain; another **had**[s] none and dried up.

4764 מָטָר *māṭār*, n.m. [38] [→ 4763, 4767]

rain [34], showers [2], downpour [+1773] [1], rain [+4763] [1]

Ex 9:33 and hail stopped, and the **rain** no longer poured down on the land.
9:34 When Pharaoh saw that the **rain** and hail and thunder had stopped,
Dt 11:11 of is a land of mountains and valleys that drinks **rain** *from* heaven.
11:14 then I will send **rain** *on* your land in its season, both autumn
11:17 he will shut the heavens so that it will not **rain** and the ground will
28:12 to send **rain** *on* your land in season and to bless all the work of
28:24 The LORD will turn the **rain** *of* your country into dust
32:2 Let my teaching fall like **rain** and my words descend like dew,
1Sa 12:17 harvest now? I will call upon the LORD to send thunder and **rain**.
12:18 the LORD, and that same day the LORD sent thunder and **rain**.
2Sa 1:21 "O mountains of Gilboa, may you have neither dew nor **rain**,
23:4 like the brightness after **rain** that brings the grass from the earth.'
1Ki 8:35 "When the heavens are shut up and there is no **rain** because your
8:36 and send **rain** on the land you gave your people for an inheritance.
17:1 there will be neither dew nor **rain** in the next few years except at
18:1 and present yourself to Ahab, and I will send **rain** on the land."
2Ch 6:26 "When the heavens are shut up and there is no **rain** because your
6:27 and send **rain** on the land you gave your people for an inheritance.
7:13 "When I shut up the heavens so that there is no **rain**, or command
Job 5:10 He bestows **rain** on the earth; he sends water upon the countryside.
28:26 when he made a decree for the **rain** and a path for the
29:23 They waited for me as for **showers** and drank in my words as the
36:27 draws up the drops of water, which distill as **rain** to the streams;
37:6 He says to the snow, 'Fall on the earth,' and to the **rain** shower,
37:6 and to the rain shower, 'Be a mighty **downpour** [+1773].'
38:28 Does the **rain** have a father? Who fathers the drops of dew?
Ps 72:6 He will be like **rain** falling on a mown field, like showers watering
135:7 he sends lightning with the **rain** and brings out the wind from his
147:8 he supplies the earth with **rain** and makes grass grow on the hills.
Pr 26:1 Like snow in summer or **rain** in harvest, honor is not fitting for a
28:3 A ruler who oppresses the poor is like a driving **rain** that leaves no
Isa 4:6 of the day, and a refuge and hiding place from the storm and **rain**.
5:6 grow there. I will command the clouds not *to* **rain** [+4763] on it."
30:23 He will also send you **rain** *for* the seed you sow in the ground,
Jer 10:13 He sends lightning with the **rain** and brings out the wind from his
51:16 He sends lightning with the **rain** and brings out the wind from his
Zec 10:1 Ask the LORD for **rain** in the springtime; it is the LORD who
10:1 He gives **showers** *of* rain to men, and plants of the field to

4765 מַטְרֵד *maṭrēd*, n.pr.f. [2] [√ 3265]

Matred [2]

Ge 36:39 and his wife's name was Mehetabel daughter of **Matred**,
1Ch 1:50 and his wife's name was Mehetabel daughter of **Matred**,

4766 מַטָּרָה *maṭṭārâ*, n.f. [16] [√ 5757]

guard [13], target [3]

1Sa 20:20 three arrows to the side of it, as though I were shooting at a **target**.
Ne 3:25 tower projecting from the upper palace near the court of the **guard**.
12:39 as far as the Sheep Gate. At the Gate of the **Guard** they stopped.
Job 16:12 seized me by the neck and crushed me. He has made me his **target**;
Jer 32:2 Jeremiah the prophet was confined in the courtyard of the **guard** in
32:8 my cousin Hanamel came to me in the courtyard of the **guard**
32:12 the deed and of all the Jews sitting in the courtyard of the **guard**.
33:1 While Jeremiah was still confined in the courtyard of the **guard**,
37:21 gave orders for Jeremiah to be placed in the courtyard of the **guard**
37:21 was gone. So Jeremiah remained in the courtyard of the **guard**.
38:6 the king's son, which was in the courtyard of the **guard**.
38:13 the cistern. And Jeremiah remained in the courtyard of the **guard**.
38:28 Jeremiah remained in the courtyard of the **guard** until the day
39:14 and had Jeremiah taken out of the courtyard of the **guard**.
39:15 While Jeremiah had been confined in the courtyard of the **guard**,
La 3:12 He drew his bow and made me the **target** for his arrows.

4767 מַטְרִי *maṭrî*, a.g. [1] [√ 4764]

Matri's [1]

1Sa 10:21 the tribe of Benjamin, clan by clan, and **Matri's** clan was chosen.

4768 מַי *may*, var. Not used in NIV/BHS [cf. 4537]

4769 מִי *mî*, p.inter. [423 / 422] [→ 4775?, 4776, 4777, 4778, 4779, 4780, 4781, 4792] See Select Index

who [285], whom [34], what [17], which [11], whose [11], if only [+5989] [9], oh [+5989] [8], anyone [7], whoever [6], *untranslated* [4], anyone [+408+2021] [3], if only [3], whose [+4200] [3], how [2], just who [+2256+4769] [2], one [2], someone [2], whoever [+408+2021] [2], whoever [+889] [2], any man [+408+2021] [1], how did it go [+905] [1], how I long for [+5761+5989] [1], I wish [+5989] [1], if only [+906+5989] [1], oh [+686+5989] [1], oh how I wish [+5989] [1], others[s] [1], what [+2296] [1]

4770 מֵי הַיַּרְקוֹן *mê hayyarqôn*, n.pr.loc. [1] [√ 4784 + 2126]

Me Jarkon [1]

Jos 19:46 **Me Jarkon** and Rakkon, with the area facing Joppa.

4771 מֵי זָהָב *mê zāhāb*, n.pr.m. [2] [√ 4784 + 2298]

Me-Zahab [2]

Ge 36:39 was Mehetabel daughter of Matred, the daughter of **Me-Zahab**.
1Ch 1:50 was Mehetabel daughter of Matred, the daughter of **Me-Zahab**.

4772 מֵידְבָא *mêdᵉbā'*, n.pr.loc. [5]

Medeba [5]

Nu 21:30 demolished them as far as Nophah, which extends to **Medeba**."
Jos 13:9 and included the whole plateau of **Medeba** as far as Dibon,
13:16 in the middle of the gorge, and the whole plateau past **Medeba**
1Ch 19:7 of Maacah with his troops, who came and camped near **Medeba**,
Isa 15:2 to its high places to weep; Moab wails over Nebo and **Medeba**.

4773 מֵידָד *mêdād*, n.pr.m. [2]

Medad [2]

Nu 11:26 However, two men, whose names were Eldad and **Medad**,
11:27 and told Moses, "Eldad and **Medad** are prophesying in the camp."

4774 מֵיטָב *mêṭāb*, n.[m.] [6] [√ 3512]

best [5], *untranslated* [1]

Ge 47:6 settle your father and your brothers in the **best** *part of* the land.
47:11 in Egypt and gave them property in the **best** *part of* the land,
Ex 22:5 [22:4] he must make restitution from the **best** *of* his own field
22:5 [22:4] from the best of his own field or **[RPH]** vineyard.
1Sa 15:9 and the army spared Agag and the **best** *of* the sheep and cattle,
15:15 they spared the **best** *of* the sheep and cattle to sacrifice to the

4775 מִיכָא *mîkā'*, n.pr.m. [4] [→ 4776?, 4777; cf. 4769?]

Mica [4]

2Sa 9:12 Mephibosheth had a young son named **Mica**, and all the members
1Ch 9:15 Bakbakkar, Heresh, Galal and Mattaniah son of **Mica**, the son of
Ne 10:11 [10:12] **Mica**, Rehob, Hashabiah,
11:22 the son of Hashabiah, the son of Mattaniah, the son of **Mica**.

4776 מִיכָאֵל *mîkā'ēl*, n.pr.m. [13] [√ 4775?; cf. 4769 + 3869 + 446]

Michael [13]

Nu 13:13 from the tribe of Asher, Sethur son of **Michael**;
1Ch 5:13 **Michael**, Meshullam, Sheba, Jorai, Jacan, Zia and Eber—seven in
5:14 the son of Jaroah, the son of Gilead, the son of **Michael**, the son of
6:40 [6:25] the son of **Michael**, the son of Baaseiah, the son of
7:3 The sons of Izrahiah: **Michael**, Obadiah, Joel and Isshiah.
8:16 **Michael**, Ishpah and Joha were the sons of Beriah.
12:20 [12:21] Jediael, **Michael**, Jozabad, Elihu and Zillethai,
27:18 Elihu, a brother of David; over Issachar: Omri son of **Michael**;
2Ch 21:2 Jehiel, Zechariah, Azariahu, **Michael** and Shephatiah.
Ezr 8:8 of Shephatiah, Zebadiah son of **Michael**, and with him 80 men;
Da 10:13 **Michael**, one of the chief princes, came to help me, because I was
10:21 (No one supports me against them except **Michael**, your prince.
12:1 "At that time **Michael**, the great prince who protects your people,

4777 מִיכָה *mîkâ*, n.pr.m. [33] [√ 4775; cf. 4769 + 3869 + 3378]

Micah [24], Micah's [6], his[s] [1], Mica [1], Micaiah [1]

Jdg 17:5 Now this man **Micah** had a shrine, and he made an ephod
17:8 On his way he came to **Micah's** house in the hill country of
17:9 **Micah** asked him, "Where are you from?" "I'm a Levite from
17:10 Then **Micah** said to him, "Live with me and be my father
17:11 **Micah** installed the Levite, and the young man became his priest
17:12 and the young man became his priest and lived in **his**[s] house.
17:13 **Micah** said, "Now I know that the LORD will be good to me,
18:2 the hill country of Ephraim and came to the house of **Micah**,
18:3 When they were near **Micah's** house, they recognized the voice of
18:4 He told them what **Micah** had done for him, and said, "He has
18:13 went on to the hill country of Ephraim and came to **Micah's** house.
18:15 and went to the house of the young Levite at **Micah's** place
18:18 When these men went into **Micah's** house and took the carved
18:22 When they had gone some distance from **Micah's** house, the men
18:22 the men who lived near **Micah** were called together and overtook

Jdg 18:23 As they shouted after them, the Danites turned and said to **Micah**,
18:26 So the Danites went their way, and **Micah**, seeing that they were
18:27 they took what **Micah** had made, and his priest, and went on to
18:31 They continued to use the idols **Micah** had made, all the time the
1Ch 5: 5 **Micah** his son, Reaiah his son, Baal his son,
8:34 The son of Jonathan: Merib-Baal, who was the father of **Micah**.
8:35 The sons of **Micah**: Pithon, Melech, Tarea and Ahaz.
9:40 The son of Jonathan: Merib-Baal, who was the father of **Micah**.
9:41 The sons of **Micah**: Pithon, Melech, Tahrea and Ahaz.
23:20 The sons of Uzziel: **Micah** the first and Isshiah the second.
24:24 The son of Uzziel: **Micah**; from the sons of Micah: Shamir.
24:24 The son of Uzziel: Micah; from the sons of **Micah**: Shamir.
24:25 The brother of **Micah**: Isshiah; from the sons of Isshiah: Zechariah.
2Ch 18:14 When he arrived, the king asked him, "**Micaiah**, shall we go to war
34:20 Abdon son of **Micah**, Shaphan the secretary and Asaiah the king's
Ne 11:17 Mattaniah son of **Mica**, the son of Zabdi, the son of Asaph,
Jer 26:18 "**Micah** [K 4779] of Moresheth prophesied in the days of
Mic 1: 1 The word of the LORD that came to **Micah** of Moresheth during

4778 מִיכָהוּ *mîkāhû*, n.pr.m. [0] [√ 4769 + 3869 + 2084]

2Ch 18: 8 ["Bring **Micaiah** [K; see Q 4781] son of Imlah at once."]

4779 מִיכָיָה *mîkāyâ*, n.pr.m. [3] [→ 4780, 4781; cf. 4769 + 3869 + 3378]

Micaiah [3]

2Ki 22:12 Acbor son of **Micaiah**, Shaphan the secretary and Asaiah the
Ne 12:35 the son of **Micaiah**, the son of Zaccur, the son of Asaph,
12:41 **Micaiah**, Elioenai, Zechariah and Hananiah with their trumpets—
Jer 26:18 ["**Micah** [K; see Q 4777] of Moresheth prophesied in the days]

4780 מִיכָיָהוּ *mîkāyāhû*, n.pr.m. & f. [2 / 1] [√ 4779; cf. 4769 + 3869 + 3378]

Micaiah [1]

2Ch 13: 2 His mother's name was <u>Maacah</u>, [BHS ***Micaiah***; NIV 5082]
17: 7 Zechariah, Nethanel and **Micaiah** to teach in the towns of Judah.

4781 מִיכָיְהוּ *mîkāyᵉhû*, n.pr.m. [21] [√ 4779; cf. 4769 + 3869 + 3378]

Micaiah [19], Micah [1], Micah's [1]

Jdg 17: 1 Now a man named **Micah** from the hill country of Ephraim
17: 4 into the image and the idol. And they were put in **Micah's** house.
1Ki 22: 8 good about me, but always bad. He is **Micaiah** son of Imlah."
22: 9 of his officials and said, "Bring **Micaiah** son of Imlah at once."
22:13 The messenger who had gone to summon **Micaiah** said to him,
22:14 **Micaiah** said, "As surely as the LORD lives, I can tell him only
22:15 When he arrived, the king asked him, "**Micaiah**, shall we go to war
22:24 son of Kenaanah went up and slapped **Micaiah** in the face.
22:25 **Micaiah** replied, "You will find out on the day you go to hide in an
22:26 "Take **Micaiah** and send him back to Amon the ruler of the city
22:28 **Micaiah** declared, "If you ever return safely, the LORD has not
2Ch 18: 7 good about me, but always bad. He is **Micaiah** son of Imlah."
18: 8 and said, "Bring **Micaiah** [K 4778] son of Imlah at once."
18:12 The messenger who had gone to summon **Micaiah** said to him,
18:13 **Micaiah** said, "As surely as the LORD lives, I can tell him only
18:23 son of Kenaanah went up and slapped **Micaiah** in the face.
18:24 **Micaiah** replied, "You will find out on the day you go to hide in an
18:25 "Take **Micaiah** and send him back to Amon the ruler of the city
18:27 **Micaiah** declared, "If you ever return safely, the LORD has not
Jer 36:11 When **Micaiah** son of Gemariah, the son of Shaphan, heard all the
36:13 After **Micaiah** told them everything he had heard Baruch read to

4782 מִיכָל *mîkāl*, n.[m.]. [1] [→ 4783]

brook [+4784] [1]

2Sa 17:20 woman answered them, "They crossed over the **brook** [+4784]."

4783 מִיכַל *mîkal*, n.pr.f. [18 / 17] [√ 4782]

Michal [17]

1Sa 14:49 his older daughter was Merab, and that of the younger was **Michal**.
18:20 Now Saul's daughter **Michal** was in love with David, and when
18:27 Then Saul gave him his daughter **Michal** in marriage.
18:28 LORD was with David and that his daughter **Michal** loved David,
19:11 **Michal**, David's wife, warned him, "If you don't run for your life
19:12 So **Michal** let David down through a window, and he fled
19:13 **Michal** took an idol and laid it on the bed, covering it with a
19:17 Saul said to **Michal**, "Why did you deceive me like this and send
19:17 he escaped?" **Michal** told him, "He said to me, 'Let me get away.
25:44 Saul had given his daughter **Michal**, David's wife, to Paltiel son of
2Sa 3:13 Do not come into my presence unless you bring **Michal** daughter
3:14 to Ish-Bosheth son of Saul, demanding, "Give me my wife **Michal**,
6:16 City of David, **Michal** daughter of Saul watched from a window.
6:20 **Michal** daughter of Saul came out to meet him and said,
6:21 David said to **Michal**, "It was before the LORD, who chose me
6:23 **Michal** daughter of Saul had no children to the day of her death.
21: 8 five sons of Saul's daughter <u>Merab</u>, [BHS ***Michal***; NIV 5266]
1Ch 15:29 City of David, **Michal** daughter of Saul watched from a window.

4784 מַיִם *mayim*, n.m. [579 / 578] [→ 72, 4770, 4771, 5387]

water [359], waters [140], *untranslated* [15], flood [3], floodwaters [+4429] [3], rain [3], springs [+5078] [3], tears [3], flowing springs [+4604] [2], river [2], sea [2], spring [+4604] [2], spring [+6524] [2], spring [2], springs [+6524] [2], that[s] [2], waterless [+401] [2], well-watered [+9272] [2], brook [+4782] [1], bubbling springs [+4432] [1], dam [1], driving rain [+2443] [1], floodwaters [+8041] [1], floodwaters [+8673] [1], flow [1], flowing streams [+3298] [1], it[s] [+2021] [1], melted [1], pool [+106] [1], pool [+1391] [1], pool [1], reservoirs [+1391] [1], reservoirs [+5224] [1], seas [1], spring [+2021+6524] [1], spring of water [1], springs [+4604] [1], stream [1], swampland [+106] [1], they[s] [+2021] [1], water supply [1], water's [1], watercourse [+7104] [1], watering [1], waves [1], well [+931] [1], wells [+931] [1]

Ge 1: 2 of the deep, and the Spirit of God was hovering over the **waters**.
1: 6 "Let there be an expanse between the **waters** to separate water
1: 6 "Let there be an expanse between the waters to separate **water**
1: 6 be an expanse between the waters to separate water from **water**."
1: 7 and separated the **water** under the expanse from the water above it.
1: 7 and separated the water under the expanse from the **water** above it.
1: 9 God said, "Let the **water** under the sky be gathered to one place,
1:10 the dry ground "land," and the gathered **waters** he called "seas."
1:20 God said, "Let the **water** teem with living creatures, and let birds
1:21 and every living and moving thing with which the **water** teems,
1:22 "Be fruitful and increase in number and fill the **water** in the seas,
6:17 I am going to bring **floodwaters** [+4429] on the earth to destroy all
7: 6 Noah was six hundred years old when the **floodwaters** [+4429]
7: 7 his sons' wives entered the ark to escape the **waters** *of* the flood.
7:10 after the seven days the **floodwaters** [+4429] came on the earth.
7:17 as the **waters** increased they lifted the ark high above the earth.
7:18 The **waters** rose and increased greatly on the earth, and the ark
7:18 on the earth, and the ark floated on the surface of the **water**.
7:19 **They**[s] [+2021] rose greatly on the earth, and all the high
7:20 The **waters** rose and covered the mountains to a depth of more
7:24 The **waters** flooded the earth for a hundred and fifty days.
8: 1 and he sent a wind over the earth, and the **waters** receded.
8: 3 The **water** receded steadily from the earth. At the end of the
8: 3 At the end of the hundred and fifty days the **water** had gone down,
8: 5 The **waters** continued to recede until the tenth month, and on the
8: 7 flying back and forth until the **water** had dried up from the earth.
8: 8 he sent out a dove to see if the **water** had receded from the surface
8: 9 its feet because there was **water** over all the surface of the earth;
8:11 Then Noah knew that the **water** had receded from the earth.
8:13 six hundred and first year, the **water** had dried up from the earth.
9:11 Never again will all life be cut off by the **waters** *of* a flood;
9:15 Never again will the **waters** become a flood to destroy all life.
16: 7 The angel of the LORD found Hagar near a **spring** [+2021+6524]
18: 4 Let a little **water** be brought, and then you may all wash your feet
21:14 took some food and a skin of **water** and gave them to Hagar.
21:15 When the **water** in the skin was gone, she put the boy under one of
21:19 God opened her eyes and she saw a well of **water**. So she went
21:19 So she went and filled the skin with **water** and gave the boy a
21:25 Abraham complained to Abimelech about a well of **water** that
24:11 He had the camels kneel down near the **well** [+931] outside the
24:13 See, I am standing beside this **spring** [+6524], and the daughters of
24:13 the daughters of the townspeople are coming out to draw **water**.
24:17 to meet her and said, "Please give me a little **water** from your jar."
24:32 for the camels, and **water** for him and his men to wash their feet.
24:43 See, I am standing beside this **spring** [+6524]; if a maiden comes
24:43 and I say to her, "Please let me drink a little **water** from your jar,"
26:18 Isaac reopened the **wells** [+931] that had been dug in the time of
26:19 dug in the valley and discovered a well of fresh **water** there.
26:20 quarreled with Isaac's herdsmen and said, "The **water** is ours!"
26:32 him about the well they had dug. They said, "We've found **water**!"
30:38 Then he placed the peeled branches in all the **watering** troughs,
37:24 the cistern. Now the cistern was empty; there was no **water** in it.
43:24 gave them **water** to wash their feet and provided fodder for their
49: 4 Turbulent as the **waters**, you will no longer excel, for you went up
Ex 2:10 She named him Moses, saying, "I drew him out of the **water**."
4: 9 take some **water** *from* the Nile and pour it on the dry ground.
4: 9 The **water** you take from the river will become blood on the
7:15 Go to Pharaoh in the morning as he goes out to the **water**.
7:17 With the staff that is in my hand I will strike the **water** of the Nile,
7:18 river will stink; the Egyptians will not be able to drink its **water**.' "
7:19 your staff and stretch out your hand over the **waters** *of* Egypt—
7:19 and canals, over the ponds and all the **reservoirs** [+5224]'—
7:20 of Pharaoh and his officials and struck the **water** of the Nile,

Ex 7:20 the water of the Nile, and all the **water** was changed into blood.
7:21 river smelled so bad that the Egyptians could not drink its **water**.
7:24 And all the Egyptians dug along the Nile to get drinking **water**,
7:24 drinking water, because they could not drink the **water** *of* the river.
8: 6 [8:2] So Aaron stretched out his hand over the **waters** *of* Egypt,
8:20 [8:16] confront Pharaoh as he goes to the **water** and say to him,
12: 9 Do not eat the meat raw or cooked in **water**, but roast it over the
14:21 east wind and turned it into dry land. The **waters** were divided,
14:22 on dry ground, with a wall of **water** on their right and on their left.
14:26 so that the **waters** may flow back over the Egyptians and their
14:28 The **water** flowed back and covered the chariots and horsemen—
14:29 on dry ground, with a wall of **water** on their right and on their left.
15: 8 By the blast of your nostrils the **waters** piled up. The surging
15:10 the sea covered them. They sank like lead in the mighty **waters**.
15:19 the LORD brought the **waters** *of* the sea back over them,
15:22 For three days they traveled in the desert without finding **water**.
15:23 to Marah, they could not drink its **water** because it was bitter.
15:25 He threw it into the **water**, and the water became sweet.
15:25 He threw it into the water, and the **water** became sweet.
15:27 where there were twelve **springs** [+6524] and seventy palm trees,
15:27 and seventy palm trees, and they camped there near the **water**.
17: 1 at Rephidim, but there was no **water** for the people to drink.
17: 2 So they quarreled with Moses and said, "Give us **water** to drink."
17: 3 the people were thirsty for **water** there, and they grumbled against
17: 6 the rock, and **water** will come out of it for the people to drink."
20: 4 in heaven above or on the earth beneath or in the **waters** below.
23:25 your God, and his blessing will be on your food and **water**.
29: 4 to the entrance to the Tent of Meeting and wash them with **water**.
30:18 it between the Tent of Meeting and the altar, and put **water** in it.
30:20 of Meeting, they shall wash with **water** so that they will not die.
32:20 scattered it on the **water** and made the Israelites drink it.
34:28 forty days and forty nights without eating bread or drinking **water**.
40: 7 between the Tent of Meeting and the altar and put **water** in it.
40:12 to the entrance to the Tent of Meeting and wash them with **water**.
40:30 the Tent of Meeting and the altar and put **water** in it for washing,
Lev 1: 9 He is to wash the inner parts and the legs with **water**, and the priest
1:13 He is to wash the inner parts and the legs with **water**, and the priest
6:28 [6:21] bronze pot, the pot is to be scoured and rinsed with **water**.
8: 6 brought Aaron and his sons forward and washed them with **water**.
8:21 He washed the inner parts and the legs with **water** and burned the
11: 9 " 'Of all the creatures living in the **water** of the seas and the
11: 9 " 'Of all the creatures living in the water **[RPH]** of the seas
11:10 **[RPH]** or among all the other living creatures in the water—
11:10 or among all the other living creatures in the **water**—
11:12 Anything living in the **water** that does not have fins and scales is
11:32 Put it in **water**; it will be unclean till evening, and then it will be
11:34 that could be eaten but has **water** on it from such a pot is unclean,
11:36 A spring, however, or a cistern for collecting **water** remains clean,
11:38 But if **water** has been put on the seed and a carcass falls on it,
11:46 every living thing that moves in the **water** and every creature that
14: 5 order that one of the birds be killed over fresh **water** in a clay pot.
14: 6 into the blood of the bird that was killed over the fresh **water**.
14: 8 must wash his clothes, shave off all his hair and bathe with **water**;
14: 9 He must wash his clothes and bathe himself with **water**, and he
14:50 He shall kill one of the birds over fresh **water** in a clay pot.
14:51 dip them into the blood of the dead bird and the fresh **water**,
14:52 the fresh **water**, the live bird, the cedar wood, the hyssop and the
15: 5 who touches his bed must wash his clothes and bathe with **water**,
15: 6 a discharge sat on must wash his clothes and bathe with **water**,
15: 7 who has a discharge must wash his clothes and bathe with **water**,
15: 8 that person must wash his clothes and bathe with **water**, and he
15:10 picks up those things must wash his clothes and bathe with **water**,
15:11 without rinsing his hands with **water** must wash his clothes
15:11 his hands with water must wash his clothes and bathe with **water**,
15:12 must be broken, and any wooden article is to be rinsed with **water**.
15:13 he must wash his clothes and bathe himself with fresh **water**,
15:16 he must bathe his whole body with **water**, and he will be unclean
15:17 or leather that has semen on it must be washed with **water**,
15:18 and there is an emission of semen, both must bathe with **water**,
15:21 touches her bed must wash his clothes and bathe with **water**,
15:22 anything she sits on must wash his clothes and bathe with **water**,
15:27 he must wash his clothes and bathe with **water**, and he will be
16: 4 so he must bathe himself with **water** before he puts them on.
16:24 He shall bathe himself with **water** in a holy place and put on his
16:26 a scapegoat must wash his clothes and bathe himself with **water**;
16:28 burns them must wash his clothes and bathe himself with **water**;
17:15 torn by wild animals must wash his clothes and bathe with **water**,
22: 6 of the sacred offerings unless he has bathed himself with **water**.
Nu 5:17 he shall take some holy **water** in a clay jar and put some dust from
5:17 and put some dust from the tabernacle floor into the **water**.
5:18 while he himself holds the bitter **water** that brings a curse.
5:19 may this bitter **water** that brings a curse not harm you.
5:22 May this **water** that brings a curse enter your body so that your
5:23 curses on a scroll and then wash them off into the bitter **water**.
5:24 He shall have the woman drink the bitter **water** that brings a curse,
5:24 a curse, and this **water** will enter her and cause bitter suffering.
5:26 it on the altar; after that, he is to have the woman drink the **water**.
5:27 then when she is made to drink the **water** that brings a curse,
5:27 when she is made to drink the water that brings a curse, **it**[s] [+2021]
8: 7 Sprinkle the **water** *of* cleansing on them; then have them shave
19: 7 the priest must wash his clothes and bathe himself with **water**.
19: 8 burns it must also wash his clothes **[RPH]** and bathe with water,
19: 8 man who burns it must also wash his clothes and bathe with **water**,
19: 9 kept by the Israelite community for use in the **water** *of* cleansing;
19:13 Because the **water** *of* cleansing has not been sprinkled on him,
19:17 purification offering into a jar and pour fresh **water** over them.
19:18 dip it in the **water** and sprinkle the tent and all the furnishings
19:19 person being cleansed must wash his clothes and bathe with **water**,
19:20 The **water** *of* cleansing has not been sprinkled on him, and he is
19:21 "The man who sprinkles the **water** *of* cleansing must also wash his
19:21 anyone who touches the **water** *of* cleansing will be unclean till
20: 2 Now there was no **water** for the community, and the people
20: 5 grapevines or pomegranates. And there is no **water** to drink!"
20: 8 Speak to that rock before their eyes and it will pour out its **water**.
20: 8 You will bring **water** out of the rock for the community so they
20:10 "Listen, you rebels, must we bring you **water** out of this rock?"
20:11 **Water** gushed out, and the community and their livestock drank.
20:13 These were the **waters** *of* Meribah, where the Israelites quarreled
20:17 go through any field or vineyard, or drink **water** *from* any well.
20:19 if we or our livestock drink any of your **water**, we will pay for it.
20:24 because both of you rebelled against my command at the **waters** *of*
21: 5 There is no bread! There is no **water**! And we detest this miserable
21:16 to Moses, "Gather the people together and I will give them **water**."
21:22 turn aside into any field or vineyard, or drink **water** *from* any well.
24: 6 like aloes planted by the LORD, like cedars beside the **waters**.
24: 7 **Water** will flow from their buckets; their seed will have abundant
24: 7 will flow from their buckets; their seed will have abundant **water**.
27:14 for when the community rebelled at the **waters** in the Desert of
27:14 (These were the **waters** *of* Meribah Kadesh, in the Desert of Zin.)
31:23 be clean. But it must also be purified with the **water** *of* cleansing.
31:23 whatever cannot withstand fire must be put through that **water**.
33: 9 where there were twelve **springs** [+6524] and seventy palm trees,
33:14 at Rephidim, where there was no **water** for the people to drink.
Dt 2: 6 pay them in silver for the food you eat and the **water** you drink.' "
2:28 Sell us food to eat and **water** to drink for their price in silver.
4:18 that moves along the ground or any fish in the **waters** below.
5: 8 in heaven above or on the earth beneath or in the **waters** below.
8: 7 a land with streams and pools of **water**, with springs flowing in the
8:15 and dreadful desert, that thirsty and **waterless** [+401] land,
8:15 and scorpions. He brought you **water** out of hard rock.
9: 9 forty days and forty nights; I ate no bread and drank no **water**.
9:18 I ate no bread and drank no **water**, because of all the sin you had
10: 7 to Gudgodah and on to Jotbathah, a land with streams of **water**.
11: 4 how he overwhelmed them with the **waters** *of* the Red Sea as they
11:11 land of mountains and valleys that drinks **[NIE]** rain from heaven.
12:16 you must not eat the blood; pour it out on the ground like **water**.
12:24 You must not eat the blood; pour it out on the ground like **water**.
14: 9 Of all the creatures living in the **water**, you may eat any that has
15:23 you must not eat the blood; pour it out on the ground like **water**.
23: 4 [23:5] and **water** on your way when you came out of Egypt,
23:11 [23:12] **[NIE]** and at sunset he may return to the camp.
29:11 [29:10] your camps who chop your wood and carry your **water**.
32:51 the Israelites at the **waters** *of* Meribah Kadesh in the Desert of Zin
33: 8 him at Massah; you contended with him at the **waters** *of* Meribah.
Jos 2:10 We have heard how the LORD dried up the **water** *of* the Red Sea
3: 8 'When you reach the edge of the Jordan's **waters**, go and stand in
3:13 set foot in **[RPH]** the Jordan, its waters flowing downstream will
3:13 its **waters** flowing downstream will be cut off and stand up in a
3:13 its waters **[RPH]** flowing downstream will be cut off and stand up
3:15 the ark reached the Jordan and their feet touched the **water's** edge,
3:16 the **water** from upstream stopped flowing. It piled up in a heap a
4: 7 tell them that the **flow** *of* the Jordan was cut off before the ark of
4: 7 When it crossed the Jordan, the **waters** *of* the Jordan were cut off.
4:18 the dry ground than the **waters** *of* the Jordan returned to their place
4:23 For the LORD your God dried up **[RPH]** the Jordan before you
5: 1 **[RPH]** the Jordan before the Israelites until we had crossed over,
7: 5 At this the hearts of the people melted and became like **water**.
9:21 them be woodcutters and **water** carriers for the entire community."
9:23 serve as woodcutters and **water** carriers for the house of my God."
9:27 the Gibeonites woodcutters and **water** carriers for the community
11: 5 joined forces and made camp together at the **Waters** *of* Merom,
11: 7 his whole army came against them suddenly at the **Waters** *of*
15: 7 It continued along to the **waters** *of* En Shemesh and came out at
15: 9 the boundary headed toward the spring of the **waters** *of* Nephtoah,
15:19 have given me land in the Negev, give me also springs of **water**."
16: 1 began at the Jordan of Jericho, east of the **waters** *of* Jericho,
18:15 the boundary came out at the spring of the **waters** *of* Nephtoah.
Jdg 1:15 have given me land in the Negev, give me also springs of **water**."

[F] Hitpael (hitpoel, hitpoal, hitpolel, hitpolal, hitpalel, hitpalal, hitpalpel, hitpalpal, hotpael, hotpaal) [G] Hiphil (hiphtil) [H] Hophal [I] Hishtaphel

Jdg 4:19 "I'm thirsty," he said. "Please give me some **water**." She opened a
5: 4 earth shook, the heavens poured, the clouds poured down **water**.
5:19 the kings of Canaan fought at Taanach by the **waters** *of* Megiddo,
5:25 He asked for **water**, and she gave him milk; in a bowl fit for nobles
6:38 squeezed the fleece and wrung out the dew—a bowlful of **water**.
7: 4 Take them down to the **water**, and I will sift them for you there.
7: 5 So Gideon took the men down to the **water**. There the LORD told
7: 5 "Separate those who lap the **water** with their tongues like a dog
7: 6 All the rest got down on their knees to drink. **[RPH]**
7:24 seize the **waters** of the Jordan ahead of them as far as Beth Barah."
7:24 and they took the **waters** of the Jordan as far as Beth Barah.
15:19 God opened up the hollow place in Lehi, and **water** came out of it.
1Sa 7: 6 at Mizpah, they drew **water** and poured it out before the LORD.
9:11 they met some girls coming out to draw **water**, and they asked
25:11 Why should I take my bread and **water**, and the meat I have
26:11 Now get the spear and **water** jug that are near his head, and let's
26:12 So David took the spear and **water** jug near Saul's head, and they
26:16 Where are the king's spear and **water** jug that were near his head?"
30:11 him to David. They gave him **water** to drink and food to eat—
30:12 eaten any food or drunk *any* **water** for three days and three nights.
2Sa 5:20 He said, "As **waters** break out, the LORD has broken out against
12:27 "I have fought against Rabbah and taken its **water supply**.
14:14 Like **water** spilled on the ground, which cannot be recovered,
17:20 woman answered them, "They crossed over the **brook** [+4782]."
17:21 They said to him, "Set out and cross the **river** at once; Ahithophel
21:10 From the beginning of the harvest till the **rain** poured down from
22:12 darkness his canopy around him—the dark **rain** clouds of the sky.
22:17 from on high and took hold of me; he drew me out of deep **waters**.
23:15 that someone would get me a drink of **water** from the well near the
23:16 drew **water** from the well near the gate of Bethlehem and carried it
1Ki 13: 8 would not go with you, nor would I eat bread or drink **water** here.
13: 9 'You must not eat bread or drink **water** or return by the way you
13:16 with you, nor can I eat bread or drink **water** with you in this place.
13:17 'You must not eat bread or drink **water** there or return by the way
13:18 he may eat bread and drink **water**.' " (But he was lying to him.)
13:19 of God returned with him and ate and drank **[RPH]** in his house.
13:22 and drank **water** in the place where he told you not to eat or drink.
13:22 **[RPH]** Therefore your body will not be buried in the tomb of
14:15 will strike Israel, so that it will be like a reed swaying in the **water**.
17:10 "Would you bring me a little **water** in a jar so I may have a drink?"
18: 4 fifty in each, and had supplied them with food and **water**.)
18: 5 "Go through the land to all the **springs** [+5078] and valleys.
18:13 in two caves, fifty in each, and supplied them with food and **water**.
18:33 [18:34] "Fill four large jars with **water** and pour it on the offering
18:35 The **water** ran down around the altar and even filled the trench.
18:35 water ran down around the altar and even filled **[RPH]** the trench.
18:38 the stones and the soil, and also licked up the **water** in the trench.
19: 6 head was a cake of bread baked over hot coals, and a jar of **water**.
22:27 and give him nothing but bread and **water** until I return safely.' "
2Ki 2: 8 Elijah took his cloak, rolled it up and struck the **water** with it.
2:14 the cloak that had fallen from him and struck the **water** with it.
2:14 When he struck the **water**, it divided to the right and to the left,
2:19 as you can see, but the **water** is bad and the land is unproductive."
2:21 Then he went out to the **spring** [+4604] and threw the salt into it,
2:21 'I have healed this **water**. Never again will it cause death or make
2:22 the **water** has remained wholesome to this day, according to the
3: 9 the army had no more **water** for themselves or for the animals with
3:11 of Shaphat is here. He used to pour **water** on the hands of Elijah."
3:17 yet this valley will be filled with **water**, and you, your cattle
3:19 will cut down every good tree, stop up all the **springs** [+5078],
3:20 there it was—**water** flowing from the direction of Edom!
3:20 from the direction of Edom! And the land was filled with **water**.
3:22 they got up early in the morning, the sun was shining on the **water**.
3:22 To the Moabites across the way, the **water** looked red—like blood.
3:25 They stopped up all the **springs** [+5078] and cut down every good
5:12 the rivers of Damascus, better than any of the **waters** *of* Israel?
6: 5 them was cutting down a tree, the iron axhead fell into the **water**.
6:22 Set food and **water** before them so that they may eat and drink
8:15 soaked it in **water** and spread it over the king's face, so that he
18:27 [their own filth and drink their own **urine**?" [Q +8079; see K 8875]]
18:31 his own vine and fig tree and drink **water** *from* his own cistern,
19:24 I have dug wells in foreign lands and drunk the **water** there.
20:20 the pool and the tunnel by which he brought **water** into the city,
1Ch 11:17 that someone would get me a drink of **water** from the well near the
11:18 drew **water** from the well near the gate of Bethlehem and carried it
14:11 He said, "As **waters** break out, God has broken out against my
2Ch 18:26 and give him nothing but bread and **water** until I return safely.' "
32: 3 military staff about blocking off the **water** *from* the springs
32: 4 "Why should the kings of Assyria come and find plenty of **water**?"
32:30 It was Hezekiah who blocked the upper outlet of the Gihon **spring**
Ezr 10: 6 While he was there, he ate no food and drank no **water**, because he
Ne 3:26 made repairs up to a point opposite the **Water** Gate toward the east
4:23 [4:17] each had his weapon, even when he went for **water**.
8: 1 people assembled as one man in the square before the **Water** Gate.
8: 3 faced the square before the **Water** Gate in the presence of the men,
8:16 the courts of the house of God and in the square by the **Water** Gate
9:11 their pursuers into the depths, like a stone into mighty **waters**.
9:15 and in their thirst you brought them **water** from the rock;
9:20 manna from their mouths, and you gave them **water** for their thirst.
12:37 passed above the house of David to the **Water** Gate on the east.
13: 2 because they had not met the Israelites with food and **water**
Job 3:24 comes to me instead of food; my groans pour out like **water**.
5:10 He bestows rain on the earth; he sends **water** upon the countryside.
8:11 tall where there is no marsh? Can reeds thrive without **water**?
9:30 [Even if I washed myself **with** [Q +928; see K 1198] soap]
11:16 will surely forget your trouble, recalling it only as **waters** gone by.
12:15 If he holds back the **waters**, there is drought; if he lets them loose,
14: 9 yet at the scent of **water** it will bud and put forth shoots like a
14:11 As **water** disappears from the sea or a riverbed becomes parched
14:19 as **water** wears away stones and torrents wash away the soil,
15:16 less man, who is vile and corrupt, who drinks up evil like **water**!
22: 7 You gave no **water** to the weary and you withheld food from the
22:11 so dark you cannot see, and why a flood of **water** covers you.
24:18 "Yet they are foam on the surface of the **water**; their portion of the
24:19 As heat and drought snatch away the **melted** snow, so the grave
26: 5 in deep anguish, those beneath the **waters** and all that live in them.
26: 8 He wraps up the **waters** in his clouds, yet the clouds do not burst
26:10 He marks out the horizon on the face of the **waters** for a boundary
27:20 Terrors overtake him like a **flood**; a tempest snatches him away in
28:25 he established the force of the wind and measured out the **waters**,
29:19 My roots will reach to the **water**, and the dew will lie all night on
34: 7 What man is like Job, who drinks scorn like **water**?
36:27 "He draws up the drops of **water**, which distill as rain to the
37:10 breath of God produces ice, and the broad **waters** become frozen.
38:30 when the **waters** become hard as stone, when the surface of the
38:34 your voice to the clouds and cover yourself with a flood of **water**?
Ps 1: 3 He is like a tree planted by streams of **water**, which yields its fruit
18:11 [18:12] his canopy around him—the dark **rain** clouds of the sky.
18:15 [18:16] The valleys of the **sea** were exposed and the foundations
18:16 [18:17] and took hold of me; he drew me out of deep **waters**.
22:14 [22:15] I am poured out like **water**, and all my bones are out of
23: 2 me lie down in green pastures, he leads me beside quiet **waters**,
29: 3 The voice of the LORD is over the **waters**; the God of glory
29: 3 of glory thunders, the LORD thunders over the mighty **waters**.
32: 6 surely when the mighty **waters** rise, they will not reach him.
33: 7 He gathers the **waters** *of* the sea into jars; he puts the deep into
42: 1 [42:2] As the deer pants for streams of **water**, so my soul pants
46: 3 [46:4] though its **waters** roar and foam and the mountains quake
58: 7 [58:8] Let them vanish like **water** that flows away; when they
63: 1 [63:2] for you, in a dry and weary land where there is no **water**.
65: 9 [65:10] The streams of God are filled with **water** to provide the
66:12 we went through fire and **water**, but you brought us to a place of
69: 1 [69:2] Save me, O God, for the **waters** have come up to my neck.
69: 2 [69:3] I have come into the deep **waters**; the floods engulf me.
69:14 [69:15] me from those who hate me, from the deep **waters**.
69:15 [69:16] Do not let the **floodwaters** [+8673] engulf me or the
73:10 their people turn to them and drink up **waters** *in* abundance.
74:13 by your power; you broke the heads of the monster in the **waters**.
77:16 [77:17] The **waters** saw you, O God, the waters saw you
77:16 [77:17] waters saw you, O God, the **waters** saw you and writhed;
77:17 [77:18] The clouds poured down **water**, the skies resounded with
77:19 [77:20] led through the sea, your way through the mighty **waters**,
78:13 and led them through; he made the **water** stand firm like a wall.
78:16 streams out of a rocky crag and made **water** flow down like rivers.
78:20 When he struck the rock, **water** gushed out, and streams flowed
79: 3 They have poured out blood like **water** all around Jerusalem,
81: 7 [81:8] of a thundercloud; I tested you at the **waters** *of* Meribah.
88:17 [88:18] All day long they surround me like a **flood**; they have
93: 4 Mightier than the thunder of the great **waters**, mightier than the
104: 3 and lays the beams of his upper chambers on their **waters**.
104: 6 the deep as with a garment; the **waters** stood above the mountains.
105:29 He turned their **waters** into blood, causing their fish to die.
105:41 He opened the rock, and **water** gushed out; like a river it flowed in
106:11 The **waters** covered their adversaries; not one of them survived.
106:32 By the **waters** *of* Meribah they angered the LORD, and trouble
107:23 out on the sea in ships; they were merchants on the mighty **waters**.
107:33 rivers into a desert, **flowing springs** [+4604] into thirsty ground,
107:35 He turned the desert into pools of **water** and the parched ground
107:35 of water and the parched ground into **flowing springs** [+4604];
109:18 it entered into his body like **water**, into his bones like oil.
114: 8 who turned the rock into a **pool** [+106], the hard rock into springs
114: 8 turned the rock into a pool, the hard rock into springs of **water**.
119:136 Streams of **tears** flow from my eyes, for your law is not obeyed.
124: 4 the **flood** would have engulfed us, the torrent would have swept
124: 5 the raging **waters** would have swept us away.
136: 6 who spread out the earth upon the **waters**, *His love endures*
144: 7 deliver me and rescue me from the mighty **waters**, from the hands
147:18 and melts them; he stirs up his breezes, and the **waters** flow.

Ps 148: 4 Praise him, you highest heavens and you **waters** above the skies.
Pr 5: 15 Drink **water** from your own cistern, running water from your own
5: 16 in the streets, your streams of **water** in the public squares?
8: 24 given birth, when there were no springs abounding with **water**;
8: 29 sea its boundary so the **waters** would not overstep his command,
9: 17 "Stolen **water** is sweet; food eaten in secret is delicious!"
17: 14 Starting a quarrel is like breaching a **dam**; so drop the matter
18: 4 The words of a man's mouth are deep **waters**, but the fountain of
20: 5 The purposes of a man's heart are deep **waters**, but a man of
21: 1 he directs it like a **watercourse** [+7104] wherever he pleases.
25: 21 give him food to eat; if he is thirsty, give him **water** to drink.
25: 25 Like cold **water** to a weary soul is good news from a distant land.
27: 19 As **water** reflects a face, so a man's heart reflects the man.
30: 4 Who has wrapped up the **waters** in his cloak? Who has established
30: 16 barren womb, land, which is never satisfied with **water**, and fire,
Ecc 2: 6 I made **reservoirs** [+1391] to water groves of flourishing trees.
11: 1 Cast your bread upon the **waters**, for after many days you will find
SS 4: 15 a well of flowing **water** streaming down from Lebanon.
5: 12 His eyes are like doves by the **water** streams, washed in milk,
8: 7 Many **waters** cannot quench love; rivers cannot wash it away.
Isa 1: 22 silver has become dross, your choice wine is diluted with **water**.
1: 30 will be like an oak with fading leaves, like a garden without **water**.
3: 1 and support: all supplies of food and all supplies of **water**,
8: 6 "Because this people has rejected the gently flowing **waters** *of*
8: 7 bring against them the mighty **floodwaters** [+8041] *of* the River—
11: 9 full of the knowledge of the LORD as the **waters** cover the sea.
12: 3 With joy you will draw **water** from the wells of salvation.
14: 23 "I will turn her into a place for owls and into **swampland** [+106];
15: 6 The **waters** *of* Nimrim are dried up and the grass is withered;
15: 9 Dimon's **waters** are full of blood, but I will bring still more upon
17: 12 uproar of the peoples—they roar like the roaring of great **waters**!
17: 13 Although the peoples roar like the roar of surging **waters**,
18: 2 which sends envoys by sea in papyrus boats over the **water**.
19: 5 The **waters** of the river will dry up, and the riverbed will be
19: 8 into the Nile; those who throw nets on the **water** will pine away.
21: 14 bring **water** for the thirsty; you who live in Tema, bring food for
22: 9 breaches in its defenses; you stored up **water** *in* the Lower Pool.
22: 11 You built a reservoir between the two walls for the **water** *of* the
23: 3 On the great **waters** came the grain of the Shihor; the harvest of
28: 2 like a **driving rain** [+2443] and a flooding downpour,
28: 17 your refuge, the lie, and **water** will overflow your hiding place.
30: 14 for taking coals from a hearth or scooping **water** out of a cistern."
30: 20 Lord gives you the bread of adversity and the **water** *of* affliction,
30: 25 streams of **water** will flow on every high mountain and every lofty
32: 2 like streams of **water** in the desert and the shadow of a great rock
32: 20 sowing your seed by every **stream**, and letting your cattle
33: 16 His bread will be supplied, and **water** will not fail him.
35: 6 **Water** will gush forth in the wilderness and streams in the desert.
35: 7 will become a pool, the thirsty ground **bubbling springs** [+4432].
36: 12 [own filth and drink their own **urine**?" [Q +8079; see K 8875]]
36: 16 his own vine and fig tree and drink **water** *from* his own cistern,
37: 25 I have dug wells in foreign lands and drunk the **water** there.
40: 12 Who has measured the **waters** in the hollow of his hand, or with
41: 17 "The poor and needy search for **water**, but there is none;
41: 18 I will turn the desert into pools of **water**, and the parched ground
41: 18 into pools of water, and the parched ground into **springs** [+4604].
43: 2 When you pass through the **waters**, I will be with you; and when
43: 16 made a way through the sea, a path through the mighty **waters**,
43: 20 because I provide **water** in the desert and streams in the wasteland,
44: 3 For I will pour **water** on the thirsty land, and streams on the dry
44: 4 grass in a meadow, like poplar trees by **flowing streams** [+3298].
44: 12 and loses his strength; he drinks no **water** and grows faint.
48: 1 and come from the <u>line</u> [BHS ***waters***; NIV 5055] *of* Judah,
48: 21 he made **water** flow for them from the rock; he split the rock
48: 21 for them from the rock; he split the rock and **water** gushed out.
49: 10 on them will guide them and lead them beside springs of **water**.
50: 2 rivers into a desert; their fish rot for lack of **water** and die of thirst.
51: 10 Was it not you who dried up the sea, the **waters** *of* the great deep,
54: 9 "To me this is like the <u>days</u> [BHS ***waters***; NIV 3427] of Noah,
54: 9 when I swore that the **waters** *of* Noah would never again cover the
55: 1 "Come, all you who are thirsty, come to the **waters**; and you who
57: 20 tossing sea, which cannot rest, whose **waves** cast up mire and mud.
58: 11 like a **spring** [+4604] whose waters never fail.
58: 11 like a well-watered garden, like a spring whose **waters** never fail.
63: 12 who divided the **waters** before them, to gain for himself
64: 2 [64:1] As when fire sets twigs ablaze and causes **water** to boil,
Jer 2: 13 They have forsaken me, the spring of living **water**, and have dug
2: 13 dug their own cisterns, broken cisterns that cannot hold **water**.
2: 18 Now why go to Egypt to drink **water** *from* the Shihor? And why
2: 18 the Shihor? And why go to Assyria to drink **water** *from* the River?
6: 7 As a well pours out its **water**, so she pours out her wickedness.
8: 14 has doomed us to perish and given us poisoned **water** to drink,
9: 1 [8:23] that my head were a **spring of water** and my eyes a
9: 15 [9:14] make this people eat bitter food and drink poisoned **water**.
9: 18 [9:17] overflow with tears and **water** streams from our eyelids.
10: 13 When he thunders, the **waters** in the heavens roar; he makes
13: 1 and put it around your waist, but do not let it touch **water**."
14: 3 The nobles send their servants for **water**; they go to the cisterns
14: 3 their servants for water; they go to the cisterns but find no **water**.
15: 18 Will you be to me like a deceptive brook, like a **spring** that fails?
17: 8 He will be like a tree planted by the **water** that sends out its roots
17: 13 because they have forsaken the LORD, the spring of living **water**.
18: 14 Do its cool **waters** from distant sources ever cease to flow?
23: 15 "I will make them eat bitter food and drink poisoned **water**,
31: 9 I will lead them beside streams of **water** on a level path where they
38: 6 it had no **water** in it, only mud, and Jeremiah sank down into the
41: 12 They caught up with him near the great **pool** in Gibeon.
46: 7 "Who is this that rises like the Nile, like rivers of surging **waters**?
46: 8 Egypt rises like the Nile, like rivers of surging **waters**. She says,
47: 2 "See how the **waters** are rising in the north; they will become an
48: 34 Eglath Shelishiyah, for even the **waters** *of* Nimrim are dried up.
50: 38 A drought on her **waters**! They will dry up. For it is a land of idols,
51: 13 You who live by many **waters** and are rich in treasures, your end
51: 16 When he thunders, the **waters** in the heavens roar; he makes
51: 55 Waves ⌞of enemies⌟ will rage like great **waters**; the roar of their
La 1: 16 "This is why I weep and my eyes overflow with **tears**. No one is
2: 19 pour out your heart like **water** in the presence of the Lord.
3: 48 Streams of **tears** flow from my eyes because my people are
3: 54 the **waters** closed over my head, and I thought I was about to be
5: 4 We must buy the **water** we drink; our wood can be had only at a
Eze 1: 24 like the roar of rushing **waters**, like the voice of the Almighty,
4: 11 Also measure out a sixth of a hin of **water** and drink it at set times.
4: 16 eat rationed food in anxiety and drink rationed **water** in despair,
4: 17 for food and **water** will be scarce. They will be appalled at the
7: 17 hand will go limp, and every knee will become as weak as **water**.
12: 18 as you eat your food, and shudder in fear as you drink your **water**.
12: 19 They will eat their food in anxiety and drink their **water** in despair,
16: 4 nor were you washed with **water** to make you clean, nor were you
16: 9 " 'I bathed you with **water** and washed the blood from you
17: 5 put it in fertile soil. He planted it like a willow by abundant **water**,
17: 8 It had been planted in good soil by abundant **water** so that it would
19: 10 mother was like a vine in your vineyard planted by the **water**;
19: 10 it was fruitful and full of branches because of abundant **water**.
21: 7 [21:12] become faint and every knee become as weak as **water**.'
24: 3 " 'Put on the cooking pot; put it on and pour **water** into it.
26: 12 fine houses and throw your stones, timber and rubble into the **sea**.
26: 19 I bring the ocean depths over you and its vast **waters** cover you,
27: 26 Your oarsmen take you out to the high **seas**. But the east wind will
27: 34 Now you are shattered by the sea in the depths of the **waters**;
31: 4 The **waters** nourished it, deep springs made it grow tall; their
31: 5 and its branches grew long, spreading because of abundant **waters**.
31: 7 its spreading boughs, for its roots went down to abundant **waters**.
31: 14 Therefore no other trees by the **waters** are ever to tower proudly
31: 14 No other trees *so* **well-watered** [+9272] are ever to reach such a
31: 15 I held back its streams, and its abundant **waters** were restrained.
31: 16 and best of Lebanon, all the trees *that were* **well-watered** [+9272],
32: 2 churning the **water** with your feet and muddying the streams.
32: 13 I will destroy all her cattle from beside abundant **waters** no longer
32: 14 Then I will let her **waters** settle and make her streams flow like oil,
34: 18 Is it not enough for you to drink clear **water**? Must you also
36: 25 I will sprinkle clean **water** on you, and you will be clean;
43: 2 His voice was like the roar of rushing **waters**, and the land was
47: 1 I saw **water** coming out from under the threshold of the temple
47: 1 The **water** was coming down from under the south side of the
47: 2 gate facing east, and the **water** was flowing from the south side.
47: 3 and then led me through **water** that was ankle-deep.
47: 3 and then led me through water **that**[s] was ankle-deep.
47: 4 thousand cubits and led me through **water** that was knee-deep.
47: 4 thousand cubits and led me through water **that**[s] was knee-deep.
47: 4 and led me through **water** that was *up to* the waist.
47: 5 because the **water** had risen and was deep enough to swim in—
47: 5 the water had risen and was **[RPH]** deep enough to swim in—
47: 8 "This **water** flows toward the eastern region and goes down into
47: 8 When it empties into the Sea, the **water** there becomes fresh.
47: 9 because this **water** flows there and makes the salt water fresh;
47: 12 will bear, because the **water** from the sanctuary flows to them.
47: 19 "On the south side it will run from Tamar as far as the **waters** *of*
48: 28 Gad will run south from Tamar to the **waters** *of* Meribah Kadesh,
Da 1: 12 ten days: Give us nothing but vegetables to eat and **water** to drink.
12: 6 to the man clothed in linen, who was above the **waters** *of* the river,
12: 7 who was above the **waters** *of* the river, lifted his right hand
Hos 2: 5 [2:7] who give me my food and my **water**, my wool and my
5: 10 I will pour out my wrath on them like a flood of **water**.
10: 7 its king will float away like a twig on the surface of the **waters**.
Joel 1: 20 the streams of **water** have dried up and fire has devoured the open
3: 18 [4:18] with milk; all the ravines of Judah will run with **water**.
Am 4: 8 People staggered from town to town for **water** but did not get
5: 8 who calls for the **waters** *of* the sea and pours them out over the

Am 5: 24 let justice roll on like a **river**, righteousness like a never-failing
8: 11 not a famine of food or a thirst for **water**, but a famine of hearing
9: 6 who calls for the **waters** *of* the sea and pours them out over the
Jnh 2: 5 [2:6] The engulfing **waters** threatened me, the deep surrounded
3: 7 or flock, taste anything; do not let them eat or **[NIE]** drink.
Mic 1: 4 like wax before the fire, like **water** rushing down a slope.
Na 2: 8 [2:9] Nineveh is like a **pool** [+1391], and its water is draining
2: 8 [2:9] Nineveh is like a pool, and its **water** is draining away.
3: 8 better than Thebes, situated on the Nile, with **water** around her?
3: 8 The river was her defense, the **waters** [BHS 4946] her wall.
3: 14 Draw **water** *for* the siege, strengthen your defenses! Work the
Hab 2: 14 knowledge of the glory of the LORD, as the **waters** cover the sea.
3: 10 Torrents of **water** swept by; the deep roared and lifted its waves on
3: 15 You trampled the sea with your horses, churning the great **waters**.
Zec 9: 11 with you, I will free your prisoners from the **waterless** [+401] pit.
14: 8 On that day living **water** will flow out from Jerusalem, half to the

4785 מִיָּמִין *miyyāmîn*, n.pr.m. [4] [√ 4975]

Mijamin [4]

1Ch 24: 9 the fifth to Malkijah, the sixth to **Mijamin**,
Ezr 10: 25 Izziah, Malkijah, **Mijamin**, Eleazar, Malkijah and Benaiah.
Ne 10: 7 [10:8] Meshullam, Abijah, **Mijamin**,
12: 5 **Mijamin**, Moadiah, Bilgah,

4786 מִין *mîn*, n.[m.]. [31] [→ 9454]

kind [18], kinds [9], *untranslated* [3], various kinds [1]

Ge 1: 11 that bear fruit with seed in it, according to their **various kinds**."
1: 12 plants bearing seed according to their **kinds** and trees bearing fruit
1: 12 and trees bearing fruit with seed in it according to their **kinds**.
1: 21 according to their **kinds**, and every winged bird according to its
1: 21 to their kinds, and every winged bird according to its **kind**.
1: 24 "Let the land produce living creatures according to their **kinds**:
1: 24 along the ground, and wild animals, each according to its **kind**."
1: 25 God made the wild animals according to their **kinds**, the livestock
1: 25 according to their kinds, the livestock according to their **kinds**,
1: 25 the creatures that move along the ground according to their **kinds**.
6: 20 Two of every **kind** *of* bird, of every kind of animal and of every
6: 20 of every **kind** *of* animal and of every kind of creature that moves
6: 20 of every **kind** *of* creature that moves along the ground will come to
7: 14 They had with them every wild animal according to its **kind**,
7: 14 animal according to its kind, all livestock according to their **kinds**,
7: 14 every creature that moves along the ground according to its **kind**
7: 14 ground according to its kind and every bird according to its **kind**,
Lev 11: 14 the red kite, any **kind** *of* black kite,
11: 15 any **kind** *of* raven,
11: 16 the horned owl, the screech owl, the gull, any **kind** *of* hawk,
11: 19 the stork, any **kind** *of* heron, the hoopoe and the bat.
11: 22 Of these you may eat any **kind** *of* locust, katydid, cricket or
11: 22 eat any kind of locust, katydid, cricket **[RPH]** or grasshopper.
11: 22 eat any kind of locust, katydid, cricket **[RPH]** or grasshopper.
11: 22 eat any kind of locust, katydid, cricket or grasshopper. **[RPH]**
11: 29 are unclean for you: the weasel, the rat, any **kind** *of* great lizard,
Dt 14: 13 the red kite, the black kite, any **kind** *of* falcon,
14: 14 any **kind** *of* raven,
14: 15 the horned owl, the screech owl, the gull, any **kind** *of* hawk,
14: 18 the stork, any **kind** *of* heron, the hoopoe and the bat.
Eze 47: 10 The fish will be of many **kinds**—like the fish of the Great Sea.

4787 מֵינֶקֶת *mêneqet*, n.[f.] *or* v.ptcp. [6] [√ 3567]

nurse [4], *untranslated* [1], nursing mothers [1]

Ge 24: 59 along with her **nurse** and Abraham's servant and his men.
35: 8 Rebekah's **nurse**, died and was buried under the oak below Bethel.
Ex 2: 7 get one of the Hebrew women **[RPH]** to nurse the baby for you?"
2Ki 11: 2 put him and his **nurse** in a bedroom to hide him from Athaliah;
2Ch 22: 11 about to be murdered and put him and his **nurse** in a bedroom.
Isa 49: 23 will be your foster fathers, and their queens your **nursing mothers**.

4788 מֵיסָךְ *mêsāk*, n.m. [0] [√ 4590]

2Ki 16: 18 [He took away the Sabbath **canopy** [K; see Q 4590] that had been]

4789 מֵיפַעַת *mêpa'at*, n.pr.loc. [4] [cf. 4602]

Mephaath [4]

Jos 13: 18 Jahaz, Kedemoth, **Mephaath**,
21: 37 Kedemoth and **Mephaath**, together with their pasturelands—
1Ch 6: 79 [6:64] Kedemoth and **Mephaath**, together with their
Jer 48: 21 come to the plateau—to Holon, Jahzah and **Mephaath**, [K 4602]

4790 מִיץ *mîṣ*, n.m. [3] [→ 5160]

churning [1], stirring up [1], twisting [1]

Pr 30: 33 For as **churning** the milk produces butter, and as twisting the nose
30: 33 as **twisting** the nose produces blood, so stirring up anger produces
30: 33 the nose produces blood, so **stirring up** anger produces strife."

4791 מֵישָׁא *mêšā'*, n.pr.m. [1]

Mesha [1]

1Ch 8: 9 By his wife Hodesh he had Jobab, Zibia, **Mesha**, Malcam,

4792 מִישָׁאֵל *mîšā'ēl*, n.pr.m. [7] [√ 4769 + 8611 + 446; Ar 10414]

Mishael [7]

Ex 6: 22 The sons of Uzziel were **Mishael**, Elzaphan and Sithri.
Lev 10: 4 Moses summoned **Mishael** and Elzaphan, sons of Aaron's uncle
Ne 8: 4 **Mishael**, Malkijah, Hashum, Hashbaddanah, Zechariah
Da 1: 6 were some from Judah: Daniel, Hananiah, **Mishael** and Azariah.
1: 7 to Hananiah, Shadrach; to **Mishael**, Meshach; and to Azariah,
1: 11 had appointed over Daniel, Hananiah, **Mishael** and Azariah,
1: 19 he found none equal to Daniel, Hananiah, **Mishael** and Azariah;

4793 מִישׁוֹר *mîšôr*, n.m. [23] [√ 3837]

plateau [9], justice [2], level ground [2], level [2], plains [2], justly [1], plain [1], plateau [+824] [1], smooth [1], straight [1], uprightness [1]

Dt 3: 10 We took all the towns on the **plateau**, and all Gilead, and all
4: 43 Bezer in the desert **plateau** [+824], for the Reubenites; Ramoth in
Jos 13: 9 and included the whole **plateau** *of* Medeba as far as Dibon,
13: 16 in the middle of the gorge, and the whole **plateau** past Medeba
13: 17 to Heshbon and all its towns on the **plateau**, including Dibon,
13: 21 —all the towns on the **plateau** and the entire realm of Sihon king of
20: 8 Bezer in the desert on the **plateau** in the tribe of Reuben,
1Ki 20: 23 if we fight them on the **plains**, surely we will be stronger than they.
20: 25 and chariot for chariot—so we can fight Israel on the **plains**.
2Ch 26: 10 because he had much livestock in the foothills and in the **plain**.
Ps 26: 12 My feet stand on **level ground**; in the great assembly I will praise
27: 11 O LORD; lead me in a **straight** path because of my oppressors.
45: 6 [45:7] a scepter of **justice** will be the scepter of your kingdom.
67: 4 [67:5] for you rule the peoples **justly** and guide the nations of the
143: 10 you are my God; may your good Spirit lead me on **level** ground.
Isa 11: 4 with **justice** he will give decisions for the poor of the earth.
40: 4 the rough ground shall become **level**, the rugged places a plain.
42: 16 darkness into light before them and make the rough places **smooth**.
Jer 21: 13 ⌞Jerusalem,⌟ you who live above this valley on the rocky **plateau**,
48: 8 The valley will be ruined and the **plateau** destroyed,
48: 21 Judgment has come to the **plateau**—to Holon, Jahzah
Zec 4: 7 Before Zerubbabel you will become **level ground**.
Mal 2: 6 He walked with me in peace and **uprightness**, and turned many

4794 מֵישַׁךְ *mêšak*, n.pr.m. [1] [→ Ar 10415]

Meshach [1]

Da 1: 7 to Hananiah, Shadrach; to Mishael, **Meshach**; and to Azariah,

4795 מֵישַׁע *mêša'*, n.pr.m. [1] [√ 3828]

Mesha [1]

2Ki 3: 4 Now **Mesha** king of Moab raised sheep, and he had to supply the

4796 מֵישָׁע *mêšā'*, n.pr.m. [1] [√ 3828]

Mesha [1]

1Ch 2: 42 **Mesha** his firstborn, who was the father of Ziph, and his son

4797 מֵישָׁרִים *mêšārîm*, n.m. [19] [√ 3837]

right [6], equity [3], fair [2], uprightly [2], alliance [1], integrity [1], justice [1], level [1], smoothly [+928] [1], straight [1]

1Ch 29: 17 my God, that you test the heart and are pleased with **integrity**.
Ps 9: 8 [9:9] in righteousness; he will govern the peoples with **justice**.
17: 2 my vindication come from you; may your eyes see *what* is **right**.
58: 1 [58:2] indeed speak justly? Do you judge **uprightly** among men?
75: 2 [75:3] "I choose the appointed time; it is I who judge **uprightly**.
96: 10 it cannot be moved; he will judge the peoples with **equity**.
98: 9 will judge the world in righteousness and the peoples with **equity**.
99: 4 The King is mighty, he loves justice—you have established **equity**;
Pr 1: 3 a disciplined and prudent life, doing what is right and just and **fair**;
2: 9 Then you will understand what is right and just and **fair**—
8: 6 I have worthy things to say; I open my lips to speak *what* is **right**.
23: 16 my inmost being will rejoice when your lips speak *what* is **right**.
23: 31 when it sparkles in the cup, when it goes down **smoothly** [+928]!
SS 1: 4 praise your love more than wine. *How* **right** they are to adore you!
7: 9 [7:10] May the wine go **straight** to my lover, flowing gently over
Isa 26: 7 The path of the righteous is **level**; O upright One, you make the
33: 15 He who walks righteously and speaks *what* is **right**, who rejects
45: 19 me in vain.' I, the LORD, speak the truth; I declare *what* is **right**.

Da 11: 6 of the South will go to the king of the North to make an **alliance**,

4798 מֵיתָר ***mêtār***, n.m. [9] [√ 3857]

ropes [7], cords [1], drawn bow [1]

Ex 35: 18 tent pegs for the tabernacle and for the courtyard, and their **ropes**;
39: 40 the **ropes** and tent pegs for the courtyard; all the furnishings for the
Nu 3: 26 the courtyard surrounding the tabernacle and altar, and the **ropes**—
3: 37 of the surrounding courtyard with their bases, tent pegs and **ropes**.
4: 26 the entrance, the **ropes** and all the equipment used in its service.
4: 32 tent pegs, **ropes**, all their equipment and everything related to their
Ps 21: 12 [21:13] turn their backs when you aim at them with **drawn bow**.
Isa 54: 2 do not hold back; lengthen your **cords**, strengthen your stakes.
Jer 10: 20 My tent is destroyed; all its **ropes** are snapped. My sons are gone

4799 מַכְאֹב ***mak'ōb***, n.m. [16] [√ 3872]

pain [7], suffering [4], sorrows [2], grief [1], pains [1], woes [1]

Ex 3: 7 of their slave drivers, and I am concerned about their **suffering**.
2Ch 6: 29 each one aware of his afflictions and **pains**, and spreading out his
Job 33: 19 Or a man may be chastened on a bed of **pain** with constant distress
Ps 32: 10 Many are the **woes** of the wicked, but the LORD's unfailing love
38: 17 [38:18] For I am about to fall, and my **pain** is ever with me.
69: 26 [69:27] you wound and talk about the **pain** *of* those you hurt.
Ecc 1: 18 wisdom comes much sorrow; the more knowledge, the more **grief**.
2: 23 All his days his work is **pain** and grief; even at night his mind does
Isa 53: 3 He was despised and rejected by men, a man of **sorrows**,
53: 4 Surely he took up our infirmities and carried our **sorrows**,
Jer 30: 15 Why do you cry out over your wound, your **pain** that has no cure?
45: 3 The LORD has added sorrow to my **pain**; I am worn out with
51: 8 Wail over her! Get balm for her **pain**; perhaps she can be healed.
La 1: 12 Is any **suffering** like my suffering that was inflicted on me,
1: 12 Is any suffering like my **suffering** that was inflicted on me,
1: 18 Listen, all you peoples; look upon my **suffering**. My young men

4800 מַכְבֵּנָה ***makbēnâ***, n.pr.loc. [1] [cf. 4801]

Macbenah [1]

1Ch 2: 49 of Madmannah and to Sheva the father of **Macbenah** and Gibea.

4801 מַכְבַּנַּי ***makbannay***, n.pr.m. [1] [cf. 4800]

Macbannai [1]

1Ch 12: 13 [12:14] Jeremiah the tenth and **Macbannai** the eleventh.

4802 מַכְבֵּר ***makbēr***, n.[m.]. [1] [→ 4803]

thick cloth [1]

2Ki 8: 15 the next day he took a **thick cloth**, soaked it in water and spread it

4803 מִכְבָּר ***mikbār***, n.m. [6] [√ 4802]

grating [6]

Ex 27: 4 Make a **grating** for it, a bronze network, and make a bronze ring at
35: 16 the altar of burnt offering with its bronze **grating**, its poles
38: 4 They made a **grating** for the altar, a bronze network, to be under
38: 5 rings to hold the poles for the four corners of the bronze **grating**.
38: 30 the bronze altar with its bronze **grating** and all its utensils,
39: 39 the bronze altar with its bronze **grating**, its poles and all its

4804 מַכָּה ***makkâ***, n.f. [48] [√ 5782]

wounds [9], wound [4], losses [3], struck down [3], *untranslated* [2], blow [2], injury [2], plagues [2], slaughter [2], afflictions [1], attack [1], beatings [1], blows [1], calamities [1], casualties [1], destroyed [+1524+4394+5782] [1], devastated [+1524+4394+5782] [1], disaster [1], disasters [1], flogged [+5782] [1], force [1], ground [1], inflicted [1], plague [1], slaughtered [1], sores [1], struck down [+928+5782] [1], victory [1]

Lev 26: 21 I will multiply your **afflictions** seven times over, as your sins
Nu 11: 33 against the people, and he struck them with a severe **plague**.
Dt 25: 3 If he *is* **flogged** [+5782] more than that, your brother will be
28: 59 the LORD will send fearful **plagues** *on* you and your
28: 59 will send fearful plagues on you and **[RPH]** your descendants,
28: 59 harsh and prolonged **disasters**, and severe and lingering illnesses.
28: 61 kind of sickness and **disaster** not recorded in this Book of the Law,
29: 22 [29:21] lands will see the **calamities** that have fallen on the land
Jos 10: 10 before Israel, who defeated them in a great **victory** at Gibeon.
10: 20 So Joshua and the Israelites **destroyed** [+1524+4394+5782] them
Jdg 11: 33 *He* **devastated** [+1524+4394+5782] twenty towns from Aroer to
15: 8 He attacked them viciously and **slaughtered** many of them.
1Sa 4: 8 who struck the Egyptians with all kinds of **plagues** in the desert.
4: 10 The **slaughter** was very great; Israel lost thirty thousand foot
6: 19 because of the heavy **blow** the LORD had dealt them,
14: 14 In that first **attack** Jonathan and his armor-bearer killed some
14: 30 Would not the **slaughter** of the Philistines have been even
19: 8 He struck them with such **force** that they fled before him.
23: 5 He inflicted heavy **losses** on the Philistines and saved the people of
1Ki 20: 21 the horses and chariots and inflicted heavy **losses** on the Arameans.
22: 35 The blood from his **wound** ran onto the floor of the chariot,
2Ki 8: 29 so King Joram returned to Jezreel to recover from the **wounds** the
9: 15 King Joram had returned to Jezreel to recover from the **wounds** the
2Ch 2: 10 [2:9] twenty thousand cors of **ground** wheat, twenty thousand
13: 17 Abijah and his men inflicted heavy **losses** on them, so that there
22: 6 so he returned to Jezreel to recover from the **wounds** they had
28: 5 hands of the king of Israel, who inflicted heavy **casualties** on him.
Est 9: 5 The Jews **struck down** all their enemies **with** [+928+5782] the
Ps 64: 7 [64:8] them with arrows; suddenly they will be **struck down**.
Pr 20: 30 wounds cleanse away evil, and **beatings** purge the inmost being.
Isa 1: 6 only wounds and welts and open **sores**, not cleansed or bandaged
10: 26 with a whip, as when he **struck down** Midian at the rock of Oreb;
14: 6 which in anger struck down peoples with unceasing **blows**,
27: 7 Has ⌊the LORD⌋ struck her as he **struck down** those who struck
30: 26 up the bruises of his people and heals the wounds he **inflicted**.
Jer 6: 7 resound in her; her sickness and **wounds** are ever before me.
10: 19 My **wound** is incurable! Yet I said to myself, "This is my sickness,
14: 17 my people—has suffered a grievous wound, a crushing **blow**.
15: 18 Why is my pain unending and my **wound** grievous and incurable?
19: 8 pass by will be appalled and will scoff because of all its **wounds**.
30: 12 " 'Your wound is incurable, your **injury** beyond healing.
30: 14 as an enemy would **[RPH]** and punished you as would the cruel,
30: 17 I will restore you to health and heal your **wounds**,' declares the
49: 17 pass by will be appalled and will scoff because of all its **wounds**.
50: 13 Babylon will be horrified and scoff because of all her **wounds**.
Mic 1: 9 For her **wound** is incurable; it has come to Judah. It has reached
Na 3: 19 Nothing can heal your wound; your **injury** is fatal. Everyone who
Zec 13: 6 If someone asks him, 'What are these **wounds** on your body?'

4805 מִכְוָה ***mikwâ***, n.f. [5] [√ 3917]

burn [4], burn [+836] [1]

Lev 13: 24 "When someone has a **burn** [+836] on his skin and a reddish-white
13: 24 a reddish-white or white spot appears in the raw flesh of the **burn**,
13: 25 it is an infectious disease that has broken out in the **burn**.
13: 28 not spread in the skin but has faded, it is a swelling from the **burn**,
13: 28 priest shall pronounce him clean; it is only a scar from the **burn**.

4806 מָכוֹן ***mākôn***, n.m. [17] [√ 3922]

place [11], foundation [2], *untranslated* [1], dwelling place [1], foundations [1], site [1]

Ex 15: 17 the **place**, O LORD, you made for your dwelling, the sanctuary,
1Ki 8: 13 a magnificent temple for you, a **place** for you to dwell forever."
8: 39 then hear from heaven, your dwelling **place**. Forgive and act;
8: 43 hear from heaven, your dwelling **place**, and do whatever the
8: 49 from heaven, your dwelling **place**, hear their prayer and their plea,
2Ch 6: 2 a magnificent temple for you, a **place** for you to dwell forever."
6: 30 hear from heaven, your dwelling **place**. Forgive, and deal with
6: 33 hear from heaven, your dwelling **place**, and do whatever the
6: 39 from heaven, your dwelling **place**, hear their prayer and their pleas,
Ezr 2: 68 offerings toward the rebuilding of the house of God on its **site**.
Ps 33: 14 from his dwelling **place** he watches all who live on earth—
89: 14 [89:15] and justice are the **foundation** *of* your throne;
97: 2 righteousness and justice are the **foundation** *of* his throne.
104: 5 He set the earth on its **foundations**; it can never be moved.
Isa 4: 5 Then the LORD will create over all of **[NIE]** Mount Zion
18: 4 "I will remain quiet and will look on from my **dwelling place**,
Da 8: 11 sacrifice from him, and the **place** *of* his sanctuary was brought low.

4807 מְכוֹנָה ***mᵉkônâ***, n.f. [25] [√ 3922]

movable stands [7], stand [6], stands [6], *untranslated* [4], foundation [1], place [1]

1Ki 7: 27 He also made ten **movable stands** of bronze; each was four cubits
7: 27 each **[RPH]** was four cubits long, four wide and three high.
7: 28 This is how the **stands** were made: They had side panels attached
7: 30 Each **stand** had four bronze wheels with bronze axles, and each
7: 32 the panels, and the axles of the wheels were attached to the **stand**.
7: 34 Each **stand** had four handles, one on each corner, projecting from
7: 34 had four handles, one on each corner, projecting from the **stand**.
7: 35 At the top of the **stand** there was a circular band half a cubit deep.
7: 35 The supports and panels were attached to the top of the **stand**.
7: 37 This is the way he made the ten **stands**. They were all cast in the
7: 38 four cubits across, one basin to go on each of the ten **stands**.
7: 38 cubits across, one basin to go on each of the ten stands. **[RPH]**
7: 39 He placed five of the **stands** on the south side of the temple
7: 43 the ten **stands** with their ten basins;
7: 43 the ten stands with their ten basins; **[RPH]**
2Ki 16: 17 the side panels and removed the basins from the **movable stands**.
25: 13 the **movable stands** and the bronze Sea that were at the temple of

2Ki 25:16 The bronze from the two pillars, the Sea and the **movable stands**,
2Ch 4:14 the **stands** with their basins;
4:14 the stands with their basins; **[RPH]**
Ezr 3:3 they built the altar on its **foundation** and sacrificed burnt offerings
Jer 27:19 the **movable stands** and the other furnishings that are left in this
52:17 the **movable stands** and the bronze Sea that were at the temple of
52:20 and the twelve bronze bulls under it, and the **movable stands**,
Zec 5:11 When it is ready, the basket will be set there in its **place**."

4808 מְכוּרָה *mᵉkûrâ*, n.f. [3] [√ 4125]
ancestry [3]
Eze 16:3 Your **ancestry** and birth were in the land of the Canaanites;
21:30 [21:35] in the land of your **ancestry**, I will judge you.
29:14 and return them to Upper Egypt, the land of their **ancestry**.

4809 מָכִי *mākî*, n.pr.m. [1]
Maki [1]
Nu 13:15 from the tribe of Gad, Geuel son of **Maki**.

4810 מָכִיר *mākîr*, n.pr.m. [22] [→ 4811]
Makir [20], Makir's [1], Makirites [1]
Ge 50:23 Also the children of **Makir** son of Manasseh were placed at birth
Nu 26:29 through **Makir**, the Makirite clan (Makir was the father of Gilead);
26:29 through Makir, the Makirite clan (**Makir** was the father of Gilead);
27:1 the son of Gilead, the son of **Makir**, the son of Manasseh,
32:39 The descendants of **Makir** son of Manasseh went to Gilead,
32:40 So Moses gave Gilead to the **Makirites**, the descendants of
36:1 The family heads of the clan of Gilead son of **Makir**, the son of
Dt 3:15 And I gave Gilead to **Makir**.
Jos 13:31 This was for the descendants of **Makir** son of Manasseh—
13:31 son of Manasseh—for half of the sons of **Makir**, clan by clan.
17:1 as Joseph's firstborn, that is, for **Makir**, Manasseh's firstborn.
17:3 the son of Gilead, the son of **Makir**, the son of Manasseh,
Jdg 5:14 From **Makir** captains came down, from Zebulun those who bear a
2Sa 9:4 "He is at the house of **Makir** son of Ammiel in Lo Debar."
9:5 brought from Lo Debar, from the house of **Makir** son of Ammiel.
17:27 **Makir** son of Ammiel from Lo Debar, and Barzillai the Gileadite
1Ch 2:21 Hezron lay with the daughter of **Makir** the father of Gilead (he had
2:23 All these were descendants of **Makir** the father of Gilead.
7:14 Aramean concubine. She gave birth to **Makir** the father of Gilead.
7:15 **Makir** took a wife from among the Huppites and Shuppites.
7:16 **Makir's** wife Maacah gave birth to a son and named him Peresh.
7:17 These were the sons of Gilead son of **Makir**, the son of Manasseh.

4811 מָכִירִי *mākîrî*, a.g. [1] [√ 4810]
Makirite [1]
Nu 26:29 through Makir, the **Makirite** clan (Makir was the father of Gilead);

4812 מָכַךְ *mākak*, v. [3] [cf. 4575]
are brought low [1], sag [1], wasted away [1]
Job 24:24 [H] *they* **are brought low** and gathered up like all others;
Ps 106:43 [A] were bent on rebellion and *they* **wasted away** in their sin.
Ecc 10:18 [C] If a man is lazy, the rafters **sag**; if his hands are idle,

4813 מִכְלָא *miklā'*, n.[m.]. [3] [√ 3973]
pens [2], pen [1]
Ps 50:9 I have no need of a bull from your stall or of goats from your **pens**,
78:70 He chose David his servant and took him from the sheep **pens**;
Hab 3:17 though there are no sheep in the **pen** and no cattle in the stalls,

4814 מִכְלוֹל *miklôl*, n.m. [2] [√ 4005]
full [1], fully [1]
Eze 23:12 governors and commanders, warriors in **full** dress,
38:4 your horses, your horsemen **fully** armed, and a great horde with

4815 מַכְלוּל *maklûl*, n.m. [1] [√ 4005]
beautiful garments [1]
Eze 27:24 In your marketplace they traded with you **beautiful garments**,

4816 מִכְלוֹת *miklôt*, n.[f.]. [1] [√ 3983]
solid [1]
2Ch 4:21 the gold floral work and lamps and tongs (they were **solid** gold);

4817 מִכְלָל *miklāl*, n.m. [1] [√ 4005]
perfect [1]
Ps 50:2 From Zion, **perfect** *in* beauty, God shines forth.

4818 מַכֹּלֶת *makkōlet*, n.f. [1] [√ 430]
food [1]
1Ki 5:11 [5:25] twenty thousand cors of wheat as **food** for his household,

4819 מִכְמָן *mikmān*, n.[m.]. [1]
treasures [1]
Da 11:43 He will gain control of the **treasures** *of* gold and silver and all the

4820 מִכְמָס *mikmās*, n.pr.loc. [2] [→ 4825; cf. 4022]
Micmash [2]
Ezr 2:27 of **Micmash** 122
Ne 7:31 of **Micmash** 122

4821 מִכְמָר *mikmār*, n.[m.]. [2] [→ 4822, 4823, 4824]
net [1], nets [1]
Ps 141:10 Let the wicked fall into their own **nets**, while I pass by in safety.
Isa 51:20 they lie at the head of every street, like antelope caught in a **net**.

4822 מַכְמֹר *makmōr*, n.[m.]. Not used in NIV/BHS [√ 4821]

4823 מִכְמֶרֶת *mikmeret*, n.f. [3] [→ 4824; cf. 4821]
dragnet [2], nets [1]
Isa 19:8 into the Nile; those who throw **nets** on the water will pine away.
Hab 1:15 he catches them in his net, he gathers them up in his **dragnet**;
1:16 Therefore he sacrifices to his net and burns incense to his **dragnet**,

4824 מִכְמֹרֶת *mikmōret*, n.f. Not used in NIV/BHS [√ 4823; cf. 4821]

4825 מִכְמָשׂ *mikmāś*, n.pr.loc. [9] [√ 4820; cf. 4022]
Micmash [9]
1Sa 13:2 two thousand were with him at **Micmash** and in the hill country of
13:5 They went up and camped at **Micmash**, east of Beth Aven.
13:11 the set time, and that the Philistines were assembling at **Micmash**,
13:16 in Gibeah in Benjamin, while the Philistines camped at **Micmash**.
13:23 a detachment of Philistines had gone out to the pass at **Micmash**.
14:5 One cliff stood to the north toward **Micmash**, the other to the south
14:31 after the Israelites had struck down the Philistines from **Micmash**
Ne 11:31 The descendants of the Benjamites from Geba lived in **Micmash**,
Isa 10:28 they pass through Migron; they store supplies at **Micmash**.

4826 מִכְמְתָת *mikmᵉtāt*, n.pr.loc. [2]
Micmethath [2]
Jos 16:6 From **Micmethath** on the north it curved eastward to Taanath
17:7 The territory of Manasseh extended from Asher to **Micmethath**

4827 מַכְנַדְבַי *maknadbay*, n.pr.m. [1]
Macnadebai [1]
Ezr 10:40 **Macnadebai**, Shashai, Sharai,

4828 מְכֹנָה *mᵉkōnâ*, n.pr.loc. [1] [√ 3922]
Meconah [1]
Ne 11:28 in Ziklag, in **Meconah** and its settlements,

4829 מִכְנָס *miknās*, n.m. [5] [√ 4043]
undergarments [4], undergarments [+965] [1]
Ex 28:42 "Make linen **undergarments** as a covering for the body, reaching
39:28 and the **undergarments** [+965] of finely twisted linen.
Lev 6:10 [6:3] linen clothes, with linen **undergarments** next to his body,
16:4 the sacred linen tunic, with linen **undergarments** next to his body;
Eze 44:18 on their heads and linen **undergarments** around their waists.

4830 מֶכֶס *mekes*, n.m. [6] [√ 4082]
tribute [6]
Nu 31:28 set apart as **tribute** for the LORD one out of every five hundred,
31:37 of which the **tribute** for the LORD was 675;
31:38 36,000 cattle, of which the **tribute** for the LORD was 72;
31:39 30,500 donkeys, of which the **tribute** for the LORD was 61;
31:40 16,000 people, of which the **tribute** for the LORD was 32.
31:41 Moses gave the **tribute** to Eleazar the priest as the LORD's part,

4831 מִכְסָה *miksâ*, n.f. [2] [√ 4082]
number [1], value [+6886] [1]
Ex 12:4 having taken into account the **number** *of* people there are.

Lev 27:23 the priest will determine its **value** [+6886] up to the Year of

4832 מִכְסֶה **mikseh**, n.[m.]. [16] [√ 4059]

covering [12], cover [+906+4059] [3], coverings [1]

Ge 8:13 Noah then removed the **covering** *from* the ark and saw that the
Ex 26:14 Make for the tent a **covering** *of* ram skins dyed red, and over that a
26:14 ram skins dyed red, and over that a **covering** *of* hides of sea cows.
35:11 the tabernacle with its tent and its **covering**, clasps, frames,
36:19 Then they made for the tent a **covering** *of* ram skins dyed red,
36:19 ram skins dyed red, and over that a **covering** *of* hides of sea cows.
39:34 the **covering** *of* ram skins dyed red, the covering of hides of sea
39:34 the **covering** *of* hides of sea cows and the shielding curtain;
40:19 the tent over the tabernacle and put the **covering** over the tent,
Nu 3:25 responsible for the care of the tabernacle and tent, its **coverings**,
4:8 **cover** [+906+4059] that with hides of sea cows and put its poles in
4:10 to wrap it and all its accessories in a **covering** *of* hides of sea cows
4:11 **cover** [+906+4059] that with hides of sea cows and put its poles in
4:12 **cover** [+906+4059] that with hides of sea cows and put them on a
4:25 its **covering** and the outer covering of hides of sea cows,
4:25 its covering and the outer **covering** *of* hides of sea cows,

4833 מְכַסֶּה **mᵉkasseh**, n.m. [4] [√ 4059]

awnings [1], clothes [1], cover [1], layer of fat [1]

Lev 9:19 the fat tail, the **layer of fat**, the kidneys and the covering of the
Isa 14:11 maggots are spread out beneath you and worms **cover** you.
23:18 who live before the LORD, for abundant food and fine **clothes**.
Eze 27:7 your **awnings** were of blue and purple from the coasts of Elishah.

4834 מַכְפֵּלָה **makpēlâ**, n.pr.loc. [6] [√ 4100]

Machpelah [6]

Ge 23:9 so he will sell me the cave of **Machpelah**, which belongs to him
23:17 So Ephron's field in **Machpelah** near Mamre—both the field
23:19 cave in the field of **Machpelah** near Mamre (which is at Hebron)
25:9 and Ishmael buried him in the cave of **Machpelah** near Mamre,
49:30 the cave in the field of **Machpelah**, near Mamre in Canaan,
50:13 of Canaan and buried him in the cave in the field of **Machpelah**,

4835 מָכַר **mākar**, v. [80] [→ 4836, 4837?, 4928, 4929]

sold [19], sell [17], selling [7], sells [7], be sold [5], sold himself [4], seller [3], sells himself [3], been sold [2], must sell [+928+2021+4084+4835] [2], were sold [2], be sold back [1], enslaved [1], hand over [+906+928+3338] [1], must be sold [+4929] [1], offer yourselves for sale [1], sell land [+4928] [1], sellers [1], sold themselves [1], sold yourself [1]

Ge 25:31 [A] Jacob replied, "First **sell** me your birthright."
25:33 [A] So he swore an oath to him, **selling** his birthright to Jacob.
31:15 [A] Not only *has he* **sold** us, but he has used up what was paid
37:27 [A] *let's* **sell** him to the Ishmaelites and not lay our hands on
37:28 [A] and **sold** him for twenty shekels of silver to the Ishmaelites,
37:36 [A] Meanwhile, the Midianites **sold** Joseph in Egypt to Potiphar,
45:4 [A] "I am your brother Joseph, the one *you* **sold** into Egypt!
45:5 [A] and do not be angry with yourselves for **selling** me here,
47:20 [A] The Egyptians, one and all, **sold** their fields,
47:22 [A] Pharaoh gave them. That is why *they did* not **sell** their land.
Ex 21:7 [A] "If a man **sells** his daughter as a servant, she is not to go free
21:8 [A] He has no right to **sell** her to foreigners, because he has
21:16 [A] "Anyone who kidnaps another and either **sells** him or still has
21:35 [A] *they are to* **sell** the live one and divide both the money
22:1 [21:37] [A] steals an ox or a sheep and slaughters it or **sells** it,
22:3 [22:2] [C] he has nothing, *he must* **be sold** to pay for his theft.
Lev 25:14 [A] " 'If *you* **sell** [+4928] **land** to one of your countrymen or buy
25:15 [A] *he is to* **sell** to you on the basis of the number of years left for
25:16 [A] because what he *is* really **selling** you is the number of crops.
25:23 [C] " 'The land *must* not **be sold** permanently, because the land
25:25 [A] countrymen becomes poor and **sells** some of his property,
25:27 [A] sold it and refund the balance to the man to whom *he* **sold** it;
25:29 [A] " 'If a man **sells** a house in a walled city, he retains the right
25:34 [C] the pastureland belonging to their towns *must* not **be sold**;
25:39 [C] becomes poor among you and **sells himself** to you,
25:42 [C] out of Egypt, *they* **must** not **be sold** [+4929] as slaves.
25:47 [C] **sells himself** to the alien living among you or to a member of
25:48 [C] he retains the right of redemption after *he has* **sold himself**.
25:50 [C] his buyer are to count the time from the year he **sold himself**
27:20 [A] or if *he has* **sold** it to someone else, it can never be
27:27 [C] to it. If he does not redeem it, *it is to* **be sold** at its set value.
27:28 [C] *may* **be sold** or redeemed; everything so devoted is most
Dt 14:21 [A] and he may eat it, or you *may* **sell** it to a foreigner.
15:12 [C] or a woman, **sells himself** to you and serves you six years,
21:14 [A] *You* **must** not **sell** [+928+2021+4084+4835] her or treat her as
21:14 [A] *You* **must** not **sell** [+928+2021+4084+4835] her or treat her as
24:7 [A] of his brother Israelites and treats him as a slave or **sells** him,
28:68 [F] There *you will* **offer yourselves for sale** to your enemies as
32:30 [A] put ten thousand to flight, unless their Rock *had* **sold** them,
Jdg 2:14 [A] *He* **sold** them to their enemies all around, whom they were
3:8 [A] so that *he* **sold** them into the hands of Cushan-Rishathaim
4:2 [A] So the LORD **sold** them into the hands of Jabin, a king of
4:9 [A] for the LORD *will* **hand** Sisera **over to** [+906+928+3338] a
10:7 [A] *He* **sold** them into the hands of the Philistines and the
Ru 4:3 [A] *is* **selling** the piece of land that belonged to our brother
1Sa 12:9 [A] so *he* **sold** them into the hand of Sisera, the commander of
1Ki 21:20 [F] "because you *have* **sold yourself** to do evil in the eyes of the
21:25 [F] who **sold himself** to do evil in the eyes of the LORD, urged
2Ki 4:7 [A] man of God, and he said, "Go, **sell** the oil and pay your debts.
17:17 [F] and **sold themselves** to do evil in the eyes of the LORD,
Ne 5:8 [C] we have bought back our Jewish brothers who **were sold** to
5:8 [A] Now you *are* **selling** your brothers, only for them to be sold
5:8 [C] selling your brothers, only for *them to* **be sold back** to us!"
10:31 [10:32] [A] bring merchandise or grain to **sell** on the Sabbath,
13:15 [A] Therefore I warned them against **selling** food on that day.
13:16 [A] **selling** them in Jerusalem on the Sabbath to the people of
13:20 [A] **sellers** *of* all kinds of goods spent the night outside
Est 7:4 [C] For I and my people *have* **been sold** for destruction
7:4 [C] If *we had* merely **been sold** as male and female slaves, I
Ps 44:12 [44:13] [A] *You* **sold** your people for a pittance, gaining
105:17 [C] and he sent a man before them—Joseph, **sold** as a slave.
Pr 23:23 [A] Buy the truth and *do* not **sell** it; get wisdom, discipline
31:24 [A] She makes linen garments and **sells** them, and supplies the
Isa 24:2 [A] for servant, for mistress as for maid, for **seller** as for buyer,
50:1 [A] Or to which of my creditors *did I* **sell** you? Because of your
50:1 [C] Because of your sins *you* **were sold**; because of your
52:3 [C] "*You were* **sold** for nothing, and without money you will be
Jer 34:14 [C] must free any fellow Hebrew who *has* **sold himself** to you.
Eze 7:12 [A] Let not the buyer rejoice nor the **seller** grieve, for wrath is
7:13 [A] The **seller** will not recover the land he has sold as long as
30:12 [A] dry up the streams of the Nile and **sell** the land to evil men;
48:14 [A] *They must* not **sell** or exchange any of it. This is the best of
Joel 3:3 [4:3] [A] *they* **sold** girls for wine that they might drink.
3:6 [4:6] [A] *You* **sold** the people of Judah and Jerusalem to the
3:7 [4:7] [A] rouse them out of the places to which *you* **sold** them,
3:8 [4:8] [A] *I will* **sell** your sons and daughters to the people of
3:8 [4:8] [A] *they will* **sell** them to the Sabeans, a nation far away."
Am 2:6 [A] They **sell** the righteous for silver, and the needy for a pair of
Na 3:4 [A] who **enslaved** nations by her prostitution and peoples by her
Zec 11:5 [A] *Those who* **sell** them say, 'Praise the LORD, I am rich!'

4836 מֶכֶר **meker**, n.m. [3] [√ 4835]

merchandise [1], pay [+5989] [1], worth [1]

Nu 20:19 our livestock drink any of your water, *we will* **pay** [+5989] *for* it.
Ne 13:16 in Jerusalem were bringing in fish and all kinds of **merchandise**
Pr 31:10 noble character who can find? She is **worth** far more than rubies.

4837 מַכָּר **makkār**, n.m. [2] [√ 4835?]

treasurers [2]

2Ki 12:5 [12:6] every priest receive the money from one of the **treasurers**,
12:7 [12:8] Take no more money from your **treasurers**, but hand it

4838 מִכְרֶה **mikreh**, n.m. [1] [√ 4125]

pits [1]

Zep 2:9 a place of weeds and salt **pits**, a wasteland forever.

4839 מְכֵרָה **mᵉkērâ**, n.[f.]. [1] [cf. 3928]

swords [1]

Ge 49:5 and Levi are brothers—their **swords** are weapons of violence.

4840 מִכְרִי **mikrî**, n.pr.m. [1]

Micri [1]

1Ch 9:8 Ibneiah son of Jeroham; Elah son of Uzzi, the son of **Micri**;

4841 מְכֵרָתִי **mᵉkērātî**, a.g. [1]

Mekerathite [1]

1Ch 11:36 Hepher the **Mekerathite**, Ahijah the Pelonite,

4842 מִכְשׁוֹל **mikšôl**, n.m. [14] [√ 4173]

stumbling block [4], obstacles [2], downfall [1], fallen [1], made fall [+2118+4200+4200] [1], make stumble [1], makes fall [1], staggering burden [+2256+7050] [1], stumble [1], stumbling blocks [1]

Lev 19:14 not curse the deaf or put a **stumbling block** in front of the blind,
1Sa 25:31 the **staggering burden** [+2256+7050] of needless bloodshed
Ps 119:165 they who love your law, and nothing can **make** them **stumble**.
Isa 8:14 stone that causes men to stumble and a rock that **makes** them **fall**.

Isa 57:14 the road! Remove the **obstacles** out of the way of my people."
Jer 6:21 "I will put **obstacles** before this people. Fathers and sons alike will
Eze 3:20 and does evil, and I put a **stumbling block** before him, he will die.
7:19 fill their stomachs with it, for it has made them **stumble** *into* sin.
14: 3 in their hearts and put wicked **stumbling blocks** before their faces.
14: 4 puts a wicked **stumbling block** before his face and then goes to a
14: 7 in his heart and puts a wicked **stumbling block** before his face and
18:30 away from all your offenses; then sin will not be your **downfall**.
21:15 [21:20] So that hearts may melt and the **fallen** be many, I have
44:12 and **made** the house of Israel **fall** [+2118+4200+4200] *into* sin,

4843 מַכְשֵׁלָה makšēlâ, n.f. [2] [√ 4173]

heap of ruins [1], heaps of rubble [1]

Isa 3: 6 have a cloak, you be our leader; take charge of this **heap of ruins**!"
Zep 1: 3 The wicked will have only **heaps of rubble** when I cut off man

4844 מִכְתָּב miktāb, n.m. [9] [√ 4180]

writing [5], *untranslated* [1], inscription [+7334] [1], letter [1], written [1]

Ex 32:16 the **writing** was the writing of God, engraved on the tablets.
32:16 the writing was the **writing** *of* God, engraved on the tablets.
39:30 and engraved on it, like an **inscription on** [+7334] a seal:
Dt 10: 4 The LORD wrote on these tablets what he had **written** before,
2Ch 21:12 Jehoram received a **letter** from Elijah the prophet, which said:
35: 4 written by David king of Israel and **[RPH]** by his son Solomon.
36:22 make a proclamation throughout his realm and to put it in **writing**:
Ezr 1: 1 make a proclamation throughout his realm and to put it in **writing**:
Isa 38: 9 A **writing** of Hezekiah king of Judah after his illness and recovery:

4845 מְכִתָּה mᵉkittâ, n.f. [1] [√ 4198]

pieces [1]

Isa 30:14 so mercilessly that among its **pieces** not a fragment will be found

4846 מִכְתָּם miktām, n.[m.]. [6] [√ 4188?]

miktam [6]

Ps 16: T [16:1] A *miktam* of David.
56: T [56:1] of, "A Dove on Distant Oaks." Of David. A *miktam*.
57: T [57:1] the tune of, "Do Not Destroy." Of David. A *miktam*.
58: T [58:1] the tune of, "Do Not Destroy." Of David. A *miktam*.
59: T [59:1] the tune of, "Do Not Destroy." Of David. A *miktam*.
60: T [60:1] A *miktam* of David. For teaching. When he fought

4847 מַכְתֵּשׁ maktēš, n.m. [3] [√ 4197]

hollow place [1], market district [1], mortar [1]

Jdg 15:19 God opened up the **hollow place** in Lehi, and water came out of it.
Pr 27:22 Though you grind a fool in a **mortar**, grinding him like grain with
Zep 1:11 Wail, you who live in the **market district**; all your merchants will

4848 מָלֵא¹ mālēʾ¹, v. [250] [→ 3550, 3551, 4849, 4850, 4851, 4852, 4853, 4854, 4859, 4864; cf. 4862; Ar 10416; *also used with compound proper names*]

filled [45], fill [38], full [33], be filled [10], over [8], wholeheartedly [7], completed [5], covered [5], fulfilled [5], was filled [4], filling [3], fills [3], ordained [+906+3338] [3], satisfy [3], set [3], *untranslated* [2], installed [+906+3338] [2], laden with [2], ordain [+3338] [2], ordination [+906+3338] [2], passed [2], aloud [1], are filled [1], at flood stage [+1536+3972+6584] [1], bathed in [1], be paid in full [1], bear [1], before elapsed [+4202] [1], came [1], come to an end [1], come [1], confirm [1], consecrate himself [+2257+3338] [1], consecrate himself [+3338] [1], consecrated [+906+3338] [1], cover [+7156] [1], cover [1], crowded [1], dared [+4213] [1], dedicate [+3338] [1], dedicated [+3338] [1], did completely [1], drenched [1], drew [+928+3338] [1], enraged [+2779] [1], enriched [1], finish [1], finished [1], fulfilling [1], fulfillment [1], give full [1], given [1], gorge [1], grant [1], have fill [1], heaping up [1], highly [1], is satisfied [1], last [1], live out [1], make succeed [1], making full [1], midst [1], mount [+4853] [1], mounted [1], numbered [1], ordain [+906+3338] [1], ordained [+3338] [1], overflowing [1], presented the full number [1], prosper [1], provide [1], racked with [1], set apart [+3338] [1], shown [1], still hunger [+1061] [1], take up [1], taking full [1], took a handful [+4090] [1], unite [1], uses [1], violent [+2805] [1], well nourished [+2692] [1], were filled [1]

Ge 1:22 [A] and increase in number and **fill** the water in the seas,
1:28 [A] and increase in number; **fill** the earth and subdue it.
6:11 [C] the earth was corrupt in God's sight and *was* **full** *of* violence.
6:13 [A] for the earth *is* **filled** *with* violence because of them.
9: 1 [A] "Be fruitful and increase in number and **fill** the earth.
21:19 [D] So she went and **filled** the skin *with* water and gave the boy a
24:16 [D] went down to the spring, **filled** her jar and came up again.
25:24 [A] When the time **came** for her to give birth, there were twin
26:15 [D] the Philistines stopped up, **filling** them *with* earth.
29:21 [A] my wife. My time *is* **completed**, and I want to lie with her."
29:27 [D] **Finish** this daughter's bridal week; then we will give you the
29:28 [D] *He* **finished** the week with Leah, and then Laban gave him
42:25 [D] Joseph gave orders *to* **fill** their bags *with* grain, to put each
44: 1 [D] "**Fill** the men's sacks *with* as much food as they can carry,
50: 3 [A] **taking** a **full** forty days, for that was the time required for
50: 3 [A] for that was **[RPH]** the time required for embalming.
Ex 1: 7 [C] exceedingly numerous, so that the land **was filled** *with* them.
2:16 [D] draw water and **fill** the troughs to water their father's flock.
7:25 [C] Seven days **passed** after the LORD struck the Nile.
8:21 [8:17] [A] The houses of the Egyptians *will be* **full** *of* flies,
10: 6 [A] *They will* **fill** your houses and those of all your officials
15: 9 [A] I will divide the spoils; *I will* **gorge** myself *on* them.
23:26 [D] or be barren in your land. *I will* **give** you *a* **full** life span.
28: 3 [D] Tell all the skilled men *to* whom *I have* **given** wisdom in
28:17 [D] **mount** [+4853] four rows of precious stones on it. In the first
28:41 [D] and his sons, anoint and **ordain** [+906+3338] them.
29: 9 [D] In this way *you shall* **ordain** [+3338] Aaron and his sons.
29:29 [D] they can be anointed and **ordained** [+906+3338] in them.
29:33 [D] atonement was made for their **ordination** [+906+3338] and
29:35 [D] commanded you, taking seven days *to* **ordain** [+3338] them.
31: 3 [D] *I have* **filled** him *with* the Spirit of God, with skill, ability
31: 5 [D] to cut and **set** stones, to work in wood, and to engage in all
32:29 [A] "You *have been* **set apart** [+3338] to the LORD today,
35:31 [D] *he has* **filled** him *with* the Spirit of God, with skill, ability
35:33 [D] to cut and **set** stones, to work in wood and to engage in all
35:35 [D] *He has* **filled** them *with* skill to do all kinds of work as
39:10 [D] *they* **mounted** four rows of precious stones on it. In the first
40:34 [A] and the glory of the LORD **filled** the tabernacle.
40:35 [A] upon it, and the glory of the LORD **filled** the tabernacle.
Lev 8:33 [A] until the days of your ordination *are* **completed**, for your
8:33 [D] for your **ordination** [+906+3338] will last seven days.
9:17 [D] He also brought the grain offering, **took a handful** [+4090]
12: 4 [A] to the sanctuary until the days of her purification *are* **over**.
12: 6 [A] the days of her purification for a son or daughter *are* **over**,
16:32 [D] **ordained** [+906+3338] to succeed his father as high priest is
19:29 [A] land will turn to prostitution and *be* **filled** *with* wickedness.
21:10 [D] *who has been* **ordained** [+906+3338] to wear the priestly
25:30 [A] If it is not redeemed before a full year *has* **passed**, the house
Nu 3: 3 [D] who *were* **ordained** [+3338] to serve as priests.
6: 5 [A] holy until the period of his separation to the LORD *is* **over**;
6:13 [A] law for the Nazirite when the period of his separation *is* **over**.
14:21 [C] and as surely as the glory of the LORD **fills** the whole earth,
14:24 [D] Caleb has a different spirit and follows me **wholeheartedly**,
32:11 [D] 'Because *they have* not followed me **wholeheartedly**,
32:12 [D] son of Nun, for *they* followed the LORD **wholeheartedly**.'
Dt 1:36 [D] feet on, because *he* followed the LORD **wholeheartedly**."
6:11 [D] filled with all kinds of good things *you did* not **provide**,
34: 9 [A] Now Joshua son of Nun *was* **filled** *with* the spirit of wisdom
Jos 3:15 [A] Now the Jordan *is* **at flood** [+1536+3972+6584] **stage** all
9:13 [D] these wineskins that *we* **filled** were new, but see how cracked
14: 8 [D] however, followed the LORD my God **wholeheartedly**.
14: 9 [D] *you have* followed the LORD my God **wholeheartedly**.'
14:14 [D] he followed the LORD, the God of Israel, **wholeheartedly**.
Jdg 16:27 [A] Now the temple *was* **crowded** *with* men and women; all the
17: 5 [D] and **installed** [+906+3338] one of his sons as his priest.
17:12 [D] Micah **installed** [+906+3338] the Levite, and the young man
1Sa 16: 1 [D] **Fill** your horn *with* oil and be on your way; I am sending you
18:26 [A] So **before** the allotted time **elapsed** [+4202],
18:27 [D] their foreskins and **presented the full number** to the king
2Sa 7:12 [A] When your days *are* **over** and you rest with your fathers, I
23: 7 [C] Whoever touches thorns **uses** a tool of iron or the shaft of a
1Ki 1:14 [D] to the king, I will come in and **confirm** what you have said."
2:27 [D] **fulfilling** the word the LORD had spoken at Shiloh about
7:14 [C] Huram *was* **highly** skilled and experienced in all kinds of
8:10 [A] the Holy Place, the cloud **filled** the temple of the LORD.
8:11 [A] of the cloud, for the glory of the LORD **filled** his temple.
8:15 [D] *who* with his own hand *has* **fulfilled** what he promised with
8:24 [D] have promised and with your hand *you have* **fulfilled** it—
11: 6 [D] *he* **did** not follow the LORD **completely**, as David his
13:33 [D] a priest *he* **consecrated** [+906+3338] for the high places.
18:33 [18:34] [D] "**Fill** four large jars *with* water and pour it on the
18:35 [D] water ran down around the altar and even **filled** the trench.
20:27 [D] flocks of goats, while the Arameans **covered** the countryside.
2Ki 3:17 [C] yet this valley *will* **be filled** *with* water, and you, your cattle
3:20 [C] the direction of Edom! And the land **was filled** *with* water.
3:25 [D] man threw a stone on every good field until it *was* **covered**.
4: 6 [A] When all the jars *were* **full**, she said to her son, "Bring me
6:17 [A] he looked and saw the hills **full** *of* horses and chariots of fire
9:24 [D] Jehu **drew** [+928+3338] his bow and shot Joram between the
10:21 [C] They crowded into the temple of Baal until it *was* **full** from
21:16 [D] so much innocent blood that *he* **filled** Jerusalem from end to

2Ki 23: 14 [D] the Asherah poles and **covered** the sites *with* human bones.
24: 4 [D] For *he had* **filled** Jerusalem *with* innocent blood,
1Ch 12: 15 [12:16] [D] first month when it *was* **overflowing** all its banks,
17: 11 [A] When your days *are* **over** and you go to be with your fathers,
29: 5 [D] to **consecrate** [+2257+3338] **himself** today to the LORD?"
2Ch 5: 13 [A] Then the temple of the LORD *was* **filled** *with* a cloud,
5: 14 [A] for the glory of the LORD **filled** the temple of God.
6: 4 [D] *who* with his hands *has* **fulfilled** what he promised with his
6: 15 [D] have promised and with your hand *you have* **fulfilled** it—
7: 1 [A] the sacrifices, and the glory of the LORD **filled** the temple.
7: 2 [A] of the LORD because the glory of the LORD **filled** it.
13: 9 [D] Whoever comes to **consecrate** [+3338] **himself** with a young
16: 14 [D] They laid him on a bier **covered** *with* spices and various
29: 31 [D] "*You have* now **dedicated** [+3338] yourselves to the
36: 21 [D] until the seventy years *were* **completed** in fulfillment of the
36: 21 [D] until the seventy years were completed *in* **fulfillment** *of* the
Ezr 9: 11 [D] By their detestable practices *they have* **filled** it with their
Est 1: 5 [A] When these days *were* **over**, the king gave a banquet,
2: 12 [A] she had to complete twelve months **[NIE]** of beauty
3: 5 [C] not kneel down or pay him honor, he *was* **enraged** [+2779].
5: 9 [C] in his presence, he **was filled** *with* rage against Mordecai.
7: 5 [A] Where is the man who *has* **dared** [+4213] to do such a
Job 3: 15 [D] with rulers who had gold, who **filled** their houses *with* silver.
8: 21 [D] *He will* yet **fill** your mouth *with* laughter and your lips with
15: 2 [D] with empty notions or **fill** his belly *with* the hot east wind?
15: 32 [C] Before his time *he will* **be paid in full**, and his branches will
16: 10 [F] they strike my cheek in scorn and **unite** together against me.
20: 11 [A] The youthful vigor *that* **fills** his bones will lie with him in
20: 22 [A] In the **midst** *of* his plenty, distress will overtake him; the full
20: 23 [D] When he has **filled** his belly, God will vent his burning anger
21: 24 [A] his body **well nourished** [+2692], his bones rich with
22: 18 [D] Yet it was he *who* **filled** their houses *with* good things, so I
23: 4 [D] state my case before him and **fill** my mouth *with* arguments.
32: 18 [A] For *I am* **full** *of* words, and the spirit within me compels me;
36: 16 [A] to the comfort of your table **laden with** choice food.
36: 17 [A] But now *you are* **laden with** the judgment due the wicked;
38: 39 [D] the prey for the lioness and **satisfy** the hunger of the lions
39: 2 [D] Do you count the months till *they* **bear**? Do you know the
41: 7 [40:31] [D] *Can you* **fill** his hide with harpoons or his head with
Ps 10: 7 [A] His mouth *is* **full** *of* curses and lies and threats; trouble
17: 14 [D] *You* **still** [+1061] *the* **hunger** *of* those you cherish; their sons
20: 4 [20:5] [D] desire of your heart and **make** all your plans **succeed**.
20: 5 [20:6] [D] of our God. *May* the LORD **grant** all your requests.
26: 10 [A] are wicked schemes, whose right hands *are* **full** *of* bribes.
33: 5 [A] and justice; the earth *is* **full** *of* his unfailing love.
38: 7 [38:8] [A] My back *is* **filled** *with* searing pain; there is no health
48: 10 [48:11] [A] your right hand *is* **filled** *with* righteousness.
71: 8 [C] My mouth *is* **filled** *with* your praise, declaring your splendor
72: 19 [C] name forever; *may* the whole earth **be filled** *with* his glory.
74: 20 [A] because haunts of violence **fill** the dark places of the land.
80: 9 [80:10] [D] the ground for it, and it took root and **filled** the land.
81: 10 [81:11] [D] of Egypt. Open wide your mouth and *I will* **fill** it.
83: 16 [83:17] [D] **Cover** their faces *with* shame so that men will seek
104: 24 [A] you made them all; the earth *is* **full** *of* your creatures.
107: 9 [D] he satisfies the thirsty and **fills** the hungry *with* good things.
110: 6 [A] **heaping up** the dead and crushing the rulers of the whole
119: 64 [A] The earth *is* **filled** *with* your love, O LORD; teach me your
126: 2 [C] Our mouths **were filled** *with* laughter, our tongues *with*
127: 5 [D] Blessed is the man whose quiver *is* **full** of them. They will
129: 7 [D] *with* it the reaper cannot **fill** his hands, nor the one who
Pr 1: 13 [D] all sorts of valuable things and **fill** our houses *with* plunder;
3: 10 [C] your barns *will* **be filled** to overflowing, and your vats will
6: 30 [D] Men do not despise a thief if he steals to **satisfy** his hunger
8: 21 [D] on those who love me and **making** their treasuries **full**.
12: 21 [A] the righteous, but the wicked **have** *their* **fill** *of* trouble.
20: 17 [C] sweet to a man, but he ends up with a mouth **full** *of* gravel.
24: 4 [C] through knowledge its rooms **are filled** *with* rare
Ecc 1: 8 [C] eye never has enough of seeing, nor the ear *its* **fill** of hearing.
6: 7 [C] efforts are for his mouth, yet his appetite **is** never **satisfied**.
8: 11 [A] the hearts of the people *are* **filled** *with* schemes to do wrong.
9: 3 [A] *are* **full** *of* evil and there is madness in their hearts while they
11: 3 [C] If clouds *are* **full** *of* water, they pour rain upon the earth.
SS 5: 2 [C] My head *is* **drenched** *with* dew, my hair with the dampness
5: 14 [E] His arms are rods of gold **set** with chrysolite. His body is like
Isa 1: 15 [A] many prayers, I will not listen. Your hands *are* **full** *of* blood;
2: 6 [A] *They are* **full** *of* superstitions from the East; they practice
2: 7 [C] Their land *is* **full** *of* silver and gold; there is no end to their
2: 7 [C] Their land *is* **full** *of* horses; there is no end to their chariots.
2: 8 [C] Their land *is* **full** *of* idols; they bow down to the work of their
6: 1 [A] high and exalted, and the train of his robe **filled** the temple.
6: 4 [C] and thresholds shook and the temple **was filled** *with* smoke.
11: 9 [A] for the earth *will be* **full** *of* the knowledge of the LORD as
13: 21 [A] But desert creatures will lie there, jackals *will* **fill** her houses;
14: 21 [A] inherit the land and **cover** [+7156] the earth *with* their cities.
15: 9 [A] Dimon's waters *are* **full** *of* blood, but I will bring still more
21: 3 [A] At this my body *is* **racked with** pain, pangs seize me,
22: 7 [A] Your choicest valleys *are* **full** *of* chariots, and horsemen are
23: 2 [D] you merchants of Sidon, whom the seafarers *have* **enriched**.
27: 6 [A] Israel will bud and blossom and **fill** all the world *with* fruit.
28: 8 [A] All the tables *are* **covered** *with* vomit and there is not a spot
30: 27 [A] his lips *are* **full** *of* wrath, and his tongue is a consuming fire.
33: 5 [D] on high; *he will* **fill** Zion *with* justice and righteousness.
34: 6 [A] The sword of the LORD *is* **bathed in** blood, it is covered
40: 2 [A] proclaim to her that her hard service *has been* **completed**,
65: 11 [D] a table for Fortune and **fill** bowls of mixed wine for Destiny,
65: 20 [D] a few days, or an old man who *does* not **live out** his years;
Jer 4: 5 [D] Cry **aloud** and say: 'Gather together! Let us flee to the
6: 11 [A] *I am* **full** *of* the wrath of the LORD, and I cannot hold it in.
13: 12 [C] of Israel, says: Every wineskin *should* **be filled** *with* wine.'
13: 12 [C] 'Don't we know that every wineskin *should* **be filled** *with*
13: 13 [D] *am going to* **fill** *with* drunkenness all who live in this land,
15: 17 [D] hand was on me and *you had* **filled** me *with* indignation.
16: 18 [A] and *have* **filled** my inheritance *with* their detestable idols."
19: 4 [A] *they have* **filled** this place *with* the blood of the innocent.
23: 10 [A] The land *is* **full** *of* adulterers; because of the curse the land
23: 24 [A] "*Do* not I **fill** heaven and earth?" declares the LORD.
25: 12 [A] "But when the seventy years *are* **fulfilled**, I will punish the
25: 34 [A] For your time to be slaughtered *has* **come**; you will fall
29: 10 [A] "When seventy years *are* **completed** for Babylon, I will
31: 25 [D] I will refresh the weary and **satisfy** the faint."
33: 5 [D] 'They *will* **be filled** *with* the dead bodies of the men I will
41: 9 [D] of Israel. Ishmael son of Nethaniah **filled** it *with* the dead.
44: 25 [D] your wives *have* **shown** by your actions what you promised
46: 12 [A] nations will hear of your shame; your cries *will* **fill** the earth.
51: 5 [A] though their land *is* **full** *of* guilt before the Holy One of
51: 11 [A] "Sharpen the arrows, **take up** the shields! The LORD has
51: 14 [D] *I will* surely **fill** you *with* men, as with a swarm of locusts,
51: 34 [D] has swallowed us and **filled** his stomach with our delicacies,
La 4: 18 [A] Our end was near, our days *were* **numbered**, for our end had
Eze 3: 3 [D] eat this scroll I am giving you and **fill** your stomach *with* it."
5: 2 [A] When the days of your siege **come to an end**, burn a third of
7: 19 [D] will not satisfy their hunger or **fill** their stomachs with it,
7: 23 [A] because the land *is* **full** *of* bloodshed and the city is full of
7: 23 [A] the land is full of bloodshed and the city *is* **full** *of* violence.
8: 17 [A] *Must they* also **fill** the land *with* violence and continually
9: 7 [D] to them, "Defile the temple and **fill** the courts *with* the slain.
9: 9 [C] the land *is* **full** *of* bloodshed and the city is full of injustice.
9: 9 [A] the land is full of bloodshed and the city *is* **full** *of* injustice.
10: 2 [D] **Fill** your hands *with* burning coals from among the cherubim
10: 3 [A] when the man went in, and a cloud **filled** the inner court.
10: 4 [C] The cloud **filled** the temple, and the court was full of the
10: 4 [A] the court *was* **full** *of* the radiance of the glory of the LORD.
11: 6 [D] many people in this city and **filled** its streets *with* the dead.
23: 33 [C] *You will* **be filled** *with* drunkenness and sorrow, the cup of
24: 4 [D] the leg and the shoulder. **Fill** it *with* the best of these bones;
26: 2 [C] swung open to me; now that she lies in ruins *I will* **prosper**,'
27: 25 [C] *You are* **filled** *with* heavy cargo in the heart of the sea.
28: 16 [A] Through your widespread trade you *were* **filled** *with*
30: 11 [A] their swords against Egypt and **fill** the land *with* the slain.
32: 5 [D] flesh on the mountains and **fill** the valleys *with* your remains.
32: 6 [C] the mountains, and the ravines *will* **be filled** with your flesh.
35: 8 [D] *I will* **fill** your mountains *with* the slain; those killed by the
43: 5 [A] inner court, and the glory of the LORD **filled** the temple.
43: 26 [D] the altar and cleanse it; thus *they will* **dedicate** [+3338] it.
44: 4 [A] saw the glory of the LORD **filling** the temple of the
Da 9: 2 [D] that the desolation of Jerusalem *would* **last** seventy years.
10: 3 [A] and I used no lotions at all until the three weeks *were* **over**.
Joel 2: 24 [A] The threshing floors *will be* **filled** *with* grain; the vats will
3: 13 [4:13] [A] for the winepress *is* **full** and the vats overflow—
Mic 3: 8 [A] *I am* **filled** *with* power, with the Spirit of the LORD,
6: 12 [A] Her rich men *are* **violent** [+2805]; her people are liars and
Na 2: 12 [2:13] [D] **filling** his lairs *with* the kill and his dens *with* the
Hab 2: 14 [C] For the earth *will* **be filled** *with* the knowledge of the glory
3: 3 [A] His glory covered the heavens and his praise **filled** the earth.
Zep 1: 9 [D] who **fill** the temple of their gods *with* violence and deceit.
Hag 2: 7 [D] *I will* **fill** this house *with* glory,' says the LORD Almighty.
Zec 8: 5 [C] The city streets *will* **be filled** *with* boys and girls playing
9: 13 [D] I will bend Judah as I bend my bow and **fill** it *with* Ephraim.
9: 15 [A] *they will be* **full** like a bowl used for sprinkling the corners

4849 ²מָלֵא *mālēʾ*², a. [63] [√ 4848]

filled [32], full [23], *untranslated* [1], abundance [1], loaded [1], loud [1], mother's[s] [1], strewn with [1], strong [1], weighed down [1]

Ge 23: 9 Ask him to sell it to me for the **full** price as a burial site among
41: 7 The thin heads of grain swallowed up the seven healthy, **full** heads.
41: 22 saw seven heads of grain, **full** and good, growing on a single stalk.
Nu 7: 13 each **filled** *with* fine flour mixed with oil as a grain offering;

Nu 7:14 one gold dish weighing ten shekels, **filled** *with* incense;
7:19 each **filled** *with* fine flour mixed with oil as a grain offering;
7:20 one gold dish weighing ten shekels, **filled** *with* incense;
7:25 each **filled** *with* fine flour mixed with oil as a grain offering;
7:26 one gold dish weighing ten shekels, **filled** *with* incense;
7:31 each **filled** *with* fine flour mixed with oil as a grain offering;
7:32 one gold dish weighing ten shekels, **filled** *with* incense;
7:37 each **filled** *with* fine flour mixed with oil as a grain offering;
7:38 one gold dish weighing ten shekels, **filled** *with* incense;
7:43 each **filled** *with* fine flour mixed with oil as a grain offering;
7:44 one gold dish weighing ten shekels, **filled** *with* incense;
7:49 each **filled** *with* fine flour mixed with oil as a grain offering;
7:50 one gold dish weighing ten shekels, **filled** *with* incense;
7:55 each **filled** *with* fine flour mixed with oil as a grain offering;
7:56 one gold dish weighing ten shekels, **filled** *with* incense;
7:61 each **filled** *with* fine flour mixed with oil as a grain offering;
7:62 one gold dish weighing ten shekels, **filled** *with* incense;
7:67 each **filled** *with* fine flour mixed with oil as a grain offering;
7:68 one gold dish weighing ten shekels, **filled** *with* incense;
7:73 each **filled** *with* fine flour mixed with oil as a grain offering;
7:74 one gold dish weighing ten shekels, **filled** *with* incense;
7:79 each **filled** *with* fine flour mixed with oil as a grain offering;
7:80 one gold dish weighing ten shekels, **filled** *with* incense;
7:86 The twelve gold dishes **filled** *with* incense weighed ten shekels
Dt 6:11 houses **filled** *with* all kinds of good things you did not provide,
33:23 abounding with the favor of the LORD and is **full** *of* his blessing;
Ru 1:21 I went away **full**, but the LORD has brought me back empty.
2Sa 23:11 banded together at a place where there was a field **full** *of* lentils,
2Ki 4:4 Pour oil into all the jars, and as each is **filled**, put it to one side."
7:15 they found the whole road **strewn with** the clothing and equipment
1Ch 11:13 At a place where there was a field **full** *of* barley, the troops fled
21:22 on the people may be stopped. Sell it to me at the **full** price."
21:24 David replied to Araunah, "No, I insist on paying the **full** price.
Ne 9:25 they took possession of houses **filled** *with* all kinds of good things,
Ps 65:9 [65:10] The streams of God are **filled** *with* water to provide the
73:10 their people turn to them and drink up waters in **abundance**.
75:8 [75:9] In the hand of the LORD is a cup **full** *of* foaming wine
144:13 Our barns will be **filled** *with* every kind of provision. Our sheep
Pr 17:1 a dry crust with peace and quiet than a house **full** *of* feasting,
Ecc 1:7 All streams flow into the sea, yet the sea is never **full**. To the place
11:5 path of the wind, or how the body is formed in a **mother's**[s] womb,
Isa 1:21 She once was **full** *of* justice; righteousness used to dwell in her—
22:2 O town **full** *of* commotion, O city of tumult and revelry?
51:20 They are **filled** *with* the wrath of the LORD and the rebuke of
Jer 4:12 a wind too **strong** for that comes from me. Now I pronounce my
5:27 Like cages **full** *of* birds, their houses are full of deceit; they have
5:27 Like cages full of birds, their houses are **full** *of* deceit; they have
6:11 will be caught in it, and the old, *those* **weighed down** *with* years.
12:6 they have betrayed you; they have raised a **loud** cry against you.
35:5 I set bowls **full** *of* wine and some cups before the men of the
Eze 1:18 and awesome, and all four rims were **full** *of* eyes all around.
10:12 their hands and their wings, were completely **full** *of* eyes,
17:3 long feathers and **full** plumage of varied colors came to Lebanon.
28:12 were the model of perfection, **full** *of* wisdom and perfect in beauty.
36:38 So will the ruined cities be **filled** *with* flocks of people. Then they
37:1 and set me in the middle of a valley; it was **full** *of* bones.
Am 2:13 I will crush you as a cart crushes when **loaded** *with* grain.
Na 1:10 from their wine; they will be consumed like dry stubble. **[NIE]**
3:1 city of blood, full of lies, **full** *of* plunder, never without victims!

4850 מְלֹא *mᵉlō'*, n.m. [38] [√ 4848]

everything in [8], all that is in [5], filled [3], full [3], handful [+4090] [2], handfuls [+2908] [2], *untranslated* [1], all that in [1], all who are in [1], all who were in [1], bowlful [+6210] [1], cover [1], fullness [1], group [1], length [1], take a handful [+7858+7859] [1], take a handful [+906+7858+7859] [1], take [1], third[s] [1], two handfuls [+2908] [1], whole band [1]

Ge 48:19 than he, and his descendants will become a **group** *of* nations."
Ex 9:8 "Take **handfuls of** [+2908] soot from a furnace and have Moses
16:32 '**Take** an omer of manna and keep it for the generations to come,
16:33 said to Aaron, "Take a jar and put an omer of **[RPH]** manna in it.
Lev 2:2 The priest *shall* **take a handful** [+7858+7859] of the fine flour
5:12 who *shall* **take a handful** [+906+7858+7859] of it as a memorial
16:12 He is to take a censer **full** *of* burning coals from the altar before the
16:12 and **two handfuls of** [+2908] finely ground fragrant incense
Nu 22:18 "Even if Balak gave me his palace **filled** *with* silver and gold,
24:13 'Even if Balak gave me his palace **filled** *with* silver and gold,
Dt 33:16 with the best gifts of the earth and its **fullness** and the favor of him
Jdg 6:38 the fleece and wrung out the dew—a **bowlful** [+6210] of water.
1Sa 28:20 Immediately Saul fell **full** length on the ground, filled with fear
2Sa 8:2 them were put to death, and the **third**[s] length was allowed to live.
1Ki 17:12 only a **handful of** [+4090] flour in a jar and a little oil in a jug.
2Ki 4:39 He gathered some of its gourds and **filled** the fold of his cloak.
1Ch 16:32 Let the sea resound, and **all that is in** it; let the fields be jubilant,
Ps 24:1 and **everything in** it, the world, and all who live in it;
50:12 I would not tell you, for the world is mine, and **all that is in** it.
89:11 [89:12] also the earth; you founded the world and **all that is in** it.
96:11 let the earth be glad; let the sea resound, and **all that is in** it;
98:7 Let the sea resound, and **everything in** it, the world, and all who
Ecc 4:6 Better *one* **handful** [+4090] with tranquillity than two handfuls
4:6 Better one handful with tranquillity than *two* **handfuls** [+2908]
Isa 6:3 holy is the LORD Almighty; the whole earth is **full** *of* his glory."
8:8 Its outspread wings will **cover** the breadth of your land,
31:4 though a **whole band** *of* shepherds is called together against him,
34:1 Let the earth hear, and **all that is in** it, the world, and all that
42:10 and **all that is in** it, you islands, and all who live in them.
Jer 8:16 They have come to devour the land and **everything in** it, the city
47:2 They will overflow the land and **everything in** it, the towns
Eze 12:19 for their land will be stripped of **everything in** it because of the
19:7 The land and **all who were in** it were terrified by his roaring.
30:12 hand of foreigners I will lay waste the land and **everything in** it.
32:15 When I make Egypt desolate and strip the land of **everything in** it,
41:8 of the side rooms. It was the **length** *of* the rod, six long cubits.
Am 6:8 his fortresses; I will deliver up the city and **everything in** it."
Mic 1:2 O peoples, all of you, listen, O earth and **all who are in** it,

4851 מִלֹּא *millō'*, n.pr.loc. Not used in NIV/BHS [√ 4864; cf. 4848]

4852 מְלֵאָה *mᵉlē'â*, n.f. [3] [√ 4848]

crops [1], granaries [1], juice [1]

Ex 22:29 [22:28] "Do not hold back offerings from your **granaries** or your
Nu 18:27 you as grain from the threshing floor or **juice** from the winepress.
Dt 22:9 not only the **crops** you plant but also the fruit of the vineyard will

4853 מִלֻּאָה *millu'â*, n.f. [3] [√ 4848]

mount [+2118] [1], mount [+4848] [1], settings [1]

Ex 28:17 **mount** [+4848] four rows of precious stones on it. In the first row
28:20 and a jasper. **Mount** [+2118] them in gold filigree settings.
39:13 and a jasper. They were mounted in gold filigree **settings**.

4854 מִלֻּאִים *millu'îm*, n.m. [15] [√ 4848]

ordination [7], mounted [3], ordination offering [2], ordination offerings [1], ordination ram [1], settings [1]

Ex 25:7 and other gems to be **mounted** on the ephod and breastpiece.
29:22 on them, and the right thigh. (This is the ram for the **ordination**.)
29:26 After you take the breast of the ram for Aaron's **ordination**,
29:27 "Consecrate those parts of the **ordination** ram that belong to
29:31 "Take the ram for the **ordination** and cook the meat in a sacred
29:34 if any of the meat of the **ordination ram** or any bread is left over
35:9 and other gems to be **mounted** on the ephod and breastpiece.
35:27 and other gems to be **mounted** on the ephod and breastpiece.
Lev 7:37 guilt offering, the **ordination offering** and the fellowship offering,
8:22 the ram for the **ordination**, and Aaron and his sons laid their hands
8:28 on the altar on top of the burnt offering as an **ordination offering**,
8:29 He also took the breast—Moses' share of the **ordination** ram—
8:31 eat it there with the bread from the basket of **ordination offerings**,
8:33 until the days of your **ordination** are completed, for your
1Ch 29:2 and wood for the wood, as well as onyx for the **settings**, turquoise,

4855 מַלְאָךְ *mal'āk*, n.m. [213] [→ 4856, 4857, 4858?; Ar 10417]

angel [98], messengers [60], messenger [23], angels [9], men [8], envoys [6], *untranslated* [1], delegation [1], he[s] [+2021] [1], he[s] [+3378] [1], men[s] [1], official [1], spies [1], the angel [+3378] [1], they[s] [+2021] [1]

Ge 16:7 The **angel** *of* the LORD found Hagar near a spring in the desert;
16:9 Then the **angel** *of* the LORD told her, "Go back to your mistress
16:10 **The angel** [+3378] added, "I will so increase your descendants that
16:11 The **angel** *of* the LORD also said to her: "You are now with child
19:1 The two **angels** arrived at Sodom in the evening, and Lot was
19:15 With the coming of dawn, the **angels** urged Lot, saying, "Hurry!
21:17 and the **angel** *of* God called to Hagar from heaven and said to her,
22:11 But the **angel** *of* the LORD called out to him from heaven,
22:15 The **angel** *of* the LORD called to Abraham from heaven a second
24:7 he will send his **angel** before you so that you can get a wife for my
24:40 will send his **angel** with you and make your journey a success,
28:12 and the **angels** *of* God were ascending and descending on it.
31:11 The **angel** *of* God said to me in the dream, 'Jacob.' I answered,
32:1 [32:2] also went on his way, and the **angels** *of* God met him.
32:3 [32:4] Jacob sent **messengers** ahead of him to his brother Esau in
32:6 [32:7] When the **messengers** returned to Jacob, they said,
48:16 the **Angel** who has delivered me from all harm—may he bless

Ex 3: 2 There the **angel** *of* the LORD appeared to him in flames of fire
14: 19 the **angel** *of* God, who had been traveling in front of Israel's army,
23: 20 I am sending an **angel** ahead of you to guard you along the way
23: 23 My **angel** will go ahead of you and bring you into the land of the
32: 34 people to the place I spoke of, and my **angel** will go before you.
33: 2 I will send an **angel** before you and drive out the Canaanites,
Nu 20: 14 Moses sent **messengers** from Kadesh to the king of Edom,
20: 16 he heard our cry and sent an **angel** and brought us out of Egypt.
21: 21 Israel sent **messengers** to say to Sihon king of the Amorites:
22: 5 sent **messengers** to summon Balaam son of Beor, who was at
22: 22 and the **angel** *of* the LORD stood in the road to oppose him.
22: 23 When the donkey saw the **angel** *of* the LORD standing in the
22: 24 the **angel** *of* the LORD stood in a narrow path between two
22: 25 When the donkey saw the **angel** *of* the LORD, she pressed close
22: 26 the **angel** *of* the LORD moved on ahead and stood in a narrow
22: 27 When the donkey saw the **angel** *of* the LORD, she lay down
22: 31 he saw the **angel** *of* the LORD standing in the road with his
22: 32 The **angel** *of* the LORD asked him, "Why have you beaten your
22: 34 Balaam said to the **angel** *of* the LORD, "I have sinned. I did not
22: 35 The **angel** *of* the LORD said to Balaam, "Go with the men,
24: 12 answered Balak, "Did I not tell the **messengers** you sent me,
Dt 2: 26 From the desert of Kedemoth I sent **messengers** to Sihon king of
Jos 6: 17 her in her house shall be spared, because she hid the **spies** we sent.
6: 25 because she hid the **men**[s] Joshua had sent as spies to Jericho—
7: 22 So Joshua sent **messengers**, and they ran to the tent, and there it
Jdg 2: 1 The **angel** *of* the LORD went up from Gilgal to Bokim and said,
2: 4 When the **angel** *of* the LORD had spoken these things to all the
5: 23 'Curse Meroz,' said the **angel** *of* the LORD. 'Curse its people
6: 11 The **angel** *of* the LORD came and sat down under the oak in
6: 12 When the **angel** *of* the LORD appeared to Gideon, he said,
6: 20 The **angel** *of* God said to him, "Take the meat and the unleavened
6: 21 the **angel** *of* the LORD touched the meat and the unleavened
6: 21 the meat and the bread. And the **angel** *of* the LORD disappeared.
6: 22 When Gideon realized that it was the **angel** *of* the LORD,
6: 22 I have seen the **angel** *of* the LORD face to face!"
6: 35 He sent **messengers** throughout Manasseh, calling them to arms,
6: 35 them to arms, and also **[RPH]** into Asher, Zebulun and Naphtali,
7: 24 Gideon sent **messengers** throughout the hill country of Ephraim,
9: 31 Under cover he sent **messengers** to Abimelech, saying, "Gaal son
11: 12 Jephthah sent **messengers** to the Ammonite king with the question:
11: 13 The king of the Ammonites answered Jephthah's **messengers**,
11: 14 Jephthah sent back **messengers** to the Ammonite king,
11: 17 Then Israel sent **messengers** to the king of Edom, saying,
11: 19 "Then Israel sent **messengers** to Sihon king of the Amorites,
13: 3 The **angel** *of* the LORD appeared to her and said, "You are sterile
13: 6 God came to me. He looked like an **angel** *of* God, very awesome.
13: 9 the **angel** *of* God came again to the woman while she was out in
13: 13 The **angel** *of* the LORD answered, "Your wife must do all that I
13: 15 Manoah said to the **angel** *of* the LORD, "We would like you to
13: 16 The **angel** *of* the LORD replied, "Even though you detain me,
13: 16 (Manoah did not realize that it was the **angel** *of* the LORD.)
13: 17 Manoah inquired of the **angel** *of* the LORD, "What is your name,
13: 18 **He**[s] [+3378] replied, "Why do you ask my name? It is beyond
13: 20 toward heaven, the **angel** *of* the LORD ascended in the flame.
13: 21 When the **angel** *of* the LORD did not show himself again to
13: 21 and his wife, Manoah realized that it was the **angel** *of* the LORD.
1Sa 6: 21 Then they sent **messengers** to the people of Kiriath Jearim,
11: 3 "Give us seven days so we can send **messengers** throughout Israel;
11: 4 When the **messengers** came to Gibeah of Saul and reported these
11: 7 and sent the pieces by **messengers** throughout Israel, proclaiming,
11: 9 They told the **messengers** who had come, "Say to the men of
11: 9 you will be delivered.' " When the **messengers** went and reported
16: 19 Saul sent **messengers** to Jesse and said, "Send me your son David,
19: 11 Saul sent **men** to David's house to watch it and to kill him in the
19: 14 When Saul sent the **men** to capture David, Michal said, "He is ill."
19: 15 Saul sent the **men** back to see David and told them, "Bring him up
19: 16 when the **men** entered, there was the idol in the bed, and at the
19: 20 so he sent **men** to capture him. But when they saw a group of
19: 20 the Spirit of God came upon Saul's **men** and they also prophesied.
19: 21 Saul was told about it, and he sent more **men**, and they prophesied
19: 21 Saul sent **men** a third time, and they also prophesied.
23: 27 a **messenger** came to Saul, saying, "Come quickly! The Philistines
25: 14 "David sent **messengers** from the desert to give our master his
25: 42 five maids, went with David's **messengers** and became his wife.
29: 9 "I know that you have been as pleasing in my eyes as an **angel** *of*
2Sa 2: 5 he sent **messengers** to the men of Jabesh Gilead to say to them,
3: 12 Then Abner sent **messengers** on his behalf to say to David,
3: 14 David sent **messengers** to Ish-Bosheth son of Saul, demanding,
3: 26 Joab then left David and sent **messengers** after Abner, and they
5: 11 Now Hiram king of Tyre sent **messengers** to David, along with
11: 4 Then David sent **messengers** to get her. She came to him,
11: 19 He instructed the **messenger**: "When you have finished giving the
11: 22 The **messenger** set out, and when he arrived he told David
11: 23 The **messenger** said to David, "The men overpowered us and came
11: 25 David told the **messenger**, "Say this to Joab: 'Don't let this upset
12: 27 Joab then sent **messengers** to David, saying, "I have fought against
14: 17 for my lord the king is like an **angel** *of* God in discerning good
14: 20 My lord has wisdom like that of an **angel** *of* God—he knows
19: 27 [19:28] My lord the king is like an **angel** *of* God; so do whatever
24: 16 When the **angel** stretched out his hand to destroy Jerusalem,
24: 16 of the calamity and said to the **angel** who was afflicting the people,
24: 16 The **angel** *of* the LORD was then at the threshing floor of
24: 17 When David saw the **angel** who was striking down the people,
1Ki 13: 18 as you are. And an **angel** said to me by the word of the LORD:
19: 2 So Jezebel sent a **messenger** to Elijah to say, "May the gods deal
19: 5 All at once an **angel** touched him and said, "Get up and eat."
19: 7 The **angel** *of* the LORD came back a second time and touched
20: 2 He sent **messengers** into the city to Ahab king of Israel, saying,
20: 5 The **messengers** came again and said, "This is what Ben-Hadad
20: 9 So he replied to Ben-Hadad's **messengers**, "Tell my lord the king,
20: 9 this demand I cannot meet.' " **They**[s] [+2021] left and took the
22: 13 The **messenger** who had gone to summon Micaiah said to him,
2Ki 1: 2 So he sent **messengers**, saying to them, "Go and consult
1: 3 But the **angel** *of* the LORD said to Elijah the Tishbite, "Go up
1: 3 "Go up and meet the **messengers** *of* the king of Samaria and ask
1: 5 When the **messengers** returned to the king, he asked them,
1: 15 The **angel** *of* the LORD said to Elijah, "Go down with him;
1: 16 to consult that you have sent **messengers** to consult Baal-Zebub,
5: 10 Elisha sent a **messenger** to say to him, "Go, wash yourself seven
6: 32 The king sent a **messenger** ahead, but before he arrived, Elisha
6: 32 Look, when the **messenger** comes, shut the door and hold it shut
6: 33 he was still talking to them, the **messenger** came down to him.
7: 15 So the **messengers** returned and reported to the king.
9: 18 The lookout reported, "The **messenger** has reached them,
10: 8 When the **messenger** arrived, he told Jehu, "They have brought the
14: 8 Then Amaziah sent **messengers** to Jehoash son of Jehoahaz,
16: 7 Ahaz sent **messengers** to say to Tiglath-Pileser king of Assyria,
17: 4 for he had sent **envoys** to So king of Egypt, and he no longer paid
19: 9 So he again sent **messengers** to Hezekiah with this word:
19: 14 Hezekiah received the letter from the **messengers** and read it.
19: 23 By your **messengers** you have heaped insults on the Lord.
19: 35 That night the **angel** *of* the LORD went out and put to death a
1Ch 14: 1 Now Hiram king of Tyre sent **messengers** to David, along with
19: 2 So David sent a **delegation** to express his sympathy to Hanun
19: 16 they sent **messengers** and had Arameans brought from beyond the
21: 12 with the **angel** *of* the LORD ravaging every part of Israel.'
21: 15 God sent an **angel** to destroy Jerusalem. But as the angel was doing
21: 15 the calamity and said to the **angel** who was destroying the people,
21: 15 The **angel** *of* the LORD was then standing at the threshing floor
21: 16 and saw the **angel** *of* the LORD standing between heaven
21: 18 Then the **angel** *of* the LORD ordered Gad to tell David to go up
21: 20 While Araunah was threshing wheat, he turned and saw the **angel**;
21: 27 the LORD spoke to the **angel**, and he put his sword back into its
21: 30 because he was afraid of the sword of the **angel** *of* the LORD.
2Ch 18: 12 The **messenger** who had gone to summon Micaiah said to him,
32: 21 the LORD sent an **angel**, who annihilated all the fighting men
35: 21 Neco sent **messengers** to him, saying, "What quarrel is there
36: 15 sent word to them through his **messengers** again and again,
36: 16 they mocked God's **messengers**, despised his words and scoffed at
Ne 6: 3 so I sent **messengers** to them with this reply: "I am carrying on a
Job 1: 14 a **messenger** came to Job and said, "The oxen were plowing
4: 18 places no trust in his servants, if he charges his **angels** with error,
33: 23 "Yet if there is an **angel** on his side as a mediator, one out of a
Ps 34: 7 [34:8] The **angel** *of* the LORD encamps around those who fear
35: 5 before the wind, with the **angel** *of* the LORD driving them away;
35: 6 and slippery, with the **angel** *of* the LORD pursuing them.
78: 49 his wrath, indignation and hostility—a band of destroying **angels**.
91: 11 For he will command his **angels** concerning you to guard you in all
103: 20 Praise the LORD, you his **angels**, you mighty ones who do his
104: 4 He makes winds his **messengers**, flames of fire his servants.
148: 2 Praise him, all his **angels**, praise him, all his heavenly hosts.
Pr 13: 17 A wicked **messenger** falls into trouble, but a trustworthy envoy
16: 14 A king's wrath is a **messenger** *of* death, but a wise man will
17: 11 bent only on rebellion; a merciless **official** will be sent against him.
Ecc 5: 6 [5:5] do not protest to the ⌞temple⌟ **messenger**, "My vow was a
Isa 14: 32 What answer shall be given to the **envoys** *of* that nation? "The
18: 2 Go, swift **messengers**, to a people tall and smooth-skinned,
30: 4 they have officials in Zoan and their **envoys** have arrived in Hanes,
33: 7 men cry aloud in the streets; the **envoys** *of* peace weep bitterly.
37: 9 When he heard it, he sent **messengers** to Hezekiah with this word:
37: 14 Hezekiah received the letter from the **messengers** and read it.
37: 36 Then the **angel** *of* the LORD went out and put to death a hundred
42: 19 Who is blind but my servant, and deaf like the **messenger** I send?
44: 26 of his servants and fulfills the predictions of his **messengers**,
63: 9 he too was distressed, and the **angel** *of* his presence saved them.
Jer 27: 3 Sidon through the **envoys** who have come to Jerusalem to
Eze 17: 15 the king rebelled against him by sending his **envoys** to Egypt to get
23: 16 she lusted after them and sent **messengers** to them in Chaldea.

Eze 23:40 "They even sent **messengers** for men who came from far away,
30: 9 " 'On that day **messengers** will go out from me in ships to frighten
Hos 12: 4 [12:5] He struggled with the **angel** and overcame him; he wept
Na 2:13 [2:14] The voices of your **messengers** will no longer be heard."
Hag 1:13 Haggai, the LORD's **messenger**, gave this message of the
Zec 1: 9 The **angel** who was talking with me answered, "I will show you
1:11 they reported to the **angel** *of* the LORD, who was standing among
1:12 the **angel** *of* the LORD said, "LORD Almighty, how long will
1:13 spoke kind and comforting words to the **angel** who talked with me.
1:14 Then the **angel** who was speaking to me said, "Proclaim this word:
1:19 [2:2] I asked the **angel** who was speaking to me, "What are
2: 3 [2:7] the **angel** who was speaking to me left, and another angel
2: 3 [2:7] speaking to me left, and another **angel** came to meet him
3: 1 he showed me Joshua the high priest standing before the **angel** *of*
3: 3 Joshua was dressed in filthy clothes as he stood before the **angel**.
3: 5 and clothed him, while the **angel** *of* the LORD stood by.
3: 6 The **angel** *of* the LORD gave this charge to Joshua:
4: 1 Then the **angel** who talked with me returned and wakened me,
4: 4 I asked the **angel** who talked with me, "What are these, my lord?"
4: 5 **He**[s] [+2021] answered, "Do you not know what these are?"
5: 5 the **angel** who was speaking to me came forward and said to me,
5:10 taking the basket?" I asked the **angel** who was speaking to me.
6: 4 I asked the **angel** who was speaking to me, "What are these,
6: 5 The **angel** answered me, "These are the four spirits of heaven,
12: 8 will be like God, like the **Angel** *of* the LORD going before them.
Mal 2: 7 because he is the **messenger** *of* the LORD Almighty.
3: 1 "See, I will send my **messenger**, who will prepare the way before
3: 1 the **messenger** *of* the covenant, whom you desire, will come,"

4856 מְלָאכָה mᵉlā'kâ, n.f. [167] [√ 4855]

work [87], regular work [+6275] [12], workers [+6913] [7], *untranslated* [4], anything [3], duties [3], task [3], workmen [+6913] [3], business [2], crafts [2], project [2], property [2], service [2], administrators [+6913] [1], anything useful [1], assist [1], been used [+928+6913] [1], building [1], craftsmanship [1], deeds [1], details [1], do [1], done [1], droves [1], everything [+2021+3972] [1], kinds [1], made [1], master craftsmen [+6913] [1], matter [1], merchants [+6913] [1], part [1], performed [1], projects [1], purpose [1], responsible [+6275] [1], responsible [1], settings [+9513] [1], something useful [1], supplies [1], these men [+2021+6913] [1], use [+6913] [1], use [+928+6913] [1], what[s] [+2021] [1], work [+6913] [1], worked [1], working [+6913] [1], workmen [+928+2021+6913] [1], workmen [1]

Ge 2: 2 By the seventh day God had finished the **work** he had been doing;
2: 2 had been doing; so on the seventh day he rested from all his **work**.
2: 3 because on it he rested from all the **work** of creating that he had
33:14 while I move along slowly at the pace of the **droves** before me
39:11 One day he went into the house to attend to his **duties**, and none of
Ex 12:16 Do no **work** at all on these days, except to prepare food for
20: 9 Six days you shall labor and do all your **work**,
20:10 On it you shall not do any **work**, neither you, nor your son
22: 8 [22:7] whether he has laid his hands on the other man's **property**.
22:11 [22:10] did not lay hands on the other person's **property**.
31: 3 of God, with skill, ability and knowledge in all kinds of **crafts**—
31: 5 to work in wood, and to engage in all kinds of **craftsmanship**.
31:14 whoever does any **work** on that day must be cut off from his
31:15 For six days, **work** is to be done, but the seventh day is a Sabbath
31:15 Whoever does any **work** on the Sabbath day must be put to death.
35: 2 For six days, **work** is to be done, but the seventh day shall be your
35: 2 to the LORD. Whoever does any **work** on it must be put to death.
35:21 brought an offering to the LORD for the **work** *on* the Tent of
35:24 everyone who had acacia wood for any **part** *of* the work brought it.
35:29 the **work** the LORD through Moses had commanded them to do.
35:31 of God, with skill, ability and knowledge in all kinds of **crafts**—
35:33 work in wood and to engage in all **kinds** *of* artistic craftsmanship.
35:35 He has filled them with skill to do all kinds of **work** *as* craftsmen,
35:35 all of them **master craftsmen** [+6913] and designers.
36: 1 ability to know how to carry out all the **work** *of* constructing the
36: 2 had given ability and who was willing to come and do the **work**.
36: 3 had brought to carry out the **work** *of* constructing the sanctuary.
36: 4 So all the skilled craftsmen who were doing all the **work** *on* the
36: 4 who were doing all the work on the sanctuary left their **work**
36: 5 "The people are bringing more than enough for doing the **work** the
36: 6 or woman is to make **anything** else as an offering for the
36: 7 because **what**[s] [+2021] they already had was more than enough to
36: 7 what they already had was more than enough to do all the **work**.
36: 8 All the skilled men among the **workmen** [+6913] made the
38:24 The total amount of the gold from the wave offering used **[RPH]**
38:24 offering used for all the **work** *on* the sanctuary was 29 talents
39:43 Moses inspected the **work** and saw that they had done it just as the
40:33 at the entrance to the courtyard. And so Moses finished the **work**.
Lev 7:24 or torn by wild animals may be used for any other **purpose**,
11:32 that article, whatever its **use** [+928+6913], will be unclean,
13:48 of linen or wool, any leather or anything **made** *of* leather—
13:51 or the leather, whatever its use, **[NIE]** it is a destructive mildew;
16:29 seventh month you must deny yourselves and not do any **work**—
23: 3 " 'There are six days when *you may* **work** [+6913], but the seventh
23: 3 You are not to do any **work**; wherever you live, it is a Sabbath to
23: 7 first day hold a sacred assembly and do no **regular work** [+6275].
23: 8 day hold a sacred assembly and do no **regular work** [+6275].' "
23:21 to proclaim a sacred assembly and do no **regular work** [+6275].
23:25 Do no **regular work** [+6275], but present an offering made to the
23:28 Do no **work** on that day, because it is the Day of Atonement,
23:30 I will destroy from among his people anyone who does any **work**
23:31 You shall do no **work** at all. This is to be a lasting ordinance for
23:35 The first day is a sacred assembly; do no **regular work** [+6275].
23:36 by fire. It is the closing assembly; do no **regular work** [+6275].
Nu 4: 3 of age who come to serve in the **work** in the Tent of Meeting.
28:18 first day hold a sacred assembly and do no **regular work** [+6275].
28:25 day hold a sacred assembly and do no **regular work** [+6275].
28:26 hold a sacred assembly and do no **regular work** [+6275].
29: 1 month hold a sacred assembly and do no **regular work** [+6275].
29: 7 a sacred assembly. You must deny yourselves and do no **work**.
29:12 hold a sacred assembly and do no **regular work** [+6275].
29:35 the eighth day hold an assembly and do no **regular work** [+6275].
Dt 5:13 Six days you shall labor and do all your **work**,
5:14 On it you shall not do any **work**, neither you, nor your son
16: 8 day hold an assembly to the LORD your God and do no **work**.
Jdg 16:11 securely with new ropes that *have* never **been used** [+928+6913],
1Sa 8:16 of your cattle and donkeys he will take for his own **use** [+6913].
15: 9 but **everything** [+2021+3972] that was despised and weak they
1Ki 5:16 [5:30] thirty-three hundred foremen who supervised the **project**
5:16 [5:30] the project and directed the **workmen** [+928+2021+6913].
7:14 was highly skilled and experienced in all kinds of bronze **work**.
7:14 He came to King Solomon and did all the **work** *assigned to* him.
7:22 the shape of lilies. And so the **work** *on* the pillars was completed.
7:40 So Huram finished all the **work** he had undertaken for King
7:51 When all the **work** King Solomon had done for the temple of the
9:23 were also the chief officials in charge of Solomon's **projects**—
9:23 550 officials supervising the men who did the **work**.
11:28 and when Solomon saw how well the young man did his **work**,
2Ki 12:11 [12:12] to the men appointed to supervise the **work** on the temple.
12:14 [12:15] it was paid to the **workmen** [+6913], who used it to repair
12:15 [12:16] whom they gave the money to pay the **workers** [+6913],
22: 5 Have them entrust it to the men appointed to supervise the **work**
22: 5 have these men pay the **workers** [+6913] who repair the temple of
22: 9 have entrusted it to the **workers** [+6913] and supervisors at the
1Ch 4:23 at Netaim and Gederah; they stayed there and **worked** for the king.
6:49 [6:34] connection with all that was **done** *in* the Most Holy Place,
9:13 were able men, **responsible** *for* ministering in the house of God.
9:19 were **responsible** [+6275] *for* guarding the thresholds of the Tent
9:33 because they were responsible for the **work** day and night.
22:15 You have many **workmen** [+6913]: stonecutters, masons and
22:15 and carpenters, as well as men skilled in every kind of **work**
23: 4 twenty-four thousand are to supervise the **work** *of* the temple of
23:24 the **workers** [+6913] twenty years old or more who served in the
25: 1 Here is the list of the men who **performed** this service:
26:29 Kenaniah and his sons were assigned **duties** away from the temple,
26:30 were responsible in Israel west of the Jordan for all the **work** *of* the
27:26 Ezri son of Kelub was in charge of the field **workers** [+6913] who
28:13 and for all the **work** *of* serving in the temple of the LORD,
28:19 and he gave me understanding in all the **details** *of* the plan."
28:20 or forsake you until all the **work** *for* the service of the temple of
28:21 every willing man skilled in any craft will help you in all the **work**.
29: 1 The **task** is great, because this palatial structure is not for man
29: 5 the silver work, and for all the **work** to be done by the craftsmen.
29: 6 and the officials in charge of the king's **work** gave willingly.
2Ch 4:11 So Huram finished the **work** he had undertaken for King Solomon
5: 1 When all the **work** Solomon had done for the temple of the
8: 9 But Solomon did not make slaves of the Israelites for his **work**;
8:16 All Solomon's **work** was carried out, from the day the foundation
13:10 serve the LORD are sons of Aaron, and the Levites **assist** them.
16: 5 heard this, he stopped building Ramah and abandoned his **work**.
17:13 had large **supplies** in the towns of Judah. He also kept experienced
24:12 Jehoiada gave it to the men who carried out the **work** required for
24:13 The men in charge of the **work** were diligent, and the repairs
24:13 work were diligent, and the repairs **[RPH]** progressed under them.
29:34 so their kinsmen the Levites helped them until the **task** was
34:10 they entrusted it to the men appointed to supervise the **work** on the
34:10 **These men**[s] [+2021+6913] paid the workers who repaired
34:12 The men did the **work** faithfully. Over them to direct them were
34:13 and supervised all the **workers** [+6913] from job to job.
34:17 and have entrusted it to the supervisors and **workers** [+6913]."
Ezr 2:69 According to their ability they gave to the treasury for this **work**
3: 8 and older to supervise the **building** *of* the house of the LORD.
3: 9 joined together in supervising those working on **[RPH]** the house
6:22 so that he assisted them in the **work** *on* the house of God,
10:13 Besides, this **matter** cannot be taken care of in a day or two,

Ne 2:16 or nobles or officials or any others who would be doing the **work**.
4:11 [4:5] among them and will kill them and put an end to the **work**."
4:15 [4:9] we all returned to the wall, each to his own **work**.
4:16 [4:10] From that day on, half of my men did the **work**,
4:17 [4:11] Those who carried materials did their **work** with one hand
4:19 [4:13] rest of the people, "The **work** is extensive and spread out,
4:21 [4:15] So we continued the **work** with half the men holding
4:22 [4:16] can serve us as guards by night and **workmen** by day."
5:16 Instead, I devoted myself to the **work** *on* this wall. All my men
5:16 All my men were assembled there for the **work**; we did not acquire
6:3 "I am carrying on a great **project** and cannot go down. Why should
6:3 Why should the **work** stop while I leave it and go down to you?"
6:9 thinking, "Their hands will get too weak for the **work**, and it will
6:16 because they realized that this **work** had been done with the help
7:70 [7:69] Some of the heads of the families contributed to the **work**.
7:71 [7:70] gave to the treasury for the **work** 20,000 drachmas of gold
10:33 [10:34] for Israel; and for all the **duties** *of* the house of our God.
11:12 and their associates, who carried on **work** for the temple—
11:16 who had charge of the outside **work** of the house of God;
11:22 who were the singers responsible for the **service** *of* the house of
13:10 singers responsible for the **service** had gone back to their own
13:30 everything foreign, and assigned them duties, each to his own **task**.
Est 3:9 into the royal treasury for the men who carry out this **business**."
9:3 and the king's **administrators** [+6913] helped the Jews,
Ps 73:28 the Sovereign LORD my refuge; I will tell of all your **deeds**.
107:23 Others went out on the sea in ships; *they were* **merchants** [+6913]
Pr 18:9 One who is slack in his **work** is brother to one who destroys.
22:29 Do you see a man skilled in his **work**? He will serve before kings;
24:27 Finish your outdoor **work** and get your fields ready; after that,
Jer 17:22 not bring a load out of your houses or do any **work** on the Sabbath,
17:24 but keep the Sabbath day holy by not doing any **work** on it,
18:3 to the potter's house, and I saw him **working** [+6913] at the wheel.
48:10 "A curse on him who is lax in doing the LORD's **work**! A curse
50:25 for the Sovereign LORD Almighty has **work** to do in the land of
Eze 15:3 Is wood ever taken from it to make **anything useful**? Do they
15:4 both ends and chars the middle, is it then useful for **anything**?
15:5 If it was not useful for **anything** when it was whole, how much
15:5 how much less can it be made into **something useful** when the fire
28:13 Your **settings** [+9513] and mountings were made of gold;
Da 8:27 for several days. Then I got up and went about the king's **business**.
Jnh 1:8 What do you **do**? Where do you come from? What is your
Hag 1:14 and began to **work** on the house of the LORD Almighty,

4857 מַלְאָכוּת mal'ākût, n.f. [1] [√ 4855]

message [1]

Hag 1:13 gave this **message** *of* the LORD to the people:

4858 מַלְאָכִי mal'ākî, n.pr.m. [1] [√ 4855?]

Malachi [1]

Mal 1:1 An oracle: The word of the LORD to Israel through **Malachi**.

4859 מִלֵּאת millē't, n.f. [1] [√ 4848]

mounted like jewels [+3782+6584] [1]

SS 5:12 washed in milk, **mounted like jewels** [+3782+6584].

4860 מַלְבּוּשׁ malbûš, n.m. [8] [√ 4252]

robes [4], clothes [3], clothing [1]

1Ki 10:5 his officials, the attending servants in their **robes**, his cupbearers,
2Ki 10:22 for all the ministers of Baal." So he brought out **robes** for them.
2Ch 9:4 the seating of his officials, the attending servants in their **robes**,
9:4 the cupbearers in their **robes** and the burnt offerings he made at the
Job 27:16 Though he heaps up silver like dust and **clothes** like piles of clay,
Isa 63:3 their blood spattered my garments, and I stained all my **clothing**.
Eze 16:13 your **clothes** were of fine linen and costly fabric and embroidered
Zep 1:8 and the king's sons and all those clad in foreign **clothes**.

4861 מַלְבֵּן malbēn, n.[m.]. [3] [√ 4246; cf. 4905]

brick pavement [1], brickmaking [1], brickwork [1]

2Sa 12:31 and axes, and he made them work at **brickmaking**. [K 4905]
Jer 43:9 bury them in clay in the **brick pavement** at the entrance to
Na 3:14 Work the clay, tread the mortar, repair the **brickwork**!

4862 מָלָה mālâ, v. Not used in NIV/BHS [cf. 4848]

4863 מִלָּה millâ, n.f. [38] [√ 4910; Ar 10418]

words [24], speaking [2], speeches [2], word [2], anything to say [1], byword [1], make fine speeches [+928+2488] [1], reply [+906+8740] [1], said [1], say [1], what say [1], what[s] [1]

2Sa 23:2 of the LORD spoke through me; his **word** was on my tongue.
Job 4:2 will you be impatient? But who can keep from **speaking**?
4:4 Your **words** have supported those who stumbled; you have
6:26 Do you mean to correct **what** I **say**, and treat the words of a
8:10 Will they not bring forth **words** from their understanding?
12:11 Does not the ear test **words** as the tongue tastes food?
13:17 Listen carefully to my **words**; let your ears take in what I say.
15:3 he argue with useless words, with **speeches** that have no value?
15:13 your rage against God and pour out *such* **words** from your mouth?
16:4 *I could* **make fine speeches** [+928+2488] against you and shake
18:2 "When will you end these **speeches**? Be sensible, and then we can
19:2 "How long will you torment me and crush me with **words**?
19:23 "Oh, that my **words** were recorded, that they were written on a
21:2 "Listen carefully to my **words**; let this be the consolation you give
23:5 I would find out **what**[s] he would answer me, and consider what he
24:25 who can prove me false and reduce my **words** to nothing?"
26:4 Who has helped you utter these **words**? And whose spirit spoke
29:9 the chief men refrained from **speaking** and covered their mouths
29:22 they spoke no more; my **words** fell gently on their ears.
30:9 their sons mock me in song; I have become a **byword** among them.
32:11 I listened to your reasoning; while you were searching for **words**,
32:14 Job has not marshaled his **words** against me, and I will not answer
32:15 are dismayed and have no more to say; **words** have failed them.
32:18 For I am full of **words**, and the spirit within me compels me;
33:1 "But now, Job, listen to my **words**; pay attention to everything I
33:8 "But you have said in my hearing—I heard the very **words**—
33:32 If you have **anything to say**, answer me; speak up, for I want you
34:2 "Hear my **words**, you wise men; listen to me, you men of learning.
34:3 For the ear tests **words** as the tongue tastes food.
34:16 "If you have understanding, hear this; listen to what I **say**.
35:4 "I *would like to* **reply to** [+906+8740] you and to your friends
35:16 mouth with empty talk; without knowledge he multiplies **words**."
36:2 and I will show you that there is more to be **said** in God's behalf.
36:4 Be assured that my **words** are not false; one perfect in knowledge
38:2 "Who is this that darkens my counsel with **words** without
Ps 19:4 [19:5] out into all the earth, their **words** to the ends of the world.
139:4 Before a **word** is on my tongue you know it completely,
Pr 23:9 not speak to a fool, for he will scorn the wisdom of your **words**.

4864 מִלּוֹא millô', n.pr.loc. [6] [→ 4851; cf. 4848]

supporting terraces [6]

2Sa 5:9 built up the area around it, from the **supporting terraces** inward.
1Ki 9:15 his own palace, the **supporting terraces**, the wall of Jerusalem,
9:24 Solomon had built for her, he constructed the **supporting terraces**.
11:27 Solomon had built the **supporting terraces** and had filled in the
1Ch 11:8 around it, from the **supporting terraces** to the surrounding wall,
2Ch 32:5 and reinforced the **supporting terraces** *of* the City of David.

4865 מַלּוּחַ mallûaḥ, n.[m.]. [1] [√ 4875]

salt herbs [1]

Job 30:4 In the brush they gathered **salt herbs**, and their food was the root

4866 מַלּוּךְ mallûk, n.pr.m. [6] [√ 4889; cf. 4887]

Malluch [6]

1Ch 6:44 [6:29] Ethan son of Kishi, the son of Abdi, the son of **Malluch**,
Ezr 10:29 Meshullam, **Malluch**, Adaiah, Jashub, Sheal and Jeremoth.
10:32 Benjamin, **Malluch** and Shemariah.
Ne 10:4 [10:5] Hattush, Shebaniah, **Malluch**,
10:27 [10:28] **Malluch**, Harim and Baanah.
12:2 Amariah, **Malluch**, Hattush,

4867 מְלוּכָה m^e^lûkâ, n.f. [24] [√ 4887]

kingdom [10], royal [7], kingship [3], dominion [1], king [1], queen [1], rule [1]

1Sa 10:16 he did not tell his uncle what Samuel had said about the **kingship**.
10:25 Samuel explained to the people the regulations of the **kingship**.
11:14 "Come, let us go to Gilgal and there reaffirm the **kingship**."
14:47 After Saul had assumed **rule** over Israel, he fought against their
18:8 me with only thousands. What more can he get but the **kingdom**?"
2Sa 12:26 against Rabbah of the Ammonites and captured the **royal** citadel.
16:8 The LORD has handed the **kingdom** over to your son Absalom.
1Ki 1:46 Moreover, Solomon has taken his seat on the **royal** throne.
2:15 "As you know," he said, "the **kingdom** was mine. All Israel looked
2:15 But things changed, and the **kingdom** has gone to my brother;
2:22 You might as well request the **kingdom** for him—after all,
11:35 I will take the **kingdom** from his son's hands and give you ten
12:21 and to regain the **kingdom** for Rehoboam son of Solomon.
21:7 Jezebel his wife said, "Is this how you act as **king** over Israel?
2Ki 25:25 who was of **royal** blood, came with ten men and assassinated
1Ch 10:14 him to death and turned the **kingdom** over to David son of Jesse.
Ps 22:28 [22:29] for **dominion** belongs to the LORD and he rules over the
Isa 34:12 Her nobles will have nothing there to be called a **kingdom**,

Isa 62: 3 in the LORD's hand, a **royal** diadem in the hand of your God.
Jer 41: 1 who was of **royal** blood and had been one of the king's officers,
Eze 16: 13 and olive oil. You became very beautiful and rose to be a **queen**.
17: 13 he took a member of the **royal** family and made a treaty with him,
Da 1: 3 to bring in some of the Israelites from the **royal** family and the
Ob 1: 21 the mountains of Esau. And the **kingdom** will be the LORD's.

4868 מַלּוּכִי mallûkî, n.pr.m. [1] [cf. 4883]

Malluch's [1]

Ne 12: 14 of **Malluch's**, [Q 4883] Jonathan; of Shecaniah's, Joseph;

4869 מָלוֹן mālôn, n.m. [8] [√ 4328]

lodging place [2], camp overnight [1], camp [1], parts [1], place where they stopped for the night [1], place where we stopped for the night [1], place [1]

Ge 42: 27 At the **place where they stopped for the night** one of them
43: 21 at the **place where we stopped for the night** we opened our sacks
Ex 4: 24 At a **lodging place** on the way, the LORD met ⌊Moses⌋ and was
Jos 4: 3 with you and put them down at the **place** where you stay tonight."
4: 8 they carried them over with them to their **camp**, where they put
2Ki 19: 23 its pines. I have reached its remotest **parts**, the finest of its forests.
Isa 10: 29 go over the pass, and say, "We will **camp overnight** at Geba."
Jer 9: 2 [9:1] Oh, that I had in the desert a **lodging place** *for* travelers,

4870 מְלוּנָה m^elûnâ, n.f. [2] [√ 4328]

hut [2]

Isa 1: 8 a vineyard, like a **hut** in a field of melons, like a city under siege.
24: 20 The earth reels like a drunkard, it sways like a **hut** in the wind;

4871 מַלּוֹתִי mallôtî, n.pr.m. [2] [√ 4910]

Mallothi [2]

1Ch 25: 4 Joshbekashah, **Mallothi**, Hothir and Mahazioth.
25: 26 the nineteenth to **Mallothi**, his sons and relatives, 12

4872 I מָלַח mālaḥ[1], v. [1] [→ 4874]

vanish [1]

Isa 51: 6 [C] the heavens *will* **vanish** like smoke, the earth will wear out

4873 II מָלַח mālaḥ[2], v.den. [4] [√ 4875]

were rubbed with salt [+4873] [2], be salted [1], season [1]

Ex 30: 35 [E] work of a perfumer. *It is to* **be salted** and pure and sacred.
Lev 2: 13 [A] **Season** all your grain offerings with salt. Do not leave the
Eze 16: 4 [H] nor **were** *you* **rubbed with salt** [+4873] or wrapped in
16: 4 [H] nor **were** *you* **rubbed with salt** [+4873] or wrapped in

4874 I מֶלַח melaḥ[1], n.[m.]. [2] [√ 4872]

clothes [2]

Jer 38: 11 He took some old rags and worn-out **clothes** from there and let
38: 12 old rags and worn-out **clothes** under your arms to pad the ropes."

4875 II מֶלַח melaḥ[2], n.m. [29] [→ 4865, 4873, 4876, 4877, 6558, 9427; Ar 10419, 10420]

salt [29]

Ge 14: 3 latter kings joined forces in the Valley of Siddim (the **Salt** Sea).
19: 26 But Lot's wife looked back, and she became a pillar of **salt**.
Lev 2: 13 Season all your grain offerings with **salt**. Do not leave the salt of
2: 13 Do not leave the **salt** *of* the covenant of your God out of your grain
2: 13 your God out of your grain offerings; add **salt** to all your offerings.
Nu 18: 19 It is an everlasting covenant of **salt** before the LORD for both you
34: 3 your southern boundary will start from the end of the **Salt** Sea,
34: 12 boundary will go down along the Jordan and end at the **Salt** Sea.
Dt 3: 17 from Kinnereth to the Sea of the Arabah (the **Salt** Sea),
29: 23 [29:22] The whole land will be a burning waste of **salt**
Jos 3: 16 while the water flowing down to the Sea of the Arabah (the **Salt**
12: 3 from the Sea of Kinnereth to the Sea of the Arabah (the **Salt** Sea),
15: 2 boundary started from the bay at the southern end of the **Salt** Sea,
15: 5 The eastern boundary is the **Salt** Sea as far as the mouth of the
15: 62 Nibshan, the City of **Salt** and En Gedi—six towns and their
18: 19 of Beth Hoglah and came out at the northern bay of the **Salt** Sea,
Jdg 9: 45 its people. Then he destroyed the city and scattered **salt** over it.
2Sa 8: 13 striking down eighteen thousand Edomites in the Valley of **Salt**.
2Ki 2: 20 "Bring me a new bowl," he said, "and put **salt** in it." So they
2: 21 Then he went out to the spring and threw the **salt** into it, saying,
14: 7 the one who defeated ten thousand Edomites in the Valley of **Salt**
1Ch 18: 12 struck down eighteen thousand Edomites in the Valley of **Salt**.
2Ch 13: 5 Israel to David and his descendants forever by a covenant of **salt**?
25: 11 then marshaled his strength and led his army to the Valley of **Salt**,
Job 6: 6 Is tasteless food eaten without **salt**, or is there flavor in the white of
Ps 60: T [60:2] down twelve thousand Edomites in the Valley of **Salt**.
Eze 43: 24 the priests are to sprinkle **salt** on them and sacrifice them as a burnt
47: 11 and marshes will not become fresh; they will be left for **salt**.
Zep 2: 9 a place of weeds and **salt** pits, a wasteland forever.

4876 מַלָּח mallāḥ, n.m. [4] [√ 4875]

mariners [2], sailors [2]

Eze 27: 9 of the sea and their **sailors** came alongside to trade for your wares.
27: 27 merchandise and wares, your **mariners**, seamen and shipwrights,
27: 29 the **mariners** and all the seamen will stand on the shore.
Jnh 1: 5 All the **sailors** were afraid and each cried out to his own god.

4877 מְלֵחָה m^elēḥâ, n.f. [3] [√ 4875]

salt flats [1], salt waste [1], salt [1]

Job 39: 6 I gave him the wasteland as his home, the **salt flats** as his habitat.
Ps 107: 34 fruitful land into a **salt waste**, because of the wickedness of those
Jer 17: 6 the parched places of the desert, in a **salt** land where no one lives.

4878 מִלְחָמָה milḥāmâ, n.f. [319] [√ 4309]

battle [135], war [73], fighting [16], fight [14], soldiers [+408] [12], wars [6], warrior [+408] [5], army [+408] [4], army [+6639] [4], battles [4], *untranslated* [3], military [3], warfare [3], at war with [+408] [2], battle formation [2], battle lines [2], fighting [+6913] [2], military age [2], armed [1], at war [+6913] [1], at war [1], attack [1], attacked [1], battle [+7372] [1], experienced fighter [+408] [1], experienced fighting men [+408+1475+2657] [1], fight [+2021+3655+4200] [1], force [+6639] [1], great soldiers [+408] [1], men ready for battle [+1522+7372] [1], ready for battle [+408+2021+4200+7372] [1], ready for battle [+928+2021+7372] [1], soldiers [+408+1505] [1], soldiers [+9530] [1], struggle [1], that[s] [1], time of war [1], wage war [+1741+2021+4200] [1], war cry [1], weapon [+3998] [1], weapon [+3998+7372] [1], weapons [+3998] [1], weapons of war [1], well-trained [+6913] [1], went to war [+906+906+6913] [1]

Ge 14: 2 **went to war** [+906+906+6913] *against* Bera king of Sodom,
14: 8 marched out and drew up their **battle** lines in the Valley of Siddim
Ex 1: 10 if **war** breaks out, will join our enemies, fight against us and leave
13: 17 For God said, "If they face **war**, they might change their minds
15: 3 The LORD is a **warrior** [+408]; the LORD is his name.
17: 16 The LORD will be at **war** against the Amalekites from generation
32: 17 he said to Moses, "There is the sound of **war** in the camp."
Nu 10: 9 When you go into **battle** in your own land against an enemy who is
21: 14 That is why the Book of the **Wars** *of* the LORD says: "Waheb in
21: 33 and his whole army marched out to meet them in **battle** at Edrei.
31: 14 commanders of hundreds—who returned from the **battle** [+7372].
31: 21 Eleazar the priest said to the soldiers who had gone into **battle**,
31: 27 Divide the spoils between the **soldiers** [+9530] who took part in
31: 28 From the **soldiers** [+408] who fought in the battle, set apart as
31: 49 "Your servants have counted the **soldiers** [+408] under our
32: 6 "Shall your countrymen go to **war** while you sit here?
32: 20 do this—if you will arm yourselves before the LORD for **battle**,
32: 27 will cross over to **fight** before the LORD, just as our lord says."
32: 29 "If the Gadites and Reubenites, every man armed for **battle**,
Dt 1: 41 So every one of you put on his **weapons** [+3998], thinking it easy
2: 9 said to me, "Do not harass the Moabites or provoke them to **war**,
2: 14 that entire generation of **fighting** men had perished from the camp,
2: 16 Now when the last of these **fighting** men among the people had
2: 24 Begin to take possession of it and engage him in **battle**.
2: 32 and all his army came out to meet us in **battle** at Jahaz,
3: 1 with his whole army marched out to meet us in **battle** at Edrei.
4: 34 by testings, by miraculous signs and wonders, by **war**, by a mighty
20: 1 When you go to **war** against your enemies and see horses
20: 2 When you are about to go into **battle**, the priest shall come forward
20: 3 O Israel, today you are going into **battle** against your enemies.
20: 5 or he may die in **battle** and someone else may dedicate it.
20: 6 him go home, or he may die in **battle** and someone else enjoy it.
20: 7 go home, or he may die in **battle** and someone else marry her."
20: 12 If they refuse to make peace and they engage you in **battle**,
20: 20 use them to build siege works until the city **at war** [+6913] with
21: 10 When you go to **war** against your enemies and the LORD your
29: 7 [29:6] and Og king of Bashan came out to **fight** against us,
Jos 4: 13 crossed over before the LORD to the plains of Jericho for **war**.
5: 4 All those who came out of Egypt—all the men of **military age**—
5: 6 the men who were of **military age** when they left Egypt had died,
6: 3 March around the city once with all the **armed** men. Do this for six
8: 1 Take the whole **army** [+6639] with you, and go up and attack Ai.
8: 3 So Joshua and the whole **army** [+6639] moved out to attack Ai.
8: 11 The entire **force** [+6639] that was with him marched up
8: 14 to meet Israel in **battle** at a certain place overlooking the Arabah.
10: 7 So Joshua marched up from Gilgal with his entire **army** [+6639],
10: 24 and said to the **army** [+408] commanders who had come with him,
11: 7 his whole **army** [+6639] came against them suddenly at the Waters

Jos 11:18 Joshua waged **war** against all these kings for a long time.
11:19 a treaty of peace with the Israelites, who took them all in **battle**.
11:20 himself who hardened their hearts to wage **war** against Israel,
11:23 according to their tribal divisions. Then the land had rest from **war**.
14:11 I'm just as vigorous to go out to **battle** now as I was then.
14:15 man among the Anakites.) Then the land had rest from **war**.
17: 1 and Bashan because the Makirites were **great soldiers** [+408].
Jdg 3: 1 Israelites who had not experienced any of the **wars** *in* Canaan
3: 2 (he did this only to teach **warfare** to the descendants of the
3:10 came upon him, so that he became Israel's judge and went to **war**.
8:13 son of Joash then returned from the **battle** by the Pass of Heres.
18:11 of the Danites, armed for **battle**, set out from Zorah and Eshtaol.
18:16 The six hundred Danites, armed for **battle**, stood at the entrance to
18:17 the six hundred armed **[RPH]** men stood at the entrance to the
20:14 at Gibeah to **fight** [+2021+3655+4200] against the Israelites.
20:17 four hundred thousand swordsmen, all of them **fighting** men.
20:18 "Who of us shall go first to **fight** against the Benjamites?"
20:20 The men of Israel went out to **fight** the Benjamites and took up
20:20 and took up **battle** positions against them at Gibeah.
20:22 again took up their positions **[RPH]** where they had stationed
20:23 They said, "Shall we go up again to **battle** against the Benjamites,
20:28 "Shall we go up again to **battle** with Benjamin our brother,
20:34 The **fighting** was so heavy that the Benjamites did not realize how
20:39 then the men of Israel would turn in the **battle**. The Benjamites had
20:39 and they said, "We are defeating them as in the first **battle**."
20:42 in the direction of the desert, but they could not escape the **battle**.
21:22 because we did not get wives for them during the **war**, and you are
1Sa 4: 1 Now the Israelites went out to **fight** against the Philistines.
4: 2 and as the **battle** spread, Israel was defeated by the Philistines,
7:10 burnt offering, the Philistines drew near to engage Israel in **battle**.
8:12 still others to make weapons of **war** and equipment for his
8:20 a king to lead us and to go out before us and fight our **battles**."
13:22 So on the day of the **battle** not a soldier with Saul and Jonathan
14:20 Then Saul and all his men assembled and went to the **battle**.
14:22 Philistines were on the run, they joined the **battle** in hot pursuit.
14:23 Israel that day, and the **battle** moved on beyond Beth Aven.
14:52 All the days of Saul there was bitter **war** with the Philistines,
16:18 He is a brave man and a **warrior** [+408]. He speaks well and is a
17: 1 Now the Philistines gathered their forces for **war** and assembled at
17: 2 Valley of Elah and drew up their **battle** line to meet the Philistines.
17: 8 the ranks of Israel, "Why do you come out and line up for **battle**?
17:13 Jesse's three oldest sons had followed Saul to the **war**: The
17:13 **[RPH]** The firstborn was Eliab; the second, Abinadab;
17:20 army was going out to its battle positions, shouting the **war cry**.
17:28 wicked your heart is; you came down only to watch the **battle**."
17:33 are only a boy, and he has been a **fighting** man from his youth."
17:47 for the **battle** is the LORD's, and he will give all of you into our
18: 5 so successfully that Saul gave him a high rank in the **army** [+408].
18:17 only serve me bravely and fight the **battles** *of* the LORD."
19: 8 Once more **war** broke out, and David went out and fought the
23: 8 Saul called up all his forces for **battle**, to go down to Keilah to
25:28 dynasty for my master, because he fights the LORD's **battles**.
26:10 time will come and he will die, or he will go into **battle** and perish.
29: 4 He must not go with us into **battle**, or he will turn against us
29: 4 go with us into battle, or he will turn against us during the **fighting**.
29: 9 commanders have said, 'He must not go up with us into **battle**.'
30:24 is to be the same as that of him who went down to the **battle**.
31: 3 The **fighting** grew fierce around Saul, and when the archers
2Sa 1: 4 David asked. "Tell me." He said, "The men fled from the **battle**.
1:25 "How the mighty have fallen in **battle**! Jonathan lies slain on your
1:27 the mighty have fallen! The weapons of **war** have perished!"
2:17 The **battle** that day was very fierce, and Abner and the men of
3: 1 The **war** between the house of Saul and the house of David lasted a
3: 6 During the **war** between the house of Saul and the house of David,
3:30 because he had killed their brother Asahel in the **battle** at Gibeon.)
8:10 in battle over Hadadezer, who had been **at war** [+408] **with** Tou.
10: 8 and drew up in **battle formation** at the entrance to their city gate,
10: 9 Joab saw that there were **battle lines** in front of him and behind
10:13 and the troops with him advanced to **fight** the Arameans,
11: 7 how Joab was, how the soldiers were and how the **war** was going.
11:15 he wrote, "Put Uriah in the front line where the **fighting** is fiercest.
11:18 Joab sent David a full account of the **battle**.
11:19 you have finished giving the king this account of the **battle**,
11:25 Press the **attack** against the city and destroy it.' Say this to
17: 8 Besides, your father is an **experienced fighter** [+408]; he will not
18: 6 to fight Israel, and the **battle** took place in the forest of Ephraim.
18: 8 The **battle** spread out over the whole countryside, and the forest
19: 3 [19:4] men steal in who are ashamed when they flee from **battle**.
19:10 [19:11] whom we anointed to rule over us, has died in **battle**.
21:15 Once again there was a **battle** between the Philistines and Israel.
21:17 to him, saying, "Never again will you go out with us to **battle**,
21:18 of time, there was another **battle** with the Philistines, at Gob.
21:19 In another **battle** with the Philistines at Gob, Elhanan son of
21:20 In still another **battle**, which took place at Gath, there was a huge
22:35 He trains my hands for **battle**; my arms can bend a bow of bronze.
22:40 You armed me with strength for **battle**; you made my adversaries
23: 9 they taunted the Philistines gathered ˻at Pas Dammim˼ for **battle**.
1Ki 2: 5 He killed them, shedding their blood in peacetime as if in **battle**,
2: 5 with **that**ˢ blood stained the belt around his waist and the sandals
5: 3 [5:17] because of the **wars** waged against my father David from
8:44 "When your people go to **war** against their enemies, wherever you
9:22 they were his **fighting** men, his government officials, his officers,
12:21 a hundred and eighty thousand **fighting** [+6913] men—
14:30 There was continual **warfare** between Rehoboam and Jeroboam.
15: 6 There was **war** between Rehoboam and Jeroboam throughout
15: 7 the kings of Judah? There was **war** between Abijah and Jeroboam.
15:16 There was **war** between Asa and Baasha king of Israel throughout
15:32 There was **war** between Asa and Baasha king of Israel throughout
20:14 commanders will do it.' " "And who will start the **battle**?"
20:18 take them alive; if they have come out for **war**, take them alive."
20:26 the Arameans and went up to Aphek to **fight** against Israel.
20:29 opposite each other, and on the seventh day the **battle** was joined.
20:39 called out to him, "Your servant went into the thick of the **battle**,
22: 1 For three years there was no **war** between Aram and Israel.
22: 4 "Will you go with me to **fight** against Ramoth Gilead?"
22: 6 and asked them, "Shall I go to **war** against Ramoth Gilead,
22:15 "Micaiah, shall we go to **war** against Ramoth Gilead, or shall I
22:30 "I will enter the **battle** in disguise, but you wear your royal robes."
22:30 So the king of Israel disguised himself and went into **battle**.
22:35 All day long the **battle** raged, and the king was propped up in his
2Ki 3: 7 Will you go with me to **fight** against Moab?" "I will go with you,"
3:26 When the king of Moab saw that the **battle** had gone against him,
8:28 Ahaziah went with Joram son of Ahab to **war** against Hazael king
13:25 Hazael the towns he had taken in **battle** from his father Jehoahaz.
14: 7 Edomites in the Valley of Salt and captured Sela in **battle**,
16: 5 Pekah son of Remaliah king of Israel marched up to **fight** against
18:20 You say you have strategy and **military** strength—but you speak
24:16 strong and fit for **war**, and a thousand craftsmen and artisans.
25: 4 the whole **army** [+408] fled at night through the gate between the
25:19 he took the officer in charge of the **fighting** men and five royal
1Ch 5:10 During Saul's reign they waged **war** against the Hagrites,
5:18 and sword, who could use a bow, and who were trained for **battle**.
5:19 They waged **war** against the Hagrites, Jetur, Naphish and Nodab.
5:20 allies over to them, because they cried out to him during the **battle**.
5:22 many others fell slain, because the **battle** was God's. And they
7: 4 they had 36,000 **men ready for battle** [+1522+7372], for they had
7:11 There were 17,200 fighting men ready to go out to **war**.
7:40 The number of men **ready for battle** [+928+2021+7372], as listed
10: 3 The **fighting** grew fierce around Saul, and when the archers
11:13 at Pas Dammim when the Philistines gathered there for **battle**.
12: 1 of Kish (they were among the warriors who helped him in **battle**;
12: 8 [12:9] brave warriors, **ready for battle** [+408+2021+4200+7372]
12:19 [12:20] when he went with the Philistines to **fight** against Saul.
12:33 [12:34] experienced soldiers prepared for **battle** with every type
12:33 [12:34] prepared for battle with every type of **weapon** [+3998],
12:35 [12:36] men of Dan, ready for **battle**—28,600;
12:36 [12:37] men of Asher, experienced soldiers prepared for **battle**—
12:37 [12:38] armed with every type of **weapon** [+3998+7372]—
12:38 [12:39] All these were **fighting** men who volunteered to serve in
14:15 of marching in the tops of the balsam trees, move out to **battle**,
18:10 in battle over Hadadezer, who had been **at war** [+408] **with** Tou.
19: 7 were mustered from their towns and moved out for **battle**.
19: 9 and drew up in **battle formation** at the entrance to their city,
19:10 Joab saw that there were **battle lines** in front of him and behind
19:14 and the troops with him advanced to **fight** the Arameans,
19:17 David formed his lines to meet the Arameans *in* **battle**, and they
20: 4 In the course of time, **war** broke out with the Philistines, at Gezer.
20: 5 In another **battle** with the Philistines, Elhanan son of Jair killed
20: 6 In still another **battle**, which took place at Gath, there was a huge
22: 8 to me: 'You have shed much blood and have fought many **wars**.
26:27 Some of the plunder taken in **battle** they dedicated for the repair of
28: 3 my Name, because you are a **warrior** [+408] and have shed blood.'
2Ch 6:34 "When your people go to **war** against their enemies, wherever you
8: 9 they were his **fighting** men, commanders of his captains,
11: 1 a hundred and eighty thousand **fighting** [+6913] men—
12:15 There was continual **warfare** *between* Rehoboam and Jeroboam.
13: 2 of Uriel of Gibeah. There was **war** between Abijah and Jeroboam.
13: 3 Abijah went into **battle** with a force of four hundred thousand able
13: 3 battle with a force of four hundred thousand able **fighting** men,
13: 3 Jeroboam drew up a **battle** line against him with eight hundred
13:14 and saw that they were being **attacked** at both front and rear.
14: 6 [14:5] No one was at **war** with him during those years,
14:10 [14:9] they took up **battle** positions in the Valley of Zephathah
15:19 There was no more **war** until the thirty-fifth year of Asa's reign.
16: 9 have done a foolish thing, and from now on you will be at **war**."
17:13 He also kept **experienced fighting men** [+408+1475+2657] in
18: 3 and my people as your people; we will join you in the **war**."
18: 5 and asked them, "Shall we go to **war** against Ramoth Gilead,

2Ch 18:14 "Micaiah, shall we go to **war** against Ramoth Gilead, or shall I
18:29 "I will enter the **battle** in disguise, but you wear your royal robes."
18:29 So the king of Israel disguised himself and went into **battle**.
18:34 All day long the **battle** raged, and the king of Israel propped
20:1 Ammonites with some of the Meunites came to make **war** on
20:15 because of this vast army. For the **battle** is not yours, but God's.
22:5 of Israel to **war** against Hazael king of Aram at Ramoth Gilead.
25:8 Even if you go and fight courageously in **battle**, God will
25:13 had not allowed to take part in the **war** raided Judean towns from
26:11 Uzziah had a **well-trained** [+6913] army, ready to go out by
26:13 their command was an army of 307,500 men trained for **war**,
27:7 Jotham's reign, including all his **wars** and the other things he did,
32:2 had come and that he intended to *make* **war** on Jerusalem,
32:6 He appointed **military** officers over the people and assembled
32:8 with us is the LORD our God to help us and to fight our **battles**."
35:21 I am attacking at this time, but the house with which I am **at war**.
Job 5:20 ransom you from death, and in **battle** from the stroke of the sword.
38:23 which I reserve for times of trouble, for days of war and **battle**?
39:25 He catches the scent of **battle** from afar, the shout of commanders
41:8 [40:32] you will remember the **struggle** and never do it again!
Ps 18:34 [18:35] He trains my hands for **battle**; my arms can bend a bow
18:39 [18:40] You armed me with strength for **battle**; you made my
24:8 The LORD strong and mighty, the LORD mighty **in battle**.
27:3 though **war** break out against me, even then will I be confident.
46:9 [46:10] He makes **wars** cease to the ends of the earth; he breaks
76:3 [76:4] the shields and the swords, the **weapons of war**.
89:43 [89:44] edge of his sword and have not supported him in **battle**.
120:7 I am a man of peace; but when I speak, they are for **war**.
140:2 [140:3] devise evil plans in their hearts and stir up **war** every day.
144:1 my Rock, who trains my hands for war, my fingers for **battle**.
Pr 20:18 Make plans by seeking advice; if you wage **war**, obtain guidance.
21:31 The horse is made ready for the day of **battle**, but victory rests
24:6 for waging **war** you need guidance, and for victory many advisers.
Ecc 3:8 to love and a time to hate, a time for **war** and a time for peace.
8:8 As no one is discharged in **time of war**, so wickedness will not
9:11 The race is not to the swift or the **battle** to the strong, nor does
SS 3:8 all of them wearing the sword, all experienced in **battle**, each with
Isa 2:4 take up sword against nation, nor will they train for **war** anymore.
3:2 the hero and **warrior** [+408], the judge and prophet, the soothsayer
3:25 Your men will fall by the sword, your warriors in **battle**.
7:1 Pekah son of Remaliah king of Israel marched up to **fight** against
13:4 The LORD Almighty is mustering an army for **war**.
21:15 the drawn sword, from the bent bow and from the heat of **battle**.
22:2 Your slain were not killed by the sword, nor did they die in **battle**.
27:4 I would march against them in **battle**; I would set them all on fire.
28:6 a source of strength to those who turn back the **battle** at the gate.
30:32 and harps, as he fights them in **battle** with the blows of his arm.
36:5 You say you have strategy and **military** strength—but you speak
41:12 Those who wage **war** *against* you will be as nothing at all.
42:13 like a mighty man, like a **warrior** [+408] he will stir up his zeal;
42:25 So he poured out on them his burning anger, the violence of **war**.
Jer 4:19 I have heard the sound of the trumpet; I have heard the **battle** cry.
6:4 "Prepare for **battle** against her! Arise, let us attack at noon!
6:23 they come like men in **battle** formation to attack you, O Daughter
8:6 Each pursues his own course like a horse charging into **battle**.
18:21 men be put to death, their young men slain by the sword in **battle**.
21:4 I am about to turn against you the weapons of **war** that are in your
28:8 times the prophets who preceded you and me have prophesied **war**,
38:4 He is discouraging the **soldiers** [+408] who are left in this city,
39:4 Zedekiah king of Judah and all the **soldiers** [+408] saw them,
41:3 as well as the Babylonian **soldiers** [+408] who were there.
41:16 the **soldiers** [+408+1505], women, children and court officials he
42:14 where we will not see **war** or hear the trumpet or be hungry for
46:3 your shields, both large and small, and march out for **battle**!
48:14 "How can you say, 'We are warriors, men valiant in **battle**'?
49:2 "when I will sound the **battle** cry against Rabbah of the
49:14 to say, "Assemble yourselves to attack it! Rise up for **battle**!"
49:26 all her **soldiers** [+408] will be silenced in that day,"
50:22 The noise of **battle** is in the land, the noise of great destruction!
50:30 all her **soldiers** [+408] will be silenced in that day,"
50:42 they come like men in **battle** formation to attack you, O Daughter
51:20 "You are my war club, my weapon for **battle**—with you I shatter
51:32 the marshes set on fire, and the **soldiers** [+408] terrified."
52:7 the city wall was broken through, and the whole **army** [+408] fled.
52:25 still in the city, he took the officer in charge of the **fighting** men,
Eze 7:14 the trumpet and get everything ready, no one will go into **battle**,
13:5 so that it will stand firm in the **battle** on the day of the LORD.
17:17 his mighty army and great horde will be of no help to him in **war**,
27:10 of Persia, Lydia and Put served as **soldiers** [+408] in your army.
27:27 and shipwrights, your merchants and all your **soldiers** [+408],
32:27 who went down to the grave with their weapons of **war**, whose
39:20 and riders, mighty men and **soldiers** [+408] of every kind,'
Da 9:26 **War** will continue until the end, and desolations have been
11:20 however, he will be destroyed, yet not in anger or in **battle**.
11:25 The king of the South *will* **wage war** [+1741+2021+4200] with a
Hos 1:7 not by bow, sword or **battle**, or by horses and horsemen, but by the
2:18 [2:20] Bow and sword and **battle** I will abolish from the land,
10:9 you have remained. Did not **war** overtake the evildoers in Gibeah?
10:14 as Shalman devastated Beth Arbel on the day of **battle**,
Joel 2:5 fire consuming stubble, like a mighty army drawn up for **battle**.
2:7 They charge like warriors; they scale walls like **soldiers** [+408].
3:9 [4:9] among the nations: Prepare for **war**! Rouse the warriors!
3:9 [4:9] the warriors! Let all the **fighting** men draw near and attack.
Am 1:14 will consume her fortresses amid war cries on the day of **battle**,
Ob 1:1 to the nations to say, "Rise, and let us go against her for **battle**"—
Mic 2:8 those who pass by without a care, like men returning from **battle**.
3:5 if he does not, they prepare to wage **war** against him.
4:3 take up sword against nation, nor will they train for **war** anymore.
Zec 9:10 the war-horses from Jerusalem, and the **battle** bow will be broken.
10:3 the house of Judah, and make them like a proud horse in **battle**.
10:4 him the tent peg, from him the **battle** bow, from him every ruler.
10:5 they will be like mighty men trampling the muddy streets in **battle**.
14:2 I will gather all the nations to Jerusalem to **fight** against it;

4879 מֶלֶט melet̩, n.[m.]. [1] [√ 4881?]

clay [1]

Jer 43:9 bury them in **clay** in the brick pavement at the entrance to

4880 מָלַט mālat̩[1], v. [95] [→ 4882; cf. 7117]

escaped [20], escape [17], save [7], flee [5], rescued [4], run [4], be delivered [3], rescue [3], saved [3], deliver [2], delivers [2], escape [+4880] [2], go free [2], got away [2], let get away [2], save [+4880] [2], be saved [1], escape [+7127] [1], escaping [1], get away [1], is kept safe [1], lay eggs [1], made escape [1], made good escape [+2256+5674] [1], release [1], retrieved [1], shoot out [1], slip out [1], slipped away [1], spared [1], were saved [1]

Ge 19:17 [C] had brought them out, one of them said, "**Flee** for your lives!
19:17 [C] the plain! **Flee** to the mountains or you will be swept away!"
19:19 [C] I can't **flee** to the mountains; this disaster will overtake me,
19:20 [C] and it is small. *Let me* **flee** to it—it is very small, isn't it?
19:22 [C] **flee** there quickly, because I cannot do anything until you
Jdg 3:26 [C] While they waited, Ehud **got away**. He passed by the idols
3:26 [C] got away. He passed by the idols and **escaped** to Seirah.
3:29 [C] all vigorous and strong; not a man **escaped**.
1Sa 19:10 [C] That night David **made good** *his* **escape** [+2256+5674].
19:11 [D] warned him, "If you don't **run** *for* your life tonight,
19:12 [C] let David down through a window, and he fled and **escaped**.
19:17 [C] me like this and send my enemy away so that *he* **escaped**?"
19:18 [C] When David had fled and **made** *his* **escape**, he went to
20:29 [C] favor in your eyes, **let** *me* **get away** to see my brothers.'
22:1 [C] David left Gath and **escaped** to the cave of Adullam.
22:20 [C] of Ahimelech son of Ahitub, **escaped** and fled to join David.
23:13 [C] When Saul was told that David *had* **escaped** from Keilah,
27:1 [C] The best thing I can do *is to* **escape** [+4880] to the land of the
27:1 [C] The best thing I can do *is to* **escape** [+4880] to the land of the
27:1 [C] for me anywhere in Israel, and *I will* **slip out** of his hand."
30:17 [C] none of them **got away**, except four hundred young men who
2Sa 1:3 [C] He answered, "*I have* **escaped** from the Israelite camp."
4:6 [C] Then Recab and his brother Baanah **slipped away**.
19:5 [19:6] [D] who *have* just **saved** your life and the lives of your
19:9 [19:10] [D] he *is* the *one who* **rescued** us from the hand of the
1Ki 1:12 [D] let me advise you how *you can* **save** your own life and the
18:40 [C] Don't **let** anyone **get away**!" They seized them, and Elijah
19:17 [C] Jehu will put to death any *who* **escape** the sword of Hazael,
19:17 [C] Elisha will put to death any *who* **escape** the sword of Jehu.
20:20 [C] Ben-Hadad king of Aram **escaped** on horseback with some
2Ki 10:24 [C] of you lets any of the men I am placing in your hands **escape**,
19:37 [C] down with the sword, and they **escaped** *to* the land of Ararat.
23:18 [D] So *they* **spared** his bones and those of the prophet who had
2Ch 16:7 [C] the army of the king of Aram *has* **escaped** from your hand.
Est 4:13 [C] are in the king's house *you* alone of all the Jews *will* **escape**.
Job 1:15 [C] and I am the only one *who has* **escaped** to tell you!"
1:16 [C] and I am the only one *who has* **escaped** to tell you!"
1:17 [C] and I am the only one *who has* **escaped** to tell you!"
1:19 [C] and I am the only one *who has* **escaped** to tell you!"
6:23 [D] **deliver** me from the hand of the enemy, ransom me from the
19:20 [F] and bones; *I have* **escaped** with only the skin of my teeth.
20:20 [D] from his craving; *he* cannot **save** *himself* by his treasure.
22:30 [D] *He will* **deliver** even one who is not innocent, who will be
22:30 [C] *who will* **be delivered** through the cleanness of your hands."
29:12 [D] because *I* **rescued** the poor who cried for help,
41:19 [41:11] [F] stream from his mouth; sparks of fire **shoot out**.
Ps 22:5 [22:6] [C] They cried to you and **were saved**; in you they
33:17 [D] for deliverance; despite all its great strength *it* cannot **save**.
41:1 [41:2] [D] the LORD **delivers** him in times of trouble.
89:48 [89:49] [D] or **save** himself from the power of the grave?

Ps 107:20 [D] his word and healed them; *he* **rescued** them from the grave.
116: 4 [D] I called on the name of the LORD: "O LORD, **save** me!"
124: 7 [C] We *have* **escaped** like a bird out of the fowler's snare;
124: 7 [C] the snare has been broken, and we *have* **escaped**.
Pr 11:21 [C] not go unpunished, but those who are righteous *will* **go free**.
19: 5 [C] go unpunished, and he who pours out lies *will* not **go free**.
28:26 [C] in himself is a fool, but he who walks in wisdom **is kept safe**.
Ecc 7:26 [C] The man who pleases God *will* **escape** her, but the sinner she
8: 8 [D] of war, so wickedness *will* not **release** those who practice it.
9:15 [D] a man poor but wise, and he **saved** the city by his wisdom.
Isa 20: 6 [C] from the king of Assyria! How then *can* we **escape**?' "
31: 5 [G] and deliver it, he will 'pass over' it and *will* **rescue** it."
34:15 [D] The owl will nest there and **lay eggs**, she will hatch them,
37:38 [C] down with the sword, and they **escaped** *to* the land of Ararat.
46: 2 [D] unable *to* **rescue** the burden, they themselves go off into
46: 4 [D] and I will carry you; I will sustain you and *I will* **rescue** you.
49:24 [C] be taken from warriors, or captives **rescued** *from* the fierce?
49:25 [C] taken from warriors, and plunder **retrieved** *from* the fierce;
66: 7 [G] before the pains come upon her, *she* **delivers** a son.
Jer 32: 4 [C] Zedekiah king of Judah *will* not **escape** out of the hands of
34: 3 [C] You *will* not **escape** from his grasp but will surely be
38:18 [C] it down; *you* yourself *will* not **escape** from their hands.' "
38:23 [C] *You* yourself *will* not **escape** from their hands but will be
39:18 [D] *I will* **save** [+4880] you; you will not fall by the sword
39:18 [D] *I will* **save** [+4880] you; you will not fall by the sword
41:15 [C] eight of his men **escaped** from Johanan and fled to the
46: 6 [C] "The swift cannot flee nor the strong **escape**. In the north by
48: 6 [D] Flee! **Run** *for* your lives; become like a bush in the desert.
48: 8 [C] will come against every town, and not a town *will* **escape**.
48:19 [C] Ask the man fleeing and the *woman* **escaping**, ask them,
51: 6 [D] **Run** *for* your lives! Do not be destroyed because of her sins.
51:45 [D] "Come out of her, my people! **Run** *for* your lives! Run from
Eze 17:15 [C] Will he succeed? *Will he* who does such things **escape**?
17:15 [C] such things escape? Will he break the treaty and yet **escape**?
17:18 [C] in pledge and yet did all these things, *he shall* not **escape**.
33: 5 [D] If he had taken warning, *he would have* **saved** himself.
Da 11:41 [C] and the leaders of Ammon *will* **be delivered** from his hand.
12: 1 [C] whose name is found written in the book—*will* **be delivered**.
Joel 2:32 [3:5] [C] who calls on the name of the LORD *will* **be saved**;
Am 2:14 [D] muster their strength, and the warrior *will* not **save** his life.
2:15 [D] stand his ground, the fleet-footed soldier *will* not **get away**,
2:15 [D] will not get away, and the horseman *will* not **save** his life.
9: 1 [C] the sword. Not one will get away, none *will* **escape** [+7127].
Zec 2: 7 [2:11] [C] **Escape**, you who live in the Daughter of Babylon!"
Mal 3:15 [C] and even those who challenge God **escape**.' "

4881 ²מָלַט **mālaṭ²**, v. Not used in NIV/BHS [→ 4879?]

4882 מְלַטְיָה **mᵉlaṭyâ**, n.pr.m. [1] [√ 4880 + 3378]

Melatiah [1]

Ne 3: 7 and Mizpah—**Melatiah** of Gibeon and Jadon of Meronoth—

4883 מְלִיכוּ **mᵉlîkû**, n.pr.m. [0] [cf. 4868]

Ne 12:14 [of **Malluch's**, [Q; see K 4868] Jonathan; of Shecaniah's,]

4884 מְלִילָה **mᵉlîlâ**, n.f. [1] [√ 4908]

kernels [1]

Dt 23:25 [23:26] you may pick **kernels** with your hands,

4885 מֵלִיץ **mēlîṣ**, n.[m.] *or* v.ptcp. [5] [√ 4329]

envoys [1], intercessor [1], interpreter [1], mediator [1], spokesmen [1]

Ge 42:23 Joseph could understand them, since he was using an **interpreter**.
2Ch 32:31 when **envoys** were sent *by* the rulers of Babylon to ask him about
Job 16:20 My **intercessor** is my friend as my eyes pour out tears to God;
33:23 "Yet if there is an angel on his side as a **mediator**, one out of a
Isa 43:27 Your first father sinned; your **spokesmen** rebelled against me.

4886 מְלִיצָה **mᵉlîṣâ**, n.[f.]. [2] [√ 4329]

parables [1], ridicule [1]

Pr 1: 6 for understanding proverbs and **parables**, the sayings and riddles
Hab 2: 6 "Will not all of them taunt him with **ridicule** and scorn, saying,

4887 ¹מָלַךְ **mālak¹**, v.den. [347] [→ 3552?, 4867 4888, 4889, 4930, 4931]

king [151], reigned [70], reign [37], made king [24], reigns [9], ruled [9], make king [7], *untranslated* [5], rule [5], proclaimed king [3], intend to reign [+4887] [2], set up king [+4889+6584] [2], surely be king [+4887] [2], acknowledged as king [1], appoint as king [1], came to power [1], confirmed as king [1], crown [1], extend [1], give king [+4200+4889] [1], king [+4889] [1], kingship [1], made king [+906+4200+4889] [1], made queen [1], make king [+906+4889] [1], put on throne [1], queen [1], reigned [+4889] [1], ruled over [1], ruling [1], set a king [+4889] [1], set up kings [1], took control [1], was made ruler [1]

Ge 36:31 [A] These were the kings who **reigned** in Edom before any
36:31 [A] who reigned in Edom before any Israelite king **reigned**:
36:32 [A] Bela son of Beor *became* **king** of Edom. His city was named
36:33 [A] Jobab son of Zerah from Bozrah succeeded him *as* **king**.
36:34 [A] from the land of the Temanites succeeded him *as* **king**.
36:35 [A] Midian in the country of Moab, succeeded him *as* **king**.
36:36 [A] Hadad died, Samlah from Masrekah succeeded him *as* **king**.
36:37 [A] Shaul from Rehoboth on the river succeeded him *as* **king**.
36:38 [A] Shaul died, Baal-Hanan son of Acbor succeeded him *as* **king**.
36:39 [A] son of Acbor died, Hadad succeeded him *as* **king**.
37: 8 [A] said to him, "*Do you* **intend to reign** [+4887] over us?
37: 8 [A] said to him, "*Do you* **intend to reign** [+4887] over us?
Ex 15:18 [A] The LORD *will* **reign** for ever and ever."
Jos 13:10 [A] who **ruled** in Heshbon, out to the border of the Ammonites.
13:12 [A] who *had* **reigned** in Ashtaroth and Edrei and had survived as
13:21 [A] realm of Sihon king of the Amorites, who **ruled** at Heshbon.
Jdg 4: 2 [A] the hands of Jabin, a king of Canaan, who **reigned** in Hazor.
9: 6 [G] great tree at the pillar in Shechem *to* **crown** Abimelech king.
9: 8 [A] for themselves. They said to the olive tree, '*Be* our **king**.'
9:10 [A] "Next, the trees said to the fig tree, 'Come and *be* our **king**.'
9:12 [A] "Then the trees said to the vine, 'Come and *be* our **king**.'
9:14 [A] all the trees said to the thornbush, 'Come and *be* our **king**.'
9:16 [G] and in good faith when *you* **made** Abimelech **king**,
9:18 [G] **made** Abimelech, the son of his slave girl, **king** over the
1Sa 8: 7 [A] they have rejected, but they have rejected me as their **king**.
8: 9 [A] let them know what the king who *will* **reign** over them will
8:11 [A] "This is what the king who *will* **reign** over you will do:
8:22 [G] "Listen to them and **give** them a **king** [+4200+4889]."
11:12 [A] "Who was it that asked, '*Shall* Saul **reign** over us?'
11:15 [G] and **confirmed** Saul **as king** in the presence of the LORD.
12: 1 [G] you said to me and *have* **set a king** [+4889] over you.
12:12 [A] you said to me, 'No, we want a king *to* **rule** over us'—
12:14 [A] the king who **reigns** over you follow the LORD your God—
13: 1 [A] Saul was ⌞thirty⌟ years old when he *became* **king**, and he
13: 1 [A] became king, and *he* **reigned** over Israel ⌞forty-⌟two years.
15:11 [G] "I am grieved that *I have* **made** Saul **king** [+906+4200+4889],
15:35 [G] the LORD was grieved that *he had* **made** Saul **king** over
16: 1 [A] for Saul, since I have rejected him as **king** over Israel?
23:17 [A] You *will be* **king** over Israel, and I will be second to you.
24:20 [24:21] [A] I know that *you will* **surely be king** [+4887] and
24:20 [24:21] [A] I know that *you will* **surely be king** [+4887] and
2Sa 2: 9 [G] *He* **made** him **king** over Gilead, Ashuri and Jezreel, and also
2:10 [A] Saul was forty years old when he *became* **king** over Israel,
2:10 [A] when he became king over Israel, and *he* **reigned** two years.
3:21 [A] and that *you may* **rule** over all that your heart desires."
5: 4 [A] David was thirty years old when he *became* **king**, and he
5: 4 [A] years old when he became king, and *he* **reigned** forty years.
5: 5 [A] In Hebron *he* **reigned** over Judah seven years and six
5: 5 [A] in Jerusalem *he* **reigned** over all Israel and Judah thirty-three
8:15 [A] David **reigned** over all Israel, doing what was just and right
10: 1 [A] Ammonites died, and his son Hanun succeeded him *as* **king**.
15:10 [A] of the trumpets, then say, 'Absalom *is* **king** in Hebron.' "
16: 8 [A] in the household of Saul, in whose place *you have* **reigned**.
1Ki 1: 5 [A] was Haggith, put himself forward and said, "I *will be* **king**."
1:11 [A] *has become* **king** without our lord David's knowing it?
1:13 [A] "Surely Solomon your son *shall be* **king** after me, and he
1:13 [A] sit on my throne"? Why then *has* Adonijah *become* **king**?'
1:17 [A] 'Solomon your son *shall be* **king** after me, and he will sit on
1:18 [A] now Adonijah *has become* **king**, and you, my lord the king,
1:24 [A] lord the king, declared that Adonijah *shall be* **king** after you,
1:30 [A] Solomon your son *shall be* **king** after me, and he will sit on
1:35 [A] he is to come and sit on my throne and **reign** in my place.
1:43 [G] "Our lord King David *has* **made** Solomon **king**.
2:11 [A] He *had* **reigned** forty years over Israel—seven years in
2:11 [A] seven years in Hebron **[RPH]** and thirty-three in Jerusalem.
2:11 [A] seven years in Hebron and thirty-three in Jerusalem. **[RPH]**
2:15 [A] All Israel looked to me as their **king**. But things changed,
3: 7 [G] you *have* **made** your servant **king** in place of my father
6: 1 [A] in the fourth year of Solomon's **reign** over Israel,
11:24 [A] went to Damascus, where they settled and **took control**.
11:25 [A] So Rezon **ruled** in Aram and was hostile toward Israel.
11:37 [A] take you, and *you will* **rule** over all that your heart desires;
11:42 [A] Solomon **reigned** in Jerusalem over all Israel forty years.
11:43 [A] his father. And Rehoboam his son succeeded him *as* **king**.
12: 1 [G] for all the Israelites had gone there to **make** him **king**.
12:17 [A] in the towns of Judah, Rehoboam *still* **ruled** over them.
12:20 [G] him to the assembly and **made** him **king** over all Israel.
14:19 [A] other events of Jeroboam's reign, his wars and how *he* **ruled**,
14:20 [A] He **reigned** for twenty-two years and then rested with his

1Ki 14:20 [A] with his fathers. And Nadab his son succeeded him *as* **king**.
14:21 [A] Rehoboam son of Solomon *was* **king** in Judah. He was
14:21 [A] He was forty-one years old when he *became* **king**, and he
14:21 [A] became king, and *he* **reigned** seventeen years in Jerusalem,
14:31 [A] an Ammonite. And Abijah his son succeeded him *as* **king**.
15: 1 [A] of Jeroboam son of Nebat, Abijah *became* **king** of Judah,
15: 2 [A] *he* **reigned** in Jerusalem three years. His mother's name was
15: 8 [A] the City of David. And Asa his son succeeded him *as* **king**.
15: 9 [A] Jeroboam king of Israel, Asa *became* **king** [+4889] *of* Judah,
15:10 [A] *he* **reigned** in Jerusalem forty-one years. His grandmother's
15:24 [A] And Jehoshaphat his son succeeded him *as* **king**.
15:25 [A] Nadab son of Jeroboam *became* **king** of Israel in the second
15:25 [A] of Asa king of Judah, and *he* **reigned** over Israel two years.
15:28 [A] third year of Asa king of Judah and succeeded him *as* **king**.
15:29 [A] As soon as he *began to* **reign**, he killed Jeroboam's whole
15:33 [A] Baasha son of Ahijah *became* **king** of all Israel in Tirzah,
16: 6 [A] buried in Tirzah. And Elah his son succeeded him *as* **king**.
16: 8 [A] Elah son of Baasha *became* **king** of Israel, and he reigned in
16:10 [A] year of Asa king of Judah. Then *he* succeeded him *as* **king**.
16:11 [A] As soon as he *began to* **reign** and was seated on the throne,
16:15 [A] of Asa king of Judah, Zimri **reigned** in Tirzah seven days.
16:16 [G] they **proclaimed** Omri, the commander of the army, **king**
16:21 [G] half supported Tibni son of Ginath for **king**, and the other
16:22 [A] Tibni son of Ginath. So Tibni died and Omri *became* **king**.
16:23 [A] Omri *became* **king** of Israel, and he reigned twelve years,
16:23 [A] of Israel, and *he* **reigned** twelve years, six of them in Tirzah.
16:28 [A] buried in Samaria. And Ahab his son succeeded him *as* **king**.
16:29 [A] Asa king of Judah, Ahab son of Omri *became* **king** of Israel,
16:29 [A] and he **reigned** in Samaria over Israel twenty-two years.
22:40 [A] his fathers. And Ahaziah his son succeeded him *as* **king**.
22:41 [A] Jehoshaphat son of Asa *became* **king** of Judah in the fourth
22:42 [A] Jehoshaphat was thirty-five years old when he *became* **king**,
22:42 [A] became king, and *he* **reigned** in Jerusalem twenty-five years.
22:50 [22:51] [A] And Jehoram his son succeeded him. **[RPH]**
22:51 [22:52] [A] Ahaziah son of Ahab *became* **king** of Israel in
22:51 [22:52] [A] king of Judah, and *he* **reigned** over Israel two years.
2Ki 1:17 [A] Joram succeeded him *as* **king** in the second year of Jehoram
3: 1 [A] Joram son of Ahab *became* **king** of Israel in Samaria in the
3: 1 [A] of Jehoshaphat king of Judah, and *he* **reigned** twelve years.
3:27 [A] he took his firstborn son, who *was to* succeed him *as* **king**,
8:15 [A] so that he died. Then Hazael succeeded him *as* **king**.
8:16 [A] Jehoram son of Jehoshaphat *began his* **reign** as king of
8:17 [A] He was thirty-two years old when he *became* **king**, and he
8:17 [A] he became king, and *he* **reigned** in Jerusalem eight years.
8:20 [G] against Judah and **set up** its own **king** [+4889+6584].
8:24 [A] City of David. And Ahaziah his son succeeded him *as* **king**.
8:25 [A] Ahaziah son of Jehoram king of Judah *began to* **reign**.
8:26 [A] Ahaziah was twenty-two years old when he *became* **king**,
8:26 [A] when he became king, and *he* **reigned** in Jerusalem one year.
9:13 [A] Then they blew the trumpet and shouted, "Jehu *is* **king**!"
9:29 [A] of Joram son of Ahab, Ahaziah *had become* **king** of Judah.)
10: 5 [G] *We will* not **appoint** anyone **as king**; you do whatever you
10:35 [A] in Samaria. And Jehoahaz his son succeeded him *as* **king**.
10:36 [A] The time that Jehu **reigned** over Israel in Samaria was
11: 3 [A] of the LORD for six years while Athaliah **ruled** the land.
11:12 [G] him with a copy of the covenant and **proclaimed** him **king**.
11:21 [12:1] [A] Joash was seven years old when he *began to* **reign**.
12: 1 [12:2] [A] In the seventh year of Jehu, Joash *became* **king**,
12: 1 [12:2] [A] and *he* **reigned** in Jerusalem forty years.
12:21 [12:22] [A] And Amaziah his son succeeded him *as* **king**.
13: 1 [A] Jehoahaz son of Jehu *became* **king** of Israel in Samaria,
13: 9 [A] in Samaria. And Jehoash his son succeeded him *as* **king**.
13:10 [A] Jehoash son of Jehoahaz *became* **king** of Israel in Samaria,
13:24 [A] Aram died, and Ben-Hadad his son succeeded him *as* **king**.
14: 1 [A] Amaziah son of Joash king of Judah *began to* **reign**.
14: 2 [A] He was twenty-five years old when he *became* **king**, and he
14: 2 [A] became king, and *he* **reigned** in Jerusalem twenty-nine years.
14:16 [A] of Israel. And Jeroboam his son succeeded him *as* **king**.
14:21 [G] years old, and **made** him **king** in place of his father Amaziah.
14:23 [A] Jeroboam son of Jehoash king of Israel *became* **king** in
14:29 [A] of Israel. And Zechariah his son succeeded him *as* **king**.
15: 1 [A] Azariah son of Amaziah king of Judah *began to* **reign**.
15: 2 [A] He was sixteen years old when he *became* **king**, and he
15: 2 [A] he became king, and *he* **reigned** in Jerusalem fifty-two years.
15: 7 [A] City of David. And Jotham his son succeeded him *as* **king**.
15: 8 [A] Zechariah son of Jeroboam *became* **king** of Israel in
15:10 [A] of the people, assassinated him and succeeded him *as* **king**.
15:13 [A] Shallum son of Jabesh *became* **king** in the thirty-ninth year
15:13 [A] Uzziah king of Judah, and *he* **reigned** in Samaria one month.
15:14 [A] in Samaria, assassinated him and succeeded him *as* **king**.
15:17 [A] Menahem son of Gadi *became* **king** of Israel, and he reigned
15:22 [A] his fathers. And Pekahiah his son succeeded him *as* **king**.
15:23 [A] Pekahiah son of Menahem *became* **king** of Israel in Samaria,
15:25 [A] So Pekah killed Pekahiah and succeeded him *as* **king**.
15:27 [A] Pekah son of Remaliah *became* **king** of Israel in Samaria,
15:30 [A] succeeded him *as* **king** in the twentieth year of Jotham son of
15:32 [A] Jotham son of Uzziah king of Judah *began to* **reign**.
15:33 [A] He was twenty-five years old when he *became* **king**, and he
15:33 [A] he became king, and *he* **reigned** in Jerusalem sixteen years.
15:38 [A] city of his father. And Ahaz his son succeeded him *as* **king**.
16: 1 [A] Ahaz son of Jotham king of Judah *began to* **reign**.
16: 2 [A] Ahaz was twenty years old when he *became* **king**, and he
16: 2 [A] he became king, and *he* **reigned** in Jerusalem sixteen years.
16:20 [A] City of David. And Hezekiah his son succeeded him *as* **king**.
17: 1 [A] Hoshea son of Elah *became* **king** of Israel in Samaria, and he
17:21 [G] of David, *they* **made** Jeroboam son of Nebat *their* **king**.
18: 1 [A] Hezekiah son of Ahaz king of Judah *began to* **reign**.
18: 2 [A] He was twenty-five years old when he *became* **king**, and he
18: 2 [A] became king, and *he* **reigned** in Jerusalem twenty-nine years.
19:37 [A] of Ararat. And Esarhaddon his son succeeded him *as* **king**.
20:21 [A] his fathers. And Manasseh his son succeeded him *as* **king**.
21: 1 [A] Manasseh was twelve years old when he *became* **king**,
21: 1 [A] he became king, and *he* **reigned** in Jerusalem fifty-five years.
21:18 [A] garden of Uzza. And Amon his son succeeded him *as* **king**.
21:19 [A] Amon was twenty-two years old when he *became* **king**,
21:19 [A] he became king, and *he* **reigned** in Jerusalem two years.
21:24 [G] King Amon, and they **made** Josiah his son **king** in his place.
21:26 [A] garden of Uzza. And Josiah his son succeeded him *as* **king**.
22: 1 [A] Josiah was eight years old when he *became* **king**, and he
22: 1 [A] became king, and *he* **reigned** in Jerusalem thirty-one years.
23:30 [G] and anointed him and **made** him **king** in place of his father.
23:31 [A] Jehoahaz was twenty-three years old when he *became* **king**,
23:31 [A] he became king, and *he* **reigned** in Jerusalem three months.
23:33 [A] the land of Hamath so that he *might* not **reign** in Jerusalem,
23:34 [G] Pharaoh Neco **made** Eliakim son of Josiah **king** in place of
23:36 [A] Jehoiakim was twenty-five years old when he *became* **king**,
23:36 [A] he became king, and *he* **reigned** in Jerusalem eleven years.
24: 6 [A] his fathers. And Jehoiachin his son succeeded him *as* **king**.
24: 8 [A] Jehoiachin was eighteen years old when he *became* **king**,
24: 8 [A] he became king, and *he* **reigned** in Jerusalem three months.
24:12 [A] In the eighth year of the **reign** of the king of Babylon,
24:17 [G] He **made** Mattaniah, Jehoiachin's uncle, **king** in his place
24:18 [A] Zedekiah was twenty-one years old when he *became* **king**,
24:18 [A] he became king, and *he* **reigned** in Jerusalem eleven years.
25: 1 [A] So in the ninth year of Zedekiah's **reign**, on the tenth day of
25:27 [A] in the year Evil-Merodach *became* **king** *of* Babylon,
1Ch 1:43 [A] These were the kings who **reigned** in Edom before any
1:43 [A] who reigned in Edom before any Israelite king **reigned**:
1:44 [A] Jobab son of Zerah from Bozrah succeeded him *as* **king**.
1:45 [A] from the land of the Temanites succeeded him *as* **king**.
1:46 [A] Midian in the country of Moab, succeeded him *as* **king**.
1:47 [A] Hadad died, Samlah from Masrekah succeeded him *as* **king**.
1:48 [A] Shaul from Rehoboth on the river succeeded him *as* **king**.
1:49 [A] Shaul died, Baal-Hanan son of Acbor succeeded him *as* **king**.
1:50 [A] When Baal-Hanan died, Hadad succeeded him *as* **king**. His
3: 4 [A] in Hebron, where *he* **reigned** seven years and six months.
3: 4 [A] six months. David **reigned** in Jerusalem thirty-three years,
4:31 [A] These were their towns until the **reign** *of* David.
11:10 [G] gave his kingship strong support to **extend** it over the whole
12:31 [12:32] [G] by name to come and **make** David **king**—
12:38 [12:39] [G] determined to **make** David **king** over all Israel.
12:38 [12:39] [G] were also of one mind to **make** David **king**.
16:31 [A] let them say among the nations, "The LORD **reigns**!"
18:14 [A] David **reigned** over all Israel, doing what was just and right
19: 1 [A] of the Ammonites died, and his son succeeded him *as* **king**.
23: 1 [G] and full of years, *he* **made** his son Solomon **king** over Israel.
28: 4 [G] from my father's sons he was pleased to **make** me **king** over
29:22 [G] *they* **acknowledged** Solomon son of David **as king** a second
29:26 [A] David son of Jesse *was* **king** over all Israel.
29:27 [A] *He* **ruled** over Israel forty years—seven in Hebron
29:27 [A] **[RPH]** seven in Hebron and thirty-three in Jerusalem.
29:27 [A] seven in Hebron and thirty-three in Jerusalem. **[RPH]**
29:28 [A] wealth and honor. His son Solomon succeeded him *as* **king**.
2Ch 1: 8 [G] to David my father and *have* **made** me **king** in his place.
1: 9 [G] for you *have* **made** me **king** over a people who are as
1:11 [G] to govern my people over whom *I have* **made** you **king**,
1:13 [A] from before the Tent of Meeting. And *he* **reigned** over Israel.
9:30 [A] Solomon **reigned** in Jerusalem over all Israel forty years.
9:31 [A] his father. And Rehoboam his son succeeded him *as* **king**.
10: 1 [G] for all the Israelites had gone there to **make** him **king**.
10:17 [A] in the towns of Judah, Rehoboam *still* **ruled** over them.
11:22 [G] chief prince among his brothers, in order to **make** him **king**.
12:13 [A] himself firmly in Jerusalem and *continued* **as king**.
12:13 [A] He was forty-one years old when he *became* **king**, and he
12:13 [A] became king, and *he* **reigned** seventeen years in Jerusalem,
12:16 [A] City of David. And Abijah his son succeeded him *as* **king**.
13: 1 [A] year of the reign of Jeroboam, Abijah *became* **king** of Judah,
13: 2 [A] *he* **reigned** in Jerusalem three years. His mother's name was

2Ch 14: 1 [13:23] [A] Asa his son succeeded him *as* **king**, and in his days
16:13 [A] in the forty-first year of his **reign** Asa died and rested with
17: 1 [A] Jehoshaphat his son succeeded him *as* **king** and strengthened
17: 7 [A] In the third year of his **reign** he sent his officials Ben-Hail,
20:31 [A] So Jehoshaphat **reigned** over Judah. He was thirty-five years
20:31 [A] He was thirty-five years old when he *became* **king** *of* Judah,
20:31 [A] of Judah, and *he* **reigned** in Jerusalem twenty-five years.
21: 1 [A] City of David. And Jehoram his son succeeded him *as* **king**.
21: 5 [A] Jehoram was thirty-two years old when he *became* **king**,
21: 5 [A] he became king, and *he* **reigned** in Jerusalem eight years.
21: 8 [G] against Judah and **set up** its own **king** [+4889+6584].
21:20 [A] Jehoram was thirty-two years old when he *became* **king**,
21:20 [A] he became king, and *he* **reigned** in Jerusalem eight years.
22: 1 [G] of Jerusalem **made** Ahaziah, Jehoram's youngest son, **king**
22: 1 [A] So Ahaziah son of Jehoram king of Judah *began to* **reign**.
22: 2 [A] Ahaziah was twenty-two years old when he *became* **king**,
22: 2 [A] when he became king, and *he* **reigned** in Jerusalem one year.
22:12 [A] temple of God for six years while Athaliah **ruled** the land.
23: 3 [A] Jehoiada said to them, "The king's son *shall* **reign**, as the
23:11 [G] him with a copy of the covenant and **proclaimed** him **king**.
24: 1 [A] Joash was seven years old when he *became* **king**, and he
24: 1 [A] he became king, and *he* **reigned** in Jerusalem forty years.
24:27 [A] of the kings. And Amaziah his son succeeded him *as* **king**.
25: 1 [A] Amaziah was twenty-five years old *when he became* **king**,
25: 1 [A] became king, and *he* **reigned** in Jerusalem twenty-nine years.
26: 1 [G] years old, and **made** him **king** in place of his father Amaziah.
26: 3 [A] Uzziah was sixteen years old when he *became* **king**, and he
26: 3 [A] he became king, and *he* **reigned** in Jerusalem fifty-two years.
26:23 [A] had leprosy." And Jotham his son succeeded him *as* **king**.
27: 1 [A] Jotham was twenty-five years old when he *became* **king**,
27: 1 [A] he became king, and *he* **reigned** in Jerusalem sixteen years.
27: 8 [A] He was twenty-five years old when he *became* **king**, and he
27: 8 [A] he became king, and *he* **reigned** in Jerusalem sixteen years.
27: 9 [A] the City of David. And Ahaz his son succeeded him *as* **king**.
28: 1 [A] Ahaz was twenty years old when he *became* **king**, and he
28: 1 [A] he became king, and *he* **reigned** in Jerusalem sixteen years.
28:27 [A] of Israel. And Hezekiah his son succeeded him *as* **king**.
29: 1 [A] Hezekiah was twenty-five years old *when he became* **king**,
29: 1 [A] became king, and *he* **reigned** in Jerusalem twenty-nine years.
29: 3 [A] In the first month of the first year of his **reign**, he opened the
32:33 [A] when he died. And Manasseh his son succeeded him *as* **king**.
33: 1 [A] Manasseh was twelve years old when he *became* **king**,
33: 1 [A] he became king, and *he* **reigned** in Jerusalem fifty-five years.
33:20 [A] in his palace. And Amon his son succeeded him *as* **king**.
33:21 [A] Amon was twenty-two years old when he *became* **king**, and
33:21 [A] he became king, and *he* **reigned** in Jerusalem two years.
33:25 [G] King Amon, and they **made** Josiah his son **king** in his place.
34: 1 [A] Josiah was eight years old when he *became* **king**, and he
34: 1 [A] became king, and *he* **reigned** in Jerusalem thirty-one years.
34: 3 [A] In the eighth year of his **reign**, while he was still young,
34: 8 [A] In the eighteenth year of Josiah's **reign**, to purify the land
36: 1 [G] and **made** him **king** in Jerusalem in place of his father.
36: 2 [A] Jehoahaz was twenty-three years old when he *became* **king**,
36: 2 [A] he became king, and *he* **reigned** in Jerusalem three months.
36: 4 [G] king of Egypt **made** Eliakim, a brother of Jehoahaz, **king**
36: 5 [A] Jehoiakim was twenty-five years old when he *became* **king**,
36: 5 [A] he became king, and *he* **reigned** in Jerusalem eleven years.
36: 8 [A] and Judah. And Jehoiachin his son succeeded him *as* **king**.
36: 9 [A] Jehoiachin was eighteen years old when he *became* **king**,
36: 9 [A] and *he* **reigned** in Jerusalem three months and ten days.
36:10 [G] and *he* **made** Jehoiachin's uncle, Zedekiah, **king** over Judah
36:11 [A] Zedekiah was twenty-one years old when he *became* **king**,
36:11 [A] he became king, and *he* **reigned** in Jerusalem eleven years.
36:20 [A] and his sons until the kingdom of Persia **came to power**.
Est 1: 1 [A] the Xerxes who **ruled over** 127 provinces stretching from
1: 3 [A] in the third year of his **reign** he gave a banquet for all his
2: 4 [A] *let* the girl who pleases the king *be* **queen** instead of Vashti."
2:17 [G] crown on her head and **made** her **queen** instead of Vashti.
Job 34:30 [A] to keep a godless man from **ruling**, from laying snares for
Ps 47: 8 [47:9] [A] God **reigns** over the nations; God is seated on his
93: 1 [A] The LORD **reigns**, he is robed in majesty; the LORD is
96:10 [A] Say among the nations, "The LORD **reigns**." The world is
97: 1 [A] The LORD **reigns**, let the earth be glad; let the distant
99: 1 [A] The LORD **reigns**, let the nations tremble; he sits enthroned
146:10 [A] The LORD **reigns** forever, your God, O Zion, for all
Pr 8:15 [A] By me kings **reign** and rulers make laws that are just;
30:22 [A] a servant *who becomes* **king**, a fool who is full of food,
Ecc 4:14 [A] The youth may have come from prison to the **kingship**, or he
Isa 7: 6 [G] and **make** the son of Tabeel **king** [+906+4889] over it."
24:23 [A] for the LORD Almighty *will* **reign** on Mount Zion and in
32: 1 [A] a king *will* **reign** in righteousness and rulers will rule with
37:38 [A] of Ararat. And Esarhaddon his son succeeded him *as* **king**.
52: 7 [A] proclaim salvation, who say to Zion, "Your God **reigns**!"
Jer 1: 2 [A] year of the **reign** *of* Josiah son of Amon king of Judah,
22:11 [A] who succeeded his father *as* **king** *of* Judah but has gone from
22:15 [A] "*Does it make you a* **king** to have more and more cedar?
23: 5 [A] a King *who will* **reign** wisely and do what is just and right in
33:21 [A] David will no longer have a descendant *to* **reign** on his
37: 1 [G] Zedekiah son of Josiah *was* **made king** of Judah *by*
37: 1 [A] *he* **reigned** [+4889] in place of Jehoiachin son of Jehoiakim.
51:59 [A] with Zedekiah king of Judah in the fourth year of his **reign**.
52: 1 [A] Zedekiah was twenty-one years old when he *became* **king**,
52: 1 [A] he became king, and *he* **reigned** in Jerusalem eleven years.
52: 4 [A] So in the ninth year of Zedekiah's **reign**, on the tenth day of
Eze 17:16 [G] in the land of the king who **put** him **on** *the* **throne**, whose
20:33 [A] *I will* **rule** over you with a mighty hand and an outstretched
Da 9: 1 [H] who **was made ruler** over the Babylonian kingdom—
9: 2 [A] in the first year of his **reign**, I, Daniel, understood from the
Hos 8: 4 [G] They **set up kings** without my consent; they choose princes
Mic 4: 7 [A] The LORD *will* **rule** over them in Mount Zion from that

4888 ²מָלַךְ **mālak²**, v. [1] [√ 4887; Ar 10422]

pondered [1]

Ne 5: 7 [C] I **pondered** them in my mind and then accused the nobles

4889 ¹מֶלֶךְ **melek¹**, n.m. [2523] [→ 4866, 4890, 4891, 4893, 4894, 4895, 4904, 4906; cf. 4887; Ar 10421; *also used with compound proper names*]

king [1840], kings [272], king's [172], royal [65], *untranslated* [51], him[s] [+2021] [29], he[s] [+2021] [26], palace [+1074] [15], his[s] [+2021] [6], king's [+4200] [4], king's [+928] [3], princes [+1201] [3], reign [3], Amaziah[s] [+2021] [2], his[s] own [+2021] [2], palace grounds [+1074] [2], ruled [2], set up king [+4887+6584] [2], give king [+4200+4887] [1], he[s] [+951] [1], him[s] [+2021+6460] [1], him[s] [+3296+4046] [1], him[s] [+951] [1], his[s] [+4200+5213] [1], his[s] [+928+2021] [1], his[s] [+951] [1], his[s] own [1], it[s] [+2021+9133] [1], king [+4887] [1], kingdom [1], kingdoms [1], made king [+906+4200+4887] [1], majesty [1], make king [+906+4887] [1], prince [+1201] [1], princess [+1426] [1], reigned [+4887] [1], rule over [1], ruled [+2118] [1], rulers [1], set a king [+4887] [1], Shalmaneser[s] [+855] [1]

Ge 14: 1 At this time Amraphel **king** *of* Shinar, Arioch king of Ellasar,
14: 1 Arioch **king** *of* Ellasar, Kedorlaomer king of Elam and Tidal king
14: 1 of Ellasar, Kedorlaomer **king** *of* Elam and Tidal king of Goiim
14: 1 of Ellasar, Kedorlaomer king of Elam and Tidal **king** *of* Goiim
14: 2 went to war against Bera **king** *of* Sodom, Birsha king of
14: 2 Birsha **king** *of* Gomorrah, Shinab king of Admah, Shemeber king
14: 2 Birsha king of Gomorrah, Shinab **king** *of* Admah, Shemeber king
14: 2 of Gomorrah, Shinab king of Admah, Shemeber **king** *of* Zeboiim,
14: 2 Shemeber king of Zeboiim, and the **king** *of* Bela (that is, Zoar).
14: 5 Kedorlaomer and the **kings** allied with him went out and defeated
14: 8 the **king** *of* Sodom, the king of Gomorrah, the king of Admah,
14: 8 the **king** *of* Gomorrah, the king of Admah, the king of Zeboiim
14: 8 the **king** *of* Admah, the king of Zeboiim and the king of Bela (that
14: 8 of Admah, the **king** *of* Zeboiim and the king of Bela (that is, Zoar)
14: 8 of Admah, the king of Zeboiim and the **king** *of* Bela (that is, Zoar)
14: 9 against Kedorlaomer **king** *of* Elam, Tidal king of Goiim, Amraphel
14: 9 Tidal **king** *of* Goiim, Amraphel king of Shinar and Arioch king of
14: 9 of Goiim, Amraphel **king** *of* Shinar and Arioch king of Ellasar—
14: 9 of Goiim, Amraphel king of Shinar and Arioch **king** *of* Ellasar—
14: 9 king of Shinar and Arioch king of Ellasar—four **kings** against five.
14:10 when the **kings** *of* Sodom and Gomorrah fled, some of the men fell
14:17 from defeating Kedorlaomer and the **kings** allied with him,
14:17 the **king** *of* Sodom came out to meet him in the Valley of Shaveh
14:17 to meet him in the Valley of Shaveh (that is, the **King's** Valley).
14:18 Then Melchizedek **king** *of* Salem brought out bread and wine.
14:21 The **king** *of* Sodom said to Abram, "Give me the people and keep
14:22 Abram said to the **king** *of* Sodom, "I have raised my hand to the
17: 6 I will make nations of you, and **kings** will come from you.
17:16 be the mother of nations; **kings** *of* peoples will come from her."
20: 2 Then Abimelech **king** *of* Gerar sent for Sarah and took her.
26: 1 and Isaac went to Abimelech **king** *of* the Philistines in Gerar.
26: 8 Abimelech **king** *of* the Philistines looked down from a window
35:11 nations will come from you, and **kings** will come from your body.
36:31 These were the **kings** who reigned in Edom before any Israelite
36:31 the kings who reigned in Edom before any Israelite **king** reigned:
39:20 him in prison, the place where the **king's** prisoners were confined.
40: 1 and the baker of the **king** *of* Egypt offended their master,
40: 1 of the king of Egypt offended their master, the **king** *of* Egypt.
40: 5 the cupbearer and the baker of the **king** *of* Egypt, who were being
41:46 years old when he entered the service of Pharaoh **king** *of* Egypt.
49:20 "Asher's food will be rich; he will provide delicacies fit for a **king**.
Ex 1: 8 a new **king**, who did not know about Joseph, came to power in
1:15 The **king** *of* Egypt said to the Hebrew midwives, whose names
1:17 and did not do what the **king** *of* Egypt had told them to do;
1:18 Then the **king** *of* Egypt summoned the midwives and asked them,

Ex 2:23 During that long period, the **king** *of* Egypt died. The Israelites
3:18 you and the elders are to go to the **king** *of* Egypt and say to him,
3:19 I know that the **king** *of* Egypt will not let you go unless a mighty
5:4 the **king** *of* Egypt said, "Moses and Aaron, why are you taking the
6:11 tell Pharaoh **king** *of* Egypt to let the Israelites go out of his
6:13 and Aaron about the Israelites and Pharaoh **king** *of* Egypt,
6:27 They were the ones who spoke to Pharaoh **king** *of* Egypt about
6:29 am the LORD. Tell Pharaoh **king** *of* Egypt everything I tell you."
14:5 When the **king** *of* Egypt was told that the people had fled,
14:8 The LORD hardened the heart of Pharaoh **king** *of* Egypt,
Nu 20:14 Moses sent messengers from Kadesh to the **king** *of* Edom,
20:17 We will travel along the **king's** highway and not turn to the right
21:1 When the Canaanite **king** *of* Arad, who lived in the Negev,
21:21 Israel sent messengers to say to Sihon **king** *of* the Amorites:
21:22 We will travel along the **king's** highway until we have passed
21:26 Heshbon was the city of Sihon **king** *of* the Amorites, who had
21:26 who had fought against the former **king** *of* Moab and had taken
21:29 and his daughters as captives to Sihon **king** *of* the Amorites.
21:33 Og **king** *of* Bashan and his whole army marched out to meet them
21:34 Do to him what you did to Sihon **king** *of* the Amorites,
22:4 So Balak son of Zippor, who was **king** of Moab at that time,
22:10 "Balak son of Zippor, **king** *of* Moab, sent me this message:
23:7 me from Aram, the **king** *of* Moab from the eastern mountains.
23:21 their God is with them; the shout of the **King** is among them.
24:7 "Their **king** will be greater than Agag; their kingdom will be
31:8 Among their **[RPH]** victims were Evi, Rekem, Zur, Hur
31:8 were Evi, Rekem, Zur, Hur and Reba—the five **kings** *of* Midian.
32:33 son of Joseph the kingdom of Sihon **king** *of* the Amorites
32:33 king of the Amorites and the kingdom of Og **king** *of* Bashan—
33:40 The Canaanite **king** *of* Arad, who lived in the Negev of Canaan,
Dt 1:4 This was after he had defeated Sihon **king** *of* the Amorites,
1:4 reigned in Heshbon, and at Edrei had defeated Og **king** *of* Bashan,
2:24 your hand Sihon the Amorite, **king** *of* Heshbon, and his country.
2:26 From the desert of Kedemoth I sent messengers to Sihon **king** *of*
2:30 But Sihon **king** *of* Heshbon refused to let us pass through.
3:1 Og **king** *of* Bashan with his whole army marched out to meet us in
3:2 Do to him what you did to Sihon **king** *of* the Amorites,
3:3 So the LORD our God also gave into our hands Og **king** *of*
3:6 as we had done with Sihon **king** *of* Heshbon, destroying every
3:8 So at that time we took from these two **kings** *of* the Amorites the
3:11 (Only Og **king** *of* Bashan was left of the remnant of the Rephaites.
3:21 eyes all that the LORD your God has done to these two **kings**.
4:46 in the land of Sihon **king** *of* the Amorites, who reigned in Heshbon
4:47 took possession of his land and the land of Og **king** *of* Bashan,
4:47 of Og king of Bashan, the two Amorite **kings** east of the Jordan.
7:8 from the land of slavery, from the power of Pharaoh **king** *of* Egypt.
7:24 He will give their **kings** into your hand, and you will wipe out their
11:3 of Egypt, both to Pharaoh **king** *of* Egypt and to his whole country;
17:14 you say, "Let us set a **king** over us like all the nations around us,"
17:15 be sure to appoint over you the **king** the LORD your God
17:15 **[RPH]** Do not place a foreigner over you, one who is not a
28:36 and the **king** you set over you to a nation unknown to you
29:7 [29:6] Sihon **king** *of* Heshbon and Og king of Bashan came out to
29:7 [29:6] and Og **king** *of* Bashan came out to fight against us,
31:4 do to them what he did to Sihon and Og, the **kings** *of* the Amorites,
33:5 He was **king** over Jeshurun when the leaders of the people
Jos 2:2 The **king** *of* Jericho was told, "Look! Some of the Israelites have
2:3 So the **king** *of* Jericho sent this message to Rahab: "Bring out the
2:10 to Sihon and Og, the two **kings** *of* the Amorites east of the Jordan,
5:1 Now when all the Amorite **kings** west of the Jordan and all the
5:1 all the Canaanite **kings** along the coast heard how the LORD had
6:2 Jericho into your hands, along with its **king** and its fighting men.
8:1 For I have delivered into your hands the **king** *of* Ai, his people,
8:2 You shall do to Ai and its **king** as you did to Jericho and its king,
8:2 You shall do to Ai and its king as you did to Jericho and its **king**,
8:14 When the **king** *of* Ai saw this, he and all the men of the city
8:23 But they took the **king** *of* Ai alive and brought him to Joshua.
8:29 He hung the **king** *of* Ai on a tree and left him there until evening.
9:1 Now when all the **kings** west of the Jordan heard about these
9:10 all that he did to the two **kings** *of* the Amorites east of the Jordan—
9:10 Sihon **king** *of* Heshbon, and Og king of Bashan, who reigned in
9:10 Sihon king of Heshbon, and Og **king** *of* Bashan, who reigned in
10:1 Now Adoni-Zedek **king** *of* Jerusalem heard that Joshua had taken
10:1 doing to Ai and its **king** as he had done to Jericho and its king,
10:1 doing to Ai and its king as he had done to Jericho and its **king**,
10:3 So Adoni-Zedek **king** *of* Jerusalem appealed to Hoham king of
10:3 So Adoni-Zedek king of Jerusalem appealed to Hoham **king** *of*
10:3 Piram **king** *of* Jarmuth, Japhia king of Lachish and Debir king of
10:3 king of Jarmuth, Japhia **king** *of* Lachish and Debir king of Eglon.
10:3 king of Jarmuth, Japhia king of Lachish and Debir **king** *of* Eglon.
10:5 Then the five **kings** *of* the Amorites—the kings of Jerusalem,
10:5 the **kings** *of* Jerusalem, Hebron, Jarmuth, Lachish and Eglon—
10:5 kings of Jerusalem, **[RPH]** Hebron, Jarmuth, Lachish and Eglon—
10:5 kings of Jerusalem, Hebron, **[RPH]** Jarmuth, Lachish and Eglon—
10:5 kings of Jerusalem, Hebron, Jarmuth, **[RPH]** Lachish and Eglon—
10:5 kings of Jerusalem, Hebron, Jarmuth, Lachish and **[RPH]** Eglon—
10:6 because all the Amorite **kings** *from* the hill country have joined
10:16 Now the five **kings** had fled and hidden in the cave at Makkedah.
10:17 When Joshua was told that the five **kings** had been found hiding in
10:22 "Open the mouth of the cave and bring those five **kings** out to me."
10:23 So they brought the five **kings** out of the cave—the kings of
10:23 the **kings** *of* Jerusalem, Hebron, Jarmuth, Lachish and Eglon.
10:23 kings of Jerusalem, **[RPH]** Hebron, Jarmuth, Lachish and Eglon.
10:23 kings of Jerusalem, Hebron, **[RPH]** Jarmuth, Lachish and Eglon.
10:23 kings of Jerusalem, Hebron, Jarmuth, **[RPH]** Lachish and Eglon.
10:23 kings of Jerusalem, Hebron, Jarmuth, Lachish and **[RPH]** Eglon.
10:24 When they had brought these **kings** to Joshua, he summoned all
10:24 "Come here and put your feet on the necks of these **kings**."
10:28 He put the city and its **king** to the sword and totally destroyed
10:28 he did to the **king** *of* Makkedah as he had done to the king of
10:28 he did to the king of Makkedah as he had done to the **king** *of*
10:30 The LORD also gave that city and its **king** into Israel's hand.
10:30 And he did to its **king** as he had done to the king of Jericho.
10:30 And he did to its king as he had done to the **king** *of* Jericho.
10:33 Meanwhile, Horam **king** *of* Gezer had come up to help Lachish,
10:37 to the sword, together with its **king**, its villages and everyone in it.
10:39 They took the city, its **king** and its villages, and put them to the
10:39 and its **king** as they had done to Libnah and its king and to Hebron.
10:39 and its king as they had done to Libnah and its **king** and to Hebron.
10:40 and the mountain slopes, together with all their **kings**.
10:42 All these **kings** and their lands Joshua conquered in one campaign,
11:1 When Jabin **king** *of* Hazor heard of this, he sent word to Jobab
11:1 he sent word to Jobab **king** *of* Madon, to the kings of Shimron
11:1 to Jobab king of Madon, to the **kings** *of* Shimron and Acshaph,
11:1 king of Madon, to the kings of Shimron and **[RPH]** Acshaph,
11:2 to the northern **kings** who were in the mountains, in the Arabah
11:5 All these **kings** joined forces and made camp together at the
11:10 turned back and captured Hazor and put its **king** to the sword.
11:12 Joshua took all these **royal** cities and their kings and put them to
11:12 all these royal cities and their **kings** and put them to the sword.
11:17 He captured all their **kings** and struck them down, putting them to
11:18 Joshua waged war against all these **kings** for a long time.
12:1 These are the **kings** *of* the land whom the Israelites had defeated
12:2 Sihon **king** *of* the Amorites, who reigned in Heshbon. He ruled
12:4 the territory of Og **king** *of* Bashan, one of the last of the Rephaites,
12:5 and half of Gilead to the border of Sihon **king** *of* Heshbon.
12:7 These are the **kings** *of* the land that Joshua and the Israelites
12:9 the **king** *of* Jericho one the king of Ai (near Bethel) one
12:9 the king of Jericho one the **king** *of* Ai (near Bethel) one
12:10 the **king** *of* Jerusalem one the king of Hebron one
12:10 the king of Jerusalem one the **king** *of* Hebron one
12:11 the **king** *of* Jarmuth one the king of Lachish one
12:11 the king of Jarmuth one the **king** *of* Lachish one
12:12 the **king** *of* Eglon one the king of Gezer one
12:12 the king of Eglon one the **king** *of* Gezer one
12:13 the **king** *of* Debir one the king of Geder one
12:13 the king of Debir one the **king** *of* Geder one
12:14 the **king** *of* Hormah one the king of Arad one
12:14 the king of Hormah one the **king** *of* Arad one
12:15 the **king** *of* Libnah one the king of Adullam one
12:15 the king of Libnah one the **king** *of* Adullam one
12:16 the **king** *of* Makkedah one the king of Bethel one
12:16 the king of Makkedah one the **king** *of* Bethel one
12:17 the **king** *of* Tappuah one the king of Hepher one
12:17 the king of Tappuah one the **king** *of* Hepher one
12:18 the **king** *of* Aphek one the king of Lasharon one
12:18 the king of Aphek one the **king** *of* Lasharon one
12:19 the **king** *of* Madon one the king of Hazor one
12:19 the king of Madon one the **king** *of* Hazor one
12:20 the **king** *of* Shimron Meron one the king of Acshaph one
12:20 the king of Shimron Meron one the **king** *of* Acshaph one
12:21 the **king** *of* Taanach one the king of Megiddo one
12:21 the king of Taanach one the **king** *of* Megiddo one
12:22 the **king** *of* Kedesh one the king of Jokneam in Carmel one
12:22 the king of Kedesh one the **king** *of* Jokneam in Carmel one
12:23 the **king** *of* Dor (in Naphoth Dor) one the king of Goyim in Gilgal
12:23 king of Dor (in Naphoth Dor) one the **king** *of* Goyim in Gilgal one
12:24 the **king** *of* Tirzah one thirty-one kings in all.
12:24 the king of Tirzah one thirty-one **kings** in all.
13:10 all the towns of Sihon **king** *of* the Amorites, who ruled in
13:21 on the plateau and the entire realm of Sihon **king** *of* the Amorites,
13:27 Zaphon with the rest of the realm of Sihon **king** *of* Heshbon (the
13:30 including all of Bashan, the entire realm of Og **king** *of* Bashan—
24:9 When Balak son of Zippor, the **king** *of* Moab, prepared to fight
24:12 which drove them out before you—also the two Amorite **kings**.
Jdg 1:7 "Seventy **kings** with their thumbs and big toes cut off have picked
3:8 so that he sold them into the hands of Cushan-Rishathaim **king** *of*
3:10 The LORD gave Cushan-Rishathaim **king** *of* Aram into the hands

Jdg 3:12 because they did this evil the LORD gave Eglon **king** *of* Moab
3:14 The Israelites were subject to Eglon **king** *of* Moab for eighteen
3:15 The Israelites sent him with tribute to Eglon **king** *of* Moab.
3:17 He presented the tribute to Eglon **king** *of* Moab, who was a very
3:19 turned back and said, "I have a secret message for you, O **king**."
4:2 into the hands of Jabin, a **king** *of* Canaan, who reigned in Hazor.
4:17 because there were friendly relations between Jabin **king** *of* Hazor
4:23 day God subdued Jabin, the Canaanite **king**, before the Israelites.
4:24 against Jabin, the Canaanite **king**, until they destroyed him.
4:24 the Canaanite king, until they destroyed **him**[s] [+3296+4046].
5:3 "Hear this, you **kings**! Listen, you rulers! I will sing to the
5:19 "**Kings** came, they fought; the kings of Canaan fought at Taanach
5:19 the **kings** *of* Canaan fought at Taanach by the waters of Megiddo,
8:5 and I am still pursuing Zebah and Zalmunna, the **kings** *of* Midian."
8:12 Zebah and Zalmunna, the two **kings** *of* Midian, fled, but he
8:18 they answered, "each one with the bearing of a **prince** [+1201]."
8:26 the pendants and the purple garments worn by the **kings** *of* Midian
9:6 the great tree at the pillar in Shechem to crown Abimelech **king**.
9:8 One day the trees went out to anoint a **king** for themselves.
9:15 'If you really want to anoint me **king** over you, come and take
11:12 Jephthah sent messengers to the Ammonite **king** with the question:
11:13 The **king** *of* the Ammonites answered Jephthah's messengers,
11:14 Jephthah sent back messengers to the Ammonite **king**,
11:17 Israel sent messengers to the **king** *of* Edom, saying, 'Give us
11:17 to go through your country,' but the **king** *of* Edom would not listen.
11:17 They sent also to the **king** *of* Moab, and he refused. So Israel
11:19 "Then Israel sent messengers to Sihon **king** *of* the Amorites,
11:19 *who* **ruled** *in* Heshbon, and said to him, 'Let us pass through your
11:25 Are you better than Balak son of Zippor, **king** *of* Moab? Did he
11:28 The **king** *of* Ammon, however, paid no attention to the message
17:6 In those days Israel had no **king**; everyone did as he saw fit.
18:1 In those days Israel had no **king**. And in those days the tribe of the
19:1 In those days Israel had no **king**. Now a Levite who lived in a
21:25 In those days Israel had no **king**; everyone did as he saw fit.
1Sa 2:10 "He will give strength to his **king** and exalt the horn of his
8:5 now appoint a **king** to lead us, such as all the other nations have."
8:6 when they said, "Give us a **king** to lead us," this displeased
8:9 let them know what the **king** who will reign over them will do."
8:10 of the LORD to the people who were asking him for a **king**.
8:11 He said, "This is what the **king** who will reign over you will do:
8:18 you will cry out for relief from the **king** you have chosen,
8:19 to listen to Samuel. "No!" they said. "We want a **king** over us.
8:20 with a **king** to lead us and to go out before us and fight our
8:22 "Listen to them and **give** them a **king** [+4200+4887]."
10:19 and distresses. And you have said, 'No, set a **king** over us.'
10:24 all the people." Then the people shouted, "Long live the **king**!"
12:1 everything you said to me and *have* **set a king** [+4887] over you.
12:2 Now you have a **king** as your leader. As for me, I am old and gray,
12:9 and into the hands of the Philistines and the **king** *of* Moab,
12:12 "But when you saw that Nahash **king** *of* the Ammonites was
12:12 against you, you said to me, 'No, we want a **king** to rule over us'—
12:12 rule over us'—even though the LORD your God was your **king**.
12:13 Now here is the **king** you have chosen, the one you asked for;
12:13 the one you asked for; see, the LORD has set a **king** over you.
12:14 and the **king** who reigns over you follow the LORD your God—
12:17 you did in the eyes of the LORD when you asked for a **king**."
12:19 we have added to all our other sins the evil of asking for a **king**."
12:25 persist in doing evil, both you and your **king** will be swept away."
14:47 Moab, the Ammonites, Edom, the **kings** *of* Zobah, and the
15:1 "I am the one the LORD sent to anoint you **king** over his people
15:8 He took Agag **king** *of* the Amalekites alive, and all his people he
15:11 "I am grieved that *I have* **made** Saul **king** [+906+4200+4887],
15:17 of the tribes of Israel? The LORD anointed you **king** over Israel.
15:20 destroyed the Amalekites and brought back Agag their **king**.
15:23 rejected the word of the LORD, he has rejected you as **king**."
15:26 the LORD, and the LORD has rejected you as **king** over Israel!"
15:32 Then Samuel said, "Bring me Agag **king** *of* the Amalekites."
16:1 to Jesse of Bethlehem. I have chosen one of his sons to be **king**."
17:25 The **king** will give great wealth to the man who kills him.
17:55 Abner replied, "As surely as you live, O **king**, I don't know."
17:56 The **king** said, "Find out whose son this young man is."
18:6 the women came out from all the towns of Israel to meet **King** Saul
18:18 in Israel, that I should become the **king's** [+4200] son-in-law?"
18:22 to David privately and say, 'Look, the **king** is pleased with you,
18:22 all like you; now become **his**[s] [+928+2021] son-in-law.' "
18:23 "Do you think it is a small matter to become the **king's** [+928]
18:25 'The **king** wants no other price for the bride than a hundred
18:25 to take revenge on **his**[s] [+2021] enemies.' " Saul's plan was to
18:26 he was pleased to become the **king's** [+928] son-in-law.
18:27 brought their foreskins and presented the full number to the **king**
18:27 to the king so that he might become the **king's** [+928] son-in-law.
19:4 and said to him, "Let not the **king** do wrong to his servant David;
20:5 is the New Moon festival, and I am supposed to dine with the **king**;
20:24 and when the New Moon festival came, the **king** sat down to eat.
20:25 **He**[s] [+2021] sat in his customary place by the wall, opposite
20:29 see my brothers.' That is why he has not come to the **king's** table."
21:2 [21:3] "The **king** charged me with a certain matter and said to me,
21:8 [21:9] other weapon, because the **king's** business was urgent."
21:10 [21:11] David fled from Saul and went to Achish **king** *of* Gath.
21:11 [21:12] said to him, "Isn't this David, the **king** *of* the land?
21:12 [21:13] and was very much afraid of Achish **king** *of* Gath.
22:3 there David went to Mizpah in Moab and said to the **king** *of* Moab,
22:4 So he left them with the **king** *of* Moab, and they stayed with him as
22:11 Then the **king** sent for the priest Ahimelech son of Ahitub
22:11 who were the priests at Nob, and they all came to the **king**.
22:14 Ahimelech answered the **king**, "Who of all your servants is as
22:14 the **king's** son-in-law, captain of your bodyguard and highly
22:15 Let not the **king** accuse your servant or any of his father's family,
22:16 the **king** said, "You will surely die, Ahimelech, you and your
22:17 the **king** ordered the guards at his side: "Turn and kill the priests of
22:17 the **king's** officials were not willing to raise a hand to strike the
22:18 The **king** then ordered Doeg, "You turn and strike down the
23:20 Now, O **king**, come down whenever it pleases you to do so,
23:20 and we will be responsible for handing him over to the **king**."
24:8 [24:9] out of the cave and called out to Saul, "My lord the **king**!"
24:14 [24:15] "Against whom has the **king** *of* Israel come out?
25:36 to Nabal, he was in the house holding a banquet like that of a **king**.
26:14 Abner?" Abner replied, "Who are you who calls to the **king**?"
26:15 is like you in Israel? Why didn't you guard your lord the **king**?
26:15 your lord the king? Someone came to destroy your lord the **king**.
26:16 Where are the **king's** spear and water jug that were near his head?"
26:17 David my son?" David replied, "Yes it is, my lord the **king**."
26:19 Now let my lord the **king** listen to his servant's words.
26:20 The **king** *of* Israel has come out to look for a flea—as one hunts a
26:22 "Here is the **king's** spear," David answered. "Let one of your
27:2 with him left and went over to Achish son of Maoch **king** *of* Gath.
27:6 him Ziklag, and it has belonged to the **kings** *of* Judah ever since.
28:13 The **king** said to her, "Don't be afraid. What do you see?"
29:3 "Is this not David, who was an officer of Saul **king** *of* Israel?
29:8 Why can't I go and fight against the enemies of my lord the **king**?"
2Sa 2:4 and there they anointed David **king** over the house of Judah.
2:7 and the house of Judah has anointed me **king** over them."
2:11 The length of time David was **king** in Hebron over the house of
3:3 Absalom the son of Maacah daughter of Talmai **king** *of* Geshur;
3:17 "For some time you have wanted to make David your **king**.
3:21 "Let me go at once and assemble all Israel for my lord the **king**,
3:23 he was told that Abner son of Ner had come to the **king** and that
3:24 So Joab went to the **king** and said, "What have you done?
3:31 in front of Abner." **King** David himself walked behind the bier.
3:32 buried Abner in Hebron, and the **king** wept aloud at Abner's tomb.
3:33 The **king** sang this lament for Abner: "Should Abner have died as
3:36 and were pleased; indeed, everything the **king** did pleased them.
3:37 all Israel knew that the **king** had no part in the murder of Abner
3:38 Then the **king** said to his men, "Do you not realize that a prince
3:39 today, though I am the anointed **king**, I am weak, and these sons of
4:8 the head of Ish-Bosheth to David at Hebron and said to the **king**,
4:8 This day the LORD has avenged my lord the **king** against Saul
5:2 In the past, while Saul was **king** over us, you were the one who led
5:3 When all the elders of Israel had come to **King** David at Hebron,
5:3 the **king** made a compact with them at Hebron before the LORD,
5:3 before the LORD, and they anointed David **king** over Israel.
5:6 The **king** and his men marched to Jerusalem to attack the Jebusites,
5:11 Now Hiram **king** *of* Tyre sent messengers to David, along with
5:12 David knew that the LORD had established him as **king** over
5:17 When the Philistines heard that David had been anointed **king** over
6:12 Now **King** David was told, "The LORD has blessed the
6:16 when she saw **King** David leaping and dancing before the LORD,
6:20 and said, "How the **king** *of* Israel has distinguished himself today,
7:1 After the **king** was settled in his palace and the LORD had given
7:2 **he**[s] [+2021] said to Nathan the prophet, "Here I am, living in a
7:3 Nathan replied to the **king**, "Whatever you have in mind, go ahead
7:18 Then **King** David went in and sat before the LORD, and he said:
8:3 Moreover, David fought Hadadezer son of Rehob, **king** *of* Zobah,
8:5 When the Arameans of Damascus came to help Hadadezer **king** *of*
8:8 to Hadadezer, **King** David took a great quantity of bronze.
8:9 When Tou **king** *of* Hamath heard that David had defeated the
8:10 he sent his son Joram to **King** David to greet him and congratulate
8:11 **King** David dedicated these articles to the LORD, as he had done
8:12 the plunder taken from Hadadezer son of Rehob, **king** *of* Zobah.
9:2 to appear before David, and the **king** said to him, "Are you Ziba?"
9:3 The **king** asked, "Is there no one still left of the house of Saul to
9:3 Ziba answered the **king**, "There is still a son of Jonathan; he is
9:4 "Where is he?" the **king** asked. Ziba answered, "He is at the house
9:4 **[RPH]** "He is at the house of Makir son of Ammiel in Lo Debar."
9:5 So **King** David had him brought from Lo Debar, from the house of
9:9 Then the **king** summoned Ziba, Saul's servant, and said to him,
9:11 Ziba said to the **king**, "Your servant will do whatever my lord the
9:11 "Your servant will do whatever my lord the **king** commands his

2Sa 9:11 So Mephibosheth ate at David's table like one of the **king's** sons.
9:13 because he always ate at the **king's** table, and he was crippled in
10:1 In the course of time, the **king** *of* the Ammonites died, and his son
10:5 The **king** said, "Stay at Jericho till your beards have grown,
10:6 and Zobah, as well as the **king** *of* Maacah with a thousand men,
10:19 When all the **kings** who were vassals of Hadadezer saw that they
11:1 In the spring, at the time when **kings** go off to war, David sent
11:2 from his bed and walked around on the roof of the **palace** [+1074].
11:8 So Uriah left the **palace** [+1074], and a gift from the king was sent
11:8 Uriah left the palace, and a gift from the **king** was sent after him.
11:9 Uriah slept at the entrance to the **palace** [+1074] with all his
11:19 "When you have finished giving the **king** this account of the battle,
11:20 the **king's** anger may flare up, and he may ask you, 'Why did you
11:24 at your servants from the wall, and some of the **king's** men died.
12:7 'I anointed you **king** over Israel, and I delivered you from the hand
12:30 He took the crown from the head of their **king**—its weight was a
13:4 do you, the **king's** son, look so haggard morning after morning?
13:6 When the **king** came to see him, Amnon said to him, "I would like
13:6 When the king came to see him, Amnon said to **him**[s] [+2021],
13:13 Please speak to the **king**; he will not keep me from being married
13:18 for this was the kind of garment the virgin daughters of the **king**
13:21 When **King** David heard all this, he was furious.
13:23 the border of Ephraim, he invited all the **king's** sons to come there.
13:24 Absalom went to the **king** and said, "Your servant has had shearers
13:24 had shearers come. Will the **king** and his officials please join me?"
13:25 "No, my son," the **king** replied. "All of us should not go; we would
13:26 with us." The **king** asked him, "Why should he go with you?"
13:27 so he sent with him Amnon and the rest of the **king's** sons.
13:29 Then all the **king's** sons got up, mounted their mules and fled.
13:30 "Absalom has struck down all the **king's** sons; not one of them is
13:31 The **king** stood up, tore his clothes and lay down on the ground;
13:32 "My lord should not think that they killed all the **princes** [+1201];
13:33 My lord the **king** should not be concerned about the report that all
13:33 not be concerned about the report that all the **king's** sons are dead.
13:34 The watchman went and told the **king**, [BHS-] "I see men in the
13:35 Jonadab said to the **king**, "See, the king's sons are here; it has
13:35 Jonadab said to the king, "See, the **king's** sons are here; it has
13:36 As he finished speaking, the **king's** sons came in, wailing loudly.
13:36 The **king**, too, and all his servants wept very bitterly.
13:37 and went to Talmai son of Ammihud, the **king** *of* Geshur.
13:39 the spirit of the **king** longed to go to Absalom, for he was consoled
14:1 Joab son of Zeruiah knew that the **king's** heart longed for
14:3 go to the **king** and speak these words to him." And Joab put the
14:4 When the woman from Tekoa went to the **king**, she fell with her
14:4 to the ground to pay him honor, and she said, "Help me, O **king**!"
14:5 The **king** asked her, "What is troubling you?" She said, "I am
14:8 The **king** said to the woman, "Go home, and I will issue an order
14:9 the woman from Tekoa said to **him**[s] [+2021], "My lord the king,
14:9 "My lord the **king**, let the blame rest on me and on my father's
14:9 father's family, and let the **king** and his throne be without guilt."
14:10 The **king** replied, "If anyone says anything to you, bring him to
14:11 "Then let the **king** invoke the LORD his God to prevent the
14:12 woman said, "Let your servant speak a word to my lord the **king**."
14:13 When the **king** says this, does he not convict himself, for the king
14:13 for the **king** has not brought back his banished son?
14:15 "And now I have come to say this to my lord the **king**
14:15 Your servant thought, 'I will speak to the **king**; perhaps he will do
14:15 to the king; perhaps **he**[s] [+2021] will do what his servant asks.
14:16 Perhaps the **king** will agree to deliver his servant from the hand of
14:17 servant says, 'May the word of my lord the **king** bring me rest,
14:17 for my lord the **king** is like an angel of God in discerning good
14:18 the **king** said to the woman, "Do not keep from me the answer to
14:18 going to ask you." "Let my lord the **king** speak," the woman said.
14:19 The **king** asked, "Isn't the hand of Joab with you in all this?"
14:19 The woman answered, "As surely as you live, my lord the **king**,
14:19 turn to the right or to the left from anything my lord the **king** says.
14:21 The **king** said to Joab, "Very well, I will do it. Go, bring back the
14:22 his face to the ground to pay him honor, and he blessed the **king**.
14:22 my lord the **king**, because the king has granted his servant's
14:22 lord the king, because the **king** has granted his servant's request."
14:24 the **king** said, "He must go to his own house; he must not see my
14:24 went to his own house and did not see the face of the **king**.
14:26 and its weight was two hundred shekels by the **royal** standard.
14:28 Absalom lived two years in Jerusalem without seeing the **king's**
14:29 Then Absalom sent for Joab in order to send him to the **king**,
14:32 and said, 'Come here so I can send you to the **king** to ask,
14:32 I want to see the **king's** face, and if I am guilty of anything,
14:33 So Joab went to the **king** and told him this. Then the king
14:33 the **king** summoned Absalom, and he came in and bowed down
14:33 and bowed down with his face to the ground before the **king**.
14:33 face to the ground before the king. And the **king** kissed Absalom.
15:2 came with a complaint to be placed before the **king** for a decision,
15:3 and proper, but there is no representative of the **king** to hear you."
15:6 toward all the Israelites who came to the **king** asking for justice,
15:7 Absalom said to the **king**, "Let me go to Hebron and fulfill a vow I
15:9 The **king** said to him, "Go in peace." So he went to Hebron.
15:15 The **king's** officials answered him, "Your servants are ready to do
15:15 The king's officials answered **him**[s] [+2021], "Your servants are
15:15 "Your servants are ready to do whatever our lord the **king**
15:16 The **king** set out, with his entire household following him;
15:16 but **he**[s] [+2021] left ten concubines to take care of the palace.
15:17 So the **king** set out, with all the people following him, and they
15:18 who had accompanied him from Gath marched before the **king**.
15:19 The **king** said to Ittai the Gittite, "Why should you come along
15:19 Go back and stay with **King** Absalom. You are a foreigner,
15:21 But Ittai replied to the **king**, "As surely as the LORD lives,
15:21 "As surely as the LORD lives, and as my lord the **king** lives,
15:21 wherever my lord the **king** may be, whether it means life or death,
15:23 The **king** also crossed the Kidron Valley, and all the people moved
15:25 the **king** said to Zadok, "Take the ark of God back into the city.
15:27 The **king** also said to Zadok the priest, "Aren't you a seer?
15:34 to the city and say to Absalom, 'I will be your servant, O **king**;
15:35 there with you? Tell them anything you hear in the **king's** palace.
16:2 The **king** asked Ziba, "Why have you brought these?" Ziba
16:2 "The donkeys are for the **king's** household to ride on, the bread
16:3 The **king** then asked, "Where is your master's grandson?"
16:3 Ziba said to **him**[s] [+2021], "He is staying in Jerusalem, because he
16:4 the **king** said to Ziba, "All that belonged to Mephibosheth is now
16:4 Ziba said. "May I find favor in your eyes, my lord the **king**."
16:5 As **King** David approached Bahurim, a man from the same clan as
16:6 He pelted David and all the **king's** officials with stones, though all
16:9 Abishai son of Zeruiah said to the **king**, "Why should this dead
16:9 to the king, "Why should this dead dog curse my lord the **king**?
16:10 the **king** said, "What do you and I have in common, you sons of
16:14 The **king** and all the people with him arrived at their destination
16:16 went to Absalom and said to him, "Long live the **king**!
16:16 and said to him, "Long live the king! Long live the **king**!"
17:2 the people with him will flee. I would strike down only the **king**
17:16 or the **king** and all the people with him will be swallowed up.' "
17:17 and inform them, and they were to go and tell **King** David,
17:21 the two climbed out of the well and went to inform **King** David.
18:2 The **king** told the troops, "I myself will surely march out with
18:4 The **king** answered, "I will do whatever seems best to you."
18:4 So the **king** stood beside the gate while all the men marched out in
18:5 The **king** commanded Joab, Abishai and Ittai, "Be gentle with the
18:5 all the troops heard the **king** giving orders concerning Absalom to
18:12 out into my hands, I would not lift my hand against the **king's** son.
18:12 In our hearing the **king** commanded you and Abishai and Ittai,
18:13 put my life in jeopardy—and nothing is hidden from the **king**—
18:18 and erected it in the **King's** Valley as a monument to himself,
18:19 take the news to the **king** that the LORD has delivered him from
18:20 but you must not do so today, because the **king's** son is dead."
18:21 Joab said to a Cushite, "Go, tell the **king** what you have seen."
18:25 The watchman called out to the **king** and reported it. The king said,
18:25 The **king** said, "If he is alone, he must have good news."
18:26 The **king** said, "He must be bringing good news, too."
18:27 "He's a good man," the **king** said. "He comes with good news."
18:28 Ahimaaz called out to the **king**, "All is well!" He bowed down
18:28 He bowed down before the **king** with his face to the ground
18:28 up the men who lifted their hands against my lord the **king**."
18:29 The **king** asked, "Is the young man Absalom safe?" Ahimaaz
18:29 "I saw great confusion just as Joab was about to send the **king's**
18:30 The **king** said, "Stand aside and wait here." So he stepped aside
18:31 the Cushite arrived and said, "My lord the **king**, hear the good
18:32 The **king** asked the Cushite, "Is the young man Absalom safe?"
18:32 "May the enemies of my lord the **king** and all who rise up to harm
18:33 [19:1] The **king** was shaken. He went up to the room over the
19:1 [19:2] "The **king** is weeping and mourning for Absalom."
19:2 [19:3] the troops heard it said, "The **king** is grieving for his son."
19:4 [19:5] The **king** covered his face and cried aloud, "O my son
19:4 [19:5] The king covered his face and cried **[RPH]** aloud, "O my
19:5 [19:6] Joab went into the house to the **king** and said, "Today you
19:8 [19:9] So the **king** got up and took his seat in the gateway.
19:8 [19:9] the men were told, "The **king** is sitting in the gateway,"
19:8 [19:9] sitting in the gateway," they all came before **him**[s] [+2021].
19:9 [19:10] "The **king** delivered us from the hand of our enemies;
19:10 [19:11] So why do you say nothing about bringing the **king**
19:11 [19:12] **King** David sent this message to Zadok and Abiathar,
19:11 [19:12] 'Why should you be the last to bring the **king** back to his
19:11 [19:12] throughout Israel has reached the **king** at his quarters?
19:12 [19:13] So why should you be the last to bring back the **king**?'
19:14 [19:15] They sent word to the **king**, "Return, you and all your
19:15 [19:16] the **king** returned and went as far as the Jordan.
19:15 [19:16] go out and meet the **king** and bring him across the Jordan.
19:15 [19:16] meet the king and bring **him**[s] [+2021] across the Jordan.
19:16 [19:17] hurried down with the men of Judah to meet **King** David.
19:17 [19:18] They rushed to the Jordan, where the **king** was.
19:18 [19:19] They crossed at the ford to take the **king's** household over

2Sa 19:18 [19:19] Gera crossed the Jordan, he fell prostrate before the **king**
19:19 [19:20] said to **him**[s] [+2021], "May my lord not hold me guilty.
19:19 [19:20] did wrong on the day my lord the **king** left Jerusalem.
19:19 [19:20] king left Jerusalem. May the **king** put it out of his mind.
19:20 [19:21] of Joseph to come down and meet my lord the **king**."
19:22 [19:23] Do I not know that today I am **king** over Israel?"
19:23 [19:24] So the **king** said to Shimei, "You shall not die."
19:23 [19:24] "You shall not die." And the **king** promised him on oath.
19:24 [19:25] Saul's grandson, also went down to meet the **king**.
19:24 [19:25] or washed his clothes from the day the **king** left until the
19:25 [19:26] When he came from Jerusalem to meet the **king**, the king
19:25 [19:26] the **king** asked him, "Why didn't you go with me,
19:26 [19:27] He said, "My lord the **king**, since I your servant am lame,
19:26 [19:27] and will ride on it, so I can go with the **king**.'
19:27 [19:28] he has slandered your servant to my lord the **king**. My
19:27 [19:28] My lord the **king** is like an angel of God; so do whatever
19:28 [19:29] deserved nothing but death from my lord the **king**,
19:28 [19:29] right do I have to make any more appeals to the **king**?"
19:29 [19:30] The **king** said to him, "Why say more? I order you
19:30 [19:31] Mephibosheth said to the **king**, "Let him take everything,
19:30 [19:31] now that my lord the **king** has arrived home safely."
19:31 [19:32] down from Rogelim to cross the Jordan with the **king**
19:32 [19:33] He had provided for the **king** during his stay in
19:33 [19:34] The **king** said to Barzillai, "Cross over with me and stay
19:34 [19:35] Barzillai answered the **king**, "How many more years will
19:34 [19:35] will I live, that I should go up to Jerusalem with the **king**?
19:35 [19:36] your servant be an added burden to my lord the **king**?
19:36 [19:37] Your servant will cross over the Jordan with the **king** for
19:36 [19:37] but why should the **king** reward me in this way?
19:37 [19:38] Let him cross over with my lord the **king**.
19:38 [19:39] The **king** said, "Kimham shall cross over with me, and I
19:39 [19:40] people crossed the Jordan, and then the **king** crossed over.
19:39 [19:40] The **king** kissed Barzillai and gave him his blessing,
19:40 [19:41] When the **king** crossed over to Gilgal, Kimham crossed
19:40 [19:41] and half the troops of Israel had taken the **king** over.
19:41 [19:42] Soon all the men of Israel were coming to the **king**
19:41 [19:42] were coming to the king and saying to **him**[s] [+2021],
19:41 [19:42] steal the **king** away and bring him and his household
19:42 [19:43] "We did this because the **king** is closely related to us.
19:42 [19:43] about it? Have we eaten any of the **king's** provisions?
19:43 [19:44] the men of Judah, "We have ten shares in the **king**;
19:43 [19:44] we not the first to speak of bringing back our **king**?"
20: 2 the men of Judah stayed by their **king** all the way from the Jordan
20: 3 When David returned to his palace in Jerusalem, **he**[s] [+2021] took
20: 4 the **king** said to Amasa, "Summon the men of Judah to come to me
20:21 of Ephraim, has lifted up his hand against the **king**, against David.
20:22 to his home. And Joab went back to the **king** in Jerusalem.
21: 2 The **king** summoned the Gibeonites and spoke to them.
21: 5 They answered the **king**, "As for the man who destroyed us
21: 6 LORD's chosen one." So the **king** said, "I will give them to you."
21: 7 The **king** spared Mephibosheth son of Jonathan, the son of Saul,
21: 8 the **king** took Armoni and Mephibosheth, the two sons of Aiah's
21:14 at Zela in Benjamin, and did everything the **king** commanded.
22:51 He gives his **king** great victories; he shows unfailing kindness to
24: 2 So the **king** said to Joab and the army commanders with him,
24: 3 Joab replied to the **king**, "May the LORD your God multiply the
24: 3 a hundred times over, and may the eyes of my lord the **king** see it.
24: 3 see it. But why does my lord the **king** want to do such a thing?"
24: 4 The **king's** word, however, overruled Joab and the army
24: 4 so they left the presence of the **king** to enroll the fighting men of
24: 9 Joab reported the number of the fighting men to the **king**:
24:20 When Araunah looked and saw the **king** and his men coming
24:20 and bowed down before the **king** with his face to the ground.
24:21 Araunah said, "Why has my lord the **king** come to his servant?"
24:22 "Let my lord the **king** take whatever pleases him and offer it up.
24:23 O **king**, Araunah gives all this to the king." Araunah also said to
24:23 O king, Araunah gives all this to the **king**." Araunah also said to
24:23 Araunah also said to **him**[s] [+2021], "May the LORD your God
24:24 But the **king** replied to Araunah, "No, I insist on paying you for it.
1Ki 1: 1 When **King** David was old and well advanced in years, he could
1: 2 "Let us look for **[RPH]** a young virgin to attend the king
1: 2 "Let us look for a young virgin to attend the **king** and take care of
1: 2 She can lie beside him so that our lord the **king** may keep warm."
1: 3 and found Abishag, a Shunammite, and brought her to the **king**.
1: 4 she took care of the **king** and waited on him, but the king had no
1: 4 and waited on him, but the **king** had no intimate relations with her.
1: 9 He invited all his brothers, the **king's** sons, and all the men of
1: 9 the king's sons, and all the men of Judah who were **royal** officials,
1:13 Go in to **King** David and say to him, 'My lord the king, did you not
1:13 Go in to King David and say to him, 'My lord the **king**, did you not
1:14 While you are still there talking to the **king**, I will come in
1:15 So Bathsheba went to see the aged **king** in his room, where
1:15 So Bathsheba went to see the aged king **[RPH]** in his room,
1:15 where Abishag the Shunammite was attending **him**[s] [+2021].
1:16 Bathsheba bowed low and knelt before the **king**. "What is it you
1:16 and knelt before the king. "What is it you want?" the **king** asked.
1:18 has become king, and you, my lord the **king**, do not know about it.
1:19 fattened calves, and sheep, and has invited all the **king's** sons,
1:20 My lord the **king**, the eyes of all Israel are on you, to learn from
1:20 to learn from you who will sit on the throne of my lord the **king**
1:21 as soon as my lord the **king** is laid to rest with his fathers,
1:22 While she was still speaking with the **king**, Nathan the prophet
1:23 they told the **king**, "Nathan the prophet is here." So he went before
1:23 So he went before the **king** and bowed with his face to the ground.
1:23 before the king and bowed **[RPH]** with his face to the ground.
1:24 Nathan said, "Have you, my lord the **king**, declared that Adonijah
1:25 He has invited all the **king's** sons, the commanders of the army
1:25 and drinking with him and saying, 'Long live **King** Adonijah!'
1:27 Is this something my lord the **king** has done without letting his
1:27 know who should sit on the throne of my lord the **king** after him?"
1:28 **King** David said, "Call in Bathsheba." So she came into the king's
1:28 So she came into the **king's** presence and stood before him.
1:28 she came into the king's presence and stood before **him**[s] [+2021].
1:29 The **king** then took an oath: "As surely as the LORD lives,
1:31 kneeling before the **king**, said, "May my lord King David live
1:31 before the king, said, "May my lord **King** David live forever!"
1:32 **King** David said, "Call in Zadok the priest, Nathan the prophet
1:32 and Benaiah son of Jehoiada." When they came before the **king**,
1:33 **he**[s] [+2021] said to them: "Take your lord's servants with you
1:34 the priest and Nathan the prophet anoint him **king** over Israel.
1:34 Blow the trumpet and shout, 'Long live **King** Solomon!'
1:36 Benaiah son of Jehoiada answered the **king**, "Amen!
1:36 May the LORD, the God of my lord the **king**, so declare it.
1:37 As the LORD was with my lord the **king**, so may he be with
1:37 his throne even greater than the throne of my lord **King** David!"
1:38 put Solomon on **King** David's mule and escorted him to Gihon.
1:39 and all the people shouted, "Long live **King** Solomon!"
1:43 "Our lord **King** David has made Solomon king.
1:44 The **king** has sent with him Zadok the priest, Nathan the prophet,
1:44 and the Pelethites, and they have put him on the **king's** mule,
1:45 and Nathan the prophet have anointed him **king** at Gihon.
1:47 the **royal** officials have come to congratulate our lord King David,
1:47 the royal officials have come to congratulate our lord **King** David,
1:47 greater than yours!' And the **king** bowed in worship on his bed
1:48 and said, **[RPH]** 'Praise be to the LORD, the God of Israel,
1:51 "Adonijah is afraid of **King** Solomon and is clinging to the horns
1:51 'Let **King** Solomon swear to me today that he will not put his
1:53 **King** Solomon sent men, and they brought him down from the
1:53 Adonijah came and bowed down to **King** Solomon, and Solomon
2:17 So he continued, "Please ask **King** Solomon—he will not refuse
2:18 "Very well," Bathsheba replied, "I will speak to the **king** for you."
2:19 When Bathsheba went to **King** Solomon to speak to him for
2:19 the **king** stood up to meet her, bowed down to her and sat down on
2:19 He had a throne brought for the **king's** mother, and she sat down at
2:20 The **king** replied, "Make it, my mother; I will not refuse you."
2:22 **King** Solomon answered his mother, "Why do you request
2:23 **King** Solomon swore by the LORD: "May God deal with me,
2:25 So **King** Solomon gave orders to Benaiah son of Jehoiada,
2:26 To Abiathar the priest the **king** said, "Go back to your fields in
2:29 **King** Solomon was told that Joab had fled to the tent of the
2:30 entered the tent of the LORD and said to Joab, "The **king** says,
2:30 Benaiah reported to the **king**, "This is how Joab answered me."
2:31 the **king** commanded Benaiah, "Do as he says. Strike him down
2:35 The **king** put Benaiah son of Jehoiada over the army in Joab's
2:35 and replaced Abiathar with Zadok the priest. **[RPH]**
2:36 the **king** sent for Shimei and said to him, "Build yourself a house
2:38 Shimei answered the **king**, "What you say is good. Your servant
2:38 say is good. Your servant will do as my lord the **king** has said."
2:39 **king** *of* Gath, and Shimei was told, "Your slaves are in Gath."
2:42 the **king** summoned Shimei and said to him, "Did I not make you
2:44 The **king** also said to Shimei, "You know in your heart all the
2:45 **King** Solomon will be blessed, and David's throne will remain
2:46 the **king** gave the order to Benaiah son of Jehoiada, and he went
3: 1 Solomon made an alliance with Pharaoh **king** *of* Egypt
3: 4 The **king** went to Gibeon to offer sacrifices, for that was the most
3:13 so that in your lifetime you will have no equal among **kings**.
3:16 Now two prostitutes came to the **king** and stood before him.
3:22 the living one is mine." And so they argued before the **king**.
3:23 The **king** said, "This one says, 'My son is alive and your son is
3:24 the **king** said, "Bring me a sword." So they brought a sword for the
3:24 "Bring me a sword." So they brought a sword for the **king**.
3:25 **He**[s] [+2021] then gave an order: "Cut the living child in two
3:26 alive was filled with compassion for her son and said to the **king**,
3:27 the **king** gave his ruling: "Give the living baby to the first woman.
3:28 When all Israel heard the verdict the **king** had given, they held the
3:28 heard the verdict the king had given, they held the **king** in awe,
4: 1 So **King** Solomon ruled over all Israel.
4: 1 So King Solomon **ruled** [+2118] over all Israel.

1Ki 4: 5 Zabud son of Nathan—a priest and personal adviser to the **king**;
4: 7 who supplied provisions for the **king** and the royal household.
4: 19 in Gilead (the country of Sihon **king** *of* the Amorites
4: 19 Sihon king of the Amorites and the country of Og **king** *of* Bashan).
4: 24 [5:4] For he ruled over all the **kingdoms** west of the River,
4: 27 [5:7] supplied provisions for **King** Solomon and all who came to
4: 27 [5:7] for King Solomon and all who came to the **king's** table.
4: 34 [5:14] sent by all the **kings** *of* the world, who had heard of his
5: 1 [5:15] When Hiram **king** *of* Tyre heard that Solomon had been
5: 1 [5:15] had been anointed **king** to succeed his father David,
5: 13 [5:27] **King** Solomon conscripted laborers from all Israel—thirty
5: 17 [5:31] At the **king's** command they removed from the quarry
6: 2 The temple that **King** Solomon built for the LORD was sixty
7: 13 **King** Solomon sent to Tyre and brought Huram,
7: 14 He came to **King** Solomon and did all the work assigned to him.
7: 40 So Huram finished all the work he had undertaken for **King**
7: 45 All these objects that Huram made for **King** Solomon for the
7: 46 The **king** had them cast in clay molds in the plain of the Jordan
7: 51 When all the work **King** Solomon had done for the temple of the
8: 1 **King** Solomon summoned into his presence at Jerusalem the elders
8: 2 All the men of Israel came together to **King** Solomon at the time of
8: 5 **King** Solomon and the entire assembly of Israel that had gathered
8: 14 Israel was standing there, the **king** turned around and blessed them.
8: 62 the **king** and all Israel with him offered sacrifices before the
8: 63 So the **king** and all the Israelites dedicated the temple of the
8: 64 On that same day the **king** consecrated the middle part of the
8: 66 They blessed the **king** and then went home, joyful and glad in heart
9: 1 finished building the temple of the LORD and the **royal** palace,
9: 10 two buildings—the temple of the LORD and the **royal** palace—
9: 11 **King** Solomon gave twenty towns in Galilee to Hiram king of
9: 11 King Solomon gave twenty towns in Galilee to Hiram **king** *of*
9: 14 Now Hiram had sent to the **king** 120 talents of gold.
9: 15 Here is the account of the forced labor **King** Solomon conscripted
9: 16 (Pharaoh **king** *of* Egypt had attacked and captured Gezer.
9: 26 **King** Solomon also built ships at Ezion Geber, which is near Elath
9: 28 back 420 talents of gold, which they delivered to **King** Solomon.
10: 3 her questions; nothing was too hard for the **king** to explain to her.
10: 6 She said to the **king**, "The report I heard in my own country about
10: 9 he has made you **king**, to maintain justice and righteousness."
10: 10 she gave the **king** 120 talents of gold, large quantities of spices,
10: 10 brought in as those the queen of Sheba gave to **King** Solomon.
10: 12 The **king** used the almugwood to make supports for the temple of
10: 12 supports for the temple of the LORD and for the **royal** palace,
10: 13 **King** Solomon gave the queen of Sheba all she desired and asked
10: 13 asked for, besides what he had given her out of his **royal** bounty.
10: 15 traders and from all the Arabian **kings** and the governors of the
10: 16 **King** Solomon made two hundred large shields of hammered gold;
10: 17 The **king** put them in the Palace of the Forest of Lebanon.
10: 18 the **king** made a great throne inlaid with ivory and overlaid with
10: 21 All **King** Solomon's goblets were gold, and all the household
10: 22 The **king** had a fleet of trading ships at sea along with the ships of
10: 23 **King** Solomon was greater in riches and wisdom than all the other
10: 23 greater in riches and wisdom than all the other **kings** *of* the earth.
10: 26 kept in the chariot cities and also with **him**[s] [+2021] in Jerusalem.
10: 27 The **king** made silver as common in Jerusalem as stones, and cedar
10: 28 and from Kue—the **royal** merchants purchased them from Kue.
10: 29 They also exported them to all the **kings** *of* the Hittites and of the
10: 29 them to all the kings of the Hittites and **[RPH]** of the Arameans.
11: 1 **King** Solomon, however, loved many foreign women besides
11: 14 an adversary, Hadad the Edomite, from the **royal** line of Edom.
11: 18 they went to Egypt, to Pharaoh **king** *of* Egypt, who gave Hadad a
11: 23 of Eliada, who had fled from his master, Hadadezer **king** *of* Zobah.
11: 26 Also, Jeroboam son of Nebat rebelled against the **king**. He was one
11: 27 Here is the account of how he rebelled against the **king**:
11: 37 rule over all that your heart desires; you will be **king** over Israel.
11: 40 to kill Jeroboam, but Jeroboam fled to Egypt, to Shishak the **king**,
12: 2 where he had fled from **King** Solomon), he returned from Egypt.
12: 6 **King** Rehoboam consulted the elders who had served his father
12: 12 as the **king** had said, "Come back to me in three days."
12: 13 The **king** answered the people harshly. Rejecting the advice given
12: 15 So the **king** did not listen to the people, for this turn of events was
12: 16 When all Israel saw that the **king** refused to listen to them,
12: 16 saw that the king refused to listen to them, they answered the **king**:
12: 18 **King** Rehoboam sent out Adoniram, who was in charge of forced
12: 18 **King** Rehoboam, however, managed to get into his chariot
12: 23 "Say to Rehoboam son of Solomon **king** *of* Judah, to the whole
12: 27 again give their allegiance to their lord, Rehoboam **king** *of* Judah.
12: 27 king of Judah. They will kill me and return to **King** Rehoboam."
12: 28 After seeking advice, the **king** made two golden calves. He said to
13: 4 When **King** Jeroboam heard what the man of God cried out against
13: 6 the **king** said to the man of God, "Intercede with the LORD your
13: 6 and the **king's** hand was restored and became as it was before.
13: 7 The **king** said to the man of God, "Come home with me and have
13: 8 the man of God answered the **king**, "Even if you were to give me
13: 11 that day. They also told their father what he had said to the **king**.
14: 2 is there—the one who told me I would be **king** over this people.
14: 14 "The LORD will raise up for himself a **king** over Israel who will
14: 19 are written in the book of the annals of the **kings** *of* Israel.
14: 25 In the fifth year of **King** Rehoboam, Shishak king of Egypt
14: 25 of King Rehoboam, Shishak **king** *of* Egypt attacked Jerusalem.
14: 26 of the temple of the LORD and the treasures of the **royal** palace.
14: 27 So **King** Rehoboam made bronze shields to replace them
14: 27 of the guard on duty at the entrance to the **royal** palace.
14: 28 Whenever the **king** went to the LORD's temple, the guards bore
14: 29 are they not written in the book of the annals of the **kings** *of*
15: 1 In the eighteenth year of the **reign** *of* Jeroboam son of Nebat,
15: 7 are they not written in the book of the annals of the **kings** *of*
15: 9 In the twentieth year of Jeroboam **king** *of* Israel, Asa became king
15: 9 of Jeroboam king of Israel, Asa *became* **king of** [+4887] Judah,
15: 16 between Asa and Baasha **king** *of* Israel throughout their reigns.
15: 17 Baasha **king** *of* Israel went up against Judah and fortified Ramah to
15: 17 anyone from leaving or entering the territory of Asa **king** *of* Judah.
15: 18 in the treasuries of the LORD's temple and of **his**[s] **own** palace.
15: 18 and sent them **[RPH]** to Ben-Hadad son of Tabrimmon,
15: 18 the son of Hezion, the **king** *of* Aram, who was ruling in Damascus.
15: 19 Now break your treaty with Baasha **king** *of* Israel so he will
15: 20 Ben-Hadad agreed with **King** Asa and sent the commanders of his
15: 22 Then **King** Asa issued an order to all Judah—no one was exempt—
15: 22 With them **King** Asa built up Geba in Benjamin, and also Mizpah.
15: 23 are they not written in the book of the annals of the **kings** *of*
15: 25 became king of Israel in the second year of Asa **king** *of* Judah,
15: 28 Baasha killed Nadab in the third year of Asa **king** *of* Judah
15: 31 are they not written in the book of the annals of the **kings** *of* Israel?
15: 32 between Asa and Baasha **king** *of* Israel throughout their reigns.
15: 33 In the third year of Asa **king** *of* Judah, Baasha son of Ahijah
16: 5 are they not written in the book of the annals of the **kings** *of* Israel?
16: 8 In the twenty-sixth year of Asa **king** *of* Judah, Elah son of Baasha
16: 10 and killed him in the twenty-seventh year of Asa **king** *of* Judah.
16: 14 are they not written in the book of the annals of the **kings** *of* Israel?
16: 15 In the twenty-seventh year of Asa **king** *of* Judah, Zimri reigned in
16: 16 Israelites in the camp heard that Zimri had plotted against the **king**
16: 18 he went into the citadel of the **royal** palace and set the palace on
16: 18 of the royal palace and set the palace on fire **[RPH]** around him.
16: 20 are they not written in the book of the annals of the **kings** *of* Israel?
16: 23 In the thirty-first year of Asa **king** *of* Judah, Omri became king of
16: 27 are they not written in the book of the annals of the **kings** *of* Israel?
16: 29 In the thirty-eighth year of Asa **king** *of* Judah, Ahab son of Omri
16: 31 he also married Jezebel daughter of Ethbaal **king** *of* the Sidonians,
16: 33 God of Israel, to anger than did all the **kings** *of* Israel before him.
19: 15 of Damascus. When you get there, anoint Hazael **king** over Aram.
19: 16 Also, anoint Jehu son of Nimshi **king** over Israel, and anoint Elisha
20: 1 Now Ben-Hadad **king** *of* Aram mustered his entire army.
20: 1 Accompanied by thirty-two **kings** with their horses and chariots,
20: 2 He sent messengers into the city to Ahab **king** *of* Israel, saying,
20: 4 The **king** *of* Israel answered, "Just as you say, my lord the king.
20: 4 The king of Israel answered, "Just as you say, my lord the **king**.
20: 7 The **king** *of* Israel summoned all the elders of the land and said to
20: 9 So he replied to Ben-Hadad's messengers, "Tell my lord the **king**,
20: 11 The **king** *of* Israel answered, "Tell him: 'One who puts on his
20: 12 this message while he and the **kings** were drinking in their tents,
20: 13 Meanwhile a prophet came to Ahab **king** *of* Israel and announced,
20: 16 and the 32 **kings** allied with him were in their tents getting drunk.
20: 16 the 32 kings allied with him **[RPH]** were in their tents getting
20: 20 Ben-Hadad **king** *of* Aram escaped on horseback with some of his
20: 21 The **king** *of* Israel advanced and overpowered the horses
20: 22 Afterward, the prophet came to the **king** *of* Israel and said,
20: 22 because next spring the **king** *of* Aram will attack you again."
20: 23 Meanwhile, the officials of the **king** *of* Aram advised him,
20: 24 Remove all the **kings** from their commands and replace them with
20: 28 The man of God came up and told the **king** *of* Israel, "This is what
20: 31 we have heard that the **kings** *of* the house of Israel are merciful.
20: 31 we have heard that the kings of the house of Israel **[RPH]** are
20: 31 Let us go to the **king** *of* Israel with sackcloth around our waists
20: 32 ropes around their heads, they went to the **king** *of* Israel and said,
20: 38 Then the prophet went and stood by the road waiting for the **king**.
20: 39 As the **king** passed by, the prophet called out to him, "Your
20: 39 As the king passed by, the prophet called out to **him**[s] [+2021],
20: 40 man disappeared." "That is your sentence," the **king** *of* Israel said.
20: 41 and the **king** *of* Israel recognized him as one of the prophets.
20: 43 and angry, the **king** *of* Israel went to his palace in Samaria.
21: 1 was in Jezreel, close to the palace of Ahab **king** *of* Samaria.
21: 10 and have them testify that he has cursed both God and the **king**.
21: 13 the people, saying, "Naboth has cursed both God and the **king**."
21: 18 "Go down to meet Ahab **king** *of* Israel, who rules in Samaria.
22: 2 in the third year Jehoshaphat **king** *of* Judah went down to see the
22: 2 Jehoshaphat king of Judah went down to see the **king** *of* Israel.
22: 3 The **king** *of* Israel had said to his officials, "Don't you know that
22: 3 and yet we are doing nothing to retake it from the **king** *of* Aram?"

1Ki 22: 4 Jehoshaphat replied to the **king** *of* Israel, "I am as you are,
22: 5 Jehoshaphat also said to the **king** *of* Israel, "First seek the counsel
22: 6 So the **king** *of* Israel brought together the prophets—about four
22: 6 they answered, "for the Lord will give it into the **king's** hand."
22: 8 The **king** *of* Israel answered Jehoshaphat, "There is still one man
22: 8 son of Imlah." "The **king** should not say that," Jehoshaphat replied.
22: 9 So the **king** *of* Israel called one of his officials and said,
22: 10 the **king** *of* Israel and Jehoshaphat king of Judah were sitting on
22: 10 Jehoshaphat **king** *of* Judah were sitting on their thrones at the
22: 12 they said, "for the LORD will give it into the **king's** hand."
22: 13 as one man the other prophets are predicting success for the **king**.
22: 15 When he arrived, the **king** asked him, "Micaiah, shall we go to war
22: 15 When he arrived, the king asked him, **[RPH]** "Micaiah, shall we
22: 15 he answered, "for the LORD will give it into the **king's** hand."
22: 16 The **king** said to him, "How many times must I make you swear to
22: 18 The **king** *of* Israel said to Jehoshaphat, "Didn't I tell you that he
22: 26 The **king** *of* Israel then ordered, "Take Micaiah and send him back
22: 26 him back to Amon the ruler of the city and to Joash the **king's** son
22: 27 and say, 'This is what the **king** says: Put this fellow in prison
22: 29 So the **king** *of* Israel and Jehoshaphat king of Judah went up to
22: 29 and Jehoshaphat **king** *of* Judah went up to Ramoth Gilead.
22: 30 The **king** *of* Israel said to Jehoshaphat, "I will enter the battle in
22: 30 So the **king** *of* Israel disguised himself and went into battle.
22: 31 Now the **king** *of* Aram had ordered his thirty-two chariot
22: 31 not fight with anyone, small or great, except the **king** *of* Israel."
22: 32 saw Jehoshaphat, they thought, "Surely this is the **king** *of* Israel."
22: 33 the chariot commanders saw that he was not the **king** *of* Israel
22: 34 and hit the **king** *of* Israel between the sections of his armor.
22: 35 and the **king** was propped up in his chariot facing the Arameans.
22: 37 So the **king** died and was brought to Samaria, and they buried him
22: 37 and was brought to Samaria, and they buried **him**[s] [+2021] there.
22: 39 are they not written in the book of the annals of the **kings** *of* Israel?
22: 41 became king of Judah in the fourth year of Ahab **king** *of* Israel.
22: 44 [22:45] Jehoshaphat was also at peace with the **king** *of* Israel.
22: 45 [22:46] written in the book of the annals of the **kings** *of* Judah?
22: 47 [22:48] There was then no **king** in Edom; a deputy ruled.
22: 47 [22:48] There was then no king in Edom; a deputy **ruled**.
22: 51 [22:52] in the seventeenth year of Jehoshaphat **king** *of* Judah,
2Ki 1: 3 "Go up and meet the messengers of the **king** *of* Samaria and ask
1: 6 "And he said to us, 'Go back to the **king** who sent you and tell him,
1: 9 and said to him, "Man of God, the **king** says, 'Come down!' "
1: 11 "Man of God, this is what the **king** says, 'Come down at once!' "
1: 15 of him." So Elijah got up and went down with him to the **king**.
1: 17 in the second year of Jehoram son of Jehoshaphat **king** *of* Judah.
1: 18 are they not written in the book of the annals of the **kings** *of* Israel?
3: 1 in Samaria in the eighteenth year of Jehoshaphat **king** *of* Judah,
3: 4 Now Mesha **king** *of* Moab raised sheep, and he had to supply the
3: 4 he had to supply the **king** *of* Israel with a hundred thousand lambs
3: 5 Ahab died, the **king** *of* Moab rebelled against the king of Israel.
3: 5 Ahab died, the king of Moab rebelled against the **king** *of* Israel.
3: 6 So at that time **King** Joram set out from Samaria and mobilized all
3: 7 He also sent this message to Jehoshaphat **king** *of* Judah: "The king
3: 7 "The **king** *of* Moab has rebelled against me. Will you go with me
3: 9 So the **king** *of* Israel set out with the king of Judah and the king of
3: 9 So the king of Israel set out with the **king** *of* Judah and the king of
3: 9 king of Israel set out with the king of Judah and the **king** *of* Edom.
3: 10 "What!" exclaimed the **king** *of* Israel. "Has the LORD called us
3: 10 "Has the LORD called us three **kings** together only to hand us
3: 11 An officer of the **king** *of* Israel answered, "Elisha son of Shaphat is
3: 12 So the **king** *of* Israel and Jehoshaphat and the king of Edom went
3: 12 and Jehoshaphat and the **king** *of* Edom went down to him.
3: 13 Elisha said to the **king** *of* Israel, "What do we have to do with each
3: 13 "No," the **king** *of* Israel answered, "because it was the LORD
3: 13 "because it was the LORD who called us three **kings** together to
3: 14 if I did not have respect for the presence of Jehoshaphat **king** *of*
3: 21 Now all the Moabites had heard that the **kings** had come to fight
3: 23 "Those **kings** must have fought and slaughtered each other.
3: 26 When the **king** *of* Moab saw that the battle had gone against him,
3: 26 seven hundred swordsmen to break through to the **king** *of* Edom,
4: 13 Can we speak on your behalf to the **king** or the commander of the
5: 1 Now Naaman was commander of the army of the **king** *of* Aram.
5: 5 "By all means, go," the **king** *of* Aram replied. "I will send a letter
5: 5 "I will send a letter to the **king** *of* Israel." So Naaman left,
5: 6 The letter that he took to the **king** *of* Israel read: "With this letter I
5: 7 As soon as the **king** *of* Israel read the letter, he tore his robes
5: 8 When Elisha the man of God heard that the **king** *of* Israel had torn
5: 8 of Israel had torn his robes, he sent **him**[s] [+2021] this message:
6: 8 Now the **king** *of* Aram was at war with Israel. After conferring
6: 9 The man of God sent word to the **king** *of* Israel: "Beware of
6: 10 So the **king** *of* Israel checked on the place indicated by the man of
6: 11 This enraged the **king** *of* Aram. He summoned his officers
6: 11 "Will you not tell me which of us is on the side of the **king** *of*
6: 12 "None of us, my lord the **king**," said one of his officers,
6: 12 tells the **king** *of* Israel the very words you speak in your bedroom."
6: 21 When the **king** *of* Israel saw them, he asked Elisha, "Shall I kill
6: 24 Ben-Hadad **king** *of* Aram mobilized his entire army and marched
6: 26 As the **king** *of* Israel was passing by on the wall, a woman cried to
6: 26 on the wall, a woman cried to him, "Help me, my lord the **king**!"
6: 28 Then **he**[s] [+2021] asked her, "What's the matter?" She answered,
6: 30 When the **king** heard the woman's words, he tore his robes.
7: 2 The officer on whose arm the **king** was leaning said to the man of
7: 6 the **king** *of* Israel has hired the Hittite and Egyptian kings to attack
7: 6 of Israel has hired the Hittite and Egyptian **kings** to attack us!"
7: 6 has hired the Hittite and Egyptian kings **[RPH]** to attack us!"
7: 9 overtake us. Let's go at once and report this to the **royal** palace."
7: 11 shouted the news, and it was reported within the **palace** [+1074].
7: 12 The **king** got up in the night and said to his officers, "I will tell you
7: 14 with their horses, and the **king** sent them after the Aramean army.
7: 15 So the messengers returned and reported to the **king**.
7: 17 Now the **king** had put the officer on whose arm he leaned in charge
7: 17 just as the man of God had foretold when the **king** came down to
7: 18 It happened as the man of God had said to the **king**: "About this
8: 3 the Philistines and went to the **king** to beg for her house and land.
8: 4 The **king** was talking to Gehazi, the servant of the man of God,
8: 5 Just as Gehazi was telling the **king** how Elisha had restored the
8: 5 Elisha had brought back to life came to beg the **king** for her house
8: 5 Gehazi said, "This is the woman, my lord the **king**, and this is her
8: 6 The **king** asked the woman about it, and she told him. Then he
8: 6 Then **he**[s] [+2021] assigned an official to her case and said to him,
8: 7 Elisha went to Damascus, and Ben-Hadad **king** *of* Aram was ill.
8: 8 **he**[s] [+2021] said to Hazael, "Take a gift with you and go to meet
8: 9 and said, "Your son Ben-Hadad **king** *of* Aram has sent me to ask,
8: 13 "The LORD has shown me that you will become **king** of Aram,"
8: 16 In the fifth year of Joram son of Ahab **king** *of* Israel,
8: 16 son of Ahab king of Israel, when Jehoshaphat was **king** *of* Judah,
8: 16 Jehoram son of Jehoshaphat began his reign as **king** *of* Judah.
8: 18 He walked in the ways of the **kings** *of* Israel, as the house of Ahab
8: 20 rebelled against Judah and **set up** its own **king** [+4887+6584].
8: 23 are they not written in the book of the annals of the **kings** *of*
8: 25 In the twelfth year of Joram son of Ahab **king** *of* Israel,
8: 25 of Israel, Ahaziah son of Jehoram **king** *of* Judah began to reign.
8: 26 name was Athaliah, a granddaughter of Omri **king** *of* Israel.
8: 28 of Ahab to war against Hazael **king** *of* Aram at Ramoth Gilead.
8: 29 so **King** Joram returned to Jezreel to recover from the wounds the
8: 29 inflicted on him at Ramoth in his battle with Hazael **king** *of* Aram.
8: 29 Ahaziah son of Jehoram **king** *of* Judah went down to Jezreel to see
9: 3 I anoint you **king** over Israel.' Then open the door and run;
9: 6 of Israel, says: 'I anoint you **king** over the LORD's people Israel.
9: 12 'This is what the LORD says: I anoint you **king** over Israel.' "
9: 14 had been defending Ramoth Gilead against Hazael **king** *of* Aram,
9: 15 **King** Joram had returned to Jezreel to recover from the wounds the
9: 15 had inflicted on him in the battle with Hazael **king** *of* Aram.)
9: 16 resting there and Ahaziah **king** *of* Judah had gone down to see him.
9: 18 rode off to meet Jehu and said, "This is what the **king** says:
9: 19 When he came to them he said, "This is what the **king** says:
9: 21 Joram **king** *of* Israel and Ahaziah king of Judah rode out, each in
9: 21 Joram king of Israel and Ahaziah **king** *of* Judah rode out, each in
9: 27 When Ahaziah **king** *of* Judah saw what had happened, he fled up
9: 34 he said, "and bury her, for she was a **king's** daughter."
10: 4 But they were terrified and said, "If two **kings** could not resist him,
10: 6 Now the **royal** princes, seventy of them, were with the leading men
10: 7 these men took the **princes** [+1201] and slaughtered all seventy of
10: 8 told Jehu, "They have brought the heads of the **princes** [+1201]."
10: 13 he met some relatives of Ahaziah **king** *of* Judah and asked,
10: 13 we have come down to greet the families of the **king** and of the
10: 34 are they not written in the book of the annals of the **kings** *of* Israel?
11: 2 the daughter of **King** Jehoram and sister of Ahaziah,
11: 2 son of Ahaziah and stole him away from among the **royal** princes,
11: 4 at the temple of the LORD. Then he showed them the **king's** son.
11: 5 on duty on the Sabbath—a third of you guarding the **royal** palace,
11: 7 go off Sabbath duty are all to guard the temple for the **king**.
11: 8 Station yourselves around the **king**, each man with his weapon in
11: 8 must be put to death. Stay close to the **king** wherever he goes."
11: 10 the spears and shields that had belonged to **King** David
11: 11 his weapon in his hand, stationed themselves around the **king**—
11: 12 Jehoiada brought out the **king's** son and put the crown on him;
11: 12 the people clapped their hands and shouted, "Long live the **king**!"
11: 14 She looked and there was the **king**, standing by the pillar,
11: 14 The officers and the trumpeters were beside the **king**, and all the
11: 16 the place where the horses enter the **palace grounds** [+1074],
11: 17 Jehoiada then made a covenant between the LORD and the **king**
11: 17 He also made a covenant between the **king** and the people.
11: 19 together they brought the **king** down from the temple of the
11: 19 from the temple of the LORD and went into the **palace** [+1074],
11: 19 of the guards. The king then took his place on the **royal** throne,
11: 20 Athaliah had been slain with the sword at the **palace** [+1074].
12: 6 [12:7] by the twenty-third year of **King** Joash the priests still had
12: 7 [12:8] Therefore **King** Joash summoned Jehoiada the priest

2Ki 12:10 [12:11] the **royal** secretary and the high priest came, counted the
12:17 [12:18] About this time Hazael **king** *of* Aram went up
12:18 [12:19] Joash **king** *of* Judah took all the sacred objects dedicated
12:18 [12:19] Jehoshaphat, Jehoram and Ahaziah, the **kings** *of* Judah—
12:18 [12:19] of the temple of the LORD and of the **royal** palace,
12:18 [12:19] he sent them to Hazael **king** *of* Aram, who then withdrew
12:19 [12:20] written in the book of the annals of the **kings** *of* Judah?
13: 1 In the twenty-third year of Joash son of Ahaziah **king** *of* Judah,
13: 3 for a long time he kept them under the power of Hazael **king** *of*
13: 4 for he saw how severely the **king** *of* Aram was oppressing Israel.
13: 7 for the **king** *of* Aram had destroyed the rest and made them like the
13: 8 are they not written in the book of the annals of the **kings** *of* Israel?
13:10 In the thirty-seventh year of Joash **king** *of* Judah, Jehoash son of
13:12 including his war against Amaziah **king** *of* Judah,
13:12 are they not written in the book of the annals of the **kings** *of* Israel?
13:13 the throne. Jehoash was buried in Samaria with the **kings** *of* Israel.
13:14 Jehoash **king** *of* Israel went down to see him and wept over him.
13:16 "Take the bow in your hands," he said to the **king** *of* Israel.
13:16 When he had taken it, Elisha put his hands on the **king's** hands.
13:18 Then he said, "Take the arrows," and the **king** took them.
13:22 Hazael **king** *of* Aram oppressed Israel throughout the reign of
13:24 Hazael **king** *of* Aram died, and Ben-Hadad his son succeeded him
14: 1 In the second year of Jehoash son of Jehoahaz **king** *of* Israel,
14: 1 king of Israel, Amaziah son of Joash **king** *of* Judah began to reign.
14: 5 he executed the officials who had murdered his father the **king**.
14: 8 son of Jehoahaz, the son of Jehu, **king** *of* Israel, with the challenge:
14: 9 But Jehoash **king** *of* Israel replied to Amaziah king of Judah:
14: 9 But Jehoash king of Israel replied to Amaziah **king** *of* Judah:
14:11 however, would not listen, so Jehoash **king** *of* Israel attacked.
14:11 Amaziah **king** *of* Judah faced each other at Beth Shemesh in
14:13 Jehoash **king** *of* Israel captured Amaziah king of Judah, the son of
14:13 Jehoash king of Israel captured Amaziah **king** *of* Judah, the son of
14:14 the temple of the LORD and in the treasuries of the **royal** palace.
14:15 including his war against Amaziah **king** *of* Judah,
14:15 are they not written in the book of the annals of the **kings** *of* Israel?
14:16 with his fathers and was buried in Samaria with the **kings** *of* Israel.
14:17 Amaziah son of Joash **king** *of* Judah lived for fifteen years after
14:17 years after the death of Jehoash son of Jehoahaz **king** *of* Israel.
14:18 are they not written in the book of the annals of the **kings** *of*
14:22 restored it to Judah after **Amaziah**[s] [+2021] rested with his fathers.
14:23 In the fifteenth year of Amaziah son of Joash **king** *of* Judah,
14:23 Jeroboam son of Jehoash **king** *of* Israel became king in Samaria,
14:28 are they not written in the book of the annals of the **kings** *of* Israel?
14:29 Jeroboam rested with his fathers, the **kings** *of* Israel.
15: 1 In the twenty-seventh year of Jeroboam **king** *of* Israel, Azariah son
15: 1 of Israel, Azariah son of Amaziah **king** *of* Judah began to reign.
15: 5 The LORD afflicted the **king** with leprosy until the day he died,
15: 5 Jotham the **king's** son had charge of the palace and governed the
15: 6 are they not written in the book of the annals of the **kings** *of*
15: 8 In the thirty-eighth year of Azariah **king** *of* Judah, Zechariah son
15:11 reign are written in the book of the annals of the **kings** *of* Israel.
15:13 became king in the thirty-ninth year of Uzziah **king** *of* Judah,
15:15 are written in the book of the annals of the **kings** *of* Israel.
15:17 In the thirty-ninth year of Azariah **king** *of* Judah, Menahem son of
15:19 Pul **king** *of* Assyria invaded the land, and Menahem gave him a
15:20 contribute fifty shekels of silver to be given to the **king** *of* Assyria.
15:20 So the **king** *of* Assyria withdrew and stayed in the land no longer.
15:21 are they not written in the book of the annals of the **kings** *of* Israel?
15:23 In the fiftieth year of Azariah **king** *of* Judah, Pekahiah son of
15:25 and Arieh, in the citadel of the **royal** palace at Samaria.
15:26 are written in the book of the annals of the **kings** *of* Israel.
15:27 In the fifty-second year of Azariah **king** *of* Judah, Pekah son of
15:29 In the time of Pekah **king** *of* Israel, Tiglath-Pileser king of Assyria
15:29 Tiglath-Pileser **king** *of* Assyria came and took Ijon, Abel Beth
15:31 are they not written in the book of the annals of the **kings** *of* Israel?
15:32 In the second year of Pekah son of Remaliah **king** *of* Israel,
15:32 king of Israel, Jotham son of Uzziah **king** *of* Judah began to reign.
15:36 are they not written in the book of the annals of the **kings** *of*
15:37 (In those days the LORD began to send Rezin **king** *of* Aram
16: 1 of Remaliah, Ahaz son of Jotham **king** *of* Judah began to reign.
16: 3 He walked in the ways of the **kings** *of* Israel and even sacrificed
16: 5 Rezin **king** *of* Aram and Pekah son of Remaliah king of Israel
16: 5 Pekah son of Remaliah **king** *of* Israel marched up to fight against
16: 6 Rezin **king** *of* Aram recovered Elath for Aram by driving out the
16: 7 Ahaz sent messengers to say to Tiglath-Pileser **king** *of* Assyria,
16: 7 Come up and save me out of the hand of the **king** *of* Aram
16: 7 me out of the hand of the king of Aram and of the **king** *of* Israel,
16: 8 in the treasuries of the **royal** palace and sent it as a gift to the king
16: 8 of the royal palace and sent it as a gift to the **king** *of* Assyria.
16: 9 The **king** *of* Assyria complied by attacking Damascus
16: 9 The king of Assyria complied by attacking **[RPH]** Damascus
16:10 **King** Ahaz went to Damascus to meet Tiglath-Pileser king of
16:10 King Ahaz went to Damascus to meet Tiglath-Pileser **king** *of*
16:10 sketch of the altar, **[RPH]** with detailed plans for its construction.
16:11 with all the plans that **King** Ahaz had sent from Damascus
16:11 sent from Damascus and finished it before **King** Ahaz returned.
16:12 When the **king** came back from Damascus and saw the altar,
16:12 the altar, **[RPH]** he approached it and presented offerings on it.
16:12 saw the altar, **he**[s] [+2021] approached it and presented offerings on
16:15 **King** Ahaz then gave these orders to Uriah the priest: "On the
16:15 grain offering, the **king's** burnt offering and his grain offering,
16:16 And Uriah the priest did just as **King** Ahaz had ordered.
16:17 **King** Ahaz took away the side panels and removed the basins from
16:18 and removed the **royal** entryway outside the temple of the LORD,
16:18 the temple of the LORD, in deference to the **king** *of* Assyria.
16:19 are they not written in the book of the annals of the **kings** *of*
17: 1 In the twelfth year of Ahaz **king** *of* Judah, Hoshea son of Elah
17: 2 of the LORD, but not like the **kings** *of* Israel who preceded him.
17: 3 Shalmaneser **king** *of* Assyria came up to attack Hoshea, who had
17: 4 But the **king** *of* Assyria discovered that Hoshea was a traitor,
17: 4 for he had sent envoys to So **king** *of* Egypt, and he no longer paid
17: 4 he no longer paid tribute to the **king** *of* Assyria, as he had done
17: 4 Therefore **Shalmaneser**[s] [+855] seized him and put him in prison.
17: 5 The **king** *of* Assyria invaded the entire land, marched against
17: 6 the **king** *of* Assyria captured Samaria and deported the Israelites to
17: 7 up out of Egypt from under the power of Pharaoh **king** *of* Egypt.
17: 8 as well as the practices that the **kings** *of* Israel had introduced.
17:24 The **king** *of* Assyria brought people from Babylon, Cuthah,
17:26 It was reported to the **king** *of* Assyria: "The people you deported
17:27 the **king** *of* Assyria gave this order: "Have one of the priests you
18: 1 In the third year of Hoshea son of Elah **king** *of* Israel,
18: 1 king of Israel, Hezekiah son of Ahaz **king** *of* Judah began to reign.
18: 5 There was no one like him among all the **kings** *of* Judah,
18: 7 He rebelled against the **king** *of* Assyria and did not serve him.
18: 9 In **King** Hezekiah's fourth year, which was the seventh year of
18: 9 which was the seventh year of Hoshea son of Elah **king** *of* Israel,
18: 9 Shalmaneser **king** *of* Assyria marched against Samaria and laid
18:10 sixth year, which was the ninth year of Hoshea **king** *of* Israel.
18:11 The **king** *of* Assyria deported Israel to Assyria and settled them in
18:13 In the fourteenth year of **King** Hezekiah's reign, Sennacherib king
18:13 Sennacherib **king** *of* Assyria attacked all the fortified cities of
18:14 So Hezekiah **king** *of* Judah sent this message to the king of Assyria
18:14 So Hezekiah king of Judah sent this message to the **king** *of* Assyria
18:14 The **king** *of* Assyria exacted from Hezekiah king of Judah three
18:14 The king of Assyria exacted from Hezekiah **king** *of* Judah three
18:15 the temple of the LORD and in the treasuries of the **royal** palace.
18:16 At this time Hezekiah **king** *of* Judah stripped off the gold with
18:16 of the temple of the LORD, and gave it to the **king** *of* Assyria.
18:17 The **king** *of* Assyria sent his supreme commander, his chief officer
18:17 with a large army, from Lachish to **King** Hezekiah at Jerusalem.
18:18 They called for the **king**; and Eliakim son of Hilkiah the palace
18:19 " 'This is what the great **king**, the king of Assyria, says:
18:19 " 'This is what the great king, the **king** *of* Assyria, says:
18:21 Such is Pharaoh **king** *of* Egypt to all who depend on him.
18:23 " 'Come now, make a bargain with my master, the **king** *of* Assyria:
18:28 in Hebrew: "Hear the word of the great **king**, the king of Assyria!
18:28 in Hebrew: "Hear the word of the great king, the **king** *of* Assyria!
18:29 This is what the **king** says: Do not let Hezekiah deceive you.
18:30 this city will not be given into the hand of the **king** *of* Assyria.'
18:31 This is what the **king** *of* Assyria says: Make peace with me
18:33 ever delivered his land from the hand of the **king** *of* Assyria?
18:36 in reply, because the **king** had commanded, "Do not answer him."
19: 1 When **King** Hezekiah heard this, he tore his clothes and put on
19: 4 whom his master, the **king** *of* Assyria, has sent to ridicule the
19: 5 When **King** Hezekiah's officials came to Isaiah,
19: 6 those words with which the underlings of the **king** *of* Assyria have
19: 8 When the field commander heard that the **king** *of* Assyria had left
19: 9 the Cushite **king** ⌞of Egypt⌟, was marching out to fight against him.
19:10 "Say to Hezekiah **king** *of* Judah: Do not let the god you depend on
19:10 'Jerusalem will not be handed over to the **king** *of* Assyria.'
19:11 Surely you have heard what the **kings** *of* Assyria have done to all
19:13 Where is the **king** *of* Hamath, the king of Arpad, the king of the
19:13 Where is the king of Hamath, the **king** *of* Arpad, the king of the
19:13 the **king** of the city of Sepharvaim, or of Hena or Ivvah?"
19:17 that the Assyrian **kings** have laid waste these nations and their
19:20 I have heard your prayer concerning Sennacherib **king** *of* Assyria.
19:32 "Therefore this is what the LORD says concerning the **king** *of*
19:36 So Sennacherib **king** *of* Assyria broke camp and withdrew.
20: 6 will deliver you and this city from the hand of the **king** *of* Assyria.
20:12 At that time Merodach-Baladan son of Baladan **king** *of* Babylon
20:14 Then Isaiah the prophet went to **King** Hezekiah and asked,
20:18 they will become eunuchs in the palace of the **king** *of* Babylon."
20:20 are they not written in the book of the annals of the **kings** *of*
21: 3 and made an Asherah pole, as Ahab **king** *of* Israel had done.
21:11 "Manasseh **king** *of* Judah has committed these detestable sins.
21:17 are they not written in the book of the annals of the **kings** *of*
21:23 conspired against him and assassinated the **king** in his palace.
21:24 the people of the land killed all who had plotted against **King**

2Ki 21:25 are they not written in the book of the annals of the **kings** *of*
22: 3 In the eighteenth year of his **reign**, King Josiah sent the secretary,
22: 3 **King** Josiah sent the secretary, Shaphan son of Azaliah, the son of
22: 9 Then Shaphan the secretary went to the **king** and reported to him:
22: 9 the secretary went to the king and reported to **him**[s] [+2021]:
22:10 Shaphan the secretary informed the **king**, "Hilkiah the priest has
22:10 me a book." And Shaphan read from it in the presence of the **king**.
22:11 When the **king** heard the words of the Book of the Law, he tore his
22:12 **He**[s] [+2021] gave these orders to Hilkiah the priest, Ahikam son of
22:12 of Micaiah, Shaphan the secretary and Asaiah the **king's** attendant:
22:16 according to everything written in the book the **king** *of* Judah has
22:18 Tell the **king** *of* Judah, who sent you to inquire of the LORD,
22:20 to bring on this place.' " So they took her answer back to the **king**.
23: 1 the **king** called together all the elders of Judah and Jerusalem.
23: 2 **He**[s] [+2021] went up to the temple of the LORD with the men of
23: 3 The **king** stood by the pillar and renewed the covenant in the
23: 4 The **king** ordered Hilkiah the high priest, the priests next in rank
23: 5 He did away with the pagan priests appointed by the **kings** *of*
23:11 the horses that the **kings** *of* Judah had dedicated to the sun.
23:12 He pulled down the altars the **kings** *of* Judah had erected on the
23:12 built in the two courts of the temple of the LORD. **He**[s] [+2021]
23:13 The **king** also desecrated the high places that were east of
23:13 the ones Solomon **king** *of* Israel had built for Ashtoreth the vile
23:19 defiled all the shrines at the high places that the **kings** *of* Israel had
23:21 The **king** gave this order to all the people: "Celebrate the Passover
23:22 nor throughout the days of the **kings** *of* Israel and the kings of
23:22 throughout the days of the kings of Israel and the **kings** *of* Judah,
23:23 in the eighteenth year of **King** Josiah, this Passover was celebrated
23:25 Neither before nor after Josiah was there a **king** like him who
23:28 are they not written in the book of the annals of the **kings** *of*
23:29 Pharaoh Neco **king** *of* Egypt went up to the Euphrates River to
23:29 Egypt went up to the Euphrates River to help the **king** *of* Assyria.
23:29 **King** Josiah marched out to meet him in battle, but Neco faced him
24: 1 Nebuchadnezzar **king** *of* Babylon invaded the land,
24: 5 are they not written in the book of the annals of the **kings** *of*
24: 7 The **king** *of* Egypt did not march out from his own country again,
24: 7 because the **king** *of* Babylon had taken all his territory, from the
24: 7 because the king of Babylon had taken all **his**[s] [+4200+5213]
24:10 At that time the officers of Nebuchadnezzar **king** *of* Babylon
24:11 Nebuchadnezzar **[RPH]** himself came up to the city while his
24:12 Jehoiachin **king** *of* Judah, his mother, his attendants, his nobles
24:12 his nobles and his officials all surrendered to **him**[s] [+951].
24:12 In the eighth year of the reign of the **king** *of* Babylon, he took
24:13 from the temple of the LORD and from the **royal** palace,
24:13 took away all the gold articles that Solomon **king** *of* Israel had
24:15 He also took from Jerusalem to Babylon the **king's** mother,
24:15 took from Jerusalem to Babylon the king's mother, **his**[s] [+2021]
24:16 The **king** *of* Babylon also deported to Babylon the entire force of
24:17 **He**[s] [+951] made Mattaniah, Jehoiachin's uncle, king in his place
24:20 his presence. Now Zedekiah rebelled against the **king** *of* Babylon.
25: 1 Nebuchadnezzar **king** *of* Babylon marched against Jerusalem with
25: 2 The city was kept under siege until the eleventh year of **King**
25: 4 through the gate between the two walls near the **king's** garden,
25: 5 the Babylonian army pursued the **king** and overtook him in the
25: 6 **he**[s] [+2021] was captured. He was taken to the king of Babylon at
25: 6 He was taken to the **king** *of* Babylon at Riblah, where sentence
25: 8 in the nineteenth year of Nebuchadnezzar **king** *of* Babylon,
25: 8 in the nineteenth year of Nebuchadnezzar king of **[RPH]**
25: 8 an official of the **king** *of* Babylon, came to Jerusalem.
25: 9 of the LORD, the **royal** palace and all the houses of Jerusalem.
25:11 the populace and those who had gone over to the **king** *of* Babylon.
25:19 the officer in charge of the fighting men and five **royal** advisers.
25:20 took them all and brought them to the **king** *of* Babylon at Riblah.
25:21 at Riblah, in the land of Hamath, the **king** had them executed.
25:22 Nebuchadnezzar **king** *of* Babylon appointed Gedaliah son of
25:23 their men heard that the **king** *of* Babylon had appointed Gedaliah
25:24 "Settle down in the land and serve the **king** *of* Babylon, and it will
25:27 In the thirty-seventh year of the exile of Jehoiachin **king** *of* Judah,
25:27 in the year Evil-Merodach became king of **[RPH]** Babylon,
25:27 he released Jehoiachin **[RPH]** from prison on the twenty-seventh
25:28 gave him a seat of honor higher than those of the other **kings** who
25:30 Day by day the **king** gave Jehoiachin a regular allowance as long
1Ch 1:43 These were the **kings** who reigned in Edom before any Israelite
1:43 the kings who reigned in Edom before any Israelite **king** reigned:
3: 2 Absalom the son of Maacah daughter of Talmai **king** *of* Geshur;
4:23 at Netaim and Gederah; they stayed there and worked for the **king**.
4:41 names were listed came in the days of Hezekiah **king** *of* Judah.
5: 6 his son, whom Tiglath-Pileser **king** *of* Assyria took into exile.
5:17 the genealogical records during the reigns of Jotham **king** *of* Judah
5:17 the reigns of Jotham king of Judah and Jeroboam **king** *of* Israel.
5:26 So the God of Israel stirred up the spirit of Pul **king** *of* Assyria
5:26 Tiglath-Pileser **king** *of* Assyria), who took the Reubenites,
9: 1 listed in the genealogies recorded in the book of the **kings** *of* Israel.
9:18 being stationed at the **King's** Gate on the east, up to the present
11: 2 In the past, even while Saul was **king**, you were the one who led
11: 3 When all the elders of Israel had come to **King** David at Hebron,
11: 3 they anointed David **king** over Israel, as the LORD had promised
14: 1 Now Hiram **king** *of* Tyre sent messengers to David, along with
14: 2 David knew that the LORD had established him as **king** over
14: 8 When the Philistines heard that David had been anointed **king** over
15:29 when she saw **King** David dancing and celebrating, she despised
16:21 allowed no man to oppress them; for their sake he rebuked **kings**:
17:16 Then **King** David went in and sat before the LORD, and he said:
18: 3 Moreover, David fought Hadadezer **king** *of* Zobah, as far as
18: 5 When the Arameans of Damascus came to help Hadadezer **king** *of*
18: 9 When Tou **king** *of* Hamath heard that David had defeated the
18: 9 David had defeated the entire army of Hadadezer **king** *of* Zobah,
18:10 he sent his son Hadoram to **King** David to greet him
18:11 **King** David dedicated these articles to the LORD, as he had done
18:17 and David's sons were chief officials at the **king's** side.
19: 1 In the course of time, Nahash **king** *of* the Ammonites died,
19: 5 The **king** said, "Stay at Jericho till your beards have grown,
19: 7 as well as the **king** *of* Maacah with his troops, who came
19: 9 while the **kings** who had come were by themselves in the open
20: 1 In the spring, at the time when **kings** go off to war, Joab led out the
20: 2 David took the crown from the head of their **king**—its weight was
21: 3 My lord the **king**, are they not all my lord's subjects? Why does
21: 4 The **king's** word, however, overruled Joab; so Joab left and went
21: 6 the numbering, because the **king's** command was repulsive to him.
21:23 Let my lord the **king** do whatever pleases him. Look, I will give
21:24 **King** David replied to Araunah, "No, I insist on paying the full
24: 6 recorded their names in the presence of the **king** and of the
24:31 in the presence of **King** David and of Zadok, Ahimelech,
25: 2 of Asaph, who prophesied under the **king's** supervision.
25: 5 All these were sons of Heman the **king's** seer. They were given
25: 6 Jeduthun and Heman were under the supervision of the **king**.
26:26 charge of all the treasuries for the things dedicated by **King** David,
26:30 Jordan for all the work of the LORD and for the **king's** service.
26:32 and **King** David put them in charge of the Reubenites, the Gadites
26:32 for every matter pertaining to God and for the affairs of the **king**.
27: 1 who served the **king** in all that concerned the army divisions that
27:24 the number was not entered in the book of the annals of **King**
27:25 Azmaveth son of Adiel was in charge of the **royal** storehouses.
27:31 All these were the officials in charge of **King** David's property.
27:32 and a scribe. Jehiel son of Hacmoni took care of the **king's** sons.
27:33 Ahithophel was the **king's** [+4200] counselor. Hushai the Arkite
27:33 was the king's counselor. Hushai the Arkite was the **king's** friend.
27:34 and by Abiathar. Joab was the commander of the **royal** army.
28: 1 the commanders of the divisions in the service of the **king**,
28: 1 of all the property and livestock belonging to the **king** and his sons,
28: 2 **King** David rose to his feet and said: "Listen to me, my brothers
28: 4 chose me from my whole family to be **king** over Israel forever.
29: 1 Then **King** David said to the whole assembly: "My son Solomon,
29: 6 and the officials in charge of the **king's** work gave willingly.
29: 9 to the LORD. David the **king** also rejoiced greatly.
29:20 they bowed low and fell prostrate before the LORD and the **king**.
29:23 So Solomon sat on the throne of the LORD as **king** in place of his
29:24 the officers and mighty men, as well as all of **King** David's sons,
29:24 of King David's sons, pledged their submission to **King** Solomon.
29:25 bestowed on him royal splendor such as no **king** over Israel ever
29:29 As for the events of **King** David's reign, from beginning to end,
2Ch 1:12 such as no **king** who was before you ever had and none after you
1:14 kept in the chariot cities and also with **him**[s] [+2021] in Jerusalem.
1:15 The **king** made silver and gold as common in Jerusalem as stones,
1:16 and from Kue—the **royal** merchants purchased them from Kue.
1:17 They also exported them to all the **kings** *of* the Hittites and of the
1:17 them to all the kings of the Hittites and **[RPH]** of the Arameans.
2: 3 [2:2] Solomon sent this message to Hiram **king** *of* Tyre:
2:11 [2:10] Hiram **king** *of* Tyre replied by letter to Solomon:
2:11 [2:10] the LORD loves his people, he has made you their **king**."
2:12 [2:11] He has given **King** David a wise son, endowed with
4:11 So Huram finished the work he had undertaken for **King** Solomon
4:16 All the objects that Huram-Abi made for **King** Solomon for the
4:17 The **king** had them cast in clay molds in the plain of the Jordan
5: 3 all the men of Israel came together to the **king** at the time of the
5: 6 **King** Solomon and the entire assembly of Israel that had gathered
6: 3 Israel was standing there, the **king** turned around and blessed them.
7: 4 the **king** and all the people offered sacrifices before the LORD.
7: 5 **King** Solomon offered a sacrifice of twenty-two thousand head of
7: 5 So the **king** and all the people dedicated the temple of God.
7: 6 which **King** David had made for praising the LORD and which
7:11 had finished the temple of the LORD and the **royal** palace,
8:10 They were also **King** Solomon's chief officials—two hundred
8:11 "My wife must not live in the palace of David **king** *of* Israel,
8:15 They did not deviate from the **king's** commands to the priests
8:18 and fifty talents of gold, which they delivered to **King** Solomon.
9: 5 She said to the **king**, "The report I heard in my own country about
9: 8 placed you on his throne as **king** to rule for the LORD your God.

2Ch 9: 8 he has made you **king** over them, to maintain justice
9: 9 she gave the **king** 120 talents of gold, large quantities of spices,
9: 9 such spices as those the queen of Sheba gave to **King** Solomon.
9: 11 The **king** used the algumwood to make steps for the temple of the
9: 11 make steps for the temple of the LORD and for the **royal** palace,
9: 12 **King** Solomon gave the queen of Sheba all she desired and asked
9: 12 asked for; he gave her more than she had brought to **him**[s] [+2021].
9: 14 Also all the **kings** *of* Arabia and the governors of the land brought
9: 15 **King** Solomon made two hundred large shields of hammered gold;
9: 16 The **king** put them in the Palace of the Forest of Lebanon.
9: 17 the **king** made a great throne inlaid with ivory and overlaid with
9: 20 All **King** Solomon's goblets were gold, and all the household
9: 21 The **king** had a fleet of trading ships manned by Hiram's men.
9: 22 **King** Solomon was greater in riches and wisdom than all the other
9: 22 greater in riches and wisdom than all the other **kings** *of* the earth.
9: 23 All the **kings** *of* the earth sought audience with Solomon to hear
9: 25 kept in the chariot cities and also with **him**[s] [+2021] in Jerusalem.
9: 26 He ruled over all the **kings** from the River to the land of the
9: 27 The **king** made silver as common in Jerusalem as stones, and cedar
10: 2 where he had fled from **King** Solomon), he returned from Egypt.
10: 6 **King** Rehoboam consulted the elders who had served his father
10: 12 as the **king** had said, "Come back to me in three days."
10: 13 The **king** answered them harshly. Rejecting the advice of the
10: 13 answered them harshly. Rejecting **[RPH]** the advice of the elders,
10: 15 So the **king** did not listen to the people, for this turn of events was
10: 16 When all Israel saw that the **king** refused to listen to them,
10: 16 saw that the king refused to listen to them, they answered the **king**:
10: 18 **King** Rehoboam sent out Adoniram, who was in charge of forced
10: 18 **King** Rehoboam, however, managed to get into his chariot
11: 3 "Say to Rehoboam son of Solomon **king** *of* Judah and to all the
12: 2 Shishak **king** *of* Egypt attacked Jerusalem in the fifth year of King
12: 2 Shishak king of Egypt attacked Jerusalem in the fifth year of **King**
12: 6 The leaders of Israel and the **king** humbled themselves and said,
12: 9 When Shishak **king** *of* Egypt attacked Jerusalem, he carried off the
12: 9 of the temple of the LORD and the treasures of the **royal** palace.
12: 10 So **King** Rehoboam made bronze shields to replace them
12: 10 of the guard on duty at the entrance to the **royal** palace.
12: 11 Whenever the **king** went to the LORD's temple, the guards went
12: 13 **King** Rehoboam established himself firmly in Jerusalem
13: 1 In the eighteenth year of the **reign** *of* Jeroboam, Abijah became
15: 16 **King** Asa also deposed his grandmother Maacah from her position
16: 1 In the thirty-sixth year of Asa's reign Baasha **king** *of* Israel went
16: 1 anyone from leaving or entering the territory of Asa **king** *of* Judah.
16: 2 of **his**[s] [+2021] **own** palace and sent it to Ben-Hadad king of
16: 2 and of his own palace and sent it to Ben-Hadad **king** *of* Aram,
16: 3 Now break your treaty with Baasha **king** *of* Israel so he will
16: 4 Ben-Hadad agreed with **King** Asa and sent the commanders of his
16: 6 **King** Asa brought all the men of Judah, and they carried away
16: 7 At that time Hanani the seer came to Asa **king** *of* Judah and said to
16: 7 "Because you relied on the **king** *of* Aram and not on the LORD
16: 7 the army of the **king** *of* Aram has escaped from your hand.
16: 11 to end, are written in the book of the **kings** of Judah and Israel.
17: 19 These were the men who served the **king**, besides those he
17: 19 besides those **he**[s] [+2021] stationed in the fortified cities
18: 3 Ahab **king** *of* Israel asked Jehoshaphat king of Judah, "Will you go
18: 3 Ahab king of Israel asked Jehoshaphat **king** *of* Judah, "Will you go
18: 4 Jehoshaphat also said to the **king** *of* Israel, "First seek the counsel
18: 5 So the **king** *of* Israel brought together the prophets—four hundred
18: 5 they answered, "for God will give it into the **king's** hand."
18: 7 The **king** *of* Israel answered Jehoshaphat, "There is still one man
18: 7 son of Imlah." "The **king** should not say that," Jehoshaphat replied.
18: 8 So the **king** *of* Israel called one of his officials and said,
18: 9 the **king** *of* Israel and Jehoshaphat king of Judah were sitting on
18: 9 Jehoshaphat **king** *of* Judah were sitting on their thrones at the
18: 11 they said, "for the LORD will give it into the **king's** hand."
18: 12 as one man the other prophets are predicting success for the **king**.
18: 14 When he arrived, **[RPH]** the king asked him, "Micaiah, shall we
18: 14 When he arrived, the **king** asked him, "Micaiah, shall we go to war
18: 15 The **king** said to him, "How many times must I make you swear to
18: 17 The **king** *of* Israel said to Jehoshaphat, "Didn't I tell you that he
18: 19 'Who will entice Ahab **king** *of* Israel into attacking Ramoth Gilead
18: 25 The **king** *of* Israel then ordered, "Take Micaiah and send him back
18: 25 him back to Amon the ruler of the city and to Joash the **king's** son,
18: 26 and say, 'This is what the **king** says: Put this fellow in prison
18: 28 So the **king** *of* Israel and Jehoshaphat king of Judah went up to
18: 28 and Jehoshaphat **king** *of* Judah went up to Ramoth Gilead.
18: 29 The **king** *of* Israel said to Jehoshaphat, "I will enter the battle in
18: 29 So the **king** *of* Israel disguised himself and went into battle.
18: 30 Now the **king** *of* Aram had ordered his chariot commanders,
18: 30 not fight with anyone, small or great, except the **king** *of* Israel."
18: 31 saw Jehoshaphat, they thought, "This is the **king** *of* Israel."
18: 32 for when the chariot commanders saw that he was not the **king** *of*
18: 33 and hit the **king** *of* Israel between the sections of his armor.
18: 34 the **king** *of* Israel propped himself up in his chariot facing the
19: 1 When Jehoshaphat **king** *of* Judah returned safely to his palace in
19: 2 the son of Hanani, went out to meet him and said to the **king**,
19: 11 tribe of Judah, will be over you in any matter concerning the **king**,
20: 15 **King** Jehoshaphat and all who live in Judah and Jerusalem!
20: 34 of Hanani, which are recorded in the book of the **kings** *of* Israel.
20: 35 Jehoshaphat **king** *of* Judah made an alliance with Ahaziah king of
20: 35 Jehoshaphat king of Judah made an alliance with Ahaziah **king** *of*
21: 2 and Shephatiah. All these were sons of Jehoshaphat **king** *of* Israel.
21: 6 He walked in the ways of the **kings** *of* Israel, as the house of Ahab
21: 8 rebelled against Judah and **set up** its own **king** [+4887+6584].
21: 12 in the ways of your father Jehoshaphat or of Asa **king** *of* Judah.
21: 13 you have walked in the ways of the **kings** *of* Israel, and you have
21: 17 invaded it and carried off all the goods found in the **king's** palace,
21: 20 was buried in the City of David, but not in the tombs of the **kings**.
22: 1 So Ahaziah son of Jehoram **king** *of* Judah began to reign.
22: 5 **king** *of* Israel to war against Hazael king of Aram at Ramoth
22: 5 of Israel to war against Hazael **king** *of* Aram at Ramoth Gilead.
22: 6 inflicted on him at Ramoth in his battle with Hazael **king** *of* Aram.
22: 6 Ahaziah son of Jehoram **king** *of* Judah went down to Jezreel to see
22: 11 Jehosheba, the daughter of **King** Jehoram, took Joash son of
22: 11 stole him away from among the **royal** princes who were about to
22: 11 the daughter of **King** Jehoram and wife of the priest Jehoiada,
23: 3 the whole assembly made a covenant with the **king** at the temple of
23: 3 Jehoiada said to them, "The **king's** son shall reign, as the LORD
23: 5 a third of you at the **royal** palace and a third at the Foundation
23: 7 The Levites are to station themselves around the **king**, each man
23: 7 must be put to death. Stay close to the **king** wherever he goes."
23: 9 and the large and small shields that had belonged to **King** David
23: 10 all the men, each with his weapon in his hand, around the **king**—
23: 11 Jehoiada and his sons brought out the **king's** son and put the crown
23: 11 him king. They anointed him and shouted, "Long live the **king**!"
23: 12 heard the noise of the people running and cheering the **king**,
23: 13 She looked, and there was the **king**, standing by his pillar at the
23: 13 The officers and the trumpeters were beside the **king**, and all the
23: 15 the entrance of the Horse Gate on the **palace grounds** [+1074],
23: 16 and the people and the **king** would be the LORD's people.
23: 20 and brought the **king** down from the temple of the LORD.
23: 20 They went into the **palace** [+1074] through the Upper Gate
23: 20 through the Upper Gate and seated the **king** on the royal throne,
24: 6 Therefore the **king** summoned Jehoiada the chief priest and said to
24: 8 At the **king's** command, a chest was made and placed outside,
24: 11 Whenever the chest was brought in by the Levites to the **king's**
24: 11 the **royal** secretary and the officer of the chief priest would come
24: 12 The **king** and Jehoiada gave it to the men who carried out the work
24: 14 they brought the rest of the money to the **king** and Jehoiada,
24: 16 He was buried with the **kings** in the City of David, because of the
24: 17 the officials of Judah came and paid homage to the **king**, and he
24: 17 and paid homage to the king, and **he**[s] [+2021] listened to them.
24: 21 by order of the **king** they stoned him to death in the courtyard of
24: 22 **King** Joash did not remember the kindness Zechariah's father
24: 23 of the people. They sent all the plunder to their **king** *in* Damascus.
24: 25 was buried in the City of David, but not in the tombs of the **kings**.
24: 27 of God are written in the annotations on the book of the **kings**.
25: 3 he executed the officials who had murdered his father the **king**.
25: 7 a man of God came to him and said, "O **king**, these troops from
25: 16 king said to him, "Have we appointed you an adviser to the **king**?
25: 17 After Amaziah **king** *of* Judah consulted his advisers, he sent this
25: 17 to Jehoash son of Jehoahaz, the son of Jehu, **king** *of* Israel:
25: 18 But Jehoash **king** *of* Israel replied to Amaziah king of Judah:
25: 18 But Jehoash king of Israel replied to Amaziah **king** *of* Judah:
25: 21 So Jehoash **king** *of* Israel attacked. He and Amaziah king of Judah
25: 21 Amaziah **king** *of* Judah faced each other at Beth Shemesh in
25: 23 Jehoash **king** *of* Israel captured Amaziah king of Judah, the son of
25: 23 Jehoash king of Israel captured Amaziah **king** *of* Judah, the son of
25: 24 together with the **palace** [+1074] treasures and the hostages,
25: 25 Amaziah son of Joash **king** *of* Judah lived for fifteen years after
25: 25 years after the death of Jehoash son of Jehoahaz **king** *of* Israel.
25: 26 are they not written in the book of the **kings** *of* Judah and Israel?
26: 2 restored it to Judah after **Amaziah**[s] [+2021] rested with his fathers.
26: 11 officer under the direction of Hananiah, one of the **royal** officials.
26: 13 for war, a powerful force to support the **king** against his enemies.
26: 18 They confronted **him**[s] [+2021+6460] and said, "It is not right for
26: 21 **King** Uzziah had leprosy until the day he died. He lived in a
26: 21 Jotham his son had charge of the **palace** [+1074] and governed the
26: 23 buried near them in a field for burial that belonged to the **kings**,
27: 5 Jotham made war on the **king** *of* the Ammonites and conquered
27: 7 he did, are written in the book of the **kings** *of* Israel and Judah.
28: 2 He walked in the ways of the **kings** *of* Israel and also made cast
28: 5 Therefore the LORD his God handed him over to the **king** *of*
28: 5 He was also given into the hands of the **king** *of* Israel, who
28: 7 Zicri, an Ephraimite warrior, killed Maaseiah the **king's** son,
28: 7 officer in charge of the palace, and Elkanah, second to the **king**.
28: 16 At that time **King** Ahaz sent to the king of Assyria for help.
28: 16 At that time King Ahaz sent to the **king** *of* Assyria for help.

2Ch 28:19 The LORD had humbled Judah because of Ahaz **king** *of* Israel,
28:20 Tiglath-Pileser **king** *of* Assyria came to him, but he gave him
28:21 from the **royal** palace and from the princes and presented them to
28:21 and from the princes and presented them to the **king** *of* Assyria,
28:22 In his time of trouble **King** Ahaz became even more unfaithful to
28:23 "Since the gods of the **kings** *of* Aram have helped them,
28:26 to end, are written in the book of the **kings** *of* Judah and Israel.
28:27 but he was not placed in the tombs of the **kings** *of* Israel.
29:15 as the **king** had ordered, following the word of the LORD.
29:18 they went in to **King** Hezekiah and reported: "We have purified the
29:19 consecrated all the articles that **King** Ahaz removed in his
29:20 Early the next morning **King** Hezekiah gathered the city officials
29:23 The goats for the sin offering were brought before the **king**
29:24 because the **king** had ordered the burnt offering and the sin
29:25 by David and Gad the **king's** seer and Nathan the prophet;
29:27 by trumpets and the instruments of David **king** *of* Israel.
29:29 the **king** and everyone present with him knelt down and worshiped.
29:30 **King** Hezekiah and his officials ordered the Levites to praise the
30: 2 The **king** and his officials and the whole assembly in Jerusalem
30: 4 The plan seemed right both to the **king** and to the whole assembly.
30: 6 At the **king's** command, couriers went throughout Israel and Judah
30: 6 and Judah with letters from the **king** and from his officials,
30: 6 are left, who have escaped from the hand of the **kings** *of* Assyria.
30:12 on the people to give them unity of mind to carry out what the **king**
30:24 Hezekiah **king** *of* Judah provided a thousand bulls and seven
30:26 for since the days of Solomon son of David **king** *of* Israel there had
31: 3 The **king** contributed from his own possessions for the morning
31:13 by appointment of **King** Hezekiah and Azariah the official in
32: 1 Sennacherib **king** *of* Assyria came and invaded Judah.
32: 4 "Why should the **kings** *of* Assyria come and find plenty of water?"
32: 7 Do not be afraid or discouraged because of the **king** *of* Assyria
32: 8 the people gained confidence from what Hezekiah the **king** *of*
32: 9 when Sennacherib **king** *of* Assyria and all his forces were laying
32: 9 officers to Jerusalem with this message for Hezekiah **king** *of* Judah
32:10 "This is what Sennacherib **king** *of* Assyria says: On what are you
32:11 'The LORD our God will save us from the hand of the **king** *of*
32:20 **King** Hezekiah and the prophet Isaiah son of Amoz cried out in
32:21 and the leaders and officers in the camp of the Assyrian **king**.
32:22 the people of Jerusalem from the hand of Sennacherib **king** *of*
32:23 for the LORD and valuable gifts for Hezekiah **king** *of* Judah.
32:32 the prophet Isaiah son of Amoz in the book of the **kings** *of* Judah
33:11 brought against them the army commanders of the **king** *of* Assyria,
33:18 the God of Israel, are written in the annals of the **kings** *of* Israel.
33:25 the people of the land killed all who had plotted against **King**
34:11 beams for the buildings that the **kings** *of* Judah had allowed to fall
34:16 Then Shaphan took the book to the **king** and reported to him:
34:16 Shaphan took the book to the king and reported to **him**[s] [+2021]:
34:18 Shaphan the secretary informed the **king**, "Hilkiah the priest has
34:18 me a book." And Shaphan read from it in the presence of the **king**.
34:19 When the **king** heard the words of the Law, he tore his robes.
34:20 **He**[s] [+2021] gave these orders to Hilkiah, Ahikam son of Shaphan,
34:20 of Micah, Shaphan the secretary and Asaiah the **king's** attendant:
34:22 those the **king** had sent with him went to speak to the prophetess
34:24 in the book that has been read in the presence of the **king** *of* Judah.
34:26 Tell the **king** *of* Judah, who sent you to inquire of the LORD,
34:28 those who live here.' " So they took her answer back to the **king**.
34:29 the **king** called together all the elders of Judah and Jerusalem.
34:30 **He**[s] [+2021] went up to the temple of the LORD with the men of
34:31 The **king** stood by his pillar and renewed the covenant in the
35: 3 ark in the temple that Solomon son of David **king** *of* Israel built.
35: 4 according to the directions written by David **king** *of* Israel
35: 7 also three thousand cattle—all from the **king's** *own* possessions.
35:10 places with the Levites in their divisions as the **king** had ordered.
35:15 prescribed by David, Asaph, Heman and Jeduthun the **king's** seer.
35:16 offerings on the altar of the LORD, as **King** Josiah had ordered.
35:18 none of the **kings** *of* Israel had ever celebrated such a Passover as
35:20 Neco **king** *of* Egypt went up to fight at Carchemish on the
35:21 "What quarrel is there between you and me, O **king** *of* Judah?
35:23 Archers shot **King** Josiah, and he told his officers, "Take me away;
35:23 King Josiah, and **he**[s] [+2021] told his officers, "Take me away;
35:27 to end, are written in the book of the **kings** *of* Israel and Judah.
36: 3 The **king** *of* Egypt dethroned him in Jerusalem and imposed on
36: 4 The **king** *of* Egypt made Eliakim, a brother of Jehoahaz, king over
36: 6 Nebuchadnezzar **king** *of* Babylon attacked him and bound him
36: 8 are written in the book of the **kings** *of* Israel and Judah.
36:10 **King** Nebuchadnezzar sent for him and brought him to Babylon,
36:13 He also rebelled against **King** Nebuchadnezzar, who had made him
36:17 He brought up against them the **king** *of* the Babylonians, who
36:18 the LORD's temple and the treasures of the **king** and his officials.
36:22 In the first year of Cyrus **king** *of* Persia, in order to fulfill the word
36:22 the LORD moved the heart of Cyrus **king** *of* Persia to make a
36:23 "This is what Cyrus **king** *of* Persia says: " 'The LORD, the God
Ezr 1: 1 In the first year of Cyrus **king** *of* Persia, in order to fulfill the word
1: 1 the LORD moved the heart of Cyrus **king** *of* Persia to make a
1: 2 "This is what Cyrus **king** *of* Persia says: " 'The LORD, the God
1: 7 **King** Cyrus brought out the articles belonging to the temple of the
1: 8 Cyrus **king** *of* Persia had them brought by Mithredath the treasurer,
2: 1 whom Nebuchadnezzar **king** *of* Babylon had taken captive to
3: 7 sea from Lebanon to Joppa, as authorized by Cyrus **king** *of* Persia.
3:10 places to praise the LORD, as prescribed by David **king** *of* Israel.
4: 2 have been sacrificing to him since the time of Esarhaddon **king** *of*
4: 3 the God of Israel, as **King** Cyrus, the king of Persia,
4: 3 God of Israel, as King Cyrus, the **king** *of* Persia, commanded us."
4: 5 frustrate their plans during the entire reign of Cyrus **king** *of* Persia
4: 5 king of Persia and down to the reign of Darius **king** *of* Persia.
4: 7 And in the days of Artaxerxes **king** *of* Persia, Bishlam, Mithredath,
6:22 them with joy by changing the attitude of the **king** *of* Assyria,
7: 1 After these things, during the reign of Artaxerxes **king** *of* Persia,
7: 6 The **king** had granted him everything he asked, for the hand of the
7: 7 also came up to Jerusalem in the seventh year of **King** Artaxerxes.
7: 8 in Jerusalem in the fifth month of the seventh year of the **king**.
7:11 This is a copy of the letter **King** Artaxerxes had given to Ezra the
7:27 who has put it into the **king's** heart to bring honor to the house of
7:28 and who has extended his good favor to me before the **king**
7:28 the king and his advisers and all the **king's** powerful officials.
8: 1 up with me from Babylon during the reign of **King** Artaxerxes:
8:22 I was ashamed to ask the **king** for soldiers and horsemen to protect
8:22 protect us from enemies on the road, because we had told the **king**,
8:25 them the offering of silver and gold and the articles that the **king**,
8:36 They also delivered the **king's** orders to the royal satraps and to the
8:36 They also delivered the king's orders to the **royal** satraps and to
9: 7 we and our **kings** and our priests have been subjected to the sword
9: 7 to pillage and humiliation at the hand of foreign **kings**, as it is
9: 9 He has shown us kindness in the sight of the **kings** *of* Persia:
Ne 1:11 favor in the presence of this man." I was cupbearer to the **king**.
2: 1 In the month of Nisan in the twentieth year of **King** Artaxerxes,
2: 1 wine was brought for him, I took the wine and gave it to the **king**.
2: 2 so the **king** asked me, "Why does your face look so sad when you
2: 3 I said to the **king**, "May the king live forever! Why should my face
2: 3 I said to the king, "May the **king** live forever! Why should my face
2: 4 The **king** said to me, "What is it you want?" Then I prayed to the
2: 5 I answered the **king**, "If it pleases the king and if your servant has
2: 5 "If it pleases the **king** and if your servant has found favor in his
2: 6 Then the **king**, with the queen sitting beside him, asked me,
2: 6 will you get back?" It pleased the **king** to send me; so I set a time.
2: 7 I also said to **him**[s] [+2021], "If it pleases the king, may I have
2: 7 I also said to him, "If it pleases the **king**, may I have letters to the
2: 8 may I have a letter to Asaph, keeper of the **king's** [+4200] forest,
2: 8 hand of my God was upon me, the **king** granted my requests.
2: 9 the governors of Trans-Euphrates and gave them the **king's** letters.
2: 9 The **king** had also sent army officers and cavalry with me.
2:14 Then I moved on toward the Fountain Gate and the **King's** Pool,
2:18 hand of my God upon me and what the **king** had said to me.
2:19 you are doing?" they asked. "Are you rebelling against the **king**?"
3:15 also repaired the wall of the Pool of Siloam, by the **King's** Garden,
3:25 the tower projecting from the upper **palace** [+1074] near the court
5: 4 "We have had to borrow money to pay the **king's** tax on our fields
5:14 Moreover, from the twentieth year of **King** Artaxerxes, when I was
6: 6 according to these reports you are about to become their **king**
6: 7 'There is a **king** in Judah!' Now this report will get back to the
6: 7 Now this report will get back to the **king**; so come, let us confer
7: 6 **king** *of* Babylon had taken captive (they returned to Jerusalem
9:22 They took over the country of Sihon **king** *of* Heshbon and the
9:22 of Sihon king of Heshbon and the country of Og **king** *of* Bashan.
9:24 along with their **kings** and the peoples of the land, to deal with
9:32 upon our **kings** and leaders, upon our priests and prophets,
9:32 all your people, from the days of the **kings** *of* Assyria until today.
9:34 Our **kings**, our leaders, our priests and our fathers did not follow
9:37 its abundant harvest goes to the **kings** you have placed over us.
11:23 The singers were under the **king's** orders, which regulated their
11:24 of Judah, was the **king's** agent in all affairs relating to the people.
13: 6 for in the thirty-second year of Artaxerxes **king** *of* Babylon I had
13: 6 year of Artaxerxes king of Babylon I had returned to the **king**.
13: 6 to the king. Some time later I asked **his**[s] [+2021] permission
13:26 because of marriages like these that Solomon **king** *of* Israel
13:26 Among the many nations there was no **king** like him. He was loved
13:26 He was loved by his God, and God made him **king** over all Israel,
Est 1: 2 At that time **King** Xerxes reigned from his royal throne in the
1: 5 these days were over, the **king** gave a banquet, lasting seven days,
1: 5 lasting seven days, in the enclosed garden of the **king's** palace,
1: 7 the royal wine was abundant, in keeping with the **king's** liberality.
1: 8 for the **king** instructed all the wine stewards to serve each man
1: 9 gave a banquet for the women in the royal palace of **King** Xerxes.
1:10 the seventh day, when **King** Xerxes was in high spirits from wine,
1:10 he commanded the seven eunuchs who served **him**[s] [+2021]—
1:11 to bring before **him**[s] [+2021] Queen Vashti, wearing her royal
1:12 when the attendants delivered the **king's** command, Queen Vashti
1:12 to come. Then the **king** became furious and burned with anger.

Est 1:13 Since it was customary for the **king** to consult experts in matters of
1:13 justice, **he**[s] [+2021] spoke with the wise men who understood the
1:14 nobles of Persia and Media who had special access to the **king**
1:15 "She has not obeyed the command of **King** Xerxes that the
1:16 Then Memucan replied in the presence of the **king** and the nobles,
1:16 not only against the **king** but also against all the nobles and the
1:16 all the nobles and the peoples of all the provinces of **King** Xerxes.
1:17 '**King** Xerxes commanded Queen Vashti to be brought before him,
1:18 conduct will respond to all the **king's** nobles in the same way.
1:19 "Therefore, if it pleases the **king**, let him issue a royal decree
1:19 that Vashti is never again to enter the presence of **King** Xerxes.
1:19 Also let the **king** give her royal position to someone else who is
1:20 when the **king's** edict is proclaimed throughout all his vast realm,
1:21 The **king** and his nobles were pleased with this advice, so the king
1:21 pleased with this advice, so the **king** did as Memucan proposed.
1:22 He sent dispatches to all parts of the **kingdom**, to each province in
2: 1 Later when the anger of **King** Xerxes had subsided,
2: 2 the **king's** personal attendants proposed, "Let a search be made for
2: 2 "Let a search be made for beautiful young virgins for the **king**.
2: 3 Let the **king** appoint commissioners in every province of his realm
2: 3 care of Hegai, the **king's** eunuch, who is in charge of the women;
2: 4 Then let the girl who pleases the **king** be queen instead of Vashti."
2: 4 of Vashti." This advice appealed to the **king**, and he followed it.
2: 6 into exile from Jerusalem by Nebuchadnezzar **king** *of* Babylon,
2: 6 among those taken captive with Jehoiachin **king** *of* Judah.
2: 8 When the **king's** order and edict had been proclaimed, many girls
2: 8 Esther also was taken to the **king's** palace and entrusted to Hegai,
2: 9 He assigned to her seven maids selected from the **king's** palace
2:12 Before a girl's turn came to go in to **King** Xerxes, she had to
2:13 this is how she would go to the **king**: Anything she wanted was
2:13 was given her to take with her from the harem to the **king's** palace.
2:14 the **king's** eunuch who was in charge of the concubines.
2:14 She would not return to the **king** unless he was pleased with her
2:14 She would not return to the king unless **he**[s] [+2021] was pleased
2:15 to go to the **king**, she asked for nothing other than what Hegai,
2:15 the **king's** eunuch who was in charge of the harem, suggested.
2:16 She was taken to **King** Xerxes in the royal residence in the tenth
2:17 Now the **king** was attracted to Esther more than to any of the other
2:18 the **king** gave a great banquet, Esther's banquet, for all his nobles
2:18 throughout the provinces and distributed gifts with **royal** liberality.
2:19 assembled a second time, Mordecai was sitting at the **king's** gate.
2:21 During the time Mordecai was sitting at the **king's** gate, Bigthana
2:21 and Teresh, two of the **king's** officers who guarded the doorway,
2:21 became angry and conspired to assassinate **King** Xerxes.
2:22 and told Queen Esther, who in turn reported it to the **king**,
2:23 was recorded in the book of the annals in the presence of the **king**.
3: 1 **King** Xerxes honored Haman son of Hammedatha, the Agagite,
3: 2 All the **royal** officials at the king's gate knelt down and paid honor
3: 2 All the royal officials at the **king's** gate knelt down and paid honor
3: 2 to Haman, for the **king** had commanded this concerning him.
3: 3 Then the **royal** officials at the king's gate asked Mordecai,
3: 3 Then the royal officials at the **king's** gate asked Mordecai,
3: 3 gate asked Mordecai, "Why do you disobey the **king's** command?"
3: 7 In the twelfth year of **King** Xerxes, in the first month, the month of
3: 8 Haman said to **King** Xerxes, "There is a certain people dispersed
3: 8 those of all other people and who do not obey the **king's** laws;
3: 8 the king's laws; it is not in the **king's** best interest to tolerate them.
3: 9 If it pleases the **king**, let a decree be issued to destroy them,
3: 9 I will put ten thousand talents of silver into the **royal** treasury for
3:10 So the **king** took his signet ring from his finger and gave it to
3:11 "Keep the money," the **king** said to Haman, "and do with the
3:12 on the thirteenth day of the first month the **royal** secretaries were
3:12 in the language of each people all Haman's orders to the **king's**
3:12 These were written in the name of **King** Xerxes himself and sealed
3:12 of King Xerxes himself and sealed with **his**[s] [+2021] **own** ring.
3:13 Dispatches were sent by couriers to all the **king's** provinces with
3:15 Spurred on by the **king's** command, the couriers went out,
3:15 The **king** and Haman sat down to drink, but the city of Susa was
4: 2 he went only as far as the **king's** gate, because no one clothed in
4: 2 no one clothed in sackcloth was allowed to enter **it**[s] [+2021+9133].
4: 3 In every province to which the edict and order of the **king** came,
4: 5 one of the **king's** eunuchs assigned to attend her,
4: 6 Mordecai in the open square of the city in front of the **king's** gate.
4: 7 to pay into the **royal** treasury for the destruction of the Jews.
4: 8 he told him to urge her to go into the **king's** presence to beg for
4:11 "All the **king's** officials and the people of the royal provinces
4:11 and the people of the **royal** provinces know that for any man
4:11 or woman who approaches the **king** in the inner court without
4:11 The only exception to this is for the **king** to extend the gold scepter
4:11 But thirty days have passed since I was called to go to the **king**."
4:13 because you are in the **king's** house you alone of all the Jews will
4:16 When this is done, I will go to the **king**, even though it is against
5: 1 her royal robes and stood in the inner court of the **palace** [+1074],
5: 1 stood in the inner court of the palace, in front of the **king's** hall.
5: 1 The **king** was sitting on his royal throne in the hall, facing the
5: 2 When **he**[s] [+2021] saw Queen Esther standing in the court,
5: 2 and **[RPH]** held out to her the gold scepter that was in his hand.
5: 3 the **king** asked, "What is it, Queen Esther? What is your request?
5: 4 "If it pleases the **king**," replied Esther, "let the king, together with
5: 4 the king," replied Esther, "let the **king**, together with Haman,
5: 5 "Bring Haman at once," the **king** said, "so that we may do what
5: 5 So the **king** and Haman went to the banquet Esther had prepared.
5: 6 the **king** again asked Esther, "Now what is your petition?
5: 8 If the **king** regards me with favor and if it pleases the king to grant
5: 8 if it pleases the **king** to grant my petition and fulfill my request,
5: 8 let the **king** and Haman come tomorrow to the banquet I will
5: 8 I will prepare for them. Then I will answer the **king's** question."
5: 9 when he saw Mordecai at the **king's** gate and observed that he
5:11 all the ways the **king** had honored him and how he had elevated
5:11 he had elevated him above the other nobles and officials. **[RPH]**
5:12 "I'm the only person Queen Esther invited to accompany the **king**
5:12 she gave. And she has invited me along with the **king** tomorrow.
5:13 as long as I see that Jew Mordecai sitting at the **king's** gate."
5:14 and ask the **king** in the morning to have Mordecai hanged on it.
5:14 go with the **king** to the dinner and be happy." This suggestion
6: 1 That night the **king** could not sleep; so he ordered the book of the
6: 1 the record of his reign, to be brought in and read to **him**[s] [+2021].
6: 2 and Teresh, two of the **king's** officers who guarded the doorway,
6: 2 the doorway, who had conspired to assassinate **King** Xerxes.
6: 3 the **king** asked. "Nothing has been done for him," his attendants
6: 3 "Nothing has been done for him," **his**[s] [+2021] attendants
6: 4 The **king** said, "Who is in the court?" Now Haman had just entered
6: 4 Now Haman had just entered the outer court of the **palace** [+1074]
6: 4 **king** about hanging Mordecai on the gallows he had erected for
6: 5 **His**[s] [+2021] attendants answered, "Haman is standing in the
6: 5 is standing in the court." "Bring him in," the **king** ordered.
6: 6 When Haman entered, the **king** asked him, "What should be done
6: 6 "What should be done for the man the **king** delights to honor?"
6: 6 "Who is there that the **king** would rather honor than me?"
6: 7 So he answered the **king**, "For the man the king delights to honor,
6: 7 So he answered the king, "For the man the **king** delights to honor,
6: 8 have them bring a royal robe the **king** has worn and a horse the
6: 8 a royal robe the king has worn and a horse the **king** has ridden,
6: 9 and horse be entrusted to one of the **king's** most noble princes.
6: 9 Let them robe the man the **king** delights to honor, and lead him on
6: 9 'This is what is done for the man the **king** delights to honor!' "
6:10 "Go at once," the **king** commanded Haman. "Get the robe
6:10 have suggested for Mordecai the Jew, who sits at the **king's** gate.
6:11 "This is what is done for the man the **king** delights to honor!"
6:12 Afterward Mordecai returned to the **king's** gate. But Haman
6:14 the **king's** eunuchs arrived and hurried Haman away to the banquet
7: 1 So the **king** and Haman went to dine with Queen Esther,
7: 2 the **king** again asked, "Queen Esther, what is your petition?
7: 3 with you, O **king**, and if it pleases your majesty, grant me my life—
7: 3 O king, and if it pleases your **majesty**, grant me my life—
7: 4 because no such distress would justify disturbing the **king**."
7: 5 **King** Xerxes asked Queen Esther, "Who is he? Where is the man
7: 6 Then Haman was terrified before the **king** and queen.
7: 7 The **king** got up in a rage, left his wine and went out into the
7: 7 But Haman, realizing that the **king** had already decided his fate,
7: 8 Just as the **king** returned from the palace garden to the banquet
7: 8 The **king** exclaimed, "Will he even molest the queen while she is
7: 8 As soon as the word left the **king's** mouth, they covered Haman's
7: 9 Then Harbona, one of the eunuchs attending the **king**, said,
7: 9 He had it made for Mordecai, who spoke up to help the **king**."
7: 9 who spoke up to help the king." The **king** said, "Hang him on it!"
7:10 he had prepared for Mordecai. Then the **king's** fury subsided.
8: 1 That same day **King** Xerxes gave Queen Esther the estate of
8: 1 Mordecai came into the presence of the **king**, for Esther had told
8: 2 The **king** took off his signet ring, which he had reclaimed from
8: 3 Esther again pleaded with the **king**, falling at his feet and weeping.
8: 4 Then the **king** extended the gold scepter to Esther and she arose
8: 4 scepter to Esther and she arose and stood before **him**[s] [+2021].
8: 5 "If it pleases the **king**," she said, "and if he regards me with favor
8: 5 regards me with favor and thinks it the right thing **[RPH]** to do,
8: 5 devised and wrote to destroy the Jews in all the **king's** provinces.
8: 7 **King** Xerxes replied to Queen Esther and to Mordecai the Jew,
8: 8 Now write another decree in the **king's** name in behalf of the Jews
8: 8 Jews as seems best to you, and seal it with the **king's** signet ring—
8: 8 for no document written in the **king's** name and sealed with his
8: 8 king's name and sealed with **his**[s] [+2021] ring can be revoked."
8: 9 At once the **royal** secretaries were summoned—
8:10 Mordecai wrote in the name of **King** Xerxes, sealed the dispatches
8:10 sealed the dispatches with the **king's** signet ring, and sent them by
8:11 The **king's** edict granted the Jews in every city the right to
8:12 of **King** Xerxes was the thirteenth day of the twelfth month,
8:14 the royal horses, raced out, spurred on by the **king's** command.
8:15 Mordecai left the **king's** presence wearing royal garments of blue

Est 8:17 wherever the edict of the **king** went, there was joy and gladness
9: 1 of Adar, the edict commanded by the **king** was to be carried out.
9: 2 The Jews assembled in their cities in all the provinces of **King**
9: 3 and the **king's** [+4200] administrators helped the Jews,
9: 4 Mordecai was prominent in the **palace** [+1074]; his reputation
9:11 slain in the citadel of Susa was reported to the **king** that same day.
9:12 The **king** said to Queen Esther, "The Jews have killed
9:12 What have they done in the rest of the **king's** provinces?
9:13 "If it pleases the **king**," Esther answered, "give the Jews in Susa
9:14 So the **king** commanded that this be done. An edict was issued in
9:16 the remainder of the Jews who were in the **king's** provinces also
9:20 he sent letters to all the Jews throughout the provinces of **King**
9:25 when the plot came to the **king's** attention, he issued written orders
10: 1 **King** Xerxes imposed tribute throughout the empire, to its distant
10: 2 of the greatness of Mordecai to which the **king** had raised him,
10: 2 are they not written in the book of the annals of the **kings** *of* Media
10: 3 Mordecai the Jew was second in rank to **King** Xerxes, preeminent
Job 3:14 with **kings** and counselors of the earth, who built for themselves
12:18 He takes off the shackles put on by **kings** and ties a loincloth
15:24 him with terror; they overwhelm him, like a **king** poised to attack,
18:14 from the security of his tent and marched off to the **king** *of* terrors.
29:25 for them and sat as their chief; I dwelt as a **king** among his troops;
34:18 Is he not the One who says to **kings**, 'You are worthless,' and to
36: 7 he enthrones them with **kings** and exalts them forever.
41:34 [41:26] on all that are haughty; he is **king** over all that are proud."
Ps 2: 2 The **kings** *of* the earth take their stand and the rulers gather
2: 6 "I have installed my **King** on Zion, my holy hill."
2:10 Therefore, you **kings**, be wise; be warned, you rulers of the earth.
5: 2 [5:3] to my cry for help, my **King** and my God, for to you I pray.
10:16 The LORD is **King** for ever and ever; the nations will perish from
18:50 [18:51] He gives his **king** great victories; he shows unfailing
20: 9 [20:10] O LORD, save the **king**! Answer us when we call!
21: 1 [21:2] O LORD, the **king** rejoices in your strength. How great is
21: 7 [21:8] For the **king** trusts in the LORD; through the unfailing
24: 7 lifted up, you ancient doors, that the **King** *of* glory may come in.
24: 8 Who is this **King** *of* glory? The LORD strong and mighty,
24: 9 them up, you ancient doors, that the **King** *of* glory may come in.
24:10 Who is he, this **King** *of* glory? The LORD Almighty—he is the
24:10 The LORD Almighty—he is the **King** *of* glory. *Selah*
29:10 over the flood; the LORD is enthroned as **King** forever.
33:16 No **king** is saved by the size of his army; no warrior escapes by his
44: 4 [44:5] You are my **King** and my God, who decrees victories for
45: 1 [45:2] stirred by a noble theme as I recite my verses for the **king**;
45: 5 [45:6] Let your sharp arrows pierce the hearts of the **king's**
45: 9 [45:10] Daughters of **kings** are among your honored women;
45:11 [45:12] The **king** is enthralled by your beauty; honor him, for he
45:13 [45:14] All glorious is the **princess** [+1426] within ⌞her chamber⌟;
45:14 [45:15] In embroidered garments she is led to the **king**; her virgin
45:15 [45:16] with joy and gladness; they enter the palace of the **king**.
47: 2 [47:3] is the LORD Most High, the great **King** over all the earth!
47: 6 [47:7] to God, sing praises; sing praises to our **King**, sing praises.
47: 7 [47:8] For God is the **King** *of* all the earth; sing to him a psalm of
48: 2 [48:3] of Zaphon is Mount Zion, the city of the Great **King**.
48: 4 [48:5] When the **kings** joined forces, when they advanced
61: 6 [61:7] Increase the days of the **king's** life, his years for many
63:11 [63:12] the **king** will rejoice in God; all who swear by God's
68:12 [68:13] "**Kings** and armies flee in haste; in the camps men divide
68:14 [68:15] When the Almighty scattered the **kings** in the land, it was
68:24 [68:25] the procession of my God and **King** into the sanctuary.
68:29 [68:30] Because of your temple at Jerusalem **kings** will bring you
72: 1 Endow the **king** with your justice, O God, the royal son with your
72: 1 with your justice, O God, the **royal** son with your righteousness.
72:10 The **kings** *of* Tarshish and of distant shores will bring tribute to
72:10 tribute to him; the **kings** *of* Sheba and Seba will present him gifts.
72:11 All **kings** will bow down to him and all nations will serve him.
74:12 you, O God, are my **king** from of old; you bring salvation upon the
76:12 [76:13] the spirit of rulers; he is feared by the **kings** *of* the earth.
84: 3 [84:4] your altar, O LORD Almighty, my **King** and my God.
89:18 [89:19] to the LORD, our **king** to the Holy One of Israel.
89:27 [89:28] my firstborn, the most exalted of the **kings** *of* the earth.
95: 3 For the LORD is the great God, the great **King** above all gods.
98: 6 of the ram's horn—shout for joy before the LORD, the **King**.
99: 4 The **King** is mighty, he loves justice—you have established equity;
102:15 [102:16] all the **kings** *of* the earth will revere your glory.
105:14 allowed no one to oppress them; for their sake he rebuked **kings**:
105:20 The **king** sent and released him, the ruler of peoples set him free.
105:30 with frogs, which went up into the bedrooms of their **rulers**.
110: 5 is at your right hand; he will crush **kings** on the day of his wrath.
119:46 I will speak of your statutes before **kings** and will not be put to
135:10 He struck down many nations and killed mighty **kings**—
135:11 Sihon **king** *of* the Amorites, Og king of Bashan and all the kings of
135:11 of the Amorites, Og **king** *of* Bashan and all the kings of Canaan—
136:17 who struck down great **kings**, *His love endures forever.*
136:18 and killed mighty **kings**—*His love endures forever.*
136:19 Sihon **king** *of* the Amorites *His love endures forever.*
136:20 and Og **king** *of* Bashan—*His love endures forever.*
138: 4 May all the **kings** *of* the earth praise you, O LORD, when they
144:10 to the One who gives victory to **kings**, who delivers his servant
145: 1 I will exalt you, my God the **King**; I will praise your name for ever
148:11 **kings** *of* the earth and all nations, you princes and all rulers on
149: 2 rejoice in their Maker; let the people of Zion be glad in their **King**.
149: 8 to bind their **kings** with fetters, their nobles with shackles of iron,
Pr 1: 1 The proverbs of Solomon son of David, **king** *of* Israel:
8:15 By me **kings** reign and rulers make laws that are just;
14:28 A large population is a **king's** glory, but without subjects a prince
14:35 A **king** delights in a wise servant, but a shameful servant incurs his
16:10 The lips of a **king** speak as an oracle, and his mouth should not
16:12 **Kings** detest wrongdoing, for a throne is established through
16:13 **Kings** take pleasure in honest lips; they value a man who speaks
16:14 A **king's** wrath is a messenger of death, but a wise man will
16:15 When a **king's** face brightens, it means life; his favor is like a rain
19:12 A **king's** rage is like the roar of a lion, but his favor is like dew on
20: 2 A **king's** wrath is like the roar of a lion; he who angers him forfeits
20: 8 When a **king** sits on his throne to judge, he winnows out all evil
20:26 A wise **king** winnows out the wicked; he drives the threshing
20:28 Love and faithfulness keep a **king** safe; through love his throne is
21: 1 The **king's** heart is in the hand of the LORD; he directs it like a
22:11 and whose speech is gracious will have the **king** for his friend.
22:29 He will serve before **kings**; he will not serve before obscure men.
24:21 Fear the LORD and the **king**, my son, and do not join with the
25: 1 of Solomon, copied by the men of Hezekiah **king** *of* Judah:
25: 2 to conceal a matter; to search out a matter is the glory of **kings**.
25: 3 and the earth is deep, so the hearts of **kings** are unsearchable.
25: 5 remove the wicked from the **king's** presence, and his throne will
25: 6 Do not exalt yourself in the **king's** presence, and do not claim a
29: 4 By justice a **king** gives a country stability, but one who is greedy
29:14 If a **king** judges the poor with fairness, his throne will always be
30:27 locusts have no **king**, yet they advance together in ranks;
30:28 lizard can be caught with the hand, yet it is found in **kings**' palaces.
30:31 a strutting rooster, a he-goat, and a **king** with his army around him.
31: 1 The sayings of **King** Lemuel—an oracle his mother taught him:
31: 3 your strength on women, your vigor on those who ruin **kings**.
31: 4 "It is not for **kings**, O Lemuel—not for kings to drink wine,
31: 4 not for **kings** to drink wine, not for rulers to crave beer,
Ecc 1: 1 The words of the Teacher, son of David, **king** in Jerusalem:
1:12 I, the Teacher, was **king** over Israel in Jerusalem.
2: 8 and gold for myself, and the treasure of **kings** and provinces.
2:12 What more can the **king's** successor do than what has already been
4:13 but foolish **king** who no longer knows how to take warning.
5: 9 [5:8] land is taken by all; the **king** himself profits from the fields.
8: 2 Obey the **king's** command, I say, because you took an oath before
8: 4 Since a **king's** word is supreme, who can say to him, "What are
9:14 a powerful **king** came against it, surrounded it and built huge
10:16 O land whose **king** was a servant and whose princes feast in the
10:17 O land whose **king** is of noble birth and whose princes eat at a
10:20 Do not revile the **king** even in your thoughts, or curse the rich in
SS 1: 4 Let the **king** bring me into his chambers. We rejoice and delight in
1:12 While the **king** was at his table, my perfume spread its fragrance.
3: 9 **King** Solomon made for himself the carriage; he made it of wood
3:11 daughters of Zion, and look at **King** Solomon wearing the crown,
7: 5 [7:6] is like royal tapestry; the **king** is held captive by its tresses.
Isa 1: 1 the reigns of Uzziah, Jotham, Ahaz and Hezekiah, **kings** *of* Judah.
6: 1 In the year that **King** Uzziah died, I saw the Lord seated on a
6: 5 and my eyes have seen the **King**, the LORD Almighty."
7: 1 the son of Uzziah, was **king** *of* Judah, King Rezin of Aram
7: 1 **King** Rezin *of* Aram and Pekah son of Remaliah king of Israel
7: 1 Pekah son of Remaliah **king** *of* Israel marched up to fight against
7: 6 and **make** the son of Tabeel **king** [+906+4887] over it."
7:16 the right, the land of the two **kings** you dread will be laid waste.
7:17 broke away from Judah—he will bring the **king** *of* Assyria."
7:20 the **king** *of* Assyria—to shave your head and the hair of your legs,
8: 4 the plunder of Samaria will be carried off by the **king** *of* Assyria."
8: 7 floodwaters of the River—the **king** *of* Assyria with all his pomp.
8:21 enraged and, looking upward, will curse their **king** and their God.
10: 8 'Are not my commanders all **kings**?' he says.
10:12 "I will punish the **king** *of* Assyria for the willful pride of his heart
14: 4 you will take up this taunt against the **king** *of* Babylon: How the
14: 9 from their thrones—all *those who* were **kings** *over* the nations.
14:18 All the **kings** *of* the nations lie in state, each in his own tomb.
14:28 This oracle came in the year **King** Ahaz died:
19: 4 a fierce **king** will rule over them," declares the Lord, the LORD
19:11 "I am one of the wise men, a disciple of the ancient **kings**"?
20: 1 sent by Sargon **king** *of* Assyria, came to Ashdod and attacked
20: 4 so the **king** *of* Assyria will lead away stripped and barefoot the
20: 6 those we fled to for help and deliverance from the **king** *of* Assyria!
23:15 Tyre will be forgotten for seventy years, the span of a **king's** life.
24:21 the powers in the heavens above and the **kings** *on* the earth below.
30:33 has long been prepared; it has been made ready for the **king**.

Isa 32: 1 a **king** will reign in righteousness and rulers will rule with justice.
33:17 Your eyes will see the **king** in his beauty and view a land that
33:22 is our judge, the LORD is our lawgiver, the LORD is our **king**;
36: 1 In the fourteenth year of **King** Hezekiah's reign, Sennacherib king
36: 1 Sennacherib **king** *of* Assyria attacked all the fortified cities of
36: 2 the **king** *of* Assyria sent his field commander with a large army
36: 2 with a large army from Lachish to **King** Hezekiah at Jerusalem.
36: 4 "Tell Hezekiah, " 'This is what the great **king**, the king of Assyria,
36: 4 " 'This is what the great king, the **king** *of* Assyria, says:
36: 6 Such is Pharaoh **king** *of* Egypt to all who depend on him.
36: 8 " 'Come now, make a bargain with my master, the **king** *of* Assyria:
36:13 in Hebrew, "Hear the words of the great **king**, the king of Assyria!
36:13 in Hebrew, "Hear the words of the great king, the **king** *of* Assyria!
36:14 This is what the **king** says: Do not let Hezekiah deceive you.
36:15 this city will not be given into the hand of the **king** *of* Assyria.'
36:16 This is what the **king** *of* Assyria says: Make peace with me
36:18 ever delivered his land from the hand of the **king** *of* Assyria?
36:21 in reply, because the **king** had commanded, "Do not answer him."
37: 1 When **King** Hezekiah heard this, he tore his clothes and put on
37: 4 whom his master, the **king** *of* Assyria, has sent to ridicule the
37: 5 When **King** Hezekiah's officials came to Isaiah,
37: 6 those words with which the underlings of the **king** *of* Assyria have
37: 8 When the field commander heard that the **king** *of* Assyria had left
37: 9 the Cushite **king** *of* Egypt, was marching out to fight against him.
37:10 "Say to Hezekiah **king** *of* Judah: Do not let the god you depend on
37:10 'Jerusalem will not be handed over to the **king** *of* Assyria.'
37:11 Surely you have heard what the **kings** *of* Assyria have done to all
37:13 Where is the **king** *of* Hamath, the king of Arpad, the king of the
37:13 Where is the king of Hamath, the **king** *of* Arpad, the king of the
37:13 the **king** of the city of Sepharvaim, or of Hena or Ivvah?"
37:18 that the Assyrian **kings** have laid waste all these peoples and their
37:21 Because you have prayed to me concerning Sennacherib **king** *of*
37:33 "Therefore this is what the LORD says concerning the **king** *of*
37:37 So Sennacherib **king** *of* Assyria broke camp and withdrew.
38: 6 will deliver you and this city from the hand of the **king** *of* Assyria.
38: 9 A writing of Hezekiah **king** *of* Judah after his illness and recovery:
39: 1 At that time Merodach-Baladan son of Baladan **king** *of* Babylon
39: 3 Then Isaiah the prophet went to **King** Hezekiah and asked,
39: 7 they will become eunuchs in the palace of the **king** *of* Babylon."
41: 2 He hands nations over to him and subdues **kings** before him.
41:21 says the LORD. "Set forth your arguments," says Jacob's **King**.
43:15 I am the LORD, your Holy One, Israel's Creator, your **King**."
44: 6 Israel's **King** and Redeemer, the LORD Almighty:
45: 1 of to subdue nations before him and to strip **kings** of their armor,
49: 7 "**Kings** will see you and rise up, princes will see and bow down,
49:23 **Kings** will be your foster fathers, and their queens your nursing
52:15 many nations, and **kings** will shut their mouths because of him.
57: 9 You went to Molech [BHS *the king*; NIV 4891] with olive oil
60: 3 will come to your light, and **kings** to the brightness of your dawn.
60:10 "Foreigners will rebuild your walls, and their **kings** will serve you.
60:11 the wealth of the nations—their **kings** led in triumphal procession.
60:16 You will drink the milk of nations and be nursed at **royal** breasts.
62: 2 The nations will see your righteousness, and all **kings** your glory;
Jer 1: 2 thirteenth year of the reign of Josiah son of Amon **king** *of* Judah,
1: 3 and through the reign of Jehoiakim son of Josiah **king** *of* Judah,
1: 3 of the eleventh year of Zedekiah son of Josiah **king** *of* Judah,
1:18 against the **kings** *of* Judah, its officials, its priests and the people of
2:26 they, their **kings** and their officials, their priests and their prophets.
3: 6 During the reign of **King** Josiah, the LORD said to me, "Have
4: 9 declares the LORD, "the **king** and the officials will lose heart,
8: 1 declares the LORD, the bones of the **kings** and officials of Judah,
8:19 "Is the LORD not in Zion? Is her **King** no longer there?"
10: 7 Who should not revere you, O **King** *of* the nations? This is your
10:10 the LORD is the true God; he is the living God, the eternal **King**.
13:13 including the **kings** who sit on David's throne, the priests,
13:18 Say to the **king** and to the queen mother, "Come down from your
15: 4 because of what Manasseh son of Hezekiah **king** *of* Judah did in
17:19 gate of the people, through which the **kings** *of* Judah go in and out;
17:20 O **kings** *of* Judah and all people of Judah and everyone living in
17:25 **kings** who sit on David's throne will come through the gates of
19: 3 word of the LORD, O **kings** *of* Judah and people of Jerusalem.
19: 4 that neither they nor their fathers nor the **kings** *of* Judah ever knew,
19:13 and those of the **kings** *of* Judah will be defiled like this place,
20: 4 I will hand all Judah over to the **king** *of* Babylon, who will carry
20: 5 all its valuables and all the treasures of the **kings** *of* Judah.
21: 1 The word came to Jeremiah from the LORD when **King** Zedekiah
21: 2 because Nebuchadnezzar **king** *of* Babylon is attacking us.
21: 4 which you are using to fight the **king** *of* Babylon and the
21: 7 I will hand over Zedekiah **king** *of* Judah, his officials
21: 7 to Nebuchadnezzar **king** *of* Babylon and to their enemies who seek
21:10 It will be given into the hands of the **king** *of* Babylon, and he will
21:11 "Moreover, say to the **royal** house of Judah, 'Hear the word of the
22: 1 "Go down to the palace of the **king** *of* Judah and proclaim this
22: 2 'Hear the word of the LORD, O **king** *of* Judah, you who sit on
22: 4 **kings** who sit on David's throne will come through the gates of
22: 6 For this is what the LORD says about the palace of the **king** *of*
22:11 who succeeded his father as king of **[RPH]** Judah but has gone
22:18 the LORD says about Jehoiakim son of Josiah **king** *of* Judah:
22:24 "even if you, Jehoiachin son of Jehoiakim **king** *of* Judah,
22:25 to Nebuchadnezzar **king** *of* Babylon and to the Babylonians.
23: 5 a **King** who will reign wisely and do what is just and right in the
24: 1 After Jehoiachin son of Jehoiakim **king** *of* Judah and the officials,
24: 1 from Jerusalem to Babylon by Nebuchadnezzar **king** *of* Babylon,
24: 8 'so will I deal with Zedekiah **king** *of* Judah, his officials and the
25: 1 Judah in the fourth year of Jehoiakim son of Josiah **king** *of* Judah,
25: 1 which was the first year of Nebuchadnezzar **king** *of* Babylon.
25: 3 from the thirteenth year of Josiah son of Amon **king** *of* Judah until
25: 9 of the north and my servant Nebuchadnezzar **king** *of* Babylon,"
25:11 and these nations will serve the **king** *of* Babylon seventy years.
25:12 I will punish the **king** *of* Babylon and his nation, the land of the
25:14 themselves will be enslaved by many nations and great **kings**;
25:18 its **kings** and officials, to make them a ruin and an object of horror
25:19 Pharaoh **king** *of* Egypt, his attendants, his officials and all his
25:20 all the foreign people there; all the **kings** *of* Uz; all the kings of the
25:20 all the **kings** *of* the Philistines (those of Ashkelon, Gaza, Ekron,
25:22 all the **kings** *of* Tyre and Sidon; the kings of the coastlands across
25:22 all the kings of Tyre and **[RPH]** Sidon; the kings of the coastlands
25:22 kings of Tyre and Sidon; the **kings** *of* the coastlands across the sea;
25:24 all the **kings** *of* Arabia and all the kings of the foreign people who
25:24 and all the **kings** *of* the foreign people who live in the desert;
25:25 all the **kings** *of* Zimri, Elam and Media;
25:25 all the kings of Zimri, **[RPH]** Elam and Media;
25:25 all the kings of Zimri, Elam and **[RPH]** Media;
25:26 and all the **kings** *of* the north, near and far, one after the other—
25:26 And after all of them, the **king** *of* Sheshach will drink it too.
26: 1 Early in the reign of Jehoiakim son of Josiah **king** *of* Judah,
26:10 they went up from the **royal** palace to the house of the LORD
26:18 "Micah of Moresheth prophesied in the days of Hezekiah **king** *of*
26:19 "Did Hezekiah **king** *of* Judah or anyone else in Judah put him to
26:21 When **King** Jehoiakim and all his officers and officials heard his
26:21 and officials heard his words, the **king** sought to put him to death.
26:22 **King** Jehoiakim, however, sent Elnathan son of Acbor to Egypt,
26:23 They brought Uriah out of Egypt and took him to **King** Jehoiakim,
27: 1 Early in the reign of Zedekiah son of Josiah **king** *of* Judah,
27: 3 Then send word to the **kings** *of* Edom, Moab, Ammon, Tyre
27: 3 **[RPH]** Moab, Ammon, Tyre and Sidon through the envoys who
27: 3 **[RPH]** Ammon, Tyre and Sidon through the envoys who have
27: 3 **[RPH]** Tyre and Sidon through the envoys who have come to
27: 3 **[RPH]** Sidon through the envoys who have come to Jerusalem to
27: 3 envoys who have come to Jerusalem to Zedekiah **king** *of* Judah.
27: 6 countries over to my servant Nebuchadnezzar **king** *of* Babylon;
27: 7 land comes; then many nations and great **kings** will subjugate him.
27: 8 or kingdom will not serve Nebuchadnezzar **king** *of* Babylon
27: 8 king of Babylon or bow its neck under **his**[s] [+951] yoke,
27: 9 sorcerers who tell you, 'You will not serve the **king** *of* Babylon.'
27:11 if any nation will bow its neck under the yoke of the **king** *of*
27:12 I gave the same message to Zedekiah **king** *of* Judah. I said,
27:12 I said, "Bow your neck under the yoke of the **king** *of* Babylon;
27:13 has threatened any nation that will not serve the **king** *of* Babylon?
27:14 'You will not serve the **king** *of* Babylon,' for they are prophesying
27:17 not listen to them. Serve the **king** *of* Babylon, and you will live.
27:18 in the palace of the **king** *of* Judah and in Jerusalem not be taken to
27:20 which Nebuchadnezzar **king** *of* Babylon did not take away when
27:20 of Jehoiakim **king** *of* Judah into exile from Jerusalem to Babylon,
27:21 and in the palace of the **king** *of* Judah and in Jerusalem:
28: 1 the fourth year, early in the reign of Zedekiah **king** *of* Judah,
28: 2 God of Israel, says: 'I will break the yoke of the **king** *of* Babylon.
28: 3 house that Nebuchadnezzar **king** *of* Babylon removed from here
28: 4 bring back to this place Jehoiachin son of Jehoiakim **king** *of* Judah
28: 4 the LORD, 'for I will break the yoke of the **king** *of* Babylon.' "
28:11 'In the same way will I break the yoke of Nebuchadnezzar **king** *of*
28:14 nations to make them serve Nebuchadnezzar **king** *of* Babylon,
29: 2 (This was after **King** Jehoiachin and the queen mother, the court
29: 3 whom Zedekiah **king** *of* Judah sent to King Nebuchadnezzar in
29: 3 whom Zedekiah king of Judah sent to **King** Nebuchadnezzar in
29:16 this is what the LORD says about the **king** who sits on David's
29:21 "I will hand them over to Nebuchadnezzar **king** *of* Babylon,
29:22 and Ahab, whom the **king** *of* Babylon burned in the fire.'
30: 9 they will serve the LORD their God and David their **king**,
32: 1 from the LORD in the tenth year of Zedekiah **king** *of* Judah,
32: 2 The army of the **king** *of* Babylon was then besieging Jerusalem,
32: 2 confined in the courtyard of the guard in the **royal** palace of Judah.
32: 3 Now Zedekiah **king** *of* Judah had imprisoned him there, saying,
32: 3 I am about to hand this city over to the **king** *of* Babylon, and he
32: 4 Zedekiah **king** *of* Judah will not escape out of the hands of the
32: 4 but will certainly be handed over to the **king** *of* Babylon,
32:28 over to the Babylonians and to Nebuchadnezzar **king** *of* Babylon,
32:32 they, their **kings** and officials, their priests and prophets, the men

Jer 32:36 and plague it will be handed over to the **king** *of* Babylon';
33: 4 the **royal** palaces of Judah that have been torn down to be used
34: 1 While Nebuchadnezzar **king** *of* Babylon and all his army and all
34: 2 Go to Zedekiah **king** *of* Judah and tell him, 'This is what the
34: 2 I am about to hand this city over to the **king** *of* Babylon, and he
34: 3 You will see the **king** *of* Babylon with your own eyes, and he will
34: 4 " 'Yet hear the promise of the LORD, O Zedekiah **king** *of* Judah.
34: 5 the former **kings** who preceded you, so they will make a fire in
34: 6 Then Jeremiah the prophet told all this to Zedekiah **king** *of* Judah,
34: 7 while the army of the **king** *of* Babylon was fighting against
34: 8 The word came to Jeremiah from the LORD after **King** Zedekiah
34:21 "I will hand Zedekiah **king** *of* Judah and his officials over to their
34:21 to the army of the **king** *of* Babylon, which has withdrawn from
35: 1 LORD during the reign of Jehoiakim son of Josiah **king** *of* Judah:
35:11 But when Nebuchadnezzar **king** *of* Babylon invaded this land,
36: 1 In the fourth year of Jehoiakim son of Josiah **king** *of* Judah,
36: 9 month of the fifth year of Jehoiakim son of Josiah **king** *of* Judah,
36:12 he went down to the secretary's room in the **royal** palace,
36:16 and said to Baruch, "We must report all these words to the **king**."
36:20 they went to the **king** in the courtyard and reported everything to
36:20 the king in the courtyard and reported everything to **him**[s] [+2021].
36:21 The **king** sent Jehudi to get the scroll, and Jehudi brought it from
36:21 and read it to the **king** and all the officials standing beside him.
36:21 it to the king and all the officials standing beside **him**[s] [+2021].
36:22 the ninth month and the **king** was sitting in the winter apartment,
36:24 The **king** and all his attendants who heard all these words showed
36:25 Delaiah and Gemariah urged the **king** not to burn the scroll,
36:26 Instead, the **king** commanded Jerahmeel, a son of the king,
36:26 a son of the **king**, Seraiah son of Azriel and Shelemiah son of
36:27 After the **king** burned the scroll containing the words that Baruch
36:28 were on the first scroll, which Jehoiakim **king** *of* Judah burned up.
36:29 Also tell Jehoiakim **king** *of* Judah, 'This is what the LORD says:
36:29 "Why did you write on it that the **king** *of* Babylon would certainly
36:30 this is what the LORD says about Jehoiakim **king** *of* Judah:
36:32 of the scroll that Jehoiakim **king** *of* Judah had burned in the fire.
37: 1 was made king of Judah by Nebuchadnezzar **king** *of* Babylon;
37: 1 *he* **reigned** [+4887] in place of Jehoiachin son of Jehoiakim.
37: 3 **King** Zedekiah, however, sent Jehucal son of Shelemiah with the
37: 7 Tell the **king** *of* Judah, who sent you to inquire of me,
37:17 **King** Zedekiah sent for him and had him brought to the palace,
37:17 him brought to the palace, where **he**[s] [+2021] asked him privately,
37:17 "you will be handed over to the **king** *of* Babylon."
37:18 Jeremiah said to **King** Zedekiah, "What crime have I committed
37:19 to you, 'The **king** *of* Babylon will not attack you or this land'?
37:20 now, my lord the **king**, please listen. Let me bring my petition
37:21 **King** Zedekiah then gave orders for Jeremiah to be placed in the
38: 3 'This city will certainly be handed over to the army of the **king** *of*
38: 4 the officials said to the **king**, "This man should be put to death.
38: 5 "He is in your hands," **King** Zedekiah answered. "The king can do
38: 5 Zedekiah answered. "The **king** can do nothing to oppose you."
38: 6 the **king's** son, which was in the courtyard of the guard.
38: 7 But Ebed-Melech, a Cushite, an official in the **royal** palace,
38: 7 into the cistern. While the **king** was sitting in the Benjamin Gate,
38: 8 Ebed-Melech went out of the **palace** [+1074] and said to him,
38: 8 Ebed-Melech went out of the palace and said to **him**[s] [+2021],
38: 9 "My lord the **king**, these men have acted wickedly in all they have
38:10 the **king** commanded Ebed-Melech the Cushite, "Take thirty men
38:11 and went to a room under the treasury in the **palace** [+1074].
38:14 **King** Zedekiah sent for Jeremiah the prophet and had him brought
38:14 "I am going to ask you something," the **king** said to Jeremiah.
38:16 **King** Zedekiah swore this oath secretly to Jeremiah: "As surely as
38:17 'If you surrender to the officers of the **king** *of* Babylon, your life
38:18 But if you will not surrender to the officers of the **king** *of* Babylon,
38:19 **King** Zedekiah said to Jeremiah, "I am afraid of the Jews who have
38:22 All the women left in the palace of the **king** *of* Judah will be
38:22 of Judah will be brought out to the officials of the **king** *of* Babylon.
38:23 from their hands but will be captured by the **king** *of* Babylon;
38:25 'Tell us what you said to the **king** and what the king said to you;
38:25 'Tell us what you said to the king and what the **king** said to you;
38:26 'I was pleading with the **king** not to send me back to Jonathan's
38:27 and he told them everything the **king** had ordered him to say.
39: 1 In the ninth year of Zedekiah **king** *of* Judah, in the tenth month,
39: 1 Nebuchadnezzar **king** *of* Babylon marched against Jerusalem with
39: 3 all the officials of the **king** *of* Babylon came and took seats in the
39: 3 a high official and all the other officials of the **king** *of* Babylon.
39: 4 When Zedekiah **king** *of* Judah and all the soldiers saw them,
39: 4 they left the city at night by way of the **king's** garden,
39: 5 took him to Nebuchadnezzar **king** *of* Babylon at Riblah in the land
39: 6 There at Riblah the **king** *of* Babylon slaughtered the sons of
39: 6 before his eyes and also killed all the nobles of Judah. **[RPH]**
39: 8 The Babylonians set fire to the **royal** palace and the houses of the
39:11 Now Nebuchadnezzar **king** *of* Babylon had given these orders
39:13 a high official and all the other officers of the **king** *of* Babylon
40: 5 whom the **king** *of* Babylon has appointed over the towns of Judah,
40: 7 their men who were still in the open country heard that the **king** *of*
40: 9 "Settle down in the land and serve the **king** *of* Babylon, and it will
40:11 all the other countries heard that the **king** *of* Babylon had left a
40:14 "Don't you know that Baalis **king** *of* the Ammonites has sent
41: 1 who was of royal blood and had been one of the **king's** officers,
41: 2 killing the one whom the **king** *of* Babylon had appointed as
41: 9 **King** Asa had made as part of his defense against Baasha king of
41: 9 Asa had made as part of his defense against Baasha **king** *of* Israel.
41:10 the **king's** daughters along with all the others who were left there,
41:18 whom the **king** *of* Babylon had appointed as governor over the
42:11 Do not be afraid of the **king** *of* Babylon, whom you now fear.
43: 6 the **king's** daughters whom Nebuzaradan commander of the
43:10 I will send for my servant Nebuchadnezzar **king** *of* Babylon,
44: 9 by the **kings** and queens *of* Judah and the wickedness committed
44:17 our **kings** and our officials did in the towns of Judah and in the
44:21 your **kings** and your officials and the people of the land?
44:30 'I am going to hand Pharaoh Hophra **king** *of* Egypt over to his
44:30 just as I handed Zedekiah **king** *of* Judah over to Nebuchadnezzar
44:30 Zedekiah king of Judah over to Nebuchadnezzar **king** *of* Babylon,
45: 1 Neriah in the fourth year of Jehoiakim son of Josiah **king** *of* Judah,
46: 2 This is the message against the army of Pharaoh Neco **king** *of*
46: 2 **king** *of* Babylon in the fourth year of Jehoiakim son of Josiah king
46: 2 in the fourth year of Jehoiakim son of Josiah **king** *of* Judah:
46:13 the coming of Nebuchadnezzar **king** *of* Babylon to attack Egypt:
46:17 they will exclaim, 'Pharaoh **king** *of* Egypt is only a loud noise;
46:18 "As surely as I live," declares the **King**, whose name is the
46:25 on Pharaoh, on Egypt and her gods and her **kings**, and on those
46:26 their lives, to Nebuchadnezzar **king** *of* Babylon and his officers.
48:15 declares the **King**, whose name is the LORD Almighty.
49:28 of Hazor, which Nebuchadnezzar **king** *of* Babylon attacked:
49:30 "Nebuchadnezzar **king** *of* Babylon has plotted against you;
49:34 concerning Elam, early in the reign of Zedekiah **king** *of* Judah:
49:38 I will set my throne in Elam and destroy her **king** and officials,"
50:17 The first to devour him was the **king** *of* Assyria; the last to crush
50:17 the last to crush his bones was Nebuchadnezzar **king** *of* Babylon."
50:18 "I will punish the **king** *of* Babylon and his land as I punished the
50:18 the king of Babylon and his land as I punished the **king** *of* Assyria.
50:41 and many **kings** are being stirred up from the ends of the earth.
50:43 The **king** *of* Babylon has heard reports about them, and his hands
51:11 The LORD has stirred up the **kings** *of* the Medes, because his
51:28 the **kings** *of* the Medes, their governors and all their officials,
51:31 messenger follows messenger to announce to the **king** *of* Babylon
51:34 "Nebuchadnezzar **king** *of* Babylon has devoured us, he has thrown
51:57 they will sleep forever and not awake," declares the **King**,
51:59 when he went to Babylon with Zedekiah **king** *of* Judah in the
52: 3 his presence. Now Zedekiah rebelled against the **king** *of* Babylon.
52: 4 Nebuchadnezzar **king** *of* Babylon marched against Jerusalem with
52: 5 The city was kept under siege until the eleventh year of **King**
52: 7 through the gate between the two walls near the **king's** garden,
52: 8 the Babylonian army pursued **King** Zedekiah and overtook him in
52: 9 **he**[s] [+2021] was captured. He was taken to the king of Babylon at
52: 9 He was taken to the **king** *of* Babylon at Riblah in the land of
52:10 There at Riblah the **king** *of* Babylon slaughtered the sons of
52:11 bound him with bronze shackles and took him **[RPH]** to Babylon,
52:12 in the nineteenth year of **[RPH]** Nebuchadnezzar king of
52:12 in the nineteenth year of Nebuchadnezzar **king** *of* Babylon,
52:12 who served the **king** *of* Babylon, came to Jerusalem.
52:13 of the LORD, the **royal** palace and all the houses of Jerusalem.
52:15 the craftsmen and those who had gone over to the **king** *of* Babylon.
52:20 which **King** Solomon had made for the temple of the LORD,
52:25 the officer in charge of the fighting men, and seven **royal** advisers.
52:26 took them all and brought them to the **king** *of* Babylon at Riblah.
52:27 at Riblah, in the land of Hamath, the **king** had them executed.
52:31 In the thirty-seventh year of the exile of Jehoiachin **king** *of* Judah,
52:31 in the year Evil-Merodach became king of **[RPH]** Babylon,
52:31 he released Jehoiachin **king** *of* Judah and freed him from prison on
52:32 gave him a seat of honor higher than those of the other **kings** who
52:34 Day by day the **king** *of* Babylon gave Jehoiachin a regular
La 2: 6 in his fierce anger he has spurned both **king** and priest.
2: 9 Her **king** and her princes are exiled among the nations, the law is
4:12 The **kings** *of* the earth did not believe, nor did any of the world's
Eze 1: 2 the month—it was the fifth year of the exile of **King** Jehoiachin—
7:27 The **king** will mourn, the prince will be clothed with despair,
17:12 'The **king** *of* Babylon went to Jerusalem and carried off her king
17:12 Babylon went to Jerusalem and carried off her **king** and her nobles,
17:16 in the land of the **king** who put him on the throne, whose oath he
19: 9 pulled him into a cage and brought him to the **king** *of* Babylon.
21:19 [21:24] mark out two roads for the sword of the **king** *of* Babylon
21:21 [21:26] For the **king** *of* Babylon will stop at the fork in the road,
24: 2 because the **king** *of* Babylon has laid siege to Jerusalem this very
26: 7 I am going to bring against Tyre Nebuchadnezzar **king** *of* Babylon,
26: 7 **king** *of* kings, with horses and chariots, with horsemen and a great
26: 7 king of **kings**, with horses and chariots, with horsemen and a great
27:33 great wealth and your wares you enriched the **kings** *of* the earth.

Eze 27:35 their **kings** shudder with horror and their faces are distorted with
28:12 take up a lament concerning the **king** *of* Tyre and say to him:
28:17 So I threw you to the earth; I made a spectacle of you before **kings**.
29: 2 set your face against Pharaoh **king** *of* Egypt and prophesy against
29: 3 " 'I am against you, Pharaoh **king** *of* Egypt, you great monster
29:18 Nebuchadnezzar **king** *of* Babylon drove his army in a hard
29:19 I am going to give Egypt to Nebuchadnezzar **king** *of* Babylon,
30:10 hordes of Egypt by the hand of Nebuchadnezzar **king** *of* Babylon.
30:21 "Son of man, I have broken the arm of Pharaoh **king** *of* Egypt.
30:22 I am against Pharaoh **king** *of* Egypt. I will break both his arms,
30:24 I will strengthen the arms of the **king** *of* Babylon and put my
30:25 I will strengthen the arms of the **king** *of* Babylon, but the arms of
30:25 when I put my sword into the hand of the **king** *of* Babylon
31: 2 "Son of man, say to Pharaoh **king** *of* Egypt and to his hordes:
32: 2 take up a lament concerning Pharaoh **king** *of* Egypt and say to
32:10 their **kings** will shudder with horror because of you when I
32:11 " 'The sword of the **king** *of* Babylon will come against you.
32:29 "Edom is there, her **kings** and all her princes; despite their power,
37:22 There will be one **king** over all of them and they will never again
37:22 **[RPH]** and they will never again be two nations or be divided into
37:24 " 'My servant David will be **king** over them, and they will all have
43: 7 neither they nor their **kings**—by their prostitution and the lifeless
43: 7 and the lifeless idols of their **kings** at their high places.
43: 9 from me their prostitution and the lifeless idols of their **kings**,
Da 1: 1 In the third year of the reign of Jehoiakim **king** *of* Judah,
1: 1 Nebuchadnezzar **king** *of* Babylon came to Jerusalem and besieged
1: 2 And the Lord delivered Jehoiakim **king** *of* Judah into his hand,
1: 3 Then the **king** ordered Ashpenaz, chief of his court officials,
1: 4 quick to understand, and qualified to serve in the **king's** palace.
1: 5 The **king** assigned them a daily amount of food and wine from the
1: 5 them a daily amount of food and wine from the **king's** table.
1: 5 for three years, and after that they were to enter the **king's** service.
1: 8 But Daniel resolved not to defile himself with the **royal** food
1:10 but the official told Daniel, "I am afraid of my lord the **king**,
1:10 your age? The **king** would then have my head because of you."
1:13 our appearance with that of the young men who eat the **royal** food,
1:15 better nourished than any of the young men who ate the **royal**
1:18 At the end of the time set by the **king** to bring them in, the chief
1:19 The **king** talked with them, and he found none equal to Daniel,
1:19 Hananiah, Mishael and Azariah; so they entered the **king's** service.
1:20 and understanding about which the **king** questioned them,
1:21 And Daniel remained there until the first year of **King** Cyrus.
2: 2 So the **king** summoned the magicians, enchanters, sorcerers
2: 2 and astrologers to tell **him**[s] [+2021] what he had dreamed.
2: 2 he had dreamed. When they came in and stood before the **king**,
2: 3 **he**[s] [+2021] said to them, "I have had a dream that troubles me
2: 4 Then the astrologers answered the **king** in Aramaic, "O king,
8: 1 In the third year of **King** Belshazzar's reign, I, Daniel, had a
8:20 The two-horned ram that you saw represents the **kings** *of* Media
8:21 The shaggy goat is the **king** *of* Greece, and the large horn between
8:21 of Greece, and the large horn between his eyes is the first **king**.
8:23 a stern-faced **king**, a master of intrigue, will arise.
8:27 for several days. Then I got up and went about the **king's** business.
9: 6 who spoke in your name to our **kings**, our princes and our fathers,
9: 8 O LORD, we and our **kings**, our princes and our fathers are
10: 1 In the third year of Cyrus **king** *of* Persia, a revelation was given to
10:13 to help me, because I was detained there with the **king** *of* Persia.
11: 2 Three more **kings** will appear in Persia, and then a fourth,
11: 3 Then a mighty **king** will appear, who will rule with great power
11: 5 "The **king** *of* the South will become strong, but one of his
11: 6 The daughter of the **king** *of* the South will go to the king of the
11: 6 The daughter of the king of the South will go to the **king** *of* the
11: 7 He will attack the forces of the **king** *of* the North and enter his
11: 8 to Egypt. For some years he will leave the **king** *of* the North alone.
11: 9 the king of the North will invade the realm of the **king** *of* the South
11:11 "Then the **king** *of* the South will march out in a rage and fight
11:11 will march out in a rage and fight against the **king** *of* the North,
11:13 For the **king** *of* the North will muster another army, larger than the
11:14 "In those times many will rise against the **king** *of* the South.
11:15 Then the **king** *of* the North will come and build up siege ramps
11:25 will stir up his strength and courage against the **king** *of* the South.
11:25 The **king** *of* the South will wage war with a large and very
11:27 The two **kings**, with their hearts bent on evil, will sit at the same
11:36 "The **king** will do as he pleases. He will exalt and magnify himself
11:40 "At the time of the end the **king** *of* the South will engage him in
11:40 and the **king** *of* the North will storm out against him with chariots
Hos 1: 1 Jotham, Ahaz and Hezekiah, **kings** *of* Judah, and during the reign
1: 1 and during the reign of Jeroboam son of Jehoash **king** *of* Israel:
3: 4 For the Israelites will live many days without **king** or prince,
3: 5 will return and seek the LORD their God and David their **king**.
5: 1 you priests! Pay attention, you Israelites! Listen, O **royal** house!
5:13 then Ephraim turned to Assyria, and sent to the great **king** for help.
7: 3 "They delight the **king** with their wickedness, the princes with
7: 5 On the day of the festival of our **king** the princes become inflamed
7: 7 their rulers. All their **kings** fall, and none of them calls on me.
8:10 will begin to waste away under the oppression of the mighty **king**.
10: 3 "We have no **king** because we did not revere the LORD.
10: 3 the LORD. But even if we had a **king**, what could he do for us?"
10: 6 It will be carried to Assyria as tribute for the great **king**.
10: 7 and its **king** will float away like a twig on the surface of the waters.
10:15 that day dawns, the **king** *of* Israel will be completely destroyed.
11: 5 "Will they not return to Egypt and will not Assyria **rule over** them
13:10 Where is your **king**, that he may save you? Where are your rulers
13:10 in all your towns, of whom you said, 'Give me a **king** and princes'?
13:11 So in my anger I gave you a **king**, and in my wrath I took him
Am 1: 1 when Uzziah was **king** *of* Judah and Jeroboam son of Jehoash was
1: 1 was king of Judah and Jeroboam son of Jehoash was **king** *of* Israel.
1:15 Her **king** will go into exile, he and his officials together,"
2: 1 Because he burned, as if to lime, the bones of Edom's **king**,
5:26 You have lifted up the shrine of your **king**, the pedestal of your
7: 1 He was preparing swarms of locusts after the **king's** *share* had
7:10 Amaziah the priest of Bethel sent a message to Jeroboam **king** *of*
7:13 because this is the **king's** sanctuary and the temple of the
Jnh 3: 6 When the news reached the **king** *of* Nineveh, he rose from his
3: 7 "By the decree of the **king** and his nobles: Do not let any man
Mic 1: 1 during the reigns of Jotham, Ahaz and Hezekiah, **kings** *of* Judah—
1:14 The town of Aczib will prove deceptive to the **kings** *of* Israel.
2:13 Their **king** will pass through before them, the LORD at their
4: 9 Why do you now cry aloud—have you no **king**? Has your
6: 5 remember what Balak **king** *of* Moab counseled and what Balaam
Na 3:18 O **king** *of* Assyria, your shepherds slumber; your nobles lie down
Hab 1:10 They deride **kings** and scoff at rulers. They laugh at all fortified
Zep 1: 1 during the reign of Josiah son of Amon **king** *of* Judah:
1: 8 and the **king's** sons and all those clad in foreign clothes.
3:15 The LORD, the **King** *of* Israel, is with you; never again will you
Hag 1: 1 In the second year of **King** Darius, on the first day of the sixth
1:15 day of the sixth month in the second year of **King** Darius.
Zec 7: 1 In the fourth year of **King** Darius, the word of the LORD came to
9: 5 will wither. Gaza will lose her **king** and Ashkelon will be deserted.
9: 9 See, your **king** comes to you, righteous and having salvation,
11: 6 "I will hand everyone over to his neighbor and his **king**.
14: 5 you fled from the earthquake in the days of Uzziah **king** *of* Judah.
14: 9 The LORD will be **king** over the whole earth. On that day there
14:10 and from the Tower of Hananel to the **royal** winepresses.
14:16 attacked Jerusalem will go up year after year to worship the **King**,
14:17 peoples of the earth do not go up to Jerusalem to worship the **King**,
Mal 1:14 For I am a great **king**," says the LORD Almighty, "and my name

4890 ²מֶלֶךְ *melek²*, n.pr.m. [2] [√ 4889; cf. 4887]

Melech [2]

1Ch 8:35 The sons of Micah: Pithon, **Melech**, Tarea and Ahaz.
9:41 The sons of Micah: Pithon, **Melech**, Tahrea and Ahaz.

4891 מֹלֶךְ *mōlek*, n.pr.[m.]. [8 / 9] [√ 4889]

Molech [9]

Lev 18:21 " 'Do not give any of your children to be sacrificed to **Molech**,
20: 2 who gives any of his children to **Molech** must be put to death.
20: 3 for by giving his children to **Molech**, he has defiled my sanctuary
20: 4 close their eyes when that man gives one of his children to **Molech**
20: 5 and all who follow him in prostituting themselves to **Molech**.
1Ki 11: 7 of Moab, and for **Molech** the detestable god of the Ammonites.
2Ki 23:10 could use it to sacrifice his son or daughter in the fire to **Molech**.
Isa 57: 9 You went to **Molech** [BHS 4889] with olive oil and increased
Jer 32:35 of Ben Hinnom to sacrifice their sons and daughters to **Molech**,

4892 מַלְכֹּדֶת *malkōdet*, n.f. [1] [√ 4334]

trap [1]

Job 18:10 A noose is hidden for him on the ground; a **trap** lies in his path.

4893 מַלְכָּה *malkâ*, n.f. [35] [√ 4889; cf. 4887; Ar 10423]

queen [30], queen's [2], queens [2], she[s] [+2021] [1]

1Ki 10: 1 When the **queen** *of* Sheba heard about the fame of Solomon
10: 4 When the **queen** *of* Sheba saw all the wisdom of Solomon
10:10 so many spices brought in as those the **queen** *of* Sheba gave to
10:13 King Solomon gave the **queen** *of* Sheba all she desired and asked
2Ch 9: 1 When the **queen** *of* Sheba heard of Solomon's fame, she came to
9: 3 When the **queen** *of* Sheba saw the wisdom of Solomon, as well as
9: 9 There had never been such spices as those the **queen** *of* Sheba
9:12 King Solomon gave the **queen** *of* Sheba all she desired and asked
Est 1: 9 **Queen** Vashti also gave a banquet for the women in the royal
1:11 to bring before him **Queen** Vashti, wearing her royal crown,
1:12 delivered the king's command, **Queen** Vashti refused to come.
1:15 "According to law, what must be done to **Queen** Vashti?"
1:16 of the king and the nobles, "**Queen** Vashti has done wrong,
1:17 For the **queen's** conduct will become known to all the women,

Est 1:17 'King Xerxes commanded **Queen** Vashti to be brought before him,
1:18 Median women of the nobility who have heard about the **queen's**
2:22 But Mordecai found out about the plot and told **Queen** Esther,
4:4 and told her about Mordecai, **she**[s] [+2021] was in great distress.
5:2 When he saw **Queen** Esther standing in the court, he was pleased
5:3 the king asked, "What is it, **Queen** Esther? What is your request?
5:12 "I'm the only person **Queen** Esther invited to accompany the king
7:1 So the king and Haman went to dine with **Queen** Esther,
7:2 the king again asked, "**Queen** Esther, what is your petition?
7:3 Then **Queen** Esther answered, "If I have found favor with you,
7:5 King Xerxes asked **Queen** Esther, "Who is he? Where is the man
7:6 Then Haman was terrified before the king and **queen**.
7:7 decided his fate, stayed behind to beg **Queen** Esther for his life.
7:8 "Will he even molest the **queen** while she is with me in the
8:1 That same day King Xerxes gave **Queen** Esther the estate of
8:7 King Xerxes replied to **Queen** Esther and to Mordecai the Jew,
9:12 The king said to **Queen** Esther, "The Jews have killed
9:29 So **Queen** Esther, daughter of Abihail, along with Mordecai the
9:31 as Mordecai the Jew and **Queen** Esther had decreed for them,
SS 6:8 Sixty **queens** there may be, and eighty concubines, and virgins
6:9 and called her blessed; the **queens** and concubines praised her.

4894 מִלְכָּה ***milkâ***, n.pr.f. [11] [√ 4889; cf. 4887]

Milcah [11]

Ge 11:29 wife was Sarai, and the name of Nahor's wife was **Milcah**;
11:29 was the daughter of Haran, the father of both **Milcah** and Iscah.
22:20 Some time later Abraham was told, "**Milcah** is also a mother;
22:23 **Milcah** bore these eight sons to Abraham's brother Nahor.
24:15 She was the daughter of Bethuel son of **Milcah**, who was the wife
24:24 "I am the daughter of Bethuel, the son that **Milcah** bore to Nahor."
24:47 'The daughter of Bethuel son of Nahor, whom **Milcah** bore to him.'
Nu 26:33 whose names were Mahlah, Noah, Hoglah, **Milcah** and Tirzah.)
27:1 of the daughters were Mahlah, Noah, Hoglah, **Milcah** and Tirzah.
36:11 Mahlah, Tirzah, Hoglah, **Milcah** and Noah—
Jos 17:3 whose names were Mahlah, Noah, Hoglah, **Milcah** and Tirzah.

4895 מַלְכוּת ***malkût***, n.f. [91] [√ 4889; cf. 4887; Ar 10424]

kingdom [36], reign [19], royal [16], realm [5], *untranslated* [2], empire [2], kingdoms [2], royal position [2], became king [1], king [1], kingship [1], palace [+1074] [1], position as king [1], royalty [1], rule [1]

Nu 24:7 king will be greater than Agag; their **kingdom** will be exalted.
1Sa 20:31 on this earth, neither you nor your **kingdom** will be established.
1Ki 2:12 the throne of his father David, and his **rule** was firmly established.
1Ch 11:10 gave his **kingship** strong support to extend it over the whole land,
12:23 [12:24] to David at Hebron to turn Saul's **kingdom** over to him,
14:2 that his **kingdom** had been highly exalted for the sake of his
17:11 one of your own sons, and I will establish his **kingdom**.
17:14 I will set him over my house and my **kingdom** forever; his throne
22:10 And I will establish the throne of his **kingdom** over Israel forever.'
26:31 In the fortieth year of David's **reign** a search was made in the
28:5 to sit on the throne of the **kingdom** *of* the LORD over Israel.
28:7 I will establish his **kingdom** forever if he is unswerving in carrying
29:25 bestowed on him **royal** splendor such as no king over Israel ever
29:30 together with the details of his **reign** and power, and the
2Ch 1:1 son of David established himself firmly over his **kingdom**,
2:1 [1:18] for the Name of the LORD and a **royal** palace for himself.
2:12 [2:11] a temple for the LORD and a **palace** [+1074] for himself.
3:2 the second day of the second month in the fourth year of his **reign**.
7:18 I will establish your **royal** throne, as I covenanted with David your
11:17 They strengthened the **kingdom** *of* Judah and supported
12:1 After Rehoboam's **position as king** was established and he had
15:10 at Jerusalem in the third month of the fifteenth year of Asa's **reign**.
15:19 There was no more war until the thirty-fifth year of Asa's **reign**.
16:1 In the thirty-sixth year of Asa's **reign** Baasha king of Israel went
16:12 In the thirty-ninth year of his **reign** Asa was afflicted with a
20:30 the **kingdom** *of* Jehoshaphat was at peace, for his God had given
29:19 that King Ahaz removed in his unfaithfulness while he was **king**.
33:13 so he brought him back to Jerusalem and to his **kingdom**.
35:19 Passover was celebrated in the eighteenth year of Josiah's **reign**.
36:20 to him and his sons until the **kingdom** *of* Persia came to power.
36:22 Cyrus king of Persia to make a proclamation throughout his **realm**
Ezr 1:1 Cyrus king of Persia to make a proclamation throughout his **realm**
4:5 king of Persia and down to the **reign** *of* Darius king of Persia.
4:6 At the beginning of the **reign** *of* Xerxes, they lodged an accusation
4:6 **[RPH]** they lodged an accusation against the people of Judah
7:1 After these things, during the **reign** *of* Artaxerxes king of Persia,
8:1 up with me from Babylon during the **reign** *of* King Artaxerxes:
Ne 9:35 Even while they were in their **kingdom**, enjoying your great
12:22 of the priests, were recorded in the **reign** *of* Darius the Persian.
Est 1:2 At that time King Xerxes reigned from his **royal** throne in the
1:4 For a full 180 days he displayed the vast wealth of his **kingdom**
1:7 one different from the other, and the **royal** wine was abundant,
1:9 Queen Vashti also gave a banquet for the women in the **royal**
1:11 to bring before him Queen Vashti, wearing her **royal** crown,
1:14 had special access to the king and were highest in the **kingdom**.
1:19 let him issue a **royal** decree and let it be written in the laws of
1:19 Also let the king give her **royal position** to someone else who is
1:20 when the king's edict is proclaimed throughout all his vast **realm**,
2:3 Let the king appoint commissioners in every province of his **realm**
2:16 She was taken to King Xerxes in the **royal** residence in the tenth
2:16 tenth month, the month of Tebeth, in the seventh year of his **reign**.
2:17 So he set a **royal** crown on her head and made her queen instead of
3:6 the Jews, throughout the whole **kingdom** *of* Xerxes.
3:8 scattered among the peoples in all the provinces of your **kingdom**
4:14 but that you have come to **royal position** for such a time as this?"
5:1 On the third day Esther put on her **royal** robes and stood in the
5:1 The king was sitting on his **royal** throne in the hall, facing the
5:1 sitting on his royal throne in the hall, **[RPH]** facing the entrance.
5:3 your request? Even up to half the **kingdom**, it will be given you."
5:6 is your request? Even up to half the **kingdom**, it will be granted."
6:8 have them bring a **royal** robe the king has worn and a horse the
6:8 horse the king has ridden, one with a **royal** crest placed on its head.
7:2 is your request? Even up to half the **kingdom**, it will be granted."
8:15 Mordecai left the king's presence wearing **royal** garments of blue
9:30 to all the Jews in the 127 provinces of the **kingdom** *of* Xerxes—
Ps 45:6 [45:7] a scepter of justice will be the scepter of your **kingdom**.
103:19 established his throne in heaven, and his **kingdom** rules over all.
145:11 They will tell of the glory of your **kingdom** and speak of your
145:12 of your mighty acts and the glorious splendor of your **kingdom**.
145:13 Your **kingdom** is an everlasting kingdom, and your dominion
145:13 Your kingdom is an everlasting **kingdom**, and your dominion
Ecc 4:14 or he may have been born in poverty within his **kingdom**.
Jer 10:7 Among all the wise men of the nations and in all their **kingdoms**,
49:34 concerning Elam, early in the **reign** *of* Zedekiah king of Judah:
52:31 in the year Evil-Merodach **became king** *of* Babylon, he released
Da 1:1 In the third year of the **reign** *of* Jehoiakim king of Judah,
1:20 better than all the magicians and enchanters in his whole **kingdom**.
2:1 In the second year of his **reign**, Nebuchadnezzar had dreams;
8:1 In the third year of King Belshazzar's **reign**, I, Daniel, had a
8:22 off represent four **kingdoms** that will emerge from his nation
8:23 "In the latter part of their **reign**, when rebels have become
9:1 by descent), who was made ruler over the Babylonian **kingdom**—
10:13 the prince of the Persian **kingdom** resisted me twenty-one days.
11:2 his wealth, he will stir up everyone against the **kingdom** *of* Greece.
11:4 his **empire** will be broken up and parceled out toward the four
11:4 because his **empire** will be uprooted and given to others.
11:9 the king of the North will invade the **realm** *of* the king of the
11:17 He will determine to come with the might of his entire **kingdom**
11:20 "His successor will send out a tax collector to maintain the **royal**
11:21 contemptible person who has not been given the honor of **royalty**.
11:21 He will invade the **kingdom** when its people feel secure, and he

4896 מַלְכִּיאֵל ***malkî'ēl***, n.pr.m. [3] [→ 4897; cf. 4889 + 446]

Malkiel [3]

Ge 46:17 Their sister was Serah. The sons of Beriah: Heber and **Malkiel**.
Nu 26:45 the Heberite clan; through **Malkiel**, the Malkielite clan.
1Ch 7:31 sons of Beriah: Heber and **Malkiel**, who was the father of Birzaith.

4897 מַלְכִּיאֵלִי ***malkî'ēlî***, a.g. [1] [√ 4896; cf. 4889 + 446]

Malkielite [1]

Nu 26:45 the Heberite clan; through Malkiel, the **Malkielite** clan.

4898 מַלְכִּיָּה ***malkiyyâ***, n.pr.m. [15] [√ 4889 + 3378]

Malkijah [15]

1Ch 6:40 [6:25] son of Michael, the son of Baaseiah, the son of **Malkijah**,
9:12 Adaiah son of Jeroham, the son of Pashhur, the son of **Malkijah**;
24:9 the fifth to **Malkijah**, the sixth to Mijamin,
Ezr 10:25 Ramiah, Izziah, **Malkijah**, Mijamin, Eleazar, Malkijah
10:25 Izziah, Malkijah, Mijamin, Eleazar, **Malkijah** and Benaiah.
10:31 of Harim: Eliezer, Ishijah, **Malkijah**, Shemaiah, Shimeon,
Ne 3:11 **Malkijah** son of Harim and Hasshub son of Pahath-Moab repaired
3:14 The Dung Gate was repaired by **Malkijah** son of Recab, ruler of
3:31 Next to him, **Malkijah**, one of the goldsmiths, made repairs as far
8:4 Mishael, **Malkijah**, Hashum, Hashbaddanah, Zechariah
10:3 [10:4] Pashhur, Amariah, **Malkijah**,
11:12 the son of Zechariah, the son of Pashhur, the son of **Malkijah**,
12:42 Shemaiah, Eleazar, Uzzi, Jehohanan, **Malkijah**, Elam and Ezer.
Jer 21:1 LORD when King Zedekiah sent to him Pashhur son of **Malkijah**
38:1 Pashhur son of **Malkijah** heard what Jeremiah was telling all the

4899 מַלְכִּיָּהוּ ***malkiyyāhû***, n.pr.m. [1] [√ 4889 + 3378]

Malkijah [1]

Jer 38:6 So they took Jeremiah and put him into the cistern of **Malkijah**,

4900 מַלְכִּי־צֶדֶק ***malkî-ṣedeq***, n.pr.m. [2] [√ 4889 + 7406]
Melchizedek [2]
Ge 14:18 Then **Melchizedek** king of Salem brought out bread and wine.
Ps 110: 4 his mind: "You are a priest forever, in the order of **Melchizedek**."

4901 מַלְכִּירָם ***malkîrām***, n.pr.m. [1] [√ 4889 + 8123]
Malkiram [1]
1Ch 3:18 **Malkiram**, Pedaiah, Shenazzar, Jekamiah, Hoshama

4902 מַלְכִּי־שׁוּעַ ***malkî-šûaʿ***, n.pr.m. [5] [√ 4889 + 8775]
Malki-Shua [5]
1Sa 14:49 Saul's sons were Jonathan, Ishvi and **Malki-Shua**. The name of his
31: 2 and they killed his sons Jonathan, Abinadab and **Malki-Shua**.
1Ch 8:33 Saul the father of Jonathan, **Malki-Shua**, Abinadab and Esh-Baal.
9:39 Saul the father of Jonathan, **Malki-Shua**, Abinadab and Esh-Baal.
10: 2 and they killed his sons Jonathan, Abinadab and **Malki-Shua**.

4903 מַלְכָּם ***malkām***, n.pr.m. [4] [√ 4889 + 4392]
Molech [3], Malcam [1]
1Ch 8: 9 By his wife Hodesh he had Jobab, Zibia, Mesha, **Malcam**,
Jer 49: 1 Has she no heirs? Why then has **Molech** taken possession of Gad?
49: 3 for **Molech** will go into exile, together with his priests
Zep 1: 5 and swear by the LORD and who also swear by **Molech**,

4904 מִלְכֹּם ***milkōm***, n.pr.[m.]. [3] [√ 4889]
Molech [3]
1Ki 11: 5 the Sidonians, and **Molech** the detestable god of the Ammonites.
11:33 **Molech** the god of the Ammonites, and have not walked in my
2Ki 23:13 and for **Molech** the detestable god of the people of Ammon.

4905 מַלְכֵּן ***malkēn***, n.[m.]. [0] [cf. 4861]
2Sa 12:31 [and he made them work at **brickmaking**. [K; see Q 4861]]

4906 מְלֶכֶת ***meleket***, n.f. [5] [√ 4889]
queen [5]
Jer 7:18 the dough and make cakes of bread for the **Queen** *of* Heaven.
44:17 We will burn incense to the **Queen** *of* Heaven and will pour out
44:18 But ever since we stopped burning incense to the **Queen** *of* Heaven
44:19 "When we burned incense to the **Queen** *of* Heaven and poured out
44:25 burn incense and pour out drink offerings to the **Queen** *of* Heaven.'

4907 מֹלֶכֶת ***mōleket***, n.pr.f. Not used in NIV/BHS [√ 2143]

4908 מָלַל¹ ***mālal¹***, v. [5] [→ 4884; cf. 581, 582]
wither [2], be blunted [1], dry [1], withers away [1]
Job 14: 2 [A] He springs up like a flower and **withers away**; like a fleeting
18:16 [A] His roots dry up below and his branches **wither** above.
Ps 37: 2 [A] for like the grass *they will* soon **wither**, like green plants
58: 7 [58:8] [F] when they draw the bow, *let* their arrows **be blunted**.
90: 6 [D] morning it springs up new, by evening *it is* **dry** and withered.

4909 מָלַל² ***mālal²***, v. [2] [cf. 4576]
are cut off [1], circumcise [1]
Jos 5: 2 [A] "Make flint knives and **circumcise** the Israelites again."
Job 24:24 [C] up like all others; *they* **are cut off** like heads of grain.

4910 מָלַל³ ***mālal³***, v. [4] [→ 4863, 4871; cf. 4911; Ar 10425]
proclaim [1], said [1], say [1], speak [1]
Ge 21: 7 [D] "Who *would have* **said** to Abraham that Sarah would nurse
Job 8: 2 [D] "How long *will you* **say** such things? Your words are a
33: 3 [D] from an upright heart; my lips sincerely **speak** what I know.
Ps 106: 2 [D] Who *can* **proclaim** the mighty acts of the LORD or fully

4911 מָלַל⁴ ***mālal⁴***, v. [1] [cf. 4910]
signals [1]
Pr 6:13 [A] his eye, **signals** with his feet and motions with his fingers,

4912 מִלְלַי ***milᵃlay***, n.pr.m. [1]
Milalai [1]
Ne 12:36 Azarel, **Milalai**, Gilalai, Maai, Nethanel, Judah and Hanani—

4913 מַלְמָד ***malmād***, n.[m.]. [1] [√ 4340]
oxgoad [+1330] [1]
Jdg 3:31 who struck down six hundred Philistines with an **oxgoad** [+1330].

4914 מָלַץ ***mālaṣ***, v. [1] [→ 6666]
sweet [1]
Ps 119:103 [C] How **sweet** *are* your words to my taste, sweeter than honey

4915 מֶלְצַר ***melṣar***, n.m. [2] [√ 5915]
guard [2]
Da 1:11 said to the **guard** whom the chief official had appointed over
1:16 So the **guard** took away their choice food and the wine they were

4916 מָלַק ***mālaq***, v. [2]
wring off [1], wring [1]
Lev 1:15 [A] it to the altar, **wring off** the head and burn it on the altar;
5: 8 [A] *He is to* **wring** its head from its neck, not severing it

4917 מַלְקוֹחַ ***malqôaḥ***, n.m. [7] [√ 4374]
spoils [4], plunder [2], all[s] [1]
Nu 31:11 They took all the plunder and **spoils**, including the people
31:12 **spoils** and plunder to Moses and Eleazar the priest and the Israelite
31:26 and the family heads of the community are to count **all**[s] the people
31:27 Divide the **spoils** between the soldiers who took part in the battle
31:32 The plunder remaining from the **spoils** that the soldiers took was
Isa 49:24 Can **plunder** be taken from warriors, or captives rescued from the
49:25 will be taken from warriors, and **plunder** retrieved from the fierce;

4918 מַלְקוֹחַיִם ***malqôḥayim***, n.[m.]. [1] [√ 4374?]
roof of mouth [1]
Ps 22:15 [22:16] and my tongue sticks to the **roof of** my **mouth**;

4919 מַלְקוֹשׁ ***malqôš***, n.m. [8] [√ 4380]
spring rains [5], rain in spring [1], spring rain [1], springtime [+6961] [1]
Dt 11:14 both autumn and **spring rains**, so that you may gather in your
Job 29:23 for me as for showers and drank in my words as the **spring rain**.
Pr 16:15 it means life; his favor is like a **rain** cloud **in spring**.
Jer 3: 3 the showers have been withheld, and no **spring rains** have fallen.
5:24 LORD our God, who gives autumn and **spring rains** in season,
Hos 6: 3 us like the winter rains, like the **spring rains** that water the earth."
Joel 2:23 you abundant showers, both autumn and **spring rains**, as before.
Zec 10: 1 Ask the LORD for rain in the **springtime** [+6961]; it is the

4920 מֶלְקָחַיִם ***melqāḥayim***, n.[m.]du. [6] [√ 4374]
tongs [3], wick trimmers [3]
Ex 25:38 Its **wick trimmers** and trays are to be of pure gold.
37:23 seven lamps, as well as its **wick trimmers** and trays, of pure gold.
Nu 4: 9 is for light, together with its lamps, its **wick trimmers** and trays,
1Ki 7:49 of the inner sanctuary); the gold floral work and lamps and **tongs**;
2Ch 4:21 the gold floral work and lamps and **tongs** (they were solid gold);
Isa 6: 6 live coal in his hand, which he had taken with **tongs** from the altar.

4921 מֶלְתָּחָה ***meltāḥâ***, n.f. [1]
wardrobe [1]
2Ki 10:22 Jehu said to the keeper of the **wardrobe**, "Bring robes for all the

4922 מַלְתָּעוֹת ***maltāʿôt***, n.f.pl. [1] [→ 5506]
fangs [1]
Ps 58: 6 [58:7] O God; tear out, O LORD, the **fangs** *of* the lions!

4923 מַמְּגוּרָה ***mammᵉgûrâ***, n.f.pl. [1] [√ 4473]
granaries [1]
Joel 1:17 the **granaries** have been broken down, for the grain has dried up.

4924 מֵמַד ***mēmād***, n.[m.]. [1] [√ 4499]
dimensions [1]
Job 38: 5 Who marked off its **dimensions**? Surely you know! Who stretched

4925 מְמוּכָן ***mᵉmûkān***, n.pr.m. [3] [→ 4584]
Memucan [3]
Est 1:14 Shethar, Admatha, Tarshish, Meres, Marsena and **Memucan**,
1:16 Then **Memucan** [K 4584] replied in the presence of the king
1:21 pleased with this advice, so the king did as **Memucan** proposed.

4926 מָמוֹת ***māmôt***, n.[m.]. [2] [√ 4637]
deadly [1], death [1]
Jer 16: 4 "They will die of **deadly** diseases. They will not be mourned

Eze 28: 8 to the pit, and you will die a violent **death** in the heart of the seas.

4927 מַמְזֵר ***mamzēr***, n.m. [2]

foreigners [1], one born of a forbidden marriage [1]

Dt 23: 2 [23:3] No **one born of a forbidden marriage** nor any of his
Zec 9: 6 **Foreigners** will occupy Ashdod, and I will cut off the pride of the

4928 מִמְכָּר ***mimkār***, n.m. [10] [√ 4835]

sold [2], what sold [2], goods [1], land sold [1], money from sale [1], release [1], sale [1], sell land [+4835] [1]

Lev 25:14 " 'If *you* **sell land** [+4835] to one of your countrymen or buy any
25:25 relative is to come and redeem **what** his countryman has **sold**.
25:27 he is to determine the value for the years since he **sold** it
25:28 **what** he **sold** will remain in the possession of the buyer until the
25:29 he retains the right of redemption a full year after its **sale**.
25:33 that is, a house **sold** in any town they hold—and is to be returned
25:50 The price for his **release** is to be based on the rate paid to a hired
Dt 18: 8 even though he has received **money from** the **sale** of family
Ne 13:20 and sellers of all kinds of **goods** spent the night outside Jerusalem.
Eze 7:13 The seller will not recover the **land** he has **sold** as long as both of

4929 מִמְכֶּרֶת ***mimkeret***, n.f. [1] [√ 4835]

must be sold [+4835] [1]

Lev 25:42 I brought out of Egypt, *they* **must** not **be sold** [+4835] as slaves.

4930 מַמְלָכָה ***mamlākâ***, n.f. [117] [√ 4887]

kingdom [58], kingdoms [45], royal [7], kings [2], kingship [2], reign [2], royal power [1]

Ge 10:10 The first centers of his **kingdom** were Babylon, Erech, Akkad
20: 9 that you have brought such great guilt upon me and my **kingdom**?
Ex 19: 6 you will be for me a **kingdom** *of* priests and a holy nation.'
Nu 32:33 the half-tribe of Manasseh son of Joseph the **kingdom** *of* Sihon
32:33 king of the Amorites and the **kingdom** *of* Og king of Bashan—
Dt 3: 4 from them—the whole region of Argob, Og's **kingdom** in Bashan.
3:10 as far as Salecah and Edrei, towns of Og's **kingdom** in Bashan.
3:13 The rest of Gilead and also all of Bashan, the **kingdom** *of* Og,
3:21 The LORD will do the same to all the **kingdoms** over there where
17:18 When he takes the throne of his **kingdom**, he is to write for
17:20 his descendants will reign a long time over his **kingdom** in Israel.
28:25 you will become a thing of horror to all the **kingdoms** *on* earth.
Jos 10: 2 because Gibeon was an important city, like one of the **royal** cities;
11:10 to the sword. (Hazor had been the head of all these **kingdoms**.)
1Sa 10:18 from the power of Egypt and all the **kingdoms** that oppressed you.'
13:13 he would have established your **kingdom** over Israel for all time.
13:14 now your **kingdom** will not endure; the LORD has sought out a
24:20 [24:21] that the **kingdom** *of* Israel will be established in your
27: 5 Why should your servant live in the **royal** city with you?"
28:17 The LORD has torn the **kingdom** out of your hands and given it
2Sa 3:10 transfer the **kingdom** from the house of Saul and establish David's
3:28 my **kingdom** are forever innocent before the LORD concerning
5:12 and had exalted his **kingdom** for the sake of his people Israel.
7:12 will come from your own body, and I will establish his **kingdom**.
7:13 my Name, and I will establish the throne of his **kingdom** forever.
7:16 Your house and your **kingdom** will endure forever before me;
1Ki 2:46 The **kingdom** was now firmly established in Solomon's hands.
4:21 [5:1] Solomon ruled over all the **kingdoms** from the River to the
9: 5 I will establish your **royal** throne over Israel forever, as I promised
10:20 Nothing like it had ever been made for any other **kingdom**.
11:11 I will most certainly tear the **kingdom** away from you and give it
11:13 Yet I will not tear the whole **kingdom** from him, but will give him
11:31 I am going to tear the **kingdom** out of Solomon's hand and give
11:34 " 'But I will not take the whole **kingdom** out of Solomon's hand;
12:26 "The **kingdom** will now likely revert to the house of David.
14: 8 I tore the **kingdom** away from the house of David and gave it to
18:10 or **kingdom** where my master has not sent someone to look for
18:10 And whenever a nation or **kingdom** claimed you were not there,
2Ki 11: 1 her son was dead, she proceeded to destroy the whole **royal** family.
14: 5 After the **kingdom** was firmly in his grasp, he executed the
15:19 to gain his support and strengthen his own hold on the **kingdom**.
19:15 you alone are God over all the **kingdoms** *of* the earth.
19:19 so that all **kingdoms** *on* earth may know that you alone, O
1Ch 16:20 wandered from nation to nation, from one **kingdom** to another.
29:11 Yours, O LORD, is the **kingdom**; you are exalted as head over
29:30 surrounded him and Israel and the **kingdoms** *of* all the other lands.
2Ch 9:19 Nothing like it had ever been made for any other **kingdom**.
11: 1 make war against Israel and to regain the **kingdom** for Rehoboam.
12: 8 between serving me and serving the **kings** *of* other lands."
13: 5 has given the **kingship** of Israel to David and his descendants
13: 8 "And now you plan to resist the **kingdom** *of* the LORD,
14: 5 [14:4] town in Judah, and the **kingdom** was at peace under him.
17: 5 The LORD established the **kingdom** under his control; and all
17:10 The fear of the LORD fell on all the **kingdoms** *of* the lands
20: 6 You rule over all the **kingdoms** *of* the nations. Power and might
20:29 The fear of God came upon all the **kingdoms** *of* the countries
21: 3 he had given the **kingdom** to Jehoram because he was his firstborn
21: 4 Jehoram established himself firmly over his father's **kingdom**,
22: 9 in the house of Ahaziah powerful enough to retain the **kingdom**.
22:10 she proceeded to destroy the whole **royal** family of the house of
23:20 through the Upper Gate and seated the king on the **royal** throne,
25: 3 After the **kingdom** was firmly in his control, he executed the
29:21 and seven male goats as a sin offering for the **kingdom**,
32:15 or **kingdom** has been able to deliver his people from my hand
36:23 has given me all the **kingdoms** *of* the earth and he has appointed
Ezr 1: 2 has given me all the **kingdoms** *of* the earth and he has appointed
Ne 9:22 "You gave them **kingdoms** and nations, allotting to them even the
Ps 46: 6 [46:7] Nations are in uproar, **kingdoms** fall; he lifts his voice,
68:32 [68:33] Sing to God, O **kingdoms** *of* the earth, sing praise to the
79: 6 acknowledge you, on the **kingdoms** that do not call on your name;
102:22 [102:23] and the **kingdoms** assemble to worship the LORD.
105:13 wandered from nation to nation, from *one* **kingdom** to another.
135:11 of the Amorites, Og king of Bashan and all the **kings** *of* Canaan—
Isa 9: 7 [9:6] He will reign on David's throne and over his **kingdom**,
10:10 As my hand seized the **kingdoms** *of* the idols, kingdoms whose
13: 4 Listen, an uproar among the **kingdoms**, like nations massing
13:19 Babylon, the jewel of **kingdoms**, the glory of the Babylonians'
14:16 "Is this the man who shook the earth and made **kingdoms** tremble,
17: 3 will disappear from Ephraim, and **royal power** from Damascus;
19: 2 against neighbor, city against city, **kingdom** against kingdom.
19: 2 against neighbor, city against city, kingdom against **kingdom**.
23:11 out his hand over the sea and made its **kingdoms** tremble.
23:17 will ply her trade with all the **kingdoms** on the face of the earth.
37:16 you alone are God over all the **kingdoms** *of* the earth.
37:20 so that all **kingdoms** *on* earth may know that you alone, O
47: 5 the Babylonians; no more will you be called queen of **kingdoms**.
60:12 For the nation or **kingdom** that will not serve you will perish;
Jer 1:10 I appoint you over nations and **kingdoms** to uproot and tear down,
1:15 I am about to summon all the peoples of the northern **kingdoms**,"
15: 4 I will make them abhorrent to all the **kingdoms** *of* the earth
18: 7 at any time I announce that a nation or **kingdom** is to be uprooted,
18: 9 I announce that a nation or **kingdom** is to be built up and planted,
24: 9 them abhorrent and an offense to all the **kingdoms** *of* the earth,
25:26 one after the other—all the **kingdoms** on the face of the earth.
27: 1 Early in the **reign** *of* Zedekiah son of Josiah king of Judah,
27: 8 or **kingdom** will not serve Nebuchadnezzar king of Babylon
28: 1 the fourth year, early in the **reign** *of* Zedekiah king of Judah,
28: 8 disaster and plague against many countries and great **kingdoms**.
29:18 and will make them abhorrent to all the **kingdoms** *of* the earth
34: 1 king of Babylon and all his army and all the **kingdoms**
34:17 I will make you abhorrent to all the **kingdoms** *of* the earth.
49:28 Concerning Kedar and the **kingdoms** *of* Hazor,
51:20 with you I shatter nations, with you I destroy **kingdoms**,
51:27 nations for battle against her; summon against her these **kingdoms**:
La 2: 2 He has brought her **kingdom** and its princes down to the ground in
Eze 17:14 so that the **kingdom** would be brought low, unable to rise again,
29:14 the land of their ancestry. There they will be a lowly **kingdom**.
29:15 It will be the lowliest of **kingdoms** and will never again exalt itself
37:22 will never again be two nations or be divided into two **kingdoms**.
Am 6: 2 Are they better off than your two **kingdoms**? Is their land larger
7:13 this is the king's sanctuary and the temple of the **kingdom**."
9: 8 the eyes of the Sovereign LORD are on the sinful **kingdom**.
Mic 4: 8 restored to you; **kingship** will come to the Daughter of Jerusalem."
Na 3: 5 show the nations your nakedness and the **kingdoms** your shame.
Zep 3: 8 to gather the **kingdoms** and to pour out my wrath on them—
Hag 2:22 I will overturn **royal** thrones and shatter the power of the foreign
2:22 royal thrones and shatter the power of the foreign **kingdoms**.

4931 מַמְלָכוּת ***mamlākût***, n.f. [9] [√ 4887]

kingdom [4], realm [3], reign [1], royal [1]

Jos 13:12 that is, the whole **kingdom** *of* Og in Bashan, who had reigned in
13:21 on the plateau and the entire **realm** *of* Sihon king of the Amorites,
13:27 Zaphon with the rest of the **realm** *of* Sihon king of Heshbon (the
13:30 including all of Bashan, the entire **realm** *of* Og king of Bashan—
13:31 and Ashtaroth and Edrei (the **royal** cities of Og in Bashan).
1Sa 15:28 "The LORD has torn the **kingdom** *of* Israel from you today
2Sa 16: 3 house of Israel will give me back my grandfather's **kingdom**.' "
Jer 26: 1 Early in the **reign** *of* Jehoiakim son of Josiah king of Judah,
Hos 1: 4 massacre at Jezreel, and I will put an end to the **kingdom** *of* Israel.

4932 מִמְסָךְ ***mimsāk***, n.m. [2] [√ 5007]

bowls of mixed wine [2]

Pr 23:30 who linger over wine, who go to sample **bowls of mixed wine**.
Isa 65:11 a table for Fortune and fill **bowls of mixed wine** for Destiny,

4933 מֶמֶר *memer*, n.[m.]. [1] [√ 5352]

bitterness [1]

Pr 17: 25 brings grief to his father and **bitterness** to the one who bore him.

4934 [1]מַמְרֵא *mamrē*[1], n.pr.loc. [8] [√ 5258?]

Mamre [8]

Ge 13: 18 and went to live near the great trees of **Mamre** at Hebron,
18: 1 The LORD appeared to Abraham near the great trees of **Mamre**
23: 17 So Ephron's field in Machpelah near **Mamre**—both the field
23: 19 cave in the field of Machpelah near **Mamre** (which is at Hebron)
25: 9 and Ishmael buried him in the cave of Machpelah near **Mamre**,
35: 27 Jacob came home to his father Isaac in **Mamre**, near Kiriath Arba
49: 30 the cave in the field of Machpelah, near **Mamre** in Canaan,
50: 13 and buried him in the cave in the field of Machpelah, near **Mamre**,

4935 [2]מַמְרֵא *mamrē*[2], n.pr.m. [2] [√ 5258?]

Mamre [2]

Ge 14: 13 Now Abram was living near the great trees of **Mamre** the Amorite,
14: 24 to the men who went with me—to Aner, Eshcol and **Mamre**.

4936 מַמְּרֹרִים *mammerōrîm*, n.m.[pl.]. [1] [√ 5352]

misery [1]

Job 9: 18 not let me regain my breath but would overwhelm me with **misery**.

4937 מִמְשַׁח *mimšaḥ*, n.[m.]. [1] [√ 5417]

anointed [1]

Eze 28: 14 You were **anointed** as a guardian cherub, for so I ordained you.

4938 מִמְשָׁל *mimšāl*, n.[m.]. [3] [√ 5440]

power [2], leaders [1]

1Ch 26: 6 who were **leaders** in their father's family because they were very
Da 11: 3 will appear, who will rule with great **power** and do as he pleases.
11: 5 stronger than he and will rule his own kingdom with great **power**.

4939 מֶמְשָׁלָה *memšālâ*, n.f. [17] [√ 5440]

dominion [4], govern [4], kingdom [3], ruled [2], authority [1], forces [1], rule [1], ruled [+3338] [1]

Ge 1: 16 the greater light to **govern** the day and the lesser light to govern the
1: 16 light to govern the day and the lesser light to **govern** the night.
1Ki 9: 19 in Jerusalem, in Lebanon and throughout all the territory he **ruled**.
2Ki 20: 13 his palace or in all his **kingdom** that Hezekiah did not show them.
2Ch 8: 6 in Jerusalem, in Lebanon and throughout all the territory he **ruled**.
32: 9 king of Assyria and all his **forces** were laying siege to Lachish,
Ps 103: 22 Praise the LORD, all his works everywhere in his **dominion**.
114: 2 Judah became God's sanctuary, Israel his **dominion**.
136: 8 the sun to **govern** the day, *His love endures forever.*
136: 9 the moon and stars to **govern** the night; *His love endures*
145: 13 and your **dominion** endures through all generations.
Isa 22: 21 fasten your sash around him and hand your **authority** over to him.
39: 2 his palace or in all his **kingdom** that Hezekiah did not show them.
Jer 34: 1 peoples in the empire he **ruled** [+3338] were fighting against
51: 28 and all their officials, and all the countries they **rule**.
Da 11: 5 stronger than he and will rule his own **kingdom** with great power.
Mic 4: 8 the Daughter of Zion, the former **dominion** will be restored to you;

4940 מִמְשַׁק *mimšaq*, n.[m.]. [1] [→ 5479]

place [1]

Zep 2: 9 a **place** *of* weeds and salt pits, a wasteland forever.

4941 מַמְתַקִּים *mamtaqqîm*, n.m.[pl.]. [2] [√ 5517]

sweet [1], sweetness [1]

Ne 8: 10 Nehemiah said, "Go and enjoy choice food and **sweet** drinks,
SS 5: 16 His mouth is **sweetness** *itself*; he is altogether lovely. This is my

4942 [1]מָן *mān*[1], n.m. [13] [cf. 4537]

manna [13]

Ex 16: 31 The people of Israel called the bread **manna**. It was white like
16: 33 Moses said to Aaron, "Take a jar and put an omer of **manna** in it.
16: 35 The Israelites ate **manna** forty years, until they came to a land that
16: 35 they ate **manna** until they reached the border of Canaan.
Nu 11: 6 we have lost our appetite; we never see anything but this **manna**!"
11: 7 The **manna** was like coriander seed and looked like resin.
11: 9 the dew settled on the camp at night, the **manna** also came down.
Dt 8: 3 causing you to hunger and then feeding you with **manna**,
8: 16 He gave you **manna** to eat in the desert, something your fathers
Jos 5: 12 The **manna** stopped the day after they ate this food from the land;
5: 12 there was no longer any **manna** for the Israelites, but that year they
Ne 9: 20 You did not withhold your **manna** from their mouths, and you
Ps 78: 24 he rained down **manna** for the people to eat, he gave them the

4943 [2]מָן *mān*[2], inter. [1] [√ 4537; Ar 10426]

what [1]

Ex 16: 15 When the Israelites saw it, they said to each other, "**What** is it?"

4944 [1]מֵן *mēn*[1], n.[m.]. [2]

music of strings [1], strings [1]

Ps 45: 8 [45:9] from palaces adorned with ivory the **music of** the **strings**
150: 4 and dancing, praise him with the **strings** and flute,

4945 [2]מֵן *mēn*[2], n.[m.]. [1] [√ 4948]

share [1]

Ps 68: 23 [68:24] while the tongues of your dogs have their **share**."

4946 מִן *min*, pp. [7522 / 7521] [→ 4403, 4406, 4424, 4425, 4514, 4644, 4974, 5088, 5136, 5456; Ar 10427] See Select Index

from [2541], *untranslated* [1138], of [592], than [182], out of [179], from [+6584] [155], some [123], in [116], on [98], at [94], from [+907] [93], more than [93], before [+7156] [82], because of [+7156] [54], too [54], by [50], outside [+2575] [49], from [+7156] [45], with [44], because of [43], any [40], for [39], to [37], from [+3338] [33], one [32], from [+6640] [25], before [+4200+7156] [24], among [23], since [21], on each side [+2256+4946+7024+7024] [20], above [+5087] [19], in addition to [+963+4200] [18], of [+7156] [17], because [16], below [+9393] [16], from [+7931] [16], from [+9348] [16], on every side [+6017] [16], not [15], as [14], above [+6584] [13], out of [+9348] [13], through [13], without [13], from [+339] [12], no [12], on both sides[s] [+2256+2296+2296+4946] [12], above [11], after [11], from [+4200+7156] [11], from among [11], part [11], away from [+6584] [10], away from [10], rather than [10], against [9], behind [+339] [9], besides [+963+4200] [9], of one piece with [9], on [+6584] [9], so [9], when [9], without [+401] [9], because [+7156] [8], off [+6584] [8], on either side [+2256+4946+7024+7024] [8], around [+6017] [7], better than [7], by [+7156] [7], north [+7600] [7], of [+907] [7], under [+9393] [7], whether [7], Israelite [+408+1074+3776] [6], over [6], before [5], far away [+8158] [5], from [+5584] [5], greater than [5], inside [+1074] [5], left [+2143] [5], long ago [+255] [5], off [5], toward [5], whenever [+1896] [5], above [+2025+4200+5087] [4], against [+3338+9393] [4], among [+7931] [4], at [+7156] [4], at either end[s] [+2256+2296+2296+4946] [4], behind [+1074] [4], beneath [+9393] [4], beyond [4], both [4], far from [4], later [+7891] [4], left [+907 +2143] [4], most [4], no [+401] [4], of [+6640] [4], of [+9348] [4], on each side [+2021+2021+2296+2296+4946+4946+4946+6298+6298] [4], out [+2575] [4], out of [+6584] [4], some [+3972] [4], south [+5582] [4], that [4], through [+907] [4], until [4], where [+402] [4], within [4], across [+6298] [3], after [+7891] [3], against [+6584] [3], against [+7156] [3], ancient [+6409] [3], apart from [+1187] [3], away from [+6640] [3], away [3], back [+9004] [3], behind [+1237] [3], belong to [3], besides [+1187] [3], between [+1068] [3], between [+2256+6330] [3], doing [+907] [3], east [+7710] [3], either [3], escape [+7156] [3], ever since [3], from [+1896] [3], higher than [+6584] [3], hold accountable [+1335+3338] [3], into [3], leave [+2143] [3], leave [+3718] [3], left [+7756] [3], malice aforethought [+4200+8533+8997+9453] [3], northern [+7600] [3], out [+9004] [3], over [+2025+4200+5087] [3], so that [3], the LORD's [+907+3378] [3], unaware of [+6623] [3], under [3], about [2], above [+4200+4946 +5087+6645] [2], along [2], as often as [+1896] [2], as well as [+963+4200] [2], at set times [+6330+6961+6961] [2], away [+725] [2], away [+9004] [2], away from [+339] [2], away from [+907] [2], back [+339] [2], before [+6584] [2], beside [+7396] [2], between [2], beyond [+2134+2256] [2], beyond [+6298] [2], bordering each side[s] [+2256+2296+2296+4946] [2], bottom [+4200+4752] [2], by [+6640] [2], cannot [2], caused by [2], dictated [+7023] [2], distant [+5305] [2], distant [+8158] [2], each year [+2025+3427+3427] [2], east [+6298] [2], even more than [2], ever [+6409] [2], ever since [+255] [2], excluded from [2], extend from [2], extended from [2], extending from [2], far and wide [+2085+2134 +2256] [2], far from [+5584] [2], flesh and blood [+2743+3655] [2], from [+6584+7156] [2], from [+9393] [2], from every side [+6017] [2], from out of [+9348] [2], future [+8158] [2], got off [+6584+7563] [2], had the habit [+8997 +9453] [2], head [+2025+2256+5087+8900] [2], in front of [+4578] [2], in regard to [2], instead of [2], Israelite [+408+1201+3776] [2], Israelites [+1201+3776] [2], just above [+5087] [2], leave [+907 +2143] [2], leave alone [+6073] [2], left [+995] [2], left of [2], less than [2], like [2], long ago [+4200+8158] [2], long ago [+6409] [2], long ago [+7710] [2], long ago [+8158] [2], made of [2], mine [+5761] [2], nearby [+5584] [2], never [2], no [+1172] [2], no [+3972+4202] [2], north [+8520] [2], not counting [+963+4200] [2], not including [+963 +4200] [2], nothing but [2], of [+4200+7156] [2], of one piece [2], on [+4578] [2], on both [+2256+2296+2296+4946] [2], on each side[s] [+2256+2296+2296+4946] [2], only [2], other than [+1187] [2], out from [2], out [2], outside [+2025+2575] [2], over [+5087] [2], over [+6584] [2], promised [+3655+7023] [2], pursuing [+339] [2], said [+3655+7023] [2], separated from [+6584] [2], since [+255] [2], so many [+8044] [2], so not [2], so that not [2], some [+7921] [2], some of [2], some time later [+3427] [2], south [+3545] [2], speak [+7023] [2], square [+2256+4946+7024+7024] [2], to [+6640] [2], top [+2025+4200+5087] [2], turning from [2], upon [2], where [+9004] [2], without [+1187] [2], your own flesh and blood [+3655+3870] [2], abandon [+3338+8332] [1], abandon [+3718] [1], about to [+6964 +7940] [1], above [+5087+6584] [1], according to [1], across from [+6298] [1], across the way [+5584] [1], after [+339] [1], after [+7895] [1], after [+7921] [1], after [+928+1896] [1], against [+3338] [1], ahead [+4200+7156] [1], all around [+6017] [1], all kinds [+3972] [1], all life [+6388] [1], all sorts [+7896] [1], all the way from [1], allots [1], along [+6298] [1], along with [+963+4200] [1], alongside [+6298] [1], aloof [+5584] [1], already [+255] [1], always [+6388] [1], am forgotten [+4213+8894] [1], among [+1068] [1], among [+907] [1], annual [+2025+3427+3427] [1], another[s] [+2021+2215+2296] [1], any [+6388] [1], any of [+907] [1], anything [+1821+1821+2021+3972] [1], anything [+1821+3972] [1], area [+2575] [1], around [+1237 +6017] [1], around [+2021+2575] [1], as long as live [+3427] [1], as long as [1], as much as [+8049] [1], Asher's [+888] [1], avert [+6296+6584] [1], avoid [+3782] [1], avoid [1], away [+6584] [1], away [+6640] [1], away [+907] [1], away from [+5584] [1], away from [+7156] [1], be without [+4162] [1], because [+889] [1], because of [+3954+7156] [1], because of [+5584] [1], because of [+6584] [1], because of [+9004] [1], before [+3270] [1], before [+6640] [1], before [+8997+9453] [1], before time [+4200+7156] [1], beforehand [+4200 +7156] [1], behind [+294] [1], belonging to [1], belongs to [1], below [+4200+9393] [1], Benjamite [+1228] [1], Benjamites [+1228] [1], Benjamites [+408+1228] [1], beside [+6584] [1], better [+3202] [1], beyond [+2134] [1], beyond [+2134+4200] [1], bodily [+1414] [1], born [+3655+8167] [1], branch of [+9348] [1], brief [+7940] [1], broke camp [+185+5825] [1], broke off [+8740] [1], brought about [+2118] [1], by [+4200] [1], by [+6298] [1], by [+6584] [1], by [+7023] [1], by [+907] [1], by [+9348] [1], by myself [+907+3276] [1], by not [1], call to account [+1335+3338] [1], call to account [+2011+6640] [1], cause [+2118] [1], causes [1], certain [1], choice lambs [+4119 +7366] [1], citizens[s] of [1], complete [+2118+4200+7891] [1], completely [+1414+2256+5883+6330] [1], concerning [1], confront [1], confronting [+7156] [1], consent [1], constant [+5584] [1], deaf [+9048] [1], defense against [+7156] [1], departing from [+339] [1], deprived of [1], descendant [+408+2446] [1], deserted [+1172+3782] [1], deserted [+132+401] [1], deserted [+339+6590] [1], deserted [+401+3782] [1], determined [+907] [1], dictate [+7023] [1], dictated [+906+7023+7924] [1], dictating [+7023] [1], dictation [+7023] [1], directed by [1], directly from [1], disappeared [+2143+6524] [1], do away with [+6073+9348] [1], do so[s] [+2006+8740] [1], down [+8031] [1], down [1], downstream [+2025+4200+5087] [1], driven from [1], due annually [+928+1896+9102+9102] [1], during [1], eastward [+7710] [1], eluded [+6015+7156] [1], entire [+7895] [1], enveloped [+6017] [1], Ephraimites [+713] [1], escaped from [1], even beyond [+6584] [1], ever [+3427] [1], ever since [+3427] [1], ever since [+4200] [1], every [+7891] [1], every kind [+448+2385+2385] [1], excelled [1], except [+1187] [1], except for [1], extends to [+4200] [1], face [+7156] [1], faced [1], facing [+5584] [1], facing [1], fail [+6073] [1], failed [+6980] [1], failed to keep [+6073] [1], far and wide [+4200+6330+8158] [1], far away [+4200+6330+8158] [1], far away [+5305] [1], few [1], follow [+339+7756] [1], for [+6584] [1], for [+7156] [1], for [+907] [1], for fear of [+7156] [1], for fear of [1], for lack of [1], for relief from [+4200+7156] [1], for sake [+7156] [1], former [+7710] [1], formerly [+919+8997] [1], forsaking [+907] [1], free from [1], from [+2296] [1], from [+255] [1], from [+4090] [1], from [+4200] [1], from [+4578] [1], from [+5584+6524] [1], from [+6017] [1], from [+6298] [1], from [+6524] [1], from [+6640+7156] [1], from [+7891] [1], from inside [1], from then on [+339+4027] [1], frontal [+5584] [1], gaunt [+9043] [1], give up [+4946+8740] [1], God's [+466] [1], gone from [+9348] [1], got off [+3718+6584] [1], had difficulty taking possession of [+3655] [1], had part in [+2118] [1], handed [+3338] [1], have no [+6] [1], have no [+6259+6524] [1], have nowhere [+6] [1], helpless [+3946] [1], high above [+2025+4200 +5087] [1], higher [+5087] [1], higher [+6584] [1], his [+5647] [1], his own [+963] [1], hold accountable [+2011+3338] [1], hold accountable [+906+2011+3338] [1], hold responsible [+1335+3338] [1], idea [+4213] [1], in [+6584] [1], in [+7931] [1], in [+9348] [1], in addition [+963+4200] [1], in deference to [+7156] [1], in front of [+7156] [1], in presence [1], in the course of time [+339+4027] [1], in the course of time [+3427+3427+4200] [1], including [1], inquire of [+907+2011] [1], inside [+1074+4200] [1], inside [+7163] [1], interior [+1074+2025] [1], Israelite [+1201+3776] [1], Israelite [+3776] [1], Israelites [+3776] [1], it[s] [+1947+2023] [1], its[s] [+5288] [1], jointed [+4200+5087+8079] [1], just [+6964] [1], keep from [1], kept distance [+3656+5584] [1], kept from [1], lacking [+1172] [1], larger share of [1], later [+339+4027] [1], later on [+3427] [1], later [1], leave [+2143+4200] [1], leave [+2143+6640] [1], leave [+2143+6643] [1], leave [+3718+9348] [1], leave [+6015] [1], leave [+6590] [1], leave [+7756] [1], leave [+9004] [1], leave alone [+2532] [1], leave alone [+6641] [1], leave [1], leaves [+907+2143] [1], leaving [+5825] [1], leaving [+6296] [1], left [+2143+6640] [1], left [+339] [1], left [+5825] [1], left [+6590] [1], left [+7756+9348] [1], left [+907] [1], left [1], lived [1], long [+6409] [1], long [+8158] [1], long [+919] [1], long ago [+3427+7710] [1], lost [+5877] [1], lost [+907+5877] [1], lost [1], lower [+9393] [1], made from [1], made up of [1], make room for [+7156] [1], make spew out [+906+3655+7023] [1], malice aforethought [+8533+8997+9453] [1], meet [+7156] [1], member [1], more than [+963+4200] [1], more [1], most of [1], much more than [1], near [+7396] [1], near [1], nearby [+7940] [1], neither [+401] [1], never [+3427+4202] [1], next to [+4578] [1], next to [+725] [1], next to [+7396] [1], no longer be [+6073] [1], no more [1], noblest [+1475] [1], none [+3972+4202] [1], none [+401] [1], none will be [+401] [1], nor [+401+2256] [1], northern [+2025+7600] [1], not [+1187] [1], not [+1194] [1], not harm [+5927] [1], nothing [+561+3972] [1], now [+255] [1], obscure [+6680+9048] [1], of [+1068] [1], of [+3338] [1], of [+3655] [1], of [+4200+8611] [1], of [+6584] [1], of [+7895] [1], of all [+9348] [1], off [+4578] [1], often [+1896] [1], old [+3427+7710] [1], older [+1524] [1], on [+907] [1], on behalf of [+907] [1], on both sides [+2256+2296+2296] [1], on high [+5087] [1], on high [+5294] [1], on terms [+6640] [1], on the basis of [1], on the other side of [+2134+2256+6298] [1], on this side of [+6298] [1], once [1], opposing [1], opposite [+5584] [1], or [1], other than [+963+4200] [1], others[s] [+2157] [1], out [+1068] [1], out [+7156] [1], out of [+1068] [1], out of [+5584] [1], out of [+7156] [1], out of [+7931] [1], out of [+907] [1], out of way [+4200+7156] [1], outer [+2025+4200+5087] [1], outnumber [+8045] [1], outnumber [+8049] [1], outside [+1946] [1], outside [+2134] [1], outweigh [+3877] [1], outweighs [+3701] [1], over [+4200+6584] [1], pad [+9393] [1], past [+6584] [1], past [+907] [1], peels [+6584] [1], permission [1], poured out [+9161] [1], presence [+6584] [1], prevent from [1], projecting from [1], protection from [+7156] [1], received from [1], recently [+2543+7940] [1], recovery [+2649+2716] [1], reject [+906+6584+7156+8938] [1], reject [+906+6584+7156+8959] [1], representative [+907] [1], represented [1], rest of [1], resting on [+9393] [1], rid [+906+6584 +8959] [1], risked [+906+5584+8959] [1], say [+3655+7023] [1], select a day [+3427+3427+4200] [1], send [+907+995] [1], sent by [+907] [1], set free [+906+3338+8938] [1], sharing [+430] [1], shed by [+3338] [1], side [+6298] [1], sides [+6017+6298] [1], since [+3427+4200] [1], since [+889] [1], so cannot [1], so that no [1], sober [+2021+3516 +3655] [1], some [+907] [1], some distance away [+8158] [1], some distance away [+8178] [1], some distance from [+7156] [1], southern [+5582] [1], southernmost [+7895] [1], southward [+9402] [1], spared from [+7156] [1], spoke the word [+7023] [1], started [1], starting out from [1], stop trusting in [+2532+4200] [1], stopped [+6590] [1], stopped up [+3877+9048] [1], stopped [1], such [+3972] [1], surely leave [+2143+2143+6584] [1], surpasses [1], surround [+2118+6017+6584] [1], take off [+3718+6584] [1], taken from [+4200+7156] [1], taken [1], than [+3463] [1], than [+889] [1], than deserved [1], the LORD's [+3378+6640] [1], their [+2157] [1], theirs [+2157] [1], there [+9004] [1], there is no [+401] [1], those[s] [1], throughout [+3972] [1], till no more [1], tilting away from [+7156] [1], to [+4200] [1], to [+6584] [1], to [+7156] [1], to [+9393] [1], to nothing [+8024] [1], told [+907+9048] [1], top of [+2025+4200+5087] [1], unaware [+6524+6623] [1], under [+3338] [1], under [+7156] [1], underneath [+1074] [1], underneath [+9393] [1], unduly [+3841] [1], unnoticed [+1172+8492] [1], unsheathed [+3655+9509] [1], untraveled [+408+1172+6296] [1], upward [+2025+4200+5087] [1], used [1], uttered [+3655] [1], utterly [1], was spent for making [+6913] [1], west [+6298] [1], when [+2118] [1], when [+255] [1], when [+3427] [1], whenever [+1896+3954] [1], where [+625] [1], wherever [+2021+3972+5226] [1], wherever [+889] [1], while [1], will [1], willingly [+4213] [1], with [+7396] [1], with the help of [+907] [1], withdrew [+2143] [1], without [+1172] [1], without [+2575] [1], without being aware [+6524] [1], without equal [+401+3202] [1], worked [1], worse than [1], yet [+889+1172] [1], your [+3871] [1], your [+4013] [1]

4947 מַנְגִּינָה ***mangînâ***, n.f. [1] [√ 5594]

mock in songs [1]

La 3:63 Look at them! Sitting or standing, they **mock** me **in** their **songs**.

4948 מָנָה¹ ***mānâ¹***, v. [28] [→ 3555, 4945, 4949, 4950, 4951, 4972, 4987, 9463?, 9464, 9466?, 9467?; Ar 10431]

counted [4], provided [4], assigned [3], count [3], be counted [2], number [2], take a census [2], appoint [1], appointed [1], counts [1], destine [1], determines [1], raise [1], was numbered [1], were assigned [1]

Ge 13:16 [A] so that if anyone could **count** the dust, then your offspring
13:16 [C] could count the dust, then your offspring *could* **be counted**.
Nu 23:10 [A] Who *can* **count** the dust of Jacob or number the fourth part
2Sa 24:1 [A] saying, "Go and **take a census** *of* Israel and Judah."
1Ki 3:8 [C] a great people, too numerous to count or **number**.
8:5 [C] and cattle that they could not be recorded or **counted**.
20:25 [A] You *must* also **raise** an army like the one you lost—horse for
2Ki 12:10 [12:11] [A] **counted** the money that had been brought into the
1Ch 9:29 [E] Others **were assigned** to take care of the furnishings and all
21:1 [A] up against Israel and incited David to **take a census** *of* Israel.
21:17 [A] "Was it not I who ordered the fighting men to *be* **counted**?
27:24 [A] Joab son of Zeruiah began to **count** the men but did not
2Ch 5:6 [C] and cattle that they could not be recorded or **counted**.
Job 7:3 [D] of futility, and nights of misery *have been* **assigned** to me.
Ps 61:7 [61:8] [D] **appoint** your love and faithfulness to protect him.
90:12 [A] Teach us to **number** our days aright, that we may gain a
147:4 [A] *He* **determines** the number of the stars and calls them each
Ecc 1:15 [C] cannot be straightened; what is lacking cannot **be counted**.
Isa 53:12 [C] life unto death, and **was numbered** with the transgressors.
65:12 [A] *I will* **destine** you for the sword, and you will all bend down
Jer 33:13 [A] flocks will again pass under the hand of the *one who* **counts**
Da 1:5 [D] The king **assigned** them a daily amount of food and wine
1:10 [D] of my lord the king, who *has* **assigned** your food and drink.
1:11 [D] said to the guard whom the chief official *had* **appointed** over
Jnh 1:17 [2:1] [D] the LORD **provided** a great fish to swallow Jonah,
4:6 [D] the LORD God **provided** a vine and made it grow up over
4:7 [D] at dawn the next day God **provided** a worm, which chewed
4:8 [D] When the sun rose, God **provided** a scorching east wind,

4949 מָנֶה ***māneh***, n.m. [5] [√ 4948; Ar 10428]

minas [4], mina [1]

1Ki 10:17 shields of hammered gold, with three **minas** of gold in each shield.
Ezr 2:69 drachmas of gold, 5,000 **minas** of silver and 100 priestly garments.
Ne 7:71 [7:70] work 20,000 drachmas of gold and 2,200 **minas** of silver.
7:72 [7:71] of gold, 2,000 **minas** of silver and 67 garments for priests.
Eze 45:12 plus twenty-five shekels plus fifteen shekels equal one **mina**.

4950 מָנָה² ***mānâ²***, n.f. [12] [√ 4948]

share [3], piece of meat [1], portion [1], portions of food [1], portions of meat [1], portions [1], presents of food [1], presents [1], some[s] [1], special food [1]

Ex 29:26 it before the LORD as a wave offering, and it will be your **share**.
Lev 7:33 of the fellowship offering shall have the right thigh as his **share**.
8:29 He also took the breast—Moses' **share** of the ordination ram—
1Sa 1:4 he would give **portions of the meat** to his wife Peninnah and to all
1:5 But to Hannah he gave a double **portion** because he loved her,
9:23 Samuel said to the cook, "Bring the **piece of meat** I gave you,
2Ch 31:19 men were designated by name to distribute **portions** to every male
Ne 8:10 sweet drinks, and send **some**[s] to those who have nothing prepared.
8:12 and drink, to send **portions of food** and to celebrate with great joy,
Est 2:9 he provided her with her beauty treatments and **special food**.
9:19 a day of joy and feasting, a day for giving **presents** to each other.
9:22 joy and giving **presents of food** to one another and gifts to the

4951 מֹנֶה ***mōneh***, n.[m.]. [2] [√ 4948]

times [2]

Ge 31:7 yet your father has cheated me by changing my wages ten **times**.
31:41 six years for your flocks, and you changed my wages ten **times**.

4952 מִנְהָג ***minhāg***, n.m. [2] [√ 5627]

driving [1], that[s] [1]

2Ki 9:20 The **driving** is like that of Jehu son of Nimshi—he drives like a
9:20 The driving is like **that**[s] *of* Jehu son of Nimshi—he drives like a

4953 מִנְהָרָה ***minhārâ***, n.f. [1]

shelters [1]

Jdg 6:2 the Israelites prepared **shelters** for themselves in mountain clefts,

4954 מָנוֹד ***mānôd***, n.[m.]. [1] [√ 5653]

shake [1]

Ps 44:14 [44:15] among the nations; the peoples **shake** their heads at us.

4955 מָנוֹחַ¹ ***mānôaḥ¹***, n.m. [7] [→ 4956, 4957, 4967; cf. 5663]

resting place [2], came to rest [1], home [1], place to set [1], places of rest [1], rest [1]

Ge 8:9 the dove could find no **place to set** its feet because there was water
Dt 28:65 you will find no repose, no **resting place** for the sole of your foot.
Ru 3:1 "My daughter, should I not try to find a **home** for you, where you
1Ch 6:31 [6:16] in the house of the LORD after the ark **came to rest** there.
Ps 116:7 Be at **rest** once more, O my soul, for the LORD has been good to
Isa 34:14 creatures will also repose and find for themselves **places of rest**.
La 1:3 She dwells among the nations; she finds no **resting place**.

4956 מָנוֹחַ² ***mānôaḥ²***, n.pr.m. [18] [√ 4955; cf. 5663]

Manoah [15], *untranslated* [2], he[s] [1]

Jdg 13:2 A certain man of Zorah, named **Manoah**, from the clan of the
13:8 Then **Manoah** prayed to the LORD: "O Lord, I beg you,
13:9 God heard **Manoah**, and the angel of God came again to the
13:9 was out in the field; but her husband **Manoah** was not with her.
13:11 **Manoah** got up and followed his wife. When he came to the man,
13:12 So **Manoah** asked him, "When your words are fulfilled, what is to
13:13 **[RPH]** "Your wife must do all that I have told her.
13:15 **Manoah** said to the angel of the LORD, "We would like you to
13:16 **[RPH]** "Even though you detain me, I will not eat any of your
13:16 (**Manoah** did not realize that it was the angel of the LORD.)
13:17 **Manoah** inquired of the angel of the LORD, "What is your name,
13:19 Then **Manoah** took a young goat, together with the grain offering,
13:19 the LORD did an amazing thing while **Manoah** and his wife
13:20 **Manoah** and his wife fell with their faces to the ground.
13:21 the angel of the LORD did not show himself again to **Manoah**
13:21 and his wife, **Manoah** realized that it was the angel of the LORD.
13:22 are doomed to die!" **he**[s] said to his wife. "We have seen God!"
16:31 him between Zorah and Eshtaol in the tomb of **Manoah** his father.

4957 מְנוּחָה ***m[e]nûḥâ***, n.f. [21] [√ 4955; cf. 5663]

rest [6], resting place [6], place of rest [2], easily [1], peace and rest [1], place to rest [1], places of rest [1], quiet [1], resting [1], staff [1]

Ge 49:15 When he sees how good is his **resting place** and how pleasant is
Nu 10:33 before them during those three days to find them a **place to rest**.
Dt 12:9 since you have not yet reached the **resting place** and the
Jdg 20:43 and **easily** overran them in the vicinity of Gibeah on the east.
Ru 1:9 May the LORD grant that each of you will find **rest** in the home
2Sa 14:17 servant says, 'May the word of my lord the king bring me **rest**,
1Ki 8:56 who has given **rest** to his people Israel just as he promised.
1Ch 22:9 But you will have a son who will be a man of **peace and rest**,
28:2 I had it in my heart to build a house as a **place of rest** for the ark of
Ps 23:2 me lie down in green pastures, he leads me beside **quiet** waters,
95:11 I declared on oath in my anger, "They shall never enter my **rest**."
132:8 and come to your **resting place**, you and the ark of your might.
132:14 "This is my **resting place** for ever and ever; here I will sit
Isa 11:10 the nations will rally to him, and his **place of rest** will be glorious.
28:12 to whom he said, "This is the **resting place**, let the weary rest";
32:18 dwelling places, in secure homes, in undisturbed **places of rest**.
66:1 the house you will build for me? Where will my **resting** place be?
Jer 45:3 to my pain; I am worn out with groaning and find no **rest**.' "
51:59 This is the message Jeremiah gave to the **staff** officer Seraiah son
Mic 2:10 For this is not your **resting place**, because it is defiled, it is ruined,
Zec 9:1 is against the land of Hadrach and will **rest** *upon* Damascus—

4958 מָנוֹל ***mānôl***, n.[m.]. Not used in NIV/BHS [cf. 4978]

4959 מָנוֹן ***mānôn***, n.m. [1]

grief [1]

Pr 29:21 man pampers his servant from youth, he will bring **grief** in the end.

4960 מָנוֹס ***mānôs***, n.m. [8] [→ 4961; cf. 5674]

refuge [4], escape [1], flee in haste [+5674] [1], flee [1], not escape [+6] [1]

2Sa 22:3 He is my stronghold, my **refuge** and my savior—from violent men
Job 11:20 But the eyes of the wicked will fail, and **escape** will elude them;
Ps 59:16 [59:17] for you are my fortress, my **refuge** in times of trouble.
142:4 [142:5] for me. I have no **refuge**; no one cares for my life.
Jer 16:19 my strength and my fortress, my **refuge** in time of distress,
25:35 The shepherds will have nowhere to **flee**, the leaders of the flock
46:5 *They* **flee in haste** [+5674] without looking back, and there is
Am 2:14 The swift *will* **not escape** [+6], the strong will not muster their

4961 מְנוּסָה ***m[e]nûsâ***, n.f. [2] [√ 4960; cf. 5674]

fleeing [1], flight [1]

Lev 26:36 They will run as though **fleeing** *from* the sword, and they will fall,
Isa 52:12 you will not leave in haste or go in **flight**; for the LORD will go

4962 מָנוֹר *mānôr*, n.m. [4]

rod [4]

1Sa 17: 7 His spear shaft was like a weaver's **rod**, and its iron point weighed
2Sa 21: 19 the Gittite, who had a spear with a shaft like a weaver's **rod**.
1Ch 11: 23 Although the Egyptian had a spear like a weaver's **rod** in his hand,
20: 5 the Gittite, who had a spear with a shaft like a weaver's **rod**.

4963 מְנוֹרָה *m^{e}nôrâ*, n.f. [42] [√ 5944]

lampstand [26], lampstands [5], each lampstand [+2256+4963] [4], *untranslated* [3], each lampstand [+4963] [2], it[s] [+2021] [1], lamp [1]

Ex 25: 31 "Make a **lampstand** of pure gold and hammer it out, base
25: 31 "Make a lampstand of pure gold and hammer **it**[s] [+2021] out,
25: 32 Six branches are to extend from the sides of the **lampstand**—
25: 32 the lampstand—three on one side and three **[RPH]** on the other.
25: 33 and the same for all six branches extending from the **lampstand**.
25: 34 on the **lampstand** there are to be four cups shaped like almond
25: 35 be under the first pair of branches extending from the **lampstand**,
26: 35 the tabernacle and put the **lampstand** opposite it on the south side.
30: 27 the table and all its articles, the **lampstand** and its accessories,
31: 8 and its articles, the pure gold **lampstand** and all its accessories,
35: 14 the **lampstand** that is *for* light with its accessories, lamps
37: 17 They made the **lampstand** of pure gold and hammered it out,
37: 17 of pure gold and hammered it out, **[RPH]** base and shaft;
37: 18 Six branches extended from the sides of the **lampstand**—three on
37: 18 the lampstand—three on one side and three **[RPH]** on the other.
37: 19 and the same for all six branches extending from the **lampstand**.
37: 20 on the **lampstand** were four cups shaped like almond flowers with
39: 37 the pure gold **lampstand** with its row of lamps and all its
40: 4 belongs on it. Then bring in the **lampstand** and set up its lamps.
40: 24 He placed the **lampstand** in the Tent of Meeting opposite the
Lev 24: 4 The lamps on the pure gold **lampstand** before the LORD must be
Nu 3: 31 for the care of the ark, the table, the **lampstand**, the altars,
4: 9 are to take a blue cloth and cover the **lampstand** that is *for* light,
8: 2 seven lamps, they are to light the area in front of the **lampstand**.' "
8: 3 he set up the lamps so that they faced forward on the **lampstand**,
8: 4 This is how the **lampstand** was made: It was made of hammered
8: 4 The **lampstand** was made exactly like the pattern the LORD had
1Ki 7: 49 the **lampstands** of pure gold (five on the right and five on the left,
2Ki 4: 10 and put in it a bed and a table, a chair and a **lamp** for him.
1Ch 28: 15 the weight of gold for the gold **lampstands** and their lamps,
28: 15 with the weight for **each lampstand** [+2256+4963] and its lamps;
28: 15 with the weight for **each lampstand** [+2256+4963] and its lamps;
28: 15 and the weight of silver for **each** silver **lampstand** [+4963]
28: 15 and the weight of silver for **each** silver **lampstand** [+4963]
28: 15 its lamps, according to the use of **each lampstand** [+2256+4963];
28: 15 its lamps, according to the use of **each lampstand** [+2256+4963];
2Ch 4: 7 He made ten gold **lampstands** according to the specifications for
4: 20 the **lampstands** of pure gold with their lamps, to burn in front of
13: 11 and light the lamps on the gold **lampstand** every evening.
Jer 52: 19 pots, **lampstands**, dishes and bowls used for drink offerings—
Zec 4: 2 "I see a solid gold **lampstand** with a bowl at the top and seven
4: 11 these two olive trees on the right and the left of the **lampstand**?"

4964 מִנְּזָר *minn^{e}zār*, n.[m.]pl. [1] [cf. 5692]

guards [1]

Na 3: 17 Your **guards** are like locusts, your officials like swarms of locusts

4965 מֻנָּח *munnāḥ*, n.m. *or* v.ptcp. [3] [√ 5663]

open area [3]

Eze 41: 9 cubits thick. The **open area** between the side rooms of the temple
41: 11 There were entrances to the side rooms from the **open area**,
41: 11 the base adjoining the **open area** was five cubits wide all around.

4966 מִנְחָה *minḥâ*, n.f. [211] [→ Ar 10432]

grain offering [92], grain offerings [42], offering [18], tribute [13], gift [11], offerings [9], gifts [8], sacrifice [5], *untranslated* [3], grain [2], it[s] [+2021] [2], offering of grain [2], sacrifices [2], evening sacrifice [+6590] [1], sacrifice [+6590] [1]

Ge 4: 3 brought some of the fruits of the soil as an **offering** to the LORD.
4: 4 his flock. The LORD looked with favor on Abel and his **offering**,
4: 5 on Cain and his **offering** he did not look with favor. So Cain was
32: 13 [32:14] from what he had with him he selected a **gift** for his
32: 18 [32:19] They are a **gift** sent to my lord Esau, and he is coming
32: 20 [32:21] "I will pacify him with these **gifts** I am sending on ahead;
32: 21 [32:22] So Jacob's **gifts** went on ahead of him, but he himself
33: 10 "If I have found favor in your eyes, accept this **gift** from me.
43: 11 of the land in your bags and take them down to the man as a **gift**—
43: 15 So the men took the **gifts** and double the amount of silver,
43: 25 They prepared their **gifts** for Joseph's arrival at noon, because they
43: 26 they presented to him the **gifts** they had brought into the house,
Ex 29: 41 Sacrifice the other lamb at twilight with the same **grain offering**
30: 9 this altar any other incense or any burnt offering or **grain offering**,
40: 29 of Meeting, and offered on it burnt offerings and **grain offerings**,
Lev 2: 1 " 'When someone brings a **grain offering** to the LORD,
2: 3 The rest of the **grain offering** belongs to Aaron and his sons;
2: 4 " 'If you bring a **grain offering** baked in an oven, it is to consist of
2: 5 If your **grain offering** is prepared on a griddle, it is to be made of
2: 6 Crumble it and pour oil on it; it is a **grain offering**.
2: 7 If your **grain offering** is cooked in a pan, it is to be made of fine
2: 8 Bring the **grain offering** made of these things to the LORD;
2: 9 He shall take out the memorial portion from the **grain offering**
2: 10 The rest of the **grain offering** belongs to Aaron and his sons;
2: 11 " 'Every **grain offering** you bring to the LORD must be made
2: 13 Season all your **grain offerings** with salt. Do not leave the salt of
2: 13 the salt of the covenant of your God out of your **grain offerings**;
2: 14 " 'If you bring a **grain offering** *of* firstfruits to the LORD,
2: 14 offer crushed heads of new grain roasted in the fire. **[RPH]**
2: 15 Put oil and incense on it; it is a **grain offering**.
5: 13 will belong to the priest, as in the case of the **grain offering**.' "
6: 14 [6:7] " 'These are the regulations for the **grain offering**:
6: 15 [6:8] The priest is to take a handful of fine flour **[RPH]** and oil,
6: 15 [6:8] and oil, together with all the incense on the **grain offering**,
6: 20 [6:13] tenth of an ephah of fine flour as a regular **grain offering**,
6: 21 [6:14] present the **grain offering** broken in pieces as an aroma
6: 23 [6:16] Every **grain offering** *of* a priest shall be burned
7: 9 Every **grain offering** baked in an oven or cooked in a pan
7: 10 every **grain offering**, whether mixed with oil or dry,
7: 37 the **grain offering**, the sin offering, the guilt offering, the
9: 4 before the LORD, together with a **grain offering** mixed with oil.
9: 17 He also brought the **grain offering**, took a handful of it and burned
10: 12 "Take the **grain offering** left over from the offerings made to the
14: 10 of an ephah of fine flour mixed with oil for a **grain offering**,
14: 20 offer it on the altar, together with the **grain offering**, and make
14: 21 tenth of an ephah of fine flour mixed with oil for a **grain offering**,
14: 31 and the other as a burnt offering, together with the **grain offering**.
23: 13 together with its **grain offering** *of* two-tenths of an ephah of fine
23: 16 and then present an **offering of** new **grain** to the LORD.
23: 18 together with their **grain offerings** and drink offerings—
23: 37 the burnt offerings and **grain offerings**, sacrifices and drink
Nu 4: 16 fragrant incense, the regular **grain offering** and the anointing oil.
5: 15 or put incense on it, because it is a **grain offering** *for* jealousy,
5: 15 for jealousy, a reminder **offering** to draw attention to guilt.
5: 18 shall loosen her hair and place in her hands the reminder **offering**,
5: 18 in her hands the reminder offering, the **grain offering** *for* jealousy,
5: 25 The priest is to take from her hands the **grain offering** *for*
5: 25 wave **it**[s] [+2021] before the LORD and bring it to the altar.
5: 26 then to take a handful of the **grain offering** as a memorial offering
6: 15 together with their **grain offerings** and drink offerings, and a
6: 17 to the LORD, together with its **grain offering** and drink offering.
7: 13 each filled with fine flour mixed with oil as a **grain offering**;
7: 19 each filled with fine flour mixed with oil as a **grain offering**;
7: 25 each filled with fine flour mixed with oil as a **grain offering**;
7: 31 each filled with fine flour mixed with oil as a **grain offering**;
7: 37 each filled with fine flour mixed with oil as a **grain offering**;
7: 43 each filled with fine flour mixed with oil as a **grain offering**;
7: 49 each filled with fine flour mixed with oil as a **grain offering**;
7: 55 each filled with fine flour mixed with oil as a **grain offering**;
7: 61 each filled with fine flour mixed with oil as a **grain offering**;
7: 67 each filled with fine flour mixed with oil as a **grain offering**;
7: 73 each filled with fine flour mixed with oil as a **grain offering**;
7: 79 each filled with fine flour mixed with oil as a **grain offering**;
7: 87 twelve male lambs a year old, together with their **grain offering**.
8: 8 Have them take a young bull with its **grain offering** *of* fine flour
15: 4 **grain offering** *of* a tenth of an ephah of fine flour mixed with a
15: 6 " 'With a ram prepare a **grain offering** *of* two-tenths of an ephah
15: 9 bring with the bull a **grain offering** *of* three-tenths of an ephah of
15: 24 along with its prescribed **grain offering** and drink offering,
16: 15 very angry and said to the LORD, "Do not accept their **offering**.
18: 9 whether **grain** or sin or guilt offerings, that part belongs to you
28: 5 together with a **grain offering** of a tenth of an ephah of fine flour
28: 8 along with the same kind of **grain offering** and drink offering that
28: 9 a **grain offering** of two-tenths of an ephah of fine flour mixed with
28: 12 With each bull there is to be a **grain offering** of three-tenths of an
28: 12 a **grain offering** of two-tenths of an ephah of fine flour mixed with
28: 13 a **grain offering** of a tenth of an ephah of fine flour mixed with oil.
28: 20 With each bull prepare a **grain offering** of three-tenths of an ephah
28: 26 when you present to the LORD an **offering of** new **grain** during
28: 28 With each bull there is to be a **grain offering** of three-tenths of an
28: 31 in addition to the regular burnt offering and its **grain offering**.
29: 3 With the bull prepare a **grain offering** of three-tenths of an ephah
29: 6 daily burnt offerings with their **grain offerings** and drink offerings
29: 6 with their grain offerings **[RPH]** and drink offerings as specified.
29: 9 With the bull prepare a **grain offering** of three-tenths of an ephah
29: 11 and the regular burnt offering with its **grain offering**,

Nu 29:14 With each of the thirteen bulls prepare a **grain offering** of
29:16 in addition to the regular burnt offering with its **grain offering**
29:18 prepare their **grain offerings** and drink offerings according to the
29:19 in addition to the regular burnt offering with its **grain offering**,
29:21 prepare their **grain offerings** and drink offerings according to the
29:22 in addition to the regular burnt offering with its **grain offering**
29:24 prepare their **grain offerings** and drink offerings according to the
29:25 in addition to the regular burnt offering with its **grain offering**
29:27 prepare their **grain offerings** and drink offerings according to the
29:28 in addition to the regular burnt offering with its **grain offering**
29:30 prepare their **grain offerings** and drink offerings according to the
29:31 in addition to the regular burnt offering with its **grain offering**
29:33 prepare their **grain offerings** and drink offerings according to the
29:34 in addition to the regular burnt offering with its **grain offering**
29:37 prepare their **grain offerings** and drink offerings according to the
29:38 in addition to the regular burnt offering with its **grain offering**
29:39 **grain offerings**, drink offerings and fellowship offerings.' "
Jos 22:23 from the LORD and to offer burnt offerings and **grain offerings**,
22:29 building an altar for burnt offerings, **grain offerings** and sacrifices,
Jdg 3:15 The Israelites sent him with **tribute** to Eglon king of Moab.
3:17 He presented the **tribute** to Eglon king of Moab, who was a very
3:18 After Ehud had presented the **tribute**, he sent on their way the men
3:18 he sent on their way the men who had carried **it** [+2021].
6:18 until I come back and bring my **offering** and set it before you."
13:19 Then Manoah took a young goat, together with the **grain offering**,
13:23 have accepted a burnt offering and **grain offering** from our hands,
1Sa 2:17 for they were treating the LORD's **offering** with contempt.
2:29 scorn my sacrifice and **offering** that I prescribed *for* my dwelling?
2:29 on the choice parts of every **offering** *made* by my people Israel?'
3:14 of Eli's house will never be atoned for by sacrifice or **offering**.' "
10:27 They despised him and brought him no **gifts**. But Saul kept silent.
26:19 has incited you against me, then may he accept an **offering**.
2Sa 8:2 So the Moabites became subject to David and brought **tribute**.
8:6 and the Arameans became subject to him and brought **tribute**.
1Ki 4:21 [5:1] These countries brought **tribute** and were Solomon's
8:64 **grain offerings** and the fat of the fellowship offerings,
8:64 the **grain offerings** and the fat of the fellowship offerings.
10:25 Year after year, everyone who came brought a **gift**—articles of
18:29 prophesying until the time for the **evening sacrifice** [+6590].
18:36 At the time of **sacrifice** [+6590], the prophet Elijah stepped
2Ki 3:20 about the time for offering the **sacrifice**, there it was—
8:8 to Hazael, "Take a **gift** with you and go to meet the man of God.
8:9 taking with him as a **gift** forty camel-loads of all the finest wares of
16:13 He offered up his burnt offering and **grain offering**, poured out his
16:15 offer the morning burnt offering and the evening **grain offering**,
16:15 grain offering, the king's burnt offering and his **grain offering**,
16:15 of the land, and their **grain offering** and their drink offering.
17:3 who had been Shalmaneser's vassal and had paid him **tribute**.
17:4 he no longer paid **tribute** to the king of Assyria, as he had done
20:12 son of Baladan king of Babylon sent Hezekiah letters and a **gift**,
1Ch 16:29 Bring an **offering** and come before him; worship the LORD in the
18:2 the Moabites, and they became subject to him and brought **tribute**.
18:6 and the Arameans became subject to him and brought **tribute**.
21:23 sledges for the wood, and the wheat for the **grain offering**.
23:29 the flour for the **grain offerings**, the unleavened wafers, the baking
2Ch 7:7 hold the burnt offerings, the **grain offerings** and the fat portions.
9:24 Year after year, everyone who came brought a **gift**—articles of
17:5 all Judah brought **gifts** to Jehoshaphat, so that he had great wealth
17:11 Some Philistines brought Jehoshaphat **gifts** and silver as tribute,
26:8 The Ammonites brought **tribute** to Uzziah, and his fame spread as
32:23 Many brought **offerings** to Jerusalem for the LORD and valuable
Ezr 9:4 of the exiles. And I sat there appalled until the evening **sacrifice**.
9:5 Then, at the evening **sacrifice**, I rose from my self-abasement,
Ne 10:33 [10:34] for the regular **grain offerings** and burnt offerings;
13:5 him with a large room formerly used to store the **grain offerings**
13:9 of the house of God, with the **grain offerings** and the incense.
Ps 20:3 [20:4] May he remember all your **sacrifices** and accept your burnt
40:6 [40:7] Sacrifice and **offering** you did not desire, but my ears you
45:12 [45:13] The Daughter of Tyre will come with a **gift**, men of
72:10 kings of Tarshish and of distant shores will bring **tribute** to him;
96:8 the glory due his name; bring an **offering** and come into his courts.
141:2 may the lifting up of my hands be like the evening **sacrifice**.
Isa 1:13 Stop bringing meaningless **offerings**! Your incense is detestable to
19:21 They will worship with sacrifices and **grain offerings**; they will
39:1 son of Baladan king of Babylon sent Hezekiah letters and a **gift**,
43:23 I have not burdened you with **grain offerings** nor wearied you
57:6 you have poured out drink offerings and offered **grain offerings**.
66:3 whoever makes a **grain** offering is like one who presents pig's
66:20 to my holy mountain in Jerusalem as an **offering** to the LORD—
66:20 "They will bring them, as the Israelites bring their **grain offerings**,
Jer 14:12 though they offer burnt offerings and **grain offerings**, I will not
17:26 **grain offerings**, incense and thank offerings to the house of the
33:18 to burn **grain offerings** and to present sacrifices.' "
41:5 bringing **grain offerings** and incense with them to the house of the
Eze 42:13 the **grain offerings**, the sin offerings and the guilt offerings—
44:29 They will eat the **grain offerings**, the sin offerings and the guilt
45:15 These will be used for the **grain offerings**, burnt offerings
45:17 **grain offerings** and drink offerings at the festivals, the New
45:17 **grain offerings**, burnt offerings and fellowship offerings to make
45:24 He is to provide as a **grain offering** an ephah for each bull
45:25 provision for sin offerings, burnt offerings, **grain offerings** and oil.
46:5 The **grain offering** given with the ram is to be an ephah,
46:5 the **grain offering** with the lambs is to be as much as he pleases,
46:7 He is to provide as a **grain offering** one ephah with the bull,
46:11 the **grain offering** is to be an ephah with a bull, an ephah with a
46:14 are also to provide with it morning by morning a **grain offering**,
46:14 The presenting of this **grain offering** to the LORD is a lasting
46:15 So the lamb and the **grain offering** and the oil shall be provided
46:20 the guilt offering and the sin offering and bake the **grain offering**,
Da 9:21 came to me in swift flight about the time of the evening **sacrifice**.
9:27 middle of the 'seven' he will put an end to sacrifice and **offering**.
Hos 10:6 It will be carried to Assyria as **tribute** for the great king.
Joel 1:9 **Grain offerings** and drink offerings are cut off from the house of
1:13 for the **grain offerings** and drink offerings are withheld from the
2:14 **grain offerings** and drink offerings for the LORD your God.
Am 5:22 Even though you bring me burnt offerings and **grain offerings**,
5:25 you bring me sacrifices and **offerings** forty years in the desert,
Zep 3:10 Cush my worshipers, my scattered people, will bring me **offerings**.
Mal 1:10 LORD Almighty, "and I will accept no **offering** from your hands.
1:11 place incense and pure **offerings** will be brought to my name,
1:13 crippled or diseased animals and offer them as **sacrifices**,
2:12 even though he brings **offerings** to the LORD Almighty.
2:13 and wail because he no longer pays attention to your **offerings**
3:3 the LORD will have men who will bring **offerings** in
3:4 the **offerings** *of* Judah and Jerusalem will be acceptable to the

4967 מְנֻחוֹת **mᵉnuḥôt**, var. [1 / 0] [√ 4955]

1Ch 2:52 Haroeh, half the Manahathites, [BHS ***Manuhoth***; NIV 4971]

4968 מְנַחֵם **mᵉnaḥēm**, n.pr.m. [8] [√ 5714]

Menahem [7], Menahem's [1]

2Ki 15:14 Then **Menahem** son of Gadi went from Tirzah up to Samaria.
15:16 At that time **Menahem**, starting out from Tirzah, attacked Tiphsah
15:17 **Menahem** son of Gadi became king of Israel, and he reigned in
15:19 **Menahem** gave him a thousand talents of silver to gain his support
15:20 **Menahem** exacted this money from Israel. Every wealthy man had
15:21 As for the other events of **Menahem's** reign, and all he did,
15:22 **Menahem** rested with his fathers. And Pekahiah his son succeeded
15:23 Pekahiah son of **Menahem** became king of Israel in Samaria,

4969 מָנַחַת[1] **mānaḥat[1]**, n.pr.m. [2] [√ 5663]

Manahath [2]

Ge 36:23 The sons of Shobal: Alvan, **Manahath**, Ebal, Shepho and Onam.
1Ch 1:40 The sons of Shobal: Alvan, **Manahath**, Ebal, Shepho and Onam.

4970 מָנַחַת[2] **mānaḥat[2]**, n.pr.loc. [1] [→ 4971; cf. 5663]

Manahath [1]

1Ch 8:6 families of those living in Geba and were deported to **Manahath**:

4971 מָנַחְתִּי **mānaḥtî**, a.g. [1 / 2] [√ 4970; cf. 5663]

Manahathites [2]

1Ch 2:52 Kiriath Jearim were: Haroeh, half the **Manahathites**, [BHS 4967]
2:54 Atroth Beth Joab, half the **Manahathites**, the Zorites,

4972 מְנִי **mᵉnî**, n.pr. [1] [√ 4948]

Destiny [1]

Isa 65:11 a table for Fortune and fill bowls of mixed wine for **Destiny**,

4973 מִנִּי[1] **minnî[1]**, n.pr.loc. [1]

Minni [1]

Jer 51:27 Ararat, **Minni** and Ashkenaz. Appoint a commander against her;

4974 מִנִּי[2] **minnî[2]**, pp. [34] [√ 4946]

from [12], *untranslated* [5], than [3], with [3], by [2], from [+4200] [2], out of [2], since [2], before [1], ever since [1], of [1]

Jdg 5:14 Some came **from** Ephraim, whose roots were in Amalek;
5:14 **From** Makir captains came down, from Zebulun those who bear a
Job 6:16 when darkened **by** thawing ice and swollen with melting snow,
7:6 "My days are swifter **than** a weaver's shuttle, and they come to an
9:3 with him, he could not answer him one time **out of** a thousand.
9:25 "My days are swifter **than** a runner; they fly away without a
11:9 Their measure is longer than the earth and wider **than** the sea.

Job 12:22 He reveals the deep things **of** darkness and brings deep shadows
14:11 As water disappears **from** the sea or a riverbed becomes parched
15:22 He despairs of escaping **[OBJ]** the darkness; he is marked for the
15:30 He will not escape **[OBJ]** the darkness; a flame will wither his
16:16 My face is red **with** weeping, deep shadows ring my eyes;
18:17 The memory of him perishes **from** the earth; he has no name in the
20: 4 "Surely you know how it has been **from** of old, ever since man
20: 4 it has been from of old, **ever since** man was placed on the earth,
28: 4 people dwell he cuts a shaft, in places forgotten **by** the foot of man;
30:30 My skin grows black and peels; my body burns **with** fever.
31: 7 if my steps have turned **from** the path, if my heart has been led by
33:18 to preserve his soul **from** the pit, his life from perishing by the
33:23 one **out of** a thousand, to tell a man what is right for him,
33:30 to turn back his soul **from** the pit, that the light of life may shine
Ps 44:10 [44:11] You made us retreat **before** the enemy, and our
44:18 [44:19] not turned back; our feet had not strayed **from** your path.
68:31 [68:32] Envoys will come **from** Egypt; Cush will submit herself
74:22 your cause; remember how fools mock you **[NIE]** all day long.
78: 2 mouth in parables, I will utter hidden things, things **from** of old—
78:42 his power—the day he redeemed them **from** the oppressor,
88: 9 [88:10] my eyes are dim **with** grief. I call to you, O LORD,
Isa 30:11 Leave **[OBJ]** this way, get off this path, and stop confronting us
30:11 Leave this way, get off **[OBJ]** this path, and stop confronting us
46: 3 you whom I have upheld **since** you were conceived, and have
46: 3 since you were conceived, and have carried **since** your birth.
Mic 7:12 In that day people will come to you **from** [+4200] Assyria
7:12 even **from** [+4200] Egypt to the Euphrates and from sea to sea

4975 מִנְיָמִין ***minyāmîn***, n.pr.m. [3] [→ 4785]

Miniamin [2], Miniamin's [1]

2Ch 31:15 Eden, **Miniamin**, Jeshua, Shemaiah, Amariah and Shecaniah
Ne 12:17 of Abijah's, Zicri; of **Miniamin's** and of Moadiah's, Piltai;
12:41 **Miniamin**, Micaiah, Elioenai, Zechariah and Hananiah with their

4976 מִנִּית ***minnît[1]***, n.pr.loc. [2]

Minnith [2]

Jdg 11:33 He devastated twenty towns from Aroer to the vicinity of **Minnith**,
Eze 27:17 they exchanged wheat from **Minnith** and confections, honey,

4977 מִנִּית ***minnît[2]***, n.pr.loc. Not used in NIV/BHS

4978 מִנְלֶה ***minleh***, n.[m.]. [1] [cf. 4958]

possessions [1]

Job 15:29 will not endure, nor will his **possessions** spread over the land.

4979 מָנַע ***mānaʿ***, v. [29] [→ 3557]

kept [4], withheld [4], withhold [4], keep [2], keeps [2], refuse [2], are denied [1], been withheld [1], denied [1], deprived [1], do not run [1], held back [1], hoards [1], keep back [1], not set [1], refused [1], restrain [1]

Ge 30: 2 [A] the place of God, who *has* **kept** you from having children?"
Nu 22:16 [C] *Do* not *let anything* **keep** *you* from coming to me,
24:11 [A] but the LORD *has* **kept** you from being rewarded."
1Sa 25:26 [A] "Now since the LORD *has* **kept** you, my master,
25:34 [A] the God of Israel, lives, who *has* **kept** me from harming you,
2Sa 13:13 [A] to the king; *he will* not **keep** me from being married to you."
1Ki 20: 7 [A] my children, my silver and my gold, *I did* not **refuse** him."
Ne 9:20 [A] *You did* not **withhold** your manna from their mouths,
Job 20:13 [A] though he cannot bear to let it go and **keeps** it in his mouth,
22: 7 [A] water to the weary and *you* **withheld** food from the hungry,
31:16 [A] "If *I have* **denied** the desires of the poor or let the eyes of the
38:15 [C] The wicked **are denied** their light, and their upraised arm is
Ps 21: 2 [21:3] [A] and *have* not **withheld** the request of his lips.
84:11 [84:12] [A] no good thing *does he* **withhold** from those whose
Pr 1:15 [A] do not go along with them, *do* **not set** foot on their paths;
3:27 [A] *Do* not **withhold** good from those who deserve it, when it is
11:26 [A] People curse the *man who* **hoards** grain, but blessing crowns
23:13 [A] *Do* not **withhold** discipline from a child; if you punish him
30: 7 [A] I ask of you, O LORD; *do* not **refuse** me before I die:
Ecc 2:10 [A] nothing my eyes desired; *I* **refused** my heart no pleasure.
Jer 2:25 [A] **Do not run** until your feet are bare and your throat is dry.
3: 3 [C] Therefore the showers *have* **been withheld**, and no spring
5:25 [A] have kept these away; your sins *have* **deprived** you of good.
31:16 [A] "**Restrain** your voice from weeping and your eyes from
42: 4 [A] the LORD says and *will* **keep** nothing **back** from you."
48:10 [A] A curse on *him who* **keeps** his sword from bloodshed!
Eze 31:15 [A] *I* **held back** its streams, and its abundant waters were
Joel 1:13 [C] drink offerings *are* **withheld** from the house of your God.
Am 4: 7 [A] "I also **withheld** rain from you when the harvest was still

4980 מַנְעוּל ***manʿûl***, n.[m.]. [6] [√ 5835]

bolts [5], lock [1]

Ne 3: 3 They laid its beams and put its doors and **bolts** and bars in place.
3: 6 They laid its beams and put its doors and **bolts** and bars in place.
3:13 They rebuilt it and put its doors and **bolts** and bars in place.
3:14 He rebuilt it and put its doors and **bolts** and bars in place.
3:15 roofing it over and putting its doors and **bolts** and bars in place.
SS 5: 5 my fingers with flowing myrrh, on the handles of the **lock**.

4981 מִנְעָל ***minʿāl***, n.m. [1] [√ 5835]

bolts of gates [1]

Dt 33:25 The **bolts of** your **gates** will be iron and bronze, and your strength

4982 מַנְעַמִּים ***manʿammîm***, n.[m.]pl. [1] [√ 5838]

delicacies [1]

Ps 141: 4 with men who are evildoers; let me not eat of their **delicacies**.

4983 מְנַעַנְעִים ***m^{e}naʿanʿîm***, n.[m.pl.]. [1] [√ 5675]

sistrums [1]

2Sa 6: 5 and with harps, lyres, tambourines, **sistrums** and cymbals.

4984 מְנַקִּית ***m^{e}naqqît***, n.f. [4] [√ 5927]

bowls [3], bowls used for drink offerings [1]

Ex 25:29 as well as its pitchers and **bowls** for the pouring out of offerings.
37:16 its plates and dishes and **bowls** and its pitchers for the pouring out
Nu 4: 7 are to spread a blue cloth and put on it the plates, dishes and **bowls**,
Jer 52:19 lampstands, dishes and **bowls used for drink offerings**—

4985 מְנַשֶּׁה ***m^{e}naššeh***, n.pr.m. [146 / 145] [→ 4986; cf. 5960]

Manasseh [130], Manasseh's [6], Manasseh [+1201] [5], Manassites [+1201] [2], *untranslated* [1], tribe of Manasseh [1]

Ge 41:51 Joseph named his firstborn **Manasseh** and said, "It is because God
46:20 **Manasseh** and Ephraim were born to Joseph by Asenath daughter
48: 1 So he took his two sons **Manasseh** and Ephraim along with him.
48: 5 Ephraim and **Manasseh** will be mine, just as Reuben and Simeon
48:13 left hand and **Manasseh** on his left toward Israel's right hand,
48:14 and crossing his arms, he put his left hand on **Manasseh's** head,
48:14 on Manasseh's head, even though **Manasseh** was the firstborn.
48:17 father's hand to move it from Ephraim's head to **Manasseh's** head.
48:20 and **Manasseh**.' " So he put Ephraim ahead of Manasseh.
48:20 and Manasseh.' " So he put Ephraim ahead of **Manasseh**.
50:23 Also the children of Makir son of **Manasseh** were placed at birth
Nu 1:10 son of Ammihud; from **Manasseh**, Gamaliel son of Pedahzur;
1:34 From the descendants of **Manasseh**: All the men twenty years old
1:35 The number from the tribe of **Manasseh** was 32,200.
2:20 The tribe of **Manasseh** will be next to them. The leader of the
2:20 The leader of the people of **Manasseh** is Gamaliel son of
7:54 the leader of the people of **Manasseh**, brought his offering.
10:23 Pedahzur was over the division of the tribe of **Manasseh** [+1201],
13:11 from the tribe of **Manasseh** (a tribe of Joseph), Gaddi son of Susi;
26:28 The descendants of Joseph by their clans through **Manasseh**
26:29 The descendants of **Manasseh**: through Makir, the Makirite clan
26:34 These were the clans of **Manasseh**; those numbered were 52,700.
27: 1 the son of Gilead, the son of Makir, the son of **Manasseh**,
27: 1 of Manasseh, belonged to the clans of **Manasseh** son of Joseph.
32:33 the half-tribe of **Manasseh** son of Joseph the kingdom of Sihon
32:39 The descendants of Makir son of **Manasseh** went to Gilead,
32:40 the Makirites, the descendants of **Manasseh**, and they settled there.
32:41 Jair, a descendant of **Manasseh**, captured their settlements
34:14 and the half-tribe of **Manasseh** have received their inheritance.
34:23 the leader from the tribe of **Manasseh** [+1201] son of Joseph;
36: 1 heads of the clan of Gilead son of Makir, the son of **Manasseh**,
36:12 They married within the clans of the descendants of **Manasseh** son
Dt 3:13 the kingdom of Og, I gave to the half tribe of **Manasseh**.
3:14 Jair, a descendant of **Manasseh**, took the whole region of Argob as
33:17 ten thousands of Ephraim; such are the thousands of **Manasseh**."
34: 2 all of Naphtali, the territory of Ephraim and **Manasseh**, all the land
Jos 1:12 the Gadites and the half-tribe of **Manasseh**, Joshua said,
4:12 Gad and the half-tribe of **Manasseh** crossed over, armed,
12: 6 the Gadites and the half-tribe of **Manasseh** to be their possession.
13: 7 among the nine tribes and half of the tribe of **Manasseh**."
13:29 This is what Moses had given to the half-tribe of **Manasseh**,
13:29 that is, to half the family of the descendants of **Manasseh**,
13:31 This was for the descendants of Makir son of **Manasseh**—
14: 4 sons of Joseph had become two tribes—**Manasseh** and Ephraim.
16: 4 So **Manasseh** and Ephraim, the descendants of Joseph,
16: 9 the Ephraimites within the inheritance of the **Manassites** [+1201].
17: 1 This was the allotment for the tribe of **Manasseh** as Joseph's
17: 1 as Joseph's firstborn, that is, for Makir, **Manasseh's** firstborn.

Jos 17: 2 So this allotment was for the rest of the people of **Manasseh**—
17: 2 These are the other male descendants of **Manasseh** son of Joseph
17: 3 of Makir, the son of **Manasseh**, had no sons but only daughters,
17: 5 **Manasseh's** share consisted of ten tracts of land besides Gilead
17: 6 because the daughters of the **tribe of Manasseh** received an
17: 6 of Gilead belonged to the rest of the descendants of **Manasseh**.
17: 7 The territory of **Manasseh** extended from Asher to Micmethath
17: 8 (**Manasseh** had the land of Tappuah, but Tappuah itself,
17: 8 Tappuah itself, on the boundary of **Manasseh**, belonged to the
17: 9 towns belonging to Ephraim lying among the towns of **Manasseh**,
17: 9 but the boundary of **Manasseh** was the northern side of the ravine
17: 10 the south the land belonged to Ephraim, on the north to **Manasseh**.
17: 11 **Manasseh** also had Beth Shan, Ibleam and the people of Dor,
17: 12 Yet the **Manassites** [+1201] were not able to occupy these towns,
17: 17 to Ephraim and **Manasseh**—"You are numerous and very
18: 7 the half-tribe of **Manasseh** have already received their inheritance
20: 8 in the tribe of Gad, and Golan in Bashan in the tribe of **Manasseh**.
21: 5 the clans of the tribes of Ephraim, Dan and half of **Manasseh**.
21: 6 Asher, Naphtali and the half-tribe of **Manasseh** in Bashan.
21: 25 From half the tribe of **Manasseh** they received Taanach and Gath
21: 27 from the half-tribe of **Manasseh**, Golan in Bashan (a city of refuge
22: 1 the Reubenites, the Gadites and the half-tribe of **Manasseh**
22: 7 (To the half-tribe of **Manasseh** Moses had given land in Bashan,
22: 9 the half-tribe of **Manasseh** left the Israelites at Shiloh in Canaan to
22: 10 the half-tribe of **Manasseh** built an imposing altar there by the
22: 11 of Canaan at Geliloth **[RPH]** near the Jordan on the Israelite side,
22: 13 land of Gilead—to Reuben, Gad and the half-tribe of **Manasseh**.
22: 15 to Reuben, Gad and the half-tribe of **Manasseh**—they said to
22: 21 the half-tribe of **Manasseh** replied to the heads of the clans of
22: 30 Gad and **Manasseh** [+1201] had to say, they were pleased.
22: 31 of Eleazar, the priest, said to Reuben, Gad and **Manasseh** [+1201],
Jdg 1: 27 **Manasseh** did not drive out the people of Beth Shan or Taanach
6: 15 My clan is the weakest in **Manasseh**, and I am the least in my
6: 35 He sent messengers throughout **Manasseh**, calling them to arms,
7: 23 Israelites from Naphtali, Asher and all **Manasseh** were called out,
11: 29 He crossed Gilead and **Manasseh**, passed through Mizpah of
12: 4 "You Gileadites are renegades from Ephraim and **Manasseh**."
18: 30 son of Gershom, the son of Moses, [BHS ***Manasseh***; NIV 5407]
1Ki 4: 13 in Ramoth Gilead (the settlements of Jair son of **Manasseh** in
2Ki 20: 21 with his fathers. And **Manasseh** his son succeeded him as king.
21: 1 **Manasseh** was twelve years old when he became king, and he
21: 9 **Manasseh** led them astray, so that they did more evil than the
21: 11 "**Manasseh** king of Judah has committed these detestable sins.
21: 16 **Manasseh** also shed so much innocent blood that he filled
21: 17 As for the other events of **Manasseh's** reign, and all he did,
21: 18 **Manasseh** rested with his fathers and was buried in his palace
21: 20 evil in the eyes of the LORD, as his father **Manasseh** had done.
23: 12 the altars **Manasseh** had built in the two courts of the temple of the
23: 26 because of all that **Manasseh** had done to provoke him to anger.
24: 3 his presence because of the sins of **Manasseh** and all he had done,
1Ch 3: 13 Ahaz his son, Hezekiah his son, **Manasseh** his son,
5: 18 the half-tribe of **Manasseh** had 44,760 men ready for military
5: 23 The people of the half-tribe of **Manasseh** were numerous;
5: 26 the Gadites and the half-tribe of **Manasseh** into exile.
6: 61 [6:46] ten towns from the clans of half the tribe of **Manasseh**.
6: 62 [6:47] from the part of the tribe of **Manasseh** that is in Bashan.
6: 70 [6:55] from half the tribe of **Manasseh** the Israelites gave Aner
6: 71 [6:56] From the clan of the half-tribe of **Manasseh** they received
7: 14 The descendants of **Manasseh**: Asriel was his descendant through
7: 17 These were the sons of Gilead son of Makir, the son of **Manasseh**.
7: 29 Along the borders of **Manasseh** [+1201] were Beth Shan,
9: 3 and from Ephraim and **Manasseh** who lived in Jerusalem were:
12: 19 [12:20] Some of the men of **Manasseh** defected to David when he
12: 20 [12:21] these were the men of **Manasseh** who defected to him:
12: 20 [12:21] and Zillethai, leaders of units of a thousand in **Manasseh**.
12: 31 [12:32] men of half the tribe of **Manasseh**, designated by name to
12: 37 [12:38] men of Reuben, Gad and the half-tribe of **Manasseh**,
27: 20 Hoshea son of Azaziah; over half the tribe of **Manasseh**: Joel son
27: 21 over the half-tribe of **Manasseh** in Gilead: Iddo son of Zechariah;
2Ch 15: 9 **Manasseh** and Simeon who had settled among them,
30: 1 and Judah and also wrote letters to Ephraim and **Manasseh**,
30: 10 The couriers went from town to town in Ephraim and **Manasseh**,
30: 11 **Manasseh** and Zebulun humbled themselves and went to
30: 18 **Manasseh**, Issachar and Zebulun had not purified themselves,
31: 1 throughout Judah and Benjamin and in Ephraim and **Manasseh**.
32: 33 him when he died. And **Manasseh** his son succeeded him as king.
33: 1 **Manasseh** was twelve years old when he became king, and he
33: 9 But **Manasseh** led Judah and the people of Jerusalem astray,
33: 10 The LORD spoke to **Manasseh** and his people, but they paid no
33: 11 who took **Manasseh** prisoner, put a hook in his nose, bound him
33: 13 and to his kingdom. Then **Manasseh** knew that the LORD is God.
33: 18 The other events of **Manasseh's** reign, including his prayer to his
33: 20 **Manasseh** rested with his fathers and was buried in his palace.
33: 22 evil in the eyes of the LORD, as his father **Manasseh** had done.
33: 22 and offered sacrifices to all the idols **Manasseh** had made.
33: 23 unlike his father **Manasseh**, he did not humble himself before the
34: 6 In the towns of **Manasseh**, Ephraim and Simeon, as far as
34: 9 were the doorkeepers had collected from the people of **Manasseh**,
Ezr 10: 30 Benaiah, Maaseiah, Mattaniah, Bezalel, Binnui and **Manasseh**.
10: 33 Mattattah, Zabad, Eliphelet, Jeremai, **Manasseh** and Shimei.
Ps 60: 7 [60:9] Gilead is mine, and **Manasseh** is mine; Ephraim is my
80: 2 [80:3] before Ephraim, Benjamin and **Manasseh**. Awaken your
108: 8 [108:9] Gilead is mine, **Manasseh** is mine; Ephraim is my
Isa 9: 21 [9:20] **Manasseh** will feed on Ephraim, and Ephraim on
9: 21 [9:20] will feed on Ephraim, and Ephraim on **Manasseh**;
Jer 15: 4 because of what **Manasseh** son of Hezekiah king of Judah did in
Eze 48: 4 "**Manasseh** will have one portion; it will border the territory of
48: 5 it will border the territory of **Manasseh** from east to west.

4986 מְנַשִּׁי *m^e naššî*, a.g. [4] [√ 4985; cf. 5960]

Manasseh [3], Manassites [1]

Dt 4: 43 for the Gadites; and Golan in Bashan, for the **Manassites**.
29: 8 [29:7] the Gadites and the half-tribe of **Manasseh**.
2Ki 10: 33 Reuben and **Manasseh**), from Aroer by the Arnon Gorge through
1Ch 26: 32 and the half-tribe of **Manasseh** for every matter pertaining to God

4987 מְנָת *m^e nāt*, n.f. [9] [√ 4948]

portions [3], portion [2], assigned [1], contributed [1], food [1], lot [+3926] [1]

2Ch 31: 3 The king **contributed** from his own possessions for the morning
31: 4 He ordered the people living in Jerusalem to give the **portion** *due*
Ne 12: 44 the storerooms the **portions** *required by* the Law for the priests
12: 47 all Israel contributed the daily **portions** *for* the singers and
13: 10 I also learned that the **portions** *assigned to* the Levites had not
Ps 11: 6 and burning sulfur; a scorching wind will be their **lot** [+3926].
16: 5 LORD, you have **assigned** me my portion and my cup; you have
63: 10 [63:11] be given over to the sword and become **food** *for* jackals.
Jer 13: 25 This is your lot, the **portion** I have decreed for you," declares the

4988 מָס *mās*, a. [1] [√ 5022]

despairing man [1]

Job 6: 14 "A **despairing man** should have the devotion of his friends,

4989 מַס *mas*, n.m. [23]

forced labor [14], slave [2], *untranslated* [1], forced laborers [1], labor force [1], laborers [1], slave labor force [1], slave labor [1], tribute [1]

Ge 49: 15 he will bend his shoulder to the burden and submit to **forced labor**.
Ex 1: 11 So they put **slave** masters over them to oppress them with forced
Dt 20: 11 all the people in it shall be subject to **forced labor** and shall work
Jos 16: 10 among the people of Ephraim but are required to do **forced labor**.
17: 13 they subjected the Canaanites to **forced labor** but did not drive
Jdg 1: 28 they pressed the Canaanites into **forced labor** but never drove
1: 30 remained among them; but they did subject them to **forced labor**.
1: 33 Beth Shemesh and Beth Anath became **forced laborers** for them.
1: 35 of Joseph increased, they too were pressed into **forced labor**.
2Sa 20: 24 Adoniram was in charge of **forced labor**; Jehoshaphat son of
1Ki 4: 6 of the palace; Adoniram son of Abda—in charge of **forced labor**.
5: 13 [5:27] King Solomon conscripted **laborers** from all Israel—thirty
5: 13 [5:27] laborers from all Israel—**[RPH]** thirty thousand men.
5: 14 [5:28] at home. Adoniram was in charge of the **forced labor**.
9: 15 Here is the account of the **forced labor** King Solomon conscripted
9: 21 these Solomon conscripted for his slave **labor force**, as it is to this
12: 18 who was in charge of **forced labor**, but all Israel stoned him to
2Ch 8: 8 these Solomon conscripted for his **slave labor force**, as it is to this
10: 18 Rehoboam sent out Adoniram, who was in charge of **forced labor**,
Est 10: 1 King Xerxes imposed **tribute** throughout the empire, to its distant
Pr 12: 24 Diligent hands will rule, but laziness ends in **slave labor**.
Isa 31: 8 before the sword and their young men will be put to **forced labor**.
La 1: 1 She who was queen among the provinces has now become a **slave**.

4990 מֵסַב *mēsab*, n.[m.]. [4] [→ 4991; cf. 6015]

around [2], surround [1], table [1]

1Ki 6: 29 On the walls all **around** the temple, in both the inner and outer
2Ki 23: 5 places of the towns of Judah and on *those* **around** Jerusalem—
Ps 140: 9 [140:10] Let the heads of *those who* **surround** me be covered
SS 1: 12 While the king was at his **table**, my perfume spread its fragrance.

4991 מְסִבָּה *m^e sibbâ*, n.[f.] (used as adv.). [1] [√ 4990; cf. 6015]

around [1]

Job 37: 12 At his direction they swirl **around** over the face of the whole earth

4992 מְסַבִּיב *missābîb*, n.pr.m. Not used in NIV/BHS [→ 4474]

4993 ¹מַסְגֵּר **masgēr[1]**, n.[m.]. [3] [→ 4994; cf. 6037]
prison [3]
Ps 142: 7 [142:8] Set me free from my **prison**, that I may praise your name.
Isa 24: 22 they will be shut up in **prison** and be punished after many days.
42: 7 to free captives from **prison** and to release from the dungeon those

4994 ²מַסְגֵּר **masgēr[2]**, n.[m.]. [4] [√ 4993; cf. 6037]
artisans [4]
2Ki 24: 14 the officers and fighting men, and all the craftsmen and **artisans**—
24: 16 strong and fit for war, and a thousand craftsmen and **artisans**.
Jer 24: 1 the **artisans** *of* Judah were carried into exile from Jerusalem to
29: 2 and the **artisans** had gone into exile from Jerusalem.)

4995 מִסְגֶּרֶת **misgeret**, n.f. [17] [√ 6037]
rim [6], panels [5], side panels [2], strongholds [2], *untranslated* [1], dens [1]
Ex 25: 25 Also make around it a **rim** a handbreadth wide and put a gold
25: 25 it a rim a handbreadth wide and put a gold molding on the **rim**.
25: 27 The rings are to be close to the **rim** to hold the poles used in
37: 12 They also made around it a **rim** a handbreadth wide and put a gold
37: 12 it a rim a handbreadth wide and put a gold molding on the **rim**.
37: 14 The rings were put close to the **rim** to hold the poles used in
2Sa 22: 46 They all lose heart; they come trembling from their **strongholds**.
1Ki 7: 28 the stands were made: They had **side panels** attached to uprights.
7: 28 were made: They had side panels **[RPH]** attached to uprights.
7: 29 On the **panels** between the uprights were lions, bulls
7: 31 was engraving. The **panels** *of* the stands were square, not round.
7: 32 The four wheels were under the **panels**, and the axles of the wheels
7: 35 The supports and **panels** were attached to the top of the stand.
7: 36 and palm trees on the surfaces of the supports and on the **panels**,
2Ki 16: 17 King Ahaz took away the **side panels** and removed the basins from
Ps 18: 45 [18:46] lose heart; they come trembling from their **strongholds**.
Mic 7: 17 They will come trembling out of their **dens**; they will turn in fear

4996 מַסַּד **massad**, n.[m.]. [1] [√ 3569]
foundation [1]
1Ki 7: 9 the outside to the great courtyard and from **foundation** to eaves,

4997 מִסְדְּרוֹן **misdᵉrôn**, n.[m.]. [1] [√ 6043?]
porch [1]
Jdg 3: 23 Ehud went out to the **porch**; he shut the doors of the upper room

4998 מָסָה **māsâ**, v. [4] [cf. 4416, 5022]
consume [1], drench [1], made melt with fear [1], melts [1]
Jos 14: 8 [G] up with me **made** the hearts of the people **melt with fear**.
Ps 6: 6 [6:7] [G] bed with weeping and **drench** my couch with tears.
39: 11 [39:12] [G] *you* **consume** their wealth like a moth—each man is
147: 18 [G] He sends his word and **melts** them; he stirs up his breezes,

4999 ¹מַסָּה **massâ[1]**, n.f. [3] [→ 5001; cf. 5814]
trials [2], testings [1]
Dt 4: 34 by **testings**, by miraculous signs and wonders, by war, by a mighty
7: 19 You saw with your own eyes the great **trials**, the miraculous signs
29: 3 [29:2] With your own eyes you saw those great **trials**, those

5000 ²מַסָּה **massâ[2]**, n.f. [1] [√ 5022]
despair [1]
Job 9: 23 brings sudden death, he mocks the **despair** *of* the innocent.

5001 ³מַסָּה **massâ[3]**, n.pr.loc. [5] [√ 4999?; cf. 5814?]
Massah [5]
Ex 17: 7 he called the place **Massah** and Meribah because the Israelites
Dt 6: 16 Do not test the LORD your God as you did at **Massah**.
9: 22 LORD angry at Taberah, at **Massah** and at Kibroth Hattaavah.
33: 8 You tested him at **Massah**; you contended with him at the waters
Ps 95: 8 as you did at Meribah, as you did that day at **Massah** in the desert,

5002 מִסָּה **missâ**, n.f. [1]
in proportion to [+889+3869] [1]
Dt 16: 10 a freewill offering **in proportion** [+889+3869] **to** the blessings the

5003 מַסְוֶה **masweh**, n.[m.]. [3] [√ 6078]
veil [3]
Ex 34: 33 When Moses finished speaking to them, he put a **veil** over his face.
34: 34 presence to speak with him, he removed the **veil** until he came out.
34: 35 Moses would put the **veil** back over his face until he went in to

5004 מסוכה מְסוּכָה **mᵉsûkâ**, n.f. [1] [→ 5379; cf. 6056]
thorn hedge [1]
Mic 7: 4 of them is like a brier, the most upright worse than a **thorn hedge**.

5005 מַסָּח **massāḥ**, n.m. *or* adv. [1] [cf. 5815?]
take turns [1]
2Ki 11: 6 at the gate behind the guard, who **take turns** guarding the temple—

5006 מִסְחָר **misḥār**, n.m. [1] [cf. 6086]
revenues [1]
1Ki 10: 15 not including the **revenues** *from* merchants and traders and from

5007 מָסַךְ **māsak**, v. [5] [→ 4932, 5008]
mixed [2], mingle [1], mixing [1], poured [1]
Ps 102: 9 [102:10] [A] ashes as my food and **mingle** my drink with tears
Pr 9: 2 [A] She has prepared her meat and **mixed** her wine; she has also
9: 5 [A] "Come, eat my food and drink the wine *I have* **mixed**.
Isa 5: 22 [A] are heroes at drinking wine and champions at **mixing** drinks,
19: 14 [A] The LORD *has* **poured** into them a spirit of dizziness; they

5008 מֶסֶךְ **mesek**, n.[m.]. [1] [√ 5007]
mixed with spices [1]
Ps 75: 8 [75:9] LORD is a cup full of foaming wine **mixed with spices**;

5009 מָסָךְ **māsāk**, n.[m.]. [25] [√ 6114]
curtain [17], shielding [3], covering [2], curtains [1], defenses [1], shields [1]
Ex 26: 36 "For the entrance to the tent make a **curtain** of blue, purple
26: 37 Make gold hooks for this **curtain** and five posts of acacia wood
27: 16 provide a **curtain** twenty cubits long, of blue, purple and scarlet
35: 12 its poles and the atonement cover and the curtain that **shields** it;
35: 15 the **curtain** *for* the doorway at the entrance to the tabernacle;
35: 17 and bases, and the **curtain** *for* the entrance to the courtyard;
36: 37 For the entrance to the tent they made a **curtain** *of* blue, purple
38: 18 The **curtain** *for* the entrance to the courtyard was of blue,
39: 34 the covering of hides of sea cows and the **shielding** curtain;
39: 38 the fragrant incense, and the **curtain** *for* the entrance to the tent;
39: 40 and bases, and the **curtain** for the entrance to the courtyard;
40: 5 and put the **curtain** *at* the entrance to the tabernacle.
40: 8 around it and put the **curtain** *at* the entrance to the courtyard.
40: 21 hung the **shielding** curtain and shielded the ark of the Testimony,
40: 28 Then he put up the **curtain** *at* the entrance to the tabernacle.
40: 33 and altar and put up the **curtain** *at* the entrance to the courtyard.
Nu 3: 25 its coverings, the **curtain** *at* the entrance to the Tent of Meeting,
3: 26 the **curtain** *at* the entrance to the courtyard surrounding the
3: 31 in ministering, the **curtain**, and everything related to their use.
4: 5 and his sons are to go in and take down the **shielding** curtain
4: 25 of sea cows, the **curtains** *for* the entrance to the Tent of Meeting,
4: 26 the **curtain** *for* the entrance, the ropes and all the equipment used
2Sa 17: 19 His wife took a **covering** and spread it out over the opening of the
Ps 105: 39 He spread out a cloud as a **covering**, and a fire to give light at
Isa 22: 8 the **defenses** *of* Judah are stripped away. And you looked in that

5010 מְסֻכָּה **mᵉsukâ**, n.f. [1] [√ 6114]
adorned [1]
Eze 28: 13 in Eden, the garden of God; every precious stone **adorned** you:

5011 ¹מַסֵּכָה **masseḵâ[1]**, n.f. [26] [√ 5818]
cast idol [5], idol cast [3], images [3], cast idols [2], cast [2], idol [2], image [2], cast images [1], cast metal [1], forming an alliance [+5818] [1], idol cast from metal [1], idols cast [1], idols made of metal [1], idols [1]
Ex 32: 4 handed him and made it into an **idol cast** in the shape of a calf,
32: 8 and have made themselves an **idol cast** in the shape of a calf.
34: 17 "Do not make **cast** idols.
Lev 19: 4 " 'Do not turn to idols or make gods of **cast metal** for yourselves.
Nu 33: 52 Destroy all their carved images and their **cast** idols, and demolish
Dt 9: 12 I commanded them and have made a **cast idol** for themselves."
9: 16 you had made for yourselves an **idol cast** in the shape of a calf.
27: 15 "Cursed is the man who carves an image or casts an **idol**—
Jdg 17: 3 to the LORD for my son to make a carved image and a **cast idol**.
17: 4 them to a silversmith, who made them into the image and the **idol**.
18: 14 an ephod, other household gods, a carved image and a **cast idol**?
18: 17 the other household gods and the **cast idol** while the priest
18: 18 the ephod, the other household gods and the **cast idol**, the priest
1Ki 14: 9 You have made for yourself other gods, **idols made of metal**;
2Ki 17: 16 and made for themselves two **idols cast** in the shape of calves,
2Ch 28: 2 kings of Israel and also made **cast idols** for worshiping the Baals.

2Ch 34: 3 of high places, Asherah poles, carved idols and **cast images**.
34: 4 and smashed the Asherah poles, the idols and the **images**.
Ne 9: 18 even when they cast for themselves an **image** of a calf and said,
Ps 106: 19 At Horeb they made a calf and worshiped an **idol cast from metal**.
Isa 30: 1 **forming an alliance** [+5818], but not by my Spirit, heaping sin
30: 22 your idols overlaid with silver and your **images** covered with gold;
42: 17 those who trust in idols, who say to **images**, 'You are our gods,'
Hos 13: 2 they make **idols** for themselves from their silver, cleverly
Na 1: 14 carved images and **cast idols** that are in the temple of your gods.
Hab 2: 18 is an idol, since a man has carved it? Or an **image** that teaches lies?

5012 ²מַסֵּכָה *massēkâ²*, n.f. [2] [√ 5819]

blanket [1], sheet [1]

Isa 25: 7 shroud that enfolds all peoples, the **sheet** that covers all nations;
28: 20 short to stretch out on, the **blanket** too narrow to wrap around you.

5013 ³מַסֵּכָה *massēkâ³*, n.f. Not used in NIV/BHS [√ 5819]

5014 מִסְכֵּן *miskēn*, a. [4] [→ 5017; cf. 6123]

poor [4]

Ecc 4: 13 Better a **poor** but wise youth than an old but foolish king who no
9: 15 Now there lived in that city a man **poor** but wise, and he saved the
9: 15 the city by his wisdom. But nobody remembered that **poor** man.
9: 16 the **poor** *man's* wisdom is despised, and his words are no longer

5015 מְסֻכָּן *mᵉsukkān*, n.[m.] *or* v.ptcp. Not used in NIV/BHS [cf. 6123]

5016 מִסְכְּנוֹת *miskᵉnôt*, n.f.pl. [7] [√ 6122]

store [6], buildings to store [1]

Ex 1: 11 and they built Pithom and Rameses as **store** cities for Pharaoh.
1Ki 9: 19 as well as all his **store** cities and the towns for his chariots
2Ch 8: 4 in the desert and all the **store** cities he had built in Hamath.
8: 6 as well as Baalath and all his **store** cities, and all the cities for his
16: 4 Dan, Abel Maim and all the **store** cities of Naphtali.
17: 12 and more powerful; he built forts and **store** cities in Judah
32: 28 He also made **buildings to store** the harvest of grain, new wine

5017 מִסְכֵּנֻת *miskēnut*, n.f. [1] [√ 5014; cf. 6123]

scarce [+430+928] [1]

Dt 8: 9 a land where bread *will* not *be* **scarce** [+430+928] and you will

5018 מַסֶּכֶת *masseket*, n.f. [2 / 3] [√ 5819]

fabric [3]

Jdg 16: 13 "If you weave the seven braids of my head into the **fabric** ꜀on the
16: 13 the seven braids of his head, wove them into the **fabric** [BHS-]
16: 14 from his sleep and pulled up the pin and the loom, with the **fabric**.

5019 מְסִלָּה *mᵉsillâ*, n.f. [27] [√ 6148]

road [10], highway [6], roads [3], highways [2], courses [1], main road [1], pilgrimage [1], steps [1], straight ahead [1], ways [1]

Nu 20: 19 "We will go along the **main road**, and if we or our livestock drink
Jdg 5: 20 the stars fought, from their **courses** they fought against Sisera.
20: 31 so that about thirty men fell in the open field and on the **roads**—
20: 32 "Let's retreat and draw them away from the city to the **roads**."
20: 45 the Israelites cut down five thousand men along the **roads**.
21: 19 of Bethel, and east of the **road** that goes from Bethel to Shechem,
1Sa 6: 12 Beth Shemesh, keeping on the **road** and lowing all the way;
2Sa 20: 12 Amasa lay wallowing in his blood in the middle of the **road**,
20: 12 he dragged him from the **road** into a field and threw a garment
20: 13 After Amasa had been removed from the **road**, all the men went on
2Ki 18: 17 of the Upper Pool, on the **road** *to* the Washerman's Field.
1Ch 26: 16 and the Shalleketh Gate on the upper **road** fell to Shuppim
26: 18 to the west, there were four at the **road** and two at the court itself.
2Ch 9: 11 The king used the algumwood to make **steps** for the temple of the
Ps 84: 5 [84:6] strength is in you, who have set their hearts on **pilgrimage**.
Pr 16: 17 The **highway** *of* the upright avoids evil; he who guards his way
Isa 7: 3 of the Upper Pool, on the **road** *to* the Washerman's Field.
11: 16 There will be a **highway** for the remnant of his people that is left
19: 23 In that day there will be a **highway** from Egypt to Assyria.
33: 8 The **highways** are deserted, no travelers are on the roads.
36: 2 of the Upper Pool, on the **road** *to* the Washerman's Field,
40: 3 make straight in the wilderness a **highway** for our God.
49: 11 all my mountains into roads, and my **highways** will be raised up.
59: 7 thoughts are evil thoughts; ruin and destruction mark their **ways**.
62: 10 Build up, build up the **highway**! Remove the stones. Raise a
Jer 31: 21 Take note of the **highway**, the road that you take. Return,
Joel 2: 8 They do not jostle each other; each marches **straight ahead**.

5020 מַסְלוּל *maslûl*, n.m. [1] [√ 6148]

highway [1]

Isa 35: 8 And a **highway** will be there; it will be called the Way of Holiness.

5021 מַסְמֵר *masmēr*, n.m. [4] [√ 6169]

nails [3], nails down [+928+2616] [1]

1Ch 22: 3 He provided a large amount of iron to make **nails** for the doors of
2Ch 3: 9 The gold **nails** weighed fifty shekels. He also overlaid the upper
Isa 41: 7 "It is good." *He* **nails** [+928+2616] **down** the idol so it will not
Jer 10: 4 and gold; they fasten it with hammer and **nails** so it will not totter.

5022 מָסַס *māsas*, v. [21] [→ 4988, 5000, 9468; cf. 4416, 4998, 5376, 5806]

melt [6], melted [3], melt with fear [+5022] [2], melted away [2], be soaked [1], disheartened [+906+4222] [1], dropped [1], made lose [1], melts [1], waste away [1], wastes away [1], weak [1]

Ex 16: 21 [C] as he needed, and when the sun grew hot, *it* **melted away**.
Dt 1: 28 [G] Our brothers *have* **made** us **lose** heart. They say, 'The people
20: 8 [C] his brothers *will* not *become* **disheartened** [+906+4222] too."
Jos 2: 11 [C] our hearts **melted** and everyone's courage failed because of
5: 1 [C] their hearts **melted** and they no longer had the courage to
7: 5 [C] At this the hearts of the people **melted** and became like
Jdg 15: 14 [C] like charred flax, and the bindings **dropped** from his hands.
1Sa 15: 9 [C] that was despised and **weak** they totally destroyed.
2Sa 17: 10 [C] heart is like the heart of a lion, *will* **melt** [+5022] **with fear**,
17: 10 [C] heart is like the heart of a lion, *will* **melt with fear** [+5022],
Ps 22: 14 [22:15] [C] has turned to wax; *it has* **melted away** within me.
68: 2 [68:3] [C] as wax **melts** before the fire, may the wicked perish
97: 5 [C] The mountains **melt** like wax before the LORD, before the
112: 10 [C] and be vexed, he will gnash his teeth and **waste away**;
Isa 10: 18 [A] it will completely destroy, as *when* a sick man **wastes away**.
13: 7 [C] of this, all hands will go limp, every man's heart *will* **melt**.
19: 1 [C] before him, and the hearts of the Egyptians **melt** within them.
34: 3 [C] up a stench; the mountains *will* **be soaked** with their blood.
Eze 21: 7 [21:12] [C] Every heart *will* **melt** and every hand go limp; every
Mic 1: 4 [C] The mountains **melt** beneath him and the valleys split apart,
Na 2: 10 [2:11] [C] Hearts **melt**, knees give way, bodies tremble, every

5023 מַסַּע *massa'*, n.[m.]. [12] [√ 5825]

journey [2], travels [2], from place to place [+4200] [1], having set out [1], order of march [1], setting out [1], stages in journey [1], traveled from place to place [1], traveling from place to place [1], way [1]

Ge 13: 3 From the Negev he went **from place** [+4200] **to place** until he
Ex 17: 1 **traveling from place to place** as the LORD commanded.
40: 36 In all the **travels** *of* the Israelites, whenever the cloud lifted from
40: 38 in the sight of all the house of Israel during all their **travels**.
Nu 10: 2 calling the community together and for **having** the camps **set out**.
10: 6 the south are to set out. The blast will be the signal for **setting out**.
10: 12 **traveled from place to place** until the cloud came to rest in the
10: 28 This was the **order of march** for the Israelite divisions as they set
33: 1 Here are the **stages in** the **journey** *of* the Israelites when they came
33: 2 LORD's command Moses recorded the stages in their **journey**.
33: 2 the stages in their journey. This is their **journey** by stages:
Dt 10: 11 "and lead the people on their **way**, so that they may enter

5024 ¹מַסָּע *massā'¹*, n.[m.]. [1] [√ 5825]

quarry [1]

1Ki 6: 7 only blocks dressed at the **quarry** were used, and no hammer,

5025 ²מַסָּע *massā'²*, n.m. [1]

dart [1]

Job 41: 26 [41:18] has no effect, nor does the spear or the **dart** or the javelin.

5026 מִסְעָד *mis'ād*, n.[m.]. [1] [√ 6184]

supports [1]

1Ki 10: 12 The king used the almugwood to make **supports** for the temple of

5027 מִסְפֵּד *mispēd*, n.m. [16] [√ 6199]

wailing [5], mourning [4], wail [2], weeping [2], howl [+6913] [1], lamented [+6199] [1], mourns [1]

Ge 50: 10 near the Jordan, *they* **lamented** [+6199] loudly and bitterly;
Est 4: 3 mourning among the Jews, with fasting, weeping and **wailing**.
Ps 30: 11 [30:12] You turned my **wailing** into dancing; you removed my
Isa 22: 12 called you on that day to weep and to **wail**, to tear out your hair
Jer 6: 26 mourn with bitter **wailing** as for an only son, for suddenly the
48: 38 in Moab and in the public squares there is nothing but **mourning**,
Eze 27: 31 will weep over you with anguish of soul and with bitter **mourning**.

Joel 2:12 me with all your heart, with fasting and weeping and **mourning**."
Am 5:16 "There will be **wailing** in all the streets and cries of anguish in
5:16 The farmers will be summoned to weep and the mourners to **wail**.
5:17 There will be **wailing** in all the vineyards, for I will pass through
Mic 1:8 and naked. *I will* **howl** [+6913] like a jackal and moan like an owl.
1:11 Beth Ezel is in **mourning**; its protection is taken from you.
Zec 12:10 and they will mourn for him as one **mourns** for an only child,
12:11 On that day the **weeping** in Jerusalem will be great,
12:11 like the **weeping** *of* Hadad Rimmon in the plain of Megiddo.

5028 מִסְפּוֹא ***mispô'***, n.m. [5]

fodder [4], feed [1]

Ge 24:25 she added, "We have plenty of straw and **fodder**, as well as room
24:32 Straw and **fodder** were brought for the camels, and water for him
42:27 the night one of them opened his sack to get **feed** for his donkey,
43:24 water to wash their feet and provided **fodder** for their donkeys.
Jdg 19:19 We have both straw and **fodder** for our donkeys and bread

5029 מִסְפָּחָה ***mispāḥâ***, n.f. [2] [√ 6202]

veils [2]

Eze 13:18 make **veils** of various lengths for their heads in order to ensnare
13:21 I will tear off your **veils** and save my people from your hands,

5030 מִסְפַּחַת ***mispaḥat***, n.f. [3] [√ 6204]

rash [3]

Lev 13:6 in the skin, the priest shall pronounce him clean; it is only a **rash**.
13:7 if the **rash** does spread in his skin after he has shown himself to the
13:8 The priest is to examine him, and if the **rash** has spread in the skin,

5031 מִסְפָּר[1] ***mispār[1]***, n.m. [134 / 133] [→ 5032?, 5033?; cf. 6219]

number [47], listed [15], *untranslated* [10], counted [8], few [7], list [6], as many as [3], how many [2], number [+5152] [2], numbered [2], numbers [2], account [1], all [1], allotted [1], any [1], bowmen [+8008] [1], census [1], count [1], counted off [+928+6296] [1], countless [+401] [1], during [1], each [+1653] [1], each[s] [+4200] [1], few [+928+5071] [1], in all [1], innumerable [+401] [1], inventory [1], length [1], life span [+3427] [1], limit [1], listing [1], many [1], measure [1], one by one [+928] [1], one for each [+3869] [1], only a few [+5493] [1], only a few [1], so many [+8041] [1], total [+3972+4200] [1], very few [+5493] [1]

Ge 34:30 We are few in **number**, and if they join forces against me
41:49 that he stopped keeping records because it was beyond **measure**.
Ex 16:16 Take an omer for **each** [+1653] person you have in your tent.' "
23:26 or be barren in your land. I will give you a full **life span** [+3427].
Lev 25:15 countryman on the basis of the **number** *of* years since the Jubilee.
25:15 he is to sell to you on the basis of the **number** *of* years left for
25:16 because what he is really selling you is the **number** *of* crops.
25:50 be based on the rate paid to a hired man for that **number** *of* years.
Nu 1:2 by their clans and families, **listing** every man by name, one by one.
1:18 and the men twenty years old or more were **listed** by name,
1:20 or more who were able to serve in the army were **listed** by name,
1:22 were able to serve in the army were counted and **listed** by name,
1:24 or more who were able to serve in the army were **listed** by name,
1:26 or more who were able to serve in the army were **listed** by name,
1:28 or more who were able to serve in the army were **listed** by name,
1:30 or more who were able to serve in the army were **listed** by name,
1:32 or more who were able to serve in the army were **listed** by name,
1:34 or more who were able to serve in the army were **listed** by name,
1:36 or more who were able to serve in the army were **listed** by name,
1:38 or more who were able to serve in the army were **listed** by name,
1:40 or more who were able to serve in the army were **listed** by name,
1:42 or more who were able to serve in the army were **listed** by name,
3:22 The **number** *of* all the males a month old or more who were
3:28 The **number** *of* all the males a month old or more was 8,600.
3:34 The **number** *of* all the males a month old or more who were
3:40 males who are a month old or more and make a **list** *of* their names.
3:43 number of firstborn males a month old or more, **listed** by name,
9:20 Sometimes the cloud was over the tabernacle **only a few** days;
14:29 of you twenty years old or more who was counted in the **census**
14:34 one year for each of the forty days **[NIE]** you explored the land—
15:12 Do this for each one, for as **many** as you prepare.
15:12 Do this for each one, for as many as you prepare. **[RPH]**
23:10 can count the dust of Jacob or **number** the fourth part of Israel?
26:53 allotted to them as an inheritance based on the **number** *of* names.
29:18 and drink offerings according to the **number** specified.
29:21 and drink offerings according to the **number** specified.
29:24 and drink offerings according to the **number** specified.
29:27 and drink offerings according to the **number** specified.
29:30 and drink offerings according to the **number** specified.
29:33 and drink offerings according to the **number** specified.
29:37 and drink offerings according to the **number** specified.
31:36 share of those who fought in the battle was: 337,500 **[NIE]** sheep,
Dt 4:27 **only a few of** [+5493] you will survive among the nations to which
25:2 have him flogged in his presence with the **number** of lashes his
32:8 he set up boundaries for the peoples according to the **number** *of*
33:6 "Let Reuben live and not die, nor his men be **few**."
Jos 4:5 according to the **number** *of* the tribes of the Israelites,
4:8 according to the **number** *of* the tribes of the Israelites, as the
Jdg 6:5 It was impossible to **count** the men and their camels; they invaded
7:6 **[NIE]** Three hundred men lapped with their hands to their
7:12 Their camels could no more be **counted** than the sand on the
7:15 When Gideon heard **[NIE]** the dream and its interpretation,
21:23 While the girls were dancing, **each**[s] [+4200] man caught one
1Sa 6:4 and five gold rats, according to the **number** *of* the Philistine rulers,
6:18 the **number** *of* the gold rats was according to the number of
27:7 **[NIE]** David lived in Philistine territory a year and four months.
2Sa 2:11 The **length** *of* time David was king in Hebron over the house of
2:15 So they stood up and *were* **counted** [+928+6296] **off**—twelve men
21:20 fingers on each hand and six toes on each foot—twenty-four **in all**.
24:2 enroll the fighting men, so that I may know **how many** there are."
24:9 Joab reported the **number** [+5152] *of* the fighting men to the king:
1Ki 18:31 Elijah took twelve stones, **one for each** [+3869] *of* the tribes
1Ch 7:2 the descendants of Tola **listed** as fighting men in their genealogy
7:40 The **number** *of* men ready for battle, as listed in their genealogy,
9:28 they **counted** them when they were brought in and when they were
9:28 when they were brought in and **[RPH]** when they were taken out.
11:11 this is the **list** *of* David's mighty men: Jashobeam, a Hacmonite,
12:23 [12:24] These are the **numbers** *of* the men armed for battle who
16:19 When they were but few in **number**, few indeed, and strangers in
21:2 Then report back to me so that I may know **how many** there are."
21:5 Joab reported the **number** [+5152] *of* the fighting men to David:
22:4 He also provided more cedar logs than could be **counted**,
22:16 in gold and silver, bronze and iron—craftsmen beyond **number**.
23:3 and the total **number** of men was thirty-eight thousand.
23:24 they were registered under their names and **counted** individually,
23:27 the Levites were **counted** from those twenty years old or more.
23:31 were to serve before the LORD regularly in the *proper* **number**
25:1 Here is the **list** *of* the men who performed this service:
25:7 and skilled in music for the LORD—they **numbered** 288.
27:1 This is the **list** *of* the Israelites—heads of families, commanders of
27:23 David did not take the **number** *of* the men twenty years old
27:24 the **number** was not entered in the book of the annals of King
27:24 number was not entered in the book [BHS ***number***; NIV 6219] *of*
2Ch 12:3 and the **innumerable** [+401] troops of Libyans,
26:11 ready to go out by divisions according to their **numbers** as
26:12 The total **number** *of* family leaders over the fighting men was
29:32 The **number** *of* burnt offerings the assembly brought was seventy
35:7 who were there a **total** [+3972+4200] of thirty thousand sheep
Ezr 1:9 This was the **inventory**: gold dishes 30 silver dishes 1,000 silver
2:2 Rehum and Baanah): The **list** *of* the men of the people of Israel:
3:4 they celebrated the Feast of Tabernacles with the required **number**
8:34 Everything was accounted for by **number** and weight,
Ne 7:7 Bigvai, Nehum and Baanah): The **list** *of* the men of Israel:
Est 9:11 The **number** *of* those slain in the citadel of Susa was reported to
Job 1:5 Early in the morning he would sacrifice a burnt offering **[NIE]** for
3:6 among the days of the year nor be entered in **any** *of* the months.
5:9 wonders that cannot be fathomed, miracles that cannot be **counted**.
9:10 wonders that cannot be fathomed, miracles that cannot be **counted**.
14:5 you have decreed the **number** *of* his months and have set limits he
15:20 the ruthless through **all** the years stored up for him.
16:22 "Only a **few** years will pass before I go on the journey of no return.
21:21 family he leaves behind when his **allotted** months come to an end?
21:33 follow after him, and a **countless** [+401] throng goes before him.
25:3 Can his forces be **numbered**? Upon whom does his light not rise?
31:37 I would give him an **account** *of* my every step; like a prince I
36:26 our understanding! The **number** *of* his years is past finding out.
38:21 for you were already born! You have lived **so many** [+8041] years!
Ps 40:12 [40:13] For troubles without **number** surround me; my sins have
104:25 vast and spacious, teeming with creatures beyond **number**—
105:12 When they were but few in **number**, few indeed, and strangers in
105:34 He spoke, and the locusts came, grasshoppers without **number**;
147:4 He determines the **number** of the stars and calls them each by
147:5 is our Lord and mighty in power; his understanding has no **limit**.
Ecc 2:3 for men to do under heaven during the **few** days of their lives.
5:18 [5:17] the sun during the **few** days of life God has given him—
6:12 during the **few** and meaningless days he passes through like a
SS 6:8 there may be, and eighty concubines, and virgins beyond **number**;
Isa 10:19 of his forests will be *so* **few** that a child could write them down.
21:17 The survivors of the **bowmen** [+8008], the warriors of Kedar,
40:26 He who brings out the starry host **one** [+928] **by one**, and calls
Jer 2:28 For you have **as many** gods **as** you have towns, O Judah.
2:32 Yet my people have forgotten me, days without **number**.
11:13 You have **as many** gods **as** you have towns, O Judah;

Jer 11:13 to that shameful god Baal are **as many as** the streets of Jerusalem.'
44:28 return to the land of Judah from Egypt will be **very few** [+5493].
46:23 They are more numerous than locusts, they cannot be **counted**.
Eze 4: 4 You are to bear their sin for the **number** *of* days you lie on your
4: 5 I have assigned you the same **number** *of* days as the years of their
4: 9 You are to eat it **during** the 390 days you lie on your side.
5: 3 take a **few** [+928+5071] strands of hair and tuck them away in the
12:16 But I will spare a **few** of them from the sword, famine and plague,
Da 9: 2 that the desolation of Jerusalem would last seventy years. **[NIE]**
Hos 1:10 [2:1] "Yet **[NIE]** the Israelites will be like the sand on the
Joel 1: 6 A nation has invaded my land, powerful and without **number**;

5032 ²מִסְפָּר *mispār²*, n.pr.m. [1] [→ 5033; cf. 5031?, 6219]
Mispar [1]
Ezr 2: 2 Mordecai, Bilshan, **Mispar**, Bigvai, Rehum and Baanah):

5033 מִסְפֶּרֶת *misperet*, n.pr.m. [1] [√ 5032; cf. 5031?]
Mispereth [1]
Ne 7: 7 Mordecai, Bilshan, **Mispereth**, Bigvai, Nehum and Baanah):

5034 מָסַר *māsar*, v. [2] [→ 5037?]
supplied [1], the means of [1]
Nu 31: 5 [C] from each tribe, *were* **supplied** from the clans of Israel.
31:16 [A] were **the means of** turning the Israelites away from the

5035 מֹסֵרוֹת *mōsērôt*, n.pr.loc. [2] [√ 673?; cf. 4594]
Moseroth [2]
Nu 33:30 They left Hashmonah and camped at **Moseroth**.
33:31 They left **Moseroth** and camped at Bene Jaakan.

5036 מֹסָרָם *mōsārām*, n.m. Not used in NIV/BHS [√ 4592; cf. 3579]

5037 מָסֹרֶת *māsōret*, n.f. [1] [√ 673? *or* 5034?]
bond [1]
Eze 20:37 under my rod, and I will bring you into the **bond** *of* the covenant.

5038 מִסַּת *missat*, n. Not used in NIV/BHS

5039 מִסְתּוֹר *mistôr*, n.[m.]. [1] [√ 6259]
hiding place [1]
Isa 4: 6 of the day, and a refuge and **hiding place** from the storm and rain.

5040 מַסְתֵּר *mastēr*, n.[m.]. [1] [√ 6259]
hide [1]
Isa 53: 3 Like *one* from whom men **hide** their faces he was despised,

5041 מִסְתָּר *mistār*, n.[m.]. [10] [√ 6259]
ambush [2], hiding [2], secret places [2], *untranslated* [1], cover [1], hiding places [1], secret [1]
Ps 10: 8 from **ambush** he murders the innocent, watching in secret for his
10: 9 He lies in wait **[RPH]** like a lion in cover; he lies in wait to catch
17:12 are like a lion hungry for prey, like a great lion crouching in **cover**.
64: 4 [64:5] They shoot from **ambush** at the innocent man; they shoot
Isa 45: 3 give you the treasures of darkness, riches stored in **secret places**,
Jer 13:17 if you do not listen, I will weep in **secret** because of your pride;
23:24 Can anyone hide in **secret places** so that I cannot see him?"
49:10 I will uncover his **hiding places**, so that he cannot conceal himself.
La 3:10 Like a bear lying in wait, like a lion in **hiding**,
Hab 3:14 as though about to devour the wretched who were in **hiding**.

5042 מַעְבָד *maᵃbād*, n.[m.]. [1] [√ 6268; Ar 10434]
deeds [1]
Job 34:25 Because he takes note of their **deeds**, he overthrows them in the

5043 מַעֲבֶה *maᵃbeh*, n.[m.]. [1] [√ 6286]
molds [1]
1Ki 7:46 The king had them cast in clay **molds** in the plain of the Jordan

5044 מַעֲבָר *maᵃbār*, n.[m.]. [3] [√ 6296]
ford [1], pass [1], stroke [1]
Ge 32:22 [32:23] and his eleven sons and crossed the **ford** *of* the Jabbok.
1Sa 13:23 Now a detachment of Philistines had gone out to the **pass** *at*
Isa 30:32 Every **stroke** the LORD lays on them with his punishing rod will

5045 מַעְבָּרָה *maʿbārâ*, n.f. [8] [√ 6296]
fords [5], pass [2], river crossings [1]
Jos 2: 7 of the spies on the road that leads to the **fords** of the Jordan,
Jdg 3:28 taking possession of the **fords** *of* the Jordan that led to Moab,
12: 5 The Gileadites captured the **fords** *of* the Jordan leading to
12: 6 they seized him and killed him at the **fords** *of* the Jordan.
1Sa 14: 4 On each side of the **pass** that Jonathan intended to cross to reach
Isa 10:29 They go over the **pass**, and say, "We will camp overnight at
16: 2 from the nest, so are the women of Moab at the **fords** of the Arnon.
Jer 51:32 the **river crossings** seized, the marshes set on fire, and the soldiers

5046 ¹מַעְגָּל *maʿgāl¹*, n.m. [3] [√ 6318]
camp [3]
1Sa 17:20 He reached the **camp** as the army was going out to its battle
26: 5 Saul was lying inside the **camp**, with the army encamped around
26: 7 lying asleep inside the **camp** with his spear stuck in the ground

5047 ²מַעְגָּל *maʿgāl²*, n.m. [13] [√ 6318]
paths [8], path [2], carts [1], way [1], ways [1]
Ps 17: 5 My steps have held to your **paths**; my feet have not slipped.
23: 3 He guides me in **paths** *of* righteousness for his name's sake.
65:11 [65:12] your bounty, and your **carts** overflow with abundance.
140: 5 [140:6] of their net and have set traps for me along my **path**.
Pr 2: 9 will understand what is right and just and fair—every good **path**.
2:15 whose paths are crooked and who are devious in their **ways**.
2:18 house leads down to death and her **paths** to the spirits of the dead.
4:11 guide you in the way of wisdom and lead you along straight **paths**.
4:26 Make level **paths** *for* your feet and take only ways that are firm.
5: 6 to the way of life; her **paths** are crooked, but she knows it not.
5:21 are in full view of the LORD, and he examines all his **paths**.
Isa 26: 7 O upright One, you make the **way** *of* the righteous smooth.
59: 8 way of peace they do not know; there is no justice in their **paths**.

5048 מָעַד *māʿad*, v. [7 / 8] [→ 4598, 5049, 5050]
turn [2], bent [1], lame [1], slip [1], slipping [1], wavering [1], wrenched [1]
2Sa 22:37 [A] broaden the path beneath me, so that my ankles *do* not **turn**.
Job 12: 5 [A] for misfortune as the fate of *those* whose feet *are* **slipping**.
Ps 18:36 [18:37] [A] the path beneath me, so that my ankles *do* not **turn**.
26: 1 [A] I have trusted in the LORD without **wavering**.
37:31 [A] The law of his God is in his heart; his feet *do* not **slip**.
69:23 [69:24] [G] so they cannot see, and their backs *be* **bent** forever.
Pr 25:19 [E] or a **lame** foot is reliance on the unfaithful in times of trouble.
Eze 29: 7 [G] you broke and their backs *were* **wrenched**. [BHS 6641]

5049 מַעֲדַי *maᵃday*, n.pr.m. [1] [→ 5050; cf. 4598, 5048 + 3378]
Maadai [1]
Ezr 10:34 From the descendants of Bani: **Maadai**, Amram, Uel,

5050 מַעַדְיָה *maʿadyâ*, n.pr.m. [1] [√ 5049; cf. 5048 + 3378]
Moadiah [1]
Ne 12: 5 Mijamin, **Moadiah**, Bilgah,

5051 מַעֲדַנּוֹת *maᵃdannôt*, n.[f.pl.]. [2] [√ 6357; cf. 6698]
beautiful [1], confidently [1]
1Sa 15:32 Agag came to him **confidently**, thinking, "Surely the bitterness of
Job 38:31 "Can you bind the **beautiful** Pleiades? Can you loose the cords of

5052 מַעֲדַנִּים *maᵃdannîm*, n.[m.pl.]. [3] [√ 6357]
delicacies [2], delight [1]
Ge 49:20 "Asher's food will be rich; he will provide **delicacies** *fit for* a king.
Pr 29:17 and he will give you peace; he will bring **delight** to your soul.
La 4: 5 Those who once ate **delicacies** are destitute in the streets.

5053 מַעְדֵּר *maʿdēr*, n.[m.]. [1] [√ 6371]
hoe [1]
Isa 7:25 As for all the hills once cultivated by the **hoe**, you will no longer

5054 מָעָה *māʿâ*, n.f. [1]
grains [1]
Isa 48:19 have been like the sand, your children like its *numberless* **grains**;

5055 מֵעֶה *mēʿeh*, n.m. [32 / 33] [→ Ar 10435]
body [4], bowels [4], heart [4], anguish [2], inside [2], stomach [2], within [2], birth [+562] [1], children [+7368] [1], flesh [1], have [+928]

[1], I [+3276] [1], inside [+928] [1], intestines [1], line [1], sons [+3665] [1], stomachs [1], tenderness [+2162] [1], within [+928+9348] [1], womb [1]

Ge 15: 4 but a son coming from your own **body** will be your heir."
25: 23 in your womb, and two peoples from **within** you will be separated;
Nu 5: 22 May this water that brings a curse enter your **body** so that your
Ru 1: 11 Am I going to **have** [+928] any more sons, who could become your
2Sa 7: 12 who will come from your own **body**, and I will establish his
16: 11 to Abishai and all his officials, "My son, who is of my own **flesh**,
20: 10 it into his belly, and his **intestines** spilled out on the ground.
2Ch 21: 15 You yourself will be very ill with a lingering disease of the **bowels**,
21: 15 of the bowels, until the disease causes your **bowels** to come out.' "
21: 18 LORD afflicted Jehoram with an incurable disease of the **bowels**.
21: 19 his **bowels** came out because of the disease, and he died in great
32: 21 of his god, some of his **sons** [+3665] cut him down with the sword.
Job 20: 14 yet his food will turn sour in his **stomach**; it will become the
30: 27 The churning **inside** me never stops; days of suffering confront me.
Ps 22: 14 [22:15] to wax; it has melted away **within** [+928+9348] me.
40: 8 [40:9] to do your will, O my God; your law is within my **heart**."
71: 6 relied on you; you brought me forth from my mother's **womb**.
SS 5: 4 hand through the latch-opening; my **heart** began to pound for him.
5: 14 His **body** is like polished ivory decorated with sapphires.
Isa 16: 11 My **heart** laments for Moab like a harp, my inmost being for Kir
48: 1 the name of Israel and come from the **line** [BHS 4784] *of* Judah,
48: 19 like the sand, your **children** [+7368] like its numberless grains;
49: 1 from my **birth** [+562] he has made mention of my name.
63: 15 Your **tenderness** [+2162] and compassion are withheld from us.
Jer 4: 19 Oh, my **anguish**, my anguish! I writhe in pain. Oh, the agony of
4: 19 Oh, my anguish, my **anguish**! I writhe in pain. Oh, the agony of
31: 20 Therefore my **heart** yearns for him; I have great compassion for
La 1: 20 O LORD, how distressed I am! **I** [+3276] am in torment within,
2: 11 My eyes fail from weeping, I am in torment **within**, my heart is
Eze 3: 3 eat this scroll I am giving you and fill your **stomach** with it."
7: 19 They will not satisfy their hunger or fill their **stomachs** with it,
Jnh 1: 17 [2:1] Jonah was **inside** [+928] the fish three days and three nights.
2: 1 [2:2] From **inside** the fish Jonah prayed to the LORD his God.

5056 מָעוֹג mā'ôg, n.[m.]. [2 / 1] [√ 6383]

bread [1]

1Ki 17: 12 LORD your God lives," she replied, "I don't have any **bread**—
Ps 35: 16 Like the ungodly *they* maliciously mocked [BHS *ungodly* ***circle*** *of mockers* ?; NIV 4353];

5057 מָעוֹז mā'ôz, n.m. [35 / 34] [→ 5058; cf. 6451]

fortress [8], refuge [8], stronghold [7], fortresses [2], helmet [+8031] [2], protection [2], height [1], mightiest fortresses [+4448] [1], protect [1], strength [1], strong [1]

Jdg 6: 26 kind of altar to the LORD your God on the top of this **height**.
2Sa 22: 33 God *who* arms [BHS *my strong* ***refuge***; NIV 273] me *with* strength
Ne 8: 10 Do not grieve, for the joy of the LORD is your **strength**."
Ps 27: 1 The LORD is the **stronghold** *of* my life—of whom shall I be
28: 8 strength of his people, a **fortress** *of* salvation for his anointed one.
31: 2 [31:3] be my rock of **refuge**, a strong fortress to save me.
31: 4 [31:5] me from the trap that is set for me, for you are my **refuge**.
37: 39 comes from the LORD; he is their **stronghold** in time of trouble.
43: 2 You are God my **stronghold**. Why have you rejected me?
52: 7 [52:9] now is the man who did not make God his **stronghold**
60: 7 [60:9] is mine; Ephraim is my **helmet** [+8031], Judah my scepter.
108: 8 [108:9] Ephraim is my **helmet** [+8031], Judah my scepter.
Pr 10: 29 The way of the LORD is a **refuge** for the righteous, but it is the
Isa 17: 9 In that day their **strong** cities, which they left because of the
17: 10 your Savior; you have not remembered the Rock, your **fortress**.
23: 4 Be ashamed, O Sidon, and you, O **fortress** *of* the sea, for the sea
23: 14 Wail, you ships of Tarshish; your **fortress** is destroyed!
25: 4 You have been a **refuge** for the poor, a refuge for the needy in his
25: 4 a **refuge** for the needy in his distress, a shelter from the storm
27: 5 Or else let them come to me for **refuge**; let them make peace with
30: 2 who look for help to Pharaoh's **protection**, to Egypt's shade for
30: 3 Pharaoh's **protection** will be to your shame, Egypt's shade will
Jer 16: 19 O LORD, my strength and my **fortress**, my refuge in time of
Eze 24: 25 on the day I take away their **stronghold**, their joy and glory,
30: 15 the **stronghold** *of* Egypt, and cut off the hordes of Thebes.
Da 11: 1 of Darius the Mede, I took my stand to support and **protect** him.)
11: 7 attack the forces of the king of the North and enter his **fortress**;
11: 10 like an irresistible flood and carry the battle as far as his **fortress**.
11: 19 he will turn back toward the **fortresses** *of* his own country
11: 31 "His armed forces will rise up to desecrate the temple **fortress**
11: 38 Instead of them, he will honor a god of **fortresses**; a god unknown
11: 39 He will attack the **mightiest fortresses** [+4448] with the help of a
Joel 3: 16 [4:16] refuge for his people, a **stronghold** for the people of Israel.
Na 1: 7 The LORD is good, a **refuge** in times of trouble. He cares for
3: 11 you will go into hiding and seek **refuge** from the enemy.

5058 מָעֻזֶן mā'ôzen, n.m. [1] [√ 5057; cf. 6451]

fortresses [1]

Isa 23: 11 He has given an order concerning Phoenicia that her **fortresses** be

5059 מָעוֹךְ mā'ôk, n.pr.m. [1] [cf. 5082]

Maoch [1]

1Sa 27: 2 with him left and went over to Achish son of **Maoch** king of Gath.

5060 ¹מָעוֹן mā'ôn[1], n.[m.]. Not used in NIV/BHS

5061 ²מָעוֹן mā'ôn[2], n.[m.]. [18] [→ 1110, 1260, 5062, 5063, 5104; cf. 6410]

dwelling [7], dwelling place [4], haunt [4], den [1], refuge [1], where live [1]

Dt 26: 15 Look down from heaven, your holy **dwelling place**, and bless your
1Sa 2: 29 scorn my sacrifice and offering that I prescribed for my **dwelling**?
2: 32 you will see distress in my **dwelling**. Although good will be done
2Ch 30: 27 for their prayer reached heaven, his holy **dwelling place**.
36: 15 because he had pity on his people and on his **dwelling place**.
Ps 26: 8 I love the house **where** you **live**, O LORD, the place where your
68: 5 [68:6] a defender of widows, is God in his holy **dwelling**.
71: 3 Be my rock of **refuge**, to which I can always go; give the
90: 1 you have been our **dwelling place** throughout all generations.
91: 9 If you make the Most High your **dwelling**—even the LORD,
Jer 9: 11 [9:10] "I will make Jerusalem a heap of ruins, a **haunt** *of* jackals;
10: 22 It will make the towns of Judah desolate, a **haunt** *of* jackals.
25: 30 he will thunder from his holy **dwelling** and roar mightily against
49: 33 "Hazor will become a **haunt** *of* jackals, a desolate place forever.
51: 37 a **haunt** *of* jackals, an object of horror and scorn, a place where no
Na 2: 11 [2:12] Where now is the lions' **den**, the place where they fed their
Zep 3: 7 her **dwelling** would not be cut off, nor all my punishments come
Zec 2: 13 [2:17] because he has roused himself from his holy **dwelling**."

5062 ³מָעוֹן mā'ôn[3], n.pr.m. & g. [3] [√ 5061]

Maon [2], Maonites [1]

Jdg 10: 12 the Amalekites and the **Maonites** oppressed you and you cried to
1Ch 2: 45 The son of Shammai was **Maon**, and Maon was the father of Beth
2: 45 son of Shammai was Maon, and **Maon** was the father of Beth Zur.

5063 ⁴מָעוֹן mā'ôn[4], n.pr.loc. [5 / 6] [√ 5061]

Maon [6]

Jos 15: 55 **Maon**, Carmel, Ziph, Juttah,
1Sa 23: 24 Now David and his men were in the Desert of **Maon**,
23: 25 he went down to the rock and stayed in the Desert of **Maon**.
23: 25 heard this, he went into the Desert of **Maon** in pursuit of David.
25: 1 Then David moved down into the Desert of **Maon**. [BHS 7000]
25: 2 A certain man in **Maon**, who had property there at Carmel,

5064 מְעוּנִים me'ûnîm, n.pr.g. [4 / 5] [cf. 5079]

Meunites [3], Meunim [2]

1Ch 4: 41 also the **Meunites** [K 5079] who were there and completely
2Ch 20: 1 Ammonites with some of the **Meunites** [BHS 6649] came to make
26: 7 against the Arabs who lived in Gur Baal and against the **Meunites**.
Ezr 2: 50 Asnah, **Meunim**, [K 5079] Nephussim,
Ne 7: 52 Besai, **Meunim**, Nephussim,

5065 מְעוֹנֹתַי me'ônōtay, n.pr.m. [1 / 2]

Meonothai [2]

1Ch 4: 13 The sons of Othniel: Hathath and **Meonothai**. [BHS-]
4: 14 **Meonothai** was the father of Ophrah. Seraiah was the father of

5066 מָעוּף mā'ûp, n.[m.]. [1] [√ 6415]

gloom [1]

Isa 8: 22 the earth and see only distress and darkness and fearful **gloom**,

5067 מָעוֹר mā'ôr, n.[m.]. [1] [√ 6423]

naked bodies [1]

Hab 2: 15 till they are drunk, so that he can gaze on their **naked bodies**.

5068 מַעַזְיָה ma'azyâ, n.pr.m. [1] [→ 5069]

Maaziah [1]

Ne 10: 8 [10:9] **Maaziah**, Bilgai and Shemaiah. These were the priests.

[F] Hitpael (hitpoel, hitpoal, hitpolel, hitpolal, hitpalel, hitpalal, hitpalpel, hitpalpal, hotpael, hotpaal) [G] Hiphil (hiphtil) [H] Hophal [I] Hishtaphel

5069 מַעַזְיָהוּ *maʿazyāhû*, n.pr.m. [1] [√ 5068]

Maaziah [1]

1Ch 24: 18 the twenty-third to Delaiah and the twenty-fourth to **Maaziah**.

5070 מָעַט *māʿaṭ*, v. [22] [→ 5071]

few [4], decrease [2], smaller [2], decreased [1], dwindles away [1], gathered little [1], give less [1], just a few [1], let diminish [1], little [1], make few in number [1], make weak [1], no less than [1], numbers decreased [1], reduce to nothing [1], small [1], trifling [1]

Ex 12: 4 [A] If any household *is* too **small** for a whole lamb, they must
16: 17 [G] did as they were told; some gathered much, some **little**.
16: 18 [G] too much, and he *who* **gathered little** did not have too little.
30: 15 [G] the poor *are* not *to* **give less** when you make the offering to
Lev 25: 16 [A] you are to increase the price, and when the years *are* **few**,
25: 16 [G] and when the years are few, *you are to* **decrease** the price,
26: 22 [G] **make** you *so* **few in number** that your roads will be
Nu 11: 32 [G] and gathered quail. **No** one gathered **less than** ten homers.
26: 54 [G] a larger inheritance, and to a smaller group a **smaller** one;
33: 54 [G] a larger inheritance, and to a smaller group a **smaller** one.
35: 8 [G] from a tribe that has many, but **few** from one that has few."
2Ki 4: 3 [G] all your neighbors for empty jars. Don't ask for **just a few**.
Ne 9: 32 [A] *do* not *let* all this hardship *seem* **trifling** in your eyes—
Ps 107: 38 [G] greatly increased, and *he did* not **let** their herds **diminish**.
107: 39 [A] *their* **numbers decreased**, and they were humbled by
Pr 13: 11 [A] Dishonest money **dwindles away**, but he who gathers money
Ecc 12: 3 [D] men stoop, when the grinders cease because *they are* **few**,
Isa 21: 17 [A] of the bowmen, the warriors of Kedar, *will be* **few**."
Jer 10: 24 [G] not in your anger, lest *you* **reduce** me **to nothing**.
29: 6 [A] and daughters. Increase in number there; *do* not **decrease**.
30: 19 [A] I will add to their numbers, and *they will* not *be* **decreased**;
Eze 29: 15 [G] *I will* **make** it *so* **weak** that it will never again rule over the

5071 מְעַט *m^{e}ʿaṭ*, subst. [101] [√ 5070]

little [33], few [12], not enough [5], only a few [5], little while [3], smaller [3], soon [+3869] [3], almost [+3869] [2], isn't enough [2], short distance [2], soon [+6388] [2], almost [+6388] [1], brief [1], brink [1], few [+3869] [1], few [+928+5031] [1], few in number [+5493] [1], fewest [1], how quickly [+3869] [1], in a moment [+3869] [1], in a very short time [+4663+6388] [1], little more [1], little while [+6388] [1], little while [+8092] [1], many [+4202] [1], might well have [+3869] [1], moment's [1], of little value [+3869] [1], only a little [1], scarcely [+3869] [1], short [1], some [+3869] [1], some [1], soon [+3869+7775] [1], too few [1], too little [1], very few [+4663] [1], very soon [+4663+6388] [1], wasn't enough [1], waste away [1]

Ge 18: 4 Let a **little** water be brought, and then you may all wash your feet
24: 17 to meet her and said, "Please give me a **little** water from your jar."
24: 43 and I say to her, "Please let me drink a **little** water from your jar,"
26: 10 One of the men **might** [+3869] **well have** slept with your wife,
30: 15 said to her, "**Wasn't** it **enough** *that* you took away my husband?
30: 30 The **little** you had before I came has increased greatly, and the
43: 2 their father said to them, "Go back and buy us a **little** more food."
43: 11 a **little** balm and a little honey, some spices and myrrh,
43: 11 a little balm and a **little** honey, some spices and myrrh,
44: 25 "Then our father said, 'Go back and buy a **little more** food.'
47: 9 My years have been **few** and difficult, and they do not equal the
Ex 17: 4 with these people? They are **almost** [+6388] ready to stone me."
23: 30 **Little** by little I will drive them out before you, until you have
23: 30 Little *by* **little** I will drive them out before you, until you have
Lev 25: 52 If **only a few** years remain until the Year of Jubilee, he is to
Nu 13: 18 the people who live there are strong or weak, **few** or many.
16: 9 **Isn't** it **enough** for you that the God of Israel has separated you
16: 13 **Isn't** it **enough** that you have brought us up out of a land flowing
26: 54 give a larger inheritance, and to a **smaller** *group* a smaller one;
26: 56 is to be distributed by lot among the larger and **smaller** groups."
33: 54 give a larger inheritance, and to a **smaller** *group* a smaller one.
35: 8 towns from a tribe that has many, but few from one that has **few**."
Dt 7: 7 than other peoples, for you were the **fewest** of all peoples.
7: 22 your God will drive out those nations before you, **little** *by* little.
7: 22 your God will drive out those nations before you, little by **little**.
26: 5 and he went down into Egypt with a **few** people and lived there
28: 38 You will sow much seed in the field but you will harvest **little**,
28: 62 as the stars in the sky will be left but **few** [+5493] **in number**,
Jos 7: 3 and do not weary all the people, for **only a few** men are there."
22: 17 Was **not** the sin of Peor **enough** for us? Up to this very day we
Jdg 4: 19 "I'm thirsty," he said. "Please give me **some** water." She opened a
Ru 2: 7 from morning till now, except for a **short** rest in the shelter."
1Sa 14: 6 can hinder the LORD from saving, whether by many or by **few**."
14: 29 See how my eyes brightened when I tasted a **little** *of* this honey.
14: 43 told him, "I merely tasted a **little** honey with the end of my staff.
17: 28 And with whom did you leave those **few** sheep in the desert?
2Sa 12: 8 if all this had been **too little**, I would have given you even more.
16: 1 When David had gone a **short distance** beyond the summit,
19: 36 [19:37] cross over the Jordan with the king for a **short distance**,
1Ki 17: 10 "Would you bring me a **little** water in a jar so I may have a drink?"
17: 12 any bread—only a handful of flour in a jar and a **little** oil in a jug.
2Ki 10: 18 all the people together and said to them, "Ahab served Baal a **little**;
1Ch 16: 19 When they were but few in number, **few** indeed, and strangers in it,
2Ch 12: 7 will not destroy them but will **soon** [+3869] give them deliverance.
29: 34 The priests, however, were **too few** to skin all the burnt offerings;
Ezr 9: 8 "But now, for a **brief** moment, the LORD our God has been
9: 8 so our God gives light to our eyes and a **little** relief in our bondage.
Ne 2: 12 I set out during the night with a **few** men. I had not told anyone
7: 4 the city was large and spacious, but there were **few** people in it,
Job 10: 20 Are not my **few** days almost over? Turn away from me so I can
10: 20 almost over? Turn away from me so I can have a **moment's** joy
15: 11 Are God's consolations **not enough** for you, words spoken gently
24: 24 *For a* **little while** they are exalted, and then they are gone;
32: 22 skilled in flattery, my Maker would **soon** [+3869] take me away.
Ps 2: 12 in your way, for his wrath can flare up **in a moment** [+3869].
8: 5 [8:6] You made him a **little** lower than the heavenly beings
37: 10 A **little** [+6388] **while**, and the wicked will be no more;
37: 16 Better the **little** that the righteous have than the wealth of many
73: 2 as for me, my feet had **almost** [+3869] slipped; I had nearly lost
81: 14 [81:15] **how quickly** [+3869] would I subdue their enemies
94: 17 me help, I would **soon** [+3869] have dwelt in the silence of death.
105: 12 When they were but few in number, **few** [+3869] indeed,
109: 8 May his days be **few**; may another take his place of leadership.
119: 87 They **almost** [+3869] wiped me from the earth, but I have not
Pr 5: 14 I have come to the **brink** of utter ruin in the midst of the whole
6: 10 A **little** sleep, a little slumber, a little folding of the hands to rest—
6: 10 A little sleep, a **little** slumber, a little folding of the hands to rest—
6: 10 A little sleep, a little slumber, a **little** folding of the hands to rest—
10: 20 choice silver, but the heart of the wicked is **of little** [+3869] **value**.
15: 16 Better a **little** with the fear of the LORD than great wealth with
16: 8 Better a **little** with righteousness than much gain with injustice.
24: 33 A **little** sleep, a little slumber, a little folding of the hands to rest—
24: 33 A little sleep, a **little** slumber, a little folding of the hands to rest—
24: 33 A little sleep, a little slumber, a **little** folding of the hands to rest—
Ecc 5: 2 [5:1] is in heaven and you are on earth, so let your words be **few**.
5: 12 [5:11] sleep of a laborer is sweet, whether he eats **little** or much,
9: 14 There was once a small city with **only a few** people in it. And a
10: 1 perfume a bad smell, so a **little** folly outweighs wisdom and honor.
SS 3: 4 **Scarcely** [+3869] had I passed them when I found the one my
Isa 1: 9 Unless the LORD Almighty had left us **some** [+3869] survivors,
7: 13 you house of David! Is it **not enough** to try the patience of men?
10: 7 his purpose is to destroy, to put an end to **many** [+4202] nations.
10: 25 **Very soon** [+4663+6388] my anger against you will end and my
16: 14 and her survivors will be **very few** [+4663] and feeble."
26: 20 hide yourselves for a **little** [+8092] **while** until his wrath has
29: 17 **In a very short** [+4663+6388] **time**, will not Lebanon be turned
Jer 42: 2 you now see, though we were once many, now **only a few** are left.
51: 33 it is trampled; the time to harvest her will **soon** [+6388] come."
Eze 5: 3 take a **few** [+928+5031] strands of hair and tuck them away in the
11: 16 yet *for* a **little while** I have been a sanctuary for them in the
16: 20 them as food to the idols. Was your prostitution **not enough**?
16: 47 in all your ways you **soon** [+3869+7775] became more depraved
34: 18 Is it **not enough** for you to feed on the good pasture? Must you
Da 11: 23 act deceitfully, and with **only a few** people he will rise to power.
11: 34 When they fall, they will receive a **little** help, and many who are
Hos 1: 4 because I will **soon** [+6388] punish the house of Jehu for the
8: 10 They will begin to **waste away** under the oppression of the mighty
Hag 1: 6 You have planted much, but have harvested **little**. You eat,
1: 9 "You expected much, but see, it turned out to be **little**. What you
2: 6 'In a **little while** I will once more shake the heavens and the earth,
Zec 1: 15 I was **only a little** angry, but they added to the calamity.'

5072 מְעֻטָּה *m^{e}ʿuṭṭâ*, var. Not used in NIV/BHS

5073 מַעֲטֶה *ma^{a}ṭeh*, n.[m.]. [1] [√ 6486]

garment [1]

Isa 61: 3 of mourning, and a **garment** *of* praise instead of a spirit of despair.

5074 מַעֲטֶפֶת *ma^{a}ṭepet*, n.f. [1] [√ 6493]

capes [1]

Isa 3: 22 the fine robes and the **capes** and cloaks, the purses

5075 מְעִי *m^{e}ʿî*, n.[m.]. [1] [√ 6505]

heap [1]

Isa 17: 1 Damascus will no longer be a city but will become a **heap** *of* ruins.

5076 מָעַי **mā'ay**, n.pr.m. [1]

Maai [1]

Ne 12:36 Azarel, Milalai, Gilalai, **Maai**, Nethanel, Judah and Hanani—

5077 מְעִיל **me'îl**, n.m. [28]

robe [20], cloak [4], robes [2], *untranslated* [1], garment [1]

Ex 28: 4 a breastpiece, an ephod, a **robe**, a woven tunic, a turban and a sash.
28:31 "Make the **robe** *of* the ephod entirely of blue cloth,
28:34 and the pomegranates are to alternate around the hem of the **robe**.
29: 5 the **robe** *of* the ephod, the ephod itself and the breastpiece.
39:22 They made the **robe** *of* the ephod entirely of blue cloth—the work
39:23 with an opening in the center of the **robe** like the opening of a
39:24 scarlet yarn and finely twisted linen around the hem of the **robe**.
39:25 attached them around the hem **[RPH]** between the pomegranates.
39:26 pomegranates alternated around the hem of the **robe** to be worn for
Lev 8: 7 around him, clothed him with the **robe** and put the ephod on him.
1Sa 2:19 Each year his mother made him a little **robe** and took it to him
15:27 to leave, Saul caught hold of the hem of his **robe**, and it tore.
18: 4 Jonathan took off the **robe** he was wearing and gave it to David,
24: 4 [24:5] crept up unnoticed and cut off a corner of Saul's **robe**.
24:11 [24:12] my father, look at this piece of your **robe** in my hand!
24:11 [24:12] I cut off the corner of your **robe** but did not kill you.
28:14 he asked. "An old man wearing a **robe** is coming up," she said.
2Sa 13:18 for this was the kind of **garment** the virgin daughters of the king
1Ch 15:27 Now David was clothed in a **robe** *of* fine linen, as were all the
Ezr 9: 3 When I heard this, I tore my tunic and **cloak**, pulled hair from my
9: 5 I rose from my self-abasement, with my tunic and **cloak** torn,
Job 1:20 At this, Job got up and tore his **robe** and shaved his head.
2:12 and they tore their **robes** and sprinkled dust on their heads.
29:14 righteousness as my clothing; justice was my **robe** and my turban.
Ps 109:29 will be clothed with disgrace and wrapped in shame as in a **cloak**.
Isa 59:17 garments of vengeance and wrapped himself in zeal as in a **cloak**.
61:10 garments of salvation and arrayed me in a **robe** *of* righteousness,
Eze 26:16 and lay aside their **robes** and take off their embroidered garments.

5078 מַעְיָן **ma'yān**, n.m. [23] [√ 6524]

springs [10], spring [5], springs [+4784] [3], fountain [2], fountains [1], well [1], wells [1]

Ge 7:11 on that day all the **springs** *of* the great deep burst forth,
8: 2 Now the **springs** *of* the deep and the floodgates of the heavens had
Lev 11:36 A **spring**, however, or a cistern for collecting water remains clean,
Jos 15: 9 From the hilltop the boundary headed toward the **spring** *of* the
18:15 the boundary came out at the **spring** *of* the waters of Nephtoah.
1Ki 18: 5 "Go through the land to all the **springs** [+4784] and valleys.
2Ki 3:19 will cut down every good tree, stop up all the **springs** [+4784],
3:25 They stopped up all the **springs** [+4784] and cut down every good
2Ch 32: 4 they blocked all the **springs** and the stream that flowed through the
Ps 74:15 It was you who opened up **springs** and streams; you dried up the
84: 6 [84:7] the Valley of Baca, they make it a place of **springs**;
87: 7 As they make music they will sing, "All my **fountains** are in you."
104:10 He makes **springs** pour water into the ravines; it flows between the
114: 8 turned the rock into a pool, the hard rock into **springs** *of* water.
Pr 5:16 Should your **springs** overflow in the streets, your streams of water
8:24 given birth, when there were no **springs** abounding with water;
25:26 Like a muddied **spring** or a polluted well is a righteous man who
SS 4:12 my sister, my bride; you are a **spring** enclosed, a sealed fountain.
4:15 You are a garden **fountain**, a well of flowing water streaming
Isa 12: 3 With joy you will draw water from the **wells** *of* salvation.
41:18 make rivers flow on barren heights, and **springs** within the valleys.
Hos 13:15 blowing in from the desert; his spring will fail and his **well** dry up.
Joel 3:18 [4:18] A **fountain** will flow out of the LORD's house and will

5079 מְעִינִים **me'înîm**, n.pr.g. [0] [cf. 5064]

1Ch 4:41 [also the **Meunites** [K; see Q 5064] who were there]
Ezr 2:50 [Asnah, **Meunim**, [K; see Q 5064] Nephussim,]

5080 מָעַךְ **mā'ak**, v. [3 / 4]

bruised [1], fondled [1], stuck [1], were fondled [1]

Lev 22:24 [B] offer to the LORD an animal whose testicles *are* **bruised**,
1Sa 26: 7 [B] lying asleep inside the camp with his spear **stuck** in the
Eze 23: 3 [E] In that land their breasts **were fondled** and their virgin
23:21 [E] was caressed and your young breasts **fondled**. [BHS 5100]

5081 מַעֲכָה **ma'akâ¹**, n.pr.g. [3] [→ 5082, 5083, 5084; *also used with compound proper names*]

Maacah [3]

2Sa 10: 6 and Zobah, as well as the king of **Maacah** with a thousand men,
10: 8 men of Tob and **Maacah** were by themselves in the open country.
1Ch 19: 7 as well as the king of **Maacah** with his troops, who came

5082 מַעֲכָה **ma'akâ²**, n.pr.m. & f. [18 / 19] [√ 5081; cf. 5059]

Maacah [19]

Ge 22:24 was Reumah, also had sons: Tebah, Gaham, Tahash and **Maacah**.
2Sa 3: 3 Absalom the son of **Maacah** daughter of Talmai king of Geshur;
1Ki 2:39 two of Shimei's slaves ran off to Achish son of **Maacah**, king of
15: 2 His mother's name was **Maacah** daughter of Abishalom.
15:10 His grandmother's name was **Maacah** daughter of Abishalom.
15:13 He even deposed his grandmother **Maacah** from her position as
1Ch 2:48 Caleb's concubine **Maacah** was the mother of Sheber
3: 2 Absalom the son of **Maacah** daughter of Talmai king of Geshur;
7:15 the Huppites and Shuppites. His sister's name was **Maacah**.
7:16 Makir's wife **Maacah** gave birth to a son and named him Peresh.
8:29 father of Gibeon lived in Gibeon. His wife's name was **Maacah**,
9:35 father of Gibeon lived in Gibeon. His wife's name was **Maacah**,
11:43 Hanan son of **Maacah**, Joshaphat the Mithnite,
27:16 son of Zicri; over the Simeonites: Shephatiah son of **Maacah**;
2Ch 11:20 he married **Maacah** daughter of Absalom, who bore him Abijah,
11:21 Rehoboam loved **Maacah** daughter of Absalom more than any of
11:22 Rehoboam appointed Abijah son of **Maacah** to be the chief prince
13: 2 His mother's name was **Maacah**, [BHS 4780] a daughter of Uriel
15:16 King Asa also deposed his grandmother **Maacah** from her position

5083 מַעֲכָת **ma'akāt**, n.pr.g. [1] [√ 5081]

they[s] [+1770+2256] [1]

Jos 13:13 so **they**[s] [+1770+2256] continue to live among the Israelites to this

5084 מַעֲכָתִי **ma'akātî**, a.g. [8] [√ 5081]

Maacah [3], Maacathite [3], Maacathite [+1201] [1], Maacathites [1]

Dt 3:14 Argob as far as the border of the Geshurites and the **Maacathites**;
Jos 12: 5 all of Bashan to the border of the people of Geshur and **Maacah**,
13:11 the territory of the people of Geshur and **Maacah**, all of Mount
13:13 the Israelites did not drive out the people of Geshur and **Maacah**,
2Sa 23:34 Eliphelet son of Ahasbai the **Maacathite** [+1201], Eliam son of
2Ki 25:23 Jaazaniah the son of the **Maacathite**, and their men.
1Ch 4:19 the father of Keilah the Garmite, and Eshtemoa the **Maacathite**.
Jer 40: 8 and Jaazaniah the son of the **Maacathite**, and their men.

5085 מָעַל **mā'al**, v. [35] [→ 5086]

unfaithful [13], unfaithful [+5086] [6], acted unfaithfully [+5086] [2], acted unfaithfully [1], betray [1], break faith [+5086] [1], broke faith [1], commits a violation [+5086] [1], forsaking [+928+5086] [1], more and more unfaithful [+5086+8049] [1], most unfaithful [+5086] [1], treachery [+5086] [1], unfaithful [+5086+6584] [1], unfaithfulness [+5086] [1], unfaithfulness guilty of [+5086] [1], unfaithfulness showed [+5086] [1], violating the ban [1]

Lev 5:15 [A] "When a person **commits a violation** [+5086] and sins
6: 2 [5:21] [A] *is* **unfaithful** [+5086] to the LORD by deceiving his
26:40 [A] their **treachery** [+5086] against me and their hostility toward
Nu 5: 6 [A] in any way and so *is* **unfaithful** [+5086] to the LORD,
5:12 [A] 'If a man's wife goes astray and *is* **unfaithful** [+5086] to him
5:27 [A] defiled herself and *been* **unfaithful** [+5086] to her husband,
Dt 32:51 [A] because *both of you* **broke faith** with me in the presence of
Jos 7: 1 [A] the Israelites **acted unfaithfully** [+5086] in regard to the
22:16 [A] 'How *could you* **break** [+5086] **faith** with the God of Israel
22:20 [A] *When* Achan son of Zerah **acted unfaithfully** [+5086]
22:31 [A] because *you have* not **acted unfaithfully** toward the LORD
1Ch 2: 7 [A] who brought trouble on Israel *by* **violating the ban** on taking
5:25 [A] *they were* **unfaithful** to the God of their fathers
10:13 [A] Saul died because he was **unfaithful** [+5086+6584] to the
2Ch 12: 2 [A] Because *they had been* **unfaithful** to the LORD,
26:16 [A] *He was* **unfaithful** to the LORD his God, and entered the
26:18 [A] Leave the sanctuary, for *you have been* **unfaithful**; and you
28:19 [A] and *had been* **most unfaithful** [+5086] to the LORD.
28:22 [A] King Ahaz became even more **unfaithful** to the LORD.
29: 6 [A] Our fathers *were* **unfaithful**; they did evil in the eyes of the
30: 7 [A] and brothers, who *were* **unfaithful** to the LORD,
36:14 [A] the people *became* **more and more unfaithful** [+5086+8049],
Ezr 10: 2 [A] "We *have been* **unfaithful** to our God by marrying foreign
10:10 [A] priest stood up and said to them, "You *have been* **unfaithful**;
Ne 1: 8 [A] saying, 'If you *are* **unfaithful**, I will scatter you among the
13:27 [A] *are being* **unfaithful** to our God by marrying foreign
Pr 16:10 [A] speak as an oracle, and his mouth *should* not **betray** justice.
Eze 14:13 [A] if a country sins against me by *being* **unfaithful** [+5086] and
15: 8 [A] land desolate because *they have been* **unfaithful** [+5086],
17:20 [A] judgment upon him there because *he was* **unfaithful** to me.
18:24 [A] Because of the **unfaithfulness** [+5086] *he is* **guilty of** and
20:27 [A] your fathers blasphemed me by **forsaking** [+928+5086] me:
39:23 [A] into exile for their sin, because *they were* **unfaithful** to me.
39:26 [A] all the **unfaithfulness** [+5086] *they* **showed** toward me when
Da 9: 7 [A] scattered us because of our **unfaithfulness** [+5086] to you.

5086 מַעַל¹ ma'al¹, n.m. [29] [√ 5085]

unfaithful [+5085] [6], unfaithfulness [6], acted unfaithfully [+5085] [2], *untranslated* [1], break faith [+5085] [1], commits a violation [+5085] [1], disobedience [1], falsehood [1], forsaking [+928+5085] [1], matter [1], more and more unfaithful [+5085+8049] [1], most unfaithful [+5085] [1], treachery [+5085] [1], turning away [1], unfaithful [+5085+6584] [1], unfaithfulness [+5085] [1], unfaithfulness guilty of [+5085] [1], unfaithfulness showed [+5085] [1]

Lev 5:15 "When a person **commits a violation** [+5085] and sins
6:2 [5:21] *is* **unfaithful** [+5085] to the LORD by deceiving his
26:40 their **treachery** [+5085] against me and their hostility toward me,
Nu 5:6 another in any way and so *is* **unfaithful** [+5085] to the LORD,
5:12 'If a man's wife goes astray and *is* **unfaithful** [+5085] to him
5:27 has defiled herself and *been* **unfaithful** [+5085] to her husband,
31:16 were the means of **turning** the Israelites **away** from the LORD in
Jos 7:1 the Israelites **acted unfaithfully** [+5085] in regard to the devoted
22:16 'How *could you* **break faith** [+5085] with the God of Israel like
22:20 *When* Achan son of Zerah **acted unfaithfully** [+5085] regarding
22:22 If this has been in rebellion or **disobedience** to the LORD,
22:31 you have not acted unfaithfully toward the LORD in this **matter**.
1Ch 9:1 were taken captive to Babylon because of their **unfaithfulness**.
10:13 Saul died because he was **unfaithful** [+5085+6584] to the LORD;
2Ch 28:19 in Judah and *had been* **most unfaithful** [+5085] to the LORD.
29:19 that King Ahaz removed in his **unfaithfulness** while he was king.
33:19 as well as all his sins and **unfaithfulness**, and the sites where he
36:14 the people *became* **more and more unfaithful** [+5085+8049],
Ezr 9:2 the leaders and officials have led the way in this **unfaithfulness**."
9:4 gathered around me because of this **unfaithfulness** *of* the exiles.
10:6 because he continued to mourn over the **unfaithfulness** *of* the
Job 21:34 your nonsense? Nothing is left of your answers but **falsehood**!"
Eze 14:13 if a country sins against me by *being* **unfaithful** [+5085] and I
15:8 the land desolate because *they have been* **unfaithful** [+5085],
17:20 judgment upon him there because **[RPH]** he was unfaithful to me.
18:24 Because of the **unfaithfulness** *he is* **guilty of** [+5085] and
20:27 In this also your fathers blasphemed me by **forsaking** [+928+5085]
39:26 all the **unfaithfulness** *they* **showed** [+5085] toward me when they
Da 9:7 have scattered us because of our **unfaithfulness** [+5085] to you.

5087 מַעַל² ma'al², subst.adv. & pp. [140] [√ 6590] See Select Index

more [+2025] [36], above [+4946] [19], *untranslated* [15], upward [+2025+4200] [6], above [+2025+4200+4946] [4], above [+2025+4200] [3], on [+2025] [3], over [+2025+4200+4946] [3], at each successive level [+2025+2025+4200+4200+5087] [2], head [+2025+2256+4946+8900] [2], higher [+2025] [2], highly [+2025+4200] [2], in ascending stages [+2025+2025+4200+4200 +5087] [2], just above [+4946] [2], over [+4946] [2], top [+2025+4200 +4946] [2], up [+2025+4200] [2], very [+2025+4200] [2], above [+4200+4946+4946+6645] [1], above [+4946+6584] [1], beyond [+2025] [1], deep [+2025] [1], depth [+2025+4200] [1], downstream [+2025+4200+4946] [1], exceedingly [+2025+4200] [1], heights [+2025+4200] [1], high above [+2025+4200+4946] [1], higher [+4946] [1], higher than [+2025+4200+8049] [1], jointed [+4200 +4946+8079] [1], magnificence [+2025] [1], more [+2025+4200] [1], more and more powerful [+1541+2025+2143+2256+4200+6330] [1], old [+2025] [1], older [+2025] [1], on high [+4946] [1], outer [+2025+4200+4946] [1], over and above [+2025+4200] [1], overturned [+2025+2200+4200] [1], project upward [+2025+4200] [1], severe [+2025+4200] [1], top [+2025] [1], top [+2025+4200] [1], top of [+2025+4200+4946] [1], top [1], upstream [+2025+4200] [1], upward [+2025+4200+4946] [1], very [+2025+4200+6330] [1], wielding [+995+2025+4200] [1]

5088 מֵעַל mē'al, pp.+pp. Not used in NIV/BHS [√ 4946 + 6584]

5089 מֹעַל mō'al, n.[m.] [1] [√ 6590]

lifted [1]

Ne 8:6 and all the people **lifted** their hands and responded, "Amen!

5090 מַעֲלֶה ma'aleh, n.m. [16] [√ 6590]

Pass [7], hill [2], way [2], ascent [1], going up [1], Mount [1], stairs [1], way up [1]

Nu 34:4 cross south of Scorpion **Pass**, continue on to Zin and go south of
Jos 10:10 Israel pursued them along the road **going up** *to* Beth Horon
15:3 crossed south of Scorpion **Pass**, continued on to Zin and went over
15:7 to Gilgal, which faces the **Pass** *of* Adummim south of the gorge.
18:17 continued to Geliloth, which faces the **Pass** *of* Adummim,
Jdg 1:36 The boundary of the Amorites was from Scorpion **Pass** to Sela
8:13 son of Joash then returned from the battle by the **Pass** *of* Heres.
1Sa 9:11 As they were going up the **hill** *to* the town, they met some girls
2Sa 15:30 But David continued up the **Mount** *of* Olives, weeping as he went;
2Ki 9:27 They wounded him in his chariot on the **way up** *to* Gur near
2Ch 20:16 They will be climbing up by the **Pass** *of* Ziz, and you will find
32:33 was buried on the **hill** *where* the tombs of David's descendants
Ne 9:4 Standing on the **stairs** were the Levites—Jeshua, Bani, Kadmiel,
12:37 directly up the steps of the City of David on the **ascent** to the wall
Isa 15:5 They go up the **way** *to* Luhith, weeping as they go; on the road to
Jer 48:5 They go up the **way** *to* Luhith, weeping bitterly as they go;

5091 מַעֲלָה¹ ma'ălâ¹, n.f. [1] [√ 6590]

what is going through [1]

Eze 11:5 O house of Israel, but I know **what is going through** your mind.

5092 מַעֲלָה² ma'ălâ², n.f. [46] [√ 6590]

steps [22], ascents [15], *untranslated* [3], stairway [2], flight of stairs [1], journey [1], lofty palace [1], most exalted [+9366] [1]

Ex 20:26 do not go up to my altar on **steps**, lest your nakedness be exposed
1Ki 10:19 The throne had six **steps**, and its back had a rounded top. On both
10:20 Twelve lions stood on the six **steps**, one at either end of each step.
2Ki 9:13 and took their cloaks and spread them under him on the bare **steps**.
20:9 Shall the shadow go forward ten **steps**, or shall it go back ten
20:9 the shadow go forward ten steps, or shall it go back ten **steps**?"
20:10 "It is a simple matter for the shadow to go forward ten **steps**,"
20:10 ten steps," said Hezekiah. "Rather, have it go back ten **steps**."
20:11 the LORD made the shadow go back the ten **steps** it had gone
20:11 go back the ten steps it had gone down on the **stairway** *of* Ahaz.
20:11 the ten steps it had gone down on the stairway of Ahaz. **[RPH]**
1Ch 17:17 looked on me as though I were the **most exalted** [+9366] *of* men,
2Ch 9:18 The throne had six **steps**, and a footstool of gold was attached to it.
9:19 Twelve lions stood on the six **steps**, one at either end of each step.
Ezr 7:9 He had begun his **journey** from Babylon on the first day of the
Ne 3:15 as far as the **steps** going down from the City of David.
12:37 At the Fountain Gate they continued directly up the **steps** *of* the
Ps 120:T [120:1] A song of **ascents**.
121:T [121:1] A song of **ascents**.
122:T [122:1] A song of **ascents**. Of David.
123:T [123:1] A song of **ascents**.
124:T [124:1] A song of **ascents**. Of David.
125:T [125:1] A song of **ascents**.
126:T [126:1] A song of **ascents**.
127:T [127:1] A song of **ascents**. Of Solomon.
128:T [128:1] A song of **ascents**.
129:T [129:1] A song of **ascents**.
130:T [130:1] A song of **ascents**.
131:T [131:1] A song of **ascents**. Of David.
132:T [132:1] A song of **ascents**.
133:T [133:1] A song of **ascents**. Of David.
134:T [134:1] A song of **ascents**.
Isa 38:8 I will make the shadow cast by the sun go back the ten **steps** it has
38:8 will make the shadow cast by the sun go back the ten steps **[RPH]**
38:8 **stairway** *of* Ahaz.'" So the sunlight went back the ten steps it had
38:8 Ahaz.'" So the sunlight went back the ten **steps** it had gone down.
38:8 So the sunlight went back the ten steps **[RPH]** it had gone down.
Eze 40:6 He climbed its **steps** and measured the threshold of the gate;
40:22 facing east. Seven **steps** led up to it, with its portico opposite them.
40:26 Seven **steps** led up to it, with its portico opposite them; it had palm
40:31 palm trees decorated its jambs, and eight **steps** led up to it.
40:34 decorated the jambs on either side, and eight **steps** led up to it.
40:37 decorated the jambs on either side, and eight **steps** led up to it.
40:49 It was reached by a **flight of stairs**, and there were pillars on each
43:17 and a gutter of a cubit all around. The **steps** *of* the altar face east."
Am 9:6 he who builds his **lofty palace** in the heavens and sets its

5093 מַעְלָה ma'lâ, adv. & pp. Not used in NIV/BHS [√ 6590]

5094 מַעֲלִיל ma'ălîl, n.m. [0] [√ 6618]

Zec 1:4 [from your evil ways and your evil **practices**.' [K; see Q 5095]]

5095 מַעֲלָל ma'ălāl, n.m. [41] [√ 6618]

deeds [16], actions [8], done [6], practices [3], dealings [1], do [1], evil practices [1], sins [1], ways [1], what doing [1], wicked deeds [1], work [1]

Dt 28:20 to sudden ruin because of the evil you have **done** in forsaking him.
Jdg 2:19 They refused to give up their **evil practices** and stubborn ways.
1Sa 25:3 but her husband, a Calebite, was surly and mean in his **dealings**.
Ne 9:35 you gave them, they did not serve you or turn from their evil **ways**.
Ps 28:4 Repay them for their deeds and for their evil **work**; repay them for
77:11 [77:12] I will remember the **deeds** *of* the LORD; yes, I will
78:7 and would not forget his **deeds** but would keep his commands.
106:29 they provoked the LORD to anger by their **wicked deeds**,

Ps 106:39 by what they did; by their **deeds** they prostituted themselves.
Pr 20:11 Even a child is known by his **actions**, by whether his conduct is
Isa 1:16 Take your evil **deeds** out of my sight! Stop doing wrong,
3: 8 their words and **deeds** are against the LORD, defying his glorious
3:10 will be well with them, for they will enjoy the fruit of their **deeds**.
Jer 4: 4 break out and burn like fire because of the evil you have **done**—
4:18 "Your own conduct and **actions** have brought this upon you.
7: 3 Reform your ways and your **actions**, and I will let you live in this
7: 5 If you really change your ways and your **actions** and deal with
11:18 I knew it, for at that time he showed me **what** they were **doing**.
17:10 according to his conduct, according to what his **deeds** deserve."
18:11 each one of you, and reform your ways and your **actions**.'
21:12 break out and burn like fire because of the evil you have **done**—
21:14 I will punish you as your **deeds** deserve, declares the LORD.
23: 2 I will bestow punishment on you for the evil you have **done**,"
23:22 have turned them from their evil ways and from their evil **deeds**.
25: 5 each of you, from your evil ways and your evil **practices**,
26: 3 the disaster I was planning because of the evil they have **done**.
26:13 Now reform your ways and your **actions** and obey the LORD
32:19 everyone according to his conduct and as his **deeds** deserve.
35:15 of you must turn from your wicked ways and reform your **actions**;
44:22 When the LORD could no longer endure your wicked **actions**
Eze 36:31 Then you will remember your evil ways and wicked **deeds**,
Hos 4: 9 punish both of them for their ways and repay them for their **deeds**.
5: 4 "Their **deeds** do not permit them to return to their God. A spirit of
7: 2 their evil deeds. Their **sins** engulf them; they are always before me.
9:15 Because of their sinful **deeds**, I will drive them out of my house.
12: 2 [12:3] to his ways and repay him according to his **deeds**.
Mic 2: 7 "Is the Spirit of the LORD angry? Does he **do** such things?"
3: 4 he will hide his face from them because of the evil they have **done**.
7:13 because of its inhabitants, as the result of their **deeds**.
Zec 1: 4 'Turn from your evil ways and your evil **practices**.' [K 5094]
1: 6 Almighty has done to us what our ways and **practices** deserve,

5096 מַעֲמָד ma'amād, n.[m.]. [5] [√ 6641]

attending [2], duty [1], places [1], position [1]

1Ki 10: 5 his officials, the **attending** servants in their robes, his cupbearers,
1Ch 23:28 The **duty** *of* the Levites was to help Aaron's descendants in the
2Ch 9: 4 the seating of his officials, the **attending** servants in their robes,
35:15 were in the **places** prescribed by David, Asaph, Heman
Isa 22:19 you from your office, and you will be ousted from your **position**.

5097 מָעֳמָד mo'omād, n.[m.]. [1] [√ 6641]

foothold [1]

Ps 69: 2 [69:3] I sink in the miry depths, where there is no **foothold**. I have

5098 מַעֲמָסָה ma'amāsâ, n.f. [1] [√ 6673]

immovable [1]

Zec 12: 3 I will make Jerusalem an **immovable** rock for all the nations.

5099 מַעֲמַקִּים ma'amaqqîm, n.m.pl. [5] [√ 6676]

depths [3], deep [2]

Ps 69: 2 [69:3] I have come into the **deep** waters; the floods engulf me.
69:14 [69:15] me from those who hate me, from the **deep** waters.
130: 1 Out of the **depths** I cry to you, O LORD;
Isa 51:10 who made a road in the **depths** *of* the sea so that the redeemed
Eze 27:34 Now you are shattered by the sea in the **depths** *of* the waters;

5100 מַ֫עַן ma'an, subst.pp.c. [272 / 271] [√ 6701]

so that [+4200] [78], to [+4200] [36], that [+4200] [24], for sake [+4200] [22], for the sake of [+4200] [22], because of [+4200] [17], so [+4200] [17], *untranslated* [14], then [+4200] [10], and [+4200] [7], for [+4200] [5], in order to [+4200] [5], therefore [+4200] [4], bent on [+4200] [1], for then [+4200] [1], in behalf of [+4200] [1], in order to [+906+4200] [1], in this way [+4200] [1], otherwise [+889+4200 +4202] [1], that is why [+4200] [1], this [+4200] [1], thus [+4200] [1], till [+4200] [1]

Ge 12:13 Say you are my sister, **so** [+4200] **that** I will be treated well for
18:19 For I have chosen him, **so** [+4200] that he will direct his children
18:19 just, **so that** [+4200] the LORD will bring about for Abraham
18:24 not spare the place **for** [+4200] **the sake of** the fifty righteous
27:25 bring me some of your game to eat, **so** [+4200] **that** I may give
37:22 Reuben said this **to** [+4200] rescue him from them and take him
50:20 God intended it for good **to** [+4200] accomplish what is now being
Ex 1:11 So they put slave masters over them **to** [+4200] oppress them with
4: 5 the LORD, "is **so** [+4200] **that** they may believe that the LORD,
8:10 [8:6] "It will be as you say, **so** [+4200] **that** you may know there
8:22 [8:18] no swarms of flies will be there, **so** [+4200] **that** you will
9:16 and **that** [+4200] my name might be proclaimed in all the earth.
9:29 there will be no more hail, **so** [+4200] you may know that the earth
10: 1 the hearts of his officials **so** [+4200] **that** I may perform these
10: 2 **that** [+4200] you may tell your children and grandchildren how I
11: 7 or animal.' **Then** [+4200] you will know that the LORD makes a
11: 9 "Pharaoh will refuse to listen to you—**so** [+4200] **that** my wonders
13: 9 a reminder on your forehead **that** [+4200] the law of the LORD is
16: 4 gather enough for that day. **In this** [+4200] **way** I will test them
16:32 keep it for the generations to come, **so** [+4200] they can see the
20:12 your mother, **so** [+4200] **that** you may live long in the land the
23:12 but on the seventh day do not work, **so** [+4200] **that** your ox
33:13 so I may know you **and** [+4200] continue to find favor with you.
Lev 17: 5 This is **so** [+4200] the Israelites will bring to the LORD the
20: 3 for by giving his children to Molech, **[NIE]** he has defiled my
23:43 **so** [+4200] your descendants will know that I had the Israelites live
Nu 15:40 **Then** [+4200] you will remember to obey all my commands
16:40 [17:5] This was to remind the Israelites **that** [+4200] no one
27:20 Give him some of your authority **so** [+4200] the whole Israelite
36: 8 must marry someone in her father's tribal clan, **so** [+4200] **that**
Dt 2:30 his heart obstinate **in order to** [+4200] give him into your hands,
3:26 But **because** [+4200] **of** you the LORD was angry with me
4: 1 Follow them **so** [+4200] **that** you may live and may go in
4:40 **that** [+4200] you may live long in the land the LORD your God
5:14 nor the alien within your gates, **so** [+4200] **that** your manservant
5:16 as the LORD your God has commanded you, **so** [+4200] **that** you
5:16 **that** [+4200] it may go well with you in the land the LORD your
5:29 keep all my commands always, **so** [+4200] **that** it might go well
5:33 that the LORD your God has commanded you, **so** [+4200] **that**
6: 2 **so** [+4200] **that** you, your children and their children after them
6: 2 that I give you, and **so** [+4200] **that** you may enjoy long life.
6:18 good in the LORD's sight, **so** [+4200] **that** it may go well with
6:23 he brought us out from there **to** [+4200] bring us in and give us the
8: 1 to follow every command I am giving you today, **so** [+4200] **that**
8: 2 God led you all the way in the desert these forty years, **to** [+4200]
8: 3 which neither you nor your fathers had known, **to** [+4200] teach
8:16 something your fathers had never known, **to** [+4200] humble
8:16 to humble and **to** [+4200] test you so that in the end it might go
8:18 **so** [+4200] confirms his covenant, which he swore to your
9: 5 the LORD your God will drive them out before you, **to** [+4200]
11: 8 therefore all the commands I am giving you today, **so** [+4200] **that**
11: 9 **so** [+4200] **that** you may live long in the land that the LORD
11:21 **so** [+4200] **that** your days and the days of your children may be
12:25 Do not eat it, **so** [+4200] **that** it may go well with you and your
12:28 to obey all these regulations I am giving you, **so** [+4200] **that**
13:17 [13:18] things shall be found in your hands, **so** [+4200] **that**
14:23 place he will choose as a dwelling for his Name, **so** [+4200] **that**
14:29 **so** [+4200] **that** the LORD your God may bless you in all the
16: 3 because you left Egypt in haste—**so** [+4200] **that** all the days of
16:20 Follow justice and justice alone, **so** [+4200] **that** you may live
17:16 or make the people return to Egypt **to** [+4200] get more of them,
17:19 he is to read it all the days of his life **so** [+4200] **that** he may learn
17:20 and turn from the law to the right or to the left. **Then** [+4200] he
20:18 **Otherwise** [+889+4200+4202], they will teach you to follow all
22: 7 be sure to let the mother go, **so** [+4200] **that** it may go well with
23:20 [23:21] not a brother Israelite, **so** [+4200] **that** the LORD your
24:19 the widow, **so** [+4200] **that** the LORD your God may bless you in
25:15 measures, **so** [+4200] **that** you may live long in the land the
27: 3 over **to** [+4200] enter the land the LORD your God is giving you,
29: 6 [29:5] I did this **so** [+4200] **that** you might know that I am the
29: 9 [29:8] follow the terms of this covenant, **so** [+4200] **that**
29:13 [29:12] **to** [+4200] confirm you this day as his people, that he
29:19 [29:18] though I persist in going my own way." **This** [+4200]
30: 6 him with all your heart and with all your soul, **and** [+4200] live.
30:19 Now choose life, **so** [+4200] **that** you and your children may live
31:12 and the aliens living in your towns—**so** [+4200] they can listen
31:12 so they can listen and **[RPH]** learn to fear the LORD your God
31:19 have them sing it, **so** [+4200] **that** it may be a witness for me
Jos 1: 7 or to the left, **that** [+4200] you may be successful wherever you
1: 8 night, **so** [+4200] **that** you may be careful to do everything written
3: 4 **Then** [+4200] you will know which way to go, since you have
4: 6 **to** [+4200] serve as a sign among you. In the future, when your
4:24 He did this **so** [+4200] **that** all the peoples of the earth might know
4:24 and **so** [+4200] **that** you might always fear the LORD your God."
11:20 hardened their hearts to wage war against Israel, **so** [+4200] **that**
11:20 destroy them totally, **[RPH]** exterminating them without mercy,
Jdg 2:22 I will use them **to** [+4200] test Israel and see whether they will
3: 2 (he did this only **to** [+4200] teach warfare to the descendants of the
1Sa 15:15 the sheep and cattle **to** [+4200] sacrifice to the LORD your God,
17:28 your heart is; you came down only **to** [+4200] watch the battle."
2Sa 13: 5 Let her prepare the food in my sight **so** [+4200] I may watch her
1Ki 2: 3 as written in the Law of Moses, **so** [+4200] **that** you may prosper
2: 4 and **that** [+4200] the LORD may keep his promise to me:
8:40 **so** [+4200] **that** they will fear you all the time they live in the land
8:41 but has come from a distant land **because** [+4200] **of** your name—
8:43 do whatever the foreigner asks of you, **so** [+4200] **that** all the
8:60 **so** [+4200] **that** all the peoples of the earth may know that the

1Ki 11:12 Nevertheless, **for** [+4200] **the sake of** David your father, I will not
11:13 will give him one tribe **for** [+4200] **the sake of** David my servant
11:13 sake of David my servant and **for** [+4200] **the sake of** Jerusalem,
11:32 **for** [+4200] **the sake of** my servant David and the city of
11:32 the sake of my servant David and **[RPH]** the city of Jerusalem,
11:34 all the days of his life **for** [+4200] **the sake of** David my servant,
11:36 I will give one tribe to his son **so** [+4200] **that** David my servant
11:39 I will humble David's descendants **because** [+4200] **of** this,
12:15 for this turn of events was from the LORD, **to** [+4200] fulfill the
15: 4 Nevertheless, **for** [+4200] David's **sake** the LORD his God gave
2Ki 8:19 Nevertheless, **for** [+4200] **the sake of** his servant David,
10:19 Jehu was acting deceptively **in order to** [+4200] destroy the
13:23 showed concern for them **because** [+4200] **of** his covenant with
19:34 I will defend this city and save it, **for** [+4200] my **sake** and for the
19:34 for my sake and **for** [+4200] **the sake of** David my servant."
20: 6 I will defend this city **for** [+4200] my **sake** and for the sake of my
20: 6 city for my sake and **for** [+4200] **the sake of** my servant David.' "
22:17 **[NIE]** provoked me to anger by all the idols their hands have
23:24 This he did **to** [+4200] fulfill the requirements of the law written in
1Ch 28: 8 to follow all the commands of the LORD your God, **that** [+4200]
2Ch 6:31 **so** [+4200] **that** they will fear you and walk in your ways all the
6:32 has come from a distant land **because** [+4200] **of** your great name
6:33 do whatever the foreigner asks of you, **so** [+4200] **that** all the
10:15 for this turn of events was from God, **to** [+4200] fulfill the word
21: 7 Nevertheless, **because** [+4200] **of** the covenant the LORD had
25:20 for God **so** [+4200] worked **that** he might hand them over to
31: 4 Levites **so** [+4200] they could devote themselves to the Law of the
32:18 and make them afraid **in order to** [+4200] capture the city.
34:25 **[NIE]** provoked me to anger by all that their hands have made,
Ezr 9:12 not seek a treaty of friendship with them at any time, **that** [+4200]
Ne 6:13 **[RPH]** He had been hired to intimidate me so that I would
6:13 He had been hired **to** [+4200] intimidate me so that I would
6:13 then they would give me a bad name **to** [+4200] discredit me.
Job 18: 4 in your anger, is the earth to be abandoned **for** [+4200] your **sake**?
19:29 and **then** [+4200] you will know that there is judgment."
40: 8 my justice? Would you condemn me **to** [+4200] justify yourself?
Ps 5: 8 [5:9] in your righteousness **because** [+4200] **of** my enemies—
6: 4 [6:5] deliver me; save me **because** [+4200] **of** your unfailing love.
8: 2 [8:3] infants you have ordained praise **because** [+4200] **of** your
9:14 [9:15] **that** [+4200] I may declare your praises in the gates of the
23: 3 guides me in paths of righteousness **for** [+4200] his name's **sake**.
25: 7 according to your love remember me, **for** [+4200] you are good,
25:11 **For** [+4200] **the sake of** your name, O LORD, forgive my
27:11 lead me in a straight path **because** [+4200] **of** my oppressors.
30:12 [30:13] **that** [+4200] my heart may sing to you and not be silent.
31: 3 [31:4] my fortress, **for** [+4200] **the sake of** your name lead and
44:26 [44:27] redeem us **because** [+4200] **of** your unfailing love.
48:11 [48:12] the villages of Judah are glad **because** [+4200] **of** your
48:13 [48:14] view her citadels, **that** [+4200] you may tell of them to
51: 4 [51:6] done what is evil in your sight, **so** [+4200] **that** you are
60: 5 [60:7] help us with your right hand, **that** [+4200] those you love
68:23 [68:24] **that** [+4200] you may plunge your feet in the blood of
69:18 [69:19] and rescue me; redeem me **because** [+4200] **of** my foes.
78: 6 **so** [+4200] the next generation would know them,
79: 9 deliver us and forgive our sins **for** [+4200] your name's **sake**.
97: 8 the villages of Judah are glad **because** [+4200] **of** your judgments,
106: 8 Yet he saved them **for** [+4200] his name's **sake**, to make his
108: 6 [108:7] help us with your right hand, **that** [+4200] those you love
109:21 deal well with me **for** [+4200] your name's **sake**;
119:11 I have hidden your word in my heart **that** [+4200] I might not sin
119:71 It was good for me to be afflicted **so** [+4200] **that** I might learn
119:80 May my heart be blameless toward your decrees, **that** [+4200] I
119:101 I have kept my feet from every evil path **so** [+4200] **that** I might
122: 8 **For** [+4200] **the sake of** my brothers and friends, I will say,
122: 9 **For** [+4200] **the sake of** the house of the LORD our God,
125: 3 not remain over the land allotted to the righteous, **for** [+4200] **then**
130: 4 with you there is forgiveness; **therefore** [+4200] you are feared.
143:11 **For** [+4200] your name's **sake**, O LORD, preserve my life;
Pr 2:20 **Thus** [+4200] you will walk in the ways of good men and keep to
15:24 The path of life leads upward for the wise **to** [+4200] keep him
19:20 and accept instruction, **and** [+4200] in the end you will be wise.
Isa 5:19 "Let God hurry, let him hasten his work **so** [+4200] we may see it.
23:16 sing many a song, **so** [+4200] **that** you will be remembered."
28:13 a little there—**so** [+4200] **that** they will go and fall backward,
30: 1 an alliance, but not by my Spirit, **[NIE]** heaping sin upon sin;
37:35 "I will defend this city and save it, **for** [+4200] my **sake** and for the
37:35 for my sake and **for** [+4200] **the sake of** David my servant!"
41:20 **so** [+4200] **that** people may see and know, may consider
42:21 It pleased the LORD **for** [+4200] **the sake of** his righteousness to
43:10 "and my servant whom I have chosen, **so** [+4200] **that** you may
43:14 the Holy One of Israel: "**For** [+4200] your **sake** I will send to
43:25 he who blots out your transgressions, **for** [+4200] my own **sake**,
43:26 the matter together; state the case for your innocence. **[NIE]**
44: 9 for them are blind; they are ignorant, **to** [+4200] their own shame.
45: 3 riches stored in secret places, **so** [+4200] **that** you may know that I
45: 4 **For** [+4200] **the sake of** Jacob my servant, of Israel my chosen,
45: 6 **so** [+4200] **that** from the rising of the sun to the place of its setting
48: 9 **For** [+4200] my own name's **sake** I delay my wrath; for the sake
48:11 **For** [+4200] my own **sake**, for my own sake, I do this. How can I
48:11 For my own sake, **for** [+4200] my own **sake**, I do this. How can I
49: 7 princes will see and bow down, **because** [+4200] **of** the LORD,
55: 5 that do not know you will hasten to you, **because** [+4200] **of**
62: 1 **For** [+4200] Zion's **sake** I will not keep silent, for Jerusalem's
62: 1 Zion's sake I will not keep silent, **for** [+4200] Jerusalem's **sake**
63:17 Return **for** [+4200] **the sake of** your servants, the tribes that are
65: 8 yet some good in it,' so will I do **in behalf** [+4200] **of** my servants;
66: 5 and exclude you **because** [+4200] **of** my name, have said,
66:11 **For** [+4200] you will nurse and be satisfied at her comforting
66:11 be satisfied at her comforting breasts; **[RPH]** you will drink
Jer 4:14 O Jerusalem, wash the evil from your heart **and** [+4200] be saved.
7:10 "We are safe"—safe **to** [+4200] do all these detestable things?
7:18 They pour out drink offerings to other gods **to** [+4200] provoke me
7:19 Are they not rather harming themselves, **to** [+4200] their own
7:23 Walk in all the ways I command you, **that** [+4200] it may go well
10:18 I will bring distress on them **so** [+4200] **that** they may be
11: 5 **Then** [+4200] I will fulfill the oath I swore to your forefathers,
14: 7 O LORD, do something **for** [+4200] **the sake of** your name.
14:21 **For** [+4200] **the sake of** your name do not despise us; do not
25: 7 declares the LORD, "**and** [+4200] you have provoked me with
27:10 They prophesy lies to you **that** [+4200] will only serve to remove
27:15 'They are prophesying lies in my name. **Therefore** [+4200],
32:14 and put them in a clay jar **so** [+4200] they will last a long time.
32:29 along with the houses where **[NIE]** the people provoked me to
32:35 should do such a detestable thing and **so** [+4200] make Judah sin.
35: 7 must always live in tents. **Then** [+4200] you will live a long time
36: 3 of Judah hear about every disaster I plan to inflict on them, **[NIE]**
42: 6 to whom we are sending you, **so** [+4200] **that** it will go well with
43: 3 Baruch son of Neriah is inciting you against us **to** [+4200] hand us
44: 8 **[NIE]** You will destroy yourselves and make yourselves an object
44: 8 and **[NIE]** make yourselves an object of cursing
44:29 declares the LORD, '**so** [+4200] **that** you will know that my
50:34 He will vigorously defend their cause **so** [+4200] **that** he may
51:39 and make them drunk, **so** [+4200] **that** they shout with laughter—
Eze 4:17 **for** [+4200] food and water will be scarce. They will be appalled at
6: 6 the high places demolished, **so** [+4200] **that** your altars will be laid
11:20 **Then** [+4200] they will follow my decrees and be careful to keep
12:16 plague, **so** [+4200] **that** in the nations where they go they may
12:19 drink their water in despair, **for** [+4200] their land will be stripped
14: 5 I will do this **to** [+4200] recapture the hearts of the people of Israel,
14:11 **Then** [+4200] the people of Israel will no longer stray from me,
16:54 **so** [+4200] **that** you may bear your disgrace and be ashamed of all
16:63 **Then** [+4200], when I make atonement for you for all you have
19: 9 They put him in prison, **so** [+4200] his roar was heard no longer on
20: 9 **for** [+4200] **the sake of** my name I did what would keep it from
20:14 **for** [+4200] **the sake of** my name I did what would keep it from
20:22 **for** [+4200] **the sake of** my name I did what would keep it from
20:26 the sacrifice of every firstborn—**that** [+4200] I might fill them
20:26 that I might fill them with horror **so** [+4200] they would know that
20:44 when I deal with you **for** [+4200] my name's **sake** and not
21:10 [21:15] sharpened **for** [+4200] the slaughter, polished to flash like
21:10 [21:15] for the slaughter, polished **to** [+4200] flash like lightning!
21:15 [21:20] **So** [+4200] **that** hearts may melt and the fallen be many,
21:28 [21:33] polished to consume and **to** [+4200] flash like lightning!
22: 6 of Israel who are in you uses his power **to** [+4200] shed blood.
22: 9 In you are slanderous men **bent** [+4200] **on** shedding blood;
22:12 In you men accept bribes **to** [+4200] shed blood; you take usury
22:27 they shed blood and kill people **to** [+4200] make unjust gain.
23:21 and your young breasts fondled. [BHS ***because of***; NIV 5080]
24:11 Then set the empty pot on the coals **till** [+4200] it becomes hot
25:10 to the people of the East as a possession, **so** [+4200] **that**
26:20 with those who go down to the pit, **and** [+4200] you will not return
31:14 **Therefore** [+4200] no other trees by the waters are ever to tower
36: 5 hearts they made my land their own possession **so** [+4200] **that**
36:22 It is not **for** [+4200] your **sake**, O house of Israel, that I am going
36:30 the crops of the field, **so** [+4200] **that** you will no longer suffer
36:32 I want you to know that I am not doing this **for** [+4200] your **sake**,
38:16 I will bring you against my land, **so** [+4200] **that** the nations may
39:12 will be burying them **in order to** [+906+4200] cleanse the land.
40: 4 to show you, for **that** [+4200] **is why** you have been brought here.
46:18 his sons their inheritance out of his own property, **so** [+4200] **that**
Da 9:17 the prayers and petitions of your servant. **For** [+4200] your **sake**,
9:19 O Lord, hear and act! **For** [+4200] your **sake**, O my God,
Hos 8: 4 gold they make idols for themselves **to** [+4200] their own
Joel 3: 6 [4:6] Jerusalem to the Greeks, **that** [+4200] you might send them
Am 1:13 pregnant women of Gilead **in order to** [+4200] extend his borders,
2: 7 and son use the same girl and **so** [+4200] profane my holy name.
5:14 Seek good, not evil, **that** [+4200] you may live. Then the LORD
9:12 **so** [+4200] **that** they may possess the remnant of Edom and all the

Ob 1: 9 will be terrified, **and** [+4200] everyone in Esau's mountains will
Mic 6: 5 Remember ⌞your journey⌟ from Shittim to Gilgal, **that** [+4200]
6: 16 you have followed their traditions. **Therefore** [+4200] I will give
Hab 2: 2 make it plain on tablets **so** [+4200] **that** a herald may run with it.
2: 15 pouring it from the wineskin till they are drunk, **so** [+4200] **that** he
Zec 12: 7 LORD will save the dwellings of Judah first, **so** [+4200] **that**
13: 4 He will not put on a prophet's garment of hair **in order to** [+4200]

5101 ¹מַעֲנֶה ***maʿaneh¹***, n.m. [7] [√ 6699]

answer [2], giving an apt reply [+7023] [1], reply [1], respond [1], say [1], way to refute [1]

Job 32: 3 because they had found no **way to refute** Job, and yet had
32: 5 But when he saw that the three men had nothing more to **say**,
Pr 15: 1 A gentle **answer** turns away wrath, but a harsh word stirs up anger.
15: 23 A man finds joy in **giving an apt reply** [+7023]—and how good is
16: 1 of the heart, but from the LORD comes the **reply** *of* the tongue.
29: 19 by mere words; though he understands, he will not **respond**.
Mic 3: 7 will all cover their faces because there is no **answer** *from* God."

5102 ²מַעֲנֶה ***maʿaneh²***, n.m. [1] [√ 6701]

ends [1]

Pr 16: 4 The LORD works out everything for his own **ends**—even the

5103 מַעֲנָה ***maʿanâ***, n.f. [2] [→ 5105; cf. 6701]

acre [+7538] [1], furrows [1]

1Sa 14: 14 killed some twenty men in an area of about half an **acre** [+7538].
Ps 129: 3 have plowed my back and made their **furrows** [Q 5105] long.

5104 מְעֹנָה ***mᵉʿōnâ***, n.f. [9] [√ 5061]

dens [5], refuge [2], den [1], dwelling place [1]

Dt 33: 27 The eternal God is your **refuge**, and underneath are the everlasting
Job 37: 8 The animals take cover; they remain in their **dens**.
38: 40 when they crouch in their **dens** or lie in wait in a thicket?
Ps 76: 2 [76:3] His tent is in Salem, his **dwelling place** in Zion.
104: 22 and they steal away; they return and lie down in their **dens**.
SS 4: 8 from the lions' **dens** and the mountain haunts of the leopards.
Jer 21: 13 who say, "Who can come against us? Who can enter our **refuge**?"
Am 3: 4 no prey? Does he growl in his **den** when he has caught nothing?
Na 2: 12 [2:13] filling his lairs with the kill and his **dens** with the prey.

5105 מַעֲנִית ***maʿanît***, var. [0] [√ 5103; cf. 6701]

Ps 129: 3 [plowed my back and made their **furrows** [Q; see K 5103] long.]

5106 מַעַץ ***maʿaṣ***, n.pr.m. [1] [→ 318]

Maaz [1]

1Ch 2: 27 sons of Ram the firstborn of Jerahmeel: **Maaz**, Jamin and Eker.

5107 מַעֲצֵבָה ***maʿaṣēbâ***, n.f. [1] [√ 6772]

torment [1]

Isa 50: 11 you shall receive from my hand: You will lie down in **torment**.

5108 מַעֲצָד ***maʿaṣād***, n.[m.]. [2]

chisel [1], tool [1]

Isa 44: 12 The blacksmith takes a **tool** and works with it in the coals;
Jer 10: 3 a tree out of the forest, and a craftsman shapes it with his **chisel**.

5109 מַעְצוֹר ***maʿṣôr***, n.[m.]. [1] [√ 6806]

hinder [1]

1Sa 14: 6 Nothing can **hinder** the LORD *from* saving, whether by many

5110 מַעְצָר ***maʿṣār***, n.[m.]. [1] [√ 6806]

self-control [+4200+8120] [1]

Pr 25: 28 Like a city whose walls are broken down is a man who lacks **self-control** [+4200+8120].

5111 מַעֲקֶה ***maʿaqeh***, n.[m.]. [1]

parapet [1]

Dt 22: 8 make a **parapet** around your roof so that you may not bring the

5112 מַעֲקַשִּׁים ***maʿaqaššîm***, n.[m.]. [1] [√ 6835]

rough places [1]

Isa 42: 16 into light before them and make the **rough places** smooth.

5113 מַעַר ***maʿar***, n.[m.]. [2] [√ 5116]

available space [1], nakedness [1]

1Ki 7: 36 of the supports and on the panels, in every **available space**,
Na 3: 5 I will show the nations your **nakedness** and the kingdoms your

5114 ¹מַעֲרָב ***maʿarāb¹***, n.m. [9] [√ 6842]

wares [8], merchants [+6842] [1]

Eze 27: 9 of the sea and their sailors came alongside to trade for your **wares**.
27: 13 they exchanged slaves and articles of bronze for your **wares**.
27: 17 from Minnith and confections, honey, oil and balm for your **wares**.
27: 19 they exchanged wrought iron, cassia and calamus for your **wares**.
27: 25 " 'The ships of Tarshish serve as carriers for your **wares**. You are
27: 27 Your wealth, merchandise and **wares**, your mariners, seamen
27: 27 and shipwrights, your **merchants** [+6842] and all your soldiers,
27: 33 great wealth and your **wares** you enriched the kings of the earth.
27: 34 your **wares** and all your company have gone down with you.

5115 ²מַעֲרָב ***maʿarāb²***, n.[m.]. [14 / 15] [√ 6845]

west [12], *untranslated* [1], place of setting [1], west [+2025] [1]

Jdg 20: 33 charged out of its place on the **west** [BHS 5116] *of* Gibeah.
1Ch 7: 28 Gezer and its villages to the **west**, and Shechem and its villages all
12: 15 [12:16] everyone living in the valleys, to the east and to the **west**.
26: 16 The lots for the **West** Gate and the Shalleketh Gate on the upper
26: 18 As for the court to the **west**, there were four at the road and two at
26: 30 were responsible in Israel west of the Jordan **[RPH]** for all the
2Ch 32: 30 channeled the water down to the **west** *side* of the City of David.
33: 14 **west** [+2025] of the Gihon spring in the valley, as far as the
Ps 75: 6 [75:7] No one from the east or the **west** or from the desert can
103: 12 as far as the east is from the **west**, so far has he removed our
107: 3 gathered from the lands, from east and **west**, from north and south.
Isa 43: 5 bring your children from the east and gather you from the **west**.
45: 6 so that from the rising of the sun to the **place of** its **setting** men
59: 19 From the **west**, men will fear the name of the LORD, and from
Da 8: 5 a goat with a prominent horn between his eyes came from the **west**,

5116 מַעֲרֶה ***maʿareh***, n.[m.]. [1 / 0] [→ 5113]

Jdg 20: 33 its place on the west [BHS *clearing* ?; NIV 5115] *of* Gibeah.

5117 ¹מְעָרָה ***mᵉʿārâ¹***, n.f. [38] [√ 6869?]

cave [30], caves [6], *untranslated* [1], den [1]

Ge 19: 30 afraid to stay in Zoar. He and his two daughters lived in a **cave**.
23: 9 so he will sell me the **cave** *of* Machpelah, which belongs to him
23: 11 to me; I give you the field, and I give you the **cave** that is in it.
23: 17 both the field and the **cave** in it, and all the trees within the borders
23: 19 Afterward Abraham buried his wife Sarah in the **cave** *in* the field
23: 20 the **cave** in it were deeded to Abraham by the Hittites as a burial
25: 9 and Ishmael buried him in the **cave** *of* Machpelah near Mamre,
49: 29 Bury me with my fathers in the **cave** in the field of Ephron the
49: 30 the **cave** in the field of Machpelah, near Mamre in Canaan,
49: 32 The field and the **cave** in it were bought from the Hittites."
50: 13 of Canaan and buried him in the **cave** *in* the field of Machpelah,
Jos 10: 16 Now the five kings had fled and hidden in the **cave** at Makkedah.
10: 17 that the five kings had been found hiding in the **cave** at Makkedah,
10: 18 he said, "Roll large rocks up to the mouth of the **cave**, and post
10: 22 "Open the mouth of the **cave** and bring those five kings out to me."
10: 22 mouth of the cave and bring those five kings out to me." **[RPH]**
10: 23 So they brought the five kings out of the **cave**—the kings of
10: 27 and threw them into the **cave** where they had been hiding.
10: 27 At the mouth of the **cave** they placed large rocks, which are there
13: 4 from Arah [BHS *cave* ?; NIV 6869] of the Sidonians
Jdg 6: 2 shelters for themselves in mountain clefts, **caves** and strongholds.
1Sa 13: 6 they hid in **caves** and thickets, among the rocks, and in pits
17: 23 [stepped out from his **lines** [K; see Q 5120] and shouted his usual]
22: 1 David left Gath and escaped to the **cave** *of* Adullam. When his
24: 3 [24:4] a **cave** was there, and Saul went in to relieve himself.
24: 3 [24:4] David and his men were far back in the **cave**.
24: 7 [24:8] to attack Saul. And Saul left the **cave** and went his way.
24: 8 [24:9] David went out of the **cave** and called out to Saul, "My
24: 10 [24:11] how the LORD delivered you into my hands in the **cave**.
2Sa 23: 13 three of the thirty chief men came down to David at the **cave** *of*
1Ki 18: 4 had taken a hundred prophets and hidden them in two **caves**,
18: 13 I hid a hundred of the LORD's prophets in two **caves**, fifty in
19: 9 There he went into a **cave** and spent the night. And the word of the
19: 13 over his face and went out and stood at the mouth of the **cave**.
1Ch 11: 15 chiefs came down to David to the rock at the **cave** *of* Adullam,
Ps 57: T [57:1] A *miktam*. When he had fled from Saul into the **cave**.
142: T [142:1] A *maskil* of David. When he was in the **cave**. A prayer.
Isa 2: 19 Men will flee to **caves** *in* the rocks and to holes in the ground from
Jer 7: 11 which bears my Name, become a **den** *of* robbers to you?
Eze 33: 27 and those in strongholds and **caves** will die of a plague.

5118 ²מְעָרָה ***m^e'ārâ^2***, n.f. [1] [→ 5125; cf. 6867]

wasteland [1]

Isa 32:14 citadel and watchtower will become a **wasteland** forever,

5119 מַעֲרָךְ ***ma'^{a}rāk***, n.[m.]. [1] [√ 6885]

plans [1]

Pr 16: 1 To man belong the **plans** *of* the heart, but from the LORD comes

5120 מַעֲרָכָה ***ma'^{a}rākâ***, n.f. [19] [√ 6885]

armies [3], battle line [3], ranks [3], lines [2], battle lines [1], battle positions [1], battlefield [+8441] [1], facing each other [+7925] [1], forces [1], it^s [+2021] [1], proper kind [1], row [1]

Ex 39:37 the pure gold lampstand with its **row** of lamps and all its
Jdg 6:26 build a **proper kind** of altar to the LORD your God on the top of
1Sa 4: 2 who killed about four thousand of them on the **battlefield** [+8441].
4:12 That same day a Benjamite ran from the **battle line** and went to
4:16 He told Eli, "I have just come from the **battle line**; I fled from it
4:16 come from the battle line; I fled from **it**^{s} [+2021] this very day."
17: 8 Goliath stood and shouted to the **ranks** *of* Israel, "Why do you
17:10 Then the Philistine said, "This day I defy the **ranks** *of* Israel!
17:20 reached the camp as the army was going out to its **battle positions**,
17:21 and the Philistines were drawing up their **lines** facing each other.
17:21 Philistines were drawing up their lines **facing each other** [+7925].
17:22 keeper of supplies, ran to the **battle lines** and greeted his brothers.
17:23 stepped out from his **lines** [K 5117] and shouted his usual
17:26 Philistine that he should defy the **armies** *of* the living God?"
17:36 one of them, because he has defied the **armies** *of* the living God.
17:45 the God of the **armies** *of* Israel, whom you have defied.
17:48 attack him, David ran quickly toward the **battle line** to meet him.
23: 3 much more, then, if we go to Keilah against the Philistine **forces**!"
1Ch 12:38 [12:39] were fighting men who volunteered to serve in the **ranks**.

5121 מַעֲרֶכֶת ***ma'^{a}reket***, n.f. [10] [√ 6885]

set out on the table [3], consecrated bread [2], row [2], rows [1], set out [1], setting out the consecrated bread [1]

Lev 24: 6 Set them in two **rows**, six in each row, on the table of pure gold
24: 6 Set them in two rows, six in each **row**, on the table of pure gold
24: 7 Along each **row** put some pure incense as a memorial portion to
1Ch 9:32 of preparing for every Sabbath the bread **set out on the table**.
23:29 They were in charge of the bread **set out on the table**, the flour for
28:16 the weight of gold for each table for **consecrated bread**;
2Ch 2: 4 [2:3] for setting out the **consecrated bread** regularly, and for
13:11 They **set out** the bread on the ceremonially clean table and light
29:18 the table for **setting out the consecrated bread**, with all its
Ne 10:33 [10:34] for the bread **set out on the table**; for the regular grain

5122 מַעֲרֹם ***ma'^{a}rōm***, n.m. [1] [√ 6867]

naked [1]

2Ch 28:15 and from the plunder they clothed all who were **naked**.

5123 מַעֲרָץ ***ma'^{a}rāṣ***, n.[m.]. Not used in NIV/BHS [√ 6907]

5124 מַעֲרָצָה ***ma'^{a}rāṣâ***, n.f. [1] [√ 6907]

great power [1]

Isa 10:33 the LORD Almighty, will lop off the boughs with **great power**.

5125 מַעֲרָת ***ma'^{a}rāt***, n.pr.loc. [1] [√ 5118?; cf. 6867]

Maarath [1]

Jos 15:59 **Maarath**, Beth Anoth and Eltekon—six towns and their villages.

5126 מַעֲשֶׂה ***ma'^{a}śeh***, n.m. [235 / 236] [→ 5127, 5128, 5129; cf. 6913]

work [60], works [17], made [14], what done [11], what made [10], deeds [8], things [7], like [+3869] [6], everything [+3972] [4], worked [4], do [3], like [3], practices [3], what^s [+2021] [3], *untranslated* [2], crops [2], deed [2], done [+6913] [2], done [2], fashioned [2], labor [2], network [+8407] [2], objects [2], occupation [2], products [2], shape [2], what deserve [+3869] [2], what did [2], working [2], accomplished [1], achievement [+4179] [1], acting [1], actions [1], acts [1], baked goods [+685+4407] [1], baking [1], basework [+4029] [1], construction [1], crafted [1], creature made [1], crime [+8288] [1], crop [1], customs [1], design [1], do [+3338] [1], does [1], duties [1], fruit [1], handiwork [+3338] [1], how made [1], idols made [1], interwoven chains [+9249] [1], is done [+6913] [1], making [1], man-made [+132+3338] [1], network [+8422+8422] [1], nothing [+4202] [1], performance [1], perfumes [+5351] [1], projects [1], property [1], sculptured [+7589] [1], shapes [+3338] [1], structure [1], that does [1], that done [1], that made [1], things did [+3338] [1], things did [1], this^s [+2021+2021+2296] [1], trouble [1], undertook [1], verses [1], way [1], well-dressed hair [+5250] [1], what do [1], what formed [1], what make [1], whatever do [1], work [+6913] [1], woven [+755] [1], wrongdoing [1]

Ge 5:29 "He will comfort us in the **labor** and painful toil of our hands
20: 9 You have done **things** to me that should not be done."
40:17 In the top basket were all kinds of **baked goods for** [+685+4407]
44:15 said to them, "What is **this**^{s} [+2021+2021+2296] you have done?
46:33 When Pharaoh calls you in and asks, 'What is your **occupation**?'
47: 3 Pharaoh asked the brothers, "What is your **occupation**?" "Your
Ex 5: 4 and Aaron, why are you taking the people away from their **labor**?
5:13 saying, "Complete the **work** *required of* you for each day,
18:20 and show them the way to live and the **duties** they are to perform.
23:12 "Six days do your **work**, but on the seventh day do not work,
23:16 "Celebrate the Feast of Harvest with the firstfruits of the **crops** you
23:16 the end of the year, when you gather in your **crops** from the field.
23:24 down before their gods or worship them or follow their **practices**.
24:10 Under his feet was *something* like a pavement **made** *of* sapphire,
26: 1 with cherubim **worked** *into* them *by* a skilled craftsman.
26:31 twisted linen, with cherubim **worked** *into* it *by* a skilled craftsman.
26:36 scarlet yarn and finely twisted linen—the **work** *of* an embroiderer.
27: 4 Make a grating for it, a bronze **network** [+8407], and make a
27:16 the **work** *of* an embroiderer—with four posts and four bases.
28: 6 and of finely twisted linen—the **work** *of* a skilled craftsman.
28: 8 Its skillfully woven waistband is to be **like** [+3869] it—of one
28:11 Engrave the names of the sons of Israel on the two stones the **way**
28:14 of pure gold, **like** a rope, and attach the chains to the settings.
28:15 breastpiece for making decisions—the **work** *of* a skilled craftsman.
28:15 Make it **like** [+3869] the ephod: of gold, and of blue, purple
28:22 "For the breastpiece make braided chains of pure gold, **like** a rope.
28:32 There shall be a **woven** [+755] edge like a collar around this
28:39 turban of fine linen. The sash is to be the **work** *of* an embroiderer.
30:25 a sacred anointing oil, a fragrant blend, the **work** *of* a perfumer.
30:35 and make a fragrant blend of incense, the **work** *of* a perfumer.
32:16 The tablets were the **work** *of* God; the writing was the writing of
34:10 The people you live among will see how awesome is the **work** that
36: 8 with cherubim **worked** *into* them *by* a skilled craftsman.
36:35 twisted linen, with cherubim **worked** *into* it *by* a skilled craftsman.
36:37 scarlet yarn and finely twisted linen—the **work** *of* an embroiderer;
37:29 and the pure, fragrant incense—the **work** *of* a perfumer.
38: 4 a bronze **network** [+8407], to be under its ledge, halfway up the
38:18 scarlet yarn and finely twisted linen—the **work** *of* an embroiderer.
39: 3 and scarlet yarn and fine linen—the **work** *of* a skilled craftsman.
39: 5 Its skillfully woven waistband was **like** [+3869] it—of one piece
39: 8 They fashioned the breastpiece—the **work** *of* a skilled craftsman.
39: 8 They **made** it like the ephod: of gold, and of blue, purple
39:15 the breastpiece they made braided chains of pure gold, **like** a rope.
39:22 robe of the ephod entirely of blue cloth—the **work** *of* a weaver—
39:27 his sons, they made tunics of fine linen—the **work** *of* a weaver—
39:29 and blue, purple and scarlet yarn—the **work** *of* an embroiderer—
Lev 18: 3 You must not do as they **do** *in* Egypt, where you used to live,
18: 3 used to live, and you must not do as they **do** *in* the land of Canaan,
Nu 8: 4 This is how the lampstand was **made**: It was made of hammered
16:28 you will know that the LORD has sent me to do all these **things**
31:20 Purify every garment as well as everything **made** *of* leather,
31:51 the priest accepted from them the gold—all the **crafted** articles.
Dt 2: 7 The LORD your God has blessed you in all the **work** *of* your
3:24 or on earth who can do the **deeds** and mighty works you do?
4:28 There you will worship **man-made** [+132+3338] gods of wood and
11: 3 the signs he performed and the **things** he **did** in the heart of Egypt,
11: 7 it was your own eyes that saw all these great **things** the LORD
14:29 your God may bless you in all the **work** [+6913] *of* your hands.
15:10 of this the LORD your God will bless you in all your **work**
16:15 will bless you in all your harvest and in all the **work** *of* your hands,
24:19 so that the LORD your God may bless you in all the **work** *of* your
27:15 detestable to the LORD, the **work** *of* the craftsman's hands—
28:12 rain on your land in season and to bless all the **work** *of* your hands.
30: 9 God will make you most prosperous in all the **work** *of* your hands
31:29 and provoke him to anger by **what** your hands have **made**."
Jos 24:31 who had experienced **everything** [+3972] the LORD had done for
Jdg 2: 7 who had seen all the great **things** the LORD had done for Israel.
2:10 who knew neither the LORD nor **what**^{s} [+2021] he had done for
13:12 are fulfilled, what is to be the rule for the boy's life and **work**?"
19:16 of the place were Benjamites), came in from his **work** in the fields.
1Sa 8: 8 As **[NIE]** they have done from the day I brought them up out of
19: 4 not wronged you, and **what** he has **done** has benefited you greatly.
20:19 go to the place where you hid when this **trouble** began,
25: 2 in Maon, who had **property** there at Carmel, was very wealthy.
1Ki 7: 8 in which he was to live, set farther back, was similar in **design**.
7:17 A **network** [+8422+8422] of interwoven chains festooned the
7:17 A network of **interwoven chains** [+9249] festooned the capitals on
7:19 The capitals on top of the pillars in the portico were in the **shape** *of*
7:22 The capitals on top were in the **shape** *of* lilies. And so the work on

1Ki 7:26 and its rim was **like** [+3869] the rim of a cup, like a lily blossom.
7:28 This is **how** the stands were **made**: They had side panels attached
7:29 and below the lions and bulls were wreaths of hammered **work**.
7:31 and with its **basework** [+4029] it measured a cubit and a half.
7:33 The wheels were **made** like chariot wheels; the axles, rims,
7:33 The wheels were made **like** [+3869] chariot wheels; the axles,
13:11 told him all that the man of God *had* **done** [+6913] there that day.
16:7 provoking him to anger by the **things** he **did** [+3338], and
2Ki 16:10 priest a sketch of the altar, with detailed plans for its **construction**.
19:18 not gods but only wood and stone, **fashioned** *by* men's hands.
22:17 and provoked me to anger by all the **idols** their hands have **made**,
23:19 Just as *he had* **done** [+6913] at Bethel, Josiah removed and defiled
1Ch 9:31 was entrusted with the responsibility for **baking** the offering bread.
23:28 and the **performance** *of* other duties at the house of God.
2Ch 3:10 In the Most Holy Place he made a pair of **sculptured** [+7589]
4:5 and its rim was **like** [+3869] the rim of a cup, like a lily blossom.
4:6 In them the **things** to be *used for* the burnt offerings were rinsed,
16:14 a bier covered with spices and various blended **perfumes** [+5351],
17:4 and followed his commands rather than the **practices** *of* Israel.
20:37 with Ahaziah, the LORD will destroy **what** you have **made**."
31:21 In **everything** [+3972] that he undertook in the service of God's
32:19 gods of the other peoples of the world—the **work** *of* men's hands.
32:30 of the City of David. He succeeded in everything he **undertook**.
34:25 and provoked me to anger by all **that** their hands have **made**,
Ezr 9:13 "What has happened to us is a result of our evil **deeds** and our
Ne 6:14 and Sanballat, O my God, because of what they have **done**;
Est 10:2 all his **acts** *of* power and might, together with a full account of the
Job 1:10 You have blessed the **work** *of* his hands, so that his flocks
14:15 answer you; you will long for the **creature** your hands have **made**.
33:17 to turn man from **wrongdoing** and keep him from pride,
34:19 favor the rich over the poor, for they are all the **work** *of* his hands?
37:7 So that all men he has **made** may know his work, he stops every
Ps 8:3 [8:4] the **work** *of* your fingers, the moon and the stars, which you
8:6 [8:7] You made him ruler over the **works** *of* your hands; you put
19:1 [19:2] the glory of God; the skies proclaim the **work** *of* his hands.
28:4 repay them for **what** their hands have **done** and bring back upon
28:5 regard for the works of the LORD and **what** his hands have **done**,
33:4 word of the LORD is right and true; he is faithful in all he **does**.
33:15 he who forms the hearts of all, who considers everything they **do**.
45:1 [45:2] My heart is stirred by a noble theme as I recite my **verses**
62:12 [62:13] will reward each person according to **what** he has **done**.
64:9 [64:10] proclaim the works of God and ponder **what** he has **done**.
66:3 Say to God, "How awesome are your **deeds**! So great is your
86:8 there is none like you, O Lord; no **deeds** can compare with yours.
90:17 establish the **work** *of* our hands for us—yes, establish the work of
90:17 work of our hands for us—yes, establish the **work** *of* our hands.
92:4 [92:5] O LORD; I sing for joy at the **works** *of* your hands.
92:5 [92:6] How great are your **works**, O LORD, how profound your
102:25 [102:26] of the earth, and the heavens are the **work** *of* your hands.
103:22 Praise the LORD, all his **works** everywhere in his dominion.
104:13 his upper chambers; the earth is satisfied by the fruit of his **work**.
104:24 How many are your **works**, O LORD! In wisdom you made them
104:31 the LORD endure forever; may the LORD rejoice in his **works**—
106:13 they soon forgot **what** he had **done** and did not wait for his
106:35 but they mingled with the nations and adopted their **customs**.
106:39 They defiled themselves by **what** they **did**; by their deeds they
107:22 sacrifice thank offerings and tell of his **works** with songs of joy.
107:24 They saw the **works** *of* the LORD, his wonderful deeds in the
111:2 Great are the **works** *of* the LORD; they are pondered by all who
111:6 He has shown his people the power of his **works**, giving them the
111:7 The **works** *of* his hands are faithful and just; all his precepts are
115:4 But their idols are silver and gold, **made** *by* the hands of men.
118:17 will not die but live, and will proclaim **what** the LORD has **done**.
135:15 idols of the nations are silver and gold, **made** *by* the hands of men.
138:8 endures forever—do not abandon the **works** *of* your hands.
139:14 your **works** are wonderful, I know that full well.
143:5 on all your works and consider **what** your hands have **done**.
145:4 One generation will commend your **works** to another; they will tell
145:9 The LORD is good to all; he has compassion on all he has **made**.
145:10 All you have **made** will praise you, O LORD; your saints will
145:13 to all his promises and loving toward all he has **made**. [BHS-]
145:17 is righteous in all his ways and loving toward all he has **made**.
Pr 16:3 Commit to the LORD **whatever** you **do**, and your plans will
16:11 are from the LORD; all the weights in the bag are of his **making**.
31:31 she has earned, and let her **works** bring her praise at the city gate.
Ecc 1:14 I have seen all the **things** that are done under the sun; all of them
2:4 I undertook great **projects**: I built houses for myself and planted
2:11 Yet when I surveyed all that my hands **[RPH]** had done and what
2:17 because the **work** that is done under the sun was grievous to me.
3:11 yet they cannot fathom **what**˜ [+2021] God has done from
3:17 for there will be a time for every activity, a time for every **deed**."
3:22 I saw that there is nothing better for a man than to enjoy his **work**,
4:3 who has not seen the evil that **is done** [+6913] under the sun.
4:4 all **achievement** [+4179] spring from man's envy of his neighbor.
5:6 [5:5] angry at what you say and destroy the **work** *of* your hands?
7:13 Consider **what** God has **done**: Who can straighten what he has
8:9 as I applied my mind to **everything** [+3972] done under the sun.
8:11 When the sentence for a **crime** [+8288] is not quickly carried out,
8:14 righteous men who get **what** the wicked **deserve** [+3869],
8:14 and wicked men who get **what** the righteous **deserve** [+3869].
8:17 I saw all **that** God has **done**. No one can comprehend what goes on
8:17 No one can comprehend **what**˜ [+2021] goes on under the sun.
9:7 with a joyful heart, for it is now that God favors **what** you **do**.
9:10 there is neither **working** nor planning nor knowledge nor wisdom.
11:5 so you cannot understand the **work** *of* God, the Maker of all
12:14 For God will bring every **deed** into judgment, including every
SS 7:1 [7:2] legs are like jewels, the **work** *of* a craftsman's hands.
Isa 2:8 they bow down to the **work** *of* their hands, to what their fingers
3:24 of a sash, a rope; instead of **well-dressed hair** [+5250], baldness;
5:12 for the deeds of the LORD, no respect for the **work** *of* his hands.
5:19 "Let God hurry, let him hasten his **work** so we may see it.
10:12 When the Lord has finished all his **work** against Mount Zion
17:8 They will not look to the altars, the **work** *of* their hands, and they
19:14 they make Egypt stagger in all **that** she **does**, as a drunkard
19:15 There is **nothing** [+4202] Egypt can do—head or tail, palm branch
19:25 Assyria my **handiwork** [+3338], and Israel my inheritance."
26:12 peace for us; all *that* we have **accomplished** you have done for us.
28:21 to do his **work**, his strange work, and perform his task, his alien
28:21 to do his work, his strange **work**, and perform his task, his alien
29:15 who do their **work** in darkness and think, "Who sees us?
29:16 Shall **what** is **formed** say to him who formed it, "He did not make
29:23 the **work** *of* my hands, they will keep my name holy;
32:17 The **fruit** *of* righteousness will be peace; the effect of
37:19 not gods but only wood and stone, **fashioned** *by* human hands.
41:29 Their **deeds** amount to nothing; their images are but wind
54:16 who fans the coals into flame and forges a weapon fit for its **work**.
57:12 I will expose your righteousness and your **works**, and they will not
59:6 for clothing; they cannot cover themselves with **what** they **make**.
59:6 Their **deeds** are evil deeds, and acts of violence are in their hands.
59:6 Their deeds are evil **deeds**, and acts of violence are in their hands.
60:21 the **work** *of* my hands, for the display of my splendor.
64:8 [64:7] you are the potter; we are all the **work** *of* your hand.
65:22 my chosen ones will long enjoy the **works** *of* their hands.
66:18 "And I, because of their **actions** and their imaginations, am about
Jer 1:16 to other gods and in worshiping **what** their hands have **made**.
7:13 While you were doing all these **things**, declares the LORD,
10:3 out of the forest, and a craftsman **shapes** [+3338] it with his chisel.
10:9 **What** the craftsman and goldsmith have **made** is then dressed in
10:9 then dressed in blue and purple—all **made** *by* skilled workers.
10:15 They are worthless, the **objects** *of* mockery; when their judgment
25:6 do not provoke me to anger with **what** your hands have **made**.
25:7 "and you have provoked me with **what** your hands have **made**,
25:14 repay them according to their deeds and the **work** *of* their hands."
32:30 done nothing but provoke me with **what** their hands have **made**,
44:8 Why provoke me to anger with **what** your hands have **made**,
48:7 Since you trust in your **deeds** and riches, you too will be taken
51:10 come, let us tell in Zion **what** the LORD our God has **done**.'
51:18 They are worthless, the **objects** *of* mockery; when their judgment
La 3:64 what they deserve, O LORD, for **what** their hands have **done**.
4:2 are now considered as pots of clay, the **work** *of* a potter's hands!
Eze 1:16 This was the appearance and **structure** *of* the wheels:
1:16 Each appeared to be **made** like a wheel intersecting a wheel.
6:6 incense altars broken down, and **what** you have **made** wiped out.
16:30 when you do all these things, **acting** *like* a brazen prostitute!
27:16 " 'Aram did business with you because of your many **products**;
27:18 because of your many **products** and great wealth of goods,
46:1 of the inner court facing east is to be shut on the six **working** days,
Da 9:14 for the LORD our God is righteous in **everything** [+3972] he
Hos 13:2 cleverly fashioned images, all of them the **work** *of* craftsmen.
14:3 [14:4] again say 'Our gods' to **what** our own hands have **made**,
Am 8:7 the Pride of Jacob: "I will never forget anything they have **done**.
Jnh 3:10 When God saw **what** they **did** and how they turned from their evil
Mic 5:13 [5:12] you will no longer bow down to the **work** *of* your hands.
6:16 the statutes of Omri and all the **practices** *of* Ahab's house,
Hab 3:17 though the olive **crop** fails and the fields produce no food,
Hag 2:14 'Whatever they **do** [+3338] and whatever they offer there is defiled.
2:17 I struck all the **work** *of* your hands with blight, mildew and hail,

5127 מַעְשַׂי **ma'śay**, n.pr.m. [1] [√ 5126 + 3378]

Maasai [1]

1Ch 9:12 **Maasai** son of Adiel, the son of Jahzerah, the son of Meshullam,

5128 מַעֲשֵׂיָה **ma'aśēyâ**, n.pr.m. [16] [√ 5126 + 3378]

Maaseiah [16]

Ezr 10:18 and his brothers: **Maaseiah**, Eliezer, Jarib and Gedaliah.
10:21 of Harim: **Maaseiah**, Elijah, Shemaiah, Jehiel and Uzziah.

Ezr 10:22 Elioenai, **Maaseiah**, Ishmael, Nethanel, Jozabad and Elasah.
10:30 Adna, Kelal, Benaiah, **Maaseiah**, Mattaniah, Bezalel, Binnui
Ne 3:23 and next to them, Azariah son of **Maaseiah**, the son of Ananiah,
8: 4 stood Mattithiah, Shema, Anaiah, Uriah, Hilkiah and **Maaseiah**;
8: 7 Hodiah, **Maaseiah**, Kelita, Azariah, Jozabad, Hanan and Pelaiah—
10:25 [10:26] Rehum, Hashabnah, **Maaseiah**,
11: 5 **Maaseiah** son of Baruch, the son of Col-Hozeh, the son of
11: 7 the son of Kolaiah, the son of **Maaseiah**, the son of Ithiel,
12:41 Eliakim, **Maaseiah**, Miniamin, Micaiah, Elioenai, Zechariah
12:42 also **Maaseiah**, Shemaiah, Eleazar, Uzzi, Jehohanan, Malkijah,
Jer 21: 1 son of Malkijah and the priest Zephaniah son of **Maaseiah**.
29:21 says about Ahab son of Kolaiah and Zedekiah son of **Maaseiah**,
29:25 to Zephaniah son of **Maaseiah** the priest, and to all the other
37: 3 son of **Maaseiah** to Jeremiah the prophet with this message:

5129 מַעֲשֵׂיָהוּ *maʿăśēyāhû*, n.pr.m. [7] [√ 5126 + 3378; cf. 6913]

Maaseiah [7]

1Ch 15:18 Jehiel, Unni, Eliab, Benaiah, **Maaseiah**, Mattithiah, Eliphelehu,
15:20 **Maaseiah** and Benaiah were to play the lyres according to
2Ch 23: 1 son of Jehohanan, Azariah son of Obed, **Maaseiah** son of Adaiah,
26:11 and **Maaseiah** the officer under the direction of Hananiah,
28: 7 Zicri, an Ephraimite warrior, killed **Maaseiah** the king's son,
34: 8 he sent Shaphan son of Azaliah and **Maaseiah** the ruler of the city,
Jer 35: 4 which was over that of **Maaseiah** son of Shallum the doorkeeper.

5130 מַעֲשֵׂר *maʿăśēr*, n.m. [32] [√ 6923]

tithe [13], tithes [13], tenth [5], setting aside a tenth [+906+6923] [1]

Ge 14:20 into your hand." Then Abram gave him a **tenth** of everything.
Lev 27:30 " 'A **tithe** *of* everything from the land, whether grain from the soil
27:31 If a man redeems any of his **tithe**, he must add a fifth of the value
27:32 The entire **tithe** *of* the herd and flock—every tenth animal that
Nu 18:21 "I give to the Levites all the **tithes** in Israel as their inheritance in
18:24 I give to the Levites as their inheritance the **tithes** that the Israelites
18:26 'When you receive from the Israelites the **tithe** I give you as your
18:26 you must present a **tenth** of that tithe as the LORD's offering.
18:26 you must present a tenth of that **tithe** as the LORD's offering.
18:28 to the LORD from all the **tithes** you receive from the Israelites.
Dt 12: 6 your burnt offerings and sacrifices, your **tithes** and special gifts,
12:11 your burnt offerings and sacrifices, your **tithes** and special gifts,
12:17 You must not eat in your own towns the **tithe** *of* your grain
14:23 Eat the **tithe** *of* your grain, new wine and oil, and the firstborn of
14:28 bring all the **tithes** of that year's produce and store it in your
26:12 When you have finished **setting aside a tenth of** [+906+6923] all
26:12 the year of the **tithe**, you shall give it to the Levite, the alien,
2Ch 31: 5 They brought a great amount, a **tithe** *of* everything.
31: 6 Judah who lived in the towns of Judah also brought a **tithe** *of* their
31: 6 and a **tithe** *of* the holy things dedicated to the LORD their God,
31:12 faithfully brought in the contributions, **tithes** and dedicated gifts.
Ne 10:37 [10:38] we will bring a **tithe** *of* our crops to the Levites, for it is
10:38 [10:39] the Levites are to bring a **tenth** *of* the tithes up to the
10:38 [10:39] the Levites are to bring a tenth of the **tithes** up to the
12:44 of the storerooms for the contributions, firstfruits and **tithes**.
13: 5 also the **tithes** *of* grain, new wine and oil prescribed for the
13:12 All Judah brought the **tithes** *of* grain, new wine and oil into the
Eze 45:11 the bath containing a **tenth** *of* a homer and the ephah a tenth of a
45:14 is a **tenth** *of* a bath from each cor (which consists of ten baths
Am 4: 4 Bring your sacrifices every morning, your **tithes** every three years.
Mal 3: 8 "But you ask, 'How do we rob you?' "In **tithes** and offerings.
3:10 Bring the whole **tithe** into the storehouse, that there may be food in

5131 מַעֲשַׁקּוֹת *maʿăšaqqôt*, n.f. [2] [√ 6921]

extortion [1], tyrannical [+8041] [1]

Pr 28:16 A **tyrannical** [+8041] ruler lacks judgment, but he who hates
Isa 33:15 who rejects gain from **extortion** and keeps his hand from accepting

5132 מֹף *mōp*, n.pr.loc. [1] [cf. 5862]

Memphis [1]

Hos 9: 6 Egypt will gather them, and **Memphis** will bury them.

5133 מִפְגָּע *mipgāʿ*, n.[m.]. [1] [√ 7003]

target [1]

Job 7:20 to you, O watcher of men? Why have you made me your **target**?

5134 מַפָּח *mappāḥ*, n.[m.]. [1] [√ 5870]

gasp [1]

Job 11:20 and escape will elude them; their hope will become a dying **gasp**."

5135 מַפֻּחַ *mappuaḥ*, n.m. [1] [√ 5870]

bellows [1]

Jer 6:29 The **bellows** blow fiercely to burn away the lead with fire,

5136 מְפִיבֹשֶׁת *mᵉpîbōšet*, מְפִי־בֹשֶׁת *mᵉpî-bōšet*, n.pr.m. [15] [√ 4946 + 7023 + 1425]

Mephibosheth [15]

2Sa 4: 4 he fell and became crippled. His name was **Mephibosheth**.)
9: 6 When **Mephibosheth** son of Jonathan, the son of Saul, came to
9: 6 David said, "**Mephibosheth**!" "Your servant," he replied.
9:10 **Mephibosheth**, grandson of your master, will always eat at my
9:11 So **Mephibosheth** ate at David's table like one of the king's sons.
9:12 **Mephibosheth** had a young son named Mica, and all the members
9:12 the members of Ziba's household were servants of **Mephibosheth**.
9:13 **Mephibosheth** lived in Jerusalem, because he always ate at the
16: 1 there was Ziba, the steward of **Mephibosheth**, waiting to meet
16: 4 said to Ziba, "All that belonged to **Mephibosheth** is now yours."
19:24 [19:25] **Mephibosheth**, Saul's grandson, also went down to meet
19:25 [19:26] "Why didn't you go with me, **Mephibosheth**?"
19:30 [19:31] **Mephibosheth** said to the king, "Let him take everything,
21: 7 The king spared **Mephibosheth** son of Jonathan, the son of Saul,
21: 8 the king took Armoni and **Mephibosheth**, the two sons of Aiah's

5137 מֻפִּים *muppîm*, n.pr.m. [1]

Muppim [1]

Ge 46:21 Ashbel, Gera, Naaman, Ehi, Rosh, **Muppim**, Huppim and Ard.

5138 מֵפִיץ *mēpîṣ*, n.m. [1] [√ 7046]

club [1]

Pr 25:18 Like a **club** or a sword or a sharp arrow is the man who gives false

5139 מַפָּל *mappāl*, n.m. [2] [→ 5142, 5143; cf. 5877]

folds [1], sweepings [1]

Job 41:23 [41:15] The **folds** *of* his flesh are tightly joined; they are firm and
Am 8: 6 for a pair of sandals, selling even the **sweepings** *with* the wheat.

5140 מִפְלָאוֹת *miplāʾôt*, n.f.[pl.]. [1] [√ 7098]

wonders [1]

Job 37:16 hang poised, *those* **wonders** *of* him who is perfect in knowledge?

5141 מִפְלַגָּה *miplaggâ*, n.f. [1] [√ 7103]

subdivisions [1]

2Ch 35:12 They set aside the burnt offerings to give them to the **subdivisions**

5142 מַפָּלָה *mappālâ*, n.f. [1] [√ 5139; cf. 5877]

ruins [1]

Isa 17: 1 Damascus will no longer be a city but will become a heap of **ruins**.

5143 מַפֵּלָה *mappēlâ*, n.f. [2] [√ 5139; cf. 5877]

ruin [2]

Isa 23:13 they stripped its fortresses bare and turned it into a **ruin**.
25: 2 You have made the city a heap of rubble, the fortified town a **ruin**,

5144 מִפְלָט *miplāṭ*, n.[m.]. [1] [√ 7117]

place of shelter [1]

Ps 55: 8 [55:9] I would hurry to my **place of shelter**, far from the tempest

5145 מִפְלֶצֶת *mipleṣet*, n.f. [4] [√ 7145]

pole^s [2], repulsive [2]

1Ki 15:13 as queen mother, because she had made a **repulsive** Asherah pole.
15:13 Asa cut the **pole**^s down and burned it in the Kidron Valley.
2Ch 15:16 as queen mother, because she had made a **repulsive** Asherah pole.
15:16 Asa cut the **pole**^s down, broke it up and burned it in the Kidron

5146 מִפְלָשׂ *miplāś*, n.[m.]. [1]

hang poised [1]

Job 37:16 Do you know how the clouds **hang poised**, those wonders of him

5147 מַפֶּלֶת *mappelet*, n.f. [8] [√ 5877]

fall [3], downfall [2], carcass [1], fallen [1], shipwreck [1]

Jdg 14: 8 back to marry her, he turned aside to look at the lion's **carcass**.
Pr 29:16 so does sin, but the righteous will see their **downfall**.
Eze 26:15 Will not the coastlands tremble at the sound of your **fall**, when the
26:18 Now the coastlands tremble on the day of your **fall**; the islands in

Eze 27: 27 will sink into the heart of the sea on the day of your **shipwreck**.
31: 13 All the birds of the air settled on the **fallen** tree, and all the beasts
31: 16 I made the nations tremble at the sound of its **fall** when I brought it
32: 10 On the day of your **downfall** each of them will tremble every

5148 מִפְעָל *mip'āl*, n.[m.]. [1] [√ 7188]

deeds [1]

Pr 8: 22 brought me forth as the first of his works, before his **deeds** of old;

5149 מִפְעָלָה *mip'ālâ*, n.[f.]. [2] [√ 7188]

what done [1], works [1]

Ps 46: 8 [46:9] Come and see the **works** *of* the LORD, the desolations he
66: 5 Come and see **what** God has **done**, how awesome his works in

5150 מַפָּץ *mappāṣ*, n.[m.]. [1] [√ 5879]

deadly [1]

Eze 9: 2 which faces north, each with a **deadly** weapon in his hand.

5151 מַפֵּץ *mappēṣ*, n.m. [1] [√ 5879]

war club [1]

Jer 51: 20 "You are my **war club**, my weapon for battle—with you I shatter

5152 מִפְקָד *mipqād*, n.[m.]. [5] [√ 7212]

number [+5031] [2], appointment [1], designated part [1], inspection [1]

2Sa 24: 9 Joab reported the **number of** [+5031] the fighting men to the king:
1Ch 21: 5 Joab reported the **number of** [+5031] the fighting men to David:
2Ch 31: 13 by **appointment** *of* King Hezekiah and Azariah the official in
Ne 3: 31 temple servants and the merchants, opposite the **Inspection** Gate,
Eze 43: 21 burn it in the **designated part** *of* the temple area outside the

5153 מִפְרָץ *miprāṣ*, n.[m.]. [1] [√ 7287]

coves [1]

Jdg 5: 17 by the ships? Asher remained on the coast and stayed in his **coves**.

5154 מַפְרֶקֶת *mapreqet*, n.f. [1] [√ 7293]

neck [1]

1Sa 4: 18 His **neck** was broken and he died, for he was an old man

5155 מִפְרָשׂ *miprāś*, n.[m.]. [2] [√ 7298]

sail [1], spreads out [1]

Job 36: 29 Who can understand how he **spreads out** the clouds, how he
Eze 27: 7 Fine embroidered linen from Egypt was your **sail** and served as

5156 מִפְשָׂעָה *mipśā'â*, n.f. [1] [cf. 7314]

buttocks [1]

1Ch 19: 4 shaved them, cut off their garments in the middle at the **buttocks**,

5157 מִפְתָּח *miptāḥ*, n.[m.]. [1] [√ 7337]

open [1]

Pr 8: 6 I have worthy things to say; I **open** my lips to speak what is right.

5158 מַפְתֵּחַ *maptēaḥ*, n.m. [3] [√ 7337]

key [2], key for opening [1]

Jdg 3: 25 open the doors of the room, they took a **key** and unlocked them.
1Ch 9: 27 and they had charge of the **key for opening** it each morning.
Isa 22: 22 I will place on his shoulder the **key** *to* the house of David;

5159 מִפְתָּן *miptān*, n.[m.]. [8] [cf. 7327]

threshold [8]

1Sa 5: 4 and hands had been broken off and were lying on the **threshold**;
5: 5 others who enter Dagon's temple at Ashdod step on the **threshold**.
Eze 9: 3 where it had been, and moved to the **threshold** *of* the temple.
10: 4 above the cherubim and moved to the **threshold** *of* the temple.
10: 18 the glory of the LORD departed from over the **threshold** *of* the
46: 2 He is to worship at the **threshold** *of* the gateway and then go out,
47: 1 I saw water coming out from under the **threshold** *of* the temple
Zep 1: 9 On that day I will punish all who avoid stepping on the **threshold**,

5160 מֵץ *mēṣ*, n.m. [1] [√ 4790]

oppressor [1]

Isa 16: 4 The **oppressor** will come to an end, and destruction will cease;

5161 מוֹץ *mōṣ*, n.m. [8]

chaff [8]

Job 21: 18 they like straw before the wind, like **chaff** swept away by a gale?
Ps 1: 4 so the wicked! They are like **chaff** that the wind blows away.
35: 5 May they be like **chaff** before the wind, with the angel of the
Isa 17: 13 driven before the wind like **chaff** *on* the hills, like tumbleweed
29: 5 will become like fine dust, the ruthless hordes like blown **chaff**.
41: 15 thresh the mountains and crush them, and reduce the hills to **chaff**.
Hos 13: 3 dew that disappears, like **chaff** swirling from a threshing floor,
Zep 2: 2 the appointed time arrives and that day sweeps on like **chaff**,

5162 מָצָא *māṣā'*, v. [454]

found [108], find [85], be found [25], finds [16], was found [12], is found [11], were [9], been found [8], were found [8], *untranslated* [7], come upon [7], meet [7], discovered [6], finding [6], is caught [6], met [6], pleased with [+928+2834+6524] [5], present [5], are [3], came upon [3], discover [3], had [+907] [3], handed [3], came [2], comprehend [2], fathom [2], happened [2], have enough [2], is found [+5162] [2], is [2], lived [2], overtook [2], prospers [+3202] [2], reach [2], still [2], survives [2], was [2], acquire [1], acquired [1], acquires [1], afford [+1896+3338] [1], are found [1], be room enough [1], be seen [1], become [1], been brought [1], before [1], bring a reward [1], brings upon [1], brings [1], came across [1], captured [1], catch [1], caught up [1], comes [1], detect [1], discover meaning [1], displease [+928+2834+4202+6524] [1], displeasing [+928+2834+4202+6524] [1], do [1], doing [1], enough [1], ever-present [+4394] [1], fall on [1], favorable toward [+928+2834 +6524] [1], find out [1], following [1], found courage [1], found out [1], found to be true [1], gain [1], gained [1], get [1], had [+4200] [1], had [1], hand over [+906+928+3338] [1], handed over [+928+3338] [1], happened to [1], has [+4200] [1], have [+928+3338] [1], have [1], here [1], hit [1], is attained [1], is captured [1], lay hold [1], lay on [1], lies [1], lift [1], looking for [1], lot [1], overcome [1], overtake [1], possess [1], probe [1], prosper [+3202] [1], reaches [1], reaped [1], regards [+4200+7156] [1], regards [+928+6524] [1], search [1], seize [1], seized [1], solved [1], spreads [1], still out [1], took [1], uncovered [1], was caught [1], were caught [1], win [1]

Ge 2: 20 [A] of the field. But for Adam no suitable helper *was* **found**.
4: 14 [A] wanderer on the earth, and whoever **finds** me will kill me."
4: 15 [A] mark on Cain so that no one *who* **found** him would kill him.
6: 8 [A] But Noah **found** favor in the eyes of the LORD.
8: 9 [A] the dove *could* **find** no place to set its feet because there was
11: 2 [A] *they* **found** a plain in Shinar and settled there.
16: 7 [A] The angel of the LORD **found** Hagar near a spring in the
18: 3 [A] He said, "If *I have* **found** favor in your eyes, my lord, do not
18: 26 [A] "If *I* **find** fifty righteous people in the city of Sodom,
18: 28 [A] "If *I* **find** forty-five there," he said, "I will not destroy it."
18: 29 [C] again he spoke to him, "What if only forty **are found** there?"
18: 30 [C] What if only thirty *can* **be found** there?" He answered,
18: 30 [A] He answered, "I will not do it if *I* **find** thirty there."
18: 31 [C] speak to the Lord, what if only twenty *can* **be found** there?"
18: 32 [C] What if only ten *can* **be found** there?" He answered, "For the
19: 11 [A] and old, with blindness so that they could not **find** the door.
19: 15 [C] Take your wife and your two daughters who *are* **here**, or you
19: 19 [A] Your servant *has* **found** favor in your eyes, and you have
26: 12 [A] crops in that land and the same year **reaped** a hundredfold,
26: 19 [A] dug in the valley and **discovered** a well of fresh water there.
26: 32 [A] the well they had dug. They said, "*We've* **found** water!"
27: 20 [A] asked his son, "How *did you* **find** it so quickly, my son?"
30: 14 [A] went out into the fields and **found** some mandrake plants,
30: 27 [A] said to him, "If *I have* **found** favor in your eyes, please stay.
31: 32 [A] But if *you* **find** anyone who has your gods, he shall not live.
31: 33 [A] into the tent of the two maidservants, but *he* **found** nothing.
31: 34 [A] searched through everything in the tent but **found** nothing.
31: 35 [A] So he searched but *could* not **find** the household gods.
31: 37 [A] what *have you* **found** that belongs to your household?
32: 5 [32:6] [A] to my lord, that I *may* **find** favor in your eyes.' "
32: 19 [32:20] [A] to say the same thing to Esau when you **meet** him.
33: 8 [A] I met?" "To **find** favor in your eyes, my lord," he said.
33: 10 [A] "If *I have* **found** favor in your eyes, accept this gift from me.
33: 15 [A] Jacob asked. "*Just let me* **find** favor in the eyes of my lord."
34: 11 [A] Dinah's father and brothers, "*Let me* **find** favor in your eyes,
36: 24 [A] This is the Anah who **discovered** the hot springs in the desert
37: 15 [A] a man **found** him wandering around in the fields and asked
37: 17 [A] Joseph went after his brothers and **found** them near Dothan.
37: 32 [A] robe back to their father and said, "*We* **found** this.
38: 20 [A] get his pledge back from the woman, but *he did* not **find** her.
38: 22 [A] So he went back to Judah and said, "*I* didn't **find** her.
38: 23 [A] I did send her this young goat, but you didn't **find** her."
39: 4 [A] Joseph **found** favor in his eyes and became his attendant.
41: 38 [A] So Pharaoh asked them, "*Can we* **find** anyone like this man,
44: 8 [A] Canaan the silver *we* **found** inside the mouths of our sacks.
44: 9 [C] If any of your servants **is found** to have *it*, he will die; and

[F] Hitpael (hitpoel, hitpoal, hitpolel, hitpolal, hitpalel, hitpalal, hitpalpel, hitpalpal, hotpael, hotpaal) [G] Hiphil (hiphtil) [H] Hophal [I] Hishtaphel

Ge 44:10 [C] Whoever **is found** to have *it* will become my slave; the rest
44:12 [C] the youngest. And the cup **was found** in Benjamin's sack.
44:16 [A] God *has* **uncovered** your servants' guilt. We are now my
44:16 [C] we ourselves and the one who **was found** to have the cup."
44:17 [C] Only the man who **was found** to have the cup will become
44:34 [A] Do not let me see the misery that *would* **come upon** my
47:14 [C] Joseph collected all the money that *was to* **be found** in Egypt
47:25 [A] "*May we* **find** favor in the eyes of our lord; we will be in
47:29 [A] and said to him, "If *I have* **found** favor in your eyes,
50: 4 [A] "If *I have* **found** favor in your eyes, speak to Pharaoh for
Ex 5:11 [A] Go and get your own straw wherever *you can* **find** it,
9:19 [C] that has not been brought in and *is* **still out** in the field,
12:19 [C] For seven days no yeast *is to* **be found** in your houses. And
15:22 [A] For three days they traveled in the desert without **finding**
16:25 [A] the LORD. *You will* not **find** any of it on the ground today.
16:27 [A] out on the seventh day to gather it, but *they* **found** none.
18: 8 [A] and about all the hardships they *had* **met** along the way
21:16 [C] or still has him *when he* **is caught** must be put to death.
22: 2 [22:1] [C] "If a thief **is caught** breaking in and is struck so that
22: 4 [22:3] [C] "If the stolen animal **is found** [+5162] alive in his
22: 4 [22:3] [C] "If the stolen animal **is found** [+5162] alive in his
22: 6 [22:5] [A] "If a fire breaks out and **spreads** *into* thornbushes
22: 7 [22:6] [C] the thief, if *he* **is caught**, must pay back double.
22: 8 [22:7] [C] if the thief **is** not **found**, the owner of the house must
33:12 [A] 'I know you by name and *you have* **found** favor with me.'
33:13 [A] If you *are* **pleased with me** [+928+2834+6524], teach me
33:13 [A] so I may know you and *continue to* **find** favor with you.
33:16 [A] know that you *are* **pleased with** [+928+2834+6524] me
33:17 [A] because I *am* **pleased with you** [+928+2834+6524] and I
34: 9 [A] "O Lord, if *I have* **found** favor in your eyes," he said,
35:23 [C] Everyone who **had** [+907] blue, purple or scarlet yarn or fine
35:24 [C] everyone who **had** [+907] acacia wood for any part of the
Lev 6: 3 [5:22] [A] or if *he* **finds** lost property and lies about it, or if he
6: 4 [5:23] [A] was entrusted to him, or the lost property *he* **found**,
9:12 [G] His sons **handed** him the blood, and he sprinkled it against
9:13 [G] *They* **handed** him the burnt offering piece by piece, including
9:18 [G] His sons **handed** him the blood, and he sprinkled it against
12: 8 [A] If she cannot **afford** [+1896+3338] a lamb, she is to bring
25:26 [A] himself prospers and **acquires** sufficient means to redeem it,
25:28 [A] if he *does* not **acquire** the means to repay him, what he sold
Nu 11:11 [A] What *have I done to* **displease** [+928+2834+4202+6524] you
11:15 [A] me to death right now—if *I have* **found** favor in your eyes—
11:22 [A] *Would* they **have enough** if flocks and herds were
11:22 [A] *Would* they **have enough** if all the fish in the sea were
15:32 [A] a man *was* **found** gathering wood on the Sabbath day.
15:33 [A] Those *who* **found** him gathering wood brought him to Moses
20:14 [A] You know about all the hardships that *have* **come upon** us.
31:50 [A] to the LORD the gold articles each of us **acquired**—
32: 5 [A] If *we have* **found** favor in your eyes," they said, "let this
32:23 [A] and you may be sure that your sin *will* **find** you **out**.
35:27 [A] the avenger of blood **finds** him outside the city, the avenger
Dt 4:29 [A] *you will* **find** him if you look for him with all your heart
4:30 [A] are in distress and all these things *have* **happened** *to* you,
17: 2 [C] **is found** doing evil in the eyes of the LORD your God in
18:10 [C] *Let* no *one* **be found** among you who sacrifices his son
19: 5 [A] a tree, the head may fly off and **hit** his neighbor and kill him.
20:11 [C] all the people **[NIE]** in it shall be subject to forced labor and
21: 1 [C] If a *man* **is found** slain, lying in a field in the land the
21:17 [C] firstborn by giving him a double share of all he **has** [+4200].
22: 3 [A] or his cloak or anything he loses. **[NIE]** Do not ignore it.
22:14 [A] when I approached her, *I did* not **find** proof of her virginity,"
22:17 [A] and said, '*I did* not **find** your daughter to be a virgin.'
22:20 [C] is true and no proof of the girl's virginity *can* **be found**,
22:22 [C] If a man **is found** sleeping with another man's wife, both the
22:23 [A] If a man *happens to* **meet** in a town a virgin pledged to be
22:25 [A] if out in the country a man *happens to* **meet** a girl pledged to
22:27 [A] for the man **found** the girl out in the country, and though the
22:28 [A] If a man *happens to* **meet** a virgin who is not pledged to be
22:28 [C] to be married and rapes her and *they are* **discovered**,
24: 1 [A] who becomes **displeasing to** [+928+2834+4202+6524] him
24: 1 [A] to him because *he* **finds** something indecent about her,
24: 7 [C] If a man **is caught** kidnapping one of his brother Israelites
31:17 [A] Many disasters and difficulties *will* **come upon** them, and on
31:17 [A] '*Have* not these disasters **come upon** us because our God is
31:21 [A] And when many disasters and difficulties **come upon** them,
32:10 [A] In a desert land *he* **found** him, in a barren and howling
Jos 2:22 [A] all along the road and returned without **finding** them.
2:23 [A] of Nun and told him everything that *had* **happened** *to* them.
10:17 [C] When Joshua was told that the five kings *had* **been found**
17:16 [C] of Joseph replied, "The hill country *is* not **enough** for us,
Jdg 1: 5 [A] It was there that *they* **found** Adoni-Bezek and fought against
5:30 [A] '*Are they* not **finding** and dividing the spoils: a girl or two
6:13 [A] "if the LORD is with us, why *has* all this **happened to** us?
6:17 [A] Gideon replied, "If now *I have* **found** favor in your eyes,
9:33 [A] come out against you, do whatever your hand **finds** to do."
14:12 [A] **[NIE]** I will give you thirty linen garments and thirty sets of
14:18 [A] with my heifer, *you would* not *have* **solved** my riddle."
15:15 [A] **Finding** a fresh jawbone of a donkey, he grabbed it
17: 8 [A] left that town *in* **search** *of* some other place to stay. On his
17: 9 [A] in Judah," he said, "and I'm **looking for** a place to stay."
20:48 [C] including the animals and everything else they **found**.
20:48 [C] they found. All the towns they **came across** they set on fire.
21:12 [A] *They* **found** among the people living in Jabesh Gilead four
21:14 [A] had been spared. But *there* **were** not enough for all of them.
Ru 1: 9 [A] May the LORD grant that each of you *will* **find** rest in the
2: 2 [A] pick up the leftover grain behind anyone in whose eyes *I* **find**
2:10 [A] "Why *have I* **found** such favor in your eyes that you notice
2:13 [A] "*May I continue to* **find** favor in your eyes, my lord,"
1Sa 1:18 [A] She said, "*May* your servant **find** favor in your eyes."
9: 4 [A] through the area around Shalisha, but *they did* not **find** them.
9: 4 [A] the territory of Benjamin, but *they did* not **find** them.
9: 8 [C] he said, "I **have** [+928+3338] a quarter of a shekel of silver.
9:11 [A] they **met** some girls coming out to draw water, and they
9:13 [A] *you will* **find** him before he goes up to the high place to eat.
9:13 [A] will eat. Go up now; *you should* **find** him about this time."
9:20 [C] days ago, do not worry about them; *they have* **been found**.
10: 2 [A] leave me today, *you will* **meet** two men near Rachel's tomb,
10: 2 [C] 'The donkeys you set out to look for *have* **been found**.
10: 3 [A] Three men going up to God at Bethel *will* **meet** you there.
10: 7 [A] do whatever your hand **finds** to do, for God is with you.
10:16 [C] "He assured us that the donkeys *had* **been found**."
10:21 [C] But when they looked for him, *he was* not *to* **be found**.
12: 5 [A] this day, that *you have* not **found** anything in my hand."
13:15 [C] in Benjamin, and Saul counted the men who **were** with him.
13:16 [C] the men **[RPH]** with them were staying in Gibeah in
13:19 [C] Not a blacksmith *could* **be found** in the whole land of Israel,
13:22 [C] with Saul and Jonathan **had** a sword or spear in his hand;
13:22 [C] his hand; only Saul and his son Jonathan **had** [+4200] them.
14:30 [A] today some of the plunder *they* **took** from their enemies.
16:22 [A] in my service, for I *am* **pleased** [+928+2834+6524] **with** *him*."
20: 3 [A] "Your father knows very well that *I have* **found** favor in
20:21 [A] I will send a boy and say, 'Go, **find** the arrows.' If I say to
20:29 [A] If *I have* **found** favor in your eyes, let me get away to see my
20:36 [A] and he said to the boy, "Run and **find** the arrows I shoot."
21: 3 [21:4] [C] me five loaves of bread, or whatever *you can* **find**."
23:17 [A] he said. "My father Saul *will* not **lay** a hand **on** you.
24:19 [24:20] [A] When a man **finds** his enemy, does he let him get
25: 8 [A] Therefore *be* **favorable toward** [+928+2834+6524] my young
25: 8 [A] and your son David whatever you *can* **find** for them.' "
25:28 [C] *Let* no wrongdoing **be found** in you as long as you live.
27: 5 [A] David said to Achish, "If *I have* **found** favor in your eyes,
29: 3 [A] the day he left Saul until now, *I have* **found** no fault in him."
29: 6 [A] *I have* **found** no fault in you, but the rulers don't approve of
29: 8 [A] "What *have you* **found** against your servant from the day I
30:11 [A] *They* **found** an Egyptian in a field and brought him to David.
31: 3 [A] when the archers **overtook** him, they wounded him critically.
31: 8 [A] *they* **found** Saul and his three sons fallen on Mount Gilboa.
2Sa 3: 8 [G] friends. *I* haven't **handed** you **over to** [+928+3338] David.
7:27 [A] So your servant *has* **found** courage to offer you this prayer.
14:22 [A] "Today your servant knows that *he has* **found** favor in your
15:25 [A] If *I* **find** favor in the LORD's eyes, he will bring me back
16: 4 [A] Ziba said. "*May I* **find** favor in your eyes, my lord the king."
17:12 [C] we will attack him wherever *he may* **be found**, and we will
17:13 [C] down to the valley until not even a piece of it *can* **be found**."
17:20 [A] The men searched but **found** no one, so they returned to
18:22 [A] You don't have any news *that will* **bring** you **a reward**."
20: 6 [A] or *he will* **find** fortified cities and escape from us."
1Ki 1: 3 [A] throughout Israel for a beautiful girl and **found** Abishag,
1:52 [C] fall to the ground; but if evil **is found** in him, he will die."
11:19 [A] Pharaoh *was* so **pleased with** [+928+2834+6524] Hadad that
11:29 [A] Ahijah the prophet of Shiloh **met** him on the way, wearing a
13:14 [A] *He* **found** him sitting under an oak tree and asked, "Are you
13:24 [A] went on his way, a lion **met** him on the road and killed him,
13:28 [A] he went out and **found** the body thrown down on the road,
14:13 [C] the LORD, the God of Israel, *has* **found** anything good.
18: 5 [A] Maybe *we can* **find** some grass to keep the horses and mules
18:10 [A] were not there, he made them swear *they could* not **find** you.
18:12 [A] If I go and tell Ahab and *he* doesn't **find** you, he will kill me.
19:19 [A] So Elijah went from there and **found** Elisha son of Shaphat.
20:36 [A] after the man went away, a lion **found** him and killed him.
20:37 [A] The prophet **found** another man and said, "Strike me,
21:20 [A] Ahab said to Elijah, "So *you have* **found** me, my enemy!"
21:20 [A] "*I have* **found** you," he answered, "because you have sold
2Ki 2:17 [A] fifty men, who searched for three days but *did* not **find** him.
4:29 [A] If *you* **meet** anyone, do not greet him, and if anyone greets
4:39 [A] out into the fields to gather herbs and **found** a wild vine.
7: 9 [A] If we wait until daylight, punishment *will* **overtake** *us*. Let's
9:21 [A] *They* **met** him at the plot of ground that had belonged to

2Ki 9:35 [A] *they* **found** nothing except her skull, her feet and her hands.
10:13 [A] he **met** some relatives of Ahaziah king of Judah and asked,
10:15 [A] After he left there, *he* **came upon** Jehonadab son of Recab,
12:5 [12:6] [C] let it be used to repair whatever damage **is found** in
12:10 [12:11] [C] counted the money that *had* **been brought** *into* the
12:18 [12:19] [C] all the gold **found** in the treasuries of the temple of
14:14 [C] and all the articles **found** *in* the temple of the LORD
16:8 [C] took the silver and gold **found** *in* the temple of the LORD
17:4 [A] But the king of Assyria **discovered** that Hoshea was a traitor,
18:15 [C] So Hezekiah gave him all the silver that **was found** *in* the
19:4 [C] has heard. Therefore pray for the remnant that *still* **survives**."
19:8 [A] he withdrew and **found** the king fighting against Libnah.
20:13 [C] his armory and everything **found** among his treasures.
22:8 [A] "*I have* **found** the Book of the Law in the temple of the
22:9 [C] "Your officials have paid out the money that **was** in the
22:13 [C] Judah about what is written in this book that *has* **been found**.
23:2 [C] which *had* **been found** in the temple of the LORD.
23:24 [A] the priest *had* **discovered** *in* the temple of the LORD.
25:19 [C] Of *those* **still** in the city, he took the officer in charge of the
25:19 [C] of the land and sixty of his men who **were found** in the city.
1Ch 4:40 [A] *They* **found** rich, good pasture, and the land was spacious,
4:41 [C] also the Meunites who **were** there and completely destroyed
10:3 [A] and when the archers **overtook** him, they wounded him.
10:8 [A] *they* **found** Saul and his sons fallen on Mount Gilboa.
17:25 [A] for him. So your servant *has* **found courage** to pray to you.
20:2 [A] its weight *was* **found** to be a talent of gold, and it was set
24:4 [C] A larger number of leaders **were found** *among* Eleazar's
26:31 [C] capable men among the Hebronites **were found** at Jazer in
28:9 [C] If you seek him, *he will* **be found** by you; but if you forsake
29:8 [C] Any who **had** [+907] precious stones gave them to the
29:17 [C] now I have seen with joy how willingly your people who **are**
2Ch 2:17 [2:16] [C] had taken; and *they* **were found** to be 153,600.
5:11 [C] All the priests who **were** there had consecrated themselves,
15:2 [C] If you seek him, *he will* **be found** by you, but if you forsake
15:4 [C] God of Israel, and sought him, and *he* **was found** by them.
15:15 [C] They sought God eagerly, and *he* **was found** by them.
19:3 [C] *There* **is**, however, some good in you, for you have rid the
20:16 [A] *you will* **find** them at the end of the gorge in the Desert of
20:25 [A] and *they* **found** among them a great amount of equipment
21:17 [C] and carried off all the goods **found** in the king's palace,
22:8 [A] *he* **found** the princes of Judah and the sons of Ahaziah's
25:5 [A] **found** that there were three hundred thousand men ready for
25:24 [C] all the articles **found** in the temple of God that had been in
29:16 [A] unclean that *they* **found** in the temple of the LORD.
29:29 [C] the king and everyone **present** with him knelt down
30:21 [C] The Israelites who *were* **present** in Jerusalem celebrated the
31:1 [C] the Israelites who **were** *there* went out to the towns of Judah,
32:4 [A] should the kings of Assyria come and **find** plenty of water?"
34:14 [A] Hilkiah the priest **found** the Book of the Law of the LORD
34:15 [A] "*I have* **found** the Book of the Law in the temple of the
34:17 [C] They have paid out the money that **was** in the temple of the
34:21 [C] Judah about what is written in this book that *has* **been found**.
34:30 [C] which *had* **been found** in the temple of the LORD.
34:32 [C] **[RPH]** the people of Jerusalem did this in accordance with
34:33 [C] he had all who *were* **present** in Israel serve the LORD their
35:7 [C] Josiah provided for all the lay people who **were** there a total
35:17 [C] The Israelites who *were* **present** celebrated the Passover at
35:18 [C] and Israel who **were** there with the people of Jerusalem.
36:8 [C] detestable things he did and all that **was found** against him,
Ezr 2:62 [C] they *could* not **find** *them* and so were excluded from the
8:15 [A] among the people and the priests, *I* **found** no Levites there.
8:25 [C] all Israel **present** there had donated for the house of our God.
10:18 [C] of the priests, *the* **following** had married foreign women:
Ne 5:8 [A] They kept quiet, because *they could* **find** nothing to say.
7:5 [A] *I* **found** the genealogical record of those who had been the
7:5 [A] been the first to return. This is what *I* **found** written there:
7:64 [C] they *could* not **find** *them* and so were excluded from the
8:14 [A] *They* **found** written in the Law, which the LORD had
9:8 [A] *You* **found** his heart faithful to you, and you made a
9:32 [A] the hardship that *has* **come upon** us, upon our kings
13:1 [C] there *it* **was found** written that no Ammonite or Moabite
Est 1:5 [C] the least to the greatest, who **were** in the citadel of Susa.
2:23 [C] And when the report was investigated and **found to be true**,
4:16 [C] "Go, gather together all the Jews who **are** in Susa, and fast
5:8 [A] If the king **regards** [+928+6524] *me with* favor and if it
6:2 [C] *It* **was found** recorded there that Mordecai had exposed
7:3 [A] "If *I have* **found** favor with you, O king, and if it pleases
8:5 [A] "and if he **regards** [+4200+7156] *me with* favor and thinks
8:6 [A] For how can I bear to see disaster **fall on** my people? How
Job 3:22 [A] filled with gladness and rejoice when *they* **reach** the grave?
11:7 [A] "*Can you* **fathom** the mysteries of God? Can you probe the
11:7 [A] of God? *Can you* **probe** the limits of the Almighty?
17:10 [A] all of you, try again! *I will* not **find** a wise man among you.
19:28 [C] we will hound him, since the root of the trouble **lies** in him,'
20:8 [A] Like a dream he flies away, no more *to be* **found**, banished
23:3 [A] If only I knew where *to* **find** him; if only I could go to his
28:12 [C] "But where *can* wisdom **be found**? Where does
28:13 [C] its worth; *it* cannot **be found** in the land of the living.
31:25 [A] over my great wealth, the fortune my hands *had* **gained**,
31:29 [A] or gloated over the trouble *that* **came** *to* him—
32:3 [A] because *they had* **found** no way to refute Job, and yet had
32:13 [A] Do not say, '*We have* **found** wisdom; let God refute him,
33:10 [A] Yet God *has* **found** fault with me; he considers me his
33:24 [A] from going down to the pit; *I have* **found** a ransom for him'—
34:11 [G] he has done; *he* **brings upon** him what his conduct deserves.
37:13 [G] *He* **brings** the clouds to punish men, or to water his earth
37:23 [A] The Almighty is beyond *our* **reach** and exalted in power;
42:15 [C] Nowhere in all the land **were** *there* **found** women as
Ps 10:15 [A] to account for his wickedness *that would* not *be* **found out**.
17:3 [A] me at night, though you test me, *you will* **find** nothing;
21:8 [21:9] [A] Your hand *will* **lay hold** on all your enemies;
21:8 [21:9] [A] your enemies; your right hand *will* **seize** your foes.
32:6 [A] everyone who is godly pray to you while you *may be* **found**;
36:2 [36:3] [A] in his own eyes he flatters himself too much to **detect**
37:36 [C] no more; though I looked for him, *he could* not **be found**.
46:1 [46:2] [C] an **ever-present** [+4394] help in trouble.
69:20 [69:21] [A] there was none, for comforters, but *I* **found** none.
76:5 [76:6] [A] last sleep; not one of the warriors *can* **lift** his hands.
84:3 [84:4] [A] Even the sparrow *has* **found** a home,
89:20 [89:21] [A] *I have* **found** David my servant; with my sacred oil
107:4 [A] **finding** no way to a city where they could settle.
116:3 [A] death entangled me, the anguish of the grave **came upon** me;
116:3 [A] came upon me; *I was* **overcome** *by* trouble and sorrow.
119:143 [A] Trouble and distress *have* **come upon** me, but your
119:162 [A] I rejoice in your promise like *one who* **finds** great spoil.
132:5 [A] till *I* **find** a place for the LORD, a dwelling for the Mighty
132:6 [A] heard it in Ephrathah, *we* **came upon** it in the fields of Jaar:
Pr 1:13 [A] *we will* **get** all sorts of valuable things and fill our houses
1:28 [A] I will not answer; they will look for me but *will* not **find** me.
2:5 [A] the fear of the LORD and **find** the knowledge of God.
3:4 [A] Then *you will* **win** favor and a good name in the sight of God
3:13 [A] Blessed is the man *who* **finds** wisdom, the man who gains
4:22 [A] for they are life to *those who* **find** them and health to a
6:31 [C] Yet if *he* **is caught**, he must pay sevenfold, though it costs
6:33 [A] Blows and disgrace *are his* **lot**, and his shame will never be
7:15 [A] came out to meet you; I looked for you and *have* **found** you!
8:9 [A] are right; they are faultless to *those who* **have** knowledge.
8:12 [A] together with prudence; *I* **possess** knowledge and discretion.
8:17 [A] I love those who love me, and those who seek me **find** me.
8:35 [A] For *whoever* **finds** me finds life and receives favor from the
8:35 [A] For whoever finds me **finds** life and receives favor from the
10:13 [C] Wisdom **is found** on the lips of the discerning, but a rod is
16:20 [A] Whoever gives heed to instruction **prospers** [+3202],
16:31 [C] hair is a crown of splendor; *it* **is attained** by a righteous life.
17:20 [A] A man of perverse heart *does* not **prosper** [+3202]; he whose
18:22 [A] *He who* **finds** a wife finds what is good and receives favor
18:22 [A] He who finds a wife **finds** what is good and receives favor
19:8 [A] own soul; he who cherishes understanding **prospers** [+3202].
20:6 [A] to have unfailing love, but a faithful man who *can* **find**?
21:21 [A] He who pursues righteousness and love **finds** life, prosperity
24:14 [A] if *you* **find** it, there is a future hope for you, and your hope
25:16 [A] If *you* **find** honey, eat just enough—too much of it, and you
28:23 [A] He who rebukes a man *will* in the end **gain** more favor than
31:10 [A] A wife of noble character who *can* **find**? She is worth far
Ecc 3:11 [A] yet they cannot **fathom** what God has done from beginning
7:14 [A] Therefore, a man cannot **discover** anything *about* his future.
7:24 [A] it is far off and most profound—who *can* **discover** it?
7:26 [A] I **find** more bitter than death the woman who is a snare,
7:27 [A] "Look," says the Teacher, "this is what *I have* **discovered**:
7:27 [A] "Adding one thing to another to **discover** the scheme of
7:28 [A] while I was still searching but not **finding**—I found one
7:28 [A] *I* **found** one ⌊upright⌋ man among a thousand, but not one
7:28 [A] but not one ⌊upright⌋ woman among them all. **[RPH]**
7:29 [A] This only *have I* **found**: God made mankind upright,
8:17 [A] No one can **comprehend** what goes on under the sun.
8:17 [A] his efforts to search it out, man cannot **discover** *its* **meaning**.
8:17 [A] wise man claims he knows, he cannot *really* **comprehend** it.
9:10 [A] Whatever your hand **finds** to do, do it with all your might,
9:15 [A] Now *there* **lived** in that city a man poor but wise, and he
11:1 [A] upon the waters, for after many days *you will* **find** it *again*.
12:10 [A] The Teacher searched to **find** just the right words, and what
SS 3:1 [A] one my heart loves; I looked for him but *did* not **find** him.
3:2 [A] one my heart loves. So I looked for him but *did* not **find** him.
3:3 [A] The watchmen **found** me as they made their rounds in the
3:4 [A] Scarcely had I passed them when *I* **found** the one my heart
5:6 [A] I looked for him but *did* not **find** him. I called him but he did
5:7 [A] The watchmen **found** me as they made their rounds in the
5:8 [A] I charge you—if *you* **find** my lover, what will you tell him?

SS 8: 1 [A] Then, if *I* **found** you outside, I would kiss you, and no one
Isa 10: 10 [A] As my hand **seized** the kingdoms of the idols, kingdoms
10: 14 [A] As *one* **reaches** into a nest, so my hand reached for the
13: 15 [C] Whoever **is captured** will be thrust through; all who are
22: 3 [C] All you *who* **were caught** were taken prisoner together,
30: 14 [C] not a fragment *will* **be found** for taking coals from a hearth
34: 14 [A] will also repose and **find** for themselves places of rest.
35: 9 [C] any ferocious beast get up on it; *they will* not **be found** there.
37: 4 [C] has heard. Therefore pray for the remnant that *still* **survives**."
37: 8 [A] he withdrew and **found** the king fighting against Libnah.
39: 2 [C] his entire armory and everything **found** among his treasures.
41: 12 [A] Though you search for your enemies, *you will* not **find** them.
51: 3 [C] Joy and gladness *will* **be found** in her, thanksgiving
55: 6 [C] Seek the LORD while he *may* **be found**; call on him while
57: 10 [A] *You* **found** renewal of your strength, and so you did not
58: 3 [A] *you* **do** as you please and exploit all your workers.
58: 13 [A] own way and not **doing** as you please or speaking idle words,
65: 1 [C] not ask for me; *I* **was found** by those who did not seek me.
65: 8 [C] "As when juice **is** *still* **found** in a cluster of grapes and men
Jer 2: 5 [A] "What fault *did* your fathers **find** in me, that they strayed
2: 24 [A] need not tire themselves; at mating time *they will* **find** her.
2: 26 [C] "As a thief is disgraced when *he* **is caught**, so the house of
2: 34 [C] On your clothes *men* **find** the lifeblood of the innocent poor,
2: 34 [A] innocent poor, though *you did* not **catch** them breaking in.
5: 1 [A] If *you can* **find** but one person who deals honestly and seeks
5: 26 [C] "Among my people **are** wicked men who lie in wait like men
6: 16 [A] way is, and walk in it, and *you will* **find** rest for your souls.
10: 18 [A] I will bring distress on them so that *they may be* **captured**."
11: 9 [C] "*There* **is** a conspiracy among the people of Judah and those
14: 3 [A] servants for water; they go to the cisterns but **find** no water.
15: 16 [C] *When* your words **came**, I ate them; they were my joy
23: 11 [A] even in my temple *I* **find** their wickedness,"
29: 13 [A] seek me and **find** me when you seek me with all your heart.
29: 14 [C] *I will* **be found** by you," declares the LORD, "and will
31: 2 [A] "The people who survive the sword *will* **find** favor in the
41: 3 [C] as well as the Babylonian soldiers who **were** there.
41: 8 [C] ten of them **[NIE]** said to Ishmael, "Don't kill us! We have
41: 12 [A] *They* **caught up** *with* him near the great pool in Gibeon.
45: 3 [A] to my pain; I am worn out with groaning and **find** no rest.' "
48: 27 [C] **Was** *she* **caught** among thieves, that you shake your head in
50: 7 [A] Whoever **found** them devoured them; their enemies said,
50: 20 [C] be none, and for the sins of Judah, but none *will* **be found**,
50: 24 [C] *you* **were found** and captured because you opposed the
52: 25 [C] Of those **still** in the city, he took the officer in charge of the
52: 25 [C] of the land and sixty of his men who **were found** in the city.
La 1: 3 [A] She dwells among the nations; *she* **finds** no resting place.
1: 6 [A] Her princes are like deer *that* **find** no pasture; in weakness
2: 9 [A] and her prophets no longer **find** visions from the LORD.
2: 16 [A] This is the day we have waited for; *we have* **lived** to see it."
Eze 3: 1 [A] to me, "Son of man, eat what *is* **before** *you*, eat this scroll;
22: 30 [A] the land so I would not have to destroy it, but *I* **found** none.
26: 21 [C] You will be sought, but *you will* never again **be found**,
28: 15 [C] the day you were created till wickedness **was found** in you.
Da 1: 19 [C] he **found** none equal to Daniel, Hananiah, Mishael
1: 20 [A] *he* **found** them ten times better than all the magicians
11: 19 [C] own country but will stumble and fall, *to* **be seen** no more.
12: 1 [C] everyone whose name **is found** written in the book—will be
Hos 2: 6 [2:8] [A] I will wall her in so that *she* cannot **find** her way.
2: 7 [2:9] [A] catch them; she will look for them but not **find** them.
5: 6 [A] and herds to seek the LORD, *they will* not **find** him;
9: 10 [A] "When *I* **found** Israel, it was like finding grapes in the
12: 4 [12:5] [A] *He* **found** him at Bethel and talked with him there—
12: 8 [12:9] [A] "I am very rich; *I have* **become** wealthy.
12: 8 [12:9] [A] With all my wealth *they will* not **find** in me any
14: 8 [14:9] [C] a green pine tree; your fruitfulness **comes** from me."
Am 8: 12 [A] for the word of the LORD, but *they will* not **find** it.
Jnh 1: 3 [A] down to Joppa, where *he* **found** a ship bound for that port.
Mic 1: 13 [C] of Zion, for the transgressions of Israel **were found** in you.
Zep 3: 13 [C] will speak no lies, nor *will* deceit **be found** in their mouths.
Zec 10: 10 [C] and Lebanon, and *there will* not **be room enough** for them.
11: 6 [G] "I *will* **hand** everyone **over to** [+906+928+3338] his
Mal 2: 6 [C] was in his mouth and nothing false **was found** on his lips.

5163 מַצָּב **maṣṣāb**, n.m. [10] [→ 5165; cf. 5893]

outpost [4], detachment [1], garrison [1], office [1], outposts [1], stood [+3922+8079] [1], stood [+8079] [1]

Jos 4: 3 of the Jordan from right where the priests **stood** [+3922+8079]
4: 9 the priests who carried the ark of the covenant had **stood** [+8079].
1Sa 13: 23 Now a **detachment** *of* Philistines had gone out to the pass at
14: 1 "Come, let's go over to the Philistine **outpost** on the other side."
14: 4 intended to cross to reach the Philistine **outpost** was a cliff;
14: 6 let's go over to the **outpost** *of* those uncircumcised fellows.
14: 11 So both of them showed themselves to the Philistine **outpost**.
14: 15 the camp and field, and those in the **outposts** and raiding parties—
2Sa 23: 14 in the stronghold, and the Philistine **garrison** was at Bethlehem.
Isa 22: 19 I will depose you from your **office**, and you will be ousted from

5164 מֻצָּב **muṣṣāb**, n.[m.]. [2] [√ 5893]

pillar [1], towers [1]

Jdg 9: 6 Beth Millo gathered beside the great tree at the **pillar** in Shechem
Isa 29: 3 I will encircle you with **towers** and set up my siege works against

5165 מַצָּבָה **maṣṣābâ**, n.f. [1] [√ 5163]

outpost [1]

1Sa 14: 12 The men of the **outpost** shouted to Jonathan and his armor-bearer,

5166 מִצָּבָה **miṣṣābâ**, n.f. [1 / 0] [√ 5893]

Zec 9: 8 my house against marauding forces. [BHS *outpost* ?; NIV 7372]

5167 מַצֵּבָה **maṣṣēbâ**, n.f. [34] [→ 5170; cf. 5893]

sacred stones [14], pillar [10], sacred stone [5], *untranslated* [1], monument [1], pillars [1], sacred pillars [1], stone pillars [1]

Ge 28: 18 under his head and set it up as a **pillar** and poured oil on top of it.
28: 22 and this stone that I have set up as a **pillar** will be God's house,
31: 13 where you anointed a **pillar** and where you made a vow to me.
31: 45 So Jacob took a stone and set it up as a **pillar**.
31: 51 this heap, and here is this **pillar** I have set up between you and me.
31: 52 This heap is a witness, and this **pillar** is a witness, that I will not go
31: 52 you will not go past this heap and **pillar** to my side to harm me.
35: 14 Jacob set up a stone **pillar** at the place where God had talked with
35: 14 talked with him, **[RPH]** and he poured out a drink offering on it;
35: 20 Over her tomb Jacob set up a **pillar**, and to this day that pillar
35: 20 set up a pillar, and to this day that **pillar** marks Rachel's tomb.
Ex 23: 24 You must demolish them and break their **sacred stones** to pieces.
24: 4 set up twelve **stone pillars** representing the twelve tribes of Israel.
34: 13 smash their **sacred stones** and cut down their Asherah poles.
Lev 26: 1 not make idols or set up an image or a **sacred stone** for yourselves,
Dt 7: 5 Break down their altars, smash their **sacred stones**, cut down their
12: 3 smash their **sacred stones** and burn their Asherah poles in the fire;
16: 22 do not erect a **sacred stone**, for these the LORD your God hates.
1Ki 14: 23 **sacred stones** and Asherah poles on every high hill and under
2Ki 3: 2 He got rid of the **sacred stone** *of* Baal that his father had made.
10: 26 They brought the **sacred stone** out of the temple of Baal
10: 27 They demolished the **sacred stone** *of* Baal and tore down the
17: 10 They set up **sacred stones** and Asherah poles on every high hill
18: 4 smashed the **sacred stones** and cut down the Asherah poles.
23: 14 Josiah smashed the **sacred stones** and cut down the Asherah poles
2Ch 14: 3 [14:2] smashed the **sacred stones** and cut down the Asherah
31: 1 smashed the **sacred stones** and cut down the Asherah poles.
Isa 19: 19 in the heart of Egypt, and a **monument** to the LORD at its border.
Jer 43: 13 the temple of the sun in Egypt he will demolish the **sacred pillars**
Eze 26: 11 with the sword, and your strong **pillars** will fall to the ground.
Hos 3: 4 days without king or prince, without sacrifice or **sacred stones**,
10: 1 more altars; as his land prospered, he adorned his **sacred stones**.
10: 2 LORD will demolish their altars and destroy their **sacred stones**.
Mic 5: 13 [5:12] carved images and your **sacred stones** from among you;

5168 מְצֹבָיָה **m^{e}ṣōbāyâ**, a.g. [1]

Mezobaite [1]

1Ch 11: 47 Eliel, Obed and Jaasiel the **Mezobaite**.

5169 מַצֶּבֶת[1] **maṣṣebet[1]**, n.f. [2] [√ 5893]

stump [1], stumps [1]

Isa 6: 13 But as the terebinth and oak leave **stumps** when they are cut down,
6: 13 they are cut down, so the holy seed will be the **stump** *in* the land."

5170 מַצֶּבֶת[2] **maṣṣebet[2]**, n.f. [2] [√ 5167; cf. 5893]

pillar [2]

2Sa 18: 18 During his lifetime Absalom had taken a **pillar** and erected it in the
18: 18 He named the **pillar** after himself, and it is called Absalom's

5171 מְצָד **m^{e}ṣād**, n.f. [11] [√ 7421; cf. 5181]

strongholds [7], fortress [2], stronghold [2]

Jdg 6: 2 shelters for themselves in mountain clefts, caves and **strongholds**.
1Sa 23: 14 David stayed in the desert **strongholds** and in the hills of the
23: 19 "Is not David hiding among us in the **strongholds** at Horesh,
23: 29 [24:1] up from there and lived in the **strongholds** *of* En Gedi.
1Ch 11: 7 David then took up residence in the **fortress**, and so it was called
12: 8 [12:9] Some Gadites defected to David at his **stronghold** in the
12: 16 [12:17] men from Judah also came to David in his **stronghold**.
Isa 33: 16 dwell on the heights, whose refuge will be the mountain **fortress**.

Jer 48:41 Kerioth will be captured and the **strongholds** taken. In that day the
51:30 warriors have stopped fighting; they remain in their **strongholds**.
Eze 33:27 and those in **strongholds** and caves will die of a plague.

5172 מָצָה māṣâ, v. [7] [cf. 5209]

be drained out [2], drain dry [1], drained to dregs [+906+9272] [1], drink down [1], drink up [1], wrung out [1]

Lev 1:15 [C] its blood *shall* **be drained out** on the side of the altar.
5:9 [C] the rest of the blood *must* **be drained out** at the base of the
Jdg 6:38 [A] he squeezed the fleece and **wrung out** the dew—a bowlful of
Ps 73:10 [C] their people turn to them and **drink up** waters in abundance.
75:8 [75:9] [A] all the wicked of the earth **drink** it **down** *to* its very
Isa 51:17 [A] *you who have* **drained to** its **dregs** [+906+9272] the goblet
Eze 23:34 [A] You will drink it and **drain** it **dry**; you will dash it to pieces

5173 מֹצָה mōṣâ, n.pr.loc. [1]

Mozah [1]

Jos 18:26 Mizpah, Kephirah, **Mozah**,

5174 מַצָּה¹ maṣṣâ[1], n.f. [53] [cf. 5209?]

unleavened bread [20], bread made without yeast [14], without yeast [5], *untranslated* [4], bread without yeast [3], bread [2], made without yeast [2], Feast of Unleavened Bread [1], prepared without yeast [1], unleavened [1]

Ge 19:3 a meal for them, baking **bread without yeast**, and they ate.
Ex 12:8 the fire, along with bitter herbs, and **bread made without yeast**.
12:15 For seven days you are to eat **bread made without yeast**.
12:17 "Celebrate the **Feast of Unleavened Bread**, because it was on this
12:18 In the first month you are to eat **bread made without yeast**,
12:20 with yeast. Wherever you live, you must eat **unleavened bread**."
12:39 had brought from Egypt, they baked cakes of **unleavened bread**.
13:6 For seven days eat **bread made without yeast** and on the seventh
13:7 Eat **unleavened bread** during those seven days; nothing with yeast
23:15 "Celebrate the Feast of **Unleavened Bread**; for seven days eat
23:15 for seven days eat **bread made without yeast**, as I commanded
29:2 **without yeast**, make bread, and cakes mixed with oil, and wafers
29:2 without yeast, make bread, and cakes **[RPH]** mixed with oil,
29:2 and cakes mixed with oil, and wafers **[RPH]** spread with oil.
29:23 From the basket of **bread made without yeast**, which is before the
34:18 "Celebrate the Feast of **Unleavened Bread**. For seven days eat
34:18 For seven days eat **bread made without yeast**, as I commanded
Lev 2:4 cakes made **without yeast** and mixed with oil, or wafers made
2:4 mixed with oil, or wafers made **without yeast** and spread with oil.
2:5 it is to be made of fine flour mixed with oil, and **without yeast**.
6:16 [6:9] rest of it, but it is to be eaten **without yeast** in a holy place;
7:12 thank offering he is to offer cakes of **bread made without yeast**
7:12 mixed with oil, wafers **made without yeast** and spread with oil,
8:2 two rams and the basket containing **bread made without yeast**,
8:26 from the basket of **bread made without yeast**, which was before
8:26 he took a cake of **bread**, and one made with oil, and a wafer;
10:12 LORD by fire and eat it **prepared without yeast** beside the altar,
23:6 of that month the LORD's Feast of **Unleavened Bread** begins;
23:6 for seven days you must eat **bread made without yeast**.
Nu 6:15 and drink offerings, and a basket of **bread made without yeast**—
6:15 of fine flour mixed with oil, and wafers **[RPH]** spread with oil.
6:17 He is to present the basket of **unleavened bread** and is to sacrifice
6:19 a cake **[RPH]** and a wafer from the basket, both made without
6:19 and a cake and a wafer from the basket, both **made without yeast**.
9:11 to eat the lamb, together with **unleavened bread** and bitter herbs.
28:17 is to be a festival; for seven days eat **bread made without yeast**.
Dt 16:3 but for seven days eat **unleavened bread**, the bread of affliction,
16:8 For six days eat **unleavened bread** and on the seventh day hold an
16:16 at the Feast of **Unleavened Bread**, the Feast of Weeks and the
Jos 5:11 of the produce of the land: **unleavened bread** and roasted grain.
Jdg 6:19 and from an ephah of flour he made **bread without yeast**.
6:20 "Take the meat and the **unleavened bread**, place them on this
6:21 angel of the LORD touched the meat and the **unleavened bread**.
6:21 Fire flared from the rock, consuming the meat and the **bread**.
1Sa 28:24 She took some flour, kneaded it and baked **bread without yeast**.
2Ki 23:9 in Jerusalem, they ate **unleavened bread** with their fellow priests.
1Ch 23:29 grain offerings, the **unleavened** wafers, the baking and the mixing,
2Ch 8:13 the Feast of **Unleavened Bread**, the Feast of Weeks and the Feast
30:13 to celebrate the Feast of **Unleavened Bread** in the second month.
30:21 Feast of **Unleavened Bread** for seven days with great rejoicing,
35:17 and observed the Feast of **Unleavened Bread** for seven days.
Ezr 6:22 days they celebrated with joy the Feast of **Unleavened Bread**,
Eze 45:21 seven days, during which you shall eat **bread made without yeast**.

5175 מַצָּה² maṣṣâ[2], n.f. [3] [√ 5897]

quarrel [1], quarrels [1], strife [1]

Pr 13:10 Pride only breeds **quarrels**, but wisdom is found in those who take
17:19 He who loves a **quarrel** loves sin; he who builds a high gate
Isa 58:4 Your fasting ends in quarreling and **strife**, and in striking each

5176 מֻצְהָב muṣhāb, n.[m.] *or* v.ptcp. Not used in NIV/BHS [√ 7410]

5177 מִצְהָלוֹת miṣhālôt, n.f.[pl.]. [2] [√ 7412]

lustful neighings [1], neighing [+7754] [1]

Jer 8:16 at the **neighing** [+7754] *of* their stallions the whole land trembles.
13:27 your adulteries and **lustful neighings**, your shameless prostitution!

5178 מָצוֹד¹ māṣôd[1], n.[m.]. [4 / 3] [√ 7421]

net [1], plunder [1], snare [1]

Job 19:6 then know that God has wronged me and drawn his **net** around me.
Pr 12:12 The wicked desire the **plunder** *of* evil men, but the root of the
Ecc 7:26 I find more bitter than death the woman who is a **snare**, whose
9:14 built huge <u>siegeworks</u> [BHS *siegeworks* ?; NIV 5189] against it.

5179 מָצוֹד² māṣôd[2], n.m. Not used in NIV/BHS [√ 7421]

5180 מְצוּדָה¹ m^e^ṣûdâ[1], n.f. [4] [√ 7421]

snare [2], prey [1], prison [1]

Ps 66:11 You brought us into **prison** and laid burdens on our backs.
Eze 12:13 I will spread my net for him, and he will be caught in my **snare**;
13:21 from your hands, and they will no longer fall **prey** to your power.
17:20 I will spread my net for him, and he will be caught in my **snare**.

5181 מְצוּדָה² m^e^ṣûdâ[2], n.f. [17] [√ 7421?; cf. 5171]

fortress [9], stronghold [7], strong fortress [+1074] [1]

1Sa 22:4 and they stayed with him as long as David was in the **stronghold**.
22:5 But the prophet Gad said to David, "Do not stay in the **stronghold**.
24:22 [24:23] but David and his men went up to the **stronghold**.
2Sa 5:7 Nevertheless, David captured the **fortress** *of* Zion, the City of
5:9 David then took up residence in the **fortress** and called it the City
5:17 but David heard about it and went down to the **stronghold**.
22:2 He said: "The LORD is my rock, my **fortress** and my deliverer;
23:14 At that time David was in the **stronghold**, and the Philistine
1Ch 11:5 Nevertheless, David captured the **fortress** *of* Zion, the City of
11:16 At that time David was in the **stronghold**, and the Philistine
Job 39:28 on a cliff and stays there at night; a rocky crag is his **stronghold**.
Ps 18:2 [18:3] The LORD is my rock, my **fortress** and my deliverer;
31:2 [31:3] my rock of refuge, a **strong fortress** [+1074] to save me.
31:3 [31:4] Since you are my rock and my **fortress**, for the sake of
71:3 the command to save me, for you are my rock and my **fortress**.
91:2 "He is my refuge and my **fortress**, my God, in whom I trust."
144:2 He is my loving God and my **fortress**, my stronghold and my

5182 מְצֹודָה¹ m^e^ṣôdâ[1], n.f. [2] [√ 7421]

net [1], prison [1]

Ecc 9:12 As fish are caught in a cruel **net**, or birds are taken in a snare,
Eze 19:9 They put him in **prison**, so his roar was heard no longer on the

5183 מְצֹודָה² m^e^ṣôdâ[2], n.f. [1] [√ 7421]

fortress [1]

Isa 29:7 that attack her and her **fortress** and besiege her, will be as it is with

5184 מִצְוָה miṣwâ, n.f. [181] [√ 7422]

commands [138], command [11], commanded [4], ordered [4], commandments [3], prescribed [3], admonition [2], instructions [2], law [2], commanded [+7422] [1], commanded [+906+7422] [1], commandment [1], gave [1], laws [1], order [1], orders [1], rules [1], terms [1], way prescribed [1], what ordered [1], what[s] [+2021+2021+2296] [1]

Ge 26:5 kept my requirements, my **commands**, my decrees and my laws."
Ex 15:26 if you pay attention to his **commands** and keep all his decrees,
16:28 "How long will you refuse to keep my **commands** and my
20:6 ⌞generations⌟ of those who love me and keep my **commandments**.
24:12 with the law and **commands** I have written for their instruction."
Lev 4:2 and does what is forbidden in any of the LORD's **commands**—
4:13 and does what is forbidden in any of the LORD's **commands**,
4:22 does what is forbidden in any of the **commands** *of* the LORD his
4:27 and does what is forbidden in any of the LORD's **commands**,
5:17 and does what is forbidden in any of the LORD's **commands**,
22:31 "Keep my **commands** and follow them. I am the LORD.
26:3 " 'If you follow my decrees and are careful to obey my **commands**,
26:14 if you will not listen to me and carry out all these **commands**,

Lev 26:15 and abhor my laws and fail to carry out all my **commands** and
27:34 These are the **commands** the LORD gave Moses on Mount Sinai
Nu 15:22 " 'Now if you unintentionally fail to keep any of these **commands**
15:31 he has despised the LORD's word and broken his **commands**,
15:39 and so you will remember all the **commands** *of* the LORD,
15:40 you will remember to obey all my **commands** and will be
36:13 These are the **commands** and regulations the LORD gave through
Dt 4: 2 but keep the **commands** *of* the LORD your God that I give you.
4:40 Keep his decrees and **commands**, which I am giving you today,
5:10 ⌊generations⌋ of those who love me and keep my **commandments**.
5:29 would be inclined to fear me and keep all my **commands** always,
5:31 you stay here with me so that I may give you all the **commands**,
6: 1 These are the **commands**, decrees and laws the LORD your God
6: 2 you live by keeping all his decrees and **commands** that I give you,
6:17 Be sure to keep the **commands** *of* the LORD your God
6:25 if we are careful to obey all this **law** before the LORD our God,
7: 9 generations of those who love him and keep his **commands**.
7:11 take care to follow the **commands**, decrees and laws I give you
8: 1 Be careful to follow every **command** I am giving you today,
8: 2 was in your heart, whether or not you would keep his **commands**.
8: 6 Observe the **commands** *of* the LORD your God, walking in his
8:11 failing to observe his **commands**, his laws and his decrees that I
10:13 to observe the LORD's **commands** and decrees that I am giving
11: 1 his requirements, his decrees, his laws and his **commands** always.
11: 8 Observe therefore all the **commands** I am giving you today,
11:13 So if you faithfully obey the **commands** I am giving you today—
11:22 If you carefully observe all these **commands** I am giving you to
11:27 the blessing if you obey the **commands** *of* the LORD your God
11:28 the curse if you disobey the **commands** *of* the LORD your God
13: 4 [13:5] Keep his **commands** and obey him; serve him and hold
13:18 [13:19] keeping all his **commands** that I am giving you today
15: 5 are careful to follow all these **commands** I am giving you today.
17:20 than his brothers and turn from the **law** to the right or to the left.
19: 9 because you carefully follow all these **laws** I command you today—
26:13 and the widow, according to all you **commanded** [+7422].
26:13 I have not turned aside from your **commands** nor have I forgotten
26:17 keep his decrees, **commands** and laws, and that you will obey him.
26:18 as he promised, and that you are to keep all his **commands**.
27: 1 the people: "Keep all these **commands** that I give you today.
27:10 Obey the LORD your God and follow his **commands** and decrees
28: 1 your God and carefully follow all his **commands** I give you today,
28: 9 if you keep the **commands** *of* the LORD your God and walk in
28:13 If you pay attention to the **commands** *of* the LORD your God
28:15 do not carefully follow all his **commands** and decrees I am giving
28:45 your God and observe the **commands** and decrees he gave you.
30: 8 the LORD and follow all his **commands** I am giving you today.
30:10 if you obey the LORD your God and keep his **commands**
30:11 Now **what**° [+2021+2021+2296] I am commanding you today is
30:16 to walk in his ways, and to keep his **commands**, decrees and laws;
31: 5 you must do to them all that *I have* **commanded** [+906+7422] you.
Jos 22: 3 but have carried out the mission the LORD your God **gave** you.
22: 5 be very careful to keep the **commandment** and the law that Moses
22: 5 to obey his **commands**, to hold fast to him and to serve him with
Jdg 2:17 had walked, the way of obedience to the LORD's **commands**.
3: 4 to see whether they would obey the LORD's **commands**,
1Sa 13:13 "You have not kept the **command** the LORD your God gave you;
1Ki 2: 3 and keep his decrees and **commands**, his laws and requirements,
2:43 your oath to the LORD and obey the **command** I gave you?"
3:14 and obey my statutes and **commands** as David your father did,
6:12 out my regulations and keep all my **commands** and obey them,
8:58 to walk in all his ways and to keep the **commands**, decrees
8:61 to live by his decrees and obey his **commands**, as at this time."
9: 6 and do not observe the **commands** and decrees I have given you
11:34 whom I chose and who observed my **commands** and statutes.
11:38 what is right in my eyes by keeping my statutes and **commands**,
13:21 and have not kept the **command** the LORD your God gave you.
14: 8 who kept my **commands** and followed me with all his heart,
18:18 You have abandoned the LORD's **commands** and have followed
2Ki 17:13 Observe my **commands** and decrees, in accordance with the entire
17:16 They forsook all the **commands** *of* the LORD their God
17:19 even Judah did not keep the **commands** *of* the LORD their God.
17:34 and **commands** that the LORD gave the descendants of Jacob,
17:37 and ordinances, the laws and **commands** he wrote for you.
18: 6 follow him; he kept the **commands** the LORD had given Moses.
18:36 because the king had **commanded**, "Do not answer him."
23: 3 to follow the LORD and keep his **commands**, regulations
1Ch 28: 7 forever if he is unswerving in carrying out my **commands**
28: 8 Be careful to follow all the **commands** *of* the LORD your God,
29:19 son Solomon the wholehearted devotion to keep your **commands**,
2Ch 7:19 and forsake the decrees and **commands** I have given you
8:13 according to the daily requirement for offerings **commanded** *by*
8:14 because this was what David the man of God had **ordered**.
8:15 They did not deviate from the king's **commands** to the priests
14: 4 [14:3] God of their fathers, and to obey his laws and **commands**.
17: 4 and followed his **commands** rather than the practices of Israel.
19:10 or other concerns of the law, **commands**, decrees or ordinances—
24:20 'Why do you disobey the LORD's **commands**? You will not
24:21 by **order** *of* the king they stoned him to death in the courtyard of
29:15 as the king had **ordered**, following the word of the LORD.
29:25 harps and lyres in the **way prescribed** *by* David and Gad the
29:25 this was **commanded** by the LORD through his prophets.
30: 6 At the king's **command**, couriers went throughout Israel and Judah
30:12 of mind to carry out **what** the king and his officials had **ordered**,
31:21 of God's temple and in obedience to the law and the **commands**,
34:31 to follow the LORD and keep his **commands**, regulations
35:10 places with the Levites in their divisions as the king had **ordered**.
35:15 were in the places **prescribed** *by* David, Asaph, Heman
35:16 offerings on the altar of the LORD, as King Josiah had **ordered**.
Ezr 7:11 a man learned in matters concerning the **commands** and decrees of
9:10 can we say after this? For we have disregarded the **commands**
9:14 Shall we again break your **commands** and intermarry with the
10: 3 of my lord and of those who fear the **commands** *of* our God.
Ne 1: 5 of love with those who love him and obey his **commands**,
1: 7 We have not obeyed the **commands**, decrees and laws you gave
1: 9 if you return to me and obey my **commands**, then even if your
9:13 that are just and right, and decrees and **commands** that are good.
9:14 known to them your holy Sabbath and gave them **commands**,
9:16 and stiff-necked, and did not obey your **commands**.
9:29 but they became arrogant and disobeyed your **commands**.
9:34 they did not pay attention to your **commands** or the warnings you
10:29 [10:30] servant of God and to obey carefully all the **commands**,
10:32 [10:33] **commands** to give a third of a shekel each year for the
11:23 The singers were under the king's **orders**, which regulated their
12:24 responding to the other, as **prescribed** *by* David the man of God.
12:45 according to the **commands** *of* David and his son Solomon.
13: 5 new wine and oil **prescribed** *for* the Levites, singers
Est 3: 3 asked Mordecai, "Why do you disobey the king's **command**?"
Job 23:12 I have not departed from the **commands** *of* his lips; I have
Ps 19: 8 [19:9] The **commands** *of* the LORD are radiant, giving light to
78: 7 and would not forget his deeds but would keep his **commands**.
89:31 [89:32] they violate my decrees and fail to keep my **commands**,
112: 1 who fears the LORD, who finds great delight in his **commands**.
119: 6 I would not be put to shame when I consider all your **commands**.
119:10 you with all my heart; do not let me stray from your **commands**.
119:19 I am a stranger on earth; do not hide your **commands** from me.
119:21 the arrogant, who are cursed and who stray from your **commands**.
119:32 I run in the path of your **commands**, for you have set my heart
119:35 Direct me in the path of your **commands**, for there I find delight.
119:47 for I delight in your **commands** because I love them.
119:48 I lift up my hands to your **commands**, which I love, and I meditate
119:60 I will hasten and not delay to obey your **commands**.
119:66 and good judgment, for I believe in your **commands**.
119:73 and formed me; give me understanding to learn your **commands**.
119:86 All your **commands** are trustworthy; help me, for men persecute
119:96 To all perfection I see a limit; but your **commands** are boundless.
119:98 Your **commands** make me wiser than my enemies, for they are
119:115 you evildoers, that I may keep the **commands** *of* my God!
119:127 Because I love your **commands** more than gold, more than pure
119:131 I open my mouth and pant, longing for your **commands**.
119:143 distress have come upon me, but your **commands** are my delight.
119:151 Yet you are near, O LORD, and all your **commands** are true.
119:166 I wait for your salvation, O LORD, and I follow your **commands**.
119:172 tongue sing of your word, for all your **commands** are righteous.
119:176 Seek your servant, for I have not forgotten your **commands**.
Pr 2: 1 if you accept my words and store up my **commands** within you,
3: 1 do not forget my teaching, but keep my **commands** in your heart,
4: 4 words with all your heart; keep my **commands** and you will live.
6:20 keep your father's **commands** and do not forsake your mother's
6:23 For these **commands** are a lamp, this teaching is a light,
7: 1 My son, keep my words and store up my **commands** within you.
7: 2 Keep my **commands** and you will live; guard my teachings as the
10: 8 The wise in heart accept **commands**, but a chattering fool comes to
13:13 will pay for it, but he who respects a **command** is rewarded.
19:16 He who obeys **instructions** guards his life, but he who is
Ecc 8: 5 Whoever obeys his **command** will come to no harm, and the wise
12:13 Fear God and keep his **commandments**, for this is the whole
Isa 29:13 Their worship of me is made up only of **rules** taught by men.
36:21 because the king had **commanded**, "Do not answer him."
48:18 If only you had paid attention to my **commands**, your peace would
Jer 32:11 the sealed copy containing the **terms** and conditions, as well as the
35:14 do not drink wine, because they obey their forefather's **command**.
35:16 Recab have carried out the **command** their forefather gave them,
35:18 'You have obeyed the **command** *of* your forefather Jonadab
35:18 have followed all his **instructions** and have done everything he
Da 9: 4 covenant of love with all who love him and obey his **commands**,
9: 5 we have turned away from your **commands** and laws.
Mal 2: 1 "And now this **admonition** is for you, O priests.
2: 4 you will know that I have sent you this **admonition** so that my

5185 מְצוֹלָה m^{e}ṣôlâ, n.f. [12] [√ 7425]

depths [9], deep [2], ravine [1]

Ex 15: 5 waters have covered them; they sank to the **depths** like a stone.
Ne 9: 11 you hurled their pursuers into the **depths**, like a stone into mighty
Job 41: 31 [41:23] He makes the **depths** churn like a boiling caldron
Ps 68: 22 [68:23] I will bring them from the **depths** *of* the sea,
69: 2 [69:3] I sink in the miry **depths**, where there is no foothold.
69: 15 [69:16] or the **depths** swallow me up or the pit close its mouth
88: 6 [88:7] You have put me in the lowest pit, in the darkest **depths**.
107: 24 saw the works of the LORD, his wonderful deeds in the **deep**.
Jnh 2: 3 [2:4] You hurled me into the **deep**, into the very heart of the seas,
Mic 7: 19 sins underfoot and hurl all our iniquities into the **depths** *of* the sea.
Zec 1: 8 He was standing among the myrtle trees in a **ravine**. Behind him
10: 11 sea will be subdued and all the **depths** *of* the Nile will dry up.

5186 מָצוֹק māṣôq, n.[m.]. [6] [→ 5188; cf. 7439]

distress [3], suffering [2], stress [1]

Dt 28: 53 Because of the **suffering** that your enemy will inflict on you during
28: 55 because of the **suffering** your enemy will inflict on you during the
28: 57 in the **distress** that your enemy will inflict on you in your cities.
1Sa 22: 2 All those who were in **distress** or in debt or discontented gathered
Ps 119: 143 Trouble and **distress** have come upon me, but your commands are
Jer 19: 9 they will eat one another's flesh during the **stress** of the siege

5187 מָצוּק māṣûq, n.m. [2] [√ 3668?]

foundations [1], stood [1]

1Sa 2: 8 "For the **foundations** *of* the earth are the LORD's; upon them he
14: 5 One cliff **stood** to the north toward Micmash, the other to the south

5188 מְצוּקָה m^{e}ṣûqâ, n.f. [7] [√ 5186; cf. 7439]

distress [4], anguish [3]

Job 15: 24 Distress and **anguish** fill him with terror; they overwhelm him,
Ps 25: 17 troubles of my heart have multiplied; free me from my **anguish**.
107: 6 LORD in their trouble, and he delivered them from their **distress**.
107: 13 the LORD in their trouble, and he saved them from their **distress**.
107: 19 the LORD in their trouble, and he saved them from their **distress**.
107: 28 LORD in their trouble, and he brought them out of their **distress**.
Zep 1: 15 a day of distress and **anguish**, a day of trouble and ruin, a day of

5189 מָצוֹר māṣôr[1], n.[m.]. [21 / 22] [√ 5190; cf. 7443]

siege [15], besieged [2], besiege [+928+995+2021+4946+7156] [1], laid siege [+928+995+2021] [1], ramparts [1], siege works [1], siegeworks [1]

Dt 20: 19 that you *should* **besiege** [+928+995+2021+4946+7156] them?
20: 20 use them to build **siege works** until the city at war with you falls.
28: 53 the suffering that your enemy will inflict on you during the **siege**,
28: 55 your enemy will inflict on you during the **siege** of all your cities.
28: 57 For she intends to eat them secretly during the **siege** and in the
2Ki 24: 10 advanced on Jerusalem and **laid siege** [+928+995+2021] *to* it,
25: 2 The city was kept under **siege** until the eleventh year of King
2Ch 32: 10 basing your confidence, that you remain in Jerusalem under **siege**?
Ps 31: 21 [31:22] his wonderful love to me when I was in a **besieged** city.
Ecc 9: 14 surrounded it and built huge **siegeworks** [BHS 5178] against it.
Jer 10: 17 up your belongings to leave the land, you who live under **siege**.
19: 9 they will eat one another's flesh during the stress of the **siege**
52: 5 The city was kept under **siege** until the eleventh year of King
Eze 4: 2 lay **siege** to it: Erect siege works against it, build a ramp up to it,
4: 3 your face toward it. It will be under **siege**, and you shall besiege it.
4: 7 Turn your face toward the **siege** *of* Jerusalem and with bared arm
4: 8 one side to the other until you have finished the days of your **siege**.
5: 2 When the days of your **siege** come to an end, burn a third of the
Mic 5: 1 [4:14] your troops, O city of troops, for a **siege** is laid against us.
Na 3: 14 Draw water for the **siege**, strengthen your defenses! Work the clay,
Hab 2: 1 I will stand at my watch and station myself on the **ramparts**;
Zec 12: 2 the surrounding peoples reeling. Judah will be **besieged** as well as

5190 מָצוֹר māṣôr[2], n.[m.]. [4] [→ 5189, 5193; cf. 7443]

fortified [2], defense [1], stronghold [1]

2Ch 8: 5 Upper Beth Horon and Lower Beth Horon as **fortified** cities,
11: 5 lived in Jerusalem and built up towns for **defense** in Judah:
Ps 60: 9 [60:11] Who will bring me to the **fortified** city? Who will lead
Zec 9: 3 Tyre has built herself a **stronghold**; she has heaped up silver like

5191 מָצוֹר māṣôr[3], n.pr.loc. [5] [√ 5213]

Egypt [5]

2Ki 19: 24 With the soles of my feet I have dried up all the streams of **Egypt**."
Isa 19: 6 canals will stink; the streams of **Egypt** will dwindle and dry up.
37: 25 With the soles of my feet I have dried up all the streams of **Egypt**.'
Mic 7: 12 day people will come to you from Assyria and the cities of **Egypt**,
7: 12 even from **Egypt** to the Euphrates and from sea to sea and from

5192 מָצוֹר māṣôr[4], n.[m.]. Not used in NIV/BHS [√ 7443]

5193 מְצוּרָה m^{e}ṣûrâ, n.f. [8] [√ 5190; cf. 7443]

fortified [5], defenses [1], fortress [1], siege works [1]

2Ch 11: 10 and Hebron. These were **fortified** cities in Judah and Benjamin.
11: 11 He strengthened their **defenses** and put commanders in them,
11: 23 the districts of Judah and Benjamin, and to all the **fortified** cities.
12: 4 he captured the **fortified** cities of Judah and came as far as
14: 6 [14:5] He built up the **fortified** cities of Judah, since the land was
21: 3 and gold and articles of value, as well as **fortified** cities in Judah,
Isa 29: 3 encircle you with towers and set up my **siege works** against you.
Na 2: 1 [2:2] Guard the **fortress**, watch the road, brace yourselves,

5194 מַצּוּת maṣṣût, n.f. [1] [√ 5897]

enemies [+408] [1]

Isa 41: 12 Though you search for your **enemies** [+408], you will not find

5195 מֵצַח mēṣaḥ, n.m. [13] [→ 5196; cf. 7458?]

forehead [8], hardened [+2617] [2], *untranslated* [1], brazen look [1], foreheads [1]

Ex 28: 38 It will be on Aaron's **forehead**, and he will bear the guilt involved
28: 38 It will be on Aaron's **forehead** continually so that they will be
1Sa 17: 49 out a stone, he slung it and struck the Philistine on the **forehead**.
17: 49 The stone sank into his **forehead**, and he fell facedown on the
2Ch 26: 19 altar in the LORD's temple, leprosy broke out on his **forehead**.
26: 20 they saw that he had leprosy on his **forehead**, so they hurried him
Isa 48: 4 the sinews of your neck were iron, your **forehead** was bronze.
Jer 3: 3 Yet you have the **brazen look** *of* a prostitute; you refuse to blush
Eze 3: 7 for the whole house of Israel is **hardened** [+2617] and obstinate.
3: 8 I will make you as unyielding and **hardened** [+2617] as they are.
3: 8 I will make you as unyielding and hardened as they are. **[RPH]**
3: 9 I will make your **forehead** like the hardest stone, harder than flint.
9: 4 of Jerusalem and put a mark on the **foreheads** *of* those who grieve

5196 מִצְחָה miṣḥâ, n.f. [1] [√ 5195; cf. 7458?]

greaves [1]

1Sa 17: 6 on his legs he wore bronze **greaves**, and a bronze javelin was slung

5197 מְצִלָּה m^{e}ṣillâ, n.f. [1] [√ 7509]

bells [1]

Zec 14: 20 HOLY TO THE LORD will be inscribed on the **bells** *of* the horses,

5198 מְצֻלָה m^{e}ṣulâ, n.f. Not used in NIV/BHS [√ 7425]

5199 מְצִלְתַּיִם m^{e}ṣiltayim, n.f.du. [13] [√ 7509]

cymbals [13]

1Ch 13: 8 and with harps, lyres, tambourines, **cymbals** and trumpets.
15: 16 accompanied by musical instruments: lyres, harps and **cymbals**.
15: 19 Asaph and Ethan were to sound the bronze **cymbals**;
15: 28 with the sounding of rams' horns and trumpets, and of **cymbals**,
16: 5 were to play the lyres and harps, Asaph was to sound the **cymbals**,
16: 42 **cymbals** and for the playing of the other instruments for sacred
25: 1 of prophesying, accompanied by harps, lyres and **cymbals**.
25: 6 with **cymbals**, lyres and harps, for the ministry at the house of
2Ch 5: 12 dressed in fine linen and playing **cymbals**, harps and lyres.
5: 13 Accompanied by trumpets, **cymbals** and other instruments,
29: 25 stationed the Levites in the temple of the LORD with **cymbals**,
Ezr 3: 10 with **cymbals**, took their places to praise the LORD, as prescribed
Ne 12: 27 with songs of thanksgiving and with the music of **cymbals**,

5200 מִצְנֶפֶת miṣnepet, n.f. [12] [√ 7571]

turban [11], *untranslated* [1]

Ex 28: 4 an ephod, a robe, a woven tunic, a **turban** and a sash.
28: 37 Fasten a blue cord to it to attach it to the **turban**; it is to be on the
28: 37 to it to attach it to the turban; it is to be on the front of the **turban**.
28: 39 "Weave the tunic of fine linen and make the **turban** *of* fine linen.
29: 6 Put the **turban** on his head and attach the sacred diadem to the
29: 6 the turban on his head and attach the sacred diadem to the **turban**.
39: 28 the **turban** *of* fine linen, the linen headbands and the
39: 31 Then they fastened a blue cord to it to attach it to the **turban**,
Lev 8: 9 Then he placed the **turban** on Aaron's head and set the gold plate,
8: 9 on the front of it, **[RPH]** as the LORD commanded Moses.
16: 4 he is to tie the linen sash around him and put on the linen **turban**.
Eze 21: 26 [21:31] Take off the **turban**, remove the crown. It will not be as it

5201 מַצָּע maṣṣāʿ, n.m. [1] [√ 3667]
bed [1]
Isa 28:20 The **bed** is too short to stretch out on, the blanket too narrow to

5202 מִצְעָד miṣʿād, n.[m.]. [3] [√ 7575]
steps [2], submission [1]
Ps 37:23 If the LORD delights in a man's way, he makes his **steps** firm;
Pr 20:24 A man's **steps** are directed by the LORD. How then can anyone
Da 11:43 the riches of Egypt, with the Libyans and Nubians in **submission**.

5203 ¹מִצְעָר miṣʿār¹, n.m. [5] [√ 7592]
small [2], humble [1], little while [1], only a few [1]
Ge 19:20 Look, here is a town near enough to run to, and it is **small**.
19:20 and it is small. Let me flee to it—it is *very* **small**, isn't it?
2Ch 24:24 Although the Aramean army had come with **only a few** men,
Job 8: 7 Your beginnings will seem **humble**, so prosperous will your future
Isa 63:18 For a **little while** your people possessed your holy place, but now

5204 ²מִצְעָר miṣʿār², n.pr.loc. [1] [√ 7592]
Mizar [1]
Ps 42: 6 [42:7] of the Jordan, the heights of Hermon—from Mount **Mizar**.

5205 ¹מִצְפֶּה miṣpeh¹, n.m. [2] [→ 2174, 5206, 5207; cf. 7595]
place that overlooks [1], watchtower [1]
2Ch 20:24 When the men of Judah came to the **place that overlooks** the
Isa 21: 8 "Day after day, my lord, I stand on the **watchtower**;

5206 ²מִצְפֶּה miṣpeh², n.pr.loc. [6 / 5] [√ 5205; cf. 7595]
Mizpah [4], there^s [+1680] [1]
Jos 11: 8 to the Valley of Mizpah [BHS *Mizpah* ?; NIV 5207] on the east,
15:38 Dilean, **Mizpah**, Joktheel,
18:26 **Mizpah**, Kephirah, Mozah,
Jdg 11:29 crossed Gilead and Manasseh, passed through **Mizpah** *of* Gilead,
11:29 and from **there**^{s} [+1680] he advanced against the Ammonites.
1Sa 22: 3 From there David went to **Mizpah** *in* Moab and said to the king of

5207 מִצְפָּה miṣpâ, n.pr.loc. [40 / 41] [√ 5205; cf. 7595]
Mizpah [39], *untranslated* [1], there^s [+928+2021] [1]
Ge 31:49 It was also called **Mizpah**, because he said, "May the LORD keep
Jos 11: 3 and to the Hivites below Hermon in the region of **Mizpah**.
11: 8 and to the Valley of **Mizpah** [BHS 5206] on the east,
Jdg 10:17 camped in Gilead, the Israelites assembled and camped at **Mizpah**.
11:11 And he repeated all his words before the LORD in **Mizpah**.
11:34 When Jephthah returned to his home in **Mizpah**, who should come
20: 1 out as one man and assembled before the LORD in **Mizpah**.
20: 3 (The Benjamites heard that the Israelites had gone up to **Mizpah**.)
21: 1 The men of Israel had taken an oath at **Mizpah**: "Not one of us
21: 5 before the LORD at **Mizpah** should certainly be put to death.
21: 8 tribes of Israel failed to assemble before the LORD at **Mizpah**?"
1Sa 7: 5 "Assemble all Israel at **Mizpah** and I will intercede with the
7: 6 When they had assembled at **Mizpah**, they drew water and poured
7: 6 against the LORD." And Samuel was leader of Israel at **Mizpah**.
7: 7 When the Philistines heard that Israel had assembled at **Mizpah**,
7:11 The men of Israel rushed out of **Mizpah** and pursued the
7:12 Then Samuel took a stone and set it up between **Mizpah** and Shen.
7:16 year to year he went on a circuit from Bethel to Gilgal to **Mizpah**,
10:17 Samuel summoned the people of Israel to the LORD at **Mizpah**
1Ki 15:22 With them King Asa built up Geba in Benjamin, and also **Mizpah**.
2Ki 25:23 Gedaliah as governor, they came to Gedaliah at **Mizpah**—
25:25 men of Judah and the Babylonians who were with him at **Mizpah**.
2Ch 16: 6 Baasha had been using. With them he built up Geba and **Mizpah**.
Ne 3: 7 to them, repairs were made by men from Gibeon and **Mizpah**—
3:15 by Shallun son of Col-Hozeh, ruler of the district of **Mizpah**.
3:19 Next to him, Ezer son of Jeshua, ruler of **Mizpah**, repaired another
Jer 40: 6 So Jeremiah went to Gedaliah son of Ahikam at **Mizpah**
40: 8 they came to Gedaliah at **Mizpah**—Ishmael son of Nethaniah,
40:10 I myself will stay at **Mizpah** to represent you before the
40:12 they all came back to the land of Judah, to Gedaliah at **Mizpah**,
40:13 officers still in the open country came to Gedaliah at **Mizpah**
40:15 Then Johanan son of Kareah said privately to Gedaliah in **Mizpah**,
41: 1 came with ten men to Gedaliah son of Ahikam at **Mizpah**.
41: 1 at Mizpah. While they were eating together there, **[RPH]**
41: 3 also killed all the Jews who were with Gedaliah at **Mizpah**,
41: 6 Ishmael son of Nethaniah went out from **Mizpah** to meet them,
41:10 made captives of all the rest of the people who were in **Mizpah**—
41:10 along with all the others who were left **there**^{s} [+928+2021],
41:14 All the people Ishmael had taken captive at **Mizpah** turned
41:16 **Mizpah** whom he had recovered from Ishmael son of Nethaniah
Hos 5: 1 You have been a snare at **Mizpah**, a net spread out on Tabor.

5208 מַצְפּוֹן maṣpôn, n.[m.]. [1] [√ 7621]
hidden treasures [1]
Ob 1: 6 But how Esau will be ransacked, his **hidden treasures** pillaged!

5209 מָצַץ māṣaṣ, v. [1] [cf. 5172?]
drink deeply [1]
Isa 66:11 [A] *you will* **drink deeply** and delight in her overflowing

5210 מֵצַר mēṣar, n.[m.]. [3] [√ 7674]
anguish [2], distress [1]
Ps 116: 3 of death entangled me, the **anguish** *of* the grave came upon me;
118: 5 In my **anguish** I cried to the LORD, and he answered by setting
La 1: 3 All who pursue her have overtaken her in the midst of her **distress**.

5211 מַצָּרָה maṣṣārâ, n.f. Not used in NIV/BHS [√ 5915]

5212 מִצְרִי miṣrî, a.g. [24] [√ 5213]
Egyptian [21], Egyptian's [2], Egyptians [1]
Ge 16: 1 no children. But she had an **Egyptian** maidservant named Hagar;
16: 3 Sarai his wife took her **Egyptian** maidservant Hagar and gave her
21: 9 Sarah saw that the son whom Hagar the **Egyptian** had borne to
25:12 whom Sarah's maidservant, Hagar the **Egyptian**, bore to Abraham.
39: 1 Potiphar, an **Egyptian** who was one of Pharaoh's officials,
39: 2 he prospered, and he lived in the house of his **Egyptian** master.
39: 5 the LORD blessed the household of the **Egyptian** because of
Ex 1:19 answered Pharaoh, "Hebrew women are not like **Egyptian** women;
2:11 He saw an **Egyptian** beating a Hebrew, one of his own people.
2:12 and seeing no one, he killed the **Egyptian** and hid him in the sand.
2:14 Are you thinking of killing me as you killed the **Egyptian**?"
2:19 They answered, "An **Egyptian** rescued us from the shepherds.
Lev 24:10 and an **Egyptian** father went out among the Israelites,
Dt 23: 7 [23:8] Do not abhor an **Egyptian**, because you lived as an alien in
1Sa 30:11 They found an **Egyptian** in a field and brought him to David.
30:13 He said, "I am an **Egyptian**, the slave of an Amalekite.
2Sa 23:21 he struck down a huge **Egyptian**. Although the Egyptian had a
23:21 Although the **Egyptian** had a spear in his hand, Benaiah went
23:21 He snatched the spear from the **Egyptian's** hand and killed him
1Ch 2:34 only daughters. He had an **Egyptian** servant named Jarha.
11:23 he struck down an **Egyptian** who was seven and a half feet tall.
11:23 Although the **Egyptian** had a spear like a weaver's rod in his hand,
11:23 He snatched the spear from the **Egyptian's** hand and killed him
Ezr 9: 1 Jebusites, Ammonites, Moabites, **Egyptians** and Amorites.

5213 מִצְרַיִם miṣrayim, n.pr.loc. & g. [687] [→ 73, 5191, 5212]
Egypt [374], Egypt [+824] [184], Egyptians [82], *untranslated* [11], Egyptian [10], Egypt's [5], Mizraim [4], Lower Egypt [+824] [2], them^s [2], country [1], Egypt [+1426] [1], Egypt [+1473] [1], Egyptians [+1201] [1], here^s [+2025] [1], his^s [+4200+4889] [1], it^s [+4722] [1], Lower Egypt [1], the Egyptians [1], there^s [+928] [1], there^s [1], they^s [1], who^s [1]
Ge 10: 6 The sons of Ham: Cush, **Mizraim**, Put and Canaan.
10:13 **Mizraim** was the father of the Ludites, Anamites, Lehabites,
12:10 Abram went down to **Egypt** to live there for a while
12:11 As he was about to enter **Egypt**, he said to his wife Sarai,
12:12 When the **Egyptians** see you, they will say, 'This is his wife.'
12:14 When Abram came to **Egypt**, the Egyptians saw that she was a
12:14 to Egypt, the **Egyptians** saw that she was a very beautiful woman.
13: 1 So Abram went up from **Egypt** to the Negev, with his wife
13:10 like the garden of the LORD, like the land of **Egypt**, toward Zoar.
15:18 from the river of **Egypt** to the great river, the Euphrates—
21:21 Desert of Paran, his mother got a wife for him from **Egypt** [+824].
25:18 to Shur, near the border of **Egypt**, as you go toward Asshur.
26: 2 LORD appeared to Isaac and said, "Do not go down to **Egypt**;
37:25 and they were on their way to take them down to **Egypt**.
37:28 twenty shekels of silver to the Ishmaelites, who took him to **Egypt**.
37:36 Meanwhile, the Midianites sold Joseph in **Egypt** to Potiphar,
39: 1 Now Joseph had been taken down to **Egypt**. Potiphar, an Egyptian
40: 1 and the baker of the king of **Egypt** offended their master,
40: 1 of the king of Egypt offended their master, the king of **Egypt**.
40: 5 the cupbearer and the baker of the king of **Egypt**, who were being
41: 8 so he sent for all the magicians and wise men of **Egypt**.
41:19 and lean. I had never seen such ugly cows in all the land of **Egypt**.
41:29 years of great abundance are coming throughout the land of **Egypt**,
41:30 Then all the abundance in **Egypt** [+824] will be forgotten,
41:33 and wise man and put him in charge of the land of **Egypt**.
41:34 the harvest of **Egypt** [+824] during the seven years of abundance.
41:36 the seven years of famine that will come upon **Egypt** [+824],
41:41 to Joseph, "I hereby put you in charge of the whole land of **Egypt**."

Ge 41:43 Thus he put him in charge of the whole land of **Egypt**.
41:44 your word no one will lift hand or foot in all **Egypt** [+824]."
41:45 to be his wife. And Joseph went throughout the land of **Egypt**.
41:46 years old when he entered the service of Pharaoh king of **Egypt**.
41:46 from Pharaoh's presence and traveled throughout **Egypt** [+824].
41:48 food produced in those seven years of abundance in **Egypt** [+824]
41:53 The seven years of abundance in **Egypt** [+824] came to an end,
41:54 all the other lands, but in the whole land of **Egypt** there was food.
41:55 When all **Egypt** [+824] began to feel the famine, the people cried
41:55 Pharaoh told all the **Egyptians**, "Go to Joseph and do what he tells
41:56 Joseph opened the storehouses and sold grain to the **Egyptians**,
41:56 the Egyptians, for the famine was severe throughout **Egypt** [+824].
41:57 And all the countries came to **Egypt** to buy grain from Joseph,
42:1 When Jacob learned that there was grain in **Egypt**, he said to his
42:2 He continued, "I have heard that there is grain in **Egypt**. Go down
42:3 Then ten of Joseph's brothers went down to buy grain from **Egypt**.
43:2 So when they had eaten all the grain they had brought from **Egypt**,
43:15 They hurried down to **Egypt** and presented themselves to Joseph.
43:32 and the **Egyptians** who ate with him by themselves,
43:32 because **Egyptians** could not eat with Hebrews, for that is
43:32 could not eat with Hebrews, for that is detestable to **Egyptians**.
45:2 he wept so loudly that the **Egyptians** heard him, and Pharaoh's
45:4 he said, "I am your brother Joseph, the one you sold into **Egypt**!
45:8 lord of his entire household and ruler of all **Egypt** [+824].
45:9 God has made me lord of all **Egypt**. Come down to me;
45:13 Tell my father about all the honor accorded me in **Egypt** and about
45:18 I will give you the best of the land of **Egypt** and you can enjoy the
45:19 Take some carts from **Egypt** [+824] for your children and your
45:20 because the best of all **Egypt** [+824] will be yours.' "
45:23 ten donkeys loaded with the best things of **Egypt**, and ten female
45:25 So they went up out of **Egypt** and came to their father Jacob in the
45:26 In fact, he is ruler of all **Egypt** [+824]." Jacob was stunned;
46:3 "Do not be afraid to go down to **Egypt**, for I will make you into a
46:4 I will go down to **Egypt** with you, and I will surely bring you back
46:6 acquired in Canaan, and Jacob and all his offspring went to **Egypt**.
46:7 He took with him to **Egypt** his sons and grandsons and his
46:8 the sons of Israel (Jacob and his descendants) who went to **Egypt**:
46:20 In **Egypt** [+824], Manasseh and Ephraim were born to Joseph by
46:26 All those who went to **Egypt** with Jacob—those who were his
46:27 With the two sons who had been born to Joseph in **Egypt**,
46:27 of Jacob's family, which went to **Egypt**, were seventy in all.
46:34 of Goshen, for all shepherds are detestable to the **Egyptians**."
47:6 the land of **Egypt** is before you; settle your father and your
47:11 So Joseph settled his father and his brothers in **Egypt** [+824]
47:13 both **Egypt** [+824] and Canaan wasted away because of the
47:14 collected all the money that was to be found in **Egypt** [+824]
47:15 When the money of the people of **Egypt** [+824] and Canaan was
47:15 was gone, all **Egypt** came to Joseph and said, "Give us food.
47:20 So Joseph bought all the land in **Egypt** for Pharaoh. The
47:20 The **Egyptians**, one and all, sold their fields, because the famine
47:21 the people to servitude, from one end of **Egypt** to the other.
47:26 So Joseph established it as a law concerning land in **Egypt**—
47:27 Now the Israelites settled in **Egypt** [+824] in the region of Goshen.
47:28 Jacob lived in **Egypt** [+824] seventeen years, and the years of his
47:29 will show me kindness and faithfulness. Do not bury me in **Egypt**,
47:30 carry me out of **Egypt** and bury me where they are buried."
48:5 your two sons born to you in **Egypt** [+824] before I came to you
48:5 before I came to you **here**[s] [+2025] will be reckoned as mine;
50:3 for embalming. And the **Egyptians** mourned for him seventy days.
50:7 the dignitaries of his court and all the dignitaries of **Egypt** [+824]—
50:11 "The **Egyptians** are holding a solemn ceremony of mourning."
50:14 After burying his father, Joseph returned to **Egypt**, together with
50:22 Joseph stayed in **Egypt**, along with all his father's family.
50:26 And after they embalmed him, he was placed in a coffin in **Egypt**.
Ex 1:1 These are the names of the sons of Israel who went to **Egypt** with
1:5 of Jacob numbered seventy in all; Joseph was already in **Egypt**.
1:8 who did not know about Joseph, came to power in **Egypt**.
1:13 and **[RPH]** worked them ruthlessly.
1:15 The king of **Egypt** said to the Hebrew midwives, whose names
1:17 and did not do what the king of **Egypt** had told them to do;
1:18 Then the king of **Egypt** summoned the midwives and asked them,
2:23 During that long period, the king of **Egypt** died. The Israelites
3:7 "I have indeed seen the misery of my people in **Egypt**.
3:8 I have come down to rescue them from the hand of the **Egyptians**
3:9 and I have seen the way the **Egyptians** are oppressing them.
3:10 you to Pharaoh to bring my people the Israelites out of **Egypt**."
3:11 that I should go to Pharaoh and bring the Israelites out of **Egypt**?"
3:12 When you have brought the people out of **Egypt**, you will worship
3:16 over you and have seen what has been done to you in **Egypt**.
3:17 I have promised to bring you up out of your misery in **Egypt** into
3:18 you and the elders are to go to the king of **Egypt** and say to him,
3:19 I know that the king of **Egypt** will not let you go unless a mighty
3:20 strike the **Egyptians** with all the wonders that I will perform
3:21 "And I will make the **Egyptians** favorably disposed toward this
3:22 your sons and daughters. And so you will plunder the **Egyptians**."
4:18 "Let me go back to my own people in **Egypt** to see if any of them
4:19 Now the LORD had said to Moses in Midian, "Go back to **Egypt**,
4:20 and sons, put them on a donkey and started back to **Egypt** [+824].
4:21 The LORD said to Moses, "When you return to **Egypt**, see that
5:4 the king of **Egypt** said, "Moses and Aaron, why are you taking the
5:12 So the people scattered all over **Egypt** [+824] to gather stubble to
6:5 whom the **Egyptians** are enslaving, and I have remembered my
6:6 and I will bring you out from under the yoke of the **Egyptians**.
6:7 who brought you out from under the yoke of the **Egyptians**.
6:11 tell Pharaoh king of **Egypt** to let the Israelites go out of his
6:13 and Aaron about the Israelites and Pharaoh king of **Egypt**,
6:13 he commanded them to bring the Israelites out of **Egypt** [+824].
6:26 "Bring the Israelites out of **Egypt** [+824] by their divisions."
6:27 They were the ones who spoke to Pharaoh king of **Egypt** about
6:27 Pharaoh king of Egypt about bringing the Israelites out of **Egypt**.
6:28 Now when the LORD spoke to Moses in **Egypt** [+824],
6:29 am the LORD. Tell Pharaoh king of **Egypt** everything I tell you."
7:3 I multiply my miraculous signs and wonders in **Egypt** [+824],
7:4 I will lay my hand on **Egypt** and with mighty acts of judgment I
7:4 I will bring out my divisions, my people the Israelites. **[RPH]**
7:5 the **Egyptians** will know that I am the LORD when I stretch out
7:5 that I am the LORD when I stretch out my hand against **Egypt**
7:11 the **Egyptian** magicians also did the same things by their secret
7:18 will stink; the **Egyptians** will not be able to drink its water.' "
7:19 your staff and stretch out your hand over the waters of **Egypt**—
7:19 Blood will be everywhere in **Egypt** [+824], even in the wooden
7:21 river smelled so bad that the **Egyptians** could not drink its water.
7:21 could not drink its water. Blood was everywhere in **Egypt** [+824].
7:22 the **Egyptian** magicians did the same things by their secret arts,
7:24 And all the **Egyptians** dug along the Nile to get drinking water,
8:5 [8:1] and ponds, and make frogs come up on the land of **Egypt**.' "
8:6 [8:2] So Aaron stretched out his hand over the waters of **Egypt**,
8:6 [8:2] and the frogs came up and covered the land. **[RPH]**
8:7 [8:3] they also made frogs come up on the land of **Egypt**.
8:16 [8:12] throughout the land of **Egypt** the dust will become gnats."
8:17 [8:13] All the dust throughout the land of **Egypt** became gnats.
8:21 [8:17] The houses of the **Egyptians** will be full of flies, and even
8:24 [8:20] throughout **Egypt** [+824] the land was ruined by the flies.
8:26 [8:22] the LORD our God would be detestable to the **Egyptians**.
8:26 [8:22] if we offer sacrifices that are detestable **[RPH]** in their
9:4 a distinction between the livestock of Israel and that of **Egypt**,
9:6 All the livestock of the **Egyptians** died, but not one animal
9:9 It will become fine dust over the whole land of **Egypt**,
9:9 will break out on men and animals throughout the land." **[RPH]**
9:11 because of the boils that were on them and on all the **Egyptians**.
9:18 I will send the worst hailstorm that has ever fallen on **Egypt**,
9:22 hand toward the sky so that hail will fall all over **Egypt** [+824]—
9:22 and on everything growing in the fields of **Egypt** [+824]."
9:23 to the ground. So the LORD rained hail on the land of **Egypt**;
9:24 It was the worst storm in all the land of **Egypt** since it had become
9:25 Throughout **Egypt** [+824] hail struck everything in the fields—
10:2 and grandchildren how I dealt harshly with the **Egyptians**
10:6 your houses and those of all your officials and all the **Egyptians**—
10:7 LORD their God. Do you not yet realize that **Egypt** is ruined?"
10:12 "Stretch out your hand over **Egypt** [+824] so that locusts will
10:12 over the land **[RPH]** and devour everything growing in the fields,
10:13 So Moses stretched out his staff over **Egypt** [+824],
10:14 they invaded all **Egypt** [+824] and settled down in every area of
10:14 and settled down in every area of the **country** in great numbers.
10:15 Nothing green remained on tree or plant in all the land of **Egypt**.
10:19 into the Red Sea. Not a locust was left anywhere in **Egypt** [+1473].
10:21 toward the sky so that darkness will spread over **Egypt** [+824]—
10:22 and total darkness covered all **Egypt** [+824] for three days.
11:1 to Moses, "I will bring one more plague on Pharaoh and on **Egypt**.
11:3 (The LORD made the **Egyptians** favorably disposed toward the
11:3 Moses himself was highly regarded in **Egypt** [+824] by Pharaoh's
11:4 the LORD says: 'About midnight I will go throughout **Egypt**.
11:5 Every firstborn son in **Egypt** [+824] will die, from the firstborn
11:6 There will be loud wailing throughout **Egypt** [+824]—worse than
11:7 you will know that the LORD makes a distinction between **Egypt**
11:9 to you—so that my wonders may be multiplied in **Egypt** [+824]."
12:1 The LORD said to Moses and Aaron in **Egypt** [+824],
12:12 "On that same night I will pass through **Egypt** [+824] and strike
12:12 and strike down every firstborn—**[RPH]** both men and animals—
12:12 and animals—and I will bring judgment on all the gods of **Egypt**.
12:13 No destructive plague will touch you when I strike **Egypt** [+824].
12:17 on this very day that I brought your divisions out of **Egypt** [+824].
12:23 the LORD goes through the land to strike down the **Egyptians**,
12:27 who passed over the houses of the Israelites in **Egypt** and spared
12:27 spared our homes when he struck down the **Egyptians**.' " Then the
12:29 the LORD struck down all the firstborn in **Egypt** [+824],
12:30 and all his officials and all the **Egyptians** got up during the night,
12:30 got up during the night, and there was loud wailing in **Egypt**,

Ex 12:33 The **Egyptians** urged the people to hurry and leave the country.
12:35 asked **the Egyptians** for articles of silver and gold and for
12:36 The LORD had made the **Egyptians** favorably disposed toward
12:36 gave them what they asked for; so they plundered the **Egyptians**.
12:39 With the dough they had brought from **Egypt**, they baked cakes of
12:39 was without yeast because they had been driven out of **Egypt**
12:40 Now the length of time the Israelite people lived in **Egypt** was 430
12:41 to the very day, all the LORD's divisions left **Egypt** [+824].
12:42 LORD kept vigil that night to bring them out of **Egypt** [+824],
12:51 brought the Israelites out of **Egypt** [+824] by their divisions.
13: 3 "Commemorate this day, the day you came out of **Egypt**, out of
13: 8 because of what the LORD did for me when I came out of **Egypt**.'
13: 9 For the LORD brought you out of **Egypt** with his mighty hand.
13:14 'With a mighty hand the LORD brought us out of **Egypt**,
13:15 the LORD killed every firstborn in **Egypt** [+824], both man
13:16 that the LORD brought us out of **Egypt** with his mighty hand."
13:17 they face war, they might change their minds and return to **Egypt**."
13:18 The Israelites went up out of **Egypt** [+824] armed for battle.
14: 4 all his army, and the **Egyptians** will know that I am the LORD."
14: 5 When the king of **Egypt** was told that the people had fled,
14: 7 along with all the other chariots of **Egypt**, with officers over all of
14: 8 The LORD hardened the heart of Pharaoh king of **Egypt**,
14: 9 The **Egyptians**—all Pharaoh's horses and chariots, horsemen
14:10 looked up, and there were the **Egyptians**, marching after them.
14:11 because there were no graves in **Egypt** that you brought us to the
14:11 to die? What have you done to us by bringing us out of **Egypt**?
14:12 Didn't we say to you in **Egypt**, 'Leave us alone; let us serve the
14:12 say to you in Egypt, 'Leave us alone; let us serve the **Egyptians**'?
14:12 It would have been better for us to serve the **Egyptians** than to die
14:13 you today. The **Egyptians** you see today you will never see again.
14:17 I will harden the hearts of the **Egyptians** so that they will go in
14:18 The **Egyptians** will know that I am the LORD when I gain glory
14:20 coming between the armies of **Egypt** and Israel. Throughout the
14:23 The **Egyptians** pursued them, and all Pharaoh's horses
14:24 and cloud at the **Egyptian** army and threw it into confusion.
14:24 cloud at the Egyptian army and threw **it**[s] [+4722] into confusion.
14:25 And the **Egyptians** said, "Let's get away from the Israelites!
14:25 the Israelites! The LORD is fighting for them against **Egypt**."
14:26 so that the waters may flow back over the **Egyptians** and their
14:27 The **Egyptians** were fleeing toward it, and the LORD swept them
14:27 were fleeing toward it, and the LORD swept **them**[s] into the sea.
14:30 day the LORD saved Israel from the hands of the **Egyptians**,
14:30 and Israel saw the **Egyptians** lying dead on the shore.
14:31 saw the great power the LORD displayed against the **Egyptians**,
15:26 not bring on you any of the diseases I brought on the **Egyptians**,
16: 1 day of the second month after they had come out of **Egypt** [+824].
16: 3 "If only we had died by the LORD's hand in **Egypt** [+824]!
16: 6 that it was the LORD who brought you out of **Egypt** [+824],
16:32 you to eat in the desert when I brought you out of **Egypt** [+824].' "
17: 3 "Why did you bring us up out of **Egypt** to make us and our
18: 1 and how the LORD had brought Israel out of **Egypt**.
18: 8 the **Egyptians** for Israel's sake and about all the hardships they had
18: 9 done for Israel in rescuing them from the hand of the **Egyptians**.
18:10 who rescued you from the hand of the **Egyptians** and of Pharaoh,
18:10 and who rescued the people from the hand of the **Egyptians**.
19: 1 In the third month after the Israelites left **Egypt** [+824]—
19: 4 'You yourselves have seen what I did to **Egypt**, and how I carried
20: 2 who brought you out of **Egypt** [+824], out of the land of slavery.
22:21 [22:20] or oppress him, for you were aliens in **Egypt** [+824].
23: 9 how it feels to be aliens, because you were aliens in **Egypt** [+824].
23:15 in the month of Abib, for in that month you came out of **Egypt**.
29:46 who brought them out of **Egypt** [+824] so that I might dwell
32: 1 As for this fellow Moses who brought us up out of **Egypt** [+824],
32: 4 are your gods, O Israel, who brought you up out of **Egypt** [+824]."
32: 7 because your people, whom you brought up out of **Egypt** [+824],
32: 8 are your gods, O Israel, who brought you up out of **Egypt** [+824].'
32:11 whom you brought out of **Egypt** [+824] with great power
32:12 Why should the **Egyptians** say, 'It was with evil intent that he
32:23 As for this fellow Moses who brought us up out of **Egypt** [+824],
33: 1 this place, you and the people you brought up out of **Egypt** [+824],
34:18 in the month of Abib, for in that month you came out of **Egypt**.
Lev 11:45 I am the LORD who brought you up out of **Egypt** [+824] to be
18: 3 You must not do as they do in **Egypt** [+824], where you used to
19:34 Love him as yourself, for you were aliens in **Egypt** [+824].
19:36 I am the LORD your God, who brought you out of **Egypt** [+824].
22:33 and who brought you out of **Egypt** [+824] to be your God.
23:43 Israelites live in booths when I brought them out of **Egypt** [+824].
25:38 who brought you out of **Egypt** [+824] to give you the land of
25:42 whom I brought out of **Egypt** [+824], they must not be sold as
25:55 They are my servants, whom I brought out of **Egypt** [+824].
26:13 who brought you out of **Egypt** [+824] so that you would no longer
26:45 out of **Egypt** [+824] in the sight of the nations to be their God.
Nu 1: 1 of the second year after the Israelites came out of **Egypt** [+824].
3:13 When I struck down all the firstborn in **Egypt** [+824], I set apart
8:17 When I struck down all the firstborn in **Egypt** [+824], I set them
9: 1 first month of the second year after they came out of **Egypt** [+824].
11: 5 We remember the fish we ate in **Egypt** at no cost—also the
11:18 "If only we had meat to eat! We were better off in **Egypt**!"
11:20 wailed before him, saying, "Why did we ever leave **Egypt**?" ' "
13:22 (Hebron had been built seven years before Zoan in **Egypt**.)
14: 2 assembly said to them, "If only we had died in **Egypt** [+824]!
14: 3 as plunder. Wouldn't it be better for us to go back to **Egypt**?"
14: 4 to each other, "We should choose a leader and go back to **Egypt**."
14:13 Moses said to the LORD, "Then the **Egyptians** will hear about it!
14:19 just as you have pardoned them from the time they left **Egypt** until
14:22 and the miraculous signs I performed in **Egypt** and in the desert
15:41 your God, who brought you out of **Egypt** [+824] to be your God.
20: 5 Why did you bring us up out of **Egypt** to this terrible place?
20:15 Our forefathers went down into **Egypt**, and we lived there many
20:15 went down into Egypt, and we lived **there**[s] [+928] many years.
20:15 there many years. The **Egyptians** mistreated us and our fathers,
20:16 he heard our cry and sent an angel and brought us out of **Egypt**.
21: 5 "Why have you brought us up out of **Egypt** to die in the desert?
22: 5 "A people has come out of **Egypt**; they cover the face of the land
22:11 'A people that has come out of **Egypt** covers the face of the land.
23:22 God brought them out of **Egypt**; they have the strength of a wild
24: 8 "God brought them out of **Egypt**; they have the strength of a wild
26: 4 These were the Israelites who came out of **Egypt** [+824]:
26:59 a descendant of Levi, who was born to the Levites in **Egypt**.
32:11 or more who came up out of **Egypt** will see the land I promised on
33: 1 out of **Egypt** [+824] by divisions under the leadership of Moses
33: 3 They marched out boldly in full view of all the **Egyptians**,
33: 4 **who**[s] were burying all their firstborn, whom the LORD had
33:38 of the fortieth year after the Israelites came out of **Egypt** [+824].
34: 5 where it will turn, join the Wadi of **Egypt** and end at the Sea.
Dt 1:27 so he brought us out of **Egypt** [+824] to deliver us into the hands
1:30 will fight for you, as he did for you in **Egypt**, before your very
4:20 out of **Egypt**, to be the people of his inheritance, as you now are.
4:34 like all the things the LORD your God did for you in **Egypt**
4:37 he brought you out of **Egypt** by his Presence and his great strength,
4:45 and laws Moses gave them when they came out of **Egypt**
4:46 defeated by Moses and the Israelites as they came out of **Egypt**.
5: 6 who brought you out of **Egypt** [+824], out of the land of slavery.
5:15 Remember that you were slaves in **Egypt** [+824] and that the
6:12 who brought you out of **Egypt** [+824], out of the land of slavery.
6:21 "We were slaves of Pharaoh in **Egypt**, but the LORD brought us
6:21 but the LORD brought us out of **Egypt** with a mighty hand.
6:22 and terrible—upon **Egypt** and Pharaoh and his whole household.
7: 8 the land of slavery, from the power of Pharaoh king of **Egypt**.
7:15 He will not inflict on you the horrible diseases you knew in **Egypt**,
7:18 well what the LORD your God did to Pharaoh and to all **Egypt**.
8:14 who brought you out of **Egypt** [+824], out of the land of slavery.
9: 7 From the day you left **Egypt** [+824] until you arrived here,
9:12 because your people whom you brought out of **Egypt** have become
9:26 by your great power and brought out of **Egypt** with a mighty hand.
10:19 who are aliens, for you yourselves were aliens in **Egypt** [+824].
10:22 Your forefathers who went down into **Egypt** were seventy in all,
11: 3 the signs he performed and the things he did in the heart of **Egypt**,
11: 3 of Egypt, both to Pharaoh king of **Egypt** and to his whole country;
11: 4 what he did to the **Egyptian** army, to its horses and chariots,
11:10 The land you are entering to take over is not like the land of **Egypt**,
13: 5 [13:6] who brought you out of **Egypt** [+824] and redeemed you
13:10 [13:11] who brought you out of **Egypt** [+824], out of the land of
15:15 Remember that you were slaves in **Egypt** [+824] and the LORD
16: 1 because in the month of Abib he brought you out of **Egypt** by
16: 3 the bread of affliction, because you left **Egypt** [+824] in haste—
16: 3 you may remember the time of your departure from **Egypt** [+824].
16: 6 sun goes down, on the anniversary of your departure from **Egypt**.
16:12 Remember that you were slaves in **Egypt**, and follow carefully
17:16 or make the people return to **Egypt** to get more of them,
20: 1 who brought you up out of **Egypt** [+824], will be with you.
23: 4 [23:5] and water on your way when you came out of **Egypt**,
24: 9 God did to Miriam along the way after you came out of **Egypt**.
24:18 Remember that you were slaves in **Egypt** and the LORD your
24:22 Remember that you were slaves in **Egypt** [+824]. That is why I
25:17 Amalekites did to you along the way when you came out of **Egypt**.
26: 5 and he went down into **Egypt** with a few people and lived there
26: 6 the **Egyptians** mistreated us and made us suffer, putting us to hard
26: 8 So the LORD brought us out of **Egypt** with a mighty hand
28:27 The LORD will afflict you with the boils of **Egypt** and with
28:60 He will bring upon you all the diseases of **Egypt** that you dreaded,
28:68 The LORD will send you back in ships to **Egypt** on a journey I
29: 2 [29:1] seen all that the LORD did in **Egypt** [+824] to Pharaoh,
29:16 [29:15] You yourselves know how we lived in **Egypt** [+824]
29:25 [29:24] with them when he brought them out of **Egypt** [+824].
34:11 and wonders the LORD sent him to do in **Egypt** [+824]—
Jos 2:10 up the water of the Red Sea for you when you came out of **Egypt**,
5: 4 All those who came out of **Egypt**—all the men of military age—

Jos 5: 4 of military age—died in the desert on the way after leaving **Egypt**.
5: 5 all the people born in the desert during the journey from **Egypt** had
5: 6 the men who were of military age when they left **Egypt** had died,
5: 9 "Today I have rolled away the reproach of **Egypt** from you."
9: 9 For we have heard reports of him: all that he did in **Egypt**,
13: 3 from the Shihor River on the east of **Egypt** to the territory of Ekron
15: 4 then passed along to Azmon and joined the Wadi of **Egypt**,
15: 47 as far as the Wadi of **Egypt** and the coastline of the Great Sea.
24: 4 of Seir to Esau, but Jacob and his sons went down to **Egypt**.
24: 5 and Aaron, and I afflicted the **Egyptians** by what I did there,
24: 6 When I brought your fathers out of **Egypt**, you came to the sea,
24: 6 the **Egyptians** pursued them with chariots and horsemen as far as
24: 7 for help, and he put darkness between you and the **Egyptians**;
24: 7 You saw with your own eyes what I did to the **Egyptians**.
24: 14 gods your forefathers worshiped beyond the River and in **Egypt**,
24: 17 himself who brought us and our fathers up out of **Egypt** [+824],
24: 32 Joseph's bones, which the Israelites had brought up from **Egypt**,
Jdg 2: 1 "I brought you up out of **Egypt** and led you into the land that I
2: 12 God of their fathers, who had brought them out of **Egypt** [+824].
6: 8 says: I brought you up out of **Egypt**, out of the land of slavery.
6: 9 I snatched you from the power of **Egypt** and from the hand of all
6: 13 when they said, 'Did not the LORD bring us up out of **Egypt**?'
10: 11 "When the **Egyptians**, the Amorites, the Ammonites, the
11: 13 "When Israel came up out of **Egypt**, they took away my land from
11: 16 when they came up out of **Egypt**, Israel went through the desert to
19: 30 not since the day the Israelites came up out of **Egypt** [+824].
1Sa 2: 27 to your father's house when they were in **Egypt** under Pharaoh?
4: 8 They are the gods who struck the **Egyptians** with all kinds of
6: 6 Why do you harden your hearts as the **Egyptians** and Pharaoh did?
8: 8 As they have done from the day I brought them up out of **Egypt**
10: 18 'I brought Israel up out of **Egypt**, and I delivered you from the
10: 18 I delivered you from the power of **Egypt** and all the kingdoms that
12: 6 and Aaron and brought your forefathers up out of **Egypt** [+824].
12: 8 "After Jacob entered **Egypt**, they cried to the LORD for help,
12: 8 who brought your forefathers out of **Egypt** and settled them in this
15: 2 did to Israel when they waylaid them as they came up from **Egypt**.
15: 6 kindness to all the Israelites when they came up out of **Egypt**."
15: 7 Amalekites all the way from Havilah to Shur, to the east of **Egypt**.
27: 8 peoples had lived in the land extending to Shur and **Egypt** [+824].)
2Sa 7: 6 from the day I brought the Israelites up out of **Egypt** to this day.
7: 23 gods from before your people, whom you redeemed from **Egypt**?
1Ki 3: 1 Solomon made an alliance with Pharaoh king of **Egypt**
4: 21 [5:1] to the land of the Philistines, as far as the border of **Egypt**.
4: 30 [5:10] men of the East, and greater than all the wisdom of **Egypt**.
6: 1 eightieth year after the Israelites had come out of **Egypt** [+824],
8: 9 a covenant with the Israelites after they came out of **Egypt** [+824].
8: 16 'Since the day I brought my people Israel out of **Egypt**, I have not
8: 21 with our fathers when he brought them out of **Egypt** [+824]."
8: 51 your people and your inheritance, whom you brought out of **Egypt**,
8: 53 O Sovereign LORD, brought our fathers out of **Egypt**."
8: 65 a vast assembly, people from Lebo Hamath to the Wadi of **Egypt**.
9: 9 who brought their fathers out of **Egypt** [+824], and have embraced
9: 16 (Pharaoh king of **Egypt** had attacked and captured Gezer.
10: 28 Solomon's horses were imported from **Egypt** and from Kue—
10: 29 They imported a chariot from **Egypt** for six hundred shekels of
11: 17 fled to **Egypt** with some Edomite officials who had served his
11: 18 they went to **Egypt**, to Pharaoh king of Egypt, who gave Hadad a
11: 18 they went to Egypt, to Pharaoh king of **Egypt**, who gave Hadad a
11: 21 While he was in **Egypt**, Hadad heard that David rested with his
11: 40 to kill Jeroboam, but Jeroboam fled to **Egypt**, to Shishak the king,
11: 40 Shishak the king, **[RPH]** and stayed there until Solomon's death.
11: 40 to Shishak the king, and stayed **there**[s] until Solomon's death.
12: 2 When Jeroboam son of Nebat heard this (he was still in **Egypt**,
12: 2 where he had fled from King Solomon), he returned from **Egypt**.
12: 28 are your gods, O Israel, who brought you up out of **Egypt** [+824]."
14: 25 of King Rehoboam, Shishak king of **Egypt** attacked Jerusalem.
2Ki 7: 6 of Israel has hired the Hittite and **Egyptian** kings to attack us!"
17: 4 for he had sent envoys to So king of **Egypt**, and he no longer paid
17: 7 who had brought them up out of **Egypt** [+824] from under the
17: 7 up out of Egypt from under the power of Pharaoh king of **Egypt**.
17: 36 who brought you up out of **Egypt** [+824] with mighty power
18: 21 Look now, you are depending on **Egypt**, that splintered reed of a
18: 21 Such is Pharaoh king of **Egypt** to all who depend on him.
18: 24 even though you are depending on **Egypt** for chariots
21: 15 from the day their forefathers came out of **Egypt** until this day."
23: 29 Pharaoh Neco king of **Egypt** went up to the Euphrates River to
23: 34 he took Jehoahaz and carried him off to **Egypt**, and there he died.
24: 7 The king of **Egypt** did not march out from his own country again,
24: 7 because the king of Babylon had taken all **his**[s] [+4200+4889]
24: 7 all his territory, from the Wadi of **Egypt** to the Euphrates River.
25: 26 with the army officers, fled to **Egypt** for fear of the Babylonians.
1Ch 1: 8 The sons of Ham: Cush, **Mizraim**, Put and Canaan.
1: 11 **Mizraim** was the father of the Ludites, Anamites, Lehabites,
13: 5 all the Israelites, from the Shihor River in **Egypt** to Lebo Hamath,
17: 21 from before your people, whom you redeemed from **Egypt**?
2Ch 1: 16 Solomon's horses were imported from **Egypt** and from Kue—
1: 17 They imported a chariot from **Egypt** for six hundred shekels of
5: 10 made a covenant with the Israelites after they came out of **Egypt**.
6: 5 'Since the day I brought my people out of **Egypt** [+824], I have not
7: 8 a vast assembly, people from Lebo Hamath to the Wadi of **Egypt**.
7: 22 the God of their fathers, who brought them out of **Egypt** [+824],
9: 26 River to the land of the Philistines, as far as the border of **Egypt**.
9: 28 Solomon's horses were imported from **Egypt** and from all other
10: 2 When Jeroboam son of Nebat heard this (he was in **Egypt**,
10: 2 where he had fled from King Solomon), he returned from **Egypt**.
12: 2 Shishak king of **Egypt** attacked Jerusalem in the fifth year of King
12: 3 of Libyans, Sukkites and Cushites that came with him from **Egypt**,
12: 9 When Shishak king of **Egypt** attacked Jerusalem, he carried off the
20: 10 not allow Israel to invade when they came from **Egypt** [+824];
26: 8 his fame spread as far as the border of **Egypt**, because he had
35: 20 Neco king of **Egypt** went up to fight at Carchemish on the
36: 3 The king of **Egypt** dethroned him in Jerusalem and imposed on
36: 4 The king of **Egypt** made Eliakim, a brother of Jehoahaz, king over
36: 4 took Eliakim's brother Jehoahaz and carried him off to **Egypt**.
Ne 9: 9 "You saw the suffering of our forefathers in **Egypt**; you heard their
9: 18 and said, 'This is your god, who brought you up out of **Egypt**,'
Ps 68: 31 [68:32] Envoys will come from **Egypt**; Cush will submit herself
78: 12 He did miracles in the sight of their fathers in the land of **Egypt**,
78: 43 the day he displayed his miraculous signs in **Egypt**, his wonders in
78: 51 He struck down all the firstborn of **Egypt**, the firstfruits of
80: 8 [80:9] You brought a vine out of **Egypt**; you drove out the nations
81: 5 [81:6] statute for Joseph when he went out against **Egypt** [+824],
81: 10 [81:11] your God, who brought you up out of **Egypt** [+824].
105: 23 Israel entered **Egypt**; Jacob lived as an alien in the land of Ham.
105: 38 **Egypt** was glad when they left, because dread of Israel had fallen
106: 7 When our fathers were in **Egypt**, they gave no thought to your
106: 21 the God who saved them, who had done great things in **Egypt**,
114: 1 When Israel came out of **Egypt**, the house of Jacob from a people
135: 8 He struck down the firstborn of **Egypt**, the firstborn of men
135: 9 into your midst, O **Egypt**, against Pharaoh and all his servants.
136: 10 to him who struck down the firstborn of **Egypt** *His love*
Pr 7: 16 I have covered my bed with colored linens from **Egypt**.
Isa 7: 18 the LORD will whistle for flies from the distant streams of **Egypt**
10: 24 beat you with a rod and lift up a club against you, as **Egypt** did.
10: 26 and he will raise his staff over the waters, as he did in **Egypt**.
11: 11 from **Lower Egypt**, from Upper Egypt, from Cush, from Elam,
11: 15 The LORD will dry up the gulf of the **Egyptian** sea; with a
11: 16 as there was for Israel when they came up from **Egypt** [+824].
19: 1 An oracle concerning **Egypt**: See, the LORD rides on a swift
19: 1 the LORD rides on a swift cloud and is coming to **Egypt**.
19: 1 The idols of **Egypt** tremble before him, and the hearts of the
19: 1 before him, and the hearts of the **Egyptians** melt within them.
19: 2 "I will stir up **Egyptian** against Egyptian—brother will fight
19: 2 "I will stir up Egyptian against **Egyptian**—brother will fight
19: 3 The **Egyptians** will lose heart, and I will bring their plans to
19: 4 I will hand the **Egyptians** over to the power of a cruel master,
19: 12 known what the LORD Almighty has planned against **Egypt**.
19: 13 the cornerstones of her peoples have led **Egypt** astray.
19: 14 they make **Egypt** stagger in all that she does, as a drunkard
19: 15 There is nothing **Egypt** can do—head or tail, palm branch
19: 16 In that day the **Egyptians** will be like women. They will shudder
19: 17 the land of Judah will bring terror to the **Egyptians**; everyone to
19: 18 In that day five cities in **Egypt** [+824] will speak the language of
19: 19 there will be an altar to the LORD in the heart of **Egypt** [+824],
19: 20 and witness to the LORD Almighty in the land of **Egypt**.
19: 21 So the LORD will make himself known to the **Egyptians**,
19: 21 the Egyptians, and in that day **they**[s] will acknowledge the LORD.
19: 22 The LORD will strike **Egypt** with a plague; he will strike them
19: 23 In that day there will be a highway from **Egypt** to Assyria.
19: 23 The Assyrians will go to **Egypt** and the Egyptians to Assyria.
19: 23 The Assyrians will go to Egypt and the **Egyptians** to Assyria.
19: 23 to Assyria. The **Egyptians** and Assyrians will worship together.
19: 24 be the third, along with **Egypt** and Assyria, a blessing on the earth.
19: 25 saying, "Blessed be **Egypt** my people, Assyria my handiwork,
20: 3 for three years, as a sign and portent against **Egypt** and Cush,
20: 4 and barefoot the **Egyptian** captives and Cushite exiles,
20: 4 young and old, with buttocks bared—to **Egypt's** shame.
20: 5 in Cush and boasted in **Egypt** will be afraid and put to shame.
23: 5 When word comes to **Egypt**, they will be in anguish at the report
27: 12 will thresh from the flowing Euphrates to the Wadi of **Egypt**,
27: 13 in Assyria and those who were exiled in **Egypt** [+824] will come
30: 2 who go down to **Egypt** without consulting me; who look for help
30: 2 look for help to Pharaoh's protection, to **Egypt's** shade for refuge.
30: 3 will be to your shame, **Egypt's** shade will bring you disgrace.
30: 7 to **Egypt**, whose help is utterly useless. Therefore I call her Rahab
31: 1 Woe to those who go down to **Egypt** for help, who rely on horses,
31: 3 But the **Egyptians** are men and not God; their horses are flesh
36: 6 Look now, you are depending on **Egypt**, that splintered reed of a

Isa 36: 6 Such is Pharaoh king of **Egypt** to all who depend on him.
36: 9 even though you are depending on **Egypt** for chariots
43: 3 I give **Egypt** for your ransom, Cush and Seba in your stead.
45: 14 "The products of **Egypt** and the merchandise of Cush, and those
52: 4 "At first my people went down to **Egypt** to live; lately, Assyria has
Jer 2: 6 who brought us up out of **Egypt** [+824] and led us through the
2: 18 Now why go to **Egypt** to drink water from the Shihor? And why
2: 36 You will be disappointed by **Egypt** as you were by Assyria.
7: 22 For when I brought your forefathers out of **Egypt** [+824]
7: 25 From the time your forefathers left **Egypt** [+824] until now,
9: 26 [9:25] **Egypt**, Judah, Edom, Ammon, Moab and all who live in
11: 4 your forefathers when I brought them out of **Egypt** [+824],
11: 7 From the time I brought your forefathers up from **Egypt** [+824]
16: 14 LORD lives, who brought the Israelites up out of **Egypt** [+824],'
23: 7 LORD lives, who brought the Israelites up out of **Egypt** [+824],'
24: 8 whether they remain in this land or live in **Egypt** [+824].
25: 19 Pharaoh king of **Egypt**, his attendants, his officials and all his
26: 21 to put him to death. But Uriah heard of it and fled in fear to **Egypt**.
26: 22 King Jehoiakim, however, sent Elnathan son of Acbor to **Egypt**,
26: 22 son of Acbor to Egypt, along with some other men. **[RPH]**
26: 23 They brought Uriah out of **Egypt** and took him to King Jehoiakim,
31: 32 when I took them by the hand to lead them out of **Egypt** [+824],
32: 20 You performed miraculous signs and wonders in **Egypt** [+824]
32: 21 You brought your people Israel out of **Egypt** [+824] with signs
34: 13 with your forefathers when I brought them out of **Egypt** [+824],
37: 5 Pharaoh's army had marched out of **Egypt**, and when the
37: 7 marched out to support you, will go back to its own land, to **Egypt**.
41: 17 at Geruth Kimham near Bethlehem on their way to **Egypt**
42: 14 if you say, 'No, we will go and live in **Egypt** [+824], where we will
42: 15 'If you are determined to go to **Egypt** and you do go to settle there,
42: 16 **[RPH]** and the famine you dread will follow you into Egypt,
42: 16 the famine you dread will follow you into **Egypt**, and there you
42: 17 all who are determined to go to **Egypt** to settle there will die by the
42: 18 so will my wrath be poured out on you when you go to **Egypt**.
42: 19 remnant of Judah, the LORD has told you, 'Do not go to **Egypt**.'
43: 2 has not sent you to say, 'You must not go to **Egypt** to settle there.'
43: 7 So they entered **Egypt** [+824] in disobedience to the LORD
43: 11 He will come and attack **Egypt** [+824], bringing death to those
43: 12 He will set fire to the temples of the gods of **Egypt**; he will burn
43: 12 so will he wrap **Egypt** [+824] around himself and depart from
43: 13 There in the temple of the sun in **Egypt** [+824] he will demolish
43: 13 and will burn down the temples of the gods of **Egypt**.' "
44: 1 Jeremiah concerning all the Jews living in **Lower Egypt** [+824]—
44: 8 burning incense to other gods in **Egypt** [+824], where you have
44: 12 Judah who were determined to go to **Egypt** [+824] to settle there.
44: 12 They will all perish in **Egypt** [+824]; they will fall by the sword
44: 13 I will punish those who live in **Egypt** [+824] with the sword,
44: 14 of Judah who have gone to live in **Egypt** [+824] will escape
44: 15 and all the people living in **Lower** and Upper **Egypt** [+824],
44: 24 the word of the LORD, all you people of Judah in **Egypt** [+824].
44: 26 But hear the word of the LORD, all Jews living in **Egypt** [+824]:
44: 26 'that no one from Judah living anywhere in **Egypt** [+824] will ever
44: 27 the Jews in **Egypt** [+824] will perish by sword and famine until
44: 28 return to the land of Judah from **Egypt** [+824] will be very few.
44: 28 the whole remnant of Judah who came to live in **Egypt** [+824] will
44: 30 'I am going to hand Pharaoh Hophra king of **Egypt** over to his
46: 2 Concerning **Egypt**: This is the message against the army of
46: 2 is the message against the army of Pharaoh Neco king of **Egypt**,
46: 8 **Egypt** rises like the Nile, like rivers of surging waters. She says,
46: 11 "Go up to Gilead and get balm, O Virgin Daughter of **Egypt**.
46: 13 of Nebuchadnezzar king of Babylon to attack **Egypt** [+824]:
46: 14 "Announce this in **Egypt**, and proclaim it in Migdol; proclaim it
46: 17 they will exclaim, 'Pharaoh king of **Egypt** is only a loud noise;
46: 19 you who live in **Egypt** [+1426], for Memphis will be laid waste
46: 20 "**Egypt** is a beautiful heifer, but a gadfly is coming against her
46: 24 The Daughter of **Egypt** will be put to shame, handed over to the
46: 25 on Pharaoh, on **Egypt** and her gods and her kings, and on those
La 5: 6 We submitted to **Egypt** and Assyria to get enough bread.
Eze 16: 26 You engaged in prostitution with the **Egyptians** [+1201],
17: 15 the king rebelled against him by sending his envoys to **Egypt** to
19: 4 trapped in their pit. They led him with hooks to the land of **Egypt**.
20: 5 the house of Jacob and revealed myself to them in **Egypt** [+824].
20: 6 them out of **Egypt** [+824] into a land I had searched out for them,
20: 7 your eyes on, and do not defile yourselves with the idols of **Egypt**.
20: 8 they had set their eyes on, nor did they forsake the idols of **Egypt**.
20: 8 wrath on them and spend my anger against them in **Egypt** [+824].
20: 9 myself to the Israelites by bringing them out of **Egypt** [+824].
20: 10 Therefore I led them out of **Egypt** [+824] and brought them into
20: 36 As I judged your fathers in the desert of the land of **Egypt**,
23: 3 They became prostitutes in **Egypt**, engaging in prostitution from
23: 8 She did not give up the prostitution she began in **Egypt**,
23: 19 the days of her youth, when she was a prostitute in **Egypt** [+824].
23: 21 when in **Egypt** your bosom was caressed and your young breasts
23: 27 a stop to the lewdness and prostitution you began in **Egypt** [+824].
23: 27 look on these things with longing or remember **Egypt** anymore.
27: 7 Fine embroidered linen from **Egypt** was your sail and served as
29: 2 set your face against Pharaoh king of **Egypt** and prophesy against
29: 2 king of Egypt and prophesy against him and against all **Egypt**.
29: 3 " 'I am against you, Pharaoh king of **Egypt**, you great monster
29: 6 Then all who live in **Egypt** will know that I am the LORD.
29: 9 **Egypt** [+824] will become a desolate wasteland. Then they will
29: 10 I will make the land of **Egypt** a ruin and a desolate waste from
29: 12 I will make the land of **Egypt** desolate among devastated lands,
29: 12 I will disperse the **Egyptians** among the nations and scatter them
29: 13 At the end of forty years I will gather the **Egyptians** from the
29: 14 I will bring **them**[s] back from captivity and return them to Upper
29: 19 I am going to give **Egypt** [+824] to Nebuchadnezzar king of
29: 20 I have given him **Egypt** [+824] as a reward for his efforts
30: 4 A sword will come against **Egypt**, and anguish will come upon
30: 4 When the slain fall in **Egypt**, her wealth will be carried away
30: 6 " 'The allies of **Egypt** will fall and her proud strength will fail.
30: 8 when I set fire to **Egypt** and all her helpers are crushed.
30: 9 Anguish will take hold of them on the day of **Egypt's** doom,
30: 10 " 'I will put an end to the hordes of **Egypt** by the hand of
30: 11 They will draw their swords against **Egypt** and fill the land with
30: 13 No longer will there be a prince in **Egypt** [+824], and I will spread
30: 13 in Egypt, and I will spread fear throughout the land. **[RPH]**
30: 15 the stronghold of **Egypt**, and cut off the hordes of Thebes.
30: 16 I will set fire to **Egypt**; Pelusium will writhe in agony. Thebes will
30: 18 Dark will be the day at Tahpanhes when I break the yoke of **Egypt**;
30: 19 So I will inflict punishment on **Egypt**, and they will know that I
30: 21 "Son of man, I have broken the arm of Pharaoh king of **Egypt**.
30: 22 I am against Pharaoh king of **Egypt**. I will break both his arms,
30: 23 I will disperse the **Egyptians** among the nations and scatter them
30: 25 of the king of Babylon and he brandishes it against **Egypt** [+824].
30: 26 I will disperse the **Egyptians** among the nations and scatter them
31: 2 "Son of man, say to Pharaoh king of **Egypt** and to his hordes:
32: 2 take up a lament concerning Pharaoh king of **Egypt** and say to
32: 12 They will shatter the pride of **Egypt**, and all her hordes will be
32: 15 When I make **Egypt** [+824] desolate and strip the land of
32: 16 for **Egypt** and all her hordes they will chant it,
32: 18 wail for the hordes of **Egypt** and consign to the earth below both
Da 9: 15 who brought your people out of **Egypt** [+824] with a mighty hand
11: 8 valuable articles of silver and gold and carry them off to **Egypt**.
11: 42 He will extend his power over many countries; **Egypt** [+824] will
11: 43 of the treasures of gold and silver and all the riches of **Egypt**,
Hos 2: 15 [2:17] her youth, as in the day she came up out of **Egypt** [+824].
7: 11 and senseless—now calling to **Egypt**, now turning to Assyria.
7: 16 insolent words. For this they will be ridiculed in the land of **Egypt**.
8: 13 their wickedness and punish their sins: They will return to **Egypt**.
9: 3 Ephraim will return to **Egypt** and eat unclean food in Assyria.
9: 6 **Egypt** will gather them, and Memphis will bury them.
11: 1 Israel was a child, I loved him, and out of **Egypt** I called my son.
11: 5 "Will they not return to **Egypt** [+824] and will not Assyria rule
11: 11 They will come trembling like birds from **Egypt**, like doves from
12: 1 [12:2] makes a treaty with Assyria and sends olive oil to **Egypt**.
12: 9 [12:10] your God, ⌞who brought you⌟ out of **Egypt** [+824];
12: 13 [12:14] LORD used a prophet to bring Israel up from **Egypt**,
13: 4 am the LORD your God, ⌞who brought you⌟ out of **Egypt** [+824].
Joel 3: 19 [4:19] **Egypt** will be desolate, Edom a desert waste, because of
Am 2: 10 "I brought you up out of **Egypt** [+824], and I led you forty years in
3: 1 against the whole family I brought up out of **Egypt** [+824]:
3: 9 to the fortresses of Ashdod and to the fortresses of **Egypt** [+824]:
4: 10 "I sent plagues among you as I did to **Egypt**. I killed your young
8: 8 the Nile; it will be stirred up and then sink like the river of **Egypt**.
9: 5 whole land rises like the Nile, then sinks like the river of **Egypt**—
9: 7 "Did I not bring Israel up from **Egypt** [+824], the Philistines from
Mic 6: 4 I brought you up out of **Egypt** [+824] and redeemed you from the
7: 15 "As in the days when you came out of **Egypt** [+824], I will show
Na 3: 9 Cush and **Egypt** were her boundless strength; Put and Libya were
Hag 2: 5 'This is what I covenanted with you when you came out of **Egypt**.
Zec 10: 10 I will bring them back from **Egypt** [+824] and gather them from
10: 11 pride will be brought down and **Egypt's** scepter will pass away.
14: 18 If the **Egyptian** people do not go up and take part, they will have
14: 19 This will be the punishment of **Egypt** and the punishment of all the

5214 מַצְרֵף *maṣrēp*, n.[m.]. [2] [√ 7671]

crucible [2]

Pr 17: 3 The **crucible** for silver and the furnace for gold, but the LORD
27: 21 The **crucible** for silver and the furnace for gold, but man is tested

5215 מַק *maq*, n.m. [2] [√ 5245]

decay [1], stench [1]

Isa 3: 24 Instead of fragrance there will be a **stench**; instead of a sash,
5: 24 so their roots will **decay** and their flowers blow away like dust;

5216 מַקֶּבֶת[1] ***maqqebet[1]***, n.f. [4] [√ 5918]
hammer [3], hammers [1]
Jdg 4:21 picked up a tent peg and a **hammer** and went quietly to him while
1Ki 6: 7 no **hammer**, chisel or any other iron tool was heard at the temple
Isa 44:12 he shapes an idol with **hammers**, he forges it with the might of his
Jer 10: 4 and gold; they fasten it with **hammer** and nails so it will not totter.

5217 מַקֶּבֶת[2] ***maqqebet[2]***, n.f. [1] [√ 5918]
quarry [+1014] [1]
Isa 51: 1 were cut and to the **quarry** [+1014] *from which* you were hewn;

5218 מַקֵּדָה ***maqqēdâ***, n.pr.loc. [9] [√ 5923]
Makkedah [9]
Jos 10:10 and cut them down all the way to Azekah and **Makkedah**.
10:16 Now the five kings had fled and hidden in the cave at **Makkedah**.
10:17 the five kings had been found hiding in the cave at **Makkedah**,
10:21 then returned safely to Joshua in the camp at **Makkedah**,
10:28 That day Joshua took **Makkedah**. He put the city and its king to
10:28 he did to the king of **Makkedah** as he had done to the king of
10:29 and all Israel with him moved on from **Makkedah** to Libnah
12:16 the king of **Makkedah** one the king of Bethel one
15:41 Gederoth, Beth Dagon, Naamah and **Makkedah**—sixteen towns

5219 מִקְדָּשׁ ***miqdāš***, n.m. [75] [√ 7727]
sanctuary [61], sanctuaries [4], holy place [2], holiest [1], holy places [1], holy things [1], it[s] [1], Most Holy Place [+7731] [1], sanctuary [+1074] [1], shrine [1], temple [1]
Ex 15:17 for your dwelling, the **sanctuary**, O Lord, your hands established.
25: 8 "Then have them make a **sanctuary** for me, and I will dwell
Lev 12: 4 or go to the **sanctuary** until the days of her purification are over.
16:33 make atonement for the **Most Holy Place** [+7731], for the Tent of
19:30 " 'Observe my Sabbaths and have reverence for my **sanctuary**.
20: 3 he has defiled my **sanctuary** and profaned my holy name.
21:12 nor leave the **sanctuary** *of* his God or desecrate it, because he has
21:12 nor leave the sanctuary of his God or desecrate **it**[s], because he has
21:23 the curtain or approach the altar, and so desecrate my **sanctuary**.
26: 2 " 'Observe my Sabbaths and have reverence for my **sanctuary**.
26:31 I will turn your cities into ruins and lay waste your **sanctuaries**,
Nu 3:38 They were responsible for the care of the **sanctuary** on behalf of
10:21 the Kohathites set out, carrying the **holy things**. The tabernacle
18: 1 are to bear the responsibility for offenses against the **sanctuary**,
18:29 portion the best and **holiest** part of everything given to you.'
19:20 because he has defiled the **sanctuary** *of* the LORD.
Jos 24:26 set it up there under the oak near the **holy place** *of* the LORD.
1Ch 22:19 Begin to build the **sanctuary** *of* the LORD God, so that you may
28:10 for the LORD has chosen you to build a temple as a **sanctuary**.
2Ch 20: 8 have lived in it and have built in it a **sanctuary** for your Name,
26:18 Leave the **sanctuary**, for you have been unfaithful; and you will
29:21 as a sin offering for the kingdom, for the **sanctuary** and for Judah.
30: 8 Come to the **sanctuary**, which he has consecrated forever.
36:17 killed their young men with the sword in the **sanctuary** [+1074],
Ne 10:39 [10:40] oil to the storerooms where the articles for the **sanctuary**
Ps 68:35 [68:36] You are awesome, O God, in your **sanctuary**; the God of
73:17 till I entered the **sanctuary** *of* God; then I understood their final
74: 7 They burned your **sanctuary** to the ground; they defiled the
78:69 He built his **sanctuary** like the heights, like the earth that he
96: 6 majesty are before him; strength and glory are in his **sanctuary**.
Isa 8:14 he will be a **sanctuary**; but for both houses of Israel he will be a
16:12 herself out; when she goes to her **shrine** to pray, it is to no avail.
60:13 and the cypress together, to adorn the place of my **sanctuary**;
63:18 but now our enemies have trampled down your **sanctuary**.
Jer 17:12 exalted from the beginning, is the place of our **sanctuary**.
51:51 because foreigners have entered the **holy places** *of* the LORD's
La 1:10 on all her treasures; she saw pagan nations enter her **sanctuary**—
2: 7 The Lord has rejected his altar and abandoned his **sanctuary**.
2:20 Should priest and prophet be killed in the **sanctuary** *of* the Lord?
Eze 5:11 because you have defiled my **sanctuary** with all your vile images
7:24 to the pride of the mighty, and their **sanctuaries** will be desecrated.
8: 6 is doing here, things that will drive me far from my **sanctuary**?
9: 6 do not touch anyone who has the mark. Begin at my **sanctuary**."
11:16 yet for a little while I have been a **sanctuary** for them in the
21: 2 [21:7] face against Jerusalem and preach against the **sanctuary**.
23:38 At that same time they defiled my **sanctuary** and desecrated my
23:39 to their idols, they entered my **sanctuary** and desecrated it.
24:21 I am about to desecrate my **sanctuary**—the stronghold in which
25: 3 over my **sanctuary** when it was desecrated and over the land of
28:18 and dishonest trade you have desecrated your **sanctuaries**.
37:26 their numbers, and I will put my **sanctuary** among them forever.
37:28 make Israel holy, when my **sanctuary** is among them forever.' "
43:21 it in the designated part of the temple area outside the **sanctuary**.
44: 1 Then the man brought me back to the outer gate of the **sanctuary**,
44: 5 to the entrance of the temple and all the exits of the **sanctuary**.
44: 7 foreigners uncircumcised in heart and flesh into my **sanctuary**,
44: 8 to my holy things, you put others in charge of my **sanctuary**.
44: 9 uncircumcised in heart and flesh is to enter my **sanctuary**,
44:11 They may serve in my **sanctuary**, having charge of the gates of the
44:15 who faithfully carried out the duties of my **sanctuary** when the
44:16 They alone are to enter my **sanctuary**; they alone are to come near
45: 3 cubits wide. In it will be the **sanctuary**, the Most Holy Place.
45: 4 who minister in the **sanctuary** and who draw near to minister
45: 4 It will be a place for their houses as well as a **holy place** for the
45: 4 a place for their houses as well as a holy place for the **sanctuary**.
45:18 are to take a young bull without defect and purify the **sanctuary**.
47:12 will bear, because the water from the **sanctuary** flows to them.
48: 8 one of the tribal portions; the **sanctuary** will be in the center of it.
48:10 south side. In the center of it will be the **sanctuary** *of* the LORD.
48:21 the sacred portion with the temple **sanctuary** will be in the center
Da 8:11 from him, and the place of his **sanctuary** was brought low.
9:17 your sake, O Lord, look with favor on your desolate **sanctuary**.
11:31 "His armed forces will rise up to desecrate the **temple** fortress
Am 7: 9 will be destroyed and the **sanctuaries** *of* Israel will be ruined;
7:13 because this is the king's **sanctuary** and the temple of the

5220 מַקְהֵל ***maqhēl***, n.[m.]. [2] [√ 7736]
great assembly [1], great congregation [1]
Ps 26:12 on level ground; in the **great assembly** I will praise the LORD.
68:26 [68:27] Praise God in the **great congregation**; praise the LORD

5221 מַקְהֵלֹת ***maqhēlôt***, n.pr.loc. [2] [√ 7736]
Makheloth [2]
Nu 33:25 They left Haradah and camped at **Makheloth**.
33:26 They left **Makheloth** and camped at Tahath.

5222 מִקְוֵא ***miqwē'***, n.pr.loc.?. Not used in NIV/BHS [cf. 7745]

5223 מִקְוֶה[1] ***miqweh[1]***, n.[m.]. [5] [√ 7747]
hope [5]
1Ch 29:15 our forefathers. Our days on earth are like a shadow, without **hope**.
Ezr 10: 2 peoples around us. But in spite of this, there is still **hope** for Israel.
Jer 14: 8 O **Hope** *of* Israel, its Savior in times of distress, why are you like a
17:13 O LORD, the **hope** *of* Israel, all who forsake you will be put to
50: 7 their true pasture, the LORD, the **hope** *of* their fathers.'

5224 מִקְוֶה[2] ***miqweh[2]***, n.[m.]. [3] [√ 7748]
collecting [1], gathered [1], reservoirs [+4784] [1]
Ge 1:10 the dry ground "land," and the **gathered** waters he called "seas."
Ex 7:19 and canals, over the ponds and all the **reservoirs** [+4784]'—
Lev 11:36 A spring, however, or a cistern for **collecting** water remains clean,

5225 מִקְוָה ***miqwâ***, n.f. [1] [√ 7748]
reservoir [1]
Isa 22:11 You built a **reservoir** between the two walls for the water of the

5226 מָקוֹם ***māqôm***, n.m. [401] [√ 7756]
place [268], home [14], *untranslated* [13], places [12], land [5], room [5], site [4], spot [4], where[s] [4], dwelling place [3], wherever [+889+928] [3], anywhere [+928+3972] [2], dwell [2], everywhere [+3972] [2], here[s] [+2021+2021+2296] [2], seat [+8699] [2], sites [2], space [2], there[s] [2], where[s] [+2021] [2], wherever [+889+928 +2021+3972] [2], area [1], base [1], channels [1], commands [1], countries [1], direction [1], dwelling [1], everywhere [+2021+3972] [1], everywhere [+928+3972] [1], haunt [1], here[s] [+2021] [1], here[s] [+928] [1], here[s] [+928+2021+2021+2296] [1], homeland [+824] [1], homeland [1], homes [1], it[s] [+2021+2021+2085] [1], it[s] [1], Nineveh[s] [+2023] [1], points [1], position [1], positions [1], post [1], proper place [+889+2118+9004] [1], regions [1], reside [1], rest [1], sanctuary [+7731] [1], seated [+4200+5989] [1], somewhere [1], suitable [1], there[s] [+2023] [1], town records [+9133] [1], town [1], way [1], where [+361] [1], where dwells [1], where lived [1], where[s] [+928] [1], where[s] [+928+2021] [1], wherever [+2021+3972+4946] [1], wherever [+285+889+928+2021] [1], wherever [+889+2021 +3972+6584] [1], wherever [+889+928+2021] [1], wherever [+928+2021+3972] [1], wherever[s] [+889] [1]
Ge 1: 9 God said, "Let the water under the sky be gathered to one **place**,
12: 6 Abram traveled through the land as far as the **site** *of* the great tree
13: 3 to the **place** between Bethel and Ai where his tent had been earlier
13: 4 **[RPH]** where he had first built an altar. There Abram called on
13:14 "Lift up your eyes from **where**[s] [+2021] you are and look north
18:24 not spare the **place** for the sake of the fifty righteous people in it?
18:26 in the city of Sodom, I will spare the whole **place** for their sake."

Ge 18:33 speaking with Abraham, he left, and Abraham returned **home**.
19:12 in the city who belongs to you? Get them out of **here**[s] [+2021],
19:13 because we are going to destroy this **place**. The outcry to the
19:14 He said, "Hurry and get out of this **place**, because the LORD is
19:27 and returned to the **place** where he had stood before the LORD.
20:11 "I said to myself, 'There is surely no fear of God in this **place**,
20:13 **Everywhere** [+2021+3972] we go, say of me, "He is my brother."
21:31 So that **place** was called Beersheba, because the two men swore an
22: 3 the burnt offering, he set out for the **place** God had told him about.
22: 4 the third day Abraham looked up and saw the **place** in the distance.
22: 9 When they reached the **place** God had told him about, Abraham
22:14 So Abraham called that **place** The LORD Will Provide. And to
24:23 is there **room** in your father's house for us to spend the night?"
24:25 of straw and fodder, as well as **room** for you to spend the night."
24:31 out here? I have prepared the house and a **place** for the camels."
26: 7 When the men of that **place** asked him about his wife, he said,
26: 7 "The men of this **place** might kill me on account of Rebekah,
28:11 When he reached a certain **place**, he stopped for the night
28:11 Taking one of the stones **there**[s], he put it under his head and lay
28:11 he put it under his head and lay down to sleep. **[RPH]**
28:16 he thought, "Surely the LORD is in this **place**, and I was not
28:17 He was afraid and said, "How awesome is this **place**! This is none
28:19 He called that **place** Bethel, though the city used to be called Luz.
29: 3 they would return the stone to its **place** over the mouth of the well.
29:22 So Laban brought together all the people of the **place** and gave a
29:26 "It is not our custom **here**[s] [+928] to give the younger daughter in
30:25 me on my way so I can go back to my own **homeland** [+824].
31:55 [32:1] and blessed them. Then he left and returned **home**.
32: 2 [32:3] is the camp of God!" So he named that **place** Mahanaim.
32:30 [32:31] So Jacob called the **place** Peniel, saying, "It is because I
33:17 shelters for his livestock. That is why the **place** is called Succoth.
35: 7 There he built an altar, and he called the **place** El Bethel, because it
35:13 God went up from him at the **place** where he had talked with him.
35:14 Jacob set up a stone pillar at the **place** where God had talked with
35:15 Jacob called the **place** where God had talked with him Bethel.
36:40 from Esau, by name, according to their clans and **regions**:
38:21 He asked the men who lived **there**[s] [+2023], "Where is the shrine
38:22 Besides, the men who lived **there**[s] said, 'There hasn't been any
39:20 him in prison, the **place** where the king's prisoners were confined.
40: 3 the guard, in the same prison **[NIE]** where Joseph was confined.
Ex 3: 5 your sandals, for the **place** where you are standing is holy ground."
3: 8 the **home** *of* the Canaanites, Hittites, Amorites, Perizzites,
16:29 stay where he is on the seventh day; no one is to go out." **[NIE]**
17: 7 he called the **place** Massah and Meribah because the Israelites
18:23 to stand the strain, and all these people will go **home** satisfied."
20:24 **Wherever** [+889+928+2021+3972] I cause my name to be
21:13 but God lets it happen, he is to flee to a **place** I will designate.
23:20 you along the way and to bring you to the **place** I have prepared.
29:31 the ram for the ordination and cook the meat in a sacred **place**.
33:21 "There is a **place** near me where you may stand on a rock.
Lev 1:16 and throw it to the east side of the altar, **where**[s] the ashes are.
4:12 he must take outside the camp to a **place** ceremonially clean,
4:24 slaughter it at the **place** where the burnt offering is slaughtered
4:29 the sin offering and slaughter it at the **place** *of* the burnt offering.
4:33 slaughter it for a sin offering at the **place** where the burnt offering
6:11 [6:4] carry the ashes outside the camp to a **place** that is
6:16 [6:9] rest of it, but it is to be eaten without yeast in a holy **place**;
6:25 [6:18] the LORD in the **place** the burnt offering is slaughtered;
6:26 [6:19] it is to be eaten in a holy **place**, in the courtyard of the Tent
6:27 [6:20] is spattered on a garment, you must wash it in a holy **place**.
7: 2 The guilt offering is to be slaughtered in the **place** where the burnt
7: 6 in a priest's family may eat it, but it must be eaten in a holy **place**;
10:13 Eat it in a holy **place**, because it is your share and your sons' share
10:14 Eat them in a ceremonially clean **place**; they have been given to
10:17 "Why didn't you eat the sin offering in the sanctuary **area**?
13:19 in the **place** where the boil was, a white swelling or reddish-white
14:13 He is to slaughter the lamb in the holy **place** where the sin offering
14:13 He is to slaughter the lamb in the holy place **[RPH]** where the sin
14:28 Some of the oil in his palm he is to put on the same **places** he put
14:40 be torn out and thrown into an unclean **place** outside the town.
14:41 the material that is scraped off dumped into an unclean **place**
14:45 and all the plaster—and taken out of the town to an unclean **place**.
16:24 He shall bathe himself with water in a holy **place** and put on his
24: 9 It belongs to Aaron and his sons, who are to eat it in a holy **place**,
Nu 9:17 **wherever** [+889+928] the cloud settled, the Israelites encamped.
10:29 "We are setting out for the **place** about which the LORD said,
11: 3 So that **place** was called Taberah, because fire from the LORD
11:34 Therefore the **place** was named Kibroth Hattaavah, because there
13:24 That **place** was called the Valley of Eshcol because of the cluster
14:40 they said. "We will go up to the **place** the LORD promised."
18:31 and your households may eat the rest of it **anywhere** [+928+3972],
19: 9 and put them in a ceremonially clean **place** outside the camp.
20: 5 Why did you bring us up out of Egypt to this terrible **place**?
20: 5 **It**[s] has no grain or figs, grapevines or pomegranates. And there is
21: 3 destroyed them and their towns; so the **place** was named Hormah.
22:26 and stood in a narrow **place** where there was no room to turn,
23:13 "Come with me to another **place** where you can see them;
23:27 Balak said to Balaam, "Come, let me take you to another **place**.
24:11 Now leave at once and go **home**! I said I would reward you
24:25 Balaam got up and returned **home** and Balak went his own way.
32: 1 the lands of Jazer and Gilead **[RPH]** were suitable for livestock.
32: 1 saw that the lands of Jazer and Gilead were **suitable** *for* livestock.
32:17 ahead of the Israelites until we have brought them to their **place**.
Dt 1:31 carries his son, all the way you went until you reached this **place**."
1:33 to search out **places** for you to camp and to show you the way you
9: 7 the day you left Egypt until you arrived **here**[s] [+2021+2021+2296],
11: 5 what he did for you in the desert until you arrived at this **place**,
11:24 Every **place** where you set your foot will be yours: Your territory
12: 2 Destroy completely all the **places** on the high mountains and on the
12: 3 the idols of their gods and wipe out their names from those **places**.
12: 5 you are to seek the **place** the LORD your God will choose from
12:11 to the **place** the LORD your God will choose as a dwelling for his
12:13 sacrifice your burnt offerings **anywhere** [+928+3972] you please.
12:14 Offer them only at the **place** the LORD will choose in one of your
12:18 LORD your God at the **place** the LORD your God will choose—
12:21 If the **place** where the LORD your God chooses to put his Name
12:26 have vowed to give, and go to the **place** the LORD will choose.
14:23 flocks in the presence of the LORD your God at the **place** he will
14:24 (because the **place** where the LORD will choose to put his Name
14:25 with you and go to the **place** the LORD your God will choose.
15:20 the presence of the LORD your God at the **place** he will choose.
16: 2 or herd at the **place** the LORD will choose as a dwelling for his
16: 6 except in the **place** he will choose as a dwelling for his Name.
16: 7 Roast it and eat it at the **place** the LORD your God will choose.
16:11 rejoice before the LORD your God at the **place** he will choose as
16:15 to the LORD your God at the **place** the LORD will choose.
16:16 appear before the LORD your God at the **place** he will choose:
17: 8 take them to the **place** the LORD your God will choose.
17:10 You must act according to the decisions they give you at the **place**
18: 6 and comes in all earnestness to the **place** the LORD will choose,
21:19 and bring him to the elders at the gate of his town. **[NIE]**
23:16 [23:17] Let him live among you **wherever** [+889+928+2021] he
26: 2 go to the **place** the LORD your God will choose as a dwelling for
26: 9 He brought us to this **place** and gave us this land, a land flowing
29: 7 [29:6] When you reached this **place**, Sihon king of Heshbon
31:11 to appear before the LORD your God at the **place** he will choose,
Jos 1: 3 I will give you every **place** where you set your foot, as I promised
3: 3 carrying it, you are to move out from your **positions** and follow it.
4:18 the dry ground than the waters of the Jordan returned to their **place**
5: 9 Egypt from you." So the **place** has been called Gilgal to this day.
5:15 off your sandals, for the **place** where you are standing is holy."
7:26 Therefore that **place** has been called the Valley of Achor ever
8:19 the men in the ambush rose quickly from their **position** and rushed
9:27 for the altar of the LORD at the **place** the LORD would choose.
20: 4 to admit him into their city and give him a **place** to live with them.
Jdg 2: 5 they called that **place** Bokim. There they offered sacrifices to the
7: 7 into your hands. Let all the other men go, each to his own **place**."
9:55 the Israelites saw that Abimelech was dead, they went **home**.
11:19 said to him, 'Let us pass through your country to our own **place**.'
15:17 he threw away the jawbone; and the **place** was called Ramath Lehi.
18:10 God has put into your hands, a **land** that lacks nothing whatever."
18:12 This is why the **place** west of Kiriath Jearim is called Mahaneh
19:13 or Ramah and spend the night in one of those **places**."
19:16 who was living in Gibeah (the men of the **place** were Benjamites),
19:28 Then the man put her on his donkey and set out for **home**.
20:22 again took up their positions **where**[s] [+928+2021] they had
20:33 All the men of Israel moved from their **places** and took up
20:33 the Israelite ambush charged out of its **place** on the west of Gibeah.
20:36 Now the men of Israel had given **way** before Benjamin,
Ru 1: 7 With her two daughters-in-law she left the **place** where she had
3: 4 When he lies down, note the **place** where he is lying. Then go
4:10 from among his family or from the **town records** [+9133].
1Sa 2:20 prayed for and gave to the LORD." Then they would go **home**.
3: 2 weak that he could barely see, was lying down in his usual **place**.
3: 9 servant is listening.' " So Samuel went and lay down in his **place**.
5: 3 of the LORD! They took Dagon and put him back in his **place**.
5:11 let it go back to its own **place**, or it will kill us and our people."
6: 2 of the LORD? Tell us how we should send it back to its **place**."
7:16 from Bethel to Gilgal to Mizpah, judging Israel in all those **places**.
9:22 **seated** [+4200+5989] them at the head of those who were invited—
12: 8 your forefathers out of Egypt and settled them in this **place**.
14:46 pursuing the Philistines, and they withdrew to their own **land**.
20:19 go to the **place** where you hid when this trouble began,
20:25 and Abner sat next to Saul, but David's **place** was empty.
20:27 the second day of the month, David's **place** was empty again.
20:37 When the boy came to the **place** where Jonathan's arrow had
21: 2 [21:3] for my men, I have told them to meet me at a certain **place**.
23:22 Find out **where**[s] David usually goes and who has seen him there.

1Sa 23:28 That is why they call this **place** Sela Hammahlekoth.
26: 5 Then David set out and went to the **place** where Saul had camped.
26: 5 He saw **where**[s] [+2021] Saul and Abner son of Ner,
26:13 the hill some distance away; there was a wide **space** between them.
26:25 So David went on his way, and Saul returned **home**.
27: 5 let a **place** be assigned to me in one of the country towns,
29: 4 the man back, that he may return to the **place** you assigned him.
30:31 to those in all the *other* **places** where David and his men had
2Sa 2:16 So that **place** in Gibeon was called Helkath Hazzurim.
2:23 every man stopped when he came to the **place** where Asahel had
5:20 my enemies before me." So that **place** was called Baal Perazim.
6: 8 out against Uzzah, and to this day that **place** is called Perez Uzzah.
6:17 and set it in its **place** inside the tent that David had pitched for it,
7:10 And I will provide a **place** for my people Israel and will plant them
11:16 he put Uriah at a **place** where he knew the strongest defenders
15:19 King Absalom. You are a foreigner, an exile from your **homeland**.
15:21 **wherever** [+889+928] my lord the king may be, whether it means
17: 9 Even now, he is hidden in a cave or some other **place**. If he should
17:12 we will attack him **wherever** [+285+889+928+2021] he may be
19:39 [19:40] gave him his blessing, and Barzillai returned to his **home**.
1Ki 4:28 [5:8] They also brought to the **proper place** [+889+2118+9004]
5: 9 [5:23] I will float them in rafts by sea to the **place** you specify.
8: 6 brought the ark of the LORD's covenant to its **place** in the inner
8: 7 The cherubim spread their wings over the **place** *of* the ark
8:21 I have provided a **place** there for the ark, in which is the covenant
8:29 toward this temple night and day, this **place** of which you said,
8:29 that you will hear the prayer your servant prays toward this **place**.
8:30 and of your people Israel when they pray toward this **place**.
8:30 Hear from heaven, your dwelling **place**, and when you hear,
8:35 and when they pray toward this **place** and confess your name
10:19 On both sides of the **seat** [+8699] were armrests, with a lion
13: 8 would I eat bread or drink water **here**[s] [+928+2021+2021+2296].
13:16 with you, nor can I eat bread or drink water with you in this **place**.
13:22 and drank water in the **place** where he told you not to eat or drink.
20:24 Remove all the kings from their **commands** and replace them with
21:19 In the **place** where dogs licked up Naboth's blood, dogs will lick
2Ki 5:11 his God, wave his hand over the **spot** and cure me of my leprosy.
6: 1 "Look, the **place** where we meet with you is too small for us.
6: 2 of us can get a pole; and let us build a **place** there for us to live."
6: 6 When he showed him the **place**, Elisha cut a stick and threw it
6: 8 he said, "I will set up my camp in such and such a **place**."
6: 9 "Beware of passing that **place**, because the Arameans are going
6:10 So the king of Israel checked on the **place** indicated by the man of
18:25 to attack and destroy this **place** without word from the LORD?
22:16 I am going to bring disaster on this **place** and its people,
22:17 my anger will burn against this **place** and will not be quenched.'
22:19 the LORD when you heard what I have spoken against this **place**
22:20 to bring on this **place**.' " So they took her answer back to the king.
23:14 down the Asherah poles and covered the **sites** with human bones.
1Ch 13:11 out against Uzzah, and to this day that **place** is called Perez Uzzah.
14:11 my enemies by my hand." So that **place** was called Baal Perazim.
15: 1 he prepared a **place** for the ark of God and pitched a tent for it.
15: 3 bring up the ark of the LORD to the **place** he had prepared for it.
16:27 and majesty are before him; strength and joy in his **dwelling place**.
17: 9 And I will provide a **place** for my people Israel and will plant them
21:22 "Let me have the **site** *of* your threshing floor so I can build an altar
21:25 So David paid Araunah six hundred shekels of gold for the **site**.
2Ch 3: 1 floor of Araunah the Jebusite, the **place** provided by David.
5: 7 brought the ark of the LORD's covenant to its **place** in the inner
5: 8 The cherubim spread their wings over the **place** *of* the ark
6:20 this **place** of which you said you would put your Name there.
6:20 May you hear the prayer your servant prays toward this **place**.
6:21 and of your people Israel when they pray toward this **place**.
6:21 Hear from heaven, your dwelling **place**; and when you hear,
6:26 and when they pray toward this **place** and confess your name
6:40 and your ears attentive to the prayers offered in this **place**.
7:12 and have chosen this **place** for myself as a temple for sacrifices.
7:15 be open and my ears attentive to the prayers offered in this **place**.
9:18 On both sides of the **seat** [+8699] were armrests, with a lion
20:26 This is why **it**[s] [+2021+2021+2085] is called the Valley of
24:11 would come and empty the chest and carry it back to its **place**.
25:10 troops who had come to him from Ephraim and sent them **home**.
25:10 They were furious with Judah and left for **home** in a great rage.
33:19 and the **sites** where he built high places and set up Asherah poles
34:24 I am going to bring disaster on this **place** and its people—
34:25 my anger will be poured out on this **place** and will not be
34:27 before God when you heard what he spoke against this **place**
34:28 eyes will not see all the disaster I am going to bring on this **place**
Ezr 1: 4 the people **[RPH]** of any place where survivors may now be
1: 4 the people of any **place** where survivors may now be living are to
8:17 **[NIE]** I told them what to say to Iddo and his kinsmen, the temple
8:17 **[NIE]** so that they might bring attendants to us for the house of
9: 8 us a remnant and giving us a firm place in his **sanctuary** [+7731],
Ne 1: 9 bring them to the **place** I have chosen as a dwelling for my Name.'
2:14 but there was not enough **room** for my mount to get through;
4:12 [4:6] "**Wherever** [+2021+3972+4946] you turn, they will attack
4:13 [4:7] behind the lowest **points** of the wall at the exposed places,
4:20 [4:14] **Wherever** [+889+928] you hear the sound of the trumpet,
12:27 the Levites were sought out from **where** they **lived** and were
Est 4: 3 In every province **[NIE]** to which the edict and order of the king
4:14 and deliverance for the Jews will arise from another **place**,
8:17 **wherever**[s] [+889] the edict of the king went, there was joy
Job 2:11 they set out from their **homes** and met together by agreement to go
6:17 flow in the dry season, and in the heat vanish from their **channels**.
7:10 never come to his house again; his **place** will know him no more.
8:18 But when it is torn from its **spot**, that place disowns it and says,
9: 6 He shakes the earth from its **place** and makes its pillars tremble.
14:18 and crumbles and as a rock is moved from its **place**,
16:18 do not cover my blood; may my cry never be laid to **rest**!
18: 4 for your sake? Or must the rocks be moved from their **place**?
18:21 of an evil man; such is the **place** *of* one who knows not God."
20: 9 him will not see him again; his **place** will look on him no more.
27:21 carries him off, and he is gone; it sweeps him out of his **place**.
27:23 It claps its hands in derision and hisses him out of his **place**.
28: 1 "There is a mine for silver and a **place** where gold is refined.
28: 6 **[NIE]** sapphires come from its rocks, and its dust contains
28:12 where can wisdom be found? Where does understanding **dwell**?
28:20 then does wisdom come from? Where does understanding **dwell**?
28:23 God understands the way to it and he alone knows **where** it **dwells**,
34:26 He punishes them for their wickedness **where**[s] [+928] everyone
37: 1 "At this my heart pounds and leaps from its **place**.
38:12 you ever given orders to the morning, or shown the dawn its **place**,
38:19 is the way to the abode of light? And where does darkness **reside**?
Ps 24: 3 ascend the hill of the LORD? Who may stand in his holy **place**?
26: 8 where you live, O LORD, the **place** where your glory dwells.
37:10 no more; though you look for **[NIE]** them, they will not be found.
44:19 [44:20] you crushed us and made us a **haunt** *for* jackals
103:16 blows over it and it is gone, and its **place** remembers it no more.
103:22 the LORD, all his works **everywhere** [+3972] in his dominion.
104: 8 went down into the valleys, to the **place** you assigned for them.
132: 5 till I find a **place** for the LORD, a dwelling for the Mighty One of
Pr 15: 3 The eyes of the LORD are **everywhere** [+928+3972], keeping
25: 6 in the king's presence, and do not claim a **place** among great men;
27: 8 a bird that strays from its nest is a man who strays from his **home**.
Ecc 1: 5 The sun rises and the sun sets, and hurries back to **where**[s] it rises.
1: 7 To the **place** the streams come from, there they return again.
3:16 In the **place** *of* judgment—wickedness was there, in the place of
3:16 wickedness was there, in the **place** *of* justice—wickedness was
3:20 All go to the same **place**; all come from dust, and to dust all return.
6: 6 but fails to enjoy his prosperity. Do not all go to the same **place**?
8:10 those who used to come and go from the holy **place** and receive
10: 4 If a ruler's anger rises against you, do not leave your **post**;
11: 3 a tree falls to the south or to the north, in the **place** where it falls,
Isa 5: 8 join field to field till no **space** is left and you live alone in the land.
7:23 in every **place** where there were a thousand vines worth a thousand
13:13 the earth will shake from its **place** at the wrath of the LORD
14: 2 Nations will take them and bring them to their own **place**.
18: 7 to Mount Zion, the **place** *of* the Name of the LORD Almighty.
22:23 I will drive him like a peg into a firm **place**; he will be a seat of
22:25 "the peg driven into the firm **place** will give way;
26:21 the LORD is coming out of his **dwelling** to punish the people of
28: 8 tables are covered with vomit and there is not a **spot** without filth.
33:21 It will be like a **place** *of* broad rivers and streams. No galley with
45:19 I have not spoken in secret, from **somewhere** *in* a land of darkness;
46: 7 it up in its place, and there it stands. From that **spot** it cannot move.
49:20 will yet say in your hearing, 'This **place** is too small for us;
54: 2 "Enlarge the **place** *of* your tent, stretch your tent curtains wide,
60:13 and the cypress together, to adorn the **place** *of* my sanctuary;
60:13 the place of my sanctuary; and I will glorify the **place** *of* my feet.
66: 1 the house you will build for me? Where will my resting **place** be?
Jer 4: 7 of nations has set out. He has left his **place** to lay waste your land.
7: 3 your ways and your actions, and I will let you live in this **place**.
7: 6 or the widow and do not shed innocent blood in this **place**,
7: 7 I will let you live in this **place**, in the land I gave your forefathers
7:12 " 'Go now to the **place** in Shiloh where I first made a dwelling for
7:14 the temple you trust in, the **place** I gave to you and your fathers.
7:20 My anger and my wrath will be poured out on this **place**, on man
7:32 for they will bury the dead in Topheth until there is no more **room**.
8: 3 **Wherever** [+928+2021+3972] I banish them, all the survivors of
13: 7 dug up the belt and took it from the **place** where I had hidden it,
14:13 suffer famine. Indeed, I will give you lasting peace in this **place**.' "
16: 2 "You must not marry and have sons or daughters in this **place**."
16: 3 daughters born in this **land** and about the women who are their
16: 9 and to the voices of bride and bridegroom in this **place**.
17:12 exalted from the beginning, is the **place** *of* our sanctuary.
19: 3 I am going to bring a disaster on this **place** that will make the ears
19: 4 For they have forsaken me and made this a **place** of foreign gods;
19: 4 and they have filled this **place** with the blood of the innocent.

Jer 19: 6 when people will no longer call this **place** Topheth or the Valley of
19: 7 " 'In this **place** I will ruin the plans of Judah and Jerusalem.
19: 11 They will bury the dead in Topheth until there is no more **room**.
19: 12 This is what I will do to this **place** and to those who live here,
19: 13 and those of the kings of Judah will be defiled like this **place**,
22: 3 or the widow, and do not shed innocent blood in this **place**.
22: 11 succeeded his father as king of Judah but has gone from this **place**:
22: 12 He will die in the **place** where they have led him captive; he will
24: 5 whom I sent away from this **place** to the land of the Babylonians.
24: 9 and cursing, **wherever** [+889+928+2021+3972] I banish them.
27: 22 'Then I will bring them back and restore them to this **place**.' "
28: 3 Within two years I will bring back to this **place** all the articles of
28: 3 king of Babylon removed from **here**[s] [+2021+2021+2296]
28: 4 I will also bring back to this **place** Jehoiachin son of Jehoiakim
28: 6 LORD's house and all the exiles back to this **place** from Babylon.
29: 10 and fulfill my gracious promise to bring you back to this **place**.
29: 14 you from all the nations and **places** where I have banished you,"
29: 14 "and will bring you back to the **place** from which I carried you into
32: 37 I will bring them back to this **place** and let them live in safety.
33: 10 'You say about this **place**, "It is a desolate waste, without men
33: 12 'In this **place**, desolate and without men or animals—in all its
40: 2 "The LORD your God decreed this disaster for this **place**.
40: 12 at Mizpah, from all the **countries** where they had been scattered.
42: 18 of condemnation and reproach; you will never see this **place** again.'
42: 22 famine and plague in the **place** where you want to go to settle."
44: 29 " 'This will be the sign to you that I will punish you in this **place**,'
45: 5 but **wherever** [+889+2021+3972+6584] you go I will let you
51: 62 Then say, 'O LORD, you have said you will destroy this **place**,
Eze 3: 12 May the glory of the LORD be praised in his **dwelling place**!—
6: 13 **places** where they offered fragrant incense to all their idols.
10: 11 The cherubim went in whatever **direction** the head faced,
12: 3 they watch, set out and go from **where**[s] you are to another place.
12: 3 as they watch, set out and go from where you are to another **place**.
17: 16 in the **land** *of* the king who put him on the throne, whose oath he
21: 30 [21:35] In the **place** where you were created, in the land of your
34: 12 I will rescue them from all the **places** where they were scattered on
38: 15 You will come from your **place** in the far north, you and many
39: 11 " 'On that day I will give Gog a burial **place** in Israel, in the valley
41: 11 the **base** *adjoining* the open area was five cubits wide all around.
42: 13 the sin offerings and the guilt offerings—for the **place** is holy.
43: 7 this is the **place** *of* my throne and the place for the soles of my feet.
43: 7 is the place of my throne and the **place** *for* the soles of my feet.
45: 4 It will be a **place** for their houses as well as a holy place for the
46: 19 belonged to the priests, and showed me a **place** at the western end.
46: 20 "This is the **place** where the priests will cook the guilt offering
Hos 1: 10 [2:1] In the **place** where it was said to them, 'You are not my
5: 15 Then I will go back to my **place** until they admit their guilt.
Joel 3: 7 [4:7] I am going to rouse them out of the **places** to which you sold
Am 4: 6 you empty stomachs in every city and lack of bread in every **town**,
8: 3 Many, many bodies—flung **everywhere** [+3972]! Silence!"
Mic 1: 3 The LORD is coming from his **dwelling place**; he comes down
Na 1: 8 overwhelming flood he will make an end of ⌞**Nineveh**[s] [+2023]⌟;
3: 17 the sun appears they fly away, and no one knows **where** [+361].
Zep 1: 4 I will cut off from this **place** every remnant of Baal, the names of
2: 11 on every shore will worship him, every one in its own **land**.
Hag 2: 9 'And in this **place** I will grant peace,' declares the LORD
Zec 14: 10 from the Benjamin Gate to the **site** *of* the First Gate, to the Corner
Mal 1: 11 In every **place** incense and pure offerings will be brought to my

5227 מָקוֹר ***māqôr***, n.m. [18] [√ 7769]

fountain [9], spring [3], assembly [1], flow [1], it[s] [1], source of [1], springs [1], well [1]

Lev 12: 7 then she will be ceremonially clean from her **flow** *of* blood.
20: 18 he has exposed the **source of** her flow, and she has also uncovered
20: 18 has exposed the source of her flow, and she has also uncovered **it**[s].
Ps 36: 9 [36:10] For with you is the **fountain** *of* life; in your light we see
68: 26 [68:27] praise the LORD in the **assembly** *of* Israel.
Pr 5: 18 May your **fountain** be blessed, and may you rejoice in the wife of
10: 11 The mouth of the righteous is a **fountain** *of* life, but violence
13: 14 The teaching of the wise is a **fountain** *of* life, turning a man from
14: 27 The fear of the LORD is a **fountain** *of* life, turning a man from
16: 22 Understanding is a **fountain** *of* life to those who have it, but folly
18: 4 are deep waters, but the **fountain** *of* wisdom is a bubbling brook.
25: 26 or a polluted **well** is a righteous man who gives way to the wicked.
Jer 2: 13 They have forsaken me, the **spring** *of* living water, and have dug
9: 1 [8:23] were a spring of water and my eyes a **fountain** *of* tears!
17: 13 because they have forsaken the LORD, the **spring** *of* living water.
51: 36 and avenge you; I will dry up her sea and make her **springs** dry.
Hos 13: 15 blowing in from the desert; his **spring** will fail and his well dry up.
Zec 13: 1 "On that day a **fountain** will be opened to the house of David

5228 מִקָּח ***miqqāḥ***, n.[m.]. [1] [√ 4374]

bribery [+8816] [1]

2Ch 19: 7 our God there is no injustice or partiality or **bribery** [+8816]."

5229 מַקָּחוֹת ***maqqāḥôt***, n.f. [1] [√ 4374]

merchandise [1]

Ne 10: 31 [10:32] "When the neighboring peoples bring **merchandise**

5230 מִקְטָר ***miqṭār***, n.m. [1] [√ 7787]

burning [1]

Ex 30: 1 "Make an altar of acacia wood for **burning** incense.

5231 מֻקְטָר ***muqṭār***, n.m. [1] [√ 7787]

incense [1]

Mal 1: 11 In every place **incense** and pure offerings will be brought to my

5232 מְקַטֶּרֶת ***m^{e}qaṭṭeret***, n.f. [1] [√ 7787]

incense altars [1]

2Ch 30: 14 the altars in Jerusalem and cleared away the **incense altars**

5233 מִקְטֶרֶת ***miqṭeret***, n.f. [2] [√ 7787]

censer [2]

2Ch 26: 19 Uzziah, who had a **censer** in his hand ready to burn incense,
Eze 8: 11 Each had a **censer** in his hand, and a fragrant cloud of incense was

5234 מַקֵּל ***maqqēl***, n.m. & f. [18]

staff [7], branches [6], branch [1], staffs [1], stick of wood [1], sticks [1], war clubs [+3338] [1]

Ge 30: 37 took fresh-cut **branches** *from* poplar, almond and plane trees
30: 37 the bark and exposing the white inner wood of the **branches**.
30: 38 Then he placed the peeled **branches** in all the watering troughs,
30: 39 they mated in front of the **branches**. And they bore young that
30: 41 Jacob would place the **branches** in the troughs in front of the
30: 41 in front of the animals so they would mate near the **branches**,
32: 10 [32:11] I had only my **staff** when I crossed this Jordan, but now I
Ex 12: 11 your belt, your sandals on your feet and your **staff** in your hand.
Nu 22: 27 down under Balaam, and he was angry and beat her with his **staff**.
1Sa 17: 40 he took his **staff** in his hand, chose five smooth stones from the
17: 43 He said to David, "Am I a dog, that you come at me with **sticks**?"
Jer 1: 11 Jeremiah?" "I see the **branch** *of* an almond tree," I replied.
48: 17 'How broken is the mighty scepter, how broken the glorious **staff**!'
Eze 39: 9 the bows and arrows, the **war clubs** [+3338] and spears.
Hos 4: 12 They consult a wooden idol and are answered by a **stick of wood**.
Zec 11: 7 Then I took two **staffs** and called one Favor and the other Union,
11: 10 I took my **staff** called Favor and broke it, revoking the covenant I
11: 14 I broke my second **staff** called Union, breaking the brotherhood

5235 מִקְלוֹת ***miqlôt***, n.pr.m. [4]

Mikloth [4]

1Ch 8: 32 **Mikloth**, who was the father of Shimeah. They too lived near their
9: 37 Gedor, Ahio, Zechariah and **Mikloth**.
9: 38 **Mikloth** was the father of Shimeam. They too lived near their
27: 4 was Dodai the Ahohite; **Mikloth** was the leader of his division.

5236 מִקְלָט ***miqlāṭ***, n.[m.]. [20] [√ 7832]

refuge [17], *untranslated* [1], place of refuge [1], protection [1]

Nu 35: 6 "Six of the towns you give the Levites will be cities of **refuge**.
35: 11 select some towns to be your cities of **refuge**, to which a person
35: 12 They will be places of **refuge** from the avenger, so that a person
35: 13 These six towns you give will be your cities of **refuge**.
35: 14 on this side of the Jordan and three in Canaan as cities of **refuge**.
35: 15 These six towns will be a **place of refuge** for Israelites, aliens
35: 25 of blood and send him back to the city *of* **refuge** to which he fled.
35: 26 goes outside the limits of the city of **refuge** to which he has fled
35: 27 **[RPH]** the avenger of blood may kill the accused without being
35: 28 The accused must stay in his city of **refuge** until the death of the
35: 32 not accept a ransom for anyone who has fled to a city of **refuge**
Jos 20: 2 "Tell the Israelites to designate the cities of **refuge**, as I instructed
20: 3 may flee there and find **protection** from the avenger of blood.
21: 13 they gave Hebron (a city of **refuge** *for* one accused of murder),
21: 21 were given Shechem (a city of **refuge** *for* one accused of murder)
21: 27 Golan in Bashan (a city of **refuge** *for* one accused of murder)
21: 32 Kedesh in Galilee (a city of **refuge** *for* one accused of murder),
21: 38 Ramoth in Gilead (a city of **refuge** *for* one accused of murder),
1Ch 6: 57 [6:42] of Aaron were given Hebron (a city of **refuge**),
6: 67 [6:52] of Ephraim they were given Shechem (a city of **refuge**),

5237 מִקְלַעַת *miqlaʿat*, n.f. [4] [√ 7844]

carved [+7844] [1], carved [+906+7844] [1], carved [1], engraving [1]

1Ki 6: 18 of the temple was cedar, **carved** *with* gourds and open flowers.
6: 29 *he* **carved** [+906+7844] cherubim, palm trees and open flowers.
6: 32 And on the two olive wood doors *he* **carved** [+7844] cherubim,
7: 31 a cubit and a half. Around its opening there was **engraving**.

5238 מִקְנֶה *miqneh*, n.m. [76] [→ 5240; cf. 7864]

livestock [45], cattle [4], flocks [4], herdsmen [+8286] [2], *untranslated* [1], acquired [1], animal [1], animals [1], bought [1], cattle [+1330] [1], droves of livestock [1], flocks [+7366] [1], flocks and herds [1], herds [+1330] [1], herds and flocks [1], herds of livestock [1], herds [1], herdsmen [1], livestock [+989] [1], owned [+2118] [1], owned [+2118+4200] [1], sheep and goats [+7366] [1], tend livestock [+408+2118] [1], tended livestock [+408+2118] [1], that[s] [1]

Ge 4: 20 he was the father of those who live in tents and raise **livestock**.
13: 2 Abram had become very wealthy in **livestock** and in silver
13: 7 And quarreling arose between Abram's **herdsmen** [+8286]
13: 7 between Abram's herdsmen and the **herdsmen of** [+8286] Lot.
26: 14 He had so many **flocks** [+7366] and herds and servants that the
26: 14 He had so many flocks and **herds** [+1330] and servants that the
29: 7 "the sun is still high; it is not time for the **flocks** to be gathered.
30: 29 worked for you and how your **livestock** has fared under my care.
31: 9 So God has taken away your father's **livestock** and has given them
31: 18 he drove all his **livestock** ahead of him, along with all the goods he
31: 18 along with all the goods **[RPH]** he had accumulated in Paddan
33: 17 he built a place for himself and made shelters for his **livestock**.
34: 5 had been defiled, his sons were in the fields with his **livestock**;
34: 23 Won't their **livestock**, their property and all their other animals
36: 6 as well as his **livestock** and all his other animals and all the goods
36: 7 staying could not support them both because of their **livestock**.
46: 6 They also took with them their **livestock** and the possessions they
46: 32 The men are shepherds; *they* **tend livestock** [+408+2118],
46: 34 'Your servants *have* **tended livestock** [+408+2118] from our
47: 6 with special ability, put them in charge of my own **livestock**."
47: 16 "Then bring your **livestock**," said Joseph. "I will sell you food in
47: 16 "I will sell you food in exchange for your **livestock**, since your
47: 17 So they brought their **livestock** to Joseph, and he gave them food
47: 17 their **sheep and goats** [+7366], their cattle and donkeys.
47: 17 their sheep and goats, their **cattle** [+1330] and donkeys.
47: 17 through that year with food in exchange for all their **livestock**.
47: 18 since our money is gone and our **livestock** [+989] belongs to you,
49: 32 The field and the cave in it were **bought** from the Hittites."
Ex 9: 3 LORD will bring a terrible plague on your **livestock** in the field—
9: 4 the LORD will make a distinction between the **livestock** *of* Israel
9: 4 a distinction between the livestock of Israel and **that**[s] *of* Egypt,
9: 6 All the **livestock** *of* the Egyptians died, but not one animal
9: 6 Egyptians died, but not one **animal** belonging to the Israelites died.
9: 7 found that not even one of the **animals** *of* the Israelites had died.
9: 19 Give an order now to bring your **livestock** and everything you have
9: 20 the LORD hurried to bring their slaves and their **livestock** inside.
9: 21 the word of the LORD left their slaves and **livestock** in the field.
10: 26 Our **livestock** too must go with us; not a hoof is to be left behind.
12: 38 as well as large **droves of livestock**, both flocks and herds.
17: 3 of Egypt to make us and our children and **livestock** die of thirst?"
34: 19 including all the firstborn males of your **livestock**, whether from
Nu 20: 19 if we or our **livestock** drink any of your water, we will pay for it.
31: 9 and took all the Midianite herds, **flocks** and goods as plunder.
32: 1 The Reubenites and Gadites, who had very large **herds and flocks**,
32: 1 saw that the lands of Jazer and Gilead were suitable for **livestock**.
32: 4 are suitable for **livestock**, and your servants have livestock.
32: 4 are suitable for livestock, and your servants have **livestock**.
32: 16 "We would like to build pens here for our **livestock** and cities for
32: 26 our **flocks** and herds will remain here in the cities of Gilead.
Dt 3: 19 and your **livestock** (I know you have much livestock)
3: 19 and your livestock (I know you have much **livestock**)
Jos 1: 14 your **livestock** may stay in the land that Moses gave you east of the
14: 4 only towns to live in, with pasturelands for their **flocks** and herds.
22: 8 with large **herds of livestock**, with silver, gold, bronze and iron,
Jdg 6: 5 They came up with their **livestock** and their tents like swarms of
18: 21 their **livestock** and their possessions in front of them, they turned
1Sa 23: 5 to Keilah, fought the Philistines and carried off their **livestock**.
30: 20 and his men drove them ahead of the other **livestock**, saying,
2Ki 3: 17 with water, and you, your **cattle** and your other animals will drink.
1Ch 5: 9 Euphrates River, because their **livestock** had increased in Gilead.
5: 21 They seized the **livestock** *of* the Hagrites—fifty thousand camels,
7: 21 men of Gath, when they went down to seize their **livestock**.
28: 1 of all the property and **livestock** belonging to the king and his sons,
2Ch 14: 15 [14:14] They also attacked the camps of the **herdsmen**
26: 10 because he had much **livestock** in the foothills and in the plain.
32: 29 He built villages and **acquired** great numbers of flocks and herds,
Job 1: 3 he **owned** [+2118] seven thousand sheep, three thousand camels,
1: 10 so that his **flocks and herds** are spread throughout the land.
36: 33 the coming storm; even the **cattle** make known its approach.
Ps 78: 48 over their cattle to the hail, their **livestock** to bolts of lightning.
Ecc 2: 7 I also **owned** [+2118+4200] more herds and flocks than anyone in
Isa 30: 23 and plentiful. In that day your **cattle** will graze in broad meadows.
Jer 9: 10 [9:9] and untraveled, and the lowing of **cattle** is not heard.
49: 32 camels will become plunder, and their large **herds** will be booty.
Eze 38: 12 rich in **livestock** and goods, living at the center of the land."
38: 13 to take away **livestock** and goods and to seize much plunder?"'

5239 מִקְנָה *miqnâ*, n.f. [15] [√ 7864]

bought [4], purchase [3], *untranslated* [2], bought [+4084] [2], price [2], paid [1], property [1]

Ge 17: 12 born in your household or **bought** *with* money from a foreigner—
17: 13 Whether born in your household or **bought** *with* your money,
17: 23 and all those born in his household or **bought** *with* his money,
17: 27 those born in his household or **bought** [+4084] from a foreigner,
23: 18 to Abraham as his **property** in the presence of all the Hittites who
Ex 12: 44 Any slave you have **bought** [+4084] may eat of it after you have
Lev 25: 16 When the years are many, you are to increase the **price**, and when
25: 16 and when the years are few, you are to decrease the **price**,
25: 51 he must pay for his redemption a larger share of the price **paid** *for*
27: 22 " 'If a man dedicates to the LORD a field he has **bought**,
Jer 32: 11 I took the deed of **purchase**—the sealed copy containing the terms
32: 12 I gave this deed **[RPH]** to Baruch son of Neriah, the son of
32: 12 **[RPH]** and of all the Jews sitting in the courtyard of the guard.
32: 14 both the sealed and unsealed copies of the deed of **purchase**,
32: 16 "After I had given the deed of **purchase** to Baruch son of Neriah,

5240 מִקְנֵיָהוּ *miqnēyāhû*, n.pr.m. [2] [√ 5238 + 3378; cf. 7864]

Mikneiah [2]

1Ch 15: 18 Eliab, Benaiah, Maaseiah, Mattithiah, Eliphelehu, **Mikneiah**,
15: 21 Eliphelehu, **Mikneiah**, Obed-Edom, Jeiel and Azaziah were to

5241 מִקְסָם *miqsām*, n.[m.]. [2] [√ 7876]

divinations [2]

Eze 12: 24 false visions or flattering **divinations** among the people of Israel.
13: 7 not seen false visions and uttered lying **divinations** when you say,

5242 מָקַץ *māqaṣ*, n.pr.loc. [1]

Makaz [1]

1Ki 4: 9 in **Makaz**, Shaalbim, Beth Shemesh and Elon Bethhanan;

5243 מִקְצוֹעַ *miqṣôaʿ*, n.m. [12] [√ 7910]

corners [5], angle [4], in each corner [+928+928+5243] [2], angle of the wall [1]

Ex 26: 24 At these two **corners** they must be double from the bottom all the
36: 29 At these two **corners** the frames were double from the bottom all
2Ch 26: 9 at the Valley Gate and at the **angle of the wall**, and he fortified
Ne 3: 19 from a point facing the ascent to the armory as far as the **angle**.
3: 20 from the **angle** to the entrance of the house of Eliashib the high
3: 24 another section, from Azariah's house to the **angle** and the corner,
3: 25 Palal son of Uzai worked opposite the **angle** and the tower
Eze 41: 22 two cubits square; its **corners**, its base and its sides were of wood.
46: 21 me to the outer court and led me around to its four **corners**,
46: 21 corners, and I saw **in each corner** [+928+928+5243] another court.
46: 21 corners, and I saw **in each corner** [+928+928+5243] another court.
46: 22 In the four **corners** *of* the outer court were enclosed courts,

5244 מַקְצֻעָה *maqṣuʿâ*, n.[f.]. [1] [√ 7909]

chisels [1]

Isa 44: 13 he roughs it out with **chisels** and marks it with compasses.

5245 מָקַק *māqaq*, v. [10] [→ 5215]

waste away [4], rot [3], be dissolved [1], fester [1], wasting away [1]

Lev 26: 39 [C] Those of you who are left *will* **waste away** in the lands of
26: 39 [C] also because of their fathers' sins *they will* **waste away**.
Ps 38: 5 [38:6] [C] My wounds **fester** and are loathsome because of my
Isa 34: 4 [C] All the stars of the heavens *will* **be dissolved** and the sky
Eze 4: 17 [C] sight of each other and *will* **waste away** because of their sin.
24: 23 [C] You will not mourn or weep but *will* **waste away** because of
33: 10 [C] weigh us down, and we *are* **wasting away** because of them.
Zec 14: 12 [G] Their flesh *will* **rot** while they are still standing on their feet,
14: 12 [C] their eyes *will* **rot** in their sockets, and their tongues will rot
14: 12 [C] rot in their sockets, and their tongues *will* **rot** in their mouths.

5246 מִקְרָא *miqrā'*, n.m. [23] [√ 7924]

assembly [15], assemblies [3], another[s] [+7731] [1], assemble [1], calling together [1], convocations [+7924] [1], read [1]

Ex 12:16 On the first day hold a sacred **assembly**, and another one on the
12:16 a sacred assembly, and **another**[s] [+7731] *one* on the seventh day.
Lev 23: 2 of the LORD, which you are to proclaim as sacred **assemblies**.
23: 3 but the seventh day is a Sabbath of rest, a day of sacred **assembly**.
23: 4 the sacred **assemblies** you are to proclaim at their appointed times:
23: 7 On the first day hold a sacred **assembly** and do no regular work.
23: 8 on the seventh day hold a sacred **assembly** and do no regular
23:21 On that same day you are to proclaim a sacred **assembly** and do no
23:24 day of rest, a sacred **assembly** commemorated with trumpet blasts.
23:27 Hold a sacred **assembly** and deny yourselves, and present an
23:35 The first day is a sacred **assembly**; do no regular work.
23:36 on the eighth day hold a sacred **assembly** and present an offering
23:37 which you are to proclaim as sacred **assemblies** for bringing
Nu 10: 2 use them for **calling** the community **together** and for having the
28:18 On the first day hold a sacred **assembly** and do no regular work.
28:25 On the seventh day hold a sacred **assembly** and do no regular
28:26 Feast of Weeks, hold a sacred **assembly** and do no regular work.
29: 1 " 'On the first day of the seventh month hold a sacred **assembly**
29: 7 " 'On the tenth day of this seventh month hold a sacred **assembly**.
29:12 seventh month, hold a sacred **assembly** and do no regular work.
Ne 8: 8 so that the people could understand what was being **read**.
Isa 1:13 New Moons, Sabbaths and **convocations** [+7924]—I cannot bear
4: 5 and over *those who* **assemble** there a cloud of smoke by day

5247 מִקְרֶה *miqreh*, n.m. [10] [√ 7936]

fate [4], destiny [2], as it turned out [+7936] [1], by chance [1], something happened [1], that[s] [1]

Ru 2: 3 **As it turned out** [+7936], she found herself working in a field
1Sa 6: 9 not his hand that struck us and that it happened to us **by chance**."
20:26 "**Something** must have **happened** to David to make him
Ecc 2:14 but I came to realize that the same **fate** overtakes them both.
2:15 I thought in my heart, "The **fate** *of* the fool will overtake me also.
3:19 Man's **fate** is like that of the animals; the same fate awaits them
3:19 Man's fate is like **that**[s] *of* the animals; the same fate awaits them
3:19 fate is like that of the animals; the same **fate** awaits them both:
9: 2 All share a common **destiny**—the righteous and the wicked,
9: 3 The same **destiny** overtakes all. The hearts of men, moreover,

5248 מְקָרֶה *m[e]qāreh*, n.[m.]. [1] [√ 7939]

rafters [1]

Ecc 10:18 If a man is lazy, the **rafters** sag; if his hands are idle, the house

5249 מְקֵרָה *m[e]qērâ*, n.f. [2] [√ 7981]

house [1], summer palace [1]

Jdg 3:20 while he was sitting alone in the upper room of his **summer palace**
3:24 "He must be relieving himself in the inner room of the **house**."

5250 מִקְשֶׁה *miqšeh*, n.[m.]. [1] [→ 5251]

well-dressed hair [+5126] [1]

Isa 3:24 of a sash, a rope; instead of **well-dressed** [+5126] **hair**, baldness;

5251 ¹מִקְשָׁה *miqšâ*[1], n.f. [9] [√ 5250]

hammered [5], hammered out [2], *untranslated* [1], hammer out [+6913] [1]

Ex 25:18 make two cherubim out of **hammered** gold at the ends of the
25:31 "Make a lampstand of pure gold and **hammer** [+6913] it **out**,
25:36 be of one piece with the lampstand, **hammered** out of pure gold.
37: 7 he made two cherubim out of **hammered** gold at the ends of the
37:17 They made the lampstand of pure gold and **hammered** it **out**,
37:22 all of one piece with the lampstand, **hammered out** *of* pure gold.
Nu 8: 4 It was made of **hammered** gold—from its base to its blossoms.
8: 4 **[RPH]** The lampstand was made exactly like the pattern the
10: 2 "Make two trumpets of **hammered** silver, and use them for calling

5252 ²מִקְשָׁה *miqšâ*[2], n.f. [2] [→ 7991]

field of melons [1], melon patch [1]

Isa 1: 8 a vineyard, like a hut in a **field of melons**, like a city under siege.
Jer 10: 5 Like a scarecrow in a **melon patch**, their idols cannot speak;

5253 ¹מַר *mar*[1], a. & subst. [37 / 38] [→ 5287; cf. 5352]

bitter [16], bitterness [7], bitterly [4], anguish [3], bitter suffering [2], deadly [1], discontented [+5883] [1], fierce [+5883] [1], hot-tempered [+5883] [1], in anguish [+5883] [1], ruthless [1]

Ge 27:34 he burst out with a loud and **bitter** cry and said to his father,
Ex 15:23 to Marah, they could not drink its water because it was **bitter**.
Nu 5:18 while he himself holds the **bitter** water that brings a curse.
5:19 may this **bitter** water that brings a curse not harm you.
5:23 curses on a scroll and then wash them off into the **bitter** water.
5:24 He shall have the woman drink the **bitter** water that brings a curse,
5:24 a curse, and this water will enter her and cause **bitter suffering**.
5:27 that brings a curse, it will go into her and cause **bitter suffering**;
Jdg 18:25 or some **hot-tempered** [+5883] men will attack you, and you
1Sa 1:10 In **bitterness** *of* soul Hannah wept much and prayed to the
15:32 him confidently, thinking, "Surely the **bitterness** *of* death is past."
22: 2 or in debt or **discontented** [+5883] gathered around him,
2Sa 2:26 devour forever? Don't you realize that this will end in **bitterness**?
17: 8 and as **fierce** [+5883] as a wild bear robbed of her cubs.
2Ki 14:26 The LORD had seen how **bitterly** [BHS 5286] everyone in
Est 4: 1 and ashes, and went out into the city, wailing loudly and **bitterly**.
Job 3:20 is light given to those in misery, and life to the **bitter** *of* soul,
7:11 anguish of my spirit, I will complain in the **bitterness** *of* my soul.
10: 1 rein to my complaint and speak out in the **bitterness** *of* my soul.
21:25 Another man dies in **bitterness** of soul, never having enjoyed
Ps 64: 3 [64:4] like swords and aim their words like **deadly** arrows.
Pr 5: 4 but in the end she is **bitter** as gall, sharp as a double-edged sword.
27: 7 loathes honey, but to the hungry even *what* is **bitter** tastes sweet.
31: 6 who are perishing, wine to *those who* are **in anguish** [+5883];
Ecc 7:26 I find more **bitter** than death the woman who is a snare, whose
Isa 5:20 light for darkness, who put **bitter** for sweet and sweet for bitter.
5:20 light for darkness, who put bitter for sweet and sweet for **bitter**.
33: 7 men cry aloud in the streets; the envoys of peace weep **bitterly**.
38:15 will walk humbly all my years because of this **anguish** *of* my soul.
38:17 Surely it was for my benefit that I suffered *such* **anguish**.
Jer 2:19 and **bitter** it is for you when you forsake the LORD your God
Eze 3:14 me away, and I went *in* **bitterness** and in the anger of my spirit,
27:30 They will raise their voice and cry **bitterly** over you; they will
27:31 They will weep over you with **anguish** *of* soul and with bitter
27:31 will weep over you with anguish of soul and with **bitter** mourning.
Am 8:10 like mourning for an only son and the end of it like a **bitter** day.
Hab 1: 6 raising up the Babylonians, that **ruthless** and impetuous people,
Zep 1:14 The cry on the day of the LORD will be **bitter**, the shouting of

5254 ²מַר *mar*[2], n.[m.]. [1]

drop [1]

Isa 40:15 Surely the nations are like a **drop** in a bucket; they are regarded as

5255 מֹר *mōr*, n.m. [12] [√ 5352]

myrrh [12]

Ex 30:23 500 shekels of liquid **myrrh**, half as much (that is, 250 shekels)
Est 2:12 six months with oil of **myrrh** and six with perfumes
Ps 45: 8 [45:9] All your robes are fragrant with **myrrh** and aloes
Pr 7:17 I have perfumed my bed with **myrrh**, aloes and cinnamon.
SS 1:13 My lover is to me a sachet of **myrrh** resting between my breasts.
3: 6 perfumed with **myrrh** and incense made from all the spices of the
4: 6 I will go to the mountain of **myrrh** and to the hill of incense.
4:14 kind of incense tree, with **myrrh** and aloes and all the finest spices.
5: 1 my sister, my bride; I have gathered my **myrrh** with my spice.
5: 5 I arose to open for my lover, and my hands dripped with **myrrh**,
5: 5 my fingers with flowing **myrrh**, on the handles of the lock.
5:13 yielding perfume. His lips are like lilies dripping with **myrrh**.

5256 ¹מָרָא *mārā'*[1], v. Not used in NIV/BHS [cf. 5286]

5257 ²מָרָא *mārā'*[2], v. [1]

spreads feathers to run [+928+2021+5294] [1]

Job 39:18 [G] Yet when *she* **spreads** [+928+2021+5294] *her* **feathers to run**,

5258 ³מָרָא *mārā'*[3], n.[m.]. Not used in NIV/BHS [→ 1344, 1374, 4934?, 4935?, 5309, 5319?]

5259 ⁴מָרָא *mārā'*[4], n.pr.f. [1] [√ 5352]

Mara [1]

Ru 1:20 "Call me **Mara**, because the Almighty has made my life very

5260 מַרְאֶה *mar'eh*, n.m. [103] [√ 8011]

untranslated [14], appearance [14], looked [10], vision [10], appears [5], beautiful [+3202] [5], appear [3], appeared [3], beautiful [+3637] [3], like [+3869] [3], that[s] [3], face [2], handsome [+3637] [2], sight [2], sleek [+3637] [2], ugly [+8273] [2], what sees [2], clearly [1], eye [1], features [1], handsome [+3202] [1], huge [1], imposing [+1524+4200] [1], look at [1], look [1], looked [+8011] [1], pattern [1], saw [+6524] [1], see [+6524] [1], see [1], seem [1], sights [+6524] [1], sights [1], similar [+2021+3869] [1], what[s] [1]

Ge 2: 9 the ground—trees that were pleasing to the **eye** and good for food.

Ge 12:11 his wife Sarai, "I know what a **beautiful** [+3637] woman you are.
24:16 The girl was very **beautiful** [+3202], a virgin; no man had ever
26:7 kill me on account of Rebekah, because she is **beautiful** [+3202]."
29:17 weak eyes, but Rachel was lovely in form, and **beautiful** [+3637].
39:6 food he ate. Now Joseph was well-built and **handsome** [+3637],
41:2 **sleek** [+3637] and fat, and they grazed among the reeds.
41:3 After them, seven other cows, **ugly** [+8273] and gaunt, came up
41:4 the cows that were **ugly** [+8273] and gaunt ate up the seven sleek,
41:4 the cows that were ugly and gaunt ate up the seven **sleek** [+3637],
41:21 could tell that they had done so; they **looked** just as ugly as before.
Ex 3:3 So Moses thought, "I will go over and see this strange **sight**—
24:17 To the Israelites the glory of the LORD **looked** like a consuming
Lev 13:3 has turned white and the sore **appears** to be more than skin deep,
13:4 on his skin is white but does not **appear** to be more than skin deep
13:12 out all over his skin and, so far as the priest can **see** [+6524],
13:20 if it **appears** to be more than skin deep and the hair in it has turned
13:25 in it has turned white, and it **appears** to be more than skin deep,
13:30 if it **appears** to be more than skin deep and the hair in it is yellow
13:31 it does not **seem** to be more than skin deep and there is no black
13:32 yellow hair in it and it does not **appear** to be more than skin deep,
13:34 not spread in the skin and **appears** to be no more than skin deep,
13:43 or forehead is reddish-white **like** [+3869] an infectious skin
14:37 or reddish depressions that **appear** to be deeper than the surface of
Nu 8:4 The lampstand was made exactly like the **pattern** the LORD had
9:15 From evening till morning the cloud above the tabernacle **looked**
9:16 to be; the cloud covered it, and at night it **looked** *like* fire.
12:8 With him I speak face to face, **clearly** and not in riddles; he sees
Dt 28:34 The **sights** [+6524] you see will drive you mad.
28:67 that will fill your hearts and the **sights** that your eyes will see.
Jos 22:10 the half-tribe of Manasseh built an **imposing** [+1524+4200] altar
Jdg 13:6 God came to me. He **looked** like an angel of God, very awesome.
13:6 to me. He looked like **[RPH]** an angel of God, very awesome.
1Sa 16:7 "Do not consider his **appearance** or his height, for I have rejected
17:42 only a boy, ruddy and **handsome** [+3637], and he despised him.
2Sa 11:2 he saw a woman bathing. The woman was very **beautiful** [+3202],
14:27 name was Tamar, and she became a **beautiful** [+3637] woman.
23:21 he struck down a **huge** Egyptian. Although the Egyptian had a
Est 1:11 her beauty to the people and nobles, for she was lovely to **look at**.
2:2 "Let a search be made for **beautiful** [+3202] young virgins for the
2:3 these **beautiful** [+3202] girls into the harem at the citadel of Susa.
2:7 who was also known as Esther, was lovely in form and **features**,
Job 4:16 It stopped, but I could not tell **what**[s] it was. A form stood before
41:9 [41:1] him is false; the mere **sight** *of* him is overpowering.
Ecc 6:9 Better **what** the eye **sees** than the roving of the appetite. This too is
11:9 Follow the ways of your heart and *whatever* your eyes **see**,
SS 2:14 on the mountainside, show me your **face**, let me hear your voice;
2:14 hear your voice; for your voice is sweet, and your **face** is lovely.
5:15 of pure gold. His **appearance** is like Lebanon, choice as its cedars.
Isa 11:3 He will not judge by **what** he **sees** *with* his eyes, or decide by what
52:14 his **appearance** was so disfigured beyond that of any man
53:2 us to him, nothing in his **appearance** that we should desire him.
Eze 1:5 four living creatures. *In* **appearance** their form was that of a man,
1:13 The **appearance** *of* the living creatures was like burning coals of
1:13 creatures was like burning coals of fire or like **[RPH]** torches.
1:14 The creatures sped back and forth like **[RPH]** flashes of lightning.
1:16 This was the **appearance** and structure of the wheels:
1:16 Each **appeared** to be made like a wheel intersecting a wheel.
1:26 Above the expanse over their heads was what **looked** like a throne
1:26 and high above on the throne was a figure like **that**[s] *of* a man.
1:27 I saw that from *what* **appeared** to be his waist up he looked like
1:27 as if **[RPH]** full of fire, and that from there down he looked like
1:27 if full of fire, and that from **[RPH]** there down he looked like fire;
1:27 as if full of fire, and that from there down he **looked** like fire;
1:28 Like the **appearance** *of* a rainbow in the clouds on a rainy day,
1:28 the clouds on a rainy day, so was **[RPH]** the radiance around him.
1:28 This was the **appearance** *of* the likeness of the glory of the
8:2 I looked, and I saw a figure like **that**[s] *of* a man. From what
8:2 From *what* **appeared** to be his waist down he was like fire,
8:2 and from there up his **appearance** was as bright as glowing metal.
8:4 glory of the God of Israel, as in the **vision** I had seen in the plain.
10:1 I saw **[RPH]** the likeness of a throne of sapphire above the
10:9 each of the cherubim; **[NIE]** the wheels sparkled like chrysolite.
10:10 As for their **appearance**, the four of them looked alike; each was
10:22 seen by the Kebar River. **[RPH]** Each one went straight ahead.
11:24 brought me to the exiles in Babylonia in the **vision** given by the
11:24 by the Spirit of God. Then the **vision** I had seen went up from me,
23:15 all of them **looked** like Babylonian chariot officers, natives of
23:16 As soon as she **saw** [+6524] them, she lusted after them and sent
40:3 me there, and I saw a man whose **appearance** was like bronze;
40:3 and I saw a man whose appearance was like **[RPH]** bronze;
41:21 the one at the front of the Most Holy Place was **[RPH]** similar.
41:21 one at the front of the Most Holy Place was **similar** [+2021+3869].
42:11 These were **like** [+3869] the rooms on the north; they had the same
43:3 **[RPH]** The vision I saw was like the vision I had seen when he
43:3 The **vision** I saw was like the vision I had seen when he came to
43:3 The vision I saw was like the **vision** I had seen when he came to
43:3 and like the visions **[RPH]** I had seen by the Kebar River,
Da 1:4 young men without any physical defect, **handsome** [+3202],
1:13 compare our **appearance** with that of the young men who eat the
1:13 compare our appearance with **that**[s] *of* the young men who eat the
1:15 At the end of the ten days they **looked** [+8011] healthier and better
8:15 to understand it, there before me stood one who **looked** like a man.
8:16 the Ulai calling, "Gabriel, tell this man the meaning of the **vision**."
8:26 "The **vision** *of* the evenings and mornings that has been given you
8:27 I was appalled by the **vision**; it was beyond understanding.
9:23 Therefore, consider the message and understand the **vision**:
10:1 The understanding of the message came to him in a **vision**.
10:6 His body was like chrysolite, his face **like** [+3869] lightning,
10:18 Again the one who **looked** like a man touched me and gave me
Joel 2:4 They have the **appearance** *of* horses; they gallop along like
2:4 the appearance of horses; **[RPH]** they gallop along like cavalry.
Na 2:4 [2:5] They **look** like flaming torches; they dart about like

5261 מַרְאָה¹ *mar'â*¹, n.f. [11] [√ 8011]

vision [5], visions [5], it[s] [+2021] [1]

Ge 46:2 And God spoke to Israel in a **vision** *at* night and said, "Jacob!
Nu 12:6 I reveal myself to him in **visions**, I speak to him in dreams.
1Sa 3:15 of the house of the LORD. He was afraid to tell Eli the **vision**,
Eze 1:1 Kebar River, the heavens were opened and I saw **visions** *of* God.
8:3 and heaven and in **visions** *of* God he took me to Jerusalem,
40:2 In **visions** *of* God he took me to the land of Israel and set me on a
43:3 destroy the city and like the **visions** I had seen by the Kebar River,
Da 10:7 I, Daniel, was the only one who saw the **vision**; the men with me
10:7 the men with me did not see **it**[s] [+2021], but such terror
10:8 So I was left alone, gazing at this great **vision**; I had no strength
10:16 "I am overcome with anguish because of the **vision**, my lord,

5262 מַרְאָה² *mar'â*², n.f. [1] [√ 8011]

mirrors [1]

Ex 38:8 its bronze stand from the **mirrors** *of* the women who served at the

5263 מֻרְאָה *mur'â*, n.f. [1] [cf. 5286]

crop [1]

Lev 1:16 He is to remove the **crop** with its contents and throw it to the east

5264 מְרוֹן *m^er'ôn*, n.pr.loc. Not used in NIV/BHS [cf. 9077]

5265 מְרַאֲשׁוֹת *m^era'ªšôt*, n.[f.]pl.den. [10] [→ 5358; cf. 8039]

near head [4], at head [2], under head [2], by head [1], heads [1]

Ge 28:11 of the stones there, he put it **under** his **head** and lay down to sleep.
28:18 next morning Jacob took the stone he had placed **under** his **head**
1Sa 19:13 it with a garment and putting some goats' hair **at the head**.
19:16 there was the idol in the bed, and **at the head** was some goats' hair.
26:7 inside the camp with his spear stuck in the ground **near** his **head**.
26:11 Now get the spear and water jug that are **near** his **head**, and let's
26:12 So David took the spear and water jug **near** Saul's **head**,
26:16 are the king's spear and water jug that were **near** his **head**?"
1Ki 19:6 and there **by** his **head** was a cake of bread baked over hot coals,
Jer 13:18 your thrones, for your glorious crowns will fall from your **heads**."

5266 מֵרַב *mērab*, n.pr.f. [3 / 4] [√ 8045]

Merab [4]

1Sa 14:49 The name of his older daughter was **Merab**, and that of the
18:17 Saul said to David, "Here is my older daughter **Merab**. I will give
18:19 So when the time came for **Merab**, Saul's daughter, to be given to
2Sa 21:8 together with the five sons of Saul's daughter **Merab**, [BHS 4783]

5267 מַרְבַד *marbad*, n.[m.]. [2] [√ 8048]

covered [+8048] [1], coverings bed [1]

Pr 7:16 *I have* **covered** my bed **with** [+8048] colored linens from Egypt.
31:22 She makes **coverings** for her **bed**; she is clothed in fine linen

5268 מִרְבָּה *mirbâ*, n.f. [1] [√ 8049]

so much [1]

Eze 23:32 and deep; it will bring scorn and derision, for it holds **so much**.

5269 מַרְבֶּה *marbeh*, n.[m.]. [2] [√ 8049]

abundance [1], increase [1]

Isa 9:7 [9:6] Of the **increase** *of* his government and peace there will be
33:23 an **abundance** *of* spoils will be divided and even the lame will

5270 מַרְבִּית marbît, n.f. [5] [√ 8049]

most [2], descendants [+1074] [1], greatness [1], profit [1]

Lev 25:37 must not lend him money at interest or sell him food at a **profit**.
1Sa 2:33 and all your **descendants** [+1074] will die in the prime of life.
1Ch 12:29 [12:30] **most** *of* whom had remained loyal to Saul's house until
2Ch 9: 6 Indeed, not even half the **greatness** *of* your wisdom was told me;
30:18 Although **most** *of* the many people who came from Ephraim,

5271 מַרְבֵּץ marbēṣ, n.[m.]. [2] [√ 8069]

lair [1], resting place [1]

Eze 25: 5 a pasture for camels and Ammon into a **resting place** *for* sheep.
Zep 2:15 What a ruin she has become, a **lair** for wild beasts! All who pass

5272 מַרְבֵּק marbēq, n.[m.]. [4]

fattened [3], stall [1]

1Sa 28:24 The woman had a **fattened** calf at the house, which she butchered
Jer 46:21 The mercenaries in her ranks are like **fattened** calves. They too
Am 6: 4 on your couches. You dine on choice lambs and **fattened** calves.
Mal 4: 2 [3:20] you will go out and leap like calves released from the **stall**.

5273 מַרְגּוֹעַ margôaʿ, n.[m.]. [1] [√ 8089]

rest [1]

Jer 6:16 good way is, and walk in it, and you will find **rest** for your souls.

5274 מַרְגְּלוֹת margᵉlôt, n.[f.]pl.den. [5] [√ 8079]

feet [4], legs [1]

Ru 3: 4 go and uncover his **feet** and lie down. He will tell you what to do."
3: 7 Ruth approached quietly, uncovered his **feet** and lay down.
3: 8 the man, and he turned and discovered a woman lying at his **feet**.
3:14 So she lay at his **feet** until morning, but got up before anyone could
Da 10: 6 his arms and **legs** like the gleam of burnished bronze,

5275 מַרְגֵּמָה margēmâ, n.f. [1] [√ 8083]

sling [1]

Pr 26: 8 Like tying a stone in a **sling** is the giving of honor to a fool.

5276 מַרְגֵּעָה margēʿâ, n.f. [1] [√ 8089]

place of repose [1]

Isa 28:12 let the weary rest"; and, "This is the **place of repose**"—

5277 מָרַד mārad, v. [25] [→ 5278, 5279?, 5280]

rebelled [12], rebel [7], revolt [2], *untranslated* [1], rebelling [1], rebellion [1], rebellious [1]

Ge 14: 4 [A] to Kedorlaomer, but in the thirteenth year *they* **rebelled**.
Nu 14: 9 [A] Only *do* not **rebel** against the LORD. And do not be afraid
Jos 22:16 [A] and build yourselves an altar in **rebellion** against him now?
22:18 [A] " 'If you **rebel** against the LORD today, tomorrow he will
22:19 [A] *do* not **rebel** against the LORD or against us by building an
22:19 [A] or against us **[RPH]** by building an altar for yourselves,
22:29 [A] "Far be it from us to **rebel** against the LORD and turn away
2Ki 18: 7 [A] *He* **rebelled** against the king of Assyria and did not serve
18:20 [A] On whom are you depending, that *you* **rebel** against me?
24: 1 [A] he changed his mind and **rebelled** against Nebuchadnezzar.
24:20 [A] Now Zedekiah **rebelled** against the king of Babylon.
2Ch 13: 6 [A] of Solomon son of David, **rebelled** against his master.
36:13 [A] *He* also **rebelled** against King Nebuchadnezzar, who had
Ne 2:19 [A] they asked. "*Are* you **rebelling** against the king?"
6: 6 [A] that you and the Jews are plotting to **revolt**, and therefore
9:26 [A] "But they were disobedient and **rebelled** against you; they
Job 24:13 [A] "There are those *who* **rebel** *against* the light, who do not
Isa 36: 5 [A] On whom are you depending, that *you* **rebel** against me?
Jer 52: 3 [A] Now Zedekiah **rebelled** against the king of Babylon.
Eze 2: 3 [A] to a **rebellious** nation that has rebelled against me;
2: 3 [A] to a rebellious nation that *has* **rebelled** against me;
17:15 [A] the king **rebelled** against him by sending his envoys to Egypt
20:38 [A] I will purge you of those *who* **revolt** and rebel against me.
Da 9: 5 [A] We have been wicked and *have* **rebelled**; we have turned
9: 9 [A] and forgiving, even though *we have* **rebelled** against him;

5278 מֶרֶד mered[1], n.[m.]. [1] [→ 5279; cf. 5277; Ar 10438]

rebellion [1]

Jos 22:22 If this has been in **rebellion** or disobedience to the LORD,

5279 ²מֶרֶד mered[2], n.pr.m. [2] [√ 5278?; cf. 5277]

Mered [2]

1Ch 4:17 The sons of Ezrah: Jether, **Mered**, Epher and Jalon. One of
4:18 children of Pharaoh's daughter Bithiah, whom **Mered** had married.

5280 מַרְדּוּת mardût, n.f. [1] [√ 5277]

rebellious [1]

1Sa 20:30 and he said to him, "You son of a perverse and **rebellious** woman!

5281 מְרֹדָךְ mᵉrōdāk, n.pr. [1] [→ 5282, 5283]

Marduk [1]

Jer 50: 2 be captured; Bel will be put to shame, **Marduk** filled with terror.

5282 מְרֹדַךְ־בַּלְאֲדָן mᵉrōdak-balʾᵃdān, n.pr.m. [1 / 2] [√ 5281 + 1156; cf. 1347]

Merodach-Baladan [2]

2Ki 20:12 At that time **Merodach-Baladan** [BHS 1347] son of Baladan
Isa 39: 1 At that time **Merodach-Baladan** son of Baladan king of Babylon

5283 מָרְדֳּכַי mordᵒkay, n.pr.m. [60] [√ 5281]

Mordecai [49], Mordecai's [5], he[s] [3], him[s] [2], he[s] [+408+2021] [1]

Ezr 2: 2 **Mordecai**, Bilshan, Mispar, Bigvai, Rehum and Baanah):
Ne 7: 7 **Mordecai**, Bilshan, Mispereth, Bigvai, Nehum and Baanah):
Est 2: 5 named **Mordecai** son of Jair, the son of Shimei, the son of Kish,
2: 7 and **Mordecai** had taken her as his own daughter when her father
2:10 family background, because **Mordecai** had forbidden her to do so.
2:11 Every day **he[s]** walked back and forth near the courtyard of the
2:15 When the turn came for Esther (the girl **Mordecai** had adopted,
2:19 assembled a second time, **Mordecai** was sitting at the king's gate.
2:20 and nationality just as **Mordecai** had told her to do,
2:20 for she continued to follow **Mordecai's** instructions as she had
2:21 During the time **Mordecai** was sitting at the king's gate, Bigthana
2:22 But **Mordecai** found out about the plot and told Queen Esther,
2:22 who in turn reported it to the king, giving credit to **Mordecai**.
3: 2 But **Mordecai** would not kneel down or pay him honor.
3: 3 Then the royal officials at the king's gate asked **Mordecai**,
3: 4 Therefore they told Haman about it to see whether **Mordecai's**
3: 5 When Haman saw that **Mordecai** would not kneel down or pay
3: 6 Yet having learned who **Mordecai's** people were, he scorned the
3: 6 people were, he scorned the idea of killing only **Mordecai**.
3: 6 Instead Haman looked for a way to destroy all **Mordecai's** people,
4: 1 When **Mordecai** learned of all that had been done, he tore his
4: 1 **he[s]** tore his clothes, put on sackcloth and ashes, and went out into
4: 4 She sent clothes for **him[s]** to put on instead of his sackcloth,
4: 5 and ordered him to find out what was troubling **Mordecai**
4: 6 So Hathach went out to **Mordecai** in the open square of the city in
4: 7 **Mordecai** told him everything that had happened to him,
4: 9 went back and reported to Esther what **Mordecai** had said.
4:10 Then she instructed him to say to **Mordecai**,
4:12 When Esther's words were reported to **Mordecai**,
4:13 **he[s]** sent back this answer: "Do not think that because you are in
4:15 Then Esther sent this reply to **Mordecai**:
4:17 So **Mordecai** went away and carried out all of Esther's
5: 9 when he saw **Mordecai** at the king's gate and observed that he
5: 9 fear in his presence, he was filled with rage against **Mordecai**.
5:13 all this gives me no satisfaction as long as I see that Jew **Mordecai**
5:14 and ask the king in the morning to have **Mordecai** hanged on it.
6: 2 It was found recorded there that **Mordecai** had exposed Bigthana
6: 3 "What honor and recognition has **Mordecai** received for this?"
6: 4 about hanging **Mordecai** on the gallows he had erected for him.
6:10 the horse and do just as you have suggested for **Mordecai** the Jew,
6:11 He robed **Mordecai**, and led him on horseback through the city
6:12 Afterward **Mordecai** returned to the king's gate. But Haman
6:13 His advisers and his wife Zeresh said to him, "Since **Mordecai**,
7: 9 He had it made for **Mordecai**, who spoke up to help the king."
7:10 they hanged Haman on the gallows he had prepared for **Mordecai**.
8: 1 **Mordecai** came into the presence of the king, for Esther had told
8: 2 he had reclaimed from Haman, and presented it to **Mordecai**.
8: 2 it to Mordecai. And Esther appointed **him[s]** over Haman's estate.
8: 7 King Xerxes replied to Queen Esther and to **Mordecai** the Jew,
8: 9 They wrote out all **Mordecai's** orders to the Jews, and to the
8:15 **Mordecai** left the king's presence wearing royal garments of blue
9: 3 helped the Jews, because fear of **Mordecai** had seized them.
9: 4 **Mordecai** was prominent in the palace; his reputation spread
9: 4 and **he[s]** [+408+2021] became more and more powerful.
9:20 **Mordecai** recorded these events, and he sent letters to all the Jews
9:23 they had begun, doing what **Mordecai** had written to them.
9:29 Queen Esther, daughter of Abihail, along with **Mordecai** the Jew,
9:31 as **Mordecai** the Jew and Queen Esther had decreed for them,
10: 2 together with a full account of the greatness of **Mordecai** to which
10: 3 **Mordecai** the Jew was second in rank to King Xerxes, preeminent

5284 מֻרְדָּף *murdāp*, n.f. & m. [1] [√ 8103]
aggression [1]
Isa 14: 6 and in fury subdued nations with relentless **aggression**.

5285 מָרָּה *morrâ*, n.f. Not used in NIV/BHS [√ 5352]

5286 ¹מָרָה *mārâ¹*, v. [45 / 44] [→ 3559, 5308, 5318?, 5361; cf. 5256, 5263]
rebelled [20], rebellious [9], rebel [3], defied [2], most rebellious [+5286] [2], rebels [2], defying [1], disobedient [1], disobeyed [1], hostility [1], rebelling [1], rebellion [1]
Nu 20: 10 [A] of the rock and Moses said to them, "Listen, you **rebels**,
20: 24 [A] because *both of you* **rebelled** against my command at the
27: 14 [A] *both of you* **disobeyed** my command to honor me as holy
Dt 1: 26 [G] *you* **rebelled** against the command of the LORD your God.
1: 43 [G] *You* **rebelled** against the LORD's command and in your
9: 7 [G] arrived here, you have been **rebellious** against the LORD.
9: 23 [G] *you* **rebelled** against the command of the LORD your God.
9: 24 [G] You have been **rebellious** against the LORD ever since I
21: 18 [A] and **rebellious** son who does not obey his father and mother
21: 20 [A] to the elders, "This son of ours is stubborn and **rebellious**.
31: 27 [G] If you have been **rebellious** against the LORD while I am
Jos 1: 18 [G] Whoever **rebels** against your word and does not obey your
1Sa 12: 14 [G] and obey him and *do* not **rebel** against his commands,
12: 15 [A] if *you* **rebel** against his commands, his hand will be against
1Ki 13: 21 [A] '*You have* **defied** the word of the LORD and have not kept
13: 26 [A] "It is the man of God who **defied** the word of the LORD.
2Ki 14: 26 [a] had seen how bitterly [BHS *rebelliously*; NIV 5253] everyone
Ne 9: 26 [G] "But *they were* **disobedient** and rebelled against you; they
Job 17: 2 [G] mockers surround me; my eyes must dwell on their **hostility**.
Ps 5: 10 [5:11] [A] their many sins, for *they have* **rebelled** against you.
78: 8 [A] a stubborn and **rebellious** generation, whose hearts were not
78: 17 [G] against him, **rebelling** in the desert *against* the Most High.
78: 40 [G] How often *they* **rebelled** *against* him in the desert
78: 56 [G] they put God to the test and **rebelled** against the Most High;
105: 28 [A] the land dark—for *had they* not **rebelled** against his words?
106: 7 [G] many kindnesses, and *they* **rebelled** by the sea, the Red Sea.
106: 33 [G] for *they* **rebelled** against the Spirit of God, and rash words
106: 43 [G] they were bent on **rebellion** and they wasted away in their
107: 11 [G] for *they had* **rebelled** *against* the words of God
Isa 1: 20 [A] if you resist and **rebel**, you will be devoured by the sword."
3: 8 [G] deeds are against the LORD, **defying** his glorious presence.
50: 5 [A] LORD has opened my ears, and I *have* not *been* **rebellious**;
63: 10 [A] Yet they **rebelled** and grieved his Holy Spirit. So he turned
Jer 4: 17 [A] because *she has* **rebelled** against me,' " declares the LORD.
5: 23 [A] these people have stubborn and **rebellious** hearts; they have
La 1: 18 [A] LORD is righteous, yet *I* **rebelled** *against* his command.
1: 20 [A] I am disturbed, for *I have been* **most rebellious** [+5286].
1: 20 [A] I am disturbed, for *I have been* **most rebellious** [+5286].
3: 42 [A] "We have sinned and **rebelled** and you have not forgiven.
Eze 5: 6 [G] Yet in her wickedness *she has* **rebelled** against my laws and
20: 8 [G] " 'But *they* **rebelled** against me and would not listen to me;
20: 13 [G] " 'Yet the people of Israel **rebelled** against me in the desert.
20: 21 [G] " 'But the children **rebelled** against me: They did not follow
Hos 13: 16 [14:1] [A] because *they have* **rebelled** against their God.
Zep 3: 1 [A] Woe to the city of oppressors, **rebellious** and defiled!

5287 ²מָרָה *mārâ²*, a. Not used in NIV/BHS [√ 5253; cf. 5352]

5288 ³מָרָה *mārâ³*, n.pr.f. [5] [→ 5300; cf. 5352]
Marah [4], its[s] [+4946] [1]
Ex 15: 23 When they came to **Marah**, they could not drink its water
15: 23 they could not drink **its**[s] [+4946] water because it was bitter.
15: 23 because it was bitter. (That is why the place is called **Marah**.)
Nu 33: 8 for three days in the Desert of Etham, they camped at **Marah**.
33: 9 They left **Marah** and went to Elim, where there were twelve

5289 מֹרָה *mōrâ*, n.f. [2] [√ 5352]
bitterness [1], source of grief [+8120] [1]
Ge 26: 35 They were a **source of grief** [+8120] to Isaac and Rebekah.
Pr 14: 10 Each heart knows its own **bitterness**, and no one else can share its

5290 מַרְהֵבָה *marhēbâ*, n.f. [0 / 1] [√ 8104; cf. 4502]
fury [1]
Isa 14: 4 has come to an end! How his **fury** [BHS 4502] has ended!

5291 מָרוּד *mārûd*, n.[m.]. [3] [√ 8113]
wandering [2], wanderer [1]
Isa 58: 7 with the hungry and to provide the poor **wanderer** with shelter—
La 1: 7 **wandering** Jerusalem remembers all the treasures that were hers in
3: 19 I remember my affliction and my **wandering**, the bitterness

5292 מֵרוֹז *mērôz*, n.pr.loc. [1]
Meroz [1]
Jdg 5: 23 'Curse **Meroz**,' said the angel of the LORD. 'Curse its people

5293 מָרוֹחַ *mārôaḥ*, n.[m.]. [1] [√ 5302]
damaged [1]
Lev 21: 20 or who has festering or running sores or **damaged** testicles.

5294 מָרוֹם *mārôm*, n.m. [54] [√ 8123]
on high [10], heights [9], heavens [4], exalted [3], high [3], on high [+928+2021] [3], pride [3], above [+928+2021] [1], arrogance [1], exalted [+6639] [1], haughty [1], heaven [1], height [1], heights [+8031] [1], heights above [1], heights of heaven [1], high positions [1], highest point [+1726] [1], highest point [1], lofty [1], on heights [1], on high [+2021] [1], on high [+2021+4200] [1], on high [+4946] [1], skies [1], spreads feathers to run [+928+2021+5257] [1]
Jdg 5: 18 risked their very lives; so did Naphtali on the **heights** *of* the field.
2Sa 22: 17 "He reached down from **on high** and took hold of me; he drew me
2Ki 19: 22 whom have you raised your voice and lifted your eyes *in* **pride**?
19: 23 "With my many chariots I have ascended the **heights** *of* the
Job 5: 11 The lowly he sets **on high**, and those who mourn are lifted to
16: 19 my witness is in heaven; my advocate is **on high** [+928+2021].
25: 2 awe belong to God; he establishes order in the **heights of heaven**.
31: 2 from God above, his heritage from the Almighty **on high** [+4946]?
39: 18 Yet when *she* **spreads** *her* **feathers to run** [+928+2021+5257],
Ps 7: 7 [7:8] gather around you. Rule over them from **on high** [+2021];
10: 5 he is **haughty** and your laws are far from him; he sneers at all his
18: 16 [18:17] He reached down from **on high** and took hold of me;
56: 2 [56:3] me all day long; many are attacking me in their **pride**.
68: 18 [68:19] When you ascended **on high** [+2021+4200], you led
71: 19 Your righteousness reaches to the **skies**, O God, you who have
73: 8 speak with malice; in their **arrogance** they threaten oppression.
75: 5 [75:6] Do not lift your horns against **heaven**; do not speak with
92: 8 [92:9] But you, O LORD, are **exalted** forever.
93: 4 breakers of the sea—the LORD **on high** [+928+2021] is mighty.
102: 19 [102:20] "The LORD looked down from his sanctuary **on high**,
144: 7 Reach down your hand from **on high**; deliver me and rescue me
148: 1 the LORD from the heavens, praise him in the **heights above**.
Pr 8: 2 On the **heights** [+8031] along the way, where the paths meet,
9: 3 her maids, and she calls from the **highest** [+1726] **point** *of* the city.
9: 14 at the door of her house, on a seat at the **highest point** *of* the city,
Ecc 10: 6 Fools are put in many **high positions**, while the rich occupy the
Isa 22: 16 hewing your grave *on* the **height** and chiseling your resting place
24: 4 and withers, the **exalted** [+6639] *of* the earth languish.
24: 18 The floodgates of the **heavens** are opened, the foundations of the
24: 21 In that day the LORD will punish the powers in the **heavens**
24: 21 LORD will punish the powers in the heavens **above** [+928+2021]
26: 5 He humbles those who dwell **on high**, he lays the lofty city low;
32: 15 till the Spirit is poured upon us from **on high**, and the desert
33: 5 The LORD is exalted, for he dwells **on high**; he will fill Zion
33: 16 this is the man who will dwell **on** the **heights**, whose refuge will be
37: 23 whom have you raised your voice and lifted your eyes *in* **pride**?
37: 24 'With my many chariots I have ascended the **heights** *of* the
37: 24 I have reached its remotest **heights**, the finest of its forests.
38: 14 My eyes grew weak as I looked to the **heavens**. I am troubled;
40: 26 Lift your eyes and look to the **heavens**: Who created all these?
57: 15 "I live in a **high** and holy place, but also with him who is contrite
58: 4 do today and expect your voice to be heard **on high** [+928+2021].
Jer 17: 12 A glorious throne, **exalted** from the beginning, is the place of our
25: 30 " 'The LORD will roar from **on high**; he will thunder from his
31: 12 They will come and shout for joy on the **heights** *of* Zion; they will
49: 16 live in the clefts of the rocks, who occupy the **heights** *of* the hill.
51: 53 Even if Babylon reaches the sky and fortifies her **lofty** stronghold,
La 1: 13 "From **on high** he sent fire, sent it down into my bones. He spread
Eze 17: 23 On the mountain **heights** *of* Israel I will plant it; it will produce
20: 40 For on my holy mountain, the **high** mountain of Israel,
34: 14 and the mountain **heights** *of* Israel will be their grazing land.
Ob 1: 3 live in the clefts of the rocks and make your home on the **heights**,
Mic 6: 6 I come before the LORD and bow down before the **exalted** God?
Hab 2: 9 to him who builds his realm by unjust gain to set his nest on **high**,

5295 מֵרוֹם *mērôm*, n.pr.loc. [2] [√ 8123]
Merom [2]
Jos 11: 5 joined forces and made camp together at the Waters of **Merom**,
11: 7 whole army came against them suddenly at the Waters of **Merom**

5296 מֵרוֹץ mērôṣ, n.[m.]. [1] [√ 8132]
race [1]
Ecc 9: 11 The **race** is not to the swift or the battle to the strong, nor does

5297 ¹מְרוּצָה m^erûṣâ¹, n.f. [4] [√ 8132]
course [2], *untranslated* [1], runs [1]
2Sa 18: 27 "It seems to me that the first one **runs** like Ahimaaz son of
18: 27 "It seems to me that the first one runs like **[RPH]** Ahimaaz son of
Jer 8: 6 Each pursues his own **course** like a horse charging into battle.
23: 10 The ⌞prophets⌟ follow an evil **course** and use their power unjustly.

5298 ²מְרוּצָה m^erûṣâ², n.f. [1] [√ 8368]
extortion [1]
Jer 22: 17 on shedding innocent blood and on oppression and **extortion**."

5299 מְרוּקִים m^erûqîm, n.[m.]. [1] [√ 5347]
beauty treatments [1]
Est 2: 12 she had to complete twelve months of **beauty treatments**

5300 מָרוֹת mārôt, n.pr.loc. [1] [√ 5288; cf. 5352]
Maroth [1]
Mic 1: 12 Those who live in **Maroth** writhe in pain, waiting for relief,

5301 מַרְזֵחַ marzēaḥ, n.m. [2]
feasting [1], funeral meal [1]
Jer 16: 5 "Do not enter a house where there is a **funeral meal**; do not go to
Am 6: 7 the first to go into exile; your **feasting** and lounging will end.

5302 מָרַח māraḥ, v. [1] [→ 5293]
apply [1]
Isa 38: 21 [A] had said, "Prepare a poultice of figs and **apply** it to the boil,

5303 מֶרְחָב merḥāb, n.[m.]. [6] [→ 5304; cf. 8143]
spacious place [3], meadow [1], setting free [1], whole [1]
2Sa 22: 20 He brought me out into a **spacious place**; he rescued me
Ps 18: 19 [18:20] He brought me out into a **spacious place**; he rescued me
31: 8 [31:9] over to the enemy but have set my feet in a **spacious place**.
118: 5 I cried to the LORD, and he answered by **setting** me **free**.
Hos 4: 16 then can the LORD pasture them like lambs in a **meadow**?
Hab 1: 6 who sweep across the **whole** earth to seize dwelling places not

5304 מֶרְחַבְיָה merḥobyâ, var. Not used in NIV/BHS [√ 5303 + 3378]

5305 מֶרְחָק merḥāq, n.m. [18] [√ 8178]
afar [4], distant [4], distant [+4946] [2], far away [2], distant lands [1], far away [+4946] [1], far-off [1], faraway [1], some distance away [1], stretches afar [1]
2Sa 15: 17 following him, and they halted at a place **some distance away**.
Ps 138: 6 he looks upon the lowly, but the proud he knows from **afar**.
Pr 25: 25 Like cold water to a weary soul is good news from a **distant** land.
31: 14 She is like the merchant ships, bringing her food from **afar**.
Isa 8: 9 you nations, and be shattered! Listen, all you **distant** lands.
10: 3 you do on the day of reckoning, when disaster comes from **afar**?
13: 5 They come from **faraway** lands, from the ends of the heavens—
17: 13 when he rebukes them they flee **far** [+4946] **away**, driven before
30: 27 See, the Name of the LORD comes from **afar**, with burning anger
33: 17 will see the king in his beauty and view a land that **stretches afar**.
46: 11 a bird of prey; from a **far-off** land, a man to fulfill my purpose.
Jer 4: 16 'A besieging army is coming from a **distant** land, raising a war cry
5: 15 the LORD, "I am bringing a **distant** [+4946] nation against you—
6: 20 about incense from Sheba or sweet calamus from a **distant** land?
8: 19 Listen to the cry of my people from a land **far away**: "Is the
31: 10 the LORD, O nations; proclaim it in **distant** [+4946] coastlands:
Eze 23: 40 "They even sent messengers for men who came from **far away**,
Zec 10: 9 among the peoples, yet in **distant lands** they will remember me.

5306 מַרְחֶשֶׁת marḥešet, n.f. [2] [√ 8180]
pan [2]
Lev 2: 7 If your grain offering is cooked in a **pan**, it is to be made of fine
7: 9 Every grain offering baked in an oven or cooked in a **pan**

5307 מָרַט māraṭ, v. [14] [→ Ar 10440, 10441]
polished [5], lost hair [+8031] [2], smooth-skinned [2], burnished [1], made raw [1], pulled out beard [1], pulled out hair [1], pulled [1]
Lev 13: 40 [C] "When a man *has* **lost** [+8031] his **hair** and is bald, he is
13: 41 [C] If *he has* **lost** [+8031] his **hair** from the front of his scalp
1Ki 7: 45 [E] for the temple of the LORD were of **burnished** bronze.
Ezr 9: 3 [A] **pulled** hair from my head and beard and sat down appalled.
Ne 13: 25 [A] on them. I beat some of the men and **pulled out** their **hair**.
Isa 18: 2 [E] Go, swift messengers, to a people tall and **smooth-skinned**,
18: 7 [E] LORD Almighty from a people tall and **smooth-skinned**,
50: 6 [A] who beat me, my cheeks to *those who* **pulled out** my **beard**;
Eze 21: 9 [21:14] [B] " 'A sword, a sword, sharpened and **polished**—
21: 10 [21:15] [E] for the slaughter, **polished** to flash like lightning!
21: 11 [21:16] [A] " 'The sword is appointed to *be* **polished**, to be
21: 11 [21:16] [E] it is sharpened and **polished**, made ready for the
21: 28 [21:33] [B] **polished** to consume and to flash like lightning!
29: 18 [B] every head was rubbed bare and every shoulder **made raw**.

5308 מְרִי m^erî, n.m. [23] [√ 5286]
rebellious [17], rebellion [3], bitter [1], rebel [+2118] [1], rebellious [+1201] [1]
Nu 17: 10 [17:25] to be kept as a sign to the **rebellious** [+1201].
Dt 31: 27 For I know how **rebellious** and stiff-necked you are. If you have
1Sa 15: 23 For **rebellion** is like the sin of divination, and arrogance like the
Ne 9: 17 in their **rebellion** appointed a leader in order to return to their
Job 23: 2 "Even today my complaint is **bitter**; his hand is heavy in spite of
Pr 17: 11 An evil man is bent only on **rebellion**; a merciless official will be
Isa 30: 9 These are **rebellious** people, deceitful children, children unwilling
Eze 2: 5 they listen or fail to listen—for they are a **rebellious** house—
2: 6 they say or terrified by them, though they are a **rebellious** house.
2: 7 whether they listen or fail to listen, for they are **rebellious**.
2: 8 listen to what I say to you. *Do* not **rebel** [+2118] like that
2: 8 Do not rebel like that **rebellious** house; open your mouth and eat
3: 9 of them or terrified by them, though they are a **rebellious** house."
3: 26 and unable to rebuke them, though they are a **rebellious** house.
3: 27 whoever will refuse let him refuse; for they are a **rebellious** house.
12: 2 "Son of man, you are living among a **rebellious** people. They have
12: 2 and ears to hear but do not hear, for they are a **rebellious** people.
12: 3 Perhaps they will understand, though they are a **rebellious** house.
12: 9 "Son of man, did not that **rebellious** house of Israel ask you,
12: 25 For in your days, you **rebellious** house, I will fulfill whatever I
17: 12 "Say to this **rebellious** house, 'Do you not know what these things
24: 3 Tell this **rebellious** house a parable and say to them: 'This is what
44: 6 Say to the **rebellious** house of Israel, 'This is what the Sovereign

5309 מְרִיא m^erî', n.[m.]. [8] [√ 5258; cf. 5263]
fattened calves [3], fattened animals [2], choice [1], fattened calf [1], yearling [1]
2Sa 6: 13 had taken six steps, he sacrificed a bull and a **fattened calf**.
1Ki 1: 9 and **fattened calves** at the Stone of Zoheleth near En Rogel.
1: 19 **fattened calves**, and sheep, and has invited all the king's sons,
1: 25 and sacrificed great numbers of cattle, **fattened calves**, and sheep.
Isa 1: 11 enough of burnt offerings, of rams and the fat of **fattened animals**;
11: 6 down with the goat, the calf and the lion and the **yearling** together;
Eze 39: 18 goats and bulls—all of them **fattened animals** *from* Bashan.
Am 5: 22 Though you bring **choice** fellowship offerings, I will have no

5310 מֵרִיב mērîb, n.pr.m. Not used in NIV/BHS [→ 5311; cf. 8189]

5311 מְרִיב בַּ֫עַל m^erîb ba'al, n.pr.m. [3] [√ 5310 + 1251; cf. 5314]
Merib-Baal [2], who^s [1]
1Ch 8: 34 The son of Jonathan: **Merib-Baal**, who was the father of Micah.
8: 34 The son of Jonathan: Merib-Baal, **who**^s was the father of Micah.
9: 40 The son of Jonathan: **Merib-Baal**, who was the father of Micah.

5312 ¹מְרִיבָה m^erîbâ¹, n.f. [2] [→ 5313, 5315; cf. 8189]
quarreling [1], rebelled [1]
Ge 13: 8 said to Lot, "Let's not have any **quarreling** between you and me,
Nu 27: 14 for when the community **rebelled** at the waters in the Desert of

5313 ²מְרִיבָה m^erîbâ², n.pr.loc. [7] [√ 5312; cf. 8189]
Meribah [7]
Ex 17: 7 the place Massah and **Meribah** because the Israelites quarreled and
Nu 20: 13 These were the waters of **Meribah**, where the Israelites quarreled
20: 24 of you rebelled against my command at the waters of **Meribah**.
Dt 33: 8 him at Massah; you contended with him at the waters of **Meribah**.

Ps 81:7 [81:8] of a thundercloud; I tested you at the waters of **Meribah**.
95:8 do not harden your hearts as you did at **Meribah**, as you did that
106:32 By the waters of **Meribah** they angered the LORD, and trouble

5314 מְרִי־בַעַל m^{e}rî-ba'al, n.pr.m. [1] [√ 5310 + 1251; cf. 5311]

who[s] [1]

1Ch 9:40 The son of Jonathan: Merib-Baal, **who**[s] was the father of Micah.

5315 מְרִיבַת קָדֵשׁ m^{e}rîbat qādēš, n.pr.loc. [4] [√ 5312 + 7729]

Meribah Kadesh [4]

Nu 27:14 (These were the waters of **Meribah Kadesh**, in the Desert of Zin.)
Dt 32:51 Israelites at the waters of **Meribah Kadesh** *in* the Desert of Zin
Eze 47:19 it will run from Tamar as far as the waters of **Meribah Kadesh**,
48:28 Gad will run south from Tamar to the waters of **Meribah Kadesh**,

5316 מְרָיָה m^{e}rāyâ, n.pr.m. [1]

Meraiah [1]

Ne 12:12 of Seraiah's family, **Meraiah**; of Jeremiah's, Hananiah;

5317 מֹרִיָּה mōriyyâ, n.pr.loc. [2]

Moriah [2]

Ge 22:2 only son, Isaac, whom you love, and go to the region of **Moriah**.
2Ch 3:1 to build the temple of the LORD in Jerusalem on Mount **Moriah**,

5318 מְרָיוֹת m^{e}rāyôt, n.pr.m. [7 / 6] [√ 5286?]

Meraioth [6]

1Ch 6:6 [5:32] the father of Zerahiah, Zerahiah the father of **Meraioth**,
6:7 [5:33] **Meraioth** the father of Amariah, Amariah the father of
6:52 [6:37] **Meraioth** his son, Amariah his son, Ahitub his son,
9:11 the son of Zadok, the son of **Meraioth**, the son of Ahitub,
Ezr 7:3 the son of Amariah, the son of Azariah, the son of **Meraioth**,
Ne 11:11 the son of Zadok, the son of **Meraioth**, the son of Ahitub,
12:15 of Meremoth's, [BHS ***Meraioth's***; NIV 5329] Helkai;

5319 מִרְיָם miryām, n.pr.f. & m. [15] [√ 5258?]

Miriam [13], her[s] [1], she[s] [1]

Ex 15:20 **Miriam** the prophetess, Aaron's sister, took a tambourine in her
15:21 **Miriam** sang to them: "Sing to the LORD, for he is highly
Nu 12:1 **Miriam** and Aaron began to talk against Moses because of his
12:4 Aaron and **Miriam**, "Come out to the Tent of Meeting, all three of
12:5 at the entrance to the Tent and summoned Aaron and **Miriam**.
12:10 When the cloud lifted from above the Tent, there stood **Miriam**—
12:10 like snow. Aaron turned toward **her**[s] and saw that she had leprosy;
12:15 So **Miriam** was confined outside the camp for seven days,
12:15 and the people did not move on till **she**[s] was brought back.
20:1 and they stayed at Kadesh. There **Miriam** died and was buried.
26:59 To Amram she bore Aaron, Moses and their sister **Miriam**.
Dt 24:9 Remember what the LORD your God did to **Miriam** along the
1Ch 4:17 One of Mered's wives gave birth to **Miriam**, Shammai and Ishbah
6:3 [5:29] Aaron, Moses and **Miriam**. The sons of Aaron: Nadab,
Mic 6:4 land of slavery. I sent Moses to lead you, also Aaron and **Miriam**.

5320 מְרִירוּת m^{e}rîrût, n.f. [1] [√ 5352]

bitter grief [1]

Eze 21:6 [21:11] Groan before them with broken heart and **bitter grief**.

5321 מְרִירִי m^{e}rîrî, a. [1] [√ 5352]

deadly [1]

Dt 32:24 famine against them, consuming pestilence and **deadly** plague;

5322 מֹרֶךְ mōrek, n.[m.]. [1] [√ 8216]

fearful [1]

Lev 26:36 *so* **fearful** in the lands of their enemies that the sound of a

5323 מֶרְכָּב merkāb, n.m. [3] [√ 8206]

chariot [1], seat [1], sits [1]

Lev 15:9 " 'Everything the man **sits** on when riding will be unclean,
1Ki 4:26 [5:6] Solomon had four thousand stalls for **chariot** horses,
SS 3:10 Its **seat** was upholstered with purple, its interior lovingly inlaid by

5324 מֶרְכָּבָה merkābâ, n.f. [44] [√ 8206]

chariots [21], chariot [20], *untranslated* [3]

Ge 41:43 He had him ride in a **chariot** *as* his second-in-command, and men
46:29 Joseph had his **chariot** made ready and went to Goshen to meet his
Ex 14:25 He made the wheels of their **chariots** come off so that they had
15:4 Pharaoh's **chariots** and his army he has hurled into the sea.
Jos 11:6 You are to hamstring their horses and burn their **chariots**."
11:9 had directed: He hamstrung their horses and burned their **chariots**.
Jdg 4:15 by the sword, and Sisera abandoned his **chariot** and fled on foot.
5:28 so long in coming? Why is the clatter of his **chariots** delayed?'
1Sa 8:11 take your sons and make them serve with his **chariots** and horses,
8:11 his chariots and horses, and they will run in front of his **chariots**.
2Sa 15:1 Absalom provided himself with a **chariot** and horses and with fifty
1Ki 7:33 The wheels were made like **chariot** wheels; the axles, rims,
10:29 They imported a **chariot** from Egypt for six hundred shekels of
12:18 however, managed to get into his **chariot** and escape to Jerusalem.
20:33 Ben-Hadad came out, Ahab had him come up into his **chariot**.
22:35 and the king was propped up in his **chariot** facing the Arameans.
2Ki 5:21 running toward him, he got down from the **chariot** to meet him.
5:26 with you when the man got down from his **chariot** to meet you?
9:27 They wounded him in his **chariot** on the way up to Gur near
10:15 your hand." So he did, and Jehu helped him up into the **chariot**.
23:11 then burned the **chariots** *dedicated to* the sun.
1Ch 28:18 He also gave him the plan for the **chariot**, that is, the cherubim of
2Ch 1:17 They imported a **chariot** from Egypt for six hundred shekels of
9:25 Solomon had four thousand stalls for horses and **chariots**,
10:18 however, managed to get into his **chariot** and escape to Jerusalem.
14:9 [14:8] against them with a vast army and three hundred **chariots**,
18:34 the king of Israel propped himself up in his **chariot** facing the
35:24 So they took him out of his **chariot**, put him in the other chariot he
SS 6:12 my desire set me among the royal **chariots** *of* my people.
Isa 2:7 Their land is full of horses; there is no end to their **chariots**.
22:18 There you will die and there your splendid **chariots** will remain—
66:15 LORD is coming with fire, and his **chariots** are like a whirlwind;
Jer 4:13 He advances like the clouds, his **chariots** come like a whirlwind,
Joel 2:5 With a noise like that of **chariots** they leap over the mountaintops,
Mic 1:13 You who live in Lachish, harness the team to the **chariot**.
5:10 [5:9] your horses from among you and demolish your **chariots**.
Na 3:2 the clatter of wheels, galloping horses and jolting **chariots**!
Hab 3:8 sea when you rode with your horses and your victorious **chariots**?
Hag 2:22 I will overthrow **chariots** and their drivers; horses and their riders
Zec 6:1 there before me were four **chariots** coming out from between two
6:2 The first **chariot** had red horses, the second black,
6:2 The first chariot had red horses, the second **[RPH]** black,
6:3 the **[RPH]** third white, and the fourth dappled—all of them
6:3 the third white, and the **[RPH]** fourth dappled—all of them

5325 מַרְכָּבוֹת markābôt, n.pr.loc. Not used in NIV/BHS [→ 1112]

5326 מַרְכֹּלֶת markōlet, n.f. [1] [√ 8217]

marketplace [1]

Eze 27:24 In your **marketplace** they traded with you beautiful garments,

5327 מִרְמָה mirmâ[1], n.f. [39] [→ 5328; cf. 8228]

deceit [12], deceitful [9], dishonest [4], lies [4], deception [3], false [3], deceitfully [+928] [2], deceitfully [1], treachery [1]

Ge 27:35 "Your brother came **deceitfully** [+928] and took your blessing."
34:13 Jacob's sons replied **deceitfully** [+928] as they spoke to Shechem
2Ki 9:23 and fled, calling out to Ahaziah, "**Treachery**, Ahaziah!"
Job 15:35 and give birth to evil; their womb fashions **deceit**."
31:5 "If I have walked in falsehood or my foot has hurried after **deceit**—
Ps 5:6 [5:7] tell lies; bloodthirsty and **deceitful** men the LORD abhors.
10:7 His mouth is full of curses and **lies** and threats; trouble and evil are
17:1 Give ear to my prayer—it does not rise from **deceitful** lips.
24:4 who does not lift up his soul to an idol or swear by *what* is **false**.
34:13 [34:14] your tongue from evil and your lips from speaking **lies**.
35:20 devise **false** accusations against those who live quietly in the land.
36:3 [36:4] The words of his mouth are wicked and **deceitful**; he has
38:12 [38:13] harm me talk of my ruin; all day long they plot **deception**.
43:1 an ungodly nation; rescue me from **deceitful** and wicked men.
50:19 You use your mouth for evil and harness your tongue to **deceit**.
52:4 [52:6] You love every harmful word, O you **deceitful** tongue!
55:11 [55:12] at work in the city; threats and **lies** never leave its streets.
55:23 [55:24] and **deceitful** men will not live out half their days.
109:2 and **deceitful** *men* have opened their mouths against me;
Pr 11:1 The LORD abhors **dishonest** scales, but accurate weights are his
12:5 of the righteous are just, but the advice of the wicked is **deceitful**.
12:17 witness gives honest testimony, but a false witness tells **lies**.
12:20 There is **deceit** in the hearts of those who plot evil, but joy for
14:8 is to give thought to their ways, but the folly of fools is **deception**.
14:25 A truthful witness saves lives, but a false witness is **deceitful**.
20:23 detests differing weights, and **dishonest** scales do not please him.
26:24 disguises himself with his lips, but in his heart he harbors **deceit**.
Isa 53:9 though he had done no violence, nor was any **deceit** in his mouth.

Jer 5:27 Like cages full of birds, their houses are full of **deceit**; they have
9: 6 [9:5] You live in the midst of **deception**; in their deceit they
9: 6 [9:5] in their **deceit** they refuse to acknowledge me,"
9: 8 [9:7] Their tongue is a deadly arrow; it speaks with **deceit**.
Da 8:25 He will cause **deceit** to prosper, and he will consider himself
11:23 After coming to an agreement with him, he will act **deceitfully**,
Hos 11:12 [12:1] surrounded me with lies, the house of Israel with **deceit**.
12: 7 [12:8] The merchant uses **dishonest** scales; he loves to defraud.
Am 8: 5 the measure, boosting the price and cheating with **dishonest** scales,
Mic 6:11 I acquit a man with dishonest scales, with a bag of **false** weights?
Zep 1: 9 who fill the temple of their gods with violence and **deceit**.

5328 ²מִרְמָה ***mirmâ²***, n.pr.m. [1] [√ 5327?; cf. 8228?]
Mirmah [1]

1Ch 8:10 Jeuz, Sakia and **Mirmah**. These were his sons, heads of families.

5329 מְרֵמוֹת ***merēmôt***, n.pr.m. [6 / 7]
Meremoth [6], Meremoth's [1]

Ezr 8:33 and the sacred articles into the hands of **Meremoth** son of Uriah,
10:36 Vaniah, **Meremoth**, Eliashib,
Ne 3: 4 **Meremoth** son of Uriah, the son of Hakkoz, repaired the next
3:21 Next to him, **Meremoth** son of Uriah, the son of Hakkoz,
10: 5 [10:6] Harim, **Meremoth**, Obadiah,
12: 3 Shecaniah, Rehum, **Meremoth**,
12:15 of Harim's, Adna; of **Meremoth's**, [BHS 5318] Helkai;

5330 מִרְמָס ***mirmās***, n.[m.]. [7] [√ 8252]
trampled underfoot [2], beaten down [1], trample down [+8492] [1], trampled [1], what trampled [+8079] [1], where run [1]

Isa 5: 5 be destroyed; I will break down its wall, and it will be **trampled**.
7:25 become places where cattle are turned loose and **where** sheep **run**.
10: 6 and to **trample** [+8492] them **down** like mud in the streets.
28:18 overwhelming scourge sweeps by, you will be **beaten down** by it.
Eze 34:19 Must my flock feed on **what** you have **trampled** [+8079]
Da 8:13 of the sanctuary and of the host that will be **trampled underfoot**?"
Mic 7:10 even now she will be **trampled underfoot** like mire in the streets.

5331 מֵרֹנֹתִי ***mērōnōtî***, a.g. [2]
Meronothite [1], of Meronoth [1]

1Ch 27:30 Jehdeiah the **Meronothite** was in charge of the donkeys.
Ne 3: 7 and Mizpah—Melatiah of Gibeon and Jadon **of Meronoth**—

5332 מֶרֶס ***meres***, n.pr.m. [1]
Meres [1]

Est 1:14 Shethar, Admatha, Tarshish, **Meres**, Marsena and Memucan,

5333 מַרְסְנָא ***marsenā'***, n.pr.m. [1]
Marsena [1]

Est 1:14 Shethar, Admatha, Tarshish, Meres, **Marsena** and Memucan,

5334 מֵרַע ***mēra'***, n.m. *or* v.ptcp. [1] [√ 8317]
evil [1]

Da 11:27 [G] The two kings, with their hearts bent on **evil**, will sit at the

5335 ¹מֵרֵעַ ***mērēa'¹***, n.[m.] *or* v.ptcp. [8] [√ 8287]
friend [3], friends [3], companions [1], personal adviser [1]

Ge 26:26 with Ahuzzath his **personal adviser** and Phicol the commander of
Jdg 14:11 When he appeared, he was given thirty **companions**.
14:20 Samson's wife was given to the **friend** who had attended him at
15: 2 you thoroughly hated her," he said, "that I gave her to your **friend**.
15: 6 Timnite's son-in-law, because his wife was given to his **friend**."
2Sa 3: 8 to the house of your father Saul and to his family and **friends**.
Job 6:14 "A despairing man should have the devotion of his **friends**,
Pr 19: 7 by all his relatives—how much more do his **friends** avoid him!

5336 ²מֵרֵעַ ***mērēa'²***, n.[m.] *or* v.ptcp. Not used in NIV/BHS [√ 8317]

5337 מִרְעֶה ***mir'eh***, n.m. [13] [√ 8286]
pasture [12], place where fed [1]

Ge 47: 4 is severe in Canaan and your servants' flocks have no **pasture**.
1Ch 4:39 Gedor to the east of the valley in search of **pasture** for their flocks.
4:40 They found rich, good **pasture**, and the land was spacious,
4:41 settled in their place, because there was **pasture** for their flocks.
Job 39: 8 He ranges the hills for his **pasture** and searches for any green
Isa 32:14 a wasteland forever, the delight of donkeys, a **pasture** *for* flocks,
La 1: 6 Her princes are like deer that find no **pasture**; in weakness they
Eze 34:14 I will tend them in a good **pasture**, and the mountain heights of
34:14 there they will feed in a rich **pasture** on the mountains of Israel.
34:18 Is it not enough for you to feed on the good **pasture**? Must you
34:18 Must you also trample the rest of your **pasture** with your feet?
Joel 1:18 The herds mill about because they have no **pasture**;
Na 2:11 [2:12] the **place where** they **fed** their young, where the lion

5338 מַרְעִית ***mar'ît***, n.f. [10] [√ 8286]
pasture [8], fed [1], flock [1]

Ps 74: 1 Why does your anger smolder against the sheep of your **pasture**?
79:13 we your people, the sheep of your **pasture**, will praise you forever;
95: 7 for he is our God and we are the people of his **pasture**, the flock
100: 3 and we are his; we are his people, the sheep of his **pasture**.
Isa 49: 9 will feed beside the roads and find **pasture** on every barren hill.
Jer 10:21 the LORD; so they do not prosper and all their **flock** is scattered.
23: 1 who are destroying and scattering the sheep of my **pasture**!"
25:36 the leaders of the flock, for the LORD is destroying their **pasture**.
Eze 34:31 You my sheep, the sheep of my **pasture**, are people, and I am your
Hos 13: 6 When I **fed** them, they were satisfied; when they were satisfied,

5339 מַרְעֲלָה ***mar'alâ***, n.pr.loc. [1] [√ 8302]
Maralah [1]

Jos 19:11 Going west it ran to **Maralah**, touched Dabbesheth, and extended

5340 ¹מַרְפֵּא ***marpē'¹***, n.m. [14] [→ 5342; cf. 8324]
healing [8], remedy [3], healed [1], health [1], incurable [+401] [1]

2Ch 21:18 the LORD afflicted Jehoram with an **incurable** [+401] disease of
36:16 LORD was aroused against his people and there was no **remedy**.
Pr 4:22 are life to those who find them and **health** to a man's whole body.
6:15 him in an instant; he will suddenly be destroyed—without **remedy**.
12:18 pierce like a sword, but the tongue of the wise brings **healing**.
13:17 falls into trouble, but a trustworthy envoy brings **healing**.
15: 4 The tongue that brings **healing** is a tree of life, but a deceitful
16:24 are a honeycomb, sweet to the soul and **healing** to the bones.
29: 1 after many rebukes will suddenly be destroyed—without **remedy**.
Jer 8:15 no good has come, for a time of **healing** but there was only terror.
14:19 Why have you afflicted us so that we cannot be **healed**? We hoped
14:19 no good has come, for a time of **healing** but there is only terror.
33: 6 " 'Nevertheless, I will bring health and **healing** to it; I will heal my
Mal 4: 2 [3:20] the sun of righteousness will rise with **healing** in its wings.

5341 ²מַרְפֵּא ***marpē'²***, n.m. [2] [√ 8332]
at peace [1], calmness [1]

Pr 14:30 A heart **at peace** gives life to the body, but envy rots the bones.
Ecc 10: 4 do not leave your post; **calmness** can lay great errors to rest.

5342 מַרְפֶּה ***marpēh***, n.m. Not used in NIV/BHS [√ 5340; cf. 8324]

5343 מִרְפָּשׂ ***mirpāś***, n.[m.]. [1] [√ 8346]
what muddied [1]

Eze 34:19 have trampled and drink **what** you have **muddied** *with* your feet?

5344 מָרַץ ***māraṣ***, v. [4]
ails [1], beyond all remedy [1], bitter [1], painful [1]

1Ki 2: 8 [C] who called down **bitter** curses on me the day I went to
Job 6:25 [C] How **painful** *are* honest words! But what do your arguments
16: 3 [G] speeches never end? What **ails** you that you keep on arguing?
Mic 2:10 [C] because it is defiled, it is ruined, **beyond all remedy**.

5345 מַרְצֵעַ ***marṣēa'***, n.[m.]. [2] [√ 8361]
awl [2]

Ex 21: 6 take him to the door or the doorpost and pierce his ear with an **awl**.
Dt 15:17 then take an **awl** and push it through his ear lobe into the door,

5346 מַרְצֶפֶת ***marṣepet***, n.f. [1] [√ 8362]
base [1]

2Ki 16:17 from the bronze bulls that supported it and set it on a stone **base**.

5347 מָרַק ***māraq***, v. [3] [→ 5299, 5348, 9475]
be scoured [1], polish [1], polished [1]

Lev 6:28 [6:21] [E] the pot *is to* **be scoured** and rinsed with water.
2Ch 4:16 [B] for the temple of the LORD were of **polished** bronze.
Pr 20:30 [g] [Blows and wounds **cleanse** [K; see Q 9475] **away** evil,]
Jer 46: 4 [A] with helmets on! **Polish** your spears, put on your armor!

5348 מָרָק māraq, n.m. [3] [√ 5347]

broth [3]

Jdg 6:19 Putting the meat in a basket and its **broth** in a pot, he brought them
6:20 place them on this rock, and pour out the **broth**."
Isa 65:4 of pigs, and whose pots hold **broth** [K 7295] *of* unclean meat;

5349 מֶרְקָח merqāḥ, n.[m.]. [1] [√ 8379]

perfume [1]

SS 5:13 His cheeks are like beds of spice yielding **perfume**. His lips are

5350 מֶרְקָחָה merqāḥâ, n.f. [2] [√ 8379]

pot of ointment [1], spices [1]

Job 41:31 [41:23] and stirs up the sea like a **pot of ointment**.
Eze 24:10 Cook the meat well, mixing in the **spices**; and let the bones be

5351 מִרְקַחַת mirqaḥat, n.f. [3] [√ 8379]

fragrant [1], perfumes [+5126] [1], took care of mixing [+4200+8379] [1]

Ex 30:25 a sacred anointing oil, a **fragrant** blend, the work of a perfumer.
1Ch 9:30 some of the priests **took care of mixing** [+4200+8379] the spices.
2Ch 16:14 a bier covered with spices and various blended **perfumes** [+5126],

5352 מָרַר mārar, v. [17] [→ 4933, 4936, 5253, 5255, 5259, 5285, 5287, 5288, 5289, 5300, 5320, 5321, 5353, 5354, 5355, 9476]

bitter [4], made bitter [2], bitter anguish [1], bitterly [1], bitterness attacked [1], furiously [1], grieve bitterly [1], grieves [1], in bitter distress [1], made taste bitterness [1], rage [1], rebel [1], suffered [1]

Ge 49:23 [D] *With* **bitterness** archers **attacked** him; they shot at him with
Ex 1:14 [D] *They* **made** their lives **bitter** with hard labor in brick
23:21 [G] *Do* not **rebel** against him; he will not forgive your rebellion,
Ru 1:13 [A] *It is* more **bitter** for me than for you, because the LORD's
1:20 [G] because the Almighty *has* **made** my life very **bitter**.
1Sa 30:6 [A] each one *was* **bitter** *in* spirit because of his sons and
2Ki 4:27 [A] She *is* **in bitter distress**, but the LORD has hidden it from
Job 27:2 [G] the Almighty, *who has* **made** me **taste bitterness** of soul,
Isa 22:4 [D] Therefore I said, "Turn away from me; *let me* weep **bitterly**.
24:9 [A] they drink wine with a song; the beer *is* **bitter** to its drinkers.
38:17 [A] Surely it was for my benefit that I **suffered** such anguish. In
Jer 4:18 [A] This is your punishment. How **bitter** *it is*! How it pierces to
La 1:4 [A] her maidens grieve, and she is in **bitter anguish**.
Da 8:7 [F] I saw him attack the ram **furiously**, striking the ram
11:11 [F] "Then the king of the South will march out *in a* **rage** and
Zec 12:10 [G] and **grieve bitterly** for him as one grieves for a firstborn son.
12:10 [G] and grieve bitterly for him as *one* **grieves** for a firstborn son.

5353 מָרֹר mārōr, n.m. [5] [√ 5352]

bitter herbs [3], bitter things [1], bitterness [1]

Ex 12:8 the fire, along with **bitter herbs**, and bread made without yeast.
Nu 9:11 to eat the lamb, together with unleavened bread and **bitter herbs**.
Dt 32:32 grapes are filled with poison, and their clusters with **bitterness**.
Job 13:26 For you write down **bitter things** against me and make me inherit
La 3:15 He has filled me with **bitter herbs** and sated me with gall.

5354 מְרֵרָה merērâ, n.f. [1] [√ 5352]

gall [1]

Job 16:13 he pierces my kidneys and spills my **gall** on the ground.

5355 מְרֹרָה merōrâ, n.f. [2] [√ 5352]

liver [1], venom [1]

Job 20:14 in his stomach; it will become the **venom** *of* serpents within him.
20:25 He pulls it out of his back, the gleaming point out of his **liver**.

5356 ¹מְרָרִי merārî[1], n.pr.m. [39] [→ 5357]

Merari [21], Merarites [+1201] [9], Merarite [+1201] [7], Merarite [2]

Ge 46:11 The sons of Levi: Gershon, Kohath and **Merari**.
Ex 6:16 their records: Gershon, Kohath and **Merari**. Levi lived 137 years.
6:19 The sons of **Merari** were Mahli and Mushi. These were the clans
Nu 3:17 were the names of the sons of Levi: Gershon, Kohath and **Merari**.
3:20 The **Merarite** [+1201] clans: Mahli and Mushi. These were the
3:33 To **Merari** belonged the clans of the Mahlites and the Mushites;
3:33 of the Mahlites and the Mushites; these were the **Merarite** clans.
3:35 The leader of the families of the **Merarite** clans was Zuriel son of
3:36 The **Merarites** [+1201] were appointed to take care of the frames
4:29 "Count the **Merarites** [+1201] by their clans and families.
4:33 This is the service of the **Merarite** [+1201] clans as they work at
4:42 The **Merarites** [+1201] were counted by their clans and families.
4:45 This was the total of those in the **Merarite** [+1201] clans.
7:8 and he gave four carts and eight oxen to the **Merarites** [+1201],
10:17 and the Gershonites and **Merarites** [+1201], who carried it,
26:57 the Kohathite clan; through **Merari**, the Merarite clan.
Jos 21:7 The descendants of **Merari**, clan by clan, received twelve towns
21:34 The **Merarite** [+1201] clans (the rest of the Levites) were given:
21:40 All the towns allotted to the **Merarite** [+1201] clans, who were the
1Ch 6:1 [5:27] The sons of Levi: Gershon, Kohath and **Merari**.
6:16 [6:1] The sons of Levi: Gershon, Kohath and **Merari**.
6:19 [6:4] The sons of **Merari**: Mahli and Mushi. These are the clans
6:29 [6:14] The descendants of **Merari**: Mahli, Libni his son,
6:44 [6:29] their associates, the **Merarites** [+1201], at his left hand:
6:47 [6:32] the son of Mushi, the son of **Merari**, the son of Levi.
6:63 [6:48] The descendants of **Merari**, clan by clan, were allotted
6:77 [6:62] The **Merarites** [+1201] (the rest of the Levites)
9:14 the son of Azrikam, the son of Hashabiah, a **Merarite** [+1201];
15:6 from the descendants of **Merari**, Asaiah the leader and 220
15:17 from their brothers the **Merarites** [+1201], Ethan son of Kushaiah;
23:6 corresponding to the sons of Levi: Gershon, Kohath and **Merari**.
23:21 The sons of **Merari**: Mahli and Mushi. The sons of Mahli:
24:26 The sons of **Merari**: Mahli and Mushi. The son of Jaaziah:
24:27 The sons of **Merari**: from Jaaziah: Beno, Shoham, Zaccur
26:10 Hosah the **Merarite** [+1201] had sons: Shimri the first (although
26:19 of the gatekeepers who were descendants of Korah and **Merari**.
2Ch 29:12 from the **Merarites** [+1201], Kish son of Abdi and Azariah son of
34:12 them were Jahath and Obadiah, Levites descended from **Merari**,
Ezr 8:19 together with Jeshaiah from the descendants of **Merari**,

5357 ²מְרָרִי merārî[2], a.g. [1] [√ 5356]

Merarite [1]

Nu 26:57 the Kohathite clan; through Merari, the **Merarite** clan.

5358 ¹מָרֵשָׁה mārēšâ[1], n.pr.loc. [6] [→ 5265, 5359?]

Mareshah [6]

Jos 15:44 Keilah, Aczib and **Mareshah**—nine towns and their villages.
2Ch 11:8 Gath, **Mareshah**, Ziph,
14:9 [14:8] and three hundred chariots, and came as far as **Mareshah**.
14:10 [14:9] battle positions in the Valley of Zephathah near **Mareshah**.
20:37 Eliezer son of Dodavahu of **Mareshah** prophesied against
Mic 1:15 I will bring a conqueror against you who live in **Mareshah**.

5359 ²מָרֵשָׁה mārēšâ[2], n.pr.m. [2] [√ 5358?]

Mareshah [2]

1Ch 2:42 his firstborn, who was the father of Ziph, and his son **Mareshah**,
4:21 Laadah the father of **Mareshah** and the clans of the linen workers

5360 מִרְשַׁעַת mirša'at, n.f. [1] [√ 8399]

wicked [1]

2Ch 24:7 Now the sons of that **wicked** *woman* Athaliah had broken into the

5361 מְרָתַיִם merātayim, n.pr.f. [1] [√ 5286]

Merathaim [1]

Jer 50:21 "Attack the land of **Merathaim** and those who live in Pekod.

5362 ¹מַשָּׂא maśśā'[1], n.m. [36] [√ 5951]

burden [8], load [7], carry [5], burdens [2], carrying [2], singing [2], what to carry [2], camel-loads [+1695] [1], carried about [1], desire [1], loads [1], oppression [1], take away [+4200+5911] [1], that[s] [1], tribute [1]

Ex 23:5 the donkey of someone who hates you fallen down under its **load**,
Nu 4:15 The Kohathites are to **carry** those things that are in the Tent of
4:19 and assign to each man his work and **what** he is **to carry**.
4:24 service of the Gershonite clans as they work and carry **burdens**:
4:27 All their service, whether **carrying** or doing other work, is to be
4:27 shall assign to them as their responsibility all they are to **carry**.
4:31 to **carry** the frames of the tabernacle, its crossbars, posts and
4:32 to their use. Assign to each man the specific things he is to **carry**.
4:47 came to do the work of serving and **carrying** the Tent of Meeting
4:49 each was assigned his work and told **what to carry**.
11:11 What have I done to displease you that you put the **burden** *of* all
11:17 They will help you carry the **burden** *of* the people so that you will
Dt 1:12 your problems and your **burdens** and your disputes all by myself?
2Sa 15:33 said to him, "If you go with me, you will be a **burden** to me.
19:35 [19:36] Why should your servant be an added **burden** to my lord
2Ki 5:17 your servant, be given as much earth as a pair of mules can **carry**,
8:9 taking with him as a gift forty **camel-loads** [+1695] of all the finest
1Ch 15:22 Kenaniah the head Levite was in charge of the **singing**; that was
15:22 **that**[s] was his responsibility because he was skillful at it.

1Ch 15: 27 and Kenaniah, who was in charge of the **singing** *of* the choirs.
2Ch 17: 11 Some Philistines brought Jehoshaphat gifts and silver as **tribute**,
20: 25 articles of value—more than *they could* **take away** [+4200+5911].
35: 3 It is not to be **carried about** on your shoulders. Now serve the
Ne 13: 15 together with wine, grapes, figs and all other kinds of **loads**.
13: 19 at the gates so that no **load** could be brought in on the Sabbath day.
Job 7: 20 have you made me your target? Have I become a **burden** to you?
Ps 38: 4 [38:5] My guilt has overwhelmed me like a **burden** too heavy to
Isa 22: 25 and will fall, and the **load** hanging on it will be cut down."
46: 1 that are carried about are burdensome, a **burden** for the weary.
46: 2 unable to rescue the **burden**, they themselves go off into captivity.
Jer 17: 21 Be careful not to carry a **load** on the Sabbath day or bring it
17: 22 Do not bring a **load** out of your houses or do any work on the
17: 24 and bring no **load** through the gates of this city on the Sabbath,
17: 27 **load** as you come through the gates of Jerusalem on the Sabbath
Eze 24: 25 their heart's **desire**, and their sons and daughters as well—
Hos 8: 10 They will begin to waste away under the **oppression** *of* the mighty

5363 ²מַשָּׂא ***maśśā'²***, n.m. [30] [√ 5951]

oracle [27], oracles [1], prophecies [1], prophecy [1]

2Ki 9: 25 Ahab his father when the LORD made this **prophecy** about him:
2Ch 24: 27 The account of his sons, the many **prophecies** about him,
Pr 30: 1 The sayings of Agur son of Jakeh—an **oracle**: This man declared
31: 1 The sayings of King Lemuel—an **oracle** his mother taught him:
Isa 13: 1 An **oracle** *concerning* Babylon that Isaiah son of Amoz saw:
14: 28 This **oracle** came in the year King Ahaz died:
15: 1 An **oracle** *concerning* Moab: Ar in Moab is ruined, destroyed in a
17: 1 An **oracle** *concerning* Damascus: "See, Damascus will no longer
19: 1 An **oracle** *concerning* Egypt: See, the LORD rides on a swift
21: 1 An **oracle** *concerning* the Desert by the Sea: Like whirlwinds
21: 11 An **oracle** *concerning* Dumah: Someone calls to me from Seir,
21: 13 An **oracle** concerning Arabia: You caravans of Dedanites,
22: 1 An **oracle** *concerning* the Valley of Vision: What troubles you
23: 1 An **oracle** *concerning* Tyre: Wail, O ships of Tarshish! For Tyre is
30: 6 An **oracle** *concerning* the animals of the Negev: Through a land of
Jer 23: 33 a prophet or a priest, ask you, 'What is the **oracle** *of* the LORD?'
23: 33 say to them, 'What **oracle**? I will forsake you,
23: 34 'This is the **oracle** *of* the LORD,' I will punish that man and his
23: 36 But you must not mention 'the **oracle** *of* the LORD' again,
23: 36 because every man's own word becomes his **oracle** and so you
23: 38 Although you claim, 'This is the **oracle** *of* the LORD,' this is what
23: 38 You used the words, 'This is the **oracle** *of* the LORD,'
23: 38 you that you must not claim, 'This is the **oracle** *of* the LORD.'
La 2: 14 The **oracles** they gave you were false and misleading.
Eze 12: 10 This **oracle** *concerns* the prince in Jerusalem and the whole house
Na 1: 1 An **oracle** *concerning* Nineveh. The book of the vision of Nahum
Hab 1: 1 The **oracle** that Habakkuk the prophet received.
Zec 9: 1 An **Oracle** The word of the LORD is against the land of Hadrach
12: 1 An **Oracle** This is the word of the LORD concerning Israel.
Mal 1: 1 An **oracle**: The word of the LORD to Israel through Malachi.

5364 ³מַשָּׂא ***maśśā'³***, n.pr.g. & loc. [2] [→ 5392?]

Massa [2]

Ge 25: 14 Mishma, Dumah, **Massa**,
1Ch 1: 30 Mishma, Dumah, **Massa**, Hadad, Tema,

5365 מַשֹּׂא ***maśśō'***, n.m. [1] [√ 5951]

partiality [+7156] [1]

2Ch 19: 7 our God there is no injustice or **partiality** [+7156] or bribery."

5366 מַשָּׂאָה ***maśśā'â***, n.f. [1] [√ 5951]

clouds of smoke [1]

Isa 30: 27 comes from afar, with burning anger and dense **clouds of smoke**;

5367 מַשְּׂאוֹת ***maś'ôt***, n.f.?. Not used in NIV/BHS [√ 5951]

5368 מַשְׂאֵת ***maś'ēt***, n.f. [15] [√ 5951]

untranslated [2], gifts [2], tax [2], burden [1], cloud [1], gift [1], lifting up [1], portion [1], portions [1], present [1], signal [1], smoke [1]

Ge 43: 34 When **portions** were served to them from Joseph's table,
43: 34 Benjamin's **portion** was five times as much as anyone else's.
43: 34 anyone else's. **[RPH]** So they feasted and drank freely with him.
Jdg 20: 38 that they should send up a great **cloud** *of* smoke from the city,
20: 40 and saw the **smoke** of the whole city going up into the sky.
2Sa 11: 8 Uriah left the palace, and a **gift** *from* the king was sent after him.
2Ch 24: 6 Jerusalem the **tax** *imposed by* Moses the servant of the LORD
24: 9 Jerusalem that they should bring to the LORD the **tax** that Moses
Est 2: 18 throughout the provinces and distributed **gifts** with royal liberality.
Ps 141: 2 may the **lifting up** *of* my hands be like the evening sacrifice.
Jer 6: 1 the trumpet in Tekoa! Raise the **signal** over Beth Hakkerem!
40: 5 the commander gave him provisions and a **present** and let him go.
Eze 20: 40 There I will require your offerings and your choice **gifts**,
Am 5: 11 You trample on the poor and force him to give you **[NIE]** grain.
Zep 3: 18 I will remove from you; they are a **burden** and a reproach to you.

5369 ¹מִשְׂגָּב ***miśgāb¹***, n.[m.]. [17] [√ 8435]

fortress [9], stronghold [5], refuge [2], high [1]

2Sa 22: 3 He is my **stronghold**, my refuge and my savior—from violent men
Ps 9: 9 [9:10] The LORD is a **refuge** for the oppressed, a stronghold in
9: 9 [9:10] refuge for the oppressed, a **stronghold** in times of trouble.
18: 2 [18:3] is my shield and the horn of my salvation, my **stronghold**.
46: 7 [46:8] Almighty is with us; the God of Jacob is our **fortress**.
46: 11 [46:12] Almighty is with us; the God of Jacob is our **fortress**.
48: 3 [48:4] is in her citadels; he has shown himself to be her **fortress**.
59: 9 [59:10] I watch for you; you, O God, are my **fortress**,
59: 16 [59:17] for you are my **fortress**, my refuge in times of trouble.
59: 17 [59:18] to you; you, O God, are my **fortress**, my loving God.
62: 2 [62:3] and my salvation; he is my **fortress**, I will never be shaken.
62: 6 [62:7] and my salvation; he is my **fortress**, I will not be shaken.
94: 22 the LORD has become my **fortress**, and my God the rock in
144: 2 and my fortress, my **stronghold** and my deliverer, my shield,
Isa 25: 12 He will bring down your **high** fortified walls and lay them low;
33: 16 dwell on the heights, whose **refuge** will be the mountain fortress.
Jer 48: 1 and captured; the **stronghold** will be disgraced and shattered.

5370 ²מִשְׂגָּב ***miśgāb²***, n.pr.loc. Not used in NIV/BHS [√ 8435]

5371 מַשֶּׂגֶת ***maśśeget***, n.[f.] *or* v.ptcp. Not used in NIV/BHS [√ 5952]

5372 מְשׂוּכָּה ***m^eśûkkâ***, n.f. [1] [√ 8504]

hedge [1]

Isa 5: 5 I will take away its **hedge**, and it will be destroyed; I will break

5373 מַשּׂוֹר ***maśśôr***, n.m. [1]

saw [1]

Isa 10: 15 him who swings it, or the **saw** boast against him who uses it?

5374 מְשׂוּרָה ***m^eśûrâ***, n.f. [4]

measure out [1], measurements of quantity [1], quantity [1], rationed [+928] [1]

Lev 19: 35 dishonest standards when measuring length, weight or **quantity**.
1Ch 23: 29 and the mixing, and all **measurements of quantity** and size.
Eze 4: 11 Also **measure out** a sixth of a hin of water and drink it at set times.
4: 16 food in anxiety and drink **rationed** [+928] water in despair,

5375 ¹מָשׂוֹשׂ ***māśôś¹***, n.m. [16] [√ 8464]

joy [6], delight [2], gaiety [2], rejoices [2], celebrations [1], joyful [1], merriment [1], rejoice greatly [+8464] [1]

Ps 48: 2 [48:3] It is beautiful in its loftiness, the **joy** *of* the whole earth.
Isa 8: 6 of Shiloah and **rejoices** over Rezin and the son of Remaliah,
24: 8 The **gaiety** *of* the tambourines is stilled, the noise of the revelers
24: 8 the noise of the revelers has stopped, the **joyful** harp is silent.
24: 11 all joy turns to gloom, all **gaiety** is banished from the earth.
32: 13 mourn for all houses of **merriment** and for this city of revelry.
32: 14 a wasteland forever, the **delight** *of* donkeys, a pasture for flocks,
60: 15 I will make you the everlasting pride and the **joy** *of* all generations.
62: 5 as a bridegroom **rejoices** over his bride, so will your God rejoice
65: 18 for I will create Jerusalem to be a delight and its people a **joy**.
66: 10 **rejoice greatly** [+8464] with her, all you who mourn over her.
Jer 49: 25 city of renown not been abandoned, the town in which I **delight**?
La 2: 15 was called the perfection of beauty, the **joy** of the whole earth?"
5: 15 **Joy** is gone from our hearts; our dancing has turned to mourning.
Eze 24: 25 their **joy** and glory, the delight of their eyes, their heart's desire,
Hos 2: 11 [2:13] I will stop all her **celebrations**: her yearly festivals,

5376 ²מָשׂוֹשׂ ***māśôś²***, n.m. [1] [cf. 5022]

withers away [1]

Job 8: 19 Surely its life **withers away**, and from the soil other plants grow.

5377 מִשְׂחָק ***miśḥāq***, n.[m.]. [1] [√ 8471]

scoff [1]

Hab 1: 10 They deride kings and **scoff** at rulers. They laugh at all fortified

5378 מַשְׂטֵמָה ***maśṭēmâ***, n.f. [2] [√ 8475]

hostility [2]

Hos 9: 7 Because your sins are so many and your **hostility** so great,

Hos 9: 8 await him on all his paths, and **hostility** in the house of his God.

5379 מְשֻׂכָה ***mᵉśukâ***, n.f. [1] [√ 5004; cf. 6056]

blocked [1]

Pr 15: 19 The way of the sluggard is **blocked** *with* thorns, but the path of the

5380 מַשְׂכִּיל ***maśkîl***, n.m. [14] [√ 8505]

maskil [13], psalm of praise [1]

Ps 32: T [32:1] Of David. A ***maskil***.
42: T [42:1] the director of music. A ***maskil*** of the Sons of Korah.
44: T [44:1] the director of music. Of the Sons of Korah. A ***maskil***.
45: T [45:1] Of the Sons of Korah. A ***maskil***. A wedding song.
47: 7 [47:8] is the King of all the earth; sing to him a **psalm of praise**.
52: T [52:1] For the director of music. A ***maskil*** of David.
53: T [53:1] of music. According to *mahalath*. A ***maskil*** of David.
54: T [54:1] of music. With stringed instruments. A ***maskil*** of David.
55: T [55:1] of music. With stringed instruments. A ***maskil*** of David.
74: T [74:1] A ***maskil*** of Asaph.
78: T [78:1] A ***maskil*** of Asaph.
88: T [88:1] A ***maskil*** of Heman the Ezrahite.
89: T [89:1] A ***maskil*** of Ethan the Ezrahite.
142: T [142:1] A ***maskil*** of David. When he was in the cave. A prayer.

5381 מַשְׂכִּית ***maśkît***, n.f. [6] [√ 8495]

carved images [1], carved [1], evil conceits [1], idol [1], imagine [+928+3869] [1], settings [1]

Lev 26: 1 do not place a **carved** stone in your land to bow down before it.
Nu 33: 52 Destroy all their **carved images** and their cast idols, and demolish
Ps 73: 7 comes iniquity; the **evil conceits** *of* their minds know no limits.
Pr 18: 11 fortified city; they **imagine** [+928+3869] it an unscalable wall.
25: 11 A word aptly spoken is like apples of gold in **settings** *of* silver.
Eze 8: 12 Israel are doing in the darkness, each at the shrine of his own **idol**?

5382 מַשְׂכֹּרֶת ***maśkōret***, n.f. [4] [√ 8509]

wages [3], rewarded [1]

Ge 29: 15 work for me for nothing? Tell me what your **wages** should be."
31: 7 yet your father has cheated me by changing my **wages** ten times.
31: 41 six years for your flocks, and you changed my **wages** ten times.
Ru 2: 12 May you be richly **rewarded** by the LORD, the God of Israel,

5383 מַשְׂמְרָה ***maśmērâ***, n.m. [1] [cf. 6169]

nails [1]

Ecc 12: 11 are like goads, their collected sayings like firmly embedded **nails**—

5384 מִשְׂפָּח ***miśpāḥ***, n.[m.]. [1] [cf. 6203]

bloodshed [1]

Isa 5: 7 And he looked for justice, but saw **bloodshed**; for righteousness,

5385 מִשְׂרָה ***miśrâ***, n.f. [2] [√ 8606]

government [2]

Isa 9: 6 [9:5] a son is given, and the **government** will be on his shoulders.
9: 7 [9:6] Of the increase of his **government** and peace there will be

5386 מִשְׂרָפוֹת ***miśrāpôt***, n.[f.pl.]. [2] [√ 8596]

burned [1], funeral fire [1]

Isa 33: 12 The peoples will be **burned** *as if to* lime; like cut thornbushes they
Jer 34: 5 As people made a **funeral fire** *in honor of* your fathers, the former

5387 מִשְׂרְפוֹת מַיִם ***miśrᵉpôt mayim***, n.pr.loc. [2] [√ 8596 + 4784]

Misrephoth Maim [2]

Jos 11: 8 to **Misrephoth Maim**, and to the Valley of Mizpah on the east,
13: 6 of the mountain regions from Lebanon to **Misrephoth Maim**,

5388 מַשְׂרֵקָה ***maśrēqâ***, n.pr.loc. [2] [√ 8601]

Masrekah [2]

Ge 36: 36 When Hadad died, Samlah from **Masrekah** succeeded him as king.
1Ch 1: 47 When Hadad died, Samlah from **Masrekah** succeeded him as king.

5389 מַשְׂרֵת ***maśrēt***, n.m. [1] [√ 8419]

pan [1]

2Sa 13: 9 she took the **pan** and served him the bread, but he refused to eat.

5390 מַשׁ ***maš***, var. [1 / 0]

Ge 10: 23 Uz, Hul, Gether and Meshech. [BHS ***Mash***; NIV 5434]

5391 מַשָּׁא ***maššā'***, n.m. [3] [√ 5957]

debts [+3338] [1], exacting of usury [1], usury [1]

Ne 5: 7 I told them, "You are exacting **usury** from your own countrymen!"
5: 10 the people money and grain. But let the **exacting of usury** stop!
10: 31 [10:32] forgo working the land and will cancel all **debts** [+3338].

5392 מֵשָׁא ***mēšā'***, n.pr.loc. [1] [√ 5364?]

Mesha [1]

Ge 10: 30 The region where they lived stretched from **Mesha** toward Sephar,

5393 מַשְׁאָב ***maš'āb***, n.[m.]. [1] [√ 8612]

watering places [1]

Jdg 5: 11 the voice of the singers at the **watering places**. They recite the

5394 מַשָּׁאָה ***maššā'â***, n.f. [2] [√ 5957]

debts [1], make a loan [+5957] [1]

Dt 24: 10 When *you* **make a loan** [+5957] of any kind to your neighbor,
Pr 22: 26 be a man who strikes hands in pledge or puts up security for **debts**;

5395 מַשֻּׁאָה ***maššu'â***, n.[f.]. Not used in NIV/BHS [√ 5958]

5396 מַשָּׁאוֹן ***maššā'ôn***, n.[m.]. [1] [√ 5958]

deception [1]

Pr 26: 26 His malice may be concealed by **deception**, but his wickedness

5397 מַשֻּׁאוֹת ***maššu'ôt***, n.f.pl. [2]

ruin [1], ruins [1]

Ps 73: 18 you place them on slippery ground; you cast them down to **ruin**.
74: 3 Turn your steps toward these everlasting **ruins**, all this destruction

5398 מִשְׁאָל ***miš'āl***, n.pr.loc. [2] [cf. 5443]

Mishal [2]

Jos 19: 26 Allammelech, Amad and **Mishal**. On the west the boundary
21: 30 from the tribe of Asher, **Mishal**, Abdon,

5399 מִשְׁאָלָה ***miš'ālâ***, n.f. [2] [√ 8626]

desires [1], requests [1]

Ps 20: 5 [20:6] name of our God. May the LORD grant all your **requests**.
37: 4 in the LORD and he will give you the **desires** *of* your heart.

5400 מִשְׁאֶרֶת ***miš'eret***, n.f. [4] [√ 8419]

kneading trough [2], kneading troughs [2]

Ex 8: 3 [7:28] your people, and into your ovens and **kneading troughs**.
12: 34 carried it on their shoulders in **kneading troughs** wrapped in
Dt 28: 5 Your basket and your **kneading trough** will be blessed.
28: 17 Your basket and your **kneading trough** will be cursed.

5401 מִשְׁבְּצוֹת ***mišbᵉṣôt***, n.f.pl. [9] [√ 8687]

filigree [3], settings [3], filigree settings [2], interwoven [1]

Ex 28: 11 engraves a seal. Then mount the stones in gold **filigree** settings
28: 13 Make gold **filigree settings**
28: 14 of pure gold, like a rope, and attach the chains to the **settings**.
28: 25 the other ends of the chains to the two **settings**, attaching them to
39: 6 They mounted the onyx stones in gold **filigree** settings
39: 13 and a jasper. They were mounted in gold **filigree** settings.
39: 16 They made two gold **filigree settings** and two gold rings,
39: 18 the other ends of the chains to the two **settings**, attaching them to
Ps 45: 13 [45:14] within ⌊her chamber⌋; her gown is **interwoven** *with* gold.

5402 מַשְׁבֵּר ***mašbēr***, n.[m.]. [3] [√ 8689]

point of birth [2], opening of the womb [+1201] [1]

2Ki 19: 3 as when children come to the **point of birth** and there is no
Isa 37: 3 as when children come to the **point of birth** and there is no
Hos 13: 13 he does not come to the **opening** [+1201] **of the womb**.

5403 מִשְׁבָּר ***mišbār***, n.[m.]. [5] [√ 8689]

waves [3], breakers [2]

2Sa 22: 5 "The **waves** *of* death swirled about me; the torrents of destruction
Ps 42: 7 [42:8] all your **waves** and breakers have swept over me.
88: 7 [88:8] upon me; you have overwhelmed me with all your **waves**.
93: 4 thunder of the great waters, mightier than the **breakers** *of* the sea—
Jnh 2: 3 [2:4] about me; all your waves and **breakers** swept over me.

5404 מִשְׁבָּת *mišbāt*, n.[m.]. [1] [√ 8697]

destruction [1]

La 1: 7 Her enemies looked at her and laughed at her **destruction**.

5405 מִשְׁגֶּה *mišgeh*, n.m. [1] [√ 8706]

mistake [1]

Ge 43: 12 put back into the mouths of your sacks. Perhaps it was a **mistake**.

5406 מָשָׁה *māšâ*, v. [3] [→ 5407; cf. 621?]

drew out [2], drew [1]

Ex 2: 10 [A] named him Moses, saying, "*I* **drew** him out of the water."
2Sa 22: 17 [G] and took hold of me; *he* **drew** me **out** of deep waters.
Ps 18: 16 [18:17] [G] took hold of me; *he* **drew** me **out** of deep waters.

5407 מֹשֶׁה *mōšeh*, n.pr.m. [766 / 767] [√ 5406]

Moses [722], he[s] [19], him[s] [17], *untranslated* [5], his[s] [3], Moses [+4200] [1]

Ex 2: 10 She named him **Moses**, saying, "I drew him out of the water."
2: 11 One day, after **Moses** had grown up, he went out to where his own
2: 14 **Moses** was afraid and thought, "What I did must have become
2: 15 When Pharaoh heard of this, he tried to kill **Moses**, but Moses fled
2: 15 but **Moses** fled from Pharaoh and went to live in Midian,
2: 17 but **Moses** got up and came to their rescue and watered their flock.
2: 21 **Moses** agreed to stay with the man, who gave his daughter
2: 21 the man, who gave his daughter Zipporah to **Moses** in marriage.
3: 1 Now **Moses** was tending the flock of Jethro his father-in-law,
3: 3 So **Moses** thought, "I will go over and see this strange sight—
3: 4 over to look, God called to him from within the bush, "**Moses**!
3: 4 God called to him from within the bush, "Moses! **Moses**!"
3: 6 At this, **Moses** hid his face, because he was afraid to look at God.
3: 11 But **Moses** said to God, "Who am I, that I should go to Pharaoh
3: 13 **Moses** said to God, "Suppose I go to the Israelites and say to them,
3: 14 God said to **Moses**, "I AM WHO I AM. This is what you are to say
3: 15 God also said to **Moses**, "Say to the Israelites, 'The LORD,
4: 1 **Moses** answered, "What if they do not believe me or listen to me
4: 3 **Moses** threw it on the ground and it became a snake, and he ran
4: 4 So **Moses** reached out and took hold of the snake and it turned
4: 10 **Moses** said to the LORD, "O Lord, I have never been eloquent,
4: 14 Then the LORD's anger burned against **Moses** and he said,
4: 18 Then **Moses** went back to Jethro his father-in-law and said to him,
4: 18 are still alive." Jethro said, **[RPH]** "Go, and I wish you well."
4: 19 Now the LORD had said to **Moses** in Midian, "Go back to Egypt,
4: 20 So **Moses** took his wife and sons, put them on a donkey and started
4: 20 started back to Egypt. And **he**[s] took the staff of God in his hand.
4: 21 The LORD said to **Moses**, "When you return to Egypt, see that
4: 27 The LORD said to Aaron, "Go into the desert to meet **Moses**."
4: 28 **Moses** told Aaron everything the LORD had sent him to say,
4: 29 **Moses** and Aaron brought together all the elders of the Israelites,
4: 30 and Aaron told them everything the LORD had said to **Moses**.
5: 1 Afterward **Moses** and Aaron went to Pharaoh and said, "This is
5: 4 the king of Egypt said, "**Moses** and Aaron, why are you taking the
5: 20 left Pharaoh, they found **Moses** and Aaron waiting to meet them,
5: 22 **Moses** returned to the LORD and said, "O Lord, why have you
6: 1 the LORD said to **Moses**, "Now you will see what I will do to
6: 2 God also said to **Moses**, "I am the LORD.
6: 9 **Moses** reported this to the Israelites, but they did not listen to him
6: 9 but they did not listen to **him**[s] because of their discouragement
6: 10 Then the LORD said to **Moses**,
6: 12 **Moses** said to the LORD, "If the Israelites will not listen to me,
6: 13 Now the LORD spoke to **Moses** and Aaron about the Israelites
6: 20 his father's sister Jochebed, who bore him Aaron and **Moses**.
6: 26 It was this same Aaron and **Moses** to whom the LORD said,
6: 27 the Israelites out of Egypt. It was the same **Moses** and Aaron.
6: 28 Now when the LORD spoke to **Moses** in Egypt,
6: 29 he said to **him**[s], "I am the LORD. Tell Pharaoh king of Egypt
6: 30 But **Moses** said to the LORD, "Since I speak with faltering lips,
7: 1 the LORD said to **Moses**, "See, I have made you like God to
7: 6 **Moses** and Aaron did just as the LORD commanded them.
7: 7 **Moses** was eighty years old and Aaron eighty-three when they
7: 8 The LORD said to **Moses** and Aaron,
7: 10 So **Moses** and Aaron went to Pharaoh and did just as the LORD
7: 14 Then the LORD said to **Moses**, "Pharaoh's heart is unyielding;
7: 19 The LORD said to **Moses**, "Tell Aaron, 'Take your staff
7: 20 **Moses** and Aaron did just as the LORD had commanded.
8: 1 [7:26] the LORD said to **Moses**, "Go to Pharaoh and say to him,
8: 5 [8:1] the LORD said to **Moses**, "Tell Aaron, 'Stretch out your
8: 8 [8:4] Pharaoh summoned **Moses** and Aaron and said, "Pray to the
8: 9 [8:5] **Moses** said to Pharaoh, "I leave to you the honor of setting
8: 12 [8:8] After **Moses** and Aaron left Pharaoh, Moses cried out to the
8: 12 [8:8] **Moses** cried out to the LORD about the frogs he had
8: 13 [8:9] the LORD did what **Moses** asked. The frogs died in the
8: 16 [8:12] the LORD said to **Moses**, "Tell Aaron, 'Stretch out your
8: 20 [8:16] the LORD said to **Moses**, "Get up early in the morning
8: 25 [8:21] Then Pharaoh summoned **Moses** and Aaron and said, "Go,
8: 26 [8:22] **Moses** said, "That would not be right. The sacrifices we
8: 29 [8:25] **Moses** answered, "As soon as I leave you, I will pray to the
8: 30 [8:26] Then **Moses** left Pharaoh and prayed to the LORD,
8: 31 [8:27] the LORD did what **Moses** asked: The flies left Pharaoh
9: 1 Then the LORD said to **Moses**, "Go to Pharaoh and say to him,
9: 8 the LORD said to **Moses** and Aaron, "Take handfuls of soot from
9: 8 and have **Moses** toss it into the air in the presence of Pharaoh.
9: 10 **Moses** tossed it into the air, and festering boils broke out on men
9: 11 The magicians could not stand before **Moses** because of the boils
9: 12 listen to Moses and Aaron, just as the LORD had said to **Moses**.
9: 13 Then the LORD said to **Moses**, "Get up early in the morning,
9: 22 the LORD said to **Moses**, "Stretch out your hand toward the sky
9: 23 When **Moses** stretched out his staff toward the sky, the LORD
9: 27 Pharaoh summoned **Moses** and Aaron. "This time I have sinned,"
9: 29 **Moses** replied, "When I have gone out of the city, I will spread out
9: 33 **Moses** left Pharaoh and went out of the city. He spread out his
9: 35 let the Israelites go, just as the LORD had said through **Moses**.
10: 1 the LORD said to **Moses**, "Go to Pharaoh, for I have hardened his
10: 3 So **Moses** and Aaron went to Pharaoh and said to him, "This is
10: 8 Then **Moses** and Aaron were brought back to Pharaoh. "Go,
10: 9 **Moses** answered, "We will go with our young and old, with our
10: 12 And the LORD said to **Moses**, "Stretch out your hand over Egypt
10: 13 So **Moses** stretched out his staff over Egypt, and the LORD made
10: 16 Pharaoh quickly summoned **Moses** and Aaron and said, "I have
10: 21 the LORD said to **Moses**, "Stretch out your hand toward the sky
10: 22 So **Moses** stretched out his hand toward the sky, and total darkness
10: 24 Pharaoh summoned **Moses** and said, "Go, worship the LORD.
10: 25 **Moses** said, "You must allow us to have sacrifices and burnt
10: 29 "Just as you say," **Moses** replied, "I will never appear before you
11: 1 Now the LORD had said to **Moses**, "I will bring one more plague
11: 3 **Moses** himself was highly regarded in Egypt by Pharaoh's officials
11: 4 So **Moses** said, "This is what the LORD says: 'About midnight I
11: 9 The LORD had said to **Moses**, "Pharaoh will refuse to listen to
11: 10 **Moses** and Aaron performed all these wonders before Pharaoh,
12: 1 The LORD said to **Moses** and Aaron in Egypt,
12: 21 Then **Moses** summoned all the elders of Israel and said to them,
12: 28 The Israelites did just what the LORD commanded **Moses**
12: 31 During the night Pharaoh summoned **Moses** and Aaron and said,
12: 35 The Israelites did as **Moses** instructed and asked the Egyptians for
12: 43 The LORD said to **Moses** and Aaron, "These are the regulations
12: 50 All the Israelites did just what the LORD had commanded **Moses**
13: 1 The LORD said to **Moses**,
13: 3 **Moses** said to the people, "Commemorate this day, the day you
13: 19 **Moses** took the bones of Joseph with him because Joseph had
14: 1 Then the LORD said to **Moses**,
14: 11 They said to **Moses**, "Was it because there were no graves in Egypt
14: 13 **Moses** answered the people, "Do not be afraid. Stand firm
14: 15 Then the LORD said to **Moses**, "Why are you crying out to me?
14: 21 **Moses** stretched out his hand over the sea, and all that night the
14: 26 the LORD said to **Moses**, "Stretch out your hand over the sea
14: 27 **Moses** stretched out his hand over the sea, and at daybreak the sea
14: 31 the LORD and put their trust in him and in **Moses** his servant.
15: 1 Then **Moses** and the Israelites sang this song to the LORD:
15: 22 **Moses** led Israel from the Red Sea and they went into the Desert of
15: 24 So the people grumbled against **Moses**, saying, "What are we to
16: 2 In the desert the whole community grumbled against **Moses**
16: 4 the LORD said to **Moses**, "I will rain down bread from heaven for
16: 6 So **Moses** and Aaron said to all the Israelites, "In the evening you
16: 8 **Moses** also said, "You will know that it was the LORD when he
16: 9 Then **Moses** told Aaron, "Say to the entire Israelite community,
16: 11 The LORD said to **Moses**,
16: 15 **Moses** said to them, "It is the bread the LORD has given you to
16: 19 **Moses** said to them, "No one is to keep any of it until morning."
16: 20 However, some of them paid no attention to **Moses**; they kept part
16: 20 of maggots and began to smell. So **Moses** was angry with them.
16: 22 and the leaders of the community came and reported this to **Moses**.
16: 24 as **Moses** commanded, and it did not stink or get maggots in it.
16: 25 "Eat it today," **Moses** said, "because today is a Sabbath to the
16: 28 the LORD said to **Moses**, "How long will you refuse to keep my
16: 32 **Moses** said, "This is what the LORD has commanded: 'Take an
16: 33 So **Moses** said to Aaron, "Take a jar and put an omer of manna in
16: 34 As the LORD commanded **Moses**, Aaron put the manna in front
17: 2 So they quarreled with **Moses** and said, "Give us water to drink."
17: 2 us water to drink." **Moses** replied, "Why do you quarrel with me?
17: 3 were thirsty for water there, and they grumbled against **Moses**.
17: 4 **Moses** cried out to the LORD, "What am I to do with these
17: 5 The LORD answered **Moses**, "Walk on ahead of the people.
17: 6 to drink." So **Moses** did this in the sight of the elders of Israel.
17: 9 **Moses** said to Joshua, "Choose some of our men and go out to
17: 10 So Joshua fought the Amalekites as **Moses** had ordered, and
17: 10 had ordered, and **Moses**, Aaron and Hur went to the top of the hill.

Ex 17:11 As long as **Moses** held up his hands, the Israelites were winning,
17:12 When **Moses**' hands grew tired, they took a stone and put it under
17:14 the LORD said to **Moses**, "Write this on a scroll as something to
17:15 **Moses** built an altar and called it The LORD is my Banner.
18: 1 Now Jethro, the priest of Midian and father-in-law of **Moses**,
18: 1 heard of everything God had done for **Moses** and for his people
18: 2 After **Moses** had sent away his wife Zipporah, his father-in-law
18: 2 sent away his wife Zipporah, **his**[s] father-in-law Jethro received her
18: 5 Jethro, **Moses**' father-in-law, together with Moses' sons and wife,
18: 5 together with Moses' sons and wife, came to **him**[s] in the desert,
18: 6 Jethro had sent word to **him**[s], "I, your father-in-law Jethro,
18: 7 So **Moses** went out to meet his father-in-law and bowed down
18: 8 **Moses** told his father-in-law about everything the LORD had
18:12 Then Jethro, **Moses**' father-in-law, brought a burnt offering
18:12 Aaron came with all the elders of Israel to eat bread with **Moses**'
18:13 The next day **Moses** took his seat to serve as judge for the people,
18:13 the people, and they stood around **him**[s] from morning till evening.
18:14 When his father-in-law saw all that **Moses** was doing for the
18:15 **Moses** answered him, "Because the people come to me to seek
18:17 **Moses**' father-in-law replied, "What you are doing is not good.
18:24 **Moses** listened to his father-in-law and did everything he said.
18:25 **He**[s] chose capable men from all Israel and made them leaders of
18:26 The difficult cases they brought to **Moses**, but the simple ones they
18:27 **Moses** sent his father-in-law on his way, and Jethro returned to his
19: 3 **Moses** went up to God, and the LORD called to him from the
19: 7 So **Moses** went back and summoned the elders of the people
19: 8 has said." So **Moses** brought their answer back to the LORD.
19: 9 The LORD said to **Moses**, "I am going to come to you in a dense
19: 9 in you." Then **Moses** told the LORD what the people had said.
19:10 the LORD said to **Moses**, "Go to the people and consecrate them
19:14 After **Moses** had gone down the mountain to the people, he
19:17 Then **Moses** led the people out of the camp to meet with God,
19:19 and louder. Then **Moses** spoke and the voice of God answered him.
19:20 top of Mount Sinai and called **Moses** to the top of the mountain.
19:20 and called Moses to the top of the mountain. So **Moses** went up
19:21 and the LORD said to **him**[s], "Go down and warn the people
19:23 **Moses** said to the LORD, "The people cannot come up Mount
19:25 So **Moses** went down to the people and told them.
20:19 and said to **Moses**, "Speak to us yourself and we will listen.
20:20 **Moses** said to the people, "Do not be afraid. God has come to test
20:21 while **Moses** approached the thick darkness where God was.
20:22 the LORD said to **Moses**, "Tell the Israelites this: 'You have seen
24: 1 Then he said to **Moses**, "Come up to the LORD, you and Aaron,
24: 2 **Moses** alone is to approach the LORD; the others must not come
24: 3 When **Moses** went and told the people all the LORD's words
24: 4 **Moses** then wrote down everything the LORD had said. He got
24: 6 **Moses** took half of the blood and put it in bowls, and the other half
24: 8 **Moses** then took the blood, sprinkled it on the people and said,
24: 9 **Moses** and Aaron, Nadab and Abihu, and the seventy elders of
24:12 The LORD said to **Moses**, "Come up to me on the mountain
24:13 **Moses** set out with Joshua his aide, and Moses went up on the
24:13 with Joshua his aide, and **Moses** went up on the mountain of God.
24:15 When **Moses** went up on the mountain, the cloud covered it,
24:16 on the seventh day the LORD called to **Moses** from within the
24:18 Then **Moses** entered the cloud as he went on up the mountain.
24:18 And **he**[s] stayed on the mountain forty days and forty nights.
25: 1 The LORD said to **Moses**,
30:11 Then the LORD said to **Moses**,
30:17 Then the LORD said to **Moses**,
30:22 Then the LORD said to **Moses**,
30:34 the LORD said to **Moses**, "Take fragrant spices—gum resin,
31: 1 Then the LORD said to **Moses**,
31:12 Then the LORD said to **Moses**,
31:18 When the LORD finished speaking to **Moses** on Mount Sinai,
32: 1 When the people saw that **Moses** was so long in coming down
32: 1 As for this fellow **Moses** who brought us up out of Egypt,
32: 7 Then the LORD said to **Moses**, "Go down, because your people,
32: 9 "I have seen these people," the LORD said to **Moses**, "and they
32:11 But **Moses** sought the favor of the LORD his God. "O LORD,"
32:15 **Moses** turned and went down the mountain with the two tablets of
32:17 he said to **Moses**, "There is the sound of war in the camp."
32:19 When **Moses** approached the camp and saw the calf
32:21 **He**[s] said to Aaron, "What did these people do to you, that you led
32:23 As for this fellow **Moses** who brought us up out of Egypt,
32:25 **Moses** saw that the people were running wild and that Aaron had
32:26 So **he**[s] stood at the entrance to the camp and said, "Whoever is for
32:28 The Levites did as **Moses** commanded, and that day about three
32:29 Then **Moses** said, "You have been set apart to the LORD today,
32:30 The next day **Moses** said to the people, "You have committed a
32:31 So **Moses** went back to the LORD and said, "Oh, what a great sin
32:33 The LORD replied to **Moses**, "Whoever has sinned against me I
33: 1 the LORD said to **Moses**, "Leave this place, you and the people
33: 5 For the LORD had said to **Moses**, "Tell the Israelites, 'You are a
33: 7 Now **Moses** used to take a tent and pitch it outside the camp some
33: 8 And whenever **Moses** went out to the tent, all the people rose
33: 8 entrances to their tents, watching **Moses** until he entered the tent.
33: 9 As **Moses** went into the tent, the pillar of cloud would come down
33: 9 and stay at the entrance, while the LORD spoke with **Moses**.
33:11 The LORD would speak to **Moses** face to face, as a man speaks
33:12 **Moses** said to the LORD, "You have been telling me, 'Lead these
33:17 the LORD said to **Moses**, "I will do the very thing you have
34: 1 The LORD said to **Moses**, "Chisel out two stone tablets like the
34: 4 So **Moses** chiseled out two stone tablets like the first ones
34: 8 **Moses** bowed to the ground at once and worshiped.
34:27 Then the LORD said to **Moses**, "Write down these words,
34:29 When **Moses** came down from Mount Sinai with the two tablets of
34:29 Mount Sinai with the two tablets of the Testimony in **his**[s] hands,
34:29 **he**[s] was not aware that his face was radiant because he had spoken
34:30 When Aaron and all the Israelites saw **Moses**, his face was radiant,
34:31 **Moses** called to them; so Aaron and all the leaders of the
34:31 of the community came back to him, and **he**[s] spoke to them.
34:33 When **Moses** finished speaking to them, he put a veil over his face.
34:34 whenever **he**[s] entered the LORD's presence to speak with him,
34:35 they saw that **his**[s] face was radiant. Then Moses would put the veil
34:35 **[RPH]** Then Moses would put the veil back over his face until he
34:35 **Moses** would put the veil back over his face until he went in to
35: 1 **Moses** assembled the whole Israelite community and said to them,
35: 4 **Moses** said to the whole Israelite community, "This is what the
35:20 the whole Israelite community withdrew from **Moses**' presence,
35:29 the work the LORD through **Moses** had commanded them to do.
35:30 **Moses** said to the Israelites, "See, the LORD has chosen Bezalel
36: 2 **Moses** summoned Bezalel and Oholiab and every skilled person to
36: 3 They received from **Moses** all the offerings the Israelites had
36: 5 said to **Moses**, "The people are bringing more than enough for
36: 6 **Moses** gave an order and they sent this word throughout the camp:
38:21 which were recorded at **Moses**' command by the Levites under the
38:22 tribe of Judah, made everything the LORD commanded **Moses**;
39: 1 sacred garments for Aaron, as the LORD commanded **Moses**.
39: 5 and with finely twisted linen, as the LORD commanded **Moses**.
39: 7 stones for the sons of Israel, as the LORD commanded **Moses**.
39:21 not swing out from the ephod—as the LORD commanded **Moses**.
39:26 to be worn for ministering, as the LORD commanded **Moses**.
39:29 the work of an embroiderer—as the LORD commanded **Moses**.
39:31 to it to attach it to the turban, as the LORD commanded **Moses**.
39:32 Israelites did everything just as the LORD commanded **Moses**.
39:33 they brought the tabernacle to **Moses**: the tent and all its
39:42 had done all the work just as the LORD had commanded **Moses**.
39:43 **Moses** inspected the work and saw that they had done it just as the
39:43 it just as the LORD had commanded. So **Moses** blessed them.
40: 1 Then the LORD said to **Moses**:
40:16 **Moses** did everything just as the LORD commanded him.
40:18 When **Moses** set up the tabernacle, he put the bases in place,
40:19 put the covering over the tent, as the LORD commanded **him**[s].
40:21 the ark of the Testimony, as the LORD commanded **him**[s].
40:23 bread on it before the LORD, as the LORD commanded **him**[s].
40:25 up the lamps before the LORD, as the LORD commanded **him**[s].
40:27 burned fragrant incense on it, as the LORD commanded **him**[s].
40:29 and grain offerings, as the LORD commanded **him**[s].
40:31 and **Moses** and Aaron and his sons used it to wash their hands
40:32 or approached the altar, as the LORD commanded **Moses**.
40:33 at the entrance to the courtyard. And so **Moses** finished the work.
40:35 **Moses** could not enter the Tent of Meeting because the cloud had
Lev 1: 1 The LORD called to **Moses** and spoke to him from the Tent of
4: 1 The LORD said to **Moses**,
5:14 The LORD said to **Moses**:
6: 1 [5:20] The LORD said to **Moses**:
6: 8 [6:1] The LORD said to **Moses**:
6:19 [6:12] The LORD also said to **Moses**,
6:24 [6:17] The LORD said to **Moses**,
7:22 The LORD said to **Moses**,
7:28 The LORD said to **Moses**,
7:38 which the LORD gave **Moses** on Mount Sinai on the day he
8: 1 The LORD said to **Moses**,
8: 4 **Moses** did as the LORD commanded him, and the assembly
8: 5 **Moses** said to the assembly, "This is what the LORD has
8: 6 **Moses** brought Aaron and his sons forward and washed them with
8: 9 on the front of it, as the LORD commanded **Moses**.
8:10 Then **Moses** took the anointing oil and anointed the tabernacle
8:13 Then **he**[s] brought Aaron's sons forward, put tunics on them,
8:13 and put headbands on them, as the LORD commanded **Moses**.
8:15 **Moses** slaughtered the bull and took some of the blood, and with
8:16 **Moses** also took all the fat around the inner parts, the covering of
8:17 he burned up outside the camp, as the LORD commanded **Moses**.
8:19 **Moses** slaughtered the ram and sprinkled the blood against the
8:20 He cut the ram into pieces and burned **[RPH]** the head, the pieces
8:21 and burned **[RPH]** the whole ram on the altar as a burnt offering,
8:21 made to the LORD by fire, as the LORD commanded **Moses**.
8:23 **Moses** slaughtered the ram and took some of its blood and put it on

[F] Hitpael (hitpoel, hitpoal, hitpolel, hitpolal, hitpalel, hitpalal, hitpalpel, hitpalpal, hotpael, hotpaal) [G] Hiphil (hiphtil) [H] Hophal [I] Hishtaphel

Lev 8: 24 **Moses** also brought Aaron's sons forward and put some of the
8: 24 right feet. Then **he**[s] sprinkled blood against the altar on all sides.
8: 28 **Moses** took them from their hands and burned them on the altar on
8: 29 **He**[s] also took the breast—Moses' share of the ordination ram—
8: 29 He also took the breast—**Moses** [+4200]' share of the ordination
8: 29 the LORD as a wave offering, as the LORD commanded **Moses**.
8: 30 **Moses** took some of the anointing oil and some of the blood from
8: 31 **Moses** then said to Aaron and his sons, "Cook the meat at the
8: 36 his sons did everything the LORD commanded through **Moses**.
9: 1 On the eighth day **Moses** summoned Aaron and his sons and the
9: 5 They took the things **Moses** commanded to the front of the Tent of
9: 6 **Moses** said, "This is what the LORD has commanded you to do,
9: 7 **Moses** said to Aaron, "Come to the altar and sacrifice your sin
9: 10 the liver from the sin offering, as the LORD commanded **Moses**;
9: 21 before the LORD as a wave offering, as **Moses** commanded.
9: 23 **Moses** and Aaron then went into the Tent of Meeting. When they
10: 3 **Moses** then said to Aaron, "This is what the LORD spoke of
10: 4 **Moses** summoned Mishael and Elzaphan, sons of Aaron's uncle
10: 5 still in their tunics, outside the camp, as **Moses** ordered.
10: 6 Then **Moses** said to Aaron and his sons Eleazar and Ithamar,
10: 7 the LORD's anointing oil is on you." So they did as **Moses** said.
10: 11 all the decrees the LORD has given them through **Moses**."
10: 12 **Moses** said to Aaron and his remaining sons, Eleazar and Ithamar,
10: 16 When **Moses** inquired about the goat of the sin offering and found
10: 19 Aaron replied to **Moses**, "Today they sacrificed their sin offering
10: 20 When **Moses** heard this, he was satisfied.
11: 1 The LORD said to **Moses** and Aaron,
12: 1 The LORD said to **Moses**,
13: 1 The LORD said to **Moses** and Aaron,
14: 1 The LORD said to **Moses**,
14: 33 The LORD said to **Moses** and Aaron,
15: 1 The LORD said to **Moses** and Aaron,
16: 1 The LORD spoke to **Moses** after the death of the two sons of
16: 2 The LORD said to **Moses**: "Tell your brother Aaron not to come
16: 34 And it was done, as the LORD commanded **Moses**.
17: 1 The LORD said to **Moses**,
18: 1 The LORD said to **Moses**,
19: 1 The LORD said to **Moses**,
20: 1 The LORD said to **Moses**,
21: 1 The LORD said to **Moses**, "Speak to the priests, the sons of
21: 16 The LORD said to **Moses**,
21: 24 So **Moses** told this to Aaron and his sons and to all the Israelites.
22: 1 The LORD said to **Moses**,
22: 17 The LORD said to **Moses**,
22: 26 The LORD said to **Moses**,
23: 1 The LORD said to **Moses**,
23: 9 The LORD said to **Moses**,
23: 23 The LORD said to **Moses**,
23: 26 The LORD said to **Moses**,
23: 33 The LORD said to **Moses**,
23: 44 So **Moses** announced to the Israelites the appointed feasts of the
24: 1 The LORD said to **Moses**,
24: 11 blasphemed the Name with a curse; so they brought him to **Moses**.
24: 13 Then the LORD said to **Moses**:
24: 23 **Moses** spoke to the Israelites, and they took the blasphemer outside
24: 23 stoned him. The Israelites did as the LORD commanded **Moses**.
25: 1 The LORD said to **Moses** on Mount Sinai,
26: 46 on Mount Sinai between himself and the Israelites through **Moses**.
27: 1 The LORD said to **Moses**,
27: 34 These are the commands the LORD gave **Moses** on Mount Sinai
Nu 1: 1 The LORD spoke to **Moses** in the Tent of Meeting in the Desert
1: 17 **Moses** and Aaron took these men whose names had been given,
1: 19 as the LORD commanded **Moses**. And so he counted them in the
1: 44 These were the men counted by **Moses** and Aaron and the twelve
1: 48 The LORD had said to **Moses**:
1: 54 The Israelites did all this just as the LORD commanded **Moses**.
2: 1 The LORD said to **Moses** and Aaron:
2: 33 along with the other Israelites, as the LORD commanded **Moses**.
2: 34 So the Israelites did everything the LORD commanded **Moses**;
3: 1 **Moses** at the time the LORD talked with Moses on Mount Sinai.
3: 1 Moses at the time the LORD talked with **Moses** on Mount Sinai.
3: 5 The LORD said to **Moses**,
3: 11 The LORD also said to **Moses**,
3: 14 The LORD said to **Moses** in the Desert of Sinai,
3: 16 So **Moses** counted them, as he was commanded by the word of the
3: 38 **Moses** and Aaron and his sons were to camp to the east of the
3: 39 number of Levites counted at the LORD's command by **Moses**
3: 40 The LORD said to **Moses**, "Count all the firstborn Israelite males
3: 42 So **Moses** counted all the firstborn of the Israelites, as the LORD
3: 44 The LORD also said to **Moses**,
3: 49 So **Moses** collected the redemption money from those who
3: 51 **Moses** gave the redemption money to Aaron and his sons,
3: 51 and his sons, as **he**[s] was commanded by the word of the LORD.
4: 1 The LORD said to **Moses** and Aaron:
4: 17 The LORD said to **Moses** and Aaron,
4: 21 The LORD said to **Moses**,
4: 34 **Moses**, Aaron and the leaders of the community counted the
4: 37 **Moses** and Aaron counted them according to the LORD's
4: 37 counted them according to the LORD's command through **Moses**.
4: 41 **Moses** and Aaron counted them according to the LORD's
4: 45 **Moses** and Aaron counted them according to the LORD's
4: 45 counted them according to the LORD's command through **Moses**.
4: 46 So **Moses**, Aaron and the leaders of Israel counted all the Levites
4: 49 At the LORD's command through **Moses**, each was assigned his
4: 49 Thus they were counted, as the LORD commanded **Moses**.
5: 1 The LORD said to **Moses**,
5: 4 the camp. They did just as the LORD had instructed **Moses**.
5: 5 The LORD said to **Moses**,
5: 11 Then the LORD said to **Moses**,
6: 1 The LORD said to **Moses**,
6: 22 The LORD said to **Moses**,
7: 1 When **Moses** finished setting up the tabernacle, he anointed it
7: 4 The LORD said to **Moses**,
7: 6 So **Moses** took the carts and oxen and gave them to the Levites.
7: 11 For the LORD had said to **Moses**, "Each day one leader is to
7: 89 When **Moses** entered the Tent of Meeting to speak with the
8: 1 The LORD said to **Moses**,
8: 3 forward on the lampstand, just as the LORD commanded **Moses**.
8: 4 was made exactly like the pattern the LORD had shown **Moses**.
8: 5 The LORD said to **Moses**:
8: 20 **Moses**, Aaron and the whole Israelite community did with the
8: 20 did with the Levites just as the LORD commanded **Moses**.
8: 22 They did with the Levites just as the LORD commanded **Moses**.
8: 23 The LORD said to **Moses**,
9: 1 The LORD spoke to **Moses** in the Desert of Sinai in the first
9: 4 So **Moses** told the Israelites to celebrate the Passover,
9: 5 Israelites did everything just as the LORD commanded **Moses**.
9: 6 of a dead body. So they came to **Moses** and Aaron that same day
9: 8 **Moses** answered them, "Wait until I find out what the LORD
9: 9 Then the LORD said to **Moses**,
9: 23 LORD's order, in accordance with his command through **Moses**.
10: 1 The LORD said to **Moses**:
10: 13 set out, this first time, at the LORD's command through **Moses**.
10: 29 Now **Moses** said to Hobab son of Reuel the Midianite,
10: 29 said to Hobab son of Reuel the Midianite, **Moses**' father-in-law,
10: 35 Whenever the ark set out, **Moses** said, "Rise up, O LORD!
11: 2 When the people cried out to **Moses**, he prayed to the LORD
11: 2 out to Moses, **he**[s] prayed to the LORD and the fire died down.
11: 10 **Moses** heard the people of every family wailing, each at the
11: 10 The LORD became exceedingly angry, and **Moses** was troubled.
11: 11 **He**[s] asked the LORD, "Why have you brought this trouble on
11: 16 The LORD said to **Moses**: "Bring me seventy of Israel's elders
11: 21 **Moses** said, "Here I am among six hundred thousand men on foot,
11: 23 The LORD answered **Moses**, "Is the LORD's arm too short?
11: 24 So **Moses** went out and told the people what the LORD had said.
11: 27 A young man ran and told **Moses**, "Eldad and Medad are
11: 28 who had been **Moses**' aide since youth, spoke up and said,
11: 28 aide since youth, spoke up and said, "**Moses**, my lord, stop them!"
11: 29 **Moses** replied, "Are you jealous for my sake? I wish that all the
11: 30 Then **Moses** and the elders of Israel returned to the camp.
12: 1 Miriam and Aaron began to talk against **Moses** because of his
12: 2 "Has the LORD spoken only through **Moses**?" they asked.
12: 3 (Now **Moses** was a very humble man, more humble than anyone
12: 4 At once the LORD said to **Moses**, Aaron and Miriam, "Come out
12: 7 this is not true of my servant **Moses**; he is faithful in all my house.
12: 8 then were you not afraid to speak against my servant **Moses**?"
12: 11 he said to **Moses**, "Please, my lord, do not hold against us the sin
12: 13 So **Moses** cried out to the LORD, "O God, please heal her!"
12: 14 The LORD replied to **Moses**, "If her father had spit in her face,
13: 1 The LORD said to **Moses**,
13: 3 So at the LORD's command **Moses** sent them out from the Desert
13: 16 These are the names of the men **Moses** sent to explore the land.
13: 16 the land. (**Moses** gave Hoshea son of Nun the name Joshua.)
13: 17 When **Moses** sent them to explore Canaan, he said, "Go up through
13: 26 They came back to **Moses** and Aaron and the whole Israelite
13: 30 Caleb silenced the people before **Moses** and said, "We should go
14: 2 All the Israelites grumbled against **Moses** and Aaron,
14: 5 **Moses** and Aaron fell facedown in front of the whole Israelite
14: 11 The LORD said to **Moses**, "How long will these people treat me
14: 13 **Moses** said to the LORD, "Then the Egyptians will hear about it!
14: 26 The LORD said to **Moses** and Aaron:
14: 36 So the men **Moses** had sent to explore the land, who returned
14: 39 When **Moses** reported this to all the Israelites, they mourned
14: 41 **Moses** said, "Why are you disobeying the LORD's command?
14: 44 though neither **Moses** nor the ark of the LORD's covenant moved
15: 1 The LORD said to **Moses**,
15: 17 The LORD said to **Moses**,
15: 22 fail to keep any of these commands the LORD gave **Moses**—

Nu 15:23 any of the LORD's commands to you through **him**[s], from the day
15:33 Those who found him gathering wood brought him to **Moses**
15:35 the LORD said to **Moses**, "The man must die. The whole
15:36 and stoned him to death, as the LORD commanded **Moses**.
15:37 The LORD said to **Moses**,
16: 2 and rose up against **Moses**. With them were 250 Israelite men,
16: 3 They came as a group to oppose **Moses** and Aaron and said to
16: 4 When **Moses** heard this, he fell facedown.
16: 8 **Moses** also said to Korah, "Now listen, you Levites!
16:12 Then **Moses** summoned Dathan and Abiram, the sons of Eliab.
16:15 **Moses** became very angry and said to the LORD, "Do not accept
16:16 **Moses** said to Korah, "You and all your followers are to appear
16:18 stood with **Moses** and Aaron at the entrance to the Tent of
16:20 The LORD said to **Moses** and Aaron,
16:23 Then the LORD said to **Moses**,
16:25 **Moses** got up and went to Dathan and Abiram, and the elders of
16:28 **Moses** said, "This is how you will know that the LORD has sent
16:36 [17:1] The LORD said to **Moses**,
16:40 [17:5] as the LORD directed him through **Moses**. This was to
16:41 [17:6] the whole Israelite community grumbled against **Moses**
16:42 [17:7] when the assembly gathered in opposition to **Moses**
16:43 [17:8] **Moses** and Aaron went to the front of the Tent of Meeting,
16:44 [17:9] and the LORD said to **Moses**,
16:46 [17:11] **Moses** said to Aaron, "Take your censer and put incense
16:47 [17:12] So Aaron did as **Moses** said, and ran into the midst of the
16:50 [17:15] Aaron returned to **Moses** at the entrance to the Tent of
17: 1 [17:16] The LORD said to **Moses**,
17: 6 [17:21] So **Moses** spoke to the Israelites, and their leaders gave
17: 7 [17:22] **Moses** placed the staffs before the LORD in the Tent of
17: 8 [17:23] The next day **Moses** entered the Tent of the Testimony
17: 9 [17:24] **Moses** brought out all the staffs from the LORD's
17:10 [17:25] The LORD said to **Moses**, "Put back Aaron's staff in
17:11 [17:26] **Moses** did just as the LORD commanded him.
17:12 [17:27] The Israelites said to **Moses**, "We will die! We are lost,
18:25 The LORD said to **Moses**,
19: 1 The LORD said to **Moses** and Aaron:
20: 2 and the people gathered in opposition to **Moses** and Aaron.
20: 3 They quarreled with **Moses** and said, "If only we had died when
20: 6 **Moses** and Aaron went from the assembly to the entrance to the
20: 7 The LORD said to **Moses**,
20: 9 So **Moses** took the staff from the LORD's presence, just as he
20:10 **He**[s] and Aaron gathered the assembly together in front of the rock
20:11 Then **Moses** raised his arm and struck the rock twice with his staff.
20:12 the LORD said to **Moses** and Aaron, "Because you did not trust
20:14 **Moses** sent messengers from Kadesh to the king of Edom,
20:23 near the border of Edom, the LORD said to **Moses** and Aaron,
20:27 **Moses** did as the LORD commanded: They went up Mount Hor
20:28 **Moses** removed Aaron's garments and put them on his son
20:28 Then **Moses** and Eleazar came down from the mountain,
21: 5 they spoke against God and against **Moses**, and said, "Why have
21: 7 The people came to **Moses** and said, "We sinned when we spoke
21: 7 take the snakes away from us." So **Moses** prayed for the people.
21: 8 The LORD said to **Moses**, "Make a snake and put it up on a pole;
21: 9 So **Moses** made a bronze snake and put it up on a pole. Then when
21:16 the well where the LORD said to **Moses**, "Gather the people
21:32 After **Moses** had sent spies to Jazer, the Israelites captured its
21:34 The LORD said to **Moses**, "Do not be afraid of him, for I have
25: 4 The LORD said to **Moses**, "Take all the leaders of these people,
25: 5 So **Moses** said to Israel's judges, "Each of you must put to death
25: 6 to his family a Midianite woman right before the eyes of **Moses**
25:10 The LORD said to **Moses**,
25:16 The LORD said to **Moses**,
26: 1 After the plague the LORD said to **Moses** and Eleazar son of
26: 3 **Moses** and Eleazar the priest spoke with them and said,
26: 4 men twenty years old or more, as the LORD commanded **Moses**."
26: 9 Abiram were the community officials who rebelled against **Moses**
26:52 The LORD said to **Moses**,
26:59 To Amram she bore Aaron, **Moses** and their sister Miriam.
26:63 These are the ones counted by **Moses** and Eleazar the priest when
26:64 Not one of them was among those counted by **Moses** and Aaron
27: 2 the entrance to the Tent of Meeting and stood before **Moses**,
27: 5 So **Moses** brought their case before the LORD
27: 6 and the LORD said to **him**[s],
27:11 for the Israelites, as the LORD commanded **Moses**.' "
27:12 the LORD said to **Moses**, "Go up this mountain in the Abarim
27:15 **Moses** said to the LORD,
27:18 So the LORD said to **Moses**, "Take Joshua son of Nun, a man in
27:22 **Moses** did as the LORD commanded him. He took Joshua
27:23 and commissioned him, as the LORD instructed through **Moses**.
28: 1 The LORD said to **Moses**,
29:40 [30:1] **Moses** told the Israelites all that the LORD commanded
29:40 [30:1] told the Israelites all that the LORD commanded **him**[s].
30: 1 [30:2] **Moses** said to the heads of the tribes of Israel: "This is
30:16 [30:17] These are the regulations the LORD gave **Moses**
31: 1 The LORD said to **Moses**,
31: 3 So **Moses** said to the people, "Arm some of your men to go to war
31: 6 **Moses** sent them into battle, a thousand from each tribe, along with
31: 7 as the LORD commanded **Moses**, and killed every man.
31:12 spoils and plunder to **Moses** and Eleazar the priest and the Israelite
31:13 **Moses**, Eleazar the priest and all the leaders of the community
31:14 **Moses** was angry with the officers of the army—the commanders
31:15 "Have you allowed all the women to live?" **he**[s] asked them.
31:21 "This is the requirement of the law that the LORD gave **Moses**:
31:25 The LORD said to **Moses**,
31:31 So **Moses** and Eleazar the priest did as the LORD commanded
31:31 and Eleazar the priest did as the LORD commanded **Moses**.
31:41 **Moses** gave the tribute to Eleazar the priest as the LORD's part,
31:41 the priest as the LORD's part, as the LORD commanded **Moses**.
31:42 which **Moses** set apart from that of the fighting men—
31:47 **Moses** selected one out of every fifty persons and animals,
31:47 every fifty persons and animals, as the LORD commanded **him**[s],
31:48 of thousands and commanders of hundreds—went to **Moses**
31:49 said to **him**[s], "Your servants have counted the soldiers under our
31:51 **Moses** and Eleazar the priest accepted from them the gold—
31:54 **Moses** and Eleazar the priest accepted the gold from the
32: 2 So they came to **Moses** and Eleazar the priest and to the leaders of
32: 6 **Moses** said to the Gadites and Reubenites, "Shall your countrymen
32:20 Then **Moses** said to them, "If you will do this—if you will arm
32:25 The Gadites and Reubenites said to **Moses**, "We your servants will
32:28 **Moses** gave orders about them to Eleazar the priest and Joshua son
32:29 **He**[s] said to them, "If the Gadites and Reubenites, every man armed
32:33 **Moses** gave to the Gadites, the Reubenites and the half-tribe of
32:40 So **Moses** gave Gilead to the Makirites, the descendants of
33: 1 they came out of Egypt by divisions under the leadership of **Moses**
33: 2 At the LORD's command **Moses** recorded the stages in their
33:50 by the Jordan across from Jericho the LORD said to **Moses**,
34: 1 The LORD said to **Moses**,
34:13 **Moses** commanded the Israelites: "Assign this land by lot as an
34:16 The LORD said to **Moses**,
35: 1 by the Jordan across from Jericho, the LORD said to **Moses**,
35: 9 Then the LORD said to **Moses**:
36: 1 came and spoke before **Moses** and the leaders, the heads of the
36: 5 at the LORD's command **Moses** gave this order to the Israelites:
36:10 So Zelophehad's daughters did as the LORD commanded **Moses**.
36:13 regulations the LORD gave through **Moses** to the Israelites on the
Dt 1: 1 These are the words **Moses** spoke to all Israel in the desert east of
1: 3 **Moses** proclaimed to the Israelites all that the LORD had
1: 5 in the territory of Moab, **Moses** began to expound this law, saying:
4:41 Then **Moses** set aside three cities east of the Jordan,
4:44 This is the law **Moses** set before the Israelites.
4:45 and laws **Moses** gave them when they came out of Egypt
4:46 who reigned in Heshbon and was defeated by **Moses**
5: 1 **Moses** summoned all Israel and said: Hear, O Israel, the decrees
27: 1 **Moses** and the elders of Israel commanded the people: "Keep all
27: 9 Then **Moses** and the priests, who are Levites, said to all Israel,
27:11 On the same day **Moses** commanded the people:
29: 1 [28:69] commanded **Moses** to make with the Israelites in Moab,
29: 2 [29:1] **Moses** summoned all the Israelites and said to them: Your
31: 1 Then **Moses** went out and spoke these words to all Israel:
31: 7 **Moses** summoned Joshua and said to him in the presence of all
31: 9 So **Moses** wrote down this law and gave it to the priests, the sons
31:10 Then **Moses** commanded them: "At the end of every seven years,
31:14 The LORD said to **Moses**, "Now the day of your death is near.
31:14 So **Moses** and Joshua came and presented themselves at the Tent
31:16 the LORD said to **Moses**: "You are going to rest with your
31:22 So **Moses** wrote down this song that day and taught it to the
31:24 After **Moses** finished writing in a book the words of this law from
31:25 **he**[s] gave this command to the Levites who carried the ark of the
31:30 **Moses** recited the words of this song from beginning to end in the
32:44 **Moses** came with Joshua son of Nun and spoke all the words of
32:45 When **Moses** finished reciting all these words to all Israel,
32:48 On that same day the LORD told **Moses**,
33: 1 This is the blessing that **Moses** the man of God pronounced on the
33: 4 the law that **Moses** gave us, the possession of the assembly of
34: 1 **Moses** climbed Mount Nebo from the plains of Moab to the top of
34: 5 And **Moses** the servant of the LORD died there in Moab,
34: 7 **Moses** was a hundred and twenty years old when he died,
34: 8 The Israelites grieved for **Moses** in the plains of Moab thirty days,
34: 8 until the time of weeping and mourning **[RPH]** was over.
34: 9 the spirit of wisdom because **Moses** had laid his hands on him.
34: 9 listened to him and did what the LORD had commanded **Moses**.
34:10 Since then, no prophet has risen in Israel like **Moses**,
34:12 or performed the awesome deeds that **Moses** did in the sight of all
Jos 1: 1 After the death of **Moses** the servant of the LORD, the LORD
1: 1 the LORD, the LORD said to Joshua son of Nun, **Moses**' aide:
1: 2 "**Moses** my servant is dead. Now then, you and all these people,
1: 3 you every place where you set your foot, as I promised **Moses**.
1: 5 As I was with **Moses**, so I will be with you; I will never leave you

[F] Hitpael (hitpoel, hitpoal, hitpolel, hitpolal, hitpalel, hitpalal, hitpalpel, hitpalpal, hotpael, hotpaal) [G] Hiphil (hiphtil) [H] Hophal [I] Hishtaphel

Jos 1: 7 Be careful to obey all the law my servant **Moses** gave you;
1: 13 "Remember the command that **Moses** the servant of the LORD
1: 14 your livestock may stay in the land that **Moses** gave you east of the
1: 15 which **Moses** the servant of the LORD gave you east of the
1: 17 Just as we fully obeyed **Moses**, so we will obey you. Only may the
1: 17 may the LORD your God be with you as he was with **Moses**.
3: 7 so they may know that I am with you as I was with **Moses**.
4: 10 Joshua was done by the people, just as **Moses** had directed Joshua.
4: 12 armed, in front of the Israelites, as **Moses** had directed them.
4: 14 revered him all the days of his life, just as they had revered **Moses**.
8: 31 as **Moses** the servant of the LORD had commanded the Israelites.
8: 31 it according to what is written in the Book of the Law of **Moses**—
8: 32 Joshua copied on stones the law of **Moses**, which he had written.
8: 33 as **Moses** the servant of the LORD had formerly commanded
8: 35 There was not a word of all that **Moses** had commanded that
9: 24 God had commanded his servant **Moses** to give you the whole land
11: 12 as **Moses** the servant of the LORD had commanded.
11: 15 As the LORD commanded his servant **Moses**, so Moses
11: 15 servant Moses, so **Moses** commanded Joshua, and Joshua did it;
11: 15 he left nothing undone of all that the LORD commanded **Moses**.
11: 20 them without mercy, as the LORD had commanded **Moses**.
11: 23 Joshua took the entire land, just as the LORD had directed **Moses**,
12: 6 **Moses**, the servant of the LORD, and the Israelites conquered
12: 6 **Moses** the servant of the LORD gave their land to the Reubenites,
13: 8 the Gadites had received the inheritance that **Moses** had given
13: 8 as **he**[s], the servant of the LORD, had assigned it to them.
13: 12 the Rephaites. **Moses** had defeated them and taken over their land.
13: 15 This is what **Moses** had given to the tribe of Reuben, clan by clan:
13: 21 **Moses** had defeated him and the Midianite chiefs, Evi, Rekem,
13: 24 This is what **Moses** had given to the tribe of Gad, clan by clan:
13: 29 This is what **Moses** had given to the half-tribe of Manasseh,
13: 32 This is the inheritance **Moses** had given when he was in the plains
13: 33 to the tribe of Levi, **Moses** had given no inheritance; the LORD,
14: 2 as the LORD had commanded through **Moses**.
14: 3 **Moses** had granted the two-and-a-half tribes their inheritance east
14: 5 divided the land, just as the LORD had commanded **Moses**.
14: 6 "You know what the LORD said to **Moses** the man of God at
14: 7 I was forty years old when **Moses** the servant of the LORD sent
14: 9 So on that day **Moses** swore to me, 'The land on which your feet
14: 10 me alive for forty-five years since the time he said this to **Moses**,
14: 11 I am still as strong today as the day **Moses** sent me out; I'm just as
17: 4 "The LORD commanded **Moses** to give us an inheritance among
18: 7 of the Jordan. **Moses** the servant of the LORD gave it to them."
20: 2 to designate the cities of refuge, as I instructed you through **Moses**,
21: 2 "The LORD commanded through **Moses** that you give us towns
21: 8 their pasturelands, as the LORD had commanded through **Moses**.
22: 2 "You have done all that **Moses** the servant of the LORD
22: 4 return to your homes in the land that **Moses** the servant of the
22: 5 and the law that **Moses** the servant of the LORD gave you:
22: 7 (To the half-tribe of Manasseh **Moses** had given land in Bashan,
22: 9 in accordance with the command of the LORD through **Moses**.
23: 6 careful to obey all that is written in the Book of the Law of **Moses**,
24: 5 " 'Then I sent **Moses** and Aaron, and I afflicted the Egyptians by
Jdg 1: 16 The descendants of **Moses**' father-in-law, the Kenite, went up from
1: 20 As **Moses** had promised, Hebron was given to Caleb, who drove
3: 4 which he had given their forefathers through **Moses**.
4: 11 other Kenites, the descendants of Hobab, **Moses**' brother-in-law,
18: 30 and Jonathan son of Gershom, the son of **Moses**, [BHS 4985]
1Sa 12: 6 "It is the LORD who appointed **Moses** and Aaron and brought
12: 8 to the LORD for help, and the LORD sent **Moses** and Aaron,
1Ki 2: 3 his laws and requirements, as written in the Law of **Moses**,
8: 9 except the two stone tablets that **Moses** had placed in it at Horeb,
8: 53 just as you declared through your servant **Moses** when you,
8: 56 failed of all the good promises he gave through his servant **Moses**.
2Ki 14: 6 in the Book of the Law of **Moses** where the LORD commanded:
18: 4 He broke into pieces the bronze snake **Moses** had made, for up to
18: 6 follow him; he kept the commands the LORD had given **Moses**.
18: 12 all that **Moses** the servant of the LORD commanded.
21: 8 and will keep the whole Law that my servant **Moses** gave them."
23: 25 and with all his strength, in accordance with all the Law of **Moses**.
1Ch 6: 3 [5:29] Aaron, **Moses** and Miriam. The sons of Aaron: Nadab,
6: 49 [6:34] in accordance with all that **Moses** the servant of God had
15: 15 as **Moses** had commanded in accordance with the word of the
21: 29 tabernacle of the LORD, which **Moses** had made in the desert,
22: 13 the decrees and laws that the LORD gave **Moses** for Israel.
23: 13 Aaron and **Moses**. Aaron was set apart, he and his descendants
23: 14 The sons of **Moses** the man of God were counted as part of the
23: 15 The sons of **Moses**: Gershom and Eliezer.
26: 24 Shubael, a descendant of Gershom son of **Moses**, was the officer in
2Ch 1: 3 which **Moses** the LORD's servant had made in the desert.
5: 10 There was nothing in the ark except the two tablets that **Moses** had
8: 13 requirement for offerings commanded by **Moses** for Sabbaths,
23: 18 the burnt offerings of the LORD as written in the Law of **Moses**,
24: 6 Jerusalem the tax imposed by **Moses** the servant of the LORD
24: 9 Jerusalem that they should bring to the LORD the tax that **Moses**
25: 4 in the Law, in the Book of **Moses**, where the LORD commanded:
30: 16 positions as prescribed in the Law of **Moses** the man of God.
33: 8 all the laws, decrees and ordinances given through **Moses**."
34: 14 of the Law of the LORD that had been given through **Moses**.
35: 6 doing what the LORD commanded through **Moses**."
35: 12 people to offer to the LORD, as is written in the Book of **Moses**.
Ezr 3: 2 in accordance with what is written in the Law of **Moses** the man of
7: 6 He was a teacher well versed in the Law of **Moses**,
Ne 1: 7 the commands, decrees and laws you gave your servant **Moses**.
1: 8 "Remember the instruction you gave your servant **Moses**,
8: 1 told Ezra the scribe to bring out the Book of the Law of **Moses**,
8: 14 in the Law, which the LORD had commanded through **Moses**,
9: 14 them commands, decrees and laws through your servant **Moses**.
10: 29 [10:30] an oath to follow the Law of God given through **Moses**
13: 1 On that day the Book of **Moses** was read aloud in the hearing of
Ps 77: 20 [77:21] You led your people like a flock by the hand of **Moses**
90: T [90:1] A prayer of **Moses** the man of God.
99: 6 **Moses** and Aaron were among his priests, Samuel was among
103: 7 He made known his ways to **Moses**, his deeds to the people of
105: 26 He sent **Moses** his servant, and Aaron, whom he had chosen.
106: 16 In the camp they grew envious of **Moses** and of Aaron, who was
106: 23 had not **Moses**, his chosen one, stood in the breach before him to
106: 32 angered the LORD, and trouble came to **Moses** because of them;
Isa 63: 11 people recalled the days of old, the days of **Moses** and his people—
63: 12 who sent his glorious arm of power to be at **Moses**' right hand,
Jer 15: 1 "Even if **Moses** and Samuel were to stand before me, my heart
Da 9: 11 the curses and sworn judgments written in the Law of **Moses**,
9: 13 Just as it is written in the Law of **Moses**, all this disaster has come
Mic 6: 4 land of slavery. I sent **Moses** to lead you, also Aaron and Miriam.
Mal 4: 4 [3:22] "Remember the law of my servant **Moses**, the decrees

5408 מַשֶּׁה *maššeh*, n.m. [1] [√ 5957]

creditor [+1251+2257+3338] [1]

Dt 15: 2 Every **creditor** [+1251+2257+3338] shall cancel the loan he has

5409 מְשׁוֹאָה *m^{e}šô'â*, n.f. [3] [√ 8735]

ruin [1], wasteland [1], wastelands [1]

Job 30: 3 they roamed the parched land in desolate **wastelands** at night.
38: 27 to satisfy a desolate **wasteland** and make it sprout with grass?
Zep 1: 15 a day of distress and anguish, a day of trouble and **ruin**, a day of

5410 מַשּׁוּאָה *maššû'â*, n.[m.]. Not used in NIV/BHS [√ 5958]

5411 מְשׁוֹבָב *m^{e}šôbāb*, n.pr.m. [1] [√ 8740]

Meshobab [1]

1Ch 4: 34 **Meshobab**, Jamlech, Joshah son of Amaziah,

5412 מְשׁוּבָה *m^{e}šûbâ*, n.f. [12 / 13] [√ 8740]

backsliding [4], faithless [4], waywardness [2], backslidings [1], turn away [1], turn from [1]

Pr 1: 32 For the **waywardness** *of* the simple will kill them,
Jer 2: 19 wickedness will punish you; your **backsliding** will rebuke you.
3: 6 said to me, "Have you seen what **faithless** Israel has done?
3: 8 I gave **faithless** Israel her certificate of divorce and sent her away
3: 11 to me, "**Faithless** Israel is more righteous than unfaithful Judah.
3: 12 " 'Return, **faithless** Israel,' declares the LORD, 'I will frown on
3: 22 "Return, faithless people; I will cure you of **backsliding**."
5: 6 for their rebellion is great and their **backslidings** many.
8: 5 Why does Jerusalem always **turn away**? They cling to deceit;
14: 7 For our **backsliding** is great; we have sinned against you.
Eze 37: 23 for I will save them from all their sinful **backsliding**, [BHS 4632]
Hos 11: 7 My people are determined to **turn from** me. Even if they call to
14: 4 [14:5] "I will heal their **waywardness** and love them freely,

5413 מְשׁוּגָה *m^{e}šûgâ*, n.f. [1] [cf. 8704, 8706]

error [1]

Job 19: 4 true that I have gone astray, my **error** remains my concern alone.

5414 מָשׁוֹט *māšôṭ*, n.[m.]. [1] [√ 8763]

oars [1]

Eze 27: 29 All who handle the **oars** will abandon their ships; the mariners

5415 מִשּׁוֹט *miššôṭ*, n.[m.]. [1] [√ 8763]

oars [1]

Eze 27: 6 Of oaks from Bashan they made your **oars**; of cypress wood from

5416 מְשִׁסָּה meśiwssâ, var. [0] [cf. 5468]

Isa 42: 24 [Who handed Jacob over to become **loot**, [K; see Q 5468]]

5417 מָשַׁח māšaḥ, v. [70 / 71] [→ 4937, 5418, 5420, 5431; Ar 10442]

anointed [33], anoint [24], spread [4], anointing [3], was anointed [2], been anointed [1], decorates [1], oil [1], rubbed [1], use [1]

Ge 31: 13 [A] where *you* **anointed** a pillar and where you made a vow to
Ex 28: 41 [A] on your brother Aaron and his sons, **anoint** and ordain them.
29: 2 [B] and cakes mixed with oil, and wafers **spread** with oil.
29: 7 [A] the anointing oil and **anoint** him by pouring it on his head.
29: 29 [A] so that they *can be* **anointed** and ordained in them.
29: 36 [A] by making atonement for it, and **anoint** it to consecrate it.
30: 26 [A] use it *to* **anoint** the Tent of Meeting, the ark of the
30: 30 [A] "**Anoint** Aaron and his sons and consecrate them so they
40: 9 [A] anointing oil and **anoint** the tabernacle and everything in it;
40: 10 [A] Then **anoint** the altar of burnt offering and all its utensils;
40: 11 [A] **Anoint** the basin and its stand and consecrate them.
40: 13 [A] **anoint** him and consecrate him so he may serve me as priest.
40: 15 [A] **Anoint** them just as you anointed their father, so they may
40: 15 [A] Anoint them just as *you* **anointed** their father, so they may
Lev 2: 4 [B] with oil, or wafers made without yeast and **spread** with oil.
6: 20 [6:13] [C] are to bring to the LORD on the day he *is* **anointed**:
7: 12 [B] with oil, wafers made without yeast and **spread** with oil,
7: 36 [A] On the day they *were* **anointed**, the LORD commanded
8: 10 [A] and **anointed** the tabernacle and everything in it,
8: 11 [A] **anointing** the altar and all its utensils and the basin with its
8: 12 [A] oil on Aaron's head and **anointed** him to consecrate him.
16: 32 [A] The priest who *is* **anointed** and ordained to succeed his
Nu 3: 3 [B] the **anointed** priests, who were ordained to serve as priests.
6: 15 [B] of fine flour mixed with oil, and wafers **spread** with oil.
7: 1 [A] *he* **anointed** it and consecrated it and all its furnishings.
7: 1 [A] *He* also **anointed** and consecrated the altar and all its
7: 10 [C] When the altar *was* **anointed**, the leaders brought their
7: 84 [C] leaders for the dedication of the altar when it **was anointed**:
7: 88 [C] offerings for the dedication of the altar after it **was anointed**.
35: 25 [A] death of the high priest, who *was* **anointed** with the holy oil.
Jdg 9: 8 [A] One day the trees went out to **anoint** a king for themselves.
9: 15 [A] 'If you really *want to* **anoint** me king over you, come
1Sa 9: 16 [A] **Anoint** him leader over my people Israel; he will deliver my
10: 1 [A] "*Has* not the LORD **anointed** you leader over his
15: 1 [A] "I am the one the LORD sent to **anoint** you king over his
15: 17 [A] tribes of Israel? The LORD **anointed** you king over Israel.
16: 3 [A] you what to do. *You are to* **anoint** for me the one I indicate."
16: 12 [A] Then the LORD said, "Rise and **anoint** him; he is the one."
16: 13 [A] horn of oil and **anointed** him in the presence of his brothers,
2Sa 1: 21 [b] the shield of Saul—no longer **rubbed** [BHS 5431] with oil.
2: 4 [A] and there *they* **anointed** David king over the house of Judah.
2: 7 [A] and the house of Judah *has* **anointed** me king over them."
3: 39 [B] today, though I *am* the **anointed** king, I am weak, and these
5: 3 [A] the LORD, and *they* **anointed** David king over Israel.
5: 17 [A] When the Philistines heard that David *had been* **anointed**
12: 7 [A] 'I **anointed** you king over Israel, and I delivered you from the
19: 10 [19:11] [A] Absalom, whom *we* **anointed** to rule over us,
1Ki 1: 34 [A] *have* Zadok the priest and Nathan the prophet **anoint** him
1: 39 [A] the horn of oil from the sacred tent and **anointed** Solomon.
1: 45 [A] and Nathan the prophet *have* **anointed** him king at Gihon.
5: 1 [5:15] [A] *had been* **anointed** king to succeed his father David,
19: 15 [A] When you get there, **anoint** Hazael king over Aram.
19: 16 [A] Also, **anoint** Jehu son of Nimshi king over Israel, and anoint
19: 16 [A] **anoint** Elisha son of Shaphat from Abel Meholah to succeed
2Ki 9: 3 [A] *I* **anoint** you king over Israel.' Then open the door and run;
9: 6 [A] says: '*I* **anoint** you king over the LORD's people Israel.
9: 12 [A] is what the LORD says: *I* **anoint** you king over Israel.' "
11: 12 [A] *They* **anointed** him, and the people clapped their hands
23: 30 [A] and **anointed** him and made him king in place of his father.
1Ch 11: 3 [A] *they* **anointed** David king over Israel, as the LORD had
14: 8 [C] When the Philistines heard that David *had* **been anointed**
29: 22 [A] **anointing** him before the LORD to be ruler and Zadok to be
2Ch 22: 7 [A] whom the LORD *had* **anointed** to destroy the house of
23: 11 [A] *They* **anointed** him and shouted, "Long live the king!"
Ps 45: 7 [45:8] [A] has set you above your companions by **anointing** you
89: 20 [89:21] [A] with my sacred oil *I have* **anointed** him.
Isa 21: 5 [A] they eat, they drink! Get up, you officers, **oil** the shields!
61: 1 [A] because the LORD *has* **anointed** me to preach good news
Jer 22: 14 [A] windows in it, panels it with cedar and **decorates** it in red.
Da 9: 24 [A] to seal up vision and prophecy and to **anoint** the most holy.
Am 6: 6 [A] You drink wine by the bowlful and **use** the finest lotions,

5418 ¹מִשְׁחָה mišḥâ¹, n.f. [21] [√ 5417]

anointing [21]

Ex 25: 6 the light; spices for the **anointing** oil and for the fragrant incense;
29: 7 Take the **anointing** oil and anoint him by pouring it on his head.
29: 21 some of the **anointing** oil and sprinkle it on Aaron and his
30: 25 Make these into a sacred **anointing** oil, a fragrant blend, the work
30: 25 the work of a perfumer. It will be the sacred **anointing** oil.
30: 31 'This is to be my sacred **anointing** oil for the generations to come.
31: 11 and the **anointing** oil and fragrant incense for the Holy Place.
35: 8 the light; spices for the **anointing** oil and for the fragrant incense;
35: 15 incense with its poles, the **anointing** oil and the fragrant incense;
35: 28 brought spices and olive oil for the light and for the **anointing** oil
37: 29 They also made the sacred **anointing** oil and the pure,
39: 38 the gold altar, the **anointing** oil, the fragrant incense, and the
40: 9 "Take the **anointing** oil and anoint the tabernacle and everything
Lev 8: 2 "Bring Aaron and his sons, their garments, the **anointing** oil,
8: 10 Then Moses took the **anointing** oil and anointed the tabernacle
8: 12 He poured some of the **anointing** oil on Aaron's head and anointed
8: 30 Moses took some of the **anointing** oil and some of the blood from
10: 7 or you will die, because the LORD's **anointing** oil is on you."
21: 10 the one among his brothers who has had the **anointing** oil poured
21: 12 because he has been dedicated by the **anointing** oil of his God.
Nu 4: 16 fragrant incense, the regular grain offering and the **anointing** oil.

5419 ²מִשְׁחָה mišḥâ², n.f. [2] [→ 5421]

untranslated [1], portion [1]

Lev 7: 35 **portion** of the offerings made to the LORD by fire that were
7: 35 **[RPH]** his sons on the day they were presented to serve the

5420 ¹מָשְׁחָה mošḥâ¹, v. [1] [√ 5417]

anointing [1]

Ex 40: 15 Their **anointing** will be to a priesthood that will continue for all

5421 ²מָשְׁחָה mošḥâ², n.f. [1] [√ 5419]

portion [1]

Nu 18: 8 me I give to you and your sons as your **portion** and regular share.

5422 מַשְׁחִית mašḥît, n.[m.]. [16] [√ 8845]

destroyer [4], destructive [2], corruption [1], deathly pale [1], destroy [1], destroyers [1], destroys [1], destruction [1], one who destroys [+1251] [1], slaughter [+2222+4200] [1], traps [1], undoing [1]

Ex 12: 13 No **destructive** plague will touch you when I strike Egypt.
12: 23 he will not permit the **destroyer** to enter your houses and strike
2Ki 23: 13 were east of Jerusalem on the south of the Hill of **Corruption**—
2Ch 22: 4 after his father's death they became his advisers, to his **undoing**.
Pr 18: 9 who is slack in his work is brother to **one who destroys** [+1251].
28: 24 and says, "It's not wrong"—he is partner to him who **destroys**.
Isa 54: 16 And it is I who have created the **destroyer** to work havoc;
Jer 4: 7 A lion has come out of his lair; a **destroyer** *of* nations has set out.
5: 26 men who snare birds and like those who set **traps** to catch men.
22: 7 I will send **destroyers** against you, each man with his weapons,
51: 1 I will stir up the spirit of a **destroyer** against Babylon and the
Eze 5: 16 I shoot at you with my deadly and **destructive** arrows of famine,
9: 6 **Slaughter** [+2222+4200] old men, young men and maidens,
21: 31 [21:36] hand you over to brutal men, men skilled in **destruction**.
25: 15 in their hearts, and with ancient hostility sought to **destroy** Judah,
Da 10: 8 no strength left, my face turned **deathly pale** and I was helpless.

5423 מִשְׁחָר mišḥār, n.[m.]. [1] [√ 8837]

dawn [1]

Ps 110: 3 from the womb of the **dawn** you will receive the dew of your

5424 מַשְׁחֵת mašḥēt, n.[m.]. [1] [√ 8845]

weapon [+3998] [1]

Eze 9: 1 guards of the city here, each with a **weapon** [+3998] in his hand."

5425 מִשְׁחַת mišḥat, n.[m.]. [1] [√ 8845]

disfigured [1]

Isa 52: 14 his appearance *was* so **disfigured** beyond that of any man

5426 מָשְׁחָת mošḥāt, n.[m.]. [1] [√ 8845]

deformed [1]

Lev 22: 25 on your behalf, because they are **deformed** and have defects.' "

5427 מִשְׁטוֹחַ mišṭôaḥ, n.[m.]. [3] [√ 8848]
place to spread [2], places for spreading [1]

Eze 26: 5 Out in the sea she will become a **place to spread** fishnets,
26: 14 you a bare rock, and you will become a **place to spread** fishnets.
47: 10 from En Gedi to En Eglaim there will be **places for spreading**

5428 מִשְׁטָר mišṭār, n.m. [1] [√ 8853]
dominion [1]

Job 38: 33 of the heavens? Can you set up ⌞God's⌟ **dominion** over the earth?

5429 מֶשִׁי mešî, n.[m.]. [2]
costly fabric [1], costly garments [1]

Eze 16: 10 I dressed you in fine linen and covered you with **costly garments**.
16: 13 clothes were of fine linen and **costly fabric** and embroidered cloth.

5430 מְשֵׁיזַבְאֵל mᵉšêzab'ēl, n.pr.m. [3] [→ Ar 10706]
Meshezabel [3]

Ne 3: 4 Meshullam son of Berekiah, the son of **Meshezabel**, made repairs,
10: 21 [10:22] **Meshezabel**, Zadok, Jaddua,
11: 24 Pethahiah son of **Meshezabel**, one of the descendants of Zerah son

5431 מָשִׁיחַ māšîaḥ, n.m. [39 / 38] [√ 5417]
anointed [38]

Lev 4: 3 " 'If the **anointed** priest sins, bringing guilt on the people,
4: 5 Then the **anointed** priest shall take some of the bull's blood
4: 16 the **anointed** priest is to take some of the bull's blood into the Tent
6: 22 [6:15] The son who is to succeed him as **anointed** priest shall
1Sa 2: 10 will give strength to his king and exalt the horn of his **anointed**."
2: 35 his house, and he will minister before my **anointed** *one* always.
12: 3 Testify against me in the presence of the LORD and his **anointed**.
12: 5 is witness against you, and also his **anointed** is witness this day,
16: 6 "Surely the LORD's **anointed** stands here before the LORD."
24: 6 [24:7] the LORD's **anointed**, or lift my hand against him;
24: 6 [24:7] hand against him; for he is the **anointed** *of* the LORD."
24: 10 [24:11] against my master, because he is the LORD's **anointed**.'
26: 9 Who can lay a hand on the LORD's **anointed** and be guiltless?
26: 11 LORD forbid that I should lay a hand on the LORD's **anointed**.
26: 16 because you did not guard your master, the LORD's **anointed**.
26: 23 hands today, but I would not lay a hand on the LORD's **anointed**.
2Sa 1: 14 not afraid to lift your hand to destroy the LORD's **anointed**?"
1: 16 against you when you said, 'I killed the LORD's **anointed**.' "
1: 21 no longer rubbed [BHS *anointed*; NIV 5417] with oil.
19: 21 [19:22] put to death for this? He cursed the LORD's **anointed**."
22: 51 he shows unfailing kindness to his **anointed**, to David and his
23: 1 the man **anointed** *by* the God of Jacob, Israel's singer of songs:
1Ch 16: 22 "Do not touch my **anointed** *ones*; do my prophets no harm."
2Ch 6: 42 O LORD God, do not reject your **anointed** *one*. Remember the
Ps 2: 2 gather together against the LORD and against his **Anointed** *One*.
18: 50 [18:51] he shows unfailing kindness to his **anointed**, to David
20: 6 [20:7] Now I know that the LORD saves his **anointed**;
28: 8 strength of his people, a fortress of salvation for his **anointed** *one*.
84: 9 [84:10] our shield, O God; look with favor on your **anointed** *one*.
89: 38 [89:39] you have been very angry with your **anointed** *one*.
89: 51 [89:52] they have mocked every step of your **anointed** *one*.
105: 15 "Do not touch my **anointed** *ones*; do my prophets no harm."
132: 10 the sake of David your servant, do not reject your **anointed** *one*.
132: 17 a horn grow for David and set up a lamp for my **anointed** *one*.
Isa 45: 1 "This is what the LORD says to his **anointed**, to Cyrus,
La 4: 20 The LORD's **anointed**, our very life breath, was caught in their
Da 9: 25 decree to restore and rebuild Jerusalem until the **Anointed** *One*,
9: 26 the **Anointed** *One* will be cut off and will have nothing.
Hab 3: 13 You came out to deliver your people, to save your **anointed** *one*.

5432 מָשַׁךְ māšak, v. [36] [→ 5433, 5436]
drew [2], tall [2], archers [+8008] [1], be delayed [1], be prolonged [1], bear [1], cheering [1], continue [1], deferred [1], delay [1], drag away [1], dragged off [1], drags away [1], drags off [1], draw along [1], drawn [1], extend [1], follow [1], go at once [1], joins [1], lead the way [1], led [1], lure [1], patient [1], planter [+2446] [1], prolong [1], pull in [1], pulled up [1], pulled [1], sound long [1], sounds a long blast [1], spread out [1], take away [1], worn [+928] [1]

Ge 37: 28 [A] his brothers **pulled** Joseph up out of the cistern and sold him
Ex 12: 21 [A] "**Go at once** and select the animals for your families
19: 13 [A] Only when the ram's horn **sounds a long blast** may they go
Dt 21: 3 [A] has never been worked and *has* never **worn** [+928] a yoke
Jos 6: 5 [A] When you hear them **sound** a **long** blast on the trumpets,
Jdg 4: 6 [A] of Naphtali and Zebulun and **lead the way** to Mount Tabor.
4: 7 [A] *I will* **lure** Sisera, the commander of Jabin's army, with his
5: 14 [A] from Zebulun *those who* **bear** a commander's staff.
20: 37 [A] into Gibeah, **spread out** and put the whole city to the sword.
1Ki 22: 34 [A] someone **drew** his bow at random and hit the king of Israel
2Ch 18: 33 [A] someone **drew** his bow at random and hit the king of Israel
Ne 9: 30 [A] For many years *you were* **patient** with them. By your Spirit
Job 21: 33 [A] all men **follow** after him, and a countless throng goes before
24: 22 [A] God **drags away** the mighty by his power; though they
41: 1 [40:25] [A] "*Can you* **pull in** the leviathan with a fishhook
Ps 10: 9 [A] he catches the helpless and **drags** them **off** in his net.
28: 3 [A] *Do* not **drag** me **away** with the wicked, with those who do
36: 10 [36:11] [A] **Continue** your love to those who know you, your
85: 5 [85:6] [A] *Will you* **prolong** your anger through all
109: 12 [A] *May* no *one* **extend** kindness to him or take pity on his
Pr 13: 12 [E] Hope **deferred** makes the heart sick, but a longing fulfilled is
Ecc 2: 3 [A] I tried **cheering** myself with wine, and embracing folly—my
SS 1: 4 [A] **Take** me **away** with you—let us hurry! Let the king bring me
Isa 5: 18 [A] Woe to *those who* **draw** sin **along** with cords of deceit,
13: 22 [C] Her time is at hand, and her days *will* not **be prolonged**.
18: 2 [E] Go, swift messengers, to a people **tall** and smooth-skinned,
18: 7 [E] will be brought to the LORD Almighty from a people **tall**
66: 19 [A] to the Libyans and Lydians (famous as **archers** [+8008]),
Jer 31: 3 [A] an everlasting love; *I have* **drawn** you *with* loving-kindness.
38: 13 [A] *they* **pulled** him **up** with the ropes and lifted him out of the
Eze 12: 25 [C] will speak what I will, and it shall be fulfilled without **delay**.
12: 28 [C] None of my words *will* **be delayed** any longer; whatever I
32: 20 [A] sword is drawn; *let* her *be* **dragged off** with all her hordes.
Hos 7: 5 [A] inflamed with wine, and he **joins** hands with the mockers.
11: 4 [A] *I* **led** them with cords of human kindness, with ties of love;
Am 9: 13 [A] and the **planter** [+2446] by the one treading grapes.

5433 מֶשֶׁךְ¹ mešek¹, n.[m.]. [2] [√ 5432]
price [1], seed to sow [+2446] [1]

Job 28: 18 are not worthy of mention; the **price** *of* wisdom is beyond rubies.
Ps 126: 6 He who goes out weeping, carrying **seed to sow** [+2446],

5434 מֶשֶׁךְ² mešek², n.pr.g. [9 / 10]
Meshech [10]

Ge 10: 2 Gomer, Magog, Madai, Javan, Tubal, **Meshech** and Tiras.
10: 23 The sons of Aram: Uz, Hul, Gether and **Meshech**. [BHS 5390]
1Ch 1: 5 Gomer, Magog, Madai, Javan, Tubal, **Meshech** and Tiras.
1: 17 and Aram. The sons of Aram: Uz, Hul, Gether and **Meshech**.
Ps 120: 5 Woe to me that I dwell in **Meshech**, that I live among the tents of
Eze 27: 13 " 'Greece, Tubal and **Meshech** traded with you; they exchanged
32: 26 "**Meshech** and Tubal are there, with all their hordes around their
38: 2 of the land of Magog, the chief prince of **Meshech** and Tubal;
38: 3 I am against you, O Gog, chief prince of **Meshech** and Tubal.
39: 1 I am against you, O Gog, chief prince of **Meshech** and Tubal.

5435 מִשְׁכָּב miškāb, n.m. [46] [√ 8886; Ar 10444]
bed [23], beds [6], bedroom [+2540] [4], lies with [2], bedding [1], bier [1], couch [1], lie in death [1], mat [1], not a virgin [+2351+3359] [1], slept with [+2351+3359] [1], slept with [+2351+3359+4200] [1], slept with [+3359] [1], slept with [+408+3359+4200] [1], taking rest [+906+8886] [1]

Ge 49: 4 for you went up onto your father's **bed**, onto my couch and defiled
Ex 8: 3 [7:28] your palace and your **bedroom** [+2540] and onto your bed,
21: 18 or with his fist and he does not die but is confined to **bed**,
Lev 15: 4 " 'Any **bed** the man with a discharge lies on will be unclean,
15: 5 Anyone who touches his **bed** must wash his clothes and bathe with
15: 21 Whoever touches her **bed** must wash his clothes and bathe with
15: 23 Whether it is the **bed** or anything she was sitting on, when anyone
15: 24 will be unclean for seven days; any **bed** he lies on will be unclean.
15: 26 Any **bed** she lies on while her discharge continues will be unclean,
15: 26 as is her **bed** during her monthly period, and anything she sits on
18: 22 " 'Do not lie with a man as one **lies with** a woman; that is
20: 13 " 'If a man lies with a man as one **lies with** a woman, both of them
Nu 31: 17 kill every woman *who has* **slept with** [+408+3359+4200] a man,
31: 18 save for yourselves every girl who *has* never **slept with** [+3359] a
31: 35 32,000 women who *had* never **slept with** [+2351+3359] a man.
Jdg 21: 11 every male and every woman *who is* **not a virgin** [+2351+3359]."
21: 12 young women who *had* never **slept with** [+2351+3359+4200] a
2Sa 4: 5 of the day while he *was* **taking** his noonday **rest** [+906+8886].
4: 7 the house while he was lying on the bed in his **bedroom** [+2540].
4: 11 killed an innocent man in his own house and on his own **bed**—
11: 2 One evening David got up from his **bed** and walked around on the
11: 13 in the evening Uriah went out to sleep on his **mat** among his
13: 5 "Go to **bed** and pretend to be ill," Jonadab said. "When your father
17: 28 brought **bedding** and bowls and articles of pottery. They also
1Ki 1: 47 greater than yours!' And the king bowed in worship on his **bed**
2Ki 6: 12 of Israel the very words you speak in your **bedroom** [+2540]."
2Ch 16: 14 They laid him on a **bier** covered with spices and various blended
Job 7: 13 my bed will comfort me and my **couch** will ease my complaint,

Job 33:15 when deep sleep falls on men as they slumber in their **beds**,
33:19 Or a man may be chastened on a **bed** of pain with constant distress
Ps 4:4 [4:5] when you are on your **beds**, search your hearts and be silent.
36:4 [36:5] Even on his **bed** he plots evil; he commits himself to a
41:3 [41:4] him on his sickbed and restore him from his **bed** of illness.
149:5 Let the saints rejoice in this honor and sing for joy on their **beds**.
Pr 7:17 I have perfumed my **bed** with myrrh, aloes and cinnamon.
22:27 the means to pay, your very **bed** will be snatched from under you.
Ecc 10:20 even in your thoughts, or curse the rich in your **bedroom** [+2540],
SS 3:1 All night long on my **bed** I looked for the one my heart loves;
Isa 57:2 walk uprightly enter into peace; they find rest as they **lie in death**.
57:7 You have made your **bed** on a high and lofty hill; there you went
57:8 Forsaking me, you uncovered your **bed**, you climbed into it
57:8 you made a pact with those whose **beds** you love, and you looked
Eze 23:17 came to her, to the **bed** *of* love, and in their lust they defiled her.
32:25 A **bed** is made for her among the slain, with all her hordes around
Hos 7:14 do not cry out to me from their hearts but wail upon their **beds**.
Mic 2:1 to those who plan iniquity, to those who plot evil on their **beds**!

5436 מֹשְׁכוֹת *mōšᵉkôt*, n.f. [1] [√ 5432]

cords [1]

Job 38:31 you bind the beautiful Pleiades? Can you loose the **cords** *of* Orion?

5437 מְשַׂכֶּלֶת *mᵉśakkelet*, n.f.abst. Not used in NIV/BHS [√ 8897]

5438 מִשְׁכָּן *miškān*, n.m. [139] [√ 8905; Ar 10445]

tabernacle [102], dwelling place [8], tents [5], dwellings [4], *untranslated* [3], dwelling [3], it[s] [+2021] [3], dwelling places [2], where dwells [2], habitat [1], homes [1], houses [1], lived [1], place where dwell [1], resting place [1], tent [1]

Ex 25:9 Make this **tabernacle** and all its furnishings exactly like the pattern
26:1 "Make the **tabernacle** with ten curtains of finely twisted linen
26:6 them to fasten the curtains together so that the **tabernacle** is a unit.
26:7 "Make curtains of goat hair for the tent over the **tabernacle**—
26:12 that is left over is to hang down at the rear of the **tabernacle**.
26:13 what is left will hang over the sides of the **tabernacle** so as to
26:15 "Make upright frames of acacia wood for the **tabernacle**.
26:17 to each other. Make all the frames of the **tabernacle** in this way.
26:18 Make twenty frames for the south side of the **tabernacle**
26:20 For the other side, the north side of the **tabernacle**, make twenty
26:22 six frames for the far end, that is, the west end of the **tabernacle**,
26:23 and make two frames for the corners **[RPH]** at the far end.
26:26 of acacia wood: five for the frames on one side of the **tabernacle**,
26:27 **[RPH]** and five for the frames on the west, at the far end of the
26:27 five for the frames on the west, at the far end of the **tabernacle**.
26:30 "Set up the **tabernacle** according to the plan shown you on the
26:35 the table outside the curtain on the north side of the **tabernacle**
27:9 "Make a courtyard for the **tabernacle**. The south side shall be a
27:19 All the other articles used in the service of the **tabernacle**,
35:11 the **tabernacle** with its tent and its covering, clasps, frames,
35:15 the curtain for the doorway at the entrance to the **tabernacle**;
35:18 the tent pegs for the **tabernacle** and for the courtyard, and their
36:8 All the skilled men among the workmen made the **tabernacle** with
36:13 the two sets of curtains together so that the **tabernacle** was a unit.
36:14 They made curtains of goat hair for the tent over the **tabernacle**—
36:20 They made upright frames of acacia wood for the **tabernacle**.
36:22 each other. They made all the frames of the **tabernacle** in this way.
36:23 They made twenty frames for the south side of the **tabernacle**
36:25 For the other side, the north side of the **tabernacle**, they made
36:27 six frames for the far end, that is, the west end of the **tabernacle**,
36:28 two frames were made for the corners of the **tabernacle** at the far
36:31 of acacia wood: five for the frames on one side of the **tabernacle**,
36:32 **[RPH]** and five for the frames on the west, at the far end of the
36:32 five for the frames on the west, at the far end of the **tabernacle**.
38:20 All the tent pegs of the **tabernacle** and of the surrounding
38:21 These are the amounts of the materials used for the **tabernacle**,
38:21 materials used for the tabernacle, the **tabernacle** *of* the Testimony,
38:31 and those for its entrance and all the tent pegs for the **tabernacle**
39:32 So all the work on the **tabernacle**, the Tent of Meeting,
39:33 they brought the **tabernacle** to Moses: the tent and all its
39:40 all the furnishings for the **tabernacle**, the Tent of Meeting;
40:2 "Set up the **tabernacle**, the Tent of Meeting, on the first day of the
40:5 and put the curtain at the entrance to the **tabernacle**.
40:6 altar of burnt offering in front of the entrance to the **tabernacle**,
40:9 the anointing oil and anoint the **tabernacle** and everything in it;
40:17 So the **tabernacle** was set up on the first day of the first month in
40:18 When Moses set up the **tabernacle**, he put the bases in place,
40:19 he spread the tent over the **tabernacle** and put the covering over
40:21 he brought the ark into the **tabernacle** and hung the shielding
40:22 of Meeting on the north side of the **tabernacle** outside the curtain
40:24 of Meeting opposite the table on the south side of the **tabernacle**
40:28 Then he put up the curtain at the entrance to the **tabernacle**.
40:29 set the altar of burnt offering near the entrance to the **tabernacle**,
40:33 Then Moses set up the courtyard around the **tabernacle** and altar
40:34 of Meeting, and the glory of the LORD filled the **tabernacle**.
40:35 settled upon it, and the glory of the LORD filled the **tabernacle**.
40:36 whenever the cloud lifted from above the **tabernacle**, they would
40:38 So the cloud of the LORD was over the **tabernacle** by day,
Lev 8:10 the anointing oil and anointed the **tabernacle** and everything in it,
15:31 will not die in their uncleanness for defiling my **dwelling place**,
17:4 offering to the LORD in front of the **tabernacle** *of* the LORD—
26:11 I will put my **dwelling place** among you, and I will not abhor you.
Nu 1:50 appoint the Levites to be in charge of the **tabernacle** *of* the
1:50 They are to carry the **tabernacle** and all its furnishings; they are to
1:50 they are to take care of it and encamp around **it**[s] [+2021].
1:51 Whenever the **tabernacle** is to move, the Levites are to take it
1:51 and whenever the **tabernacle** is to be set up, the Levites shall do it.
1:53 are to set up their tents around the **tabernacle** *of* the Testimony
1:53 The Levites are to be responsible for the care of the **tabernacle** *of*
3:7 at the Tent of Meeting by doing the work of the **tabernacle**.
3:8 obligations of the Israelites by doing the work of the **tabernacle**.
3:23 Gershonite clans were to camp on the west, behind the **tabernacle**.
3:25 the Gershonites were responsible for the care of the **tabernacle**
3:26 curtain at the entrance to the courtyard surrounding the **tabernacle**
3:29 Kohathite clans were to camp on the south side of the **tabernacle**.
3:35 of Abihail; they were to camp on the north side of the **tabernacle**.
3:36 were appointed to take care of the frames of the **tabernacle**,
3:38 and Aaron and his sons were to camp to the east of the **tabernacle**,
4:16 He is to be in charge of the entire **tabernacle** and everything in it,
4:25 They are to carry the curtains of the **tabernacle**, the Tent of
4:26 the curtains of the courtyard surrounding the **tabernacle** and altar,
4:31 to carry the frames of the **tabernacle**, its crossbars, posts and
5:17 and put some dust from the **tabernacle** floor into the water.
7:1 When Moses finished setting up the **tabernacle**, he anointed it
7:3 a cart from every two. These they presented before the **tabernacle**.
9:15 On the day the **tabernacle**, the Tent of the Testimony, was set up,
9:15 Tent of the Testimony, was set up, the cloud covered **it**[s] [+2021].
9:15 From evening till morning the cloud above the **tabernacle** looked
9:18 As long as the cloud stayed over the **tabernacle**, they remained in
9:19 When the cloud remained over the **tabernacle** a long time,
9:20 Sometimes the cloud was over the **tabernacle** only a few days;
9:22 Whether the cloud stayed over the **tabernacle** for two days
10:11 the cloud lifted from above the **tabernacle** *of* the Testimony.
10:17 Then the **tabernacle** was taken down, and the Gershonites
10:17 the Gershonites and Merarites, who carried **it**[s] [+2021], set out.
10:21 holy things. The **tabernacle** was to be set up before they arrived.
16:9 you near himself to do the work at the LORD's **tabernacle**
16:24 'Move away from the **tents** *of* Korah, Dathan and Abiram.' "
16:27 So they moved away from the **tents** *of* Korah, Dathan and Abiram.
17:13 [17:28] Anyone who even comes near the **tabernacle** *of* the
19:13 and fails to purify himself defiles the LORD's **tabernacle**.
24:5 beautiful are your tents, O Jacob, your **dwelling places**, O Israel!
31:30 who are responsible for the care of the LORD's **tabernacle**."
31:47 who were responsible for the care of the LORD's **tabernacle**.
Jos 22:19 where the LORD's **tabernacle** stands, and share the land with us.
22:29 the altar of the LORD our God that stands before his **tabernacle**."
2Sa 7:6 have been moving from place to place with a tent as my **dwelling**.
1Ch 6:32 [6:17] They ministered with music before the **tabernacle**,
6:48 [6:33] were assigned to all the other duties of the **tabernacle**,
16:39 his fellow priests before the **tabernacle** *of* the LORD at the high
17:5 from one tent site to another, from one **dwelling place** to another.
21:29 The **tabernacle** *of* the LORD, which Moses had made in the
23:26 the Levites no longer need to carry the **tabernacle** or any of the
2Ch 1:5 had made was in Gibeon in front of the **tabernacle** *of* the LORD;
29:6 They turned their faces away from the LORD's **dwelling place**
Job 18:21 Surely such is the **dwelling** *of* an evil man; such is the place of one
21:28 now is the great man's house, the tents where wicked men **lived**?'
39:6 I gave him the wasteland as his home, the salt flats as his **habitat**.
Ps 26:8 where you live, O LORD, the place **where** your glory **dwells**.
43:3 bring me to your holy mountain, to the **place where** you **dwell**.
46:4 [46:5] city of God, the holy place **where** the Most High **dwells**.
49:11 [49:12] houses forever, their **dwellings** for endless generations,
74:7 to the ground; they defiled the **dwelling place** *of* your Name.
78:28 He made them come down inside their camp, all around their **tents**.
78:60 He abandoned the **tabernacle** *of* Shiloh, the tent he had set up
84:1 [84:2] How lovely is your **dwelling place**, O LORD Almighty!
87:2 the LORD loves the gates of Zion more than all the **dwellings** *of*
132:5 a place for the LORD, a **dwelling** for the Mighty One of Jacob."
132:7 "Let us go to his **dwelling place**; let us worship at his footstool—
SS 1:8 and graze your young goats by the **tents** *of* the shepherds.
Isa 22:16 grave on the height and chiseling your **resting place** in the rock?
32:18 dwelling places, in secure **homes**, in undisturbed places of rest.
54:2 of your tent, stretch your **tent** curtains wide, do not hold back;
Jer 9:19 [9:18] We must leave our land because our **houses** are in ruins.' "
30:18 fortunes of Jacob's tents and have compassion on his **dwellings**;

Jer 51:30 Her **dwellings** are set on fire; the bars of her gates are broken.
Eze 25: 4 They will set up their camps and pitch their **tents** among you;
37:27 My **dwelling place** will be with them; I will be their God,
Hab 1: 6 who sweep across the whole earth to seize **dwelling places** not

5439 [1]מָשַׁל ***māšal*[1]**, v. [17] [→ 5441, 5442, 5444, 5446]

be like [2], is like [2], quote [2], tell [2], become like [1], byword [1], liken [1], poets [1], quote proverb [1], quotes proverbs [1], quoting [1], reduced to [1], telling [1]

Nu 21:27 [A] That is why the **poets** say: "Come to Heshbon and let it be
Job 17: 6 [A] "God has made me a **byword** to everyone, a man in whose
30:19 [F] throws me into the mud, and *I am* **reduced to** dust and ashes.
Ps 28: 1 [C] *I will* **be like** those who have gone down to the pit.
49:12 [49:13] [C] does not endure; *he* **is like** the beasts that perish.
49:20 [49:21] [C] A man who has riches without understanding **is like**
143: 7 [C] face from me or *I will* **be like** those who go down to the pit.
Isa 14:10 [C] have become weak, as we are; *you have* **become like** us."
46: 5 [G] To whom *will you* **liken** me that we may be compared?
Eze 12:23 [A] to this proverb, and *they will* no longer **quote** it in Israel.'
16:44 [A] " 'Everyone who **quotes proverbs** will quote this proverb
16:44 [A] " 'Everyone who quotes proverbs *will* **quote** *this* **proverb**
17: 2 [A] set forth an allegory and **tell** the house of Israel a parable.
18: 2 [A] "What do you people mean *by* **quoting** this proverb about
18: 3 [A] you *will* no longer **quote** this proverb in Israel.
20:49 [21:5] [D] are saying of me, 'Isn't he *just* **telling** parables?' "
24: 3 [A] **Tell** this rebellious house a parable and say to them: 'This is

5440 [2]מָשַׁל ***māšal*[2]**, v. [80] [→ 4938, 4939, 5445]

rule [28], ruler [16], rules [7], ruled [6], rulers [4], ruler's [3], actually rule [+928+5440] [2], govern [2], ruling [2], *untranslated* [1], controls [1], dominion [1], exercised [1], gain control [1], has right [1], in charge [1], made ruler [1], make rulers [1], master [1]

Ge 1:18 [A] to **govern** the day and the night, and to separate light from
3:16 [A] desire will be for your husband, and he *will* **rule** over you."
4: 7 [A] at your door; it desires to have you, but you *must* **master** it."
24: 2 [A] the *one* **in charge** of all that he had, "Put your hand under
37: 8 [A] *Will you* **actually rule** [+928+5440] us?" And they hated
37: 8 [A] *Will you* **actually rule** [+928+5440] us?" And they hated
45: 8 [A] lord of his entire household and **ruler** of all Egypt.
45:26 [A] In fact, he *is* **ruler** of all Egypt." Jacob was stunned; he did
Ex 21: 8 [A] *He* **has** no **right** to sell her to foreigners, because he has
Dt 15: 6 [A] *You will* **rule** over many nations but none will rule over you.
15: 6 [A] You will rule over many nations but none *will* **rule** over you.
Jos 12: 2 [A] *He* **ruled** from Aroer on the rim of the Arnon Gorge—from
12: 5 [A] *He* **ruled** over Mount Hermon, Salecah, all of Bashan to the
Jdg 8:22 [A] The Israelites said to Gideon, "**Rule** over us—you, your son
8:23 [A] Gideon told them, "I *will* not **rule** over you, nor will my son
8:23 [A] "I will not rule over you, nor *will* my son **rule** over you.
8:23 [A] will my son rule over you. The LORD *will* **rule** over you."
9: 2 [A] *to have* all seventy of Jerub-Baal's sons **rule** over you,
9: 2 [A] one man?' **[RPH]** Remember, I am your flesh and blood."
14: 4 [A] the Philistines; for at that time they *were* **ruling** over Israel.)
15:11 [A] "Don't you realize that the Philistines *are* **rulers** over us?
2Sa 23: 3 [A] '*When one* **rules** over men *in* righteousness, when he rules in
23: 3 [A] over men in righteousness, *when he* **rules** *in* the fear of God,
1Ki 4:21 [5:1] [A] Solomon **ruled** over all the kingdoms from the River
1Ch 29:12 [A] and honor come from you; you *are* the **ruler** of all things.
2Ch 7:18 [A] I said, 'You shall never fail to have a man *to* **rule** over Israel.'
9:26 [A] He **ruled** over all the kings from the River to the land of the
20: 6 [A] You **rule** over all the kingdoms of the nations. Power
23:20 [A] the **rulers** of the people and all the people of the land
Ne 9:37 [A] *They* **rule** over our bodies and our cattle as they please. We
Job 25: 2 [G] "**Dominion** and awe belong to God; he establishes order in
Ps 8: 6 [8:7] [G] *You* **made** him **ruler** over the works of your hands;
19:13 [19:14] [A] also from willful sins; *may they* not **rule** over me.
22:28 [22:29] [A] to the LORD and *he* **rules** over the nations.
59:13 [59:14] [A] to the ends of the earth that God **rules** over Jacob.
66: 7 [A] *He* **rules** forever by his power, his eyes watch the nations—
89: 9 [89:10] [A] You **rule** over the surging sea; when its waves
103:19 [A] his throne in heaven, and his kingdom **rules** over all.
105:20 [A] king sent and released him, the **ruler** *of* peoples set him free.
105:21 [A] him master of his household, **ruler** over all he possessed,
106:41 [A] them over to the nations, and their foes **ruled** over them.
Pr 6: 7 [A] It has no commander, no overseer or **ruler**,
12:24 [A] Diligent hands *will* **rule**, but laziness ends in slave labor.
16:32 [A] a *man who* **controls** his temper than one who takes a city.
17: 2 [A] A wise servant *will* **rule** over a disgraceful son, and will
19:10 [A] in luxury—how much worse for a slave *to* **rule** over princes!
22: 7 [A] The rich **rule** over the poor, and the borrower is servant to
23: 1 [A] When you sit to dine with a **ruler**, note well what is before
28:15 [A] or a charging bear is a wicked man **ruling** over a helpless
29: 2 [A] the people rejoice; when the wicked **rule**, the people groan.
29:12 [A] If a **ruler** listens to lies, all his officials become wicked.
29:26 [A] Many seek an audience with a **ruler**, but it is from the
Ecc 9:17 [A] are more to be heeded than the shouts of a **ruler** of fools.
10: 4 [A] If a **ruler's** anger rises against you, do not leave your post;
Isa 3: 4 [A] make boys their officials; mere children *will* **govern** them.
3:12 [A] Youths oppress my people, women **rule** over them. O my
14: 5 [A] has broken the rod of the wicked, the scepter of the **rulers**,
16: 1 [A] Send lambs as tribute to the **ruler** *of* the land, from Sela,
19: 4 [A] a fierce king *will* **rule** over them," declares the Lord,
28:14 [A] the LORD, you scoffers *who* **rule** this people in Jerusalem.
40:10 [A] LORD comes with power, and his arm **rules** for him.
49: 7 [A] and abhorred by the nation, to the servant of **rulers**:
52: 5 [A] and *those who* **rule** them mock," declares the LORD.
63:19 [A] *you have* not **ruled** over them, they have not been called by
Jer 22:30 [A] will sit on the throne of David or **rule** anymore in Judah."
30:21 [A] be one of their own; their **ruler** will arise from among them.
33:26 [A] will not choose one of his sons *to* **rule** over the descendants
51:46 [A] rumors of violence in the land and of **ruler** against ruler.
51:46 [A] rumors of violence in the land and of ruler against **ruler**.
La 5: 8 [A] Slaves **rule** over us, and there is none to free us from their
Eze 19:11 [A] Its branches were strong, fit for a **ruler's** scepter. It towered
19:14 [A] No strong branch is left on it fit for a **ruler's** scepter.' This is
Da 11: 3 [A] *who will* **rule** *with* great power and do as he pleases.
11: 4 [A] to his descendants, nor will it have the power *he* **exercised**,
11: 5 [A] than he and *will* **rule** his own kingdom *with* great power.
11:39 [G] *He will* **make** them **rulers** over many people and will
11:43 [A] *He will* **gain control** of the treasures of gold and silver
Mic 5: 2 [5:1] [A] out of you will come for me one who will be **ruler**
Hab 1:14 [A] men like fish in the sea, like sea creatures that have no **ruler**.
Zec 6:13 [A] be clothed with majesty and will sit and **rule** on his throne.

5441 [3]מָשַׁל ***māšal*[3]**, v.den. Not used in NIV/BHS [√ 5439]

5442 [1]מָשָׁל ***māšāl*[1]**, n.m. [40] [√ 5439]

oracle [7], proverb [7], proverbs [7], byword [6], discourse [2], parable [2], parables [2], saying [2], make sport of [+2118+4200 +4200] [1], object of scorn [1], ridicule [+5951+6584] [1], taunt [+4200+5951+6584] [1], taunt [1]

Nu 23: 7 Then Balaam uttered his **oracle**: "Balak brought me from Aram,
23:18 Then he uttered his **oracle**: "Arise, Balak, and listen; hear me,
24: 3 and he uttered his **oracle**: "The oracle of Balaam son of Beor,
24:15 Then he uttered his **oracle**: "The oracle of Balaam son of Beor,
24:20 Balaam saw Amalek and uttered his **oracle**: "Amalek was first
24:21 he saw the Kenites and uttered his **oracle**: "Your dwelling place is
24:23 Then he uttered his **oracle**: "Ah, who can live when God does this?
Dt 28:37 You will become a thing of horror and an **object of scorn**
1Sa 10:12 there answered, "And who is their father?" So it became a **saying**:
24:13 [24:14] As the old **saying** goes, 'From evildoers come evil deeds,'
1Ki 4:32 [5:12] He spoke three thousand **proverbs** and his songs numbered
9: 7 Israel will then become a **byword** and an object of ridicule among
2Ch 7:20 I will make it a **byword** and an object of ridicule among all
Job 13:12 Your maxims are **proverbs** *of* ashes; your defenses are defenses of
27: 1 And Job continued his **discourse**:
29: 1 Job continued his **discourse**:
Ps 44:14 [44:15] You have made us a **byword** among the nations;
49: 4 [49:5] I will turn my ear to a **proverb**; with the harp I will
69:11 [69:12] people **make sport** [+2118+4200+4200] **of** *me*.
78: 2 I will open my mouth in **parables**, I will utter hidden things,
Pr 1: 1 The **proverbs** *of* Solomon son of David, king of Israel:
1: 6 for understanding **proverbs** and parables, the sayings and riddles
10: 1 The **proverbs** *of* Solomon: A wise son brings joy to his father,
25: 1 These are more **proverbs** *of* Solomon, copied by the men of
26: 7 Like a lame man's legs that hang limp is a **proverb** in the mouth of
26: 9 Like a thornbush in a drunkard's hand is a **proverb** in the mouth of
Ecc 12: 9 He pondered and searched out and set in order many **proverbs**.
Isa 14: 4 you will take up this **taunt** against the king of Babylon: How the
Jer 24: 9 a reproach and a **byword**, an object of ridicule and cursing,
Eze 12:22 "Son of man, what is this **proverb** you have in the land of Israel:
12:23 I am going to put an end to this **proverb**, and they will no longer
14: 8 my face against that man and make him an example and a **byword**.
17: 2 set forth an allegory and tell the house of Israel a **parable**.
18: 2 "What do you people mean by quoting this **proverb** about the land
18: 3 Sovereign LORD, you will no longer quote this **proverb** in Israel.
20:49 [21:5] They are saying of me, 'Isn't he just telling **parables**?' "
24: 3 Tell this rebellious house a **parable** and say to them: 'This is what
Joel 2:17 your inheritance an object of scorn, a **byword** among the nations.
Mic 2: 4 In that day *men will* **ridicule** [+5951+6584] you; they will taunt
Hab 2: 6 "*Will* not all of them **taunt** [+4200+5951+6584] him with ridicule

5443 [2]מָשָׁל ***māšāl*[2]**, n.pr.loc. [1] [cf. 5398]

Mashal [1]

1Ch 6:74 [6:59] from the tribe of Asher they received **Mashal**, Abdon,

5444 ¹מֹשֶׁל mōšel¹, n.[m.]. [1] [√ 5439]

equal [1]

Job 41:33 [41:25] Nothing on earth is his **equal**—a creature without fear.

5445 ²מֹשֶׁל mōšel², n.[m.]. [2] [√ 5440]

power [1], rule [1]

Da 11: 4 not go to his descendants, nor will it have the **power** he exercised,
Zec 9:10 His **rule** will extend from sea to sea and from the River to the ends

5446 מְשֹׁל mᵉšōl, n.[m.]. Not used in NIV/BHS [√ 5439]

5447 מִשְׁלוֹחַ mišlôaḥ, n.[m.]. [3] [√ 8938]

giving [2], lay [1]

Est 9:19 a day of joy and feasting, a day for **giving** presents to each other.
9:22 joy and **giving** presents of food to one another and gifts to the
Isa 11:14 They *will* **lay** hands *on* Edom and Moab, and the Ammonites will

5448 מִשְׁלָח mišlāḥ, n.[m.]. [7] [√ 8938]

put to [6], places where turned loose [1]

Dt 12: 7 and shall rejoice in everything you have **put** your hand **to**,
12:18 before the LORD your God in everything you **put** your hand **to**.
15:10 bless you in all your work and in everything you **put** your hand **to**.
23:20 [23:21] *you* **put** your hand **to** in the land you are entering to
28: 8 a blessing on your barns and on everything you **put** your hand **to**.
28:20 confusion and rebuke in everything you **put** your hand **to**,
Isa 7:25 they will become **places where** cattle are **turned loose** and where

5449 מִשְׁלַחַת mišlaḥat, n.f. [2] [√ 8938]

band [1], discharged [1]

Ps 78:49 his wrath, indignation and hostility—a **band** *of* destroying angels.
Ecc 8: 8 As no one is **discharged** in time of war, so wickedness will not

5450 מְשֻׁלָּם mᵉšullām, n.pr.m. [25] [→ 5452, 5453; cf. 8966]

Meshullam [25]

2Ki 22: 3 Shaphan son of Azaliah, the son of **Meshullam**, to the temple of
1Ch 3:19 and Shimei. The sons of Zerubbabel: **Meshullam** and Hananiah.
5:13 Michael, **Meshullam**, Sheba, Jorai, Jacan, Zia and Eber—
8:17 Zebadiah, **Meshullam**, Hizki, Heber,
9: 7 Sallu son of **Meshullam**, the son of Hodaviah, the son of
9: 8 **Meshullam** son of Shephatiah, the son of Reuel, the son of Ibnijah.
9:11 the son of **Meshullam**, the son of Zadok, the son of Meraioth,
9:12 the son of Jahzerah, the son of **Meshullam**, the son of
2Ch 34:12 and Zechariah and **Meshullam**, descended from Kohath.
Ezr 8:16 Elnathan, Jarib, Elnathan, Nathan, Zechariah and **Meshullam**,
10:15 supported by **Meshullam** and Shabbethai the Levite, opposed this.
10:29 **Meshullam**, Malluch, Adaiah, Jashub, Sheal and Jeremoth.
Ne 3: 4 Next to him **Meshullam** son of Berekiah, the son of Meshezabel,
3: 6 by Joiada son of Paseah and **Meshullam** son of Besodeiah.
3:30 **Meshullam** son of Berekiah made repairs opposite his living
6:18 his son Jehohanan had married the daughter of **Meshullam** son of
8: 4 Malkijah, Hashum, Hashbaddanah, Zechariah and **Meshullam**.
10: 7 [10:8] **Meshullam**, Abijah, Mijamin,
10:20 [10:21] Magpiash, **Meshullam**, Hezir,
11: 7 Sallu son of **Meshullam**, the son of Joed, the son of Pedaiah,
11:11 the son of **Meshullam**, the son of Zadok, the son of Meraioth,
12:13 of Ezra's, **Meshullam**; of Amariah's, Jehohanan;
12:16 of Iddo's, Zechariah; of Ginnethon's, **Meshullam**;
12:25 **Meshullam**, Talmon and Akkub were gatekeepers who guarded
12:33 along with Azariah, Ezra, **Meshullam**,

5451 מְשִׁלֵּמוֹת mᵉšillēmôt, n.pr.m. [2] [→ 5454; cf. 8966]

Meshillemoth [2]

2Ch 28:12 Berekiah son of **Meshillemoth**, Jehizkiah son of Shallum,
Ne 11:13 the son of Ahzai, the son of **Meshillemoth**, the son of Immer,

5452 מְשֶׁלֶמְיָה mᵉšelemyâ, n.pr.m. [1] [√ 5450 + 3378]

Meshelemiah [1]

1Ch 9:21 Zechariah son of **Meshelemiah** was the gatekeeper at the entrance

5453 מְשֶׁלֶמְיָהוּ mᵉšelemyāhû, n.pr.m. [3] [√ 5450 + 3378]

Meshelemiah [3]

1Ch 26: 1 **Meshelemiah** son of Kore, one of the sons of Asaph.
26: 2 **Meshelemiah** had sons: Zechariah the firstborn,
26: 9 **Meshelemiah** had sons and relatives, who were able men—

5454 מְשִׁלֵּמִית mᵉšillēmît, n.pr.m. [1] [√ 5451; cf. 8966]

Meshillemith [1]

1Ch 9:12 the son of Meshullam, the son of **Meshillemith**, the son of Immer.

5455 מְשֻׁלֶּמֶת mᵉšullemet, n.pr.f. [1] [√ 8966]

Meshullemeth [1]

2Ki 21:19 His mother's name was **Meshullemeth** daughter of Haruz;

5456 מִשְׁלֹשׁ mišlōš, n.[m.]. Not used in NIV/BHS [√ 4946 + 8993]

5457 מְשַׁמָּה mᵉšammâ, n.f. [7] [√ 9037]

waste [4], dried up [2], object of horror [1]

Isa 15: 6 The waters of Nimrim are **dried up** and the grass is withered;
Jer 48:34 Eglath Shelishiyah, for even the waters of Nimrim are **dried up**.
Eze 5:15 an **object of horror** to the nations around you when I inflict
6:14 and make the land a desolate **waste** from the desert to Diblah—
33:28 I will make the land a desolate **waste**, and her proud strength will
33:29 when I have made the land a desolate **waste** because of all the
35: 3 stretch out my hand against you and make you a desolate **waste**.

5458 מִשְׁמָן mišmān, n.[m.]. [4 / 5] [√ 9043]

fat [2], richest [1], sturdiest [1], sturdy [1]

1Sa 15: 9 of the sheep and cattle, the **fat** [BHS 5467] *calves* and lambs—
Ps 78:31 he put to death the **sturdiest** among them, cutting down the young
Isa 10:16 will send a wasting disease upon his **sturdy** *warriors*;
17: 4 the glory of Jacob will fade; the **fat** *of* his body will waste away.
Da 11:24 When the **richest** provinces feel secure, he will invade them

5459 מִשְׁמַנָּה mišmannâ, n.pr.m. [1] [√ 9043]

Mishmannah [1]

1Ch 12:10 [12:11] **Mishmannah** the fourth, Jeremiah the fifth,

5460 מַשְׁמַנִּים mašmannîm, n.[m.]. [1] [√ 9043]

choice food [1]

Ne 8:10 Nehemiah said, "Go and enjoy **choice food** and sweet drinks,

5461 ¹מִשְׁמָע mišmāʿ¹, n.[m.]. [1] [→ 5462; cf. 9048]

what hears [1]

Isa 11: 3 he sees with his eyes, or decide by **what** he **hears** *with* his ears;

5462 ²מִשְׁמָע mišmāʿ², n.pr.m. [4] [√ 5461; cf. 9048]

Mishma [4]

Ge 25:14 **Mishma**, Dumah, Massa,
1Ch 1:30 **Mishma**, Dumah, Massa, Hadad, Tema,
4:25 Shallum was Shaul's son, Mibsam his son and **Mishma** his son.
4:26 The descendants of **Mishma**: Hammuel his son, Zaccur his son

5463 מִשְׁמַעַת mišmaʿat, n.f. [4] [√ 9048]

bodyguard [3], subject to [1]

1Sa 22:14 captain of your **bodyguard** and highly respected in your
2Sa 23:23 among the Three. And David put him in charge of his **bodyguard**.
1Ch 11:25 among the Three. And David put him in charge of his **bodyguard**.
Isa 11:14 on Edom and Moab, and the Ammonites will be **subject to** them.

5464 ¹מִשְׁמָר mišmār¹, n.[m.]. [22] [√ 9068]

custody [6], guard [4], else[s] [1], guarded [+928+9068] [1], guards [+408] [1], guards [1], imprisoned [+906+906+928+5989] [1], other[s] [1], posts [1], prison [+1074] [1], section [1], services [1], take command [+2118+4200] [1], under guard [+6584] [1]

Ge 40: 3 and put them in **custody** *in* the house of the captain of the guard,
40: 4 he attended them. After they had been in **custody** for some time,
40: 7 So he asked Pharaoh's officials who were in **custody** with him *in*
41:10 and *he* **imprisoned** [+906+906+928+5989] me and the chief baker
42:17 And he put them all in **custody** for three days.
42:19 honest men, let one of your brothers stay here in **prison** [+1074],
Lev 24:12 They put him in **custody** until the will of the LORD should be
Nu 15:34 they kept him in **custody**, because it was not clear what should be
1Ch 26:16 road fell to Shuppim and Hosah. **Guard** was alongside of guard:
26:16 road fell to Shuppim and Hosah. Guard was alongside of **guard**:
Ne 4: 9 [4:3] we prayed to our God and posted a **guard** day and night to
4:22 [4:16] so they can serve us as **guards** by night and workmen by
4:23 [4:17] I nor my brothers nor my men nor the **guards** [+408]
7: 3 as guards, some at their **posts** and some near their own houses."
12:24 give praise and thanksgiving, *one* **section** responding to the other,
12:24 give praise and thanksgiving, one section responding to the **other**[s],

Ne 12:25 Akkub were gatekeepers *who* **guarded** [+928+9068] the
13:14 so faithfully done for the house of my God and its **services**.
Job 7:12 or the monster of the deep, that you put me **under guard** [+6584]?
Pr 4:23 Above all **else**ˢ, guard your heart, for it is the wellspring of life.
Jer 51:12 Reinforce the **guard**, station the watchmen, prepare an ambush!
Eze 38: 7 gathered about you, and **take command** [+2118+4200] of them.

5465 ²מִשְׁמָר *mišmār²*, n.[m.]. Not used in NIV/BHS [√ 9068]

5466 מִשְׁמֶרֶת *mišmeret*, n.f. [78] [√ 9068]

duties [10], requirements [7], *untranslated* [5], care [5], responsibilities [4], kept [3], responsible [3], service [3], duty [2], have charge of [+9068] [2], keep [2], order [2], responsible for care [2], what requires [2], assigned [1], guard [+906+9068] [1], guard [1], guarding [+906+9068] [1], guarding [+9068] [1], guarding [1], guards [1], in charge [1], lead [1], loyal [+9068] [1], mission [1], obligations [1], on behalf of [+4200] [1], positions [1], post [1], responsibility [1], responsible [+9068] [1], safe [1], services [1], serving [1], specific things [+3998] [1], take care of [+2118+4200+4200] [1], take care of [1], under guard [1], use [1], watch [1]

Ge 26: 5 because Abraham obeyed me and kept my **requirements**,
Ex 12: 6 **Take care** [+2118+4200+4200] **of** them until the fourteenth day of the month, when all the people of the community of Israel must
16:23 want to boil. Save whatever is left and **keep** it until morning.' "
16:32 'Take an omer of manna and **keep** it for the generations to come,
16:33 place it before the LORD to be **kept** for the generations to come."
16:34 put the manna in front of the Testimony, that it might be **kept**.
Lev 8:35 and night for seven days and do **what** the LORD **requires**,
18:30 Keep my **requirements** and do not follow any of the detestable
22: 9 " 'The priests are to keep my **requirements** so that they do not
Nu 1:53 The Levites are to be responsible for the **care** *of* the tabernacle of
3: 7 They are to perform **duties** *for* him and for the whole community
3: 7 **[RPH]** for the whole community at the Tent of Meeting by doing
3: 8 fulfilling the **obligations** *of* the Israelites by doing the work of the
3:25 the Gershonites were **responsible for** the **care** *of* the tabernacle
3:28 The Kohathites were **responsible** *for* the care of the sanctuary.
3:31 They were **responsible for** the **care** *of* the ark, the table,
3:32 He was appointed over those who were **responsible** *for* the care of
3:36 The Merarites were appointed to **take care of** the frames of the
3:38 They were **responsible** *for* the care of the sanctuary on behalf of
3:38 for the care of the sanctuary **on behalf** [+4200] **of** the Israelites.
4:27 You shall assign to them as their **responsibility** all they are to
4:28 Their **duties** are to be under the direction of Ithamar son of Aaron,
4:31 This is their **duty** as they perform service at the Tent of Meeting:
4:32 Assign to each man the **specific things** [+3998] he is to carry.
8:26 They may assist their brothers in performing their **duties** at the
8:26 is how you are to assign the **responsibilities** of the Levites."
9:19 the Israelites obeyed the LORD's **order** and did not set out.
9:23 They obeyed the LORD's **order**, in accordance with his
17:10 [17:25] of the Testimony, to be **kept** as a sign to the rebellious.
18: 3 *They are to be* **responsible to** [+9068] you and are to perform all
18: 3 be responsible to you and are to perform all the **duties** *of* the Tent,
18: 4 join you and be responsible for the **care** *of* the Tent of Meeting—
18: 5 "You are to be responsible for the **care** *of* the sanctuary and the
18: 5 be responsible for the care of the sanctuary and **[RPH]** the altar,
18: 8 "I myself have put you **in charge** *of* the offerings presented to me;
19: 9 They shall be kept by the Israelite community for **use** in the water
31:30 who are responsible for the **care** *of* the LORD's tabernacle."
31:47 who were responsible for the **care** *of* the LORD's tabernacle.
Dt 11: 1 Love the LORD your God and keep his **requirements**, his
Jos 22: 3 but have carried out the **mission** the LORD your God gave you.
1Sa 22:23 seeking your life is seeking mine also. You will be **safe** with me."
2Sa 20: 3 to take care of the palace and put them in a house **under guard**.
1Ki 2: 3 observe **what** the LORD your God **requires**: Walk in his ways,
2Ki 11: 5 on the Sabbath—a third of you **guarding** [+9068] the royal palace,
11: 6 the guard, *who* take turns **guarding** [+906+9068] the temple—
11: 7 duty *are* all *to* **guard** [+906+9068] the temple for the king.
1Ch 9:23 their descendants were in charge of **guarding** the gates of the
9:27 stationed around the house of God, because they had to **guard** it;
12:29 [12:30] most of whom *had remained* **loyal to** [+9068] Saul's
23:32 so the Levites carried out their **responsibilities** *for* the Tent of
23:32 **[RPH]** for the Holy Place and, under their brothers the
23:32 of Aaron, for **[RPH]** the service of the temple of the LORD.
25: 8 and old alike, teacher as well as student, cast lots *for* their **duties**.
26:12 chief men, had **duties** for ministering in the temple of the LORD,
2Ch 7: 6 The priests took their **positions**, as did the Levites with the
8:14 the Levites to **lead** the praise and to assist the priests according to
13:11 We are observing the **requirements** *of* the LORD our God.
23: 6 all the other men are to guard *what* the LORD has **assigned** to
31:16 according to their **responsibilities** and their divisions.
31:17 or more, according to their **responsibilities** and their divisions.
35: 2 He appointed the priests to their **duties** and encouraged them in the
Ne 7: 3 Also appoint residents of Jerusalem as **guards**, some at their posts
12: 9 and Unni, their associates, stood opposite them in the **services**.
12:45 They performed the **service** *of* their God and the service of
12:45 performed the service of their God and the **service** *of* purification,
13:30 everything foreign, and assigned them **duties**, each to his own task.
Isa 21: 8 my lord, I stand on the watchtower; every night I stay at my **post**.
Eze 40:45 south is for the priests *who* **have charge of** [+9068] the temple,
40:46 north is for the priests *who* **have charge of** [+9068] the altar.
44: 8 Instead of carrying out your **duty** *in regard to* my holy things,
44: 8 my holy things, you put others in charge of **[RPH]** my sanctuary.
44:14 Yet I will put them in charge of the **duties** *of* the temple and all the
44:15 who faithfully carried out the **duties** *of* my sanctuary when the
44:16 come near my table to minister before me and perform my **service**.
48:11 who were faithful in **serving** me and did not go astray as the
Hab 2: 1 I will stand at my **watch** and station myself on the ramparts;
Zec 3: 7 'If you will walk in my ways and keep my **requirements**,
Mal 3:14 What did we gain by carrying out his **requirements** and going

5467 מִשְׁנֶה *mišneh*, n.[m.]. [35 / 34] [√ 9101]

second [8], next in rank [5], double [4], twice as much [4], Second District [3], double portion [2], copied [+906+4180] [1], copy [1], matching [1], New Quarter [1], other [1], second in rank [1], second-in-command [1], twice [1]

Ge 41:43 He had him ride in a chariot as his **second-in-command**, and men
43:12 Take **double** *the amount of* silver with you, for you must return
43:15 So the men took the gifts and **double** *the amount of* silver,
Ex 16: 5 and that is to be **twice as much** as they gather on the other days."
16:22 On the sixth day, they gathered **twice as much**—two omers for
Dt 15:18 six years has been worth **twice as much** *as* that of a hired hand.
17:18 he is to write for himself on a scroll a **copy** *of* this law, taken from
Jos 8:32 Joshua **copied** [+906+4180] on stones the law of Moses, which he
1Sa 8: 2 of his firstborn was Joel and the name of his **second** was Abijah,
15: 9 the fat [BHS ***grown bulls*** ?; NIV 5458] *calves* and lambs—
17:13 was Eliab; the **second**, Abinadab; and the third, Shammah.
23:17 You will be king over Israel, and I will be **second** to you. Even my
2Sa 3: 3 his **second**, Kileab the son of Abigail the widow of Nabal of
2Ki 22:14 of the wardrobe. She lived in Jerusalem, in the **Second District**.
23: 4 the priests **next in rank** and the doorkeepers to remove from the
25:18 Zephaniah the priest **next in rank** and the three doorkeepers.
1Ch 5:12 the chief, Shapham the **second**, then Janai and Shaphat, in Bashan.
15:18 and with them their brothers **next in rank**: Zechariah, Jaaziel,
16: 5 Zechariah **second**, then Jeiel, Shemiramoth, Jehiel, Mattithiah,
2Ch 28: 7 officer in charge of the palace, and Elkanah, **second** *to* the king.
31:12 in charge of these things, and his brother Shimei was **next in rank**.
34:22 of the wardrobe. She lived in Jerusalem, in the **Second District**.
35:24 put him in the **other** chariot he had and brought him to Jerusalem,
Ezr 1:10 gold bowls 30 **matching** silver bowls 410 other articles 1,000
Ne 11: 9 Judah son of Hassenuah was over the **Second District** of the city.
11:17 and prayer; Bakbukiah, **second** among his associates;
Est 10: 3 Mordecai the Jew was **second in rank** to King Xerxes, preeminent
Job 42:10 prosperous again and gave him **twice** as much as he had before.
Isa 61: 7 Instead of their shame my people will receive a **double portion**,
61: 7 so they will inherit a **double portion** in their land, and everlasting
Jer 16:18 I will repay them **double** for their wickedness and their sin,
17:18 on them the day of disaster; destroy them with **double** destruction.
52:24 Zephaniah the priest **next in rank** and the three doorkeepers.
Zep 1:10 wailing from the **New Quarter**, and a loud crash from the hills.
Zec 9:12 even now I announce that I will restore **twice as much** to you.

5468 מְשִׁסָּה *mᵉšissâ*, n.f. [6] [√ 9116; cf. 5416]

plundered [3], loot [2], victim [1]

2Ki 21:14 their enemies. They will be looted and **plundered** by all their foes,
Isa 42:22 they have been made **loot**, with no one to say, "Send them back."
42:24 Who handed Jacob over to become **loot**, [K 5416] and Israel to the
Jer 30:16 Those who plunder you will be **plundered**; all who make spoil of
Hab 2: 7 and make you tremble? Then you will become their **victim**.
Zep 1:13 Their wealth will be **plundered**, their houses demolished.

5469 מִשְׁעוֹל *miš'ôl*, n.m. [1] [√ 9123]

narrow path [1]

Nu 22:24 the angel of the LORD stood in a **narrow path** *between* two

5470 מִשְׁעִי *miš'î*, n.f. [1]

make clean [1]

Eze 16: 4 nor were you washed with water to **make** you **clean**, nor were you

5471 מִשְׁעָם *miš'ām*, n.pr.m. [1]

Misham [1]

1Ch 8:12 Eber, **Misham**, Shemed (who built Ono and Lod with its

5472 מִשְׁעָן miš'ān, n.[m.]. [4] [√ 9128]
supplies [2], support [2]

2Sa 22:19 me in the day of my disaster, but the LORD was my **support**.
Ps 18:18 [18:19] the day of my disaster, but the LORD was my **support**.
Isa 3:1 and support: all **supplies** *of* food and all supplies of water,
3:1 and support: all supplies of food and all **supplies** *of* water,

5473 מַשְׁעֵן maš'ēn, n.f. [1] [√ 9128]
supply [1]

Isa 3:1 about to take from Jerusalem and Judah both **supply** and support:

5474 מַשְׁעֵנָה maš'ēnâ, n.f. [1] [√ 9128]
support [1]

Isa 3:1 about to take from Jerusalem and Judah both supply and **support**:

5475 מִשְׁעֶנֶת miš'enet, n.f. [11] [√ 9128]
staff [9], cane [1], staffs [1]

Ex 21:19 if the other gets up and walks around outside with his **staff**;
Nu 21:18 nobles of the people sank—the nobles with scepters and **staffs**."
Jdg 6:21 With the tip of the **staff** that was in his hand, the angel of the
2Ki 4:29 your cloak into your belt, take my **staff** in your hand and run.
4:29 anyone greets you, do not answer. Lay my **staff** on the boy's face."
4:31 Gehazi went on ahead and laid the **staff** on the boy's face,
18:21 that splintered reed of a **staff**, which pierces a man's hand
Ps 23:4 for you are with me; your rod and your **staff**, they comfort me.
Isa 36:6 that splintered reed of a **staff**, which pierces a man's hand
Eze 29:6 " 'You have been a **staff** *of* reed for the house of Israel.
Zec 8:4 the streets of Jerusalem, each with **cane** in hand because of his age.

5476 מִשְׁפָּחָה mišpāḥâ, n.f. [303] [√ 9148]
clan [131], clans [124], *untranslated* [12], peoples [8], families [7], family [7], clan by clan [+4200] [2], each clan [+5476] [2], every family [+2256+5476] [2], people [2], clan [+3+1074] [1], kinds [1], kingdoms [1], Levites [+4291] [1], nation [1], one kind after another [+2157+4200] [1]

Ge 8:19 came out of the ark, **one kind** [+2157+4200] **after another**.
10:5 spread out into their territories by their **clans** within their nations,
10:18 Zemarites and Hamathites. Later the Canaanite **clans** scattered
10:20 These are the sons of Ham by their **clans** and languages, in their
10:31 These are the sons of Shem by their **clans** and languages, in their
10:32 These are the **clans** *of* Noah's sons, according to their lines of
12:3 I will curse; and all **peoples** *on* earth will be blessed through you."
24:38 go to my father's family and to my own **clan**, and get a wife for
24:40 so that you can get a wife for my son from my own **clan** and from
24:41 Then, when you go to my **clan**, you will be released from my oath
28:14 All **peoples** *on* earth will be blessed through you and your
36:40 from Esau, by name, according to their **clans** and regions:
Ex 6:14 and Pallu, Hezron and Carmi. These were the **clans** *of* Reuben.
6:15 the son of a Canaanite woman. These were the **clans** *of* Simeon.
6:17 The sons of Gershon, by **clans**, were Libni and Shimei.
6:19 These were the **clans** *of* Levi according to their records.
6:24 were Assir, Elkanah and Abiasaph. These were the Korahite **clans**.
6:25 These were the heads of the Levite families, clan by **clan**.
12:21 "Go at once and select the animals for your **families** and slaughter
Lev 20:5 I will set my face against that man and his **family** and will cut off
25:10 of you is to return to his family property and each to his own **clan**.
25:41 he will go back to his own **clan** and to the property of his
25:45 living among you and members of their **clans** born in your country,
25:47 to the alien living among you or to a member of the alien's **clan**,
25:49 or a cousin or any blood relative in his **clan** may redeem him.
Nu 1:2 "Take a census of the whole Israelite community by their **clans**
1:18 The people indicated their ancestry by their **clans** and families,
1:20 one by one, according to the records of their **clans** and families.
1:22 one by one, according to the records of their **clans** and families.
1:24 listed by name, according to the records of their **clans** and families.
1:26 listed by name, according to the records of their **clans** and families.
1:28 listed by name, according to the records of their **clans** and families.
1:30 listed by name, according to the records of their **clans** and families.
1:32 listed by name, according to the records of their **clans** and families.
1:34 listed by name, according to the records of their **clans** and families.
1:36 listed by name, according to the records of their **clans** and families.
1:38 listed by name, according to the records of their **clans** and families.
1:40 listed by name, according to the records of their **clans** and families.
1:42 listed by name, according to the records of their **clans** and families.
2:34 and that is the way they set out, each with his **clan** and family.
3:15 "Count the Levites by their families and **clans**. Count every male a
3:18 These were the names of the Gershonite **clans**: Libni and Shimei.
3:19 The Kohathite **clans**: Amram, Izhar, Hebron and Uzziel.
3:20 The Merarite **clans**: Mahli and Mushi. These were the Levite clans,
3:20 These were the Levite **clans**, according to their families.
3:21 To Gershon belonged the **clans** *of* the Libnites and Shimeites;
3:21 Gershon belonged the clans of the Libnites and **[RPH]** Shimeites;
3:21 of the Libnites and Shimeites; these were the Gershonite **clans**.
3:23 The Gershonite **clans** were to camp on the west,
3:27 To Kohath belonged the **clans** *of* the Amramites, Izharites,
3:27 of the Amramites, **[RPH]** Izharites, Hebronites and Uzzielites;
3:27 of the Amramites, Izharites, **[RPH]** Hebronites and Uzzielites;
3:27 of the Amramites, Izharites, Hebronites and **[RPH]** Uzzielites;
3:27 Hebronites and Uzzielites; these were the Kohathite **clans**.
3:29 The Kohathite **clans** were to camp on the south side of the
3:30 The leader of the families of the Kohathite **clans** was Elizaphan
3:33 To Merari belonged the **clans** *of* the Mahlites and the Mushites;
3:33 belonged the clans of the Mahlites and **[RPH]** the Mushites;
3:33 of the Mahlites and the Mushites; these were the Merarite **clans**.
3:35 The leader of the families of the Merarite **clans** was Zuriel son of
3:39 LORD's command by Moses and Aaron according to their **clans**,
4:2 a census of the Kohathite branch of the Levites by their **clans**
4:18 "See that the Kohathite tribal **clans** are not cut off from the
4:22 "Take a census also of the Gershonites by their families and **clans**.
4:24 "This is the service of the Gershonite **clans** as they work and carry
4:28 This is the service of the Gershonite **clans** at the Tent of Meeting.
4:29 "Count the Merarites by their **clans** and families.
4:33 This is the service of the Merarite **clans** as they work at the Tent of
4:34 the leaders of the community counted the Kohathites by their **clans**
4:36 counted by **clans**, were 2,750.
4:37 This was the total of all those in the Kohathite **clans** who served in
4:38 The Gershonites were counted by their **clans** and families.
4:40 counted by their **clans** and families, were 2,630.
4:41 This was the total of those in the Gershonite **clans** who served at
4:42 The **[RPH]** Merarites were counted by their clans and families.
4:42 The Merarites were counted by their **clans** and families.
4:44 counted by their **clans**, were 3,200.
4:45 This was the total of those in the Merarite **clans**. Moses and Aaron
4:46 and the leaders of Israel counted all the Levites by their **clans**
11:10 Moses heard the people of every **family** wailing, each at the
26:5 through Hanoch, the Hanochite **clan**; through Pallu, the Palluite
26:5 the Hanochite clan; through Pallu, the Palluite **clan**;
26:6 through Hezron, the Hezronite **clan**; through Carmi, the Carmite
26:6 the Hezronite clan; through Carmi, the Carmite **clan**.
26:7 These were the **clans** *of* Reuben; those numbered were 43,730.
26:12 The descendants of Simeon by their **clans** were: through Nemuel,
26:12 through Nemuel, the Nemuelite **clan**; through Jamin, the Jaminite
26:12 through Jamin, the Jaminite **clan**; through Jakin, the Jakinite clan;
26:12 through Jamin, the Jaminite clan; through Jakin, the Jakinite **clan**;
26:13 through Zerah, the Zerahite **clan**; through Shaul, the Shaulite clan.
26:13 through Zerah, the Zerahite clan; through Shaul, the Shaulite **clan**.
26:14 These were the **clans** *of* Simeon; there were 22,200 men.
26:15 The descendants of Gad by their **clans** were: through Zephon,
26:15 through Zephon, the Zephonite **clan**; through Haggi, the Haggite
26:15 through Haggi, the Haggite **clan**; through Shuni, the Shunite clan;
26:15 through Haggi, the Haggite clan; through Shuni, the Shunite **clan**;
26:16 through Ozni, the Oznite **clan**; through Eri, the Erite clan;
26:16 through Ozni, the Oznite clan; through Eri, the Erite **clan**;
26:17 through Arodi, the Arodite **clan**; through Areli, the Arelite clan.
26:17 through Arodi, the Arodite clan; through Areli, the Arelite **clan**.
26:18 These were the **clans** *of* Gad; those numbered were 40,500.
26:20 The descendants of Judah by their **clans** were: through Shelah,
26:20 through Shelah, the Shelanite **clan**; through Perez, the Perezite
26:20 through Perez, the Perezite **clan**; through Zerah, the Zerahite clan.
26:20 through Perez, the Perezite clan; through Zerah, the Zerahite **clan**.
26:21 through Hezron, the Hezronite **clan**; through Hamul, the Hamulite
26:21 the Hezronite clan; through Hamul, the Hamulite **clan**.
26:22 These were the **clans** *of* Judah; those numbered were 76,500.
26:23 The descendants of Issachar by their **clans** were: through Tola,
26:23 through Tola, the Tolaite **clan**; through Puah, the Puite clan;
26:23 through Tola, the Tolaite clan; through Puah, the Puite **clan**;
26:24 through Jashub, the Jashubite **clan**; through Shimron,
26:24 the Jashubite clan; through Shimron, the Shimronite **clan**.
26:25 These were the **clans** *of* Issachar; those numbered were 64,300.
26:26 The descendants of Zebulun by their **clans** were: through Sered,
26:26 through Sered, the Seredite **clan**; through Elon, the Elonite clan;
26:26 through Elon, the Elonite **clan**; through Jahleel, the Jahleelite clan.
26:26 through Elon, the Elonite clan; through Jahleel, the Jahleelite **clan**.
26:27 These were the **clans** *of* Zebulun; those numbered were 60,500.
26:28 The descendants of Joseph by their **clans** through Manasseh
26:29 through Makir, the Makirite **clan** (Makir was the father of Gilead);
26:29 was the father of Gilead); through Gilead, the Gileadite **clan**.
26:30 through Iezer, the Iezerite **clan**; through Helek, the Helekite clan;
26:30 through Iezer, the Iezerite clan; through Helek, the Helekite **clan**;
26:31 through Asriel, the Asrielite **clan**; through Shechem,
26:31 the Asrielite clan; through Shechem, the Shechemite **clan**;
26:32 through Shemida, the Shemidaite **clan**; through Hepher,
26:32 the Shemidaite clan; through Hepher, the Hepherite **clan**.
26:34 These were the **clans** *of* Manasseh; those numbered were 52,700.

Nu 26:35 These were the descendants of Ephraim by their **clans**:
26:35 through Shuthelah, the Shuthelahite **clan**; through Beker,
26:35 through Beker, the Bekerite **clan**; through Tahan, the Tahanite
26:35 the Bekerite clan; through Tahan, the Tahanite **clan**.
26:36 were the descendants of Shuthelah: through Eran, the Eranite **clan**.
26:37 These were the **clans** *of* Ephraim; those numbered were 32,500.
26:37 were 32,500. These were the descendants of Joseph by their **clans**.
26:38 The descendants of Benjamin by their **clans** were: through Bela,
26:38 through Bela, the Belaite **clan**; through Ashbel, the Ashbelite clan;
26:38 through Bela, the Belaite clan; through Ashbel, the Ashbelite **clan**;
26:38 the Ashbelite clan; through Ahiram, the Ahiramite **clan**;
26:39 through Shupham, the Shuphamite **clan**; through Hupham,
26:39 the Shuphamite clan; through Hupham, the Huphamite **clan**.
26:40 through Ard, the Ardite **clan**; through Naaman, the Naamite clan.
26:40 through Ard, the Ardite clan; through Naaman, the Naamite **clan**.
26:41 These were the **clans** *of* Benjamin; those numbered were 45,600.
26:42 These were the descendants of Dan by their **clans**:
26:42 through Shuham, the Shuhamite **clan**. These were the clans of
26:42 the Shuhamite clan. These were the **clans** *of* Dan:
26:42 the Shuhamite clan. These were the clans of Dan: **[RPH]**
26:43 All of them were Shuhamite **clans**; and those numbered were
26:44 The descendants of Asher by their **clans** were: through Imnah,
26:44 through Imnah, the Imnite **clan**; through Ishvi, the Ishvite clan;
26:44 through Ishvi, the Ishvite **clan**; through Beriah, the Beriite clan;
26:44 through Ishvi, the Ishvite clan; through Beriah, the Beriite **clan**;
26:45 through Heber, the Heberite **clan**; through Malkiel, the Malkielite
26:45 the Heberite clan; through Malkiel, the Malkielite **clan**.
26:47 These were the **clans** *of* Asher; those numbered were 53,400.
26:48 The descendants of Naphtali by their **clans** were: through Jahzeel,
26:48 through Jahzeel, the Jahzeelite **clan**; through Guni, the Gunite clan;
26:48 through Jahzeel, the Jahzeelite clan; through Guni, the Gunite **clan**;
26:49 through Jezer, the Jezerite **clan**; through Shillem, the Shillemite
26:49 the Jezerite clan; through Shillem, the Shillemite **clan**.
26:50 These were the **clans** *of* Naphtali; those numbered were 45,400.
26:50 were the clans of Naphtali; **[RPH]** those numbered were 45,400.
26:57 These were the Levites who were counted by their **clans**:
26:57 through Gershon, the Gershonite **clan**; through Kohath,
26:57 through Kohath, the Kohathite **clan**; through Merari, the Merarite
26:57 the Kohathite clan; through Merari, the Merarite **clan**.
26:58 These also were Levite **clans**: the Libnite clan, the Hebronite clan,
26:58 the Libnite **clan**, the Hebronite clan, the Mahlite clan, the Mushite
26:58 the Libnite clan, the Hebronite **clan**, the Mahlite clan, the Mushite
26:58 the Mahlite **clan**, the Mushite clan, the Korahite clan.
26:58 the Mahlite clan, the Mushite **clan**, the Korahite clan.
26:58 the Mahlite clan, the Mushite clan, the Korahite **clan**.
27:1 of Manasseh, belonged to the **clans** *of* Manasseh son of Joseph.
27:4 Why should our father's name disappear from his **clan** because he
27:11 give his inheritance to the nearest relative in his **clan**, that he may
33:54 Distribute the land by lot, according to your **clans**. To a larger
36:1 The family heads of the **clan** *of* Gilead son of Makir, the son of
36:1 who were from the **clans** *of* the descendants of Joseph, came
36:6 please as long as they marry within the tribal **clan** *of* their father.
36:8 any Israelite tribe must marry someone in her father's tribal **clan**,
36:12 They married within the **clans** *of* the descendants of Manasseh son
36:12 and their inheritance remained in their father's **clan** and tribe.
Dt 29:18 [29:17] **clan** or tribe among you today whose heart turns away
Jos 6:23 They brought out her entire **family** and put them in a place outside
7:14 The tribe that the LORD takes shall come forward clan by **clan**;
7:14 the **clan** that the LORD takes shall come forward family by
7:17 The **clans** *of* Judah came forward, and he took the Zerahites.
7:17 clans of Judah came forward, and he took **[RPH]** the Zerahites.
7:17 He had the **clan** *of* the Zerahites come forward by families,
13:15 This is what Moses had given to the tribe of Reuben, clan by **clan**:
13:23 their villages were the inheritance of the Reubenites, clan by **clan**.
13:24 This is what Moses had given to the tribe of Gad, clan by **clan**:
13:28 and their villages were the inheritance of the Gadites, clan by **clan**.
13:29 to half the family of the descendants of Manasseh, clan by **clan**:
13:31 son of Manasseh—for half of the sons of Makir, clan by **clan**.
15:1 The allotment for the tribe of Judah, clan by **clan**, extended down
15:12 are the boundaries around the people of Judah by their **clans**.
15:20 This is the inheritance of the tribe of Judah, clan by **clan**:
16:5 This was the territory of Ephraim, clan by **clan**: The boundary of
16:8 was the inheritance of the tribe of the Ephraimites, clan by **clan**.
17:2 **[RPH]** the clans of Abiezer, Helek, Asriel, Shechem, Hepher
17:2 other male descendants of Manasseh son of Joseph by their **clans**.
18:11 The lot came up for the tribe of Benjamin, clan by **clan**. Their
18:20 marked out the inheritance of the **clans** *of* Benjamin on all sides.
18:21 The tribe of Benjamin, clan by **clan**, had the following cities:
18:28 their villages. This was the inheritance of Benjamin for its **clans**.
19:1 The second lot came out for the tribe of Simeon, clan by **clan**.
19:8 was the inheritance of the tribe of the Simeonites, clan by **clan**.
19:10 The third lot came up for Zebulun, clan by **clan**: The boundary of
19:16 and their villages were the inheritance of Zebulun, clan by **clan**.
19:17 The fourth lot came out for Issachar, clan by **clan**.
19:23 villages were the inheritance of the tribe of Issachar, clan by **clan**.
19:24 The fifth lot came out for the tribe of Asher, clan by **clan**.
19:31 villages were the inheritance of the tribe of Asher, clan by **clan**.
19:32 The sixth lot came out for Naphtali, clan by **clan**:
19:39 villages were the inheritance of the tribe of Naphtali, clan by **clan**.
19:40 The seventh lot came out for the tribe of Dan, clan by **clan**.
19:48 their villages were the inheritance of the tribe of Dan, clan by **clan**.
21:4 The first lot came out for the Kohathites, clan by **clan**. The Levites
21:5 were allotted ten towns from the **clans** *of* the tribes of Ephraim,
21:6 allotted thirteen towns from the **clans** *of* the tribes of Issachar,
21:7 The descendants of Merari, clan by **clan**, received twelve towns
21:10 of Aaron who were from the Kohathite **clans** of the Levites,
21:20 The rest of the Kohathite **clans** *of* the Levites were allotted towns
21:26 their pasturelands were given to the rest of the Kohathite **clans**.
21:27 The Levite **clans** of the Gershonites were given: from the half-tribe
21:33 All the towns of the Gershonite **clans** were thirteen, together with
21:34 The Merarite **clans** (the rest of the Levites) were given: from the
21:40 All the towns allotted to the Merarite **clans**, who were the rest of
21:40 who were the rest of the **Levites** [+4291], were twelve.
Jdg 1:25 put the city to the sword but spared the man and his whole **family**.
9:1 and said to them and to all his mother's **clan** [+3+1074],
13:2 man of Zorah, named Manoah, from the **clan** *of* the Danites,
17:7 Bethlehem in Judah, who had been living within the **clan** *of* Judah,
18:2 out the land and explore it. These men represented all their **clans**.
18:11 six hundred men from the **clan** *of* the Danites, armed for battle,
18:19 and **clan** in Israel as priest rather than just one man's household?"
21:24 Israelites left that place and went home to their tribes and **clans**,
Ru 2:1 from the **clan** *of* Elimelech, a man of standing, whose name was
2:3 in a field belonging to Boaz, who was from the **clan** *of* Elimelech.
1Sa 9:21 is not my **clan** the least of all the clans of the tribe of Benjamin?
9:21 is not my clan the least of all the **clans** *of* the tribe of Benjamin?
10:21 the tribe of Benjamin, clan by **clan**, and Matri's clan was chosen.
10:21 the tribe of Benjamin, clan by clan, and Matri's **clan** was chosen.
18:18 "Who am I, and what is my family or my father's **clan** in Israel,
20:6 because an annual sacrifice is being made there for his whole **clan**.'
20:29 because our **family** is observing a sacrifice in the town and my
2Sa 14:7 Now the whole **clan** has risen up against your servant; they say,
16:5 a man from the *same* **clan** *as* Saul's family came out from there.
1Ch 2:53 and the **clans** *of* Kiriath Jearim: the Ithrites, Puthites, Shumathites
2:55 and the **clans** *of* scribes who lived at Jabez: the Tirathites,
4:2 of Ahumai and Lahad. These were the **clans** *of* the Zorathites.
4:8 and Hazzobebah and of the **clans** *of* Aharhel son of Harum.
4:21 of Mareshah and the **clans** *of* the linen workers at Beth Ashbea,
4:27 so their entire **clan** did not become as numerous as the people of
4:38 The men listed above by name were leaders of their **clans**.
5:7 Their relatives by **clans**, listed according to their genealogical
6:19 [6:4] These are the **clans** *of* the Levites listed according to their
6:54 [6:39] descendants of Aaron who were from the Kohathite **clan**,
6:60 [6:45] which were distributed among the Kohathite **clans**,
6:61 [6:46] ten towns from the **clans** *of* half the tribe of Manasseh.
6:62 [6:47] The descendants of Gershon, **clan** [+4200] **by clan**, were
6:63 [6:48] The descendants of Merari, **clan** [+4200] **by clan**, were
6:66 [6:51] Some of the Kohathite **clans** were given as their territory
6:70 [6:55] with their pasturelands, to the rest of the Kohathite **clans**.
6:71 [6:56] From the **clan** *of* the half-tribe of Manasseh they received
7:5 The relatives who were fighting men belonging to all the **clans** *of*
16:28 Ascribe to the LORD, O **families** *of* nations, ascribe to the
Ne 4:13 [4:7] posting them by **families**, with their swords, spears and
Est 9:28 and observed in every generation by **every family** [+2256+5476],
9:28 and observed in every generation by **every family** [+2256+5476],
Job 31:34 and so dreaded the contempt of the **clans** that I kept silent
32:2 But Elihu son of Barakel the Buzite, of the **family** *of* Ram,
Ps 22:27 [22:28] all the **families** *of* the nations will bow down before him,
96:7 Ascribe to the LORD, O **families** *of* nations, ascribe to the
107:41 out of their affliction and increased their **families** like flocks.
Jer 1:15 I am about to summon all the **peoples** *of* the northern kingdoms,"
2:4 the LORD, O house of Jacob, all you **clans** *of* the house of Israel.
3:14 I will choose you—one from a town and two from a **clan**—
8:3 all the survivors of this evil **nation** will prefer death to life,
10:25 acknowledge you, on the **peoples** who do not call on your name.
15:3 "I will send four **kinds** of destroyers against them,"
25:9 I will summon all the **peoples** *of* the north and my servant
31:1 declares the LORD, "I will be the God of all the **clans** *of* Israel,
33:24 are saying, 'The LORD has rejected the two **kingdoms** he chose'?
Eze 20:32 like the **peoples** *of* the world, who serve wood and stone."
Am 3:1 of Israel—against the whole **family** I brought up out of Egypt:
3:2 "You only have I chosen of all the **families** *of* the earth; therefore I
Mic 2:3 "I am planning disaster against this **people**, from which you cannot
Na 3:4 enslaved nations by her prostitution and **peoples** by her witchcraft.
Zec 12:12 The land will mourn, **each clan** [+5476] by itself, with their wives
12:12 The land will mourn, **each clan** [+5476] by itself, with their wives
12:12 the **clan** *of* the house of David and their wives, the clan of the
12:12 and their wives, the **clan** *of* the house of Nathan and their wives,
12:13 the **clan** *of* the house of Levi and their wives, the clan of Shimei

Zec 12: 13 house of Levi and their wives, the **clan** *of* Shimei and their wives,
12: 14 and all the rest of the **clans** and their wives.
12: 14 and all the rest of the clans **[RPH]** and their wives.
12: 14 and all the rest of the clans **[RPH]** and their wives.
14: 17 If any of the **peoples** *of* the earth do not go up to Jerusalem to
14: 18 If the Egyptian **people** do not go up and take part, they will have

5477 מִשְׁפָּט **mišpāṭ**, n.m. [421] [→ 6535; cf. 9149]

justice [94], laws [83], just [28], judgment [24], right [13], cause [11], judgments [11], regulations [11], specified [8], ordinances [7], punishment [6], law [5], sentence [5], case [4], prescribed [4], rights [4], standards [4], decision [3], injustice [+4202] [3], ordinance [3], prescribed way [3], requirements [3], what requires [3], *untranslated* [2], commands [2], court [2], custom [2], decisions [2], judge [2], judging [2], justly [2], legal [2], practice [2], practices [2], proper procedure [2], sentenced [2], specifications [2], trial [2], verdict [+1821] [2], what do[s] [2], accuser [+1251] [1], accuses [+907+2021 +4200+7756] [1], always do [1], bloodshed [+1947] [1], capital offense [+4638] [1], charges [1], customs [1], decided [1], defense [1], deserve [1], deserving [1], dimensions [1], disputes decided [1], do [1], due [1], honest [1], honestly [1], inquiring [1], judge [+906+9149] [1], judges [+6913] [1], justice of cause [1], kind [1], lawsuits [1], like [+3869] [1], making decisions [1], manner [1], means of making decisions [1], place of judgment [1], plan [1], precepts [1], prescribed [+3869] [1], proper place [1], punish [+928+6913] [1], quotas [+3869] [1], regulation [1], regulations prescribed [1], render judgment [+9149] [1], right way [1], rightfully [1], rule [1], share [1], standards measuring [1], statutes [1], unjust [+4202] [1], verdict [1], vindication [1], way prescribed [1]

Ge 18: 19 him to keep the way of the LORD by doing what is right and **just**,
18: 25 Far be it from you! Will not the Judge of all the earth do **right**?"
40: 13 in his hand, just as you used to **do** when you were his cupbearer.
Ex 15: 25 There the LORD made a decree and a **law** for them, and there he
21: 1 "These are the **laws** you are to set before them:
21: 9 selects her for his son, he must grant her the **rights** *of* a daughter.
21: 31 This **law** also applies if the bull gores a son or daughter.
23: 6 "Do not deny **justice** *to* your poor people in their lawsuits.
24: 3 Moses went and told the people all the LORD's words and **laws**,
26: 30 "Set up the tabernacle according to the **plan** shown you on the
28: 15 "Fashion a breastpiece for **making decisions**—the work of a
28: 29 of **decision** as a continuing memorial before the LORD.
28: 30 **[RPH]** so they may be over Aaron's heart whenever he enters the
28: 30 Thus Aaron will always bear the **means of making decisions** *for*
Lev 5: 10 then offer the other as a burnt offering in the **prescribed way**
9: 16 He brought the burnt offering and offered it in the **prescribed way**.
18: 4 You must obey my **laws** and be careful to follow my decrees.
18: 5 Keep my decrees and **laws**, for the man who obeys them will live
18: 26 But you must keep my decrees and my **laws**. The native-born
19: 15 " 'Do not pervert **justice**; do not show partiality to the poor
19: 35 " 'Do not use dishonest **standards** when **measuring** length,
19: 37 " 'Keep all my decrees and all my **laws** and follow them. I am the
20: 22 " 'Keep all my decrees and **laws** and follow them, so that the land
24: 22 You are to have the same **law** for the alien and the native-born.
25: 18 " 'Follow my decrees and be careful to obey my **laws**, and you will
26: 15 if you reject my decrees and abhor my **laws** and fail to carry out all
26: 43 their sins because they rejected my **laws** and abhorred my decrees.
26: 46 the **laws** and the regulations that the LORD established on Mount
Nu 9: 3 of this month, in accordance with all its rules and **regulations**."
9: 14 Passover must do so in accordance with its rules and **regulations**.
15: 16 The same laws and **regulations** will apply both to you and to the
15: 24 along with its **prescribed** grain offering and drink offering,
27: 5 So Moses brought their **case** before the LORD
27: 11 This is to be a **legal** requirement for the Israelites, as the LORD
27: 21 who will obtain decisions for him by **inquiring** *of* the Urim before
29: 6 with their grain offerings and drink offerings as **specified**.
29: 18 and drink offerings according to the number **specified**.
29: 21 and drink offerings according to the number **specified**.
29: 24 and drink offerings according to the number **specified**.
29: 27 and drink offerings according to the number **specified**.
29: 30 and drink offerings according to the number **specified**.
29: 33 and drink offerings according to the number **specified**.
29: 37 and drink offerings according to the number **specified**.
35: 12 of murder may not die before he stands **trial** before the assembly.
35: 24 and the avenger of blood according to these **regulations**.
35: 29 " 'These are to be **legal** requirements for you throughout the
36: 13 **regulations** the LORD gave through Moses to the Israelites on
Dt 1: 17 Do not show partiality in **judging**; hear both small and great alike.
1: 17 Do not be afraid of any man, for **judgment** belongs to God.
4: 1 Hear now, O Israel, the decrees and **laws** I am about to teach you.
4: 5 you decrees and **laws** as the LORD my God commanded me,
4: 8 and **laws** as this body of laws I am setting before you today?
4: 14 **laws** you are to follow in the land that you are crossing the Jordan
4: 45 and **laws** Moses gave them when they came out of Egypt
5: 1 O Israel, the decrees and **laws** I declare in your hearing today.
5: 31 **laws** you are to teach them to follow in the land I am giving them
6: 1 **laws** the LORD your God directed me to teach you to observe in
6: 20 decrees and **laws** the LORD our God has commanded you?"
7: 11 care to follow the commands, decrees and **laws** I give you today.
7: 12 If you pay attention to these **laws** and are careful to follow them,
8: 11 his **laws** and his decrees that I am giving you this day.
10: 18 He defends the **cause** *of* the fatherless and the widow, and loves
11: 1 his requirements, his decrees, his **laws** and his commands always.
11: 32 you obey all the decrees and **laws** I am setting before you today.
12: 1 **laws** you must be careful to follow in the land that the LORD,
16: 18 is giving you, and *they shall* **judge** [+906+9149] the people fairly.
16: 19 Do not pervert **justice** or show partiality. Do not accept a bribe,
17: 8 come before your courts that are too difficult for you to **judge**—
17: 9 Inquire of them and they will give you the **verdict** [+1821].
17: 11 to the law they teach you and the **decisions** they give you.
18: 3 This is the **share** *due* the priests from the people who sacrifice a
19: 6 is too great, and kill him even though he is not **deserving** *of* death,
21: 17 of his father's strength. The **right** *of* the firstborn belongs to him.
21: 22 If a man guilty of a **capital offense** [+4638] is put to death
24: 17 Do not deprive the alien or the fatherless of **justice**, or take the
25: 1 they are to take it to **court** and the judges will decide the case,
26: 16 God commands you this day to follow these decrees and **laws**;
26: 17 keep his decrees, commands and **laws**, and that you will obey him.
27: 19 "Cursed is the man who withholds **justice** *from* the alien,
30: 16 to walk in his ways, and to keep his commands, decrees and **laws**;
32: 4 He is the Rock, his works are perfect, and all his ways are **just**.
32: 41 I sharpen my flashing sword and my hand grasps it in **judgment**,
33: 10 He teaches your **precepts** to Jacob and your law to Israel.
33: 21 LORD's righteous will, and his **judgments** concerning Israel."
Jos 6: 15 and marched around the city seven times in the same **manner**,
20: 6 He is to stay in that city until he has stood **trial** before the
24: 25 and there at Shechem he drew up for them decrees and **laws**.
Jdg 4: 5 and the Israelites came to her to have their **disputes decided**.
13: 12 are fulfilled, what is to be the **rule** *for* the boy's life and work?"
18: 7 in safety, **like** [+3869] the Sidonians, unsuspecting and secure.
1Sa 2: 13 Now it was the **practice** *of* the priests with the people that
8: 3 after dishonest gain and accepted bribes and perverted **justice**.
8: 9 let them know **what** the king who will reign over them will **do**[s]."
8: 11 He said, "This is **what** the king who will reign over you will **do**[s]:
10: 25 Samuel explained to the people the **regulations** *of* the kingship.
27: 11 'This is what David did.' " And such was his **practice** as long as he
30: 25 made this a statute and **ordinance** for Israel from that day to this.
2Sa 8: 15 over all Israel, doing what was **just** and right for all his people.
15: 2 came with a complaint to be placed before the king for a **decision**,
15: 4 Then everyone who has a complaint or **case** could come to me
15: 6 toward all the Israelites who came to the king asking for **justice**,
22: 23 All his **laws** are before me; I have not turned away from his
1Ki 2: 3 and keep his decrees and commands, his **laws** and requirements,
3: 11 death of your enemies but for discernment in administering **justice**,
3: 28 When all Israel heard the **verdict** the king had given, they held the
3: 28 they saw that he had wisdom from God to administer **justice**.
4: 28 [5:8] They also brought to the proper place their **quotas** [+3869]
6: 12 carry out my **regulations** and keep all my commands and obey
6: 38 temple was finished in all its details according to its **specifications**.
7: 7 He built the throne hall, the Hall of **Justice**, where he was to judge,
8: 45 from heaven their prayer and their plea, and uphold their **cause**.
8: 49 hear their prayer and their plea, and uphold their **cause**.
8: 58 keep the commands, decrees and **regulations** he gave our fathers.
8: 59 that he may uphold the **cause** *of* his servant and the cause of his
8: 59 and the **cause** *of* his people Israel according to each day's need,
9: 4 father did, and do all I command and observe my decrees and **laws**,
10: 9 he has made you king, to maintain **justice** and righteousness."
11: 33 nor kept my statutes and **laws** as David, Solomon's father,
18: 28 slashed themselves with swords and spears, as was their **custom**,
20: 40 man disappeared." "That is your **sentence**," the king of Israel said.
2Ki 1: 7 "What **kind** *of* man was it who came to meet you and told you
11: 14 and there was the king, standing by the pillar, as the **custom** was.
17: 26 of Samaria do not know **what** the god of that country **requires**.
17: 26 them off, because the people do not know **what** he **requires**."
17: 27 live there and teach the people **what** the god of the land **requires**."
17: 33 they also served their own gods in accordance with the **customs** *of*
17: 34 To this day they persist in their former **practices**. They neither
17: 34 worship the LORD nor adhere to the decrees and **ordinances**,
17: 37 You must always be careful to keep the decrees and **ordinances**,
17: 40 would not listen, however, but persisted in their former **practices**.
25: 6 of Babylon at Riblah, where **sentence** was pronounced on him.
1Ch 6: 32 [6:17] duties according to the **regulations** *laid down* for them.
15: 13 did not inquire of him about how to do it in the **prescribed way**."
16: 12 he has done, his miracles, and the **judgments** he pronounced,
16: 14 He is the LORD our God; his **judgments** are in all the earth.
18: 14 over all Israel, doing *what* was **just** and right for all his people.
22: 13 the decrees and **laws** that the LORD gave Moses for Israel.
23: 31 in the proper number and in the **way prescribed** for them.

1Ch 24: 19 according to the **regulations prescribed** *for* them by their
28: 7 if he is unswerving in carrying out my commands and **laws**,
2Ch 4: 7 He made ten gold lampstands according to the **specifications** *for*
4: 20 their lamps, to burn in front of the inner sanctuary as **prescribed**;
6: 35 from heaven their prayer and their plea, and uphold their **cause**.
6: 39 hear their prayer and their pleas, and uphold their **cause**.
7: 17 and do all I command, and observe my decrees and **laws**,
8: 14 In keeping with the **ordinance** *of* his father David, he appointed
9: 8 made you king over them, to maintain **justice** and righteousness."
19: 6 who is with you whenever you give a **verdict** [+1821].
19: 8 and heads of Israelite families to administer the **law** *of* the LORD
19: 10 or other concerns of the law, commands, decrees or **ordinances**—
30: 16 they took up their regular positions as **prescribed** in the Law of
33: 8 all the laws, decrees and **ordinances** given through Moses."
35: 13 They roasted the Passover animals over the fire as **prescribed**,
Ezr 3: 4 number of burnt offerings **prescribed** [+3869] *for* each day.
7: 10 Law of the LORD, and to teaching its decrees and **laws** in Israel.
Ne 1: 7 the commands, decrees and **laws** you gave your servant Moses.
8: 18 and on the eighth day, in accordance with the **regulation**,
9: 13 You gave them **regulations** and laws that are just and right,
9: 29 They sinned against your **ordinances**, by which a man will live if
10: 29 [10:30] **regulations** and decrees of the LORD our Lord.
Job 8: 3 Does God pervert **justice**? Does the Almighty pervert what is
9: 19 is mighty! And if it is a matter of **justice**, who will summon him?
9: 32 I might answer him, that we might confront each other in **court**.
13: 18 Now that I have prepared my **case**, I know I will be vindicated.
14: 3 eye on such a one? Will you bring him before you for **judgment**?
19: 7 I get no response; though I call for help, there is no **justice**.
22: 4 for your piety that he rebukes you and brings **charges** against you?
23: 4 I would state my **case** before him and fill my mouth with
27: 2 "As surely as God lives, who has denied me **justice**, the Almighty,
29: 14 righteousness as my clothing; **justice** was my robe and my turban.
31: 13 "If I have denied **justice** to my menservants and maidservants
32: 9 old who are wise, not only the aged who understand *what* is **right**.
34: 4 Let us discern for ourselves *what* is **right**; let us learn together
34: 5 "Job says, 'I am innocent, but God denies me **justice**.
34: 6 Although I am **right**, I am considered a liar; although I am
34: 12 that God would do wrong, that the Almighty would pervert **justice**.
34: 17 Can he who hates **justice** govern? Will you condemn the just
34: 23 men further, that they should come before him for **judgment**.
35: 2 "Do you think this is **just**? You say, 'I will be cleared by God.'
36: 6 does not keep the wicked alive but gives the afflicted their **rights**.
36: 17 due the wicked; judgment and **justice** have taken hold of you.
37: 23 in his **justice** and great righteousness, he does not oppress.
40: 8 "Would you discredit my **justice**? Would you condemn me to
Ps 1: 5 Therefore the wicked will not stand in the **judgment**, nor sinners
7: 6 [7:7] the rage of my enemies. Awake, my God; decree **justice**.
9: 4 [9:5] For you have upheld my **right** and my cause; you have sat
9: 7 [9:8] reigns forever; he has established his throne for **judgment**.
9: 16 [9:17] The LORD is known by his **justice**; the wicked are
10: 5 he is haughty and your **laws** are far from him; he sneers at all his
17: 2 May my **vindication** come from you; may your eyes see what is
18: 22 [18:23] All his **laws** are before me; I have not turned away from
19: 9 [19:10] The **ordinances** *of* the LORD are sure and altogether
25: 9 He guides the humble in what is **right** and teaches them his way.
33: 5 The LORD loves righteousness and **justice**; the earth is full of his
35: 23 Awake, and rise to my **defense**! Contend for me, my God
36: 6 [36:7] like the mighty mountains, your **justice** like the great deep.
37: 6 like the dawn, the **justice of** your **cause** like the noonday sun.
37: 28 For the LORD loves the **just** and will not forsake his faithful
37: 30 righteous man utters wisdom, and his tongue speaks *what* is **just**.
48: 11 [48:12] the villages of Judah are glad because of your **judgments**.
72: 1 Endow the king with your **justice**, O God, the royal son with your
72: 2 your people in righteousness, your afflicted ones with **justice**.
76: 9 [76:10] when you, O God, rose up to **judge**, to save all the
81: 4 [81:5] is a decree for Israel, an **ordinance** of the God of Jacob.
89: 14 [89:15] and **justice** are the foundation of your throne;
89: 30 [89:31] his sons forsake my law and do not follow my **statutes**,
94: 15 **Judgment** will again be founded on righteousness, and all the
97: 2 righteousness and **justice** are the foundation of his throne.
97: 8 and the villages of Judah are glad because of your **judgments**,
99: 4 The King is mighty, he loves **justice**—you have established equity;
99: 4 established equity; in Jacob you have done *what* is **just** and right.
101: 1 I will sing of your love and **justice**; to you, O LORD, I will sing
103: 6 The LORD works righteousness and **justice** for all the oppressed.
105: 5 he has done, his miracles, and the **judgments** he pronounced,
105: 7 He is the LORD our God; his **judgments** are in all the earth.
106: 3 Blessed are they who maintain **justice**, who constantly do what is
111: 7 The works of his hands are faithful and **just**; all his precepts are
112: 5 is generous and lends freely, who conducts his affairs with **justice**.
119: 7 will praise you with an upright heart as I learn your righteous **laws**.
119: 13 With my lips I recount all the **laws** *that come from* your mouth.
119: 20 My soul is consumed with longing for your **laws** at all times.
119: 30 I have chosen the way of truth; I have set my heart on your **laws**.
119: 39 Take away the disgrace I dread, for your **laws** are good.
119: 43 word of truth from my mouth, for I have put my hope in your **laws**.
119: 52 I remember your ancient **laws**, O LORD, and I find comfort in
119: 62 At midnight I rise to give you thanks for your righteous **laws**.
119: 75 I know, O LORD, that your **laws** are righteous, and in
119: 84 servant wait? When *will you* **punish** [+928+6913] my persecutors?
119: 91 Your **laws** endure to this day, for all things serve you.
119: 102 I have not departed from your **laws**, for you yourself have taught
119: 106 an oath and confirmed it, that I will follow your righteous **laws**.
119: 108 the willing praise of my mouth, and teach me your **laws**.
119: 120 My flesh trembles in fear of you; I stand in awe of your **laws**.
119: 121 I have done what is righteous and **just**; do not leave me to my
119: 132 have mercy on me, as you **always do** to those who love your name.
119: 137 Righteous are you, O LORD, and your **laws** are right.
119: 149 your love; preserve my life, O LORD, according to your **laws**.
119: 156 is great, O LORD; preserve my life according to your **laws**.
119: 160 All your words are true; all your righteous **laws** are eternal.
119: 164 Seven times a day I praise you for your righteous **laws**.
119: 175 Let me live that I may praise you, and may your **laws** sustain me.
122: 5 There the thrones for **judgment** stand, the thrones of the house of
140: 12 [140:13] justice for the poor and upholds the **cause** *of* the needy.
143: 2 Do not bring your servant into **judgment**, for no one living is
146: 7 He upholds the **cause** of the oppressed and gives food to the
147: 19 He has revealed his word to Jacob, his **laws** and decrees to Israel.
147: 20 He has done this for no other nation; they do not know his **laws**.
149: 9 to carry out the **sentence** written against them. This is the glory of
Pr 1: 3 a disciplined and prudent life, doing what is right and **just** and fair;
2: 8 for he guards the course of the **just** and protects the way of his
2: 9 Then you will understand what is right and **just** and fair—
8: 20 I walk in the way of righteousness, along the paths of **justice**,
12: 5 The plans of the righteous are **just**, but the advice of the wicked is
13: 23 may produce abundant food, but **injustice** [+4202] sweeps it away.
16: 8 a little with righteousness than much gain with **injustice** [+4202].
16: 10 a king speak as an oracle, and his mouth should not betray **justice**.
16: 11 **Honest** scales and balances are from the LORD; all the weights in
16: 33 lot is cast into the lap, but its every **decision** is from the LORD.
17: 23 man accepts a bribe in secret to pervert the course of **justice**.
18: 5 to be partial to the wicked or to deprive the innocent of **justice**.
19: 28 A corrupt witness mocks at **justice**, and the mouth of the wicked
21: 3 is right and **just** is more acceptable to the LORD than sacrifice.
21: 7 wicked will drag them away, for they refuse to do *what* is **right**.
21: 15 When **justice** is done, it brings joy to the righteous but terror to
24: 23 are sayings of the wise: To show partiality in **judging** is not good:
28: 5 Evil men do not understand **justice**, but those who seek the
29: 4 By **justice** a king gives a country stability, but one who is greedy
29: 26 with a ruler, but it is from the LORD that man gets **justice**.
Ecc 3: 16 In the place of **judgment**—wickedness was there, in the place of
5: 8 [5:7] **justice** and rights denied, do not be surprised at such things;
8: 5 and the wise heart will know the **proper** time and **procedure**.
8: 6 For there is a **proper** time and **procedure** for every matter,
11: 9 but know that for all these things God will bring you to **judgment**.
12: 14 For God will bring every deed into **judgment**, including every
Isa 1: 17 learn to do right! Seek **justice**, encourage the oppressed. Defend
1: 21 She once was full of **justice**; righteousness used to dwell in her—
1: 27 Zion will be redeemed with **justice**, her penitent ones with
3: 14 The LORD enters into **judgment** against the elders and leaders of
4: 4 cleanse the bloodstains from Jerusalem by a spirit of **judgment**
5: 7 And he looked for **justice**, but saw bloodshed; for righteousness,
5: 16 the LORD Almighty will be exalted by his **justice**, and the holy
9: 7 [9:6] establishing and upholding it with **justice** and righteousness
10: 2 their rights and withhold **justice** from the oppressed of my people,
16: 5 one who in judging seeks **justice** and speeds the cause of
26: 8 Yes, LORD, walking in the way of your **laws**, we wait for you;
26: 9 When your **judgments** come upon the earth, the people of the
28: 6 He will be a spirit of **justice** to him who sits in judgment, a source
28: 6 He will be a spirit of justice to him who sits in **judgment**,
28: 17 I will make **justice** the measuring line and righteousness the plumb
28: 26 His God instructs him and teaches him the **right way**.
30: 18 For the LORD is a God of **justice**. Blessed are all who wait for
32: 1 a king will reign in righteousness and rulers will rule with **justice**.
32: 7 destroy the poor with lies, even when the plea of the needy is **just**.
32: 16 **Justice** will dwell in the desert and righteousness live in the fertile
33: 5 he dwells on high; he will fill Zion with **justice** and righteousness.
34: 5 see, it descends in **judgment** on Edom, the people I have totally
40: 14 consult to enlighten him, and who taught him the **right** way?
40: 27 is hidden from the LORD; my **cause** is disregarded by my God"?
41: 1 and speak; let us meet together at the **place of judgment**.
42: 1 I will put my Spirit on him and he will bring **justice** to the nations.
42: 3 he will not snuff out. In faithfulness he will bring forth **justice**;
42: 4 will not falter or be discouraged till he establishes **justice** on earth.
49: 4 Yet *what* is **due** me is in the LORD's hand, and my reward is
50: 8 each other! Who is my **accuser** [+1251]? Let him confront me!
51: 4 will go out from me; my **justice** will become a light to the nations.
53: 8 By oppression and **judgment** he was taken away. And who can

Isa 54:17 refute every tongue *that* **accuses** [+907+2021+4200+7756] you.
56:1 "Maintain **justice** and do what is right, for my salvation is close at
58:2 does what is right and has not forsaken the **commands** *of* its God.
58:2 They ask me for just **decisions** and seem eager for God to come
59:8 way of peace they do not know; there is no **justice** in their paths.
59:9 So **justice** is far from us, and righteousness does not reach us.
59:11 We look for **justice**, but find none; for deliverance, but it is far
59:14 So **justice** is driven back, and righteousness stands at a distance;
59:15 The LORD looked and was displeased that there was no **justice**.
61:8 "For I, the LORD, love **justice**; I hate robbery and iniquity.
Jer 1:16 I will pronounce my **judgments** on my people because of their
4:2 if in a truthful, **just** and righteous way you swear, 'As surely as the
4:12 comes from me. Now I pronounce my **judgments** against them."
5:1 If you can find but one person who deals **honestly** and seeks the
5:4 not know the way of the LORD, the **requirements** *of* their God.
5:5 know the way of the LORD, the **requirements** *of* their God."
5:28 the fatherless to win it, they do not defend the **rights** *of* the poor.
7:5 change your ways and your actions and deal with each other **justly**,
8:7 But my people do not know the **requirements** *of* the LORD.
9:24 [9:23] **justice** and righteousness on earth, for in these I delight,"
10:24 Correct me, LORD, but only with **justice**—not in your anger,
12:1 a case before you. Yet I would speak with you about your **justice**:
17:11 did not lay is the man who gains riches by **unjust** [+4202] means.
21:12 " 'Administer **justice** every morning; rescue from the hand of his
22:3 This is what the LORD says: Do *what* is **just** and right. Rescue
22:13 his upper rooms by **injustice** [+4202], making his countrymen
22:15 He did *what* was **right** and just, so all went well with him.
23:5 who will reign wisely and do *what* is **just** and right in the land.
26:11 "This man should be **sentenced** *to* death because he has
26:16 and the prophets, "This man should not be **sentenced** *to* death!
30:11 I will discipline you but only with **justice**; I will not let you go
30:18 rebuilt on her ruins, and the palace will stand in its **proper place**.
32:7 because as nearest relative it is your **right** and duty to buy it.'
32:8 Since it is your **right** to redeem it and possess it, buy it for
33:15 from David's line; he will do *what* is **just** and right in the land.
39:5 in the land of Hamath, where he pronounced **sentence** on him.
46:28 I will discipline you but only with **justice**; I will not let you go
48:21 **Judgment** has come to the plateau—to Holon, Jahzah
48:47 to come," declares the LORD. Here ends the **judgment** *on* Moab.
49:12 "If those who do not **deserve** to drink the cup must drink it,
51:9 and each go to his own land, for her **judgment** reaches to the skies,
52:9 in the land of Hamath, where he pronounced **sentence** on him.
La 3:35 to deny a man his **rights** before the Most High,
3:59 have seen, O LORD, the wrong done to me. Uphold my **cause**!
Eze 5:6 Yet in her wickedness she has rebelled against my **laws**
5:6 She has rejected my **laws** and has not followed my decrees.
5:7 around you and have not followed my decrees or kept my **laws**.
5:7 You have not even conformed to the **standards** *of* the nations
5:8 and I will inflict **punishment** on you in the sight of the nations.
7:23 because the land is full of **bloodshed** [+1947] and the city is full of
7:27 to their conduct, and by their own **standards** I will judge them.
11:12 for you have not followed my decrees or kept my **laws** but have
11:12 but have conformed to the **standards** *of* the nations around you."
11:20 Then they will follow my decrees and be careful to keep my **laws**.
16:38 I will sentence you to the **punishment** *of* women who commit
18:5 "Suppose there is a righteous man who does *what* is **just** and right.
18:8 doing wrong and **judges** [+6913] fairly between man and man.
18:9 He follows my decrees and faithfully keeps my **laws**. That man is
18:17 or excessive interest. He keeps my **laws** and follows my decrees.
18:19 Since the son has done *what* is **just** and right and has been careful
18:21 and keeps all my decrees and does *what* is **just** and right,
18:27 the wickedness he has committed and does *what* is **just** and right,
20:11 I gave them my decrees and made known to them my **laws**,
20:13 They did not follow my decrees but rejected my **laws**—
20:16 because they rejected my **laws** and did not follow my decrees
20:18 your fathers or keep their **laws** or defile yourselves with their idols.
20:19 your God; follow my decrees and be careful to keep my **laws**.
20:21 did not follow my decrees, they were not careful to keep my **laws**—
20:24 because they had not obeyed my **laws** but had rejected my decrees
20:25 over to statutes that were not good and **laws** they could not live by;
21:27 [21:32] be restored until he comes to whom it **rightfully** belongs;
22:29 the poor and needy and mistreat the alien, denying them **justice**.
23:24 I will turn you over to them for **punishment**, and they will punish
23:24 and they will punish you according to their **standards**.
23:45 righteous men will sentence them to the **punishment** *of* women
23:45 of women who commit adultery and **[RPH]** shed blood,
33:14 then turns away from his sin and does *what* is **just** and right—
33:16 against him. He has done *what* is **just** and right; he will surely live.
33:19 turns away from his wickedness and does *what* is **just** and right,
34:16 and the strong I will destroy. I will shepherd the flock with **justice**.
36:27 move you to follow my decrees and be careful to keep my **laws**.
37:24 They will follow my **laws** and be careful to keep my decrees.
39:21 all the nations will see the **punishment** I inflict and the hand I lay
42:11 had the same length and width, with similar exits and **dimensions**.
44:24 [the priests are to serve as **judges** [Q; see K 9149] and decide]
44:24 are to serve as judges and decide it according to my **ordinances**.
45:9 up your violence and oppression and do *what* is **just** and right.
Da 9:5 we have turned away from your commands and **laws**.
Hos 2:19 [2:21] I will betroth you in righteousness and **justice**, in love
5:1 Listen, O royal house! This **judgment** is against you:
5:11 Ephraim is oppressed, trampled in **judgment**, intent on pursuing
6:5 of my mouth; my **judgments** flashed like lightning upon you.
10:4 therefore **lawsuits** spring up like poisonous weeds in a plowed
12:6 [12:7] maintain love and **justice**, and wait for your God always.
Am 5:7 You who turn **justice** into bitterness and cast righteousness to the
5:15 Hate evil, love good; maintain **justice** in the courts.
5:24 let **justice** roll on like a river, righteousness like a never-failing
6:12 you have turned **justice** into poison and the fruit of righteousness
Mic 3:1 you rulers of the house of Israel. Should you not know **justice**,
3:8 with the Spirit of the LORD, and with **justice** and might,
3:9 the house of Israel, who despise **justice** and distort all that is right;
6:8 To act **justly** and to love mercy and to walk humbly with your
7:9 LORD's wrath, until he pleads my case and establishes my **right**.
Hab 1:4 Therefore the law is paralyzed, and **justice** never prevails.
1:4 The wicked hem in the righteous, so that **justice** is perverted.
1:7 they are a **law** to themselves and promote their own honor.
1:12 O LORD, you have appointed them to execute **judgment**;
Zep 2:3 all you humble of the land, you who do what he **commands**.
3:5 Morning by morning he dispenses his **justice**, and every new day
3:8 I have **decided** to assemble the nations, to gather the kingdoms
3:15 The LORD has taken away your **punishment**, he has turned back
Zec 7:9 'Administer true **justice**; show mercy and compassion to one
8:16 and **render** true and sound **judgment** [+9149] in your courts;
Mal 2:17 and he is pleased with them" or "Where is the God of **justice**?"
3:5 "So I will come near to you for **judgment**. I will be quick to testify
4:4 [3:22] the decrees and **laws** I gave him at Horeb for all Israel.

5478 מִשְׁפְּתַיִם *mišpᵉtayim*, n.[m.]du. [2] [√ 9189]

campfires [1], two saddlebags [1]

Ge 49:14 is a rawboned donkey lying down between **two saddlebags**.
Jdg 5:16 Why did you stay among the **campfires** to hear the whistling for

5479 מֶשֶׁק *mešeq*, n.[m.]. [1] [√ 4940]

one who will inherit [+1201] [1]

Ge 15:2 the **one who will inherit** [+1201] my estate is Eliezer of

5480 מַשָּׁק *maššāq*, n.[m.]. [1] [√ 9212]

swarm [1]

Isa 33:4 as by young locusts; like a **swarm** *of* locusts men pounce on it.

5481 מְשֻׁקָּד *mᵉšuqqād*, n.m. [6] [√ 9195; cf. 9193]

shaped like almond flowers [4], *untranslated* [2]

Ex 25:33 Three cups **shaped like almond flowers** with buds and blossoms
25:33 are to be on one branch, three **[RPH]** on the next branch,
25:34 there are to be four cups **shaped like almond flowers** with buds
37:19 Three cups **shaped like almond flowers** with buds and blossoms
37:19 three **[RPH]** on the next branch and the same for all six branches
37:20 on the lampstand were four cups **shaped like almond flowers** with

5482 ¹מַשְׁקֶה *mašqeh¹*, n.m. [19] [√ 9197]

cupbearer [10], cupbearers [2], goblets [+3998] [2], liquid [1], position [1], water [1], well watered [1], well-watered [1]

Ge 13:10 and saw that the whole plain of the Jordan *was* **well watered**,
40:1 the **cupbearer** and the baker *of* the king of Egypt offended their
40:2 with his two officials, the chief **cupbearer** and the chief baker,
40:5 the **cupbearer** and the baker of the king of Egypt, who were being
40:9 So the chief **cupbearer** told Joseph his dream. He said to him,
40:13 in his hand, just as you used to do when you were his **cupbearer**.
40:20 He lifted up the heads of the chief **cupbearer** and the chief baker
40:21 He restored the chief **cupbearer** to his position, so that he once
40:21 He restored the chief cupbearer to his **position**, so that he once
40:23 The chief **cupbearer**, however, did not remember Joseph;
41:9 the chief **cupbearer** said to Pharaoh, "Today I am reminded of my
Lev 11:34 is unclean, and any **liquid** that could be drunk from it is unclean.
1Ki 10:5 his officials, the attending servants in their robes, his **cupbearers**,
10:21 All King Solomon's **goblets** [+3998] were gold, and all the
2Ch 9:4 the **cupbearers** in their robes and the burnt offerings he made at
9:20 All King Solomon's **goblets** [+3998] were gold, and all the
Ne 1:11 favor in the presence of this man." I was **cupbearer** to the king.
Isa 32:6 hungry he leaves empty and from the thirsty he withholds **water**.
Eze 45:15 flock of two hundred from the **well-watered** pastures *of* Israel.

5483 ²מַשְׁקֶה *mašqeh²*, n.m. Not used in NIV/BHS [√ 9197]

5484 מִשְׁקוֹל ***mišqôl***, n.[m.]. [1] [√ 9202]

weigh out [1]

Eze 4:10 **Weigh out** twenty shekels of food to eat each day and eat it at set

5485 מַשְׁקוֹף ***mašqôp***, n.[m.]. [3] [√ 9207]

top [2], tops [1]

Ex 12: 7 and **tops** of the doorframes of the houses where they eat the lambs.
12:22 it into the blood in the basin and put some of the blood on the **top**
12:23 he will see the blood on the **top** and sides of the doorframe

5486 מִשְׁקָל ***mišqāl***, n.m. [49] [√ 9202]

weight [20], weighing [16], weighed [6], *untranslated* [1], exact weight [1], force [1], paid [+4200+5989] [1], rationed [+928] [1], set of scales [+4404] [1], weighed out [1]

Ge 24:22 the man took out a gold nose ring **weighing** a beka and two gold
24:22 ring weighing a beka and two gold bracelets **weighing** ten shekels.
43:21 us found his silver—the **exact weight**—in the mouth of his sack.
Lev 19:35 dishonest standards when measuring length, **weight** or quantity.
26:26 your bread in one oven, and they will dole out the bread by **weight**.
Nu 7:13 His offering was one silver plate **weighing** a hundred and thirty
7:19 The offering he brought was one silver plate **weighing** a hundred
7:25 His offering was one silver plate **weighing** a hundred and thirty
7:31 His offering was one silver plate **weighing** a hundred and thirty
7:37 His offering was one silver plate **weighing** a hundred and thirty
7:43 His offering was one silver plate **weighing** a hundred and thirty
7:49 His offering was one silver plate **weighing** a hundred and thirty
7:55 His offering was one silver plate **weighing** a hundred and thirty
7:61 His offering was one silver plate **weighing** a hundred and thirty
7:67 His offering was one silver plate **weighing** a hundred and thirty
7:73 His offering was one silver plate **weighing** a hundred and thirty
7:79 His offering was one silver plate **weighing** a hundred and thirty
Jos 7:21 shekels of silver and a wedge of gold **weighing** fifty shekels,
Jdg 8:26 The **weight** *of* the gold rings he asked for came to seventeen
1Sa 17: 5 wore a coat of scale armor of bronze **weighing** five thousand
2Sa 12:30 its **weight** was a talent of gold, and it was set with precious
21:16 whose bronze spearhead **weighed** three hundred shekels and who
21:16 hundred shekels **[RPH]** and who was armed with a new ⌞sword⌟,
1Ki 7:47 there were so many; the **weight** *of* the bronze was not determined.
10:14 The **weight** *of* the gold that Solomon received yearly was 666
2Ki 25:16 for the temple of the LORD, was more than could be **weighed**.
1Ch 20: 2 its **weight** was found to be a talent of gold, and it was set with
21:25 So David **paid** [+4200+5989] Araunah six hundred shekels of gold
22: 3 and for the fittings, and more bronze than could be **weighed**.
22:14 quantities of bronze and iron too great to be **weighed**, and wood
28:14 He designated the **weight** of gold for all the gold articles to be used
28:14 the **weight** of silver for all the silver articles to be used in various
28:15 the **weight** of gold for the gold lampstands and their lamps,
28:15 and their lamps, with the **weight** *for* each lampstand and its lamps;
28:15 and the **weight** of silver for each silver lampstand and its lamps,
28:16 the **weight** of gold for each table for consecrated bread; the weight
28:17 and pitchers; the **weight** of gold for each gold dish;
28:17 of gold for each gold dish; the **weight** of silver for each silver dish;
28:18 and the **weight** of the refined gold for the altar of incense.
2Ch 3: 9 The gold nails **weighed** fifty shekels. He also overlaid the upper
4:18 so much that the **weight** *of* the bronze was not determined.
9:13 The **weight** *of* the gold that Solomon received yearly was 666
Ezr 8:30 sacred articles that had been **weighed out** to be taken to the house
8:34 Everything was accounted for by number and **weight**,
8:34 and weight, and the entire **weight** was recorded at that time.
Job 28:25 When he established the **force** of the wind and measured out the
Jer 52:20 for the temple of the LORD, was more than could be **weighed**.
Eze 4:16 The people will eat **rationed** [+928] food in anxiety and drink
5: 1 Then take a **set of scales** [+4404] and divide up the hair.

5487 מִשְׁקֶלֶת ***mišqelet***, n.f. [2] [√ 9202?]

plumb line [2]

2Ki 21:13 and the **plumb line** *used against* the house of Ahab.
Isa 28:17 make justice the measuring line and righteousness the **plumb line**;

5488 מִשְׁקָע ***mišqāʿ***, n.[m.]. [1] [√ 9205]

clear [1]

Eze 34:18 Is it not enough for you to drink **clear** water? Must you also muddy

5489 מִשְׁרָה ***mišrâ***, n.f. [1] [√ 9223]

juice [1]

Nu 6: 3 He must not drink grape **juice** or eat grapes or raisins.

5490 מִשְׁרָעִי ***mišrāʿî***, a.g. [1]

Mishraites [1]

1Ch 2:53 Kiriath Jearim: the Ithrites, Puthites, Shumathites and **Mishraites**.

5491 מָשַׁשׁ ***māšaš***, v. [9] [cf. 3560, 4630]

grope [2], searched through [2], *untranslated* [1], felt [1], grope about [1], touched [1], touches [1]

Ge 27:12 [A] What if my father **touches** me? I would appear to be tricking
27:22 [A] *who* **touched** him and said, "The voice is the voice of Jacob,
31:34 [D] Laban **searched through** everything in the tent but found
31:37 [D] Now that *you have* **searched through** all my goods,
Ex 10:21 [G] darkness will spread over Egypt—darkness *that can be* **felt**."
Dt 28:29 [D] At midday *you will* **grope about** like a blind man in the
28:29 [D] At midday you will grope about like **[RPH]** a blind man in
Job 5:14 [D] upon them in the daytime; at noon *they* **grope** as in the night.
12:25 [D] *They* **grope** *in* darkness with no light; he makes them

5492 מִשְׁתֶּה ***mišteh***, n.m. [46] [√ 9272; Ar 10447]

banquet [12], feast [12], feasting [8], drink [3], *untranslated* [2], drinking [2], banquet [+3516] [1], banquets [1], dinner [1], feasts [1], meal [1], table [1], that[s] [1]

Ge 19: 3 He prepared a **meal** for them, baking bread without yeast,
21: 8 and on the day Isaac was weaned Abraham held a great **feast**.
26:30 Isaac then made a **feast** for them, and they ate and drank.
29:22 Laban brought together all the people of the place and gave a **feast**.
40:20 was Pharaoh's birthday, and he gave a **feast** for all his officials.
Jdg 14:10 Samson made a **feast** there, as was customary for bridegrooms.
14:12 "If you can give me the answer within the seven days of the **feast**,
14:17 She cried the whole seven days of the **feast**. So on the seventh day
1Sa 25:36 he was in the house holding a **banquet** like that of a king.
25:36 he was in the house holding a banquet like **that**[s] *of* a king.
2Sa 3:20 to David at Hebron, David prepared a **feast** for him and his men.
1Ki 3:15 and fellowship offerings. Then he gave a **feast** for all his court.
Ezr 3: 7 and gave food and **drink** and oil to the people of Sidon and Tyre,
Est 1: 3 in the third year of his reign he gave a **banquet** for all his nobles
1: 5 these days were over, the king gave a **banquet**, lasting seven days,
1: 9 Queen Vashti also gave a **banquet** *for* the women in the royal
2:18 the king gave a great **banquet**, Esther's banquet, for all his nobles
2:18 a great banquet, Esther's **banquet**, for all his nobles and officials.
5: 4 with Haman, come today to a **banquet** I have prepared for him."
5: 5 So the king and Haman went to the **banquet** Esther had prepared.
5: 6 As they were **drinking** wine, the king again asked Esther,
5: 8 and Haman come tomorrow to the **banquet** I will prepare for them.
5:12 Esther invited to accompany the king to the **banquet** she gave.
5:14 go with the king to the **dinner** and be happy." This suggestion
6:14 and hurried Haman away to the **banquet** Esther had prepared.
7: 2 as they were **drinking** wine on that second day, the king again
7: 7 left **[RPH]** his wine and went out into the palace garden.
7: 8 king returned from the palace garden to the **banquet** [+3516] hall,
8:17 and gladness among the Jews, with **feasting** and celebrating.
9:17 on the fourteenth they rested and made it a day of **feasting** and joy.
9:18 on the fifteenth they rested and made it a day of **feasting** and joy.
9:19 the fourteenth of the month of Adar as a day of joy and **feasting**,
9:22 He wrote them to observe the days as days of **feasting** and joy
Job 1: 4 His sons used to take turns holding **feasts** in their homes, and they
1: 5 When a period of **feasting** had run its course, Job would send
Pr 15:15 are wretched, but the cheerful heart has a continual **feast**.
Ecc 7: 2 to go to a house of mourning than to go to a house of **feasting**,
Isa 5:12 They have harps and lyres at their **banquets**, tambourines
25: 6 On this mountain the LORD Almighty will prepare a **feast** *of* rich
25: 6 a feast of rich food for all peoples, a **banquet** *of* aged wine—
Jer 16: 8 "And do not enter a house where there is **feasting** and sit down to
51:39 are aroused, I will set out a **feast** *for* them and make them drunk,
Da 1: 5 them a daily amount of food and wine from the king's **table**.
1: 8 **[NIE]** and he asked the chief official for permission not to defile
1:10 afraid of my lord the king, who has assigned your food and **drink**.
1:16 and the wine they were to **drink** and gave them vegetables instead.

5493 מְתִי ***mōt[1]***, n.m. [22 / 20] [→ 1432, 5500]

men [11], few [3], few in number [+5071] [1], friends [1], little [1], only a few [+5031] [1], people [1], very few [+5031] [1]

Ge 34:30 We are **few** *in* number, and if they join forces against me
Dt 2:34 and completely destroyed them—**men**, women and children.
3: 6 of Heshbon, destroying every city—**men**, women and children.
4:27 **only a few** [+5031] *of* you will survive among the nations to which
26: 5 and he went down into Egypt with a few **people** and lived there
28:62 as the stars in the sky will be left but **few in number** [+5071],
33: 6 "Let Reuben live and not die, nor his **men** be few."
1Ch 16:19 When they were but **few** *in* number, few indeed, and strangers in it,
Job 11: 3 Will your idle talk reduce **men** to silence? Will no one rebuke you
11:11 Surely he recognizes deceitful **men**; and when he sees evil,

Job 19: 19 All my intimate **friends** detest me; those I love have turned against
22: 15 Will you keep to the old path that evil **men** have trod?
24: 12 The groans of the dying [BHS *men*; NIV 4637] rise from the city,
31: 31 if the **men** *of* my household have never said, 'Who has not had his
Ps 17: 14 O LORD, by your hand save me from such **men**, from men of this
17: 14 such men, from **men** of this world whose reward is in this life.
26: 4 I do not sit with deceitful **men**, nor do I consort with hypocrites;
105: 12 When they were but **few** *in* number, few indeed, and strangers in it,
Isa 3: 25 Your **men** will fall by the sword, your warriors in battle.
5: 13 their men of rank *will* die [BHS *are men*; NIV 4637] *of* hunger
41: 14 Do not be afraid, O worm Jacob, O **little** Israel, for I myself will
Jer 44: 28 return to the land of Judah from Egypt will be **very few** [+5031].

5494 ²מֹת **mōt²**, n.m. Not used in NIV/BHS

5495 מַתְבֵּן **matbēn**, n.[m.]. [1] [√ 9320]

straw [1]

Isa 25: 10 Moab will be trampled under him as **straw** is trampled down in the

5496 מֶתֶג **meteg**, n.m. [4] [→ 5497]

bit [3], halter [1]

2Ki 19: 28 I will put my hook in your nose and my **bit** in your mouth,
Ps 32: 9 must be controlled by **bit** and bridle or they will not come to you.
Pr 26: 3 A whip for the horse, a **halter** for the donkey, and a rod for the
Isa 37: 29 I will put my hook in your nose and my **bit** in your mouth,

5497 מֶתֶג הָאַמָּה **meteg hā'ammâ**, n.pr.loc. [1] [√ 5496 + 2021 + 585]

Metheg Ammah [1]

2Sa 8: 1 and he took **Metheg Ammah** from the control of the Philistines.

5498 מָתוֹק **mātôq**, a. [12] [√ 5517]

sweet [10], sweeter [2]

Jdg 14: 14 of the eater, something to eat; out of the strong, *something* **sweet**."
14: 18 day the men of the town said to him, "What is **sweeter** than honey?
Ps 19: 10 [19:11] they are **sweeter** than honey, than honey from the comb.
Pr 16: 24 words are a honeycomb, **sweet** to the soul and healing to the bones.
24: 13 for it is good; honey from the comb is **sweet** to your taste.
27: 7 loathes honey, but to the hungry even what is bitter tastes **sweet**.
Ecc 5: 12 [5:11] The sleep of a laborer is **sweet**, whether he eats little
11: 7 Light is **sweet**, and it pleases the eyes to see the sun.
SS 2: 3 I delight to sit in his shade, and his fruit is **sweet** to my taste.
Isa 5: 20 light for darkness, who put bitter for **sweet** and sweet for bitter.
5: 20 light for darkness, who put bitter for sweet and **sweet** for bitter.
Eze 3: 3 with it." So I ate it, and it tasted as **sweet** as honey in my mouth.

5499 מְתוּשָׁאֵל **metûšā'ēl**, n.pr.m. [2] [√ 4637 + 8611 + 446]

Methushael [2]

Ge 4: 18 father of Mehujael, and Mehujael was the father of **Methushael**,
4: 18 father of Methushael, and **Methushael** was the father of Lamech.

5500 מְתוּשֶׁלַח **metûšelaḥ**, n.pr.m. [6] [√ 5493 + 8938?]

Methuselah [6]

Ge 5: 21 Enoch had lived 65 years, he became the father of **Methuselah**.
5: 22 after he became the father of **Methuselah**, Enoch walked with God
5: 25 When **Methuselah** had lived 187 years, he became the father of
5: 26 **Methuselah** lived 782 years and had other sons and daughters.
5: 27 Altogether, **Methuselah** lived 969 years, and then he died.
1Ch 1: 3 Enoch, **Methuselah**, Lamech, Noah.

5501 מָתַח **mātaḥ**, v. [1] [→ 623, 5502]

spreads out [1]

Isa 40: 22 [A] like a canopy, and **spreads** them **out** like a tent to live in.

5502 מִתְחָה **mitḥâ**, n.[f.]. Not used in NIV/BHS [√ 5501]

5503 מָתַי **mātay**, adv.inter. [43]

how long [+6330] [27], when [11], how long [2], for how long [+6330] [1], how long [+339+6388] [1], setting the time [+4200] [1]

Ge 30: 30 But now, **when** may I do something for my own household?"
Ex 8: 9 [8:5] "I leave to you the honor of **setting the time** [+4200] for me
10: 3 says: '**How long** [+6330] will you refuse to humble yourself before
10: 7 Pharaoh's officials said to him, "**How long** [+6330] will this man
Nu 14: 27 "**How long** [+6330] will this wicked community grumble against
1Sa 1: 14 said to her, "**How long** [+6330] will you keep on getting drunk?
16: 1 The LORD said to Samuel, "**How long** [+6330] will you mourn
2Sa 2: 26 you realize that this will end in bitterness? **How long** [+6330]
1Ki 18: 21 said, "**How long** [+6330] will you waver between two opinions?
Ne 2: 6 asked me, "**How long** [+6330] will your journey take, and when
2: 6 "How long will your journey take, and **when** will you get back?"
Job 7: 4 When I lie down I think, '**How long** *before* I get up?' The night
Ps 6: 3 [6:4] My soul is in anguish. **How long** [+6330], O LORD,
41: 5 [41:6] of me in malice, "**When** will he die and his name perish?"
42: 2 [42:3] for the living God. **When** can I go and meet with God?
74: 10 **How long** [+6330] will the enemy mock you, O God? Will the foe
80: 4 [80:5] O LORD God Almighty, **how long** [+6330] will your
82: 2 "**How long** [+6330] will you defend the unjust and show partiality
90: 13 Relent, O LORD! **How long** [+6330] will it be? Have compassion
94: 3 **How long** [+6330] will the wicked, O LORD, how long will the
94: 3 O LORD, **how long** [+6330] will the wicked be jubilant?
94: 8 ones among the people; you fools, **when** will you become wise?
101: 2 be careful to lead a blameless life—**when** will you come to me?
119: 82 looking for your promise; I say, "**When** will you comfort me?"
119: 84 must your servant wait? **When** will you punish my persecutors?
Pr 1: 22 "**How long** [+6330] will you simple ones love your simple ways?
6: 9 **How long** [+6330] will you lie there, you sluggard? When will you
6: 9 lie there, you sluggard? **When** will you get up from your sleep?
23: 35 I don't feel it! **When** will I wake up so I can find another drink?"
Isa 6: 11 Then I said, "**For how long** [+6330], O Lord?" And he answered:
Jer 4: 14 and be saved. **How long** [+6330] will you harbor wicked thoughts?
4: 21 **How long** [+6330] must I see the battle standard and hear the
12: 4 **How long** [+6330] will the land lie parched and the grass in every
13: 27 O Jerusalem! **How long** [+339+6388] will you be unclean?"
23: 26 **How long** [+6330] will this continue in the hearts of these lying
31: 22 **How long** [+6330] will you wander, O unfaithful daughter?
47: 5 O remnant on the plain, **how long** [+6330] will you cut
Da 8: 13 another holy one said to him, "**How long** [+6330] will it take *for*
12: 6 who was above the waters of the river, "**How long** [+6330] will it
Hos 8: 5 burns against them. **How long** will they be incapable of purity?
Am 8: 5 "**When** will the New Moon be over that we may sell grain,
Hab 2: 6 himself wealthy by extortion! **How long** [+6330] must this go on?'
Zec 1: 12 "LORD Almighty, **how long** [+6330] will you withhold mercy

5504 מַתְכֹּנֶת **matkōnet**, n.f. [5] [√ 9419]

formula [2], number [1], original design [1], standard measure [1]

Ex 5: 8 But require them to make the same **number** *of* bricks as before;
30: 32 it on men's bodies and do not make any oil with the same **formula**.
30: 37 Do not make any incense with this **formula** for yourselves;
2Ch 24: 13 They rebuilt the temple of God according to its **original design**
Eze 45: 11 of a homer; the homer is to be the **standard measure** *for* both.

5505 מַתְּלָאָה **mattelā'â**, p.indef.+n.f. Not used in NIV/BHS [√ 4537 + 9430]

5506 מְתַלְּעוֹת **metallee'ôt**, n.f.pl. [3] [√ 4922]

fangs [2], jaws [1]

Job 29: 17 I broke the **fangs** *of* the wicked and snatched the victims from their
Pr 30: 14 whose **jaws** are set with knives to devour the poor from the earth,
Joel 1: 6 without number; it has the teeth of a lion, the **fangs** *of* a lioness.

5507 מְתֹם **metōm**, n.[m.]. [4] [√ 9462]

health [2], all [1], soundness [1]

Jdg 20: 48 of Israel went back to Benjamin and put **all** the towns to the sword,
Ps 38: 3 [38:4] Because of your wrath there is no **health** in my body;
38: 7 [38:8] is filled with searing pain; there is no **health** in my body.
Isa 1: 6 sole of your foot to the top of your head there is no **soundness**—

5508 ¹מַתָּן **mattān¹**, n.m.col. [5] [→ 5509, 5513, 5514, 5515; cf. 5989; Ar 10448]

gift [3], gifts [2]

Ge 34: 12 price for the bride and the **gift** I am to bring as great as you like,
Nu 18: 11 whatever is set aside from the **gifts** of all the wave offerings of the
Pr 18: 16 A **gift** opens the way for the giver and ushers him into the presence
19: 6 with a ruler, and everyone is the friend of a man who gives **gifts**.
21: 14 A **gift** given in secret soothes anger, and a bribe concealed in the

5509 ²מַתָּן **mattān²**, n.pr.m. [3] [√ 5508; cf. 5989]

Mattan [3]

2Ki 11: 18 to pieces and killed **Mattan** the priest of Baal in front of the altars.
2Ch 23: 17 and idols and killed **Mattan** the priest of Baal in front of the altars.
Jer 38: 1 Shephatiah son of **Mattan**, Gedaliah son of Pashhur, Jehucal son

5510 ¹מַתָּנָה **mattānâ¹**, n.f. [17] [→ 5511; cf. 5989]

gifts [9], gift [5], bribe [1], bribes [1], given [1]

Ge 25: 6 he gave **gifts** to the sons of his concubines and sent them away
Ex 28: 38 sacred gifts the Israelites consecrate, whatever their **gifts** may be.

Lev 23:38 and in addition to your **gifts** and whatever you have vowed
Nu 18: 6 your fellow Levites from among the Israelites as a **gift** to you,
18: 7 the curtain. I am giving you the service of the priesthood as a **gift**.
18:29 portion the best and holiest part of everything **given** *to* you.'
Dt 16:17 Each of you must bring a **gift** in proportion to the way the LORD
2Ch 21: 3 Their father had given them many **gifts** of silver and gold
Est 9:22 and giving presents of food to one another and **gifts** to the poor.
Ps 68:18 [68:19] you received **gifts** from men, even from the rebellious—
Pr 15:27 man brings trouble to his family, but he who hates **bribes** will live.
Ecc 7: 7 turns a wise man into a fool, and a **bribe** corrupts the heart.
Eze 20:26 I let them become defiled through their **gifts**—the sacrifice of
20:31 When you offer your **gifts**—the sacrifice of your sons in the fire—
20:39 and no longer profane my holy name with your **gifts** and idols.
46:16 If the prince makes a **gift** from his inheritance to one of his sons,
46:17 he makes a **gift** from his inheritance to one of his servants,

5511 ²מַתָּנָה *mattānâ²*, n.pr.loc. [2] [√ 5510; cf. 5989]

Mattanah [2]

Nu 21:18 and staffs." Then they went from the desert to **Mattanah**,
21:19 from **Mattanah** to Nahaliel, from Nahaliel to Bamoth,

5512 מִתְנִי *mitnî*, a.g. [1] [√ 5516?]

Mithnite [1]

1Ch 11:43 Hanan son of Maacah, Joshaphat the **Mithnite**,

5513 מַתְּנַי *mattᵉnay*, n.pr.m. [3] [√ 5508 + 3378]

Mattenai [3]

Ezr 10:33 **Mattenai**, Mattattah, Zabad, Eliphelet, Jeremai, Manasseh
10:37 Mattaniah, **Mattenai** and Jaasu.
Ne 12:19 of Joiarib's, **Mattenai**; of Jedaiah's, Uzzi;

5514 מַתַּנְיָה *mattanyâ*, n.pr.m. [13] [√ 5508 + 3378]

Mattaniah [13]

2Ki 24:17 He made **Mattaniah**, Jehoiachin's uncle, king in his place
1Ch 9:15 Bakbakkar, Heresh, Galal and **Mattaniah** son of Mica, the son of
2Ch 20:14 of Jeiel, the son of **Mattaniah**, a Levite and descendant of Asaph,
Ezr 10:26 **Mattaniah**, Zechariah, Jehiel, Abdi, Jeremoth and Elijah.
10:27 Elioenai, Eliashib, **Mattaniah**, Jeremoth, Zabad and Aziza.
10:30 Benaiah, Maaseiah, **Mattaniah**, Bezalel, Binnui and Manasseh.
10:37 **Mattaniah**, Mattenai and Jaasu.
Ne 11:17 **Mattaniah** son of Mica, the son of Zabdi, the son of Asaph,
11:22 the son of Hashabiah, the son of **Mattaniah**, the son of Mica.
12: 8 Binnui, Kadmiel, Sherebiah, Judah, and also **Mattaniah**, who,
12:25 **Mattaniah**, Bakbukiah, Obadiah, Meshullam, Talmon and Akkub
12:35 the son of **Mattaniah**, the son of Micaiah, the son of Zaccur,
13:13 made Hanan son of Zaccur, the son of **Mattaniah**, their assistant,

5515 מַתַּנְיָהוּ *mattanyāhû*, n.pr.m. [3] [√ 5508 + 3378]

Mattaniah [3]

1Ch 25: 4 Bukkiah, **Mattaniah**, Uzziel, Shubael and Jerimoth; Hananiah,
25:16 the ninth to **Mattaniah**, his sons and relatives, 12
2Ch 29:13 from the descendants of Asaph, Zechariah and **Mattaniah**;

5516 מָתְנַיִם *motnayim*, n.m.du. [47] [→ 5512?]

waist [16], side [4], waists [4], backs [3], body [2], loins [2], there[s] [2], tuck cloak into belt [+2520] [2], armor [1], belt [+258] [1], bodies [1], brace yourselves [+2616] [1], cloak tucked into belt [+2520] [1], get ready [+273] [1], heart [1], make wear [+6584+6590] [1], put on [+928+8492] [1], sets about work [+2520] [1], strutting rooster [+2435] [1], tucking cloak into belt [+9113] [1]

Ge 37:34 **put on** [+928+8492] sackcloth and mourned for his son many
Ex 12:11 with your **cloak tucked into** your **belt** [+2520], your sandals on
28:42 as a covering for the body, reaching from the **waist** to the thigh.
Dt 33:11 Smite the **loins** *of* those who rise up against him; strike his foes till
2Sa 20: 8 strapped over it at his **waist** was a belt with a dagger in its sheath.
1Ki 2: 5 with that blood stained the belt around his **waist** and the sandals on
12:10 tell them, 'My little finger is thicker than my father's **waist**.
18:46 **tucking** his **cloak into** *his* **belt** [+9113], he ran ahead of Ahab all
20:31 Let us go to the king of Israel with sackcloth around our **waists**
20:32 Wearing sackcloth around their **waists** and ropes around their
2Ki 1: 8 with a garment of hair and with a leather belt around his **waist**."
4:29 Elisha said to Gehazi, "**Tuck** your **cloak into** your **belt** [+2520],
9: 1 and said to him, "**Tuck** *your* **cloak into** your **belt** [+2520],
2Ch 10:10 tell them, 'My little finger is thicker than my father's **waist**.
Ne 4:18 [4:12] each of the builders wore his sword at his **side** as he
Job 12:18 the shackles put on by kings and ties a loincloth around their **waist**.
40:16 What strength he has in his **loins**, what power in the muscles of his
Ps 66:11 You brought us into prison and laid burdens on our **backs**.
69:23 [69:24] so they cannot see, and their **backs** be bent forever.
Pr 30:31 a **strutting rooster** [+2435], a he-goat, and a king with his army
31:17 *She* **sets about** her **work** [+2520] vigorously; her arms are strong
Isa 11: 5 Righteousness will be his **belt** [+258] and faithfulness the sash
20: 2 "Take off the sackcloth from your **body** and the sandals from your
21: 3 At this my **body** is racked with pain, pangs seize me, like those of
45: 1 of to subdue nations before him and to strip kings of their **armor**,
Jer 1:17 "**Get** yourself **ready** [+273]! Stand up and say to them whatever I
13: 1 "Go and buy a linen belt and put it around your **waist**, but do not
13: 2 bought a belt, as the LORD directed, and put it around my **waist**.
13: 4 "Take the belt you bought and are wearing around your **waist**,
13:11 For as a belt is bound around a man's **waist**, so I bound the whole
48:37 every hand is slashed and every **waist** is covered with sackcloth.
Eze 1:27 I saw that from what appeared to be his **waist** up he looked like
1:27 as if full of fire, and that from **there**[s] down he looked like fire;
8: 2 From what appeared to be his **waist** down he was like fire,
8: 2 and from **there**[s] up his appearance was as bright as glowing metal.
9: 2 them was a man clothed in linen who had a writing kit at his **side**.
9: 3 to the man clothed in linen who had the writing kit at his **side**
9:11 the man in linen with the writing kit at his **side** brought back word,
21: 6 [21:11] Groan before them with broken **heart** and bitter grief.
23:15 with belts around their **waists** and flowing turbans on their heads;
29: 7 they leaned on you, you broke and their **backs** were wrenched.
44:18 on their heads and linen undergarments around their **waists**.
47: 4 and led me through water that was up to the **waist**.
Da 10: 5 dressed in linen, with a belt of the finest gold around his **waist**.
Am 8:10 *I will* **make** all of you **wear** [+6584+6590] sackcloth and shave
Na 2: 1 [2:2] the fortress, watch the road, **brace yourselves** [+2616],
2:10 [2:11] Hearts melt, knees give way, **bodies** tremble, every face

5517 מָתַק *mātaq*, v. [6] [→ 4941, 5498, 5518, 5519, 5520?]

sweet [4], enjoyed sweet [1], feasts on [1]

Ex 15:25 [A] He threw it into the water, and the water *became* **sweet**.
Job 20:12 [G] "Though evil *is* **sweet** in his mouth and he hides it under his
21:33 [A] The soil in the valley *is* **sweet** to him; all men follow after
24:20 [A] The womb forgets them, the worm **feasts on** them; evil men
Ps 55:14 [55:15] [G] with whom *I once* **enjoyed sweet** fellowship as we
Pr 9:17 [A] "Stolen water *is* **sweet**; food eaten in secret is delicious!"

5518 מֶתֶק *mātēq*, n.m. [2] [√ 5517]

pleasant [1], pleasantness [1]

Pr 16:21 are called discerning, and **pleasant** words promote instruction.
27: 9 the **pleasantness** *of* one's friend springs from his earnest counsel.

5519 מֹתֶק *mōteq*, n.[m.]. [1] [√ 5517]

sweet [1]

Jdg 9:11 the fig tree replied, 'Should I give up my fruit, so good and **sweet**,

5520 מִתְקָה *mitqâ*, n.pr.loc. [2] [√ 5517?]

Mithcah [2]

Nu 33:28 They left Terah and camped at **Mithcah**.
33:29 They left **Mithcah** and camped at Hashmonah.

5521 מִתְרְדָת *mitrᵉdāt*, n.pr.m. [2]

Mithredath [2]

Ezr 1: 8 Cyrus king of Persia had them brought by **Mithredath** the
4: 7 **Mithredath**, Tabeel and the rest of his associates wrote a letter to

5522 מַתַּת *mattat*, n.f. [6] [→ 5524, 5525; cf. 5989]

gift [3], as much as pleases [+3338] [2], gifts he does not give [+9214] [1]

1Ki 13: 7 with me and have something to eat, and I will give you a **gift**."
Pr 25:14 rain is a man who boasts of **gifts** [+9214] **he does not give**.
Ecc 3:13 and find satisfaction in all his toil—this is the **gift** *of* God.
5:19 [5:18] his lot and be happy in his work—this is a **gift** *of* God.
Eze 46: 5 offering with the lambs is to be **as much as** he **pleases** [+3338],
46:11 with a ram, and with the lambs **as much as** one **pleases** [+3338],

5523 מַתַּתָּה *mattattâ*, n.pr.m. [1] [√ 5989]

Mattattah [1]

Ezr 10:33 Mattenai, **Mattattah**, Zabad, Eliphelet, Jeremai, Manasseh

5524 מַתִּתְיָה *mattityâ*, n.pr.m. [4] [√ 5522 + 3378]

Mattithiah [4]

1Ch 9:31 A Levite named **Mattithiah**, the firstborn son of Shallum the
16: 5 Jehiel, **Mattithiah**, Eliab, Benaiah, Obed-Edom and Jeiel.
Ezr 10:43 Jeiel, **Mattithiah**, Zabad, Zebina, Jaddai, Joel and Benaiah.
Ne 8: 4 Beside him on his right stood **Mattithiah**, Shema, Anaiah,

5525 מַתִּתְיָהוּ ***mattityāhû***, n.pr.m. [4] [√ 5522 + 3378]

Mattithiah [4]

1Ch 15: 18 Jehiel, Unni, Eliab, Benaiah, Maaseiah, **Mattithiah**, Eliphelehu,
15: 21 and **Mattithiah**, Eliphelehu, Mikneiah, Obed-Edom, Jeiel
25: 3 Zeri, Jeshaiah, Shimei, Hashabiah and **Mattithiah**, six in all,
25: 21 the fourteenth to **Mattithiah**, his sons and relatives, 12

נ, *n*

5526 נ ***n***, letter. Not used in NIV/BHS [→ Ar 10449]

5527 נָ- ***-ān***, נְ- ***-n***, p.f.pl.suf. [36] [√ 2023, 2401] Not indexed

untranslated [12], their [9], they [5], them [4], each [2], the creatures[s] [1], the rooms[s] [1], the[s] [1], you [1]

5528 נָא[1] ***nāʼ¹***, pt. [405] [→ 626, 629] See Select Index

untranslated [297], please [59], now [22], I beg you [5], then [4], come now [+6964] [3], I would like [2], all right [1], but [1], I pray [1], if you will [1], O [1], please [+1065] [1], please [+3283] [1], quick [1], right now [1], so [1], therefore [1], very well [+2180] [1], we pray [1]

5529 נָא[2] ***nāʼ²***, a. [1]

raw [1]

Ex 12: 9 Do not eat the meat **raw** or cooked in water, but roast it over the

5530 נֹא ***nōʼ***, n.pr.loc. [4] [→ 5531]

Thebes [4]

Jer 46: 25 "I am about to bring punishment on Amon god of **Thebes**,
Eze 30: 14 Upper Egypt, set fire to Zoan and inflict punishment on **Thebes**.
30: 15 the stronghold of Egypt, and cut off the hordes of **Thebes**.
30: 16 **Thebes** will be taken by storm; Memphis will be in constant

5531 נֹא אָמוֹן ***nōʼ ʼāmôn***, n.pr.loc. [1] [√ 5530 + 572]

Thebes [1]

Na 3: 8 Are you better than **Thebes**, situated on the Nile, with water

5532 נֹאד ***nōʼd***, n.m. [6 / 7]

skin [2], wineskins [+3516] [2], jars [1], scroll [1], wineskin [1]

Jos 9: 4 were loaded with worn-out sacks and old **wineskins** [+3516],
9: 13 these **wineskins** [+3516] that we filled were new, but see how
Jdg 4: 19 She opened a **skin** *of* milk, gave him a drink, and covered him up.
1Sa 16: 20 a **skin** *of* wine and a young goat and sent them with his son David
Ps 33: 7 He gathers the waters of the sea into **jars**; [BHS 5603] he puts the
56: 8 [56:9] Record my lament; list my tears on your **scroll**—are they
119: 83 Though I am like a **wineskin** in the smoke, I do not forget your

5533 נָאָה ***nāʼâ***, v. [3] [→ 5534; cf. 5658]

beautiful [2], adorns [1]

Ps 93: 5 [D] holiness **adorns** your house for endless days, O LORD.
SS 1: 10 [A] Your cheeks *are* **beautiful** with earrings, your neck with
Isa 52: 7 [D] How **beautiful** on the mountains *are* the feet of those who

5534 נָאוֶה ***nāʼweh***, a. [10] [√ 5533]

fitting [4], lovely [4], beautiful [1], unsuited [+4202] [1]

Ps 33: 1 you righteous; it is **fitting** for the upright to praise him.
147: 1 to sing praises to our God, how pleasant and **fitting** to praise him!
Pr 17: 7 Arrogant lips are **unsuited** [+4202] to a fool—how much worse
19: 10 It is not **fitting** for a fool to live in luxury—how much worse for a
26: 1 snow in summer or rain in harvest, honor is not **fitting** for a fool.
SS 1: 5 Dark am I, yet **lovely**, O daughters of Jerusalem, dark like the tents
2: 14 hear your voice; for your voice is sweet, and your face is **lovely**.
4: 3 Your lips are like a scarlet ribbon; your mouth is **lovely**.
6: 4 You are beautiful, my darling, as Tirzah, **lovely** as Jerusalem,
Jer 6: 2 I will destroy the Daughter of Zion, so **beautiful** and delicate.

5535 נָאַם ***nāʼam***, v.den. [1] [→ 5536]

declare [1]

Jer 23: 31 [A] the prophets who wag their own tongues and yet **declare**,

5536 נְאֻם ***nᵉʼum***, n.m. [376] [√ 5535]

declares [363], oracle [9], says [3], declared [1]

Ge 22: 16 **declares** the LORD, that because you have done this and have not
Nu 14: 28 So tell them, 'As surely as I live, **declares** the LORD, I will do to
24: 3 "The **oracle** *of* Balaam son of Beor, the oracle of one whose eye
24: 3 of Balaam son of Beor, the **oracle** *of* one whose eye sees clearly,
24: 4 the **oracle** *of* one who hears the words of God, who sees a vision
24: 15 "The **oracle** *of* Balaam son of Beor, the oracle of one whose eye
24: 15 of Balaam son of Beor, the **oracle** *of* one whose eye sees clearly,
24: 16 the **oracle** *of* one who hears the words of God, who has knowledge
1Sa 2: 30 "Therefore the LORD, the God of Israel, **declares**: 'I promised
2: 30 now the LORD **declares**: 'Far be it from me! Those who honor
2Sa 23: 1 "The **oracle** *of* David son of Jesse, the oracle of the man exalted by
23: 1 son of Jesse, the **oracle** *of* the man exalted by the Most High,
2Ki 9: 26 blood of Naboth and the blood of his sons, **declares** the LORD,
9: 26 make you pay for it on this plot of ground, **declares** the LORD.'
19: 33 he will return; he will not enter this city, **declares** the LORD.
22: 19 and wept in my presence, I have heard you, **declares** the LORD.
2Ch 34: 27 and wept in my presence, I have heard you, **declares** the LORD.
Ps 36: 1 [36:2] An **oracle** is within my heart *concerning* the sinfulness of
110: 1 The LORD **says** to my Lord: "Sit at my right hand until I make
Pr 30: 1 an oracle: This man **declared** to Ithiel, to Ithiel and to Ucal:
Isa 1: 24 the LORD Almighty, the Mighty One of Israel, **declares**:
3: 15 the faces of the poor?" **declares** the Lord, the LORD Almighty.
14: 22 "I will rise up against them," **declares** the LORD Almighty.
14: 22 her offspring and descendants," **declares** the LORD.
14: 23 with the broom of destruction," **declares** the LORD Almighty.
17: 3 be like the glory of the Israelites," **declares** the LORD Almighty.
17: 6 on the fruitful boughs," **declares** the LORD, the God of Israel.
19: 4 will rule over them," **declares** the Lord, the LORD Almighty.
22: 25 "In that day," **declares** the LORD Almighty, "the peg driven into
30: 1 "Woe to the obstinate children," **declares** the LORD, "to those
31: 9 **declares** the LORD, whose fire is in Zion, whose furnace is in
37: 34 he will return; he will not enter this city," **declares** the LORD.
41: 14 **declares** the LORD, your Redeemer, the Holy One of Israel.
43: 10 "You are my witnesses," **declares** the LORD, "and my servant
43: 12 You are my witnesses," **declares** the LORD, "that I am God.
49: 18 As surely as I live," **declares** the LORD, "you will wear them all
52: 5 "And now what do I have here?" **declares** the LORD. "For my
52: 5 for nothing, and those who rule them mock," **declares** the LORD.
54: 17 and this is their vindication from me," **declares** the LORD.
55: 8 neither are your ways my ways," **declares** the LORD.
56: 8 The Sovereign LORD **declares**—he who gathers the exiles of
59: 20 to those in Jacob who repent of their sins," **declares** the LORD.
66: 2 **declares** the LORD. "This is the one I esteem: he who is humble
66: 17 they will meet their end together," **declares** the LORD.
66: 22 **declares** the LORD, "so will your name and descendants endure.
Jer 1: 8 for I am with you and will rescue you," **declares** the LORD.
1: 15 all the peoples of the northern kingdoms," **declares** the LORD.
1: 19 for I am with you and will rescue you," **declares** the LORD.
2: 3 held guilty, and disaster overtook them,' " **declares** the LORD.
2: 9 I bring charges against you again," **declares** the LORD.
2: 12 O heavens, and shudder with great horror," **declares** the LORD.
2: 19 and have no awe of me," **declares** the Lord, the LORD Almighty.
2: 22 of your guilt is still before me," **declares** the Sovereign LORD.
2: 29 You have all rebelled against me," **declares** the LORD.
3: 1 would you now return to me?" **declares** the LORD.
3: 10 me with all her heart, but only in pretense," **declares** the LORD.
3: 12 " 'Return, faithless Israel,' **declares** the LORD, 'I will frown on
3: 12 for I am merciful,' **declares** the LORD, 'I will not be angry
3: 13 spreading tree, and have not obeyed me,' " **declares** the LORD.
3: 14 "Return, faithless people," **declares** the LORD, "for I am your
3: 16 **declares** the LORD, "men will no longer say, 'The ark of the
3: 20 been unfaithful to me, O house of Israel," **declares** the LORD.
4: 1 "If you will return, O Israel, return to me," **declares** the LORD.
4: 9 **declares** the LORD, "the king and the officials will lose heart,
4: 17 because she has rebelled against me,' " **declares** the LORD.
5: 9 Should I not punish them for this?" **declares** the LORD.
5: 11 of Judah have been utterly unfaithful to me," **declares** the LORD.
5: 15 O house of Israel," **declares** the LORD, "I am bringing a distant
5: 18 "Yet even in those days," **declares** the LORD, "I will not destroy
5: 22 Should you not fear me?" **declares** the LORD. "Should you not
5: 29 Should I not punish them for this?" **declares** the LORD.
6: 12 my hand against those who live in the land," **declares** the LORD.
7: 11 robbers to you? But I have been watching! **declares** the LORD.
7: 13 **declares** the LORD, I spoke to you again and again, but you did
7: 19 But am I the one they are provoking? **declares** the LORD.
7: 30 people of Judah have done evil in my eyes, **declares** the LORD.
7: 32 So beware, the days are coming, **declares** the LORD,
8: 1 " 'At that time, **declares** the LORD, the bones of the kings
8: 3 nation will prefer death to life, **declares** the LORD Almighty.'
8: 13 " 'I will take away their harvest, **declares** the LORD. There will
8: 17 cannot be charmed, and they will bite you," **declares** the LORD.
9: 3 [9:2] they do not acknowledge me," **declares** the LORD.
9: 6 [9:5] they refuse to acknowledge me," **declares** the LORD.
9: 9 [9:8] Should I not punish them for this?" **declares** the LORD.
9: 22 [9:21] Say, "This is what the LORD **declares**: " 'The dead
9: 24 [9:23] on earth, for in these I delight," **declares** the LORD.

Jer 9:25 [9:24] "The days are coming," **declares** the LORD, "when I will
12:17 I will completely uproot and destroy it," **declares** the LORD.
13:11 **declares** the LORD, 'to be my people for my renown and praise
13:14 one against the other, fathers and sons alike, **declares** the LORD.
13:25 **declares** the LORD, "because you have forgotten me and trusted
15: 3 **declares** the LORD, "the sword to kill and the dogs to drag away
15: 6 You have rejected me," **declares** the LORD. "You keep on
15: 9 survivors to the sword before their enemies," **declares** the LORD.
15:20 for I am with you to rescue and save you," **declares** the LORD.
16: 5 my love and my pity from this people," **declares** the LORD.
16:11 **declares** the LORD, 'and followed other gods and served
16:14 "However, the days are coming," **declares** the LORD,
16:16 many fishermen," **declares** the LORD, "and they will catch them.
17:24 if you are careful to obey me, **declares** the LORD, and bring no
18: 6 **declares** the LORD. "Like clay in the hand of the potter,
19: 6 So beware, the days are coming, **declares** the LORD,
19:12 do to this place and to those who live here, **declares** the LORD.
21: 7 After that, **declares** the LORD, I will hand over Zedekiah king of
21:10 to do this city harm and not good, **declares** the LORD.
21:13 live above this valley on the rocky plateau, **declares** the LORD—
21:14 I will punish you as your deeds deserve, **declares** the LORD.
22: 5 But if you do not obey these commands, **declares** the LORD,
22:16 Is that not what it means to know me?" **declares** the LORD.
22:24 "As surely as I live," **declares** the LORD, "even if you,
23: 1 and scattering the sheep of my pasture!" **declares** the LORD.
23: 2 on you for the evil you have done," **declares** the LORD.
23: 4 or terrified, nor will any be missing," **declares** the LORD.
23: 5 "The days are coming," **declares** the LORD, "when I will raise
23: 7 "So then, the days are coming," **declares** the LORD,
23:11 even in my temple I find their wickedness," **declares** the LORD.
23:12 on them in the year they are punished," **declares** the LORD.
23:23 a God nearby," **declares** the LORD, "and not a God far away?
23:24 **declares** the LORD. "Do not I fill heaven and earth?"
23:24 "Do not I fill heaven and earth?" **declares** the LORD.
23:28 For what has straw to do with grain?" **declares** the LORD.
23:29 "Is not my word like fire," **declares** the LORD, "and like a
23:30 "Therefore," **declares** the LORD, "I am against the prophets who
23:31 Yes," **declares** the LORD, "I am against the prophets who wag
23:31 wag their own tongues and yet declare, 'The LORD **declares**.'
23:32 against those who prophesy false dreams," **declares** the LORD.
23:32 do not benefit these people in the least," **declares** the LORD.
23:33 to them, 'What oracle? I will forsake you, **declares** the LORD.'
25: 7 "But you did not listen to me," **declares** the LORD, "and you
25: 9 **declares** the LORD, "and I will bring them against this land
25:12 the land of the Babylonians, for their guilt," **declares** the LORD,
25:29 upon all who live on the earth, **declares** the LORD Almighty.'
25:31 and put the wicked to the sword,' " **declares** the LORD.
27: 8 famine and plague, **declares** the LORD, until I destroy it by his
27:11 in its own land to till it and to live there, **declares** the LORD." ' "
27:15 'I have not sent them,' **declares** the LORD. 'They are prophesying
27:22 will remain until the day I come for them,' **declares** the LORD.
28: 4 **declares** the LORD, 'for I will break the yoke of the king of
29: 9 to you in my name. I have not sent them," **declares** the LORD.
29:11 **declares** the LORD, "plans to prosper you and not to harm you,
29:14 I will be found by you," **declares** the LORD, "and will bring you
29:14 and places where I have banished you," **declares** the LORD,
29:19 **declares** the LORD, "words that I sent to them again and again
29:19 And you exiles have not listened either," **declares** the LORD.
29:23 them to do. I know it and am a witness to it," **declares** the LORD.
29:32 **declares** the LORD, because he has preached rebellion against
30: 3 The days are coming,' **declares** the LORD, 'when I will bring my
30: 8 " 'In that day,' **declares** the LORD Almighty, 'I will break the
30:10 my servant; do not be dismayed, O Israel,' **declares** the LORD.
30:11 I am with you and will save you,' **declares** the LORD. 'Though I
30:17 restore you to health and heal your wounds,' **declares** the LORD,
30:21 who will devote himself to be close to me?' **declares** the LORD.
31: 1 "At that time," **declares** the LORD, "I will be the God of all the
31:14 my people will be filled with my bounty," **declares** the LORD.
31:16 from tears, for your work will be rewarded," **declares** the LORD.
31:17 So there is hope for your future," **declares** the LORD. "Your
31:20 for him; I have great compassion for him," **declares** the LORD.
31:27 "The days are coming," **declares** the LORD, "when I will plant
31:28 I will watch over them to build and to plant," **declares** the LORD.
31:31 "The time is coming," **declares** the LORD, "when I will make a
31:32 though I was a husband to them," **declares** the LORD.
31:33 with the house of Israel after that time," **declares** the LORD.
31:34 from the least of them to the greatest," **declares** the LORD.
31:36 if these decrees vanish from my sight," **declares** the LORD,
31:37 of Israel because of all they have done," **declares** the LORD.
31:38 "The days are coming," **declares** the LORD, "when this city will
32: 5 where he will remain until I deal with him, **declares** the LORD.
32:30 me with what their hands have made, **declares** the LORD.
32:44 because I will restore their fortunes, **declares** the LORD."
33:14 " 'The days are coming,' **declares** the LORD, 'when I will fulfill
34: 5 O master!" I myself make this promise, **declares** the LORD.' "
34:17 So I now proclaim 'freedom' for you, **declares** the LORD—
34:22 I am going to give the order, **declares** the LORD, and I will bring
35:13 you not learn a lesson and obey my words?' **declares** the LORD.
39:17 I will rescue you on that day, **declares** the LORD; you will not be
39:18 with your life, because you trust in me, **declares** the LORD.' "
42:11 **declares** the LORD, for I am with you and will save you
44:29 to you that I will punish you in this place,' **declares** the LORD,
45: 5 For I will bring disaster on all people, **declares** the LORD,
46: 5 and there is terror on every side," **declares** the LORD.
46:18 "As surely as I live," **declares** the King, whose name is the
46:23 chop down her forest," **declares** the LORD, "dense though it be.
46:26 Egypt will be inhabited as in times past," **declares** the LORD.
46:28 O Jacob my servant, for I am with you," **declares** the LORD.
48:12 days are coming," **declares** the LORD, "when I will send men
48:15 **declares** the King, whose name is the LORD Almighty.
48:25 Moab's horn is cut off; her arm is broken," **declares** the LORD.
48:30 I know her insolence but it is futile," **declares** the LORD,
48:35 high places and burn incense to their gods," **declares** the LORD.
48:38 broken Moab like a jar that no one wants," **declares** the LORD.
48:43 and snare await you, O people of Moab," **declares** the LORD.
48:44 upon Moab the year of her punishment," **declares** the LORD.
48:47 the fortunes of Moab in days to come," **declares** the LORD.
49: 2 the days are coming," **declares** the LORD, "when I will sound the
49: 5 all those around you," **declares** the Lord, the LORD Almighty.
49: 6 will restore the fortunes of the Ammonites," **declares** the LORD.
49:13 I swear by myself," **declares** the LORD, "that Bozrah will
49:16 from there I will bring you down," **declares** the LORD.
49:26 will be silenced in that day," **declares** the LORD Almighty.
49:30 Stay in deep caves, you who live in Hazor," **declares** the LORD.
49:31 a nation at ease, which lives in confidence," **declares** the LORD,
49:32 will bring disaster on them from every side," **declares** the LORD.
49:37 disaster upon them, even my fierce anger," **declares** the LORD.
49:38 and destroy her king and officials," **declares** the LORD.
49:39 the fortunes of Elam in days to come," **declares** the LORD.
50: 4 "In those days, at that time," **declares** the LORD, "the people of
50:10 all who plunder her will have their fill," **declares** the LORD.
50:20 In those days, at that time," **declares** the LORD, "search will be
50:21 Pursue, kill and completely destroy them," **declares** the LORD.
50:30 all her soldiers will be silenced in that day," **declares** the LORD.
50:31 "See, I am against you, O arrogant one," **declares** the Lord,
50:35 **declares** the LORD—"against those who live in Babylon
50:40 **declares** the LORD, "so no one will live there;
51:24 for all the wrong they have done in Zion," **declares** the LORD.
51:25 you who destroy the whole earth," **declares** the LORD.
51:26 for you will be desolate forever," **declares** the LORD.
51:39 then sleep forever and not awake," **declares** the LORD.
51:48 out of the north destroyers will attack her," **declares** the LORD.
51:52 "But days are coming," **declares** the LORD, "when I will punish
51:53 I will send destroyers against her," **declares** the LORD.
51:57 they will sleep forever and not awake," **declares** the King,
Eze 5:11 Therefore as surely as I live, **declares** the Sovereign LORD,
11: 8 is what I will bring against you, **declares** the Sovereign LORD.
11:21 own heads what they have done, **declares** the Sovereign LORD."
12:25 I will fulfill whatever I say, **declares** the Sovereign LORD.' "
12:28 whatever I say will be fulfilled, **declares** the Sovereign LORD.' "
13: 6 They say, "The LORD **declares**," when the LORD has not sent
13: 7 when you say, "The LORD **declares**," though I have not spoken?
13: 8 lying visions, I am against you, **declares** the Sovereign LORD.
13:16 her when there was no peace, **declares** the Sovereign LORD." '
14:11 and I will be their God, **declares** the Sovereign LORD.' "
14:14 themselves by their righteousness, **declares** the Sovereign LORD.
14:16 as surely as I live, **declares** the Sovereign LORD, even if these
14:18 as surely as I live, **declares** the Sovereign LORD, even if these
14:20 **declares** the Sovereign LORD, even if Noah, Daniel and Job
14:23 done nothing in it without cause, **declares** the Sovereign LORD."
15: 8 they have been unfaithful, **declares** the Sovereign LORD."
16: 8 with you, **declares** the Sovereign LORD, and you became mine.
16:14 you made your beauty perfect, **declares** the Sovereign LORD.
16:19 That is what happened, **declares** the Sovereign LORD.
16:23 " 'Woe! Woe to you, **declares** the Sovereign LORD. In addition
16:30 " 'How weak-willed you are, **declares** the Sovereign LORD,
16:43 on your head what you have done, **declares** the Sovereign LORD.
16:48 **declares** the Sovereign LORD, your sister Sodom and her
16:58 your lewdness and your detestable practices, **declares** the LORD.
16:63 because of your humiliation, **declares** the Sovereign LORD.' "
17:16 " 'As surely as I live, **declares** the Sovereign LORD, he shall die
18: 3 "As surely as I live, **declares** the Sovereign LORD, you will no
18: 9 is righteous; he will surely live, **declares** the Sovereign LORD.
18:23 **declares** the Sovereign LORD. Rather, am I not pleased when
18:30 each one according to his ways, **declares** the Sovereign LORD.
18:32 pleasure in the death of anyone, **declares** the Sovereign LORD.
20: 3 I will not let you inquire of me, **declares** the Sovereign LORD.'
20:31 As surely as I live, **declares** the Sovereign LORD, I will not let

Eze 20:33 As surely as I live, **declares** the Sovereign LORD, I will rule over
20:36 land of Egypt, so I will judge you, **declares** the Sovereign LORD.
20:40 the high mountain of Israel, **declares** the Sovereign LORD,
20:44 O house of Israel, **declares** the Sovereign LORD.' "
21:7 [21:12] It will surely take place, **declares** the Sovereign LORD."
21:13 [21:18] does not continue? **declares** the Sovereign LORD.'
22:12 And you have forgotten me, **declares** the Sovereign LORD.
22:31 own heads all they have done, **declares** the Sovereign LORD."
23:34 tear your breasts. I have spoken, **declares** the Sovereign LORD.
24:14 your conduct and your actions, **declares** the Sovereign LORD.' "
25:14 they will know my vengeance, **declares** the Sovereign LORD.' "
26:5 spread fishnets, for I have spoken, **declares** the Sovereign LORD.
26:14 for I the LORD have spoken, **declares** the Sovereign LORD.
26:21 you will never again be found, **declares** the Sovereign LORD."
28:10 of foreigners. I have spoken, **declares** the Sovereign LORD.' "
29:20 and his army did it for me, **declares** the Sovereign LORD.
30:6 will fall by the sword within her, **declares** the Sovereign LORD.
31:18 is Pharaoh and all his hordes, **declares** the Sovereign LORD.' "
32:8 bring darkness over your land, **declares** the Sovereign LORD.
32:14 make her streams flow like oil, **declares** the Sovereign LORD.
32:16 all her hordes they will chant it, **declares** the Sovereign LORD."
32:31 that were killed by the sword, **declares** the Sovereign LORD.
32:32 with those killed by the sword, **declares** the Sovereign LORD."
33:11 Say to them, 'As surely as I live, **declares** the Sovereign LORD,
34:8 As surely as I live, **declares** the Sovereign LORD, because my
34:15 and have them lie down, **declares** the Sovereign LORD.
34:30 the house of Israel, are my people, **declares** the Sovereign LORD.
34:31 are people, and I am your God, **declares** the Sovereign LORD.' "
35:6 therefore as surely as I live, **declares** the Sovereign LORD,
35:11 therefore as surely as I live, **declares** the Sovereign LORD,
36:14 or make your nation childless, **declares** the Sovereign LORD.
36:15 or cause your nation to fall, **declares** the Sovereign LORD.' "
36:23 will know that I am the LORD, **declares** the Sovereign LORD,
36:32 I am not doing this for your sake, **declares** the Sovereign LORD.
37:14 LORD have spoken, and I have done it, **declares** the LORD.' "
38:18 my hot anger will be aroused, **declares** the Sovereign LORD.
38:21 against Gog on all my mountains, **declares** the Sovereign LORD.
39:5 the open field, for I have spoken, **declares** the Sovereign LORD.
39:8 It will surely take place, **declares** the Sovereign LORD.
39:10 and loot those who looted them, **declares** the Sovereign LORD.
39:13 be a memorable day for them, **declares** the Sovereign LORD.
39:20 and soldiers of every kind,' **declares** the Sovereign LORD.
39:29 my Spirit on the house of Israel, **declares** the Sovereign LORD."
43:19 come near to minister before me, **declares** the Sovereign LORD.
43:27 the altar. Then I will accept you, **declares** the Sovereign LORD."
44:12 bear the consequences of their sin, **declares** the Sovereign LORD.
44:15 offer sacrifices of fat and blood, **declares** the Sovereign LORD.
44:27 to offer a sin offering for himself, **declares** the Sovereign LORD.
45:9 Stop dispossessing my people, **declares** the Sovereign LORD.
45:15 to make atonement for the people, **declares** the Sovereign LORD.
47:23 are to give him his inheritance," **declares** the Sovereign LORD.
48:29 and these will be their portions," **declares** the Sovereign LORD.
Hos 2:13 [2:15] after her lovers, but me she forgot," **declares** the LORD.
2:16 [2:18] "In that day," **declares** the LORD, "you will call me 'my
2:21 [2:23] "In that day I will respond," **declares** the LORD—"I will
11:11 I will settle them in their homes," **declares** the LORD.
Joel 2:12 "Even now," **declares** the LORD, "return to me with all your
Am 2:11 Is this not true, people of Israel?" **declares** the LORD.
2:16 bravest warriors will flee naked on that day," **declares** the LORD.
3:10 **declares** the LORD, "who hoard plunder and loot in their
3:13 the house of Jacob," **declares** the Lord, the LORD God Almighty.
3:15 and the mansions will be demolished," **declares** the LORD.
4:3 and you will be cast out toward Harmon," **declares** the LORD.
4:5 for this is what you love to do," **declares** the Sovereign LORD.
4:6 yet you have not returned to me," **declares** the LORD.
4:8 to drink, yet you have not returned to me," **declares** the LORD.
4:9 olive trees, yet you have not returned to me," **declares** the LORD.
4:10 yet you have not returned to me," **declares** the LORD.
4:11 the fire, yet you have not returned to me," **declares** the LORD.
6:8 has sworn by himself—the LORD God Almighty **declares**:
6:14 For the LORD God Almighty **declares**, "I will stir up a nation
8:3 "In that day," **declares** the Sovereign LORD, "the songs in the
8:9 "In that day," **declares** the Sovereign LORD, "I will make the sun
8:11 "The days are coming," **declares** the Sovereign LORD, "when I
9:7 **declares** the LORD. "Did I not bring Israel up from Egypt,
9:8 I will not totally destroy the house of Jacob," **declares** the LORD.
9:12 bear my name," **declares** the LORD, who will do these things.
9:13 "The days are coming," **declares** the LORD, "when the reaper
Ob 1:4 the stars, from there I will bring you down," **declares** the LORD.
1:8 "In that day," **declares** the LORD, "will I not destroy the wise
Mic 4:6 "In that day," **declares** the LORD, "I will gather the lame;
5:10 [5:9] "In that day," **declares** the LORD, "I will destroy your
Na 2:13 [2:14] "I am against you," **declares** the LORD Almighty. "I will
3:5 "I am against you," **declares** the LORD Almighty. "I will lift
Zep 1:2 away everything from the face of the earth," **declares** the LORD.
1:3 I cut off man from the face of the earth," **declares** the LORD.
1:10 "On that day," **declares** the LORD, "a cry will go up from the
2:9 surely as I live," **declares** the LORD Almighty, the God of Israel,
3:8 Therefore wait for me," **declares** the LORD, "for the day I will
Hag 1:9 I blew away. Why?" **declares** the LORD Almighty.
1:13 the LORD to the people: "I am with you," **declares** the LORD.
2:4 now be strong, O Zerubbabel,' **declares** the LORD. 'Be strong,
2:4 all you people of the land,' **declares** the LORD, 'and work.
2:4 'and work. For I am with you,' **declares** the LORD Almighty.
2:8 is mine and the gold is mine,' **declares** the LORD Almighty.
2:9 in this place I will grant peace,' **declares** the LORD Almighty."
2:14 with this people and this nation in my sight,' **declares** the LORD.
2:17 and hail, yet you did not turn to me,' **declares** the LORD.
2:23 " 'On that day,' **declares** the LORD Almighty, 'I will take you,
2:23 my servant Zerubbabel son of Shealtiel,' **declares** the LORD,
2:23 for I have chosen you,' **declares** the LORD Almighty."
Zec 1:3 'Return to me,' **declares** the LORD Almighty, 'and I will return to
1:4 they would not listen or pay attention to me, **declares** the LORD.
1:16 be stretched out over Jerusalem,' **declares** the LORD Almighty.
2:5 [2:9] **declares** the LORD, 'and I will be its glory within.'
2:6 [2:10] Flee from the land of the north," **declares** the LORD,
2:6 [2:10] you to the four winds of heaven," **declares** the LORD.
2:10 [2:14] and I will live among you," **declares** the LORD.
3:9 and I will engrave an inscription on it,' **says** the LORD Almighty,
3:10 to sit under his vine and fig tree,' **declares** the LORD Almighty."
5:4 The LORD Almighty **declares**, 'I will send it out, and it will enter
8:6 but will it seem marvelous to me?" **declares** the LORD Almighty.
8:11 of this people as I did in the past," **declares** the LORD Almighty.
8:17 do not love to swear falsely. I hate all this," **declares** the LORD.
10:12 the LORD and in his name they will walk," **declares** the LORD.
11:6 longer have pity on the people of the land," **declares** the LORD.
12:1 of the earth, and who forms the spirit of man within him, **declares**:
12:4 horse with panic and its rider with madness," **declares** the LORD.
13:2 will be remembered no more," **declares** the LORD Almighty.
13:7 **declares** the LORD Almighty. "Strike the shepherd,
13:8 In the whole land," **declares** the LORD, "two-thirds will be
Mal 1:2 Esau Jacob's brother?" the LORD **says**. "Yet I have loved Jacob,

5537 נָאַף *nāʾap*, v. [31] [→ 5538, 5539; cf. 5677]

commit adultery [7], adulterers [6], committed adultery [5], adulteress [3], adulterer [2], adulterous [2], adultery [2], commits adultery [2], *untranslated* [1], adulteries [1]

Ex 20:14 [A] "*You shall* not **commit adultery**.
Lev 20:10 [A] " 'If a man **commits adultery** with another man's wife—
20:10 [A] **[RPH]** with the wife of his neighbor—both the adulterer
20:10 [A] both the **adulterer** and the adulteress must be put to death.
20:10 [A] both the adulterer and the **adulteress** must be put to death.
Dt 5:18 [A] "*You shall* not **commit adultery**.
Job 24:15 [A] The eye of the **adulterer** watches for dusk; he thinks,
Ps 50:18 [D] you join with him; you throw in your lot with **adulterers**.
Pr 6:32 [A] *a man who* **commits adultery** lacks judgment;
30:20 [D] "This is the way of an **adulteress**: She eats and wipes her
Isa 57:3 [D] of a sorceress, you offspring of **adulterers** and prostitutes!
Jer 3:8 [D] of divorce and sent her away because of all *her* **adulteries**.
3:9 [A] the land and **committed adultery** with stone and wood.
5:7 [A] yet *they* **committed adultery** and thronged to the houses of
7:9 [A] " 'Will you steal and murder, **commit adultery** and perjury,
9:2 [9:1] [D] they *are* all **adulterers**, a crowd of unfaithful people.
23:10 [D] The land is full of **adulterers**; because of the curse the land
23:14 [A] They **commit adultery** and live a lie. They strengthen the
29:23 [D] *they have* **committed adultery** with their neighbors' wives
Eze 16:32 [D] " 'You **adulterous** wife! You prefer strangers to your own
16:38 [A] you to the punishment of *women who* **commit adultery**
23:37 [D] for *they have* **committed adultery** and blood is on their
23:37 [D] *They* **committed adultery** with their idols; they even
23:45 [A] them to the punishment of *women who* **commit adultery**
23:45 [A] because they *are* **adulterous** and blood is on their hands.
Hos 3:1 [D] though she is loved by another and *is an* **adulteress**.
4:2 [A] is only cursing, lying and murder, stealing and **adultery**;
4:13 [D] turn to prostitution and your daughters-in-law *to* **adultery**.
4:14 [D] nor your daughters-in-law when *they* **commit adultery**,
7:4 [D] They *are* all **adulterers**, burning like an oven whose fire the
Mal 3:5 [D] quick to testify against sorcerers, **adulterers** and perjurers,

5538 נַאֲפוּפִים *naʾapûpîm*, n.[m.pl.]. [1] [√ 5537]

unfaithfulness [1]

Hos 2:2 [2:4] her face and the **unfaithfulness** from between her breasts.

5539 נִאֻפִים ni'upîm, n.[m.]. [2] [√ 5537]
adulteries [1], adultery [1]
Jer 13:27 your **adulteries** and lustful neighings, your shameless prostitution!
Eze 23:43 I said about the one worn out by **adultery**, 'Now let them use her

5540 נָאַץ nā'aṣ, v. [24] [→ 5541, 5542]
spurned [5], despise [4], made show utter contempt [+906+5540] [2], revile [2], treated with contempt [2], despised [1], is blasphemed [1], rejected [1], rejecting [1], reviled [1], reviles [1], spurns [1], treat with contempt [1], treating with contempt [1]
Nu 14:11 [D] "How long *will* these people **treat** me **with contempt**?
14:23 [D] No one *who has* **treated** me **with contempt** will ever see it.
16:30 [D] that these men *have* **treated** the LORD **with contempt**."
Dt 31:20 [D] and worship them, **rejecting** me and breaking my covenant.
32:19 [A] The LORD saw this and **rejected** them because he was
1Sa 2:17 [D] they *were* **treating** the LORD's offering **with contempt**.
2Sa 12:14 [D] *you have* **made** the enemies of the LORD **show utter contempt** [+906+5540],
12:14 [D] *you have* **made** the enemies of the LORD **show utter contempt** [+906+5540],
Ps 10:3 [D] of his heart; he blesses the greedy and **reviles** the LORD.
10:13 [D] Why *does* the wicked man **revile** God? Why does he say to
74:10 [D] mock you, O God? *Will* the foe **revile** your name forever?
74:18 [D] O LORD, how foolish people *have* **reviled** your name.
107:11 [A] the words of God and **despised** the counsel of the Most High.
Pr 1:30 [A] they would not accept my advice and **spurned** my rebuke,
5:12 [A] "How I hated discipline! How my heart **spurned** correction!
15:5 [A] A fool **spurns** his father's discipline, but whoever heeds
Isa 1:4 [D] *they have* **spurned** the Holy One of Israel and turned their
5:24 [D] and **spurned** the word of the Holy One of Israel.
52:5 [F] "And all day long my name **is** constantly **blasphemed**.
60:14 [D] all *who* **despise** you will bow down at your feet and will call
Jer 14:21 [A] For the sake of your name *do* not **despise** us; do not dishonor
23:17 [D] They keep saying to *those who* **despise** me, 'The LORD
33:24 [A] So *they* **despise** my people and no longer regard them as a
La 2:6 [A] in his fierce anger *he has* **spurned** both king and priest.

5541 נְאָצָה ne'āṣâ, n.f. [2] [√ 5540]
disgrace [2]
2Ki 19:3 This day is a day of distress and rebuke and **disgrace**, as when
Isa 37:3 This day is a day of distress and rebuke and **disgrace**, as when

5542 נֶאָצָה ne'āṣâ, n.f. [3] [√ 5540]
blasphemies [2], contemptible things [1]
Ne 9:18 you up out of Egypt,' or when they committed awful **blasphemies**.
9:26 to turn them back to you; they committed awful **blasphemies**.
Eze 35:12 **contemptible things** you have said against the mountains of Israel.

5543 נָאַק nā'aq, v. [2] [→ 5544; cf. 650]
groan [+5544] [1], groans [1]
Job 24:12 [A] *The* **groans** of the dying *rise* from the city, and the souls of
Eze 30:24 [A] *he will* **groan** [+5544] before him like a mortally wounded

5544 נְאָקָה ne'āqâ, n.f. [4] [√ 5543; cf. 650]
groaning [2], groan [+5543] [1], groaned [1]
Ex 2:24 God heard their **groaning** and he remembered his covenant with
6:5 Moreover, I have heard the **groaning** *of* the Israelites,
Jdg 2:18 for the LORD had compassion on them as they **groaned** under
Eze 30:24 *he will* **groan** [+5543] before him like a mortally wounded man.

5545 נֵאַר nā'ar, v. [2]
abandoned [1], renounced [1]
Ps 89:39 [89:40] [D] *You have* **renounced** the covenant with your
La 2:7 [D] The Lord has rejected his altar and **abandoned** his sanctuary.

5546 נֹב nōb, n.pr.loc. [6]
Nob [6]
1Sa 21:1 [21:2] David went to **Nob**, to Ahimelech the priest. Ahimelech
22:9 "I saw the son of Jesse come to Ahimelech son of Ahitub at **Nob**.
22:11 who were the priests at **Nob**, and they all came to the king.
22:19 He also put to the sword **Nob**, the town of the priests, with its men
Ne 11:32 in Anathoth, **Nob** and Ananiah,
Isa 10:32 This day they will halt at **Nob**; they will shake their fist at the

5547 נָבָא nābā', v.den. [115] [√ 5566; Ar 10451]
prophesy [47], prophesying [28], prophesied [26], prophesies [8], *untranslated* [2], acts like a prophet [1], frantic prophesying [1], poses as a prophet [1], prophetic [1]
Nu 11:25 [F] on them, *they* **prophesied**, but they did not do so again.
11:26 [F] Spirit also rested on them, and *they* **prophesied** in the camp.
11:27 [F] "Eldad and Medad *are* **prophesying** in the camp."
1Sa 10:5 [F] being played before them, and they *will be* **prophesying**.
10:6 [F] come upon you in power, and *you will* **prophesy** with them;
10:10 [F] came upon him in power, and *he* joined in their **prophesying**.
10:11 [C] known him saw him **prophesying** with the prophets,
10:13 [F] After Saul stopped **prophesying**, he went to the high place.
18:10 [F] *He was* **prophesying** in his house, while David was playing
19:20 [C] when they saw a group of prophets **prophesying**,
19:20 [F] of God came upon Saul's men and they also **prophesied**.
19:21 [F] told about it, and he sent more men, and they **prophesied** too.
19:21 [F] Saul sent men a third time, and they also **prophesied**.
19:23 [F] and he walked along **prophesying** until he came to Naioth.
19:24 [F] off his robes and also **prophesied** in Samuel's presence.
1Ki 18:29 [F] *they continued their* **frantic prophesying** until the time for
22:8 [F] because *he* never **prophesies** anything good about me,
22:10 [F] of Samaria, with all the prophets **prophesying** before them.
22:12 [C] All the other prophets *were* **prophesying** the same thing.
22:18 [F] "Didn't I tell you that *he* never **prophesies** anything good
1Ch 25:1 [C] and Jeduthun for the ministry of **prophesying**, [K 5566]
25:2 [C] of Asaph, who **prophesied** under the king's supervision.
25:3 [C] who **prophesied**, using the harp in thanking and praising the
2Ch 18:7 [F] he never **prophesies** anything good about me, but always
18:9 [F] of Samaria, with all the prophets **prophesying** before them.
18:11 [C] All the other prophets *were* **prophesying** the same thing.
18:17 [F] that *he* never **prophesies** anything good about me, but only
20:37 [F] Eliezer son of Dodavahu of Mareshah **prophesied** against
Jer 2:8 [C] The prophets **prophesied** by Baal, following worthless idols.
5:31 [C] The prophets **prophesy** lies, the priests rule by their own
11:21 [C] '*Do* not **prophesy** in the name of the LORD or you will die
14:14 [C] said to me, "The prophets *are* **prophesying** lies in my name.
14:14 [F] They *are* **prophesying** to you false visions, divinations,
14:15 [C] says about the prophets who *are* **prophesying** in my name:
14:16 [C] the people they *are* **prophesying** to will be thrown out into
19:14 [C] from Topheth, where the LORD had sent him to **prophesy**,
20:1 [C] of the LORD, heard Jeremiah **prophesying** these things,
20:6 [C] and all your friends to whom *you have* **prophesied** lies.' "
23:13 [C] *They* **prophesied** by Baal and led my people Israel astray.
23:16 [C] "Do not listen to what the prophets *are* **prophesying** to you;
23:21 [C] I did not speak to them, yet they *have* **prophesied**.
23:25 [C] "I have heard what the prophets say who **prophesy** lies in my
23:26 [C] **[RPH]** who prophesy the delusions of their own minds?
23:32 [C] Indeed, I am against *those who* **prophesy** false dreams,"
25:13 [C] this book and **prophesied** *by* Jeremiah against all the nations.
25:30 [C] "Now **prophesy** all these words against them and say to
26:9 [C] Why *do you* **prophesy** in the LORD's name that this house
26:11 [C] to death because *he has* **prophesied** against this city.
26:12 [C] LORD sent me to **prophesy** against this house and this city
26:18 [C] "Micah of Moresheth **prophesied** in the days of Hezekiah
26:20 [F] another man *who* **prophesied** in the name of the LORD;
26:20 [C] *he* **prophesied** the same things against this city and this land
27:10 [C] They **prophesy** lies to you that will only serve to remove you
27:14 [C] the king of Babylon,' for they *are* **prophesying** lies to you.
27:15 [C] 'They *are* **prophesying** lies in my name. Therefore, I will
27:15 [C] both you and the prophets who **prophesy** to you.' "
27:16 [C] Do not listen to the prophets **[RPH]** who say, 'Very soon
27:16 [C] back from Babylon.' They *are* **prophesying** lies to you.
28:6 [C] May the LORD fulfill the words *you have* **prophesied** by
28:8 [C] me *have* **prophesied** war, disaster and plague against many
28:9 [C] the prophet who **prophesies** peace will be recognized as one
29:9 [C] They *are* **prophesying** lies to you in my name. I have not
29:21 [C] of Maaseiah, who *are* **prophesying** lies to you in my name:
29:26 [F] you should put any madman *who* **acts like a prophet** into the
29:27 [F] from Anathoth, who **poses as a prophet** among you?
29:31 [C] Because Shemaiah *has* **prophesied** to you, even though I did
32:3 [C] him there, saying, "Why *do* you **prophesy** as you do?
37:19 [C] Where are your prophets who **prophesied** to you, 'The king
Eze 4:7 [C] siege of Jerusalem and with bared arm **prophesy** against her.
6:2 [C] face against the mountains of Israel; **prophesy** against them
11:4 [C] Therefore **prophesy** against them; prophesy, son of man."
11:4 [C] Therefore prophesy against them; **prophesy**, son of man."
11:13 [C] Now as I *was* **prophesying**, Pelatiah son of Benaiah died.
12:27 [C] years from now, and he **prophesies** about the distant future.'
13:2 [C] **prophesy** against the prophets of Israel who are now
13:2 [C] against the prophets of Israel who *are now* **prophesying**.
13:16 [C] those prophets of Israel who **prophesied** to Jerusalem
13:17 [F] of your people who **prophesy** out of their own imagination.
13:17 [C] out of their own imagination. **Prophesy** against them

Eze 20:46 [21:2] [C] and **prophesy** against the forest of the southland.
21: 2 [21:7] [C] the sanctuary. **Prophesy** against the land of Israel
21: 9 [21:14] [C] "Son of man, **prophesy** and say, 'This is what the
21:14 [21:19] [C] of man, **prophesy** and strike your hands together.
21:28 [21:33] [C] "And you, son of man, **prophesy** and say, 'This is
25: 2 [C] your face against the Ammonites and **prophesy** against them.
28:21 [C] of man, set your face against Sidon; **prophesy** against her
29: 2 [C] of Egypt and **prophesy** against him and against all Egypt.
30: 2 [C] "Son of man, **prophesy** and say: 'This is what the Sovereign
34: 2 [C] "Son of man, **prophesy** against the shepherds of Israel;
34: 2 [C] against the shepherds of Israel; **prophesy** and say to them:
35: 2 [C] set your face against Mount Seir; **prophesy** against it
36: 1 [C] "Son of man, **prophesy** to the mountains of Israel and say,
36: 3 [C] Therefore **prophesy** and say, 'This is what the Sovereign
36: 6 [C] Therefore **prophesy** concerning the land of Israel and say to
37: 4 [C] to me, "**Prophesy** to these bones and say to them, 'Dry bones,
37: 7 [C] So *I* **prophesied** as I was commanded. And as I was
37: 7 [C] as I *was* **prophesying**, there was a noise, a rattling sound,
37: 9 [C] he said to me, "**Prophesy** to the breath; prophesy, son of
37: 9 [C] **prophesy**, son of man, and say to it, 'This is what the
37:10 [C] So *I* **prophesied** as he commanded me, and breath entered
37:12 [C] Therefore **prophesy** and say to them: 'This is what the
38: 2 [C] chief prince of Meshech and Tubal; **prophesy** against him
38:14 [C] "Therefore, son of man, **prophesy** and say to Gog: 'This is
38:17 [C] At that time they **prophesied** for years that I would bring you
39: 1 [C] "Son of man, **prophesy** against Gog and say: 'This is what
Joel 2:28 [3:1] [C] Your sons and daughters *will* **prophesy**, your old men
Am 2:12 [C] drink wine and commanded the prophets not *to* **prophesy**.
3: 8 [C] The Sovereign LORD has spoken—who *can* but **prophesy**?
7:12 [C] Earn your bread there and *do your* **prophesying** there.
7:13 [C] Don't **prophesy** anymore at Bethel, because this is the king's
7:15 [C] the flock and said to me, 'Go, **prophesy** to my people Israel.'
7:16 [C] You say, " '*Do* not **prophesy** against Israel, and stop
Zec 13: 3 [C] if anyone still **prophesies**, his father and mother, to whom he
13: 3 [C] When he **prophesies**, his own parents will stab him.
13: 4 [C] "On that day every prophet will be ashamed of his **prophetic**

5548 נָבַב *nābab*, v. Not used in NIV/BHS [→ 5554]

5549 נְבוֹ[1] n^{e}*bô*[1], n.pr.loc. [11]

Nebo [11]

Nu 32: 3 Jazer, Nimrah, Heshbon, Elealeh, Sebam, **Nebo** and Beon—
32:38 as well as **Nebo** and Baal Meon (these names were changed)
33:47 and camped in the mountains of Abarim, near **Nebo**.
Dt 32:49 "Go up into the Abarim Range to Mount **Nebo** in Moab, across
34: 1 Moses climbed Mount **Nebo** from the plains of Moab to the top of
1Ch 5: 8 They settled in the area from Aroer to **Nebo** and Baal Meon.
Ezr 2:29 of **Nebo** 52
Ne 7:33 of the other **Nebo** 52
Isa 15: 2 to its high places to weep; Moab wails over **Nebo** and Medeba.
Jer 48: 1 the God of Israel, says: "Woe to **Nebo**, for it will be ruined.
48:22 to Dibon, **Nebo** and Beth Diblathaim,

5550 נְבוֹ[2] n^{e}*bô*[2], n.pr.[m.]. [1] [→ 5551, 5589; *also used with compound proper names*]

Nebo [1]

Isa 46: 1 Bel bows down, **Nebo** stoops low; their idols are borne by beasts

5551 נְבוֹ[3] n^{e}*bô*[3], n.pr.m. [1] [√ 5550]

Nebo [1]

Ezr 10:43 From the descendants of **Nebo**: Jeiel, Mattithiah, Zabad, Zebina,

5552 נְבוּ שַׂר־סְכִים n^{e}*bû śar-s*^{e}*kîm*, n.pr.m. [1] [√ 5550 + 8569; cf. 8593]

Nebo-Sarsekim [1]

Jer 39: 3 Nergal-Sharezer of Samgar, **Nebo-Sarsekim** a chief officer,

5553 נְבוּאָה n^{e}*bû'â*, n.f. [3] [√ 5566; Ar 10452]

prophecy [2], prophesied [+1819] [1]

2Ch 9:29 in the **prophecy** *of* Ahijah the Shilonite and in the visions of Iddo
15: 8 these words and the **prophecy** of Azariah son of Oded the prophet,
Ne 6:12 but that *he had* **prophesied** [+1819] against me because Tobiah

5554 נָבוּב *nābûb*, n.m. *or* v.ptcp. [4] [√ 5548]

hollow [3], witless [1]

Ex 27: 8 Make the altar **hollow**, out of boards. It is to be made just as you
38: 7 of the altar for carrying it. They made it **hollow**, *out of* boards.
Job 11:12 a **witless** man can no more become wise than a wild donkey's colt
Jer 52:21 cubits in circumference; each was four fingers thick, and **hollow**.

5555 נְבוּזַרְאֲדָן n^{e}*bûzar*^{a}*dān*, נְבוּזַר־אֲדָן n^{e}*bûzar-*^{a}*dān*, n.pr.m. [15] [√ 5550 + 2445]

Nebuzaradan [15]

2Ki 25: 8 **Nebuzaradan** commander of the imperial guard, an official of the
25:11 **Nebuzaradan** the commander of the guard carried into exile the
25:20 **Nebuzaradan** the commander took them all and brought them to
Jer 39: 9 **Nebuzaradan** commander of the imperial guard carried into exile
39:10 **Nebuzaradan** the commander of the guard left behind in the land
39:11 Jeremiah through **Nebuzaradan** commander of the imperial guard:
39:13 So **Nebuzaradan** the commander of the guard, Nebushazban a
40: 1 The word came to Jeremiah from the LORD after **Nebuzaradan**
41:10 over whom **Nebuzaradan** commander of the imperial guard had
43: 6 the king's daughters whom **Nebuzaradan** commander of the
52:12 **Nebuzaradan** commander of the imperial guard, who served the
52:15 **Nebuzaradan** the commander of the guard carried into exile some
52:16 **Nebuzaradan** left behind the rest of the poorest people of the land
52:26 **Nebuzaradan** the commander took them all and brought them to
52:30 745 Jews taken into exile by **Nebuzaradan** the commander of the

5556 נְבוּכַדְנֶאצַּר n^{e}*bûkadne'ṣṣar*, נְבוּכַדְנֶצַּר n^{e}*bûkadneṣṣar*, נְבוּכַדְנֶצּוֹר n^{e}*bûkadneṣṣôr*, n.pr.m. [27] [√ 5550; Ar 10453]

Nebuchadnezzar [26], his[s] [1]

2Ki 24: 1 **Nebuchadnezzar** king of Babylon invaded the land,
24:10 At that time the officers of **Nebuchadnezzar** king of Babylon
24:11 **Nebuchadnezzar** himself came up to the city while his officers
25: 1 **Nebuchadnezzar** king of Babylon marched against Jerusalem with
25: 8 in the nineteenth year of **Nebuchadnezzar** king of Babylon,
25:22 **Nebuchadnezzar** king of Babylon appointed Gedaliah son of
1Ch 6:15 [5:41] and Jerusalem into exile by the hand of **Nebuchadnezzar**.
2Ch 36: 6 **Nebuchadnezzar** king of Babylon attacked him and bound him
36: 7 **Nebuchadnezzar** also took to Babylon articles from the temple of
36:10 King **Nebuchadnezzar** sent for him and brought him to Babylon,
36:13 He also rebelled against King **Nebuchadnezzar**, who had made
Ezr 1: 7 which **Nebuchadnezzar** had carried away from Jerusalem
2: 1 whom **Nebuchadnezzar** king of Babylon had taken captive to
Ne 7: 6 **Nebuchadnezzar** king of Babylon had taken captive (they
Est 2: 6 into exile from Jerusalem by **Nebuchadnezzar** king of Babylon,
Jer 27: 6 countries over to my servant **Nebuchadnezzar** king of Babylon;
27: 8 or kingdom will not serve **Nebuchadnezzar** king of Babylon
27:20 which **Nebuchadnezzar** king of Babylon did not take away when
28: 3 house that **Nebuchadnezzar** king of Babylon removed from here
28:11 'In the same way will I break the yoke of **Nebuchadnezzar** king of
28:14 nations to make them serve **Nebuchadnezzar** king of Babylon,
29: 1 all the other people **Nebuchadnezzar** had carried into exile from
29: 3 whom Zedekiah king of Judah sent to King **Nebuchadnezzar** in
Da 1: 1 **Nebuchadnezzar** king of Babylon came to Jerusalem and besieged
1:18 them in, the chief official presented them to **Nebuchadnezzar**.
2: 1 In the second year of **his**[s] reign, Nebuchadnezzar had dreams;
2: 1 In the second year of his reign, **Nebuchadnezzar** had dreams;

5557 נְבוּכַדְרֶאצַּר n^{e}*bûkadre'ṣṣar*, נְבוּכַדְרֶאצּוֹר *nebûkadre'ṣṣôr*, n.pr.m. [33] [√ 5550; Ar 10453]

Nebuchadnezzar [31], his[s] [+4200] [1], Nebuchadnezzar's [+4200] [1]

Jer 21: 2 because **Nebuchadnezzar** king of Babylon is attacking us.
21: 7 to **Nebuchadnezzar** king of Babylon and to their enemies who
22:25 to **Nebuchadnezzar** king of Babylon and to the Babylonians.
24: 1 from Jerusalem to Babylon by **Nebuchadnezzar** king of Babylon,
25: 1 which was the first year of **Nebuchadnezzar** king of Babylon.
25: 9 of the north and my servant **Nebuchadnezzar** king of Babylon,"
29:21 "I will hand them over to **Nebuchadnezzar** king of Babylon,
32: 1 king of Judah, which was the eighteenth year of **Nebuchadnezzar**.
32:28 over to the Babylonians and to **Nebuchadnezzar** king of Babylon,
34: 1 While **Nebuchadnezzar** king of Babylon and all his army
35:11 But when **Nebuchadnezzar** king of Babylon invaded this land,
37: 1 was made king of Judah by **Nebuchadnezzar** king of Babylon;
39: 1 **Nebuchadnezzar** king of Babylon marched against Jerusalem with
39: 5 took him to **Nebuchadnezzar** king of Babylon at Riblah in the
39:11 Now **Nebuchadnezzar** king of Babylon had given these orders
43:10 I will send for my servant **Nebuchadnezzar** king of Babylon,
44:30 just as I handed Zedekiah king of Judah over to **Nebuchadnezzar**
46: 2 **Nebuchadnezzar** king of Babylon in the fourth year of Jehoiakim
46:13 the coming of **Nebuchadnezzar** king of Babylon to attack Egypt:
46:26 their lives, to **Nebuchadnezzar** king of Babylon and his officers.
49:28 of Hazor, which **Nebuchadnezzar** king of Babylon attacked:
49:30 "**Nebuchadnezzar** king of Babylon has plotted against you;
50:17 the last to crush his bones was **Nebuchadnezzar** king of Babylon."
51:34 "**Nebuchadnezzar** king of Babylon has devoured us, he has
52: 4 **Nebuchadnezzar** king of Babylon marched against Jerusalem with
52:12 in the nineteenth year of **Nebuchadnezzar** king of Babylon,

Jer 52:28 This is the number of the people **Nebuchadnezzar** carried into
52:29 in **Nebuchadnezzar's** [+4200] eighteenth year, 832 people from
52:30 in **his**[s] [+4200] twenty-third year, 745 Jews taken into exile by
Eze 26: 7 From the north I am going to bring against Tyre **Nebuchadnezzar**
29:18 **Nebuchadnezzar** king of Babylon drove his army in a hard
29:19 I am going to give Egypt to **Nebuchadnezzar** king of Babylon,
30:10 hordes of Egypt by the hand of **Nebuchadnezzar** king of Babylon.

5558 נְבוּשַׁזְבָּן *nebûšazbān*, נְבוּשַׁז־בָּן *nebûšaz-bān*, n.pr.m. [1] [√ 5550]

Nebushazban [1]

Jer 39:13 **Nebushazban** a chief officer, Nergal-Sharezer a high official

5559 נָבוֹת *nābôt*, n.pr.m. [22]

Naboth [17], Naboth's [4], he[s] [1]

1Ki 21: 1 incident involving a vineyard belonging to **Naboth** the Jezreelite.
21: 2 Ahab said to **Naboth**, "Let me have your vineyard to use for a
21: 3 **Naboth** replied, "The LORD forbid that I should give you the
21: 4 sullen and angry because **Naboth** the Jezreelite had said,
21: 6 He answered her, "Because I said to **Naboth** the Jezreelite,
21: 7 Cheer up. I'll get you the vineyard of **Naboth** the Jezreelite."
21: 8 them to the elders and nobles who lived in **Naboth's** city with him.
21: 9 of fasting and seat **Naboth** in a prominent place among the people.
21:12 and seated **Naboth** in a prominent place among the people.
21:13 and brought charges against **Naboth** before the people,
21:13 the people, saying, "**Naboth** has cursed both God and the king."
21:14 they sent word to Jezebel: "**Naboth** has been stoned and is dead."
21:15 As soon as Jezebel heard that **Naboth** had been stoned to death,
21:15 take possession of the vineyard of **Naboth** the Jezreelite that he
21:15 that he refused to sell you. **He**[s] is no longer alive, but dead."
21:16 When Ahab heard that **Naboth** was dead, he got up and went down
21:16 he got up and went down to take possession of **Naboth's** vineyard.
21:18 He is now in **Naboth's** vineyard, where he has gone to take
21:19 In the place where dogs licked up **Naboth's** blood, dogs will lick
2Ki 9:21 They met him at the plot of ground that had belonged to **Naboth**
9:25 and throw him on the field that belonged to **Naboth** the Jezreelite.
9:26 'Yesterday I saw the blood of **Naboth** and the blood of his sons,

5560 נָבַח *nābaḥ*, v. [1] [→ 5561?]

bark [1]

Isa 56:10 [A] they are all mute dogs, they cannot **bark**; they lie around

5561 ¹נֹבַח *nōbaḥ*[1], n.pr.m. [1] [√ 5560?]

Nobah [1]

Nu 32:42 And **Nobah** captured Kenath and its surrounding settlements

5562 ²נֹבַח *nōbaḥ*[2], n.pr.loc. [2]

Nobah [2]

Nu 32:42 and its surrounding settlements and called it **Nobah** after himself.
Jdg 8:11 Gideon went up by the route of the nomads east of **Nobah**

5563 נִבְחַז *nibḥaz*, n.pr.[m.]. [1]

Nibhaz [1]

2Ki 17:31 the Avvites made **Nibhaz** and Tartak, and the Sepharvites burned

5564 נָבַט *nābaṭ*, v. [69] [→ 4438, 5565]

look [20], looked [7], consider [6], see [3], tolerate [3], gaze [2], have regard for [2], look down [2], look up [2], looks [2], seen [2], detect [1], esteem [1], have regard for [+4200] [1], let look [1], look around [1], look on [1], look with favor [+7156] [1], looked around [1], looked over [1], looks down [1], observe [1], sees [1], stare [1], viewed [1], views [1], watch [1], watches over [1], watching [1]

Ge 15: 5 [G] and said, "**Look up** at the heavens and count the stars—
19:17 [G] Don't **look** back, and don't stop anywhere in the plain!
19:26 [G] But Lot's wife **looked** back, and she became a pillar of salt.
Ex 3: 6 [G] Moses hid his face, because he was afraid *to* **look** at God.
33: 8 [G] to their tents, **watching** Moses until he entered the tent.
Nu 12: 8 [G] clearly and not in riddles; *he* **sees** the form of the LORD.
21: 9 [G] anyone was bitten by a snake and **looked** at the bronze snake,
23:21 [G] "No misfortune *is* **seen** in Jacob, no misery observed in
1Sa 2:32 [G] *you will* **see** distress in my dwelling. Although good will be
16: 7 [G] "*Do* not **consider** his appearance or his height, for I have
17:42 [G] He **looked** David **over** and saw that he was only a boy, ruddy
24: 8 [24:9] [G] When Saul **looked** behind him, David bowed down
1Ki 18:43 [G] "Go and **look** toward the sea," he told his servant. And he
18:43 [G] the sea," he told his servant. And he went up and **looked**.
19: 6 [G] *He* **looked around**, and there by his head was a cake of
2Ki 3:14 [G] king of Judah, *I would* not **look** at you or even notice you.
1Ch 21:21 [G] David approached, and when Araunah **looked** and saw him,
Job 6:19 [G] The caravans of Tema **look** for water, the traveling
28:24 [G] for he **views** the ends of the earth and sees everything under
35: 5 [G] **Look up** *at* the heavens and see; gaze at the clouds so high
36:25 [G] All mankind has seen it; men **gaze** *on* it from afar.
39:29 [G] From there he seeks out his food; his eyes **detect** it from afar.
Ps 10:14 [G] do see trouble and grief; *you* **consider** it to take it in hand.
13: 3 [13:4] [G] **Look** *on* me and answer, O LORD my God.
22:17 [22:18] [G] count all my bones; people **stare** and gloat over me.
33:13 [G] From heaven the LORD **looks down** and sees all mankind;
34: 5 [34:6] [G] *Those who* **look** to him are radiant; their faces are
74:20 [G] **Have regard** [+4200] **for** your covenant, because haunts of
80:14 [80:15] [G] O God Almighty! **Look down** from heaven and see!
84: 9 [84:10] [G] **look** [+7156] **with favor** *on* your anointed one.
91: 8 [G] *You will* only **observe** with your eyes and see the
92:11 [92:12] [G] My eyes *have* **seen** the defeat of my adversaries;
94: 9 [G] the ear not hear? *Does he* who formed the eye not **see**?
102:19 [102:20] [G] on high, from heaven *he* **viewed** the earth,
104:32 [G] he *who* **looks** at the earth, and it trembles, who touches the
119: 6 [G] I would not be put to shame when I **consider** all your
119:15 [G] I meditate on your precepts and **consider** your ways.
119:18 [G] Open my eyes that *I may* **see** wonderful things in your law.
142: 4 [142:5] [G] **Look** *to* my right and see; no one is concerned for
Pr 4:25 [G] **Let** your eyes **look** straight ahead, fix your gaze directly
Isa 5:12 [G] but *they* **have** no **regard for** the deeds of the LORD,
5:30 [D] if *one* **looks** at the land, he will see darkness and distress;
8:22 [G] Then *they will* **look** toward the earth and see only distress
18: 4 [G] will remain quiet and *will* **look on** from my dwelling place,
22: 8 [G] *you* **looked** in that day to the weapons in the Palace of the
22:11 [G] *you did* not **look** to the One who made it, or have regard for
38:11 [G] no longer *will I* **look** *on* mankind, or be with those who now
42:18 [G] "Hear, you deaf; **look**, *you* blind, and see!
51: 1 [G] **Look** to the rock from which you were cut and to the quarry
51: 2 [G] **look** to Abraham, your father, and to Sarah, who gave you
51: 6 [G] Lift up your eyes to the heavens, **look** at the earth beneath;
63: 5 [G] *I* **looked**, but there was no one to help, I was appalled that no
63:15 [G] **Look down** from heaven and see from your lofty throne,
64: 9 [64:8] [G] **look** *upon* us, we pray, for we are all your people.
66: 2 [G] "This is the one *I* **esteem**: he who is humble and contrite in
La 1:11 [G] "Look, O LORD, and **consider**, for I am despised."
1:12 [G] nothing to you, all you who pass by? **Look around** and see.
2:20 [G] "Look, O LORD, and **consider**: Whom have you ever
3:63 [G] **Look** *at* them! Sitting or standing, they mock me in their
4:16 [G] himself has scattered them; he no longer **watches over** them.
5: 1 [G] what has happened to us; **look**, and see our disgrace.
Am 5:22 [G] choice fellowship offerings, *I will* **have** no **regard for** them.
Jnh 2: 4 [2:5] [G] yet I will **look** again toward your holy temple.'
Hab 1: 3 [G] Why *do you* **tolerate** wrong? Destruction and violence are
1: 5 [G] "Look at the nations and **watch**—and be utterly amazed. For
1:13 [G] eyes are too pure to look on evil; you cannot **tolerate** wrong.
1:13 [G] tolerate wrong. Why then *do you* **tolerate** the treacherous?
2:15 [G] till they are drunk, so that *he can* **gaze** on their naked bodies.
Zec 12:10 [G] *They will* **look** on me, the one they have pierced, and they

5565 נְבָט *nebāṭ*, n.pr.m. [25] [√ 5564]

Nebat [25]

1Ki 11:26 Also, Jeroboam son of **Nebat** rebelled against the king. He was one
12: 2 When Jeroboam son of **Nebat** heard this (he was still in Egypt,
12:15 spoken to Jeroboam son of **Nebat** through Ahijah the Shilonite.
15: 1 In the eighteenth year of the reign of Jeroboam son of **Nebat**,
16: 3 and I will make your house like that of Jeroboam son of **Nebat**.
16:26 He walked in all the ways of Jeroboam son of **Nebat** and in his sin,
16:31 considered it trivial to commit the sins of Jeroboam son of **Nebat**,
21:22 I will make your house like that of Jeroboam son of **Nebat**
22:52 [22:53] and mother and in the ways of Jeroboam son of **Nebat**,
2Ki 3: 3 Nevertheless he clung to the sins of Jeroboam son of **Nebat**,
9: 9 make the house of Ahab like the house of Jeroboam son of **Nebat**
10:29 he did not turn away from the sins of Jeroboam son of **Nebat**,
13: 2 of the LORD by following the sins of Jeroboam son of **Nebat**,
13:11 did not turn away from any of the sins of Jeroboam son of **Nebat**,
14:24 did not turn away from any of the sins of Jeroboam son of **Nebat**,
15: 9 He did not turn away from the sins of Jeroboam son of **Nebat**,
15:18 reign he did not turn away from the sins of Jeroboam son of **Nebat**,
15:24 He did not turn away from the sins of Jeroboam son of **Nebat**,
15:28 He did not turn away from the sins of Jeroboam son of **Nebat**,
17:21 the house of David, they made Jeroboam son of **Nebat** their king.
23:15 the altar at Bethel, the high place made by Jeroboam son of **Nebat**,
2Ch 9:29 in the visions of Iddo the seer concerning Jeroboam son of **Nebat**?
10: 2 When Jeroboam son of **Nebat** heard this (he was in Egypt,
10:15 spoken to Jeroboam son of **Nebat** through Ahijah the Shilonite.
13: 6 Yet Jeroboam son of **Nebat**, an official of Solomon son of David,

5566 נָבִיא ***nābîʾ***, n.m. [315 / 314] [→ 5547, 5553, 5567; Ar 10455]

prophet [152], prophets [150], *untranslated* [1], he[s] [+2021+3758] [1], him[s] [+2021+3759] [1], his[s] [+2021] [1], his[s] own [+2021+2021+2418] [1], one[s] [+2021] [1], prophecy [1], prophesy [1], prophet's [1], them[s] [+2021] [1], these men[s] [+1201+2021] [1], those who prophesy [1]

Ge 20: 7 for he is a **prophet**, and he will pray for you and you will live.
Ex 7: 1 like God to Pharaoh, and your brother Aaron will be your **prophet**.
Nu 11:29 I wish that all the LORD's people were **prophets** and that the
12: 6 "When a **prophet** *of* the LORD is *among* you, I reveal myself to
Dt 13: 1 [13:2] If a **prophet**, or one who foretells by dreams, appears
13: 3 [13:4] you must not listen to the words of that **prophet**
13: 5 [13:6] That **prophet** or dreamer must be put to death, because he
18:15 The LORD your God will raise up for you a **prophet** like me
18:18 I will raise up for them a **prophet** like you from among their
18:20 a **prophet** who presumes to speak in my name anything I have not
18:20 or a **prophet** who speaks in the name of other gods, must be put to
18:22 If what a **prophet** proclaims in the name of the LORD does not
18:22 That **prophet** has spoken presumptuously. Do not be afraid of him.
34:10 Since then, no **prophet** has risen in Israel like Moses,
Jdg 6: 8 he sent them a **prophet**, who said, "This is what the LORD,
1Sa 3:20 recognized that Samuel was attested as a **prophet** of the LORD.
9: 9 to the seer," because the **prophet** of today used to be called a seer.)
10: 5 you will meet a procession of **prophets** coming down from the
10:10 When they arrived at Gibeah, a procession of **prophets** met him;
10:11 had formerly known him saw him prophesying with the **prophets**,
10:11 happened to the son of Kish? Is Saul also among the **prophets**?"
10:12 So it became a saying: "Is Saul also among the **prophets**?"
19:20 when they saw a group of **prophets** prophesying, with Samuel
19:24 This is why people say, "Is Saul also among the **prophets**?"
22: 5 But the **prophet** Gad said to David, "Do not stay in the stronghold.
28: 6 the LORD did not answer him by dreams or Urim or **prophets**.
28:15 He no longer answers me, either by **prophets** or by dreams.
2Sa 7: 2 he said to Nathan the **prophet**, "Here I am, living in a palace of
12:25 he sent word through Nathan the **prophet** to name him Jedidiah.
24:11 the word of the LORD had come to Gad the **prophet**,
1Ki 1: 8 Nathan the **prophet**, Shimei and Rei and David's special guard did
1:10 he did not invite Nathan the **prophet** or Benaiah or the special
1:22 she was still speaking with the king, Nathan the **prophet** arrived.
1:23 they told the king, "Nathan the **prophet** is here." So he went
1:32 the priest, Nathan the **prophet** and Benaiah son of Jehoiada."
1:34 the priest and Nathan the **prophet** anoint him king over Israel.
1:38 So Zadok the priest, Nathan the **prophet**, Benaiah son of Jehoiada,
1:44 Nathan the **prophet**, Benaiah son of Jehoiada, the Kerethites
1:45 and Nathan the **prophet** have anointed him king at Gihon.
11:29 Ahijah the **prophet** of Shiloh met him on the way, wearing a new
13:11 Now there was a certain old **prophet** living in Bethel, whose sons
13:18 The old prophet answered, "I too am a **prophet**, as you are.
13:20 the word of the LORD came to the old **prophet** who had brought
13:23 the **prophet** who had brought him back saddled his donkey for
13:25 they went and reported it in the city where the old **prophet** lived.
13:26 When the **prophet** who had brought him back from his journey
13:29 So the **prophet** picked up the body of the man of God, laid it on
13:29 brought it back to **his**[s] [+2021+2021+2418] **own** city to mourn for
14: 2 Ahijah the **prophet** is there—the one who told me I would be king
14:18 as the LORD had said through his servant the **prophet** Ahijah.
16: 7 the word of the LORD came through the **prophet** Jehu son of
16:12 of the LORD spoken against Baasha through the **prophet** Jehu—
18: 4 While Jezebel was killing off the LORD's **prophets**, Obadiah had
18: 4 Obadiah had taken a hundred **prophets** and hidden them in two
18:13 what I did while Jezebel was killing the **prophets** *of* the LORD?
18:13 I hid a hundred of the LORD's **prophets** in two caves, fifty in
18:19 bring the four hundred and fifty **prophets** *of* Baal and the four
18:19 fifty prophets of Baal and the four hundred **prophets** *of* Asherah,
18:20 all Israel and assembled the **prophets** on Mount Carmel.
18:22 said to them, "I am the only one of the LORD's **prophets** left,
18:22 prophets left, but Baal has four hundred and fifty **prophets**.
18:25 Elijah said to the **prophets** *of* Baal, "Choose one of the bulls
18:36 time of sacrifice, the **prophet** Elijah stepped forward and prayed:
18:40 Then Elijah commanded them, "Seize the **prophets** *of* Baal.
19: 1 had done and how he had killed all the **prophets** with the sword.
19:10 down your altars, and put your **prophets** to death with the sword.
19:14 down your altars, and put your **prophets** to death with the sword.
19:16 son of Shaphat from Abel Meholah to succeed you as **prophet**.
20:13 Meanwhile a **prophet** came to Ahab king of Israel and announced,
20:22 Afterward, the **prophet** came to the king of Israel and said,
20:35 By the word of the LORD one of the sons of the **prophets** said to
20:38 Then the **prophet** went and stood by the road waiting for the king.
20:41 and the king of Israel recognized him as one of the **prophets**.
22: 6 So the king of Israel brought together the **prophets**—about four
22: 7 "Is there not a **prophet** of the LORD here whom we can inquire
22:10 gate of Samaria, with all the **prophets** prophesying before them.
22:12 All the other **prophets** were prophesying the same thing. "Attack
22:13 as one man the other **prophets** are predicting success for the king.
22:22 will go out and be a lying spirit in the mouths of all his **prophets**,'
22:23 has put a lying spirit in the mouths of all these **prophets** *of* yours.
2Ki 2: 3 The company of the **prophets** at Bethel came out to Elisha
2: 5 The company of the **prophets** at Jericho went up to Elisha
2: 7 Fifty men of the company of the **prophets** went and stood at a
2:15 The company of the **prophets** from Jericho, who were watching,
3:11 But Jehoshaphat asked, "Is there no **prophet** of the LORD here,
3:13 Go to the **prophets** *of* your father and the prophets of your
3:13 to the prophets of your father and the **prophets** *of* your mother."
4: 1 The wife of a man from the company of the **prophets** cried out to
4:38 While the company of the **prophets** was meeting with him,
4:38 the large pot and cook some stew for **these men**[s] [+1201+2021]."
5: 3 "If only my master would see the **prophet** who is in Samaria!
5: 8 come to me and he will know that there is a **prophet** in Israel."
5:13 "My father, if the **prophet** had told you to do some great thing,
5:22 'Two young men from the company of the **prophets** have just
6: 1 The company of the **prophets** said to Elisha, "Look, the place
6:12 said one of his officers, "but Elisha, the **prophet** who is in Israel,
9: 1 The **prophet** Elisha summoned a man from the company of the
9: 1 Elisha summoned a man from the company of the **prophets**
9: 4 So the young man, the **prophet**, went to Ramoth Gilead.
9: 7 I will avenge the blood of my servants the **prophets** and the blood
10:19 Now summon all the **prophets** *of* Baal, all his ministers and all his
14:25 his servant Jonah son of Amittai, the **prophet** from Gath Hepher.
17:13 and Judah through all his **prophets** and seers:
17:13 and that I delivered to you through my servants the **prophets**."
17:23 as he had warned through all his servants the **prophets**.
19: 2 all wearing sackcloth, to the **prophet** Isaiah son of Amoz.
20: 1 The **prophet** Isaiah son of Amoz went to him and said, "This is
20:11 the **prophet** Isaiah called upon the LORD, and the LORD made
20:14 Then Isaiah the **prophet** went to King Hezekiah and asked,
21:10 The LORD said through his servants the **prophets**:
23: 2 of Judah, the people of Jerusalem, the priests and the **prophets**—
23:18 his bones and those of the **prophet** who had come from Samaria.
24: 2 the word of the LORD proclaimed by his servants the **prophets**.
1Ch 16:22 "Do not touch my anointed ones; do my **prophets** no harm."
17: 1 he said to Nathan the **prophet**, "Here I am, living in a palace of
25: 1 [for the ministry of **prophesying**, [K; see Q 5547] accompanied by]
29:29 the records of Nathan the **prophet** and the records of Gad the seer,
2Ch 9:29 are they not written in the records of Nathan the **prophet**,
12: 5 the **prophet** Shemaiah came to Rehoboam and to the leaders of
12:15 are they not written in the records of Shemaiah the **prophet**
13:22 what he said, are written in the annotations of the **prophet** Iddo.
15: 8 these words and the prophecy of Azariah son of Oded the **prophet**,
18: 5 So the king of Israel brought together the **prophets**—four hundred
18: 6 "Is there not a **prophet** of the LORD here whom we can inquire
18: 9 gate of Samaria, with all the **prophets** prophesying before them.
18:11 All the other **prophets** were prophesying the same thing. "Attack
18:12 as one man the other **prophets** are predicting success for the king.
18:21 " 'I will go and be a lying spirit in the mouths of all his **prophets**,'
18:22 has put a lying spirit in the mouths of these **prophets** *of* yours.
20:20 be upheld; have faith in his **prophets** and you will be successful."
21:12 Jehoram received a letter from Elijah the **prophet**, which said:
24:19 Although the LORD sent **prophets** to the people to bring them
25:15 he sent a **prophet** to him, who said, "Why do you consult this
25:16 So the **prophet** stopped but said, "I know that God has determined
26:22 beginning to end, are recorded by the **prophet** Isaiah son of Amoz.
28: 9 a **prophet** of the LORD named Oded was there, and he went out
29:25 by David and Gad the king's seer and Nathan the **prophet**;
29:25 this was commanded by the LORD through his **prophets**.
32:20 the **prophet** Isaiah son of Amoz cried out in prayer to heaven
32:32 his acts of devotion are written in the vision of the **prophet** Isaiah
35:18 observed like this in Israel since the days of the **prophet** Samuel;
36:12 and did not humble himself before Jeremiah the **prophet**,
36:16 scoffed at his **prophets** until the wrath of the LORD was aroused
Ezr 9:11 you gave through your servants the **prophets** when you said:
Ne 6: 7 have even appointed **prophets** to make this proclamation about
6:14 the rest of the **prophets** who have been trying to intimidate me.
9:26 They killed your **prophets**, who had admonished them in order to
9:30 By your Spirit you admonished them through your **prophets**.
9:32 upon our kings and leaders, upon our priests and **prophets**,
Ps 51: T [51:2] When the **prophet** Nathan came to him after David had
74: 9 no **prophets** are left, and none of us knows how long this will be.
105:15 "Do not touch my anointed ones; do my **prophets** no harm."
Isa 3: 2 the hero and warrior, the judge and **prophet**, the soothsayer
9:15 [9:14] men are the head, the **prophets** who teach lies are the tail.
28: 7 Priests and **prophets** stagger from beer and are befuddled with
29:10 He has sealed your eyes (the **prophets**); he has covered your heads
37: 2 all wearing sackcloth, to the **prophet** Isaiah son of Amoz.
38: 1 The **prophet** Isaiah son of Amoz went to him and said, "This is
39: 3 Then Isaiah the **prophet** went to King Hezekiah and asked,
Jer 1: 5 born I set you apart; I appointed you as a **prophet** to the nations."

Jer 2: 8 The **prophets** prophesied by Baal, following worthless idols.
2: 26 their kings and their officials, their priests and their **prophets**.
2: 30 Your sword has devoured your **prophets** like a ravening lion.
4: 9 the priests will be horrified, and the **prophets** will be appalled."
5: 13 The **prophets** are but wind and the word is not in them; so let what
5: 31 The **prophets** prophesy lies, the priests rule by their own authority,
6: 13 are greedy for gain; **prophets** and priests alike, all practice deceit.
7: 25 day after day, again and again I sent you my servants the **prophets**.
8: 1 and officials of Judah, the bones of the priests and **prophets**,
8: 10 are greedy for gain; **prophets** and priests alike, all practice deceit.
13: 13 the priests, the **prophets** and all those living in Jerusalem.
14: 13 I said, "Ah, Sovereign LORD, the **prophets** keep telling them,
14: 14 said to me, "The **prophets** are prophesying lies in my name.
14: 15 this is what the LORD says about the **prophets** who are
14: 15 this land.' Those same **prophets** will perish by sword and famine.
14: 18 Both **prophet** and priest have gone to a land they know not.' "
18: 18 nor will counsel from the wise, nor the word from the **prophets**.
20: 2 he had Jeremiah the **prophet** beaten and put in the stocks at the
23: 9 Concerning the **prophets**: My heart is broken within me; all my
23: 11 "Both **prophet** and priest are godless; even in my temple I find
23: 13 "Among the **prophets** *of* Samaria I saw this repulsive thing:
23: 14 among the **prophets** *of* Jerusalem I have seen something horrible:
23: 15 this is what the LORD Almighty says concerning the **prophets**:
23: 15 because from the **prophets** *of* Jerusalem ungodliness has spread
23: 16 "Do not listen to what the **prophets** are prophesying to you;
23: 21 I did not send these **prophets**, yet they have run with their
23: 25 "I have heard what the **prophets** say who prophesy lies in my
23: 26 How long will this continue in the hearts of these lying **prophets**,
23: 26 lying prophets, *who* **prophesy** the delusions of their own minds?
23: 28 Let the **prophet** who has a dream tell his dream, but let the one
23: 30 "I am against the **prophets** who steal from one another words
23: 31 "I am against the **prophets** who wag their own tongues and yet
23: 33 "When these people, or a **prophet** or a priest, ask you, 'What is the
23: 34 If a **prophet** or a priest or anyone else claims, 'This is the oracle of
23: 37 This is what you keep saying to a **prophet**: 'What is the LORD's
25: 2 So Jeremiah the **prophet** said to all the people of Judah and to all
25: 4 though the LORD has sent all his servants the **prophets** to you
26: 5 and if you do not listen to the words of my servants the **prophets**,
26: 7 the **prophets** and all the people heard Jeremiah speak these words
26: 8 the priests, the **prophets** and all the people seized him and said,
26: 11 the priests and the **prophets** said to the officials and all the people,
26: 16 the officials and all the people said to the priests and the **prophets**,
27: 9 So do not listen to your **prophets**, your diviners, your interpreters
27: 14 Do not listen to the words of the **prophets** who say to you,
27: 15 will perish, both you and the **prophets** who prophesy to you.' "
27: 16 Do not listen to the **prophets** who say, 'Very soon now the articles
27: 18 If they are **prophets** and have the word of the LORD, let them
28: 1 the **prophet** Hananiah son of Azzur, who was from Gibeon,
28: 5 the **prophet** Jeremiah replied to the prophet Hananiah before the
28: 5 the prophet Jeremiah replied to the **prophet** Hananiah before the
28: 6 **He**[s] [+2021+3758] said, "Amen! May the LORD do so!
28: 8 From early times the **prophets** who preceded you and me have
28: 9 the **prophet** who prophesies peace will be recognized as one truly
28: 9 prophet who prophesies peace will be recognized as **one**[s] [+2021]
28: 9 sent by the LORD only if **his**[s] [+2021] prediction comes true."
28: 10 the **prophet** Hananiah took the yoke off the neck of the prophet
28: 10 the prophet Hananiah took the yoke off the neck of the **prophet**
28: 11 within two years.' " At this, the **prophet** Jeremiah went on his way.
28: 12 Shortly after the **prophet** Hananiah had broken the yoke off the
28: 12 had broken the yoke off the neck of the **prophet** Jeremiah,
28: 15 Then the **prophet** Jeremiah said to Hananiah the prophet,
28: 15 Then the prophet Jeremiah said to Hananiah the **prophet**,
28: 17 the seventh month of that same year, Hananiah the **prophet** died.
29: 1 This is the text of the letter that the **prophet** Jeremiah sent from
29: 1 the **prophets** and all the other people Nebuchadnezzar had carried
29: 8 "Do not let the **prophets** and diviners among you deceive you.
29: 15 may say, "The LORD has raised up **prophets** for us in Babylon,"
29: 19 that I sent to them again and again by my servants the **prophets**.
29: 29 the priest, however, read the letter to Jeremiah the **prophet**.
32: 2 Jeremiah the **prophet** was confined in the courtyard of the guard in
32: 32 they, their kings and officials, their priests and **prophets**, the men
34: 6 Then Jeremiah the **prophet** told all this to Zedekiah king of Judah,
35: 15 Again and again I sent all my servants the **prophets** to you.
36: 8 Baruch son of Neriah did everything Jeremiah the **prophet** told
36: 26 of Abdeel to arrest Baruch the scribe and Jeremiah the **prophet**.
37: 2 the words the LORD had spoken through Jeremiah the **prophet**.
37: 3 son of Maaseiah to Jeremiah the **prophet** with this message:
37: 6 Then the word of the LORD came to Jeremiah the **prophet**:
37: 13 the son of Hananiah, arrested **him**[s] [+2021+3759] and said,
37: 19 Where are your **prophets** who prophesied to you, 'The king of
38: 9 have acted wickedly in all they have done to Jeremiah the **prophet**.
38: 10 and lift Jeremiah the **prophet** out of the cistern before he dies."
38: 14 King Zedekiah sent for Jeremiah the **prophet** and had him brought
42: 2 Jeremiah the **prophet** and said to him, "Please hear our petition
42: 4 "I have heard you," replied Jeremiah the **prophet**. "I will certainly
43: 6 of Shaphan, and Jeremiah the **prophet** and Baruch son of Neriah.
44: 4 Again and again I sent my servants the **prophets**, who said,
45: 1 This is what Jeremiah the **prophet** told Baruch son of Neriah in the
46: 1 This is the word of the LORD that came to Jeremiah the **prophet**
46: 13 This is the message the LORD spoke to Jeremiah the **prophet**
47: 1 This is the word of the LORD that came to Jeremiah the **prophet**
49: 34 This is the word of the LORD that came to Jeremiah the **prophet**
50: 1 This is the word the LORD spoke through Jeremiah the **prophet**
51: 59 This is the message Jeremiah **[NIE]** gave to the staff officer
La 2: 9 and her **prophets** no longer find visions from the LORD.
2: 14 The visions of your **prophets** were false and worthless; they did
2: 20 Should priest and **prophet** be killed in the sanctuary of the Lord?
4: 13 it happened because of the sins of her **prophets** and the iniquities
Eze 2: 5 they will know that a **prophet** has been among them.
7: 26 They will try to get a vision from the **prophet**; the teaching of the
13: 2 prophesy against the **prophets** *of* Israel who are now prophesying.
13: 2 Say to **those who prophesy** out of their own imagination:
13: 3 Woe to the foolish **prophets** who follow their own spirit and have
13: 4 Your **prophets**, O Israel, are like jackals among ruins.
13: 9 My hand will be against the **prophets** who see false visions
13: 16 those **prophets** *of* Israel who prophesied to Jerusalem and saw
14: 4 stumbling block before his face and then goes to a **prophet**,
14: 7 block before his face and then goes to a **prophet** to inquire of me,
14: 9 " 'And if the **prophet** is enticed to utter a prophecy, I the LORD
14: 9 I the LORD have enticed that **prophet**, and I will stretch out my
14: 10 the **prophet** will be as guilty as the one who consults him.
22: 25 There is a conspiracy of her princes [BHS *prophets*; NIV 5954]
22: 28 Her **prophets** whitewash these deeds for them by false visions
33: 33 then they will know that a **prophet** has been among them."
38: 17 I spoke of in former days by my servants the **prophets** *of* Israel?
Da 9: 2 to the word of the LORD given to Jeremiah the **prophet**,
9: 6 We have not listened to your servants the **prophets**, who spoke in
9: 10 or kept the laws he gave us through his servants the **prophets**.
9: 24 to seal up vision and **prophecy** and to anoint the most holy.
Hos 4: 5 You stumble day and night, and the **prophets** stumble with you.
6: 5 Therefore I cut you in pieces with my **prophets**, I killed you with
9: 7 and your hostility so great, the **prophet** is considered a fool,
9: 8 The **prophet**, along with my God, is the watchman over Ephraim,
12: 10 [12:11] I spoke to the **prophets**, gave them many visions and told
12: 10 [12:11] many visions and told parables through **them**[s] [+2021]."
12: 13 [12:14] The LORD used a **prophet** to bring Israel up from
12: 13 [12:14] Israel up from Egypt, by a **prophet** he cared for him.
Am 2: 11 I also raised up **prophets** from among your sons and Nazirites
2: 12 drink wine and commanded the **prophets** not to prophesy.
3: 7 nothing without revealing his plan to his servants the **prophets**.
7: 14 "I was neither a **prophet** nor a prophet's son, but I was a shepherd,
7: 14 "I was neither a prophet nor a **prophet's** son, but I was a shepherd,
Mic 3: 5 "As for the **prophets** who lead my people astray, if one feeds
3: 6 The sun will set for the **prophets**, and the day will go dark for
3: 11 priests teach for a price, and her **prophets** tell fortunes for money.
Hab 1: 1 The oracle that Habakkuk the **prophet** received.
3: 1 A prayer of Habakkuk the **prophet**. On *shigionoth*.
Zep 3: 4 Her **prophets** are arrogant; they are treacherous men. Her priests
Hag 1: 1 the word of the LORD came through the **prophet** Haggai to
1: 3 Then the word of the LORD came through the **prophet** Haggai:
1: 12 of the LORD their God and the message of the **prophet** Haggai,
2: 1 the word of the LORD came through the **prophet** Haggai:
2: 10 of Darius, the word of the LORD came to the **prophet** Haggai:
Zec 1: 1 the word of the LORD came to the **prophet** Zechariah son of
1: 4 be like your forefathers, to whom the earlier **prophets** proclaimed:
1: 5 are your forefathers now? And the **prophets**, do they live forever?
1: 6 and my decrees, which I commanded my servants the **prophets**,
1: 7 the word of the LORD came to the **prophet** Zechariah son of
7: 3 the priests of the house of the LORD Almighty and the **prophets**,
7: 7 LORD proclaimed through the earlier **prophets** when Jerusalem
7: 12 Almighty had sent by his Spirit through the earlier **prophets**.
8: 9 "You who now hear these words spoken by the **prophets** who
13: 2 "I will remove both the **prophets** and the spirit of impurity from
13: 4 "On that day every **prophet** will be ashamed of his prophetic
13: 5 He will say, 'I am not a **prophet**. I am a farmer; the land has been
Mal 4: 5 [3:23] I will send you the **prophet** Elijah before that great

5567 נְבִיאָה n^e^bî'â, n.f. [6] [√ 5566]

prophetess [6]

Ex 15: 20 Miriam the **prophetess**, Aaron's sister, took a tambourine in her
Jdg 4: 4 Deborah, a **prophetess**, the wife of Lappidoth, was leading Israel
2Ki 22: 14 Shaphan and Asaiah went to speak to the **prophetess** Huldah,
2Ch 34: 22 those the king had sent with him went to speak to the **prophetess**
Ne 6: 14 remember also the **prophetess** Noadiah and the rest of the prophets
Isa 8: 3 I went to the **prophetess**, and she conceived and gave birth to a

5568 נְבָיוֹת ***n[e]bāyôt***, n.pr.g. [5]

Nebaioth [5]

Ge 25:13 **Nebaioth** the firstborn of Ishmael, Kedar, Adbeel, Mibsam,
28: 9 the sister of **Nebaioth** and daughter of Ishmael son of Abraham,
36: 3 also Basemath daughter of Ishmael and sister of **Nebaioth**.
1Ch 1:29 **Nebaioth** the firstborn of Ishmael, Kedar, Adbeel, Mibsam,
Isa 60: 7 will be gathered to you, the rams of **Nebaioth** will serve you;

5569 נֵבֶךְ ***nēbek***, n.[m.]. [1]

springs [1]

Job 38:16 "Have you journeyed to the **springs** *of* the sea or walked in the

5570 נָבֵל ***nābēl[1]***, v. [20] [→ 5577, 5578?]

fading [3], fall [3], wither [3], lose heart [2], only wear out [+5570] [2], withers [2], crumbles [1], die away [1], shrivel up [1], shriveled [1], withered [1]

Ex 18:18 [A] who come to you *will* **only wear** [+5570] *yourselves* **out**.
18:18 [A] who come to you *will* **only wear** *yourselves* **out** [+5570].
2Sa 22:46 [A] They all **lose heart**; they come trembling from their
Job 14:18 [A] "But as a mountain erodes and **crumbles** and as a rock is
Ps 1: 3 [A] yields its fruit in season and whose leaf *does* not **wither**.
18:45 [18:46] [A] They all **lose heart**; they come trembling from their
37: 2 [A] will soon wither, like green plants *they will* soon **die away**.
Isa 1:30 [A] You will be like an oak with **fading** leaves, like a garden
24: 4 [A] The earth dries up and **withers**, the world languishes and
24: 4 [A] earth dries up and withers, the world languishes and **withers**,
28: 1 [A] to the **fading** flower, his glorious beauty,
28: 4 [A] That **fading** flower, his glorious beauty, set on the head of a
34: 4 [A] all the starry host *will* **fall** like withered leaves from the vine,
34: 4 [A] all the starry host will fall like **withered** leaves from the
34: 4 [A] leaves from the vine, like **shriveled** figs from the fig tree.
40: 7 [A] The grass withers and the flowers **fall**, because the breath of
40: 8 [A] The grass withers and the flowers **fall**, but the word of our
64: 6 [64:5] [A] we all **shrivel up** like a leaf, and like the wind our
Jer 8:13 [A] There will be no figs on the tree, and their leaves *will* **wither**.
Eze 47:12 [A] Their leaves *will* not **wither**, nor will their fruit fail.

5571 [2]נָבַל ***nābal[2]***, v. [5] [→ 5572, 5573, 5576]

dishonor [1], dishonors [1], played the fool [1], rejected [1], treat with contempt [1]

Dt 32:15 [D] the God who made him and **rejected** the Rock his Savior.
Pr 30:32 [A] "If *you have* **played the fool** and exalted yourself, or if you
Jer 14:21 [D] do not despise us; *do* not **dishonor** your glorious throne.
Mic 7: 6 [D] For a son **dishonors** his father, a daughter rises up against
Na 3: 6 [D] *I will* **treat** you **with contempt** and make you a spectacle.

5572 נָבָל ***nābāl[1]***, a. [19] [→ 5573; cf. 5571]

fool [9], foolish [4], fools [2], base [1], lawless [1], no understanding [1], wicked fools [1]

Dt 32: 6 this the way you repay the LORD, O **foolish** and unwise people?
32:21 I will make them angry by a nation that has **no understanding**.
1Sa 25:25 is just like his name—his name is **Fool**, and folly goes with him.
2Sa 3:33 this lament for Abner: "Should Abner have died as the **lawless** die?
13:13 about you? You would be like one of the **wicked fools** in Israel.
Job 2:10 He replied, "You are talking like a **foolish** *woman*. Shall we accept
30: 8 A **base** and nameless brood, they were driven out of the land.
Ps 14: 1 The **fool** says in his heart, "There is no God." They are corrupt,
39: 8 [39:9] all my transgressions; do not make me the scorn of **fools**.
53: 1 [53:2] The **fool** says in his heart, "There is no God." They are
74:18 O LORD, how **foolish** people have reviled your name.
74:22 defend your cause; remember how **fools** mock you all day long.
Pr 17: 7 Arrogant lips are unsuited to a **fool**—how much worse lying lips to
17:21 a fool for a son brings grief; there is no joy for the father of a **fool**.
30:22 a servant who becomes king, a **fool** who is full of food,
Isa 32: 5 No longer will the **fool** be called noble nor the scoundrel be highly
32: 6 For the **fool** speaks folly, his mind is busy with evil: He practices
Jer 17:11 they will desert him, and in the end he will prove to be a **fool**.
Eze 13: 3 Woe to the **foolish** prophets who follow their own spirit and have

5573 [2]נָבָל ***nābāl[2]***, n.pr.m. [21] [√ 5572; cf. 5571]

Nabal [18], Nabal's [2], he[s] [1]

1Sa 25: 3 His name was **Nabal** and his wife's name was Abigail. She was an
25: 4 David was in the desert, he heard that **Nabal** was shearing sheep.
25: 5 to them, "Go up to **Nabal** at Carmel and greet him in my name.
25: 9 men arrived, they gave **Nabal** this message in David's name.
25:10 **Nabal** answered David's servants, "Who is this David? Who is this
25:14 One of the servants told **Nabal's** wife Abigail: "David sent
25:19 on ahead; I'll follow you." But she did not tell her husband **Nabal**.
25:25 May my lord pay no attention to that wicked man **Nabal**. He is just
25:26 your enemies and all who intend to harm my master be like **Nabal**.
25:34 not one male belonging to **Nabal** would have been left alive by
25:36 When Abigail went to **Nabal**, he was in the house holding a
25:36 **He**[s] was in high spirits and very drunk. So she told him nothing
25:37 in the morning, when **Nabal** was sober, his wife told him all these
25:38 About ten days later, the LORD struck **Nabal** and he died.
25:39 When David heard that **Nabal** was dead, he said, "Praise be to the
25:39 who has upheld my cause against **Nabal** for treating me with
25:39 and has brought **Nabal's** wrongdoing down on his own head."
27: 3 Ahinoam of Jezreel and Abigail of Carmel, the widow of **Nabal**.
30: 5 Ahinoam of Jezreel and Abigail, the widow of **Nabal** of Carmel.
2Sa 2: 2 Ahinoam of Jezreel and Abigail, the widow of **Nabal** of Carmel.
3: 3 Kileab the son of Abigail the widow of **Nabal** of Carmel;

5574 [1]נֵבֶל ***nēbel[1]***, n.m. [11] [→ 4429, 5575?]

skin [3], wineskin [2], jars [1], jugs [1], pots [1], pottery [+3450] [1], skins [1], water jars [1]

1Sa 1:24 with a three-year-old bull, an ephah of flour and a **skin** *of* wine,
10: 3 another three loaves of bread, and another a **skin** *of* wine.
25:18 two **skins** *of* wine, five dressed sheep, five seahs of roasted grain,
2Sa 16: 1 cakes of raisins, a hundred cakes of figs and a **skin** *of* wine.
Job 38:37 count the clouds? Who can tip over the **water jars** *of* the heavens
Isa 22:24 and offshoots—all its lesser vessels, from the bowls to all the **jars**.
30:14 It will break in pieces like **pottery** [+3450], shattered so
Jer 13:12 the God of Israel, says: Every **wineskin** should be filled with wine.'
13:12 'Don't we know that every **wineskin** should be filled with wine?'
48:12 they will pour her out; they will empty her jars and smash her **jugs**.
La 4: 2 are now considered as **pots** *of* clay, the work of a potter's hands!

5575 [2]נֵבֶל ***nēbel[2]***, n.m. [27] [√ 5574?]

lyres [15], lyre [7], harps [4], harp [1]

1Sa 10: 5 of prophets coming down from the high place with **lyres**,
2Sa 6: 5 and with harps, **lyres**, tambourines, sistrums and cymbals.
1Ki 10:12 for the royal palace, and to make harps and **lyres** for the musicians.
1Ch 13: 8 and with harps, **lyres**, tambourines, cymbals and trumpets.
15:16 accompanied by musical instruments: **lyres**, harps and cymbals.
15:20 and Benaiah were to play the **lyres** according to *alamoth,*
15:28 and trumpets, and of cymbals, and the playing of **lyres** and harps.
16: 5 They were to play the **lyres** and harps, Asaph was to sound the
25: 1 of prophesying, accompanied by harps, **lyres** and cymbals.
25: 6 with cymbals, **lyres** and harps, for the ministry at the house of
2Ch 5:12 dressed in fine linen and playing cymbals, harps and **lyres**.
9:11 for the royal palace, and to make harps and **lyres** for the musicians.
20:28 and went to the temple of the LORD with **harps** and lutes
29:25 harps and **lyres** in the way prescribed by David and Gad the king's
Ne 12:27 of thanksgiving and with the music of cymbals, harps and **lyres**.
Ps 33: 2 LORD with the harp; make music to him on the ten-stringed **lyre**.
57: 8 [57:9] Awake, my soul! Awake, harp and **lyre**! I will awaken the
71:22 I will praise you with the **harp** for your faithfulness, O my God;
81: 2 [81:3] strike the tambourine, play the melodious harp and **lyre**.
92: 3 [92:4] to the music of the ten-stringed **lyre** and the melody of the
108: 2 [108:3] Awake, harp and **lyre**! I will awaken the dawn.
144: 9 O God; on the ten-stringed **lyre** I will make music to you,
150: 3 the sounding of the trumpet, praise him with the harp and **lyre**,
Isa 5:12 They have harps and **lyres** at their banquets, tambourines
14:11 brought down to the grave, along with the noise of your **harps**;
Am 5:23 noise of your songs! I will not listen to the music of your **harps**.
6: 5 You strum away on your **harps** like David and improvise on

5576 נְבָלָה ***n[e]bālâ***, n.f. [13] [√ 5571]

disgraceful thing [4], folly [3], disgraceful [2], vileness [2], outrageous things [1], wicked thing [1]

Ge 34: 7 because Shechem had done a **disgraceful thing** in Israel by lying
Dt 22:21 She has done a **disgraceful thing** in Israel by being promiscuous
Jos 7:15 of the LORD and has done a **disgraceful thing** in Israel!' "
Jdg 19:23 Since this man is my guest, don't do this **disgraceful thing**.
19:24 you wish. But to this man, don't do such a **disgraceful** thing."
20: 6 because they committed this lewd and **disgraceful** act in Israel.
20:10 it can give them what they deserve for all this **vileness** done in
1Sa 25:25 is just like his name—his name is Fool, and **folly** goes with him.
2Sa 13:12 a thing should not be done in Israel! Don't do this **wicked thing**.
Job 42: 8 accept his prayer and not deal with you according to your **folly**.
Isa 9:17 [9:16] is ungodly and wicked, every mouth speaks **vileness**.
32: 6 For the fool speaks **folly**, his mind is busy with evil: He practices
Jer 29:23 For they have done **outrageous things** in Israel; they have

5577 נְבֵלָה ***n[e]bēlâ***, n.f. [48] [√ 5570]

body [13], carcasses [13], carcass [5], dead bodies [5], anything found dead [3], *untranslated* [2], it[s] [+2021] [2], already dead [1], animal found dead [1], bodies [1], found dead [1], lifeless forms [1]

Lev 5: 2 whether the **carcasses** *of* unclean wild animals or of unclean

Lev 5: 2 carcasses of unclean wild animals or **[RPH]** of unclean livestock
5: 2 or **[RPH]** of unclean creatures that move along the ground—
7: 24 The fat of an **animal found dead** or torn by wild animals may be
11: 8 You must not eat their meat or touch their **carcasses**; they are
11: 11 you must not eat their meat and you must detest their **carcasses**.
11: 24 whoever touches their **carcasses** will be unclean till evening.
11: 25 Whoever picks up one of their **carcasses** must wash his clothes,
11: 27 whoever touches their **carcasses** will be unclean till evening.
11: 28 Anyone who picks up their **carcasses** must wash his clothes,
11: 35 Anything that one of their **carcasses** falls on becomes unclean;
11: 36 but anyone who touches one of these **carcasses** is unclean.
11: 37 If a **carcass** falls on any seeds that are to be planted, they remain
11: 38 But if water has been put on the seed and a **carcass** falls on it,
11: 39 anyone who touches the **carcass** will be unclean till evening.
11: 40 Anyone who eats some of the **carcass** must wash his clothes,
11: 40 Anyone who picks up the **carcass** must wash his clothes, and he
17: 15 who eats **anything found dead** or torn by wild animals must wash
22: 8 He must not eat **anything found dead** or torn by wild animals,
Dt 14: 8 the cud. You are not to eat their meat or touch their **carcasses**.
14: 21 Do not eat anything you find **already dead**. You may give it to an
21: 23 you must not leave his **body** on the tree overnight. Be sure to bury
28: 26 Your **carcasses** will be food for all the birds of the air and the
Jos 8: 29 Joshua ordered them to take his **body** from the tree and throw it
1Ki 13: 22 Therefore your **body** will not be buried in the tomb of your
13: 24 and killed him, and his **body** was thrown down on the road,
13: 24 with both the donkey and the lion standing beside **it**ˢ [+2021].
13: 25 Some people who passed by saw the **body** thrown down there,
13: 25 with the lion standing beside the **body**, and they went and reported
13: 28 Then he went out and found the **body** thrown down on the road,
13: 28 the road, with the donkey and the lion standing beside **it**ˢ [+2021].
13: 28 The lion had neither eaten the **body** nor mauled the donkey.
13: 29 So the prophet picked up the **body** *of* the man of God, laid it on the
13: 30 he laid the **body** in his own tomb, and they mourned over him
2Ki 9: 37 Jezebel's **body** will be like refuse on the ground in the plot at
Ps 79: 2 They have given the **dead bodies** *of* your servants as food to the
Isa 5: 25 mountains shake, and the **dead bodies** are like refuse in the streets.
26: 19 your dead will live; their **bodies** will rise. You who dwell in the
Jer 7: 33 the **carcasses** *of* this people will become food for the birds of the
9: 22 [9:21] " 'The **dead bodies** *of* men will lie like refuse on the open
16: 4 and their **dead bodies** will become food for the birds of the air
16: 18 because they have defiled my land with the **lifeless forms** *of* their
19: 7 and I will give their **carcasses** as food to the birds of the air
26: 23 and his **body** thrown into the burial place of the common people.)
34: 20 Their **dead bodies** will become food for the birds of the air
36: 30 his **body** will be thrown out and exposed to the heat by day
Eze 4: 14 From my youth until now I have never eaten **anything found dead**
44: 31 eat anything, bird or animal, **found dead** or torn by wild animals.

5578 נַבְלוּת *nablût*, n.f. [1] [√ 5570?]

lewdness [1]

Hos 2: 10 [2:12] So now I will expose her **lewdness** before the eyes of her

5579 נְבַלָּט *nᵉballāṭ*, n.pr.loc. [1]

Neballat [1]

Ne 11: 34 in Hadid, Zeboim and **Neballat**,

5580 נָבַע *nābaʿ*, v. [11] [→ 81, 4432]

gushes [2], bubbling [1], celebrate [+2352] [1], give a bad smell [+944] [1], overflow [1], pour forth [1], pour out [1], poured out [1], spew [1], utter [1]

Ps 19: 2 [19:3] [G] Day after day *they* **pour forth** speech; night after
59: 7 [59:8] [G] See what *they* **spew** from their mouths—they spew
78: 2 [G] in parables, *I will* **utter** hidden things, things from of old—
94: 4 [G] *They* **pour out** arrogant words; all the evildoers are full of
119:171 [G] *May* my lips **overflow** *with* praise, for you teach me your
145: 7 [G] *They will* **celebrate** [+2352] your abundant goodness
Pr 1: 23 [G] *I would have* **poured out** my heart to you and made my
15: 2 [G] but the mouth of the fool **gushes** folly.
15: 28 [G] weighs its answers, but the mouth of the wicked **gushes** evil.
18: 4 [A] deep waters, but the fountain of wisdom is a **bubbling** brook.
Ecc 10: 1 [G] As dead flies **give** perfume **a bad smell** [+944], so a little

5581 נִבְשָׁן *nibšān*, n.pr.loc. [1]

Nibshan [1]

Jos 15: 62 **Nibshan**, the City of Salt and En Gedi—six towns and their

5582 נֶגֶב *negeb*, n.[pr.m.]. [111] [→ 8241]

south [38], Negev [36], south [+2025] [9], southern [6], south [+4946] [4], south [+2025+9402] [3], southern [+2025] [3], Negev [+824] [2], south [+2025+2025+9402] [2], south [+9402] [2], southeast [+2025 +2025+7711] [1], southeast [+2025+7711] [1], southern [+448+6991] [1], southern [+4946] [1], southland [+8441] [1], southland [1]

Ge 12: 9 Then Abram set out and continued toward the **Negev**.
13: 1 So Abram went up from Egypt to the **Negev**, with his wife
13: 3 From the **Negev** he went from place to place until he came to
13: 14 your eyes from where you are and look north and **south** [+2025],
20: 1 Now Abraham moved on from there into the region of the **Negev**
24: 62 come from Beer Lahai Roi, for he was living in the **Negev** [+824].
28: 14 spread out to the west and to the east, to the north and to the **south**.
Ex 26: 18 Make twenty frames for the **south** [+2025+2025+9402] side of the
27: 9 The **south** [+2025+9402] side shall be a hundred cubits long
36: 23 They made twenty frames for the **south** [+2025+9402] side of the
38: 9 The **south** [+2025+9402] side was a hundred cubits long and had
40: 24 opposite the table on the **south** [+2025] side of the tabernacle
Nu 13: 17 he said, "Go up through the **Negev** and on into the hill country.
13: 22 They went up through the **Negev** and came to Hebron, where
13: 29 The Amalekites live in the **Negev** [+824]; the Hittites, Jebusites
21: 1 When the Canaanite king of Arad, who lived in the **Negev**,
33: 40 The Canaanite king of Arad, who lived in the **Negev** of Canaan,
34: 3 " 'Your **southern** side will include some of the Desert of Zin along
34: 3 your **southern** boundary will start from the end of the Salt Sea,
34: 4 cross **south** of Scorpion Pass, continue on to Zin and go south of
34: 4 Scorpion Pass, continue on to Zin and go **south** of Kadesh Barnea.
35: 5 three thousand on the **south** side, three thousand on the west
Dt 1: 7 in the western foothills, in the **Negev** and along the coast,
34: 3 the **Negev** and the whole region from the Valley of Jericho,
Jos 10: 40 the **Negev**, the western foothills and the mountain slopes,
11: 2 in the Arabah **south** *of* Kinnereth, in the western foothills
11: 16 the hill country, all the **Negev**, the whole region of Goshen,
12: 8 the Arabah, the mountain slopes, the desert and the **Negev**—
15: 1 of Edom, to the Desert of Zin in the extreme **south** [+9402].
15: 2 Their **southern** boundary started from the bay at the southern end
15: 2 started from the bay at the **southern** [+2025] end of the Salt Sea,
15: 3 crossed **south** of Scorpion Pass, continued on to Zin and went over
15: 3 continued on to Zin and went over to the **south** of Kadesh Barnea.
15: 4 Wadi of Egypt, ending at the sea. This is their **southern** boundary.
15: 7 which faces the Pass of Adummim **south** [+4946] of the gorge.
15: 8 it ran up the Valley of Ben Hinnom along the **southern** [+4946]
15: 19 Since you have given me land in the **Negev**, give me also springs
15: 21 The southernmost towns of the tribe of Judah in the **Negev** toward
17: 9 Then the boundary continued **south** [+2025] to the Kanah Ravine.
17: 10 On the **south** the land belonged to Ephraim, on the north to
18: 5 Judah is to remain in its territory on the **south** and the house of
18: 13 From there it crossed to the **south** slope of Luz (that is, Bethel)
18: 13 went down to Ataroth Addar on the hill **south** [+4946] of Lower
18: 14 From the hill facing Beth Horon on the **south** the boundary turned
18: 14 south the boundary turned **south** [+2025] along the western side
18: 15 The **southern** [+2025] side began at the outskirts of Kiriath Jearim
18: 16 It continued down the Hinnom Valley along the **southern** [+2025]
18: 19 bay of the Salt Sea, at the mouth of the Jordan in the **south**.
18: 19 mouth of the Jordan in the south. This was the **southern** boundary.
19: 8 around these towns as far as Baalath Beer (Ramah in the **Negev**).
19: 34 It touched Zebulun on the **south**, Asher on the west and the Jordan
Jdg 1: 9 living in the hill country, the **Negev** and the western foothills.
1: 15 Since you have given me land in the **Negev**, give me also springs
1: 16 among the people of the Desert of Judah in the **Negev** *near* Arad.
21: 19 that goes from Bethel to Shechem, and to the **south** of Lebonah."
1Sa 14: 5 to the north toward Micmash, the other to the **south** toward Geba.
20: 41 David got up from the **south** side ⌞of the stone⌟ and bowed down
27: 10 "Against the **Negev** *of* Judah" or "Against the Negev of
27: 10 the Negev of Judah" or "Against the **Negev** *of* Jerahmeel"
27: 10 the Negev of Jerahmeel" or "Against the **Negev** *of* the Kenites."
30: 1 Now the Amalekites had raided the **Negev** and Ziklag. They had
30: 14 We raided the **Negev** *of* the Kerethites and the territory belonging
30: 14 and the territory belonging to Judah and the **Negev** *of* Caleb.
2Sa 24: 7 Finally, they went on to Beersheba in the **Negev** *of* Judah.
1Ki 7: 25 three facing west, three facing **south** [+2025] and three facing east.
7: 39 the south side, at the **southeast** [+2025+7711] corner of the temple.
1Ch 9: 24 were on the four sides: east, west, north and **south** [+2025].
26: 15 The lot for the **South** Gate fell to Obed-Edom, and the lot for the
26: 17 four a day on the **south** [+2025] and two at a time at the
2Ch 4: 4 three facing west, three facing **south** [+2025] and three facing east.
4: 10 on the south side, at the **southeast** [+2025+2025+7711] corner.
28: 18 had raided towns in the foothills and in the **Negev** of Judah.
Ps 126: 4 Restore our fortunes, O LORD, like streams in the **Negev**.
Isa 21: 1 Like whirlwinds sweeping through the **southland**, an invader
30: 6 An oracle concerning the animals of the **Negev**: Through a land of
Jer 13: 19 The cities in the **Negev** will be shut up, and there will be no one to
17: 26 from the hill country and the **Negev**, bringing burnt offerings
32: 44 towns of the hill country, of the western foothills and of the **Negev**,
33: 13 of the western foothills and of the **Negev**, in the territory of
Eze 20: 46 [21:2] and prophesy against the forest of the **southland** [+8441].
20: 47 [21:3] Say to the **southern** forest: 'Hear the word of the LORD.

Eze 20:47 [21:3] and every face from **south** to north will be scorched by it.
21: 4 [21:9] my sword will be unsheathed against everyone from **south**
40: 2 on whose **south** [+4946] *side* were some buildings that looked like
46: 9 whoever enters by the north gate to worship is to go out the **south**
46: 9 and whoever enters by the **south** gate is to go out the north gate.
47: 1 down from under the south side of the temple, **south** [+4946]
47:19 "On the **south** [+9402] side it will run from Tamar as far as the
47:19 This will be the **south** [+2025+2025+9402] boundary.
48:10 wide on the east side and 25,000 cubits long on the **south** *side*.
48:16 4,500 cubits, the **south** side 4,500 cubits, the east side 4,500 cubits,
48:17 250 cubits on the **south**, 250 cubits on the east, and 250 cubits on
48:28 "The **southern** [+448+6991] boundary of Gad will run south from
48:33 "On the **south** side, which measures 4,500 cubits, will be three
Da 8: 4 the ram as he charged toward the west and the north and the **south**.
8: 9 which started small but grew in power to the **south** and to the east
11: 5 "The king of the **South** will become strong, but one of his
11: 6 The daughter of the king of the **South** will go to the king of the
11: 9 the king of the North will invade the realm of the king of the **South**
11:11 "Then the king of the **South** will march out in a rage and fight
11:14 "In those times many will rise against the king of the **South**.
11:15 The forces of the **South** will be powerless to resist; even their best
11:25 will stir up his strength and courage against the king of the **South**.
11:25 The king of the **South** will wage war with a large and very
11:29 "At the appointed time he will invade the **South** again, but this
11:40 "At the time of the end the king of the **South** will engage him in
Ob 1:19 People from the **Negev** will occupy the mountains of Esau,
1:20 who are in Sepharad will possess the towns of the **Negev**.
Zec 7: 7 and the **Negev** and the western foothills were settled?' "
14: 4 half of the mountain moving north and half moving **south** [+2025].
14:10 The whole land, from Geba to Rimmon, **south** *of* Jerusalem,

5583 נָגַד *nāgad*, v. [370 / 371] [→ 5584, 5592; Ar 10457]

tell [93], told [87], was told [23], reported [15], declare [14], proclaim [11], announce [8], explain [6], report [5], answered [4], give [4], inform [4], revealed [4], said [4], *untranslated* [3], declared [3], explained [3], foretold [3], show [3], assured [+4200+5583] [2], be sure to tell [+4200+5583] [2], been told about [+4200+5583] [2], brought report [2], denounces [2], foretell [2], give answer [+906+4200+5583] [2], heard [2], informed [2], messenger [2], must report [+906+5583] [2], speak [2], telling [2], tells [2], warned [2], were clearly told [+906+4200+5583] [2], admit [1], announces [1], announcing [1], been brought to attention [+2256+4200+9048] [1], been shown [1], been told [1], confess [1], confront [1], declares [1], declaring [1], describe [1], disclose [1], do[S] so [1], explaining [1], expose [1], exposed [1], give an answer [1], kept secret [+401+906] [1], learn [1], learned [+906+4200] [1], let know [1], made clear [1], make known [1], message [1], messenger[S] [1], parade [1], proclaiming [1], report came back [1], reveals [1], sent word [+2256+8938] [1], showed [1], shown [1], speak up [1], spoke [1], tell answer [1], tell the news [1], testify [1], testimony [1], told answer [1], utter [1], was reported [1], word came [1]

Ge 3:11 [G] he said, "Who **told** you that you were naked? Have you eaten
9:22 [G] saw his father's nakedness and **told** his two brothers outside.
12:18 [G] to me?" he said. "Why didn't *you* **tell** me she was your wife?
14:13 [G] had escaped came and **reported** this to Abram the Hebrew.
21:26 [G] You *did* not **tell** me, and I heard about it only today."
22:20 [H] Some time later Abraham **was told**, "Milcah is also a mother;
24:23 [G] Please **tell** me, is there room in your father's house for us to
24:28 [G] girl ran and **told** her mother's household about these things.
24:49 [G] will show kindness and faithfulness to my master, **tell** me;
24:49 [G] and if not, **tell** me, so I may know which way to turn."
26:32 [G] servants came and **told** him about the well they had dug.
27:42 [H] When Rebekah **was told** what her older son Esau had said,
29:12 [G] He *had* **told** Rachel that he was a relative of her father and a
29:12 [G] and a son of Rebekah. So she ran and **told** her father.
29:15 [G] for me for nothing? **Tell** me what your wages should be."
31:20 [G] Jacob deceived Laban the Aramean by not **telling** him he
31:22 [H] On the third day Laban **was told** that Jacob had fled.
31:27 [G] Why didn't *you* **tell** me, so I could send you away with joy
32: 5 [32:6] [G] Now I am sending *this* **message** to my lord, that I
32:29 [32:30] [G] Jacob said, "Please **tell** me your name." But he
37: 5 [G] Joseph had a dream, and when *he* **told** it to his brothers, they
37:16 [G] *Can you* **tell** me where they are grazing their flocks?"
38:13 [H] When Tamar **was told**, "Your father-in-law is on his way to
38:24 [H] About three months later Judah **was told**, "Your
41:24 [G] I told this to the magicians, but none *could* **explain** it to me."
41:25 [G] God *has* **revealed** to Pharaoh what he is about to do.
42:29 [G] land of Canaan, *they* **told** him all that had happened to them.
43: 6 [G] "Why did you bring this trouble on me by **telling** the man
43: 7 [G] have another brother?' *We* simply **answered** his questions.
44:24 [G] your servant my father, *we* **told** him what my lord had said.
45:13 [G] **Tell** my father *about* all the honor accorded me in Egypt and
45:26 [G] *They* **told** him, "Joseph is still alive! In fact, he is ruler of all
46:31 [G] "I will go up and **speak** to Pharaoh and will say to him,
47: 1 [G] Joseph went and **told** Pharaoh, "My father and brothers, with
48: 2 [G] When Jacob *was* **told**, "Your son Joseph has come to you,"
49: 1 [G] so *I can* **tell** you what will happen to you in days to come.
Ex 4:28 [G] **told** Aaron everything the LORD had sent him to say, and also
13: 8 [G] On that day **tell** your son, 'I do this because of what the
14: 5 [H] When the king of Egypt **was told** that the people had fled,
16:22 [G] leaders of the community came and **reported** this to Moses.
19: 3 [G] house of Jacob and what *you are to* **tell** the people of Israel:
19: 9 [G] Then Moses **told** the LORD what the people had said.
Lev 5: 1 [G] because *he does* not **speak up** when he hears a public charge
14:35 [G] the owner of the house must go and **tell** the priest, 'I have
Nu 11:27 [G] A young man ran and **told** Moses, "Eldad and Medad are
23: 3 [G] Whatever he reveals to me *I will* **tell** you." Then he went off
Dt 4:13 [G] *He* **declared** to you his covenant, the Ten Commandments,
5: 5 [G] and you to **declare** to you the word of the LORD,
17: 4 [H] *this has* **been brought to** your **attention** [+2256+4200+9048],
17: 9 [G] that time. Inquire of them and *they will* **give** you the verdict.
17:10 [G] You must act according to the decisions *they* **give** you at the
17:11 [G] Do not turn aside from what *they* **tell** you, to the right or to
26: 3 [G] "*I* **declare** today to the LORD your God that I have come to
30:18 [G] *I* **declare** to you this day that you will certainly be destroyed.
32: 7 [G] Ask your father and *he will* **tell** you, your elders, and they
Jos 2:14 [G] "If *you* don't **tell** what we are doing, we will treat you kindly
2:20 [G] if *you* **tell** what we are doing, we will be released from the
7:19 [G] **Tell** me what you have done; do not hide it from me."
9:24 [H] "Your servants **were clearly told** [+906+4200+5583] how
9:24 [H] "Your servants **were clearly told** [+906+4200+5583] how
10:17 [H] When Joshua **was told** that the five kings had been found
Jdg 4:12 [G] When *they* **told** Sisera that Barak son of Abinoam had gone
9: 7 [G] When Jotham *was* **told** *about* this, he climbed up on the top
9:25 [H] who passed by, and *this* **was reported** to Abimelech.
9:42 [G] went out to the fields, and this *was* **reported** to Abimelech.
9:47 [H] When Abimelech **heard** that they had assembled there,
13: 6 [G] ask him where he came from, and *he* didn't **tell** me his name.
13:10 [G] The woman hurried *to* **tell** her husband, "He's here! The man
14: 2 [G] When he returned, *he* **said** to his father and mother, "I have
14: 6 [G] *he* **told** neither his father nor his mother what he had done.
14: 9 [G] *he did* not **tell** them that he had taken the honey from the
14:12 [G] "If *you can* **give** me *the* **answer** [+906+4200+5583] within the
14:12 [G] "If *you can* **give** me *the* **answer** [+906+4200+5583] within the
14:13 [G] If you can't **tell** me *the* **answer**, you must give me thirty
14:14 [G] For three days they could not **give** the answer.
14:15 [G] "Coax your husband into **explaining** the riddle for us, or we
14:16 [G] my people a riddle, but *you* haven't **told** me *the* **answer**."
14:16 [G] "*I* haven't even **explained** it to my father or mother," he
14:16 [G] or mother," he replied, "so *why should I* **explain** it to you?"
14:17 [G] So on the seventh day *he* finally **told** her, because she
14:17 [G] to press him. *She* in turn **explained** the riddle to her people.
14:19 [G] gave their clothes to *those who had* **explained** the riddle.
16: 6 [G] "**Tell** me the secret of your great strength and how you can
16:10 [G] you lied to me. Come now, **tell** me how you can be tied."
16:13 [G] **Tell** me how you can be tied." He replied, "If you weave the
16:15 [G] of me and haven't **told** me the secret of your great strength."
16:17 [G] So *he* **told** her everything. "No razor has ever been used on
16:18 [G] When Delilah saw that *he had* **told** her everything, she sent
16:18 [G] "Come back once more; *he has* **told** me everything."
Ru 2:11 [H] "I've **been told** [+4200+5583] all **about** what you have done
2:11 [H] "I've **been told** all **about** [+4200+5583] what you have done
2:19 [G] Ruth **told** her mother-in-law *about* the one at whose place
3: 4 [G] uncover his feet and lie down. He *will* **tell** you what to do."
3:16 [G] Then *she* **told** her everything Boaz had done for her
4: 4 [G] redeem it, do so. But if you will not, **tell** me, so I will know.
1Sa 3:13 [G] For *I* **told** him that I would judge his family forever
3:15 [G] the house of the LORD. He was afraid *to* **tell** Eli the vision,
3:18 [G] So Samuel **told** him everything, hiding nothing from him.
4:13 [G] When the man entered the town and **told** what had happened,
4:14 [G] of this uproar?" The man hurried over **[RPH]** to Eli,
8: 9 [G] **let** them **know** what the king who will reign over them will
9: 6 [G] go there now. Perhaps *he will* **tell** us what way to take."
9: 8 [G] it to the man of God so that *he will* **tell** us what way to take."
9:18 [G] "*Would you* please **tell** me where the seer's house is?"
9:19 [G] I will let you go and *will* **tell** you all that is in your heart.
10:15 [G] Saul's uncle said, "**Tell** me what Samuel said to you."
10:16 [G] "*He* **assured** [+4200+5583] us that the donkeys had been
10:16 [G] "*He* **assured** [+4200+5583] us that the donkeys had been
10:16 [G] *he did* not **tell** his uncle what Samuel had said about the
11: 9 [G] the messengers went and **reported** this to the men of Jabesh,
14: 1 [G] outpost on the other side." But *he did* not **tell** his father.
14:33 [G] *someone* **said** to Saul, "Look, the men are sinning against the
14:43 [G] Then Saul said to Jonathan, "**Tell** me what you have done."
14:43 [G] So Jonathan **told** him, "I merely tasted a little honey with the
15:12 [H] Samuel got up and went to meet Saul, but he **was told**,
15:16 [G] "*Let me* **tell** you what the LORD said to me last night."

1Sa 17:31 [G] What David said was overheard and **reported** to Saul,
18:20 [G] and when *they* **told** Saul *about* it, he was pleased.
18:24 [G] When Saul's servants **told** him what David had said,
18:26 [G] When the attendants **told** David these things, he was pleased
19: 2 [G] **warned** him, "My father Saul is looking for a chance to kill
19: 3 [G] I'll speak to him about you and *will* **tell** you what I find out."
19: 7 [G] Jonathan called David and **told** him the whole conversation.
19:11 [G] Michal, David's wife, **warned** him, "If you don't run for
19:18 [G] Samuel at Ramah and **told** him all that Saul had done to him.
19:19 [H] **Word came** to Saul: "David is in Naioth at Ramah";
19:21 [G] Saul *was* **told** *about* it, and he sent more men, and they
20: 9 [G] my father was determined to harm you, wouldn't *I* **tell** you?"
20:10 [G] "Who *will* **tell** me if your father answers you harshly?"
22:21 [G] He **told** David that Saul had killed the priests of the LORD.
22:22 [G] I knew *he would* **be sure to tell** [+4200+5583] Saul.
22:22 [G] I knew *he would* **be sure to tell** [+4200+5583] Saul.
23: 1 [G] When David *was* **told**, "Look, the Philistines are fighting
23: 7 [H] Saul *was* **told** that David had gone to Keilah, and he said,
23:11 [G] O LORD, God of Israel, **tell** your servant." And the LORD
23:13 [H] When Saul **was told** that David had escaped from Keilah,
23:25 [G] and when David *was* **told** *about* it, he went down to the rock
24: 1 [24:2] [G] he *was* **told**, "David is in the Desert of En Gedi."
24:18 [24:19] [G] *have* just now **told** me *of* the good you did to me;
25: 8 [G] Ask your own servants and *they will* **tell** you. Therefore be
25:12 [G] went back. When they arrived, *they* **reported** every word.
25:14 [G] One of the servants **told** Nabal's wife Abigail: "David sent
25:19 [G] I'll follow you." But *she did* not **tell** her husband Nabal.
25:36 [G] and very drunk. So *she* **told** him nothing until daybreak.
25:37 [G] when Nabal was sober, his wife **told** him all these things,
27: 4 [H] When Saul **was told** that David had fled to Gath, he no
27:11 [G] to Gath, for he thought, "*They* might **inform** on us and say,
2Sa 1: 4 [G] "**Tell** me." He said, "The men fled from the battle.
1: 5 [G] David said to the young man who **brought** him *the* **report**,
1: 6 [G] the young man **[RPH]** said, "and there was Saul, leaning on
1:13 [G] David said to the young man who **brought** him *the* **report**,
1:20 [G] "**Tell** it not in Gath, proclaim it not in the streets of
2: 4 [G] When David *was* **told** that it was the men of Jabesh Gilead
3:23 [G] he *was* **told** that Abner son of Ner had come to the king
4:10 [G] when a *man* **told** me, 'Saul is dead,' and thought he was
6:12 [H] Now King David **was told**, "The LORD has blessed the
7:11 [G] " 'The LORD **declares** to you that the LORD himself will
10: 5 [G] When David **was told** *about* this, he sent messengers to meet
10:17 [H] When David **was told** *of* this, he gathered all Israel, crossed
11: 5 [G] woman conceived and **sent word** [+2256+8938] to David,
11:10 [G] When David *was* **told**, "Uriah did not go home," he asked
11:18 [G] Joab sent **[NIE]** David a full account of the battle.
11:22 [G] when he arrived *he* **told** David everything Joab had sent him
12:18 [G] David's servants were afraid to **tell** him that the child was
13: 4 [G] Won't *you* **tell** me?" Amnon said to him, "I'm in love with
13:34 [g] The watchman went and **told** [BHS-] the king, "I see men in
14:33 [G] So Joab went to the king and **told** him this. Then the king
15:13 [G] A **messenger** came and told David, "The hearts of the men
15:28 [G] in the desert until word comes from you to **inform** me."
15:31 [G] Now David *had been* **told**, "Ahithophel is among the
15:35 [G] with you? **Tell** them anything you hear in the king's palace.
17:16 [G] Now send a message immediately and **tell** David, 'Do not
17:17 [G] A servant girl was to go and **inform** them, and they were to
17:17 [G] and inform them, and they were to go and **tell** King David,
17:18 [G] a young man saw them and **told** Absalom. So the two of
17:21 [G] two climbed out of the well and went *to* **inform** King David.
18:10 [G] When one of the men saw this, *he* **told** Joab, "I just saw
18:11 [G] Joab said to the man who *had* **told** him this, "What! You saw
18:21 [G] said to a Cushite, "Go, **tell** the king what you have seen."
18:25 [G] The watchman called out to the king and **reported** it. The
19: 1 [19:2] [H] Joab **was told**, "The king is weeping and mourning
19: 6 [19:7] [G] *You have* **made** *it* **clear** today that the commanders
19: 8 [19:9] [G] When the men *were* **told**, "The king is sitting in the
21:11 [H] When David **was told** what Aiah's daughter Rizpah,
24:13 [G] So Gad went to David and **said** to him, "Shall there come
1Ki 1:20 [G] to **learn** from you who will sit on the throne of my lord the
1:23 [G] *they* **told** the king, "Nathan the prophet is here." So he went
1:51 [H] Solomon **was told**, "Adonijah is afraid of King Solomon
2:29 [H] King Solomon **was told** that Joab had fled to the tent of the
2:39 [G] king of Gath, and Shimei *was* **told**, "Your slaves are in
2:41 [H] When Solomon **was told** that Shimei had gone from
10: 3 [G] Solomon **answered** all her questions; nothing was too hard
10: 3 [G] nothing was too hard for the king *to* **explain** to her.
10: 7 [H] Indeed, not even half **was told** me; in wisdom and wealth
14: 3 [G] and go to him. He *will* **tell** you what will happen to the boy."
18:12 [G] If I go and **tell** Ahab and he doesn't find you, he will kill me.
18:13 [H] Haven't you **heard**, my lord, what I did while Jezebel was
18:16 [G] So Obadiah went to meet Ahab and **told** him, and Ahab went
19: 1 [G] Now Ahab **told** Jezebel everything Elijah had done and how
20:17 [G] *who* **reported**, "Men are advancing from Samaria."
2Ki 4: 2 [G] can I help you? **Tell** me, what do you have in your house?"
4: 7 [G] She went and **told** the man of God, and he said, "Go, sell the
4:27 [G] the LORD has hidden it from me and *has* not **told** me why."
4:31 [G] So Gehazi went back to meet Elisha and **told** him, "The boy
5: 4 [G] to his master and **told** him what the girl from Israel had said.
6:11 [G] "*Will you* not **tell** me which of us is on the side of the king
6:12 [G] **tells** the king of Israel the very words you speak in your
6:13 [H] I can send men and capture him." *The* **report came back**:
7: 9 [G] Let's go at once and **report** this *to* the royal palace."
7:10 [G] and called out to the city gatekeepers and **told** them,
7:11 [G] shouted the news, and *it was* **reported** within the palace.
7:12 [G] "*I will* **tell** you what the Arameans have done to us.
7:15 [G] So the messengers returned and **reported** to the king.
8: 7 [H] When the king **was told**, "The man of God has come all the
9:12 [G] they said. "**Tell** us." Jehu said, "Here is what he told me:
9:15 [G] anyone slip out of the city to go and **tell the news** in Jezreel."
9:18 [G] The lookout **reported**, "The messenger has reached them,
9:20 [G] The lookout **reported**, "He has reached them, but he isn't
9:36 [G] They went back and **told** Jehu, who said, "This is the word of
10: 8 [G] When the messenger arrived, *he* **told** Jehu, "They have
18:37 [G] and **told** him what the field commander had said.
22:10 [G] Shaphan the secretary **informed** the king, "Hilkiah the priest
1Ch 17:10 [G] " '*I* **declare** to you that the LORD will build a house for
19: 5 [G] When someone came and **told** David about the men, he sent
19:17 [H] When David **was told** *of* this, he gathered all Israel
2Ch 9: 2 [G] Solomon **answered** all her questions; nothing was too hard
9: 2 [G] nothing was too hard for him *to* **explain** to her.
9: 6 [H] not even half the greatness of your wisdom **was told** me;
20: 2 [G] Some men came and **told** Jehoshaphat, "A vast army is
34:18 [G] Shaphan the secretary **informed** the king, "Hilkiah the priest
Ezr 2:59 [G] they could not **show** that their families were descended from
Ne 2:12 [G] *I had* not **told** anyone what my God had put in my heart to
2:16 [G] because as yet *I had* **said** nothing to the Jews or the priests
2:18 [G] *I* also **told** them *about* the gracious hand of my God upon
7:61 [G] they could not **show** that their families were descended from
Est 2:10 [G] Esther *had* not **revealed** her nationality and family
2:10 [G] because Mordecai had forbidden her *to* **do**ˢ **so**.
2:20 [G] *had* **kept secret** [+401+906] her family background and
2:22 [G] Mordecai found out about the plot and **told** Queen Esther,
3: 4 [G] Therefore *they* **told** Haman *about* it to see whether
3: 4 [G] would be tolerated, for *he had* **told** them he was a Jew.
3: 6 [G] Yet *having* **learned** [+906+4200] who Mordecai's people
4: 4 [G] and eunuchs came and **told** her *about* Mordecai,
4: 7 [G] **told** him everything that had happened to him, including
4: 8 [G] published in Susa, to show to Esther and **explain** it to her,
4: 9 [G] went back and **reported** to Esther what Mordecai had said.
4:12 [G] When Esther's words *were* **reported** to Mordecai,
6: 2 [G] It was found recorded there that Mordecai *had* **exposed**
8: 1 [G] of the king, for Esther *had* **told** how he was related to her.
Job 1:15 [G] and I am the only one who has escaped to **tell** you!"
1:16 [G] and I am the only one who has escaped to **tell** you!"
1:17 [G] and I am the only one who has escaped to **tell** you!"
1:19 [G] are dead, and I am the only one who has escaped to **tell** you!"
11: 6 [G] **disclose** to you the secrets of wisdom, for true wisdom has
12: 7 [G] will teach you, or the birds of the air, and *they will* **tell** you;
15:18 [G] what wise men *have* **declared**, hiding nothing received from
17: 5 [G] If *a man* **denounces** his friends for reward, the eyes of his
21:31 [G] Who **denounces** his conduct to his face? Who repays him for
26: 4 [G] Who has helped *you* **utter** these words? And whose spirit
31:37 [G] *I would* **give** him an account of my every step; like a prince I
33:23 [G] one out of a thousand, to **tell** a man what is right for him,
36: 9 [G] *he* **tells** them what they have done—that they have sinned
36:33 [G] **announces** the coming storm; even the cattle make known
38: 4 [G] I laid the earth's foundation? **Tell** me, if you understand.
38:18 [G] the vast expanses of the earth? **Tell** me, if you know all this.
42: 3 [G] Surely *I* **spoke** *of* things I did not understand, things too
Ps 9:11 [9:12] [G] **proclaim** among the nations what he has done.
19: 1 [19:2] [G] of God; the skies **proclaim** the work of his hands.
22:31 [22:32] [G] *They will* **proclaim** his righteousness to a people
30: 9 [30:10] [G] dust praise you? *Will it* **proclaim** your faithfulness?
38:18 [38:19] [G] *I* **confess** my iniquity; I am troubled by my sin.
40: 5 [40:6] [G] *were I to* **speak** and tell of them, they would be too
50: 6 [G] the heavens **proclaim** his righteousness, for God himself is
51:15 [51:17] [G] my lips, and my mouth *will* **declare** your praise.
52: T [52:2] [G] Doeg the Edomite had gone to Saul and **told** him:
64: 9 [64:10] [G] *they will* **proclaim** the works of God and ponder
71:17 [G] taught me, and to this day *I* **declare** your marvelous deeds.
71:18 [G] O God, till *I* **declare** your power to the next generation,
75: 9 [75:10] [G] As for me, *I will* **declare** this forever; I will sing
92: 2 [92:3] [G] to **proclaim** your love in the morning and your
92:15 [92:16] [G] **proclaiming**, "The LORD is upright; he is my
97: 6 [G] The heavens **proclaim** his righteousness, and all the peoples
111: 6 [G] *He has* **shown** his people the power of his works, giving
142: 2 [142:3] [G] complaint before him; before him *I* **tell** my trouble.

Ps 145: 4 [G] your works to another; *they will* **tell** *of* your mighty acts.
147: 19 [G] *He has* **revealed** his word to Jacob, his laws and decrees to
Pr 12: 17 [G] A truthful witness gives honest **testimony**, but a false
29: 24 [G] is his own enemy; he is put under oath and *dare* not **testify**.
Ecc 6: 12 [G] Who *can* **tell** him what will happen under the sun after he is
8: 7 [G] no man knows the future, who *can* **tell** him what is to come?
10: 14 [G] is coming—who *can* **tell** him what will happen after him?
10: 20 [G] and a bird on the wing *may* **report** what you say.
SS 1: 7 [G] **Tell** me, you whom I love, where you graze your flock
5: 8 [G] I charge you—if you find my lover, what *will you* **tell** him?
Isa 3: 9 [G] *they* **parade** their sin like Sodom; they do not hide it.
7: 2 [H] Now the house of David **was told**, "Aram has allied itself
19: 12 [G] *Let them* **show** you and make known what the LORD
21: 2 [H] A dire vision *has* **been shown** to me: The traitor betrays,
21: 6 [G] "Go, post a lookout and *have him* **report** what he sees.
21: 10 [G] *I* **tell** you what I have heard from the LORD Almighty,
36: 22 [G] and **told** him what the field commander had said.
40: 21 [H] you not heard? *Has it* not **been told** you from the beginning?
41: 22 [G] "Bring in ⌞your idols⌟ *to* **tell** us what is going to happen.
41: 22 [G] **Tell** us what the former things were, so that we may consider
41: 23 [G] **tell** us what the future holds, so we may know that you are
41: 26 [G] Who **told** *of* this from the beginning, so we could know,
41: 26 [G] No *one* **told** *of* this, no one foretold it, no one heard any
42: 9 [G] the former things have taken place, and new things I **declare**;
42: 12 [G] glory to the LORD and **proclaim** his praise in the islands.
43: 9 [G] Which of them **foretold** this and proclaimed to us the former
43: 12 [G] I *have* **revealed** and saved and proclaimed—I, and not some
44: 7 [G] *Let him* **declare** and lay out before me what has happened
44: 7 [G] what is yet to come—yes, *let him* **foretell** what will come.
44: 8 [G] not be afraid. Did I not proclaim this and **foretell** it long ago?
45: 19 [G] I, the LORD, speak the truth; I **declare** what is right.
45: 21 [G] **Declare** what is to be, present it—let them take counsel
45: 21 [G] foretold this long ago, *who* **declared** it from the distant past?
46: 10 [G] I **make known** the end from the beginning, from ancient
48: 3 [G] *I* **foretold** the former things long ago, my mouth announced
48: 5 [G] Therefore *I* **told** you these things long ago; before they
48: 6 [G] these things; look at them all. *Will* you not **admit** them?
48: 14 [G] and listen: Which of ⌞the idols⌟ *has* **foretold** these things?
48: 20 [G] **Announce** this with shouts of joy and proclaim it.
57: 12 [G] I *will* **expose** your righteousness and your works, and they
58: 1 [G] **Declare** to my people their rebellion and to the house of
66: 19 [G] my glory. *They will* **proclaim** my glory among the nations.
Jer 4: 5 [G] "**Announce** in Judah and proclaim in Jerusalem and say:
4: 15 [G] A voice *is* **announcing** from Dan, proclaiming disaster from
5: 20 [G] "**Announce** this to the house of Jacob and proclaim it in
9: 12 [9:11] [G] been instructed by the LORD and *can* **explain** it?
16: 10 [G] "When *you* **tell** these people all this and they ask you, 'Why
20: 10 [G] "Terror on every side! **Report** him! Let's report him!"
20: 10 [G] "Terror on every side! Report him! *Let's* **report** him!"
31: 10 [G] of the LORD, O nations; **proclaim** it in distant coastlands:
33: 3 [G] 'Call to me and I will answer you and **tell** you great
36: 13 [G] After Micaiah **told** them everything he had heard Baruch
36: 16 [G] "*We* **must report** [+906+5583] all these words to the king."
36: 16 [G] "*We* **must report** [+906+5583] all these words to the king."
36: 17 [G] they asked Baruch, "**Tell** us, how did you come to write all
36: 20 [G] to the king in the courtyard and **reported** everything to him.
38: 15 [G] to Zedekiah, "If *I* **give** you **an answer**, will you not kill me?
38: 25 [G] '**Tell** us what you said to the king and what the king said to
38: 27 [G] and *he* **told** them everything the king had ordered him to say.
42: 3 [G] the LORD your God *will* **tell** us where we should go and
42: 4 [G] *I will* **tell** you everything the LORD says and will keep
42: 20 [G] our God for us; **tell** us everything he says and we will do it.'
42: 21 [G] *I have* **told** you today, but you still have not obeyed the
46: 14 [G] "**Announce** this in Egypt, and proclaim it in Migdol;
48: 20 [G] and cry out! **Announce** by the Arnon that Moab is destroyed.
50: 2 [G] "**Announce** and proclaim among the nations, lift up a banner
50: 28 [G] refugees from Babylon **declaring** in Zion how the LORD
51: 31 [G] **messenger** follows messenger to announce to the king of
51: 31 [G] messenger follows **messenger** to announce to the king of
51: 31 [G] messenger follows messenger to **announce** to the king of
Eze 23: 36 [G] Then **confront** them *with* their detestable practices,
24: 19 [G] "Won't *you* **tell** us what these things have to do with us?"
37: 18 [G] ask you, 'Won't *you* **tell** us what you mean by this?'
40: 4 [G] brought here. **Tell** the house of Israel everything you see."
43: 10 [G] "Son of man, **describe** the temple *to* the people of Israel,
Da 2: 2 [G] sorcerers and astrologers to **tell** him what he had dreamed.
9: 23 [G] an answer was given, which I have come to **tell** you, for you
10: 21 [G] but first *I will* **tell** you what is written in the Book of Truth.
11: 2 [G] "Now then, *I* **tell** you the truth: Three more kings will appear
Hos 4: 12 [G] consult a wooden idol and *are* **answered** *by* a stick of wood.
Am 4: 13 [G] creates the wind, and **reveals** his thoughts to man,
Jnh 1: 8 [G] So they asked him, "**Tell** us, who is responsible for making
1: 10 [G] from the LORD, because *he had already* **told** them so.)
Mic 1: 10 [G] **Tell** it not in Gath; weep not at all. In Beth Ophrah roll in the
3: 8 [G] with justice and might, to **declare** to Jacob his transgression,
6: 8 [G] *He has* **showed** you, O man, what is good. And what does
Zec 9: 12 [G] even now I **announce** that I will restore twice as much to

5584 נֶגֶד *neged*, subst. & adv. & pp. [151] [√ 5583; Ar 10458]
before [29], opposite [15], before [+4200] [13], in the presence of [7], in front of [6], from [+4946] [5], *untranslated* [3], facing [3], in [3], near [3], presence [3], before [+7156] [2], by [2], distance [2], far from [+4946] [2], in [+4200] [2], in front of [+4200] [2], in presence [+4200+6524] [2], in the presence of [+2025] [2], in the sight of [2], nearby [+4946] [2], opposite [+4200] [2], regard [+4200+8492] [2], straight in [2], accompany [+2143+4200] [1], across the way [+4946] [1], against [1], aloof [+4946] [1], away from [+4946] [1], because of [+4946] [1], before [+4200+6524] [1], bent on [+7156] [1], beyond [1], constant [+4946] [1], defend [+6641] [1], directly [1], facing [+4946] [1], from [+4946+6524] [1], frontal [+4946] [1], in broad daylight [+2021+9087] [1], in sight [1], in the face of [+4200] [1], kept distance [+3656+4946] [1], known to [1], next to [+4200] [1], opposite [+4946] [1], out of [+4946] [1], resisted [+4200+6641] [1], responsible for [+4200] [1], right before [+4200] [1], risked [+906+4946+8959] [1], some distance [1], straight through [1], straight [1], succeed against [+4200] [1], suitable [+3869] [1], suitable for [+3869] [1], to [1], with [1]

Ge 2: 18 man to be alone. I will make a helper **suitable for** [+3869] him."
2: 20 of the field. But for Adam no **suitable** [+3869] helper was found.
21: 16 she went off and sat down **nearby** [+4946], about a bowshot away,
21: 16 boy die." And as she sat there **nearby** [+4946], she began to sob.
31: 32 **In the presence of** our relatives, see for yourself whether there is
31: 37 Put it here **in front of** your relatives and mine, and let them judge
33: 12 "Let us be on our way; *I'll* **accompany** [+2143+4200] you."
47: 15 and said, "Give us food. Why should we die **before** your eyes?
Ex 10: 10 your women and children! Clearly you are **bent** [+7156] **on** evil.
19: 2 and Israel camped there in the desert **in front of** the mountain.
34: 10 **Before** all your people I will do wonders never before done in any
Nu 2: 2 are to camp around the Tent of Meeting **some distance** from it,
22: 32 oppose you because your path is a reckless one **before** [+4200] me.
25: 4 kill them and expose them **in** broad daylight before the LORD,
Dt 28: 66 You will live in **constant** [+4946] suspense, filled with dread both
31: 11 will choose, you shall read this law **before** them in their hearing.
32: 52 Therefore, you will see the land only from a **distance**; you will not
Jos 3: 16 completely cut off. So the people crossed over **opposite** Jericho.
5: 13 saw a man standing **in front** [+4200] **of** him with a drawn sword in
6: 5 will collapse and the people will go up, every man **straight in**."
6: 20 so every man charged **straight in**, and they took the city.
8: 11 him marched up and approached the city and arrived **in front of** it.
8: 33 ark of the covenant of the LORD, **facing** those who carried it—
8: 35 that Joshua did not read **to** the whole assembly of Israel,
Jdg 9: 17 my father fought for you, **risked** [+906+4946+8959] his life to
20: 34 ten thousand of Israel's finest men made a **frontal** [+4946] attack
Ru 4: 4 and suggest that you buy it **in the presence of** these seated here
4: 4 these seated here and **in the presence of** the elders of my people.
1Sa 12: 3 Testify against me **in the presence of** the LORD and his
12: 3 me in the presence of the LORD and **[RPH]** his anointed.
15: 30 please honor me **before** the elders of my people and before Israel;
15: 30 please honor me before the elders of my people and **before** Israel;
16: 6 "Surely the LORD's anointed stands here **before** the LORD."
26: 20 Now do not let my blood fall to the ground **far from** [+4946] the
2Sa 12: 12 I will do this thing **in broad daylight** [+2021+9087] before all
12: 12 but I will do this thing in broad daylight **before** all Israel.' "
18: 13 you *would have* **kept** *your* **distance from** [+3656+4946] me."
22: 13 Out of the brightness of his **presence** bolts of lightning blazed
22: 23 All his laws are **before** [+4200] me; I have not turned away from
22: 25 my righteousness, according to my cleanness **in** [+4200] his sight.
1Ki 8: 22 Solomon stood before the altar of the LORD **in front of** the
20: 27 The Israelites camped **opposite** them like two small flocks of
21: 10 seat two scoundrels **opposite** him and have them testify that he has
21: 13 two scoundrels came and sat **opposite** him and brought charges
21: 13 and brought charges against Naboth **before** the people,
2Ki 1: 13 third captain went up and fell on his knees **before** [+4200] Elijah.
2: 7 and stood at a distance, **facing** [+4946] the place where Elijah
2: 15 who were watching, **[RPH]** said, "The spirit of Elijah is resting
3: 22 To the Moabites **across** [+4946] **the way**, the water looked red—
4: 25 When he saw her in the **distance**, the man of God said to his
1Ch 5: 11 The Gadites lived **next** [+4200] **to** them in Bashan, as far as
8: 32 father of Shimeah. They too lived **near** their relatives in Jerusalem.
9: 38 of Shimeam. They too lived **near** their relatives in Jerusalem.
2Ch 6: 12 Solomon stood before the altar of the LORD **in front of** the
6: 13 and then knelt down **before** the whole assembly of Israel
7: 6 **Opposite** the Levites, the priests blew their trumpets, and all the
8: 14 to assist **[OBJ]** the priests according to each day's requirement.
Ne 3: 10 Jedaiah son of Harumaph made repairs **opposite** his house,
3: 16 made repairs up to a point **opposite** the tombs of David, as far as
3: 19 from a point **facing** the ascent to the armory as far as the angle.
3: 23 Benjamin and Hasshub made repairs **in front of** their house;

Ne 3:25 Palal son of Uzai worked **opposite** [+4946] the angle and the tower
3:26 made repairs up to a point **opposite** the Water Gate toward the east
3:27 **from** [+4946] the great projecting tower to the wall of Ophel.
3:28 the priests made repairs, each **in front** [+4200] **of** his own house.
3:29 to them, Zadok son of Immer made repairs **opposite** his house.
3:30 Meshullam son of Berekiah made repairs **opposite** his living
3:31 temple servants and the merchants, **opposite** the Inspection Gate,
4: 5 [3:37] for they have thrown insults **in the face** [+4200] **of** the
7: 3 as guards, some at their posts and some **near** their own houses."
8: 3 faced the square before the Water Gate **in the presence of** the men,
11:22 who were the singers **responsible** [+4200] **for** the service of the
12: 9 their associates, stood **opposite** [+4200] them in the services.
12:24 who stood **opposite** [+4200] them to give praise and thanksgiving,
12:37 At the Fountain Gate they continued **directly** up the steps of the
13:21 I warned them and said, "Why do you spend the night **by** the wall?
Job 4:16 A form stood **before** [+4200] my eyes, and I heard a hushed voice:
10:17 You bring new witnesses **against** me and increase your anger
26: 6 Death is naked **before** God; Destruction lies uncovered.
Ps 5: 5 [5:6] The arrogant cannot stand **in** your **presence** [+4200+6524];
10: 5 he is haughty and your laws are **far from** [+4946] him; he sneers at
16: 8 I have set the LORD always **before** [+4200] me. Because he is at
18:12 [18:13] Out of the brightness of his **presence** clouds advanced,
18:22 [18:23] All his laws are **before** [+4200] me; I have not turned
18:24 [18:25] according to the cleanness of my hands **in** [+4200] his
22:25 [22:26] **before** those who fear you will I fulfill my vows.
23: 5 You prepare a table before me **in the presence of** my enemies.
26: 3 for your love is ever **before** [+4200+6524] me, and I walk
31:19 [31:20] which you bestow **in the sight of** men on those who take
31:22 [31:23] my alarm I said, "I am cut off **from** [+4946] your sight!"
36: 1 [36:2] There is no fear of God **before** [+4200] his eyes.
38: 9 [38:10] All my longings lie open **before** you, O Lord; my sighing
38:11 [38:12] companions avoid me **because of** [+4946] my wounds;
38:17 [38:18] For I am about to fall, and my pain is ever **with** me.
39: 1 [39:2] on my mouth as long as the wicked are in my **presence**."
39: 5 [39:6] the span of my years is as nothing **before** you.
44:15 [44:16] My disgrace is **before** me all day long, and my face is
50: 8 or your burnt offerings, which are ever **before** [+4200] me.
51: 3 [51:5] I know my transgressions, and my sin is always **before** me.
52: 9 [52:11] is good. I will praise you **in the presence of** your saints.
54: 3 [54:5] seek my life—men without **regard for** [+4200+8492] God.
69:19 [69:20] and shamed; all my enemies are **before** you.
78:12 He did miracles **in the sight of** their fathers in the land of Egypt,
86:14 men seeks my life—men without **regard for** [+4200+8492] you.
88: 1 [88:2] the God who saves me, day and night I cry out **before** you.
89:36 [89:37] and his throne endure **before** me like the sun;
90: 8 You have set our iniquities **before** [+4200] you, our secret sins in
101: 3 I will set **before** [+4200] my eyes no vile thing. The deeds of
101: 7 who speaks falsely will stand **in** my **presence** [+4200+6524].
109:15 May their sins always remain **before** the LORD, that he may cut
116:14 I will fulfill my vows to the LORD **in the presence** [+2025] **of** all
116:18 I will fulfill my vows to the LORD **in the presence** [+2025] **of** all
119:46 I will speak of your statutes **before** kings and will not be put to
119:168 your precepts and your statutes, for all my ways are **known to** you.
138: 1 with all my heart; **before** the "gods" I will sing your praise.
Pr 4:25 your eyes look straight ahead, fix your gaze directly **before** you.
14: 7 Stay **away from** [+4946] a foolish man, for you will not find
15:11 Death and Destruction lie open **before** the LORD—how much
21:30 no insight, no plan that can **succeed against** [+4200] the LORD.
Ecc 4:12 one may be overpowered, two *can* **defend themselves** [+6641].
6: 8 poor man gain by knowing how to conduct himself **before** others?
SS 6: 5 Turn your eyes **from** [+4946] me; they overwhelm me. Your hair
Isa 1: 7 your fields are being stripped by foreigners **right before** [+4200]
1:16 Take your evil deeds **out of** [+4946] my sight! Stop doing wrong,
5:21 those who are wise in their own eyes and clever **in** their own sight.
24:23 on Mount Zion and in Jerusalem, and **before** its elders, gloriously.
40:17 **Before** him all the nations are as nothing; they are regarded by him
47:14 Here are no coals to warm anyone; here is no fire to sit **by**.
49:16 you on the palms of my hands; your walls are ever **before** me.
59:12 For our offenses are many **in** your **sight**, and our sins testify
61:11 will make righteousness and praise spring up **before** all nations.
Jer 16:17 hidden from me, nor is their sin concealed **from** [+4946] my eyes.
31:39 The measuring line will stretch from there **straight** to the hill of
La 3:35 to deny a man his rights **before** [+7156] the Most High,
Eze 40:13 twenty-five cubits from one parapet opening to the **opposite** one.
40:23 There was a gate to the inner court **facing** the north gate, just as
41:16 everything **beyond** and including the threshold was covered with
42: 1 and brought me to the rooms **opposite** the temple courtyard
42: 1 the temple courtyard and **opposite** the outer wall on the north side.
42: 3 Both **in** the section twenty cubits from the inner court and in the
42: 3 and in the section **opposite** the pavement of the outer court,
Da 8:15 there **before** [+4200] me stood one who looked like a man.
10:13 the prince of the Persian kingdom **resisted** [+4200+6641] me
10:16 I said to the one standing **before** [+4200] me, "I am overcome with
Hos 7: 2 Their sins engulf them; they are always **before** [+7156] me.
Joel 1:16 Has not the food been cut off **before** our very eyes—joy
Am 4: 3 You will each go **straight** out **through** breaks in the wall,
9: 3 Though they hide **from** [+4946+6524] me at the bottom of the sea,
Ob 1:11 On the day you stood **aloof** [+4946] while strangers carried off his
Jnh 2: 4 [2:5] I said, 'I have been banished **from** [+4946] your sight; yet I
Hab 1: 3 Destruction and violence are **before** [+4200] me; there is strife,

5585 נָגַה *nāgah*, v. [6] [→ 5586, 5587, 5588]

turns into light [2], burning [1], dawned [1], give [1], shine [1]

2Sa 22:29 [G] O LORD; the LORD **turns** my darkness **into light**.
Job 18: 5 [A] wicked is snuffed out; the flame of his fire stops **burning**.
22:28 [A] decide on will be done, and light *will* **shine** on your ways.
Ps 18:28 [18:29] [G] my God **turns** my darkness **into light**.
Isa 9: 2 [9:1] [A] in the land of the shadow of death a light *has* **dawned**.
13:10 [G] sun will be darkened and the moon *will* not **give** its light.

5586 נֹגַהּ *nōgah*[1], n.f. [19] [→ 5587; cf. 5585; Ar 10459]

brightness [5], brilliant light [2], dawn [2], no longer shine [+665] [2], radiance [2], bright [1], flashing [1], glow [1], light [1], ray of brightness [1], splendor [1]

2Sa 22:13 Out of the **brightness** *of* his presence bolts of lightning blazed
23: 4 like the **brightness** after rain that brings the grass from the earth.'
Ps 18:12 [18:13] Out of the **brightness** *of* his presence clouds advanced,
Pr 4:18 The path of the righteous is like the first gleam of **dawn**, shining
Isa 4: 5 there a cloud of smoke by day and a **glow** *of* flaming fire by night;
50:10 Let him who walks in the dark, who has no **light**, trust in the name
60: 3 will come to your light, and kings to the **brightness** *of* your dawn.
60:19 light by day, nor will the **brightness** *of* the moon shine on you,
62: 1 till her righteousness shines out like the **dawn**, her salvation like a
Eze 1: 4 cloud with flashing lightning and surrounded by **brilliant light**.
1:13 among the creatures; it was **bright**, and lightning flashed out of it.
1:27 there down he looked like fire; and **brilliant light** surrounded him.
1:28 in the clouds on a rainy day, so was the **radiance** around him.
10: 4 and the court was full of the **radiance** *of* the glory of the LORD.
Joel 2:10 and moon are darkened, and the stars **no longer shine** [+665].
3:15 [4:15] will be darkened, and the stars **no longer shine** [+665].
Am 5:20 be darkness, not light—pitch-dark, without a **ray of brightness**?
Hab 3: 4 His **splendor** was like the sunrise; rays flashed from his hand,
3:11 glint of your flying arrows, at the lightning of your **flashing** spear.

5587 ²נֹגַהּ *nōgah*[2], n.pr.m. [2] [√ 5586; cf. 5585]

Nogah [2]

1Ch 3: 7 **Nogah**, Nepheg, Japhia,
14: 6 **Nogah**, Nepheg, Japhia,

5588 נְגֹהָה *n^{e}gōhâ*, n.f. [1] [√ 5585]

brightness [1]

Isa 59: 9 but all is darkness; for **brightness**, but we walk in deep shadows.

5589 נְגוֹ *n^{e}gô*, n.pr.m. Not used in NIV/BHS [√ 6269 + 5550]

5590 נָגַח *nāgaḥ*, v. [11] [→ 5591]

gore [3], gores [3], *untranslated* [1], butting [1], charged [1], engage in battle [1], push back [1]

Ex 21:28 [A] "If a bull **gores** a man or a woman to death, the bull must be
21:31 [A] This law also applies if the bull **gores** a son or daughter.
21:31 [A] law also applies if the bull gores a son or daughter. **[RPH]**
21:32 [A] If the bull **gores** a male or female slave, the owner must pay
Dt 33:17 [D] With them *he will* **gore** the nations, even those at the ends of
1Ki 22:11 [D] 'With these *you will* **gore** the Arameans until they are
2Ch 18:10 [D] 'With these *you will* **gore** the Arameans until they are
Ps 44: 5 [44:6] [D] Through you *we* **push back** our enemies;
Eze 34:21 [D] **butting** all the weak sheep with your horns until you have
Da 8: 4 [D] I watched the ram *as he* **charged** toward the west
11:40 [F] of the end the king of the South *will* **engage** him **in battle**,

5591 נַגָּח *naggāḥ*, a. [2] [√ 5590]

goring [2]

Ex 21:29 the bull has had the habit of **goring** and the owner has been warned
21:36 However, if it was known that the bull had the habit of **goring**,

5592 נָגִיד *nāgîd*, n.m. [44] [√ 5583]

leader [13], ruler [12], prince [3], in charge [2], officers [2], official in charge [2], administrators [1], chief [1], commanders [1], leaders [1], nobles [1], officer in charge [1], officer [1], rulers [1], supervisor [1], worthy things [1]

1Sa 9:16 Anoint him **leader** over my people Israel; he will deliver my
10: 1 "Has not the LORD anointed you **leader** over his inheritance?
13:14 a man after his own heart and appointed him **leader** of his people,

1Sa 25:30 concerning him and has appointed him **leader** over Israel,
2Sa 5: 2 shepherd my people Israel, and you will become their **ruler**.' "
6:21 or anyone from his house when he appointed me **ruler** over the
7: 8 and from following the flock to be **ruler** over my people Israel.
1Ki 1:35 in my place. I have appointed him **ruler** over Israel and Judah."
14: 7 among the people and made you a **leader** over my people Israel.
16: 2 you up from the dust and made you **leader** of my people Israel,
2Ki 20: 5 "Go back and tell Hezekiah, the **leader** *of* my people, 'This is what
1Ch 5: 2 Judah was the strongest of his brothers and a **ruler** came from him,
9:11 the son of Ahitub, the **official in charge** *of* the house of God;
9:20 In earlier times Phinehas son of Eleazar was **in charge** of the
11: 2 shepherd my people Israel, and you will become their **ruler**.' "
12:27 [12:28] **leader** of the family of Aaron, with 3,700 men,
13: 1 David conferred with each of his **officers**, the commanders of
17: 7 and from following the flock, to be **ruler** over my people Israel.
26:24 Gershom son of Moses, was the **officer** in charge of the treasuries.
27: 4 was Dodai the Ahohite; Mikloth was the **leader** of his division.
27:16 The **officers** over the tribes of Israel: over the Reubenites:
28: 4 He chose Judah as **leader**, and from the house of Judah he chose
29:22 anointing him before the LORD to be **ruler** and Zadok to be
2Ch 6: 5 nor have I chosen anyone to be the **leader** over my people Israel.
11:11 He strengthened their defenses and put **commanders** in them,
11:22 Rehoboam appointed Abijah son of Maacah to be the chief **prince**
19:11 and Zebadiah son of Ishmael, the **leader** of the tribe of Judah,
28: 7 Azrikam the **officer in charge** *of* the palace, and Elkanah,
31:12 Conaniah, a Levite, was **in charge** of these things, and his brother
31:13 and Azariah the **official in charge** *of* the temple of God.
32:21 who annihilated all the fighting men and the **leaders** and officers in
35: 8 Zechariah and Jehiel, the **administrators** *of* God's temple,
Ne 11:11 of Meraioth, the son of Ahitub, **supervisor** *in* the house of God,
Job 29:10 the voices of the **nobles** were hushed, and their tongues stuck to
31:37 account of my every step; like a **prince** I would approach him.)—
Ps 76:12 [76:13] He breaks the spirit of **rulers**; he is feared by the kings of
Pr 8: 6 Listen, for I have **worthy things** to say; I open my lips to speak
28:16 A tyrannical **ruler** lacks judgment, but he who hates ill-gotten gain
Isa 55: 4 a witness to the peoples, a **leader** and commander of the peoples.
Jer 20: 1 son of Immer, the **chief** officer in the temple of the LORD,
Eze 28: 2 "Son of man, say to the **ruler** *of* Tyre, 'This is what the Sovereign
Da 9:25 the **ruler**, comes, there will be seven 'sevens,' and sixty-two
9:26 The people of the **ruler** who will come will destroy the city
11:22 before him; both it and a **prince** *of* the covenant will be destroyed.

5593 נְגִינָה n^e^gînâ, n.f. [14] [√ 5594]

stringed instruments [9], mock in song [2], music [1], song [1], songs [1]

Job 30: 9 "And now their sons **mock** me **in song**; I have become a byword
Ps 4: T [4:1] of music. With **stringed instruments**. A psalm of David.
6: T [6:1] For the director of music. With **stringed instruments**.
54: T [54:1] With **stringed instruments**. A *maskil* of David.
55: T [55:1] With **stringed instruments**. A *maskil* of David.
61: T [61:1] director of music. With **stringed instruments**. Of David.
67: T [67:1] of music. With **stringed instruments**. A psalm. A song.
69:12 [69:13] at the gate mock me, and I am the **song** *of* the drunkards.
76: T [76:1] With **stringed instruments**. A psalm of Asaph. A song.
77: 6 [77:7] I remembered my **songs** in the night. My heart mused
Isa 38:20 we will sing with **stringed instruments** all the days of our lives in
La 3:14 of all my people; they **mock** me **in song** all day long.
5:14 gone from the city gate; the young men have stopped their **music**.
Hab 3:19 For the director of music. On my **stringed instruments**.

5594 נָגַן nāgan, v. [15] [→ 4947, 5593]

harpist [2], play [+928+3338] [2], play the harp [2], play [2], playing the harp [+928+3338] [2], musicians [1], playing [1], plays an instrument [1], plays [1], sing [1]

1Sa 16:16 [D] servants here to search for someone who can **play** the harp.
16:16 [D] He *will* **play** [+928+3338] when the evil spirit from God
16:17 [D] "Find someone *who* **plays** well and bring him to me."
16:18 [D] son of Jesse of Bethlehem who knows how *to* **play the harp**.
16:23 [D] upon Saul, David would take his harp and **play** [+928+3338].
18:10 [D] while David *was* **playing** [+928+3338] **the harp**, as he
19: 9 [D] his hand. While David *was* **playing** [+928+3338] **the harp**,
2Ki 3:15 [D] But now bring me a **harpist**." While the harpist was playing,
3:15 [D] While the **harpist** was playing, the hand of the LORD
3:15 [D] While the harpist was **playing**, the hand of the LORD came
Ps 33: 3 [D] Sing to him a new song; **play** skillfully, and shout for joy.
68:25 [68:26] [A] In front are the singers, after them the **musicians**;
Isa 23:16 [D] **play the harp** well, sing many a song, so that you will be
38:20 [D] *we will* **sing** *with* stringed instruments all the days of our
Eze 33:32 [D] songs with a beautiful voice and **plays an instrument** well,

5595 נָגַע nāga', v. [150] [→ 5596]

touches [43], touched [24], touch [17], came [6], come [4], reached [4], arrived [3], reaches [3], struck [3], afflicted [2], get [2], reach [2], reaching [2], strike [2], strikes [2], *untranslated* [1], add [1], afford [+1896+3338] [1], approach [1], are plagued [1], attack [1], befall [1], bother [1], bring down [1], brought down [1], casts down [1], draws near [1], drew near [1], extend [1], follows [1], happened [1], inflicted [1], is [1], laid [1], let themselves be driven back [1], level [1], molest [1], molests [1], near [1], pierces [1], plagued [1], put [1], seize [1], stricken [1], touching [1], went [1]

Ge 3: 3 [A] of the garden, and *you must* not **touch** it, or you will die.' "
12:17 [D] the LORD **inflicted** serious diseases *on* Pharaoh and his
20: 6 [A] sinning against me. That is why I did not let you **touch** her.
26:11 [A] "Anyone *who* **molests** this man or his wife shall surely be
26:29 [A] just as *we did* not **molest** you but always treated you well
28:12 [G] with its top **reaching** to heaven, and the angels of God were
32:25 [32:26] [A] *he* **touched** the socket of Jacob's hip so that his hip
32:32 [32:33] [A] because the socket of Jacob's hip *was* **touched** near
Ex 4:25 [G] cut off her son's foreskin and **touched** ⌞Moses'⌟ feet with it.
12:22 [G] the blood in the basin and **put** some of the blood on the top
19:12 [A] that you do not go up the mountain or **touch** the foot of it.
19:12 [A] Whoever **touches** the mountain shall surely be put to death.
19:13 [A] or shot with arrows; not a hand *is to be* **laid** on him.
29:37 [A] altar will be most holy, and whatever **touches** it will be holy.
30:29 [A] will be most holy, and whatever **touches** them will be holy.
Lev 5: 2 [A] **touches** anything ceremonially unclean—whether the
5: 3 [A] " 'Or if *he* **touches** human uncleanness—anything that would
5: 7 [G] " 'If he cannot **afford** [+1896+3338] a lamb, he is to bring
6:18 [6:11] [A] Whatever **touches** them will become holy.' "
6:27 [6:20] [A] Whatever **touches** any of the flesh will become holy,
7:19 [A] " 'Meat that **touches** anything ceremonially unclean must not
7:21 [A] **touches** something unclean—whether human uncleanness or
11: 8 [A] You must not eat their meat or **touch** their carcasses; they are
11:24 [A] whoever **touches** their carcasses will be unclean till evening.
11:26 [A] whoever **touches** ⌞the carcass of⌟ any of them will be
11:27 [A] whoever **touches** their carcasses will be unclean till evening.
11:31 [A] Whoever **touches** them when they are dead will be unclean
11:36 [A] but *anyone who* **touches** one of these carcasses is unclean.
11:39 [A] anyone *who* **touches** the carcass will be unclean till evening.
12: 4 [A] *She must* not **touch** anything sacred or go to the sanctuary
15: 5 [A] Anyone who **touches** his bed must wash his clothes
15: 7 [A] " 'Whoever **touches** the man who has a discharge must wash
15:10 [A] whoever **touches** any of the things that were under him will
15:11 [A] " 'Anyone the man with a discharge **touches** without rinsing
15:12 [A] " 'A clay pot that the man **touches** must be broken, and any
15:19 [A] and anyone who **touches** her will be unclean till evening.
15:21 [A] Whoever **touches** her bed must wash his clothes and bathe
15:22 [A] Whoever **touches** anything she sits on must wash his clothes
15:23 [A] or anything she was sitting on, when anyone **touches** it,
15:27 [A] Whoever **touches** them will be unclean; he must wash his
22: 4 [A] He will also be unclean if he **touches** something defiled by a
22: 5 [A] if he **touches** any crawling thing that makes him unclean, or
22: 6 [A] The one who **touches** any such thing will be unclean till
Nu 4:15 [A] But *they must* not **touch** the holy things or they will die.
16:26 [A] *Do* not **touch** anything belonging to them, or you will be
19:11 [A] "Whoever **touches** the dead body of anyone will be unclean
19:13 [A] Whoever **touches** the dead body of anyone and fails to purify
19:16 [A] **touches** someone who has been killed with a sword or
19:18 [A] anyone *who has* **touched** a human bone or a grave or
19:21 [A] anyone *who* **touches** the water of cleansing will be unclean
19:22 [A] Anything that an unclean person **touches** becomes unclean,
19:22 [A] and anyone who **touches** it becomes unclean till evening."
31:19 [A] or **touched** anyone who was killed must stay outside the
Dt 14: 8 [A] You are not to eat their meat or **touch** their carcasses.
Jos 8:15 [C] and all Israel **let themselves be driven back** before them,
9:19 [A] the God of Israel, and we cannot **touch** them now.
Jdg 6:21 [A] the angel of the LORD **touched** the meat and the
20:34 [A] that the Benjamites did not realize how **near** disaster *was*.
20:41 [A] because they realized that disaster *had* **come** upon them.
Ru 2: 9 [A] I have told the men not *to* **touch** you. And whenever you are
1Sa 6: 9 [A] we will know that it was not his hand that **struck** us and that
10:26 [A] accompanied by valiant men whose hearts God *had* **touched**.
14: 9 [G] If they say to us, 'Wait there until we **come** to you,' we will
2Sa 5: 8 [A] *will have to* use the water shaft *to* **reach** those 'lame and
14:10 [A] to you, bring him to me, and *he will* not **bother** you again."
23: 7 [A] Whoever **touches** thorns uses a tool of iron or the shaft of a
1Ki 6:27 [A] The wing of one cherub **touched** one wall, while the wing of
6:27 [A] one wall, while the wing of the other **touched** the other wall,
6:27 [A] their wings **touched** each other in the middle of the room.
19: 5 [A] All at once an angel **touched** him and said, "Get up and eat."
19: 7 [A] LORD came back a second time and **touched** him and said,
2Ki 13:21 [A] When the body **touched** Elisha's bones, the man came to life
15: 5 [D] The LORD **afflicted** the king *with* leprosy until the day he
1Ch 16:22 [A] "*Do* not **touch** my anointed ones; do my prophets no harm."
2Ch 3:11 [G] cherub was five cubits long and **touched** the temple wall,
3:11 [G] also five cubits long, **touched** the wing of the other cherub.

2Ch 3:12 [G] was five cubits long and **touched** the other temple wall,
26:20 [D] was eager to leave, because the LORD *had* **afflicted** him.
28: 9 [G] you have slaughtered them in a rage *that* **reaches** to heaven.
Ezr 3: 1 [A] When the seventh month **came** and the Israelites had settled
Ne 7:73 [7:72] [A] When the seventh month **came** and the Israelites had
Est 2:12 [G] Before a girl's turn **came** to go in to King Xerxes, she had to
2:15 [G] When the turn **came** *for* Esther (the girl Mordecai had
4: 3 [G] province to which the edict and order of the king **came**,
4:14 [G] that *you have* **come** to royal position for such a time as
5: 2 [A] So Esther approached and **touched** the tip of the scepter.
6:14 [G] the king's eunuchs **arrived** and hurried Haman away to the
8:17 [G] wherever the edict of the king **went**, there was joy
9: 1 [G] **[RPH]** the edict commanded by the king was to be carried
9:26 [G] of what they had seen and what *had* **happened** to them,
Job 1:11 [A] stretch out your hand and **strike** everything he has, and he
1:19 [A] in from the desert and **struck** the four corners of the house.
2: 5 [A] stretch out your hand and **strike** his flesh and bones, and he
4: 5 [A] you are discouraged; *it* **strikes** you, and you are dismayed.
5:19 [A] he will rescue you; in seven no harm *will* **befall** you.
6: 7 [A] I refuse to **touch** it; such food makes me ill.
19:21 [A] my friends, have pity, for the hand of God *has* **struck** me.
20: 6 [G] pride reaches to the heavens and his head **touches** the clouds,
Ps 32: 6 [G] surely when the mighty waters rise, *they will* not **reach** him.
73: 5 [E] common to man; *they* **are** not **plagued** by human ills.
73:14 [B] All day long I have been **plagued**; I have been punished
88: 3 [88:4] [G] is full of trouble and my life **draws near** the grave.
104:32 [A] and it trembles, *who* **touches** the mountains, and they smoke.
105:15 [A] "*Do* not **touch** my anointed ones; do my prophets no harm."
107:18 [G] They loathed all food and **drew near** the gates of death.
144: 5 [A] and come down; **touch** the mountains, so that they smoke.
Pr 6:29 [A] man's wife; no one who **touches** her will go unpunished.
Ecc 8:14 [G] righteous men who **get** what the wicked deserve, and wicked
8:14 [G] and wicked men who **get** what the righteous deserve.
12: 1 [G] of trouble come and the years **approach** when you will say,
SS 2:12 [G] the season of singing *has* **come**, the cooing of doves is heard
Isa 5: 8 [G] Woe to you *who* **add** house to house and join field to field
6: 7 [G] With it *he* **touched** my mouth and said, "See, this has
6: 7 [A] my mouth and said, "See, this *has* **touched** your lips;
8: 8 [G] over it, passing through it and **reaching** up to the neck.
16: 8 [A] *which once* **reached** Jazer and spread toward the desert.
25:12 [G] *he will* **bring** them **down** to the ground, to the very dust.
26: 5 [G] he levels it to the ground and **casts** it **down** to the dust.
30: 4 [G] officials in Zoan and their envoys *have* **arrived** *in* Hanes,
52:11 [A] **Touch** no unclean thing! Come out from it and be pure,
53: 4 [B] yet we considered him **stricken** *by* God, smitten by him,
Jer 1: 9 [G] reached out his hand and **touched** my mouth and said to me,
4:10 [A] 'You will have peace,' when the sword **is** at our throats."
4:18 [A] How bitter it is! How *it* **pierces** to the heart!"
12:14 [A] "As for all my wicked neighbors who **seize** the inheritance I
48:32 [A] as far as the sea; *they* **reached** as far as the sea of Jazer.
51: 9 [A] go to his own land, for her judgment **reaches** to the skies,
La 2: 2 [G] *He has* **brought** her kingdom and its princes **down** to the
4:14 [A] so defiled with blood that no one dares *to* **touch** their
4:15 [A] "Away! Away! Don't **touch** us!" When they flee and wander
Eze 7:12 [G] The time has come, the day *has* **arrived**. Let not the buyer
13:14 [G] *will* **level** it to the ground so that its foundation will be laid
17:10 [A] Will it not wither completely when the east wind **strikes** it—
Da 8: 5 [A] crossing the whole earth without **touching** the ground.
8: 7 [G] I saw him **attack** the ram furiously, striking the ram
8:18 [A] to the ground. Then *he* **touched** me and raised me to my feet.
9:21 [A] **came** to me in swift flight about the time of the evening
10:10 [A] A hand **touched** me and set me trembling on my hands
10:16 [A] *one* who looked like a man **touched** my lips, and I opened
10:18 [A] Again *the one* who looked like a man **touched** me and gave
12:12 [G] the one who waits for and **reaches** the end of the 1,335 days.
Hos 4: 2 [A] they break all bounds, and bloodshed **follows** bloodshed.
Am 9: 5 [A] the LORD Almighty, he *who* **touches** the earth and it melts,
Jnh 3: 6 [A] When the news **reached** the king of Nineveh, he rose from
Mic 1: 9 [A] *It has* **reached** the very gate of my people, even to Jerusalem
Hag 2:12 [A] that fold **touches** some bread or stew, some wine, oil or other
2:13 [A] "If a person defiled by contact with a dead body **touches** one
Zec 2: 8 [2:12] [A] whoever **touches** you touches the apple of his eye—
2: 8 [2:12] [A] whoever touches you **touches** the apple of his eye—
14: 5 [G] will flee by my mountain valley, for it *will* **extend** to Azel.

5596 נֶ֫גַע *nega'*, n.m. [78] [√ 5595]

mildew [15], infectious [11], sore [11], *untranslated* [3], contamination [3], disaster [3], infected person [3], it[s] [+2021] [3], affected article [2], afflictions [2], assaults [+4200+5596] [2], contaminated [2], diseases [2], article[s] [1], assault [1], blows [1], contaminated article [1], flogging [1], floggings [1], infected person [+5999] [1], infection [1], person[s] [1], plague [1], scourge [1], sores [1], spreading mildew [+7669] [1], stricken [1], this kind of sore [+2021+5999] [1], wounds [1]

Ge 12:17 the LORD inflicted serious **diseases** on Pharaoh and his
Ex 11: 1 to Moses, "I will bring one more **plague** on Pharaoh and on Egypt.
Lev 13: 2 or a bright spot on his skin that may become an **infectious** skin
13: 3 The priest is to examine the **sore** on his skin, and if the hair in the
13: 3 if the hair in the **sore** has turned white and the sore appears to be
13: 3 has turned white and the **sore** appears to be more than skin deep,
13: 3 appears to be more than skin deep, it is an **infectious** skin disease.
13: 4 the priest is to put the **infected person** in isolation for seven days.
13: 5 if he sees that the **sore** is unchanged and has not spread in the skin,
13: 5 that the sore is unchanged and has not spread **[RPH]** in the skin,
13: 6 if the **sore** has faded and has not spread in the skin, the priest shall
13: 6 and if the sore has faded and has not spread **[RPH]** in the skin,
13: 9 "When anyone has an **infectious** skin disease, he must be brought
13:12 it covers all the skin of the **infected person** from head to foot,
13:13 covered his whole body, he shall pronounce that **person**[s] clean.
13:17 The priest is to examine him, and if the **sores** have turned white,
13:17 turned white, the priest shall pronounce the **infected person** clean;
13:20 It is an **infectious** skin disease that has broken out where the boil
13:22 in the skin, the priest shall pronounce him unclean; it is **infectious**.
13:25 priest shall pronounce him unclean; it is an **infectious** skin disease.
13:27 priest shall pronounce him unclean; it is an **infectious** skin disease.
13:29 "If a man or woman has a **sore** on the head or on the chin,
13:30 the priest is to examine the **sore**, and if it appears to be more than
13:31 when the priest examines **this kind of sore** [+2021+5999],
13:31 the priest is to put the **infected** [+5999] **person** in isolation for
13:32 On the seventh day the priest is to examine the **sore**, and if the itch
13:42 But if he has a reddish-white **sore** on his bald head or forehead,
13:43 if the swollen **sore** on his head or forehead is reddish-white like an
13:44 shall pronounce him unclean because of the **sore** on his head.
13:45 "The person with such an **infectious** disease must wear torn
13:46 As long as he has the **infection** he remains unclean. He must live
13:47 "If any clothing is **contaminated** *with* mildew—any woolen
13:49 and if the **contamination** in the clothing, or leather, or woven
13:49 it is a **[RPH]** spreading mildew and must be shown to the priest.
13:50 The priest is to examine the **mildew** and isolate the affected article
13:50 examine the mildew and isolate the **affected article** for seven days.
13:51 On the seventh day he is to examine **it**[s] [+2021], and if the mildew
13:51 and if the **mildew** has spread in the clothing, or the woven
13:51 whatever its use, it is a destructive mildew; the **article**[s] is unclean.
13:52 or linen, or any leather article that has the **contamination** in it,
13:53 the **mildew** has not spread in the clothing, or the woven or knitted
13:54 he shall order that the **contaminated article** be washed. Then he is
13:55 After the **affected article** has been washed, the priest is to examine
13:55 is to examine it, and if the **mildew** has not changed its appearance,
13:55 even though **it**[s] [+2021] has not spread, it is unclean.
13:56 the **mildew** has faded after the article has been washed,
13:57 and whatever has the **mildew** must be burned with fire.
13:58 any leather article that has been washed and is rid of the **mildew**,
13:59 These are the regulations concerning **contamination** *by* mildew in
14: 3 If the person has been healed of his **infectious** skin disease,
14:32 These are the regulations for anyone who has an **infectious** skin
14:34 and I put a **spreading mildew** [+7669] in a house in that land,
14:35 'I have seen something that looks like **mildew** in my house.'
14:36 the house to be emptied before he goes in to examine the **mildew**,
14:37 He is to examine the **mildew** on the walls, and if it has greenish
14:37 if **it**[s] [+2021] has greenish or reddish depressions that appear to be
14:39 return to inspect the house. If the **mildew** has spread on the walls,
14:40 he is to order that the **contaminated** stones be torn out and thrown
14:43 "If the **mildew** reappears in the house after the stones have been
14:44 and examine it and, if the **mildew** has spread in the house,
14:48 and the **mildew** has not spread after the house has been plastered,
14:48 he shall pronounce the house clean, because the **mildew** is gone.
14:54 These are the regulations for any **infectious** skin disease, for an
Dt 17: 8 whether bloodshed, lawsuits or **assaults** [+4200+5596]—take them
17: 8 whether bloodshed, lawsuits or **assaults** [+4200+5596]—take them
21: 5 name of the LORD and to decide all cases of dispute and **assault**.
24: 8 In cases of leprous **diseases** be very careful to do exactly as the
2Sa 7:14 punish him with the rod of men, with **floggings** *inflicted by* men.
1Ki 8:37 them in any of their cities, whatever **disaster** or disease may come,
8:38 each one aware of the **afflictions** *of* his own heart, and spreading
2Ch 6:28 them in any of their cities, whatever **disaster** or disease may come,
6:29 each one aware of his **afflictions** and pains, and spreading out his
Ps 38:11 [38:12] and companions avoid me because of my **wounds**;
39:10 [39:11] Remove your **scourge** from me; I am overcome by the
89:32 [89:33] punish their sin with the rod, their iniquity with **flogging**;
91:10 then no harm will befall you, no **disaster** will come near your tent.
Pr 6:33 **Blows** and disgrace are his lot, and his shame will never be wiped
Isa 53: 8 of the living; for the transgression of my people he was **stricken**.

5597 נָגַף *nāgap*, v. [49] [→ 4487, 5598]

be defeated [5], strike [5], been defeated [4], strike down [3], struck down [3], were defeated [3], afflicted [2], been routed [2], defeating [+4200+5597+7156] [2], struck [2], stumble [2], was defeated [2], was routed [2], bring defeat upon [1], defeated [1], defeating [1], hit [1], inflicts [1], injures [1], plague [1], routed [1], strike with a plague [1], struck with a plague [1], were beaten [1], were routed [1]

Ex 8: 2 [7:27] [A] I *will* **plague** your whole country with frogs.
12: 23 [A] When the LORD goes through the land to **strike down** the
12: 23 [A] the destroyer to enter your houses and **strike** you **down**.
12: 27 [A] spared our homes when he **struck down** the Egyptians.' "
21: 22 [A] "If men who are fighting **hit** a pregnant woman and she gives
21: 35 [A] "If a man's bull **injures** the bull of another and it dies, they
32: 35 [A] the LORD **struck** the people **with a plague** because of
Lev 26: 17 [C] against you so that *you will* **be defeated** by your enemies;
Nu 14: 42 [C] is not with you. *You will* **be defeated** by your enemies,
Dt 1: 42 [C] not be with you. *You will* **be defeated** by your enemies.' "
28: 7 [C] enemies who rise up against you *will* **be defeated** before you.
28: 25 [C] The LORD will cause you *to* **be defeated** before your
Jos 24: 5 [A] and Aaron, and *I* **afflicted** the Egyptians by what I did there,
Jdg 20: 32 [C] "We *are* **defeating** them as before," the Israelites were
20: 35 [A] The LORD **defeated** Benjamin before Israel, and on that
20: 36 [C] the Benjamites saw that *they* **were beaten**. Now the men of
20: 39 [C] "We *are* **defeating** [+4200+5597+7156] them as in the first
20: 39 [C] "We *are* **defeating** [+4200+5597+7156] them as in the first
1Sa 4: 2 [C] as the battle spread, Israel **was defeated** by the Philistines,
4: 3 [A] "Why *did* the LORD **bring defeat upon** us today before
4: 10 [C] the Israelites **were defeated** and every man fled to his tent.
7: 10 [C] threw them into such a panic that *they* **were routed** before
25: 38 [A] About ten days later, the LORD **struck** Nabal and he died.
26: 10 [A] LORD lives," he said, "the LORD *himself will* **strike** him;
2Sa 2: 17 [C] and the men of Israel **were defeated** by David's men.
10: 15 [C] After the Arameans saw that *they had* **been routed** by Israel,
10: 19 [C] of Hadadezer saw that *they had* **been defeated** by Israel,
12: 15 [A] the LORD **struck** the child that Uriah's wife had borne to
18: 7 [C] There the army of Israel **was defeated** by David's men,
1Ki 8: 33 [C] "When your people Israel *have* **been defeated** by an enemy
2Ki 14: 12 [C] Judah **was routed** by Israel, and every man fled to his home.
1Ch 19: 16 [C] After the Arameans saw that *they had* **been routed** by Israel,
19: 19 [C] of Hadadezer saw that *they had* **been defeated** by Israel,
2Ch 6: 24 [C] "When your people Israel *have* **been defeated** by an enemy
13: 15 [A] God **routed** Jeroboam and all Israel before Abijah and Judah.
13: 20 [A] of Abijah. And the LORD **struck** him **down** and he died.
14: 12 [14:11] [A] The LORD **struck down** the Cushites before Asa
20: 22 [C] Seir who were invading Judah, and *they* **were defeated**.
21: 14 [A] *is about to* **strike** your people, your sons, your wives and
21: 18 [A] the LORD **afflicted** Jehoram with an incurable disease of
25: 22 [C] Judah **was routed** by Israel, and every man fled to his home.
Ps 89: 23 [89:24] [A] foes before him and **strike down** his adversaries.
91: 12 [A] so that *you will* not **strike** your foot against a stone.
Pr 3: 23 [A] go on your way in safety, and your foot *will* not **stumble**;
Isa 19: 22 [A] The LORD *will* **strike** Egypt **with a plague**; he will strike
19: 22 [A] Egypt with a plague; *he will* **strike** them and heal them.
Jer 13: 16 [F] the darkness, before your feet **stumble** on the darkening hills.
Zec 14: 12 [A] This is the plague with which the LORD *will* **strike** all the
14: 18 [A] The LORD will bring on them the plague *he* **inflicts** on the

5598 נֶגֶף *negep*, n.m. [7] [√ 5597]

plague [6], causes to stumble [1]

Ex 12: 13 No destructive **plague** will touch you when I strike Egypt.
30: 12 Then no **plague** will come on them when you number them.
Nu 8: 19 so that no **plague** will strike the Israelites when they go near the
16: 46 [17:11] has come out from the LORD; the **plague** has started."
16: 47 [17:12] The **plague** had already started among the people,
Jos 22: 17 even though a **plague** fell on the community of the LORD!
Isa 8: 14 both houses of Israel he will be a stone that **causes** men **to stumble**

5599 נָגַר *nāgar*, v. [10] [→ 5600; cf. 1760]

rushing [2], delivered over [1], flow [1], given over [+3338+6584] [1], hand over [1], pour [1], pours out [1], spilled [1], stretched out [1]

2Sa 14: 14 [C] Like water **spilled** on the ground, which cannot be recovered,
Job 20: 28 [C] off his house, **rushing** waters on the day of God's wrath.
Ps 63: 10 [63:11] [G] They *will be* **given** [+3338+6584] **over** *to* the
75: 8 [75:9] [G] *he* **pours** it **out**, and all the wicked of the earth drink
77: 2 [77:3] [C] at night I **stretched out** untiring hands and my soul
Jer 18: 21 [G] over to famine; **hand** them **over** to the power of the sword.
La 3: 49 [C] My eyes *will* **flow** unceasingly, without relief,
Eze 35: 5 [G] **delivered** the Israelites **over** to the sword at the time of their
Mic 1: 4 [H] like wax before the fire, like water **rushing** down a slope.
1: 6 [G] *I will* **pour** her stones into the valley and lay bare her

5600 נִגֶּרֶת *niggeret*, n.[f.] *or* v.ptcp. Not used in NIV/BHS [√ 5599]

5601 נָגַשׂ *nāgaś*, v. [23] [cf. 5602]

slave drivers [5], oppressor [3], require payment [2], ruler [2], driver's [1], exacted [1], exploit [1], hard pressed [1], in distress [1], oppress each other [1], oppress [1], oppressors [1], slave driver's [1], tax collector [1], was oppressed [1]

Ex 3: 7 [A] I have heard them crying out because of their **slave drivers**,
5: 6 [A] That same day Pharaoh gave this order to the **slave drivers**
5: 10 [A] the **slave drivers** and the foremen went out and said to the
5: 13 [A] The **slave drivers** kept pressing them, saying,
5: 14 [A] The Israelite foremen appointed by Pharaoh's **slave drivers**
Dt 15: 2 [A] *He shall* not **require payment** *from* his fellow Israelite or
15: 3 [A] *You may* **require payment** *from* a foreigner, but you must
1Sa 13: 6 [C] situation was critical and that their army *was* **hard pressed**,
14: 24 [C] Now the men of Israel *were* **in distress** that day,
2Ki 23: 35 [A] **exacted** the silver and gold *from* the people of the land
Job 3: 18 [A] enjoy their ease; they no longer hear the **slave driver's** shout.
39: 7 [A] commotion in the town; he does not hear a **driver's** shout.
Isa 3: 5 [C] People *will* **oppress each other**—man against man, neighbor
3: 12 [A] Youths **oppress** my people, women rule over them. O my
9: 4 [9:3] [A] bar across their shoulders, the rod of their **oppressor**.
14: 2 [A] captives of their captors and rule over their **oppressors**.
14: 4 [A] How the **oppressor** has come to an end! How his fury has
53: 7 [C] He **was oppressed** and afflicted, yet he did not open his
58: 3 [A] you do as you please and **exploit** all your workers.
60: 17 [A] will make peace your governor and righteousness your **ruler**.
Da 11: 20 [A] "His successor will send out a **tax collector** to maintain the
Zec 9: 8 [A] Never again will an **oppressor** overrun my people, for now I
10: 4 [A] the tent peg, from him the battle bow, from him every **ruler**.

5602 נָגַשׁ *nāgaš*, v. [125] [cf. 5601]

approached [12], bring [11], come near [11], brought [7], came [7], approach [6], went up [5], come [4], take [4], went [3], advanced [2], brought close [2], came up [2], close [2], come close [2], come forward [2], come here [2], get so close [2], go up [2], go [2], presented [2], abstain from sexual relations [+440+448+851] [1], assemble [+3481] [1], be brought [1], be overtaken [1], bring in [1], bring near [1], brings [1], came forward [1], came near [1], came over [1], confront [1], done[s] so [1], draw near [1], drew near [1], get out [1], give more space [1], go near [1], march out [1], moved forward [1], offered [1], overtake [1], place [1], present [1], sacrifice [1], set forth [1], set [1], step forward [1], stepped forward [1], took [1], touch [1], went close [1], went over [1], were fettered [+4200+5733] [1]

Ge 18: 23 [A] Abraham **approached** him and said: "Will you sweep away
19: 9 [A] "**Get out** *of* our way," they replied. And they said,
19: 9 [A] pressure on Lot and **moved forward** to break down the door.
27: 21 [A] Isaac said to Jacob, "**Come near** so I can touch you, my son,
27: 22 [A] Jacob **went close** to his father Isaac, who touched him
27: 25 [G] Then he said, "My son, **bring** me some of your game to eat,
27: 25 [G] Jacob **brought** it to him and he ate; and he brought some
27: 26 [A] father Isaac said to him, "**Come here**, my son, and kiss me."
27: 27 [A] So *he* **went** to him and kissed him. When Isaac caught the
29: 10 [A] he **went over** and rolled the stone away from the mouth of
33: 3 [A] bowed down to the ground seven times as he **approached** his
33: 6 [A] and their children **approached** and bowed down.
33: 7 [A] Next, Leah and her children **came** and bowed down. Last of
33: 7 [C] Last of all **came** Joseph and Rachel, and they too bowed
43: 19 [A] So *they* **went up** to Joseph's steward and spoke to him at the
44: 18 [A] Judah **went up** to him and said: "Please, my lord, let your
45: 4 [A] Joseph said to his brothers, "**Come close** to me." When they
45: 4 [A] When *they had* **done**[s] so, he said, "I am your brother Joseph,
48: 10 [G] So Joseph **brought** his sons **close** to him, and his father
48: 13 [G] toward Israel's right hand, and **brought** them **close** to him.
Ex 19: 15 [A] **Abstain** [+440+448+851] **from sexual relations**."
19: 22 [C] Even the priests, who **approach** the LORD,
20: 21 [C] while Moses **approached** the thick darkness where God was.
21: 6 [G] his master *must* **take** him before the judges. He shall take
21: 6 [G] *He shall* **take** him to the door or the doorpost and pierce his
24: 2 [C] Moses alone *is to* **approach** the LORD; the others must not
24: 2 [A] is to approach the LORD; the others *must* not **come near**.
24: 14 [A] with you, and anyone involved in a dispute *can* **go** to them."
28: 43 [A] or **approach** the altar to minister in the Holy Place,
30: 20 [A] when they **approach** the altar to minister by presenting an
32: 6 [G] burnt offerings and **presented** fellowship offerings.
34: 30 [A] his face was radiant, and they were afraid *to* **come near** him.
34: 32 [C] Afterward all the Israelites **came near** him, and he gave them
Lev 2: 8 [G] present it to the priest, *who shall* **take** it to the altar.
8: 14 [G] *He* then **presented** the bull for the sin offering, and Aaron
21: 21 [A] *is to* **come near** to present the offerings made to the LORD
21: 21 [A] *he must* not **come near** to offer the food of his God.
21: 23 [A] he must not go near the curtain or **approach** the altar, and
Nu 4: 19 [A] and not die when they **come near** the most holy things,
8: 19 [A] so that no plague will strike the Israelites when they **go near**

Nu 32: 16 [A] *they* **came up** to him and said, "We would like to build pens
Dt 20: 2 [C] the priest *shall* **come forward** and address the army.
21: 5 [C] The priests, the sons of Levi, *shall* **step forward**,
25: 1 [C] *they are to* **take** it to court and the judges will decide the
25: 9 [C] his brother's widow *shall* **go up** to him in the presence of the
Jos 3: 9 [A] "**Come** here and listen to the words of the LORD your God.
8: 11 [A] and **approached** the city and arrived in front of it.
14: 6 [A] Now the men of Judah **approached** Joshua at Gilgal,
21: 1 [A] **approached** Eleazar the priest, Joshua son of Nun, and
Jdg 6: 19 [G] he brought them out and **offered** them *to* him under the oak.
9: 52 [A] *as he* **approached** the entrance to the tower to set it on fire,
20: 23 [A] "Shall we **go up** again to battle against the Benjamites,
Ru 2: 14 [A] At mealtime Boaz said to her, "**Come** over here. Have some
1Sa 7: 10 [C] the Philistines **drew near** to engage Israel in battle.
9: 18 [A] Saul **approached** Samuel in the gateway and asked,
13: 9 [G] "**Bring** me the burnt offering and the fellowship offerings."
14: 18 [G] Saul said to Ahijah, "**Bring** the ark of God." (At that time it
14: 34 [G] and tell them, 'Each of you **bring** me your cattle and sheep,
14: 34 [G] with blood still in it.' " So everyone **brought** his ox that night
14: 38 [A] Saul therefore said, "**Come** here, all you who are leaders of
15: 32 [G] Then Samuel said, "**Bring** me Agag king of the Amalekites."
17: 16 [A] For forty days the Philistine **came forward** every morning
17: 40 [A] with his sling in his hand, **approached** the Philistine.
23: 9 [G] he said to Abiathar the priest, "**Bring** the ephod."
28: 25 [G] *she* **set** it before Saul and his men, and they ate. That same
30: 7 [G] the priest, the son of Ahimelech, "**Bring** me the ephod."
30: 7 [G] "Bring me the ephod." Abiathar **brought** it to him,
30: 21 [A] As David and his men **approached**, he greeted them.
2Sa 1: 15 [A] David called one of his men and said, "**Go**, strike him
3: 34 [H] were not bound, your feet **were** not **fettered** [+4200+5733].
10: 13 [A] and the troops with him **advanced** to fight the Arameans,
11: 20 [C] may ask you, 'Why *did you* **get so close** to the city to fight?
11: 21 [C] Why *did you* **get so close** to the wall?' If he asks you this,
13: 11 [G] But when *she* **took** it to him to eat, he grabbed her and said,
17: 28 [17:29] [G] *They* also **brought** wheat and barley, flour
1Ki 4: 21 [5:1] [G] *These* countries **brought** tribute and were Solomon's
18: 21 [A] Elijah **went** before the people and said, "How long will you
18: 30 [A] Elijah said to all the people, "**Come here** to me." They came
18: 30 [A] They **came** to him, and he repaired the altar of the LORD,
18: 36 [A] of sacrifice, the prophet Elijah **stepped forward** and prayed:
20: 13 [C] Meanwhile a prophet **came** to Ahab king of Israel
20: 22 [A] Afterward, the prophet **came** to the king of Israel and said,
20: 28 [A] The man of God **came up** and told the king of Israel, "This is
22: 24 [A] Zedekiah son of Kenaanah **went up** and slapped Micaiah in
2Ki 2: 5 [A] The company of the prophets at Jericho **went up** to Elisha
4: 5 [G] her sons. They **brought** the jars to her and she kept pouring.
4: 6 [G] jars were full, she said to her son, "**Bring** me another one."
4: 27 [A] Gehazi **came over** to push her away, but the man of God
5: 13 [A] Naaman's servants **went** to him and said, "My father,
1Ch 19: 14 [A] and the troops with him **advanced** to fight the Arameans,
2Ch 18: 23 [A] Zedekiah son of Kenaanah **went up** and slapped Micaiah in
29: 23 [G] The goats for the sin offering *were* **brought** before the king
29: 31 [A] **Come** and bring sacrifices and thank offerings to the temple
Ezr 4: 2 [A] *they* **came** to Zerubbabel and to the heads of the families
9: 1 [C] the leaders **came** to me and said, "The people of Israel,
Job 40: 19 [G] of God, yet his Maker *can* **approach** him with his sword.
41: 16 [41:8] [A] each *is so* **close** to the next that no air can pass
Ps 91: 7 [A] thousand at your right hand, but *it will* not **come near** you.
Isa 29: 13 [C] "These people **come near** to me with their mouth and honor
41: 1 [A] *Let them* **come forward** and speak; let us meet together at
41: 21 [G] the LORD. "**Set forth** your arguments," says Jacob's King.
41: 22 [G] "**Bring in** ⌞your idols⌟ to tell us what is going to happen.
45: 20 [F] and come; **assemble** [+3481], *you* fugitives from the nations.
45: 21 [G] Declare what is to be, **present** it—let them take counsel
49: 20 [A] 'This place is too small for us; **give** us **more space** to live in.'
50: 8 [A] face each other! Who is my accuser? *Let him* **confront** me!
65: 5 [A] don't **come near** me, for I am too sacred for you!'
Jer 30: 21 [C] I will bring him near and *he will* **come close** to me, for who
30: 21 [A] for who is he who will devote himself to *be* **close** to me?'
42: 1 [A] and all the people from the least to the greatest **approached**
46: 3 [A] your shields, both large and small, and **march out** for battle!
Eze 9: 6 [A] and children, but *do* not **touch** anyone who has the mark.
44: 13 [A] *They are* not *to* **come near** to serve me as priests or come
44: 13 [A] or **come near** any of my holy things or my most holy
Joel 3: 9 [4:9] [A] *Let* all the fighting men **draw near** and attack.
Am 5: 25 [G] "*Did you* **bring** me sacrifices and offerings forty years in the
6: 3 [G] You put off the evil day and **bring near** a reign of terror.
9: 10 [G] all those who say, 'Disaster *will* not **overtake** or meet us.'
9: 13 [C] "when the reaper *will* **be overtaken** by the plowman
Mal 1: 7 [G] "*You* **place** defiled food on my altar. "But you ask, 'How
1: 8 [G] When *you* **bring** blind animals for sacrifice, is that not
1: 8 [G] When *you* **sacrifice** crippled or diseased animals, is that not
1: 11 [H] and pure offerings *will* **be brought** to my name,
2: 12 [G] even though *he* **brings** offerings to the LORD Almighty.
3: 3 [G] the LORD will have *men who will* **bring** offerings in

5603 נֵד *nēd*, n.m. [5 / 4]

heap [2], wall [2]

Ex 15: 8 The surging waters stood firm like a **wall**; the deep waters
Jos 3: 13 waters flowing downstream will be cut off and stand up in a **heap**."
3: 16 It piled up in a **heap** a great distance away, at a town called Adam
Ps 33: 7 He gathers the waters of the sea into jars; [BHS *a heap*; NIV 5532]
78: 13 and led them through; he made the water stand firm like a **wall**.

5604 נָדָא *nādā'*, v. [0] [cf. 5610, 5612, 5653]

2Ki 17: 21 [g] [Jeroboam **enticed** [K; see Q 5615] Israel away from]

5605 נָדַב *nādab*, v. [17] [→ 5606, 5607, 5618, 5619; Ar 10219, 10461; *also used with compound proper names*]

brought as freewill offerings [+5607] [1], freewill offerings [1], gave freewill offerings [1], gave willingly [1], give generously [1], given freely [1], given willingly [1], prompts to give [1], volunteered himself for service [1], volunteered [1], willing [+906+4213] [1], willing [+906+8120] [1], willing response [1], willing volunteers [1], willing [1], willingly given [1], willingly offer themselves [1]

Ex 25: 2 [A] for me from each man whose heart **prompts** him **to give**.
35: 21 [A] everyone who *was* **willing** [+906+8120] and whose heart
35: 29 [A] women who *were* **willing** [+906+4213] brought to the
Jdg 5: 2 [F] take the lead, when the people **willingly offer themselves**—
5: 9 [F] with the **willing volunteers** among the people.
1Ch 29: 5 [F] who *is* **willing** to consecrate himself today to the LORD?"
29: 6 [F] and the officials in charge of the king's work **gave willingly**.
29: 9 [F] The people rejoiced at the **willing response** *of* their leaders,
29: 9 [F] for *they had* **given freely** and wholeheartedly to the LORD.
29: 14 [F] that we should be able to **give** as **generously** as this?
29: 17 [F] All these things *have* I **given willingly** and with honest
29: 17 [F] how **willingly** your people who are here *have* **given** to you.
2Ch 17: 16 [F] who **volunteered himself for** *the* **service** of the LORD,
Ezr 1: 6 [F] with valuable gifts, in addition to all the **freewill offerings**.
2: 68 [F] some of the heads of the families **gave freewill offerings**
3: 5 [F] as well as those **brought as freewill** [+5607] **offerings** to the
Ne 11: 2 [F] The people commended all the men who **volunteered** to live

5606 נָדָב *nādāb*, n.pr.m. [20] [→ 5608; cf. 5605]

Nadab [19], Nadab's [1]

Ex 6: 23 and she bore him **Nadab** and Abihu, Eleazar and Ithamar.
24: 1 "Come up to the LORD, you and Aaron, **Nadab** and Abihu,
24: 9 Moses and Aaron, **Nadab** and Abihu, and the seventy elders of
28: 1 along with his sons **Nadab** and Abihu, Eleazar and Ithamar,
Lev 10: 1 Aaron's sons **Nadab** and Abihu took their censers, put fire in them
Nu 3: 2 The names of the sons of Aaron were **Nadab** the firstborn
3: 4 **Nadab** and Abihu, however, fell dead before the LORD when
26: 60 Aaron was the father of **Nadab** and Abihu, Eleazar and Ithamar.
26: 61 **Nadab** and Abihu died when they made an offering before the
1Ki 14: 20 rested with his fathers. And **Nadab** his son succeeded him as king.
15: 25 **Nadab** son of Jeroboam became king of Israel in the second year
15: 27 a Philistine town, while **Nadab** and all Israel were besieging it.
15: 31 As for the other events of **Nadab's** reign, and all he did, are they
1Ch 2: 28 Shammai and Jada. The sons of Shammai: **Nadab** and Abishur.
2: 30 The sons of **Nadab**: Seled and Appaim. Seled died without
6: 3 [5:29] The sons of Aaron: **Nadab**, Abihu, Eleazar and Ithamar.
8: 30 son was Abdon, followed by Zur, Kish, Baal, Ner, **Nadab**,
9: 36 son was Abdon, followed by Zur, Kish, Baal, Ner, **Nadab**,
24: 1 The sons of Aaron were **Nadab**, Abihu, Eleazar and Ithamar.
24: 2 **Nadab** and Abihu died before their father did, and they had no

5607 נְדָבָה *nᵉdābâ*, n.f. [26] [√ 5605]

freewill offerings [10], freewill offering [7], freely [2], willing [2], *untranslated* [1], abundant [1], brought as freewill offerings [+5605] [1], freewill [1], voluntarily [1]

Ex 35: 29 women who were willing brought to the LORD **freewill offerings**
36: 3 the people continued to bring **freewill offerings** morning after
Lev 7: 16 his offering is the result of a vow or is a **freewill** offering,
22: 18 to the LORD, either to fulfill a vow or as a **freewill offering**,
22: 21 to the LORD to fulfill a special vow or as a **freewill offering**,
22: 23 present as a **freewill offering** an ox or a sheep that is deformed
23: 38 have vowed and all the **freewill offerings** you give to the LORD.)
Nu 15: 3 for special vows or **freewill offerings** or festival offerings—
29: 39 " 'In addition to what you vow and your **freewill offerings**,
Dt 12: 6 what you have vowed to give and your **freewill offerings**,
12: 17 you have vowed to give, or your **freewill offerings** or special gifts.
16: 10 **freewill offering** in proportion to the blessings the LORD your
23: 23 [23:24] because you made your vow **freely** to the LORD your
2Ch 31: 14 East Gate, was in charge of the **freewill offerings** *given to* God,

2Ch 35: 8 His officials also contributed **voluntarily** to the people and the
Ezr 1: 4 and with **freewill offerings** for the temple of God in Jerusalem.' "
3: 5 as well as those **brought as freewill offerings** [+5605] to the
8: 28 The silver and gold are a **freewill offering** to the LORD,
Ps 54: 6 [54:8] I will sacrifice a **freewill offering** to you; I will praise your
68: 9 [68:10] You gave **abundant** showers, O God; you refreshed your
110: 3 Your troops will be **willing** on your day of battle. Arrayed in holy
119: 108 Accept, O LORD, the **willing** praise *of* my mouth, and teach me
Eze 46: 12 When the prince provides a **freewill offering** to the LORD—
46: 12 When the prince provides a freewill offering **[RPH]** to the
Hos 14: 4 [14:5] "I will heal their waywardness and love them **freely**,
Am 4: 5 bread as a thank offering and brag about your **freewill offerings**—

5608 נְדַבְיָה **n^{e}dabyâ**, n.pr.m. [1] [√ 5606; cf. 5605 + 3378]

Nedabiah [1]

1Ch 3: 18 Shenazzar, Jekamiah, Hoshama and **Nedabiah**.

5609 נִדְגָּלוֹת **nidgālôt**, n.?. Not used in NIV/BHS [√ 1840]

5610 נָדַד **nādad**, v. [28] [→ 5611; cf. 5604, 5612, 5653; Ar 10463]

flee [5], fled [3], banished [2], flee in haste [+5610] [2], fugitives [2], strays [2], be cast aside [1], could not [1], flapped [1], flown away [1], fluttering [1], fly away [1], in flight [1], nothing [1], refugees [1], strayed [1], wanderers [1], wanders about [1]

Ge 31: 40 [A] and the cold at night, and sleep **fled** from my eyes.
2Sa 23: 6 [H] evil men are all *to* **be cast aside** like thorns, which are not
Est 6: 1 [A] That night the king **could not** sleep; so he ordered the book
Job 15: 23 [A] He **wanders about**—food for vultures; he knows the day of
18: 18 [G] from light into darkness and *is* **banished** from the world.
20: 8 [H] no more to be found, **banished** like a vision of the night.
Ps 31: 11 [31:12] [A] those who see me on the street **flee** from me.
55: 7 [55:8] [A] I would **flee** far away and stay in the desert; *Selah*
68: 12 [68:13] [A] "Kings and armies **flee** [+5610] **in haste**; in the
68: 12 [68:13] [A] "Kings and armies **flee in haste** [+5610]; in the
Pr 27: 8 [A] Like a bird *that* **strays** from its nest is a man who strays
27: 8 [A] Like a bird that strays from its nest is a man *who* **strays** from
Isa 10: 14 [A] not *one* **flapped** a wing, or opened its mouth to chirp.' "
10: 31 [A] Madmenah *is* **in flight**; the people of Gebim take cover.
16: 2 [A] Like **fluttering** birds pushed from the nest, so are the women
16: 3 [A] at high noon. Hide the fugitives, do not betray the **refugees**.
17: 11 [A] yet the harvest *will be as* **nothing** in the day of disease and
21: 14 [A] you who live in Tema, bring food for the **fugitives**.
21: 15 [A] *They* **flee** from the sword, from the drawn sword, from the
22: 3 [A] All your leaders *have* **fled** together; they have been captured
33: 3 [A] At the thunder of your voice, the peoples **flee**; when you rise
Jer 4: 25 [A] there were no people; every bird in the sky *had* **flown away**.
9: 10 [9:9] [A] birds of the air *have* **fled** and the animals are gone.
49: 5 [A] you will be driven away, and no one will gather the **fugitives**.
Hos 7: 13 [A] Woe to them, because *they have* **strayed** from me!
9: 17 [A] not obeyed him; they will be **wanderers** among the nations.
Na 3: 7 [A] All who see you *will* **flee** from you and say, 'Nineveh is in
3: 17 [D] when the sun appears *they* **fly away**, and no one knows

5611 נְדֻדִים **n^{e}dudîm**, n.[m.pl.]. [1] [√ 5610]

toss [+8425] [1]

Job 7: 4 before I get up?' The night drags on, and *I* **toss** [+8425] till dawn.

5612 נָדָה **nādâ**, v. [2] [→ 5614, 5765; cf. 5604, 5610, 5653]

exclude [1], put off [1]

Isa 66: 5 [D] **exclude** you because of my name, have said, 'Let the LORD
Am 6: 3 [D] *You* **put off** the evil day and bring near a reign of terror.

5613 נֵדֶה **nēdeh**, n.m. [1]

fee [1]

Eze 16: 33 Every prostitute receives a **fee**, but you give gifts to all your lovers,

5614 נִדָּה **niddâ**, n.[m.]. [29] [→ 5765; cf. 5612]

period [7], cleansing [6], monthly period [3], unclean thing [3], act of impurity [1], corruption [1], defilement [1], impurity of monthly period [1], impurity [1], monthly flow [1], monthly period [+1864] [1], monthly period [+1865] [1], polluted [1], woman's monthly uncleanness [+2021+3240] [1]

Lev 12: 2 just as she is unclean during her **monthly period** [+1864].
12: 5 for two weeks the woman will be unclean, as during her **period**.
15: 19 the **impurity of** her **monthly period** will last seven days,
15: 20 " 'Anything she lies on during her **period** will be unclean,
15: 24 " 'If a man lies with her and her **monthly flow** touches him,
15: 25 of blood for many days at a time other than her **monthly period**
15: 25 or has a discharge that continues beyond her **period**,
15: 25 as long as she has the discharge, just as in the days of her **period**.
15: 26 as is her bed during her **monthly period**, and anything she sits on
15: 26 and anything she sits on will be unclean, as during her **period**.
15: 33 for a *woman* in her **monthly period** [+1865], for a man or a
18: 19 sexual relations during the uncleanness of her **monthly period**.
20: 21 " 'If a man marries his brother's wife, it is an **act of impurity**;
Nu 19: 9 kept by the Israelite community for use in the water of **cleansing**;
19: 13 Because the water of **cleansing** has not been sprinkled on him,
19: 20 The water of **cleansing** has not been sprinkled on him, and he is
19: 21 "The man who sprinkles the water of **cleansing** must also wash his
19: 21 anyone who touches the water of **cleansing** will be unclean till
31: 23 be clean. But it must also be purified with the water of **cleansing**.
2Ch 29: 5 God of your fathers. Remove *all* **defilement** from the sanctuary.
Ezr 9: 11 'The land you are entering to possess is a land **polluted** by the
9: 11 to possess is a land polluted by the **corruption** *of* its peoples.
La 1: 17 his foes; Jerusalem has become an **unclean thing** among them.
Eze 7: 19 their silver into the streets, and their gold will be an **unclean thing**.
7: 20 Therefore I will turn these into an **unclean thing** for them.
18: 6 defile his neighbor's wife or lie with a woman *during* her **period**.
22: 10 in you are those who violate women during their **period**,
36: 17 like a **woman's monthly uncleanness** [+2021+3240] in my sight.
Zec 13: 1 inhabitants of Jerusalem, to cleanse them from sin and **impurity**.

5615 נָדַח **nādaḥ[1]**, v. [53] [→ 4505; cf. 1866, 1890, 1891, 5616]

banish [6], banished [5], exiles [5], been scattered [3], drive [2], fugitives [2], led astray [2], strays [2], are drawn away [1], be driven away [1], be enticed [1], be thrust [1], been banished [1], been driven [1], chased away [1], disperses [1], drive out [1], driven away [1], driven [1], enticed [1], estranged [1], exiled [1], hunted [1], outcast [1], pushing [1], scatter [1], scattered [1], seduced [1], spewed out [1], straying [1], topple [1], turn away [1], turn [1], were exiled [1]

Dt 4: 19 [C] *do* not **be enticed** *into* bowing down to them and worshiping
13: 5 [13:6] [G] *he has tried* to **turn** you from the way the LORD
13: 10 [13:11] [G] because he tried to **turn** you **away** from the LORD
13: 13 [13:14] [G] and *have* **led** the people of their town **astray**,
22: 1 [C] If you see your brother's ox or sheep **straying**, do not ignore
30: 1 [G] the LORD your God **disperses** you among the nations,
30: 4 [C] Even if you *have* **been banished** to the most distant land
30: 17 [C] if *you* **are drawn away** to bow down to other gods
2Sa 14: 13 [C] for the king has not brought back his **banished** son?
14: 14 [C] so that a **banished** *person* may not remain estranged from
14: 14 [C] so that a banished person *may* not *remain* **estranged** from
2Ki 17: 21 [G] Jeroboam **enticed** [K 5604] Israel away from following the
2Ch 13: 9 [G] didn't *you* **drive out** the priests of the LORD, the sons of
21: 11 [G] Jerusalem to prostitute themselves and *had* **led** Judah **astray**.
Ne 1: 9 [C] then even if your **exiled** *people* are at the farthest horizon,
Job 6: 13 [C] to help myself, now that success *has* **been driven** from me?
Ps 5: 10 [5:11] [G] **Banish** them for their many sins, for they have
62: 4 [62:5] [G] They fully intend to **topple** him from his lofty place;
147: 2 [C] LORD builds up Jerusalem; he gathers the **exiles** *of* Israel.
Pr 7: 21 [G] she led him astray; *she* **seduced** him with her smooth talk.
Isa 8: 22 [E] fearful gloom, and *they will* **be thrust** *into* utter darkness.
11: 12 [C] raise a banner for the nations and gather the **exiles** *of* Israel;
13: 14 [H] Like a **hunted** gazelle, like sheep without a shepherd,
16: 3 [C] at high noon. Hide the **fugitives**, do not betray the refugees.
16: 4 [C] Let the Moabite **fugitives** stay with you; be their shelter from
27: 13 [C] in Assyria and those *who* **were exiled** in Egypt will come
56: 8 [C] LORD declares—he who gathers the **exiles** *of* Israel:
Jer 8: 3 [G] Wherever *I* **banish** them, all the survivors of this evil nation
16: 15 [G] and out of all the countries where *he had* **banished** them.'
23: 2 [G] and **driven** them **away** and have not bestowed care on them,
23: 3 [G] my flock out of all the countries where *I have* **driven** them
23: 8 [G] and out of all the countries where *he had* **banished** them.'
24: 9 [G] an object of ridicule and cursing, wherever *I* **banish** them.
27: 10 [G] far from your lands; *I will* **banish** you and you will perish.
27: 15 [G] I *will* **banish** you and you will perish, both you
29: 14 [G] from all the nations and places where *I have* **banished** you,"
29: 18 [G] and reproach, among all the nations where *I* **drive** them.
30: 17 [C] declares the LORD, 'because you are called an **outcast**,
32: 37 [G] I will surely gather them from all the lands where *I* **banish**
40: 12 [C] from all the countries where *they had* **been scattered**.
43: 5 [C] of Judah from all the nations where *they had* **been scattered**.
46: 28 [G] destroy all the nations among which *I* **scatter** you,
49: 5 [C] "Every one of *you will* **be driven away**, and no one will
49: 36 [C] and there will not be a nation where Elam's **exiles** do not go.
50: 17 [G] "Israel is a scattered flock that lions *have* **chased away**.
51: 34 [G] his stomach with our delicacies, and then *has* **spewed** us **out**.
Eze 4: 13 [G] eat defiled food among the nations where *I will* **drive** them."
34: 4 [C] You have not brought back the **strays** or searched for the
34: 16 [C] I will search for the lost and bring back the **strays**. I will bind
Da 9: 7 [G] in all the countries where *you have* **scattered** us because of

Joel 2:20 [G] army far from you, **pushing** it into a parched and barren land,
Mic 4: 6 [C] I will assemble the **exiles** and those I have brought to grief.
Zep 3:19 [C] rescue the lame and gather those *who have* **been scattered**.

5616 ²נָדַח nāḏaḥ², v. [3] [cf. 5615]

bring [1], putting [1], swings [1]

Dt 19: 5 [C] and as he **swings** his ax to fell a tree, the head may fly off
20:19 [A] do not destroy its trees by **putting** an ax to them,
2Sa 15:14 [G] and **bring** ruin upon us and put the city to the sword."

5617 נֹדִי nōḏî, n.[m.]. Not used in NIV/BHS

5618 נָדִיב nāḏîḇ, a. (used as noun). [27] [→ 5619; cf. 5605]

nobles [8], princes [5], willing [3], noble [2], ruler [2], willing [+4213] [2], great man's [1], nobleman [1], officials [1], prince's [1], royal [1]

Ex 35: 5 Everyone who is **willing** [+4213] is to bring to the LORD an
35:22 All who were **willing** [+4213], men and women alike, came
Nu 21:18 the well that the princes dug, that the **nobles** *of* the people sank—
1Sa 2: 8 he seats them with **princes** and has them inherit a throne of honor.
1Ch 28:21 every **willing** *man* skilled in any craft will help you in all the
2Ch 29:31 and all whose hearts were **willing** brought burnt offerings.
Job 12:21 He pours contempt on **nobles** and disarms the mighty.
21:28 You say, 'Where now is the **great man's** house, the tents where
34:18 says to kings, 'You are worthless,' and to **nobles**, 'You are wicked,'
Ps 47: 9 [47:10] The **nobles** *of* the nations assemble as the people of the
51:12 [51:14] me the joy of your salvation and grant me a **willing** spirit,
83:11 [83:12] Make their **nobles** like Oreb and Zeeb, all their princes
107:40 he who pours contempt on **nobles** made them wander in a trackless
113: 8 he seats them with **princes**, with the princes of their people.
113: 8 he seats them with princes, with the **princes** *of* their people.
118: 9 It is better to take refuge in the LORD than to trust in **princes**.
146: 3 Do not put your trust in **princes**, in mortal men, who cannot save.
Pr 8:16 by me princes govern, and all **nobles** who rule on earth.
17: 7 lips are unsuited to a fool—how much worse lying lips to a **ruler**!
17:26 to punish an innocent man, or to flog **officials** for their integrity.
19: 6 Many curry favor with a **ruler**, and everyone is the friend of a man
25: 7 "Come up here," than for him to humiliate you before a **nobleman**.
SS 6:12 my desire set me among the **royal** chariots of my people.
7: 1 [7:2] How beautiful your sandaled feet, O **prince's** daughter!
Isa 13: 2 shout to them; beckon to them to enter the gates of the **nobles**.
32: 5 No longer will the fool be called **noble** nor the scoundrel be highly
32: 8 the **noble** *man* makes noble plans, and by noble deeds he stands.

5619 נְדִיבָה nᵉḏîḇâ, n.f. [3] [√ 5618; cf. 5605]

noble [2], dignity [1]

Job 30:15 my **dignity** is driven away as by the wind, my safety vanishes like
Isa 32: 8 the noble man makes **noble** plans, and by noble deeds he stands.
32: 8 the noble man makes noble plans, and by **noble** *deeds* he stands.

5620 ¹נָדָן nāḏān¹, n.[m.]. [1] [→ Ar 10464]

sheath [1]

1Ch 21:27 spoke to the angel, and he put his sword back into its **sheath**.

5621 ²נָדָן nāḏān², n.[m.]. [1] [cf. 5989]

gifts [1]

Eze 16:33 Every prostitute receives a fee, but you give **gifts** to all your lovers,

5622 נָדַף nāḏap, v. [9]

windblown [3], blow away [2], blows away [1], fleeting [1], is blown away [1], refute [1]

Lev 26:36 [C] that the sound of a **windblown** leaf will put them to flight.
Job 13:25 [C] Will you torment a **windblown** leaf? Will you chase after dry
32:13 [A] 'We have found wisdom; *let* God **refute** him, not man.'
Ps 1: 4 [A] so the wicked! They are like chaff that the wind **blows away**.
68: 2 [68:3] [C] As smoke **is blown away** by the wind, may you blow
68: 2 [68:3] [A] blown away by the wind, *may you* **blow** them **away**;
Pr 21: 6 [C] A fortune made by a lying tongue is a **fleeting** vapor and a
Isa 19: 7 [C] Nile will become parched, *will* **blow away** and be no more.
41: 2 [C] to dust with his sword, to **windblown** chaff with his bow.

5623 נָדַר nāḏar, v. [31] [→ 5624; cf. 5692, 5693, 5694]

made a vow [+5624] [4], vowed [+5624] [3], made vow [+5624] [2], make a vow [+5624] [2], makes a vow [+5624] [2], vow made [+5624] [2], vow [2], made a vow [1], made vow [1], made vows [+5624] [1], make a special vow [+7098] [1], make a vow [1], make vows [+5624] [1], make vows [1], makes a vow [1], making a vow [1], making vow [1], vowed [1], vows made [+5624] [1], vows to give [1], vows [1]

Ge 28:20 [A] Jacob **made a vow** [+5624], saying, "If God will be with me
31:13 [A] anointed a pillar and where *you* **made a vow** [+5624] to me.
Lev 27: 8 [A] him according to what the *man* **making** *the* **vow** can afford.
Nu 6: 2 [A] 'If a man or woman *wants* to **make a special vow** [+7098],
6:21 [A] " 'This is the law of the Nazirite who **vows** his offering to the
6:21 [A] He must fulfill the **vow** *he has* **made** [+5624], according to
21: 2 [A] Israel **made** *this* **vow** [+5624] to the LORD: "If you will
30: 2 [30:3] [A] When a man **makes a vow** [+5624] to the LORD
30: 3 [30:4] [A] father's house **makes a vow** [+5624] to the LORD
30:10 [30:11] [A] "If a woman living with her husband **makes a vow**
Dt 12:11 [A] all the choice possessions you *have* **vowed** [+5624] to the
12:17 [A] and flocks, or whatever you *have* **vowed** [+5624] to give,
23:21 [23:22] [A] If *you* **make a vow** [+5624] to the LORD your
23:22 [23:23] [A] if you refrain from **making a vow**, you will not be
23:23 [23:24] [A] because *you* **made** *your* **vow** freely to the LORD
Jdg 11:30 [A] Jephthah **made a vow** [+5624] to the LORD: "If you give
11:39 [A] to her father and he did to her as he *had* **vowed** [+5624].
1Sa 1:11 [A] *she* **made a vow** [+5624], saying, "O LORD Almighty,
2Sa 15: 7 [A] to Hebron and fulfill a **vow** *I* **made** [+5624] to the LORD.
15: 8 [A] was living at Geshur in Aram, *I* **made** *this* **vow** [+5624]:
Ps 76:11 [76:12] [A] **Make vows** to the LORD your God and fulfill
132: 2 [A] to the LORD and **made a vow** to the Mighty One of Jacob:
Ecc 5: 4 [5:3] [A] When *you* **make a vow** [+5624] to God, do not delay
5: 4 [5:3] [A] He has no pleasure in fools; fulfill *your* **vow**.
5: 5 [5:4] [A] It is better not *to* **vow** than to make a vow and not
5: 5 [5:4] [A] It is better not to vow than *to* **make a vow** and not
Isa 19:21 [A] *they will* **make vows** [+5624] to the LORD and keep them.
Jer 44:25 [A] 'We will certainly carry out the **vows** [+5624] *we* **made** to
Jnh 1:16 [A] a sacrifice to the LORD and **made vows** [+5624] to him.
2: 9 [2:10] [A] to you. What *I have* **vowed** I will make good.
Mal 1:14 [A] who has an acceptable male in his flock and **vows to give** it,

5624 נֶדֶר nēḏer, n.m. [60] [√ 5623]

vows [21], vow [13], made a vow [+5623] [4], vowed [+5623] [3], vowed [3], made vow [+5623] [2], make a vow [+5623] [2], makes a vow [+5623] [2], vow made [+5623] [2], fulfill a special vow [+7098] [1], made vows [+5623] [1], make vows [+5623] [1], makes a special vow [+7098] [1], special vow [+7098] [1], special vows [+7098] [1], vows made [+5623] [1], what promised [1]

Ge 28:20 Then Jacob **made a vow** [+5623], saying, "If God will be with me
31:13 you anointed a pillar and where *you* **made a vow** [+5623] to me.
Lev 7:16 his offering is the result of a **vow** or is a freewill offering,
22:18 to the LORD, either to fulfill a **vow** or as a freewill offering,
22:21 fellowship offering to the LORD to **fulfill a special vow** [+7098]
22:23 or stunted, but it will not be accepted in fulfillment of a **vow**.
23:38 and in addition to your gifts and whatever you have **vowed**
27: 2 'If anyone **makes a special vow** [+7098] to dedicate persons to the
Nu 6: 2 a special vow, a **vow** *of* separation to the LORD as a Nazirite,
6: 5 " 'During the entire period of his **vow** *of* separation no razor may
6:21 He must fulfill the **vow** [+5623] *he has* **made**, according to the
15: 3 for **special vows** [+7098] or freewill offerings or festival
15: 8 for a **special vow** [+7098] or a fellowship offering to the LORD,
21: 2 Israel **made** *this* **vow** [+5623] to the LORD: "If you will deliver
29:39 " 'In addition to *what* you **vow** and your freewill offerings,
30: 2 [30:3] When a man **makes a vow** [+5623] to the LORD or takes
30: 3 [30:4] in her father's house **makes a vow** [+5623] to the LORD
30: 4 [30:5] her father hears about her **vow** or pledge but says nothing
30: 4 [30:5] all her **vows** and every pledge by which she obligated
30: 5 [30:6] none of her **vows** or the pledges by which she obligated
30: 6 [30:7] "If she marries after she makes a **vow** or after her lips utter
30: 7 [30:8] her **vows** or the pledges by which she obligated herself will
30: 8 [30:9] he nullifies the **vow** that obligates her or the rash promise
30: 9 [30:10] "Any **vow** or obligation taken by a widow or divorced
30:11 [30:12] all her **vows** or the pledges by which she obligated herself
30:12 [30:13] none of the **vows** or pledges that came from her lips will
30:13 [30:14] Her husband may confirm or nullify any **vow** she makes
30:14 [30:15] he confirms all her **vows** or the pledges binding on her.
Dt 12: 6 *what* you have **vowed** to give and your freewill offerings,
12:11 all the choice possessions you *have* **vowed** [+5623] to the LORD.
12:17 and flocks, or whatever you *have* **vowed** [+5623] to give,
12:26 your consecrated things and whatever you have **vowed** to give,
23:18 [23:19] into the house of the LORD your God to pay any **vow**,
23:21 [23:22] If *you* **make a vow** [+5623] to the LORD your God,
Jdg 11:30 Jephthah **made a vow** [+5623] to the LORD: "If you give the
11:39 returned to her father and he did to her as he *had* **vowed** [+5623].
1Sa 1:11 And *she* **made a vow** [+5623], saying, "O LORD Almighty,
1:21 to offer the annual sacrifice to the LORD and to fulfill his **vow**,
2Sa 15: 7 me go to Hebron and fulfill a **vow** [+5623] *I* **made** to the LORD.
15: 8 servant was living at Geshur in Aram, *I* **made** *this* **vow** [+5623]:
Job 22:27 pray to him, and he will hear you, and you will fulfill your **vows**.
Ps 22:25 [22:26] before those who fear you will I fulfill my **vows**.
50:14 thank offerings to God, fulfill your **vows** to the Most High,
56:12 [56:13] I am under **vows** *to* you, O God; I will present my thank
61: 5 [61:6] For you have heard my **vows**, O God; you have given me
61: 8 [61:9] sing praise to your name and fulfill my **vows** day after day.

Ps 65: 1 [65:2] O God, in Zion; to you our **vows** will be fulfilled.
66: 13 to your temple with burnt offerings and fulfill my **vows** to you—
116: 14 I will fulfill my **vows** to the LORD in the presence of all his
116: 18 I will fulfill my **vows** to the LORD in the presence of all his
Pr 7: 14 "I have fellowship offerings at home; today I fulfilled my **vows**.
20: 25 to dedicate something rashly and only later to consider his **vows**.
31: 2 "O my son, O son of my womb, O son of my **vows**,
Ecc 5: 4 [5:3] When *you* **make a vow** [+5623] to God, do not delay in
Isa 19: 21 *they will* **make vows** [+5623] to the LORD and keep them.
Jer 44: 25 'We will certainly carry out the **vows** *we* **made** [+5623] to burn
44: 25 "Go ahead then, do **what** you **promised**! Keep your vows!
44: 25 "Go ahead then, do what you promised! Keep your **vows**!
Jnh 1: 16 offered a sacrifice to the LORD and **made vows** [+5623] to him.
Na 1: 15 [2:1] Celebrate your festivals, O Judah, and fulfill your **vows**.

5625 נֹהַּ ***nōah***, n.[m.]. [1]

value [1]

Eze 7: 11 will be left, none of that crowd—no wealth, nothing *of* **value**.

5626 נָה- ***-nâ***, p.f.s.suf. [211 / 212] [√ 2023] Not indexed

it [84], *untranslated* [53], her [22], them [9], its [6], which[s] [5], they [4], she [3], that [3], the lampstand[s] [3], him [2], the[s] [2], this [2], everything [+3972] [1], himself [1], incense[s] [1], one [1], so[s] [1], the animal[s] [1], the city[s] [1], the flock[s] [1], the food[s] [1], the land[s] [1], their [1], themselves [1], which [1], widow[s] [1]

5627 ¹נָהַג ***nāhag¹***, v. [30] [→ 4952]

carried off [3], guiding [3], lead [3], led [3], drive [2], guide [2], drive away [1], driven away [1], drives [1], driving [1], drove ahead [1], drove [1], guided [1], lead away [1], lead on [+2143+2256] [1], led forth [1], led in triumphal procession [1], led out [1], made blow [1], take [1]

Ge 31: 18 [A] *he* **drove** all his livestock **ahead** *of him*, along with all the
31: 26 [D] and *you've* **carried off** my daughters like captives in war.
Ex 3: 1 [A] *he* **led** the flock *to* the far side of the desert and came to
10: 13 [D] the LORD **made** an east wind **blow** across the land all that
14: 25 [D] of their chariots come off so that *they* had difficulty **driving**.
Dt 4: 27 [D] among the nations to which the LORD *will* **drive** you.
28: 37 [D] ridicule to all the nations where the LORD *will* **drive** you.
1Sa 23: 5 [A] fought the Philistines and **carried off** their livestock.
30: 2 [A] of them, but **carried** them **off** as they went on their way.
30: 20 [A] and his men **drove** them ahead of the other livestock, saying,
30: 22 [A] However, each man *may* **take** his wife and children and go."
2Sa 6: 3 [A] and Ahio, sons of Abinadab, *were* **guiding** the new cart
2Ki 4: 24 [A] the donkey and said to her servant, "**Lead** [+2143+2256] **on**;
9: 20 [A] like that of Jehu son of Nimshi—*he* **drives** like a madman."
1Ch 13: 7 [A] house on a new cart, with Uzzah and Ahio **guiding** it.
20: 1 [A] when kings go off to war, Joab **led out** the armed forces.
2Ch 25: 11 [A] marshaled his strength and **led** his army to the Valley of Salt,
Job 24: 3 [A] *They* **drive away** the orphan's donkey and take the widow's
Ps 48: 14 [48:15] [D] and ever; he *will be* our **guide** even to the end.
78: 26 [D] from the heavens and **led forth** the south wind by his power.
78: 52 [D] out like a flock; *he* **led** them like sheep through the desert.
80: 1 [80:2] [A] Shepherd of Israel, you *who* **lead** Joseph like a flock;
Ecc 2: 3 [A] embracing folly—my mind *still* **guiding** me with wisdom.
SS 8: 2 [A] *I would* **lead** you and bring you to my mother's house—
Isa 11: 6 [A] and the yearling together; and a little child *will* **lead** them.
20: 4 [A] *will* **lead away** stripped and barefoot the Egyptian captives and
49: 10 [D] He who has compassion on them *will* **guide** them and lead
60: 11 [B] of the nations—their kings **led in triumphal procession**.
63: 14 [D] This is how *you* **guided** your people to make for yourself a
La 3: 2 [A] *He has* **driven** me **away** and made me walk in darkness

5628 ²נָהַג ***nāhag²***, v. [1] [cf. 5640]

moan [1]

Na 2: 7 [2:8] [D] Its slave girls **moan** like doves and beat upon their

5629 ¹נָהָה ***nāhâ¹***, v. [3] [→ 5631, 5632, 5760]

mourned [1], taunt [1], wail [1]

1Sa 7: 2 [C] all the people of Israel **mourned** and sought after the
Eze 32: 18 [A] **wail** for the hordes of Egypt and consign to the earth below
Mic 2: 4 [A] ridicule you; *they will* **taunt** you *with* this mournful song:

5630 ²נָהָה ***nāhâ²***, v. Not used in NIV/BHS

5631 נְהִי ***nehî***, n.[m.]. [7] [→ 5760; cf. 5629]

wail [2], mourners [+3359] [1], mournful song [1], mourning [1], wail [+5951] [1], wailing [1]

Jer 9: 10 [9:9] I will weep and **wail** for the mountains and take up a lament
9: 18 [9:17] and **wail** [+5951] over us till our eyes overflow with tears
9: 19 [9:18] The sound of **wailing** is heard from Zion: 'How ruined we
9: 20 [9:19] Teach your daughters how to **wail**; teach one another a
31: 15 "A voice is heard in Ramah, **mourning** and great weeping,
Am 5: 16 will be summoned to weep and the **mourners** [+3359] to wail.
Mic 2: 4 will ridicule you; they will taunt you with this **mournful song**:

5632 נִהְיָה ***nihyâ***, n.f. Not used in NIV/BHS [√ 5629]

5633 נָהַל ***nāhal***, v. [10] [→ 5634, 5635, 5636]

guide [3], brought [1], gently leads [1], lead [1], leads [1], move along [1], put [1], took care of [1]

Ge 33: 14 [F] while I **move along** slowly at the pace of the droves before
47: 17 [D] *he* **brought** them through that year with food in exchange for
Ex 15: 13 [D] In your strength *you will* **guide** them to your holy dwelling.
2Ch 28: 15 [D] All those who were weak *they* **put** on donkeys.
32: 22 [D] the hand of all others. *He* **took care of** them on every side.
Ps 23: 2 [D] lie down in green pastures, *he* **leads** me beside quiet waters,
31: 3 [31:4] [D] for the sake of your name lead and **guide** me.
Isa 40: 11 [D] close to his heart; *he* **gently leads** those that have young.
49: 10 [D] them will guide them and **lead** them beside springs of water.
51: 18 [D] Of all the sons she bore there was none *to* **guide** her; of all

5634 נַהֲלָל ***nahalāl***, n.pr.loc. [2] [√ 5633]

Nahalal [2]

Jos 19: 15 Included were Kattath, **Nahalal**, Shimron, Idalah and Bethlehem.
21: 35 Dimnah and **Nahalal**, together with their pasturelands—

5635 ¹נַהֲלֹל ***nahălōl¹***, n.m. [1] [→ 5636; cf. 5633]

water holes [1]

Isa 7: 19 in the rocks, on all the thornbushes and at all the **water holes**.

5636 ²נַהֲלֹל ***nahălōl²***, n.pr.loc. [1] [√ 5635; cf. 5633]

Nahalol [1]

Jdg 1: 30 did Zebulun drive out the Canaanites living in Kitron or **Nahalol**,

5637 נָהַם ***nāham***, v. [5] [→ 5638, 5639; cf. 2101, 2159, 2169]

groan [2], growl [1], roar [1], roaring [1]

Pr 5: 11 [A] At the end of your life *you will* **groan**, when your flesh
28: 15 [A] Like a **roaring** lion or a charging bear is a wicked man ruling
Isa 5: 29 [A] *they* **growl** as they seize their prey and carry it off with no
5: 30 [A] In that day *they will* **roar** over it like the roaring of the sea.
Eze 24: 23 [A] because of your sins and **groan** among yourselves.

5638 נַהַם ***naham***, n.[m.]. [2] [√ 5637]

roar [2]

Pr 19: 12 A king's rage is like the **roar** *of* a lion, but his favor is like dew on
20: 2 A king's wrath is like the **roar** *of* a lion; he who angers him

5639 נְהָמָה ***nehāmâ***, n.f. [2] [√ 5637]

anguish [1], roaring [1]

Ps 38: 8 [38:9] am feeble and utterly crushed; I groan in **anguish** *of* heart.
Isa 5: 30 In that day they will roar over it like the **roaring** *of* the sea.

5640 נָהַק ***nāhaq***, v. [2] [cf. 5628]

bray [1], brayed [1]

Job 6: 5 [A] *Does* a wild donkey **bray** when it has grass, or an ox bellow
30: 7 [A] *They* **brayed** among the bushes and huddled in the

5641 ¹נָהַר ***nāhar¹***, v. [3] [√ 5643]

stream [3]

Isa 2: 2 [A] be raised above the hills, and all nations *will* **stream** to it.
Jer 51: 44 [A] The nations *will* no longer **stream** to him. And the wall of
Mic 4: 1 [A] it will be raised above the hills, and peoples *will* **stream** to it.

5642 ²נָהַר ***nāhar²***, v. [3] [→ 5644; cf. 5944]

radiant [2], rejoice [1]

Ps 34: 5 [34:6] [A] Those who look to him *are* **radiant**; their faces are
Isa 60: 5 [A] you will look and *be* **radiant**, your heart will throb and swell
Jer 31: 12 [A] *they will* **rejoice** in the bounty of the LORD—the grain,

5643 נָהָר ***nāhār***, n.m. [119] [→ 808, 5641, 5645; Ar 10468]

river [58], rivers [23], streams [12], *untranslated* [5], Trans-Euphrates [+2021+6298] [4], canal [3], seas [3], Euphrates[s] [2], flood [2], riverbed [2], waters [2], canals [1], currents [1], rivers [+5707] [1]

Ge 2: 10 A **river** watering the garden flowed from Eden; from there it was
2: 13 The name of the second **river** is the Gihon; it winds through the
2: 14 The name of the third **river** is the Tigris; it runs along the east side

Ge 2:14 the east side of Asshur. And the fourth **river** is the Euphrates.
15:18 from the **river** *of* Egypt to the great river, the Euphrates—
15:18 from the river of Egypt to the great **river**, the Euphrates—
15:18 from the river of Egypt to the great river, **[RPH]** the Euphrates—
31:21 So he fled with all he had, and crossing the **River**, he headed for
36:37 Shaul from Rehoboth on the **river** succeeded him as king.
Ex 7:19 over the **streams** and canals, over the ponds and all the
8:5 [8:1] 'Stretch out your hand with your staff over the **streams**
23:31 Sea to the Sea of the Philistines, and from the desert to the **River**.
Nu 22:5 son of Beor, who was at Pethor, near the **River**, in his native land.
24:6 "Like valleys they spread out, like gardens beside a **river**,
Dt 1:7 and to Lebanon, as far as the great **river**, the Euphrates.
1:7 and to Lebanon, as far as the great river, the Euphrates. **[RPH]**
11:24 and from the **[RPH]** Euphrates River to the western sea.
11:24 to Lebanon, and from the Euphrates **River** to the western sea.
Jos 1:4 the desert to Lebanon, and from the great **river**, the Euphrates—
1:4 to Lebanon, and from the great river, **[RPH]** the Euphrates—
24:2 and Nahor, lived beyond the **River** and worshiped other gods.
24:3 But I took your father Abraham from the land beyond the **River**
24:14 Throw away the gods your forefathers worshiped beyond the **River**
24:15 whether the gods your forefathers served beyond the **River**,
2Sa 8:3 when he went to restore his control along the Euphrates **River**.
10:16 Hadadezer had Arameans brought from beyond the **River**;
1Ki 4:21 [5:1] Solomon ruled over all the kingdoms from the **River** to the
4:24 [5:4] For he ruled over all the kingdoms west of the **River**,
4:24 [5:4] from Tiphsah to Gaza, **[RPH]** and had peace on all sides.
14:15 that he gave to their forefathers and scatter them beyond the **River**,
2Ki 5:12 Are not Abana and Pharpar, the **rivers** *of* Damascus, better than
17:6 in Gozan on the Habor **River** and in the towns of the Medes.
18:11 in Halah, in Gozan on the Habor **River** and in towns of the Medes.
23:29 Pharaoh Neco king of Egypt went up to the Euphrates **River** to
24:7 all his territory, from the Wadi of Egypt to the Euphrates **River**.
1Ch 1:48 Shaul from Rehoboth on the **river** succeeded him as king.
5:9 up to the edge of the desert that extends to the Euphrates **River**,
5:26 He took them to Halah, Habor, Hara and the **river** *of* Gozan,
18:3 when he went to establish his control along the Euphrates **River**.
19:16 and had Arameans brought from beyond the **River**,
2Ch 9:26 He ruled over all the kings from the **River** to the land of the
Ezr 8:15 I assembled them at the **canal** that flows toward Ahava, and we
8:21 There, by the Ahava **Canal**, I proclaimed a fast, so that we might
8:31 first month we set out from the Ahava **Canal** to go to Jerusalem.
8:36 They also delivered the king's orders to the royal satraps and to the governors of **Trans-Euphrates** [+2021+6298], who then gave
Ne 2:7 I also said to him, "If it pleases the king, may I have letters to the governors of **Trans-Euphrates** [+2021+6298], so that they will
2:9 So I went to the governors of **Trans-Euphrates** [+2021+6298] and gave them the king's letters. The king had also sent army officers
3:7 Melatiah of Gibeon and Jadon of Meronoth—places under the authority of the governor of **Trans-Euphrates** [+2021+6298].
Job 14:11 disappears from the sea or a **riverbed** becomes parched and dry,
20:17 the streams, the **rivers** [+5707] *flowing with* honey and cream.
22:16 off before their time, their foundations washed away by a **flood**.
28:11 He searches the sources of the **rivers** and brings hidden things to
40:23 When the **river** rages, he is not alarmed; he is secure,
Ps 24:2 for he founded it upon the seas and established it upon the **waters**.
46:4 [46:5] There is a **river** whose streams make glad the city of God,
66:6 the sea into dry land, they passed through the **waters** on foot—
72:8 rule from sea to sea and from the **River** to the ends of the earth.
74:15 up springs and streams; you dried up the ever flowing **rivers**.
78:16 streams out of a rocky crag and made water flow down like **rivers**.
80:11 [80:12] out its boughs to the Sea, its shoots as far as the **River**.
89:25 [89:26] set his hand over the sea, his right hand over the **rivers**.
93:3 The **seas** have lifted up, O LORD, the seas have lifted up their
93:3 seas have lifted up, O LORD, the **seas** have lifted up their voice;
93:3 lifted up their voice; the **seas** have lifted up their pounding waves.
98:8 Let the **rivers** clap their hands, let the mountains sing together for
105:41 the rock, and water gushed out; like a **river** it flowed in the desert.
107:33 He turned **rivers** into a desert, flowing springs into thirsty ground,
137:1 By the **rivers** *of* Babylon we sat and wept when we remembered
SS 8:7 Many waters cannot quench love; **rivers** cannot wash it away.
Isa 7:20 In that day the Lord will use a razor hired from beyond the **River**—
8:7 about to bring against them the mighty floodwaters of the **River**—
11:15 a scorching wind he will sweep his hand over the Euphrates **River**.
18:1 Woe to the land of whirring wings along the **rivers** *of* Cush,
18:2 nation of strange speech, whose land is divided by **rivers**.
18:7 nation of strange speech, whose land is divided by **rivers**—
19:5 of the river will dry up, and the **riverbed** will be parched and dry.
19:6 The **canals** will stink; the streams of Egypt will dwindle and dry
27:12 In that day the LORD will thresh from the flowing **Euphrates**[s] to
33:21 It will be like a place of broad **rivers** and streams. No galley with
41:18 I will make **rivers** flow on barren heights, and springs within the
42:15 their vegetation; I will turn **rivers** into islands and dry up the pools.
43:2 when you pass through the **rivers**, they will not sweep over you.
43:19 I am making a way in the desert and **streams** in the wasteland.
43:20 because I provide water in the desert and **streams** in the wasteland,
44:27 says to the watery deep, 'Be dry, and I will dry up your **streams**,'
47:2 Lift up your skirts, bare your legs, and wade through the **streams**.
48:18 your peace would have been like a **river**, your righteousness like
50:2 By a mere rebuke I dry up the sea, I turn **rivers** into a desert;
59:19 For he will come like a pent-up **flood** that the breath of the LORD
66:12 "I will extend peace to her like a **river**, and the wealth of nations
Jer 2:18 the Shihor? And why go to Assyria to drink water from the **River**?
46:2 which was defeated at Carchemish on the Euphrates **River** by
46:6 In the north by the **River** Euphrates they stumble and fall.
46:7 "Who is this that rises like the Nile, like **rivers** *of* surging waters?
46:8 Egypt rises like the Nile, like **rivers** *of* surging waters. She says,
46:10 will offer sacrifice in the land of the north by the **River** Euphrates.
Eze 1:1 while I was among the exiles by the Kebar **River**, the heavens
1:3 the son of Buzi, by the Kebar **River** in the land of the Babylonians.
3:15 I came to the exiles who lived at Tel Abib near the Kebar **River**.
3:23 like the glory I had seen by the Kebar **River**, and I fell facedown.
10:15 These were the living creatures I had seen by the Kebar **River**.
10:20 creatures I had seen beneath the God of Israel by the Kebar **River**,
10:22 had the same appearance as those I had seen by the Kebar **River**.
31:4 their **streams** flowed all around its base and sent their channels to
31:15 I held back its **streams**, and its abundant waters were restrained.
32:2 you are like a monster in the seas thrashing about in your **streams**,
32:2 churning the water with your feet and muddying the **streams**.
32:14 I will let her waters settle and make her **streams** flow like oil,
43:3 destroy the city and like the visions I had seen by the Kebar **River**,
Da 10:4 as I was standing on the bank of the great **river**, the Tigris,
Jnh 2:3 [2:4] very heart of the seas, and the **currents** swirled about me;
Mic 7:12 even from Egypt to the **Euphrates**[s] and from sea to sea and from
Na 1:4 He rebukes the sea and dries it up; he makes all the **rivers** run dry.
2:6 [2:7] The **river** gates are thrown open and the palace collapses.
Hab 3:8 Were you angry with the **rivers**, O LORD? Was your wrath
3:8 with the rivers, O LORD? Was your wrath against the **streams**?
3:9 called for many arrows. *Selah* You split the earth with **rivers**;
Zep 3:10 From beyond the **rivers** *of* Cush my worshipers, my scattered
Zec 9:10 extend from sea to sea and from the **River** to the ends of the earth.

5644 נְהָרָה *nehārâ*, n.f. [1] [√ 5642; Ar 10465, 10466, 10467]

light [1]

Job 3:4 may God above not care about it; may no **light** shine upon it.

5645 נַהֲרַיִם *naharayim*, n.pr.loc. Not used in NIV/BHS [→ 808; cf. 5643]

5646 נוּ- *-nû*[1], p.com.pl.suf. [1647] [√ 3276] Not indexed

us [701], our [670], we [94], *untranslated* [91], our [+4200] [22], our own [12], ourselves [10], ours [7], the[s] [6], it [5], we [+5883] [5], me [3], ourselves [+5883] [3], us [+5883] [3], ours [+4200] [2], a[s] [1], each other [+9109] [1], he[s] [+466+3378] [1], here[s] [1], one [1], ours [+4200+7156] [1], that [1], us [+6524] [1], us deserve [1], we [+3972] [1], we're [1], what[s] [1], you [1]

5647 נוּ- *-nû*[2], נוֹ- *-nô*, p.m.s.suf. [511 / 512] [√ 2023] Not indexed

him [175], *untranslated* [109], it [85], them [48], he [24], his [10], my wrath[s] [8], they [8], animal[s] [2], its [2], the altar[s] [2], the ephod[s] [2], the servant[s] [2], themselves [2], whom [2], Abimelech[s] [1], Absalom[s] [1], all[s] he has [1], all[s] [1], another[s] [1], any[s] [1], drink[s] [1], Edom[s] [1], hers [1], his [+4946] [1], his own [1], Jeremiah[s] [1], Judah[s] [1], man[s] [1], manna[s] [1], one [1], the blood[s] [1], the man[s] [1], the meat[s] [1], the oil[s] [1], the roof[s] [1], the sacred[s] portion [1], the wicked[s] [1], their own [1], their [1], there[s] [1], these tithes[s] [1], this bread[s] [1], those[s] [1], what [1], who [1]

5648 נוא *nû'*, v. [8] [→ 9481]

forbids [2], discourage [+906+4213] [1], discouraged [+906+4213] [1], forbid [1], forbidden [1], refuse [1], thwarts [1]

Nu 30:5 [30:6] [G] if her father **forbids** her when he hears about it,
30:5 [30:6] [G] release her because her father *has* **forbidden** her.
30:8 [30:9] [G] if her husband **forbids** her when he hears about it, he
30:11 [30:12] [G] but says nothing to her and *does* not **forbid** her,
32:7 [G] Why *do you* **discourage** [+906+4213] the Israelites from going
32:9 [G] *they* **discouraged** [+906+4213] the Israelites from entering the
Ps 33:10 [G] plans of the nations; *he* **thwarts** the purposes of the peoples.
141:5 [G] rebuke me—it is oil on my head. My head *will* not **refuse** it.

5649 נוּב *nûb*, v. [4] [→ 1973, 5650, 5762, 9482]

bear fruit [1], brings forth [1], increase [1], make thrive [1]

Ps 62:10 [62:11] [A] though your riches **increase**, do not set your heart
92:14 [92:15] [A] *They will* still **bear fruit** in old age, they will stay

Pr 10:31 [A] The mouth of the righteous **brings forth** wisdom, but a
Zec 9:17 [D] Grain *will* **make** the young men **thrive**, and new wine the

5650 נֹוב nôb, n.[m.]. [0] [√ 5649]

Isa 57:19 [creating **praise** [K; see Q 5762] *on* the lips of the mourners]

5651 נֹובָי nôbāy, n.pr.m. [0] [cf. 5763]

Ne 10:19 [10:20] [Hariph, Anathoth, **Nebai**, [K; see Q 5763]]

5652 נוּג nûg, n.[m.]. [1]

sorrows [1]

Zep 3:18 "The **sorrows** for the appointed feasts I will remove from you;

5653 נוּד nûd, v. [25] [→ 4954, 5654, 5655, 5764; cf. 5604, 5610, 5612; Ar 10469]

flee [3], mourn [3], wanderer [2], away [1], comfort [1], comforted [1], drive away [1], fluttering [1], go astray [1], make wander [1], moaning [1], mourn loss [1], shake head in scorn [1], shake heads in scorn [1], shake [1], show sympathy [1], swaying [1], sways [1], sympathize [1], sympathy [1]

Ge 4:12 [A] crops for you. You will be a restless **wanderer** on the earth."
4:14 [A] I will be a restless **wanderer** on the earth, and whoever finds
1Ki 14:15 [A] so that it will be like a reed **swaying** in the water.
2Ki 21:8 [G] I will not again **make** the feet of the Israelites **wander** from
Job 2:11 [A] agreement to go and **sympathize** with him and comfort him.
42:11 [A] *They* **comforted** and consoled him over all the trouble the
Ps 11:1 [A] then can you say to me: "**Flee** like a bird *to* your mountain.
36:11 [36:12] [G] nor the hand of the wicked **drive** me **away**.
64:8 [64:9] [F] all who see them *will* **shake** *their* **heads in scorn**.
69:20 [69:21] [A] I looked for **sympathy**, but there was none, for
Pr 26:2 [A] Like a **fluttering** sparrow or a darting swallow, an
Isa 24:20 [F] earth reels like a drunkard, *it* **sways** like a hut in the wind;
51:19 [A] who *can* **comfort** you?—ruin and destruction, famine
Jer 4:1 [A] detestable idols out of my sight and no longer **go astray**,
15:5 [A] have pity on you, O Jerusalem? Who *will* **mourn** for you?
16:5 [A] do not go to mourn or **show sympathy**, because I have
18:16 [G] all who pass by will be appalled and *will* **shake** their heads.
22:10 [A] Do not weep for the dead ˹king˺ or **mourn** his **loss**; rather,
31:18 [F] "I have surely heard Ephraim's **moaning**: 'You disciplined
48:17 [A] **Mourn** for her, all who live around her, all who know her
48:27 [F] that *you* **shake** *your* **head in scorn** whenever you speak of
49:30 [A] "Flee quickly **away**! Stay in deep caves, you who live in
50:3 [A] No one will live in it; both men and animals *will* **flee** away.
50:8 [A] "**Flee** out of Babylon; leave the land of the Babylonians,
Na 3:7 [A] and say, 'Nineveh is in ruins—who *will* **mourn** for her?'

5654 נוֹד nôd[1], n.[m.]. [1] [√ 5653]

lament [1]

Ps 56:8 [56:9] Record my **lament**; list my tears on your scroll—are they

5655 נוֹד nôd[2], n.pr.loc. [1] [√ 5653]

Nod [1]

Ge 4:16 went out from the LORD's presence and lived in the land of **Nod**,

5656 נוֹדָב nôdāb, n.pr.g. [1]

Nodab [1]

1Ch 5:19 They waged war against the Hagrites, Jetur, Naphish and **Nodab**.

5657 נָוָה nāwā[1], v.den. [1] [√ 5659]

at rest [1]

Hab 2:5 [A] indeed, wine betrays him; he is arrogant and never **at rest**.

5658 נָוָה nāwā[2], v. [1] [cf. 5533]

praise [1]

Ex 15:2 [G] He is my God, and *I will* **praise** him, my father's God, and I

5659 נָוֶה nāweh[1], n.m. [32] [→ 5657, 5661]

pasture [9], dwelling [3], house [3], grazing land [2], homeland [2], pastureland [2], abode [1], dwelling place [1], dwelling places [1], haunt [1], haunts [1], home [1], land [1], pastures [1], pleasant place [1], property [1], settlement [1]

Ex 15:13 In your strength you will guide them to your holy **dwelling**.
2Sa 7:8 I took you from the **pasture** and from following the flock to be
15:25 will bring me back and let me see it and his **dwelling place** again.
1Ch 17:7 I took you from the **pasture** and from following the flock,
Job 5:3 have seen a fool taking root, but suddenly his **house** was cursed.
5:24 you will take stock of your **property** and find nothing missing.
18:15 resides in his tent; burning sulfur is scattered over his **dwelling**.
Ps 79:7 for they have devoured Jacob and destroyed his **homeland**.
Pr 3:33 the house of the wicked, but he blesses the **home** *of* the righteous.
21:20 In the **house** *of* the wise are stores of choice food and oil, but a
24:15 Do not lie in wait like an outlaw against a righteous man's **house**,
Isa 27:10 stands desolate, an abandoned **settlement**, forsaken like the desert;
32:18 My people will live in peaceful **dwelling places**, in secure homes,
33:20 your eyes will see Jerusalem, a peaceful **abode**, a tent that will not
34:13 She will become a **haunt** *for* jackals, a home for owls.
35:7 In the **haunts** where jackals once lay, grass and reeds and papyrus
65:10 Sharon will become a **pasture** *for* flocks, and the Valley of Achor
Jer 10:25 they have devoured him completely and destroyed his **homeland**.
23:3 I have driven them and will bring them back to their **pasture**,
25:30 thunder from his holy dwelling and roar mightily against his **land**.
31:23 'The LORD bless you, O righteous **dwelling**, O sacred mountain.'
33:12 in all its towns there will again be **pastures** *for* shepherds to rest
49:19 a lion coming up from Jordan's thickets to a rich **pastureland**,
49:20 he will completely destroy their **pasture** because of them.
50:7 their true **pasture**, the LORD, the hope of their fathers.'
50:19 I will bring Israel back to his own **pasture** and he will graze on
50:44 a lion coming up from Jordan's thickets to a rich **pastureland**,
50:45 he will completely destroy their **pasture** because of them.
Eze 25:5 I will turn Rabbah into a **pasture** *for* camels and Ammon into a
34:14 and the mountain heights of Israel will be their **grazing land**.
34:14 There they will lie down in good **grazing land**, and there they will
Hos 9:13 I have seen Ephraim, like Tyre, planted in a **pleasant place**.

5660 נָוֶה nāweh[2], a. Not used in NIV/BHS [√ 5659; cf. 5533]

5661 נָוָה nāwā[3], n.f. [15] [√ 5959]

pastures [7], camps [+1074] [1], dwell [1], dwellings [1], grasslands [1], haunts [1], meadows [1], pasturelands [1], place [1]

Job 8:6 rouse himself on your behalf and restore you to your rightful **place**.
Ps 23:2 He makes me lie down in green **pastures**, he leads me beside quiet
65:12 [65:13] The **grasslands** *of* the desert overflow; the hills are
68:12 [68:13] in haste; in the **camps** [+1074] men divide the plunder.
74:20 because **haunts** *of* violence fill the dark places of the land.
83:12 [83:13] "Let us take possession of the **pasturelands** *of* God."
Jer 9:10 [9:9] and take up a lament concerning the desert **pastures**.
23:10 the land lies parched and the **pastures** *in* the desert are withered.
25:37 The peaceful **meadows** will be laid waste because of the fierce
La 2:2 Without pity the Lord has swallowed up all the **dwellings** *of* Jacob;
Joel 1:19 for fire has devoured the open **pastures** and flames have burned up
1:20 of water have dried up and fire has devoured the open **pastures**.
2:22 O wild animals, for the open **pastures** are becoming green.
Am 1:2 the **pastures** *of* the shepherds dry up, and the top of Carmel
Zep 2:6 The land by the sea, *where* the Kerethites **dwell**, will be a place for

5662 נָוֹת nāwôt, n.pr.loc. [0] [cf. 5766]

1Sa 20:1 [David fled from **Naioth** [K; see Q 5766] at Ramah and went to]

5663 נוּחַ nûaḥ[1], v. [139] [→ 2182, 3562, 3563, 4955, 4956, 4957, 4965, 4969, 4970, 4971, 5665, 5666?, 5739, 5740, 5767]

leave [11], given rest [8], put [8], rest [7], left [5], rested [5], set [5], at rest [4], give rest [4], kept [4], leave alone [4], place [4], placed [4], find rest [3], gave rest [3], gives rest [3], settle [3], subside [3], allowed [2], came to rest [2], granted rest [2], laid [2], put down [2], set up [2], allied [1], allowed to remain [1], be set [1], cast [1], comes to rest [1], deposited [1], forsake [1], get relief [1], give peace [1], gives relief [1], giving rest [1], got relief [1], have rest [1], lay to rest [1], lay [1], lays [1], left unweighed [1], let be idle [1], let go [+906+3338] [1], let remain [1], lowered [1], permits [1], remain [1], reposes [1], resides [1], resting [1], safely [1], save [1], saved [1], set down [1], settled down [1], store up [1], store [1], subsided [1], throw [1], tolerate [1], touch [1], wait patiently [1], waited [1]

Ge 2:15 [G] **put** him in the Garden of Eden to work it and take care of it.
8:4 [A] month the ark **came to rest** on the mountains of Ararat.
19:16 [G] and of his two daughters and led them **safely** out of the city,
39:16 [G] *She* **kept** his cloak beside her until his master came home.
42:33 [G] **Leave** one of your brothers here with me, and take food for
Ex 10:14 [A] **settled down** in every area of the country in great numbers.
16:23 [G] to boil. **Save** whatever is left and keep it until morning.' "
16:24 [G] So *they* **saved** it until morning, as Moses commanded, and it
16:33 [G] **place** it before the LORD to be kept for the generations to
16:34 [G] Aaron **put** the manna in front of the Testimony, that it might
17:11 [G] Israelites were winning, but whenever *he* **lowered** his hands,
20:11 [A] and all that is in them, but *he* **rested** on the seventh day.
23:12 [A] so that your ox and your donkey *may* **rest** and the slave born
32:10 [G] Now **leave** me **alone** so that my anger may burn against them
33:14 [G] "My Presence will go with you, and *I will* **give** you **rest**."

[F] Hitpael (hitpoel, hitpoal, hitpolel, hitpolal, hitpalel, hitpalal, hitpalpel, hitpalpal, hotpael, hotpaal) [G] Hiphil (hiphtil) [H] Hophal [I] Hishtaphel

Lev 7:15 [G] on the day it is offered; *he must* **leave** none of it till morning.
16:23 [G] entered the Most Holy Place, and *he is to* **leave** them there.
24:12 [G] *They* **put** him in custody until the will of the LORD should
Nu 10:36 [A] Whenever it **came to rest**, he said, "Return, O LORD,
11:25 [A] When the Spirit **rested** on them, they prophesied, but they
11:26 [A] Yet the Spirit also **rested** on them, and they prophesied in the
15:34 [G] *they* **kept** him in custody, because it was not clear what
17: 4 [17:19] [G] **Place** them in the Tent of Meeting in front of the
17: 7 [17:22] [G] Moses **placed** the staffs before the LORD in the
19: 9 [G] and **put** them in a ceremonially clean place outside the camp.
32:15 [G] he will again **leave** all this people in the desert,
Dt 3:20 [G] until the LORD **gives rest** to your brothers as he has to you,
5:14 [A] so that your manservant and maidservant *may* **rest**, as you
12:10 [G] and *he will* **give** you **rest** from all your enemies around you
14:28 [G] the tithes of that year's produce and **store** it in your towns,
25:19 [G] When the LORD your God **gives** you **rest** from all the
26: 4 [G] and **set** it **down** in front of the altar of the LORD your God.
26:10 [G] **Place** the basket before the LORD your God and bow down
Jos 1:13 [G] 'The LORD your God *is* **giving** you **rest** and has granted
1:15 [G] until the LORD **gives** them **rest**, as he has done for you,
3:13 [A] **set** foot in the Jordan, its waters flowing downstream will be
4: 3 [G] and **put** them **down** at the place where you stay tonight."
4: 8 [G] over with them to their camp, where *they* **put** them **down**.
6:23 [G] and **put** them in a place outside the camp of Israel.
21:44 [G] The LORD **gave** them **rest** on every side, just as he had
22: 4 [G] Now that the LORD your God *has* **given** your brothers **rest**
23: 1 [G] the LORD *had* **given** Israel **rest** from all their enemies
Jdg 2:23 [G] The LORD *had* **allowed** those nations **to remain**; he did
3: 1 [G] These are the nations the LORD **left** to test all those
6:18 [G] I come back and bring my offering and **set** it before you."
6:20 [G] **place** them on this rock, and pour out the broth."
16:26 [G] "**Put** me where I can feel the pillars that support the temple,
1Sa 6:18 [G] The large rock, on which *they* **set** the ark of the LORD, is a
10:25 [G] them down on a scroll and **deposited** it before the LORD.
25: 9 [A] gave Nabal this message in David's name. Then *they* **waited**.
2Sa 7: 1 [G] the LORD *had* **given** him **rest** from all his enemies around
7:11 [G] people Israel. *I will* also **give** you **rest** from all your enemies.
16:11 [G] **Leave** him **alone**; let him curse, for the LORD has told him
16:21 [G] "Lie with your father's concubines whom *he* **left** to take care
20: 3 [G] he took the ten concubines *he had* **left** to take care of the
21:10 [A] she did not let the birds of the air **touch** them by day or the
1Ki 5: 4 [5:18] [G] now the LORD my God *has* **given** me **rest** on every
7:47 [G] Solomon **left** all these things **unweighed**, because there were
8: 9 [G] the two stone tablets that Moses *had* **placed** *in* it at Horeb,
13:29 [G] **laid** it on the donkey, and brought it back to his own city to
13:30 [G] *he* **laid** the body in his own tomb, and they mourned over
13:31 [G] the man of God is buried; **lay** my bones beside his bones.
19: 3 [G] he came to Beersheba in Judah, *he* **left** his servant there,
2Ki 2:15 [A] said, "The spirit of Elijah *is* **resting** on Elisha."
17:29 [G] **set** them **up** in the shrines the people of Samaria had made at
23:18 [G] "**Leave** it **alone**," he said. "Don't let anyone disturb his
1Ch 16:21 [G] *He* **allowed** no man to oppress them; for their sake he
22: 9 [G] and *I will* **give** him **rest** from all his enemies on every side.
22:18 [G] with you? And *has he* not **granted** you **rest** on every side?
23:25 [G] *has* **granted rest** to his people and has come to dwell in
2Ch 1:14 [G] which *he* **kept** in the chariot cities and also with him in
4: 8 [G] He made ten tables and **placed** them in the temple, five on
9:25 [G] which *he* **kept** in the chariot cities and also with him in
14: 6 [14:5] [G] during those years, for the LORD **gave** him **rest**.
14: 7 [14:6] [G] sought him and *he has* **given** us **rest** on every side."
15:15 [G] found by them. So the LORD **gave** them **rest** on every side.
20:30 [G] was at peace, for his God *had* **given** him **rest** on every side.
Ne 9:28 [A] "But as soon as they *were* **at rest**, they again did what was
Est 3: 8 [G] it is not in the king's best interest to **tolerate** them.
9:16 [A] to protect themselves and **get relief** from their enemies.
9:17 [A] on the fourteenth they **rested** and made it a day of feasting
9:18 [A] then on the fifteenth they **rested** and made it a day of
9:22 [A] as the time when the Jews **got relief** from their enemies,
Job 3:13 [A] would be lying down in peace; I would be asleep and **at rest**
3:17 [A] wicked cease from turmoil, and there the weary *are* **at rest**.
3:26 [A] no peace, no quietness; *I* **have** no **rest**, but only turmoil."
Ps 17:14 [G] sons have plenty, and *they* **store up** wealth for their children.
105:14 [G] *He* **allowed** no one to oppress them; for their sake he
119:121 [G] what is righteous and just; *do* not **leave** me to my oppressors.
125: 3 [A] The scepter of the wicked *will* not **remain** over the land
Pr 14:33 [A] Wisdom **reposes** in the heart of the discerning and even
21:16 [A] of understanding **comes to rest** in the company of the dead.
29:17 [G] Discipline your son, and *he will* **give** you **peace**; he will
Ecc 2:18 [G] because *I must* **leave** them to the one who comes after me.
5:12 [5:11] [G] the abundance of a rich man **permits** him no sleep.
7: 9 [A] provoked in your spirit, for anger **resides** in the lap of fools.
7:18 [G] to grasp the one and not **let** [+906+3338] **go** of the other.
10: 4 [G] If a ruler's anger rises against you, *do* not **leave** your post;
10: 4 [G] do not leave your post; calmness *can* **lay** great errors **to rest**.
11: 6 [G] in the morning, and at evening **let** not your hands **be idle**,
Isa 7: 2 [A] of David was told, "Aram *has* **allied** *itself* with Ephraim";
7:19 [A] They will all come and **settle** in the steep ravines and in the
11: 2 [A] The Spirit of the LORD *will* **rest** on him—the Spirit of
14: 1 [G] he will choose Israel and *will* **settle** them in their own land.
14: 3 [G] On the day the LORD **gives** you **relief** from suffering and
14: 7 [A] All the lands *are* **at rest** and at peace; they break into
23:12 [A] "Up, cross over to Cyprus; even there you *will* **find** no **rest**."
25:10 [A] The hand of the LORD *will* **rest** on this mountain;
28: 2 [G] flooding downpour, *he will* **throw** it forcefully to the ground.
28:12 [G] whom he said, "This is the resting place, *let* the weary **rest**";
30:32 [G] Every stroke the LORD **lays** on them *with* his punishing
46: 7 [G] and carry it; *they* **set** it **up** in its place, and there it stands.
57: 2 [A] uprightly enter into peace; *they* **find rest** as they lie in death.
63:14 [G] the plain, they *were* **given rest** *by* the Spirit of the LORD.
65:15 [G] *You will* **leave** your name to my chosen ones as a curse;
Jer 14: 9 [G] O LORD, and we bear your name; *do* not **forsake** us!
27:11 [G] *I will* **let** that nation **remain** in its own land to till it and to
43: 6 [G] of the imperial guard *had* **left** with Gedaliah son of Ahikam,
La 5: 5 [H] pursue us are at our heels; we are weary and **find** no **rest**.
Eze 5:13 [G] my anger will cease and my wrath against them *will* **subside**,
16:39 [G] and take your fine jewelry and **leave** you naked and bare.
16:42 [G] my wrath against you *will* **subside** and my jealous anger will
21:17 [21:22] [G] my hands together, and my wrath *will* **subside**.
22:20 [G] and my wrath and **put** you inside the city and melt you.
24:13 [G] not be clean again until my wrath against you *has* **subsided**.
37: 1 [G] the Spirit of the LORD and **set** me in the middle of a valley;
37:14 [G] and you will live, and *I will* **settle** you in your own land.
40: 2 [G] me to the land of Israel and **set** me on a very high mountain,
40:42 [G] On them *were* **placed** the utensils for slaughtering the burnt
42:13 [G] There *they will* **put** the most holy offerings—the grain
42:14 [G] they are not to go into the outer court until *they* **leave** behind
44:19 [G] ministering in and *are to* **leave** them in the sacred rooms,
44:30 [G] ground meal so that a blessing *may* **rest** on your household.
Da 12:13 [A] *You will* **rest**, and then at the end of the days you will rise to
Hos 4:17 [G] Ephraim is joined to idols; **leave him alone**!
Am 5: 7 [G] justice into bitterness and **cast** righteousness to the ground
Hab 3:16 [A] Yet *I will* **wait patiently** for the day of calamity to come on
Zec 5:11 [H] When it is ready, the basket *will* **be set** there in its place."
6: 8 [G] country *have* **given** my Spirit **rest** in the land of the north."

5664 ²נוּחַ nûaḥ², v. Not used in NIV/BHS [cf. 634]

5665 נֹחַ nôaḥ, n.f. [1] [→ 5666; cf. 5663]

resting place [1]

2Ch 6:41 and come to your **resting place**, you and the ark of your might.

5666 נוֹחָה nôḥâ, n.pr.m. [1] [√ 5665?; cf. 5663?]

Nohah [1]

1Ch 8: 2 **Nohah** the fourth and Rapha the fifth.

5667 נוּט nûṭ, v. [1]

shake [1]

Ps 99: 1 [A] he sits enthroned between the cherubim, *let* the earth **shake**.

5668 נָוִית nāwît, n.pr.loc. [0] [cf. 5766]

1Sa 19:18 [he and Samuel went to **Naioth** [K; see Q 5766] and stayed there.]
19:19 ["David is in **Naioth** [K; see Q 5766] at Ramah";]
19:22 ["Over in **Naioth** [K; see Q 5766] at Ramah," they said.]
19:23 [So Saul went to **Naioth** [K; see Q 5766] at Ramah.]
19:23 [prophesying until he came to **Naioth**. [K; see Q 5766]]

5669 נָוֶל nāwel, n. Not used in NIV/BHS

5670 נוּם nûm, v. [6] [→ 3564?, 3565?, 5671, 9484]

slumber [3], sleep [2], slumbers [1]

Ps 76: 5 [76:6] [A] Valiant men lie plundered, *they* **sleep** their last sleep;
121: 3 [A] your foot slip—he who watches over you *will* not **slumber**;
121: 4 [A] he who watches over Israel *will* neither **slumber** nor sleep.
Isa 5:27 [A] of them grows tired or stumbles, not *one* **slumbers** or sleeps;
56:10 [A] cannot bark; they lie around and dream, they love to **sleep**.
Na 3:18 [A] O king of Assyria, your shepherds **slumber**; your nobles lie

5671 נוּמָה nûmâ, n.f. [1] [√ 5670]

drowsiness [1]

Pr 23:21 and gluttons become poor, and **drowsiness** clothes them in rags.

5672 נוּן ***nûn¹***, v. [1] [cf. 5673?, 5768]
continue [1]
Ps 72:17 [C] his name endure forever; *may* it **continue** as long as the sun.

5673 נוּן ***nûn²***, n.pr.m. [30] [cf. 5672?]
Nun [30]
Ex 33:11 but his young aide Joshua son of **Nun** did not leave the tent.
Nu 11:28 Joshua son of **Nun**, who had been Moses' aide since youth,
13:8 from the tribe of Ephraim, Hoshea son of **Nun**;
13:16 the land. (Moses gave Hoshea son of **Nun** the name Joshua.)
14:6 Joshua son of **Nun** and Caleb son of Jephunneh, who were among
14:30 your home, except Caleb son of Jephunneh and Joshua son of **Nun**.
14:38 only Joshua son of **Nun** and Caleb son of Jephunneh survived.
26:65 was left except Caleb son of Jephunneh and Joshua son of **Nun**.
27:18 "Take Joshua son of **Nun**, a man in whom is the spirit, and lay
32:12 Caleb son of Jephunneh the Kenizzite and Joshua son of **Nun**,
32:28 Joshua son of **Nun** and to the family heads of the Israelite tribes.
34:17 you as an inheritance: Eleazar the priest and Joshua son of **Nun**.
Dt 1:38 your assistant, Joshua son of **Nun**, will enter it. Encourage him,
31:23 The LORD gave this command to Joshua son of **Nun**: "Be strong
32:44 Moses came with Joshua son of **Nun** and spoke all the words of
34:9 Now Joshua son of **Nun** was filled with the spirit of wisdom
Jos 1:1 the LORD, the LORD said to Joshua son of **Nun**, Moses' aide:
2:1 Then Joshua son of **Nun** secretly sent two spies from Shittim.
2:23 forded the river and came to Joshua son of **Nun** and told him
6:6 So Joshua son of **Nun** called the priests and said to them, "Take up
14:1 Joshua son of **Nun** and the heads of the tribal clans of Israel
17:4 to Eleazar the priest, Joshua son of **Nun**, and the leaders and said,
19:49 the Israelites gave Joshua son of **Nun** an inheritance among them,
19:51 Joshua son of **Nun** and the heads of the tribal clans of Israel
21:1 Joshua son of **Nun**, and the heads of the other tribal families of
24:29 After these things, Joshua son of **Nun**, the servant of the LORD,
Jdg 2:8 Joshua son of **Nun**, the servant of the LORD, died at the age of a
1Ki 16:34 with the word of the LORD spoken by Joshua son of **Nun**.
1Ch 7:27 **Nun** his son and Joshua his son.
Ne 8:17 From the days of Joshua son of **Nun** until that day, the Israelites

5674 נוּס ***nûs***, v. [159] [→ 4960, 4961, 5771]
fled [63], flee [38], flees [7], ran [7], fleeing [6], run [5], escape [3], flee away [3], escaped [2], forced to flee [+5674] [2], fugitives [2], get away [+5674] [2], draining away [1], drives along [1], fled back [1], fled up [1], flee in haste [+4960] [1], flight [1], fugitive [1], get away [1], gone [1], hurried to bring [1], keep [1], leave [1], made good escape [+2256+4880] [1], on the run [1], put to flight [1], retreat [1], routed [1], running away [1], turned and ran [1]
Ge 14:10 [A] when the kings of Sodom and Gomorrah **fled**, some of the
14:10 [A] some of the men fell into them and the rest **fled** to the hills.
19:20 [A] Look, here is a town near enough to **run** to, and it is small.
39:12 [A] But he left his cloak in her hand and **ran** out of the house.
39:13 [A] had left his cloak in her hand and *had* **run** out of the house,
39:15 [A] he left his cloak beside me and **ran** out of the house."
39:18 [A] he left his cloak beside me and **ran** out of the house."
Ex 4:3 [A] it on the ground and it became a snake, and *he* **ran** from it.
9:20 [G] the word of the LORD **hurried to bring** their slaves and
14:25 [A] And the Egyptians said, "*Let's* **get away** from the Israelites!
14:27 [A] The Egyptians *were* **fleeing** toward it, and the LORD swept
21:13 [A] God lets it happen, *he is to* **flee** to a place I will designate.
Lev 26:17 [A] and *you will* **flee** even when no one is pursuing you.
26:36 [A] *They will* **run** as though fleeing from the sword, and they
Nu 10:35 [A] your enemies be scattered; *may* your foes **flee** before you."
16:34 [A] At their cries, all the Israelites around them **fled**, shouting,
35:6 [A] to which a person who has killed someone *may* **flee**.
35:11 [A] a person who has killed someone accidentally *may* **flee**.
35:15 [A] so that anyone who has killed another accidentally *can* **flee**
35:25 [A] and send him back to the city of refuge to which *he* **fled**.
35:26 [A] outside the limits of the city of refuge to which *he has* **fled**
35:32 [A] " 'Do not accept a ransom for *anyone who has* **fled** to a city
Dt 4:42 [A] to which anyone who had killed a person *could* **flee** if he had
4:42 [A] *He could* **flee** into one of these cities and save his life.
19:3 [A] so that anyone who kills a man *may* **flee** there.
19:4 [A] the man who kills another and **flees** there to save his life—
19:5 [A] That man *may* **flee** to one of these cities and save his life.
19:11 [A] assaults and kills him, and then **flees** to one of these cities,
28:7 [A] come at you from one direction but **flee** from you in seven.
28:25 [A] come at them from one direction but **flee** from them in seven,
32:30 [G] or two **put** ten thousand **to flight**, unless their Rock had sold
34:7 [A] he died, yet his eyes were not weak nor his strength **gone**.
Jos 7:4 [A] men went up; but *they were* **routed** by the men of Ai,
8:5 [A] out against us, as they did before, *we will* **flee** from them.
8:6 [A] '*They are* **running away** from us as they did before.'
8:6 [A] from us as they did before.' So when *we* **flee** from them,
8:15 [A] be driven back before them, and *they* **fled** toward the desert.
8:20 [A] the sky, but they had no chance to **escape** in any direction,
8:20 [A] for the Israelites who *had been* **fleeing** *toward* the desert
10:11 [A] As they **fled** before Israel on the road down from Beth Horon
10:16 [A] Now the five kings *had* **fled** and hidden in the cave at
20:3 [A] kills a person accidentally and unintentionally *may* **flee** there
20:4 [A] "When *he* **flees** to one of these cities, he is to stand in the
20:6 [A] go back to his own home in the town from which *he* **fled**."
20:9 [A] someone accidentally *could* **flee** to these designated cities
Jdg 1:6 [A] Adoni-Bezek **fled**, but they chased him and caught him,
4:15 [A] the sword, and Sisera abandoned his chariot and **fled** on foot.
4:17 [A] Sisera, however, **fled** on foot to the tent of Jael, the wife of
6:11 [G] wheat in a winepress to **keep** it from the Midianites.
7:21 [A] the camp, all the Midianites ran, crying out as *they* **fled**.
7:22 [A] The army **fled** to Beth Shittah toward Zererah as far as the
8:12 [A] of Midian, **fled**, but he pursued them and captured them,
9:21 [A] Jotham **fled**, escaping to Beer, and he lived there because he
9:40 [A] chased him, and many fell wounded *in the* **flight**—
9:51 [A] all the men and women—all the people of the city—**fled**.
20:32 [A] "*Let's* **retreat** and draw them away from the city to the
20:45 [A] and **fled** toward the desert to the rock of Rimmon,
20:47 [A] men turned and **fled** into the desert to the rock of Rimmon,
1Sa 4:10 [A] the Israelites were defeated and every man **fled** to his tent.
4:16 [A] just come from the battle line; I **fled** from it this very day."
4:17 [A] "Israel **fled** before the Philistines, and the army has suffered
14:22 [A] of Ephraim heard that the Philistines *were* **on the run**,
17:24 [A] Israelites saw the man, *they* all **ran** from him in great fear.
17:51 [A] saw that their hero was dead, *they* **turned and ran**.
19:8 [A] He struck them with such force that *they* **fled** before him.
19:10 [A] That night David **made good** *his* **escape** [+2256+4880].
30:17 [A] four hundred young men who rode off on camels and **fled**.
31:1 [A] the Israelites **fled** before them, and many fell slain on Mount
31:7 [A] those across the Jordan saw that the Israelite army *had* **fled**
31:7 [A] and his sons had died, they abandoned their towns and **fled**.
2Sa 1:4 [A] "Tell me." He said, "The men **fled** from the battle.
4:4 [A] His nurse picked him up and **fled**, but as she hurried to leave,
4:4 [A] but as she hurried to **leave**, he fell and became crippled.
10:13 [A] advanced to fight the Arameans, and *they* **fled** before him.
10:14 [A] When the Ammonites saw that the Arameans *were* **fleeing**,
10:14 [A] *they* **fled** before Abishai and went inside the city.
10:18 [A] they **fled** before Israel, and David killed seven hundred of
13:29 [A] all the king's sons got up, mounted their mules and **fled**.
17:2 [A] him with terror, and then all the people with him *will* **flee**.
18:3 [A] if *we are* **forced to flee** [+5674], they won't care about us.
18:3 [A] if *we are* **forced to flee** [+5674], they won't care about us.
18:17 [A] over him. Meanwhile, all the Israelites **fled** to their homes.
19:3 [19:4] [A] steal in who are ashamed when they **flee** from battle.
19:8 [19:9] [A] Meanwhile, the Israelites *had* **fled** to their homes.
23:11 [A] was a field full of lentils, Israel's troops **fled** from them.
24:13 [A] Or three months of **fleeing** from your enemies while they
1Ki 2:28 [A] he **fled** to the tent of the LORD and took hold of the horns
2:29 [A] King Solomon was told that Joab *had* **fled** to the tent of the
12:18 [A] managed to get into his chariot and **escape** *to* Jerusalem.
20:20 [A] At that, the Arameans **fled**, with the Israelites in pursuit.
20:30 [A] The rest of them **escaped** to the city of Aphek, where the
20:30 [A] And Ben-Hadad **fled** to the city and hid in an inner room.
2Ki 3:24 [A] the Israelites rose up and fought them until *they* **fled**.
7:7 [A] So they got up and **fled** in the dusk and abandoned their tents
7:7 [A] They left the camp as it was and **ran** for their lives.
8:21 [A] broke through by night; his army, however, **fled back** home.
9:3 [A] king over Israel.' Then open the door and **run**; don't delay!"
9:10 [A] no one will bury her.' " Then he opened the door and **ran**.
9:23 [A] Joram turned about and **fled**, calling out to Ahaziah,
9:27 [A] saw what had happened, *he* **fled up** the road to Beth Haggan.
9:27 [A] Gur near Ibleam, but *he* **escaped** *to* Megiddo and died there.
14:12 [A] Judah was routed by Israel, and every man **fled** to his home.
14:19 [A] *he* **fled** to Lachish, but they sent men after him to Lachish
1Ch 10:1 [A] the Israelites **fled** before them, and many fell slain on Mount
10:7 [A] all the Israelites in the valley saw that the army *had* **fled**
10:7 [A] and his sons had died, they abandoned their towns and **fled**.
11:13 [A] was a field full of barley, the troops **fled** from the Philistines.
19:14 [A] advanced to fight the Arameans, and *they* **fled** before him.
19:15 [A] When the Ammonites saw that the Arameans *were* **fleeing**,
19:15 [A] they too **fled** before his brother Abishai and went inside the
19:18 [A] they **fled** before Israel, and David killed seven thousand of
2Ch 10:18 [A] managed to get into his chariot and **escape** *to* Jerusalem.
13:16 [A] The Israelites **fled** before Judah, and God delivered them into
14:12 [14:11] [A] Cushites before Asa and Judah. The Cushites **fled**,
25:22 [A] Judah was routed by Israel, and every man **fled** to his home.
25:27 [A] conspired against him in Jerusalem and *he* **fled** to Lachish,
Ps 68:1 [68:2] [A] enemies be scattered; *may* his foes **flee** before him.
104:7 [A] at your rebuke the waters **fled**, at the sound of your thunder
114:3 [A] The sea looked and **fled**, the Jordan turned back;
114:5 [A] Why was it, O sea, that *you* **fled**, O Jordan, that you turned

Pr 28: 1 [A] The wicked man **flees** though no one pursues,
28: 17 [A] A man tormented by the guilt of murder *will be a* **fugitive** till
SS 2: 17 [A] Until the day breaks and the shadows **flee**, turn, my lover,
4: 6 [A] Until the day breaks and the shadows **flee**, I will go to the
Isa 10: 3 [A] disaster comes from afar? To whom *will you* **run** for help?
10: 29 [A] overnight at Geba." Ramah trembles; Gibeah of Saul **flees**.
13: 14 [A] return to his own people, each *will* **flee** to his native land.
17: 13 [A] when he rebukes them *they* **flee** far away, driven before the
20: 6 [A] those *we* **fled** *to* for help and deliverance from the king of
24: 18 [A] Whoever **flees** at the sound of terror will fall into a pit;
30: 16 [A] You said, 'No, *we will* **flee** on horses.' Therefore you will
30: 16 [A] Therefore *you will* **flee**! You said, 'We will ride off on swift
30: 17 [A] at the threat of five *you will all* **flee away**, till you are left
31: 8 [A] *They will* **flee** before the sword and their young men will be
35: 10 [A] will overtake them, and sorrow and sighing *will* **flee away**.
51: 11 [A] will overtake them, and sorrow and sighing *will* **flee away**.
59: 19 [D] a pent-up flood that the breath of the LORD **drives along**.
Jer 46: 5 [A] *They* **flee** [+4960] **in haste** without looking back, and there
46: 6 [A] "The swift cannot **flee** nor the strong escape. In the north by
46: 21 [A] They too will turn and **flee** together, they will not stand their
48: 6 [A] **Flee**! Run for your lives; become like a bush in the desert.
48: 19 [A] Ask the *man* **fleeing** and the woman escaping, ask them,
48: 44 [A] "Whoever **flees** [K 5771] from the terror will fall into a pit,
48: 45 [A] "In the shadow of Heshbon the **fugitives** stand helpless, for a
49: 8 [A] Turn and **flee**, hide in deep caves, you who live in Dedan,
49: 24 [A] she has turned to **flee** and panic has gripped her;
49: 30 [A] "**Flee** quickly away! Stay in deep caves, you who live in
50: 16 [A] return to his own people, *let* everyone **flee** to his own land.
50: 28 [A] Listen to the **fugitives** and refugees from Babylon declaring
51: 6 [A] "**Flee** from Babylon! Run for your lives! Do not be destroyed
Am 2: 16 [A] Even the bravest warriors *will* **flee** naked on that day,"
5: 19 [A] It will be as though a man **fled** from a lion only to meet a
9: 1 [A] the sword. Not one *will* **get away** [+5674], none will escape.
9: 1 [A] the sword. Not one *will* **get away** [+5674], none will escape.
Na 2: 8 [2:9] [A] Nineveh is like a pool, and its water *is* **draining away**.
Zec 2: 6 [2:10] [A] **Flee** from the land of the north,"
14: 5 [A] *You will* **flee** *by* my mountain valley, for it will extend to
14: 5 [A] *You will* **flee** as you fled from the earthquake in the days of
14: 5 [A] You will flee as *you* **fled** from the earthquake in the days of

5675 נוּעַ *nûaʻ*, v. [40] [→ 4983]

shake [5], hold sway [3], shaken [3], make wander about [2], reels [+5675] [2], restless [2], stagger [2], staggered [2], tosses [2], wander about [2], wandering [+5675] [2], crooked [1], disturb [1], grope [1], is shaken [1], made wander [1], moving [1], set trembling [1], shaking [1], shook [1], sways [1], tremble [1], trembled [1], wander [1]

Ge 4: 12 [A] crops for you. You will be a **restless** wanderer on the earth."
4: 14 [A] I will be a **restless** wanderer on the earth, and whoever finds
Ex 20: 18 [A] and saw the mountain in smoke, they **trembled** with fear.
Nu 32: 13 [G] and *he* **made** them **wander** in the desert forty years,
Jdg 9: 9 [A] both gods and men are honored, to **hold sway** over the trees?'
9: 11 [A] up my fruit, so good and sweet, to **hold sway** over the trees?'
9: 13 [A] cheers both gods and men, to **hold sway** over the trees?'
1Sa 1: 13 [A] and her lips *were* **moving** but her voice was not heard.
2Sa 15: 20 [G] today *shall I* **make** you **wander about** with us, when I do
2Ki 19: 21 [G] The Daughter of Jerusalem **tosses** her head as you flee.
23: 18 [G] it alone," he said. "Don't *let* anyone **disturb** his bones."
Job 16: 4 [G] make fine speeches against you and **shake** my head at you.
28: 4 [A] by the foot of man; far from men he dangles and **sways**.
Ps 22: 7 [22:8] [G] me mock me; they hurl insults, **shaking** their heads:
59: 11 [59:12] [G] In your might **make** them **wander about**, and bring
59: 15 [59:16] [A] They **wander about** for food and howl if not
107: 27 [A] They reeled and **staggered** like drunken men; they were at
109: 10 [A] *May* his children *be* **wandering** [+5675] beggars; may they
109: 10 [A] *May* his children *be* **wandering** [+5675] beggars; may they
109: 25 [G] to my accusers; when they see me, *they* **shake** their heads.
Pr 5: 6 [A] the way of life; her paths *are* **crooked**, but she knows it not.
Isa 6: 4 [A] and thresholds **shook** and the temple was filled with smoke.
7: 2 [A] so the hearts of Ahaz and his people *were* **shaken**,
7: 2 [A] as the trees of the forest *are* **shaken** by the wind.
19: 1 [A] The idols of Egypt **tremble** before him, and the hearts of the
24: 20 [A] The earth **reels** [+5675] like a drunkard, it sways like a hut in
24: 20 [A] The earth **reels** [+5675] like a drunkard, it sways like a hut in
29: 9 [A] be drunk, but not from wine, **stagger**, but not from beer.
37: 22 [G] The Daughter of Jerusalem **tosses** her head as you flee.
Jer 14: 10 [A] "They greatly love to **wander**; they do not restrain their feet.
La 2: 15 [G] and **shake** their heads at the Daughter of Jerusalem:
4: 14 [A] Now *they* **grope** through the streets like men who are blind.
4: 15 [A] When they flee and **wander about**, people among the
Da 10: 10 [G] touched me and **set** me **trembling** on my hands and knees.
Am 4: 8 [A] People **staggered** from town to town for water but did not
8: 12 [A] *Men will* **stagger** from sea to sea and wander from north to
9: 9 [G] *I will* **shake** the house of Israel among all the nations as
9: 9 [C] of Israel among all the nations as grain **is shaken** in a sieve,
Na 3: 12 [C] when *they are* **shaken**, the figs fall into the mouth of the
Zep 2: 15 [G] wild beasts! All who pass by her scoff and **shake** their fists.

5676 נוֹעַדְיָה *nôʻadyâ*, n.pr.m. & f. [2] [√ 3585 + 3378]

Noadiah [2]

Ezr 8: 33 the Levites Jozabad son of Jeshua and **Noadiah** son of Binnui.
Ne 6: 14 remember also the prophetess **Noadiah** and the rest of the prophets

5677 נוּף[1] *nûp*[1], v. [35] [→ 2185, 5864, 9485; cf. 5537]

wave [12], waved [4], presented [3], present [2], use [2], beckon [+3338] [1], put [1], raise [1], raised [1], raises [1], shake [1], shakes [1], sweep [1], used [1], uses [1], was waved [+9485] [1], wield [1]

Ex 20: 25 [G] dressed stones, for you will defile it if *you* **use** a tool on it.
29: 24 [G] and **wave** them before the LORD as a wave offering.
29: 26 [G] **wave** it before the LORD as a wave offering, and it will be
29: 27 [H] the breast that **was waved** [+9485] and the thigh that was
35: 22 [G] They all **presented** their gold as a wave offering to the
Lev 7: 30 [G] and **wave** the breast before the LORD as a wave offering.
8: 27 [G] and **waved** them before the LORD as a wave offering.
8: 29 [G] **waved** it before the LORD as a wave offering, as the
9: 21 [G] Aaron **waved** the breasts and the right thigh before the
10: 15 [G] by fire, to *be* **waved** before the LORD as a wave offering.
14: 12 [G] *he shall* **wave** them before the LORD as a wave offering.
14: 24 [G] of oil, and **wave** them before the LORD as a wave offering.
23: 11 [G] *He is to* **wave** the sheaf before the LORD so it will be
23: 11 [G] the priest *is to* **wave** it on the day after the Sabbath.
23: 12 [G] On the day you **wave** the sheaf, you must sacrifice as a burnt
23: 20 [G] The priest *is to* **wave** the two lambs before the LORD as a
Nu 5: 25 [G] **wave** it before the LORD and bring it to the altar.
6: 20 [G] The priest *shall* then **wave** them before the LORD as a
8: 11 [G] Aaron *is to* **present** the Levites before the LORD as a wave
8: 13 [G] and then **present** them as a wave offering to the LORD.
8: 15 [G] purified the Levites and **presented** them as a wave offering,
8: 21 [G] Aaron **presented** them as a wave offering before the LORD
Dt 23: 25 [23:26] [G] but *you must* not **put** a sickle to his standing grain.
27: 5 [G] an altar of stones. *Do* not **use** any iron tool upon them.
Jos 8: 31 [G] altar of uncut stones, on which no iron tool *had been* **used**.
2Ki 5: 11 [G] **wave** his hand over the spot and cure me of my leprosy.
Job 31: 21 [G] if *I have* **raised** my hand against the fatherless, knowing that
Isa 10: 15 [G] him who swings it, or the saw boast against *him who* **uses** it?
10: 15 [G] As if a rod *were to* **wield** him who lifts it up, or a club
10: 32 [D] *they will* **shake** their fist at the mount of the Daughter of
11: 15 [G] with a scorching wind *he will* **sweep** his hand over the
13: 2 [G] **beckon** [+3338] *to* them to enter the gates of the nobles.
19: 16 [G] uplifted hand that the LORD Almighty **raises** against them.
30: 28 [G] He **shakes** the nations in the sieve of destruction; he places in
Zec 2: 9 [2:13] [G] I *will* surely **raise** my hand against them so that their

5678 נוּף[2] *nûp*[2], v. [2] [→ 5885]

gave [1], perfumed [1]

Ps 68: 9 [68:10] [G] *You* **gave** abundant showers, O God; you refreshed
Pr 7: 17 [A] *I have* **perfumed** my bed *with* myrrh, aloes and cinnamon.

5679 נוֹף *nôp*, n.[m.]. [1] [→ 5865, 5868, 5869, 5884]

loftiness [1]

Ps 48: 2 [48:3] It is beautiful in its **loftiness**, the joy of the whole earth.

5680 נוּץ *nûṣ*, v. [1]

flee [1]

La 4: 15 [A] When *they* **flee** and wander about, people among the nations

5681 נוֹצָה *nôṣâ*, n.f. [3] [cf. 5901, 5902]

plumage [2], feathers [1]

Job 39: 13 but they cannot compare with the pinions and **feathers** of the stork.
Eze 17: 3 long feathers and full **plumage** of varied colors came to Lebanon.
17: 7 was another great eagle with powerful wings and full **plumage**.

5682 נוּק *nûq*, v. Not used in NIV/BHS [cf. 3567]

5683 נוּשׁ *nûš*, v. [1] [cf. 631]

helpless [1]

Ps 69: 20 [69:21] [A] has broken my heart and *has left me* **helpless**;

5684 נָזָה¹ ***nāzâ¹***, v. [24]

sprinkle [17], spattered [2], sprinkled [2], *untranslated* [1], is spattered [1], sprinkles [1]

Ex 29:21 [G] and **sprinkle** it on Aaron and his garments and on his sons
Lev 4: 6 [G] and **sprinkle** some of it seven times before the LORD,
4:17 [G] **sprinkle** it before the LORD seven times in front of the
5: 9 [G] *is to* **sprinkle** some of the blood of the sin offering against
6:27 [6:20] [A] if any of the blood **is spattered** on a garment,
6:27 [6:20] [A] a garment, you must wash it **[RPH]** in a holy place.
8:11 [G] *He* **sprinkled** some of the oil on the altar seven times,
8:30 [G] **sprinkled** them on Aaron and his garments and on his sons
14: 7 [G] Seven times *he shall* **sprinkle** the one to be cleansed of the
14:16 [G] with his finger **sprinkle** some of it before the LORD seven
14:27 [G] with his right forefinger **sprinkle** some of the oil from his
14:51 [G] and the fresh water, and **sprinkle** the house seven times.
16:14 [G] with his finger **sprinkle** it on the front of the atonement
16:14 [G] *he shall* **sprinkle** some of it with his finger seven times
16:15 [G] *He shall* **sprinkle** it on the atonement cover and in front of it.
16:19 [G] *He shall* **sprinkle** some of the blood on it with his finger
Nu 8: 7 [G] **Sprinkle** the water of cleansing on them; then have them
19: 4 [G] **sprinkle** it seven times toward the front of the Tent of
19:18 [G] **sprinkle** the tent and all the furnishings and the people who
19:19 [G] The man who is clean *is to* **sprinkle** the unclean person on
19:21 [G] "The *man who* **sprinkles** the water of cleansing must also
2Ki 9:33 [A] some of her blood **spattered** the wall and the horses as they
Isa 52:15 [G] so *will he* **sprinkle** many nations, and kings will shut their
63: 3 [A] their blood **spattered** my garments, and I stained all my

5685 נָזָה² ***nāzâ²***, v. Not used in NIV/BHS

5686 נָזִיד ***nāzîd***, n.[m.]. [6] [√ 2326]

stew [6]

Ge 25:29 Once when Jacob was cooking *some* **stew**, Esau came in from the
25:34 Then Jacob gave Esau some bread and *some* lentil **stew**. He ate
2Ki 4:38 "Put on the large pot and cook *some* **stew** for these men."
4:39 When he returned, he cut them up into the pot of **stew**, though no
4:40 The **stew** was poured out for the men, but as they began to eat it,
Hag 2:12 that fold touches some bread or **stew**, some wine, oil or other food,

5687 נָזִיר ***nāzîr***, n.m. [16] [√ 5693]

Nazirite [8], Nazirites [2], prince [2], untended vines [2], princes [1], separation [1]

Ge 49:26 the head of Joseph, on the brow of the **prince** *among* his brothers.
Lev 25: 5 what grows of itself or harvest the grapes of your **untended vines**.
25:11 and do not reap what grows of itself or harvest the **untended vines**.
Nu 6: 2 a special vow, a vow of **separation** to the LORD as a Nazirite,
6:13 " 'Now this is the law for the **Nazirite** when the period of his
6:18 of Meeting, the **Nazirite** must shave off the hair that he dedicated.
6:19 " 'After the **Nazirite** has shaved off the hair of his dedication,
6:20 thigh that was presented. After that, the **Nazirite** may drink wine.
6:21 " 'This is the law of the **Nazirite** who vows his offering to the
Dt 33:16 the head of Joseph, on the brow of the **prince** *among* his brothers.
Jdg 13: 5 because the boy is to be a **Nazirite**, *set apart to* God from birth,
13: 7 because the boy will be a **Nazirite** *of* God from birth until the day
16:17 "because I have been a **Nazirite** *set apart to* God since birth.
La 4: 7 Their **princes** were brighter than snow and whiter than milk,
Am 2:11 from among your sons and **Nazirites** from among your young men.
2:12 "But you made the **Nazirites** drink wine and commanded the

5688 נָזַל ***nāzal***, v. [10] [→ 5689]

flow [3], descend [1], made flow [1], pour down moisture [1], shower down [1], spread abroad [1], streaming down [1], streams [1]

Nu 24: 7 [A] Water *will* **flow** from their buckets; their seed will have
Dt 32: 2 [A] my teaching fall like rain and my words **descend** like dew,
Job 36:28 [A] the clouds **pour down** *their* **moisture** and abundant showers
Ps 147:18 [A] and melts them; he stirs up his breezes, and the waters **flow**.
SS 4:15 [A] a well of flowing water **streaming down** from Lebanon.
4:16 [A] Blow on my garden, that its fragrance *may* **spread abroad**.
Isa 45: 8 [A] rain down righteousness; *let* the clouds **shower** it **down**.
48:21 [G] *he* **made** water **flow** for them from the rock; he split the rock
Jer 9:18 [9:17] [A] with tears and water **streams** *from* our eyelids.
18:14 [A] Do its cool waters from distant sources ever cease *to* **flow**?

5689 נֹזֵל ***nōzēl***, n.[m.] *or* v.ptcp. [5] [√ 5688]

streams [3], running water [1], surging [1]

Ex 15: 8 The **surging** waters stood firm like a wall; the deep waters
Ps 78:16 he brought **streams** out of a rocky crag and made water flow down
78:44 their rivers to blood; they could not drink from their **streams**.
Pr 5:15 water from your own cistern, **running water** from your own well.
Isa 44: 3 will pour water on the thirsty land, and **streams** on the dry ground;

5690 נֶזֶם ***nezem***, n.m. [17]

ring [5], earrings [4], rings [4], earring [2], nose ring [2]

Ge 24:22 the man took out a gold **nose ring** weighing a beka and two gold
24:30 As soon as he had seen the **nose ring**, and the bracelets on his
24:47 "Then I put the **ring** in her nose and the bracelets on her arms,
35: 4 gave Jacob all the foreign gods they had and the **rings** in their ears,
Ex 32: 2 "Take off the gold **earrings** that your wives, your sons and your
32: 3 So all the people took off their **earrings** and brought them to
35:22 gold jewelry of all kinds: brooches, **earrings**, rings and ornaments.
Jdg 8:24 that each of you give me an **earring** *from* your share of the
8:24 (It was the custom of the Ishmaelites to wear gold **earrings**.)
8:25 out a garment, and each man threw a **ring** *from* his plunder onto it.
8:26 The weight of the gold **rings** he asked for came to seventeen
Job 42:11 upon him, and each one gave him a piece of silver and a gold **ring**.
Pr 11:22 Like a gold **ring** in a pig's snout is a beautiful woman who shows
25:12 Like an **earring** *of* gold or an ornament of fine gold is a wise
Isa 3:21 the signet rings and nose **rings**,
Eze 16:12 I put a **ring** on your nose, earrings on your ears and a beautiful
Hos 2:13 [2:15] she decked herself with **rings** and jewelry, and went after

5691 נֵזֶק ***nēzeq***, n.[m.]. [1] [→ Ar 10472]

disturbing [1]

Est 7: 4 because no such distress would justify **disturbing** the king."

5692 נָזַר¹ ***nāzar¹***, v. [5] [→ 5693; cf. 4964, 5623]

consecrated themselves [1], fast [1], keep separate [1], separates himself [1], treat with respect [1]

Lev 15:31 [G] " '*You must* **keep** the Israelites **separate** from things that
22: 2 [C] his sons *to* **treat with respect** the sacred offerings the
Eze 14: 7 [C] or any alien living in Israel **separates himself** from me
Hos 9:10 [C] *they* **consecrated themselves** to that shameful idol
Zec 7: 3 [C] the prophets, "Should I mourn and **fast** in the fifth month,

5693 נָזַר² ***nāzar²***, v.den. [5] [→ 5687, 5692, 5694; cf. 5623]

separation [2], abstain [1], dedicate [1], Nazirite [1]

Nu 6: 2 [G] a vow of separation to the LORD as a **Nazirite**,
6: 3 [G] *he must* **abstain** from wine and other fermented drink
6: 5 [G] He must be holy until the period of *his* **separation** to the
6: 6 [G] Throughout the period of his **separation** to the LORD he
6:12 [G] *He must* **dedicate** *himself* to the LORD for the period of

5694 נֵזֶר ***nēzer***, n.m. [25] [√ 5693; cf. 5623]

crown [7], separation [6], dedicated [3], diadem [3], Nazirite [2], *untranslated* [1], dedication [1], hair [1], symbol of separation [1]

Ex 29: 6 the turban on his head and attach the sacred **diadem** to the turban.
39:30 the plate, the sacred **diadem**, out of pure gold and engraved on it,
Lev 8: 9 and set the gold plate, the sacred **diadem**, on the front of it,
21:12 because he has been **dedicated** *by* the anointing oil of his God.
Nu 6: 4 As long as he is a **Nazirite**, he must not eat anything that comes
6: 5 " 'During the entire period of his vow of **separation** no razor may
6: 7 because the **symbol of** his **separation** *to* God is on his head.
6: 8 Throughout the period of his **separation** he is consecrated to the
6: 9 suddenly in his presence, thus defiling the hair he has **dedicated**,
6:12 dedicate himself to the LORD for the period of his **separation**
6:12 do not count, because he became defiled during his **separation**.
6:13 the law for the Nazirite when the period of his **separation** is over.
6:18 of Meeting, the Nazirite must shave off the hair that he **dedicated**.
6:18 **[RPH]** and put it in the fire that is under the sacrifice of the
6:19 " 'After the Nazirite has shaved off the hair of his **dedication**,
6:21 his offering to the LORD in accordance with his **separation**,
6:21 the vow he has made, according to the law of the **Nazirite**.' "
2Sa 1:10 And I took the **crown** that was on his head and the band on his arm
2Ki 11:12 Jehoiada brought out the king's son and put the **crown** on him;
2Ch 23:11 and his sons brought out the king's son and put the **crown** on him;
Ps 89:39 [89:40] with your servant and have defiled his **crown** in the dust.
132:18 with shame, but the **crown** on his head will be resplendent."
Pr 27:24 not endure forever, and a **crown** is not secure for all generations.
Jer 7:29 Cut off your **hair** and throw it away; take up a lament on the
Zec 9:16 of his people. They will sparkle in his land like jewels in a **crown**.

5695 נֹחַ ***nōaḥ***, n.pr.m. [46 / 47] [√ 5714]

Noah [40], Noah's [3], he[s] [2], his[s] [2]

Ge 5:29 He named him **Noah** and said, "He will comfort us in the labor
5:30 After **Noah** was born, Lamech lived 595 years and had other sons
5:32 After **Noah** was 500 years old, he became the father of Shem,
5:32 500 years old, **he**[s] became the father of Shem, Ham and Japheth.
6: 8 But **Noah** found favor in the eyes of the LORD.
6: 9 This is the account of **Noah**. Noah was a righteous man,
6: 9 **Noah** was a righteous man, blameless among the people of his

[F] Hitpael (hitpoel, hitpoal, hitpolel, hitpolal, hitpalel, hitpalal, hitpalpel, hitpalpal, hotpael, hotpaal) [G] Hiphil (hiphtil) [H] Hophal [I] Hishtaphel

Ge 6: 9 blameless among the people of his time, and **he**[s] walked with God.
6: 10 **Noah** had three sons: Shem, Ham and Japheth.
6: 13 So God said to **Noah**, "I am going to put an end to all people,
6: 22 **Noah** did everything just as God commanded him.
7: 1 The LORD then said to **Noah**, "Go into the ark, you and your
7: 5 And **Noah** did all that the LORD commanded him.
7: 6 **Noah** was six hundred years old when the floodwaters came on the
7: 7 **Noah** and his sons and his wife and his sons' wives entered the ark
7: 9 male and female, came to **Noah** and entered the ark, as God had
7: 9 came to Noah and entered the ark, as God had commanded **Noah**.
7: 11 In the six hundredth year of **Noah's** life, on the seventeenth day of
7: 13 On that very day **Noah** and his sons, Shem, Ham and Japheth,
7: 13 On that very day Noah and **his**[s] sons, Shem, Ham and Japheth,
7: 13 together with **his**[s] wife and the wives of his three sons,
7: 15 of all creatures that have the breath of life in them came to **Noah**
7: 23 from the earth. Only **Noah** was left, and those with him in the ark.
8: 1 God remembered **Noah** and all the wild animals and the livestock
8: 6 After forty days **Noah** opened the window he had made in the ark
8: 11 Then **Noah** knew that the water had receded from the earth.
8: 13 **Noah** then removed the covering from the ark and saw that the
8: 15 Then God said to **Noah**,
8: 18 So **Noah** came out, together with his sons and his wife and his
8: 20 **Noah** built an altar to the LORD and, taking some of all the clean
9: 1 Then God blessed **Noah** and his sons, saying to them, "Be fruitful
9: 8 Then God said to **Noah** and to his sons with him:
9: 17 So God said to **Noah**, "This is the sign of the covenant I have
9: 18 The sons of **Noah** who came out of the ark were Shem, Ham
9: 19 These were the three sons of **Noah**, and from them came the
9: 20 **Noah**, a man of the soil, proceeded to plant a vineyard.
9: 24 When **Noah** awoke from his wine and found out what his youngest
9: 28 After the flood **Noah** lived 350 years.
9: 29 Altogether, **Noah** lived 950 years, and then he died.
10: 1 This is the account of Shem, Ham and Japheth, **Noah's** sons,
10: 32 These are the clans of **Noah's** sons, according to their lines of
1Ch 1: 3 Enoch, Methuselah, Lamech, **Noah**. [BHS-]
1: 4 The sons of **Noah**: Shem, Ham and Japheth.
Isa 54: 9 "To me this is like the days of **Noah**, when I swore that the waters
54: 9 when I swore that the waters of **Noah** would never again cover the
Eze 14: 14 **Noah**, Daniel and Job—were in it, they could save only themselves
14: 20 the Sovereign LORD, even if **Noah**, Daniel and Job were in it,

5696 נַחְבִּי *naḥbî*, n.pr.m. [1]

Nahbi [1]

Nu 13: 14 from the tribe of Naphtali, **Nahbi** son of Vophsi;

5697 נָחָה *nāḥâ*[1], v. [39]

lead [11], guide [9], led [6], guided [4], guides [2], brought [1], disperses [1], kept [1], lead out [1], left [1], settled [1], ushers [1]

Ge 24: 27 [A] the LORD *has* **led** me on the journey *to* the house of my
24: 48 [G] who *had* **led** me on the right road to get the granddaughter of
Ex 13: 17 [A] God *did* not **lead** them *on* the road through the Philistine
13: 21 [A] ahead of them in a pillar of cloud to **guide** them *on* their way
15: 13 [A] "In your unfailing love *you will* **lead** the people you have
32: 34 [A] Now go, **lead** the people to the place I spoke of, and my
Nu 23: 7 [G] "Balak **brought** me from Aram, the king of Moab from the
Dt 32: 12 [G] The LORD alone **led** him; no foreign god was with him.
1Sa 22: 4 [G] So *he* **left** them with the king of Moab, and they stayed with
1Ki 10: 26 [G] which *he* **kept** in the chariot cities and also with him in
2Ki 18: 11 [G] Assyria deported Israel to Assyria and **settled** them in Halah,
Ne 9: 12 [G] By day *you* **led** them with a pillar of cloud, and by night with
9: 19 [G] By day the pillar of cloud did not cease to **guide** them on
Job 12: 23 [G] and destroys them; he enlarges nations, and **disperses** them.
31: 18 [G] as would a father, and from my birth *I* **guided** the widow—
38: 32 [G] in their seasons or **lead out** the Bear with its cubs?
Ps 5: 8 [5:9] [A] **Lead** me, O LORD, in your righteousness because of
23: 3 [G] *He* **guides** me in paths of righteousness for his name's sake.
27: 11 [A] **lead** me in a straight path because of my oppressors.
31: 3 [31:4] [G] for the sake of your name **lead** and guide me.
43: 3 [G] Send forth your light and your truth, *let* them **guide** me;
60: 9 [60:11] [A] me to the fortified city? Who *will* **lead** me to Edom?
61: 2 [61:3] [G] grows faint; **lead** me to the rock that is higher than I.
67: 4 [67:5] [G] the peoples justly and **guide** the nations of the earth.
73: 24 [G] *You* **guide** me with your counsel, and afterward you will
77: 20 [77:21] [A] *You* **led** your people like a flock by the hand of
78: 14 [G] *He* **guided** them with the cloud by day and with light from
78: 53 [G] *He* **guided** them safely, so they were unafraid; but the sea
78: 72 [G] them with integrity of heart; with skillful hands *he* **led** them.
107: 30 [G] it grew calm, and *he* **guided** them to their desired haven.
108: 10 [108:11] [A] to the fortified city? Who *will* **lead** me to Edom?
139: 10 [G] even there your hand *will* **guide** me, your right hand will
139: 24 [A] any offensive way in me, and **lead** me in the way everlasting.
143: 10 [G] are my God; *may* your good Spirit **lead** me on level ground.
Pr 6: 22 [G] When you walk, *they will* **guide** you; when you sleep,
11: 3 [G] The integrity of the upright **guides** them, but the unfaithful
18: 16 [G] for the giver and **ushers** him into the presence of the great.
Isa 57: 18 [G] I will heal him; *I will* **guide** him and restore comfort to him,
58: 11 [A] The LORD *will* **guide** you always; he will satisfy your

5698 [2]נָחָה *nāḥâ*[2], v. Not used in NIV/BHS

5699 נַחוּם *naḥûm*, n.pr.m. [1] [√ 5714]

Nahum [1]

Na 1: 1 The book of the vision of **Nahum** the Elkoshite.

5700 נְחוּם *nᵉḥûm*, n.pr.m. [1] [cf. 8156]

Nehum [1]

Ne 7: 7 Mordecai, Bilshan, Mispereth, Bigvai, **Nehum** and Baanah):

5701 נָחוֹר *nāḥôr*, n.pr.m. [18]

Nahor [16], Nahor's [2]

Ge 11: 22 When Serug had lived 30 years, he became the father of **Nahor**.
11: 23 And after he became the father of **Nahor**, Serug lived 200 years
11: 24 When **Nahor** had lived 29 years, he became the father of Terah.
11: 25 of Terah, **Nahor** lived 119 years and had other sons and daughters.
11: 26 lived 70 years, he became the father of Abram, **Nahor** and Haran.
11: 27 of Terah. Terah became the father of Abram, **Nahor** and Haran.
11: 29 Abram and **Nahor** both married. The name of Abram's wife was
11: 29 wife was Sarai, and the name of **Nahor's** wife was Milcah;
22: 20 is also a mother; she has borne sons to your brother **Nahor**:
22: 23 Milcah bore these eight sons to Abraham's brother **Nahor**.
24: 10 out for Aram Naharaim and made his way to the town of **Nahor**.
24: 15 son of Milcah, who was the wife of Abraham's brother **Nahor**.
24: 24 "I am the daughter of Bethuel, the son that Milcah bore to **Nahor**."
24: 47 "She said, 'The daughter of Bethuel son of **Nahor**, whom Milcah
29: 5 He said to them, "Do you know Laban, **Nahor's** grandson?"
31: 53 May the God of Abraham and the God of **Nahor**, the God of their
Jos 24: 2 including Terah the father of Abraham and **Nahor**, lived beyond
1Ch 1: 26 Serug, **Nahor**, Terah

5702 נָחוּשׁ *nāḥûš*, a. [1] [√ 5733]

bronze [1]

Job 6: 12 Do I have the strength of stone? Is my flesh **bronze**?

5703 נְחוּשָׁה *nᵉḥûšâ*, n.f. [10] [√ 5733; Ar 10473]

bronze [8], bronze-tipped [1], copper [1]

Lev 26: 19 sky above you like iron and the ground beneath you like **bronze**.
2Sa 22: 35 He trains my hands for battle; my arms can bend a bow of **bronze**.
Job 20: 24 he flees from an iron weapon, a **bronze-tipped** arrow pierces him.
28: 2 Iron is taken from the earth, and **copper** is smelted from ore.
40: 18 His bones are tubes of **bronze**, his limbs like rods of iron.
41: 27 [41:19] Iron he treats like straw and **bronze** like rotten wood.
Ps 18: 34 [18:35] my hands for battle; my arms can bend a bow of **bronze**.
Isa 45: 2 I will break down gates of **bronze** and cut through bars of iron.
48: 4 the sinews of your neck were iron, your forehead was **bronze**.
Mic 4: 13 I will give you hoofs of **bronze** and you will break to pieces many

5704 נְחִילוֹת *nᵉḥîlôt*, n.f. [1] [√ 2720?; cf. 2726?]

flutes [1]

Ps 5: T [5:1] For the director of music. For **flutes**. A psalm of David.

5705 נָחִיר *nāḥîr*, n.[m.]. [1] [√ 5723]

nostrils [1]

Job 41: 20 [41:12] Smoke pours from his **nostrils** as from a boiling pot over

5706 נָחַל *nāḥal*, v.den. [59] [→ 5709]

inherit [6], assign as an inheritance [2], distribute [2], gave inheritance [2], giving as an inheritance [2], inheritance [2], lead to inherit [2], receive inheritance [2], received inheritance [2], received [2], *untranslated* [1], allotted [1], assign inheritance [1], assigned [1], been allotted [1], bestowing [1], cause to inherit [1], divide as inheritance [1], divide for an inheritance [1], divide [1], dividing [1], gave [1], get inheritance [1], give as an inheritance [1], give inheritance [1], has inherit [1], have inheritance [+5709] [1], have inheritance [1], help assign [1], heritage [1], inherit land [1], inheritance given [1], inherits [1], leaves an inheritance [1], pass on as an inheritance [1], possess [1], possessed [1], reassign [1], receive inheritance [+5709] [1], receive [1], received as an inheritance [1], take as inheritance [1], take possession [1], will [1], wills [1]

Ex 23: 30 [A] until you have increased enough *to* **take possession** *of* the
32: 13 [A] I promised them, and *it will be their* **inheritance** forever.' "

Ex 34: 9 [A] and our sin, and **take us as** *your* **inheritance**."
Lev 25:46 [F] *You can* **will** them to your children as inherited property
Nu 18:20 [A] said to Aaron, "*You will* **have** no **inheritance** in their land,
18:23 [A] *They will* **receive** no **inheritance** [+5709] among the
18:24 [A] '*They will* **have** no **inheritance** [+5709] among the
26:55 [A] What each group **inherits** will be according to the names for
32:18 [F] our homes until every Israelite *has* **received** his inheritance.
32:19 [A] *We will* not **receive** *any* **inheritance** with them on the other
33:54 [F] **Distribute** the land by lot, according to your clans. To a
33:54 [F] will be theirs. **Distribute** it according to your ancestral tribes.
34:13 [F] the Israelites: "**Assign** this land by lot **as an inheritance**.
34:17 [A] men who *are to* **assign** the land for you **as an inheritance**:
34:18 [A] appoint one leader from each tribe to **help assign** the land.
34:29 [D] **assign** *the* **inheritance** *to* the Israelites in the land of
35: 8 [A] tribe that has many, but few from one that has few." **[NIE]**
Dt 1:38 [G] Encourage him, because he *will* **lead** Israel **to inherit** it.
3:28 [G] and *will* **cause** them **to inherit** the land that you will see."
12:10 [G] land the LORD your God *is* **giving** you **as an inheritance**,
19: 3 [G] land the LORD your God *is* **giving** you **as an inheritance**,
19:14 [A] *you* **receive** in the land the LORD your God is giving you
21:16 [G] when he **wills** his property *to* his sons, he must not give the
31: 7 [G] and you *must* **divide** it *among* them **as** their **inheritance**.
32: 8 [G] When the Most High **gave** the nations their **inheritance**,
Jos 1: 6 [G] because you *will* **lead** these people **to inherit** the land I
13:32 [D] This is *the* **inheritance** Moses *had* **given** when he was in the
14: 1 [A] Israelites **received as an inheritance** in the land of Canaan,
14: 1 [D] and the heads of the tribal clans of Israel **allotted** *to* them.
16: 4 [A] the descendants of Joseph, **received** *their* **inheritance**.
17: 6 [A] because the daughters of the tribe of Manasseh **received** an
19: 9 [A] So the Simeonites **received** *their* **inheritance** within the
19:49 [A] When they had finished **dividing** the land into its allotted
19:51 [D] the heads of the tribal clans of Israel **assigned** by lot at
Jdg 11: 2 [A] "*You are* not *going to* **get** *any* **inheritance** in our family,"
1Sa 2: 8 [G] them with princes and **has** them **inherit** a throne of honor.
1Ch 28: 8 [G] **pass** *it* **on as an inheritance** to your descendants forever.
Job 7: 3 [H] so I *have* **been allotted** months of futility, and nights of
Ps 69:36 [69:37] [A] the children of his servants *will* **inherit** it, and those
82: 8 [A] judge the earth, for all the nations *are* your **inheritance**.
119:111 [A] Your statutes *are my* **heritage** forever; they are the joy of
Pr 3:35 [A] The wise **inherit** honor, but fools he holds up to shame.
8:21 [G] **bestowing** wealth on those who love me and making their
11:29 [A] He who brings trouble on his family *will* **inherit** only wind,
13:22 [G] A good man **leaves an inheritance** *for* his children's
14:18 [A] The simple **inherit** folly, but the prudent are crowned with
28:10 [A] own trap, but the blameless *will* **receive** a good **inheritance**.
Isa 14: 2 [F] the house of Israel *will* **possess** the nations as menservants
49: 8 [G] to restore the land and to **reassign** its desolate inheritances,
57:13 [A] But the man who makes me his refuge *will* **inherit** the land
Jer 3:18 [G] land to the land *I* **gave** your forefathers *as an* **inheritance**.
12:14 [G] neighbors who seize the inheritance *I* **gave** my people Israel,
16:19 [A] and say, "Our fathers **possessed** nothing but false gods,
Eze 46:18 [G] *He is to* **give** his sons their **inheritance** out of his own
47:13 [F] *you are to* **divide** the land **for an inheritance** among the
47:14 [A] *You are to* **divide** it equally among them. Because I swore
Zep 2: 9 [A] the survivors of my nation *will* **inherit** their **land**."
Zec 2:12 [2:16] [A] The LORD *will* **inherit** Judah as his portion in the
8:12 [G] *I will* **give** all these things **as an inheritance** *to* the remnant

5707 נַ֫חַל¹ *naḥal¹*, n.m. [139] [→ 5708?, 5711, 5712]

valley [34], gorge [19], river [17], streams [12], ravine [11], ravines [9], stream [8], Wadi [7], brook [5], torrent [3], torrents [2], valleys [2], *untranslated* [1], course [1], intermittent streams [1], poplars [+6857] [1], rivers [+5643] [1], rivers [1], shaft [1], stream beds [1], streams [+692] [1], there[s] [+928+7724] [1]

Ge 26:17 from there and encamped in the **Valley** *of* Gerar and settled there.
26:19 Isaac's servants dug in the **valley** and discovered a well of fresh
32:23 [32:24] After he had sent them across the **stream**, he sent over all
Lev 11: 9 all the creatures living in the water of the seas and the **streams**,
11:10 creatures in the seas or **streams** that do not have fins and scales—
23:40 palm fronds, leafy branches and **poplars** [+6857], and rejoice
Nu 13:23 When they reached the **Valley** *of* Eshcol, they cut off a branch
13:24 That place was called the **Valley** *of* Eshcol because of the cluster
21:12 From there they moved on and camped in the Zered **Valley**.
21:14 the LORD says: "Waheb in Suphah and the **ravines**, the Arnon
21:15 the slopes of the **ravines** that lead to the site of Ar and lie along the
24: 6 "Like **valleys** they spread out, like gardens beside a river,
32: 9 After they went up to the **Valley** *of* Eshcol and viewed the land,
34: 5 where it will turn, join the **Wadi** *of* Egypt and end at the Sea.
Dt 1:24 the hill country, and came to the **Valley** *of* Eshcol and explored it.
2:13 And the LORD said, "Now get up and cross the Zered **Valley**."
2:13 get up and cross the Zered Valley." So we crossed the **valley**.
2:14 the time we left Kadesh Barnea until we crossed the Zered **Valley**.
2:24 "Set out now and cross the Arnon **Gorge**. See, I have given into
2:36 From Aroer on the rim of the Arnon **Gorge**, and from the town in
2:36 from the town in the **gorge**, even as far as Gilead, not one town
2:37 neither the land along the **course** *of* the Jabbok nor that around the
3: 8 east of the Jordan, from the Arnon **Gorge** as far as Mount Hermon.
3:12 and the Gadites the territory north of Aroer by the Arnon **Gorge**,
3:16 to the Arnon **Gorge** (the middle of the gorge being the border)
3:16 to the Arnon Gorge (the middle of the **gorge** being the border)
3:16 out to the Jabbok **River**, which is the border of the Ammonites.
4:48 This land extended from Aroer on the rim of the Arnon **Gorge** to
8: 7 a land with **streams** and pools *of* water, with springs flowing in the
9:21 and threw the dust into a **stream** that flowed down the mountain.
10: 7 to Gudgodah and on to Jotbathah, a land with **streams** *of* water.
21: 4 and lead her down to a **valley** that has not been plowed or planted
21: 4 There in the **valley** they are to break the heifer's neck.
21: 6 their hands over the heifer whose neck was broken in the **valley**,
Jos 12: 1 from the Arnon **Gorge** to Mount Hermon, including all the eastern
12: 2 He ruled from Aroer on the rim of the Arnon **Gorge**—from the
12: 2 from the middle of the **gorge**—to the Jabbok River, which is the
12: 2 to the Jabbok **River**, which is the border of the Ammonites.
13: 9 It extended from Aroer on the rim of the Arnon **Gorge**, and from
13: 9 of the Arnon Gorge, and from the town in the middle of the **gorge**,
13:16 The territory from Aroer on the rim of the Arnon **Gorge**, and from
13:16 from the town in the middle of the **gorge**, and the whole plateau
15: 4 then passed along to Azmon and joined the **Wadi** *of* Egypt,
15: 7 to Gilgal, which faces the Pass of Adummim south of the **gorge**.
15:47 as far as the **Wadi** *of* Egypt and the coastline of the Great Sea.
16: 8 From Tappuah the border went west to the Kanah **Ravine**
17: 9 Then the boundary continued south to the Kanah **Ravine**.
17: 9 There were towns **[RPH]** belonging to Ephraim lying among the
17: 9 but the boundary of Manasseh was the northern side of the **ravine**
19:11 touched Dabbesheth, and extended to the **ravine** near Jokneam.
Jdg 4: 7 with his chariots and his troops to the Kishon **River** and give him
4:13 the men with him, from Harosheth Haggoyim to the Kishon **River**.
5:21 The **river** Kishon swept them away, the age-old river, the river
5:21 river Kishon swept them away, the age-old **river**, the river Kishon.
5:21 river Kishon swept them away, the age-old river, the **river** Kishon.
16: 4 he fell in love with a woman in the **Valley** *of* Sorek whose name
1Sa 15: 5 Saul went to the city of Amalek and set an ambush in the **ravine**.
17:40 his staff in his hand, chose five smooth stones from the **stream**,
30: 9 and the six hundred men with him came to the Besor **Ravine**,
30:10 for two hundred men were too exhausted to cross the **ravine**.
30:21 to follow him and who were left behind at the Besor **Ravine**.
2Sa 15:23 The king also crossed the Kidron **Valley**, and all the people moved
17:13 we will drag it down to the **valley** until not even a piece of it can
22: 5 swirled about me; the **torrents** *of* destruction overwhelmed me.
23:30 Benaiah the Pirathonite, Hiddai from the **ravines** *of* Gaash,
24: 5 south of the town in the **gorge**, and then went through Gad
1Ki 2:37 The day you leave and cross the Kidron **Valley**, you can be sure
8:65 a vast assembly, people from Lebo Hamath to the **Wadi** *of* Egypt.
15:13 Asa cut the pole down and burned it in the Kidron **Valley**.
17: 3 "Leave here, turn eastward and hide in the Kerith **Ravine**,
17: 4 You will drink from the **brook**, and I have ordered the ravens to
17: 5 He went to the Kerith **Ravine**, east of the Jordan, and stayed there.
17: 6 and bread and meat in the evening, and he drank from the **brook**.
17: 7 Some time later the **brook** dried up because there had been no rain
18: 5 to Obadiah, "Go through the land to all the springs and **valleys**.
18:40 Elijah had them brought down to the Kishon **Valley**
2Ki 3:16 "This is what the LORD says: Make this **valley** full of ditches.
3:17 yet this **valley** will be filled with water, and you, your cattle
10:33 from Aroer by the Arnon **Gorge** through Gilead to Bashan.
23: 6 the temple of the LORD to the Kidron **Valley** outside Jerusalem
23: 6 Valley outside Jerusalem and burned it **there**[s] [+928+7724].
23:12 them to pieces and threw the rubble into the Kidron **Valley**.
24: 7 all his territory, from the **Wadi** *of* Egypt to the Euphrates River.
1Ch 11:32 Hurai from the **ravines** *of* Gaash, Abiel the Arbathite,
2Ch 7: 8 a vast assembly, people from Lebo Hamath to the **Wadi** *of* Egypt.
15:16 cut the pole down, broke it up and burned it in the Kidron **Valley**.
20:16 you will find them at the end of the **gorge** in the Desert of Jeruel.
29:16 The Levites took it and carried it out to the Kidron **Valley**.
30:14 away the incense altars and threw them into the Kidron **Valley**.
32: 4 all the springs and the **stream** that flowed through the land.
33:14 west of the Gihon spring in the **valley**, as far as the entrance of the
Ne 2:15 so I went up the **valley** by night, examining the wall. Finally,
Job 6:15 But my brothers are as undependable as **intermittent streams**,
6:15 as intermittent streams, as the **streams** [+692] that overflow
20:17 the streams, the **rivers** *flowing* **with** [+5643] honey and cream.
21:33 The soil in the **valley** is sweet to him; all men follow after him,
22:24 nuggets to the dust, your gold of Ophir to the rocks in the **ravines**,
28: 4 Far from where people dwell he cuts a **shaft**, in places forgotten by
30: 6 They were forced to live in the dry **stream beds**, among the rocks
40:22 him in their shadow; the poplars by the **stream** surround him.
Ps 18: 4 [18:5] the **torrents** *of* destruction overwhelmed me.
36: 8 [36:9] you give them drink from your **river** *of* delights.
74:15 It was you who opened up springs and **streams**; you dried up the

Ps 78:20 struck the rock, water gushed out, and **streams** flowed abundantly.
83:9 [83:10] as you did to Sisera and Jabin at the **river** Kishon,
104:10 He makes springs pour water into the **ravines**; it flows between the
110:7 He will drink from a **brook** beside the way; therefore he will lift up
124:4 would have engulfed us, the **torrent** would have swept over us,
Pr 18:4 are deep waters, but the fountain of wisdom is a bubbling **brook**.
30:17 will be pecked out by the ravens of the **valley**, will be eaten by the
Ecc 1:7 All **streams** flow into the sea, yet the sea is never full. To the place
1:7 To the place the **streams** come from, there they return again.
SS 6:11 to the grove of nut trees to look at the new growth in the **valley**,
Isa 7:19 They will all come and settle in the steep **ravines** and in the
11:15 He will break it up into seven **streams** so that men can cross over
15:7 and stored up they carry away over the **Ravine** *of* the Poplars.
27:12 will thresh from the flowing Euphrates to the **Wadi** *of* Egypt,
30:28 His breath is like a rushing **torrent**, rising up to the neck.
30:33 of the LORD, like a **stream** *of* burning sulfur, sets it ablaze.
34:9 Edom's **streams** will be turned into pitch, her dust into burning
35:6 Water will gush forth in the wilderness and **streams** in the desert.
57:5 you sacrifice your children in the **ravines** and under the
57:6 ⌊The idols⌋ among the smooth stones of the **ravines** are your
66:12 to her like a river, and the wealth of nations like a flooding **stream**;
Jer 31:9 I will lead them beside **streams** *of* water on a level path where they
31:40 all the terraces out to the Kidron **Valley** on the east as far as the
47:2 are rising in the north; they will become an overflowing **torrent**.
La 2:18 the Daughter of Zion, let your tears flow like a **river** day and night;
Eze 47:5 now it was a **river** that I could not cross, because the water had
47:5 and was deep enough to swim in—a **river** that no one could cross.
47:6 do you see this?" Then he led me back to the bank of the **river**.
47:7 I saw a great number of trees on each side of the **river**.
47:9 Swarms of living creatures will live wherever the **river** flows.
47:9 the salt water fresh; so where the **river** flows everything will live.
47:12 Fruit trees of all kinds will grow on both banks of the **river**.
Joel 3:18 [4:18] of the LORD's house and will water the **valley** *of* acacias.
Am 5:24 roll on like a river, righteousness like a never-failing **stream**!
6:14 you all the way from Lebo Hamath to the **valley** *of* the Arabah."
Mic 6:7 be pleased with thousands of rams, with ten thousand **rivers** *of* oil?

5708 ²נַחַל **naḥal**[2], n.[m.]. Not used in NIV/BHS [√ 5707?]

5709 ¹נַחֲלָה **naḥ^{a}lâ**[1], n.f. [222] [√ 5706]

inheritance [185], heritage [5], inherit [3], part [3], property [3], *untranslated* [2], inheritances [2], one[s] [2], territory [2], that[s] [2], ancestral property [1], estate [1], have inheritance [+5706] [1], inherited [1], it[s] [1], land inherited [1], land inherits [1], land [1], lands [1], place [1], receive inheritance [+5706] [1], territories [1], territory inherit [1]

Ge 31:14 "Do we still have any share in the **inheritance** *of* our father's
48:6 in the **territory** they **inherit** they will be reckoned under the names
Ex 15:17 them in and plant them on the mountain of your **inheritance**—
Nu 16:14 and honey or given us an **inheritance** *of* fields and vineyards.
18:20 I am your share and your **inheritance** among the Israelites.
18:21 "I give to the Levites all the tithes in Israel as their **inheritance** in
18:23 *They will* **receive** no **inheritance** [+5706] among the Israelites.
18:24 I give to the Levites as their **inheritance** the tithes that the
18:24 '*They will* **have** no **inheritance** [+5706] among the Israelites.' "
18:26 receive from the Israelites the tithe I give you as your **inheritance**,
26:53 "The land is to be allotted to them as an **inheritance** based on the
26:54 To a larger group give a larger **inheritance**, and to a smaller group
26:54 give a larger inheritance, and to a smaller group a smaller **one**[s];
26:54 each is to receive its **inheritance** according to the number of those
26:56 Each **inheritance** is to be distributed by lot among the larger
26:62 other Israelites because they received no **inheritance** among them.
27:7 You must certainly give them property as an **inheritance** among
27:7 father's relatives and turn their father's **inheritance** over to them.
27:8 and leaves no son, turn his **inheritance** over to his daughter.
27:9 If he has no daughter, give his **inheritance** to his brothers.
27:10 If he has no brothers, give his **inheritance** to his father's brothers.
27:11 give his **inheritance** to the nearest relative in his clan, that he may
32:18 to our homes until every Israelite has received his **inheritance**.
32:19 because our **inheritance** has come to us on the east side of the
32:32 but the property we **inherit** will be on this side of the Jordan."
33:54 To a larger group give a larger **inheritance**, and to a smaller group
33:54 give a larger inheritance, and to a smaller group a smaller **one**[s].
34:2 the land that will be allotted to you as an **inheritance** will have
34:14 and the half-tribe of Manasseh have received their **inheritance**.
34:15 a half tribes have received their **inheritance** on the east side of the
35:2 towns to live in from the **inheritance** the Israelites will possess.
35:8 are to be given in proportion to the **inheritance** *of* each tribe:
36:2 my lord to give the land as an **inheritance** to the Israelites by lot,
36:2 he ordered you to give the **inheritance** *of* our brother Zelophehad
36:3 then their **inheritance** will be taken from our ancestral inheritance
36:3 then their inheritance will be taken from our ancestral **inheritance**
36:3 and added to **that**[s] *of* the tribe they marry into.
36:3 so part of the **inheritance** allotted *to* us will be taken away.
36:4 their **inheritance** will be added to that of the tribe into which they
36:4 their inheritance will be added to **that**[s] *of* the tribe into which they
36:4 their **property** will be taken from the tribal inheritance of our
36:4 their property will be taken from the tribal **inheritance** *of* our
36:7 No **inheritance** in Israel is to pass from tribe to tribe, for every
36:7 for every Israelite shall keep the tribal **land inherited** *from* his
36:8 Every daughter who inherits **land** in any Israelite tribe must marry
36:8 so that every Israelite will possess the **inheritance** *of* his fathers.
36:9 No **inheritance** may pass from tribe to tribe, for each Israelite tribe
36:9 tribe to tribe, for each Israelite tribe is to keep the **land it inherits**."
36:12 and their **inheritance** remained in their father's clan and tribe.
Dt 4:20 out of Egypt, to be the people of his **inheritance**, as you now are.
4:21 good land the LORD your God is giving you as your **inheritance**.
4:38 to bring you into their land to give it to you for your **inheritance**,
9:26 your own **inheritance** that you redeemed by your great power
9:29 your **inheritance** that you brought out by your great power
10:9 the Levites have no share or **inheritance** among their brothers;
10:9 the LORD is their **inheritance**, as the LORD your God told
12:9 and the **inheritance** the LORD your God is giving you.
12:12 your towns, who have no allotment or **inheritance** *of* their own.
14:27 for they have no allotment or **inheritance** of their own.
14:29 the Levites (who have no allotment or **inheritance** of their own)
15:4 the LORD your God is giving you to possess as your **inheritance**,
18:1 tribe of Levi—are to have no allotment or **inheritance** with Israel.
18:1 offerings made to the LORD by fire, for that is their **inheritance**.
18:2 They shall have no **inheritance** among their brothers; the LORD
18:2 the LORD is their **inheritance**, as he promised them.
19:10 which the LORD your God is giving you as your **inheritance**,
19:14 **inheritance** you receive in the land the LORD your God is giving
20:16 the nations the LORD your God is giving you as an **inheritance**,
21:23 the land the LORD your God is giving you as an **inheritance**.
24:4 the land the LORD your God is giving you as an **inheritance**.
25:19 you in the land he is giving you to possess as an **inheritance**,
26:1 the land the LORD your God is giving you as an **inheritance**
29:8 [29:7] their land and gave it as an **inheritance** to the Reubenites,
32:9 the LORD's portion is his people, Jacob his allotted **inheritance**.
Jos 11:23 he gave it as an **inheritance** to Israel according to their tribal
13:6 Be sure to allocate this land to Israel for an **inheritance**, as I have
13:7 divide it as an **inheritance** among the nine tribes and half of the
13:8 the Gadites had received the **inheritance** that Moses had given
13:14 to the tribe of Levi he gave no **inheritance**, since the offerings
13:14 the God of Israel, are their **inheritance**, as he promised them.
13:23 and their villages were the **inheritance** *of* the Reubenites,
13:28 These towns and their villages were the **inheritance** *of* the Gadites,
13:33 But to the tribe of Levi, Moses had given no **inheritance**;
13:33 the LORD, the God of Israel, is their **inheritance**, as he promised
14:2 Their **inheritances** were assigned by lot to the nine-and-a-half
14:3 Moses had granted the two-and-a-half tribes their **inheritance** east
14:3 but had not granted the Levites an **inheritance** among the rest,
14:9 'The land on which your feet have walked will be your **inheritance**
14:13 Caleb son of Jephunneh and gave him Hebron as his **inheritance**.
14:14 to Caleb son of Jephunneh the Kenizzite **[RPH]** ever since,
15:20 This is the **inheritance** *of* the tribe of Judah, clan by clan:
16:5 The boundary of their **inheritance** went from Ataroth Addar in the
16:8 This was the **inheritance** *of* the tribe of the Ephraimites, clan by
16:9 aside for the Ephraimites within the **inheritance** *of* the Manassites.
17:4 "The LORD commanded Moses to give us an **inheritance** among
17:4 So Joshua gave them an **inheritance** along with the brothers of
17:6 of the tribe of Manasseh received an **inheritance** among the sons.
17:14 given us only one allotment and one portion for an **inheritance**?
18:2 seven Israelite tribes who had not yet received their **inheritance**.
18:4 to write a description of it, according to the **inheritance** *of* each.
18:7 because the priestly service of the LORD is their **inheritance**.
18:7 the half-tribe of Manasseh have already received their **inheritance**
18:20 These were the boundaries that marked out the **inheritance** of the
18:28 their villages. This was the **inheritance** *of* Benjamin for its clans.
19:1 clan by clan. Their **inheritance** lay within the territory of Judah.
19:1 clan by clan. Their inheritance lay within the **territory** *of* Judah.
19:2 **It**[s] included: Beersheba (or Sheba), Moladah,
19:8 This was the **inheritance** *of* the tribe of the Simeonites, clan by
19:9 The **inheritance** *of* the Simeonites was taken from the share of
19:9 So the Simeonites received their inheritance within the **territory** *of*
19:10 by clan: The boundary of their **inheritance** went as far as Sarid.
19:16 These towns and their villages were the **inheritance** *of* Zebulun,
19:23 and their villages were the **inheritance** *of* the tribe of Issachar,
19:31 and their villages were the **inheritance** *of* the tribe of Asher,
19:39 and their villages were the **inheritance** *of* the tribe of Naphtali,
19:41 The territory of their **inheritance** included: Zorah, Eshtaol,
19:48 and their villages were the **inheritance** *of* the tribe of Dan,
19:49 the Israelites gave Joshua son of Nun an **inheritance** among them,
19:51 These are the **territories** that Eleazar the priest, Joshua son of Nun
21:3 the following towns and pasturelands out of their own **inheritance**:
23:4 Remember how I have allotted as an **inheritance** for your tribes all
24:28 Then Joshua sent the people away, each to his own **inheritance**.

Jos 24:30 they buried him in the land of his **inheritance**, at Timnath Serah in
24:32 of Shechem. This became the **inheritance** of Joseph's descendants.
Jdg 2: 6 went to take possession of the land, each to his own **inheritance**.
2: 9 they buried him in the land of his **inheritance**, at Timnath Heres in
18: 1 in those days the tribe of the Danites was seeking a **place** of their
18: 1 because they had not yet come into an **inheritance** among the
20: 6 and sent one piece to each region of Israel's **inheritance**,
21:23 Then they returned to their **inheritance** and rebuilt the towns
21:24 went home to their tribes and clans, each to his own **inheritance**.
Ru 4: 5 in order to maintain the name of the dead with his **property**."
4: 6 "Then I cannot redeem it because I might endanger my own **estate**.
4:10 in order to maintain the name of the dead with his **property**,
1Sa 10: 1 "Has not the LORD anointed you leader over his **inheritance**?
26:19 have now driven me from my share in the LORD's **inheritance**
2Sa 14:16 to cut off both me and my son from the **inheritance** God gave us.'
20: 1 and shouted, "We have no share in David, no **part** in Jesse's son!
20:19 Why do you want to swallow up the LORD's **inheritance**?"
21: 3 I make amends so that you will bless the LORD's **inheritance**?"
1Ki 8:36 and send rain on the land you gave your people for an **inheritance**.
8:51 for they are your people and your **inheritance**, whom you brought
8:53 out from all the nations of the world to be your own **inheritance**,
12:16 "What share do we have in David, what **part** in Jesse's son?
21: 3 "The LORD forbid that I should give you the **inheritance** *of* my
21: 4 had said, "I will not give you the **inheritance** *of* my fathers."
2Ki 21:14 I will forsake the remnant of my **inheritance** and hand them over
1Ch 16:18 you I will give the land of Canaan as the portion you will **inherit**."
2Ch 6:27 and send rain on the land you gave your people for an **inheritance**.
10:16 "What share do we have in David, what **part** in Jesse's son?
Ne 11:20 were in all the towns of Judah, each on his **ancestral property**.
Job 20:29 God allots the wicked, the **heritage** appointed for them by God."
27:13 the **heritage** a ruthless man receives from the Almighty:
31: 2 lot from God above, his **heritage** *from* the Almighty on high?
42:15 their father granted them an **inheritance** along with their brothers.
Ps 2: 8 Ask of me, and I will make the nations your **inheritance**, the ends
16: 6 for me in pleasant places; surely I have a delightful **inheritance**.
28: 9 Save your people and bless your **inheritance**; be their shepherd
33:12 whose God is the LORD, the people he chose for his **inheritance**.
37:18 known to the LORD, and their **inheritance** will endure forever.
47: 4 [47:5] He chose our **inheritance** for us, the pride of Jacob,
68: 9 [68:10] O God; you refreshed your weary **inheritance**.
74: 2 of old, the tribe of your **inheritance**, whom you redeemed—
78:55 before them and allotted their lands to them as an **inheritance**;
78:62 people over to the sword; he was very angry with his **inheritance**.
78:71 to be the shepherd of his people Jacob, of Israel his **inheritance**.
79: 1 O God, the nations have invaded your **inheritance**; they have
94: 5 crush your people, O LORD; they oppress your **inheritance**.
94:14 will not reject his people; he will never forsake his **inheritance**.
105:11 you I will give the land of Canaan as the portion you *will* **inherit**."
106: 5 the joy of your nation and join your **inheritance** in giving praise.
106:40 LORD was angry with his people and abhorred his **inheritance**.
111: 6 the power of his works, giving them the **lands** *of* other nations.
127: 3 Sons are a **heritage** *from* the LORD, children a reward from him.
135:12 he gave their land as an **inheritance**, an inheritance to his people
135:12 their land as an inheritance, an **inheritance** to his people Israel.
136:21 gave their land as an **inheritance**, *His love endures*
136:22 an **inheritance** to his servant Israel; *His love endures*
Pr 17: 2 and will share the **inheritance** as one of the brothers.
19:14 Houses and wealth are **inherited** *from* parents, but a prudent wife
20:21 An **inheritance** quickly gained at the beginning will not be blessed
Ecc 7:11 Wisdom, like an **inheritance**, is a good thing and benefits those
Isa 19:25 my people, Assyria my handiwork, and Israel my **inheritance**."
47: 6 I was angry with my people and desecrated my **inheritance**;
49: 8 to restore the land and to reassign its desolate **inheritances**,
54:17 This is the **heritage** *of* the servants of the LORD, and this is their
58:14 of the land and to feast on the **inheritance** *of* your father Jacob."
63:17 for the sake of your servants, the tribes that are your **inheritance**.
Jer 2: 7 and defiled my land and made my **inheritance** detestable.
3:19 you a desirable land, the most beautiful **inheritance** *of* any nation.'
10:16 Maker of all things, including Israel, the tribe of his **inheritance**—
12: 7 "I will forsake my house, abandon my **inheritance**; I will give the
12: 8 My **inheritance** has become to me like a lion in the forest.
12: 9 Has not my **inheritance** become to me like a speckled bird of prey
12:14 "As for all my wicked neighbors who seize the **inheritance** I gave
12:15 will bring each of them back to his own **inheritance** and his own
16:18 and have filled my **inheritance** with their detestable idols."
17: 4 Through your own fault you will lose the **inheritance** I gave you.
50:11 you rejoice and are glad, you who pillage my **inheritance**,
51:19 is the Maker of all things, including the tribe of his **inheritance**—
La 5: 2 Our **inheritance** has been turned over to aliens, our homes to
Eze 35:15 Because you rejoiced when the **inheritance** *of* the house of Israel
36:12 They will possess you, and you will be their **inheritance**;
44:28 **[RPH]** " 'I am to be the only inheritance the priests have.
44:28 " 'I am to be the only **inheritance** the priests have. You are to give
45: 1 " 'When you allot the land as an **inheritance**, you are to present to
46:16 If the prince makes a gift from his **inheritance** to one of his sons,
46:16 belong to his descendants; it is to be their property by **inheritance**.
46:17 he makes a gift from his **inheritance** to one of his servants,
46:17 to the prince. His **inheritance** belongs to his sons only; it is theirs.
46:18 The prince must not take any of the **inheritance** *of* the people,
47:14 give it to your forefathers, this land will become your **inheritance**.
47:22 You are to allot it as an **inheritance** for yourselves and for the
47:22 along with you they are to be allotted an **inheritance** among the
47:23 there you are to give him his **inheritance**," declares the Sovereign
48:29 "This is the land you are to allot as an **inheritance** to the tribes of
Joel 2:17 Do not make your **inheritance** an object of scorn, a byword among
3: 2 [4:2] into judgment against them concerning my **inheritance**,
Mic 2: 2 They defraud a man of his home, a fellowman of his **inheritance**.
7:14 the flock of your **inheritance**, which lives by itself in a forest,
7:18 and forgives the transgression of the remnant of his **inheritance**?
Mal 1: 3 into a wasteland and left his **inheritance** to the desert jackals."

5710 נַחֲלָה[2] **naḥalâ[2]**, n.[m.] *or* v.ptcp. [1] [√ 2703]

disease [1]

Isa 17:11 yet the harvest will be as nothing in the day of **disease** and

5711 נַחֲלָה[3] **naḥalâ[3]**, n.[pr.loc.?]. [2] [→ 5712; cf. 5707]

Wadi [2]

Eze 47:19 Meribah Kadesh, then along the **Wadi** ⌞of Egypt⌟ to the Great Sea.
48:28 Meribah Kadesh, then along the **Wadi** ⌞of Egypt⌟ to the Great Sea.

5712 נַחֲלִיאֵל **naḥalîʾēl**, n.pr.loc. [2] [√ 5711 + 446]

Nahaliel [2]

Nu 21:19 from Mattanah to **Nahaliel**, from Nahaliel to Bamoth,
21:19 from Mattanah to Nahaliel, from **Nahaliel** to Bamoth,

5713 נֶחֱלָמִי **neḥelāmî**, a.g. [3]

Nehelamite [3]

Jer 29:24 Tell Shemaiah the **Nehelamite**,
29:31 'This is what the LORD says about Shemaiah the **Nehelamite**:
29:32 I will surely punish Shemaiah the **Nehelamite** and his descendants.

5714 נָחַם **nāḥam**, v. [108] [→ 4968, 5695, 5699, 5700, 5715, 5716, 5717, 5718, 5719, 5720, 9487, 9488, 9489]

comfort [23], comforted [5], express sympathy [5], relent [5], be comforted [4], change mind [4], comforts [4], was grieved [4], console [3], grieved [3], have compassion [3], relented [3], am grieved [2], be consoled [2], comforter [2], comforters [2], compassion [2], consoled [2], give comfort [2], relents [2], be avenged [1], change minds [1], consoling himself [1], find comfort [1], get relief [1], given comfort [1], giving comfort [1], had compassion [1], have pity [1], look with compassion [1], pity [1], reassured [1], reconsider [1], recovered from grief [1], relent and do not bring [1], relent and not bring [1], relent so that not bring [1], relented and did not [1], repent [1], repented [1], repents [1], show compassion [1], showed pity [1], was comforted [1], was consoled [1], were consoled [1]

Ge 5:29 [D] "He *will* **comfort** us in the labor and painful toil of our hands
6: 6 [C] The LORD **was grieved** that he had made man on the earth,
6: 7 [C] birds of the air—for *I* **am grieved** that I have made them."
24:67 [C] loved her; and Isaac **was comforted** after his mother's death.
27:42 [F] "Your brother Esau *is* **consoling himself** with the thought of
37:35 [D] All his sons and daughters came to **comfort** him, but he
37:35 [F] came to comfort him, but he refused to **be comforted**.
38:12 [C] When Judah *had* **recovered from** *his* **grief**, he went up to
50:21 [D] And *he* **reassured** them and spoke kindly to them.
Ex 13:17 [C] they might **change** *their* **minds** and return to Egypt."
32:12 [C] **relent and do not bring** disaster on your people.
32:14 [C] the LORD **relented and did not** bring on his people the
Nu 23:19 [F] nor a son of man, that *he should* **change** *his* **mind**.
Dt 32:36 [F] **have compassion** on his servants when he sees their strength
Jdg 2:18 [C] for the LORD **had compassion** *on* them as they groaned
21: 6 [C] Now the Israelites **grieved** for their brothers, the Benjamites.
21:15 [C] The people **grieved** for Benjamin, because the LORD had
Ru 2:13 [D] "*You have* **given** me **comfort** and have spoken kindly to
1Sa 15:11 [C] "*I* **am grieved** that I have made Saul king, because he has
15:29 [C] who is the Glory of Israel does not lie or **change** *his* **mind**;
15:29 [C] for he is not a man, that *he should* **change** *his* **mind**."
15:35 [C] the LORD **was grieved** that he had made Saul king over
2Sa 10: 2 [D] So David sent a delegation to **express** his **sympathy** to
10: 3 [D] your father by sending men to you *to* **express sympathy**?
12:24 [D] David **comforted** his wife Bathsheba, and he went to her
13:39 [C] to Absalom, for *he* **was consoled** concerning Amnon's death.
24:16 [C] the LORD **was grieved** because of the calamity and said to
1Ch 7:22 [D] for them many days, and his relatives came to **comfort** him.
19: 2 [D] So David sent a delegation to **express** his **sympathy** *to*

1Ch 19: 2 [D] in the land of the Ammonites to **express sympathy** *to* him,
19: 3 [D] your father by sending men to you *to* **express sympathy**?
21: 15 [C] the LORD saw it and **was grieved** because of the calamity
Job 2: 11 [D] agreement to go and sympathize with him and **comfort** him.
7: 13 [D] When I think my bed *will* **comfort** me and my couch will
16: 2 [D] many things like these; miserable **comforters** are you all!
21: 34 [D] "So how *can you* **console** me *with* your nonsense? Nothing
29: 25 [D] among his troops; I was like *one who* **comforts** mourners.
42: 6 [C] Therefore I despise myself and **repent** in dust and ashes."
42: 11 [D] **consoled** him over all the trouble the LORD had brought
Ps 23: 4 [D] you are with me; your rod and your staff, they **comfort** me.
69: 20 [69:21] [D] there was none, for **comforters**, but I found none.
71: 21 [D] You will increase my honor and **comfort** me once again.
77: 2 [77:3] [C] untiring hands and my soul refused *to* **be comforted**.
86: 17 [D] for you, O LORD, have helped me and **comforted** me.
90: 13 [C] How long will it be? **Have compassion** on your servants.
106: 45 [C] his covenant and out of his great love *he* **relented**.
110: 4 [C] The LORD has sworn and *will* not **change** *his* **mind**:
119: 52 [F] your ancient laws, O LORD, and *I* **find comfort** in them.
119: 76 [D] May your unfailing love be my **comfort**, according to your
119: 82 [D] for your promise; I say, "When *will you* **comfort** me?"
135: 14 [F] vindicate his people and **have compassion** on his servants.
Ecc 4: 1 [D] saw the tears of the oppressed—and they have no **comforter**;
4: 1 [D] on the side of their oppressors—and they have no **comforter**.
Isa 1: 24 [C] *I will* **get relief** from my foes and avenge myself on my
12: 1 [D] your anger has turned away and *you have* **comforted** me.
22: 4 [D] Do not try to **console** me over the destruction of my people."
40: 1 [D] **Comfort**, comfort my people, says your God.
40: 1 [D] Comfort, **comfort** my people, says your God.
49: 13 [D] For the LORD **comforts** his people and will have
51: 3 [D] The LORD *will* surely **comfort** Zion and will look with
51: 3 [D] and *will* **look with compassion** *on* all her ruins;
51: 12 [D] "I, even I, am he *who* **comforts** you. Who are you that you
51: 19 [D] and destruction, famine and sword—who *can* **console** you?
52: 9 [D] of Jerusalem, for the LORD *has* **comforted** his people,
54: 11 [E] "O afflicted city, lashed by storms and not **comforted**, I will
57: 6 [C] grain offerings. In the light of these things, *should I* **relent**?
61: 2 [D] the day of vengeance of our God, to **comfort** all who mourn,
66: 13 [D] As a mother **comforts** her child, so will I comfort you;
66: 13 [D] As a mother comforts her child, so *will* I **comfort** you;
66: 13 [E] I comfort you; and *you will* **be comforted** over Jerusalem."
Jer 4: 28 [C] because I have spoken and *will* not **relent**, I have decided
8: 6 [C] No one **repents** of his wickedness, saying, "What have I
15: 6 [C] on you and destroy you; I can no longer **show compassion**.
16: 7 [D] No one will offer food to **comfort** those who mourn for the
18: 8 [C] *I will* **relent** and not inflict on it the disaster I had planned.
18: 10 [C] then *I will* **reconsider** the good I had intended to do for it.
20: 16 [C] man be like the towns the LORD overthrew without **pity**.
26: 3 [C] *I will* **relent** and not bring on them the disaster I was
26: 13 [C] the LORD *will* **relent and not bring** the disaster he has
26: 19 [C] *did* not the LORD **relent**, **so that** he *did* **not bring** the
31: 13 [D] *I will* **give** them **comfort** and joy instead of sorrow.
31: 15 [C] weeping for her children and refusing to **be comforted**,
31: 19 [C] After I strayed, *I* **repented**; after I came to understand, I beat
42: 10 [C] for *I am* **grieved** over the disaster I have inflicted on you.
La 1: 2 [D] Among all her lovers there is none *to* **comfort** her.
1: 9 [D] Her fall was astounding; there was none *to* **comfort** her.
1: 16 [D] No one is near *to* **comfort** me, no one to restore my spirit.
1: 17 [D] stretches out her hands, but there is no *one to* **comfort** her.
1: 21 [D] have heard my groaning, but there is no *one to* **comfort** me.
2: 13 [D] To what can I liken you, that *I may* **comfort** you, O Virgin
Eze 5: 13 [F] my wrath against them will subside, and *I will* **be avenged**.
14: 22 [C] *you will* **be consoled** regarding the disaster I have brought
14: 23 [D] You *will be* **consoled** when you see their conduct and their
16: 54 [D] be ashamed of all you have done in **giving** them **comfort**.
24: 14 [C] I will not hold back; I will not have pity, nor *will I* **relent**.
31: 16 [C] that were well-watered, **were consoled** in the earth below.
32: 31 [C] *he will* **be consoled** for all his hordes that were killed by the
Joel 2: 13 [C] and abounding in love, and *he* **relents** from sending calamity.
2: 14 [C] He may turn and **have pity** and leave behind a blessing—
Am 7: 3 [C] So the LORD **relented**. "This will not happen," the LORD
7: 6 [C] So the LORD **relented**. "This will not happen either,"
Jnh 3: 9 [C] yet relent and *with* **compassion** turn from his fierce anger
3: 10 [C] he *had* **compassion** and did not bring upon them the
4: 2 [C] in love, a God *who* **relents** from sending calamity.
Na 3: 7 [D] mourn for her?' Where can I find *anyone to* **comfort** you?"
Zec 1: 17 [D] the LORD *will* again **comfort** Zion and choose
8: 14 [C] and **showed** no **pity** when your fathers angered me,"
10: 2 [D] they tell dreams that are false, *they* **give comfort** in vain.

5715 נָחַם naḥam, n.pr.m. [1] [√ 5714]

Naham [1]

1Ch 4: 19 The sons of Hodiah's wife, the sister of **Naham**: the father of

5716 נֹחַם nōḥam, n.m. [1] [√ 5714]

compassion [1]

Hos 13: 14 O grave, is your destruction? "I will have no **compassion**,

5717 נֶחָמָה neḥāmâ, n.f. [2] [√ 5714]

comfort [1], consolation [1]

Job 6: 10 I would still have this **consolation**—my joy in unrelenting pain—
Ps 119: 50 My **comfort** in my suffering is this: Your promise preserves my

5718 נְחֶמְיָה n^{e}ḥemyâ, n.pr.m. [8] [√ 5714 + 3378]

Nehemiah [8]

Ezr 2: 2 Jeshua, **Nehemiah**, Seraiah, Reelaiah, Mordecai, Bilshan,
Ne 1: 1 The words of **Nehemiah** son of Hacaliah: In the month of Kislev
3: 16 Beyond him, **Nehemiah** son of Azbuk, ruler of a half-district of
7: 7 Jeshua, **Nehemiah**, Azariah, Raamiah, Nahamani, Mordecai,
8: 9 **Nehemiah** the governor, Ezra the priest and scribe, and the Levites
10: 1 [10:2] **Nehemiah** the governor, the son of Hacaliah. Zedekiah,
12: 26 and in the days of **Nehemiah** the governor and of Ezra the priest
12: 47 So in the days of Zerubbabel and of **Nehemiah**, all Israel

5719 נִחוּמִים niḥumîm, n.m.[pl.]. [3] [√ 5714]

comfort [1], comforting [1], compassion [1]

Isa 57: 18 but I will heal him; I will guide him and restore **comfort** to him,
Hos 11: 8 My heart is changed within me; all my **compassion** is aroused.
Zec 1: 13 and **comforting** words to the angel who talked with me.

5720 נַחֲמָנִי naḥ^{a}mānî, n.pr.m. [1] [√ 5714]

Nahamani [1]

Ne 7: 7 Azariah, Raamiah, **Nahamani**, Mordecai, Bilshan, Mispereth,

5721 נַחְנוּ naḥnû, p.com.pl. [6] [√ 636] Not indexed

we [5], *untranslated* [1]

5722 נָחַץ nāḥaṣ, v. [1] [cf. 4315]

urgent [1]

1Sa 21: 8 [21:9] [B] because the king's business was **urgent**."

5723 נָחַר nāḥar, v. [2] [→ 5705, 5724, 5725]

angry [1], blow fiercely [1]

SS 1: 6 [D] My mother's sons *were* **angry** with me and made me take
Jer 6: 29 [A] The bellows **blow fiercely** to burn away the lead with fire,

5724 נַחַר naḥar, n.[m.]. [1] [√ 5723]

snorting [1]

Job 39: 20 him leap like a locust, striking terror with his proud **snorting**?

5725 נַחֲרָה naḥ^{a}râ, n.f. [1] [√ 5723]

snorting [1]

Jer 8: 16 The **snorting** *of* the enemy's horses is heard from Dan; at the

5726 נַחְרַי naḥray, n.pr.m. [2]

Naharai [2]

2Sa 23: 37 Zelek the Ammonite, **Naharai** the Beerothite, the armor-bearer of
1Ch 11: 39 Zelek the Ammonite, **Naharai** the Berothite, the armor-bearer of

5727 נָחַשׁ nāḥaš, v.den. [11] [→ 5728; cf. 4317]

divination [2], find things out by divination [+5727] [2], uses for divination [+928+5727] [2], interprets omens [1], learned by divination [1], practice divination [1], sorcery [1], took as a good sign [1]

Ge 30: 27 [D] *I have* **learned by divination** that the LORD has blessed
44: 5 [D] drinks from and also **uses for divination** [+928+5727]?
44: 5 [D] drinks from and also **uses for divination** [+928+5727]?
44: 15 [D] a man like me *can* **find things out by divination** [+5727]?"
44: 15 [D] a man like me *can* **find things out by divination** [+5727]?"
Lev 19: 26 [D] the blood still in it. " '*Do* not **practice divination** or sorcery.
Dt 18: 10 [D] who practices divination or sorcery, **interprets omens**,
1Ki 20: 33 [D] The men **took** *this* **as a good sign** and were quick to pick up
2Ki 17: 17 [D] They practiced divination and **sorcery** and sold themselves
21: 6 [D] practiced sorcery and **divination**, and consulted mediums
2Ch 33: 6 [D] practiced sorcery, **divination** and witchcraft, and consulted

5728 נַחַשׁ naḥaš, n.[m.]. [2] [√ 5727]

sorcery [2]

Nu 23: 23 There is no **sorcery** against Jacob, no divination against Israel.
24: 1 he did not resort to **sorcery** as at other times, but turned his face

5729 [1]נָחָשׁ ***nāḥāš***[1], n.m. [31] [→ 5731, 5732]

snake [14], serpent [11], snakes [3], serpent's [2], venomous snakes [1]

Ge 3: 1 Now the **serpent** was more crafty than any of the wild animals the
3: 2 The woman said to the **serpent**, "We may eat fruit from the trees
3: 4 "You will not surely die," the **serpent** said to the woman.
3: 13 The woman said, "The **serpent** deceived me, and I ate."
3: 14 So the LORD God said to the **serpent**, "Because you have done
49: 17 Dan will be a **serpent** by the roadside, a viper along the path,
Ex 4: 3 Moses threw it on the ground and it became a **snake**, and he ran
7: 15 and take in your hand the staff that was changed into a **snake**.
Nu 21: 6 the LORD sent venomous **snakes** among them; they bit the
21: 7 Pray that the LORD will take the **snakes** away from us."
21: 9 So Moses made a bronze **snake** and put it up on a pole. Then when
21: 9 when anyone was bitten by a **snake** and looked at the bronze
21: 9 anyone was bitten by a snake and looked at the bronze **snake**,
Dt 8: 15 and waterless land, with its venomous **snakes** and scorpions.
2Ki 18: 4 He broke into pieces the bronze **snake** Moses had made, for up to
Job 26: 13 breath the skies became fair; his hand pierced the gliding **serpent**.
Ps 58: 4 [58:5] Their venom is like the venom of a **snake**, like that of a
140: 3 [140:4] They make their tongues as sharp as a **serpent's**;
Pr 23: 32 In the end it bites like a **snake** and poisons like a viper.
30: 19 the way of an eagle in the sky, the way of a **snake** on a rock,
Ecc 10: 8 into it; whoever breaks through a wall may be bitten by a **snake**.
10: 11 If a **snake** bites before it is charmed, there is no profit for the
Isa 14: 29 from the root of that **snake** will spring up a viper, its fruit will be a
27: 1 great and powerful sword, Leviathan the gliding **serpent**,
27: 1 Leviathan the gliding serpent, Leviathan the coiling **serpent**;
65: 25 lion will eat straw like the ox, but dust will be the **serpent's** food.
Jer 8: 17 "See, I will send **venomous snakes** among you, vipers that cannot
46: 22 Egypt will hiss like a fleeing **serpent** as the enemy advances in
Am 5: 19 and rested his hand on the wall only to have a **snake** bite him.
9: 3 bottom of the sea, there I will command the **serpent** to bite them.
Mic 7: 17 They will lick dust like a **snake**, like creatures that crawl on the

5730 [2]נָחָשׁ ***nāḥāš***[2], n.pr.loc. Not used in NIV/BHS [√ 5733; cf. 5736]

5731 [3]נָחָשׁ ***nāḥāš***[3], n.pr.m. [9] [√ 5729]

Nahash [8], him[s] [1]

1Sa 11: 1 **Nahash** the Ammonite went up and besieged Jabesh Gilead.
11: 1 And all the men of Jabesh said to **him**[s], "Make a treaty with us,
11: 2 **Nahash** the Ammonite replied, "I will make a treaty with you only
12: 12 "But when you saw that **Nahash** king of the Ammonites was
2Sa 10: 2 David thought, "I will show kindness to Hanun son of **Nahash**,
17: 25 the daughter of **Nahash** and sister of Zeruiah the mother of Joab.
17: 27 Shobi son of **Nahash** from Rabbah of the Ammonites,
1Ch 19: 1 In the course of time, **Nahash** king of the Ammonites died,
19: 2 David thought, "I will show kindness to Hanun son of **Nahash**,

5732 נַחְשׁוֹן ***naḥšôn***, n.pr.m. [10] [√ 5729]

Nahshon [10]

Ex 6: 23 daughter of Amminadab and sister of **Nahshon**, and she bore him
Nu 1: 7 from Judah, **Nahshon** son of Amminadab;
2: 3 The leader of the people of Judah is **Nahshon** son of Amminadab.
7: 12 The one who brought his offering on the first day was **Nahshon**
7: 17 This was the offering of **Nahshon** son of Amminadab.
10: 14 their standard. **Nahshon** son of Amminadab was in command.
Ru 4: 20 Amminadab the father of **Nahshon**, Nahshon the father of Salmon,
4: 20 Amminadab the father of Nahshon, **Nahshon** the father of Salmon,
1Ch 2: 10 Amminadab the father of **Nahshon**, the leader of the people of
2: 11 **Nahshon** was the father of Salmon, Salmon the father of Boaz,

5733 [1]נְחֹשֶׁת ***nᵉḥōšet***[1], n.m. [140] [→ 5702, 5703, 5730; cf. 5736; Ar 10473]

bronze [128], bronze shackles [5], copper [4], chains [1], wealth [1], were fettered [+4200+5602] [1]

Ge 4: 22 Tubal-Cain, who forged all kinds of tools out of **bronze** and iron.
Ex 25: 3 offerings you are to receive from them: gold, silver and **bronze**;
26: 11 make fifty **bronze** clasps and put them in the loops to fasten the
26: 37 wood overlaid with gold. And cast five **bronze** bases for them.
27: 2 and the altar are of one piece, and overlay the altar with **bronze**.
27: 3 Make all its utensils of **bronze**—its pots to remove the ashes,
27: 4 Make a grating for it, a **bronze** network, and make a bronze ring at
27: 4 and make a **bronze** ring at each of the four corners of the network.
27: 6 poles of acacia wood for the altar and overlay them with **bronze**.
27: 10 with twenty posts and twenty **bronze** bases and with silver hooks
27: 11 with twenty posts and twenty **bronze** bases and with silver hooks
27: 17 courtyard are to have silver bands and hooks, and **bronze** bases.
27: 18 of finely twisted linen five cubits high, and with **bronze** bases.
27: 19 the tent pegs for it and those for the courtyard, are to be of **bronze**.
30: 18 "Make a **bronze** basin, with its bronze stand, for washing.
30: 18 "Make a bronze basin, with its **bronze** stand, for washing.
31: 4 to make artistic designs for work in gold, silver and **bronze**,
35: 5 is to bring to the LORD an offering of gold, silver and **bronze**;
35: 16 the altar of burnt offering with its **bronze** grating, its poles
35: 24 of silver or **bronze** brought it as an offering to the LORD,
35: 32 to make artistic designs for work in gold, silver and **bronze**,
36: 18 They made fifty **bronze** clasps to fasten the tent together as a unit.
36: 38 and their bands with gold and made their five bases of **bronze**.
38: 2 the altar were of one piece, and they overlaid the altar with **bronze**.
38: 3 They made all its utensils of **bronze**—its pots, shovels, sprinkling
38: 4 a **bronze** network, to be under its ledge, halfway up the altar.
38: 5 rings to hold the poles for the four corners of the **bronze** grating.
38: 6 made the poles of acacia wood and overlaid them with **bronze**.
38: 8 They made the **bronze** basin and its bronze stand from the mirrors
38: 8 its **bronze** stand from the mirrors of the women who served at the
38: 10 with twenty posts and twenty **bronze** bases, and with silver hooks
38: 11 cubits long and had twenty posts and twenty **bronze** bases,
38: 17 The bases for the posts were **bronze**. The hooks and bands on the
38: 19 with four posts and four **bronze** bases. Their hooks and bands were
38: 20 of the tabernacle and of the surrounding courtyard were **bronze**.
38: 29 The **bronze** *from* the wave offering was 70 talents and 2,400
38: 30 the **bronze** altar with its bronze grating and all its utensils,
38: 30 the bronze altar with its **bronze** grating and all its utensils,
39: 39 the **bronze** altar with its bronze grating, its poles and all its
39: 39 the bronze altar with its **bronze** grating, its poles and all its
Lev 6: 28 [6:21] but if it is cooked in a **bronze** pot, the pot is to be scoured
Nu 16: 39 [17:4] So Eleazar the priest collected the **bronze** censers brought
21: 9 So Moses made a **bronze** snake and put it up on a pole. Then when
21: 9 anyone was bitten by a snake and looked at the **bronze** snake,
31: 22 Gold, silver, **bronze**, iron, tin, lead
Dt 8: 9 where the rocks are iron and you can dig **copper** out of the hills.
28: 23 The sky over your head will be **bronze**, the ground beneath you
33: 25 The bolts of your gates will be iron and **bronze**, and your strength
Jos 6: 19 All the silver and gold and the articles of **bronze** and iron are
6: 24 but they put the silver and gold and the articles of **bronze**
22: 8 with large herds of livestock, with silver, gold, **bronze** and iron,
Jdg 16: 21 Binding him with **bronze** *shackles*, they set him to grinding in the
1Sa 17: 5 He had a **bronze** helmet on his head and wore a coat of scale
17: 5 wore a coat of scale armor of **bronze** weighing five thousand
17: 6 on his legs he wore **bronze** greaves, and a bronze javelin was slung
17: 6 wore bronze greaves, and a **bronze** javelin was slung on his back.
17: 38 He put a coat of armor on him and a **bronze** helmet on his head.
2Sa 3: 34 hands were not bound, your feet **were** not **fettered** [+4200+5602].
8: 8 to Hadadezer, King David took a great quantity of **bronze**.
8: 10 Joram brought with him articles of silver and gold and **bronze**.
21: 16 whose **bronze** spearhead weighed three hundred shekels and who
1Ki 4: 13 in Bashan and its sixty large walled cities with **bronze** gate bars);
7: 14 and whose father was a man of Tyre and a craftsman in **bronze**.
7: 14 was highly skilled and experienced in all kinds of **bronze** work.
7: 15 He cast two **bronze** pillars, each eighteen cubits high and twelve
7: 16 He also made two capitals of cast **bronze** to set on the tops of the
7: 27 He also made ten movable stands of **bronze**; each was four cubits
7: 30 Each stand had four **bronze** wheels with bronze axles, and each
7: 30 Each stand had four bronze wheels with **bronze** axles, and each
7: 38 He then made ten **bronze** basins, each holding forty baths
7: 45 Solomon for the temple of the LORD were of burnished **bronze**.
7: 47 there were so many; the weight of the **bronze** was not determined.
8: 64 because the **bronze** altar before the LORD was too small to hold
14: 27 So King Rehoboam made **bronze** shields to replace them
2Ki 16: 14 The **bronze** altar that stood before the LORD he brought from the
16: 15 But I will use the **bronze** altar for seeking guidance."
16: 17 He removed the Sea from the **bronze** bulls that supported it
18: 4 He broke into pieces the **bronze** snake Moses had made, for up to
25: 7 bound him with **bronze shackles** and took him to Babylon.
25: 13 The Babylonians broke up the **bronze** pillars, the movable stands
25: 13 and the **bronze** Sea that were at the temple of the LORD
25: 13 the temple of the LORD and they carried the **bronze** to Babylon.
25: 14 dishes and all the **bronze** articles used in the temple service.
25: 16 The **bronze** *from* the two pillars, the Sea and the movable stands,
25: 17 The **bronze** capital on top of one pillar was four and a half feet
25: 17 decorated with a network and pomegranates of **bronze** all around.
1Ch 15: 19 Asaph and Ethan were to sound the **bronze** cymbals;
18: 8 that belonged to Hadadezer, David took a great quantity of **bronze**,
18: 8 which Solomon used to make the **bronze** Sea, the pillars
18: 8 to make the bronze Sea, the pillars and various **bronze** articles.
18: 10 brought all kinds of articles of gold and silver and **bronze**.
22: 3 and for the fittings, and more **bronze** than could be weighed.
22: 14 quantities of **bronze** and iron too great to be weighed, and wood
22: 16 in gold and silver, **bronze** and iron—craftsmen beyond number.
29: 2 **bronze** for the bronze, iron for the iron and wood for the wood,
29: 2 bronze for the **bronze**, iron for the iron and wood for the wood,
29: 7 eighteen thousand talents of **bronze** and a hundred thousand talents
2Ch 1: 5 But the **bronze** altar that Bezalel son of Uri, the son of Hur,

2Ch 1: 6 Solomon went up to the **bronze** altar before the LORD in the
2: 7 [2:6] a man skilled to work in gold and silver, **bronze** and iron,
2: 14 [2:13] work in gold and silver, **bronze** and iron, stone and wood,
4: 1 He made a **bronze** altar twenty cubits long, twenty cubits wide
4: 9 and the doors for the court, and overlaid the doors with **bronze**.
4: 16 Solomon for the temple of the LORD were of polished **bronze**.
4: 18 so much that the weight of the **bronze** was not determined.
6: 13 Now he had made a **bronze** platform, five cubits long, five cubits
7: 7 because the **bronze** altar he had made could not hold the burnt
12: 10 So King Rehoboam made **bronze** shields to replace them
24: 12 and also workers in iron and **bronze** to repair the temple.
33: 11 bound him with **bronze shackles** and took him to Babylon.
36: 6 and bound him with **bronze shackles** to take him to Babylon.
Ezr 8: 27 and two fine articles of polished **bronze**, as precious as gold.
Ps 107: 16 for he breaks down gates of **bronze** and cuts through bars of iron.
Isa 60: 17 Instead of **bronze** I will bring you gold, and silver in place of iron.
60: 17 Instead of wood I will bring you **bronze**, and iron in place of
Jer 1: 18 an iron pillar and a **bronze** wall to stand against the whole land—
6: 28 about to slander. They are **bronze** and iron; they all act corruptly.
15: 12 "Can a man break iron—iron from the north—or **bronze**?
15: 20 I will make you a wall to this people, a fortified wall of **bronze**;
39: 7 and bound him with **bronze shackles** to take him to Babylon.
52: 11 bound him with **bronze shackles** and took him to Babylon,
52: 17 The Babylonians broke up the **bronze** pillars, the movable stands
52: 17 and the **bronze** Sea that were at the temple of the LORD
52: 17 temple of the LORD and they carried all the **bronze** to Babylon.
52: 18 dishes and all the **bronze** articles used in the temple service.
52: 20 The **bronze** *from* the two pillars, the Sea and the twelve bronze
52: 20 the Sea and the twelve **bronze** bulls under it, and the movable
52: 22 The **bronze** capital on top of the one pillar was five cubits high
52: 22 decorated with a network and pomegranates of **bronze** all around.
La 3: 7 so I cannot escape; he has weighed me down with **chains**.
Eze 1: 7 feet were like those of a calf and gleamed like burnished **bronze**.
9: 2 kit at his side. They came in and stood beside the **bronze** altar.
16: 36 Because you poured out your **wealth** and exposed your nakedness
22: 18 all of them are the **copper**, tin, iron and lead left inside a furnace.
22: 20 **copper**, iron, lead and tin into a furnace to melt it with a fiery
24: 11 its **copper** glows so its impurities may be melted and its deposit
27: 13 they exchanged slaves and articles of **bronze** for your wares.
40: 3 me there, and I saw a man whose appearance was like **bronze**;
Da 10: 6 his arms and legs like the gleam of burnished **bronze**,
Zec 6: 1 coming out from between two mountains—mountains of **bronze**!

5734 ²נְחֹשֶׁת **nᵉḥōšet²**, n.[f.]. Not used in NIV/BHS

5735 נְחֻשְׁתָּא **nᵉḥuštā'**, n.pr.f. [1]

Nehushta [1]

2Ki 24: 8 His mother's name was **Nehushta** daughter of Elnathan; she was

5736 נְחֻשְׁתָּן **nᵉḥuštān**, n.pr. [1] [cf. 5730, 5733]

Nehushtan [1]

2Ki 18: 4 had been burning incense to it. (It was called **Nehushtan**.)

5737 נחת **nāḥat**, v. [10] [→ 5738, 5741; cf. 9393; Ar 10474]

bend [2], bring down [1], come down [1], come [1], descend [1], go down [1], impresses [1], level [1], pierced [+928] [1]

2Sa 22: 35 [D] my hands for battle; my arms *can* **bend** a bow of bronze.
Job 17: 16 [A] the gates of death? *Will we* **descend** together into the dust?"
21: 13 [A] their years in prosperity and **go down** *to* the grave in peace.
Ps 18: 34 [18:35] [D] for battle; my arms *can* **bend** a bow of bronze.
38: 2 [38:3] [C] For your arrows *have* **pierced** [+928] me, and your
38: 2 [38:3] [A] pierced me, and your hand *has* **come down** upon me.
65: 10 [65:11] [D] You drench its furrows and **level** its ridges;
Pr 17: 10 [A] A rebuke **impresses** a man of discernment more than a
Jer 21: 13 [A] the LORD—you who say, "Who *can* **come** against us?
Joel 3: 11 [4:11] [G] **Bring down** your warriors, O LORD!

5738 ¹נַחַת **naḥat¹**, n.[m.]. [1] [√ 5737]

coming down [1]

Isa 30: 30 and will make them see his arm **coming down** with raging anger

5739 ²נַחַת **naḥat²**, n.f. & m. [6] [→ 5740; cf. 5663]

rest [2], comfort [1], peace [1], quiet [1], tranquillity [1]

Job 36: 16 to the **comfort** *of* your table laden with choice food.
Pr 29: 9 court with a fool, the fool rages and scoffs, and there is no **peace**.
Ecc 4: 6 Better one handful with **tranquillity** than two handfuls with toil
6: 5 the sun or knew anything, it has more **rest** than does that man—
9: 17 The **quiet** words of the wise are more to be heeded than the shouts
Isa 30: 15 "In repentance and **rest** is your salvation, in quietness and trust is

5740 ³נַחַת **naḥat³**, n.pr.m. [5] [√ 5739; cf. 5663]

Nahath [5]

Ge 36: 13 The sons of Reuel: **Nahath**, Zerah, Shammah and Mizzah.
36: 17 Esau's son Reuel: Chiefs **Nahath**, Zerah, Shammah and Mizzah.
1Ch 1: 37 The sons of Reuel: **Nahath**, Zerah, Shammah and Mizzah.
6: 26 [6:11] Elkanah his son, Zophai his son, **Nahath** his son,
2Ch 31: 13 Jehiel, Azaziah, **Nahath**, Asahel, Jerimoth, Jozabad, Eliel,

5741 נָחֵת **nāḥēt**, a. [1] [√ 5737]

going down [1]

2Ki 6: 9 passing that place, because the Arameans are **going down** there."

5742 נָטָה **nāṭâ**, v. [215] [→ 4750, 4751, 4752, 4753, 4754, 4755; cf. 352]

stretch out [22], stretched out [20], outstretched [18], turn [12], pitched [10], turned [7], give ear [+265] [6], pay attention [+265+906] [6], stretches out [5], upraised [5], deprive [4], deny [3], pervert [3], spread out [3], took aside [3], turn aside [3], turned away [3], deprive of justice [2], evening [2], extended [2], held out [2], listen [+265] [2], parted [2], pitch [2], spread [2], swerve [2], *untranslated* [1], afternoon [+2021+3427] [1], applying [1], be stretched out [1], bend [1], bent down [1], brandishes [1], conspired [1], did^s this [+2257+3338] [1], directs [1], extend [1], get back on [1], get off [1], giving [1], go ahead [1], go forward [1], grow long [1], hear [+265] [1], hold out [1], inclined [+4213] [1], kept away [1], lay [1], lead [1], leaning [1], led astray [+906+4213] [1], led astray [1], let be drawn [1], let down [1], lie down [1], listen closely [+265] [1], listen well [+265] [1], measures [1], misleads [1], outspread [1], paid any attention [+265+906+4200+9048] [1], paid attention [+265+906] [1], part [1], pay attention [+265] [1], perverted [1], plot [1], pushed [1], raised [1], set [1], shakes [1], showed [1], shown [1], siding [1], slipped [1], spreads out [1], stay [1], stays only a night [+4328] [1], strayed [1], stretch wide [1], stretched [1], throw [1], thrust [1], turn away [1], turned aside [1], turning aside [1], turning [1], went over [1], withholds [1], won over [1], yield [1]

Ge 12: 8 [A] went on toward the hills east of Bethel and **pitched** his tent,
24: 14 [G] 'Please **let down** your jar that I may have a drink,' and she
26: 25 [A] There *he* **pitched** his tent, and there his servants dug a well.
33: 19 [A] of Shechem, the plot of ground where *he* **pitched** his tent.
35: 21 [A] moved on again and **pitched** his tent beyond Migdal Eder.
38: 1 [A] and went down *to* **stay** with a man of Adullam named Hirah.
38: 16 [A] *he* **went over** to her by the roadside and said, "Come now,
39: 21 [A] *he* **showed** him kindness and granted him favor in the eyes of
49: 15 [A] *he will* **bend** his shoulder to the burden and submit to forced
Ex 6: 6 [B] I will redeem you with an **outstretched** arm and with mighty
7: 5 [A] I am the LORD when I **stretch out** my hand against Egypt
7: 19 [A] and **stretch out** your hand over the waters of Egypt—
8: 5 [8:1] [A] '**Stretch out** your hand with your staff over the
8: 6 [8:2] [A] So Aaron **stretched out** his hand over the waters of
8: 16 [8:12] [A] '**Stretch out** your staff and strike the dust of the
8: 17 [8:13] [A] when Aaron **stretched out** his hand with the staff
9: 22 [A] "**Stretch out** your hand toward the sky so that hail will fall
9: 23 [A] When Moses **stretched out** his staff toward the sky,
10: 12 [A] "**Stretch out** your hand over Egypt so that locusts will
10: 13 [A] So Moses **stretched out** his staff over Egypt,
10: 21 [A] "**Stretch out** your hand toward the sky so that darkness will
10: 22 [A] So Moses **stretched out** his hand toward the sky, and total
14: 16 [A] and **stretch out** your hand over the sea to divide the water
14: 21 [A] Moses **stretched out** his hand over the sea, and all that night
14: 26 [A] "**Stretch out** your hand over the sea so that the waters may
14: 27 [A] Moses **stretched out** his hand over the sea, and at daybreak
15: 12 [A] *You* **stretched out** your right hand and the earth swallowed
23: 2 [G] in a lawsuit, *do* not **pervert** justice by siding with the crowd,
23: 2 [A] in a lawsuit, do not pervert justice by **siding** with the crowd,
23: 6 [G] "*Do* not **deny** justice to your poor people in their lawsuits.
33: 7 [A] take a tent and **pitch** it outside the camp some distance away,
Nu 20: 17 [A] will travel along the king's highway and not **turn** *to* the right
20: 21 [A] go through their territory, Israel **turned** away from them.
21: 15 [A] the slopes of the ravines that **lead** to the site of Ar and lie
21: 22 [A] *We will* not **turn aside** into any field or vineyard, or drink
22: 23 [A] drawn sword in his hand, she **turned** off the road into a field.
22: 23 [G] into a field. Balaam beat her to **get** her **back on** the road.
22: 26 [A] stood in a narrow place where there was no room to **turn**,
22: 33 [A] donkey saw me and **turned away** from me these three times.
22: 33 [A] If *she had* not **turned away**, I would certainly have killed
24: 6 [C] "Like valleys *they* **spread out**, like gardens beside a river,
Dt 4: 34 [B] by war, by a mighty hand and an **outstretched** arm, or by
5: 15 [B] out of there with a mighty hand and an **outstretched** arm.
7: 19 [B] and wonders, the mighty hand and **outstretched** arm,
9: 29 [B] out by your great power and your **outstretched** arm."
11: 2 [B] his majesty, his mighty hand, his **outstretched** arm;

Dt 16: 19 [G] *Do* not **pervert** justice or show partiality. Do not accept a
24: 17 [G] *Do* not **deprive** the alien or the fatherless *of* justice, or take
26: 8 [B] us out of Egypt with a mighty hand and an **outstretched** arm,
27: 19 [G] "Cursed is the man *who* **withholds** justice from the alien,
Jos 8: 18 [A] "**Hold out** toward Ai the javelin that is in your hand,
8: 18 [A] deliver the city." So Joshua **held out** his javelin toward Ai.
8: 19 [A] As soon as *he* **did**[s] [+2257+3338] **this**, the men in the
8: 26 [A] For Joshua did not draw back the hand that **held out** his
24: 23 [G] that are among you and **yield** your hearts to the LORD,
Jdg 4: 11 [A] **pitched** his tent by the great tree in Zaanannim near Kedesh.
9: 3 [A] they *were* **inclined** [+4213] to follow Abimelech, for they
16: 30 [A] *he* **pushed** with all his might, and down came the temple on
19: 8 [A] "Refresh yourself. Wait till **afternoon** [+2021+3427]!"
1Sa 8: 3 [A] *They* **turned aside** after dishonest gain and accepted bribes
8: 3 [G] dishonest gain and accepted bribes and **perverted** justice.
14: 7 [A] "**Go ahead**; I am with you heart and soul."
2Sa 2: 19 [A] **turning** neither to the right nor to the left as he pursued him.
2: 21 [A] Abner said to him, "**Turn aside** to the right or to the left;
3: 27 [G] returned to Hebron, Joab **took** him **aside** into the gateway,
6: 10 [G] he **took** it **aside** *to* the house of Obed-Edom the Gittite.
6: 17 [A] set it in its place inside the tent that David *had* **pitched** for it,
16: 22 [G] So *they* **pitched** a tent for Absalom on the roof, and he lay
19: 14 [19:15] [G] *He* **won over** the hearts of all the men of Judah as
21: 10 [G] Aiah took sackcloth and **spread** it **out** for herself on a rock.
22: 10 [A] *He* **parted** the heavens and came down; dark clouds were
1Ki 2: 28 [A] who *had* **conspired** with Adonijah though not with Absalom,
2: 28 [A] who had conspired with Adonijah though not **[RPH]** with
8: 42 [B] and your mighty hand and your **outstretched** arm—
8: 58 [G] *May he* **turn** our hearts to him, to walk in all his ways and to
11: 2 [G] because *they will* surely **turn** your hearts after their gods."
11: 3 [G] and his wives **led** him **astray** [+906+4213].
11: 4 [G] grew old, his wives **turned** his heart after other gods,
11: 9 [A] because his heart *had* **turned away** from the LORD,
2Ki 17: 36 [B] up out of Egypt with mighty power and **outstretched** arm,
19: 16 [G] **Give ear** [+265], O LORD, and hear; open your eyes,
20: 10 [A] "It is a simple matter for the shadow to **go forward** ten
21: 13 [A] *I will* **stretch out** over Jerusalem the measuring line used
1Ch 13: 13 [G] *he* **took** it **aside** to the house of Obed-Edom the Gittite.
15: 1 [A] prepared a place for the ark of God and **pitched** a tent for it.
16: 1 [A] and set it inside the tent that David *had* **pitched** for it,
21: 10 [A] is what the LORD says: I *am* **giving** you three options.
21: 16 [B] with a drawn sword in his hand **extended** over Jerusalem.
2Ch 1: 4 [A] for it, because *he had* **pitched** a tent for it in Jerusalem.
6: 32 [B] and your mighty hand and your **outstretched** arm—
Ezr 7: 28 [G] and *who has* **extended** his good favor to me before the king
9: 9 [G] *He has* **shown** us kindness in the sight of the kings of Persia:
Job 9: 8 [A] He alone **stretches out** the heavens and treads on the waves
15: 25 [A] because *he* **shakes** his fist at God and vaunts himself against
15: 29 [A] not endure, nor *will* his possessions **spread** over the land.
23: 11 [G] his steps; I have kept to his way without **turning aside**.
24: 4 [G] *They* **thrust** the needy from the path and force all the poor of
26: 7 [A] *He* **spreads out** the northern ⌞skies⌟ over empty space;
31: 7 [A] if my steps *have* **turned** from the path, if my heart has been
36: 18 [G] entices you by riches; *do* not *let* a large bribe **turn** you **aside**.
38: 5 [A] Surely you know! Who **stretched** a measuring line across it?
Ps 17: 6 [G] for you will answer me; **give ear** [+265] to me and hear my
17: 11 [A] surround me, with eyes alert, to **throw** me to the ground.
18: 9 [18:10] [A] *He* **parted** the heavens and came down; dark clouds
21: 11 [21:12] [A] Though *they* **plot** evil against you and devise
27: 9 [G] your face from me, *do* not **turn** your servant **away** in anger;
31: 2 [31:3] [G] **Turn** your ear to me, come quickly to my rescue;
40: 1 [40:2] [A] for the LORD; *he* **turned** to me and heard my cry.
44: 18 [44:19] [A] our feet *had* not **strayed** from your path.
45: 10 [45:11] [G] Listen, O daughter, consider and **give ear** [+265]:
49: 4 [49:5] [G] *I will* **turn** my ear to a proverb; with the harp I will
62: 3 [62:4] [B] him down—this **leaning** wall, this tottering fence?
71: 2 [G] me in your righteousness; **turn** your ear to me and save me.
73: 2 [A] as for me, my feet *had* almost **slipped**; I had nearly lost my
78: 1 [G] hear my teaching; **listen** [+265] to the words of my mouth.
86: 1 [G] **Hear** [+265], O LORD, and answer me, for I am poor
88: 2 [88:3] [G] my prayer come before you; **turn** your ear to my cry.
102: 2 [102:3] [G] **Turn** your ear to me; when I call, answer me
102: 11 [102:12] [B] My days are like the **evening** shadow; I wither
104: 2 [A] as with a garment; *he* **stretches out** the heavens like a tent
109: 23 [A] I fade away like an **evening** shadow; I am shaken off like a
116: 2 [G] Because *he* **turned** his ear to me, I will call on him as long as
119: 36 [G] **Turn** my heart toward your statutes and not toward selfish
119: 51 [A] mock me without restraint, but *I do* not **turn** from your law.
119:112 [A] My heart *is* **set** *on* keeping your decrees to the very end.
119:157 [A] who persecute me, but *I have* not **turned** from your statutes.
125: 5 [G] those *who* **turn** *to* crooked ways the LORD will banish
136: 12 [B] with a mighty hand and **outstretched** arm; *His love*
141: 4 [G] **Let** not my heart **be drawn** to what is evil, to take part in
144: 5 [G] **Part** your heavens, O LORD, and come down; touch the
Pr 1: 24 [A] and no one gave heed *when I* **stretched out** my hand,
2: 2 [G] ear to wisdom and **applying** your heart to understanding,
4: 5 [A] do not forget my words or **swerve** from them.
4: 20 [G] pay attention to what I say; **listen closely** [+265] to my
4: 27 [A] *Do* not **swerve** *to* the right or the left; keep your foot from
5: 1 [G] pay attention to my wisdom, **listen well** [+265] to my words
5: 13 [G] not obey my teachers or **listen** [+265] to my instructors.
7: 21 [G] With persuasive words *she* **led** him **astray**; she seduced him
17: 23 [G] A wicked man accepts a bribe in secret to **pervert** the course
18: 5 [G] be partial to the wicked or to **deprive** the innocent of justice.
21: 1 [G] *he* **directs** it like a watercourse wherever he pleases.
22: 17 [G] **Pay attention** [+265] and listen to the sayings of the wise;
Isa 3: 16 [B] walking along with **outstretched** necks, flirting with their
5: 25 [A] his people; his hand *is* **raised** and he strikes them down.
5: 25 [B] his anger is not turned away, his hand *is* still **upraised**.
8: 8 [H] Its **outspread** wings will cover the breadth of your land,
9: 12 [9:11] [B] anger is not turned away, his hand *is* still **upraised**.
9: 17 [9:16] [B] anger is not turned away, his hand *is* still **upraised**.
9: 21 [9:20] [B] anger is not turned away, his hand *is* still **upraised**.
10: 2 [G] to **deprive** the poor of their rights and withhold justice from
10: 4 [B] his anger is not turned away, his hand *is* still **upraised**.
14: 26 [B] whole world; this is the hand **stretched out** over all nations.
14: 27 [B] His hand *is* **stretched out**, and who can turn it back?
23: 11 [A] The LORD *has* **stretched out** his hand over the sea
29: 21 [G] and with false testimony **deprive** the innocent of justice.
30: 11 [G] Leave this way, **get off** this path, and stop confronting us
31: 3 [G] When the LORD **stretches out** his hand, he who helps will
34: 11 [A] God *will* **stretch out** over Edom the measuring line of chaos
37: 17 [G] **Give ear** [+265], O LORD, and hear; open your eyes,
40: 22 [A] He **stretches out** the heavens like a canopy, and spreads
42: 5 [A] he who created the heavens and **stretched** them **out**,
44: 13 [A] The carpenter **measures** *with* a line and makes an outline
44: 20 [G] He feeds on ashes, a deluded heart **misleads** him; he cannot
44: 24 [A] has made all things, *who* alone **stretched out** the heavens,
45: 12 [A] My own hands **stretched out** the heavens; I marshaled their
51: 13 [A] *who* **stretched out** the heavens and laid the foundations of
54: 2 [G] your tent, **stretch** your tent curtains **wide**, do not hold back;
55: 3 [G] **Give ear** [+265] and come to me; hear me, that your soul
66: 12 [A] "I *will* **extend** peace to her like a river, and the wealth of
Jer 5: 25 [G] Your wrongdoings *have* **kept** these **away**; your sins have
6: 4 [C] daylight is fading, and the shadows of evening **grow long**.
6: 12 [G] when *I* **stretch out** my hand against those who live in the
7: 24 [G] But they did not listen or **pay attention** [+265+906]; instead,
7: 26 [G] But they did not listen to me or **pay attention** [+265+906].
10: 12 [A] and **stretched out** the heavens by his understanding.
10: 20 [A] no one is left now *to* **pitch** my tent or to set up my shelter.
11: 8 [G] But they did not listen or **pay attention** [+265+906]; instead,
14: 8 [A] in the land, like a traveler *who* **stays only a night** [+4328]?
15: 6 [G] So *I will* **lay** hands on you and destroy you; I can no longer
17: 23 [G] Yet they did not listen or **pay attention** [+265+906]; they
21: 5 [B] I myself will fight against you with an **outstretched** hand
25: 4 [G] not listened or **paid any attention** [+265+906+4200+9048].
27: 5 [B] and **outstretched** arm I made the earth and its people
32: 17 [B] and the earth by your great power and **outstretched** arm.
32: 21 [B] by a mighty hand and an **outstretched** arm and with great
34: 14 [G] did not listen to me or **pay attention** [+265+906] to me.
35: 15 [G] *you have* not **paid attention** [+265+906] or listened to me.
43: 10 [A] buried here; *he will* **spread** his royal canopy above them.
44: 5 [G] they did not listen or **pay attention** [+265+906]; they did not
51: 15 [A] and **stretched out** the heavens by his understanding.
51: 25 [A] "*I will* **stretch out** my hand against you, roll you off the
La 2: 8 [A] *He* **stretched out** a measuring line and did not withhold his
3: 35 [G] to **deny** a man his rights before the Most High,
Eze 1: 22 [B] **Spread out** above the heads of the living creatures was what
6: 14 [A] *I will* **stretch out** my hand against them and make the land a
14: 9 [A] *I will* **stretch out** my hand against him and destroy him from
14: 13 [A] and *I* **stretch out** my hand against it to cut off its food supply
16: 27 [A] So *I* **stretched out** my hand against you and reduced your
20: 33 [B] and an **outstretched** arm and with outpoured wrath.
20: 34 [B] with a mighty hand and an **outstretched** arm and with
25: 7 [A] therefore I *will* **stretch out** my hand against you and give
25: 13 [A] *I will* **stretch out** my hand against Edom and kill its men
25: 16 [A] I *am about to* **stretch out** my hand against the Philistines,
30: 25 [A] of the king of Babylon and *he* **brandishes** it against Egypt.
35: 3 [A] *I will* **stretch out** my hand against you and make you a
Da 9: 18 [G] **Give ear** [+265], O God, and hear; open your eyes and see
Hos 11: 4 [A] *I* lifted the yoke from their neck and **bent down** to feed
Am 2: 7 [G] the dust of the ground and **deny** justice to the oppressed.
2: 8 [G] *They* **lie down** beside every altar on garments taken in
5: 12 [G] take bribes and *you* **deprive** the poor **of justice** in the courts.
Zep 1: 4 [A] "*I will* **stretch out** my hand against Judah and against all
2: 13 [A] *He will* **stretch out** his hand against the north and destroy
Zec 1: 16 [C] the measuring line *will* **be stretched out** over Jerusalem,'
12: 1 [A] The LORD, *who* **stretches out** the heavens, who lays the

[F] Hitpael (hitpoel, hitpoal, hitpolel, hitpolal, hitpalel, hitpalal, hitpalpel, hitpalpal, hotpael, hotpaal) [G] Hiphil (hiphtil) [H] Hophal [I] Hishtaphel

Mal 3: 5 [G] the widows and the fatherless, and **deprive** aliens **of justice**,

5743 נְטוֹפָתִי *n*ᵉ*ṭôpātî*, a.g. [11] [√ 5756; cf. 5752]
Netophathite [8], Netophathites [3]

2Sa 23:28 Zalmon the Ahohite, Maharai the **Netophathite**,
23:29 Heled son of Baanah the **Netophathite**, Ithai son of Ribai from
2Ki 25:23 son of Kareah, Seraiah son of Tanhumeth the **Netophathite**,
1Ch 2:54 Bethlehem, the **Netophathites**, Atroth Beth Joab, half the
9:16 the son of Elkanah, who lived in the villages of the **Netophathites**.
11:30 Maharai the **Netophathite**, Heled son of Baanah the Netophathite,
11:30 Maharai the Netophathite, Heled son of Baanah the **Netophathite**,
27:13 for the tenth month, was Maharai the **Netophathite**, a Zerahite.
27:15 The twelfth, for the twelfth month, was Heldai the **Netophathite**,
Ne 12:28 region around Jerusalem—from the villages of the **Netophathites**,
Jer 40: 8 Seraiah son of Tanhumeth, the sons of Ephai the **Netophathite**,

5744 נָטִיל *nāṭîl*, a. [1] [√ 5747]
who trade with [1]

Zep 1:11 will be wiped out, all **who trade with** silver will be ruined.

5745 נָטִיעַ *nāṭîa'*, n.[m.]. [1] [√ 5749]
plants [1]

Ps 144:12 Then our sons in their youth will be like well-nurtured **plants**,

5746 נְטִישׁוֹת *n*ᵉ*ṭîšôt*, n.f. [3] [√ 5759]
branches [2], spreading branches [1]

Isa 18: 5 and cut down and take away the **spreading branches**.
Jer 5:10 Strip off her **branches**, for these people do not belong to the
48:32 Your **branches** spread as far as the sea; they reached as far as the

5747 נָטַל *nāṭal*, v. [4] [→ 5744, 5748; Ar 10475]
giving [1], laid [1], lifted up [1], weighs [1]

2Sa 24:12 [A] 'This is what the LORD says: I am **giving** you three options.
Isa 40:15 [A] *he* **weighs** the islands as though they were fine dust.
63: 9 [D] *he* **lifted** them **up** and carried them all the days of old.
La 3:28 [A] him sit alone in silence, for the LORD *has* **laid** it on him.

5748 נֵטֶל *nēṭel*, n.[m.]. [1] [√ 5747]
burden [1]

Pr 27: 3 Stone is heavy and sand a **burden**, but provocation by a fool is

5749 נָטַע *nāṭa'*, v. [58] [→ 4760, 5745, 5750, 5751]
plant [28], planted [19], *untranslated* [1], are planted [1], farmers [1], firmly embedded [1], implanted [1], pitch [1], plants [1], replanted [1], set in place [1], set out [1], set up [1]

Ge 2: 8 [A] Now the LORD God *had* **planted** a garden in the east,
9:20 [A] Noah, a man of the soil, proceeded *to* **plant** a vineyard.
21:33 [A] Abraham **planted** a tamarisk tree in Beersheba, and there he
Ex 15:17 [A] and **plant** them on the mountain of your inheritance—
Lev 19:23 [A] " 'When you enter the land and **plant** any kind of fruit tree,
Nu 24: 6 [A] gardens beside a river, like aloes **planted** *by* the LORD,
Dt 6:11 [A] not dig, and vineyards and olive groves *you did* not **plant**—
16:21 [A] *Do* not **set up** any wooden Asherah pole beside the altar you
20: 6 [A] *Has* anyone **planted** a vineyard and not begun to enjoy it?
28:30 [A] *You will* **plant** a vineyard, but you will not even begin to
28:39 [A] *You will* **plant** vineyards and cultivate them but you will not
Jos 24:13 [A] eat from vineyards and olive groves that you *did* not **plant**.'
2Sa 7:10 [A] *will* **plant** them so that they can have a home of their own
2Ki 19:29 [A] third year sow and reap, **plant** vineyards and eat their fruit.
1Ch 17: 9 [A] *will* **plant** them so that they can have a home of their own
Ps 44: 2 [44:3] [A] you drove out the nations and **planted** our fathers;
80: 8 [80:9] [A] of Egypt; you drove out the nations and **planted** it.
80:15 [80:16] [A] the root your right hand *has* **planted**, the son you
94: 9 [A] Does he *who* **implanted** the ear not hear? Does he who
104:16 [A] are well watered, the cedars of Lebanon that *he* **planted**.
107:37 [A] and **planted** vineyards that yielded a fruitful harvest;
Pr 31:16 [A] a field and buys it; out of her earnings *she* **plants** a vineyard.
Ecc 2: 4 [A] I built houses for myself and **planted** vineyards.
2: 5 [A] and parks and **planted** all kinds of fruit trees in them.
3: 2 [A] and a time to die, a time to **plant** and a time to uproot,
3: 2 [B] a time to die, a time to plant and a time to uproot, **[RPH]**
12:11 [B] their collected sayings like **firmly embedded** nails—
Isa 5: 2 [A] cleared it of stones and **planted** it with the choicest vines.
17:10 [A] *though you* **set out** the finest plants and plant imported
37:30 [A] third year sow and reap, **plant** vineyards and eat their fruit.
40:24 [C] No sooner **are** *they* **planted**, no sooner are they sown, no
44:14 [A] of the forest, or **planted** a pine, and the rain made it grow.
51:16 [A] I *who* **set** the heavens **in place**, who laid the foundations of
65:21 [A] dwell in them; *they will* **plant** vineyards and eat their fruit.
65:22 [A] build houses and others live in them, or **plant** and others eat.
Jer 1:10 [A] tear down, to destroy and overthrow, to build and to **plant**."
2:21 [A] I *had* **planted** you like a choice vine of sound and reliable
11:17 [A] The LORD Almighty, who **planted** you, has decreed
12: 2 [A] *You have* **planted** them, and they have taken root; they grow
18: 9 [A] that a nation or kingdom is to be built up and **planted**,
24: 6 [A] not tear them down; *I will* **plant** them and not uproot them.
29: 5 [A] and settle down; **plant** gardens and eat what they produce.
29:28 [A] and settle down; **plant** gardens and eat what they produce.' "
31: 5 [A] Again *you will* **plant** vineyards on the hills of Samaria;
31: 5 [A] of Samaria; the **farmers** will plant them and enjoy their fruit.
31: 5 [A] of Samaria; the farmers *will* **plant** them and enjoy their fruit.
31:28 [A] so I will watch over them to build and to **plant**,"
32:41 [A] and *will* assuredly **plant** them in this land with all my heart
35: 7 [A] you must never build houses, sow seed or **plant** vineyards;
42:10 [A] *I will* **plant** you and not uproot you, for I am grieved over
45: 4 [A] overthrow what I have built and uproot what *I have* **planted**,
Eze 28:26 [A] there in safety and will build houses and **plant** vineyards;
36:36 [A] what was destroyed and *have* **replanted** what was desolate.
Da 11:45 [A] *He will* **pitch** his royal tents between the seas at the beautiful
Am 5:11 [A] though *you have* **planted** lush vineyards, you will not drink
9:14 [A] *They will* **plant** vineyards and drink their wine; they will
9:15 [A] *I will* **plant** Israel in their own land, never again to be
Zep 1:13 [A] in them; *they will* **plant** vineyards but not drink the wine.

5750 נֶטַע *neṭa'*, n.[m.]. [4] [√ 5749]
garden [1], plant [1], plants [1], set out [1]

Job 14: 9 at the scent of water it will bud and put forth shoots like a **plant**.
Isa 5: 7 house of Israel, and the men of Judah are the **garden** *of* his delight.
17:10 though you set out the finest **plants** and plant imported vines,
17:11 though on the day you **set** them **out**, you make them grow,

5751 נְטָעִים *n*ᵉ*ṭā'îm*, n.pr.loc. [1] [√ 5749]
Netaim [1]

1Ch 4:23 They were the potters who lived at **Netaim** and Gederah;

5752 נָטַף *nāṭap*, v. [18] [→ 3213, 5743, 5753, 5754, 5755, 5756]
drip [3], prophesy [3], preach [2], dripped [1], dripping [1], drop [1], fell gently [1], poured down rain [1], poured down [1], poured [1], preaching [1], prophet [1], prophets say [1]

Jdg 5: 4 [A] the earth shook, the heavens **poured**, the clouds poured down
5: 4 [A] the heavens poured, the clouds **poured down** water.
Job 29:22 [A] they spoke no more; my words **fell gently** on their ears.
Ps 68: 8 [68:9] [A] the heavens **poured down rain**, before God,
Pr 5: 3 [A] For the lips of an adulteress **drip** honey, and her speech is
SS 4:11 [A] Your lips **drop** sweetness as the honeycomb, my bride; milk
5: 5 [A] to open for my lover, and my hands **dripped** *with* myrrh,
5:13 [A] His lips are like lilies **dripping** *with* myrrh.
Eze 20:46 [21:2] [G] **preach** against the south and prophesy against the
21: 2 [21:7] [G] against Jerusalem and **preach** against the sanctuary.
Joel 3:18 [4:18] [A] "In that day the mountains *will* **drip** new wine,
Am 7:16 [G] against Israel, and stop **preaching** against the house of Isaac.'
9:13 [G] New wine *will* **drip** *from* the mountains and flow from all
Mic 2: 6 [G] "*Do* not **prophesy**," their prophets say. "Do not prophesy
2: 6 [G] "Do not prophesy," their **prophets say**. "Do not prophesy
2: 6 [G] "*Do* not **prophesy** about these things; disgrace will not
2:11 [G] and says, '*I will* **prophesy** for you plenty of wine and beer,'
2:11 [G] and beer,' he would be just the **prophet** *for* this people!

5753 נָטָף *nāṭāp*, n.[m.]. [1] [√ 5752]
gum resin [1]

Ex 30:34 **gum resin**, onycha and galbanum—and pure frankincense,

5754 נֶטֶף *neṭep*, n.m. [1] [√ 5752]
drops [1]

Job 36:27 "He draws up the **drops** *of* water, which distill as rain to the

5755 נְטִפָה *n*ᵉ*ṭipâ*, n.[f.]. [2] [√ 5752]
earrings [1], pendants [1]

Jdg 8:26 the **pendants** and the purple garments worn by the kings of Midian
Isa 3:19 the **earrings** and bracelets and veils,

5756 נְטֹפָה *n*ᵉ*ṭōpâ*, n.pr.loc. [2] [√ 5743; cf. 5752]
Netophah [2]

Ezr 2:22 of **Netophah** 56
Ne 7:26 the men of Bethlehem and **Netophah** 188

5757 ¹נָטַר ***nāṭar***[1], v. [9] [→ 4766; cf. 5758, 5915]

angry [2], bear a grudge against [1], harbor anger [1], maintains wrath [1], neglected [+4202] [1], take care of [1], tenants [1], tend [1]

Lev 19: 18 [A] seek revenge or **bear a grudge against** one of your people,
Ps 103: 9 [A] not always accuse, nor *will he* **harbor** *his* **anger** forever;
SS 1: 6 [A] were angry with me and made me **take care of** the vineyards;
1: 6 [A] the vineyards; my own vineyard *I have* **neglected** [+4202].
8: 11 [A] a vineyard in Baal Hamon; he let out his vineyard to **tenants**.
8: 12 [A] and two hundred are for *those who* **tend** its fruit.
Jer 3: 5 [A] *will you* always *be* **angry**? Will your wrath continue
3: 12 [A] declares the LORD, '*I will* not *be* **angry** forever.
Na 1: 2 [A] on his foes and **maintains** *his* **wrath** against his enemies.

5758 ²נָטַר ***nāṭar***[2], v. Not used in NIV/BHS [cf. 5757]

5759 נָטַשׁ ***nāṭaš***, v. [40] [→ 5746]

abandoned [5], forsake [5], left [4], leave [3], reject [3], spread out [3], abandon [1], be abandoned [1], brought down [1], cast out [1], deserted [1], drawn [1], drop [1], forgo [1], hangs loose [1], let [1], rejected [1], scattered [1], spread [1], spreading out [1], stopped thinking [1], throw [1], unused [1]

Ge 31: 28 [A] *You* didn't even **let** me kiss my grandchildren and my
Ex 23: 11 [A] the seventh year let the land lie unplowed and **unused**.
Nu 11: 31 [A] *It* **brought** them **down** all around the camp to about three
Dt 32: 15 [A] *He* **abandoned** the God who made him and rejected the
Jdg 6: 13 [A] now the LORD *has* **abandoned** us and put us into the hand
15: 9 [C] went up and camped in Judah, **spreading out** near Lehi.
1Sa 4: 2 [A] *as* the battle **spread**, Israel was defeated by the Philistines,
10: 2 [A] now your father *has* **stopped thinking** *about* them and is
12: 22 [A] For the sake of his great name the LORD *will* not **reject** his
17: 20 [A] Early in the morning David **left** the flock with a shepherd,
17: 22 [A] David **left** his things with the keeper of supplies, ran to the
17: 28 [A] And with whom *did you* **leave** those few sheep in the desert?
30: 16 [B] **scattered** over the countryside, eating, drinking and reveling
2Sa 5: 18 [C] had come and **spread out** in the Valley of Rephaim;
5: 22 [C] came up and **spread out** in the Valley of Rephaim;
1Ki 8: 57 [A] was with our fathers; may he never leave us nor **forsake** us.
2Ki 21: 14 [A] *I will* **forsake** the remnant of my inheritance and hand them
Ne 10: 31 [10:32] [A] Every seventh year *we will* **forgo** working the land
Ps 27: 9 [A] *Do* not **reject** me or forsake me, O God my Savior.
78: 60 [A] *He* **abandoned** the tabernacle of Shiloh, the tent he had set
94: 14 [A] For the LORD *will* not **reject** his people; he will never
Pr 1: 8 [A] and *do* not **forsake** your mother's teaching.
6: 20 [A] and *do* not **forsake** your mother's teaching.
17: 14 [A] a dam; so **drop** the matter before a dispute breaks out.
Isa 2: 6 [A] *You have* **abandoned** your people, the house of Jacob. They
16: 8 [C] Their shoots **spread out** and went as far as the sea.
21: 15 [B] from the **drawn** sword, from the bent bow and from the heat
32: 14 [E] The fortress *will* **be abandoned**, the noisy city deserted;
33: 23 [C] Your rigging **hangs loose**: The mast is not held secure,
Jer 7: 29 [A] and **abandoned** this generation that is under his wrath.
12: 7 [A] "I will forsake my house, **abandon** my inheritance; I will
15: 6 [A] You *have* **rejected** me," declares the LORD. "You keep on
23: 33 [A] 'What oracle? *I will* **forsake** you, declares the LORD.'
23: 39 [A] **cast** you **out** of my presence along with the city I gave to you
Eze 29: 5 [A] *I will* **leave** you in the desert, you and all the fish of your
31: 12 [A] the most ruthless of foreign nations cut it down and **left** it.
31: 12 [A] nations of the earth came out from under its shade and **left** it.
32: 4 [A] *I will* **throw** you on the land and hurl you on the open field.
Hos 12: 14 [12:15] [A] his Lord *will* **leave** upon him the guilt of his
Am 5: 2 [C] is Virgin Israel, never to rise again, **deserted** in her own land,

5760 נִי ***nî***, n.[m.]. [1] [√ 5631; cf. 5629]

wail [1]

Eze 27: 32 As they **wail** and mourn over you, they will take up a lament

5761 ־ִי ***-nî***, p.com.s.suf. [1308 / 1306] [√ 3276] Not indexed

me [1010], I [203], *untranslated* [43], my [28], us [12], myself [3], mine [+4946] [2], we [2], him [1], how I long for [+4769+5989] [1], I'll [1]

5762 נִיב ***nîb***, n.[m.]. [2] [√ 5649]

it^{s} [1], praise [1]

Isa 57: 19 creating **praise** [K 5650] *on* the lips of the mourners in Israel.
Mal 1: 12 the Lord's table, 'It is defiled,' and of its food, '**It**^{s} is contemptible.'

5763 נֵיבָי ***nêbāy***, n.pr.m. [1] [√ 5651?]

Nebai [1]

Ne 10: 19 [10:20] Hariph, Anathoth, **Nebai**, [K 5651]

5764 נִיד ***nîd***, n.m. [1] [√ 5653]

comfort [1]

Job 16: 5 encourage you; **comfort** *from* my lips would bring you relief.

5765 נִידָה ***nîdâ***, n.f. [1] [√ 5614; cf. 5612]

unclean [1]

La 1: 8 Jerusalem has sinned greatly and so has become **unclean**.

5766 נָיוֹת ***nāyôt***, n.pr.loc. [6] [cf. 5662, 5668]

Naioth [6]

1Sa 19: 18 Then he and Samuel went to **Naioth** [K 5668] and stayed there.
19: 19 Word came to Saul: "David is in **Naioth** [K 5668] at Ramah";
19: 22 and David?" "Over in **Naioth** [K 5668] at Ramah," they said.
19: 23 So Saul went to **Naioth** [K 5668] at Ramah. But the Spirit of God
19: 23 he walked along prophesying until he came to **Naioth**. [K 5668]
20: 1 David fled from **Naioth** [K 5662] at Ramah and went to Jonathan

5767 נִיחֹחַ ***nîḥōaḥ***, n.[m.]. [43] [√ 5663; Ar 10478]

pleasing [39], fragrant incense [+8194] [4]

Ge 8: 21 The LORD smelled the **pleasing** aroma and said in his heart:
Ex 29: 18 It is a burnt offering to the LORD, a **pleasing** aroma, an offering
29: 25 burn them on the altar along with the burnt offering for a **pleasing**
29: 41 a **pleasing** aroma, an offering made to the LORD by fire.
Lev 1: 9 an offering made by fire, an aroma **pleasing** to the LORD.
1: 13 an offering made by fire, an aroma **pleasing** to the LORD.
1: 17 an offering made by fire, an aroma **pleasing** to the LORD.
2: 2 an offering made by fire, an aroma **pleasing** to the LORD.
2: 9 altar as an offering made by fire, an aroma **pleasing** to the LORD.
2: 12 but they are not to be offered on the altar as a **pleasing** aroma.
3: 5 as an offering made by fire, an aroma **pleasing** to the LORD.
3: 16 on the altar as food, an offering made by fire, a **pleasing** aroma.
4: 31 the priest shall burn it on the altar as an aroma **pleasing** to the
6: 15 [6:8] burn the memorial portion on the altar as an aroma **pleasing**
6: 21 [6:14] broken in pieces as an aroma **pleasing** to the LORD.
8: 21 a **pleasing** aroma, an offering made to the LORD by fire,
8: 28 a **pleasing** aroma, an offering made to the LORD by fire.
17: 6 of Meeting and burn the fat as an aroma **pleasing** to the LORD.
23: 13 an offering made to the LORD by fire, a **pleasing** aroma—
23: 18 an offering made by fire, an aroma **pleasing** to the LORD.
26: 31 and I will take no delight in the **pleasing** aroma of your offerings.
Nu 15: 3 from the herd or the flock, as an aroma **pleasing** to the LORD—
15: 7 as a drink offering. Offer it as an aroma **pleasing** to the LORD.
15: 10 will be an offering made by fire, an aroma **pleasing** to the LORD.
15: 13 an offering made by fire as an aroma **pleasing** to the LORD.
15: 14 an offering made by fire as an aroma **pleasing** to the LORD,
15: 24 bull for a burnt offering as an aroma **pleasing** to the LORD,
18: 17 fat as an offering made by fire, an aroma **pleasing** to the LORD.
28: 2 food for my offerings made by fire, as an aroma **pleasing** *to* me.'
28: 6 burnt offering instituted at Mount Sinai as a **pleasing** aroma,
28: 8 This is an offering made by fire, an aroma **pleasing** to the LORD.
28: 13 This is for a burnt offering, a **pleasing** aroma, an offering made to
28: 24 fire every day for seven days as an aroma **pleasing** to the LORD;
28: 27 seven male lambs a year old as an aroma **pleasing** to the LORD.
29: 2 As an aroma **pleasing** to the LORD, prepare a burnt offering of
29: 6 They are offerings made to the LORD by fire—a **pleasing** aroma.
29: 8 Present as an aroma **pleasing** to the LORD a burnt offering of one
29: 13 Present an offering made by fire as an aroma **pleasing** to the
29: 36 Present an offering made by fire as an aroma **pleasing** to the
Eze 6: 13 places where they offered **fragrant incense** [+8194] to all their
16: 19 you to eat—you offered as **fragrant incense** [+8194] before them.
20: 28 presented their **fragrant incense** [+8194] and poured out their
20: 41 I will accept you as **fragrant incense** [+8194] when I bring you

5768 ¹נִין ***nîn***[1], v. Not used in NIV/BHS [→ 5769; cf. 5672]

5769 ²נִין ***nîn***[2], n.[m.]. [3] [√ 5768]

offspring [2], children [1]

Ge 21: 23 will not deal falsely with me or my **children** or my descendants.
Job 18: 19 He has no **offspring** or descendants among his people, no survivor
Isa 14: 22 Babylon her name and survivors, her **offspring** and descendants,"

5770 נִינְוֵה ***nîn^{e}wēh***, n.pr.loc. [17]

Nineveh [16], Ninevites [+408] [1]

Ge 10: 11 he went to Assyria, where he built **Nineveh**, Rehoboth Ir, Calah
10: 12 Resen, which is between **Nineveh** and Calah; that is the great city.
2Ki 19: 36 and withdrew. He returned to **Nineveh** and stayed there.
Isa 37: 37 and withdrew. He returned to **Nineveh** and stayed there.
Jnh 1: 2 "Go to the great city of **Nineveh** and preach against it, because its
3: 2 "Go to the great city of **Nineveh** and proclaim to it the message I

[F] Hitpael (hitpoel, hitpoal, hitpolel, hitpolal, hitpalel, hitpalal, hitpalpel, hitpalpal, hotpael, hotpaal) [G] Hiphil (hiphtil) [H] Hophal [I] Hishtaphel

Jnh 3: 3 Jonah obeyed the word of the LORD and went to **Nineveh**.
3: 3 Now **Nineveh** was a very important city—a visit required three
3: 4 "Forty more days and **Nineveh** will be overturned."
3: 5 The **Ninevites** [+408] believed God. They declared a fast,
3: 6 When the news reached the king of **Nineveh**, he rose from his
3: 7 he issued a proclamation in **Nineveh**: "By the decree of the king
4: 11 **Nineveh** has more than a hundred and twenty thousand people who
Na 1: 1 An oracle concerning **Nineveh**. The book of the vision of Nahum
2: 8 [2:9] **Nineveh** is like a pool, and its water is draining away.
3: 7 All who see you will flee from you and say, '**Nineveh** is in ruins—
Zep 2: 13 leaving **Nineveh** utterly desolate and dry as the desert.

5771 נִיס *nîs*, n.m. *or* v. [0] [√ 5674]

Jer 48: 44 ["Whoever **flees** [K; see Q 5674] from the terror will fall into]

5772 נִיסָן *nîsān*, n.pr. [2]

Nisan [2]

Ne 2: 1 In the month of **Nisan** in the twentieth year of King Artaxerxes,
Est 3: 7 in the first month, the month of **Nisan**, they cast the *pur* (that is,

5773 נִיצוֹץ *nîṣôṣ*, n.[m.]. [1] [√ 5913]

spark [1]

Isa 1: 31 The mighty man will become tinder and his work a **spark**;

5774 נִיר¹ *nîr¹*, v. [2] [→ 5776]

break up [2]

Jer 4: 3 [A] "**Break up** your unplowed ground and do not sow among
Hos 10: 12 [A] fruit of unfailing love, and **break up** your unplowed ground;

5775 נִיר² *nîr²*, n.[m.]. [5] [√ 5944]

lamp [5]

1Ki 11: 36 so that David my servant may always have a **lamp** before me in
15: 4 for David's sake the LORD his God gave him a **lamp** in
2Ki 8: 19 He had promised to maintain a **lamp** for David and his descendants
2Ch 21: 7 He had promised to maintain a **lamp** for him and his descendants
Pr 21: 4 Haughty eyes and a proud heart, the **lamp** *of* the wicked, are sin!

5776 נִיר³ *nîr³*, n.[m.]. [3] [√ 5774]

unplowed ground [2], field [1]

Pr 13: 23 A poor man's **field** may produce abundant food, but injustice
Jer 4: 3 "Break up your **unplowed ground** and do not sow among thorns.
Hos 10: 12 the fruit of unfailing love, and break up your **unplowed ground**;

5777 נָכָא¹ *nākā'¹*, v. [1] [→ 5778, 5779, 5780?; cf. 5782]

were driven out [1]

Job 30: 8 [C] and nameless brood, *they* **were driven out** of the land.

5778 נָכָא² *nākā'²*, a. [1] [√ 5777]

grieve [1]

Isa 16: 7 together for Moab. Lament and **grieve** for the men of Kir Hareseth.

5779 נָכֵא *nākē'*, a. [3] [√ 5777]

crushed [2], crushes [1]

Pr 15: 13 heart makes the face cheerful, but heartache **crushes** the spirit.
17: 22 heart is good medicine, but a **crushed** spirit dries up the bones.
18: 14 spirit sustains him in sickness, but a **crushed** spirit who can bear?

5780 נְכֹאת *nᵉkō't*, n.f. [2] [√ 5777?]

spices [2]

Ge 37: 25 Their camels were loaded with **spices**, balm and myrrh, and they
43: 11 a little balm and a little honey, *some* **spices** and myrrh,

5781 נֶכֶד *neked*, n.[m.]. [3]

descendants [3]

Ge 21: 23 will not deal falsely with me or my children or my **descendants**.
Job 18: 19 He has no offspring or **descendants** among his people, no survivor
Isa 14: 22 Babylon her name and survivors, her offspring and **descendants**,"

5782 נָכָה *nākâ*, v. [499 / 500] [→ 4804, 5783, 5784, 5787; cf. 5777]

struck down [57], killed [39], struck [34], defeated [32], strike [28], put [24], attacked [21], kill [15], attack [13], beat [10], kills [10], strike down [9], inflicted [7], conquered [5], cut down [5], destroy [5], afflict [4], afflicted [4], attacks [4], fought [4], hits [4], murdered [4], slain [4], subdued [4], take [4], *untranslated* [3], assassinated [3], defeat [3], hit [3], killing [3], pin [3], punished [3], put to death [3], slaughtered [3], stabbed [3], strikes [3], beaten [2], broke through [2], conscience-stricken [+906+4213] [2], defeating [2], destroyed [2], flog [2], had beaten [2], indeed defeated [+906+5782] [2], inflict [2], kill [+5883] [2], must certainly put [+906+5782] [2], overpowered [2], punish [2], slapped [2], slaughtering [2], strike together [2], striking down [2], striking [2], struck [+5782] [2], takes life [+5883] [2], victory [2], were destroyed [2], wounded [2], annihilate [1], assailant [1], assassinated [+906+906+906+2256+4637] [1], assassins [1], attacked viciously [+906+3751+6584+8797] [1], attackers [1], be beaten [1], be struck down [1], beat down [1], beating [1], beats [1], being beaten [1], blazed [1], blighted [1], blind [+928+2021+6427] [1], break up [1], chewed [1], clapped [1], conquers [1], dealt [1], destroyed [+1524+4394+4804] [1], devastated [+1524+4394+4804] [1], drove [1], executed [+906+2256+4637] [1], executed [1], fall [1], fallen [1], fell upon [1], flogged [+4804] [1], give lashes [1], had executed [+906+2256+4637] [1], had struck down [1], harm [1], have flogged [1], him[s] [+2021] [1], hitting [1], inflicted casualties [1], injured [1], is blighted [1], is struck [1], killed [+4637] [1], killed [+8357] [1], killed [+906+2995+4200+7023] [1], killed off [1], kills [+2256+4637 +5883] [1], lashes [1], overthrow [1], person[s] [1], plunge [1], plunged [1], putting to death [1], putting to rout [1], routed [1], sacked [1], send down [1], shot [1], slay [1], smash [1], smitten [1], strikes down [1], strikes the blow [1], struck down [+928+4804] [1], struck the blow [1], tear down [1], thrust [1], was killed [1], was put to death [1], were afflicted [1], were beaten [1], wound [1], wounds was given [1]

Ge 4: 15 [G] mark on Cain so that no one who found him *would* **kill** him.
8: 21 [G] never again *will I* **destroy** all living creatures, as I have done.
14: 5 [G] **defeated** the Rephaites in Ashteroth Karnaim, the Zuzites in
14: 7 [G] *they* **conquered** the whole territory of the Amalekites, as well
14: 15 [G] Abram divided his men to attack them and *he* **routed** them,
14: 17 [G] After Abram returned from **defeating** Kedorlaomer and the
19: 11 [G] Then *they* **struck** the men who were at the door of the house,
32: 8 [32:9] [G] He thought, "If Esau comes and **attacks** one group,
32: 11 [32:12] [G] for I am afraid he will come and **attack** me,
34: 30 [G] if they join forces against me and **attack** me, I and my
36: 35 [G] son of Bedad, who **defeated** Midian in the country of Moab,
37: 21 [G] him from their hands. "*Let's* not **take** his life," he said.
Ex 2: 11 [G] He saw an Egyptian **beating** a Hebrew, one of his own
2: 12 [G] no one, *he* **killed** the Egyptian and hid him in the sand.
2: 13 [G] in the wrong, "Why *are you* **hitting** your fellow Hebrew?"
3: 20 [G] **strike** the Egyptians with all the wonders that I will perform
5: 14 [H] foremen appointed by Pharaoh's slave drivers **were beaten**
5: 16 [H] Your servants *are* **being beaten**, but the fault is with your
7: 17 [G] With the staff that is in my hand I *will* **strike** the water of the
7: 20 [G] of Pharaoh and his officials and **struck** the water of the Nile,
7: 25 [G] Seven days passed after the LORD **struck** the Nile.
8: 16 [8:12] [G] out your staff and **strike** the dust of the ground,'
8: 17 [8:13] [G] hand with the staff and **struck** the dust of the ground,
9: 15 [G] **struck** you and your people with a plague that would have
9: 25 [G] Throughout Egypt hail **struck** everything in the fields—both
9: 25 [G] it **beat down** everything growing in the fields and stripped
9: 31 [E] (The flax and barley **were destroyed**, since the barley had
9: 32 [E] The wheat and spelt, however, **were** not **destroyed**,
12: 12 [G] I will pass through Egypt and **strike down** every firstborn—
12: 13 [G] No destructive plague will touch you when I **strike** Egypt.
12: 29 [G] At midnight the LORD **struck down** all the firstborn in
17: 5 [G] take in your hand the staff with which *you* **struck** the Nile,
17: 6 [G] **Strike** the rock, and water will come out of it for the people
21: 12 [G] "*Anyone who* **strikes** a man and kills him shall surely be put
21: 15 [G] "*Anyone who* **attacks** his father or his mother must be put to
21: 18 [G] and one **hits** the other with a stone or with his fist
21: 19 [G] the *one who* **struck the blow** will not be held responsible if
21: 20 [G] "If a man **beats** his male or female slave with a rod
21: 26 [G] "If a man **hits** a manservant or maidservant *in* the eye and
22: 2 [22:1] [H] is caught breaking in and **is struck** so that he dies,
Lev 24: 17 [G] " 'If anyone **takes** the **life of** [+5883] a human being, he must
24: 18 [G] *Anyone who* **takes** the **life of** [+5883] someone's animal
24: 21 [G] *Whoever* **kills** an animal must make restitution, but whoever
24: 21 [G] but *whoever* **kills** a man must be put to death.
26: 24 [G] and *will* **afflict** you for your sins seven times over.
Nu 3: 13 [G] When I **struck down** all the firstborn in Egypt, I set apart for
8: 17 [G] When I **struck down** all the firstborn in Egypt, I set them
11: 33 [G] against the people, and he **struck** them *with* a severe plague.
14: 12 [G] *I will* **strike** them **down** with a plague and destroy them,
14: 45 [G] **attacked** them and beat them down all the way to Hormah.
20: 11 [G] raised his arm and **struck** the rock twice with his staff.
21: 24 [G] **put** him to the sword and took over his land from the Arnon
21: 35 [G] So *they* **struck** him **down**, together with his sons and his
22: 6 [G] Perhaps then I will be able *to* **defeat** them and drive them out
22: 23 [G] road into a field. Balaam **beat** her to get her back on the road.
22: 25 [G] crushing Balaam's foot against it. So *he* **beat** her again.
22: 27 [G] under Balaam, and he was angry and **beat** her with his staff.

Nu 22:28 [G] "What have I done to you *to make you* **beat** me these three
22:32 [G] "Why *have you* **beaten** your donkey these three times?
25:14 [H] The name of the Israelite **[RPH]** who was killed with the
25:14 [H] The name of the Israelite who *was* **killed** with the Midianite
25:15 [H] the name of the Midianite woman who **was put to death** was
25:17 [G] "Treat the Midianites as enemies and **kill** them,
25:18 [H] the *woman who* **was killed** when the plague came as a result
32: 4 [G] the land the LORD **subdued** before the people of Israel—
33: 4 [G] whom the LORD *had* **struck down** among them;
35:11 [G] to which *a person who has* **killed** [+8357] someone
35:15 [G] so that anyone *who has* **killed** another accidentally can flee
35:16 [G] " 'If *a man* **strikes** someone with an iron object so that he
35:17 [G] and *he* **strikes** someone so that he dies, he is a murderer;
35:18 [G] and *he* **hits** someone so that he dies, he is a murderer;
35:21 [G] or if in hostility *he* **hits** him with his fist so that he dies,
35:21 [G] his fist so that he dies, that **person**[s] shall be put to death;
35:24 [G] the assembly must judge between **him**[s] [+2021] and the
35:30 [G] " 'Anyone *who* **kills** a person is to be put to death as a
Dt 1: 4 [G] *had* **defeated** Sihon king of the Amorites, who reigned in
2:33 [G] *we* **struck** him **down**, together with his sons and his whole
3: 3 [G] all his army. *We* **struck** them **down**, leaving no survivors.
4:46 [G] who reigned in Heshbon and *was* **defeated** *by* Moses
7: 2 [G] has delivered them over to you and *you have* **defeated** them,
13:15 [13:16] [G] *you* **must certainly put** [+906+5782] to the sword
13:15 [13:16] [G] *you* **must certainly put** [+906+5782] to the sword
19: 4 [G] *one* who **kills** his neighbor unintentionally, without malice
19: 6 [G] **kill** [+5883] him even though he is not deserving of death,
19:11 [G] in wait for him, assaults and **kills** [+2256+4637+5883] him,
20:13 [G] delivers it into your hand, **put** to the sword all the men in it.
21: 1 [G] is giving you to possess, and it is not known who **killed** him,
25: 2 [G] If the guilty man deserves *to be* **beaten**, the judge shall make
25: 2 [G] **have** him **flogged** in his presence with the number of lashes
25: 3 [G] *he must* not **give** him more than forty **lashes**. If he is flogged
25: 3 [G] If he *is* **flogged** [+4804] more than that, your brother will be
25:11 [G] one of them comes to rescue her husband from his **assailant**,
27:24 [G] "Cursed is the man *who* **kills** his neighbor secretly." Then all
27:25 [G] "Cursed is the man who accepts a bribe to **kill** [+5883] an
28:22 [G] The LORD *will* **strike** you with wasting disease, with fever
28:27 [G] The LORD *will* **afflict** you with the boils of Egypt and with
28:28 [G] The LORD *will* **afflict** you with madness, blindness
28:35 [G] The LORD *will* **afflict** your knees and legs with painful
29: 7 [29:6] [G] came out to fight against us, but *we* **defeated** them.
Jos 7: 3 [G] Send two or three thousand men *to* **take** it and do not weary
7: 5 [G] who **killed** about thirty-six of them. They chased the
7: 5 [G] as the stone quarries and **struck** them **down** on the slopes.
8:21 [G] the city, they turned around and **attacked** the men of Ai.
8:22 [G] Israel **cut** them **down**, leaving them neither survivors nor
8:24 [G] to Ai and **killed** [+906+2995+4200+7023] those who were in it.
9:18 [G] the Israelites *did* not **attack** them, because the leaders of the
10: 4 [G] "Come up and help me **attack** Gibeon," he said, "because it
10:10 [G] *who* **defeated** them in a great victory at Gibeon.
10:10 [G] and **cut** them **down** all the way to Azekah and Makkedah.
10:20 [G] So Joshua and the Israelites **destroyed** [+1524+4394+4804]
10:26 [G] Joshua **struck** and killed the kings and hung them on five
10:28 [G] *He* **put** the city and its king to the sword and totally
10:30 [G] The city and everyone in it Joshua **put** to the sword. He left
10:32 [G] The city and everyone in it *he* **put** to the sword, just as he
10:33 [G] up to help Lachish, but Joshua **defeated** him and his army—
10:35 [G] They captured it that same day and **put** it to the sword
10:37 [G] and **put** it to the sword, together with its king, its villages
10:39 [G] the city, its king and its villages, and **put** them to the sword.
10:40 [G] **subdued** the whole region, including the hill country,
10:41 [G] Joshua **subdued** them from Kadesh Barnea to Gaza and from
11: 8 [G] *They* **defeated** them and pursued them all the way to Greater
11: 8 [G] of Mizpah on the east, **[NIE]** until no survivors were left.
11:10 [G] and captured Hazor and **put** its king to the sword.
11:11 [G] Everyone in it *they* **put** to the sword. They totally destroyed
11:12 [G] these royal cities and their kings and **put** them to the sword.
11:14 [G] all the people *they* **put** to the sword until they completely
11:17 [G] He captured all their kings and **struck** them **down**, putting
12: 1 [G] are the kings of the land whom the Israelites *had* **defeated**
12: 6 [G] servant of the LORD, and the Israelites **conquered** them.
12: 7 [G] and the Israelites **conquered** on the west side of the Jordan,
13:12 [G] Moses *had* **defeated** them and taken over their land.
13:21 [G] *had* **defeated** him and the Midianite chiefs, Evi, Rekem, Zur,
15:16 [G] Acsah in marriage to the man who **attacks** and captures
19:47 [G] attacked Leshem, took it, **put** it to the sword and occupied it.
20: 3 [G] so that anyone *who* **kills** a person accidentally
20: 5 [G] because *he* **killed** his neighbor unintentionally and without
20: 9 [G] or any alien living among them *who* **killed** someone
Jdg 1: 4 [G] and *they* **struck down** ten thousand men at Bezek.
1: 5 [G] against him, **putting to rout** the Canaanites and Perizzites.
1: 8 [G] and took it. *They* **put** the city to the sword and set it on fire.
1:10 [G] Kiriath Arba) and **defeated** Sheshai, Ahiman and Talmai.
1:12 [G] give my daughter Acsah in marriage to the man who **attacks**
1:17 [G] their brothers and **attacked** the Canaanites living in Zephath,
1:25 [G] *they* **put** the city to the sword but spared the man and his
3:13 [G] and Amalekites to join him, Eglon came and **attacked** Israel,
3:29 [G] At that time *they* **struck down** about ten thousand Moabites,
3:31 [G] *who* **struck down** six hundred Philistines with an oxgoad.
6:16 [G] and *you will* **strike down** all the Midianites together."
7:13 [G] *It* **struck** the tent with such force that the tent overturned and
8:11 [G] of Nobah and Jogbehah and **fell upon** the unsuspecting army.
9:43 [G] the people coming out of the city, he rose *to* **attack** them.
9:44 [G] rushed upon those in the fields and **struck** them **down**.
11:21 [G] and all his men into Israel's hands, and *they* **defeated** them.
11:33 [G] *He* **devastated** [+1524+4394+4804] twenty towns from Aroer
12: 4 [G] The Gileadites **struck** them **down** because the Ephraimites
14:19 [G] He went down to Ashkelon, **struck down** thirty of their men,
15: 8 [G] *He* **attacked** [+906+3751+6584+8797] them **viciously** and
15:15 [G] of a donkey, he grabbed it and **struck down** a thousand men.
15:16 [G] With a donkey's jawbone *I have* **killed** a thousand men."
18:27 [G] *They* **attacked** them with the sword and burned down their
20:31 [G] They began to **inflict** casualties on the Israelites as before,
20:37 [G] into Gibeah, spread out and **put** the whole city to the sword.
20:39 [G] The Benjamites had begun to **inflict** casualties on the men of
20:45 [G] as far as Gidom and **struck down** two thousand more.
20:48 [G] went back to Benjamin and **put** all the towns to the sword,
21:10 [G] go to Jabesh Gilead and **put** to the sword those living there,
1Sa 2:14 [G] *He would* **plunge** it into the pan or kettle or caldron or pot,
4: 2 [G] *who* **killed** about four thousand of them on the battlefield.
4: 8 [G] They are the gods who **struck** the Egyptians with all kinds of
5: 6 [G] devastation upon them and **afflicted** them with tumors.
5: 9 [G] *He* **afflicted** the people of the city, both young and old, with
5:12 [H] Those who did not die **were afflicted** with tumors, and the
6:19 [G] But God **struck down** some of the men of Beth Shemesh,
6:19 [G] **putting** seventy of them **to death** because they had looked
6:19 [G] because of the heavy blow the LORD *had* **dealt** them,
7:11 [G] **slaughtering** them along the way to a point below Beth Car.
11:11 [G] and **slaughtered** them until the heat of the day.
13: 3 [G] Jonathan **attacked** the Philistine outpost at Geba,
13: 4 [G] "Saul *has* **attacked** the Philistine outpost, and now Israel has
14:14 [G] his armor-bearer **killed** some twenty men in an area of about
14:31 [G] after the Israelites *had* **struck down** the Philistines from
14:48 [G] He fought valiantly and **defeated** the Amalekites, delivering
15: 3 [G] **attack** the Amalekites and totally destroy everything that
15: 7 [G] Saul **attacked** the Amalekites all the way from Havilah to
17: 9 [G] If he is able to fight and **kill** me, we will become your
17: 9 [G] if I overcome him and **kill** him, you will become our subjects
17:25 [G] The king will give great wealth to the man who **kills** him.
17:26 [G] "What will be done for the man who **kills** this Philistine
17:27 [G] "This is what will be done for the man who **kills** him."
17:35 [G] went after it, **struck** it and rescued the sheep from its mouth.
17:35 [G] it turned on me, I seized it by its hair, **struck** it and killed it.
17:36 [G] Your servant *has* **killed** both the lion and the bear; this
17:46 [G] over to me, and *I'll* **strike** you **down** and cut off your head.
17:49 [G] a stone, he slung it and **struck** the Philistine on the forehead.
17:50 [G] without a sword in his hand *he* **struck down** the Philistine
17:57 [G] As soon as David returned from **killing** the Philistine, Abner
18: 6 [G] When the men were returning home after David *had* **killed**
18: 7 [G] "Saul *has* **slain** his thousands, and David his tens of
18:11 [G] he hurled it, saying to himself, "*I'll* **pin** David to the wall."
18:27 [G] and his men went out and **killed** two hundred Philistines.
19: 5 [G] He took his life in his hands when *he* **killed** the Philistine.
19: 8 [G] *He* **struck** them *with* such force that they fled before him.
19:10 [G] Saul tried to **pin** him to the wall with his spear, but David
19:10 [G] but David eluded him as Saul **drove** the spear into the wall.
20:33 [G] Saul hurled his spear at him to **kill** him. Then Jonathan knew
21: 9 [21:10] [G] whom *you* **killed** in the Valley of Elah, is here;
21:11 [21:12] [G] " 'Saul *has* **slain** his thousands, and David his tens
22:19 [G] *He* also **put** to the sword Nob, the town of the priests,
23: 2 [G] saying, "Shall I go and **attack** these Philistines?"
23: 2 [G] answered him, "Go, **attack** the Philistines and save Keilah."
23: 5 [G] He **inflicted** heavy losses on the Philistines and saved the
24: 5 [24:6] [G] David *was* **conscience-stricken** [+906+4213] for having
26: 8 [G] Now *let me* **pin** him to the ground with one thrust of my
27: 9 [G] Whenever David **attacked** an area, he did not leave a man
29: 5 [G] " 'Saul *has* **slain** his thousands, and David his tens of
30: 1 [G] and Ziklag. *They had* **attacked** Ziklag and burned it,
30:17 [G] David **fought** them from dusk until the evening of the next
31: 2 [G] and they **killed** his sons Jonathan, Abinadab and Malki-Shua.
2Sa 1: 1 [G] David returned from **defeating** the Amalekites and stayed in
1:15 [G] strike him down!" So *he* **struck** him **down**, and he died.
2:22 [G] "Stop chasing me! Why *should I* **strike** you down?
2:23 [G] so Abner **thrust** the butt of his spear into Asahel's stomach,
2:31 [G] David's men *had* **killed** [+4637] three hundred and sixty
3:27 [G] Joab **stabbed** him *in* the stomach, and he died.
4: 6 [G] if to get some wheat, and *they* **stabbed** him in the stomach.

[F] Hitpael (hitpoel, hitpoal, hitpolel, hitpolal, hitpalel, hitpalal, hitpalpel, hitpalpal, hotpael, hotpaal) [G] Hiphil (hiphtil) [H] Hophal [I] Hishtaphel

2Sa 4: 7 [G] After *they* **stabbed** and killed him, they cut off his head.
5: 8 [G] "Anyone *who* **conquers** the Jebusites will have to use the
5:20 [G] So David went to Baal Perazim, and there he **defeated** them.
5:24 [G] has gone out in front of you to **strike** the Philistine army."
5:25 [G] *he* **struck down** the Philistines all the way from Gibeon to
6: 7 [G] therefore God **struck** him **down** and he died there beside the
8: 1 [G] of time, David **defeated** the Philistines and subdued them,
8: 2 [G] David also **defeated** the Moabites. He made them lie down
8: 3 [G] Moreover, David **fought** Hadadezer son of Rehob, king of
8: 5 [G] of Zobah, David **struck down** twenty-two thousand of them.
8: 9 [G] When Tou king of Hamath heard that David *had* **defeated**
8:10 [G] congratulate him on *his* **victory** in battle over Hadadezer,
8:13 [G] David became famous after he returned from **striking down**
10:18 [G] *He* also **struck down** Shobach the commander of their army,
11:15 [C] withdraw from him so *he will* **be struck down** and die."
11:21 [G] Who **killed** Abimelech son of Jerub-Besheth? Didn't a
12: 9 [G] *You* **struck down** Uriah the Hittite with the sword and took
13:28 [G] and I say to you, '**Strike** Amnon **down**,' then kill him.
13:30 [G] "Absalom *has* **struck down** all the king's sons; not one of
14: 6 [G] there to separate them. One **struck** the other and killed him.
14: 7 [G] they say, 'Hand over the *one who* **struck** his brother **down**,
15:14 [G] and bring ruin upon us and **put** the city to the sword."
17: 2 [G] with him will flee. *I would* **strike down** only the king
18:11 [G] Why didn't *you* **strike** him to the ground right there?
18:15 [G] surrounded Absalom, **struck** him and killed him.
20:10 [G] Joab **plunged** it into his belly, and his intestines spilled out
21: 2 [G] in his zeal for Israel and Judah had tried to **annihilate** them.)
21:12 [G] had hung them after they **struck** Saul **down** on Gilboa.)
21:16 [G] was armed with a new ⌞sword⌟, said he *would* **kill** David.
21:17 [G] *he* **struck** the Philistine **down** and killed him.
21:18 [G] At that time Sibbecai the Hushathite **killed** Saph, one of the
21:19 [G] Elhanan son of Jaare-Oregim the Bethlehemite **killed** Goliath
21:21 [G] Jonathan son of Shimeah, David's brother, **killed** him.
23:10 [G] **struck down** the Philistines till his hand grew tired and froze
23:12 [G] He defended it and **struck** the Philistines **down**, and the
23:20 [G] great exploits. He **struck down** two of Moab's best men.
23:20 [G] also went down into a pit on a snowy day and **killed** a lion.
23:21 [G] he **struck down** a huge Egyptian. Although the Egyptian had
24:10 [G] David *was* **conscience-stricken** [+906+4213] after he had
24:17 [G] When David saw the angel who *was* **striking down** the
1Ki 11:15 [G] up to bury the dead, *had* **struck down** all the men in Edom.
14:15 [G] the LORD *will* **strike** Israel, so that it will be like a reed
15:20 [G] *He* **conquered** Ijon, Dan, Abel Beth Maacah and all
15:27 [G] he **struck** him **down** at Gibbethon, a Philistine town,
15:29 [G] as he began to reign, *he* **killed** Jeroboam's whole family.
16: 7 [G] the house of Jeroboam—and also because *he* **destroyed** it.
16:10 [G] **struck** him **down** and killed him in the twenty-seventh year
16:11 [G] seated on the throne, *he* **killed off** Baasha's whole family.
16:16 [G] that Zimri had plotted against the king and **murdered** him,
20:20 [G] each one **struck down** his opponent. At that, the Arameans
20:21 [G] of Israel advanced and **overpowered** the horses and chariots
20:21 [G] and chariots and **inflicted** heavy losses on the Arameans.
20:29 [G] The Israelites **inflicted** a hundred thousand **casualties** *on* the
20:35 [G] "**Strike** me with your weapon," but the man refused.
20:35 [G] "Strike me with your weapon," but the man refused. **[RPH]**
20:36 [G] the LORD, as soon as you leave me a lion *will* **kill** you."
20:36 [G] after the man went away, a lion found him and **killed** him.
20:37 [G] prophet found another man and said, "**Strike** me, please."
20:37 [G] please." So the man **struck** [+5782] him and wounded him.
20:37 [G] please." So the man **struck** [+5782] him and wounded him.
22:24 [G] son of Kenaanah went up and **slapped** Micaiah in the face.
22:34 [G] and **hit** the king of Israel between the sections of his armor.
2Ki 2: 8 [G] took his cloak, rolled it up and **struck** the water with it.
2:14 [G] cloak that had fallen from him and **struck** the water *with* it.
2:14 [G] When *he* **struck** the water, it divided to the right and to the
3:19 [G] *You will* **overthrow** every fortified city and every major
3:23 [G] "Those kings must have fought and **slaughtered** each other.
3:24 [G] the Israelites rose up and **fought** them until they fled.
3:24 [a] [And the Israelites **invaded** [+928] [Q; see K 995] the land]
3:24 [G] the Israelites invaded the land and **slaughtered** the Moabites.
3:25 [G] men armed with slings surrounded it and **attacked** it as well.
6:18 [G] prayed to the LORD, "**Strike** these people with blindness."
6:18 [G] So *he* **struck** them with blindness, as Elisha had asked.
6:21 [G] saw them, he asked Elisha, "*Shall I* **kill** them, my father?
6:21 [G] "Shall I kill them, my father? *Shall I* **kill** them?"
6:22 [G] "*Do* not **kill** them," he answered. "Would you kill men you
6:22 [G] "*Would* you **kill** men you have captured with your own
8:21 [G] but he rose up and **broke through** by night;
8:28 [G] of Aram at Ramoth Gilead. The Arameans **wounded** Joram;
8:29 [G] *had* **inflicted** *on* him at Ramoth in his battle with Hazael
9: 7 [G] *You are to* **destroy** the house of Ahab your master, and I
9:15 [G] *had* **inflicted** *on* him in the battle with Hazael king of
9:24 [G] Jehu drew his bow and **shot** Joram between the shoulders.
9:27 [G] to Beth Haggan. Jehu chased him, shouting, "**Kill** him too!"
10: 9 [G] against my master and killed him, but who **killed** all these?
10:11 [G] So Jehu **killed** everyone in Jezreel who remained of the
10:17 [G] *he* **killed** all who were left there of Ahab's family;
10:25 [G] and officers: "Go in and **kill** them; let no one escape."
10:25 [G] So *they* **cut** them **down** with the sword. The guards
10:32 [G] Hazael **overpowered** the Israelites throughout their territory
11:12 [G] and the people **clapped** their hands and shouted,
12:20 [12:21] [G] against him and **assassinated** him *at* Beth Millo,
12:21 [12:22] [G] The officials *who* **murdered** him were Jozabad son
13:17 [G] "*You will* completely **destroy** the Arameans at Aphek."
13:18 [G] Elisha told him, "**Strike** the ground." He struck it three times
13:18 [G] "Strike the ground." *He* **struck** it three times and stopped.
13:19 [G] "You *should have* **struck** the ground five or six times;
13:19 [G] *you would have* **defeated** Aram and completely destroyed it.
13:19 [G] destroyed it. But now *you will* **defeat** it only three times."
13:25 [G] Three times Jehoash **defeated** him, and so he recovered the
14: 5 [G] *he* **executed** the officials who had murdered his father the
14: 5 [G] he executed the officials who *had* **murdered** his father the
14: 6 [G] Yet he did not put the sons of the **assassins** to death, in
14: 7 [G] He was the *one who* **defeated** ten thousand Edomites in the
14:10 [G] *You have* **indeed defeated** [+906+5782] Edom and now you
14:10 [G] *You have* **indeed defeated** [+906+5782] Edom and now you
15:10 [G] *He* **attacked** him in front of the people, assassinated him
15:14 [G] *He* **attacked** Shallum son of Jabesh in Samaria, assassinated
15:16 [G] **attacked** Tiphsah and everyone in the city and its vicinity,
15:16 [G] *He* **sacked** Tiphsah and ripped open all the pregnant women.
15:25 [G] *he* **assassinated** Pekahiah, along with Argob and Arieh,
15:30 [G] *He* **attacked** and assassinated him, and then succeeded him
18: 8 [G] he **defeated** the Philistines, as far as Gaza and its territory.
19:35 [G] angel of the LORD went out and **put to death** a hundred
19:37 [G] and Sharezer **cut** him **down** with the sword,
21:24 [G] the people of the land **killed** all who had plotted against King
25:21 [G] of Hamath, the king *had* them **executed** [+906+2256+4637].
25:25 [G] **assassinated** [+906+906+906+2256+4637] Gedaliah and also
1Ch 1:46 [G] son of Bedad, who **defeated** Midian in the country of Moab,
4:41 [G] *They* **attacked** the Hamites in their dwellings and also the
4:43 [G] *They* **killed** the remaining Amalekites who had escaped,
10: 2 [G] and they **killed** his sons Jonathan, Abinadab and Malki-Shua.
11: 6 [G] "Whoever leads the **attack** *on* the Jebusites will become
11:14 [G] They defended it and **struck** the Philistines **down**,
11:22 [G] great exploits. He **struck down** two of Moab's best men.
11:22 [G] also went down into a pit on a snowy day and **killed** a lion.
11:23 [G] he **struck down** an Egyptian who was seven and a half feet
13:10 [G] *he* **struck** him **down** because he had put his hand on the ark.
14:11 [G] men went up to Baal Perazim, and there *he* **defeated** them.
14:15 [G] has gone out in front of you to **strike** the Philistine army."
14:16 [G] *they* **struck down** the Philistine army, all the way from
18: 1 [G] David **defeated** the Philistines and subdued them, and he
18: 2 [G] David also **defeated** the Moabites, and they became subject
18: 3 [G] Moreover, David **fought** Hadadezer king of Zobah, as far as
18: 5 [G] of Zobah, David **struck down** twenty-two thousand of them.
18: 9 [G] When Tou king of Hamath heard that David *had* **defeated**
18:10 [G] congratulate him on *his* **victory** in battle over Hadadezer,
18:12 [G] Abishai son of Zeruiah **struck down** eighteen thousand
20: 1 [G] in Jerusalem. Joab **attacked** Rabbah and left it in ruins.
20: 4 [G] At that time Sibbecai the Hushathite **killed** Sippai, one of the
20: 5 [G] Elhanan son of Jair **killed** Lahmi the brother of Goliath the
20: 7 [G] Jonathan son of Shimea, David's brother, **killed** him.
21: 7 [G] was also evil in the sight of God; so *he* **punished** Israel.
2Ch 13:17 [G] Abijah and his men **inflicted** heavy losses on them, so that
14:14 [14:13] [G] *They* **destroyed** all the villages around Gerar,
14:15 [14:14] [G] *They* also **attacked** the camps of the herdsmen
16: 4 [G] *They* **conquered** Ijon, Dan, Abel Maim and all the store
18:23 [G] son of Kenaanah went up and **slapped** Micaiah in the face.
18:33 [G] and **hit** the king of Israel between the sections of his armor.
21: 9 [G] but he rose up and **broke through** by night.
22: 5 [G] of Aram at Ramoth Gilead. The Arameans **wounded** Joram;
22: 6 [G] *they had* **inflicted** *on* him at Ramoth in his battle with
25: 3 [G] he executed the officials who *had* **murdered** his father the
25:11 [G] the Valley of Salt, where *he* **killed** ten thousand men of Seir.
25:13 [G] *They* **killed** three thousand people and carried off great
25:14 [G] When Amaziah returned from **slaughtering** the Edomites,
25:16 [G] Stop! Why *be* **struck down**?" So the prophet stopped
25:19 [G] You say to yourself that *you have* **defeated** Edom, and now
28: 5 [G] The Arameans **defeated** him and took many of his people as
28: 5 [G] of the king of Israel, *who* **inflicted** heavy casualties on him.
28:17 [G] again come and **attacked** Judah and carried away prisoners,
28:23 [G] sacrifices to the gods of Damascus, who *had* **defeated** him;
33:25 [G] the people of the land **killed** all who had plotted against King
Ne 13:25 [G] on them. *I* **beat** some of the men and pulled out their hair.
Est 9: 5 [G] The Jews **struck** [+928+4804] **down** all their enemies *with*
Job 1:15 [G] *They* **put** the servants to the sword, and I am the only one
1:17 [G] *They* **put** the servants to the sword, and I am the only one
2: 7 [G] **afflicted** Job with painful sores from the soles of his feet to

Job 16:10 [G] *they* **strike** my cheek in scorn and unite together against me.
Ps 3:7 [3:8] [G] **Strike** all my enemies *on* the jaw; break the teeth of
35:15 [a] **attackers** [BHS 5784] gathered against me when I was
60: T [60:2] [G] **struck down** twelve thousand Edomites in the Valley
69:26 [69:27] [G] For they persecute those you **wound** and talk about
78:20 [G] When *he* **struck** the rock, water gushed out, and streams
78:51 [G] *He* **struck down** all the firstborn of Egypt, the firstfruits of
78:66 [G] *He* **beat** back his enemies; he put them to everlasting shame.
102:4 [102:5] [H] My heart **is blighted** and withered like grass; I
105:33 [G] *he* **struck down** their vines and fig trees and shattered the
105:36 [G] *he* **struck down** all the firstborn in their land, the firstfruits
121:6 [G] the sun *will* not **harm** you by day, nor the moon by night.
135:8 [G] He **struck down** the firstborn of Egypt, the firstborn of men
135:10 [G] He **struck down** many nations and killed mighty kings—
136:10 [G] to *him who* **struck down** the firstborn of Egypt *His*
136:17 [G] *who* **struck down** great kings, *His love endures*
Pr 17:10 [G] a man of discernment more than a hundred **lashes** a fool.
17:26 [G] punish an innocent man, or to **flog** officials for their integrity.
19:25 [G] **Flog** a mocker, and the simple will learn prudence; rebuke a
23:13 [G] from a child; if *you* **punish** him with the rod, he will not die.
23:14 [G] **Punish** him with the rod and save his soul from death.
23:35 [G] "*They* **hit** me," you will say, "but I'm not hurt! They beat
SS 5:7 [G] *They* **beat** me, they bruised me; they took away my cloak,
Isa 1:5 [H] Why *should you* **be beaten** anymore? Why do you persist in
5:25 [G] his people; his hand is raised and *he* **strikes** them **down**.
9:13 [9:12] [G] the people have not returned to him *who* **struck**
10:20 [G] will no longer rely on *him who* **struck** them **down** but will
10:24 [G] *who* **beat** you with a rod and lift up a club against you,
11:4 [G] *He will* **strike** the earth with the rod of his mouth; with the
11:15 [G] *He will* **break** it **up** into seven streams so that men can cross
14:6 [G] *which* in anger **struck down** peoples *with* unceasing blows,
14:29 [G] all you Philistines, that the rod *that* **struck** you is broken;
27:7 [G] *Has* ⌊the LORD⌋ **struck** her as he struck down those who
27:7 [G] LORD⌋ struck her as he struck down *those who* **struck** her?
30:31 [G] shatter Assyria; with his scepter *he will* **strike** them **down**.
37:36 [G] angel of the LORD went out and **put to death** a hundred
37:38 [G] and Sharezer **cut** him **down** with the sword,
49:10 [G] nor thirst, nor *will* the desert heat or the sun **beat** *upon* them.
50:6 [G] I offered my back to *those who* **beat** me, my cheeks to those
53:4 [H] him stricken by God, **smitten** *by* him, and afflicted.
57:17 [G] *I* **punished** him, and hid my face in anger, yet he kept on in
58:4 [G] and strife, and *in* **striking** *each other* with wicked fists.
60:10 [G] Though in anger *I* **struck** you, in favor I will show you
66:3 [G] But whoever sacrifices a bull is like *one who* **kills** a man,
Jer 2:30 [G] "In vain *I* **punished** your people; they did not respond to
5:3 [G] *You* **struck** them, but they felt no pain; you crushed them,
5:6 [G] Therefore a lion from the forest *will* **attack** them, a wolf
14:19 [G] Why *have you* **afflicted** us so that we cannot be healed? We
18:18 [G] *let's* **attack** him with our tongues and pay no attention to
18:21 [H] be put to death, their young men **slain** *by* the sword in battle.
20:2 [G] he **had** Jeremiah the prophet **beaten** and put in the stocks at
20:4 [G] will carry them away to Babylon or **put** them to the sword.
21:6 [G] *I will* **strike down** those who live in this city—both men and
21:7 [G] *He will* **put** them to the sword; he will show them no mercy
26:23 [G] *who* **had** him **struck down** with a sword and his body
29:21 [G] and *he will* **put** them **to death** before your very eyes.
30:14 [G] *I have* **struck** you as an enemy would and punished you as
33:5 [G] filled with the dead bodies of the men *I will* **slay** in my anger
37:10 [G] Even if *you were to* **defeat** the entire Babylonian army that
37:15 [G] They were angry with Jeremiah and **had** him **beaten** and
40:14 [G] has sent Ishmael son of Nethaniah to **take** your life?"
40:15 [G] "Let me go and **kill** Ishmael son of Nethaniah, and no one
40:15 [G] Why *should he* **take** your life and cause all the Jews who are
41:2 [G] with him got up and **struck down** Gedaliah son of Ahikam,
41:3 [G] **killed** all the Jews who were with Gedaliah at Mizpah, as well
41:9 [G] *he had* **killed** along with Gedaliah was the one King Asa had
41:16 [G] after *he had* **assassinated** Gedaliah son of Ahikam:
41:18 [G] because Ishmael son of Nethaniah *had* **killed** Gedaliah son
43:11 [G] and **attack** Egypt, bringing death to those destined for death,
46:2 [G] **defeated** at Carchemish on the Euphrates River *by*
46:13 [G] coming of Nebuchadnezzar king of Babylon to **attack** Egypt:
47:1 [G] concerning the Philistines before Pharaoh **attacked** Gaza:
49:28 [G] of Hazor, which Nebuchadnezzar king of Babylon **attacked**:
52:27 [G] of Hamath, the king **had** them **executed** [+906+2256+4637].
La 3:30 [G] Let him offer his cheek to *one who would* **strike** him, and let
Eze 5:2 [G] Take a third and **strike** it with the sword all around the city.
6:11 [G] **Strike** your hands **together** and stamp your feet and cry out
7:9 [G] you will know that it is I the LORD *who* **strikes the blow**.
9:5 [G] he said to the others, "Follow him through the city and **kill**,
9:7 [G] Go!" So they went out and *began* **killing** throughout the city.
9:8 [G] While they *were* **killing** and I was left alone, I fell facedown,
21:14 [21:19] [G] of man, prophesy and **strike** your hands together.
21:17 [21:22] [G] I too *will* **strike** my hands together, and my wrath
22:13 [G] " '*I will* surely **strike** my hands **together** at the unjust gain
32:15 [G] of everything in it, when I **strike down** all who live there,
33:21 [H] from Jerusalem came to me and said, "The city *has* **fallen**!"
39:3 [G] *I will* **strike** your bow from your left hand and make your
40:1 [H] of the month, in the fourteenth year after the **fall** *of* the city—
Da 8:7 [G] ram furiously, **striking** the ram and shattering his two horns.
Hos 6:1 [G] heal us; *he has* **injured** us but he will bind up our wounds.
9:16 [H] Ephraim *is* **blighted**, their root is withered, they yield no
14:5 [14:6] [G] Like a cedar of Lebanon *he will* **send down** his roots;
Am 3:15 [G] *I will* **tear down** the winter house along with the summer
4:9 [G] "Many times *I* **struck** your gardens and vineyards, I struck
6:11 [G] *he will* **smash** the great house *into* pieces and the small
9:1 [G] "**Strike** the tops of the pillars so that the thresholds shake.
Jnh 4:7 [G] provided a worm, *which* **chewed** the vine so that it withered.
4:8 [G] and the sun **blazed** on Jonah's head so that he grew faint.
Mic 5:1 [4:14] [G] *They will* **strike** Israel's ruler on the cheek with a
6:13 [G] Therefore, I have begun *to* **destroy** you, to ruin you
Hag 2:17 [G] *I* **struck** all the work of your hands with blight, mildew
Zec 9:4 [G] take away her possessions and **destroy** her power on the sea,
10:11 [G] through the sea of trouble; the surging sea *will be* **subdued**
12:4 [G] On that day *I will* **strike** every horse with panic and its rider
12:4 [G] but *I will* **blind** [+928+2021+6427] all the horses of the nations.
13:6 [H] 'The **wounds** *I* **was given** at the house of my friends.'
13:7 [G] "**Strike** the shepherd, and the sheep will be scattered, and I
Mal 4:6 [3:24] [G] or else I will come and **strike** the land *with* a curse."

5783 נָכֶה nākeh, a. [3] [√ 5782]

contrite [1], crippled [1], lame [1]

2Sa 4:4 (Jonathan son of Saul had a son who was **lame** *in* both feet.
9:3 "There is still a son of Jonathan; he is **crippled** *in* both feet."
Isa 66:2 he who is humble and **contrite** *in* spirit, and trembles at my word.

5784 נֵכֶה nēkeh, a. [1 / 0] [√ 5782]

Ps 35:15 attackers [BHS *the stricken*; NIV 5782] gathered against me

5785 נְכֹה n^e^kōh, n.pr.m. [4] [→ 5786]

Neco [3], *untranslated* [1]

2Ki 23:29 Pharaoh **Neco** king of Egypt went up to the Euphrates River to
23:33 Pharaoh **Neco** put him in chains at Riblah in the land of Hamath
23:34 Pharaoh **Neco** made Eliakim son of Josiah king in place of his
23:35 the people of the land according to their assessments. **[RPH]**

5786 נְכוֹ n^e^kô, n.pr.m. [4] [√ 5785]

Neco [4]

2Ch 35:20 **Neco** king of Egypt went up to fight at Carchemish on the
35:22 He would not listen to what **Neco** had said at God's command
36:4 **Neco** took Eliakim's brother Jehoahaz and carried him off to
Jer 46:2 This is the message against the army of Pharaoh **Neco** king of

5787 נָכוֹן nākôn[1], n.[m.]. [1] [√ 5782]

fate [1]

Job 12:5 Men at ease have contempt for misfortune as the **fate** of those

5788 נָכוֹן nākôn[2], a. *or* v.ptcp. Not used in NIV/BHS [√ 3922]

5789 נָכוֹן nākôn[3], n.pr.m. [1] [√ 3922]

Nacon [1]

2Sa 6:6 When they came to the threshing floor of **Nacon**, Uzzah reached

5790 נֹכַח nōkaḥ, subst. (used as pp. & adv.). [25] [→ 5791]

opposite [5], before [3], facing [3], faces [2], approval [1], directly in front of [+4200] [1], directly opposite [+4200+7156] [1], in front of [1], in full view [+6524] [1], in the presence of [+7156] [1], on behalf of [+4200] [1], open before [+7156] [1], straight ahead [+4200] [1], toward [+448] [1], toward [+6330] [1], vicinity [1]

Ge 25:21 Isaac prayed to the LORD **on behalf** [+4200] **of** his wife,
30:38 so that they would be **directly in front** [+4200] **of** the flocks when
Ex 14:2 encamp by the sea, **directly opposite** [+4200+7156] Baal Zephon.
26:35 the tabernacle and put the lampstand **opposite** it on the south side.
40:24 He placed the lampstand in the Tent of Meeting **opposite** the table
Nu 19:4 sprinkle it seven times **toward** [+448] the front of the Tent of
Jos 15:7 to Gilgal, which **faces** the Pass of Adummim south of the gorge.
18:17 continued to Geliloth, which **faces** the Pass of Adummim,
Jdg 18:6 "Go in peace. Your journey has the LORD's **approval**."
19:10 the man left and went **toward** [+6330] Jebus (that is, Jerusalem),
20:43 and easily overran them in the **vicinity** *of* Gibeah on the east.
1Ki 20:29 For seven days they camped **opposite** each other, and on the
22:35 and the king was propped up in his chariot **facing** the Arameans.
2Ch 18:34 the king of Israel propped himself up in his chariot **facing** the
Est 5:1 stood in the inner court of the palace, **in front of** the king's hall.

[F] Hitpael (hitpoel, hitpoal, hitpolel, hitpolal, hitpalel, hitpalal, hitpalpel, hitpalpal, hotpael, hotpaal) [G] Hiphil (hiphtil) [H] Hophal [I] Hishtaphel

Est 5: 1 king was sitting on his royal throne in the hall, **facing** the entrance.
Pr 4: 25 Let your eyes look **straight ahead** [+4200], fix your gaze directly
5: 21 For a man's ways are **in full view of** [+6524] the LORD,
Jer 17: 16 day of despair. What passes my lips is **open before** [+7156] you.
La 2: 19 pour out your heart like water **in the presence of** [+7156] the Lord.
Eze 14: 3 in their hearts and put wicked stumbling blocks **before** their faces.
14: 4 puts a wicked stumbling block **before** his face and then goes to a
14: 7 in his heart and puts a wicked stumbling block **before** his face and
46: 9 gate by which he entered, but each is to go out the **opposite** gate.
47: 20 the Great Sea will be the boundary to a point **opposite** Lebo

5791 נָכֹחַ nākōaḥ, a. & subst. [8] [√ 5790]

right [3], honest [1], honesty [1], proper [1], uprightly [1], uprightness [1]

2Sa 15: 3 would say to him, "Look, your claims are valid and **proper**,
Pr 8: 9 To the discerning all of them are **right**; they are faultless to those
24: 26 An **honest** answer is like a kiss on the lips.
Isa 26: 10 even in a land of **uprightness** they go on doing evil and regard not
30: 10 and to the prophets, "Give us no more visions of *what* is **right**!
57: 2 Those who walk **uprightly** enter into peace; they find rest as they
59: 14 a distance; truth has stumbled in the streets, **honesty** cannot enter.
Am 3: 10 "They do not know how to do **right**," declares the LORD,

5792 נָכַל nākal, v. [4] [→ 3964?, 5793]

cheat [1], conspire [1], deceived [+928+4200+5793] [1], plotted [1]

Ge 37: 18 [F] and before he reached them, *they* **plotted** to kill him.
Nu 25: 18 [D] because they treated you as enemies when they **deceived** [+928+4200+5793] you in the affair of Peor and their sister Cozbi,
Ps 105: 25 [F] he turned to hate his people, to **conspire** against his servants.
Mal 1: 14 [A] "Cursed is the **cheat** who has an acceptable male in his flock

5793 נֶכֶל nēkel, n.[m.]. [1] [√ 5792]

deceived [+928+4200+5792] [1]

Nu 25: 18 when they **deceived** [+928+4200+5792] you in the affair of Peor

5794 נְכָסִים nᵉkāsîm, n.m.[pl.]. [5] [→ Ar 10479]

possessions [2], riches [2], wealth [1]

Jos 22: 8 saying, "Return to your homes with your great **wealth**—with large
2Ch 1: 11 for wealth, **riches** or honor, nor for the death of your enemies,
1: 12 I will also give you wealth, **riches** and honor, such as no king who
Ecc 5: 19 [5:18] when God gives any man wealth and **possessions**,
6: 2 God gives a man wealth, **possessions** and honor, so that he lacks

5795 נָכַר¹ nākar¹, v. [44] [→ 2129, 5798; cf. 5796]

recognized [9], recognize [5], acknowledge [4], show partiality [+7156] [4], know [2], are recognized [1], concerned [1], disguises himself [1], distinguish [1], examine to see [1], favor [1], is known [1], know how [1], make friends with [1], misunderstand [1], notice [1], paid regard [1], realized [1], regard [1], remembers [1], see [1], takes note of [1], tell [1], took note [1], took notice [1]

Ge 27: 23 [G] *He did* not **recognize** him, for his hands were hairy like
31: 32 [G] **see** for yourself whether there is anything of yours here with
37: 32 [G] found this. **Examine** it **to see** whether it is your son's robe."
37: 33 [G] *He* **recognized** it and said, "It is my son's robe!
38: 25 [G] "*See if you* **recognize** whose seal and cord and staff these
38: 26 [G] Judah **recognized** them and said, "She is more righteous than
42: 7 [G] *he* **recognized** them, but he pretended to be a stranger and
42: 8 [G] Although Joseph **recognized** his brothers, they did not
42: 8 [G] Joseph recognized his brothers, they *did* not **recognize** him.
Dt 1: 17 [G] *Do* not **show partiality** [+7156] in judging; hear both small
16: 19 [G] Do not pervert justice or **show partiality** [+7156]. Do not
21: 17 [G] *He must* **acknowledge** the son of his unloved wife as the
32: 27 [D] lest the adversary **misunderstand** and say, 'Our hand has
33: 9 [G] *He did* not **recognize** his brothers or acknowledge his own
Jdg 18: 3 [G] they **recognized** the voice of the young Levite;
Ru 2: 10 [G] "Why have I found such favor in your eyes that you **notice**
2: 19 [G] did you work? Blessed be the *man who* **took notice** *of* you!"
3: 14 [G] but got up before anyone *could be* **recognized**;
1Sa 26: 17 [G] Saul **recognized** David's voice and said, "Is that your voice,
2Sa 3: 36 [G] All the people **took note** and were pleased; indeed,
1Ki 18: 7 [G] Obadiah **recognized** him, bowed down to the ground, and
20: 41 [G] and the king of Israel **recognized** him as one of the prophets.
Ezr 3: 13 [G] No one *could* **distinguish** the sound of the shouts of joy from
Ne 6: 12 [G] *I* **realized** that God had not sent him, but that he had
13: 24 [G] and *did* not **know how** to speak the language of Judah.
Job 2: 12 [G] saw him from a distance, *they could* hardly **recognize** him;
4: 16 [G] It stopped, but *I could* not **tell** what it was. A form stood
7: 10 [G] come to his house again; his place *will* **know** him no more.
21: 29 [D] who travel? *Have you* **paid** no **regard** *to* their accounts—
24: 13 [G] the light, *who do* not **know** its ways or stay in its paths.
24: 17 [G] *they* **make friends with** the terrors of darkness.
34: 19 [D] to princes and *does* not **favor** the rich over the poor,
34: 25 [G] Because *he* **takes note of** their deeds, he overthrows them in
Ps 103: 16 [G] over it and it is gone, and its place **remembers** it no more.
142: 4 [142:5] [G] Look to my right and see; no *one is* **concerned** for
Pr 20: 11 [F] Even a child **is known** by his actions, by whether his conduct
24: 23 [G] the wise: *To* **show partiality** [+7156] in judging is not good:
26: 24 [C] A malicious man **disguises himself** with his lips, but in his
28: 21 [G] *To* **show partiality** [+7156] is not good—yet a man will do
Isa 61: 9 [G] All who see them *will* **acknowledge** that they are a people
63: 16 [G] though Abraham does not know us or Israel **acknowledge** us;
Jer 24: 5 [G] these good figs, *I* **regard** as good the exiles from Judah,
La 4: 8 [C] are blacker than soot; *they* **are** not **recognized** in the streets.
Da 11: 39 [G] and will greatly honor *those who* **acknowledge** him.

5796 ²נָכַר nākar², v.den. [5] [→ 5797, 5799; cf. 5795]

handed over [+906+928+3338] [1], made foreign [1], pretend to be someone else [1], pretended to be a stranger [1], pretense [1]

Ge 42: 7 [F] *he* **pretended to be a stranger** and spoke harshly to them.
1Sa 23: 7 [D] "God *has* **handed** him **over to** [+906+928+3338] me,
1Ki 14: 5 [F] When she arrives, she *will* **pretend to be someone else**."
14: 6 [F] he said, "Come in, wife of Jeroboam. Why this **pretense**?
Jer 19: 4 [D] have forsaken me and **made** this a place of **foreign** gods;

5797 נֵכָר nēkār, n.[m.]. [36] [√ 5796]

foreign [16], foreigners [+1201] [10], foreigner [+1201] [5], they[s] [+1201] [2], alien [1], foreigner [+1201+2021] [1], foreigners [+1201+2021] [1]

Ge 17: 12 your household or bought with money from a **foreigner** [+1201]—
17: 27 those born in his household or bought from a **foreigner** [+1201],
35: 2 "Get rid of the **foreign** gods you have with you, and purify
35: 4 So they gave Jacob all the **foreign** gods they had and the rings in
Ex 12: 43 regulations for the Passover: "No **foreigner** [+1201] is to eat of it.
Lev 22: 25 must not accept such animals from the hand of a **foreigner** [+1201]
Dt 31: 16 these people will soon prostitute themselves to the **foreign** gods of
32: 12 The LORD alone led him; no **foreign** god was with him.
Jos 24: 20 If you forsake the LORD and serve **foreign** gods, he will turn
24: 23 "throw away the **foreign** gods that are among you and yield your
Jdg 10: 16 they got rid of the **foreign** gods among them and served the
1Sa 7: 3 then rid yourselves of the **foreign** gods and the Ashtoreths
2Sa 22: 45 **foreigners** [+1201] come cringing to me; as soon as they hear me,
22: 46 **They**[s] [+1201] *all* lose heart; they come trembling from their
2Ch 14: 3 [14:2] He removed the **foreign** altars and the high places,
33: 15 He got rid of the **foreign** gods and removed the image from the
Ne 9: 2 descent had separated themselves from all **foreigners** [+1201].
13: 30 So I purified the priests and the Levites of everything **foreign**,
Ps 18: 44 [18:45] they obey me; **foreigners** [+1201] cringe before me.
18: 45 [18:46] **They**[s] [+1201] *all* lose heart; they come trembling from
81: 9 [81:10] god among you; you shall not bow down to an **alien** god.
137: 4 How can we sing the songs of the LORD while in a **foreign** land?
144: 7 me from the mighty waters, from the hands of **foreigners** [+1201]
144: 11 rescue me from the hands of **foreigners** [+1201] whose mouths are
Isa 56: 3 Let no **foreigner** [+1201+2021] who has bound himself to the
56: 6 And **foreigners** [+1201+2021] who bind themselves to the LORD
60: 10 "**Foreigners** [+1201] will rebuild your walls, and their kings will
61: 5 Aliens will shepherd your flocks; **foreigners** [+1201] will work
62: 8 never again will **foreigners** [+1201] drink the new wine for which
Jer 5: 19 you have forsaken me and served **foreign** gods in your own land,
8: 19 me to anger with their images, with their worthless **foreign** idols?"
Eze 44: 7 you brought **foreigners** [+1201] uncircumcised in heart and flesh
44: 9 No **foreigner** [+1201] uncircumcised in heart and flesh is to enter
44: 9 not even the **foreigners** [+1201] who live among the Israelites.
Da 11: 39 He will attack the mightiest fortresses with the help of a **foreign**
Mal 2: 11 the LORD loves, by marrying the daughter of a **foreign** god.

5798 נֵכֶר nēker, n.[m.]. [2] [√ 5795]

disaster [1], misfortune [1]

Job 31: 3 Is it not ruin for the wicked, **disaster** for those who do wrong?
Ob 1: 12 should not look down on your brother in the day of his **misfortune**,

5799 נָכְרִי nokrî, a. [45] [√ 5796]

foreign [14], foreigner [10], wayward [6], alien [4], foreigners [4], another man's [1], another [1], foreigners [+6639] [1], pagans [+3529] [1], someone else [1], stranger [1], wild [1]

Ge 31: 15 Does he not regard us as **foreigners**? Not only has he sold us,
Ex 2: 22 him Gershom, saying, "I have become an alien in a **foreign** land."
18: 3 for Moses said, "I have become an alien in a **foreign** land";
21: 8 He has no right to sell her to **foreigners** [+6639], because he has
Dt 14: 21 of your towns, and he may eat it, or you may sell it to a **foreigner**.
15: 3 You may require payment from a **foreigner**, but you must cancel
17: 15 Do not place a **foreigner** over you, one who is not a brother
23: 20 [23:21] You may charge a **foreigner** interest, but not a brother

Dt 29:22 [29:21] **foreigners** who come from distant lands will see the
Jdg 19:12 We won't go into an **alien** city, whose people are not Israelites.
Ru 2:10 I found such favor in your eyes that you notice me—a **foreigner**?"
2Sa 15:19 King Absalom. You are a **foreigner**, an exile from your homeland.
1Ki 8:41 "As for the **foreigner** who does not belong to your people Israel
8:43 your dwelling place, and do whatever the **foreigner** asks of you,
11:1 loved many **foreign** women besides Pharaoh's daughter—
11:8 He did the same for all his **foreign** wives, who burned incense
2Ch 6:32 "As for the **foreigner** who does not belong to your people Israel
6:33 your dwelling place, and do whatever the **foreigner** asks of you,
Ezr 10:2 "We have been unfaithful to our God by marrying **foreign** women
10:10 you have married **foreign** women, adding to Israel's guilt.
10:11 from the peoples around you and from your **foreign** wives."
10:14 let everyone in our towns who has married a **foreign** woman come
10:17 finished dealing with all the men who had married **foreign** women.
10:18 of the priests, the following had married **foreign** women:
10:44 All these had married **foreign** women, and some of them had
Ne 13:26 over all Israel, but even he was led into sin by **foreign** women.
13:27 and are being unfaithful to our God by marrying **foreign** women?"
Job 19:15 maidservants count me a stranger; they look upon me as an **alien**.
Ps 69:8 [69:9] stranger to my brothers, an **alien** to my own mother's sons;
Pr 2:16 the adulteress, from the **wayward** *wife* with her seductive words,
5:10 feast on your wealth and your toil enrich **another man's** house.
5:20 an adulteress? Why embrace the bosom of **another** *man's wife*?
6:24 immoral woman, from the smooth tongue of the **wayward** *wife*.
7:5 the adulteress, from the **wayward** *wife* with her seductive words.
20:16 a stranger; hold it in pledge if he does it for a **wayward** *woman*.
23:27 for a prostitute is a deep pit and a **wayward** *wife* is a narrow well.
27:2 and not your own mouth; **someone else**, and not your own lips.
27:13 a stranger; hold it in pledge if he does it for a **wayward** *woman*.
Ecc 6:2 not enable him to enjoy them, and a **stranger** enjoys them instead.
Isa 2:6 like the Philistines and clasp hands with **pagans** [+3529].
28:21 do his work, his strange work, and perform his task, his **alien** task.
Jer 2:21 How then did you turn against me into a corrupt, **wild** vine?
La 5:2 has been turned over to aliens, our homes to **foreigners**.
Ob 1:11 and **foreigners** entered his gates and cast lots for Jerusalem,
Zep 1:8 and the king's sons and all those clad in **foreign** clothes.

5800 נְכֹת *nᵉkōt*, n.[f.]. [2]

storehouses [+1074] [2]

2Ki 20:13 and showed them all that was in his **storehouses** [+1074]—
Isa 39:2 and showed them what was in his **storehouses** [+1074]—

5801 נָלָה *nālâ*, v. [1] [cf. 3983]

stop [1]

Isa 33:1 [G] be destroyed; when you **stop** betraying, you will be betrayed.

5802 נְמִבְזָה *nᵉmibzâ*, var. Not used in NIV/BHS [√ 1022]

5803 נְמוּאֵל *nᵉmû'ēl*, n.pr.m. [3] [→ 5804; cf. 3543, 5832?]

Nemuel [3]

Nu 26:9 the sons of Eliab were **Nemuel**, Dathan and Abiram. The same
26:12 through **Nemuel**, the Nemuelite clan; through Jamin, the Jaminite
1Ch 4:24 descendants of Simeon: **Nemuel**, Jamin, Jarib, Zerah and Shaul;

5804 נְמוּאֵלִי *nᵉmû'ēlî*, a.g. [1] [√ 5803]

Nemuelite [1]

Nu 26:12 through Nemuel, the **Nemuelite** clan; through Jamin, the Jaminite

5805 נְמָלָה *nᵉmālâ*, n.f. [2]

ant [1], ants [1]

Pr 6:6 Go to the **ant**, you sluggard; consider its ways and be wise!
30:25 **Ants** are creatures of little strength, yet they store up their food in

5806 נָמֵס *nāmēs*, v. Not used in NIV/BHS [√ 5022]

5807 נָמֵר *nāmēr*, n.m. [6] [→ Ar 10480]

leopard [4], leopards [2]

SS 4:8 from the lions' dens and the mountain haunts of the **leopards**.
Isa 11:6 the **leopard** will lie down with the goat, the calf and the lion
Jer 5:6 a **leopard** will lie in wait near their towns to tear to pieces any who
13:23 Can the Ethiopian change his skin or the **leopard** its spots?
Hos 13:7 come upon them like a lion, like a **leopard** I will lurk by the path.
Hab 1:8 Their horses are swifter than **leopards**, fiercer than wolves at dusk.

5808 נִמְרֹד *nimrōd*, n.pr.m. [4]

Nimrod [4]

Ge 10:8 Cush was the father of **Nimrod**, who grew to be a mighty warrior
10:9 that is why it is said, "Like **Nimrod**, a mighty hunter before the
1Ch 1:10 Cush was the father of **Nimrod**, who grew to be a mighty warrior
Mic 5:6 [5:5] with the sword, the land of **Nimrod** with drawn sword.

5809 נִמְרָה *nimrâ*, n.pr.loc. [1] [→ 1113, 5810]

Nimrah [1]

Nu 32:3 "Ataroth, Dibon, Jazer, **Nimrah**, Heshbon, Elealeh, Sebam,

5810 נִמְרִים *nimrîm*, n.pr.loc. [2] [√ 5809]

Nimrim [2]

Isa 15:6 The waters of **Nimrim** are dried up and the grass is withered;
Jer 48:34 Eglath Shelishiyah, for even the waters of **Nimrim** are dried up.

5811 נִמְשִׁי *nimšî*, n.pr.m. [5]

Nimshi [5]

1Ki 19:16 Also, anoint Jehu son of **Nimshi** king over Israel, and anoint Elisha
2Ki 9:2 you get there, look for Jehu son of Jehoshaphat, the son of **Nimshi**.
9:14 son of Jehoshaphat, the son of **Nimshi**, conspired against Joram.
9:20 The driving is like that of Jehu son of **Nimshi**—he drives like a
2Ch 22:7 he went out with Joram to meet Jehu son of **Nimshi**,

5812 נֵס *nēs*, n.[m.]. [21] [√ 5824; cf. 5823, 5824]

banner [14], battle standard [2], pole [2], sail [1], signal [1], warning sign [1]

Ex 17:15 Moses built an altar and called it The LORD is my **Banner**.
Nu 21:8 The LORD said to Moses, "Make a snake and put it up on a **pole**;
21:9 So Moses made a bronze snake and put it up on a **pole**. Then when
26:10 the fire devoured the 250 men. And they served as a **warning sign**.
Ps 60:4 [60:6] you have raised a **banner** to be unfurled against the bow.
Isa 5:26 He lifts up a **banner** for the distant nations, he whistles for those at
11:10 In that day the Root of Jesse will stand as a **banner** *for* the
11:12 He will raise a **banner** for the nations and gather the exiles of
13:2 Raise a **banner** on a bare hilltop, shout to them; beckon to them to
18:3 when a **banner** is raised on the mountains, you will see it,
30:17 are left like a flagstaff on a mountaintop, like a **banner** on a hill."
31:9 at sight of the **battle standard** their commanders will panic,"
33:23 hangs loose: The mast is not held secure, the **sail** is not spread.
49:22 will beckon to the Gentiles, I will lift up my **banner** to the peoples;
62:10 the highway! Remove the stones. Raise a **banner** for the nations.
Jer 4:6 Raise the **signal** to go to Zion! Flee for safety without delay!
4:21 How long must I see the **battle standard** and hear the sound of the
50:2 and proclaim among the nations, lift up a **banner** and proclaim it;
51:12 Lift up a **banner** against the walls of Babylon!
51:27 "Lift up a **banner** in the land! Blow the trumpet among the
Eze 27:7 linen from Egypt was your sail and served as your **banner**;

5813 נְסִבָּה *nᵉsibbâ*, n.f. [1] [√ 6015]

turn of events [1]

2Ch 10:15 did not listen to the people, for this **turn of events** was from God,

5814 נָסָה *nāsâ*, v. [36] [→ 4999, 5001?]

test [14], tested [8], put to the test [6], used to [2], did[s] [1], testing [1], tried [1], try [1], venture [1], ventures [1]

Ge 22:1 [D] Some time later God **tested** Abraham. He said to him,
Ex 15:25 [D] made a decree and a law for them, and there *he* **tested** them.
16:4 [D] In this way *I will* **test** them and see whether they will follow
17:2 [D] quarrel with me? Why *do you* **put** the LORD **to the test**?"
17:7 [D] and because they **tested** the LORD saying,
20:20 [D] God has come to **test** you, so that the fear of God will be
Nu 14:22 [D] the desert but who disobeyed me and **tested** me ten times—
Dt 4:34 [D] *Has* any god *ever* **tried** to take for himself one nation out of
6:16 [D] *Do* not **test** the LORD your God as you did at Massah.
6:16 [D] Do not test the LORD your God as *you* **did**[s] at Massah.
8:2 [D] and to **test** you in order to know what was in your heart,
8:16 [D] to humble and to **test** you so that in the end it might go well
13:3 [13:4] [D] The LORD your God *is* **testing** you to find out
28:56 [D] gentle that *she would* not **venture** to touch the ground with
33:8 [D] *You* **tested** him at Massah; you contended with him at the
Jdg 2:22 [D] I will use them to **test** Israel and see whether they will keep
3:1 [D] These are the nations the LORD left to **test** all those
3:4 [D] They were left to **test** the Israelites to see whether they would
6:39 [D] *Allow me* one more **test** with the fleece. This time make the
1Sa 17:39 [D] and tried walking around, because *he was* not **used to** them.
17:39 [D] in these," he said to Saul, "because *I am* not **used to** them."
1Ki 10:1 [D] of the LORD, she came to **test** him with hard questions.
2Ch 9:1 [D] she came to Jerusalem to **test** him with hard questions.
32:31 [D] God left him to **test** him and to know everything that was in
Job 4:2 [D] "If *someone* **ventures** a word with you, will you be
Ps 26:2 [D] Test me, O LORD, and **try** me, examine my heart and my

Ps 78: 18 [D] *They* willfully **put** God **to the test** by demanding the food
78: 41 [D] Again and again *they* **put** God **to the test**; they vexed the
78: 56 [D] *they* **put** God **to the test** and rebelled against the Most High;
95: 9 [D] where your fathers **tested** and tried me, though they had seen
106: 14 [D] in to their craving; in the wasteland *they* **put** God **to the test.**
Ecc 2: 1 [D] *I will* **test** you with pleasure to find out what is good."
7: 23 [D] All this *I* **tested** by wisdom and I said, "I am determined to
Isa 7: 12 [D] "I will not ask; *I will* not **put** the LORD **to the test.**"
Da 1: 12 [D] "Please **test** your servants for ten days: Give us nothing
1: 14 [D] So he agreed to this and **tested** them for ten days.

5815 נָסַח **nāsaḥ**, v. [4] [cf. 5005?; Ar 10481]

be uprooted [1], tear [1], tears down [1], torn [1]

Dt 28: 63 [C] *You will* **be uprooted** from the land you are entering to
Ps 52: 5 [52:7] [A] He will snatch you up and **tear** you from your tent;
Pr 2: 22 [A] cut off from the land, and the unfaithful *will be* **torn** from it.
15: 25 [A] The LORD **tears down** the proud man's house but he keeps

5816 ¹נָסִיךְ **nāsîk[1]**, n.m. [2] [→ 5817; cf. 5818]

drink offerings [1], metal images [1]

Dt 32: 38 fat of their sacrifices and drank the wine of their **drink offerings**?
Da 11: 8 their **metal images** and their valuable articles of silver and gold

5817 ²נָסִיךְ **nāsîk[2]**, n.m. [4] [√ 5816; cf. 5818, 5820]

princes [3], leaders [1]

Jos 13: 21 Rekem, Zur, Hur and Reba—**princes** *allied with* Sihon—
Ps 83: 11 [83:12] and Zeeb, all their **princes** like Zebah and Zalmunna,
Eze 32: 30 "All the **princes** *of* the north and all the Sidonians are there;
Mic 5: 5 [5:4] against him seven shepherds, even eight **leaders** *of* men.

5818 ¹נָסַךְ **nāsak[1]**, v. [23] [→ 5011, 5816, 5817, 5821, 5822; cf. 3575, 6057; Ar 10482]

poured out [7], pour out [6], pouring out [3], casts [2], brought [1], forming an alliance [+5011] [1], pour [1], pouring out of drink offerings [1], pouring out of offerings [1]

Ge 35: 14 [G] talked with him, and *he* **poured out** a drink offering on it;
Ex 25: 29 [H] as its pitchers and bowls *for the* **pouring out of offerings.**
30: 9 [A] or grain offering, and *do* not **pour** a drink offering on it.
37: 16 [H] and its pitchers for the **pouring out of drink offerings.**
Nu 28: 7 [G] **Pour out** the drink offering to the LORD at the sanctuary.
2Sa 23: 16 [G] to drink it; instead, *he* **poured** it **out** before the LORD.
2Ki 16: 13 [G] and grain offering, **poured out** his drink offering,
1Ch 11: 18 [D] to drink it; instead, *he* **poured** it **out** before the LORD.
Ps 16: 4 [G] *I will* not **pour out** their libations of blood or take up their
Isa 29: 10 [A] The LORD *has* **brought** over you a deep sleep: He has
30: 1 [A] **forming an alliance** [+5011], but not by my Spirit, heaping
40: 19 [A] As for an idol, a craftsman **casts** it, and a goldsmith overlays
44: 10 [A] Who shapes a god and **casts** an idol, which can profit him
Jer 7: 18 [G] *They* **pour out** drink offerings to other gods to provoke me
19: 13 [G] starry hosts and **poured out** drink offerings to other gods.' "
32: 29 [G] to Baal and by **pouring out** drink offerings to other gods.
44: 17 [G] *will* **pour out** drink offerings to her just as we and our
44: 18 [G] the Queen of Heaven and **pouring out** drink offerings to her,
44: 19 [G] the Queen of Heaven and **poured out** drink offerings to her,
44: 19 [G] like her image and **pouring out** drink offerings to her?"
44: 25 [G] and **pour out** drink offerings to the Queen of Heaven.'
Eze 20: 28 [G] their fragrant incense and **poured out** their drink offerings.
Hos 9: 4 [A] *They will* not **pour out** wine offerings to the LORD, nor

5819 ²נָסַךְ **nāsak[2]**, v. [1] [→ 5012, 5013, 5018; cf. 6115, 8455, 8504]

covers [1]

Isa 25: 7 [B] that enfolds all peoples, the sheet that **covers** all nations;

5820 ³נָסַךְ **nāsak[3]**, v. [2] [cf. 5817, 6057]

installed [1], was appointed [1]

Ps 2: 6 [A] "I *have* **installed** my King on Zion, my holy hill."
Pr 8: 23 [C] *I* **was appointed** from eternity, from the beginning, before

5821 ¹נֶסֶךְ **nesek[1]**, n.m. [60] [√ 5818; Ar 10483]

drink offerings [32], drink offering [27], libations [1]

Ge 35: 14 God had talked with him, and he poured out a **drink offering** on it;
Ex 29: 40 pressed olives, and a quarter of a hin of wine as a **drink offering.**
29: 41 the same grain offering and its **drink offering** as in the morning—
30: 9 or grain offering, and do not pour a **drink offering** on it.
Lev 23: 13 and its **drink offering** *of* a quarter of a hin of wine.
23: 18 together with their grain offerings and **drink offerings**—
23: 37 sacrifices and **drink offerings** required for each day.
Nu 4: 7 on it the plates, dishes and bowls, and the jars for **drink offerings**;
6: 15 together with their grain offerings and **drink offerings**, and a
6: 17 to the LORD, together with its grain offering and **drink offering.**
15: 5 the sacrifice, prepare a quarter of a hin of wine as a **drink offering.**
15: 7 a third of a hin of wine as a **drink offering**. Offer it as an aroma
15: 10 Also bring half a hin of wine as a **drink offering**. It will be an
15: 24 along with its prescribed grain offering and **drink offering,**
28: 7 The accompanying **drink offering** is to be a quarter of a hin of
28: 7 Pour out the **drink offering** to the LORD at the sanctuary.
28: 8 grain offering and **drink offering** that you prepare in the morning.
28: 9 together with its **drink offering** and a grain offering of two-tenths
28: 10 in addition to the regular burnt offering and its **drink offering.**
28: 14 With each bull there is to be a **drink offering** of half a hin of wine;
28: 15 Besides the regular burnt offering with its **drink offering,**
28: 24 in addition to the regular burnt offering and its **drink offering.**
28: 31 Prepare these together with their **drink offerings**, in addition to the
29: 6 with their grain offerings and **drink offerings** as specified.
29: 11 burnt offering with its grain offering, and their **drink offerings.**
29: 16 regular burnt offering with its grain offering and **drink offering.**
29: 18 and **drink offerings** according to the number specified.
29: 19 burnt offering with its grain offering, and their **drink offerings.**
29: 21 and **drink offerings** according to the number specified.
29: 22 regular burnt offering with its grain offering and **drink offering.**
29: 24 and **drink offerings** according to the number specified.
29: 25 regular burnt offering with its grain offering and **drink offering.**
29: 27 and **drink offerings** according to the number specified.
29: 28 regular burnt offering with its grain offering and **drink offering.**
29: 30 and **drink offerings** according to the number specified.
29: 31 regular burnt offering with its grain offering and **drink offering.**
29: 33 and **drink offerings** according to the number specified.
29: 34 regular burnt offering with its grain offering and **drink offering.**
29: 37 and **drink offerings** according to the number specified.
29: 38 regular burnt offering with its grain offering and **drink offering.**
29: 39 grain offerings, **drink offerings** and fellowship offerings.' "
2Ki 16: 13 burnt offering and grain offering, poured out his **drink offering,**
16: 15 of the land, and their grain offering and their **drink offering.**
1Ch 29: 21 and a thousand male lambs, together with their **drink offerings,**
2Ch 29: 35 and the **drink offerings** that accompanied the burnt offerings.
Ps 16: 4 I will not pour out their **libations** of blood or take up their names
Isa 57: 6 to them you have poured out **drink offerings** and offered grain
Jer 7: 18 They pour out **drink offerings** to other gods to provoke me to
19: 13 the starry hosts and poured out **drink offerings** to other gods.' "
32: 29 the roofs to Baal and by pouring out **drink offerings** to other gods.
44: 17 and will pour out **drink offerings** to her just as we and our fathers,
44: 18 to the Queen of Heaven and pouring out **drink offerings** to her,
44: 19 to the Queen of Heaven and poured out **drink offerings** to her,
44: 19 cakes like her image and pouring out **drink offerings** to her?"
44: 25 and pour out **drink offerings** to the Queen of Heaven.'
Eze 20: 28 their fragrant incense and poured out their **drink offerings.**
45: 17 grain offerings and **drink offerings** at the festivals, the New
Joel 1: 9 and **drink offerings** are cut off from the house of the LORD.
1: 13 and **drink offerings** are withheld from the house of your God.
2: 14 grain offerings and **drink offerings** for the LORD your God.

5822 ²נֶסֶךְ **nesek[2]**, n.m. [4] [√ 5818]

images [3], metal god [1]

Isa 41: 29 deeds amount to nothing; their **images** are but wind and confusion.
48: 5 idols did them; my wooden image and **metal god** ordained them.'
Jer 10: 14 by his idols. His **images** are a fraud; they have no breath in them.
51: 17 by his idols. His **images** are a fraud; they have no breath in them.

5823 ¹נָסַס **nāsas[1]**, v. [1] [cf. 5812, 5824]

sick [1]

Isa 10: 18 [A] it will completely destroy, as when a **sick** *man* wastes away.

5824 ²נָסַס **nāsas[2]**, v. [2] [→ 5812; cf. 5812, 5823]

be unfurled [1], sparkle [1]

Ps 60: 4 [60:6] [F] have raised a banner to **be unfurled** against the bow.
Zec 9: 16 [F] *They will* **sparkle** in his land like jewels in a crown.

5825 נָסַע **nāsa'**, v. [146] [→ 5023, 5024]

set out [49], left [43], moved on [6], traveled [5], went [5], move [3], broke camp [2], brought out [2], move on [2], moved [2], pulled up [2], withdrew [2], *untranslated* [1], advance [1], are pulled up [1], be on way [+2143+2256] [1], been pulled down [1], broke camp [+185+4946] [1], journeyed [1], leaving [+4946] [1], led [1], left [+4946] [1], let loose [1], marching [1], move about [1], move out [1], out [1], put to one side [1], quarries [1], removed from quarry [1], setting out [1], tore loose [1], uproots [1], wander [1], went out [1]

Ge 11: 2 [A] As men **moved** eastward, they found a plain in Shinar
12: 9 [A] Then Abram **set out** and continued toward the Negev.

Ge 12: 9 [A] Abram set out and continued **[RPH]** toward the Negev.
13: 11 [A] the whole plain of the Jordan and **set out** toward the east.
20: 1 [A] Now Abraham **moved on** from there into the region of the
33: 12 [A] Esau said, "*Let us* **be on** *our* **way** [+2143+2256]; I'll
33: 17 [A] Jacob, however, **went** to Succoth, where he built a place for
35: 5 [A] *they* **set out**, and the terror of God fell upon the towns all
35: 16 [A] *they* **moved on** from Bethel. While they were still some
35: 21 [A] Israel **moved on** again and pitched his tent beyond Migdal
37: 17 [A] "*They have* **moved on** from here," the man answered. "I
46: 1 [A] So Israel **set out** with all that was his, and when he reached
Ex 12: 37 [A] The Israelites **journeyed** from Rameses to Succoth.
13: 20 [A] After **leaving** [+4946] Succoth they camped at Etham on the
14: 10 [A] and there were the Egyptians, **marching** after them.
14: 15 [A] are you crying out to me? Tell the Israelites *to* **move on**.
14: 19 [A] in front of Israel's army, **withdrew** and went behind them.
14: 19 [A] The pillar of cloud also **moved** from in front and stood
15: 22 [G] Moses **led** Israel from the Red Sea and they went into the
16: 1 [A] The whole Israelite community **set out** from Elim and came
17: 1 [A] The whole Israelite community **set out** from the Desert of
19: 2 [A] After *they* **set out** from Rephidim, they entered the Desert of
40: 36 [A] cloud lifted from above the tabernacle, *they would* **set out**;
40: 37 [A] if the cloud did not lift, *they did* not **set out**—until the day it
Nu 1: 51 [A] Whenever the tabernacle *is to* **move**, the Levites are to take it
2: 9 [A] to their divisions, number 186,400. *They will* **set out** first.
2: 16 [A] to their divisions, number 151,450. *They will* **set out** second.
2: 17 [A] the camp of the Levites *will* **set out** in the middle of the
2: 17 [A] *They will* **set out** in the same order as they encamp, each in
2: 24 [A] to their divisions, number 108,100. *They will* **set out** third.
2: 31 [A] *They will* **set out** last, under their standards.
2: 34 [A] that is the way *they* **set out**, each with his clan and family.
4: 5 [A] When the camp *is to* **move**, Aaron and his sons are to go in
4: 15 [A] all the holy articles, and when the camp *is ready to* **move**,
9: 17 [A] the cloud lifted from above the Tent, the Israelites **set out**;
9: 18 [A] At the LORD's command the Israelites **set out**, and at his
9: 19 [A] the Israelites obeyed the LORD's order and *did* not **set out**.
9: 20 [A] would encamp, and then at his command *they would* **set out**.
9: 21 [A] till morning, and when it lifted in the morning, *they* **set out**.
9: 21 [A] by day or by night, whenever the cloud lifted, *they* **set out**.
9: 22 [A] a year, the Israelites would remain in camp and not **set out**;
9: 22 [A] and not set out; but when it lifted, *they would* **set out**.
9: 23 [A] they encamped, and at the LORD's command *they* **set out**.
10: 5 [A] is sounded, the tribes camping on the east *are to* **set out**.
10: 6 [A] of a second blast, the camps on the south *are to* **set out**.
10: 12 [A] the Israelites **set out** from the Desert of Sinai and traveled
10: 13 [A] *They* **set out**, this first time, at the LORD's command
10: 14 [A] The divisions of the camp of Judah **went** first, under their
10: 17 [A] and the Gershonites and Merarites, who carried it, **set out**.
10: 18 [A] The divisions of the camp of Reuben **went** next, under their
10: 21 [A] the Kohathites **set out**, carrying the holy things. The
10: 22 [A] The divisions of the camp of Ephraim **went** next, under their
10: 25 [A] the divisions of the camp of Dan **set out**, under their
10: 28 [A] the order of march for the Israelite divisions as *they* **set out**.
10: 29 [A] "We *are* **setting out** for the place about which the LORD
10: 33 [A] So *they* **set out** from the mountain of the LORD
10: 33 [A] The ark of the covenant of the LORD **went** before them
10: 34 [A] was over them by day when they **set out** from the camp.
10: 35 [A] Whenever the ark **set out**, Moses said, "Rise up, O LORD!
11: 31 [A] Now a wind **went out** from the LORD and drove quail in
11: 35 [A] From Kibroth Hattaavah the people **traveled** *to* Hazeroth
12: 15 [A] and the people *did* not **move on** till she was brought back.
12: 16 [A] the people **left** [+4946] Hazeroth and encamped in the Desert
14: 25 [A] **set out** *toward* the desert along the route to the Red Sea."
20: 22 [A] The whole Israelite community **set out** from Kadesh
21: 4 [A] *They* **traveled** from Mount Hor *along* the route to the Red
21: 10 [A] The Israelites **moved on** and camped at Oboth.
21: 11 [A] Then *they* **set out** from Oboth and camped in Iye Abarim,
21: 12 [A] From there *they* **moved on** and camped in the Zered Valley.
21: 13 [A] *They* **set out** from there and camped alongside the Arnon,
22: 1 [A] the Israelites **traveled** to the plains of Moab and camped
33: 3 [A] The Israelites **set out** from Rameses on the fifteenth day of
33: 5 [A] The Israelites **left** Rameses and camped at Succoth.
33: 6 [A] *They* **left** Succoth and camped at Etham, on the edge of the
33: 7 [A] *They* **left** Etham, turned back to Pi Hahiroth, to the east of
33: 8 [A] *They* **left** Pi Hahiroth and passed through the sea into the
33: 9 [A] *They* **left** Marah and went to Elim, where there were twelve
33: 10 [A] *They* **left** Elim and camped by the Red Sea.
33: 11 [A] *They* **left** the Red Sea and camped in the Desert of Sin.
33: 12 [A] *They* **left** the Desert of Sin and camped at Dophkah.
33: 13 [A] *They* **left** Dophkah and camped at Alush.
33: 14 [A] *They* **left** Alush and camped at Rephidim, where there was
33: 15 [A] *They* **left** Rephidim and camped in the Desert of Sinai.
33: 16 [A] *They* **left** the Desert of Sinai and camped at Kibroth
33: 17 [A] *They* **left** Kibroth Hattaavah and camped at Hazeroth.
33: 18 [A] *They* **left** Hazeroth and camped at Rithmah.
33: 19 [A] *They* **left** Rithmah and camped at Rimmon Perez.
33: 20 [A] *They* **left** Rimmon Perez and camped at Libnah.
33: 21 [A] *They* **left** Libnah and camped at Rissah.
33: 22 [A] *They* **left** Rissah and camped at Kehelathah.
33: 23 [A] *They* **left** Kehelathah and camped at Mount Shepher.
33: 24 [A] *They* **left** Mount Shepher and camped at Haradah.
33: 25 [A] *They* **left** Haradah and camped at Makheloth.
33: 26 [A] *They* **left** Makheloth and camped at Tahath.
33: 27 [A] *They* **left** Tahath and camped at Terah.
33: 28 [A] *They* **left** Terah and camped at Mithcah.
33: 29 [A] *They* **left** Mithcah and camped at Hashmonah.
33: 30 [A] *They* **left** Hashmonah and camped at Moseroth.
33: 31 [A] *They* **left** Moseroth and camped at Bene Jaakan.
33: 32 [A] *They* **left** Bene Jaakan and camped at Hor Haggidgad.
33: 33 [A] *They* **left** Hor Haggidgad and camped at Jotbathah.
33: 34 [A] *They* **left** Jotbathah and camped at Abronah.
33: 35 [A] *They* **left** Abronah and camped at Ezion Geber.
33: 36 [A] *They* **left** Ezion Geber and camped at Kadesh, in the Desert
33: 37 [A] *They* **left** Kadesh and camped at Mount Hor, on the border
33: 41 [A] *They* **left** Mount Hor and camped at Zalmonah.
33: 42 [A] *They* **left** Zalmonah and camped at Punon.
33: 43 [A] *They* **left** Punon and camped at Oboth.
33: 44 [A] *They* **left** Oboth and camped at Iye Abarim, on the border of
33: 45 [A] *They* **left** Iyim and camped at Dibon Gad.
33: 46 [A] *They* **left** Dibon Gad and camped at Almon Diblathaim.
33: 47 [A] *They* **left** Almon Diblathaim and camped in the mountains of
33: 48 [A] *They* **left** the mountains of Abarim and camped on the plains
Dt 1: 7 [A] and **advance** *into* the hill country of the Amorites;
1: 19 [A] *we* **set out** from Horeb and went toward the hill country of
1: 40 [A] **set out** toward the desert *along* the route to the Red Sea."
2: 1 [A] and **set out** toward the desert *along* the route to the Red Sea,
2: 24 [A] "*Set* **out** now and cross the Arnon Gorge. See, I have given
10: 6 [A] (The Israelites **traveled** from the wells of the Jaakanites to
10: 7 [A] From there *they* **traveled** *to* Gudgodah and on to Jotbathah,
Jos 3: 1 [A] all the Israelites **set out** from Shittim and went to the Jordan,
3: 3 [A] you *are to* **move out** from your positions and follow it.
3: 14 [A] So when the people **broke** [+185+4946] **camp** to cross the
9: 17 [A] So the Israelites **set out** and on the third day came to their
Jdg 16: 3 [A] together with the two posts, and **tore** them **loose**, bar and all.
16: 14 [A] his sleep and **pulled up** the pin and the loom, with the fabric.
18: 11 [A] armed for battle, **set out** from Zorah and Eshtaol.
1Ki 5: 17 [5:31] [G] *they* **removed from** the **quarry** large blocks of
2Ki 3: 27 [A] was great; *they* **withdrew** and returned to their own land.
4: 4 [G] oil into all the jars, and as each is filled, **put it to one side**."
19: 8 [A] commander heard that the king of Assyria *had* **left** Lachish,
19: 36 [A] So Sennacherib king of Assyria **broke camp** and withdrew.
Ezr 8: 31 [A] On the twelfth day of the first month *we* **set out** from the
Job 4: 21 [C] **Are** not the cords of their tent **pulled up**, so that they die
19: 10 [G] on every side till I am gone; *he* **uproots** my hope like a tree.
Ps 78: 26 [G] *He* **let loose** the east wind from the heavens and led forth the
78: 52 [G] *he* **brought** his people **out** like a flock; he led them like
80: 8 [80:9] [G] *You* **brought** a vine **out** of Egypt; you drove out the
Ecc 10: 9 [G] *Whoever* **quarries** stones may be injured by them;
Isa 33: 20 [A] its stakes *will* never *be* **pulled up**, nor any of its ropes
37: 8 [A] commander heard that the king of Assyria *had* **left** Lachish,
37: 37 [A] So Sennacherib king of Assyria **broke camp** and withdrew.
38: 12 [C] Like a shepherd's tent my house *has* **been pulled down**
Jer 4: 7 [A] has come out of his lair; a destroyer of nations *has* **set out**.
31: 24 [A] farmers and *those who* **move about** with their flocks.
Zec 10: 2 [A] Therefore *the people* **wander** like sheep oppressed for lack

5826 נָסַק *nāsaq*, v. Not used in NIV/BHS

5827 נִסְרֹךְ *nisrōk*, n.pr.[m.]. [2]

Nisroch [2]

2Ki 19: 37 while he was worshiping in the temple of his god **Nisroch**,
Isa 37: 38 while he was worshiping in the temple of his god **Nisroch**,

5828 נֵעָה *nē'â*, n.pr.loc. [1]

Neah [1]

Jos 19: 13 and Eth Kazin; it came out at Rimmon and turned toward **Neah**.

5829 נֹעָה *nō'â*, n.pr.f. [4]

Noah [4]

Nu 26: 33 whose names were Mahlah, **Noah**, Hoglah, Milcah and Tirzah.)
27: 1 of the daughters were Mahlah, **Noah**, Hoglah, Milcah and Tirzah.
36: 11 Mahlah, Tirzah, Hoglah, Milcah and **Noah**—
Jos 17: 3 whose names were Mahlah, **Noah**, Hoglah, Milcah and Tirzah.

5830 נְעוּרִים **ne'ûrîm**, n.[m.]pl. [46] [√ 5849]

youth [37], young [5], childhood [3], boyhood [1]

Ge 8:21 even though every inclination of his heart is evil from **childhood**.
46:34 'Your servants have tended livestock from our **boyhood** on,
Lev 22:13 and she returns to live in her father's house as in her **youth**,
Nu 30:3 [30:4] "When a **young** woman still living in her father's house
30:16 [30:17] a father and his **young** daughter still living in his house.
1Sa 12:2 with you. I have been your leader from my **youth** until this day.
17:33 are only a boy, and he has been a fighting man from his **youth**."
2Sa 19:7 [19:8] that have come upon you from your **youth** till now."
1Ki 18:12 Yet I your servant have worshiped the LORD since my **youth**.
Job 13:26 bitter things against me and make me inherit the sins of my **youth**.
31:18 from my **youth** I reared him as would a father, and from my birth I
Ps 25:7 Remember not the sins of my **youth** and my rebellious ways;
71:5 my hope, O Sovereign LORD, my confidence since my **youth**.
71:17 Since my **youth**, O God, you have taught me, and to this day I
103:5 with good things so that your **youth** is renewed like the eagle's.
127:4 Like arrows in the hands of a warrior are sons born in one's **youth**.
129:1 They have greatly oppressed me from my **youth**—let Israel say—
129:2 they have greatly oppressed me from my **youth**, but they have not
144:12 Then our sons in their **youth** will be like well-nurtured plants,
Pr 2:17 who has left the partner of her **youth** and ignored the covenant she
5:18 fountain be blessed, and may you rejoice in the wife of your **youth**.
Isa 47:12 your many sorceries, which you have labored at since **childhood**.
47:15 these you have labored with and trafficked with since **childhood**.
54:6 a wife who married **young**, only to be rejected," says your God.
Jer 2:2 " 'I remember the devotion of your **youth**, how as a bride you
3:4 you not just called to me: 'My Father, my friend from my **youth**,
3:24 From our **youth** shameful gods have consumed the fruits of our
3:25 from our **youth** till this day we have not obeyed the LORD our
22:21 This has been your way from your **youth**; you have not obeyed me.
31:19 and humiliated because I bore the disgrace of my **youth**.'
48:11 "Moab has been at rest from **youth**, like wine left on its dregs,
La 3:27 It is good for a man to bear the yoke while he is **young**.
Eze 4:14 From my **youth** until now I have never eaten anything found dead
16:22 your prostitution you did not remember the days of your **youth**,
16:43 " 'Because you did not remember the days of your **youth**
16:60 remember the covenant I made with you in the days of your **youth**,
23:3 prostitutes in Egypt, engaging in prostitution from their **youth**.
23:8 when during her **youth** men slept with her, caressed her virgin
23:19 and more promiscuous as she recalled the days of her **youth**,
23:21 So you longed for the lewdness of your **youth**, when in Egypt your
23:21 Egypt your bosom was caressed and your **young** breasts fondled.
Hos 2:15 [2:17] There she will sing as in the days of her **youth**, as in the
Joel 1:8 like a virgin in sackcloth grieving for the husband of her **youth**.
Zec 13:5 I am a farmer; the land has been my livelihood since my **youth**.'
Mal 2:14 is acting as the witness between you and the wife of your **youth**,
2:15 in your spirit, and do not break faith with the wife of your **youth**.

5831 נְעוּרוֹת **ne'ûrôt**, n.[f.]pl. [1] [√ 5853]

youth [1]

Jer 32:30 and Judah have done nothing but evil in my sight from their **youth**;

5832 נְעִיאֵל **ne'î'ēl**, n.pr.loc. [1] [cf. 5803?]

Neiel [1]

Jos 19:27 and went north to Beth Emek and **Neiel**, passing Cabul on the left.

5833 ¹נָעִים **nā'îm[1]**, a. [11] [√ 5838]

pleasant [4], beautiful [1], charming [1], compliments [+1821] [1], contentment [1], gracious [1], pleasing [1], pleasures [1]

2Sa 1:23 in life they were loved and **gracious**, and in death they were not
Job 36:11 the rest of their days in prosperity and their years in **contentment**.
Ps 16:6 The boundary lines have fallen for me in **pleasant** *places*;
16:11 joy in your presence, with eternal **pleasures** at your right hand.
133:1 How good and **pleasant** it is when brothers live together in unity!
135:3 the LORD is good; sing praise to his name, for that is **pleasant**.
147:1 to sing praises to our God, how **pleasant** and fitting to praise him!
Pr 22:18 for it is **pleasing** when you keep them in your heart and have all of
23:8 you have eaten and will have wasted your **compliments** [+1821].
24:4 knowledge its rooms are filled with rare and **beautiful** treasures.
SS 1:16 How handsome you are, my lover! Oh, how **charming**! And our

5834 ²נָעִים **nā'îm[2]**, a. [2] [√ 5838]

melodious [1], singer [1]

2Sa 23:1 the man anointed by the God of Jacob, Israel's **singer** *of* songs:
Ps 81:2 [81:3] strike the tambourine, play the **melodious** harp and lyre.

5835 ¹נָעַל **nā'al[1]**, v. [6] [→ 4980, 4981; cf. 5837]

locked [2], bolt [1], bolted [1], locked up [1], sealed [1]

Jdg 3:23 [A] the doors of the upper room behind him and **locked** them.
3:24 [B] servants came and found the doors of the upper room **locked**.
2Sa 13:17 [A] "Get this woman out of here and **bolt** the door after her."
13:18 [A] So his servant put her out and **bolted** the door after her. She
SS 4:12 [B] You are a garden **locked up**, my sister, my bride; you are a
4:12 [B] my bride; you are a spring enclosed, a **sealed** fountain.

5836 ²נָעַל **nā'al[2]**, v.den. [2] [√ 5837]

put sandals on [1], sandals [1]

2Ch 28:15 [G] They provided them with clothes and **sandals**, food and
Eze 16:10 [A] with an embroidered dress and **put** leather **sandals on** you.

5837 נַעַל **na'al**, n.f. [22] [→ 5836; cf. 5835]

sandals [14], sandal [6], sandaled [+928+2021] [1], unsandaled [+2740] [1]

Ge 14:23 not even a thread or the thong of a **sandal**, so that you will never
Ex 3:5 "Take off your **sandals**, for the place where you are standing is
12:11 your belt, your **sandals** on your feet and your staff in your hand.
Dt 25:9 of the elders, take off one of his **sandals**, spit in his face and say,
25:10 be known in Israel as The Family of the **Unsandaled** [+2740].
29:5 [29:4] clothes did not wear out, nor did the **sandals** on your feet.
Jos 5:15 "Take off your **sandals**, for the place where you are standing is
9:5 The men put worn and patched **sandals** on their feet and wore old
9:13 our clothes and **sandals** are worn out by the very long journey."
Ru 4:7 become final, one party took off his **sandal** and gave it to the other.
4:8 said to Boaz, "Buy it yourself." And he removed his **sandal**.
1Ki 2:5 blood stained the belt around his waist and the **sandals** on his feet.
Ps 60:8 [60:10] Moab is my washbasin, upon Edom I toss my **sandal**;
108:9 [108:10] Moab is my washbasin, upon Edom I toss my **sandal**;
SS 7:1 [7:2] How beautiful your **sandaled** [+928+2021] feet, O prince's
Isa 5:27 not a belt is loosened at the waist, not a **sandal** thong is broken.
11:15 it up into seven streams so that men can cross over in **sandals**.
20:2 off the sackcloth from your body and the **sandals** from your feet."
Eze 24:17 Keep your turban fastened and your **sandals** on your feet;
24:23 keep your turbans on your heads and your **sandals** on your feet.
Am 2:6 sell the righteous for silver, and the needy for a *pair of* **sandals**.
8:6 buying the poor with silver and the needy for a *pair of* **sandals**,

5838 נָעֵם **nā'ēm**, v. [8] [→ 45, 321, 534, 4982, 5833, 5834, 5839, 5840, 5841, 5842, 5843, 5844, 5845, 5846]

pleasant [2], dear [1], delicious [1], go well [1], more favored [1], pleasing [1], well [1]

Ge 49:15 [A] how good is his resting place and how **pleasant** *is* his land,
2Sa 1:26 [A] for you, Jonathan my brother; *you were* very **dear** to me.
Ps 141:6 [A] and the wicked will learn that my words *were* **well** spoken.
Pr 2:10 [A] your heart, and knowledge *will be* **pleasant** to your soul.
9:17 [A] "Stolen water is sweet; food eaten in secret *is* **delicious**!"
24:25 [A] *it will* **go well** with those who convict the guilty, and rich
SS 7:6 [7:7] [A] How beautiful you are and how **pleasing**, O love,
Eze 32:19 [A] Say to them, '*Are you* **more favored** than others? Go down

5839 נַעַם **na'am**, n.pr.m. [1] [√ 5838]

Naam [1]

1Ch 4:15 son of Jephunneh: Iru, Elah and **Naam**. The son of Elah: Kenaz.

5840 נֹעַם **nō'am**, n.m. [7] [→ 45, 321, 534; cf. 5838]

favor [3], pleasant [2], beauty [1], pleasing [1]

Ps 27:4 to gaze upon the **beauty** *of* the LORD and to seek him in his
90:17 May the **favor** *of* the Lord our God rest upon us; establish the work
Pr 3:17 Her ways are **pleasant** ways, and all her paths are peace.
15:26 thoughts of the wicked, but those of the pure are **pleasing** to him.
16:24 **Pleasant** words are a honeycomb, sweet to the soul and healing to
Zec 11:7 Then I took two staffs and called one **Favor** and the other Union,
11:10 I took my staff called **Favor** and broke it, revoking the covenant I

5841 ¹נַעֲמָה **na'amâ[1]**, n.pr.f. [4] [√ 5838]

Naamah [4]

Ge 4:22 of tools out of bronze and iron. Tubal-Cain's sister was **Naamah**.
1Ki 14:21 His mother's name was **Naamah**; she was an Ammonite.
14:31 His mother's name was **Naamah**; she was an Ammonite.
2Ch 12:13 His mother's name was **Naamah**; she was an Ammonite.

5842 ²נַעֲמָה **na'amâ[2]**, n.pr.loc. [1] [√ 5838]

Naamah [1]

Jos 15:41 Gederoth, Beth Dagon, **Naamah** and Makkedah—sixteen towns

5843 נָעֳמִי ***no'omî***, n.pr.f. [21] [√ 5838]

Naomi [19], Naomi's [1], she^s^ [1]

Ru 1: 2 The man's name was Elimelech, his wife's name **Naomi**,
1: 3 Now Elimelech, **Naomi's** husband, died, and she was left with her
1: 8 **Naomi** said to her two daughters-in-law, "Go back, each of you,
1: 11 **Naomi** said, "Return home, my daughters. Why would you come
1: 19 because of them, and the women exclaimed, "Can this be **Naomi**?"
1: 20 "Don't call me **Naomi**," she told them. "Call me Mara,
1: 21 Why call me **Naomi**? The LORD has afflicted me; the Almighty
1: 22 So **Naomi** returned from Moab accompanied by Ruth the
2: 1 Now **Naomi** had a relative on her husband's side, from the clan of
2: 2 And Ruth the Moabitess said to **Naomi**, "Let me go to the fields
2: 6 "She is the Moabitess who came back from Moab with **Naomi**.
2: 20 "The LORD bless him!" **Naomi** said to her daughter-in-law.
2: 20 **She**^s^ added, "That man is our close relative; he is one of our
2: 22 **Naomi** said to Ruth her daughter-in-law, "It will be good for you,
3: 1 One day **Naomi** her mother-in-law said to her, "My daughter,
4: 3 the kinsman-redeemer, "**Naomi**, who has come back from Moab,
4: 5 "On the day you buy the land from **Naomi** and from Ruth the
4: 9 "Today you are witnesses that I have bought from **Naomi** all the
4: 14 The women said to **Naomi**: "Praise be to the LORD, who this day
4: 16 Then **Naomi** took the child, laid him in her lap and cared for him.
4: 17 The women living there said, "**Naomi** has a son." And they named

5844 נַעֲמִי ***na'ªmî***, a.g. [1] [√ 5843; cf. 5838]

Naamite [1]

Nu 26: 40 through Ard, the Ardite clan; through Naaman, the **Naamite** clan.

5845 נַעֲמָן ***na'ªmān***, n.pr.m. [16] [→ 5844; cf. 5838]

Naaman [14], Naaman's [2]

Ge 46: 21 Bela, Beker, Ashbel, Gera, **Naaman**, Ehi, Rosh, Muppim,
Nu 26: 40 The descendants of Bela through Ard and **Naaman** were:
26: 40 through Ard, the Ardite clan; through **Naaman**, the Naamite clan.
2Ki 5: 1 Now **Naaman** was commander of the army of the king of Aram.
5: 2 captive a young girl from Israel, and she served **Naaman's** wife.
5: 6 "With this letter I am sending my servant **Naaman** to you
5: 9 So **Naaman** went with his horses and chariots and stopped at the
5: 11 **Naaman** went away angry and said, "I thought that he would
5: 17 "If you will not," said **Naaman**, "please let me, your servant,
5: 20 to himself, "My master was too easy on **Naaman**, this Aramean,
5: 21 So Gehazi hurried after **Naaman**. When Naaman saw him running
5: 21 When **Naaman** saw him running toward him, he got down from
5: 23 "By all means, take two talents," said **Naaman**. He urged Gehazi
5: 27 **Naaman's** leprosy will cling to you and to your descendants
1Ch 8: 4 Abishua, **Naaman**, Ahoah,
8: 7 **Naaman**, Ahijah, and Gera, who deported them and who was the

5846 נַעֲמָנִים ***na'ªmānîm***, n.[m.]. [1] [√ 5838]

finest [1]

Isa 17: 10 though you set out the **finest** plants and plant imported vines,

5847 נַעֲמָתִי ***na'ªmātî***, a.g. [4]

Naamathite [4]

Job 2: 11 the Temanite, Bildad the Shuhite and Zophar the **Naamathite**,
11: 1 Then Zophar the **Naamathite** replied:
20: 1 Then Zophar the **Naamathite** replied:
42: 9 and Zophar the **Naamathite** did what the LORD told them;

5848 נַעֲצוּץ ***na'ªṣûṣ***, n.[m.]. [2]

thornbush [1], thornbushes [1]

Isa 7: 19 in the rocks, on all the **thornbushes** and at all the water holes.
55: 13 Instead of the **thornbush** will grow the pine tree, and instead of

5849 ¹נער ***nā'ar¹***, v. [1] [→ 5830, 5852?, 5853?]

growl [1]

Jer 51: 38 [A] people all roar like young lions, *they* **growl** like lion cubs.

5850 ²נער ***nā'ar²***, v. [11] [→ 5861]

swept [2], am shaken off [1], drop leaves [1], keeps [1], shake myself free [1], shake off [1], shake out [1], shake [1], shaken out [1], shook out [1]

Ex 14: 27 [D] fleeing toward it, and the LORD **swept** them into the sea.
Jdg 16: 20 [C] and thought, "I'll go out as before and **shake myself free**."
Ne 5: 13 [A] *I* also **shook out** the folds of my robe and said, "In this way
5: 13 [D] "In this way *may* God **shake out** of his house
5: 13 [B] So may such a man be **shaken out** and emptied!" At this the
Job 38: 13 [C] take the earth by the edges and **shake** the wicked out of it?
Ps 109: 23 [C] away like an evening shadow; *I* **am shaken off** like a locust.
136: 15 [D] **swept** Pharaoh and his army into the Red Sea; *His love*
Isa 33: 9 [A] like the Arabah, and Bashan and Carmel **drop** *their* **leaves**.
33: 15 [A] from extortion and **keeps** his hand from accepting bribes,
52: 2 [F] **Shake off** your dust; rise up, sit enthroned, O Jerusalem.

5851 ³נַעַר ***nā'ar³***, v. Not used in NIV/BHS

5852 ¹נֹעַר ***na'ar¹***, n.[m.]. Not used in NIV/BHS [√ 5849?]

5853 ²נַעַר ***na'ar²***, n.m. [240] [→ 5831, 5854, 5855, 5856, 5859?; cf. 5849?]

boy [48], servant [29], young [25], young man [23], men [21], servants [14], child [13], young men [11], *untranslated* [9], boy's [4], boys [4], young officers [4], children [3], youth [3], foreman [+5893] [2], him^s^ [+2021] [2], steward [2], them^s^ [+2021] [2], underlings [2], aide [1], assistants [1], attendants [+9250] [1], attendants [1], boy [+7783] [1], child's [1], he^s^ [+2021] [1], he^s^ [1], helper [1], Jether^s^ [+2021] [1], man [1], men's [1], personal attendants [+9250] [1], personal servant [+9250] [1], servant's [1], sons [1], workers [1], youths [+7783] [1], youths [1]

Ge 14: 24 I will accept nothing but what my **men** have eaten and the share
18: 7 and selected a choice, tender calf and gave it to a **servant**,
19: 4 of the city of Sodom—both **young** and old—surrounded the house.
21: 12 "Do not be so distressed about the **boy** and your maidservant.
21: 17 God heard the **boy** crying, and the angel of God called to Hagar
21: 17 Do not be afraid; God has heard the **boy** crying as he lies there.
21: 18 Lift the **boy** up and take him by the hand, for I will make him into
21: 19 she went and filled the skin with water and gave the **boy** a drink.
21: 20 God was with the **boy** as he grew up. He lived in the desert
22: 3 He took with him two of his **servants** and his son Isaac.
22: 5 He said to his **servants**, "Stay here with the donkey while I
22: 5 "Stay here with the donkey while I and the **boy** go over there.
22: 12 "Do not lay a hand on the **boy**," he said. "Do not do anything to
22: 19 Abraham returned to his **servants**, and they set off together for
25: 27 The **boys** grew up, and Esau became a skillful hunter, a man of the
34: 19 The **young man**, who was the most honored of all his father's
37: 2 Joseph, a **young man** of seventeen, was tending the flocks with his
41: 12 Now a **young** Hebrew was there with us, a servant of the captain of
43: 8 "Send the **boy** along with me and we will go at once, so that we
44: 22 And we said to my lord, 'The **boy** cannot leave his father;
44: 30 if the **boy** is not with us when I go back to your servant my father
44: 31 sees that the **boy** isn't there, he will die. Your servants will bring
44: 32 Your servant guaranteed the **boy's** safety to my father. I said,
44: 33 let your servant remain here as my lord's slave in place of the **boy**,
44: 33 slave in place of the boy, and let the **boy** return with his brothers.
44: 34 How can I go back to my father if the **boy** is not with me?
48: 16 who has delivered me from all harm—may he bless these **boys**.
Ex 2: 6 and saw the baby. **He**^s^ was crying, and she felt sorry for him.
10: 9 "We will go with our **young** and old, with our sons and daughters,
24: 5 Then he sent **young** Israelite **men**, and they offered burnt offerings
33: 11 but his **young** aide Joshua son of Nun did not leave the tent.
Nu 11: 27 A **young man** ran and told Moses, "Eldad and Medad are
22: 22 was riding on his donkey, and his two **servants** were with him.
Dt 22: 15 [the **girl's** [K; see Q 5855] father and mother shall bring proof that]
22: 15 [shall bring proof that **she**^s^ [+2021] [K; see Q 5855] was a virgin]
22: 16 [The **girl's** [K; see Q 5855] father will say to the elders, "I gave]
22: 20 [no proof of the **girl's** [+4200] [K; see Q 5855] virginity can be]
22: 21 [**she**^s^ [+2021] [K; see Q 5855] shall be brought to the door of her]
22: 23 [If a man happens to meet in a town a virgin **[RPH]** pledged to be]
22: 24 [the **girl** [K; see Q 5855] because she was in a town and did not]
22: 25 [if out in the country a man happens to meet a **girl** [K; see Q 5855]]
22: 26 [Do nothing to the **girl**; [K; see Q 5855] she has committed no sin]
22: 26 [**she**^s^ [K; see Q 5855] has committed no sin deserving death.]
22: 27 [though the betrothed **girl** [K; see Q 5855] screamed, there was no]
22: 28 [If a man happens to meet a **[RPH]** virgin who is not pledged to be]
22: 29 [he shall pay the **girl's** [K; see Q 5855] father fifty shekels of]
28: 50 nation without respect for the old or pity for the **young**.
Jos 6: 21 men and women, **young** and old, cattle, sheep and donkeys.
6: 23 So the **young men** who had done the spying went in and brought
Jdg 7: 10 are afraid to attack, go down to the camp with your **servant** Purah
7: 11 and Purah his **servant** went down to the outposts of the camp.
8: 14 He caught a **young** man of Succoth and questioned him,
8: 20 **Jether**^s^ [+2021] did not draw his sword, because he was only a
8: 20 did not draw his sword, because he was only a **boy** and was afraid.
9: 54 **[NIE]** "Draw your sword and kill me, so that they can't say,
9: 54 'A woman killed him.' " So his **servant** ran him through, and he
13: 5 because the **boy** is to be a Nazirite, set apart to God from birth,
13: 7 because the **boy** will be a Nazirite of God from birth until the day
13: 8 come again to teach us how to bring up the **boy** who is to be born."
13: 12 are fulfilled, what is to be the rule for the **boy's** life and work?"
13: 24 named him Samson. **He**^s^ [+2021] grew and the LORD blessed
16: 26 Samson said to the **servant** who held his hand, "Put me where I

Jdg 17: 7 A **young** Levite from Bethlehem in Judah, who had been living
17: 11 live with him, and the **young man** was to him like one of his sons.
17: 12 and the **young man** became his priest and lived in his house.
18: 3 Micah's house, they recognized the voice of the **young** Levite;
18: 15 and went to the house of the **young** Levite at Micah's place
19: 3 He had with him his **servant** and two donkeys. She took him into
19: 9 with his concubine and his **servant**, got up to leave, his
19: 11 the day was almost gone, the **servant** said to his master, "Come,
19: 13 He added, **[RPH]** "Come, let's try to reach Gibeah or Ramah
19: 19 your servants—me, your maidservant, and the **young man** with us.
Ru 2: 5 Boaz asked the **foreman** [+5893] of his harvesters, "Whose young
2: 6 The **foreman** [+5893] replied, "She is the Moabitess who came
2: 9 I have told the **men** not to touch you. And whenever you are
2: 9 go and get a drink from the water jars the **men** have filled."
2: 15 As she got up to glean, Boaz gave orders to his **men**, "Even if she
2: 21 'Stay with my **workers** until they finish harvesting all my grain.' "
1Sa 1: 22 "After the **boy** is weaned, I will take him and present him before
1: 24 After he was weaned, she took the **boy** with her, young as he was,
1: 24 After he was weaned, she took the boy with her, **young** as he was,
1: 25 When they had slaughtered the bull, they brought the **boy** to Eli,
1: 27 I prayed for this **child**, and the LORD has granted me what I
2: 11 but the **boy** ministered before the LORD under Eli the priest.
2: 13 the **servant** *of* the priest would come with a three-pronged fork in
2: 15 the **servant** *of* the priest would come and say to the man who was
2: 17 This sin of the **young men** was very great in the LORD's sight,
2: 18 was ministering before the LORD—a **boy** wearing a linen ephod.
2: 21 the **boy** Samuel grew up in the presence of the LORD.
2: 26 the **boy** Samuel continued to grow in stature and in favor with the
3: 1 The **boy** Samuel ministered before the LORD under Eli.
3: 8 called me." Then Eli realized that the LORD was calling the **boy**.
4: 21 She named the **boy** Ichabod, saying, "The glory has departed from
9: 3 "Take one of the **servants** with you and go and look for the
9: 5 Saul said to the **servant** who was with him, "Come, let's go back,
9: 7 Saul said to his **servant**, "If we go, what can we give the man?
9: 8 The **servant** answered him again. "Look," he said, "I have a
9: 10 "Good," Saul said to his **servant**. "Come, let's go." So they set out
9: 22 Samuel brought Saul and his **servant** into the hall and seated them
9: 27 Samuel said to Saul, "Tell the **servant** to go on ahead of us"—
10: 14 Now Saul's uncle asked him and his **servant**, "Where have you
14: 1 One day Jonathan son of Saul said to the **young man** bearing his
14: 6 Jonathan said to his **young** armor-bearer, "Come, let's go over to
16: 11 So he asked Jesse, "Are these all the **sons** you have?" "There is
16: 18 One of the **servants** answered, "I have seen a son of Jesse of
17: 33 you are only a **boy**, and he has been a fighting man from his
17: 42 He looked David over and saw that he was only a **boy**, ruddy
17: 55 commander of the army, "Abner, whose son is that **young man**?"
17: 58 "Whose son are you, **young man**?" Saul asked him. David said,
20: 21 I will send a **boy** and say, 'Go, find the arrows.' If I say to him,
20: 21 If I say to **him**[s] [+2021], 'Look, the arrows are on this side of you;
20: 35 the field for his meeting with David. He had a small **boy** with him,
20: 36 and he said to the **boy**, "Run and find the arrows I shoot."
20: 36 the arrows I shoot." As the **boy** ran, he shot an arrow beyond him.
20: 37 When the **boy** came to the place where Jonathan's arrow had
20: 37 Jonathan called out after **him**[s] [+2021], "Isn't the arrow beyond
20: 38 Then he shouted, **[RPH]** "Hurry! Go quickly! Don't stop!"
20: 38 The **boy** picked up the arrow and returned to his master.
20: 39 (The **boy** knew nothing of all this; only Jonathan and David knew.)
20: 40 Then Jonathan gave his weapons to the **boy** and said, "Go,
20: 41 After the **boy** had gone, David got up from the south side ⌊of the
21: 2 [21:3] As for my **men**, I have told them to meet me at a certain
21: 4 [21:5] provided the **men** have kept themselves from women."
21: 5 [21:6] The **men's** things are holy even on missions that are not
25: 5 So he sent ten **young men** and said to them, "Go up to Nabal at
25: 5 So he sent ten young men and said to **them**[s] [+2021], "Go up to
25: 8 Ask your own **servants** and they will tell you. Therefore be
25: 8 Therefore be favorable toward my **young men**, since we come at a
25: 9 When David's **men** arrived, they gave Nabal this message in
25: 12 David's **men** turned around and went back. When they arrived,
25: 14 One **[RPH]** of the servants told Nabal's wife Abigail: "David sent
25: 14 One of the **servants** told Nabal's wife Abigail: "David sent
25: 19 Then she told her **servants**, "Go on ahead; I'll follow you."
25: 25 But as for me, your servant, I did not see the **men** my master sent.
25: 27 has brought to my master, be given to the **men** who follow you.
26: 22 "Let one of your **young men** come over and get it.
30: 13 He said, "I am an **[NIE]** Egyptian, the slave of an Amalekite.
30: 17 except four hundred **young** men who rode off on camels and fled.
2Sa 1: 5 Then David said to the **young man** who brought him the report,
1: 6 the **young man** said, "and there was Saul, leaning on his spear,
1: 13 David said to the **young man** who brought him the report,
1: 15 David called one of his **men** and said, "Go, strike him down!"
2: 14 "Let's have *some* of the **young men** get up and fight hand to hand
2: 21 take on one of the **young men** and strip him of his weapons."
4: 12 So David gave an order to his **men**, and they killed them. They cut
9: 9 Then the king summoned Ziba, Saul's **servant**, and said to him,
12: 16 David pleaded with God for the **child**. He fasted and went into his
13: 17 He called his **personal servant** [+9250] and said, "Get this woman
13: 28 Absalom ordered his **men**, "Listen! When Amnon is in high spirits
13: 29 So Absalom's **men** did to Amnon what Absalom had ordered.
13: 32 "My lord should not think that they killed all the **[NIE]** princes;
13: 34 Now the **man** standing watch looked up and saw many people on
14: 21 "Very well, I will do it. Go, bring back the **young man** Absalom."
16: 1 there was Ziba, the **steward** *of* Mephibosheth, waiting to meet
16: 2 household to ride on, the bread and fruit are for the **men** to eat,
17: 18 a **young man** saw them and told Absalom. So the two of them left
18: 5 and Ittai, "Be gentle with the **young man** Absalom for my sake."
18: 12 and Ittai, 'Protect the **young man** Absalom for my sake.'
18: 15 And ten of Joab's armor-bearers surrounded **[NIE]** Absalom,
18: 29 The king asked, "Is the **young man** Absalom safe?" Ahimaaz
18: 32 The king asked the Cushite, "Is the **young man** Absalom safe?"
18: 32 and all who rise up to harm you be like that **young man**."
19: 17 [19:18] along with Ziba, the **steward** *of* Saul's household, and his
20: 11 One of Joab's **men** stood beside Amasa and said, "Whoever favors
1Ki 3: 7 I am only a little **child** and do not know how to carry out my
11: 17 Hadad, still only a **boy** [+7783], fled to Egypt with some Edomite
11: 28 and when Solomon saw how well the **young man** did his work,
14: 3 and go to him. He will tell you what will happen to the **boy**."
14: 17 soon as she stepped over the threshold of the house, the **boy** died.
18: 43 "Go and look toward the sea," he told his **servant**. And he went up
19: 3 When he came to Beersheba in Judah, he left his **servant** there,
20: 14 'The **young officers** *of* the provincial commanders will do it.' "
20: 15 So Ahab summoned the **young officers** *of* the provincial
20: 17 The **young officers** *of* the provincial commanders went out first.
20: 19 The **young officers** *of* the provincial commanders marched out of
2Ki 2: 23 *some* **youths** [+7783] came out of the town and jeered at him.
4: 12 He said to his **servant** Gehazi, "Call the Shunammite." So he
4: 19 to his father. His father told a **servant**, "Carry him to his mother."
4: 22 "Please send me one of the **servants** and a donkey so I can go to
4: 24 She saddled the donkey and said to her **servant**, "Lead on;
4: 25 in the distance, the man of God said to his **servant** Gehazi, "Look!
4: 29 anyone greets you, do not answer. Lay my staff on the **boy's** face."
4: 30 But the **child's** mother said, "As surely as the LORD lives
4: 31 Gehazi went on ahead and laid the staff on the **boy's** face,
4: 31 back to meet Elisha and told him, "The **boy** has not awakened."
4: 32 reached the house, there was the **boy** lying dead on his couch.
4: 35 him once more. The **boy** sneezed seven times and opened his eyes.
4: 35 The boy sneezed seven times and opened his eyes. **[RPH]**
4: 38 he said to his **servant**, "Put on the large pot and cook some stew
5: 14 his flesh was restored and became clean like that of a young **boy**.
5: 20 Gehazi, the **servant** *of* Elisha the man of God, said to himself,
5: 22 'Two **young men** from the company of the prophets have just come
5: 23 He gave them to two of his **servants**, and they carried them ahead
6: 15 the city. "Oh, my lord, what shall we do?" the **servant** asked.
6: 17 Then the LORD opened the **servant's** eyes, and he looked
8: 4 talking to Gehazi, the **servant** *of* the man of God, and had said,
9: 4 So the **young man**, the prophet, went to Ramoth Gilead.
9: 4 So the young man, **[RPH]** the prophet, went to Ramoth Gilead.
19: 6 those words with which the **underlings** *of* the king of Assyria have
1Ch 12: 28 [12:29] Zadok, a brave **young** warrior, with 22 officers from his
22: 5 David said, "My son Solomon is **young** and inexperienced,
29: 1 the one whom God has chosen, is **young** and inexperienced.
2Ch 13: 7 and opposed Rehoboam son of Solomon when he was **young**
34: 3 In the eighth year of his reign, while he was still **young**, he began
Ne 4: 16 [4:10] From that day on, half of my **men** did the work,
4: 22 [4:16] every man and his **helper** stay inside Jerusalem at night,
4: 23 [4:17] Neither I nor my brothers nor my **men** nor the guards with
5: 10 and my **men** are also lending the people money and grain.
5: 15 to food and wine. Their **assistants** also lorded it over the people.
5: 16 All my **men** were assembled there for the work; we did not acquire
6: 5 the fifth time, Sanballat sent his **aide** to me with the same message,
13: 19 I stationed some of my own **men** at the gates so that no load could
Est 2: 2 the king's **personal attendants** [+9250] proposed, "Let a search be
3: 13 **young** and old, women and little children—on a single day,
6: 3 has been done for him," his **attendants** [+9250] answered.
6: 5 His **attendants** answered, "Haman is standing in the court."
Job 1: 15 They put the **servants** to the sword, and I am the only one who has
1: 16 of God fell from the sky and burned up the sheep and the **servants**,
1: 17 They put the **servants** to the sword, and I am the only one who has
1: 19 It collapsed on **them**[s] [+2021] and they are dead, and I am the only
24: 5 of foraging food; the wasteland provides food for their **children**.
29: 5 the Almighty was still with me and my **children** were around me,
29: 8 the **young men** saw me and stepped aside and the old men rose to
Ps 37: 25 I was **young** and now I am old, yet I have never seen the righteous
119: 9 How can a **young man** keep his way pure? By living according to
148: 12 young men and maidens, old men and **children**.
Pr 1: 4 prudence to the simple, knowledge and discretion to the **young**—
7: 7 I noticed among the young men, a **youth** who lacked judgment.
20: 11 Even a **child** is known by his actions, by whether his conduct is
22: 6 Train a **child** in the way he should go, and when he is old he will

Pr 22:15 Folly is bound up in the heart of a **child**, but the rod of discipline
23:13 Do not withhold discipline from a **child**; if you punish him with
29:15 imparts wisdom, but a **child** left to himself disgraces his mother.
Ecc 10:16 O land whose king was a **servant** and whose princes feast in the
Isa 3:4 I will make **boys** their officials; mere children will govern them.
3:5 The **young** will rise up against the old, the base against the
7:16 before the **boy** knows enough to reject the wrong and choose the
8:4 Before the **boy** knows how to say 'My father' or 'My mother,'
10:19 of his forests will be so few that a **child** could write them down.
11:6 and the yearling together; and a little **child** will lead them.
13:18 Their bows will strike down the **young men**; they will have no
20:4 barefoot the Egyptian captives and Cushite exiles, **young** and old,
37:6 those words with which the **underlings** *of* the king of Assyria have
40:30 Even **youths** grow tired and weary, and young men stumble
65:20 his years; he who dies at a hundred will be thought a *mere* **youth**;
Jer 1:6 I said, "I do not know how to speak; I am only a **child**."
1:7 But the LORD said to me, "Do not say, 'I am only a **child**.'
51:22 I shatter man and woman, with you I shatter old man and **youth**,
La 2:21 "**Young** and old lie together in the dust of the streets; my young
5:13 men toil at the millstones; **boys** stagger under loads of wood.
Hos 11:1 "When Israel was a **child**, I loved him, and out of Egypt I called
Zec 2:4 [2:8] "Run, tell that **young man**, 'Jerusalem will be a city without
11:16 or seek the **young**, or heal the injured, or feed the healthy,

5854 נֹ֫עַר ***nō'ar***, n.m. [4] [√ 5853]

youth [3], child's [1]

Job 33:25 his flesh is renewed like a **child's**; it is restored as in the days of
36:14 They die in their **youth**, among male prostitutes of the shrines.
Ps 88:15 [88:16] From my **youth** I have been afflicted and close to death;
Pr 29:21 If a man pampers his servant from **youth**, he will bring grief in the

5855 [1]נַעֲרָה ***na'ărâ***[1], n.f. [63] [→ 5856; cf. 5853]

girl [19], girl's [10], maids [7], servant girls [5], *untranslated* [4], girls [4], she[s] [+2021] [3], young [3], her[s] [+2021] [2], young woman [2], attendants [1], girl's [+4200] [1], girls [+1435] [1], she[s] [1]

Ge 24:14 May it be that when I say to a **girl**, 'Please let down your jar that I
24:16 The **girl** was very beautiful, a virgin; no man had ever lain with
24:28 The **girl** ran and told her mother's household about these things.
24:55 and her mother replied, "Let the **girl** remain with us ten days or so;
24:57 Then they said, "Let's call the **girl** and ask her about it."
24:61 Then Rebekah and her **maids** got ready and mounted their camels
34:3 daughter of Jacob, and he loved the **girl** and spoke tenderly to her.
34:3 of Jacob, and he loved the girl and spoke tenderly to **her**[s] [+2021].
34:12 I'll pay whatever you ask me. Only give me the **girl** as my wife."
Ex 2:5 to bathe, and her **attendants** were walking along the river bank.
Dt 22:15 the **girl's** [K 5853] father and mother shall bring proof that she
22:15 mother shall bring proof that **she**[s] [+2021] [K 5853] was a virgin
22:16 The **girl's** [K 5853] father will say to the elders, "I gave my
22:19 him a hundred shekels of silver and give them to the **girl's** father,
22:20 no proof of the **girl's** [+4200] [K 5853] virginity can be found,
22:21 **she**[s] [+2021] [K 5853] shall be brought to the door of her father's
22:23 If a man happens to meet in a town a virgin **[RPH]** pledged to be
22:24 the **girl** [K 5853] because she was in a town and did not scream
22:25 if out in the country a man happens to meet a **girl** [K 5853]
22:26 Do nothing to the **girl**; [K 5853] she has committed no sin
22:26 to the girl; **she**[s] [K 5853] has committed no sin deserving death.
22:27 though the betrothed **girl** [K 5853] screamed, there was no one to
22:28 If a man happens to meet a **[RPH]** virgin who is not pledged to be
22:29 he shall pay the **girl's** [K 5853] father fifty shekels of silver.
Jdg 19:3 and when **her**[s] [+2021] father saw him, he gladly welcomed him.
19:4 His father-in-law, the **girl's** father, prevailed upon him to stay;
19:5 he prepared to leave, but the **girl's** father said to his son-in-law,
19:6 Afterward the **girl's** father said, "Please stay tonight and enjoy
19:8 when he rose to go, the **girl's** father said, "Refresh yourself.
19:9 up to leave, his father-in-law, the **girl's** father, said, "Now look,
21:12 four hundred **young** women who had never slept with a man,
Ru 2:5 the foreman of his harvesters, "Whose **young woman** is that?"
2:6 **[RPH]** "She is the Moabitess who came back from Moab with
2:8 and don't go away from here. Stay here with my **servant girls**.
2:22 "It will be good for you, my daughter, to go with his **girls**,
2:23 So Ruth stayed close to the **servant girls** *of* Boaz to glean until the
3:2 Is not Boaz, with whose **servant girls** you have been, a kinsman of
4:12 the offspring the LORD gives you by this **young woman**,
1Sa 9:11 they met *some* **girls** coming out to draw water, and they asked
25:42 attended by her five **maids**, went with David's messengers
1Ki 1:2 "Let us look for a **young** virgin to attend the king and take care of
1:3 they searched throughout Israel for a beautiful **girl** and found
1:4 The **girl** was very beautiful; she took care of the king and waited
2Ki 5:2 Aram had gone out and had taken captive a young **girl** from Israel,
5:4 went to his master and told him what the **girl** from Israel had said.
Est 2:2 "Let a search be made for beautiful **young** virgins for the king.
2:3 these beautiful **girls** [+1435] into the harem at the citadel of Susa.
2:4 Then let the **girl** who pleases the king be queen instead of Vashti."
2:7 This **girl**, who was also known as Esther, was lovely in form
2:8 many **girls** were brought to the citadel of Susa and put under the
2:9 The **girl** pleased him and won his favor. Immediately he provided
2:9 He assigned to her seven **maids** selected from the king's palace
2:9 and moved her and her **maids** into the best place in the harem.
2:12 Before a **girl's** turn came to go in to King Xerxes, she had to
2:12 Before a girl's turn came **[RPH]** to go in to King Xerxes,
2:13 this is how **she**[s] [+2021] would go to the king: Anything she
4:4 When Esther's **maids** and eunuchs came and told her about
4:16 for three days, night or day. I and my **maids** will fast as you do.
Job 41:5 [40:29] pet of him like a bird or put him on a leash for your **girls**?
Pr 9:3 She has sent out her **maids**, and she calls from the highest point of
27:27 to feed you and your family and to nourish your **servant girls**.
31:15 she provides food for her family and portions for her **servant girls**.
Am 2:7 Father and son use the same **girl** and so profane my holy name.

5856 [2]נַעֲרָה ***na'ărâ***[2], n.pr.f. [3] [→ 5855, 5858?; cf. 5853, 5857?]

Naarah [3]

1Ch 4:5 Ashhur the father of Tekoa had two wives, Helah and **Naarah**.
4:6 **Naarah** bore him Ahuzzam, Hepher, Temeni and Haahashtari.
4:6 Temeni and Haahashtari. These were the descendants of **Naarah**.

5857 [3]נַעֲרָה ***na'ărâ***[3], n.pr.loc. [1] [cf. 5856?, 5858?, 5860]

Naarah [1]

Jos 16:7 it went down from Janoah to Ataroth and **Naarah**, touched Jericho

5858 נַעֲרַי ***na'ăray***, n.pr.m. [1] [cf. 5856?, 5857?]

Naarai [1]

1Ch 11:37 Hezro the Carmelite, **Naarai** son of Ezbai,

5859 נְעַרְיָה ***n^{e}'aryâ***, n.pr.m. [3] [√ 5853? + 3378]

Neariah [3]

1Ch 3:22 his sons: Hattush, Igal, Bariah, **Neariah** and Shaphat—six in all.
3:23 The sons of **Neariah**: Elioenai, Hizkiah and Azrikam—three in all.
4:42 led by Pelatiah, **Neariah**, Rephaiah and Uzziel, the sons of Ishi,

5860 נַעֲרָן ***na'ărān***, n.pr.loc. [1] [cf. 5857]

Naaran [1]

1Ch 7:28 **Naaran** to the east, Gezer and its villages to the west,

5861 נְעֹרֶת ***n^{e}'ōret***, n.f. [2] [√ 5850]

piece of string [+7348] [1], tinder [1]

Jdg 16:9 he snapped the thongs as easily as a **piece of string** [+7348] snaps
Isa 1:31 The mighty man will become **tinder** and his work a spark;

5862 נֹף ***nōp***, n.pr.loc. [7] [cf. 5132]

Memphis [7]

Isa 19:13 of Zoan have become fools, the leaders of **Memphis** are deceived;
Jer 2:16 the men of **Memphis** and Tahpanhes have shaved the crown of
44:1 in Migdol, Tahpanhes and **Memphis**—and in Upper Egypt:
46:14 it in Migdol; proclaim it also in **Memphis** and Tahpanhes:
46:19 for **Memphis** will be laid waste and lie in ruins without inhabitant.
Eze 30:13 will destroy the idols and put an end to the images in **Memphis**.
30:16 will be taken by storm; **Memphis** will be in constant distress.

5863 נֶ֫פֶג ***nepeg***, n.pr.m. [4]

Nepheg [4]

Ex 6:21 The sons of Izhar were Korah, **Nepheg** and Zicri.
2Sa 5:15 Ibhar, Elishua, **Nepheg**, Japhia,
1Ch 3:7 Nogah, **Nepheg**, Japhia,
14:6 Nogah, **Nepheg**, Japhia,

5864 [1]נָפָה ***nāpâ***[1], n.f. [1] [√ 5677]

sieve [1]

Isa 30:28 He shakes the nations in the **sieve** *of* destruction; he places in the

5865 [2]נָפָה ***nāpâ***[2], n.f. Not used in NIV/BHS [√ 5679; cf. 5868]

5866 נְפוּסִים ***n^{e}pûsîm***, n.pr.[g.?]. [1] [→ 5867, 5873, 5875]

Nephussim [1]

Ezr 2:50 Asnah, Meunim, **Nephussim**, [K 5873]

5867 נְפוּשְׁסִים ***nᵉpûššîm***, n.pr.[g.?]. [1] [√ 5866]

Nephussim [1]

Ne 7:52 Besai, Meunim, **Nephussim**, [Q 5875]

5868 נָפוֹת ***nāpôt***, n.pr.loc. [0 / 1] [√ 5679; cf. 5865]

Naphoth [1]

Jos 17:11 settlements (the third in the list is **Naphoth**). [BHS 5884]

5869 נָפוֹת דֹּאר ***nāpôt dōʾr***, נָפוֹת דּוֹר ***nāpôt dôr***, n.pr.loc. [3] [√ 5679 + 1799]

Naphoth Dor [3]

Jos 11: 2 in the western foothills and in **Naphoth Dor** on the west;
12:23 the king of Dor (in **Naphoth Dor**) one the king of Goyim in
1Ki 4:11 in **Naphoth Dor** (he was married to Taphath daughter of

5870 נָפַח ***nāpaḥ***, v. [12] [→ 5134, 5135, 9515; cf. 7031]

boiling [2], blast [1], blew away [1], blow [1], breathe last [+5883] [1], breathe [1], breathed [1], broken [1], fans [1], sniff contemptuously [1], unfanned [+4202] [1]

Ge 2: 7 [A] the ground and **breathed** into his nostrils the breath of life,
Job 20:26 [E] A fire **unfanned** [+4202] will consume him and devour what
31:39 [G] its yield without payment or **broken** the spirit of its tenants,
41:20 [41:12] [B] Smoke pours from his nostrils as from a **boiling** pot
Isa 54:16 [A] it is I who created the blacksmith *who* **fans** the coals *into*
Jer 1:13 [B] "I see a **boiling** pot, tilting away from the north," I answered.
15: 9 [A] of seven will grow faint and **breathe** [+5883] her **last**.
Eze 22:20 [A] iron, lead and tin into a furnace to melt it with a fiery **blast**,
22:21 [A] I will gather you and *I will* **blow** on you with my fiery wrath,
37: 9 [A] O breath, and **breathe** into these slain, that they may live.' "
Hag 1: 9 [A] to be little. What you brought home, *I* **blew away**. Why?"
Mal 1:13 [G] *you* **sniff** *at* it **contemptuously**," says the LORD Almighty.

5871 נֹפַח ***nōpaḥ***, n.pr.loc. [1]

Nophah [1]

Nu 21:30 We have demolished them as far as **Nophah**, which extends to

5872 נְפִילִים ***nᵉpîlîm***, n.m.pl. [3] [√ 5877]

Nephilim [3]

Ge 6: 4 The **Nephilim** were on the earth in those days—and also
Nu 13:33 We saw the **Nephilim** there (the descendants of Anak come from
13:33 there (the descendants of Anak come from the **Nephilim**).

5873 נְפִיסִים ***nᵉpîsîm***, n.pr.g.?. [0] [√ 5866]

Ezr 2:50 [Asnah, Meunim, **Nephussim**, [K; see Q 5866]]

5874 נָפִישׁ ***nāpîš***, n.pr.m. [3] [√ 5882]

Naphish [3]

Ge 25:15 Hadad, Tema, Jetur, **Naphish** and Kedemah.
1Ch 1:31 Jetur, **Naphish** and Kedemah. These were the sons of Ishmael.
5:19 They waged war against the Hagrites, Jetur, **Naphish** and Nodab.

5875 נְפִישְׁסִים ***nᵉpîšᵉsîm***, n.pr.g.?. [0] [√ 5866]

Ne 7:52 [Besai, Meunim, **Nephussim**, [Q; see K 5867]]

5876 נֹפֶךְ ***nōpek***, n.[m.]. [4]

turquoise [4]

Ex 28:18 in the second row a **turquoise**, a sapphire and an emerald;
39:11 in the second row a **turquoise**, a sapphire and an emerald;
Eze 27:16 they exchanged **turquoise**, purple fabric, embroidered work,
28:13 chrysolite, onyx and jasper, sapphire, **turquoise** and beryl.

5877 נָפַל ***nāpal***, v. [434] [→ 5139, 5142, 5143, 5147, 5872, 5878; Ar 10484]

fall [102], fell [67], fallen [40], falls [23], cast [13], allotted [4], collapsed [4], down [4], downfall [4], failed [4], gone over [4], make fall [4], allot [3], bring down [3], came [3], cut down [3], fall down [3], falling [3], fell down [3], put [3], bring [2], brought down [2], defected [2], deserting [2], downcast [2], falls prostrate [2], fell prostrate [2], going to death [2], got down [2], have cut down [2], inferior [2], lay [2], lie fallen [2], lying [2], seized [+6584] [2], surely come to ruin [+5877] [2], surrender [2], those[s] [+2021] [2], threw arms around [+6584+7418] [2], threw down [2], threw [2], waste away [2], *untranslated* [1], afraid [+6584+7065] [1], allocate [1], allots [1], assail [+6584] [1], attack [+928] [1], attacked [+928] [1], attacked [1], become [1], bowed down [+6584+7156] [1], bowed down to the ground [+6584+7156] [1], brings on [1], cast down [1], casting [1], cause to fall [1], caused to fall [1], collapse [1], collapses [1], come into [+928+4200] [1], come over [1], confined [1], consisted of [1], cracked [+7288] [1], crumble [1], cutting down [1], defeated [1], deserts [1], died [1], do not count [1], down came [1], dropped out [1], drops [1], erodes [1], fail [+824+2025+4946] [1], fall in battle [+2728] [1], fall limp [1], fallen down [1], falls down [1], fell dead [1], frown [+7156] [1], give birth [1], give up [1], given birth [1], gone down [1], happens [1], have fall [1], hear [+4200+7156] [1], hurtling down [1], killed [1], knocks out [1], lay prostrate [1], left [1], let fall [1], lie [1], lived in hostility toward [+6584+7156] [1], lose [1], lost [+4946] [1], lost [+907+4946] [1], lost self-confidence [+928+4394+6524] [1], made come down [1], make drop [1], make lie down [1], make [1], making [1], neglect [1], overpower [1], overwhelmed [+6584] [1], perish [1], pleading [+9382] [1], plunge [1], precious [+4202] [1], present [+4200+7156] [1], reach [1], settled [1], settles [1], sink [1], slaughter [1], slay [1], someone[s] [+2021] [1], stilled [1], strewn [1], stumble [1], such force[s] [1], surrenders [1], those[s] [1], threw arms around [+6584] [1], throw in [1], throw [1], throwing himself down [1], thrown [1], tumbles [1], wastes away [1], were[s] [1]

Ge 2:21 [G] So the LORD God **caused** the man **to fall** *into* a deep sleep;
4: 5 [A] So Cain was very angry, and his face *was* **downcast**.
4: 6 [A] to Cain, "Why are you angry? Why *is* your face **downcast**?
14:10 [A] *some of the men* **fell** into them and the rest fled to the hills.
15:12 [A] As the sun was setting, Abram **fell** *into* a deep sleep, and a
15:12 [A] deep sleep, and a thick and dreadful darkness **came** over him.
17: 3 [A] Abram **fell** facedown, and God said to him,
17:17 [A] Abraham **fell** facedown; he laughed and said to himself,
24:64 [A] also looked up and saw Isaac. *She* **got down** from her camel
25:18 [A] *they* **lived in hostility** [+6584+7156] **toward** all their
33: 4 [A] *he* **threw** [+6584] *his* **arms around** his neck and kissed him.
43:18 [F] He wants to attack us and **overpower** us and seize us as
44:14 [A] and *they* **threw** *themselves* to the ground before him.
45:14 [A] *he* **threw** [+6584+7418] *his* **arms around** his brother
46:29 [A] *he* **threw** [+6584+7418] *his* **arms around** his father
49:17 [A] bites the horse's heels so that its rider **tumbles** backward.
50: 1 [A] Joseph **threw** *himself* upon his father and wept over him
50:18 [A] then came and **threw** *themselves* **down** before him.
Ex 15:16 [A] terror and dread *will* **fall** upon them. By the power of your
19:21 [A] way through to see the LORD and many of them **perish**.
21:18 [A] or with his fist and he does not die but *is* **confined** to bed,
21:27 [G] if *he* **knocks out** the tooth of a manservant or maidservant,
21:33 [A] and fails to cover it and an ox or a donkey **falls** into it,
32:28 [A] and that day about three thousand of the people **died**.
Lev 9:24 [A] all the people saw it, they shouted for joy and **fell** facedown.
11:32 [A] When one of them dies and **falls** on something, that article,
11:33 [A] If one of them **falls** into a clay pot, everything in it will be
11:35 [A] Anything that one of their carcasses **falls** on becomes
11:37 [A] If a carcass **falls** on any seeds that are to be planted,
11:38 [A] But if water has been put on the seed and a carcass **falls** on it,
26: 7 [A] your enemies, and *they will* **fall** by the sword before you.
26: 8 [A] and your enemies *will* **fall** by the sword before you.
26:36 [A] and *they will* **fall**, even though no one is pursuing them.
Nu 5:21 [A] and denounce you when he causes your thigh *to* **waste away**
5:22 [G] so that your abdomen swells and your thigh **wastes away**."
5:27 [A] her abdomen will swell and her thigh **waste away**, and she
6:12 [A] The previous days **do not count**, because he became defiled
14: 3 [A] Why is the LORD bringing us to this land only to *let us* **fall**
14: 5 [A] Aaron **fell** facedown in front of the whole Israelite assembly
14:29 [A] In this desert your bodies *will* **fall**—every one of you twenty
14:32 [A] But you—your bodies *will* **fall** in this desert.
14:43 [A] he will not be with you and *you will* **fall** by the sword."
16: 4 [A] When Moses heard this, *he* **fell** facedown.
16:22 [A] But Moses and Aaron **fell** facedown and cried out, "O God,
16:45 [17:10] [A] an end to them at once." And *they* **fell** facedown.
20: 6 [A] to the entrance to the Tent of Meeting and **fell** facedown,
24: 4 [A] *who* **falls prostrate**, and whose eyes are opened:
24:16 [A] *who* **falls prostrate**, and whose eyes are opened:
34: 2 [A] the land that *will be* **allotted** to you as an inheritance will
35:23 [G] **drops** a stone on him that could kill him, and he dies,
Dt 9:18 [F] once again *I* **fell prostrate** before the LORD for forty days
9:25 [F] *I* **lay prostrate** before the LORD those forty days and forty
9:25 [F] **[RPH]** because the LORD had said he would destroy you.
21: 1 [A] **lying** in a field in the land the LORD your God is giving
22: 4 [A] If you see your brother's donkey or his ox **fallen** on the road,
22: 8 [A] on your house if **someone**[s] [+2021] falls from the roof.
22: 8 [A] of bloodshed on your house if someone **falls** from the roof.
25: 2 [G] the judge *shall* **make** him **lie down** and have him flogged in
Jos 2: 9 [A] this land to you and that a great fear of you *has* **fallen** on us,
5:14 [A] Joshua **fell** facedown to the ground in reverence, and asked
6: 5 [A] the wall of the city *will* **collapse** and the people will go up,
6:20 [A] when the people gave a loud shout, the wall **collapsed**;
7: 6 [A] **fell** facedown to the ground before the ark of the LORD,
7:10 [A] "Stand up! What *are* you *doing* **down** on your face?

Jos 8:24 [A] when every one of them *had been* **put** to the sword, all the
8:25 [A] Twelve thousand men and women **fell** that day—
11:7 [A] suddenly at the Waters of Merom and **attacked** [+928] them,
13:6 [G] Be sure *to* **allocate** this land to Israel for an inheritance, as I
17:5 [A] Manasseh's share **consisted of** ten tracts of land besides
21:45 [A] all the LORD's good promises to the house of Israel **failed**;
23:4 [G] *I have* **allotted** as an inheritance for your tribes all the land
23:14 [A] good promises the LORD your God gave you *has* **failed**.
23:14 [A] Every promise has been fulfilled; not one *has* **failed**.
Jdg 2:19 [G] *They* refused *to* **give up** their evil practices and stubborn
3:25 [A] There they saw their lord **fallen** to the floor, dead.
4:16 [A] All the troops of Sisera **fell** by the sword; not a man was left.
4:22 [A] and there **lay** Sisera with the tent peg through his temple—
5:27 [A] At her feet he sank, *he* **fell**; there he lay. At her feet he sank,
5:27 [A] At her feet he sank, *he* **fell**; where he sank, there he fell—
5:27 [A] her feet he sank, he fell; where he sank, there *he* **fell**—dead.
7:12 [A] and all the other eastern peoples *had* **settled** in the valley,
7:13 [A] It struck the tent with **such force**[s] that the tent overturned
7:13 [A] tent with such force that the tent overturned and **collapsed**."
8:10 [A] a hundred and twenty thousand swordsmen *had* **fallen**.
9:40 [A] chased him, and many **fell** wounded in the flight—
12:6 [A] Forty-two thousand Ephraimites *were* **killed** at that time.
13:20 [A] Manoah and his wife **fell** with their faces to the ground.
15:18 [A] die of thirst and **fall** into the hands of the uncircumcised?"
16:30 [A] **down came** the temple on the rulers and all the people in it.
18:1 [A] because they *had* not yet **come** [+928+4200] **into** an
19:26 [A] **fell down** *at* the door and lay there until daylight.
19:27 [A] there lay his concubine, **fallen** *in* the doorway of the house,
20:44 [A] Eighteen thousand Benjamites **fell**, all of them valiant
20:46 [A] On that day twenty-five thousand Benjamite swordsmen **fell**,
Ru 2:10 [A] At this, she bowed **down** with her face to the ground. She
3:18 [A] "Wait, my daughter, until you find out what **happens**.
1Sa 3:19 [G] he grew up, and *he* **let** none of his words **fall** to the ground.
4:10 [A] very great; Israel **lost** [+4946] thirty thousand foot soldiers.
4:18 [A] of God, Eli **fell** backward off his chair by the side of the gate.
5:3 [A] **fallen** on his face on the ground before the ark of the
5:4 [A] **fallen** on his face on the ground before the ark of the
11:7 [A] the terror of the LORD **fell** on the people, and they turned
14:13 [A] The Philistines **fell** before Jonathan, and his armor-bearer
14:42 [G] Saul said, "**Cast** the lot between me and Jonathan my son."
14:45 [A] LORD lives, not a hair of his head *will* **fall** to the ground,
17:32 [A] to Saul, "*Let* no one **lose** heart on account of this Philistine;
17:49 [A] sank into his forehead, and *he* **fell** facedown on the ground.
17:52 [A] Their dead *were* **strewn** along the Shaaraim road to Gath
18:25 [G] plan was to **have** David **fall** by the hands of the Philistines.
19:24 [A] *He* **lay** that way all that day and night. This is why people
20:41 [A] ⌞of the stone⌟ and bowed **down** before Jonathan three times,
25:23 [A] and bowed **down** before David with her face to the ground.
25:24 [A] *She* **fell** at his feet and said: "My lord, let the blame be on me
26:12 [A] because the LORD *had* **put** them *into* a deep sleep.
26:20 [A] Now *do* not *let* my blood **fall** to the ground far from the
28:20 [A] Immediately Saul **fell** full length on the ground, filled with
29:3 [A] from the day he **left** Saul until now, I have found no fault in
31:1 [A] fled before them, and *many* **fell** slain on Mount Gilboa.
31:4 [A] would not do it; so Saul took his own sword and **fell** on it.
31:5 [A] Saul was dead, he too **fell** on his sword and died with him.
31:8 [A] they found Saul and his three sons **fallen** on Mount Gilboa.
2Sa 1:2 [A] he came to David, *he* **fell** to the ground to pay him honor.
1:4 [A] Many of them **fell** and died. And Saul and his son Jonathan
1:10 [A] because I knew that after he *had* **fallen** he could not survive.
1:12 [A] the house of Israel, because *they had* **fallen** by the sword.
1:19 [A] lies slain on your heights. How the mighty *have* **fallen**!
1:25 [A] "How the mighty *have* **fallen** in battle! Jonathan lies slain on
1:27 [A] "How the mighty *have* **fallen**! The weapons of war have
2:16 [A] dagger into his opponent's side, and *they* **fell down** together.
2:23 [A] came out through his back. *He* **fell** there and died on the spot.
2:23 [A] stopped when he came to the place where Asahel *had* **fallen**
3:29 [A] on a crutch or *who* **falls** by the sword or who lacks food."
3:34 [A] were not fettered. *You* **fell** as one falls before wicked men."
3:34 [A] were not fettered. You fell as *one* **falls** before wicked men."
3:38 [A] that a prince and a great man *has* **fallen** in Israel this day?
4:4 [A] but as she hurried to leave, *he* **fell** and became crippled.
9:6 [A] to David, *he* **bowed** [+6584+7156] **down** to pay him honor.
11:17 [A] fought against Joab, some of the men in David's army **fell**;
14:4 [A] *she* **fell** with her face to the ground to pay him honor, and she
14:11 [A] "not one hair of your son's head *will* **fall** to the ground."
14:22 [A] Joab **fell** with his face to the ground to pay him honor, and he
17:9 [A] If *he should* **attack** [+928] your troops first, whoever hears
17:12 [A] and we will fall on him as dew **settles** on the ground.
19:18 [19:19] [A] the Jordan, *he* **fell prostrate** before the king
20:8 [A] As he stepped forward, *it* **dropped out** *of* its sheath.
20:15 [G] While they were battering the wall to **bring** it **down**,
21:9 [A] All seven of them **fell** together; they were put to death during
21:22 [A] in Gath, and *they* **fell** at the hands of David and his men.
22:39 [A] and they could not rise; *they* **fell** beneath my feet.
24:14 [A] *Let us* **fall** into the hands of the LORD, for his mercy is
24:14 [A] mercy is great; but *do* not *let me* **fall** into the hands of men."
1Ki 1:52 [A] a worthy man, not a hair of his head *will* **fall** to the ground;
8:56 [A] Not one word *has* **failed** of all the good promises he gave
18:7 [A] **bowed** [+6584+7156] **down to the ground**, and said, "Is it
18:38 [A] Then the fire of the LORD **fell** and burned up the sacrifice,
18:39 [A] people saw this, *they* **fell** prostrate and cried, "The LORD—
20:25 [A] must also raise an army like the one you **lost** [+907+4946]—
20:30 [A] where the wall **collapsed** on twenty-seven thousand of them.
22:20 [A] into attacking Ramoth Gilead and **going to** *his* **death** there?'
2Ki 1:2 [A] Now Ahaziah *had* **fallen** through the lattice of his upper
2:13 [A] He picked up the cloak that *had* **fallen** from Elijah and went
2:14 [A] he took the cloak that *had* **fallen** from him and struck the
3:19 [G] *You will* **cut down** every good tree, stop up all the springs,
3:25 [G] stopped up all the springs and **cut down** every good tree.
4:37 [A] She came in, **fell** at his feet and bowed to the ground.
5:21 [A] toward him, *he* **got down** from the chariot to meet him.
6:5 [G] As one of them was **cutting down** a tree, the iron axhead fell
6:5 [A] was cutting down a tree, the iron axhead **fell** into the water.
6:6 [A] The man of God asked, "Where *did it* **fall**?" When he
7:4 [A] So let's go over to the camp of the Arameans and **surrender**.
10:10 [A] against the house of Ahab *will* **fail** [+824+2025+4946].
14:10 [A] Why ask for trouble and *cause* your own **downfall** and that
19:7 [G] and there *I will* **have** him **cut down** with the sword.' "
25:11 [A] **those**[s] [+2021] who had gone over to the king of Babylon.
25:11 [A] and those who *had* **gone over** to the king of Babylon.
1Ch 5:10 [A] war against the Hagrites, *who were* **defeated** at their hands;
5:22 [A] many others **fell** slain, because the battle was God's.
10:1 [A] fled before them, and *many* **fell** slain on Mount Gilboa.
10:4 [A] would not do it; so Saul took his own sword and **fell** on it.
10:5 [A] saw that Saul was dead, he too **fell** on his sword and died.
10:8 [A] they found Saul and his sons **fallen** on Mount Gilboa.
12:19 [12:20] [A] Some of *the men* of Manasseh **defected** to David
12:19 [12:20] [A] "It will cost us our heads *if he* **deserts** to his master
12:20 [12:21] [A] were *the men* of Manasseh *who* **defected** to him:
20:8 [A] in Gath, and *they* **fell** at the hands of David and his men.
21:13 [A] *Let me* **fall** into the hands of the LORD, for his mercy is
21:13 [A] is very great; but *do* not *let me* **fall** into the hands of men."
21:14 [A] on Israel, and seventy thousand men of Israel **fell dead**.
21:16 [A] and the elders, clothed in sackcloth, **fell** facedown.
24:31 [G] They also **cast** lots, just as their brothers the descendants of
25:8 [G] old alike, teacher as well as student, **cast** lots for their duties.
26:13 [G] Lots *were* **cast** for each gate, according to their families,
26:14 [A] The lot for the East Gate **fell** to Shelemiah. Then lots were
26:14 [G] Then lots *were* **cast** *for* his son Zechariah, a wise counselor,
2Ch 13:17 [A] so that *there* **were**[s] five hundred thousand casualties among
14:13 [14:12] [A] Such a great number of Cushites **fell** that they could
15:9 [A] for large numbers *had* **come over** to him from Israel when
18:19 [A] into attacking Ramoth Gilead and **going to** *his* **death** there?'
20:18 [A] and Jerusalem **fell down** in worship before the LORD.
20:24 [A] vast army, they saw only dead bodies **lying** on the ground;
25:19 [A] Why ask for trouble and *cause* your own **downfall** and that
29:9 [A] This is why our fathers *have* **fallen** by the sword and why
32:21 [G] of his god, some of his sons **cut** him **down** with the sword.
Ezr 10:1 [F] and **throwing himself down** before the house of God,
Ne 6:16 [A] and **lost** [+928+4394+6524] their **self-confidence**,
10:34 [10:35] [G] the priests, the Levites and the people—*have* **cast**
11:1 [G] the rest of the people **cast** lots to bring one out of every ten to
Est 3:7 [G] the month of Nisan, *they* **cast** the *pur* (that is, the lot)
6:10 [G] *Do* not **neglect** anything you have recommended."
6:13 [A] "Since Mordecai, before whom your **downfall** has started,
6:13 [A] stand against him—*you will* **surely come to ruin** [+5877]!"
6:13 [A] stand against him—*you will* **surely come to ruin** [+5877]!"
7:8 [A] Haman *was* **falling** on the couch where Esther was reclining.
8:3 [A] again pleaded with the king, **falling** at his feet and weeping.
8:17 [A] because fear of the Jews *had* **seized** [+6584] them.
9:2 [A] all the other nationalities *were* **afraid of** [+6584+7065] them.
9:3 [A] the Jews, because fear of Mordecai *had* **seized** [+6584] them.
9:24 [G] the Jews to destroy them and *had* **cast** the *pur* (that is,
Job 1:15 [A] the Sabeans **attacked** and carried them off. They put the
1:16 [A] "The fire of God **fell** from the sky and burned up the sheep
1:19 [A] *It* **collapsed** on them and they are dead, and I am the only
1:20 [A] and shaved his head. Then *he* **fell** to the ground in worship
4:13 [A] dreams in the night, when deep sleep **falls** on men,
6:27 [G] *You would* even **cast** lots for the fatherless and barter away
12:3 [A] But I have a mind as well as you; I *am* not **inferior** to you.
13:2 [A] What you know, I also know; I *am* not **inferior** to you.
13:11 [A] terrify you? *Would* not the dread of him **fall** on you?
14:18 [A] "But as a mountain **erodes** and crumbles and as a rock is
29:24 [G] the light of my face *was* **precious** [+4202] *to them*.
31:22 [A] *let* my arm **fall** from the shoulder, let it be broken off at the
33:15 [A] when deep sleep **falls** on men as they slumber in their beds,
Ps 5:10 [5:11] [A] O God! *Let* their intrigues *be their* **downfall**.

Ps 7: 15 [7:16] [A] a hole and scoops it out **falls** into the pit he has made.
10: 10 [A] are crushed, they collapse; *they* **fall** under his strength.
16: 6 [A] The boundary lines *have* **fallen** for me in pleasant places;
18: 38 [18:39] [A] that they could not rise; *they* **fell** beneath my feet.
20: 8 [20:9] [A] They are brought to their knees and **fall**, but we rise
22: 18 [22:19] [G] garments among them and **cast** lots for my clothing.
27: 2 [A] and my foes attack me, they will stumble and **fall**.
35: 8 [A] hid entangle them, *may they* **fall** into the pit, to their ruin.
36: 12 [36:13] [A] See how the evildoers **lie fallen**—thrown down, not
37: 14 [G] and bend the bow to **bring down** the poor and needy,
37: 24 [A] though *he* **stumble**, he will not fall, for the LORD upholds
45: 5 [45:6] [A] king's enemies; *let* the nations **fall** beneath your feet.
55: 4 [55:5] [A] within me; the terrors of death **assail** [+6584] me.
57: 6 [57:7] [A] in my path—but *they have* **fallen** into it *themselves*.
69: 9 [69:10] [A] and the insults of those who insult you **fall** on me.
73: 18 [G] place them on slippery ground; *you* **cast** them **down** to ruin.
78: 28 [G] *He* **made** them **come down** inside their camp, all around
78: 55 [G] and **allotted** their lands *to* them as an inheritance;
78: 64 [A] their priests *were* **put** to the sword, and their widows could
82: 7 [A] will die like mere men; *you will* **fall** like every other ruler."
91: 7 [A] A thousand *may* **fall** at your side, ten thousand at your right
105: 38 [A] when they left, because dread of Israel *had* **fallen** on them.
106: 26 [G] uplifted hand that he *would* **make** them **fall** in the desert,
106: 27 [G] **make** their descendants **fall** among the nations and scatter
118: 13 [A] I was pushed back and *about to* **fall**, but the LORD helped
140: 10 [140:11] [G] *may* they *be* **thrown** into the fire, into miry pits,
141: 10 [A] *Let* the wicked **fall** into their own nets, while I pass by in
145: 14 [A] The LORD upholds all those *who* **fall** and lifts up all who
Pr 1: 14 [G] **throw in** your lot with us, and we will share a common
7: 26 [G] Many are the victims *she has* **brought down**; her slain are a
11: 5 [A] but the wicked *are* **brought down** by their own wickedness.
11: 14 [A] For lack of guidance a nation **falls**, but many advisers make
11: 28 [A] Whoever trusts in his riches *will* **fall**, but the righteous will
13: 17 [A] A wicked messenger **falls** into trouble, but a trustworthy
17: 20 [A] not prosper; he whose tongue is deceitful **falls** into trouble.
19: 15 [G] Laziness **brings on** deep sleep, and the shiftless man goes
22: 14 [A] deep pit; he who is under the LORD's wrath *will* **fall** *into* it.
24: 16 [A] for though a righteous man **falls** seven times, he rises again,
24: 17 [A] Do not gloat when your enemy **falls**; when he stumbles,
26: 27 [A] If a man digs a pit, *he will* **fall** into it; if a man rolls a stone,
28: 10 [A] He who leads the upright along an evil path *will* **fall** into his
28: 14 [A] the LORD, but he who hardens his heart **falls** into trouble.
28: 18 [A] kept safe, but he whose ways are perverse *will* suddenly **fall**.
Ecc 4: 10 [A] If one **falls down**, his friend can help him up. But pity the
4: 10 [A] But pity the man who **falls** and has no one to help him up!
9: 12 [A] so men are trapped by evil times that **fall** unexpectedly upon
10: 8 [A] Whoever digs a pit *may* **fall** into it; whoever breaks through
11: 3 [A] Whether a tree **falls** to the south or to the north, in the place
11: 3 [A] falls to the south or to the north, in the place where it **falls**,
Isa 3: 8 [A] Jerusalem staggers, Judah *is* **falling**; their words and deeds
3: 25 [A] Your men *will* **fall** by the sword, your warriors in battle.
8: 15 [A] *they will* **fall** and be broken, they will be snared
9: 8 [9:7] [A] has sent a message against Jacob; *it will* **fall** on Israel.
9: 10 [9:9] [A] "The bricks *have* **fallen down**, but we will rebuild
10: 4 [A] but to cringe among the captives or **fall** among the slain.
10: 34 [A] thickets with an ax; Lebanon *will* **fall** before the Mighty One.
13: 15 [A] be thrust through; all who are caught *will* **fall** by the sword.
14: 12 [A] How *you have* **fallen** from heaven, O morning star, son of
16: 9 [A] your ripened fruit and over your harvests *have been* **stilled**.
21: 9 [A] he gives back the answer: 'Babylon *has* **fallen**, has fallen!
21: 9 [A] he gives back the answer: 'Babylon has fallen, *has* **fallen**!
22: 25 [A] it will be sheared off and *will* **fall**, and the load hanging on it
24: 18 [A] Whoever flees at the sound of terror *will* **fall** into a pit;
24: 20 [A] so heavy upon it is the guilt of its rebellion that *it* **falls**—
26: 18 [A] to the earth; *we have* not **given birth** *to* people of the world.
26: 19 [G] the dew of the morning; the earth *will* **give birth** *to* her dead.
30: 13 [A] **cracked** [+7288] and bulging, that collapses suddenly, in an
30: 25 [A] In the day of great slaughter, when the towers **fall**, streams of
31: 3 [A] he who helps will stumble, he who is helped *will* **fall**;
31: 8 [A] "Assyria *will* **fall** by a sword that is not of man; a sword,
34: 17 [G] He **allots** their portions; his hand distributes them by
37: 7 [G] and there *I will* **have** him **cut down** with the sword.' "
47: 11 [A] A calamity *will* **fall** upon you that you cannot ward off with a
54: 15 [A] not be my doing; whoever attacks you *will* **surrender** to you.
Jer 3: 12 [G] '*I will* **frown** [+7156] on you no longer, for I am merciful,'
6: 15 [A] So *they will* **fall** among the fallen; they will be brought down
6: 15 [A] So they will fall among the **fallen**; they will be brought down
8: 4 [A] " 'When *men* **fall down**, do they not get up? When a man
8: 12 [A] So *they will* **fall** among the fallen; they will be brought down
8: 12 [A] So they will fall among the **fallen**; they will be brought down
9: 22 [9:21] [A] " 'The dead bodies of men *will* **lie** like refuse on the
15: 8 [G] suddenly *I will* **bring down** on them anguish and terror.
19: 7 [G] *I will* **make** them **fall** by the sword before their enemies, at
20: 4 [A] with your own eyes you will see *them* **fall** by the sword of
21: 9 [A] **surrenders** to the Babylonians who are besieging you will
22: 7 [G] cut up your fine cedar beams and **throw** them into the fire.
23: 12 [A] they will be banished to darkness and there *they will* **fall**.
25: 27 [A] **fall** to rise no more because of the sword I will send among
25: 34 [A] has come; you *will* **fall** and be shattered like fine pottery.
36: 7 [A] Perhaps they *will* **bring** their petition before the LORD,
37: 13 [A] and said, "You *are* **deserting** to the Babylonians!"
37: 14 [A] Jeremiah said. "I *am* not **deserting** to the Babylonians."
37: 20 [A] the king, please listen. *Let* me **bring** my petition before you:
38: 19 [A] "I am afraid of the Jews who *have* **gone over** to the
38: 26 [G] 'I *was* **pleading** [+9382] with the king not to send me back
39: 9 [A] along with **those**[s] [+2021] who had gone over to him,
39: 9 [A] along with those who *had* **gone over** to him, and the rest of
39: 18 [A] *you will* not **fall** by the sword but will escape with your life,
42: 2 [A] "Please **hear** [+4200+7156] our petition and pray to the
42: 9 [G] to whom you sent me to **present** [+4200+7156] your
44: 12 [A] in Egypt; *they will* **fall** by the sword or die from famine.
46: 6 [A] In the north by the River Euphrates they stumble and **fall**.
46: 12 [A] will stumble over another; both *will* **fall down** together."
46: 16 [A] They will stumble repeatedly; *they will* **fall** over each other.
48: 32 [A] The destroyer *has* **fallen** on your ripened fruit and grapes.
48: 44 [A] "Whoever flees from the terror *will* **fall** into a pit, whoever
49: 21 [A] At the sound of their **fall** the earth will tremble; their cry will
49: 26 [A] Surely, her young men *will* **fall** in the streets; all her soldiers
50: 15 [A] She surrenders, her towers **fall**, her walls are torn down.
50: 30 [A] Therefore, her young men *will* **fall** in the streets; all her
50: 32 [A] one will stumble and **fall** and no one will help her up;
51: 4 [A] *They will* **fall down** slain in Babylon, fatally wounded in her
51: 8 [A] Babylon *will* suddenly **fall** and be broken. Wail over her!
51: 44 [A] no longer stream to him. And the wall of Babylon *will* **fall**.
51: 47 [A] will be disgraced and her slain *will* all **lie fallen** within her.
51: 49 [A] "Babylon *must* **fall** because of Israel's slain, just as the slain
51: 49 [A] just as the slain in all the earth *have* **fallen** because of
52: 15 [A] and **those**[s] who had gone over to the king of Babylon.
52: 15 [A] and those who *had* **gone over** to the king of Babylon.
La 1: 7 [A] When her people **fell** into enemy hands, there was no one to
2: 21 [A] my young men and maidens *have* **fallen** by the sword.
5: 16 [A] The crown *has* **fallen** from our head. Woe to us, for we have
Eze 1: 28 [A] When I saw it, *I* **fell** facedown, and I heard the voice of one
3: 23 [A] the glory I had seen by the Kebar River, and *I* **fell** facedown.
5: 12 [A] inside you; a third *will* **fall** by the sword outside your walls;
6: 4 [G] and *I will* **slay** your people in front of your idols.
6: 7 [A] Your *people will* **fall** slain among you, and you will know
6: 11 [A] of Israel, for *they will* **fall** by the sword, famine and plague.
6: 12 [A] and he that is near *will* **fall** by the sword, and he that survives
8: 1 [A] the hand of the Sovereign LORD **came** upon me there.
9: 8 [A] *I* **fell** facedown, crying out, "Ah, Sovereign LORD!
11: 5 [A] the Spirit of the LORD **came** upon me, and he told me to
11: 10 [A] *You will* **fall** by the sword, and I will execute judgment on
11: 13 [A] *I* **fell** facedown and cried out in a loud voice, "Ah,
13: 11 [A] tell those who cover it with whitewash that *it is going to* **fall**.
13: 11 [A] come in torrents, and I will send hailstones **hurtling down**,
13: 12 [A] When the wall **collapses**, will people not ask you, "Where is
13: 14 [A] When *it* **falls**, you will be destroyed in it; and you will know
17: 21 [A] All his fleeing troops *will* **fall** by the sword,
23: 25 [A] and those of you who are left *will* **fall** by the sword.
24: 6 [A] Empty it piece by piece without **casting** lots for them.
24: 21 [A] and daughters you left behind *will* **fall** by the sword.
25: 13 [A] and from Teman to Dedan *they will* **fall** by the sword.
27: 27 [A] everyone else on board *will* **sink** into the heart of the sea on
27: 34 [A] your wares and all your company *have* **gone down** with you.
28: 23 [D] The slain *will* **fall** within her, with the sword against her on
29: 5 [A] *You will* **fall** on the open field and not be gathered or picked
30: 4 [A] When the slain **fall** in Egypt, her wealth will be carried away
30: 5 [A] the people of the covenant land *will* **fall** by the sword along
30: 6 [A] " 'The allies of Egypt *will* **fall** and her proud strength will
30: 6 [A] From Migdol to Aswan *they will* **fall** by the sword within
30: 17 [A] young men of Heliopolis and Bubastis *will* **fall** by the sword,
30: 22 [G] as the broken one, and **make** the sword **fall** from his hand.
30: 25 [A] the king of Babylon, but the arms of Pharaoh *will* **fall limp**.
31: 12 [A] Its boughs **fell** on the mountains and in all the valleys; its
32: 12 [G] *I will* **cause** your hordes **to fall** by the swords of mighty
32: 20 [A] *They will* **fall** among those killed by the sword. The sword is
32: 22 [A] the graves of all her slain, all who *have* **fallen** by the sword.
32: 23 [A] terror in the land of the living are slain, **fallen** by the sword.
32: 24 [A] around her grave. All of them are slain, **fallen** by the sword.
32: 27 [A] lie with the other uncircumcised warriors *who have* **fallen**,
33: 27 [A] as I live, those who are left in the ruins *will* **fall** by the sword,
35: 8 [A] those killed by the sword *will* **fall** on your hills and in your
38: 20 [A] the cliffs *will* **crumble** and every wall will fall to the ground.
38: 20 [A] the cliffs will crumble and every wall *will* **fall** to the ground.
39: 3 [G] left hand and **make** your arrows **drop** from your right hand.
39: 4 [A] On the mountains of Israel *you will* **fall**, you and all your
39: 5 [A] *You will* **fall** in the open field, for I have spoken,

Eze 39:23 [A] them over to their enemies, and they all **fell** by the sword.
43: 3 [A] visions I had seen by the Kebar River, and *I* **fell** facedown.
44: 4 [A] filling the temple of the LORD, and *I* **fell** facedown.
45: 1 [G] " 'When you **allot** the land as an inheritance, you are to
47:14 [A] it to your forefathers, this land *will* **become** your inheritance.
47:22 [G] *You are to* **allot** it as an inheritance for yourselves and for
47:22 [A] along with you *they are to be* **allotted** an inheritance among
48:29 [G] "This is the land *you are to* **allot** as an inheritance to the
Da 8:10 [G] *it* **threw** some of the starry host **down** to the earth
8:17 [A] place where I was standing, I was terrified and **fell** prostrate.
9:18 [G] We *do* not **make** requests of you because we are righteous,
9:20 [G] **making** my request to the LORD my God for his holy hill—
10: 7 [A] but such terror **overwhelmed** [+6584] them that they fled
11:12 [G] will be filled with pride and *will* **slaughter** many thousands,
11:19 [A] the fortresses of his own country but will stumble and **fall**,
11:26 [A] will be swept away, and many *will* **fall** [+2728] **in battle**.
Hos 7: 7 [A] All their kings **fall**, and none of them calls on me.
7:16 [A] Their leaders *will* **fall** by the sword because of their insolent
10: 8 [A] to the mountains, "Cover us!" and to the hills, "**Fall** on us!"
13:16 [14:1] [A] *They will* **fall** by the sword; their little ones will be
Joel 2: 8 [A] *They* **plunge** through defenses without breaking ranks.
Am 3: 5 [A] *Does* a bird **fall** into a trap on the ground where no snare has
3:14 [A] the horns of the altar will be cut off and **fall** to the ground.
5: 2 [A] "**Fallen** *is* Virgin Israel, never to rise again, deserted in her
7:17 [A] the city, and your sons and daughters *will* **fall** by the sword.
8:14 [A] god of Beersheba lives'—*they will* **fall**, never to rise again."
9: 9 [A] is shaken in a sieve, and not a pebble *will* **reach** the ground.
9:11 [A] "In that day I will restore David's **fallen** tent. I will repair its
Jnh 1: 7 [G] *let us* **cast** lots to find out who is responsible for this
1: 7 [G] for this calamity." *They* **cast** lots and the lot fell on Jonah.
1: 7 [A] for this calamity." They cast lots and the lot **fell** on Jonah.
Mic 7: 8 [A] gloat over me, my enemy! Though *I have* **fallen**, I will rise.
Na 3:12 [A] they are shaken, the figs **fall** into the mouth of the eater.
Zec 11: 2 [A] Wail, O pine tree, for the cedar *has* **fallen**; the stately trees

5878 נֵ֫פֶל *nēpel*, n.m. [3] [√ 5877]

stillborn child [2], stillborn child [+851] [1]

Job 3:16 Or why was I not hidden in the ground like a **stillborn child**,
Ps 58: 8 [58:9] like a **stillborn** [+851] **child**, may they not see the sun.
Ecc 6: 3 proper burial, I say that a **stillborn child** is better off than he.

5879 [1]נָפַץ *nāpaṣ[1]*, v. [18] [→ 5150, 5151, 5881; cf. 5880, 7046, 7207]

shatter [9], broken [2], smash [2], broke [1], crushed to pieces [1], dash to pieces [1], dashes [1], separate [1]

Jdg 7:19 [A] their trumpets and **broke** the jars that were in their hands.
1Ki 5: 9 [5:23] [D] *I will* **separate** them and you can take them away.
Ps 2: 9 [D] an iron scepter; *you will* **dash** them **to pieces** like pottery."
137: 9 [D] who seizes your infants and **dashes** them against the rocks.
Isa 27: 9 [E] all the altar stones to be like chalk stones **crushed to pieces**,
Jer 13:14 [D] *I will* **smash** them one against the other, fathers and sons
22:28 [B] Jehoiachin a despised, **broken** pot, an object no one wants?
48:12 [D] pour her out; they will empty her jars and **smash** her jugs.
51:20 [D] with you *I* **shatter** nations, with you I destroy kingdoms,
51:21 [D] with you *I* **shatter** horse and rider, with you I shatter chariot
51:21 [D] shatter horse and rider, with you *I* **shatter** chariot and driver,
51:22 [D] with you *I* **shatter** man and woman, with you I shatter old
51:22 [D] and woman, with you *I* **shatter** old man and youth,
51:22 [D] and youth, with you *I* **shatter** young man and maiden,
51:23 [D] with you *I* **shatter** shepherd and flock, with you I shatter
51:23 [D] and flock, with you *I* **shatter** farmer and oxen,
51:23 [D] and oxen, with you *I* **shatter** governors and officials.
Da 12: 7 [D] When the power of the holy people *has been* finally **broken**,

5880 [2]נָפַץ *nāpaṣ[2]*, v. [3] [cf. 5879]

scatter [1], scattered [1], scattering [1]

Ge 9:19 [A] from them came *the people who were* **scattered** *over* the
1Sa 13:11 [A] Saul replied, "When I saw that the men *were* **scattering**, and
Isa 33: 3 [A] the peoples flee; when you rise up, the nations **scatter**.

5881 נֶ֫פֶץ *nepeṣ*, n.[m.]. [1] [√ 5879]

cloudburst [1]

Isa 30:30 and consuming fire, with **cloudburst**, thunderstorm and hail.

5882 נָפַשׁ *nāpaš*, v.den. [3] [→ 5874, 5883]

be refreshed [1], refreshed himself [1], rested [1]

Ex 23:12 [C] in your household, and the alien as well, *may* **be refreshed**.
31:17 [C] on the seventh day he abstained from work and **rested**.' "
2Sa 16:14 [C] their destination exhausted. And there *he* **refreshed himself**.

5883 נֶ֫פֶשׁ *nepeš*, n.f. [754] [√ 5882]

life [129], soul [105], *untranslated* [43], lives [36], me [+3276] [35], I [+3276] [29], person [22], you [+3870] [21], himself [+2257] [18], heart [16], yourselves [+4013] [12], people [11], myself [+3276] [9], themselves [+4392] [9], anyone [7], everyone [+2021+3972] [7], he [+2257] [7], herself [+2023] [7], appetite [6], creatures [6], spirit [5], them [+4392] [5], we [+5646] [5], body [4], creature [4], dead body [4], death [4], hearts [4], man [4], my [+3276] [4], one [4], souls [4], they [+4392] [4], you [+3871] [4], yourself [+3870] [4], breath [3], dead [3], desire [3], lifeblood [+1947] [3], needs [3], ourselves [+5646] [3], persons [3], someone [3], those[s] [3], us [+5646] [3], anyone [+2021+3972] [2], anyone [+3972] [2], as surely as live [+2644] [2], desires [2], everyone [+3972] [2], he[s] [+2021+2021 +2085] [2], hunger [2], hungry [+8281] [2], kill [+4374] [2], kill [+5782] [2], long [+906+5951] [2], members [2], mind [2], neck [2], she [+2023] [2], takes life [+5782] [2], thing [2], you [+4013] [2], yourselves [+3870] [2], affection [1], alive [+928] [1], all [1], another[s] [1], appetites [1], as surely as live [+2256+2644+2644] [1], be a willing party [+5951] [1], being [1], breathe last [+5870] [1], breathed her last [+3655] [1], closest friend [+889+3869+3870+8276] [1], completely [+1414+2256+4946+6330] [1], corpse [1], cost [1], counting on [+448+906+5951] [1], courage [1], craved [1], craving [+205] [1], craving [1], descendants [+3655+3751] [1], die [1], discontented [+5253] [1], dying [1], earnest [1], earnestness [+205] [1], enemies [+8533] [1], faint [+1790] [1], feel [1], fierce [+5253] [1], given to gluttony [+1251] [1], greed [1], greedy man [+8146] [1], guilt of murder [+1947] [1], he[s] [1], heart's [1], herself [1], him [+2257] [1], him[s] [1], his own [+2257] [1], hot-tempered [+5253] [1], how it feels [1], hunger [+8199] [1], impatient [+7918] [1], in all[s] [1], in anguish [+5253] [1], its own [+2257] [1], just what wanted [1], keep themselves alive [+8740] [1], keep themselves alive [+906+4392 +8740] [1], kidnapping [+1704] [1], kill [1], kills [+2256+4637+5782] [1], livelihood [1], living soul [1], made a fatal mistake [+928+9494] [1], member [1], minds [1], mortal [+928] [1], murders [+8357] [1], none [+3972+4202] [1], people [+132] [1], perfume [1], personal vows [+6886] [1], pleased [1], plunder [+906+7693] [1], relish [+448+5951] [1], slave [1], slaves [+132] [1], stouthearted [+6437] [1], that[s] [1], the flock[s] [+4392] [1], themselves [+2257] [1], these[s] [1], they [+2257] [1], thirst [1], thirsty [+8799] [1], thoughts [+928+6783] [1], threatened [+6330] [1], throats [1], wait to kill [+9068] [1], wanted [+906+8626] [1], wanted to kill [+906+1335] [1], weary [+6546] [1], willing [1], wished [1], wishes [1], yourself [+2257] [1], zeal [1]

Ge 1:20 And God said, "Let the water teem with living **creatures**,
1:21 and every living and moving **thing** with which the water teems,
1:24 "Let the land produce living **creatures** according to their kinds:
1:30 everything that has the **breath** *of* life in it—I give every green
2: 7 his nostrils the breath of life, and the man became a living **being**.
2:19 whatever the man called each living **creature**, that was its name.
9: 4 "But you must not eat meat that has its **lifeblood** [+1947] still in it.
9: 5 for your **lifeblood** [+1947] I will surely demand an accounting.
9: 5 I will demand an accounting for the **life** of his fellow man.
9:10 and with every living **creature** that was with you—the birds,
9:12 making between me and you and every living **creature** with you,
9:15 between me and you and all living **creatures** of every kind.
9:16 between God and all living **creatures** of every kind on the earth."
12: 5 they had accumulated and the **people** they had acquired in Haran,
12:13 well for your sake and my **life** will be spared because of you."
14:21 to Abram, "Give me the **people** and keep the goods for yourself."
17:14 will be cut off from his people; **he**[s] [+2021+2021+2085] has
19:17 they had brought them out, one of them said, "Flee for your **lives**!
19:19 and you have shown great kindness to me in sparing my **life**.
19:20 flee to it—it is very small, isn't it? Then my **life** will be spared."
23: 8 He said to them, "If you are **willing** to let me bury my dead,
27: 4 so that **I** [+3276] may give you my blessing before I die."
27:19 some of my game so that **you** [+3870] may give me your blessing."
27:25 of your game to eat, so that **I** [+3276] may give you my blessing."
27:31 of my game, so that **you** [+3870] may give me your blessing."
32:30 [32:31] I saw God face to face, and yet my **life** was spared."
34: 3 His **heart** was drawn to Dinah daughter of Jacob, and he loved the
34: 8 said to them, "My son Shechem has his **heart** set on your daughter.
35:18 As she **breathed** [+3655] **her last**—for she was dying—she named
36: 6 and sons and daughters and all the **members** *of* his household,
37:21 to rescue him from their hands. "Let's not take his **life**," he said.
42:21 saw how distressed he was when he pleaded with us for his **life**,
44:30 and if my father, whose **life** is closely bound up with the boy's life,
44:30 and if my father, whose life is closely bound up with the boy's **life**,
46:15 **These**[s] sons and daughters of his were thirty-three in all.
46:18 whom Laban had given to his daughter Leah—sixteen *in* **all**.
46:22 sons of Rachel who were born to Jacob—**[RPH]** fourteen in all.
46:25 Laban had given to his daughter Rachel—seven in all. **[RPH]**
46:26 All **those**[s] who went to Egypt with Jacob—those who were his
46:26 not counting his sons' wives—numbered sixty-six **persons**.
46:27 **[RPH]** the members of Jacob's family, which went to Egypt,

Ge 46:27 the **members** of Jacob's family, which went to Egypt,
49: 6 Let **me** [+3276] not enter their council, let me not join their
Ex 1: 5 The **descendants of** [+3655+3751] Jacob numbered seventy in all;
1: 5 numbered seventy in all; **[RPH]** Joseph was already in Egypt.
4:19 for all the men who **wanted to kill** [+906+1335] you are dead."
12: 4 having taken into account the number of **people** there are.
12:15 first day through the seventh **[NIE]** must be cut off from Israel.
12:16 on these days, except to prepare food for **everyone** [+3972] to eat—
12:19 whoever eats anything with yeast in it **[NIE]** must be cut off from
15: 9 I will divide the spoils; I will gorge **myself** [+3276] on them.
16:16 he needs. Take an omer for each **person** you have in your tent.' "
21:23 But if there is serious injury, you are to take **life** for life,
21:23 But if there is serious injury, you are to take life for **life**,
21:30 of him, he may redeem his **life** by paying whatever is demanded.
23: 9 you yourselves know **how it feels** to be aliens, because you were
30:12 each one must pay the LORD a ransom for his **life** at the time he
30:15 when you make the offering to the LORD to atone for your **lives**.
30:16 Israelites before the LORD, making atonement for your **lives**."
31:14 whoever does any work on that day must be cut off **[NIE]** from
Lev 2: 1 " 'When **someone** brings a grain offering to the LORD,
4: 2 'When **anyone** sins unintentionally and does what is forbidden in
4:27 " 'If a **member** of the community sins unintentionally and does
5: 1 " 'If a **person** sins because he does not speak up when he hears a
5: 2 " 'Or if a **person** touches anything ceremonially unclean—
5: 4 " 'Or if a **person** thoughtlessly takes an oath to do anything,
5:15 "When a **person** commits a violation and sins unintentionally in
5:17 "If a **person** sins and does what is forbidden in any of the
6: 2 [5:21] "If **anyone** sins and is unfaithful to the LORD by
7:18 it is impure; the **person** who eats any of it will be held responsible.
7:20 if **anyone** who is unclean eats any meat of the fellowship offering
7:20 to the LORD, that **person** must be cut off from his people.
7:21 If **anyone** touches something unclean—whether human
7:21 to the LORD, that **person** must be cut off from his people.' "
7:25 be made to the LORD must be cut off **[RPH]** from his people.
7:27 If **anyone** [+3972] eats blood, that person must be cut off from his
7:27 anyone eats blood, that **person** must be cut off from his people.' "
11:10 or among all the other living **creatures** in the water—
11:43 Do not defile **yourselves** [+4013] by any of these creatures.
11:44 Do not make **yourselves** [+4013] unclean by any creature that
11:46 every living **thing** that moves in the water and every creature that
11:46 in the water and every **creature** that moves about on the ground.
16:29 tenth day of the seventh month you must deny **yourselves** [+4013]
16:31 It is a sabbath of rest, and you must deny **yourselves** [+4013];
17:10 I will set my face against that **person** who eats blood and will cut
17:11 For the **life** *of* a creature is in the blood, and I have given it to you
17:11 I have given it to you to make atonement for **yourselves** [+4013]
17:11 on the altar; it is the blood that makes atonement for one's **life**.
17:12 Therefore I say to the Israelites, "**None** [+3972+4202] of you may
17:14 because the **life** *of* every creature is its blood. That is why I have
17:14 **[RPH]** That is why I have said to the Israelites, "You must not eat
17:14 of any creature, because the **life** *of* every creature is its blood;
17:15 " '**Anyone** [+3972], whether native-born or alien, who eats
18:29 detestable things—such **persons** must be cut off from their people.
19: 8 is holy to the LORD; that **person** must be cut off from his people.
19:28 " 'Do not cut your bodies for the **dead** or put tattoo marks on
20: 6 " 'I will set my face against **[RPH]** the person who turns to
20: 6 " 'I will set my face against the **person** who turns to mediums
20:25 Do not defile **yourselves** [+4013] by any animal or bird
21: 1 make himself ceremonially unclean for any of his people who **die**,
21:11 He must not enter a place where there is a dead **body**. He must not
22: 3 to the LORD, that **person** must be cut off from my presence.
22: 4 will also be unclean if he touches something defiled by a **corpse**
22: 6 The **one** who touches any such thing will be unclean till evening.
22:11 if a priest buys a **slave** with money, or if a slave is born in his
23:27 Hold a sacred assembly and deny **yourselves** [+4013], and present
23:29 **Anyone** [+2021+3972] who does not deny himself on that day
23:30 I will destroy **[RPH]** from among his people anyone who does
23:30 I will destroy from among his people **anyone** [+2021+3972] who
23:32 a sabbath of rest for you, and you must deny **yourselves** [+4013].
24:17 " 'If anyone **takes** the **life** [+5782] *of* a human being, he must be
24:18 *Anyone who* **takes** the **life** [+5782] *of* someone's animal must
24:18 the life of someone's animal must make restitution—**life** for life.
24:18 the life of someone's animal must make restitution—life for **life**.
26:11 my dwelling place among you, and **I** [+3276] will not abhor you.
26:15 if **you** [+4013] reject my decrees and abhor my laws and fail to
26:16 and fever that will destroy your sight and drain away your **life**.
26:30 on the lifeless forms of your idols, and **I** [+3276] will abhor you.
26:43 because **they** [+4392] rejected my laws and abhorred my decrees.
27: 2 'If anyone makes a special vow to dedicate **persons** to the LORD
Nu 5: 2 any kind, or who is ceremonially unclean because of a **dead body**.
5: 6 any way and so is unfaithful to the LORD, that **person** is guilty
6: 6 of his separation to the LORD he must not go near a dead **body**.
6:11 because he sinned by being in the presence of the **dead body**.
9: 6 because they were ceremonially unclean on account of a **dead**
9: 7 said to Moses, "We have become unclean because of a **dead** body,
9:10 are unclean because of a **dead body** or are away on a journey,
9:13 that **person** must be cut off from his people because he did not
11: 6 But now we have lost our **appetite**; we never see anything
15:27 " 'But if just one **person** sins unintentionally, he must bring a
15:28 The priest is to make atonement before the LORD for the **one**
15:30 " 'But **anyone** who sins defiantly, whether native-born or alien,
15:30 the LORD, and that **person** must be cut off from his people.
15:31 and broken his commands, that **person** must surely be cut off;
16:38 [17:3] the censers of the men who sinned at the cost of their **lives**.
19:11 "Whoever touches the dead **body** of anyone will be unclean for
19:13 Whoever touches the dead **body** *of* anyone and fails to purify
19:13 the LORD's tabernacle. That **person** must be cut off from Israel.
19:18 the tent and all the furnishings and the **people** who were there.
19:20 who is unclean does not purify himself, **he**[s] [+2021+2021+2085]
19:22 and **anyone** who touches it becomes unclean till evening."
21: 4 around Edom. But the people *grew* **impatient** [+7918] on the way;
21: 5 There is no water! And **we** [+5646] detest this miserable food!"
23:10 Let **me** [+3276] die the death of the righteous, and may my end be
29: 7 You must deny **yourselves** [+4013] and do no work.
30: 2 [30:3] or takes an oath to obligate **himself** [+2257] by a pledge,
30: 4 [30:5] about her vow or pledge **[RPH]** but says nothing to her,
30: 4 [30:5] every pledge by which she obligated **herself** [+2023] will
30: 5 [30:6] or the pledges by which she obligated **herself** [+2023] will
30: 6 [30:7] a rash promise by which she obligates **herself** [+2023]
30: 7 [30:8] or the pledges by which she obligated **herself** [+2023] will
30: 8 [30:9] the rash promise by which she obligates **herself** [+2023],
30: 9 [30:10] "Any vow or obligation taken by **[RPH]** a widow
30:10 [30:11] or obligates **herself** [+2023] by a pledge under oath
30:11 [30:12] or the pledges by which she obligated **herself** [+2023]
30:12 [30:13] or pledges **[RPH]** that came from her lips will stand.
30:13 [30:14] any vow she makes or any sworn pledge to deny **herself**.
31:19 "All of you who have killed **anyone** or touched anyone who was
31:28 set apart as tribute for the LORD one **[NIE]** out of every five
31:35 and 32,000 **[NIE]** women who had never slept with a man.
31:35 and 32,000 women who had never slept with a **man**.
31:40 16,000 **[NIE]** people, of which the tribute for the LORD was 32.
31:40 of which the tribute for the LORD was 32. **[NIE]**
31:46 and 16,000 **[NIE]** people.
31:50 to make atonement for **ourselves** [+5646] before the LORD."
35:11 to which a person who has killed **someone** accidentally may flee.
35:15 so that anyone who has killed **another**[s] accidentally can flee there.
35:30 " 'Anyone who kills a **person** is to be put to death as a murderer
35:30 no **one** is to be put to death on the testimony of only one witness.
35:31 " 'Do not accept a ransom for the **life** *of* a murderer, who deserves
Dt 4: 9 watch **yourselves** [+3870] closely so that you do not forget the
4:15 out of the fire. Therefore watch **yourselves** [+4013] very carefully,
4:29 him if you look for him with all your heart and with all your **soul**.
6: 5 all your heart and with all your **soul** and with all your strength.
10:12 the LORD your God with all your heart and with all your **soul**,
10:22 Your forefathers who went down into Egypt were seventy **in all**[s],
11:13 and to serve him with all your heart and with all your **soul**—
11:18 Fix these words of mine in your hearts and **minds**; tie them as
12:15 of your towns and eat as much of the meat as **you** [+3870] want,
12:20 and **you** [+3870] crave meat and say, "I would like some meat,"
12:20 some meat," then you may eat as much of it as **you** [+3870] want.
12:21 in your own towns you may eat as much of them as **you** [+3870]
12:23 But be sure you do not eat the blood, because the blood is the **life**,
12:23 the blood is the life, and you must not eat the **life** with the meat.
13: 3 [13:4] you love him with all your heart and with all your **soul**.
13: 6 [13:7] or your **closest friend** [+889+3869+3870+8276] secretly
14:26 Use the silver to buy whatever **you** [+3870] like: cattle, sheep,
14:26 wine or other fermented drink, or anything **you** [+3870] wish.
18: 6 comes in all **earnestness** [+205] to the place the LORD will
19: 6 and **kill** [+5782] him even though he is not deserving of death,
19:11 lies in wait for him, assaults and **kills** [+2256+4637+5782] him,
19:21 **life** for life, eye for eye, tooth for tooth, hand for hand, foot for
19:21 life for **life**, eye for eye, tooth for tooth, hand for hand, foot for
21:14 If you are not pleased with her, let her go wherever she **wishes**.
22:26 that of someone who attacks and **murders** [+8357] his neighbor,
23:24 [23:25] you may eat all the grapes **you** [+3870] want, but do not
24: 6 because that would be taking a man's **livelihood** as security.
24: 7 If a man is caught **kidnapping** [+1704] one of his brother Israelites
24:15 because he is poor and *is* **counting on** [+448+906+5951] it.
26:16 carefully observe them with all your heart and with all your **soul**.
27:25 "Cursed is the man who accepts a bribe to **kill** [+5782] an innocent
28:65 an anxious mind, eyes weary with longing, and a despairing **heart**.
30: 2 with all your **soul** according to everything I command you today,
30: 6 so that you may love him with all your heart and with all your **soul**,
30:10 to the LORD your God with all your heart and with all your **soul**.
Jos 2:13 belong to them, and that you will save **us** [+5646] from death."
2:14 "Our **lives** for your lives!" the men assured her. "If you don't tell
9:24 So we feared for our **lives** because of you, and that is why we did
10:28 to the sword and totally destroyed **everyone** [+2021+3972] in it.

Jos 10:30 and **everyone** [+2021+3972] in it Joshua put to the sword.
10:32 The city and **everyone** [+2021+3972] in it he put to the sword,
10:35 it to the sword and totally destroyed **everyone** [+2021+3972] in it,
10:37 with its king, its villages and **everyone** [+2021+3972] in it.
10:37 they totally destroyed it and **everyone** [+2021+3972] in it.
10:39 **Everyone** [+3972] in it they totally destroyed.
11:11 **Everyone** [+2021+3972] in it they put to the sword.
20: 3 so that anyone who kills a **person** accidentally and unintentionally
20: 9 or any alien living among them who killed **someone** accidentally
22: 5 fast to him and to serve him with all your heart and all your **soul**."
23:11 So be very careful **[NIE]** to love the LORD your God.
23:14 **soul** that not one of all the good promises the LORD your God
Jdg 5:18 The people of Zebulun risked their very **lives**; so did Naphtali on
5:21 the age-old river, the river Kishon. March on, my **soul**; be strong!
9:17 for you, risked his **life** to rescue you from the hand of Midian
10:16 the LORD. And **he** [+2257] could bear Israel's misery no longer.
12: 3 I took my **life** in my hands and crossed over to fight the
16:16 With such nagging she prodded him day after day until **he** [+2257]
16:30 Samson said, "Let **me** [+3276] die with the Philistines!" Then he
18:25 or some **hot-tempered** [+5253] men will attack you, and you
18:25 men will attack you, and you and your family will lose your **lives**."
18:25 attack you, and you and your family will lose your lives." **[RPH]**
Ru 4:15 He will renew your **life** and sustain you in your old age. For your
1Sa 1:10 In bitterness of **soul** Hannah wept much and prayed to the LORD.
1:15 drinking wine or beer; I was pouring out my **soul** to the LORD.
1:26 and she said to him, "**As surely as** you **live** [+2644], my lord,
2:16 and then take whatever **you** [+3870] want," the servant would
2:33 spared only to blind your eyes with tears and to grieve your **heart**,
2:35 who will do according to what is in my heart and **mind**.
17:55 Abner replied, "As surely as **you** [+3870] live, O king, I don't
18: 1 **[RPH]** Jonathan became one in spirit with David, and he loved
18: 1 Jonathan became one in **spirit** with David, and he loved him as
18: 1 one in spirit with David, and he loved him as **himself** [+2257].
18: 3 a covenant with David because he loved him as **himself** [+2257].
19: 5 He took his **life** in his hands when he killed the Philistine.
19:11 David's wife, warned him, "If you don't run for your **life** tonight,
20: 1 How have I wronged your father, that he is trying to take my **life**?"
20: 3 Yet as surely as the LORD lives and as **you** [+3870] live,
20: 4 to David, "Whatever **you** [+3870] want me to do, I'll do for you."
20:17 of love for him, because he loved him as he loved **himself** [+2257].
22: 2 or in debt or **discontented** [+5253] gathered around him,
22:22 I am responsible for the **death** *of* your father's whole family.
22:23 be afraid; the man who is seeking your **life** is seeking mine also.
22:23 the man who is seeking your life is seeking mine **[RPH]** also.
23:15 Desert of Ziph, he learned that Saul had come out to take his **life**.
23:20 O king, come down whenever it pleases **you** [+3870] to do so,
24:11 [24:12] but you are hunting me down to take my **life**.
25:26 as surely as the LORD lives and as **you** [+3870] live, may your
25:29 Even though someone is pursuing you to take your **life**, the life of
25:29 the **life** *of* my master will be bound securely in the bundle of the
25:29 the **lives** *of* your enemies he will hurl away as from the pocket of a
26:21 Because you considered my **life** precious today, I will not try to
26:24 As surely as I valued your **life** today, so may the LORD value my
26:24 so may the LORD value my **life** and deliver me from all trouble."
28: 9 Why have you set a trap for my **life** to bring about my death?"
28:21 I took my **life** in my hands and did what you told me to do.
30: 6 each one was bitter in **spirit** because of his sons and daughters.
2Sa 1: 9 and kill me! I am in the throes of death, but I'm still **alive** [+928].'
3:21 with you, and that you may rule over all that your **heart** desires."
4: 8 Ish-Bosheth son of Saul, your enemy, who tried to take your **life**.
4: 9 the LORD lives, who has delivered **me** [+3276] out of all trouble,
5: 8 to reach those 'lame and blind' *who are* David's **enemies** [+8533]."
11:11 **As surely as** you **live** [+2256+2644+2644], I will not do such a
14: 7 so that we may put him to death for the **life** *of* his brother whom he
14:14 But God does not take away **life**; instead, he devises ways
14:19 "**As surely as** you **live** [+2644], my lord the king,
16:11 "My son, who is of my own flesh, is trying to take my **life**.
17: 8 and as **fierce** [+5253] as a wild bear robbed of her cubs.
18:13 if I had put my **life** in jeopardy—and nothing is hidden from the
19: 5 [19:6] who have just saved your **life** and the lives of your sons
19: 5 [19:6] the **lives** *of* your sons and daughters and the lives of your
19: 5 [19:6] and daughters and the **lives** *of* your wives and concubines.
19: 5 [19:6] and the lives of your wives and **[RPH]** concubines.
23:17 "Is it not the blood of men who went at the risk of their **lives**?"
1Ki 1:12 let me advise you how you can save your own **life** and the life of
1:12 how you can save your own life and the **life** *of* your son Solomon.
1:29 LORD lives, who has delivered **me** [+3276] out of every trouble,
2: 4 and if they walk faithfully before me with all their heart and **soul**,
2:23 so severely, if Adonijah does not pay with his **life** for this request!
3:11 nor have asked for the **death** *of* your enemies but for discernment
8:48 and **soul** in the land of their enemies who took them captive,
11:37 I will take you, and you will rule over all that your **heart** desires;
17:21 the LORD, "O LORD my God, let this boy's **life** return to him!"
17:22 heard Elijah's cry, and the boy's **life** returned to him, and he lived.
19: 2 if by this time tomorrow I do not make your **life** like that of one of
19: 2 if by this time tomorrow I do not make your life like **that**[s] *of* one
19: 3 Elijah was afraid and ran for his **life**. When he came to Beersheba
19: 4 sat down under it and prayed that **he** [+2257] might die.
19: 4 he said. "Take my **life**; I am no better than my ancestors."
19:10 the only one left, and now they are trying to **kill** [+4374] me too."
19:14 the only one left, and now they are trying to **kill** [+4374] me too."
20:31 and ropes around our heads. Perhaps he will spare your **life**."
20:32 'Please let **me** [+3276] live.' " The king answered, "Is he still alive?
20:39 If he is missing, it will be your **life** for his life, or you must pay a
20:39 If he is missing, it will be your life for his **life**, or you must pay a
20:42 Therefore it is your **life** for his life, your people for his people.' "
20:42 Therefore it is your life for his **life**, your people for his people.' "
2Ki 1:13 "please have respect for my **life** and the lives of these fifty men,
1:13 "please have respect for my life and the **lives** *of* these fifty men,
1:14 two captains and all their men. But now have respect for my **life**!"
2: 2 "As surely as the LORD lives and as **you** [+3870] live,
2: 4 he replied, "As surely as the LORD lives and as **you** [+3870] live,
2: 6 he replied, "As surely as the LORD lives and as **you** [+3870] live,
4:27 of God said, "Leave her alone! **She** [+2023] is in bitter distress,
4:30 "As surely as the LORD lives and as **you** [+3870] live, I will not
7: 7 and donkeys. They left the camp as it was and ran for their **lives**.
9:15 Jehu said, "If this is the way you **feel**, don't let anyone slip out of
10:24 I am placing in your hands escape, it will be your **life** for his life."
10:24 I am placing in your hands escape, it will be your life for his **life**."
12: 4 [12:5] the money received from **personal vows** [+6886] and the
23: 3 and decrees with all his heart and all his **soul**,
23:25 with all his heart and with all his **soul** and with all his strength,
1Ch 5:21 They also took one hundred thousand **people** [+132] captive,
11:19 I drink the blood of these men who went at the risk of their **lives**?"
11:19 Because they risked their **lives** to bring it back, David would not
22:19 Now devote your heart and **soul** to seeking the LORD your God.
28: 9 serve him with wholehearted devotion and with a willing **mind**,
2Ch 1:11 for wealth, riches or honor, nor for the **death** *of* your enemies,
6:38 and **soul** in the land of their captivity where they were taken,
15:12 the LORD, the God of their fathers, with all their heart and **soul**.
34:31 and decrees with all his heart and all his **soul**,
Est 4:13 "Do not think **[NIE]** that because you are in the king's house you
7: 3 with you, O king, and if it pleases your majesty, grant me my **life**—
7: 7 decided his fate, stayed behind to beg Queen Esther for his **life**.
8:11 in every city the right to assemble and protect **themselves** [+4392];
9:16 the king's provinces also assembled to protect **themselves** [+4392]
9:31 as they had established for **themselves** [+4392] and their
Job 2: 4 Satan replied. "A man will give all he has for his own **life**.
2: 6 "Very well, then, he is in your hands; but you must spare his **life**."
3:20 "Why is light given to those in misery, and life to the bitter of **soul**,
6: 7 **I** [+3276] refuse to touch it; such food makes me ill.
6:11 still hope? What prospects, that **I** [+3276] should be patient?
7:11 anguish of my spirit, I will complain in the bitterness of my **soul**.
7:15 so that **I** [+3276] prefer strangling and death, rather than this body
9:21 "Although I am blameless, I have no concern for **myself** [+3276];
10: 1 "**I** [+3276] loathe my very life; therefore I will give free rein to my
10: 1 rein to my complaint and speak out in the bitterness of my **soul**.
11:20 and escape will elude them; their hope will become a **dying** gasp."
12:10 In his hand is the **life** *of* every creature and the breath of all
13:14 Why do I put myself in jeopardy and take my **life** in my hands?
14:22 the pain of his own body and mourns only for **himself** [+2257]."
16: 4 I also could speak like you, if **you** [+4013] were in my place;
16: 4 I also could speak like you, if you were in **my** [+3276] place;
18: 4 You who tear **yourself** [+2257] to pieces in your anger, is the earth
19: 2 "How long will you torment **me** [+3276] and crush me with
21:25 Another man dies in bitterness of **soul**, never having enjoyed
23:13 and who can oppose him? He does whatever **he** [+2257] pleases.
24:12 rise from the city, and the **souls** *of* the wounded cry out for help.
27: 2 the Almighty, who has made me taste bitterness of **soul**,
27: 8 has the godless when he is cut off, when God takes away his **life**?
30:16 "And now my **life** ebbs away; days of suffering grip me.
30:25 wept for those in trouble? Has not my **soul** grieved for the poor?
31:30 not allowed my mouth to sin by invoking a curse against his **life**—
31:39 its yield without payment or broken the **spirit** *of* its tenants,
32: 2 became very angry with Job for justifying **himself** [+2257] rather
33:18 to preserve his **soul** from the pit, his life from perishing by the
33:20 being finds food repulsive and his **soul** loathes the choicest meal.
33:22 His **soul** draws near to the pit, and his life to the messengers of
33:28 He redeemed my **soul** from going down to the pit, and I will live to
33:30 to turn back his **soul** from the pit, that the light of life may shine on
36:14 **They** [+4392] die in their youth, among male prostitutes of the
41:21 [41:13] His **breath** sets coals ablaze, and flames dart from his
Ps 3: 2 [3:3] Many are saying of **me** [+3276], "God will not deliver him."
6: 3 [6:4] My **soul** is in anguish. How long, O LORD, how long?
6: 4 [6:5] Turn, O LORD, and deliver **me** [+3276]; save me because
7: 2 [7:3] or they will tear **me** [+3276] like a lion and rip me to pieces
7: 5 [7:6] let my enemy pursue and overtake **me** [+3276]; let him
10: 3 He boasts of the cravings of his **heart**; he blesses the greedy

Ps 11: 1 In the LORD I take refuge. How then can you say to **me** [+3276]:
11: 5 but the wicked and those who love violence his **soul** hates.
13: 2 [13:3] How long must I wrestle with my **thoughts** [+928+6783]
16: 10 because you will not abandon **me** [+3276] to the grave, nor will
17: 9 who assail me, from my **mortal** [+928] enemies who surround me.
17: 13 them down; rescue **me** [+3276] from the wicked by your sword.
19: 7 [19:8] The law of the LORD is perfect, reviving the **soul**.
22: 20 [22:21] Deliver my **life** from the sword, my precious life from the
22: 29 [22:30] those who cannot keep **themselves** [+2257] alive.
23: 3 he restores my **soul**. He guides me in paths of righteousness for his
24: 4 who does not lift up his **soul** to an idol or swear by what is false.
25: 1 To you, O LORD, I lift up my **soul**;
25: 13 **He** [+2257] will spend his days in prosperity, and his descendants
25: 20 Guard my **life** and rescue me; let me not be put to shame, for I take
26: 9 Do not take away my **soul** along with sinners, my life with
27: 12 Do not turn me over to the **desire** *of* my foes, for false witnesses
30: 3 [30:4] O LORD, you brought **me** [+3276] up from the grave;
31: 7 [31:8] you saw my affliction and knew the anguish of my **soul**.
31: 9 [31:10] grow weak with sorrow, my **soul** and my body with grief.
31: 13 [31:14] they conspire against me and plot to take my **life**.
33: 19 to deliver **them** [+4392] from death and keep them alive in famine.
33: 20 **We** [+5646] wait in hope for the LORD; he is our help and our
34: 2 [34:3] My **soul** will boast in the LORD; let the afflicted hear
34: 22 [34:23] The LORD redeems **[NIE]** his servants; no one will be
35: 3 those who pursue me. Say to my **soul**, "I am your salvation."
35: 4 May those who seek my **life** be disgraced and put to shame;
35: 7 for me without cause and without cause dug a pit for **me** [+3276],
35: 9 my **soul** will rejoice in the LORD and delight in his salvation.
35: 12 They repay me evil for good and leave my **soul** forlorn.
35: 13 I put on sackcloth and humbled **myself** [+3276] with fasting.
35: 17 Rescue my **life** from their ravages, my precious life from these
35: 25 Do not let them think, "Aha, **just what** we **wanted**!" or say,
38: 12 [38:13] Those who seek my **life** set their traps, those who would
40: 14 [40:15] May all who seek to take my **life** be put to shame
41: 2 [41:3] in the land and not surrender him to the **desire** *of* his foes.
41: 4 [41:5] on me; heal **me** [+3276], for I have sinned against you."
42: 1 [42:2] for streams of water, so my **soul** pants for you, O God.
42: 2 [42:3] My **soul** thirsts for God, for the living God. When can I go
42: 4 [42:5] These things I remember as I pour out my **soul**: how I used
42: 5 [42:6] Why are you downcast, O my **soul**? Why so disturbed
42: 6 [42:7] My **soul** is downcast within me; therefore I will remember
42: 11 [42:12] Why are you downcast, O my **soul**? Why so disturbed
43: 5 Why are you downcast, O my **soul**? Why so disturbed within me?
44: 25 [44:26] **We** [+5646] are brought down to the dust; our bodies
49: 8 [49:9] the ransom for a **life** is costly, no payment is ever enough—
49: 15 [49:16] God will redeem my **life** from the grave; he will surely
49: 18 [49:19] Though while he lived he counted **himself** [+2257]
54: 3 [54:5] Strangers are attacking me; ruthless men seek my **life**—
54: 4 [54:6] is my help; the Lord is the one who sustains **me** [+3276].
55: 18 [55:19] He ransoms **me** [+3276] unharmed from the battle waged
56: 6 [56:7] they lurk, they watch my steps, eager to take my **life**.
56: 13 [56:14] For you have delivered **me** [+3276] from death and my
57: 1 [57:2] O God, have mercy on me, for in you my **soul** takes refuge.
57: 4 [57:5] **I** [+3276] am in the midst of lions; I lie among ravenous
57: 6 [57:7] They spread a net for my feet—**I** [+3276] was bowed down
59: 3 [59:4] See how they lie in wait for **me** [+3276]! Fierce men
62: 1 [62:2] My **soul** finds rest in God alone; my salvation comes from
62: 5 [62:6] Find rest, O my **soul**, in God alone; my hope comes from
63: 1 [63:2] my **soul** thirsts for you, my body longs for you, in a dry
63: 5 [63:6] My **soul** will be satisfied as with the richest of foods; with
63: 8 [63:9] My **soul** clings to you; your right hand upholds me.
63: 9 [63:10] They who seek my **life** will be destroyed; they will go
66: 9 he has preserved our **lives** and kept our feet from slipping.
66: 16 who fear God; let me tell you what he has done for **me** [+3276].
69: 1 [69:2] Save me, O God, for the waters have come up to my **neck**.
69: 10 [69:11] When I weep and fast, **[NIE]** I must endure scorn;
69: 18 [69:19] Come near and rescue **me** [+3276]; redeem me because of
70: 2 [70:3] May those who seek my **life** be put to shame
71: 10 against me; *those who* **wait to kill** [+9068] me conspire together.
71: 13 May **my** [+3276] accusers perish in shame; may those who want to
71: 23 My lips will shout for joy when I sing praise to you—**I** [+3276],
72: 13 pity on the weak and the needy and save the needy from **death**.
72: 14 He will rescue **them** [+4392] from oppression and violence,
74: 19 Do not hand over the **life** *of* your dove to wild beasts; do not forget
77: 2 [77:3] out untiring hands and my **soul** refused to be comforted.
78: 18 willfully put God to the test by demanding the food they **craved**.
78: 50 he did not spare **them** [+4392] from death but gave them over to
84: 2 [84:3] My **soul** yearns, even faints, for the courts of the LORD;
86: 2 Guard my **life**, for I am devoted to you. You are my God;
86: 4 Bring joy to **[RPH]** your servant, for to you, O Lord, I lift up my
86: 4 Bring joy to your servant, for to you, O Lord, I lift up my **soul**.
86: 13 you have delivered **me** [+3276] from the depths of the grave.
86: 14 are attacking me, O God; a band of ruthless men seeks my **life**—
88: 3 [88:4] For my **soul** is full of trouble and my life draws near the
88: 14 [88:15] do you reject **me** [+3276] and hide your face from me?
89: 48 [89:49] or save **himself** [+2257] from the power of the grave?
94: 17 Unless the LORD had given me help, **I** [+3276] would soon have
94: 19 was great within me, your consolation brought joy to my **soul**.
94: 21 They band together against **[NIE]** the righteous and condemn the
97: 10 for he guards the **lives** *of* his faithful ones and delivers them from
103: 1 Praise the LORD, O my **soul**; all my inmost being, praise his holy
103: 2 Praise the LORD, O my **soul**, and forget not all his benefits—
103: 22 works everywhere in his dominion. Praise the LORD, O my **soul**.
104: 1 Praise the LORD, O my **soul**. O LORD my God, you are very
104: 35 be no more. Praise the LORD, O my **soul**. Praise the LORD.
105: 18 They bruised his feet with shackles, his **neck** was put in irons,
105: 22 to instruct his princes as he **pleased** and teach his elders wisdom.
106: 15 they asked for, but sent a wasting disease upon **them** [+4392].
107: 5 They were hungry and thirsty, and their **lives** ebbed away.
107: 9 for he satisfies the **thirsty** [+8799] and fills the hungry with good
107: 9 satisfies the thirsty and fills the **hungry** [+8281] with good things.
107: 18 **They** [+4392] loathed all food and drew near the gates of death.
107: 26 went down to the depths; in their peril their **courage** melted away.
109: 20 payment to my accusers, to those who speak evil of **me** [+3276].
109: 31 of the needy one, to save his **life** from those who condemn him.
116: 4 called on the name of the LORD: "O LORD, save **me** [+3276]!"
116: 7 Be at rest once more, O my **soul**, for the LORD has been good to
116: 8 For you, O LORD, have delivered my **soul** from death, my eyes
119: 20 My **soul** is consumed with longing for your laws at all times.
119: 25 **I** [+3276] am laid low in the dust; preserve my life according to
119: 28 My **soul** is weary with sorrow; strengthen me according to your
119: 81 My **soul** faints with longing for your salvation, but I have put my
119:109 Though I constantly take my **life** in my hands, I will not forget
119:129 Your statutes are wonderful; therefore **I** [+3276] obey them.
119:167 **I** [+3276] obey your statutes, for I love them greatly.
119:175 Let **me** [+3276] live that I may praise you, and may your laws
120: 2 Save **me** [+3276], O LORD, from lying lips and from deceitful
120: 6 Too long have **I** [+3276] lived among those who hate peace.
121: 7 LORD will keep you from all harm—he will watch over your **life**;
123: 4 **We** [+5646] have endured much ridicule from the proud, much
124: 4 have engulfed us, the torrent would have swept over **us** [+5646],
124: 5 the raging waters would have swept **us** [+5646] away.
124: 7 **We** [+5646] have escaped like a bird out of the fowler's snare;
130: 5 I wait for the LORD, my **soul** waits, and in his word I put my
130: 6 My **soul** waits for the Lord more than watchmen wait for the
131: 2 I have stilled and quieted my **soul**; like a weaned child with its
131: 2 child with its mother, like a weaned child is my **soul** within me.
138: 3 you answered me; you made me bold and **stouthearted** [+6437].
139: 14 your works are wonderful, **I** [+3276] know that full well.
141: 8 in you I take refuge—do not give **me** [+3276] over to death.
142: 4 [142:5] for me. I have no refuge; no one cares for my **life**.
142: 7 [142:8] Set **me** [+3276] free from my prison, that I may praise
143: 3 The enemy pursues **me** [+3276], he crushes me to the ground;
143: 6 out my hands to you; my **soul** thirsts for you like a parched land.
143: 8 Show me the way I should go, for to you I lift up my **soul**.
143: 11 my life; in your righteousness, bring **me** [+3276] out of trouble.
143: 12 my enemies; destroy all **my** [+3276] foes, for I am your servant.
146: 1 Praise the LORD. Praise the LORD, O my **soul**.
Pr 1: 18 in wait for their own blood; they waylay only **themselves** [+4392]!
1: 19 go after ill-gotten gain; it takes away the **lives** *of* those who get it.
2: 10 will enter your heart, and knowledge will be pleasant to your **soul**.
3: 22 they will be life for **you** [+3870], an ornament to grace your neck.
6: 16 things the LORD hates, seven that are detestable to **him** [+2257]:
6: 26 you to a loaf of bread, and the adulteress preys upon your very **life**.
6: 30 Men do not despise a thief if he steals to satisfy his **hunger** when
6: 32 lacks judgment; whoever does so destroys **himself** [+2257].
7: 23 a bird darting into a snare, little knowing it will cost him his **life**.
8: 36 whoever fails to find me harms **himself** [+2257]; all who hate me
10: 3 go hungry **[NIE]** but he thwarts the craving of the wicked.
11: 17 A kind man benefits **himself** [+2257], but a cruel man brings
11: 25 A generous **man** will prosper; he who refreshes others will himself
11: 30 of the righteous is a tree of life, and he who wins **souls** is wise.
12: 10 A righteous man cares for the **needs** *of* his animal, but the kindest
13: 2 enjoys good things, but the unfaithful have a **craving** *for* violence.
13: 3 He who guards his lips guards his **life**, but he who speaks rashly
13: 4 **[RPH]** but the desires of the diligent are fully satisfied.
13: 4 and gets nothing, but the **desires** *of* the diligent are fully satisfied.
13: 8 A man's riches may ransom his **life**, but a poor man hears no
13: 19 A longing fulfilled is sweet to the **soul**, but fools detest turning
13: 25 The righteous eat to their **hearts'** content, but the stomach of the
14: 10 Each heart knows **its own** [+2257] bitterness, and no one else can
14: 25 A truthful witness saves **lives**, but a false witness is deceitful.
15: 32 He who ignores discipline despises **himself** [+2257], but whoever
16: 17 of the upright avoids evil; he who guards his way guards his **life**.
16: 24 words are a honeycomb, sweet to the **soul** and healing to the bones.
16: 26 The laborer's **appetite** works for him; his hunger drives him on.
18: 7 A fool's mouth is his undoing, and his lips are a snare to his **soul**.
19: 2 It is not good to have **zeal** without knowledge, nor to be hasty

Pr 19: 8 He who gets wisdom loves his own **soul**; he who cherishes
19: 15 Laziness brings on deep sleep, and the shiftless **man** goes hungry.
19: 16 He who obeys instructions guards his **life**, but he who is
19: 18 that there is hope; *do* not **be a willing party** [+5951] to his death.
20: 2 wrath is like the roar of a lion; he who angers him forfeits his **life**.
21: 10 The wicked **man** craves evil; his neighbor gets no mercy from him.
21: 23 his mouth and his tongue keeps **himself** [+2257] from calamity.
22: 5 and snares, but he who guards his **soul** stays far from them.
22: 23 their case and *will* **plunder** [+906+7693] those who plunder them.
22: 25 or you may learn his ways and get **yourself** [+3870] ensnared.
23: 2 and put a knife to your throat if you are **given to gluttony** [+1251].
23: 7 for he is the kind of man who is always thinking about the **cost**.
23: 14 Punish him with the rod and save his **soul** from death.
24: 12 the heart perceive it? Does not he who guards your **life** know it?
24: 14 Know also that wisdom is sweet to your **soul**; if you find it,
25: 13 to those who send him; he refreshes the **spirit** *of* his masters.
25: 25 Like cold water to a weary **soul** is good news from a distant land.
27: 7 **He**[s] who is full loathes honey, but to the hungry even what is bitter
27: 7 but to the **[RPH]** hungry even what is bitter tastes sweet.
27: 9 the pleasantness of one's friend springs from his **earnest** counsel.
28: 17 A man tormented by the **guilt of murder** [+1947] will be a
28: 25 A **greedy man** [+8146] stirs up dissension, but he who trusts in the
29: 10 men hate a man of integrity and seek to **kill** the upright.
29: 17 and he will give you peace; he will bring delight to your **soul**.
29: 24 The accomplice of a thief is **his own** [+2257] enemy; he is put
31: 6 who are perishing, wine to *those who* are **in anguish** [+5253];
Ecc 2: 24 than to eat and drink and find **[NIE]** satisfaction in his work.
4: 8 he asked, "and why am I depriving **myself** [+3276] of enjoyment?"
6: 2 possessions and honor, so that he lacks nothing his **heart** desires,
6: 3 if **he** [+2257] cannot enjoy his prosperity and does not receive
6: 7 man's efforts are for his mouth, yet his **appetite** is never satisfied.
6: 9 Better what the eye sees than the roving of the **appetite**. This too is
7: 28 while **I** [+3276] was still searching but not finding—I found one
SS 1: 7 Tell me, you whom **I** [+3276] love, where you graze your flock
3: 1 All night long on my bed I looked for the one my **heart** loves;
3: 2 its streets and squares; I will search for the one my **heart** loves.
3: 3 their rounds in the city. "Have you seen the one my **heart** loves?"
3: 4 Scarcely had I passed them when I found the one my **heart** loves.
5: 6 but my lover had left; he was gone. My **heart** sank at his departure.
6: 12 my **desire** set me among the royal chariots of my people.
Isa 1: 14 Your New Moon festivals and your appointed feasts my **soul** hates.
3: 9 their sin like Sodom; they do not hide it. Woe to **them** [+4392]!
3: 20 and ankle chains and sashes, the **perfume** bottles and charms,
5: 14 Therefore the grave enlarges its **appetite** and opens its mouth
10: 18 fertile fields it will **completely** [+1414+2256+4946+6330] destroy,
15: 4 the armed men of Moab cry out, and their **hearts** are faint.
19: 10 will be dejected, and all the wage earners will be sick at **heart**.
26: 8 wait for you; your name and renown are the desire of our **hearts**.
26: 9 My **soul** yearns for you in the night; in the morning my spirit longs
29: 8 that he is eating, but he awakens, and his **hunger** [+8199] remains;
29: 8 he is drinking, but he awakens faint, with his **thirst** unquenched.
32: 6 the **hungry** [+8281] he leaves empty and from the thirsty he
38: 15 will walk humbly all my years because of this anguish of my **soul**.
38: 17 In your love you kept **me** [+3276] from the pit of destruction;
42: 1 whom I uphold, my chosen one in whom **I** [+3276] delight;
43: 4 men in exchange for you, and people in exchange for your **life**.
44: 20 he cannot save **himself** [+2257], or say, "Is not this thing in my
46: 2 rescue the burden, they **themselves** [+4392] go off into captivity.
47: 14 They cannot even save **themselves** [+4392] from the power of the
49: 7 to **him**[s] who was despised and abhorred by the nation,
51: 23 who said to **you** [+3871], 'Fall prostrate that we may walk over
53: 10 to suffer, and though the LORD makes his **life** a guilt offering,
53: 11 After the suffering of his **soul**, he will see the light ⌞of life⌟
53: 12 because he poured out his **life** unto death, and was numbered with
55: 2 eat what is good, and your **soul** will delight in the richest of fare.
55: 3 Give ear and come to me; hear me, that your **soul** may live.
56: 11 They are dogs with mighty **appetites**; they never have enough.
58: 3 Why have we humbled **ourselves** [+5646], and you have not
58: 5 I have chosen, only a day for a man to humble **himself** [+2257]?
58: 10 and if you spend **yourselves** [+3870] in behalf of the hungry
58: 10 in behalf of the hungry and satisfy the **needs** *of* the oppressed,
58: 11 he will satisfy your **needs** in a sun-scorched land and will
61: 10 I delight greatly in the LORD; my **soul** rejoices in my God.
66: 3 their own ways, and their **souls** delight in their abominations;
Jer 2: 24 accustomed to the desert, sniffing the wind in her **craving** [+205]—
2: 34 On your clothes men find the **lifeblood** [+1947] *of* the innocent
3: 11 "Faithless Israel is more righteous than **[NIE]** unfaithful Judah.
4: 10 'You will have peace,' when the sword is at our **throats**."
4: 19 For **I** [+3276] have heard the sound of the trumpet; I have heard
4: 30 yourself in vain. Your lovers despise you; they seek your **life**.
4: 31 "Alas! I am fainting; my **life** is given over to murderers."
5: 9 "Should I not avenge **myself** [+3276] on such a nation as this?
5: 29 "Should I not avenge **myself** [+3276] on such a nation as this?
6: 8 or **I** [+3276] will turn away from you and make your land desolate
6: 16 good way is, and walk in it, and you will find rest for your **souls**.
9: 9 [9:8] "Should I not avenge **myself** [+3276] on such a nation as
11: 21 LORD says about the men of Anathoth who are seeking your **life**
12: 7 I will give the one **I** [+3276] love into the hands of her enemies.
13: 17 if you do not listen, **I** [+3276] will weep in secret because of your
14: 19 Do **you** [+3870] despise Zion? Why have you afflicted us
15: 1 were to stand before me, my **heart** would not go out to this people.
15: 9 The mother of seven will grow faint and **breathe** her **last** [+5870].
17: 21 Be careful **[NIE]** not to carry a load on the Sabbath day or bring it
18: 20 good be repaid with evil? Yet they have dug a pit for **me** [+3276].
19: 7 before their enemies, at the hands of those who seek their **lives**,
19: 9 of the siege imposed on them by the enemies who seek their **lives**.'
20: 13 He rescues the **life** *of* the needy from the hands of the wicked.
21: 7 king of Babylon and to their enemies who seek their **lives**.
21: 9 who are besieging you will live; he will escape with his **life**.
22: 25 I will hand you over to those who seek your **life**, those you fear—
22: 27 You will never come back to the land you **long** [+906+5951] to
26: 19 We are about to bring a terrible disaster on **ourselves** [+5646]!"
31: 12 and herds. **They** [+4392] will be like a well-watered garden,
31: 14 I will satisfy **[NIE]** the priests with abundance, and my people
31: 25 I will refresh the **weary** [+6546] and satisfy the faint."
31: 25 I will refresh the weary and satisfy the **faint** [+1790]."
32: 41 will assuredly plant them in this land with all my heart and **soul**.
34: 16 and female slaves you had set free to go where they **wished**.
34: 20 I will hand over to their enemies who seek their **lives**. Their dead
34: 21 and his officials over to their enemies who seek their **lives**,
37: 9 Do not deceive **yourselves** [+4013], thinking, 'The Babylonians
38: 2 the Babylonians will live. He will escape with his **life**; he will live.'
38: 16 "As surely as the LORD lives, who has given us **breath**,
38: 16 kill you nor hand you over to those who are seeking your **life**."
38: 17 your **life** will be spared and this city will not be burned down;
38: 20 Then it will go well with you, and your **life** will be spared.
39: 18 you will not fall by the sword but will escape with your **life**,
40: 14 Ammonites has sent Ishmael son of Nethaniah to take your **life**?"
40: 15 Why should he take your **life** and cause all the Jews who are
42: 20 that *you* **made a fatal mistake** [+928+9494] when you sent me to
43: 6 the king's daughters **[NIE]** whom Nebuzaradan commander of
44: 7 Why bring such great disaster on **yourselves** [+4013] by cutting
44: 14 land of Judah, to which they **long** [+906+5951] to return and live;
44: 30 Hophra king of Egypt over to his enemies who seek his **life**,
44: 30 king of Babylon, the enemy who was seeking his **life**.' "
45: 5 but wherever you go I will let you escape with your **life**.' "
46: 26 I will hand them over to those who seek their **lives**, to
48: 6 Flee! Run for your **lives**; become like a bush in the desert.
49: 37 shatter Elam before their foes, before those who seek their **lives**;
50: 19 his **appetite** will be satisfied on the hills of Ephraim and Gilead.
51: 6 Run for your **lives**! Do not be destroyed because of her sins.
51: 14 The LORD Almighty has sworn by **himself** [+2257]: I will surely
51: 45 "Come out of her, my people! Run for your **lives**! Run from the
52: 29 in Nebuchadnezzar's eighteenth year, 832 **people** from Jerusalem;
52: 30 745 **[RPH]** Jews taken into exile by Nebuzaradan the commander
52: 30 commander of the imperial guard. There were 4,600 **people** in all.
La 1: 11 barter their treasures for food to **keep themselves alive** [+8740].
1: 16 No one is near to comfort me, no one to restore my **spirit**.
1: 19 searched for food *to* **keep themselves alive** [+906+4392+8740].
2: 12 streets of the city, as their **lives** ebb away in their mothers' arms.
2: 19 Lift up your hands to him for the **lives** *of* your children, who faint
3: 17 **I** [+3276] have been deprived of peace; I have forgotten what
3: 20 I well remember them, and my **soul** is downcast within me.
3: 24 I say to **myself** [+3276], "The LORD is my portion; therefore I
3: 25 is good to those whose hope is in him, to the **one** who seeks him;
3: 51 What I see brings grief to my **soul** because of all the women of my
3: 58 O Lord, you took up **my** [+3276] case; you redeemed my life.
5: 9 We get our bread at the risk of our **lives** because of the sword in
Eze 3: 19 he will die for his sin; but you will have saved **yourself** [+3870].
3: 21 he took warning, and you will have saved **yourself** [+3870]."
4: 14 "Not so, Sovereign LORD! I have never defiled **myself** [+3276].
7: 19 They will not satisfy their **hunger** or fill their stomachs with it,
13: 18 veils of various lengths for their heads in order to ensnare **people**.
13: 18 Will you ensnare the **lives** of my people but preserve your own?
13: 18 ensnare the lives of my people but **[RPH]** preserve your own?
13: 19 you have killed **those**[s] who should not have died and have spared
13: 19 should not have died and have spared **those**[s] who should not live.
13: 20 I am against your magic charms with which you ensnare **people**
13: 20 your arms; I will set free the **people** that you ensnare like birds.
13: 20 I will set free the people that you ensnare **[RPH]** like birds.
14: 14 they could save only **themselves** [+4392] by their righteousness,
14: 20 They would save only **themselves** [+4392] by their righteousness.
16: 5 for on the day you were born **you** [+3871] were despised.
16: 27 I gave you over to the **greed** *of* your enemies, the daughters of the
17: 17 ramps are built and siege works erected to destroy many **lives**.
18: 4 For every **living soul** belongs to me, the father as well as the son—
18: 4 living soul belongs to me, **[RPH]** the father as well as the son—
18: 4 living soul belongs to me, the father as well as **[RPH]** the son—

Eze 18: 4 both alike belong to me. The **soul** who sins is the one who will die.
18: 20 The **soul** who sins is the one who will die. The son will not share
18: 27 has committed and does what is just and right, he will save his **life**.
22: 25 they devour **people**, take treasures and precious things and make
22: 27 their prey; they shed blood and kill **people** to make unjust gain.
23: 17 After she had been defiled by them, **she** [+2023] turned away from
23: 18 exposed her nakedness, **I** [+3276] turned away from her in disgust,
23: 18 her in disgust, just as **I** [+3276] had turned away from her sister.
23: 22 lovers against you, those **you** [+3871] turned away from in disgust,
23: 28 those you hate, to those **you** [+3871] turned away from in disgust.
24: 21 take pride, the delight of your eyes, the object of your **affection**.
24: 25 their **heart's** desire, and their sons and daughters as well—
25: 6 rejoicing with all the malice of your **heart** against the land of
25: 15 acted in vengeance and took revenge with malice in their **hearts**,
27: 13 they exchanged **slaves** [+132] and articles of bronze for your
27: 31 They will weep over you with anguish of **soul** and with bitter
32: 10 your downfall each of them will tremble every moment for his **life**.
33: 5 If he had taken warning, he would have saved **himself** [+2257].
33: 6 the people and the sword comes and takes the **life** of one of them,
33: 9 he will die for his sin, but you will have saved **yourself** [+3870].
36: 5 with malice in their hearts **[RPH]** they made my land their own
47: 9 Swarms of living **creatures** will live wherever the river flows.
Hos 4: 8 on the sins of my people and **relish** [+448+5951] their wickedness.
9: 4 This food will be for **themselves** [+4392]; it will not come into the
Am 2: 14 will not muster their strength, and the warrior will not save his **life**.
2: 15 soldier will not get away, and the horseman will not save his **life**.
6: 8 The Sovereign LORD has sworn by **himself** [+2257]—
Jnh 1: 14 "O LORD, please do not let us die for taking this man's **life**.
2: 5 [2:6] The engulfing waters **threatened** [+6330] me, the deep
2: 7 [2:8] "When my **life** was ebbing away, I remembered you,
4: 3 Now, O LORD, take away my **life**, for it is better for me to die
4: 8 He **wanted** [+906+8626] to die, and said, "It would be better for
Mic 6: 7 for my transgression, the fruit of my body for the sin of my **soul**?
7: 1 cluster of grapes to eat, none of the early figs that **I** [+3276] crave.
7: 3 accepts bribes, the powerful dictate what **they** [+2257] desire—
Hab 2: 4 "See, he is puffed up; his **desires** are not upright—but the
2: 5 Because **he** [+2257] is as greedy as the grave and like death is
2: 10 of many peoples, shaming your own house and forfeiting your **life**.
Hag 2: 13 "If a person defiled by contact with a **dead body** touches one of
Zec 11: 8 **The flock**[*] [+4392] detested me, and I grew weary of them
11: 8 The flock detested me, and **I** [+3276] grew weary of them

5884 נֹפֶת **nepet**, n.f. [1 / 0] [√ 5679]

Jos 17: 11 (the third in the list is Naphoth). [BHS *Nepheth* ?; NIV 5868]

5885 נֹפֶת **nōpet**, n.m. [5] [√ 5678]

honey [3], honey from the comb [1], sweetness as the honeycomb [1]

Ps 19: 10 [19:11] they are sweeter than honey, than **honey** *from* the comb.
Pr 5: 3 For the lips of an adulteress drip **honey**, and her speech is
24: 13 for it is good; **honey from the comb** is sweet to your taste.
27: 7 He who is full loathes **honey**, but to the hungry even what is bitter
SS 4: 11 Your lips drop **sweetness as the honeycomb**, my bride; milk

5886 נֶפְתּוֹחַ **neptôaḥ**, n.pr.loc. [2]

Nephtoah [2]

Jos 15: 9 the boundary headed toward the spring of the waters of **Nephtoah**,
18: 15 the boundary came out at the spring of the waters of **Nephtoah**.

5887 נַפְתּוּלִים **naptûlîm**, n.[m.pl.]. [1] [√ 7349]

had a struggle [+7349] [1]

Ge 30: 8 "*I have* **had a** great **struggle** [+7349] with my sister, and I have

5888 נַפְתֻּחִים **naptuḥîm**, n.pr.loc. & a.g. [2]

Naphtuhites [2]

Ge 10: 13 was the father of the Ludites, Anamites, Lehabites, **Naphtuhites**,
1Ch 1: 11 was the father of the Ludites, Anamites, Lehabites, **Naphtuhites**,

5889 נַפְתָּלִי **naptālî**, n.pr.m. [51] [√ 7349?]

Naphtali [44], Naphtali [+1201] [5], *untranslated* [1], Naphtali [+824] [1]

Ge 30: 8 with my sister, and I have won." So she named him **Naphtali**.
35: 25 The sons of Rachel's maidservant Bilhah: Dan and **Naphtali**.
46: 24 The sons of **Naphtali**: Jahziel, Guni, Jezer and Shillem.
49: 21 "**Naphtali** is a doe set free that bears beautiful fawns.
Ex 1: 4 Dan and **Naphtali**; Gad and Asher.
Nu 1: 15 from **Naphtali**, Ahira son of Enan."
1: 42 From the descendants of **Naphtali**: All the men twenty years old
1: 43 The number from the tribe of **Naphtali** was 53,400.
2: 29 The tribe of **Naphtali** will be next. The leader of the people of
2: 29 The leader of the people of **Naphtali** is Ahira son of Enan.
7: 78 the leader of the people of **Naphtali**, brought his offering.
10: 27 son of Enan was over the division of the tribe of **Naphtali** [+1201].
13: 14 from the tribe of **Naphtali**, Nahbi son of Vophsi;
26: 48 The descendants of **Naphtali** by their clans were: through Jahzeel,
26: 50 These were the clans of **Naphtali**; those numbered were 45,400.
34: 28 son of Ammihud, the leader from the tribe of **Naphtali** [+1201]."
Dt 27: 13 Reuben, Gad, Asher, Zebulun, Dan and **Naphtali**.
33: 23 About **Naphtali** he said: "Naphtali is abounding with the favor of
33: 23 "**Naphtali** is abounding with the favor of the LORD and is full of
34: 2 all of **Naphtali**, the territory of Ephraim and Manasseh, all the land
Jos 19: 32 The sixth lot came out for **Naphtali** [+1201], clan by clan:
19: 32 The sixth lot came out for Naphtali, clan by clan: **[RPH]**
19: 39 their villages were the inheritance of the tribe of **Naphtali** [+1201],
20: 7 So they set apart Kedesh in Galilee in the hill country of **Naphtali**,
21: 6 Asher, **Naphtali** and the half-tribe of Manasseh in Bashan.
21: 32 from the tribe of **Naphtali**, Kedesh in Galilee (a city of refuge for
Jdg 1: 33 Neither did **Naphtali** drive out those living in Beth Shemesh
4: 6 She sent for Barak son of Abinoam from Kedesh in **Naphtali**
4: 6 take with you ten thousand men of **Naphtali** [+1201] and Zebulun
4: 10 where he summoned Zebulun and **Naphtali**. Ten thousand men
5: 18 risked their very lives; so did **Naphtali** on the heights of the field.
6: 35 calling them to arms, and also into Asher, Zebulun and **Naphtali**,
7: 23 Israelites from **Naphtali**, Asher and all Manasseh were called out,
1Ki 4: 15 in **Naphtali** (he had married Basemath daughter of Solomon);
7: 14 whose mother was a widow from the tribe of **Naphtali** and whose
15: 20 Beth Maacah and all Kinnereth in addition to **Naphtali** [+824].
2Ki 15: 29 He took Gilead and Galilee, including all the land of **Naphtali**,
1Ch 2: 2 Dan, Joseph, Benjamin, **Naphtali**, Gad and Asher.
6: 62 [6:47] towns from the tribes of Issachar, Asher and **Naphtali**,
6: 76 [6:61] from the tribe of **Naphtali** they received Kedesh in Galilee,
7: 13 The sons of **Naphtali**: Jahziel, Guni, Jezer and Shillem—
12: 34 [12:35] men of **Naphtali**—1,000 officers, together with 37,000
12: 40 [12:41] Zebulun and **Naphtali** came bringing food on donkeys,
27: 19 over Zebulun: Ishmaiah son of Obadiah; over **Naphtali**:
2Ch 16: 4 Dan, Abel Maim and all the store cities of **Naphtali**.
34: 6 the towns of Manasseh, Ephraim and Simeon, as far as **Naphtali**,
Ps 68: 27 [68:28] and there the princes of Zebulun and of **Naphtali**.
Isa 9: 1 [8:23] he humbled the land of Zebulun and the land of **Naphtali**,
Eze 48: 3 "**Naphtali** will have one portion; it will border the territory of
48: 4 it will border the territory of **Naphtali** from east to west.
48: 34 the gate of Gad, the gate of Asher and the gate of **Naphtali**.

5890 נֵץ **nēṣ**[1], n.m. [2] [√ 5914]

blossomed [+6590] [1], flowers [1]

Ge 40: 10 As soon as it budded, it **blossomed** [+6590], and its clusters
SS 2: 12 **Flowers** appear on the earth; the season of singing has come,

5891 נֵץ **nēṣ**[2], n.m. [3] [√ 5892]

hawk [3]

Lev 11: 16 the horned owl, the screech owl, the gull, any kind of **hawk**,
Dt 14: 15 the horned owl, the screech owl, the gull, any kind of **hawk**,
Job 39: 26 "Does the **hawk** take flight by your wisdom and spread his wings

5892 נָצָא **nāṣā'**, v. Not used in NIV/BHS [→ 5891; cf. 5899]

5893 נָצַב **nāṣab**[1], v. [74] [→ 2205, 5163, 5164, 5165, 5166, 5167, 5169, 5170, 5895, 5896, 5907, 5908; cf. 3656, 5894]

standing [14], set up [9], set [5], stood [5], stand [3], *untranslated* [2], district officers [2], foreman [+5853] [2], officials [2], attendants [1], attending [1], decreed [1], deputy [1], district governors [1], erected as a monument [1], establish [1], foremen [+8569] [1], healthy [1], is [1], keeps intact [1], leader [1], life [1], made stand firm [1], made [1], piled up [1], present yourself [1], presides [1], ready [1], repointing [1], resting [1], stands firm [1], stay [1], stood by [1], stood firm [1], stood upright [1], takes place [1], takes stand [1], wait [1], waiting [1]

Ge 18: 2 [C] Abraham looked up and saw three men **standing** nearby.
21: 28 [G] Abraham **set** apart seven ewe lambs from the flock,
21: 29 [G] "What is the meaning of these seven ewe lambs *you have* **set**
24: 13 [C] See, I *am* **standing** beside this spring, and the daughters of
24: 43 [C] See, I *am* **standing** beside this spring; if a maiden comes out
28: 12 [H] He had a dream in which he saw a stairway **resting** on the
28: 13 [C] There above it **stood** the LORD, and he said: "I am the
33: 20 [G] There *he* **set up** an altar and called it El Elohe Israel.
35: 14 [G] Jacob **set up** a stone pillar at the place where God had talked
35: 20 [G] Over her tomb Jacob **set up** a pillar, and to this day that pillar
37: 7 [C] in the field when suddenly my sheaf rose and **stood upright**,
45: 1 [C] could no longer control himself before all his **attendants**,
Ex 5: 20 [C] they found Moses and Aaron **waiting** to meet them,
7: 15 [C] **Wait** on the bank of the Nile to meet him, and take in your
15: 8 [C] The surging waters **stood firm** like a wall; the deep waters
17: 9 [C] Tomorrow I *will* **stand** on top of the hill with the staff of God
18: 14 [C] while all these people **stand** around you from morning till

Ex 33: 8 [C] all the people rose and **stood** at the entrances to their tents,
33: 21 [C] "There is a place near me where *you may* **stand** on a rock.
34: 2 [C] **Present yourself** to me there on top of the mountain.
Nu 16: 27 [C] Abiram had come out and *were* **standing** with their wives,
22: 23 [C] When the donkey saw the angel of the LORD **standing** in
22: 31 [C] he saw the angel of the LORD **standing** in the road with his
22: 34 [C] I did not realize you *were* **standing** in the road to oppose me.
23: 6 [C] back to him and found *him* **standing** beside his offering,
23: 17 [C] he went to him and found him **standing** beside his offering,
Dt 29: 10 [29:9] [C] All of you *are* **standing** today in the presence of the
32: 8 [G] *he* **set up** boundaries for the peoples according to the number
Jos 6: 26 [G] at the cost of his youngest *will he* **set up** its gates."
Jdg 18: 16 [C] armed for battle, **stood** *at* the entrance to the gate.
18: 17 [C] the six hundred armed men **stood** *at* the entrance to the gate.
Ru 2: 5 [C] Boaz asked the **foreman** [+5853] of his harvesters, "Whose
2: 6 [C] The **foreman** [+5853] replied, "She is the Moabitess who
1Sa 1: 26 [C] I am the woman who **stood** here beside you praying to the
4: 20 [C] was dying, the *women* **attending** her said, "Don't despair;
13: 21 [G] for sharpening forks and axes and for **repointing** goads.
15: 12 [G] There *he has* **set up** a monument in his own honor and has
19: 20 [C] with Samuel standing there *as* their **leader**, the Spirit of God
22: 6 [C] the hill at Gibeah, with all his officials **standing** around him.
22: 7 [C] Saul said to them, **[RPH]** "Listen, men of Benjamin! Will
22: 9 [C] the Edomite, who *was* **standing** with Saul's officials, said,
22: 17 [C] Then the king ordered the guards **[NIE]** at his side: "Turn
2Sa 13: 31 [C] and all his servants **stood by** with their clothes torn.
18: 17 [G] pit in the forest and **piled up** a large heap of rocks over him.
18: 18 [G] **erected** it in the King's Valley **as a monument** to himself,
1Ki 4: 5 [C] in charge of the **district officers**; Zabud son of Nathan—
4: 7 [C] Solomon also had twelve **district governors** over all Israel,
4: 27 [5:7] [C] The **district officers**, each in his month,
5: 16 [5:30] [C] as well as thirty-three hundred **foremen** [+8569] who
9: 23 [C] They were also the chief **officials** in charge of Solomon's
16: 34 [G] and *he* **set up** its gates at the cost of his youngest son Segub,
22: 47 [22:48] [C] There was then no king in Edom; a **deputy** ruled.
2Ki 17: 10 [G] *They* **set up** sacred stones and Asherah poles on every high
1Ch 18: 3 [G] when he went to **establish** his control along the Euphrates
2Ch 8: 10 [C] They were also King Solomon's chief **officials**—[K 5907]
Ps 39: 5 [39:6] [C] before you. Each man's **life** is but a breath. *Selah*
41: 12 [41:13] [G] you uphold me and **set** me in your presence forever.
45: 9 [45:10] [C] at your right hand **is** the royal bride in gold of Ophir.
74: 17 [G] It was you *who* **set** all the boundaries of the earth; you made
78: 13 [G] led them through; *he* **made** the water **stand firm** like a wall.
82: 1 [C] God **presides** in the great assembly; he gives judgment
119: 89 [C] O LORD, is eternal; *it* **stands firm** in the heavens.
Pr 8: 2 [C] along the way, where the paths meet, *she* **takes** *her* **stand**;
15: 25 [G] man's house but *he* **keeps** the widow's boundaries **intact**.
Isa 3: 13 [C] The LORD **takes** *his* **place** in court; he rises to judge the
21: 8 [C] I stand on the watchtower; every night I **stay** at my post.
Jer 5: 26 [G] who snare birds and like *those who* **set** traps to catch men.
31: 21 [G] "**Set up** road signs; put up guideposts. Take note of the
La 2: 4 [C] Like an enemy he has strung his bow; his right hand *is* **ready**.
3: 12 [G] He drew his bow and **made** me the target for his arrows.
Am 7: 7 [C] The Lord *was* **standing** by a wall that had been built true to
9: 1 [C] I saw the Lord **standing** by the altar, and he said:
Na 2: 7 [2:8] [H] *It is* **decreed** that ˻the city˼ be exiled and carried
Zec 11: 16 [C] or seek the young, or heal the injured, or feed the **healthy**,

5894 ²נָצַב **nāṣab²**, v. Not used in NIV/BHS [cf. 5893]

5895 ¹נִצָּב **niṣṣāb¹**, n.[m.] *or* v.ptcp. Not used in NIV/BHS [√ 5893; cf. 3656]

5896 ²נִצָּב **niṣṣāb²**, n.m. [1] [√ 5893]

handle [1]

Jdg 3: 22 Even the **handle** sank in after the blade, which came out his back.

5897 ¹נָצָה **nāṣâ¹**, v. [8] [→ 5175, 5194]

fighting [3], rebelled [2], fight broke out [1], fought [1], got into a fight [1]

Ex 2: 13 [C] The next day he went out and saw two Hebrews **fighting**.
21: 22 [C] "If men *who are* **fighting** hit a pregnant woman and she
Lev 24: 10 [C] a **fight broke out** in the camp between him and an Israelite.
Nu 26: 9 [G] Abiram were the community officials who **rebelled** against
26: 9 [G] were among Korah's followers when they **rebelled** against
Dt 25: 11 [C] If two men *are* **fighting** and the wife of one of them comes to
2Sa 14: 6 [C] *They* **got into a fight** *with* each other in the field, and no one
Ps 60: T [60:2] [G] When he **fought** Aram Naharaim and Aram Zobah,

5898 ²נָצָה **nāṣâ²**, v. [6 / 8]

laid waste [+3655] [2], lie in ruins [2], piles of stone [+1643] [2], desolate [1], laid waste [1]

2Ki 19: 25 [C] you have turned fortified cities into **piles of stone** [+1643].
Isa 37: 26 [C] you have turned fortified cities into **piles of stone** [+1643].
Jer 4: 7 [A] your land. Your towns *will* **lie in ruins** without inhabitant.
9: 10 [9:9] [C] *They are* **desolate** and untraveled, and the lowing of
9: 12 [9:11] [C] and **laid waste** like a desert that no one can cross?
46: 19 [C] will be laid waste and **lie in ruins** without inhabitant.
48: 9 [a] for *she will be* **laid waste** [+5898]; [BHS 3655]
48: 9 [a] for *she will be* **laid waste** [+5898]; [BHS 3655]

5899 ³נָצָה **nāṣâ³**, v. Not used in NIV/BHS [→ 5902; cf. 5892]

5900 נִצָּה **niṣṣâ**, n.f. [2] [√ 5914]

blossoms [1], flower [1]

Job 15: 33 of its unripe grapes, like an olive tree shedding its **blossoms**.
Isa 18: 5 the blossom is gone and the **flower** becomes a ripening grape,

5901 ¹נֹצָה **nōṣâ¹**, n.f. [1] [cf. 5681, 5902]

contents [1]

Lev 1: 16 He is to remove the crop with its **contents** and throw it to the east

5902 ²נֹצָה **nōṣâ²**, n.f. Not used in NIV/BHS [√ 5899; cf. 5681, 5901]

5903 נְצוּרִים **nᵉṣûrîm**, n.[m.]. Not used in NIV/BHS [√ 5915]

5904 נָצַח **nāṣaḥ**, v. [65] [→ 5905, 5909; Ar 10488]

director of music [56], foremen [2], supervise [2], direct [1], directing [1], does always [1], supervised [1], supervising [1]

1Ch 15: 21 [D] were to play the harps, **directing** according to *sheminith*.
23: 4 [D] twenty-four thousand are to **supervise** the work of the temple
2Ch 2: 2 [2:1] [D] the hills and thirty-six hundred as **foremen** over them.
2: 18 [2:17] [D] with 3,600 **foremen** over them to keep the people
34: 12 [D] Over them to **direct** them were Jahath and Obadiah, Levites
34: 13 [D] the laborers and **supervised** all the workers from job to job.
Ezr 3: 8 [D] older to **supervise** the building of the house of the LORD.
3: 9 [D] joined together in **supervising** those working on the house of
Ps 4: T [4:1] [D] For the **director of music**. With stringed instruments.
5: T [5:1] [D] For the **director of music**. For flutes. A psalm of
6: T [6:1] [D] For the **director of music**. With stringed instruments.
8: T [8:1] [D] For the **director of music**. According to *gittith*.
9: T [9:1] [D] For the **director of music**. To ˻the tune of˼ "The
11: T [11:1] [D] For the **director of music**. Of David.
12: T [12:1] [D] For the **director of music**. According to *sheminith*.
13: T [13:1] [D] For the **director of music**. A psalm of David.
14: T [14:1] [D] For the **director of music**. Of David.
18: T [18:1] [D] For the **director of music**. Of David the servant of
19: T [19:1] [D] For the **director of music**. A psalm of David.
20: T [20:1] [D] For the **director of music**. A psalm of David.
21: T [21:1] [D] For the **director of music**. A psalm of David.
22: T [22:1] [D] For the **director of music**. To ˻the tune of˼ "The Doe
31: T [31:1] [D] For the **director of music**. A psalm of David.
36: T [36:1] [D] For the **director of music**. Of David the servant of
39: T [39:1] [D] For the **director of music**. For Jeduthun. A psalm of
40: T [40:1] [D] For the **director of music**. Of David. A psalm.
41: T [41:1] [D] For the **director of music**. A psalm of David.
42: T [42:1] [D] For the **director of music**. A *maskil* of the Sons of
44: T [44:1] [D] For the **director of music**. Of the Sons of Korah.
45: T [45:1] [D] For the **director of music**. To ˻the tune of˼ "Lilies."
46: T [46:1] [D] For the **director of music**. Of the Sons of Korah.
47: T [47:1] [D] For the **director of music**. Of the Sons of Korah.
49: T [49:1] [D] For the **director of music**. Of the Sons of Korah.
51: T [51:1] [D] For the **director of music**. A psalm of David.
52: T [52:1] [D] For the **director of music**. A *maskil* of David.
53: T [53:1] [D] For the **director of music**. According to *mahalath*.
54: T [54:1] [D] For the **director of music**. With stringed instruments.
55: T [55:1] [D] For the **director of music**. With stringed instruments.
56: T [56:1] [D] For the **director of music**. To ˻the tune of˼ "A Dove
57: T [57:1] [D] For the **director of music**. ˻To the tune of˼ "Do Not
58: T [58:1] [D] For the **director of music**. ˻To the tune of˼ "Do Not
59: T [59:1] [D] For the **director of music**. ˻To the tune of˼ "Do Not
60: T [60:1] [D] For the **director of music**. To ˻the tune of˼ "The Lily
61: T [61:1] [D] For the **director of music**. With stringed instruments.
62: T [62:1] [D] For the **director of music**. For Jeduthun. A psalm of
64: T [64:1] [D] For the **director of music**. A psalm of David.
65: T [65:1] [D] For the **director of music**. A psalm of David.
66: T [66:1] [D] For the **director of music**. A song. A psalm.
67: T [67:1] [D] For the **director of music**. With stringed instruments.

Ps 68: T [68:1] [D] For the **director of music**. Of David. A psalm.
69: T [69:1] [D] For the **director of music**. To ⌞the tune of⌟ "Lilies."
70: T [70:1] [D] For the **director of music**. Of David. A petition.
75: T [75:1] [D] For the **director of music**. ⌞To the tune of⌟ "Do Not
76: T [76:1] [D] For the **director of music**. With stringed instruments.
77: T [77:1] [D] For the **director of music**. For Jeduthun. Of Asaph.
80: T [80:1] [D] For the **director of music**. To ⌞the tune of⌟ "The
81: T [81:1] [D] For the **director of music**. According to *gittith*.
84: T [84:1] [D] For the **director of music**. According to *gittith*.
85: T [85:1] [D] For the **director of music**. Of the Sons of Korah.
88: T [88:1] [D] of the Sons of Korah. For the **director of music**.
109: T [109:1] [D] For the **director of music**. Of David. A psalm.
139: T [139:1] [D] For the **director of music**. Of David. A psalm.
140: T [140:1] [D] For the **director of music**. A psalm of David.
Jer 8: 5 [C] Why **does** Jerusalem **always** turn away? They cling to deceit;
Hab 3: 19 [D] For the **director of music**. On my stringed instruments.

5905 ¹נֵ֫צַח nēṣaḥ[1], n.m. [43] [√ 5904]

forever [+4200] [18], always [+4200] [4], never [+4200+4202] [3], ever again [+4200+5905] [2], never [+1153+4200] [2], endless [+4200] [1], eternal [1], everlasting [+4200] [1], everlasting [1], flamed unchecked [+9068] [1], forever [1], glory [1], majesty [1], never [+4202+6330] [1], never [+561+4200] [1], once for all [+4200] [1], splendor [1], unending [1], utmost [1]

1Sa 15: 29 He who is the **Glory** *of* Israel does not lie or change his mind;
2Sa 2: 26 called out to Joab, "Must the sword devour **forever** [+4200]?
1Ch 29: 11 is the greatness and the power and the glory and the **majesty**
Job 4: 20 they are broken to pieces; unnoticed, they perish **forever** [+4200].
14: 20 You overpower him **once** [+4200] **for all**, and he is gone;
20: 7 he will perish **forever** [+4200], like his own dung; those who have
23: 7 and I would be delivered **forever** [+4200] from my judge.
34: 36 that Job might be tested to the **utmost** for answering like a wicked
36: 7 he enthrones them with kings and exalts them **forever** [+4200].
Ps 9: 6 [9:7] **Endless** [+4200] ruin has overtaken the enemy, you have
9: 18 [9:19] the needy will not **always** [+4200] be forgotten,
10: 11 has forgotten; he covers his face and **never** [+1153+4200] sees."
13: 1 [13:2] How long, O LORD? Will you forget me **forever**? How
16: 11 joy in your presence, with **eternal** pleasures at your right hand.
44: 23 [44:24] Rouse yourself! Do not reject us **forever** [+4200].
49: 9 [49:10] that he should live on **forever** [+4200] and not see decay.
49: 19 [49:20] who will **never** [+4202+6330] see the light ⌞of life⌟.
52: 5 [52:7] Surely God will bring you down to **everlasting** [+4200]
68: 16 [68:17] where the LORD himself will dwell **forever** [+4200]?
74: 1 Why have you rejected us **forever** [+4200], O God? Why does
74: 3 Turn your steps toward these **everlasting** ruins, all this destruction
74: 10 mock you, O God? Will the foe revile your name **forever** [+4200]?
74: 19 do not forget the lives of your afflicted people **forever** [+4200].
77: 8 [77:9] Has his unfailing love vanished **forever** [+4200]? Has his
79: 5 How long, O LORD? Will you be angry **forever** [+4200]?
89: 46 [89:47] O LORD? Will you hide yourself **forever** [+4200]?
103: 9 He will not **always** [+4200] accuse, nor will he harbor his anger
Pr 21: 28 and whoever listens to him will be destroyed **forever** [+4200].
Isa 13: 20 She will **never** [+4200+4202] be inhabited or lived in through all
25: 8 he will swallow up death **forever** [+4200]. The Sovereign LORD
28: 28 to make bread; so one does not go on threshing it **forever** [+4200].
33: 20 its stakes will **never** [+1153+4200] be pulled up, nor any of its
34: 10 lie desolate; no one will **ever** [+4200+5905] pass through it **again**.
34: 10 lie desolate; no one will **ever** pass through it **again** [+4200+5905].
57: 16 nor will I **always** [+4200] be angry, for then the spirit of man
Jer 3: 5 Will your wrath continue **forever** [+4200]?' This is how you talk,
15: 18 Why is my pain **unending** and my wound grievous and incurable?
50: 39 It will **never** [+4200+4202] again be inhabited or lived in from
La 3: 18 "My **splendor** is gone and all that I had hoped from the LORD."
5: 20 Why do you **always** [+4200] forget us? Why do you forsake us
Am 1: 11 anger raged continually and his fury **flamed unchecked** [+9068],
8: 7 "I will **never** [+561+4200] forget anything they have done.
Hab 1: 4 the law is paralyzed, and justice **never** [+4200+4202] prevails.

5906 ²נֵ֫צַח nēṣaḥ[2], n.m. [2]

blood [2]

Isa 63: 3 their **blood** spattered my garments, and I stained all my clothing.
63: 6 wrath I made them drunk and poured their **blood** on the ground."

5907 ¹נְצִיב n^{e}ṣîb[1], n.m. [11] [→ 5908; cf. 5893]

garrisons [4], outpost [3], *untranslated* [1], garrison [1], governor [1], pillar [1]

Ge 19: 26 But Lot's wife looked back, and she became a **pillar** *of* salt.
1Sa 10: 5 you will go to Gibeah of God, where there is a Philistine **outpost**.
13: 3 Jonathan attacked the Philistine **outpost** at Geba,
13: 4 "Saul has attacked the Philistine **outpost**, and now Israel has
2Sa 8: 6 He put **garrisons** in the Aramean kingdom of Damascus,
8: 14 He put **garrisons** throughout Edom, and all the Edomites became
8: 14 **[RPH]** and all the Edomites became subject to David.
1Ki 4: 19 of Og king of Bashan). He was the only **governor** over the district.
1Ch 11: 16 in the stronghold, and the Philistine **garrison** was at Bethlehem.
18: 13 He put **garrisons** in Edom, and all the Edomites became subject to
2Ch 8: 10 [They were also King Solomon's chief **officials**—[K; see Q 5893]]
17: 2 troops in all the fortified cities of Judah and put **garrisons** in Judah

5908 ²נְצִיב n^{e}ṣîb[2], n.pr.loc. [1] [√ 5907; cf. 5893]

Nezib [1]

Jos 15: 43 Iphtah, Ashnah, **Nezib**,

5909 נְצִיחַ n^{e}ṣîaḥ, n.pr.m. [2] [√ 5904]

Neziah [2]

Ezr 2: 54 **Neziah** and Hatipha
Ne 7: 56 **Neziah** and Hatipha

5910 נָצִיר nāṣîr, a. [0] [√ 5915]

Isa 49: 6 [and bring back *those of* Israel I *have* **kept**. [K; see Q 5915]]

5911 נָצַל nāṣal, v. [213] [→ 2208; Ar 10489]

rescue [42], deliver [40], save [32], delivered [17], rescued [12], delivers [6], saved [6], surely deliver [+5911] [4], be saved [3], snatched [3], be delivered [2], defended [2], escape [2], ever delivered [+906+5911] [2], free yourself [2], protect [2], recovered [2], rescued at all [+906+5911] [2], rescues [2], saves [2], succeed in the rescue [+5911] [2], *untranslated* [1], be rescued [1], come to rescue [1], defender [1], deliverance [1], delivering [1], ease [1], escapes [1], free [1], plunder [1], plundered [1], protected [1], rescuing [1], retake [1], safe [1], separate [+1068] [1], snatch [1], spared [1], stripped off [1], take away [+4200+5362] [1], take back [1], take [1], taken away [1], taken refuge [1], took away [1], was spared [1]

Ge 31: 9 [G] So God *has* **taken away** your father's livestock and has
31: 16 [G] Surely all the wealth that God **took away** from our father
32: 11 [32:12] [G] **Save** me, I pray, from the hand of my brother Esau,
32: 30 [32:31] [C] saw God face to face, and yet my life **was spared**."
37: 21 [G] Reuben heard this, *he tried to* **rescue** him from their hands.
37: 22 [G] Reuben said this to **rescue** him from them and take him back
Ex 2: 19 [G] "An Egyptian **rescued** us from the shepherds.
3: 8 [G] So I have come down to **rescue** them from the hand of the
3: 22 [D] and daughters. And so *you will* **plunder** the Egyptians."
5: 23 [G] and *you have* not **rescued** [+906+5911] your people **at all**."
5: 23 [G] and *you have* not **rescued** your people **at all** [+906+5911]."
6: 6 [G] *I will* **free** you from being slaves to them, and I will redeem
12: 27 [G] **spared** our homes when he struck down the Egyptians.' "
12: 36 [D] them what they asked for; so *they* **plundered** the Egyptians.
18: 4 [G] was my helper; *he* **saved** me from the sword of Pharaoh."
18: 8 [G] had met along the way and how the LORD *had* **saved** them.
18: 9 [G] for Israel in **rescuing** them from the hand of the Egyptians.
18: 10 [G] who **rescued** you from the hand of the Egyptians and of
18: 10 [G] and who **rescued** the people from the hand of the Egyptians.
33: 6 [F] So the Israelites **stripped off** their ornaments at Mount
Nu 35: 25 [G] The assembly *must* **protect** the one accused of murder from
Dt 23: 14 [23:15] [G] your God moves about in your camp to **protect** you
23: 15 [23:16] [C] If a slave *has* **taken refuge** with you, do not hand
25: 11 [G] the wife of one of them comes to **rescue** her husband from
32: 39 [G] and I will heal, and no *one can* **deliver** out of my hand.
Jos 2: 13 [G] who belong to them, and that *you will* **save** us from death."
9: 26 [G] So Joshua **saved** them from the Israelites, and they did not
22: 31 [G] Now *you have* **rescued** the Israelites from the LORD's
24: 10 [G] you again and again, and *I* **delivered** you out of his hand.
Jdg 6: 9 [G] *I* **snatched** you from the power of Egypt and from the hand
8: 34 [G] who *had* **rescued** them from the hands of all their enemies
9: 17 [G] risked his life *to* **rescue** you from the hand of Midian
10: 15 [G] with us whatever you think best, but please **rescue** us now."
11: 26 [G] the Arnon. Why didn't *you* **retake** them during that time?
18: 28 [G] There was no *one to* **rescue** them because they lived a long
1Sa 4: 8 [G] Who *will* **deliver** us from the hand of these mighty gods?
7: 3 [G] and *he will* **deliver** you out of the hand of the Philistines."
7: 14 [G] Israel **delivered** the neighboring territory from the power of
10: 18 [G] *I* **delivered** you from the power of Egypt and all the
12: 10 [G] now **deliver** us from the hands of our enemies, and we will
12: 11 [G] *he* **delivered** you from the hands of your enemies on every
12: 21 [G] no good, nor *can they* **rescue** you, because they are useless.
14: 48 [G] **delivering** Israel from the hands of those who had plundered
17: 35 [G] went after it, struck it and **rescued** the sheep from its mouth.
17: 37 [G] The LORD who **delivered** me from the paw of the lion
17: 37 [G] the paw of the bear *will* **deliver** me from the hand of this
26: 24 [G] the LORD value my life and **deliver** me from all trouble."
30: 8 [G] certainly overtake them and **succeed in the rescue** [+5911]."
30: 8 [G] certainly overtake them and **succeed in the rescue** [+5911]."

1Sa 30:18 [G] **recovered** everything the Amalekites had taken, including
30:18 [G] the Amalekites had taken, including his two wives. **[RPH]**
30:22 [G] we will not share with them the plunder *we* **recovered**.
2Sa 12: 7 [G] king over Israel, and I **delivered** you from the hand of Saul.
14: 6 [G] in the field, and no *one was there to* **separate** [+1068] them.
14:16 [G] Perhaps the king will agree to **deliver** his servant from the
19: 9 [19:10] [G] king **delivered** us from the hand of our enemies;
20: 6 [G] or he will find fortified cities and **escape** *from* us."
22: 1 [G] the LORD **delivered** him from the hand of all his enemies
22:18 [G] *He* **rescued** me from my powerful enemy, from my foes,
22:49 [G] me above my foes; from violent men *you* **rescued** me.
23:12 [G] *He* **defended** it and struck the Philistines down, and the
2Ki 17:39 [G] it is he *who will* **deliver** you from the hand of all your
18:29 [G] Hezekiah deceive you. He cannot **deliver** you from my hand.
18:30 [G] when he says, 'The LORD *will* **surely deliver** [+5911] us;
18:30 [G] when he says, 'The LORD *will* **surely deliver** [+5911] us;
18:32 [G] misleading you when he says, 'The LORD *will* **deliver** us.'
18:33 [G] *Has* the god of any nation **ever delivered** [+906+5911] his
18:33 [G] *Has* the god of any nation **ever delivered** [+906+5911] his
18:34 [G] and Ivvah? *Have they* **rescued** Samaria from my hand?
18:35 [G] Who of all the gods of these countries *has been able to* **save**
18:35 [G] then *can* the LORD **deliver** Jerusalem from my hand?"
19:11 [C] destroying them completely. And *will* you **be delivered**?
19:12 [G] the nations that were destroyed by my forefathers **deliver** them:
20: 6 [G] *I will* **deliver** you and this city from the hand of the king of
1Ch 11:14 [G] *They* **defended** it and struck the Philistines down,
16:35 [G] gather us and **deliver** us from the nations, that we may give
2Ch 20:25 [D] of value—more than *they could* **take** [+4200+5362] **away**.
25:15 [G] which *could* not **save** their own people from your hand?"
32:11 [G] 'The LORD our God *will* **save** us from the hand of the king
32:13 [G] Were the gods of those nations ever able to **deliver** their land
32:14 [G] fathers destroyed has been able to **save** his people from me?
32:14 [G] How then can your god **deliver** you from my hand?
32:15 [G] or kingdom has been able to **deliver** his people from my
32:15 [G] How much less *will* your god **deliver** you from my hand!"
32:17 [G] of the other lands *did* not **rescue** their people from my hand,
32:17 [G] so the god of Hezekiah *will* not **rescue** his people from my
Ezr 8:31 [G] *he* **protected** us from enemies and bandits along the way.
Ne 9:28 [G] and in your compassion *you* **delivered** them time after time.
Job 5: 4 [G] are far from safety, crushed in court without a **defender**.
5:19 [G] From six calamities *he will* **rescue** you; in seven no harm
10: 7 [G] not guilty and that no *one can* **rescue** me from your hand?
Ps 7: 1 [7:2] [G] in you; save and **deliver** me from all who pursue me,
7: 2 [7:3] [G] a lion and rip me to pieces with no *one to* **rescue** me.
18: T [18:1] [G] **delivered** him from the hand of all his enemies
18:17 [18:18] [G] *He* **rescued** me from my powerful enemy, from my
18:48 [18:49] [G] above my foes; from violent men *you* **rescued** me.
22: 8 [22:9] [G] *Let him* **deliver** him, since he delights in him."
22:20 [22:21] [G] **Deliver** my life from the sword, my precious life
25:20 [G] Guard my life and **rescue** me; let me not be put to shame,
31: 2 [31:3] [G] Turn your ear to me, **come** quickly **to** my **rescue**;
31:15 [31:16] [G] **deliver** me from my enemies and from those who
33:16 [C] the size of his army; no warrior **escapes** by his great strength.
33:19 [G] to **deliver** them from death and keep them alive in famine.
34: 4 [34:5] [G] he answered me; *he* **delivered** me from all my fears.
34:17 [34:18] [G] hears them; *he* **delivers** them from all their troubles.
34:19 [34:20] [G] but the LORD **delivers** him from them all;
35:10 [G] You **rescue** the poor from those too strong for them, the poor
39: 8 [39:9] [G] **Save** me from all my transgressions; do not make me
40:13 [40:14] [G] Be pleased, O LORD, to **save** me; O LORD,
50:22 [G] forget God, or I will tear you to pieces, with none *to* **rescue**:
51:14 [51:16] [G] **Save** me from bloodguilt, O God, the God who
54: 7 [54:9] [G] For *he has* **delivered** me from all my troubles,
56:13 [56:14] [G] For *you have* **delivered** me from death and my feet
59: 1 [59:2] [G] **Deliver** me from my enemies, O God; protect me
59: 2 [59:3] [G] **Deliver** me from evildoers and save me from
69:14 [69:15] [G] **Rescue** me from the mire, do not let me sink;
69:14 [69:15] [C] **deliver** *me* from those who hate me, from the deep
70: 1 [70:2] [G] Hasten, O God, to **save** me; O LORD, come quickly
71: 2 [G] **Rescue** me and deliver me in your righteousness; turn your
71:11 [G] pursue him and seize him, for no *one will* **rescue** him."
72:12 [G] For *he will* **deliver** the needy who cry out, the afflicted who
79: 9 [G] **deliver** us and forgive our sins for your name's sake.
82: 4 [G] and needy; **deliver** them from the hand of the wicked.
86:13 [G] *you have* **delivered** me from the depths of the grave.
91: 3 [G] Surely he *will* **save** you from the fowler's snare and from the
97:10 [G] faithful ones and **delivers** them from the hand of the wicked.
106:43 [G] Many times *he* **delivered** them, but they were bent on
107: 6 [G] in their trouble, and *he* **delivered** them from their distress.
109:21 [G] name's sake; out of the goodness of your love, **deliver** me.
119:43 [G] *Do* not **snatch** the word of truth from my mouth, for I have
119:170 [G] come before you; **deliver** me according to your promise.
120: 2 [G] **Save** me, O LORD, from lying lips and from deceitful
142: 6 [142:7] [G] **rescue** me from those who pursue me, for they are
143: 9 [G] **Rescue** me from my enemies, O LORD, for I hide myself in
144: 7 [G] deliver me and **rescue** me from the mighty waters,
144:11 [G] **rescue** me from the hands of foreigners whose mouths are
Pr 2:12 [G] Wisdom *will* **save** you from the ways of wicked men,
2:16 [G] It *will* **save** you also from the adulteress, from the wayward
6: 3 [C] do this, my son, *to* **free yourself**, since you have fallen into
6: 5 [C] **Free yourself**, like a gazelle from the hand of the hunter, like
10: 2 [G] are of no value, but righteousness **delivers** from death.
11: 4 [G] in the day of wrath, but righteousness **delivers** from death.
11: 6 [G] The righteousness of the upright **delivers** them,
12: 6 [G] in wait for blood, but the speech of the upright **rescues** them.
14:25 [G] A truthful witness **saves** lives, but a false witness is deceitful.
19:19 [G] the penalty; if *you* **rescue** him, you will have to do it again.
23:14 [G] Punish him with the rod and **save** his soul from death.
24:11 [G] **Rescue** those being led away to death; hold back those
Isa 5:29 [G] they seize their prey and carry it off with no *one to* **rescue**.
19:20 [G] send them a savior and defender, and *he will* **rescue** them.
20: 6 [C] we fled to for help and **deliverance** from the king of Assyria!
31: 5 [G] he will shield it and **deliver** it, he will 'pass over' it and will
36:14 [G] Do not let Hezekiah deceive you. He cannot **deliver** you!
36:15 [G] when he says, 'The LORD *will* **surely deliver** [+5911] us;
36:15 [G] when he says, 'The LORD *will* **surely deliver** [+5911] us;
36:18 [G] mislead you when he says, 'The LORD *will* **deliver** us.'
36:18 [G] *Has* the god of any nation *ever* **delivered** his land from the
36:19 [G] of Sepharvaim? *Have they* **rescued** Samaria from my hand?
36:20 [G] Who of all the gods of these countries *has been able to* **save**
36:20 [G] then *can* the LORD **deliver** Jerusalem from my hand?"
37:11 [C] destroying them completely. And *will* you **be delivered**?
37:12 [G] nations that were destroyed by my forefathers **deliver** them—
38: 6 [G] *I will* **deliver** you and this city from the hand of the king of
42:22 [G] They have become plunder, with no *one to* **rescue** them;
43:13 [G] No *one can* **deliver** out of my hand. When I act, who can
44:17 [G] He prays to it and says, "**Save** me; you are my god."
44:20 [G] *he* cannot **save** himself, or say, "Is not this thing in my right
47:14 [G] *They* cannot even **save** themselves from the power of the
50: 2 [G] Do I lack the strength to **rescue** you? By a mere rebuke I dry
57:13 [G] you cry out for help, *let* your collection ˻of idols˼ **save** you!
Jer 1: 8 [G] for I am with you and *will* **rescue** you," declares the LORD.
1:19 [G] for I am with you and *will* **rescue** you," declares the LORD.
7:10 [C] this house, which bears my Name, and say, "*We are* **safe**"—
15:20 [G] for I am with you to rescue and **save** you,"
15:21 [G] "*I will* **save** you from the hands of the wicked and redeem
20:13 [G] *He* **rescues** the life of the needy from the hands of the
21:12 [G] **rescue** from the hand of his oppressor the one who has been
22: 3 [G] **Rescue** from the hand of his oppressor the one who has been
39:17 [G] *I will* **rescue** you on that day, declares the LORD; you will
42:11 [G] with you and will save you and **deliver** you from his hands.
Eze 3:19 [G] he will die for his sin; but you *will have* **saved** yourself.
3:21 [G] because he took warning, and you *will have* **saved** yourself."
7:19 [G] gold will not be able to **save** them in the day of the LORD's
13:21 [G] will tear off your veils and **save** my people from your hands,
13:23 [G] *I will* **save** my people from your hands. And then you will
14:14 [D] in it, they *could* **save** only themselves by their righteousness,
14:16 [G] were in it, *they could* not **save** their own sons or daughters.
14:16 [C] They alone *would* **be saved**, but the land would be desolate.
14:18 [G] were in it, *they could* not **save** their own sons or daughters.
14:18 [C] their own sons or daughters. They alone *would* **be saved**.
14:20 [G] and Job were in it, *they could* **save** neither son nor daughter.
14:20 [G] They *would* **save** only themselves by their righteousness.
33: 9 [G] he will die for his sin, but you *will have* **saved** yourself.
33:12 [G] 'The righteousness of the righteous man *will* not **save** him
34:10 [G] *I will* **rescue** my flock from their mouths, and it will no
34:12 [G] *I will* **rescue** them from all the places where they were
34:27 [G] and **rescue** them from the hands of those who enslaved them.
Da 8: 4 [G] stand against him, and none *could* **rescue** from his power.
8: 7 [G] on him, and none *could* **rescue** the ram from his power.
Hos 2: 9 [2:11] [G] *I will* **take back** my wool and my linen, intended to
2:10 [2:12] [G] of her lovers; no one *will* **take** her out of my hands.
5:14 [G] go away; I will carry them off, with no *one to* **rescue** them.
Am 3:12 [G] "As a shepherd **saves** from the lion's mouth only two leg
3:12 [C] leg bones or a piece of an ear, so *will* the Israelites **be saved**,
4:11 [H] You were like a burning stick **snatched** from the fire, yet you
Jnh 4: 6 [G] made it grow up over Jonah to give shade for his head to **ease**
Mic 4:10 [C] You will go to Babylon; there *you will* **be rescued**.
5: 6 [5:5] [G] *He will* **deliver** us from the Assyrian when he invades
5: 8 [5:7] [G] and mangles as it goes, and no *one can* **rescue**.
Hab 2: 9 [C] gain to set his nest on high, to **escape** the clutches of ruin!
Zep 1:18 [G] Neither their silver nor their gold will be able to **save** them
Zec 3: 2 [H] Is not this man a burning stick **snatched** from the fire?"
11: 6 [G] the land, and *I will* not **rescue** them from their hands."

5912 נִצָּנִים *niṣṣānîm*, n.[m.]. Not used in NIV/BHS [√ 5914]

5913 ¹נָצַץ nāṣaṣ¹, v. [1] [→ 5773; cf. 5914]

gleamed [1]

Eze 1: 7 [A] were like those of a calf and **gleamed** like burnished bronze.

5914 ²נָצַץ nāṣaṣ², v.den. [3] [→ 5890, 5900, 5912; cf. 5913]

in bloom [2], blossoms [1]

Ecc 12: 5 [G] when the almond tree **blossoms** and the grasshopper drags
SS 6: 11 [G] if the vines had budded or the pomegranates *were* **in bloom**.
7: 12 [7:13] [G] have opened, and if the pomegranates *are* **in bloom**—

5915 נָצַר nāṣar, v. [61 / 60] [→ 4915, 5211, 5903, 5910, 5917; cf. 5757; Ar 10476]

keep [15], protect [8], guards [5], guard [4], obey [4], guarded [2], preserve [2], watch over [2], watchtower [+4463] [2], crafty [1], guard well [1], hidden [1], is spared [1], keep safe [1], keep watch over [1], keeping secret vigil [1], keeps [1], kept [1], maintaining [1], observe [1], preserves [1], tends [1], watcher [1], watchman [1], watchmen [1]

Ex 34: 7 [A] **maintaining** love to thousands, and forgiving wickedness,
Dt 32: 10 [A] and cared for him; *he* **guarded** him as the apple of his eye,
33: 9 [A] but he watched over your word and **guarded** your covenant.
2Ki 17: 9 [A] From **watchtower** [+4463] to fortified city they built
18: 8 [A] From **watchtower** [+4463] to fortified city, he defeated the
Job 7: 20 [A] I have sinned, what have I done to you, O **watcher** *of* men?
27: 18 [A] is like a moth's cocoon, like a hut made by a **watchman**.
Ps 12: 7 [12:8] [A] us safe and **protect** us from such people forever.
25: 10 [A] and faithful for *those who* **keep** the demands of his covenant.
25: 21 [A] *May* integrity and uprightness **protect** me, because my hope
31: 23 [31:24] [A] The LORD **preserves** the faithful, but the proud he
32: 7 [A] *you will* **protect** me from trouble and surround me with
34: 13 [34:14] [A] **keep** your tongue from evil and your lips from
40: 11 [40:12] [A] *may* your love and your truth always **protect** me.
61: 7 [61:8] [A] appoint your love and faithfulness *to* **protect** him.
64: 1 [64:2] [A] **protect** my life from the threat of the enemy.
78: 7 [A] would not forget his deeds but *would* **keep** his commands.
105: 45 [A] that they might keep his precepts and **observe** his laws.
119: 2 [A] Blessed are *they who* **keep** his statutes and seek him with all
119: 22 [A] from me scorn and contempt, for *I* **keep** your statutes.
119: 33 [A] to follow your decrees; then *I will* **keep** them to the end.
119: 34 [A] and *I will* **keep** your law and obey it with all my heart.
119: 56 [A] This has been my practice: *I* **obey** your precepts.
119: 69 [A] smeared me with lies, I **keep** your precepts with all my heart.
119:100 [A] more understanding than the elders, for *I* **obey** your precepts.
119:115 [A] you evildoers, that *I may* **keep** the commands of my God!
119:129 [A] Your statutes are wonderful; therefore I **obey** them.
119:145 [A] answer me, O LORD, and *I will* **obey** your decrees.
140: 1 [140:2] [A] from evil men; **protect** me from men of violence,
140: 4 [140:5] [A] **protect** me from men of violence who plan to trip
Pr 2: 8 [A] for he **guards** the course of the just and protects the way of
2: 11 [A] will protect you, and understanding *will* **guard** you.
3: 1 [A] forget my teaching, but **keep** my commands *in* your heart,
3: 21 [A] My son, **preserve** sound judgment and discernment, do not
4: 6 [A] she will protect you; love her, and *she will* **watch over** you.
4: 13 [A] do not let it go; **guard** it **well**, for it is your life.
4: 23 [A] Above all else, **guard** your heart, for it is the wellspring of
5: 2 [A] maintain discretion and your lips *may* **preserve** knowledge.
6: 20 [A] **keep** your father's commands and do not forsake your
7: 10 [B] to meet him, dressed like a prostitute and with **crafty** intent.
13: 3 [A] *He who* **guards** his lips guards his life, but he who speaks
13: 6 [A] Righteousness **guards** the man of integrity, but wickedness
16: 17 [A] upright avoids evil; *he who* **guards** his way guards his life.
20: 28 [A] Love and faithfulness **keep** a king **safe**; through love his
22: 12 [A] The eyes of the LORD **keep watch over** knowledge, but he
23: 26 [A] me your heart and *let* your eyes **keep** [K 8354] *to* my ways,
24: 12 [A] heart perceive it? Does not he *who* **guards** your life know it?
27: 18 [A] *He who* **tends** a fig tree will eat its fruit, and he who looks
28: 7 [A] *He who* **keeps** the law is a discerning son, but a companion
Isa 26: 3 [A] *You will* **keep** *in* perfect peace him whose mind is steadfast,
27: 3 [A] I, the LORD, **watch over** it; I water it continually. I guard it
27: 3 [A] *I* **guard** it day and night so that no one may harm it.
42: 6 [A] *I will* **keep** you and will make you to be a covenant for the
48: 6 [B] tell you of new things, of **hidden** *things* unknown to you.
49: 6 [B] and bring back *those of* Israel I *have* **kept**. [K 5910]
49: 8 [A] *I will* **keep** you and will make you to be a covenant for the
65: 4 [B] the graves and spend their nights **keeping secret vigil**;
Jer 4: 16 [a] 'A besieging [BHS *watching*; NIV 7443] *army* is coming
31: 6 [A] There will be a day when **watchmen** cry out on the hills of
Eze 6: 12 [B] and he that survives and **is spared** will die of famine.
Na 2: 1 [2:2] [A] **Guard** the fortress, watch the road, brace yourselves,

5916 נֵצֶר nēṣer, n.m. [4]

branch [2], family line [+9247] [1], shoot [1]

Isa 11: 1 up from the stump of Jesse; from his roots a **Branch** will bear fruit.
14: 19 you are cast out of your tomb like a rejected **branch**; you are
60: 21 They are the **shoot** I have planted, the work of my hands,
Da 11: 7 "One from her **family line** [+9247] will arise to take her place.

5917 נִצְּרָה niṣṣ^erâ, n.f. *or* v.ptcp. [1] [√ 5915 not in KB]

watch [1]

Ps 141: 3 over my mouth, O LORD; keep **watch** over the door of my lips.

5918 ¹נָקַב nāqab¹, v. [16] [→ 2186, 5216, 5217, 5920, 5921, 5922; cf. 3676, 5919, 7686]

designated [3], pierce [2], pierces [2], been given [1], bestow [1], bored [1], holes [1], name [1], notable [1], pierced [1], were designated [1], were registered [1]

Ge 30: 28 [A] He added, "**Name** your wages, and I will pay them."
Nu 1: 17 [C] and Aaron took these men whose names *had* **been given**,
2Ki 12: 9 [12:10] [A] the priest took a chest and **bored** a hole in its lid.
18: 21 [A] *which* **pierces** a man's hand and wounds him if he leans on
1Ch 12: 31 [12:32] [C] **designated** by name to come and make David
16: 41 [C] and **designated** by name to give thanks to the LORD,
2Ch 28: 15 [C] The men **designated** by name took the prisoners, and from
31: 19 [C] men **were designated** by name to distribute portions to every
Ezr 8: 20 [C] to assist the Levites. All **were registered** by name.
Job 40: 24 [A] capture him by the eyes, or trap him and **pierce** his nose?
41: 2 [40:26] [A] through his nose or **pierce** his jaw with a hook?
Isa 36: 6 [A] *which* **pierces** a man's hand and wounds him if he leans on
62: 2 [A] by a new name that the mouth of the LORD *will* **bestow**.
Am 6: 1 [B] *you* **notable** *men of* the foremost nation, to whom the people
Hab 3: 14 [A] With his own spear *you* **pierced** his head when his warriors
Hag 1: 6 [B] You earn wages, only to put them in a purse *with* **holes** in it."

5919 ²נָקַב nāqab², v. [3] [cf. 5918, 7686]

blasphemes [2], blasphemed [1]

Lev 24: 11 [A] The son of the Israelite woman **blasphemed** the Name with a
24: 16 [A] *anyone who* **blasphemes** the name of the LORD must be
24: 16 [A] an alien or native-born, when he **blasphemes** the Name,

5920 ¹נֶקֶב neqeb¹, n.[m.]. [1] [√ 5918]

mountings [1]

Eze 28: 13 Your settings and **mountings** were made of gold; on the day you

5921 ²נֶקֶב neqeb², n.pr.loc. Not used in NIV/BHS [√ 5918]

5922 נְקֵבָה n^eqēbâ, n.f. [22] [√ 5918]

female [16], woman [3], daughter [1], girl [1], women [1]

Ge 1: 27 image of God he created him; male and **female** he created them.
5: 2 He created them male and **female** and blessed them. And when
6: 19 all living creatures, male and **female**, to keep them alive with you.
7: 3 also seven of every kind of bird, male and **female**, to keep their
7: 9 male and **female**, came to Noah and entered the ark, as God had
7: 16 The animals going in were male and **female** of every living thing,
Lev 3: 1 and he offers an animal from the herd, whether male or **female**,
3: 6 to the LORD, he is to offer a male or **female** without defect.
4: 28 he must bring as his offering for the sin he committed a **female**
4: 32 a lamb as his sin offering, he is to bring a **female** without defect.
5: 6 he must bring to the LORD a **female** lamb or goat from the flock
12: 5 If she gives birth to a **daughter**, for two weeks the woman will be
12: 7 the regulations for the woman who gives birth to a boy or a **girl**.
15: 33 in her monthly period, for a man or a **woman** with a discharge,
27: 4 and if it is a **female**, set her value at thirty shekels.
27: 5 value of a male at twenty shekels and of a **female** at ten shekels.
27: 6 five shekels of silver and that of a **female** at three shekels of silver.
27: 7 value of a male at fifteen shekels and of a **female** at ten shekels.
Nu 5: 3 Send away male and **female** alike; send them outside the camp
31: 15 "Have you allowed all the **women** to live?" he asked them.
Dt 4: 16 an image of any shape, whether formed like a man or a **woman**,
Jer 31: 22 will create a new thing on earth—a **woman** will surround a man."

5923 נָקֹד nāqōd, a. [9] [→ 5218, 5925, 5926]

speckled [9]

Ge 30: 32 and remove from them every **speckled** or spotted sheep,
30: 32 every dark-colored lamb and every spotted or **speckled** goat.
30: 33 Any goat in my possession that is not **speckled** or spotted,
30: 35 all the **speckled** or spotted female goats (all that had white on
30: 39 And they bore young that were streaked or **speckled** or spotted.
31: 8 If he said, 'The **speckled** *ones* will be your wages,' then all the

Ge 31: 8 be your wages,' then all the flocks gave birth to **speckled** *young*;
31: 10 goats mating with the flock were streaked, **speckled** or spotted.
31: 12 **speckled** or spotted, for I have seen all that Laban has been doing

5924 נֹקֵד *nōqēd*, n.m. [2]

raised sheep [1], shepherds [1]

2Ki 3: 4 Now Mesha king of Moab **raised sheep**, and he had to supply the
Am 1: 1 The words of Amos, one of the **shepherds** of Tekoa—what he saw

5925 נְקֻדָּה *neqqudâ*, n.f. [1] [√ 5923]

studded [1]

SS 1: 11 We will make you earrings of gold, **studded** with silver.

5926 נִקֻּדִים *niqqudîm*, n.[m.]. [3] [√ 5923]

moldy [2], cakes [1]

Jos 9: 5 old clothes. All the bread of their food supply was dry and **moldy**.
9: 12 day we left to come to you. But now see how dry and **moldy** it is.
1Ki 14: 3 of bread with you, *some* **cakes** and a jar of honey, and go to him.

5927 נָקָה *nāqâ*, v. [44] [→ 4984, 5929, 5930, 5931]

go unpunished [9], leave the guilty unpunished [+5927] [6], let go entirely unpunished [+5927] [4], innocent [3], be banished [2], be released [2], go unpunished [+5927] [2], hold guiltless [2], indeed go unpunished [+5927] [2], be cleared of guilt [1], consider innocent [1], destitute [1], forgive [1], guiltless [1], have a right to get even [1], hold innocent [1], let go unpunished [1], not be held responsible [1], not harm [+4946] [1], pardon [1], pardoned [1]

Ge 24: 8 [C] with you, then *you will* **be released** from this oath of mine.
24: 41 [C] *you will* **be released** from my oath even if they refuse to give
Ex 20: 7 [D] for the LORD *will* not **hold** anyone **guiltless** who misuses
21: 19 [C] the one who struck the blow *will* **not be held responsible** if
34: 7 [D] Yet *he does* not **leave the guilty unpunished** [+5927]; he
34: 7 [D] Yet *he does* not **leave the guilty unpunished** [+5927]; he
Nu 5: 19 [C] *may* this bitter water that brings a curse **not harm** [+4946] *you*.
5: 28 [C] she *will* **be cleared of guilt** and will be able to have children.
5: 31 [C] The husband *will be* **innocent** of any wrongdoing,
14: 18 [D] Yet *he does* not **leave the guilty unpunished** [+5927]; he
14: 18 [D] Yet *he does* not **leave the guilty unpunished** [+5927]; he
Dt 5: 11 [D] for the LORD *will* not **hold** anyone **guiltless** who misuses
Jdg 15: 3 [C] "This time *I* **have a right to get even** with the Philistines;
1Sa 26: 9 [C] can lay a hand on the LORD's anointed and *be* **guiltless**?
1Ki 2: 9 [D] now, *do* not **consider** him **innocent**. You are a man of
Job 9: 28 [D] all my sufferings, for I know *you will* not **hold** me **innocent**.
10: 14 [D] watching me and *would* not **let** my offense **go unpunished**.
Ps 19: 12 [19:13] [D] can discern his errors? **Forgive** my hidden faults.
19: 13 [19:14] [C] will I be blameless, **innocent** of great transgression.
Pr 6: 29 [C] man's wife; no one who touches her *will* **go unpunished**.
11: 21 [C] The wicked *will* not **go unpunished**, but those who are
16: 5 [C] proud of heart. Be sure of this: *They will* not **go unpunished**.
17: 5 [C] whoever gloats over disaster *will* not **go unpunished**.
19: 5 [C] A false witness *will* not **go unpunished**, and he who pours
19: 9 [C] A false witness *will* not **go unpunished**, and he who pours
28: 20 [C] but one eager to get rich *will* not **go unpunished**.
Isa 3: 26 [C] will lament and mourn; **destitute**, she will sit on the ground.
Jer 2: 35 [C] you say, '*I am* **innocent**; he is not angry with me.' But I will
25: 29 [C] my Name, and *will* you **indeed go unpunished** [+5927]?
25: 29 [C] my Name, and *will* you **indeed go unpunished** [+5927]?
25: 29 [C] *You will* not **go unpunished**, for I am calling down a sword
30: 11 [D] *I will* not **let** you **go entirely unpunished** [+5927].'
30: 11 [D] *I will* not **let** you **go entirely unpunished** [+5927].'
46: 28 [D] *I will* not **let** you **go entirely unpunished** [+5927]."
46: 28 [D] *I will* not **let** you **go entirely unpunished** [+5927]."
49: 12 [C] cup must drink it, why *should* you **go unpunished** [+5927]?
49: 12 [A] cup must drink it, why *should* you **go unpunished** [+5927]?
49: 12 [C] *You will* not **go unpunished**, but must drink it.
Joel 3: 21 [4:21] [D] which *I have* not **pardoned**, I will pardon."
3: 21 [4:21] [D] which I have not pardoned, *I will* **pardon**."
Na 1: 3 [D] the LORD *will* not **leave the guilty unpunished** [+5927].
1: 3 [D] the LORD *will* not **leave the guilty unpunished** [+5927].
Zec 5: 3 [C] to what it says on one side, every thief *will* **be banished**,
5: 3 [C] on the other, everyone who swears falsely *will* **be banished**.

5928 נְקוֹדָא *neqôdā'*, n.pr.m. [4]

Nekoda [4]

Ezr 2: 48 Rezin, **Nekoda**, Gazzam,
2: 60 The descendants of Delaiah, Tobiah and **Nekoda** 652
Ne 7: 50 Reaiah, Rezin, **Nekoda**,
7: 62 the descendants of Delaiah, Tobiah and **Nekoda** 642

5929 נָקִי *nāqî*, a. [43] [√ 5927]

innocent [30], released [2], clean [1], exempt [1], free from blame [1], free from obligation [1], free [1], harmless soul [+2855] [1], innocent man [+1947] [1], not binding [1], not held responsible [1], not responsible [1], without guilt [1]

Ge 24: 41 refuse to give her to you—you will be **released** from my oath.'
44: 10 it will become my slave; the rest of you will be **free from blame**."
Ex 21: 28 be eaten. But the owner of the bull will **not** be **held responsible**.
23: 7 false charge and do not put an **innocent** or honest person to death,
Nu 32: 22 and be **free from** your **obligation** to the LORD and to Israel.
Dt 19: 10 Do this so that **innocent** blood will not be shed in your land,
19: 13 You must purge from Israel the guilt of shedding **innocent** blood,
21: 8 do not hold your people guilty of the blood of an **innocent** *man*."
21: 9 So you will purge from yourselves the guilt of shedding **innocent**
24: 5 For one year he is to be **free** to stay at home and bring happiness to
27: 25 "Cursed is the man who accepts a bribe to kill an **innocent**
Jos 2: 17 to her, "This oath you made us swear will **not** be **binding** *on* us
2: 19 his blood will be on his own head; we will **not** be **responsible**.
2: 20 are doing, we will be **released** from the oath you made us swear."
1Sa 19: 5 would you do wrong to an **innocent** [+1947] **man** like David by
2Sa 3: 28 my kingdom are forever **innocent** before the LORD concerning
14: 9 father's family, and let the king and his throne be **without guilt**."
1Ki 15: 22 Then King Asa issued an order to all Judah—no one was **exempt**—
2Ki 21: 16 so much **innocent** blood that he filled Jerusalem from end to end—
24: 4 including the shedding of **innocent** blood. For he had filled
24: 4 For he had filled Jerusalem with **innocent** blood, and the LORD
Job 4: 7 "Consider now: Who, being **innocent**, has ever perished?
9: 23 scourge brings sudden death, he mocks the despair of the **innocent**.
17: 8 are appalled at this; the **innocent** are aroused against the ungodly.
22: 19 see their ruin and rejoice; the **innocent** mock them, saying,
22: 30 He will deliver even *one who* is not **innocent**, who will be
27: 17 up the righteous will wear, and the **innocent** will divide his silver.
Ps 10: 8 from ambush he murders the **innocent**, watching in secret for his
15: 5 without usury and does not accept a bribe against the **innocent**.
24: 4 *He who* has **clean** hands and a pure heart, who does not lift up his
94: 21 together against the righteous and condemn the **innocent** to death.
106: 38 They shed **innocent** blood, the blood of their sons and daughters,
Pr 1: 11 for someone's blood, let's waylay some **harmless** [+2855] **soul**;
6: 17 haughty eyes, a lying tongue, hands that shed **innocent** blood,
Isa 59: 7 Their feet rush into sin; they are swift to shed **innocent** blood.
Jer 2: 34 On your clothes men find the lifeblood of the **innocent** poor,
7: 6 or the widow and do not shed **innocent** blood in this place,
19: 4 and they have filled this place with the blood of the **innocent**.
22: 3 or the widow, and do not shed **innocent** blood in this place.
22: 17 on shedding **innocent** blood and on oppression and extortion."
26: 15 you will bring the guilt of **innocent** blood on yourselves and on
Joel 3: 19 [4:19] people of Judah, in whose land they shed **innocent** blood.
Jnh 1: 14 Do not hold us accountable for killing an **innocent** *man*, for you,

5930 נָקִיא *nāqî'*, a. Not used in NIV/BHS [√ 5927; Ar 10490]

5931 נִקָּיוֹן *niqqāyôn*, n.[m.]. [5] [√ 5927]

innocence [2], clean [1], empty stomachs [+9094] [1], purity [1]

Ge 20: 5 I have done this with a clear conscience and **clean** hands."
Ps 26: 6 I wash my hands in **innocence**, and go about your altar, O LORD,
73: 13 kept my heart pure; in vain have I washed my hands in **innocence**.
Hos 8: 5 burns against them. How long will they be incapable of **purity**?
Am 4: 6 "I gave you **empty stomachs** [+9094] in every city and lack of

5932 נָקִיק *nāqîq*, n.m. [3]

crevices [2], crevice [1]

Isa 7: 19 and settle in the steep ravines and in the **crevices** in the rocks,
Jer 13: 4 and go now to Perath and hide it there in a **crevice** *in* the rocks."
16: 16 on every mountain and hill and from the **crevices** *of* the rocks.

5933 נָקַם *nāqam*, v. [35] [→ 5934, 5935]

avenge [6], must be punished [+5933] [2], takes vengeance [2], took revenge [+5934] [2], avenge [+5934] [1], avenge [+906+5935] [1], avenge myself [1], avenge themselves [1], avenge wrongs [1], avenged myself [1], avenged [1], avenger [1], avenging [1], be punished [1], bent on revenge [1], doing so [1], get revenge [+5934] [1], get revenge [1], is avenged [1], punished [1], seek revenge [1], suffer vengeance [1], take revenge [+5934] [1], take revenge [1], take vengeance [+5935] [1], take vengeance [1], vengeance [1]

Ge 4: 15 [H] kills Cain, *he will* **suffer vengeance** seven times over."
4: 24 [H] If Cain **is avenged** seven times, then Lamech seventy-seven
Ex 21: 20 [C] slave dies as a direct result, *he* **must be punished** [+5933],
21: 20 [A] slave dies as a direct result, *he* **must be punished** [+5933],
21: 21 [H] but *he is* not *to* **be punished** if the slave gets up after a day
Lev 19: 18 [A] " '*Do* not **seek revenge** or bear a grudge against one of your

Lev 26:25 [A] I will bring the sword upon you *to* **avenge** [+5934] the
Nu 31: 2 [A] "**Take vengeance** [+5935] on the Midianites *for* the
Dt 32:43 [A] with his people, for *he will* **avenge** the blood of his servants;
Jos 10:13 [A] moon stopped, till the nation **avenged** *itself on* its enemies,
Jdg 15: 7 [C] acted like this, I won't stop until *I* **get** *my* **revenge** on you."
16:28 [C] *let me with* one blow **get revenge** [+5934] on the Philistines
1Sa 14:24 [C] before *I have* **avenged myself** on my enemies!"
18:25 [C] to **take revenge** on his enemies.' " Saul's plan was to have
24:12 [24:13] [A] *may* the LORD **avenge** *the* **wrongs** you have *done to*
2Ki 9: 7 [D] *I will* **avenge** the blood of my servants the prophets
Est 8:13 [C] be ready on that day to **avenge themselves** on their enemies.
Ps 8: 2 [8:3] [F] of your enemies, to silence the foe and the **avenger**.
44:16 [44:17] [F] because of the enemy, *who is* **bent on revenge**.
99: 8 [A] Israel a forgiving God, though you **punished** their misdeeds.
Isa 1:24 [C] get relief from my foes and **avenge myself** on my enemies.
Jer 5: 9 [F] "*Should I* not **avenge** myself on such a nation as this?
5:29 [F] "*Should I* not **avenge** myself on such a nation as this?
9: 9 [9:8] [F] "*Should I* not **avenge** myself on such a nation as this?"
15:15 [C] and care for me. **Avenge** me on my persecutors.
46:10 [C] a day of vengeance, for **vengeance** on his foes.
50:15 [C] this is the vengeance of the LORD, **take vengeance** on her;
51:36 [D] "See, I will defend your cause and **avenge** [+906+5935] you;
Eze 24: 8 [A] and **take revenge** [+5934] I put her blood on the bare rock,
25:12 [A] 'Because Edom **took revenge** [+5934] on the house of Judah
25:12 [C] on the house of Judah and became very guilty *by* **doing so**,
25:15 [C] and **took revenge** [+5934] with malice in their hearts,
Na 1: 2 [A] The LORD is a jealous and **avenging** God; the LORD
1: 2 [A] the LORD **takes vengeance** and is filled with wrath.
1: 2 [A] The LORD **takes vengeance** on his foes and maintains his

5934 נָקָם *nāqām*, n.m. [17] [→ 5935; cf. 5933]

vengeance [7], take vengeance [+8740] [2], took revenge [+5933] [2], avenge [+5933] [1], avenge [1], avenged [1], get revenge [+5933] [1], revenge [1], take revenge [+5933] [1]

Lev 26:25 I will bring the sword upon you *to* **avenge** [+5933] the breaking of
Dt 32:35 It is mine to **avenge**; I will repay. In due time their foot will slip;
32:41 my hand grasps it in judgment, *I will* **take vengeance** [+8740] on
32:43 avenge the blood of his servants; *he will* **take vengeance** [+8740]
Jdg 16:28 *let me with* one blow **get revenge** [+5933] on the Philistines for
Ps 58:10 [58:11] The righteous will be glad when they are **avenged**,
Pr 6:34 husband's fury, and he will show no mercy when he takes **revenge**.
Isa 34: 8 For the LORD has a day of **vengeance**, a year of retribution,
35: 4 do not fear; your God will come, he will come with **vengeance**;
47: 3 your shame uncovered. I will take **vengeance**; I will spare no one."
59:17 he put on the garments of **vengeance** and wrapped himself in zeal
61: 2 year of the LORD's favor and the day of **vengeance** of our God,
63: 4 For the day of **vengeance** was in my heart, and the year of my
Eze 24: 8 and **take revenge** [+5933] I put her blood on the bare rock,
25:12 'Because Edom **took revenge** [+5933] on the house of Judah
25:15 and **took revenge** [+5933] with malice in their hearts,
Mic 5:15 [5:14] I will take **vengeance** in anger and wrath upon the nations

5935 נְקָמָה *n^eqāmâ*, n.f. [27] [√ 5934; cf. 5933]

vengeance [17], avenges [+4200+5989] [2], avenges [2], avenge [+906+5933] [1], avenge [1], avenged [+4200+5989] [1], avenged [+4200+6913] [1], revenge [1], take vengeance [+5933] [1]

Nu 31: 2 "**Take vengeance** on the Midianites **for** [+5933] the Israelites.
31: 3 the Midianites and to carry out the LORD's **vengeance** on them.
Jdg 11:36 now that the LORD *has* **avenged** [+4200+6913] you of your
2Sa 4: 8 This day the LORD *has* **avenged** [+4200+5989] my lord the king
22:48 He is the God who **avenges** [+4200+5989] me, who puts the
Ps 18:47 [18:48] He is the God who **avenges** [+4200+5989] me, who
79:10 make known among the nations that *you* **avenge** the outpoured
94: 1 O LORD, the God who **avenges**, O God who avenges,
94: 1 the God who avenges, O God who **avenges**, shine forth.
149: 7 to inflict **vengeance** on the nations and punishment on the peoples,
Jer 11:20 and test the heart and mind, let me see your **vengeance** upon them,
20:10 then we will prevail over him and take our **revenge** on him."
20:12 probe the heart and mind, let me see your **vengeance** upon them,
46:10 a day of **vengeance**, for vengeance on his foes.
50:15 Since this is the **vengeance** *of* the LORD, take vengeance on her;
50:28 declaring in Zion how the LORD our God has taken **vengeance**,
50:28 LORD our God has taken vengeance, **vengeance** *for* his temple.
51: 6 It is time for the LORD's **vengeance**; he will pay her what she
51:11 The LORD will take **vengeance**, vengeance for his temple.
51:11 The LORD will take vengeance, **vengeance** *for* his temple.
51:36 "See, I will defend your cause and **avenge** [+906+5933] you;
La 3:60 You have seen the depth of their **vengeance**, all their plots against
Eze 25:14 I will take **vengeance** on Edom by the hand of my people Israel,
25:14 they will know my **vengeance**, declares the Sovereign LORD.' "
25:15 'Because the Philistines acted in **vengeance** and took revenge with
25:17 I will carry out great **vengeance** on them and punish them in my
25:17 know that I am the LORD, when I take **vengeance** on them.' "

5936 נָקַע *nāqa'*, v. [3] [cf. 3697]

turned away in disgust [2], turned away [1]

Eze 23:18 [A] her in disgust, just as I *had* **turned away** from her sister.
23:22 [A] lovers against you, those you **turned away** from **in disgust**,
23:28 [A] to those you hate, to those you **turned away** from **in disgust**.

5937 נָקַף[1] *nāqap*[1], v. [2] [→ 5939]

cut down [1], destroyed [1]

Job 19:26 [D] after my skin *has been* **destroyed**, yet in my flesh I will see
Isa 10:34 [D] *He will* **cut down** the forest thickets with an ax; Lebanon

5938 נָקַף[2] *nāqap*[2], v. [17] [→ 5940; cf. 9543]

untranslated [2], surrounded [2], circling [1], cut hair [1], cycle go on [1], drawn [1], echoes along [1], encircled [1], engulfed [1], go around [1], march around [+906+906+6015] [1], run course [1], station themselves [1], station yourselves [1], surround [1]

Lev 19:27 [G] " '*Do* not **cut** the **hair** at the sides of your head or clip off the
Jos 6: 3 [G] **March around** [+906+906+6015] the city once with all the
6:11 [G] ark of the LORD carried around the city, **circling** it once.
1Ki 7:24 [G] **[RPH]** The gourds were cast in two rows in one piece with
2Ki 6:14 [G] force there. They went by night and **surrounded** the city.
11: 8 [G] **Station yourselves** around the king, each man with his
2Ch 4: 3 [G] **[NIE]** The bulls were cast in two rows in one piece with the
23: 7 [G] The Levites *are to* **station themselves** around the king,
Job 1: 5 [G] When a period of feasting *had* **run** *its* **course**, Job would
19: 6 [G] that God has wronged me and **drawn** his net around me.
Ps 17: 9 [G] who assail me, from my mortal enemies *who* **surround** me.
22:16 [22:17] [G] a band of evil men *has* **encircled** me, they have
48:12 [48:13] [G] Walk about Zion, **go around** her, count her towers,
88:17 [88:18] [G] me like a flood; *they have* completely **engulfed** me.
Isa 15: 8 [G] Their outcry **echoes along** the border of Moab; their wailing
29: 1 [A] Add year to year and *let* your **cycle** of festivals **go on**.
La 3: 5 [G] and **surrounded** me *with* bitterness and hardship.

5939 נֹקֶף *nōqep*, n.[m.] [2] [√ 5937]

beaten [2]

Isa 17: 6 as when an olive tree is **beaten**, leaving two or three olives on the
24:13 the earth and among the nations, as when an olive tree is **beaten**,

5940 נִקְפָּה *niqpâ*, n.f. [1] [√ 5938]

rope [1]

Isa 3:24 instead of a sash, a **rope**; instead of well-dressed hair, baldness;

5941 נָקַר *nāqar*, v. [6] [→ 5942]

gouge out [2], gouged out [1], pecked out [1], pierces [1], were hewn [1]

Nu 16:14 [D] *Will you* **gouge out** the eyes of these men? No, we will not
Jdg 16:21 [D] seized him, **gouged out** his eyes and took him down to Gaza.
1Sa 11: 2 [A] condition that I **gouge out** the right eye of every one of you
Job 30:17 [D] Night **pierces** my bones; my gnawing pains never rest.
Pr 30:17 [A] *will be* **pecked out** *by* the ravens of the valley, will be eaten
Isa 51: 1 [E] you were cut and to the quarry from which *you* **were hewn**;

5942 נְקָרָה *n^eqārâ*, n.f. [2] [√ 5941]

caverns [1], cleft [1]

Ex 33:22 I will put you in a **cleft** *in* the rock and cover you with my hand
Isa 2:21 They will flee to **caverns** *in* the rocks and to the overhanging crags

5943 נָקַשׁ *nāqaš*, v. [5 / 4] [cf. 3704, 7772; Ar 10491]

be ensnared [1], seize [1], set a trap [1], set traps [1]

Dt 12:30 [C] be careful not *to* **be ensnared** by inquiring about their gods,
1Sa 28: 9 [F] Why *have* you **set a trap** for my life to bring about my
Ps 9:16 [9:17] [a] the wicked **are** ensnared [BHS ***set traps***; NIV 3704]
38:12 [38:13] [D] Those who seek my life **set** *their* **traps**, those who
109:11 [D] *May* a creditor **seize** all he has; may strangers plunder the

5944 נֵר[1] *nēr*[1], n.m. [44] [→ 46, 79, 4963, 5775, 5945, 5949, 5950; cf. 5642; Ar 10471]

lamps [23], lamp [16], *untranslated* [2], lights [2], them[s] [1]

Ex 25:37 "Then make its seven **lamps** and set them up on it so that they light
25:37 "Then make its seven lamps and set **them**[s] up on it so that they
27:20 pressed olives for the light so that the **lamps** may be kept burning.
30: 7 incense on the altar every morning when he tends the **lamps**.
30: 8 He must burn incense again when he lights the **lamps** at twilight
35:14 that is for light with its accessories, **lamps** and oil for the light;
37:23 They made its seven **lamps**, as well as its wick trimmers and trays,

[A] Qal [B] Qal passive [C] Niphal [D] Piel (poel, polel, pilel, pilal, pealal, pilpel) [E] Pual (poal, polal, poalal, pulal, pualal)

Ex 39:37 the pure gold lampstand with its row *of* **lamps** and all its
39:37 lampstand with its row of lamps **[RPH]** and all its accessories,
40: 4 belongs on it. Then bring in the lampstand and set up its **lamps**.
40:25 set up the **lamps** before the LORD, as the LORD commanded
Lev 24: 2 for the light so that the **lamps** may be kept burning continually.
24: 4 The **lamps** on the pure gold lampstand before the LORD must be
Nu 4: 9 is for light, together with its **lamps**, its wick trimmers and trays,
8: 2 to Aaron and say to him, 'When you set up the seven **lamps**,
8: 2 they are to light the area in front of the lampstand.' " **[RPH]**
8: 3 he set up the **lamps** so that they faced forward on the lampstand,
1Sa 3: 3 The **lamp** *of* God had not yet gone out, and Samuel was lying
2Sa 21:17 us to battle, so that the **lamp** *of* Israel will not be extinguished."
22:29 You are my **lamp**, O LORD; the LORD turns my darkness into
1Ki 7:49 of the inner sanctuary); the gold floral work and **lamps** and tongs;
1Ch 28:15 the weight of gold for the gold lampstands and their **lamps**,
28:15 and their lamps, with the weight for each lampstand and its **lamps**;
28:15 and the weight of silver for each silver lampstand and its **lamps**,
2Ch 4:20 the lampstands of pure gold with their **lamps**, to burn in front of
4:21 the gold floral work and **lamps** and tongs (they were solid gold);
13:11 and light the **lamps** on the gold lampstand every evening.
29: 7 They also shut the doors of the portico and put out the **lamps**.
Job 18: 6 The light in his tent becomes dark; the **lamp** beside him goes out.
21:17 "Yet how often is the **lamp** *of* the wicked snuffed out? How often
29: 3 when his **lamp** shone upon my head and by his light I walked
Ps 18:28 [18:29] You, O LORD, keep my **lamp** burning; my God turns
119:105 Your word is a **lamp** to my feet and a light for my path.
132:17 a horn grow for David and set up a **lamp** for my anointed one.
Pr 6:23 For these commands are a **lamp**, this teaching is a light,
13: 9 shines brightly, but the **lamp** *of* the wicked is snuffed out.
20:20 or mother, his **lamp** will be snuffed out in pitch darkness.
20:27 The **lamp** *of* the LORD searches the spirit of a man; it searches
24:20 has no future hope, and the **lamp** *of* the wicked will be snuffed out.
31:18 that her trading is profitable, and her **lamp** does not go out at night.
Jer 25:10 and bridegroom, the sound of millstones and the light of the **lamp**.
Zep 1:12 At that time I will search Jerusalem with **lamps** and punish those
Zec 4: 2 solid gold lampstand with a bowl at the top and seven **lights** on it,
4: 2 at the top and seven lights on it, with seven channels to the **lights**.

5945 ²נֵר ***nēr²***, n.pr.m. [16 / 17] [√ 5944]

Ner [17]

1Sa 14:50 The name of the commander of Saul's army was Abner son of **Ner**,
14:51 Saul's father Kish and Abner's father **Ner** were sons of Abiel.
26: 5 He saw where Saul and Abner son of **Ner**, the commander of the
26:14 He called out to the army and to Abner son of **Ner**, "Aren't you
2Sa 2: 8 Meanwhile, Abner son of **Ner**, the commander of Saul's army,
2:12 Abner son of **Ner**, together with the men of Ish-Bosheth son of
3:23 he was told that Abner son of **Ner** had come to the king and that
3:25 You know Abner son of **Ner**; he came to deceive you and observe
3:28 before the LORD concerning the blood of Abner son of **Ner**.
3:37 knew that the king had no part in the murder of Abner son of **Ner**.
1Ki 2: 5 of Israel's armies, Abner son of **Ner** and Amasa son of Jether.
2:32 Abner son of **Ner**, commander of Israel's army, and Amasa son of
1Ch 8:30 son was Abdon, followed by Zur, Kish, Baal, **Ner**, [BHS-] Nadab,
8:33 **Ner** was the father of Kish, Kish the father of Saul, and Saul the
9:36 son was Abdon, followed by Zur, Kish, Baal, **Ner**, Nadab,
9:39 **Ner** was the father of Kish, Kish the father of Saul, and Saul the
26:28 by Saul son of Kish, Abner son of **Ner** and Joab son of Zeruiah,

5946 נֵרְגַל ***nērᵉgal***, n.pr. [1] [→ 5947]

Nergal [1]

2Ki 17:30 the men from Cuthah made **Nergal**, and the men from Hamath

5947 נֵרְגַל שַׂר־אֶצֶר ***nērgal śar-'eṣer***, n.pr.m. [3] [√ 5946 + 8570]

Nergal-Sharezer [3]

Jer 39: 3 **Nergal-Sharezer** *of* Samgar, Nebo-Sarsekim a chief officer,
39: 3 **Nergal-Sharezer** a high official and all the other officials of the
39:13 **Nergal-Sharezer** a high official and all the other officers of the

5948 נֵרְדְּ ***nērd***, n.m. [3]

nard [2], perfume [1]

SS 1:12 While the king was at his table, my **perfume** spread its fragrance.
4:13 orchard of pomegranates with choice fruits, with henna and **nard**,
4:14 **nard** and saffron, calamus and cinnamon, with every kind of

5949 נֵרִיָּה ***nēriyyâ***, n.pr.m. [7] [→ 4950; cf. 5944 + 3378]

Neriah [7]

Jer 32:12 and I gave this deed to Baruch son of **Neriah**, the son of Mahseiah,
32:16 "After I had given the deed of purchase to Baruch son of **Neriah**,
36: 4 So Jeremiah called Baruch son of **Neriah**, and while Jeremiah
36: 8 Baruch son of **Neriah** did everything Jeremiah the prophet told
43: 3 Baruch son of **Neriah** is inciting you against us to hand us over to
45: 1 This is what Jeremiah the prophet told Baruch son of **Neriah** in the
51:59 message Jeremiah gave to the staff officer Seraiah son of **Neriah**,

5950 נֵרִיָּהוּ ***nēriyyāhû***, n.pr.m. [3] [√ 5949; cf. 5944 + 3378]

Neriah [3]

Jer 36:14 So Baruch son of **Neriah** went to them with the scroll in his hand.
36:32 took another scroll and gave it to the scribe Baruch son of **Neriah**,
43: 6 of Shaphan, and Jeremiah the prophet and Baruch son of **Neriah**.

5951 נָשָׂא ***nāśā'***, v. [654 / 652] [→ 5362, 5363, 5365, 5366, 5367, 5368, 5953, 5954, 5955, 8420, 8421, 8480?, 8481?; Ar 10492]

carry [36], bear [35], lift up [32], carried [26], carrying [26], up [26], armor-bearer [+3998] [18], lifted up [16], take up [14], took [12], forgive [10], raise [10], brought [8], *untranslated* [7], held responsible [+6411] [7], lifted [7], take [7], uttered [+606+2256] [7], bring [6], carried off [6], took up [6], aloud [+906+7754] [5], bearing [5], carries [5], lift [5], look [+6524] [5], swore with uplifted [5], take a census [+906+8031] [5], take away [5], aloud [+7754] [4], carry off [4], endure [4], exalted [4], get [4], loaded [4], lofty [4], pick up [4], picks up [4], rose [4], show partiality [+7156] [4], spread [4], suffer [4], accept [+7156] [3], be carried off [3], bore [3], forgiving [3], looked [+6524] [3], married [3], offer [3], picked up [3], put [3], share [+928] [3], sworn with uplifted [3], armor-bearers [+3998] [2], arrogant [+4213] [2], at all forgive [+4200+5951] [2], be lifted up [2], be raised [2], bearer [2], brought back [2], carried away [2], forgave [2], held responsible [+2628] [2], long [+906+5883] [2], misuse [+906+2021+4200+8736] [2], misuses [+906+2021+4200+8736] [2], must be carried [+5951] [2], pay [2], pray [+9525] [2], receive [2], released [+906+8031] [2], rise up [2], rise [2], shows partiality [+7156] [2], spare [2], suffered [2], support [2], taken anything [+5951] [2], taken [2], wear [2], with uplifted swore [2], won [+4200+7156] [2], abounds [1], accept [+4946+7156] [1], accept [1], accepted [+906+7156] [1], are forgiven [1], armed [1], be a willing party [+5883] [1], be carried [1], be exalted [1], be forgiven [1], be raised up [1], bear up [1], bear with [1], beckon [+3338] [1], become guilty [+2628+6584] [1], been exalted [1], began [+906+7754] [1], begin [1], borne fruit [1], bring upon [1], carried [+928+6673] [1], carriers [+6025] [1], carries off [1], carry about [1], carry away [1], carry back [1], casts [1], caught up [1], chose [1], clothed with [1], containing [1], continued on journey [+8079] [1], count [+906+928 +928+8031] [1], counted [+906+8031] [1], counting on [+448+906 +5883] [1], cry out [+606+4200] [1], disdainful [1], ease [1], elevated [1], elevating [1], equipped [1], exalt itself [1], exalted yourself [1], gather [1], gave assistance [1], grant [+4200+7156] [1], granted request [+7156] [1], guilty [+2628] [1], guilty [1], had [1], handle [1], have respect for [1], helped [1], high [1], highly regarded [+7156] [1], honored [+7156] [1], include in the census [+906+8031] [1], incur [1], is carried off [1], is exalted [1], let shine [1], lifts up [1], loaded up [1], look in the face [+448+7156] [1], look with longing [+6524] [1], looked about [+6524] [1], looks [+6524] [1], loudly [+7754] [1], made [1], make [1], man of rank [+7156] [1], married [+851+4200] [1], misuse [+2021+4200+8736] [1], mount up [1], mourn [+7806] [1], moved [1], out [+906] [1], out [1], pardon [1], pardoned [1], pardons [1], partial [+7156] [1], placed [1], pleased with [+928+2834+6524] [1], prepare [1], produce [1], prominent [+7156] [1], provide [1], pull up [1], put himself forward [1], put in jeopardy [+928+1414+9094] [1], raised [+906+2256+5989] [1], raised [1], raising [1], rear [1], rebel [1], receive [+7156] [1], relish [+448+5883] [1], respect [+7156] [1], responsible for [1], ridicule [+5442+6584] [1], rise again [1], rises high [1], rouse themselves [1], saw [+906+6524] [1], served [1], set yourselves [1], share in [+6584] [1], shout [1], shouted [+2256+7754 +7924] [1], showed partiality [+7156] [1], shown honor [+7156] [1], shown partiality [+7156] [1], sing [1], snatch up [1], suffer for [1], suffering for [1], supplied [1], swear with uplifted [1], sweep away [1], sweeps away [1], swore [+3338] [1], sworn [+906+3338] [1], take in marriage [1], taken as wives [1], taken away [1], taken up [1], takes up [1], takes [1], taunt [+4200+5442+6584] [1], toil [1], too heavy a burden to carry [+906+3523+4202] [1], took away [1], took notice [+906+6524] [1], transport [1], trembles [1], turn [1], uplifted [1], wail [+5631] [1], was highly regarded [1], was raised [1], wearing [1], weep [+1140] [1], willing [+4213] [1], willing [+906+4213] [1], won [+928+6524] [1], wore [1]

Ge 4:13 [A] to the LORD, "My punishment is more than I *can* **bear**.
7:17 [A] as the waters increased *they* **lifted** the ark high above the
13: 6 [A] the land *could* not **support** them while they stayed together,
13:10 [A] Lot looked **up** and saw that the whole plain of the Jordan was
13:14 [A] "**Lift up** your eyes from where you are and look north and
18: 2 [A] Abraham looked **up** and saw three men standing nearby.
18:24 [A] not **spare** the place for the sake of the fifty righteous people
18:26 [A] city of Sodom, *I will* **spare** the whole place for their sake."
19:21 [A] "Very well, *I will* **grant** [+4200+7156] this request too;

Ge 21:16 [A] And as she sat there nearby, *she* **began** [+906+7754] to sob.
21:18 [A] **Lift** the boy **up** and take him by the hand, for I will make
22:4 [A] On the third day Abraham looked **up** and saw the place in the
22:13 [A] Abraham looked **up** and there in a thicket he saw a ram
24:63 [A] and as he looked **up**, he saw camels approaching.
24:64 [A] Rebekah also looked **up** and saw Isaac. She got down from
27:3 [A] Now then, **get** your weapons—your quiver and bow—and go
27:38 [A] Bless me too, my father!" Then Esau wept **aloud** [+7754].
29:1 [A] Jacob **continued** [+8079] **on** his **journey** and came to the
29:11 [A] Jacob kissed Rachel and began to weep **aloud** [+906+7754].
31:10 [A] "In breeding season I once had a dream in which I looked **up**
31:12 [A] 'Look **up** and see that all the male goats mating with the
31:17 [A] Then Jacob **put** his children and his wives on camels,
32:20 [32:21] [A] I see him, perhaps *he will* **receive** [+7156] me."
33:1 [A] Jacob looked **up** and there was Esau, coming with his four
33:5 [A] Esau looked **up** and saw the women and children. "Who are
36:7 [A] the land where they were staying could not **support** them
37:25 [A] they looked **up** and saw a caravan of Ishmaelites coming
37:25 [A] Their camels *were* **loaded** *with* spices, balm and myrrh,
39:7 [A] after a while his master's wife **took notice** [+906+6524] of
40:13 [A] Within three days Pharaoh *will* **lift up** your head and restore
40:19 [A] Within three days Pharaoh *will* **lift** off your head and hang
40:20 [A] *He* **lifted up** the heads of the chief cupbearer and the chief
42:26 [A] *they* **loaded** their grain on their donkeys and left.
43:29 [A] As he **looked about** [+6524] and saw his brother Benjamin,
43:34 [A] When portions *were* **served** to them from Joseph's table,
44:1 [A] "Fill the men's sacks with as much food as they can **carry**,
45:19 [A] your children and your wives, and **get** your father and come.
45:23 [A] ten donkeys **loaded** with the best things of Egypt, and ten
45:23 [A] ten female donkeys **loaded** *with* grain and bread and other
45:27 [A] when he saw the carts Joseph had sent to **carry** him **back**,
46:5 [A] Israel's sons **took** their father Jacob and their children and
46:5 [A] their wives in the carts that Pharaoh had sent to **transport**
47:30 [A] **carry** me out of Egypt and bury me where they are buried."
50:13 [A] They **carried** him to the land of Canaan and buried him in
50:17 [A] I ask you to **forgive** your brothers the sins and the wrongs
50:17 [A] Now please **forgive** the sins of the servants of the God of
Ex 6:8 [A] I will bring you to the land I **swore with uplifted** hand to
10:13 [A] all that night. By morning the wind *had* **brought** the locusts;
10:17 [A] Now **forgive** my sin once more and pray to the LORD your
10:19 [A] *which* **caught up** the locusts and carried them into the Red
12:34 [A] So the people **took** their dough before the yeast was added,
14:10 [A] As Pharaoh approached, the Israelites looked **up**, and there
18:22 [A] make your load lighter, because *they will* **share** it with you.
19:4 [A] how *I* **carried** you on eagles' wings and brought you to
20:7 [A] "*You shall* not **misuse** [+906+2021+4200+8736] the name of
20:7 [A] guiltless who **misuses** [+906+2021+4200+8736] his name.
23:1 [A] "*Do* not **spread** false reports. Do not help a wicked man by
23:21 [A] *he will* not **forgive** your rebellion, since my Name is in him.
25:14 [A] the poles into the rings on the sides of the chest to **carry** it.
25:27 [A] close to the rim to hold the poles *used in* **carrying** the table.
25:28 [C] overlay them with gold and **carry** the table with them.
27:7 [A] so they will be on two sides of the altar when it *is* **carried**.
28:12 [A] Aaron *is to* **bear** the names on his shoulders as a memorial
28:29 [A] he *will* **bear** the names of the sons of Israel over his heart on
28:30 [A] Thus Aaron *will* always **bear** the means of making decisions
28:38 [A] he *will* **bear** the guilt involved in the sacred gifts the
28:43 [A] in the Holy Place, so that *they will* not **incur** guilt and die.
30:4 [A] two on opposite sides—to hold the poles used to **carry** it.
30:12 [A] "When *you* **take a census** [+906+8031] *of* the Israelites to
32:32 [A] now, please **forgive** their sin—but if not, then blot me out of
34:7 [A] to thousands, and **forgiving** wickedness, rebellion and sin.
35:21 [A] everyone who was willing and whose heart **moved** him came
35:26 [A] all the women who *were* **willing** [+906+4213] and had the
36:2 [A] and who *was* **willing** [+4213] to come and do the work.
37:5 [A] the poles into the rings on the sides of the ark to **carry** it.
37:14 [A] close to the rim to hold the poles used in **carrying** the table.
37:15 [A] The poles for **carrying** the table were made of acacia wood
37:27 [A] two on opposite sides—to hold the poles used to **carry** it.
38:7 [A] so they would be on the sides of the altar for **carrying** it.
Lev 5:1 [A] or learned about, he *will be* **held responsible** [+6411].
5:17 [A] know it, he is guilty and *will be* **held responsible** [+6411].
7:18 [A] person who eats any of it *will be* **held responsible** [+6411].
9:22 [A] Aaron **lifted** his hands toward the people and blessed them.
10:4 [A] **carry** your cousins outside the camp, away from the front of
10:5 [A] So they came and **carried** them, still in their tunics, outside
10:17 [A] it was given to you to **take away** the guilt of the community
11:25 [A] Whoever **picks up** one of their carcasses must wash his
11:28 [A] Anyone *who* **picks up** their carcasses must wash his clothes,
11:40 [A] Anyone *who* **picks up** the carcass must wash his clothes,
15:10 [A] whoever **picks up** those things must wash his clothes
16:22 [A] The goat *will* **carry** on itself all their sins to a solitary place;
17:16 [A] and bathe himself, he *will be* **held responsible** [+6411].' "
19:8 [A] Whoever eats it *will be* **held responsible** [+6411] because he
19:15 [A] *do* not **show partiality** [+7156] *to* the poor or favoritism to
19:17 [A] neighbor frankly so *you will* not **share** [+6584] **in** his guilt.
20:17 [A] dishonored his sister and *will be* **held responsible** [+6411].
20:19 [A] both of you *would be* **held responsible** [+6411].
20:20 [A] They *will be* **held responsible** [+2628]; they will die
22:9 [A] so that they *do* not **become guilty** [+2628+6584] and die for
22:16 [G] and so **bring upon** them guilt requiring payment.
24:15 [A] anyone curses his God, he *will be* **held responsible** [+2628];
Nu 1:2 [A] "**Take a census** [+906+8031] *of* the whole Israelite
1:49 [A] or **include** them **in the census** [+906+8031] of the other
1:50 [A] They *are to* **carry** the tabernacle and all its furnishings; they
3:40 [A] who are a month old or more and **make** a list of their names.
4:2 [A] "**Take a census** [+906+8031] *of* the Kohathite branch of the
4:15 [A] to move, the Kohathites are to come to *do the* **carrying**.
4:22 [A] "**Take a census** [+906+8031] also *of* the Gershonites by
4:25 [A] *They are to* **carry** the curtains of the tabernacle, the Tent of
5:31 [A] but the woman *will* **bear** the consequences of her sin.' "
6:26 [A] the LORD **turn** his face toward you and give you peace." '
7:9 [A] because *they were* to **carry** on their shoulders the holy
9:13 [A] That man *will* **bear** the consequences of his sin.
10:17 [A] and the Gershonites and Merarites, *who* **carried** it, set out.
10:21 [A] the Kohathites set out, **carrying** the holy things. The
11:12 [A] Why do you tell me *to* **carry** them in my arms, as a nurse
11:12 [A] me to carry them in my arms, as a nurse **carries** an infant,
11:14 [A] I cannot **carry** all these people by myself; the burden is too
11:17 [A] *They will* help you **carry** the burden of the people so that
11:17 [A] of the people so that you *will* not *have to* **carry** it alone.
13:23 [A] Two of them **carried** it on a pole between them, along with
14:1 [A] the community **raised** [+906+2256+5989] their voices and
14:18 [A] to anger, abounding in love and **forgiving** sin and rebellion.
14:19 [A] just as *you have* **pardoned** them from the time they left
14:30 [A] Not one of you will enter the land I **swore with uplifted**
14:33 [A] **suffering for** your unfaithfulness, until the last of your
14:34 [A] *you will* **suffer for** your sins and know what it is like to have
16:3 [F] then *do you* **set yourselves** above the LORD's assembly?"
16:15 [A] *I have* not **taken** so much as a donkey from them, nor have I
18:1 [A] your father's family *are to* **bear** the responsibility for
18:1 [A] your sons alone *are to* **bear** the responsibility for offenses
18:22 [A] or they *will* **bear** the consequences of their sin and will die.
18:23 [A] of Meeting and **bear** the responsibility for offenses against it.
18:32 [A] best part of it *you will* not *be* **guilty** [+2628] in this matter;
23:7 [A] Balaam **uttered** [+606+2256] his oracle: "Balak brought me
23:18 [A] *he* **uttered** [+606+2256] his oracle: "Arise, Balak, and listen;
23:24 [F] *they* **rouse themselves** like a lion that does not rest till he
24:2 [A] When Balaam looked **out** and saw Israel encamped tribe by
24:3 [A] *he* **uttered** [+606+2256] his oracle: "The oracle of Balaam
24:7 [F] will be greater than Agag; their kingdom *will* **be exalted**.
24:15 [A] *he* **uttered** [+606+2256] his oracle: "The oracle of Balaam
24:20 [A] Balaam saw Amalek and **uttered** [+606+2256] his oracle:
24:21 [A] he saw the Kenites and **uttered** [+606+2256] his oracle:
24:23 [A] *he* **uttered** [+606+2256] his oracle: "Ah, who can live when
26:2 [A] "**Take a census** [+906+8031] *of* the whole Israelite
30:15 [30:16] [A] about them, then *he is* **responsible for** her guilt."
31:26 [A] heads of the community *are to* **count** [+906+928+928+8031]
31:49 [A] "Your servants *have* **counted** [+906+8031] the soldiers
Dt 1:9 [A] *are* **too heavy a burden** for me **to carry** [+906+3523+4202]
1:12 [A] how *can I* **bear** your problems and your burdens and your
1:31 [A] There you saw how the LORD your God **carried** you, as a
1:31 [A] as a father **carries** his son, all the way you went until you
3:27 [A] and **look** [+6524] west and north and south and east.
4:19 [A] And when you look **up** to the sky and see the sun, the moon
5:11 [A] "*You shall* not **misuse** [+906+2021+4200+8736] the name of
5:11 [A] guiltless *who* **misuses** [+906+2021+4200+8736] his name.
10:8 [A] At that time the LORD set apart the tribe of Levi to **carry**
10:17 [A] who **shows** no **partiality** [+7156] and accepts no bribes.
12:26 [A] **take** your consecrated things and whatever you have vowed
14:24 [A] blessed by the LORD your God and cannot **carry** your tithe
24:15 [A] because he is poor and *is* **counting** [+448+906+5883] **on** it.
28:49 [A] The LORD *will* **bring** a nation against you from far away,
28:50 [A] a fierce-looking nation without **respect** [+7156] for the old
31:9 [A] of Levi, who **carried** the ark of the covenant of the LORD,
31:25 [A] he gave this command to the Levites *who* **carried** the ark of
32:11 [A] its wings to catch them and **carries** them on its pinions.
32:40 [A] *I* **lift** my hand to heaven and declare: As surely as I live
33:3 [A] feet they all bow down, and from you **receive** instruction,
Jos 3:3 [A] the priests, who are Levites, **carrying** it, you are to move out
3:6 [A] "**Take up** the ark of the covenant and pass on ahead of the
3:6 [A] of the people." So *they* **took** it **up** and went ahead of them.
3:8 [A] Tell the priests *who* **carry** the ark of the covenant: 'When
3:13 [A] as soon as the priests *who* **carry** the ark of the LORD—
3:14 [A] the priests **carrying** the ark of the covenant went ahead of
3:15 [A] Yet as soon as the priests *who* **carried** the ark reached the
3:15 [A] Yet as soon as the priests who carried the ark **[RPH]**
3:17 [A] The priests *who* **carried** the ark of the covenant of the

Jos 4: 3 [A] tell them *to* **take up** twelve stones from the middle of the
4: 8 [A] *They* **took** twelve stones from the middle of the Jordan,
4: 9 [A] the priests *who* **carried** the ark of the covenant had stood.
4: 10 [A] Now the priests *who* **carried** the ark remained standing in
4: 16 [A] "Command the priests **carrying** the ark of the Testimony to
4: 18 [A] the priests came up out of the river **carrying** the ark of the
5: 13 [A] he looked **up** and saw a man standing in front of him with a
6: 4 [A] *Have* seven priests **carry** trumpets of rams' horns in front of
6: 6 [A] "**Take up** the ark of the covenant of the LORD and have
6: 6 [A] and *have* seven priests **carry** trumpets in front of it."
6: 8 [A] the seven priests **carrying** the seven trumpets before the
6: 12 [A] next morning and the priests **took up** the ark of the LORD.
6: 13 [A] The seven priests **carrying** the seven trumpets went forward,
8: 33 [A] of the covenant of the LORD, facing *those who* **carried** it—
24: 19 [A] *He will* not **forgive** your rebellion and your sins.
Jdg 2: 4 [A] to all the Israelites, the people wept **aloud** [+906+7754],
3: 18 [A] the tribute, he sent on their way the men *who had* **carried** it.
8: 28 [A] subdued before the Israelites and *did* not **raise** its head again.
9: 7 [A] and **shouted** [+2256+7754+7924] to them, "Listen to me,
9: 48 [A] and cut off some branches, which *he* **lifted** to his shoulders.
9: 54 [A] Hurriedly he called to his **armor-bearer** [+3998], "Draw
16: 31 [A] and his father's whole family went down *to* **get** him.
19: 17 [A] When *he* **looked** [+6524] and saw the traveler in the city
21: 2 [A] God until evening, **raising** their voices and weeping bitterly.
21: 23 [A] each man caught one and **carried** her **off** to be his wife.
Ru 1: 4 [A] *They* **married** [+851+4200] Moabite women, one named
1: 9 [A] Then she kissed them and they wept **aloud** [+7754]
1: 14 [A] At this **[RPH]** they wept again. Then Orpah kissed her
2: 18 [A] *She* **carried** it back to town, and her mother-in-law saw how
1Sa 2: 28 [A] to burn incense, and to **wear** an ephod in my presence.
4: 4 [A] *they* **brought** back the ark of the covenant of the LORD
6: 13 [A] when they looked **up** and saw the ark, they rejoiced at the
10: 3 [A] One *will be* **carrying** three young goats, another three loaves
10: 3 [A] another **[RPH]** three loaves of bread, and another a skin of
10: 3 [A] three loaves of bread, and another **[RPH]** a skin of wine.
11: 4 [A] these terms to the people, they all wept **aloud** [+906+7754].
14: 1 [A] One day Jonathan son of Saul said to the young man **bearing**
14: 3 [A] among whom was Ahijah, *who was* **wearing** an ephod.
14: 6 [A] Jonathan said to his young **armor-bearer** [+3998], "Come,
14: 7 [A] all that you have in mind," his **armor-bearer** [+3998] said.
14: 12 [A] outpost shouted to Jonathan and his **armor-bearer** [+3998],
14: 12 [A] So Jonathan said to his **armor-bearer** [+3998], "Climb up
14: 13 [A] and feet, with his **armor-bearer** [+3998] right behind him.
14: 13 [A] his **armor-bearer** [+3998] followed and killed behind him.
14: 14 [A] his **armor-bearer** [+3998] killed some twenty men in an
14: 17 [A] and his **armor-bearer** [+3998] who were not there.
15: 25 [A] Now I beg you, **forgive** my sin and come back with me,
16: 21 [A] and David became one of his **armor-bearers** [+3998].
17: 7 [A] six hundred shekels. His shield **bearer** went ahead of him.
17: 20 [A] with a shepherd, **loaded up** and set out, as Jesse had directed.
17: 34 [A] a lion or a bear came and **carried off** a sheep from the flock,
17: 41 [A] the Philistine, with his shield **bearer** in front of him,
22: 18 [A] That day he killed eighty-five men *who* **wore** the linen
24: 16 [24:17] [A] David my son?" And he wept **aloud** [+7754].
25: 28 [A] Please **forgive** your servant's offense, for the LORD will
25: 35 [A] I have heard your words and **granted** [+7156] your **request**."
30: 4 [A] his men wept **aloud** [+906+7754] until they had no strength
31: 4 [A] Saul said to his **armor-bearer** [+3998], "Draw your sword
31: 4 [A] his **armor-bearer** [+3998] was terrified and would not do it;
31: 5 [A] When the **armor-bearer** [+3998] saw that Saul was dead,
31: 6 [A] So Saul and his three sons and his **armor-bearer** [+3998]
2Sa 2: 22 [A] *could I* **look** your brother Joab **in the face** [+448+7156]?"
2: 32 [A] *They* **took** Asahel and buried him in his father's tomb at
3: 32 [A] and the king wept **aloud** [+906+7754] at Abner's tomb.
4: 4 [A] His nurse **picked** him **up** and fled, but as she hurried to
5: 12 [D] *had* **exalted** his kingdom for the sake of his people Israel.
5: 21 [A] their idols there, and David and his men **carried** them **off**.
6: 3 [A] on a new cart and **brought** it from the house of Abinadab,
6: 4 [a] [BHS+ *and* ***brought*** *it from the house of Abinadab*] with the ark
6: 13 [A] When *those who were* **carrying** the ark of the LORD had
8: 2 [A] the Moabites became subject to David and **brought** tribute.
8: 6 [A] the Arameans became subject to him and **brought** tribute.
13: 34 [A] Now the man standing watch looked **up** and saw many
13: 36 [A] the king's sons came in, wailing **loudly** [+7754].
14: 14 [A] But God *does* not **take away** life; instead, he devises ways
15: 24 [A] all the Levites who were with him *were* **carrying** the ark of
17: 13 [G] into a city, then all Israel *will* **bring** ropes to that city,
18: 15 [A] ten of Joab's **armor-bearers** [+3998] surrounded Absalom,
18: 24 [A] As he looked **out** [+906], he saw a man running alone.
18: 28 [A] He has delivered up the men who **lifted** their hands against
19: 42 [19:43] [C] *Have we* **taken** [+5951] **anything** for ourselves?"
19: 42 [19:43] [C] *Have we* **taken anything** [+5951] for ourselves?"
20: 21 [A] *has* **lifted up** his hand against the king, against David.
23: 16 [A] near the gate of Bethlehem and **carried** it back to David.
23: 37 [A] the **armor-bearer** [+3998] *of* Joab son of Zeruiah,
1Ki 1: 5 [F] was Haggith, **put himself forward** and said, "I will be king."
2: 26 [A] because *you* **carried** the ark of the Sovereign LORD before
5: 9 [5:23] [A] I will separate them and you *can* **take** them **away**.
5: 15 [5:29] [A] Solomon had seventy thousand **carriers** [+6025] and
8: 3 [A] the elders of Israel had arrived, the priests **took up** the ark,
9: 11 [D] because Hiram *had* **supplied** him with all the cedar and pine
10: 2 [A] with camels **carrying** spices, large quantities of gold,
10: 11 [A] (Hiram's ships **brought** gold from Ophir; and from there
10: 22 [A] **carrying** gold, silver and ivory, and apes and baboons.
13: 29 [A] So the prophet **picked up** the body of the man of God, laid it
14: 28 [A] went to the LORD's temple, the guards **bore** the shields,
15: 22 [A] *they* **carried away** from Ramah the stones and timber
18: 12 [A] I don't know where the Spirit of the LORD *may* **carry** you
2Ki 2: 16 [A] Perhaps the Spirit of the LORD *has* **picked** him **up** and set
3: 14 [A] if I *did* not **have respect for** the presence of Jehoshaphat
4: 19 [A] His father told a servant, "**Carry** him to his mother."
4: 20 [A] After the servant *had* **lifted** him **up** and carried him to his
4: 36 [A] And he did. When she came, he said, "**Take** your son."
4: 37 [A] bowed to the ground. Then *she* **took** her son and went out.
5: 1 [B] man in the sight of his master and **highly regarded** [+7156],
5: 23 [A] two of his servants, and *they* **carried** them ahead of Gehazi.
7: 8 [A] and drank, and **carried** away silver, gold and clothes,
7: 8 [A] another tent and **took** some things from it and hid them also.
9: 25 [A] "**Pick** him **up** and throw him on the field that belonged to
9: 25 [A] his father when the LORD **made** this prophecy about him:
9: 26 [A] Now then, **pick** him **up** and throw him on that plot,
9: 32 [A] He looked **up** at the window and called out, "Who is on my
14: 10 [A] indeed defeated Edom and now you *are* **arrogant** [+4213].
14: 20 [A] *He was* **brought back** by horse and was buried in Jerusalem
18: 14 [A] from me, and *I will* **pay** whatever you demand of me."
19: 4 [A] Therefore **pray** [+9525] for the remnant that still survives."
19: 22 [A] have you raised your voice and **lifted** your eyes in pride?
20: 17 [C] have stored up until this day, *will* **be carried off** to Babylon.
23: 4 [A] the fields of the Kidron Valley and **took** the ashes *to* Bethel.
25: 13 [A] of the LORD and *they* **carried** the bronze to Babylon.
25: 27 [A] *he* **released** [+906+8031] Jehoiachin from prison on the
1Ch 5: 18 [A] able-bodied men *who could* **handle** shield and sword, who
10: 4 [A] Saul said to his **armor-bearer** [+3998], "Draw your sword
10: 4 [A] his **armor-bearer** [+3998] was terrified and would not do it;
10: 5 [A] When the **armor-bearer** [+3998] saw that Saul was dead,
10: 9 [A] They stripped him and **took** his head and his armor, and sent
10: 12 [A] valiant men went and **took** the bodies of Saul and his sons
11: 18 [A] near the gate of Bethlehem and **carried** it back to David.
11: 39 [A] the **armor-bearer** [+3998] *of* Joab son of Zeruiah,
12: 24 [12:25] [A] men of Judah, **carrying** shield and spear—
14: 2 [C] that his kingdom *had* **been** highly **exalted** for the sake of his
15: 2 [A] "No one but the Levites *may* **carry** the ark of God,
15: 2 [A] because the LORD chose them to **carry** the ark of the
15: 15 [A] the Levites **carried** the ark of God with the poles on their
15: 26 [A] Because God had helped the Levites *who were* **carrying** the
15: 27 [A] as were all the Levites who *were* **carrying** the ark, and as
16: 29 [A] **Bring** an offering and come before him; worship the LORD
18: 2 [A] and they became subject to him and **brought** tribute.
18: 6 [A] the Arameans became subject to him and **brought** tribute.
18: 11 [A] with the silver and gold *he had* **taken** from all these nations:
21: 16 [A] David looked **up** and saw the angel of the LORD standing
21: 24 [A] *I will* not **take** for the LORD what is yours, or sacrifice a
23: 22 [A] Their cousins, the sons of Kish, **married** them.
23: 26 [A] the Levites no *longer need* to **carry** the tabernacle or any of
27: 23 [A] David *did* not **take** the number of the men twenty years old
29: 11 [F] O LORD, is the kingdom; you *are* **exalted** as head over all.
2Ch 5: 4 [A] the elders of Israel had arrived, the Levites **took up** the ark,
9: 1 [A] with camels **carrying** spices, large quantities of gold,
9: 21 [A] **carrying** gold, silver and ivory, and apes and baboons.
11: 21 [A] In all, *he* **had** eighteen wives and sixty concubines,
12: 11 [A] the guards went with him, **bearing** the shields,
13: 21 [A] *He* **married** fourteen wives and had twenty-two sons
14: 8 [14:7] [A] **equipped** *with* large shields and *with* spears,
14: 8 [14:7] [A] **armed** *with* small shields and with bows.
14: 13 [14:12] [A] men of Judah **carried off** a large amount of plunder.
16: 6 [A] *they* **carried away** from Ramah the stones and timber
24: 3 [A] Jehoiada **chose** two wives for him, and he had sons
24: 11 [A] and empty the chest and **carry** it back to its place.
25: 19 [A] and now you *are* **arrogant** [+4213] and proud.
25: 28 [A] He *was* **brought back** by horse and was buried with his
32: 23 [F] then on *he* **was highly regarded** by all the nations.
Ezr 1: 4 [D] survivors may now be living *are to* **provide** him with silver
8: 36 [D] *who* then **gave assistance** *to* the people and *to* the house of
9: 2 [A] *They have* **taken** some of their daughters **as wives** for
9: 12 [A] marriage to their sons or **take** their daughters for your sons.
10: 44 [A] All these *had* **married** foreign women, and some of them
Ne 2: 1 [A] was brought for him, *I* **took** the wine and gave it to the king.
4: 17 [4:11] [A] Those *who* **carried** [+928+6673] materials did their

Ne 9:15 [A] take possession of the land *you had* **sworn with uplifted**
13:25 [A] nor *are you to* **take** their daughters **in marriage** for your
Est 2: 9 [A] The girl pleased him and **won** [+4200+7156] his favor.
2:15 [A] Esther **won** [+928+6524] the favor of everyone who saw her.
2:17 [A] *she* **won** [+4200+7156] his favor and approval more than any
3: 1 [D] **elevating** him and giving him a seat of honor higher than that
5: 2 [A] he *was* **pleased with her** [+928+2834+6524] and held out to
5:11 [D] how *he had* **elevated** him above the other nobles
9: 3 [D] the governors and the king's administrators **helped** the Jews,
Job 2:12 [A] When *they* **saw** [+906+6524] him from a distance, they
2:12 [A] they began to weep **aloud** [+7754], and they tore their robes
6: 2 [A] could be weighed and all my misery *be* **placed** on the scales!
7:13 [A] bed will comfort me and my couch *will* **ease** my complaint,
7:21 [A] Why *do you* not **pardon** my offenses and forgive my sins?
10:15 [A] *I* cannot **lift** my head, for I am full of shame and drowned in
11:15 [A] *you will* **lift up** your face without shame; you will stand firm
13: 8 [A] *Will you* **show** him **partiality** [+7156]? Will you argue the
13:10 [A] surely rebuke you if *you* secretly **showed partiality** [+7156].
13:14 [A] Why *do I* **put** myself **in jeopardy** [+928+1414+9094] and take
21: 3 [A] **Bear with** me while I speak, and after I have spoken,
21:12 [A] *They* **sing** to the music of tambourine and harp; they make
22: 8 [B] owning land—an **honored** [+7156] *man*, living on it.
22:26 [A] delight in the Almighty and *will* **lift up** your face to God.
24:10 [A] go about naked; *they* **carry** the sheaves, but still go hungry.
27: 1 [A] And Job continued **[NIE]** his discourse:
27:21 [A] The east wind **carries** him **off**, and he is gone; it sweeps him
29: 1 [A] Job continued **[NIE]** his discourse:
30:22 [A] *You* **snatch** me **up** and drive me before the wind; you toss
31:36 [A] Surely *I would* **wear** it on my shoulder, I would put it on like
32:21 [A] *I will* **show partiality** [+7156] *to* no one, nor will I flatter
32:22 [A] skilled in flattery, my Maker *would* soon **take** me **away**.
34:19 [A] who **shows** no **partiality** [+7156] *to* princes and does not
34:31 [A] a man says to God, '*I am* **guilty** but will offend no more.
36: 3 [A] *I* **get** my knowledge from afar; I will ascribe justice to my
40:20 [A] The hills **bring** him their produce, and all the wild animals
42: 8 [A] *I will* **accept** [+7156] his prayer and not deal with you
42: 9 [A] and the LORD **accepted** [+906+7156] Job's prayer.
Ps 4: 6 [4:7] [A] **Let** the light of your face **shine** upon us, O LORD.
7: 6 [7:7] [C] in your anger; **rise up** against the rage of my enemies.
10:12 [A] Arise, LORD! **Lift up** your hand, O God. Do not forget the
15: 3 [A] his neighbor no wrong and **casts** no slur on his fellowman,
16: 4 [A] their libations of blood or **take up** their names on my lips.
24: 4 [A] who *does* not **lift up** his soul to an idol or swear by what is
24: 5 [A] *He will* **receive** blessing from the LORD and vindication
24: 7 [A] **Lift up** your heads, O you gates; be lifted up, you ancient
24: 7 [C] **be lifted up**, *you* ancient doors, that the King of glory may
24: 9 [A] **Lift up** your heads, O you gates; lift them up, you ancient
24: 9 [A] **lift** them **up**, *you* ancient doors, that the King of glory may
25: 1 [A] To you, O LORD, *I* **lift up** my soul;
25:18 [A] my affliction and my distress and **take away** all my sins.
28: 2 [A] for help, as I **lift up** my hands toward your Most Holy Place.
28: 9 [D] your inheritance; be their shepherd and **carry** them forever.
32: 1 [B] Blessed is *he whose* transgressions **are forgiven**, whose sins
32: 5 [A] to the LORD"—and you **forgave** the guilt of my sin.
50:16 [A] you to recite my laws or **take** my covenant on your lips?
55:12 [55:13] [A] If an enemy were insulting me, *I could* **endure** it;
63: 4 [63:5] [A] as I live, and in your name *I will* **lift up** my hands.
69: 7 [69:8] [A] For *I* **endure** scorn for your sake, and shame covers
72: 3 [A] The mountains *will* **bring** prosperity to the people, the hills
81: 2 [81:3] [A] **Begin** the music, strike the tambourine,
82: 2 [A] the unjust and **show partiality** [+7156] *to* the wicked?
83: 2 [83:3] [A] enemies are astir, how your foes **rear** their heads.
85: 2 [85:3] [A] *You* **forgave** the iniquity of your people and covered
86: 4 [A] joy to your servant, for to you, O Lord, *I* **lift up** my soul.
88:15 [88:16] [A] *I have* **suffered** your terrors and am in despair.
89: 9 [89:10] [A] when its waves **mount up**, you still them.
89:50 [89:51] [A] how I **bear** in my heart the taunts of all the nations,
91:12 [A] *they will* **lift** you **up** in their hands, so that you will not strike
93: 3 [A] The seas *have* **lifted up**, O LORD, the seas have lifted up
93: 3 [A] have lifted up, O LORD, the seas *have* **lifted up** their voice;
93: 3 [A] up their voice; the seas *have* **lifted up** their pounding waves.
94: 2 [C] **Rise up**, O Judge of the earth; pay back to the proud what
96: 8 [A] due his name; **bring** an offering and come into his courts.
99: 8 [A] you were to Israel a **forgiving** God, though you punished
102:10 [102:11] [A] for *you have* **taken** me **up** and thrown me aside.
106:26 [A] So *he* **swore** to them **with uplifted** hand that he would make
116:13 [A] *I will* **lift up** the cup of salvation and call on the name of the
119:48 [A] *I* **lift up** my hands to your commands, which I love, and I
121: 1 [A] *I* **lift up** my eyes to the hills—where does my help come
123: 1 [A] *I* **lift up** my eyes to you, to you whose throne is in heaven.
126: 6 [A] He who goes out weeping, **carrying** seed to sow, will return
126: 6 [A] will return with songs of joy, **carrying** sheaves with him.
134: 2 [A] **Lift up** your hands in the sanctuary and praise the LORD.
139: 9 [A] If *I* **rise** *on* the wings of the dawn, if I settle on the far side of
139:20 [A] your adversaries **misuse** [+2021+4200+8736] your name.
143: 8 [A] Show me the way I should go, for to you *I* **lift up** my soul.
Pr 6:35 [A] *He will* not **accept** [+7156] any compensation; he will refuse
9:12 [A] will reward you; if you are a mocker, you alone *will* **suffer**."
18: 5 [A] It is not good *to be* **partial** [+7156] *to* the wicked or to
18:14 [A] sustains him in sickness, but a crushed spirit who *can* **bear**?
19:18 [A] there is hope; *do* not **be a willing party** [+5883] to his death.
19:19 [A] A hot-tempered man *must* **pay** the penalty; if you rescue
30:13 [C] eyes are ever so haughty, whose glances *are* so **disdainful**;
30:21 [A] three things the earth trembles, under four it cannot **bear up**:
30:32 [F] "If you have played the fool and **exalted yourself**, or if you
Ecc 5:15 [5:14] [A] *He* **takes** nothing from his labor that he can carry in
5:19 [5:18] [A] to **accept** his lot and be happy in his work—
SS 5: 7 [A] *they* **took** away my cloak, those watchmen of the walls!
Isa 1:14 [A] have become a burden to me; I am weary of **bearing** them.
2: 2 [C] *it will* **be raised** above the hills, and all nations will stream to
2: 4 [A] Nation *will* not **take up** sword against nation, nor will they
2: 9 [A] be brought low and mankind humbled—*do* not **forgive** them.
2:12 [C] and lofty, for all *that* **is exalted** (and they will be humbled),
2:13 [C] cedars of Lebanon, tall and **lofty**, and all the oaks of Bashan,
2:14 [C] for all the towering mountains and all the **high** hills,
3: 3 [B] the captain of fifty and **man of rank** [+7156], the counselor,
3: 7 [A] in that day *he will* **cry out** [+606+4200], "I have no remedy.
5:26 [A] *He* **lifts up** a banner for the distant nations, he whistles for
6: 1 [C] I saw the Lord seated on a throne, high and **exalted**,
8: 4 [C] the plunder of Samaria *will* **be carried off** by the king of
9:15 [9:14] [B] the elders and **prominent** [+7156] *men* are the head,
10:24 [A] who beat you with a rod and **lift up** a club against you,
10:26 [A] and *he will* **raise** his staff over the waters, as he did in Egypt.
11:12 [A] *He will* **raise** a banner for the nations and gather the exiles of
13: 2 [A] **Raise** a banner on a bare hilltop, shout to them; beckon to
14: 4 [A] *you will* **take up** this taunt against the king of Babylon: How
15: 7 [A] stored up *they* **carry away** over the Ravine of the Poplars.
18: 3 [A] when a banner *is* **raised** on the mountains, you will see it,
22: 6 [A] Elam **takes up** the quiver, with her charioteers and horses;
24:14 [A] They **raise** their voices, they shout for joy; from the west
30: 6 [A] the envoys **carry** their riches on donkeys' backs,
30:25 [C] water will flow on every high mountain and every **lofty** hill.
33:10 [C] the LORD. "Now will I be exalted; now *will I* **be lifted up**.
33:24 [B] and the sins of those who dwell there *will* **be forgiven**.
37: 4 [A] Therefore **pray** [+9525] for the remnant that still survives."
37:23 [A] have you raised your voice and **lifted** your eyes in pride?
38:21 [A] had said, "**Prepare** a poultice of figs and apply it to the boil,
39: 6 [C] have stored up until this day, *will* **be carried off** to Babylon.
40: 4 [C] Every valley *shall* **be raised up**, every mountain and hill
40:11 [A] the lambs in his arms and **carries** them close to his heart;
40:24 [A] they wither, and a whirlwind **sweeps** them **away** like chaff.
40:26 [A] **Lift** your eyes and look to the heavens: Who created all
41:16 [A] You will winnow them, the wind *will* **pick** them **up**, and a
42: 2 [A] He will not shout or cry out, or **raise** his voice in the streets.
42:11 [A] *Let* the desert and its towns **raise** their voices;
45:20 [A] Ignorant are those *who* **carry about** idols of wood, who pray
46: 3 [B] since you were conceived, and *have* **carried** since your birth.
46: 4 [A] I have made you and I *will* **carry** you; I will sustain you
46: 7 [A] *They* **lift** it to their shoulders and carry it; they set it up in its
49:18 [A] **Lift up** your eyes and look around; all your sons gather
49:22 [A] "See, I *will* **beckon** [+3338] to the Gentiles, I will lift up my
49:22 [C] in their arms and **carry** your daughters on their shoulders.
51: 6 [A] **Lift up** your eyes to the heavens, look at the earth beneath;
52: 8 [A] Your watchmen **lift up** their voices; together they shout for
52:11 [A] and be pure, you *who* **carry** the vessels of the LORD.
52:13 [C] act wisely; he will be raised and **lifted up** and highly exalted.
53: 4 [A] Surely he **took up** our infirmities and carried our sorrows,
53:12 [A] For he **bore** the sin of many, and made intercession for the
57: 7 [C] You have made your bed on a high and **lofty** hill; there you
57:13 [A] The wind *will* **carry** all of them **off**, a mere breath will blow
57:15 [C] For this is what the high and **lofty** One says—he who lives
60: 4 [A] "**Lift up** your eyes and look about you: All assemble
60: 6 [A] **bearing** gold and incense and proclaiming the praise of the
63: 9 [D] he lifted them up and **carried** them all the days of old.
64: 6 [64:5] [A] like a leaf, and like the wind our sins **sweep** us **away**.
66:12 [C] you will nurse and **be carried** on her arm and dandled on her
Jer 3: 2 [A] "Look **up** to the barren heights and see. Is there any place
4: 6 [A] **Raise** the signal to go to Zion! Flee for safety without delay!
6: 1 [A] the trumpet in Tekoa! **Raise** the signal over Beth Hakkerem!
7:16 [A] "So do not pray for this people nor **offer** any plea or petition
7:29 [A] **take up** a lament on the barren heights, for the LORD has
9:10 [9:9] [A] *I will* **weep** [+1140] and wail for the mountains
9:18 [9:17] [A] **wail** [+5631] over us till our eyes overflow with tears
10: 5 [C] *they* **must be carried** [+5951] because they cannot walk.
10: 5 [A] *they* **must be carried** [+5951] because they cannot walk.
10:19 [A] I said to myself, "This is my sickness, and *I must* **endure** it."
11:14 [A] "Do not pray for this people nor **offer** any plea or petition for
13:20 [A] **Lift up** your eyes and see those who are coming from the

Jer 15:15 [A] take me away; think of *how* I **suffer** reproach for your sake.
17:21 [A] Be careful not *to* **carry** a load on the Sabbath day or bring it
17:27 [A] **carrying** any load as you come through the gates of
22:27 [D] You will never come back to the land you **long** [+906+5883]
31:19 [A] and humiliated because *I* **bore** the disgrace of my youth.'
44:14 [D] of Judah, to which they **long** [+906+5883] to return and live;
44:22 [A] When the LORD could no longer **endure** your wicked
49:29 [A] their shelters *will be* **carried off** with all their goods
50: 2 [A] proclaim among the nations, **lift up** a banner and proclaim it;
51: 9 [C] judgment reaches to the skies, *it* **rises** as **high** as the clouds.'
51:12 [A] **Lift up** a banner against the walls of Babylon!
51:27 [A] "**Lift up** a banner in the land! Blow the trumpet among the
52:17 [A] of the LORD and *they* **carried** all the bronze to Babylon.
52:31 [A] *he* **released** [+906+8031] Jehoiachin king of Judah and freed
La 2:19 [A] **Lift up** your hands to him for the lives of your children,
3:27 [A] It is good for a man *to* **bear** the yoke while he is young.
3:41 [A] *Let us* **lift up** our hearts and our hands to God in heaven,
4:16 [A] The priests *are* **shown** no **honor** [+7156], the elders no
5:13 [A] Young men **toil** *at* the millstones; boys stagger under loads
Eze 1:19 [C] when the living creatures **rose** from the ground, the wheels
1:19 [C] living creatures rose from the ground, the wheels also **rose**.
1:20 [C] they would go, and the wheels *would* **rise** along with them,
1:21 [C] when the creatures **rose** from the ground, the wheels rose
1:21 [C] rose from the ground, the wheels **rose** along with them,
3:12 [A] the Spirit **lifted** me **up**, and I heard behind me a loud
3:14 [A] The Spirit then **lifted** me **up** and took me away, and I went in
4: 4 [A] *You are to* **bear** their sin for the number of days you lie on
4: 5 [A] So for 390 days *you will* **bear** the sin of the house of Israel.
4: 6 [A] on your right side, and **bear** the sin of the house of Judah.
8: 3 [A] The Spirit **lifted** me **up** between earth and heaven and in
8: 5 [A] he said to me, "Son of man, **look** [+6524] toward the north."
8: 5 [A] So I **looked** [+6524], and in the entrance north of the gate of
10: 7 [A] *He* **took up** some of it and put it into the hands of the man in
10:16 [A] when the cherubim **spread** their wings to rise from the
10:19 [A] the cherubim **spread** their wings and rose from the ground,
11: 1 [A] the Spirit **lifted** me **up** and brought me to the gate of the
11:22 [A] with the wheels beside them, **spread** their wings,
11:24 [A] The Spirit **lifted** me **up** and brought me to the exiles in
12: 6 [A] **Put** them on your shoulder as they are watching and carry
12: 7 [A] at dusk, **carrying** them on my shoulders while they watched.
12:12 [A] "The prince among them *will* **put** his things on his shoulder
14:10 [A] *They will* **bear** their guilt—the prophet will be as guilty as
16:52 [A] **Bear** your disgrace, for you have furnished some justification
16:52 [A] So then, be ashamed and **bear** your disgrace, for you have
16:54 [A] so that *you may* **bear** your disgrace and be ashamed of all
16:58 [A] You *will* **bear** the consequences of your lewdness and your
17: 8 [A] produce branches, **bear** fruit and become a splendid vine.'
17: 9 [A] take a strong arm or many people to **pull** it **up** by the roots.
17:14 [F] unable *to* **rise again**, surviving only by keeping his treaty.
17:23 [A] *it will* **produce** branches and bear fruit and become a
18: 6 [A] or **look** [+6524] to the idols of the house of Israel.
18:12 [A] He does not return what he took in pledge. He **looks** [+6524]
18:15 [A] or **look** [+6524] to the idols of the house of Israel.
18:19 [A] 'Why *does* the son not **share** [+928] the guilt of his father?'
18:20 [A] The son *will* not **share** [+928] the guilt of the father, nor will
18:20 [A] nor *will* the father **share** [+928] the guilt of the son.
19: 1 [A] "**Take up** a lament concerning the princes of Israel
20: 5 [A] I **swore with uplifted** hand to the descendants of the house
20: 5 [A] *With* **uplifted** hand I said to them, "I am the LORD your
20: 6 [A] On that day *I* **swore** [+3338] to them that I would bring them
20:15 [A] Also **with uplifted** hand I **swore** to them in the desert that I
20:23 [A] Also **with uplifted** hand I **swore** to them in the desert that I
20:28 [A] When I brought them into the land I *had* **sworn** [+906+3338]
20:31 [A] When you **offer** your gifts—the sacrifice of your sons in the
20:42 [A] the land I *had* **sworn with uplifted** hand to give to your
23:27 [A] You *will* not **look** on these things **with longing** [+6524] or
23:35 [A] you *must* **bear** the consequences of your lewdness and
23:49 [A] and **bear** the consequences of your sins of idolatry.
26:17 [A] *they will* **take up** a lament concerning you and say to you:
27: 2 [A] "Son of man, **take up** a lament concerning Tyre.
27:32 [A] As they wail and **mourn** [+7806] over you, they will take up
28:12 [A] **take up** a lament concerning the king of Tyre and say to him:
29:15 [F] and *will* never again **exalt itself** above the other nations.
29:19 [A] king of Babylon, and *he will* **carry off** its wealth.
32: 2 [A] **take up** a lament concerning Pharaoh king of Egypt and say
32:24 [A] *They* **bear** their shame with those who go down to the pit.
32:25 [A] *they* **bear** their shame with those who go down to the pit;
32:30 [A] and **bear** their shame with those who go down to the pit.
33:25 [A] still in it and **look** [+6524] to your idols and shed blood,
34:29 [A] victims of famine in the land or **bear** the scorn of the nations.
36: 6 [A] because *you have* **suffered** the scorn of the nations.
36: 7 [A] I **swear with uplifted** hand that the nations around you will
36: 7 [A] hand that the nations around you *will* also **suffer** scorn.
36: 8 [A] will produce branches and fruit **[RPH]** for my people Israel,
36:15 [A] no longer *will you* **suffer** the scorn of the peoples or cause
38:13 [A] to **carry off** silver and gold, to take away livestock
39:10 [A] *They will* not *need to* **gather** wood from the fields or cut it
39:26 [a] *They will* forget [BHS ***bear***; NIV 5960] their shame
43: 5 [A] the Spirit **lifted** me **up** and brought me into the inner court,
44:10 [A] who wandered from me after their idols *must* **bear** the
44:12 [A] therefore I *have* **sworn with uplifted** hand that they must
44:12 [A] hand that *they must* **bear** the consequences of their sin,
44:13 [A] *they must* **bear** the shame of their detestable practices.
45:11 [A] the bath **containing** a tenth of a homer and the ephah a tenth
47:14 [A] Because I **swore with uplifted** hand to give it to your
Da 1:16 [A] So the guard **took away** their choice food and the wine they
8: 3 [A] I looked **up**, and there before me was a ram with two horns,
10: 5 [A] I looked **up** and there before me was a man dressed in linen,
11:12 [C] When the army **is carried off**, the king of the South will be
11:14 [F] The violent men among your own people *will* **rebel** in
Hos 1: 6 [A] of Israel, that *I should* **at all forgive** [+4200+5951] them.
1: 6 [A] of Israel, that *I should* **at all forgive** [+4200+5951] them.
4: 8 [A] sins of my people and **relish** [+448+5883] their wickedness.
5:14 [A] go away; *I will* **carry** them **off**, with no one to rescue them.
13: 1 [A] Ephraim spoke, men trembled; he *was* **exalted** in Israel.
14: 2 [14:3] [A] "**Forgive** all our sins and receive us graciously,
Joel 2:22 [A] The trees *are* **bearing** their fruit; the fig tree and the vine
Am 4: 2 [D] "The time will surely come when you *will be* **taken away**
5: 1 [A] O house of Israel, this lament I **take up** concerning you:
5:26 [A] *You have* **lifted up** the shrine of your king, the pedestal of
6:10 [A] if a relative who is to burn the bodies comes *to* **carry** them
Jnh 1:12 [A] "**Pick** me **up** and throw me into the sea," he replied, "and it
1:15 [A] *they* **took** Jonah and threw him overboard, and the raging sea
Mic 2: 2 [A] They covet fields and seize them, and houses, and **take** them.
2: 4 [A] In that day *men will* **ridicule** [+5442+6584] you; they will
4: 1 [C] it *will* **be raised** above the hills, and peoples will stream to it.
4: 3 [A] Nation *will* not **take up** sword against nation, nor will they
6:16 [A] people to derision; *you will* **bear** the scorn of the nations."
7: 9 [A] *I will* **bear** the LORD's wrath, until he pleads my case
7:18 [A] *who* **pardons** sin and forgives the transgression of the
Na 1: 5 [A] The earth **trembles** at his presence, the world and all who
Hab 1: 3 [A] violence are before me; there is strife, and conflict **abounds**.
2: 6 [A] "*Will* not all of them **taunt** [+4200+5442+6584] him with
3:10 [A] water swept by; the deep roared and **lifted** its waves on high.
Hag 2:12 [A] If a person **carries** consecrated meat in the fold of his
2:19 [A] the pomegranate and the olive tree *have* not **borne fruit**.
Zec 1:18 [2:1] [A] I looked **up**—and there before me were four horns!
1:21 [2:4] [A] scattered Judah so that no one *could* **raise** his head,
1:21 [2:4] [A] throw down these horns of the nations who **lifted up**
2: 1 [2:5] [A] I looked **up**—and there before me was a man with a
5: 1 [A] I **looked** [+6524] again—and there before me was a flying
5: 5 [A] said to me, "Look **up** and see what this is that is appearing."
5: 7 [C] the cover of lead **was raised**, and there in the basket sat a
5: 9 [A] Then I looked **up**—and there before me were two women,
5: 9 [A] and *they* **lifted up** the basket between heaven and earth.
6: 1 [A] I looked **up** again—and there before me were four chariots
6:13 [A] he *will be* **clothed with** majesty and will sit and rule on his
Mal 1: 8 [A] *Would he* **accept** [+7156] you?" says the LORD Almighty.
1: 9 [A] from your hands, *will he* **accept** [+4946+7156] you?"—
2: 3 [A] your festival sacrifices, and you *will be* **carried off** with it.
2: 9 [A] but *have* **shown partiality** [+7156] in matters of the law."

5952 נָשַׂג *nāśag*, v. [50 / 49] [→ 5371]

overtake [14], afford [+3338] [6], overtook [6], catch up [2], certainly overtake [+5952] [2], continue until [2], overtaken [2], prospers [+3338] [2], accompany [1], afford [+3338+4200+4200] [1], attain [1], catch [1], caught up [1], equal [1], move [1], overtaking [1], put [1], reach [1], reaches [1], rich [+3338] [1], wants to give [+3338] [1]

Ge 31:25 [G] tent in the hill country of Gilead when Laban **overtook** him,
44: 4 [G] men at once, and when *you* **catch up** *with* them, say to them,
44: 6 [G] When *he* **caught up** *with* them, he repeated these words to
47: 9 [G] *they do* not **equal** the years of the pilgrimage of my fathers."
Ex 14: 9 [G] **overtook** them as they camped by the sea near Pi Hahiroth,
15: 9 [G] "The enemy boasted, 'I will pursue, *I will* **overtake** them.
Lev 5:11 [G] he cannot **afford** [+3338+4200+4200] two doves or two young
14:21 [G] "If, however, he is poor and cannot **afford** [+3338] these,
14:22 [G] which he *can* **afford** [+3338], one for a sin offering
14:30 [G] or the young pigeons, which the person *can* **afford** [+3338],
14:31 [g] [BHS+ *such as the person can* ***afford***] one as a sin offering
14:32 [G] who cannot **afford** [+3338] the regular offerings for his
25:26 [G] no one to redeem it for him but *he* himself **prospers** [+3338]
25:47 [G] or a temporary resident among you *becomes* **rich** [+3338]
25:49 [G] Or if he **prospers** [+3338], he may redeem himself.
26: 5 [G] Your threshing *will* **continue until** grape harvest
26: 5 [G] and the grape harvest *will* **continue until** planting,
27: 8 [G] to what the man making the vow *can* **afford** [+3338].
Nu 6:21 [G] in addition to whatever else he *can* **afford** [+3338].

Dt 19: 6 [G] him in a rage, **overtake** him if the distance is too great,
28: 2 [G] and **accompany** you if you obey the LORD your God:
28: 15 [G] all these curses will come upon you and **overtake** you:
28: 45 [G] will pursue you and **overtake** you until you are destroyed,
Jos 2: 5 [G] Go after them quickly. *You may* **catch up** *with* them."
1Sa 14: 26 [G] yet no *one* **put** his hand to his mouth, because they feared the
30: 8 [G] *Will I* **overtake** them?" "Pursue them," he answered.
30: 8 [G] "*You will* **certainly overtake** [+5952] them and succeed in
30: 8 [G] "*You will* **certainly overtake** [+5952] them and succeed in
2Sa 15: 14 [G] or he will move quickly *to* **overtake** us and bring ruin upon
2Ki 25: 5 [G] pursued the king and **overtook** him in the plains of Jericho.
1Ch 21: 12 [G] with their swords **overtaking** you, or three days of the sword
Job 24: 2 [G] *Men* **move** boundary stones; they pasture flocks they have
27: 20 [G] Terrors **overtake** him like a flood; a tempest snatches him
41: 26 [41:18] [G] The sword *that* **reaches** him has no effect, nor does
Ps 7: 5 [7:6] [G] let my enemy pursue and **overtake** me; let him
18: 37 [18:38] [G] I pursued my enemies and **overtook** them; I did not
40: 12 [40:13] [G] my sins *have* **overtaken** me, and I cannot see.
69: 24 [69:25] [G] wrath on them; *let* your fierce anger **overtake** them.
Pr 2: 19 [G] None who go to her return or **attain** the paths of life.
Isa 35: 10 [G] Gladness and joy *will* **overtake** them, and sorrow
51: 11 [G] Gladness and joy *will* **overtake** them, and sorrow
59: 9 [G] justice is far from us, and righteousness *does* not **reach** us.
Jer 39: 5 [G] and **overtook** Zedekiah in the plains of Jericho.
42: 16 [G] the sword you fear *will* **overtake** you there, and the famine
52: 8 [G] King Zedekiah and **overtook** him in the plains of Jericho.
La 1: 3 [G] All who pursue her *have* **overtaken** her in the midst of her
Eze 46: 7 [G] and with the lambs as much as he **wants to give** [+3338],
Hos 2: 7 [2:9] [G] She will chase after her lovers but not **catch** them; she
10: 9 [G] *Did* not war **overtake** the evildoers in Gibeah?
Zec 1: 6 [G] *did* not my words and my decrees, which I commanded my servants the prophets, **overtake**

5953 נְשׂוּאָה nᵉśû'â, n.f. [1] [√ 5951]

images that are carried about [1]

Isa 46: 1 The **images that are carried about** are burdensome, a burden for

5954 נָשִׂיא nāśî', n.m. [130 / 131] [√ 5951]

leader [43], leaders [30], prince [29], princes [10], *untranslated* [6], chiefs [3], ruler [3], chief leader [+5954] [2], rulers [2], chief [1], himself[s] [1], they[s] [+2021] [1]

Ge 17: 20 He will be the father of twelve **rulers**, and I will make him into a
23: 6 "Sir, listen to us. You are a mighty **prince** among us. Bury your
25: 16 these are the names of the twelve tribal **rulers** according to their
34: 2 the **ruler** *of* that area, saw her, he took her and violated her.
Ex 16: 22 the **leaders** *of* the community came and reported this to Moses.
22: 28 [22:27] "Do not blaspheme God or curse the **ruler** of your people.
34: 31 so Aaron and all the **leaders** of the community came back to him,
35: 27 The **leaders** brought onyx stones and other gems to be mounted on
Lev 4: 22 " 'When a **leader** sins unintentionally and does what is forbidden
Nu 1: 16 from the community, the **leaders** *of* their ancestral tribes.
1: 44 men counted by Moses and Aaron and the twelve **leaders** *of* Israel,
2: 3 The **leader** of the people of Judah is Nahshon son of Amminadab.
2: 5 The **leader** of the people of Issachar is Nethanel son of Zuar.
2: 7 The **leader** of the people of Zebulun is Eliab son of Helon.
2: 10 The **leader** of the people of Reuben is Elizur son of Shedeur.
2: 12 The **leader** of the people of Simeon is Shelumiel son of
2: 14 The **leader** of the people of Gad is Eliasaph son of Deuel.
2: 18 The **leader** of the people of Ephraim is Elishama son of Ammihud.
2: 20 The **leader** of the people of Manasseh is Gamaliel son of
2: 22 The **leader** of the people of Benjamin is Abidan son of Gideoni.
2: 25 The **leader** of the people of Dan is Ahiezer son of Ammishaddai.
2: 27 The **leader** of the people of Asher is Pagiel son of Ocran.
2: 29 The **leader** of the people of Naphtali is Ahira son of Enan.
3: 24 The **leader** *of* the families of the Gershonites was Eliasaph son of
3: 30 The **leader** *of* the families of the Kohathite clans was Elizaphan
3: 32 The **chief leader** [+5954] *of* the Levites was Eleazar son of Aaron,
3: 32 The **chief leader of** [+5954] the Levites was Eleazar son of Aaron,
3: 35 The **leader** *of* the families of the Merarite clans was Zuriel son of
4: 34 the **leaders** *of* the community counted the Kohathites by their clans
4: 46 and the **leaders** *of* Israel counted all the Levites by their clans
7: 2 the **leaders** *of* Israel, the heads of families who were the tribal
7: 2 the heads of families who were the tribal **leaders** in charge of those
7: 3 twelve oxen—an ox from each **leader** and a cart from every two.
7: 10 the **leaders** brought their offerings for its dedication and presented
7: 10 for its dedication and presented them **[RPH]** before the altar.
7: 11 "Each day one **leader** is to bring his offering for the dedication of
7: 11 "Each day one leader **[RPH]** is to bring his offering for the
7: 18 Nethanel son of Zuar, the **leader** *of* Issachar, brought his offering.
7: 24 third day, Eliab son of Helon, the **leader** of the people of Zebulun,
7: 30 the **leader** of the people of Reuben, brought his offering.
7: 36 the **leader** of the people of Simeon, brought his offering.
7: 42 son of Deuel, the **leader** of the people of Gad, brought his offering.
7: 48 the **leader** of the people of Ephraim, brought his offering.
7: 54 the **leader** of the people of Manasseh, brought his offering.
7: 60 the **leader** of the people of Benjamin, brought his offering.
7: 66 the **leader** of the people of Dan, brought his offering.
7: 72 of Ocran, the **leader** of the people of Asher, brought his offering.
7: 78 the **leader** of the people of Naphtali, brought his offering.
7: 84 These were the offerings of the Israelite **leaders** for the dedication
10: 4 If only one is sounded, the **leaders**—the heads of the clans of
13: 2 to the Israelites. From each ancestral tribe send one of its **leaders**."
16: 2 well-known community **leaders** who had been appointed members
17: 2 [17:17] one from the **leader** *of* each of their ancestral tribes.
17: 6 [17:21] to the Israelites, and their **leaders** gave him twelve staffs,
17: 6 [17:21] one for the **leader** of each of their ancestral tribes, and
17: 6 [17:21] **[RPH]** and Aaron's staff was among them.
25: 14 woman was Zimri son of Salu, the **leader** of a Simeonite family.
25: 18 and their sister Cozbi, the daughter of a Midianite **leader**,
27: 2 Eleazar the priest, the **leaders** and the whole assembly, and said,
31: 13 all the **leaders** *of* the community went to meet them outside the
32: 2 and Eleazar the priest and to the **leaders** *of* the community,
34: 18 And appoint one **leader** from each tribe to help assign the land.
34: 18 appoint one leader **[RPH]** from each tribe to help assign the land.
34: 22 Bukki son of Jogli, the **leader** from the tribe of Dan;
34: 23 son of Ephod, the **leader** from the tribe of Manasseh son of Joseph;
34: 24 of Shiphtan, the **leader** from the tribe of Ephraim son of Joseph;
34: 25 Elizaphan son of Parnach, the **leader** from the tribe of Zebulun;
34: 26 Paltiel son of Azzan, the **leader** from the tribe of Issachar;
34: 27 Ahihud son of Shelomi, the **leader** from the tribe of Asher;
34: 28 Pedahel son of Ammihud, the **leader** from the tribe of Naphtali."
36: 1 came and spoke before Moses and the **leaders**, the heads of the
Jos 9: 15 to let them live, and the **leaders** *of* the assembly ratified it by oath.
9: 18 because the **leaders** *of* the assembly had sworn an oath to them by
9: 18 God of Israel. The whole assembly grumbled against the **leaders**,
9: 19 all the **leaders** answered, "We have given them our oath by the
9: 21 **They**[s] [+2021] continued, "Let them live, but let them be
9: 21 the entire community." So the **leaders**' promise to them was kept.
13: 21 Moses had defeated him and the Midianite **chiefs**, Evi, Rekem,
17: 4 to Eleazar the priest, Joshua son of Nun, and the **leaders** and said,
22: 14 With him they sent ten of the **chief** *men*, one for each of the tribes
22: 14 ten of the chief men, one **[RPH]** for each of the tribes of Israel,
22: 14 ten of the chief men, one **[RPH]** for each of the tribes of Israel,
22: 30 When Phinehas the priest and the **leaders** *of* the community—
22: 32 the **leaders** returned to Canaan from their meeting with the
1Ki 8: 1 all the heads of the tribes and the **chiefs** of the Israelite families,
11: 34 I have made him **ruler** all the days of his life for the sake of David
1Ch 2: 10 the father of Nahshon, the **leader** *of* the people of Judah.
4: 38 The men listed above by name were **leaders** of their clans.
5: 6 of Assyria took into exile. Beerah was a **leader** of the Reubenites.
7: 40 of families, choice men, brave warriors and outstanding **leaders**.
2Ch 1: 2 to the judges and to all the **leaders** in Israel, the heads of families—
5: 2 all the heads of the tribes and the **chiefs** of the Israelite families,
Ezr 1: 8 who counted them out to Sheshbazzar the **prince** of Judah.
Eze 7: 27 The king will mourn, the **prince** will be clothed with despair,
12: 10 This oracle concerns the **prince** in Jerusalem and the whole house
12: 12 "The **prince** among them will put his things on his shoulder at
19: 1 "Take up a lament concerning the **princes** *of* Israel
21: 12 [21:17] is against my people; it is against all the **princes** *of* Israel.
21: 25 [21:30] " 'O profane and wicked **prince** *of* Israel, whose day has
22: 6 " 'See how each of the **princes** *of* Israel who are in you uses his
22: 25 There is a conspiracy of her **princes** [BHS 5566] within her like a
26: 16 Then all the **princes** *of* the coast will step down from their thrones
27: 21 " 'Arabia and all the **princes** *of* Kedar were your customers;
30: 13 No longer will there be a **prince** in Egypt, and I will spread fear
32: 29 "Edom is there, her kings and all her **princes**; despite their power,
34: 24 be their God, and my servant David will be **prince** among them.
37: 25 there forever, and David my servant will be their **prince** forever.
38: 2 of the land of Magog, the chief **prince** *of* Meshech and Tubal;
38: 3 I am against you, O Gog, chief **prince** *of* Meshech and Tubal.
39: 1 I am against you, O Gog, chief **prince** *of* Meshech and Tubal.
39: 18 and drink the blood of the **princes** *of* the earth as if they were rams
44: 3 The **prince** himself is the only one who may sit inside the gateway
44: 3 The prince **himself**[s] is the only one who may sit inside the gateway
45: 7 " 'The **prince** will have the land bordering each side of the area
45: 8 my **princes** will no longer oppress my people but will allow the
45: 9 You have gone far enough, O **princes** *of* Israel! Give up your
45: 16 participate in this special gift for the use of the **prince** in Israel.
45: 17 It will be the duty of the **prince** to provide the burnt offerings,
45: 22 On that day the **prince** is to provide a bull as a sin offering for
46: 2 The **prince** is to enter from the outside through the portico of the
46: 4 The burnt offering the **prince** brings to the LORD on the Sabbath
46: 8 When the **prince** enters, he is to go in through the portico of the
46: 10 The **prince** is to be among them, going in when they go in
46: 12 When the **prince** provides a freewill offering to the LORD—
46: 16 If the **prince** makes a gift from his inheritance to one of his sons,

Eze 46:17 keep it until the year of freedom; then it will revert to the **prince**.
46:18 The **prince** must not take any of the inheritance of the people,
48:21 the sacred portion and the city property will belong to the **prince**.
48:21 running the length of the tribal portions will belong to the **prince**,
48:22 the city will lie in the center of the area that belongs to the **prince**.
48:22 The area belonging to the **prince** will lie between the border of

5955 ²נָשִׂיא **nāśî'²**, n.[m.]. [4] [√ 5951]

clouds [4]

Ps 135:7 He makes **clouds** rise from the ends of the earth; he sends lightning
Pr 25:14 Like **clouds** and wind without rain is a man who boasts of gifts he
Jer 10:13 the heavens roar; he makes **clouds** rise from the ends of the earth.
51:16 the heavens roar; he makes **clouds** rise from the ends of the earth.

5956 נָשַׂק **nāśaq**, v. [3] [cf. 8519]

broke out [1], burn up [1], kindles a fire [1]

Ps 78:21 [C] his fire **broke out** against Jacob, and his wrath rose against
Isa 44:15 [G] and warms himself, *he* **kindles a fire** and bakes bread.
Eze 39:9 [G] **burn** them **up**—the small and large shields, the bows and

5957 ¹נָשָׁא **nāšā'¹**, v. [18] [→ 5391, 5394, 5408, 5963; cf. 5961, 5968, 8735]

creditor [3], required [+460+928] [2], borrowed [+928] [1], creditors [1], debtor [+928] [1], exacting [1], in debt [+4200] [1], lending [1], lent [1], loan made [1], make a loan [+5394] [1], making loan [1], moneylender [1], subject to tribute [1], usury charging [1]

Ex 22:25 [22:24] [A] you who is needy, do not be like a **moneylender**;
Dt 15:2 [G] Every creditor shall cancel *the* **loan** *he has* **made** to his
24:10 [G] When *you* **make a loan** [+5394] of any kind to your
24:11 [A] let the man to whom you *are* **making** *the* **loan** bring the
1Sa 22:2 [A] All those who were in distress or **in debt** [+4200] or
1Ki 8:31 [A] and *is* **required** [+460+928] to take an oath and he comes
2Ki 4:1 [A] now his **creditor** is coming to take my two boys as his
2Ch 6:22 [A] and *is* **required** [+460+928] to take an oath and he comes
Ne 5:7 [A] "You *are* **exacting** usury from your own countrymen!"
5:10 [A] and my men *are* also **lending** the people money and grain.
5:11 [A] and houses, and also *the* **usury** you *are* **charging** them—
Ps 89:22 [89:23] [G] No enemy *will* **subject** him **to tribute**; no wicked
109:11 [A] May a **creditor** seize all he has; may strangers plunder the
Isa 24:2 [A] for borrower as for lender, for **debtor** [+928] as for creditor.
24:2 [A] for borrower as for lender, for debtor as for **creditor**.
50:1 [A] Or to which of my **creditors** did I sell you? Because of your
Jer 15:10 [A] *I have* neither **lent** nor borrowed, yet everyone curses me.
15:10 [A] I have neither lent nor **borrowed** [+928], yet everyone curses

5958 ²נָשָׁא **nāšā'²**, v. [15] [→ 5395, 5396, 5410; cf. 8735]

deceive [5], deceived [3], let deceive [3], completely deceived [+4200+4200+5958] [2], are deceived [1], take by surprise [1]

Ge 3:13 [G] The woman said, "The serpent **deceived** me, and I ate."
2Ki 18:29 [G] This is what the king says: *Do* not **let** Hezekiah **deceive** you.
19:10 [G] *Do* not **let** the god you depend on **deceive** you when he says,
2Ch 32:15 [G] Now *do* not *let* Hezekiah **deceive** you and mislead you like
Ps 55:15 [55:16] [G] *Let* death **take** my enemies **by surprise**; [K 3812]
Isa 19:13 [C] have become fools, the leaders of Memphis **are deceived**;
36:14 [G] *Do* not **let** Hezekiah **deceive** you. He cannot deliver you!
37:10 [G] Do not let the god you depend on **deceive** you when he says,
Jer 4:10 [G] how **completely** *you have* **deceived** [+4200+4200+5958] this
4:10 [G] how **completely** *you have* **deceived** [+4200+4200+5958] this
29:8 [G] "*Do* not *let* the prophets and diviners among you **deceive**
37:9 [G] *Do* not **deceive** yourselves, thinking, 'The Babylonians will
49:16 [G] you inspire and the pride of your heart *have* **deceived** you,
Ob 1:3 [G] The pride of your heart *has* **deceived** you, you who live in
1:7 [G] to the border; your friends *will* **deceive** and overpower you;

5959 נָשַׁב **nāšab**, v. [3] [√ 876; cf. 5971, 5973]

blows [1], drove away [1], stirs up [1]

Ge 15:11 [G] came down on the carcasses, but Abram **drove** them **away**.
Ps 147:18 [G] and melts them; *he* **stirs up** his breezes, and the waters flow.
Isa 40:7 [A] because the breath of the LORD **blows** on them.

5960 ¹נָשָׁה **nāšâ¹**, v. [7 / 9] [→ 4985, 4986, 5964; cf. 8861]

forget [3], forgotten [2], surely forget [+906+5960] [2], made forget [1], not endow [1]

Ge 41:51 [D] because God *has* **made** me **forget** all my trouble and all my
Job 11:6 [G] Know this: God *has* even **forgotten** some of your sin.
39:17 [G] for God *did* **not endow** her *with* wisdom or give her a share
Isa 44:21 [C] you are my servant; O Israel, I *will* not **forget** *you*.
Jer 23:39 [A] I *will* **surely forget** [+906+5960] you and cast you out of my
23:39 [A] I *will* **surely forget** [+906+5960] you and cast you out of my
La 3:17 [A] been deprived of peace; *I have* **forgotten** what prosperity is.
Eze 39:26 [a] *They will* **forget** [BHS 5951] their shame and all the
Mic 6:10 [a] *Am I* still *to* **forget**, [BHS 838] O wicked house,

5961 ²נָשָׁה **nāšâ²**, v. Not used in NIV/BHS [cf. 5957]

5962 נָשֶׁה **nāšeh**, n.[m.]. [2]

tendon [+1630] [2]

Ge 32:32 [32:33] eat the **tendon** [+1630] attached to the socket of the hip,
32:32 [32:33] of Jacob's hip was touched near the **tendon** [+1630].

5963 נְשִׁי **nešî**, n.[m.]. [1] [√ 5957]

debts [1]

2Ki 4:7 the man of God, and he said, "Go, sell the oil and pay your **debts**.

5964 נְשִׁיָּה **nešiyyâ**, n.f. [1] [√ 5960]

oblivion [1]

Ps 88:12 [88:13] or your righteous deeds in the land of **oblivion**?

5965 נְשִׁיקָה **nešîqâ**, n.f. [2] [√ 5975]

kisses [2]

Pr 27:6 from a friend can be trusted, but an enemy multiplies **kisses**.
SS 1:2 Let him kiss me with the **kisses** *of* his mouth—for your love is

5966 ¹נָשַׁךְ **nāšak¹**, v. [11] [cf. 5968]

bite [3], bites [3], bitten [2], bit [1], feeds [+928+9094] [1], is bitten [1]

Ge 49:17 [A] that **bites** the horse's heels so that its rider tumbles backward.
Nu 21:6 [D] among them; *they* **bit** the people and many Israelites died.
21:8 [B] it up on a pole; anyone who **is bitten** can look at it and live."
21:9 [A] when anyone *was* **bitten** *by* a snake and looked at the bronze
Pr 23:32 [A] In the end *it* **bites** like a snake and poisons like a viper.
Ecc 10:8 [A] whoever breaks through a wall *may be* **bitten** *by* a snake.
10:11 [A] If a snake **bites** before it is charmed, there is no profit for the
Jer 8:17 [D] be charmed, and *they will* **bite** you," declares the LORD.
Am 5:19 [A] rested his hand on the wall only to have a snake **bite** him.
9:3 [A] of the sea, there I will command the serpent *to* **bite** them.
Mic 3:5 [A] if one **feeds** [+928+9094] them, they proclaim 'peace';

5967 ²נָשַׁךְ **nāšak²**, v.den. [5] [√ 5968]

untranslated [1], charge interest [+4200+5968] [1], charge interest [1], debtors [1], earn interest [1]

Dt 23:19 [23:20] [G] *Do* not **charge** your brother **interest** [+4200+5968],
23:19 [23:20] [A] or food or anything else that *may* **earn interest**.
23:20 [23:21] [G] *You may* **charge** a foreigner **interest**, but not a
23:20 [23:21] [G] but not **[RPH]** a brother Israelite,
Hab 2:7 [A] Will not your **debtors** suddenly arise? Will they not wake up

5968 נֶשֶׁךְ **nešek**, n.[m.]. [12] [→ 5967; cf. 5957, 5966]

usury [5], *untranslated* [2], interest [2], charge interest [+4200+5967] [1], exorbitant interest [+2256+9552] [1], interest of any kind [+2256+9552] [1]

Ex 22:25 [22:24] do not be like a moneylender; charge him no **interest**.
Lev 25:36 Do not take **interest** [+2256+9552] **of any kind** from him,
25:37 You must not lend him money at **interest** or sell him food at a
Dt 23:19 [23:20] *Do* not **charge** your brother **interest** [+4200+5967],
23:19 [23:20] whether on money or **[RPH]** food or anything else that
23:19 [23:20] or food or **[RPH]** anything else that may earn interest.
Ps 15:5 who lends his money without **usury** and does not accept a bribe
Pr 28:8 He who increases his wealth by **exorbitant interest** [+2256+9552]
Eze 18:8 He does not lend at **usury** or take excessive interest. He withholds
18:13 He lends at **usury** and takes excessive interest. Will such a man
18:17 his hand from sin and takes no **usury** or excessive interest.
22:12 you take **usury** and excessive interest and make unjust gain from

5969 נִשְׁכָּה **niškâ**, n.f. [3] [cf. 4384]

living quarters [1], room [1], storerooms [+238+4200] [1]

Ne 3:30 son of Berekiah made repairs opposite his **living quarters**.
12:44 appointed to be in charge of the **storerooms** [+238+4200] for the
13:7 in providing Tobiah a **room** in the courts of the house of God.

5970 נָשַׁל **nāšal**, v. [7]

take off [2], drive out [1], drives out [1], driving out [1], drop off [1], fly off [1]

Ex 3:5 [A] "**Take off** your sandals, for the place where you are standing
Dt 7:1 [A] entering to possess and **drives out** before you many nations—
7:22 [A] The LORD your God *will* **drive out** those nations before
19:5 [A] a tree, the head *may* **fly off** and hit his neighbor and kill him.

Dt 28:40 [A] but you will not use the oil, because the olives *will* **drop off.**
Jos 5:15 [A] "**Take off** your sandals, for the place where you are standing
2Ki 16:6 [D] recovered Elath for Aram *by* **driving out** the men of Judah.

5971 נָשַׁם nāšam, v. [1] [→ 5972, 9491, 9492; cf. 5959, 5973]
gasp [1]

Isa 42:14 [A] like a woman in childbirth, I cry out, *I* **gasp** and pant.

5972 נְשָׁמָה nᵉšāmâ, n.f. [24] [√ 5971; Ar 10494]
breath [11], breathed [4], blast [2], spirit [2], breath [+8120] [1], breathes [1], breathing [1], can hardly breathe [+928+4202+8636] [1], life [1]

Ge 2:7 dust of the ground and breathed into his nostrils the **breath** *of* life,
7:22 Everything on dry land that had the **breath** [+8120] *of* life in its
Dt 20:16 you as an inheritance, do not leave alive anything that **breathes.**
Jos 10:40 He totally destroyed all who **breathed,** just as the LORD,
11:11 They totally destroyed them, not sparing anything that **breathed,**
11:14 they completely destroyed them, not sparing anyone that **breathed.**
2Sa 22:16 the rebuke of the LORD, at the **blast** *of* breath from his nostrils.
1Ki 15:29 He did not leave Jeroboam anyone that **breathed,** but destroyed
17:17 He grew worse and worse, and finally stopped **breathing.**
Job 4:9 At the **breath** *of* God they are destroyed; at the blast of his anger
26:4 you utter these words? And whose **spirit** spoke from your mouth?
27:3 as long as I have **life** within me, the breath of God in my nostrils,
32:8 it is the spirit in a man, the **breath** *of* the Almighty, that gives him
33:4 of God has made me; the **breath** *of* the Almighty gives me life.
34:14 If it were his intention and he withdrew his spirit and **breath,**
37:10 The **breath** *of* God produces ice, and the broad waters become
Ps 18:15 [18:16] O LORD, at the **blast** *of* breath from your nostrils.
150:6 Let everything that has **breath** praise the LORD.
Pr 20:27 The lamp of the LORD searches the **spirit** *of* a man; it searches
Isa 2:22 Stop trusting in man, who has but a **breath** in his nostrils.
30:33 the **breath** *of* the LORD, like a stream of burning sulfur,
42:5 and all that comes out of it, who gives **breath** to its people,
57:16 grow faint before me—the **breath** of man that I have created.
Da 10:17 My strength is gone and I **can hardly breathe** [+928+4202+8636]."

5973 נָשַׁף nāšap, v. [2] [→ 3568, 5974; cf. 5959, 5971]
blew [1], blows [1]

Ex 15:10 [A] But *you* **blew** with your breath, and the sea covered them.
Isa 40:24 [A] root in the ground, than *he* **blows** on them and they wither,

5974 נֶשֶׁף nešep, n.m. [12] [√ 5973]
dusk [4], twilight [3], dawn [2], darkening [1], morning [1], night [1]

1Sa 30:17 David fought them from **dusk** until the evening of the next day,
2Ki 7:5 At **dusk** they got up and went to the camp of the Arameans.
7:7 So they got up and fled in the **dusk** and abandoned their tents
Job 3:9 May its **morning** stars become dark; may it wait for daylight in
7:4 long before I get up?' The night drags on, and I toss till **dawn.**
24:15 The eye of the adulterer watches for **dusk;** he thinks, 'No eye will
Ps 119:147 I rise before **dawn** and cry for help; I have put my hope in your
Pr 7:9 at **twilight,** as the day was fading, as the dark of night set in.
Isa 5:11 who stay up late at **night** till they are inflamed with wine.
21:4 me tremble; the **twilight** I longed for has become a horror to me.
59:10 At midday we stumble as if it were **twilight;** among the strong,
Jer 13:16 the darkness, before your feet stumble on the **darkening** hills.

5975 נָשַׁק nāšaq¹, v. [30] [→ 5965]
kissed [17], kiss [9], kiss good-by [2], kissed good-by [1], offered a kiss of homage [+4200+7023] [1]

Ge 27:26 [A] father Isaac said to him, "Come here, my son, and **kiss** me."
27:27 [A] So he went to him and **kissed** him. When Isaac caught the
29:11 [A] Then Jacob **kissed** Rachel and began to weep aloud.
29:13 [D] He embraced him and **kissed** him and brought him to his
31:28 [D] let me **kiss** my grandchildren and my daughters **good-by.**
31:55 [32:1] [D] the next morning Laban **kissed** his grandchildren and
33:4 [A] he threw his arms around his neck and **kissed** him.
45:15 [D] *he* **kissed** all his brothers and wept over them. Afterward his
48:10 [A] close to him, and his father **kissed** them and embraced them.
50:1 [A] himself upon his father and wept over him and **kissed** him.
Ex 4:27 [A] So he met Moses at the mountain of God and **kissed** him.
18:7 [A] to meet his father-in-law and bowed down and **kissed** him.
Ru 1:9 [A] Then *she* **kissed** them and they wept aloud
1:14 [A] Orpah **kissed** her mother-in-law **good-by,** but Ruth clung to
1Sa 10:1 [A] a flask of oil and poured it on Saul's head and **kissed** him,
20:41 [A] *they* **kissed** each other and wept together—but David wept
2Sa 14:33 [A] to the ground before the king. And the king **kissed** Absalom.
15:5 [A] would reach out his hand, take hold of him and **kiss** him.
19:39 [19:40] [A] The king **kissed** Barzillai and gave him his blessing,
20:9 [A] Joab took Amasa by the beard with his right hand to **kiss**
1Ki 19:18 [A] down to Baal and all whose mouths *have* not **kissed** him."
19:20 [A] "*Let me* **kiss** my father and mother **good-by,**" he said, "and
Job 31:27 [A] and my hand **offered** them **a kiss** [+4200+7023] **of homage,**
Ps 2:12 [D] **Kiss** the Son, lest he be angry and you be destroyed in your
85:10 [85:11] [A] righteousness and peace **kiss** *each other.*
Pr 7:13 [A] She took hold of him and **kissed** him and with a brazen face
24:26 [A] An honest answer *is* like *a* **kiss** *on* the lips.
SS 1:2 [A] *Let him* **kiss** me with the kisses of his mouth—for your love
8:1 [A] Then, if I found you outside, *I would* **kiss** you, and no one
Hos 13:2 [A] "They offer human sacrifice and **kiss** the calf-idols."

5976 ²נָשַׁק nāšaq², v. [5] [√ 5977]
armed [2], armed [+8227] [1], brushing [1], submit [1]

Ge 41:40 [A] of my palace, and all my people are *to* **submit** to your orders.
1Ch 12:2 [A] *they were* **armed** *with* bows and were able to shoot arrows
2Ch 17:17 [A] with 200,000 *men* **armed** *with* bows and shields;
Ps 78:9 [A] The men of Ephraim, though **armed** [+8227] *with* bows,
Eze 3:13 [G] the sound of the wings of the living creatures **brushing**

5977 ¹נֶשֶׁק nešeq¹, n.[m.]. [10] [→ 5976]
weapons [6], armory [1], battle [1], fray [1], weapon [1]

1Ki 10:25 articles of silver and gold, robes, **weapons** and spices, and horses
2Ki 10:2 and you have chariots and horses, a fortified city and **weapons,**
2Ch 9:24 articles of silver and gold, and robes, **weapons** and spices,
Ne 3:19 from a point facing the ascent to the **armory** as far as the angle.
Job 20:24 Though he flees from an iron **weapon,** a bronze-tipped arrow
39:21 paws fiercely, rejoicing in his strength, and charges into the **fray.**
Ps 140:7 [140:8] who shields my head in the day of **battle**—
Isa 22:8 you looked in that day to the **weapons** *in* the Palace of the Forest;
Eze 39:9 Israel will go out and use the **weapons** for fuel and burn them up—
39:10 cut it from the forests, because they will use the **weapons** for fuel.

5978 ²נֶשֶׁק nešeq², n.[m.]. Not used in NIV/BHS

5979 נֶשֶׁר nešer, n.m. [26] [→ Ar 10495]
eagle [15], eagles [6], eagle's [2], vulture [2], vultures [+1201] [1]

Ex 19:4 and how I carried you on **eagles'** wings and brought you to myself.
Lev 11:13 they are detestable: the **eagle,** the vulture, the black vulture,
Dt 14:12 But these you may not eat: the **eagle,** the vulture, the black vulture,
28:49 from the ends of the earth, like an **eagle** swooping down, a nation
32:11 like an **eagle** that stirs up its nest and hovers over its young,
2Sa 1:23 They were swifter than **eagles,** they were stronger than lions.
Job 9:26 like boats of papyrus, like **eagles** swooping down on their prey.
39:27 Does the **eagle** soar at your command and build his nest on high?
Ps 103:5 with good things so that your youth is renewed like the **eagle's.**
Pr 23:5 they will surely sprout wings and fly off to the sky like an **eagle.**
30:17 by the ravens of the valley, will be eaten by the **vultures** [+1201].
30:19 the way of an **eagle** in the sky, the way of a snake on a rock,
Isa 40:31 They will soar on wings like **eagles;** they will run and not grow
Jer 4:13 chariots come like a whirlwind, his horses are swifter than **eagles.**
48:40 An **eagle** is swooping down, spreading its wings over Moab.
49:16 Though you build your nest as high as the **eagle's,** from there I will
49:22 An **eagle** will soar and swoop down, spreading its wings over
La 4:19 Our pursuers were swifter than **eagles** *in* the sky; they chased us
Eze 1:10 and on the left the face of an ox; each also had the face of an **eagle.**
10:14 the third the face of a lion, and the fourth the face of an **eagle.**
17:3 A great **eagle** with powerful wings, long feathers and full plumage
17:7 " 'But there was another great **eagle** with powerful wings and full
Hos 8:1 An **eagle** is over the house of the LORD because the people have
Ob 1:4 Though you soar like the **eagle** and make your nest among the
Mic 1:16 make yourselves as bald as the **vulture,** for they will go from you
Hab 1:8 come from afar. They fly like a **vulture** swooping to devour;

5980 נָשַׁת nāšat, v. [3 / 4]
cease [1], dry up [1], exhausted [1], parched [1]

Isa 19:5 [C] The waters of the river *will* **dry up,** and the riverbed will be
41:17 [A] but there is none; their tongues *are* **parched** with thirst.
Jer 18:14 [c] *Do* its cool waters from distant sources *ever* **cease** [BHS 6004]
51:30 [A] Their strength *is* **exhausted;** they have become like women.

5981 נִשְׁתְּוָן ništᵉwān, n.[m.]. [5] [→ Ar 10496]
letter [4], written reply [1]

Ezr 4:7 The **letter** was written in Aramaic script and in the Aramaic
4:18 The **letter** you sent us has been read and translated in my presence.
4:23 As soon as the copy of the **letter** of King Artaxerxes was read to
5:5 until a report could go to Darius and his **written reply** be received.
7:11 This is a copy of the **letter** King Artaxerxes had given to Ezra the

5982 נְתוּנִים nᵉtûnîm, v.ptcp. *or* n.m.[pl.]. Not used in NIV/BHS [√ 5987; cf. 5989]

5983 נָתַח nātaḥ, v. [9] [→ 5984]

cut into pieces [4], cut [4], cut up [1]

Ex 29:17 [D] **Cut** the ram into pieces and wash the inner parts and the legs,
Lev 1: 6 [D] He is to skin the burnt offering and **cut** it into pieces.
1:12 [D] *He is to* **cut** it into pieces, and the priest shall arrange them,
8:20 [D] *He* **cut** the ram into pieces and burned the head, the pieces
Jdg 19:29 [D] he took a knife and **cut up** his concubine, limb by limb, into
20: 6 [D] **cut** her **into pieces** and sent one piece to each region of
1Sa 11: 7 [D] He took a pair of oxen, **cut** them **into pieces**, and sent the
1Ki 18:23 [D] *let them* **cut** it **into pieces** and put it on the wood but not set
18:33 [D] the wood, **cut** the bull **into pieces** and laid it on the wood.

5984 נֵתַח nētaḥ, n.m. [13] [√ 5983]

pieces [8], piece [2], parts [1], piece by piece [+4200] [1], pieces of meat [1]

Ex 29:17 Cut the ram into **pieces** and wash the inner parts and the legs,
29:17 and the legs, putting them with the head and the *other* **pieces**.
Lev 1: 6 He is to skin the burnt offering and cut it into **pieces**.
1: 8 Aaron's sons the priests shall arrange the **pieces**, including the
1:12 He is to cut it into **pieces**, and the priest shall arrange them,
8:20 He cut the ram into **pieces** and burned the head, the pieces
8:20 cut the ram into pieces and burned the head, the **pieces** and the fat.
9:13 They handed him the burnt offering **piece by piece** [+4200],
Jdg 19:29 into twelve **parts** and sent them into all the areas of Israel.
Eze 24: 4 Put into it the **pieces of meat**, all the choice pieces—the leg
24: 4 Put into it the pieces of meat, all the choice **pieces**—the leg
24: 6 not go away! Empty it **piece** by piece without casting lots for them.
24: 6 not go away! Empty it piece by **piece** without casting lots for them.

5985 נָתִיב nātîb, n.m. [5] [→ 5986]

path [3], hidden path [1], wake [1]

Job 18:10 A noose is hidden for him on the ground; a trap lies in his **path**.
28: 7 No bird of prey knows that **hidden path**, no falcon's eye has seen
41:32 [41:24] Behind him he leaves a glistening **wake**; one would think
Ps 78:50 He prepared a **path** for his anger; he did not spare them from death
119:35 Direct me in the **path** *of* your commands, for there I find delight.

5986 נְתִיבָה nᵉtîbâ, n.f. [21] [√ 5985]

paths [11], path [3], way [2], bypaths [1], road [1], roads [1], streets [1], travelers [+2143] [1]

Jdg 5: 6 roads were abandoned; **travelers** [+2143] took to winding paths.
Job 19: 8 my way so I cannot pass; he has shrouded my **paths** in darkness.
24:13 against the light, who do not know its ways or stay in its **paths**.
30:13 They break up my **road**; they succeed in destroying me—
38:20 them to their places? Do you know the **paths** *to* their dwellings?
Ps 119:105 Your word is a lamp to my feet and a light for my **path**.
142: 3 [142:4] spirit grows faint within me, it is you who know my **way**.
Pr 1:15 my son, do not go along with them, do not set foot on their **paths**;
3:17 Her ways are pleasant ways, and all her **paths** are peace.
7:25 Do not let your heart turn to her ways or stray into her **paths**.
8: 2 heights along the way, where the **paths** meet, she takes her stand;
8:20 I walk in the way of righteousness, along the **paths** *of* justice,
12:28 way of righteousness there is life; along that **path** is immortality.
Isa 42:16 they have not known, along unfamiliar **paths** I will guide them;
43:16 made a way through the sea, a **path** through the mighty waters,
58:12 Repairer of Broken Walls, Restorer of **Streets** with Dwellings.
59: 8 They have turned them into crooked **roads**; no one who walks in
Jer 6:16 ask for the ancient **paths**, ask where the good way is, and walk in
18:15 They made them walk in **bypaths** and on roads not built up.
La 3: 9 my way with blocks of stone; he has made my **paths** crooked.
Hos 2: 6 [2:8] I will wall her in so that she cannot find her **way**.

5987 נָתִין nātîn, n.m. [17] [→ 5982; cf. 5989; Ar 10497]

temple servants [15], *untranslated* [1], themˢ [+2021] [1]

1Ch 9: 2 towns were some Israelites, priests, Levites and **temple servants**.
Ezr 2:43 The **temple servants**: the descendants of Ziha, Hasupha, Tabbaoth,
2:58 The **temple servants** and the descendants of the servants of
2:70 and the **temple servants** settled in their own towns,
7: 7 Levites, singers, gatekeepers and **temple servants**,
8:17 and his kinsmen, the **temple servants** [K 5989] in Casiphia,
8:20 They also brought 220 of the **temple servants**—a body that David
8:20 to assist the Levites. **[RPH]** All were registered by name.
Ne 3:26 the **temple servants** living on the hill of Ophel made repairs up to
3:31 made repairs as far as the house of the **temple servants**
7:46 The **temple servants**: the descendants of Ziha, Hasupha, Tabbaoth,
7:60 The **temple servants** and the descendants of the servants of
7:73 [7:72] the gatekeepers, the singers and the **temple servants**,
10:28 [10:29] **temple servants** and all who separated themselves from
11: 3 **temple servants** and descendants of Solomon's servants lived in
11:21 The **temple servants** lived on the hill of Ophel, and Ziha
11:21 of Ophel, and Ziha and Gishpa were in charge of **them**ˢ [+2021].

5988 נָתַךְ nātak, v. [21] [→ 2247]

poured out [7], be melted [3], melt [2], paid out [2], pour out [2], poured down [2], be poured out [1], been poured out [1], is poured out [1]

Ex 9:33 [C] and the rain no *longer* **poured down** on the land.
2Sa 21:10 [C] From the beginning of the harvest till the rain **poured down**
2Ki 22: 9 [G] "Your officials *have* **paid out** the money that was in the
2Ch 12: 7 [A] My wrath *will* not *be* **poured out** on Jerusalem through
34:17 [G] *They have* **paid out** the money that was in the temple of the
34:21 [C] Great is the LORD's anger that **is poured out** on us
34:25 [A] my anger *will be* **poured out** on this place and will not be
Job 3:24 [A] comes to me instead of food; my groans **pour out** like water.
10:10 [G] *Did you* not **pour** me **out** like milk and curdle me like
Jer 7:20 [C] My anger and my wrath *will* **be poured out** on this place,
42:18 [C] wrath *have* **been poured out** on those who lived in
42:18 [A] so *will* my wrath *be* **poured out** on you when you go to
44: 6 [A] Therefore, my fierce anger *was* **poured out**; it raged against
Eze 22:20 [G] iron, lead and tin into a furnace to **melt** it with a fiery blast,
22:20 [G] and my wrath and put you inside the city and **melt** you.
22:21 [C] you with my fiery wrath, and *you will* **be melted** inside her.
22:22 [H] is melted in a furnace, so *you will* **be melted** inside her,
24:11 [C] its copper glows so its impurities *may* **be melted** and its
Da 9:11 [A] the servant of God, *have been* **poured out** on us, because we
9:27 [A] until the end that is decreed *is* **poured out** on him."
Na 1: 6 [C] His wrath *is* **poured out** like fire; the rocks are shattered

5989 נָתַן nātan, v. [2012] [→ 921, 924, 925, 5508, 5509, 5510, 5511, 5522, 5523, 5987, 5990; cf. 3852, 4501, 5621; Ar 10498; *also used with compound proper names*]

give [344], gave [231], put [169], given [147], giving [58], make [55], gives [45], made [37], set [36], *untranslated* [29], placed [23], let [19], be given [18], hand over [+906+928+3338] [18], grant [14], hand over [+928+3338] [14], pay [14], place [14], handed over [+928+3338] [13], yield [13], bring [12], delivered [12], granted [11], appointed [10], if only [+4769] [9], send [9], spread [9], assigned [8], be handed over [+928+3338] [8], entrusted [8], hand over [8], oh [+4769] [8], deliver [7], exchanged [7], give over [7], handed over [+906+928+3338] [7], sent [7], lay [6], offered [6], repay [6], sell [6], allow [5], attach [5], gave in marriage [+851+906+4200] [5], get [5], give in marriage [+851+906+4200] [5], give in marriage [5], give up [5], paid [5], set up [5], show [5], take [5], allowed [4], be given wholly [+5989] [4], been given [4], bring down [4], certainly be handed over [+928+3338+5989] [4], fasten [4], fastened [4], gave over [4], makes [4], offer [4], provide [4], provided [4], provides [4], setting [4], thunders [+7754] [4], was given [4], applied [3], attached [3], bringing down [3], brought [3], cause [3], caused [3], deal [3], establish [3], give back [3], laid [3], paying [3], produce [3], resounded [3], stationed [3], surrender [3], treat [3], turn [3], turned [3], was issued [3], appoint [2], are given [2], are laid [2], are [2], attaching [2], avenges [+4200+5935] [2], be issued [2], been put [2], bestows [2], causes [2], contributed [2], dedicated [2], deliver [+906+5989] [2], deliver over [2], delivered over [2], delivers [2], direct [2], distributing [2], do [2], doˢ so [2], entrust [2], established [2], gifts [2], give [+906+5989] [2], give generously [+5989] [2], given over [2], glad to give [+5989] [2], hand over [+906+906+906+906 +928+3338] [2], handed over [+906+906+906+928+3338] [2], handed over [2], hang [2], is given [2], kept [2], left [2], lend [2], lends [2], lifting [2], made turn [2], maintain [2], making [2], must certainly give [+4200+5989] [2], permit [2], presented [2], prevent [+1194] [2], proclaim [2], providing [2], puts [2], putting [2], raised [2], received [2], reported [2], reward [2], surely hand over [+906+928+3338 +5989] [2], thrown [2], thunder [+7754] [2], turn into [2], turn over [2], wrap [2], yields [2], abandoned [1], allotted [+906+906+928+1598 +2021] [1], allotted [+906+928+1598+2021] [1], allotted [1], allow to possess [1], allowing [1], allows [1], announced [1], announces [1], appoints [1], are put [1], arranged [1], ascribe [1], avenged [+4200+5935] [1], barter [1], be bought [1], be defeated [+928+3338] [1], be given in marriage [+851+906+4200] [1], be handed over [1], be injured [1], be left [1], be supplied [1], be [1], bears [1], became [1], been allotted [1], been committed [1], been given over [1], been handed over [+928+3338] [1], been published [1], been subjected [1], bestow [1], bestowed [1], bless [+906+1388] [1], blessed [+1388+4200] [1], blessed [+1388+6584] [1], bow [1], bowed [1], breeds [1], bringing [1], brings [1], bury [1], buy [1], called together [1], came [1], carry out [1], cast [1], charge [1], charging [1], choose [1], committed [1], confirm [1], consign [1], costs [1], cover

[+4062+6584] [1], credited [1], cry aloud [+7754] [1], cut [+928+8582] [1], demand [1], designate [1], designated [1], despoil [+1020+4200] [1], destined [1], devote [1], devoted [1], did[s] [+2257+3338] [1], dispenses [1], display [1], distribute [1], distributed [1], do[s] [1], does [1], drop [1], dry up [+3000] [1], enabled [1], endow [1], exchange [1], falls [1], filled [1], flourishes [1], from [1], gave in marriage [+851+906+4200+4200] [1], gave in marriage [1], gave in pledge [1], gave up [1], gave victory [+928+3338] [1], give [+851+4200+4200] [1], give [+928+3338] [1], give away [1], give in marriage [+408+906+4200] [1], give in marriage [+851+2021+4200] [1], give in marriage [+851+4200] [1], give permission [1], given in pledge [1], given up [1], gives gifts [1], gives over [1], granted requests [1], granting [1], grants [1], growl [+7754] [1], growled [+7754] [1], hand over [+906+906+928+3338] [1], hand over to [+906+928+3338] [1], handed [+906+906+928+3338] [1], handed over [+906+906+928+3338] [1], handing over [+906+928+3338] [1], hands over [1], has sexual relations [+8888] [1], have [+4200] [1], have sexual relations [+2446+4200+8888] [1], have sexual relations [+8888] [1], have [1], healing [+8337] [1], hold accountable [+6584] [1], hold [1], honor [+3883+4200] [1], how I long for [+4769+5761] [1], I wish [+4769] [1], if only [+906+4769] [1], imparts [1], imposed [1], imprisoned [+657+906+1074+2021] [1], imprisoned [+906+906 +928+5464] [1], inflict [1], injured [+928+4583] [1], injures [+928+4583] [1], inserted [1], inspire [+906+928+4222] [1], instruct [1], is drawn [1], is thrown [1], issued [1], join [1], keep [1], leave [1], let be heard [1], let have [1], let out [1], lifts [1], made face [+448+7156] [1], made ready [1], make restitution [1], make turn [+448+906] [1], marry [1], oh [+686+4769] [1], oh how I wish [+4769] [1], open [+7341] [1], ordained [1], paid [+4200+5486] [1], pay [+4084+4200] [1], pay [+4836] [1], pay [+906+8510] [1], pay [+924] [1], perform [1], permitted to do [1], pile [1], piled [1], pitch [1], plant [1], pledged [+3338] [1], pour out [1], pour [1], produces [1], producing [1], prove to be [1], pulled [1], push [1], put in place [1], put on [+4230] [1], put out [1], put up [1], raise [1], raised [+906+2256+5951] [1], raises [1], raising [1], receive [1], receives [+4200] [1], reduced [1], reflected on [+448+906+4213] [1], replaced [+906+9393] [1], resolved [+906+7156] [1], resound [1], respect [+3702+4200] [1], reward [+7190] [1], rewarded [+8510] [1], rises [1], roared [+7754] [1], roars [+928+7754] [1], sacrificed [+906+928 +6296] [1], seated [+4200+5226] [1], sell [+906+928+4084+4200] [1], sell [+928+4084+4200] [1], send down [1], send out [1], share [1], shares [1], sing [+7754] [1], slander [+928+1984] [1], sleeping with [+906+928+8888] [1], sparkles [+6524] [1], spend [1], spreads [1], stained [1], store [1], stored [1], strike [1], subjected [1], submit [+3338] [1], submitted [+3338] [1], suffer [+6584] [1], supplied [1], supplies [1], supply [1], surrenders [+3338] [1], take for [+906+4200 +7156] [1], think [+4213] [1], think [+906+4222] [1], thunders [+928+7754] [1], tie [+6584] [1], tie up [1], traded [1], treated [1], turned [+906+7156] [1], turned into [1], turned over [1], turns [1], use [1], was entrusted [1], was given in marriage [+851+4200] [1], was left hanging [1], wept so loudly [+906+928+1140+7754] [1], were assigned [1], were given over [1], were given [1], wins [1]

Ge 1:17 [A] God **set** them in the expanse of the sky to give light on the
1:29 [A] "*I* **give** you every seed-bearing plant on the face of the whole
3: 6 [A] *She* also **gave** some to her husband, who was with her,
3:12 [A] The man said, "The woman *you* **put** here with me—she gave
3:12 [A] with me—she **gave** me some fruit from the tree, and I ate it."
4:12 [A] you work the ground, *it will* no longer **yield** its crops for you.
9: 2 [C] upon all the fish of the sea; *they* **are given** into your hands.
9: 3 [A] Just as *I* **gave** you the green plants, I now give you
9:12 [A] "This is the sign of the covenant I *am* **making** between me
9:13 [A] *I have* **set** my rainbow in the clouds, and it will be the sign of
12: 7 [A] to Abram and said, "To your offspring *I will* **give** this land."
13:15 [A] All the land that you see *I will* **give** to you and your offspring
13:17 [A] the length and breadth of the land, for *I am* **giving** it to you."
14:20 [A] into your hand." Then Abram **gave** him a tenth of everything.
14:21 [A] "**Give** me the people and keep the goods for yourself."
15: 2 [A] what *can you* **give** me since I remain childless and the one
15: 3 [A] Abram said, "*You have* **given** me no children; so a servant in
15: 7 [A] who brought you out of Ur of the Chaldeans to **give** you this
15:10 [A] them in two and **arranged** the halves opposite each other;
15:18 [A] with Abram and said, "To your descendants *I* **give** this land,
16: 3 [A] and **gave** her to her husband to be his wife.
16: 5 [A] I **put** my servant in your arms, and now that she knows she is
17: 2 [A] *I will* **confirm** my covenant between me and you and will
17: 5 [A] be Abraham, for *I have* **made** you a father of many nations.
17: 6 [A] *I will* **make** nations *of* you, and kings will come from you.
17: 8 [A] whole land of Canaan, where you are now an alien, *I will* **give**
17:16 [A] I will bless her and *will* surely **give** you a son by her. I will
17:20 [A] of twelve rulers, and *I will* **make** him into a great nation.
18: 7 [A] and selected a choice, tender calf and **gave** it to a servant,
18: 8 [A] the calf that had been prepared, and **set** these before them.
20: 6 [A] sinning against me. That is why *I did* not **let** you touch her.
20:14 [A] and male and female slaves and **gave** them to Abraham,
20:16 [A] "*I am* **giving** your brother a thousand shekels of silver.
21:14 [A] took some food and a skin of water and **gave** them to Hagar.
21:27 [A] brought sheep and cattle and **gave** them to Abimelech,
23: 4 [A] **Sell** me some property for a burial site here so I can bury my
23: 9 [A] so *he will* **sell** me the cave of Machpelah, which belongs to
23: 9 [A] Ask him *to* **sell** it to me for the full price as a burial site
23:11 [A] *I* **give** you the field, and I give you the cave that is in it.
23:11 [A] I give you the field, and *I* **give** you the cave that is in it.
23:11 [A] *I* **give** it to you in the presence of my people. Bury your
23:13 [A] "Listen to me, if you will. *I will* **pay** the price of the field.
24: 7 [A] me on oath, saying, 'To your offspring *I will* **give** this land'—
24:32 [A] Straw and fodder *were* **brought** for the camels, and water for
24:35 [A] *He has* **given** him sheep and cattle, silver and gold,
24:36 [A] son in her old age, and *he has* **given** him everything he owns.
24:41 [A] you will be released from my oath even if *they* refuse *to* **give**
24:53 [A] and articles of clothing and **gave** them to Rebekah;
24:53 [A] *he* also **gave** costly gifts to her brother and to her mother.
25: 5 [A] Abraham **left** everything he owned to Isaac.
25: 6 [A] he **gave** gifts to the sons of his concubines and sent them
25:34 [A] Jacob **gave** Esau some bread and some lentil stew. He ate
26: 3 [A] For to you and your descendants *I will* **give** all these lands
26: 4 [A] as the stars in the sky and *will* **give** them all these lands,
27:17 [A] Then *she* **handed to** [+906+906+928+3338] her son Jacob the
27:28 [A] *May* God **give** you of heaven's dew and of earth's richness—
27:37 [A] lord over you and *have* **made** all his relatives his servants,
28: 4 [A] *May he* **give** you and your descendants the blessing given to
28: 4 [A] you now live as an alien, the land God **gave** to Abraham."
28:13 [A] *I will* **give** you and your descendants the land on which you
28:20 [A] I am taking and *will* **give** me food to eat and clothes to wear
28:22 [A] and of all that *you* **give** me I will give you a tenth."
29:19 [A] "It's better *that* I **give** her to you than to some other man.
29:19 [A] "It's better that I give her to you than **[RPH]** to some other
29:24 [A] Laban **gave** his servant girl Zilpah to his daughter *as* her
29:26 [A] **give** the younger daughter **in marriage** before the older one.
29:27 [A] *we will* **give** you the younger one also, in return for another
29:28 [A] and then Laban **gave** him his daughter Rachel to be his wife.
29:29 [A] Laban **gave** his servant girl Bilhah to his daughter Rachel as
29:33 [A] LORD heard that I am not loved, *he* **gave** me this one too."
30: 4 [A] So *she* **gave** him her servant Bilhah as a wife. Jacob slept
30: 6 [A] he has listened to my plea and **given** me a son."
30: 9 [A] took her maidservant Zilpah and **gave** her to Jacob as a wife.
30:14 [A] to Leah, "Please **give** me some of your son's mandrakes."
30:18 [A] "God *has* **rewarded** [+8510] me for giving my maidservant
30:18 [A] "God has rewarded me for **giving** my maidservant to my
30:26 [A] **Give** me my wives and children, for whom I have served
30:28 [A] He added, "Name your wages, and *I will* **pay** them."
30:31 [A] "What *shall I* **give** you?" he asked. "Don't give me
30:31 [A] he asked. "Don't **give** me anything," Jacob replied.
30:35 [A] and *he* **placed** them in the care of his sons.
30:40 [A] **made** the rest **face** [+448+7156] the streaked
31: 7 [A] ten times. However, God *has* not **allowed** him to harm me.
31: 9 [A] taken away your father's livestock and *has* **given** them to me.
32:16 [32:17] [A] *He* **put** them in the care of his servants, each herd
34: 8 [A] heart set on your daughter. Please **give** her to him as his wife.
34: 9 [A] **give** us your daughters and take our daughters for yourselves.
34:11 [A] favor in your eyes, and *I will* **give** you whatever you ask.
34:12 [A] bring as great as you like, and *I'll* **pay** whatever you ask me.
34:12 [A] pay whatever you ask me. Only **give** me the girl as my wife."
34:14 [A] we can't **give** our sister to a man who is not circumcised.
34:16 [A] *we will* **give** you our daughters and take your daughters for
34:21 [A] We can marry their daughters and they *can* **marry** ours.
35: 4 [A] So *they* **gave** Jacob all the foreign gods they had and the
35:12 [A] The land *I* **gave** to Abraham and Isaac I also give to you,
35:12 [A] The land I gave to Abraham and Isaac *I* also **give** to you,
35:12 [A] and *I will* **give** this land to your descendants after you."
38: 9 [A] he spilled his semen on the ground to keep from **producing**
38:14 [C] now grown up, she *had* not **been given** to him as his wife.
38:16 [A] "And what *will you* **give** me to sleep with you?" she asked.
38:17 [A] "*Will you* **give** me something *as* a pledge until you send it?"
38:18 [A] He said, "What pledge *should I* **give** you?" "Your seal
38:18 [A] So *he* **gave** them to her and slept with her, and she became
38:26 [A] righteous than I, since *I* wouldn't **give** her to my son Shelah."
38:28 [A] As she was giving birth, *one of them* **put out** his hand;
39: 4 [A] and *he* **entrusted** to his care everything he owned.
39: 8 [A] the house; everything he owns *he has* **entrusted** to my care.
39:20 [A] Joseph's master took him and **put** him in prison, the place
39:21 [A] and **granted** him favor in the eyes of the prison warden.
39:22 [A] So the warden **put** Joseph in charge of all those held in the
40: 3 [A] **put** them in custody in the house of the captain of the guard,
40:11 [A] them into Pharaoh's cup and **put** the cup in his hand."
40:13 [A] to your position, and *you will* **put** Pharaoh's cup in his hand,
40:21 [A] so that *he once again* **put** the cup into Pharaoh's hand,
41:10 [A] and *he* **imprisoned** me … **in** [+906+906+928+5464] the house

Ge 41:41 [A] "*I hereby* **put** you in charge of the whole land of Egypt."
41:42 [A] his signet ring from his finger and **put** it on Joseph's finger.
41:43 [A] Thus *he* **put** him in charge of the whole land of Egypt.
41:45 [A] and **gave** him Asenath daughter of Potiphera, priest of On,
41:48 [A] seven years of abundance in Egypt and **stored** it in the cities.
41:48 [A] In each city *he* **put** the food grown in the fields surrounding
42:25 [A] in his sack, and to **give** them provisions for their journey.
42:27 [A] night one of them opened his sack to **get** feed for his donkey,
42:30 [A] to us and **treated** us as though we were spying on the land.
42:34 [A] *I will* **give** your brother **back** to you, and you can trade in
42:37 [A] to you. **Entrust** him to my care, and I will bring him back."
43:14 [A] And *may* God Almighty **grant** you mercy before the man
43:23 [A] the God of your father, *has* **given** you treasure in your sacks;
43:24 [A] **gave** them water to wash their feet and provided fodder for
43:24 [A] to wash their feet and **provided** fodder for their donkeys.
45: 2 [A] And he **wept so loudly** [+906+928+1140+7754] that the
45:18 [A] *I will* **give** you the best of the land of Egypt and you can
45:21 [A] Joseph **gave** them carts, as Pharaoh had commanded, and he
45:21 [A] and *he* also **gave** them provisions for their journey.
45:22 [A] To each of them *he* **gave** new clothing, but to Benjamin he
45:22 [A] to Benjamin *he* **gave** three hundred shekels of silver and five
46:18 [A] by Zilpah, whom Laban *had* **given** to his daughter Leah—
46:25 [A] by Bilhah, whom Laban *had* **given** to his daughter Rachel—
47:11 [A] in Egypt and **gave** them property in the best part of the land,
47:16 [A] "*I will* **sell** you food in exchange for your livestock,
47:17 [A] he **gave** them food in exchange for their horses, their sheep
47:19 [A] **Give** us seed so that we may live and not die, and that the
47:22 [A] and had food enough from the allotment Pharaoh **gave** them.
47:24 [A] when the crop comes in, **give** a fifth of it to Pharaoh. The
48: 4 [A] *I will* **make** you a community of peoples, and I will give this
48: 4 [A] *I will* **give** this land as an everlasting possession to your
48: 9 [A] "They are the sons God *has* **given** me here," Joseph said to
48:22 [A] I **give** the ridge of land I took from the Amorites with my
49:20 [A] food will be rich; he *will* **provide** delicacies fit for a king.
49:21 [A] "Naphtali is a doe set free that **bears** beautiful fawns.
Ex 2: 9 [A] and nurse him for me, and I *will* **pay** [+906+8510] you."
2:21 [A] *who* **gave** his daughter Zipporah to Moses **in marriage**.
3:19 [A] I know that the king of Egypt *will* not **let** you go unless a
3:21 [A] "And *I will* **make** the Egyptians favorably disposed toward
5: 7 [A] "You are no longer to **supply** the people *with* straw for
5:10 [A] is what Pharaoh says: 'I *will* not **give** you any more straw.
5:16 [C] Your servants **are given** no straw, yet we are told, 'Make
5:18 [C] You *will* not **be given** any straw, yet you must produce your
5:18 [A] any straw, yet *you must* **produce** your full quota of bricks."
5:21 [A] his officials and *have* **put** a sword in their hand to kill us."
6: 4 [A] I also established my covenant with them to **give** them the
6: 8 [A] I will bring you to the land I swore with uplifted hand to **give**
6: 8 [A] to Isaac and to Jacob. *I will* **give** it to you as a possession.
7: 1 [A] said to Moses, "See, *I have* **made** you like God to Pharaoh,
7: 4 [A] *I will* **lay** my hand on Egypt and with mighty acts of
7: 9 [A] '**Perform** a miracle,' then say to Aaron, 'Take your staff
9:23 [A] the LORD **sent** thunder and hail, and lightning flashed
10:25 [A] "You *must* **allow** us to have sacrifices and burnt offerings to
11: 3 [A] (The LORD **made** the Egyptians favorably disposed toward
12: 7 [A] they are to take some of the blood and **put** it on the sides
12:23 [A] he *will* not **permit** the destroyer to enter your houses
12:25 [A] When you enter the land that the LORD *will* **give** you as he
12:36 [A] The LORD *had* **made** the Egyptians favorably disposed
13: 5 [A] the land he swore to your forefathers to **give** you, a land
13:11 [A] brings you into the land of the Canaanites and **gives** it to you,
16: 3 [A] "**If only** [+4769] we had died by the LORD's hand in
16: 8 [A] "You will know that it was the LORD when *he* **gives** you
16:15 [A] to them, "It is the bread the LORD *has* **given** you to eat.
16:29 [A] Bear in mind that the LORD *has* **given** you the Sabbath;
16:29 [A] that is why on the sixth day he **gives** you bread for two days.
16:33 [A] said to Aaron, "Take a jar and **put** an omer of manna in it.
17: 2 [A] quarreled with Moses and said, "**Give** us water to drink."
18:25 [A] men from all Israel and **made** them leaders of the people,
20:12 [A] live long in the land the LORD your God *is* **giving** you.
21: 4 [A] If his master **gives** him a wife and she bears him sons
21:19 [A] *he must* **pay** the injured man *for* the loss of his time and see
21:22 [A] the woman's husband demands and the court **allows**.
21:23 [A] But if there is serious injury, *you are to* **take** life for life,
21:30 [A] he may redeem his life *by* **paying** whatever is demanded.
21:32 [A] the owner *must* **pay** thirty shekels of silver to the master of
22: 7 [22:6] [A] "If a man **gives** his neighbor silver or goods for
22:10 [22:9] [A] "If a man **gives** a donkey, an ox, a sheep or any other
22:17 [22:16] [A] If her father absolutely refuses to **give** her to him,
22:29 [22:28] [A] "*You must* **give** me the firstborn of your sons.
22:30 [22:29] [A] seven days, but **give** them to me on the eighth day.
23:27 [A] *I will* **make** [+448+906] all your enemies **turn** their backs
23:31 [A] *I will* **hand over to** [+906+928+3338] you the people who
24:12 [A] *I will* **give** you the tablets of stone, with the law
25:12 [A] Cast four gold rings for it and **fasten** them to its four feet,
25:16 [A] Then **put** in the ark the Testimony, which I will give you.
25:16 [A] Then put in the ark the Testimony, which *I will* **give** you.
25:21 [A] **Place** the cover on top of the ark and put in the ark the
25:21 [A] the cover on top of the ark and **put** in the ark the Testimony,
25:21 [A] and put in the ark the Testimony, which *I will* **give** you.
25:26 [A] gold rings for the table and **fasten** them to the four corners,
25:30 [A] **Put** the bread of the Presence on this table to be before me at
26:32 [A] **Hang** it *with* gold hooks on four posts of acacia wood
26:33 [A] **Hang** the curtain from the clasps and place the ark of the
26:34 [A] **Put** the atonement cover on the ark of the Testimony in the
26:35 [A] and **put** the lampstand opposite it on the south side.
27: 5 [A] **Put** it under the ledge of the altar so that it is halfway up the
28:14 [A] pure gold, like a rope, and **attach** the chains to the settings.
28:23 [A] rings for it and **fasten** them to two corners of the breastpiece.
28:24 [A] **Fasten** the two gold chains to the rings at the corners of the
28:25 [A] and the other ends of the chains **[RPH]** to the two settings,
28:25 [A] **attaching** them to the shoulder pieces of the ephod at the
28:27 [A] **attach** them to the bottom of the shoulder pieces on the front
28:30 [A] Also **put** the Urim and the Thummim in the breastpiece, so
29: 3 [A] **Put** them in a basket and present them in it—along with the
29: 6 [A] on his head and **attach** the sacred diadem to the turban.
29:12 [A] and **put** it on the horns of the altar with your finger,
29:17 [A] the legs, **putting** them with the head and the other pieces.
29:20 [A] **put** it on the lobes of the right ears of Aaron and his sons,
30: 6 [A] **Put** the altar in front of the curtain that is before the ark of
30:12 [A] each one *must* **pay** the LORD a ransom for his life at the
30:13 [A] one who crosses over to those already counted *is to* **give**
30:14 [A] years old or more, *are to* **give** an offering to the LORD.
30:15 [A] the poor are not to give less when *you* **make** the offering to
30:16 [A] and **use** it for the service of the Tent of Meeting.
30:18 [A] **Place** it between the Tent of Meeting and the altar, and put
30:18 [A] the Tent of Meeting and the altar, and **put** water in it.
30:33 [A] whoever **puts** it on anyone other than a priest must be cut off
30:36 [A] and **place** it in front of the Testimony in the Tent of Meeting,
31: 6 [A] Moreover, I *have* **appointed** Oholiab son of Ahisamach,
31: 6 [A] Also *I have* **given** skill to all the craftsmen to make
31:18 [A] *he* **gave** him the two tablets of the Testimony, the tablets of
32:13 [A] *I will* **give** your descendants all this land I promised them,
32:24 [A] *they* **gave** me the gold, and I threw it into the fire, and out
32:29 [A] and he *has* **blessed** [+1388+6584] you this day."
33: 1 [A] Isaac and Jacob, saying, '*I will* **give** it to your descendants.'
34:33 [A] Moses finished speaking to them, *he* **put** a veil over his face.
35:34 [A] *he has* **given** both him and Oholiab son of Ahisamach,
36: 1 [A] and every skilled person to whom the LORD *has* **given** skill
36: 2 [A] every skilled person *to* whom the LORD *had* **given** ability
37:13 [A] rings for the table and **fastened** them to the four corners,
39:16 [A] **fastened** the rings to two of the corners of the breastpiece.
39:17 [A] *They* **fastened** the two gold chains to the rings at the corners
39:18 [A] and the other ends of the chains **[RPH]** to the two settings,
39:18 [A] **attaching** them to the shoulder pieces of the ephod at the
39:20 [A] **attached** them to the bottom of the shoulder pieces on the
39:25 [A] **attached** them around the hem between the pomegranates.
39:31 [A] Then *they* **fastened** a blue cord to it to attach it to the turban,
39:31 [A] Then they fastened a blue cord to it to **attach** it to the turban,
40: 5 [A] **Place** the gold altar of incense in front of the ark of the
40: 6 [A] "**Place** the altar of burnt offering in front of the entrance to
40: 7 [A] **place** the basin between the Tent of Meeting and the altar
40: 7 [A] between the Tent of Meeting and the altar and **put** water in it.
40: 8 [A] around it and **put** the curtain at the entrance to the courtyard.
40:18 [A] *he* **put** the bases **in place**, erected the frames, inserted the
40:18 [A] the frames, **inserted** the crossbars and set up the posts.
40:20 [A] He took the Testimony and **placed** it in the ark, attached the
40:20 [A] the poles to the ark and **put** the atonement cover over it.
40:22 [A] Moses **placed** the table in the Tent of Meeting on the north
40:30 [A] Tent of Meeting and the altar and **put** water in it for washing,
40:33 [A] and **put up** the curtain at the entrance to the courtyard.
Lev 1: 7 [A] The sons of Aaron the priest *are to* **put** fire on the altar
2: 1 [A] is to be of fine flour. He is to pour oil on it, **put** incense on it
2:15 [A] **Put** oil and incense on it; it is a grain offering.
4: 7 [A] The priest *shall* then **put** some of the blood on the horns of
4:18 [A] *He is to* **put** some of the blood on the horns of the altar that
4:25 [A] **put** it on the horns of the altar of burnt offering and pour out
4:30 [A] **put** it on the horns of the altar of burnt offering and pour out
4:34 [A] **put** it on the horns of the altar of burnt offering and pour out
5:11 [A] He must not put oil or **[RPH]** incense on it, because it is a
5:16 [A] add a fifth of the value to that and **give** it all to the priest,
6: 5 [5:24] [A] **give** it all to the owner on the day he presents his
6:17 [6:10] [A] *I have* **given** it as their share of the offerings made to
7:32 [A] *You are to* **give** the right thigh of your fellowship offerings
7:34 [A] that is presented and *have* **given** them to Aaron the priest
7:36 [A] the LORD commanded that the Israelites **give** this to them
8: 7 [A] *He* **put** the tunic on Aaron, tied the sash around him, clothed
8: 7 [A] clothed him with the robe and **put** the ephod on him.
8: 8 [A] on him and **put** the Urim and Thummim in the breastpiece.

Lev 8:15 [A] with his finger *he* **put** it on all the horns of the altar to purify
8:23 [A] some of its blood and **put** it on the lobe of Aaron's right ear,
8:24 [A] and **put** some of the blood on the lobes of their right ears,
8:27 [A] *He* **put** all these in the hands of Aaron and his sons
9:9 [A] his finger into the blood and **put** it on the horns of the altar;
10:1 [A] Abihu took their censers, **put** fire in them and added incense;
10:14 [C] *they have* **been given** *to* you and your children as your share
10:17 [A] it *was* **given** to you to take away the guilt of the community
11:38 [H] if water *has* **been put** on the seed and a carcass falls on it,
14:14 [A] **put** it on the lobe of the right ear of the one to be cleansed,
14:17 [A] The priest *is to* **put** some of the oil remaining in his palm on
14:18 [A] The rest of the oil in his palm the priest *shall* **put** on the head
14:25 [A] **put** it on the lobe of the right ear of the one to be cleansed,
14:28 [A] Some of the oil in his palm he *is to* **put** on the same places he
14:29 [A] The rest of the oil in his palm the priest *shall* **put** on the head
14:34 [A] land of Canaan, which I *am* **giving** you as your possession,
14:34 [A] and *I* **put** a spreading mildew in a house in that land,
15:14 [A] entrance to the Tent of Meeting and **give** them to the priest.
16:8 [A] He *is to* **cast** lots for the two goats—one lot for the LORD
16:13 [A] *He is to* **put** the incense on the fire before the LORD,
16:18 [A] of the goat's blood and **put** it on all the horns of the altar.
16:21 [A] all their sins—and **put** them on the goat's head.
17:10 [A] *I will* **set** my face against that person who eats blood and will
17:11 [A] I *have* **given** it to you to make atonement for yourselves on
18:20 [A] " '*Do* not **have sexual** [+2446+4200+8888] **relations** with
18:21 [A] " '*Do* not **give** any of your children to be sacrificed to
18:23 [A] " '*Do* not **have sexual** [+8888] **relations** with an animal
19:14 [A] curse the deaf or **put** a stumbling block in front of the blind,
19:20 [C] but who has not been ransomed or **given** her freedom,
19:28 [A] " '*Do* not **cut** [+928+8582] your bodies for the dead or put
19:28 [A] your bodies for the dead or **put** tattoo marks on yourselves.
20:2 [A] or any alien living in Israel who **gives** any of his children to
20:3 [A] I *will* **set** my face against that man and I will cut him off
20:3 [A] for *by* **giving** his children to Molech, he has defiled my
20:4 [A] their eyes when that man **gives** one of his children to Molech
20:6 [A] " '*I will* **set** my face against the person who turns to mediums
20:15 [A] " 'If a man **has sexual** [+8888] **relations** with an animal,
20:24 [A] I *will* **give** it to you as an inheritance, a land flowing with
22:14 [A] *he must* **make restitution** to the priest *for* the offering
22:22 [A] *Do* not **place** any of these on the altar as an offering made to
23:10 [A] 'When you enter the land I *am going to* **give** you and you
23:38 [A] and all the freewill offerings *you* **give** to the LORD.)
24:7 [A] Along each row **put** some pure incense as a memorial
24:19 [A] If anyone **injures** [+928+4583] his neighbor, whatever he
24:20 [A] As *he has* **injured** [+928+4583] the other, so he is to be
24:20 [C] for tooth. As he has injured the other, so he *is to* **be injured**.
25:2 [A] 'When you enter the land I *am going to* **give** you, the land
25:19 [A] Then the land *will* **yield** its fruit, and you will eat your fill
25:24 [A] *you must* **provide** *for* the redemption of the land.
25:37 [A] *You must* not **lend** him money at interest or sell him food at
25:37 [A] not lend him money at interest or **sell** him food at a profit.
25:38 [A] who brought you out of Egypt to **give** you the land of Canaan
26:1 [A] *do* not **place** a carved stone in your land to bow down before
26:4 [A] *I will* **send** you rain in its season, and the ground will yield
26:4 [A] the ground *will* **yield** its crops and the trees of the field their
26:4 [A] yield its crops and the trees of the field **[RPH]** their fruit.
26:6 [A] " '*I will* **grant** peace in the land, and you will lie down
26:11 [A] *I will* **put** my dwelling place among you, and I will not abhor
26:17 [A] *I will* **set** my face against you so that you will be defeated by
26:19 [A] **make** the sky above you like iron and the ground beneath
26:20 [A] be spent in vain, because your soil *will* not **yield** its crops,
26:20 [A] yield its crops, nor *will* the trees of the land **yield** their fruit.
26:25 [C] plague among you, and *you will* **be given** into enemy hands.
26:30 [A] and **pile** your dead bodies on the lifeless forms of your idols,
26:31 [A] *I will* **turn** your cities **into** ruins and lay waste your
26:46 [A] the regulations that the LORD **established** on Mount Sinai
27:9 [A] such an animal **given** to the LORD becomes holy.
27:23 [A] the man *must* **pay** its value on that day as something holy to
Nu 3:9 [A] **Give** the Levites to Aaron and his sons; they are the Israelites
3:9 [B] they are the Israelites *who are to* **be given** [+5989] **wholly** to
3:9 [A] they are the Israelites *who are to* **be given wholly** [+5989] to
3:48 [A] **Give** the money for the redemption of the additional
3:51 [A] Moses **gave** the redemption money to Aaron and his sons,
4:6 [A] *they are to* **cover** this **with** [+4062+6584] hides of sea cows,
4:7 [A] **put** on it the plates, dishes and bowls, and the jars for drink
4:10 [A] *they are to* **wrap** it and all its accessories in a covering of
4:10 [A] covering of hides of sea cows and **put** it on a carrying frame.
4:12 [A] **wrap** them in a blue cloth, cover that with hides of sea cows
4:12 [A] with hides of sea cows and **put** them on a carrying frame.
4:14 [A] *they are to* **place** on it all the utensils used for ministering at
5:7 [A] one fifth to it and **give** it all to the person he has wronged.
5:10 [A] but what he **gives** to the priest will belong to the priest.' "
5:15 [A] He must not pour oil on it or **put** incense on it, because it is a
5:17 [A] and **put** some dust from the tabernacle floor into the water.
5:18 [A] loosen her hair and **place** in her hands the reminder offering,
5:20 [A] defiled yourself *by* **sleeping** [+906+928+8888] **with** a man
5:21 [A] "*may* the LORD **cause** your people to curse and denounce
5:21 [A] denounce you when he **causes** your thigh to waste away and
6:18 [A] **put** it in the fire that is under the sacrifice of the fellowship
6:19 [A] the priest *is to* **place** in his hands a boiled shoulder of the
7:5 [A] **Give** them to the Levites as each man's work requires."
7:6 [A] Moses took the carts and oxen and **gave** them to the Levites.
7:7 [A] *He* **gave** two carts and four oxen to the Gershonites, as their
7:8 [A] *he* **gave** four carts and eight oxen to the Merarites, as their
7:9 [A] Moses *did* not **give** any to the Kohathites, because they were
8:16 [B] They are the Israelites *who are to* **be given** [+5989] **wholly**
8:16 [B] They are the Israelites *who are to* **be given wholly** [+5989]
8:19 [A] *I have* **given** the Levites as gifts to Aaron and his sons to do
8:19 [B] I have given the Levites as **gifts** to Aaron and his sons to do
10:29 [A] the place about which the LORD said, '*I will* **give** it to you.'
11:13 [A] Where *can* I **get** meat for all these people? They keep
11:13 [A] these people? They keep wailing to me, '**Give** us meat to eat!'
11:18 [A] Now the LORD *will* **give** you meat, and you will eat it.
11:21 [A] and you say, '*I will* **give** them meat to eat for a whole month!'
11:25 [A] that was on him and **put** the Spirit on the seventy elders.
11:29 [A] "Are you jealous for my sake? **I wish that** [+4769] all the
11:29 [A] and that the LORD *would* **put** his Spirit on them!"
13:2 [A] the land of Canaan, which I *am* **giving** to the Israelites.
14:1 [A] of the community **raised** [+906+2256+5951] their voices and
14:4 [A] "*We should* **choose** a leader and go back to Egypt."
14:8 [A] a land flowing with milk and honey, and *will* **give** it to us.
15:2 [A] to them: 'After you enter the land I *am* **giving** you as a home
15:21 [A] Throughout the generations to come *you are to* **give** this
15:38 [A] of your garments, with **[NIE]** a blue cord on each tassel.
16:7 [A] tomorrow **put** fire and incense in them before the LORD.
16:14 [A] and honey or **given** us an inheritance of fields and vineyards.
16:17 [A] Each man is to take his censer and **put** incense in it—
16:18 [A] **put** fire and incense in it, and stood with Moses and Aaron at
16:46 [17:11] [A] to Aaron, "Take your censer and **put** incense in it,
16:47 [17:12] [A] Aaron **offered** the incense and made atonement for
17:6 [17:21] [A] and their leaders **gave** him twelve staffs,
18:6 [B] **dedicated** to the LORD to do the work at the Tent of
18:7 [A] *I am* **giving** you the service of the priesthood as a gift.
18:8 [A] "*I* myself *have* **put** you in charge of the offerings presented
18:8 [A] all the holy offerings the Israelites give me *I* **give** to you
18:11 [A] *I* **give** this to you and your sons and daughters as your
18:12 [A] "*I* **give** you all the finest olive oil and all the finest new wine
18:12 [A] grain *they* **give** the LORD as the firstfruits of their harvest.
18:19 [A] offerings the Israelites present to the LORD *I* **give** to you
18:21 [A] "*I* **give** to the Levites all the tithes in Israel as their
18:24 [A] *I* **give** to the Levites as their inheritance the tithes that the
18:26 [A] 'When you receive from the Israelites the tithe *I* **give** you as
18:28 [A] From these tithes *you must* **give** the LORD's portion to
19:3 [A] **Give** it to Eleazar the priest; it is to be taken outside the camp
19:17 [A] offering into a jar and **pour** fresh water over them.
20:8 [A] to that rock before their eyes and *it will* **pour out** its water.
20:12 [A] you will not bring this community into the land *I* **give** them."
20:19 [A] livestock drink any of your water, *we will* **pay for** [+4836] it.
20:21 [A] Since Edom refused *to* **let** them go through their territory,
20:24 [A] He will not enter the land *I* **give** the Israelites, because both
21:2 [A] "If *you will* **deliver** [+906+5989] these people into our
21:2 [A] "If *you will* **deliver** [+906+5989] these people into our
21:3 [A] to Israel's plea and **gave** the Canaanites **over** to them.
21:16 [A] "Gather the people together and *I will* **give** them water."
21:23 [A] Sihon *would* not **let** Israel pass through his territory. He
21:29 [A] *He has* **given up** his sons as fugitives and his daughters as
21:34 [A] *I have* **handed** him **over to** [+906+906+906+928+3338] you,
22:13 [A] for the LORD has refused to **let** me go with you."
22:18 [A] "Even if Balak **gave** me his palace filled with silver and gold,
24:13 [A] 'Even if Balak **gave** me his palace filled with silver and gold,
25:12 [A] Therefore tell him I *am* **making** my covenant of peace with
26:54 [B] each *is to* **receive** its inheritance according to the number of
26:62 [C] because they **received** no inheritance among them.
27:4 [A] had no son? **Give** us property among our father's relatives."
27:7 [A] *You* **must certainly give** [+4200+5989] them property as an
27:7 [A] *You* **must certainly give** [+4200+5989] them property as an
27:9 [A] If he has no daughter, **give** his inheritance to his brothers.
27:10 [A] has no brothers, **give** his inheritance to his father's brothers.
27:11 [A] **give** his inheritance to the nearest relative in his clan, that he
27:12 [A] the Abarim range and see the land *I have* **given** the Israelites.
27:20 [A] **Give** him some of your authority so the whole Israelite
31:3 [A] and to **carry out** the LORD's vengeance on them.
31:29 [A] and **give** it to Eleazar the priest as the LORD's part.
31:30 [A] **Give** them to the Levites, who are responsible for the care of
31:41 [A] Moses **gave** the tribute to Eleazar the priest as the LORD's
31:47 [A] the LORD commanded him, and **gave** them to the Levites,
32:5 [B] "*let* this land **be given** to your servants as our possession.
32:7 [A] from going over into the land the LORD *has* **given** them?

Nu 32: 9 [A] Israelites from entering the land the LORD *had* **given** them.
32: 29 [A] before you, **give** them the land of Gilead as their possession.
32: 33 [A] **gave** to the Gadites, the Reubenites and the half-tribe of
32: 40 [A] So Moses **gave** Gilead to the Makirites, the descendants of
33: 53 [A] and settle in it, for *I have* **given** you the land to possess.
34: 13 [A] The LORD has ordered that it *be* **given** to the nine and a
35: 2 [A] "Command the Israelites *to* **give** the Levites towns to live in
35: 2 [A] will possess. And **give** them pasturelands around the towns.
35: 4 [A] "The pasturelands around the towns that *you* **give** the Levites
35: 6 [A] "Six of the towns *you* **give** the Levites will be cities of
35: 6 [A] "Six of the towns you give the Levites will be **[RPH]** cities
35: 6 [A] may flee. In addition, **give** them forty-two other towns.
35: 7 [A] *you must* **give** the Levites forty-eight towns, together with
35: 8 [A] The towns *you* **give** the Levites from the land the Israelites
35: 8 [A] *are to be* **given** in proportion to the inheritance of each tribe:
35: 13 [A] These six towns *you* **give** will be your cities of refuge.
35: 14 [A] **Give** three on this side of the Jordan and three in Canaan as
35: 14 [A] of the Jordan and **[RPH]** three in Canaan as cities of refuge.
36: 2 [A] "When the LORD commanded my lord to **give** the land as
36: 2 [A] he ordered you to **give** the inheritance of our brother
Dt 1: 8 [A] See, *I have* **given** you this land. Go in and take possession of
1: 8 [A] land that the LORD swore *he would* **give** to your fathers—
1: 15 [A] and **appointed** them to have authority over you—
1: 20 [A] of the Amorites, which the LORD our God *is* **giving** us.
1: 21 [A] See, the LORD your God *has* **given** you the land. Go up
1: 25 [A] "It is a good land that the LORD our God *is* **giving** us."
1: 27 [A] so he brought us out of Egypt to **deliver** us into the hands of
1: 35 [A] shall see the good land I swore to **give** your forefathers,
1: 36 [A] *I will* **give** him and his descendants the land he set his feet
1: 39 [A] *I will* **give** it to them and they will take possession of it.
2: 5 [A] them to war, for *I will* not **give** you any of their land,
2: 5 [A] *I have* **given** Esau the hill country of Seir as his own.
2: 9 [A] them to war, for *I will* not **give** you any part of their land.
2: 9 [A] *I have* **given** Ar to the descendants of Lot as a possession."
2: 12 [A] just as Israel did in the land the LORD **gave** them as their
2: 19 [A] for *I will* not **give** you possession *of* any land belonging to
2: 19 [A] *I have* **given** it as a possession to the descendants of Lot."
2: 24 [A] *I have* **given** into your hand Sihon the Amorite, king of
2: 25 [A] This very day I will begin *to* **put** the terror and fear of you on
2: 28 [A] price in silver. **[RPH]** Only let us pass through on foot—
2: 29 [A] the Jordan into the land the LORD our God *is* **giving** us."
2: 30 [A] and his heart obstinate in order to **give** him into your hands,
2: 31 [A] I have begun *to* **deliver** Sihon and his country **over** to you.
2: 33 [A] the LORD our God **delivered** him **over** to us and we struck
2: 36 [A] too strong for us. The LORD our God **gave** us all of them.
3: 2 [A] *I have* **handed** him **over to** [+906+906+906+928+3338] you
3: 3 [A] our God also **gave** into our hands Og king of Bashan and
3: 12 [A] the land that we took over at that time, *I* **gave** the Reubenites
3: 13 [A] the kingdom of Og, *I* **gave** to the half tribe of Manasseh.
3: 15 [A] And *I* **gave** Gilead to Makir.
3: 16 [A] the Gadites *I* **gave** the territory extending from Gilead down
3: 18 [A] "The LORD your God *has* **given** you this land to take
3: 19 [A] much livestock) may stay in the towns *I have* **given** you,
3: 20 [A] taken over the land that the LORD your God *is* **giving** them,
3: 20 [A] each of you may go back to the possession *I have* **given**
4: 1 [A] land that the LORD, the God of your fathers, *is* **giving** you.
4: 8 [A] and laws as this body of laws I *am* **setting** before you today?
4: 21 [A] enter the good land the LORD your God *is* **giving** you as
4: 38 [A] to bring you into their land to **give** it to you for your
4: 40 [A] long in the land the LORD your God **gives** you for all time.
5: 16 [A] with you in the land the LORD your God *is* **giving** you.
5: 22 [A] he wrote them on two stone tablets and **gave** them to me.
5: 29 [A] **Oh** [+4769], that their hearts would be inclined to fear me
5: 31 [A] laws you are to teach them to follow in the land I *am* **giving**
6: 10 [A] to your fathers, to Abraham, Isaac and Jacob, to **give** you—
6: 22 [A] Before our eyes the LORD **sent** miraculous signs
6: 23 [A] **give** us the land that he promised on oath to our forefathers.
7: 2 [A] when the LORD your God *has* **delivered** them **over** to you
7: 3 [A] *Do* not **give** your daughters to their sons or take their
7: 13 [A] in the land that he swore to your forefathers to **give** you.
7: 15 [A] knew in Egypt, but *he will* **inflict** them on all who hate you.
7: 16 [A] all the peoples the LORD your God **gives over** to you.
7: 23 [A] the LORD your God *will* **deliver** them **over** to you,
7: 24 [A] *He will* **give** their kings into your hand, and you will wipe
8: 10 [A] praise the LORD your God for the good land *he has* **given**
8: 18 [A] for it is he who **gives** you the ability to produce wealth, and
9: 6 [A] LORD your God *is* **giving** you this good land to possess,
9: 10 [A] The LORD **gave** me two stone tablets inscribed by the
9: 11 [A] and forty nights, the LORD **gave** me the two stone tablets,
9: 23 [A] "Go up and take possession of the land *I have* **given** you."
10: 4 [A] the day of the assembly. And the LORD **gave** them to me.
10: 11 [A] possess the land that I swore to their fathers to **give** them."
10: 18 [A] the widow, and loves the alien, **giving** him food and clothing.
11: 9 [A] that the LORD swore to your forefathers to **give** to them
11: 14 [A] then *I will* **send** rain on your land in its season, both autumn
11: 15 [A] *I will* **provide** grass in the fields for your cattle, and you will
11: 17 [A] so that it will not rain and the ground *will* **yield** no produce,
11: 17 [A] soon perish from the good land the LORD *is* **giving** you.
11: 21 [A] in the land that the LORD swore to **give** your forefathers,
11: 25 [A] *will* **put** the terror and fear of you on the whole land,
11: 26 [A] See, I *am* **setting** before you today a blessing and a curse—
11: 29 [A] *you are to* **proclaim** on Mount Gerizim the blessings, and on
11: 31 [A] take possession of the land the LORD your God *is* **giving**
11: 32 [A] obey all the decrees and laws I *am* **setting** before you today.
12: 1 [A] the God of your fathers, *has* **given** you to possess—
12: 9 [A] and the inheritance the LORD your God *is* **giving** you.
12: 15 [A] according to the blessing the LORD your God **gives** you.
12: 21 [A] from the herds and flocks the LORD *has* **given** you,
13: 1 [13:2] [A] and **announces** to you a miraculous sign or wonder,
13: 12 [13:13] [A] towns the LORD your God *is* **giving** you to live in
13: 17 [13:18] [A] *he will* **show** you mercy, have compassion on you,
14: 21 [A] *You may* **give** it to an alien living in any of your towns,
14: 25 [A] **exchange** your tithe for silver, and take the silver with you
14: 26 [A] *Use* the silver *to* **buy** whatever you like: cattle, sheep, wine or
15: 4 [A] for in the land the LORD your God *is* **giving** you to possess
15: 7 [A] towns of the land that the LORD your God *is* **giving** you,
15: 9 [A] ill will toward your needy brother and **give** him nothing.
15: 10 [A] **Give** [+5989] **generously** to him and do so without a
15: 10 [A] **Give generously** [+5989] to him and do so without a
15: 10 [A] Give generously to him and **do**˚ **so** without a grudging heart;
15: 14 [A] **Give** to him as the LORD your God has blessed you.
15: 17 [A] take an awl and **push** it through his ear lobe into the door,
16: 5 [A] the Passover in any town the LORD your God **gives** you
16: 10 [A] the Feast of Weeks to the LORD your God *by* **giving**
16: 17 [A] way the LORD your God *has* **blessed** [+1388+4200] you.
16: 18 [A] **Appoint** judges and officials for each of your tribes in every
16: 18 [A] tribes in every town the LORD your God *is* **giving** you,
16: 20 [A] and possess the land the LORD your God *is* **giving** you.
17: 2 [A] **gives** you is found doing evil in the eyes of the LORD your
17: 14 [A] When you enter the land the LORD your God *is* **giving** you
17: 15 [A] *Do* not **place** a foreigner over you, one who is not a brother
18: 3 [A] a sheep: **[RPH]** the shoulder, the jowls and the inner parts.
18: 4 [A] *You are to* **give** them the firstfruits of your grain, new wine
18: 9 [A] When you enter the land the LORD your God *is* **giving** you,
18: 14 [A] the LORD your God *has* not **permitted** you **to do** so.
18: 18 [A] *I will* **put** my words in his mouth, and he will tell them
19: 1 [A] God has destroyed the nations whose land he *is* **giving** you,
19: 2 [A] in the land the LORD your God *is* **giving** you to possess.
19: 8 [A] and **gives** you the whole land he promised them,
19: 8 [A] and gives you the whole land he promised **[RPH]** them,
19: 10 [A] which the LORD your God *is* **giving** you as your
19: 12 [A] **hand** him **over to** [+906+928+3338] the avenger of blood to
19: 14 [A] in the land the LORD your God *is* **giving** you to possess.
20: 13 [A] When the LORD your God **delivers** it into your hand, put to
20: 14 [A] you may use the plunder the LORD your God **gives** you
20: 16 [A] in the cities of the nations the LORD your God *is* **giving**
21: 1 [A] lying in a field in the land the LORD your God *is* **giving**
21: 8 [A] *do* not **hold** your people guilty of the blood of an innocent
21: 10 [A] the LORD your God **delivers** them into your hands and you
21: 17 [A] as the firstborn by **giving** him a double share of all he has.
21: 23 [A] land the LORD your God *is* **giving** you as an inheritance.
22: 16 [A] "*I* **gave** [+851+906+4200] my daughter **in marriage** to this
22: 19 [A] a hundred shekels of silver and **give** them to the girl's father,
22: 29 [A] he *shall* **pay** the girl's father fifty shekels of silver. He must
23: 14 [23:15] [A] to protect you and to **deliver** your enemies to you.
23: 24 [23:25] [A] grapes you want, but *do* not **put** any in your basket.
24: 1 [A] of divorce, **gives** it to her and sends her from his house,
24: 3 [A] **gives** it to her and sends her from his house, or if he dies,
24: 4 [A] land the LORD your God *is* **giving** you as an inheritance.
24: 15 [A] **Pay** him his wages each day before sunset, because he is
25: 15 [A] live long in the land the LORD your God *is* **giving** you.
25: 19 [A] you in the land he *is* **giving** you to possess as an inheritance,
26: 1 [A] the land the LORD your God *is* **giving** you as an inheritance
26: 2 [A] from the soil of the land the LORD your God *is* **giving** you
26: 3 [A] to the land the LORD swore to our forefathers to **give** us."
26: 6 [A] mistreated us and made us suffer, **putting** us *to* hard labor.
26: 9 [A] He brought us to this place and **gave** us this land, a land
26: 10 [A] the firstfruits of the soil that *you*, O LORD, *have* **given**
26: 11 [A] in all the good things the LORD your God *has* **given** to you
26: 12 [A] *you shall* **give** it to the Levite, the alien, the fatherless
26: 13 [A] my house the sacred portion and *have* **given** it to the Levite,
26: 14 [A] while I was unclean, nor *have I* **offered** any of it to the dead.
26: 15 [A] the land *you have* **given** us as you promised on oath to our
26: 19 [A] He has declared that he *will* **set** you in praise, fame
27: 2 [A] the Jordan into the land the LORD your God *is* **giving** you,
27: 3 [A] over to enter the land the LORD your God *is* **giving** you,
28: 1 [A] the LORD your God *will* **set** you high above all the nations
28: 7 [A] The LORD *will* **grant** that the enemies who rise up against

Dt 28: 8 [A] The LORD your God will bless you in the land *he is* **giving**
28: 11 [A] in the land he swore to your forefathers to **give** you.
28: 12 [A] to **send** rain on your land in season and to bless all the work
28: 13 [A] The LORD *will* **make** you the head, not the tail. If you pay
28: 24 [A] The LORD *will* **turn** the rain of your country **into** dust
28: 25 [A] The LORD *will* **cause** you to be defeated before your
28: 31 [B] Your sheep *will* **be given** to your enemies, and no one will
28: 32 [B] Your sons and daughters *will* **be given** to another nation,
28: 48 [A] *He will* **put** an iron yoke on your neck until he has destroyed
28: 52 [A] throughout the land the LORD your God *is* **giving** you.
28: 53 [A] the sons and daughters the LORD your God *has* **given** you.
28: 55 [A] he *will* not **give** to one of them any of the flesh of his
28: 65 [A] There the LORD *will* **give** you an anxious mind, eyes weary
28: 67 [A] the morning you will say, "**If only** [+4769] it were evening!"
28: 67 [A] in the evening, "**If only** [+4769] it were morning!"—
29: 4 [29:3] [A] to this day the LORD *has* not **given** you a mind that
29: 8 [29:7] [A] and **gave** it as an inheritance to the Reubenites,
30: 1 [A] and curses *I have* **set** before you come upon you
30: 7 [A] The LORD your God *will* **put** all these curses on your
30: 15 [A] *I* **set** before you today life and prosperity, death and
30: 19 [A] earth as witnesses against you that *I have* **set** before you life
30: 20 [A] he will give you many years in the land he swore to **give** to
31: 5 [A] The LORD *will* **deliver** them to you, and you must do to
31: 7 [A] land that the LORD swore to their forefathers to **give** them,
31: 9 [A] So Moses wrote down this law and **gave** it to the priests,
32: 49 [A] the land I *am* **giving** the Israelites as their own possession.
32: 52 [A] you will not enter the land I *am* **giving** to the people of
34: 4 [A] and Jacob when I said, '*I will* **give** it to your descendants.'
Jos 1: 2 [A] the Jordan River into the land I *am about to* **give** to them—
1: 3 [A] *I will* **give** you every place where you set your foot, as I
1: 6 [A] to inherit the land I swore to their forefathers to **give** them.
1: 11 [A] take possession of the land the LORD your God *is* **giving**
1: 13 [A] your God is giving you rest and *has* **granted** you this land.'
1: 14 [A] your livestock may stay in the land that Moses **gave** you east
1: 15 [A] of the land that the LORD your God *is* **giving** them.
1: 15 [A] which Moses the servant of the LORD **gave** you east of the
2: 9 [A] "I know that the LORD *has* **given** this land to you and that
2: 12 [A] because I have shown kindness to you. **Give** me a sure sign
2: 14 [A] and faithfully when the LORD **gives** us the land."
2: 24 [A] "The LORD *has* surely **given** the whole land into our
5: 6 [A] land that he had solemnly promised their fathers to **give** us,
6: 2 [A] *I have* **delivered** Jericho into your hands, along with its king
6: 16 [A] the people, "Shout! For the LORD *has* **given** you the city!
6: 24 [A] *they* **put** the silver and gold and the articles of bronze and iron
7: 7 [A] to **deliver** us into the hands of the Amorites to destroy us?
7: 19 [A] to the LORD, the God of Israel, and **give** him the praise.
8: 1 [A] For *I have* **delivered** into your hands the king of Ai, his
8: 7 [A] the city. The LORD your God *will* **give** it into your hand.
8: 18 [A] is in your hand, for into your hand *I will* **deliver** the city."
9: 24 [A] commanded his servant Moses to **give** you the whole land
9: 27 [A] That day he **made** the Gibeonites woodcutters and water
10: 8 [A] "Do not be afraid of them; *I have* **given** them into your hand.
10: 12 [A] On the day the LORD **gave** the Amorites **over** to Israel,
10: 19 [A] them from the rear and don't **let** them reach their cities,
10: 19 [A] for the LORD your God *has* **given** them into your hand."
10: 30 [A] The LORD also **gave** that city and its king into Israel's
10: 32 [A] The LORD **handed** Lachish **over to** [+906+928+3338]
11: 6 [A] because by this time tomorrow I *will* **hand** all of them **over**
11: 8 [A] the LORD **gave** them into the hand of Israel. They defeated
11: 23 [A] he **gave** it as an inheritance to Israel according to their tribal
12: 6 [A] Moses the servant of the LORD **gave** their land to the
12: 7 [A] which rises toward Seir (their lands Joshua **gave** as an
13: 8 [A] Gadites had received the inheritance that Moses *had* **given**
13: 8 [A] as he, the servant of the LORD, *had* **assigned** it to them.
13: 14 [A] to the tribe of Levi *he* **gave** no inheritance,
13: 15 [A] This is what Moses *had* **given** to the tribe of Reuben, clan by
13: 24 [A] This is what Moses *had* **given** to the tribe of Gad, clan by
13: 29 [A] This is what Moses *had* **given** to the half-tribe of Manasseh,
13: 33 [A] to the tribe of Levi, Moses *had* **given** no inheritance;
14: 3 [A] Moses *had* **granted** the two-and-a-half tribes their
14: 3 [A] *had* not **granted** the Levites an inheritance among the rest,
14: 4 [A] The Levites **received** no share of the land but only towns to
14: 12 [A] Now **give** me this hill country that the LORD promised me
14: 13 [A] son of Jephunneh and **gave** him Hebron as his inheritance.
15: 13 [A] Joshua **gave** to Caleb son of Jephunneh a portion in Judah—
15: 16 [A] "*I will* **give** [+851+906+4200] my daughter Acsah **in marriage**
15: 17 [A] **gave** [+851+906+4200] his daughter Acsah to him **in marriage**.
15: 19 [A] She replied, "**Do** me a special favor. Since you have given
15: 19 [A] Since *you have* **given** me land in the Negev, give me also
15: 19 [A] given me land in the Negev, **give** me also springs of water."
15: 19 [A] of water." So Caleb **gave** her the upper and lower springs.
17: 4 [A] "The LORD commanded Moses to **give** us an inheritance
17: 4 [A] So Joshua **gave** them an inheritance along with the brothers
17: 13 [A] *they* **subjected** the Canaanites to forced labor but did not
17: 14 [A] "Why *have you* **given** us only one allotment and one portion
18: 3 [A] that the LORD, the God of your fathers, *has* **given** you?
18: 7 [A] Moses the servant of the LORD **gave** it to them."
19: 49 [A] the Israelites **gave** Joshua son of Nun an inheritance among
19: 50 [A] *They* **gave** him the town he asked for—Timnath Serah in the
20: 2 [A] "Tell the Israelites *to* **designate** the cities of refuge, as I
20: 4 [A] him into their city and **give** him a place to live with them.
20: 8 [A] *they* **designated** Bezer in the desert on the plateau in the tribe
21: 2 [A] "The LORD commanded through Moses that you **give** us
21: 3 [A] the Israelites **gave** the Levites the following towns and
21: 8 [A] So the Israelites **allotted** [+906+906+928+1598+2021] to the
21: 9 [A] and Simeon *they* **allotted** the following towns by name
21: 11 [A] *They* **gave** them Kiriath Arba (that is, Hebron), with its
21: 12 [A] the fields and villages around the city *they had* **given** to
21: 13 [A] So to the descendants of Aaron the priest *they* **gave** Hebron
21: 21 [A] In the hill country of Ephraim they *were* **given** Shechem (a
21: 43 [A] So the LORD **gave** Israel all the land he had sworn to give
21: 43 [A] So the LORD gave Israel all the land he had sworn to **give**
21: 44 [A] **handed** all their enemies **over to** [+906+928+3338] them.
22: 4 [A] of the LORD **gave** you on the other side of the Jordan.
22: 7 [A] (To the half-tribe of Manasseh Moses *had* **given** land in
22: 7 [A] to the other half of the tribe Joshua **gave** land on the west
22: 25 [A] The LORD *has* **made** the Jordan a boundary between us
23: 13 [A] this good land, which the LORD your God *has* **given** you.
23: 15 [A] until he has destroyed you from this good land he *has* **given**
23: 16 [A] you will quickly perish from the good land *he has* **given**
24: 3 [A] and gave him many descendants. *I* **gave** him Isaac,
24: 4 [A] to Isaac *I* **gave** Jacob and Esau. I assigned the hill country of
24: 4 [A] *I* **assigned** the hill country of Seir to Esau, but Jacob and his
24: 8 [A] They fought against you, but *I* **gave** them into your hands.
24: 11 [A] and Jebusites, but *I* **gave** them into your hands.
24: 13 [A] So *I* **gave** you a land on which you did not toil and cities you
24: 33 [C] which *had* **been allotted** to his son Phinehas in the hill
Jdg 1: 2 [A] "Judah is to go; *I have* **given** the land into their hands."
1: 4 [A] the LORD **gave** the Canaanites and Perizzites into their
1: 12 [A] "*I will* **give** [+851+906+4200] my daughter Acsah **in marriage**
1: 13 [A] **gave** [+851+906+4200] his daughter Acsah to him **in marriage**.
1: 15 [A] Since *you have* **given** me land *in* the Negev, give me also
1: 15 [A] given me land in the Negev, **give** me also springs of water."
1: 15 [A] of water." Then Caleb **gave** her the upper and lower springs.
1: 20 [A] As Moses had promised, Hebron *was* **given** to Caleb, who
1: 34 [A] hill country, not **allowing** them to come down into the plain.
2: 14 [A] **handed** them **over to** [+928+3338] raiders who plundered
2: 23 [A] he did not drive them out at once *by* **giving** them into the
3: 6 [A] in marriage and **gave** their own daughters to their sons,
3: 10 [A] The LORD **gave** Cushan-Rishathaim king of Aram into the
3: 28 [A] he ordered, "for the LORD *has* **given** Moab, your enemy,
3: 28 [A] Jordan that led to Moab, *they* **allowed** no one to cross over.
4: 7 [A] troops to the Kishon River and **give** him into your hands.' "
4: 14 [A] This is the day the LORD *has* **given** Sisera into your hands.
5: 25 [A] He asked for water, and *she* **gave** him milk; in a bowl fit for
6: 1 [A] for seven years he **gave** them into the hands of the
6: 9 [A] I drove them from before you and **gave** you their land.
6: 13 [A] has abandoned us and **put** us into the hand of Midian."
7: 2 [A] "You have too many men for me *to* **deliver** Midian into their
7: 7 [A] I will save you and **give** the Midianites into your hands.
7: 9 [A] the camp, because *I am going to* **give** it into your hands.
7: 14 [A] God *has* **given** the Midianites and the whole camp into his
7: 15 [A] The LORD *has* **given** the Midianite camp into your hands."
7: 16 [A] *he* **placed** trumpets and empty jars in the hands of all of
8: 3 [A] God **gave** Oreb and Zeeb, the Midianite leaders, into your
8: 5 [A] He said to the men of Succoth, "**Give** my troops some bread;
8: 6 [A] your possession? Why *should we* **give** bread to your troops?"
8: 7 [A] when the LORD *has* **given** Zebah and Zalmunna into my
8: 15 [A] Why *should we* **give** bread to your exhausted men?' "
8: 24 [A] that each of you **give** me an earring from your share of the
8: 25 [A] They answered, "*We'll be* **glad to give** [+5989] them."
8: 25 [A] They answered, "*We'll be* **glad to give** [+5989] them."
9: 4 [A] *They* **gave** him seventy shekels of silver from the temple of
9: 29 [A] **If only** [+906+4769] this people were under my command!
11: 9 [A] to fight the Ammonites and the LORD **gives** them to me—
11: 21 [A] God of Israel, **gave** Sihon and all his men into Israel's hands,
11: 30 [A] "If *you* **give** [+906+5989] the Ammonites into my hands,
11: 30 [A] "If *you* **give** [+906+5989] the Ammonites into my hands,
11: 32 [A] the Ammonites, and the LORD **gave** them into his hands.
12: 3 [A] the LORD **gave** [+928+3338] me the **victory** *over* them.
13: 1 [A] so the LORD **delivered** them into the hands of the
14: 9 [A] rejoined his parents, *he* **gave** them some, and they too ate it.
14: 12 [A] *I will* **give** you thirty linen garments and thirty sets of
14: 13 [A] you *must* **give** me thirty linen garments and thirty sets of
14: 19 [A] and **gave** their clothes to those who had explained the riddle.
15: 1 [A] to my wife's room." But her father *would* not **let** him go in.
15: 2 [A] hated her," he said, "that *I* **gave** her to your friend.
15: 6 [A] because his wife *was* **given** to his friend."

Jdg 15:12 [A] you up and **hand** you **over to** [+928+3338] the Philistines."
15:13 [A] only tie you up and **hand** you **over to** [+928+3338] them.
15:18 [A] the LORD, "You *have* **given** your servant this great victory.
16: 5 [A] Each one of us *will* **give** you eleven hundred shekels of
16:23 [A] saying, "Our god *has* **delivered** Samson, our enemy, into our
16:24 [A] saying, "Our god *has* **delivered** our enemy into our hands,
17: 4 [A] two hundred shekels of silver and **gave** them to a silversmith,
17:10 [A] and priest, and I'll **give** you ten shekels of silver a year,
18:10 [A] and a spacious land that God *has* **put** into your hands,
20:13 [A] Now **surrender** those wicked men of Gibeah so that we may
20:28 [A] "Go, for tomorrow *I will* **give** them into your hands."
20:36 [A] Now the men of Israel *had* **given** way before Benjamin,
21: 1 [A] *will* **give** [+851+4200] his daughter **in marriage** to a
21: 7 [A] *to* **give** [+851+4200+4200] them any of our daughters in
21:14 [A] *were* **given** the women of Jabesh Gilead who had been
21:18 [A] We can't **give** them our daughters as wives, since we
21:18 [A] 'Cursed be *anyone who* **gives** a wife to a Benjamite.'
21:22 [A] since you *did* not **give** your daughters to them.' "
Ru 1: 6 [A] come to the aid of his people by **providing** food for them,
1: 9 [A] *May* the LORD **grant** that each of you will find rest in the
2:18 [A] **gave** her what she had left over after she had eaten enough.
3:17 [A] "*He* **gave** me these six measures of barley, saying,
4: 7 [A] one party took off his sandal and **gave** it to the other.
4:11 [A] *May* the LORD **make** the woman who is coming into your
4:12 [A] Through the offspring the LORD **gives** you by this young
4:13 [A] he went to her, and the LORD **enabled** her to conceive,
1Sa 1: 4 [A] *he would* **give** portions of the meat to his wife Peninnah
1: 5 [A] to Hannah *he* **gave** a double portion because he loved her,
1:11 [A] remember me, and not forget your servant but **give** her a son,
1:11 [A] then *I will* **give** him to the LORD for all the days of his life,
1:16 [A] *Do* not **take** [+906+4200+7156] your servant **for** a wicked
1:17 [A] *may* the God of Israel **grant** you what you have asked of
1:27 [A] and the LORD *has* **granted** me what I asked of him.
2:10 [A] "*He will* **give** strength to his king and exalt the horn of his
2:15 [A] who was sacrificing, "**Give** the priest some meat to roast;
2:16 [A] the servant would then answer, "No, **hand** it **over** now;
2:28 [A] *I* also **gave** your father's house all the offerings made with
6: 5 [A] are destroying the country, and **pay** honor to Israel's god.
6: 8 [A] Take the ark of the LORD and **put** it on the cart, and in a
8: 6 [A] when they said, "**Give** us a king to lead us," this displeased
8:14 [A] and olive groves and **give** them to his attendants.
8:15 [A] and of your vintage and **give** it to his officials and attendants.
9: 8 [A] *I will* **give** it to the man of God so that he will tell us what
9:22 [A] **seated** [+4200+5226] them at the head of those who were
9:23 [A] said to the cook, "**Bring** the piece of meat I gave you,
9:23 [A] said to the cook, "Bring the piece of meat *I* **gave** you,
10: 4 [A] They will greet you and **offer** you two loaves of bread, which
11:12 [A] **Bring** these men to us and we will put them to death."
12:13 [A] one you asked for; see, the LORD *has* **set** a king over you.
12:17 [A] I will call upon the LORD *to* **send** thunder and rain.
12:18 [A] and that same day the LORD **sent** thunder and rain.
14:10 [A] because that will be our sign that the LORD *has* **given** them
14:12 [A] the LORD *has* **given** them into the hand of Israel."
14:37 [A] *Will you* **give** them into Israel's hand?" But God did not
15:28 [A] from you today and *has* **given** it to one of your neighbors—
17:10 [A] ranks of Israel! **Give** me a man and let us fight each other."
17:25 [A] *He will* also **give** him his daughter **in marriage** and will
17:38 [A] of armor on him and **[RPH]** a bronze helmet on his head.
17:44 [A] "and *I'll* **give** your flesh to the birds of the air and the beasts
17:46 [A] Today *I will* **give** the carcasses of the Philistine army to the
17:47 [A] is the LORD's, and *he will* **give** all of you into our hands."
18: 2 [A] with him and *did* not **let** him return to his father's house.
18: 4 [A] took off the robe he was wearing and **gave** it to David,
18: 8 [A] "*They have* **credited** David *with* tens of thousands,"
18: 8 [A] he thought, "but me with **[RPH]** only thousands.
18:17 [A] *I will* **give** [+851+906+4200] her to you **in marriage**; only
18:19 [A] time came for Merab, Saul's daughter, *to be* **given** to David,
18:19 [C] she **was given** [+851+4200] **in marriage** to Adriel of
18:21 [A] "*I will* **give** her to him," he thought, "so that she may be a
18:27 [A] Then Saul **gave** [+851+906+4200+4200] him his daughter
Michal **in marriage**.
20:40 [A] Then Jonathan **gave** his weapons to the boy and said, "Go,
21: 3 [21:4] [A] **Give** [+928+3338] me five loaves of bread,
21: 6 [21:7] [A] So the priest **gave** him the consecrated bread,
21: 9 [21:10] [A] David said, "There is none like it; **give** it to me."
22: 7 [A] *Will* the son of Jesse **give** all of you fields and vineyards?
22:10 [A] *he* also **gave** him provisions and the sword of Goliath the
22:10 [A] and the sword of Goliath the Philistine." **[RPH]**
22:13 [A] **giving** him bread and a sword and inquiring of God for him,
23: 4 [A] for I *am going to* **give** the Philistines into your hand."
23:14 [A] searched for him, but God *did* not **give** David into his hands.
24: 4 [24:5] [A] 'I *will* **give** your enemy into your hands for you to
24: 7 [24:8] [A] his men and *did* not **allow** them to attack Saul.
24:10 [24:11] [A] LORD **delivered** you into my hands in the cave.
25: 8 [A] Please **give** your servants and your son David whatever you
25:11 [A] and **give** it to men coming from who knows where?"
25:27 [C] this gift, which your servant has brought to my master, **be given**
25:44 [A] Saul *had* **given** his daughter Michal, David's wife, to Paltiel
26:23 [A] The LORD **delivered** you into my hands today, but I would
27: 5 [A] *let* a place *be* **assigned** to me in one of the country towns,
27: 6 [A] So on that day Achish **gave** him Ziklag, and it has belonged
28:17 [A] out of your hands and **given** it to one of your neighbors—
28:19 [A] *will* **hand over** both Israel and you **to** [+906+928+3338]
28:19 [A] *will* also **hand over** the army of Israel **to** [+906+928+3338]
30:11 [A] to David. *They* **gave** him water to drink and food to eat—
30:12 [A] **[RPH]** part of a cake of pressed figs and two cakes of
30:22 [A] *we will* not **share** with them the plunder we recovered.
30:23 [A] you must not do that with what the LORD *has* **given** us.
30:23 [A] **handed over to** [+906+928+3338] us the forces that came
2Sa 3:14 [A] son of Saul, demanding, "**Give** me my wife Michal,
4: 8 [A] This day the LORD *has* **avenged** [+4200+5935] my lord
4:10 [A] in Ziklag. That was the reward I **gave** him for his news!
5:19 [A] the Philistines? *Will you* **hand** them **over to** [+928+3338]
5:19 [A] The LORD answered him, "Go, for *I will* **surely hand** the
Philistines **over to** [+906+928+3338+5989] you."
5:19 [A] The LORD answered him, "Go, for *I will* **surely hand** the
Philistines **over to** [+906+928+3338+5989] you."
9: 9 [A] "*I have* **given** your master's grandson everything that
10:10 [A] *He* **put** the rest of the men under the command of Abishai his
11:16 [A] *he* **put** Uriah at a place where he knew the strongest
12: 8 [A] *I* **gave** your master's house to you, and your master's wives
12: 8 [A] *I* **gave** you the house of Israel and Judah. And if all this had
12:11 [A] take your wives and **give** them to one who is close to you,
14: 7 [A] they say, '**Hand over** the one who struck his brother down,
16: 8 [A] *has* **handed** the kingdom **over to** [+906+928+3338] your son
18: 9 [H] *He* **was left hanging** in midair, while the mule he was riding
18:11 [A] I would have had to **give** you ten shekels of silver and a
18:33 [19:1] [A] **If only** [+4769] I had died instead of you—O
20: 3 [A] take care of the palace and **put** them *in* a house under guard.
20:21 [A] **Hand over** this one man, and I'll withdraw from the city."
21: 6 [H] *let* seven of his male descendants **be given** to us to be killed
21: 6 [A] chosen one." So the king said, "I *will* **give** them to you."
21: 9 [A] *He* **handed** them **over to** [+928+3338] the Gibeonites, who
21:10 [A] *she did* not **let** the birds of the air touch them by day or the
22:14 [A] from heaven; the voice of the Most High **resounded**.
22:33 [a] me with strength and **makes** [BHS 6001] my way perfect.
22:36 [A] *You* **give** me your shield of victory; you stoop down to make
22:41 [A] *You* **made** my enemies **turn** their backs in flight, and I
22:48 [A] He is the God who **avenges** [+4200+5935] me, who puts the
24: 9 [A] Joab **reported** the number of the fighting men to the king:
24:15 [A] So the LORD **sent** a plague on Israel from that morning
24:23 [A] O king, Araunah **gives** all this to the king." Araunah also said
1Ki 1:48 [A] who *has* **allowed** my eyes to see a successor on my throne
2: 5 [A] *with* that blood **stained** the belt around his waist and the
2:17 [A] *to* **give** me Abishag the Shunammite as my wife."
2:21 [H] the Shunammite **be given** [+851+906+4200] **in marriage**
2:35 [A] The king **put** Benaiah son of Jehoiada over the army in
2:35 [A] and **replaced** [+906+9393] Abiathar *with* Zadok the priest.
3: 5 [A] and God said, "Ask for whatever you want *me to* **give** you."
3: 6 [A] and *have* **given** him a son to sit on his throne this very day.
3: 9 [A] So **give** your servant a discerning heart to govern your people
3:12 [A] *I will* **give** you a wise and discerning heart, so that there will
3:13 [A] Moreover, *I will* **give** you what you have not asked for—
3:25 [A] living child in two and **give** half to one and half to the other."
3:26 [A] said to the king, "Please, my lord, **give** her the living baby!
3:27 [A] "**Give** the living baby to the first woman. Do not kill him;
4:29 [5:9] [A] God **gave** Solomon wisdom and very great insight,
5: 3 [5:17] [A] God until the LORD **put** his enemies under his feet.
5: 5 [5:19] [A] 'Your son whom *I will* **put** on the throne in your
5: 6 [5:20] [A] *I will* **pay** you for your men whatever wages you set.
5: 7 [5:21] [A] for *he has* **given** David a wise son to rule over this
5: 9 [5:23] [A] you are to grant my wish by **providing** food *for* my
5:10 [5:24] [A] In this way Hiram *kept* Solomon **supplied** *with* all
5:11 [5:25] [A] Solomon **gave** Hiram twenty thousand cors of wheat
5:11 [5:25] [A] Solomon *continued to* **do**[s] this for Hiram year after
5:12 [5:26] [A] The LORD **gave** Solomon wisdom, just as he had
6: 6 [A] *He* **made** offset ledges around the outside of the temple
6:19 [A] He prepared the inner sanctuary within the temple to **set** the
6:27 [A] *He* **placed** the cherubim inside the innermost room of the
7:16 [A] He also made two capitals of cast bronze to **set** on the tops of
7:39 [A] *He* **placed** five of the stands on the south side of the temple
7:39 [A] *He* **placed** the Sea on the south side, at the southeast corner
7:51 [A] and *he* **placed** them in the treasuries of the LORD's temple.
8:32 [A] and **bringing down** on his own head what he has done.
8:32 [A] the innocent not guilty, and so **establish** his innocence.
8:34 [A] and bring them back to the land *you* **gave** to their fathers.
8:36 [A] **send** rain on the land you gave your people for an
8:36 [A] send rain on the land *you* **gave** your people for an

1Ki 8:39 [A] **deal** with each man according to all he does, since you know
8:40 [A] you all the time they live in the land *you* **gave** our fathers.
8:46 [A] become angry with them and **give** them **over** to the enemy,
8:48 [A] pray to you toward the land *you* **gave** their fathers,
8:50 [A] against you, and **cause** their conquerors to show them mercy;
8:56 [A] who *has* **given** rest to his people Israel just as he promised.
9:6 [A] and decrees *I have* **given** you and go off to serve other gods
9:7 [A] I will cut off Israel from the land *I have* **given** them and will
9:11 [A] King Solomon **gave** twenty towns in Galilee to Hiram king
9:12 [A] from Tyre to see the towns that Solomon *had* **given** him,
9:13 [A] "What kind of towns are these *you have* **given** me,
9:16 [A] and then **gave** it as a wedding gift to his daughter,
9:22 [A] But Solomon did not **make** slaves of any of the Israelites;
10:9 [A] has delighted in you and **placed** you on the throne of Israel.
10:10 [A] *she* **gave** the king 120 talents of gold, large quantities of
10:10 [A] so many spices brought in as those the queen of Sheba **gave**
10:13 [A] King Solomon **gave** the queen of Sheba all she desired and
10:13 [A] besides what *he had* **given** her out of his royal bounty.
10:17 [A] The king **put** them in the Palace of the Forest of Lebanon.
10:24 [A] with Solomon to hear the wisdom God *had* **put** in his heart.
10:27 [A] The king **made** silver as common in Jerusalem as stones, and
10:27 [A] cedar **[RPH]** as plentiful as sycamore-fig trees in the
11:11 [A] away from you and **give** it to one of your subordinates.
11:13 [A] but *will* **give** him one tribe for the sake of David my servant
11:18 [A] *who* **gave** Hadad a house and land and provided him with
11:18 [A] Hadad a house and land **[RPH]** and provided him with food.
11:19 [A] *he* **gave** [+851+906+4200] him a sister … **in marriage**.
11:31 [A] the kingdom out of Solomon's hand and **give** you ten tribes.
11:35 [A] the kingdom from his son's hands and **give** you ten tribes.
11:36 [A] *I will* **give** one tribe to his son so that David my servant may
11:38 [A] as the one I built for David and *will* **give** Israel to you.
12:4 [A] now lighten the harsh labor and the heavy yoke he **put** on us,
12:9 [A] who say to me, 'Lighten the yoke your father **put** on us'?"
12:29 [A] One he set up in Bethel, and the other **[RPH]** in Dan.
13:3 [A] That same day the man of God **gave** a sign: "This is the sign
13:5 [A] its ashes poured out according to the sign **given** *by* the man
13:7 [A] and have something to eat, and *I will* **give** you a gift."
13:8 [A] "Even if *you were to* **give** me half your possessions, I would
13:26 [A] The LORD *has* **given** him **over** to the lion, which has
14:7 [A] the people and **made** you a leader over my people Israel.
14:8 [A] kingdom away from the house of David and **gave** it to you,
14:15 [A] He will uproot Israel from this good land that *he* **gave** to
14:16 [A] *he will* **give** Israel **up** because of the sins Jeroboam has
15:4 [A] for David's sake the LORD his God **gave** him a lamp in
15:17 [A] fortified Ramah to **prevent** [+1194] anyone *from* leaving
15:18 [A] *He* **entrusted** it to his officials and sent them to Ben-Hadad
16:2 [A] up from the dust and **made** you leader of my people Israel,
16:3 [A] *I will* **make** your house like that of Jeroboam son of Nebat.
17:14 [A] the jug of oil will not run dry until the day the LORD **gives**
17:19 [A] "**Give** me your son," Elijah replied. He took him from her
17:23 [A] *He* **gave** him to his mother and said, "Look, your son is
18:1 [A] present yourself to Ahab, and *I will* **send** rain on the land."
18:9 [A] *are* **handing** your servant **over to** [+906+928+3338] Ahab to
18:23 [A] **Get** two bulls for us. Let them choose one for themselves,
18:23 [A] the other bull and **put** it on the wood but not set fire to it.
18:26 [A] So they took the bull **given** them and prepared it. Then they
19:21 [A] equipment to cook the meat and **gave** it to the people,
20:5 [A] your silver and gold, your wives and your children. **[NIE]**
20:13 [A] I *will* **give** it into your hand today, and then you will know
20:28 [A] of the valleys, *I will* **deliver** this vast army into your hands,
21:2 [A] "**Let** me **have** your vineyard to use for a vegetable garden,
21:2 [A] In exchange *I will* **give** you a better vineyard or, if you
21:2 [A] *I will* **pay** [+4084+4200] you whatever it is worth."
21:3 [A] "The LORD forbid that I *should* **give** you the inheritance of
21:4 [A] had said, "*I will* not **give** you the inheritance of my fathers."
21:6 [A] the Jezreelite, '**Sell** [+906+928+4084+4200] me your vineyard;
21:6 [A] or if you prefer, *I will* **give** you another vineyard in its place.'
21:6 [A] in its place.' But he said, '*I will* not **give** you my vineyard.' "
21:7 [A] Cheer up. I'll **get** you the vineyard of Naboth the Jezreelite."
21:15 [A] the Jezreelite that he refused to **sell** [+928+4084+4200] you.
21:22 [A] *I will* **make** your house like that of Jeroboam son of Nebat
22:6 [A] "for the Lord *will* **give** it into the king's hand."
22:12 [A] they said, "for the LORD *will* **give** it into the king's hand."
22:15 [A] "for the LORD *will* **give** it into the king's hand."
22:23 [A] "So now the LORD *has* **put** a lying spirit in the mouths of
2Ki 3:10 [A] together only to **hand** us **over to** [+906+928+3338] Moab?"
3:13 [A] kings together to **hand** us **over to** [+906+928+3338] Moab."
3:18 [A] *he will* also **hand** Moab **over to** [+906+928+3338]
4:42 [A] of new grain. "**Give** it to the people to eat," Elisha said.
4:43 [A] "How *can I* **set** this before a hundred men?" his servant
4:43 [A] But Elisha answered, "**Give** it to the people to eat.
4:44 [A] *he* **set** it before them, and they ate and had some left over,
5:1 [A] because through him the LORD *had* **given** victory to Aram.
5:17 [H] "please *let me*, your servant, **be given** as much earth as a pair
5:22 [A] Please **give** them a talent of silver and two sets of clothing.' "
5:23 [A] *He* **gave** them to two of his servants, and they carried them
6:28 [A] said to me, '**Give up** your son so we may eat him today,
6:29 [A] '**Give up** your son so we may eat him,' but she had hidden
8:6 [A] he **assigned** an official to her case and said to him,
8:19 [A] He had promised to **maintain** a lamp for David and his
9:9 [A] *I will* **make** the house of Ahab like the house of Jeroboam
10:15 [A] "If so," said Jehu, "**give** me your hand." So he did, and Jehu
10:15 [A] So *he* **did**[s] [+2257+3338], and Jehu helped him up into the
11:10 [A] he **gave** the commanders the spears and shields that had
11:12 [A] **put** the crown on him; he presented him with a copy of the
12:7 [12:8] [A] but **hand** it **over** for repairing the temple."
12:9 [12:10] [A] *He* **placed** it beside the altar, on the right side as
12:9 [12:10] [A] **put** into the chest all the money that was brought to
12:11 [12:12] [A] *they* **gave** the money to the men appointed to
12:14 [12:15] [A] it *was* **paid** to the workmen, who used it to repair
12:15 [12:16] [A] to whom *they* **gave** the money to pay the workers,
12:15 [12:16] [A] to whom they gave the money to **pay** the workers,
13:3 [A] for a long time *he* **kept** them under the power of Hazael king
13:5 [A] The LORD **provided** a deliverer for Israel, and they
14:9 [A] '**Give** [+851+906+4200] your daughter to my son **in marriage**.'
15:19 [A] Menahem **gave** him a thousand talents of silver to gain his
15:20 [A] fifty shekels of silver to *be* **given** to the king of Assyria.
16:14 [A] of the LORD—and **put** it on the north side of the new altar.
16:17 [A] the bronze bulls that supported it and **set** it on a stone base.
17:20 [A] he afflicted them and **gave** them into the hands of plunderers,
18:14 [A] from me, and I will pay whatever *you* **demand** of me."
18:15 [A] So Hezekiah **gave** him all the silver that was found in the
18:16 [A] the temple of the LORD, and **gave** it to the king of Assyria.
18:23 [A] *I will* **give** you two thousand horses—if you can put riders on
18:23 [A] you two thousand horses—if you can **put** riders on them!
18:30 [C] this city *will* not **be given** into the hand of the king of
19:7 [A] I *am going to* **put** such a spirit in him that when he hears a
19:10 [C] 'Jerusalem *will* not **be handed over to** [+928+3338] the king
19:18 [A] *They have* **thrown** their gods into the fire and destroyed
21:8 [A] the Israelites wander from the land *I* **gave** their forefathers,
21:14 [A] and **hand** them **over to** [+928+3338] their enemies.
22:5 [A] *Have them* **entrust** it to the men appointed to supervise the
22:5 [A] *have these men* **pay** the workers who repair the temple of
22:7 [C] But they need not account for the money **entrusted** to them,
22:8 [A] temple of the LORD." He **gave** it to Shaphan, who read it.
22:9 [A] *have* **entrusted** it to the workers and supervisors at the
22:10 [A] informed the king, "Hilkiah the priest *has* **given** me a book."
23:5 [A] He did away with the pagan priests **appointed** *by* the kings
23:11 [A] the horses that the kings of Judah *had* **dedicated** to the sun.
23:33 [A] *he* **imposed** on Judah a levy of a hundred talents of silver
23:35 [A] Jehoiakim **paid** Pharaoh Neco the silver and gold he
23:35 [A] In order to **do**[s] **so**, he taxed the land and exacted the silver
23:35 [A] people of the land according to their assessments. **[RPH]**
25:28 [A] **gave** him a seat of honor higher than those of the other kings
25:30 [C] Day by day the king **gave** Jehoiachin a regular allowance as
1Ch 2:35 [A] Sheshan **gave** [+851+906+4200] his daughter **in marriage** to
5:1 [C] his rights as firstborn **were given** to the sons of Joseph son of
5:20 [C] **handed** the Hagrites and all their allies **over to** [+928+3338]
6:48 [6:33] [B] Their fellow Levites **were assigned** to all the other
6:55 [6:40] [A] They *were* **given** Hebron in Judah with its
6:56 [6:41] [A] the fields and villages around the city *were* **given** to
6:57 [6:42] [A] the descendants of Aaron *were* **given** Hebron (a city of
6:64 [6:49] [A] So the Israelites **gave** the Levites these towns and
6:65 [6:50] [A] Benjamin *they* **allotted** [+906+928+1598+2021] the
6:67 [6:52] [A] they *were* **given** Shechem (a city of refuge), and
12:18 [12:19] [A] and **made** them leaders of his raiding bands.
14:10 [A] the Philistines? *Will you* **hand** them **over to** [+928+3338]
14:10 [A] "Go, *I will* **hand** them **over to** [+928+3338] you."
14:17 [A] every land, and the LORD **made** all the nations fear him.
16:4 [A] *He* **appointed** some of the Levites to minister before the ark
16:7 [A] That day David first **committed** to Asaph and his associates
16:18 [A] "To you *I will* **give** the land of Canaan as the portion you
17:22 [A] *You* **made** your people Israel your very own forever,
19:11 [A] *He* **put** the rest of the men under the command of Abishai his
21:5 [A] Joab **reported** the number of the fighting men to David: In
21:14 [A] So the LORD **sent** a plague on Israel, and seventy thousand
21:22 [A] "*Let* me **have** the site of your threshing floor so I can build
21:22 [A] on the people may be stopped. **Sell** it to me at the full price."
21:23 [A] Look, *I will* **give** the oxen for the burnt offerings,
21:23 [A] and the wheat for the grain offering. *I will* **give** all this."
21:25 [A] So David **paid** [+4200+5486] Araunah six hundred shekels
22:9 [A] and *I will* **grant** Israel peace and quiet during his reign.
22:12 [A] *May* the LORD **give** you discretion and understanding
22:18 [A] *he has* **handed** the inhabitants of the land **over to** [+906+928+3338]
22:19 [A] Now **devote** your heart and soul to seeking the LORD your
25:5 [A] God **gave** Heman fourteen sons and three daughters.
28:5 [A] Of all my sons—and the LORD *has* **given** me many—he
28:11 [A] David **gave** his son Solomon the plans for the portico of the

1Ch 29: 3 [A] in my devotion to the temple of my God *I now* **give** my
29: 7 [A] *They* **gave** toward the work on the temple of God five
29: 8 [A] Any who had precious stones **gave** them to the treasury of
29: 14 [A] and *we have* **given** you only what comes from your hand.
29: 19 [A] **give** my son Solomon the wholehearted devotion to keep
29: 24 [A] **pledged** [+3338] their submission to King Solomon.
29: 25 [A] **bestowed** on him royal splendor such as no king over Israel
2Ch 1: 7 [A] said to him, "Ask for whatever you want *me to* **give** you."
1: 10 [A] **Give** me wisdom and knowledge, that I may lead this people,
1: 12 [B] therefore wisdom and knowledge *will* **be given** you. And I
1: 12 [A] *I will* also **give** you wealth, riches and honor, such as no king
1: 15 [A] **made** silver and gold as common in Jerusalem as stones, and
1: 15 [A] cedar as plentiful **[RPH]** as sycamore-fig trees in the
2: 10 [2:9] [A] *I will* **give** your servants, the woodsmen who cut the
2: 11 [2:10] [A] loves his people, *he has* **made** you their king."
2: 12 [2:11] [A] *He has* **given** King David a wise son, endowed with
2: 14 [2:13] [C] and can execute any design **given** to him.
3: 16 [A] made interwoven chains and **put** them on top of the pillars.
3: 16 [A] a hundred pomegranates and **attached** them to the chains.
4: 6 [A] and **placed** five on the south side and five on the north.
4: 7 [A] to the specifications for them and **placed** them in the temple,
4: 10 [A] *He* **placed** the Sea on the south side, at the southeast corner.
5: 1 [A] and *he* **placed** them in the treasuries of God's temple.
5: 10 [A] except the two tablets that Moses *had* **placed** in it at Horeb,
6: 13 [A] cubits high, and *had* **placed** it in the center of the outer court.
6: 23 [A] repaying the guilty by **bringing down** on his own head what
6: 23 [A] the innocent not guilty and so **establish** his innocence.
6: 25 [A] bring them back to the land *you* **gave** to them and their
6: 27 [A] **send** rain on the land you gave your people for an
6: 27 [A] send rain on the land *you* **gave** your people for an
6: 30 [A] Forgive, and **deal** with each man according to all he does,
6: 31 [A] walk in your ways all the time they live in the land *you* **gave**
6: 36 [A] become angry with them and **give** them **over** to the enemy,
6: 38 [A] pray toward the land *you* **gave** their fathers, toward the city
7: 19 [A] and forsake the decrees and commands *I have* **given** you
7: 20 [A] I will uproot Israel from my land, which *I have* **given** them,
7: 20 [A] *I will* **make** it a byword and an object of ridicule among all
8: 2 [A] Solomon rebuilt the villages that Hiram *had* **given** him,
8: 9 [A] Solomon *did* not **make** slaves of the Israelites for his work;
9: 8 [A] **placed** you on his throne as king to rule for the LORD your
9: 8 [A] *he has* **made** you king over them, to maintain justice
9: 9 [A] *she* **gave** the king 120 talents of gold, large quantities of
9: 9 [A] spices as those the queen of Sheba **gave** to King Solomon.
9: 12 [A] King Solomon **gave** the queen of Sheba all she desired and
9: 16 [A] The king **put** them in the Palace of the Forest of Lebanon.
9: 23 [A] with Solomon to hear the wisdom God *had* **put** in his heart.
9: 27 [A] The king **made** silver as common in Jerusalem as stones, and
9: 27 [A] cedar **[RPH]** as plentiful as sycamore-fig trees in the
10: 4 [A] now lighten the harsh labor and the heavy yoke he **put** on us,
10: 9 [A] who say to me, 'Lighten the yoke your father **put** on us'?"
11: 11 [A] He strengthened their defenses and **put** commanders in them,
11: 16 [A] Those from every tribe of Israel who **set** their hearts on
11: 23 [A] *He* **gave** them abundant provisions and took many wives for
12: 7 [A] I will not destroy them but *will* soon **give** them deliverance.
13: 5 [A] *has* **given** the kingship of Israel to David and his descendants
13: 16 [A] fled before Judah, and God **delivered** them into their hands.
16: 1 [A] fortified Ramah to **prevent** [+1194] anyone *from* leaving
16: 8 [A] you relied on the LORD, *he* **delivered** them into your hand.
16: 10 [A] because of this; he was so enraged that *he* **put** him *in* prison.
17: 2 [A] *He* **stationed** troops in all the fortified cities of Judah and put
17: 2 [A] in all the fortified cities of Judah and **put** garrisons in Judah
17: 5 [A] all Judah **brought** gifts to Jehoshaphat, so that he had great
17: 19 [A] besides those he **stationed** in the fortified cities throughout
18: 5 [A] they answered, "for God *will* **give** it into the king's hand."
18: 11 [A] they said, "for the LORD *will* **give** it into the king's hand."
18: 14 [C] he answered, "for *they will* **be given** into your hand."
18: 22 [A] "So now the LORD *has* **put** a lying spirit in the mouths of
20: 3 [A] Jehoshaphat **resolved** [+906+7156] to inquire of the LORD,
20: 7 [A] **give** it forever to the descendants of Abraham your friend?
20: 10 [A] whose territory *you would* not **allow** Israel to invade when
20: 22 [A] the LORD **set** ambushes against the men of Ammon
21: 3 [A] Their father *had* **given** them many gifts of silver and gold
21: 3 [A] *he had* **given** the kingdom to Jehoram because he was his
21: 7 [A] He had promised to **maintain** a lamp for him and his
22: 11 [A] to be murdered and **put** him and his nurse in a bedroom.
23: 9 [A] **gave** the commanders of units of a hundred the spears and the
23: 11 [A] **put** the crown on him; they presented him with a copy of the
24: 8 [A] the king's command, a chest was made and **placed** outside,
24: 9 [A] A proclamation *was* then **issued** in Judah and Jerusalem that
24: 12 [A] Jehoiada **gave** it to the men who carried out the work
24: 24 [A] the LORD **delivered** into their hands a much larger army.
25: 9 [A] "But what about the hundred talents *I* **paid** for these Israelite
25: 9 [A] "The LORD *can* **give** you much more than that."
25: 16 [A] said to him, "*Have we* **appointed** you an adviser to the king?
25: 18 [A] '**Give** [+851+906+4200] your daughter to my son **in marriage**.'
25: 20 [A] so worked that he *might* **hand** them **over** [+928+3338] to
26: 8 [A] The Ammonites **brought** tribute to Uzziah, and his fame
27: 5 [A] That year the Ammonites **paid** him a hundred talents of
28: 5 [A] his God **handed** him **over to** [+928+3338] the king of Aram.
28: 5 [C] *He* **was** also **given** into the hands of the king of Israel, who
28: 9 [A] was angry with Judah, *he* **gave** them into your hand.
28: 21 [A] from the princes and **presented** them to the king of Assyria,
29: 6 [A] the LORD's dwelling place and **turned** their backs on him.
29: 8 [A] *he has* **made** them an object of dread and horror and scorn,
30: 7 [A] so that *he* **made** them an object of horror, as you see.
30: 8 [A] as your fathers were; **submit** [+3338] to the LORD.
30: 12 [A] Also in Judah the hand of God was on the people to **give**
31: 4 [A] He ordered the people living in Jerusalem to **give** the portion
31: 6 [A] to the LORD their God, and *they* **piled** them in heaps.
31: 14 [A] **distributing** the contributions made to the LORD and also
31: 15 [A] **distributing** to their fellow priests according to their
31: 19 [A] men were designated by name to **distribute** portions to every
32: 6 [A] *He* **appointed** military officers over the people
32: 11 [A] he is misleading you, to **let** you die of hunger and thirst.
32: 24 [A] who answered him and **gave** him a miraculous sign.
32: 29 [A] of flocks and herds, for God *had* **given** him very great riches.
34: 9 [A] **gave** him the money that had been brought into the temple of
34: 10 [A] *they* **entrusted** it to the men appointed to supervise the work
34: 10 [A] These men **paid** the workers who repaired and restored the
34: 11 [A] *They* also **gave** money to the carpenters and builders to
34: 15 [A] Law in the temple of the LORD." He **gave** it to Shaphan.
34: 16 [C] are doing everything that *has* **been committed** to them.
34: 17 [A] and *have* **entrusted** it to the supervisors and workers."
34: 18 [A] informed the king, "Hilkiah the priest *has* **given** me a book."
35: 3 [A] "**Put** the sacred ark in the temple that Solomon son of David
35: 8 [A] **gave** the priests twenty-six hundred Passover offerings
35: 12 [A] They set aside the burnt offerings to **give** them to the
35: 25 [A] These **became** a tradition in Israel and are written in the
36: 7 [A] the temple of the LORD and **put** them in his temple there.
36: 17 [A] God **handed** all of them **over to** [+928+3338]
36: 23 [A] *has* **given** me all the kingdoms of the earth and he has
Ezr 1: 2 [A] *has* **given** me all the kingdoms of the earth and he has
1: 7 [A] from Jerusalem and *had* **placed** in the temple of his god.
2: 69 [A] According to their ability *they* **gave** to the treasury for this
3: 7 [A] *they* **gave** money to the masons and carpenters, and gave
7: 6 [A] of Moses, which the LORD, the God of Israel, *had* **given**.
7: 6 [A] The king *had* **granted** him everything he asked, for the hand
7: 11 [A] This is a copy of the letter King Artaxerxes *had* **given** to
7: 27 [A] who *has* **put** it into the king's heart to bring honor to the
8: 17 [b] [his kinsmen, the **temple servants** [K; see Q 5987] in Casiphia,]
8: 20 [A] and the officials *had* **established** to assist the Levites.
8: 36 [A] *They* also **delivered** the king's orders to the royal satraps
9: 7 [C] our priests *have* **been subjected** to the sword and captivity,
9: 8 [A] us a remnant and **giving** us a firm place in his sanctuary,
9: 8 [A] light to our eyes and **[RPH]** a little relief in our bondage.
9: 9 [A] He *has* **granted** us new life to rebuild the house of our God
9: 9 [A] he *has* **given** us a wall of protection in Judah and Jerusalem.
9: 12 [A] *do* not **give** your daughters **in marriage** to their sons or take
9: 13 [A] our sins have deserved and *have* **given** us a remnant like this.
10: 11 [A] Now **make** confession to the LORD, the God of your
10: 19 [A] (*They all* **gave** their hands **in pledge** to put away their wives,
Ne 1: 11 [A] Give your servant success today *by* **granting** him favor in
2: 1 [A] was brought for him, I took the wine and **gave** it to the king.
2: 6 [A] you get back?" It pleased the king to send me; so *I* **set** a time.
2: 7 [A] *may* I **have** [+4200] letters to the governors of
2: 8 [A] so *he will* **give** me timber to make beams for the gates of the
2: 8 [A] of my God was upon me, the king **granted** my **requests**.
2: 9 [A] of Trans-Euphrates and **gave** them the king's letters.
2: 12 [A] I had not told anyone what my God *had* **put** in my heart to
4: 4 [3:36] [A] **Give** them **over** as plunder in a land of captivity.
5: 7 [A] So *I* **called together** a large meeting to deal with them
7: 5 [A] So my God **put** it into my heart to assemble the nobles, the
7: 70 [7:69] [A] Some of the heads of the families **contributed** to the
7: 70 [7:69] [A] The governor **gave** to the treasury 1,000 drachmas of
7: 71 [7:70] [A] Some of the heads of the families **gave** to the treasury
7: 72 [7:71] [A] The total **given** *by* the rest of the people was 20,000
9: 8 [A] you made a covenant with him to **give** to his descendants the
9: 8 [A] you made a covenant with him to give **[RPH]** to his
9: 10 [A] *You* **sent** miraculous signs and wonders against Pharaoh,
9: 13 [A] *You* **gave** them regulations and laws that are just and right,
9: 15 [A] In their hunger *you* **gave** them bread from heaven and in
9: 15 [A] of the land you had sworn with uplifted hand to **give** them.
9: 17 [A] in their rebellion **appointed** a leader in order to return to
9: 20 [A] *You* **gave** your good Spirit to instruct them. You did not
9: 20 [A] from their mouths, and *you* **gave** them water for their thirst.
9: 22 [A] "*You* **gave** them kingdoms and nations, allotting to them
9: 24 [A] *you* **handed** the Canaanites **over to** [+906+906+928+3338]
9: 27 [A] So *you* **handed** them **over to** [+928+3338] their enemies,

Ne 9:27 [A] and in your great compassion *you* **gave** them deliverers,
9:29 [A] Stubbornly *they* **turned** their backs on you, became
9:30 [A] so *you* **handed** them **over to** [+928+3338] the neighboring
9:35 [A] enjoying your great goodness **[RPH]** to them in the
9:35 [A] to them in the spacious and fertile land *you* **gave** them,
9:36 [A] slaves in the land *you* **gave** our forefathers so they could eat
9:37 [A] its abundant harvest goes to the kings *you have* **placed** over
10:29 [10:30] [C] an oath to follow the Law of God **given** through
10:30 [10:31] [A] "We promise not *to* **give** our daughters **in marriage**
10:32 [10:33] [A] **give** a third of a shekel each year for the service of
12:47 [A] all Israel **contributed** the daily portions for the singers and
13: 4 [B] Eliashib the priest *had* **been put** in charge of the storerooms
13: 5 [A] with a large room formerly used *to* **store** the grain offerings
13:10 [C] portions assigned to the Levites *had* not **been given** to them,
13:25 [A] "*You are* not *to* **give** your daughters **in marriage** to their
13:26 [A] loved by his God, and God **made** him king over all Israel,
Est 1:19 [A] Also *let* the king **give** her royal position to someone else who
1:20 [A] all the women *will* **respect** [+3702+4200] their husbands,
2: 3 [A] of the women; and *let* beauty treatments *be* **given** *to* them.
2: 9 [A] Immediately he **provided** her *with* her beauty treatments
2: 9 [A] He **assigned** to her seven maids selected from the king's
2:13 [C] Anything she wanted **was given** her to take with her from the
2:18 [A] the provinces and **distributed** gifts with royal liberality.
3:10 [A] from his finger and **gave** it to Haman son of Hammedatha,
3:11 [B] "**Keep** the money," the king said to Haman, "and do with the
3:14 [C] A copy of the text of the edict *was to* **be issued** *as* law in
3:15 [C] went out, and the edict **was issued** in the citadel of Susa.
4: 8 [A] *He* also **gave** him a copy of the text of the edict for their
4: 8 [C] which *had* **been published** in Susa, to show to Esther
5: 3 [C] Even up to half the kingdom, *it will* **be given** you."
5: 6 [C] *It will* **be given** you. And what is your request?
5: 8 [A] if it pleases the king to **grant** my petition and fulfill my
6: 8 [C] the king has ridden, one with a royal crest **placed** on its head.
6: 9 [A] *let* the robe and horse *be* **entrusted** to one of the king's most
7: 2 [C] "Queen Esther, what is your petition? *It will* **be given** you.
7: 3 [C] O king, and if it pleases your majesty, **grant** me my life—
8: 1 [A] That same day King Xerxes **gave** Queen Esther the estate of
8: 2 [A] he had reclaimed from Haman, and **presented** it to Mordecai.
8: 7 [A] Haman attacked the Jews, *I have* **given** his estate to Esther,
8:11 [A] The king's edict **granted** the Jews in every city the right to
8:13 [C] A copy of the text of the edict *was* to **be issued** *as* law in
8:14 [C] And the edict **was** also **issued** in the citadel of Susa.
9:12 [C] *It will* **be given** you. What is your request? It will also be
9:13 [C] "**give** the Jews in Susa **permission** to carry out this day's
9:14 [C] An edict **was issued** in Susa, and they hanged the ten sons of
Job 1:21 [A] The LORD **gave** and the LORD has taken away;
1:22 [A] all this, Job did not sin *by* **charging** God *with* wrongdoing.
2: 4 [A] Satan replied. "A man *will* **give** all he has for his own life.
3:20 [A] "Why *is* light **given** to those in misery, and life to the bitter
5:10 [A] He **bestows** rain on the earth; he sends water upon the
6: 8 [A] "**Oh** [+4769], that I might have my request, that God would
6: 8 [A] have my request, that God *would* **grant** what I hope for,
9:18 [A] *He would* not **let** me regain my breath but would overwhelm
9:24 [C] When a land **falls** into the hands of the wicked, he blindfolds
11: 5 [A] **Oh, how I wish** [+4769] that God would speak, that he
13: 5 [A] **If only** [+4769] you would be altogether silent! For you,
14: 4 [A] Who *can* **bring** what is pure from the impure? No one!
14:13 [A] "**If only** [+4769] you would hide me in the grave and conceal
15:19 [C] (to whom alone the land **was given** when no alien passed
19:23 [A] "**Oh** [+686+4769], that my words were recorded, that they
19:23 [A] were recorded, **[RPH]** that they were written on a scroll,
23: 3 [A] **If only** [+4769] I knew where to find him; if only I could go
24:23 [A] *He may* **let** them rest in a feeling of security, but his eyes are
28:15 [H] It cannot **be bought** *with* the finest gold, nor can its price be
29: 2 [A] "**How I long for** [+4769+5761] the months gone by,
31:30 [A] *I have* not **allowed** my mouth to sin by invoking a curse
31:31 [A] never said, 'Who **[NIE]** has not had his fill of Job's meat?'—
31:35 [A] ("**Oh** [+4769], that I had someone to hear me! I sign now my
35: 7 [A] If you are righteous, what *do you* **give** to him, or what does
35:10 [A] 'Where is God my Maker, *who* **gives** songs in the night,
36: 3 [A] my knowledge from afar; *I will* **ascribe** justice to my Maker.
36: 6 [A] not keep the wicked alive but **gives** the afflicted their rights.
36:31 [A] way he governs the nations and **provides** food in abundance.
37:10 [A] The breath of God **produces** ice, and the broad waters
38:36 [A] the heart with wisdom or **gave** understanding to the mind?
39:19 [A] "*Do you* **give** the horse his strength or clothe his neck with a
42:11 [A] and each one **gave** him a piece of silver and a gold ring.
42:15 [A] their father **granted** them an inheritance along with their
Ps 1: 3 [A] which **yields** its fruit in season and whose leaf does not
2: 8 [A] Ask of me, and *I will* **make** the nations your inheritance,
4: 7 [4:8] [A] *You have* **filled** my heart *with* greater joy than when
8: 1 [8:2] [A] the earth! *You have* **set** your glory above the heavens.
10:14 [A] do see trouble and grief; you consider it to **take** it in hand.
14: 7 [A] **Oh** [+4769], that salvation for Israel would come out of
15: 5 [A] *who* **lends** his money without usury and does not accept a
16:10 [A] me to the grave, nor *will you* **let** your Holy One see decay.
18:13 [18:14] [A] the voice of the Most High **resounded**.
18:32 [18:33] [A] arms me with strength and **makes** my way perfect.
18:35 [18:36] [A] *You* **give** me your shield of victory, and your right
18:40 [18:41] [A] *You* **made** my enemies **turn** their backs in flight,
18:47 [18:48] [A] He is the God who **avenges** [+4200+5935] me, who
20: 4 [20:5] [A] *May he* **give** you the desire of your heart and make
21: 2 [21:3] [A] *You have* **granted** him the desire of his heart
21: 4 [21:5] [A] He asked you for life, and *you* **gave** it to him—
27:12 [A] *Do* not **turn** me **over** to the desire of my foes, for false
28: 4 [A] **Repay** them for their deeds and for their evil work;
28: 4 [A] **repay** them for what their hands have done and bring back
29:11 [A] The LORD **gives** strength to his people; the LORD blesses
33: 7 [A] waters of the sea into jars; *he* **puts** the deep into storehouses.
37: 4 [A] in the LORD and *he will* **give** you the desires of your heart.
37:21 [A] and do not repay, but the righteous **give** generously;
39: 5 [39:6] [A] *You have* **made** my days a mere handbreadth;
40: 3 [40:4] [A] *He* **put** a new song in my mouth, a hymn of praise to
41: 2 [41:3] [A] and not **surrender** him to the desire of his foes.
44:11 [44:12] [A] *You* **gave** us **up** to be devoured like sheep and have
46: 6 [46:7] [A] kingdoms fall; *he* **lifts** his voice, the earth melts.
49: 7 [49:8] [A] the life of another or **give** to God a ransom for him—
50:20 [A] and **slander** [+928+1984] your own mother's son.
51:16 [51:18] [A] You do not delight in sacrifice, or *I would* **bring** it;
53: 6 [53:7] [A] **Oh** [+4769], that salvation for Israel would come out
55: 6 [55:7] [A] I said, "**Oh** [+4769], that I had the wings of a dove!
55:22 [55:23] [A] will sustain you; *he will* never **let** the righteous fall.
60: 4 [60:6] [A] *you have* **raised** a banner to be unfurled against the
61: 5 [61:6] [A] *you have* **given** me the heritage of those who fear
66: 9 [A] he has preserved our lives and **kept** our feet from slipping.
67: 6 [67:7] [A] the land *will* **yield** its harvest, and God, our God,
68:11 [68:12] [A] The Lord **announced** the word, and great was the
68:33 [68:34] [A] skies above, *who* **thunders with** [+928+7754]
68:34 [68:35] [A] **Proclaim** the power of God, whose majesty is over
68:35 [68:36] [A] of Israel **gives** power and strength to his people.
69:11 [69:12] [A] when *I* **put** [+4230] **on** sackcloth, people make
69:21 [69:22] [A] *They* **put** gall in my food and gave me vinegar for
69:27 [69:28] [A] **Charge** them *with* crime upon crime; do not let
72: 1 [A] **Endow** the king *with* your justice, O God, the royal son *with*
72:15 [A] Long may he live! *May* gold from Sheba *be* **given** him. May
74:14 [A] and **gave** him as food to the creatures of the desert.
74:19 [A] *Do* not **hand over** the life of your dove to wild beasts; do not
77:17 [77:18] [A] down water, the skies **resounded** *with* thunder;
78:20 [A] streams flowed abundantly. But can he also **give** us food?
78:24 [A] for the people to eat, *he* **gave** them the grain of heaven.
78:46 [A] *He* **gave** their crops to the grasshopper, their produce to the
78:61 [A] *He* **sent** ⌞the ark of⌟ his might into captivity, his splendor into
78:66 [A] He beat back his enemies; *he* **put** them to everlasting shame.
79: 2 [A] *They have* **given** the dead bodies of your servants as food to
81: 2 [81:3] [A] Begin the music, **strike** the tambourine,
84:11 [84:12] [A] and shield; the LORD **bestows** favor and honor;
85: 7 [85:8] [A] O LORD, and **grant** us your salvation.
85:12 [85:13] [A] The LORD *will* indeed **give** what is good, and our
85:12 [85:13] [A] what is good, and our land *will* **yield** its harvest.
86:16 [A] **grant** your strength to your servant and save the son of your
89:27 [89:28] [A] I *will* also **appoint** him my firstborn, the most
99: 7 [A] of cloud; they kept his statutes and the decrees *he* **gave** them.
104:12 [A] The birds of the air nest by the waters; *they* **sing** [+7754]
104:27 [A] These all look to you to **give** them their food at the proper
104:28 [A] *When you* **give** it to them, they gather it up; when you open
105:11 [A] "To you *I will* **give** the land of Canaan as the portion you
105:32 [A] *He* **turned** their rain **into** hail, with lightning throughout
105:44 [A] *he* **gave** them the lands of the nations, and they fell heir to
106:15 [A] So *he* **gave** them what they asked for, but sent a wasting
106:41 [A] *He* **handed** them **over to** [+928+3338] the nations, and their
106:46 [A] *He* **caused** them to be pitied by all who held them captive.
111: 5 [A] *He* **provides** food for those who fear him; he remembers his
111: 6 [A] power of his works, **giving** them the lands of other nations.
112: 9 [A] He has scattered abroad *his* **gifts** to the poor,
115: 1 [A] Not to us, O LORD, not to us but to your name **be** the glory,
115:16 [A] belong to the LORD, but the earth *he has* **given** to man.
118:18 [A] me severely, but *he has* not **given** me **over** to death.
119:110 [A] The wicked *have* **set** a snare for me, but I have not strayed
120: 3 [A] What *will he* **do** to you, and what more besides, O deceitful
121: 3 [A] *He will* not **let** your foot slip—he who watches over you will
124: 6 [A] be to the LORD, who *has* not **let** us be torn by their teeth.
127: 2 [A] toiling for food to eat—for *he* **grants** sleep to those he loves.
132: 4 [A] *I will* **allow** no sleep to my eyes, no slumber to my eyelids,
135:12 [A] *he* **gave** their land as an inheritance, an inheritance to his
136:21 [A] **gave** their land as an inheritance, *His love endures*
136:25 [A] *who* **gives** food to every creature. *His love endures*
140: 8 [140:9] [A] *do* not **grant** the wicked their desires, O LORD;
144:10 [A] to the *One who* **gives** victory to kings, who delivers his

Ps 145:15 [A] look to you, and you **give** them their food at the proper time.
146: 7 [A] the cause of the oppressed and **gives** food to the hungry.
147: 9 [A] *He* **provides** food for the cattle and for the young ravens
147:16 [A] He **spreads** the snow like wool and scatters the frost like
148: 6 [A] for ever and ever; *he* **gave** a decree that will never pass away.
Pr 1: 4 [A] for **giving** prudence to the simple, knowledge and discretion
1:20 [A] aloud in the street, *she* **raises** her voice in the public squares;
2: 3 [A] call out for insight and **cry aloud** [+7754] for understanding,
2: 6 [A] For the LORD **gives** wisdom, and from his mouth come
3:28 [A] to your neighbor, "Come back later; *I'll* **give** it tomorrow"—
3:34 [A] He mocks proud mockers but **gives** grace to the humble.
4: 2 [A] *I* **give** you sound learning, so do not forsake my teaching.
4: 9 [A] *She will* **set** a garland of grace on your head and present you
5: 9 [A] lest *you* **give** your best strength to others and your years to
6: 4 [A] **Allow** no sleep to your eyes, no slumber to your eyelids.
6:31 [A] though *it* **costs** *him* all the wealth of his house.
8: 1 [A] wisdom call out? *Does* not understanding **raise** her voice?
9: 9 [A] **Instruct** a wise man and he will be wiser still; teach a
10:10 [A] He who winks maliciously **causes** grief, and a chattering fool
10:24 [A] will overtake him; what the righteous desire *will be* **granted**.
12:12 [A] plunder of evil men, but the root of the righteous **flourishes**.
13:10 [A] Pride only **breeds** quarrels, but wisdom is found in those
13:15 [A] Good understanding **wins** favor, but the way of the unfaithful
21:26 [A] he craves for more, but the righteous **give** without sparing.
22: 9 [A] will himself be blessed, for *he* **shares** his food with the poor.
22:16 [A] to increase his wealth and *he who* **gives gifts** to the rich—
23:26 [A] **give** me your heart and let your eyes keep to my ways,
23:31 [A] when *it* **sparkles** [+6524] in the cup, when it goes down
26: 8 [A] Like tying a stone in a sling is the **giving** *of* honor to a fool.
28:27 [A] *He who* **gives** to the poor will lack nothing, but he who
29:15 [A] The rod of correction **imparts** wisdom, but a child left to
29:17 [A] he will give you peace; *he will* **bring** delight to your soul.
29:25 [A] Fear of man *will* **prove to be** a snare, but whoever trusts in
30: 8 [A] **give** me neither poverty nor riches, but give me only my
31: 3 [A] *do* not **spend** your strength on women, your vigor on those
31: 6 [A] **Give** beer to those who are perishing, wine to those who are
31:15 [A] *she* **provides** food for her family and portions for her servant
31:24 [A] and sells them, and **supplies** the merchants *with* sashes.
31:31 [A] **Give** her the reward she has earned, and let her works bring
Ecc 1:13 [A] *I* **devoted** myself to study and to explore by wisdom all that
1:13 [A] under heaven. What a heavy burden God *has* **laid** on men!
1:17 [A] *I* **applied** myself to the understanding of wisdom, and also of
2:21 [A] *he must* **leave** all he owns to someone who has not worked
2:26 [A] pleases him, God **gives** wisdom, knowledge and happiness,
2:26 [A] to the sinner *he* **gives** the task of gathering and storing up
2:26 [A] storing up wealth to **hand** it **over** to the one who pleases
3:10 [A] I have seen the burden God *has* **laid** on men.
3:11 [A] *He has* also **set** eternity in the hearts of men; yet they cannot
5: 1 [4:17] [A] Go near to listen rather than *to* **offer** the sacrifice of
5: 6 [5:5] [A] *Do* not **let** your mouth lead you into sin. And do not
5:18 [5:17] [A] sun during the few days of life God *has* **given** him—
5:19 [5:18] [A] when God **gives** any man wealth and possessions,
6: 2 [A] God **gives** a man wealth, possessions and honor, so that he
7: 2 [A] the destiny of every man; the living *should* **take** this to heart.
7:21 [A] Do not **pay** attention to every word people say, or you may
8: 9 [A] as I **applied** my mind to everything done under the sun.
8:15 [A] all the days of the life God *has* **given** him under the sun.
8:16 [A] When *I* **applied** my mind to know wisdom and to observe
9: 1 [A] So *I* **reflected** [+448+906+4213] **on** all this and concluded that
9: 9 [A] all the days of this meaningless life that God *has* **given** you
10: 6 [C] Fools **are put** in many high positions, while the rich occupy
11: 2 [A] **Give** portions to seven, yes to eight, for you do not know
12: 7 [A] it came from, and the spirit returns to God who **gave** it.
12:11 [C] sayings like firmly embedded nails—**given** by one Shepherd.
SS 1:12 [A] the king was at his table, my perfume **spread** its fragrance.
2:13 [A] its early fruit; the blossoming vines **spread** their fragrance.
7:12 [7:13] [A] are in bloom—there *I will* **give** you my love.
7:13 [7:14] [A] The mandrakes **send out** their fragrance, and at our
8: 1 [A] **If only** [+4769] you were to me like a brother, who was
8: 7 [A] If one *were to* **give** all the wealth of his house for love,
8:11 [A] a vineyard in Baal Hamon; *he* **let out** his vineyard to tenants.
Isa 3: 4 [A] *I will* **make** boys their officials; mere children will govern
7:14 [A] Therefore the Lord himself *will* **give** you a sign: The virgin
8:18 [A] Here am I, and the children the LORD *has* **given** me.
9: 6 [9:5] [C] For to us a child is born, to us a son **is given**,
22:21 [A] and **hand** your authority **over to** [+928+3338] him.
22:22 [A] *I will* **place** on his shoulder the key to the house of David;
27: 4 [A] **If only** [+4769] there were briers and thorns confronting me!
29:11 [A] if *you* **give** the scroll to someone who can read, and say to
29:12 [C] Or if you **give** the scroll to someone who cannot read,
30:20 [A] Although the Lord **gives** you the bread of adversity
30:23 [A] *He will* also **send** you rain for the seed you sow in the
33:16 [C] His bread *will* **be supplied**, and water will not fail him.
34: 2 [A] will totally destroy them, *he will* **give** them **over** to slaughter.
35: 2 [C] The glory of Lebanon *will* **be given** to it, the splendor of
36: 8 [A] *I will* **give** you two thousand horses—if you can put riders on
36: 8 [A] you two thousand horses—if you can **put** riders on them!
36:15 [C] this city *will* not **be given** into the hand of the king of
37: 7 [A] I *am going to* **put** a spirit in him so that when he hears a
37:10 [C] 'Jerusalem *will* not **be handed over to** [+928+3338] the king
37:19 [A] They *have* **thrown** their gods into the fire and destroyed
40:23 [A] He **brings** princes to naught and reduces the rulers of this
40:29 [A] *He* **gives** strength to the weary and increases the power of the
41: 2 [A] *He* **hands** nations **over** *to* him and subdues kings before him.
41: 2 [A] *He* **turns** them to dust *with* his sword, to windblown chaff
41:19 [A] *I will* **put** in the desert the cedar and the acacia, the myrtle
41:27 [A] they are!' *I* **gave** to Jerusalem a messenger of good tidings.
42: 1 [A] *I will* **put** my Spirit on him and he will bring justice to the
42: 5 [A] and all that comes out of it, *who* **gives** breath to its people,
42: 6 [A] *will* **make** you to be a covenant for the people and a light for
42: 8 [A] *I will* not **give** my glory to another or my praise to idols.
42:24 [A] Who **handed** Jacob **over** to become loot, and Israel to the
43: 3 [A] *I* **give** Egypt for your ransom, Cush and Seba in your stead.
43: 4 [A] and because I love you, *I will* **give** men in exchange for you,
43: 6 [A] I will say to the north, '**Give** them **up**!' and to the south,
43: 9 [A] *Let them* **bring** *in* their witnesses to prove they were right,
43:16 [A] he *who* **made** a way through the sea, a path through the
43:20 [A] because *I* **provide** water in the desert and streams in the
43:28 [A] and *I will* **consign** Jacob to destruction and Israel to scorn.
45: 3 [A] *I will* **give** you the treasures of darkness, riches stored in
46:13 [A] *I will* **grant** salvation to Zion, my splendor to Israel.
47: 6 [A] *I* **gave** them into your hand, and you showed them no mercy.
48:11 [A] I let myself be defamed? *I will* not **yield** my glory to another.
49: 6 [A] *I will* also **make** you a light for the Gentiles, that you may
49: 8 [A] keep you and *will* **make** you to be a covenant for the people,
50: 4 [A] The Sovereign LORD *has* **given** me an instructed tongue,
50: 6 [A] *I* **offered** my back to those who beat me, my cheeks to those
51:12 [C] that you fear mortal men, the sons of men, *who* **are** but grass,
53: 9 [A] He *was* **assigned** a grave with the wicked, and with the rich
55: 4 [A] See, *I have* **made** him a witness to the peoples, a leader
55:10 [A] so that *it* **yields** seed for the sower and bread for the eater,
56: 5 [A] to them *I will* **give** within my temple and its walls a
56: 5 [A] *I will* **give** them an everlasting name that will not be cut off.
61: 3 [A] to **bestow** on them a crown of beauty instead of ashes, the oil
61: 8 [A] In my faithfulness *I will* **reward** [+7190] them and make an
62: 7 [A] **give** him no rest till he establishes Jerusalem and makes her
62: 8 [A] "Never again *will I* **give** your grain as food for your enemies,
Jer 1: 5 [A] I set you apart; *I* **appointed** you as a prophet to the nations."
1: 9 [A] and said to me, "Now, *I have* **put** my words in your mouth.
1:15 [A] **set up** their thrones in the entrance of the gates of Jerusalem;
1:18 [A] Today I *have* **made** you a fortified city, an iron pillar and a
2:15 [A] Lions have roared; *they have* **growled** [+7754] at him. They
3: 8 [A] *I* **gave** faithless Israel her certificate of divorce and sent her
3:15 [A] *I will* **give** you shepherds after my own heart, who will lead
3:19 [A] would I treat you like sons and **give** you a desirable land,
4:16 [A] a distant land, **raising** a war cry against the cities of Judah.
5:14 [A] I *will* **make** my words in your mouth a fire and these people
5:24 [A] our God, who **gives** autumn and spring rains in season,
6:21 [A] "I *will* **put** obstacles before this people. Fathers and sons
6:27 [A] "*I have* **made** you a tester of metals and my people the ore,
7: 7 [A] in the land *I* **gave** your forefathers for ever and ever.
7:14 [A] temple you trust in, the place *I* **gave** to you and your fathers.
8:10 [A] Therefore *I will* **give** their wives to other men and their fields
8:13 [A] What *I have* **given** them will be taken from them.' "
9: 1 [8:23] [A] **Oh** [+4769], that my head were a spring of water
9: 2 [9:1] [A] **Oh** [+4769], that I had in the desert a lodging place for
9:11 [9:10] [A] "*I will* **make** Jerusalem a heap of ruins, a haunt of
9:11 [9:10] [A] *I will* **lay** waste the towns of Judah so no one can live
9:13 [9:12] [A] they have forsaken my law, which *I* **set** before them;
10:13 [A] When he **thunders** [+7754], the waters in the heavens roar;
11: 5 [A] to **give** them a land flowing with milk and honey'—
12: 7 [A] *I will* **give** the one I love into the hands of her enemies.
12: 8 [A] to me like a lion in the forest. *She* **roars** [+928+7754]
12:10 [A] *they will* **turn** my pleasant field into a desolate wasteland.
13:16 [A] **Give** glory to the LORD your God before he brings the
13:20 [C] Where is the flock *that* **was entrusted** to you, the sheep of
14:13 [A] Indeed, *I will* **give** you lasting peace in this place.' "
14:22 [A] *Do* the skies *themselves* **send down** showers? No, it is you,
15: 4 [A] *I will* **make** them abhorrent to all the kingdoms of the earth
15: 9 [A] *I will* **put** the survivors to the sword before their enemies,"
15:13 [A] Your wealth and your treasures *I will* **give** as plunder,
15:20 [A] *I will* **make** you a wall to this people, a fortified wall of
16:13 [A] serve other gods day and night, for *I will* **show** you no favor.'
16:15 [A] For I will restore them to the land *I* **gave** their forefathers.
17: 3 [A] and all your treasures *I will* **give away** as plunder,
17: 4 [A] Through your own fault you will lose the inheritance *I* **gave**
17:10 [A] the mind, to **reward** a man according to his conduct,
18:21 [A] So **give** their children **over** to famine; hand them over to the

Jer 19: 7 [A] and *I will* **give** their carcasses as food to the birds of the air
19: 12 [A] declares the LORD. I *will* **make** this city like Topheth.
20: 2 [A] **put** in the stocks at the Upper Gate of Benjamin at the
20: 4 [A] 'I *will* **make** you a terror to yourself and to all your friends;
20: 4 [A] *I will* **hand** all Judah **over to** [+906+928+3338]
20: 5 [A] **[RPH]** I will hand over to their enemies all the wealth of
20: 5 [A] *I will* **hand over to** [+906+906+906+906+928+3338] their
21: 7 [A] *I will* **hand over** [+906+906+906+906+928+3338] Zedekiah
21: 8 [A] I *am* **setting** before you the way of life and the way of death.
21: 10 [C] *It will* **be given** into the hands of the king of Babylon, and he
22: 13 [A] work for nothing, not **paying** them *for* their labor.
22: 20 [A] to Lebanon and cry out, **let** your voice **be heard** in Bashan,
22: 25 [A] *I will* **hand** you **over to** [+928+3338] those who seek your
23: 39 [A] cast you out of my presence along with the city *I* **gave** to you
23: 40 [A] *I will* **bring** upon you everlasting disgrace—everlasting
24: 7 [A] *I will* **give** them a heart to know me, that I am the LORD.
24: 8 [A] 'so *will I* **deal** with Zedekiah king of Judah, his officials
24: 9 [A] *I will* **make** them abhorrent and an offense to all the kingdoms
24: 10 [A] them until they are destroyed from the land *I* **gave** to them
25: 5 [A] you can stay in the land the LORD **gave** to you and your
25: 18 [A] to **make** them a ruin and an object of horror and scorn and
25: 30 [A] LORD will roar from on high; *he will* **thunder** [+7754]
25: 31 [A] and **put** the wicked to the sword,' " declares the LORD.
26: 4 [A] listen to me and follow my law, which *I have* **set** before you,
26: 6 [A] *I will* **make** this house like Shiloh and this city an object of
26: 6 [A] this city **[RPH]** an object of cursing among all the nations
26: 15 [A] you *will* **bring** the guilt of innocent blood on yourselves
26: 24 [A] so he *was* not **handed over to** [+906+928+3338] the people
27: 2 [A] a yoke out of straps and crossbars and **put** it on your neck.
27: 5 [A] and the animals that are on it, and *I* **give** it to anyone I please.
27: 6 [A] I *will* **hand** all your countries **over to** [+906+928+3338] my
27: 6 [A] *I will* **make** even the wild animals subject to him.
27: 8 [A] king of Babylon or **bow** its neck under his yoke,
28: 14 [A] *I will* **put** an iron yoke on the necks of all these nations to
28: 14 [A] *I will* even **give** him control over the wild animals.' "
29: 6 [A] and **give** [+408+906+4200] your daughters **in marriage**,
29: 11 [A] and not to harm you, plans to **give** you hope and a future.
29: 17 [A] against them and *I will* **make** them like poor figs that are
29: 18 [A] *will* **make** them abhorrent to all the kingdoms of the earth and
29: 21 [A] "I *will* **hand** them **over to** [+906+928+3338]
29: 26 [A] 'The LORD *has* **appointed** you priest in place of Jehoiada
29: 26 [A] *you should* **put** any madman who acts like a prophet into the
30: 3 [A] restore them to the land *I* **gave** their forefathers to possess,'
30: 16 [A] all who make spoil of you *I will* **despoil** [+1020+4200].
31: 33 [A] "*I will* **put** my law in their minds and write it on their hearts.
31: 35 [A] *he who* **appoints** the sun to shine by day, who decrees the
32: 3 [A] I *am about to* **hand** this city **over to** [+906+928+3338] the
32: 4 [C] *will* **certainly be handed over to** [+928+3338+5989] the
32: 4 [C] *will* **certainly be handed over to** [+928+3338+5989] the
32: 12 [A] *I* **gave** this deed to Baruch son of Neriah, the son of
32: 14 [A] and **put** them in a clay jar so they will last a long time.
32: 16 [A] "After I *had* **given** the deed of purchase to Baruch son of
32: 19 [A] you **reward** everyone according to his conduct and as his
32: 22 [A] *You* **gave** them this land you had sworn to give their
32: 22 [A] You gave them this land you had sworn to **give** their
32: 24 [C] the city *will* **be handed over to** [+928+3338] the
32: 25 [C] though the city *will* **be handed over to** [+928+3338] the
32: 28 [A] I *am about to* **hand** this city **over to** [+906+928+3338] the
32: 36 [C] plague *it will* **be handed over to** [+928+3338] the king of
32: 39 [A] *I will* **give** them singleness of heart and action, so that they
32: 40 [A] and *I will* **inspire** [+906+928+4222] them to fear me, so that
32: 43 [C] for *it has* **been handed over to** [+928+3338] the
34: 2 [A] I *am about to* **hand** this city **over to** [+906+928+3338] the
34: 3 [C] surely be captured and **handed over to** [+928+3338] him.
34: 17 [A] *I will* **make** you abhorrent to all the kingdoms of the earth.
34: 18 [A] *I will* **treat** *like* the calf they cut in two and then walked
34: 20 [A] *I will* **hand over to** [+906+928+3338] their enemies who
34: 21 [A] "*I will* **hand** Zedekiah … **over to** [+906+906+928+3338]
34: 22 [A] *I will* **lay** waste the towns of Judah so no one can live there."
35: 5 [A] *I* **set** bowls full of wine and some cups before the men of the
35: 15 [A] you will live in the land *I have* **given** to you and your
36: 32 [A] another scroll and **gave** it to the scribe Baruch son of Neriah,
37: 4 [A] go among the people, for he *had* not yet *been* **put** *in* prison.
37: 15 [A] beaten and **imprisoned** [+657+906+1074+2021] *in* the house
37: 17 [C] Jeremiah replied, "*you will* **be handed over to** [+928+3338]
37: 18 [A] your officials or this people, that *you have* **put** me in prison?
37: 21 [A] **given** bread from the street of the bakers each day until all
38: 3 [C] *will* **certainly be handed over to** [+928+3338+5989] the
38: 3 [C] *will* **certainly be handed over to** [+928+3338+5989] the
38: 7 [A] heard that *they had* **put** Jeremiah into the cistern.
38: 16 [A] I will neither kill you nor **hand** you **over to** [+928+3338]
38: 18 [C] this city *will* **be handed over to** [+928+3338] the
38: 19 [A] for the Babylonians *may* **hand** me **over to** [+906+928+3338]
38: 20 [A] "*They will* not **hand** you **over**," Jeremiah replied. "Obey the
39: 10 [A] and at that time *he* **gave** them vineyards and fields.
39: 14 [A] *They* **turned** him **over** to Gedaliah son of Ahikam, the son
39: 17 [C] the LORD; *you will* not **be handed over to** [+928+3338]
40: 5 [A] the commander **gave** him provisions and a present and let
40: 11 [A] all the other countries heard that the king of Babylon *had* **left**
42: 12 [A] *I will* **show** you compassion so that he will have compassion
43: 3 [A] us to **hand** us **over to** [+906+928+3338] the Babylonians,
44: 10 [A] my law and the decrees *I* **set** before you and your fathers.
44: 30 [A] 'I *am going to* **hand** Pharaoh … **over to** [+906+928+3338]
44: 30 [A] *I* **handed** Zedekiah king of Judah **over to** [+906+928+3338]
45: 5 [A] but wherever you go *I will* **let** you escape with your life.' "
46: 24 [C] of Egypt will be put to shame, **handed over to** [+928+3338]
46: 26 [A] *I will* **hand** them **over to** [+928+3338] those who seek their
48: 9 [A] **Put** salt on Moab, for she will be laid waste; her towns will
48: 34 [A] "The sound of their cry **rises** from Heshbon to Elealeh
49: 15 [A] "Now *I will* **make** you small among the nations,
50: 15 [A] *She* **surrenders** [+3338], her towers fall, her walls are torn
51: 16 [A] When he **thunders** [+7754], the waters in the heavens roar;
51: 25 [A] roll you off the cliffs, and **make** you a burned-out mountain.
51: 55 [C] rage like great waters; the roar of their voices *will* **resound**.
52: 11 [A] where *he* **put** him in prison till the day of his death.
52: 32 [A] **gave** him a seat of honor higher than those of the other kings
52: 34 [C] Day by day the king of Babylon **gave** Jehoiachin a regular
La 1: 11 [A] *they* **barter** their treasures for food to keep themselves alive.
1: 13 [A] turned me back. *He* **made** me desolate, faint all the day long.
1: 14 [A] my strength. *He has* **handed** me **over to** [+928+3338]
2: 7 [A] *they have* **raised** a shout in the house of the LORD as on
2: 18 [A] river day and night; **give** yourself no relief, your eyes no rest.
3: 29 [A] *Let him* **bury** his face in the dust—there may yet be hope.
3: 30 [A] *Let him* **offer** his cheek to one who would strike him, and let
3: 65 [A] **Put** a veil over their hearts, and may your curse be on them!
5: 6 [A] *We* **submitted** [+3338] *to* Egypt and Assyria to get enough
Eze 2: 8 [A] rebellious house; open your mouth and eat what I **give** you."
3: 3 [A] eat this scroll I *am* **giving** you and fill your stomach with it."
3: 8 [A] But *I will* **make** you as unyielding and hardened as they are.
3: 9 [A] *I will* **make** your forehead like the hardest stone, harder than
3: 17 [A] of man, *I have* **made** you a watchman for the house of Israel;
3: 20 [A] and *I* **put** a stumbling block before him, he will die.
3: 25 [A] you, son of man, *they will* **tie** [+6584] *with* ropes; you will
4: 1 [A] **put** it in front of you and draw the city of Jerusalem on it.
4: 2 [A] **lay** siege to it: Erect siege works against it, build a ramp up
4: 2 [A] to it, **set up** camps against it and put battering rams around it.
4: 3 [A] **place** it as an iron wall between you and the city and turn
4: 5 [A] I *have* **assigned** you the same number of days as the years of
4: 6 [A] of Judah. *I have* **assigned** you 40 days, a day for each year.
4: 8 [A] *I will* **tie** you **up** *with* ropes so that you cannot turn from one
4: 9 [A] **put** them in a storage jar and use them to make bread for
4: 15 [A] "*I will* **let** you bake your bread over cow manure instead of
5: 14 [A] "*I will* **make** you a ruin and a reproach among the nations
6: 5 [A] *I will* **lay** the dead bodies of the Israelites in front of their
6: 13 [A] places where *they* **offered** fragrant incense to all their idols.
6: 14 [A] **make** the land a desolate waste from the desert to Diblah—
7: 3 [A] your conduct and **repay** you *for* all your detestable practices.
7: 4 [A] *I will* surely **repay** you *for* your conduct and the detestable
7: 8 [A] your conduct and **repay** you *for* all your detestable practices.
7: 9 [A] *I will* **repay** you in accordance with your conduct
7: 20 [A] Therefore *I will* **turn** these into an unclean thing for them.
7: 21 [A] *I will* **hand** it all **over** as plunder **to** [+928+3338] foreigners
9: 10 [A] *I will* **bring down** on their own heads what they have done."
10: 7 [A] up some of it and **put** it into the hands of the man in linen,
11: 9 [A] the city and **hand** you **over to** [+906+928+3338] foreigners
11: 15 [C] the LORD; this land **was given** to us as our possession.'
11: 17 [A] and *I will* **give** you **back** the land of Israel again.'
11: 19 [A] *I will* **give** them an undivided heart and put a new spirit in
11: 19 [A] give them an undivided heart and **put** a new spirit in them;
11: 19 [A] from them their heart of stone and **give** them a heart of flesh.
11: 21 [A] *I will* **bring down** on their own heads what they have done,
12: 6 [A] the land, for *I have* **made** you a sign to the house of Israel."
13: 11 [A] come in torrents, and *I will* **send** hailstones hurtling down,
14: 3 [A] and **put** wicked stumbling blocks before their faces.
14: 8 [A] *I will* **set** my face against that man and make him an example
15: 4 [C] after *it* **is thrown** on the fire as fuel and the fire burns both
15: 6 [A] As *I have* **given** the wood of the vine among the trees of the
15: 6 [A] for the fire, so *will I* **treat** the people living in Jerusalem.
15: 7 [A] *I will* **set** my face against them. Although they have come
15: 8 [A] *I will* **make** the land desolate because they have been
16: 7 [A] *I* **made** you grow like a plant of the field. You grew up
16: 11 [A] *I* **put** bracelets on your arms and a necklace around your
16: 12 [A] *I* **put** a ring on your nose, earrings on your ears and a
16: 17 [A] You also took the fine jewelry *I* **gave** you, the jewelry made
16: 18 [A] on them, and *you* **offered** my oil and incense before them.
16: 19 [A] Also the food *I* **provided** for you—the fine flour, olive oil
16: 19 [A] you to eat—*you* **offered** as fragrant incense before them.
16: 21 [A] You slaughtered my children and **sacrificed** [+906+928+6296]

[A] Qal [B] Qal passive [C] Niphal [D] Piel (poel, polel, pilel, pilal, pealal, pilpel) [E] Pual (poal, polal, poalal, pulal, pualal)

Eze 16:27 [A] *I* **gave** you **over** to the greed of your enemies, the daughters
16:33 [A] Every prostitute **receives** [+4200] a fee, but you give gifts to
16:33 [A] prostitute receives a fee, but you **give** gifts to all your lovers,
16:34 [A] for you **give** payment and none is given to you.
16:34 [C] for you give payment and none **is given** to you.
16:36 [A] and because *you* **gave** them your children's blood,
16:38 [A] *I will* **bring** *upon* you the blood vengeance of my wrath
16:39 [A] Then *I will* **hand** you **over to** [+906+928+3338] your lovers,
16:41 [A] and *you will* no longer **pay** [+924] your lovers.
16:43 [A] I *will* surely **bring down** on your head what you have done,
16:61 [A] *I will* **give** them to you as daughters, but not on the basis of
17: 5 [A] took some of the seed of your land and **put** it in fertile soil.
17:15 [A] against him by sending his envoys to Egypt to **get** horses
17:18 [A] Because *he had* **given** his hand **in pledge** and yet did all
17:19 [A] *I will* **bring down** on his head my oath that he despised
17:22 [A] will take a shoot from the very top of a cedar and **plant** it;
18: 7 [A] He does not commit robbery but **gives** his food to the hungry
18: 8 [A] *He does* not **lend** at usury or take excessive interest.
18:13 [A] *He* **lends** at usury and takes excessive interest. Will such a
18:16 [A] He does not commit robbery but **gives** his food to the hungry
19: 8 [A] the nations **came** against him, those from regions round
19: 9 [A] With hooks *they* **pulled** him into a cage and brought him to
20:11 [A] *I* **gave** them my decrees and made known to them my laws,
20:12 [A] Also *I* **gave** them my Sabbaths as a sign between us, so they
20:15 [A] that I would not bring them into the land *I had* **given** them—
20:25 [A] I also **gave** them **over** *to* statutes that were not good and laws
20:28 [A] When I brought them into the land I had sworn to **give** them
20:28 [A] **made** offerings that provoked me to anger, presented their
20:42 [A] the land I had sworn with uplifted hand to **give** to your
21:11 [21:16] [A] " 'The sword *is* **appointed** to be polished, to be
21:11 [21:16] [A] **made ready** for the hand of the slayer.
21:15 [21:20] [A] *I have* **stationed** the sword for slaughter at all their
21:27 [21:32] [A] to whom it rightfully belongs; to him *I will* **give** it.'
21:29 [21:34] [A] it *will be* **laid** on the necks of the wicked who are to
21:31 [21:36] [A] against you; *I will* **hand** you **over to** [+928+3338]
22: 4 [A] Therefore *I will* **make** you an object of scorn to the nations
22:31 [A] **bringing down** on their own heads all they have done,
23: 7 [A] *She* **gave** herself as a prostitute to all the elite of the
23: 9 [A] "Therefore *I* **handed** her **over to** [+928+3338] her lovers,
23:24 [A] *I will* **turn** you **over** to them for punishment, and they will
23:25 [A] *I will* **direct** my jealous anger against you, and they will deal
23:28 [A] I *am about to* **hand** you **over to** [+928+3338] those you
23:31 [A] the way of your sister; so *I will* **put** her cup into your hand.
23:42 [A] *they* **put** bracelets on the arms of the woman and her sister
23:46 [A] a mob against them and **give** them **over** to terror and plunder.
23:49 [A] You *will* **suffer** [+6584] the penalty for your lewdness
24: 8 [A] up wrath and take revenge *I* **put** her blood on the bare rock,
25: 4 [A] therefore I *am going to* **give** you to the people of the East as
25: 4 [A] They will set up their camps and **pitch** their tents among you;
25: 5 [A] *I will* **turn** Rabbah into a pasture for camels and Ammon
25: 7 [A] my hand against you and **give** you as plunder to the nations.
25:10 [A] *I will* **give** Moab along with the Ammonites to the people of
25:13 [A] *I will* **lay** it waste, and from Teman to Dedan they will fall
25:14 [A] *I will* **take** vengeance on Edom by the hand of my people
25:17 [A] that I am the LORD, when I **take** vengeance on them.' "
26: 4 [A] I will scrape away her rubble and **make** her a bare rock.
26: 8 [A] *he will* **set up** siege works against you, build a ramp up to
26: 9 [A] *He will* **direct** the blows of his battering rams against your
26:14 [A] *I will* **make** you a bare rock, and you will become a place to
26:17 [A] and your citizens; *you* **put** your terror on all who lived there.
26:19 [A] When I **make** you a desolate city, like cities no longer
26:20 [f] or take *your* place [BHS ***return***; NIV 3656] in the land
26:21 [A] *I will* **bring** you *to* a horrible end and you will be no more.
27:10 [A] and helmets on your walls, **bringing** you splendor.
27:12 [A] *they* **exchanged** silver, iron, tin and lead for your
27:13 [A] *they* **exchanged** slaves and articles of bronze for your wares.
27:14 [A] Togarmah **exchanged** work horses, war horses and mules *for*
27:16 [A] *they* **exchanged** turquoise, purple fabric, embroidered work,
27:17 [A] *they* **exchanged** wheat from Minnith and confections, honey,
27:19 [A] *they* **exchanged** wrought iron, cassia and calamus for your
27:22 [A] for your merchandise *they* **exchanged** the finest of all kinds
28: 2 [A] a god, though *you* **think** [+4213] you are as wise as a god.
28: 6 [A] " 'Because you **think** [+906+4222] you are wise, as wise as a
28:14 [A] were anointed as a guardian cherub, for so *I* **ordained** you.
28:17 [A] you to the earth; *I* **made** a spectacle of you before kings.
28:18 [A] *I* **reduced** you to ashes on the ground in the sight of all who
28:25 [A] will live in their own land, which *I* **gave** to my servant Jacob.
29: 4 [A] *I will* **put** hooks in your jaws and make the fish of your
29: 5 [A] *I will* **give** you as food to the beasts of the earth and the birds
29:10 [A] *I will* **make** the land of Egypt a ruin and a desolate waste
29:12 [A] *I will* **make** the land of Egypt desolate among devastated
29:19 [A] I *am going to* **give** Egypt to Nebuchadnezzar king of
29:20 [A] *I have* **given** him Egypt as a reward for his efforts because
29:21 [A] of Israel, and *I will* **open** [+7341] your mouth among them.
30: 8 [A] when I **set** fire to Egypt and all her helpers are crushed.
30:12 [A] *I will* **dry up** [+3000] the streams of the Nile and sell the
30:13 [A] a prince in Egypt, and *I will* **spread** fear throughout the land.
30:14 [A] **set** fire to Zoan and inflict punishment on Thebes.
30:16 [A] *I will* **set** fire to Egypt; Pelusium will writhe in agony.
30:21 [A] It has not been bound up for **healing** [+8337] or put in a
30:24 [A] arms of the king of Babylon and **put** my sword in his hand,
30:25 [A] when I **put** my sword into the hand of the king of Babylon
31:10 [A] **lifting** its top above the thick foliage, and because it was
31:11 [A] *I* **handed** it **over** to the ruler of the nations, for him to deal
31:14 [A] proudly on high, **lifting** their tops above the thick foliage.
31:14 [C] they *are* all **destined** for death, for the earth below,
32: 5 [A] *I will* **spread** your flesh on the mountains and fill the valleys
32: 8 [A] *I will* **bring** darkness over your land, declares the Sovereign
32:15 [A] When I **make** Egypt desolate and strip the land of everything
32:20 [C] The sword **is drawn**; let her be dragged off with all her
32:23 [C] Their graves **are** in the depths of the pit and her army lies
32:23 [A] All who *had* **spread** terror in the land of the living are slain,
32:24 [A] All who *had* **spread** terror in the land of the living went
32:25 [A] A bed *is* **made** for her among the slain, with all her hordes
32:25 [C] Because their terror *had* **spread** in the land of the living, they
32:25 [C] those who go down to the pit; *they* **are laid** among the slain.
32:26 [A] because *they* **spread** their terror in the land of the living.
32:27 [A] of war, whose swords *were* **placed** under their heads?
32:29 [C] their power, *they* **are laid** with those killed by the sword.
32:32 [A] Although *I had* him **spread** terror in the land of the living,
33: 2 [A] land choose one of their men and **make** him their watchman,
33: 7 [A] of man, *I have* **made** you a watchman for the house of Israel;
33:24 [C] surely the land *has* **been given** to us as our possession.'
33:27 [A] those out in the country *I will* **give** to the wild animals to be
33:28 [A] *I will* **make** the land a desolate waste, and her proud strength
33:29 [A] when I *have* **made** the land a desolate waste because of all
34:26 [A] *I will* **bless** [+906+1388] them and the places surrounding
34:27 [A] The trees of the field *will* **yield** their fruit and the ground will
34:27 [A] field will yield their fruit and the ground *will* **yield** its crops;
35: 3 [A] out my hand against you and **make** you a desolate waste.
35: 7 [A] *I will* **make** Mount Seir a desolate waste and cut off from it
35: 9 [A] *I will* **make** you desolate forever; your towns will not be
35:12 [C] been laid waste and *have* **been given over** to us to devour."
36: 5 [A] with malice in their hearts *they* **made** my land their own
36: 8 [A] *will* **produce** branches and fruit for my people Israel,
36:26 [A] *I will* **give** you a new heart and put a new spirit in you; I will
36:26 [A] I will give you a new heart and **put** a new spirit in you; I will
36:26 [A] from you your heart of stone and **give** you a heart of flesh.
36:27 [A] *I will* **put** my Spirit in you and move you to follow my
36:28 [A] You will live in the land *I* **gave** your forefathers; you will be
36:29 [A] and make it plentiful and *will* not **bring** famine upon you.
37: 6 [A] *I will* **attach** tendons to you and make flesh come upon you
37: 6 [A] with skin; *I will* **put** breath in you, and you will come to life.
37:14 [A] *I will* **put** my Spirit in you and you will live, and I will settle
37:19 [A] **join** it to Judah's stick, making them a single stick of wood,
37:25 [A] They will live in the land *I* **gave** to my servant Jacob,
37:26 [A] *I will* **establish** them and increase their numbers, and I will
37:26 [A] and *I will* **put** my sanctuary among them forever.
38: 4 [A] **put** hooks in your jaws and bring you out with your whole
39: 4 [A] *I will* **give** you as food to all kinds of carrion birds and to the
39:11 [A] " 'On that day *I will* **give** Gog a burial place in Israel,
39:21 [A] "*I will* **display** my glory among the nations, and all the
39:23 [A] and **handed** them **over to** [+928+3338] their enemies,
43: 8 [A] When they **placed** their threshold next to my threshold
43:19 [A] *You are to* **give** a young bull as a sin offering to the priests,
43:20 [A] some of its blood and **put** it on the four horns of the altar
44:14 [A] Yet *I will* **put** them in charge of the duties of the temple
44:28 [A] *You are to* **give** them no possession in Israel; I will be their
44:30 [A] *You are to* **give** them the first portion of your ground meal
45: 6 [A] " '*You are to* **give** the city as its property an area 5,000
45: 8 [A] *will* **allow** the house of Israel **to possess** the land according
45:19 [A] of the sin offering and **put** it on the doorposts of the temple,
46:16 [A] If the prince **makes** a gift *from* his inheritance to one of his
46:17 [A] *he* **makes** a gift from his inheritance to one of his servants,
47:11 [C] and marshes will not become fresh; *they will* **be left** for salt.
47:14 [A] Because I swore with uplifted hand to **give** it to your
47:23 [A] there *you are to* **give** him his inheritance,"
Da 1: 2 [A] the Lord **delivered** Jehoiakim king of Judah into his hand,
1: 9 [A] Now God *had* **caused** the official to show favor and
1:12 [A] **Give** us nothing but vegetables to eat and water to drink.
1:16 [A] wine they were to drink and **gave** them vegetables instead.
1:17 [A] To these four young men God **gave** knowledge
8:12 [C] ⌞of the saints⌟ and the daily sacrifice **were given over** to it.
8:13 [A] the **surrender** *of* the sanctuary and of the host that will be
9: 3 [A] So *I* **turned** [+906+7156] to the Lord God and pleaded with
9:10 [A] or kept the laws *he* **gave** us through his servants the prophets.
10:12 [A] Since the first day that *you* **set** your mind to gain
10:15 [A] *I* **bowed** with my face toward the ground and was speechless.

Da 11: 6 [C] In those days she *will* **be handed over**, together with her
11: 11 [C] will raise a large army, but it *will* **be defeated** [+928+3338].
11: 17 [A] *he will* **give** [+851+2021+4200] him a daughter **in marriage**
11: 21 [A] person who *has* not *been* **given** the honor of royalty.
11: 31 [A] Then *they will* **set up** the abomination that causes desolation.
12: 11 [A] and the abomination that causes desolation *is* **set up**,
Hos 2: 5 [2:7] [A] *who* **give** me my food and my water, my wool and my
2: 8 [2:10] [A] that I was the *one who* **gave** her the grain,
2: 12 [2:14] [A] which she said were her pay **from** her lovers;
2: 15 [2:17] [A] *I will* **give** her **back** her vineyards, and will make
5: 4 [A] "Their deeds *do* not **permit** them to return to their God. A
9: 14 [A] **Give** them, O LORD—what will you give them? Give them
9: 14 [A] Give them, O LORD—what *will you* **give** them? Give them
9: 14 [A] what will you give them? **Give** them wombs that miscarry
11: 8 [A] "How *can I* **give** you **up**, Ephraim? How can I hand you
11: 8 [A] I hand you over, Israel? How *can I* **treat** you like Admah?
13: 10 [A] your towns, of whom you said, '**Give** me a king and princes'?
13: 11 [A] So in my anger *I* **gave** you a king, and in my wrath I took
Joel 2: 11 [A] The LORD **thunders** [+7754] at the head of his army; his
2: 17 [A] *Do* not **make** your inheritance an object of scorn, a byword
2: 19 [A] never again *will I* **make** you an object of scorn to the nations.
2: 22 [A] bearing their fruit; the fig tree and the vine **yield** their riches.
2: 23 [A] for *he has* **given** you the autumn rains in righteousness.
2: 30 [3:3] [A] *I will* **show** wonders in the heavens and on the earth,
3: 3 [4:3] [A] lots for my people and **traded** boys for prostitutes;
3: 16 [4:16] [A] roar from Zion and **thunder** [+7754] from Jerusalem;
Am 1: 2 [A] roars from Zion and **thunders** [+7754] from Jerusalem;
3: 4 [A] *Does* he **growl** [+7754] in his den when he has caught
4: 6 [A] "I **gave** you empty stomachs in every city and lack of bread
9: 15 [A] never again to be uprooted from the land *I have* **given** them,"
Ob 1: 2 [A] "See, *I will* **make** you small among the nations; you will be
Jnh 1: 3 [A] After **paying** the fare, he went aboard and sailed for Tarshish
1: 14 [A] *Do* not **hold** [+6584] us **accountable** *for* killing an innocent
Mic 1: 14 [A] Therefore *you will* **give** parting gifts to Moresheth Gath. The
3: 5 [A] if *he* **does** not, they prepare to wage war against him.
5: 3 [5:2] [A] Therefore Israel *will be* **abandoned** until the time
6: 7 [A] *Shall I* **offer** my firstborn for my transgression, the fruit of
6: 14 [A] save nothing, because what you save *I will* **give** to the sword.
6: 16 [A] Therefore I *will* **give** you **over** to ruin and your people to
7: 20 [A] *You will be* true to Jacob, and **show** mercy to Abraham,
Hab 3: 10 [A] the deep **roared** [+7754] and lifted its waves on high.
Zep 3: 5 [A] Morning by morning *he* **dispenses** his justice, and every new
3: 20 [A] *I will* **give** you honor and praise among all the peoples of the
Hag 2: 9 [A] 'And in this place *I will* **grant** peace,' declares the LORD
Zec 3: 7 [A] and *I will* **give** you a place among these standing here.
3: 9 [A] See, the stone *I have* **set** in front of Joshua! There are seven
7: 11 [A] stubbornly *they* **turned** their backs and stopped up their ears.
8: 12 [A] "The seed will grow well, the vine *will* **yield** its fruit,
8: 12 [A] the vine will yield its fruit, the ground *will* **produce** its crops,
8: 12 [A] will produce its crops, and the heavens *will* **drop** their dew.
10: 1 [A] *He* **gives** showers of rain to men, and plants of the field to
Mal 2: 2 [A] if you do not set your heart to **honor** [+3883+4200] my
2: 5 [A] a covenant of life and peace, and *I* **gave** them to him;
2: 9 [A] "So I *have* **caused** you to be despised and humiliated before

5990 נָתָן nātān, n.pr.m. [42] [√ 5989]

Nathan [42]

2Sa 5: 14 children born to him there: Shammua, Shobab, **Nathan**, Solomon,
7: 2 he said to **Nathan** the prophet, "Here I am, living in a palace of
7: 3 **Nathan** replied to the king, "Whatever you have in mind,
7: 4 That night the word of the LORD came to **Nathan**, saying:
7: 17 **Nathan** reported to David all the words of this entire revelation.
12: 1 The LORD sent **Nathan** to David. When he came to him,
12: 5 David burned with anger against the man and said to **Nathan**,
12: 7 **Nathan** said to David, "You are the man! This is what the LORD,
12: 13 Then David said to **Nathan**, "I have sinned against the LORD."
12: 13 **Nathan** replied, "The LORD has taken away your sin. You are
12: 15 After **Nathan** had gone home, the LORD struck the child that
12: 25 he sent word through **Nathan** the prophet to name him Jedidiah.
23: 36 Igal son of **Nathan** from Zobah, the son of Hagri,
1Ki 1: 8 **Nathan** the prophet, Shimei and Rei and David's special guard did
1: 10 he did not invite **Nathan** the prophet or Benaiah or the special
1: 11 **Nathan** asked Bathsheba, Solomon's mother, "Have you not heard
1: 22 she was still speaking with the king, **Nathan** the prophet arrived.
1: 23 they told the king, "**Nathan** the prophet is here." So he went before
1: 24 **Nathan** said, "Have you, my lord the king, declared that Adonijah
1: 32 the priest, **Nathan** the prophet and Benaiah son of Jehoiada."
1: 34 the priest and **Nathan** the prophet anoint him king over Israel.
1: 38 So Zadok the priest, **Nathan** the prophet, Benaiah son of Jehoiada,
1: 44 **Nathan** the prophet, Benaiah son of Jehoiada, the Kerethites
1: 45 and **Nathan** the prophet have anointed him king at Gihon.
4: 5 Azariah son of **Nathan**—in charge of the district officers;
4: 5 Zabud son of **Nathan**—a priest and personal adviser to the king;
1Ch 2: 36 Attai was the father of **Nathan**, Nathan the father of Zabad,
2: 36 Attai was the father of Nathan, **Nathan** the father of Zabad,
3: 5 born to him there: Shammua, Shobab, **Nathan** and Solomon.
11: 38 Joel the brother of **Nathan**, Mibhar son of Hagri,
14: 4 children born to him there: Shammua, Shobab, **Nathan**, Solomon,
17: 1 he said to **Nathan** the prophet, "Here I am, living in a palace of
17: 2 **Nathan** replied to David, "Whatever you have in mind, do it,
17: 3 That night the word of God came to **Nathan**, saying:
17: 15 **Nathan** reported to David all the words of this entire revelation.
29: 29 the records of **Nathan** the prophet and the records of Gad the seer,
2Ch 9: 29 are they not written in the records of **Nathan** the prophet,
29: 25 by David and Gad the king's seer and **Nathan** the prophet;
Ezr 8: 16 Elnathan, Jarib, Elnathan, **Nathan**, Zechariah and Meshullam,
10: 39 Shelemiah, **Nathan**, Adaiah,
Ps 51: T [51:2] When the prophet **Nathan** came to him after David had
Zec 12: 12 and their wives, the clan of the house of **Nathan** and their wives,

5991 נְתַנְאֵל n^e^tan'ēl, n.pr.m. [14] [√ 5889 + 446]

Nethanel [14]

Nu 1: 8 from Issachar, **Nethanel** son of Zuar;
2: 5 The leader of the people of Issachar is **Nethanel** son of Zuar.
7: 18 On the second day **Nethanel** son of Zuar, the leader of Issachar,
7: 23 fellowship offering. This was the offering of **Nethanel** son of Zuar.
10: 15 **Nethanel** son of Zuar was over the division of the tribe of Issachar,
1Ch 2: 14 the fourth **Nethanel**, the fifth Raddai,
15: 24 Joshaphat, **Nethanel**, Amasai, Zechariah, Benaiah and Eliezer the
24: 6 The scribe Shemaiah son of **Nethanel**, a Levite, recorded their
26: 4 the second, Joah the third, Sacar the fourth, **Nethanel** the fifth,
2Ch 17: 7 Zechariah, **Nethanel** and Micaiah to teach in the towns of Judah.
35: 9 Also Conaniah along with Shemaiah and **Nethanel**, his brothers,
Ezr 10: 22 Elioenai, Maaseiah, Ishmael, **Nethanel**, Jozabad and Elasah.
Ne 12: 21 of Hilkiah's, Hashabiah; of Jedaiah's, **Nethanel**.
12: 36 Azarel, Milalai, Gilalai, Maai, **Nethanel**, Judah and Hanani—

5992 נְתַנְיָה n^e^tanyâ, n.pr.m. [15] [√ 5989 + 3378]

Nethaniah [15]

2Ki 25: 23 Ishmael son of **Nethaniah**, Johanan son of Kareah, Seraiah son of
25: 25 however, Ishmael son of **Nethaniah**, the son of Elishama,
1Ch 25: 2 From the sons of Asaph: Zaccur, Joseph, **Nethaniah** and Asarelah.
Jer 40: 14 Ammonites has sent Ishmael son of **Nethaniah** to take your life?"
40: 15 "Let me go and kill Ishmael son of **Nethaniah**, and no one will
41: 1 In the seventh month Ishmael son of **Nethaniah**, the son of
41: 2 Ishmael son of **Nethaniah** and the ten men who were with him got
41: 6 Ishmael son of **Nethaniah** went out from Mizpah to meet them,
41: 7 Ishmael son of **Nethaniah** and the men who were with him
41: 10 Ishmael son of **Nethaniah** took them captive and set out to cross
41: 11 about all the crimes Ishmael son of **Nethaniah** had committed,
41: 12 took all their men and went to fight Ishmael son of **Nethaniah**.
41: 15 Ishmael son of **Nethaniah** and eight of his men escaped from
41: 16 of **Nethaniah** after he had assassinated Gedaliah son of Ahikam:
41: 18 because Ishmael son of **Nethaniah** had killed Gedaliah son of

5993 נְתַנְיָהוּ n^e^tanyāhû, n.pr.m. [5] [√ 5989 + 3378]

Nethaniah [5]

1Ch 25: 12 the fifth to **Nethaniah**, his sons and relatives, 12
2Ch 17: 8 Shemaiah, **Nethaniah**, Zebadiah, Asahel, Shemiramoth,
Jer 36: 14 all the officials sent Jehudi son of **Nethaniah**, the son of
40: 8 Ishmael son of **Nethaniah**, Johanan and Jonathan the sons of
41: 9 king of Israel. Ishmael son of **Nethaniah** filled it with the dead.

5994 נְתַן־מֶלֶךְ n^e^tan-melek, n.pr.m. [1] [√ 5989 + 4889]

Nathan-Melech [1]

2Ki 23: 11 in the court near the room of an official named **Nathan-Melech**.

5995 נָתַס nātas, v. [1] [cf. 5996, 5997, 6004]

break up [1]

Job 30: 13 [A] *They* **break up** my road; they succeed in destroying me—

5996 נָתַע nāta', v. [1] [cf. 5995, 5997, 6004]

are broken [1]

Job 4: 10 [C] and growl, yet the teeth of the great lions **are broken**.

5997 נָתַץ nātaṣ, v. [42] [cf. 5995, 5996, 6004]

broke down [6], tore down [6], break down [4], demolished [4], tear down [3], torn down [3], demolish [2], destroyed [2], pulled down [2], be broken up [1], been torn down [1], breaks down [1], bring down to ruin [1], broken down [1], destroy [1], lay in ruins [1], shattered [1], tear out [1], tears down [1]

Ex 34: 13 [A] **Break down** their altars, smash their sacred stones and cut

Lev 11:35 [H] an oven or cooking pot *must* **be broken up**.
14:45 [A] It *must be* **torn down**—its stones, timbers and all the
Dt 7: 5 [A] **Break down** their altars, smash their sacred stones, cut down
12: 3 [D] **Break down** their altars, smash their sacred stones and burn
Jdg 2: 2 [A] people of this land, but *you shall* **break down** their altars.'
6:28 [E] there was Baal's altar, **demolished**, with the Asherah pole
6:30 [A] because *he has* **broken down** Baal's altar and cut down the
6:31 [A] he can defend himself when *someone* **breaks down** his
6:32 [A] contend with him," because *he* **broke down** Baal's altar.
8: 9 [A] "When I return in triumph, *I will* **tear down** this tower."
8:17 [A] *He* also **pulled down** the tower of Peniel and killed the men
9:45 [A] Then *he* **destroyed** the city and scattered salt over it.
2Ki 10:27 [A] *They* **demolished** the sacred stone of Baal and tore down the
10:27 [A] the sacred stone of Baal and **tore down** the temple of Baal,
11:18 [A] of the land went to the temple of Baal and **tore** it **down**.
23: 7 [A] *He* also **tore down** the quarters of the male shrine prostitutes,
23: 8 [A] *He* **broke down** the shrines at the gates—at the entrance to
23:12 [A] *He* **pulled down** the altars the kings of Judah had erected on
23:15 [A] Israel to sin—even that altar and high place *he* **demolished**.
25:10 [A] the imperial guard, **broke down** the walls around Jerusalem.
2Ch 23:17 [A] All the people went to the temple of Baal and **tore it down**.
31: 1 [D] *They* **destroyed** the high places and the altars throughout
33: 3 [D] rebuilt the high places his father Hezekiah *had* **demolished**;
34: 4 [D] Under his direction the altars of the Baals *were* **torn down**;
34: 7 [D] *he* **tore down** the altars and the Asherah poles and crushed
36:19 [D] fire to God's temple and **broke down** the wall of Jerusalem;
Job 19:10 [A] *He* **tears** me **down** on every side till I am gone; he uproots
Ps 52: 5 [52:7] [A] Surely God *will* **bring** you **down to** everlasting **ruin**:
58: 6 [58:7] [A] O God; **tear out**, O LORD, the fangs of the lions!
Isa 22:10 [A] in Jerusalem and **tore down** houses to strengthen the wall.
Jer 1:10 [A] you over nations and kingdoms to uproot and **tear down**,
4:26 [C] all its towns **lay in ruins** before the LORD, before his fierce
18: 7 [A] or kingdom is to be uprooted, **torn down** and destroyed,
31:28 [A] Just as I watched over them to uproot and **tear down**, and to
33: 4 [B] the royal palaces of Judah that *have* **been torn down** to be
39: 8 [A] houses of the people and **broke down** the walls of Jerusalem.
52:14 [A] imperial guard **broke down** all the walls around Jerusalem.
Eze 16:39 [D] will tear down your mounds and **destroy** your lofty shrines.
26: 9 [A] your walls and **demolish** your towers with his weapons.
26:12 [A] and **demolish** your fine houses and throw your stones,
Na 1: 6 [C] is poured out like fire; the rocks *are* **shattered** before him.

5998 נָתַק nātaq, v. [27] [→ 5999]

break [2], broken [2], snapped [2], are purged out [1], are shattered [1], are snapped [1], broke away [1], drag off [1], draw away [1], is broken [1], is torn [1], lured away [1], pull off [1], set [1], snaps [1], tear away [1], tear off [1], tear [1], torn off [1], torn [1], uprooted [+906+9247] [1], were drawn away [1], were lured away [1]

Lev 22:24 [B] an animal whose testicles are bruised, crushed, **torn** or cut.
Jos 4:18 [C] No sooner *had* they **set** their feet on the dry ground than the
8: 6 [G] They will pursue us until *we have* **lured** them **away** from the
8:16 [C] and they pursued Joshua and **were lured away** from the city.
Jdg 16: 9 [D] *he* **snapped** the thongs as easily as a piece of string snaps
16: 9 [C] he snapped the thongs as easily as a piece of string **snaps**
16:12 [D] *he* **snapped** the ropes off his arms as if they were threads.
20:31 [H] came out to meet them and **were drawn away** from the city.
20:32 [A] and **draw** them **away** from the city to the roads."
Job 17:11 [C] my plans **are shattered**, and so are the desires of my heart.
18:14 [C] He **is torn** from the security of his tent and marched off to
Ps 2: 3 [D] "*Let us* **break** their chains," they say, "and throw off their
107:14 [D] and the deepest gloom and **broke away** their chains.
Ecc 4:12 [C] A cord of three strands **is** not quickly **broken**.
Isa 5:27 [C] a belt is loosened at the waist, not a sandal thong *is* **broken**.
33:20 [C] stakes will never be pulled up, nor any of its ropes **broken**.
58: 6 [D] of the yoke, to set the oppressed free and **break** every yoke?
Jer 2:20 [D] "Long ago you broke off your yoke and **tore off** your bonds;
5: 5 [D] they too had broken off the yoke and **torn off** the bonds.
6:29 [C] the refining goes on in vain; the wicked **are** not **purged out**.
10:20 [C] My tent is destroyed; all its ropes **are snapped**. My sons are
12: 3 [G] about you. **Drag** them **off** like sheep to be butchered!
22:24 [A] a signet ring on my right hand, *I would* still **pull** you **off**.
30: 8 [D] break the yoke off their necks and *will* **tear off** their bonds;
Eze 17: 9 [D] *Will* it not *be* **uprooted** [+906+9247] and stripped of its fruit
23:34 [D] drain it dry; you will dash it to pieces and **tear** your breasts.
Na 1:13 [D] their yoke from your neck and **tear** your shackles **away**."

5999 נֶתֶק neteq, n.m. [14] [√ 5998]

itch [7], it[s] [+2021] [3], diseased area [1], him[s] [+2021] [1], infected person [+5596] [1], this kind of sore [+2021+5596] [1]

Lev 13:30 it is an **itch**, an infectious disease of the head or chin.
13:31 when the priest examines **this kind of sore** [+2021+5596],
13:31 the priest is to put the **infected person** [+5596] in isolation for
13:32 and if the **itch** has not spread and there is no yellow hair in it
13:32 and **it**[s] [+2021] does not appear to be more than skin deep,
13:33 he must be shaved except for the **diseased area**, and the priest is to
13:33 the priest is to keep **him**[s] [+2021] in isolation another seven days.
13:34 On the seventh day the priest is to examine the **itch**, and if it has
13:34 if **it**[s] [+2021] has not spread in the skin and appears to be no more
13:35 But if the **itch** does spread in the skin after he is pronounced clean,
13:36 the priest is to examine him, and if the **itch** has spread in the skin,
13:37 in his judgment **it**[s] [+2021] is unchanged and black hair has grown
13:37 it is unchanged and black hair has grown in it, the **itch** is healed.
14:54 are the regulations for any infectious skin disease, for an **itch**,

6000 ¹נָתַר nātar[1], v. [1] [cf. 6002]

let loose [1]

Job 6: 9 [G] be willing to crush me, *to* **let loose** his hand and cut me off!

6001 ²נָתַר nātar[2], v. [3]

hopping [1], leaps [1], made tremble [1]

Lev 11:21 [D] those that have jointed legs for **hopping** on the ground.
Job 37: 1 [A] "At this my heart pounds and **leaps** from its place.
Hab 3: 6 [G] shook the earth; he looked, and **made** the nations **tremble**.

6002 ³נָתַר nātar[3], v. [4 / 3] [cf. 6000]

released [1], sets free [1], untie [1]

2Sa 22:33 [g] and makes [BHS *sets free*; NIV 5989] my way perfect.
Ps 105:20 [G] The king sent and **released** him, the ruler of peoples set him
146: 7 [G] gives food to the hungry. The LORD **sets** prisoners **free**,
Isa 58: 6 [G] loose the chains of injustice and **untie** the cords of the yoke,

6003 נֶתֶר neter, n.[m.]. [2]

soda [2]

Pr 25:20 or like vinegar poured on **soda**, is one who sings songs to a heavy
Jer 2:22 Although you wash yourself with **soda** and use an abundance of

6004 נָתַשׁ nātaš, v. [21 / 20] [cf. 5995, 5996, 5997]

uproot [11], be uprooted [3], uprooted [3], completely uproot [+906+6004] [2], was uprooted [1]

Dt 29:28 [29:27] [A] in great wrath the LORD **uprooted** them from
1Ki 14:15 [A] *He will* **uproot** Israel from this good land that he gave to
2Ch 7:20 [A] *I will* **uproot** Israel from my land, which I have given them,
Ps 9: 6 [9:7] [A] overtaken the enemy, *you have* **uprooted** their cities;
Jer 1:10 [A] you over nations and kingdoms to **uproot** and tear down,
12:14 [A] I *will* **uproot** them from their lands and I will uproot the
12:14 [A] and *I will* **uproot** the house of Judah from among them.
12:15 [A] after I **uproot** them, I will again have compassion and will
12:17 [A] *I will* **completely uproot** [+906+6004] and destroy it,"
12:17 [A] *I will* **completely uproot** [+906+6004] and destroy it,"
18: 7 [A] time I announce that a nation or kingdom *is to be* **uprooted**,
18:14 [c] cool waters … *ever* cease [BHS *be uprooted* ?; NIV 5980]
24: 6 [A] not tear them down; I will plant them and not **uproot** them.
31:28 [A] Just as I watched over them to **uproot** and tear down, and to
31:40 [C] The city *will* never again **be uprooted** or demolished."
42:10 [A] I will plant you and not **uproot** you, for I am grieved over
45: 4 [A] overthrow what I have built and **uproot** what I have planted,
Eze 19:12 [H] *it* **was uprooted** in fury and thrown to the ground. The east
Da 11: 4 [C] because his empire *will* **be uprooted** and given to others.
Am 9:15 [C] never again *to* **be uprooted** from the land I have given
Mic 5:14 [5:13] [A] *I will* **uproot** from among you your Asherah poles

ס, s

6005 ס s, letter. Not used in NIV/BHS [→ 6163; Ar 10500]

6006 סְאָה sᵉ'â, n.f. [9]

seahs [6], seah [3]

Ge 18: 6 "get three **seahs** *of* fine flour and knead it and bake some bread."
1Sa 25:18 two skins of wine, five dressed sheep, five **seahs** of roasted grain,
1Ki 18:32 he dug a trench around it large enough to hold *two* **seahs** *of* seed.
2Ki 7: 1 a **seah** *of* flour will sell for a shekel and two seahs of barley for a
7: 1 and *two* **seahs** of barley for a shekel at the gate of Samaria."
7:16 So a **seah** *of* flour sold for a shekel, and two seahs of barley sold
7:16 and *two* **seahs** *of* barley sold for a shekel, as the LORD had said.
7:18 a **seah** *of* flour will sell for a shekel and two seahs of barley for a
7:18 and *two* **seahs** of barley for a shekel at the gate of Samaria."

6007 סְאוֹן ***seʼôn***, n.[m.]. [1] [→ 6008]

boot [1]

Isa 9: 5 [9:4] Every warrior's **boot** used in battle and every garment rolled

6008 סָאַן ***sāʼan***, v.den. [1] [√ 6007]

warrior's [1]

Isa 9: 5 [9:4] [A] Every **warrior's** boot used in battle and every garment

6009 סַאסְּאָה ***saʼsseʼâ***, n.f. [1]

warfare [1]

Isa 27: 8 By **warfare** and exile you contend with her—with his fierce blast

6010 סָבָא ***sābāʼ***[1], v. [6? / 5] [√ 6011]

drink fill [1], drink too much [1], drunk [1], drunkard [1], drunkards [1]

Dt 21:20 [A] He will not obey us. He is a profligate and a **drunkard**."
Pr 23:20 [A] Do not join *those who* **drink too much** wine or gorge
23:21 [A] for **drunkards** and gluttons become poor, and drowsiness
Isa 56:12 [A] one cries, "let me get wine! *Let us* **drink** *our* **fill** *of* beer!
Eze 23:42 [a] Sabeans [BHS K (& Q?) *drunkards*; NIV 6014] were brought]
Na 1:10 [B] will be entangled among thorns and **drunk** from their wine;

6011 סֹבֶא ***sōbeʼ***, n.m. [3] [→ 6010]

choice wine [1], drinks [1], wine [1]

Isa 1:22 silver has become dross, your **choice wine** is diluted with water.
Hos 4:18 Even when their **drinks** are gone, they continue their prostitution;
Na 1:10 They will be entangled among thorns and drunk from their **wine**;

6012 סָבָא ***sābāʼ***[2], n.m. Not used in NIV/BHS [√ 6015?]

6013 סְבָא ***sebāʼ***, n.pr.m. [4] [→ 6014]

Seba [4]

Ge 10: 7 The sons of Cush: **Seba**, Havilah, Sabtah, Raamah and Sabteca.
1Ch 1: 9 The sons of Cush: **Seba**, Havilah, Sabta, Raamah and Sabteca.
Ps 72:10 tribute to him; the kings of Sheba and **Seba** will present him gifts.
Isa 43: 3 I give Egypt for your ransom, Cush and **Seba** in your stead.

6014 סְבָאִי ***sebāʼî***, n.pl.g. [1 / 2] [√ 6013]

Sabeans [2]

Isa 45:14 of Egypt and the merchandise of Cush, and those tall **Sabeans**—
Eze 23:42 **Sabeans** [BHS K (& Q?) 6010] were brought from the desert

6015 סָבַב ***sābab***, v. [162 / 163] [→ 4585, 4990, 4991, 5813, 6012?, 6016, 6017]

surrounded [15], turned [12], surround [10], turn [9], changed [4], go about [3], moved [3], prowl about [3], turning [3], circle around [2], coiled around [2], curved [2], fall in [+448] [2], led around [2], made rounds [2], made way around [2], march around [2], marched around [2], measure around [+906+6017] [2], pass [2], round [2], settings [2], turn about [2], turned around [2], turned away [2], turns [2], went around [2], winds through [2], *untranslated* [1], all around [1], around [1], be turned over [1], become [1], began [1], bring back [1], bring over [1], brought around [1], carried around [1], change [1], changing [1], circled [1], circuit [1], circumference [+2562] [1], coming around [1], cross [1], curved around [1], dragged [1], eluded [+4946+7156] [1], encircled [+906+6017] [1], encircled [+906+6017+6017] [1], encircling [1], engulf [1], gather around [1], gathered around [1], go around [1], go [1], hinged [1], is rolled [1], leave [+4946] [1], march around [+906+906+5938] [1], on every side [1], once again [1], put around [1], responsible for [+928] [1], returned home [1], roundabout [1], sent around [1], shielded [1], sit down [1], skirted [1], stand aside [1], stepped aside [1], sulking [+906+7156] [1], surrounding [1], surrounds [1], swarmed around [1], swirled about [1], swung open [1], took away [1], turn against [1], turn away [+7156] [1], turn over [1], turned [+7156] [1], turned over [1], waged against from all sides [1], walk about [1], walk through [1], went throughout [1], went [1], were changed [1], were mounted [1]

Ge 2:11 [A] it **winds through** the entire land of Havilah, where there is
2:13 [A] river is the Gihon; it **winds through** the entire land of Cush.
19: 4 [C] city of Sodom—both young and old—**surrounded** the house.
37: 7 [A] while your sheaves **gathered around** mine and bowed down
42:24 [A] *He* **turned away** from them and began to weep, but
Ex 13:18 [G] So God **led** the people **around** *by* the desert road *toward* the
28:11 [H] a seal. Then mount the stones in gold filigree **settings**
39: 6 [H] They mounted the onyx stones in gold filigree **settings**
39:13 [H] and a jasper. *They* **were mounted** in gold filigree settings.
Nu 21: 4 [A] Hor along the route to the Red Sea, to **go around** Edom.
32:38 [H] as well as Nebo and Baal Meon (these names **were changed**)
34: 4 [C] **cross** south of Scorpion Pass, continue on to Zin and go
34: 5 [C] where it *will* **turn**, join the Wadi of Egypt and end at the Sea.
36: 7 [A] No inheritance in Israel *is to* **pass** from tribe to tribe,
36: 9 [A] No inheritance *may* **pass** from tribe to tribe, for each Israelite
Dt 2: 1 [A] For a long time *we* **made** *our* **way around** the hill country of
2: 3 [A] "You *have* **made** *your* **way around** this hill country long
32:10 [D] *He* **shielded** him and cared for him; he guarded him as the
Jos 6: 3 [A] **March around** [+906+906+5938] the city once with all the
6: 4 [A] On the seventh day, **march around** the city seven times,
6: 7 [A] **March around** the city, with the armed guard going ahead of
6:11 [G] So *he had* the ark of the LORD **carried around** the city,
6:14 [A] So on the second day *they* **marched around** the city once
6:15 [A] **marched around** the city seven times in the same manner,
6:15 [A] except that on that day *they* **circled** the city seven times.
7: 9 [C] *they will* **surround** us and wipe out our name from the earth.
15: 3 [C] it ran past Hezron up to Addar and **curved around** to Karka.
15:10 [C] it **curved** westward from Baalah to Mount Seir, ran along the
16: 6 [C] From Micmethath on the north it **curved** eastward to Taanath
18:14 [C] the boundary turned **[RPH]** south along the western side
19:14 [C] There the boundary **went around** on the north to Hannathon
Jdg 11:18 [A] through the desert, **skirted** the lands of Edom and Moab,
16: 2 [A] So *they* **surrounded** the place and lay in wait for him all
18:23 [G] after them, the Danites **turned** [+7156] and said to Micah,
19:22 [C] some of the wicked men of the city **surrounded** the house.
20: 5 [A] the men of Gibeah came after me and **surrounded** the house,
1Sa 5: 8 [A] "*Have* the ark of the god of Israel **moved** *to* Gath."
5: 8 [G] moved to Gath." So *they* **moved** the ark of the God of Israel.
5: 9 [G] after *they had* **moved** it, the LORD's hand was against that
5:10 [G] "*They have* **brought** the ark of the god of Israel **around** to
7:16 [A] year he went *on a* **circuit** *from* Bethel *to* Gilgal *to* Mizpah,
15:12 [A] his own honor and *has* **turned** and gone on down to Gilgal."
15:27 [A] As Samuel **turned** to leave, Saul caught hold of the hem of
16:11 [A] "Send for him; *we will* not **sit down** until he arrives."
17:30 [A] *He* then **turned** away to someone else and brought up the
18:11 [A] to the wall." But David **eluded** [+4946+7156] him twice.
22:17 [A] "**Turn** and kill the priests of the LORD, because they too
22:18 [A] then ordered Doeg, "You **turn** and strike down the priests."
22:18 [A] So Doeg the Edomite **turned** and struck them down.
22:22 [A] I *am* **responsible** [+928] **for** the death of your father's whole
2Sa 3:12 [G] with me, and I will help you **bring** all Israel **over** to you."
5:23 [G] **circle around** behind them and attack them in front of the
14:20 [D] Your servant Joab did this to **change** the present situation.
14:24 [A] the king said, "*He must* **go** to his own house; he must not see
14:24 [A] So Absalom **went** to his own house and did not see the face
18:15 [A] ten of Joab's armor-bearers **surrounded** Absalom, struck
18:30 [A] The king said, "**Stand aside** and wait here." So he stepped
18:30 [A] and wait here." So *he* **stepped aside** and stood there.
20:12 [G] *he* **dragged** him from the road *into* a field and threw a
22: 6 [A] The cords of the grave **coiled around** me; the snares of death
1Ki 2:15 [A] *things* **changed**, and the kingdom has gone to my brother;
5: 3 [5:17] [A] wars **waged against** my father David **from all sides**,
7:15 [A] each eighteen cubits high and twelve cubits **around**, by line.
7:23 [A] a line of thirty cubits *to* **measure around** [+906+6017] it.
7:24 [A] Below the rim, gourds **encircled** [+906+6017] it—ten to a
8:14 [G] standing there, the king **turned around** and blessed them.
18:37 [G] are God, and that you *are* **turning** their hearts back again."
21: 4 [G] He lay on his bed **sulking** [+906+7156] and refused to eat.
2Ki 3: 9 [A] After a **roundabout** march of seven days, the army had no
3:25 [A] men armed with slings **surrounded** it and attacked it as well.
6:15 [A] an army with horses and chariots *had* **surrounded** the city.
8:21 [A] The Edomites **surrounded** him and his chariot commanders,
9:18 [A] Jehu replied. "**Fall** [+448] **in** behind me." The lookout
9:19 [A] do you have to do with peace? **Fall** [+448] **in** behind me."
16:18 [G] *He* **took away** the Sabbath canopy that had been built at the
20: 2 [G] Hezekiah **turned** his face to the wall and prayed to the
23:34 [G] his father Josiah and **changed** Eliakim's name *to* Jehoiakim.
24:17 [G] king in his place and **changed** his name *to* Zedekiah.
1Ch 10:14 [G] to death and **turned** the kingdom **over** to David son of Jesse.
12:23 [12:24] [G] at Hebron to **turn** Saul's kingdom **over** to him,
13: 3 [G] *Let us* **bring** the ark of our God **back** to us, for we did not
14:14 [G] **circle around** them and attack them in front of the balsam
16:43 [A] his own home, and David **returned home** to bless his family.
2Ch 4: 2 [A] a line of thirty cubits *to* **measure around** [+906+6017] it.
4: 3 [A] Below the rim, figures of bulls **encircled** [+906+6017+6017] it
6: 3 [G] standing there, the king **turned around** and blessed them.
13:13 [G] Now Jeroboam *had* **sent** troops **around** to the rear, so that
14: 7 [14:6] [G] "and **put** walls **around** them, with towers, gates
17: 9 [A] *they* **went around** to all the towns of Judah and taught the
18:31 [A] So *they* **turned** to attack him, but Jehoshaphat cried out,
21: 9 [A] The Edomites **surrounded** him and his chariot commanders,
23: 2 [A] *They* **went throughout** Judah and gathered the Levites
29: 6 [G] *They* **turned** their faces **away** from the LORD's dwelling
33:14 [A] entrance of the Fish Gate and **encircling** the hill of Ophel;
35:22 [G] Josiah, however, *would* not **turn** [+7156] **away** from him,

2Ch 36: 4 [G] and Jerusalem and **changed** Eliakim's name *to* Jehoiakim.
Ezr 6:22 [G] because the LORD had filled them with joy *by* **changing**
Job 10: 8 [A] Will you now **turn** [BHS 6017] and destroy me?
16:13 [A] his archers **surround** me. Without pity, he pierces my
40:22 [A] in their shadow; the poplars by the stream **surround** him.
Ps 7: 7 [7:8] [D] *Let* the assembled peoples **gather around** you. Rule
17:11 [A] *they* now **surround** me, with eyes alert, to throw me to the
18: 5 [18:6] [A] The cords of the grave **coiled around** me; the snares
22:12 [22:13] [A] Many bulls **surround** me; strong bulls of Bashan
22:16 [22:17] [A] Dogs *have* **surrounded** me; a band of evil men has
26: 6 [D] my hands in innocence, and **go about** your altar, O LORD,
32: 7 [D] from trouble and **surround** me *with* songs of deliverance.
32:10 [D] the LORD's unfailing love **surrounds** the man who trusts
48:12 [48:13] [A] **Walk about** Zion, go around her, count her towers,
49: 5 [49:6] [A] days come, *when* wicked deceivers **surround** me—
55:10 [55:11] [D] Day and night *they* **prowl about** on its walls;
59: 6 [59:7] [D] snarling like dogs, and **prowl about** the city.
59:14 [59:15] [D] snarling like dogs, and **prowl about** the city.
71:21 [A] You will increase my honor and comfort me **once again**.
88:17 [88:18] [A] All day long *they* **surround** me like a flood;
109: 3 [A] *With* words of hatred *they* **surround** me; they attack me
114: 3 [A] The sea looked and fled, the Jordan **turned** back;
114: 5 [A] was it, O sea, that you fled, O Jordan, that *you* **turned** back,
118:10 [A] All the nations **surrounded** me, but in the name of the
118:11 [A] *They* **surrounded** me on every side, but in the name of the
118:11 [A] They surrounded me **on every side**, but in the name of the
118:12 [A] *They* **swarmed around** me like bees, but they died out as
Pr 26:14 [A] As a door **turns** on its hinges, so a sluggard turns on his bed.
Ecc 1: 6 [A] The wind blows to the south and **turns** to the north; round
1: 6 [A] **round** and round it goes, ever returning on its course.
1: 6 [A] round and **round** it goes, ever returning on its course.
2:20 [A] So my heart **began** to despair over all my toilsome labor
7:25 [A] So I **turned** my mind to understand, to investigate and to
9:14 [A] **surrounded** it and built huge siegeworks against it.
12: 5 [A] goes to his eternal home and mourners **go about** the streets.
SS 2:17 [A] **turn**, my lover, and be like a gazelle or like a young stag on
3: 2 [D] I will get up now and **go about** the city, through its streets
3: 3 [A] The watchmen found me *as* they **made** *their* **rounds** in the
5: 7 [A] The watchmen found me *as* they **made** *their* **rounds** in the
6: 5 [G] **Turn** your eyes from me; they overwhelm me. Your hair is
Isa 23:16 [A] "Take up a harp, **walk through** the city, O prostitute
28:27 [H] with a sledge, nor **is** a cartwheel **rolled** over cummin;
38: 2 [G] Hezekiah **turned** his face to the wall and prayed to the
Jer 6:12 [C] Their houses *will* **be turned over** to others, together with
21: 4 [G] I *am about to* **turn against** you the weapons of war that are
31:22 [D] a new thing on earth—a woman *will* **surround** a man."
31:39 [C] there straight to the hill of Gareb and then **turn** to Goah.
41:14 [A] All the people Ishmael had taken captive at Mizpah **turned**
52:21 [A] cubits high and twelve cubits *in* **circumference** [+2562];
Eze 1: 9 [C] one went straight ahead; *they did* not **turn** as they moved.
1:12 [C] would go, they would go, without **turning** as they went.
1:17 [C] the wheels *did* not **turn about** as the creatures went.
7:22 [G] *I will* **turn** my face away from them, and they will desecrate
10:11 [C] the wheels *did* not **turn about** as the cherubim went.
10:11 [C] direction the head faced, without **turning** as they went.
10:16 [C] from the ground, the wheels *did* not **leave** [+4946] their side.
26: 2 [C] the nations is broken, and its doors *have* **swung open** to me;
41: 7 [C] The side rooms **all around** the temple were wider at each
41: 7 [H] The *structure* **surrounding** the temple was built in
41:24 [H] Each door had two leaves—two **hinged** leaves for each door.
42:19 [A] *he* **turned** to the west side and measured; it was five hundred
47: 2 [G] and **led** me **around** the outside to the outer gate facing east,
Hos 7: 2 [A] Their sins **engulf** them; they are always before me.
11:12 [12:1] [A] Ephraim *has* **surrounded** me with lies, the house of
Jnh 2: 3 [2:4] [D] heart of the seas, and the currents **swirled about** me;
2: 5 [2:6] [D] waters threatened me, the deep **surrounded** me;
Hab 2:16 [A] The cup from the LORD's right hand *is* **coming around** to
Zec 14:10 [A] south of Jerusalem, *will* **become** like the Arabah.

6016 סִבָּה *sibbâ*, n.f. [1] [√ 6015]

turn of events [1]

1Ki 12:15 listen to the people, for this **turn of events** was from the LORD,

6017 סָבִיב *sābîb*, subst. (used as pp. & adv.). [335 / 334] [√ 6015]

around [108], all around [+6017] [34], surrounding [27], all around [23], *untranslated* [17], on every side [+4946] [16], on all sides [13], on every side [9], around [+4946] [7], around [+6017] [6], all [5], neighbors [5], surround [5], every side [4], surrounded [4], about [2], all over [+6017+6584] [2], back and forth [+6017] [2], circular in shape [+6318] [2], completely surrounding [+4200+6017] [2], covered with [+6017+8470] [2], encircled [+906+6015+6017] [2], from every side [+4946] [2], measure around [+906+6015] [2], neighboring [2], surrounding [+6017] [2], surrounds [2], throughout [+928] [2], all around [+4946] [1], along [1], area around [1], around [+1237+4946] [1], circular band [+6318] [1], completely [1], course [1], encircled [+906+6015] [1], encircling [1], enveloped [+4946] [1], escorted by [1], everything around [1], everywhere [1], from [+4946] [1], full [+1074] [1], in [1], on [1], outside walls [1], overrun [1], ringed about [1], round about [1], sides [+4946+6298] [1], stationed around [1], surround [+2118+4946+6584] [1], went over [+2118] [1]

Ge 23:17 cave in it, and all the trees within the borders **[NIE]** of the field—
35: 5 and the terror of God fell upon the towns **all around** them
41:48 In each city he put the food grown in the fields **surrounding** it.
Ex 7:24 And all the Egyptians dug **along** the Nile to get drinking water,
16:13 and in the morning there was a layer of dew **around** the camp.
19:12 Put limits for the people **around** the mountain and tell them,
25:11 pure gold, both inside and out, and make a gold molding **around** it.
25:24 Overlay it with pure gold and make a gold molding **around** it.
25:25 Also make **around** it a rim a handbreadth wide and put a gold
25:25 it a rim a handbreadth wide and put a gold molding **on** the rim.
27:17 All the posts **around** the courtyard are to have silver bands
28:32 There shall be a woven edge like a collar **around** this opening,
28:33 of blue, purple and scarlet yarn **around** the hem of the robe,
28:33 the hem of the robe, with gold bells between them. **[RPH]**
28:34 and the pomegranates are to alternate **around** the hem of the robe.
29:16 and take the blood and sprinkle it against the altar **on all sides**.
29:20 their right feet. Then sprinkle blood against the altar **on all sides**.
30: 3 Overlay the top and **all** the sides and the horns with pure gold,
30: 3 and the horns with pure gold, and make a gold molding **around** it.
37: 2 pure gold, both inside and out, and made a gold molding **around** it.
37:11 they overlaid it with pure gold and made a gold molding **around** it.
37:12 They also made **around** it a rim a handbreadth wide and put a gold
37:12 a handbreadth wide and put a gold molding on the rim. **[RPH]**
37:26 They overlaid the top and **all** the sides and the horns with pure
37:26 and the horns with pure gold, and made a gold molding **around** it.
38:16 All the curtains **around** the courtyard were of finely twisted linen.
38:20 of the tabernacle and of the **surrounding** courtyard were bronze.
38:31 the bases for the **surrounding** courtyard and those for its entrance
38:31 pegs for the tabernacle and those for the **surrounding** courtyard.
39:23 and a band **around** this opening, so that it would not tear.
39:25 and attached them **around** the hem between the pomegranates.
39:26 pomegranates alternated **around** the hem of the robe to be worn
40: 8 Set up the courtyard **around** it and put the curtain at the entrance
40:33 Then Moses set up the courtyard **around** the tabernacle and altar
Lev 1: 5 sprinkle it against the altar **on all sides** at the entrance to the Tent
1:11 the priests shall sprinkle its blood against the altar **on all sides**.
3: 2 the priests shall sprinkle the blood against the altar **on all sides**.
3: 8 Aaron's sons shall sprinkle its blood against the altar **on all sides**.
3:13 Aaron's sons shall sprinkle its blood against the altar **on all sides**.
7: 2 and its blood is to be sprinkled against the altar **on all sides**.
8:15 with his finger he put it on **all** the horns of the altar to purify the
8:19 the ram and sprinkled the blood against the altar **on all sides**.
8:24 right feet. Then he sprinkled blood against the altar **on all sides**.
9:12 him the blood, and he sprinkled it against the altar **on all sides**.
9:18 him the blood, and he sprinkled it against the altar **on all sides**.
14:41 He must have **all** the inside walls of the house scraped and the
16:18 and some of the goat's blood and put it on **all** the horns of the altar.
25:31 houses in villages without walls **around** them are to be considered
25:44 and female slaves are to come from the nations **around** you;
Nu 1:50 all its furnishings; they are to take care of it and encamp **around** it.
1:53 are to set up their tents **around** the tabernacle of the Testimony
2: 2 "The Israelites are to camp **around** the Tent of Meeting some
3:26 the curtain at the entrance to the courtyard **surrounding** the
3:37 as well as the posts of the **surrounding** courtyard with their bases,
4:26 the curtains of the courtyard **surrounding** the tabernacle and altar,
4:32 as well as the posts of the **surrounding** courtyard with their bases,
11:24 seventy of their elders and had them stand **around** the Tent.
11:31 It brought them down **all around** the camp to about three feet
11:32 than ten homers. Then they spread them out **all around** the camp.
16:24 'Move away **from** [+4946] the tents of Korah, Dathan
16:27 **[RPH]** Dathan and Abiram had come out and were standing with
16:34 At their cries, all the Israelites **around** them fled, shouting,
22: 4 "This horde is going to lick up everything **around** us, as an ox
32:33 the whole land with its cities and the territory **around** them.
34:12 " 'This will be your land, with its boundaries **on every side**.' "
35: 2 will possess. And give them pasturelands **around** the towns.
35: 4 "The pasturelands **around** the towns that you give the Levites will
Dt 6:14 Do not follow other gods, the gods of the peoples **around** you;
12:10 he will give you rest from all your enemies **around** [+4946] you
13: 7 [13:8] gods of the peoples **around** you, whether near or far, from
17:14 you say, "Let us set a king over us like all the nations **around** us,"
21: 2 and measure the distance from the body to the **neighboring** towns.
25:19 **around** [+4946] you in the land he is giving you to possess as an
Jos 15:12 These are the boundaries **around** the people of Judah by their

Jos 18:20 marked out the inheritance of the clans of Benjamin **on all sides**.
19: 8 all the villages **around** these towns as far as Baalath Beer (Ramah
21:11 Hebron), with its **surrounding** pastureland, in the hill country of
21:42 Each of these towns had pasturelands **surrounding** it; this was true
21:44 The LORD gave them rest on **every side**, just as he had sworn to
23: 1 had given Israel rest from all their enemies **around** [+4946] them,
Jdg 2:12 and worshiped various gods of the peoples **around** them.
2:14 He sold them to their enemies **all around** [+4946], whom they
7:18 from all **around** the camp blow yours and shout, 'For the LORD
7:21 While each man held his position **around** the camp, all the
8:34 them from the hands of all their enemies **on every** [+4946] **side**.
20:29 Then Israel set an ambush **around** Gibeah.
1Sa 12:11 he delivered you from the hands of your enemies on **every side**,
14:21 had gone up with them to their camp **went over** [+2118] to the
14:47 rule over Israel, he fought against their enemies **on every side**:
26: 5 was lying inside the camp, with the army encamped **around** him.
26: 7 near his head. Abner and the soldiers were lying **around** him.
31: 9 they sent messengers **throughout** [+928] the land of the Philistines
2Sa 5: 9 He built up the **area around** it, from the supporting terraces
7: 1 had given him rest from all his enemies **around** [+4946] him,
22:12 He made darkness his canopy **around** him—the dark rain clouds
24: 6 of Tahtim Hodshi, and on to Dan Jaan and **around** toward Sidon.
1Ki 3: 1 and the temple of the LORD, and the wall **around** Jerusalem.
4:24 [5:4] Tiphsah to Gaza, and had peace on all **sides** [+4946+6298].
4:31 [5:11] And his fame spread to all the **surrounding** nations.
5: 4 [5:18] now the LORD my God has given me rest on **every side**,
6: 5 and inner sanctuary he built a structure **around** the building,
6: 5 around the building, **[RPH]** in which there were side rooms.
6: 5 a structure around the building, **in** which there were side rooms.
6: 6 He made offset ledges **around** the outside of the temple so that
7:12 The great courtyard was **surrounded** *by* a wall of three courses of
7:18 He made pomegranates in two rows **encircling** each network to
7:20 were the two hundred pomegranates in rows **all around**.
7:23 He made the Sea of cast metal, **circular in shape** [+6318],
7:23 It took a line of thirty cubits *to* **measure around** [+906+6015] it.
7:24 Below the rim, gourds **encircled** [+906+6015] it—ten to a cubit.
7:24 **[RPH]** The gourds were cast in two rows in one piece with the
7:35 At the top of the stand there was a **circular band** [+6318] half a
7:36 on the panels, in every available space, with wreaths **all around**.
18:32 he dug a trench **around** it large enough to hold two seahs of seed.
18:35 The water ran down **around** the altar and even filled the trench.
2Ki 6:17 saw the hills full of horses and chariots of fire **all around** Elisha.
11: 8 Station yourselves **around** the king, each man with his weapon in
11:11 his weapon in his hand, stationed themselves **around** the king—
17:15 They imitated the nations **around** them although the LORD had
25: 1 He encamped outside the city and built siege works **all around** it.
25: 4 king's garden, though the Babylonians were **surrounding** the city.
25:10 of the imperial guard, broke down the walls **around** Jerusalem.
25:17 decorated with a network and pomegranates of bronze all **around**.
1Ch 4:33 all the villages **around** these towns as far as Baalath. These were
6:55 [6:40] They were given Hebron in Judah with its **surrounding**
9:27 They would spend the night **stationed around** the house of God,
10: 9 sent messengers **throughout** [+928] the land of the Philistines to
11: 8 He built up the city **around** it, from the supporting terraces to the
11: 8 around it, from the supporting terraces to the **surrounding** *wall*,
22: 9 I will give him rest from all his enemies **on every** [+4946] **side**.
22:18 with you? And has he not granted you rest **on every** [+4946] **side**?
28:12 courts of the temple of the LORD and all the **surrounding** rooms,
2Ch 4: 2 He made the Sea of cast metal, **circular in shape** [+6318],
4: 2 It took a line of thirty cubits *to* **measure around** [+906+6015] it.
4: 3 Below the rim, figures of bulls **encircled** [+906+6015+6017] ite
4: 3 Below the rim, figures of bulls **encircled** [+906+6015+6017] it
4: 3 **[RPH]** The bulls were cast in two rows in one piece with the Sea.
14: 7 [14:6] and he has given us rest **on every** [+4946] **side**."
14:14 [14:13] They destroyed all the villages **around** Gerar,
15:15 by them. So the LORD gave them rest **on every** [+4946] **side**.
17:10 LORD fell on all the kingdoms of the lands **surrounding** Judah,
20:30 at peace, for his God had given him rest **on every** [+4946] **side**.
23: 7 The Levites are to station themselves **around** the king, each man
23:10 all the men, each with his weapon in his hand, **around** the king—
32:22 the hand of all others. He took care of them **on every** [+4946] **side**.
34: 6 and Simeon, as far as Naphtali, and in the ruins **around** them,
Ezr 1: 6 All their **neighbors** assisted them with articles of silver and gold,
Ne 5:17 as well as those who came to us from the **surrounding** nations.
6:16 all the **surrounding** nations were afraid and lost their
12:28 The singers also were brought together from the region **around**
12:29 for the singers had built villages for themselves **around** Jerusalem.
Job 1:10 "Have you not put a hedge **around** [+1237+4946] him and his
10: 8 Will you now turn [BHS *around*; NIV 6015] and destroy me?
18:11 Terrors startle him **on every side** and dog his every step.
19:10 He tears me down **on every side** till I am gone; he uproots my
19:12 they build a siege ramp against me and encamp **around** my tent.
22:10 That is why snares are **all around** you, why sudden peril terrifies
29: 5 the Almighty was still with me and my children were **around** me,
41:14 [41:6] doors of his mouth, **ringed about** *with* his fearsome teeth?
Ps 3: 6 [3:7] the tens of thousands drawn up against me **on every side**.
12: 8 [12:9] The wicked freely strut **about** when what is vile is honored
18:11 [18:12] He made darkness his covering, his canopy **around** him—
27: 6 my head will be exalted above the enemies *who* **surround** me;
31:13 [31:14] there is terror **on every** [+4946] **side**; they conspire
34: 7 [34:8] The angel of the LORD encamps **around** those who fear
44:13 [44:14] our neighbors, the scorn and derision of *those* **around** us.
50: 3 a fire devours before him, and **around** him a tempest rages.
76:11 [76:12] let all the **neighboring** *lands* bring gifts to the One to be
78:28 made them come down inside their camp, **all around** their tents.
79: 3 They have poured out blood like water **all around** Jerusalem,
79: 4 to our neighbors, of scorn and derision to *those* **around** us.
89: 7 [89:8] he is more awesome than all *who* **surround** him.
89: 8 [89:9] O LORD, and your faithfulness **surrounds** you.
97: 2 Clouds and thick darkness **surround** him; righteousness
97: 3 Fire goes before him and consumes his foes **on every side**.
125: 2 As the mountains **surround** Jerusalem, so the LORD surrounds
125: 2 so the LORD **surrounds** his people both now and forevermore.
128: 3 your house; your sons will be like olive shoots **around** your table.
Ecc 1: 6 to the north; round and round it goes, ever returning on its **course**.
SS 3: 7 **escorted by** sixty warriors, the noblest of Israel,
Isa 42:25 It **enveloped** [+4946] them in flames, yet they did not understand;
49:18 Lift up your eyes and look **around**; all your sons gather and come
60: 4 "Lift up your eyes and look **about** you: All assemble and come to
Jer 1:15 they will come against all her **surrounding** walls and against all
4:17 *They* **surround** [+2118+4946+6584] her like men guarding a field,
6: 3 they will pitch their tents **around** her, each tending his own
6:25 the enemy has a sword, and there is terror **on every** [+4946] **side**.
12: 9 me like a speckled bird of prey that other birds of prey **surround**
17:26 the towns of Judah and the villages **around** [+4946] Jerusalem,
20:10 I hear many whispering, "Terror **on every** [+4946] **side**!
21:14 a fire in your forests that will consume everything **around** you.' "
25: 9 and its inhabitants and against all the **surrounding** nations.
32:44 in the villages **around** Jerusalem, in the towns of Judah and in the
33:13 in the villages **around** Jerusalem and in the towns of Judah,
46: 5 and there is terror **on every** [+4946] **side**," declares the LORD.
46:14 and get ready, for the sword devours *those* **around** you.'
48:17 Mourn for her, all who live **around** her, all who know her fame;
48:39 an object of ridicule, an object of horror to all *those* **around** her."
49: 5 I will bring terror on you from all *those* **around** you,"
49:29 Men will shout to them, 'Terror **on every** [+4946] **side**!'
50:14 "Take up your positions **around** Babylon, all you who draw the
50:15 Shout against her **on every side**! She surrenders, her towers fall,
50:29 Encamp **all around** her; let no one escape. Repay her for her
50:32 a fire in her towns that will consume all who are **around** her."
51: 2 they will oppose her **on every** [+4946] **side** in the day of her
52: 4 They camped outside the city and built siege works **all around** it.
52: 7 king's garden, though the Babylonians were **surrounding** the city.
52:14 of the imperial guard broke down all the walls **around** Jerusalem.
52:22 decorated with a network and pomegranates of bronze all **around**.
52:23 the total number of pomegranates above the **surrounding** network
La 1:17 The LORD has decreed for Jacob that his **neighbors** become his
2: 3 in Jacob like a flaming fire that consumes **everything around** it.
2:22 so you summoned against me terrors **on every** [+4946] **side**.
Eze 1: 4 cloud with flashing lightning and **surrounded** *by* brilliant light.
1:18 and awesome, and all four rims were full of eyes **all around**.
1:27 as if **full of** [+1074] fire, and that from there down he looked like
1:27 there down he looked like fire; and brilliant light **surrounded** him.
1:28 in the clouds on a rainy day, so was the radiance **around** him.
4: 2 up to it, set up camps against it and put battering rams **around** it.
5: 2 Take a third and strike it with the sword **all around** the city.
5: 5 have set in the center of the nations, with countries **all around** her.
5: 6 and decrees more than the nations and countries **around** her.
5: 7 You have been more unruly than the nations **around** you and have
5: 7 not even conformed to the standards of the nations **around** you.
5:12 inside you; a third will fall by the sword **outside** your **walls**;
5:14 make you a ruin and a reproach among the nations **around** you,
5:15 an object of horror to the nations **around** you when I inflict
6: 5 of their idols, and I will scatter your bones **around** your altars.
6:13 when their people lie slain among their idols **around** their altars,
8:10 I saw portrayed **all** [+6017+6584] **over** the walls all kinds of
8:10 I saw portrayed **all over** [+6017+6584] the walls all kinds of
10:12 their hands and their wings, were **completely** full of eyes,
11:12 but have conformed to the standards of the nations **around** you."
12:14 I will scatter to the winds all those **around** him—his staff
16:33 bribing them to come to you from **everywhere** for your illicit
16:37 I will gather them against you from **all around** and will strip you
16:57 and all her **neighbors** and the daughters of the Philistines—
16:57 of the Philistines—all *those* **around** you who despise you.
19: 8 the nations came against him, those from regions **round about**.
23:22 in disgust, and I will bring them against you from **every side**—
23:24 they will take up positions against you **on every side** with large
27:11 Men of Arvad and Helech manned your walls **on every side**;

Eze 27: 11 They hung their shields **around** your walls; they brought your
28: 23 fall within her, with the sword against her **on every** [+4946] **side**.
28: 24 " 'No longer will the people of Israel have malicious **neighbors**
28: 26 I inflict punishment on all their **neighbors** who maligned them.
31: 4 their streams flowed **all around** its base and sent their channels to
32: 22 she is **surrounded** *by* the graves of all her slain, all who have
32: 23 are in the depths of the pit and her army lies **around** her grave.
32: 24 "Elam is there, with all her hordes **around** her grave. All of them
32: 25 for her among the slain, with all her hordes **around** her grave.
32: 26 and Tubal are there, with all their hordes **around** their graves.
34: 26 I will bless them and the *places* **surrounding** my hill. I will send
36: 3 Because they ravaged and hounded you **from every** [+4946] **side**
36: 4 and ridiculed by the rest of the nations **around** [+4946] you—
36: 7 I swear with uplifted hand that the nations **around** [+4946] you
36: 36 the nations **around** you that remain will know that I the LORD
37: 2 He led me **back** [+6017] **and forth** among them, and I saw a great
37: 2 He led me **back and forth** [+6017] among them, and I saw a great
37: 21 I will gather them from **all around** and bring them back into their
39: 17 come together from **all around** to the sacrifice I am preparing for
40: 5 I saw a wall **completely surrounding** [+4200+6017] the temple
40: 5 I saw a wall **completely surrounding** [+4200+6017] the temple
40: 14 the projecting walls **all around** [+6017] the inside of the gateway—
40: 14 the projecting walls **all around** [+6017] the inside of the gateway—
40: 16 were surmounted by narrow parapet openings **all around** [+6017],
40: 16 were surmounted by narrow parapet openings **all around** [+6017],
40: 16 as was the portico; the openings **all around** [+6017] faced inward.
40: 16 as was the portico; the openings **all around** [+6017] faced inward.
40: 17 a pavement that had been constructed **all around** [+6017] the
40: 17 a pavement that had been constructed **all around** [+6017] the
40: 25 and its portico had narrow openings **all around** [+6017],
40: 25 and its portico had narrow openings **all around** [+6017],
40: 29 The gateway and its portico had openings **all around** [+6017].
40: 29 The gateway and its portico had openings **all around** [+6017].
40: 30 (The porticoes of the gateways **around** [+6017] the inner court
40: 30 (The porticoes of the gateways **around** [+6017] the inner court
40: 33 The gateway and its portico had openings **all around** [+6017].
40: 33 The gateway and its portico had openings **all around** [+6017].
40: 36 and its portico, and it had openings **all around** [+6017].
40: 36 and its portico, and it had openings **all around** [+6017].
40: 43 a handbreadth long, were attached to the wall **all around** [+6017].
40: 43 a handbreadth long, were attached to the wall **all around** [+6017].
41: 5 each side room **around** [+6017] the temple was four cubits wide.
41: 5 each side room **around** [+6017] the temple was four cubits wide.
41: 5 each side room around the temple was four cubits wide. **[RPH]**
41: 6 There were ledges **all around** [+6017] the wall of the temple to
41: 6 There were ledges **all around** [+6017] the wall of the temple to
41: 7 **[RPH]** so that the rooms widened as one went upward.
41: 7 **[RPH]** so that the rooms widened as one went upward.
41: 8 I saw that the temple had a raised base **all around** [+6017] it,
41: 8 I saw that the temple had a raised base **all around** [+6017] it,
41: 10 the ⌞priests'⌟ rooms was twenty cubits wide **all around** [+6017] the
41: 10 the ⌞priests'⌟ rooms was twenty cubits wide **all around** [+6017] the
41: 10 the ⌞priests'⌟ rooms was twenty cubits wide all around **[RPH]** the
41: 11 adjoining the open area was five cubits wide **all around** [+6017].
41: 11 adjoining the open area was five cubits wide **all around** [+6017].
41: 12 The wall of the building was five cubits thick **all around** [+6017],
41: 12 The wall of the building was five cubits thick **all around** [+6017],
41: 16 and the narrow windows and galleries **around** the three of them—
41: 16 including the threshold was **covered with** [+6017+8470] wood.
41: 16 including the threshold was **covered with** [+6017+8470] wood.
41: 17 and on the walls at regular intervals **all around** [+6017] the inner
41: 17 and on the walls at regular intervals **all around** [+6017] the inner
41: 19 the other. They were carved **all around** [+6017] the whole temple.
41: 19 the other. They were carved **all around** [+6017] the whole temple.
42: 15 me out by the east gate and measured the area **all around** [+6017]:
42: 15 me out by the east gate and measured the area **all around** [+6017]:
42: 16 side with the measuring rod; it was five hundred cubits. **[NIE]**
42: 17 **[NIE]** He measured the north side; it was five hundred cubits by
42: 20 It had a wall **around** [+6017] it, five hundred cubits long and five
42: 20 It had a wall **around** [+6017] it, five hundred cubits long and five
43: 12 All the **surrounding** [+6017] area on top of the mountain will be
43: 12 All the **surrounding** [+6017] area on top of the mountain will be
43: 13 and a cubit wide, with a rim of one span **around** the edge.
43: 17 with a rim of half a cubit and a gutter of a cubit **all around**.
43: 17 of a cubit all around. **[RPH]** The steps of the altar face east."
43: 20 and on the four corners of the upper ledge and **all around** the rim,
45: 1 and 20,000 cubits wide; the entire area will be holy. **[NIE]**
45: 2 for the sanctuary, **[RPH]** with 50 cubits around it for open land.
45: 2 is to be for the sanctuary, with 50 cubits **around** it for open land.
46: 23 **Around** the inside of each of the four courts was a ledge of stone,
46: 23 **[RPH]** with places for fire built all around under the ledge.
46: 23 of stone, with places for fire built **all around** under the ledge.
48: 35 "The distance **all around** will be 18,000 cubits. "And the name of
Da 9: 16 and your people an object of scorn to all *those* **around** us.
Joel 3: 11 [4:11] Come quickly, all you nations **from every** [+4946] **side**,
3: 12 [4:12] I will sit to judge all the nations **on every** [+4946] **side**.
Am 3: 11 "An enemy will **overrun** the land; he will pull down your
Na 3: 8 better than Thebes, situated on the Nile, with water **around** her?
Zec 2: 5 [2:9] I myself will be a wall of fire **around** it,'
7: 7 and its **surrounding** towns were at rest and prosperous,
12: 2 Jerusalem a cup that sends all the **surrounding** peoples reeling.
12: 6 They will consume right and left all the **surrounding** peoples,
14: 14 The wealth of all the **surrounding** nations will be collected—

6018 סָבַךְ *sābak*, v. [2] [→ 6019, 6020; cf. 8449]

entangled [1], entwines [1]

Job 8: 17 [E] *it* **entwines** its roots around a pile of rocks and looks for a
Na 1: 10 [B] *They will be* **entangled** among thorns and drunk from their

6019 סְבָךְ *sᵉbak*, n.[m.]. [3] [√ 6018]

thickets [2], thicket [1]

Ge 22: 13 looked up and there in a **thicket** he saw a ram caught by its horns.
Isa 9: 18 [9:17] and thorns, it sets the forest **thickets** ablaze,
10: 34 He will cut down the forest **thickets** with an ax; Lebanon will fall

6020 סְבֹךְ *sᵉbōk*, n.[m.]. [2] [√ 6018]

lair [1], thicket [1]

Ps 74: 5 They behaved like men wielding axes to cut through a **thicket** *of*
Jer 4: 7 A lion has come out of his **lair**; a destroyer of nations has set out.

6021 סִבְּכַי *sibbᵉkay*, n.pr.m. [4]

Sibbecai [4]

2Sa 21: 18 At that time **Sibbecai** the Hushathite killed Saph, one of the
1Ch 11: 29 **Sibbecai** the Hushathite, Ilai the Ahohite,
20: 4 At that time **Sibbecai** the Hushathite killed Sippai, one of the
27: 11 for the eighth month, was **Sibbecai** the Hushathite, a Zerahite.

6022 סָבַל *sābal*, v. [9] [→ 6023, 6024, 6025, 6026; cf. 2290; Ar 10502]

bear [2], sustain [2], burden [1], carried [1], carry [1], drags himself along [1], draw heavy loads [1]

Ge 49: 15 [A] he will bend his shoulder to the **burden** and submit to forced
Ps 144: 14 [E] our oxen *will* **draw heavy loads**. There will be no breaching
Ecc 12: 5 [F] the grasshopper **drags himself along** and desire no longer is
Isa 46: 4 [A] old age and gray hairs I am he, I am he *who will* **sustain** you.
46: 4 [A] and I will carry you; I *will* **sustain** you and I will rescue you.
46: 7 [A] They lift it to their shoulders and **carry** it; they set it up in its
53: 4 [A] Surely he took up our infirmities and **carried** our sorrows,
53: 11 [A] servant will justify many, and he *will* **bear** their iniquities.
La 5: 7 [A] and are no more, and we **bear** their punishment.

6023 סֵבֶל *sēbel*, n.[m.]. [3] [√ 6022]

burden [1], labor force [1], materials [1]

1Ki 11: 28 he put him in charge of the whole **labor force** *of* the house of
Ne 4: 17 [4:11] Those who carried **materials** did their work with one hand
Ps 81: 6 [81:7] He says, "I removed the **burden** from their shoulders;

6024 סֹבֶל *sōbel*, n.m. [3] [√ 6022]

burden [2], burdens [1]

Isa 9: 4 [9:3] you have shattered the yoke that **burdens** them, the bar
10: 27 In that day their **burden** will be lifted from your shoulders,
14: 25 from my people, and his **burden** removed from their shoulders."

6025 סַבָּל *sabbāl*, n.[m.]. [5] [√ 6022]

carriers [2], laborers [2], carriers [+5951] [1]

1Ki 5: 15 [5:29] Solomon had seventy thousand **carriers** [+5951] and
2Ch 2: 2 [2:1] He conscripted seventy thousand men as **carriers** and eighty
2: 18 [2:17] He assigned 70,000 of them to be **carriers** and 80,000 to
34: 13 had charge of the **laborers** and supervised all the workers from job
Ne 4: 10 [4:4] "The strength of the **laborers** is giving out, and there is

6026 סִבְלוֹת *siblôt*, n.f. [6] [√ 6022]

yoke [2], forced labor [1], hard labor [1], work [1], working [1]

Ex 1: 11 put slave masters over them to oppress them with **forced labor**,
2: 11 where his own people were and watched them at their **hard labor**.
5: 4 taking the people away from their labor? Get back to your **work**!"
5: 5 are now numerous, and you are stopping them from **working**."
6: 6 and I will bring you out from under the **yoke** *of* the Egyptians.
6: 7 who brought you out from under the **yoke** *of* the Egyptians.

[F] Hitpael (hitpoel, hitpoal, hitpolel, hitpolal, hitpalel, hitpalal, hitpalpel, hitpalpal, hotpael, hotpaal) [G] Hiphil (hiphtil) [H] Hophal [I] Hishtaphel

6027 סִבֹּלֶת sibbōlet, n.f. [1] [cf. 8672, 8673]
Sibboleth [1]

Jdg 12: 6 they said, "All right, say 'Shibboleth.' " If he said, "**Sibboleth,**"

6028 סִבְרַיִם sibrayim, n.pr.loc. [1]
Sibraim [1]

Eze 47: 16 and **Sibraim** (which lies on the border between Damascus

6029 סַבְתָּא sabtā', n.pr.g. [1] [→ 6030]
Sabta [1]

1Ch 1: 9 The sons of Cush: Seba, Havilah, **Sabta**, Raamah and Sabteca.

6030 סַבְתָּה sabtâ, n.pr.g. [1] [√ 6029]
Sabtah [1]

Ge 10: 7 The sons of Cush: Seba, Havilah, **Sabtah**, Raamah and Sabteca.

6031 סַבְתְּכָא sabtᵉkā', n.pr.g. [2]
Sabteca [2]

Ge 10: 7 The sons of Cush: Seba, Havilah, Sabtah, Raamah and **Sabteca**.
1Ch 1: 9 The sons of Cush: Seba, Havilah, Sabta, Raamah and **Sabteca**.

6032 סָגַד sāgad, v. [4] [→ Ar 10504]
bow down [2], bows down [2]

Isa 44: 15 [A] a god and worships it; he makes an idol and **bows down** to it.
44: 17 [A] he makes a god, his idol; *he* **bows down** to it and worships.
44: 19 [A] from what is left? *Shall I* **bow down** to a block of wood?"
46: 6 [A] to make it into a god, and *they* **bow down** and worship it.

6033 סְגוֹר sᵉgôr, n.[m.]. [2 / 1] [√ 6037]
rip open [+4213+7973] [1]

Job 28: 15 bought with the finest gold, [BHS *enclosure* ?; NIV 6034]
Hos 13: 8 I will attack them and **rip** them **open** [+4213+7973].

6034 סָגוּר sāgûr, n.m. [8 / 9] [cf. 6037?]
pure [8], finest gold [1]

1Ki 6: 20 He overlaid the inside with **pure** gold, and he also overlaid the
6: 21 Solomon covered the inside of the temple with **pure** gold,
7: 49 the lampstands of **pure** gold (five on the right and five on the left,
7: 50 the **pure** gold basins, wick trimmers, sprinkling bowls, dishes
10: 21 articles in the Palace of the Forest of Lebanon were **pure** gold.
2Ch 4: 20 the lampstands of **pure** gold with their lamps, to burn in front of
4: 22 the **pure** gold wick trimmers, sprinkling bowls, dishes and censers;
9: 20 articles in the Palace of the Forest of Lebanon were **pure** gold.
Job 28: 15 It cannot be bought with the **finest gold**, [BHS 6033] nor can its

6035 סְגֻלָּה sᵉgullâ, n.f. [8]
treasured possession [6], personal treasures [1], treasure [1]

Ex 19: 5 then out of all nations you will be my **treasured possession**.
Dt 7: 6 on the face of the earth to be his people, his **treasured possession**.
14: 2 the LORD has chosen you to be his **treasured possession**.
26: 18 his **treasured possession** as he promised, and that you are to keep
1Ch 29: 3 the temple of my God I now give my **personal treasures** of gold
Ps 135: 4 chosen Jacob to be his own, Israel to be his **treasured possession**.
Ecc 2: 8 and gold for myself, and the **treasure** *of* kings and provinces.
Mal 3: 17 "in the day when I make up my **treasured possession**.

6036 סֶגֶן segen, n.m. [17] [cf. 6122, 6125; Ar 10505]
officials [12], commanders [3], officers [1], rulers [1]

Ezr 9: 2 the leaders and **officials** have led the way in this unfaithfulness."
Ne 2: 16 The **officials** did not know where I had gone or what I was doing,
2: 16 or the priests or nobles or **officials** or any others who would be
4: 14 [4:8] said to the nobles, the **officials** and the rest of the people,
4: 19 [4:13] the **officials** and the rest of the people, "The work is
5: 7 them in my mind and then accused the nobles and **officials**.
5: 17 Furthermore, a hundred and fifty Jews and **officials** ate at my table,
7: 5 the **officials** and the common people for registration by families.
12: 40 in the house of God; so did I, together with half the **officials**,
13: 11 So I rebuked the **officials** and asked them, "Why is the house of
Isa 41: 25 He treads on **rulers** as if they were mortar, as if he were a potter
Jer 51: 23 shatter farmer and oxen, with you I shatter governors and **officials**.
51: 28 the kings of the Medes, their governors and all their **officials**,
51: 57 and wise men drunk, her governors, **officers** and warriors as well;
Eze 23: 6 clothed in blue, governors and **commanders**, all of them handsome
23: 12 governors and **commanders**, warriors in full dress,
23: 23 all of them governors and **commanders**, chariot officers and men

6037 סָגַר sāgar, v. [83 / 82] [→ 4993, 4994, 4995, 6033, 6050; cf. 6034?, 6126; Ar 10506]
shut [21], put in isolation [5], be shut [4], gave over [3], be shut up [2], close up [2], close [2], closed up [2], closed [2], delivered [2], hand over [+928+3338] [2], hand over [2], handed over [+928+3338] [2], isolate [2], keep in isolation [2], sold [2], surrender [2], tightly shut up [+2256+6037] [2], are closed [1], closed in [1], confine [1], confined [1], confines in prison [1], deliver up [1], delivered up [1], filled in [1], given up [1], handing over [+928+3338] [1], hemmed in [1], imprisoned himself [1], imprisons [1], is barred [1], locked [1], sealed together [+2597] [1], shut yourself [1], shuts [1], surrender [+906+928+3338] [1], turned over [1], will[s] [1]

Ge 2: 21 [A] one of the man's ribs and **closed up** the place *with* flesh.
7: 16 [A] God had commanded Noah. Then the LORD **shut** him in.
19: 6 [A] Lot went outside to meet them and **shut** the door behind him
19: 10 [A] and pulled Lot back into the house and **shut** the door.
Ex 14: 3 [A] around the land in confusion, **hemmed in** *by* the desert.'
Lev 13: 4 [G] the priest *is to* **put** the infected person **in isolation** for seven
13: 5 [G] the skin, he *is to* **keep** him **in isolation** another seven days.
13: 11 [G] *He is* not *to* **put** him **in isolation**, because he is already
13: 21 [G] then the priest *is to* **put** him **in isolation** for seven days.
13: 26 [G] then the priest *is to* **put** him **in isolation** for seven days.
13: 31 [G] the priest *is to* **put** the infected person **in isolation** for seven
13: 33 [G] and the priest *is to* **keep** him **in isolation** another seven days.
13: 50 [G] the mildew and **isolate** the affected article for seven days.
13: 54 [G] be washed. Then *he is to* **isolate** it for another seven days.
14: 38 [G] out the doorway of the house and **close** it **up** for seven days.
14: 46 [G] "Anyone who goes into the house while it *is* **closed up** will
Nu 12: 14 [C] **Confine** *her* outside the camp for seven days; after that she
12: 15 [C] So Miriam *was* **confined** outside the camp for seven days,
Dt 23: 15 [23:16] [G] with you, *do* not **hand** him **over** to his master.
32: 30 [G] Rock had sold them, unless the LORD *had* **given** them **up**?
Jos 2: 5 [A] At dusk, when it was time to **close** the city gate, the men left.
2: 7 [A] and as soon as the pursuers had gone out, the gate *was* **shut**.
6: 1 [A] Now Jericho *was* **tightly shut** [+2256+6037] **up** because of
6: 1 [E] Now Jericho *was* **tightly shut up** [+2256+6037] because of
20: 5 [G] *they must* not **surrender** [+906+928+3338] the one accused,
Jdg 3: 22 [A] Ehud did not pull the sword out, and the fat **closed in** over it.
3: 23 [A] *he* **shut** the doors of the upper room behind him and locked
9: 51 [A] *They* **locked** themselves in and climbed up on the tower
1Sa 1: 5 [A] because he loved her, and the LORD *had* **closed** her womb.
1: 6 [A] because the LORD *had* **closed** her womb, her rival kept
17: 46 [D] This day the LORD *will* **hand** you **over to** [+928+3338]
23: 7 [C] for David *has* **imprisoned himself** by entering a town with
23: 11 [G] *Will* the citizens of Keilah **surrender** me to him? Will Saul
23: 12 [G] "*Will* the citizens of Keilah **surrender** me and my men to
23: 12 [G] and my men to Saul?" And the LORD said, "*They* **will**[s]."
23: 20 [G] responsible for **handing** him **over to** [+928+3338] the king."
24: 18 [24:19] [D] the LORD **delivered** me into your hands, but you
26: 8 [D] "Today God *has* **delivered** your enemy into your hands.
30: 15 [G] will not kill me or **hand** me **over to** [+928+3338] my master,
2Sa 18: 28 [D] *He has* **delivered up** the men who lifted their hands against
1Ki 11: 27 [A] *had* **filled in** the gap in the wall of the city of David his
2Ki 4: 4 [A] Then go inside and **shut** the door behind you and your sons.
4: 5 [A] She left him and afterward **shut** the door behind her and her
4: 21 [A] the bed of the man of God, then **shut** the door and went out.
4: 33 [A] **shut** the door on the two of them and prayed to the LORD.
6: 32 [A] messenger comes, **shut** the door and hold it shut against him.
2Ch 28: 24 [A] *He* **shut** the doors of the LORD's temple and set up altars at
29: 7 [A] *They* also **shut** the doors of the portico and put out the
Ne 6: 10 [A] of God, inside the temple, and *let us* **close** the temple doors,
13: 19 [C] I ordered the doors *to* **be shut** and not opened until the
Job 3: 10 [A] for *it did* not **shut** the doors of the womb *on* me to hide
11: 10 [G] "If he comes along and **confines** you **in prison** and convenes
12: 14 [A] cannot be rebuilt; the man *he* **imprisons** cannot be released.
16: 11 [G] God *has* **turned** me **over** to evil men and thrown me into the
41: 15 [41:7] [B] has rows of shields tightly **sealed together** [+2597];
Ps 17: 10 [A] *They* **close up** their callous hearts, and their mouths speak
31: 8 [31:9] [G] *You have* not **handed** me **over to** [+928+3338] the
35: 3 [a] Brandish spear and javelin [BHS ***block the way***; NIV 6038]
78: 48 [G] *He* **gave over** their cattle to the hail, their livestock to bolts
78: 50 [G] not spare them from death but **gave** them **over** to the plague.
78: 62 [G] *He* **gave** his people **over** to the sword; he was very angry
Ecc 12: 4 [E] when the doors to the street **are closed** and the sound of
Isa 22: 22 [A] what he opens no *one can* **shut**, and what he shuts no one
22: 22 [A] opens no one can shut, and what *he* **shuts** no one can open.
24: 10 [E] city lies desolate; the entrance to every house **is barred**.
24: 22 [E] *they will* **be shut up** in prison and be punished after many
26: 20 [A] my people, enter your rooms and **shut** the doors behind you;
45: 1 [C] to open doors before him so that gates *will* not **be shut**:
60: 11 [C] will always stand open, *they will* never **be shut**, day or night,
Jer 13: 19 [E] The cities in the Negev *will* **be shut up**, and there will be no

La 2: 7 [G] his sanctuary. *He has* **handed over to** [+928+3338]
Eze 3: 24 [C] spoke to me and said: "Go, **shut yourself** inside your house.
44: 1 [B] gate of the sanctuary, the one facing east, and it *was* **shut**.
44: 2 [B] The LORD said to me, "This gate is to remain **shut**. It must
44: 2 [B] It is to remain **shut** because the LORD, the God of Israel,
46: 1 [B] The gate of the inner court facing east is to be **shut** on the six
46: 2 [C] and then go out, but the gate *will* not **be shut** until evening.
46: 12 [A] shall go out, and after he has gone out, the gate *will be* **shut**.
Am 1: 6 [G] she took captive whole communities and **sold** them to Edom,
1: 9 [G] Because she **sold** whole communities of captives to Edom,
6: 8 [G] his fortresses; *I will* **deliver up** the city and everything in it."
Ob 1: 14 [G] nor **hand over** their survivors in the day of their trouble.
Mal 1: 10 [A] "Oh, that one of you *would* **shut** the temple doors, so that

6038 סָגָר **sāgār**, n.m. [0 / 1]

javelin [1]

Ps 35: 3 and **javelin** [BHS 6037] against those who pursue me.

6039 סַגְרִיר **sagrîr**, n.[m.]. [1]

rainy [1]

Pr 27: 15 A quarrelsome wife is like a constant dripping on a **rainy** day;

6040 סַד **sad**, n.[m.]. [2] [cf. 8440]

shackles [2]

Job 13: 27 You fasten my feet in **shackles**; you keep close watch on all my
33: 11 He fastens my feet in **shackles**; he keeps close watch on all my

6041 סָדִין **sādîn**, n.[m.]. [4]

linen garments [4]

Jdg 14: 12 I will give you thirty **linen garments** and thirty sets of clothes.
14: 13 you must give me thirty **linen garments** and thirty sets of clothes."
Pr 31: 24 She makes **linen garments** and sells them, and supplies the
Isa 3: 23 and mirrors, and the **linen garments** and tiaras and shawls.

6042 סְדֹם **sᵉdōm**, n.pr.loc. [39]

Sodom [38], the city[s] [1]

Ge 10: 19 and then toward **Sodom**, Gomorrah, Admah and Zeboiim,
13: 10 (This was before the LORD destroyed **Sodom** and Gomorrah.)
13: 12 among the cities of the plain and pitched his tents near **Sodom**.
13: 13 Now the men of **Sodom** were wicked and were sinning greatly
14: 2 went to war against Bera king of **Sodom**, Birsha king of
14: 8 the king of **Sodom**, the king of Gomorrah, the king of Admah,
14: 10 when the kings of **Sodom** and Gomorrah fled, some of the men fell
14: 11 The four kings seized all the goods of **Sodom** and Gomorrah
14: 12 nephew Lot and his possessions, since he was living in **Sodom**.
14: 17 the king of **Sodom** came out to meet him in the Valley of Shaveh
14: 21 The king of **Sodom** said to Abram, "Give me the people and keep
14: 22 Abram said to the king of **Sodom**, "I have raised my hand to the
18: 16 When the men got up to leave, they looked down toward **Sodom**,
18: 20 "The outcry against **Sodom** and Gomorrah is so great and their sin
18: 22 The men turned away and went toward **Sodom**, but Abraham
18: 26 LORD said, "If I find fifty righteous people in the city of **Sodom**,
19: 1 The two angels arrived at **Sodom** in the evening, and Lot was
19: 1 in the evening, and Lot was sitting in the gateway of **the city**[s].
19: 4 gone to bed, all the men from every part of the city of **Sodom**—
19: 24 the LORD rained down burning sulfur on **Sodom**
19: 28 He looked down toward **Sodom** and Gomorrah, toward all the land
Dt 29: 23 [29:22] It will be like the destruction of **Sodom** and Gomorrah,
32: 32 Their vine comes from the vine of **Sodom** and from the fields of
Isa 1: 9 we would have become like **Sodom**, we would have been like
1: 10 Hear the word of the LORD, you rulers of **Sodom**; listen to the
3: 9 against them; they parade their sin like **Sodom**; they do not hide it.
13: 19 will be overthrown by God like **Sodom** and Gomorrah.
Jer 23: 14 They are all like **Sodom** to me; the people of Jerusalem are like
49: 18 As **Sodom** and Gomorrah were overthrown, along with their
50: 40 As God overthrew **Sodom** and Gomorrah along with their
La 4: 6 The punishment of my people is greater than that of **Sodom**,
Eze 16: 46 who lived to the south of you with her daughters, was **Sodom**.
16: 48 your sister **Sodom** and her daughters never did what you and your
16: 49 " 'Now this was the sin of your sister **Sodom**: She and her
16: 53 I will restore the fortunes of **Sodom** and her daughters and of
16: 55 **Sodom** with her daughters and Samaria with her daughters,
16: 56 You would not even mention your sister **Sodom** in the day of your
Am 4: 11 "I overthrew some of you as I overthrew **Sodom** and Gomorrah.
Zep 2: 9 the God of Israel, "surely Moab will become like **Sodom**,

6043 סֵדֶר **sēder**, n.[m.]. [1] [→ 4997?; cf. 8444]

disorder [+4202] [1]

Job 10: 22 to the land of deepest night, of deep shadow and **disorder** [+4202],

6044 סַהַר **sahar**, n.[m.]. [1] [→ 6045]

rounded [1]

SS 7: 2 [7:3] Your navel is a **rounded** goblet that never lacks blended

6045 סֹהַר **sōhar**, n.[m.]. [8] [√ 6044]

prison [+1074+2021] [6], *untranslated* [2]

Ge 39: 20 Joseph's master took him and put him in **prison** [+1074+2021],
39: 20 But while Joseph was there in *the* **prison** [+1074+2021],
39: 21 granted him favor in the eyes of the **prison** [+1074+2021] warden.
39: 22 So the warden **[RPH]** put Joseph in charge of all those held in the
39: 22 put Joseph in charge of all those held in the **prison** [+1074+2021],
39: 23 The warden **[RPH]** paid no attention to anything under Joseph's
40: 3 in the same **prison** [+1074+2021] where Joseph was confined.
40: 5 the king of Egypt, who were being held in **prison** [+1074+2021]—

6046 סוֹא **sô'**, n.pr.m. [1]

So [1]

2Ki 17: 4 for he had sent envoys to **So** king of Egypt, and he no longer paid

6047 ¹סוּג **sûg¹**, v. [24] [cf. 6048, 6092, 8450, 8485]

be turned [5], move [4], deserted [+294] [1], disloyal [1], drawn back [+294] [1], faithless [+4213] [1], is driven back [+294] [1], moves [1], overtake [1], retreating [+294] [1], store up [1], turn away [1], turn back [1], turn [1], turned away [1], turned [1], turning [1]

Dt 19: 14 [G] *Do* not **move** your neighbor's boundary stone set up by your
27: 17 [G] "Cursed is the man *who* **moves** his neighbor's boundary
2Sa 1: 22 [C] flesh of the mighty, the bow of Jonathan *did* not **turn** back,
Ps 35: 4 [C] *may* those who plot my ruin **be turned** back in dismay.
40: 14 [40:15] [C] *may* all who desire my ruin **be turned** back in
44: 18 [44:19] [C] Our hearts *had* not **turned** back; our feet had not
53: 3 [53:4] [A] Everyone *has* **turned away**, they have together
70: 2 [70:3] [C] *may* all who desire my ruin **be turned** back in
78: 57 [C] Like their fathers *they were* **disloyal** and faithless,
80: 18 [80:19] [A] *we will* not **turn away** from you; revive us, and we
129: 5 [C] *May* all who hate Zion **be turned** back in shame.
Pr 14: 14 [A] The **faithless** [+4213] will be fully repaid for their ways,
22: 28 [G] *Do* not **move** an ancient boundary stone set up by your
23: 10 [G] *Do* not **move** an ancient boundary stone or encroach on the
Isa 42: 17 [C] 'You are our gods,' *will* **be turned** back in utter shame.
50: 5 [C] I have not been rebellious; *I have* not **drawn** [+294] **back**.
59: 13 [C] **turning** our backs *on* our God, fomenting oppression
59: 14 [H] So justice **is driven back** [+294], and righteousness stands at
Jer 38: 22 [C] are sunk in the mud; your friends *have* **deserted** [+294] you.'
46: 5 [C] They are terrified, *they are* **retreating** [+294], their warriors
Hos 5: 10 [G] Judah's leaders are like *those who* **move** boundary stones.
Mic 2: 6 [C] prophesy about these things; disgrace *will* not **overtake** us."
6: 14 [G] *You will* **store up** but save nothing, because what you save I
Zep 1: 6 [C] those *who* **turn back** from following the LORD and neither

6048 ²סוּג **sûg²**, v. [1] [cf. 6047, 8451?]

encircled [1]

SS 7: 2 [7:3] [B] Your waist is a mound of wheat **encircled** by lilies.

6049 ³סוּג **sûg³**, n.[m.]. [0] [cf. 6092]

Eze 22: 18 [the house of Israel has become **dross** [K; see Q 6092] to me;]

6050 סוּגַר **sûgar**, n.[m.]. [1] [√ 6037]

cage [1]

Eze 19: 9 With hooks they pulled him into a **cage** and brought him to the

6051 סוֹד **sôd**, n.[m.]. [21] [→ 1233; cf. 3570]

council [7], confidence [4], company [1], confides [1], conspiracy [1], conspire [1], counsel [1], fellowship [1], gathered [1], intimate friendship [1], intimate [1], plan [1]

Ge 49: 6 Let me not enter their **council**, let me not join their assembly,
Job 15: 8 Do you listen in on God's **council**? Do you limit wisdom to
19: 19 All my **intimate** friends detest me; those I love have turned against
29: 4 in my prime, when God's **intimate friendship** blessed my house,
Ps 25: 14 The LORD **confides** in those who fear him; he makes his
55: 14 [55:15] with whom I once enjoyed sweet **fellowship** as we
64: 2 [64:3] Hide me from the **conspiracy** *of* the wicked, from that
83: 3 [83:4] With cunning they **conspire** against your people; they plot
89: 7 [89:8] In the **council** *of* the holy ones God is greatly feared; he is
111: 1 I will extol the LORD with all my heart in the **council** *of* the
Pr 3: 32 detests a perverse man but takes the upright into his **confidence**.
11: 13 A gossip betrays a **confidence**, but a trustworthy man keeps a
15: 22 Plans fail for lack of **counsel**, but with many advisers they succeed.
20: 19 A gossip betrays a **confidence**; so avoid a man who talks too

Pr 25: 9 case with a neighbor, do not betray another man's **confidence**,
Jer 6: 11 the children in the street and on the young men **gathered** together;
15: 17 I never sat in the **company** *of* revelers, never made merry with
23: 18 But which of them has stood in the **council** *of* the LORD to see
23: 22 if they had stood in my **council**, they would have proclaimed my
Eze 13: 9 They will not belong to the **council** *of* my people or be listed in the
Am 3: 7 nothing without revealing his **plan** to his servants the prophets.

6052 סוֹדִי sôdî, n.pr.m. [1]

Sodi [1]

Nu 13: 10 from the tribe of Zebulun, Gaddiel son of **Sodi**;

6053 סוּחַ sûaḥ, n.pr.m. [1]

Suah [1]

1Ch 7: 36 The sons of Zophah: **Suah**, Harnepher, Shual, Beri, Imrah,

6054 סוּחָה sûḥâ, n.f. [1] [→ 6082; cf. 8472]

refuse [1]

Isa 5: 25 mountains shake, and the dead bodies are like **refuse** in the streets.

6055 סוֹטַי sôṭay, n.pr.m. [2]

Sotai [2]

Ezr 2: 55 of Solomon: the descendants of **Sotai**, Hassophereth, Peruda,
Ne 7: 57 servants of Solomon: the descendants of **Sotai**, Sophereth, Perida,

6056 סוּךְ¹ sûk[1], v. [2] [→ 5004, 5379; cf. 8504]

spurred on [1], stir up [1]

Isa 9: 11 [9:10] [D] foes against them and *has* **spurred** their enemies **on**.
19: 2 [D] "*I will* **stir up** Egyptian against Egyptian—brother will fight

6057 סוּךְ² sûk[2], v. [10] [→ 655; cf. 3575, 5818, 5820]

use [3], used lotions at all [+6057] [2], healing balm [1], perfume [1], pour [1], put on lotions [1], put on [1]

Ex 30: 32 [H] *Do* not **pour** it on men's bodies and do not make any oil with
Dt 28: 40 [A] trees throughout your country but *you will* not **use** the oil,
Ru 3: 3 [A] Wash and **perfume** *yourself*, and put on your best clothes.
2Sa 12: 20 [G] After he had washed, **put on lotions** and changed his clothes,
14: 2 [A] in mourning clothes, and don't **use** any cosmetic lotions.
2Ch 28: 15 [A] with clothes and sandals, food and drink, and **healing balm**.
Eze 16: 9 [A] and washed the blood from you and **put** ointments **on** you.
Da 10: 3 [A] *I* **used** no **lotions** [+6057] **at all** until the three weeks were
10: 3 [A] *I* **used** no **lotions at all** [+6057] until the three weeks were
Mic 6: 15 [A] you will press olives but not **use** the oil *on yourselves*, you

6058 סוּךְ³ sûk[3], v. Not used in NIV/BHS [cf. 8455]

6059 סְוֵנֵה s[e]wēnēh, n.pr.loc. [2 / 3] [→ 6060]

Aswan [3]

Isa 49: 12 from the west, some from the region of **Aswan**." [BHS 6100]
Eze 29: 10 land of Egypt a ruin and a desolate waste from Migdol to **Aswan**,
30: 6 From Migdol to **Aswan** they will fall by the sword within her,

6060 סְוֵנִים s[e]wēnîm, n.pr.pl. Not used in NIV/BHS [√ 6059; cf. 6100]

6061 סוּס¹ sûs[1], n.m. [137 / 138] [→ 6063, 6064]

horses [90], horse [30], *untranslated* [3], horseman [+8206] [3], horseback [2], mounted [+8206] [2], war-horses [2], horse's [1], horsemen [+8206] [1], mounted [+928+2021] [1], stallions [1], them[s] [1], work horses [1]

Ge 47: 17 and he gave them food in exchange for their **horses**, their sheep
49: 17 that bites the **horse's** heels so that its rider tumbles backward.
Ex 9: 3 on your **horses** and donkeys and camels and on your cattle
14: 9 all Pharaoh's **horses** and chariots, horsemen and troops—
14: 23 all Pharaoh's **horses** and chariots and horsemen followed them into
15: 1 is highly exalted. The **horse** and its rider he has hurled into the sea.
15: 19 When Pharaoh's **horses**, chariots and horsemen went into the sea,
15: 21 highly exalted. The **horse** and its rider he has hurled into the sea."
Dt 11: 4 what he did to the Egyptian army, to its **horses** and chariots,
17: 16 must not acquire great numbers of **horses** for himself or make the
17: 16 or make the people return to Egypt to get more of **them**[s],
20: 1 and see **horses** and chariots and an army greater than yours,
Jos 11: 4 with all their troops and a large number of **horses** and chariots—
11: 6 You are to hamstring their **horses** and burn their chariots."
11: 9 had directed: He hamstrung their **horses** and burned their chariots.
Jdg 5: 22 thundered the **horses**' hoofs—galloping, galloping go his mighty
2Sa 15: 1 with a chariot and **horses** and with fifty men to run ahead of him.
1Ki 4: 26 [5:6] Solomon had four thousand stalls for chariot **horses**,
4: 28 [5:8] and straw for the chariot horses and the other **horses**.
10: 25 and gold, robes, weapons and spices, and **horses** and mules.
10: 28 Solomon's **horses** were imported from Egypt and from Kue—
10: 29 six hundred shekels of silver, and a **horse** for a hundred and fifty.
18: 5 Maybe we can find some grass to keep the **horses** and mules alive
20: 1 Accompanied by thirty-two kings with their **horses** and chariots,
20: 20 Ben-Hadad king of Aram escaped on **horseback** with some of his
20: 21 king of Israel advanced and overpowered the **horses** and chariots
20: 25 **horse** for horse and chariot for chariot—so we can fight Israel on
20: 25 horse for **horse** and chariot for chariot—so we can fight Israel on
22: 4 as you are, my people as your people, my **horses** as your horses."
22: 4 as you are, my people as your people, my horses as your **horses**."
2Ki 2: 11 suddenly a chariot of fire and **horses** *of* fire appeared and separated
3: 7 as you are, my people as your people, my **horses** as your horses."
3: 7 as you are, my people as your people, my horses as your **horses**."
5: 9 So Naaman went with his **horses** and chariots and stopped at the
6: 14 Then he sent **horses** and chariots and a strong force there.
6: 15 an army with **horses** and chariots had surrounded the city.
6: 17 he looked and saw the hills full of **horses** and chariots of fire all
7: 6 to hear the sound of chariots and **horses** and a great army,
7: 7 the dusk and abandoned their tents and their **horses** and donkeys.
7: 10 only tethered **horses** and donkeys, and the tents left just as they
7: 13 "Have some men take five of the **horses** that are left in the city.
7: 14 So they selected two chariots with their **horses**, and the king sent
9: 18 The **horseman** [+8206] rode off to meet Jehu and said, "This is
9: 19 So the king sent out a second **horseman** [+8206]. When he came
9: 33 spattered the wall and the **horses** as they trampled her underfoot.
10: 2 your master's sons are with you and you have chariots and **horses**,
11: 16 So they seized her as she reached the place where the **horses** enter
14: 20 He was brought back by **horse** and was buried in Jerusalem with
18: 23 I will give you two thousand **horses**—if you can put riders on
23: 11 the **horses** that the kings of Judah had dedicated to the sun.
2Ch 1: 16 Solomon's **horses** were imported from Egypt and from Kue—
1: 17 six hundred shekels of silver, and a **horse** for a hundred and fifty.
9: 24 and gold, and robes, weapons and spices, and **horses** and mules.
9: 25 Solomon had four thousand stalls for **horses** and chariots,
9: 28 Solomon's **horses** were imported from Egypt and from all other
23: 15 So they seized her as she reached the entrance of the **Horse** Gate
25: 28 He was brought back by **horse** and was buried with his fathers in
Ezr 2: 66 They had 736 **horses**, 245 mules,
Ne 3: 28 Above the **Horse** Gate, the priests made repairs, each in front of
7: 68 [7:67] There were 736 **horses**, [BHS-] 245 mules,
Est 6: 8 a royal robe the king has worn and a **horse** the king has ridden,
6: 9 and **horse** be entrusted to one of the king's most noble princes.
6: 9 lead him on the **horse** through the city streets, proclaiming before
6: 10 "Get the robe and the **horse** and do just as you have suggested for
6: 11 So Haman got the robe and the **horse**. He robed Mordecai,
8: 10 signet ring, and sent them by **mounted** [+928+2021] couriers,
Job 39: 18 when she spreads her feathers to run, she laughs at **horse** and rider.
39: 19 "Do you give the **horse** his strength or clothe his neck with a
Ps 20: 7 [20:8] Some trust in chariots and some in **horses**, but we trust in
32: 9 Do not be like the **horse** or the mule, which have no understanding
33: 17 A **horse** is a vain hope for deliverance; despite all its great strength
76: 6 [76:7] O God of Jacob, both **horse** and chariot lie still.
147: 10 His pleasure is not in the strength of the **horse**, nor his delight in
Pr 21: 31 The **horse** is made ready for the day of battle, but victory rests
26: 3 A whip for the **horse**, a halter for the donkey, and a rod for the
Ecc 10: 7 I have seen slaves on **horseback**, while princes go on foot like
Isa 2: 7 Their land is full of **horses**; there is no end to their chariots.
5: 28 their **horses**' hoofs seem like flint, their chariot wheels like a
30: 16 You said, 'No, we will flee on **horses**.' Therefore you will flee!
31: 1 who rely on **horses**, who trust in the multitude of their chariots
31: 3 are men and not God; their **horses** are flesh and not spirit.
36: 8 I will give you two thousand **horses**—if you can put riders on
43: 17 who drew out the chariots and **horses**, the army and reinforcements
63: 13 the depths? Like a **horse** in open country, they did not stumble;
66: 20 on **horses**, in chariots and wagons, and on mules and camels,"
Jer 4: 13 chariots come like a whirlwind, his **horses** are swifter than eagles.
5: 8 They are well-fed, lusty **stallions**, each neighing for another man's
6: 23 They sound like the roaring sea as they ride on their **horses**;
8: 6 Each pursues his own course like a **horse** charging into battle.
8: 16 The snorting of the enemy's **horses** is heard from Dan; at the
12: 5 and they have worn you out, how can you compete with **horses**?
17: 25 and their officials will come riding in chariots and on **horses**,
22: 4 riding in chariots and on **horses**, accompanied by their officials
31: 40 Kidron Valley on the east as far as the corner of the **Horse** Gate,
46: 4 Harness the **horses**, mount the steeds! Take your positions with
46: 9 Charge, O **horses**! Drive furiously, O charioteers! March on,
50: 37 A sword against her **horses** and chariots and all the foreigners in
50: 42 They sound like the roaring sea as they ride on their **horses**;
51: 21 with you I shatter **horse** and rider, with you I shatter chariot
51: 27 a commander against her; send up **horses** like a swarm of locusts.
Eze 17: 15 rebelled against him by sending his envoys to Egypt to get **horses**

Eze 23: 6 of them handsome young men, and **mounted** [+8206] horsemen.
23: 12 warriors in full dress, **mounted** [+8206] horsemen,
23: 20 like those of donkeys and whose emission was like that of **horses**.
23: 23 chariot officers and men of high rank, all mounted on **horses**.
26: 7 king of kings, with **horses** and chariots, with horsemen and a great
26: 10 His **horses** will be so many that they will cover you with dust.
26: 11 The hoofs of his **horses** will trample all your streets; he will kill
27: 14 " 'Men of Beth Togarmah exchanged **work horses**, war horses
38: 4 your **horses**, your horsemen fully armed, and a great horde with
38: 15 all of them riding on **horses**, a great horde, a mighty army.
39: 20 At my table you will eat your fill of **horses** and riders, mighty men
Hos 1: 7 not by bow, sword or battle, or by **horses** and horsemen, but by the
14: 3 [14:4] Assyria cannot save us; we will not mount **war-horses**. We
Joel 2: 4 They have the appearance of **horses**; they gallop along like
Am 2: 15 will not get away, and the **horseman** [+8206] will not save his life.
4: 10 your young men with the sword, along with your captured **horses**.
6: 12 Do **horses** run on the rocky crags? Does one plow there with oxen?
Mic 5: 10 [5:9] "I will destroy your **horses** from among you and demolish
Na 3: 2 the clatter of wheels, galloping **horses** and jolting chariots!
Hab 1: 8 Their **horses** are swifter than leopards, fiercer than wolves at dusk.
3: 8 Did you rage against the sea when you rode with your **horses**
3: 15 You trampled the sea with your **horses**, churning the great waters.
Hag 2: 22 **horses** and their riders will fall, each by the sword of his brother.
Zec 1: 8 I had a vision—and there before me was a man riding a red **horse**!
1: 8 trees in a ravine. Behind him were red, brown and white **horses**.
6: 2 The first chariot had red **horses**, the second black,
6: 2 The first chariot had red horses, the second **[RPH]** black,
6: 3 the third **[RPH]** white, and the fourth dappled—all of them
6: 3 the third white, and the fourth **[RPH]** dappled—all of them
6: 6 The one with the black **horses** is going toward the north country,
9: 10 the chariots from Ephraim and the **war-horses** from Jerusalem,
10: 3 the house of Judah, and make them like a proud **horse** in battle.
10: 5 is with them, they will fight and overthrow the **horsemen** [+8206].
12: 4 On that day I will strike every **horse** with panic and its rider with
12: 4 the house of Judah, but I will blind all the **horses** *of* the nations.
14: 15 A similar plague will strike the **horses** and mules, the camels
14: 20 TO THE LORD will be inscribed on the bells of the **horses**,

6062 ²סוּס **sûs²**, n.[m.]. [1 / 0] [cf. 6101]

Isa 38: 14 I cried like a swift [BHS *swift* ?; NIV 6101] or thrush,
Jer 8: 7 [the **swift** [K; see Q 6101] and the thrush observe the time]

6063 סוּסָה **sûsâ**, n.f. [1] [→ 2963; cf. 6061]

mare [1]

SS 1: 9 my darling, to a **mare** harnessed to one of the chariots of Pharaoh.

6064 סוּסִי **sûsî**, n.f. [1] [√ 6061]

Susi [1]

Nu 13: 11 from the tribe of Manasseh (a tribe of Joseph), Gaddi son of **Susi**;

6065 סוּסִים **sûsîm**, n.pr.loc. Not used in NIV/BHS [→ 2964]

6066 ¹סוּף **sûp¹**, v. [7 / 6] [→ 6067, 6070; Ar 10508]

sweep away [2], demolished [1], die out [1], meet end [1], sweep away [+665] [1]

Est 9: 28 [A] nor *should* the memory of them **die out** among their
Isa 66: 17 [A] *they will* **meet** *their* **end** together," declares the LORD.
Jer 8: 13 [g] will take away their harvest, [BHS *utterly take away*; NIV 658]
Am 3: 15 [A] will be destroyed and the mansions *will be* **demolished**,"
Zep 1: 2 [G] "*I will* **sweep** [+665] **away** everything from the face of the
1: 3 [G] "*I will* **sweep away** both men and animals; I will sweep
1: 3 [G] *I will* **sweep away** the birds of the air and the fish of the sea.

6067 סוֹף **sôp**, n.m. [5] [√ 6066; Ar 10509]

end [2], conclusion [1], destiny [1], rear [1]

2Ch 20: 16 you will find them at the **end** *of* the gorge in the Desert of Jeruel.
Ecc 3: 11 yet they cannot fathom what God has done from beginning to **end**.
7: 2 to go to a house of feasting, for death is the **destiny** *of* every man;
12: 13 Now all has been heard; here is the **conclusion** *of* the matter:
Joel 2: 20 into the eastern sea and *those in the* **rear** into the western sea.

6068 ²סוּף **sûp²**, n.m. [28] [→ 6069, 6071]

Red [24], reeds [2], rushes [1], seaweed [1]

Ex 2: 3 child in it and put it among the **reeds** along the bank of the Nile.
2: 5 She saw the basket among the **reeds** and sent her slave girl to get
10: 19 which caught up the locusts and carried them into the **Red** Sea.
13: 18 So God led the people around by the desert road toward the **Red**
15: 4 The best of Pharaoh's officers are drowned in the **Red** Sea.
15: 22 Moses led Israel from the **Red** Sea and they went into the Desert of
23: 31 "I will establish your borders from the **Red** Sea to the Sea of the
Nu 14: 25 and set out toward the desert along the route to the **Red** Sea."
21: 4 They traveled from Mount Hor along the route to the **Red** Sea,
33: 10 They left Elim and camped by the **Red** Sea.
33: 11 They left the **Red** Sea and camped in the Desert of Sin.
Dt 1: 40 and set out toward the desert along the route to the **Red** Sea."
2: 1 and set out toward the desert along the route to the **Red** Sea,
11: 4 how he overwhelmed them with the waters of the **Red** Sea as they
Jos 2: 10 We have heard how the LORD dried up the water of the **Red** Sea
4: 23 **Red** Sea when he dried it up before us until we had crossed over.
24: 6 pursued them with chariots and horsemen as far as the **Red** Sea.
Jdg 11: 16 Israel went through the desert to the **Red** Sea and on to Kadesh.
1Ki 9: 26 which is near Elath in Edom, on the shore of the **Red** Sea.
Ne 9: 9 of our forefathers in Egypt; you heard their cry at the **Red** Sea.
Ps 106: 7 your many kindnesses, and they rebelled by the sea, the **Red** Sea.
106: 9 He rebuked the **Red** Sea, and it dried up; he led them through the
106: 22 miracles in the land of Ham and awesome deeds by the **Red** Sea.
136: 13 to him who divided the **Red** Sea asunder *His love endures*
136: 15 swept Pharaoh and his army into the **Red** Sea; *His love*
Isa 19: 6 Egypt will dwindle and dry up. The reeds and **rushes** will wither,
Jer 49: 21 fall the earth will tremble; their cry will resound to the **Red** Sea.
Jnh 2: 5 [2:6] surrounded me; **seaweed** was wrapped around my head.

6069 ³סוּף **sûp³**, n.pr.loc. [1] [√ 6068]

Suph [1]

Dt 1: 1 opposite **Suph**, between Paran and Tophel, Laban, Hazeroth

6070 ¹סוּפָה **sûpâ¹**, n.f. [15] [√ 6066]

whirlwind [6], gale [2], storm [2], tempest [2], stormy [1], whirlwinds [1], windstorm [1]

Job 21: 18 they like straw before the wind, like chaff swept away by a **gale**?
27: 20 him like a flood; a **tempest** snatches him away in the night.
37: 9 The **tempest** comes out from its chamber, the cold from the
Ps 83: 15 [83:16] them with your tempest and terrify them with your **storm**.
Pr 1: 27 when disaster sweeps over you like a **whirlwind**, when distress
10: 25 When the **storm** has swept by, the wicked are gone,
Isa 5: 28 horses' hoofs seem like flint, their chariot wheels like a **whirlwind**.
17: 13 the wind like chaff on the hills, like tumbleweed before a **gale**.
21: 1 Like **whirlwinds** sweeping through the southland, an invader
29: 6 with **windstorm** and tempest and flames of a devouring fire.
66: 15 LORD is coming with fire, and his chariots are like a **whirlwind**;
Jer 4: 13 He advances like the clouds, his chariots come like a **whirlwind**,
Hos 8: 7 "They sow the wind and reap the **whirlwind**. The stalk has no
Am 1: 14 war cries on the day of battle, amid violent winds on a **stormy** day.
Na 1: 3 His way is in the **whirlwind** and the storm, and clouds are the dust

6071 ²סוּפָה **sûpâ²**, n.pr.loc. [1] [√ 6068]

Suphah [1]

Nu 21: 14 the LORD says: "Waheb in **Suphah** and the ravines, the Arnon

6072 סֹפֶרֶת **sôperet**, n.pr.m. [1] [√ 6219]

Sophereth [1]

Ne 7: 57 servants of Solomon: the descendants of Sotai, **Sophereth**, Perida,

6073 ¹סוּר **sûr¹**, v. [300] [→ 6239; cf. 6074, 6075]

removed [31], remove [28], turn away [22], turn [10], turned away [10], away [7], take away [7], cut off [6], leave [6], turn aside [6], take [5], turned [5], depart [4], got rid of [4], left [4], shuns [4], stop [4], took off [4], turned aside [4], get rid of [3], keep [3], lifted [3], taken away [3], turning aside [3], turning [3], avoids [2], cease [2], come in [2], come [2], deny [2], departed [2], deposed [2], go [2], gone [2], is removed [2], leave alone [+4946] [2], put away [2], rejected [2], rid [2], shun [2], stopped [2], stray [2], take off [2], throw away [2], took away [2], took [2], turned in [2], *untranslated* [1], abolish [1], banish [1], been removed [1], broke away [1], carry away [1], circumcise [+6889] [1], clear [1], cleared away [1], come over [1], denied [1], denies [1], deprives [1], dethroned [1], deviate [1], did away with [1], do away with [+4946+9348] [1], dragged [1], end [1], entered [+448] [1], escape [1], expelled [1], fail [+4946] [1], failed to keep [+4946] [1], far [1], give up pursuit [1], give up [1], go away [1], go over [1], gone over [1], hardened rebels [+6253] [1], instead of [1], is abolished [1], keep free [1], lay aside [1], led astray [1], left undone [1], made come off [1], make leave [1], move back [1], move [1], moved away [1], no longer be [+4946] [1], pass away [1], past [1], put aside [1], put out [1], removal [1], removes [1], return [1], sent away [1], set aside [1], shows no [1], shunned [1], silences [1], slip [1], snatch away [1], stay [1], strip off [1], take back [1], taken [1], turns away [1], turns [1], vanish [1], ward off [1], went over [1], went up [1]

Ge 8: 13 [G] Noah then **removed** the covering from the ark and saw that
19: 2 [A] he said, "please **turn aside** to your servant's house.
19: 3 [A] he insisted so strongly that *they did* **go** with him and entered

Ge 30:32 [G] and **remove** from them every speckled or spotted sheep,
30:35 [G] *he* **removed** all the male goats that were streaked or spotted,
35: 2 [G] "**Get rid of** the foreign gods you have with you, and purify
38:14 [G] *she* **took off** her widow's clothes, covered herself with a veil
38:19 [G] *she* **took off** her veil and put on her widow's clothes again.
41:42 [G] Pharaoh **took** his signet ring from his finger and put it on
48:17 [G] so he took hold of his father's hand to **move** it from
49:10 [A] The scepter *will* not **depart** from Judah, nor the ruler's staff
Ex 3: 3 [A] Moses thought, "*I will* **go over** and see this strange sight—
3: 4 [A] When the LORD saw that *he had* **gone over** to look, God
8: 8 [8:4] [G] "Pray to the LORD *to* **take** the frogs **away** from me
8:11 [8:7] [A] *will* **leave** you and your houses, your officials and
8:29 [8:25] [A] the flies *will* **leave** Pharaoh and his officials and
8:31 [8:27] [A] The flies **left** Pharaoh and his officials and his
10:17 [G] your God *to* **take** this deadly plague **away** from me."
14:25 [G] *He* **made** the wheels of their chariots **come off** so that they
23:25 [G] and water. *I will* **take away** sickness from among you,
25:15 [A] remain in the rings of this ark; *they are* not *to be* **removed**.
32: 8 [A] They have been quick *to* **turn away** from what I commanded
33:23 [G] *I will* **remove** my hand and you will see my back; but my
34:34 [G] to speak with him, *he* **removed** the veil until he came out.
Lev 1:16 [G] *He is to* **remove** the crop with its contents and throw it to the
3: 4 [G] covering of the liver, which *he will* **remove** with the kidneys.
3: 9 [G] **cut off** close to the backbone, all the fat that covers the inner
3:10 [G] covering of the liver, which *he will* **remove** with the kidneys.
3:15 [G] covering of the liver, which *he will* **remove** with the kidneys.
4: 9 [G] of the liver, which *he will* **remove** with the kidneys—
4:31 [G] *He shall* **remove** all the fat, just as the fat is removed from
4:31 [H] just as the fat **is removed** from the fellowship offering,
4:35 [G] *He shall* **remove** all the fat, just as the fat is removed from
4:35 [H] just as the fat **is removed** from the lamb of the fellowship
7: 4 [G] of the liver, which *is to be* **removed** with the kidneys.
13:58 [A] leather article that has been washed and *is* **rid** of the mildew,
Nu 12:10 [A] When the cloud **lifted** from above the Tent, there stood
14: 9 [A] Their protection *is* **gone**, but the LORD is with us. Do not
16:26 [A] "**Move back** from the tents of these wicked men!
21: 7 [G] Pray that the LORD *will* **take** the snakes **away** from us."
Dt 2:27 [A] main road; *we will* not **turn aside** *to* the right or *to* the left.
4: 9 [A] or *let them* **slip** from your heart as long as you live.
5:32 [A] commanded you; *do* not **turn aside** *to* the right or to the left.
7: 4 [G] for *they will* **turn** your sons **away** from following me to
7:15 [G] The LORD *will* **keep** you **free** from every disease. He will
9:12 [A] *They have* **turned away** quickly from what I commanded
9:16 [A] *You had* **turned aside** quickly from the way that the
11:16 [A] or you will be enticed *to* **turn away** and worship other gods
11:28 [A] **turn** from the way that I command you today by following
17:11 [A] *Do* not **turn aside** from what they tell you, to the right or to
17:17 [A] He must not take many wives, or his heart *will be* **led astray**.
17:20 [A] his brothers and **turn** from the law to the right or to the left.
21:13 [G] and **put aside** the clothes she was wearing when captured.
28:14 [A] *Do* not **turn aside** from any of the commands I give you
31:29 [A] and *to* **turn** from the way I have commanded you.
Jos 1: 7 [A] *do* not **turn** from it to the right or to the left, that you may be
7:13 [G] You cannot stand against your enemies until you **remove** it.
11:15 [G] *he* **left** nothing **undone** of all that the LORD commanded
23: 6 [A] of Moses, without **turning aside** to the right or to the left.
24:14 [G] **Throw away** the gods your forefathers worshiped beyond
24:23 [G] "**throw away** the foreign gods that are among you and yield
Jdg 2:17 [A] *they* quickly **turned** from the way in which their fathers had
4:18 [A] meet Sisera and said to him, "**Come**, my lord, come right in.
4:18 [A] meet Sisera and said to him, "Come, my lord, **come** right in.
4:18 [A] So *he* **entered** [+448] her tent, and she put a covering over
9:29 [G] *I would* **get rid of** him. I would say to Abimelech, 'Call out
10:16 [G] *they* **got rid of** the foreign gods among them and served the
14: 8 [A] to marry her, *he* **turned aside** to look at the lion's carcass.
16:17 [A] If my head were shaved, my strength *would* **leave** me, and I
16:19 [A] and so began to subdue him. And his strength **left** him.
16:20 [A] But he did not know that the LORD *had* **left** him.
18: 3 [A] so *they* **turned in** there and asked him, "Who brought you
18:15 [A] So *they* **turned in** there and went to the house of the young
19:11 [A] *let's* **stop** at this city of the Jebusites and spend the night."
19:12 [A] *We* won't **go** into an alien city, whose people are not
19:15 [A] There *they* **stopped** to spend the night. They went and sat in
20: 8 [A] us will go home. No, not one of *us will* **return** to his house.
Ru 4: 1 [A] Boaz said, "**Come over** here, my friend, and sit down."
4: 1 [A] my friend, and sit down." So *he* **went over** and sat down.
1Sa 1:14 [G] long will you keep on getting drunk? **Get rid of** your wine."
6: 3 [A] you will know why his hand *has* not *been* **lifted** from you."
6:12 [A] all the way; *they did* not **turn** *to* the right or *to* the left.
7: 3 [G] then **rid** yourselves *of* the foreign gods and the Ashtoreths
7: 4 [G] So the Israelites **put away** their Baals and Ashtoreths,
12:20 [A] yet *do* not **turn away** from the LORD, but serve the
12:21 [A] *Do* not **turn away** after useless idols. They can do you no
15: 6 [A] "Go **away**, leave the Amalekites so that I do not destroy you
15: 6 [A] of Egypt." So the Kenites **moved away** from the Amalekites.
15:32 [A] thinking, "Surely the bitterness of death *is* **past**."
16:14 [A] Now the Spirit of the LORD *had* **departed** from Saul,
16:23 [A] he would feel better, and the evil spirit *would* **leave** him.
17:26 [G] kills this Philistine and **removes** this disgrace from Israel?
17:39 [G] "because I am not used to them." So he **took** them **off**.
17:46 [G] over to me, and I'll strike you down and **cut off** your head.
18:12 [A] because the LORD was with David but *had* **left** Saul.
18:13 [G] So he **sent** David **away** from him and gave him command
21: 6 [21:7] [H] that *had* **been removed** from before the LORD
28: 3 [G] Saul *had* **expelled** the mediums and spiritists from the land.
28:15 [A] are fighting against me, and God *has* **turned away** from me.
28:16 [A] now that the LORD *has* **turned away** from you
2Sa 2:21 [A] of his weapons." But Asahel would not **stop** chasing him.
2:22 [A] Again Abner warned Asahel, "**Stop** chasing me! Why should
2:23 [A] Asahel refused to **give up** *the* **pursuit**; so Abner thrust the
4: 7 [G] After they stabbed and killed him, *they* **cut off** his head.
5: 6 [G] get in here; even the blind and the lame *can* **ward** you **off**."
6:10 [G] He was not willing to **take** the ark of the LORD to be with
7:15 [A] my love *will* never *be* **taken away** from him, as I took it
7:15 [G] as *I* **took** it **away** from Saul, whom I removed from before
7:15 [G] I took it away from Saul, whom *I* **removed** from before you.
12:10 [A] therefore, the sword *will* never **depart** from your house,
16: 9 [G] my lord the king? Let me go over and **cut off** his head."
22:23 [A] are before me; *I have* not **turned away** from his decrees.
1Ki 2:31 [G] so **clear** me and my father's house *of* the guilt of the
15: 5 [A] *had* not **failed** [+4946] **to keep** any of the LORD's
15:12 [G] the land and **got rid of** all the idols his fathers had made.
15:13 [G] *He* even **deposed** his grandmother Maacah from her position
15:14 [A] Although *he did* not **remove** the high places, Asa's heart was
20:24 [G] **Remove** all the kings from their commands and replace them
20:39 [A] someone **[NIE]** came to me with a captive and said,
20:41 [A] the prophet quickly **removed** the headband from his eyes,
22:32 [A] So *they* **turned** to attack him, but when Jehoshaphat cried
22:43 [A] in the ways of his father Asa and *did* not **stray** from them;
22:43 [22:44] [A] The high places, however, *were* not **removed**,
2Ki 3: 2 [G] *He* **got rid of** the sacred stone of Baal that his father had
3: 3 [A] caused Israel to commit; *he did* not **turn away** from them.
4: 8 [A] for a meal. So whenever he came by, *he* **stopped** there to eat.
4:10 [A] for him. Then *he can* **stay** there whenever he comes to us."
4:11 [A] Elisha came, *he* **went up** to his room and lay down there.
6:32 [G] how this murderer is sending someone to **cut off** my head?
10:29 [A] he *did* not **turn away** from the sins of Jeroboam son of
10:31 [A] *He did* not **turn away** from the sins of Jeroboam, which he
12: 3 [12:4] [A] The high places, however, *were* not **removed**;
13: 2 [A] Israel to commit, and *he did* not **turn away** from them.
13: 6 [A] *they did* not **turn away** from the sins of the house of
13:11 [A] *did* not **turn away** from any of the sins of Jeroboam son of
14: 4 [A] The high places, however, *were* not **removed**; the people
14:24 [A] *did* not **turn away** from any of the sins of Jeroboam son of
15: 4 [A] The high places, however, *were* not **removed**; the people
15: 9 [A] *He did* not **turn away** from the sins of Jeroboam son of
15:18 [A] During his entire reign *he did* not **turn away** from the sins of
15:24 [A] *He did* not **turn away** from the sins of Jeroboam son of
15:28 [A] *He did* not **turn away** from the sins of Jeroboam son of
15:35 [A] The high places, however, *were* not **removed**; the people
16:17 [G] side panels and **removed** the basins from the movable stands.
17:18 [G] very angry with Israel and **removed** them from his presence.
17:22 [A] in all the sins of Jeroboam and *did* not **turn away** from them
17:23 [G] until the LORD **removed** them from his presence, as he had
18: 4 [G] He **removed** the high places, smashed the sacred stones
18: 6 [A] He held fast to the LORD and *did* not **cease** to follow him;
18:22 [G] he the one whose high places and altars Hezekiah **removed**,
22: 2 [A] his father David, not **turning aside** *to* the right or *to* the left.
23:19 [G] Josiah **removed** and defiled all the shrines at the high places
23:27 [G] "*I will* **remove** Judah also from my presence as I removed
23:27 [G] "I will remove Judah also from my presence as *I* **removed**
24: 3 [G] in order to **remove** them from his presence because of the
1Ch 13:13 [G] He *did* not **take** the ark to be with him in the City of David.
17:13 [G] *I will* never **take** my love **away** from him, as I took it away
17:13 [G] away from him, as *I* **took** it **away** from your predecessor.
2Ch 8:15 [A] *They did* not **deviate** *from* the king's commands to the
14: 3 [14:2] [G] *He* **removed** the foreign altars and the high places,
14: 5 [14:4] [G] *He* **removed** the high places and incense altars in
15:16 [G] King Asa also **deposed** his grandmother Maacah from her
15:17 [A] Although *he did* not **remove** the high places from Israel,
17: 6 [G] *he* **removed** the high places and the Asherah poles from
20:10 [A] so *they* **turned away** from them and did not destroy them.
20:32 [A] in the ways of his father Asa and *did* not **stray** from them;
20:33 [A] The high places, however, *were* not **removed**, and the people
25:27 [A] From the time that Amaziah **turned away** from following the
30: 9 [G] *He will* not **turn** his face from you if you return to him."
30:14 [G] *They* **removed** the altars in Jerusalem and cleared away the
30:14 [G] the altars in Jerusalem and **cleared away** the incense altars

2Ch 32:12 [G] *Did* not Hezekiah himself **remove** this god's high places and
33: 8 [G] I will not again **make** the feet of the Israelites **leave** the land
33:15 [G] *He* **got rid of** the foreign gods and removed the image from
34: 2 [A] his father David, not **turning aside** *to* the right or *to* the left.
34:33 [G] Josiah **removed** all the detestable idols from all the territory
34:33 [A] as he lived, *they did* not **fail** [+4946] to follow the LORD,
35:12 [G] *They* **set aside** the burnt offerings to give them to the
35:15 [A] The gatekeepers at each gate *did* not *need to* **leave** their
36: 3 [G] The king of Egypt **dethroned** him in Jerusalem and imposed
Ne 9:19 [A] By day the pillar of cloud *did* not **cease** to guide them on
Est 3:10 [G] So the king **took** his signet ring from his finger and gave it to
4: 4 [G] She sent clothes for him to put on **instead of** his sackcloth,
8: 2 [G] The king **took off** his signet ring, which he had reclaimed
Job 1: 1 [A] was blameless and upright; he feared God and **shunned** evil.
1: 8 [A] and upright, a man who fears God and **shuns** evil."
2: 3 [A] and upright, a man who fears God and **shuns** evil.
9:34 [G] *someone to* **remove** God's rod from me, so that his terror
12:20 [G] *He* **silences** the lips of trusted advisers and takes away the
12:24 [G] *He* **deprives** the leaders of the earth *of* their reason; he sends
15:30 [A] *He will* not **escape** the darkness; a flame will wither his
15:30 [A] and the breath of God's mouth *will* **carry** *him* **away**.
19: 9 [G] me of my honor and **removed** the crown from my head.
21:14 [A] Yet they say to God, '**Leave** us **alone** [+4946]! We have no
22:17 [A] They said to God, '**Leave** us **alone** [+4946]! What can the
27: 2 [G] as God lives, *who has* **denied** me justice, the Almighty,
27: 5 [G] you are in the right; till I die, *I will* not **deny** my integrity.
28:28 [A] that is wisdom, and *to* **shun** evil is understanding.' "
33:17 [G] to **turn** man *from* wrongdoing and keep him from pride,
34: 5 [G] "Job says, 'I am innocent, but God **denies** me justice.
34:20 [G] pass away; the mighty *are* **removed** without human hand.
34:27 [A] because *they* **turned** from following him and had no regard
Ps 6: 8 [6:9] [A] **Away** from me, all you who do evil, for the LORD
14: 3 [A] All *have* **turned aside**, they have together become corrupt;
18:22 [18:23] [G] *I have* not **turned away** from his decrees.
34:14 [34:15] [A] **Turn** from evil and do good; seek peace and pursue
37:27 [A] **Turn** from evil and do good; then you will dwell in the land
39:10 [39:11] [G] **Remove** your scourge from me; I am overcome by
66:20 [G] who *has* not **rejected** my prayer or withheld his love from
81: 6 [81:7] [G] He says, "*I* **removed** the burden from their
101: 4 [A] Men of perverse heart *shall be* **far** from me; I will have
119:29 [G] **Keep** me from deceitful ways; be gracious to me through
119:102 [A] *I have* not **departed** from your laws, for you yourself have
119:115 [A] **Away** from me, *you* evildoers, that I may keep the
139:19 [A] the wicked, O God! **Away** from me, *you* bloodthirsty men!
Pr 3: 7 [A] not be wise in your own eyes; fear the LORD and **shun** evil.
4:24 [G] **Put away** perversity from your mouth; keep corrupt talk far
4:27 [G] not swerve to the right or the left; **keep** your foot from evil.
5: 7 [A] my sons, listen to me; *do* not **turn aside** from what I say.
9: 4 [A] "*Let all* who are simple **come in** here!" she says to those
9:16 [A] "*Let all* who are simple **come in** here!" she says to those
11:22 [A] a pig's snout is a beautiful woman *who* **shows no** discretion.
13:14 [A] is a fountain of life, **turning** a man from the snares of death.
13:19 [A] is sweet to the soul, but fools detest **turning** from evil.
14:16 [A] A wise man fears the LORD and **shuns** evil, but a fool is
14:27 [A] is a fountain of life, **turning** a man from the snares of death.
15:24 [A] The path of life leads upward for the wise to **keep** him from
16: 6 [A] through the fear of the LORD *a man* **avoids** evil.
16:17 [A] The highway of the upright **avoids** evil; he who guards his
22: 6 [A] he should go, and when he is old *he will* not **turn** from it.
27:22 [A] grain with a pestle, *you will* not **remove** his folly from him.
28: 9 [G] If *anyone* **turns** a deaf ear to the law, even his prayers are
Ecc 11:10 [G] **banish** anxiety from your heart and cast off the troubles of
Isa 1:16 [G] **Take** your evil deeds out of my sight! Stop doing wrong,
1:25 [G] purge away your dross and **remove** all your impurities.
3: 1 [G] *is about to* **take** from Jerusalem and Judah both supply
3:18 [G] In that day the Lord *will* **snatch away** their finery:
5: 5 [G] I *will* **take away** its hedge, and it will be destroyed; I will
5:23 [G] acquit the guilty for a bribe, but **deny** justice to the innocent.
6: 7 [A] your lips; your guilt *is* **taken away** and your sin atoned for."
7:17 [A] a time unlike any since Ephraim **broke away** from Judah—
10:13 [G] *I* **removed** the boundaries of nations, I plundered their
10:27 [A] In that day their burden *will be* **lifted** from your shoulders,
11:13 [A] Ephraim's jealousy *will* **vanish**, and Judah's enemies will be
14:25 [A] His yoke *will be* **taken** from my people, and his burden
14:25 [A] my people, and his burden **removed** from their shoulders."
17: 1 [H] Damascus *will* **no longer be** [+4946] a city but will become
18: 5 [G] and cut down and **take away** the spreading branches.
25: 8 [G] *he will* **remove** the disgrace of his people from all the earth.
27: 9 [G] and this will be the full fruitage of the **removal** *of* his sin:
30:11 [A] **Leave** this way, get off this path, and stop confronting us
31: 2 [G] and can bring disaster; *he does* not **take back** his words.
36: 7 [G] he the one whose high places and altars Hezekiah **removed**,
49:21 [B] I was bereaved and barren; I was exiled and **rejected**.
52:11 [A] **Depart**, depart, go out from there! Touch no unclean thing!
52:11 [A] Depart, **depart**, go out from there! Touch no unclean thing!
58: 9 [G] "If *you* **do away** [+4946+9348] **with** the yoke of oppression,
59:15 [A] to be found, and *whoever* **shuns** evil becomes a prey.
Jer 4: 1 [G] "If *you* **put** your detestable idols **out** of my sight and no
4: 4 [G] **circumcise** [+6889] your hearts, *you* men of Judah
5:10 [G] **Strip off** her branches, for these people do not belong to the
5:23 [A] rebellious hearts; *they have* **turned aside** and gone away.
6:28 [A] They are all **hardened rebels** [+6253], going about to
15: 5 [A] Who will mourn for you? Who *will* **stop** to ask how you are?
17: 5 [A] his strength and whose heart **turns away** from the LORD.
17:13 [B] *Those who* **turn away** *from* you will be written in the dust
32:31 [G] my anger and wrath that I *must* **remove** it from my sight.
32:40 [A] them to fear me, so that they *will* never **turn away** from me.
La 3:11 [D] *he* **dragged** me *from* the path and mangled me and left me
4:15 [A] "**Go away**! You are unclean!" men cry to them. "Away!
4:15 [A] "**Away**! Away! Don't touch us!" When they flee and wander
4:15 [A] "Away! **Away**! Don't touch us!" When they flee and wander
Eze 6: 9 [A] which *have* **turned** away from me, and by their eyes,
11:18 [G] to it and **remove** all its vile images and detestable idols.
11:19 [G] *I will* **remove** from them their heart of stone and give them a
16:42 [A] will subside and my jealous anger *will* **turn away** from you;
16:50 [G] Therefore *I* **did away with** them as you have seen.
21:26 [21:31] [G] **Take off** the turban, remove the crown. It will not
23:25 [G] *They will* **cut off** your noses and your ears, and those of you
26:16 [G] **lay aside** their robes and take off their embroidered
36:26 [G] *I will* **remove** from you your heart of stone and give you a
45: 9 [G] **Give up** your violence and oppression and do what is just
Da 9: 5 [A] we *have* **turned away** from your commands and laws.
9:11 [A] All Israel has transgressed your law and **turned away**,
11:31 [G] the temple fortress and *will* **abolish** the daily sacrifice.
12:11 [H] "From the time that the daily sacrifice **is abolished**
Hos 2: 2 [2:4] [G] *Let her* **remove** the adulterous look from her face
2:17 [2:19] [G] *I will* **remove** the names of the Baals from her lips;
4:18 [A] Even when their drinks *are* **gone**, they continue their
7:14 [A] together for grain and new wine but **turn away** from me.
9:12 [A] of every one. Woe to them when **I turn away** from them!
Am 5:23 [G] **Away** *with* the noise of your songs! I will not listen to the
6: 7 [A] the first to go into exile; your feasting and lounging *will* **end**.
Zep 3:11 [G] because *I will* **remove** from this city those who rejoice in
3:15 [G] The LORD *has* **taken away** your punishment, he has turned
Zec 3: 4 [G] who were standing before him, "**Take off** his filthy clothes."
9: 7 [G] *I will* **take** the blood from their mouths, the forbidden food
10:11 [A] will be brought down and Egypt's scepter *will* **pass away**.
Mal 2: 8 [A] you *have* **turned** from the way and by your teaching have
3: 7 [A] of your forefathers *you have* **turned away** from my decrees

6074 [2]סוּר sûr[2], a.vbl. [1] [cf. 6073]

corrupt [1]

Jer 2:21 How then did you turn against me into a **corrupt**, wild vine?

6075 [3]סוּר sûr[3], n.pr.loc. [1] [cf. 6073]

Sur [1]

2Ki 11: 6 a third at the **Sur** Gate, and a third at the gate behind the guard,

6076 סוֹרִי sôrî, a. Not used in NIV/BHS

6077 [1]סוּת sût[1], v. [18]

incited [4], urged [3], entices [2], misleading [2], drew away [1], inciting [1], let mislead [1], mislead [1], misled [1], urged on [1], wooing [1]

Dt 13: 6 [13:7] [G] or your closest friend secretly **entices** you, saying,
Jos 15:18 [G] came to Othniel, *she* **urged** him to ask her father for a field.
Jdg 1:14 [G] came to Othniel, *she* **urged** him to ask her father for a field.
1Sa 26:19 [G] If the LORD *has* **incited** you against me, then may he
2Sa 24: 1 [G] *he* **incited** David against them, saying, "Go and take a census
1Ki 21:25 [G] evil in the eyes of the LORD, **urged on** *by* Jezebel his wife.
2Ki 18:32 [G] listen to Hezekiah, for *he is* **misleading** you when he says,
1Ch 21: 1 [G] up against Israel and **incited** David to take a census of Israel.
2Ch 18: 2 [G] the people with him and **urged** him to attack Ramoth Gilead.
18:31 [G] the LORD helped him. God **drew** them **away** from him,
32:11 [G] *he is* **misleading** you, to let you die of hunger and thirst.
32:15 [G] do not let Hezekiah deceive you and **mislead** you like this.
Job 2: 3 [G] though *you* **incited** me against him to ruin him without any
36:16 [G] "*He is* **wooing** you from the jaws of distress to a spacious
36:18 [G] Be careful that no *one* **entices** you by riches; do not let a
Isa 36:18 [G] "*Do* not **let** Hezekiah **mislead** you when he says,
Jer 38:22 [G] " '*They* **misled** you and overcame you—those trusted friends
43: 3 [G] Baruch son of Neriah *is* **inciting** you against us to hand us

6078 סוּת² **sût²**, n.[m.]. [1] [→ 5003]

robes [1]

Ge 49: 11 will wash his garments in wine, his **robes** in the blood of grapes.

6079 סָחַב **sāḥab**, v. [5] [→ 6080]

dragged away [3], drag away [1], drag down [1]

2Sa 17: 13 [A] *we will* **drag** it **down** to the valley until not even a piece of it
Jer 15: 3 [A] "the sword to kill and the dogs to **drag away** and the birds of
22: 19 [A] **dragged away** and thrown outside the gates of Jerusalem."
49: 20 [A] The young of the flock *will be* **dragged away**; he will
50: 45 [A] The young of the flock *will be* **dragged away**; he will

6080 סְחָבָה **s^eḥābâ**, n.f. [2] [√ 6079]

rags [2]

Jer 38: 11 He took *some* old **rags** and worn-out clothes from there and let
38: 12 "Put these old **rags** and worn-out clothes under your arms to pad

6081 סָחָה **sāḥâ**, v. [1] [cf. 6082]

scrape away [1]

Eze 26: 4 [A] *I will* **scrape away** her rubble and make her a bare rock.

6082 סְחִי **s^eḥî**, n.[m.]. [1] [√ 6054; cf. 6081]

scum [1]

La 3: 45 You have made us **scum** and refuse among the nations.

6083 סְחִיפָה **s^eḥîpâ**, n.[m.]. Not used in NIV/BHS [√ 6085]

6084 סָחִישׁ **sāḥîš**, n.[m.]. [1] [cf. 8826]

what springs from [1]

2Ki 19: 29 what grows by itself, and the second year **what springs from** *that.*

6085 סָחַף **sāḥap**, v. [2] [→ 6083]

be laid low [1], driving [1]

Pr 28: 3 [A] A ruler who oppresses the poor is like a **driving** rain that
Jer 46: 15 [C] Why *will* your warriors **be laid low**? They cannot stand,

6086 סָחַר **sāḥar**, v. [21] [→ 6087, 6088; cf. 5006]

merchants [8], did business with [4], trade [3], customers [+3338] [1], gone [1], merchant [1], pounds [1], traders [1], trafficked [1]

Ge 23: 16 [A] according to the weight current among the **merchants**.
34: 10 [A] to you. Live in it, **trade** *in* it, and acquire property in it."
34: 21 [A] "Let them live in our land and **trade** *in* it; the land has plenty
37: 28 [A] So when the Midianite **merchants** came by, his brothers
42: 34 [A] your brother back to you, and *you can* **trade** *in* the land.' "
1Ki 10: 28 [A] from Kue—the royal **merchants** purchased them from Kue.
2Ch 1: 16 [A] from Kue—the royal **merchants** purchased them from Kue.
9: 14 [A] including the revenues brought in by merchants and **traders**.
Ps 38: 10 [38:11] [D] My heart **pounds**, my strength fails me;
Pr 31: 14 [A] She is like the **merchant** ships, bringing her food from afar.
Isa 23: 2 [A] you people of the island and you **merchants** *of* Sidon,
23: 8 [A] the bestower of crowns, whose **merchants** are princes,
47: 15 [A] you have labored with and **trafficked** *with* since childhood.
Jer 14: 18 [A] and priest *have* **gone** to a land they know not.' "
Eze 27: 12 [A] " 'Tarshish **did business with** you because of your great
27: 16 [A] " 'Aram **did business with** you because of your many
27: 18 [A] **did business with** you in wine from Helbon and wool from
27: 21 [A] and all the princes of Kedar were your **customers** [+3338];
27: 21 [A] *they* **did business with** you in lambs, rams and goats.
27: 36 [A] The **merchants** among the nations hiss at you; you have
38: 13 [A] Sheba and Dedan and the **merchants** *of* Tarshish and all her

6087 סַחַר **saḥar**, n.m. [7] [√ 6086]

untranslated [1], marketplace [1], merchandise [1], profit [1], profitable [+3202] [1], profits [1], trading [1]

Pr 3: 14 for she is more **profitable** [+3202] than silver and yields better
3: 14 for she is more profitable than **[RPH]** silver and yields better
31: 18 She sees that her **trading** is profitable, and her lamp does not go
Isa 23: 3 revenue of Tyre, and she became the **marketplace** *of* the nations.
23: 18 Yet her **profit** and her earnings will be set apart for the LORD;
23: 18 Her **profits** will go to those who live before the LORD,
45: 14 "The products of Egypt and the **merchandise** *of* Cush, and those

6088 סְחֹרָה **s^eḥōrâ**, n.f. [1] [√ 6086]

customers [+3338] [1]

Eze 27: 15 with you, and many coastlands were your **customers** [+3338];

6089 סֹחֵרָה **sōḥērâ**, n.f. [1]

rampart [1]

Ps 91: 4 will find refuge; his faithfulness will be your shield and **rampart**.

6090 סֹחֶרֶת **sōḥeret**, n.f. [1]

costly stones [1]

Est 1: 6 of porphyry, marble, mother-of-pearl and other **costly stones**.

6091 סֵט **sēṭ**, n.[m.]. [1] [cf. 8454]

faithless [1]

Ps 101: 3 The deeds of **faithless** *men* I hate; they will not cling to me.

6092 סִיג **sîg**, n.[m.]. [8 / 7] [cf. 6047, 6049, 6213, 8485]

dross [7]

Ps 119: 119 All the wicked of the earth you discard like **dross**; therefore I love
Pr 25: 4 Remove the **dross** from the silver, and out comes material for the
26: 23 a coating of glaze [BHS *silver dross*; NIV 6213] over earthenware
Isa 1: 22 Your silver has become **dross**, your choice wine is diluted with
1: 25 I will thoroughly purge away your **dross** and remove all your
Eze 22: 18 of man, the house of Israel has become **dross** [K 6049] to me;
22: 18 and lead left inside a furnace. They are but the **dross** *of* silver.
22: 19 'Because you have all become **dross**, I will gather you into

6093 סִיד **sîd**, n.[m.]. Not used in NIV/BHS [cf. 6167, 8487]

6094 סִיוָן **sîwān**, n.pr. [1]

Sivan [1]

Est 8: 9 on the twenty-third day of the third month, the month of **Sivan**.

6095 סִיחוֹן **sîḥôn**, n.pr.m. [37]

Sihon [34], he[s] [2], Sihon's [1]

Nu 21: 21 Israel sent messengers to say to **Sihon** king of the Amorites:
21: 23 **Sihon** would not let Israel pass through his territory. He mustered
21: 23 **He**[s] mustered his entire army and marched out into the desert
21: 26 Heshbon was the city of **Sihon** king of the Amorites, who had
21: 27 to Heshbon and let it be rebuilt; let **Sihon's** city be restored.
21: 28 "Fire went out from Heshbon, a blaze from the city of **Sihon**.
21: 29 and his daughters as captives to **Sihon** king of the Amorites.
21: 34 Do to him what you did to **Sihon** king of the Amorites,
32: 33 the half-tribe of Manasseh son of Joseph the kingdom of **Sihon**
Dt 1: 4 This was after he had defeated **Sihon** king of the Amorites,
2: 24 See, I have given into your hand **Sihon** the Amorite, king of
2: 26 From the desert of Kedemoth I sent messengers to **Sihon** king of
2: 30 But **Sihon** king of Heshbon refused to let us pass through.
2: 31 I have begun to deliver **Sihon** and his country over to you.
2: 32 When **Sihon** and all his army came out to meet us in battle at
3: 2 Do to him what you did to **Sihon** king of the Amorites,
3: 6 as we had done with **Sihon** king of Heshbon, destroying every
4: 46 in the land of **Sihon** king of the Amorites, who reigned in Heshbon
29: 7 [29:6] **Sihon** king of Heshbon and Og king of Bashan came out to
31: 4 And the LORD will do to them what he did to **Sihon** and Og,
Jos 2: 10 what you did to **Sihon** and Og, the two kings of the Amorites east
9: 10 **Sihon** king of Heshbon, and Og king of Bashan, who reigned in
12: 2 **Sihon** king of the Amorites, who reigned in Heshbon. He ruled
12: 5 and half of Gilead to the border of **Sihon** king of Heshbon.
13: 10 all the towns of **Sihon** king of the Amorites, who ruled in
13: 21 on the plateau and the entire realm of **Sihon** king of the Amorites,
13: 21 Evi, Rekem, Zur, Hur and Reba—princes allied with **Sihon**—
13: 27 Zaphon with the rest of the realm of **Sihon** king of Heshbon (the
Jdg 11: 19 "Then Israel sent messengers to **Sihon** king of the Amorites,
11: 20 **Sihon**, however, did not trust Israel to pass through his territory.
11: 20 **He**[s] mustered all his men and encamped at Jahaz and fought with
11: 21 the God of Israel, gave **Sihon** and all his men into Israel's hands,
1Ki 4: 19 in Gilead (the country of **Sihon** king of the Amorites
Ne 9: 22 They took over the country of **Sihon** king of Heshbon and the
Ps 135: 11 **Sihon** king of the Amorites, Og king of Bashan and all the kings of
136: 19 **Sihon** king of the Amorites *His love endures forever.*
Jer 48: 45 a fire has gone out from Heshbon, a blaze from the midst of **Sihon**;

6096 סִין¹ **sîn¹**, n.pr.loc. [2]

Pelusium [2]

Eze 30: 15 I will pour out my wrath on **Pelusium**, the stronghold of Egypt,
30: 16 I will set fire to Egypt; **Pelusium** will writhe in agony. Thebes will

6097 סִין² **sîn²**, n.pr.loc. [4]

Sin [4]

Ex 16: 1 community set out from Elim and came to the Desert of **Sin**,
17: 1 The whole Israelite community set out from the Desert of **Sin**,

Nu 33:11 They left the Red Sea and camped in the Desert of **Sin**.
33:12 They left the Desert of **Sin** and camped at Dophkah.

6098 סִינִי *sînî*, a.g. [2]

Sinites [2]

Ge 10:17 Hivites, Arkites, **Sinites**,
1Ch 1:15 Hivites, Arkites, **Sinites**,

6099 סִינַי *sînay*, n.pr.loc. [35]

Sinai [35]

Ex 16: 1 and came to the Desert of Sin, which is between Elim and **Sinai**,
19: 1 left Egypt—on the very day—they came to the Desert of **Sinai**.
19: 2 After they set out from Rephidim, they entered the Desert of **Sinai**,
19:11 because on that day the LORD will come down on Mount **Sinai**
19:18 Mount **Sinai** was covered with smoke, because the LORD
19:20 The LORD descended to the top of Mount **Sinai** and called
19:23 said to the LORD, "The people cannot come up Mount **Sinai**,
24:16 the glory of the LORD settled on Mount **Sinai**. For six days the
31:18 When the LORD finished speaking to Moses on Mount **Sinai**,
34: 2 Be ready in the morning, and then come up on Mount **Sinai**.
34: 4 like the first ones and went up Mount **Sinai** early in the morning,
34:29 When Moses came down from Mount **Sinai** with the two tablets of
34:32 all the commands the LORD had given him on Mount **Sinai**.
Lev 7:38 which the LORD gave Moses on Mount **Sinai** on the day he
7:38 to bring their offerings to the LORD, in the Desert of **Sinai**.
25: 1 The LORD said to Moses on Mount **Sinai**,
26:46 the regulations that the LORD established on Mount **Sinai**
27:34 These are the commands the LORD gave Moses on Mount **Sinai**
Nu 1: 1 **Sinai** on the first day of the second month of the second year after
1:19 And so he counted them in the Desert of **Sinai**:
3: 1 Moses at the time the LORD talked with Moses on Mount **Sinai**.
3: 4 offering with unauthorized fire before him in the Desert of **Sinai**.
3:14 The LORD said to Moses in the Desert of **Sinai**,
9: 1 The LORD spoke to Moses in the Desert of **Sinai** in the first
9: 5 so in the Desert of **Sinai** at twilight on the fourteenth day of the
10:12 the Israelites set out from the Desert of **Sinai** and traveled from
26:64 the priest when they counted the Israelites in the Desert of **Sinai**.
28: 6 This is the regular burnt offering instituted at Mount **Sinai** as a
33:15 They left Rephidim and camped in the Desert of **Sinai**.
33:16 They left the Desert of **Sinai** and camped at Kibroth Hattaavah.
Dt 33: 2 "The LORD came from **Sinai** and dawned over them from Seir;
Jdg 5: 5 the One of **Sinai**, before the LORD, the God of Israel.
Ne 9:13 "You came down on Mount **Sinai**; you spoke to them from heaven.
Ps 68: 8 [68:9] before God, the One of **Sinai**, before God, the God of
68:17 [68:18] the Lord ˌhas comeˌ from **Sinai** into his sanctuary.

6100 סִינִים *sînîm*, a.g.pl. [1 / 0] [cf. 6060]

Isa 49:12 some some from the region of Aswan." [BHS *Sinim*; NIV 6059]

6101 סִיס *sîs*, n.[m.]. [1 / 2] [cf. 6062]

swift [2]

Isa 38:14 I cried like a **swift** [BHS 6062] or thrush, I moaned like a
Jer 8: 7 the **swift** [K 6062] and the thrush observe the time of their

6102 סִיסְרָא *sîs^erā'*, n.pr.m. [21]

Sisera [20], Sisera's [1]

Jdg 4: 2 The commander of his army was **Sisera**, who lived in Harosheth
4: 7 I will lure **Sisera**, the commander of Jabin's army, with his
4: 9 not be yours, for the LORD will hand **Sisera** over to a woman."
4:12 When they told **Sisera** that Barak son of Abinoam had gone up to
4:13 **Sisera** gathered together his nine hundred iron chariots and all the
4:14 This is the day the LORD has given **Sisera** into your hands.
4:15 the LORD routed **Sisera** and all his chariots and army by the
4:15 by the sword, and **Sisera** abandoned his chariot and fled on foot.
4:16 All the troops of **Sisera** fell by the sword; not a man was left.
4:17 **Sisera**, however, fled on foot to the tent of Jael, the wife of Heber
4:18 Jael went out to meet **Sisera** and said to him, "Come, my lord,
4:22 Barak came by in pursuit of **Sisera**, and Jael went out to meet him.
4:22 and there lay **Sisera** with the tent peg through his temple—
5:20 the stars fought, from their courses they fought against **Sisera**.
5:26 She struck **Sisera**, she crushed his head, she shattered and pierced
5:28 "Through the window peered **Sisera's** mother; behind the lattice
5:30 or two for each man, colorful garments as plunder for **Sisera**,
1Sa 12: 9 so he sold them into the hand of **Sisera**, the commander of the
Ezr 2:53 Barkos, **Sisera**, Temah,
Ne 7:55 Barkos, **Sisera**, Temah,
Ps 83: 9 [83:10] as you did to **Sisera** and Jabin at the river Kishon,

6103 סִיעָא *sî'ā'*, n.pr.m. [1] [→ 6104]

Sia [1]

Ne 7:47 Keros, **Sia**, Padon,

6104 סִיעֲהָא *sî'ahā'*, n.pr.m. [1] [√ 6103]

Siaha [1]

Ezr 2:44 Keros, **Siaha**, Padon,

6105 סִיר *sîr*, n.m. & f. [29] [√ 6106?]

pot [11], pots [11], cooking pot [2], washbasin [+8176] [2], caldron [1], cooking pots [1], pan [1]

Ex 16: 3 There we sat around **pots** *of* meat and ate all the food we wanted,
27: 3 its **pots** to remove the ashes, and its shovels, sprinkling bowls,
38: 3 its **pots**, shovels, sprinkling bowls, meat forks and firepans.
1Ki 7:45 the **pots**, shovels and sprinkling bowls. All these objects that
2Ki 4:38 "Put on the large **pot** and cook some stew for these men."
4:39 When he returned, he cut them up into the **pot** *of* stew, though no
4:40 to eat it, they cried out, "O man of God, there is death in the **pot**!"
4:41 He put it into the **pot** and said, "Serve it to the people to eat."
4:41 it to the people to eat." And there was nothing harmful in the **pot**.
25:14 They also took away the **pots**, shovels, wick trimmers, dishes
2Ch 4:11 He also made the **pots** and shovels and sprinkling bowls.
4:16 the **pots**, shovels, meat forks and all related articles. All the objects
35:13 boiled the holy offerings in **pots**, caldrons and pans and served
Job 41:31 [41:23] He makes the depths churn like a boiling **caldron**
Ps 58: 9 [58:10] Before your **pots** can feel ˌthe heat ofˌ the thorns—
60: 8 [60:10] Moab is my **washbasin** [+8176], upon Edom I toss my
108: 9 [108:10] Moab is my **washbasin** [+8176], upon Edom I toss my
Ecc 7: 6 Like the crackling of thorns under the **pot**, so is the laughter of
Jer 1:13 "I see a boiling **pot**, tilting away from the north," I answered.
52:18 They also took away the **pots**, shovels, wick trimmers, sprinkling
52:19 **pots**, lampstands, dishes and bowls used for drink offerings—
Eze 11: 3 to build houses? This city is a **cooking pot**, and we are the meat.'
11: 7 bodies you have thrown there are the meat and this city is the **pot**,
11:11 This city will not be a **pot** for you, nor will you be the meat in it;
24: 3 " 'Put on the **cooking pot**; put it on and pour water into it.
24: 6 " 'Woe to the city of bloodshed, to the **pot** now encrusted,
Mic 3: 3 who chop them up like meat for the **pan**, like flesh for the pot?"
Zec 14:20 the **cooking pots** in the LORD's house will be like the sacred
14:21 Every **pot** in Jerusalem and Judah will be holy to the LORD

6106 סִירָה *sîrâ*, n.[m.]. [5] [√ 6105?; cf. 6241]

thorns [3], fishhooks [+1855] [1], thornbushes [1]

Ecc 7: 6 Like the crackling of **thorns** under the pot, so is the laughter of
Isa 34:13 **Thorns** will overrun her citadels, nettles and brambles her
Hos 2: 6 [2:8] Therefore I will block her path with **thornbushes**; I will
Am 4: 2 be taken away with hooks, the last of you with **fishhooks** [+1855].
Na 1:10 They will be entangled among **thorns** and drunk from their wine;

6107 סָךְ *sāk*, n.[m.]. [1] [√ 6115]

multitude [1]

Ps 42: 4 [42:5] how I used to go with the **multitude**,

6108 סֹךְ *sōk*, n.[m.]. [4] [→ 6109, 6111; cf. 8494]

cover [1], dwelling [1], lair [1], tent [1]

Ps 10: 9 He lies in wait like a lion in **cover**; he lies in wait to catch the
27: 5 For in the day of trouble he will keep me safe in his **dwelling**;
76: 2 [76:3] His **tent** is in Salem, his dwelling place in Zion.
Jer 25:38 Like a lion he will leave his **lair**, and their land will become

6109 סֻכָּה *sukkâ*, n.f. [31 / 32] [→ 6111; cf. 6108]

Tabernacles [9], booths [7], shelter [3], tents [3], canopy [2], dwelling [1], hut [1], pavilion [1], shelters [1], shrine [1], tent [1], them[s] [+2021] [1], thicket [1]

Ge 33:17 he built a place for himself and made **shelters** for his livestock.
Lev 23:34 of the seventh month the LORD's Feast of **Tabernacles** begins,
23:42 Live in **booths** for seven days: All native-born Israelites are to live
23:42 for seven days: All native-born Israelites are to live in **booths**
23:43 had the Israelites live in **booths** when I brought them out of Egypt.
Dt 16:13 Celebrate the Feast of **Tabernacles** for seven days after you have
16:16 the Feast of Weeks and the Feast of **Tabernacles**.
31:10 in the year for canceling debts, during the Feast of **Tabernacles**,
2Sa 11:11 "The ark and Israel and Judah are staying in **tents**, and my master
22:12 He made darkness his **canopy** around him—the dark rain clouds of
1Ki 20:12 this message while he and the kings were drinking in their **tents**,
20:16 and the 32 kings allied with him were in their **tents** getting drunk.
2Ch 8:13 the Feast of Weeks and the Feast of **Tabernacles**.
Ezr 3: 4 they celebrated the Feast of **Tabernacles** with the required number
Ne 8:14 that the Israelites were to live in **booths** during the feast of the

Ne 8:15 and from myrtles, palms and shade trees, to make **booths**"—
8:16 back branches and built themselves **booths** on their own roofs,
8:17 The whole company that had returned from exile built **booths**
8:17 had returned from exile built booths and lived in **them**[s] [+2021].
Job 27:18 he builds is like a moth's cocoon, like a **hut** made by a watchman.
36:29 how he spreads out the clouds, how he thunders from his **pavilion**?
38:40 when they crouch in their dens or lie in wait in a **thicket**?
Ps 18:11 [18:12] He made darkness his covering, his **canopy** around him—
31:20 [31:21] in your **dwelling** you keep them safe from accusing
Isa 1: 8 The Daughter of Zion is left like a **shelter** in a vineyard, like a hut
4: 6 It will be a **shelter** and shade from the heat of the day, and a refuge
Am 5:26 You have lifted up the **shrine** [BHS 6110] *of* your king,
9:11 "In that day I will restore David's fallen **tent**. I will repair its
Jnh 4: 5 There he made himself a **shelter**, sat in its shade and waited to see
Zec 14:16 the LORD Almighty, and to celebrate the Feast of **Tabernacles**.
14:18 the nations that do not go up to celebrate the Feast of **Tabernacles**.
14:19 the nations that do not go up to celebrate the Feast of **Tabernacles**.

6110 סִכּוּת *sikkût*, n.pr.?. [1 / 0]

Am 5:26 have lifted up the shrine *of* [BHS *Sikkuth*; NIV 6109] your king,

6111 סֻכּוֹת *sukkôt*, n.pr.loc. [18] [√ 6109; cf. 6108]

Succoth [18]

Ge 33:17 Jacob, however, went to **Succoth**, where he built a place for
33:17 shelters for his livestock. That is why the place is called **Succoth**.
Ex 12:37 The Israelites journeyed from Rameses to **Succoth**. There were
13:20 After leaving **Succoth** they camped at Etham on the edge of the
Nu 33: 5 The Israelites left Rameses and camped at **Succoth**.
33: 6 They left **Succoth** and camped at Etham, on the edge of the desert.
Jos 13:27 **Succoth** and Zaphon with the rest of the realm of Sihon king of
Jdg 8: 5 He said to the men of **Succoth**, "Give my troops some bread;
8: 6 the officials of **Succoth** said, "Do you already have the hands of
8: 8 request of them, but they answered as the men of **Succoth** had.
8:14 He caught a young man of **Succoth** and questioned him,
8:14 down for him the names of the seventy-seven officials of **Succoth**,
8:15 Gideon came and said to the men of **Succoth**, "Here are Zebah
8:16 taught the men of **Succoth** a lesson by punishing them with desert
1Ki 7:46 them cast in clay molds in the plain of the Jordan between **Succoth**
2Ch 4:17 them cast in clay molds in the plain of the Jordan between **Succoth**
Ps 60: 6 [60:8] out Shechem and measure off the Valley of **Succoth**.
108: 7 [108:8] out Shechem and measure off the Valley of **Succoth**.

6112 סֻכּוֹת בְּנוֹת *sukkôt benôt*, n.pr. [1] [cf. 1219]

Succoth Benoth [1]

2Ki 17:30 The men from Babylon made **Succoth Benoth**, the men from

6113 סֻכִּיִּים *sukkiyyîm*, n.pr.m.pl. [1]

Sukkites [1]

2Ch 12: 3 of Libyans, **Sukkites** and Cushites that came with him from Egypt,

6114 ¹סָכַךְ *sākak[1]*, v. [18] [→ 4590, 5009, 5010, 6116, 6117; cf. 8503]

covered [2], guardian [2], overshadowing [2], conceal [1], cover [1], hedged in [1], overshadowed [1], relieve himself [+906+2257+8079] [1], relieving himself [+906+2257+8079] [1], shelter [1], shield [1], shielded [1], shields [1], shut up [1], spread protection [1]

Ex 25:20 [A] wings spread upward, **overshadowing** the cover with them.
37: 9 [A] wings spread upward, **overshadowing** the cover with them.
40: 3 [A] ark of the Testimony in it and **shield** the ark *with* the curtain.
40:21 [G] the shielding curtain and **shielded** the ark of the Testimony,
Jdg 3:24 [G] "He *must be* **relieving** [+906+2257+8079] **himself** in the inner
1Sa 24: 3 [24:4] [G] and Saul went in to **relieve** [+906+2257+8079] **himself**.
1Ki 8: 7 [A] of the ark and **overshadowed** the ark and its carrying poles.
1Ch 28:18 [A] and **shelter** the ark of the covenant of the LORD.
Job 3:23 [G] to a man whose way is hidden, whom God *has* **hedged in**?
38: 8 [G] "Who **shut up** the sea behind doors when it burst forth from
40:22 [A] The lotuses **conceal** him in their shadow; the poplars by the
Ps 5:11 [5:12] [G] **Spread** *your* **protection** over them, that those who
91: 4 [G] *He will* **cover** you with his feathers, and under his wings you
140: 7 [140:8] [A] *who* **shields** my head in the day of battle—
La 3:43 [A] "*You have* **covered** yourself with anger and pursued us;
3:44 [A] *You have* **covered** yourself with a cloud so that no prayer
Eze 28:14 [A] You were anointed as a **guardian** cherub, for so I ordained
28:16 [A] I expelled you, O **guardian** cherub, from among the fiery

6115 ²סָכַךְ *sākak[2]*, v. [2] [→ 6107; cf. 5819, 8455, 8504]

knit together [2]

Job 10:11 [D] and flesh and **knit** me **together** with bones and sinews?
Ps 139:13 [A] inmost being; *you* **knit** me **together** in my mother's womb.

6116 סֹכֵךְ *sōkēk*, n.[m.]. [1] [√ 6114]

protective shield [1]

Na 2: 5 [2:6] dash to the city wall; the **protective shield** is put in place.

6117 סְכָכָה *sekākâ*, n.pr.loc. [1] [√ 6114]

Secacah [1]

Jos 15:61 In the desert: Beth Arabah, Middin, **Secacah**,

6118 סָכַל *sākal*, v. [8] [→ 6119, 6120, 6121]

done a foolish thing [3], acted foolishly [1], acted like a fool [1], foolish [1], turn into foolishness [1], turns into nonsense [1]

Ge 31:28 [G] and my daughters good-by. You have done a **foolish** *thing*.
1Sa 13:13 [C] "*You* **acted foolishly**," Samuel said. "You have not kept the
26:21 [G] Surely *I have* **acted like a fool** and have erred greatly."
2Sa 15:31 [D] "O LORD, **turn** Ahithophel's counsel **into foolishness**."
24:10 [C] the guilt of your servant. *I have* **done a** very **foolish thing**."
1Ch 21: 8 [C] the guilt of your servant. *I have* **done a** very **foolish thing**."
2Ch 16: 9 [C] *You have* **done a foolish thing**, and from now on you will be
Isa 44:25 [D] the learning of the wise and **turns** it **into nonsense**,

6119 סָכָל *sākāl*, n.m. [7] [√ 6118]

fool [4], foolish [1], senseless [1], stupid [1]

Ecc 2:19 And who knows whether he will be a wise man or a **fool**?
7:17 Do not be overwicked, and do not be a **fool**—why die before your
10: 3 the **fool** lacks sense and shows everyone how stupid he is.
10: 3 the fool lacks sense and shows everyone *how* **stupid** he is.
10:14 and the **fool** multiplies words. No one knows what is coming—
Jer 4:22 know me. They are **senseless** children; they have no understanding.
5:21 Hear this, you **foolish** and senseless people, who have eyes

6120 סֶכֶל *sekel*, n.m. [1] [√ 6118]

fools [1]

Ecc 10: 6 **Fools** are put in many high positions, while the rich occupy the low

6121 סִכְלוּת *siklût*, n.f. [6] [√ 6118; cf. 8508]

folly [6]

Ecc 2: 3 I tried cheering myself with wine, and embracing **folly**—my mind
2:12 my thoughts to consider wisdom, and also madness and **folly**.
2:13 I saw that wisdom is better than **folly**, just as light is better than
7:25 to understand the stupidity of wickedness and the madness of **folly**.
10: 1 perfume a bad smell, so a little **folly** outweighs wisdom and honor.
10:13 At the beginning his words are **folly**; at the end they are wicked

6122 ¹סָכַן *sākan[1]*, v. [9] [→ 5016, 6125; cf. 6036]

been in the habit of [+6122] [2], be of benefit [1], benefit [1], familiar with [1], profit [1], profits [1], submit [1], useless [+4202] [1]

Nu 22:30 [G] *Have I* **been in the habit** [+6122] **of** doing this to you?"
22:30 [G] *Have I* **been in the habit of** [+6122] doing this to you?"
Job 15: 3 [A] Would he argue with **useless** [+4202] words, with speeches
22: 2 [A] "*Can* a man **be of benefit** to God? Can even a wise man
22: 2 [A] be of benefit to God? *Can* even a wise man **benefit** him?
22:21 [G] "**Submit** to God and be at peace with him; in this way
34: 9 [A] '*It* **profits** a man nothing when he tries to please God.'
35: 3 [A] Yet you ask him, 'What **profit** *is it* to me, and what do I gain
Ps 139: 3 [G] and my lying down; *you are* **familiar with** all my ways.

6123 ²סָכַן *sākan[2]*, v. [1] [cf. 5014, 5017]

too poor [1]

Isa 40:20 [E] A *man* **too poor** *to* present such an offering selects wood that

6124 ³סָכַן *sākan[3]*, v. [1]

be endangered [1]

Ecc 10: 9 [C] by them; whoever splits logs *may* **be endangered** by them.

6125 סֹכֵן *sōkēn*, n.[m.] *or* v.ptcp. [3] [√ 6122; cf. 6036]

steward [1], take care of [+2118+4200] [1], took care of [+2118+4200] [1]

1Ki 1: 2 virgin to attend the king and **take care** [+2118+4200] **of** him.
1: 4 The girl was very beautiful; *she* **took care** [+2118+4200] **of** the
Isa 22:15 "Go, say to this **steward**, to Shebna, who is in charge of the

6126 ¹סָכַר *sākar[1]*, v. [2] [cf. 6037, 6127]

be silenced [1], been closed [1]

Ge 8: 2 [C] the deep and the floodgates of the heavens *had* **been closed**,
Ps 63:11 [63:12] [C] while the mouths of liars *will* **be silenced**.

6127 ²סָכַר ***sākar²***, v. [1] [cf. 6126]

hand over [1]

Isa 19: 4 [D] *I will* **hand** the Egyptians **over** to the power of a cruel

6128 ³סָכַר ***sākar³***, v. [1] [cf. 8509]

hired [1]

Ezr 4: 5 [A] *They* **hired** counselors to work against them and frustrate

6129 סָכַת ***sākat***, v. [1]

silent [1]

Dt 27: 9 [G] are Levites, said to all Israel, "*Be* **silent**, O Israel, and listen!

6130 סַל ***sal***, n.m. [15]

basket [12], baskets [2], it[s] [+2021] [1]

Ge 40: 16 "I too had a dream: On my head were three **baskets** *of* bread.
40: 17 In the top **basket** were all kinds of baked goods for Pharaoh,
40: 17 but the birds were eating them out of the **basket** on my head."
40: 18 is what it means," Joseph said. "The three **baskets** are three days.
Ex 29: 3 Put them in a **basket** and present them in it—along with the bull
29: 3 Put them in a basket and present them in **it**[s] [+2021]—along with
29: 23 From the **basket** *of* bread made without yeast, which is before the
29: 32 are to eat the meat of the ram and the bread that is in the **basket**.
Lev 8: 2 the two rams and the **basket** *containing* bread made without yeast,
8: 26 from the **basket** *of* bread made without yeast, which was before
8: 31 eat it there with the bread from the **basket** *of* ordination offerings,
Nu 6: 15 and drink offerings, and a **basket** *of* bread made without yeast—
6: 17 He is to present the **basket** *of* unleavened bread and is to sacrifice
6: 19 and a cake and a wafer from the **basket**, both made without yeast.
Jdg 6: 19 Putting the meat in a **basket** and its broth in a pot, he brought them

6131 סָלָא ***sālā'***, v. [1] [→ 6139, 6140?, 6141?,; cf. 6137]

worth their weight [1]

La 4: 2 [E] the precious sons of Zion, once **worth their weight** in gold,

6132 סַלֻּא ***sallu'***, n.pr.m. [2] [√ 6140?]

Sallu [2]

1Ch 9: 7 **Sallu** son of Meshullam, the son of Hodaviah, the son of
Ne 11: 7 **Sallu** son of Meshullam, the son of Joed, the son of Pedaiah,

6133 סִלָּא ***sillā'***, n.pr.loc. [1]

Silla [1]

2Ki 12: 20 [12:21] assassinated him at Beth Millo, on the road down to **Silla**.

6134 סָלַד ***sālad***, v. [1] [→ 6135?]

joy [1]

Job 6: 10 [D] still have this consolation—*my* **joy** in unrelenting pain—

6135 סֶלֶד ***seled***, n.pr.m. [2] [√ 6134?]

Seled [2]

1Ch 2: 30 The sons of Nadab: **Seled** and Appaim. Seled died without
2: 30 sons of Nadab: Seled and Appaim. **Seled** died without children.

6136 ¹סָלָה ***sālâ¹***, v. [2]

reject [1], rejected [1]

Ps 119:118 [A] *You* **reject** all who stray from your decrees, for their
La 1: 15 [D] "The Lord *has* **rejected** all the warriors in my midst; he has

6137 ²סָלָה ***sālâ²***, v. [2] [cf. 6131]

be bought [2]

Job 28: 16 [E] *It* cannot **be bought** with the gold of Ophir, with precious
28: 19 [E] cannot compare with it; *it* cannot **be bought** with pure gold.

6138 סֶלָה ***selâ***, n.[f.] [74] [cf. 6148?]

Selah [74]

Ps 3: 2 [3:3] are saying of me, "God will not deliver him." ***Selah***
3: 4 [3:5] I cry aloud, and he answers me from his holy hill. ***Selah***
3: 8 [3:9] May your blessing be on your people. ***Selah***
4: 2 [4:3] long will you love delusions and seek false gods? ***Selah***
4: 4 [4:5] are on your beds, search your hearts and be silent. ***Selah***
7: 5 [7:6] life to the ground and make me sleep in the dust. ***Selah***
9: 16 [9:17] ensnared by the work of their hands. *Higgaion.* ***Selah***
9: 20 [9:21] O LORD; let the nations know they are but men. ***Selah***
20: 3 [20:4] your sacrifices and accept your burnt offerings. ***Selah***
21: 2 [21:3] and have not withheld the request of his lips. ***Selah***
24: 6 those who seek him, who seek your face, O God of Jacob. ***Selah***
24: 10 The LORD Almighty—he is the King of glory. ***Selah***
32: 4 my strength was sapped as in the heat of summer. ***Selah***
32: 5 to the LORD"—and you forgave the guilt of my sin. ***Selah***
32: 7 from trouble and surround me with songs of deliverance. ***Selah***
39: 5 [39:6] before you. Each man's life is but a breath. ***Selah***
39: 11 [39:12] wealth like a moth—each man is but a breath. ***Selah***
44: 8 [44:9] day long, and we will praise your name forever. ***Selah***
46: 3 [46:4] and the mountains quake with their surging. ***Selah***
46: 7 [46:8] is with us; the God of Jacob is our fortress. ***Selah***
46: 11 [46:12] is with us; the God of Jacob is our fortress. ***Selah***
47: 4 [47:5] for us, the pride of Jacob, whom he loved. ***Selah***
48: 8 [48:9] city of our God: God makes her secure forever. ***Selah***
49: 13 [49:14] of their followers, who approve their sayings. ***Selah***
49: 15 [49:16] the grave; he will surely take me to himself. ***Selah***
50: 6 proclaim his righteousness, for God himself is judge. ***Selah***
52: 3 [52:5] falsehood rather than speaking the truth. ***Selah***
52: 5 [52:7] he will uproot you from the land of the living. ***Selah***
54: 3 [54:5] men seek my life—men without regard for God. ***Selah***
55: 7 [55:8] I would flee far away and stay in the desert; ***Selah***
55: 19 [55:20] ***Selah*** men who never change their ways and have no
57: 3 [57:4] ***Selah*** God sends his love and his faithfulness.
57: 6 [57:7] my path—but they have fallen into it themselves. ***Selah***
59: 5 [59:6] all the nations; show no mercy to wicked traitors. ***Selah***
59: 13 [59:14] the ends of the earth that God rules over Jacob. ***Selah***
60: 4 [60:6] raised a banner to be unfurled against the bow. ***Selah***
61: 4 [61:5] and take refuge in the shelter of your wings. ***Selah***
62: 4 [62:5] mouths they bless, but in their hearts they curse. ***Selah***
62: 8 [62:9] pour out your hearts to him, for God is our refuge. ***Selah***
66: 4 they sing praise to you, they sing praise to your name." ***Selah***
66: 7 the nations—let not the rebellious rise up against him. ***Selah***
66: 15 and an offering of rams; I will offer bulls and goats. ***Selah***
67: 1 [67:2] and bless us and make his face shine upon us, ***Selah***
67: 4 [67:5] peoples justly and guide the nations of the earth. ***Selah***
68: 7 [68:8] when you marched through the wasteland, ***Selah***
68: 19 [68:20] to God our Savior, who daily bears our burdens. ***Selah***
68: 32 [68:33] O kingdoms of the earth, sing praise to the Lord, ***Selah***
75: 3 [75:4] its people quake, it is I who hold its pillars firm. ***Selah***
76: 3 [76:4] the shields and the swords, the weapons of war. ***Selah***
76: 9 [76:10] up to judge, to save all the afflicted of the land. ***Selah***
77: 3 [77:4] and I groaned; I mused, and my spirit grew faint. ***Selah***
77: 9 [77:10] Has he in anger withheld his compassion?" ***Selah***
77: 15 [77:16] the descendants of Jacob and Joseph. ***Selah***
81: 7 [81:8] I tested you at the waters of Meribah. ***Selah***
82: 2 you defend the unjust and show partiality to the wicked? ***Selah***
83: 8 [83:9] them to lend strength to the descendants of Lot. ***Selah***
84: 4 [84:5] dwell in your house; they are ever praising you. ***Selah***
84: 8 [84:9] God Almighty; listen to me, O God of Jacob. ***Selah***
85: 2 [85:3] iniquity of your people and covered all their sins. ***Selah***
87: 3 Glorious things are said of you, O city of God: ***Selah***
87: 6 the register of the peoples: "This one was born in Zion." ***Selah***
88: 7 [88:8] you have overwhelmed me with all your waves. ***Selah***
88: 10 [88:11] Do those who are dead rise up and praise you? ***Selah***
89: 4 [89:5] make your throne firm through all generations.' " ***Selah***
89: 37 [89:38] like the moon, the faithful witness in the sky." ***Selah***
89: 45 [89:46] you have covered him with a mantle of shame. ***Selah***
89: 48 [89:49] or save himself from the power of the grave? ***Selah***
140: 3 [140:4] a serpent's; the poison of vipers is on their lips. ***Selah***
140: 5 [140:6] and have set traps for me along my path. ***Selah***
140: 8 [140:9] their plans succeed, or they will become proud. ***Selah***
143: 6 hands to you; my soul thirsts for you like a parched land. ***Selah***
Hab 3: 3 ***Selah*** His glory covered the heavens and his praise filled the
3: 9 called for many arrows. ***Selah*** You split the earth with rivers;
3: 13 land of wickedness, you stripped him from head to foot. ***Selah***

6139 סַלּוּ ***sallû***, n.pr.m. [1 / 2] [√ 6131; cf. 6144]

Sallu [1], Sallu's [1]

Ne 12: 7 **Sallu**, Amok, Hilkiah and Jedaiah. These were the leaders of the
12: 20 of **Sallu's**, [BHS 6144] Kallai; of Amok's, Eber;

6140 סָלוּא ***sālû'***, n.pr.m. [1] [√ 6131? *or* 6132?]

Salu [1]

Nu 25: 14 who was killed with the Midianite woman was Zimri son of **Salu**,

6141 סִלּוֹן ***sillôn***, n.m. [2] [√ 6131?]

briers [1], thorns [1]

Eze 2: 6 though briers and **thorns** are all around you and you live among
28: 24 people of Israel have malicious neighbors who are painful **briers**

6142 סָלַח **sālaḥ**, v. [46] [→ 6143, 6145]

forgive [26], be forgiven [13], release [3], forgiven [2], forgives [1], pardon [1]

Ex 34: 9 [A] **forgive** our wickedness and our sin, and take us as your
Lev 4:20 [C] will make atonement for them, and they *will* **be forgiven**.
4:26 [C] make atonement for the man's sin, and he *will* **be forgiven**.
4:31 [C] priest will make atonement for him, and he *will* **be forgiven**.
4:35 [C] him for the sin he has committed, and *he will* **be forgiven**.
5:10 [C] him for the sin he has committed, and he *will* **be forgiven**.
5:13 [C] any of these sins he has committed, and he *will* **be forgiven**.
5:16 [C] him with the ram as a guilt offering, and he *will* **be forgiven**.
5:18 [C] he has committed unintentionally, and he *will* **be forgiven**.
6: 7 [5:26] [C] he *will* **be forgiven** for any of these things he did that
19:22 [C] for the sin he has committed, and his sin *will* **be forgiven**.
Nu 14:19 [A] with your great love, **forgive** the sin of these people,
14:20 [A] The LORD replied, "*I have* **forgiven** them, as you asked.
15:25 [C] they *will* **be forgiven**, for it was not intentional and they have
15:26 [C] community and the aliens living among them *will* **be forgiven**,
15:28 [C] when atonement has been made for him, he *will* **be forgiven**.
30: 5 [30:6] [A] the LORD *will* **release** her because her father has
30: 8 [30:9] [A] obligates herself, and the LORD *will* **release** her.
30:12 [30:13] [A] has nullified them, and the LORD *will* **release** her.
Dt 29:20 [29:19] [A] The LORD will never be willing *to* **forgive** him;
1Ki 8:30 [A] your dwelling place, and when you hear, **forgive**.
8:34 [A] hear from heaven and **forgive** the sin of your people Israel
8:36 [A] then hear from heaven and **forgive** the sin of your servants,
8:39 [A] **Forgive** and act; deal with each man according to all he does,
8:50 [A] **forgive** your people, who have sinned against you; forgive
2Ki 5:18 [A] But *may* the LORD **forgive** your servant for this one thing:
5:18 [A] of Rimmon, *may* the LORD **forgive** your servant for this."
24: 4 [A] innocent blood, and the LORD was not willing to **forgive**.
2Ch 6:21 [A] your dwelling place; and when you hear, **forgive**.
6:25 [A] hear from heaven and **forgive** the sin of your people Israel
6:27 [A] then hear from heaven and **forgive** the sin of your servants,
6:30 [A] **Forgive**, and deal with each man according to all he does,
6:39 [A] And **forgive** your people, who have sinned against you.
7:14 [A] and *will* **forgive** their sin and will heal their land.
Ps 25:11 [A] O LORD, **forgive** my iniquity, though it is great.
103: 3 [A] who **forgives** all your sins and heals all your diseases,
Isa 55: 7 [A] mercy on him, and to our God, for he will freely **pardon**.
Jer 5: 1 [A] deals honestly and seeks the truth, *I will* **forgive** this city.
5: 7 [A] "Why *should I* **forgive** you? Your children have forsaken me
31:34 [A] "For *I will* **forgive** their wickedness and will remember their
33: 8 [A] and *will* **forgive** all their sins of rebellion against me.
36: 3 [A] then *I will* **forgive** their wickedness and their sin."
50:20 [A] but none will be found, for *I will* **forgive** the remnant I spare.
La 3:42 [A] "We have sinned and rebelled and you *have* not **forgiven**.
Da 9:19 [A] O Lord, listen! O Lord, **forgive**! O Lord, hear and act! For
Am 7: 2 [A] the land clean, I cried out, "Sovereign LORD, **forgive**!

6143 סַלָּח **sallāḥ**, a. [1] [√ 6142]

forgiving [1]

Ps 86: 5 You are **forgiving** and good, O Lord, abounding in love to all who

6144 סַלַּי **sallay**, n.pr.m. [2 / 1] [cf. 6139]

Sallai [1]

Ne 11: 8 and his followers, Gabbai and **Sallai**—928 men.
12:20 of Sallu's, [BHS *Sallai's*; NIV 6139] Kallai;

6145 סְלִיחָה **s^e^lîḥâ**, n.f. [3] [√ 6142]

forgiving [2], forgiveness [1]

Ne 9:17 But you are a **forgiving** God, gracious and compassionate,
Ps 130: 4 But with you there is **forgiveness**; therefore you are feared.
Da 9: 9 The Lord our God is merciful and **forgiving**, even though we have

6146 סַלְכָה **salkâ**, n.pr.loc. [4]

Salecah [4]

Dt 3:10 and all Gilead, and all Bashan as far as **Salecah** and Edrei,
Jos 12: 5 He ruled over Mount Hermon, **Salecah**, all of Bashan to the border
13:11 all of Mount Hermon and all Bashan as far as **Salecah**—
1Ch 5:11 The Gadites lived next to them in Bashan, as far as **Salecah**:

6147 ¹סָלַל **sālal**[1], v. [2] [cf. 6148]

esteem [1], set yourself [1]

Ex 9:17 [F] You still **set yourself** against my people and will not let them
Pr 4: 8 [D] **Esteem** her, and she will exalt you; embrace her, and she will

6148 ²סָלַל **sālal**[2], v. [10] [→ 5019, 5020, 6149, 6150, 6151; cf. 6138?, 6147]

build up [4], build [2], built up [1], extol [1], is a highway [1], pile up [1]

Job 19:12 [A] *they* **build** a siege ramp against me and encamp around my
30:12 [A] snares for my feet, *they* **build** their siege ramps against me.
Ps 68: 4 [68:5] [A] to his name, **extol** him who rides on the clouds—
Pr 15:19 [B] blocked with thorns, but the path of the upright **is a highway**.
Isa 57:14 [A] And it will be said: "**Build up**, build up, prepare the road!
57:14 [A] And it will be said: "Build up, **build up**, prepare the road!
62:10 [A] **Build up**, build up the highway! Remove the stones. Raise a
62:10 [A] Build up, **build up** the highway! Remove the stones. Raise a
Jer 18:15 [B] They made them walk in bypaths and on roads not **built up**.
50:26 [A] Break open her granaries; **pile** her **up** like heaps of grain.

6149 סֹלְלָה **sōl^e^lâ**, n.f. [11] [√ 6148; cf. 2360]

siege ramps [4], ramp [3], siege ramp [3], ramps [1]

2Sa 20:15 They built a **siege ramp** up to the city, and it stood against the
2Ki 19:32 will not come before it with shield or build a **siege ramp** against it.
Isa 37:33 will not come before it with shield or build a **siege ramp** against it.
Jer 6: 6 "Cut down the trees and build **siege ramps** against Jerusalem.
32:24 "See how the **siege ramps** are built up to take the city. Because of
33: 4 Judah that have been torn down to be used against the **siege ramps**
Eze 4: 2 build a **ramp** up to it, set up camps against it and put battering
17:17 when **ramps** are built and siege works erected to destroy many
21:22 [21:27] the gates, to build a **ramp** and to erect siege works.
26: 8 build a **ramp** up to your walls and raise his shields against you.
Da 11:15 and build up **siege ramps** and will capture a fortified city.

6150 סֻלָּם **sullām**, n.m. [1] [√ 6148]

stairway [1]

Ge 28:12 He had a dream in which he saw a **stairway** resting on the earth,

6151 סַלְסִלָּה **salsillâ**, n.[f.]. [1] [√ 6148]

branches [1]

Jer 6: 9 pass your hand over the **branches** again, like one gathering

6152 סֶלַע **sela**[c1], n.m. [58] [→ 6153, 6154, 6255?]

rock [30], rocks [9], crags [4], *untranslated* [2], cliff [2], cliffs [2], mountain [2], cliff [+9094] [1], rocky crag [1], rocky crags [1], rocky [1], stone [1], stronghold [1], where[s] [+928+8234] [1]

Nu 20: 8 Speak to that **rock** before their eyes and it will pour out its water.
20: 8 You will bring water out of the **rock** for the community so they
20:10 and Aaron gathered the assembly together in front of the **rock**
20:10 "Listen, you rebels, must we bring you water out of this **rock**?"
20:11 Then Moses raised his arm and struck the **rock** twice with his staff.
24:21 "Your dwelling place is secure, your nest is set in a **rock**;
Dt 32:13 He nourished him with honey from the **rock**, and with oil from the
Jdg 6:20 place them on this **rock**, and pour out the broth."
15: 8 Then he went down and stayed in a cave in the **rock** *of* Etam.
15:11 men from Judah went down to the cave in the **rock** *of* Etam
15:13 they bound him with two new ropes and led him up from the **rock**.
20:45 As they turned and fled toward the desert to the **rock** *of* Rimmon,
20:47 men turned and fled into the desert to the **rock** *of* Rimmon,
20:47 fled into the desert to the rock of Rimmon, **where**[s] [+928+8234]
21:13 sent an offer of peace to the Benjamites at the **rock** *of* Rimmon.
1Sa 13: 6 hid in caves and thickets, among the **rocks**, and in pits and cisterns.
14: 4 to cross to reach the Philistine outpost was a **cliff** [+9094];
14: 4 was a cliff; **[RPH]** one was called Bozez, and the other Seneh.
23:25 he went down to the **rock** and stayed in the Desert of Maon.
2Sa 22: 2 He said: "The LORD is my **rock**, my fortress and my deliverer;
1Ki 19:11 the mountains apart and shattered the **rocks** before the LORD,
2Ch 25:12 took them to the top of a **cliff** and threw them down so that all were
25:12 and threw them down **[RPH]** so that all were dashed to pieces.
Ne 9:15 and in their thirst you brought them water from the **rock**;
Job 39: 1 "Do you know when the **mountain** goats give birth? Do you watch
39:28 He dwells on a **cliff** and stays there at night; a rocky crag is his
39:28 on a cliff and stays there at night; a **rocky** crag is his stronghold.
Ps 18: 2 [18:3] The LORD is my **rock**, my fortress and my deliverer;
31: 3 [31:4] Since you are my **rock** and my fortress, for the sake of
40: 2 [40:3] he set my feet on a **rock** and gave me a firm place to stand.
42: 9 [42:10] I say to God my **Rock**, "Why have you forgotten me?
71: 3 the command to save me, for you are my **rock** and my fortress.
78:16 he brought streams out of a **rocky crag** and made water flow down
104:18 belong to the wild goats; the **crags** are a refuge for the coneys.
137: 9 he who seizes your infants and dashes them against the **rocks**.
141: 6 their rulers will be thrown down from the **cliffs**, and the wicked
Pr 30:26 are creatures of little power, yet they make their home in the **crags**;
SS 2:14 My dove in the clefts of the **rock**, in the hiding places on the
Isa 2:21 to the overhanging **crags** from dread of the LORD and the
7:19 and settle in the steep ravines and in the crevices in the **rocks**,

Isa 22:16 grave on the height and chiseling your resting place in the **rock**?
31: 9 Their **stronghold** will fall because of terror; at sight of the battle
32: 2 water in the desert and the shadow of a great **rock** in a thirsty land.
33:16 dwell on the heights, whose refuge will be the **mountain** fortress.
57: 5 your children in the ravines and under the overhanging **crags**.
Jer 5: 3 They made their faces harder than **stone** and refused to repent.
13: 4 and go now to Perath and hide it there in a crevice in the **rocks**."
16:16 on every mountain and hill and from the crevices of the **rocks**.
23:29 the LORD, "and like a hammer that breaks a **rock** in pieces?
48:28 Abandon your towns and dwell among the **rocks**, you who live in
49:16 you who live in the clefts of the **rocks**, who occupy the heights of
51:25 roll you off the **cliffs**, and make you a burned-out mountain.
Eze 24: 7 She poured it on the bare **rock**; she did not pour it on the ground,
24: 8 To stir up wrath and take revenge I put her blood on the bare **rock**,
26: 4 I will scrape away her rubble and make her a bare **rock**.
26:14 I will make you a bare **rock**, and you will become a place to spread
Am 6:12 Do horses run on the **rocky crags**? Does one plow there with
Ob 1: 3 you who live in the clefts of the **rocks** and make your home on the

6153 ²סֶלַע *sela'²*, n.pr.loc. [4] [√ 6152]

Sela [4]

Jdg 1:36 The boundary of the Amorites was from Scorpion Pass to **Sela**
2Ki 14: 7 Edomites in the Valley of Salt and captured **Sela** in battle,
Isa 16: 1 from **Sela**, across the desert, to the mount of the Daughter of Zion.
42:11 Let the people of **Sela** sing for joy; let them shout from the

6154 סֶלַע הַמַּחְלְקוֹת *sela' hammaḥleqôt*, n.pr.loc. [1] [√ 6152 + 2165; cf. 4712]

Sela Hammahlekoth [1]

1Sa 23:28 That is why they call this place **Sela Hammahlekoth**.

6155 סָלְעָם *sol'ām*, n.m. [1] [√ 6152?]

katydid [1]

Lev 11:22 you may eat any kind of locust, **katydid**, cricket or grasshopper.

6156 סָלַף *sālap*, v. [7] [→ 6157]

overthrows [2], twists [2], brings to ruin [+2021+4200+8273] [1], frustrates [1], ruins [1]

Ex 23: 8 [D] blinds those who see and **twists** the words of the righteous.
Dt 16:19 [D] the eyes of the wise and **twists** the words of the righteous.
Job 12:19 [D] priests away stripped and **overthrows** men long established.
Pr 13: 6 [D] the man of integrity, but wickedness **overthrows** the sinner.
19: 3 [D] A man's own folly **ruins** his life, yet his heart rages against
21:12 [D] and **brings** the wicked **to ruin** [+2021+4200+8273].
22:12 [D] but *he* **frustrates** the words of the unfaithful.

6157 סֶלֶף *selep*, n.m. [2] [√ 6156]

deceitful [1], duplicity [1]

Pr 11: 3 guides them, but the unfaithful are destroyed by their **duplicity**.
15: 4 healing is a tree of life, but a **deceitful** tongue crushes the spirit.

6158 סָלַק *sālaq*, v. [1] [→ Ar 10513]

go up [1]

Ps 139: 8 [A] If *I* **go up** *to* the heavens, you are there; if I make my bed in

6159 סֹלֶת *sōlet*, n.f. [53]

fine flour [46], flour [6], fine [1]

Ge 18: 6 "get three seahs of **fine** flour and knead it and bake some bread."
Ex 29: 2 from **fine** wheat **flour**, without yeast, make bread, and cakes mixed
29:40 With the first lamb offer a tenth of an ephah of **fine flour** mixed
Lev 2: 1 a grain offering to the LORD, his offering is to be of **fine flour**.
2: 2 The priest shall take a handful of the **fine flour** and oil, together
2: 4 a grain offering baked in an oven, it is to consist of **fine flour**:
2: 5 it is to be made of **fine flour** mixed with oil, and without yeast.
2: 7 offering is cooked in a pan, it is to be made of **fine flour** and oil.
5:11 for his sin a tenth of an ephah of **fine flour** for a sin offering.
6:15 [6:8] The priest is to take a handful of **fine flour** and oil, together
6:20 [6:13] a tenth of an ephah of **fine flour** as a regular grain offering,
7:12 with oil, and cakes of **fine flour** well-kneaded and mixed with oil.
14:10 with three-tenths of an ephah of **fine flour** mixed with oil *for*
14:21 together with a tenth of an ephah of **fine flour** mixed with oil for a
23:13 offering of two-tenths of an ephah of **fine flour** mixed with oil—
23:17 bring two loaves made of two-tenths of an ephah of **fine flour**,
24: 5 "Take **fine flour** and bake twelve loaves of bread, using two-tenths
Nu 6:15 cakes made of **fine flour** mixed with oil, and wafers spread with
7:13 each filled with **fine flour** mixed with oil as a grain offering;
7:19 each filled with **fine flour** mixed with oil as a grain offering;
7:25 each filled with **fine flour** mixed with oil as a grain offering;
7:31 each filled with **fine flour** mixed with oil as a grain offering;
7:37 each filled with **fine flour** mixed with oil as a grain offering;
7:43 each filled with **fine flour** mixed with oil as a grain offering;
7:49 each filled with **fine flour** mixed with oil as a grain offering;
7:55 each filled with **fine flour** mixed with oil as a grain offering;
7:61 each filled with **fine flour** mixed with oil as a grain offering;
7:67 each filled with **fine flour** mixed with oil as a grain offering;
7:73 each filled with **fine flour** mixed with oil as a grain offering;
7:79 each filled with **fine flour** mixed with oil as a grain offering;
8: 8 Have them take a young bull with its grain offering of **fine flour**
15: 4 tenth of an ephah of **fine flour** mixed with a quarter of a hin of oil.
15: 6 of an ephah of **fine flour** mixed with a third of a hin of oil,
15: 9 three-tenths of an ephah of **fine flour** mixed with half a hin of oil.
28: 5 together with a grain offering of a tenth of an ephah of **fine flour**
28: 9 a grain offering of two-tenths of an ephah of **fine flour** mixed with
28:12 offering of three-tenths of an ephah of **fine flour** mixed with oil;
28:12 a grain offering of two-tenths of an ephah of **fine flour** mixed with
28:13 a grain offering of a tenth of an ephah of **fine flour** mixed with oil.
28:20 offering of three-tenths of an ephah of **fine flour** mixed with oil;
28:28 offering of three-tenths of an ephah of **fine flour** mixed with oil;
29: 3 offering of three-tenths of an ephah of **fine flour** mixed with oil;
29: 9 offering of three-tenths of an ephah of **fine flour** mixed with oil;
29:14 offering of three-tenths of an ephah of **fine flour** mixed with oil;
1Ki 4:22 [5:2] Solomon's daily provisions were thirty cors of **fine flour**
2Ki 7: 1 a seah of **flour** will sell for a shekel and two seahs of barley for a
7:16 So a seah of **flour** sold for a shekel, and two seahs of barley sold
7:18 a seah of **flour** will sell for a shekel and two seahs of barley for a
1Ch 9:29 as well as the **flour** and wine, and the oil, incense and spices.
23:29 the **flour** for the grain offerings, the unleavened wafers, the baking
Eze 16:13 embroidered cloth. Your food was **fine flour**, honey and olive oil.
16:19 for you—the **fine flour**, olive oil and honey I gave you to eat—
46:14 a sixth of an ephah with a third of a hin of oil to moisten the **flour**.

6160 סַם *sam*, n.m. [16] [√ 6167]

fragrant [14], *untranslated* [1], fragrant spices [1]

Ex 25: 6 the light; spices for the anointing oil and for the **fragrant** incense;
30: 7 "Aaron must burn **fragrant** incense on the altar every morning
30:34 Then the LORD said to Moses, "Take **fragrant spices**—
30:34 **[RPH]** and pure frankincense, all in equal amounts,
31:11 and the anointing oil and **fragrant** incense for the Holy Place.
35: 8 the light; spices for the anointing oil and for the **fragrant** incense;
35:15 incense with its poles, the anointing oil and the **fragrant** incense;
35:28 for the light and for the anointing oil and for the **fragrant** incense.
37:29 also made the sacred anointing oil and the pure, **fragrant** incense—
39:38 the gold altar, the anointing oil, the **fragrant** incense, and the
40:27 burned **fragrant** incense on it, as the LORD commanded him.
Lev 4: 7 put some of the blood on the horns of the altar of **fragrant** incense
16:12 two handfuls of finely ground **fragrant** incense and take them
Nu 4:16 the **fragrant** incense, the regular grain offering and the anointing
2Ch 2: 4 [2:3] to dedicate it to him for burning **fragrant** incense before
13:11 they present burnt offerings and **fragrant** incense to the LORD.

6161 סַמְגַּר *samgar*, n.pr.m. [1] [→ 6162]

Samgar [1]

Jer 39: 3 Nergal-Sharezer of **Samgar**, Nebo-Sarsekim a chief officer,

6162 סַמְגַּר־נְבוֹ *samgar-nebô*, n.pr.m. Not used in NIV/BHS [√ 6161 + 5550]

6163 סְמָדַר *semādar*, n.m. [3] [√ 6005 + *]

blossoming [1], blossoms [1], in bloom [1]

SS 2:13 forms its early fruit; the **blossoming** vines spread their fragrance.
2:15 little foxes that ruin the vineyards, our vineyards that are **in bloom**.
7:12 [7:13] if their **blossoms** have opened, and if the pomegranates are

6164 סָמַךְ *sāmak*, v. [48] [→ 322, 3577, 6165; cf. 8527]

lay [17], laid [6], sustained [3], upholds [3], leans [2], steadfast [2], sustain [2], sustains [2], allies [1], bracing [1], gained confidence [1], gave support [1], laid siege [1], lies heavily [1], relied [1], rely [1], rested [1], secure [1], strengthen [1]

Ge 27:37 [A] and *I have* **sustained** him *with* grain and new wine.
Ex 29:10 [A] and Aaron and his sons *shall* **lay** their hands on its head.
29:15 [A] and Aaron and his sons *shall* **lay** their hands on its head.
29:19 [A] and Aaron and his sons *shall* **lay** their hands on its head.
Lev 1: 4 [A] *He is to* **lay** his hand on the head of the burnt offering, and it
3: 2 [A] *He is to* **lay** his hand on the head of his offering
3: 8 [A] *He is to* **lay** his hand on the head of his offering
3:13 [A] *He is to* **lay** his hand on its head and slaughter it in front of
4: 4 [A] *He is to* **lay** his hand on its head and slaughter it before the
4:15 [A] The elders of the community *are to* **lay** their hands on the

Lev 4:24 [A] *He is to* **lay** his hand on the goat's head and slaughter it at
4:29 [A] *He is to* **lay** his hand on the head of the sin offering
4:33 [A] *He is to* **lay** his hand on its head and slaughter it for a sin
8:14 [A] and Aaron and his sons **laid** their hands on its head.
8:18 [A] and Aaron and his sons **laid** their hands on its head.
8:22 [A] and Aaron and his sons **laid** their hands on its head.
16:21 [A] He *is to* **lay** both hands on the head of the live goat
24:14 [A] All those who heard him *are to* **lay** their hands on his head,
Nu 8:10 [A] the LORD, and the Israelites *are to* **lay** their hands on them.
8:12 [A] "After the Levites **lay** their hands on the heads of the bulls,
27:18 [A] a man in whom is the spirit, and **lay** your hand on him.
27:23 [A] *he* **laid** his hands on him and commissioned him, as the
Dt 34:9 [A] spirit of wisdom because Moses *had* **laid** his hands on him.
Jdg 16:29 [C] **Bracing** *himself* against them, his right hand on the one
2Ki 18:21 [C] pierces a man's hand and wounds him if *he* **leans** on it!
2Ch 29:23 [A] the king and the assembly, and *they* **laid** their hands on them.
32:8 [C] the people **gained confidence** from what Hezekiah the king
Ps 3:5 [3:6] [A] I wake again, because the LORD **sustains** me.
37:17 [A] will be broken, but the LORD **upholds** the righteous.
37:24 [A] he will not fall, for the LORD **upholds** him *with* his hand.
51:12 [51:14] [A] and grant me a willing spirit, *to* **sustain** me.
54:4 [54:6] [A] is my help; the Lord is the *one who* **sustains** me.
71:6 [C] From birth *I have* **relied** on you; you brought me forth from
88:7 [88:8] [A] Your wrath **lies heavily** upon me; you have
111:8 [B] *They are* **steadfast** for ever and ever, done in faithfulness
112:8 [B] His heart *is* **secure**, he will have no fear; in the end he will
119:116 [A] **Sustain** me according to your promise, and I will live; do not
145:14 [A] The LORD **upholds** all those who fall and lifts up all who
SS 2:5 [D] **Strengthen** me with raisins, refresh me with apples, for I am
Isa 26:3 [B] You will keep in perfect peace him whose mind *is* **steadfast**,
36:6 [C] pierces a man's hand and wounds him if *he* **leans** on it!
48:2 [C] citizens of the holy city and **rely** on the God of Israel—
59:16 [A] salvation for him, and his own righteousness **sustained** him.
63:5 [A] was no one to help, I was appalled that no *one* **gave support**;
63:5 [A] worked salvation for me, and my own wrath **sustained** me.
Eze 24:2 [A] because the king of Babylon *has* **laid siege** to Jerusalem this
30:6 [A] " 'The **allies** *of* Egypt will fall and her proud strength will
Am 5:19 [A] **rested** his hand on the wall only to have a snake bite him.

6165 סְמַכְיָהוּ *sᵉmakyāhû*, n.pr.m. [1] [√ 6164]

Semakiah [1]

1Ch 26:7 and Elzabad; his relatives Elihu and **Semakiah** were also able men.

6166 סֶמֶל *semel*, n.m. [5]

idol [2], image [2], shape [1]

Dt 4:16 an image of any **shape**, whether formed like a man or a woman,
2Ch 33:7 He took the carved **image** he had made and put it in God's temple,
33:15 and removed the **image** from the temple of the LORD,
Eze 8:3 of the inner court, where the **idol** that provokes to jealousy stood.
8:5 in the entrance north of the gate of the altar I saw this **idol** *of*

6167 סָמַם *sāmam*, v. Not used in NIV/BHS [→ 6160; cf. 6093, 8487, 8531]

6168 סָמַן *sāman*, v. [1]

plot [1]

Isa 28:25 [C] wheat in its place, barley *in its* **plot**, and spelt in its field?

6169 סָמַר *sāmar*, v. [2] [→ 5021, 6170; cf. 5383]

stood on end [1], trembles [1]

Job 4:15 [D] glided past my face, and the hair on my body **stood on end**.
Ps 119:120 [A] My flesh **trembles** in fear of you; I stand in awe of your

6170 סָמָר *sāmār*, a. [1] [√ 6169]

swarm [1]

Jer 51:27 a commander against her; send up horses like a **swarm** of locusts.

6171 סְנָאָה *sᵉnā'â*, n.pr.m. [2] [√ 8533, cf. 6176]

Senaah [2]

Ezr 2:35 of **Senaah** 3,630
Ne 7:38 of **Senaah** 3,930

6172 סַנְבַלַּט *sanballaṭ*, n.pr.m. [10]

Sanballat [10]

Ne 2:10 When **Sanballat** the Horonite and Tobiah the Ammonite official
2:19 But when **Sanballat** the Horonite, Tobiah the Ammonite official
4:1 [3:33] When **Sanballat** heard that we were rebuilding the wall, he
4:7 [4:1] when **Sanballat**, Tobiah, the Arabs, the Ammonites
6:1 When word came to **Sanballat**, Tobiah, Geshem the Arab
6:2 **Sanballat** and Geshem sent me this message: "Come, let us meet
6:5 fifth time, **Sanballat** sent his aide to me with the same message,
6:12 against me because Tobiah and **Sanballat** had hired him.
6:14 Remember Tobiah and **Sanballat**, O my God, because of what
13:28 Eliashib the high priest was son-in-law to **Sanballat** the Horonite.

6173 סַנָּה *sannâ*, n.pr.loc. Not used in NIV/BHS [→ 7962]

6174 סְנֶה *sᵉneh*, n.m. [6]

bush [5], it[s] [+2021] [1]

Ex 3:2 the LORD appeared to him in flames of fire from within a **bush**.
3:2 Moses saw that though the **bush** was on fire it did not burn up.
3:2 Moses saw that though the bush was on fire **it**[s] [+2021] did not
3:3 and see this strange sight—why the **bush** does not burn up."
3:4 over to look, God called to him from within the **bush**, "Moses!
Dt 33:16 its fullness and the favor of him who dwelt in the burning **bush**.

6175 סֶנֶּה *senneh*, n.pr.loc. [1]

Seneh [1]

1Sa 14:4 outpost was a cliff; one was called Bozez, and the other **Seneh**.

6176 סְנוּאָה *sᵉnû'â*, n.pr.m. Not used in NIV/BHS [√ 8533; cf. 2190, 6171]

6177 סַנְוֵרִים *sanwērîm*, n.[m.pl.]. [3]

blindness [3]

Ge 19:11 and old, with **blindness** so that they could not find the door.
2Ki 6:18 Elisha prayed to the LORD, "Strike these people with **blindness**."
6:18 So he struck them with **blindness**, as Elisha had asked.

6178 סַנְחֵרִיב *sanḥērîb*, n.pr.m. [13]

Sennacherib [13]

2Ki 18:13 **Sennacherib** king of Assyria attacked all the fortified cities of
19:16 listen to the words **Sennacherib** has sent to insult the living God.
19:20 I have heard your prayer concerning **Sennacherib** king of Assyria.
19:36 So **Sennacherib** king of Assyria broke camp and withdrew.
2Ch 32:1 **Sennacherib** king of Assyria came and invaded Judah.
32:2 When Hezekiah saw that **Sennacherib** had come and that he
32:9 when **Sennacherib** king of Assyria and all his forces were laying
32:10 "This is what **Sennacherib** king of Assyria says: On what are you
32:22 the people of Jerusalem from the hand of **Sennacherib** king of
Isa 36:1 **Sennacherib** king of Assyria attacked all the fortified cities of
37:17 listen to all the words **Sennacherib** has sent to insult the living
37:21 Because you have prayed to me concerning **Sennacherib** king of
37:37 So **Sennacherib** king of Assyria broke camp and withdrew.

6179 סַנְסַנָּה *sansannâ*, n.pr.loc. [1]

Sansannah [1]

Jos 15:31 Ziklag, Madmannah, **Sansannah**,

6180 סַנְסִנָּה *sansinnâ*, n.[m.]pl. [1]

fruit [1]

SS 7:8 [7:9] "I will climb the palm tree; I will take hold of its **fruit**."

6181 סְנַפִּיר *sᵉnappîr*, n.[m.]. [5]

fins [5]

Lev 11:9 and the streams, you may eat any that have **fins** and scales.
11:10 creatures in the seas or streams that do not have **fins** and scales—
11:12 Anything living in the water that does not have **fins** and scales is to
Dt 14:9 living in the water, you may eat any that has **fins** and scales.
14:10 But anything that does not have **fins** and scales you may not eat;

6182 סָס *sās*, n.m. [1]

worm [1]

Isa 51:8 eat them up like a garment; the **worm** will devour them like wool.

6183 סִסְמַי *sismay*, n.pr.m. [2]

Sismai [2]

1Ch 2:40 Eleasah the father of **Sismai**, Sismai the father of Shallum,
2:40 Eleasah the father of Sismai, **Sismai** the father of Shallum,

6184 סָעַד sā'ad, v. [12] [→ 5026; Ar 10514]

refresh [2], sustains [2], grant support [1], have something to eat [1], made secure [1], refreshed [+4213] [1], supported [1], sustain [1], uphold [1], upholding [1]

Ge 18: 5 [A] so you *can be* **refreshed** [+4213] and then go on your way—
Jdg 19: 5 [A] to his son-in-law, "**Refresh** yourself *with* something to eat;
19: 8 [A] when he rose to go, the girl's father said, "**Refresh** yourself.
1Ki 13: 7 [A] "Come home with me and **have something to eat**, and I will
Ps 18:35 [18:36] [A] shield of victory, and your right hand **sustains** me;
20: 2 [20:3] [A] the sanctuary and **grant** you **support** from Zion.
41: 3 [41:4] [A] The LORD *will* **sustain** him on his sickbed and
94:18 [A] "My foot is slipping," your love, O LORD, **supported** me.
104:15 [A] oil to make his face shine, and bread *that* **sustains** his heart.
119:117 [A] **Uphold** me, and I will be delivered; I will always have
Pr 20:28 [A] keep a king safe; through love his throne *is* **made secure**.
Isa 9: 7 [9:6] [A] establishing and **upholding** it with justice

6185 סָעָה sā'â, v. [1]

tempest [+8120] [1]

Ps 55: 8 [55:9] [A] of shelter, far from the **tempest** [+8120] and storm."

6186 סָעִיף¹ sā'îp¹, n.[m.]. [4] [→ 6187, 6188, 6189, 6190, 6191; cf. 6187]

cave [2], overhanging [2]

Jdg 15: 8 Then he went down and stayed in a **cave** *in* the rock of Etam.
15:11 three thousand men from Judah went down to the **cave** *in* the rock
Isa 2:21 to the **overhanging** crags from dread of the LORD and the
57: 5 your children in the ravines and under the **overhanging** crags.

6187 סָעִיף² sā'îp², n.[m.]. [2] [→ 6188, 6190, 6250; cf. 6186]

boughs [1], branches [1]

Isa 17: 6 four or five on the fruitful **boughs**," declares the LORD,
27:10 the calves graze, there they lie down; they strip its **branches** bare.

6188 סָעַף sā'ap, v.den. [1] [√ 6187; cf. 6186]

lop off [1]

Isa 10:33 [D] LORD Almighty, *will* **lop off** the boughs with great power.

6189 סֵעֵף sē'ēp, a. [1] [→ 6191; cf. 6186]

double-minded [1]

Ps 119:113 I hate **double-minded** *men*, but I love your law.

6190 סְעַפָּה se'appâ, n.f. [2] [√ 6187; cf. 6186]

boughs [2]

Eze 31: 6 All the birds of the air nested in its **boughs**, all the beasts of the
31: 8 of God could not rival it, nor could the pine trees equal its **boughs**,

6191 סְעִפִּים se'ippîm, n.f. [1] [√ 6189; cf. 6186]

opinions [1]

1Ki 18:21 and said, "How long will you waver between two **opinions**?

6192 סָעַר sā'ar, v. [7] [→ 6193, 6194; cf. 8548]

enraged [+4213+6584] [1], grew even wilder [+2143+2256+6584] [1], lashed by storms [1], rougher and rougher [+2143+2256] [1], scattered with a whirlwind [1], stormed out [1], swirling [1]

2Ki 6:11 [C] This **enraged** [+4213+6584] the king of Aram. He
Isa 54:11 [E] "O afflicted city, **lashed by storms** and not comforted, I will
Hos 13: 3 [D] that disappears, like chaff **swirling** from a threshing floor,
Jnh 1:11 [A] The sea *was getting* **rougher** [+2143+2256] **and rougher**.
1:13 [A] for the sea **grew even wilder** [+2143+2256+6584] than before.
Hab 3:14 [A] pierced his head when his warriors **stormed out** to scatter us,
Zec 7:14 [D] '*I* **scattered** them **with a whirlwind** among all the nations,

6193 סַעַר sa'ar, n.m. [8] [→ 6194; cf. 6192]

storm [4], tempest [1], violent winds [1], whirlwind [1], wind [1]

Ps 55: 8 [55:9] to my place of shelter, far from the tempest and **storm**."
83:15 [83:16] so pursue them with your **tempest** and terrify them with
Jer 23:19 in wrath, a **whirlwind** swirling down on the heads of the wicked.
25:32 to nation; a mighty **storm** is rising from the ends of the earth."
30:23 a driving **wind** swirling down on the heads of the wicked.
Am 1:14 war cries on the day of battle, amid **violent winds** on a stormy day.
Jnh 1: 4 and such a violent **storm** arose that the ship threatened to break up.
1:12 I know that it is my fault that this great **storm** has come upon you."

6194 סְעָרָה se'ārâ, n.f. [16] [√ 6193; cf. 6192]

storm [5], whirlwind [3], gale [1], storms [1], stormy [1], tempest [+8120] [1], tempest [1], violent wind [+8120] [1], violent winds [+8120] [1], windstorm [+8120] [1]

2Ki 2: 1 the LORD was about to take Elijah up to heaven in a **whirlwind**,
2:11 the two of them, and Elijah went up to heaven in a **whirlwind**.
Job 38: 1 Then the LORD answered Job out of the **storm**. He said:
40: 6 Then the LORD spoke to Job out of the **storm**:
Ps 107:25 and stirred up a **tempest** [+8120] that lifted high the waves.
107:29 He stilled the **storm** to a whisper; the waves of the sea were
148: 8 and hail, snow and clouds, **stormy** winds that do his bidding,
Isa 29: 6 with windstorm and **tempest** and flames of a devouring fire.
40:24 and they wither, and a **whirlwind** sweeps them away like chaff.
41:16 the wind will pick them up, and a **gale** will blow them away.
Jer 23:19 See, the **storm** *of* the LORD will burst out in wrath, a whirlwind
30:23 See, the **storm** *of* the LORD will burst out in wrath, a driving
Eze 1: 4 and I saw a **windstorm** [+8120] coming out of the north—
13:11 hurtling down, and **violent winds** [+8120] will burst forth.
13:13 In my wrath I will unleash a **violent wind** [+8120], and in my
Zec 9:14 will sound the trumpet; he will march in the **storms** *of* the south,

6195 סַף¹ sap¹, n.m. [7] [cf. 6196]

basins [3], *untranslated* [1], basin [1], bowls [1], cup [1]

Ex 12:22 dip it into the blood in the **basin** and put some of the blood on the
12:22 the blood in the basin and put some of the blood **[RPH]** on the top
2Sa 17:28 brought bedding and **bowls** and articles of pottery. They also
1Ki 7:50 the pure gold **basins**, wick trimmers, sprinkling bowls, dishes
2Ki 12:13 [12:14] into the temple was not spent for making silver **basins**,
Jer 52:19 The commander of the imperial guard took away the **basins**,
Zec 12: 2 "I am going to make Jerusalem a **cup** *that sends* all the

6196 סַף² sap², n.m. Not used in NIV/BHS [cf. 6195]

6197 סַף³ sap³, n.m. [25 / 24] [→ 6214]

threshold [7], doorkeepers [+9068] [5], thresholds [5], doorway [2], doorframes [1], doorkeeper [+9068] [1], doors [1], doorways [1], entrance [1]

Jdg 19:27 in the doorway of the house, with her hands on the **threshold**.
1Ki 14:17 As soon as she stepped over the **threshold** *of* the house, the boy
2Ki 12: 9 [12:10] The priests who guarded the **entrance** put into the chest
22: 4 which the **doorkeepers** [+9068] have collected from the people.
23: 4 the **doorkeepers** [+9068] to remove from the temple of the
25:18 the priest next in rank and the three **doorkeepers** [+9068].
1Ch 9:19 were responsible for guarding the **thresholds** of the Tent just as
9:22 those chosen to be gatekeepers at the **thresholds** numbered 212.
2Ch 3: 7 **doorframes**, walls and doors of the temple with gold,
23: 4 are going on duty on the Sabbath are to keep watch at the **doors**,
34: 9 which the Levites *who were* the **doorkeepers** [+9068] had
Est 2:21 and Teresh, two of the king's officers who guarded the **doorway**,
6: 2 and Teresh, two of the king's officers who guarded the **doorway**,
Isa 6: 4 and **thresholds** shook and the temple was filled with smoke.
Jer 35: 4 over that of Maaseiah son of Shallum the **doorkeeper** [+9068].
52:24 the priest next in rank and the three **doorkeepers** [+9068].
Eze 40: 6 He climbed its steps and measured the **threshold** *of* the gate;
40: 6 it was one rod deep. [BHS+ *the first* **threshold**,]
40: 7 the **threshold** *of* the gate next to the portico facing the temple was
41:16 as well as the **thresholds** and the narrow windows and galleries
41:16 and including the **threshold** was covered with wood.
43: 8 When they placed their **threshold** next to my threshold and their
43: 8 When they placed their threshold next to my **threshold** and their
Am 9: 1 "Strike the tops of the pillars so that the **thresholds** shake.
Zep 2:14 rubble will be in the **doorways**, the beams of cedar will be

6198 סַף⁴ sap⁴, n.pr.m. [1] [cf. 6205]

Saph [1]

2Sa 21:18 At that time Sibbecai the Hushathite killed **Saph**, one of the

6199 סָפַד sāpad, v. [30] [→ 5027, 6252?]

mourn [12], mourned [8], lament [3], be mourned [2], beat [1], lamented [+5027] [1], mourners [1], walk in mourning [1], weep [1]

Ge 23: 2 [A] and Abraham went to **mourn** for Sarah and to weep over her.
50:10 [A] near the Jordan, *they* **lamented** [+5027] loudly and bitterly;
1Sa 25: 1 [A] Samuel died, and all Israel assembled and **mourned** for him;
28: 3 [A] all Israel *had* **mourned** for him and buried him in his own
2Sa 1:12 [A] *They* **mourned** and wept and fasted till evening for Saul
3:31 [A] put on sackcloth and **walk in mourning** in front of Abner."
11:26 [A] wife heard that her husband was dead, *she* **mourned** for him.
1Ki 13:29 [A] brought it back to his own city to **mourn** *for* him and bury
13:30 [A] and *they* **mourned** over him and said, "Oh, my brother!"
14:13 [A] All Israel *will* **mourn** for him and bury him. He is the only

1Ki 14: 18 [A] They buried him, and all Israel **mourned** for him,
Ecc 3: 4 [A] and a time to laugh, a time *to* **mourn** and a time to dance,
12: 5 [A] goes to his eternal home and **mourners** go about the streets.
Isa 32: 12 [A] **Beat** your breasts for the pleasant fields, for the fruitful
Jer 4: 8 [A] So put on sackcloth, **lament** and wail, for the fierce anger of
16: 4 [C] *They will* not **be mourned** or buried but will be like refuse
16: 5 [A] do not go to **mourn** or show sympathy, because I have
16: 6 [A] They will not be buried or **mourned**, and no one will cut
22: 18 [A] "*They will* not **mourn** for him: 'Alas, my brother! Alas,
22: 18 [A] *They will* not **mourn** for him: 'Alas, my master! Alas,
25: 33 [C] *They will* not **be mourned** or gathered up or buried, but will
34: 5 [A] so they will make a fire in your honor and **lament**, "Alas,
49: 3 [A] Put on sackcloth and **mourn**; rush here and there inside the
Eze 24: 16 [A] of your eyes. Yet *do* not **lament** or weep or shed any tears.
24: 23 [A] *You will* not **mourn** or weep but will waste away because of
Joel 1: 13 [A] Put on sackcloth, O priests, and **mourn**; wail, you who
Mic 1: 8 [A] Because of this *I will* **weep** and wail; I will go about barefoot
Zec 7: 5 [A] 'When you fasted and **mourned** in the fifth and seventh
12: 10 [A] *they will* **mourn** for him as one mourns for an only child,
12: 12 [A] The land *will* **mourn**, each clan by itself, with their wives by

6200 סָפָה sāpâ, v. [17 / 16]

be swept away [4], sweep away [2], are caught [1], be destroyed [1], being swept away [1], bring disaster [1], perish [1], perished [1], sweeps away [1], swept away [1], take off [1], take [1]

Ge 18: 23 [A] "*Will you* **sweep away** the righteous with the wicked?
18: 24 [A] *Will you* really **sweep** it **away** and not spare the place for the
19: 15 [C] or *you will* **be swept away** when the city is punished."
19: 17 [C] the plain! Flee to the mountains or *you will* **be swept away**!"
Nu 16: 26 [C] to them, or *you will* **be swept away** because of all their sins."
Dt 29: 19 [29:18] [A] This *will* **bring disaster** *on* the watered land as well
32: 23 [g] "*I will* heap [BHS *sweep*; NIV 3578] calamities upon them
1Sa 12: 25 [C] in doing evil, both you and your king *will* **be swept away**."
26: 10 [C] and he will die, or he will go into battle and **perish**.
27: 1 [C] "One of these days *I will* **be destroyed** by the hand of Saul.
1Ch 21: 12 [C] three months of **being swept away** before your enemies,
Ps 40: 14 [40:15] [A] May all who seek to **take** my life be put to shame
73: 19 [A] are they destroyed, completely **swept away** by terrors!
Pr 13: 23 [C] may produce abundant food, but injustice **sweeps** it **away**.
Isa 7: 20 [A] and the hair of your legs, and *to* **take off** your beards also.
13: 15 [C] be thrust through; all who **are caught** will fall by the sword.
Jer 12: 4 [A] live in it are wicked, the animals and birds *have* **perished**.

6201 סָפוֹן sāpôn, n.[m.]. Not used in NIV/BHS [√ 6211]

6202 ¹סָפַח sāpaḥ¹, v. [4] [→ 5029, 6206, 6207; cf. 8558?, 9148]

appoint [1], huddled [1], share [1], unite [1]

1Sa 2: 36 [A] "**Appoint** me to some priestly office so I can have food to
26: 19 [F] They have now driven me from my **share** in the LORD's
Job 30: 7 [E] brayed among the bushes and **huddled** in the undergrowth.
Isa 14: 1 [C] Aliens will join them and **unite** with the house of Jacob.

6203 ²סָפַח sāpaḥ², v. [1] [cf. 5384, 8558?, 9148]

pouring [1]

Hab 2: 15 [D] **pouring** it *from* the wineskin till they are drunk, so that he

6204 סַפַּחַת sappaḥat, n.f. [2] [→ 5030]

rash [2]

Lev 13: 2 "When anyone has a swelling or a **rash** or a bright spot on his skin
14: 56 and for a swelling, a **rash** or a bright spot,

6205 סִפַּי sippay, n.pr.m. [1] [cf. 6198]

Sippai [1]

1Ch 20: 4 At that time Sibbecai the Hushathite killed **Sippai**, one of the

6206 ¹סָפִיחַ sāpîaḥ¹, n.[m.]. [4] [√ 6202]

what grows by itself [2], what grows of itself [2]

Lev 25: 5 Do not reap **what grows of itself** or harvest the grapes of your
25: 11 do not sow and do not reap **what grows of itself** or harvest the
2Ki 19: 29 "This year you will eat **what grows by itself**, and the second year
Isa 37: 30 "This year you will eat **what grows by itself**, and the second year

6207 ²סָפִיחַ sāpîaḥ², n.[m.]. [1] [√ 6202]

torrents [1]

Job 14: 19 as water wears away stones and **torrents** wash away the soil,

6208 סְפִינָה sᵉpînâ, n.f. [1] [√ 6211]

below deck [+2021+3752] [1]

Jnh 1: 5 But Jonah had gone **below deck** [+2021+3752], where he lay down

6209 סַפִּיר sappîr, n.[m.]. [11]

sapphires [5], sapphire [4], sapphire [+74] [2]

Ex 24: 10 Under his feet was something like a pavement made of **sapphire**,
28: 18 in the second row a turquoise, a **sapphire** and an emerald;
39: 11 in the second row a turquoise, a **sapphire** and an emerald;
Job 28: 6 **sapphires** come from its rocks, and its dust contains nuggets of
28: 16 be bought with the gold of Ophir, with precious onyx or **sapphires**.
SS 5: 14 His body is like polished ivory decorated with **sapphires**.
Isa 54: 11 you with stones of turquoise, your foundations with **sapphires**.
La 4: 7 bodies more ruddy than rubies, their appearance like **sapphires**.
Eze 1: 26 over their heads was what looked like a throne of **sapphire** [+74],
10: 1 I saw the likeness of a throne of **sapphire** [+74] above the expanse
28: 13 chrysolite, onyx and jasper, **sapphire**, turquoise and beryl.

6210 סֵפֶל sēpel, n.[m.]. [2]

bowl [1], bowlful [+4850] [1]

Jdg 5: 25 him milk; in a **bowl** *fit for* nobles she brought him curdled milk.
6: 38 the fleece and wrung out the dew—a **bowlful** [+4850] of water.

6211 סָפַן sāpan, v. [6] [→ 6201, 6208, 6212; cf. 8561]

covered [1], paneled [1], panels [1], roofing [1], was kept [1], was roofed [1]

Dt 33: 21 [B] best land for himself; the leader's portion **was kept** for him.
1Ki 6: 9 [A] and completed it, **roofing** it *with* beams and cedar planks.
7: 3 [B] *It* **was roofed** with cedar above the beams that rested on the
7: 7 [B] to judge, and *he* **covered** it with cedar from floor to ceiling.
Jer 22: 14 [B] windows in it, **panels** it with cedar and decorates it in red.
Hag 1: 4 [B] "Is it a time for you yourselves to be living in your **paneled**

6212 סִפֻּן sippun, n.[m.]. [1] [√ 6211]

ceiling [1]

1Ki 6: 15 paneling them from the floor of the temple to the **ceiling**,

6213 סַפְסִיג sapsîg, n.[m.]. [0 / 1] [cf. 6092]

glaze [1]

Pr 26: 23 Like a coating of **glaze** [BHS 6092] over earthenware are fervent

6214 סָפַף sāpap, v.den. [1] [√ 6197]

doorkeeper [1]

Ps 84: 10 [84:11] [F] I would rather be *a* **doorkeeper** in the house of my

6215 ¹סָפַק sāpaq¹, v. [6] [cf. 6216, 8562]

beat [2], clap [1], punishes [1], scornfully claps hands [1], struck together [1]

Nu 24: 10 [A] *He* **struck** his hands **together** and said to him, "I summoned
Job 34: 26 [A] *He* **punishes** them for their wickedness where everyone can
34: 37 [A] **scornfully** *he* **claps** *his* **hands** among us and multiplies his
Jer 31: 19 [A] I repented; after I came to understand, *I* **beat** my breast.
La 2: 15 [A] All who pass your way **clap** their hands at you; they scoff
Eze 21: 12 [21:17] [A] along with my people. Therefore **beat** your breast.

6216 ²סָפַק sāpaq², v. [1] [cf. 6215]

wallow [1]

Jer 48: 26 [A] *Let* Moab **wallow** in her vomit; let her be an object of

6217 סֶפֶק sepeq, n.[m.]. [1] [cf. 8563]

riches [1]

Job 36: 18 Be careful that no one entices you by **riches**; do not let a large

6218 סָפַר sāpar, v. [105] [√ 6219]

tell [18], told [17], count [12], count off [6], declare [6], proclaim [4], counted [3], telling [3], be recorded [2], be told [2], recount [2], talk [2], were told [2], *untranslated* [1], acknowledge [1], appraised [1], be counted [1], boasted [1], census taken [+6222] [1], conscripted [1], counted out [1], declared [1], gave account [1], inform [1], is declared [1], keeping records [1], make countless [+889+906+906+4202 +8049] [1], proclaimed [1], recite [1], record [1], recounted [1], repeated [1], speak [1], state [1], took a census [1], utter [1], wait [1], were counted [1], write [1]

Ge 15: 5 [A] and said, "Look up at the heavens and **count** the stars—
15: 5 [A] and count the stars—if indeed you can **count** them."
16: 10 [C] your descendants that *they will be* too numerous *to* **count**."

Ge 24:66 [D] Then the servant **told** Isaac all he had done.
29:13 [D] him to his home, and there Jacob **told** him all these things.
32:12 [32:13] [C] the sand of the sea, which cannot **be counted**.' "
37:9 [D] Then he had another dream, and *he* **told** it to his brothers.
37:10 [D] When *he* **told** his father as well as his brothers, his father
40:8 [D] not interpretations belong to God? **Tell** me your dreams."
40:9 [D] So the chief cupbearer **told** Joseph his dream. He said to him,
41:8 [D] Pharaoh **told** them his dreams, but no one could interpret
41:12 [D] *We* **told** him our dreams, and he interpreted them for us,
41:49 [A] it was so much that he stopped **keeping records** because it
Ex 9:16 [D] and that my name *might be* **proclaimed** in all the earth.
10:2 [D] that *you may* **tell** your children and grandchildren how I
18:8 [D] **told** his father-in-law *about* everything the LORD had done to
24:3 [D] and **told** the people all the LORD's words and laws,
Lev 15:13 [A] *he is to* **count off** seven days for his ceremonial cleansing;
15:28 [A] cleansed from her discharge, *she must* **count off** seven days,
23:15 [A] the sheaf of the wave offering, **count off** seven full weeks.
23:16 [A] **Count off** fifty days up to the day after the seventh Sabbath,
25:8 [A] " '**Count off** seven sabbaths of years—seven times seven
Nu 13:27 [D] *They* **gave** Moses *this* **account**: "We went into the land to
Dt 16:9 [A] **Count off** seven weeks from the time you begin to put the
16:9 [A] you begin to put the sickle to the standing grain. **[RPH]**
Jos 2:23 [D] of Nun and **told** him everything that had happened to them.
Jdg 6:13 [D] Where are all his wonders that our fathers **told** us *about*
7:13 [D] Gideon arrived just as a man *was* **telling** a friend his dream.
1Sa 11:5 [D] Then *they* **repeated** to him what the men of Jabesh had said.
2Sa 24:10 [A] David was conscience-stricken after *he had* **counted** the
1Ki 3:8 [C] a great people, too numerous *to* **count** or number.
8:5 [C] and cattle that *they could* not **be recorded** or counted.
13:11 [D] and **told** him all that the man of God had done there that day.
13:11 [D] *They* also **told** their father what he had said to the king.
2Ki 8:4 [D] "**Tell** me *about* all the great things Elisha has done."
8:5 [D] Just as Gehazi was **telling** the king how Elisha had restored
8:6 [D] The king asked the woman about it, and *she* **told** him.
1Ch 16:24 [D] **Declare** his glory among the nations, his marvelous deeds
21:2 [A] "Go and **count** the Israelites from Beersheba to Dan.
23:3 [C] The Levites thirty years old or more **were counted**, and the
2Ch 2:2 [2:1] [A] He **conscripted** seventy thousand men as carriers
2:17 [2:16] [A] Solomon **took a census** *of* all the aliens who were in
2:17 [2:16] [A] after the **census** [+6222] his father David *had* **taken**;
5:6 [C] and cattle that *they could* not **be recorded** or counted.
Ezr 1:8 [A] *who* **counted** them **out** to Sheshbazzar the prince of Judah.
Est 5:11 [D] **boasted** to them *about* his vast wealth, his many sons, and all
6:13 [D] **told** Zeresh his wife and all his friends everything that had
Job 12:8 [D] and it will teach you, or *let* the fish of the sea **inform** you.
14:16 [A] Surely then *you will* **count** my steps but not keep track of my
15:17 [D] and I will explain to you; *let me* **tell** you what I have seen,
28:27 [D] then he looked at wisdom and **appraised** it; he confirmed it
31:4 [A] Does he not see my ways and **count** my every step?
37:20 [E] *Should* he **be told** that I want to speak? Would any man ask
38:37 [D] Who has the wisdom *to* **count** the clouds? Who can tip over
39:2 [A] *Do you* **count** the months till they bear? Do you know the
Ps 2:7 [D] *I will* **proclaim** the decree of the LORD: He said to me,
9:1 [9:2] [D] with all my heart; *I will* **tell** *of* all your wonders.
9:14 [9:15] [D] that *I may* **declare** your praises in the gates of the
19:1 [19:2] [D] The heavens **declare** the glory of God; the skies
22:17 [22:18] [D] *I can* **count** all my bones; people stare and gloat
22:22 [22:23] [D] *I will* **declare** your name to my brothers; in the
22:30 [22:31] [E] future generations *will* **be told** about the Lord.
26:7 [D] aloud your praise and **telling** *of* all your wonderful deeds.
40:5 [40:6] [D] and tell of them, they would be too many *to* **declare**.
44:1 [44:2] [D] our fathers *have* **told** us what you did in their days,
48:12 [48:13] [A] Walk about Zion, go around her, **count** her towers,
48:13 [48:14] [D] that *you may* **tell** of them to the next generation.
50:16 [D] "What right have you to **recite** my laws or take my covenant
56:8 [56:9] [A] **Record** my lament; list my tears on your scroll—are
59:12 [59:13] [D] in their pride. For the curses and lies *they* **utter**,
64:5 [64:6] [D] in evil plans, *they* **talk** *about* hiding their snares;
66:16 [D] you who fear God; *let me* **tell** you what he has done for me.
69:26 [69:27] [D] and **talk** about the pain of those you hurt.
71:15 [D] My mouth *will* **tell** *of* your righteousness, *of* your salvation
73:15 [D] If I had said, "*I will* **speak** thus," I would have betrayed your
73:28 [D] Sovereign LORD my refuge; I *will* **tell** *of* all your deeds.
75:1 [75:2] [D] Name is near; *men* **tell** *of* your wonderful deeds.
78:3 [D] we have heard and known, what our fathers *have* **told** us.
78:4 [D] we *will* **tell** the next generation the praiseworthy deeds of the
78:6 [D] yet to be born, and *they* in turn *would* **tell** their children.
79:13 [D] from generation to generation *we will* **recount** your praise.
87:6 [A] The LORD *will* **write** in the register of the peoples:
88:11 [88:12] [E] **Is** your love **declared** in the grave, your faithfulness
96:3 [D] **Declare** his glory among the nations, his marvelous deeds
102:21 [102:22] [D] So the name of the LORD *will be* **declared** in
107:22 [D] thank offerings and **tell** *of* his works with songs of joy.
118:17 [D] but live, and *will* **proclaim** what the LORD has done.
119:13 [D] With my lips *I* **recount** all the laws that come from your
119:26 [D] *I* **recounted** my ways and you answered me; teach me your
139:18 [A] *Were I to* **count** them, they would outnumber the grains of
145:6 [D] your awesome works, and *I will* **proclaim** your great deeds.
Isa 22:10 [A] *You* **counted** the buildings in Jerusalem and tore down
43:21 [D] the people I formed for myself *that they may* **proclaim** my
43:26 [D] argue the matter together; **state** the case for your innocence.
52:15 [E] For what they **were** not **told**, they will see, and what they
Jer 23:27 [D] They think the dreams *they* **tell** one another will make my
23:28 [D] *Let* the prophet who has a dream **tell** his dream, but let the
23:32 [D] "*They* **tell** them and lead my people astray with their
33:22 [C] *I will* **make** the descendants of David … and the Levites who minister before me as **countless** [+889+906+906+4202+8049]
51:10 [D] come, *let us* **tell** in Zion what the LORD our God has done.'
Eze 12:16 [D] so that in the nations where they go *they may* **acknowledge**
44:26 [A] After he is cleansed, *he must* **wait** seven days.
Hos 1:10 [2:1] [C] the seashore, which cannot be measured or **counted**.
Joel 1:3 [D] **Tell** it to your children, and let your children tell it to their
Hab 1:5 [E] your days that you would not believe, even if *you* **were told**.

6219 סֵ֫פֶר **sēper[1]**, n.m. [185 / 186] [→ 2191, 5031, 5032?, 5033, 6072, 6218, 6221, 6222, 6225, 6228, 6229, 6230, 7963; cf. 6220; Ar 10515]

book [104], scroll [23], letter [12], letters [10], deed [6], certificate [4], dispatches [4], scroll [+4479] [4], it[s] [+2021] [3], literature [2], written [2], *untranslated* [1], books [1], can read [+3359] [1], cannot read [+3359+4202] [1], deeds [1], documents [1], indictment [1], know how to read [+3359] [1], record [1], records [1], Scriptures [1], them[s] [1]

Ge 5:1 This is the **written** account of Adam's line. When God created
Ex 17:14 "Write this on a **scroll** as something to be remembered and make
24:7 Then he took the **Book** *of* the Covenant and read it to the people.
32:32 but if not, then blot me out of the **book** you have written."
32:33 "Whoever has sinned against me I will blot out of my **book**.
Nu 5:23 " 'The priest is to write these curses on a **scroll** and then wash them
21:14 That is why the **Book** *of* the Wars of the LORD says: "Waheb in
Dt 17:18 he is to write for himself on a **scroll** a copy of this law, taken from
24:1 he writes her a **certificate** *of* divorce, gives it to her and sends her
24:3 second husband dislikes her and writes her a **certificate** *of* divorce,
28:58 which are written in this **book**, and do not revere this glorious
28:61 kind of sickness and disaster not recorded in this **Book** *of* the Law,
29:20 [29:19] All the curses written in this **book** will fall upon him,
29:21 [29:20] curses of the covenant written in this **Book** *of* the Law.
29:27 [29:26] so that he brought on it all the curses written in this **book**.
30:10 his commands and decrees that are written in this **Book** *of* the Law
31:24 After Moses finished writing in a **book** the words of this law from
31:26 "Take this **Book** *of* the Law and place it beside the ark of the
Jos 1:8 Do not let this **Book** *of* the Law depart from your mouth; meditate
8:31 He built it according to what is written in the **Book** *of* the Law of
8:34 and the curses—just as it is written in the **Book** *of* the Law.
10:13 avenged itself on its enemies, as it is written in the **Book** *of* Jashar.
18:9 They wrote its description on a **scroll**, town by town, in seven
23:6 be careful to obey all that is written in the **Book** *of* the Law of
24:26 And Joshua recorded these things in the **Book** *of* the Law of God.
1Sa 10:25 He wrote them down on a **scroll** and deposited it before the
2Sa 1:18 taught this lament of the bow (it is written in the **Book** *of* Jashar):
11:14 In the morning David wrote a **letter** to Joab and sent it with Uriah.
11:15 In **it**[s] [+2021] he wrote, "Put Uriah in the front line where the
1Ki 11:41 are they not written in the **book** *of* the annals of Solomon?
14:19 are written in the **book** *of* the annals of the kings of Israel.
14:29 are they not written in the **book** *of* the annals of the kings of
15:7 are they not written in the **book** *of* the annals of the kings of
15:23 are they not written in the **book** *of* the annals of the kings of
15:31 are they not written in the **book** *of* the annals of the kings of Israel?
16:5 are they not written in the **book** *of* the annals of the kings of Israel?
16:14 are they not written in the **book** *of* the annals of the kings of Israel?
16:20 are they not written in the **book** *of* the annals of the kings of Israel?
16:27 are they not written in the **book** *of* the annals of the kings of Israel?
21:8 So she wrote **letters** in Ahab's name, placed his seal on them,
21:8 sent **them**[s] to the elders and nobles who lived in Naboth's city
21:9 In those **letters** she wrote: "Proclaim a day of fasting and seat
21:11 city did as Jezebel directed in the **letters** she had written to them.
22:39 are they not written in the **book** *of* the annals of the kings of Israel?
22:45 [22:46] are they not written in the **book** *of* the annals of the kings
2Ki 1:18 are they not written in the **book** *of* the annals of the kings of Israel?
5:5 "I will send a **letter** to the king of Israel." So Naaman left,
5:6 The **letter** that he took to the king of Israel read: "With this letter I
5:6 "With this **letter** I am sending my servant Naaman to you
5:7 As soon as the king of Israel read the **letter**, he tore his robes
8:23 are they not written in the **book** *of* the annals of the kings of
10:1 So Jehu wrote **letters** and sent them to Samaria: to the officials of
10:2 "As soon as this **letter** reaches you, since your master's sons are
10:6 Jehu wrote them a second **letter**, saying, "If you are on my side

2Ki 10: 7 When the **letter** arrived, these men took the princes and
10: 34 are they not written in the **book** *of* the annals of the kings of Israel?
12: 19 [12:20] are they not written in the **book** *of* the annals of the kings
13: 8 are they not written in the **book** *of* the annals of the kings of Israel?
13: 12 are they not written in the **book** *of* the annals of the kings of Israel?
14: 6 in accordance with what is written in the **Book** *of* the Law of
14: 15 are they not written in the **book** *of* the annals of the kings of Israel?
14: 18 are they not written in the **book** *of* the annals of the kings of
14: 28 are they not written in the **book** *of* the annals of the kings of Israel?
15: 6 are they not written in the **book** *of* the annals of the kings of
15: 11 The other events of Zechariah's reign are written in the **book** *of* the
15: 15 are written in the **book** *of* the annals of the kings of Israel.
15: 21 are they not written in the **book** *of* the annals of the kings of Israel?
15: 26 are written in the **book** *of* the annals of the kings of Israel.
15: 31 are they not written in the **book** *of* the annals of the kings of Israel?
15: 36 are they not written in the **book** *of* the annals of the kings of
16: 19 are they not written in the **book** *of* the annals of the kings of
19: 14 Hezekiah received the **letter** from the messengers and read it.
20: 12 son of Baladan king of Babylon sent Hezekiah **letters**
20: 20 are they not written in the **book** *of* the annals of the kings of
21: 17 are they not written in the **book** *of* the annals of the kings of
21: 25 are they not written in the **book** *of* the annals of the kings of
22: 8 "I have found the **Book** *of* the Law in the temple of the LORD."
22: 8 of the LORD." He gave **it**[s] [+2021] to Shaphan, who read it.
22: 10 informed the king, "Hilkiah the priest has given me a **book**."
22: 11 When the king heard the words of the **Book** *of* the Law, he tore his
22: 13 for all Judah about what is written in this **book** that has been
22: 13 because our fathers have not obeyed the words of this **book**;
22: 16 according to everything written in the **book** the king of Judah has
23: 2 He read in their hearing all the words of the **Book** *of* the Covenant,
23: 3 thus confirming the words of the covenant written in this **book**.
23: 21 LORD your God, as it is written in this **Book** *of* the Covenant."
23: 24 **book** that Hilkiah the priest had discovered in the temple of the
23: 28 are they not written in the **book** *of* the annals of the kings of
24: 5 are they not written in the **book** *of* the annals of the kings of
1Ch 9: 1 All Israel was listed in the genealogies recorded in the **book** *of* the
27: 24 the number was not entered in the **book** [BHS 5031] *of* the annals
2Ch 16: 11 to end, are written in the **book** *of* the kings of Judah and Israel.
17: 9 taking with them the **Book** *of* the Law of the LORD;
20: 34 of Hanani, which are recorded in the **book** *of* the kings of Israel.
24: 27 of God are written in the annotations on the **book** *of* the kings.
25: 4 in the Law, in the **Book** *of* Moses, where the LORD commanded:
25: 26 are they not written in the **book** *of* the kings of Judah and Israel?
27: 7 he did, are written in the **book** *of* the kings of Israel and Judah.
28: 26 to end, are written in the **book** *of* the kings of Judah and Israel.
32: 17 The king also wrote **letters** insulting the LORD, the God of
32: 32 the prophet Isaiah son of Amoz in the **book** *of* the kings of Judah
34: 14 Hilkiah the priest found the **Book** *of* the Law of the LORD that
34: 15 "I have found the **Book** *of* the Law in the temple of the LORD."
34: 15 in the temple of the LORD." He gave **it**[s] [+2021] to Shaphan.
34: 16 Then Shaphan took the **book** to the king and reported to him:
34: 18 informed the king, "Hilkiah the priest has given me a **book**."
34: 21 and Judah about what is written in this **book** that has been found.
34: 21 have not acted in accordance with all that is written in this **book**."
34: 24 all the curses written in the **book** that has been read in the presence
34: 30 He read in their hearing all the words of the **Book** *of* the Covenant,
34: 31 and to obey the words of the covenant written in this **book**.
35: 12 people to offer to the LORD, as is written in the **Book** *of* Moses.
35: 27 to end, are written in the **book** *of* the kings of Israel and Judah.
36: 8 are written in the **book** *of* the kings of Israel and Judah.
Ne 7: 5 I found the genealogical **record** *of* those who had been the first to
8: 1 They told Ezra the scribe to bring out the **Book** *of* the Law of
8: 3 And all the people listened attentively to the **Book** *of* the Law.
8: 5 Ezra opened the **book**. All the people could see him because he
8: 8 They read from the **Book** of the Law of God, making it clear
8: 18 first day to the last, Ezra read from the **Book** *of* the Law of God.
9: 3 read from the **Book** *of* the Law of the LORD their God for a
12: 23 of Johanan son of Eliashib were recorded in the **book** *of* the annals.
13: 1 On that day the **Book** *of* Moses was read aloud in the hearing of
Est 1: 22 He sent **dispatches** to all parts of the kingdom, to each province in
2: 23 All this was recorded in the **book** *of* the annals in the presence of
3: 13 **Dispatches** were sent by couriers to all the king's provinces with
6: 1 so he ordered the **book** *of* the chronicles, the record of his reign,
8: 5 let an order be written overruling the **dispatches** that Haman son of
8: 10 sealed the **dispatches** with the king's signet ring, and sent them by
9: 20 he sent **letters** to all the Jews throughout the provinces of King
9: 25 he issued **written** orders that the evil scheme Haman had devised
9: 30 Mordecai sent **letters** to all the Jews in the 127 provinces of the
9: 32 regulations about Purim, and it was written down in the **records**.
10: 2 are they not written in the **book** *of* the annals of the kings of Media
Job 19: 23 that my words were recorded, that they were written on a **scroll**,
31: 35 Almighty answer me; let my accuser put his **indictment** in writing.
Ps 40: 7 [40:8] I have come—it is written about me in the **scroll** [+4479].
69: 28 [69:29] May they be blotted out of the **book** *of* life and not be
139: 16 All the days ordained for me were written in your **book** before one
Ecc 12: 12 Of making many **books** there is no end, and much study wearies
Isa 29: 11 For you this whole vision is nothing but words sealed in a **scroll**.
29: 11 And if you give the scroll to *someone who* **can read** [+3359],
29: 12 Or if you give the **scroll** to someone who cannot read, and say,
29: 12 if you give the scroll to someone *who* **cannot read** [+3359+4202],
29: 12 please," he will answer, "*I* don't **know how to read** [+3359]."
29: 18 In that day the deaf will hear the words of the **scroll**, and out of
30: 8 Go now, write it on a tablet for them, inscribe it on a **scroll**,
34: 4 of the heavens will be dissolved and the sky rolled up like a **scroll**;
34: 16 Look in the **scroll** *of* the LORD and read: None of these will be
37: 14 Hezekiah received the **letter** from the messengers and read it.
39: 1 son of Baladan king of Babylon sent Hezekiah **letters**
50: 1 "Where is your mother's **certificate** *of* divorce with which I sent
Jer 3: 8 I gave faithless Israel her **certificate** *of* divorce and sent her away
25: 13 all that are written in this **book** and prophesied by Jeremiah against
29: 1 This is the text of the **letter** that the prophet Jeremiah sent from
29: 25 You sent **letters** in your own name to all the people in Jerusalem,
29: 29 the priest, however, read the **letter** to Jeremiah the prophet.
30: 2 says: 'Write in a **book** all the words I have spoken to you.
32: 10 I signed and sealed the **deed**, had it witnessed, and weighed out the
32: 11 I took the **deed** *of* purchase—the sealed copy containing the terms
32: 12 and I gave this **deed** to Baruch son of Neriah, the son of Mahseiah,
32: 12 my cousin Hanamel and of the witnesses who had signed the **deed**
32: 14 Take these **documents**, both the sealed and unsealed copies of the
32: 14 the sealed and **[RPH]** unsealed copies of the deed of purchase,
32: 14 both the sealed and unsealed copies of the **deed** *of* purchase,
32: 16 "After I had given the **deed** *of* purchase to Baruch son of Neriah,
32: 44 **deeds** will be signed, sealed and witnessed in the territory of
36: 2 "Take a **scroll** [+4479] and write on it all the words I have spoken
36: 4 had spoken to him, Baruch wrote them on the **scroll** [+4479].
36: 8 LORD's temple he read the words of the LORD from the **scroll**.
36: 10 at the LORD's temple the words of Jeremiah from the **scroll**.
36: 11 son of Shaphan, heard all the words of the LORD from the **scroll**,
36: 13 everything he had heard Baruch read to the people from the **scroll**,
36: 18 all these words to me, and I wrote them in ink on the **scroll**."
36: 32 Baruch wrote on it all the words of the **scroll** that Jehoiakim king
45: 1 after Baruch had written on a **scroll** the words Jeremiah was
51: 60 Jeremiah had written on a **scroll** about all the disasters that would
51: 63 When you finish reading this **scroll**, tie a stone to it and throw it
Eze 2: 9 and I saw a hand stretched out to me. In it was a **scroll** [+4479],
Da 1: 4 was to teach them the language and **literature** *of* the Babylonians.
1: 17 and understanding of all kinds of **literature** and learning.
9: 2 first year of his reign, I, Daniel, understood from the **Scriptures**,
12: 1 everyone whose name is found written in the **book**—will be
12: 4 close up and seal the words of the **scroll** until the time of the end.
Na 1: 1 The **book** *of* the vision of Nahum the Elkoshite.
Mal 3: 16 A **scroll** *of* remembrance was written in his presence concerning

6220 ²סֵ֫פֶר ***sēper²***, n.m. Not used in NIV/BHS [cf. 6219]

6221 סֹפֵר ***sōpēr***, n.m. [56] [√ 6219; Ar 10516]

secretary [28], scribe [11], secretaries [4], scribes [2], teacher [2], writing [2], chief officer [1], commander's [1], man learned [1], officer in charge [1], scribe's [1], secretary's [1], writer [1]

Jdg 5: 14 came down, from Zebulun those who bear a **commander's** staff.
2Sa 8: 17 Ahimelech son of Abiathar were priests; Seraiah was **secretary**;
20: 25 Sheva was **secretary**; Zadok and Abiathar were priests;
1Ki 4: 3 Elihoreph and Ahijah, sons of Shisha—**secretaries**;
2Ki 12: 10 [12:11] the royal **secretary** and the high priest came, counted the
18: 18 son of Hilkiah the palace administrator, Shebna the **secretary**,
18: 37 Shebna the **secretary** and Joah son of Asaph the recorder went to
19: 2 Shebna the **secretary** and the leading priests, all wearing
22: 3 King Josiah sent the **secretary**, Shaphan son of Azaliah, the son of
22: 8 Hilkiah the high priest said to Shaphan the **secretary**, "I have
22: 9 Then Shaphan the **secretary** went to the king and reported to him:
22: 10 Shaphan the **secretary** informed the king, "Hilkiah the priest has
22: 12 Shaphan the **secretary** and Asaiah the king's attendant:
25: 19 He also took the **secretary** who was chief officer in charge of
1Ch 2: 55 and the clans of **scribes** who lived at Jabez: the Tirathites,
18: 16 Ahimelech son of Abiathar were priests; Shavsha was **secretary**;
24: 6 The **scribe** Shemaiah son of Nethanel, a Levite, recorded their
27: 32 David's uncle, was a counselor, a man of insight and a **scribe**.
2Ch 24: 11 the royal **secretary** and the officer of the chief priest would come
26: 11 according to their numbers as mustered by Jeiel the **secretary**
34: 13 Some of the Levites were **secretaries**, scribes and doorkeepers.
34: 15 Hilkiah said to Shaphan the **secretary**, "I have found the Book of
34: 18 Shaphan the **secretary** informed the king, "Hilkiah the priest has
34: 20 of Micah, Shaphan the **secretary** and Asaiah the king's attendant:
Ezr 7: 6 He was a **teacher** well versed in the Law of Moses,
7: 11 the letter King Artaxerxes had given to Ezra the priest and **teacher**,
7: 11 a **man learned** *in* matters concerning the commands and decrees
Ne 8: 1 They told Ezra the **scribe** to bring out the Book of the Law of

Ne 8: 4 Ezra the **scribe** stood on a high wooden platform built for the
8: 9 Nehemiah the governor, Ezra the priest and **scribe**, and the Levites
8: 13 gathered around Ezra the **scribe** to give attention to the words of
12: 26 days of Nehemiah the governor and of Ezra the priest and **scribe**.
12: 36 David the man of God. Ezra the **scribe** led the procession.
13: 13 I put Shelemiah the priest, Zadok the **scribe**, and a Levite named
Est 3: 12 on the thirteenth day of the first month the royal **secretaries** were
8: 9 At once the royal **secretaries** were summoned—
Ps 45: 1 [45:2] for the king; my tongue is the pen of a skillful **writer**.
Isa 33: 18 "Where is that **chief officer**? Where is the one who took the
33: 18 took the revenue? Where is the **officer in charge** *of* the towers?"
36: 3 son of Hilkiah the palace administrator, Shebna the **secretary**,
36: 22 son of Hilkiah the palace administrator, Shebna the **secretary**,
37: 2 Shebna the **secretary**, and the leading priests, all wearing
Jer 8: 8 when actually the lying pen of the **scribes** has handled it falsely?
36: 10 From the room of Gemariah son of Shaphan the **secretary**,
36: 12 he went down to the **secretary's** room in the royal palace,
36: 12 Elishama the **secretary**, Delaiah son of Shemaiah, Elnathan son of
36: 20 After they put the scroll in the room of Elishama the **secretary**,
36: 21 and Jehudi brought it from the room of Elishama the **secretary**
36: 23 the king cut them off with a **scribe's** knife and threw them into the
36: 26 of Azriel and Shelemiah son of Abdeel to arrest Baruch the **scribe**
36: 32 took another scroll and gave it to the **scribe** Baruch son of Neriah,
37: 15 him beaten and imprisoned in the house of Jonathan the **secretary**,
37: 20 Do not send me back to the house of Jonathan the **secretary**,
52: 25 He also took the **secretary** who was chief officer in charge of
Eze 9: 2 With them was a man clothed in linen who had a **writing** kit at his
9: 3 the LORD called to the man clothed in linen who had the **writing**

6222 ¹סְפָר *s^epār¹*, n.[m.]. [1] [√ 6219]

census taken [+6218] [1]

2Ch 2: 17 [2:16] after the **census** his father David *had* **taken** [+6218];

6223 ²סְפָר *s^epār²*, n.pr.loc. [1] [cf. 9184]

Sephar [1]

Ge 10: 30 The region where they lived stretched from Mesha toward **Sephar**,

6224 סְפָרַד *s^epārad*, n.pr.loc. [1]

Sepharad [1]

Ob 1: 20 the exiles from Jerusalem who are in **Sepharad** will possess the

6225 סִפְרָה *siprâ*, n.f. [1] [√ 6219]

record [1]

Ps 56: 8 [56:9] list my tears on your scroll—are they not in your **record**?

6226 סְפַרְוַיִם *s^eparwayim*, n.pr.loc. [6] [→ 6227]

Sepharvaim [6]

2Ki 17: 24 Hamath and **Sepharvaim** and settled them in the towns of Samaria
17: 31 to Adrammelech and Anammelech, the gods of **Sepharvaim**.
18: 34 and Arpad? Where are the gods of **Sepharvaim**, Hena and Ivvah?
19: 13 the king of the city of **Sepharvaim**, or of Hena or Ivvah?"
Isa 36: 19 gods of Hamath and Arpad? Where are the gods of **Sepharvaim**?
37: 13 the king of the city of **Sepharvaim**, or of Hena or Ivvah?"

6227 סְפַרְוִים *s^eparwîm*, a.g. [1] [√ 6226]

Sepharvites [1]

2Ki 17: 31 the **Sepharvites** burned their children in the fire as sacrifices to

6228 סְפֹרוֹת *s^epōrôt*, n.f. [1] [√ 6219]

measure [1]

Ps 71: 15 of your salvation all day long, though I know not its **measure**.

6229 סֹפְרִים *sōp^erîm*, n.[m.pl.] *or* v.ptcp. Not used in NIV/BHS [√ 6219]

6230 סֹפֶרֶת *sōperet*, n.pr.m. Not used in NIV/BHS [√ 6219]

6231 סֶפֶת *sepet*, v. Not used in NIV/BHS [√ 3578]

6232 סָקַל *sāqal*, v. [22]

stone [5], be stoned [2], been stoned [2], must be stoned to death [+6232] [2], stone [+74+928+2021] [2], surely be stoned [+6232] [2], cleared of stones [1], pelted [1], remove [1], stoned [+74+906+928 +2021] [1], stoned [+74+928+2021] [1], stoning [1], throwing [1]

Ex 8: 26 [8:22] [A] are detestable in their eyes, *will they* not **stone** us?
17: 4 [A] do with these people? *They are* almost *ready to* **stone** me."
19: 13 [C] *He shall* **surely be stoned** [+6232] or shot with arrows; not a
19: 13 [A] *He shall* **surely be stoned** [+6232] or shot with arrows; not a
21: 28 [C] a woman to death, the bull **must be stoned** [+6232] **to death**,
21: 28 [A] a woman to death, the bull **must be stoned to death** [+6232],
21: 29 [C] the bull *must* **be stoned** and the owner also must be put to
21: 32 [C] silver to the master of the slave, and the bull *must* **be stoned**.
Dt 13: 10 [13:11] [A] **Stone** him to death, because he tried to turn you
17: 5 [A] city gate and **stone** [+74+928+2021] that person to death.
22: 21 [A] there the men of her town *shall* **stone** [+74+928+2021] her to
22: 24 [A] **stone** them to death—the girl because she was in a town and
Jos 7: 25 [A] and after *they had* **stoned** [+74+906+928+2021] the rest,
1Sa 30: 6 [A] because the men were talking of **stoning** him;
2Sa 16: 6 [D] *He* **pelted** David and all the king's officials with stones,
16: 13 [D] cursing as he went and **throwing** stones at him
1Ki 21: 10 [A] and the king. Then take him out and **stone** him to death."
21: 13 [A] outside the city and **stoned** [+74+928+2021] him to death.
21: 14 [E] sent word to Jezebel: "Naboth *has* **been stoned** and is dead."
21: 15 [E] As soon as Jezebel heard that Naboth *had* **been stoned** to
Isa 5: 2 [D] He dug it up and **cleared** it **of stones** and planted it with the
62: 10 [D] Build up, build up the highway! **Remove** the stones. Raise a

6233 סָר *sār*, n.m. [1] [√ 6254; cf. 8606]

captain [1]

1Sa 22: 14 **captain** of your bodyguard and highly respected in your

6234 סַר *sar*, a. [3] [√ 6253]

sullen [3]

1Ki 20: 43 **Sullen** and angry, the king of Israel went to his palace in Samaria.
21: 4 **sullen** and angry because Naboth the Jezreelite had said,
21: 5 His wife Jezebel came in and asked him, "Why are you so **sullen**?

6235 סָרָב *sārāb*, n.m. [1]

briers [1]

Eze 2: 6 though **briers** and thorns are all around you and you live among

6236 סַרְגוֹן *sargôn*, n.pr.m. [1]

Sargon [1]

Isa 20: 1 sent by **Sargon** king of Assyria, came to Ashdod and attacked

6237 סֶרֶד *sered*, n.pr.m. [2] [→ 6238]

Sered [2]

Ge 46: 14 The sons of Zebulun: **Sered**, Elon and Jahleel.
Nu 26: 26 through **Sered**, the Seredite clan; through Elon, the Elonite clan;

6238 סַרְדִּי *sardî*, a.g. [1] [√ 6237]

Seredite [1]

Nu 26: 26 through Sered, the **Seredite** clan; through Elon, the Elonite clan;

6239 ¹סָרָה *sārâ¹*, n.f. [1] [√ 6073]

unceasing [+1194] [1]

Isa 14: 6 which in anger struck down peoples with **unceasing** [+1194]

6240 ²סָרָה *sārâ²*, n.f. [7] [√ 6253]

rebellion [4], crime [1], revolt [1], revolted against [1]

Dt 13: 5 [13:6] because he preached **rebellion** against the LORD your
19: 16 If a malicious witness takes the stand to accuse a man of a **crime**,
Isa 1: 5 Why do you persist in **rebellion**? Your whole head is injured,
31: 6 Return to him you have so greatly **revolted against**, O Israelites.
59: 13 turning our backs on our God, fomenting oppression and **revolt**,
Jer 28: 16 because you have preached **rebellion** against the LORD.' "
29: 32 the LORD, because he has preached **rebellion** against me.' "

6241 סִרָה *sirâ*, n.pr.[loc.]. [1] [→ 1015; cf. 6106]

Sirah [1]

2Sa 3: 26 after Abner, and they brought him back from the well of **Sirah**.

6242 סָרוּחַ *sārûah*, a. *or* v.ptcp. [2] [√ 6243]

flowing [1], lounging [1]

Eze 23: 15 with belts around their waists and **flowing** turbans on their heads;
Am 6: 7 the first to go into exile; your feasting and **lounging** will end.

6243 ¹סָרַח *sārah¹*, v. [4] [→ 6242, 6245; cf. 8580]

hang down [1], hang [1], lounge [1], spreading [1]

Ex 26: 12 [A] the half curtain that is left over *is to* **hang down** at the rear of
26: 13 [B] what is left *will* **hang** over the sides of the tabernacle so as to
Eze 17: 6 [A] it sprouted and became a low, **spreading** vine. Its branches
Am 6: 4 [B] lie on beds inlaid with ivory and **lounge** on your couches.

6244 ²סָרַח **sāraḥ²**, v. [1]

decayed [1]

Jer 49: 7 [C] perished from the prudent? *Has* their wisdom **decayed**?

6245 סֶרַח **seraḥ**, n.m. [1] [√ 6243]

length [1]

Ex 26:12 As for the additional **length** of the tent curtains, the half curtain

6246 סִרְיוֹן **siryôn**, n.[m.]. [2] [cf. 8590, 9234]

armor [2]

Jer 46: 4 positions with helmets on! Polish your spears, put on your **armor**!
51: 3 Let not the archer string his bow, nor let him put on his **armor**.

6247 סָרִיס **sārîs**, n.m. [45] [→ 8060]

eunuchs [10], official [9], officials [9], officer [5], court officials [4], eunuch [4], officers [2], attendants [1], palace officials [1]

Ge 37:36 to Potiphar, *one of* Pharaoh's **officials**, the captain of the guard.
39: 1 Potiphar, an Egyptian who was one of Pharaoh's **officials**,
40: 2 Pharaoh was angry with his two **officials**, the chief cupbearer
40: 7 So he asked Pharaoh's **officials** who were in custody with him in
1Sa 8:15 and of your vintage and give it to his **officials** and attendants.
1Ki 22: 9 So the king of Israel called one of his **officials** and said,
2Ki 8: 6 he assigned an **official** to her case and said to him, "Give back
9:32 is on my side? Who?" Two or three **eunuchs** looked down at him.
18:17 his chief **officer** and his field commander with a large army,
20:18 they will become **eunuchs** in the palace of the king of Babylon."
23:11 They were in the court near the room of an **official** named
24:12 his attendants, his nobles and his **officials** all surrendered to him.
24:15 his wives, his **officials** and the leading men of the land.
25:19 he took the **officer** in charge of the fighting men and five royal
1Ch 28: 1 to the king and his sons, together with the **palace officials**,
2Ch 18: 8 So the king of Israel called one of his **officials** and said,
Est 1:10 from wine, he commanded the seven **eunuchs** who served him—
1:12 when the **attendants** delivered the king's command, Queen Vashti
1:15 has not obeyed the command of King Xerxes that the **eunuchs**
2: 3 care of Hegai, the king's **eunuch**, who is in charge of the women;
2:14 the king's **eunuch** who was in charge of the concubines.
2:15 the king's **eunuch** who was in charge of the harem, suggested.
2:21 and Teresh, two of the king's **officers** who guarded the doorway,
4: 4 When Esther's maids and **eunuchs** came and told her about
4: 5 one of the king's **eunuchs** assigned to attend her,
6: 2 and Teresh, two of the king's **officers** who guarded the doorway,
6:14 the king's **eunuchs** arrived and hurried Haman away to the
7: 9 Then Harbona, one of the **eunuchs** attending the king, said,
Isa 39: 7 they will become **eunuchs** in the palace of the king of Babylon."
56: 3 And let not any **eunuch** complain, "I am only a dry tree."
56: 4 "To the **eunuchs** who keep my Sabbaths, who choose what pleases
Jer 29: 2 the **court officials** and the leaders of Judah and Jerusalem,
34:19 the **court officials**, the priests and all the people of the land who
38: 7 But Ebed-Melech, a Cushite, an **official** in the royal palace,
39: 3 Nergal-Sharezer of Samgar, Nebo-Sarsekim a chief **officer**,
39:13 Nebushazban a chief **officer**, Nergal-Sharezer a high official
41:16 women, children and **court officials** he had brought from Gibeon.
52:25 still in the city, he took the **officer** in charge of the fighting men,
Da 1: 3 Then the king ordered Ashpenaz, chief of his **court officials**,
1: 7 The chief **official** gave them new names: to Daniel, the name
1: 8 he asked the chief **official** for permission not to defile himself this
1: 9 Now God had caused the **official** to show favor and sympathy to
1:10 but the **official** told Daniel, "I am afraid of my lord the king,
1:11 said to the guard whom the chief **official** had appointed over
1:18 them in, the chief **official** presented them to Nebuchadnezzar.

6248 ¹סֶרֶן **seren¹**, n.[m.]. [1]

axles [1]

1Ki 7:30 Each stand had four bronze wheels with bronze **axles**, and each

6249 ²סֶרֶן **seren²**, n.m. [21]

rulers [21]

Jos 13: 3 as Canaanite (the territory of the five Philistine **rulers** *in* Gaza,
Jdg 3: 3 the five **rulers** *of* the Philistines, all the Canaanites, the Sidonians,
16: 5 The **rulers** *of* the Philistines went to her and said, "See if you can
16: 8 the **rulers** *of* the Philistines brought her seven fresh thongs that had
16:18 she sent word to the **rulers** *of* the Philistines, "Come back once
16:18 So the **rulers** *of* the Philistines returned with the silver in their
16:23 Now the **rulers** *of* the Philistines assembled to offer a great
16:27 all the **rulers** *of* the Philistines were there, and on the roof were
16:30 and down came the temple on the **rulers** and all the people in it.
1Sa 5: 8 So they called together all the **rulers** *of* the Philistines and asked
5:11 So they called together all the **rulers** *of* the Philistines and said,
6: 4 and five gold rats, according to the number of the Philistine **rulers**,
6: 4 because the same plague has struck both you and your **rulers**.
6:12 The **rulers** *of* the Philistines followed them as far as the border of
6:16 The five **rulers** *of* the Philistines saw all this and then returned that
6:18 to the number of Philistine towns belonging to the five **rulers**—
7: 7 at Mizpah, the **rulers** *of* the Philistines came up to attack them.
29: 2 As the Philistine **rulers** marched with their units of hundreds
29: 6 I have found no fault in you, but the **rulers** don't approve of you.
29: 7 and go in peace; do nothing to displease the Philistine **rulers**."
1Ch 12:19 [12:20] after consultation, their **rulers** sent him away.

6250 סַרְעַפָּה **sar'appâ**, n.f. [1] [√ 6187]

boughs [1]

Eze 31: 5 its **boughs** increased and its branches grew long, spreading

6251 סָרַף **sārap**, v. [1] [cf. 8596]

burn [1]

Am 6:10 [D] if a relative *who is to* **burn** the bodies comes to carry them

6252 סִרְפָּד **sirpād**, n.[m.]. [1] [√ 6199?]

briers [1]

Isa 55:13 will grow the pine tree, and instead of **briers** the myrtle will grow.

6253 ¹סָרַר **sārar¹** v. [17] [→ 6234, 6240; cf. 6254]

stubborn [6], rebellious [4], obstinate [2], stubbornly [2], defiant [1], hardened rebels [+6073] [1], rebels [1]

Dt 21:18 [A] If a man has a **stubborn** and rebellious son who does not
21:20 [A] to the elders, "This son of ours *is* **stubborn** and rebellious.
Ne 9:29 [A] **Stubbornly** they turned their backs on you, became
Ps 66: 7 [A] watch the nations—let not the **rebellious** rise up against him.
68: 6 [68:7] [A] but the **rebellious** live in a sun-scorched land.
68:18 [68:19] [A] received gifts from men, even from the **rebellious**—
78: 8 [A] a **stubborn** and rebellious generation, whose hearts were not
Pr 7:11 [A] (She is loud and **defiant**, her feet never stay at home;
Isa 1:23 [A] Your rulers *are* **rebels**, companions of thieves; they all love
30: 1 [A] "Woe to the **obstinate** children," declares the LORD,
65: 2 [A] All day long I have held out my hands to an **obstinate**
Jer 5:23 [A] these people have **stubborn** and rebellious hearts; they have
6:28 [A] They are all **hardened rebels** [+6073], going about to
Hos 4:16 [A] The Israelites *are* **stubborn**, like a stubborn heifer. How
4:16 [A] The Israelites are stubborn, like a **stubborn** heifer. How
9:15 [A] I will no longer love them; all their leaders *are* **rebellious**.
Zec 7:11 [A] **stubbornly** they turned their backs and stopped up their ears.

6254 ²סָרַר **sārar²**, v.den. [1] [→ 6233; cf. 6253, 8569, 8606]

in charge [1]

1Ch 15:22 [A] Kenaniah the head Levite *was* **in charge** of the singing; that

6255 סְתָו **s^e^tāw**, n.m. [1] [cf. 6257]

winter [1]

SS 2:11 The **winter** [Q 6257] is past; the rains are over and gone.

6256 סְתוּר **s^e^tûr**, n.pr.m. [1] [√ 6259]

Sethur [1]

Nu 13:13 from the tribe of Asher, **Sethur** son of Michael;

6257 סְתָיו **s^e^tāyw**, n.m. [0] [cf. 6255]

SS 2:11 [The **winter** [Q; see K 6255] is past; the rains are over and gone.]

6258 סָתַם **sātam**, v. [12] [cf. 8608]

stopped up [3], blocked [2], being closed [1], blocking off [1], close up [1], closed up [1], inmost place [1], seal up [1], stop up [1]

Ge 26:15 [D] the Philistines **stopped up**, filling them with earth.
26:18 [D] which the Philistines *had* **stopped up** after Abraham died,
2Ki 3:19 [A] You will cut down every good tree, **stop up** all the springs,
3:25 [A] *They* **stopped up** all the springs and cut down every good
2Ch 32: 3 [A] military staff about **blocking off** the water from the springs
32: 4 [A] *they* **blocked** all the springs and the stream that flowed
32:30 [A] It was Hezekiah *who* **blocked** the upper outlet of the Gihon
Ne 4: 7 [4:1] [C] had gone ahead and that the gaps *were* **being closed**,
Ps 51: 6 [51:8] [B] you teach me wisdom in the **inmost place**.
Da 8:26 [A] but **seal up** the vision, for it concerns the distant future."
12: 4 [A] **close up** and seal the words of the scroll until the time of the
12: 9 [B] because the words *are* **closed up** and sealed until the time of

6259 סָתַר ***sātar***, v. [82] [→ 5039, 5040, 5041, 6256, 6260, 6261; Ar 10519]

hide [35], hidden [10], hid [9], hiding [4], certainly hide [+6259] [2], conceal [2], concealed [2], is hidden [2], secret [2], are hidden [1], away [1], be sheltered [1], covers [1], go into hiding [1], have no [+4946+6524] [1], hide yourself [1], hides himself [1], hides [1], hiding place [1], take refuge [1], takes refuge [1], undetected [1], vanish [1]

Ge 4:14 [C] me from the land, and *I will be* **hidden** from your presence;
31:49 [C] between you and me when *we are* **away** from each other.
Ex 3:6 [G] At this, Moses **hid** his face, because he was afraid to look at
Nu 5:13 [C] her impurity *is* **undetected** (since there is no witness against
Dt 7:20 [C] until even the survivors who **hide** from you have perished.
29:29 [29:28] [C] The **secret** *things* belong to the LORD our God,
31:17 [G] *I will* **hide** my face from them, and they will be destroyed.
31:18 [G] I *will* **certainly hide** [+6259] my face on that day because of
31:18 [G] I *will* **certainly hide** [+6259] my face on that day because of
32:20 [G] "*I will* **hide** my face from them," he said, "and see what their
1Sa 20:2 [G] in me. Why *would* he **hide** this from me? It's not so!"
20:5 [C] **hide** in the field until the evening of the day after tomorrow.
20:19 [C] go to the place where *you* **hid** when this trouble began,
20:24 [C] So David **hid** in the field, and when the New Moon festival
23:19 [F] "*Is* not David **hiding** among us in the strongholds at Horesh,
26:1 [F] and said, "*Is* not David **hiding** on the hill of Hakilah,
1Ki 17:3 [C] "Leave here, turn eastward and **hide** in the Kerith Ravine,
2Ki 11:2 [G] and his nurse in a bedroom *to* **hide** him from Athaliah;
2Ch 22:11 [G] *she* **hid** the child from Athaliah so she could not kill him.
Job 3:10 [G] for it did not shut the doors of the womb on me *to* **hide**
3:23 [C] Why is life given to a man whose way *is* **hidden**, whom God
13:20 [C] these two things, O God, and then *I will* not **hide** from you:
13:24 [G] Why *do you* **hide** your face and consider me your enemy?
14:13 [G] me in the grave and **conceal** me till your anger has passed!
28:21 [C] every living thing, **concealed** even from the birds of the air.
34:22 [C] is no dark place, no deep shadow, where evildoers *can* **hide**.
34:29 [G] If *he* **hides** his face, who can see him? Yet he is over man
Ps 10:11 [G] "God has forgotten; *he* **covers** his face and never sees."
13:1 [13:2] [G] How long *will you* **hide** your face from me?
17:8 [G] the apple of your eye; **hide** me in the shadow of your wings
19:6 [19:7] [C] circuit to the other; nothing **is hidden** from its heat.
19:12 [19:13] [C] can discern his errors? Forgive my **hidden** *faults*.
22:24 [22:25] [G] *he has* not **hidden** his face from him but has
27:5 [G] *he will* **hide** me in the shelter of his tabernacle and set me
27:9 [G] *Do* not **hide** your face from me, do not turn your servant
30:7 [30:8] [G] but *when you* **hid** your face, I was dismayed.
31:20 [31:21] [G] In the shelter of your presence *you* **hide** them from
38:9 [38:10] [C] O Lord; my sighing **is** not **hidden** from you.
44:24 [44:25] [G] Why *do you* **hide** your face and forget our misery
51:9 [51:11] [G] **Hide** your face from my sins and blot out all my
54:T [54:2] [F] to Saul and said, "*Is* not David **hiding** among us?"
55:12 [55:13] [C] raising himself against me, *I could* **hide** from him.
64:2 [64:3] [G] **Hide** me from the conspiracy of the wicked,
69:17 [69:18] [G] *Do* not **hide** your face from your servant;
88:14 [88:15] [G] do you reject me and **hide** your face from me?
89:46 [89:47] [C] How long, O LORD? *Will you* **hide yourself**
102:2 [102:3] [G] *Do* not **hide** your face from me when I am in
104:29 [G] *When you* **hide** your face, they are terrified; when you take
119:19 [G] am a stranger on earth; *do* not **hide** your commands from me.
143:7 [G] *Do* not **hide** your face from me or I will be like those who go
Pr 22:3 [C] A prudent man sees danger and **takes refuge**, but the simple
25:2 [G] It is the glory of God *to* **conceal** a matter; to search out a
27:5 [E] Better is open rebuke than **hidden** love.
27:12 [C] The prudent see danger and **take refuge**, but the simple keep
28:28 [C] When the wicked rise to power, people **go into hiding**;
Isa 8:17 [G] the LORD, who *is* **hiding** his face from the house of Jacob.
16:3 [D] at high noon. **Hide** the fugitives, do not betray the refugees.
28:15 [C] have made a lie our refuge and falsehood *our* **hiding place**."
29:14 [F] will perish, the intelligence of the intelligent *will* **vanish**."
29:15 [G] Woe to those who go to great depths to **hide** their plans from
40:27 [C] O Israel, "My way *is* **hidden** from the LORD;
45:15 [F] Truly you are a God *who* **hides himself**, O God and Savior of
49:2 [G] me into a polished arrow and **concealed** me in his quiver.
50:6 [G] my beard; *I did* not **hide** my face from mocking and spitting.
54:8 [G] In a surge of anger *I* **hid** my face from you for a moment,
57:17 [G] I punished him, and **hid** my face in anger, yet he kept on in
59:2 [G] your sins *have* **hidden** his face from you, so that he will not
64:7 [64:6] [G] for *you have* **hidden** your face from us and made us
65:16 [C] the past troubles will be forgotten and **hidden** from my eyes.
Jer 16:17 [C] *they* **are** not **hidden** from me, nor is their sin concealed from
23:24 [C] *Can* anyone **hide** in secret places so that I cannot see him?"
33:5 [G] *I will* **hide** my face from this city because of all its
36:19 [C] the officials said to Baruch, "You and Jeremiah, go and **hide**.
36:26 [G] and Jeremiah the prophet. But the LORD *had* **hidden** them.
Eze 28:3 [B] Are you wiser than Daniel? Is no **secret** hidden from you?
39:23 [G] So *I* **hid** my face from them and handed them over to their
39:24 [G] and their offenses, and *I* **hid** my face from them.
39:29 [G] *I will* no longer **hide** my face from them, for I will pour out
Hos 13:14 [C] your destruction? "I *will* **have no** [+4946+6524] compassion,
Am 9:3 [C] Though *they* **hide** from me at the bottom of the sea, there I
Mic 3:4 [G] At that time *he will* **hide** his face from them because of the
Zep 2:3 [C] perhaps *you will* **be sheltered** on the day of the LORD's

6260 סֵתֶר ***sēter***, n.[m.]. [35] [→ 6261; cf. 6259]

secret [8], secretly [+928+2021] [6], shelter [5], hiding place [2], privately [+928+2021] [2], refuge [2], concealed [1], covering [1], hidden [1], hiding places [1], hiding [1], ravine [1], secret place [1], sly [1], thundercloud [+8308] [1], veil [1]

Dt 13:6 [13:7] or your closest friend **secretly** [+928+2021] entices you,
27:15 the work of the craftsman's hands—and sets it up in **secret**."
27:24 "Cursed is the man who kills his neighbor **secretly** [+928+2021]."
28:57 For she intends to eat them **secretly** [+928+2021] during the siege
Jdg 3:19 turned back and said, "I have a **secret** message for you, O king."
1Sa 19:2 on your guard tomorrow morning; go into **hiding** and stay there.
25:20 As she came riding her donkey into a mountain **ravine**, there were
2Sa 12:12 You did it in **secret**, but I will do this thing in broad daylight
Job 13:10 He would surely rebuke you if you **secretly** [+928+2021] showed
22:14 Thick clouds **veil** him, so he does not see us as he goes about in the
24:15 he thinks, 'No eye will see me,' and he keeps his face **concealed**.
31:27 so that my heart was **secretly** [+928+2021] enticed and my hand
40:21 the lotus plants he lies, **hidden** *among* the reeds in the marsh.
Ps 18:11 [18:12] He made darkness his **covering**, his canopy around him—
27:5 he will hide me in the **shelter** *of* his tabernacle and set me high
31:20 [31:21] In the **shelter** *of* your presence you hide them from the
32:7 You are my **hiding place**; you will protect me from trouble
61:4 [61:5] tent forever and take refuge in the **shelter** *of* your wings.
81:7 [81:8] I answered you out of a **thundercloud** [+8308];
91:1 He who dwells in the **shelter** *of* the Most High will rest in the
101:5 Whoever slanders his neighbor in **secret**, him will I put to silence;
119:114 You are my **refuge** and my shield; I have put my hope in your
139:15 was not hidden from you when I was made in the **secret place**.
Pr 9:17 "Stolen water is sweet; food eaten in **secret** is delicious!"
21:14 A gift given in **secret** soothes anger, and a bribe concealed in the
25:23 As a north wind brings rain, so a **sly** tongue brings angry looks.
SS 2:14 in the **hiding places** *on* the mountainside, show me your face,
Isa 16:4 fugitives stay with you; be their **shelter** from the destroyer."
28:17 your refuge, the lie, and water will overflow your **hiding place**.
32:2 will be like a shelter from the wind and a **refuge** *from* the storm,
45:19 I have not spoken in **secret**, from somewhere in a land of darkness;
48:16 "From the first announcement I have not spoken in **secret**;
Jer 37:17 brought to the palace, where he asked him **privately** [+928+2021],
38:16 King Zedekiah swore this oath **secretly** [+928+2021] to Jeremiah:
40:15 Johanan son of Kareah said **privately** [+928+2021] to Gedaliah in

6261 סִתְרָה ***sitrâ***, n.f. [1] [√ 6260; cf. 6259]

give shelter [+2118+6584] [1]

Dt 32:38 rise up to help you! *Let them* **give** you **shelter** [+2118+6584]!

6262 סִתְרִי ***sitrî***, n.pr.m. [1]

Sithri [1]

Ex 6:22 The sons of Uzziel were Mishael, Elzaphan and **Sithri**.

ע,

6263 ע ', letter. Not used in NIV/BHS [→ Ar 10521]

6264 עָב[1] ***'āb[1]***, n.m. [3]

overhang [1], overhanging roof [1], overhangs [1]

1Ki 7:6 and in front of that were pillars and an **overhanging roof**.
Eze 41:25 and there was a wooden **overhang** on the front of the portico.
41:26 on each side. The side rooms of the temple also had **overhangs**.

6265 עָב[2] ***'āb[2]***, n.m. [30 / 31] [√ 6380]

clouds [19], cloud [7], clouds of the sky [+8836] [2], dense [1], cloudless [+4202] [1], thick clouds [1]

Ex 19:9 to Moses, "I am going to come to you in a **dense** cloud,
Jdg 5:4 earth shook, the heavens poured, the **clouds** poured down water.
2Sa 22:12 his canopy around him—the dark rain **clouds of the sky** [+8836].
23:4 he is like the light of morning at sunrise on a **cloudless** [+4202]
1Ki 18:44 "A **cloud** as small as a man's hand is rising from the sea."
18:45 Meanwhile, the sky grew black with **clouds**, the wind rose,
Job 20:6 his pride reaches to the heavens and his head touches the **clouds**,

Job 22: 14 **Thick clouds** veil him, so he does not see us as he goes about in
26: 8 He wraps up the waters in his **clouds**, yet the clouds do not burst
30: 15 is driven away as by the wind, my safety vanishes like a **cloud**.
36: 29 Who can understand how he spreads out the **clouds**, how he
37: 11 He loads the **clouds** with moisture; he scatters his lightning
37: 16 Do you know how the **clouds** hang poised, those wonders of him
38: 34 "Can you raise your voice to the **clouds** and cover yourself with a
Ps 18: 11 [18:12] around him—the dark rain **clouds of the sky** [+8836].
18: 12 [18:13] Out of the brightness of his presence **clouds** advanced,
68: 4 [68:5] extol him who rides on the **clouds**—[BHS 6858]
77: 17 [77:18] The **clouds** poured down water, the skies resounded with
104: 3 He makes the **clouds** his chariot and rides on the wings of the
147: 8 He covers the sky with **clouds**; he supplies the earth with rain
Pr 16: 15 face brightens, it means life; his favor is like a rain **cloud** in spring.
Ecc 11: 3 If **clouds** are full of water, they pour rain upon the earth. Whether a
11: 4 the wind will not plant; whoever looks at the **clouds** will not reap.
12: 2 and the stars grow dark, and the **clouds** return after the rain;
Isa 5: 6 will grow there. I will command the **clouds** not to rain on it."
14: 14 I will ascend above the tops of the **clouds**; I will make myself like
18: 4 heat in the sunshine, like a **cloud** *of* dew in the heat of harvest."
19: 1 the LORD rides on a swift **cloud** and is coming to Egypt.
25: 5 as heat is reduced by the shadow of a **cloud**, so the song of the
44: 22 I have swept away your offenses like a **cloud**, your sins like the
60: 8 "Who are these that fly along like **clouds**, like doves to their nests?

6266 עָב³ *'āb³*, n.m. [1] [√ 6380?]

thickets [1]

Jer 4: 29 Some go into the **thickets**; some climb up among the rocks.

6267 עָב *'ab*, n.[m.]. Not used in NIV/BHS [√ 6286]

6268 עָבַד *'ābad*, v. [287 / 291] [→ 5042, 6269, 6271, 6272, 6275, 6276, 6285, 6381; *also used with compound proper names*; Ar 10522]

serve [88], worship [37], served [28], worshiped [13], do [11], work [10], serving [8], subject to [8], ministers [6], *untranslated* [3], enslave [3], enslaved [3], labor [3], subject [3], work for [3], worked for [3], worked [3], worshiping [3], burdened [2], farm [2], hold in bondage [2], serves [2], till [2], used [2], workers [2], works [2], be cultivated [1], be plowed [1], been plowed [1], been worked [1], been° [1], bondage [+6275] [1], cultivate [1], do work [1], do° [1], doing [1], done [1], drove [1], efforts [1], enslaving [1], farmer [+141+408] [1], fulfilling by doing [1], keep working [1], laborer [1], led [1], made work [1], make slaves [1], make work [1], making work [1], observe [1], perform [1], profits [1], put to work [1], reduced to servitude [+906+906+4200+6551] [1], servant [1], serve as slaves [1], services [1], slave [1], subjects [1], subjugate [1], submit [1], to subject [1], work [+6275] [1], work [+906+6275] [1], worship [+906+6275] [1]

Ge 2: 5 [A] rain on the earth and there was no man to **work** the ground,
2: 15 [A] put him in the Garden of Eden to **work** it and take care of it.
3: 23 [A] of Eden to **work** the ground from which he had been taken.
4: 2 [A] Now Abel kept flocks, and Cain **worked** the soil.
4: 12 [A] When *you* **work** the ground, it will no longer yield its crops
14: 4 [A] *For* twelve years *they had been* **subject to** Kedorlaomer,
15: 13 [A] and they *will be* **enslaved** and mistreated four hundred years.
15: 14 [A] I will punish the nation *they* **serve as slaves**, and afterward
25: 23 [A] than the other, and the older *will* **serve** the younger."
27: 29 [A] *May* nations **serve** you and peoples bow down to you.
27: 40 [A] You will live by the sword and *you will* **serve** your brother.
29: 15 [A] are a relative of mine, *should you* **work for** me for nothing?
29: 18 [A] "*I'll* **work for** you seven years in return for your younger
29: 20 [A] So Jacob **served** seven years to get Rachel, but they seemed
29: 25 [A] *I* **served** you for Rachel, didn't I? Why have you deceived
29: 27 [A] one also, in return for another seven years of work." **[NIE]**
29: 30 [A] than Leah. And *he* **worked** for Laban another seven years.
30: 26 [A] me my wives and children, for whom *I have* **served** you,
30: 26 [A] on my way. You know how much work I've **done** *for* you."
30: 29 [A] "You know how *I have* **worked for** you and how your
31: 6 [A] You know that *I've* **worked for** your father with all my
31: 41 [A] *I* **worked for** you fourteen years for your two daughters
47: 21 [G] Joseph **reduced** the people **to servitude** [+906+906 +4200+6551], [BHS 6296]
49: 15 [A] bend his shoulder to the burden and **submit** to forced labor.
Ex 1: 13 [G] and **worked** them ruthlessly.
1: 14 [A] in all their hard labor the Egyptians **used** them ruthlessly.
3: 12 [A] out of Egypt, *you will* **worship** God on this mountain."
4: 23 [A] I told you, "Let my son go, so *he may* **worship** me." But you
5: 18 [A] Now get *to* **work**. You will not be given any straw, yet you
6: 5 [G] whom the Egyptians *are* **enslaving**, and I have remembered
7: 16 [A] my people go, so that *they may* **worship** me in the desert.
8: 1 [7:26] [A] Let my people go, so that *they may* **worship** me.
8: 20 [8:16] [A] Let my people go, so that *they may* **worship** me.
9: 1 [A] says: "Let my people go, so that *they may* **worship** me."
9: 13 [A] says: Let my people go, so that *they may* **worship** me,
10: 3 [A] before me? Let my people go, so that *they may* **worship** me.
10: 7 [A] people go, so that *they may* **worship** the LORD their God.
10: 8 [A] "Go, **worship** the LORD your God," he said. "But just who
10: 11 [A] **worship** the LORD, since that's what you have been asking
10: 24 [A] summoned Moses and said, "Go, **worship** the LORD.
10: 26 [A] We have to use some of them in **worshiping** the LORD our
10: 26 [A] will not know what *we are to use to* **worship** the LORD."
12: 31 [A] Go, **worship** the LORD as you have requested.
13: 5 [A] and honey—*you are to* **observe** this ceremony in this month:
14: 5 [A] We have let the Israelites go and *have* lost *their* **services**!"
14: 12 [A] to you in Egypt, 'Leave us alone; *let us* **serve** the Egyptians'?
14: 12 [A] It would have been better for us *to* **serve** the Egyptians than
20: 5 [H] You shall not bow down to them or **worship** them; for I,
20: 9 [A] Six days *you shall* **labor** and do all your work,
21: 2 [A] you buy a Hebrew servant, *he is to* **serve** you for six years.
21: 6 [A] his ear with an awl. Then *he will be* his **servant** for life.
23: 24 [H] before their gods or **worship** them or follow their practices.
23: 25 [A] **Worship** the LORD your God, and his blessing will be on
23: 33 [A] because the **worship** *of* their gods will certainly be a snare to
34: 21 [A] "Six days *you shall* **labor**, but on the seventh day you shall
Lev 25: 39 [A] and sells himself to you, *do* not **make** him **work** as a slave.
25: 40 [A] among you; *he is to* **work** for you until the Year of Jubilee.
25: 46 [A] as inherited property and *can* **make** them **slaves** for life,
Nu 3: 7 [A] for the whole community at the Tent of Meeting by **doing** the
3: 8 [A] **fulfilling** the obligations of the Israelites **by doing** the work
4: 23 [A] come to serve in the **work** [+6275] at the Tent of Meeting.
4: 24 [A] "This is the service of the Gershonite clans *as* they **work**
4: 26 [A] The Gershonites *are to* **do** all that needs to be done with
4: 30 [A] to serve in the **work** [+906+6275] *at* the Tent of Meeting.
4: 37 [A] in the Kohathite clans who **served** in the Tent of Meeting.
4: 41 [A] in the Gershonite clans who **served** at the Tent of Meeting.
4: 47 [A] All the men from thirty to fifty years of age who came to **do**
7: 5 [A] that they may be **used** *in* the work at the Tent of Meeting.
8: 11 [A] so that they may be ready to **do** the work of the LORD.
8: 15 [A] they are to come to **do** *their* **work** at the Tent of Meeting.
8: 19 [A] his sons to **do** the work at the Tent of Meeting on behalf of
8: 22 [A] the Levites came to **do** their work at the Tent of Meeting
8: 25 [A] must retire from their regular service and **work** no longer.
8: 26 [A] Tent of Meeting, but *they themselves must* not **do** the work.
16: 9 [A] brought you near himself to **do** the work at the LORD's
18: 6 [A] dedicated to the LORD to **do** the work at the Tent of
18: 7 [A] **[RPH]** I am giving you the service of the priesthood as a
18: 21 [A] for the work they **do** while serving at the Tent of Meeting.
18: 23 [A] It is the Levites *who are to* **do** the work at the Tent of
Dt 4: 19 [A] **worshiping** things the LORD your God has apportioned to
4: 28 [A] There *you will* **worship** man-made gods of wood and stone,
5: 9 [H] You shall not bow down to them or **worship** them; for I,
5: 13 [A] Six days *you shall* **labor** and do all your work,
6: 13 [A] your God, **serve** him only and take your oaths in his name.
7: 4 [A] for they will turn your sons away from following me *to* **serve**
7: 16 [A] Do not look on them with pity and *do* not **serve** their gods,
8: 19 [A] and follow other gods and **worship** and bow down to them,
10: 12 [A] to **serve** the LORD your God with all your heart and with
10: 20 [A] Fear the LORD your God and **serve** him. Hold fast to him
11: 13 [A] and to **serve** him with all your heart and with all your soul—
11: 16 [A] to turn away and **worship** other gods and bow down to them.
12: 2 [A] where the nations you are dispossessing **worship** their gods.
12: 30 [A] their gods, saying, "How *do* these nations **serve** their gods?
13: 2 [13:3] [H] you have not known) "and *let us* **worship** them,"
13: 4 [13:5] [A] and obey him; **serve** him and hold fast to him.
13: 6 [13:7] [A] **worship** other gods" (gods that neither you nor your
13: 13 [13:14] [A] **worship** other gods" (gods you have not known),
15: 12 [A] or a woman, sells himself to you and **serves** you six years,
15: 19 [A] *Do* not **put** the firstborn of your oxen **to work**, and do not
17: 3 [A] contrary to my command *has* **worshiped** other gods, bowing
20: 11 [A] in it shall be subject to forced labor and *shall* **work for** you.
21: 3 [E] the body shall take a heifer that *has* never **been worked**
21: 4 [C] lead her down to a valley that *has* not **been plowed** or
28: 14 [A] or to the left, following other gods and **serving** them.
28: 36 [A] There *you will* **worship** other gods, gods of wood and stone.
28: 39 [A] You will plant vineyards and **cultivate** them but you will not
28: 47 [A] Because *you did* not **serve** the LORD your God joyfully
28: 48 [A] *you will* **serve** the enemies the LORD sends against you.
28: 64 [A] There *you will* **worship** other gods—gods of wood
29: 18 [29:17] [A] God to go and **worship** the gods of those nations;
29: 26 [29:25] [A] They went off and **worshiped** other gods
30: 17 [A] drawn away to bow down to other gods and **worship** them,
31: 20 [A] and thrive, they will turn to other gods and **worship** them,
Jos 16: 10 [A] the people of Ephraim but are required *to* **do** forced labor.
22: 5 [A] to hold fast to him and to **serve** him with all your heart
22: 27 [A] that we *will* **worship** [+906+6275] the LORD at his

Jos 23: 7 [A] by them. *You must* not **serve** them or bow down to them.
23: 16 [A] and go and **serve** other gods and bow down to them,
24: 2 [A] lived beyond the River and **worshiped** other gods.
24: 14 [A] "Now fear the LORD and **serve** him with all faithfulness.
24: 14 [A] Throw away the gods your forefathers **worshiped** beyond the
24: 14 [A] beyond the River and in Egypt, and **serve** the LORD.
24: 15 [A] if **serving** the LORD seems undesirable to you, then choose
24: 15 [A] choose for yourselves this day whom *you will* **serve**, whether
24: 15 [A] whether the gods your forefathers **served** beyond the River,
24: 15 [A] But as for me and my household, *we will* **serve** the LORD."
24: 16 [A] "Far be it from us to forsake the LORD to **serve** other gods!
24: 18 [A] We too *will* **serve** the LORD, because he is our God."
24: 19 [A] said to the people, "You are not able to **serve** the LORD.
24: 20 [A] If you forsake the LORD and **serve** foreign gods, he will
24: 21 [A] the people said to Joshua, "No! *We will* **serve** the LORD."
24: 22 [A] yourselves that you have chosen to **serve** the LORD."
24: 24 [A] "*We will* **serve** the LORD our God and obey him."
24: 31 [A] Israel **served** the LORD throughout the lifetime of Joshua
Jdg 2: 7 [A] The people **served** the LORD throughout the lifetime of
2: 11 [A] did evil in the eyes of the LORD and **served** the Baals.
2: 13 [A] they forsook him and **served** Baal and the Ashtoreths.
2: 19 [A] following other gods and **serving** and worshiping them.
3: 6 [A] gave their own daughters to their sons, and **served** their gods.
3: 7 [A] LORD their God and **served** the Baals and the Asherahs.
3: 8 [A] king of Aram Naharaim, **to** whom the Israelites *were* **subject**
3: 14 [A] The Israelites *were* **subject to** Eglon king of Moab for
9: 28 [A] and who is Shechem, that *we should be* **subject to** him?
9: 28 [A] his deputy? **Serve** the men of Hamor, Shechem's father!
9: 28 [A] Shechem's father! Why *should* we **serve** Abimelech?
9: 38 [A] 'Who is Abimelech that *we should be* **subject to** him?'
10: 6 [A] *They* **served** the Baals and the Ashtoreths, and the gods of
10: 6 [A] the Israelites forsook the LORD and no longer **served** him,
10: 10 [A] against you, forsaking our God and **serving** the Baals."
10: 13 [A] you have forsaken me and **served** other gods, so I will no
10: 16 [A] rid of the foreign gods among them and **served** the LORD.
1Sa 4: 9 [A] Be men, or *you will be* **subject** to the Hebrews, as they have
4: 9 [A] will be subject to the Hebrews, as *they have* **been**' to you.
7: 3 [A] and commit yourselves to the LORD and **serve** him only,
7: 4 [A] their Baals and Ashtoreths, and **served** the LORD only.
8: 8 [A] forsaking me and **serving** other gods, so they are doing to
11: 1 [A] "Make a treaty with us, and *we will be* **subject to** you."
12: 10 [A] the LORD and **served** the Baals and the Ashtoreths.
12: 10 [A] us from the hands of our enemies, and *we will* **serve** you.'
12: 14 [A] If you fear the LORD and **serve** and obey him and do not
12: 20 [A] from the LORD, but **serve** the LORD with all your heart.
12: 24 [A] fear the LORD and **serve** him faithfully with all your heart;
17: 9 [A] and kill him, you will become our subjects and **serve** us."
26: 19 [A] LORD's inheritance and have said, 'Go, **serve** other gods.'
2Sa 9: 10 [A] and your sons and your servants *are to* **farm** the land for him
10: 19 [A] made peace with the Israelites and *became* **subject** *to* them.
12: 31 [G] and *he* **made** them **work** [BHS 6296] at brickmaking.
15: 8 [A] back to Jerusalem, *I will* **worship** the LORD in Hebron.' "
16: 19 [A] Furthermore, whom *should* I **serve**? Should I not serve the
16: 19 [A] the son? Just as *I* **served** your father, so I will serve you."
22: 44 [A] the head of nations. People I did not know *are* **subject to** me,
1Ki 4: 21 [5:1] [A] and *were* Solomon's **subjects** all his life.
9: 6 [A] given you and go off *to* **serve** other gods and worship them,
9: 9 [A] have embraced other gods, worshiping and **serving** them—
9: 21 [A] these Solomon conscripted for his **slave** labor force, as it is to
12: 4 [A] and the heavy yoke he put on us, and *we will* **serve** you."
12: 7 [A] and **serve** them and give them a favorable answer,
16: 31 [A] of the Sidonians, and began *to* **serve** Baal and worship him.
22: 53 [22:54] [A] *He* **served** and worshiped Baal and provoked the
2Ki 10: 18 [A] people together and said to them, "Ahab **served** Baal a little;
10: 18 [A] "Ahab served Baal a little; Jehu *will* **serve** him much.
10: 19 [A] all the prophets of Baal, all his **ministers** and all his priests.
10: 19 [A] acting deceptively in order to destroy the **ministers** *of* Baal.
10: 21 [A] word throughout Israel, and all the **ministers** *of* Baal came;
10: 22 [A] of the wardrobe, "Bring robes for all the **ministers** *of* Baal."
10: 23 [A] Jehu said to the **ministers** *of* Baal, "Look around and see that
10: 23 [A] of the LORD are here with you—only **ministers** *of* Baal."
17: 12 [A] *They* **worshiped** idols, though the LORD had said, "You
17: 16 [A] down to all the starry hosts, and *they* **worshiped** Baal.
17: 33 [A] *they* also **served** their own gods in accordance with the
17: 35 [A] or bow down to them, **serve** them or sacrifice to them.
17: 41 [A] were worshiping the LORD, they were **serving** their idols.
18: 7 [A] rebelled against the king of Assyria and *did* not **serve** him.
21: 3 [A] He bowed down to all the starry hosts and **worshiped** them.
21: 21 [A] *he* **worshiped** the idols his father had worshiped, and bowed
21: 21 [A] he worshiped the idols his father *had* **worshiped**, and bowed
25: 24 [A] "Settle down in the land and **serve** the king of Babylon,
1Ch 19: 19 [A] they made peace with David and *became* **subject** *to* him.
28: 9 [A] **serve** him with wholehearted devotion and with a willing
2Ch 2: 18 [2:17] [G] foremen over them to **keep** the people **working**.
7: 19 [A] given you and go off *to* **serve** other gods and worship them,
7: 22 [A] have embraced other gods, worshiping and **serving** them—
10: 4 [A] and the heavy yoke he put on us, and *we will* **serve** you."
24: 18 [A] God of their fathers, and **worshiped** Asherah poles and idols.
30: 8 [A] **Serve** the LORD your God, so that his fierce anger will turn
33: 3 [A] He bowed down to all the starry hosts and **worshiped** them.
33: 16 [A] on it, and told Judah to **serve** the LORD, the God of Israel.
33: 22 [A] Amon **worshiped** and offered sacrifices to all the idols
34: 33 [A] he had all who were present in Israel serve **[RPH]** the
35: 3 [A] Now **serve** the LORD your God and his people Israel.
Ne 9: 35 [A] *they did* not **serve** you or turn from their evil ways.
Job 21: 15 [A] Who is the Almighty, that *we should* **serve** him? What
36: 11 [A] If they obey and **serve** him, they will spend the rest of their
39: 9 [A] "Will the wild ox consent *to* **serve** you? Will he stay by your
Ps 2: 11 [A] **Serve** the LORD with fear and rejoice with trembling.
18: 43 [18:44] [A] of nations; people I did not know *are* **subject to** me.
22: 30 [22:31] [A] Posterity *will* **serve** him; future generations will be
72: 11 [A] kings will bow down to him and all nations *will* **serve** him.
97: 7 [A] All *who* **worship** images are put to shame, those who boast
100: 2 [A] **Worship** the LORD with gladness; come before him with
102: 22 [102:23] [A] the kingdoms assemble to **worship** the LORD.
106: 36 [A] *They* **worshiped** their idols, which became a snare to them.
Pr 12: 11 [A] *He who* **works** his land will have abundant food, but he who
28: 19 [A] *He who* **works** his land will have abundant food, but the one
Ecc 5: 9 [5:8] [C] taken by all; the king *himself* **profits** from the fields.
5: 12 [5:11] [A] The sleep of a **laborer** is sweet, whether he eats little
Isa 14: 3 [E] relief from suffering and turmoil and cruel **bondage** [+6275],
19: 9 [A] *Those who* **work** *with* combed flax will despair, the weavers
19: 21 [A] *They will* **worship** *with* sacrifices and grain offerings; they
19: 23 [A] The Egyptians and Assyrians *will* **worship** together.
23: 10 [A] **Till** [BHS 6296] your land as along the Nile, O Daughter of
28: 21 [A] his strange work, and **perform** his task, his alien task.
30: 24 [A] The oxen and donkeys *that* **work** the soil will eat fodder
43: 23 [G] *I have* not **burdened** you with grain offerings nor wearied
43: 24 [G] *you have* **burdened** me with your sins and wearied me with
60: 12 [A] For the nation or kingdom that *will* not **serve** you will perish;
Jer 2: 20 [A] off your bonds; you said, '*I will* not **serve** [Q 6296] you!'
5: 19 [A] have forsaken me and **served** foreign gods in your own land,
5: 19 [A] so now *you will* **serve** foreigners in a land not your own.'
8: 2 [A] which they have loved and **served** and which they have
11: 10 [A] They have followed other gods to **serve** them. Both the house
13: 10 [A] and go after other gods to **serve** and worship them,
15: 14 [G] *I will* **enslave** [BHS 6296] you *to* your enemies in a land
16: 11 [A] 'and followed other gods and **served** and worshiped them.
16: 13 [A] there *you will* **serve** other gods day and night, for I will show
17: 4 [G] *I will* **enslave** you *to* your enemies in a land you do not
22: 9 [A] their God and have worshiped and **served** other gods.' "
22: 13 [A] by injustice, **making** his countrymen **work** for nothing,
25: 6 [A] Do not follow other gods to **serve** and worship them; do not
25: 11 [A] these nations *will* **serve** the king of Babylon seventy years.
25: 14 [A] *They* themselves *will be* **enslaved** by many nations and great
27: 6 [A] I will make even the wild animals **subject to** him.
27: 7 [A] All nations *will* **serve** him and his son and his grandson until
27: 7 [A] then many nations and great kings *will* **subjugate** him.
27: 8 [A] or kingdom *will* not **serve** Nebuchadnezzar king of Babylon
27: 9 [A] who tell you, '*You will* not **serve** the king of Babylon.'
27: 11 [A] neck under the yoke of the king of Babylon and **serve** him,
27: 11 [A] I will let that nation remain in its own land *to* **till** it and to
27: 12 [A] king of Babylon; **serve** him and his people, and you will live.
27: 13 [A] any nation that *will* not **serve** the king of Babylon?
27: 14 [A] '*You will* not **serve** the king of Babylon,' for they are
27: 17 [A] listen to them. **Serve** the king of Babylon, and you will live.
28: 14 [A] to *make* them **serve** Nebuchadnezzar king of Babylon,
28: 14 [A] Nebuchadnezzar king of Babylon, and *they will* **serve** him.
30: 8 [A] tear off their bonds; no longer *will* foreigners **enslave** them.
30: 9 [A] *they will* **serve** the LORD their God and David their king,
34: 9 [A] and female; no one was *to* **hold** a fellow Jew **in bondage**.
34: 10 [A] and female slaves and no longer **hold** them **in bondage**.
34: 14 [A] After *he has* **served** you six years, you must let him go free.'
35: 15 [A] reform your actions; do not follow other gods to **serve** them.
40: 9 [A] "Do not be afraid *to* **serve** the Babylonians," he said.
40: 9 [A] "Settle down in the land and **serve** the king of Babylon,
44: 3 [A] by **worshiping** other gods that neither they nor you nor your
Eze 20: 39 [A] LORD says: Go and **serve** your idols, every one of you!
20: 40 [A] there in the land the entire house of Israel *will* **serve** me,
29: 18 [G] Nebuchadnezzar king of Babylon **drove** his army *in* a hard
29: 18 [A] his army got no reward from the campaign *he* **led** against
29: 20 [A] I have given him Egypt as a reward for *his* **efforts** because
34: 27 [A] and rescue them from the hands of those *who* **enslaved** them.
36: 9 [C] will look on you with favor; *you will* **be plowed** and sown,
36: 34 [C] The desolate land *will* **be cultivated** instead of lying desolate
48: 18 [A] Its produce will supply food for the **workers** *of* the city.
48: 19 [A] The **workers** *from* the city who farm it will come from all
48: 19 [A] The workers from the city *who* **farm** it will come from all

Hos 12: 12 [12:13] [A] Israel **served** to get a wife, and to pay for her he
Zep 3: 9 [A] the name of the LORD and **serve** him shoulder to shoulder.
Zec 13: 5 [A] I am a **farmer** [+141+408]; the land has been my livelihood
Mal 3: 14 [A] "You have said, 'It is futile *to* **serve** God. What did we gain
3: 17 [A] just as in compassion a man spares his son who **serves** him.
3: 18 [A] between *those who* **serve** God and those who do not.
3: 18 [A] between those who serve God and *those* who **do**ˢ not.

6269 עֶבֶד¹ ***'ebed¹***, n.m. [801 / 802] [→ 5589, 6268, 6270, 6277, 6278, 6279, 6280; Ar 10523; *also used with compound proper names*]

servant [325], servants [157], officials [77], men [48], slaves [30], officers [16], menservants [15], slave [15], attendants [14], slavery [14], manservant [8], male slaves [7], servant's [7], subject [7], *untranslated* [5], official [4], subjects [3], attendant [2], in bondage [2], lowest of slaves [+6269] [2], male slave [2], officer [2], retinue [2], serve [2], slaves [+2256+9148] [2], themˢ [+2257] [2], theyˢ [+2257] [2], vassal [2], vassals [2], as a slave [+6275] [1], court [1], delegation [+928+3338] [1], enslaved [+2256+3899+4200+4200 +9148] [1], envoys [1], fellow officers [+123] [1], government officials [1], heˢ [+3870] [1], himˢ [+3870] [1], Iˢ [+3870] [1], in service [1], make men slaves [+3899+4200+4200] [1], meˢ [+3870] [1], messengers [1], reduced to servitude [+906+906+4200+6296] [1], servants [+4200] [1], servants men [1], servants the [1], served [1], service [1], slaves [+563+2256] [1], slaves male [1], subordinates [1], themˢ [+1192] [1], theyˢ [+8620] [1], worship [1]

Ge 9: 25 The **lowest of slaves** [+6269] will he be to his brothers."
9: 25 The **lowest of slaves** [+6269] will he be to his brothers."
9: 26 the LORD, the God of Shem! May Canaan be the **slave** of Shem.
9: 27 Japheth live in the tents of Shem, and may Canaan be his **slave**."
12: 16 and female donkeys, **menservants** and maidservants, and camels.
14: 15 During the night Abram divided his **men** to attack them and he
18: 3 found favor in your eyes, my lord, do not pass your **servant** by.
18: 5 then go on your way—now that you have come to your **servant**."
19: 2 "My lords," he said, "please turn aside to your **servant's** house.
19: 19 Your **servant** has found favor in your eyes, and you have shown
20: 8 Early the next morning Abimelech summoned all his **officials**,
20: 14 and cattle and **male** and female **slaves** and gave them to Abraham,
21: 25 about a well of water that Abimelech's **servants** had seized.
24: 2 He said to the chief **servant** in his household, the one in charge of
24: 5 The **servant** asked him, "What if the woman is unwilling to come
24: 9 So the **servant** put his hand under the thigh of his master Abraham
24: 10 Then the **servant** took ten of his master's camels and left,
24: 14 let her be the one you have chosen for your **servant** Isaac.
24: 17 The **servant** hurried to meet her and said, "Please give me a little
24: 34 So he said, "I am Abraham's **servant**.
24: 35 and cattle, silver and gold, **menservants** and maidservants,
24: 52 When Abraham's **servant** heard what they said, he bowed down to
24: 53 the **servant** brought out gold and silver jewelry and articles of
24: 59 along with her nurse and Abraham's **servant** and his men.
24: 61 and went back with the man. So the **servant** took Rebekah and left.
24: 65 asked the **servant**, "Who is that man in the field coming to meet
24: 65 "He is my master," the **servant** answered. So she took her veil
24: 66 Then the **servant** told Isaac all he had done.
26: 15 So all the wells that his father's **servants** had dug in the time of his
26: 19 Isaac's **servants** dug in the valley and discovered a well of fresh
26: 24 number of your descendants for the sake of my **servant** Abraham."
26: 25 There he pitched his tent, and there his **servants** dug a well.
26: 32 That day Isaac's **servants** came and told him about the well they
27: 37 him lord over you and have made all his relatives his **servants**,
30: 43 and maidservants and **menservants**, and camels and donkeys.
32: 4 [32:5] 'Your **servant** Jacob says, I have been staying with Laban
32: 5 [32:6] sheep and goats, **menservants** and maidservants.
32: 10 [32:11] and faithfulness you have shown your **servant**.
32: 16 [32:17] He put them in the care of his **servants**, each herd by
32: 16 [32:17] herd by itself, and said to his **servants**, "Go ahead of me,
32: 18 [32:19] you are to say, 'They belong to your **servant** Jacob.
32: 20 [32:21] 'Your **servant** Jacob is coming behind us.' " For he
33: 5 "They are the children God has graciously given your **servant**."
33: 14 So let my lord go on ahead of his **servant**, while I move along
39: 17 "That Hebrew **slave** you brought us came to me to make sport of
39: 19 saying, "This is how your **slave** treated me," he burned with anger.
40: 20 was Pharaoh's birthday, and he gave a feast for all his **officials**.
40: 20 chief cupbearer and the chief baker in the presence of his **officials**:
41: 10 Pharaoh was once angry with his **servants**, and he imprisoned me
41: 12 Hebrew was there with us, a **servant** of the captain of the guard.
41: 37 The plan seemed good to Pharaoh and to all his **officials**.
41: 38 So Pharaoh asked **them**ˢ [+2257], "Can we find anyone like this
42: 10 my lord," they answered. "Your **servants** have come to buy food.
42: 11 all the sons of one man. Your **servants** are honest men, not spies."
42: 13 they replied, "Your **servants** were twelve brothers, the sons of one
43: 18 He wants to attack us and overpower us and seize us as **slaves**
43: 28 They replied, "Your **servant** our father is still alive and well."
44: 7 such things? Far be it from your **servants** to do anything like that!
44: 9 If any of your **servants** is found to have it, he will die; and the rest
44: 9 he will die; and the rest of us will become my lord's **slaves**."
44: 10 Whoever is found to have it will become my **slave**; the rest of you
44: 16 God has uncovered your **servants**' guilt. We are now my lord's
44: 16 We are now my lord's **slaves**—we ourselves and the one who was
44: 17 the man who was found to have the cup will become my **slave**.
44: 18 "Please, my lord, let your **servant** speak a word to my lord.
44: 18 Do not be angry with your **servant**, though you are equal to
44: 19 My lord asked his **servants**, 'Do you have a father or a brother?'
44: 21 "Then you said to your **servants**, 'Bring him down to me so I can
44: 23 you told your **servants**, 'Unless your youngest brother comes down
44: 24 When we went back to your **servant** my father, we told him what
44: 27 "Your **servant** my father said to us, 'You know that my wife bore
44: 30 if the boy is not with us when I go back to your **servant** my father
44: 31 Your **servants** will bring the gray head of our father down to the
44: 31 Your servants will bring the gray head of our father down **[RPH]**
44: 32 Your **servant** guaranteed the boy's safety to my father. I said,
44: 33 please let your **servant** remain here as my lord's slave in place of
44: 33 please let your servant remain here as my lord's **slave** in place of
45: 16 brothers had come, Pharaoh and all his **officials** were pleased.
46: 34 'Your **servants** have tended livestock from our boyhood on,
47: 3 "Your **servants** are shepherds," they replied to Pharaoh, "just as
47: 4 in Canaan and your **servants** [+4200]' flocks have no pasture.
47: 4 no pasture. So now, please let your **servants** settle in Goshen."
47: 19 for food, and we with our land will be **in bondage** to Pharaoh.
47: 21 Joseph **reduced** the people **to servitude** [+906+906+4200+6296], [BHS 6551]
47: 25 favor in the eyes of our lord; we will be **in bondage** to Pharaoh."
50: 2 Joseph directed the physicians **in** his **service** to embalm his father
50: 7 All Pharaoh's **officials** accompanied him—the dignitaries of his
50: 17 Now please forgive the sins of the **servants** *of* the God of your
50: 18 themselves down before him. "We are your **slaves**," they said.
Ex 4: 10 neither in the past nor since you have spoken to your **servant**.
5: 15 to Pharaoh: "Why have you treated your **servants** this way?
5: 16 Your **servants** are given no straw, yet we are told, 'Make bricks!'
5: 16 Your **servants** are being beaten, but the fault is with your own
5: 21 You have made us a stench to Pharaoh and his **officials** and have
7: 10 Aaron threw his staff down in front of Pharaoh and his **officials**,
7: 20 of Pharaoh and his **officials** and struck the water of the Nile,
8: 3 [7:28] into the houses of your **officials** and on your people,
8: 4 [7:29] will go up on you and your people and all your **officials**.' "
8: 9 [8:5] your **officials** and your people that you and your houses may
8: 11 [8:7] leave you and your houses, your **officials** and your people;
8: 21 [8:17] I will send swarms of flies on you and your **officials**, on
8: 24 [8:20] into Pharaoh's palace and into the houses of his **officials**,
8: 29 [8:25] the flies will leave Pharaoh and his **officials** and his people.
8: 31 [8:27] The flies left Pharaoh and his **officials** and his people; not a
9: 14 my plagues against you and against your **officials** and your people,
9: 20 Those **officials** *of* Pharaoh who feared the word of the LORD
9: 20 who feared the word of the LORD hurried to bring their **slaves**
9: 21 But those who ignored the word of the LORD left their **slaves**
9: 30 know that you and your **officials** still do not fear the LORD God."
9: 34 he sinned again: He and his **officials** hardened their hearts.
10: 1 for I have hardened his heart and the hearts of his **officials**
10: 6 your houses and those of all your **officials** and all the Egyptians—
10: 7 Pharaoh's **officials** said to him, "How long will this man be a snare
11: 3 Moses himself was highly regarded in Egypt by Pharaoh's **officials**
11: 8 All these **officials** *of* yours will come to me, bowing down before
12: 30 Pharaoh and all his **officials** and all the Egyptians got up during the
12: 44 Any **slave** you have bought may eat of it after you have
13: 3 the day you came out of Egypt, out of the land of **slavery**,
13: 14 the LORD brought us out of Egypt, out of the land of **slavery**.
14: 5 Pharaoh and his **officials** changed their minds about them
14: 31 the LORD and put their trust in him and in Moses his **servant**.
20: 2 who brought you out of Egypt, out of the land of **slavery**.
20: 10 nor your son or daughter, nor your **manservant** or maidservant,
20: 17 or his **manservant** or maidservant, his ox or donkey,
21: 2 "If you buy a Hebrew **servant**, he is to serve you for six years.
21: 5 "But if the **servant** declares, 'I love my master and my wife
21: 7 his daughter as a servant, she is not to go free as **menservants** do.
21: 20 "If a man beats his **male** or female **slave** with a rod and the slave
21: 26 "If a man hits a **manservant** or maidservant in the eye and
21: 27 And if he knocks out the tooth of a **manservant** or maidservant,
21: 32 If the bull gores a **male** or female **slave**, the owner must pay thirty
32: 13 Remember your **servants** Abraham, Isaac and Israel, to whom you
Lev 25: 6 for yourself, your **manservant** and maidservant, and the hired
25: 39 and sells himself to you, do not make him work **as a slave** [+6275].
25: 42 Because the Israelites are my **servants**, whom I brought out of
25: 42 whom I brought out of Egypt, they must not be sold as **slaves**.
25: 44 " 'Your **male** and female **slaves** are to come from the nations
25: 44 nations around you; from them you may buy **slaves** [+563+2256].
25: 55 for the Israelites belong to me as **servants**. They are my servants,

Lev 25:55 They are my **servants**, whom I brought out of Egypt. I am the
26:13 of Egypt so that you would no longer be **slaves** to the Egyptians;
Nu 11:11 the LORD, "Why have you brought this trouble on your **servant**?
12: 7 this is not true of my **servant** Moses; he is faithful in all my house.
12: 8 then were you not afraid to speak against my **servant** Moses?"
14:24 because my **servant** Caleb has a different spirit and follows me
22:18 Balaam answered **them**[s] [+1192], "Even if Balak gave me his
31:49 "Your **servants** have counted the soldiers under our command,
32: 4 are suitable for livestock, and your **servants** have livestock.
32: 5 "let this land be given to your **servants** as our possession.
32:25 said to Moses, "We your **servants** will do as our lord commands.
32:27 your **servants**, every man armed for battle, will cross over to fight
32:31 "Your **servants** will do what the LORD has said.
Dt 3:24 you have begun to show to your **servant** your greatness and your
5: 6 who brought you out of Egypt, out of the land of **slavery**.
5:14 nor your son or daughter, nor your **manservant** or maidservant,
5:14 so that your **manservant** and maidservant may rest, as you do.
5:15 Remember that you were **slaves** in Egypt and that the LORD your
5:21 or land, his **manservant** or maidservant, his ox or donkey,
6:12 who brought you out of Egypt, out of the land of **slavery**.
6:21 "We were **slaves** of Pharaoh in Egypt, but the LORD brought us
7: 8 with a mighty hand and redeemed you from the land of **slavery**,
8:14 who brought you out of Egypt, out of the land of **slavery**.
9:27 Remember your **servants** Abraham, Isaac and Jacob. Overlook the
12:12 your sons and daughters, your **menservants** and maidservants,
12:18 your sons and daughters, your **menservants** and maidservants,
13: 5 [13:6] out of Egypt and redeemed you from the land of **slavery**;
13:10 [13:11] who brought you out of Egypt, out of the land of **slavery**.
15:15 Remember that you were **slaves** in Egypt and the LORD your
15:17 his ear lobe into the door, and he will become your **servant** for life.
15:18 because his **service** *to* you these six years has been worth twice as
16:11 your sons and daughters, your **menservants** and maidservants,
16:12 Remember that you were **slaves** in Egypt, and follow carefully
16:14 your sons and daughters, your **menservants** and maidservants,
23:15 [23:16] If a **slave** has taken refuge with you, do not hand him over
24:18 Remember that you were **slaves** in Egypt and the LORD your
24:22 Remember that you were **slaves** in Egypt. That is why I command
28:68 yourselves for sale to your enemies as **male** and female **slaves**,
29: 2 [29:1] in Egypt to Pharaoh, to all his **officials** and to all his land.
32:36 have compassion on his **servants** when he sees their strength is
32:43 with his people, for he will avenge the blood of his **servants**;
34: 5 And Moses the **servant** *of* the LORD died there in Moab,
34:11 in Egypt—to Pharaoh and to all his **officials** and to his whole land.
Jos 1: 1 After the death of Moses the **servant** *of* the LORD, the LORD
1: 2 "Moses my **servant** is dead. Now then, you and all these people,
1: 7 Be careful to obey all the law my **servant** Moses gave you;
1:13 "Remember the command that Moses the **servant** *of* the LORD
1:15 which Moses the **servant** *of* the LORD gave you east of the
5:14 asked him, "What message does my Lord have for his **servant**?"
8:31 as Moses the **servant** *of* the LORD had commanded the Israelites.
8:33 as Moses the **servant** *of* the LORD had formerly commanded
9: 8 "We are your **servants**," they said to Joshua. But Joshua asked,
9: 9 "Your **servants** have come from a very distant country because of
9:11 go and meet them and say to them, "We are your **servants**;
9:23 You will never cease to **serve** as woodcutters and water carriers for
9:24 "Your **servants** were clearly told how the LORD your God had
9:24 had commanded his **servant** Moses to give you the whole land
10: 6 "Do not abandon your **servants**. Come up to us quickly and save
11:12 as Moses the **servant** *of* the LORD had commanded.
11:15 As the LORD commanded his **servant** Moses, so Moses
12: 6 Moses, the **servant** *of* the LORD, and the Israelites conquered
12: 6 Moses the **servant** *of* the LORD gave their land to the
13: 8 as he, the **servant** *of* the LORD, had assigned it to them.
14: 7 I was forty years old when Moses the **servant** *of* the LORD sent
18: 7 of the Jordan. Moses the **servant** *of* the LORD gave it to them."
22: 2 "You have done all that Moses the **servant** *of* the LORD
22: 4 return to your homes in the land that Moses the **servant** *of* the
22: 5 and the law that Moses the **servant** *of* the LORD gave you:
24:17 and our fathers up out of Egypt, from that land of **slavery**,
24:29 After these things, Joshua son of Nun, the **servant** *of* the LORD,
Jdg 2: 8 Joshua son of Nun, the **servant** *of* the LORD, died at the age of a
3:24 the **servants** came and found the doors of the upper room locked.
6: 8 says: I brought you up out of Egypt, out of the land of **slavery**.
6:27 So Gideon took ten of his **servants** and did as the LORD told
15:18 to the LORD, "You have given your **servant** this great victory.
19:19 for our donkeys and bread and wine for ourselves your **servants**—
1Sa 3: 9 for your **servant** is listening.' " So Samuel went and lay down in
3:10 Then Samuel said, "Speak, for your **servant** is listening."
8:14 and vineyards and olive groves and give them to his **attendants**.
8:15 and of your vintage and give it to his officials and **attendants**.
8:16 Your **menservants** and maidservants and the best of your cattle
8:17 a tenth of your flocks, and you yourselves will become his **slaves**.
12:19 "Pray to the LORD your God for your **servants** so that we will
16:15 Saul's **attendants** said to him, "See, an evil spirit from God is
16:16 Let our lord command his **servants** here to search for someone
16:17 So Saul said to his **attendants**, "Find someone who plays well
17: 8 Am I not a Philistine, and are you not the **servants** of Saul?
17: 9 If he is able to fight and kill me, we will become your **subjects**;
17: 9 and kill him, you will become our **subjects** and serve us."
17:32 on account of this Philistine; your **servant** will go and fight him."
17:34 said to Saul, "Your **servant** has been keeping his father's sheep.
17:36 Your **servant** has killed both the lion and the bear; this
17:58 David said, "I am the son of your **servant** Jesse of Bethlehem."
18: 5 the army. This pleased all the people, and Saul's **officers** as well.
18:22 Then Saul ordered his **attendants**: "Speak to David privately
18:22 the king is pleased with you, and his **attendants** all like you;
18:23 **They**[s] [+8620] repeated these words to David. But David said,
18:24 When Saul's **servants** told him what David had said,
18:26 When the **attendants** told David these things, he was pleased to
18:30 David met with more success than the rest of Saul's **officers**,
19: 1 Saul told his son Jonathan and all the **attendants** to kill David.
19: 4 and said to him, "Let not the king do wrong to his **servant** David;
20: 7 If he says, 'Very well,' then your **servant** is safe. But if he loses his
20: 8 As for you, show kindness to your **servant**, for you have brought
20: 8 for you have brought **him**[s] [+3870] into a covenant with you
21: 7 [21:8] Now one of Saul's **servants** was there that day,
21:11 [21:12] But the **servants** *of* Achish said to him, "Isn't this David,
21:14 [21:15] Achish said to his **servants**, "Look at the man! He is
22: 6 on the hill at Gibeah, with all his **officials** standing around him.
22: 7 Saul said to **them**[s] [+2257], "Listen, men of Benjamin! Will the
22: 8 or tells me that my son has incited my **servant** to lie in wait for
22: 9 Doeg the Edomite, who was standing with Saul's **officials**, said,
22:14 "Who of all your **servants** is as loyal as David, the king's
22:15 Let not the king accuse your **servant** or any of his father's family,
22:15 for your **servant** knows nothing at all about this whole affair."
22:17 the king's **officials** were not willing to raise a hand to strike the
23:10 your **servant** has heard definitely that Saul plans to come to Keilah
23:11 Will Saul come down, as your **servant** has heard? O LORD,
23:11 O LORD, God of Israel, tell your **servant**." And the LORD said,
25: 8 Please give your **servants** and your son David whatever you can
25:10 Nabal answered David's **servants**, "Who is this David? Who is
25:10 Many **servants** are breaking away from their masters these days.
25:39 He has kept his **servant** from doing wrong and has brought
25:40 His **servants** went to Carmel and said to Abigail, "David has sent
25:41 ready to serve you and wash the feet of my master's **servants**."
26:18 he added, "Why is my lord pursuing his **servant**? What have I
26:19 Now let my lord the king listen to his **servant's** words.
27: 5 Why should your **servant** live in the royal city with you?"
27:12 to his people, the Israelites, that he will be my **servant** forever."
28: 2 "Then you will see for yourself what your **servant** can do."
28: 7 Saul then said to his **attendants**, "Find me a woman who is a
28: 7 and inquire of her." "There is one in Endor," **they**[s] [+2257] said.
28:23 his **men** joined the woman in urging him, and he listened to them.
28:25 she set it before Saul and his **men**, and they ate. That same night
29: 3 "Is this not David, who was an **officer** *of* Saul king of Israel?
29: 8 "What have you found against your **servant** from the day I came to
29:10 along with your master's **servants** who have come with you,
30:13 He said, "I am an Egyptian, the **slave** of an Amalekite.
2Sa 2:12 together with the **men** *of* Ish-Bosheth son of Saul, left Mahanaim
2:13 Joab son of Zeruiah and David's **men** went out and met them at the
2:15 and Ish-Bosheth son of Saul, and twelve **[NIE]** for David.
2:17 and Abner and the men of Israel were defeated by David's **men**.
2:30 Besides Asahel, nineteen of David's **men** were found missing.
2:31 David's **men** had killed three hundred and sixty Benjamites who
3:18 'By my **servant** David I will rescue my people Israel from the hand
3:22 Just then David's **men** and Joab returned from a raid and brought
3:38 Then the king said to his **men**, "Do you not realize that a prince
6:20 disrobing in the sight of the slave girls of his **servants** as any
7: 5 "Go and tell my **servant** David, 'This is what the LORD says:
7: 8 "Now then, tell my **servant** David, 'This is what the LORD
7:19 have also spoken about the future of the house of your **servant**.
7:20 say to you? For you know your **servant**, O Sovereign LORD.
7:21 you have done this great thing and made it known to your **servant**.
7:25 keep forever the promise you have made concerning your **servant**
7:26 the house of your **servant** David will be established before you.
7:27 God of Israel, you have revealed this to your **servant**, saying,
7:27 So your **servant** has found courage to offer you this prayer.
7:28 and you have promised these good things to your **servant**.
7:29 Now be pleased to bless the house of your **servant**, that it may
7:29 with your blessing the house of your **servant** will be blessed
8: 2 So the Moabites became **subject** to David and brought tribute.
8: 6 and the Arameans became **subject** to him and brought tribute.
8: 7 David took the gold shields that belonged to the **officers** *of*
8:14 throughout Edom, and all the Edomites became **subject** to David.
9: 2 Now there was a **servant** of Saul's household named Ziba.
9: 2 the king said to him, "Are you Ziba?" "Your **servant**," he replied.
9: 6 David said, "Mephibosheth!" "Your **servant**," he replied.
9: 8 Mephibosheth bowed down and said, "What is your **servant**,

2Sa 9:10 and your sons and your **servants** are to farm the land for him
9:10 eat at my table." (Now Ziba had fifteen sons and twenty **servants**.)
9:11 "Your **servant** will do whatever my lord the king commands his
9:11 will do whatever my lord the king commands his **servant** to do."
9:12 all the members of Ziba's household were **servants** of
10:2 So David sent a **delegation** [+928+3338] to express his sympathy
10:2 his father. When David's **men** came to the land of the Ammonites,
10:3 "Do you think David is honoring your father by sending **men** to
10:4 So Hanun seized David's **men**, shaved off half of each man's
10:19 When all the kings who were **vassals** *of* Hadadezer saw that they
11:1 David sent Joab out with the king's **men** and the whole Israelite
11:9 slept at the entrance to the palace with all his master's **servants**
11:11 my master Joab and my lord's **men** are camped in the open fields.
11:13 Uriah went out to sleep on his mat among his master's **servants**;
11:17 and fought against Joab, some of the **men** *in* David's army fell;
11:21 then say to him, 'Also, your **servant** Uriah the Hittite is dead.' "
11:24 Then the archers shot arrows at your **servants** from the wall,
11:24 at your servants from the wall, and some of the king's **men** died.
11:24 men died. Moreover, your **servant** Uriah the Hittite is dead."
12:18 David's **servants** were afraid to tell him that the child was dead,
12:19 David noticed that his **servants** were whispering among
12:19 child dead?" he asked. **[RPH]** "Yes," they replied, "he is dead."
12:21 His **servants** asked him, "Why are you acting this way? While the
13:24 went to the king and said, "Your **servant** has had shearers come.
13:24 had shearers come. Will the king and his **officials** please join me?"
13:24 Will the king and his officials please join **me**[s] [+3870]?"
13:31 on the ground; and all his **servants** stood by with their clothes torn.
13:35 the king's sons are here; it has happened just as your **servant** said."
13:36 The king, too, and all his **servants** wept very bitterly.
14:19 it was your **servant** Joab who instructed me to do this and who put
14:20 Your **servant** Joab did this to change the present situation.
14:22 "Today your **servant** knows that he has found favor in your eyes,
14:22 lord the king, because the king has granted his **servant's** request."
14:30 Then he said to his **servants**, "Look, Joab's field is next to mine,
14:30 and set it on fire." So Absalom's **servants** set the field on fire.
14:31 and he said to him, "Why have your **servants** set my field on fire?"
15:2 would answer, "Your **servant** is from one of the tribes of Israel."
15:8 While your **servant** was living at Geshur in Aram, I made this
15:14 David said to all his **officials** who were with him in Jerusalem,
15:15 The king's **officials** answered him, "Your servants are ready to do
15:15 "Your **servants** are ready to do whatever our lord the king
15:18 All his **men** marched past him, along with all the Kerethites
15:21 whether it means life or death, there will your **servant** be."
15:34 to the city and say to Absalom, 'I will be your **servant**, O king;
15:34 I was your father's **servant** in the past, but now I will be your
15:34 your father's servant in the past, but now I will be your **servant**,'
16:6 He pelted David and all the king's **officials** with stones, though all
16:11 David then said to Abishai and all his **officials**, "My son, who is of
17:20 When Absalom's **men** came to the woman at the house, they
18:7 There the army of Israel was defeated by David's **men**,
18:9 Now Absalom happened to meet David's **men**. He was riding his
18:29 great confusion just as Joab was about to send the king's **servant**
18:29 as Joab was about to send the king's servant and me, your **servant**,
19:5 [19:6] and said, "Today you have humiliated all your **men**,
19:6 [19:7] that the commanders and their **men** mean nothing to you.
19:7 [19:8] Now go out and encourage your **men**. I swear by the
19:14 [19:15] sent word to the king, "Return, you and all your **men**."
19:17 [19:18] and his fifteen sons and twenty **servants**.
19:19 [19:20] Do not remember how your **servant** did wrong on the day
19:20 [19:21] For I your **servant** know that I have sinned, but today I
19:26 [19:27] "My lord the king, since I your **servant** am lame, I said,
19:26 [19:27] the king, since I your servant am lame, **I**[s] [+3870] said,
19:26 [19:27] I can go with the king.' But Ziba my **servant** betrayed me.
19:27 [19:28] he has slandered your **servant** to my lord the king. My
19:28 [19:29] you gave your **servant** a place among those who sat at
19:35 [19:36] is not? Can your **servant** taste what he eats and drinks?
19:35 [19:36] Why should your **servant** be an added burden to my lord
19:36 [19:37] Your **servant** will cross over the Jordan with the king for
19:37 [19:38] Let your **servant** return, that I may die in my own town
19:37 [19:38] my father and mother. But here is your **servant** Kimham.
20:6 Take your master's **men** and pursue him, or he will find fortified
21:15 David went down with his **men** to fight against the Philistines,
21:22 of Rapha in Gath, and they fell at the hands of David and his **men**.
24:10 O LORD, I beg you, take away the guilt of your **servant**.
24:20 Araunah looked and saw the king and his **men** coming toward him,
24:21 Araunah said, "Why has my lord the king come to his **servant**?"
1Ki 1:2 So his **servants** said to him, "Let us look for a young virgin to
1:9 the king's sons, and all the men of Judah who were royal **officials**,
1:19 of the army, but he has not invited Solomon your **servant**.
1:26 me your **servant**, and Zadok the priest, and Benaiah son of
1:26 son of Jehoiada, and your **servant** Solomon he did not invite.
1:27 **servants** know who should sit on the throne of my lord the king
1:33 "Take your lord's **servants** with you and set Solomon my son on
1:47 the royal **officials** have come to congratulate our lord King David,
1:51 today that he will not put his **servant** to death with the sword.' "
2:38 say is good. Your **servant** will do as my lord the king has said."
2:39 two of Shimei's **slaves** ran off to Achish son of Maacah, king of
2:39 king of Gath, and Shimei was told, "Your **slaves** are in Gath."
2:40 his donkey and went to Achish at Gath in search of his **slaves**.
2:40 So Shimei went away and brought the **slaves** back from Gath.
3:6 "You have shown great kindness to your **servant**, my father David,
3:7 you have made your **servant** king in place of my father David.
3:8 Your **servant** is here among the people you have chosen, a great
3:9 So give your **servant** a discerning heart to govern your people
3:15 and fellowship offerings. Then he gave a feast for all his **court**.
5:1 [5:15] he sent his **envoys** to Solomon, because he had always
5:6 [5:20] My **men** will work with yours, and I will pay you for your
5:6 [5:20] **[RPH]** and I will pay you for your men whatever wages
5:6 [5:20] and I will pay you for your **men** whatever wages you set.
5:9 [5:23] My **men** will haul them down from Lebanon to the sea,
8:23 you who keep your covenant of love with your **servants** who
8:24 You have kept your promise to your **servant** David my father;
8:25 keep for your **servant** David my father the promises you made to
8:26 let your word that you promised your **servant** David my father
8:28 Yet give attention to your **servant's** prayer and his plea for mercy,
8:28 the prayer that your **servant** is praying in your presence this day.
8:29 so that you will hear the prayer your **servant** prays toward this
8:30 Hear the supplication of your **servant** and of your people Israel
8:32 Judge between your **servants**, condemning the guilty and bringing
8:36 then hear from heaven and forgive the sin of your **servants**,
8:52 "May your eyes be open to your **servant's** plea and to the plea of
8:53 just as you declared through your **servant** Moses when you,
8:56 failed of all the good promises he gave through his **servant** Moses.
8:59 that he may uphold the cause of his **servant** and the cause of his
8:66 for all the good things the LORD had done for his **servant** David
9:22 But Solomon *did* not make **slaves** of any of the Israelites;
9:22 fighting men, his **government officials**, his officers, his captains,
9:27 Hiram sent his **men**—sailors who knew the sea—to serve in the
9:27 who knew the sea—to serve in the fleet with Solomon's **men**.
10:5 the food on his table, the seating of his **officials**, the attending
10:8 How happy your **officials**, who continually stand before you
10:13 Then she left and returned with her **retinue** to her own country.
11:11 kingdom away from you and give it to one of your **subordinates**.
11:13 but will give him one tribe for the sake of David my **servant**
11:17 fled to Egypt with some Edomite officials who had **served** his
11:26 He was one of Solomon's **officials**, an Ephraimite from Zeredah,
11:32 But for the sake of my **servant** David and the city of Jerusalem,
11:34 him ruler all the days of his life for the sake of David my **servant**,
11:36 so that David my **servant** may always have a lamp before me in
11:38 by keeping my statutes and commands, as David my **servant** did,
12:7 "If today you will be a **servant** to these people and serve them
12:7 give them a favorable answer, they will always be your **servants**."
14:8 and gave it to you, but you have not been like my **servant** David,
14:18 as the LORD had said through his **servant** the prophet Ahijah.
15:18 He entrusted it to his **officials** and sent them to Ben-Hadad son of
15:29 according to the word of the LORD given through his **servant**
16:9 Zimri, one of his **officials**, who had command of half his chariots,
18:9 "that you are handing your **servant** over to Ahab to be put to
18:12 Yet I your **servant** have worshiped the LORD since my youth.
18:36 known today that you are God in Israel and that I am your **servant**
20:6 about this time tomorrow I am going to send my **officials** to search
20:6 my officials to search your palace and the houses of your **officials**.
20:9 the king, 'Your **servant** will do all you demanded the first time,
20:12 and the kings were drinking in their tents, and he ordered his **men**:
20:23 Meanwhile, the **officials** *of* the king of Aram advised him,
20:31 His **officials** said to him, "Look, we have heard that the kings of
20:32 to the king of Israel and said, "Your **servant** Ben-Hadad says:
20:39 called out to him, "Your **servant** went into the thick of the battle,
20:40 While your **servant** was busy here and there, the man
22:3 The king of Israel had said to his **officials**, "Don't you know that
22:49 [22:50] "Let my **men** sail with your men," but Jehoshaphat
22:49 [22:50] "Let my men sail with your **men**," but Jehoshaphat
2Ki 1:13 respect for my life and the lives of these fifty men, your **servants**!
2:16 "Look," they said, "we your **servants** have fifty able men.
3:11 An **officer** *of* the king of Israel answered, "Elisha son of Shaphat is
4:1 "Your **servant** my husband is dead, and you know that he revered
4:1 is dead, and you know that **he**[s] [+3870] revered the LORD.
4:1 But now his creditor is coming to take my two boys as his **slaves**."
5:6 "With this letter I am sending my **servant** Naaman to you
5:13 Naaman's **servants** went to him and said, "My father,
5:15 except in Israel. Please accept now a gift from your **servant**."
5:17 "If you will not," said Naaman, "please let me, your **servant**,
5:17 for your **servant** will never again make burnt offerings
5:18 But may the LORD forgive your **servant** for this one thing:
5:18 of Rimmon, may the LORD forgive your **servant** for this."
5:25 "Your **servant** didn't go anywhere," Gehazi answered.
5:26 vineyards, flocks, herds, or **menservants** and maidservants?
6:3 one of them said, "Won't you please come with your **servants**?"

2Ki 6: 8 After conferring with his **officers**, he said, "I will set up my camp
6: 11 He summoned his **officers** and demanded of them, "Will you not
6: 12 of us, my lord the king," said one of his **officers**, "but Elisha,
7: 12 The king got up in the night and said to his **officers**, "I will tell you
7: 13 One of his **officers** answered, "Have some men take five of the
8: 13 Hazael said, "How could your **servant**, a mere dog,
8: 19 Nevertheless, for the sake of his **servant** David, the LORD was
9: 7 I will avenge the blood of my **servants** the prophets and the blood
9: 7 and the blood of all the LORD's **servants** shed by Jezebel.
9: 11 When Jehu went out to his **fellow officers** [+123], one of them
9: 28 His **servants** took him by chariot to Jerusalem and buried him with
9: 36 "This is the word of the LORD that he spoke through his **servant**
10: 5 "We are your **servants** and we will do anything you say. We will
10: 10 The LORD has done what he promised through his **servant**
10: 23 and see that no **servants** *of* the LORD are here with you—
12: 20 [12:21] His **officials** conspired against him and assassinated him
12: 21 [12:22] The **officials** who murdered him were Jozabad son of
14: 5 he executed the **officials** who had murdered his father the king.
14: 25 God of Israel, spoken through his **servant** Jonah son of Amittai,
16: 7 to Tiglath-Pileser king of Assyria, "I am your **servant** and vassal.
17: 3 who had been Shalmaneser's **vassal** and had paid him tribute.
17: 13 and that I delivered to you through my **servants** the prophets."
17: 23 as he had warned through all his **servants** the prophets.
18: 12 all that Moses the **servant** *of* the LORD commanded.
18: 24 can you repulse one officer of the least *of* my master's **officials**,
18: 26 "Please speak to your **servants** in Aramaic, since we understand it.
19: 5 When King Hezekiah's **officials** came to Isaiah,
19: 34 and save it, for my sake and for the sake of David my **servant**."
20: 6 this city for my sake and for the sake of my **servant** David.' "
21: 8 and will keep the whole Law that my **servant** Moses gave them."
21: 10 The LORD said through his **servants** the prophets:
21: 23 Amon's **officials** conspired against him and assassinated the king
22: 9 "Your **officials** have paid out the money that was in the temple of
22: 12 Shaphan the secretary and Asaiah the king's **attendant**:
23: 30 Josiah's **servants** brought his body in a chariot from Megiddo to
24: 1 invaded the land, and Jehoiakim became his **vassal** for three years.
24: 2 the word of the LORD proclaimed by his **servants** the prophets.
24: 10 At that time the **officers** *of* Nebuchadnezzar king of Babylon
24: 11 Nebuchadnezzar himself came up to the city while his **officers**
24: 12 his **attendants**, his nobles and his officials all surrendered to him.
25: 8 an **official** *of* the king of Babylon, came to Jerusalem.
25: 24 their men. "Do not be afraid of the Babylonian **officials**," he said.
1Ch 2: 34 only daughters. He had an Egyptian **servant** named Jarha.
2: 35 Sheshan gave his daughter in marriage to his **servant** Jarha,
6: 49 [6:34] in accordance with all that Moses the **servant** *of* God had
16: 13 O descendants of Israel his **servant**, O sons of Jacob, his chosen
17: 4 "Go and tell my **servant** David, 'This is what the LORD says:
17: 7 "Now then, tell my **servant** David, 'This is what the LORD
17: 17 you have spoken about the future of the house of your **servant**.
17: 18 "What more can David say to you for honoring your **servant**?
17: 18 say to you for honoring your servant? For you know your **servant**,
17: 19 For the sake of your **servant** and according to your will, you have
17: 23 let the promise you have made concerning your **servant** and his
17: 24 the house of your **servant** David will be established before you.
17: 25 have revealed to your **servant** that you will build a house for him.
17: 25 a house for him. So your **servant** has found courage to pray to you.
17: 26 are God! You have promised these good things to your **servant**.
17: 27 Now you have been pleased to bless the house of your **servant**,
18: 2 the Moabites, and they became **subject** to him and brought tribute.
18: 6 and the Arameans became **subject** to him and brought tribute.
18: 7 David took the gold shields carried by the **officers** *of* Hadadezer
18: 13 garrisons in Edom, and all the Edomites became **subject** to David.
19: 2 When David's **men** came to Hanun in the land of the Ammonites
19: 3 Haven't his **men** come to you to explore and spy out the country
19: 4 So Hanun seized David's **men**, shaved them, cut off their garments
19: 19 When the **vassals** *of* Hadadezer saw that they had been defeated by
20: 8 of Rapha in Gath, and they fell at the hands of David and his **men**.
21: 3 My lord the king, are they not all my lord's **subjects**? Why does
21: 8 Now, I beg you, take away the guilt of your **servant**. I have done a
2Ch 1: 3 which Moses the LORD's **servant** had made in the desert.
2: 8 [2:7] for I know that your **men** are skilled in cutting timber there.
2: 8 [2:7] in cutting timber there. My **men** will work with yours
2: 8 [2:7] cutting timber there. My men will work with yours **[RPH]**
2: 10 [2:9] I will give your **servants**, the woodsmen who cut the timber,
2: 15 [2:14] "Now let my lord send his **servants** the wheat and barley
6: 14 you who keep your covenant of love with your **servants** who
6: 15 You have kept your promise to your **servant** David my father;
6: 16 keep for your **servant** David my father the promises you made to
6: 17 let your word that you promised your **servant** David come true.
6: 19 Yet give attention to your **servant's** prayer and his plea for mercy,
6: 19 and the prayer that your **servant** is praying in your presence.
6: 20 May you hear the prayer your **servant** prays toward this place.
6: 21 Hear the supplications of your **servant** and of your people Israel
6: 23 Judge between your **servants**, repaying the guilty by bringing
6: 27 then hear from heaven and forgive the sin of your **servants**,
6: 42 Remember the great love promised to David your **servant**."
8: 9 But Solomon did not make **slaves** of the Israelites for his work;
8: 18 And Hiram sent him ships commanded by his own **officers**,
8: 18 him ships commanded by his own officers, **men** who knew the sea.
8: 18 These, with Solomon's **men**, sailed to Ophir and brought back four
9: 4 the food on his table, the seating of his **officials**, the attending
9: 7 How happy your **officials**, who continually stand before you
9: 10 (The **men** *of* Hiram and the men of Solomon brought gold from
9: 10 men of Hiram and the **men** *of* Solomon brought gold from Ophir;
9: 12 Then she left and returned with her **retinue** to her own country.
9: 21 The king had a fleet of trading ships manned by Hiram's **men**.
10: 7 give them a favorable answer, they will always be your **servants**."
12: 8 They will, however, become **subject** to him, so that they may learn
13: 6 an **official** *of* Solomon son of David, rebelled against his master.
24: 6 Jerusalem the tax imposed by Moses the **servant** *of* the LORD
24: 9 that Moses the **servant** *of* God had required of Israel in the desert.
24: 25 His **officials** conspired against him for murdering the son of
25: 3 he executed the **officials** who had murdered his father the king.
28: 10 intend to **make** the **men** … your **slaves** [+3899+4200+4200].
32: 9 he sent his **officers** to Jerusalem with this message for Hezekiah
32: 16 Sennacherib's **officers** spoke further against the LORD God
32: 16 further against the LORD God and against his **servant** Hezekiah.
33: 24 Amon's **officials** conspired against him and assassinated him in his
34: 16 "Your **officials** are doing everything that has been committed to
34: 20 of Micah, Shaphan the secretary and Asaiah the king's **attendant**:
35: 23 Archers shot King Josiah, and he told his **officers**, "Take me away;
35: 24 So **they**[s] [+2257] took him out of his chariot, put him in the other
36: 20 they became **servants** to him and his sons until the kingdom of
Ezr 2: 55 The descendants of the **servants** *of* Solomon: the descendants of
2: 58 and the descendants of the **servants** *of* Solomon 392
2: 65 besides their 7,337 **menservants** and maidservants; and they also
9: 9 Though we are **slaves**, our God has not deserted us in our bondage.
9: 11 you gave through your **servants** the prophets when you said:
Ne 1: 6 your eyes open to hear the prayer your **servant** is praying before
1: 6 your servant is praying before you day and night for your **servants**,
1: 7 the commands, decrees and laws you gave your **servant** Moses.
1: 8 "Remember the instruction you gave your **servant** Moses,
1: 10 "They are your **servants** and your people, whom you redeemed by
1: 11 let your ear be attentive to the prayer of this your **servant**
1: 11 to the prayer of your **servants** who delight in revering your name.
1: 11 Give your **servant** success today by granting him favor in the
2: 5 it pleases the king and if your **servant** has found favor in his sight,
2: 10 the Horonite and Tobiah the Ammonite **official** heard about this,
2: 19 Tobiah the Ammonite **official** and Geshem the Arab heard about it,
2: 20 We his **servants** will start rebuilding, but as for you, you have no
5: 5 as theirs, yet we have to subject our sons and daughters to **slavery**.
7: 57 The descendants of the **servants** *of* Solomon: the descendants of
7: 60 and the descendants of the **servants** *of* Solomon 392
7: 67 besides their 7,337 **menservants** and maidservants; and they also
9: 10 against all his **officials** and all the people of his land,
9: 14 them commands, decrees and laws through your **servant** Moses.
9: 36 "But see, we are **slaves** today, slaves in the land you gave our
9: 36 **slaves** in the land you gave our forefathers so they could eat its
10: 29 [10:30] the Law of God given through Moses the **servant** *of* God
11: 3 descendants of Solomon's **servants** lived in the towns of Judah,
Est 1: 3 year of his reign he gave a banquet for all his nobles and **officials**.
2: 18 a great banquet, Esther's banquet, for all his nobles and **officials**.
3: 2 All the royal **officials** at the king's gate knelt down and paid honor
3: 3 Then the royal **officials** at the king's gate asked Mordecai,
4: 11 "All the king's **officials** and the people of the royal provinces
5: 11 and how he had elevated him above the other nobles and **officials**.
7: 4 If we had merely been sold as **male** and female **slaves**, I would
Job 1: 8 the LORD said to Satan, "Have you considered my **servant** Job?
2: 3 the LORD said to Satan, "Have you considered my **servant** Job?
3: 19 and the great are there, and the **slave** is freed from his master.
4: 18 If God places no trust in his **servants**, if he charges his angels with
7: 2 Like a **slave** longing for the evening shadows, or a hired man
19: 16 I summon my **servant**, but he does not answer, though I beg him
31: 13 "If I have denied justice to my **menservants** and maidservants
41: 4 [40:28] with you for you to take him as your **slave** for life?
42: 7 you have not spoken of me what is right, as my **servant** Job has.
42: 8 So now take seven bulls and seven rams and go to my **servant** Job
42: 8 My **servant** Job will pray for you, and I will accept his prayer
42: 8 You have not spoken of me what is right, as my **servant** Job has."
Ps 18: T [18:1] the director of music. Of David the **servant** *of* the LORD.
19: 11 [19:12] By them is your **servant** warned; in keeping them there is
19: 13 [19:14] Keep your **servant** also from willful sins; may they not
27: 9 hide your face from me, do not turn your **servant** away in anger;
31: 16 [31:17] Let your face shine on your **servant**; save me in your
34: 22 [34:23] The LORD redeems his **servants**; no one will be
35: 27 LORD be exalted, who delights in the well-being of his **servant**."
36: T [36:1] the director of music. Of David the **servant** *of* the LORD.
69: 17 [69:18] Do not hide your face from your **servant**; answer me

Ps 69:36 [69:37] the children of his **servants** will inherit it, and those who
78:70 He chose David his **servant** and took him from the sheep pens;
79: 2 They have given the dead bodies of your **servants** as food to the
79:10 the nations that you avenge the outpoured blood of your **servants**.
86: 2 to you. You are my God; save your **servant** who trusts in you.
86: 4 Bring joy to your **servant**, for to you, O Lord, I lift up my soul.
86:16 grant your strength to your **servant** and save the son of your
89: 3 [89:4] with my chosen one, I have sworn to David my **servant**,
89:20 [89:21] I have found David my **servant**; with my sacred oil I have
89:39 [89:40] You have renounced the covenant with your **servant**
89:50 [89:51] Remember, Lord, how your **servant** has been mocked,
90:13 How long will it be? Have compassion on your **servants**.
90:16 May your deeds be shown to your **servants**, your splendor to their
102:14 [102:15] For her stones are dear to your **servants**; her very dust
102:28 [102:29] The children of your **servants** will live in your presence;
105: 6 O descendants of Abraham his **servant**, O sons of Jacob,
105:17 and he sent a man before them—Joseph, sold as a **slave**.
105:25 he turned to hate his people, to conspire against his **servants**.
105:26 He sent Moses his **servant**, and Aaron, whom he had chosen.
105:42 For he remembered his holy promise given to his **servant**
109:28 they attack they will be put to shame, but your **servant** will rejoice.
113: 1 Praise, O **servants** *of* the LORD, praise the name of the LORD.
116:16 O LORD, truly I am your **servant**; I am your servant, the son of
116:16 I am your servant; I am your **servant**, the son of your maidservant;
119:17 Do good to your **servant**, and I will live; I will obey your word.
119:23 and slander me, your **servant** will meditate on your decrees.
119:38 Fulfill your promise to your **servant**, so that you may be feared.
119:49 Remember your word to your **servant**, for you have given me
119:65 Do good to your **servant** according to your word, O LORD.
119:76 love be my comfort, according to your promise to your **servant**.
119:84 How long must your **servant** wait? When will you punish my
119:91 Your laws endure to this day, for all things **serve** you.
119:122 Ensure your **servant's** well-being; let not the arrogant oppress me.
119:124 Deal with your **servant** according to your love and teach me your
119:125 I am your **servant**; give me discernment that I may understand
119:135 Make your face shine upon your **servant** and teach me your
119:140 have been thoroughly tested, and your **servant** loves them.
119:176 Seek your **servant**, for I have not forgotten your commands.
123: 2 As the eyes of **slaves** look to the hand of their master, as the eyes
132:10 For the sake of David your **servant**, do not reject your anointed
134: 1 all you **servants** *of* the LORD who minister by night in the house
135: 1 the name of the LORD; praise him, you **servants** *of* the LORD,
135: 9 into your midst, O Egypt, against Pharaoh and all his **servants**.
135:14 will vindicate his people and have compassion on his **servants**.
136:22 an inheritance to his **servant** Israel; *His love endures*
143: 2 Do not bring your **servant** into judgment, for no one living is
143:12 silence my enemies; destroy all my foes, for I am your **servant**.
144:10 to kings, who delivers his **servant** David from the deadly sword.
Pr 11:29 will inherit only wind, and the fool will be **servant** to the wise.
12: 9 yet have a **servant** than pretend to be somebody and have no food.
14:35 A king delights in a wise **servant**, but a shameful servant incurs his
17: 2 A wise **servant** will rule over a disgraceful son, and will share the
19:10 live in luxury—how much worse for a **slave** to rule over princes!
22: 7 rich rule over the poor, and the borrower is **servant** to the lender.
29:19 A **servant** cannot be corrected by mere words; though he
29:21 If a man pampers his **servant** from youth, he will bring grief in the
30:10 "Do not slander a **servant** to his master, or he will curse you,
30:22 a **servant** who becomes king, a fool who is full of food,
Ecc 2: 7 I bought **male** and female **slaves** and had other slaves who were
7:21 word people say, or you may hear your **servant** cursing you—
10: 7 I have seen **slaves** on horseback, while princes go on foot like
10: 7 seen slaves on horseback, while princes go on foot like **slaves**.
Isa 14: 2 And the house of Israel will possess the nations as **menservants**
20: 3 "Just as my **servant** Isaiah has gone stripped and barefoot for three
22:20 "In that day I will summon my **servant**, Eliakim son of Hilkiah.
24: 2 for master as for **servant**, for mistress as for maid, for seller as for
36: 9 can you repulse one officer of the least of my master's **officials**,
36:11 "Please speak to your **servants** in Aramaic, since we understand it.
37: 5 When King Hezekiah's **officials** came to Isaiah,
37:24 By your **messengers** you have heaped insults on the Lord.
37:35 and save it, for my sake and for the sake of David my **servant**!"
41: 8 "But you, O Israel, my **servant**, Jacob, whom I have chosen,
41: 9 I said, 'You are my **servant**'; I have chosen you and have not
42: 1 "Here is my **servant**, whom I uphold, my chosen one in whom I
42:19 Who is blind but my **servant**, and deaf like the messenger I send?
42:19 the one committed to me, blind like the **servant** *of* the LORD?
43:10 declares the LORD, "and my **servant** whom I have chosen,
44: 1 "But now listen, O Jacob, my **servant**, Israel, whom I have chosen.
44: 2 Do not be afraid, O Jacob, my **servant**, Jeshurun, whom I have
44:21 these things, O Jacob, for you are my **servant**, O Israel.
44:21 I have made you, you are my **servant**; O Israel, I will not forget
44:26 who carries out the words of his **servants** and fulfills the
45: 4 For the sake of Jacob my **servant**, of Israel my chosen, I summon
48:20 of the earth; say, "The LORD has redeemed his **servant** Jacob."
49: 3 He said to me, "You are my **servant**, Israel, in whom I will display
49: 5 he who formed me in the womb to be his **servant** to bring Jacob
49: 6 "It is too small a thing for you to be my **servant** to restore the
49: 7 was despised and abhorred by the nation, to the **servant** *of* rulers:
50:10 among you fears the LORD and obeys the word of his **servant**?
52:13 See, my **servant** will act wisely; he will be raised and lifted up
53:11 by his knowledge my righteous **servant** will justify many,
54:17 This is the heritage of the **servants** *of* **the** LORD, and this is their
56: 6 to love the name of the LORD, and to **worship** him, all who keep
63:17 Return for the sake of your **servants**, the tribes that are your
65: 8 there is yet some good in it,' so will I do in behalf of my **servants**;
65: 9 chosen people will inherit them, and there will my **servants** live.
65:13 "My **servants** will eat, but you will go hungry; my servants will
65:13 will go hungry; my **servants** will drink, but you will go thirsty;
65:13 go thirsty; my **servants** will rejoice, but you will be put to shame.
65:14 My **servants** will sing out of the joy of their hearts, but you will
65:15 put you to death, but to his **servants** he will give another name.
66:14 the hand of the LORD will be made known to his **servants**,
Jer 2:14 Is Israel a **servant**, a slave by birth? Why then has he become
7:25 day after day, again and again I sent you my **servants** the prophets.
21: 7 his **officials** and the people in this city who survive the plague,
22: 2 your **officials** and your people who come through these gates.
22: 4 and on horses, accompanied by their **officials** and their people.
25: 4 though the LORD has sent all his **servants** the prophets to you
25: 9 of the north and my **servant** Nebuchadnezzar king of Babylon,"
25:19 king of Egypt, his **attendants**, his officials and all his people,
26: 5 and if you do not listen to the words of my **servants** the prophets,
27: 6 Now I will hand all your countries over to my **servant**
29:19 that I sent to them again and again by my **servants** the prophets.
30:10 " 'So do not fear, O Jacob my **servant**; do not be dismayed,
33:21 my covenant with David my **servant**—and my covenant with the
33:22 I will make the descendants of David my **servant** and the Levites
33:26 then I will reject the descendants of Jacob and David my **servant**
34: 9 Everyone was to free his Hebrew **slaves**, both **male** and female;
34:10 covenant agreed that they would free their **male** and female **slaves**
34:11 took back the **slaves** [+2256+9148] they had freed and enslaved
34:11 and **enslaved** [+2256+3899+4200+4200+9148] them again.
34:13 when I brought them out of Egypt, out of the land of **slavery**.
34:16 each of you has taken back the **male** and female **slaves** you had set
34:16 You have forced them to become your **slaves** [+2256+9148] again.
35:15 Again and again I sent all my **servants** the prophets to you.
36:24 and all his **attendants** who heard all these words showed no fear,
36:31 and his children and his **attendants** for their wickedness;
37: 2 Neither he nor his **attendants** nor the people of the land paid any
37:18 have I committed against you or your **officials** or this people,
43:10 I will send for my **servant** Nebuchadnezzar king of Babylon,
44: 4 Again and again I sent my **servants** the prophets, who said,
46:26 their lives, to Nebuchadnezzar king of Babylon and his **officers**.
46:27 "Do not fear, O Jacob my **servant**; do not be dismayed, O Israel.
46:28 Do not fear, O Jacob my **servant**, for I am with you,"
La 5: 8 **Slaves** rule over us, and there is none to free us from their hands.
Eze 28:25 they will live in their own land, which I gave to my **servant** Jacob.
34:23 over them one shepherd, my **servant** David, and he will tend them;
34:24 be their God, and my **servant** David will be prince among them.
37:24 " 'My **servant** David will be king over them, and they will all have
37:25 They will live in the land I gave to my **servant** Jacob, the land
37:25 there forever, and David my **servant** will be their prince forever.
38:17 Are you not the one I spoke of in former days by my **servants** the
46:17 he makes a gift from his inheritance to one of his **servants**,
Da 1:12 "Please test your **servants** for ten days: Give us nothing
1:13 and treat your **servants** in accordance with what you see."
9: 6 We have not listened to your **servants** the prophets, who spoke in
9:10 or kept the laws he gave us through his **servants** the prophets.
9:11 the **servant** *of* God, have been poured out on us, because we have
9:17 "Now, our God, hear the prayers and petitions of your **servant**.
10:17 How can I, your **servant**, talk with you, my lord? My strength is
Joel 2:29 [3:2] Even on my **servants**, both **men** and women, I will pour out
Am 3: 7 nothing without revealing his plan to his **servants** the prophets.
Mic 6: 4 you up out of Egypt and redeemed you from the land of **slavery**.
Hag 2:23 'I will take you, my **servant** Zerubbabel son of Shealtiel,'
Zec 1: 6 and my decrees, which I commanded my **servants** the prophets,
2: 9 [2:13] hand against them so that their **slaves** will plunder them.
3: 8 of things to come: I am going to bring my **servant**, the Branch.
Mal 1: 6 "A son honors his father, and a **servant** his master. If I am a father,
4: 4 [3:22] "Remember the law of my **servant** Moses, the decrees

6270 [2]עֶבֶד *'ebed*[2], n.pr.m. [6] [√ 6269]

Ebed [6]

Jdg 9:26 Now Gaal son of **Ebed** moved with his brothers into Shechem,
9:28 Gaal son of **Ebed** said, "Who is Abimelech, and who is Shechem,
9:30 When Zebul the governor of the city heard what Gaal son of **Ebed**
9:31 "Gaal son of **Ebed** and his brothers have come to Shechem
9:35 Now Gaal son of **Ebed** had gone out and was standing at the

Ezr 8: 6 descendants of Adin, **Ebed** son of Jonathan, and with him 50 men;

6271 עָבָד ***ᵃbād***, n.m. [1] [√ 6268]

what do [1]

Ecc 9: 1 the righteous and the wise and **what** they **do** are in God's hands,

6272 עַבְדָּא ***'abdā'***, n.pr.m. [2] [√ 6268]

Abda [2]

1Ki 4: 6 Ahishar—in charge of the palace; Adoniram son of **Abda**—
Ne 11: 17 and **Abda** son of Shammua, the son of Galal, the son of Jeduthun.

6273 עֹבֵד־אֱדוֹם ***'ōbēd-ᵉdôm***, n.pr.m. [20] [√ 6268 + 139]

Obed-Edom [18], him[s] [1], his[s] [1]

2Sa 6: 10 Instead, he took it aside to the house of **Obed-Edom** the Gittite.
6: 11 The ark of the LORD remained in the house of **Obed-Edom** the
6: 11 and the LORD blessed **him**[s] and his entire household.
6: 12 "The LORD has blessed the household of **Obed-Edom** and
6: 12 brought up the ark of God from the house of **Obed-Edom** to the
1Ch 13: 13 Instead, he took it aside to the house of **Obed-Edom** the Gittite.
13: 14 The ark of God remained with the family of **Obed-Edom** in his
13: 14 and the LORD blessed **his**[s] household and everything he had.
15: 18 Mattithiah, Eliphelehu, Mikneiah, **Obed-Edom** and Jeiel,
15: 21 Mikneiah, **Obed-Edom**, Jeiel and Azaziah were to play the harps,
15: 24 **Obed-Edom** and Jehiah were also to be doorkeepers for the ark.
15: 25 ark of the covenant of the LORD from the house of **Obed-Edom**,
16: 5 Jehiel, Mattithiah, Eliab, Benaiah, **Obed-Edom** and Jeiel.
16: 38 He also left **Obed-Edom** and his sixty-eight associates to minister
16: 38 **Obed-Edom** son of Jeduthun, and also Hosah, were gatekeepers.
26: 4 **Obed-Edom** also had sons: Shemaiah the firstborn,
26: 8 All these were descendants of **Obed-Edom**; they and their sons
26: 8 strength to do the work—descendants of **Obed-Edom**, 62 in all.
26: 15 The lot for the South Gate fell to **Obed-Edom**, and the lot for the
2Ch 25: 24 in the temple of God that had been in the care of **Obed-Edom**,

6274 עַבְדְּאֵל ***'abdᵉ'ēl***, n.pr.m. [1] [√ 6269 + 446; cf. 6280]

Abdeel [1]

Jer 36: 26 of Azriel and Shelemiah son of **Abdeel** to arrest Baruch the scribe

6275 עֲבֹדָה ***ᵃbōdâ***, n.f. [145] [√ 6268; Ar 10525]

work [39], service [24], regular work [+4856] [12], labor [7], duties [5], serving [5], use [5], various kinds of service [+2256+6275] [4], ceremony [3], ministering [3], *untranslated* [2], campaign [2], constructing [2], job [2], ministry [2], slavery [2], task [2], as a slave [+6269] [1], assist [1], bondage [+6268] [1], bondage [1], by [1], craft [1], cultivate [1], demands [1], doing work [1], doing [1], effect [1], farmed [1], posts [1], regular service [+7372] [1], required [1], responsible [+4856] [1], responsible [1], served [1], slaves [1], tasks [1], work [+6268] [1], work [+906+6268] [1], workers [+1074] [1], worship [+906+6268] [1]

Ge 29: 27 the younger one also, in return for another seven years of **work**."
30: 26 will be on my way. You know how much **work** I've done for you."
Ex 1: 14 They made their lives bitter with hard **labor** in brick and mortar
1: 14 labor in brick and mortar and with all kinds of **work** in the fields;
1: 14 in all their hard **labor** the Egyptians used them ruthlessly.
2: 23 The Israelites groaned in their **slavery** and cried out, and their cry
2: 23 and their cry for help because of their **slavery** went up to God.
5: 9 Make the **work** harder for the men so that they keep working
5: 11 you can find it, but your **work** will not be reduced at all.' "
6: 6 I will free you from being **slaves** to them, and I will redeem you
6: 9 listen to him because of their discouragement and cruel **bondage**.
12: 25 the LORD will give you as he promised, observe this **ceremony**.
12: 26 your children ask you, 'What does this **ceremony** mean to you?'
13: 5 and honey—you are to observe this **ceremony** in this month:
27: 19 All the other articles used in the **service** *of* the tabernacle,
30: 16 from the Israelites and use it for the **service** *of* the Tent of Meeting.
35: 21 Tent of Meeting, for all its **service**, and for the sacred garments.
35: 24 everyone who had acacia wood for any part of the **work** brought it.
36: 1 ability to know how to carry out all the work of **constructing** the
36: 3 had brought to carry out the work of **constructing** the sanctuary.
36: 5 "The people are bringing more than enough for **doing** the work the
38: 21 which were recorded at Moses' command **by** the Levites under the
39: 32 So all the **work** *on* the tabernacle, the Tent of Meeting,
39: 40 all the furnishings for **[RPH]** the tabernacle, the Tent of Meeting;
39: 42 The Israelites had done all the **work** just as the LORD had
Lev 23: 7 first day hold a sacred assembly and do no **regular work** [+4856].
23: 8 day hold a sacred assembly and do no **regular work** [+4856].' "
23: 21 to proclaim a sacred assembly and do no **regular work** [+4856].
23: 25 Do no **regular work** [+4856], but present an offering made to the
23: 35 The first day is a sacred assembly; do no **regular work** [+4856].
23: 36 by fire. It is the closing assembly; do no **regular work** [+4856].
25: 39 and sells himself to you, do not make him work **as a slave** [+6269].
Nu 3: 7 at the Tent of Meeting by doing the **work** *of* the tabernacle.
3: 8 fulfilling the obligations of the Israelites by doing the **work** *of* the
3: 26 and altar, and the ropes—and everything related to their **use**.
3: 31 used in ministering, the curtain, and everything related to their **use**.
3: 36 bases, all its equipment, and everything related to their **use**,
4: 4 "This is the **work** *of* the Kohathites in the Tent of Meeting:
4: 19 and assign to each man his **work** and what he is to carry.
4: 23 who come to serve in the **work** [+6268] at the Tent of Meeting.
4: 24 "This is the **service** *of* the Gershonite clans as they work and carry
4: 26 the entrance, the ropes and all the equipment used in its **service**.
4: 27 All their **service**, whether carrying or doing other work, is to be
4: 27 All their service, whether carrying or **doing** other **work**, is to be
4: 28 This is the **service** *of* the Gershonite clans at the Tent of Meeting.
4: 30 come to serve in the **work at** [+906+6268] the Tent of Meeting.
4: 31 This is their duty as they perform **service** at the Tent of Meeting:
4: 32 ropes, all their equipment and everything related to their **use**.
4: 33 This is the **service** *of* the Merarite clans as they work at the Tent of
4: 33 This is the service of the Merarite clans as they **work** at the Tent of
4: 35 years of age who came to serve in the **work** in the Tent of Meeting,
4: 39 years of age who came to serve in the **work** at the Tent of Meeting,
4: 43 years of age who came to serve in the **work** at the Tent of Meeting,
4: 47 thirty to fifty years of age who came to do the **work** *of* serving
4: 47 thirty to fifty years of age who came to do the work of **serving**
4: 47 do the work of serving and **[RPH]** carrying the Tent of Meeting
4: 49 through Moses, each was assigned his **work** and told what to carry.
7: 5 that they may be used in the **work** *at* the Tent of Meeting.
7: 5 Give them to the Levites as each man's **work requires**."
7: 7 two carts and four oxen to the Gershonites, as their **work** required,
7: 8 four carts and eight oxen to the Merarites, as their **work** required.
7: 9 their shoulders the holy things, *for* which they were **responsible**.
8: 11 so that they may be ready to do the **work** *of* the LORD.
8: 19 his sons to do the **work** at the Tent of Meeting *on behalf of* the
8: 22 the Levites came to do their **work** at the Tent of Meeting under the
8: 24 or more shall come to take part in the **work** *at* the Tent of Meeting,
8: 25 they must retire from their **regular service** [+7372] and work no
8: 26 at the Tent of Meeting, but they themselves must not do the **work**.
16: 9 brought you near himself to do the **work** *at* the LORD's
18: 4 all the **work** *at* the Tent—and no one else may come near where
18: 6 dedicated to the LORD to do the **work** *at* the Tent of Meeting.
18: 7 the curtain. I am giving you the **service** *of* the priesthood as a gift.
18: 21 return for the **work** they do while serving at the Tent of Meeting.
18: 21 return for the work they do while **serving** *at* the Tent of Meeting.
18: 23 It is the Levites who are to do the **work** *at* the Tent of Meeting
18: 31 for it is your wages for your **work** at the Tent of Meeting.
28: 18 first day hold a sacred assembly and do no **regular work** [+4856].
28: 25 day hold a sacred assembly and do no **regular work** [+4856].
28: 26 hold a sacred assembly and do no **regular work** [+4856].
29: 1 month hold a sacred assembly and do no **regular work** [+4856].
29: 12 hold a sacred assembly and do no **regular work** [+4856].
29: 35 the eighth day hold an assembly and do no **regular work** [+4856].
Dt 26: 6 mistreated us and made us suffer, putting us to hard **labor**.
Jos 22: 27 that we *will* **worship** [+906+6268] the LORD at his sanctuary
1Ki 12: 4 but now lighten the harsh **labor** and the heavy yoke he put on us,
1Ch 4: 21 and the clans of the linen **workers** [+1074] at Beth Ashbea,
6: 32 [6:17] They performed their **duties** according to the regulations
6: 48 [6:33] were assigned to all the other **duties** *of* the tabernacle,
9: 13 were able men, responsible for **ministering** *in* the house of God.
9: 19 were **responsible for** [+4856] guarding the thresholds of the Tent
9: 28 of them were in charge of the articles used in the temple **service**;
23: 24 twenty years old or more *who* **served** *in* the temple of the LORD.
23: 26 to carry the tabernacle or any of the articles used in its **service**."
23: 28 Aaron's descendants in the **service** *of* the temple of the LORD:
23: 28 and the performance of *other* **duties** *at* the house of God.
23: 32 descendants of Aaron, for the **service** *of* the temple of the LORD.
24: 3 them into divisions for their appointed order of **ministering**.
24: 19 This was their appointed order of **ministering** when they entered
25: 1 Heman and Jeduthun for the **ministry** of prophesying,
25: 1 Here is the list of the men who performed this **service**:
25: 6 lyres and harps, for the **ministry** *at* the house of God.
26: 8 their relatives were capable men with the strength to do the **work**—
26: 30 Jordan for all the work of the LORD and for the king's **service**.
27: 26 Ezri son of Kelub was in charge of the field workers who **farmed**
28: 13 and for all the work of **serving** *in* the temple of the LORD,
28: 13 the LORD, as well as for all the articles to be used in its **service**.
28: 14 gold articles to be used in **various kinds of service** [+2256+6275],
28: 14 gold articles to be used in **various kinds of service** [+2256+6275],
28: 14 articles to be used in **various kinds of service** [+2256+6275]:
28: 14 articles to be used in **various kinds of service** [+2256+6275]:
28: 15 and its lamps, according to the **use** of each lampstand;
28: 20 or forsake you until all the work for the **service** *of* the temple of
28: 21 and Levites are ready for all the **work** *on* the temple of God,
28: 21 every willing man skilled in any **craft** will help you in all the
29: 7 They gave toward the **work** *on* the temple of God five thousand

2Ch 8:14 he appointed the divisions of the priests for their **duties**,
10:4 but now lighten the harsh **labor** and the heavy yoke he put on us,
12:8 so that they may learn the difference between **serving** me
12:8 between serving me and **serving** the kings of other lands."
24:12 Jehoiada gave it to the men who carried out the work **required** *for*
29:35 So the **service** *of* the temple of the LORD was reestablished.
31:2 each of them according to their **duties** as priests or Levites—
31:16 of the LORD to perform the daily duties of their *various* **tasks**,
31:21 In everything that he undertook in the **service** *of* God's temple
34:13 of the laborers and supervised all the workers from **job** to job.
34:13 of the laborers and supervised all the workers from job to **job**.
35:2 and encouraged them in the **service** *of* the LORD's temple.
35:10 The **service** was arranged and the priests stood in their places with
35:15 The gatekeepers at each gate did not need to leave their **posts**,
35:16 So at that time the entire **service** *of* the LORD was carried out for
Ezr 8:20 that David and the officials had established to **assist** the Levites.
Ne 3:5 their nobles would not put their shoulders to the **work** *under* their
5:18 to the governor, because the **demands** were heavy on these people.
10:32 [10:33] shekel each year for the **service** *of* the house of our God:
10:37 [10:38] who collect the tithes in all the towns where we **work**.
Ps 104:14 makes grass grow for the cattle, and plants for man to **cultivate**—
104:23 Then man goes out to his work, to his **labor** until evening.
Isa 14:3 you relief from suffering and turmoil and cruel **bondage** [+6268],
28:21 do his work, his strange work, and perform his **task**, his alien task.
28:21 do his work, his strange work, and perform his task, his alien **task**.
32:17 the **effect** *of* righteousness will be quietness and confidence
La 1:3 After affliction and harsh **labor**, Judah has gone into exile.
Eze 29:18 king of Babylon drove his army in a hard **campaign** against Tyre;
29:18 his army got no reward from the **campaign** he led against Tyre.
44:14 of the duties of the temple and all the **work** that is to be done in it.

6276 עֲבֻדָּה *ᵃbuddâ*, n.f. [2] [√ 6268]

servants [2]

Ge 26:14 and herds and **servants** that the Philistines envied him.
Job 1:3 and five hundred donkeys, and had a large number of **servants**.

6277 עַבְדּוֹן[1] *ʿabdôn[1]*, n.pr.m. [6] [√ 6278; cf. 6269]

Abdon [6]

Jdg 12:13 After him, **Abdon** son of Hillel, from Pirathon, led Israel.
12:15 **Abdon** son of Hillel died, and was buried at Pirathon in Ephraim,
1Ch 8:23 **Abdon**, Zicri, Hanan,
8:30 and his firstborn son was **Abdon**, followed by Zur, Kish, Baal,
9:36 and his firstborn son was **Abdon**, followed by Zur, Kish, Baal,
2Ch 34:20 **Abdon** son of Micah, Shaphan the secretary and Asaiah the king's

6278 עַבְדּוֹן[2] *ʿabdôn[2]*, n.pr.loc. [2 / 3] [√ 6277; cf. 6269]

Abdon [3]

Jos 19:28 It went to **Abdon**, [BHS 6306] Rehob, Hammon and Kanah,
21:30 from the tribe of Asher, Mishal, **Abdon**,
1Ch 6:74 [6:59] from the tribe of Asher they received Mashal, **Abdon**,

6279 עַבְדִּי *ʿabdî*, n.pr.m. [3] [√ 6280?]

Abdi [3]

1Ch 6:44 [6:29] Ethan son of Kishi, the son of **Abdi**, the son of Malluch,
2Ch 29:12 the Merarites, Kish son of **Abdi** and Azariah son of Jehallelel;
Ezr 10:26 of Elam: Mattaniah, Zechariah, Jehiel, **Abdi**, Jeremoth and Elijah.

6280 עַבְדִּיאֵל *ʿabdîʾēl*, n.pr.m. [1] [→ 6274, 6279?; cf. 6269 + 446, 6274]

Abdiel [1]

1Ch 5:15 Ahi son of **Abdiel**, the son of Guni, was head of their family.

6281 עֹבַדְיָה *ʿōbadyâ*, n.pr.m. [11] [√ 6268 + 3378]

Obadiah [11]

1Ch 3:21 and the sons of Rephaiah, of Arnan, of **Obadiah** and of Shecaniah.
7:3 The sons of Izrahiah: Michael, **Obadiah**, Joel and Isshiah.
8:38 Azrikam, Bokeru, Ishmael, Sheariah, **Obadiah** and Hanan.
9:16 **Obadiah** son of Shemaiah, the son of Galal, the son of Jeduthun;
9:44 Azrikam, Bokeru, Ishmael, Sheariah, **Obadiah** and Hanan.
12:9 [12:10] **Obadiah** the second in command, Eliab the third,
2Ch 17:7 **Obadiah**, Zechariah, Nethanel and Micaiah to teach in the towns
Ezr 8:9 of Joab, **Obadiah** son of Jehiel, and with him 218 men;
Ne 10:5 [10:6] Harim, Meremoth, **Obadiah**,
12:25 Mattaniah, Bakbukiah, **Obadiah**, Meshullam, Talmon and Akkub
Ob 1:1 The vision of **Obadiah**. This is what the Sovereign LORD says

6282 עֹבַדְיָהוּ *ʿōbadyāhû*, n.pr.m. [9] [√ 6268 + 3378]

Obadiah [9]

1Ki 18:3 Ahab had summoned **Obadiah**, who was in charge of his palace.
18:3 of his palace. (**Obadiah** was a devout believer in the LORD.
18:4 **Obadiah** had taken a hundred prophets and hidden them in two
18:5 Ahab had said to **Obadiah**, "Go through the land to all the springs
18:6 to cover, Ahab going in one direction and **Obadiah** in another.
18:7 As **Obadiah** was walking along, Elijah met him. Obadiah
18:16 So **Obadiah** went to meet Ahab and told him, and Ahab went to
1Ch 27:19 over Zebulun: Ishmaiah son of **Obadiah**; over Naphtali:
2Ch 34:12 Over them to direct them were Jahath and **Obadiah**, Levites

6283 עֶבֶד־מֶלֶךְ *ʿebed-melek*, n.pr.m. [6] [√ 6269 + 4889]

Ebed-Melech [6]

Jer 38:7 But **Ebed-Melech**, a Cushite, an official in the royal palace,
38:8 **Ebed-Melech** went out of the palace and said to him,
38:10 the king commanded **Ebed-Melech** the Cushite, "Take thirty men
38:11 So **Ebed-Melech** took the men with him and went to a room under
38:12 **Ebed-Melech** the Cushite said to Jeremiah, "Put these old rags
39:16 "Go and tell **Ebed-Melech** the Cushite, 'This is what the LORD

6284 עֲבֵד נְגוֹ *ᵃbēd nᵉgô*, n.pr.m. [1] [√ 6269 + 5550; Ar 10460, 10524]

Abednego [1]

Da 1:7 Shadrach; to Mishael, Meshach; and to Azariah, **Abednego**.

6285 עַבְדֻת *ʿabdut*, n.f. [3] [√ 6268]

bondage [2], slavery [1]

Ezr 9:8 our God gives light to our eyes and a little relief in our **bondage**.
9:9 we are slaves, our God has not deserted us in our **bondage**.
Ne 9:17 their rebellion appointed a leader in order to return to their **slavery**.

6286 עָבָה *ʿābâ*, v. [3] [→ 5043, 6267, 6295]

thicker [2], heavy [1]

Dt 32:15 [A] and kicked; filled with food, *he became* **heavy** and sleek.
1Ki 12:10 [A] tell them, 'My little finger *is* **thicker** than my father's waist.
2Ch 10:10 [A] tell them, 'My little finger *is* **thicker** than my father's waist.

6287 עֲבוֹט *ᵃbôṭ*, n.[m.]. [4] [→ 6292, 6294]

pledge [2], *untranslated* [1], offering as a pledge [1]

Dt 24:10 do not go into his house to get *what* he is **offering as a pledge**.
24:11 let the man to whom you are making the loan bring the **pledge** out
24:12 man is poor, do not go to sleep with his **pledge** in your possession.
24:13 Return **[RPH]** his cloak to him by sunset so that he may sleep in

6288 עֲבוּר[1] *ᵃbûr[1]*, pp. & c. [49] [→ 1236]

for the sake of [+928] [11], because of [+928] [6], so that [+928] [5], for sake [+928] [4], to [+928] [4], because [+928] [3], for [+928] [2], in order to [+928] [2], on account of [+928] [2], so [+928] [2], that [+928] [2], *untranslated* [2], for this purpose [+928] [1], then [+928] [1], to [+928+4200] [1], while [+928] [1]

Ge 3:17 must not eat of it,' "Cursed is the ground **because** [+928] **of** you;
8:21 "Never again will I curse the ground **because** [+928] **of** man,
12:13 so that I will be treated well **for** [+928] your **sake** and my life will
12:16 He treated Abram well **for** [+928] her **sake**, and Abram acquired
18:26 city of Sodom, I will spare the whole place **for** [+928] their **sake**."
18:29 He said, "**For** [+928] **the sake of** forty, I will not do it."
18:31 He said, "**For** [+928] **the sake of** twenty, I will not destroy it."
18:32 He answered, "**For** [+928] **the sake of** ten, I will not destroy it."
21:30 "Accept these seven lambs from my hand **[NIE]** as a witness that
26:24 of your descendants for [+928] **the sake of** my servant Abraham."
27:4 bring it to me to eat, **so** [+928] **that** I may give you my blessing
27:10 take it to your father to eat, **so** [+928] that he may give you his
27:19 eat some of my game **so** [+928] **that** you may give me your
27:31 eat some of my game, **so** [+928] **that** you may give me your
46:34 just as our fathers did.' **Then** [+928] you will be allowed to settle
Ex 9:14 your people, **so** [+928] you may know that there is no one like me
9:16 I have raised you up **for** [+928] **this** very **purpose**, that I might
9:16 I have raised you up for this very purpose, **that** [+928] I might
13:8 'I do this **because** [+928] **of** what the LORD did for me when I
19:9 "I am going to come to you in a dense cloud, **so** [+928] **that** the
20:20 God has come **to** [+928+4200] test you, so that the fear of God will
20:20 God has come to test you, **so** [+928] **that** the fear of God will be
1Sa 1:6 her rival kept provoking her **in order to** [+928] irritate her.
12:22 **For** [+928] **the sake of** his great name the LORD will not reject
23:10 to come to Keilah and destroy the town **on account** [+928] **of** me.
2Sa 5:12 had exalted his kingdom **for** [+928] **the sake of** his people Israel.
6:12 and everything he has, **because** [+928] **of** the ark of God."

2Sa 7:21 **For** [+928] **the sake of** your word and according to your will,
9: 1 of Saul to whom I can show kindness **for** [+928] Jonathan's **sake**?"
9: 7 "for I will surely show you kindness **for** [+928] **the sake of** your
10: 3 Hasn't David sent them to you **to** [+928] explore the city and spy it
12:21 "Why are you acting this way? **While** [+928] the child was alive,
12:25 **because** [+928] the LORD loved him, he sent word through
13: 2 to the point of illness **on account** [+928] **of** his sister Tamar,
14:20 Your servant Joab did this **to** [+928] change the present situation.
17:14 of Ahithophel **in order to** [+928] bring disaster on Absalom.
18:18 "I have no son **to** [+928] carry on the memory of my name."
1Ch 14: 2 that his kingdom had been highly exalted **for** [+928] **the sake of**
17:19 O LORD. **For** [+928] **the sake of** your servant and according to
19: 3 Haven't his men come to you **to** [+928] explore and spy out the
2Ch 28:19 The LORD had humbled Judah **because** [+928] **of** Ahaz king of
Job 20: 2 "My troubled thoughts prompt me to answer **because** [+928] I am
Ps 105:45 **that** [+928] they might keep his precepts and observe his laws.
106:32 the LORD, and trouble came to Moses **because** [+928] **of** them;
132:10 **For** [+928] **the sake of** David your servant, do not reject your
Jer 14: 4 The **[NIE]** ground is cracked because there is no rain in the land;
Am 2: 6 the righteous for silver, and the needy **for** [+928] a pair of sandals.
8: 6 the poor with silver and the needy **for** [+928] a pair of sandals,
Mic 2:10 For this is not your resting place, **because** [+928] it is defiled,

6289 ²עֲבוּר *ʿᵃbûr²*, n.[m.]. [2] [√ 6296]

food [1], produce [1]

Jos 5:11 that very day, they ate some of the **produce** *of* the land:
5:12 The manna stopped the day after they ate this **food** *from* the land;

6290 ¹עָבֹת *ʿābôt¹*, a. [4] [√ 6309]

leafy [3], shade [1]

Lev 23:40 palm fronds, **leafy** branches and poplars, and rejoice before the
Ne 8:15 and from myrtles, palms and **shade** trees, to make booths"—
Eze 6:13 the mountaintops, under every spreading tree and every **leafy** oak—
20:28 sworn to give them and they saw any high hill or any **leafy** tree,

6291 ²עֲבוֹת *ʿābôt²*, n.m. & f. [5] [√ 6309]

thick foliage [4], boughs [1]

Ps 118:27 With **boughs** in hand, join in the festal procession up to the horns
Eze 19:11 It towered high above the **thick foliage**, conspicuous for its height
31: 3 the forest; it towered on high, its top above the **thick foliage**.
31:10 lifting its top above the **thick foliage**, and because it was proud of
31:14 to tower proudly on high, lifting their tops above the **thick foliage**.

6292 ¹עָבַט *ʿābaṭ¹*, v.den. [5] [√ 6287]

freely lend [+6292] [2], borrow [1], get [1], lend [1]

Dt 15: 6 [G] you *will* **lend** *to* many nations but will borrow from none.
15: 6 [A] you will lend to many nations but *will* **borrow** from none.
15: 8 [G] and **freely lend** [+6292] him whatever he needs.
15: 8 [G] and **freely lend** [+6292] him whatever he needs.
24:10 [A] do not go into his house to **get** what he is offering as a

6293 ²עָבַט *ʿābaṭ²*, v.den. [1]

swerving [1]

Joel 2: 7 [D] They all march in line, not **swerving** *from* their course.

6294 עַבְטִיט *ʿabṭîṭ*, n.[m.]intens. [1] [√ 6287]

extortion [1]

Hab 2: 6 piles up stolen goods and makes himself wealthy *by* **extortion**!

6295 עֲבִי *ʿᵃbî*, n.[m.]. [5] [√ 6286]

thick [2], thickness [2], molds [1]

1Ki 7:26 It was a handbreadth *in* **thickness**, and its rim was like the rim of a
2Ch 4: 5 It was a handbreadth *in* **thickness**, and its rim was like the rim of a
4:17 The king had them cast in clay **molds** in the plain of the Jordan
Job 15:26 defiantly charging against him with a **thick**, strong shield.
Jer 52:21 cubits in circumference; each was four fingers **thick**, and hollow.

6296 ¹עָבַר *ʿābar¹*, v. [547 / 543] [→ 5044, 5045, 6289, 6298, 6299, 6300, 6302, 6305]

crossed [31], pass [30], cross [28], cross over [23], passed [21], crossed over [17], go [17], crossing [12], went [10], passed by [9], pass by [8], pass through [8], went on [8], go over [7], sacrificed [6], violated [6], come [5], go on [5], moved on [5], swept [5], *untranslated* [4], pass by [+2006] [4], sacrifice [4], take away [4], advanced [3], came along [3], come over [3], continued [3], going [3], led [3], over [3], pass away [3], passed through [3], spread [3], traveled [3], bring across [+906+906+6296] [2], bring across [2], broken [2], came by [2], comes [2], cross over without fail [+6296] [2], disobey [2], get through [2], go beyond [2], go on way [2], go past [2], going down [2], gone by [2], gone [2], had pass [2], journey [2], led through [2], make [2], marched [2], pass on [2], passed along [2], passer-by [2], passes [2], passing by [2], passing through [2], past [2], put [2], send [2], spare [2], sweep through [2], sweeps by [2], swept by [2], taken away [2], travel [2], travelers [2], travels [2], turn over [2], walked [2], according to the weight current [1], advance [1], avert [+4946+6584] [1], be over [1], been [1], beyond [1], blown [1], blows [1], breed [1], brought over [1], brought [1], came to the other side [1], carried over [1], carry over [1], cast off [1], cause to pass [1], cease [1], census [+408] [1], coming over [1], coming [1], continue on [1], continued along [1], continued on [1], counted off [+928+5031] [1], cover [+6584] [1], cover [1], crosses over [1], crossing over [1], did[s] so [1], disobeyed [1], disobeying [1], disregarded [1], driven [1], enter [1], exceed [1], expelled [1], explored [+906+928+9365] [1], extended [1], fail [1], fall [1], felt [1], fleeting [1], flowing [1], follow [+339] [1], forded [1], forgive [1], forgives [1], forth [1], give over [1], go away [1], goes across [1], goes through [1], goes [1], going over [1], gone on [1], had pass by [1], have no limit [1], have shave [+6584+9509] [1], have sounded [1], invade [+928] [1], invade [1], irresistible [1], issued [1], jealous [+6584+7863+8120] [1], kept on going [1], know no limits [1], laid [1], lead across [+4200+7156] [1], leaving [+4946] [1], led around [1], let pass [1], make cross [1], marauding [+2256+8740] [1], march on [1], marched on [1], marched past [+3338+6584] [1], marching [1], missed [1], moved on ahead [1], moved on beyond [1], moves on [1], on the way [1], on way [1], outran [1], over going [1], overcome [1], overflow [1], overlook [1], overrun [1], overstep [1], overwhelmed [+8031] [1], overwhelming [1], pass into other hands [1], passed away [1], passes by [1], passing [1], perish [1], perishing [1], provide safe-conduct [1], put a yoke [1], put an end [1], ran past [1], ran [1], reclaimed [1], remove [1], removed [1], repealed [1], roam [1], sacrificed [+906+928+5989] [1], sacrifices [1], sail [1], seafarers [+3542] [1], send out [1], sent across [1], sent over [1], sent throughout [1], sent [1], set free [1], shave [1], sin [1], sound [1], spreading among [1], surrounded [1], sweep [1], sweeps on [1], swept away [1], swim [1], take note as pass [1], take over [1], taken from [1], taken over [1], them[s] [+2021] [1], they[s] [+2021] [1], through [1], took off [1], took [1], transfer [1], transgressed [1], travel [+2006] [1], traveled along [1], traveling through [1], turn away [1], turned aside [1], untraveled [+408+1172+4946] [1], used [1], vanishes [1], violate [1], violation [1], wade through [1], walk on [1], walk over [1], walked over [1], went as far as [1], went away [1], went forward [1], went over [1], went up [1]

Ge 8: 1 [G] and he **sent** a wind over the earth, and the waters receded.
12: 6 [A] Abram **traveled** through the land as far as the site of the
15:17 [A] with a blazing torch appeared and **passed** between the pieces.
18: 3 [A] favor in your eyes, my lord, *do* not **pass** your servant by.
18: 5 [A] to eat, so you can be refreshed and then **go on** *your* **way**—
18: 5 [A] go on your way—now that *you have* **come** to your servant."
23:16 [A] **according to the weight current** among the merchants.
30:32 [A] *Let me* **go** through all your flocks today and remove from
31:21 [A] So he fled with all he had, and **crossing** the River, he headed
31:52 [A] that I *will* not **go past** this heap to your side to harm you
31:52 [A] that you *will* not **go past** this heap and pillar to my side to
32:10 [32:11] [A] I had only my staff *when I* **crossed** this Jordan,
32:16 [32:17] [A] by itself, and said to his servants, "**Go** ahead of me,
32:21 [32:22] [A] So Jacob's gifts **went on** ahead of him, but he
32:22 [32:23] [A] his eleven sons and **crossed** the ford of the Jabbok.
32:23 [32:24] [G] After *he had* **sent** them **across** the stream, he sent
32:23 [32:24] [G] across the stream, *he* **sent over** all his possessions.
32:31 [32:32] [A] The sun rose above him as *he* **passed** Peniel, and he
33: 3 [A] *He* himself **went on** ahead and bowed down to the ground
33:14 [A] So *let* my lord **go on** ahead of his servant, while I move
37:28 [A] So when the Midianite merchants **came by**, his brothers
41:46 [A] out from Pharaoh's presence and **traveled** throughout Egypt.
47:21 [g] Joseph reduced [BHS *moved*; NIV 6268] the people to
50: 4 [A] When the days of mourning *had* **passed**, Joseph said to
Ex 12:12 [A] "On that same night *I will* **pass** through Egypt and strike
12:23 [A] When the LORD **goes through** the land to strike down the
13:12 [G] *you are to* **give over** to the LORD the first offspring of
15:16 [A] until your people **pass by**, O LORD, until the people you
15:16 [A] pass by, O LORD, until the people you bought **pass by**.
17: 5 [A] LORD answered Moses, "**Walk on** ahead of the people.
30:13 [A] Each *one* who **crosses over** to those already counted is to
30:14 [A] All who **cross over**, those twenty years old or more, are to
32:27 [A] and **forth** through the camp from one end to the other,
33:19 [G] "I *will* **cause** all my goodness **to pass** in front of you,
33:22 [A] When my glory **passes by**, I will put you in a cleft in the rock
33:22 [A] the rock and cover you with my hand until I *have* **passed by**.
34: 6 [A] he **passed** in front of Moses, proclaiming, "The LORD,
36: 6 [G] gave an order and *they* **sent** this word **throughout** the camp:
38:26 [A] from everyone who *had* **crossed over** to those counted,
Lev 18:21 [G] " 'Do not give any of your children to *be* **sacrificed** to

Lev 25: 9 [G] **have** the trumpet **sounded** everywhere on the tenth day of
25: 9 [G] on the Day of Atonement **sound** the trumpet throughout your
26: 6 [A] the land, and the sword *will* not **pass** through your country.
27:32 [A] every tenth animal that **passes** under the shepherd's rod—
Nu 5:14 [A] if feelings of jealousy **come** over her husband and he
5:14 [A] or if he *is* **jealous** [+6584+7863+8120] and suspects her even
5:30 [A] or when feelings of jealousy **come** over a man because he
6: 5 [A] of his vow of separation no razor *may be* **used** on his head.
8: 7 [G] **have** *them* **shave** [+6584+9509] their whole bodies
13:32 [A] "The land *we* **explored** [+906+928+9365] devours those living
14: 7 [A] "The land *we* **passed** through and explored is exceedingly
14:41 [A] "Why *are* you **disobeying** the LORD's command?
20:17 [A] Please *let us* **pass** through your country. We will not go
20:17 [A] *We will* not **go** through any field or vineyard, or drink water
20:17 [A] or to the left until *we have* **passed through** your territory."
20:18 [A] "*You may* not **pass** through here; if you try, we will march
20:19 [A] *We* only *want to* **pass through** on foot—nothing else."
20:20 [A] Again they answered: "*You may* not **pass through**."
20:21 [A] Since Edom refused to let them **go** through their territory,
21:22 [A] "*Let us* **pass** through your country. We will not turn aside
21:22 [A] highway until *we have* **passed through** your territory."
21:23 [A] Sihon would not let Israel **pass** through his territory. He
22:18 [A] or small to **go beyond** the command of the LORD my God.
22:26 [A] the angel of the LORD **moved on ahead** and stood in a
24:13 [A] good or bad, *to* **go beyond** the command of the LORD—
27: 7 [G] and **turn** their father's inheritance **over** to them.
27: 8 [G] and leaves no son, **turn** his inheritance **over** to his daughter.
31:23 [G] anything else that can withstand fire *must be* **put** through the
31:23 [G] whatever cannot withstand fire *must be* **put** through that
32: 5 [G] as our possession. *Do* not **make** us **cross** the Jordan."
32: 7 [A] Why do you discourage the Israelites from **going over** into
32:21 [A] if all of you *will* **go** armed **over** the Jordan before the
32:27 [A] *will* **cross over** to fight before the LORD, just as our lord
32:29 [A] for battle, **cross over** the Jordan with you before the LORD,
32:30 [A] if *they do* not **cross over** with you armed, they must accept
32:32 [A] We *will* **cross over** before the LORD *into* Canaan armed,
33: 8 [A] left Pi Hahiroth and **passed** through the sea into the desert,
33:51 [A] and say to them: 'When you **cross** the Jordan into Canaan,
34: 4 [A] **continue on** to Zin and go south of Kadesh Barnea.
34: 4 [A] Then it will go to Hazar Addar and **over** to Azmon,
35:10 [A] and say to them: 'When you **cross** the Jordan into Canaan,
Dt 2: 4 [A] 'You *are about to* **pass** through the territory of your brothers
2: 8 [A] So *we* **went on** past our brothers the descendants of Esau,
2: 8 [A] Ezion Geber, and **traveled along** the desert road of Moab.
2:13 [A] the LORD said, "Now get up and **cross** the Zered Valley."
2:13 [A] get up and cross the Zered Valley." So *we* **crossed** the valley.
2:14 [A] we left Kadesh Barnea until *we* **crossed** the Zered Valley.
2:18 [A] "Today you *are to* **pass by** the region of Moab at Ar.
2:24 [A] "Set out now and **cross** the Arnon Gorge. See, I have given
2:27 [A] "*Let us* **pass** through your country. We will stay on the main
2:28 [A] for their price in silver. Only *let us* **pass through** on foot—
2:29 [A] until *we* **cross** the Jordan into the land the LORD our God
2:30 [G] But Sihon king of Heshbon refused *to* **let** us **pass** through.
3:18 [A] for battle, *must* **cross over** ahead of your brother Israelites.
3:21 [A] same to all the kingdoms **over** there where you *are* **going**.
3:25 [A] *Let me* **go over** and see the good land beyond the Jordan—
3:27 [A] your own eyes, since *you are* not *going to* **cross** this Jordan.
3:28 [A] for he *will* **lead** this people **across** [+4200+7156] and will
4:14 [A] laws you are to follow in the land that you *are* **crossing** the
4:21 [A] he solemnly swore that I *would* not **cross** the Jordan
4:22 [A] I will die in this land; I *will* not **cross** the Jordan; but you are
4:22 [A] you *are about to* **cross over** and take possession of that good
4:26 [A] from the land that you *are* **crossing** the Jordan to possess.
6: 1 [A] in the land that you *are* **crossing** the Jordan to possess,
9: 1 [A] You *are* now *about to* **cross** the Jordan to go in
9: 3 [A] the *one who* **goes across** ahead of you like a devouring fire.
11: 8 [A] take over the land that you *are* **crossing** the Jordan to
11:11 [A] the land you *are* **crossing** the Jordan to take possession of is
11:31 [A] You *are about to* **cross** the Jordan to enter and take
12:10 [A] *you will* **cross** the Jordan and settle in the land the LORD
17: 2 [A] eyes of the LORD your God in **violation** *of* his covenant,
18:10 [G] Let no one be found among you *who* **sacrifices** his son
24: 5 [A] must not be sent to war or *have* any other duty **laid** on him.
26:13 [A] *I have* not **turned aside** from your commands nor have I
27: 2 [A] When *you have* **crossed** the Jordan into the land the LORD
27: 3 [A] *have* **crossed over** to enter the land the LORD your God is
27: 4 [A] when you *have* **crossed** the Jordan, set up these stones on
27:12 [A] When you *have* **crossed** the Jordan, these tribes shall stand
29:12 [29:11] [A] You are standing here in order to **enter** into a
29:16 [29:15] [A] how *we* **passed** through the countries on the way
29:16 [29:15] [A] how we passed through the countries **on the way**
30:13 [A] "Who *will* **cross** the sea to get it and proclaim it to us so we
30:18 [A] You will not live long in the land you *are* **crossing** the
31: 2 [A] The LORD has said to me, '*You shall* not **cross** the Jordan.'
31: 3 [A] The LORD your God himself *will* **cross over** ahead of you.
31: 3 [A] Joshua also *will* **cross over** ahead of you, as the LORD
31:13 [A] you live in the land you *are* **crossing** the Jordan to possess."
32:47 [A] By them you will live long in the land you *are* **crossing** the
34: 4 [A] see it with your eyes, but *you will* not **cross over** into it."
Jos 1: 2 [A] get ready *to* **cross** the Jordan River into the land I am about
1:11 [A] "**Go** through the camp and tell the people, 'Get your supplies
1:11 [A] Three days from now you *will* **cross** the Jordan here to go in
1:14 [A] fully armed, *must* **cross over** ahead of your brothers.
2:23 [A] **forded** the river and came to Joshua son of Nun and told him
3: 1 [A] went to the Jordan, where they camped before **crossing over**.
3: 2 [A] After three days the officers **went** throughout the camp,
3: 4 [A] which way to go, since *you have* never **been** this way before.
3: 6 [A] up the ark of the covenant and **pass on** ahead of the people."
3:11 [A] the ark of the covenant of the Lord of all the earth *will* **go**
3:14 [A] So when the people broke camp to **cross** the Jordan,
3:16 [A] cut off. So the people **crossed over** opposite Jericho.
3:17 [A] while all Israel **passed by** until the whole nation had
3:17 [A] the whole nation had completed the **crossing** on dry ground.
4: 1 [A] When the whole nation had finished **crossing** the Jordan,
4: 3 [G] *to* **carry** them **over** with you and put them down at the place
4: 5 [A] "**Go over** before the ark of the LORD your God into the
4: 7 [A] When it **crossed** the Jordan, the waters of the Jordan were
4: 8 [G] *they* **carried** them **over** with them to their camp, where they
4:10 [A] just as Moses had directed Joshua. The people hurried **over**,
4:11 [A] as soon as all of them *had* **crossed**, the ark of the LORD
4:11 [A] the priests **came to the other side** while the people watched.
4:12 [A] and the half-tribe of Manasseh **crossed over**, armed,
4:13 [A] About forty thousand armed for battle **crossed over** before
4:22 [A] tell them, 'Israel **crossed** the Jordan on dry ground.'
4:23 [A] dried up the Jordan before you until you *had* **crossed over**.
4:23 [A] Sea when he dried it up before us until we *had* **crossed over**.
5: 1 [A] up the Jordan before the Israelites until we *had* **crossed over**,
6: 7 [A] he ordered the people, "**Advance**! March around the city,
6: 7 [A] with the armed guard **going** ahead of the ark of the LORD."
6: 8 [A] the seven trumpets before the LORD **went forward**,
7: 7 [G] why *did you ever* **bring** this people **across** [+906+906+6296]
7: 7 [G] why *did you ever* **bring** this people **across** [+906+906+6296]
7:11 [A] *they have* **violated** my covenant, which I commanded them
7:15 [A] *He has* **violated** the covenant of the LORD and has done a
10:29 [A] and all Israel with him **moved on** from Makkedah to Libnah
10:31 [A] and all Israel with him **moved on** from Libnah to Lachish;
10:34 [A] and all Israel with him **moved on** from Lachish to Eglon;
15: 3 [A] **continued on** to Zin and went over to the south of Kadesh
15: 3 [A] *it* **ran past** Hezron up to Addar and curved around to Karka.
15: 4 [A] *It* then **passed along** to Azmon and joined the Wadi of
15: 6 [A] **continued** north of Beth Arabah to the Stone of Bohan son of
15: 7 [A] It **continued along** to the waters of En Shemesh and came
15:10 [A] **ran** along the northern slope of Mount Jearim (that is,
15:10 [A] continued down to Beth Shemesh and **crossed** *to* Timnah.
15:11 [A] **passed along** *to* Mount Baalah and reached Jabneel.
16: 2 [A] Luz), **crossed over** to the territory of the Arkites in Ataroth,
16: 6 [A] to Taanath Shiloh, **passing by** it to Janoah on the east.
18: 9 [A] So the men left and **went** through the land. They wrote its
18:13 [A] From there it **crossed** to the south slope of Luz (that is,
18:18 [A] *It* **continued** to the northern slope of Beth Arabah and on
18:19 [A] It then **went** to the northern slope of Beth Hoglah and came
19:13 [A] Then *it* **continued** eastward to Gath Hepher and Eth Kazin;
22:19 [A] land you possess is defiled, **come over** to the LORD's land,
23:16 [A] If you **violate** the covenant of the LORD your God,
24:11 [A] " 'Then *you* **crossed** the Jordan and came to Jericho. The
24:17 [A] and among all the nations through which *we* **traveled**.
Jdg 2:20 [A] "Because this nation *has* **violated** the covenant that I laid
3:26 [A] got away. He **passed by** the idols and escaped to Seirah.
3:28 [A] Jordan that led to Moab, they allowed no one to **cross over**.
6:33 [A] **crossed over** the Jordan and camped in the Valley of Jezreel.
8: 4 [A] yet keeping up the pursuit, came to the Jordan and **crossed** it.
9:25 [A] on the hilltops to ambush and rob everyone who **passed** by,
9:26 [A] Now Gaal son of Ebed moved with his brothers **[NIE]** into
10: 9 [A] The Ammonites also **crossed** the Jordan to fight against
11:17 [A] saying, '*Give us permission to* **go** through your country,'
11:19 [A] to him, '*Let us* **pass** through your country to our own place.'
11:20 [A] however, did not trust Israel *to* **pass** through his territory.
11:29 [A] *He* **crossed** Gilead and Manasseh, passed through Mizpah of
11:29 [A] and Manasseh, **passed through** Mizpah of Gilead,
11:29 [A] and from there *he* **advanced** *against* the Ammonites.
11:32 [A] Jephthah **went** over to fight the Ammonites, and the LORD
12: 1 [A] their forces, **crossed over** to Zaphon and said to Jephthah,
12: 1 [A] "Why *did you* **go** to fight the Ammonites without calling us
12: 3 [A] life in my hands and **crossed** over to fight the Ammonites,
12: 5 [A] "*Let me* **cross over**," the men of Gilead asked him, "Are you
18:13 [A] From there *they* **went on** *to* the hill country of Ephraim
19:12 [A] whose people are not Israelites. *We will* **go on** to Gibeah."
19:14 [A] So *they* **went on**, and the sun set as they neared Gibeah in

Jdg 19:18 [A] "We *are* **on** our **way** from Bethlehem in Judah to a remote
Ru 2: 8 [A] and glean in another field and don't **go away** from here.
4: 1 [A] When the kinsman-redeemer he had mentioned **came along**,
1Sa 2:24 [G] it is not a good report that I hear **spreading among** the
9: 4 [A] So *he* **passed** through the hill country of Ephraim
9: 4 [A] of Ephraim and **[RPH]** through the area around Shalisha,
9: 4 [A] *They* **went on** into the district of Shaalim, but the donkeys
9: 4 [A] *he* **passed** through the territory of Benjamin, but they did not
9:27 [A] said to Saul, "Tell the servant *to* **go on** ahead of us"—
9:27 [A] the servant **did**[s] **so**—"but you stay here awhile, so that I may
13: 7 [A] Some Hebrews even **crossed** the Jordan *to* the land of Gad
14: 1 [A] *let's* **go over** to the Philistine outpost on the other side."
14: 4 [A] On each side of the pass that Jonathan intended to **cross** to
14: 6 [A] *let's* **go over** to the outpost of those uncircumcised fellows.
14: 8 [A] then; we *will* **cross over** toward the men and let them see us.
14:23 [A] Israel that day, and the battle **moved on beyond** Beth Aven.
15:12 [A] his own honor and has turned and **gone on** down to Gilgal."
15:24 [A] *I* **violated** the LORD's command and your instructions.
16: 8 [G] Jesse called Abinadab and **had** him **pass** in front of Samuel.
16: 9 [G] Jesse then **had** Shammah **pass by**, but Samuel said, "Nor has
16:10 [G] Jesse **had** seven of his sons **pass** before Samuel, but Samuel
20:36 [G] I shoot." As the boy ran, he shot an arrow **beyond** him.
25:19 [A] Then she told her servants, "**Go on** ahead; I'll follow you."
26:13 [A] David **crossed over** *to* the other side and stood on top of the
26:22 [A] "*Let* one of your young men **come over** and get it.
27: 2 [A] him left and **went over** to Achish son of Maoch king of Gath.
29: 2 [A] As the Philistine rulers **marched** with their units of hundreds
29: 2 [A] David and his men *were* **marching** at the rear with Achish.
30:10 [A] for two hundred men were too exhausted *to* **cross** the ravine.
2Sa 2: 8 [G] son of Saul and **brought** him **over** *to* Mahanaim.
2:15 [A] So they stood up and *were* **counted off** [+928+5031]—
2:29 [A] *They* **crossed** the Jordan, continued through the whole
3:10 [G] **transfer** the kingdom from the house of Saul and establish
10:17 [A] he gathered all Israel, **crossed** the Jordan and went to Helam.
11:27 [A] After the time of mourning *was* **over**, David had her brought
12:13 [G] Nathan replied, "The LORD *has* **taken away** your sin.
12:31 [g] *he* made them work [BHS ***made … pass through***; NIV 6268]
15:18 [A] All his men **marched past** [+3338+6584] him, along with all
15:18 [A] had accompanied him from Gath **marched** before the king.
15:22 [A] David said to Ittai, "Go ahead, **march on**." So Ittai the Gittite
15:22 [A] So Ittai the Gittite **marched on** with all his men and the
15:23 [A] whole countryside wept aloud as all the people **passed by**.
15:23 [A] The king also **crossed** the Kidron Valley, and all the people
15:23 [A] and all the people **moved on** toward the desert.
15:24 [A] until all the people had finished **leaving** [+4946] the city.
15:33 [A] David said to him, "If *you* **go** with me, you will be a burden
16: 1 [A] When David *had* **gone** a short distance beyond the summit,
16: 9 [A] my lord the king? *Let me* **go over** and cut off his head."
17:16 [A] **cross** [+6296] **over without fail**, or the king and all the
17:16 [A] **cross over without fail** [+6296], or the king and all the
17:20 [A] The woman answered them, "*They* **crossed over** the brook."
17:21 [A] They said to him, "Set out and **cross** the river at once;
17:22 [A] and all the people with him set out and **crossed** the Jordan.
17:22 [A] no one was left who *had* not **crossed** the Jordan.
17:24 [A] and Absalom **crossed** the Jordan with all the men of Israel.
18: 9 [A] in midair, while the mule he was riding **kept on going**.
18:23 [A] Ahimaaz ran by way of the plain and **outran** the Cushite.
19:15 [19:16] [G] and meet the king and **bring** him **across** the Jordan.
19:18 [19:19] [A] *They* **crossed** *at* the ford to take the king's
19:18 [19:19] [G] at the ford to **take** the king's household **over**
19:18 [19:19] [A] When Shimei son of Gera **crossed** the Jordan,
19:31 [19:32] [A] from Rogelim *to* **cross** the Jordan with the king
19:33 [19:34] [A] "**Cross over** with me and stay with me in
19:36 [19:37] [A] Your servant *will* **cross over** the Jordan with the
19:37 [19:38] [A] *Let him* **cross over** with my lord the king.
19:38 [19:39] [A] The king said, "Kimham *shall* **cross over** with me,
19:39 [19:40] [A] So all the people **crossed** the Jordan, and
19:39 [19:40] [A] crossed the Jordan, and then the king **crossed over**.
19:40 [19:41] [A] When the king **crossed over** to Gilgal, Kimham
19:40 [19:41] [A] crossed over to Gilgal, Kimham **crossed** with him.
19:40 [19:41] [G] half the troops of Israel *had* **taken** the king **over**.
19:41 [19:42] [G] and **bring** him and his household **across** the Jordan,
20:13 [A] all the men **went on** with Joab to pursue Sheba son of Bicri.
20:14 [A] Sheba **passed** through all the tribes of Israel to Abel Beth
24: 5 [A] After **crossing** the Jordan, they camped near Aroer, south of
24:10 [G] O LORD, I beg you, **take away** the guilt of your servant.
24:20 [A] and saw the king and his men **coming** toward him,
1Ki 2:37 [A] The day you leave and **cross** the Kidron Valley, you can be
6:21 [D] *he* **extended** gold chains across the front of the inner
9: 8 [A] all *who* **pass** by will be appalled and will scoff and say,
13:25 [A] Some people *who* **passed by** saw the body thrown down
15:12 [G] *He* **expelled** the male shrine prostitutes from the land and got
18: 6 [A] So they divided the land they *were* to **cover**, Ahab going in
18:29 [A] Midday **passed**, and they continued their frantic prophesying
19:11 [A] of the LORD, for the LORD *is about to* **pass by**."
19:19 [A] Elijah **went up** to him and threw his cloak around him.
20:39 [A] As the king **passed by**, the prophet called out to him, "Your
22:24 [A] "Which way *did* the spirit from the LORD **go** when he went
22:36 [A] As the sun was setting, a cry **spread** through the army:
2Ki 2: 8 [A] to the left, and the two of them **crossed over** on dry ground.
2: 9 [A] When they *had* **crossed**, Elijah said to Elisha, "Tell me,
2:14 [A] it divided to the right and to the left, and he **crossed over**.
4: 8 [A] One day Elisha **went** to Shunem. And a well-to-do woman
4: 8 [A] for a meal. So whenever he **came by**, he stopped there to eat.
4: 9 [A] "I know that this man *who* often **comes** our way is a holy
4:31 [A] Gehazi **went on** ahead and laid the staff on the boy's face,
6: 9 [A] "Beware of **passing** that place, because the Arameans are
6:26 [A] As the king of Israel was **passing by** on the wall, a woman
6:30 [A] As he **went** along the wall, the people looked, and there,
8:21 [A] So Jehoram **went** to Zair with all his chariots. The Edomites
12: 4 [12:5] [A] the money collected in the **census** [+408], the money
14: 9 [A] a wild beast in Lebanon **came along** and trampled the thistle
16: 3 [G] of the kings of Israel and even **sacrificed** his son in the fire,
17:17 [G] *They* **sacrificed** their sons and daughters in the fire. They
18:12 [A] the LORD their God, but *had* **violated** his covenant—
21: 6 [G] *He* **sacrificed** his own son in the fire, practiced sorcery and
23:10 [G] so no one *could use* it *to* **sacrifice** his son or daughter in the
1Ch 12:15 [12:16] [A] It was they who **crossed** the Jordan in the first
19:17 [A] told of this, he gathered all Israel and **crossed** the Jordan;
21: 8 [G] Now, I beg you, **take away** the guilt of your servant. I have
29:30 [A] the circumstances that **surrounded** him and Israel and the
2Ch 7:21 [A] so imposing, all *who* **pass** by will be appalled and say,
15: 8 [G] *He* **removed** the detestable idols from the whole land of
18:23 [A] "Which way *did* the spirit from the LORD **go** when he went
21: 9 [A] So Jehoram **went** there with his officers and all his chariots.
24:20 [A] 'Why *do* you **disobey** the LORD's commands? You will not
25:18 [A] a wild beast in Lebanon **came along** and trampled the thistle
30: 5 [G] They decided to **send** a proclamation throughout Israel,
30:10 [A] The couriers **went** from town to town in Ephraim
33: 6 [G] He **sacrificed** his sons in the fire in the Valley of Ben
35:23 [G] shot King Josiah, and he told his officers, "**Take** me **away**;
35:24 [G] So they **took** him out of his chariot, put him in the other
36:22 [G] the LORD moved the heart of Cyrus king of Persia *to* **make**
Ezr 1: 1 [G] the LORD moved the heart of Cyrus king of Persia *to* **make**
10: 7 [G] A proclamation *was* then **issued** throughout Judah
Ne 2: 7 [G] so that *they will* **provide** me **safe-conduct** until I arrive in
2:14 [A] *I* **moved on** toward the Fountain Gate and the King's Pool,
2:14 [A] but there was not enough room for my mount to **get through**;
8:15 [G] and **spread** it throughout their towns and in Jerusalem:
9:11 [A] before them, so that *they* **passed** through it on dry ground,
Est 1:19 [A] in the laws of Persia and Media, *which* cannot *be* **repealed**,
3: 3 [A] "Why *do* you **disobey** the king's command?"
4:17 [A] So Mordecai **went away** and carried out all of Esther's
8: 2 [G] which *he had* **reclaimed** from Haman, and presented it to
8: 3 [G] She begged him to **put an end** *to* the evil plan of Haman the
9:27 [A] all who join them *should* without **fail** observe these two days
9:28 [A] these days of Purim *should* never **cease** to be celebrated by
Job 6:15 [A] as intermittent streams, as the streams *that* **overflow**
7:21 [G] Why do you not pardon my offenses and **forgive** my sins?
9:11 [A] When *he* **passes** me, I cannot see him; when he goes by, I
11:16 [A] forget your trouble, recalling it only as waters **gone by**.
13:13 [A] and let me speak; then *let* **come** to me what may.
14: 5 [A] number of his months and have set limits *he* cannot **exceed**.
15:19 [A] (to whom alone the land was given when no alien **passed**
17:11 [A] My days *have* **passed**, my plans are shattered, and so are the
19: 8 [A] He has blocked my way so *I* cannot **pass**; he has shrouded
21:10 [D] Their bulls never fail *to* **breed**; their cows calve and do not
21:29 [A] Have you never questioned *those who* **travel** [+2006]? Have
30:15 [A] driven away as by the wind, my safety **vanishes** like a cloud.
33:18 [A] his soul from the pit, his life from **perishing** by the sword.
33:28 [A] He redeemed my soul from **going down** to the pit, and I will
34:20 [A] of the night; the people are shaken and *they* **pass away**;
36:12 [A] *they will* **perish** by the sword and die without knowledge.
37:21 [A] bright as it is in the skies after the wind *has* **swept** them
Ps 8: 8 [8:9] [A] the fish of the sea, all *that* **swim** the paths of the seas.
17: 3 [A] will find nothing; I have resolved that my mouth *will* not **sin**.
18:12 [18:13] [A] of the brightness of his presence clouds **advanced**,
37:36 [A] *he soon* **passed away** and was no more; though I looked for
38: 4 [38:5] [A] My guilt *has* **overwhelmed** [+8031] me like a burden
42: 4 [42:5] [A] how *I used to* **go** with the multitude,
42: 7 [42:8] [A] all your waves and breakers *have* **swept** over me.
48: 4 [48:5] [A] kings joined forces, when *they* **advanced** together,
57: 1 [57:2] [A] shadow of your wings until the disaster *has* **passed**.
66: 6 [A] sea into dry land, *they* **passed** through the waters on foot—
73: 7 [A] the evil conceits of their minds **know no limits**.
78:13 [G] He divided the sea and **led** them **through**; he made the water
80:12 [80:13] [A] so that all *who* **pass** [+2006] **by** pick its grapes?
81: 6 [81:7] [A] their hands *were* **set free** from the basket.

Ps 84: 6 [84:7] [A] *As they* **pass** through the Valley of Baca, they make
88: 16 [88:17] [A] Your wrath *has* **swept** over me; your terrors have
89: 41 [89:42] [A] All *who* **pass** [+2006] **by** have plundered him;
90: 4 [A] years in your sight are like a day that *has just* **gone by**,
103: 16 [A] the wind **blows** over it and it is gone, and its place
104: 9 [A] You set a boundary *they* cannot **cross**; never again will they
119: 37 [G] **Turn** my eyes **away** from worthless things; preserve my life
119: 39 [G] **Take away** the disgrace I dread, for your laws are good.
124: 4 [A] have engulfed us, the torrent *would have* **swept** over us,
124: 5 [A] the raging waters *would have* **swept** us **away**.
129: 8 [A] May those *who* **pass by** not say, "The blessing of the
136: 14 [A] **brought** Israel through the midst of it, *His love*
141: 10 [A] the wicked fall into their own nets, while I **pass by** in safety.
144: 4 [A] Man is like a breath; his days are like a **fleeting** shadow.
148: 6 [A] and ever; he gave a decree *that will* never **pass away**.
Pr 4: 15 [A] Avoid it, *do* not **travel** on it; turn from it and go on your
4: 15 [A] do not travel on it; turn from it and **go on** *your* **way**.
7: 8 [A] *He was* **going down** the street near her corner, walking
8: 29 [A] its boundary so the waters *would* not **overstep** his command,
9: 15 [A] calling out to *those who* **pass** [+2006] **by**, who go straight on
10: 25 [A] When the storm *has* **swept by**, the wicked are gone,
19: 11 [A] gives him patience; it is to his glory *to* **overlook** an offense.
22: 3 [A] and takes refuge, but the simple *keep* **going** and suffer for it.
24: 30 [A] I **went** past the field of the sluggard, past the vineyard of the
26: 10 [A] wounds at random is he who hires a fool or any **passer-by**.
26: 17 [A] Like one who seizes a dog by the ears is a **passer-by** who
27: 12 [A] and take refuge, but the simple *keep* **going** and suffer for it.
Ecc 11: 10 [G] from your heart and **cast off** the troubles of your body,
SS 2: 11 [A] See! The winter *is* **past**; the rains are over and gone.
3: 4 [A] Scarcely *had I* **passed** them when I found the one my heart
5: 5 [A] my fingers with **flowing** myrrh, on the handles of the lock.
5: 6 [A] I opened for my lover, but my lover had left; *he was* **gone**.
5: 13 [A] His lips are like lilies dripping with myrrh. **[NIE]**
Isa 8: 8 [A] over it, **passing through** it and reaching up to the neck.
8: 21 [A] Distressed and hungry, *they will* **roam** through the land;
10: 28 [A] They enter Aiath; *they* **pass** through Migron; they store
10: 29 [A] *They* **go over** the pass, and say, "We will camp overnight at
16: 8 [A] Their shoots spread out and **went as far as** the sea.
23: 2 [A] of Sidon, whom the **seafarers** [+3542] have enriched.
23: 6 [A] **Cross over** to Tarshish; wail, *you* people of the island.
23: 10 [a] Till [BHS *Go through*; NIV 6268] your land as along the Nile,
23: 12 [A] "Up, **cross over** *to* Cyprus; even there you will find no rest."
24: 5 [A] *they have* **disobeyed** the laws, violated the statutes
26: 20 [A] yourselves for a little while until his wrath *has* **passed by**.
28: 15 [A] When an overwhelming scourge **sweeps by**, it cannot touch
28: 18 [A] When the overwhelming scourge **sweeps by**, you will be
28: 19 [A] As often as it **comes** it will carry you away; morning after
28: 19 [A] after morning, by day and by night, *it will* **sweep through**."
29: 5 [A] become like fine dust, the ruthless hordes like **blown** chaff.
31: 9 [A] Their stronghold *will* **fall** because of terror; at sight of the
33: 8 [A] The highways are deserted, no **travelers** are *on* the roads.
33: 21 [A] with oars will ride them, no mighty ship *will* **sail** them.
34: 10 [A] it will lie desolate; no *one will* ever **pass** through it again.
35: 8 [A] The unclean *will* not **journey** *on* it; it will be for those who
40: 27 [A] from the LORD; my cause *is* **disregarded** by my God"?
41: 3 [A] He pursues them and **moves on** unscathed, by a path his feet
43: 2 [A] When *you* **pass** through the waters, I will be with you;
45: 14 [A] tall Sabeans—*they will* **come over** to you and will be yours;
45: 14 [A] they will trudge behind you, **coming over** to you in chains.
47: 2 [A] your skirts, bare your legs, and **wade through** the streams.
51: 10 [A] the depths of the sea so that the redeemed *might* **cross over**?
51: 23 [A] who said to you, 'Fall prostrate that *we may* **walk over** you.'
51: 23 [A] your back like the ground, like a street to *be* **walked over**."
54: 9 [A] waters of Noah *would* never again **cover** [+6584] the earth.
60: 15 [A] been forsaken and hated, with no *one* **traveling through**,
62: 10 [A] **Pass through**, pass through the gates! Prepare the way for
62: 10 [A] Pass through, **pass through** the gates! Prepare the way for
Jer 2: 6 [A] and darkness, a land where no one **travels** and no one lives?'
2: 10 [A] **Cross over** *to* the coasts of Kittim and look, send to Kedar
2: 20 [a] [you said, '*I will* not **serve** [Q; see K 6268] you!']
5: 22 [A] a boundary for the sea, an everlasting barrier *it* cannot **cross**.
5: 22 [A] they cannot prevail; they may roar, but *they* cannot **cross** it.
5: 28 [A] Their evil deeds **have no limit**; they do not plead the case of
8: 13 [A] What I have given them *will be* **taken from** them.' "
8: 20 [A] "The harvest *is* **past**, the summer has ended, and we are not
9: 10 [9:9] [A] They are desolate and **untraveled** [+408+1172+4946],
9: 12 [9:11] [A] and laid waste like a desert that no *one can* **cross**?
11: 15 [G] *Can* consecrated meat **avert** [+4946+6584] ˪your
13: 24 [A] "I will scatter you like chaff **driven** by the desert wind.
15: 14 [g] *I will* enslave [BHS ***cause to bring***; NIV 6268] you *to* your
18: 16 [A] all *who* **pass** by will be appalled and will shake their heads.
19: 8 [A] all *who* **pass** by will be appalled and will scoff because of all
22: 8 [A] "People from many nations *will* **pass** by this city and will ask
23: 9 [A] like a man **overcome** *by* wine, because of the LORD
32: 35 [G] Baal in the Valley of Ben Hinnom to **sacrifice** their sons and
33: 13 [A] flocks *will* again **pass** under the hand of the one who counts
34: 18 [A] The men who *have* **violated** my covenant and have not
34: 18 [A] the calf they cut in two and then **walked** between its pieces.
34: 19 [A] all the people of the land who **walked** between the pieces of
41: 10 [A] them captive and set out to **cross over** to the Ammonites.
46: 17 [G] of Egypt is only a loud noise; *he has* **missed** his opportunity.'
48: 32 [A] Your branches **spread** as far as the sea; they reached as far as
49: 17 [A] all *who* **pass** by will be appalled and will scoff because of all
50: 13 [A] All *who* **pass** Babylon will be horrified and scoff because of
51: 43 [A] a land where no one lives, through which no man **travels**.
La 1: 12 [A] "Is it nothing to you, all you *who* **pass** [+2006] **by**? Look
2: 15 [A] All *who* **pass** your way clap their hands at you; they scoff
3: 44 [A] yourself with a cloud so that no prayer *can* **get through**.
4: 21 [A] But to you also the cup *will be* **passed**; you will be drunk
Eze 5: 1 [G] use it as a barber's razor *to* **shave** your head and your beard.
5: 14 [A] the nations around you, in the sight of all *who* **pass by**.
5: 17 [A] Plague and bloodshed *will* **sweep** through you, and I will
9: 4 [A] "**Go** throughout the city of Jerusalem and put a mark on the
9: 5 [A] to the others, "**Follow** [+339] him through the city and kill,
14: 15 [G] "Or if *I* **send** wild beasts through that country and they leave
14: 15 [A] so that no *one can* **pass through** it because of the beasts,
14: 17 [A] and say, '*Let* the sword **pass** throughout the land,'
16: 6 [A] " 'Then *I* **passed** by and saw you kicking about in your
16: 8 [A] " 'Later *I* **passed** by, and when I looked at you and saw that
16: 15 [A] You lavished your favors on anyone *who* **passed by**
16: 21 [G] You slaughtered my children and **sacrificed** [+906+928+5989]
16: 25 [A] body with increasing promiscuity to anyone *who* **passed by**.
20: 26 [G] the **sacrifice** *of* every firstborn—that I might fill them with
20: 31 [G] you offer your gifts—the **sacrifice** *of* your sons in the fire—
20: 37 [G] *I will* **take note** *of* you **as** you pass under my rod, and I will
23: 37 [G] *they* even **sacrificed** their children, whom they bore to me,
29: 11 [A] No foot of man or animal *will* **pass** through it; no one will
29: 11 [A] pass through it; **[RPH]** no one will live there for forty years.
33: 28 [A] of Israel will become desolate so that no *one will* **cross** them.
35: 7 [A] a desolate waste and cut off from it *all who* **come** and go.
36: 34 [A] of lying desolate in the sight of all *who* **pass through** it.
37: 2 [G] *He* **led** me back and forth among them, and I saw a great
39: 11 [A] in the valley of those *who* **travel** east toward the Sea.
39: 11 [A] It will block the way of **travelers**, because Gog and all his
39: 14 [A] *Some will* **go** throughout the land and, in addition to them,
39: 14 [A] go throughout the land and, in addition to **them**[s] [+2021],
39: 15 [A] As **they**[s] [+2021] go through the land and one of them sees a
39: 15 [A] As they **go** through the land and one of them sees a human
46: 21 [G] me to the outer court and **led** me **around** to its four corners,
47: 3 [G] and then **led** me through water that was ankle-deep.
47: 4 [G] and **led** me through water that was knee-deep.
47: 4 [G] and **led** me **through** water that was up to the waist.
47: 5 [A] now it was a river that I could not **cross**, because the water
47: 5 [C] deep enough to swim in—a river that no *one could* **cross**.
48: 14 [G] is the best of the land and *must* not **pass into other hands**,
Da 9: 11 [A] All Israel *has* **transgressed** your law and turned away,
11: 10 [A] which will sweep on like an **irresistible** flood and carry the
11: 20 [G] "His successor *will* **send out** a tax collector to maintain the
11: 40 [A] invade many countries and **sweep through** them like a flood.
Hos 6: 7 [A] Like Adam, they *have* **broken** the covenant—they were
8: 1 [A] because the people *have* **broken** my covenant and rebelled
10: 11 [A] that loves to thresh; so I *will* **put a yoke** on her fair neck.
Joel 3: 17 [4:17] [A] never again *will* foreigners **invade** [+928] her.
Am 5: 5 [A] do not go to Gilgal, *do* not **journey** *to* Beersheba.
5: 17 [A] for *I will* **pass** through your midst," says the LORD.
6: 2 [A] **Go** *to* Calneh and look at it; go from there to great Hamath,
7: 8 [A] line among my people Israel; *I will* **spare** them no longer.
8: 2 [A] time is ripe for my people Israel; *I will* **spare** them no longer.
8: 5 [A] "When *will* the New Moon **be over** that we may sell grain,
Jnh 2: 3 [2:4] [A] about me; all your waves and breakers **swept** over me.
3: 6 [G] he rose from his throne, **took off** his royal robes, covered
Mic 1: 11 [A] **Pass on** in nakedness and shame, you who live in Shaphir.
2: 8 [A] You strip off the rich robe from *those who* **pass by** without a
2: 13 [A] up before them; they will break **through** the gate and go out.
2: 13 [A] Their king *will* **pass through** before them, the LORD at
5: 8 [5:7] [A] which mauls and mangles as *it* **goes**, and no one can
7: 18 [A] **forgives** the transgression of the remnant of his inheritance?
Na 1: 8 [A] with an **overwhelming** flood he will make an end of
1: 12 [A] and are numerous, they will be cut off and **pass away**.
1: 15 [2:1] [A] No more *will* the wicked **invade** you; they will be
3: 19 [A] hands at your fall, for who *has* not **felt** your endless cruelty?
Hab 1: 11 [A] Then they sweep past like the wind and **go on**—guilty men,
3: 10 [A] Torrents of water **swept by**; the deep roared and lifted its
Zep 2: 2 [A] the appointed time arrives and that day **sweeps on** like chaff,
2: 15 [A] wild beasts! All *who* **pass** by her scoff and shake their fists.
3: 6 [A] have left their streets deserted, with no *one* **passing through**.
Zec 3: 4 [G] Then he said to Joshua, "See, *I have* **taken away** your sin,
7: 14 [A] so desolate behind them that no one could come or **go**.

Zec 9: 8 [A] defend my house against **marauding** [+2256+8740] forces.
9: 8 [A] Never again *will* an oppressor **overrun** my people, for now I
10: 11 [A] *They will* **pass** through the sea of trouble; the surging sea
13: 2 [G] "*I will* **remove** both the prophets and the spirit of impurity

6297 ²עָבַר *'ābar²*, v.den. [8] [→ 6301]

very angry [4], angers [1], angry [1], hotheaded [1], meddles [1]

Dt 3: 26 [F] because of you the LORD *was* **angry** with me and would
Ps 78: 21 [F] When the LORD heard them, *he was* **very angry**; his fire
78: 59 [F] When God heard them, *he was* **very angry**; he rejected Israel
78: 62 [F] over to the sword; *he was* **very angry** with his inheritance.
89: 38 [89:39] [F] *you have been* **very angry** with your anointed one.
Pr 14: 16 [F] and shuns evil, but a fool *is* **hotheaded** and reckless.
20: 2 [F] is like the roar of a lion; *he who* **angers** him forfeits his life.
26: 17 [F] the ears is a passer-by *who* **meddles** in a quarrel not his own.

6298 ¹עֵבֶר *'ēber¹*, n.m. [90] [√ 6296; Ar 10526]

east [+928] [9], side [9], other side [6], beyond [+928] [5], *untranslated* [4], across [+928] [4], beyond [4], Trans-Euphrates [+2021+5643] [4], across [+4946] [3], straight ahead [+448+7156] [3], beyond [+4946] [2], east [+4946] [2], near [+928] [2], next to [+448] [2], on each side [+2021+2021+2296+2296+4946+4946 +4946+4946+6298] [2], across from [+4946] [1], along [+4946] [1], along [+928] [1], along [1], alongside [+4946] [1], at [+928] [1], by [+4946] [1], east [+2025+4667] [1], east [+928+2025+4667] [1], east [+928+2025+4667+9087] [1], east [+928+4667+9087] [1], east side [1], east [1], from [+4946] [1], goes on [1], land beyond [1], next to [+4200] [1], on the other side of [+2134+2256+4946] [1], on this side of [+4946] [1], over here [+285+4200] [1], over there [+285+4200] [1], side [+4946] [1], sides [+4946+6017] [1], sides [1], space [1], this side [1], west [+4946] [1], west [+928] [1], west [1]

Ge 50: 10 **near** [+928] the Jordan, they lamented loudly and bitterly;
50: 11 That is why that place **near** [+928] the Jordan is called Abel
Ex 25: 37 and set them up on it so that they light the **space** in front of it.
28: 26 of the breastpiece on the inside edge **next** [+448] **to** the ephod.
32: 15 in his hands. They were inscribed on both **sides**, front and back.
39: 19 of the breastpiece on the inside edge **next** [+448] **to** the ephod.
Nu 21: 13 They set out from there and camped **alongside** [+4946] the Arnon,
22: 1 and camped along the Jordan **across** [+4946] **from** Jericho.
32: 19 with them **on the other side** [+2134+2256+4946] **of** the Jordan,
32: 19 because our inheritance has come to us on the east **side** [+4946] *of*
32: 32 the property we inherit will be **on this side** [+4946] **of** the Jordan."
34: 15 a half tribes have received their inheritance on the east **side** of the
35: 14 Give three on **this side** of the Jordan and three in Canaan as cities
Dt 1: 1 Moses spoke to all Israel in the desert **east** [+928] *of* the Jordan—
1: 5 **East** [+928] *of* the Jordan in the territory of Moab, Moses began to
3: 8 two kings of the Amorites the territory **east** [+928] *of* the Jordan,
3: 20 the land that the LORD your God is giving them, **across** [+928]
3: 25 Let me go over and see the good land **beyond** [+928] the Jordan—
4: 41 set aside three cities **east of** [+928+2025+4667+9087] the Jordan,
4: 46 and were in the valley near Beth Peor **east** [+928] *of* the Jordan,
4: 47 the two Amorite kings **east of** [+928+4667+9087] the Jordan.
4: 49 and included all the Arabah **east of** [+2025+4667] the Jordan,
11: 30 As you know, these mountains are **across** [+928] the Jordan,
30: 13 Nor is it **beyond** [+4946] the sea, so that you have to ask,
30: 13 "Who will cross **[RPH]** the sea to get it and proclaim it to us
Jos 1: 14 stay in the land that Moses gave you **east** [+928] *of* the Jordan,
1: 15 which Moses the servant of the LORD gave you **east** [+928] *of*
2: 10 and Og, the two kings of the Amorites **east** [+928] *of* the Jordan,
5: 1 Now when all the Amorite kings west of **[NIE]** the Jordan
7: 7 If only we had been content to stay on the **other side** *of* the Jordan!
9: 1 Now when all the kings **west** [+928] *of* the Jordan heard about
9: 10 all that he did to the two kings of the Amorites **east** [+928] *of* the
12: 1 and whose territory they took over **[NIE]** east of the Jordan,
12: 7 and the Israelites conquered on the west **side** *of* the Jordan,
13: 8 that Moses had given them **east** [+928+2025+4667] of the Jordan,
13: 27 of the realm of Sihon king of Heshbon (the east **side** *of* the Jordan,
13: 32 in the plains of Moab **across** [+4946] the Jordan east of Jericho.
14: 3 two-and-a-half tribes their inheritance **east** [+4946] of the Jordan
17: 5 of land besides Gilead and Bashan **east** [+4946] of the Jordan,
18: 7 already received their inheritance on the east **side** of the Jordan.
20: 8 On the east **side** of the Jordan of Jericho they designated Bezer in
22: 4 servant of the LORD gave you on the **other side** *of* the Jordan.
22: 7 to the other half of the tribe Joshua gave land on the west **side** *of*
22: 11 border of Canaan at Geliloth near the Jordan on the Israelite **side**,
24: 2 lived **beyond** [+928] the River and worshiped other gods.
24: 3 But I took your father Abraham from the **land beyond** the River
24: 8 to the land of the Amorites who lived **east** [+928] *of* the Jordan.
24: 14 Throw away the gods your forefathers worshiped **beyond** [+928]
24: 15 whether the gods your forefathers served **beyond** [+928] the River,
Jdg 5: 17 Gilead stayed **beyond** [+928] the Jordan. And Dan, why did he
7: 25 of Oreb and Zeeb to Gideon, who was **by** [+4946] the Jordan.
10: 8 oppressed all the Israelites on the **east side** *of* the Jordan in Gilead,
11: 18 the country of Moab, and camped on the **other side** *of* the Arnon.
1Sa 14: 1 "Come, let's go over to the Philistine outpost on the **other side**."
14: 4 **On each side** [+2021+2021+2296+2296+4946+4946+ 4946+4946+6298] *of* the pass that Jonathan intended to cross
14: 4 **On each side of** [+2021+2021+2296+2296+4946+4946 +4946+4946+6298] the pass that Jonathan intended to cross
14: 40 then said to all the Israelites, "You stand **over there** [+285+4200];
14: 40 and Jonathan my son will stand **over here** [+285+4200]."
26: 13 David crossed over to the **other side** and stood on top of the hill
31: 7 When the Israelites **along** [+928] the valley and those across the
31: 7 those **across** [+928] the Jordan saw that the Israelite army had fled
2Sa 10: 16 Hadadezer had Arameans brought from **beyond** the River;
1Ki 4: 12 from Beth Shan to Abel Meholah **across** [+4946] to Jokmeam;
4: 24 [5:4] For he ruled over all the kingdoms **west** *of* the River,
4: 24 [5:4] from Tiphsah to Gaza, **[RPH]** and had peace on all sides.
4: 24 [5:4] Tiphsah to Gaza, and had peace on all **sides** [+4946+6017].
7: 20 above the bowl-shaped part **next** [+4200] **to** the network,
7: 30 a basin resting on four supports, cast with wreaths on each **side**.
14: 15 to their forefathers and scatter them **beyond** [+4946] the River,
1Ch 6: 78 [6:63] from the tribe of Reuben **across** [+4946] the Jordan east of
12: 37 [12:38] from **east** of the Jordan, men of Reuben, Gad
19: 16 and had Arameans brought from **beyond** the River,
26: 30 were responsible in Israel **west** [+4946] of the Jordan for all the
2Ch 20: 2 is coming against you from Edom, from the **other side** of the Sea.
Ezr 8: 36 and to the governors of **Trans-Euphrates** [+2021+5643],
Ne 2: 7 I have letters to the governors of **Trans-Euphrates** [+2021+5643],
2: 9 So I went to the governors of **Trans-Euphrates** [+2021+5643] and
3: 7 the authority of the governor of **Trans-Euphrates** [+2021+5643].
Job 1: 19 when suddenly a mighty wind swept in **from** [+4946] the desert
Isa 7: 20 In that day the Lord will use a razor hired from **beyond** the River—
9: 1 [8:23] of the Gentiles, by the way of the sea, **along** the Jordan—
18: 1 Woe to the land of whirring wings **along** [+4946] the rivers of
47: 15 Each of them **goes on** in his error; there is not one that can save
Jer 25: 22 and Sidon; the kings of the coastlands **across** [+928] the sea;
48: 28 Be like a dove that makes its nest **at** [+928] the mouth of a cave.
49: 32 in distant places and will bring disaster on them from every **side**,"
Eze 1: 9 Each one went **straight ahead** [+448+7156]; they did not turn as
1: 12 Each one went **straight ahead** [+448+7156]. Wherever the spirit
10: 22 by the Kebar River. Each one went **straight ahead** [+448+7156].
Zep 3: 10 From **beyond** the rivers of Cush my worshipers, my scattered

6299 ²עֵבֶר *'ēber²*, n.pr.m. [15] [√ 6296]

Eber [15]

Ge 10: 21 was Japheth; Shem was the ancestor of all the sons of **Eber**.
10: 24 Arphaxad was the father of Shelah, and Shelah the father of **Eber**.
10: 25 Two sons were born to **Eber**: One was named Peleg, because in his
11: 14 When Shelah had lived 30 years, he became the father of **Eber**.
11: 15 And after he became the father of **Eber**, Shelah lived 403 years
11: 16 When **Eber** had lived 34 years, he became the father of Peleg.
11: 17 of Peleg, **Eber** lived 430 years and had other sons and daughters.
Nu 24: 24 they will subdue Asshur and **Eber**, but they too will come to ruin."
1Ch 1: 18 Arphaxad was the father of Shelah, and Shelah the father of **Eber**.
1: 19 Two sons were born to **Eber**: One was named Peleg, because in his
1: 25 **Eber**, Peleg, Reu,
5: 13 Michael, Meshullam, Sheba, Jorai, Jacan, Zia and **Eber**—
8: 12 **Eber**, Misham, Shemed (who built Ono and Lod with its
8: 22 Ishpan, **Eber**, Eliel,
Ne 12: 20 of Sallu's, Kallai; of Amok's, **Eber**;

6300 עָבָר *'ābār*, n.pr.loc. Not used in NIV/BHS [√ 6296]

6301 עֶבְרָה *'ebrâ*, n.f. [34] [√ 6297]

wrath [21], anger [4], fury [4], insolence [2], rage [2], overweening pride [+2295] [1]

Ge 49: 7 Cursed be their anger, so fierce, and their **fury**, so cruel! I will
Job 21: 30 the day of calamity, that he is delivered from the day of **wrath**?
40: 11 Unleash the **fury** *of* your wrath, look at every proud man and bring
Ps 7: 6 [7:7] in your anger; rise up against the **rage** *of* my enemies.
78: 49 against them his hot anger, his **wrath**, indignation and hostility—
85: 3 [85:4] You set aside all your **wrath** and turned from your fierce
90: 9 All our days pass away under your **wrath**; we finish our years with
90: 11 your anger? For your **wrath** is as great as the fear that is due you.
Pr 11: 4 Wealth is worthless in the day of **wrath**, but righteousness delivers
11: 23 ends only in good, but the hope of the wicked only in **wrath**.
14: 35 delights in a wise servant, but a shameful servant incurs his **wrath**.
21: 24 is his name; he behaves with **overweening pride** [+2295].
22: 8 wickedness reaps trouble, and the rod of his **fury** will be destroyed.
Isa 9: 19 [9:18] By the **wrath** *of* the LORD Almighty the land will be
10: 6 I dispatch him against a people who **anger** me, to seize loot
13: 9 a cruel day, with **wrath** and fierce anger—to make the land
13: 13 the earth will shake from its place at the **wrath** *of* the LORD

[F] Hitpael (hitpoel, hitpoal, hitpolel, hitpolal, hitpalel, hitpalal, hitpalpel, hitpalpal, hotpael, hotpaal) [G] Hiphil (hiphtil) [H] Hophal [I] Hishtaphel

Isa 14: 6 which in **anger** struck down peoples with unceasing blows,
16: 6 her overweening pride and conceit, her pride and her **insolence**—
Jer 7: 29 has rejected and abandoned this generation that is under his **wrath**.
48: 30 I know her **insolence** but it is futile," declares the LORD,
La 2: 2 in his **wrath** he has torn down the strongholds of the Daughter of
3: 1 I am the man who has seen affliction by the rod of his **wrath**.
Eze 7: 19 will not be able to save them in the day of the LORD's **wrath**.
21: 31 [21:36] upon you and breathe out my fiery **anger** against you;
22: 21 I will gather you and I will blow on you with my fiery **wrath**,
22: 31 out my wrath on them and consume them with my fiery **anger**,
38: 19 fiery **wrath** I declare that at that time there shall be a great
Hos 5: 10 I will pour out my **wrath** on them like a flood of water.
13: 11 in my anger I gave you a king, and in my **wrath** I took him away.
Am 1: 11 his anger raged continually and his **fury** flamed unchecked,
Hab 3: 8 Did you **rage** against the sea when you rode with your horses
Zep 1: 15 That day will be a day of **wrath**, a day of distress and anguish,
1: 18 gold will be able to save them on the day of the LORD's **wrath**.

6302 עֲבָרָה ʿabārâ, n.f. [2 / 3] [→ 6305; cf. 6296]

fords [2], ford [1]

2Sa 15: 28 I will wait at the **fords** [Q 6858] *in* the desert until word comes
17: 16 'Do not spend the night at the **fords** [BHS 6858] *in* the desert;
19: 18 [19:19] They crossed at the **ford** to take the king's household over

6303 עִבְרִי ʿibrî[1], a. & n.g. [34] [→ 6304]

Hebrew [16], Hebrews [16], *untranslated* [1], woman[s] [1]

Ge 14: 13 who had escaped came and reported this to Abram the **Hebrew**.
39: 14 "this **Hebrew** has been brought to us to make sport of us!
39: 17 "That **Hebrew** slave you brought us came to me to make sport of
40: 15 For I was forcibly carried off from the land of the **Hebrews**,
41: 12 Now a young **Hebrew** was there with us, a servant of the captain
43: 32 because Egyptians could not eat with **Hebrews**, for that is
Ex 1: 15 The king of Egypt said to the **Hebrew** midwives, whose names
1: 16 "When you help the **Hebrew** *women* in childbirth and observe
1: 19 answered Pharaoh, "**Hebrew** *women* are not like Egyptian women;
2: 6 felt sorry for him. "This is one of the **Hebrew** babies," she said.
2: 7 and get one of the **Hebrew** women to nurse the baby for you?"
2: 11 He saw an Egyptian beating a **Hebrew**, one of his own people.
2: 13 The next day he went out and saw two **Hebrews** fighting.
3: 18 of Egypt and say to him, 'The LORD, the God of the **Hebrews**,
5: 3 Then they said, "The God of the **Hebrews** has met with us.
7: 16 say to him, 'The LORD, the God of the **Hebrews**, has sent me to
9: 1 to him, 'This is what the LORD, the God of the **Hebrews**, says:
9: 13 to him, 'This is what the LORD, the God of the **Hebrews**, says:
10: 3 "This is what the LORD, the God of the **Hebrews**, says:
21: 2 "If you buy a **Hebrew** servant, he is to serve you for six years.
Dt 15: 12 If a fellow **Hebrew**, a *man* or a woman, sells himself to you
15: 12 a man or a **woman**[s], sells himself to you and serves you six years,
1Sa 4: 6 Philistines asked, "What's all this shouting in the **Hebrew** camp?"
4: 9 Be men, or you will be subject to the **Hebrews**, as they have been
13: 3 blown throughout the land and said, "Let the **Hebrews** hear!"
13: 7 *Some* **Hebrews** even crossed the Jordan to the land of Gad
13: 19 had said, "Otherwise the **Hebrews** will make swords or spears!"
14: 11 "The **Hebrews** are crawling out of the holes they were hiding in."
14: 21 Those **Hebrews** who had previously been with the Philistines
29: 3 of the Philistines asked, "What about these **Hebrews**?"
Jer 34: 9 Everyone was to free his **Hebrew** slaves, both male and female;
34: 9 and female; **[RPH]** no one was to hold a fellow Jew in bondage.
34: 14 'Every seventh year each of you must free any fellow **Hebrew** who
Jnh 1: 9 He answered, "I am a **Hebrew** and I worship the LORD,

6304 [2]עִבְרִי ʿibrî[2], n.pr.m. [1] [√ 6303]

Ibri [1]

1Ch 24: 27 The sons of Merari: from Jaaziah: Beno, Shoham, Zaccur and **Ibri**.

6305 עֲבָרִים ʿabārîm, n.pr.loc. [5] [√ 6302; cf. 6296]

Abarim [5]

Nu 27: 12 "Go up this mountain in the **Abarim** range and see the land I have
33: 47 left Almon Diblathaim and camped in the mountains of **Abarim**,
33: 48 They left the mountains of **Abarim** and camped on the plains of
Dt 32: 49 "Go up into the **Abarim** Range to Mount Nebo in Moab, across
Jer 22: 20 in Bashan, cry out from **Abarim**, for all your allies are crushed.

6306 עֶבְרֹן ʿebrōn, n.pr.loc. [1 / 0] [cf. 6278]

Jos 19: 28 It went to Abdon, [BHS *Ebron*; NIV 6278] Rehob, Hammon and

6307 עַבְרֹנָה ʿabrōnâ, n.pr.loc. [2]

Abronah [2]

Nu 33: 34 They left Jotbathah and camped at **Abronah**.
33: 35 They left **Abronah** and camped at Ezion Geber.

6308 עָבַשׁ ʿābaš, v. [1]

shriveled [1]

Joel 1: 17 [A] The seeds *are* **shriveled** beneath the clods. The storehouses

6309 עָבַת ʿābat, v. [1] [→ 6290, 6291, 6310]

conspire [1]

Mic 7: 3 [D] dictate what they desire—*they all* **conspire** *together*.

6310 עֲבֹת ʿabōt, n.m. [19] [√ 6309]

ropes [7], chains [4], rope [3], chains [+9249] [1], cords [1], fetters [1], harness [1], ties [1]

Ex 28: 14 of pure gold, like a **rope**, and attach the chains to the settings.
28: 14 like a rope, and attach the **chains** [+9249] to the settings.
28: 22 "For the breastpiece make braided chains of pure gold, like a **rope**.
28: 24 Fasten the two gold **chains** to the rings at the corners of the
28: 25 the other ends of the **chains** to the two settings, attaching them to
39: 15 the breastpiece they made braided chains of pure gold, like a **rope**.
39: 17 They fastened the two gold **chains** to the rings at the corners of the
39: 18 the other ends of the **chains** to the two settings, attaching them to
Jdg 15: 13 So they bound him with two new **ropes** and led him up from the
15: 14 The **ropes** on his arms became like charred flax, and the bindings
16: 11 "If anyone ties me securely with new **ropes** that have never been
16: 12 So Delilah took new **ropes** and tied him with them. Then,
Job 39: 10 Can you hold him to the furrow with a **harness**? Will he till the
Ps 2: 3 "Let us break their chains," they say, "and throw off their **fetters**."
129: 4 is righteous; he has cut me free from the **cords** *of* the wicked.
Isa 5: 18 sin along with cords of deceit, and wickedness as with cart **ropes**,
Eze 3: 25 And you, son of man, they will tie with **ropes**; you will be bound
4: 8 I will tie you up with **ropes** so that you cannot turn from one side
Hos 11: 4 I led them with cords of human kindness, with **ties** *of* love;

6311 עָגַב ʿāgab, v. [7] [→ 6312, 6311; cf. 6385]

lusted after [+6584] [3], lovers [1], lusted after [+448] [1], lusted after [1], lusted [1]

Jer 4: 30 [A] in vain. Your **lovers** despise you; they seek your life.
Eze 23: 5 [A] *she* **lusted** [+6584] **after** her lovers, the Assyrians—
23: 7 [A] defiled herself with all the idols of everyone *she* **lusted after**.
23: 9 [A] her over to her lovers, the Assyrians, for whom *she* **lusted**.
23: 12 [A] *She* too **lusted** [+448] **after** the Assyrians—governors
23: 16 [A] *she* **lusted** [+6584] **after** them and sent messengers to them
23: 20 [A] There *she* **lusted** [+6584] **after** her lovers, whose genitals

6312 עֲגָבָה ʿagābâ, n.f. [1] [√ 6311]

lust [1]

Eze 23: 11 yet *in* her **lust** and prostitution she was more depraved than her

6313 עֲגָבִים ʿagābîm, n.[m.]. [2] [√ 6311]

devotion [1], love [1]

Eze 33: 31 With their mouths they express **devotion**, but their hearts are
33: 32 to them you are nothing more than one who sings **love** songs with a

6314 עֻגָה ʿugâ, n.f. [7] [√ 6383]

cake of bread [2], cakes [2], bread [1], cake [1], flat cake [1]

Ge 18: 6 "get three seahs of fine flour and knead it and bake *some* **bread**."
Ex 12: 39 had brought from Egypt, they baked **cakes** *of* unleavened bread.
Nu 11: 8 it in a mortar. They cooked it in a pot or made it into **cakes**.
1Ki 17: 13 But first make a small **cake of bread** for me from what you have
19: 6 and there by his head was a **cake of bread** baked over hot coals,
Eze 4: 12 Eat the food as you would a barley **cake**; bake it in the sight of the
Hos 7: 8 mixes with the nations; Ephraim is a **flat cake** not turned over.

6315 עָגוּר ʿāgûr, n.[m.]. [2]

thrush [2]

Isa 38: 14 I cried like a swift or **thrush**, I moaned like a mourning dove.
Jer 8: 7 the swift and the **thrush** observe the time of their migration.

6316 עָגִיל ʿāgîl, n.[m.]. [2] [√ 6318]

earrings [2]

Nu 31: 50 armlets, bracelets, signet rings, **earrings** and necklaces—to make
Eze 16: 12 **earrings** on your ears and a beautiful crown on your head.

6317 עֲגִלָה ʿagîlâ, n.f. [0 / 1] [√ 6318]

shields [1]

Ps 46: 9 [46:10] the spear, he burns the **shields** [BHS 6322] with fire.

6318 עָגֹל *'āgōl*, a. [6] [→ 5046, 5047, 6316, 6317, 6319, 6320, 6321, 6322, 6323]

circular in shape [+6017] [2], round [2], circular band [+6017] [1], rounded [1]

1Ki 7:23 He made the Sea of cast metal, **circular** [+6017] **in shape**,
7:31 This opening was **round**, and with its basework it measured a cubit
7:31 was engraving. The panels of the stands were square, not **round**.
7:35 At the top of the stand there was a **circular** [+6017] **band** half a
10:19 The throne had six steps, and its back had a **rounded** top.
2Ch 4:2 He made the Sea of cast metal, **circular** [+6017] **in shape**,

6319 עֵגֶל *'ēgel*, n.m. [36] [√ 6318]

calf [19], calves [10], shape of a calf [3], calf-idol [2], calf-idols [1], shape of calves [1]

Ex 32:4 handed him and made it into an idol cast in the **shape of a calf**,
32:8 and have made themselves an idol cast in the **shape of a calf**.
32:19 Moses approached the camp and saw the **calf** and the dancing,
32:20 And he took the **calf** they had made and burned it in the fire;
32:24 me the gold, and I threw it into the fire, and out came this **calf**!"
32:35 a plague because of what they did with the **calf** Aaron had made.
Lev 9:2 "Take a bull **calf** for your sin offering and a ram for your burnt
9:3 'Take a male goat for a sin offering, a **calf** and a lamb—both a year
9:8 to the altar and slaughtered the **calf** as a sin offering for himself.
Dt 9:16 you had made for yourselves an idol cast in the **shape of a calf**.
9:21 thing of yours, the **calf** you had made, and burned it in the fire.
1Sa 28:24 The woman had a fattened **calf** at the house, which she butchered
1Ki 12:28 After seeking advice, the king made two golden **calves**. He said to
12:32 This he did in Bethel, sacrificing to the **calves** he had made.
2Ki 10:29 to commit—the worship of the golden **calves** at Bethel and Dan.
17:16 and made for themselves two idols cast in the **shape of calves**,
2Ch 11:15 for the high places and for the goat and **calf** idols he had made.
13:8 have with you the golden **calves** that Jeroboam made to be your
Ne 9:18 even when they cast for themselves an image of a **calf** and said,
Ps 29:6 He makes Lebanon skip like a **calf**, Sirion like a young wild ox.
68:30 [68:31] the herd of bulls among the **calves** *of* the nations.
106:19 At Horeb they made a **calf** and worshiped an idol cast from metal.
Isa 11:6 down with the goat, the **calf** and the lion and the yearling together;
27:10 forsaken like the desert; there the **calves** graze, there they lie down;
Jer 31:18 'You disciplined me like an unruly **calf**, and I have been
34:18 I will treat like the **calf** they cut in two and then walked between its
34:19 the people of the land who walked between the pieces of the **calf**,
46:21 The mercenaries in her ranks are like fattened **calves**. They too will
Eze 1:7 their feet were like those of a **calf** and gleamed like burnished
Hos 8:5 Throw out your **calf-idol**, O Samaria! My anger burns against
8:6 it is not God. It will be broken in pieces, that **calf** *of* Samaria.
10:5 The people who live in Samaria fear for the **calf-idol** *of* Beth
13:2 these people, "They offer human sacrifice and kiss the **calf-idols**."
Am 6:4 on your couches. You dine on choice lambs and fattened **calves**.
Mic 6:6 I come before him with burnt offerings, with **calves** a year old?
Mal 4:2 [3:20] you will go out and leap like **calves** released *from* the stall.

6320 עֶגְלָה¹ *'eglâ*[1], n.f. [11] [→ 6321; cf. 6318]

heifer [6], heifer [+1330] [2], heifer's [1], her[s] [+2021] [1], young cow [+1330] [1]

Ge 15:9 "Bring me a **heifer**, a goat and a ram, each three years old,
Dt 21:3 the elders of the town nearest the body shall take a **heifer** [+1330]
21:4 and lead **her**[s] [+2021] down to a valley that has not been plowed
21:4 There in the valley they are to break the **heifer's** neck.
21:6 their hands over the **heifer** whose neck was broken in the valley,
Jdg 14:18 Samson said to them, "If you had not plowed with my **heifer**,
1Sa 16:2 The LORD said, "Take a **heifer** [+1330] with you and say,
Isa 7:21 a man will keep alive a **young cow** [+1330] and two goats.
Jer 46:20 "Egypt is a beautiful **heifer**, but a gadfly is coming against her
50:11 because you frolic like a **heifer** threshing grain and neigh like
Hos 10:11 Ephraim is a trained **heifer** that loves to thresh; so I will put a yoke

6321 עֶגְלָה² *'eglâ*[2], n.pr.f. [2] [√ 6320]

Eglah [2]

2Sa 3:5 the sixth, Ithream the son of David's wife **Eglah**. These were born
1Ch 3:3 the son of Abital; and the sixth, Ithream, by his wife **Eglah**.

6322 עֲגָלָה *'ᵃgālâ*, n.f. [25 / 24] [√ 6318]

cart [13], carts [8], cartwheel [+236] [1], it[s] [+2021] [1], threshing cart [1]

Ge 45:19 Take *some* **carts** from Egypt for your children and your wives,
45:21 Joseph gave them **carts**, as Pharaoh had commanded, and he also
45:27 and when he saw the **carts** Joseph had sent to carry him back,
46:5 and their wives in the **carts** that Pharaoh had sent to transport him.
Nu 7:3 They brought as their gifts before the LORD six covered **carts**
7:3 twelve oxen—an ox from each leader and a **cart** from every two.
7:6 So Moses took the **carts** and oxen and gave them to the Levites.
7:7 He gave two **carts** and four oxen to the Gershonites, as their work
7:8 he gave four **carts** and eight oxen to the Merarites, as their work
1Sa 6:7 "Now then, get a new **cart** ready, with two cows that have calved
6:7 Hitch the cows to the **cart**, but take their calves away and pen them
6:8 Take the ark of the LORD and put it on the **cart**, and in a chest
6:10 They took two such cows and hitched them to the **cart** and penned
6:11 They placed the ark of the LORD on the **cart** and along with it
6:14 The **cart** came to the field of Joshua of Beth Shemesh, and there it
6:14 The people chopped up the wood of the **cart** and sacrificed the
2Sa 6:3 They set the ark of God on a new **cart** and brought it from the
6:3 Uzzah and Ahio, sons of Abinadab, were guiding the new **cart**
1Ch 13:7 They moved the ark of God from Abinadab's house on a new **cart**,
13:7 house on a new cart, with Uzzah and Ahio guiding **it**[s] [+2021].
Ps 46:9 [46:10] he burns the <u>shields</u> [BHS *chariots*; NIV 6317] with fire.
Isa 5:18 sin along with cords of deceit, and wickedness as with **cart** ropes,
28:27 with a sledge, nor is a **cartwheel** [+236] rolled over cummin;
28:28 Though he drives the wheels of his **threshing cart** over it,
Am 2:13 I will crush you as a **cart** crushes when loaded with grain.

6323 עֶגְלוֹן¹ *'eglôn*[1], n.pr.m. [5] [√ 6318]

Eglon [4], who[s] [1]

Jdg 3:12 because they did this evil the LORD gave **Eglon** king of Moab
3:14 The Israelites were subject to **Eglon** king of Moab for eighteen
3:15 The Israelites sent him with tribute to **Eglon** king of Moab.
3:17 He presented the tribute to **Eglon** king of Moab, who was a very
3:17 the tribute to Eglon king of Moab, **who**[s] was a very fat man.

6324 עֶגְלוֹן² *'eglôn*[2], n.pr.loc. [8]

Eglon [8]

Jos 10:3 king of Jarmuth, Japhia king of Lachish and Debir king of **Eglon**.
10:5 the kings of Jerusalem, Hebron, Jarmuth, Lachish and **Eglon**—
10:23 the kings of Jerusalem, Hebron, Jarmuth, Lachish and **Eglon**.
10:34 and all Israel with him moved on from Lachish to **Eglon**;
10:36 Then Joshua and all Israel with him went up from **Eglon** to Hebron
10:37 Just as at **Eglon**, they totally destroyed it and everyone in it.
12:12 the king of **Eglon** one the king of Gezer one
15:39 Lachish, Bozkath, **Eglon**,

6325 עֶגְלַיִם *'eglayim*, n.pr.loc. Not used in NIV/BHS [→ 6536]

6326 עֶגְלַת שְׁלִשִׁיָּה *'eglat šᵉlišiyyâ*, n.pr.loc. [2] [cf. 8999]

Eglath Shelishiyah [2]

Isa 15:5 her fugitives flee as far as Zoar, as far as **Eglath Shelishiyah**.
Jer 48:34 and Jahaz, from Zoar as far as Horonaim and **Eglath Shelishiyah**,

6327 עָגַם *'āgam*, v. [1] [cf. 108]

grieved [1]

Job 30:25 [A] for those in trouble? *Has* not my soul **grieved** for the poor?

6328 עָגַן *'āgan*, v. [1]

remain unmarried [+408+1194+2118+4200+4200] [1]

Ru 1:13 [C] *Would you* **remain unmarried** [+408+1194+2118+4200+4200]

6329 עַד¹ *'ad*[1], n.m. [48]

ever [16], forever [+4200] [12], forever [+6330] [3], ancient [2], eternal [+4200] [2], ever [+4200] [2], ever and ever [2], everlasting [2], always [+4200] [1], continually [+4200] [1], eternal [1], ever [+6330] [1], forever [1], never [+1153+2256+6409] [1], of old [1]

Ge 49:26 blessings are greater than the blessings of the **ancient** mountains,
Ex 15:18 The LORD will reign for ever and **ever**."
1Ch 28:9 but if you forsake him, he will reject you **forever** [+4200].
Job 19:24 with an iron tool on lead, or engraved in rock **forever** [+4200]!
20:4 "Surely you know how it has been from **of old**, ever since man was
Ps 9:5 [9:6] you have blotted out their name for ever and **ever**.
9:18 [9:19] nor the hope of the afflicted **ever** [+4200] perish.
10:16 The LORD is King for ever and **ever**; the nations will perish from
19:9 [19:10] fear of the LORD is pure, enduring **forever** [+4200].
21:4 [21:5] and you gave it to him—length of days, for ever and **ever**.
21:6 [21:7] Surely you have granted him **eternal** [+4200] blessings
22:26 [22:27] will praise him—may your hearts live **forever** [+4200]!
37:29 the righteous will inherit the land and dwell in it **forever** [+4200].
45:6 [45:7] Your throne, O God, will last for ever and **ever**; a scepter
45:17 [45:18] therefore the nations will praise you for ever and **ever**.
48:14 [48:15] For this God is our God for ever and **ever**; he will be our
52:8 [52:10] of God; I trust in God's unfailing love for ever and **ever**.
61:8 [61:9] will I **ever** [+4200] sing praise to your name and fulfill my
83:17 [83:18] May they **ever** [+6330] be ashamed and dismayed; may

Ps 89:29 [89:30] I will establish his line **forever** [+4200], his throne as
92: 7 [92:8] evildoers flourish, they will be **forever** [+6330] destroyed.
104: 5 on its foundations; it can **never** [+1153+2256+6409] be moved.
111: 3 are his deeds, and his righteousness endures **forever** [+4200].
111: 8 They are steadfast for **ever** and ever, done in faithfulness
111:10 have good understanding. To him belongs **eternal** [+4200] praise.
112: 3 are in his house, and his righteousness endures **forever** [+4200].
112: 9 his gifts to the poor, his righteousness endures **forever** [+4200];
119:44 I will always obey your law, for ever and **ever**.
132:12 then their sons will sit on your throne for **ever and ever**."
132:14 "This is my resting place for **ever and ever**; here I will sit
145: 1 my God the King; I will praise your name for ever and **ever**.
145: 2 Every day I will praise you and extol your name for ever and **ever**.
145:21 Let every creature praise his holy name for ever and **ever**.
148: 6 He set them in place for **ever** and ever; he gave a decree that will
Pr 12:19 Truthful lips endure **forever** [+4200], but a lying tongue lasts only
29:14 the poor with fairness, his throne will **always** [+4200] be secure.
Isa 9: 6 [9:5] Mighty God, **Everlasting** Father, Prince of Peace.
26: 4 Trust in the LORD **forever** [+6330], for the LORD, the LORD,
45:17 you will never be put to shame or disgraced, to ages **everlasting**.
47: 7 You said, 'I will continue forever—the **eternal** queen!' But you did
57:15 and lofty One says—he who lives **forever**, whose name is holy:
64: 9 [64:8] O LORD; do not remember our sins **forever** [+4200].
65:18 But be glad and rejoice **forever** [+6330] in what I will create,
Da 12: 3 who lead many to righteousness, like the stars for ever and **ever**.
Am 1:11 because his anger raged **continually** [+4200] and his fury flamed
Mic 4: 5 will walk in the name of the LORD our God for ever and **ever**.
7:18 You do not stay angry **forever** [+4200] but delight to show mercy.
Hab 3: 6 The **ancient** mountains crumbled and the age-old hills collapsed.

6330 ²עַד ***'ad²***, pp. [1262 / 1261] [→ 1187, 6364; cf. 6334?; Ar 10527] See Select Index

to [322], until [224], till [94], *untranslated* [90], as far as [70], forever [+6409] [44], until [+889] [30], how long [+5503] [27], up to [21], and [13], all the way to [12], how long [+625+2025] [12], reached [+995] [10], before [9], at [8], or [8], as [7], by [7], for [6], until [+8611] [6], very [+4394] [6], ever [+6409] [5], forevermore [+6409] [5], while [5], after [4], approached [+995] [4], even [4], from [4], how long [+4537] [4], still [4], always [+6409] [3], among [3], and alike [3], before [+889+4202] [3], between [+2256+4946] [3], beyond measure [+4394] [3], but [3], ever since [+2021+2021+2296+3427] [3], forever [+6329] [3], out to [3], reaches to [3], through [3], until [+3954] [3], until [+561] [3], when [3], abundantly [+889+3907+6330] [2], as far away as [2], at set times [+4946+6961+6961] [2], come to [2], down to [2], enough [2], everlasting [+6409] [2], forever [+2021+6409] [2], forever [+4200+6409] [2], from beginning to [2], how many [+3869 +4537] [2], in the end [2], in [2], lasts [2], meanwhile [+2256+3907 +3907+6330] [2], more [+6409] [2], never [+4202+6409] [2], of [2], reach [+995] [2], still [+2021+2021+2296+3427] [2], this far [+2151] [2], till [+8611] [2], until [+561+889] [2], up [2], utterly [+4394] [2], with [2], against [+928] [1], all the way to [+995] [1], all the way to [+995+3870] [1], all the way up [1], almost to a man [+4392+9462] [1], and [+2256] [1], arrive [+995] [1], arrived [+995] [1], as long as [1], at the point of [1], before [+4202] [1], by then [1], completely [+1414+2256+4946+5883] [1], completely [+3983] [1], completely destroyed [+3983] [1], down to [+9462] [1], end [1], endless [+6409] [1], ends [1], entered [+2143] [1], entering [+995] [1], even as far as [1], even enough [1], ever [+6329] [1], extends to [1], far and wide [+4200+4946+8158] [1], far and wide [+8158] [1], far away [+4200 +4946+8158] [1], finally [+889] [1], for an instant [+1180+8371] [1], for how long [+5503] [1], forevermore [+2021+6409] [1], founded on [1], here [+2178] [1], hold back overnight [+907+1332+4328] [1], how long [+625] [1], huge [+1524+4200+4394] [1], in the end [+889] [1], including [1], into [1], join [+995] [1], lasted so long [1], lasting [+2021+2021+2296+3427] [1], lasting [+6409] [1], led to [1], loud [+1524+4394] [1], more and more powerful [+1541+2025+2143 +2256+4200+5087] [1], much [+4394] [1], near [1], never [+4202+5905] [1], never [+561+6409] [1], on [+6964] [1], only [1], over [1], prior [1], reach to [1], reached [+1540] [1], reached [+448+995] [1], reached height [+8003] [1], reaching to [1], reduces to [1], since [+2178] [1], since [1], so much that [1], so much [1], still in force [1], swiftly [+4559] [1], that [+889] [1], this far [+7024] [1], though [1], threatened [+5883] [1], thus far [+2178] [1], till [+3954] [1], till [+561] [1], till [+6961] [1], till [+889] [1], to the point of [1], to the vicinity of [+995+3870] [1], together with [+2256] [1], toward [+5790] [1], toward [1], trembled violently [+1524+3006+3010+4394] [1], until the end of [1], until the time for [1], very [+2025+4200+5087] [1], waited [1], when [+4537] [1], when [+625+2025] [1], when [+8611] [1], while [+8611] [1], while still [1], without [+401] [1], without restraint [+4394] [1], yet [+2021+2021+2085+3427] [1], yet [+2021+2021+2156+3427] [1], yet [+2178] [1], yet [+6964] [1], yet [1]

6331 ³עַד ***'ad³***, n.[m.]. [2 / 1] [√ 6334]

prey [1]

Ge 49:27 in the morning he devours the **prey**, in the evening he divides the
Zep 3: 8 I will stand up to testify. [BHS *plunder*; NIV 6332]

6332 עֵד ***'ēd***, n.m. [69 / 73] [→ 3444; cf. 6386]

witness [38], witnesses [18], *untranslated* [3], testify [3], testimony [3], call in as witnesses [+906+906+6386] [1], evidence [1], had witnessed [+6386] [1], have the transaction witnessed [+6386] [1], testify [+2118] [1], testify [+4200+6699] [1], those who speak up for [1], witnessed [+6386] [1]

Ge 31:44 a covenant, you and I, and let it serve as a **witness** between us."
31:48 Laban said, "This heap is a **witness** between you and me today."
31:50 is with us, remember that God is a **witness** between you and me."
31:52 This heap is a **witness**, and this pillar is a witness, that I will not go
Ex 20:16 "You shall not give false **testimony** against your neighbor.
22:13 [22:12] he shall bring in the remains as **evidence** and he will not
23: 1 Do not help a wicked man by being a malicious **witness**.
Lev 5: 1 he hears a public charge to **testify** regarding something he has seen
Nu 5:13 her impurity is undetected (since there is no **witness** against her
35:30 be put to death as a murderer only on the testimony of **witnesses**.
35:30 no one is to be put to death on the testimony of only one **witness**.
Dt 5:20 "You shall not give false **testimony** against your neighbor.
17: 6 the testimony of two or three **witnesses** a man shall be put to death,
17: 6 of two or three witnesses **[RPH]** a man shall be put to death,
17: 6 no one shall be put to death on the testimony of only one **witness**.
17: 7 The hands of the **witnesses** must be the first in putting him to
19:15 One **witness** is not enough to convict a man accused of any crime
19:15 be established by the testimony of two **[RPH]** or three witnesses.
19:15 must be established by the testimony of two or three **witnesses**.
19:16 If a malicious **witness** takes the stand to accuse a man of a crime,
19:18 if the **witness** proves to be a liar, giving false testimony against his
19:18 to be a liar, **[RPH]** giving false testimony against his brother,
31:19 have them sing it, so that it may be a **witness** for me against them.
31:21 upon them, this song *will* **testify** [+4200+6699] against them,
31:26 LORD your God. There it will remain as a **witness** against you.
Jos 22:27 it is to be a **witness** between us and you and the generations that
22:28 and sacrifices, but as a **witness** between us and you.'
22:34 altar this name: A **Witness** Between Us that the LORD is God.
24:22 "You are **witnesses** against yourselves that you have chosen to
24:22 to serve the LORD." "Yes, we are **witnesses**," they replied.
Ru 4: 9 "Today you are **witnesses** that I have bought from Naomi all the
4:10 his family or from the town records. Today you are **witnesses**!"
4:11 Then the elders and all those at the gate said, "We are **witnesses**.
1Sa 6:18 is a **witness** [BHS 6330] to this day in the field of Joshua of Beth
12: 5 Samuel said to them, "The LORD is **witness** against you,
12: 5 is witness against you, and also his anointed is **witness** this day,
12: 5 have not found anything in my hand." "He is **witness**," they said.
Job 10:17 You bring new **witnesses** against me and increase your anger
16: 8 it has become a **witness**; my gauntness rises up and testifies against
16:19 Even now my **witness** is in heaven; my advocate is on high.
Ps 27:12 for false **witnesses** rise up against me, breathing out violence.
35:11 Ruthless **witnesses** come forward; they question me on things I
89:37 [89:38] forever like the moon, the faithful **witness** in the sky."
Pr 6:19 a false **witness** who pours out lies and a man who stirs up
12:17 witness gives honest testimony, but a false **witness** tells lies.
14: 5 A truthful **witness** does not deceive, but a false witness pours out
14: 5 truthful witness does not deceive, but a false **witness** pours out lies.
14:25 A truthful **witness** saves lives, but a false witness is deceitful.
19: 5 A false **witness** will not go unpunished, and he who pours out lies
19: 9 A false **witness** will not go unpunished, and he who pours out lies
19:28 A corrupt **witness** mocks at justice, and the mouth of the wicked
21:28 A false **witness** will perish, and whoever listens to him will be
24:28 *Do* not **testify** [+2118] against your neighbor without cause,
25:18 or a sharp arrow is the man who gives false **testimony** against his
Isa 8: 2 And *I will* **call in** Uriah the priest and Zechariah son of Jeberekiah **as** reliable **witnesses** [+906+906+6386] for me."
19:20 and **witness** to the LORD Almighty in the land of Egypt.
30: 8 for the days to come it may be an everlasting **witness**. [BHS 6330]
33: 8 its **witnesses** [BHS 6551] are despised, no one is respected.
43: 9 Let them bring in their **witnesses** to prove they were right,
43:10 "You are my **witnesses**," declares the LORD, "and my servant
43:12 You are my **witnesses**," declares the LORD, "that I am God.
44: 8 I not proclaim this and foretell it long ago? You are my **witnesses**.
44: 9 **Those who** would **speak up for** them are blind; they are ignorant,
55: 4 See, I have made him a **witness** *to* the peoples, a leader
Jer 29:23 them to do. I know it and am a **witness** *to* it," declares the LORD.
32:10 I signed and sealed the deed, **had** it **witnessed** [+6386], and
32:12 my cousin Hanamel and of the **witnesses** who had signed the deed
32:25 field with silver and **have the transaction witnessed** [+6386].' "
32:44 sealed and **witnessed** [+6386] in the territory of Benjamin,
42: 5 faithful **witness** against us if we do not act in accordance with

Mic 1: 2 who are in it, that the Sovereign LORD may **witness** against you,
Zep 3: 8 the LORD, "for the day I will stand up to **testify**. [BHS 6331]
Mal 3: 5 I will be quick to **testify** against sorcerers, adulterers and perjurers,

6333 עִדֹּא ***'iddō'***, n.pr.m. [1] [√ 6341]

Iddo [1]

1Ki 4: 14 Ahinadab son of **Iddo**—in Mahanaim;

6334 ¹עָדָה ***'ādâ¹***, v. [2] [→ 3586?, 3588?, 6330?, 6331; Ar 10528]

prowls [1], takes away [1]

Job 28: 8 [A] Proud beasts do not set foot on it, and no lion **prowls** there.
Pr 25: 20 [G] Like *one who* **takes away** a garment on a cold day, or like

6335 ²עָדָה ***'ādâ²***, v. [8] [→ 538, 3586?, 3587, 3588?, 6336, 6344]

adorned [2], adorn [1], adorns [1], decked [1], put on jewelry [+6344] [1], put on [1], take up [1]

Job 40: 10 [A] **adorn** *yourself with* glory and splendor, and clothe yourself
Isa 61: 10 [A] like a priest, and as a bride **adorns** *herself with* her jewels.
Jer 4: 30 [A] Why dress yourself in scarlet and **put on** jewels of gold?
31: 4 [A] Again *you will* **take up** your tambourines and go out to
Eze 16: 11 [A] *I* **adorned** you *with* jewelry: I put bracelets on your arms
16: 13 [A] So *you were* **adorned** *with* gold and silver; your clothes
23: 40 [A] painted your eyes and **put on** *your* **jewelry** [+6344].
Hos 2: 13 [2:15] [A] *she* **decked** herself *with* rings and jewelry, and went

6336 ³עָדָה ***'ādâ³***, n.pr.f. [8] [√ 6344; cf. 6335]

Adah [8]

Ge 4: 19 married two women, one named **Adah** and the other Zillah.
4: 20 **Adah** gave birth to Jabal; he was the father of those who live in
4: 23 Lamech said to his wives, "**Adah** and Zillah, listen to me;
36: 2 **Adah** daughter of Elon the Hittite, and Oholibamah daughter of
36: 4 **Adah** bore Eliphaz to Esau, Basemath bore Reuel,
36: 10 Eliphaz, the son of Esau's wife **Adah**, and Reuel, the son of Esau's
36: 12 bore him Amalek. These were grandsons of Esau's wife **Adah**.
36: 16 descended from Eliphaz in Edom; they were grandsons of **Adah**.

6337 ¹עֵדָה ***'ēdâ¹***, n.f. [148] [cf. 3585]

community [69], assembly [50], followers [10], *untranslated* [4], people [4], band [2], company [2], assembled [1], community's [1], flocking together [1], herd [1], household [1], swarm [1], whole assembly [+2256+7736] [1]

Ex 12: 3 Tell the whole **community** *of* Israel that on the tenth day of this
12: 6 when all the people of the **community** *of* Israel must slaughter
12: 19 with yeast in it must be cut off from the **community** *of* Israel,
12: 47 The whole **community** *of* Israel must celebrate it.
16: 1 The whole Israelite **community** set out from Elim and came to the
16: 2 In the desert the whole **community** grumbled against Moses
16: 9 Then Moses told Aaron, "Say to the entire Israelite **community**,
16: 10 While Aaron was speaking to the whole Israelite **community**,
16: 22 the leaders of the **community** came and reported this to Moses.
17: 1 The whole Israelite **community** set out from the Desert of Sin,
34: 31 so Aaron and all the leaders of the **community** came back to him,
35: 1 Moses assembled the whole Israelite **community** and said to them,
35: 4 Moses said to the whole Israelite **community**, "This is what the
35: 20 the whole Israelite **community** withdrew from Moses' presence,
38: 25 The silver obtained from those of the **community** who were
Lev 4: 13 " 'If the whole Israelite **community** sins unintentionally and does
4: 15 The elders of the **community** are to lay their hands on the bull's
8: 3 gather the entire **assembly** at the entrance to the Tent of Meeting."
8: 4 and the **assembly** gathered at the entrance to the Tent of Meeting.
8: 5 Moses said to the **assembly**, "This is what the LORD has
9: 5 and the entire **assembly** came near and stood before the LORD.
10: 6 and the LORD will be angry with the whole **community**.
10: 17 it was given to you to take away the guilt of the **community** by
16: 5 From the Israelite **community** he is to take two male goats for a
19: 2 "Speak to the entire **assembly** *of* Israel and say to them: 'Be holy
24: 14 their hands on his head, and the entire **assembly** is to stone him.
24: 16 The entire **assembly** must stone him. Whether an alien
Nu 1: 2 "Take a census of the whole Israelite **community** by their clans
1: 16 These were the men appointed from the **community**, the leaders of
1: 18 they called the whole **community** together on the first day of the
1: 53 so that wrath will not fall on the Israelite **community**.
3: 7 for the whole **community** at the Tent of Meeting by doing the
4: 34 the leaders of the **community** counted the Kohathites by their
8: 9 the Tent of Meeting and assemble the whole Israelite **community**.
8: 20 the whole Israelite **community** did with the Levites just as the
10: 2 use them for calling the **community** together and for having the
10: 3 the whole **community** is to assemble before you at the entrance to
13: 26 the whole Israelite **community** at Kadesh in the Desert of Paran.
13: 26 There they reported to them and to the whole **assembly**
14: 1 That night all the people of the **community** raised their voices
14: 2 against Moses and Aaron, and the whole **assembly** said to them,
14: 5 Aaron fell facedown in front of the whole Israelite **assembly**
14: 7 said to the entire Israelite **assembly**, "The land we passed through
14: 10 the whole **assembly** talked about stoning them. Then the glory of
14: 27 "How long will this wicked **community** grumble against me?
14: 35 and I will surely do these things to this whole wicked **community**,
14: 36 made the whole **community** grumble against him by spreading a
15: 24 if this is done unintentionally without the **community** being aware
15: 24 the whole **community** is to offer a young bull for a burnt offering
15: 25 priest is to make atonement for the whole Israelite **community**,
15: 26 The whole Israelite **community** and the aliens living among them
15: 33 wood brought him to Moses and Aaron and the whole **assembly**,
15: 35 must die. The whole **assembly** must stone him outside the camp."
15: 36 So the **assembly** took him outside the camp and stoned him to
16: 2 well-known **community** leaders who had been appointed members
16: 3 The whole **community** is holy, every one of them, and the LORD
16: 5 he said to Korah and all his **followers**: "In the morning the LORD
16: 6 You, Korah, and all your **followers** are to do this: Take censers
16: 9 Israel has separated you from the rest of the Israelite **community**
16: 9 and to stand before the **community** and minister to them?
16: 11 the LORD that you and all your **followers** have banded together.
16: 16 and all your **followers** are to appear before the LORD tomorrow—
16: 19 When Korah had gathered all his **followers** in opposition to them
16: 19 the glory of the LORD appeared to the entire **assembly**.
16: 21 "Separate yourselves from this **assembly** so I can put an end to
16: 22 will you be angry with the entire **assembly** when only one man
16: 24 "Say to the **assembly**, 'Move away from the tents of Korah,
16: 26 He warned the **assembly**, "Move back from the tents of these
16: 40 [17:5] or he would become like Korah and his **followers**.
16: 41 [17:6] The next day the whole Israelite **community** grumbled
16: 42 [17:7] when the **assembly** gathered in opposition to Moses
16: 45 [17:10] "Get away from this **assembly** so I can put an end to them
16: 46 [17:11] and hurry to the **assembly** to make atonement for them.
19: 9 They shall be kept by the Israelite **community** for use in the water
20: 1 In the first month the whole Israelite **community** arrived at the
20: 2 Now there was no water for the **community**, and the people
20: 8 and you and your brother Aaron gather the **assembly** together.
20: 8 You will bring water out of the rock for the **community** so they
20: 11 Water gushed out, and the **community** and their livestock drank.
20: 22 The whole Israelite **community** set out from Kadesh and came to
20: 27 They went up Mount Hor in the sight of the whole **community**.
20: 29 and when the whole **community** learned that Aaron had died,
25: 6 the whole **assembly** *of* Israel while they were weeping at the
25: 7 the son of Aaron, the priest, saw this, he left the **assembly**,
26: 2 "Take a census of the whole Israelite **community** by families—
26: 9 Abiram were the **community** officials who rebelled against Moses
26: 9 were among Korah's **followers** when they rebelled against the
26: 10 whose **followers** died when the fire devoured the 250 men.
27: 2 Eleazar the priest, the leaders and the whole **assembly**, and said,
27: 3 He was not among Korah's **followers**, who banded together
27: 3 the LORD, **[RPH]** but he died for his own sin and left no sons.
27: 14 for when the **community** rebelled at the waters in the Desert of
27: 16 of the spirits of all mankind, appoint a man over this **community**
27: 17 so the LORD's **people** will not be like sheep without a shepherd."
27: 19 and the entire **assembly** and commission him in their presence.
27: 20 of your authority so the whole Israelite **community** will obey him.
27: 21 and the entire **community** of the Israelites will go out,
27: 22 had him stand before Eleazar the priest and the whole **assembly**.
31: 12 and the Israelite **assembly** at their camp on the plains of Moab,
31: 13 all the leaders of the **community** went to meet them outside the
31: 16 happened at Peor, so that a plague struck the LORD's **people**.
31: 26 and the family heads of the **community** are to count all the people
31: 27 soldiers who took part in the battle and the rest of the **community**.
31: 43 the **community's** half—was 337,500 sheep,
32: 2 and Eleazar the priest and to the leaders of the **community**,
32: 4 the land the LORD subdued before the **people** *of* Israel—
35: 12 of murder may not die before he stands trial before the **assembly**.
35: 24 the **assembly** must judge between him and the avenger of blood
35: 25 The **assembly** must protect the one accused of murder from the
35: 25 and **[RPH]** send him back to the city of refuge to which he fled.
Jos 9: 15 to let them live, and the leaders of the **assembly** ratified it by oath.
9: 18 because the leaders of the **assembly** had sworn an oath to them by
9: 18 God of Israel. The whole **assembly** grumbled against the leaders,
9: 19 **[RPH]** "We have given them our oath by the LORD, the God of
9: 21 them be woodcutters and water carriers for the entire **community**."
9: 27 the Gibeonites woodcutters and water carriers for the **community**
18: 1 The whole **assembly** *of* the Israelites gathered at Shiloh and set up
20: 6 is to stay in that city until he has stood trial before the **assembly**
20: 9 by the avenger of blood prior to standing trial before the **assembly**.
22: 12 the whole **assembly** *of* Israel gathered at Shiloh to go to war

Jos 22:16 "The whole **assembly** *of* the LORD says: 'How could you break
22:17 even though a plague fell on the **community** *of* the LORD!
22:18 tomorrow he will be angry with the whole **community** *of* Israel.
22:20 did not wrath come upon the whole **community** *of* Israel?
22:30 When Phinehas the priest and the leaders of the **community**—
Jdg 14: 8 at the lion's carcass. In it was a **swarm** *of* bees and some honey,
20: 1 as one man and assembled **[NIE]** before the LORD in Mizpah.
21:10 So the **assembly** sent twelve thousand fighting men with
21:13 the whole **assembly** sent an offer of peace to the Benjamites at the
21:16 the elders of the **assembly** said, "With the women of Benjamin
1Ki 8: 5 the entire **assembly** *of* Israel that had gathered about him were
12:20 they sent and called him to the **assembly** and made him king over
2Ch 5: 6 the entire **assembly** *of* Israel that had gathered about him were
Job 15:34 For the **company** *of* the godless will be barren, and fire will
16: 7 you have worn me out; you have devastated my entire **household**.
Ps 1: 5 stand in the judgment, nor sinners in the **assembly** *of* the righteous.
7: 7 [7:8] Let the **assembled** peoples gather around you. Rule over
22:16 [22:17] a **band** *of* evil men has encircled me, they have pierced
68:30 [68:31] the **herd** *of* bulls among the calves of the nations.
74: 2 Remember the **people** you purchased of old, the tribe of your
82: 1 God presides in the great **assembly**; he gives judgment among the
86:14 are attacking me, O God; a **band** *of* ruthless men seeks my life—
106:17 and swallowed Dathan; it buried the **company** *of* Abiram.
106:18 Fire blazed among their **followers**; a flame consumed the wicked.
111: 1 with all my heart in the council of the upright and in the **assembly**.
Pr 5:14 utter ruin in the midst of the **whole assembly** [+2256+7736]."
Jer 30:20 in days of old, and their **community** will be established before me;
Hos 7:12 of the air. When I hear them **flocking together**, I will catch them.

6338 ²עֵדָה *'ēdâ²*, n.f. [5] [√ 6386]

witness [4], witnesses [1]

Ge 21:30 "Accept these seven lambs from my hand as a **witness** that I dug
31:52 This heap is a witness, and this pillar is a **witness**, that I will not go
Jos 24:27 he said to all the people. "This stone will be a **witness** against us.
24:27 It will be a **witness** against you if you are untrue to your God."
Jer 6:18 O nations; observe, O **witnesses**, what will happen to them.

6339 ³עֵדָה *'ēdâ³*, n.f. Not used in NIV/BHS [√ 6386]

6340 עִדָּה *'iddâ*, n.f. [1]

filthy [1]

Isa 64: 6 [64:5] is unclean, and all our righteous acts are like **filthy** rags;

6341 עִדּוֹ *'iddô*, n.pr.m. [4] [→ 6333, 6342; Ar 10529]

Iddo [4]

1Ch 6:21 [6:6] Joah his son, **Iddo** his son, Zerah his son and Jeatherai his
2Ch 12:15 the prophet and of **Iddo** the seer that deal with genealogies?
13:22 what he said, are written in the annotations of the prophet **Iddo**.
Zec 1: 1 came to the prophet Zechariah son of Berekiah, the son of **Iddo**:

6342 עִדּוֹא *'iddô'*, n.pr.m. [3] [√ 6341; Ar 10529]

Iddo [2], Iddo's [1]

Ne 12: 4 **Iddo**, Ginnethon, Abijah,
12:16 of **Iddo's**, [K 6345] Zechariah; of Ginnethon's, Meshullam;
Zec 1: 7 came to the prophet Zechariah son of Berekiah, the son of **Iddo**.

6343 עֵדוּת *'ēdût*, n.f. [83] [√ 6386]

Testimony [37], statutes [29], stipulations [4], copy of covenant [2], Covenant [2], regulations [2], requirements [2], statute [2], demands [1], warnings gave [+928+6386] [1], warnings given [+906+928+6386] [1]

Ex 16:34 Aaron put the manna in front of the **Testimony**, that it might be
25:16 Then put in the ark the **Testimony**, which I will give you.
25:21 Place the cover on top of the ark and put in the ark the **Testimony**,
25:22 between the two cherubim that are over the ark of the **Testimony**,
26:33 the clasps and place the ark of the **Testimony** behind the curtain.
26:34 Put the atonement cover on the ark of the **Testimony** in the Most
27:21 outside the curtain that is in front of the **Testimony**, Aaron
30: 6 in front of the curtain that is before the ark of the **Testimony**—
30: 6 before the atonement cover that is over the **Testimony**—where I
30:26 use it to anoint the Tent of Meeting, the ark of the **Testimony**,
30:36 and place it in front of the **Testimony** in the Tent of Meeting,
31: 7 the ark of the **Testimony** with the atonement cover on it,
31:18 he gave him the two tablets of the **Testimony**, the tablets of stone
32:15 went down the mountain with the two tablets of the **Testimony** in
34:29 Mount Sinai with the two tablets of the **Testimony** in his hands,
38:21 materials used for the tabernacle, the tabernacle of the **Testimony**,
39:35 the ark of the **Testimony** with its poles and the atonement cover;
40: 3 Place the ark of the **Testimony** in it and shield the ark with the
40: 5 Place the gold altar of incense in front of the ark of the **Testimony**
40:20 He took the **Testimony** and placed it in the ark, attached the poles
40:21 hung the shielding curtain and shielded the ark of the **Testimony**,
Lev 16:13 incense will conceal the atonement cover above the **Testimony**,
24: 3 Outside the curtain of the **Testimony** in the Tent of Meeting,
Nu 1:50 the Levites to be in charge of the tabernacle of the **Testimony**—
1:53 are to set up their tents around the tabernacle of the **Testimony**
1:53 to be responsible for the care of the tabernacle of the **Testimony**."
4: 5 the shielding curtain and cover the ark of the **Testimony** with it.
7:89 cherubim above the atonement cover on the ark of the **Testimony**.
9:15 the Tent of the **Testimony**, was set up, the cloud covered it.
10:11 the cloud lifted from above the tabernacle of the **Testimony**.
17: 4 [17:19] them in the Tent of Meeting in front of the **Testimony**,
17: 7 [17:22] staffs before the LORD in the Tent of the **Testimony**.
17: 8 [17:23] The next day Moses entered the Tent of the **Testimony**
17:10 [17:25] "Put back Aaron's staff in front of the **Testimony**,
18: 2 and your sons minister before the Tent of the **Testimony**.
Dt 4:45 These are the **stipulations**, decrees and laws Moses gave them
6:17 your God and the **stipulations** and decrees he has given you.
6:20 "What is the meaning of the **stipulations**, decrees and laws the
Jos 4:16 "Command the priests carrying the ark of the **Testimony** to come
1Ki 2: 3 and keep his decrees and commands, his laws and **requirements**,
2Ki 11:12 he presented him with a **copy of** the **covenant** and proclaimed him
17:15 and the **warnings** *he had* **given** [+906+928+6386] them.
23: 3 **regulations** and decrees with all his heart and all his soul,
1Ch 29:19 **requirements** and decrees and to do everything to build the
2Ch 23:11 they presented him with a **copy of** the **covenant** and proclaimed
24: 6 and by the assembly of Israel for the Tent of the **Testimony**?"
34:31 **regulations** and decrees with all his heart and all his soul,
Ne 9:34 to your commands or the **warnings** *you* **gave** [+928+6386] them.
Ps 19: 7 [19:8] The **statutes** *of* the LORD are trustworthy, making wise
25:10 and faithful for those who keep the **demands** of his covenant.
60: T [60:1] To ˛the tune of˛ "The Lily of the **Covenant**." A *miktam*
78: 5 He decreed **statutes** for Jacob and established the law in Israel,
78:56 and rebelled against the Most High; they did not keep his **statutes**.
80: T [80:1] To ˛the tune of˛ "The Lilies of the **Covenant**." Of Asaph.
81: 5 [81:6] He established it as a **statute** for Joseph when he went out
93: 5 Your **statutes** stand firm; holiness adorns your house for endless
99: 7 of cloud; they kept his **statutes** and the decrees he gave them.
119: 2 Blessed are they who keep his **statutes** and seek him with all their
119:14 I rejoice in following your **statutes** as one rejoices in great riches.
119:22 Remove from me scorn and contempt, for I keep your **statutes**.
119:24 Your **statutes** are my delight; they are my counselors.
119:31 I hold fast to your **statutes**, O LORD; do not let me be put to
119:36 Turn my heart toward your **statutes** and not toward selfish gain.
119:46 I will speak of your **statutes** before kings and will not be put to
119:59 considered my ways and have turned my steps to your **statutes**.
119:79 who fear you turn to me, those who understand your **statutes**.
119:88 according to your love, and I will obey the **statutes** *of* your mouth.
119:95 wicked are waiting to destroy me, but I will ponder your **statutes**.
119:99 more insight than all my teachers, for I meditate on your **statutes**.
119:111 Your **statutes** are my heritage forever; they are the joy of my heart.
119:119 of the earth you discard like dross; therefore I love your **statutes**.
119:125 give me discernment that I may understand your **statutes**.
119:129 Your **statutes** are wonderful; therefore I obey them.
119:138 The **statutes** you have laid down are righteous; they are fully
119:144 Your **statutes** are forever right; give me understanding that I may
119:146 I call out to you; save me and I will keep your **statutes**.
119:152 Long ago I learned from your **statutes** that you established them to
119:157 foes who persecute me, but I have not turned from your **statutes**.
119:167 I obey your **statutes**, for I love them greatly.
119:168 I obey your precepts and your **statutes**, for all my ways are known
122: 4 to praise the name of the LORD according to the **statute** given to
132:12 if your sons keep my covenant and the **statutes** I teach them,
Jer 44:23 obeyed him or followed his law or his decrees or his **stipulations**,

6344 עֲדִי *'adî*, n.[m.]. [14] [√ 3587, 6336, 6346, 6348; cf. 6335; *also used with compound proper names*]

ornaments [5], jewelry [2], most beautiful of jewels [+6344] [2], beautiful jewelry [+7382] [1], bridle [+8270] [1], desires [1], jewels [1], put on jewelry [+6335] [1]

Ex 33: 4 they began to mourn and no one put on any **ornaments**.
33: 5 Now take off your **ornaments** and I will decide what to do with
33: 6 So the Israelites stripped off their **ornaments** at Mount Horeb.
2Sa 1:24 and finery, who adorned your garments with **ornaments** *of* gold.
Ps 32: 9 must be controlled by bit and **bridle** [+8270] or they will not come
103: 5 who satisfies your **desires** with good things so that your youth is
Isa 49:18 declares the LORD, "you will wear them all as **ornaments**;
Jer 2:32 Does a maiden forget her **jewelry**, a bride her wedding ornaments?
4:30 Why dress yourself in scarlet and put on **jewels** *of* gold?
Eze 7:20 They were proud of their **beautiful jewelry** [+7382] and used it to
16: 7 and developed and became the **most beautiful of jewels** [+6344].
16: 7 and developed and became the **most beautiful of jewels** [+6344].
16:11 I adorned you with **jewelry**: I put bracelets on your arms and a

Eze 23:40 for them, painted your eyes and **put on** *your* **jewelry** [+6335].

6345 עֲדָיָא ***ʿadāyā'***, n.pr.m. [0] [cf. 6347]

Ne 12:16 [of **Iddo's**, [K; see Q 6342] Zechariah; of Ginnethon's,]

6346 עֲדִיאֵל ***ʿadî'ēl***, n.pr.m. [3] [√ 6344 + 446]

Adiel [3]

1Ch 4:36 Jaakobah, Jeshohaiah, Asaiah, **Adiel**, Jesimiel, Benaiah,
9:12 Maasai son of **Adiel**, the son of Jahzerah, the son of Meshullam,
27:25 Azmaveth son of **Adiel** was in charge of the royal storehouses.

6347 עֲדָיָה ***ʿadāyâ***, n.pr.m. [8] [√ 6344 + 3378; cf. 6345]

Adaiah [8]

2Ki 22:1 His mother's name was Jedidah daughter of **Adaiah**; she was from
1Ch 6:41 [6:26] the son of Ethni, the son of Zerah, the son of **Adaiah**,
8:21 **Adaiah**, Beraiah and Shimrath were the sons of Shimei.
9:12 **Adaiah** son of Jeroham, the son of Pashhur, the son of Malkijah;
Ezr 10:29 Meshullam, Malluch, **Adaiah**, Jashub, Sheal and Jeremoth.
10:39 Shelemiah, Nathan, **Adaiah**,
Ne 11:5 the son of Hazaiah, the son of **Adaiah**, the son of Joiarib, the son
11:12 **Adaiah** son of Jeroham, the son of Pelaliah, the son of Amzi,

6348 עֲדָיָהוּ ***ʿadāyāhû***, n.pr.m. [1] [√ 6344 + 3378]

Adaiah [1]

2Ch 23:1 son of Jehohanan, Azariah son of Obed, Maaseiah son of **Adaiah**,

6349 [1]עָדִין ***ʿādîn¹***, a. [1] [√ 6357]

wanton [1]

Isa 47:8 "Now then, listen, you **wanton** *creature*, lounging in your security

6350 [2]עָדִין ***ʿādîn²***, n.pr.m. [4] [√ 6357]

Adin [4]

Ezr 2:15 of **Adin** 454
8:6 of the descendants of **Adin**, Ebed son of Jonathan, and with him 50
Ne 7:20 of **Adin** 655
10:16 [10:17] Adonijah, Bigvai, **Adin**,

6351 עֲדִינָא ***ʿadînā'***, n.pr.m. [1] [√ 6357]

Adina [1]

1Ch 11:42 **Adina** son of Shiza the Reubenite, who was chief of the

6352 עֲדִינוֹ ***ʿadînô***, n.pr.m. [1 / 0]

2Sa 23:8 was chief of the Three; he raised [BHS *Adino*; NIV 6424]

6353 עֲדִיתַיִם ***ʿadîtayim***, n.pr.loc. [1]

Adithaim [1]

Jos 15:36 Shaaraim, **Adithaim** and Gederah (or Gederothaim)—

6354 עַדְלַי ***ʿadlay***, n.pr.m. [1]

Adlai [1]

1Ch 27:29 Shaphat son of **Adlai** was in charge of the herds in the valleys.

6355 עֲדֻלָּם ***ʿadullām***, n.pr.loc. [8] [→ 6356]

Adullam [8]

Jos 12:15 the king of Libnah one the king of **Adullam** one
15:35 Jarmuth, **Adullam**, Socoh, Azekah,
1Sa 22:1 David left Gath and escaped to the cave of **Adullam**. When his
2Sa 23:13 the thirty chief men came down to David at the cave of **Adullam**,
1Ch 11:15 chiefs came down to David to the rock at the cave of **Adullam**,
2Ch 11:7 Beth Zur, Soco, **Adullam**,
Ne 11:30 Zanoah, **Adullam** and their villages, in Lachish and its fields,
Mic 1:15 in Mareshah. He who is the glory of Israel will come to **Adullam**.

6356 עֲדֻלָּמִי ***ʿadullāmî***, a.g. [3] [√ 6355]

Adullamite [2], of Adullam [1]

Ge 38:1 and went down to stay with a man **of Adullam** named Hirah.
38:12 his sheep, and his friend Hirah the **Adullamite** went with him.
38:20 Meanwhile Judah sent the young goat by his friend the **Adullamite**

6357 עָדַן ***ʿādan***, v.den. [1] [→ 5051, 5052, 6349, 6350, 6351, 6366; cf. 6367?]

reveled [1]

Ne 9:25 [F] were well-nourished; *they* **reveled** in your great goodness.

6358 [1]עֵדֶן ***ʿēden¹***, n.[m.]. [3] [→ 6360, 6365; cf. 6363]

delicacies [1], delights [1], finery [1]

2Sa 1:24 of Israel, weep for Saul, who clothed you in scarlet and **finery**,
Ps 36:8 [36:9] you give them drink from your river of **delights**.
Jer 51:34 he has swallowed us and filled his stomach with our **delicacies**,

6359 [2]עֵדֶן ***ʿēden²***, n.pr.loc. [14]

Eden [14]

Ge 2:8 Now the LORD God had planted a garden in the east, in **Eden**;
2:10 A river watering the garden flowed from **Eden**; from there it was
2:15 and put him in the Garden of **Eden** to work it and take care of it.
3:23 So the LORD God banished him from the Garden of **Eden** to
3:24 he placed on the east side of the Garden of **Eden** cherubim
4:16 the LORD's presence and lived in the land of Nod, east of **Eden**.
Isa 51:3 he will make her deserts like **Eden**, her wastelands like the garden
Eze 28:13 You were in **Eden**, the garden of God; every precious stone
31:9 the envy of all the trees of **Eden** in the garden of God.
31:16 Then all the trees of **Eden**, the choicest and best of Lebanon,
31:18 " 'Which of the trees of **Eden** can be compared with you in
31:18 will be brought down with the trees of **Eden** to the earth below;
36:35 "This land that was laid waste has become like the garden of **Eden**;
Joel 2:3 Before them the land is like the garden of **Eden**, behind them,

6360 [3]עֵדֶן ***ʿēden³***, n.pr.m. [2] [√ 6358]

Eden [2]

2Ch 29:12 from the Gershonites, Joah son of Zimmah and **Eden** son of Joah;
31:15 **Eden**, Miniamin, Jeshua, Shemaiah, Amariah and Shecaniah

6361 עֶדֶן ***ʿeden***, n.pr.loc. [3] [→ 1114]

Eden [3]

2Ki 19:12 Haran, Rezeph and the people of **Eden** who were in Tel Assar?
Isa 37:12 Haran, Rezeph and the people of **Eden** who were in Tel Assar?
Eze 27:23 Canneh and **Eden** and merchants of Sheba, Asshur and Kilmad

6362 עֲדֶן ***ʿaden***, adv. [1]

yet [1]

Ecc 4:3 better than both is he who has not **yet** been, who has not seen the

6363 עַדְנָא ***ʿadnā'***, n.pr.m. [2] [cf. 6358, 6365]

Adna [2]

Ezr 10:30 **Adna**, Kelal, Benaiah, Maaseiah, Mattaniah, Bezalel, Binnui
Ne 12:15 of Harim's, **Adna**; of Meremoth's, Helkai;

6364 עֲדֶנָּה ***ʿadenâ***, adv. [1] [√ 6330 + 2178]

still [1]

Ecc 4:2 had already died, are happier than the living, who are **still** alive.

6365 עַדְנָה ***ʿadnâ***, n.pr.m. [1] [√ 6358; cf. 6363]

Adnah [1]

2Ch 17:14 units of 1,000: **Adnah** the commander, with 300,000 fighting men;

6366 עֶדְנָה ***ʿednâ***, n.f. [1] [√ 6357]

pleasure [1]

Ge 18:12 am worn out and my master is old, will I now have this **pleasure**?"

6367 עַדְנַח ***ʿadnaḥ***, n.pr.m. [1] [cf. 6357?]

Adnah [1]

1Ch 12:20 [12:21] **Adnah**, Jozabad, Jediael, Michael, Jozabad, Elihu

6368 עַדְעָדָה ***ʿadʿādâ***, n.pr.loc. [1]

Adadah [1]

Jos 15:22 Kinah, Dimonah, **Adadah**,

6369 עָדַף ***ʿādap***, v. [9]

additional [2], left [2], balance [1], exceed number [1], exceeded number [1], have too much [1], left over [1]

Ex 16:18 [G] by the omer, he who gathered much *did* not **have too much**,
16:23 [A] to boil. Save whatever *is* **left** and keep it until morning.' "
26:12 [A] As for the **additional** length of the tent curtains, the half
26:12 [A] the half curtain that *is* **left over** is to hang down at the rear of
26:13 [A] what *is* **left** will hang over the sides of the tabernacle so as to
Lev 25:27 [A] sold it and refund the **balance** to the man to whom he sold it;
Nu 3:46 [A] firstborn Israelites who **exceed** the **number** *of* the Levites,
3:48 [A] Give the money for the redemption of the **additional**
3:49 [A] those *who* **exceeded** the **number** redeemed by the Levites.

6370 ¹עָדַר ***ʿādar¹***, v. [2] [cf. 6468]

help [1], volunteered to serve [1]

1Ch 12:33 [12:34] [A] of weapon, to **help** David with undivided loyalty—
12:38 [12:39] [A] men *who* **volunteered to serve** *in* the ranks.

6371 ²עָדַר ***ʿādar²***, v. [2] [→ 5053]

cultivated [2]

Isa 5: 6 [C] neither pruned nor **cultivated**, and briers and thorns will
7:25 [C] As for all the hills *once* **cultivated** by the hoe, you will no

6372 ³עָדַר ***ʿādar³***, v. [7] [→ 6373]

missing [3], fail [1], left [1], nowhere to be found [1], saw to it that was lacking [1]

1Sa 30:19 [C] Nothing *was* **missing**: young or old, boy or girl, plunder or
2Sa 17:22 [C] no one *was* **left** who had not crossed the Jordan.
1Ki 4:27 [5:7] [D] king's table. *They* **saw to it that** nothing **was lacking**.
Isa 34:16 [C] None of these *will be* **missing**, not one will lack her mate.
40:26 [C] great power and mighty strength, not one of them *is* **missing**.
59:15 [C] Truth is **nowhere to be found**, and whoever shuns evil
Zep 3: 5 [C] every new day *he does* not **fail**, yet the unrighteous know no

6373 ¹עֵדֶר ***ʿēder¹***, n.m. [39] [→ 6372]

flock [15], flocks [15], herds [3], each herd [+6373] [2], *untranslated* [1], flocks and herds [1], herds [+1330] [1], sheep [1]

Ge 29: 2 with three **flocks** *of* sheep lying near it because the flocks were
29: 2 sheep lying near it because the **flocks** were watered from that well.
29: 3 When all the **flocks** were gathered there, the shepherds would roll
29: 8 "until all the **flocks** are gathered and the stone has been rolled
30:40 Thus he made separate **flocks** for himself and did not put them
32:16 [32:17] **each herd** [+6373] by itself, and said to his servants,
32:16 [32:17] **each herd** [+6373] by itself, and said to his servants,
32:16 [32:17] ahead of me, and keep some space between the **herds**."
32:16 [32:17] of me, and keep some space between the herds." **[RPH]**
32:19 [32:20] the third and all the others who followed the **herds**:
Jdg 5:16 you stay among the campfires to hear the whistling for the **flocks**?
1Sa 17:34 When a lion or a bear came and carried off a sheep from the **flock**,
2Ch 32:28 he made stalls for various kinds of cattle, and pens for the **flocks**.
Job 24: 2 Men move boundary stones; they pasture **flocks** they have stolen.
Ps 78:52 people out like a flock; he led them like **sheep** through the desert.
Pr 27:23 the condition of your flocks, give careful attention to your **herds**;
SS 1: 7 Why should I be like a veiled woman beside the **flocks** *of* your
4: 1 Your hair is like a **flock** *of* goats descending from Mount Gilead.
4: 2 Your teeth are like a **flock** *of* sheep just shorn, coming up from the
6: 5 Your hair is like a **flock** *of* goats descending from Gilead.
6: 6 Your teeth are like a **flock** *of* sheep coming up from the washing.
Isa 17: 2 The cities of Aroer will be deserted and left to **flocks**, which will
32:14 a wasteland forever, the delight of donkeys, a pasture for **flocks**,
40:11 He tends his **flock** like a shepherd: He gathers the lambs in his
Jer 6: 3 Shepherds with their **flocks** will come against her; they will pitch
13:17 with tears, because the LORD's **flock** will be taken captive.
13:20 Where is the **flock** that was entrusted to you, the sheep of which
31:10 will gather them and will watch over his **flock** like a shepherd.'
31:24 all its towns—farmers and those who move about with their **flocks**.
51:23 with you I shatter shepherd and **flock**, with you I shatter farmer
Eze 34:12 As a shepherd looks after his scattered **flock** when he is with them,
Joel 1:18 The **herds** [+1330] mill about because they have no pasture;
1:18 they have no pasture; even the **flocks** *of* sheep are suffering.
Mic 2:12 bring them together like sheep in a pen, like a **flock** in its pasture;
4: 8 As for you, O watchtower of the **flock**, O stronghold of the
5: 8 [5:7] like a young lion among **flocks** *of* sheep, which mauls
Zep 2:14 **Flocks and herds** will lie down there, creatures of every kind.
Zec 10: 3 for the LORD Almighty will care for his **flock**, the house of
Mal 1:14 "Cursed is the cheat who has an acceptable male in his **flock**

6374 ²עֵדֶר ***ʿēder²***, n.pr.m. [2] [→ 4468, 6375?, 6376, 6377]

Eder [2]

1Ch 23:23 The sons of Mushi: Mahli, **Eder** and Jerimoth—three in all.
24:30 the sons of Mushi: Mahli, **Eder** and Jerimoth. These were the

6375 ³עֵדֶר ***ʿēder³***, n.pr.loc. [1] [√ 6374?]

Eder [1]

Jos 15:21 Negev toward the boundary of Edom were: Kabzeel, **Eder**, Jagur,

6376 עֵדֶר ***ʿeder***, n.pr.m. [1] [√ 6374]

Eder [1]

1Ch 8:15 Zebadiah, Arad, **Eder**,

6377 עַדְרִיאֵל ***ʿadrîʾēl***, n.pr.m. [2] [√ 6374 + 446]

Adriel [2]

1Sa 18:19 given to David, she was given in marriage to **Adriel** of Meholah.
2Sa 21: 8 whom she had borne to **Adriel** son of Barzillai the Meholathite.

6378 עֲדָשִׁים ***ᵃdāšîm***, n.f. [4]

lentils [3], lentil [1]

Ge 25:34 Then Jacob gave Esau some bread and some **lentil** stew. He ate
2Sa 17:28 and barley, flour and roasted grain, beans and **lentils**,
23:11 banded together at a place where there was a field full of **lentils**,
Eze 4: 9 "Take wheat and barley, beans and **lentils**, millet and spelt;

6379 עַוָּא ***ʿawwāʾ***, n.pr.loc. [1] [cf. 6393]

Avva [1]

2Ki 17:24 Cuthah, **Avva**, Hamath and Sepharvaim and settled them in the

6380 עוּב ***ʿûb***, v.den. [1] [→ 6266?]

covered with the cloud [1]

La 2: 1 [G] *has* **covered** the Daughter of Zion **with the cloud** of his

6381 עוֹבֵד ***ʿôbēd***, n.pr.m. [10] [√ 6268]

Obed [10]

Ru 4:17 living there said, "Naomi has a son." And they named him **Obed**.
4:21 Salmon the father of Boaz, Boaz the father of **Obed**,
4:22 **Obed** the father of Jesse, and Jesse the father of David.
1Ch 2:12 Boaz the father of **Obed** and Obed the father of Jesse.
2:12 Boaz the father of Obed and **Obed** the father of Jesse.
2:37 Zabad the father of Ephlal, Ephlal the father of **Obed**,
2:38 **Obed** the father of Jehu, Jehu the father of Azariah,
11:47 Eliel, **Obed** and Jaasiel the Mezobaite.
26: 7 Othni, Rephael, **Obed** and Elzabad; his relatives Elihu
2Ch 23: 1 son of Jehohanan, Azariah son of **Obed**, Maaseiah son of Adaiah,

6382 עוֹבָל ***ʿôbāl***, n.pr.g. [1 / 2] [cf. 6508]

Obal [2]

Ge 10:28 **Obal**, Abimael, Sheba,
1Ch 1:22 **Obal**, [BHS 6508] Abimael, Sheba,

6383 עוּג ***ʿûg***, v.den. [1] [→ 5056, 6314]

bake [1]

Eze 4:12 [A] **bake** it in the sight of the people, using human excrement for

6384 עוֹג ***ʿôg***, n.pr.m. [22]

Og [20], Og's [2]

Nu 21:33 **Og** king of Bashan and his whole army marched out to meet them
32:33 king of the Amorites and the kingdom of **Og** king of Bashan—
Dt 1: 4 reigned in Heshbon, and at Edrei had defeated **Og** king of Bashan,
3: 1 **Og** king of Bashan with his whole army marched out to meet us in
3: 3 So the LORD our God also gave into our hands **Og** king of
3: 4 from them—the whole region of Argob, **Og's** kingdom in Bashan.
3:10 as far as Salecah and Edrei, towns of **Og's** kingdom in Bashan.
3:11 (Only **Og** king of Bashan was left of the remnant of the Rephaites.
3:13 The rest of Gilead and also all of Bashan, the kingdom of **Og**,
4:47 took possession of his land and the land of **Og** king of Bashan,
29: 7 [29:6] and **Og** king of Bashan came out to fight against us,
31: 4 And the LORD will do to them what he did to Sihon and **Og**,
Jos 2:10 what you did to Sihon and **Og**, the two kings of the Amorites east
9:10 Sihon king of Heshbon, and **Og** king of Bashan, who reigned in
12: 4 the territory of **Og** king of Bashan, one of the last of the Rephaites,
13:12 that is, the whole kingdom of **Og** in Bashan, who had reigned in
13:30 including all of Bashan, the entire realm of **Og** king of Bashan—
13:31 and Ashtaroth and Edrei (the royal cities of **Og** in Bashan).
1Ki 4:19 Sihon king of the Amorites and the country of **Og** king of Bashan).
Ne 9:22 of Sihon king of Heshbon and the country of **Og** king of Bashan.
Ps 135:11 of the Amorites, **Og** king of Bashan and all the kings of Canaan—
136:20 and **Og** king of Bashan—*His love endures forever.*

6385 עוּגָב ***ʿûgāb***, n.m. [4] [cf. 6311]

flute [4]

Ge 4:21 was Jubal; he was the father of all who play the harp and **flute**.
Job 21:12 of tambourine and harp; they make merry to the sound of the **flute**.
30:31 harp is tuned to mourning, and my **flute** to the sound of wailing.
Ps 150: 4 with tambourine and dancing, praise him with the strings and **flute**,

6386 עוּד[1] *'ûd*[1], v.den. [44] [→ 537, 6332, 6338, 6339, 6343, 6388, 6389, 9496; cf. 6387]
warned [5], warn [4], testify [3], admonished [2], call as witnesses [2], sustains [2], warn solemnly [+928+6386] [2], warned [+928+6386] [2], warned solemnly [+928+6386] [2], *untranslated* [1], acting as witness [1], been warned [1], bind [1], brought charges against [1], call in as witnesses [+906+906+6332] [1], call to testify [1], commended [1], gave charge [1], give warning [1], had witnessed [+6332] [1], have testify [1], have the transaction witnessed [+6332] [1], say [1], solemnly declared [1], stand firm [1], testified [1], warnings gave [+928+6343] [1], warnings given [+906+928+6343] [1], witnessed [+6332] [1]

Ge 43: 3 [G] said to him, "The man **warned** [+928+6386] us **solemnly**,
43: 3 [G] said to him, "The man **warned** us **solemnly** [+928+6386],
Ex 19:21 [G] "Go down and **warn** the people so they do not force their
19:23 [G] because *you* yourself **warned** us, 'Put limits around the
21:29 [H] the owner *has* **been warned** but has not kept it penned up
Dt 4:26 [G] *I* **call** heaven and earth **as witnesses** against you this day that
8:19 [G] *I* **testify** against you today that you will surely be destroyed.
30:19 [G] This day *I* **call** heaven and earth **as witnesses** against you
31:28 [G] and **call** heaven and earth **to testify** against them.
32:46 [G] "Take to heart all the words I *have* **solemnly declared** to you
1Sa 8: 9 [G] **warn** [+928+6386] them **solemnly** and let them know what
8: 9 [G] **warn** them **solemnly** [+928+6386] and let them know what
1Ki 2:42 [G] "Did I not make you swear by the LORD and **warn** you,
21:10 [G] **have** *them* **testify** that he has cursed both God and the king.
21:13 [G] and **brought charges against** Naboth before the people,
2Ki 17:13 [G] The LORD **warned** Israel and Judah through all his
17:15 [G] and the **warnings** [+906+928+6343] *he had* **given** them.
2Ch 24:19 [G] and though *they* **testified** against them, they would not listen.
Ne 9:26 [G] who *had* **admonished** them in order to turn them back to
9:29 [G] "*You* **warned** them to return to your law, but they became
9:30 [G] By your Spirit *you* **admonished** them through your prophets.
9:34 [G] or the **warnings** [+928+6343] *you* **gave** them.
13:15 [G] Therefore *I* **warned** them *against* selling food on that day.
13:21 [G] *I* **warned** them and said, "Why do you spend the night by the
Job 29:11 [G] spoke well of me, and those who saw me **commended** me,
Ps 20: 8 [20:9] [F] to their knees and fall, but we rise up and **stand firm**.
50: 7 [G] and I will speak, O Israel, and *I will* **testify** against you:
81: 8 [81:9] [G] "Hear, O my people, and *I will* **warn** you—if you
119:61 [D] Though the wicked **bind** me *with* ropes, I will not forget
146: 9 [D] over the alien and **sustains** the fatherless and the widow,
147: 6 [D] The LORD **sustains** the humble but casts the wicked to the
Isa 8: 2 [G] And *I will* **call in** Uriah the priest and Zechariah son of Jeberekiah **as** reliable **witnesses** [+906+906+6332] for me."
Jer 6:10 [G] To whom can I speak and **give warning**? Who will listen to
11: 7 [G] *I* **warned** [+928+6386] them again and again, saying,
11: 7 [G] *I* **warned** [+928+6386] them again and again, saying,
11: 7 [G] I warned them again and again, **[RPH]** saying, "Obey me."
32:10 [G] I signed and sealed the deed, **had** it **witnessed** [+6332], and
32:25 [G] with silver and **have the transaction witnessed** [+6332].' "
32:44 [G] sealed and **witnessed** [+6332] in the territory of Benjamin,
42:19 [G] 'Do not go to Egypt.' Be sure of this: *I* **warn** you today
La 2:13 [G] What *can I* **say** *for* you? With what can I compare you,
Am 3:13 [G] "Hear this and **testify** against the house of Jacob,"
Zec 3: 6 [G] The angel of the LORD **gave** *this* **charge** to Joshua:
Mal 2:14 [G] because the LORD *is* **acting as** *the* **witness** between you

6387 עוּד[2] *'ûd*[2], v. Not used in NIV/BHS [cf. 6386]

6388 עוֹד *'ôd*, subst. (used as adv.). [490] [√ 6386; Ar 10531]
longer [74], again [72], still [54], more [35], *untranslated* [28], again [+3578] [22], while still [16], other [11], another [9], anymore [8], continued [8], yet [7], further [6], more [+3578] [6], within [+928] [6], longer [+3578] [5], never [+4202] [5], also [4], anymore [+3578] [4], besides [4], once again [4], another [+337] [3], any longer [3], any more [3], else [3], all the more [+3578] [2], as long as [+3972] [2], as long as live [+928] [2], even [2], ever [2], left [2], more [+337] [2], once again [+3578] [2], once more [+3578] [2], overwhelmed [+928+2118+4202+8120] [2], remain [2], remained [2], remains [2], soon [+5071] [2], still another [2], while [2], added [1], all life [+4946] [1], almost [+5071] [1], always [+4946] [1], another [+3578] [1], any [+4946] [1], any longer [+3578] [1], as long as [+561] [1], as long as [+928] [1], as long as [1], awaits [1], back [+3578] [1], back [1], before [+4202] [1], but also [1], continue [1], continued [+3578] [1], do again [+3578] [1], even as [1], even more [1], ever again [1], failed [+4202+7756] [1], for [1], from now [+928] [1], from now on [1], furthermore [+2256] [1], how long [+339+5503] [1], in a very short time [+4663+5071] [1], in [1], kept on [1], left now [1], little while [+5071] [1], long time [1], make again [+3578] [1], more [+3578+4200] [1], moreover [1], next [1], not enough [+7781] [1], now [1], on [1], once more [1], only [1], others [1], reappears [+8011] [1], reconsider [+8740] [1], regain [+6806] [1], return [+995] [1], since then [1], something else [1], stands [1], still [+3972] [1], still [+8636] [1], still another [+3578] [1], stopped [+3578+4202] [1], time [1], very soon [+4663+5071] [1], were added [+3578] [1], yet to come [1]

Ge 4:25 Adam lay with his wife **again**, and she gave birth to a son
7: 4 Seven days from **now** I will send rain on the earth for forty days
8:10 He waited seven **more** [+337] days and again sent out the dove
8:12 He waited seven **more** [+337] days and sent the dove out again,
8:12 He waited seven more days and sent the dove out **again**, but this
8:21 "Never **again** [+3578] will I curse the ground because of man,
8:21 And never **again** [+3578] will I destroy all living creatures,
8:22 "**As long** [+3972] **as** the earth endures, seedtime and harvest,
9:11 Never **again** will all life be cut off by the waters of a flood;
9:11 of a flood; never **again** will there be a flood to destroy the earth."
9:15 Never **again** will the waters become a flood to destroy all life.
17: 5 No **longer** will you be called Abram; your name will be Abraham,
18:22 but Abraham **remained** standing before the LORD.
18:29 **Once again** [+3578] he spoke to him, "What if only forty are
19:12 The two men said to Lot, "Do you have anyone **else** here—
24:20 ran **back** to the well to draw more water, and drew enough for all
25: 6 while he was **still** living, he gave gifts to the sons of his concubines
29: 7 "Look," he said, "the sun is **still** high; it is not time for the flocks to
29: 9 **While** he was **still** talking with them, Rachel came with her
29:27 one also, in return for **another** [+337] seven years of work."
29:30 than Leah. And he worked for Laban **another** [+337] seven years.
29:33 She conceived **again**, and when she gave birth to a son she said,
29:34 **Again** she conceived, and when she gave birth to a son she said,
29:35 She conceived **again**, and when she gave birth to a son she said,
30: 7 Rachel's servant Bilhah conceived **again** and bore Jacob a second
30:19 Leah conceived **again** and bore Jacob a sixth son.
31:14 "Do we **still** have any share in the inheritance of our father's
32:28 [32:29] man said, "Your name will no **longer** be Jacob, but Israel,
35: 9 from Paddan Aram, God appeared to him **again** and blessed him.
35:10 "Your name is Jacob, but you will no **longer** be called Jacob;
35:16 While they were **still** some distance from Ephrath, Rachel began to
37: 5 he told it to his brothers, they hated him **all the more** [+3578].
37: 8 And they hated him **all the more** [+3578] because of his dream
37: 9 Then he had **another** [+337] dream, and he told it to his brothers.
37: 9 "Listen," he said, "I had **another** dream, and this time the sun
38: 4 She conceived **again** and gave birth to a son and named him Onan.
38: 5 She gave birth to **still another** [+3578] son and named him Shelah.
38:26 to my son Shelah." And he did not sleep with her **again** [+3578].
40:13 **Within** [+928] three days Pharaoh will lift up your head
40:19 **Within** [+928] three days Pharaoh will lift off your head and hang
43: 6 this trouble on me by telling the man you had **another** brother?"
43: 7 and our family. 'Is your father **still** living?' he asked us.
43:27 "How is your aged father you told me about? Is he **still** living?"
43:28 They replied, "Your servant our father is **still** alive and well."
44:14 Joseph was **still** in the house when Judah and his brothers came in,
45: 3 Joseph said to his brothers, "I am Joseph! Is my father **still** living?"
45: 6 and for the **next** five years there will not be plowing and reaping.
45:11 for you there, because five years of famine are **still** *to come*.
45:26 They told him, "Joseph is **still** alive! In fact, he is ruler of all
45:28 My son Joseph is **still** alive. I will go and see him before I die."
46:29 he threw his arms around his father and wept *for a* **long time**.
46:30 ready to die, since I have seen for myself that you are **still** alive."
48: 7 to my sorrow Rachel died in the land of Canaan while we were **still**
48:15 the God who has been my shepherd **all** my **life** [+4946] to this day,
Ex 2: 3 when she could hide him no **longer**, she got a papyrus basket for
3:15 God **also** said to Moses, "Say to the Israelites, 'The LORD,
4: 6 Then the LORD said, **[NIE]** "Put your hand inside your cloak."
4:18 to my own people in Egypt to see if any of them are **still** alive."
9: 2 If you refuse to let them go and **continue** to hold them back,
9:17 You **still** set yourself against my people and will not let them go.
9:29 The thunder will stop and there will be no **more** hail, so you may
10:29 Moses replied, "I will never appear before you **again** [+3578]."
11: 1 to Moses, "I will bring one **more** plague on Pharaoh and on Egypt.
14:13 The Egyptians you see today you will never see **again** [+3578].
17: 4 with these people? They are **almost** [+5071] ready to stone me."
36: 3 the people **continued** to bring freewill offerings morning after
36: 6 or woman is to make anything **else** as an offering for the
Lev 13:57 But if *it* **reappears** [+8011] in the clothing, or in the woven
17: 7 They must no **longer** offer any of their sacrifices to the goat idols
25:51 If many years **remain**, he must pay for his redemption a larger
27:20 he has sold it to someone else, it can **never** [+4202] be redeemed.
Nu 8:25 they must retire from their regular service and work no **longer**.
11:33 **while** the meat was **still** between their teeth and before it could be
18: 5 and the altar, so that wrath will not fall on the Israelites **again**.
18:22 **From now on** the Israelites must not go near the Tent of Meeting,
19:13 sprinkled on him, he is unclean; his uncleanness **remains** on him.
22:15 Balak sent **other** princes, more numerous and more distinguished
22:30 own donkey, which you have **always** [+4946] ridden, to this day?
32:14 your fathers and making the LORD **even** more angry with Israel.

[F] Hitpael (hitpoel, hitpoal, hitpolel, hitpolal, hitpalel, hitpalal, hitpalpel, hitpalpal, hotpael, hotpaal) [G] Hiphil (hiphtil) [H] Hophal [I] Hishtaphel

Nu 32: 15 he *will* **again** [+3578] leave all this people in the desert,
Dt 3: 26 "Do not speak to me **anymore** [+3578] about this matter.
4: 35 might know that the LORD is God; besides him there is no **other**.
4: 39 is God in heaven above and on the earth below. There is no **other**.
5: 25 if we hear the voice of the LORD our God **any longer** [+3578].
10: 16 your hearts, therefore, and do not be stiff-necked **any longer**.
13: 16 [13:17] It is to remain a ruin forever, **never** [+4202] to be rebuilt.
17: 13 will hear and be afraid, and will not be contemptuous **again**.
17: 16 has told you, "You are not to go back that way **again** [+3578]."
18: 16 of the LORD our God nor see this great fire **anymore** [+3578],
19: 9 then you are to set aside three **more** [+3578+4200] cities.
19: 20 never **again** [+3578] will such an evil thing be done among you.
28: 68 Egypt on a journey I said you *should* never **make again** [+3578].
31: 2 and twenty years old and I am no **longer** able to lead you.
31: 27 If you have been rebellious against the LORD while I am **still**
34: 10 **Since then**, no prophet has risen in Israel like Moses,
Jos 1: 11 Three days **from now** [+928] you will cross the Jordan here to go
2: 11 and everyone's courage **failed** [+4202+7756] because of you,
5: 1 and they no **longer** had the courage to face the Israelites.
5: 12 there was no **longer** any manna for the Israelites, but that year they
14: 11 I am **still** as strong today as the day Moses sent me out; I'm just as
Jdg 2: 14 their enemies all around, whom they were no **longer** able to resist.
6: 24 LORD is Peace. To this day it **stands** in Ophrah of the Abiezrites.
7: 4 But the LORD said to Gideon, "There are **still** too many men.
8: 20 did not draw his sword, because he was **only** a boy and was afraid.
9: 37 Gaal spoke up **again** [+3578]: "Look, people are coming down
11: 14 Jephthah sent **back** [+3578] messengers to the Ammonite king,
13: 8 let the man of God you sent to us come **again** to teach us how to
13: 9 the angel of God came **again** to the woman while she was out in
13: 21 the angel of the LORD *did* not show himself **again** [+3578]
18: 24 gods I made, and my priest, and went away. What **else** do I have?
20: 25 they cut down **another** eighteen thousand Israelites, all of them
20: 28 "*Shall we* go up **again** [+3578] to battle with Benjamin our
Ru 1: 11 Am I going to have **any more** sons, who could become your
1: 14 At this they wept **again**. Then Orpah kissed her mother-in-law
1Sa 1: 18 her way and ate something, and her face was no **longer** downcast.
3: 6 **Again** [+3578] the LORD called, "Samuel!" And Samuel got up
7: 13 were subdued and did not invade Israelite territory **again** [+3578].
10: 22 So they inquired **further** of the LORD, "Has the man come here
10: 22 inquired further of the LORD, "Has the man come here **yet**?"
13: 7 Saul **remained** at Gilgal, and all the troops with him were quaking
16: 11 "*There is* **still** [+8636] the youngest," Jesse answered, "but he is
18: 8 me with only thousands. What **more** can he get but the kingdom?"
18: 29 Saul became **still** more afraid of him, and he remained his enemy
20: 3 David took an oath **[NIE]** and said, "Your father knows very well
20: 14 unfailing kindness like that of the LORD **as long** [+561] **as** I live,
23: 4 **Once again** [+3578] David inquired of the LORD,
23: 22 Go and make **further** preparation. Find out where David usually
26: 21 considered my life precious today, I will not try to harm you **again**.
27: 1 Saul will give up searching for me **[NIE]** anywhere in Israel,
27: 4 David had fled to Gath, *he* no **longer** [+3578] searched for him.
28: 15 He no **longer** answers me, either by prophets or by dreams.
2Sa 1: 9 and kill me! I am in the throes of death, but I'm **still** [+3972] alive.'
2: 22 **Again** [+3578] Abner warned Asahel, "Stop chasing me! Why
2: 28 *they* no **longer** pursued Israel, nor did they fight anymore.
2: 28 no longer pursued Israel, nor *did they* fight **anymore** [+3578].
3: 11 Ish-Bosheth did not dare to say **another** word to Abner, because he
3: 35 all came and urged David to eat something while it was **still** day;
5: 13 David took **more** concubines and wives in Jerusalem, and more
5: 13 in Jerusalem, and **more** sons and daughters were born to him.
5: 22 **Once more** [+3578] the Philistines came up and spread out in the
6: 1 David **again** brought together out of Israel chosen men,
6: 22 I will become **even** more undignified than this, and I will be
7: 10 that they can have a home of their own and no **longer** be disturbed.
7: 19 as if this *were* **not enough** [+7781] in your sight, O Sovereign
7: 20 "What **more** [+3578] can David say to you? For you know your
9: 1 "Is there anyone **still** left of the house of Saul to whom I can show
9: 3 "Is there no one **still** left of the house of Saul to whom I can show
9: 3 Ziba answered the king, "There is **still** a son of Jonathan; he is
10: 19 So the Arameans were afraid to help the Ammonites **anymore**.
12: 22 He answered, "While the child was **still** alive, I fasted and wept.
12: 23 Can I bring him back **again**? I will go to him, but he will not return
14: 10 bring him to me, and he will not bother you **again** [+3578]."
14: 29 to come to him. So he sent a second **time**, but he refused to come.
14: 32 It would be better for me if I were **still** there!" ' Now then,
18: 14 plunged them into Absalom's heart **while** Absalom was **still** alive
18: 22 Ahimaaz son of Zadok **again** [+3578] said to Joab, "Come what
19: 28 [19:29] So what right do I have **[RPH]** to make any more
19: 28 [19:29] So what right do I have to make **any more** appeals to the
19: 29 [19:30] The king said to him, "Why say **more**? I order you
19: 35 [19:36] Can I **still** hear the voices of men and women singers?
19: 35 [19:36] Why should your servant be an **added** burden to my lord
21: 15 **Once again** there was a battle between the Philistines and Israel.
21: 17 to him, saying, "Never **again** will you go out with us to battle,
21: 18 of time, there was **another** battle with the Philistines, at Gob.
21: 19 In **another** battle with the Philistines at Gob, Elhanan son of
21: 20 In **still another** battle, which took place at Gath, there was a huge
1Ki 1: 14 **While** you are **still** there talking to the king, I will come in
1: 22 **While** she was **still** speaking with the king, Nathan the prophet
1: 42 **Even as** he was speaking, Jonathan son of Abiathar the priest
8: 60 earth may know that the LORD is God and that there is no **other**.
10: 5 of the LORD, she *was* **overwhelmed** [+928+2118+4202+8120].
10: 10 Never **again** were so many spices brought in as those the queen of
12: 2 When Jeroboam son of Nebat heard this (he was **still** in Egypt,
12: 5 "Go away **for** three days and then come back to me."
20: 32 'Please let me live.' " The king answered, "Is he **still** alive?
22: 7 "Is there not a prophet of the LORD here **[NIE]** whom we can
22: 8 "There is **still** one man through whom we can inquire of the
22: 43 [22:44] the people **continued** to offer sacrifices and burn incense
2Ki 2: 12 and horsemen of Israel!" And Elisha saw him no **more**.
2: 21 Never **again** will it cause death or make the land unproductive.' "
4: 6 all the jars were full, she said to her son, "Bring me **another** one."
4: 6 "Bring me another one." But he replied, "There is not a jar **left**."
5: 17 for your servant will never **again** make burnt offerings
6: 23 So the bands from Aram **stopped** [+3578+4202] raiding Israel's
6: 33 **While** he was **still** talking to them, the messenger came down to
6: 33 from the LORD. Why should I wait for the LORD **any longer**?"
12: 3 [12:4] the people **continued** to offer sacrifices and burn incense
14: 4 the people **continued** to offer sacrifices and burn incense there.
15: 4 the people **continued** to offer sacrifices and burn incense there.
15: 35 the people **continued** to offer sacrifices and burn incense there.
24: 7 of Egypt did not march out from his own country **again** [+3578],
1Ch 12: 1 **while** he was banished from the presence of Saul son of Kish (they
14: 3 In Jerusalem David took **more** wives and became the father of
14: 3 more wives and became the father of **more** sons and daughters.
14: 13 **Once more** [+3578] the Philistines raided the valley;
14: 14 so David inquired of God **again**, and God answered him, "Do not
17: 9 that they can have a home of their own and no **longer** be disturbed.
17: 18 "What **more** [+3578] can David say to you for honoring your
19: 19 the Arameans were not willing to help the Ammonites **anymore**.
20: 5 In **another** battle with the Philistines, Elhanan son of Jair killed
20: 6 In **still another** battle, which took place at Gath, there was a huge
29: 3 **Besides**, in my devotion to the temple of my God I now give my
2Ch 9: 4 of the LORD, she *was* **overwhelmed** [+928+2118+4202+8120].
10: 5 Rehoboam answered, "Come back to me **in** three days."
13: 20 Jeroboam *did* not **regain** [+6806] power during the time of Abijah.
14: 7 [14:6] The land is **still** ours, because we have sought the LORD
17: 6 was devoted to the ways of the LORD; **furthermore** [+2256],
18: 6 "Is there not a prophet of the LORD here **[NIE]** whom we can
18: 7 "There is **still** one man through whom we can inquire of the
20: 33 the people **still** had not set their hearts on the God of their fathers.
27: 2 The people, however, **continued** their corrupt practices.
28: 17 The Edomites had **again** come and attacked Judah and carried
32: 16 Sennacherib's officers spoke **further** against the LORD God
33: 17 The people, however, **continued** to sacrifice at the high places,
34: 3 In the eighth year of his reign, **while** he was **still** young, he began
34: 16 Shaphan took the book to the king and reported to **[NIE]** him:
Ne 2: 17 the wall of Jerusalem, and we will no **longer** be in disgrace."
Est 2: 14 *She would* not **return** [+995] to the king unless he was pleased
6: 14 **While** they were **still** talking with him, the king's eunuchs arrived
9: 12 It will be given you. What is your request? It will **also** be granted."
Job 1: 16 **While** he was **still** speaking, another messenger came and said,
1: 17 **While** he was **still** speaking, another messenger came and said,
2: 3 he **still** maintains his integrity, though you incited me against him
2: 9 His wife said to him, "Are you **still** holding on to your integrity?
6: 10 I would **still** have this consolation—my joy in unrelenting pain—
6: 29 do not be unjust; **reconsider** [+8740], for my integrity is at stake.
7: 10 He will never come to his house **again**; his place will know him no
7: 10 never come to his house again; his place will know him no **more**.
8: 12 **While still** growing and uncut, they wither more quickly than
14: 7 If it is cut down, it will sprout **again**, and its new shoots will not
20: 9 him will not see him again; his place will look on him no **more**.
24: 20 evil men are no **longer** remembered but are broken like a tree.
27: 3 **as long** [+3972] **as** I have life within me, the breath of God in my
29: 5 when the Almighty was **still** with me and my children were around
32: 15 "They are dismayed and have no **more** to say; words have failed
32: 16 they are silent, now that they stand there with no reply? **[NIE]**
34: 23 God has no need to examine men **further**, that they should come
36: 2 and I will show you that there is **more** to be said in God's behalf.
Ps 10: 18 order that man, who is of the earth, may terrify no **more** [+3578].
37: 10 A **little while** [+5071], and the wicked will be no more;
39: 1 [39:2] I will put a muzzle on my mouth **as long** [+928] **as** the
42: 5 [42:6] your hope in God, for I will **yet** praise him, my Savior and
42: 11 [42:12] in God, for I will **yet** praise him, my Savior and my God.
43: 5 hope in God, for I will **yet** praise him, my Savior and my God.
49: 9 [49:10] that he should live **on** forever and not see decay.
74: 9 no prophets are **left**, and none of us knows how long this will be.
77: 7 [77:8] Will he never show his favor **again** [+3578]?

Ps 78:17 *they* **continued** [+3578] to sin against him, rebelling in the desert
78:30 from the food they craved, even **while** it was **still** in their mouths,
78:32 In spite of all this, they **kept on** sinning; in spite of his wonders,
83:4 [83:5] a nation, that the name of Israel be remembered no **more**."
84:4 [84:5] those who dwell in your house; they are **ever** praising you.
88:5 [88:6] whom you remember no **more**, who are cut off from your
92:14 [92:15] They will **still** bear fruit in old age, they will stay fresh
103:16 blows over it and it is gone, and its place remembers it no **more**.
104:33 all my life; I will sing praise to my God **as long** [+928] **as I live**.
104:35 But may sinners vanish from the earth and the wicked be no **more**.
139:18 outnumber the grains of sand. When I awake, I am **still** with you.
141:5 not refuse it. Yet my prayer is **ever** against the deeds of evildoers;
146:2 all my life; I will sing praise to my God **as long** [+928] **as I live**.
Pr 9:9 Instruct a wise man and he will be wiser **still**; teach a righteous
11:24 One man gives freely, yet gains **even more**; another withholds
19:19 if you rescue him, *you will have to* **do** it **again** [+3578].
23:35 When will I wake up so I can find **another** [+3578] drink?"
31:7 and forget their poverty and remember their misery no **more**.
31:15 She gets up while it is **still** dark; she provides food for her family
Ecc 3:16 I saw **something else** under the sun: In the place of judgment—
4:13 but foolish king who no **longer** knows how to take warning.
7:28 **while** I was **still** searching but not finding—I found one ⌞upright⌟
9:5 they have no **further** reward, and even the memory of them is
9:6 never **again** will they have a part in anything that happens under
12:9 the Teacher wise, **but also** he imparted knowledge to the people.
Isa 1:5 Why should you be beaten **anymore**? Why do you persist in
2:4 take up sword against nation, nor will they train for war **anymore**.
5:4 What **more** could have been done for my vineyard than I have
5:25 for all this, his anger is not turned away, his hand is **still** upraised.
6:13 And though a tenth **remains** in the land, it will again be laid waste.
7:8 **Within** [+928] sixty-five years Ephraim will be too shattered to be
8:5 The LORD spoke to me **again** [+3578]:
9:12 [9:11] his anger is not turned away, his hand is **still** upraised.
9:17 [9:16] his anger is not turned away, his hand is **still** upraised.
9:21 [9:20] his anger is not turned away, his hand is **still** upraised.
10:4 for all this, his anger is not turned away, his hand is **still** upraised.
10:20 *will* no **longer** [+3578] rely on him who struck them down
10:25 **Very soon** [+4663+5071] my anger against you will end and my
10:32 This day **[NIE]** they will halt at Nob; they will shake their fist at
14:1 **once again** he will choose Israel and will settle them in their own
21:16 "**Within** [+928] one year, as a servant bound by contract would
23:10 O Daughter of Tarshish, for you no **longer** have a harbor.
23:12 He said, "No **more of** [+3578] your reveling, O Virgin Daughter of
26:21 the blood shed upon her; she will conceal her slain no **longer**.
28:4 as soon as someone sees it and takes **[NIE]** it in his hand,
29:17 **In a very short time** [+4663+5071], will not Lebanon be turned
30:20 and the water of affliction, your teachers will be hidden no **more**;
32:5 No **longer** will the fool be called noble nor the scoundrel be highly
38:11 no **longer** will I look on mankind, or be with those who now dwell
45:5 I am the LORD, and there is no **other**; apart from me there is no
45:6 there is none besides me. I am the LORD, and there is no **other**.
45:14 with you, saying, 'Surely God is with you, and there is no **other**;
45:18 to be inhabited—he says: "I am the LORD, and there is no **other**.
45:21 And there is no **[RPH]** God apart from me, a righteous God
45:22 all you ends of the earth; for I am God, and there is no **other**.
46:9 I am God, and there is no **other**; I am God, and there is none like
47:8 and saying to yourself, 'I am, and there is none **besides** me.
47:10 you when you say to yourself, 'I am, and there is none **besides** me.'
49:20 The children born during your bereavement will **yet** say in your
51:22 from that cup, the goblet of my wrath, you will never drink **again**.
52:1 The uncircumcised and defiled will not enter you **again** [+3578].
54:4 and remember no **more** the reproach of your widowhood.
54:9 when I swore that the waters of Noah would never **again** cover the
56:8 "I will gather *still* **others** to them besides those already gathered."
60:18 No **longer** will violence be heard in your land, nor ruin
60:19 The sun will no **more** be your light by day, nor will the brightness
60:20 Your sun will never set **again**, and your moon will wane no more;
62:4 No **longer** will they call you Deserted, or name your land Desolate.
62:4 **[RPH]** But you will be called Hephzibah, and your land Beulah;
62:8 "Never **again** will I give your grain as food for your enemies,
65:19 the sound of weeping and of crying will be heard in it no **more**.
65:20 "Never **again** will there be in it an infant who lives but a few days,
65:24 they call I will answer; **while** they are **still** speaking I will hear.
Jer 2:9 "Therefore I bring charges against you **again**,"
2:31 people say, 'We are free to roam; we will come to you no **more**'?
3:1 and marries another man, should he return to her **again**?
3:16 declares the LORD, "men will no **longer** say, 'The ark of the
3:16 it will not be missed, nor will **another** one be made.
3:17 No **longer** will they follow the stubbornness of their evil hearts.
7:32 when people will no **longer** call it Topheth or the Valley of Ben
10:20 no one is **left now** to pitch my tent or to set up my shelter.
11:19 the land of the living, that his name be remembered no **more**."
13:27 O Jerusalem! **How long** [+339+5503] will you be unclean?"
15:9 Her sun will set while it is **still** day; she will be disgraced
16:14 are coming," declares the LORD, "when men will no **longer** say,
19:6 when people will no **longer** call this place Topheth or the Valley of
19:11 **[NIE]** They will bury the dead in Topheth until there is no more
20:9 if I say, "I will not mention him or speak **any more** in his name,"
22:10 because he will **never** [+4202] return nor see his native land again.
22:11 but has gone from this place: "He will **never** [+4202] return.
22:12 where they have led him captive; he will not see this land **again**."
22:30 none will sit on the throne of David or rule **anymore** in Judah."
23:4 they will no **longer** be afraid or terrified, nor will any be missing,"
23:7 declares the LORD, "when people will no **longer** say,
23:36 But you must not mention 'the oracle of the LORD' **again**,
28:3 **Within** [+928] two years I will bring back to this place all the
28:11 off the neck of all the nations **within** [+928] two years.' " At this,
30:8 will tear off their bonds; no **longer** will foreigners enslave them.
31:4 I will build you up **again** and you will be rebuilt, O Virgin Israel.
31:4 **Again** you will take up your tambourines and go out to dance with
31:5 **Again** you will plant vineyards on the hills of Samaria; the farmers
31:12 like a well-watered garden, and *they will* sorrow no **more** [+3578].
31:20 I delight? Though I often speak against him, I **still** remember him.
31:23 the land of Judah and in its towns will **once again** use these words:
31:29 "In those days people will no **longer** say, 'The fathers have eaten
31:34 No **longer** will a man teach his neighbor, or a man his brother,
31:34 forgive their wickedness and will remember their sins no **more**."
31:39 The measuring line will stretch **[NIE]** from there straight to the
31:40 the LORD. The city will never **again** be uprooted or demolished."
32:15 Houses, fields and vineyards will **again** be bought in this land.'
33:1 **While** Jeremiah was **still** confined in the courtyard of the guard,
33:10 by neither men nor animals, there will be heard **once more**
33:12 in all its towns there will **again** be pastures for shepherds to rest
33:13 flocks will **again** pass under the hand of the one who counts them,'
33:24 So they despise my people and no **longer** regard them as a nation.
34:10 their male and female slaves and no **longer** hold them in bondage.
36:32 in the fire. And many similar words **were added** [+3578] to them.
38:9 where he will starve to death when there is no **longer** any bread in
40:5 However, **before** [+4202] Jeremiah turned to go, Nebuzaradan
42:18 and reproach; you will never see this place **again**.'
44:22 When the LORD could no **longer** endure your wicked actions
44:26 'that no one from Judah living anywhere in Egypt will **ever again**
48:2 Moab will be praised no **more**; in Heshbon men will plot her
49:7 "Is there no **longer** wisdom in Teman? Has counsel perished from
50:39 It will never **again** be inhabited or lived in from generation to
51:33 it is trampled; the time to harvest her will **soon** [+5071] come."
51:44 The nations will no **longer** stream to him. And the wall of Babylon
La 4:17 **Moreover**, our eyes failed, looking in vain for help; from our
Eze 5:4 **Again**, take a few of these and throw them into the fire and burn
5:9 do to you what I have never done before and will never do **again**.
7:13 The seller will not recover the land he has sold **as long as** both of
8:6 But **[NIE]** you will see things that are even more detestable."
8:13 **[NIE]** "You will see them doing things that are even more
8:15 **[NIE]** You will see things that are even more detestable than
12:23 an end to this proverb, and they will no **longer** quote it in Israel.'
12:24 For there will be no **more** false visions or flattering divinations
12:25 **[RPH]** For in your days, you rebellious house, I will fulfill
12:28 None of my words will be delayed **any longer**; whatever I say will
13:21 from your hands, and they will no **longer** fall prey to your power.
13:23 therefore you will no **longer** see false visions or practice
14:11 the people of Israel will no **longer** stray from me, nor will they
14:11 nor will they defile themselves **anymore** with all their sins.
15:5 how much less can it be made **[NIE]** into something useful when
16:41 a stop to your prostitution, and you will no **longer** pay your lovers.
16:42 anger will turn away from you; I will be calm and no **longer** angry.
16:63 will remember and be ashamed and never **again** open your mouth
18:3 Sovereign LORD, you will no **longer** quote this proverb in Israel.
19:9 so his roar was heard no **longer** on the mountains of Israel.
20:27 In this **also** your fathers blasphemed me by forsaking me:
20:39 and no **longer** profane my holy name with your gifts and idols.
21:5 [21:10] my sword from its scabbard; it will not return **again**.'
23:27 look on these things with longing or remember Egypt **anymore**.
23:38 They have **also** done this to me: At that same time they defiled my
24:13 you will not be clean **again** until my wrath against you has
24:27 be opened; you will speak with him and will no **longer** be silent.
26:13 noisy songs, and the music of your harps will be heard no **more**.
26:14 You will **never** [+4202] be rebuilt, for I the LORD have spoken,
26:21 You will be sought, but you will never **again** be found, declares
28:24 " 'No **longer** will the people of Israel have malicious neighbors
29:15 and will never **again** exalt itself above the other nations.
29:16 Egypt will no **longer** be a source of confidence for the people of
30:13 No **longer** will there be a prince in Egypt, and I will spread fear
32:13 I will destroy all her cattle from beside abundant waters no **longer**
33:22 the morning. So my mouth was opened and I was no **longer** silent.
34:10 the flock so that the shepherds can no **longer** feed themselves.
34:22 I will save my flock, and they will no **longer** be plundered.
34:28 They will no **longer** be plundered by the nations, nor will wild
34:29 they will no **longer** be victims of famine in the land or bear the

Eze 34:29 of famine in the land or bear **[RPH]** the scorn of the nations.
36:12 *you will* never **again** [+3578] deprive them of their children.
36:14 therefore you will no **longer** devour men or make your nation
36:14 your nation childless, **[RPH]** declares the Sovereign LORD.
36:15 No **longer** will I make you hear the taunts of the nations, and no
36:15 no **longer** will you suffer the scorn of the peoples or cause your
36:15 your nation to fall, **[NIE]** declares the Sovereign LORD.' "
36:30 so that you will no **longer** suffer disgrace among the nations
36:37 Once **again** I will yield to the plea of the house of Israel and do
37:22 they will never **again** be two nations or be divided into two
37:22 again be two nations or be divided **[RPH]** into two kingdoms.
37:22 again be two nations or be divided into two kingdoms. **[RPH]**
37:23 They will no **longer** defile themselves with their idols and vile
39:7 I will no **longer** let my holy name be profaned, and the nations will
39:28 gather them to their own land, not leaving **any** [+4946] behind.
39:29 I will no **longer** hide my face from them, for I will pour out my
43:7 The house of Israel will never **again** defile my holy name—
45:8 my princes will no **longer** oppress my people but will allow the
Da 9:20 **While** I was speaking and praying, confessing my sin and the sin
9:21 **while** I was **still** in prayer, Gabriel, the man I had seen in the
10:14 people in the future, for the vision concerns a time **yet to come**."
11:2 Three **more** kings will appear in Persia, and then a fourth,
11:27 to no avail, because an end will **still** come at the appointed time.
11:35 until the time of the end, for it will **still** come at the appointed time.
Hos 1:4 because I will **soon** [+5071] punish the house of Jehu for the
1:6 Gomer conceived **again** and gave birth to a daughter.
1:6 for I will no **longer** [+3578] show love to the house of Israel,
2:16 [2:18] me 'my husband'; you will no **longer** call me 'my master.'
2:17 [2:19] Baals from her lips; no **longer** will their names be invoked.
3:1 The LORD said to me, "Go, show your love to your wife **again**,
11:12 [12:1] Judah **[NIE]** is unruly against God, even against the
12:9 [12:10] I will make you live in tents **again**, as in the days of your
14:3 [14:4] We will never **again** say 'Our gods' to what our own hands
14:8 [14:9] O Ephraim, what **more** have I to do with idols? I will
Joel 2:19 never **again** will I make you an object of scorn to the nations.
2:27 that I am the LORD your God, and that there is no **other**;
3:17 [4:17] will be holy; never **again** will foreigners invade her.
Am 4:7 "I also withheld rain from you when the harvest was **still** three
6:10 to carry them out of the house and asks anyone **still** hiding there,
7:8 line among my people Israel; I will spare them no **longer** [+3578].
7:13 Don't prophesy **anymore** [+3578] at Bethel, because this is the
8:2 is ripe for my people Israel; I will spare them no **longer** [+3578].
8:14 as the god of Beersheba lives'—they will fall, never to rise **again**."
9:15 never **again** to be uprooted from the land I have given them,"
Jnh 3:4 "Forty **more** days and Nineveh will be overturned."
Mic 1:15 **[NIE]** I will bring a conqueror against you who live in Mareshah.
4:3 take up sword against nation, nor will they train for war **anymore**.
5:13 [5:12] you will no **longer** bow down to the work of your hands.
6:10 Am I **still** to forget, O wicked house, your ill-gotten treasures
Na 1:12 I have afflicted you, ⌞O Judah,⌟ I will afflict you no **more**.
1:14 **[NIE]** I will destroy the carved images and cast idols that are in
1:15 [2:1] No **more** [+3578] will the wicked invade you; they will be
2:13 [2:14] The voices of your messengers will no **longer** be heard."
Hab 2:3 For the revelation **awaits** an appointed time; it speaks of the end
Zep 2:15 She said to herself, "I am, and there is none **besides** me." What a
3:11 Never **again** [+3578] will you be haughty on my holy hill.
3:15 the King of Israel, is with you; never **again** will you fear any harm.
Hag 2:6 'In a little while I will once **more** shake the heavens and the earth,
2:19 Is there **yet** any seed left in the barn? Until now, the vine
Zec 1:17 "Proclaim **further**: This is what the LORD Almighty says:
1:17 'My towns will **again** overflow with prosperity, and the LORD
1:17 and the LORD will **again** comfort Zion and choose Jerusalem.' "
1:17 LORD will again comfort Zion and **[RPH]** choose Jerusalem.' "
2:12 [2:16] portion in the holy land and will **again** choose Jerusalem.
8:4 "**Once again** men and women of ripe old age will sit in the streets
8:20 "Many peoples and the inhabitants of many cities will **yet** come,
9:8 Never **again** will an oppressor overrun my people, for now I am
11:6 For I will no **longer** have pity on the people of the land,"
11:15 said to me, "Take **again** the equipment of a foolish shepherd.
12:6 surrounding peoples, but Jerusalem will **remain** intact in her place.
13:2 they will be remembered no **more**," declares the LORD
13:3 if anyone **still** prophesies, his father and mother, to whom he was
14:11 It will be inhabited; never **again** will it be destroyed. Jerusalem
14:21 on that day there will no **longer** be a Canaanite in the house of the
Mal 2:13 and wail because he no **longer** pays attention to your offerings

6389 עֹדֵד ***'ôdēd***, n.pr.m. [3] [√ 6386]
Oded [3]

2Ch 15:1 The Spirit of God came upon Azariah son of **Oded**.
15:8 these words and the prophecy of Azariah son of **Oded** the prophet,
28:9 a prophet of the LORD named **Oded** was there, and he went out

6390 עָוָה[1] ***'āwâ***[1], v. [17] [→ 6392, 6411, 6412, 6413, 6505; cf. 6391]
done wrong [6], perverted [2], am staggered [1], bowed down [1], did wrong [1], does wrong [1], made crooked [1], perverse [1], ruin [1], sinning [1], warped [1]

1Sa 20:30 [C] said to him, "You son of a **perverse** and rebellious *woman*!
2Sa 7:14 [G] When he **does wrong**, I will punish him with the rod of men,
19:19 [19:20] [G] Do not remember how your servant **did wrong** on
24:17 [G] the LORD, "I am the one who has sinned and **done wrong**.
1Ki 8:47 [G] and say, 'We have sinned, *we have* **done wrong**,
2Ch 6:37 [G] 'We have sinned, *we have* **done wrong** and acted wickedly';
Est 1:16 [A] of the king and the nobles, "Queen Vashti *has* **done wrong**,
Job 33:27 [G] to men and says, 'I sinned, and **perverted** what was right,
Ps 38:6 [38:7] [C] *I am* **bowed down** and brought very low; all day
106:6 [G] as our fathers did; *we have* **done wrong** and acted wickedly.
Pr 12:8 [C] to his wisdom, but *men with* **warped** minds are despised.
Isa 21:3 [C] ***I am* staggered** by what I hear, I am bewildered by what I
24:1 [D] devastate it; *he will* **ruin** its face and scatter its inhabitants—
Jer 3:21 [G] because *they have* **perverted** their ways and have forgotten
9:5 [9:4] [G] tongues to lie; they weary themselves with **sinning**.
La 3:9 [D] way with blocks of stone; *he has* **made** my paths **crooked**.
Da 9:5 [A] we have sinned and **done wrong**. We have been wicked and

6391 עָוָה[2] ***'āwâ***[2], v.den. Not used in NIV/BHS [cf. 6390]

6392 עַוָּה[1] ***'awwâ***[1], n.f. [3] [→ 6504, 6509; cf. 6390]
ruin [3]

Eze 21:27 [21:32] A **ruin**! A ruin! I will make it a ruin! It will not be
21:27 [21:32] A ruin! A **ruin**! I will make it a ruin! It will not be
21:27 [21:32] A ruin! A ruin! I will make it a **ruin**! It will not be

6393 עַוָּה[2] ***'awwâ***[2], n.pr.loc. Not used in NIV/BHS [→ 6398, 6399; cf. 6379]

6394 עִוָּה ***'iwwâ***, n.pr.loc. [3] [√ 6399]
Ivvah [3]

2Ki 18:34 and Arpad? Where are the gods of Sepharvaim, Hena and **Ivvah**?
19:13 the king of the city of Sepharvaim, or of Hena or **Ivvah**?"
Isa 37:13 the king of the city of Sepharvaim, or of Hena or **Ivvah**?"

6395 עוּז ***'ûz***, v. [5] [→ 6437; cf. 6451]
flee for safety [2], bring to a place of shelter [1], look for help [1], take cover [1]

Ex 9:19 [G] *to* **bring** your livestock … **to a place of shelter**,
Isa 10:31 [G] Madmenah is in flight; the people of Gebim **take cover**.
30:2 [A] *who* **look for help** to Pharaoh's protection, to Egypt's shade
Jer 4:6 [G] Raise the signal to go to Zion! **Flee for safety** without delay!
6:1 [G] "**Flee for safety**, people of Benjamin! Flee from Jerusalem!

6396 עֲוִיל[1] ***'ᵃwîl***[1], n.m. [2] [√ 6402]
children [1], little boys [1]

Job 19:18 Even the **little boys** scorn me; when I appear, they ridicule me.
21:11 They send forth their **children** as a flock; their little ones dance

6397 עֲוִיל[2] ***'ᵃwîl***[2], n.m. [1] [√ 6401]
evil men [1]

Job 16:11 God has turned me over to **evil men** and thrown me into the

6398 עַוִּים[1] ***'awwîm***[1], a.g. [3] [√ 6393]
Avvites [3]

Dt 2:23 And as for the **Avvites** who lived in villages as far as Gaza,
Jos 13:3 Ashdod, Ashkelon, Gath and Ekron—that of the **Avvites**);
2Ki 17:31 the **Avvites** made Nibhaz and Tartak, and the Sepharvites burned

6399 עַוִּים[2] ***'awwîm***[2], n.pr.loc. [1] [√ 6393; cf. 6394]
Avvim [1]

Jos 18:23 **Avvim**, Parah, Ophrah,

6400 עֲוִית ***'ᵃwît***, n.pr.loc. [2] [cf. 6511]
Avith [2]

Ge 36:35 of Moab, succeeded him as king. His city was named **Avith**.
1Ch 1:46 succeeded him as king. His city was named **Avith**. [K 6511]

6401 עָוַל¹ ***'āwal¹***, v.den. [2] [→ 6397, 6404, 6405, 6406, 6637]
doing evil [1], evil [1]

Ps 71: 4 [D] the hand of the wicked, from the grasp of **evil** and cruel men.
Isa 26: 10 [D] even in a land of uprightness *they go on* **doing evil**

6402 עוּל² ***'ûl²***, v. [5] [→ 6396, 6403, 6407, 6408]
calved [1], have young [1], nursing young [1], sheep [1], such[s] [1]

Ge 33: 13 [A] care for the ewes and cows *that are* **nursing** *their* **young**.
1Sa 6: 7 [A] with two cows *that have* **calved** and have never been yoked.
6: 10 [A] They took two **such**[s] cows and hitched them to the cart
Ps 78: 71 [A] from tending the **sheep** he brought him to be the shepherd of
Isa 40: 11 [A] close to his heart; he gently leads *those that* **have young**.

6403 עוּל³ ***'ûl³***, n.m. [2 / 3] [√ 6402]
infant [2], baby at breast [1]

Job 24: 9 the breast; the **infant** [BHS 6584] *of* the poor is seized for a debt.
Isa 49: 15 "Can a mother forget the **baby at** her **breast** and have no
65: 20 "Never again will there be in it an **infant** who lives but a few days,

6404 עָוֶל ***'āwel***, n.m. [21 / 22] [√ 6401]
evil [5], sin [4], dishonest [3], wrong [3], dishonestly [1], doing wrong [1], fault [1], guilt [1], pervert [+928+6913] [1], unjust [1], ways [1]

Lev 19: 15 " '*Do* not **pervert** [+928+6913] justice; do not show partiality to
19: 35 " 'Do not use **dishonest** standards when measuring length,
Dt 25: 16 anyone who does these things, anyone who deals **dishonestly**.
32: 4 A faithful God who does no **wrong**, upright and just is he.
Job 34: 10 Far be it from God to do evil, from the Almighty to do **wrong**.
34: 32 me what I cannot see; if I have done **wrong**, I will not do so again.'
Ps 7: 3 [7:4] my God, if I have done this and there is **guilt** on my hands—
53: 1 [53:2] They are corrupt, and their **ways** are vile; there is no one
82: 2 "How long will you defend the **unjust** and show partiality to the
Pr 29: 27 The righteous detest the **dishonest**; the wicked detest the upright.
Jer 2: 5 "What **fault** did your fathers find in me, that they strayed so far
Eze 3: 20 when a righteous man turns from his righteousness and does **evil**,
18: 8 He withholds his hand from **doing wrong** and judges fairly
18: 17 He withholds his hand from **sin** [BHS 6714] and takes no usury
18: 24 if a righteous man turns from his righteousness and commits **sin**
18: 26 If a righteous man turns from his righteousness and commits **sin**,
18: 26 he will die for it; because of the **sin** he has committed he will die.
28: 18 and **dishonest** trade you have desecrated your sanctuaries.
33: 13 surely live, but then he trusts in his righteousness and does **evil**,
33: 13 has done will be remembered; he will die for the **evil** he has done.
33: 15 the decrees that give life, and does no **evil**, he will surely live;
33: 18 If a righteous man turns from his righteousness and does **evil**,

6405 עַוָּל ***'awwāl***, n.m. [5] [√ 6401]
wicked [2], evil man [1], unjust [1], unrighteous [1]

Job 18: 21 Surely such is the dwelling of an **evil man**; such is the place of one
27: 7 my enemies be like the wicked, my adversaries like the **unjust**!
29: 17 I broke the fangs of the **wicked** and snatched the victims from their
31: 3 Is it not ruin for the **wicked**, disaster for those who do wrong?
Zep 3: 5 new day he does not fail, yet the **unrighteous** know no shame.

6406 עַוְלָה ***'awlâ***, n.f. & m. [32] [√ 6401; cf. 6593, 6637]
wicked [7], wickedness [7], evil [5], wrong [5], injustice [3], crime [1], false [1], iniquity [1], unjust [1], wickedly [1]

2Sa 3: 34 feet were not fettered. You fell as one falls before **wicked** men."
7: 10 **Wicked** people will not oppress them anymore, as they did at the
1Ch 17: 9 **Wicked** people will not oppress them anymore, as they did at the
2Ch 19: 7 for with the LORD our God there is no **injustice** or partiality
Job 6: 29 Relent, do not be **unjust**; reconsider, for my integrity is at stake.
6: 30 Is there any **wickedness** on my lips? Can my mouth not discern
11: 14 the sin that is in your hand and allow no **evil** to dwell in your tent,
13: 7 Will you speak **wickedly** on God's behalf? Will you speak
15: 16 less man, who is vile and corrupt, who drinks up **evil** like water!
22: 23 you will be restored: If you remove **wickedness** far from your tent
24: 20 **evil** *men* are no longer remembered but are broken like a tree.
27: 4 my lips will not speak **wickedness**, and my tongue will utter no
36: 23 his ways for him, or said to him, 'You have done **wrong**'?
Ps 37: 1 because of evil men or be envious of those who do **wrong**;
43: 1 an ungodly nation; rescue me from deceitful and **wicked** men.
58: 2 [58:3] No, in your heart you devise **injustice**, and your hands
64: 6 [64:7] They plot **injustice** and say, "We have devised a perfect
89: 22 [89:23] subject him to tribute; no **wicked** man will oppress him.
92: 15 [92:16] my Rock, and there is no **wickedness** [K 6637] in him."
107: 42 The upright see and rejoice, but all the **wicked** shut their mouths.
119: 3 They do nothing **wrong**; they walk in his ways.
125: 3 for then the righteous might use their hands to do **evil**.
Pr 22: 8 He who sows **wickedness** reaps trouble, and the rod of his fury
Isa 59: 3 lips have spoken lies, and your tongue mutters **wicked** *things*.
61: 8 "For I, the LORD, love justice; I hate robbery and **iniquity**.
Eze 28: 15 from the day you were created till **wickedness** was found in you.
Hos 10: 13 you have planted wickedness, you have reaped **evil**, you have eaten
Mic 3: 10 who build Zion with bloodshed, and Jerusalem with **wickedness**.
Hab 2: 12 who builds a city with bloodshed and establishes a town by **crime**!
Zep 3: 5 The LORD within her is righteous; he does no **wrong**. Morning
3: 13 The remnant of Israel will do no **wrong**; they will speak no lies,
Mal 2: 6 was in his mouth and nothing **false** was found on his lips.

6407 עוֹלֵל ***'ôlēl***, n.m. [11] [√ 6402]
children [7], infant [1], infants [1], little children [1], little ones [1]

1Sa 15: 3 **children** and infants, cattle and sheep, camels and donkeys.' "
22: 19 with its men and women, its **children** and infants, and its cattle,
2Ki 8: 12 young men with the sword, dash their **little children** to the ground,
Job 3: 16 a stillborn child, like an **infant** who never saw the light of day?
Ps 8: 2 [8:3] From the lips of **children** and infants you have ordained
17: 14 their sons have plenty, and they store up wealth for their **children**.
Isa 13: 16 Their **infants** will be dashed to pieces before their eyes;
Jer 44: 7 the **children** and infants, and so leave yourselves without a
La 2: 11 because **children** and infants faint in the streets of the city.
2: 20 women eat their offspring, the **children** they have cared for?
Hos 13: 16 [14:1] their **little ones** will be dashed to the ground, their pregnant

6408 עוֹלָל ***'ôlāl***, n.m. [9] [√ 6402]
children [7], infants [2]

Ps 137: 9 he who seizes your **infants** and dashes them against the rocks.
Jer 6: 11 "Pour it out on the **children** in the street and on the young men
9: 21 [9:20] it has cut off the **children** from the streets and the young
La 1: 5 Her **children** have gone into exile, captive before the foe.
2: 19 Lift up your hands to him for the lives of your **children**, who faint
4: 4 its mouth; the **children** beg for bread, but no one gives it to them.
Joel 2: 16 bring together the elders, gather the **children**, those nursing at the
Mic 2: 9 You take away my blessing from their **children** forever.
Na 3: 10 Her **infants** were dashed to pieces at the head of every street.

6409 עוֹלָם ***'ôlām***, n.m. [438 / 439] [cf. 6518; Ar 10550]
forever [+4200] [137], everlasting [56], forever [+6330] [44], lasting [26], forever [21], ancient [13], ever [9], regular [9], never [+4200+4202] [8], of old [7], eternal [5], ever [+4200] [5], ever [+6330] [5], for ever [5], forevermore [+6330] [5], long ago [4], always [+6330] [3], always [3], ancient [+4946] [3], eternal [+4200] [3], old [3], age-old [2], always [+4200] [2], ancient times [2], eternity [2], ever [+4946] [2], everlasting [+6330] [2], for life [2], forever [+2021+6330] [2], forever [+4200+6330] [2], long ago [+4946] [2], long [2], more [+6330] [2], never [+1153+4200] [2], never [+4202+6330] [2], never [+440+4200] [2], never again [+4200+4202] [2], permanent [2], *untranslated* [1], again [+4200] [1], ages [1], all eternity [1], all time [1], any time [1], as long as live [+3427+3972 +4200] [1], continue [1], continued [1], early times [1], endless [+6330] [1], everlasting [+3972] [1], everlasting [+4200] [1], for life [+4200] [1], forevermore [+2021+6330] [1], gone by [1], lasting [+4200] [1], lasting [+6330] [1], lasting [+9458] [1], life [1], long [+4200] [1], long [+4946] [1], long ago [+4200] [1], long time [1], never [+1153+2256+6329] [1], never [+401+4200] [1], never [+4202] [1], never [+561+6330] [1], to come [1], to the very end [+4200+6813] [1], used to be [+3427] [1]

Ge 3: 22 take also from the tree of life and eat, and live **forever** [+4200]."
6: 3 "My Spirit will not contend with man **forever** [+4200], for he is
6: 4 had children by them. They were the heroes of **old**, men of renown.
9: 12 living creature with you, a covenant for all generations **to come**:
9: 16 I will see it and remember the **everlasting** covenant between God
13: 15 that you see I will give to you and your offspring **forever** [+6330].
17: 7 I will establish my covenant as an **everlasting** covenant between
17: 8 I will give as an **everlasting** possession to you and your
17: 13 My covenant in your flesh is to be an **everlasting** covenant.
17: 19 I will establish my covenant with him as an **everlasting** covenant
21: 33 there he called upon the name of the LORD, the **Eternal** God.
48: 4 I will give this land as an **everlasting** possession to your
49: 26 of the ancient mountains, than the bounty of the **age-old** hills.
Ex 3: 15 This is my name **forever** [+4200], the name by which I am to be
12: 14 shall celebrate it as a festival to the LORD—a **lasting** ordinance.
12: 17 Celebrate this day as a **lasting** ordinance for the generations to
12: 24 "Obey these instructions as a **lasting** [+6330] ordinance for you
14: 13 The Egyptians you see today you will **never** [+4202+6330] see
15: 18 The LORD will reign for **ever** and ever."
19: 9 speaking with you and will **always** [+4200] put their trust in you."
21: 6 his ear with an awl. Then he will be his servant **for life** [+4200].
27: 21 This is to be a **lasting** ordinance among the Israelites for the
28: 43 "This is to be a **lasting** ordinance for Aaron and his descendants.
29: 9 and his sons. The priesthood is theirs by a **lasting** ordinance.

Ex 29:28 This is **always** to be the regular share from the Israelites for Aaron
30:21 This is to be a **lasting** ordinance for Aaron and his descendants for
31:16 celebrating it for the generations to come as a **lasting** covenant.
31:17 It will be a sign between me and the Israelites **forever** [+4200],
32:13 promised them, and it will be their inheritance **forever** [+4200].' "
40:15 Their anointing will be to a priesthood that will **continue** for all
Lev 3:17 " 'This is a **lasting** ordinance for the generations to come,
6:18 [6:11] It is his **regular** share of the offerings made to the LORD
6:22 [6:15] It is the LORD's **regular** share and is to be burned
7:34 the priest and his sons as their **regular** share from the Israelites.' "
7:36 this to them as their **regular** share for the generations to come.
10:9 will die. This is a **lasting** ordinance for the generations to come.
10:15 This will be the **regular** share for you and your children, as the
16:29 "This is to be a **lasting** ordinance for you: On the tenth day of the
16:31 of rest, and you must deny yourselves; it is a **lasting** ordinance.
16:34 "This is to be a **lasting** ordinance for you: Atonement is to be made
17:7 This is to be a **lasting** ordinance for them and for the generations to
23:14 This is to be a **lasting** ordinance for the generations to come,
23:21 This is to be a **lasting** ordinance for the generations to come,
23:31 This is to be a **lasting** ordinance for the generations to come,
23:41 This is to be a **lasting** ordinance for the generations to come;
24:3 This is to be a **lasting** ordinance for the generations to come.
24:8 after Sabbath, on behalf of the Israelites, as a **lasting** covenant.
24:9 because it is a most holy part of their **regular** share of the offerings
25:32 " 'The Levites **always** have the right to redeem their houses in the
25:34 to their towns must not be sold; it is their **permanent** possession.
25:46 children as inherited property and can make them slaves for **life**,
Nu 10:8 This is to be a **lasting** ordinance for you and the generations to
15:15 among you; this is a **lasting** ordinance for the generations to come.
18:8 me I give to you and your sons as your portion and **regular** share.
18:11 give this to you and your sons and daughters as your **regular** share.
18:19 I give to you and your sons and daughters as your **regular** share.
18:19 It is an **everlasting** covenant of salt before the LORD for both
18:23 against it. This is a **lasting** ordinance for the generations to come.
19:10 This will be a **lasting** ordinance both for the Israelites and for the
19:21 This is a **lasting** ordinance for them. "The man who sprinkles the
25:13 and his descendants will have a covenant of a **lasting** priesthood,
Dt 5:29 that it might go well with them and their children **forever** [+4200]!
12:28 so that it may **always** [+6330] go well with you and your children
13:16 [13:17] It is to remain a ruin **forever**, never to be rebuilt.
15:17 his ear lobe into the door, and he will become your servant **for life**.
23:3 [23:4] of the LORD, even down to the tenth generation. **[NIE]**
23:6 [23:7] Do not seek a treaty of friendship with them **as long as** you **live** [+3427+3972+4200].
28:46 and a wonder to you and your descendants **forever** [+6330].
29:29 [29:28] belong to us and to our children **forever** [+6330],
32:7 Remember the days **of old**; consider the generations long past.
32:40 hand to heaven and declare: As surely as I live **forever** [+4200],
33:15 the ancient mountains and the fruitfulness of the **everlasting** hills;
33:27 God is your refuge, and underneath are the **everlasting** arms.
Jos 4:7 are to be a memorial to the people of Israel **forever** [+6330]."
8:28 So Joshua burned Ai and made it a **permanent** heap of ruins,
14:9 will be your inheritance and that of your children **forever** [+6330],
24:2 the God of Israel, says: '**Long** [+4946] **ago** your forefathers,
Jdg 2:1 I said, 'I will **never** [+4200+4202] break my covenant with you,
1Sa 1:22 him before the LORD, and he will live there **always** [+6330]."
2:30 your father's house would minister before me **forever** [+6330].'
3:13 For I told him that I would judge his family **forever** [+6330]
3:14 'The guilt of Eli's house will **never** [+561+6330] be atoned for by
13:13 he would have established your kingdom over Israel for **all time**.
20:15 and do not **ever** [+6330] cut off your kindness from my family—
20:23 the LORD is witness between you and me **forever** [+6330]."
20:42 and my descendants **forever** [+6330].' " Then David left,
27:8 (From **ancient times** these peoples had lived in the land extending
27:12 to his people, the Israelites, that he will be my servant **forever**."
2Sa 3:28 my kingdom are **forever** [+6330] innocent before the LORD
7:13 and I will establish the throne of his kingdom **forever** [+6330].
7:16 and your kingdom will endure **forever** [+6330] before me;
7:16 before me; your throne will be established **forever** [+6330].' "
7:24 established your people Israel as your very own **forever** [+6330],
7:25 keep **forever** [+6330] the promise you have made concerning your
7:26 so that your name will be great **forever** [+6330]. Then men will
7:29 of your servant, that it may continue **forever** [+4200] in your sight;
7:29 the house of your servant will be blessed **forever** [+4200]."
12:10 the sword will **never** [+4202+6330] depart from your house,
22:51 to his anointed, to David and his descendants **forever** [+6330]."
23:5 Has he not made with me an **everlasting** covenant, arranged
1Ki 1:31 the king, said, "May my lord King David live **forever** [+4200]!"
2:33 rest on the head of Joab and his descendants **forever** [+4200].
2:33 his throne, may there be the LORD's peace **forever** [+6330]."
2:45 throne will remain secure before the LORD **forever** [+6330]."
8:13 a magnificent temple for you, a place for you to dwell **forever**."
9:3 which you have built, by putting my Name there **forever** [+6330].
9:5 I will establish your royal throne over Israel **forever** [+4200],
10:9 Because of the LORD's **eternal** [+4200] love for Israel, he has
2Ki 5:27 will cling to you and to your descendants **forever** [+4200]."
21:7 out of all the tribes of Israel, I will put my Name **forever** [+4200].
1Ch 15:2 ark of the LORD and to minister before him **forever** [+6330]."
16:15 He remembers his covenant **forever** [+4200], the word he
16:17 it to Jacob as a decree, to Israel as an **everlasting** covenant:
16:34 to the LORD, for he is good; his love endures **forever** [+4200].
16:36 to the LORD, the God of Israel, from **everlasting** to everlasting.
16:36 to the LORD, the God of Israel, from everlasting to **everlasting**.
16:41 give thanks to the LORD, "for his love endures **forever** [+4200]."
17:12 a house for me, and I will establish his throne **forever** [+6330].
17:14 set him over my house and my kingdom **forever** [+2021+6330];
17:14 his throne will be established **forever** [+6330].' "
17:22 You made your people Israel your very own **forever** [+6330],
17:23 your servant and his house be established **forever** [+6330].
17:24 be established and that your name will be great **forever** [+6330].
17:27 of your servant, that it may continue **forever** [+4200] in your sight;
17:27 have blessed it, and it will be blessed **forever** [+4200]."
22:10 establish the throne of his kingdom over Israel **forever** [+6330].'
23:13 Aaron was set apart, he and his descendants **forever** [+6330],
23:13 and to pronounce blessings in his name **forever** [+6330].
23:25 and has come to dwell in Jerusalem **forever** [+4200+6330],
28:4 me from my whole family to be king over Israel **forever** [+4200].
28:7 I will establish his kingdom **forever** [+4200+6330] if he is
28:8 pass it on as an inheritance to your descendants **forever** [+6330].
29:10 God of our father Israel, from **everlasting** to everlasting.
29:10 God of our father Israel, from everlasting to **everlasting**.
29:18 keep this desire in the hearts of your people **forever** [+4200],
2Ch 2:4 [2:3] our God. This is a **lasting** [+4200] ordinance for Israel.
5:13 and sang: "He is good; his love endures **forever** [+4200]."
6:2 a magnificent temple for you, a place for you to dwell **forever**."
7:3 saying, "He is good; his love endures **forever** [+4200]."
7:6 when he gave thanks, saying, "His love endures **forever** [+4200]."
7:16 this temple so that my Name may be there **forever** [+6330].
9:8 your God for Israel and his desire to uphold them **forever** [+4200],
13:5 and his descendants **forever** [+4200] by a covenant of salt?
20:7 give it **forever** [+4200] to the descendants of Abraham your
20:21 thanks to the LORD, for his love endures **forever** [+4200]."
30:8 Come to the sanctuary, which he has consecrated **forever** [+4200].
33:4 had said, "My Name will remain in Jerusalem **forever** [+4200]."
33:7 I will put my Name **forever** [+4200]. [BHS 6518]
Ezr 3:11 "He is good; his love to Israel endures **forever** [+4200]."
9:12 Do not seek a treaty of friendship with them at **any time**, that you
9:12 leave it to your children as an **everlasting** [+6330] inheritance.'
Ne 2:3 but I said to the king, "May the king live **forever** [+4200]!
9:5 the LORD your God, who is from **everlasting** to everlasting."
9:5 the LORD your God, who is from everlasting to **everlasting**."
13:1 or Moabite should **ever** [+6330] be admitted into the assembly of
Job 7:16 I despise my life; I would not live **forever** [+4200]. Let me alone;
22:15 Will you keep to the **old** path that evil men have trod?
41:4 [40:28] with you for you to take him as your slave **for life**?
Ps 5:11 [5:12] refuge in you be glad; let them **ever** [+4200] sing for joy.
9:5 [9:6] you have blotted out their name for **ever** and ever.
9:7 [9:8] The LORD reigns **forever** [+4200]; he has established his
10:16 The LORD is King **for ever** and ever; the nations will perish
12:7 [12:8] us safe and protect us from such people **forever** [+4200].
15:5 He who does these things will **never** [+4200+4202] be shaken.
18:50 [18:51] to David and his descendants **forever** [+6330].
21:4 [21:5] and you gave it to him—length of days, **for ever** and ever.
24:7 be lifted up, you **ancient** doors, that the King of glory may come
24:9 lift them up, you **ancient** doors, that the King of glory may come
25:6 O LORD, your great mercy and love, for they are from **of old**.
28:9 be their shepherd and carry them **forever** [+2021+6330].
29:10 over the flood; the LORD is enthroned as King **forever** [+4200].
30:6 [30:7] felt secure, I said, "I will **never** [+1153+4200] be shaken."
30:12 [30:13] LORD my God, I will give you thanks **forever** [+4200].
31:1 [31:2] taken refuge; let me **never** [+440+4200] be put to shame;
33:11 the plans of the LORD stand firm **forever** [+4200], the purposes
37:18 to the LORD, and their inheritance will endure **forever** [+4200].
37:27 and do good; then you will dwell in the land **forever** [+4200].
37:28 They will be protected **forever** [+4200], but the offspring of the
41:12 [41:13] uphold me and set me in your presence **forever** [+4200].
41:13 [41:14] the God of Israel, from **everlasting** to everlasting.
41:13 [41:14] the God of Israel, from everlasting to **everlasting**.
44:8 [44:9] day long, and we will praise your name **forever** [+4200].
45:2 [45:3] with grace, since God has blessed you **forever** [+4200].
45:6 [45:7] Your throne, O God, will last **for ever** and ever; a scepter
45:17 [45:18] therefore the nations will praise you for **ever** and ever.
48:8 [48:9] our God: God makes her secure **forever** [+6330]. *Selah*
48:14 [48:15] For this God is our God **for ever** and ever; he will be our
49:8 [49:9] for a life is costly, no payment is **ever** [+4200] enough—
49:11 [49:12] Their tombs will remain their houses **forever** [+4200],
52:8 [52:10] of God; I trust in God's unfailing love **for ever** and ever.
52:9 [52:11] I will praise you **forever** [+4200] for what you have done;

Ps 55:22 [55:23] he will **never** [+4200+4202] let the righteous fall.
61: 4 [61:5] I long to dwell in your tent **forever** and take refuge in the
61: 7 [61:8] May he be enthroned in God's presence **forever**;
66: 7 He rules **forever** by his power, his eyes watch the nations—
71: 1 I have taken refuge; let me **never** [+440+4200] be put to shame.
72:17 May his name endure **forever** [+4200]; may it continue as long as
72:19 Praise be to his glorious name **forever** [+4200]; may the whole
73:12 the wicked are like—**always** carefree, they increase in wealth.
73:26 God is the strength of my heart and my portion **forever** [+4200].
75: 9 [75:10] As for me, I will declare this **forever** [+4200]; I will sing
77: 5 [77:6] I thought about the former days, the years of **long ago**;
77: 7 [77:8] "Will the Lord reject **forever** [+4200]? Will he never show
78:66 He beat back his enemies; he put them to **everlasting** shame.
78:69 like the heights, like the earth that he established **forever** [+4200].
79:13 the sheep of your pasture, will praise you **forever** [+4200];
81:15 [81:16] and their punishment would last **forever** [+4200].
85: 5 [85:6] Will you be angry with us **forever** [+4200]? Will you
86:12 with all my heart; I will glorify your name **forever** [+4200].
89: 1 [89:2] I will sing of the LORD's great love **forever**; with my
89: 2 [89:3] I will declare that your love stands firm **forever**, that you
89: 4 [89:5] 'I will establish your line **forever** [+6330] and make your
89:28 [89:29] I will maintain my love to him **forever** [+4200], and my
89:36 [89:37] that his line will continue **forever** [+4200] and his throne
89:37 [89:38] it will be established **forever** like the moon, the faithful
89:52 [89:53] Praise be to the LORD **forever** [+4200]! Amen
90: 2 and the world, from **everlasting** to everlasting you are God.
90: 2 and the world, from everlasting to **everlasting** you are God.
92: 8 [92:9] But you, O LORD, are exalted **forever** [+4200].
93: 2 Your throne was established long ago; you are from **all eternity**.
100: 5 For the LORD is good and his love endures **forever** [+4200];
102:12 [102:13] you, O LORD, sit enthroned **forever** [+4200]; your
103: 9 not always accuse, nor will he harbor his anger **forever** [+4200];
103:17 from **everlasting** to everlasting the LORD's love is with those
103:17 from everlasting to **everlasting** the LORD's love is with those
104: 5 on its foundations; it can **never** [+1153+2256+6329] be moved.
104:31 May the glory of the LORD endure **forever** [+4200];
105: 8 He remembers his covenant **forever** [+4200], the word he
105:10 it to Jacob as a decree, to Israel as an **everlasting** covenant:
106: 1 to the LORD, for he is good; his love endures **forever** [+4200].
106:31 This was credited to him as righteousness for **endless** [+6330]
106:48 to the LORD, the God of Israel, from **everlasting** to everlasting.
106:48 to the LORD, the God of Israel, from everlasting to **everlasting**.
107: 1 to the LORD, for he is good; his love endures **forever** [+4200].
110: 4 "You are a priest **forever** [+4200], in the order of Melchizedek."
111: 5 those who fear him; he remembers his covenant **forever** [+4200].
111: 8 They are steadfast for ever and **ever** [+4200], done in faithfulness
111: 9 he ordained his covenant **forever** [+4200]—holy and awesome is
112: 6 Surely he will **never** [+4200+4202] be shaken; a righteous man
112: 6 will never be shaken; a righteous man will be remembered **forever**.
113: 2 of the LORD be praised, both now and **forevermore** [+6330].
115:18 is we who extol the LORD, both now and **forevermore** [+6330].
117: 2 and the faithfulness of the LORD endures **forever** [+4200].
118: 1 to the LORD, for he is good; his love endures **forever** [+4200].
118: 2 Let Israel say: "His love endures **forever** [+4200]."
118: 3 Let the house of Aaron say: "His love endures **forever** [+4200]."
118: 4 who fear the LORD say: "His love endures **forever** [+4200]."
118:29 to the LORD, for he is good; his love endures **forever** [+4200].
119:44 I will always obey your law, for **ever** and ever.
119:52 I remember your **ancient** [+4946] laws, O LORD, and I find
119:89 Your word, O LORD, is **eternal** [+4200]; it stands firm in the
119:93 I will **never** [+4200+4202] forget your precepts, for by them you
119:98 me wiser than my enemies, for they are **ever** [+4200] with me.
119:111 Your statutes are my heritage **forever** [+4200]; they are the joy of
119:112 is set on keeping your decrees **to the very end** [+4200+6813].
119:142 Your righteousness is **everlasting** [+4200] and your law is true.
119:144 Your statutes are **forever** [+4200] right; give me understanding
119:152 your statutes that you established them to last **forever** [+4200].
119:160 your words are true; all your righteous laws are **eternal** [+4200].
121: 8 over your coming and going both now and **forevermore** [+6330].
125: 1 Mount Zion, which cannot be shaken but endures **forever** [+4200].
125: 2 LORD surrounds his people both now and **forevermore** [+6330].
131: 3 put your hope in the LORD both now and **forevermore** [+6330].
133: 3 LORD bestows his blessing, even life **forevermore** [+2021+6330].
135:13 Your name, O LORD, endures **forever** [+4200], your renown,
136: 1 for he is good. *His love endures* ***forever*** [+4200].
136: 2 to the God of gods. *His love endures* ***forever*** [+4200].
136: 3 to the Lord of lords: *His love endures* ***forever*** [+4200].
136: 4 does great wonders, *His love endures* ***forever*** [+4200].
136: 5 made the heavens, *His love endures* ***forever*** [+4200].
136: 6 earth upon the waters, *His love endures* ***forever*** [+4200].
136: 7 the great lights—*His love endures* ***forever*** [+4200].
136: 8 sun to govern the day, *His love endures* ***forever*** [+4200].
136: 9 to govern the night; *His love endures* ***forever*** [+4200].
136:10 the firstborn of Egypt *His love endures* ***forever*** [+4200].
136:11 out from among them *His love endures* ***forever*** [+4200].
136:12 and outstretched arm; *His love endures* ***forever*** [+4200].
136:13 the Red Sea asunder *His love endures* ***forever*** [+4200].
136:14 the midst of it, *His love endures* ***forever*** [+4200].
136:15 into the Red Sea; *His love endures* ***forever*** [+4200].
136:16 through the desert, *His love endures* ***forever*** [+4200].
136:17 down great kings, *His love endures* ***forever*** [+4200].
136:18 killed mighty kings—*His love endures* ***forever*** [+4200].
136:19 king of the Amorites *His love endures* ***forever*** [+4200].
136:20 Og king of Bashan—*His love endures* ***forever*** [+4200].
136:21 as an inheritance, *His love endures* ***forever*** [+4200].
136:22 to his servant Israel; *His love endures* ***forever*** [+4200].
136:23 us in our low estate *His love endures* ***forever*** [+4200].
136:24 us from our enemies, *His love endures* ***forever*** [+4200].
136:25 to every creature. *His love endures* ***forever*** [+4200].
136:26 to the God of heaven. *His love endures* ***forever*** [+4200].
138: 8 your love, O LORD, endures **forever** [+4200]—do not abandon
139:24 is any offensive way in me, and lead me in the way **everlasting**.
143: 3 to the ground; he makes me dwell in darkness like those **long** dead.
145: 1 my God the King; I will praise your name for **ever** and ever.
145: 2 Every day I will praise you and extol your name for **ever** and ever.
145:13 Your kingdom is an **everlasting** [+3972] kingdom, and your
145:21 Let every creature praise his holy name for **ever** and ever.
146: 6 in them—the LORD, who remains faithful **forever** [+4200].
146:10 The LORD reigns **forever** [+4200], your God, O Zion, for all
148: 6 He set them in place for ever and **ever** [+4200]; he gave a decree
Pr 8:23 I was appointed from **eternity**, from the beginning, before the
10:25 the wicked are gone, but the righteous stand firm **forever**.
10:30 The righteous will **never** [+1153+4200] be uprooted,
22:28 Do not move an **ancient** boundary stone set up by your forefathers.
23:10 Do not move an **ancient** boundary stone or encroach on the fields
27:24 for riches do not endure **forever** [+4200], and a crown is not secure
Ecc 1: 4 and generations go, but the earth remains **forever** [+4200].
1:10 It was here already, **long** [+4200] **ago**; it was here before our time.
2:16 the wise man, like the fool, will not be **long** [+4200] remembered;
3:11 He has also set **eternity** in the hearts of men; yet they cannot
3:14 I know that everything God does will endure **forever** [+4200];
9: 6 **never** [+401+4200] again will they have a part in anything that
12: 5 man goes to his **eternal** home and mourners go about the streets.
Isa 9: 7 [9:6] and righteousness from that time on and **forever** [+6330].
14:20 offspring of the wicked will never be mentioned **again** [+4200].
24: 5 violated the statutes and broken the **everlasting** covenant.
25: 2 stronghold a city no more; it will **never** [+4200+4202] be rebuilt.
26: 4 LORD forever, for the LORD, the LORD, is the Rock **eternal**.
30: 8 that for the days to come it may be an **everlasting** [+6330] witness.
32:14 and watchtower will become a wasteland **forever** [+6330],
32:17 of righteousness will be quietness and confidence **forever** [+6330].
33:14 consuming fire? Who of us can dwell with **everlasting** burning?"
34:10 be quenched night and day; its smoke will rise **forever** [+4200].
34:17 They will possess it **forever** [+6330] and dwell there from
35:10 enter Zion with singing; **everlasting** joy will crown their heads.
40: 8 the flowers fall, but the word of our God stands **forever** [+4200]."
40:28 The LORD is the **everlasting** God, the Creator of the ends of the
42:14 "For a **long time** I have kept silent, I have been quiet and held
44: 7 me what has happened since I established my **ancient** people,
45:17 Israel will be saved by the LORD with an **everlasting** salvation;
45:17 you will never be put to shame or disgraced, to **ages** everlasting.
46: 9 Remember the former things, those of **long ago**; I am God,
47: 7 You said, 'I will continue **forever** [+4200]—the eternal queen!'
51: 6 my salvation will last **forever** [+4200], my righteousness will
51: 8 my righteousness will last **forever** [+4200], my salvation through
51: 9 of the LORD; awake, as in days gone by, as in generations **of old**.
51:11 enter Zion with singing; **everlasting** joy will crown their heads.
54: 8 but with **everlasting** kindness I will have compassion on you,"
55: 3 I will make an **everlasting** covenant with you, my faithful love
55:13 for an **everlasting** sign, which will not be destroyed."
56: 5 I will give them an **everlasting** name that will not be cut off.
57:11 because I have **long** [+4946] been silent that you do not fear me?
57:16 I will not accuse **forever** [+4200], nor will I always be angry,
58:12 Your people will rebuild the **ancient** ruins and will raise up the
59:21 of their descendants from this time on and **forever** [+6330],"
60:15 I will make you the **everlasting** pride and the joy of all
60:19 for the LORD will be your **everlasting** light, and your God will
60:20 the LORD will be your **everlasting** light, and your days of sorrow
60:21 be righteous and they will possess the land **forever** [+4200].
61: 4 They will rebuild the **ancient** ruins and restore the places long
61: 7 a double portion in their land, and **everlasting** joy will be theirs.
61: 8 I will reward them and make an **everlasting** covenant with them.
63: 9 he lifted them up and carried them all the days **of old**.
63:11 Then his people recalled the days **of old**, the days of Moses
63:12 the waters before them, to gain for himself **everlasting** renown,
63:16 O LORD, are our Father, our Redeemer from **of old** is your name.
63:19 We are yours from **of old**; but you have not ruled over them,
64: 4 [64:3] Since **ancient times** no one has heard, no ear has

Isa 64: 5 [64:4] when we **continued** to sin against them, you were angry.
Jer 2: 20 "**Long** [+4946] **ago** you broke off your yoke and tore off your
3: 5 will you **always** [+4200] be angry? Will your wrath continue
3: 12 declares the LORD, 'I will not be angry **forever** [+4200].
5: 15 an **ancient** [+4946] and enduring nation, a people whose language
5: 22 sand a boundary for the sea, an **everlasting** barrier it cannot cross.
6: 16 ask for the **ancient** paths, ask where the good way is, and walk in
7: 7 in the land I gave your forefathers for **ever** [+4946] and ever.
7: 7 in the land I gave your forefathers for ever and **ever** [+6330].
10: 10 the LORD is the true God; he is the living God, the **eternal** King.
17: 4 for you have kindled my anger, and it will burn **forever** [+6330]."
17: 25 in Jerusalem, and this city will be inhabited **forever** [+4200].
18: 15 which made them stumble in their ways and in the **ancient** paths.
18: 16 Their land will be laid waste, an object of **lasting** scorn; all who
20: 11 their dishonor will **never** [+4202] be forgotten.
20: 17 with my mother as my grave, her womb enlarged **forever**.
23: 40 I will bring upon you **everlasting** disgrace—everlasting shame that
23: 40 **everlasting** shame that will not be forgotten."
25: 5 LORD gave to you and your fathers for **ever** [+4946] and ever.
25: 5 LORD gave to you and your fathers for ever and **ever** [+6330].
25: 9 make them an object of horror and scorn, and an **everlasting** ruin.
25: 12 declares the LORD, "and will make it desolate **forever**.
28: 8 From **early times** the prophets who preceded you and me have
31: 3 "I have loved you with an **everlasting** love; I have drawn you with
31: 40 The city will **never** [+4200+4202] again be uprooted or
32: 40 I will make an **everlasting** covenant with them: I will never stop
33: 11 for the LORD is good; his love endures **forever** [+4200]."
35: 6 'Neither you nor your descendants must **ever** [+6330] drink wine.
49: 13 and of cursing; and all its towns will be in ruins **forever**."
49: 33 will become a haunt of jackals, a desolate place **forever** [+6330].
49: 36 [there will not be a nation where **Elam's** [K; see Q 6520] exiles]
50: 5 bind themselves to the LORD in an **everlasting** covenant that will
51: 26 for you will be desolate **forever**," declares the LORD.
51: 39 then sleep **forever** and not awake," declares the LORD.
51: 57 they will sleep **forever** and not awake," declares the King,
51: 62 neither man nor animal will live in it; it will be desolate **forever**.'
La 3: 6 He has made me dwell in darkness like those **long** dead.
3: 31 For men are not cast off by the Lord **forever** [+4200].
5: 19 You, O LORD, reign **forever** [+4200]; your throne endures from
Eze 16: 60 your youth, and I will establish an **everlasting** covenant with you.
25: 15 in their hearts, and with **ancient** hostility sought to destroy Judah,
26: 20 down with those who go down to the pit, to the people of **long ago**.
26: 20 as in **ancient** [+4946] ruins, with those who go down to the pit,
26: 21 will be sought, but you will **never** [+4200+4202] again be found,
27: 36 you have come to a horrible end and will be no **more** [+6330].' "
28: 19 you have come to a horrible end and will be no **more** [+6330].' "
35: 5 " 'Because you harbored an **ancient** hostility and delivered the
35: 9 I will make you desolate **forever**; your towns will not be inhabited.
36: 2 "Aha! The **ancient** heights have become our possession." '
37: 25 and their children's children will live there **forever** [+6330],
37: 25 and David my servant will be their prince **forever** [+4200].
37: 26 a covenant of peace with them; it will be an **everlasting** covenant.
37: 26 and I will put my sanctuary among them **forever** [+4200].
37: 28 Israel holy, when my sanctuary is among them **forever** [+4200].' "
43: 7 This is where I will live among the Israelites **forever** [+4200].
43: 9 idols of their kings, and I will live among them **forever** [+4200].
46: 14 of this grain offering to the LORD is a **lasting** [+9458] ordinance.
Da 9: 24 to bring in **everlasting** righteousness, to seal up vision
12: 2 some to **everlasting** life, others to shame and everlasting contempt.
12: 2 some to everlasting life, others to shame and **everlasting** contempt.
12: 3 who lead many to righteousness, like the stars for **ever** and ever.
12: 7 I heard him swear by him who lives **forever**, saying, "It will be for
Hos 2: 19 [2:21] I will betroth you to me **forever** [+4200]; I will betroth you
Joel 2: 2 such as never was of **old** nor ever will be in ages to come.
2: 26 for you; **never again** [+4200+4202] will my people be shamed.
2: 27 is no other; **never again** [+4200+4202] will my people be shamed.
3: 20 [4:20] Judah will be inhabited **forever** [+4200] and Jerusalem
Am 9: 11 restore its ruins, and build it as it **used to be** [+3427],
Ob 1: 10 be covered with shame; you will be destroyed **forever** [+4200].
Jnh 2: 6 [2:7] sank down; the earth beneath barred me in **forever** [+4200].
Mic 2: 9 You take away my blessing from their children **forever** [+4200].
4: 5 we will walk in the name of the LORD our God for **ever**
4: 7 rule over them in Mount Zion from that day and **forever** [+6330].
5: 2 [5:1] whose origins are from of old, from **ancient** times."
7: 14 Let them feed in Bashan and Gilead as in days **long ago**.
Hab 3: 6 The ancient mountains crumbled and the **age-old** hills collapsed.
3: 6 and the age-old hills collapsed. His ways are **eternal**.
Zep 2: 9 a place of weeds and salt pits, a wasteland **forever** [+6330].
Zec 1: 5 forefathers now? And the prophets, do they live **forever** [+4200]?
Mal 1: 4 a people **always** [+6330] under the wrath of the LORD.
3: 4 acceptable to the LORD, as in days **gone by**, as in former years.

6410 עוּן *'ûn*, v. Not used in NIV/BHS [→ 5061]

6411 עָוֺן *'āwōn*, n.m. [232 / 233] [√ 6390; Ar 10532]

sin [59], sins [49], guilt [35], wickedness [13], iniquity [12], iniquities [10], punishment [9], held responsible [+5951] [7], crime [4], guilty [4], wicked [4], consequences of sin [3], responsibility for offenses [3], blame [2], offense [2], sinful [2], wrong [2], *untranslated* [1], affliction [1], crimes [1], evil deeds [1], faults [1], offenses [1], punished [+7936] [1], punished [1], punishment for sins [1], sins [+1821] [1], wrongdoing [1], wrongdoings [1], wrongs [1]

Ge 4: 13 Cain said to the LORD, "My **punishment** is more than I can bear.
15: 16 for the **sin** *of* the Amorites has not yet reached its full measure."
19: 15 are here, or you will be swept away when the city is **punished**."
44: 16 God has uncovered your servants' **guilt**. We are now my lord's
Ex 20: 5 punishing the children for the **sin** *of* the fathers to the third
28: 38 he will bear the **guilt** *involved in* the sacred gifts the Israelites
28: 43 minister in the Holy Place, so that they will not incur **guilt** and die.
34: 7 love to thousands, and forgiving **wickedness**, rebellion and sin.
34: 7 their children for the **sin** *of* the fathers to the third and fourth
34: 9 forgive our **wickedness** and our sin, and take us as your
Lev 5: 1 he has seen or learned about, he *will be* **held responsible** [+5951].
5: 17 not know it, he is guilty and *will be* **held responsible** [+5951].
7: 18 the person who eats any of it *will be* **held responsible** [+5951].
10: 17 it was given to you to take away the **guilt** *of* the community by
16: 21 confess over it all the **wickedness** and rebellion of the Israelites—
16: 22 The goat will carry on itself all their **sins** to a solitary place;
17: 16 and bathe himself, he *will be* **held responsible** [+5951].' "
18: 25 so I punished it for its **sin**, and the land vomited out its inhabitants.
19: 8 Whoever eats it *will be* **held responsible** [+5951] because he has
20: 17 He has dishonored his sister and *will be* **held responsible** [+5951].
20: 19 a close relative; both of you *would be* **held responsible** [+5951].
22: 16 sacred offerings and so bring upon them **guilt** requiring payment.
26: 39 will waste away in the lands of their enemies because of their **sins**;
26: 39 their sins; also because of their fathers' **sins** they will waste away.
26: 40 " 'But if they will confess their **sins** and the sins of their fathers—
26: 40 " 'But if they will confess their sins and the **sins** *of* their fathers—
26: 41 their uncircumcised hearts are humbled and they pay for their **sin**,
26: 43 They will pay for their **sins** because they rejected my laws
Nu 5: 15 offering for jealousy, a reminder offering to draw attention to **guilt**.
5: 31 The husband will be innocent of any **wrongdoing**, but the woman
5: 31 but the woman will bear the **consequences of** her **sin**.' "
14: 18 is slow to anger, abounding in love and forgiving **sin** and rebellion.
14: 18 he punishes the children for the **sin** *of* the fathers to the third
14: 19 In accordance with your great love, forgive the **sin** *of* these people,
14: 34 you will suffer for your **sins** and know what it is like to have me
15: 31 that person must surely be cut off; his **guilt** remains on him.' "
18: 1 are to bear the **responsibility for offenses** *against* the sanctuary,
18: 1 your sons alone are to bear the **responsibility for offenses** *against*
18: 23 of Meeting and bear the **responsibility for offenses** *against* it.
30: 15 [30:16] he hears about them, then he is responsible for her **guilt**."
Dt 5: 9 punishing the children for the **sin** *of* the fathers to the third
19: 15 One witness is not enough to convict a man accused of any **crime**
Jos 22: 17 Was not the **sin** *of* Peor enough for us? Up to this very day we
22: 20 of Israel? He was not the only one who died for his **sin**.' "
1Sa 3: 13 I would judge his family forever because of the **sin** he knew about;
3: 14 'The **guilt** *of* Eli's house will never be atoned for by sacrifice
20: 1 to Jonathan and asked, "What have I done? What is my **crime**?
20: 8 If I am **guilty**, then kill me yourself! Why hand me over to your
25: 24 fell at his feet and said: "My lord, let the **blame** be on me alone.
28: 10 as the LORD lives, you *will* not *be* **punished** [+7936] for this."
2Sa 3: 8 Yet now you accuse me of an **offense** *involving* this woman!
14: 9 let the **blame** rest on me and on my father's family, and let the
14: 32 and if I am **guilty** of anything, let him put me to death."
16: 12 [the LORD will see my distress [BHS K *sin*, Q 6524; NIV 6715]]
19: 19 [19:20] said to him, "May my lord not hold me **guilty**. Do not
22: 24 I have been blameless before him and have kept myself from **sin**.
24: 10 O LORD, I beg you, take away the **guilt** *of* your servant.
1Ki 17: 18 of God? Did you come to remind me of my **sin** and kill my son?"
2Ki 7: 9 If we wait until daylight, **punishment** will overtake us. Let's go at
1Ch 21: 8 Now, I beg you, take away the **guilt** *of* your servant. I have done a
Ezr 9: 6 because our **sins** are higher than our heads and our guilt has
9: 7 Because of our **sins**, we and our kings and our priests have been
9: 13 you have punished us less than our **sins** have deserved and have
Ne 4: 5 [3:37] Do not cover up their **guilt** or blot out their sins from your
9: 2 and confessed their sins and the **wickedness** *of* their fathers.
Job 7: 21 Why do you not pardon my offenses and forgive my **sins**?
10: 6 that you must search out my **faults** and probe after my sin—
10: 14 be watching me and would not let my **offense** go unpunished.
11: 6 two sides. Know this: God has even forgotten some of your **sin**.
13: 23 How many **wrongs** and sins have I committed? Show me my
13: 26 bitter things against me and make me inherit the **sins** *of* my youth.
14: 17 My offenses will be sealed up in a bag; you will cover over my **sin**.
15: 5 Your **sin** prompts your mouth; you adopt the tongue of the crafty.
19: 29 for wrath will bring **punishment** *by* the sword, and then you will
20: 27 The heavens will expose his **guilt**; the earth will rise up against

Job 22: 5 Is not your wickedness great? Are not your **sins** endless?
31: 11 For that would have been shameful, a **sin** to be judged.
31: 28 these also would be **sins** to be judged, for I would have been
31: 33 have concealed my sin as men do, by hiding my **guilt** in my heart
33: 9 'I am pure and without sin; I am clean and free from **guilt**.
Ps 18: 23 [18:24] been blameless before him and have kept myself from **sin**.
25: 11 of your name, O LORD, forgive my **iniquity**, though it is great.
31: 10 [31:11] my strength fails because of my **affliction**, and my bones
32: 2 Blessed is the man whose **sin** the LORD does not count against
32: 5 I acknowledged my sin to you and did not cover up my **iniquity**.
32: 5 to the LORD"—and you forgave the **guilt** *of* my sin.
36: 2 [36:3] eyes he flatters himself too much to detect or hate his **sin**.
38: 4 [38:5] My **guilt** has overwhelmed me like a burden too heavy to
38: 18 [38:19] I confess my **iniquity**; I am troubled by my sin.
39: 11 [39:12] You rebuke and discipline men for their **sin**; you consume
40: 12 [40:13] my **sins** have overtaken me, and I cannot see.
49: 5 [49:6] evil days come, when **wicked** deceivers surround me—
51: 2 [51:4] Wash away all my **iniquity** and cleanse me from my sin.
51: 5 [51:7] Surely I was **sinful** at birth, sinful from the time my mother
51: 9 [51:11] Hide your face from my sins and blot out all my **iniquity**.
59: 4 [59:5] I have done no **wrong**, yet they are ready to attack me.
65: 3 [65:4] When we were overwhelmed by **sins** [+1821], you forgave
69: 27 [69:28] Charge them with **crime** upon crime; do not let them
69: 27 [69:28] Charge them with crime upon **crime**; do not let them
73: 7 From their callous hearts comes **iniquity**; [BHS 6524] the evil
78: 38 was merciful; he forgave their **iniquities** and did not destroy them.
79: 8 Do not hold against us the **sins** *of* the fathers; may your mercy
85: 2 [85:3] You forgave the **iniquity** *of* your people and covered all
89: 32 [89:33] punish their sin with the rod, their **iniquity** with flogging;
90: 8 You have set our **iniquities** before you, our secret sins in the light
103: 3 who forgives all your **sins** and heals all your diseases,
103: 10 treat us as our sins deserve or repay us according to our **iniquities**.
106: 43 but they were bent on rebellion and they wasted away in their **sin**.
107: 17 rebellious ways and suffered affliction because of their **iniquities**.
109: 14 May the **iniquity** *of* his fathers be remembered before the LORD;
130: 3 If you, O LORD, kept a record of **sins**, O Lord, who could stand?
130: 8 He himself will redeem Israel from all their **sins**.
Pr 5: 22 The **evil deeds** *of* a wicked man ensnare him; the cords of his sin
16: 6 Through love and faithfulness **sin** is atoned for; through the fear of
Isa 1: 4 Ah, sinful nation, a people loaded with **guilt**, a brood of evildoers,
5: 18 Woe to those who draw **sin** along with cords of deceit,
6: 7 your lips; your **guilt** is taken away and your sin atoned for."
13: 11 I will punish the world for its evil, the wicked for their **sins**.
14: 21 Prepare a place to slaughter his sons for the **sins** *of* their
22: 14 "Till your dying day this **sin** will not be atoned for," says the Lord,
26: 21 out of his dwelling to punish the people of the earth for their **sins**.
27: 9 By this, then, will Jacob's **guilt** be atoned for, and this will be the
30: 13 this **sin** will become for you like a high wall, cracked and bulging,
33: 24 "I am ill"; and the **sins** of those who dwell there will be forgiven.
40: 2 her hard service has been completed, that her **sin** has been paid for,
43: 24 burdened me with your sins and wearied me with your **offenses**.
50: 1 Because of your **sins** you were sold; because of your transgressions
53: 5 pierced for our transgressions, he was crushed for our **iniquities**;
53: 6 own way; and the LORD has laid on him the **iniquity** *of* us all.
53: 11 servant will justify many, and he will bear their **iniquities**.
57: 17 I was enraged by his **sinful** greed; I punished him, and hid my face
59: 2 your **iniquities** have separated you from your God; your sins have
59: 3 For your hands are stained with blood, your fingers with **guilt**.
59: 12 Our offenses are ever with us, and we acknowledge our **iniquities**:
64: 6 [64:5] up like a leaf, and like the wind our **sins** sweep us away.
64: 7 [64:6] face from us and made us waste away because of our **sins**.
64: 9 [64:8] O LORD; do not remember our **sins** forever.
65: 7 both your **sins** and the sins of your fathers," says the LORD.
65: 7 both your sins and the **sins** *of* your fathers," says the LORD.
Jer 2: 22 an abundance of soap, the stain of your **guilt** is still before me,"
3: 13 Only acknowledge your **guilt**—you have rebelled against the
5: 25 Your **wrongdoings** have kept these away; your sins have deprived
11: 10 They have returned to the **sins** *of* their forefathers, who refused to
13: 22 because of your many **sins** that your skirts have been torn off
14: 7 Although our **sins** testify against us, O LORD, do something for
14: 10 he will now remember their **wickedness** and punish them for their
14: 20 we acknowledge our wickedness and the **guilt** *of* our fathers;
16: 10 What **wrong** have we done? What sin have we committed against
16: 17 are not hidden from me, nor is their **sin** concealed from my eyes.
16: 18 I will repay them double for their **wickedness** and their sin,
18: 23 Do not forgive their **crimes** or blot out their sins from your sight.
25: 12 the land of the Babylonians, for their **guilt**," declares the LORD,
30: 14 the cruel, because your **guilt** is so great and your sins so many.
30: 15 Because of your great **guilt** and many sins I have done these things
31: 30 Instead, everyone will die for his own **sin**; whoever eats sour
31: 34 "For I will forgive their **wickedness** and will remember their sins
32: 18 bring the punishment for the fathers' **sins** into the laps of their
33: 8 I will cleanse them from all the **sin** they have committed against
33: 8 against me and will forgive all their **sins** of rebellion against me.
36: 3 his wicked way; then I will forgive their **wickedness** and their sin."
36: 31 and his children and his attendants for their **wickedness**;
50: 20 declares the LORD, "search will be made for Israel's **guilt**,
51: 6 Run for your lives! Do not be destroyed because of her **sins**.
La 2: 14 they did not expose your **sin** to ward off your captivity.
4: 6 The **punishment** *of* my people is greater than that of Sodom,
4: 13 because of the sins of her prophets and the **iniquities** *of* her priests,
4: 22 O Daughter of Zion, your **punishment** will end; he will not
4: 22 of Edom, he will punish your **sin** and expose your wickedness.
5: 7 fathers sinned and are no more, and we bear their **punishment**.
Eze 3: 18 that wicked man will die for his **sin**, and I will hold you
3: 19 from his wickedness or from his evil ways, he will die for his **sin**;
4: 4 your left side and put the **sin** *of* the house of Israel upon yourself.
4: 4 You are to bear their **sin** for the number of days you lie on your
4: 5 assigned you the same number of days as the years of their **sin**.
4: 5 So for 390 days you will bear the **sin** *of* the house of Israel.
4: 6 this time on your right side, and bear the **sin** *of* the house of Judah.
4: 17 at the sight of each other and will waste away because of their **sin**.
7: 13 Because of their **sins**, not one of them will preserve his life.
7: 16 moaning like doves of the valleys, each because of his **sins**.
7: 19 or fill their stomachs with it, for it has made them stumble into **sin**.
9: 9 "The **sin** *of* the house of Israel and Judah is exceedingly great;
14: 3 in their hearts and put **wicked** stumbling blocks before their faces.
14: 4 puts a **wicked** stumbling block before his face and then goes to a
14: 7 in his heart and puts a **wicked** stumbling block before his face and
14: 10 They will bear their **guilt**—the prophet will be as guilty as the one
14: 10 the prophet will be as **guilty** as the one who consults him.
14: 10 the prophet will be as guilty as **[RPH]** the one who consults him.
16: 49 " 'Now this was the **sin** *of* your sister Sodom: She and her
18: 17 my decrees. He will not die for his father's **sin**; he will surely live.
18: 18 his father will die for his own **sin**, because he practiced extortion,
18: 19 "Yet you ask, 'Why does the son not share the **guilt** *of* his father?'
18: 20 The son will not share the **guilt** *of* the father, nor will the father
18: 20 the guilt of the father, nor will the father share the **guilt** *of* the son.
18: 30 away from all your offenses; then **sin** will not be your downfall.
21: 23 [21:28] he will remind them of their **guilt** and take them captive.
21: 24 [21:29] 'Because you people have brought to mind your **guilt** by
21: 25 [21:30] whose time of **punishment** has reached its climax,
21: 29 [21:34] whose time of **punishment** has reached its climax.
24: 23 will not mourn or weep but will waste away because of your **sins**
28: 18 By your many **sins** and dishonest trade you have desecrated your
29: 16 but will be a reminder of their **sin** in turning to her for help.
32: 27 The **punishment for** their **sins** rested on their bones,
33: 6 life of one of them, that man will be taken away because of his **sin**,
33: 8 that wicked man will die for his **sin**, and I will hold you
33: 9 to turn from his ways and he does not do so, he will die for his **sin**,
35: 5 of their calamity, the time their **punishment** reached its climax,
36: 31 you will loathe yourselves for your **sins** and detestable practices.
36: 33 On the day I cleanse you from all your **sins**, I will resettle your
39: 23 will know that the people of Israel went into exile for their **sin**,
43: 10 to the people of Israel, that they may be ashamed of their **sins**.
44: 10 from me after their idols must bear the **consequences of** their **sin**.
44: 12 presence of their idols and made the house of Israel fall into **sin**,
44: 12 uplifted hand that they must bear the **consequences of** their **sin**,
Da 9: 13 sought the favor of the LORD our God by turning from our **sins**
9: 16 Our sins and the **iniquities** *of* our fathers have made Jerusalem
9: 24 to put an end to sin, to atone for **wickedness**, to bring in
Hos 4: 8 They feed on the sins of my people and relish their **wickedness**.
5: 5 the Israelites, even Ephraim, stumble in their **sin**; Judah also
7: 1 the **sins** *of* Ephraim are exposed and the crimes of Samaria
8: 13 Now he will remember their **wickedness** and punish their sins:
9: 7 Because your **sins** are so many and your hostility so great,
9: 9 God will remember their **wickedness** and punish them for their
10: 10 be gathered against them to put them in bonds for their double **sin**.
12: 8 [12:9] With all my wealth they will not find in me any **iniquity**
13: 12 The **guilt** *of* Ephraim is stored up, his sins are kept on record.
14: 1 [14:2] the LORD your God. Your **sins** have been your downfall!
14: 2 [14:3] "Forgive all our **sins** and receive us graciously, that we
Am 3: 2 families of the earth; therefore I will punish you for all your **sins**."
Mic 7: 18 who pardons **sin** and forgives the transgression of the remnant of
7: 19 you will tread our **sins** underfoot and hurl all our iniquities into the
Zec 3: 4 Then he said to Joshua, "See, I have taken away your **sin**,
3: 9 'and I will remove the **sin** *of* this land in a single day.
5: 6 "This is the **iniquity** [BHS 6524] *of* the people throughout the
Mal 2: 6 with me in peace and uprightness, and turned many from **sin**.

6412 עוֹנָה ***'ônâ***, n.f. Not used in NIV/BHS [√ 6390]

6413 עִוְעִים ***'iw'îm***, n.pl.abst. [1] [√ 6390]
dizziness [1]

Isa 19: 14 The LORD has poured into them a spirit of **dizziness**; they make

6414 עוּף[1] ***'ûp*[1]**, v. [24] [→ 6416]

fly away [4], darting [3], flew [3], fly [3], flying [3], flies [2], cast [1], flies away [1], fly along [1], fly off [1], hovering overhead [1], swoop down [1]

Ge 1:20 [D] *let* birds **fly** above the earth across the expanse of the sky."
Dt 4:17 [A] or like any animal on earth or any bird that **flies** in the air,
2Sa 22:11 [A] He mounted the cherubim and **flew**; he soared on the wings
Job 5: 7 [A] Yet man is born to trouble as surely as sparks **fly** upward.
20: 8 [A] Like a dream *he* **flies away**, no more to be found, banished
Ps 18:10 [18:11] [A] He mounted the cherubim and **flew**; he soared on
55: 6 [55:7] [A] wings of a dove! *I would* **fly away** and be at rest—
90:10 [A] and sorrow, for they quickly pass, and *we* **fly away**.
91: 5 [A] not fear the terror of night, nor the arrow *that* **flies** by day,
Pr 23: 5 [G] **Cast** but a glance at riches, and they are gone, for they will
23: 5 [A] for they will surely sprout wings and **fly off** to the sky
26: 2 [A] Like a fluttering sparrow or a **darting** swallow, an
Isa 6: 2 [D] two they covered their feet, and with two *they were* **flying**.
6: 6 [A] one of the seraphs **flew** to me with a live coal in his hand,
11:14 [A] *They will* **swoop down** on the slopes of Philistia to the west;
14:29 [D] up a viper, its fruit will be a **darting**, venomous serpent.
30: 6 [D] of lions and lionesses, of adders and **darting** snakes,
31: 5 [A] Like birds **hovering overhead**, the LORD Almighty will
60: 8 [A] "Who are these *that* **fly along** like clouds, like doves to their
Hos 9:11 [F] Ephraim's glory *will* **fly away** like a bird—no birth, no
Na 3:16 [A] the sky, but like locusts they strip the land and then **fly away**.
Hab 1: 8 [A] come from afar. *They* **fly** like a vulture swooping to devour;
Zec 5: 1 [A] I looked again—and there before me was a **flying** scroll!
5: 2 [A] I answered, "I see a **flying** scroll, thirty feet long and fifteen

6415 עוּף[2] ***'ûp*[2]**, v. Not used in NIV/BHS [→ 4599, 5066, 6757, 9507; cf. 6547]

6416 עוֹף ***'ôp***, n.m. [71] [√ 6414; Ar 10533]

birds [54], bird [12], flying [2], winged [2], winged creature [1]

Ge 1:20 and let **birds** fly above the earth across the expanse of the sky."
1:21 to their kinds, and every winged **bird** according to its kind.
1:22 fill the water in the seas, and let the **birds** increase on the earth."
1:26 and let them rule over the fish of the sea and the **birds** *of* the air,
1:28 Rule over the fish of the sea and the **birds** *of* the air and over every
1:30 And to all the beasts of the earth and all the **birds** *of* the air
2:19 of the ground all the beasts of the field and all the **birds** *of* the air.
2:20 all the livestock, the **birds** *of* the air and all the beasts of the field.
6: 7 and creatures that move along the ground, and **birds** *of* the air—
6:20 Two of every kind of **bird**, of every kind of animal and of every
7: 3 also seven of every kind of **bird**, male and female, to keep their
7: 8 of **birds** and of all creatures that move along the ground,
7:14 ground according to its kind and every **bird** according to its kind,
7:21 **birds**, livestock, wild animals, all the creatures that swarm over the
7:23 the ground and the **birds** *of* the air were wiped from the earth.
8:17 the **birds**, the animals, and all the creatures that move along the
8:19 and all the creatures that move along the ground and all the **birds**—
8:20 taking some of all the clean animals and clean **birds**, he sacrificed
9: 2 will fall upon all the beasts of the earth and all the **birds** *of* the air,
9:10 the **birds**, the livestock and all the wild animals, all those that
40:17 but the **birds** were eating them out of the basket on my head."
40:19 and hang you on a tree. And the **birds** will eat away your flesh."
Lev 1:14 " 'If the offering to the LORD is a burnt offering of **birds**,
7:26 you live, you must not eat the blood of any **bird** or animal.
11:13 " 'These are the **birds** you are to detest and not eat because they are
11:20 " 'All **flying** insects that walk on all fours are to be detestable to
11:21 some **winged** creatures that walk on all fours that you may eat:
11:23 But all other **winged** creatures that have four legs you are to detest.
11:46 **birds**, every living thing that moves in the water and every
17:13 or **bird** that may be eaten must drain out the blood and cover it
20:25 and unclean animals and between unclean and clean **birds**.
20:25 Do not defile yourselves by any animal or **bird** or anything that
Dt 14:19 All **flying** insects that swarm are unclean to you; do not eat them.
14:20 But any **winged creature** that is clean you may eat.
28:26 Your carcasses will be food for all the **birds** *of* the air and the
1Sa 17:44 "and I'll give your flesh to the **birds** *of* the air and the beasts of the
17:46 will give the carcasses of the Philistine army to the **birds** *of* the air
2Sa 21:10 she did not let the **birds** *of* the air touch them by day or the wild
1Ki 4:33 [5:13] He also taught about animals and **birds**, reptiles and fish.
14:11 and the **birds** *of* the air will feed on those who die in the country.
16: 4 and the **birds** *of* the air will feed on those who die in the country."
21:24 and the **birds** *of* the air will feed on those who die in the country."
Job 12: 7 they will teach you, or the **birds** *of* the air, and they will tell you;
28:21 of every living thing, concealed even from the **birds** *of* the air.
35:11 beasts of the earth and makes us wiser than the **birds** *of* the air'?
Ps 50:11 I know every **bird** *in* the mountains, and the creatures of the field
78:27 down on them like dust, flying **birds** like sand on the seashore.
79: 2 the dead bodies of your servants as food to the **birds** *of* the air,
104:12 The **birds** *of* the air nest by the waters; they sing among the
Ecc 10:20 in your bedroom, because a **bird** *of* the air may carry your words,
Isa 16: 2 Like fluttering **birds** pushed from the nest, so are the women of
Jer 4:25 and there were no people; every **bird** *in* the sky had flown away.
5:27 Like cages full of **birds**, their houses are full of deceit; they have
7:33 the carcasses of this people will become food for the **birds** *of* the
9:10 [9:9] The **birds** *of* the air have fled and the animals are gone.
12: 4 who live in it are wicked, the animals and **birds** have perished.
15: 3 sword to kill and the dogs to drag away and the **birds** *of* the air
16: 4 and their dead bodies will become food for the **birds** *of* the air
19: 7 and I will give their carcasses as food to the **birds** *of* the air
34:20 Their dead bodies will become food for the **birds** *of* the air
Eze 29: 5 give you as food to the beasts of the earth and the **birds** *of* the air.
31: 6 All the **birds** *of* the air nested in its boughs, all the beasts of the
31:13 All the **birds** *of* the air settled on the fallen tree, and all the beasts
32: 4 I will let all the **birds** *of* the air settle on you and all the beasts of
38:20 The fish of the sea, the **birds** *of* the air, the beasts of the field,
44:31 eat anything, **bird** or animal, found dead or torn by wild animals.
Hos 2:18 [2:20] the **birds** *of* the air and the creatures that move along the
4: 3 the beasts of the field and the **birds** *of* the air and the fish of the
7:12 my net over them; I will pull them down like **birds** *of* the air.
9:11 Ephraim's glory will fly away like a **bird**—no birth, no pregnancy,
Zep 1: 3 I will sweep away the **birds** *of* the air and the fish of the sea.

6417 עֹפַי ***'ôpay***, n.pr.m. [0] [cf. 6550]

Jer 40: 8 [the sons of **Ephai** [K; see Q 6550] the Netophathite,]

6418 עוּץ[1] ***'ûṣ*[1]**, v. [2] [cf. 3619]

consider [1], devise [1]

Jdg 19:30 [A] of Egypt. Think about it! **Consider** it! Tell us what to do!"
Isa 8:10 [A] **Devise** your strategy, but it will be thwarted; propose your

6419 עוּץ[2] ***'ûṣ*[2]**, n.pr.m. [5]

Uz [5]

Ge 10:23 The sons of Aram: **Uz**, Hul, Gether and Meshech.
22:21 **Uz** the firstborn, Buz his brother, Kemuel (the father of Aram),
36:28 The sons of Dishan: **Uz** and Aran.
1Ch 1:17 and Aram. The sons of Aram: **Uz**, Hul, Gether and Meshech.
1:42 Bilhan, Zaavan and Akan. The sons of Dishan: **Uz** and Aran.

6420 עוּץ[3] ***'ûṣ*[3]**, n.pr.loc. [3]

Uz [2], Uz [+824] [1]

Job 1: 1 In the land of **Uz** there lived a man whose name was Job. This man
Jer 25:20 and all the foreign people there; all the kings of **Uz** [+824];
La 4:21 and be glad, O Daughter of Edom, you who live in the land of **Uz**.

6421 עוּק ***'ûq***, v. [2] [→ 4601?, 6821]

crush [1], crushes [1]

Am 2:13 [G] I *will* **crush** you as a cart crushes when loaded with grain.
2:13 [A] I will crush you as a cart **crushes** when loaded with grain.

6422 עָוַר[1] ***'āwar*[1]**, v. [5] [→ 6426, 6427, 6428]

put out [3], blinds [2]

Ex 23: 8 [D] for a bribe **blinds** those who see and twists the words of the
Dt 16:19 [D] for a bribe **blinds** the eyes of the wise and twists the words of
2Ki 25: 7 [D] Then *they* **put out** his eyes, bound him with bronze shackles
Jer 39: 7 [D] *he* **put out** Zedekiah's eyes and bound him with bronze
52:11 [D] *he* **put out** Zedekiah's eyes, bound him with bronze shackles

6423 עוּר[2] ***'ûr*[2]**, v. [1] [→ 5067, 6425?; cf. 6867]

uncovered [+6880] [1]

Hab 3: 9 [C] *You* **uncovered** [+6880] your bow, you called for many

6424 עוּר[3] ***'ûr*[3]**, v. [81 / 82] [→ 3600, 6552, 6555, 6749, 6841, 6878, 6879]

awake [16], stir up [8], awaken [6], rouse [6], stirred up [6], wake up [5], raised [4], arouse [3], moved [3], arise [2], aroused [2], be roused [2], stirs up [2], wakens [2], being stirred up [1], gloated [1], is wakened [1], lament [+2411] [1], lash [1], raise up [1], rising [1], roused himself [1], roused [1], rouses [1], stir [1], strives [1], thrive [1], wakened [1], whoever he may be [+2256+6699] [1]

Dt 32:11 [G] like an eagle *that* **stirs up** its nest and hovers over its young,
Jdg 5:12 [A] '**Wake up**, wake up, Deborah! Wake up, wake up, break out
5:12 [A] 'Wake up, **wake up**, Deborah! Wake up, wake up, break out
5:12 [A] **Wake up**, wake up, break out in song! Arise, O Barak!
5:12 [A] Wake up, **wake up**, break out in song! Arise, O Barak!
2Sa 23: 8 [D] he **raised** [BHS 6352] his spear against eight hundred men,
23:18 [D] He **raised** his spear against three hundred men, whom he

1Ch 5:26 [G] So the God of Israel **stirred up** the spirit of Pul king of
11:11 [D] he **raised** his spear against three hundred men, whom he
11:20 [D] He **raised** his spear against three hundred men, whom he
2Ch 21:16 [G] The LORD **aroused** against Jehoram the hostility of the
36:22 [G] the LORD **moved** the heart of Cyrus king of Persia to make
Ezr 1: 1 [G] the LORD **moved** the heart of Cyrus king of Persia to make
1: 5 [G] and Levites—everyone whose heart God *had* **moved**—
Job 3: 8 [D] days curse that day, those who are ready *to* **rouse** Leviathan.
8: 6 [G] even now *he will* **rouse** *himself* on your behalf and restore
14:12 [C] no more, men will not awake or **be roused** from their sleep.
17: 8 [F] at this; the innocent *are* **aroused** against the ungodly.
31:29 [F] or **gloated** *over* the trouble that came to him—
41:10 [41:2] [A] No one is fierce enough *to* **rouse** him. Who then is
Ps 7: 6 [7:7] [A] rage of my enemies. **Awake**, my God; decree justice.
35:23 [G] **Awake**, and rise to my defense! Contend for me, my God
44:23 [44:24] [A] **Awake**, O Lord! Why do you sleep?
57: 8 [57:9] [A] **Awake**, my soul! Awake, harp and lyre! I will
57: 8 [57:9] [A] Awake, my soul! **Awake**, harp and lyre! I will
57: 8 [57:9] [G] Awake, harp and lyre! *I will* **awaken** the dawn.
59: 4 [59:5] [A] to attack me. **Arise** to help me; look on my plight!
72:16 [G] flourish like Lebanon; *let it* **thrive** like the grass of the field.
73:20 [G] As a dream when one awakes, so when you **arise**, O Lord,
78:38 [G] he restrained his anger and *did* not **stir up** his full wrath.
80: 2 [80:3] [D] **Awaken** your might; come and save us.
108: 2 [108:3] [A] **Awake**, harp and lyre! I will awaken the dawn.
108: 2 [108:3] [A] Awake, harp and lyre! *I will* **awaken** the dawn.
Pr 10:12 [D] Hatred **stirs up** dissension, but love covers over all wrongs.
SS 2: 7 [G] of the field: *Do* not **arouse** or awaken love until it so desires.
2: 7 [D] of the field: Do not arouse or **awaken** love until it so desires.
3: 5 [G] of the field: *Do* not **arouse** or awaken love until it so desires.
3: 5 [D] of the field: Do not arouse or **awaken** love until it so desires.
4:16 [A] **Awake**, north wind, and come, south wind! Blow on my
5: 2 [A] I slept but my heart *was* **awake**. Listen! My lover is
8: 4 [G] charge you: *Do* not **arouse** or awaken love until it so desires.
8: 4 [D] charge you: Do not arouse or **awaken** love until it so desires.
8: 5 [D] Under the apple tree *I* **roused** you; there your mother
Isa 10:26 [D] The LORD Almighty *will* **lash** them *with* a whip, as when
13:17 [G] See, I *will* **stir up** against them the Medes, who do not care
14: 9 [D] *it* **rouses** the spirits of the departed to greet you—all those
15: 5 [D] on the road to Horonaim *they* **lament** [+2411] their
41: 2 [G] "Who *has* **stirred up** one from the east, calling him in
41:25 [G] "*I have* **stirred up** one from the north, and he comes—
42:13 [G] out like a mighty man, like a warrior *he will* **stir up** his zeal;
45:13 [G] I *will* **raise up** Cyrus in my righteousness: I will make all his
50: 4 [G] *He* **wakens** me morning by morning, wakens my ear to listen
50: 4 [G] by morning, **wakens** my ear to listen like one being taught.
51: 9 [A] **Awake**, awake! Clothe yourself with strength, O arm of the
51: 9 [A] Awake, **awake**! Clothe yourself with strength, O arm of the
51: 9 [A] **awake**, as in days gone by, as in generations of old.
51:17 [F] **Awake**, awake! Rise up, O Jerusalem, you who have drunk
51:17 [F] Awake, **awake**! Rise up, O Jerusalem, you who have drunk
52: 1 [A] **Awake**, awake, O Zion, clothe yourself with strength. Put on
52: 1 [A] Awake, **awake**, O Zion, clothe yourself with strength. Put on
64: 7 [64:6] [F] No one calls on your name or **strives** to lay hold of
Jer 6:22 [C] a great nation *is being* **stirred up** from the ends of the earth.
25:32 [C] a mighty storm *is* **rising** from the ends of the earth."
50: 9 [G] For I *will* **stir up** and bring against Babylon an alliance of
50:41 [C] many kings *are* **being stirred up** from the ends of the earth.
51: 1 [G] I *will* **stir up** the spirit of a destroyer against Babylon and the
51:11 [G] The LORD *has* **stirred up** the kings of the Medes,
Eze 23:22 [G] I *will* **stir up** your lovers against you, those you turned away
Da 11: 2 [G] *he will* **stir up** everyone against the kingdom of Greece.
11:25 [G] "With a large army *he will* **stir up** his strength and courage
Hos 7: 4 [G] burning like an oven whose fire the baker need not **stir** from
Joel 3: 7 [4:7] [G] I *am going to* **rouse** them out of the places to which
3: 9 [4:9] [G] the nations: Prepare for war! **Rouse** the warriors!
3:12 [4:12] [C] "*Let* the nations **be roused**; let them advance into the
Hab 2:19 [A] says to wood, 'Come to life!' Or to lifeless stone, '**Wake up**!'
Hag 1:14 [G] **stirred up** the spirit of Zerubbabel son of Shealtiel, governor
Zec 2:13 [2:17] [C] *he has* **roused himself** from his holy dwelling."
4: 1 [G] the angel who talked with me returned and **wakened** me,
4: 1 [C] and wakened me, as a man **is wakened** from his sleep.
9:13 [D] *I will* **rouse** your sons, O Zion, against your sons, O Greece,
13: 7 [A] "**Awake**, O sword, against my shepherd, against the man
Mal 2:12 [A] the man who does this, **whoever he may be** [+2256+6699],

6425 עוֹר *'ôr*, n.m. [99] [√ 6423?]

skin [39], leather [14], hides [13], hide [8], skin [+1414] [8], skins [6], *untranslated* [3], face [+7156] [3], body [1], flesh [1], goatskins [+1531+6436] [1], its[s] [+2021] [1], nothing but skin [+1414+2256] [1]

Ge 3:21 The LORD God made garments of **skin** for Adam and his wife
27:16 and the smooth part of his neck with the **goatskins** [+1531+6436].
Ex 22:27 [22:26] because his cloak is the only covering he has for his **body**.
25: 5 ram **skins** dyed red and hides of sea cows; acacia wood;
25: 5 ram skins dyed red and **hides** *of* sea cows; acacia wood;
26:14 Make for the tent a covering of ram **skins** dyed red, and over that a
26:14 ram skins dyed red, and over that a covering of **hides** *of* sea cows.
29:14 But burn the bull's flesh and its **hide** and its offal outside the camp.
34:29 he was not aware that his **face** [+7156] was radiant because he had
34:30 and all the Israelites saw Moses, his **face** [+7156] was radiant,
34:35 they saw that his **face** [+7156] was radiant. Then Moses would put
35: 7 ram **skins** dyed red and hides of sea cows; acacia wood;
35: 7 ram skins dyed red and **hides** *of* sea cows; acacia wood;
35:23 or goat hair, ram **skins** dyed red or hides of sea cows brought them.
35:23 or goat hair, ram skins dyed red or **hides** *of* sea cows brought them.
36:19 Then they made for the tent a covering of ram **skins** dyed red,
36:19 ram skins dyed red, and over that a covering of **hides** *of* sea cows.
39:34 the covering of ram **skins** dyed red, the covering of hides of sea
39:34 the covering of **hides** *of* sea cows and the shielding curtain;
Lev 4:11 But the **hide** *of* the bull and all its flesh, as well as the head
7: 8 offers a burnt offering for anyone may keep its **hide** for himself.
8:17 the bull with its **hide** and its flesh and its offal he burned up
9:11 the flesh and the **hide** he burned up outside the camp.
11:32 be unclean, whether it is made of wood, cloth, **hide** or sackcloth.
13: 2 or a bright spot on his **skin** [+1414] that may become an infectious
13: 2 or a bright spot on his skin that may become **[RPH]** an infectious
13: 3 The priest is to examine the sore on his **skin** [+1414], and if the
13: 3 and the sore appears to be more than **skin** [+1414] deep,
13: 4 If the spot on his **skin** [+1414] is white but does not appear to be
13: 4 on his skin is white but does not appear to be more than **skin** deep
13: 5 if he sees that the sore is unchanged and has not spread in the **skin**,
13: 6 if the sore has faded and has not spread in the **skin**, the priest shall
13: 7 if the rash does spread in his **skin** after he has shown himself to the
13: 8 The priest is to examine him, and if the rash has spread in the **skin**,
13:10 if there is a white swelling in the **skin** that has turned the hair white
13:11 skin disease **[RPH]** and the priest shall pronounce him unclean.
13:12 "If the disease breaks out all over his **skin** and, so far as the priest
13:12 it covers all the **skin** *of* the infected person from head to foot,
13:18 "When someone has a boil on his **skin** [+1414] and it heals,
13:20 if it appears to be more than **skin** deep and the hair in it has turned
13:21 no white hair in it and it is not more than **skin** deep and has faded,
13:22 If it is spreading in the **skin**, the priest shall pronounce him
13:24 "When someone has a burn on his **skin** [+1414] and a
13:25 in it has turned white, and it appears to be more than **skin** deep,
13:26 hair in the spot and if it is not more than **skin** deep and has faded,
13:27 if it is spreading in the **skin**, the priest shall pronounce him
13:28 the spot is unchanged and has not spread in the **skin** but has faded,
13:30 if it appears to be more than **skin** deep and the hair in it is yellow
13:31 it does not seem to be more than **skin** deep and there is no black
13:32 yellow hair in it and it does not appear to be more than **skin** deep,
13:34 if it has not spread in the **skin** and appears to be no more than skin
13:34 not spread in the skin and appears to be no more than **skin** deep,
13:35 But if the itch does spread in the **skin** after he is pronounced clean,
13:36 the priest is to examine him, and if the itch has spread in the **skin**,
13:38 "When a man or woman has white spots on the **skin** [+1414],
13:39 **[RPH]** it is a harmless rash that has broken out on the skin;
13:39 are dull white, it is a harmless rash that has broken out on the **skin**;
13:43 or forehead is reddish-white like an infectious **skin** [+1414]
13:48 of linen or wool, any **leather** or anything made of leather—
13:48 of linen or wool, any leather or anything made of **leather**—
13:49 or **leather**, or woven or knitted material, or any leather article,
13:49 or knitted material, or any **leather** article, is greenish or reddish,
13:51 or the woven or knitted material, or the **leather**, whatever its use,
13:51 or knitted material, or the leather, whatever **its**[s] [+2021] use,
13:52 or linen, or any **leather** article that has the contamination in it,
13:53 or the woven or knitted material, or the **leather** article,
13:56 out of the clothing, or the **leather**, or the woven or knitted material.
13:57 or knitted material, or in the **leather** article, it is spreading,
13:58 or any **leather** article that has been washed and is rid of the
13:59 or linen clothing, woven or knitted material, or any **leather** article,
15:17 or **leather** that has semen on it must be washed with water,
16:27 outside the camp; their **hides**, flesh and offal are to be burned up.
Nu 4: 6 they are to cover this with **hides** *of* sea cows, spread a cloth of
4: 8 cover that with **hides** *of* sea cows and put its poles in place.
4:10 to wrap it and all its accessories in a covering of **hides** *of* sea cows
4:11 and cover that with **hides** *of* sea cows and put its poles in place.
4:12 cover that with **hides** *of* sea cows and put them on a carrying
4:14 Over it they are to spread a covering of **hides** *of* sea cows
19: 5 the heifer is to be burned—its **hide**, flesh, blood and offal.
31:20 Purify every garment as well as everything made of **leather**,
2Ki 1: 8 with a garment of hair and with a **leather** belt around his waist."
Job 2: 4 "**Skin** for skin!" Satan replied. "A man will give all he has for his
2: 4 "Skin for **skin**!" Satan replied. "A man will give all he has for his
7: 5 is clothed with worms and scabs, my **skin** is broken and festering.
10:11 clothe me with **skin** and flesh and knit me together with bones
18:13 It eats away parts of his **skin**; death's firstborn devours his limbs.
19:20 I am **nothing but skin** [+1414+2256] and bones; I have escaped

Job 19:20 and bones; I have escaped with only the **skin** *of* my teeth.
19:26 after my **skin** has been destroyed, yet in my flesh I will see God;
30:30 My **skin** grows black and peels; my body burns with fever.
41: 7 [40:31] Can you fill his **hide** with harpoons or his head with
Jer 13:23 Can the Ethiopian change his **skin** or the leopard its spots?
La 3: 4 He has made my skin and my **flesh** grow old and has broken my
4: 8 Their **skin** has shriveled on their bones; it has become as dry as a
5:10 Our **skin** is hot as an oven, feverish from hunger.
Eze 37: 6 to you and make flesh come upon you and cover you with **skin**;
37: 8 and tendons and flesh appeared on them and **skin** covered them,
Mic 3: 2 who tear the **skin** from my people and the flesh from their bones;
3: 3 people's flesh, strip off their **skin** and break their bones in pieces;

6426 עִוֵּר *ʿiwwēr*, a. [26] [√ 6422]

blind [26]

Ex 4:11 him deaf or mute? Who gives him sight or makes him **blind**?
Lev 19:14 not curse the deaf or put a stumbling block in front of the **blind**,
21:18 come near: no man who is **blind** or lame, disfigured or deformed;
Dt 15:21 If an animal has a defect, is lame or **blind**, or has any serious flaw,
27:18 "Cursed is the man who leads the **blind** astray on the road."
28:29 At midday you will grope about like a **blind** *man* in the dark.
2Sa 5: 6 will not get in here; even the **blind** and the lame can ward you off."
5: 8 shaft to reach those 'lame and **blind**' who are David's enemies."
5: 8 is why they say, "The '**blind** and lame' will not enter the palace."
Job 29:15 I was eyes to the **blind** and feet to the lame.
Ps 146: 8 the LORD gives sight to the **blind**, the LORD lifts up those who
Isa 29:18 and out of gloom and darkness the eyes of the **blind** will see.
35: 5 will the eyes of the **blind** be opened and the ears of the deaf
42: 7 to open eyes that are **blind**, to free captives from prison and to
42:16 I will lead the **blind** by ways they have not known,
42:18 "Hear, you deaf; look, you **blind**, and see!
42:19 Who is **blind** but my servant, and deaf like the messenger I send?
42:19 Who is **blind** like the one committed to me, blind like the servant
42:19 the one committed to me, **blind** like the servant of the LORD?
43: 8 Lead out those who have eyes but are **blind**, who have ears
56:10 Israel's watchmen are **blind**, they all lack knowledge; they are all
59:10 Like the **blind** we grope along the wall, feeling our way like men
Jer 31: 8 Among them will be the **blind** and the lame, expectant mothers
La 4:14 Now they grope through the streets like *men who* are **blind**.
Zep 1:17 will bring distress on the people and they will walk like **blind** *men*,
Mal 1: 8 When you bring **blind** *animals* for sacrifice, is that not wrong?

6427 עִוָּרוֹן *ʿiwwārôn*, n.[m.] [2] [√ 6422]

blind [+928+2021+5782] [1], blindness [1]

Dt 28:28 will afflict you with madness, **blindness** and confusion of mind.
Zec 12: 4 but *I will* **blind** [+928+2021+5782] all the horses of the nations.

6428 עַוֶּרֶת *ʿawweret*, n.f. [1] [√ 6422]

blind [1]

Lev 22:22 Do not offer to the LORD the **blind**, the injured or the maimed,

6429 עוּשׁ *ʿûš*, v. [1] [→ 3447, 3593, 3601; cf. 6431]

quickly [1]

Joel 3:11 [4:11] [A] Come **quickly**, all you nations from every side,

6430 עָוַת *ʿāwat*, v. [11] [→ 6432]

pervert [3], cheating [1], deprive [1], frustrates [1], is twisted [1], made crooked [1], stoop [1], wronged [1], wronging [1]

Job 8: 3 [D] *Does* God **pervert** justice? Does the Almighty pervert what
8: 3 [D] pervert justice? *Does* the Almighty **pervert** what is right?
19: 6 [D] know that God *has* **wronged** me and drawn his net around
34:12 [D] would do wrong, that the Almighty *would* **pervert** justice.
Ps 119:78 [D] May the arrogant be put to shame for **wronging** me without
146: 9 [D] and the widow, but *he* **frustrates** the ways of the wicked.
Ecc 1:15 [E] *What* **is twisted** cannot be straightened; what is lacking
7:13 [D] has done: Who can straighten what *he has* **made crooked**?
12: 3 [F] the strong men **stoop**, when the grinders cease because they
La 3:36 [D] to **deprive** a man of justice—would not the Lord see such
Am 8: 5 [D] boosting the price and **cheating** *with* dishonest scales,

6431 עוּת *ʿût*, v. [1] [√ 6433; cf. 6429]

sustains [1]

Isa 50: 4 [A] instructed tongue, to know the word *that* **sustains** the weary.

6432 עַוָּתָה *ʿawwātâ*, n.f. [1] [√ 6430]

wrong done [1]

La 3:59 You have seen, O LORD, the **wrong done** *to* me. Uphold my

6433 עוּתַי *ʿûtay*, n.pr.m. [2] [√ 6431]

Uthai [2]

1Ch 9: 4 **Uthai** son of Ammihud, the son of Omri, the son of Imri, the son
Ezr 8:14 descendants of Bigvai, **Uthai** and Zaccur, and with them 70 men.

6434 עַז *ʿaz*, a. [23] [→ 6456?; cf. 6451]

strong [5], mighty [4], fierce [3], powerful [3], fierce-looking [+7156] [1], fortified [1], great [1], harshly [1], stern-faced [+7156] [1], strength [1], stronger [1], stronghold [1]

Ge 49: 7 Cursed be their anger, so **fierce**, and their fury, so cruel! I will
Ex 14:21 all that night the LORD drove the sea back with a **strong** east
Nu 13:28 the people who live there are **powerful**, and the cities are fortified
21:24 only as far as the Ammonites, because their border was **fortified**.
Dt 28:50 a **fierce-looking** [+7156] nation without respect for the old
Jdg 14:14 of the eater, something to eat; out of the **strong**, something sweet."
14:18 What is **stronger** than a lion?" Samson said to them, "If you had
2Sa 22:18 He rescued me from my **powerful** enemy, from my foes, who were
Ne 9:11 their pursuers into the depths, like a stone into **mighty** waters.
Ps 18:17 [18:18] He rescued me from my **powerful** enemy, from my foes,
59: 3 [59:4] **Fierce** *men* conspire against me for no offense or sin of
Pr 18:23 A poor man pleads for mercy, but a rich man answers **harshly**.
21:14 and a bribe concealed in the cloak pacifies **great** wrath.
30:25 Ants are creatures of little **strength**, yet they store up their food in
SS 8: 6 for love is as **strong** as death, its jealousy unyielding as the grave.
Isa 19: 4 a **fierce** king will rule over them," declares the Lord, the LORD
25: 3 Therefore **strong** peoples will honor you; cities of ruthless nations
26: 1 We have a **strong** city; God makes salvation its walls
43:16 made a way through the sea, a path through the **mighty** waters,
56:11 They are dogs with **mighty** appetites; they never have enough.
Eze 7:24 I will put an end to the pride of the **mighty**, and their sanctuaries
Da 8:23 a **stern-faced** [+7156] king, a master of intrigue, will arise.
Am 5: 9 he flashes destruction on the **stronghold** and brings the fortified

6435 עָז *ʿāz*, n.m. [1] [√ 6451]

power [1]

Ge 49: 3 first sign of my strength, excelling in honor, excelling in **power**.

6436 עֵז *ʿēz*, n.m. [74] [√ 6451?; Ar 10535]

male goat [+8538] [24], goats [12], goat [8], goat hair [7], young goat [+1531] [7], goat [+7618] [2], goat [+8538] [2], goat [+8544] [2], goats hair [+3889] [2], male goats [+8538] [2], goat [+8445] [1], goats [+1201] [1], goatskins [+1531+6425] [1], male goats [+7618] [1], young goat [1], young goats [+1531] [1]

Ge 15: 9 "Bring me a heifer, a **goat** and a ram, each three years old,
27: 9 Go out to the flock and bring me two choice **young goats** [+1531],
27:16 and the smooth part of his neck with the **goatskins** [+1531+6425].
30:32 every dark-colored lamb and every spotted or speckled **goat**.
30:33 Any **goat** in my possession that is not speckled or spotted,
30:35 the speckled or spotted female **goats** (all that had white on them)
31:38 Your sheep and **goats** have not miscarried, nor have I eaten rams
32:14 [32:15] two hundred female **goats** and twenty male goats,
37:31 slaughtered a **goat** [+8538] and dipped the robe in the blood.
38:17 "I'll send you a **young goat** [+1531] from my flock," he said.
38:20 Meanwhile Judah sent the **young goat** [+1531] by his friend the
Ex 12: 5 and you may take them from the sheep or the **goats**.
25: 4 blue, purple and scarlet yarn and fine linen; **goat hair**;
26: 7 "Make curtains of **goat hair** for the tent over the tabernacle—
35: 6 blue, purple and scarlet yarn and fine linen; **goat hair**;
35:23 purple or scarlet yarn or fine linen, or **goat hair**, ram skins dyed
35:26 the women who were willing and had the skill spun the **goat hair**.
36:14 They made curtains of **goat hair** for the tent over the tabernacle—
Lev 1:10 from either the sheep or the **goats**, he is to offer a male without
3:12 " 'If his offering is a **goat**, he is to present it before the LORD.
4:23 he must bring as his offering a male **goat** [+8538] without defect.
4:28 for the sin he committed a female **goat** [+8544] without defect.
5: 6 a female lamb or **goat** [+8544] from the flock as a sin offering;
7:23 to the Israelites: 'Do not eat any of the fat of cattle, sheep or **goats**.
9: 3 'Take a **male goat** [+8538] for a sin offering, a calf and a lamb—
16: 5 From the Israelite community he is to take two **male goats** [+8538]
17: 3 who sacrifices an ox, a lamb or a **goat** in the camp or outside of it
22:19 sheep or **goats** in order that it may be accepted on your behalf.
22:27 "When a calf, a lamb or a **goat** is born, it is to remain with its
23:19 sacrifice one **male goat** [+8538] for a sin offering and two lambs,
Nu 7:16 one **male goat** [+8538] for a sin offering;
7:22 one **male goat** [+8538] for a sin offering;
7:28 one **male goat** [+8538] for a sin offering;
7:34 one **male goat** [+8538] for a sin offering;
7:40 one **male goat** [+8538] for a sin offering;
7:46 one **male goat** [+8538] for a sin offering;
7:52 one **male goat** [+8538] for a sin offering;
7:58 one **male goat** [+8538] for a sin offering;

Nu 7:64 one **male goat** [+8538] for a sin offering;
7:70 one **male goat** [+8538] for a sin offering;
7:76 one **male goat** [+8538] for a sin offering;
7:82 one **male goat** [+8538] for a sin offering;
7:87 Twelve **male goats** [+8538] were used for the sin offering.
15:11 Each bull or ram, each lamb or **young goat**, is to be prepared in
15:24 and drink offering, and a **male goat** [+8538] for a sin offering.
15:27 he must bring a year-old female **goat** for a sin offering.
18:17 "But you must not redeem the firstborn of an ox, a sheep or a **goat**;
28:15 one **male goat** [+8538] is to be presented to the LORD as a sin
28:30 Include one **male goat** [+8538] to make atonement for you.
29:5 Include one **male goat** [+8538] as a sin offering to make
29:11 Include one **male goat** [+8538] as a sin offering, in addition to the
29:16 Include one **male goat** [+8538] as a sin offering, in addition to the
29:19 Include one **male goat** [+8538] as a sin offering, in addition to the
29:25 Include one **male goat** [+8538] as a sin offering, in addition to the
31:20 garment as well as everything made of leather, **goat hair** or wood."
Dt 14:4 are the animals you may eat: the ox, the sheep, the **goat** [+8445],
Jdg 6:19 Gideon went in, prepared a **young goat** [+1531], and from an
13:15 "We would like you to stay until we prepare a **young goat** [+1531]
13:19 Manoah took a **young goat** [+1531], together with the grain
15:1 Samson took a **young goat** [+1531] and went to visit his wife.
1Sa 16:20 a skin of wine and a **young goat** [+1531] and sent them with his
19:13 it with a garment and putting some **goats** [+3889]' **hair** at the head.
19:16 the idol in the bed, and at the head was some **goats** [+3889]' **hair**.
25:2 He had a thousand **goats** and three thousand sheep, which he was
1Ki 20:27 Israelites camped opposite them like two small flocks of **goats**,
2Ch 29:21 and seven **male goats** [+7618] as a sin offering for the kingdom,
35:7 thirty thousand sheep and **goats** [+1201] for the Passover offerings,
Pr 27:27 You will have plenty of **goats**' milk to feed you and your family
SS 4:1 Your hair is like a flock of **goats** descending from Mount Gilead.
6:5 Your hair is like a flock of **goats** descending from Gilead.
Eze 43:22 "On the second day you are to offer a **male goat** [+8538] without
45:23 offering to the LORD, and a **male goat** [+8538] for a sin offering.
Da 8:5 suddenly a **goat** [+7618] with a prominent horn between his eyes
8:8 The **goat** [+7618] became very great, but at the height of his power

6437 עֹז *'ōz*, n.m. [92 / 93] [→ 6454, 6459, 6460; cf. 6395, 6451]

strength [38], strong [12], power [11], mighty [8], might [6], fortified [3], stronghold [3], praise [2], feeble [+4202] [1], firm [1], fortress [1], great power [1], great [1], hard [1], stouthearted [+5883] [1], strongholds [1], stubborn [1], vigorously [+928] [1]

Ex 15:2 The LORD is my **strength** and my song; he has become my
15:13 In your **strength** you will guide them to your holy dwelling.
Lev 26:19 I will break down your **stubborn** pride and make the sky above
Jdg 5:21 the age-old river, the river Kishon. March on, my soul; be **strong**!
9:51 Inside the city, however, was a **strong** tower, to which all the men
1Sa 2:10 "He will give **strength** to his king and exalt the horn of his
2Sa 6:5 celebrating with all their **might** [BHS 6770] before the LORD,
6:14 a linen ephod, danced before the LORD with all his **might**,
1Ch 13:8 all the Israelites were celebrating with all their **might** before God,
16:11 Look to the LORD and his **strength**; seek his face always.
16:27 and majesty are before him; **strength** and joy in his dwelling place.
16:28 O families of nations, ascribe to the LORD glory and **strength**,
2Ch 6:41 and come to your resting place, you and the ark of your **might**.
30:21 every day, accompanied by the LORD's instruments of **praise**.
Ezr 8:22 looks to him, but his **great** anger is against all who forsake him."
Job 12:16 To him belong **strength** and victory; both deceived and deceiver
26:2 the powerless! How you have saved the arm that is **feeble** [+4202]!
37:6 and to the rain shower, 'Be a **mighty** downpour.'
41:22 [41:14] **Strength** resides in his neck; dismay goes before him.
Ps 8:2 [8:3] the lips of children and infants you have ordained **praise**
21:1 [21:2] O LORD, the king rejoices in your **strength**. How great is
21:13 [21:14] Be exalted, O LORD, in your **strength**; we will sing
28:7 The LORD is my **strength** and my shield; my heart trusts in him,
28:8 The LORD is the **strength** of his people, a fortress of salvation
29:1 O mighty ones, ascribe to the LORD glory and **strength**.
29:11 The LORD gives **strength** to his people; the LORD blesses his
30:7 [30:8] when you favored me, you made my mountain stand **firm**;
46:1 [46:2] God is our refuge and **strength**, an ever-present help in
59:9 [59:10] O my **Strength**, I watch for you; you, O God, are my
59:16 [59:17] I will sing of your **strength**, in the morning I will sing of
59:17 [59:18] O my **Strength**, I sing praise to you; you, O God, are my
61:3 [61:4] you have been my refuge, a **strong** tower against the foe.
62:7 [62:8] honor depend on God; he is my **mighty** rock, my refuge.
62:11 [62:12] two things have I heard: that you, O God, are **strong**,
63:2 [63:3] in the sanctuary and beheld your **power** and your glory.
66:3 So great is your **power** that your enemies cringe before you.
68:28 [68:29] Summon your **power**, O God; show us your strength,
68:33 [68:34] the ancient skies above, who thunders with **mighty** voice.
68:34 [68:35] Proclaim the **power** of God, whose majesty is over Israel,
68:34 [68:35] whose majesty is over Israel, whose **power** is in the skies.
68:35 [68:36] the God of Israel gives **power** and strength to his people.
71:7 have become like a portent to many, but you are my **strong** refuge.
74:13 It was you who split open the sea by your **power**; you broke the
77:14 [77:15] you display your **power** among the peoples.
78:26 wind from the heavens and led forth the south wind by his **power**.
78:61 He sent ⌞the ark of⌟ his **might** into captivity, his splendor into the
81:1 [81:2] Sing for joy to God our **strength**; shout aloud to the God of
84:5 [84:6] Blessed are those whose **strength** is in you, who have set
86:16 grant your **strength** to your servant and save the son of your
89:10 [89:11] with your **strong** arm you scattered your enemies.
89:17 [89:18] For you are their glory and **strength**, and by your favor
90:11 Who knows the **power** *of* your anger? For your wrath is as great as
93:1 the LORD is robed in majesty and is armed with **strength**.
96:6 majesty are before him; **strength** and glory are in his sanctuary.
96:7 O families of nations, ascribe to the LORD glory and **strength**.
99:4 The King is **mighty**, he loves justice—you have established equity;
105:4 Look to the LORD and his **strength**; seek his face always.
110:2 The LORD will extend your **mighty** scepter from Zion; you will
118:14 The LORD is my **strength** and my song; he has become my
132:8 and come to your resting place, you and the ark of your **might**.
138:3 you answered me; you made me bold and **stouthearted** [+5883].
140:7 [140:8] O Sovereign LORD, my **strong** deliverer, who shields
150:1 Praise God in his sanctuary; praise him in his **mighty** heavens.
Pr 10:15 The wealth of the rich is their **fortified** city, but poverty is the ruin
14:26 He who fears the LORD has a secure **fortress**, and for his
18:10 The name of the LORD is a **strong** tower; the righteous run to it
18:11 The wealth of the rich is their **fortified** city; they imagine it an
18:19 An offended brother is more unyielding than a **fortified** city,
21:22 of the mighty and pulls down the **stronghold** in which they trust.
24:5 A wise man has **great power**, and a man of knowledge increases
31:17 She sets about her work **vigorously** [+928]; her arms are strong for
31:25 She is clothed with **strength** and dignity; she can laugh at the days
Ecc 8:1 Wisdom brightens a man's face and changes its **hard** appearance.
Isa 12:2 The LORD, the LORD, is my **strength** and my song; he has
45:24 and **strength**.' " All who have raged against him will come to him
49:5 in the eyes of the LORD and my God has been my **strength**—
51:9 Clothe yourself with **strength**, O arm of the LORD; awake,
52:1 Awake, awake, O Zion, clothe yourself with **strength**. Put on your
62:8 The LORD has sworn by his right hand and by his **mighty** arm:
Jer 16:19 O LORD, my **strength** and my fortress, my refuge in time of
48:17 say, 'How broken is the **mighty** scepter, how broken the glorious
51:53 Even if Babylon reaches the sky and fortifies her lofty **stronghold**,
Eze 19:11 Its branches were **strong**, fit for a ruler's scepter. It towered high
19:12 of its fruit; its **strong** branches withered and fire consumed them.
19:14 No **strong** branch is left on it fit for a ruler's scepter.' This is a
24:21 the **stronghold** *in which* you take pride, the delight of your eyes,
26:11 with the sword, and your **strong** pillars will fall to the ground.
30:6 " 'The allies of Egypt will fall and her proud **strength** will fail.
30:18 the yoke of Egypt; there her proud **strength** will come to an end.
33:28 land a desolate waste, and her proud **strength** will come to an end,
Am 3:11 he will pull down your **strongholds** and plunder your fortresses."
Mic 5:4 [5:3] and shepherd his flock in the **strength** *of* the LORD,
Hab 3:4 rays flashed from his hand, where his **power** was hidden.

6438 עֻזָּא *'uzzā'*, n.pr.m. [11] [→ 6446]

Uzzah [6], Uzza [5]

2Sa 6:3 **Uzzah** and Ahio, sons of Abinadab, were guiding the new cart
6:6 **Uzzah** reached out and took hold of the ark of God, because the
2Ki 21:18 and was buried in his palace garden, the garden of **Uzza**.
21:26 He was buried in his grave in the garden of **Uzza**. And Josiah his
1Ch 8:7 who deported them and who was the father of **Uzza** and Ahihud.
13:7 Abinadab's house on a new cart, with **Uzzah** and Ahio guiding it.
13:9 **Uzzah** reached out his hand to steady the ark, because the oxen
13:10 The LORD's anger burned against **Uzzah**, and he struck him
13:11 because the LORD's wrath had broken out against **Uzzah**,
Ezr 2:49 **Uzza**, Paseah, Besai,
Ne 7:51 Gazzam, **Uzza**, Paseah,

6439 עֲזָאזֵל *'ᵃzā'zēl*, n.[m. *or* pr.]. [4]

scapegoat [4]

Lev 16:8 two goats—one lot for the LORD and the other for the **scapegoat**.
16:10 the goat chosen by lot as the **scapegoat** shall be presented alive
16:10 for making atonement by sending it into the desert as a **scapegoat**.
16:26 "The man who releases the goat as a **scapegoat** must wash his

6440 עָזַב¹ *'āzab¹*, v. [212] [→ 6442, 6447, 6448]

forsake [37], forsaken [34], leave [28], left [19], abandoned [18], deserted [11], forsook [8], abandon [6], forsaking [5], free [5], rejected [4], neglect [3], desert [2], deserts [2], fails [2], leaves [2], rejecting [2], be abandoned [1], be laid waste [1], be left [1], been abandoned [1], change [1], commits [1], disregarded [1], forfeit [1], forsakes [1], gave up [1], give free rein [1], give up [1], go [1], ignores

[1], is forsaken [1], is neglected [1], lays [1], left behind [1], left destitute [1], renounces [1], stop [1], stopped showing [1], turn from [1], vanish [1]

Ge 2:24 [A] For this reason a man *will* **leave** his father and mother and be
24:27 [A] who *has* not **abandoned** his kindness and faithfulness to my
28:15 [A] *I will* not **leave** you until I have done what I have promised
39:6 [A] So *he* **left** in Joseph's care everything he had; with Joseph in
39:12 [A] But *he* **left** his cloak in her hand and ran out of the house.
39:13 [A] When she saw that *he had* **left** his cloak in her hand and had
39:15 [A] *he* **left** his cloak beside me and ran out of the house."
39:18 [A] *he* **left** his cloak beside me and ran out of the house."
44:22 [A] And we said to my lord, 'The boy cannot **leave** his father;
44:22 [A] cannot leave his father; if *he* **leaves** him, his father will die.'
50:8 [A] their children and their flocks and herds *were* **left** in Goshen.
Ex 2:20 [A] is he?" he asked his daughters. "Why *did you* **leave** him?
9:21 [A] who ignored the word of the LORD **left** their slaves and
23:5 [A] hates you fallen down under its load, do not **leave** it there;
Lev 19:10 [A] **Leave** them for the poor and the alien. I am the LORD your
23:22 [A] **Leave** them for the poor and the alien. I am the LORD
26:43 [C] For the land *will be* **deserted** by them and will enjoy its
Nu 10:31 [A] Moses said, "Please *do* not **leave** us. You know where we
Dt 12:19 [A] Be careful not *to* **neglect** the Levites as long as you live in
14:27 [A] *do* not **neglect** the Levites living in your towns, for they have
28:20 [A] because of the evil you have done *in* **forsaking** him.
29:25 [29:24] [A] because this people **abandoned** the covenant of the
31:6 [A] goes with you; he will never leave you nor **forsake** you."
31:8 [A] will be with you; he will never leave you nor **forsake** you.
31:16 [A] *They will* **forsake** me and break the covenant I made with
31:17 [A] that day I will become angry with them and **forsake** them;
32:36 [B] he sees their strength is gone and no one is left, slave or **free**.
Jos 1:5 [A] so I will be with you; I will never leave you nor **forsake** you.
8:17 [A] *They* **left** the city open and went in pursuit of Israel.
22:3 [A] *you have* not **deserted** your brothers but have carried out the
24:16 [A] "Far be it from us *to* **forsake** the LORD to serve other
24:20 [A] If *you* **forsake** the LORD and serve foreign gods, he will
Jdg 2:12 [A] *They* **forsook** the LORD, the God of their fathers, who had
2:13 [A] because *they* **forsook** him and served Baal and the
2:21 [A] out before them any of the nations Joshua **left** when he died.
10:6 [A] because the Israelites **forsook** the LORD and no longer
10:10 [A] against you, **forsaking** our God and serving the Baals."
10:13 [A] you *have* **forsaken** me and served other gods, so I will no
Ru 1:16 [A] "Don't urge me to **leave** you or to turn back from you.
2:11 [A] how *you* **left** your father and mother and your homeland
2:16 [A] for her from the bundles and **leave** them for her to pick up,
2:20 [A] "He *has* not **stopped showing** his kindness *to* the living and
1Sa 8:8 [A] **forsaking** me and serving other gods, so they are doing to
12:10 [A] *we have* **forsaken** the LORD and served the Baals and the
30:13 [A] My master **abandoned** me when I became ill three days ago.
31:7 [A] and his sons had died, *they* **abandoned** their towns and fled.
2Sa 5:21 [A] The Philistines **abandoned** their idols there, and David
15:16 [A] but he **left** ten concubines to take care of the palace.
1Ki 6:13 [A] among the Israelites and *will* not **abandon** my people Israel."
8:57 [A] was with our fathers; *may he* never **leave** us nor forsake us.
9:9 [A] 'Because *they have* **forsaken** the LORD their God,
11:33 [A] I will do this because *they have* **forsaken** me and worshiped
12:8 [A] Rehoboam **rejected** the advice the elders gave him
12:13 [A] people harshly. **Rejecting** the advice given him by the elders,
14:10 [B] off from Jeroboam every last male in Israel—slave or **free**.
18:18 [A] You *have* **abandoned** the LORD's commands and have
19:10 [A] The Israelites *have* **rejected** your covenant, broken down
19:14 [A] The Israelites *have* **rejected** your covenant, broken down
19:20 [A] Elisha then **left** his oxen and ran after Elijah. "Let me kiss
21:21 [B] cut off from Ahab every last male in Israel—slave or **free**.
2Ki 2:2 [A] as the LORD lives and as you live, *I will* not **leave** you."
2:4 [A] as the LORD lives and as you live, *I will* not **leave** you."
2:6 [A] as the LORD lives and as you live, *I will* not **leave** you."
4:30 [A] as the LORD lives and as you live, *I will* not **leave** you."
7:7 [A] and **abandoned** their tents and their horses and donkeys.
8:6 [A] including all the income from her land from the day *she* **left**
9:8 [B] cut off from Ahab every last male in Israel—slave or **free**.
14:26 [B] everyone in Israel, whether slave or **free**, was suffering;
17:16 [A] *They* **forsook** all the commands of the LORD their God
21:22 [A] *He* **forsook** the LORD, the God of his fathers, and did not
22:17 [A] Because *they have* **forsaken** me and burned incense to other
1Ch 10:7 [A] and his sons had died, *they* **abandoned** their towns and fled.
14:12 [A] The Philistines *had* **abandoned** their gods there, and David
16:37 [A] David **left** Asaph and his associates before the ark of the
28:9 [A] by you; but if *you* **forsake** him, he will reject you forever.
28:20 [A] or **forsake** you until all the work for the service of the temple
2Ch 7:19 [A] "But if you turn away and **forsake** the decrees
7:22 [A] will answer, 'Because *they have* **forsaken** the LORD,
10:8 [A] Rehoboam **rejected** the advice the elders gave him
10:13 [A] answered them harshly. **Rejecting** the advice of the elders,
11:14 [A] The Levites even **abandoned** their pasturelands
12:1 [A] *he* and all Israel with him **abandoned** the law of the LORD.
12:5 [A] "This is what the LORD says, 'You *have* **abandoned** me;
12:5 [A] abandoned me; therefore, I now **abandon** you to Shishak.' "
13:10 [A] the LORD is our God, and *we have* not **forsaken** him.
13:11 [A] of the LORD our God. But you *have* **forsaken** him.
15:2 [A] be found by you, but if *you* **forsake** him, he will forsake you.
15:2 [A] be found by you, but if you forsake him, *he will* **forsake** you.
21:10 [A] because Jehoram *had* **forsaken** the LORD, the God of his
24:18 [A] *They* **abandoned** the temple of the LORD, the God of their
24:20 [A] Because *you have* **forsaken** the LORD, he has forsaken
24:20 [A] you have forsaken the LORD, *he has* **forsaken** you.' "
24:24 [A] Because Judah *had* **forsaken** the LORD, the God of their
24:25 [A] the Arameans withdrew, *they* **left** Joash severely wounded.
28:6 [A] because Judah *had* **forsaken** the LORD, the God of their
28:14 [A] So the soldiers **gave up** the prisoners and plunder in the
29:6 [A] did evil in the eyes of the LORD our God and **forsook** him.
32:31 [A] God **left** him to test him and to know everything that was in
34:25 [A] Because *they have* **forsaken** me and burned incense to other
Ezr 8:22 [A] to him, but his great anger is against all *who* **forsake** him."
9:9 [A] we are slaves, our God *has* not **deserted** us in our bondage.
9:10 [A] we say after this? For *we have* **disregarded** the commands
Ne 5:10 [A] people money and grain. But *let* the exacting of usury **stop**!
9:17 [A] and abounding in love. Therefore *you did* not **desert** them,
9:19 [A] "Because of your great compassion you *did* not **abandon**
9:28 [A] *you* **abandoned** them to the hand of their enemies so that
9:31 [A] mercy you did not put an end to them or **abandon** them,
10:39 [10:40] [A] "*We will* not **neglect** the house of our God."
13:11 [C] and asked them, "Why **is** the house of God **neglected**?"
Job 6:14 [A] even though *he* **forsakes** the fear of the Almighty.
9:27 [A] my complaint, *I will* **change** my expression, and smile,'
10:1 [A] therefore *I will* **give free rein** to my complaint and speak out
18:4 [C] in your anger, *is* the earth *to* **be abandoned** for your sake?
20:13 [A] though he cannot bear *to let* it **go** and keeps it in his mouth,
20:19 [A] For he has oppressed the poor and **left** them **destitute**; he has
39:11 [A] his great strength? *Will you* **leave** your heavy work to him?
39:14 [A] *She* **lays** her eggs on the ground and lets them warm in the
Ps 9:10 [9:11] [A] for *you*, LORD, *have* never **forsaken** those who
10:14 [A] The victim **commits** *himself* to you; you are the helper of the
16:10 [A] because *you will* not **abandon** me to the grave, nor will you
22:1 [22:2] [A] My God, my God, why *have you* **forsaken** me?
27:9 [A] Do not reject me or **forsake** me, O God my Savior.
27:10 [A] Though my father and mother **forsake** me, the LORD will
37:8 [A] Refrain from anger and **turn from** wrath; do not fret—
37:25 [C] yet I have never seen the righteous **forsaken** or their children
37:28 [A] LORD loves the just and *will* not **forsake** his faithful ones.
37:33 [A] the LORD *will* not **leave** them in their power or let them be
38:10 [38:11] [A] My heart pounds, my strength **fails** me;
38:21 [38:22] [A] O LORD, *do* not **forsake** me; be not far from me,
40:12 [40:13] [A] the hairs of my head, and my heart **fails** *within* me.
49:10 [49:11] [A] alike perish and **leave** their wealth to others.
71:9 [A] when I am old; *do* not **forsake** me when my strength is gone.
71:11 [A] They say, "God *has* **forsaken** him; pursue him and seize
71:18 [A] Even when I am old and gray, *do* not **forsake** me, O God,
89:30 [89:31] [A] "If his sons **forsake** my law and do not follow my
94:14 [A] not reject his people; *he will* never **forsake** his inheritance.
119:8 [A] I will obey your decrees; *do* not utterly **forsake** me.
119:53 [A] because of the wicked, *who have* **forsaken** your law.
119:87 [A] me from the earth, but I *have* not **forsaken** your precepts.
Pr 2:13 [A] who **leave** the straight paths to walk in dark ways,
2:17 [A] who *has* **left** the partner of her youth and ignored the
3:3 [A] *Let* love and faithfulness never **leave** you; bind them around
4:2 [A] I give you sound learning, so *do* not **forsake** my teaching.
4:6 [A] *Do* not **forsake** wisdom, and she will protect you; love her,
9:6 [A] **Leave** your simple ways and you will live; walk in the way
10:17 [A] to life, but *whoever* **ignores** correction leads others astray.
15:10 [A] Stern discipline awaits *him who* **leaves** the path; he who
27:10 [A] *Do* not **forsake** your friend and the friend of your father,
28:4 [A] *Those who* **forsake** the law praise the wicked, but those who
28:13 [A] but whoever confesses and **renounces** them finds mercy.
Isa 1:4 [A] *They have* **forsaken** the LORD; they have spurned the
1:28 [A] be broken, and *those who* **forsake** the LORD will perish.
6:12 [B] has sent everyone far away and the land **is** utterly **forsaken**.
7:16 [C] the land of the two kings you dread *will* **be laid waste**.
10:3 [A] will you run for help? Where *will you* **leave** your riches?
10:14 [B] as men gather **abandoned** eggs, so I gathered all the
17:2 [B] The cities of Aroer *will be* **deserted** and left to flocks, which
17:9 [A] their strong cities, which *they* **left** because of the Israelites,
17:9 [B] will be like *places* **abandoned** *to* thickets and undergrowth.
18:6 [C] *They will* all **be left** to the mountain birds of prey and to the
27:10 [C] an abandoned settlement, **forsaken** like the desert;
32:14 [E] The fortress will be abandoned, the noisy city **deserted**;
41:17 [A] will answer them; *I*, the God of Israel, *will* not **forsake** them.
42:16 [A] These are the things I will do; *I will* not **forsake** them.

Isa 49: 14 [A] Zion said, "The LORD *has* **forsaken** me, the Lord has
54: 6 [B] LORD will call you back as if you were a wife **deserted**
54: 7 [A] "For a brief moment *I* **abandoned** you, but with deep
55: 7 [A] *Let* the wicked **forsake** his way and the evil man his
58: 2 [A] what is right and *has* not **forsaken** the commands of its God.
60: 15 [B] "Although you have been **forsaken** and hated, with no one
62: 4 [B] No longer will they call you **Deserted**, or name your land
62: 12 [C] will be called Sought After, the City No *Longer* **Deserted**.
65: 11 [A] "But as for you *who* **forsake** the LORD and forget my holy
Jer 1: 16 [A] on my people because of their wickedness *in* **forsaking** me,
2: 13 [A] *They have* **forsaken** me, the spring of living water, and have
2: 17 [A] Have you not brought this on yourselves *by* **forsaking** the
2: 19 [A] bitter it is for you *when* you **forsake** the LORD your God
4: 29 [B] the rocks. All the towns *are* **deserted**; no one lives in them.
5: 7 [A] Your children *have* **forsaken** me and sworn by gods that are
5: 19 [A] 'As *you have* **forsaken** me and served foreign gods in your
9: 2 [9:1] [A] that *I might* **leave** my people and go away from them;
9: 13 [9:12] [A] "It is because they *have* **forsaken** my law,
9: 19 [9:18] [A] *We must* **leave** our land because our houses are in
12: 7 [A] "*I will* **forsake** my house, abandon my inheritance; I will
14: 5 [A] Even the doe in the field **deserts** her newborn fawn
16: 11 [A] say to them, 'It is because your fathers **forsook** me,'
16: 11 [A] worshiped them. *They* **forsook** me and did not keep my law.
17: 11 [A] When his life is half gone, *they will* **desert** him, and in the
17: 13 [A] the hope of Israel, all *who* **forsake** you will be put to shame.
17: 13 [A] written in the dust because *they have* **forsaken** the LORD,
18: 14 [A] *Does* the snow of Lebanon *ever* **vanish** from its rocky
19: 4 [A] For *they have* **forsaken** me and made this a place of foreign
22: 9 [A] 'Because *they have* **forsaken** the covenant of the LORD
25: 38 [A] Like a lion *he will* **leave** his lair, and their land will become
48: 28 [A] **Abandon** your towns and dwell among the rocks, you who
49: 11 [A] **Leave** your orphans; I will protect their lives. Your widows
49: 25 [E] Why *has* the city of renown not **been abandoned**, the town
51: 9 [A] *let us* **leave** her and each go to his own land, for her
La 5: 20 [A] do you always forget us? Why *do you* **forsake** us so long?
Eze 8: 12 [A] does not see us; the LORD *has* **forsaken** the land.' "
9: 9 [A] They say, 'The LORD *has* **forsaken** the land; the LORD
20: 8 [A] set their eyes on, nor *did they* **forsake** the idols of Egypt.
23: 8 [A] *She did* not **give up** the prostitution she began in Egypt,
23: 29 [A] *They will* **leave** you naked and bare, and the shame of your
24: 21 [A] and daughters *you* **left behind** will fall by the sword.
36: 4 [C] and the **deserted** towns that have been plundered
Da 11: 30 [A] and show favor to *those who* **forsake** the holy covenant.
Hos 4: 10 [A] because *they have* **deserted** the LORD to give themselves
Jnh 2: 8 [2:9] [A] "Those who cling to worthless idols **forfeit** the grace
Zep 2: 4 [B] Gaza will be **abandoned** and Ashkelon left in ruins.
Zec 11: 17 [A] "Woe to the worthless shepherd, *who* **deserts** the flock!
Mal 4: 1 [3:19] [A] "Not a root or a branch *will be* **left** to them.

6441 ²עָזַב *'āzab²*, v. [4]

be sure help [+6441] [2], restore wall [1], restored [1]

Ex 23: 5 [A] do not leave it there; **be sure** *you* **help** [+6441] him with it.
23: 5 [A] do not leave it there; **be sure** *you* **help** [+6441] him with it.
Ne 3: 8 [A] to that. *They* **restored** Jerusalem as far as the Broad Wall.
4: 2 [3:34] [A] *Will they* **restore** their **wall**? Will they offer

6442 עִזְבוֹנִים *'izbônîm*, n.[m.]. [7] [√ 6440]

merchandise [7]

Eze 27: 12 they exchanged silver, iron, tin and lead for your **merchandise**.
27: 14 work horses, war horses and mules for your **merchandise**.
27: 16 fine linen, coral and rubies for your **merchandise**.
27: 19 " 'Danites and Greeks from Uzal bought your **merchandise**;
27: 22 for your **merchandise** they exchanged the finest of all kinds of
27: 27 Your wealth, **merchandise** and wares, your mariners, seamen
27: 33 When your **merchandise** went out on the seas, you satisfied many

6443 עַזְבּוּק *'azbûq*, n.pr.m. [1] [√ 1011?]

Azbuk [1]

Ne 3: 16 Beyond him, Nehemiah son of **Azbuk**, ruler of a half-district of

6444 עַזְגָּד *'azgād*, n.pr.m. [4]

Azgad [4]

Ezr 2: 12 of **Azgad** 1,222
8: 12 of the descendants of **Azgad**, Johanan son of Hakkatan, and with
Ne 7: 17 of **Azgad** 2,322
10: 15 [10:16] Bunni, **Azgad**, Bebai,

6445 עַזָּה *'azzâ*, n.pr.loc. [20] [→ 6484]

Gaza [20]

Ge 10: 19 of Canaan reached from Sidon toward Gerar as far as **Gaza**,
Dt 2: 23 And as for the Avvites who lived in villages as far as **Gaza**,
Jos 10: 41 Joshua subdued them from Kadesh Barnea to **Gaza** and from the
11: 22 Israelite territory; only in **Gaza**, Gath and Ashdod did any survive.
15: 47 and **Gaza**, its settlements and villages, as far as the Wadi of Egypt
Jdg 1: 18 The men of Judah also took **Gaza**, Ashkelon and Ekron—
6: 4 They camped on the land and ruined the crops all the way to **Gaza**
16: 1 One day Samson went to **Gaza**, where he saw a prostitute.
16: 21 seized him, gouged out his eyes and took him down to **Gaza**.
1Sa 6: 17 one each for Ashdod, **Gaza**, Ashkelon, Gath and Ekron.
1Ki 4: 24 [5:4] the River, from Tiphsah to **Gaza**, and had peace on all sides.
2Ki 18: 8 he defeated the Philistines, as far as **Gaza** and its territory.
Jer 25: 20 (those of Ashkelon, **Gaza**, Ekron, and the people left at Ashdod);
47: 1 prophet concerning the Philistines before Pharaoh attacked **Gaza**:
47: 5 **Gaza** will shave her head in mourning; Ashkelon will be silenced.
Am 1: 6 "For three sins of **Gaza**, even for four, I will not turn back ⌊my
1: 7 I will send fire upon the walls of **Gaza** that will consume her
Zep 2: 4 **Gaza** will be abandoned and Ashkelon left in ruins. At midday
Zec 9: 5 **Gaza** will writhe in agony, and Ekron too, for her hope will wither.
9: 5 will wither. **Gaza** will lose her king and Ashkelon will be deserted.

6446 עֻזָּה *'uzzâ*, n.pr.m. [3] [→ 7290; cf. 6438]

Uzzah [3]

2Sa 6: 7 The LORD's anger burned against **Uzzah** because of his
6: 8 because the LORD's wrath had broken out against **Uzzah**,
1Ch 6: 29 [6:14] Mahli, Libni his son, Shimei his son, **Uzzah** his son,

6447 ¹עֲזוּבָה *'ᵃzûbâ¹*, n.f. Not used in NIV/BHS [√ 6440]

6448 ²עֲזוּבָה *'ᵃzûbâ²*, n.pr.f. [4] [√ 6440]

Azubah [4]

1Ki 22: 42 His mother's name was **Azubah** daughter of Shilhi.
1Ch 2: 18 Caleb son of Hezron had children by his wife **Azubah** (and by
2: 19 When **Azubah** died, Caleb married Ephrath, who bore him Hur.
2Ch 20: 31 His mother's name was **Azubah** daughter of Shilhi.

6449 עֱזוּז *'ᵉzûz*, n.[m.]. [3] [√ 6451]

power [2], violence [1]

Ps 78: 4 deeds of the LORD, his **power**, and the wonders he has done.
145: 6 They will tell of the **power** *of* your awesome works, and I will
Isa 42: 25 So he poured out on them his burning anger, the **violence** *of* war.

6450 עִזּוּז *'izzûz*, a. [2] [√ 6451]

reinforcements [1], strong [1]

Ps 24: 8 The LORD **strong** and mighty, the LORD mighty in battle.
Isa 43: 17 out the chariots and horses, the army and **reinforcements** together,

6451 עָזַז *'āzaz*, v. [11] [→ 5057, 5058, 6434, 6435, 6436?, 6449, 6450, 6452, 6453, 6456, 6461, 6464; cf. 3594, 6395, 6437]

strong [2], brazen [1], fixed securely [1], makes powerful [1], oppressive [1], overpowered [+3338+6584] [1], puts up a bold front [+928+7156] [1], show strength [1], triumph [1], triumphant [1]

Jdg 3: 10 [A] the hands of Othniel, who **overpowered** [+3338+6584] him.
6: 2 [A] Because the power of Midian *was so* **oppressive**, the
Ps 9: 19 [9:20] [A] Arise, O LORD, *let* not man **triumph**;
52: 7 [52:9] [A] great wealth and *grew* **strong** by destroying others!"
68: 28 [68:29] [A] **show** us *your* **strength**, O God, as you have done
89: 13 [89:14] [A] your hand *is* **strong**, your right hand exalted.
Pr 7: 13 [G] hold of him and kissed him and *with* a **brazen** face she said:
8: 28 [A] clouds above and **fixed securely** the fountains of the deep,
21: 29 [G] A wicked man **puts up a bold** [+928+7156] **front**, but an
Ecc 7: 19 [A] Wisdom **makes** one wise man more **powerful** than ten rulers
Da 11: 12 [A] many thousands, yet *he will* not *remain* **triumphant**.

6452 עָזָז *'āzāz*, n.pr.m. [1] [√ 6451]

Azaz [1]

1Ch 5: 8 Bela son of **Azaz**, the son of Shema, the son of Joel. They settled

6453 עֲזַזְיָהוּ *'ᵃzazyāhû*, n.pr.m. [3] [√ 6451 + 3378]

Azaziah [3]

1Ch 15: 21 Mikneiah, Obed-Edom, Jeiel and **Azaziah** were to play the harps,
27: 20 Hoshea son of **Azaziah**; over half the tribe of Manasseh: Joel son
2Ch 31: 13 Jehiel, **Azaziah**, Nahath, Asahel, Jerimoth, Jozabad, Eliel,

6454 עֻזִּי *'uzzî*, n.pr.m. [11] [√ 6437]

Uzzi [11]

1Ch 6: 5 [5:31] Abishua the father of Bukki, Bukki the father of **Uzzi**,

1Ch 6: 6 [5:32] **Uzzi** the father of Zerahiah, Zerahiah the father of
6: 51 [6:36] Bukki his son, **Uzzi** his son, Zerahiah his son,
7: 2 **Uzzi**, Rephaiah, Jeriel, Jahmai, Ibsam and Samuel—heads of their
7: 3 The son of **Uzzi**: Izrahiah. The sons of Izrahiah: Michael, Obadiah,
7: 7 Ezbon, **Uzzi**, Uzziel, Jerimoth and Iri, heads of families—
9: 8 Ibneiah son of Jeroham; Elah son of **Uzzi**, the son of Micri;
Ezr 7: 4 the son of Zerahiah, the son of **Uzzi**, the son of Bukki,
Ne 11: 22 The chief officer of the Levites in Jerusalem was **Uzzi** son of Bani,
12: 19 of Joiarib's, Mattenai; of Jedaiah's, **Uzzi**;
12: 42 Shemaiah, Eleazar, **Uzzi**, Jehohanan, Malkijah, Elam and Ezer.

6455 עֻזִּיָּא *'uzziyyā'*, n.pr.m. [1] [cf. 6459]

Uzzia [1]

1Ch 11: 44 **Uzzia** the Ashterathite, Shama and Jeiel the sons of Hotham the

6456 עֲזִיאֵל *'ᵃzî'ēl*, n.pr.m. [1] [√ 6434? + 446?]

Aziel [1]

1Ch 15: 20 Zechariah, **Aziel**, Shemiramoth, Jehiel, Unni, Eliab, Maaseiah

6457 עֻזִּיאֵל *'uzzî'ēl*, n.pr.m. [16] [→ 6458; cf. 6437 + 446]

Uzziel [16]

Ex 6: 18 The sons of Kohath were Amram, Izhar, Hebron and **Uzziel**.
6: 22 The sons of **Uzziel** were Mishael, Elzaphan and Sithri.
Lev 10: 4 summoned Mishael and Elzaphan, sons of Aaron's uncle **Uzziel**,
Nu 3: 19 The Kohathite clans: Amram, Izhar, Hebron and **Uzziel**.
3: 30 of the families of the Kohathite clans was Elizaphan son of **Uzziel**.
1Ch 4: 42 led by Pelatiah, Neariah, Rephaiah and **Uzziel**, the sons of Ishi,
6: 2 [5:28] The sons of Kohath: Amram, Izhar, Hebron and **Uzziel**.
6: 18 [6:3] The sons of Kohath: Amram, Izhar, Hebron and **Uzziel**.
7: 7 Ezbon, Uzzi, **Uzziel**, Jerimoth and Iri, heads of families—
15: 10 from the descendants of **Uzziel**, Amminadab the leader and 112
23: 12 sons of Kohath: Amram, Izhar, Hebron and **Uzziel**—four in all.
23: 20 The sons of **Uzziel**: Micah the first and Isshiah the second.
24: 24 The son of **Uzziel**: Micah; from the sons of Micah: Shamir.
25: 4 Bukkiah, Mattaniah, **Uzziel**, Shubael and Jerimoth; Hananiah,
2Ch 29: 14 from the descendants of Jeduthun, Shemaiah and **Uzziel**.
Ne 3: 8 **Uzziel** son of Harhaiah, one of the goldsmiths, repaired the next

6458 עָזִּיאֵלִי *'ozzî'ēlî*, a.g. [2] [√ 6457; cf. 6437 + 446]

Uzzielites [2]

Nu 3: 27 the clans of the Amramites, Izharites, Hebronites and **Uzzielites**;
1Ch 26: 23 the Amramites, the Izharites, the Hebronites and the **Uzzielites**:

6459 עֻזִּיָּה *'uzziyyâ*, n.pr.m. [8] [√ 6437 + 3378; cf. 6455]

Uzziah [8]

2Ki 15: 13 became king in the thirty-ninth year of **Uzziah** king of Judah,
15: 30 him as king in the twentieth year of Jotham son of **Uzziah**.
1Ch 6: 24 [6:9] his son, Uriel his son, **Uzziah** his son and Shaul his son.
Ezr 10: 21 of Harim: Maaseiah, Elijah, Shemaiah, Jehiel and **Uzziah**.
Ne 11: 4 Athaiah son of **Uzziah**, the son of Zechariah, the son of Amariah,
Hos 1: 1 that came to Hosea son of Beeri during the reigns of **Uzziah**,
Am 1: 1 when **Uzziah** was king of Judah and Jeroboam son of Jehoash was
Zec 14: 5 you fled from the earthquake in the days of **Uzziah** king of Judah.

6460 עֻזִּיָּהוּ *'uzziyyāhû*, n.pr.m. [19] [√ 6437 + 3378]

Uzziah [17], him[s] [+2021+4889] [1], Uzziah's [1]

2Ki 15: 32 king of Israel, Jotham son of **Uzziah** king of Judah began to reign.
15: 34 right in the eyes of the LORD, just as his father **Uzziah** had done.
1Ch 27: 25 Jonathan son of **Uzziah** was in charge of the storehouses in the
2Ch 26: 1 all the people of Judah took **Uzziah**, who was sixteen years old,
26: 3 **Uzziah** was sixteen years old when he became king, and he
26: 8 The Ammonites brought tribute to **Uzziah**, and his fame spread as
26: 9 **Uzziah** built towers in Jerusalem at the Corner Gate, at the Valley
26: 11 **Uzziah** had a well-trained army, ready to go out by divisions
26: 14 **Uzziah** provided shields, spears, helmets, coats of armor, bows
26: 18 They confronted **him**[s] [+2021+4889] and said, "It is not right for
26: 18 They confronted him and said, "It is not right for you, **Uzziah**,
26: 19 **Uzziah**, who had a censer in his hand ready to burn incense,
26: 21 King **Uzziah** had leprosy until the day he died. He lived in a
26: 22 The other events of **Uzziah's** reign, from beginning to end,
26: 23 **Uzziah** rested with his fathers and was buried near them in a field
27: 2 right in the eyes of the LORD, just as his father **Uzziah** had done,
Isa 1: 1 that Isaiah son of Amoz saw during the reigns of **Uzziah**,
6: 1 In the year that King **Uzziah** died, I saw the Lord seated on a
7: 1 the son of **Uzziah**, was king of Judah, King Rezin of Aram

6461 עֲזִיזָא *'ᵃzîzā'*, n.pr.m. [1] [√ 6451]

Aziza [1]

Ezr 10: 27 Elioenai, Eliashib, Mattaniah, Jeremoth, Zabad and **Aziza**.

6462 עַזְמָוֶת *'azmāwet*[1], n.pr.m. [6] [→ 1115, 6463]

Azmaveth [6]

2Sa 23: 31 Abi-Albon the Arbathite, **Azmaveth** the Barhumite,
1Ch 8: 36 **Azmaveth** and Zimri, and Zimri was the father of Moza.
9: 42 of Jadah, Jadah was the father of Alemeth, **Azmaveth** and Zimri,
11: 33 **Azmaveth** the Baharumite, Eliahba the Shaalbonite,
12: 3 Jeziel and Pelet the sons of **Azmaveth**; Beracah, Jehu the
27: 25 **Azmaveth** son of Adiel was in charge of the royal storehouses.

6463 עַזְמָוֶת *'azmāwet*[2], n.pr.loc. [2] [√ 6462]

Azmaveth [2]

Ezr 2: 24 of **Azmaveth** 42
Ne 12: 29 from Beth Gilgal, and from the area of Geba and **Azmaveth**,

6464 עַזָּן *'azzān*, n.pr.m. [1] [√ 6451]

Azzan [1]

Nu 34: 26 Paltiel son of **Azzan**, the leader from the tribe of Issachar;

6465 עָזְנִיָּה *'ozniyyâ*, n.f. [2]

black vulture [2]

Lev 11: 13 they are detestable: the eagle, the vulture, the **black vulture**,
Dt 14: 12 these you may not eat: the eagle, the vulture, the **black vulture**,

6466 עָזַק *'āzaq*, v. [1]

dug up [1]

Isa 5: 2 [D] *He* **dug it up** and cleared it of stones and planted it with the

6467 עֲזֵקָה *'ᵃzēqâ*, n.pr.loc. [7]

Azekah [7]

Jos 10: 10 and cut them down all the way to **Azekah** and Makkedah.
10: 11 fled before Israel on the road down from Beth Horon to **Azekah**,
15: 35 Jarmuth, Adullam, Socoh, **Azekah**,
1Sa 17: 1 pitched camp at Ephes Dammim, between Socoh and **Azekah**.
2Ch 11: 9 Adoraim, Lachish, **Azekah**,
Ne 11: 30 in Lachish and its fields, and in **Azekah** and its settlements.
Jer 34: 7 cities of Judah that were still holding out—Lachish and **Azekah**.

6468 עָזַר *'āzar*, v. [81] [→ 540, 3597, 6469, 6470, 6474, 6475, 6478, 6479, 6481; cf. 6370]

help [42], helped [12], helps [6], helper [2], added [1], allied with [1], allies [1], am helped [1], assist [1], came to rescue [1], cohorts [1], gave support [+339] [1], give support [1], helpers [1], helping [1], is helped [1], protect [1], receive help [+6469] [1], support [1], supported [1], sustain [1], was helped [1], were helped [1]

Ge 49: 25 [A] your father's God, *who* **helps** you, because of the Almighty,
Dt 32: 38 [A] Let them rise up *to* **help** you! Let them give you shelter!
Jos 1: 14 [A] over ahead of your brothers. *You are to* **help** your brothers
10: 4 [A] "Come up and **help** me attack Gibeon," he said, "because it
10: 6 [A] **Help** us, because all the Amorite kings from the hill country
10: 33 [A] Horam king of Gezer had come up to **help** Lachish,
1Sa 7: 12 [A] it Ebenezer, saying, "Thus far *has* the LORD **helped** us."
2Sa 8: 5 [A] When the Arameans of Damascus came to **help** Hadadezer
18: 3 [A] It would be better now for you to **give** us **support** from the
21: 17 [A] Abishai son of Zeruiah **came to** David's **rescue**; he struck
1Ki 1: 7 [A] Abiathar the priest, and *they* **gave** him *their* **support** [+339].
20: 16 [A] the 32 kings **allied with** him were in their tents getting
2Ki 14: 26 [A] or free, was suffering; there was no *one to* **help** them.
1Ch 5: 20 [C] *They* **were helped** *in* fighting them, and God handed the
12: 1 [A] (they were among the warriors *who* **helped** him *in* battle;
12: 17 [12:18] [A] "If you have come to me in peace, to **help** me,
12: 18 [12:19] [A] success to you, and success to *those who* **help** you,
12: 18 [12:19] [A] to those who help you, for your God *will* **help** you."
12: 19 [12:20] [A] (*He and his men did* not **help** the Philistines
12: 21 [12:22] [A] They **helped** David against raiding bands, for all of
12: 22 [12:23] [A] Day after day men came to **help** David, until he had
15: 26 [A] Because God *had* **helped** the Levites who were carrying the
18: 5 [A] When the Arameans of Damascus came to **help** Hadadezer
22: 17 [A] David ordered all the leaders of Israel to **help** his son
2Ch 14: 11 [14:10] [A] there is no one like you to **help** the powerless
14: 11 [14:10] [A] **Help** us, O LORD our God, for we rely on you,
18: 31 [A] but Jehoshaphat cried out, and the LORD **helped** him.
19: 2 [A] "*Should you* **help** the wicked and love those who hate the
20: 23 [A] the men from Seir, *they* **helped** to destroy one another.
25: 8 [A] the enemy, for God has the power to **help** or to overthrow."
26: 7 [A] God **helped** him against the Philistines and against the Arabs
26: 13 [A] a powerful force to **support** the king against his enemies.
26: 15 [C] for he **was** greatly **helped** until he became powerful.
28: 16 [A] At that time King Ahaz sent to the king of Assyria for **help**.

2Ch 28:23 [G] "Since the gods of the kings of Aram *have* **helped** them,
28:23 [A] helped them, I will sacrifice to them so *they will* **help** me."
32: 3 [A] water from the springs outside the city, and *they* **helped** him.
32: 8 [A] with us is the LORD our God to **help** us and to fight our
Ezr 8:22 [A] and horsemen to **protect** us from enemies on the road,
10:15 [A] **supported** *by* Meshullam and Shabbethai the Levite,
Job 9:13 [A] his anger; even the **cohorts** *of* Rahab cowered at his feet.
26: 2 [A] "How *you have* **helped** the powerless! How you have saved
29:12 [A] cried for help, and the fatherless who had none *to* **assist** him.
30:13 [A] succeed in destroying me—without *anyone's* **helping** them.
Ps 10:14 [A] commits himself to you; you are the **helper** of the fatherless.
22:11 [22:12] [A] for trouble is near and there is no *one to* **help**.
28: 7 [C] and my shield; my heart trusts in him, and *I* **am helped**.
30:10 [30:11] [A] and be merciful to me; O LORD, be my **help**."
37:40 [A] The LORD **helps** them and delivers them; he delivers them
46: 5 [46:6] [A] she will not fall; God *will* **help** her at break of day.
54: 4 [54:6] [A] Surely God *is* my **help**; the Lord is the one who
72:12 [A] needy who cry out, the afflicted who have no *one to* **help**.
79: 9 [A] **Help** us, O God our Savior, for the glory of your name;
86:17 [A] for you, O LORD, *have* **helped** me and comforted me.
107:12 [A] to bitter labor; they stumbled, and there was no *one to* **help**.
109:26 [A] **Help** me, O LORD my God; save me in accordance with
118: 7 [A] The LORD is with me; *he is* my **helper**. I will look in
118:13 [A] pushed back and about to fall, but the LORD **helped** me.
119:86 [A] **help** me, for men persecute me without cause.
119:173 [A] May your hand be ready to **help** me, for I have chosen your
119:175 [A] live that I may praise you, and *may* your laws **sustain** me.
Isa 30: 7 [A] to Egypt, *whose* **help** is utterly useless. Therefore I call her
31: 3 [A] *he who* **helps** will stumble, he who is helped will fall;
31: 3 [B] he who helps will stumble, *he who* **is helped** will fall;
41: 6 [A] each **helps** the other and says to his brother, "Be strong!"
41:10 [A] I will strengthen you and **help** you; I will uphold you with
41:13 [A] your right hand and says to you, Do not fear; I *will* **help** you.
41:14 [A] O worm Jacob, O little Israel, for *I* myself *will* **help** you,"
44: 2 [A] who formed you in the womb, and *who will* **help** you:
49: 8 [A] I will answer you, and in the day of salvation *I will* **help** you;
50: 7 [A] Because the Sovereign LORD **helps** me, I will not be
50: 9 [A] It is the Sovereign LORD *who* **helps** me. Who is he that
63: 5 [A] I looked, but there was no *one to* **help**, I was appalled that no
Jer 47: 4 [A] and to cut off all survivors *who could* **help** Tyre and Sidon.
La 1: 7 [A] people fell into enemy hands, there was no *one to* **help** her.
Eze 30: 8 [A] when I set fire to Egypt and all her **helpers** are crushed.
32:21 [A] the grave the mighty leaders will say of Egypt and her **allies**,
Da 10:13 [A] Michael, one of the chief princes, came to **help** me, because I
11:34 [C] When they fall, *they will* **receive** a little **help** [+6469], and
11:45 [A] Yet he will come to his end, and no *one will* **help** him.
Zec 1:15 [A] I was only a little angry, but they **added** to the calamity.'

6469 ¹עֵזֶר **'ēzer¹**, n.m. [21] [→ 2193, 6470, 6471, 6472, 6476, 6477; cf. 6468; *also used with compound proper names*]

help [13], helper [5], receive help [+6468] [1], staff [1], strength [1]

Ge 2:18 for the man to be alone. I will make a **helper** suitable for him."
2:20 the beasts of the field. But for Adam no suitable **helper** was found.
Ex 18: 4 was named Eliezer, for he said, "My father's God was my **helper**;
Dt 33: 7 own hands he defends his cause. Oh, be his **help** against his foes!"
33:26 who rides on the heavens to **help** you and on the clouds in his
33:29 He is your shield and **helper** and your glorious sword.
Ps 20: 2 [20:3] May he send you **help** from the sanctuary and grant you
33:20 We wait in hope for the LORD; he is our **help** and our shield.
70: 5 [70:6] You are my **help** and my deliverer; O LORD, do not
89:19 [89:20] "I have bestowed **strength** on a warrior; I have exalted a
115: 9 O house of Israel, trust in the LORD—he is their **help** and shield.
115:10 O house of Aaron, trust in the LORD—he is their **help** and shield.
115:11 who fear him, trust in the LORD—he is their **help** and shield.
121: 1 I lift up my eyes to the hills—where does my **help** come from?
121: 2 My **help** comes from the LORD, the Maker of heaven and earth.
124: 8 Our **help** is in the name of the LORD, the Maker of heaven
146: 5 Blessed is he whose **help** is the God of Jacob, whose hope is in the
Isa 30: 5 who bring neither **help** nor advantage, but only shame and
Eze 12:14 his **staff** and all his troops—and I will pursue them with drawn
Da 11:34 When they fall, *they will* **receive** a little **help** [+6468], and many
Hos 13: 9 O Israel, because you are against me, against your **helper**.

6470 ²עֵזֶר **'ēzer²**, n.pr.m. [4] [√ 6469; cf. 6468]

Ezer [4]

1Ch 4: 4 Penuel was the father of Gedor, and **Ezer** the father of Hushah.
7:21 **Ezer** and Elead were killed by the native-born men of Gath,
12: 9 [12:10] **Ezer** was the chief, Obadiah the second in command,
Ne 3:19 Next to him, **Ezer** son of Jeshua, ruler of Mizpah, repaired another

6471 ¹עֶזֶר **'ezer¹**, n.pr.loc. Not used in NIV/BHS [√ 6469]

6472 ²עֶזֶר **'ezer²**, n.pr.m. [1] [√ 6469]

Ezer [1]

Ne 12:42 Shemaiah, Eleazar, Uzzi, Jehohanan, Malkijah, Elam and **Ezer**.

6473 עַזֻּר **'azzur**, n.pr.m. [3]

Azzur [3]

Ne 10:17 [10:18] Ater, Hezekiah, **Azzur**,
Jer 28: 1 the prophet Hananiah son of **Azzur**, who was from Gibeon,
Eze 11: 1 I saw among them Jaazaniah son of **Azzur** and Pelatiah son of

6474 עֶזְרָא **'ezrā'**, n.pr.m. [22] [√ 6468; Ar 10537]

Ezra [21], Ezra's [1]

Ezr 7: 1 **Ezra** son of Seraiah, the son of Azariah, the son of Hilkiah,
7: 6 this **Ezra** came up from Babylon. He was a teacher well versed in
7:10 For **Ezra** had devoted himself to the study and observance of the
7:11 This is a copy of the letter King Artaxerxes had given to **Ezra** the
10: 1 While **Ezra** was praying and confessing, weeping and throwing
10: 2 son of Jehiel, one of the descendants of Elam, said to **Ezra**,
10: 5 So **Ezra** rose up and put the leading priests and Levites and all
10: 6 **Ezra** withdrew from before the house of God and went to the room
10:10 **Ezra** the priest stood up and said to them, "You have been
10:16 **Ezra** the priest selected men who were family heads, one from
Ne 8: 1 They told **Ezra** the scribe to bring out the Book of the Law of
8: 2 So on the first day of the seventh month **Ezra** the priest brought
8: 4 **Ezra** the scribe stood on a high wooden platform built for the
8: 5 **Ezra** opened the book. All the people could see him because he
8: 6 **Ezra** praised the LORD, the great God; and all the people lifted
8: 9 Nehemiah the governor, **Ezra** the priest and scribe, and the Levites
8:13 gathered around **Ezra** the scribe to give attention to the words of
12: 1 son of Shealtiel and with Jeshua: Seraiah, Jeremiah, **Ezra**,
12:13 of **Ezra's**, Meshullam; of Amariah's, Jehohanan;
12:26 days of Nehemiah the governor and of **Ezra** the priest and scribe.
12:33 along with Azariah, **Ezra**, Meshullam,
12:36 David the man of God. **Ezra** the scribe led the procession.

6475 עֲזַרְאֵל **'ᵃzar'ēl**, n.pr.m. [6] [√ 6468 + 446]

Azarel [6]

1Ch 12: 6 [12:7] **Azarel**, Joezer and Jashobeam the Korahites;
25:18 the eleventh to **Azarel**, his sons and relatives, 12
27:22 over Dan: **Azarel** son of Jeroham. These were the officers over the
Ezr 10:41 **Azarel**, Shelemiah, Shemariah,
Ne 11:13 Amashsai son of **Azarel**, the son of Ahzai, the son of
12:36 **Azarel**, Milalai, Gilalai, Maai, Nethanel, Judah and Hanani—

6476 ¹עֶזְרָה **'ezrâ¹**, n.f. [26] [→ 6477; cf. 6469]

help [19], aid [3], allies [1], helper [1], influence [1], support [1]

Jdg 5:23 its people bitterly, because they did not come to **help** the LORD,
5:23 come to help the LORD, to **help** the LORD against the mighty.'
2Ch 28:21 presented them to the king of Assyria, but that did not **help** him.
Job 6:13 Do I have any power to **help** myself, now that success has been
31:21 hand against the fatherless, knowing that I had **influence** in court,
Ps 22:19 [22:20] be not far off; O my Strength, come quickly to **help** me.
27: 9 do not turn your servant away in anger; you have been my **helper**.
35: 2 Take up shield and buckler; arise and come to my **aid**.
38:22 [38:23] Come quickly to **help** me, O Lord my Savior.
40:13 [40:14] to save me; O LORD, come quickly to **help** me.
40:17 [40:18] You are my **help** and my deliverer; O my God, do not
44:26 [44:27] Rise up and **help** us; redeem us because of your unfailing
46: 1 [46:2] is our refuge and strength, an ever-present **help** in trouble.
60:11 [60:13] Give us **aid** against the enemy, for the help of man is
63: 7 [63:8] Because you are my **help**, I sing in the shadow of your
70: 1 [70:2] O God, to save me; O LORD, come quickly to **help** me.
71:12 Be not far from me, O God; come quickly, O my God, to **help** me.
94:17 Unless the LORD had given me **help**, I would soon have dwelt in
108:12 [108:13] Give us **aid** against the enemy, for the help of man is
Isa 10: 3 when disaster comes from afar? To whom will you run for **help**?
20: 6 those we fled to for **help** and deliverance from the king of Assyria!
31: 1 Woe to those who go down to Egypt for **help**, who rely on horses,
31: 2 against the house of the wicked, against *those who* **help** evildoers.
Jer 37: 7 'Pharaoh's army, which has marched out to **support** you, will go
La 4:17 Moreover, our eyes failed, looking in vain for **help**; from our
Na 3: 9 were her boundless strength; Put and Libya were among her **allies**.

6477 ²עֶזְרָה **'ezrâ²**, n.pr.m. [1] [√ 6476]

Ezrah [1]

1Ch 4:17 The sons of **Ezrah**: Jether, Mered, Epher and Jalon. One of

6478 עֲזָרָה ***ᵃzārâ***, n.f. [9] [√ 6468]
ledge [6], court [2], outer court [1]

2Ch 4: 9 the large **court** and the doors for the court, and overlaid the doors
4: 9 the large court and the doors for the **court**, and overlaid the doors
6: 13 three cubits high, and had placed it in the center of the **outer court**.
Eze 43: 14 From the gutter on the ground up to the lower **ledge** it is two cubits
43: 14 from the smaller **ledge** up to the larger ledge it is four cubits high
43: 14 from the smaller ledge up to the larger **ledge** it is four cubits high
43: 17 The upper **ledge** also is square, fourteen cubits long and fourteen
43: 20 and on the four corners of the upper **ledge** and all around the rim,
45: 19 on the four corners of the upper **ledge** of the altar and on the

6479 עֶזְרִי ***ʿezrî***, n.pr.m. [1] [√ 6468 + 3378? *or* 3276?]
Ezri [1]

1Ch 27: 26 **Ezri** son of Kelub was in charge of the field workers who farmed

6480 עַזְרִיאֵל ***ʿazrîʾēl***, n.pr.m. [3] [√ 6469 + 446]
Azriel [3]

1Ch 5: 24 Epher, Ishi, Eliel, **Azriel**, Jeremiah, Hodaviah and Jahdiel.
27: 19 Ishmaiah son of Obadiah; over Naphtali: Jerimoth son of **Azriel**;
Jer 36: 26 Seraiah son of **Azriel** and Shelemiah son of Abdeel to arrest

6481 עֲזַרְיָה ***ᵃzaryâ***, n.pr.m. [32] [√ 6468 + 3378; Ar 10538]
Azariah [31], Azariah's [1]

2Ki 14: 21 all the people of Judah took **Azariah**, who was sixteen years old,
15: 1 of Israel, **Azariah** son of Amaziah king of Judah began to reign.
15: 7 **Azariah** rested with his fathers and was buried near them in the
15: 17 In the thirty-ninth year of **Azariah** king of Judah, Menahem son of
15: 23 In the fiftieth year of **Azariah** king of Judah, Pekahiah son of
15: 27 In the fifty-second year of **Azariah** king of Judah, Pekah son of
1Ch 2: 8 The son of Ethan: **Azariah**.
2: 38 Obed the father of Jehu, Jehu the father of **Azariah**,
2: 39 **Azariah** the father of Helez, Helez the father of Eleasah,
3: 12 Amaziah his son, **Azariah** his son, Jotham his son,
6: 9 [5:35] Ahimaaz the father of **Azariah**, Azariah the father of
6: 9 [5:35] the father of Azariah, **Azariah** the father of Johanan,
6: 10 [5:36] Johanan the father of **Azariah** (it was he who served as
6: 11 [5:37] **Azariah** the father of Amariah, Amariah the father of
6: 13 [5:39] the father of Hilkiah, Hilkiah the father of **Azariah**,
6: 14 [5:40] **Azariah** the father of Seraiah, and Seraiah the father of
6: 36 [6:21] the son of Elkanah, the son of Joel, the son of **Azariah**,
9: 11 **Azariah** the son of Hilkiah, the son of Meshullam, the son of Zadok,
2Ch 21: 2 were **Azariah**, Jehiel, Zechariah, Azariahu, Michael
Ezr 7: 1 Ezra son of Seraiah, the son of **Azariah**, the son of Hilkiah,
7: 3 the son of Amariah, the son of **Azariah**, the son of Meraioth,
Ne 3: 23 and next to them, **Azariah** son of Maaseiah, the son of Ananiah,
3: 24 another section, from **Azariah's** house to the angle and the corner,
7: 7 **Azariah**, Raamiah, Nahamani, Mordecai, Bilshan, Mispereth,
8: 7 Maaseiah, Kelita, **Azariah**, Jozabad, Hanan and Pelaiah—
10: 2 [10:3] Seraiah, **Azariah**, Jeremiah,
12: 33 along with **Azariah**, Ezra, Meshullam,
Jer 43: 2 **Azariah** son of Hoshaiah and Johanan son of Kareah and all the
Da 1: 6 were some from Judah: Daniel, Hananiah, Mishael and **Azariah**.
1: 7 Shadrach; to Mishael, Meshach; and to **Azariah**, Abednego.
1: 11 had appointed over Daniel, Hananiah, Mishael and **Azariah**,
1: 19 he found none equal to Daniel, Hananiah, Mishael and **Azariah**;

6482 עֲזַרְיָהוּ ***ᵃzaryāhû***, n.pr.m. [16] [√ 6469 + 3378]
Azariah [14], Azariah's [1], Azariahu [1]

1Ki 4: 2 these were his chief officials: **Azariah** son of Zadok—the priest;
4: 5 **Azariah** son of Nathan—in charge of the district officers;
2Ki 15: 6 As for the other events of **Azariah's** reign, and all he did,
15: 8 In the thirty-eighth year of **Azariah** king of Judah, Zechariah son
2Ch 15: 1 The Spirit of God came upon **Azariah** son of Oded.
15: 8 and the prophecy of **Azariah** [BHS-] son of Oded the prophet,
21: 2 Jehiel, Zechariah, **Azariahu**, Michael and Shephatiah.
22: 6 Ahaziah [BHS *Azariah*; NIV 302] son of Jehoram king of Judah
23: 1 **Azariah** son of Jeroham, Ishmael son of Jehohanan, Azariah son
23: 1 son of Jehohanan, **Azariah** son of Obed, Maaseiah son of Adaiah,
26: 17 **Azariah** the priest with eighty other courageous priests of the
26: 20 When **Azariah** the chief priest and all the other priests looked at
28: 12 **Azariah** son of Jehohanan, Berekiah son of Meshillemoth,
29: 12 the Kohathites, Mahath son of Amasai and Joel son of **Azariah**;
29: 12 the Merarites, Kish son of Abdi and **Azariah** son of Jehallelel;
31: 10 and **Azariah** the chief priest, from the family of Zadok, answered,
31: 13 and **Azariah** the official in charge of the temple of God.

6483 עַזְרִיקָם ***ʿazrîqām***, n.pr.m. [6] [√ 6469 + 7756]
Azrikam [6]

1Ch 3: 23 The sons of Neariah: Elioenai, Hizkiah and **Azrikam**—three in all.
8: 38 **Azrikam**, Bokeru, Ishmael, Sheariah, Obadiah and Hanan.
9: 14 of Hasshub, the son of **Azrikam**, the son of Hashabiah, a Merarite;
9: 44 **Azrikam**, Bokeru, Ishmael, Sheariah, Obadiah and Hanan.
2Ch 28: 7 **Azrikam** the officer in charge of the palace, and Elkanah,
Ne 11: 15 the son of **Azrikam**, the son of Hashabiah, the son of Bunni;

6484 עַזָּתִי ***ʿazzātî***, a.g. [2] [√ 6445]
Gaza [1], people of Gaza [1]

Jos 13: 3 as Canaanite (the territory of the five Philistine rulers in **Gaza**,
Jdg 16: 2 The **people of Gaza** were told, "Samson is here!" So they

6485 עֵט ***ʿēṭ***, n.m. [4]
pen [2], tool [2]

Job 19: 24 that they were inscribed with an iron **tool** on lead, or engraved in
Ps 45: 1 [45:2] for the king; my tongue is the **pen** *of* a skillful writer.
Jer 8: 8 when actually the lying **pen** *of* the scribes has handled it falsely?
17: 1 "Judah's sin is engraved with an iron **tool**, inscribed with a flint

6486 ¹עָטָה ***ʿāṭâ¹***, v. [15] [→ 5073; cf. 3598]
cover [5], wrapped [2], covered with a mantle [1], covered [1], veiled [1], wearing [1], wrap around himself [1], wrapped himself [1], wraps around him [1], wraps himself [1]

Lev 13: 45 [A] **cover** the lower part of his face and cry out, 'Unclean!
1Sa 28: 14 [A] "An old man **wearing** a robe is coming up," she said.
Ps 71: 13 [A] *may* those who want to harm me *be* **covered** *with* scorn
84: 6 [84:7] [G] of springs; the autumn rains also **cover** it *with* pools.
89: 45 [89:46] [G] *you have* **covered** him **with a mantle** *of* shame.
104: 2 [A] *He* **wraps himself** *in* light as with a garment; he stretches
109: 19 [A] May it be like a cloak **wrapped** about him, like a belt tied
109: 29 [A] clothed with disgrace and **wrapped** *in* shame as in a cloak.
SS 1: 7 [A] Why should I be like a **veiled** *woman* beside the flocks of
Isa 59: 17 [A] of vengeance and **wrapped himself** *in* zeal as in a cloak.
Jer 43: 12 [A] As a shepherd **wraps** his garment **around him**, so will he
43: 12 [A] so *will he* **wrap** Egypt **around himself** and depart from there
Eze 24: 17 [A] *do* not **cover** the lower part of your face or eat the customary
24: 22 [A] *You will* not **cover** the lower part of your face or eat the
Mic 3: 7 [A] They *will* all **cover** their faces because there is no answer

6487 ²עָטָה ***ʿāṭâ²***, v. [3]
take firm hold [+6487] [2], is grasped [1]

Isa 22: 17 [A] the LORD *is about to* **take firm hold** [+6487] *of* you
22: 17 [A] the LORD *is about to* **take firm hold of** [+6487] you
Eze 21: 15 [21:20] [E] to flash like lightning, *it* **is grasped** for slaughter.

6488 עָטוּף ***ʿāṭûp***, a. *or* v.ptcp. [2] [√ 6494]
faint [1], weak [1]

Ge 30: 42 So the **weak** animals went to Laban and the strong ones to Jacob.
La 2: 19 of your children, who **faint** from hunger at the head of every street.

6489 עֲטִין ***ᵃṭîn***, n.[m.]. [1]
body [1]

Job 21: 24 his **body** well nourished, his bones rich with marrow.

6490 עֲטִישָׁה ***ᵃṭîšâ***, n.f. [1]
snorting [1]

Job 41: 18 [41:10] His **snorting** throws out flashes of light; his eyes are like

6491 עֲטַלֵּף ***ᵃṭallēp***, n.[m.]. [3] [√ 6493 + 4200]
bat [2], bats [1]

Lev 11: 19 the stork, any kind of heron, the hoopoe and the **bat**.
Dt 14: 18 the stork, any kind of heron, the hoopoe and the **bat**.
Isa 2: 20 away to the rodents and **bats** their idols of silver and idols of gold,

6492 עָטָם ***ʿāṭām***, n.f. Not used in NIV/BHS [√ 6793]

6493 ¹עָטַף ***ʿāṭap¹***, v. [3] [→ 5074, 6491; cf. 6495]
clothe [+4200+8884] [1], mantled [1], turns [1]

Job 23: 9 [A] when *he* **turns** *to* the south, I catch no glimpse of him.
Ps 65: 13 [65:14] [A] with flocks and the valleys *are* **mantled** *with* grain;
73: 6 [A] *they* **clothe** [+4200+8884] themselves *with* violence.

6494 ²עָטַף **'āṭap²**, v. [11] [→ 6488]

faint [8], ebbed away [1], ebbing away [1], weak [1]

Ge 30:42 [G] but if the animals *were* **weak**, he would not place them there.
Ps 61: 2 [61:3] [A] the earth I call to you, I call as my heart *grows* **faint**;
77: 3 [77:4] [F] and I groaned; I mused, and my spirit *grew* **faint**.
102: T [102:1] [A] When *he is* **faint** and pours out his lament before
107: 5 [F] They were hungry and thirsty, and their lives **ebbed away**.
142: 3 [142:4] [F] When my spirit *grows* **faint** within me, it is you
143: 4 [F] So my spirit *grows* **faint** within me; my heart within me is
Isa 57:16 [A] for then the spirit of man *would grow* **faint** before me—
La 2:11 [C] because children and infants **faint** in the streets of the city.
2:12 [F] as they **faint** like wounded men in the streets of the city,
Jnh 2: 7 [2:8] [F] "When my life *was* **ebbing away**, I remembered you,

6495 ³עָטַף **'āṭap³**, v. Not used in NIV/BHS [cf. 6493]

6496 ¹עָטַר **'āṭar¹**, v. [2] [→ 6497, 6498, 6499, 6500, 6501, 6502, 6503]

closing in [1], surround [1]

1Sa 23:26 [A] As Saul and his forces *were* **closing in** on David and his men
Ps 5:12 [5:13] [A] *you* **surround** them *with* your favor as with a shield.

6497 ²עָטַר **'āṭar²**, v.den. [5] [√ 6496]

crowned [2], bestower of crowns [1], crown [1], crowns [1]

Ps 8: 5 [8:6] [D] and **crowned** him *with* glory and honor.
65:11 [65:12] [D] *You* **crown** the year with your bounty, and your
103: 4 [D] life from the pit and **crowns** you *with* love and compassion,
SS 3:11 [D] the crown with which his mother **crowned** him on the day of
Isa 23: 8 [G] the **bestower of crowns**, whose merchants are princes,

6498 ¹עֲטָרָה **'ᵃṭārâ¹**, n.f. [23] [√ 6496]

crown [18], wreath [3], crowns [2]

2Sa 12:30 He took the **crown** from the head of their king—its weight was a
1Ch 20: 2 David took the **crown** from the head of their king—its weight was
Est 8:15 and white, a large **crown** *of* gold and a purple robe of fine linen.
Job 19: 9 stripped me of my honor and removed the **crown** *from* my head.
31:36 I would wear it on my shoulder, I would put it on like a **crown**.
Ps 21: 3 [21:4] rich blessings and placed a **crown** *of* pure gold on his head.
Pr 4: 9 of grace on your head and present you with a **crown** *of* splendor."
12: 4 A wife of noble character is her husband's **crown**, but a
14:24 The wealth of the wise is their **crown**, but the folly of fools yields
16:31 Gray hair is a **crown** *of* splendor; it is attained by a righteous life.
17: 6 Children's children are a **crown** *to* the aged, and parents are the
SS 3:11 daughters of Zion, and look at King Solomon wearing the **crown**,
Isa 28: 1 Woe to that **wreath**, the pride of Ephraim's drunkards, to the
28: 3 That **wreath**, the pride of Ephraim's drunkards, will be trampled
28: 5 a glorious crown, a beautiful **wreath** for the remnant of his people.
62: 3 You will be a **crown** *of* splendor in the LORD's hand, a royal
Jer 13:18 your thrones, for your glorious **crowns** will fall from your heads."
La 5:16 The **crown** has fallen *from* our head. Woe to us, for we have
Eze 16:12 earrings on your ears and a beautiful **crown** on your head.
21:26 [21:31] Take off the turban, remove the **crown**. It will not be as it
23:42 of the woman and her sister and beautiful **crowns** on their heads.
Zec 6:11 Take the silver and gold and make a **crown**, and set it on the head
6:14 The **crown** will be given to Heldai, Tobijah, Jedaiah and Hen son

6499 ²עֲטָרָה **'ᵃṭārâ²**, n.pr.f. [1] [√ 6496]

Atarah [1]

1Ch 2:26 Jerahmeel had another wife, whose name was **Atarah**; she was the

6500 עֲטָרוֹת **'ᵃṭārôt**, n.pr.loc. [4] [→ 6501, 6502; cf. 6496]

Ataroth [4]

Nu 32: 3 "**Ataroth**, Dibon, Jazer, Nimrah, Heshbon, Elealeh, Sebam,
32:34 The Gadites built up Dibon, **Ataroth**, Aroer,
Jos 16: 2 Luz), crossed over to the territory of the Arkites in **Ataroth**,
16: 7 it went down from Janoah to **Ataroth** and Naarah, touched Jericho

6501 עַטְרוֹת אַדָּר **'aṭrôt 'addār**, n.pr.loc. [2] [√ 6500 + 162]

Ataroth Addar [2]

Jos 16: 5 The boundary of their inheritance went from **Ataroth Addar** in
18:13 went down to **Ataroth Addar** on the hill south of Lower Beth

6502 עַטְרוֹת בֵּית יוֹאָב **'aṭrôt bêt yô'āb**, n.pr.loc. [1] [√ 6500 + 1074 + 3405]

Atroth Beth Joab [1]

1Ch 2:54 Bethlehem, the Netophathites, **Atroth Beth Joab**, half the

6503 עַטְרוֹת שׁוֹפָן **'aṭrôt šôpān**, n.pr.loc. [1] [√ 6496 + 8794]

Atroth Shophan [1]

Nu 32:35 **Atroth Shophan**, Jazer, Jogbehah,

6504 עַי **'ay**, n.pr.loc. [38] [→ 6509; cf. 6392]

Ai [36], city[s] [1], who[s] [+408+2021] [1]

Ge 12: 8 and pitched his tent, with Bethel on the west and **Ai** on the east.
13: 3 to the place between Bethel and **Ai** where his tent had been earlier
Jos 7: 2 Now Joshua sent men from Jericho to **Ai**, which is near Beth Aven
7: 2 and spy out the region." So the men went up and spied out **Ai**.
7: 3 they said, "Not all the people will have to go up against **Ai**.
7: 4 thousand men went up; but they were routed by the men of **Ai**,
7: 5 **who**[s] [+408+2021] killed about thirty-six of them. They chased the
8: 1 Take the whole army with you, and go up and attack **Ai**.
8: 1 For I have delivered into your hands the king of **Ai**, his people,
8: 2 You shall do to **Ai** and its king as you did to Jericho and its king,
8: 3 So Joshua and the whole army moved out to attack **Ai**. He chose
8: 9 to the place of ambush and lay in wait between Bethel and **Ai**,
8: 9 and lay in wait between Bethel and Ai, to the west of **Ai**—
8:10 and he and the leaders of Israel marched before them to **Ai**.
8:11 They set up camp north of **Ai**, with the valley between them
8:11 up camp north of Ai, with the valley between them and the **city**[s].
8:12 five thousand men and set them in ambush between Bethel and **Ai**,
8:14 When the king of **Ai** saw this, he and all the men of the city hurried
8:16 All the men of **Ai** [K 6551] were called to pursue them, and they
8:17 Not a man remained in **Ai** or Bethel who did not go after Israel.
8:18 said to Joshua, "Hold out toward **Ai** the javelin that is in your hand,
8:20 The men of **Ai** looked back and saw the smoke of the city rising
8:21 up from the city, they turned around and attacked the men of **Ai**.
8:23 But they took the king of **Ai** alive and brought him to Joshua.
8:24 When Israel had finished killing all the men of **Ai** in the fields
8:24 all the Israelites returned to **Ai** and killed those who were in it.
8:25 thousand men and women fell that day—all the people of **Ai**.
8:26 that held out his javelin until he had destroyed all who lived in **Ai**.
8:28 So Joshua burned **Ai** and made it a permanent heap of ruins,
8:29 He hung the king of **Ai** on a tree and left him there until evening.
9: 3 people of Gibeon heard what Joshua had done to Jericho and **Ai**,
10: 1 Adoni-Zedek king of Jerusalem heard that Joshua had taken **Ai**
10: 1 doing to **Ai** and its king as he had done to Jericho and its king,
10: 2 it was larger than **Ai**, and all its men were good fighters.
12: 9 the king of Jericho one the king of **Ai** (near Bethel) one
Ezr 2:28 of Bethel and **Ai** 223
Ne 7:32 of Bethel and **Ai** 123
Jer 49: 3 "Wail, O Heshbon, for **Ai** is destroyed! Cry out, O inhabitants of

6505 עִי **'î**, n.[m.]. [5] [→ 1247, 5075, 6510, 6516, 6517; cf. 6390]

heap of rubble [3], broken man [1], rubble [1]

Job 30:24 "Surely no one lays a hand on a **broken man** when he cries for
Ps 79: 1 defiled your holy temple, they have reduced Jerusalem to **rubble**.
Jer 26:18 be plowed like a field, Jerusalem will become a **heap of rubble**,
Mic 1: 6 "Therefore I will make Samaria a **heap of rubble**, a place for
3:12 be plowed like a field, Jerusalem will become a **heap of rubble**,

6506 ¹עֵיבָל **'êbāl¹**, n.pr.loc. [4] [→ 6507]

Ebal [4]

Dt 27: 4 set up these stones on Mount **Ebal**, as I command you today,
27:13 And these tribes shall stand on Mount **Ebal** to pronounce curses:
Jos 8:30 Joshua built on Mount **Ebal** an altar to the LORD, the God of
8:33 front of Mount Gerizim and half of them in front of Mount **Ebal**,

6507 ²עֵיבָל **'êbāl²**, n.pr.m. & g. [3] [√ 6506]

Ebal [3]

Ge 36:23 The sons of Shobal: Alvan, Manahath, **Ebal**, Shepho and Onam.
Dt 11:29 on Mount Gerizim the blessings, and on Mount **Ebal** the curses.
1Ch 1:40 The sons of Shobal: Alvan, Manahath, **Ebal**, Shepho and Onam.

6508 ³עֵיבָל **'êbāl³**, n.pr.m. [1 / 0] [cf. 6382]

1Ch 1:22 Obal, [BHS *Ebal*; NIV 6382] Abimael, Sheba,

6509 עַיָּה **'ayyâ**, n.pr.loc. [2] [√ 6504; cf. 6569]

Aija [1], Ayyah [1]

1Ch 7:28 and Shechem and its villages all the way to **Ayyah** and its villages.
Ne 11:31 from Geba lived in Micmash, **Aija**, Bethel and its settlements,

6510 עִיּוֹן ***ʿiyyôn***, n.pr.loc. [3] [√ 6505]

Ijon [3]

1Ki 15:20 He conquered **Ijon**, Dan, Abel Beth Maacah and all Kinnereth in
2Ki 15:29 Tiglath-Pileser king of Assyria came and took **Ijon**, Abel Beth
2Ch 16: 4 They conquered **Ijon**, Dan, Abel Maim and all the store cities of

6511 עֲיוֹת ***ʿayôt***, n.pr.loc. [0] [cf. 6400]

1Ch 1:46 [His city was named **Avith**. [K; see Q 6400]]

6512 עִיט ***ʿîṭ*[1]**, v. [1] [cf. 6513]

hurled insults [1]

1Sa 25:14 [A] give our master his greetings, but *he* **hurled insults** at them.

6513 ²עִיט ***ʿîṭ*[2]**, v.den. [2] [→ 6514, 6515?; cf. 6512]

pounce [1], pounced [1]

1Sa 14:32 [A] They **pounced** [K 6913] on the plunder and, taking sheep,
15:19 [A] Why *did you* **pounce** on the plunder and do evil in the eyes

6514 עַיִט ***ʿayiṭ***, n.m. [8] [→ 6515?; cf. 6513]

bird of prey [3], birds of prey [3], birds [1], carrion birds [+7606] [1]

Ge 15:11 **birds of prey** came down on the carcasses, but Abram drove them
Job 28: 7 No **bird of prey** knows that hidden path, no falcon's eye has seen
Isa 18: 6 They will all be left to the mountain **birds of prey** and to the wild
18: 6 the **birds** will feed on them all summer, the wild animals all
46:11 From the east I summon a **bird of prey**; from a far-off land,
Jer 12: 9 Has not my inheritance become to me like a speckled **bird of prey**
12: 9 to me like a speckled bird of prey that other **birds of prey** surround
Eze 39: 4 I will give you as food to all kinds of **carrion birds** [+7606]

6515 עֵיטָם ***ʿêṭām***, n.pr.loc. [5] [√ 6514? + 4392?]

Etam [5]

Jdg 15: 8 Then he went down and stayed in a cave in the rock of **Etam**.
15:11 men from Judah went down to the cave in the rock of **Etam**
1Ch 4: 3 These were the sons of **Etam**: Jezreel, Ishma and Idbash. Their
4:32 Their surrounding villages were **Etam**, Ain, Rimmon, Token
2Ch 11: 6 Bethlehem, **Etam**, Tekoa,

6516 עִיֵּי הָעֲבָרִים ***ʿiyyê hāʿabārîm***, n.pr.loc. [2] [√ 6505 + 2192]

Iye Abarim [2]

Nu 21:11 Then they set out from Oboth and camped in **Iye Abarim**,
33:44 They left Oboth and camped at **Iye Abarim**, on the border of

6517 עִיִּים ***ʿiyyîm***, n.pr.loc. [2] [√ 6505]

Iim [1], Iyim [1]

Nu 33:45 They left **Iyim** and camped at Dibon Gad.
Jos 15:29 Baalah, **Iim**, Ezem,

6518 עֵילוֹם ***ʿêlôm***, n.m. [1 / 0] [cf. 6409]

2Ch 33: 7 I will put my Name forever. [BHS *forever* ?; NIV 6409]

6519 עִילַי ***ʿîlay***, n.pr.m. [1]

Ilai [1]

1Ch 11:29 Sibbecai the Hushathite, **Ilai** the Ahohite,

6520 ¹עֵילָם ***ʿêlām*[1]**, n.pr.g. & loc. [15] [→ 6521; Ar 10551]

Elam [14], Elam's [1]

Ge 14: 1 of Ellasar, Kedorlaomer king of **Elam** and Tidal king of Goiim
14: 9 against Kedorlaomer king of **Elam**, Tidal king of Goiim, Amraphel
Isa 11:11 from Cush, from **Elam**, from Babylonia, from Hamath and from
21: 2 the looter takes loot. **Elam**, attack! Media, lay siege!
22: 6 **Elam** takes up the quiver, with her charioteers and horses;
Jer 25:25 all the kings of Zimri, **Elam** and Media;
49:34 of the LORD that came to Jeremiah the prophet concerning **Elam**,
49:35 "See, I will break the bow of **Elam**, the mainstay of their might.
49:36 I will bring against **Elam** the four winds from the four quarters of
49:36 there will not be a nation where **Elam's** [K 6409] exiles do not go.
49:37 I will shatter **Elam** before their foes, before those who seek their
49:38 I will set my throne in **Elam** and destroy her king and officials,"
49:39 "Yet I will restore the fortunes of **Elam** in days to come,"
Eze 32:24 "**Elam** is there, with all her hordes around her grave. All of them
Da 8: 2 vision I saw myself in the citadel of Susa in the province of **Elam**;

6521 ²עֵילָם ***ʿêlām*[2]**, n.pr.m. [13] [√ 6520; Ar 10551]

Elam [13]

Ge 10:22 The sons of Shem: **Elam**, Asshur, Arphaxad, Lud and Aram.
1Ch 1:17 **Elam**, Asshur, Arphaxad, Lud and Aram. The sons of Aram:
8:24 Hananiah, **Elam**, Anthothijah,
26: 3 **Elam** the fifth, Jehohanan the sixth and Eliehoenai the seventh.
Ezr 2: 7 of **Elam** 1,254
2:31 of the other **Elam** 1,254
8: 7 of the descendants of **Elam**, Jeshaiah son of Athaliah, and with
10: 2 son of Jehiel, one of the descendants of **Elam**, said to Ezra,
10:26 From the descendants of **Elam**: Mattaniah, Zechariah, Jehiel,
Ne 7:12 of **Elam** 1,254
7:34 of the other **Elam** 1,254
10:14 [10:15] of the people: Parosh, Pahath-Moab, **Elam**, Zattu, Bani,
12:42 Shemaiah, Eleazar, Uzzi, Jehohanan, Malkijah, **Elam** and Ezer.

6522 עֲיָם ***ʿayām***, n.[m.] [1]

scorching [1]

Isa 11:15 with a **scorching** wind he will sweep his hand over the Euphrates

6523 עָיַן ***ʿāyan***, v.den. [1] [√ 6524]

kept jealous eye on [1]

1Sa 18: 9 [A] And from that time on Saul **kept** a **jealous eye on** David.

6524 ¹עַיִן ***ʿayin*[1]**, n.f. & m. [885] [→ 5078, 6523, 6526, 6543, 6544; cf. 6525; Ar 10540; *also used with compound proper names*]

eyes [437], sight [63], eye [36], *untranslated* [25], looked [25], presence [14], seems [+928] [10], spring [10], seemed [+928] [8], think [+928] [8], pleased [+928+3512] [7], face [6], look with pity [+2571] [6], look [6], before [+4200] [5], displeased [+928+8317] [5], look [+5951] [5], pleased with [+928+2834+5162] [5], pleases [+928+3202] [5], seem [+928] [4], to [+928] [4], with [+928] [4], favorably disposed toward [+928+2834] [3], fountain [3], like [+928+3202] [3], looked [+5951] [3], saw [+928] [3], watch [+4200] [3], watched [+4200] [3], watching [3], appearance [2], by [+928] [2], distressed [+928+8317] [2], full view [2], have respect for [+928+3700] [2], in presence [+4200+5584] [2], looked with pity [+2571] [2], on forehead [+1068] [2], on foreheads [+1068] [2], please [+928+3202] [2], please [+928+3837] [2], pleased [+928+3202] [2], pleased [+928+3837] [2], sees [+928] [2], show pity [+2571] [2], show pity [+2571+6584] [2], sparkled [2], spring [+4784] [2], springs [+4784] [2], thought [+928] [2], to [+4200] [2], watching [+4200] [2], angry [+928+3013] [1], appealed to [+928+3512] [1], appear [+928+2118+3869] [1], approve of [+928+3202] [1], before [+4200+5584] [1], begrudge [+928+928+928+8317] [1], by [+4200] [1], consider [+928] [1], considered [+928] [1], cover the offense [+4064] [1], despise [+928+1022] [1], despise [+928+7837] [1], despises [+928+1022] [1], despises [+928+7837] [1], disappeared [+2143+4946] [1], disapprove [+928+8317] [1], displease [+928+2834+4202+5162] [1], displease [+928+8273] [1], displeasing [+928+2834+4202+5162] [1], displeasing [+928+8273] [1], downcast [+8814] [1], eyebrows [+1461] [1], eyes [+1426] [1], eyesight [1], favorable toward [+928+2834+5162] [1], for [+928] [1], fountains [1], from [+4946] [1], from [+4946+5584] [1], from [+928] [1], front of heads [+1068] [1], galled [+928+8317] [1], generous man [+3202] [1], glad [+928+3512] [1], glance [1], gleam [1], have no [+4946+6259] [1], have no compassion [+8317] [1], in broad daylight [+2021+2021+2296+4200+9087] [1], in front of [+4200] [1], in full view [+5790] [1], judgment [1], keeping watch [+928+8011] [1], like [+3869] [1], liked [+928+3837] [1], look [+928] [1], look after [+6584+8492] [1], look after [+906+6584+8492] [1], look carefully [+928+8011] [1], look with compassion [+2571] [1], look with longing [+5951] [1], looked [+906] [1], looked [+928+2118] [1], looked about [+5951] [1], looks [+5951] [1], lost self-confidence [+928+4394 +5877] [1], never [+440] [1], not please [+928+8317] [1], not want [+928+8273] [1], outward appearance [1], please [+928+2256+3202 +3838] [1], please [+928+3838] [1], pleased [+928+3201] [1], pleased [+928+3838] [1], pleased with [+928+2834+5951] [1], pleased with [+928+3202] [1], pleased with [+928+3512] [1], pleased with [+928+3837] [1], pleases [+928+3512] [1], pools [1], prefer [+928+3202] [1], regards [+928+5162] [1], satisfied [+928+3512] [1], saw [+5260] [1], saw [+906+5951] [1], scorned the idea [+928+1022] [1], see [+4200] [1], see [+448] [1], see [+5260] [1], see [+6584 +8492] [1], see [+906+2021+4200+8011] [1], see [+906+8011] [1], see for yourselves [+4013+8011] [1], see to it [+4200] [1], seem [+928+2118+4200] [1], seem [+928+4017] [1], seemed [+928+2118] [1], show ill will [+8317] [1], show [1], showing pity [+2571] [1], sights [+5260] [1], sparkles [+5989] [1], sparkling [1], spring [+2021+4784] [1], springs [1], stay awake [+7219] [1], stingy [+8273] [1], stingy man

[+8273] [1], those[s] [1], took notice [+906+5951] [1], troubled [+928+8273] [1], unaware [+4946+6623] [1], upset [+906+928+8317] [1], us [+5646] [1], value [+4718] [1], value [+928+1540] [1], valued [+928+1540] [1], wanted to do [+928+3202] [1], watch [+928] [1], watch [1], watches [1], well [1], what see [1], winks maliciously [+7975] [1], wish [+928+3202] [1], wish [+928+3512] [1], wished [+928+3202] [1], without being aware [+4946] [1], won [+928+5951] [1]

Ge 3: 5 "For God knows that when you eat of it your **eyes** will be opened,
3: 6 that the fruit of the tree was good for food and pleasing to the **eye**,
3: 7 the **eyes** *of* both of them were opened, and they realized they were
6: 8 But Noah found favor in the **eyes** *of* the LORD.
13: 10 Lot **looked** up and saw that the whole plain of the Jordan was well
13: 14 "Lift up your **eyes** from where you are and look north and south,
16: 4 she was pregnant, *she began to* **despise** [+928+7837] her mistress.
16: 5 now that she knows she is pregnant, she **despises me** [+928+7837].
16: 6 Abram said. "Do with her whatever you **think** [+928] best."
16: 7 The angel of the LORD found Hagar near a **spring** [+2021+4784]
16: 7 in the desert; it was the **spring** that is beside the road to Shur.
18: 2 Abraham **looked** up and saw three men standing nearby. When he
18: 3 He said, "If I have found favor in your **eyes**, my lord, do not pass
19: 8 out to you, and you can do what you **like** [+928+3202] with them.
19: 14 the city!" But his sons-in-law **thought** [+928] he was joking.
19: 19 Your servant has found favor in your **eyes**, and you have shown
20: 15 "My land is before you; live wherever you **like** [+928+3202]."
20: 16 This is to **cover the offense** [+4064] against you before all who are
21: 11 The matter **distressed** [+928+8317] Abraham greatly because it
21: 12 "*Do* not *be so* **distressed** [+928+8317] about the boy and your
21: 19 God opened her **eyes** and she saw a well of water. So she went
22: 4 On the third day Abraham **looked** up and saw the place in the
22: 13 Abraham **looked** up and there in a thicket he saw a ram caught by
23: 11 I give it to you in the **presence** *of* my people. Bury your dead."
23: 18 to Abraham as his property in the **presence** of all the Hittites who
24: 13 See, I am standing beside this **spring** [+4784], and the daughters of
24: 16 She went down to the **spring**, filled her jar and came up again.
24: 29 brother named Laban, and he hurried out to the man at the **spring**.
24: 30 to the man and found him standing by the camels near the **spring**.
24: 42 "When I came to the **spring** today, I said, 'O LORD, God of my
24: 43 See, I am standing beside this **spring** [+4784]; if a maiden comes
24: 45 She went down to the **spring** and drew water, and I said to her,
24: 63 to meditate, and *as* he **looked** up, he saw camels approaching.
24: 64 Rebekah also **looked** up and saw Isaac. She got down from her
27: 1 When Isaac was old and his **eyes** were so weak that he could no
27: 12 *I would* **appear** [+928+2118+3869] to be tricking him and would
28: 8 **displeasing** the Canaanite women were **to** [+928+8273] his father
29: 17 Leah had weak **eyes**, but Rachel was lovely in form, and beautiful.
29: 20 but *they* **seemed** [+928+2118] like only a few days *to* him
30: 27 Laban said to him, "If I have found favor in your **eyes**, please stay.
30: 41 Jacob would place the branches in the troughs **in front** [+4200] **of**
31: 10 "In breeding season I once had a dream in which I **looked** up
31: 12 '**Look** up and see that all the male goats mating with the flock are
31: 35 Rachel said to her father, "Don't *be* **angry** [+928+3013], my lord,
31: 40 in the daytime and the cold at night, and sleep fled from my **eyes**.
32: 5 [32:6] message to my lord, that I may find favor in your **eyes**.' "
33: 1 Jacob **looked** up and there was Esau, coming with his four hundred
33: 5 Esau **looked** up and saw the women and children. "Who are these
33: 8 droves I met?" "To find favor in *your* **eyes**, my lord," he said.
33: 10 "If I have found favor in your **eyes**, accept this gift from me.
33: 15 Jacob asked. "Just let me find favor in the **eyes** *of* my lord."
34: 11 to Dinah's father and brothers, "Let me find favor in your **eyes**,
34: 18 Their proposal **seemed** [+928] good to Hamor and his son
34: 18 proposal seemed good to Hamor and **[RPH]** his son Shechem.
37: 25 they **looked** up and saw a caravan of Ishmaelites coming from
38: 7 But Er, Judah's firstborn, was wicked in the LORD's **sight**;
38: 10 What he did was wicked in the LORD's **sight**; so he put him to
39: 4 Joseph found favor in his **eyes** and became his attendant. Potiphar
39: 7 after a while his master's wife **took notice** [+906+5951] of Joseph
39: 21 and granted him favor in the **eyes** *of* the prison warden.
41: 37 The plan **seemed** [+928] good *to* Pharaoh and to all his officials.
41: 37 The plan seemed good to Pharaoh and to **[RPH]** all his officials.
42: 24 He had Simeon taken from them and bound before their **eyes**.
43: 29 As he **looked** [+5951] **about** and saw his brother Benjamin,
44: 21 'Bring him down to me so *I can* **see** [+6584+8492] him for myself.'
45: 5 and do not be angry **with** [+928] yourselves for selling me here,
45: 12 "*You can* **see for yourselves** [+4013+8011], and so can my brother
45: 12 can see for yourselves, and so can **[RPH]** my brother Benjamin,
45: 16 had come, Pharaoh and all his officials *were* **pleased** [+928+3512].
45: 16 had come, Pharaoh and all his officials were pleased. **[RPH]**
45: 20 **Never** [+440] mind about your belongings, because the best of all
46: 4 you back again. And Joseph's own hand will close your **eyes**."
47: 19 Why should we perish before your **eyes**—we and our land as well?
47: 25 "May we find favor in the **eyes** *of* our lord; we will be in bondage
47: 29 his son Joseph and said to him, "If I have found favor in your **eyes**,
48: 10 Now Israel's **eyes** were failing because of old age, and he could
48: 17 his right hand on Ephraim's head he *was* **displeased** [+928+8317];
49: 12 His **eyes** will be darker than wine, his teeth whiter than milk.
49: 22 "Joseph is a fruitful vine, a fruitful vine near a **spring**,
50: 4 "If I have found favor in your **eyes**, speak to Pharaoh for me.
Ex 3: 21 Egyptians **favorably disposed toward** [+928+2834] this people,
4: 30 to Moses. He also performed the signs **before** [+4200] the people,
5: 21 You have made us a stench **to** [+928] Pharaoh and his officials
5: 21 You have made us a stench to Pharaoh and **[RPH]** his officials
7: 20 He raised his staff in the **presence** *of* Pharaoh and his officials
7: 20 and **[RPH]** his officials and struck the water of the Nile,
8: 26 [8:22] And if we offer sacrifices that are detestable in their **eyes**,
9: 8 and have Moses toss it into the air in the **presence** *of* Pharaoh.
10: 5 They will cover the **face** *of* the ground so that it cannot be seen.
10: 15 They covered **[NIE]** all the ground until it was black. They
11: 3 Egyptians **favorably disposed toward** [+928+2834] the people,
11: 3 Moses himself was highly regarded in Egypt **by** [+928] Pharaoh's
11: 3 in Egypt by Pharaoh's officials and **by** [+928] the people.)
12: 36 Egyptians **favorably disposed toward** [+928+2834] the people,
13: 9 a reminder **on** your **forehead** [+1068] that the law of the LORD
13: 16 a symbol **on** your **forehead** [+1068] that the LORD brought us
14: 10 As Pharaoh approached, the Israelites **looked** up, and there were
15: 26 the voice of the LORD your God and do what is right in his **eyes**,
15: 27 where there were twelve **springs** [+4784] and seventy palm trees,
17: 6 to drink." So Moses did this in the **sight** *of* the elders of Israel.
19: 11 will come down on Mount Sinai in the **sight** *of* all the people.
21: 8 If *she does* **not please** [+928+8317] the master who has selected
21: 24 **eye** for eye, tooth for tooth, hand for hand, foot for foot,
21: 24 eye for **eye**, tooth for tooth, hand for hand, foot for foot,
21: 26 a man hits a manservant or maidservant in the **eye** and destroys it,
21: 26 a manservant or maidservant in the eye **[RPH]** and destroys it,
21: 26 he must let the servant go free to compensate for the **eye**.
24: 17 **To** [+4200] the Israelites the glory of the LORD looked like a
33: 12 'I know you by name and you have found favor **with** [+928] me.'
33: 13 If you *are* **pleased with me** [+928+2834+5162], teach me your
33: 13 so I may know you and continue to find favor **with** [+928] you.
33: 16 anyone know that you *are* **pleased with** [+928+2834+5162] me
33: 17 because I *am* **pleased with you** [+928+2834+5162] and I know
34: 9 "O Lord, if I have found favor in your **eyes**," he said, "then let the
40: 38 in the **sight** *of* all the house of Israel during all their travels.
Lev 4: 13 even though the community *is* **unaware of** [+4946+6623] the
10: 19 *Would* the LORD *have been* **pleased** [+928+3512] if I had eaten
10: 20 When Moses heard this, he *was* **satisfied** [+928+3512].
13: 5 if he **sees** [+928] that the sore is unchanged and has not spread in
13: 12 out all over his skin and, so far as the priest can **see** [+5260],
13: 37 in his **judgment** it is unchanged and black hair has grown in it,
13: 55 is to examine it, and if the mildew has not changed its **appearance**,
14: 9 his head, his beard, his **eyebrows** [+1461] and the rest of his hair.
20: 4 If the people of the community close their **eyes** when that man
20: 17 is a disgrace. They must be cut off before the **eyes** *of* their people.
21: 20 or who is hunchbacked or dwarfed, or who has any **eye** defect,
24: 20 fracture for fracture, **eye** for eye, tooth for tooth. As he has injured
24: 20 fracture for fracture, eye for **eye**, tooth for tooth. As he has injured
25: 53 you must **see** [+4200] **to it** that his owner does not rule over him
26: 16 wasting diseases and fever that will destroy your **sight** and drain
26: 45 I brought out of Egypt in the **sight** *of* the nations to be their God.
Nu 5: 13 this is hidden **from** [+4946] her husband and her impurity is
10: 31 where we should camp in the desert, and you can be our **eyes**.
11: 6 lost our appetite; we never **see** [+448] anything but this manna!"
11: 7 The manna was like coriander seed and **looked** like resin.
11: 7 The manna was like coriander seed and looked like **[RPH]** resin.
11: 10 became exceedingly angry, and Moses was **troubled** [+928+8273].
11: 11 What *have I done to* **displease** [+928+2834+4202+5162] you that
11: 15 put me to death right now—if I have found favor in your **eyes**—
13: 33 We seemed like grasshoppers in our own **eyes**, and we looked the
13: 33 in our own eyes, and *we* **looked** [+928+2118] the same *to* them."
14: 14 these people and that you, O LORD, have been seen **face** to face,
14: 14 these people and that you, O LORD, have been seen face to **face**,
15: 24 unintentionally **without** the community **being aware** [+4946] *of* it,
15: 39 yourselves by going after the lusts of your own hearts and **eyes**.
16: 14 Will you gouge out the **eyes** *of* these men? No, we will not come!"
19: 5 While he **watches**, the heifer is to be burned—its hide, flesh,
20: 8 Speak to that rock before their **eyes** and it will pour out its water.
20: 12 in me enough to honor me as holy in the **sight** *of* the Israelites,
20: 27 They went up Mount Hor in the **sight** *of* the whole community.
22: 5 they cover the **face** *of* the land and have settled next to me.
22: 11 'A people that has come out of Egypt covers the **face** *of* the land.
22: 31 the LORD opened Balaam's **eyes**, and he saw the angel of the
22: 34 Now if you *are* **displeased** [+928+8317], I will go back."
23: 27 Perhaps *it will* **please** [+928+3837] God to let you curse them for
24: 1 Now when Balaam saw that *it* **pleased** [+928+3201] the LORD to
24: 2 When Balaam **looked** out and saw Israel encamped tribe by tribe,
24: 3 of Balaam son of Beor, the oracle of one whose **eye** sees clearly,
24: 4 the Almighty, who falls prostrate, and whose **eyes** are opened:
24: 15 of Balaam son of Beor, the oracle of one whose **eye** sees clearly,

Nu 24:16 the Almighty, who falls prostrate, and whose **eyes** are opened:
25: 6 to his family a Midianite woman right before the **eyes** *of* Moses
25: 6 **[RPH]** the whole assembly of Israel while they were weeping at
27:14 disobeyed my command to honor me as holy before their **eyes**."
27:19 and the entire assembly and commission him in their **presence**.
32: 5 If we have found favor in your **eyes**," they said, "let this land be
32:13 until the whole generation of those who had done evil in his **sight**
33: 3 They marched out boldly in **full view** *of* all the Egyptians,
33: 9 where there were twelve **springs** [+4784] and seventy palm trees,
33:55 those you allow to remain will become barbs in your **eyes**
36: 6 They may marry anyone they **please** [+928+3202] as long as they
Dt 1:23 The idea **seemed** [+928] good *to* me; so I selected twelve of you,
1:30 fight for you, as he did for you in Egypt, before your very **eyes**,
3:21 "You have seen with your own **eyes** all that the LORD your God
3:27 top of Pisgah and **look** [+5951] west and north and south and east.
3:27 Look at the land with your own **eyes**, since you are not going to
4: 3 You saw with your own **eyes** what the LORD did at Baal Peor.
4: 6 for this will **show** your wisdom and understanding to the nations,
4: 9 so that you do not forget the things your **eyes** have seen
4:19 And when you **look** up to the sky and see the sun, the moon
4:25 doing evil in the **eyes** *of* the LORD your God and provoking him
4:34 the LORD your God did for you in Egypt before your very **eyes**?
6: 8 symbols on your hands and bind them **on** your **foreheads** [+1068].
6:18 Do what is right and good in the LORD's **sight**, so that it may go
6:22 Before our **eyes** the LORD sent miraculous signs and wonders—
7:16 *Do* not **look** on them **with pity** [+2571] and do not serve their
7:19 You saw with your own **eyes** the great trials, the miraculous signs
8: 7 a land with streams and **pools** of water, with springs flowing in the
9:17 them out of my hands, breaking them to pieces before your **eyes**.
9:18 doing what was evil in the LORD's **sight** and so provoking him
10:21 those great and awesome wonders you saw with your own **eyes**.
11: 7 it was your own **eyes** that saw all these great things the LORD has
11:12 the **eyes** *of* the LORD your God are continually on it from the
11:18 symbols on your hands and bind them **on** your **foreheads** [+1068].
12: 8 are not to do as we do here today, everyone as he **sees** [+928] fit,
12:25 because you will be doing what is right in the **eyes** *of* the LORD.
12:28 doing what is good and right in the **eyes** *of* the LORD your God.
13: 8 [13:9] to him or listen to him. **Show** him no **pity** [+2571+6584].
13:18 [13:19] I am giving you today and doing what is right in his **eyes**.
14: 1 or shave the **front of** your **heads** [+1068] for the dead,
15: 9 so that you *do* not **show ill will** [+8317] toward your needy brother
15:18 *Do* not **consider** [+928] it a hardship to set your servant free,
16:19 for a bribe blinds the **eyes** *of* the wise and twists the words of the
17: 2 in the **eyes** *of* the LORD your God in violation of his covenant,
19:13 **Show** him no **pity** [+2571+6584]. You must purge from Israel the
19:21 **Show** no **pity** [+2571]: life for life, eye for eye, tooth for tooth,
19:21 life for life, **eye** for eye, tooth for tooth, hand for hand, foot for
19:21 life for life, eye for **eye**, tooth for tooth, hand for hand, foot for
21: 7 "Our hands did not shed this blood, nor did our **eyes** see it done.
21: 9 since you have done what is right in the **eyes** *of* the LORD.
24: 1 who becomes **displeasing to** [+928+2834+4202+5162] him
25: 3 flogged more than that, your brother will be degraded in your **eyes**.
25: 9 his brother's widow shall go up to him in the **presence** *of* the
25:12 you shall cut off her hand. **Show** her no **pity** [+2571].
28:31 Your ox will be slaughtered before your **eyes**, but you will eat none
28:32 and you will wear out your **eyes** watching for them day after day,
28:34 The **sights** [+5260] you see will drive you mad.
28:54 sensitive man among you *will* **have no compassion** [+8317] on his
28:56 *will* **begrudge** [+928+928+928+8317] the husband she loves and
28:65 an anxious mind, **eyes** weary with longing, and a despairing heart.
28:67 that will fill your hearts and the sights that your **eyes** will see.
29: 2 [29:1] Your **eyes** have seen all that the LORD did in Egypt to
29: 3 [29:2] With your own **eyes** you saw those great trials, those
29: 4 [29:3] a mind that understands or **eyes** that see or ears that hear.
31: 7 summoned Joshua and said to him in the **presence** *of* all Israel,
31:29 fall upon you because you will do evil in the **sight** *of* the LORD
32:10 and cared for him; he guarded him as the apple of his **eye**,
33:28 Jacob's **spring** is secure in a land of grain and new wine, where the
34: 4 I have let you see it with your **eyes**, but you will not cross over into
34: 7 old when he died, yet his **eyes** were not weak nor his strength gone.
34:12 or performed the awesome deeds that Moses did in the **sight** *of* all
Jos 3: 7 to Joshua, "Today I will begin to exalt you in the **eyes** *of* all Israel,
4:14 That day the LORD exalted Joshua in the **sight** *of* all Israel;
5:13 he **looked** up and saw a man standing in front of him with a drawn
9:25 Do to us whatever **seems** [+928] good and right *to* you."
10:12 over to Israel, Joshua said to the LORD in the **presence** *of* Israel:
22:30 and Manasseh had to say, they *were* **pleased** [+928+3512].
22:33 They *were* **glad** [+928+3512] to hear the report and praised God.
23:13 and traps for you, whips on your backs and thorns in your **eyes**,
24: 7 You saw with your own **eyes** what I did to the Egyptians.
24:15 But if serving the LORD **seems** [+928] undesirable *to* you,
24:17 land of slavery, and performed those great signs before our **eyes**.
Jdg 2:11 the Israelites did evil in the **eyes** *of* the LORD and served the
3: 7 The Israelites did evil in the **eyes** *of* the LORD; they forgot the
3:12 Once again the Israelites did evil in the **eyes** *of* the LORD,
3:12 because they did this evil **[RPH]** the LORD gave Eglon king of
4: 1 the Israelites once again did evil in the **eyes** *of* the LORD.
6: 1 Again the Israelites did evil in the **eyes** *of* the LORD, and for
6:17 Gideon replied, "If now I have found favor in your **eyes**, give me a
6:21 And the angel of the LORD **disappeared** [+2143+4946].
7: 1 (that is, Gideon) and all his men camped at the **spring** *of* Harod.
10: 6 Again the Israelites did evil in the **eyes** *of* the LORD. They served
10:15 Do with us whatever you **think** [+928] best, but please rescue us
13: 1 Again the Israelites did evil in the **eyes** *of* the LORD,
14: 3 to his father, "Get her for me. She's the right one **for** [+928] me."
14: 7 and talked with the woman, and he **liked** [+928+3837] her.
16:21 seized him, gouged out his **eyes** and took him down to Gaza.
16:28 me with one blow get revenge on the Philistines for my two **eyes**."
17: 6 In those days Israel had no king; everyone did as he **saw** [+928] fit.
19:17 When *he* **looked** [+5951] and saw the traveler in the city square,
19:24 you can use them and do to them whatever you **wish** [+928+3202].
21:25 In those days Israel had no king; everyone did as he **saw** [+928] fit.
Ru 2: 2 pick up the leftover grain behind anyone in whose **eyes** I find
2: 9 **Watch** [+928] the field where the men are harvesting, and follow
2:10 "Why have I found such favor in your **eyes** that you notice me—
2:13 "May I continue to find favor in your **eyes**, my lord," she said.
1Sa 1:18 She said, "May your servant find favor in your **eyes**." Then she
1:23 "Do what **seems** [+928] best *to* you," Elkanah her husband told
2:33 off from my altar will be spared only to blind your **eyes** with tears
3: 2 whose **eyes** were becoming so weak that he could barely see,
3:18 Eli said, "He is the LORD; let him do what is good in his **eyes**."
4:15 years old and whose **eyes** were set so that he could not see.
6:13 when they **looked** up and saw the ark, they rejoiced at the sight.
8: 6 "Give us a king to lead us," this **displeased** [+928+8317] Samuel;
11: 2 on the condition that I gouge out the right **eye** of every one of you
11:10 and you can do to us whatever **seems** [+928] good *to* you."
12: 3 whose hand have I accepted a bribe to make me shut my **eyes**?
12:16 see this great thing the LORD is about to do before your **eyes**!
12:17 you will realize what an evil thing you did in the **eyes** *of* the
14:27 He raised his hand to his mouth, and his **eyes** brightened.
14:29 See how my **eyes** brightened when I tasted a little of this honey.
14:36 "Do whatever **seems** [+928] best *to* you," they replied.
14:40 over here." "Do what **seems** [+928] best *to* you," the men replied.
15:17 Samuel said, "Although you were once small in your own **eyes**,
15:19 you pounce on the plunder and do evil in the **eyes** *of* the LORD?"
16: 7 Man looks at the **outward appearance**, but the LORD looks at
16:12 He was ruddy, with a fine **appearance** and handsome features.
16:22 in my service, for I *am* **pleased with him** [+928+2834+5162]."
18: 5 *This* **pleased** [+928+3512] all the people, and Saul's officers as
18: 5 This pleased all the people, and **[RPH]** Saul's officers as well.
18: 8 Saul was very angry; this refrain **galled** [+928+8317] him.
18:20 and when they told Saul about it, he *was* **pleased** [+928+3837].
18:23 "Do you **think** [+928] it is a small matter to become the king's
18:26 he *was* **pleased** [+928+3837] to become the king's son-in-law.
20: 3 "Your father knows very well that I have found favor in your **eyes**,
20:29 If I have found favor in your **eyes**, let me get away to see my
21:13 [21:14] So he pretended to be insane in their **presence**; and while
24: 4 [24:5] you **wish** [+928+3512].' " Then David crept up unnoticed
24:10 [24:11] This day you have seen with your own **eyes** how the
25: 8 Therefore *be* **favorable toward** [+928+2834+5162] my young
26:21 Because you **considered** [+928] my life precious today, I will not
26:24 As surely as I **valued** [+928+1540] your life today, so may the
26:24 so *may* the LORD **value** [+928+1540] my life and deliver me
27: 5 Then David said to Achish, "If I have found favor in your **eyes**,
29: 1 their forces at Aphek, and Israel camped by the **spring** in Jezreel.
29: 6 I would be **pleased** [+928+3202] to have you serve with me in the
29: 6 no fault in you, but the rulers don't **approve of** [+928+3202] you.
29: 7 do nothing to **displease** [+928+8273] the Philistine rulers."
29: 9 "I know that you have been as pleasing in my **eyes** as an angel of
2Sa 3:19 and the whole house of Benjamin **wanted to do** [+928+3202].
3:19 that Israel and the whole house of Benjamin wanted to do. **[RPH]**
3:36 All the people took note and *were* **pleased** [+928+3512]; indeed,
3:36 indeed, everything the king did **pleased** [+928+3202] them.
4:10 and **thought** [+928] he was bringing good news, I seized him
6:20 disrobing in the **sight** *of* the slave girls of his servants as any
6:22 undignified than this, and I will be humiliated in my own **eyes**.
7:19 And as if this were not enough in your **sight**, O Sovereign LORD,
10: 3 "Do you **think** [+928] David is honoring your father by sending
10:12 cities of our God. The LORD will do what is good in his **sight**."
11:25 'Don't *let* this **upset** [+906+928+8317] you; the sword devours one
11:27 the thing David had done **displeased** [+928+8317] the LORD.
12: 9 despise the word of the LORD by doing what is evil in his **eyes**?
12:11 Before your very **eyes** I will take your wives and give them to one
12:11 your wives **in broad daylight** [+2021+2021+2296+4200+9087].
13: 2 and it **seemed** [+928] impossible for him to do anything to her.
13: 5 Let her prepare the food in my **sight** so I may watch her and
13: 6 my sister Tamar to come and make some special bread in my **sight**,
13: 8 some dough, kneaded it, made the bread in his **sight** and baked it.

2Sa 13:34 Now the man standing watch **looked** [+906] up and saw many
14:22 "Today your servant knows that he has found favor in your **eyes**,
15:25 If I find favor in the LORD's **eyes**, he will bring me back
15:26 I am ready; let him do to me whatever **seems** [+928] good *to* him."
16: 4 Ziba said. "May I find favor in your **eyes**, my lord the king."
16:12 [the LORD will see my distress [BHS Q, K 6411 *sin*; NIV 6715]]
16:22 and he lay with his father's concubines in the **sight** *of* all Israel.
17: 4 This plan **seemed** [+928] good *to* Absalom and to all the elders of
17: 4 seemed good to Absalom and to **[RPH]** all the elders of Israel.
18: 4 The king answered, "I will do whatever **seems** [+928] best *to* you."
18:24 by the wall. As he **looked** out, he saw a man running alone.
19: 6 [19:7] I see that you would be **pleased** [+928+3838] if Absalom
19:18 [19:19] and to do whatever he **wished** [+928+3202].
19:27 [19:28] angel of God; so do whatever **pleases** [+928+3202] you.
19:37 [19:38] the king. Do for him whatever **pleases** [+928+3202] you."
19:38 [19:39] and I will do for him whatever **pleases** [+928+3202] you.
20: 6 or he will find fortified cities and escape from **us** [+5646]."
22:25 to my righteousness, according to my cleanness in his **sight**.
22:28 the humble, but your **eyes** are on the haughty to bring them low.
24: 3 a hundred times over, and may the **eyes** *of* my lord the king see it.
24:22 "Let my lord the king take whatever **pleases** [+928+3202] him
1Ki 1:20 My lord the king, the **eyes** *of* all Israel are on you, to learn from
1:48 who has allowed my **eyes** to see a successor on my throne
3:10 The Lord *was* **pleased** [+928+3512] that Solomon had asked for
8:29 May your **eyes** be open toward this temple night and day, this place
8:52 "May your **eyes** be open to your servant's plea and to the plea of
9: 3 Name there forever. My **eyes** and my heart will always be there.
9:12 had given him, he *was* not **pleased with** [+928+3837] them.
10: 7 not believe these things until I came and saw with my own **eyes**.
11: 6 So Solomon did evil in the **eyes** *of* the LORD; he did not follow
11:19 Pharaoh *was* so **pleased with** [+928+2834+5162] Hadad that he
11:33 nor done what is right in my **eyes**, nor kept my statutes and laws as
11:38 do what is right in my **eyes** by keeping my statutes and commands,
14: 4 Now Ahijah could not see; his **sight** was gone because of his age.
14: 8 me with all his heart, doing only what was right in my **eyes**.
14:22 Judah did evil in the **eyes** *of* the LORD. By the sins they
15: 5 For David had done what was right in the **eyes** *of* the LORD
15:11 Asa did what was right in the **eyes** *of* the LORD, as his father
15:26 He did evil in the **eyes** *of* the LORD, walking in the ways of his
15:34 He did evil in the **eyes** *of* the LORD, walking in the ways of
16: 7 because of all the evil he had done in the **eyes** *of* the LORD,
16:19 doing evil in the **eyes** *of* the LORD and walking in the ways of
16:25 Omri did evil in the **eyes** *of* the LORD and sinned more than all
16:30 Ahab son of Omri did more evil in the **eyes** *of* the LORD than
20: 6 They will seize everything you **value** [+4718] and carry it away.' "
20:38 He disguised himself with his headband down over his **eyes**.
20:41 Then the prophet quickly removed the headband from his **eyes**,
21: 2 if you **prefer** [+928+3202], I will pay you whatever it is worth."
21:20 "because you have sold yourself to do evil in the **eyes** *of* the
21:25 who sold himself to do evil in the **eyes** *of* the LORD, urged on by
22:43 stray from them; he did what was right in the **eyes** *of* the LORD.
22:52 [22:53] He did evil in the **eyes** *of* the LORD, because he walked
2Ki 1:13 "please **have respect for** [+928+3700] my life and the lives of
1:14 all their men. But now **have respect for** [+928+3700] my life!"
3: 2 He did evil in the **eyes** *of* the LORD, but not as his father
3:18 This is an easy thing in the **eyes** *of* the LORD; he will also hand
4:34 lay upon the boy, mouth to mouth, **eyes** to eyes, hands to hands.
4:34 lay upon the boy, mouth to mouth, eyes to **eyes**, hands to hands.
4:35 him once more. The boy sneezed seven times and opened his **eyes**.
6:17 And Elisha prayed, "O LORD, open his **eyes** so he may see."
6:17 Then the LORD opened the servant's **eyes**, and he looked
6:20 Elisha said, "LORD, open the **eyes** *of* these men so they can see."
6:20 the LORD opened their **eyes** and they looked, and there they
7: 2 "You will see it with your own **eyes**," answered Elisha, "but you
7:19 The man of God had replied, "You will see it with your own **eyes**,
8:18 married a daughter of Ahab. He did evil in the **eyes** *of* the LORD.
8:27 ways of the house of Ahab and did evil in the **eyes** *of* the LORD,
9:30 she painted her **eyes**, arranged her hair and looked out of a
10: 5 appoint anyone as king; you do whatever you **think** [+928] best."
10:30 you have done well in accomplishing what is right in my **eyes**
12: 2 [12:3] Joash did what was right in the **eyes** *of* the LORD all the
13: 2 He did evil in the **eyes** *of* the LORD by following the sins of
13:11 He did evil in the **eyes** *of* the LORD and did not turn away from
14: 3 He did what was right in the **eyes** *of* the LORD, but not as his
14:24 He did evil in the **eyes** *of* the LORD and did not turn away from
15: 3 He did what was right in the **eyes** *of* the LORD, just as his father
15: 9 He did evil in the **eyes** *of* the LORD, as his fathers had done.
15:18 He did evil in the **eyes** *of* the LORD. During his entire reign he
15:24 Pekahiah did evil in the **eyes** *of* the LORD. He did not turn away
15:28 He did evil in the **eyes** *of* the LORD. He did not turn away from
15:34 He did what was right in the **eyes** *of* the LORD, just as his father
16: 2 he did not do what was right in the **eyes** *of* the LORD his God.
17: 2 He did evil in the **eyes** *of* the LORD, but not like the kings of
17:17 and sold themselves to do evil in the **eyes** *of* the LORD,
18: 3 He did what was right in the **eyes** *of* the LORD, just as his father
19:16 O LORD, and hear; open your **eyes**, O LORD, and see;
19:22 whom have you raised your voice and lifted your **eyes** in pride?
20: 3 wholehearted devotion and have done what is good in your **eyes**."
21: 2 He did evil in the **eyes** *of* the LORD, following the detestable
21: 6 He did much evil in the **eyes** *of* the LORD, provoking him to
21:15 because they have done evil in my **eyes** and have provoked me to
21:16 Judah to commit, so that they did evil in the **eyes** *of* the LORD.
21:20 He did evil in the **eyes** *of* the LORD, as his father Manasseh had
22: 2 He did what was right in the **eyes** *of* the LORD and walked in all
22:20 Your **eyes** will not see all the disaster I am going to bring on this
23:32 He did evil in the **eyes** *of* the LORD, just as his fathers had done.
23:37 he did evil in the **eyes** *of* the LORD, just as his fathers had done.
24: 9 He did evil in the **eyes** *of* the LORD, just as his father had done.
24:19 He did evil in the **eyes** *of* the LORD, just as Jehoiakim had done.
25: 7 They killed the sons of Zedekiah before his **eyes**. Then they put out
25: 7 Then they put out his **eyes**, bound him with bronze shackles
1Ch 2: 3 Er, Judah's firstborn, was wicked in the LORD's **sight**;
13: 4 agreed to do this, because it **seemed** [+928] right *to* all the people.
17:17 as if this were not enough in your **sight**, O God, you have spoken
19: 3 "Do you **think** [+928] David is honoring your father by sending
19:13 cities of our God. The LORD will do what is good in his **sight**."
21: 7 This command was also evil in the **sight** *of* God; so he punished
21:16 David **looked** up and saw the angel of the LORD standing
21:23 Let my lord the king do whatever **pleases** [+928+3202] him.
28: 8 "So now I charge you in the **sight** *of* all Israel and of the assembly
29:10 David praised the LORD in the **presence** *of* the whole assembly,
29:25 The LORD highly exalted Solomon in the **sight** *of* all Israel
2Ch 6:20 May your **eyes** be open toward this temple day and night, this place
6:40 may your **eyes** be open and your ears attentive to the prayers
7:15 Now my **eyes** will be open and my ears attentive to the prayers
7:16 may be there forever. My **eyes** and my heart will always be there.
9: 6 not believe what they said until I came and saw with my own **eyes**.
14: 2 [14:1] was good and right in the **eyes** *of* the LORD his God.
16: 9 For the **eyes** *of* the LORD range throughout the earth to
20:12 We do not know what to do, but our **eyes** are upon you."
20:32 stray from them; he did what was right in the **eyes** *of* the LORD.
21: 6 married a daughter of Ahab. He did evil in the **eyes** *of* the LORD.
22: 4 He did evil in the **eyes** *of* the LORD, as the house of Ahab had
24: 2 Joash did what was right in the **eyes** *of* the LORD all the years of
25: 2 He did what was right in the **eyes** *of* the LORD, but not
26: 4 He did what was right in the **eyes** *of* the LORD, just as his father
27: 2 He did what was right in the **eyes** *of* the LORD, just as his father
28: 1 his father, he did not do what was right in the **eyes** *of* the LORD.
29: 2 He did what was right in the **eyes** *of* the LORD, just as his father
29: 6 they did evil in the **eyes** *of* the LORD our God and forsook him.
29: 8 of dread and horror and scorn, as you can see with your own **eyes**.
30: 4 The plan **seemed** [+928] right both *to* the king and to the whole
30: 4 seemed right both to the king and to **[RPH]** the whole assembly.
32: 3 military staff about blocking off the water from the **springs** outside
32:23 then on he was highly regarded **by** [+4200] all the nations.
33: 2 He did evil in the **eyes** *of* the LORD, following the detestable
33: 6 He did much evil in the **eyes** *of* the LORD, provoking him to
33:22 He did evil in the **eyes** *of* the LORD, as his father Manasseh had
34: 2 He did what was right in the **eyes** *of* the LORD and walked in the
34:28 Your **eyes** will not see all the disaster I am going to bring on this
36: 5 eleven years. He did evil in the **eyes** *of* the LORD his God.
36: 9 three months and ten days. He did evil in the **eyes** *of* the LORD.
36:12 He did evil in the **eyes** *of* the LORD his God and did not humble
Ezr 3:12 wept aloud when they **saw** [+928] the foundation of this temple
9: 8 so our God gives light to our **eyes** and a little relief in our bondage.
Ne 1: 6 your **eyes** open to hear the prayer your servant is praying before
2:13 night I went out through the Valley Gate toward the Jackal **Well**
2:14 Then I moved on toward the **Fountain** Gate and the King's Pool,
3:15 The **Fountain** Gate was repaired by Shallun son of Col-Hozeh,
6:16 were afraid and **lost** their **self-confidence** [+928+4394+5877],
8: 5 All the people could **see** [+4200] him because he was standing
12:37 At the **Fountain** Gate they continued directly up the steps of the
Est 1:17 and so they *will* **despise** [+928+1022] their husbands and say,
1:21 and his nobles *were* **pleased with** [+928+3512] this advice,
2: 4 let the girl who **pleases** [+928+3512] the king be queen instead of
2: 4 This advice **appealed to** [+928+3512] the king, and he followed it.
2: 9 The girl **pleased** [+928+3512] him and won his favor. Immediately
2:15 And Esther **won** [+928+5951] the favor of everyone who saw her.
3: 6 he **scorned the idea** [+928+1022] of killing only Mordecai.
3:11 to Haman, "and do with the people as you **please** [+928+3202]."
5: 2 he *was* **pleased with her** [+928+2834+5951] and held out to her
5: 8 If the king **regards** *me* **with** [+928+5162] favor and if it pleases
7: 3 "If I have found favor **with** [+928] you, O king, and if it pleases
8: 5 it the right thing to do, and if he is **pleased with** [+928+3202] me,
8: 8 the king's name in behalf of the Jews as **seems** [+928] best *to* you,
Job 2:12 When *they* **saw** [+906+5951] him from a distance, they could
3:10 shut the doors of the womb on me to hide trouble from my **eyes**.
4:16 A form stood before my **eyes**, and I heard a hushed voice:

Job 7: 7 that my life is but a breath; my **eyes** will never see happiness again.
7: 8 The **eye** that now sees me will see me no longer; you will look for
7: 8 will see me no longer; you will **look** for me, but I will be no more.
10: 4 Do you have **eyes** *of* flesh? Do you see as a mortal sees?
10: 18 me out of the womb? I wish I had died before any **eye** saw me.
11: 4 say to God, 'My beliefs are flawless and I am pure in your **sight**.'
11: 20 But the **eyes** *of* the wicked will fail, and escape will elude them;
13: 1 "My **eyes** have seen all this, my ears have heard and understood it.
14: 3 Do you fix your **eye** on such a one? Will you bring him before you
15: 12 Why has your heart carried you away, and why do your **eyes** flash,
15: 15 trust in his holy ones, if even the heavens are not pure in his **eyes**,
16: 9 his teeth at me; my opponent fastens on me his piercing **eyes**.
16: 20 My intercessor is my friend as my **eyes** pour out tears to God;
17: 2 mockers surround me; my **eyes** must dwell on their hostility.
17: 5 denounces his friends for reward, the **eyes** *of* his children will fail.
17: 7 My **eyes** have grown dim with grief; my whole frame is but a
18: 3 Why are we regarded as cattle and considered stupid in your **sight**?
19: 15 count me a stranger; they **look** [+928] *upon* me as an alien.
19: 27 I myself will see him with my own **eyes**—I, and not another.
20: 9 The **eye** that saw him will not see him again; his place will look on
21: 8 children established around them, their offspring before their **eyes**.
21: 20 Let his own **eyes** see his destruction; let him drink of the wrath of
22: 29 you say, 'Lift them up!' then he will save the **downcast** [+8814].
24: 15 The **eye** *of* the adulterer watches for dusk; he thinks, 'No eye will
24: 15 he thinks, 'No **eye** will see me,' and he keeps his face concealed.
24: 23 let them rest in a feeling of security, but his **eyes** are on their ways.
25: 5 If even the moon is not bright and the stars are not pure in his **eyes**,
27: 19 but will do so no more; when he opens his **eyes**, all is gone.
28: 7 No bird of prey knows that hidden path, no falcon's **eye** has seen it.
28: 10 He tunnels through the rock; his **eyes** see all its treasures.
28: 21 It is hidden from the **eyes** *of* every living thing, concealed even
29: 11 me spoke well of me, and **those**[s] who saw me commended me,
29: 15 I was **eyes** to the blind and feet to the lame.
31: 1 "I made a covenant with my **eyes** not to look lustfully at a girl.
31: 7 if my heart has been led by my **eyes**, or if my hands have been
31: 16 the desires of the poor or let the **eyes** *of* the widow grow weary,
32: 1 stopped answering Job, because he was righteous in his own **eyes**.
34: 21 "His **eyes** are on the ways of men; he sees their every step.
36: 7 He does not take his **eyes** off the righteous; he enthrones them with
39: 29 From there he seeks out his food; his **eyes** detect it from afar.
40: 24 Can anyone capture him by the **eyes**, or trap him and pierce his
41: 18 [41:10] out flashes of light; his **eyes** are like the rays of dawn.
42: 5 My ears had heard of you but now my **eyes** have seen you.
Ps 5: 5 [5:6] The arrogant cannot stand **in** your **presence** [+4200+5584];
6: 7 [6:8] My **eyes** grow weak with sorrow; they fail because of all my
10: 8 he murders the innocent, **watching** in secret for his victims.
11: 4 He **[RPH]** observes the sons of men; his eyes examine them.
13: 3 [13:4] my God. Give light to my **eyes**, or I will sleep in death;
15: 4 *who* **despises** [+928+1022] a vile man but honors those who fear
17: 2 my vindication come from you; may your **eyes** see what is right.
17: 8 Keep me as the apple of your **eye**; hide me in the shadow of your
17: 11 they now surround me, with **eyes** alert, to throw me to the ground.
18: 24 [18:25] according to the cleanness of my hands in his **sight**.
18: 27 [18:28] the humble but bring low those whose **eyes** are haughty.
19: 8 [19:9] of the LORD are radiant, giving light to the **eyes**.
25: 15 My **eyes** are ever on the LORD, for only he will release my feet
26: 3 for your love is ever **before** [+4200+5584] me, and I walk
31: 9 [31:10] my **eyes** grow weak with sorrow, my soul and my body
31: 22 [31:23] In my alarm I said, "I am cut off from your **sight**!"
32: 8 in the way you should go; I will counsel you and **watch** over you.
33: 18 the **eyes** *of* the LORD are on those who fear him, on those whose
34: 15 [34:16] The **eyes** *of* the LORD are on the righteous and his ears
35: 19 let not those who hate me without reason maliciously wink the **eye**.
35: 21 and say, "Aha! Aha! With our own **eyes** we have seen it."
36: 1 [36:2] of the wicked: There is no fear of God before his **eyes**.
36: 2 [36:3] For in his own **eyes** he flatters himself too much to detect
38: 10 [38:11] strength fails me; even the light has gone from my **eyes**.
50: 21 like you. But I will rebuke you and accuse you to your **face**.
51: 4 [51:6] you only, have I sinned and done what is evil in your **sight**,
54: 7 [54:9] and my **eyes** have looked in triumph on my foes.
66: 7 He rules forever by his power, his **eyes** watch the nations—
69: 3 [69:4] my throat is parched. My **eyes** fail, looking for my God.
69: 23 [69:24] May their **eyes** be darkened so they cannot see, and their
72: 14 and violence, for precious is their blood in his **sight**.
73: 7 callous hearts comes iniquity; [BHS *Their* **eyes** *bulge*; NIV 6411]
73: 16 When I tried to understand all this, it was oppressive **to** [+928] me
77: 4 [77:5] You kept my **eyes** from closing; I was too troubled to
79: 10 Before our **eyes**, make known among the nations that you avenge
88: 9 [88:10] my **eyes** are dim with grief. I call to you, O LORD,
90: 4 For a thousand years in your **sight** are like a day that has just gone
91: 8 You will only observe with your **eyes** and see the punishment of
92: 11 [92:12] My **eyes** have seen the defeat of my adversaries; my ears
94: 9 implanted the ear not hear? Does he who formed the **eye** not see?
98: 2 and revealed his righteousness **to** [+4200] the nations.
101: 3 I will set before my **eyes** no vile thing. The deeds of faithless men I
101: 5 whoever has haughty **eyes** and a proud heart, him will I not endure.
101: 6 My **eyes** will be on the faithful in the land, that they may dwell
101: 7 who speaks falsely will stand **in** my **presence** [+4200+5584].
115: 5 They have mouths, but cannot speak, **eyes**, but they cannot see;
116: 8 my soul from death, my **eyes** from tears, my feet from stumbling,
116: 15 Precious in the **sight** *of* the LORD is the death of his saints.
118: 23 the LORD has done this, and it is marvelous in our **eyes**.
119: 18 Open my **eyes** that I may see wonderful things in your law.
119: 37 Turn my **eyes** away from worthless things; preserve my life
119: 82 My **eyes** fail, looking for your promise; I say, "When will you
119: 123 My **eyes** fail, looking for your salvation, looking for your righteous
119: 136 Streams of tears flow from my **eyes**, for your law is not obeyed.
119: 148 My **eyes** stay open through the watches of the night, that I may
121: 1 I lift up my **eyes** to the hills—where does my help come from?
123: 1 I lift up my **eyes** to you, to you whose throne is in heaven.
123: 2 As the **eyes** *of* slaves look to the hand of their master, as the eyes
123: 2 as the **eyes** *of* a maid look to the hand of her mistress, so our eyes
123: 2 so our **eyes** look to the LORD our God, till he shows us his
131: 1 My heart is not proud, O LORD, my **eyes** are not haughty;
132: 4 I will allow no sleep to my **eyes**, no slumber to my eyelids,
135: 16 They have mouths, but cannot speak, **eyes**, but they cannot see;
139: 16 your **eyes** saw my unformed body. All the days ordained for me
141: 8 my **eyes** are fixed on you, O Sovereign LORD; in you I take
145: 15 The **eyes** *of* all look to you, and you give them their food at the
Pr 1: 17 How useless to spread a net in **full view** *of* all the birds!
3: 4 you will win favor and a good name in the **sight** *of* God and man.
3: 7 Do not be wise in your own **eyes**; fear the LORD and shun evil.
3: 21 and discernment, do not let them out of your **sight**;
4: 21 Do not let them out of your **sight**, keep them within your heart;
4: 25 Let your **eyes** look straight ahead, fix your gaze directly before
5: 21 For a man's ways are **in full view** [+5790] *of* the LORD,
6: 4 Allow no sleep to your **eyes**, no slumber to your eyelids.
6: 13 who winks with his **eye**, signals with his feet and motions with his
6: 17 haughty **eyes**, a lying tongue, hands that shed innocent blood,
7: 2 and you will live; guard my teachings as the apple of your **eye**.
8: 28 the clouds above and fixed securely the **fountains** *of* the deep,
10: 10 *He who* **winks maliciously** [+7975] causes grief, and a chattering
10: 26 As vinegar to the teeth and smoke to the **eyes**, so is a sluggard to
12: 15 The way of a fool **seems** [+928] right *to* him, but a wise man
15: 3 The **eyes** *of* the LORD are everywhere, keeping watch on the
15: 30 A cheerful **look** brings joy to the heart, and good news gives health
16: 2 All a man's ways **seem** [+928] innocent *to* him, but motives are
16: 30 He who winks with his **eye** is plotting perversity; he who purses
17: 8 A bribe is a charm **to** [+928] the one who gives it; wherever he
17: 24 wisdom in view, but a fool's **eyes** wander to the ends of the earth.
20: 8 sits on his throne to judge, he winnows out all evil with his **eyes**.
20: 12 Ears that hear and **eyes** that see—the LORD has made them both.
20: 13 grow poor; **stay awake** [+7219] and you will have food to spare.
21: 2 All a man's ways **seem** [+928] right *to* him, but the LORD
21: 4 Haughty **eyes** and a proud heart, the lamp of the wicked, are sin!
21: 10 man craves evil; his neighbor gets no mercy **from** [+928] him.
22: 9 A **generous man** [+3202] will himself be blessed, for he shares his
22: 12 The **eyes** *of* the LORD keep watch over knowledge, but he
23: 5 Cast but a **glance** at riches, and they are gone, for they will surely
23: 6 Do not eat the food of a **stingy man** [+8273], do not crave his
23: 26 My son, give me your heart and let your **eyes** keep to my ways,
23: 29 Who has needless bruises? Who has bloodshot **eyes**?
23: 31 when *it* **sparkles** [+5989] in the cup, when it goes down smoothly!
23: 33 Your **eyes** will see strange sights and your mind imagine confusing
24: 18 the LORD will see and **disapprove** [+928+8317] and turn his wrath
25: 7 you before a nobleman. What you have seen with your **eyes**
26: 5 a fool according to his folly, or he will be wise in his own **eyes**.
26: 12 Do you see a man wise in his own **eyes**? There is more hope for a
26: 16 The sluggard is wiser in his own **eyes** than seven men who answer
27: 20 Destruction are never satisfied, and neither are the **eyes** *of* man.
28: 11 A rich man may be wise in his own **eyes**, but a poor man who has
28: 22 A **stingy** [+8273] man is eager to get rich and is unaware that
28: 27 but he who closes his **eyes** to them receives many curses.
29: 13 have this in common: The LORD gives sight to the **eyes** *of* both.
30: 12 those who are pure in their own **eyes** and yet are not cleansed of
30: 13 those whose **eyes** are ever so haughty, whose glances are
30: 17 "The **eye** that mocks a father, that scorns obedience to a mother,
Ecc 1: 8 The **eye** never has enough of seeing, nor the ear its fill of hearing.
2: 10 I denied myself nothing my **eyes** desired; I refused my heart no
2: 14 The wise man has **eyes** in his head, while the fool walks in the
4: 8 no end to his toil, yet his **eyes** were not content with his wealth.
5: 11 [5:10] what benefit are they to the owner except to feast his **eyes**
6: 9 Better what the **eye** sees than the roving of the appetite. This too is
8: 16 man's labor on earth—his **eyes** not seeing sleep day or night—
11: 7 Light is sweet, and it pleases the **eyes** to see the sun.
11: 9 Follow the ways of your heart and whatever your **eyes** see,
SS 1: 15 you are, my darling! Oh, how beautiful! Your **eyes** are doves.
4: 1 Oh, how beautiful! Your **eyes** behind your veil are doves.

SS 4: 9 you have stolen my heart with one glance of your **eyes**, with one
5: 12 His **eyes** are like doves by the water streams, washed in milk,
6: 5 Turn your **eyes** from me; they overwhelm me. Your hair is like a
7: 4 [7:5] Your **eyes** are the pools of Heshbon by the gate of Bath
8: 10 Thus I have become in his **eyes** like one bringing contentment.
Isa 1: 15 you spread out your hands in prayer, I will hide my **eyes** from you;
1: 16 Take your evil deeds out of my **sight**! Stop doing wrong,
2: 11 The **eyes** *of* the arrogant man will be humbled and the pride of men
3: 8 and deeds are against the LORD, defying his glorious **presence**.
3: 16 flirting with their **eyes**, tripping along with mincing steps,
5: 15 and mankind humbled, the **eyes** *of* the arrogant humbled.
5: 21 Woe to those who are wise in their own **eyes** and clever in their
6: 5 and my **eyes** have seen the King, the LORD Almighty."
6: 10 of this people calloused; make their ears dull and close their **eyes**.
6: 10 Otherwise they might see with their **eyes**, hear with their ears,
10: 12 for the willful pride of his heart and the haughty look in his **eyes**.
11: 3 He will not judge by what he sees with his **eyes**, or decide by what
13: 16 Their infants will be dashed to pieces before their **eyes**;
13: 18 infants nor *will* they **look with compassion** [+2571] on children.
17: 7 look to their Maker and turn their **eyes** to the Holy One of Israel.
29: 10 He has sealed your **eyes** (the prophets); he has covered your heads
29: 18 and out of gloom and darkness the **eyes** *of* the blind will see.
30: 20 will be hidden no more; with your own **eyes** you will see them.
32: 3 the **eyes** *of* those who see will no longer be closed, and the ears of
33: 15 plots of murder and shuts his **eyes** against contemplating evil—
33: 17 Your **eyes** will see the king in his beauty and view a land that
33: 20 your **eyes** will see Jerusalem, a peaceful abode, a tent that will not
35: 5 will the **eyes** *of* the blind be opened and the ears of the deaf
37: 17 O LORD, and hear; open your **eyes**, O LORD, and see;
37: 23 whom have you raised your voice and lifted your **eyes** in pride?
38: 3 wholehearted devotion and have done what is good in your **eyes**."
38: 14 My **eyes** grew weak as I looked to the heavens. I am troubled;
40: 26 Lift your **eyes** and look to the heavens: Who created all these?
42: 7 to open **eyes** that are blind, to free captives from prison and to
43: 4 Since you are precious and honored in my **sight**, and because I
43: 8 Lead out those who have **eyes** but are blind, who have ears
44: 18 their **eyes** are plastered over so they cannot see, and their minds
49: 5 for I am honored in the **eyes** *of* the LORD and my God has been
49: 18 Lift up your **eyes** and look around; all your sons gather and come
51: 6 Lift up your **eyes** to the heavens, look at the earth beneath;
52: 8 returns to Zion, they will see it **[RPH]** with their own eyes.
52: 8 the LORD returns to Zion, they will see it with their own **eyes**.
52: 10 The LORD will lay bare his holy arm in the **sight** *of* all the
59: 10 we grope along the wall, feeling our way like men without **eyes**.
59: 15 and *was* **displeased** [+928+8317] that there was no justice.
60: 4 "Lift up your **eyes** and look about you: All assemble and come to
64: 4 [64:3] no ear has perceived, no **eye** has seen any God besides you,
65: 12 not listen. You did evil in my **sight** and chose what displeases me."
65: 16 For the past troubles will be forgotten and hidden from my **eyes**.
66: 4 They did evil in my **sight** and chose what displeases me."
Jer 3: 2 "**Look** up to the barren heights and see. Is there any place where
4: 30 and put on jewels of gold? Why shade your **eyes** with paint?
5: 3 O LORD, do not your **eyes** look for truth? You struck them,
5: 21 who have **eyes** but do not see, who have ears but do not hear:
7: 11 which bears my Name, become a den of robbers **to** [+928] you?
7: 30 " 'The people of Judah have done evil in my **eyes**,
9: 1 [8:23] were a spring of water and my **eyes** a fountain of tears!
9: 18 [9:17] and wail over us till our **eyes** overflow with tears
13: 17 my **eyes** will weep bitterly, overflowing with tears,
13: 20 Lift up your **eyes** and see those who are coming from the north.
14: 6 and pant like jackals; their **eyesight** fails for lack of pasture."
14: 17 " 'Let my **eyes** overflow with tears night and day without ceasing;
16: 9 Before your **eyes** and in your days I will bring an end to the sounds
16: 17 My **eyes** are on all their ways; they are not hidden from me,
16: 17 are not hidden from me, nor is their sin concealed from my **eyes**.
18: 4 it into another pot, shaping it as **seemed** [+928] best *to* him.
18: 10 if it does evil in my **sight** and does not obey me, then I will
19: 10 "Then break the jar while those who go with you are **watching**,
20: 4 with your own **eyes** you will see them fall by the sword of their
22: 17 "But your **eyes** and your heart are set only on dishonest gain,
24: 6 My **eyes** will watch over them for their good, and I will bring them
26: 14 do with me whatever you **think** [+928] is good and right.
27: 5 that are on it, and I give it to anyone I **please** [+928+3837].
28: 1 said to me in the house of the LORD in the **presence** *of* the
28: 5 replied to the prophet Hananiah **before** [+4200] the priests
28: 5 **[RPH]** all the people who were standing in the house of the
28: 11 he said **before** [+4200] all the people, "This is what the LORD
29: 21 of Babylon, and he will put them to death before your very **eyes**.
31: 16 "Restrain your voice from weeping and your **eyes** from tears,
32: 4 with him face to face and see **[RPH]** him with his own eyes.
32: 4 will speak with him face to face and see him with his own **eyes**.
32: 12 in the **presence** *of* my cousin Hanamel and of the witnesses who
32: 12 and **[RPH]** of the witnesses who had signed the deed
32: 12 and **[RPH]** of all the Jews sitting in the courtyard of the guard.
32: 13 "In their **presence** I gave Baruch these instructions:
32: 19 Your **eyes** are open to all the ways of men; you reward everyone
32: 30 and Judah have done nothing but evil in my **sight** from their youth;
34: 3 You will see the king of Babylon with **[RPH]** your own eyes,
34: 3 You will see the king of Babylon with your own **eyes**, and he will
34: 15 Recently you repented and did what is right in my **sight**: Each of
39: 6 king of Babylon slaughtered the sons of Zedekiah before his **eyes**
39: 7 he put out Zedekiah's **eyes** and bound him with bronze shackles to
39: 12 "Take him and **look** [+6584+8492] **after** him; don't harm him
40: 4 me to Babylon, if you **like** [+928+3202], and I will look after you;
40: 4 if you like, and I *will* **look** [+906+6584+8492] **after** you;
40: 4 but if you do **not want** [+928+8273] to, then don't come.
40: 4 before you; go wherever you **please** [+928+2256+3202+3838]."
40: 5 among the people, or go anywhere else you **please** [+928+3838]."
42: 2 For as you now **see** [+906+8011], though we were once many,
43: 9 "While the Jews are **watching**, take some large stones with you
51: 24 "Before your **eyes** I will repay Babylon and all who live in
52: 2 He did evil in the **eyes** *of* the LORD, just as Jehoiakim had done.
52: 10 king of Babylon slaughtered the sons of Zedekiah before his **eyes**;
52: 11 Then he put out Zedekiah's **eyes**, bound him with bronze shackles
La 1: 16 "This is why I weep **[RPH]** and my eyes overflow with tears.
1: 16 "This is why I weep and my **eyes** overflow with tears. No one is
2: 4 Like a foe he has slain all who were pleasing to the **eye**; he has
2: 11 My **eyes** fail from weeping, I am in torment within, my heart is
2: 18 and night; give yourself no relief, your **eyes** [+1426] no rest.
3: 48 Streams of tears flow from my **eyes** because my people are
3: 49 My **eyes** will flow unceasingly, without relief,
3: 51 **What I see** brings grief to my soul because of all the women of my
4: 17 Moreover, our **eyes** failed, looking in vain for help; from our
5: 17 this our hearts are faint, because of these things our **eyes** grow dim
Eze 1: 4 by brilliant light. The center of the fire **looked** like glowing metal,
1: 7 like those of a calf and gleamed **like** [+3869] burnished bronze.
1: 16 They **sparkled** like chrysolite, and all four looked alike.
1: 18 and awesome, and all four rims were full of **eyes** all around.
1: 22 was what looked like an expanse, **sparkling** like ice, and awesome.
1: 27 I saw that from what appeared to be his waist up he **looked** like
4: 12 bake it in the **sight** *of* the people, using human excrement for fuel."
5: 8 and I will inflict punishment on you in the **sight** *of* the nations.
5: 11 my favor; I *will* not **look** *on* you **with pity** [+2571] or spare you.
5: 14 among the nations around you, in the **sight** *of* all who pass by.
6: 9 which have turned away from me, and by their **eyes**, which have
7: 4 I *will* not **look** on you **with pity** [+2571] or spare you; I will surely
7: 9 I *will* not **look** *on* you **with pity** [+2571] or spare you; I will repay
8: 2 from there up his appearance was as bright as **[NIE]** glowing
8: 5 Then he said to me, "Son of man, **look** [+5951] toward the north."
8: 5 So I **looked** [+5951], and in the entrance north of the gate of the
8: 18 in anger; I *will* not **look** *on* them **with pity** [+2571] or spare them.
9: 5 the city and kill, without **showing pity** [+2571] or compassion.
9: 10 So I *will* not **look** on them **with pity** [+2571] or spare them,
10: 2 scatter them over the city." And as I **watched** [+4200], he went in.
10: 9 beside each of the cherubim; the wheels **sparkled** like chrysolite.
10: 12 their hands and their wings, were completely full of **eyes**,
10: 19 While I **watched** [+4200], the cherubim spread their wings
12: 2 They have **eyes** to see but do not see and ears to hear but do not
12: 3 as they **watch** [+4200], set out and go from where you are to
12: 3 **[RPH]** Perhaps they will understand, though they are a rebellious
12: 4 During the daytime, while they **watch** [+4200], bring out your
12: 4 in the evening, while they are **watching** [+4200], go out like those
12: 5 While they **watch** [+4200], dig through the wall and take your
12: 6 Put them on your shoulder as they are **watching** [+4200] and carry
12: 7 carrying them on my shoulders while they **watched** [+4200].
12: 12 so that *he* cannot **see** [+906+2021+4200+8011] the land.
16: 5 No *one* **looked** on you **with pity** [+2571] or had compassion
16: 41 and inflict punishment on you in the **sight** *of* many women.
18: 6 or **look** [+5951] to the idols of the house of Israel.
18: 12 He does not return what he took in pledge. He **looks** [+5951] to the
18: 15 or **look** [+5951] to the idols of the house of Israel.
20: 7 "Each of you, get rid of the vile images you have set your **eyes** on,
20: 8 they did not get rid of the vile images they had set their **eyes** on,
20: 9 it from being profaned in the **eyes** *of* the nations they lived among
20: 9 in whose **sight** I had revealed myself to the Israelites by bringing
20: 14 in the **eyes** *of* the nations in whose sight I had brought them out.
20: 14 in the eyes of the nations in whose **sight** I had brought them out.
20: 17 Yet I **looked** on them **with pity** [+2571] and did not destroy them
20: 22 in the **eyes** *of* the nations in whose sight I had brought them out.
20: 22 in the eyes of the nations in whose **sight** I had brought them out.
20: 24 my Sabbaths, and their **eyes** ⌞lusted⌟ after their fathers' idols.
20: 41 and I will show myself holy among you in the **sight** *of* the nations.
21: 6 [21:11] Groan **before** [+4200] them with broken heart and bitter
21: 23 [21:28] *It will* **seem** [+928+2118+4200] like a false omen *to* those
22: 16 When you have been defiled in the **eyes** *of* the nations, you will
22: 26 they shut their **eyes** to the keeping of my Sabbaths, so that I am
23: 16 As soon as she **saw** [+5260] them, she lusted after them and sent
23: 27 You *will* not **look** [+5951] on these things **with longing** or

Eze 23: 40 yourself for them, painted your **eyes** and put on your jewelry.
24: 16 blow I am about to take away from you the delight of your **eyes**.
24: 21 take pride, the delight of your **eyes**, the object of your affection.
24: 25 their joy and glory, the delight of their **eyes**, their heart's desire,
28: 18 I reduced you to ashes on the ground in the **sight** *of* all who were
28: 25 I will show myself holy among them in the **sight** *of* the nations.
33: 25 the blood still in it and **look** [+5951] to your idols and shed blood,
36: 23 when I show myself holy through you before their **eyes**.
36: 34 instead of lying desolate in the **sight** *of* all who pass through it.
37: 20 Hold before their **eyes** the sticks you have written on
38: 16 know me when I show myself holy through you before their **eyes**.
38: 23 and I will make myself known in the **sight** *of* many nations.
39: 27 I will show myself holy through them in the **sight** *of* many nations.
40: 4 look with your **eyes** and hear with your ears and pay attention to
43: 11 Write these down **before** [+4200] them so that they may be faithful
44: 5 **look carefully** [+928+8011], listen closely and give attention to
Da 8: 3 I **looked** up, and there before me was a ram with two horns,
8: 5 suddenly a goat with a prominent horn between his **eyes** came from
8: 21 of Greece, and the large horn between his **eyes** is the first king.
9: 18 open your **eyes** and see the desolation of the city that bears your
10: 5 I **looked** up and there before me was a man dressed in linen,
10: 6 his **eyes** like flaming torches, his arms and legs like the gleam of
10: 6 his arms and legs like the **gleam** *of* burnished bronze,
Hos 2: 10 [2:12] So now I will expose her lewdness before the **eyes** *of* her
13: 14 is your destruction? "I *will* **have no** [+4946+6259] compassion,
Joel 1: 16 Has not the food been cut off before our very **eyes**—joy
Am 9: 3 Though they hide **from** [+4946+5584] me at the bottom of the sea,
9: 4 slay them. I will fix my **eyes** upon them for evil and not for good."
9: 8 "Surely the **eyes** *of* the Sovereign LORD are on the sinful
Jnh 2: 4 [2:5] I said, 'I have been banished from your **sight**; yet I will look
Mic 4: 11 They say, "Let her be defiled, let our **eyes** gloat over Zion!"
7: 10 My **eyes** will see her downfall; even now she will be trampled
Hab 1: 13 Your **eyes** are too pure to look on evil; you cannot tolerate wrong.
Zep 3: 20 of the earth when I restore your fortunes before your very **eyes**,"
Hag 2: 3 to you now? Does it not **seem** [+928+4017] *to* you like nothing?
Zec 1: 18 [2:1] Then I **looked** up—and there before me were four horns!
2: 1 [2:5] I **looked** up—and there before me was a man with a
2: 8 [2:12] for whoever touches you touches the apple of his **eye**—
3: 9 There are seven **eyes** on that one stone, and I will engrave an
4: 10 "(These seven are the **eyes** *of* the LORD, which range throughout
5: 1 I **looked** [+5951] again—and there before me was a flying scroll!
5: 5 and said to me, "**Look** up and see what this is that is appearing."
5: 6 "This is the iniquity [BHS *appearance*; NIV 6411] *of* the people
5: 9 Then I **looked** up—and there before me were two women,
6: 1 I **looked** up again—and there before me were four chariots coming
8: 6 "It may **seem** [+928] marvelous *to* the remnant of this people at
8: 6 this people at that time, but will it **seem** [+928] marvelous *to* me?"
9: 1 for the **eyes** *of* men and all the tribes of Israel are on the LORD—
9: 8 overrun my people, for now I *am* **keeping watch** [+928+8011].
11: 12 I told them, "If you **think** [+928] it best, give me my pay;
11: 17 deserts the flock! May the sword strike his arm and his right **eye**!
11: 17 May his arm be completely withered, his right **eye** totally blinded!"
12: 4 "I will keep a watchful **eye** over the house of Judah, but I will blind
14: 12 their **eyes** will rot in their sockets, and their tongues will rot in their
Mal 1: 5 You will see it with your own **eyes** and say, 'Great is the LORD—
2: 17 By saying, "All who do evil are good in the **eyes** *of* the LORD,

6525 עַ֫יִן ² *'ayin²*, n.f. Not used in NIV/BHS [cf. 6524]

6526 עַ֫יִן ³ *'ayin³*, n.pr.loc. [5] [√ 6524]

Ain [5]

Nu 34: 11 will go down from Shepham to Riblah on the east side of **Ain**
Jos 15: 32 Lebaoth, Shilhim, **Ain** and Rimmon—a total of twenty-nine towns
19: 7 **Ain**, Rimmon, Ether and Ashan—four towns and their villages—
21: 16 **Ain**, Juttah and Beth Shemesh, together with their pasturelands—
1Ch 4: 32 villages were Etam, **Ain**, Rimmon, Token and Ashan—

6527 עֵין גֶּדִי *'ên gedî*, n.pr.loc. [6] [√ 6524 + 1531]

En Gedi [6]

Jos 15: 62 Nibshan, the City of Salt and **En Gedi**—six towns and their
1Sa 23: 29 [24:1] up from there and lived in the strongholds of **En Gedi**.
24: 1 [24:2] he was told, "David is in the Desert of **En Gedi**."
2Ch 20: 2 side of the Sea. It is already in Hazazon Tamar" (that is, **En Gedi**).
SS 1: 14 to me a cluster of henna blossoms from the vineyards of **En Gedi**.
Eze 47: 10 from **En Gedi** to En Eglaim there will be places for spreading nets.

6528 עֵין גַּנִּים *'ên gannîm*, n.pr.loc. [3] [√ 6524 + 1712]

En Gannim [3]

Jos 15: 34 Zanoah, **En Gannim**, Tappuah, Enam,
19: 21 Remeth, **En Gannim**, En Haddah and Beth Pazzez.
21: 29 Jarmuth and **En Gannim**, together with their pasturelands—

6529 עֵין־דֹּאר *'ên-dō'r*, עֵין־דּוֹר *'ên-dôr*, n.pr.loc. [3] [√ 6524 + 1799]

Endor [3]

Jos 17: 11 Ibleam and the people of Dor, **Endor**, Taanach and Megiddo,
1Sa 28: 7 I may go and inquire of her." "There is one in **Endor**," they said.
Ps 83: 10 [83:11] who perished at **Endor** and became like refuse on the

6530 עֵין הַקּוֹרֵא *'ên haqqôrē'*, n.pr.loc. [1] [√ 6524 + 2213]

En Hakkore [1]

Jdg 15: 19 So the spring was called **En Hakkore**, and it is still there in Lehi.

6531 עֵין הַתַּנִּין *'ên hattannîn*, n.pr.loc. Not used in NIV/BHS [√ 6524 + 2021 + 9490]

6532 עֵין חַדָּה *'ên ḥaddâ*, n.pr.loc. [1] [√ 6524 + 2528]

En Haddah [1]

Jos 19: 21 Remeth, En Gannim, **En Haddah** and Beth Pazzez.

6533 עֵין חָצוֹר *'ên ḥāṣôr*, n.pr.loc. [1] [√ 6524 + 2937]

En Hazor [1]

Jos 19: 37 Kedesh, Edrei, **En Hazor**,

6534 עֵין חֲרֹד *'ên ḥ^a^rōd*, n.pr.loc. Not used in NIV/BHS [√ 6524 + 3008]

6535 עֵין מִשְׁפָּט *'ên mišpāṭ*, n.pr.loc. [1] [√ 6524 + 5477]

En Mishpat [1]

Ge 14: 7 Then they turned back and went to **En Mishpat** (that is, Kadesh),

6536 עֵין עֶגְלַיִם *'ên 'eglayim*, n.pr.loc. [1] [√ 6524 + 6325]

En Eglaim [1]

Eze 47: 10 from En Gedi to **En Eglaim** there will be places for spreading nets.

6537 עֵין רֹגֵל *'ên rōgēl*, n.pr.loc. [4] [√ 6524 + 8080]

En Rogel [4]

Jos 15: 7 along to the waters of En Shemesh and came out at **En Rogel**.
18: 16 along the southern slope of the Jebusite city and so to **En Rogel**.
2Sa 17: 17 Jonathan and Ahimaaz were staying at **En Rogel**. A servant girl
1Ki 1: 9 and fattened calves at the Stone of Zoheleth near **En Rogel**.

6538 עֵין רִמּוֹן *'ên rimmôn*, n.pr.loc. [1] [√ 6524 + 8235]

En Rimmon [1]

Ne 11: 29 in **En Rimmon**, in Zorah, in Jarmuth,

6539 עֵין שֶׁמֶשׁ *'ên šemeš*, n.pr.loc. [2] [√ 6524 + 9087]

En Shemesh [2]

Jos 15: 7 It continued along to the waters of **En Shemesh** and came out at
18: 17 It then curved north, went to **En Shemesh**, continued to Geliloth,

6540 עֵין תַּפּוּחַ *'ên tappûaḥ*, n.pr.loc. [1] [√ 6524 + 9517]

En Tappuah [1]

Jos 17: 7 southward from there to include the people living at **En Tappuah**.

6541 עֵינוֹן *'ênôn*, n.pr.loc. Not used in NIV/BHS [→ 2965]

6542 עֵינַיִם *'ênayim*, n.pr.loc. [2] [cf. 6543?]

Enaim [2]

Ge 38: 14 then sat down at the entrance to **Enaim**, which is on the road to
38: 21 is the shrine prostitute who was beside the road at **Enaim**?"

6543 עֵינָם *'ênām*, n.pr.loc. [1] [√ 6524 + 4392; cf. 6542?]

Enam [1]

Jos 15: 34 Zanoah, En Gannim, Tappuah, **Enam**,

6544 עֵינָן *'ênān*, n.pr.m. [5] [→ 2966; cf. 6524 + 5527]

Enan [5]

Nu 1: 15 from Naphtali, Ahira son of **Enan**."
2: 29 The leader of the people of Naphtali is Ahira son of **Enan**.
7: 78 On the twelfth day Ahira son of **Enan**, the leader of the people of
7: 83 a fellowship offering. This was the offering of Ahira son of **Enan**.
10: 27 Ahira son of **Enan** was over the division of the tribe of Naphtali.

6545 עִיף 'îp, v. [5] [→ 6546; cf. 3615]

exhausted [2], exhausted [+4394] [1], faint [1], fainting [1]

Jdg 4:21 [A] and went quietly to him while he lay fast asleep, **exhausted**.
1Sa 14:28 [A] man who eats food today!' That is why the men *are* **faint**."
14:31 [A] from Micmash to Aijalon, *they were* **exhausted** [+4394].
2Sa 21:15 [A] to fight against the Philistines, and he *became* **exhausted**.
Jer 4:31 [A] "Alas! I *am* **fainting**; my life is given over to murderers."

6546 עָיֵף 'āyēp, a. [17] [√ 6545; cf. 3615]

weary [6], exhausted [2], famished [2], tired [2], faint [1], parched [1], thirsty [1], weary [+5883] [1], worn out [1]

Ge 25:29 some stew, Esau came in from the open country, **famished**.
25:30 "Quick, let me have some of that red stew! I'm **famished**!"
Dt 25:18 When you were **weary** and worn out, they met you on your
Jdg 8:4 **exhausted** yet keeping up the pursuit, came to the Jordan
8:5 they are **worn out**, and I am still pursuing Zebah and Zalmunna,
2Sa 16:14 and all the people with him arrived at their destination **exhausted**.
17:29 people have become hungry and **tired** and thirsty in the desert."
Job 22:7 You gave no water to the **weary** and you withheld food from the
Ps 63:1 [63:2] for you, in a dry and **weary** land where there is no water.
143:6 out my hands to you; my soul thirsts for you like a **parched** land.
Pr 25:25 Like cold water to a **weary** soul is good news from a distant land.
Isa 5:27 Not *one* of them grows **tired** or stumbles, not one slumbers
28:12 to whom he said, "This is the resting place, let the **weary** rest";
29:8 he is drinking, but he awakens **faint**, with his thirst unquenched.
32:2 water in the desert and the shadow of a great rock in a **thirsty** land.
46:1 that are carried about are burdensome, a burden for the **weary**.
Jer 31:25 I will refresh the **weary** [+5883] and satisfy the faint."

6547 ¹עֵיפָה 'êpā¹, n.f. [2] [→ 6548, 6549; cf. 6415]

darkness [1], deepest night [+694+4017] [1]

Job 10:22 to the land of **deepest night** [+694+4017], of deep shadow
Am 4:13 and reveals his thoughts to man, he who turns dawn to **darkness**,

6548 ²עֵיפָה 'êpā², n.pr.g. [1] [√ 6549; cf. 6547]

Ephah [1]

Isa 60:6 camels will cover your land, young camels of Midian and **Ephah**.

6549 ³עֵיפָה 'êpā³, n.pr.m. & f. [4] [→ 6548; cf. 6547]

Ephah [4]

Ge 25:4 The sons of Midian were **Ephah**, Epher, Hanoch, Abida
1Ch 1:33 The sons of Midian: **Ephah**, Epher, Hanoch, Abida and Eldaah.
2:46 Caleb's concubine **Ephah** was the mother of Haran, Moza
2:47 sons of Jahdai: Regem, Jotham, Geshan, Pelet, **Ephah** and Shaaph.

6550 עֵיפַי 'êpay, n.pr.m. [1] [cf. 6417]

Ephai [1]

Jer 40:8 son of Tanhumeth, the sons of **Ephai** [K 6417] the Netophathite,

6551 ¹עִיר 'îr¹, n.f. [1092 / 1090] [→ 6840?; *also found with compound proper names*]

city [512], towns [262], cities [126], town [100], *untranslated* [44], it[s] [+2021] [10], villages [8], hometown [3], cities [+2256+6551] [2], each town [+2256+6551] [2], each towns [+6551] [2], every city [+2256+6551] [2], Ai[s] [+2021] [1], another[s] [1], citadel [1], fellow townsmen [+408] [1], inner shrine [1], it[s] [+2021+2021+2296] [1], its[s] [+928+2021] [1], its[s] [1], places [1], them[s] [+3972] [1], them[s] [+824+2021] [1], them[s] [1], there[s] [+928+2021] [1], townspeople [+408] [1], villages [+7252] [1], which[s] [1], Ziklag[s] [+2021] [1]

Ge 4:17 Cain was then building a **city**, and he named it after his son Enoch.
4:17 then building a city, and he named **it**[s] [+2021] after his son Enoch.
10:12 which is between Nineveh and Calah; that is the great **city**.
11:4 they said, "Come, let us build ourselves a **city**, with a tower that
11:5 the LORD came down to see the **city** and the tower that the men
11:8 from there over all the earth, and they stopped building the **city**.
13:12 while Lot lived among the **cities** *of* the plain and pitched his tents
18:24 What if there are fifty righteous people in the **city**? Will you really
18:26 LORD said, "If I find fifty righteous people in the **city** of Sodom,
18:28 Will you destroy the whole **city** because of five people?" "If I find
19:4 gone to bed, all the men from every part of the **city** *of* Sodom—
19:12 or daughters, or anyone else in the **city** who belongs to you?
19:14 out of this place, because the LORD is about to destroy the **city**!"
19:15 are here, or you will be swept away when the **city** is punished."
19:16 and of his two daughters and led them safely out of the **city**,
19:20 Look, here is a **town** near enough to run to, and it is small.
19:21 grant this request too; I will not overthrow the **town** you speak of.
19:22 until you reach it." (That is why the **town** was called Zoar.)
19:25 Thus he overthrew those **cities** and the entire plain, including all
19:25 and the entire plain, including all those living in the **cities**—
19:29 So when God destroyed the **cities** *of* the plain, he remembered
19:29 he brought Lot out of the catastrophe that overthrew the **cities**
23:10 the hearing of all the Hittites who had come to the gate of his **city**.
23:18 presence of all the Hittites who had come to the gate of the **city**.
24:10 out for Aram Naharaim and made his way to the **town** *of* Nahor.
24:11 He had the camels kneel down near the well outside the **town**;
24:13 the daughters of the **townspeople** [+408] are coming out to draw
26:33 and to this day the name of the **town** has been Beersheba.
28:19 He called that place Bethel, though the **city** used to be called Luz.
33:18 he arrived safely at the **city** *of* Shechem in Canaan and camped
33:18 the city of Shechem in Canaan and camped within sight of the **city**.
34:20 his son Shechem went to the gate of their **city** to speak to their
34:20 to the gate of their city to speak to their **fellow townsmen** [+408].
34:24 All the men who went out of the **city** gate agreed with Hamor
34:24 and his son Shechem, and every male in the **city** was circumcised.
34:25 took their swords and attacked the unsuspecting **city**,
34:27 dead bodies and looted the **city** where their sister had been defiled.
34:28 and herds and donkeys and everything else of theirs in the **city**
35:5 and the terror of God fell upon the **towns** all around them
36:32 son of Beor became king of Edom. His **city** was named Dinhabah.
36:35 of Moab, succeeded him as king. His **city** was named Avith.
36:39 His **city** was named Pau, and his wife's name was Mehetabel
41:35 under the authority of Pharaoh, to be kept in the **cities** for food.
41:48 those seven years of abundance in Egypt and stored it in the **cities**.
41:48 In each **city** he put the food grown in the fields surrounding it.
44:4 They had not gone far from the **city** when Joseph said to his
44:13 Then they all loaded their donkeys and returned to the **city**.
47:21 Joseph reduced the people to **servitude** [BHS *the cities*, NIV 6269],
Ex 1:11 and they built Pithom and Rameses as store **cities** for Pharaoh.
9:29 Moses replied, "When I have gone out of the **city**, I will spread out
9:33 Moses left Pharaoh and went out of the **city**. He spread out his
Lev 14:40 be torn out and thrown into an unclean place outside the **town**.
14:41 that is scraped off dumped into an unclean place outside the **town**.
14:45 and all the plaster—and taken out of the **town** to an unclean place.
14:53 he is to release the live bird in the open fields outside the **town**.
25:29 " 'If a man sells a house in a walled **city**, he retains the right of
25:30 the house in the walled **city** shall belong permanently to the buyer
25:32 have the right to redeem their houses in the Levitical **towns**,
25:32 to redeem their houses in the Levitical towns, **which**[s] they possess.
25:33 that is, a house sold in any **town** they hold—and is to be returned
25:33 because the houses in the **towns** *of* the Levites are their property
25:34 But the pastureland belonging to their **towns** must not be sold;
26:25 When you withdraw into your **cities**, I will send a plague among
26:31 I will turn your **cities** into ruins and lay waste your sanctuaries,
26:33 Your land will be laid waste, and your **cities** will lie in ruins.
Nu 13:19 Is it good or bad? What kind of **towns** do they live in? Are they
13:28 live there are powerful, and the **cities** are fortified and very large.
20:16 "Now we are here at Kadesh, a **town** on the edge of your territory.
21:2 these people into our hands, we will totally destroy their **cities**."
21:3 They completely destroyed them and their **towns**; so the place was
21:25 Israel captured all the **cities** *of* the Amorites and occupied them,
21:25 Israel captured all the cities of the Amorites and occupied **them**[s],
21:26 Heshbon was the **city** *of* Sihon king of the Amorites, who had
21:27 "Come to Heshbon and let it be rebuilt; let Sihon's **city** be restored.
22:36 he went out to meet him at the Moabite **town** on the Arnon border,
24:19 ruler will come out of Jacob and destroy the survivors of the **city**."
31:10 They burned all the **towns** where the Midianites had settled,
32:16 pens here for our livestock and **cities** for our women and children.
32:17 Meanwhile our women and children will live in fortified **cities**,
32:24 Build **cities** for your women and children, and pens for your flocks,
32:26 our flocks and herds will remain here in the **cities** *of* Gilead.
32:33 the whole land with its **cities** and the territory around them.
32:33 land with its cities and the territory around **them**[s] [+824+2021].
32:36 Beth Nimrah and Beth Haran as fortified **cities**, and built pens for
32:38 and Sibmah. They gave names to the **cities** they rebuilt.
35:2 "Command the Israelites to give the Levites **towns** to live in from
35:2 will possess. And give them pasturelands around the **towns**.
35:3 they will have **towns** to live in and pasturelands for their cattle,
35:4 "The pasturelands around the **towns** that you give the Levites will
35:4 Levites will extend out fifteen hundred feet from the **town** wall.
35:5 Outside the **town**, measure three thousand feet on the east side,
35:5 and three thousand on the north, with the **town** in the center.
35:5 in the center. They will have this area as pastureland for the **towns**.
35:6 "Six of the **towns** you give the Levites will be cities of refuge,
35:6 "Six of the towns you give the Levites will be **cities** *of* refuge,
35:6 someone may flee. In addition, give them forty-two other **towns**.
35:7 In all you must give the Levites forty-eight **towns**, together with
35:7 forty-eight towns, together with their pasturelands. **[RPH]**
35:8 The **towns** you give the Levites from the land the Israelites possess
35:8 Take many **towns** from a tribe that has many, but few from one
35:11 select *some* **towns** to be your cities of refuge, to which a person
35:11 select some towns to be your **cities** *of* refuge, to which a person
35:12 They will be **places** of refuge from the avenger, so that a person

Nu 35:13 These six **towns** you give will be your cities of refuge.
35:13 These six towns you give will be your **cities** *of* refuge.
35:14 Give three **[RPH]** on this side of the Jordan and three in Canaan
35:14 side of the Jordan and three **[RPH]** in Canaan as cities of refuge.
35:14 on this side of the Jordan and three in Canaan as **cities** *of* refuge.
35:15 These six **towns** will be a place of refuge for Israelites, aliens
35:25 of blood and send him back to the **city** *of* refuge to which he fled.
35:26 " 'But if the accused ever goes outside the limits of the **city** *of*
35:27 the avenger of blood finds him outside the **city**, the avenger of
35:28 The accused must stay in his **city** *of* refuge until the death of the
35:32 " 'Do not accept a ransom for anyone who has fled to a **city** *of*
Dt 1:22 about the route we are to take and the **towns** we will come to."
1:28 and taller than we are; the **cities** are large, with walls up to the sky.
2:34 At that time we took all his **towns** and completely destroyed
2:34 we took all his towns and completely destroyed **them**[s] [+3972]—
2:35 the plunder from the **towns** we had captured we carried off for
2:36 from the **town** in the gorge, even as far as Gilead, not one town
2:37 the course of the Jabbok nor that around the **towns** *in* the hills.
3:4 At that time we took all his **cities**. There was not one of the sixty
3:4 There was not one of the sixty **cities** that we did not take from
3:5 All these **cities** were fortified with high walls and with gates
3:5 and bars, and there were also a great many unwalled **villages**.
3:6 we had done with Sihon king of Heshbon, destroying every **city**—
3:7 and the plunder from their **cities** we carried off for ourselves.
3:10 We took all the **towns** *on* the plateau, and all Gilead, and all
3:10 as far as Salecah and Edrei, **towns** *of* Og's kingdom in Bashan.
3:12 including half the hill country of Gilead, together with its **towns**.
3:19 you have much livestock) may stay in the **towns** I have given you,
4:41 Then Moses set aside three **cities** east of the Jordan,
4:42 He could flee into one of these **cities** and save his life.
6:10 to give you—a land with large, flourishing **cities** you did not build,
9:1 stronger than you, with large **cities** that have walls up to the sky.
13:12 [13:13] If you hear it said about one of the **towns** the LORD
13:13 [13:14] among you and have led the people of their **town** astray,
13:15 [13:16] must certainly put to the sword all who live in that **town**.
13:16 [13:17] completely burn the **town** and all its plunder as a whole
19:1 you have driven them out and settled in their **towns** and houses,
19:2 set aside for yourselves three **cities** centrally located in the land the
19:5 That man may flee to one of these **cities** and save his life.
19:7 This is why I command you to set aside for yourselves three **cities**.
19:9 always in his ways—then you are to set aside three more **cities**.
19:11 assaults and kills him, and then flees to one of these **cities**,
19:12 the elders of his **town** shall send for him, bring him back from the
20:10 When you march up to attack a **city**, make its people an offer of
20:14 the children, the livestock and everything else in the **city**,
20:15 This is how you are to treat all the **cities** that are at a distance from
20:15 distance from you and do not belong to **[RPH]** the nations nearby.
20:16 in the **cities** *of* the nations the LORD your God is giving you as
20:19 When you lay siege to a **city** for a long time, fighting against it to
20:20 use them to build siege works until the **city** at war with you falls.
21:2 and measure the distance from the body to the neighboring **towns**.
21:3 the elders of the **town** nearest the body shall take a heifer that has
21:3 the elders of the town **[RPH]** nearest the body shall take a heifer
21:4 and lead her down **[RPH]** to a valley that has not been plowed
21:6 all the elders of the **town** nearest the body shall wash their hands
21:19 hold of him and bring him to the elders at the gate of his **town**.
21:20 to the elders, **[RPH]** "This son of ours is stubborn and rebellious.
21:21 all the men of his **town** shall stone him to death. You must purge
22:15 mother shall bring proof that she was a virgin to the **town** elders at
22:17 her parents shall display the cloth before the elders of the **town**,
22:18 and the elders shall take **[RPH]** the man and punish him.
22:21 and there the men of her **town** shall stone her to death.
22:23 If a man happens to meet in a **town** a virgin pledged to be married
22:24 you shall take both of them to the gate of that **town** and stone them
22:24 the girl because she was in a **town** and did not scream for help,
25:8 Then the elders of his **town** shall summon him and talk to him.
28:3 You will be blessed in the **city** and blessed in the country.
28:16 You will be cursed in the **city** and cursed in the country.
34:3 from the Valley of Jericho, the **City** *of* Palms, as far as Zoar.
Jos 3:16 distance away, at a **town** called Adam in the vicinity of Zarethan,
6:3 March around the **city** once with all the armed men. Do this for six
6:3 the city once with all the armed men. **[RPH]** Do this for six days.
6:4 On the seventh day, march around the **city** seven times,
6:5 then the wall of the **city** will collapse and the people will go up,
6:7 March around the **city**, with the armed guard going ahead of the
6:11 So he had the ark of the LORD carried around the **city**, circling it
6:14 So on the second day they marched around the **city** once
6:15 and marched around the **city** seven times in the same manner,
6:15 except that on that day they circled the **city** seven times.
6:16 the people, "Shout! For the LORD has given you the **city**!
6:17 The **city** and all that is in it are to be devoted to the LORD.
6:20 so every man charged straight in, **[RPH]** and they took the city.
6:20 so every man charged straight in, and they took the **city**.
6:21 They devoted the **city** to the LORD and destroyed with the sword
6:24 they burned the whole **city** and everything in it, but they put the
6:26 before the LORD is the man who undertakes to rebuild this **city**,
8:1 into your hands the king of Ai, his people, his **city** and his land.
8:2 and livestock for yourselves. Set an ambush behind the **city**."
8:4 "Listen carefully. You are to set an ambush behind the **city**.
8:4 **[RPH]** Don't go very far from it. All of you be on the alert.
8:4 Don't go very far from **it**[s] [+2021]. All of you be on the alert.
8:5 I and all those with me will advance on the **city**, and when the men
8:6 They will pursue us until we have lured them away from the **city**,
8:7 you are to rise up from ambush and take the **city**. The LORD your
8:8 When you have taken the **city**, set it on fire. Do what the LORD
8:8 When you have taken the city, set **it**[s] [+2021] on fire. Do what the
8:11 him marched up and approached the **city** and arrived in front of it.
8:12 set them in ambush between Bethel and Ai, to the west of the **city**.
8:13 all those in the camp to the north of the **city** and the ambush to the
8:13 to the north of the city and the ambush to the west of **it**[s] [+2021].
8:14 all the men of the **city** hurried out early in the morning to meet
8:14 not know that an ambush had been set against him behind the **city**.
8:16 [All the men of **Ai** [K; see Q 6504] were called to pursue them,]
8:16 and they pursued Joshua and were lured away from the **city**.
8:17 go after Israel. They left the **city** open and went in pursuit of Israel.
8:18 the city." So Joshua held out his javelin toward **Ai**[s] [+2021].
8:19 They entered the **city** and captured it and quickly set it on fire.
8:19 entered the city and captured it and quickly set **it**[s] [+2021] on fire.
8:20 looked back and saw the smoke of the **city** rising against the sky,
8:21 when Joshua and all Israel saw that the ambush had taken the **city**
8:21 had taken the city and that smoke was going up from the **city**,
8:22 The men of the ambush also came out of the **city** against them,
8:27 did carry off for themselves the livestock and plunder of this **city**,
8:29 from the tree and throw it down at the entrance of the **city** gate.
9:17 So the Israelites set out and on the third day came to their **cities**:
9:17 their cities: **[RPH]** Gibeon, Kephirah, Beeroth and Kiriath Jearim.
10:2 because Gibeon was an important **city**, like one of the royal cities;
10:2 because Gibeon was an important city, like one of the royal **cities**;
10:19 attack them from the rear and don't let them reach their **cities**,
10:20 to a man—but the few who were left reached their fortified **cities**.
10:37 to the sword, together with its king, its **villages** and everyone in it.
10:39 They took the city, its king and its **villages**, and put them to the
11:12 Joshua took all these royal **cities** and their kings and put them to
11:13 Yet Israel did not burn any of the **cities** built on their mounds—
11:14 off for themselves all the plunder and livestock of these **cities**,
11:19 not one **city** made a treaty of peace with the Israelites, who took
11:21 country of Israel. Joshua totally destroyed them and their **towns**.
13:9 of the Arnon Gorge, and from the **town** in the middle of the gorge,
13:10 all the **towns** *of* Sihon king of the Amorites, who ruled in
13:16 from the **town** in the middle of the gorge, and the whole plateau
13:17 to Heshbon and all its **towns** on the plateau, including Dibon,
13:21 —all the **towns** *on* the plateau and the entire realm of Sihon king of
13:23 These **towns** and their villages were the inheritance of the
13:25 all the **towns** *of* Gilead and half the Ammonite country as far as
13:28 These **towns** and their villages were the inheritance of the Gadites,
13:30 king of Bashan—all the settlements of Jair in Bashan, sixty **towns**,
13:31 and Ashtaroth and Edrei (the royal **cities** *of* Og in Bashan).
14:4 The Levites received no share of the land but only **towns** to live in,
14:12 the Anakites were there and their **cities** were large and fortified,
15:9 came out at the **towns** *of* Mount Ephron and went down toward
15:21 The southernmost **towns** of the tribe of Judah in the Negev toward
15:32 and Rimmon—a total of twenty-nine **towns** and their villages.
15:36 and Gederah (or Gederothaim)—fourteen **towns** and their villages.
15:41 Naamah and Makkedah—sixteen **towns** and their villages.
15:44 Keilah, Aczib and Mareshah—nine **towns** and their villages.
15:51 Goshen, Holon and Giloh—eleven **towns** and their villages.
15:54 Arba (that is, Hebron) and Zior—nine **towns** and their villages.
15:57 Kain, Gibeah and Timnah—ten **towns** and their villages.
15:59 Maarath, Beth Anoth and Eltekon—six **towns** and their villages.
15:60 Kiriath Jearim) and Rabbah—two **towns** and their villages.
15:62 Nibshan, the **City** *of* Salt and En Gedi—six towns and their
15:62 the City of Salt and En Gedi—six **towns** and their villages.
16:9 It also included all the **towns** and their villages that were set aside
16:9 **[RPH]** and their villages that were set aside for the Ephraimites
17:9 There were **towns** belonging to Ephraim lying among the towns of
17:9 There were towns belonging to Ephraim lying among the **towns** *of*
17:12 Yet the Manassites were not able to occupy these **towns**,
18:9 wrote its description on a scroll, town by **town**, in seven parts,
18:14 Baal (that is, Kiriath Jearim), a **town** *of* the people of Judah.
18:21 The tribe of Benjamin, clan by clan, had the following **cities**:
18:24 Ophni and Geba—twelve **towns** and their villages.
18:28 Jerusalem), Gibeah and Kiriath—fourteen **towns** and their villages.
19:6 Beth Lebaoth and Sharuhen—thirteen **towns** and their villages;
19:7 Rimmon, Ether and Ashan—four **towns** and their villages—
19:8 all the villages around these **towns** as far as Baalath Beer (Ramah
19:15 and Bethlehem. There were twelve **towns** and their villages.
19:16 These **towns** and their villages were the inheritance of Zebulun,
19:22 ended at the Jordan. There were sixteen **towns** and their villages.

Jos 19:23 These **towns** and their villages were the inheritance of the tribe of
19:29 turned back toward Ramah and went to the fortified **city** *of* Tyre,
19:30 and Rehob. There were twenty-two **towns** and their villages.
19:31 These **towns** and their villages were the inheritance of the tribe of
19:35 The fortified **cities** were Ziddim, Zer, Hammath, Rakkath,
19:38 and Beth Shemesh. There were nineteen **towns** and their villages.
19:39 These **towns** and their villages were the inheritance of the tribe of
19:48 These **towns** and their villages were the inheritance of the tribe of
19:50 They gave him the **town** he asked for—Timnath Serah in the hill
19:50 country of Ephraim. And he built up the **town** and settled there.
20: 2 "Tell the Israelites to designate the **cities** *of* refuge, as I instructed
20: 4 "When he flees to one of these **cities**, he is to stand in the entrance
20: 4 he is to stand in the entrance of the **city** gate and state his case
20: 4 of the city gate and state his case before the elders of that **city**.
20: 4 they are to admit him into their **city** and give him a place to live
20: 6 He is to stay in that **city** until he has stood trial before the assembly
20: 6 he may go back **[RPH]** to his own home in the town from which
20: 6 he may go back to his own home in the **town** from which he fled."
20: 9 killed someone accidentally could flee to these designated **cities**
21: 2 "The LORD commanded through Moses that you give us **towns**
21: 3 the Israelites gave the Levites the following **towns**
21: 4 the priest were allotted thirteen **towns** from the tribes of Judah,
21: 5 The rest of Kohath's descendants were allotted ten **towns** from the
21: 6 The descendants of Gershon were allotted thirteen **towns** from the
21: 7 received twelve **towns** from the tribes of Reuben, Gad
21: 8 So the Israelites allotted to the Levites these **towns** and their
21: 9 of Judah and Simeon they allotted the following **towns** by name
21:12 villages around the **city** they had given to Caleb son of Jephunneh
21:13 they gave Hebron (a **city** *of* refuge for one accused of murder),
21:16 with their pasturelands—nine **towns** from these two tribes.
21:18 and Almon, together with their pasturelands—four **towns**.
21:19 All the **towns** *for* the priests, the descendants of Aaron,
21:19 of Aaron, were thirteen, **[RPH]** together with their pasturelands.
21:20 The rest of the Kohathite clans of the Levites were allotted **towns**
21:21 In the hill country of Ephraim they were given Shechem (a **city** *of*
21:22 and Beth Horon, together with their pasturelands—four **towns**.
21:24 and Gath Rimmon, together with their pasturelands—four **towns**.
21:25 and Gath Rimmon, together with their pasturelands—two **towns**.
21:26 All these ten **towns** and their pasturelands were given to the rest of
21:27 Golan in Bashan (a **city** *of* refuge for one accused of murder)
21:27 and Be Eshtarah, together with their pasturelands—two **towns**;
21:29 and En Gannim, together with their pasturelands—four **towns**;
21:31 and Rehob, together with their pasturelands—four **towns**;
21:32 Kedesh in Galilee (a **city** *of* refuge for one accused of murder),
21:32 and Kartan, together with their pasturelands—three **towns**.
21:33 All the **towns** *of* the Gershonite clans were thirteen, together with
21:33 clans were thirteen, **[RPH]** together with their pasturelands.
21:35 and Nahalal, together with their pasturelands—four **towns**;
21:37 and Mephaath, together with their pasturelands—four **towns**;
21:38 Ramoth in Gilead (a **city** *of* refuge for one accused of murder),
21:39 and Jazer, together with their pasturelands—four **towns** in all.
21:40 All the **towns** allotted to the Merarite clans, who were the rest of
21:40 who were the rest of the Levites, were **[RPH]** twelve.
21:41 The **towns** *of* the Levites in the territory held by the Israelites were
21:41 the territory held by the Israelites were **[RPH]** forty-eight in all,
21:42 **Each** of these **towns** [+6551] had pasturelands surrounding it;
21:42 **Each** of these **towns** [+6551] had pasturelands surrounding it;
21:42 Each of these towns **[RPH]** had pasturelands surrounding it;
21:42 had pasturelands surrounding it; this was true for all these **towns**.
24:13 you a land on which you did not toil and **cities** you did not build;
Jdg 1: 8 and took it. They put the **city** to the sword and set it on fire.
1:16 went up from the **City** *of* Palms with the men of Judah to live
1:17 Canaanites living in Zephath, and they totally destroyed the **city**.
1:23 When they sent men to spy out Bethel (formerly called **[RPH]**
1:24 the spies saw a man coming out of the **city** and they said to him,
1:24 "Show us how to get into the **city** and we will see that you are
1:25 **[RPH]** and they put the city to the sword but spared the man
1:25 they put the **city** to the sword but spared the man and his whole
1:26 where he built a **city** and called it Luz, which is its name to this
3:13 and attacked Israel, and they took possession of the **City** *of* Palms.
6:27 because he was afraid of his family and the men of the **town**,
6:28 In the morning when the men of the **town** got up, there was Baal's
6:30 The men of the **town** demanded of Joash, "Bring out your son.
8:16 He took the elders of the **town** and taught the men of Succoth a
8:17 pulled down the tower of Peniel and killed the men of the **town**.
8:27 made the gold into an ephod, which he placed in Ophrah, his **town**.
9:30 When Zebul the governor of the **city** heard what Gaal son of Ebed
9:31 have come to Shechem and are stirring up the **city** against you.
9:33 In the morning at sunrise, advance against the **city**. When Gaal
9:35 and was standing at the entrance to the **city** gate just as Abimelech
9:43 When he saw the people coming out of the **city**, he rose to attack
9:44 him rushed forward to a position at the entrance to the **city** gate.
9:45 All that day Abimelech pressed his attack against the **city** until he
9:45 pressed his attack against the city until he had captured **it**[s] [+2021]
9:45 its people. Then he destroyed the **city** and scattered salt over it.
9:51 Inside the **city**, however, was a strong tower, to which all the men
9:51 to which all the men and women—all the people of the **city**—fled.
10: 4 They controlled thirty **towns** in Gilead, which to this day are called
11:26 the surrounding settlements and all the **towns** along the Arnon.
11:33 He devastated twenty **towns** from Aroer to the vicinity of Minnith,
12: 7 Jephthah the Gileadite died, and was buried in a **town** *in* Gilead.
14:18 Before sunset on the seventh day the men of the **town** said to him,
16: 2 the place and lay in wait for him all night at the **city** gate.
16: 3 Then he got up and took hold of the doors of the **city** gate,
17: 8 left that **town** in search of some other place to stay. On his way he
18:27 They attacked them with the sword and burned down their **city**.
18:28 near Beth Rehob. The Danites rebuilt the **city** and settled there.
18:29 They named **it**[s] [+2021] Dan after their forefather Dan, who was
18:29 who was born to Israel—though the **city** used to be called Laish.
19:11 let's stop at this **city** *of* the Jebusites and spend the night."
19:12 We won't go into an alien **city**, whose people are not Israelites.
19:15 They went and sat in the **city** square, but no one took them into his
19:17 When he looked and saw the traveler in the **city** square, the old
19:22 some of the wicked men of the **city** surrounded the house.
20:11 men of Israel got together and united as one man against the **city**.
20:14 From their **towns** they came together at Gibeah to fight against the
20:15 mobilized twenty-six thousand swordsmen from their **towns**,
20:31 came out to meet them and were drawn away from the **city**.
20:32 "Let's retreat and draw them away from the **city** to the roads."
20:37 dash into Gibeah, spread out and put the whole **city** to the sword.
20:38 that they should send up a great cloud of smoke from the **city**,
20:40 But when the column of smoke began to rise from the **city**,
20:40 and saw the smoke of the whole **city** going up into the sky.
20:42 the men of Israel who came out of the **towns** cut them down there.
20:48 of Israel went back to Benjamin and put all the **towns** to the sword,
20:48 else they found. All the **towns** they came across they set on fire.
21:23 to their inheritance and rebuilt the **towns** and settled in them.
Ru 1:19 the whole **town** was stirred because of them, and the women
2:18 She carried it back to **town**, and her mother-in-law saw how much
3:15 measures of barley and put it on her. Then he went back to **town**.
4: 2 Boaz took ten of the elders of the **town** and said, "Sit here,"
1Sa 1: 3 Year after year this man went up from his **town** to worship
4:13 When the man entered the **town** and told what had happened,
4:13 and told what had happened, the whole **town** sent up a cry.
5: 9 after they had moved it, the LORD's hand was against that **city**,
5: 9 He afflicted the people of the **city**, both young and old, with an
5:11 For death had filled the **city** with panic; God's hand was very
5:12 afflicted with tumors, and the outcry of the **city** went up to heaven.
6:18 to the number of Philistine **towns** belonging to the five rulers—
6:18 to the five rulers—the fortified **towns** with their country villages.
7:14 The **towns** from Ekron to Gath that the Philistines had captured
8:22 Samuel said to the men of Israel, "Everyone go back to his **town**."
9: 6 But the servant replied, "Look, in this **town** there is a man of God;
9:10 let's go." So they set out for the **town** where the man of God was.
9:11 As they were going up the hill to the **town**, they met some girls
9:12 he has just come to our **town** today, for the people have a sacrifice
9:13 As soon as you enter the **town**, you will find him before he goes up
9:14 They went up to the **town**, and as they were entering it, there was
9:14 the town, and as they were entering **it**[s] [+2021], there was Samuel,
9:25 After they came down from the high place to the **town**, Samuel
9:27 As they were going down to the edge of the **town**, Samuel said to
10: 5 As you approach the **town**, you will meet a procession of prophets
15: 5 Saul went to the **city** *of* Amalek and set an ambush in the ravine.
16: 4 at Bethlehem, the elders of the **town** trembled when they met him.
18: 6 the women came out from all the **towns** *of* Israel to meet King Saul
20: 6 asked my permission to hurry to Bethlehem, his **hometown**,
20:29 because our family is observing a sacrifice in the **town** and my
20:40 his weapons to the boy and said, "Go, carry them back to **town**."
20:42 [21:1] Then David left, and Jonathan went back to the **town**.
22:19 the **town** *of* the priests, with its men and women, its children
23: 7 for David has imprisoned himself by entering a **town** *with* gates
23:10 plans to come to Keilah and destroy the **town** on account of me.
27: 5 let a place be assigned to me in one of the country **towns**,
27: 5 Why should your servant live in the royal **city** with you?"
28: 3 had mourned for him and buried him in his own **town** of Ramah.
30: 3 When David and his men came to **Ziklag**[s] [+2021], they found it
30:29 to those in the **towns** *of* the Jerahmeelites and the Kenites;
30:29 to those in the towns of the Jerahmeelites and **[RPH]** the Kenites;
31: 7 and his sons had died, they abandoned their **towns** and fled.
2Sa 2: 1 "Shall I go up to one of the **towns** *of* Judah?" he asked. The
2: 3 each with his family, and they settled in Hebron and its **towns**.
5: 7 David captured the fortress of Zion, the **City** *of* David.
5: 9 took up residence in the fortress and called it the **City** *of* David.
6:10 to take the ark of the LORD to be with him in the **City** *of* David.
6:12 from the house of Obed-Edom to the **City** *of* David with rejoicing.
6:16 As the ark of the LORD was entering the **City** *of* David,
8: 8 From Tebah and Berothai, **towns** *that belonged to* Hadadezer,
10: 3 Hasn't David sent them to you to explore the **city** and spy it out

2Sa 10: 12 and let us fight bravely for our people and the **cities** *of* our God.
10: 14 were fleeing, they fled before Abishai and went inside the **city**.
11: 16 So while Joab had the **city** under siege, he put Uriah at a place
11: 17 When the men of the **city** came out and fought against Joab,
11: 20 and he may ask you, 'Why did you get so close to the **city** to fight?
11: 25 Press the attack against the **city** and destroy it.' Say this to
12: 1 he said, "There were two men in a certain **town**, one rich
12: 26 against Rabbah of the Ammonites and captured the royal **citadel**.
12: 27 "I have fought against Rabbah and taken **its**ˢ water supply.
12: 28 muster the rest of the troops and besiege the **city** and capture it.
12: 28 Otherwise I will take the **city**, and it will be named after me."
12: 30 on David's head. He took a great quantity of plunder from the **city**
12: 31 He did this to all the Ammonite **towns**. Then David and his entire
15: 2 Absalom would call out to him, "What **town** are you from?"
15: 12 David's counselor, to come from Giloh, his **hometown**.
15: 14 overtake us and bring ruin upon us and put the **city** to the sword."
15: 24 offered sacrifices until all the people had finished leaving the **city**.
15: 25 the king said to Zadok, "Take the ark of God back into the **city**.
15: 27 Go back to the **city** in peace, with your son Ahimaaz and Jonathan
15: 34 if you return to the **city** and say to Absalom, 'I will be your servant,
15: 37 Hushai arrived at Jerusalem as Absalom was entering the **city**.
17: 13 If he withdraws into a **city**, then all Israel will bring ropes to that
17: 13 he withdraws into a city, then all Israel will bring ropes to that **city**,
17: 17 King David, for they could not risk being seen entering the **city**.
17: 23 he saddled his donkey and set out for his house in his **hometown**.
18: 3 It would be better now for you to give us support from the **city**."
19: 3 [19:4] The men stole into the **city** that day as men steal in who are
19: 37 [19:38] that I may die in my own **town** near the tomb of my father
20: 6 and pursue him, or he will find fortified **cities** and escape from us."
20: 15 They built a siege ramp up to the **city**, and it stood against the outer
20: 16 a wise woman called from the **city**, "Listen! Listen! Tell Joab to
20: 19 in Israel. You are trying to destroy a **city** that is a mother in Israel.
20: 21 Hand over this one man, and I'll withdraw from the **city**."
20: 22 and his men dispersed from the **city**, each returning to his home.
24: 5 south of the **town** in the gorge, and then went through Gad
24: 7 fortress of Tyre and all the **towns** *of* the Hivites and Canaanites.
1Ki 2: 10 David rested with his fathers and was buried in the **City** *of* David.
3: 1 He brought her to the **City** *of* David until he finished building his
4: 13 in Bashan and its sixty large walled **cities** with bronze gate bars);
8: 1 up the ark of the LORD's covenant from Zion, the **City** *of* David.
8: 16 I have not chosen a **city** in any tribe of Israel to have a temple built
8: 44 when they pray to the LORD toward the **city** you have chosen
8: 48 toward the **city** you have chosen and the temple I have built for
9: 11 King Solomon gave twenty **towns** in Galilee to Hiram king of
9: 12 when Hiram went from Tyre to see the **towns** that Solomon had
9: 13 "What kind of **towns** are these you have given me, my brother?"
9: 16 He killed **its**ˢ [+928+2021] Canaanite inhabitants and then gave it
9: 19 as well as all his store **cities** and the towns for his chariots
9: 19 his store cities and the **towns** *for* his chariots and for his horses—
9: 19 and the towns for his chariots and for **[RPH]** his horses—
9: 24 After Pharaoh's daughter had come up from the **City** *of* David to
10: 26 which he kept in the chariot **cities** and also with him in Jerusalem.
11: 27 and had filled in the gap in the wall of the **city** *of* David his father.
11: 32 But for the sake of my servant David and the **city** of Jerusalem,
11: 36 before me in Jerusalem, the **city** where I chose to put my Name.
11: 43 with his fathers and was buried in the **city** *of* David his father.
12: 17 But as for the Israelites who were living in the **towns** *of* Judah,
13: 25 they went and reported it in the **city** where the old prophet lived.
13: 29 and brought it back to his own **city** to mourn for him and bury him.
13: 32 against all the shrines on the high places in the **towns** *of* Samaria
14: 11 Dogs will eat those belonging to Jeroboam who die in the **city**,
14: 12 go back home. When you set foot in your **city**, the boy will die.
14: 21 the **city** the LORD had chosen out of all the tribes of Israel in
14: 31 with his fathers and was buried with them in the **City** *of* David.
15: 8 Abijah rested with his fathers and was buried in the **City** *of* David.
15: 20 and sent the commanders of his forces against the **towns** *of* Israel.
15: 23 Asa's reign, all his achievements, all he did and the **cities** he built,
15: 24 and was buried with them in the **city** *of* his father David.
16: 4 Dogs will eat those belonging to Baasha who die in the **city**,
16: 18 When Zimri saw that the **city** was taken, he went into the citadel of
16: 24 from Shemer for two talents of silver and built a **city** on the hill,
17: 10 When he came to the **town** gate, a widow was there gathering
20: 2 He sent messengers into the **city** to Ahab king of Israel, saying,
20: 12 his men: "Prepare to attack." So they prepared to attack the **city**.
20: 19 commanders marched out of the **city** with the army behind them
20: 30 The rest of them escaped to the **city** of Aphek, where the wall
20: 30 And Ben-Hadad fled to the **city** and hid in an inner room.
20: 34 "I will return the **cities** my father took from your father,"
21: 8 them to the elders and nobles who lived in Naboth's **city** with him.
21: 11 nobles who lived in Naboth's **city** did as Jezebel directed in the
21: 11 nobles who lived in Naboth's city did **[RPH]** as Jezebel directed
21: 13 So they took him outside the **city** and stoned him to death.
21: 24 "Dogs will eat those belonging to Ahab who die in the **city**,
22: 26 "Take Micaiah and send him back to Amon the ruler of the **city**
22: 36 through the army: "Every man to his **town**; everyone to his land!"
22: 39 the palace he built and inlaid with ivory, and the **cities** he fortified,
22: 50 [22:51] and was buried with them in the **city** *of* David his father.
2Ki 2: 19 The men of the **city** said to Elisha, "Look, our lord, this town is
2: 19 "Look, our lord, this **town** is well situated, as you can see,
2: 23 the road, some youths came out of the **town** and jeered at him.
3: 19 You will overthrow every fortified **city** and every major town.
3: 19 You will overthrow every fortified city and every major **town**.
3: 25 They destroyed the **towns**, and each man threw a stone on every
6: 14 a strong force there. They went by night and surrounded the **city**.
6: 15 an army with horses and chariots had surrounded the **city**.
6: 19 Elisha told them, "This is not the road and this is not the **city**.
7: 4 If we say, 'We'll go into the **city**'—the famine is there, and we will
7: 4 into the city'—the famine is **there**ˢ [+928+2021], and we will die.
7: 10 So they went and called out to the **city** gatekeepers and told them,
7: 12 **[RPH]** and then we will take them alive and get into the city.' "
7: 12 come out, and then we will take them alive and get into the **city**.' "
8: 24 with his fathers and was buried with them in the **City** *of* David.
9: 15 don't let anyone slip out of the **city** to go and tell the news in
9: 28 and buried him with his fathers in his tomb in the **City** *of* David.
10: 2 and you have chariots and horses, a fortified **city** and weapons,
10: 5 the **city** governor, the elders and the guardians sent this message to
10: 6 seventy of them, were with the leading men of the **city**,
10: 25 bodies out and then entered the **inner shrine** *of* the temple of Baal.
11: 20 the **city** was quiet, because Athaliah had been slain with the sword
12: 21 [12:22] and was buried with his fathers in the **City** *of* David.
13: 25 Hazael the **towns** he had taken in battle from his father Jehoahaz.
13: 25 Jehoash defeated him, and so he recovered the Israelite **towns**.
14: 20 and was buried in Jerusalem with his fathers, in the **City** *of* David.
15: 7 with his fathers and was buried near them in the **City** *of* David.
15: 38 with his fathers and was buried with them in the **City** *of* David,
16: 20 with his fathers and was buried with them in the **City** *of* David.
17: 6 in Gozan on the Habor River and in the **towns** *of* the Medes.
17: 9 From watchtower to fortified **city** they built themselves high places
17: 9 to fortified city they built themselves high places in all their **towns**.
17: 24 and settled them in the **towns** *of* Samaria to replace the Israelites.
17: 24 the Israelites. They took over Samaria and lived in its **towns**.
17: 26 resettled in the **towns** *of* Samaria do not know what the god of that
17: 29 each national group made its own gods in the *several* **towns** where
18: 8 From watchtower to fortified **city**, he defeated the Philistines,
18: 11 in Halah, in Gozan on the Habor River and in **towns** *of* the Medes.
18: 13 Sennacherib king of Assyria attacked all the fortified **cities** *of*
18: 30 this **city** will not be given into the hand of the king of Assyria.'
19: 13 the king of the **city** *of* Sepharvaim, or of Hena or Ivvah?"
19: 25 it to pass, that you have turned fortified **cities** into piles of stone.
19: 32 "He will not enter this **city** or shoot an arrow here. He will not
19: 33 he will return; he will not enter this **city**, declares the LORD.
19: 34 I will defend this **city** and save it, for my sake and for the sake of
20: 4 [Before Isaiah had left the middle **court**, [K +2021; see Q 2958]]
20: 6 will deliver you and this **city** from the hand of the king of Assyria.
20: 6 I will defend this **city** for my sake and for the sake of my servant
20: 20 the pool and the tunnel by which he brought water into the **city**,
23: 5 of Judah to burn incense on the high places of the **towns** *of* Judah
23: 8 Josiah brought all the priests from the **towns** *of* Judah
23: 8 of Joshua, the **city** governor, which is on the left of the city gate.
23: 8 of Joshua, the city governor, which is on the left of the **city** gate.
23: 17 The men of the **city** said, "It marks the tomb of the man of God
23: 19 in the **towns** *of* Samaria that had provoked the LORD to anger.
23: 27 the **city** I chose, and this temple, about which I said,
24: 10 of Babylon advanced on Jerusalem and laid siege to **it**ˢ [+2021],
24: 11 Nebuchadnezzar himself came up to the **city** while his officers
25: 2 The **city** was kept under siege until the eleventh year of King
25: 3 By the ninth day of the ⌞fourth⌟ month the famine in the **city** had
25: 4 the **city** wall was broken through, and the whole army fled at night
25: 4 king's garden, though the Babylonians were surrounding the **city**.
25: 11 of the guard carried into exile the people who remained in the **city**,
25: 19 Of **[RPH]** those still in the city, he took the officer in charge of
25: 19 Of those still in the **city**, he took the officer in charge of the
25: 19 people of the land and sixty of his men who were found in the **city**.
1Ch 1: 43 king reigned: Bela son of Beor, whose **city** was named Dinhabah.
1: 46 of Moab, succeeded him as king. His **city** was named Avith.
1: 50 His **city** was named Pau, and his wife's name was Mehetabel
2: 22 the father of Jair, who controlled twenty-three **towns** in Gilead.
2: 23 as well as Kenath with its surrounding settlements—sixty **towns**.)
4: 31 and Shaaraim. These were their **towns** until the reign of David.
4: 32 were Etam, Ain, Rimmon, Token and Ashan—five **towns**—
4: 33 all the villages around these **towns** as far as Baalath. These were
6: 56 [6:41] villages around the **city** were given to Caleb son of
6: 57 [6:42] So the descendants of Aaron were given Hebron (a **city** *of*
6: 60 [6:45] These **towns**, which were distributed among the Kohathite
6: 60 [6:45] among the Kohathite clans, were thirteen **[RPH]** in all.
6: 61 [6:46] The rest of Kohath's descendants were allotted ten **towns**
6: 62 [6:47] were allotted thirteen **towns** from the tribes of Issachar,
6: 63 [6:48] were allotted twelve **towns** from the tribes of Reuben, Gad

1Ch 6:64 [6:49] So the Israelites gave the Levites these **towns** and their
6:65 [6:50] and Benjamin they allotted the previously named **towns**.
6:66 [6:51] given as their territory **towns** from the tribe of Ephraim.
6:67 [6:52] of Ephraim they were given Shechem (a **city** *of* refuge),
9: 2 Now the first to resettle on their own property in their own **towns**
10: 7 and his sons had died, they abandoned their **towns** and fled.
11: 5 David captured the fortress of Zion, the **City** *of* David.
11: 7 up residence in the fortress, and so it was called the **City** *of* David.
11: 8 He built up the **city** around it, from the supporting terraces to the
11: 8 to the surrounding wall, while Joab restored the rest of the **city**.
13: 2 and Levites who are with them in their **towns** and pasturelands,
13:13 He did not take the ark to be with him in the **City** *of* David.
15: 1 After David had constructed buildings for himself in the **City** *of*
15:29 As the ark of the covenant of the LORD was entering the **City** *of*
18: 8 From Tebah and Cun, **towns** *that belonged to* Hadadezer,
19: 7 while the Ammonites were mustered from their **towns** and moved
19: 9 and drew up in battle formation at the entrance to their **city**,
19:13 and let us fight bravely for our people and the **cities** *of* our God.
19:15 they too fled before his brother Abishai and went inside the **city**.
20: 2 on David's head. He took a great quantity of plunder from the **city**
20: 3 iron picks and axes. David did this to all the Ammonite **towns**.
27:25 outlying districts, in the **towns**, the villages and the watchtowers.
2Ch 1:14 which he kept in the chariot **cities** and also with him in Jerusalem.
5: 2 up the ark of the LORD's covenant from Zion, the **City** *of* David.
6: 5 I have not chosen a **city** in any tribe of Israel to have a temple built
6:34 and when they pray to you toward this **city** you have chosen
6:38 toward the **city** you have chosen and toward the temple I have built
8: 2 Solomon rebuilt the **villages** that Hiram had given him, and settled
8: 4 Tadmor in the desert and all the store **cities** he had built in Hamath.
8: 5 Upper Beth Horon and Lower Beth Horon as fortified **cities**,
8: 6 as well as Baalath and all his store **cities**, and all the cities for his
8: 6 store cities, and all the **cities** *for* his chariots and for his horses—
8: 6 and all the cities for his chariots and **[RPH]** for his horses—
8:11 Solomon brought Pharaoh's daughter up from the **City** *of* David to
9:25 which he kept in the chariot **cities** and also with him in Jerusalem.
9:31 with his fathers and was buried in the **city** *of* David his father.
10:17 But as for the Israelites who were living in the **towns** *of* Judah,
11: 5 lived in Jerusalem and built up **towns** for defense in Judah:
11:10 and Hebron. These were fortified **cities** in Judah and Benjamin.
11:12 He put shields and spears in all the **cities** [+2256+6551], and made
11:12 He put shields and spears in all the **cities** [+2256+6551], and made
11:23 the districts of Judah and Benjamin, and to all the fortified **cities**.
12: 4 he captured the fortified **cities** of Judah and came as far as
12:13 the **city** the LORD had chosen out of all the tribes of Israel in
12:16 rested with his fathers and was buried in the **City** *of* David.
13:19 Abijah pursued Jeroboam and took from him the **towns** of Bethel,
14: 1 [13:23] with his fathers and was buried in the **City** *of* David.
14: 5 [14:4] the high places and incense altars in every **town** *in* Judah,
14: 6 [14:5] He built up the fortified **cities** of Judah, since the land was
14: 7 [14:6] "Let us build up these **towns**," he said to Judah, "and put
14:14 [14:13] They destroyed all the **villages** around Gerar,
14:14 [14:13] They plundered all these **villages**, since there was much
15: 6 One nation was being crushed by another and *one* **city** by another,
15: 6 nation was being crushed by another and one city by **another**[s],
15: 8 and from the **towns** he had captured in the hills of Ephraim.
16: 4 and sent the commanders of his forces against the **towns** *of* Israel.
16: 4 Dan, Abel Maim and all the store **cities** *of* Naphtali.
16:14 in the tomb that he had cut out for himself in the **City** *of* David.
17: 2 He stationed troops in all the fortified **cities** *of* Judah and put
17: 2 and in the **towns** *of* Ephraim that his father Asa had captured.
17: 7 Zechariah, Nethanel and Micaiah to teach in the **towns** *of* Judah.
17: 9 they went around to all the **towns** *of* Judah and taught the people.
17:12 and more powerful; he built forts and store **cities** in Judah
17:13 had large supplies in the **towns** *of* Judah. He also kept experienced
17:19 besides those he stationed in the fortified **cities** throughout Judah.
18:25 "Take Micaiah and send him back to Amon the ruler of the **city**
19: 5 judges in the land, in each of the fortified **cities** *of* Judah.
19: 5 judges in the land, in each of the fortified cities of Judah. **[RPH]**
19: 5 judges in the land, in each of the fortified cities of Judah. **[RPH]**
19:10 before you from your fellow countrymen who live in the **cities**—
20: 4 indeed, they came from every **town** *in* Judah to seek him.
21: 1 with his fathers and was buried with them in the **City** *of* David.
21: 3 and gold and articles of value, as well as fortified **cities** in Judah,
21:20 to no one's regret, and was buried in the **City** *of* David,
23: 2 the Levites and the heads of Israelite families from all the **towns**.
23:21 the **city** was quiet, because Athaliah had been slain with the sword.
24: 5 "Go to the **towns** *of* Judah and collect the money due annually
24:16 He was buried with the kings in the **City** *of* David, because of the
24:25 So he died and was buried in the **City** *of* David, but not in the
25:13 had not allowed to take part in the war raided Judean **towns** from
25:28 back by horse and was buried with his fathers in the **City** *of* Judah.
26: 6 He then rebuilt **towns** near Ashdod and elsewhere among the
27: 4 He built **towns** in the Judean hills and forts and towers in the
27: 9 Jotham rested with his fathers and was buried in the **City** *of* David.
28:15 countrymen at Jericho, the **City** *of* Palms, and returned to Samaria.
28:18 while the Philistines had raided **towns** *in* the foothills and *in* the
28:25 In every **town** in Judah he built high places to burn sacrifices to
28:25 In every town **[RPH]** in Judah he built high places to burn
28:27 rested with his fathers and was buried in the **city** of Jerusalem,
29:20 Early the next morning King Hezekiah gathered the **city** officials
30:10 The couriers went from **town** to town in Ephraim and Manasseh,
30:10 The couriers went from town to **town** in Ephraim and Manasseh,
31: 1 the Israelites who were there went out to the **towns** *of* Judah,
31: 1 the Israelites returned to their own **towns** and to their own
31: 6 Judah who lived in the **towns** *of* Judah also brought a tithe of their
31:15 and Shecaniah assisted him faithfully in the **towns** *of* the priests,
31:19 who lived on the farm lands around their **towns** or in any other
31:19 lived on the farm lands around their towns or in any other **towns**,
31:19 **[RPH]** men were designated by name to distribute portions to
32: 1 He laid siege to the fortified **cities**, thinking to conquer them for
32: 3 staff about blocking off the water from the springs outside the **city**,
32: 5 and reinforced the supporting terraces of the **City** *of* David.
32: 6 and assembled them before him in the square at the **city** gate
32:18 to terrify them and make them afraid in order to capture the **city**.
32:29 He built **villages** and acquired great numbers of flocks and herds,
32:30 channeled the water down to the west side of the **City** *of* David.
33:14 Afterward he rebuilt the outer wall of the **City** *of* David, west of
33:14 He stationed military commanders in all the fortified **cities** in
33:15 the temple hill and in Jerusalem; and he threw them out of the **city**.
34: 6 In the **towns** *of* Manasseh, Ephraim and Simeon, as far as
34: 8 he sent Shaphan son of Azaliah and Maaseiah the ruler of the **city**,
Ezr 2: 1 (they returned to Jerusalem and Judah, each to his own **town**,
2:70 the gatekeepers and the temple servants settled in their own **towns**,
2:70 the other people, and the rest of the Israelites settled in their **towns**.
3: 1 seventh month came and the Israelites had settled in their **towns**,
10:14 let everyone in our **towns** who has married a foreign woman come
10:14 along with the elders and judges of **each town** [+2256+6551],
10:14 along with the elders and judges of **each town** [+2256+6551],
Ne 2: 3 Why should my face not look sad when the **city** where my fathers
2: 5 let him send me to the **city** in Judah where my fathers are buried
2: 8 and for the **city** wall and for the residence I will occupy?"
3:15 as far as the steps going down from the **City** *of* David.
7: 4 Now the **city** was large and spacious, but there were few people in
7: 6 (they returned to Jerusalem and Judah, each to his own **town**,
7:73 [7:72] and the rest of the Israelites, settled in their own **towns**.
7:73 [7:72] month came and the Israelites had settled in their **towns**,
8:15 this word and spread it throughout their **towns** and in Jerusalem:
9:25 They captured fortified **cities** and fertile land; they took possession
10:37 [10:38] who collect the tithes in all the **towns** *where* we work.
11: 1 the holy **city**, while the remaining nine were to stay in their own
11: 1 while the remaining nine were to stay in their own **towns**.
11: 3 descendants of Solomon's servants lived in the **towns** *of* Judah,
11: 3 towns of Judah, each on his own property in the *various* **towns**,
11: 9 Judah son of Hassenuah was over the Second District of the **city**.
11:18 The Levites in the holy **city** totaled 284.
11:20 with the priests and Levites, were in all the **towns** *of* Judah,
12:37 directly up the steps of the **City** *of* David on the ascent to the wall
12:44 From the fields around the **towns** they were to bring into the
13:18 that our God brought all this calamity upon us and upon this **city**?
Est 3:15 and Haman sat down to drink, but the **city** *of* Susa was bewildered.
4: 1 put on sackcloth and ashes, and went out into the **city**, wailing
4: 6 So Hathach went out to Mordecai in the open square of the **city** in
6: 9 lead him on the horse through the **city** streets, proclaiming before
6:11 robed Mordecai, and led him on horseback through the **city** streets,
8:11 The king's edict granted the Jews in every **city** the right to
8:11 The king's edict granted the Jews in every city **[RPH]** the right to
8:15 robe of fine linen. And the **city** *of* Susa held a joyous celebration.
8:17 In every province and in every **city**, wherever the edict of the king
8:17 **[RPH]** wherever the edict of the king went, there was joy
9: 2 The Jews assembled in their **cities** in all the provinces of King
9:19 That is why rural Jews—those living in **villages** [+7252]—
9:28 and in every province and in **every city** [+2256+6551].
9:28 and in every province and in **every city** [+2256+6551].
Job 15:28 he will inhabit ruined **towns** and houses where no one lives,
24:12 The groans of the dying rise from the **city**, and the souls of the
Ps 9: 6 [9:7] has overtaken the enemy, you have uprooted their **cities**;
31:21 [31:22] his wonderful love to me when I was in a besieged **city**.
46: 4 [46:5] There is a river whose streams make glad the **city** *of* God,
48: 1 [48:2] worthy of praise, in the **city** *of* our God, his holy mountain.
48: 8 [48:9] so have we seen in the **city** *of* the LORD Almighty,
48: 8 [48:9] in the city of the LORD Almighty, in the **city** *of* our God:
55: 9 [55:10] their speech, for I see violence and strife in the **city**.
59: 6 [59:7] at evening, snarling like dogs, and prowl about the **city**.
59:14 [59:15] at evening, snarling like dogs, and prowl about the **city**.
60: 9 [60:11] Who will bring me to the fortified **city**? Who will lead me
69:35 [69:36] for God will save Zion and rebuild the **cities** *of* Judah.
87: 3 Glorious things are said of you, O **city** *of* God: *Selah*
101: 8 the land; I will cut off every evildoer from the **city** *of* the LORD.

Ps 107: 4 desert wastelands, finding no way to a **city** where they could settle.
107: 7 He led them by a straight way to a **city** where they could settle.
107:36 the hungry to live, and they founded a **city** where they could settle.
108:10 [108:11] Who will bring me to the fortified **city**? Who will lead
122: 3 Jerusalem is built like a **city** that is closely compacted together.
127: 1 Unless the LORD watches over the **city**, the watchmen stand
Pr 1:21 she cries out, in the gateways of the **city** she makes her speech:
16:32 a man who controls his temper than one who takes a **city**.
21:22 A wise man attacks the **city** *of* the mighty and pulls down the
25:28 Like a **city** whose walls are broken down is a man who lacks
Ecc 7:19 makes one wise man more powerful than ten rulers in a **city**.
8:10 the holy place and receive praise in the **city** where they did this.
9:14 There was once a small **city** with only a few people in it. And a
9:15 that city a man poor but wise, and he saved the **city** by his wisdom.
10:15 A fool's work wearies him; he does not know the way to **town**.
SS 3: 2 I will get up now and go about the **city**, through its streets
3: 3 The watchmen found me as they made their rounds in the **city**.
5: 7 The watchmen found me as they made their rounds in the **city**.
Isa 1: 7 Your country is desolate, your **cities** burned with fire; your fields
1: 8 a vineyard, like a hut in a field of melons, like a **city** under siege.
1:26 Afterward you will be called the **City** *of* Righteousness,
6:11 "Until the **cities** lie ruined and without inhabitant, until the houses
14:17 who overthrew its **cities** and would not let his captives go home?"
14:21 not to rise to inherit the land and cover the earth with their **cities**.
14:31 Wail, O gate! Howl, O **city**! Melt away, all you Philistines!
17: 1 Damascus will no longer be a **city** but will become a heap of ruins.
17: 2 The **cities** *of* Aroer will be deserted and left to flocks, which will
17: 9 In that day their strong **cities**, which they left because of the
19: 2 neighbor against neighbor, **city** against city, kingdom against
19: 2 neighbor against neighbor, city against **city**, kingdom against
19:18 In that day five **cities** in Egypt will speak the language of Canaan
19:18 One of them will be called the **City** *of* Destruction.
22: 2 O **town** full of commotion, O city of tumult and revelry?
22: 9 you saw that the **City** *of* David had many breaches in its defenses;
23:16 "Take up a harp, walk through the **city**, O prostitute forgotten;
24:12 The **city** is left in ruins, its gate is battered to pieces.
25: 2 You have made the **city** a heap of rubble, the fortified town a ruin,
25: 2 the fortified town a ruin, the foreigners' stronghold a **city** no more;
26: 1 We have a strong **city**; God makes salvation its walls and ramparts.
27:10 The fortified **city** stands desolate, an abandoned settlement,
32:14 The fortress will be abandoned, the noisy **city** deserted; citadel
32:19 Though hail flattens the forest and the **city** is leveled completely,
33: 8 its witnesses [BHS ***the cities***; NIV 6332] are despised,
36: 1 Sennacherib king of Assyria attacked all the fortified **cities** *of*
36:15 this **city** will not be given into the hand of the king of Assyria.'
37:13 the king of the **city** *of* Sepharvaim, or of Hena or Ivvah?"
37:26 it to pass, that you have turned fortified **cities** into piles of stone.
37:33 "He will not enter this **city** or shoot an arrow here. He will not
37:34 he will return; he will not enter this **city**," declares the LORD.
37:35 "I will defend this **city** and save it, for my sake and for the sake of
38: 6 will deliver you and this **city** from the hand of the king of Assyria.
38: 6 city from the hand of the king of Assyria. I will defend this **city**.
40: 9 do not be afraid; say to the **towns** *of* Judah, "Here is your God!"
42:11 Let the desert and its **towns** raise their voices; let the settlements
44:26 of the **towns** *of* Judah, 'They shall be built,' and of their ruins,
45:13 He will rebuild my **city** and set my exiles free, but not for a price
48: 2 you who call yourselves citizens of the holy **city** and rely on the
52: 1 Put on your garments of splendor, O Jerusalem, the holy **city**.
54: 3 will dispossess nations and settle in their desolate **cities**.
60:14 bow down at your feet and will call you the **City** *of* the LORD,
61: 4 they will renew the ruined **cities** that have been devastated for
62:12 and you will be called Sought After, the **City** No Longer Deserted.
64:10 [64:9] Your sacred **cities** have become a desert; even Zion is a
66: 6 Hear that uproar from the **city**, hear that noise from the temple!
Jer 1:15 all her surrounding walls and against all the **towns** *of* Judah.
1:18 Today I have made you a fortified **city**, an iron pillar and a bronze
2:15 They have laid waste his land; his **towns** are burned and deserted.
2:28 For you have as many gods as you have **towns**, O Judah.
3:14 I will choose you—one from a **town** and two from a clan—
4: 5 and say: 'Gather together! Let us flee to the fortified **cities**!'
4: 7 waste your land. Your **towns** will lie in ruins without inhabitant.
4:16 from a distant land, raising a war cry against the **cities** *of* Judah.
4:26 all its **towns** lay in ruins before the LORD, before his fierce
4:29 At the sound of horsemen and archers every **town** takes to flight.
4:29 among the rocks. All the **towns** are deserted; no one lives in them.
5: 6 a leopard will lie in wait near their **towns** to tear to pieces any who
5:17 With the sword they will destroy the fortified **cities** in which you
6: 6 This **city** must be punished; it is filled with oppression.
7:17 Do you not see what they are doing in the **towns** *of* Judah
7:34 and to the voices of bride and bridegroom in the **towns** *of* Judah
8:14 Gather together! Let us flee to the fortified **cities** and perish there!
8:16 the land and everything in it, the **city** and all who live there."
9:11 [9:10] I will lay waste the **towns** *of* Judah so no one can live
10:22 It will make the **towns** *of* Judah desolate, a haunt of jackals.
11: 6 "Proclaim all these words in the **towns** *of* Judah and in the streets
11:12 The **towns** *of* Judah and the people of Jerusalem will go and cry
11:13 You have as many gods as you have **towns**, O Judah; and the altars
13:19 The **cities** *in* the Negev will be shut up, and there will be no one to
14:18 slain by the sword; if I go into the **city**, I see the ravages of famine.
17:24 and bring no load through the gates of this **city** on the Sabbath,
17:25 throne will come through the gates of this **city** with their officials.
17:25 those living in Jerusalem, and this **city** will be inhabited forever.
17:26 People will come from the **towns** *of* Judah and the villages around
19: 8 I will devastate this **city** and make it an object of scorn; all who
19:11 this **city** just as this potter's jar is smashed and cannot be repaired.
19:12 live here, declares the LORD. I will make this **city** like Topheth.
19:15 I am going to bring on this **city** and the villages around it every
19:15 the **villages** around it every disaster I pronounced against them,
20: 5 I will hand over to their enemies all the wealth of this **city**—
20:16 May that man be like the **towns** the LORD overthrew without
21: 4 the wall besieging you. And I will gather them inside this **city**.
21: 6 I will strike down those who live in this **city**—both men
21: 7 his officials and the people in this **city** who survive the plague,
21: 9 Whoever stays in this **city** will die by the sword, famine or plague.
21:10 I have determined to do this **city** harm and not good,
22: 6 I will surely make you like a desert, like **towns** not inhabited.
22: 8 "People from many nations will pass by this **city** and will ask one
22: 8 'Why has the LORD done such a thing to this great **city**?'
23:39 and cast you out of my presence along with the **city** I gave to you
25:18 Jerusalem and the **towns** *of* Judah, its kings and officials, to make
25:29 I am beginning to bring disaster on the **city** that bears my Name,
26: 2 speak to all the people of the **towns** *of* Judah who come to worship
26: 6 this **city** an object of cursing among all the nations of the earth.' "
26: 9 will be like Shiloh and this **city** will be desolate and deserted?"
26:11 be sentenced to death because he has prophesied against this **city**.
26:12 against this house and this **city** all the things you have heard.
26:15 blood on yourselves and on this **city** and on those who live in it,
26:20 he prophesied the same things against this **city** and this land as
27:17 of Babylon, and you will live. Why should this **city** become a ruin?
27:19 movable stands and the other furnishings that are left in this **city**,
29: 7 and prosperity of the **city** to which I have carried you into exile.
29:16 sits on David's throne and all the people who remain in this **city**,
30:18 the **city** will be rebuilt on her ruins, and the palace will stand in its
31:21 road that you take. Return, O Virgin Israel, return to your **towns**.
31:23 the land of Judah and in its **towns** will once again use these words:
31:24 People will live together in Judah and all its **towns**—farmers
31:38 "when this **city** will be rebuilt for me from the Tower of Hananel
32: 3 I am about to hand this **city** over to the king of Babylon, and he
32:24 "See how the siege ramps are built up to take the **city**. Because of
32:24 the **city** will be handed over to the Babylonians who are attacking
32:25 And though the **city** will be handed over to the Babylonians,
32:28 I am about to hand this **city** over to the Babylonians and to
32:29 The Babylonians who are attacking this **city** will come in and set it
32:29 this city will come in and set **it**[s] [+2021+2021+2296] on fire;
32:31 this **city** has so aroused my anger and wrath that I must remove it
32:36 "You are saying about this **city**, 'By the sword, famine and plague
32:44 in the **towns** *of* Judah and in the towns of the hill country,
32:44 in the towns of Judah and in the **towns** *of* the hill country,
32:44 the hill country, **[RPH]** of the western foothills and of the Negev,
32:44 the hill country, of the western foothills and **[RPH]** of the Negev,
33: 4 says about the houses in this **city** and the royal palaces of Judah
33: 5 I will hide my face from this **city** because of all its wickedness.
33:10 Yet in the **towns** *of* Judah and the streets of Jerusalem that are
33:12 in all its **towns** there will again be pastures for shepherds to rest
33:13 In the **towns** *of* the hill country, of the western foothills and of the
33:13 **[RPH]** of the western foothills and of the Negev, in the territory
33:13 of the western foothills and **[RPH]** of the Negev, in the territory
33:13 in the villages around Jerusalem and in the **towns** *of* Judah,
34: 1 were fighting against Jerusalem and all its surrounding **towns**,
34: 2 I am about to hand this **city** over to the king of Babylon, and he
34: 7 and the other **cities** *of* Judah that were still holding out—
34: 7 and Azekah. These were the only fortified **cities** left in Judah.
34: 7 These were the only fortified cities left in **[RPH]** Judah.
34:22 declares the LORD, and I will bring them back to this **city**.
34:22 And I will lay waste the **towns** *of* Judah so no one can live there."
36: 6 them to all the people of Judah who come in from their **towns**.
36: 9 in Jerusalem and those who had come from the **towns** *of* Judah.
37: 8 the Babylonians will return and attack this **city**; they will capture it
37:10 left in their tents, they would come out and burn this **city** down."
37:21 of the bakers each day until all the bread in the **city** was gone.
38: 2 'Whoever stays in this **city** will die by the sword, famine or plague,
38: 3 'This **city** will certainly be handed over to the army of the king of
38: 4 He is discouraging the soldiers who are left in this **city**, as well as
38: 9 will starve to death when there is no longer any bread in the **city**."
38:17 your life will be spared and this **city** will not be burned down;
38:18 this **city** will be handed over to the Babylonians and they will burn
38:23 by the king of Babylon; and this **city** will be burned down."
39: 2 of Zedekiah's eleventh year, the **city** wall was broken through.

Jer 39: 4 they left the **city** at night by way of the king's garden,
39: 9 carried into exile to Babylon the people who remained in the **city**,
39:16 I am about to fulfill my words against this **city** through disaster,
40: 5 whom the king of Babylon has appointed over the **towns** *of* Judah,
40:10 in your storage jars, and live in the **towns** you have taken over."
41: 7 When they went into the **city**, Ishmael son of Nethaniah and the
44: 2 disaster I brought on Jerusalem and on all the **towns** *of* Judah.
44: 6 it raged against the **towns** *of* Judah and the streets of Jerusalem
44:17 our kings and our officials did in the **towns** *of* Judah and in the
44:21 and think about the incense burned in the **towns** *of* Judah
46: 8 and cover the earth; I will destroy **cities** and their people.'
47: 2 and everything in it, the **towns** and those who live in them.
48: 8 The destroyer will come against every **town**, and not a town will
48: 8 will come against every town, and not a **town** will escape.
48: 9 her **towns** will become desolate, with no one to live in them.
48:15 Moab will be destroyed and her **towns** invaded; her finest young
48:24 to Kerioth and Bozrah—to all the **towns** *of* Moab, far and near.
48:28 Abandon your **towns** and dwell among the rocks, you who live in
49: 1 taken possession of Gad? Why do his people live in its **towns**?
49:13 and of cursing; and all its **towns** will be in ruins forever."
49:25 Why has the **city** *of* renown not been abandoned, the town in
50:32 I will kindle a fire in her **towns** that will consume all who are
51:31 to announce to the king of Babylon that his entire **city** is captured,
51:43 Her **towns** will be desolate, a dry and desert land, a land where no
52: 5 The **city** was kept under siege until the eleventh year of King
52: 6 By the ninth day of the fourth month the famine in the **city** had
52: 7 Then the **city** wall was broken through, and the whole army fled.
52: 7 They left the **city** at night through the gate between the two walls
52: 7 king's garden, though the Babylonians were surrounding the **city**.
52:15 some of the poorest people and those who remained in the **city**,
52:25 Of **[RPH]** those still in the city, he took the officer in charge of
52:25 Of those still in the **city**, he took the officer in charge of the
52:25 people of the land and sixty of his men who were found in the **city**.
La 1: 1 How deserted lies the **city**, once so full of people! How like a
1:19 my elders perished in the **city** while they searched for food to keep
2:12 as they faint like wounded men in the streets of the **city**, as their
2:15 "Is this the **city** that was called the perfection of beauty, the joy of
3:51 I see brings grief to my soul because of all the women of my **city**.
5:11 have been ravished in Zion, and virgins in the **towns** *of* Judah.
Eze 4: 1 put it in front of you and draw the **city** of Jerusalem on it.
4: 3 an iron wall between you and the **city** and turn your face toward it.
5: 2 come to an end, burn a third of the hair with fire inside the **city**.
6: 6 the **towns** will be laid waste and the high places demolished,
7:15 and those in the **city** will be devoured by famine and plague.
7:23 the land is full of bloodshed and the **city** is full of violence.
9: 1 "Bring the guards of the **city** here, each with a weapon in his
9: 4 "Go throughout the **city** *of* Jerusalem and put a mark on the
9: 5 he said to the others, "Follow him through the **city** and kill,
9: 7 Go!" So they went out and began killing throughout the **city**.
9: 9 the land is full of bloodshed and the **city** is full of injustice.
10: 2 coals from among the cherubim and scatter them over the **city**."
11: 2 the men who are plotting evil and giving wicked advice in this **city**.
11: 6 You have killed many people in this **city** and filled its streets with
11:23 The glory of the LORD went up from within the **city** and stopped
11:23 within the city and stopped above the mountain east of **it** [+2021].
12:20 The inhabited **towns** will be laid waste and the land will be
17: 4 to a land of merchants, where he planted it in a **city** *of* traders.
19: 7 He broke down their strongholds and devastated their **towns**.
21:19 [21:24] Make a signpost where the road branches off to the **city**.
22: 2 will you judge her? Will you judge this **city** *of* bloodshed?
22: 3 O **city** that brings on herself doom by shedding blood in her midst
24: 6 " 'Woe to the **city** *of* bloodshed, to the pot now encrusted,
24: 9 " 'Woe to the **city** *of* bloodshed! I, too, will pile the wood high.
25: 9 expose the flank of Moab, beginning **[RPH]** at its frontier towns—
25: 9 I will expose the flank of Moab, beginning at its frontier **towns**—
26:10 chariots when he enters your gates as men enter a **city** whose walls
26:17 " 'How you are destroyed, O **city** *of* renown, peopled by men of the
26:19 When I make you a desolate **city**, like cities no longer inhabited,
26:19 When I make you a desolate city, like **cities** no longer inhabited,
29:12 and her **cities** will lie desolate forty years among ruined cities.
29:12 and her cities will lie desolate forty years among ruined **cities**.
30: 7 among desolate lands, and their **cities** will lie among ruined cities.
30: 7 among desolate lands, and their cities will lie among ruined **cities**.
33:21 from Jerusalem came to me and said, "The **city** has fallen!"
35: 4 I will turn your **towns** into ruins and you will be desolate.
35: 9 I will make you desolate forever; your **towns** will not be inhabited.
36: 4 the desolate ruins and the deserted **towns** that have been plundered
36:10 house of Israel. The **towns** will be inhabited and the ruins rebuilt.
36:33 your sins, I will resettle your **towns**, and the ruins will be rebuilt.
36:35 the **cities** that were lying in ruins, desolate and destroyed,
36:38 So will the ruined **cities** be filled with flocks of people. Then they
39: 9 " 'Then those who live in the **towns** *of* Israel will go out and use
39:16 (Also a **town** called Hamonah will be there.) And so they will
40: 1 tenth of the month, in the fourteenth year after the fall of the **city**—
40: 2 on whose south side were some buildings that looked like a **city**.
43: 3 was like the vision I had seen when he came to destroy the **city**
45: 5 in the temple, as their possession for **towns** [BHS 6929] to live in.
45: 6 " 'You are to give the **city** as its property an area 5,000 cubits wide
45: 7 the area formed by the sacred district and the property of the **city**.
45: 7 **[RPH]** It will extend westward from the west side and eastward
48:15 will be for the common use of the **city**, for houses and for
48:15 for houses and for pastureland. The **city** will be in the center of it
48:17 The pastureland for the **city** will be 250 cubits on the north,
48:18 west side. Its produce will supply food for the workers of the **city**.
48:19 The workers from the **city** who farm it will come from all the tribes
48:20 set aside the sacred portion, along with the property of the **city**.
48:21 the sacred portion and the **city** property will belong to the prince.
48:22 the property of the **city** will lie in the center of the area that
48:30 "These will be the exits of the **city**: Beginning on the north side,
48:31 the gates of the **city** will be named after the tribes of Israel.
48:35 "And the name of the **city** from that time on will be: THE LORD
Da 9:16 and your wrath from Jerusalem, your **city**, your holy hill.
9:18 your eyes and see the desolation of the **city** that bears your Name.
9:19 do not delay, because your **city** and your people bear your Name."
9:24 decreed for your people and your holy **city** to finish transgression,
9:26 The people of the ruler who will come will destroy the **city**
11:15 and build up siege ramps and will capture a fortified **city**.
Hos 8:14 his Maker and built palaces; Judah has fortified many **towns**.
8:14 I will send fire upon their **cities** that will consume their fortresses."
11: 6 Swords will flash in their **cities**, will destroy the bars of their gates
13:10 Where are your rulers in all your **towns**, of whom you said,
Joel 2: 9 They rush upon the **city**; they run along the wall. They climb into
Am 3: 6 When a trumpet sounds in a **city**, do not the people tremble?
3: 6 When disaster comes to a **city**, has not the LORD caused it?
4: 6 "I gave you empty stomachs in every **city** and lack of bread in
4: 7 I sent rain on one **town**, but withheld it from another. One field had
4: 7 **[RPH]** One field had rain; another had none and dried up.
4: 8 People staggered from **town** to town for water but did not get
4: 8 People staggered from town to **town** for water but did not get
5: 3 "The **city** that marches out a thousand strong for Israel will have
6: 8 detest his fortresses; I will deliver up the **city** and everything in it."
7:17 " 'Your wife will become a prostitute in the **city**, and your sons
9:14 people Israel; they will rebuild the ruined **cities** and live in them.
Ob 1:20 who are in Sepharad will possess the **towns** *of* the Negev.
Jnh 1: 2 "Go to the great **city** of Nineveh and preach against it, because its
3: 2 "Go to the great **city** *of* Nineveh and proclaim to it the message I
3: 3 Now Nineveh was a very important **city**—a visit required three
3: 4 On the first day, Jonah started into the **city**. He proclaimed:
4: 5 Jonah went out **[RPH]** and sat down at a place east of the city.
4: 5 Jonah went out and sat down at a place east of the **city**. There he
4: 5 sat in its shade and waited to see what would happen to the **city**.
4:11 cattle as well. Should I not be concerned about that great **city**?"
Mic 5:11 [5:10] I will destroy the **cities** *of* your land and tear down all your
5:14 [5:13] among you your Asherah poles and demolish your **cities**.
6: 9 The LORD is calling to the **city**—and to fear your name is
7:12 day people will come to you from Assyria and the **cities** *of* Egypt,
Na 3: 1 Woe to the **city** *of* blood, full of lies, full of plunder, never without
Hab 2:12 "Woe to him who builds a **city** with bloodshed and establishes a
Zep 1:16 a day of trumpet and battle cry against the fortified **cities**
2:15 This is the carefree **city** that lived in safety. She said to herself,
3: 1 Woe to the **city** *of* oppressors, rebellious and defiled!
3: 6 Their **cities** are destroyed; no one will be left—no one at all.
Zec 1:12 you withhold mercy from Jerusalem and from the **towns** *of* Judah,
1:17 'My **towns** will again overflow with prosperity, and the LORD
7: 7 and its surrounding **towns** were at rest and prosperous,
8: 3 Jerusalem will be called the **City** *of* Truth, and the mountain of the
8: 5 The **city** streets will be filled with boys and girls playing there."
8:20 "Many peoples and the inhabitants of many **cities** will yet come,
14: 2 the **city** will be captured, the houses ransacked, and the women
14: 2 Half of the **city** will go into exile, but the rest of the people will not
14: 2 into exile, but the rest of the people will not be taken from the **city**.

6552 [2]עִיר *ʿîr*[2], n.[m.]. [2] [√ 6424]
anguish [1], wrath [1]

Jer 15: 8 suddenly I will bring down on them **anguish** and terror.
Hos 11: 9 and not man—the Holy One among you. I will not come in **wrath**.

6553 [3]עִיר *ʿîr*[3], n.pr.m. [1] [√ 6554]
Ir [1]

1Ch 7:12 The Shuppites and Huppites were the descendants of **Ir**,

6554 [4]עִיר *ʿîr*[4], n.m. [1] [→ 6553, 6562, 6565, 6566]
donkey [1]

Ge 49:11 He will tether his **donkey** to a vine, his colt to the choicest branch;

6555 עַיִר ***'ayir***, n.m. [7] [√ 6424]

donkeys [4], colt [2], male donkeys [1]

Ge 32:15 [32:16] and twenty female donkeys and ten **male donkeys**.
Jdg 10: 4 He had thirty sons, who rode thirty **donkeys**. They controlled thirty
12:14 had forty sons and thirty grandsons, who rode on seventy **donkeys**.
Job 11:12 a witless man can no more become wise than a wild donkey's **colt**
Isa 30: 6 darting snakes, the envoys carry their riches on **donkeys**' backs,
30:24 The oxen and **donkeys** that work the soil will eat fodder and mash,
Zec 9: 9 gentle and riding on a donkey, on a **colt**, the foal of a donkey.

6556 עִיר הַהֶרֶס ***'îr haheres***, n.pr.loc. Not used in NIV/BHS [√ 6551 + 2021 + 2239]

6557 עִיר הַחֶרֶס ***'îr haḥeres***, n.pr.loc. Not used in NIV/BHS [√ 6551 + 2021 + 3064]

6558 עִיר הַמֶּלַח ***'îr hammelaḥ***, n.pr.loc. Not used in NIV/BHS [√ 6551 + 2021 + 4875]

6559 עִיר הַתְּמָרִים ***'îr hatt^e^mārîm***, n.pr.loc. Not used in NIV/BHS [√ 6551 + 2021 + 9469]

6560 עִיר נָחָשׁ ***'îr nāḥāš***, n.pr.loc. [1] [√ 6551 + 5730]

Ir Nahash [1]

1Ch 4:12 of Beth Rapha, Paseah and Tehinnah the father of **Ir Nahash**.

6561 עִיר שֶׁמֶשׁ ***'îr šemeš***, n.pr.loc. [1] [√ 6551 + 9087]

Ir Shemesh [1]

Jos 19:41 territory of their inheritance included: Zorah, Eshtaol, **Ir Shemesh**,

6562 עִירָא ***'îrā'***, n.pr.m. [6] [√ 6554]

Ira [6]

2Sa 20:26 and **Ira** the Jairite was David's priest.
23:26 Helez the Paltite, **Ira** son of Ikkesh from Tekoa,
23:38 **Ira** the Ithrite, Gareb the Ithrite
1Ch 11:28 **Ira** son of Ikkesh from Tekoa, Abiezer from Anathoth,
11:40 **Ira** the Ithrite, Gareb the Ithrite,
27: 9 for the sixth month, was **Ira** the son of Ikkesh the Tekoite.

6563 עִירָד ***'îrād***, n.pr.m. [2] [√ 6871]

Irad [2]

Ge 4:18 To Enoch was born **Irad**, and Irad was the father of Mehujael,
4:18 To Enoch was born Irad, and **Irad** was the father of Mehujael,

6564 עִירוּ ***'îrû***, n.pr.m. [1]

Iru [1]

1Ch 4:15 son of Jephunneh: **Iru**, Elah and Naam. The son of Elah: Kenaz.

6565 עִירִי ***'îrî***, n.pr.m. [1] [√ 6554]

Iri [1]

1Ch 7: 7 Ezbon, Uzzi, Uzziel, Jerimoth and **Iri**, heads of families—

6566 עִירָם ***'îrām***, n.pr.m. [2] [√ 6554 + 4392]

Iram [2]

Ge 36:43 Magdiel and **Iram**. These were the chiefs of Edom, according to
1Ch 1:54 Magdiel and **Iram**. These were the chiefs of Edom.

6567 עֵירֹם ***'êrōm***, a. (used as noun). [10] [√ 6867]

naked [9], nakedness [1]

Ge 3: 7 of both of them were opened, and they realized they were **naked**;
3:10 "I heard you in the garden, and I was afraid because I was **naked**;
3:11 he said, "Who told you that you were **naked**? Have you eaten from
Dt 28:48 therefore in hunger and thirst, in **nakedness** and dire poverty,
Eze 16: 7 were formed and your hair grew, you who were **naked** and bare.
16:22 when you were **naked** and bare, kicking about in your blood.
16:39 and take your fine jewelry and leave you **naked** and bare.
18: 7 gives his food to the hungry and provides clothing for the **naked**.
18:16 gives his food to the hungry and provides clothing for the **naked**.
23:29 They will leave you **naked** and bare, and the shame of your

6568 עַיִשׁ ***'ayiš***, n.f. [1] [→ 6933]

bear [1]

Job 38:32 constellations in their seasons or lead out the **Bear** with its cubs?

6569 עַיַּת ***'ayyat***, n.pr.loc. [1] [cf. 6509]

Aiath [1]

Isa 10:28 They enter **Aiath**; they pass through Migron; they store supplies at

6570 עַכְבּוֹר ***'akbôr***, n.pr.m. [7] [√ 6572]

Acbor [7]

Ge 36:38 Shaul died, Baal-Hanan son of **Acbor** succeeded him as king.
36:39 When Baal-Hanan son of **Acbor** died, Hadad succeeded him as
2Ki 22:12 **Acbor** son of Micaiah, Shaphan the secretary and Asaiah the
22:14 **Acbor**, Shaphan and Asaiah went to speak to the prophetess
1Ch 1:49 Shaul died, Baal-Hanan son of **Acbor** succeeded him as king.
Jer 26:22 King Jehoiakim, however, sent Elnathan son of **Acbor** to Egypt,
36:12 the secretary, Delaiah son of Shemaiah, Elnathan son of **Acbor**,

6571 עַכָּבִישׁ ***'akkābîš***, n.m. [2]

spider's [2]

Job 8:14 What he trusts in is fragile; what he relies on is a **spider's** web.
Isa 59: 5 They hatch the eggs of vipers and spin a **spider's** web.

6572 עַכְבָּר ***'akbār***, n.m. [6] [→ 6570]

rats [5], rat [1]

Lev 11:29 are unclean for you: the weasel, the **rat**, any kind of great lizard,
1Sa 6: 4 They replied, "Five gold tumors and five gold **rats**, according to
6: 5 of the tumors and of the **rats** that are destroying the country,
6:11 along with it the chest containing the gold **rats** and the models of
6:18 the number of the gold **rats** was according to the number of
Isa 66:17 who eat the flesh of pigs and **rats** and other abominable things—

6573 עַכּוֹ ***'akkô***, n.pr.loc. [1]

Acco [1]

Jdg 1:31 Nor did Asher drive out those living in **Acco** or Sidon or Ahlab

6574 עָכוֹר ***'ākôr***, n.pr.loc. [5] [√ 6579]

Achor [5]

Jos 7:24 and sheep, his tent and all that he had, to the Valley of **Achor**.
7:26 Therefore that place has been called the Valley of **Achor** ever
15: 7 The boundary then went up to Debir from the Valley of **Achor**
Isa 65:10 the Valley of **Achor** a resting place for herds, for my people who
Hos 2:15 [2:17] and will make the Valley of **Achor** a door of hope.

6575 עָכָן ***'ākān***, n.pr.m. [6]

Achan [6]

Jos 7: 1 **Achan** son of Carmi, the son of Zimri, the son of Zerah,
7:18 and **Achan** son of Carmi, the son of Zimri, the son of Zerah,
7:19 Then Joshua said to **Achan**, "My son, give glory to the LORD,
7:20 **Achan** replied, "It is true! I have sinned against the LORD,
7:24 took **Achan** son of Zerah, the silver, the robe, the gold wedge,
22:20 When **Achan** son of Zerah acted unfaithfully regarding the devoted

6576 עָכַס ***'ākas***, v.den. [1 / 2] [→ 6577, 6578]

ornaments jingling [1], stepping [1]

Pr 7:22 [D] the slaughter, like a deer **stepping** [BHS 6577] into a noose
Isa 3:16 [D] with mincing steps, with **ornaments jingling** on their ankles.

6577 עֶכֶס ***'ekes***, n.[m.]. [2 / 1] [√ 6576]

bangles [1]

Pr 7:22 like a deer stepping [BHS *fetters* ?; NIV 6576] into a noose
Isa 3:18 their finery: the **bangles** and headbands and crescent necklaces,

6578 עַכְסָה ***'aksâ***, n.pr.f. [5] [√ 6576]

Acsah [5]

Jos 15:16 "I will give my daughter **Acsah** in marriage to the man who attacks
15:17 took it; so Caleb gave his daughter **Acsah** to him in marriage.
Jdg 1:12 "I will give my daughter **Acsah** in marriage to the man who attacks
1:13 took it; so Caleb gave his daughter **Acsah** to him in marriage.
1Ch 2:49 the father of Macbenah and Gibea. Caleb's daughter was **Acsah**.

6579 עָכַר ***'ākar***, v. [14] [→ 6574, 6580, 6581]

brings trouble [4], brought trouble [3], bring trouble [2], made trouble [2], increased [1], troubler [1], wretched [1]

Ge 34:30 [A] "*You have* **brought trouble** *on* me by making me a stench
Jos 6:18 [A] camp of Israel liable to destruction and **bring trouble** *on* it.
7:25 [A] Joshua said, "Why *have you* **brought** *this* **trouble** *on* us?
7:25 [A] The LORD *will* **bring trouble** *on* you today." Then all
Jdg 11:35 [A] You have made me miserable and **wretched**, because I have
1Sa 14:29 [A] Jonathan said, "My father *has* **made trouble** *for* the country.

[A] Qal [B] Qal passive [C] Niphal [D] Piel (poel, polel, pilel, pilal, pealal, pilpel) [E] Pual (poal, polal, poalal, pulal, pualal)

1Ki 18: 17 [A] he said to him, "Is that you, you **troubler** *of* Israel?"
18: 18 [A] "*I have* not **made trouble** *for* Israel," Elijah replied.
1Ch 2: 7 [A] who **brought trouble** *on* Israel by violating the ban on
Ps 39: 2 [39:3] [C] even saying anything good, my anguish **increased**.
Pr 11: 17 [A] benefits himself, but a cruel man **brings trouble** *on* himself.
11: 29 [A] *He who* **brings trouble** *on* his family will inherit only wind,
15: 6 [C] but the income of the wicked **brings** them **trouble**.
15: 27 [A] A greedy man **brings trouble** *to* his family, but he who hates

6580 עָכָר *'ākār*, n.pr.m. [1] [√ 6579]

Achar [1]

1Ch 2: 7 **Achar**, who brought trouble on Israel by violating the ban on

6581 עָכְרָן *'okrān*, n.pr.m. [5] [√ 6579]

Ocran [5]

Nu 1: 13 from Asher, Pagiel son of **Ocran**;
2: 27 The leader of the people of Asher is Pagiel son of **Ocran**.
7: 72 On the eleventh day Pagiel son of **Ocran**, the leader of the people
7: 77 fellowship offering. This was the offering of Pagiel son of **Ocran**.
10: 26 Pagiel son of **Ocran** was over the division of the tribe of Asher,

6582 עַכְשׁוּב *'akšûb*, n.m. [1]

vipers [1]

Ps 140: 3 [140:4] sharp as a serpent's; the poison of **vipers** is on their lips.

6583 ¹עַלִי *'al¹*, subst. [4] [√ 6590; cf. 6584; Ar 10546]

Most High [4]

2Sa 23: 1 son of Jesse, the oracle of the man exalted by the **Most High**,
Ps 7: 10 [7:11] My shield is God **Most High**, who saves the upright in
Hos 7: 16 They do not turn to the **Most High**; they are like a faulty bow.
11: 7 Even if they call to the **Most High**, he will by no means exalt

6584 ²עַל *'al²*, pp. & c. [5772 / 5771] [→ 5088, 6586, 6629; cf. 6583; Ar 10542] See Select Index

on [1150], *untranslated* [904], against [400], over [376], to [319], for [250], in [248], upon [166], from [+4946] [155], at [128], by [92], with [79], of [61], because of [57], about [53], therefore [+4027] [52], above [45], in charge of [43], that is why [+4027] [34], concerning [31], along [29], because [29], around [27], near [26], beside [25], so [+4027] [25], into [24], according to [18], from [18], facedown [+7156] [15], under [15], because [+889] [14], above [+4946] [13], on [+7156] [13], why [+4537] [13], to [+3338] [12], attack [10], away from [+4946] [10], bears [+7924] [10], border [10], over [+7156] [10], within [10], on [+4946] [9], toward [9], after [8], along with [8], as [8], before [8], near [+7156] [8], off [+4946] [8], on top of [8], together with [8], administrator[s] [+889] [7], next to [+3338] [7], wearing [7], attacked [+6590] [6], because [+3954] [6], because of [+1821] [6], in [+7156] [6], in front of [+7156] [6], next to [6], there[s] [+2023] [6], among [5], attack [+6590] [5], attack [+995] [5], because [+4027] [5], before [+7156] [5], east [+7156] [5], for sake [5], had charge of [5], next section [+3338] [5], this is why [+4027] [5], across [4], bear [+7924] [4], because of [+128] [4], connected to [4], enter [+6590] [4], have [4], in accordance with [4], in addition to [4], in command [+7372] [4], out of [+4946] [4], than [4], upon [+7156] [4], about [+128] [3], according to [+7023] [3], against [+4946] [3], attacking [+7756] [3], because [+1821] [3], burning [+836+2021] [3], concerning [+1821] [3], covered with [3], faces [+7156] [3], facing [+7156] [3], had to [3], higher than [+4946] [3], in opposition to [3], in spite of [3], invaded [+6590] [3], lusted after [+6311] [3], next [+3338] [3], on account of [3], oppose [3], past [3], responsible for [3], rested on [3], so [+2296] [3], tenderly [+4213] [3], throughout [3], top [3], toward [+7156] [3], up to [3], wear [+2118] [3], when [3], about [+1821] [2], according to [+3869] [2], across [+7156] [2], across from [+7156] [2], along [+3338] [2], and [2], as for [2], as though [2], as well as [2], attached to [2], attacked [+995] [2], await [2], before [+4946] [2], besides [2], besiege [+2837] [2], by [+3338] [2], cover [2], crown [2], decorated with [2], defied [+1540] [2], enter [+995] [2], fighting [2], for [+1821] [2], for [+3954+4027] [2], from [+4946+7156] [2], from [+7156] [2], got off [+4946+7563] [2], in behalf [2], in front of [2], inner [2], lying on [+7156] [2], mating with [+6590] [2], more than [2], no wonder [+4027] [2], on behalf [2], onto [2], outside [2], over [+4946] [2], prostrate [+7156] [2], protect [+6641] [2], responsibility for [2], rests on [2], rule [+2118] [2], rule over [2], seized [+5877] [2], separated from [+4946] [2], set on [2], so that [+4027] [2], the steward[s] [+889] [2], therefore [+2296] [2], though [2], threw arms around [+5877+7418] [2], to [+7931] [2], too [2], which way [+196+3545+6584+8520] [2], wore [2], above [+1068] [1], above [+4946+5087] [1], above [+7156] [1], accompanied by [+3338] [1], accuse [+7212] [1], add [1], adjoining [+3338] [1], adjoining section [+3338] [1], adorned [+6590] [1], afraid [+5877+7065] [1], against [+7156] [1], against side [1], ahead [+7156] [1], all over [+6017 +6017] [1], all the way to [1], although [1], and [+4027] [1], and alike [1], and so [+4027] [1], anoint [1], apart from [1], aptly [+698] [1], aroused [+2118+4200] [1], as a result of [+1821] [1], as far as [1], as for [+1826] [1], as part of [1], as prescribed by [+3338] [1], assail [+5877] [1], assaults [+7756] [1], assistant [+3338] [1], assisted [+3338] [1], assume the responsibility for carrying out [+6641] [1], at [+6813] [1], at [+7156] [1], at flood stage [+1536+3972] [1], at flood stage [+1536+3972+4848] [1], at heels [+7418] [1], at side [1], attack [+3338+6590] [1], attacked [+7756] [1], attacked viciously [+906+3751+5782+8797] [1], attacking [+995] [1], attacking [1], attacks [+7756] [1], attacks [+995] [1], attendants [+6641] [1], avert [+4946+6296] [1], away [+4946] [1], because [+1826] [1], because [+3954+4027] [1], because of [+3970] [1], because of [+4027] [1], because of [+4946] [1], because of [+6813] [1], because of this [+4027] [1], become guilty [+2628+5951] [1], been under [+6590] [1], below [+141+2021] [1], beside [+3338] [1], beside [+4946] [1], beside [+7156] [1], besieged [+1215] [1], besieged [+2837] [1], better than [1], between [1], beyond [1], binding on [1], blessed [1], bordering [1], borne on [+7156] [1], bowed down [+5877+7156] [1], bowed down to the ground [+5877+7156] [1], bracelets [+3338+7543] [1], by [+4946] [1], by [+7023] [1], care for [1], cares [+4213+8492] [1], carried by [+2118] [1], carry on [+7756] [1], charged against [1], commander in chief [+2021+7372] [1], confronted [+6641] [1], confronted [+7756] [1], conquered [+2616] [1], consider [+4213+8492] [1], contribute [1], corresponding to [+7156] [1], could not [+2118] [1], cover [+6296] [1], credited to [1], crossing [+7156] [1], crowns [1], deal with [1], decide [+2118+7023] [1], demanded [+7023] [1], depend on [1], directed to [1], do anything that endangers life [+1947+6641] [1], do not know where am going [+889+2143+2143] [1], don't say a word [+3338+7023+8492] [1], drove back [+2118] [1], during [1], east [+7156+7710] [1], embraced [+7418] [1], encircle [+7443] [1], encourage [+1819+4213] [1], encouraged [+1819+4222] [1], encouragingly [+4213] [1], entered [+995] [1], even beyond [+4946] [1], expressed [+7023] [1], extend toward [1], extended [+7156] [1], falsely [+9214] [1], feed on [1], fight [1], follows [+7925] [1], for [+1386] [1], for [+3338] [1], for [+4946] [1], for [+889] [1], for sake [+128] [1], gave a high rank in [+8492] [1], given over [+3338+5599] [1], got off [+3718+4946] [1], governor[s] [+889] [1], had [+2118] [1], had to [+2118] [1], had [1], hanging on [1], has [1], have [+2118] [1], help [1], here[s] [+3276] [1], here[s] [+3870] [1], higher [+4946] [1], highest [+8031] [1], his [+2257] [1], hold accountable [+5989] [1], how [+4027] [1], how [1], in [+4946] [1], in accordance with [+7023] [1], in behalf [+3208] [1], in behalf of [+1821] [1], in behalf of [1], in charge [+6641] [1], in control [1], in hands [1], in hostility toward [+7156] [1], in little more than [+3427] [1], in preference to [+7156] [1], in presence of [1], in presence [1], in store for [1], in the light of [1], in the presence of [1], in the way should go [+2006+7023] [1], including [1], increase [+3578] [1], instead of [+4030] [1], invade [+6590] [1], invaded [+995] [1], its [+2023] [1], jealous [+6296+7863+8120] [1], join [+2143] [1], join [+2616] [1], keeper[s] [+889] [1], kneeling [+1386+4156] [1], knelt down [+1384+1386] [1], laid siege to [+2837] [1], leader [1], leads to [1], lie with [+995] [1], lingering [+3427+3427] [1], little by little [+3338] [1], lived in hostility toward [+5877+7156] [1], load [1], loaded with [1], longed for [1], look after [+6524+8492] [1], look after [+906+6524+8492] [1], make wear [+5516+6590] [1], manned [1], marched past [+3338+6296] [1], more and more [+3578+3972] [1], mounted like jewels [+3782+4859] [1], near [+3338] [1], nearby [+3338] [1], nearby [1], nearest [+7156] [1], object of malicious talk [+4383+6590+8557] [1], obligates [1], of [+4946] [1], on [+7023] [1], on behalf of [1], on foot [+824+2021] [1], on side [1], opposed [+599] [1], opposed [+6641] [1], over [+4200+4946] [1], over higher [1], overflow [+6590] [1], overpower [+4309] [1], overpowered [+3338+6451] [1], overruled [+2616] [1], overwhelm [+995] [1], overwhelmed [+5877] [1], part of [1], part [1], past [+4946] [1], peels [+4946] [1], persuade [+1819+4213] [1], placed on [1], presence [+4946] [1], protects [+6641] [1], put in charge [+3338+6641] [1], put in charge of the storerooms [+238+732] [1], reaches to [1], reason [1], received gladly [+8523] [1], reclining [1], regarding [1], reign over [1], reject [+906+4946+7156+8938] [1], reject [+906+4946+7156+8959] [1], repay [+906+8031+8740] [1], required [+2011] [1], required of [1], resolved [+4213+8492] [1], responsible [1], rest on [1], rid [+906+4946+8959] [1], ring [1], ruled over [1], serve [+6641] [1], set against [1], share in [+5951] [1], shave [+7947] [1], simply [+7023] [1], since [+3954+4027] [1], since [+4027] [1], since [1], sleep with [+4156] [1], so [+3869] [1], spoken kindly [+1819+4213] [1], stand up [+6641+6642] [1], steward[s] [+408+889+1074+2021] [1], steward[s] [+889+1074] [1], strike [1], succeeded [+4030+6641] [1], successor [+4030+6641] [1], suffer [+5989] [1], supervised [1], supporting [1], surely leave [+2143+2143+4946] [1], take [+995] [1], take care of [1], take off [+3718+4946] [1], takes [+3782] [1], that [+4027] [1], that's why [+4027] [1], the duty of [1], their [+2157] [1], their[s] [+3776] [1], then

[+4027] [1], there [+2157] [1], therefore [+1826+8611] [1], think [+4222+6590] [1], think about [+4213+6590] [1], this is why [+465] [1], threw arms around [+5877] [1], throughout [+3972+7156] [1], tie [+5989] [1], to [+4200+7156] [1], to [+4946] [1], to reach [1], took up [+6641] [1], touches [+2118] [1], toward [+2006] [1], toward [+2006+7156] [1], under guard [+5464] [1], upside down [+7156] [1], used for [1], used [1], using [1], voluntarily [+408+4213+6590] [1], watch over [+8492] [1], wear [+6590] [1], wearing around [1], weigh down [1], what [+4537] [1], when [+889] [1], where[s] [+2157] [1], where[s] [+6642] [1], wherever [+889+2021+3972+5226] [1], wherever [+889+3972] [1], while still alive [+7156] [1], why [+2296] [1], will [+7023] [1], with [+3338] [1], with [+7156] [1], worn [1], yet [1], your [+3871] [1], your [+4013] [1]

6585 עֹל 'ōl, n.m. [40] [√ 6619]

yoke [36], it[s] [3], yoked [+6584+6590] [1]

Ge 27:40 you grow restless, you will throw his **yoke** from off your neck."
Lev 26:13 I broke the bars of your **yoke** and enabled you to walk with heads
Nu 19: 2 without defect or blemish and that has never been under a **yoke**.
Dt 21: 3 a heifer that has never been worked and has never worn a **yoke**
28:48 He will put an iron **yoke** on your neck until he has destroyed you.
1Sa 6: 7 cows that have calved and *have* never *been* **yoked** [+6584+6590].
1Ki 12: 4 "Your father put a heavy **yoke** *on* us, but now lighten the harsh
12: 4 but now lighten the harsh labor and the heavy **yoke** he put on us,
12: 9 people who say to me, 'Lighten the **yoke** your father put on us'?"
12:10 'Your father put a heavy **yoke** *on* us, but make our yoke lighter'—
12:11 My father laid on you a heavy **yoke**; I will make it even heavier.
12:11 My father laid on you a heavy yoke; I will make **it**[s] even heavier.
12:14 of the young men and said, "My father made your **yoke** heavy;
12:14 "My father made your yoke heavy; I will make **it**[s] even heavier.
2Ch 10: 4 "Your father put a heavy **yoke** *on* us, but now lighten the harsh
10: 4 but now lighten the harsh labor and the heavy **yoke** he put on us,
10: 9 people who say to me, 'Lighten the **yoke** your father put on us'?"
10:10 'Your father put a heavy **yoke** *on* us, but make our yoke lighter'—
10:11 My father laid on you a heavy **yoke**; I will make it even heavier.
10:11 My father laid on you a heavy yoke; I will make **it**[s] even heavier.
10:14 of the young men and said, "My father made your **yoke** heavy;
Isa 9: 4 [9:3] you have shattered the **yoke** *that* burdens them, the bar
10:27 will be lifted from your shoulders, their **yoke** from your neck;
10:27 your neck; the **yoke** will be broken because you have grown so fat.
14:25 His **yoke** will be taken from my people, and his burden removed
47: 6 them no mercy. Even on the aged you laid a very heavy **yoke**.
Jer 2:20 "Long ago you broke off your **yoke** and tore off your bonds;
5: 5 with one accord they too had broken off the **yoke** and torn off the
27: 8 Nebuchadnezzar king of Babylon or bow its neck under his **yoke**,
27:11 if any nation will bow its neck under the **yoke** *of* the king of
27:12 I said, "Bow your neck under the **yoke** *of* the king of Babylon;
28: 2 God of Israel, says: 'I will break the **yoke** *of* the king of Babylon.
28: 4 the LORD, 'for I will break the **yoke** *of* the king of Babylon.' "
28:11 'In the same way will I break the **yoke** *of* Nebuchadnezzar king of
28:14 I will put an iron **yoke** on the necks of all these nations to make
30: 8 'I will break the **yoke** off their necks and will tear off their bonds;
La 1:14 "My sins have been bound into a **yoke**; by his hands they were
3:27 It is good for a man to bear the **yoke** while he is young.
Eze 34:27 when I break the bars of their **yoke** and rescue them from the hands
Hos 11: 4 I lifted the **yoke** from their neck and bent down to feed them.

6586 עַל־כֵּן 'al-kēn, pp.+adv. Not used in NIV/BHS [→ 3956; cf. 6584 + 4027]

6587 עֻלָּא 'ullā', n.pr.m. [1] [√ 6590]

Ulla [1]

1Ch 7:39 The sons of **Ulla**: Arah, Hanniel and Rizia.

6588 עַלְבוֹן 'albôn, n.pr.m. Not used in NIV/BHS [→ 50]

6589 עִלֵּג 'illēg, a. [1] [cf. 4352]

stammering [1]

Isa 32: 4 and the **stammering** tongue will be fluent and clear.

6590 עָלָה 'ālâ, v. [892] [→ 541, 5087, 5089, 5090, 5091, 5092, 5093, 6583, 6587, 6591, 6592, 6595, 6597, 6603, 6604, 6605, 6606, 6607, 6608, 6609, 6610, 9498?, 9499]

went up [111], go up [76], brought up [46], came up [31], go [24], bring up [23], come up [23], offered [14], *untranslated* [13], come [13], sacrificed [13], offer [12], up [12], attack [11], sacrifice [11], gone up [10], bring [9], coming up [9], lifted [9], rise [8], rises [8], went [8], climbed [7], attacked [+6584] [6], led up [6], marched up [6], set up [6], ascended [5], attack [+6584] [5], attacked [5], came [5], chews [5], marched [5], presented [5], rising [5], sacrificing [5], take up [5], ascend [4], attack [+448] [4], brought [4], chew [4], climb up [4], conscripted [4], enter [+6584] [4], goes up [4], going up [4], grow [4], return [4], rose [4], send up [4], took [4], climbed up [3], grew up [3], growing [3], invaded [+6584] [3], lying on [3], makes rise [3], march [3], offered sacrifices [3], offerings [3], present [3], returned [3], used [3], withdraw [3], withdrew [3], advance [2], advances [2], aroused [2], assemble [2], attacking [2], carried up [2], carried [2], carry up [2], climb [2], climbs [2], daybreak [+2021+8840] [2], get [2], go back [2], go on up [2], go straight up [2], gone [2], got on [2], imported [+2256+3655] [2], invaded [2], is [2], lift [2], made [2], mating with [+6584] [2], offered up [2], offering [2], raged [2], reached [2], reaches [2], sets up [2], should go up [+6590] [2], soar [2], spring up [2], sprinkled [2], surely bring back [+6590] [2], take [2], taken [2], withdrawn [2], accompanied [+907] [1], adorned [+6584] [1], advanced [1], appeared [1], approach [1], are exalted [1], are recorded [1], ascending [1], ascent [1], assemble [+928+2021+7736] [1], at [+928] [1], attack [+3338+6584] [1], attacked [+928] [1], attacking [+448] [1], attacks [1], back [1], been under [+6584] [1], billowed up [1], blazed up [1], blossomed [+5890] [1], blow away [1], blowing in [1], bring back [1], bringing up [1], brought along [1], brought back [1], building [1], burning [1], burnt offerings [1], carried away [1], casting up [1], charge [1], charged [1], charging [1], chosen [1], climbed in [1], climbing up [1], come back [1], comes out [1], comes [1], coming out [1], coming [1], consider [1], continued up [1], continued [1], decorated [1], deserted [+339+4946] [1], drag away [1], entered [1], evening sacrifice [+4966] [1], exalted [1], falls [1], filled [1], first light of dawn [+8840] [1], flare up [1], flared [1], flowed over [1], followed [+928+8079] [1], gathered [1], get up [1], goes [1], going [1], gone ahead [1], grow up [1], had come up [1], had go up [1], haul up [1], have [1], headed [1], helped up [1], invade [+6584] [1], invade [+928] [1], invaded [+448] [1], invaded [+928] [1], is on way [1], kept burning [1], lead [1], leading to [1], leave [+4946] [1], left [+4946] [1], lights [1], made come up [1], made grow up [1], make come up [1], make come [1], make offerings [1], make wear [+5516+6584] [1], makes offering [1], making [1], mount [1], mounted up [1], move away [1], moved away [1], moved up [1], object of malicious talk [+4383+6584+8557] [1], offer up [1], offers [1], on way up [1], on way [1], on [1], overflow [+6584] [1], overgrown [1], overrun [1], paid [1], passed [1], presented offerings [1], progressed [1], pull out [1], pulls up [1], put on [1], raises up [1], ran up [1], ran [1], reached [+448] [1], restore [1], retreated [1], sacrifice [+4966] [1], sacrifice [+6592] [1], scale [1], send [1], serve [1], sprinkle [1], stepped out [1], steps [1], stir up [1], stirs up [1], stopped [+4946] [1], surpass [1], swarm [1], take away [1], taken up [1], think [+4222+6584] [1], think about [+4213+6584] [1], took up [1], upper [1], voluntarily [+408+4213+6584] [1], walking [1], wear [+6584] [1], wear [1], weighed [1], went back [1], went off [1], went over [1], worked [1], yoked [+6584+6585] [1]

Ge 2: 6 [A] streams **came up** from the earth and watered the whole
8:20 [G] and clean birds, *he* **sacrificed** burnt offerings on it.
13: 1 [A] So Abram **went up** from Egypt to the Negev, with his wife
17:22 [A] finished speaking with Abraham, God **went up** from him.
19:15 [A] With the **coming** *of* dawn, the angels urged Lot, saying,
19:28 [A] he saw dense smoke **rising** from the land, like smoke from a
19:30 [A] Lot and his two daughters **left** [+4946] Zoar and settled in the
22: 2 [G] **Sacrifice** him there as a burnt offering on one of the
22:13 [G] and **sacrificed** it as a burnt offering instead of his son.
24:16 [A] went down to the spring, filled her jar and **came up** again.
26:23 [A] From there *he* **went up** *to* Beersheba.
28:12 [A] and the angels of God *were* **ascending** and descending on it.
31:10 [A] saw that the male goats **mating** [+6584] **with** the flock were
31:12 [A] see that all the male goats **mating** [+6584] **with** the flock are
32:24 [32:25] [A] and a man wrestled with him till **[NIE]** daybreak.
32:26 [32:27] [A] the man said, "Let me go, for *it* **is** daybreak."
35: 1 [A] Then God said to Jacob, "Go **up** *to* Bethel and settle there,
35: 3 [A] come, *let us* **go up** *to* Bethel, where I will build an altar to
35:13 [A] God **went up** from him at the place where he had talked with
37:28 [A] his brothers pulled Joseph **up** out of the cistern and sold him
38:12 [A] *he* **went up** to Timnah, to the men who were shearing his
38:13 [A] "Your father-in-law **is on** *his* **way** to Timnah to shear his
40:10 [A] As soon as it budded, it **blossomed** [+5890], and its clusters
41: 2 [A] when out of the river *there* **came up** seven cows, sleek and
41: 3 [A] **came up** out of the Nile and stood beside those on the
41: 5 [A] of grain, healthy and good, *were* **growing** on a single stalk.
41:18 [A] when out of the river *there* **came up** seven cows, fat and
41:19 [A] After them, seven other cows **came up**—scrawny and very
41:22 [A] heads of grain, full and good, **growing** on a single stalk.
41:27 [A] ugly cows that **came up** afterward are seven years, and so are
44:17 [A] my slave. The rest of you, **go back** to your father in peace."
44:24 [A] When *we* **went back** to your servant my father, we told him
44:33 [A] in place of the boy, and *let* the boy **return** with his brothers.
44:34 [A] How *can I* **go back** to my father if the boy is not with me?
45: 9 [A] Now hurry **back** to my father and say to him, 'This is what

Ge 45:25 [A] So *they* **went up** out of Egypt and came to their father Jacob
46: 4 [G] with you, and I *will* **surely bring** [+6590] you **back** again.
46: 4 [A] with you, and I *will* **surely bring** you **back** [+6590] again.
46:29 [A] made ready and **went** to Goshen to meet his father Israel.
46:31 [A] "*I will* **go up** and speak to Pharaoh and will say to him,
49: 4 [A] for *you* **went up** *onto* your father's bed, onto my couch
49: 4 [A] onto your father's bed, **[RPH]** onto my couch and defiled it.
49: 9 [A] are a lion's cub, O Judah; *you* **return** from the prey, my son.
50: 5 [A] Now *let me* **go up** and bury my father; then I will return.' "
50: 6 [A] Pharaoh said, "**Go up** and bury your father, as he made you
50: 7 [A] So Joseph **went up** to bury his father. All Pharaoh's officials
50: 7 [A] All Pharaoh's officials **accompanied** [+907] him—
50: 9 [A] Chariots and horsemen also **went up** with him. It was a very
50:14 [A] and all the *others who had* **gone** with him to bury his father.
50:24 [G] **take** you **up** out of this land to the land he promised on oath
50:25 [G] and then *you must* **carry** my bones **up** from this place."
Ex 1:10 [A] our enemies, fight against us and **leave** [+4946] the country."
2:23 [A] their cry for help because of their slavery **went up** to God.
3: 8 [G] to **bring** them **up** out of that land into a good and spacious
3:17 [G] I have promised *to* **bring** you **up** out of your misery in Egypt
8: 3 [7:28] [A] They will come **up** into your palace and your
8: 4 [7:29] [A] The frogs *will* **go up** on you and your people and all
8: 5 [8:1] [G] and **make** frogs **come up** on the land of Egypt.' "
8: 6 [8:2] [A] of Egypt, and the frogs **came up** and covered the land.
8: 7 [8:3] [G] *they* also **made** frogs **come up** on the land of Egypt.
10:12 [A] hand over Egypt so that locusts *will* **swarm** over the land
10:14 [A] they **invaded** [+6584] all Egypt and settled down in every
12:38 [A] Many other people **went up** with them, as well as large
13:18 [A] The Israelites **went up** out of Egypt armed for battle.
13:19 [G] then *you must* **carry** my bones **up** with you from this place."
16:13 [A] That evening quail **came** and covered the camp, and in the
16:14 [A] When the dew *was* **gone**, thin flakes like frost on the ground
17: 3 [G] "Why *did you* **bring** us **up** out of Egypt to make us and our
17:10 [A] and Moses, Aaron and Hur **went** *to* the top of the hill.
19: 3 [A] Moses **went up** to God, and the LORD called to him from
19:12 [A] 'Be careful that you *do* not **go up** the mountain or touch the
19:13 [A] horn sounds a long blast *may* they **go up** to the mountain."
19:18 [A] The smoke **billowed up** *from* it like smoke from a furnace,
19:20 [A] called Moses to the top of the mountain. So Moses **went up**
19:23 [A] to the LORD, "The people cannot **come up** Mount Sinai,
19:24 [A] LORD replied, "Go down and *bring* Aaron **up** with you.
19:24 [A] the people must not force their way through to **come up** to
20:26 [A] *do* not **go up** to my altar on steps, lest your nakedness be
24: 1 [A] "**Come up** to the LORD, you and Aaron, Nadab and Abihu,
24: 2 [A] not come near. And the people *may* not **come up** with him."
24: 5 [G] *they* **offered** burnt offerings and sacrificed young bulls as
24: 9 [A] Nadab and Abihu, and the seventy elders of Israel **went up**
24:12 [A] to Moses, "**Come up** to me on the mountain and stay here,
24:13 [A] Joshua his aide, and Moses **went up** on the mountain of God.
24:15 [A] When Moses **went up** on the mountain, the cloud covered it,
24:18 [A] Moses entered the cloud as *he* **went** on **up** the mountain.
25:37 [G] "Then make its seven lamps and **set** them **up** *on* it so that
27:20 [G] olives for the light so that the lamps *may be* kept **burning**.
30: 8 [G] He must burn incense again when he **lights** the lamps at
30: 9 [G] *Do* not **offer** on this altar any other incense or any burnt
32: 1 [G] As for this fellow Moses who **brought** us **up** out of Egypt,
32: 4 [G] are your gods, O Israel, who **brought** you **up** out of Egypt."
32: 6 [G] **sacrificed** burnt offerings and presented fellowship offerings.
32: 7 [G] because your people, whom *you* **brought up** out of Egypt,
32: 8 [G] are your gods, O Israel, who **brought** you **up** out of Egypt.'
32:23 [G] As for this fellow Moses who **brought** us **up** out of Egypt,
32:30 [A] now *I will* **go up** to the LORD; perhaps I can make
33: 1 [G] this place, you and the people *you* **brought up** out of Egypt,
33: 1 [A] and **go up** to the land I promised on oath to Abraham, Isaac
33: 3 [A] *I will* not **go** with you, because you are a stiff-necked people
33: 5 [A] *If I were to* **go** with you even for a moment, I might destroy
33:12 [G] the LORD, "You have been telling me, '**Lead** these people,'
33:15 [G] Presence does not go with us, *do* not **send** us **up** from here.
34: 2 [A] Be ready in the morning, and then **come up** on Mount Sinai.
34: 3 [A] No one *is to* **come** with you or be seen anywhere on the
34: 4 [A] the first ones and **went up** Mount Sinai early in the morning,
34:24 [A] no one will covet your land when you **go up** three times each
40: 4 [G] on it. Then bring in the lampstand and **set up** its lamps.
40:25 [G] **set up** the lamps before the LORD, as the LORD
40:29 [G] and **offered** on it burnt offerings and grain offerings,
40:36 [C] whenever the cloud **lifted** from above the tabernacle,
40:37 [C] if the cloud *did* not **lift**, they did not set out—until the day it
40:37 [C] cloud did not lift, they did not set out—until the day it **lifted**.
Lev 2:12 [A] *they are* not *to be* **offered** on the altar as a pleasing aroma.
11: 3 [G] has a split hoof completely divided and *that* **chews** the cud.
11: 4 [G] " 'There are some *that* only **chew** the cud or only have a split
11: 4 [G] The camel, though it **chews** the cud, does not have a split
11: 5 [G] The coney, though it **chews** the cud, does not have a split
11: 6 [G] The rabbit, though it **chews** the cud, does not have a split
11:26 [G] or *that does* not **chew** the cud is unclean for you;
11:45 [G] I am the LORD who **brought** you **up** out of Egypt to be
14:20 [G] **offer** it on the altar, together with the grain offering,
16: 9 [A] Aaron shall bring the goat whose lot **falls** to the LORD
16:10 [A] the goat **chosen** *by* lot as the scapegoat shall be presented
17: 8 [G] or any alien living among them who **offers** a burnt offering
19:19 [G] " '*Do* not **wear** clothing woven of two kinds of material.
24: 2 [G] the light so that the lamps *may be* **kept burning** continually.
Nu 8: 2 [G] to Aaron and say to him, 'When you **set up** the seven lamps,
8: 3 [G] *he* **set up** the lamps so that they faced forward on the
9:17 [C] Whenever the cloud **lifted** from above the Tent, the Israelites
9:21 [C] till morning, and when it **lifted** in the morning, they set out.
9:21 [C] Whether by day or by night, whenever the cloud **lifted**, they
9:22 [C] and not set out; but when it **lifted**, they would set out.
10:11 [C] the cloud **lifted** from above the tabernacle of the Testimony.
13:17 [A] "**Go up** through the Negev and on into the hill country.
13:17 [A] "Go up through the Negev and **on** *into* the hill country.
13:21 [A] So *they* **went up** and explored the land from the Desert of
13:22 [A] *They* **went up** through the Negev and came to Hebron,
13:30 [A] "*We* **should go up** [+6590] and take possession of the land,
13:30 [A] "*We* **should go up** [+6590] and take possession of the land,
13:31 [A] the men who *had* **gone up** with him said, "We can't attack
13:31 [A] up with him said, "We can't **attack** [+448] those people;
14:13 [G] By your power *you* **brought** these people **up** from among
14:40 [A] Early the next morning *they* **went up** toward the high hill
14:40 [A] "*We will* **go up** to the place the LORD promised."
14:42 [A] *Do* not **go up**, because the LORD is not with you. You will
14:44 [A] in their presumption *they* **went up** toward the high hill
16:12 [A] the sons of Eliab. But they said, "*We will* not **come**!
16:13 [G] Isn't it enough that *you have* **brought** us **up** out of a land
16:14 [A] gouge out the eyes of these men? No, *we will* not **come**!"
16:24 [C] '**Move away** from the tents of Korah, Dathan and Abiram.' "
16:27 [C] So *they* **moved away** from the tents of Korah, Dathan
19: 2 [A] or blemish and that *has* never **been under** [+6584] a yoke.
20: 5 [G] Why *did you* **bring** us **up** out of Egypt to this terrible place?
20:19 [A] "*We will* **go** along the main road, and if we or our livestock
20:25 [G] Get Aaron and his son Eleazar and **take** them **up** Mount Hor.
20:27 [A] *They* **went up** Mount Hor in the sight of the whole
21: 5 [G] "Why *have you* **brought** us **up** out of Egypt to die in the
21:17 [A] Israel sang this song: "**Spring up**, O well! Sing about it,
21:33 [A] they turned and **went up** *along* the road toward Bashan,
22:41 [G] The next morning Balak took Balaam **up** *to* Bamoth Baal,
23: 2 [G] and the two of them **offered** a bull and a ram on each altar.
23: 4 [G] and on each altar *I have* **offered** a bull and a ram."
23:14 [G] built seven altars and **offered** a bull and a ram on each altar.
23:30 [G] Balaam had said, and **offered** a bull and a ram on each altar.
27:12 [A] "**Go up** this mountain in the Abarim range and see the land I
32: 9 [A] After *they* **went up** to the Valley of Eshcol and viewed the
32:11 [A] or more who **came up** out of Egypt will see the land I
33:38 [A] At the LORD's command Aaron the priest **went up** Mount
Dt 1:21 [A] **Go up** and take possession of it as the LORD, the God of
1:22 [A] bring back a report about the route *we are to* **take** and the
1:24 [A] They left and **went up** into the hill country, and came to the
1:26 [A] you were unwilling to **go up**; you rebelled against the
1:28 [A] Where *can* we **go**? Our brothers have made us lose heart.
1:41 [A] We *will* **go up** and fight, as the LORD our God commanded
1:41 [A] his weapons, thinking it easy to **go up** into the hill country.
1:42 [A] the LORD said to me, "Tell them, '*Do* not **go up** and fight,
1:43 [A] and in your arrogance *you* **marched up** into the hill country.
3: 1 [A] Next we turned and **went up** *along* the road toward Bashan,
3:27 [A] **Go up** *to* the top of Pisgah and look west and north and south
5: 5 [A] you were afraid of the fire and *did* not **go up** the mountain.)
9: 9 [A] When I **went up** on the mountain to receive the tablets of
9:23 [A] "**Go up** and take possession of the land I have given you."
10: 1 [A] like the first ones and **come up** to me on the mountain.
10: 3 [A] *I* **went up** on the mountain with the two tablets in my hands.
12:13 [G] Be careful not *to* **sacrifice** your burnt offerings anywhere
12:14 [G] **Offer** them only at the place the LORD will choose in one
14: 6 [G] that has a split hoof divided in two and that **chews** the cud.
14: 7 [G] of *those that* **chew** the cud or that have a split hoof
14: 7 [G] Although they **chew** the cud, they do not have a split hoof;
17: 8 [A] **take** them to the place the LORD your God will choose.
20: 1 [G] who **brought** you **up** out of Egypt, will be with you.
25: 7 [A] she *shall* **go** to the elders at the town gate and say,
27: 6 [G] and **offer** burnt offerings on it to the LORD your God.
28:43 [A] The alien who lives among you *will* **rise** above you higher
29:23 [29:22] [A] nothing sprouting, no vegetation **growing** on it.
30:12 [A] "Who *will* **ascend** into heaven to get it and proclaim it to us
32:49 [A] "**Go up** into the Abarim Range to Mount Nebo in Moab,
32:50 [A] There on the mountain that you *have* **climbed** you will die
34: 1 [A] Moses **climbed** Mount Nebo from the plains of Moab to the
Jos 2: 6 [G] (But she *had* **taken** them **up** to the roof and hidden them
2: 8 [A] the spies lay down for the night, she **went up** on the roof
4:16 [A] the ark of the Testimony *to* **come up** out of the Jordan."

Jos 4:17 [A] Joshua commanded the priests, "**Come up** out of the Jordan."
4:18 [A] the priests **came up** out of the river carrying the ark of the
4:19 [A] On the tenth day of the first month the people **went up** from
6: 5 [A] the wall of the city will collapse and the people *will* **go up**,
6:15 [A] On the seventh day, they got up at **daybreak** [+2021+8840]
6:20 [A] so every man **charged** straight in, and they took the city.
7: 2 [A] of Bethel, and told them, "**Go up** and spy out the region."
7: 2 [A] spy out the region." So the men **went up** and spied out Ai.
7: 3 [A] they said, "Not all the people *will have to* **go up** *against* Ai.
7: 3 [A] **Send** two or three thousand men to take it and do not weary
7: 4 [A] So about three thousand men **went up**; but they were routed
7: 6 [G] of Israel did the same, and **sprinkled** dust on their heads.
7:24 [G] his tent and all that he had, **[RPH]** to the Valley of Achor.
8: 1 [A] Take the whole army with you, and go up and **attack** Ai.
8: 3 [A] So Joshua and the whole army moved out to **attack** Ai. He
8:10 [A] and he and the leaders of Israel **marched** before them to Ai.
8:11 [A] The entire force that was with him **marched up**
8:20 [A] and saw the smoke of the city **rising** against the sky,
8:21 [A] taken the city and that smoke *was* **going up** *from* the city,
8:31 [A] On it *they* **offered** to the LORD burnt offerings
10: 4 [A] "**Come up** and help me attack Gibeon," he said, "because it
10: 5 [A] They **moved up** with all their troops and took up positions
10: 6 [A] **Come up** to us quickly and save us! Help us, because all the
10: 7 [A] So Joshua **marched up** from Gilgal with his entire army,
10: 9 [A] After an all-night **march** from Gilgal, Joshua took them by
10:33 [A] Horam king of Gezer *had* **come up** to help Lachish,
10:36 [A] and all Israel with him **went up** from Eglon to Hebron
11:17 [A] from Mount Halak, which **rises** *toward* Seir, to Baal Gad in
12: 7 [A] which **rises** toward Seir (their lands Joshua gave as an
14: 8 [A] my brothers who **went up** with me made the hearts of the
15: 3 [A] on to Zin and **went over** to the south of Kadesh Barnea.
15: 3 [A] it ran past Hezron **up** to Addar and curved around to Karka.
15: 6 [A] **went up** *to* Beth Hoglah and continued north of Beth Arabah
15: 6 [A] continued north of Beth Arabah **[RPH]** to the Stone of
15: 7 [A] then **went up** to Debir from the Valley of Achor
15: 8 [A] it **ran up** the Valley of Ben Hinnom along the southern slope
15: 8 [A] From there it **climbed** to the top of the hill west of the
15:15 [A] From there *he* **marched** against the people living in Debir
16: 1 [A] **went up** from there through the desert into the hill country of
17:15 [A] **go up** into the forest and clear land for yourselves there in
18:11 [A] The lot **came up** for the tribe of Benjamin, clan by clan.
18:12 [A] **passed** the northern slope of Jericho and headed west into the
18:12 [A] slope of Jericho and **headed** west into the hill country,
19:10 [A] The third lot **came up** for Zebulun, clan by clan: The
19:11 [A] Going west it **ran** *to* Maralah, touched Dabbesheth,
19:12 [A] of Kisloth Tabor and went on to Daberath and **up** *to* Japhia.
19:47 [A] so they **went up** and attacked Leshem, took it, put it to the
22:12 [A] the whole assembly of Israel gathered at Shiloh to **go** to war
22:23 [G] the LORD and to **offer** burnt offerings and grain offerings,
22:33 [A] they talked no more about **going** to war against them to
24:17 [G] LORD our God himself who **brought** us and our fathers **up**
24:32 [G] which the Israelites *had* **brought up** from Egypt,
Jdg 1: 1 [A] "Who will be the first *to* **go up** and fight for us against the
1: 2 [A] The LORD answered, "Judah *is to* **go**; I have given the land
1: 3 [A] "**Come up** with us into the territory allotted to us, to fight
1: 4 [A] When Judah **attacked**, the LORD gave the Canaanites
1:16 [A] **went up** from the City of Palms with the men of Judah to
1:22 [A] Now the house of Joseph **attacked** Bethel, and the LORD
2: 1 [A] The angel of the LORD **went up** from Gilgal to Bokim
2: 1 [G] "*I* **brought** you **up** out of Egypt and led you into the land
4: 5 [A] and the Israelites **came** to her to have their disputes decided.
4:10 [A] Ten thousand men **followed** [+928+8079] him, and Deborah
4:10 [A] men followed him, and Deborah also **went** with him.
4:12 [A] that Barak son of Abinoam *had* **gone up** *to* Mount Tabor,
6: 3 [A] and other eastern peoples **[RPH]** invaded the country.
6: 3 [A] and other eastern peoples **invaded** [+6584] the country.
6: 5 [A] They **came up** with their livestock and their tents like
6: 8 [G] I **brought** you **up** out of Egypt, out of the land of slavery.
6:13 [G] they said, '*Did* not the LORD **bring** us **up** out of Egypt?'
6:21 [A] Fire **flared** from the rock, consuming the meat and the bread.
6:26 [G] that you cut down, **offer** the second bull as a burnt offering."
6:28 [H] and the second bull **sacrificed** on the newly built altar!
6:35 [A] and Naphtali, so that *they* too **went up** to meet them.
8: 8 [A] From there *he* **went up** *to* Peniel and made the same request
8:11 [A] Gideon **went up** *by* the route of the nomads east of Nobah
9:48 [A] he and all his men **went up** Mount Zalmon. He took an ax
9:51 [A] locked themselves in and **climbed up** on the tower roof.
11:13 [A] "When Israel **came up** out of Egypt, they took away my land
11:16 [A] when they **came up** out of Egypt, Israel went through the
11:31 [G] be the LORD's, and *I will* **sacrifice** it as a burnt offering."
12: 3 [A] over them. Now why *have you* **come up** today to fight me?"
13: 5 [A] No razor *may be* **used** on his head, because the boy is to be a
13:16 [G] But if you prepare a burnt offering, **offer** it to the LORD."
13:19 [G] the grain offering, and **sacrificed** it on a rock to the LORD.
13:20 [A] As the flame **blazed up** from the altar toward heaven,
13:20 [A] the angel of the LORD **ascended** in the flame.
14: 2 [A] When *he* **returned**, he said to his father and mother, "I have
14:19 [A] Burning with anger, *he* **went up** *to* his father's house.
15: 6 [A] So the Philistines **went up** and burned her and her father to
15: 9 [A] The Philistines **went up** and camped in Judah, spreading out
15:10 [A] The men of Judah asked, "Why *have you* **come** to fight us?"
15:10 [A] "*We have* **come** to take Samson prisoner," they answered,
15:13 [G] him with two new ropes and **led** him **up** from the rock.
16: 3 [G] and **carried** them to the top of the hill that faces Hebron.
16: 5 [A] The rulers of the Philistines **went** to her and said, "See if you
16: 8 [G] the rulers of the Philistines **brought** her seven fresh thongs
16:17 [A] "No razor *has ever been* **used** on my head," he said,
16:18 [A] word to the rulers of the Philistines, "**Come back** once more;
16:18 [A] So the rulers of the Philistines **returned** with the silver in
16:18 [G] So the rulers of the Philistines returned with **[RPH]** the
16:31 [G] *They* **brought** him **back** and buried him between Zorah
18: 9 [A] They answered, "Come on, *let's* **attack** [+6584] them! We
18:12 [A] **On** *their* **way** they set up camp near Kiriath Jearim in Judah.
18:17 [A] **[RPH]** The five men who had spied out the land went inside
19:25 [A] her throughout the night, and **at** [+928] dawn they let her go.
19:30 [A] not since the day the Israelites **came up** out of Egypt.
20: 3 [A] (The Benjamites heard that the Israelites *had* **gone up** *to*
20:18 [A] The Israelites **went up** *to* Bethel and inquired of God. They
20:18 [A] "Who of us *shall* **go** first to fight against the Benjamites?"
20:23 [A] The Israelites **went up** and wept before the LORD until
20:23 [A] our brothers?" The LORD answered, "**Go up** against them."
20:26 [A] the Israelites, all the people, **went up** to Bethel, and there
20:26 [G] fasted that day until evening and **presented** burnt offerings
20:28 [A] The LORD responded, "**Go**, for tomorrow I will give them
20:30 [A] They **went up** against the Benjamites on the third day
20:31 [A] the one **leading to** Bethel and the other to Gibeah.
20:38 [G] they *should* **send up** a great cloud of smoke from the city,
20:40 [A] But when the column of smoke began to **rise** from the city,
20:40 [A] and saw the smoke of the whole city **going up** into the sky.
21: 4 [G] and **presented** burnt offerings and fellowship offerings.
21: 5 [A] *has* failed *to* **assemble** [+928+2021+7736] before the LORD?"
21: 5 [A] *to* **assemble** before the LORD at Mizpah should certainly
21: 8 [A] "Which one of the tribes of Israel failed *to* **assemble** before
21:19 [A] and east of the road that **goes** from Bethel to Shechem,
Ru 4: 1 [A] Meanwhile Boaz **went up** *to* the town gate and sat there.
1Sa 1: 3 [A] Year after year this man **went up** from his town to worship
1: 7 [A] Whenever Hannah **went up** to the house of the LORD, her
1:11 [A] days of his life, and no razor *will ever be* **used** on his head."
1:21 [A] When the man Elkanah **went up** with all his family to offer
1:22 [A] Hannah *did* not **go**. She said to her husband, "After the boy
1:24 [G] he was weaned, *she* **took** the boy with her, young as he was,
2: 6 [G] and makes alive; he brings down to the grave and **raises up**.
2:14 [G] priest would take for himself whatever the fork **brought up**.
2:19 [G] **took** it to him when she went up with her husband to offer
2:19 [A] took it to him when she **went up** with her husband to offer
2:28 [A] to **go up** to my altar, to burn incense, and to wear an ephod in
5:12 [A] with tumors, and the outcry of the city **went up** *to* heaven.
6: 7 [A] that have calved and *have* never *been* **yoked** [+6584+6585].
6: 9 [A] If *it* **goes up** to its own territory, toward Beth Shemesh, then
6:14 [G] and **sacrificed** the cows as a burnt offering to the LORD.
6:15 [G] On that day the people of Beth Shemesh **offered** burnt
6:20 [A] this holy God? To whom *will* the ark **go up** from here?"
6:21 [G] of the LORD. Come down and **take** it **up** to your place."
7: 1 [G] of Kiriath Jearim came and **took up** the ark of the LORD.
7: 7 [A] the rulers of the Philistines **came up** to attack them.
7: 9 [G] and **offered** it **up** as a whole burnt offering to the LORD.
7:10 [G] While Samuel was **sacrificing** the burnt offering,
8: 8 [G] As they have done from the day *I* **brought** them **up** out of
9:11 [A] As they *were* **going up** the hill to the town, they met some
9:13 [A] you will find him before *he* **goes up** to the high place to eat.
9:13 [A] will eat. **Go up** now; you should find him about this time."
9:14 [A] *They* **went up** *to* the town, and as they were entering it, there
9:14 [A] coming toward them **on** *his* **way up** *to* the high place.
9:19 [A] "**Go up** ahead of me *to* the high place, for today you are to
9:26 [A] They rose about **daybreak** [+2021+8840] and Samuel called to
10: 3 [A] Three men **going up** to God at Bethel will meet you there.
10: 8 [G] I will surely come down to you to **sacrifice** burnt offerings
10:18 [G] 'I **brought** Israel **up** out of Egypt, and I delivered you from
11: 1 [A] Nahash the Ammonite **went up** and besieged Jabesh Gilead.
12: 6 [G] and Aaron and **brought** your forefathers **up** out of Egypt.
13: 5 [A] *They* **went up** and camped at Micmash, east of Beth Aven.
13: 9 [G] And Saul **offered up** the burnt offering.
13:10 [G] Just as he finished **making** the offering, Samuel arrived,
13:12 [G] So I felt compelled *to* **offer** the burnt offering."
13:15 [A] Then Samuel left Gilgal and **went up** *to* Gibeah in Benjamin,
14: 9 [A] to you,' we will stay where we are and not **go up** to them.
14:10 [A] if they say, '**Come up** to us,' we will climb up, because that
14:10 [A] if they say, 'Come up to us,' *we will* **climb up**, because that

[A] Qal [B] Qal passive [C] Niphal [D] Piel (poel, polel, pilel, pilal, pealal, pilpel) [E] Pual (poal, polal, poalal, pulal, pualal)

1Sa 14:12 [A] "**Come up** to us and we'll teach you a lesson."
14:12 [A] So Jonathan said to his armor-bearer, "**Climb up** after me;
14:13 [A] Jonathan **climbed up**, using his hands and feet, with his
14:21 [A] *had* **gone up** with them to their camp went over to the
14:46 [A] Saul **stopped** [+4946] pursuing the Philistines, and they
15: 2 [A] Israel when they waylaid them as they **came up** from Egypt.
15: 6 [A] to all the Israelites when they **came up** out of Egypt."
15:34 [A] for Ramah, but Saul **went up** to his home in Gibeah of Saul.
17:23 [A] **stepped out** from his lines and shouted his usual defiance,
17:25 [A] been saying, "Do you see how this man *keeps* **coming out**?
17:25 [A] this man keeps coming out? *He* **comes out** to defy Israel.
19:15 [G] "**Bring** him **up** to me in his bed so that I may kill him."
23:19 [A] The Ziphites **went up** to Saul at Gibeah and said, "Is not
23:29 [24:1] [A] David **went up** from there and lived in the
24:22 [24:23] [A] but David and his men **went up** to the stronghold.
25: 5 [A] "Go **up** to Nabal at Carmel and greet him in my name.
25:13 [A] About four hundred men **went up** with David, while two
25:35 [A] hand what she had brought him and said, "**Go** home in peace.
27: 8 [A] Now David and his men **went up** and raided the Geshurites,
28: 8 [G] for me," he said, "and **bring up** for me the one I name."
28:11 [G] Then the woman asked, "Whom *shall I* **bring up** for you?"
28:11 [G] shall I bring up for you?" "**Bring up** Samuel," he said.
28:13 [A] woman said, "I see a spirit **coming up** out of the ground."
28:14 [A] "An old man wearing a robe *is* **coming up**," she said.
28:15 [G] to Saul, "Why have you disturbed me by **bringing** me **up**?"
29: 9 [A] have said, '*He must* not **go up** with us into battle.'
29:11 [A] land of the Philistines, and the Philistines **went up** *to* Jezreel.
2Sa 1:24 [G] who **adorned** [+6584] your garments *with* ornaments of
2: 1 [A] "*Shall I* **go up** to one of the towns of Judah?" he asked. The
2: 1 [A] he asked. The LORD said, "**Go up**." David asked,
2: 1 [A] LORD said, "Go up." David asked, "Where *shall I* **go**?"
2: 2 [A] So David **went up** there with his two wives, Ahinoam of
2: 3 [G] David also **took** the men who were with him, each with his
2:27 [C] the men *would have* **continued** the pursuit of their brothers
5:17 [A] they **went up** in full force to search for him, but David heard
5:19 [A] of the LORD, "*Shall I* **go** and attack the Philistines?
5:19 [A] The LORD answered him, "**Go**, for I will surely hand the
5:22 [A] Once more the Philistines **came up** and spread out in the
5:23 [A] he answered, "*Do* not **go straight up**, but circle around
6: 2 [G] from Baalah of Judah to **bring up** from there the ark of God,
6:12 [G] **brought up** the ark of God from the house of Obed-Edom to
6:15 [G] the entire house of Israel **brought up** the ark of the LORD
6:17 [G] David **sacrificed** burnt offerings and fellowship offerings
6:18 [G] After he had finished **sacrificing** the burnt offerings
7: 6 [G] the day I **brought** the Israelites **up** out of Egypt to this day.
11:20 [A] the king's anger *may* **flare up**, and he may ask you,
15:24 [G] Abiathar **offered sacrifices** until all the people had finished
15:30 [A] David *continued* **up** the Mount of Olives, weeping as he
15:30 [A] continued up the Mount of Olives, weeping as *he* **went**;
15:30 [A] covered their heads too and were weeping as *they* **went up**.
15:30 [A] their heads too and were weeping as they went up. **[RPH]**
17:21 [A] the two **climbed** out of the well and went to inform King
18:33 [19:1] [A] *He* **went up** to the room over the gateway and wept.
19:34 [19:35] [A] that *I should* **go up** *to* Jerusalem with the king?
20: 2 [A] So all the men of Israel **deserted** [+339+4946] David to
21:13 [G] David **brought** the bones of Saul and his son Jonathan from
22: 9 [A] Smoke **rose** from his nostrils; consuming fire came from his
23: 9 [A] Pas Dammim, for battle. Then the men of Israel **retreated**,
24:18 [A] "**Go up** and build an altar to the LORD on the threshing
24:19 [A] So David **went up**, as the LORD had commanded through
24:22 [G] my lord the king take whatever pleases him and **offer it up**.
24:24 [G] *I will* not **sacrifice** to the LORD my God burnt offerings
24:25 [G] and **sacrificed** burnt offerings and fellowship offerings.
1Ki 1:35 [A] *you are to* **go up** with him, and he is to come and sit on my
1:40 [A] all the people **went up** after him, playing flutes and rejoicing
1:45 [A] From there *they have* **gone up** cheering, and the city
2:34 [A] So Benaiah son of Jehoiada **went up** and struck down Joab
3: 4 [G] and Solomon **offered** a thousand burnt offerings on that altar.
3:15 [G] and **sacrificed** burnt offerings and fellowship offerings.
5:13 [5:27] [G] King Solomon **conscripted** laborers from all Israel—
6: 8 [A] a stairway *led* **up** to the middle level and from there to the
8: 1 [G] to **bring up** the ark of the LORD's covenant from Zion,
8: 4 [G] *they* **brought up** the ark of the LORD and the Tent of Meeting
8: 4 [G] furnishings in it. The priests and Levites **carried** them **up**,
9:15 [G] King Solomon **conscripted** to build the LORD's temple,
9:16 [A] (Pharaoh king of Egypt *had* **attacked** and captured Gezer.
9:21 [G] these Solomon **conscripted** for his slave labor force, as it is
9:24 [A] After Pharaoh's daughter *had* **come up** from the City of
9:25 [G] Three times a year Solomon **sacrificed** burnt offerings
10: 5 [G] and the burnt offerings *he* **made** at the temple of the LORD,
10:16 [A] six hundred bekas of gold **went** into each shield.
10:17 [A] with three minas of gold **[RPH]** in each shield.
10:29 [A] *They* **imported** [+2256+3655] a chariot from Egypt for six
11:15 [A] commander of the army, *who had* **gone up** to bury the dead,
12:18 [A] managed to **get** into his chariot and escape to Jerusalem.
12:24 [A] *Do* not **go up** to fight against your brothers, the Israelites.
12:27 [A] If these people **go up** to offer sacrifices at the temple of the
12:28 [A] to the people, "It is too much for you *to* **go up** *to* Jerusalem.
12:28 [G] are your gods, O Israel, who **brought** you **up** out of Egypt."
12:32 [G] the festival held in Judah, and **offered sacrifices** on the altar.
12:33 [G] *he* **offered sacrifices** on the altar he had built at Bethel.
12:33 [A] for the Israelites and **went up** to the altar to make offerings.
14:25 [A] Shishak king of Egypt **attacked** [+6584] Jerusalem.
15:17 [A] Baasha king of Israel **went up** against Judah and fortified
15:19 [A] with Baasha king of Israel so *he will* **withdraw** from me."
16:17 [A] and all the Israelites with him **withdrew** from Gibbethon
17:19 [G] **carried** him to the upper room where he was staying,
18:29 [A] prophesying until the time for the **evening sacrifice** [+4966].
18:36 [A] At the time of **sacrifice** [+4966], the prophet Elijah stepped
18:41 [A] Elijah said to Ahab, "**Go**, eat and drink, for there is the sound
18:42 [A] So Ahab **went off** to eat and drink, but Elijah climbed to the
18:42 [A] off to eat and drink, but Elijah **climbed** to the top of Carmel,
18:43 [A] "**Go** and look toward the sea," he told his servant. And he
18:43 [A] the sea," he told his servant. And *he* **went up** and looked.
18:44 [A] "A cloud as small as a man's hand *is* **rising** from the sea."
18:44 [A] So Elijah said, "**Go** and tell Ahab, 'Hitch up your chariot
20: 1 [A] *he* **went up** and besieged Samaria and attacked it.
20:22 [A] because next spring the king of Aram *will* **attack** [+6584]
20:26 [A] the Arameans and **went up** to Aphek to fight against Israel.
20:33 [G] came out, Ahab **had** him **come up** into his chariot.
22: 6 [A] "**Go**," they answered, "for the Lord will give it into the
22:12 [A] "**Attack** Ramoth Gilead and be victorious," they said,
22:15 [A] "**Attack** and be victorious," he answered, "for the LORD
22:20 [A] 'Who will entice Ahab into **attacking** Ramoth Gilead and
22:29 [A] and Jehoshaphat king of Judah **went up** *to* Ramoth Gilead.
22:35 [A] All day long the battle **raged**, and the king was propped up in
2Ki 1: 3 [A] "**Go up** and meet the messengers of the king of Samaria
1: 4 [A] LORD says: 'You will not leave the bed *you are* **lying on**.
1: 6 [A] "A man **came** to meet us," they replied. "And he said to us,
1: 6 [A] Therefore you will not leave the bed *you are* **lying on**.
1: 7 [A] "What kind of man was it who **came** to meet you and told
1: 9 [A] The captain **went up** to Elijah, who was sitting on the top of
1:13 [A] This third captain **went up** and fell on his knees before
1:16 [A] done this, you will never leave the bed *you are* **lying on**.
2: 1 [G] When the LORD *was about to* **take** Elijah **up** to heaven in
2:11 [A] two of them, and Elijah **went up** *to* heaven in a whirlwind.
2:23 [A] From there Elisha **went up** *to* Bethel. As he was walking
2:23 [A] As he *was* **walking** along the road, some youths came out of
2:23 [A] "**Go on up**, *you* baldhead!" they said. "Go on up,
2:23 [A] on up, you baldhead!" they said. "**Go on up**, *you* baldhead!"
3: 7 [A] "*I will* **go** with you," he replied. "I am as you are, my people
3: 8 [A] "By what route *shall we* **attack**?" he asked. "Through the
3:20 [G] about the time for **offering** the sacrifice, there it was—
3:21 [A] Now all the Moabites had heard that the kings *had* **come** to
3:27 [G] him as king, and **offered** him as a sacrifice on the city wall.
4:21 [A] *She* **went up** and laid him on the bed of the man of God,
4:34 [A] *he* **got on** the bed and lay upon the boy, mouth to mouth,
4:35 [A] walked back and forth in the room and then **got on** the bed
6:24 [A] his entire army and **marched up** and laid siege to Samaria.
10:15 [G] So he did, and Jehu **helped** him **up** into the chariot.
12: 4 [12:5] [A] brought **voluntarily** [+408+4213+6584] to the temple.
12:10 [12:11] [A] the royal secretary and the high priest **came**,
12:17 [12:18] [A] About this time Hazael king of Aram **went up**
12:17 [12:18] [A] Then he turned to **attack** [+6584] Jerusalem.
12:18 [12:19] [A] king of Aram, *who* then **withdrew** from Jerusalem.
14:11 [A] would not listen, so Jehoash king of Israel **attacked**.
15:14 [A] Then Menahem son of Gadi went from Tirzah **up** *to* Samaria.
16: 5 [A] king of Israel **marched up** to fight *against* Jerusalem
16: 7 [A] **Come up** and save me out of the hand of the king of Aram
16: 9 [A] The king of Assyria complied by **attacking** [+448]
16:12 [G] saw the altar, he approached it and **presented offerings** on it.
17: 3 [A] Shalmaneser king of Assyria **came up** to attack Hoshea, who
17: 4 [G] *he* no *longer* **paid** tribute to the king of Assyria, as he had
17: 5 [A] The king of Assyria **invaded** [+928] the entire land, marched
17: 5 [A] **marched** *against* Samaria and laid siege to it for three years.
17: 7 [G] who *had* **brought** them **up** out of Egypt from under the
17:36 [G] who **brought** you **up** out of Egypt with mighty power
18: 9 [A] Shalmaneser king of Assyria **marched** against Samaria
18:13 [A] Sennacherib king of Assyria **attacked** [+6584] all the
18:17 [A] They came **up** *to* Jerusalem and stopped at the aqueduct of
18:17 [A] **[RPH]** and stopped at the aqueduct of the Upper Pool,
18:25 [A] *have I* **come** to attack and destroy this place without word
18:25 [A] The LORD himself told me *to* **march** against this country
19:14 [A] he **went up** *to* the temple of the LORD and spread it out
19:23 [A] "With my many chariots I *have* **ascended** the heights of the
19:28 [A] rage against me and your insolence *has* **reached** my ears,
20: 5 [A] On the third day from now *you will* **go up** *to* the temple of
20: 8 [A] that *I will* **go up** *to* the temple of the LORD on the third day

2Ki 22: 4 [A] "**Go up** to Hilkiah the high priest and have him get ready the
23: 2 [A] He **went up** *to* the temple of the LORD with the men of
23: 9 [A] Although the priests of the high places *did* not **serve** at the
23:29 [A] Pharaoh Neco king of Egypt **went up** to the Euphrates River
24: 1 [A] Nebuchadnezzar king of Babylon **invaded** the land,
24:10 [A] of Nebuchadnezzar king of Babylon **advanced** *on* Jerusalem
25: 6 [G] He *was* **taken** to the king of Babylon at Riblah, where
1Ch 11: 6 [A] Joab son of Zeruiah **went up** first, and so he received the
13: 6 [A] all the Israelites with him **went** to Baalah of Judah (Kiriath
13: 6 [G] to **bring up** from there the ark of God the LORD, who is
14: 8 [A] they **went up** in full force to search for him, but David heard
14:10 [A] inquired of God: "*Shall I* **go** and attack the Philistines?
14:10 [A] The LORD answered him, "**Go**, I will hand them over to
14:11 [A] So David and *his men* **went up** to Baal Perazim, and there he
14:14 [A] "*Do* not **go straight up**, but circle around them and attack
15: 3 [G] David assembled all Israel in Jerusalem to **bring up** the ark
15:12 [G] to consecrate yourselves and **bring up** the ark of the LORD,
15:14 [G] Levites consecrated themselves in order to **bring up** the ark
15:25 [G] the commanders of units of a thousand went to **bring up** the
15:28 [G] So all Israel **brought up** the ark of the covenant of the
16: 2 [G] After David had finished **sacrificing** the burnt offerings
16:40 [G] to **present** burnt offerings to the LORD on the altar of burnt
17: 5 [G] I have not dwelt in a house from the day *I* **brought** Israel **up**
21:18 [A] the angel of the LORD ordered Gad to tell David *to* **go up**
21:19 [A] So David **went up** in obedience to the word that Gad had
21:24 [G] is yours, or **sacrifice** a burnt offering that costs me nothing."
21:26 [G] and **sacrificed** burnt offerings and fellowship offerings.
23:31 [G] whenever burnt offerings *were* **presented** to the LORD on
26:16 [A] and the Shalleketh Gate on the **upper** road fell to Shuppim
27:24 [A] the number *was* not **entered** in the book of the annals of
29:21 [G] to the LORD and **presented** burnt offerings to him:
2Ch 1: 4 [G] Now David *had* **brought up** the ark of God from Kiriath
1: 6 [A] Solomon **went up** to the bronze altar before the LORD in
1: 6 [G] Tent of Meeting and **offered** a thousand burnt offerings on it.
1:17 [G] *They* **imported** [+2256+3655] a chariot from Egypt for six
2:16 [2:15] [G] to Joppa. You *can* then **take** them **up** *to* Jerusalem."
3: 5 [G] fine gold and **decorated** it *with* palm tree and chain designs.
3:14 [G] crimson yarn and fine linen, with cherubim **worked** into it.
5: 2 [G] to **bring up** the ark of the LORD's covenant from Zion,
5: 5 [G] *they* **brought up** the ark and the Tent of Meeting and all the
5: 5 [G] in it. The priests, who were Levites, **carried** them **up**;
8: 8 [G] these Solomon **conscripted** for his slave labor force, as it is
8:11 [G] Solomon **brought** Pharaoh's daughter **up** from the City of
8:12 [G] Solomon **sacrificed** burnt offerings to the LORD,
8:13 [G] according to the daily requirement for **offerings** commanded
9: 4 [G] and the burnt offerings *he* **made** at the temple of the LORD,
9:15 [A] six hundred bekas of hammered gold **went** into each shield.
9:16 [A] with three hundred bekas of gold **[RPH]** in each shield.
10:18 [A] managed to **get** into his chariot and escape to Jerusalem.
11: 4 [A] *Do* not **go up** to fight against your brothers. Go home,
12: 2 [A] Shishak king of Egypt **attacked** [+6584] Jerusalem in the
12: 9 [A] When Shishak king of Egypt **attacked** [+6584] Jerusalem,
16: 1 [A] of Asa's reign Baasha king of Israel **went up** against Judah
16: 3 [A] with Baasha king of Israel so *he will* **withdraw** from me."
18: 2 [A] with him and urged him to **attack** [+448] Ramoth Gilead.
18: 5 [A] "**Go**," they answered, "for God will give it into the king's
18:11 [A] "**Attack** Ramoth Gilead and be victorious," they said,
18:14 [A] "**Attack** and be victorious," he answered, "for they will be
18:19 [A] 'Who will entice Ahab king of Israel into **attacking** Ramoth
18:28 [A] and Jehoshaphat king of Judah **went up** to Ramoth Gilead.
18:34 [A] All day long the battle **raged**, and the king of Israel propped
20:16 [A] They *will be* **climbing up** by the Pass of Ziz, and you will
20:34 [H] which **are recorded** in the book of the kings of Israel.
21:17 [A] *They* **attacked** [+928] Judah, invaded it and carried off all
23:18 [G] to **present** the burnt offerings of the LORD as written in the
24:13 [A] work were diligent, and the repairs **progressed** under them.
24:14 [G] articles for the service and for the **burnt offerings**, and also
24:14 [G] burnt offerings were **presented** continually in the temple of
24:23 [A] turn of the year, the army of Aram **marched** against Joash;
25:21 [A] So Jehoash king of Israel **attacked**. He and Amaziah king of
29: 7 [G] or **present** any burnt offerings at the sanctuary to the God of
29:20 [A] officials together and **went up** *to* the temple of the LORD.
29:21 [G] of Aaron, to **offer** these on the altar of the LORD.
29:27 [G] Hezekiah gave the order to **sacrifice** the burnt offering on the
29:29 [G] When the **offerings** were finished, the king and everyone
32: 5 [G] all the broken sections of the wall and **building** towers on it.
34:30 [A] He **went up** *to* the temple of the LORD with the men of
35:14 [G] *were* **sacrificing** the burnt offerings and the fat portions until
35:16 [G] the **offering** *of* burnt offerings on the altar of the LORD,
35:20 [A] Neco king of Egypt **went up** to fight at Carchemish on the
36: 6 [A] Nebuchadnezzar king of Babylon **attacked** [+6584] him
36:16 [A] the wrath of the LORD *was* **aroused** against his people
36:17 [G] *He* **brought up** against them the king of the Babylonians,
36:23 [A] may the LORD his God be with him, and *let him* **go up**.' "
Ezr 1: 3 [A] *let him* **go up** to Jerusalem in Judah and build the temple of
1: 5 [A] prepared to **go up** and build the house of the LORD in
1:11 [G] Sheshbazzar **brought** all these **along** when the exiles came
1:11 [C] Sheshbazzar brought all these along when the exiles **came up**
2: 1 [A] Now these are the people of the province who **came up** from
2:59 [A] The following **came up** from the towns of Tel Melah, Tel
3: 2 [G] the altar of the God of Israel to **sacrifice** burnt offerings on it,
3: 3 [G] and **sacrificed** burnt offerings on it to the LORD,
3: 6 [G] On the first day of the seventh month they began to **offer**
4: 2 [G] time of Esarhaddon king of Assyria, who **brought** us here."
7: 6 [A] this Ezra **came up** from Babylon. He was a teacher well
7: 7 [A] also **came up** to Jerusalem in the seventh year of King
7:28 [A] and gathered leading men from Israel to **go up** with me.
8: 1 [A] those registered with them who **came up** with me from
Ne 2:15 [A] so *I* **went up** the valley by night, examining the wall. Finally,
3:19 [A] from a point facing the **ascent** *to* the armory as far as the
4: 3 [3:35] [A] if even a fox **climbed up** on it, he would break down
4: 7 [4:1] [A] that the repairs to Jerusalem's walls *had* **gone ahead**
4:21 [4:15] [A] from the **first light of dawn** [+8840] till the stars
7: 5 [A] record of those *who had been* the first *to* **return**.
7: 6 [A] These are the people of the province who **came up** from the
7:61 [A] The following **came up** from the towns of Tel Melah, Tel
9:18 [G] 'This is your god, who **brought** you **up** out of Egypt,'
10:38 [10:39] [G] the Levites *are to* **bring** a tenth of the tithes **up** to
12: 1 [A] and Levites who **returned** with Zerubbabel son of Shealtiel
12:31 [G] *I* **had** the leaders of Judah **go up** on top of the wall. I also
12:37 [A] At the Fountain Gate *they* **continued** directly **up** the steps of
Job 1: 5 [G] Early in the morning *he would* **sacrifice** a burnt offering *for*
5:26 [A] to the grave in full vigor, like sheaves **gathered** in season.
6:18 [A] from their routes; *they* **go up** into the wasteland and perish.
7: 9 [A] is gone, so he who goes down to the grave *does* not **return**.
20: 6 [A] Though his pride **reaches** to the heavens and his head
36:20 [A] long for the night, to **drag** people **away** *from* their homes.
36:33 [A] the coming storm; even the cattle make known *its* **approach**.
42: 8 [G] my servant Job and **sacrifice** a burnt offering for yourselves.
Ps 18: 8 [18:9] [A] Smoke **rose** from his nostrils; consuming fire came
24: 3 [A] Who *may* **ascend** the hill of the LORD? Who may stand in
30: 3 [30:4] [G] O LORD, *you* **brought** me **up** from the grave;
40: 2 [40:3] [G] *He* **lifted** me out of the slimy pit, out of the mud
47: 5 [47:6] [A] God *has* **ascended** amid shouts of joy, the LORD
47: 9 [47:10] [C] of the earth belong to God; *he is* greatly **exalted**.
51:19 [51:21] [G] delight you; then bulls *will be* **offered** on your altar.
62: 9 [62:10] [A] but a lie; if **weighed** on a balance, they are nothing;
66:15 [G] *I will* **sacrifice** [+6592] fat animals to you and an offering of
68:18 [68:19] [A] *When you* **ascended** on high, you led captives in
71:20 [G] from the depths of the earth you will again **bring** me **up**.
74:23 [A] the uproar of your enemies, *which* **rises** continually.
78:21 [A] broke out against Jacob, and his wrath **rose** against Israel,
78:31 [A] God's anger **rose** against them; he put to death the sturdiest
81:10 [81:11] [G] your God, who **brought** you **up** out of Egypt.
97: 9 [C] High over all the earth; *you* **are exalted** far above all gods.
102:24 [102:25] [G] "*Do* not **take** me **away**, O my God, in the midst of
104: 8 [A] *they* **flowed over** the mountains, they went down into the
107:26 [A] *They* **mounted up** *to* the heavens and went down to the
122: 4 [A] That is where the tribes **go up**, the tribes of the LORD,
132: 3 [A] "I will not enter my house or **go** to my bed—
135: 7 [G] *He* **makes** clouds **rise** from the ends of the earth; he sends
137: 6 [G] if *I do* not **consider** Jerusalem my highest joy.
Pr 15: 1 [G] answer turns away wrath, but a harsh word **stirs up** anger.
21:22 [A] A wise man **attacks** the city of the mighty and pulls down
24:31 [A] thorns *had* **come up** everywhere, the ground was covered
25: 7 [A] it is better for him to say to you, "**Come up** here," than for
26: 9 [A] Like a thornbush **[NIE]** in a drunkard's hand is a proverb in
30: 4 [A] Who *has* **gone up** *to* heaven and come down? Who has
31:29 [A] "Many women do noble things, but you **surpass** them all."
Ecc 3:21 [A] Who knows if the spirit of man **rises** upward and if the spirit
10: 4 [A] If a ruler's anger **rises** against you, do not leave your post;
SS 3: 6 [A] Who is this **coming up** from the desert like a column of
4: 2 [A] a flock of sheep just shorn, **coming up** from the washing.
6: 6 [A] Your teeth are like a flock of sheep **coming up** from the
7: 8 [7:9] [A] I said, "*I will* **climb** the palm tree; I will take hold of
8: 5 [A] Who is this **coming up** from the desert leaning on her lover?
Isa 2: 3 [A] and say, "Come, *let us* **go up** to the mountain of the LORD,
5: 6 [A] pruned nor cultivated, and briers and thorns *will* **grow** there.
5:24 [A] their roots will decay and their flowers **blow away** like dust;
7: 1 [A] Pekah son of Remaliah king of Israel **marched up** to fight
7: 6 [A] "*Let us* **invade** [+928] Judah; let us tear it apart and divide it
8: 7 [G] *is about to* **bring** against them the mighty floodwaters of the
8: 7 [A] *It will* **overflow** [+6584] all its channels, run over all its
11:16 [A] as there was for Israel when they **came up** from Egypt.
14: 8 [A] have been laid low, no woodsman **comes** to cut us down."
14:13 [A] You said in your heart, "*I will* **ascend** *to* heaven; I will raise
14:14 [A] *I will* **ascend** above the tops of the clouds; I will make
15: 2 [A] Dibon **goes up** *to* its temple, *to* its high places to weep;

Isa 15: 5 [A] *They* **go up** the way to Luhith, weeping as they go; on the
21: 2 [A] the looter takes loot. Elam, **attack**! Media, lay siege!
22: 1 [A] troubles you now, that you *have* all **gone up** on the roofs,
24: 18 [A] a pit; whoever **climbs** out of the pit will be caught in a snare.
32: 13 [A] of my people, a land **overgrown** *with* thorns and briers—
34: 3 [A] will be thrown out, their dead bodies *will* **send up** a stench;
34: 10 [A] not be quenched night and day; its smoke *will* **rise** forever.
34: 13 [A] Thorns *will* **overrun** her citadels, nettles and brambles her
35: 9 [A] lion will be there, nor *will* any ferocious beast **get up** *on* it;
36: 1 [A] Sennacherib king of Assyria **attacked** [+6584] all the
36: 10 [A] *have I* **come** to attack and destroy this land without the
36: 10 [A] The LORD himself told me *to* **march** against this country
37: 14 [A] he **went up** *to* the temple of the LORD and spread it out
37: 24 [A] 'With my many chariots I *have* **ascended** the heights of the
37: 29 [A] against me and because your insolence *has* **reached** my ears,
38: 22 [A] "What will be the sign that *I will* **go up** *to* the temple of the
40: 9 [A] who bring good tidings to Zion, **go up** on a high mountain.
40: 31 [A] *They will* **soar** *on* wings like eagles; they will run and not
53: 2 [A] *He* **grew up** before him like a tender shoot, and like a root
55: 13 [A] Instead of the thornbush *will* **grow** the pine tree, and instead
55: 13 [A] grow the pine tree, and instead of briers the myrtle *will* **grow**.
57: 6 [G] have poured out drink offerings and **offered** grain offerings.
57: 7 [A] and lofty hill; there *you* **went up** to offer your sacrifices.
57: 8 [A] uncovered your bed, *you* **climbed** *into* it and opened it wide;
60: 7 [G] *they will be* accepted *as* **offerings** *on* my altar, and I will
63: 11 [G] where is he *who* **brought** them through the sea,
65: 17 [A] things will not be remembered, nor *will they* **come** to mind.
66: 3 [G] *whoever* **makes** a grain **offering** is like one who presents
Jer 2: 6 [G] who **brought** us **up** out of Egypt and led us through the
3: 16 [A] *It will* never **enter** [+6584] their minds or be remembered;
4: 7 [A] A lion *has* **come** out of his lair; a destroyer of nations has set
4: 13 [A] *He* **advances** like the clouds, his chariots come like a
4: 29 [A] Some go into the thickets; *some* **climb up** among the rocks.
5: 10 [A] "**Go** through her vineyards and ravage them, but do not
6: 4 [A] Arise, *let us* **attack** at noon! But, alas, the daylight is fading,
6: 5 [A] So arise, *let us* **attack** at night and destroy her fortresses!"
7: 31 [A] I did not command, nor *did it* **enter** [+6584] my mind.
8: 22 [A] Why then **is** *there* no healing for the wound of my people?
9: 21 [9:20] [A] Death *has* **climbed in** through our windows and has
10: 13 [G] *he* **makes** clouds **rise** from the ends of the earth.
11: 7 [G] From the time I **brought** your forefathers **up** from Egypt
14: 2 [A] they wail for the land, and a cry **goes up** from Jerusalem.
14: 12 [G] though *they* **offer** burnt offerings and grain offerings, I will
16: 14 [G] LORD lives, who **brought** the Israelites **up** out of Egypt,'
16: 15 [G] who **brought** the Israelites **up** out of the land of the north
19: 5 [A] not command or mention, nor *did it* **enter** [+6584] my mind.
21: 2 [A] for us as in times past so that *he will* **withdraw** from us."
22: 20 [A] "**Go up** *to* Lebanon and cry out, let your voice be heard in
23: 7 [G] LORD lives, who **brought** the Israelites **up** out of Egypt,'
23: 8 [G] who **brought** the descendants of Israel **up** out of the land of
26: 10 [A] *they* **went up** from the royal palace *to* the house of the
27: 22 [G] 'Then *I will* **bring** them **back** and restore them to this
30: 17 [G] *I will* **restore** you to health and heal your wounds,' declares
31: 6 [A] 'Come, *let us* **go up** *to* Zion, to the LORD our God.' "
32: 35 [A] I never commanded, nor *did it* **enter** [+6584] my mind,
33: 6 [G] " 'Nevertheless, I *will* **bring** health and healing to it; I will
33: 18 [G] a man to stand before me continually *to* **offer** burnt offerings,
34: 21 [A] of the king of Babylon, which *has* **withdrawn** from you.
35: 11 [A] when Nebuchadnezzar king of Babylon **invaded** [+448] this
37: 5 [C] heard the report about them, *they* **withdrew** from Jerusalem.
37: 11 [C] After the Babylonian army *had* **withdrawn** from Jerusalem
38: 10 [G] **lift** Jeremiah the prophet out of the cistern before he dies."
38: 13 [G] pulled him up with the ropes and **lifted** him out of the cistern.
39: 5 [G] **took** him to Nebuchadnezzar king of Babylon at Riblah in
44: 21 [A] **think about** [+4213+6584] the incense burned in the towns
46: 4 [A] Harness the horses, **mount** the steeds! Take your positions
46: 7 [A] "Who is this *that* **rises** like the Nile, like rivers of surging
46: 8 [A] Egypt **rises** like the Nile, like rivers of surging waters. She
46: 8 [A] She says, '*I will* **rise** and cover the earth; I will destroy cities
46: 9 [A] **Charge**, O horses! Drive furiously, O charioteers! March on,
46: 11 [A] "**Go up** *to* Gilead and get balm, O Virgin Daughter of Egypt.
47: 2 [A] "See how the waters *are* **rising** in the north; they will
48: 5 [A] *They* **go up** the way to Luhith, weeping bitterly as they go;
48: 15 [A] Moab will be destroyed and her towns **invaded**; her finest
48: 18 [A] for he who destroys Moab *will* **come up** against you and ruin
48: 35 [G] In Moab I will put an end to *those who* **make offerings** *on*
48: 44 [A] a pit, whoever **climbs** out of the pit will be caught in a snare;
49: 19 [A] "Like a lion **coming up** from Jordan's thickets to a rich
49: 22 [A] An eagle *will* **soar** and swoop down, spreading its wings
49: 28 [A] and **attack** [+448] Kedar and destroy the people of the East.
49: 31 [A] "Arise and **attack** [+448] a nation at ease, which lives in
50: 3 [A] A nation from the north *will* **attack** [+6584] her and lay
50: 9 [G] **bring** against Babylon an alliance of great nations from the
50: 21 [A] "**Attack** [+6584] the land of Merathaim and those who live
50: 44 [A] Like a lion **coming up** from Jordan's thickets to a rich
51: 3 [F] not the archer string his bow, nor *let him* **put on** his armor.
51: 16 [G] *he* **makes** clouds **rise** from the ends of the earth.
51: 27 [G] against her; **send up** horses like a swarm of locusts.
51: 42 [A] The sea *will* **rise** over Babylon; its roaring waves will cover
51: 50 [G] in a distant land, and **think on** [+4222+6584] Jerusalem."
51: 53 [A] Even if Babylon **reaches** the sky and fortifies her lofty
52: 9 [G] He *was* **taken** to the king of Babylon at Riblah in the land of
La 1: 14 [A] *They have* **come** upon my neck and the Lord has sapped my
2: 10 [G] *they have* **sprinkled** dust on their heads and put on
Eze 8: 11 [A] in his hand, and a fragrant cloud of incense *was* **rising**.
9: 3 [C] Now the glory of the God of Israel **went up** from above the
11: 23 [A] The glory of the LORD **went up** from within the city
11: 24 [A] Spirit of God. Then the vision I had seen **went up** from me,
13: 5 [A] *You have* not **gone up** to the breaks in the wall to repair it
14: 3 [G] these men *have* **set up** idols in their hearts and put wicked
14: 4 [G] When any Israelite **sets up** idols in his heart and puts a
14: 7 [G] **sets up** idols in his heart and puts a wicked stumbling block
16: 40 [G] *They will* **bring** a mob against you, who will stone you
19: 3 [G] *She* **brought up** one of her cubs, and he became a strong
20: 32 [A] and stone." But what you **have** in mind will never happen.
23: 46 [G] **Bring** a mob against them and give them over to terror
24: 8 [G] To **stir up** wrath and take revenge I put her blood on the bare
26: 3 [G] O Tyre, and *I will* **bring** many nations against you,
26: 3 [G] many nations against you, like the sea **casting up** its waves.
26: 19 [G] when I **bring** the ocean depths over you and its vast waters
27: 30 [G] *they will* **sprinkle** dust on their heads and roll in ashes.
29: 4 [G] *I will* **pull** you **out** from among your streams, with all the
32: 3 [G] cast my net over you, and *they will* **haul** you **up** in my net.
36: 3 [C] and *the* **object of** people's **malicious talk** [+4383+6584+8557]
37: 6 [G] and **make** flesh **come** upon you and cover you with skin;
37: 8 [A] tendons and flesh **appeared** on them and skin covered them,
37: 12 [G] I am going to open your graves and **bring** you **up** from them;
37: 13 [G] when I open your graves and **bring** you **up** from them.
38: 9 [A] all your troops and the many nations with you *will* **go up**,
38: 10 [A] On that day thoughts *will* **come** into your mind and you will
38: 11 [A] will say, "*I will* **invade** [+6584] a land of unwalled villages;
38: 16 [A] *You will* **advance** against my people Israel like a cloud that
38: 18 [A] my hot anger *will be* **aroused**, declares the Sovereign
39: 2 [G] *I will* **bring** you from the far north and send you against the
40: 6 [A] *He* **climbed** its steps and measured the threshold of the gate;
40: 22 [A] Seven steps **led up** to it, with its portico opposite them.
40: 26 [A] Seven steps **led up** *to* it, with its portico opposite them; it had
40: 31 [G] palm trees decorated its jambs, and eight steps **led up** *to* it.
40: 34 [G] the jambs on either side, and eight steps **led up** *to* it.
40: 37 [G] the jambs on either side, and eight steps **led up** *to* it.
40: 40 [A] near the **steps** at the entrance to the north gateway were two
40: 49 [A] It *was* **reached** [+448] by a flight of stairs, and there were
41: 7 [A] A stairway **went up** from the lowest floor to the top floor
43: 18 [G] These will be the regulations for **sacrificing** burnt offerings
43: 24 [G] and **sacrifice** them as a burnt offering to the LORD.
44: 17 [G] they *must* not **wear** [+6584] any woolen garment while
47: 12 [A] Fruit trees of all kinds *will* **grow** on both banks of the river.
Da 8: 3 [A] One of the horns was longer than the other but **grew up** later.
8: 8 [A] in its place four prominent horns **grew up** toward the four
11: 23 [A] and with only a few people *he will* **rise** to power.
Hos 1: 11 [2:2] [A] appoint one leader and *will* **come up** out of the land,
2: 15 [2:17] [A] of her youth, as in the day she **came up** out of Egypt.
4: 15 [A] "Do not go to Gilgal; *do* not **go up** *to* Beth Aven. And do not
8: 9 [A] For they *have* **gone up** *to* Assyria like a wild donkey •
10: 8 [A] Thorns and thistles *will* **grow up** and cover their altars.
12: 13 [12:14] [G] The LORD used a prophet *to* **bring** Israel **up** from
13: 15 [A] from the LORD will come, **blowing in** from the desert;
Joel 1: 6 [A] A nation *has* **invaded** [+6584] my land, powerful
2: 7 [A] They charge like warriors; *they* **scale** walls like soldiers.
2: 9 [A] *They* **climb** into the houses; like thieves they enter through
2: 20 [A] its stench *will* **go up**; its smell will rise." Surely he has done
2: 20 [A] its stench will go up; its smell *will* **rise**." Surely he has done
3: 9 [4:9] [A] Let all the fighting men draw near and **attack**.
3: 12 [4:12] [A] *let them* **advance** into the Valley of Jehoshaphat,
Am 2: 10 [G] "I **brought** you **up** out of Egypt, and I led you forty years in
3: 1 [G] against the whole family *I* **brought up** out of Egypt:
3: 5 [A] *Does* a trap **spring up** from the earth when there is nothing
4: 10 [G] *I* **filled** your nostrils *with* the stench of your camps, yet you
5: 22 [G] Even though *you* **bring** me burnt offerings and grain
7: 1 [A] been harvested and just as the second crop *was* **coming up**.
8: 8 [A] The whole land *will* **rise** like the Nile; it will be stirred up
8: 10 [G] *I will* **make** all of you **wear** [+5516+6584] sackcloth and
9: 2 [A] Though *they* **climb up** *to* the heavens, from there I will bring
9: 5 [A] the whole land **rises** like the Nile, then sinks like the river of
9: 7 [G] "*Did I* not **bring** Israel **up** from Egypt, the Philistines from
Ob 1: 21 [A] Deliverers *will* **go up** on Mount Zion to govern the
Jnh 1: 2 [A] against it, because its wickedness *has* **come up** before me."
2: 6 [2:7] [G] *you* **brought** my life **up** from the pit, O LORD my

Jnh 4: 6 [G] **made** it **grow up** over Jonah to give shade for his head to
4: 7 [A] at **[NIE]** dawn the next day God provided a worm,
Mic 2: 13 [A] One who breaks open the way *will* **go up** before them;
4: 2 [A] and say, "Come, *let us* **go up** to the mountain of the LORD,
6: 4 [G] *I* **brought** you **up** out of Egypt and redeemed you from the
Na 2: 1 [2:2] [A] An attacker **advances** against you, ⌞Nineveh⌟.
2: 7 [2:8] [H] is decreed that ⌞the city⌟ be exiled and **carried away**.
3: 3 [G] **Charging** cavalry, flashing swords and glittering spears!
Hab 1: 15 [G] The wicked foe **pulls** all of them **up** with hooks, he catches
3: 16 [A] Yet I will wait patiently for the day of calamity to **come** on
Hag 1: 8 [A] **Go up** *into* the mountains and bring down timber and build
Zec 14: 13 [A] of another, and they *will* **attack** [+3338+6584] each other.
14: 16 [A] Jerusalem *will* **go up** year after year to worship the King,
14: 17 [A] If any of the peoples of the earth *do* not **go up** to Jerusalem
14: 18 [A] If the Egyptian people *do* not **go up** and take part, they will
14: 18 [A] that *do* not **go up** to celebrate the Feast of Tabernacles.
14: 19 [A] the punishment of all the nations that *do* not **go up** to

6591 עָלֶה *'āleh*, n.m. [18] [√ 6590]

leaves [7], leaf [5], *untranslated* [4], branches [1], green leaf [1]

Ge 3: 7 so they sewed fig **leaves** together and made coverings for
8: 11 in the evening, there in its beak was a freshly plucked olive **leaf**!
Lev 26: 36 enemies that the sound of a windblown **leaf** will put them to flight.
Ne 8: 15 and bring back **branches** *from* olive and wild olive trees,
8: 15 and bring back branches from olive and **[RPH]** wild olive trees,
8: 15 from **[RPH]** myrtles, palms and shade trees, to make booths"—
8: 15 from myrtles, **[RPH]** palms and shade trees, to make booths"—
8: 15 from myrtles, palms and **[RPH]** shade trees, to make booths"—
Job 13: 25 Will you torment a windblown **leaf**? Will you chase after dry
Ps 1: 3 which yields its fruit in season and whose **leaf** does not wither.
Pr 11: 28 in his riches will fall, but the righteous will thrive like a **green leaf**.
Isa 1: 30 You will be like an oak with fading **leaves**, like a garden without
34: 4 all the starry host will fall like withered **leaves** from the vine,
64: 6 [64:5] we all shrivel up like a **leaf**, and like the wind our sins
Jer 8: 13 There will be no figs on the tree, and their **leaves** will wither.
17: 8 It does not fear when heat comes; its **leaves** are always green.
Eze 47: 12 Their **leaves** will not wither, nor will their fruit fail. Every month
47: 12 Their fruit will serve for food and their **leaves** for healing."

6592 עֹלָה *'ōlâ*[1], n.f. [286 / 287] [√ 6590; Ar 10545]

burnt offering [159], burnt offerings [108], offering [7], *untranslated* [4], sacrifice [2], burnt [1], it[s] [+2021] [1], its[s] [+2021] [1], offerings [1], sacrifice [+6590] [1], sacrifices [1], them[s] [1]

Ge 8: 20 clean animals and clean birds, he sacrificed **burnt offerings** on it.
22: 2 Sacrifice him there as a **burnt offering** on one of the mountains I
22: 3 When he had cut enough wood for the **burnt offering**, he set out
22: 6 Abraham took the wood for the **burnt offering** and placed it on his
22: 7 Isaac said, "but where is the lamb for the **burnt offering**?"
22: 8 "God himself will provide the lamb for the **burnt offering**,
22: 13 the ram and sacrificed it as a **burnt offering** instead of his son.
Ex 10: 25 and **burnt offerings** to present to the LORD our God.
18: 12 brought a **burnt offering** and other sacrifices to God,
20: 24 and sacrifice on it your **burnt offerings** and fellowship offerings,
24: 5 they offered **burnt offerings** and sacrificed young bulls as
29: 18 It is a **burnt offering** to the LORD, a pleasing aroma, an offering
29: 25 burn them on the altar along with the **burnt offering** for a pleasing
29: 42 "For the generations to come this **burnt offering** is to be made
30: 9 this altar any other incense or any **burnt offering** or grain offering,
30: 28 the altar of **burnt offering** and all its utensils, and the basin with
31: 9 the altar of **burnt offering** and all its utensils, the basin with its
32: 6 and sacrificed **burnt offerings** and presented fellowship offerings.
35: 16 the altar of **burnt offering** with its bronze grating, its poles
38: 1 They built the altar of **burnt offering** *of* acacia wood, three cubits
40: 6 "Place the altar of **burnt offering** in front of the entrance to the
40: 10 Then anoint the altar of **burnt offering** and all its utensils;
40: 29 He set the altar of **burnt offering** near the entrance to the
40: 29 of Meeting, and offered on it **burnt offerings** and grain offerings,
Lev 1: 3 " 'If the offering is a **burnt offering** from the herd, he is to offer a
1: 4 He is to lay his hand on the head of the **burnt offering**, and it will
1: 6 He is to skin the **burnt offering** and cut it into pieces.
1: 9 It is a **burnt offering**, an offering made by fire, an aroma pleasing
1: 10 " 'If the offering is a **burnt offering** from the flock, from either the
1: 13 It is a **burnt offering**, an offering made by fire, an aroma pleasing
1: 14 " 'If the offering to the LORD is a **burnt offering** of birds,
1: 17 It is a **burnt offering**, an offering made by fire, an aroma pleasing
3: 5 sons are to burn it on the altar on top of the **burnt offering**
4: 7 the altar of **burnt offering** at the entrance to the Tent of Meeting.
4: 10 Then the priest shall burn them on the altar of **burnt offering**.
4: 18 the altar of **burnt offering** at the entrance to the Tent of Meeting.
4: 24 slaughter it at the place where the **burnt offering** is slaughtered
4: 25 put it on the horns of the altar of **burnt offering** and pour out the
4: 25 and pour out the rest of the blood at the base of the altar. **[RPH]**
4: 29 the sin offering and slaughter it at the place of the **burnt offering**.
4: 30 put it on the horns of the altar of **burnt offering** and pour out the
4: 33 slaughter it for a sin offering at the place where the **burnt offering**
4: 34 put it on the horns of the altar of **burnt offering** and pour out the
5: 7 his sin—one for a sin offering and the other for a **burnt offering**.
5: 10 then offer the other as a **burnt offering** in the prescribed way
6: 9 [6:2] 'These are the regulations for the **burnt offering**:
6: 9 [6:2] The **burnt offering** is to remain on the altar hearth
6: 10 [6:3] shall remove the ashes of the **burnt offering** that the fire has
6: 12 [6:5] is to add firewood and arrange the **burnt offering** on the fire
6: 25 [6:18] the LORD in the place the **burnt offering** is slaughtered;
7: 2 slaughtered in the place where the **burnt offering** is slaughtered,
7: 8 The priest who offers a **burnt offering** *for* anyone may keep its
7: 8 a burnt offering for anyone may keep **its**[s] [+2021] hide for himself.
7: 37 These, then, are the regulations for the **burnt offering**, the grain
8: 18 He then presented the ram for the **burnt** *offering*, and Aaron
8: 21 and burned the whole ram on the altar as a **burnt offering**,
8: 28 burned them on the altar on top of the **burnt offering** as an
9: 2 a bull calf for your sin offering and a ram for your **burnt offering**,
9: 3 both a year old and without defect—for a **burnt offering**,
9: 7 to the altar and sacrifice your sin offering and your **burnt offering**
9: 12 he slaughtered the **burnt offering**. His sons handed him the blood,
9: 13 They handed him the **burnt offering** piece by piece, including the
9: 14 and burned them on top of the **burnt offering** on the altar.
9: 16 He brought the **burnt offering** and offered it in the prescribed
9: 17 burned it on the altar in addition to the morning's **burnt offering**.
9: 22 the **burnt offering** and the fellowship offering, he stepped down.
9: 24 and consumed the **burnt offering** and the fat portions on the altar.
10: 19 their sin offering and their **burnt offering** before the LORD,
12: 6 to the Tent of Meeting a year-old lamb for a **burnt offering**
12: 8 one for a **burnt offering** and the other for a sin offering.
14: 13 where the sin offering and the **burnt offering** are slaughtered.
14: 19 After that, the priest shall slaughter the **burnt offering**
14: 20 and offer **it**[s] [+2021] on the altar, together with the grain offering,
14: 22 one for a sin offering and the other for a **burnt offering**.
14: 31 one as a sin offering and the other as a **burnt offering**,
15: 15 the one for a sin offering and the other for a **burnt offering**.
15: 30 sacrifice one for a sin offering and the other for a **burnt offering**.
16: 3 with a young bull for a sin offering and a ram for a **burnt offering**.
16: 5 two male goats for a sin offering and a ram for a **burnt offering**.
16: 24 he shall come out and sacrifice the **burnt offering** *for* himself
16: 24 burnt offering for himself and the **burnt offering** *for* the people,
17: 8 or any alien living among them who offers a **burnt offering**
22: 18 presents a gift for a **burnt offering** to the LORD, either to fulfill
23: 12 you must sacrifice as a **burnt offering** to the LORD a lamb a year
23: 18 They will be a **burnt offering** to the LORD, together with their
23: 37 the **burnt offerings** and grain offerings, sacrifices and drink
Nu 6: 11 and the other as a **burnt offering** to make atonement for him
6: 14 a year-old male lamb without defect for a **burnt offering**,
6: 16 the LORD and make the sin offering and the **burnt offering**.
7: 15 one ram and one male lamb a year old, for a **burnt offering**;
7: 21 one ram and one male lamb a year old, for a **burnt offering**;
7: 27 one ram and one male lamb a year old, for a **burnt offering**;
7: 33 one ram and one male lamb a year old, for a **burnt offering**;
7: 39 one ram and one male lamb a year old, for a **burnt offering**;
7: 45 one ram and one male lamb a year old, for a **burnt offering**;
7: 51 one ram and one male lamb a year old, for a **burnt offering**;
7: 57 one ram and one male lamb a year old, for a **burnt offering**;
7: 63 one ram and one male lamb a year old, for a **burnt offering**;
7: 69 one ram and one male lamb a year old, for a **burnt offering**;
7: 75 one ram and one male lamb a year old, for a **burnt offering**;
7: 81 one ram and one male lamb a year old, for a **burnt offering**;
7: 87 The total number of animals for the **burnt offering** came to twelve
8: 12 for a sin offering to the LORD and the other for a **burnt offering**,
10: 10 you are to sound the trumpets over your **burnt offerings**
15: 3 whether **burnt offerings** or sacrifices, for special vows or freewill
15: 5 With each lamb for the **burnt offering** or the sacrifice, prepare a
15: 8 " 'When you prepare a young bull as a **burnt offering** or sacrifice,
15: 24 the whole community is to offer a young bull for a **burnt offering**
23: 3 said to Balak, "Stay here beside your **offering** while I go aside.
23: 6 he went back to him and found him standing beside his **offering**,
23: 15 "Stay here beside your **offering** while I meet with him over there."
23: 17 So he went to him and found him standing beside his **offering**,
28: 3 a year old without defect, as a regular **burnt offering** each day.
28: 6 This is the regular **burnt offering** instituted at Mount Sinai as a
28: 10 This is the **burnt offering** *for* every Sabbath, in addition to the
28: 10 in addition to the regular **burnt offering** and its drink offering.
28: 11 present to the LORD a **burnt offering** of two young bulls,
28: 13 This is for a **burnt offering**, a pleasing aroma, an offering made to
28: 14 This is the monthly **burnt offering** to be made at each new moon
28: 15 Besides the regular **burnt offering** with its drink offering,
28: 19 a **burnt offering** of two young bulls, one ram and seven male
28: 23 Prepare these in addition to the regular morning **burnt offering**.
28: 23 these in addition to the regular morning burnt offering. **[RPH]**

Nu 28:24 it is to be prepared in addition to the regular **burnt offering**
28:27 Present a **burnt offering** of two young bulls, one ram and seven
28:31 in addition to the regular **burnt offering** and its grain offering.
29: 2 prepare a **burnt offering** of one young bull, one ram and seven
29: 6 daily **burnt offerings** with their grain offerings and drink offerings
29: 6 and daily burnt offerings **[RPH]** with their grain offerings
29: 8 Present as an aroma pleasing to the LORD a **burnt offering** of
29:11 and the regular **burnt offering** with its grain offering,
29:13 a **burnt offering** of thirteen young bulls, two rams and fourteen
29:16 in addition to the regular **burnt offering** with its grain offering
29:19 in addition to the regular **burnt offering** with its grain offering,
29:22 in addition to the regular **burnt offering** with its grain offering
29:25 in addition to the regular **burnt offering** with its grain offering
29:28 in addition to the regular **burnt offering** with its grain offering
29:31 in addition to the regular **burnt offering** with its grain offering
29:34 in addition to the regular **burnt offering** with its grain offering
29:36 a **burnt offering** of one bull, one ram and seven male lambs a year
29:38 in addition to the regular **burnt offering** with its grain offering
29:39 your **burnt offerings**, grain offerings, drink offerings and
Dt 12: 6 there bring your **burnt offerings** and sacrifices, your tithes
12:11 your **burnt offerings** and sacrifices, your tithes and special gifts,
12:13 Be careful not to sacrifice your **burnt offerings** anywhere you
12:14 Offer **them**[s] only at the place the LORD will choose in one of
12:27 Present your **burnt offerings** on the altar of the LORD your God,
27: 6 and offer **burnt offerings** on it to the LORD your God.
Jos 8:31 On it they offered to the LORD **burnt offerings** and sacrificed
22:23 from the LORD and to offer **burnt offerings** and grain offerings,
22:26 and build an altar—but not for **burnt offerings** or sacrifices.'
22:27 will worship the LORD at his sanctuary with our **burnt offerings**,
22:28 which our fathers built, not for **burnt offerings** and sacrifices,
22:29 turn away from him today by building an altar for **burnt offerings**,
Jdg 6:26 pole that you cut down, offer the second bull as a **burnt offering**."
11:31 will be the LORD's, and I will sacrifice it as a **burnt offering**."
13:16 But if you prepare a **burnt offering**, offer it to the LORD."
13:23 he would not have accepted a **burnt offering** and grain offering
20:26 They fasted that day until evening and presented **burnt offerings**
21: 4 an altar and presented **burnt offerings** and fellowship offerings.
1Sa 6:14 and sacrificed the cows as a **burnt offering** to the LORD.
6:15 On that day the people of Beth Shemesh offered **burnt offerings**
7: 9 and offered it up as a whole **burnt offering** to the LORD.
7:10 While Samuel was sacrificing the **burnt offering**, the Philistines
10: 8 I will surely come down to you to sacrifice **burnt offerings**
13: 9 "Bring me the **burnt offering** and the fellowship offerings."
13: 9 the fellowship offerings." And Saul offered up the **burnt offering**.
13:10 Just as he finished making the **offering**, Samuel arrived, and Saul
13:12 LORD's favor.' So I felt compelled to offer the **burnt offering**."
15:22 "Does the LORD delight in **burnt offerings** and sacrifices as
2Sa 6:17 David sacrificed **burnt offerings** and fellowship offerings before
6:18 After he had finished sacrificing the **burnt offerings**
24:22 Here are oxen for the **burnt offering**, and here are threshing
24:24 I will not sacrifice to the LORD my God **burnt offerings** that
24:25 and sacrificed **burnt offerings** and fellowship offerings.
1Ki 3: 4 and Solomon offered a thousand **burnt offerings** on that altar.
3:15 and sacrificed **burnt offerings** and fellowship offerings.
8:64 there he offered **burnt offerings**, grain offerings and the fat of the
8:64 altar before the LORD was too small to hold the **burnt offerings**,
9:25 Three times a year Solomon sacrificed **burnt offerings**
10: 5 and the **burnt offerings** he made at the temple of the LORD,
18:33 [18:34] with water and pour it on the **offering** and on the wood."
18:38 Then the fire of the LORD fell and burned up the **sacrifice**,
2Ki 3:27 him as king, and offered him as a **sacrifice** on the city wall.
5:17 for your servant will never again make **burnt offerings**
10:24 So they went in to make sacrifices and **burnt offerings**. Now Jehu
10:25 As soon as Jehu had finished making the **burnt offering**, he
16:13 He offered up his **burnt offering** and grain offering, poured out his
16:15 offer the morning **burnt offering** and the evening grain offering,
16:15 grain offering, the king's **burnt offering** and his grain offering,
16:15 grain offering, and the **burnt offering** *of* all the people of the land,
16:15 Sprinkle on the altar all the blood of the **burnt offerings**
1Ch 6:49 [6:34] who presented offerings on the altar of **burnt offering**
16: 1 they presented **burnt offerings** and fellowship offerings before
16: 2 After David had finished sacrificing the **burnt offerings**
16:40 to present **burnt offerings** to the LORD on the altar of burnt
16:40 offerings to the LORD on the altar of **burnt offering** regularly,
21:23 Look, I will give the oxen for the **burnt offerings**, the threshing
21:24 what is yours, or sacrifice a **burnt offering** that costs me nothing."
21:26 and sacrificed **burnt offerings** and fellowship offerings.
21:26 answered him with fire from heaven on the altar of **burnt offering**.
21:29 the altar of **burnt offering** were at that time on the high place at
22: 1 God is to be here, and also the altar of **burnt offering** for Israel."
23:31 whenever **burnt offerings** were presented to the LORD on
29:21 sacrifices to the LORD and presented **burnt offerings** to him:
2Ch 1: 6 the Tent of Meeting and offered a thousand **burnt offerings** on it.
2: 4 [2:3] and for making **burnt offerings** every morning and evening
4: 6 In them the things to be used for the **burnt offerings** were rinsed,
7: 1 from heaven and consumed the **burnt offering** and the sacrifices,
7: 7 there he offered **burnt offerings** and the fat of the fellowship
7: 7 the bronze altar he had made could not hold the **burnt offerings**,
8:12 of the portico, Solomon sacrificed **burnt offerings** to the LORD,
9: 4 the **burnt offerings** [BHS 6608] he made at the temple of the
13:11 Every morning and evening they present **burnt offerings**
23:18 to present the **burnt offerings** *of* the LORD as written in the Law
24:14 **burnt offerings** were presented continually in the temple of the
29: 7 or present any **burnt offerings** at the sanctuary to the God of
29:18 the altar of **burnt offering** with all its utensils, and the table for
29:24 because the king had ordered the **burnt offering** and the sin
29:27 Hezekiah gave the order to sacrifice the **burnt offering** on the
29:27 As the **offering** began, singing to the LORD began also,
29:28 All this continued until the sacrifice of the **burnt offering** was
29:31 and all whose hearts were willing brought **burnt offerings**.
29:32 The number of **burnt offerings** the assembly brought was seventy
29:32 male lambs—all of them for **burnt offerings** to the LORD.
29:34 The priests, however, were too few to skin all the **burnt offerings**;
29:35 There were **burnt offerings** in abundance, together with the fat of
29:35 and the drink offerings that accompanied the **burnt offerings**.
30:15 and brought **burnt offerings** to the temple of the LORD.
31: 2 to offer **burnt offerings** and fellowship offerings, to minister,
31: 3 evening **burnt offerings** and for the burnt offerings on the
31: 3 **[RPH]** and for the burnt offerings on the Sabbaths,
31: 3 burnt offerings and for the **burnt offerings** on the Sabbaths,
35:12 They set aside the **burnt offerings** to give them to the subdivisions
35:14 were sacrificing the **burnt offerings** and the fat portions until
35:16 and the offering of **burnt offerings** on the altar of the LORD,
Ezr 3: 2 the altar of the God of Israel to sacrifice **burnt offerings** on it,
3: 3 its foundation and sacrificed **burnt offerings** on it to the LORD,
3: 3 on it to the LORD, both the morning and evening **sacrifices**.
3: 4 the required number of **burnt offerings** prescribed for each day.
3: 5 After that, they presented the regular **burnt offerings**, the New
3: 6 seventh month they began to offer **burnt offerings** to the LORD,
8:35 from captivity sacrificed **burnt offerings** to the God of Israel:
8:35 twelve male goats. All this was a **burnt offering** to the LORD.
Ne 10:33 [10:34] for the regular grain offerings and **burnt offerings**;
Job 1: 5 Early in the morning he would sacrifice a **burnt offering** for each
42: 8 go to my servant Job and sacrifice a **burnt offering** for yourselves.
Ps 20: 3 [20:4] all your sacrifices and accept your **burnt offerings**.
40: 6 [40:7] **burnt offerings** and sin offerings you did not require.
50: 8 I do not rebuke you for your sacrifices or your **burnt offerings**,
51:16 [51:18] bring it; you do not take pleasure in **burnt offerings**.
51:19 [51:21] whole **burnt offerings** to delight you;
66:13 I will come to your temple with **burnt offerings** and fulfill my
66:15 *I will* **sacrifice** [+6590] fat animals to you and an offering of rams;
Isa 1:11 "I have more than enough of **burnt offerings**, of rams and the fat
40:16 for altar fires, nor its animals enough for **burnt offerings**.
43:23 You have not brought me sheep for **burnt offerings**, nor honored
56: 7 Their **burnt offerings** and sacrifices will be accepted on my altar;
Jer 6:20 Your **burnt offerings** are not acceptable; your sacrifices do not
7:21 add your **burnt offerings** to your other sacrifices and eat the meat
7:22 I did not just give them commands about **burnt offerings**
14:12 though they offer **burnt offerings** and grain offerings, I will not
17:26 and the Negev, bringing **burnt offerings** and sacrifices,
19: 5 places of Baal to burn their sons in the fire as **offerings** to Baal—
33:18 a man to stand before me continually to offer **burnt offerings**,
Eze 40:38 of the inner gateways, where the **burnt offerings** were washed.
40:39 on which the **burnt offerings**, sin offerings and guilt offerings
40:42 were also four tables of dressed stone for the **burnt offerings**,
40:42 them were placed the utensils for slaughtering the **burnt offerings**
43:18 These will be the regulations for sacrificing **burnt offerings**
43:24 salt on them and sacrifice them as a **burnt offering** to the LORD.
43:27 the priests are to present your **burnt offerings** and fellowship
44:11 they may slaughter the **burnt offerings** and sacrifices for the
45:15 **burnt offerings** and fellowship offerings to make atonement for
45:17 It will be the duty of the prince to provide the **burnt offerings**,
45:17 **burnt offerings** and fellowship offerings to make atonement for
45:23 and seven rams without defect as a **burnt offering** to the LORD,
45:25 for sin offerings, **burnt offerings**, grain offerings and oil.
46: 2 The priests are to sacrifice his **burnt offering** and his fellowship
46: 4 The **burnt offering** the prince brings to the LORD on the Sabbath
46:12 whether a **burnt offering** or fellowship offerings—the gate facing
46:12 He shall offer his **burnt offering** or his fellowship offerings as he
46:13 a year-old lamb without defect for a **burnt offering** to the LORD;
46:15 be provided morning by morning for a regular **burnt offering**.
Hos 6: 6 and acknowledgment of God rather than **burnt offerings**.
Am 5:22 Even though you bring me **burnt offerings** and grain offerings,
Mic 6: 6 Shall I come before him with **burnt offerings**, with calves a year

6593 עֹלָה[2] **'ōlâ[2]**, n.f. Not used in NIV/BHS [cf. 6406]

[F] Hitpael (hitpoel, hitpoal, hitpolel, hitpolal, hitpalel, hitpalal, hitpalpel, hitpalpal, hotpael, hotpaal) [G] Hiphil (hiphtil) [H] Hophal [I] Hishtaphel

6594 עַלְוָה *'alwâ¹*, n.f. [1]

evildoers [+1201] [1]

Hos 10: 9 Did not war overtake the **evildoers** [+1201] in Gibeah?

6595 עַלְוָה *'alwâ²*, n.pr.m. [2] [√ 6590]

Alvah [2]

Ge 36: 40 according to their clans and regions: Timna, **Alvah**, Jetheth,
1Ch 1: 51 The chiefs of Edom were: Timna, **Alvah**, [K 6607] Jetheth,

6596 עֲלוּמִים *'alûmîm*, n.pl.abst. [4] [→ 3609, 6624, 6625, 6628]

youth [3], youthful vigor [1]

Job 20: 11 The **youthful vigor** that fills his bones will lie with him in the dust.
33: 25 is renewed like a child's; it is restored as in the days of his **youth**.
Ps 89: 45 [89:46] You have cut short the days of his **youth**; you have
Isa 54: 4 You will forget the shame of your **youth** and remember no more

6597 עַלְוָן *'alwān*, n.pr.m. [1 / 2] [√ 6590; cf. 6615]

Alvan [2]

Ge 36: 23 The sons of Shobal: **Alvan**, Manahath, Ebal, Shepho and Onam.
1Ch 1: 40 **Alvan**, [BHS 6615] Manahath, Ebal, Shepho and Onam.

6598 עֲלוּקָה *'alûqâ*, n.f. [1]

leech [1]

Pr 30: 15 "The **leech** has two daughters. 'Give! Give!' they cry. "There are

6599 עָלוֹת *'ālôt*, n.pr.loc. [1]

Aloth [1]

1Ki 4: 16 Baana son of Hushai—in Asher and in **Aloth**;

6600 עָלַז *'ālaz*, v. [16] [→ 6601, 6611; cf. 6632]

rejoice [7], jubilant [2], triumph [2], glad [1], leaps for joy [1], made merry [1], reveling [1], shout with laughter [1]

2Sa 1: 20 [A] be glad, lest the daughters of the uncircumcised **rejoice**.
Ps 28: 7 [A] My heart **leaps for joy** and I will give thanks to him in song.
60: 6 [60:8] [A] "*In* **triumph** I will parcel out Shechem and measure
68: 4 [68:5] [A] his name is the LORD—and **rejoice** before him.
94: 3 [A] O LORD, how long *will* the wicked *be* **jubilant**?
96: 12 [A] *let* the fields *be* **jubilant**, and everything in them. Then all
108: 7 [108:8] [A] "*In* **triumph** I will parcel out Shechem and measure
149: 5 [A] *Let* the saints **rejoice** in this honor and sing for joy on their
Pr 23: 16 [A] my inmost being *will* **rejoice** when your lips speak what is
Isa 23: 12 [A] He said, "No more of your **reveling**, O Virgin Daughter of
Jer 11: 15 [A] When you engage in your wickedness, then *you* **rejoice**."
15: 17 [A] in the company of revelers, never **made merry** with them;
50: 11 [A] "Because you rejoice and *are* **glad**, you who pillage my
51: 39 [A] and make them drunk, so that *they* **shout with laughter**—
Hab 3: 18 [A] yet I *will* **rejoice** in the LORD, I will be joyful in God my
Zep 3: 14 [A] Be glad and **rejoice** with all your heart, O Daughter of

6601 עָלֵז *'ālēz*, a. (used as n.). [1] [√ 6600]

revelers [1]

Isa 5: 14 their nobles and masses with all their brawlers and **revelers**.

6602 עֲלָטָה *'alāṭâ*, n.f. [4]

dusk [3], darkness [1]

Ge 15: 17 When the sun had set and **darkness** had fallen, a smoking firepot
Eze 12: 6 on your shoulder as they are watching and carry them out at **dusk**.
12: 7 I took my belongings out at **dusk**, carrying them on my shoulders
12: 12 prince among them will put his things on his shoulder at **dusk**

6603 עֵלִי *'ēlî¹*, n.pr.m. [33] [√ 3378 *or* 446 + 6590]

Eli [27], Eli's [4], *untranslated* [1], who[s] [1]

1Sa 1: 3 where Hophni and Phinehas, the two sons of **Eli**, were priests of
1: 9 Now **Eli** the priest was sitting on a chair by the doorpost of the
1: 12 As she kept on praying to the LORD, **Eli** observed her mouth.
1: 13 but her voice was not heard. **Eli** thought she was drunk
1: 14 said to her, **[RPH]** "How long will you keep on getting drunk?
1: 17 **Eli** answered, "Go in peace, and may the God of Israel grant you
1: 25 When they had slaughtered the bull, they brought the boy to **Eli**,
2: 11 but the boy ministered before the LORD under **Eli** the priest.
2: 12 **Eli's** sons were wicked men; they had no regard for the LORD.
2: 20 **Eli** would bless Elkanah and his wife, saying, "May the LORD
2: 22 Now **Eli**, who was very old, heard about everything his sons were
2: 27 Now a man of God came to **Eli** and said to him, "This is what the
3: 1 The boy Samuel ministered before the LORD under **Eli**.
3: 2 One night **Eli**, whose eyes were becoming so weak that he could
3: 5 he ran to **Eli** and said, "Here I am; you called me." But Eli said,
3: 6 Samuel got up and went to **Eli** and said, "Here I am; you called
3: 8 and Samuel got up and went to **Eli** and said, "Here I am;
3: 8 called me." Then **Eli** realized that the LORD was calling the boy.
3: 9 So **Eli** told Samuel, "Go and lie down, and if he calls you,
3: 12 At that time I will carry out against **Eli** everything I spoke against
3: 14 Therefore, I swore to the house of **Eli**, 'The guilt of Eli's house will
3: 14 'The guilt of **Eli's** house will never be atoned for by sacrifice
3: 15 of the house of the LORD. He was afraid to tell **Eli** the vision,
3: 16 but **Eli** called him and said, "Samuel, my son." Samuel answered,
4: 4 **Eli's** two sons, Hophni and Phinehas, were there with the ark of
4: 11 God was captured, and **Eli's** two sons, Hophni and Phinehas, died.
4: 13 there was **Eli** sitting on his chair by the side of the road, watching,
4: 14 **Eli** heard the outcry and asked, "What is the meaning of this
4: 14 "What is the meaning of this uproar?" The man hurried over to **Eli**,
4: 15 **who**[s] was ninety-eight years old and whose eyes were set
4: 16 He told **Eli**, "I have just come from the battle line; I fled from it
14: 3 son of Phinehas, the son of **Eli**, the LORD's priest in Shiloh.
1Ki 2: 27 the word the LORD had spoken at Shiloh about the house of **Eli**.

6604 עֱלִי *'ēlî²*, n.[m.]. [0 / 1] [√ 6590; Ar 10546]

Most High [1]

Ps 7: 8 [7:9] according to my integrity, O **Most High**. [BHS 6584]

6605 עֱלִי *'ᵉlî*, n.[m.]. [1] [√ 6590]

pestle [1]

Pr 27: 22 you grind a fool in a mortar, grinding him like grain with a **pestle**,

6606 עִלִּי *'illî*, a. [2] [√ 6590; Ar 10547]

upper [2]

Jos 15: 19 springs of water." So Caleb gave her the **upper** and lower springs.
Jdg 1: 15 of water." Then Caleb gave her the **upper** and lower springs.

6607 עַלְיָה *'alyâ*, n.pr.m. [0] [√ 6590]

1Ch 1: 51 [The chiefs of Edom were: Timna, **Alvah**, [K; see Q 6595] Jetheth,]

6608 עֲלִיָּה *'aliyyâ*, n.f. [20 / 19] [√ 6590; Ar 10547]

upper room [6], room [4], room above [2], upper chambers [2], upper parts [2], upper rooms [2], room over [1]

Jdg 3: 20 approached him while he was sitting alone in the **upper room** *of*
3: 23 he shut the doors of the **upper room** behind him and locked them.
3: 24 the servants came and found the doors of the **upper room** locked.
3: 25 but when he did not open the doors of the **room**, they took a key
2Sa 18: 33 [19:1] He went up to the **room over** the gateway and wept. As he
1Ki 17: 19 carried him to the **upper room** where he was staying, and laid him
17: 23 up the child and carried him down from the **room** into the house.
2Ki 1: 2 Now Ahaziah had fallen through the lattice of his **upper room** in
4: 10 Let's make a small **room** *on* the roof and put in it a bed and a
4: 11 day when Elisha came, he went up to his **room** and lay down there.
23: 12 of Judah had erected on the roof near the **upper room** *of* Ahaz,
1Ch 28: 11 its buildings, its storerooms, its **upper parts**, its inner rooms
2Ch 3: 9 weighed fifty shekels. He also overlaid the **upper parts** with gold.
9: 4 the burnt offerings [BHS *ascent*; NIV 6592] he made at the temple
Ne 3: 31 the Inspection Gate, and as far as the **room above** the corner;
3: 32 between the **room above** the corner and the Sheep Gate the
Ps 104: 3 and lays the beams of his **upper chambers** on their waters.
104: 13 He waters the mountains from his **upper chambers**; the earth is
Jer 22: 13 his **upper rooms** by injustice, making his countrymen work for
22: 14 'I will build myself a great palace with spacious **upper rooms**.'

6609 עֶלְיוֹן *'elyôn¹*, a. [22] [√ 6590; Ar 10548]

upper [15], high [2], imposing [2], top [2], most exalted [1]

Ge 40: 17 In the **top** basket were all kinds of baked goods for Pharaoh,
Dt 26: 19 fame and honor **high** above all the nations he has made and that
28: 1 the LORD your God will set you **high** above all the nations on
Jos 16: 5 went from Ataroth Addar in the east to **Upper** Beth Horon
1Ki 9: 8 though this temple is now **imposing**, all who pass by will be
2Ki 15: 35 Jotham rebuilt the **Upper** Gate of the temple of the LORD.
18: 17 up to Jerusalem and stopped at the aqueduct of the **Upper** Pool,
1Ch 7: 24 who built Lower and **Upper** Beth Horon as well as Uzzen Sheerah.
2Ch 7: 21 though this temple is now *so* **imposing**, all who pass by will be
8: 5 He rebuilt **Upper** Beth Horon and Lower Beth Horon as fortified
23: 20 They went into the palace through the **Upper** Gate and seated the
27: 3 Jotham rebuilt the **Upper** Gate of the temple of the LORD
32: 30 It was Hezekiah who blocked the **upper** outlet of the Gihon spring
Ne 3: 25 the tower projecting from the **upper** palace near the court of the
Ps 89: 27 [89:28] my firstborn, the **most exalted** of the kings of the earth.
Isa 7: 3 to meet Ahaz at the end of the aqueduct of the **Upper** Pool,
36: 2 When the commander stopped at the aqueduct of the **Upper** Pool,

Jer 20: 2 put in the stocks at the **Upper** Gate of Benjamin at the LORD's
36: 10 which was in the **upper** courtyard at the entrance of the New Gate
Eze 9: 2 And I saw six men coming from the direction of the **upper** gate,
41: 7 A stairway went up from the lowest floor to the **top** *floor* through
42: 5 Now the **upper** rooms were narrower, for the galleries took more

6610 [2]עֶלְיוֹן ʿelyôn[2], n.m. [31] [√ 6590; Ar 10546, 10548]

Most High [31]

Ge 14: 18 brought out bread and wine. He was priest of God **Most High**,
14: 19 saying, "Blessed be Abram by God **Most High**, Creator of heaven
14: 20 blessed be God **Most High**, who delivered your enemies into your
14: 22 God **Most High**, Creator of heaven and earth, and have taken an
Nu 24: 16 who has knowledge from the **Most High**, who sees a vision from
Dt 32: 8 When the **Most High** gave the nations their inheritance, when he
2Sa 22: 14 thundered from heaven; the voice of the **Most High** resounded.
Ps 7: 17 [7:18] and will sing praise to the name of the LORD **Most High**.
9: 2 [9:3] in you; I will sing praise to your name, O **Most High**.
18: 13 [18:14] from heaven; the voice of the **Most High** resounded.
21: 7 [21:8] through the unfailing love of the **Most High** he will not be
46: 4 [46:5] city of God, the holy place where the **Most High** dwells.
47: 2 [47:3] How awesome is the LORD **Most High**, the great King
50: 14 thank offerings to God, fulfill your vows to the **Most High**,
57: 2 [57:3] I cry out to God **Most High**, to God, who fulfills ⌊his
73: 11 "How can God know? Does the **Most High** have knowledge?"
77: 10 [77:11] the years of the right hand of the **Most High**."
78: 17 to sin against him, rebelling in the desert against the **Most High**.
78: 35 that God was their Rock, that God **Most High** was their Redeemer.
78: 56 But they put God to the test and rebelled against the **Most High**;
82: 6 "I said, 'You are "gods"; you are all sons of the **Most High**.'
83: 18 [83:19] that you alone are the **Most High** over all the earth.
87: 5 were born in her, and the **Most High** himself will establish her."
91: 1 He who dwells in the shelter of the **Most High** will rest in the
91: 9 If you make the **Most High** your dwelling—even the LORD,
92: 1 [92:2] the LORD and make music to your name, O **Most High**,
97: 9 For you, O LORD, are the **Most High** over all the earth;
107: 11 the words of God and despised the counsel of the **Most High**.
Isa 14: 14 the tops of the clouds; I will make myself like the **Most High**."
La 3: 35 to deny a man his rights before the **Most High**,
3: 38 Is it not from the mouth of the **Most High** that both calamities

6611 עַלִּיז ʿallîz, a. [7] [√ 6600; cf. 6616]

revelry [3], rejoice [2], carefree [1], revelers [1]

Isa 13: 3 warriors to carry out my wrath—*those who* **rejoice** *in* my triumph.
22: 2 O town full of commotion, O city of tumult and **revelry**?
23: 7 Is this your city of **revelry**, the old, old city, whose feet have taken
24: 8 the noise of the **revelers** has stopped, the joyful harp is silent.
32: 13 mourn for all houses of merriment and for this city of **revelry**.
Zep 2: 15 This is the **carefree** city that lived in safety. She said to herself,
3: 11 because I will remove from this city *those who* **rejoice** *in* their

6612 עֲלִיל ʿalîl, n.[m.]. [1] [√ 6619]

furnace [1]

Ps 12: 6 [12:7] like silver refined in a **furnace** of clay, purified seven

6613 עֲלִילָה ʿalîlâ, n.f. [24] [√ 6618]

actions [6], what done [5], deeds [4], did [1], do [1], done [1], mighty deeds [1], misdeeds [1], practices [1], slandered [+1821+8492] [1], slanders [+1821+4200+8492] [1], works [1]

Dt 22: 14 **slanders** [+1821+4200+8492] her and gives her a bad name,
22: 17 Now he *has* **slandered** [+1821+8492] her and said, 'I did not find
1Sa 2: 3 the LORD is a God who knows, and by him **deeds** are weighed.
1Ch 16: 8 on his name; make known among the nations **what** he has **done**.
Ps 9: 11 [9:12] in Zion; proclaim among the nations **what** he has **done**.
14: 1 They are corrupt, their **deeds** are vile; there is no one who does
66: 5 see what God has done, how awesome his **works** in man's behalf!
77: 12 [77:13] on all your works and consider all your **mighty deeds**.
78: 11 They forgot **what** he had **done**, the wonders he had shown them.
99: 8 to Israel a forgiving God, though you punished their **misdeeds**.
103: 7 made known his ways to Moses, his **deeds** to the people of Israel:
105: 1 on his name; make known among the nations **what** he has **done**.
141: 4 is evil, to take part in wicked **deeds** with men who are evildoers;
Isa 12: 4 make known among the nations **what** he has **done**, and proclaim
Eze 14: 22 come to you, and when you see their conduct and their **actions**,
14: 23 You will be consoled when you see their conduct and their **actions**,
20: 43 and all the **actions** by which you have defiled yourselves,
20: 44 and not according to your evil ways and your corrupt **practices**,
21: 24 [21:29] open rebellion, revealing your sins in all *that* you **do**—
24: 14 You will be judged according to your conduct and your **actions**,
36: 17 in their own land, they defiled it by their conduct and their **actions**.
36: 19 I judged them according to their conduct and their **actions**.
Zep 3: 7 upon her. But they were still eager to act corruptly in all they **did**.
3: 11 will not be put to shame for all the wrongs you have **done** to me,

6614 עֲלִילִיָּה ʿalîliyyâ, n.f. [1]

deeds [1]

Jer 32: 19 great are your purposes and mighty are your **deeds**. Your eyes are

6615 עַלְיָן ʿalyān, n.pr.m. [1 / 0] [cf. 6597]

1Ch 1: 40 The sons of Shobal: Alvan, [BHS *Alian*; NIV 6597]

6616 עָלִיץ ʿālîṣ, a. Not used in NIV/BHS [cf. 6611]

6617 עֲלִיצֻת ʿalîṣut, n.f. [1] [√ 6636; cf. 6632]

gloating [1]

Hab 3: 14 **gloating** as though about to devour the wretched who were in

6618 [1]עָלַל ʿālal[1], v. [18] [→ 5094, 5095, 6613, 6622, 9500; cf. 6621]

abuse [2], glean thoroughly [+6618] [2], abused [1], brings grief [1], cut down [1], deal [1], dealt harshly [1], dealt [1], go over a second time [1], go over the vines again [+339] [1], made a fool [1], mistreat [1], take part in [1], treated harshly [1], treated [1], was inflicted [1]

Ex 10: 2 [F] and grandchildren how *I* **dealt harshly** with the Egyptians
Lev 19: 10 [D] *Do* not **go over** your vineyard **a second time** or pick up the
Nu 22: 29 [F] Balaam answered the donkey, "*You have* **made a fool** of me!
Dt 24: 21 [D] in your vineyard, *do* not **go** [+339] **over the vines again**.
Jdg 19: 25 [F] they raped her and **abused** her throughout the night, and at
20: 45 [D] the Israelites **cut down** five thousand men along the roads.
1Sa 6: 6 [F] When *he* **treated** them **harshly**, did they not send the
31: 4 [F] fellows will come and run me through and **abuse** me."
1Ch 10: 4 [F] or these uncircumcised fellows will come and **abuse** me."
Ps 141: 4 [F] to **take part in** wicked deeds with men who are evildoers;
Jer 6: 9 [D] "*Let them* **glean** [+6618] the remnant of Israel as **thoroughly**
6: 9 [D] "*Let them* **glean** the remnant of Israel as **thoroughly** [+6618]
38: 19 [F] may hand me over to them and *they will* **mistreat** me."
La 1: 12 [E] Is any suffering like my suffering that **was inflicted** on me,
1: 22 [D] **deal** with them as you have dealt with me because of all my
1: 22 [D] deal with them as *you have* **dealt** with me because of all my
2: 20 [D] and consider: Whom *have you ever* **treated** like this?
3: 51 [D] What I see **brings grief** to my soul because of all the women

6619 [2]עָלַל ʿālal[2], v. [1] [→ 6585, 6612; Ar 10549]

buried [1]

Job 16: 15 [D] sackcloth over my skin and **buried** my brow in the dust.

6620 [3]עָלַל ʿālal[3], v.den. [1]

youths [1]

Isa 3: 12 [D] **Youths** oppress my people, women rule over them. O my

6621 [4]עָלַל ʿālal[4], v.den. Not used in NIV/BHS [cf. 6618]

6622 עֹלֵלוֹת ʿōlēlôt, n.f.pl.intens. [6] [√ 6618]

few grapes [2], gleanings [2], gleaning [1], gleanings of grapes [1]

Jdg 8: 2 Aren't the **gleanings of** Ephraim's **grapes** better than the full grape
Isa 17: 6 Yet *some* **gleanings** will remain, as when an olive tree is beaten,
24: 13 tree is beaten, or as when **gleanings** are left after the grape harvest.
Jer 49: 9 If grape pickers came to you, would they not leave a **few grapes**?
Ob 1: 5 If grape pickers came to you, would they not leave a **few grapes**?
Mic 7: 1 I am like one who gathers summer fruit at the **gleaning** *of* the

6623 עָלַם ʿālam, v. [29] [→ 9501, 9502]

hidden [4], ignore [4], unaware of [+4946] [3], close [+906+4946 +6623] [2], hard [2], hide [2], bring [1], close [1], closes [1], hiding [1], hypocrites [1], make shut [1], obscures [1], secret [1], shut [1], swollen [1], turn away [1], unaware [+4946+6524] [1]

Lev 4: 13 [C] even though the community *is* **unaware** [+4946+6524] *of* the
5: 2 [C] even though he *is* **unaware** [+4946] **of** *it*, he has become
5: 3 [C] even though he *is* **unaware** [+4946] **of** *it*, when he learns of
5: 4 [C] even though he *is* **unaware** [+4946] **of** *it*, in any case when
20: 4 [G] people of the community **close** [+906+4946+6623] their eyes
20: 4 [G] people of the community **close** [+906+4946+6623] their eyes
Nu 5: 13 [C] *this is* **hidden** from her husband and her impurity is
Dt 22: 1 [F] *do* not **ignore** it but be sure to take it back to him.
22: 3 [F] or his cloak or anything he loses. *Do* not **ignore** it.
22: 4 [F] or his ox fallen on the road, *do* not **ignore** it.
28: 61 [G] The LORD *will* also **bring** on you every kind of sickness
1Sa 12: 3 [G] From whose hand have I accepted a bribe *to* **make** *me* **shut**
1Ki 10: 3 [C] nothing was too **hard** for the king to explain to her.
2Ki 4: 27 [G] the LORD *has* **hidden** it from me and has not told me

2Ch 9: 2 [C] nothing *was* too **hard** for him to explain to her.
Job 6: 16 [F] darkened by thawing ice and **swollen** with melting snow,
28: 21 [C] *It is* **hidden** from the eyes of every living thing,
42: 3 [G] ⌞You asked,⌟ 'Who is this *that* **obscures** my counsel without
Ps 10: 1 [G] stand far off? *Why do you* **hide** *yourself* in times of trouble?
26: 4 [C] not sit with deceitful men, nor do I consort with **hypocrites**;
55: 1 [55:2] [F] Listen to my prayer, O God, *do* not **ignore** my plea;
90: 8 [B] before you, our **secret** sins in the light of your presence.
Pr 28: 27 [G] but *he who* **closes** his eyes to them receives many curses.
Ecc 12: 14 [C] including every **hidden** *thing*, whether it is good or evil.
Isa 1: 15 [G] out your hands in prayer, *I will* **hide** my eyes from you;
58: 7 [F] and not *to* **turn away** from your own flesh and blood?
La 3: 56 [G] heard my plea: "*Do* not **close** your ears to my cry for relief."
Eze 22: 26 [G] *they* **shut** their eyes to the keeping of my Sabbaths, so that I
Na 3: 11 [C] you will go into **hiding** and seek refuge from the enemy.

6624 עֶלֶם *'elem*, n.m. [2] [√ 6596]

boy [1], young man [1]

1Sa 17: 56 The king said, "Find out whose son this **young man** is."
20: 22 But if I say to the **boy**, 'Look, the arrows are beyond you,'

6625 עַלְמָה *'almâ*, n.f. [7] [√ 6596; cf. 6628]

maiden [2], maidens [2], girl [1], virgin [1], virgins [1]

Ge 24: 43 if a **maiden** comes out to draw water and I say to her, "Please let
Ex 2: 8 she answered. And the **girl** went and got the baby's mother.
Ps 68: 25 [68:26] with them are the **maidens** playing tambourines.
Pr 30: 19 of a ship on the high seas, and the way of a man with a **maiden**.
SS 1: 3 is like perfume poured out. No wonder the **maidens** love you!
6: 8 there may be, and eighty concubines, and **virgins** beyond number;
Isa 7: 14 The **virgin** will be with child and will give birth to a son, and will

6626 עַלְמוֹן *'almôn*, n.pr.loc. [1] [→ 6627]

Almon [1]

Jos 21: 18 Anathoth and **Almon**, together with their pasturelands—

6627 עַלְמוֹן דִּבְלָתָיְמָה *'almôn diblātayim*, n.pr.loc. [2] [√ 6626 + 1814]

Almon Diblathaim [2]

Nu 33: 46 They left Dibon Gad and camped at **Almon Diblathaim**.
33: 47 They left **Almon Diblathaim** and camped in the mountains of

6628 עֲלָמוֹת *'ălāmôt*, n.f. [2] [√ 6596; cf. 6625]

alamoth [2]

1Ch 15: 20 and Benaiah were to play the lyres according to ***alamoth***,
Ps 46: T [46:1] Of the Sons of Korah. According to ***alamoth***. A song.

6629 עַל־מוּת *'al-mût*, tt. [1 / 0] [√ 6584 + 4637]

Ps 9: T [9:1] To … "The Death [BHS ***Almuth***; NIV 6584] of the Son."

6630 ¹עָלֶמֶת *'ālemet¹*, n.pr.loc. [1] [√ 6631?]

Alemeth [1]

1Ch 6: 60 [6:45] Geba, **Alemeth** and Anathoth, together with their

6631 ²עָלֶמֶת *'ālemet²*, n.pr.m. [3] [√ 6630?]

Alemeth [3]

1Ch 7: 8 Elioenai, Omri, Jeremoth, Abijah, Anathoth and **Alemeth**.
8: 36 Jehoaddah was the father of **Alemeth**, Azmaveth and Zimri,
9: 42 of Jadah, Jadah was the father of **Alemeth**, Azmaveth and Zimri,

6632 עָלַס *'ālas*, v. [3] [cf. 6600, 6617, 6636]

enjoy ourselves [1], enjoy [1], flap joyfully [1]

Job 20: 18 [A] back uneaten; *he will* not **enjoy** the profit from his trading.
39: 13 [C] "The wings of the ostrich **flap joyfully**, but they cannot
Pr 7: 18 [F] deep of love till morning; *let's* **enjoy ourselves** with love!

6633 עָלַע *'ālaʿ*, v. [1] [cf. 4363]

feast on [1]

Job 39: 30 [D] His young ones **feast on** blood, and where the slain are,

6634 עָלַף *'ālap*, v. [6]

faint [2], decorated [1], disguise herself [1], fainted [1], withered away [1]

Ge 38: 14 [F] covered herself with a veil *to* **disguise herself**, and then sat
SS 5: 14 [E] His body is like polished ivory **decorated** *with* sapphires.
Isa 51: 20 [E] Your sons *have* **fainted**; they lie at the head of every street,
Eze 31: 15 [E] with gloom, and all the trees of the field **withered away**.
Am 8: 13 [F] and strong young men *will* **faint** because of thirst.
Jnh 4: 8 [F] and the sun blazed on Jonah's head so that *he grew* **faint**.

6635 עֻלְפֶּה *'ulpeh*, var. Not used in NIV/BHS

6636 עָלַץ *'ālaṣ*, v. [8] [→ 6617; cf. 6632]

rejoice [3], rejoices [2], triumph [2], jubilant [1]

1Sa 2: 1 [A] "My heart **rejoices** in the LORD; in the LORD my horn is
1Ch 16: 32 [A] is in it; *let* the fields *be* **jubilant**, and everything in them!
Ps 5: 11 [5:12] [A] that those who love your name *may* **rejoice** in you.
9: 2 [9:3] [A] I will be glad and **rejoice** in you; I will sing praise to
25: 2 [A] me be put to shame, nor *let* my enemies **triumph** over me.
68: 3 [68:4] [A] may the righteous be glad and **rejoice** before God;
Pr 11: 10 [A] When the righteous prosper, the city **rejoices**; when the
28: 12 [A] When the righteous **triumph**, there is great elation; but when

6637 עֹלָתָה *'ōlātâ*, n.f. [1] [√ 6401; cf. 6406]

injustice [1]

Job 5: 16 So the poor have hope, and **injustice** shuts its mouth.
Ps 92: 15 [92:16] [and there is no **wickedness** [K; see Q 6406] in him."]

6638 ¹עַם *'am¹*, n.[m.]. Not used in NIV/BHS [√ 6639; Ar 10553]

6639 ²עַם *'am²*, n.m. [1868] [→ 6638; Ar 10553; *also used with compound proper names*]

people [1293], peoples [100], nations [90], men [72], army [48], *untranslated* [35], troops [31], they[s] [+2021] [28], them[s] [+2021] [19], people [+1426] [14], soldiers [10], nation [9], people [+1201] [8], people's [7], countrymen [+1201] [6], each people [+2256+6639] [6], fighting men [6], those[s] [+2021] [5], army [+4878] [4], Israelites[s] [4], nationality [4], others[s] [4], common people [+1201] [2], creatures [2], everyone [+2021+3972] [2], humble [+6714] [2], lay people [+1201] [2], lives [2], one of the other peoples [+2256+6639] [2], one[s] [+2021] [2], their[s] [+2021] [2], them[s] [+2021+3972] [2], they[s] [+824+2021] [2], those[s] [2], various peoples [+2256+6639] [2], anyone[s] else [1], army [+2256+7736] [1], common people [1], community [+824+2021] [1], everyone [1], exalted [+5294] [1], fellow townsmen [+9133] [1], followers [+339+889+2021] [1], following [+907] [1], force [+4878] [1], force of men [1], forces [1], foreigners [+5799] [1], guests [1], Israel [+3776] [1], Israelites [+1201+3776] [1], it[s] [+2021] [1], leaders [+8031] [1], man [1], merchants [+4047] [1], multitude [1], nationalities [1], native [+1201] [1], one another [+2021] [1], other nationalities [+824+2021] [1], people's [+4200] [1], person [1], population [1], soldier [1], soldiers [+7372] [1], someone [+285+2021] [1], their[s] [+3276+3776] [1], their[s] [+824+2021] [1], them[s] [+2021+2021+2296] [1], them[s] [+2257] [1], them[s] [+3276] [1], they[s] [+2021+3972] [1], they[s] [1], those[s] [+339+889+2021] [1]

Ge 11: 6 "If as one **people** speaking the same language they have begun to
14: 16 and his possessions, together with the women and the other **people**.
17: 14 not been circumcised in the flesh, will be cut off from his **people**;
17: 16 be the mother of nations; kings of **peoples** will come from her."
19: 4 of Sodom—both young and old—**[RPH]** surrounded the house.
23: 7 Abraham rose and bowed down before the **people** *of* the land,
23: 11 I give it to you in the presence of my **people** [+1201]. Bury your
23: 12 Again Abraham bowed down before the **people** *of* the land
23: 13 he said to Ephron in **their**[s] [+824+2021] hearing, "Listen to me,
25: 8 an old man and full of years; and he was gathered to his **people**.
25: 17 He breathed his last and died, and he was gathered to his **people**.
26: 10 One of the **men** might well have slept with your wife, and you
26: 11 So Abimelech gave orders to all the **people**: "Anyone who molests
27: 29 May **nations** serve you and peoples bow down to you. Be lord over
28: 3 increase your numbers until you become a community of **peoples**.
32: 7 [32:8] distress Jacob divided the **people** who were with him into
33: 15 Esau said, "Then let me leave some of my **men** with you."
34: 16 We'll settle among you and become one **people** with you.
34: 22 the men will consent to live with us as one **people** only on the
35: 6 Jacob and all the **people** with him came to Luz (that is, Bethel)
35: 29 Then he breathed his last and died and was gathered to his **people**,
41: 40 of my palace, and all my **people** are to submit to your orders.
41: 55 began to feel the famine, the **people** cried to Pharaoh for food.
42: 6 the governor of the land, the one who sold grain to all its **people**.
47: 21 Joseph reduced the **people** to servitude, from one end of Egypt to
47: 23 Joseph said to the **people**, "Now that I have bought you and your
48: 4 I will make you a community of **peoples**, and I will give this land
48: 19 He too will become a **people**, and he too will become great.
49: 10 comes to whom it belongs and the obedience of the **nations** is his.
49: 16 "Dan will provide justice for his **people** as one of the tribes of
49: 29 them these instructions: "I am about to be gathered to my **people**.
49: 33 up into the bed, breathed his last and was gathered to his **people**.

Ge 50:20 to accomplish what is now being done, the saving of many **lives**.
Ex 1: 9 "Look," he said to his **people**, "the Israelites have become much
1: 9 "the **Israelites** [+1201+3776] have become much too numerous for
1:20 So God was kind to the midwives and the **people** increased
1:22 Pharaoh gave this order to all his **people**: "Every boy that is born
3: 7 "I have indeed seen the misery of my **people** in Egypt.
3:10 I am sending you to Pharaoh to bring my **people** the Israelites out
3:12 When you have brought the **people** out of Egypt, you will worship
3:21 I will make the Egyptians favorably disposed toward this **people**,
4:16 He will speak to the **people** for you, and it will be as if he were
4:21 But I will harden his heart so that he will not let the **people** go.
4:30 had said to Moses. He also performed the signs before the **people**,
4:31 **they**[s] [+2021] believed. And when they heard that the LORD was
5: 1 'Let my **people** go, so that they may hold a festival to me in the
5: 4 and Aaron, why are you taking the **people** away from their labor?
5: 5 Pharaoh said, "Look, the **people** *of* the land are now numerous,
5: 6 this order to the slave drivers and foremen in charge of the **people**:
5: 7 "You are no longer to supply the **people** with straw for making
5:10 the slave drivers **[RPH]** and the foremen went out and said to the
5:10 the slave drivers and the foremen went out and said to the **people**,
5:12 So the **people** scattered all over Egypt to gather stubble to use for
5:16 servants are being beaten, but the fault is with your own **people**."
5:22 "O Lord, why have you brought trouble upon this **people**?
5:23 he has brought trouble upon this **people**, and you have not rescued
5:23 upon this people, and you have not rescued your **people** at all."
6: 7 I will take you as my own **people**, and I will be your God.
7: 4 of judgment I will bring out my divisions, my **people** the Israelites.
7:14 "Pharaoh's heart is unyielding; he refuses to let the **people** go.
7:16 Let my **people** go, so that they may worship me in the desert.
8: 1 [7:26] Let my **people** go, so that they may worship me.
8: 3 [7:28] into the houses of your officials and on your **people**,
8: 4 [7:29] will go up on you and your **people** and all your officials.' "
8: 8 [8:4] the LORD to take the frogs away from me and my **people**,
8: 8 [8:4] I will let your **people** go to offer sacrifices to the LORD."
8: 9 [8:5] your officials and your **people** that you and your houses may
8:11 [8:7] leave you and your houses, your officials and your **people**;
8:20 [8:16] Let my **people** go, so that they may worship me.
8:21 [8:17] If you do not let my **people** go, I will send swarms of flies
8:21 [8:17] and your officials, on your **people** and into your houses.
8:22 [8:18] differently with the land of Goshen, where my **people** live;
8:23 [8:19] I will make a distinction between my **people** and your
8:23 [8:19] make a distinction between my people and your **people**.
8:29 [8:25] flies will leave Pharaoh and his officials and his **people**.
8:29 [8:25] not letting the **people** go to offer sacrifices to the LORD."
8:31 [8:27] The flies left Pharaoh and his officials and his **people**;
8:32 [8:28] hardened his heart and would not let the **people** go.
9: 1 says: "Let my **people** go, so that they may worship me."
9: 7 Yet his heart was unyielding and he would not let the **people** go.
9:13 says: Let my **people** go, so that they may worship me,
9:14 my plagues against you and against your officials and your **people**,
9:15 your **people** with a plague that would have wiped you off the earth.
9:17 You still set yourself against my **people** and will not let them go.
9:27 "The LORD is in the right, and I and my **people** are in the wrong.
10: 3 before me? Let my **people** go, so that they may worship me.
10: 4 If you refuse to let **them**[s] [+3276] go, I will bring locusts into your
11: 2 Tell the **people** that men and women alike are to ask their
11: 3 LORD made the Egyptians favorably disposed toward the **people**,
11: 3 highly regarded in Egypt by Pharaoh's officials and by the **people**.)
11: 8 and saying, 'Go, you and all the **people** who follow you!'
12:27 he struck down the Egyptians.' " Then the **people** bowed down
12:31 Leave my **people**, you and the Israelites! Go, worship the LORD
12:33 The Egyptians urged the **people** to hurry and leave the country.
12:34 So the **people** took their dough before the yeast was added,
12:36 had made the Egyptians favorably disposed toward the **people**,
13: 3 Moses said to the **people**, "Commemorate this day, the day you
13:17 When Pharaoh let the **people** go, God did not lead them on the
13:17 "If they face war, **they**[s] [+2021] might change their minds
13:18 So God led the **people** around by the desert road toward the Red
13:22 nor the pillar of fire by night left its place in front of the **people**.
14: 5 When the king of Egypt was told that the **people** had fled,
14: 5 and his officials changed their minds about **them**[s] [+2021]
14: 6 So he had his chariot made ready and took his **army** with him.
14:13 Moses answered the **people**, "Do not be afraid. Stand firm
14:31 the **people** feared the LORD and put their trust in him and in
15:13 "In your unfailing love you will lead the **people** you have
15:14 The **nations** will hear and tremble; anguish will grip the people of
15:16 until your **people** pass by, O LORD, until the people you bought
15:16 people pass by, O LORD, until the **people** you bought pass by.
15:24 So the **people** grumbled against Moses, saying, "What are we to
16: 4 The **people** are to go out each day and gather enough for that day.
16:27 some of the **people** went out on the seventh day to gather it,
16:30 So the **people** rested on the seventh day.
17: 1 at Rephidim, but there was no water for the **people** to drink.
17: 2 So **they**[s] [+2021] quarreled with Moses and said, "Give us water to
17: 3 the **people** were thirsty for water there, and they grumbled against
17: 3 thirsty for water there, and **they**[s] [+2021] grumbled against Moses.
17: 4 cried out to the LORD, "What am I to do with these **people**?
17: 5 The LORD answered Moses, "Walk on ahead of the **people**.
17: 6 the rock, and water will come out of it for the **people** to drink."
17:13 So Joshua overcame the Amalekite **army** with the sword.
18: 1 of everything God had done for Moses and for his **people** Israel,
18:10 and who rescued the **people** from the hand of the Egyptians.
18:13 The next day Moses took his seat to serve as judge for the **people**,
18:13 and **they**[s] [+2021] stood around him from morning till evening.
18:14 his father-in-law saw all that Moses was doing for the **people**,
18:14 for the people, he said, "What is this you are doing for the **people**?
18:14 while all these **people** stand around you from morning till
18:15 "Because the **people** come to me to seek God's will.
18:18 and these **people** who come to you will only wear yourselves out.
18:19 You must be the **people's** [+4200] representative before God
18:21 But select capable men from all the **people**—men who fear God,
18:22 Have them serve as judges for the **people** at all times, but have
18:23 to stand the strain, and all these **people** will go home satisfied."
18:25 capable men from all Israel and made them leaders of the **people**,
18:26 They served as judges for the **people** at all times. The difficult
19: 5 then out of all **nations** you will be my treasured possession.
19: 7 So Moses went back and summoned the elders of the **people**
19: 8 The **people** all responded together, "We will do everything the
19: 8 So Moses brought **their**[s] [+2021] answer back to the LORD.
19: 9 so that the **people** will hear me speaking with you and will always
19: 9 in you." Then Moses told the LORD what the **people** had said.
19:10 "Go to the **people** and consecrate them today and tomorrow.
19:11 will come down on Mount Sinai in the sight of all the **people**.
19:12 Put limits for the **people** around the mountain and tell them,
19:14 After Moses had gone down the mountain to the **people**, he
19:14 he consecrated **them**[s] [+2021], and they washed their clothes.
19:15 Then he said to the **people**, "Prepare yourselves for the third day.
19:16 loud trumpet blast. **Everyone** [+2021+3972] in the camp trembled.
19:17 Then Moses led the **people** out of the camp to meet with God,
19:21 "Go down and warn the **people** so they do not force their way
19:23 said to the LORD, "The **people** cannot come up Mount Sinai,
19:24 the **people** must not force their way through to come up to the
19:25 So Moses went down to the **people** and told them.
20:18 When the **people** saw the thunder and lightning and heard the
20:18 and saw the mountain in smoke, **they**[s] [+2021] trembled with fear.
20:20 Moses said to the **people**, "Do not be afraid. God has come to test
20:21 The **people** remained at a distance, while Moses approached the
21: 8 He has no right to sell her to **foreigners** [+5799], because he has
22:25 [22:24] "If you lend money to one of my **people** among you who
22:28 [22:27] "Do not blaspheme God or curse the ruler of your **people**.
23:11 the poor among your **people** may get food from it, and the wild
23:27 of you and throw into confusion every **nation** you encounter.
24: 2 must not come near. And the **people** may not come up with him."
24: 3 Moses went and told the **people** all the LORD's words and laws,
24: 3 and laws, **they**[s] [+2021] responded with one voice,
24: 7 Then he took the Book of the Covenant and read it to the **people**.
24: 8 Moses then took the blood, sprinkled it on the **people** and said,
30:33 it on anyone other than a priest must be cut off from his **people**.' "
30:38 any like it to enjoy its fragrance must be cut off from his **people**."
31:14 does any work on that day must be cut off from his **people**.
32: 1 When the **people** saw that Moses was so long in coming down
32: 1 so long in coming down from the mountain, **they**[s] [+2021]
32: 3 So all the **people** took off their earrings and brought them to
32: 6 So the next day the **people** rose early and sacrificed burnt offerings
32: 7 Then the LORD said to Moses, "Go down, because your **people**,
32: 9 "I have seen these **people**," the LORD said to Moses, "and they
32: 9 the LORD said to Moses, "and they are a stiff-necked **people**.
32:11 he said, "why should your anger burn against your **people**,
32:12 your fierce anger; relent and do not bring disaster on your **people**.
32:14 and did not bring on his **people** the disaster he had threatened.
32:17 When Joshua heard the noise of the **people** shouting, he said to
32:21 He said to Aaron, "What did these **people** do to you, that you led
32:22 Aaron answered. "You know how prone these **people** are to evil.
32:25 Moses saw that the **people** were running wild and that Aaron had
32:28 and that day about three thousand of the **people** died.
32:30 The next day Moses said to the **people**, "You have committed a
32:31 and said, "Oh, what a great sin these **people** have committed!
32:34 Now go, lead the **people** to the place I spoke of, and my angel will
32:35 the LORD struck the **people** with a plague because of what they
33: 1 "Leave this place, you and the **people** you brought up out of Egypt,
33: 3 because you are a stiff-necked **people** and I might destroy you on
33: 4 When the **people** heard these distressing words, they began to
33: 5 said to Moses, "Tell the Israelites, 'You are a stiff-necked **people**.
33: 8 all the **people** rose and stood at the entrances to their tents,
33:10 Whenever the **people** saw the pillar of cloud standing at the
33:10 pillar of cloud standing at the entrance to the tent, **they**[s] [+2021]
33:12 to the LORD, "You have been telling me, 'Lead these **people**,'
33:13 to find favor with you. Remember that this nation is your **people**."

Ex 33:16 are pleased with me and with your **people** unless you go with us?
33:16 and your **people** from all the other people on the face of the earth?"
33:16 and your people from all the other **people** on the face of the earth?"
34: 9 Although this is a stiff-necked **people**, forgive our wickedness
34:10 Before all your **people** I will do wonders never before done in any
34:10 The **people** you live among will see how awesome is the work that
36: 5 "The **people** are bringing more than enough for doing the work the
36: 6 And so the **people** were restrained from bringing more,
Lev 4: 3 " 'If the anointed priest sins, bringing guilt on the **people**,
4:27 " 'If a member of the **community** [+824+2021] sins unintentionally
7:20 to the LORD, that person must be cut off from his **people**.
7:21 to the LORD, that person must be cut off from his **people**.' "
7:25 fire may be made to the LORD must be cut off from his **people**.
7:27 anyone eats blood, that person must be cut off from his **people**.' "
9: 7 burnt offering and make atonement for yourself and the **people**;
9: 7 sacrifice the offering that is for the **people** and make atonement for
9:15 Aaron then brought the offering that was for the **people**. He took
9:15 He took the goat for the **people's** sin offering and slaughtered it
9:18 the ox and the ram as the fellowship offering for the **people**.
9:22 Then Aaron lifted his hands toward the **people** and blessed them.
9:23 When they came out, they blessed the **people**; and the glory of the
9:23 the people; and the glory of the LORD appeared to all the **people**.
9:24 when all the **people** saw it, they shouted for joy and fell facedown.
10: 3 in the sight of all the **people** I will be honored.' " Aaron remained
16:15 "He shall then slaughter the goat for the sin offering for the **people**
16:24 the burnt offering for himself and the burnt offering for the **people**,
16:24 for the people, to make atonement for himself and for the **people**.
16:33 the altar, and for the priests and all the **people** *of* the community.
17: 4 he has shed blood and must be cut off from his **people**.
17: 9 it to the LORD—that man must be cut off from his **people**.
17:10 that person who eats blood and will cut him off from his **people**.
18:29 detestable things—such persons must be cut off from their **people**.
19: 8 is holy to the LORD; that person must be cut off from his **people**.
19:16 " 'Do not go about spreading slander among your **people**. " 'Do not
19:18 not seek revenge or bear a grudge against one of your **people**,
20: 2 be put to death. The **people** *of* the community are to stone him.
20: 3 my face against that man and I will cut him off from his **people**;
20: 4 If the **people** *of* the community close their eyes when that man
20: 5 and his family and will cut off from their **people** both him
20: 6 himself by following them, and I will cut him off from his **people**.
20:17 They must be cut off before the eyes of their **people** [+1201].
20:18 also uncovered it. Both of them must be cut off from their **people**.
20:24 am the LORD your God, who has set you apart from the **nations**.
20:26 am holy, and I have set you apart from the **nations** to be my own.
21: 1 make himself ceremonially unclean for any of his **people** who die,
21: 4 He must not make himself unclean for **people** related to him by
21:14 defiled by prostitution, but only a virgin from his own **people**,
21:15 so he will not defile his offspring among his **people**. I am the
23:29 does not deny himself on that day must be cut off from his **people**.
23:30 I will destroy from among his **people** anyone who does any work
26:12 will walk among you and be your God, and you will be my **people**.
Nu 5:21 "may the LORD cause your **people** to curse and denounce you
5:27 waste away, and she will become accursed among her **people**.
9:13 that person must be cut off from his **people** because he did not
11: 1 Now the **people** complained about their hardships in the hearing of
11: 2 When the **people** cried out to Moses, he prayed to the LORD
11: 8 The **people** went around gathering it, and then ground it in a
11:10 Moses heard the **people** of every family wailing, each at the
11:11 to displease you that you put the burden of all these **people** on me?
11:12 Did I conceive all these **people**? Did I give them birth? Why do
11:13 Where can I get meat for all these **people**? They keep wailing to
11:14 I cannot carry all these **people** by myself; the burden is too heavy
11:16 who are known to you as leaders and officials among the **people**.
11:17 They will help you carry the burden of the **people** so that you will
11:18 "Tell the **people**: 'Consecrate yourselves in preparation for
11:21 "Here I am among six hundred thousand **men** on foot, and you say,
11:24 So Moses went out and told the **people** what the LORD had said.
11:24 He brought together seventy of **their**[s] [+2021] elders and had them
11:29 I wish that all the LORD's **people** were prophets and that the
11:32 All that day and night and all the next day the **people** went out
11:33 be consumed, the anger of the LORD burned against the **people**,
11:33 the people, and he struck **them**[s] [+2021] with a severe plague.
11:34 because there they buried the **people** who had craved other food.
11:35 From Kibroth Hattaavah the **people** traveled to Hazeroth
12:15 and the **people** did not move on till she was brought back.
12:16 the **people** left Hazeroth and encamped in the Desert of Paran.
13:18 and whether the **people** who live there are strong or weak,
13:28 the **people** who live there are powerful, and the cities are fortified
13:30 Caleb silenced the **people** before Moses and said, "We should go
13:31 who had gone up with him said, "We can't attack those **people**;
13:32 those living in it. All the **people** we saw there are of great size.
14: 1 That night all the **people** of the community raised their voices
14: 9 do not be afraid of the **people** *of* the land, because we will swallow
14:11 to Moses, "How long will these **people** treat me with contempt?
14:13 By your power you brought these **people** up from among them.
14:14 O LORD, are with these **people** and that you, O LORD,
14:15 If you put these **people** to death all at one time, the nations who
14:16 'The LORD was not able to bring these **people** into the land he
14:19 In accordance with your great love, forgive the sin of these **people**,
14:19 just as you have pardoned **them**[s] [+2021+2021+2296] from the
14:39 When Moses reported this to all the Israelites, **they**[s] [+2021]
15:26 because all the **people** were involved in the unintentional wrong.
15:30 the LORD, and that person must be cut off from his **people**.
16:41 [17:6] "You have killed the LORD's **people**," they said.
16:47 [17:12] The plague had already started among the **people**,
16:47 [17:12] the incense and made atonement for **them**[s] [+2021].
20: 1 arrived at the Desert of Zin, and **they**[s] [+2021] stayed at Kadesh.
20: 3 **They**[s] [+2021] quarreled with Moses and said, "If only we had
20:20 Edom came out against them with a large and powerful **army**.
20:24 "Aaron will be gathered to his **people**. He will not enter the land I
21: 2 "If you will deliver these **people** into our hands, we will totally
21: 4 to go around Edom. But the **people** grew impatient on the way;
21: 5 **they**[s] [+2021] spoke against God and against Moses, and said,
21: 6 Then the LORD sent venomous snakes among **them**[s] [+2021];
21: 6 snakes among them; they bit the **people** and many Israelites died.
21: 6 among them; they bit the people and many **[RPH]** Israelites died.
21: 7 The **people** came to Moses and said, "We sinned when we spoke
21: 7 take the snakes away from us." So Moses prayed for the **people**.
21:16 to Moses, "Gather the **people** together and I will give them water."
21:18 the well that the princes dug, that the nobles of the **people** sank—
21:23 He mustered his entire **army** and marched out into the desert
21:29 Woe to you, O Moab! You are destroyed, O **people** *of* Chemosh!
21:33 and his whole **army** marched out to meet them in battle at Edrei.
21:34 I have handed him over to you, with his whole **army** and his land.
21:35 they struck him down, together with his sons and his whole **army**,
22: 3 and Moab was terrified because there were so many **people**.
22: 5 who was at Pethor, near the River, in his **native** [+1201] land.
22: 5 "A **people** has come out of Egypt; they cover the face of the land
22: 6 Now come and put a curse on these **people**, because they are too
22:11 'A **people** that has come out of Egypt covers the face of the land.
22:12 You must not put a curse on those **people**, because they are
22:17 whatever you say. Come and put a curse on these **people** for me."
22:41 up to Bamoth Baal, and from there he saw part of the **people**.
23: 9 I see a **people** who live apart and do not consider themselves one
23:24 The **people** rise like a lioness; they rouse themselves like a lion
24:14 Now I am going back to my **people**, but come, let me warn you of
24:14 let me warn you of what this **people** will do to your people in days
24:14 let me warn you of what this people will do to your **people** in days
25: 1 the **men** began to indulge in sexual immorality with Moabite
25: 2 who invited **them**[s] [+2021] to the sacrifices to their gods.
25: 2 to their gods. The **people** ate and bowed down before these gods.
25: 4 "Take all the leaders of these **people**, kill them and expose them in
27:13 After you have seen it, you too will be gathered to your **people**,
31: 2 for the Israelites. After that, you will be gathered to your **people**."
31: 3 So Moses said to the **people**, "Arm some of your men to go to war
31:32 The plunder remaining from the spoils that the **soldiers** [+7372]
32:15 following him, he will again leave all this **people** in the desert,
33:14 at Rephidim, where there was no water for the **people** to drink.
Dt 1:28 They say, 'The **people** are stronger and taller than we are;
2: 4 Give the **people** these orders: 'You are about to pass through the
2:10 a **people** strong and numerous, and as tall as the Anakites.
2:16 Now when the last of these fighting men among the **people** had
2:21 They were a **people** strong and numerous, and as tall as the
2:25 to put the terror and fear of you on all the **nations** under heaven.
2:32 and all his **army** came out to meet us in battle at Jahaz,
2:33 we struck him down, together with his sons and his whole **army**.
3: 1 Og king of Bashan with his whole **army** marched out to meet us in
3: 2 for I have handed him over to you with his whole **army** and his
3: 3 God also gave into our hands Og king of Bashan and all his **army**.
3:28 for he will lead this **people** across and will cause them to inherit
4: 6 for this will show your wisdom and understanding to the **nations**,
4: 6 "Surely this great nation is a wise and understanding **people**."
4:10 "Assemble the **people** before me to hear my words so that they
4:19 LORD your God has apportioned to all the **nations** under heaven.
4:20 out of Egypt, to be the **people** *of* his inheritance, as you now are.
4:27 The LORD will scatter you among the **peoples**, and only a few of
4:33 Has any other **people** heard the voice of God speaking out of fire,
5:28 the LORD said to me, "I have heard what this **people** said to you.
6:14 Do not follow other gods, the gods of the **peoples** around you;
7: 6 For you are a **people** holy to the LORD your God. The LORD
7: 6 The LORD your God has chosen you out of all the **peoples** on the
7: 6 you out of all the peoples on the face of the earth to be his **people**,
7: 7 choose you because you were more numerous than other **peoples**,
7: 7 than other peoples, for you were the fewest of all **peoples**.
7:14 You will be blessed more than any other **people**; none of your men
7:16 You must destroy all the **peoples** the LORD your God gives over
7:19 The LORD your God will do the same to all the **peoples** you now
9: 2 The **people** are strong and tall—Anakites! You know about them

Dt 9: 6 you this good land to possess, for you are a stiff-necked **people**.
9: 12 because your **people** whom you brought out of Egypt have become
9: 13 the LORD said to me, "I have seen this **people**, and they are a
9: 13 "I have seen this people, and they are a stiff-necked **people** indeed!
9: 26 and said, "O Sovereign LORD, do not destroy your **people**,
9: 27 Overlook the stubbornness of this **people**, their wickedness
9: 29 they are your **people**, your inheritance that you brought out by
10: 11 "and lead the **people** on their way, so that they may enter
10: 15 chose you, their descendants, above all the **nations**, as it is today.
13: 7 [13:8] gods of the **peoples** around you, whether near or far, from
13: 9 [13:10] putting him to death, and then the hands of all the **people**.
14: 2 for you are a **people** holy to the LORD your God. Out of all the
14: 2 Out of all the **peoples** on the face of the earth, the LORD has
14: 2 LORD has chosen you to be his treasured possession. **[RPH]**
14: 21 to a foreigner. But you are a **people** holy to the LORD your God.
16: 18 your God is giving you, and they shall judge the **people** fairly.
17: 7 first in putting him to death, and then the hands of all the **people**.
17: 13 All the **people** will hear and be afraid, and will not be
17: 16 or make the **people** return to Egypt to get more of them,
18: 3 This is the share due the priests from the **people** who sacrifice a
20: 1 and see horses and chariots and an **army** greater than yours,
20: 2 go into battle, the priest shall come forward and address the **army**.
20: 5 The officers shall say to the **army**: "Has anyone built a new house
20: 8 the officers shall add, **[RPH]** "Is any man afraid or fainthearted?
20: 9 When the officers have finished speaking to the **army**, they shall
20: 9 to the army, they shall appoint commanders over **it**[s] [+2021].
20: 11 all the **people** in it shall be subject to forced labor and shall work
20: 16 in the cities of the **nations** the LORD your God is giving you as
21: 8 Accept this atonement for your **people** Israel, whom you have
21: 8 do not hold your **people** guilty of the blood of an innocent man."
26: 15 bless your **people** Israel and the land you have given us as you
26: 18 And the LORD has declared this day that you are his **people**,
26: 19 and that you will be a **people** holy to the LORD your God,
27: 1 Moses and the elders of Israel commanded the **people**: "Keep all
27: 9 You have now become the **people** of the LORD your God.
27: 11 On the same day Moses commanded the **people**:
27: 12 these tribes shall stand on Mount Gerizim to bless the **people**:
27: 15 and sets it up in secret." Then all the **people** shall say, "Amen!"
27: 16 his father or his mother." Then all the **people** shall say, "Amen!"
27: 17 boundary stone." Then all the **people** shall say, "Amen!"
27: 18 blind astray on the road." Then all the **people** shall say, "Amen!"
27: 19 or the widow." Then all the **people** shall say, "Amen!"
27: 20 dishonors his father's bed." Then all the **people** shall say, "Amen!"
27: 21 relations with any animal." Then all the **people** shall say, "Amen!"
27: 22 daughter of his mother." Then all the **people** shall say, "Amen!"
27: 23 with his mother-in-law." Then all the **people** shall say, "Amen!"
27: 24 kills his neighbor secretly." Then all the **people** shall say, "Amen!"
27: 25 to kill an innocent person." Then all the **people** shall say, "Amen!"
27: 26 law by carrying them out." Then all the **people** shall say, "Amen!"
28: 9 The LORD will establish you as his holy **people**, as he promised
28: 10 all the **peoples** *on* earth will see that you are called by the name of
28: 32 Your sons and daughters will be given to another **nation**, and you
28: 33 A **people** that you do not know will eat what your land and labor
28: 37 and ridicule to all the **nations** where the LORD will drive you.
28: 64 the LORD will scatter you among all **nations**, from one end of
29: 13 [29:12] to confirm you this day as his **people**, that he may be your
30: 3 and gather you again from all the **nations** where he scattered you.
31: 7 for you must go with this **people** into the land that the LORD
31: 12 Assemble the **people**—men, women and children, and the aliens
31: 16 these **people** will soon prostitute themselves to the foreign gods of
32: 6 this the way you repay the LORD, O foolish and unwise **people**?
32: 8 he set up boundaries for the **peoples** according to the number of
32: 9 For the LORD's portion is his **people**, Jacob his allotted
32: 21 I will make them envious by those who are not a **people**; I will
32: 36 The LORD will judge his **people** and have compassion on his
32: 43 Rejoice, O nations, with his **people**, for he will avenge the blood of
32: 43 on his enemies and make atonement for his land and **people**.
32: 44 and spoke all the words of this song in the hearing of the **people**.
32: 50 that you have climbed you will die and be gathered to your **people**,
32: 50 brother Aaron died on Mount Hor and was gathered to his **people**.
33: 3 Surely it is you who love the **people**; all the holy ones are in your
33: 5 He was king over Jeshurun when the leaders of the **people**
33: 7 "Hear, O LORD, the cry of Judah; bring him to his **people**.
33: 17 With them he will gore the **nations**, even those at the ends of the
33: 19 They will summon **peoples** to the mountain and there offer
33: 21 When the heads of the **people** assembled, he carried out the
33: 29 O Israel! Who is like you, a **people** saved by the LORD?
Jos 1: 2 Now then, you and all these **people**, get ready to cross the Jordan
1: 6 because you will lead these **people** to inherit the land I swore to
1: 10 So Joshua ordered the officers of the **people**:
1: 11 "Go through the camp and tell the **people**, 'Get your supplies
3: 3 giving orders to the **people**: "When you see the ark of the covenant
3: 5 Joshua told the **people**, "Consecrate yourselves, for tomorrow the
3: 6 "Take up the ark of the covenant and pass on ahead of the **people**."
3: 6 the people." So they took it up and went ahead of **them**[s] [+2021].
3: 14 So when the **people** broke camp to cross the Jordan, the priests
3: 14 carrying the ark of the covenant went ahead of **them**[s] [+2021].
3: 16 completely cut off. So the **people** crossed over opposite Jericho.
4: 2 "Choose twelve men from among the **people**, one from each tribe,
4: 10 the LORD had commanded Joshua was done by the **people**,
4: 10 just as Moses had directed Joshua. The **people** hurried over,
4: 11 as soon as all of **them**[s] [+2021] had crossed, the ark of the LORD
4: 11 and the priests came to the other side while the **people** watched.
4: 19 On the tenth day of the first month the **people** went up from the
4: 24 so that all the **peoples** *of* the earth might know that the hand of the
5: 4 All **those**[s] [+2021] who came out of Egypt—all the men of
5: 5 All the **people** that came out had been circumcised, but all the
5: 5 all the **people** born in the desert during the journey from Egypt had
6: 5 a long blast on the trumpets, have all the **people** give a loud shout;
6: 5 then the wall of the city will collapse and the **people** will go up,
6: 7 And he ordered the **people**, "Advance! March around the city,
6: 8 When Joshua had spoken to the **people**, the seven priests carrying
6: 10 But Joshua had commanded the **people**, "Do not give a war cry,
6: 16 sounded the trumpet blast, Joshua commanded the **people**, "Shout!
6: 20 When the trumpets sounded, the **people** shouted, and at the sound
6: 20 the people shouted, and at **[RPH]** the sound of the trumpet,
6: 20 the trumpet, when the **people** gave a loud shout, the wall collapsed;
6: 20 so every **man** charged straight in, and they took the city.
7: 3 they said, "Not all the **people** will have to go up against Ai.
7: 3 or three thousand men to take it and do not weary all the **people**,
7: 4 men went up; **[RPH]** but they were routed by the men of Ai,
7: 5 At this the hearts of the **people** melted and became like water.
7: 7 why did you ever bring this **people** across the Jordan to deliver us
7: 13 "Go, consecrate the **people**. Tell them, 'Consecrate yourselves in
8: 1 Take the whole **army** [+4878] with you, and go up and attack Ai.
8: 1 into your hands the king of Ai, his **people**, his city and his land.
8: 3 So Joshua and the whole **army** [+4878] moved out to attack Ai.
8: 5 I and all **those**[s] [+2021] with me will advance on the city,
8: 9 to the west of Ai—but Joshua spent that night with the **people**.
8: 10 Early the next morning Joshua mustered his **men**, and he
8: 10 and the leaders of Israel marched before **them**[s] [+2021] to Ai.
8: 11 The entire **force** [+4878] that was with him marched up
8: 13 They had the **soldiers** take up their positions—all those in the
8: 14 all the men of **[RPH]** the city hurried out early in the morning to
8: 16 All the **men** of Ai were called to pursue them, and they pursued
8: 20 for the **Israelites**[s] who had been fleeing toward the desert had
8: 33 when he gave instructions to bless the **people** *of* Israel.
10: 7 So Joshua marched up from Gilgal with his entire **army** [+4878],
10: 21 The whole **army** then returned safely to Joshua in the camp at
10: 33 come up to help Lachish, but Joshua defeated him and his **army**—
11: 4 a huge **army**, as numerous as the sand on the seashore.
11: 7 his whole **army** [+4878] came against them suddenly at the Waters
14: 8 my brothers who went up with me made the hearts of the **people**
17: 14 We are a numerous **people** and the LORD has blessed us
17: 15 "If you are so **[RPH]** numerous," Joshua answered, "and if the
17: 17 and Manasseh—"You are numerous **[RPH]** and very powerful.
24: 2 Joshua said to all the **people**, "This is what the LORD, the God of
24: 16 the **people** answered, "Far be it from us to forsake the LORD to
24: 17 and among all the **nations** through which we traveled.
24: 18 the LORD drove out before us all the **nations**, including the
24: 19 Joshua said to the **people**, "You are not able to serve the LORD.
24: 21 But the **people** said to Joshua, "No! We will serve the LORD."
24: 22 **[RPH]** "You are witnesses against yourselves that you have
24: 24 the **people** said to Joshua, "We will serve the LORD our God
24: 25 On that day Joshua made a covenant for the **people**, and there at
24: 27 "See!" he said to all the **people**. "This stone will be a witness
24: 28 Then Joshua sent the **people** away, each to his own inheritance.
Jdg 1: 16 among the **people** of the Desert of Judah in the Negev near Arad.
2: 4 had spoken these things to all the Israelites, the **people** wept aloud,
2: 6 After Joshua had dismissed the Israelites, **they**[s] [+2021] went to
2: 7 The **people** served the LORD throughout the lifetime of Joshua
2: 12 and worshiped various gods of the **peoples** around them.
3: 18 the tribute, he sent on their way the **men** who had carried it.
4: 13 together his nine hundred iron chariots and all the **men** with him,
5: 2 Israel take the lead, when the **people** willingly offer themselves—
5: 9 Israel's princes, with the willing volunteers among the **people**.
5: 11 "Then the **people** *of* the LORD went down to the city gates.
5: 13 the nobles; the **people** *of* the LORD came to me with the mighty.
5: 14 were in Amalek; Benjamin was with the **people** who followed you.
5: 18 The **people** of Zebulun risked their very lives; so did Naphtali on
7: 1 (that is, Gideon) and all his **men** camped at the spring of Harod.
7: 2 "You have too many **men** for me to deliver Midian into their
7: 3 announce now to the **people**, 'Anyone who trembles with fear may
7: 3 and leave Mount Gilead.' " So twenty-two thousand **men** left,
7: 4 But the LORD said to Gideon, "There are still too many **men**.
7: 5 So Gideon took the **men** down to the water. There the LORD told
7: 6 their mouths. All the rest **[RPH]** got down on their knees to drink.
7: 7 into your hands. Let all the other **men** go, each to his own place."

[F] Hitpael (hitpoel, hitpoal, hitpolel, hitpolal, hitpalel, hitpalal, hitpalpel, hitpalpal, hotpael, hotpaal) [G] Hiphil (hiphtil) [H] Hophal [I] Hishtaphel

Jdg 7: 8 who took over the provisions and trumpets of the **others**[s].
8: 5 He said to the men of Succoth, "Give my **troops** some bread;
9: 29 If only this **people** were under my command! Then I would get rid
9: 32 during the night you and your **men** should come and lie in wait in
9: 33 When Gaal and his **men** come out against you, do whatever your
9: 34 So Abimelech and all his **troops** set out by night and took up
9: 35 as Abimelech and his **soldiers** came out from their hiding place.
9: 36 When Gaal saw **them**[s] [+2021], he said to Zebul, "Look,
9: 36 **people** are coming down from the tops of the mountains!"
9: 37 "Look, **people** are coming down from the center of the land,
9: 38 Aren't these the **men** you ridiculed? Go out and fight them!"
9: 42 The next day the **people** of Shechem went out to the fields,
9: 43 So he took his **men**, divided them into three companies and set an
9: 43 When he saw the **people** coming out of the city, he rose to attack
9: 45 attack against the city until he had captured it and killed its **people**.
9: 48 he and all his **men** went up Mount Zalmon. He took an ax
9: 48 he lifted to his shoulders. He ordered the **men** with him, "Quick!
9: 49 So all the **men** cut branches and followed Abimelech. They piled
10: 18 The leaders of the **people** of Gilead said to each other, "Whoever
11: 11 and the **people** made him head and commander over them.
11: 20 He mustered all his **men** and encamped at Jahaz and fought with
11: 21 the God of Israel, gave Sihon and all his **men** into Israel's hands,
11: 23 God of Israel, has driven the Amorites out before his **people** Israel,
12: 2 my **people** were engaged in a great struggle with the Ammonites,
14: 3 acceptable woman among your relatives or among all our **people**?
14: 16 You've given my **people** [+1201] a riddle, but you haven't told me
14: 17 press him. She in turn explained the riddle to her **people** [+1201].
16: 24 When the **people** saw him, they praised their god, saying,
16: 30 and down came the temple on the rulers and all the **people** in it.
18: 7 where they saw that the **people** were living in safety, like the
18: 10 you will find an unsuspecting **people** and a spacious land that God
18: 20 and the carved image and went along with the **people**.
18: 27 and went on to Laish, against a peaceful and unsuspecting **people**.
20: 2 The leaders of all the **people** *of* the tribes of Israel took their places
20: 2 of Israel took their places in the assembly of the **people** *of* God,
20: 8 All the **people** rose as one man, saying, "None of us will go home.
20: 10 and a thousand from ten thousand, to get provisions for the **army**.
20: 16 Among all these **soldiers** there were seven hundred chosen men
20: 22 the men of Israel encouraged **one another** [+2021] and again took
20: 26 the Israelites, all the **people**, went up to Bethel, and there they sat
20: 31 The Benjamites came out to meet **them**[s] [+2021] and were drawn
20: 31 They began to inflict casualties on the **Israelites**[s] as before,
21: 2 The **people** went to Bethel, where they sat before God until
21: 4 Early the next day the **people** built an altar and presented burnt
21: 9 For when they counted the **people**, they found that none of the
21: 15 The **people** grieved for Benjamin, because the LORD had made a
Ru 1: 6 had come to the aid of his **people** by providing food for them,
1: 10 and said to her, "We will go back with you to your **people**."
1: 15 "your sister-in-law is going back to her **people** and her gods.
1: 16 I will stay. Your **people** will be my people and your God my God.
1: 16 I will stay. Your people will be my **people** and your God my God.
2: 11 and came to live with a **people** you did not know before.
3: 11 All my **fellow townsmen** [+9133] know that you are a woman of
4: 4 of these seated here and in the presence of the elders of my **people**.
4: 9 Boaz announced to the elders and all the **people**, "Today you are
4: 11 the elders and all **those**[s] [+2021] at the gate said, "We are
1Sa 2: 13 Now it was the practice of the priests with the **people** that
2: 23 I hear from all the **people** about these wicked deeds of yours.
2: 24 a good report that I hear spreading among the LORD's **people**.
2: 29 on the choice parts of every offering made by my **people** Israel?'
4: 3 When the **soldiers** returned to camp, the elders of Israel asked,
4: 4 So the **people** sent men to Shiloh, and they brought back the ark of
4: 17 fled before the Philistines, and the **army** has suffered heavy losses.
5: 10 the ark of the god of Israel around to us to kill us and our **people**."
5: 11 let it go back to its own place, or it will kill us and our **people**."
6: 19 putting seventy of **them**[s] [+2021] to death because they had looked
6: 19 The **people** mourned because of the heavy blow the LORD had
6: 19 because of the heavy blow the LORD had dealt **them**[s] [+2021],
8: 7 "Listen to all that the **people** are saying to you; it is not you they
8: 10 Samuel told all the words of the LORD to the **people** who were
8: 19 But the **people** refused to listen to Samuel. "No!" they said.
8: 21 When Samuel heard all that the **people** said, he repeated it before
9: 2 equal among the Israelites—a head taller than any of the **others**[s].
9: 12 to our town today, for the **people** have a sacrifice at the high place.
9: 13 The **people** will not begin eating until he comes, because he must
9: 16 Anoint him leader over my **people** Israel; he will deliver my
9: 16 he will deliver my **people** from the hand of the Philistines.
9: 16 I have looked upon my **people**, for their cry has reached me."
9: 17 "This is the man I spoke to you about; he will govern my **people**."
9: 24 'I have invited **guests**.' " And Saul dined with Samuel that day.
10: 11 known him saw him prophesying with the prophets, **they**[s] [+2021]
10: 17 Samuel summoned the **people** of Israel to the LORD at Mizpah
10: 23 as he stood among the **people** he was a head taller than any of the
10: 23 among the people he was a head taller than any of the **others**[s].
10: 24 Samuel said to all the **people**, "Do you see the man the LORD
10: 24 There is no one like him among all the **people**." Then the people
10: 24 all the people." Then the **people** shouted, "Long live the king!"
10: 25 Samuel explained to the **people** the regulations of the kingship.
10: 25 Then Samuel dismissed the **people**, each to his own home.
11: 4 came to Gibeah of Saul and reported these terms to the **people**,
11: 4 reported these terms to the people, **they**[s] [+2021] all wept aloud.
11: 5 behind his oxen, and he asked, "What is wrong with the **people**?
11: 7 the terror of the LORD fell on the **people**, and they turned out as
11: 11 The next day Saul separated his **men** into three divisions; during
11: 12 The **people** then said to Samuel, "Who was it that asked,
11: 14 Then Samuel said to the **people**, "Come, let us go to Gilgal
11: 15 So all the **people** went to Gilgal and confirmed Saul as king in the
12: 6 Samuel said to the **people**, "It is the LORD who appointed Moses
12: 18 So all the **people** stood in awe of the LORD and of Samuel.
12: 19 The **people** all said to Samuel, "Pray to the LORD your God for
12: 20 **[RPH]** "You have done all this evil; yet do not turn away from
12: 22 the sake of his great name the LORD will not reject his **people**,
12: 22 because the LORD was pleased to make you his own. **[RPH]**
13: 2 in Benjamin. The rest of the **men** he sent back to their homes.
13: 4 And the **people** were summoned to join Saul at Gilgal.
13: 5 and **soldiers** as numerous as the sand on the seashore.
13: 6 their situation was critical and that their **army** was hard pressed,
13: 6 and that their army was hard pressed, **they**[s] [+2021] hid in caves
13: 7 at Gilgal, and all the **troops** with him were quaking with fear.
13: 8 Samuel did not come to Gilgal, and Saul's **men** began to scatter.
13: 11 Saul replied, "When I saw that the **men** were scattering, and that
13: 14 a man after his own heart and appointed him leader of his **people**,
13: 15 in Benjamin, and Saul counted the **men** who were with him.
13: 16 and the **men** with them were staying in Gibeah in Benjamin,
13: 22 So on the day of the battle not a **soldier** with Saul and Jonathan
14: 2 tree in Migron. **[RPH]** With him were about six hundred men,
14: 3 priest in Shiloh. No **one**[s] [+2021] was aware that Jonathan had left.
14: 15 Then panic struck the whole **army**—those in the camp and field,
14: 17 Then Saul said to the **men** who were with him, "Muster the forces
14: 20 Then Saul and all his **men** assembled and went to the battle.
14: 24 because Saul had bound the **people** under an oath, saying,
14: 24 myself on my enemies!" So none of the **troops** tasted food.
14: 26 When **they**[s] [+2021] went into the woods, they saw the honey
14: 26 put his hand to his mouth, because **they**[s] [+2021] feared the oath.
14: 27 Jonathan had not heard that his father had bound the **people** with
14: 28 one of the **soldiers** told him, "Your father bound the army under a
14: 28 told him, "Your father bound the **army** under a strict oath, saying,
14: 28 be any man who eats food today!' That is why the **men** are faint."
14: 30 How much better it would have been if the **men** had eaten today
14: 31 after the **Israelites**[s] had struck down the Philistines from Micmash
14: 32 **They**[s] [+2021] pounced on the plunder and, taking sheep,
14: 32 cattle and calves, **they**[s] [+2021] butchered them on the ground
14: 33 the **men** are sinning against the LORD by eating meat that has
14: 34 he said, "Go out among the **men** and tell them, 'Each of you bring
14: 34 still in it.' " So **everyone** [+2021+3972] brought his ox that night
14: 38 therefore said, "Come here, all you who are leaders of the **army**,
14: 39 son Jonathan, he must die." But not one of the **men** said a word.
14: 40 stand over here." "Do what seems best to you," the **men** replied.
14: 41 and Saul were taken by lot, and the **men** were cleared.
14: 45 the **men** said to Saul, "Should Jonathan die—he who has brought
14: 45 So the **men** rescued Jonathan, and he was not put to death.
15: 1 "I am the one the LORD sent to anoint you king over his **people**
15: 4 So Saul summoned the **men** and mustered them at Telaim—
15: 8 and all his **people** he totally destroyed with the sword.
15: 9 But Saul and the **army** spared Agag and the best of the sheep
15: 15 Saul answered, "The **soldiers** brought them from the Amalekites;
15: 21 The **soldiers** took sheep and cattle from the plunder, the best of
15: 24 I was afraid of the **people** and so I gave in to them.
15: 30 please honor me before the elders of my **people** and before Israel;
17: 27 They repeated to him what **they**[s] [+2021] had been saying
17: 30 brought up the same matter, and the **men** answered him as before.
18: 5 the army. This pleased all the **people**, and Saul's officers as well.
18: 13 over a thousand men, and David led the **troops** in their campaigns.
23: 8 Saul called up all his **forces** for battle, to go down to Keilah to
26: 5 was lying inside the camp, with the **army** encamped around him.
26: 7 So David and Abishai went to the **army** by night, and there was
26: 7 near his head. Abner and the **soldiers** were lying around him.
26: 14 He called out to the **army** and to Abner son of Ner, "Aren't you
26: 15 **Someone** [+285+2021] came to destroy your lord the king.
27: 12 to himself, "He has become so odious to his **people**, the Israelites,
30: 4 and his **men** wept aloud until they had no strength left to weep.
30: 6 greatly distressed because the **men** were talking of stoning him;
30: 6 each **[RPH]** one was bitter in spirit because of his sons and
30: 21 They came out to meet David and the **people** with him. As David
30: 21 with him. As David and his **men** approached, he greeted them.
31: 9 the news in the temple of their idols and among their **people**.
2Sa 1: 4 David asked. "Tell me." He said, "The **men** fled from the battle.
1: 4 Many of **them**[s] [+2021] fell and died. And Saul and his son

2Sa 1:12 and for the **army** *of* the LORD and the house of Israel,
2:26 How long before you order your **men** to stop pursuing their
2:27 the **men** would have continued the pursuit of their brothers until
2:28 So Joab blew the trumpet, and all the **men** came to a halt;
2:30 Joab returned from pursuing Abner and assembled all his **men**.
3:18 'By my servant David I will rescue my **people** Israel from the hand
3:31 David said to Joab and all the **people** with him, "Tear your clothes
3:32 and the king wept aloud at Abner's tomb. All the **people** wept also.
3:34 falls before wicked men." And all the **people** wept over him again.
3:35 **they**[s] [+2021] all came and urged David to eat something while it
3:36 All the **people** took note and were pleased; indeed, everything the
3:36 indeed, everything the king did pleased **them**[s] [+2021+3972].
3:37 So on that day all the **people** and all Israel knew that the king had
5: 2 And the LORD said to you, 'You will shepherd my **people** Israel,
5:12 and had exalted his kingdom for the sake of his **people** Israel.
6: 2 all his **men** set out from Baalah of Judah to bring up from there the
6:18 he blessed the **people** in the name of the LORD Almighty.
6:19 a cake of raisins to each **person** in the whole crowd of Israelites,
6:19 both men and women. And all the **people** went to their homes.
6:21 when he appointed me ruler over the LORD's **people** Israel—
7: 7 of their rulers whom I commanded to shepherd my **people** Israel,
7: 8 and from following the flock to be ruler over my **people** Israel.
7:10 And I will provide a place for my **people** Israel and will plant them
7:11 have done ever since the time I appointed leaders over my **people**
7:23 who is like your **people** Israel—the one nation on earth that God
7:23 the one nation on earth that God went out to redeem as a **people**
7:23 by driving out nations and their gods from before your **people**,
7:24 You have established your **people** Israel as your very own forever,
7:24 You have established your people Israel as your very own **[RPH]**
8:15 over all Israel, doing what was just and right for all his **people**.
10:10 He put the rest of the **men** under the command of Abishai his
10:12 Be strong and let us fight bravely for our **people** and the cities of
10:13 and the **troops** with him advanced to fight the Arameans,
11: 7 how Joab was, how the **soldiers** were and how the war was going.
11:17 and fought against Joab, some of the men in David's **army** fell;
12:28 Now muster the rest of the **troops** and besiege the city and capture
12:29 So David mustered the entire **army** and went to Rabbah,
12:31 brought out the **people** who were there, consigning them to labor
12:31 Then David and his entire **army** returned to Jerusalem.
13:34 watch looked up and saw many **people** on the road west of him,
14:13 then have you devised a thing like this against the **people** *of* God?
14:15 this to my lord the king because the **people** have made me afraid.
15:12 and Absalom's **following** [+907] kept on increasing.
15:17 So the king set out, with all the **people** following him, and they
15:23 The whole countryside wept aloud as all the **people** passed by.
15:23 the Kidron Valley, and all the **people** moved on toward the desert.
15:24 Abiathar offered sacrifices until all the **people** had finished leaving
15:30 All the **people** with him covered their heads too and were weeping
16: 6 though all the **troops** and the special guard were on David's right
16:14 and all the **people** with him arrived at their destination exhausted.
16:15 Meanwhile, Absalom and all the **men** *of* Israel came to Jerusalem,
16:18 by the LORD, by these **people**, and by all the men of Israel—
17: 2 strike him with terror, and then all the **people** with him will flee.
17: 3 bring all the **people** back to you. The death of the man you seek
17: 3 seek will mean the return of all; all the **people** will be unharmed."
17: 8 an experienced fighter; he will not spend the night with the **troops**.
17: 9 'There has been a slaughter among the **troops** who follow
17:16 or the king and all the **people** with him will be swallowed up.' "
17:22 So David and all the **people** with him set out and crossed the
17:29 and cheese from cows' milk for David and his **people** to eat.
17:29 "The **people** have become hungry and tired and thirsty in the
18: 1 David mustered the **men** who were with him and appointed over
18: 2 David sent the **troops** out—a third under the command of Joab,
18: 2 The king told the **troops**, "I myself will surely march out with
18: 3 But the **men** said, "You must not go out; if we are forced to flee,
18: 4 So the king stood beside the gate while all the **men** marched out in
18: 5 all the **troops** heard the king giving orders concerning Absalom to
18: 6 The **army** marched into the field to fight Israel, and the battle took
18: 7 There the **army** *of* Israel was defeated by David's men,
18: 8 and the forest claimed more **lives** that day than the sword.
18:16 and the **troops** stopped pursuing Israel, for Joab halted them.
18:16 the troops stopped pursuing Israel, for Joab halted **them**[s] [+2021].
19: 2 [19:3] for the whole **army** the victory that day was turned into
19: 2 [19:3] because on that day the **troops** heard it said, "The king is
19: 3 [19:4] The **men** stole into the city that day as men steal in who are
19: 3 [19:4] The men stole into the city that day as **men** steal in who are
19: 8 [19:9] When the **men** were told, "The king is sitting in the
19: 8 [19:9] "The king is sitting in the gateway," **they**[s] [+2021] all
19: 9 [19:10] the **people** were all arguing with each other, saying,
19:39 [19:40] So all the **people** crossed the Jordan, and then the king
19:40 [19:41] All the **troops** *of* Judah and half the troops of Israel had
19:40 [19:41] and half the **troops** *of* Israel had taken the king over.
20:12 the road, and the man saw that all the **troops** came to a halt there.
20:15 All the **troops** with Joab came and besieged Sheba in Abel Beth
20:22 Then the woman went to all the **people** with her wise advice,
22:28 You save the **humble** [+6714], but your eyes are on the haughty to
22:44 "You have delivered me from the attacks of my **people**; you have
22:44 me as the head of nations. **People** I did not know are subject to me,
22:48 He is the God who avenges me, who puts the **nations** under me,
23:10 The **troops** returned to Eleazar, but only to strip the dead.
23:11 there was a field full of lentils, Israel's **troops** fled from them.
24: 2 tribes of Israel from Dan to Beersheba and enroll the **fighting men**,
24: 2 fighting men, so that I may know how many **[RPH]** there are."
24: 3 "May the LORD your God multiply the **troops** a hundred times
24: 4 so they left the presence of the king to enroll the **fighting men** *of*
24: 9 Joab reported the number of the **fighting men** to the king:
24:10 was conscience-stricken after he had counted the **fighting men**,
24:15 and seventy thousand of the **people** from Dan to Beersheba died.
24:16 of the calamity and said to the angel who was afflicting the **people**,
24:17 When David saw the angel who was striking down the **people**,
24:21 to the LORD, that the plague on the **people** may be stopped."
1Ki 1:39 Then they sounded the trumpet and all the **people** shouted,
1:40 all the **people** went up after him, playing flutes and rejoicing
1:40 went up after him, **[RPH]** playing flutes and rejoicing greatly,
3: 2 The **people**, however, were still sacrificing at the high places,
3: 8 Your servant is here among the **people** you have chosen, a great
3: 8 you have chosen, a great **people**, too numerous to count or number.
3: 9 So give your servant a discerning heart to govern your **people**
3: 9 and wrong. For who is able to govern this great **people** *of* yours?"
4:34 [5:14] Men of all **nations** came to listen to Solomon's wisdom,
5: 7 [5:21] has given David a wise son to rule over this great **nation**."
5:16 [5:30] supervised the project and directed **[RPH]** the workmen.
6:13 live among the Israelites and will not abandon my **people** Israel."
8:16 'Since the day I brought my **people** Israel out of Egypt, I have not
8:16 to be there, but I have chosen David to rule my **people** Israel.'
8:30 and of your **people** Israel when they pray toward this place.
8:33 "When your **people** Israel have been defeated by an enemy
8:34 then hear from heaven and forgive the sin of your **people** Israel
8:36 and forgive the sin of your servants, your **people** Israel.
8:36 and send rain on the land you gave your **people** for an inheritance.
8:38 and when a prayer or plea is made by any of your **people** Israel—
8:41 "As for the foreigner who does not belong to your **people** Israel
8:43 so that all the **peoples** *of* the earth may know your name and fear
8:43 may know your name and fear you, as do your own **people** Israel,
8:44 "When your **people** go to war against their enemies, wherever you
8:50 forgive your **people**, who have sinned against you; forgive all the
8:51 for they are your **people** and your inheritance, whom you brought
8:52 open to your servant's plea and to the plea of your **people** Israel,
8:53 For you singled them out from all the **nations** *of* the world to be
8:56 who has given rest to his **people** Israel just as he promised.
8:59 and the cause of his **people** Israel according to each day's need,
8:60 so that all the **peoples** *of* the earth may know that the LORD is
8:66 On the following day he sent the **people** away. They blessed the
8:66 the LORD had done for his servant David and his **people** Israel.
9: 7 then become a byword and an object of ridicule among all **peoples**.
9:20 All the **people** left from the Amorites, Hittites, Perizzites,
9:23 550 officials supervising the **men** who did the work.
12: 5 three days and then come back to me." So the **people** went away.
12: 6 "How would you advise me to answer these **people**?" he asked.
12: 7 "If today you will be a servant to these **people** and serve them
12: 9 How should we answer these **people** who say to me, 'Lighten the
12:10 "Tell these **people** who have said to you, 'Your father put a heavy
12:12 days later Jeroboam and all the **people** returned to Rehoboam,
12:13 The king answered the **people** harshly. Rejecting the advice given
12:15 So the king did not listen to the **people**, for this turn of events was
12:16 all Israel saw that the king refused to listen to them, **they**[s] [+2021]
12:23 whole house of Judah and Benjamin, and to the rest of the **people**,
12:27 If these **people** go up to offer sacrifices at the temple of the
12:27 sacrifices at the temple of the LORD in Jerusalem, **they**[s] [+2021]
12:30 the **people** went even as far as Dan to worship the one there.
12:31 on high places and appointed priests from all sorts of **people**,
13:33 more appointed priests for the high places from all sorts of **people**.
14: 2 is there—the one who told me I would be king over this **people**.
14: 7 'I raised you up from among the **people** and made you a leader
14: 7 among the people and made you a leader over my **people** Israel.
16: 2 you up from the dust and made you leader of my **people** Israel,
16: 2 in the ways of Jeroboam and caused my **people** Israel to sin
16:15 The **army** was encamped near Gibbethon, a Philistine town.
16:16 When the **Israelites**[s] in the camp heard that Zimri had plotted
16:21 the **people** *of* Israel were split into two factions; half supported
16:21 half **[RPH]** supported Tibni son of Ginath for king, and the other
16:22 But Omri's **followers** [+339+889+2021] proved stronger than
16:22 stronger than **those**[s] [+339+889+2021] *of* Tibni son of Ginath.
18:21 Elijah went before the **people** and said, "How long will you waver
18:21 if Baal is God, follow him." But the **people** said nothing.
18:22 Elijah said to **them**[s] [+2021], "I am the only one of the LORD's
18:24 he is God." Then all the **people** said, "What you say is good."
18:30 Elijah said to all the **people**, "Come here to me." They came to

1Ki 18:30 the people, "Come here to me." **They**[s] [+2021+3972] came to him,
18:37 so these **people** will know that you, O LORD, are God,
18:39 When all the **people** saw this, they fell prostrate and cried,
19:21 the plowing equipment to cook the meat and gave it to the **people**,
20: 8 The elders and the **people** all answered, "Don't listen to him
20:10 if enough dust remains in Samaria to give each of my **men** a
20:15 Then he assembled the rest of **[RPH]** the Israelites, 7,000 in all.
20:42 Therefore it is your life for his life, your **people** for his people.' "
20:42 Therefore it is your life for his life, your people for his **people**.' "
21: 9 of fasting and seat Naboth in a prominent place among the **people**.
21:12 and seated Naboth in a prominent place among the **people**.
21:13 and brought charges against Naboth before the **people**,
22: 4 "I am as you are, my **people** as your people, my horses as your
22: 4 "I am as you are, my people as your **people**, my horses as your
22:28 through me." Then he added, "Mark my words, all you **people**!"
22:43 [22:44] the **people** continued to offer sacrifices and burn incense
2Ki 3: 7 "I am as you are, my **people** as your people, my horses as your
3: 7 "I am as you are, my people as your **people**, my horses as your
4:13 the army?' " She replied, "I have a home among my own **people**."
4:41 He put it into the pot and said, "Serve it to the **people** to eat."
4:42 heads of new grain. "Give it to the **people** to eat," Elisha said.
4:43 servant asked. But Elisha answered, "Give it to the **people** to eat.
6:30 he went along the wall, the **people** looked, and there, underneath,
7:16 the **people** went out and plundered the camp of the Arameans.
7:17 and the **people** trampled him in the gateway, and he died,
7:20 to him, for the **people** trampled him in the gateway, and he died.
8:21 and broke through by night; his **army**, however, fled back home.
9: 6 of Israel, says: 'I anoint you king over the LORD's **people** Israel.
10: 9 He stood before all the **people** and said, "You are innocent.
10:18 Then Jehu brought all the **people** together and said to them,
11:13 When Athaliah heard the noise made by the guards and the **people**,
11:13 the people, she went to the **people** at the temple of the LORD.
11:14 and all the **people** *of* the land were rejoicing and blowing trumpets.
11:17 and the king and **people** that they would be the LORD's people.
11:17 and the king and people that they would be the LORD's **people**.
11:17 He also made a covenant between the king and the **people**.
11:18 All the **people** *of* the land went to the temple of Baal and tore it
11:19 of hundreds, the Carites, the guards and all the **people** *of* the land,
11:20 and all the **people** *of* the land rejoiced. And the city was quiet,
12: 3 [12:4] the **people** continued to offer sacrifices and burn incense
12: 8 [12:9] they would not collect any more money from the **people**
13: 7 Nothing had been left of the **army** of Jehoahaz except fifty
14: 4 the **people** continued to offer sacrifices and burn incense there.
14:21 all the **people** *of* Judah took Azariah, who was sixteen years old,
15: 4 the **people** continued to offer sacrifices and burn incense there.
15: 5 son had charge of the palace and governed the **people** *of* the land.
15:10 He attacked him in front of the **people**, assassinated him
15:35 the **people** continued to offer sacrifices and burn incense there.
16:15 grain offering, and the burnt offering of all the **people** *of* the land,
18:26 Don't speak to us in Hebrew in the hearing of the **people** on the
18:36 the **people** remained silent and said nothing in reply, because the
20: 5 "Go back and tell Hezekiah, the leader of my **people**, 'This is what
21:24 the **people** *of* the land killed all who had plotted against King
21:24 and **they**[s] [+824+2021] made Josiah his son king in his place.
22: 4 which the doorkeepers have collected from the **people**.
22:13 "Go and inquire of the LORD for me and for the **people** and for
23: 2 and the prophets—all the **people** from the least to the greatest.
23: 3 this book. Then all the **people** pledged themselves to the covenant.
23: 6 scattered the dust over the graves of the **common people** [+1201].
23:21 The king gave this order to all the **people**: "Celebrate the Passover
23:30 the **people** *of* the land took Jehoahaz son of Josiah and anointed
23:35 gold from the **people** *of* the land according to their assessments.
24:14 total of ten thousand. Only the poorest **people** *of* the land were left.
25: 3 had become so severe that there was no food for the **people** to eat.
25:11 of the guard carried into exile the **people** who remained in the city,
25:19 was chief officer in charge of conscripting the **people** *of* the land
25:19 people of the land and sixty of his **men** who were found in the city.
25:22 son of Shaphan, to be over the **people** he had left behind in Judah.
25:26 At this, all the **people** from the least to the greatest, together with
1Ch 5:25 and prostituted themselves to the gods of the **peoples** *of* the land,
10: 9 to proclaim the news among their idols and their **people**.
11: 2 'You will shepherd my **people** Israel, and you will become their
11: 2 people Israel, and you will become **their**[s] [+3276+3776] ruler.' "
11:13 there was a field full of barley, the **troops** fled from the Philistines.
13: 4 agreed to do this, because it seemed right to all the **people**.
14: 2 that his kingdom had been highly exalted for the sake of his **people**
16: 2 he blessed the **people** in the name of the LORD.
16: 8 on his name; make known among the **nations** what he has done.
16:20 from nation to nation, from one kingdom to **[RPH]** another.
16:24 glory among the nations, his marvelous deeds among all **peoples**.
16:26 For all the gods of the **nations** are idols, but the LORD made the
16:28 Ascribe to the LORD, O families of **nations**, ascribe to the
16:36 Then all the **people** said "Amen" and "Praise the LORD."
16:43 all the **people** left, each for his own home, and David returned
17: 6 to any of their leaders whom I commanded to shepherd my **people**,
17: 7 and from following the flock, to be ruler over my **people** Israel.
17: 9 And I will provide a place for my **people** Israel and will plant them
17:10 have done ever since the time I appointed leaders over my **people**
17:21 who is like your **people** Israel—the one nation on earth whose God
17:21 the one nation on earth whose God went out to redeem a **people** for
17:21 awesome wonders by driving out nations from before your **people**,
17:22 You made your **people** Israel your very own forever, and you,
17:22 You made your people Israel your very own **[RPH]** forever,
18:14 over all Israel, doing what was just and right for all his **people**.
19: 7 as well as the king of Maacah with his **troops**, who came
19:11 He put the rest of the **men** under the command of Abishai his
19:13 Be strong and let us fight bravely for our **people** and the cities of
19:14 and the **troops** with him advanced to fight the Arameans,
20: 3 brought out the **people** who were there, consigning them to labor
20: 3 Then David and his entire **army** returned to Jerusalem.
21: 2 So David said to Joab and the commanders of the **troops**,
21: 3 "May the LORD multiply his **troops** a hundred times over.
21: 5 Joab reported the number of the **fighting men** to David: In all
21:17 "Was it not I who ordered the **fighting men** to be counted?
21:17 and my family, but do not let this plague remain on your **people**."
21:22 altar to the LORD, that the plague on the **people** may be stopped.
22:18 to me, and the land is subject to the LORD and to his **people**.
23:25 has granted rest to his **people** and has come to dwell in Jerusalem
28: 2 to his feet and said: "Listen to me, my brothers and my **people**.
28:21 The officials and all the **people** will obey your every command."
29: 9 The **people** rejoiced at the willing response of their leaders,
29:14 "But who am I, and who are my **people**, that we should be able to
29:17 now I have seen with joy how willingly your **people** who are here
29:18 and Israel, keep this desire in the hearts of your **people** forever,
2Ch 1: 9 for you have made me king over a **people** who are as numerous as
1:10 Give me wisdom and knowledge, that I may lead this **people**,
1:10 this people, for who is able to govern this great **people** *of* yours?"
1:11 knowledge to govern my **people** over whom I have made you king,
2:11 [2:10] "Because the LORD loves his **people**, he has made you
2:18 [2:17] with 3,600 foremen over them to keep the **people** working.
6: 5 'Since the day I brought my **people** out of Egypt, I have not chosen
6: 5 nor have I chosen anyone to be the leader over my **people** Israel.
6: 6 to be there, and I have chosen David to rule my **people** Israel.'
6:21 and of your **people** Israel when they pray toward this place.
6:24 "When your **people** Israel have been defeated by an enemy
6:25 then hear from heaven and forgive the sin of your **people** Israel
6:27 and forgive the sin of your servants, your **people** Israel.
6:27 and send rain on the land you gave your **people** for an inheritance.
6:29 and when a prayer or plea is made by any of your **people** Israel—
6:32 "As for the foreigner who does not belong to your **people** Israel
6:33 so that all the **peoples** *of* the earth may know your name and fear
6:33 may know your name and fear you, as do your own **people** Israel,
6:34 "When your **people** go to war against their enemies, wherever you
6:39 And forgive your **people**, who have sinned against you.
7: 4 the king and all the **people** offered sacrifices before the LORD.
7: 5 So the king and all the **people** dedicated the temple of God.
7:10 On the twenty-third day of the seventh month he sent the **people** to
7:10 had done for David and Solomon and for his **people** Israel.
7:13 locusts to devour the land or send a plague among my **people**,
7:14 if my **people**, who are called by my name, will humble themselves
7:20 will make it a byword and an object of ridicule among all **peoples**.
8: 7 All the **people** left from the Hittites, Amorites, Perizzites,
8:10 two hundred and fifty officials supervising the **men**.
10: 5 "Come back to me in three days." So the **people** went away.
10: 6 "How would you advise me to answer these **people**?" he asked.
10: 7 "If you will be kind to these **people** and please them and give them
10: 9 How should we answer these **people** who say to me, 'Lighten the
10:10 "Tell the **people** who have said to you, 'Your father put a heavy
10:12 days later Jeroboam and all the **people** returned to Rehoboam,
10:15 So the king did not listen to the **people**, for this turn of events was
10:16 all Israel saw that the king refused to listen to them, **they**[s] [+2021]
12: 3 sixty thousand horsemen and the innumerable **troops** of Libyans,
13: 9 and make priests of your own as the **peoples** *of* other lands do?
13:17 Abijah and his **men** inflicted heavy losses on them, so that there
14:13 [14:12] Asa and his **army** pursued them as far as Gerar. Such a
16:10 At the same time Asa brutally oppressed some of the **people**.
17: 9 they went around to all the towns of Judah and taught the **people**.
18: 2 slaughtered many sheep and cattle for him and the **people** with him
18: 3 "I am as you are, and my **people** as your people;
18: 3 "I am as you are, and my people as your **people**;
18:27 through me." Then he added, "Mark my words, all you **people**!"
19: 4 he went out again among the **people** from Beersheba to the hill
20: 7 not drive out the inhabitants of this land before your **people** Israel
20:21 After consulting the **people**, Jehoshaphat appointed men to sing to
20:25 So Jehoshaphat and his **men** went to carry off their plunder,
20:33 the **people** still had not set their hearts on the God of their fathers.
21:14 So now the LORD is about to strike your **people**, your sons,
21:19 His **people** made no fire in his honor, as they had for his fathers.

2Ch 23: 5 all the other **men** are to be in the courtyards of the temple of the
23: 6 all the other **men** are to guard what the LORD has assigned to
23: 10 He stationed all the **men**, each with his weapon in his hand,
23: 12 When Athaliah heard the noise of the **people** running and cheering
23: 12 the king, she went to **them**[s] [+2021] at the temple of the LORD.
23: 13 and all the **people** *of* the land were rejoicing and blowing trumpets,
23: 16 Jehoiada then made a covenant that he and the **people** and the king
23: 16 and the people and the king would be the LORD's **people**.
23: 17 All the **people** went to the temple of Baal and tore it down.
23: 20 the rulers of the **people** and all the people of the land and brought
23: 20 the rulers of the people and all the **people** *of* the land and brought
23: 21 and all the **people** *of* the land rejoiced. And the city was quiet,
24: 10 the officials and all the **people** brought their contributions gladly,
24: 20 He stood before the **people** and said, "This is what God says:
24: 23 and Jerusalem and killed all the leaders of the **people**.
24: 23 **[RPH]** They sent all the plunder to their king in Damascus.
25: 11 then marshaled his strength and led his **army** to the Valley of Salt,
25: 15 prophet to him, who said, "Why do you consult this **people's** gods,
25: 15 which could not save their own **people** from your hand?"
26: 1 all the **people** *of* Judah took Uzziah, who was sixteen years old,
26: 21 son had charge of the palace and governed the **people** *of* the land.
27: 2 The **people**, however, continued their corrupt practices.
29: 36 all the **people** rejoiced at what God had brought about for his
29: 36 the people rejoiced at what God had brought about for his **people**,
30: 3 and the **people** had not assembled in Jerusalem.
30: 13 A very large crowd of **people** assembled in Jerusalem to celebrate
30: 18 Although most of the many **people** who came from Ephraim,
30: 20 And the LORD heard Hezekiah and healed the **people**.
30: 27 The priests and the Levites stood to bless the **people**, and God
31: 4 He ordered the **people** living in Jerusalem to give the portion due
31: 8 the heaps, they praised the LORD and blessed his **people** Israel.
31: 10 and plenty to spare, because the LORD has blessed his **people**,
32: 4 A large **force of men** assembled, and they blocked all the springs
32: 6 He appointed military officers over the **people** and assembled them
32: 8 the **people** gained confidence from what Hezekiah the king of
32: 13 and my fathers have done to all the **peoples** *of* the other lands?
32: 14 my fathers destroyed has been able to save his **people** from me?
32: 15 or kingdom has been able to deliver his **people** from my hand
32: 17 of the other lands did not rescue their **people** from my hand,
32: 17 so the god of Hezekiah will not rescue his **people** from my hand."
32: 18 they called out in Hebrew to the **people** *of* Jerusalem who were on
32: 19 as they did about the gods of the other **peoples** *of* the world—
33: 10 The LORD spoke to Manasseh and his **people**, but they paid no
33: 17 The **people**, however, continued to sacrifice at the high places,
33: 25 the **people** *of* the land killed all who had plotted against King
33: 25 and **they**[s] [+824+2021] made Josiah his son king in his place.
34: 30 and the Levites—all the **people** from the least to the greatest.
35: 3 Now serve the LORD your God and his **people** Israel.
35: 5 of the families of your fellow countrymen, the **lay people** [+1201].
35: 7 Josiah provided for all the **lay people** [+1201] who were there a
35: 8 His officials also contributed voluntarily to the **people** and the
35: 12 of the families of the **people** [+1201] to offer to the LORD,
35: 13 and pans and served them quickly to all the **people** [+1201].
36: 1 the **people** *of* the land took Jehoahaz son of Josiah and made him
36: 14 of the priests and the **people** became more and more unfaithful,
36: 15 because he had pity on his **people** and on his dwelling place.
36: 16 until the wrath of the LORD was aroused against his **people**
36: 23 Anyone of his **people** among you—may the LORD his God be
Ezr 1: 3 Anyone of his **people** among you—may his God be with him,
2: 2 Rehum and Baanah): The list of the men of the **people** *of* Israel:
2: 70 along with some of the other **people**, and the rest of the Israelites
3: 1 in their towns, the **people** assembled as one man in Jerusalem.
3: 3 Despite their fear of the **peoples** around them, they built the altar
3: 11 And all the **people** gave a great shout of praise to the LORD,
3: 13 No **one**[s] [+2021] could distinguish the sound of the shouts of joy
3: 13 of weeping, **[RPH]** because the people made so much noise.
3: 13 the sound of weeping, because the **people** made so much noise.
4: 4 the **peoples** around them set out to discourage the people of Judah
4: 4 the peoples around them set out to discourage the **people** *of* Judah
8: 15 When I checked among the **people** and the priests, I found no
8: 36 who then gave assistance to the **people** and to the house of God.
9: 1 the leaders came to me and said, "The **people** of Israel,
9: 1 have not kept themselves separate from the neighboring **peoples**
9: 2 and have mingled the holy race with the **peoples** around them.
9: 11 to possess is a land polluted by the corruption of its **peoples**.
9: 14 intermarry with the **peoples** *who commit* such detestable
10: 1 gathered around him. **They**[s] [+2021] too wept bitterly.
10: 2 our God by marrying foreign women from the **peoples** around us.
10: 9 all the **people** were sitting in the square before the house of God,
10: 11 Separate yourselves from the **peoples** around you and from your
10: 13 But there are many **people** here and it is the rainy season;
Ne 1: 8 'If you are unfaithful, I will scatter you among the **nations**,
1: 10 "They are your servants and your **people**, whom you redeemed by
4: 6 [3:38] half its height, for the **people** worked with all their heart.
4: 13 [4:7] Therefore I stationed *some of* the **people** behind the lowest
4: 14 [4:8] said to the nobles, the officials and the rest of the **people**,
4: 19 [4:13] the officials and the rest of the **people**, "The work is
4: 22 [4:16] At that time I also said to the **people**, "Have every man
5: 1 Now the **men** and their wives raised a great outcry against their
5: 13 and praised the LORD. And the **people** did as they had promised.
5: 15 placed a heavy burden on the **people** and took forty shekels of
5: 15 to food and wine. Their assistants also lorded it over the **people**.
5: 18 to the governor, because the demands were heavy on these **people**.
5: 19 me with favor, O my God, for all I have done for these **people**.
7: 4 the city was large and spacious, but there were few **people** in it,
7: 5 the officials and the **common people** for registration by families.
7: 7 Nehum and Baanah): The list of the men of **Israel** [+3776]:
7: 72 [7:71] The total given by the rest of the **people** was 20,000
7: 73 [7:72] along with certain of the **people** and the rest of the
8: 1 all the **people** assembled as one man in the square before the Water
8: 3 And all the **people** listened attentively to the Book of the Law.
8: 5 All the **people** could see him because he was standing above them;
8: 5 see him because he was standing above **them**[s] [+2021+3972];
8: 5 standing above them; and as he opened it, the **people** all stood up.
8: 6 and all the **people** lifted their hands and responded, "Amen!
8: 7 instructed the **people** in the Law while the people were standing
8: 7 instructed the people in the Law while the **people** were standing
8: 9 and the Levites who were instructing the **people** said to them all,
8: 9 the Levites who were instructing the people said to **them**[s] [+2021]
8: 9 For all the **people** had been weeping as they listened to the words
8: 11 The Levites calmed all the **people**, saying, "Be still, for this is a
8: 12 all the **people** went away to eat and drink, to send portions of food
8: 13 of all the families, **[RPH]** along with the priests and the Levites,
8: 16 So the **people** went out and brought back branches and built
9: 10 against all his officials and all the **people** *of* his land,
9: 22 "You gave them kingdoms and **nations**, allotting to them even the
9: 24 along with their kings and the **peoples** *of* the land, to deal with
9: 30 no attention, so you handed them over to the neighboring **peoples**.
9: 32 our priests and prophets, upon our fathers and all your **people**,
10: 14 [10:15] The leaders of the **people**: Parosh, Pahath-Moab, Elam,
10: 28 [10:29] "The rest of the **people**—priests, Levites, gatekeepers,
10: 28 [10:29] the neighboring **peoples** for the sake of the Law of God,
10: 30 [10:31] to give our daughters in marriage to the **peoples** around us
10: 31 [10:32] "When the neighboring **peoples** bring merchandise
10: 34 [10:35] "We—the priests, the Levites and the **people**—have cast
11: 1 Now the leaders of the **people** settled in Jerusalem, and the rest of
11: 1 the rest of the **people** cast lots to bring one out of every ten to live
11: 2 The **people** commended all the men who volunteered to live in
11: 24 of Judah, was the king's agent in all affairs relating to the **people**.
12: 30 they purified the **people**, the gates and the wall.
12: 38 I followed them on top of the wall, together with half the **people**—
13: 1 day the Book of Moses was read aloud in the hearing of the **people**
13: 24 or the language of **one of the other peoples** [+2256+6639],
13: 24 or the language of **one of the other peoples** [+2256+6639],
Est 1: 5 for all the **people** from the least to the greatest, who were in the
1: 11 in order to display her beauty to the **people** and nobles,
1: 16 all the nobles and the **peoples** of all the provinces of King Xerxes.
1: 22 own script and to **each people** [+2256+6639] in its own language,
1: 22 own script and to **each people's** [+2256+6639] in its own language,
1: 22 proclaiming in each **people's** tongue that every man should be
2: 10 Esther had not revealed her **nationality** and family background,
2: 20 and **nationality** just as Mordecai had told her to do,
3: 6 Yet having learned who Mordecai's **people** were, he scorned the
3: 6 Instead Haman looked for a way to destroy all Mordecai's **people**,
3: 8 "There is a certain **people** dispersed and scattered among the
3: 8 scattered among the **peoples** in all the provinces of your kingdom
3: 8 whose customs are different from those of all other **people**
3: 11 the king said to Haman, "and do with the **people** as you please."
3: 12 in the language of **each people** [+2256+6639] all Haman's orders
3: 12 in the language of **each people** [+2256+6639] all Haman's orders
3: 12 and the nobles of the **various peoples** [+2256+6639].
3: 12 and the nobles of the **various peoples** [+2256+6639].
3: 14 made known to the **people** of every nationality so they would be
4: 8 presence to beg for mercy and plead with him for her **people**.
4: 11 and the **people** *of* the royal provinces know that for any man
7: 3 this is my petition. And spare my **people**—this is my request.
7: 4 For I and my **people** have been sold for destruction and slaughter
8: 6 For how can I bear to see disaster fall on my **people**? How can I
8: 9 the language of **each people** [+2256+6639] and also to the Jews in
8: 9 the language of **each people** [+2256+6639] and also to the Jews in
8: 11 kill and annihilate any armed force of any **nationality** or province
8: 13 every province and made known to the people of every **nationality**
8: 17 many people of **other nationalities** [+824+2021] became Jews
9: 2 because the people of all the other **nationalities** were afraid of
10: 3 because he worked for the good of his **people** and spoke up for the
Job 12: 2 "Doubtless you are the **people**, and wisdom will die with you!
12: 24 He deprives the **leaders of** [+8031] the earth of their reason;
17: 6 "God has made me a byword to **everyone**, a man in whose face

Job 18:19 He has no offspring or descendants among his **people**, no survivor
34:20 the middle of the night; the **people** are shaken and they pass away;
34:30 keep a godless man from ruling, from laying snares for the **people**.
36:20 Do not long for the night, to drag **people** away from their homes.
36:31 This is the way he governs the **nations** and provides food in
Ps 3:6 [3:7] I will not fear the tens of thousands **[NIE]** drawn up against
3:8 [3:9] May your blessing be on your **people**. *Selah*
7:8 [7:9] let the LORD judge the **peoples**. Judge me, O LORD,
9:11 [9:12] in Zion; proclaim among the **nations** what he has done.
14:4 those who devour my **people** as men eat bread and who do not call
14:7 When the LORD restores the fortunes of his **people**, let Jacob
18:27 [18:28] You save the **humble** [+6714] but bring low those whose
18:43 [18:44] You have delivered me from the attacks of the **people**;
18:43 [18:44] head of nations; **people** I did not know are subject to me.
18:47 [18:48] God who avenges me, who subdues **nations** under me,
22:6 [22:7] and not a man, scorned by men and despised by the **people**.
22:31 [22:32] They will proclaim his righteousness to a **people** yet
28:9 Save your **people** and bless your inheritance; be their shepherd
29:11 The LORD gives strength to his **people**; the LORD blesses his
29:11 strength to his people; the LORD blesses his **people** with peace.
33:10 the plans of the nations; he thwarts the purposes of the **peoples**.
33:12 whose God is the LORD, the **people** he chose for his inheritance.
35:18 in the great assembly; among throngs of **people** I will praise you.
44:12 [44:13] You sold your **people** for a pittance, gaining nothing from
45:5 [45:6] the king's enemies; let the **nations** fall beneath your feet.
45:10 [45:11] and give ear: Forget your **people** and your father's house.
45:12 [45:13] will come with a gift, **men** of wealth will seek your favor.
45:17 [45:18] therefore the **nations** will praise you for ever and ever.
47:1 [47:2] Clap your hands, all you **nations**; shout to God with cries
47:3 [47:4] He subdued **nations** under us, peoples under our feet.
47:9 [47:10] The nobles of the **nations** assemble as the people of the
47:9 [47:10] The nobles of the nations assemble as the **people** *of* the
49:1 [49:2] Hear this, all you **peoples**; listen, all who live in this world,
50:4 the heavens above, and the earth, that he may judge his **people**:
50:7 "Hear, O my **people**, and I will speak, O Israel, and I will testify
53:4 [53:5] those who devour my **people** as men eat bread and who do
53:6 [53:7] When God restores the fortunes of his **people**, let Jacob
56:7 [56:8] in your anger, O God, bring down the **nations**.
57:9 [57:10] I will praise you, O Lord, among the **nations**; I will sing
59:11 [59:12] not kill them, O Lord our shield, or my **people** will forget.
60:3 [60:5] You have shown your **people** desperate times; you have
62:8 [62:9] Trust in him at all times, O **people**; pour out your hearts to
66:8 Praise our God, O **peoples**, let the sound of his praise be heard;
67:3 [67:4] May the **peoples** praise you, O God; may all the peoples
67:3 [67:4] peoples praise you, O God; may all the **peoples** praise you.
67:4 [67:5] for you rule the **peoples** justly and guide the nations of the
67:5 [67:6] May the **peoples** praise you, O God; may all the peoples
67:5 [67:6] peoples praise you, O God; may all the **peoples** praise you.
68:7 [68:8] When you went out before your **people**, O God, when you
68:30 [68:31] the herd of bulls among the calves of the **nations**.
68:30 [68:31] bars of silver. Scatter the **nations** who delight in war.
68:35 [68:36] the God of Israel gives power and strength to his **people**.
72:2 He will judge your **people** in righteousness, your afflicted ones
72:3 The mountains will bring prosperity to the **people**, the hills the
72:4 He will defend the afflicted among the **people** and save the
73:10 Therefore their **people** turn to them and drink up waters in
74:14 and gave him as food **[RPH]** to the creatures of the desert.
74:18 O LORD, how foolish **people** have reviled your name.
77:14 [77:15] you display your power among the **peoples**.
77:15 [77:16] With your mighty arm you redeemed your **people**,
77:20 [77:21] You led your **people** like a flock by the hand of Moses
78:1 O my **people**, hear my teaching; listen to the words of my mouth.
78:20 But can he also give us food? Can he supply meat for his **people**?"
78:52 he brought his **people** out like a flock; he led them like sheep
78:62 He gave his **people** over to the sword; he was very angry with his
78:71 the sheep he brought him to be the shepherd of his **people** Jacob,
79:13 we your **people**, the sheep of your pasture, will praise you forever;
80:4 [80:5] your anger smolder against the prayers of your **people**?
81:8 [81:9] "Hear, O my **people**, and I will warn you—if you would
81:11 [81:12] "But my **people** would not listen to me; Israel would not
81:13 [81:14] "If my **people** would but listen to me, if Israel would
83:3 [83:4] With cunning they conspire against your **people**; they plot
85:2 [85:3] You forgave the iniquity of your **people** and covered all
85:6 [85:7] not revive us again, that your **people** may rejoice in you?
85:8 [85:9] he promises peace to his **people**, his saints—but let them
87:6 The LORD will write in the register of the **peoples**: "This one
89:15 [89:16] Blessed are **those**[s] [+2021] who have learned to acclaim
89:19 [89:20] I have exalted a young man from among the **people**.
89:50 [89:51] how I bear in my heart the taunts of all the **nations**,
94:5 They crush your **people**, O LORD; they oppress your inheritance.
94:8 Take heed, you senseless ones among the **people**; you fools,
94:14 For the LORD will not reject his **people**; he will never forsake his
95:7 for he is our God and we are the **people** *of* his pasture, the flock
95:10 I said, "They are a **people** *whose* hearts go astray, and they have
96:3 glory among the nations, his marvelous deeds among all **peoples**.
96:5 For all the gods of the **nations** are idols, but the LORD made the
96:7 Ascribe to the LORD, O families of **nations**, ascribe to the
96:10 it cannot be moved; he will judge the **peoples** with equity.
96:13 will judge the world in righteousness and the **peoples** in his truth.
97:6 proclaim his righteousness, and all the **peoples** see his glory.
98:9 will judge the world in righteousness and the **peoples** with equity.
99:1 The LORD reigns, let the **nations** tremble; he sits enthroned
99:2 Great is the LORD in Zion; he is exalted over all the **nations**.
100:3 and we are his; we are his **people**, the sheep of his pasture.
102:18 [102:19] that a **people** not yet created may praise the LORD:
102:22 [102:23] when the **peoples** and the kingdoms assemble to worship
105:1 on his name; make known among the **nations** what he has done.
105:13 from nation to nation, from one kingdom to **[RPH]** another.
105:20 The king sent and released him, the ruler of **peoples** set him free.
105:24 The LORD made his **people** very fruitful; he made them too
105:25 whose hearts he turned to hate his **people**, to conspire against his
105:43 He brought out his **people** with rejoicing, his chosen ones with
106:4 Remember me, O LORD, when you show favor to your **people**,
106:34 They did not destroy the **peoples** as the LORD had commanded
106:40 Therefore the LORD was angry with his **people** and abhorred his
106:48 to everlasting. Let all the **people** say, "Amen!" Praise the LORD.
107:32 Let them exalt him in the assembly of the **people** and praise him in
108:3 [108:4] I will praise you, O LORD, among the **nations**; I will
110:3 Your **troops** will be willing on your day of battle. Arrayed in holy
111:6 He has shown his **people** the power of his works, giving them the
111:9 He provided redemption for his **people**; he ordained his covenant
113:8 he seats them with princes, with the princes of their **people**.
114:1 out of Egypt, the house of Jacob from a **people** *of* foreign tongue,
116:14 fulfill my vows to the LORD in the presence of all his **people**.
116:18 fulfill my vows to the LORD in the presence of all his **people**,
125:2 so the LORD surrounds his **people** both now and forevermore.
135:12 their land as an inheritance, an inheritance to his **people** Israel.
135:14 For the LORD will vindicate his **people** and have compassion on
136:16 to him who led his **people** through the desert, *His love*
144:2 my shield, in whom I take refuge, who subdues **peoples** under me.
144:15 Blessed are the **people** of whom this is true; blessed are the people
144:15 this is true; blessed are the **people** whose God is the LORD.
148:14 He has raised up for his **people** a horn, the praise of all his saints,
148:14 the praise of all his saints, of Israel, the **people** close to his heart.
149:4 For the LORD takes delight in his **people**; he crowns the humble
Pr 11:14 For lack of guidance a **nation** falls, but many advisers make
14:28 A large **population** is a king's glory, but without subjects a prince
24:24 are innocent"—**peoples** will curse him and nations denounce him.
28:15 or a charging bear is a wicked man ruling over a helpless **people**.
29:2 When the righteous thrive, the **people** rejoice; when the wicked
29:2 the people rejoice; when the wicked rule, the **people** groan.
29:18 Where there is no revelation, the **people** cast off restraint;
30:25 Ants are **creatures** of little strength, yet they store up their food in
30:26 coneys are **creatures** of little power, yet they make their home in
Ecc 4:16 There was no end to all the **people** who were before them.
12:9 the Teacher wise, but also he imparted knowledge to the **people**.
SS 6:12 my desire set me among the royal chariots of my **people**.
Isa 1:3 but Israel does not know, my **people** do not understand."
1:4 Ah, sinful nation, a **people** loaded with guilt, a brood of evildoers,
1:10 of Sodom; listen to the law of our God, you **people** *of* Gomorrah!
2:3 Many **peoples** will come and say, "Come, let us go up to the
2:4 between the nations and will settle disputes for many **peoples**.
2:6 You have abandoned your **people**, the house of Jacob. They are
3:5 **People** will oppress each other—man against man, neighbor
3:7 or clothing in my house; do not make me the leader of the **people**."
3:12 Youths oppress my **people**, women rule over them. O my people,
3:12 O my **people**, your guides lead you astray; they turn you from the
3:13 The LORD takes his place in court; he rises to judge the **people**.
3:14 enters into judgment against the elders and leaders of his **people**:
3:15 What do you mean by crushing my **people** and grinding the faces
5:13 Therefore my **people** will go into exile for lack of understanding;
5:25 Therefore the LORD's anger burns against his **people**; his hand is
6:5 a man of unclean lips, and I live among a **people** *of* unclean lips,
6:9 He said, "Go and tell this **people**: " 'Be ever hearing, but never
6:10 Make the heart of this **people** calloused; make their ears dull
7:2 so the hearts of Ahaz and his **people** were shaken, as the trees of
7:8 sixty-five years Ephraim will be too shattered to be a **people**.
7:17 The LORD will bring on you and on your **people** and on the
8:6 "Because this **people** has rejected the gently flowing waters of
8:9 Raise the war cry, you **nations**, and be shattered! Listen, all you
8:11 hand upon me, warning me not to follow the way of this **people**.
8:12 "Do not call conspiracy everything that these **people** call
8:19 who whisper and mutter, should not a **people** inquire of their God?
9:2 [9:1] The **people** walking in darkness have seen a great light;
9:9 [9:8] All the **people** will know it—Ephraim and the inhabitants of
9:13 [9:12] But the **people** have not returned to him who struck them,
9:16 [9:15] Those who guide this **people** mislead them, and those who
9:19 [9:18] will be scorched and the **people** will be fuel for the fire;

Isa 10: 2 their rights and withhold justice from the oppressed of my **people**,
10: 6 I dispatch him against a **people** who anger me, to seize loot
10: 13 I removed the boundaries of **nations**, I plundered their treasures;
10: 14 into a nest, so my hand reached for the wealth of the **nations**;
10: 22 Though your **people**, O Israel, be like the sand by the sea,
10: 24 "O my **people** who live in Zion, do not be afraid of the Assyrians,
11: 10 In that day the Root of Jesse will stand as a banner for the **peoples**;
11: 11 time to reclaim the remnant that is left of his **people** from Assyria,
11: 16 There will be a highway for the remnant of his **people** that is left
12: 4 make known among the **nations** what he has done, and proclaim
13: 4 Listen, a noise on the mountains, like that of a great **multitude**!
13: 14 like sheep without a shepherd, each will return to his own **people**,
14: 2 **Nations** will take them and bring them to their own place.
14: 6 which in anger struck down **peoples** with unceasing blows,
14: 20 in burial, for you have destroyed your land and killed your **people**.
14: 32 established Zion, and in her his afflicted **people** will find refuge."
17: 12 Oh, the raging of many **nations**—they rage like the raging sea!
18: 2 a people tall and smooth-skinned, to a **people** feared far and wide,
18: 7 gifts will be brought to the LORD Almighty from a **people** tall
18: 7 people tall and smooth-skinned, from a **people** feared far and wide,
19: 25 saying, "Blessed be Egypt my **people**, Assyria my handiwork,
22: 4 not try to console me over the destruction of my **people** [+1426]."
23: 13 the land of the Babylonians, this **people** that is now of no account!
24: 2 it will be the same for priest as for **people**, for master as for
24: 4 and withers, the **exalted of** [+5294] the earth languish.
24: 13 So will it be on the earth and among the **nations**, as when an olive
25: 3 Therefore strong **peoples** will honor you; cities of ruthless nations
25: 6 LORD Almighty will prepare a feast of rich food for all **peoples**,
25: 7 this mountain he will destroy the shroud that enfolds all **peoples**,
25: 8 he will remove the disgrace of his **people** from all the earth.
26: 11 Let them see your zeal for your **people** and be put to shame;
26: 20 Go, my **people**, enter your rooms and shut the doors behind you;
27: 11 For this is a **people** without understanding; so their Maker has no
28: 5 a glorious crown, a beautiful wreath for the remnant of his **people**.
28: 11 foreign lips and strange tongues God will speak to this **people**,
28: 14 of the LORD, you scoffers who rule this **people** in Jerusalem.
29: 13 "These **people** come near to me with their mouth and honor me
29: 14 Therefore once more I will astound these **people** with wonder upon
30: 5 everyone will be put to shame because of a **people** useless to them,
30: 6 their treasures on the humps of camels, to that unprofitable **nation**,
30: 9 These are rebellious **people**, deceitful children, children unwilling
30: 19 O **people** of Zion, who live in Jerusalem, you will weep no more.
30: 26 when the LORD binds up the bruises of his **people** and heals the
30: 28 he places in the jaws of the **peoples** a bit that leads them astray.
32: 13 and for the land of my **people**, a land overgrown with thorns
32: 18 My **people** will live in peaceful dwelling places, in secure homes,
33: 3 At the thunder of your voice, the **peoples** flee; when you rise up,
33: 12 The **peoples** will be burned as if to lime; like cut thornbushes they
33: 19 You will see those arrogant **people** no more, those people of an
33: 19 those **people** *of* an obscure speech, with their strange,
33: 24 and the sins of **those**[s] [+2021] who dwell there will be forgiven.
34: 5 in judgment on Edom, the **people** I have totally destroyed.
36: 11 Don't speak to us in Hebrew in the hearing of the **people** on the
40: 1 Comfort, comfort my **people**, says your God.
40: 7 breath of the LORD blows on them. Surely the **people** are grass.
42: 5 and all that comes out of it, who gives breath to its **people**,
42: 6 I will keep you and will make you to be a covenant for the **people**
42: 22 this is a **people** plundered and looted, all of them trapped in pits
43: 8 Lead out **those**[s] who have eyes but are blind, who have ears
43: 20 streams in the wasteland, to give drink to my **people**, my chosen,
43: 21 the **people** I formed for myself that they may proclaim my praise.
44: 7 me what has happened since I established my ancient **people**,
47: 6 I was angry with my **people** and desecrated my inheritance;
49: 8 I will keep you and will make you to be a covenant for the **people**,
49: 13 For the LORD comforts his **people** and will have compassion on
49: 22 will beckon to the Gentiles, I will lift up my banner to the **peoples**;
51: 4 "Listen to me, my **people**; hear me, my nation: The law will go out
51: 4 will go out from me; my justice will become a light to the **nations**.
51: 5 is on the way, and my arm will bring justice to the **nations**.
51: 7 know what is right, you **people** who have my law in your hearts:
51: 16 of the earth, and who say to Zion, 'You are my **people**.' "
51: 22 your Sovereign LORD says, your God, who defends his **people**:
52: 4 "At first my **people** went down to Egypt to live; lately, Assyria has
52: 5 "For my **people** have been taken away for nothing, and those who
52: 6 Therefore my **people** will know my name; therefore in that day
52: 9 you ruins of Jerusalem, for the LORD has comforted his **people**,
53: 8 of the living; for the transgression of my **people** he was stricken.
56: 3 "The LORD will surely exclude me from his **people**."
56: 7 for my house will be called a house of prayer for all **nations**."
57: 14 the road! Remove the obstacles out of the way of my **people**."
58: 1 Declare to my **people** their rebellion and to the house of Jacob
60: 21 will all your **people** be righteous and they will possess the land
61: 9 known among the nations and their offspring among the **peoples**.
62: 10 Prepare the way for the **people**. Build up, build up the highway!
62: 10 the highway! Remove the stones. Raise a banner for the **nations**.
62: 12 They will be called the Holy **People**, the Redeemed of the LORD;
63: 3 trodden the winepress alone; from the **nations** no one was with me.
63: 6 I trampled the **nations** in my anger; in my wrath I made them
63: 8 He said, "Surely they are my **people**, sons who will not be false to
63: 11 people recalled the days of old, the days of Moses and his **people**—
63: 14 This is how you guided your **people** to make for yourself a
63: 18 For a little while your **people** possessed your holy place, but now
64: 9 [64:8] look upon us, we pray, for we are all your **people**.
65: 2 All day long I have held out my hands to an obstinate **people**,
65: 3 a **people** who continually provoke me to my very face,
65: 10 of Achor a resting place for herds, for my **people** who seek me.
65: 18 for I will create Jerusalem to be a delight and its **people** a joy.
65: 19 I will rejoice over Jerusalem and take delight in my **people**;
65: 22 For as the days of a tree, so will be the days of my **people**;
Jer 1: 18 kings of Judah, its officials, its priests and the **people** *of* the land.
2: 11 But my **people** have exchanged their Glory for worthless idols.
2: 13 "My **people** have committed two sins: They have forsaken me,
2: 31 Why do my **people** say, 'We are free to roam; we will come to you
2: 32 Yet my **people** have forgotten me, days without number.
4: 10 how completely you have deceived this **people** and Jerusalem by
4: 11 At that time this **people** and Jerusalem will be told, "A scorching
4: 11 the barren heights in the desert blows toward my **people** [+1426],
4: 22 "My **people** are fools; they do not know me. They are senseless
5: 14 words in your mouth a fire and these **people** the wood it consumes.
5: 21 Hear this, you foolish and senseless **people**, who have eyes
5: 23 these **people** have stubborn and rebellious hearts; they have turned
5: 26 "Among my **people** are wicked men who lie in wait like men who
5: 31 priests rule by their own authority, and my **people** love it this way.
6: 14 They dress the wound of my **people** as though it were not serious.
6: 19 I am bringing disaster on this **people**, the fruit of their schemes,
6: 21 "I will put obstacles before this **people**. Fathers and sons alike will
6: 22 "Look, an **army** is coming from the land of the north; a great
6: 26 O my **people** [+1426], put on sackcloth and roll in ashes; mourn
6: 27 "I have made you a tester of metals and my **people** the ore,
7: 12 see what I did to it because of the wickedness of my **people** Israel.
7: 16 "So do not pray for this **people** nor offer any plea or petition for
7: 23 Obey me, and I will be your God and you will be my **people**.
7: 33 the carcasses of this **people** will become food for the birds of the
8: 5 Why then have these **people** turned away? Why does Jerusalem
8: 7 But my **people** do not know the requirements of the LORD.
8: 11 They dress the wound of my **people** [+1426] as though it were not
8: 19 Listen to the cry of my **people** [+1426] from a land far away:
8: 21 Since my **people** [+1426] are crushed, I am crushed; I mourn,
8: 22 then is there no healing for the wound of my **people** [+1426]?
9: 1 [8:23] weep day and night for the slain of my **people** [+1426].
9: 2 [9:1] so that I might leave my **people** and go away from them;
9: 7 [9:6] what else can I do because of the sin of my **people** [+1426]?
9: 15 [9:14] I will make this **people** eat bitter food and drink poisoned
10: 3 For the customs of the **peoples** are worthless; they cut a tree out of
11: 4 command you, and you will be my **people**, and I will be your God.
11: 14 "Do not pray for this **people** nor offer any plea or petition for
12: 14 neighbors who seize the inheritance I gave my **people** Israel,
12: 16 if they learn well the ways of my **people** and swear by my name,
12: 16 even as they once taught my **people** to swear by Baal—
12: 16 to swear by Baal—then they will be established among my **people**.
13: 10 These wicked **people**, who refuse to listen to my words,
13: 11 the LORD, 'to be my **people** for my renown and praise and honor.
14: 10 This is what the LORD says about this **people**: "They greatly love
14: 11 LORD said to me, "Do not pray for the well-being of this **people**.
14: 16 the **people** they are prophesying to will be thrown out into the
14: 17 and day without ceasing; for my virgin daughter—my **people**—
15: 1 were to stand before me, my heart would not go out to this **people**.
15: 7 I will bring bereavement and destruction on my **people**, for they
15: 20 I will make you a wall to this **people**, a fortified wall of bronze;
16: 5 my love and my pity from this **people**," declares the LORD.
16: 10 "When you tell these **people** all this and they ask you, 'Why has
17: 19 "Go and stand at the gate of the **people** [+1201], through which the
18: 15 Yet my **people** have forgotten me; they burn incense to worthless
19: 1 Take along some of the elders of the **people** and of the priests
19: 11 I will smash this **nation** and this city just as this potter's jar is
19: 14 in the court of the LORD's temple and said to all the **people**,
21: 7 his officials and the **people** in this city who survive the plague,
21: 8 "Furthermore, tell the **people**, 'This is what the LORD says:
22: 2 your officials and your **people** who come through these gates.
22: 4 and on horses, accompanied by their officials and their **people**.
23: 2 the God of Israel, says to the shepherds who tend my **people**:
23: 13 They prophesied by Baal and led my **people** Israel astray.
23: 22 they would have proclaimed my words to my **people** and would
23: 27 They think the dreams they tell one another will make my **people**
23: 32 "They tell them and lead my **people** astray with their reckless lies,
23: 32 They do not benefit these **people** in the least," declares the
23: 33 "When these **people**, or a prophet or a priest, ask you, 'What is the
23: 34 If a prophet or a priest or **anyone**[s] **else** claims, 'This is the oracle of

Jer 24: 7 They will be my **people**, and I will be their God, for they will
25: 1 The word came to Jeremiah concerning all the **people** *of* Judah in
25: 2 So Jeremiah the prophet said to all the **people** *of* Judah and to all
25: 19 king of Egypt, his attendants, his officials and all his **people**,
26: 7 all the **people** heard Jeremiah speak these words in the house of the
26: 8 as soon as Jeremiah finished telling all the **people** everything the
26: 8 the priests, the prophets and all the **people** seized him and said,
26: 9 all the **people** crowded around Jeremiah in the house of the
26: 11 the priests and the prophets said to the officials and all the **people**,
26: 12 Jeremiah said to all the officials and all the **people**: "The LORD
26: 16 the officials and all the **people** said to the priests and the prophets,
26: 17 the land stepped forward and said to the entire assembly of **people**,
26: 18 He told all the **people** *of* Judah, 'This is what the LORD Almighty
26: 23 body thrown into the burial place of the **common people** [+1201].)
26: 24 so he was not handed over to the **people** to be put to death.
27: 12 the king of Babylon; serve him and his **people**, and you will live.
27: 13 Why will you and your **people** die by the sword, famine
27: 16 I said to the priests and all these **people**, "This is what the LORD
28: 1 of the LORD in the presence of the priests and all the **people**:
28: 5 and all the **people** who were standing in the house of the LORD.
28: 7 I have to say in your hearing and in the hearing of all the **people**:
28: 11 and he said before all the **people**, "This is what the LORD says:
28: 15 has not sent you, yet you have persuaded this **nation** to trust in lies.
29: 1 all the other **people** Nebuchadnezzar had carried into exile from
29: 16 sits on David's throne and all the **people** who remain in this city,
29: 25 You sent letters in your own name to all the **people** in Jerusalem,
29: 32 He will have no one left among this **people**, nor will he see the
29: 32 nor will he see the good things I will do for my **people**,
30: 3 'when I will bring my **people** Israel and Judah back from captivity
30: 22 " 'So you will be my **people**, and I will be your God.' "
31: 1 be the God of all the clans of Israel, and they will be my **people**."
31: 2 "The **people** who survive the sword will find favor in the desert;
31: 7 and say, 'O LORD, save your **people**, the remnant of Israel.'
31: 14 my **people** will be filled with my bounty," declares the LORD.
31: 33 it on their hearts. I will be their God, and they will be my **people**.
32: 21 You brought your **people** Israel out of Egypt with signs
32: 38 They will be my **people**, and I will be their God.
32: 42 As I have brought all this great calamity on this **people**, so I will
33: 24 "Have you not noticed that these **people** are saying, 'The LORD
33: 24 So they despise my **people** and no longer regard them as a nation.
34: 1 and **peoples** *in* the empire he ruled were fighting against Jerusalem
34: 8 all the **people** in Jerusalem to proclaim freedom for the slaves.
34: 10 **people** who entered into this covenant agreed that they would free
34: 19 all the **people** *of* the land who walked between the pieces of the
35: 16 their forefather gave them, but these **people** have not obeyed me.'
36: 6 read to the **people** from the scroll the words of the LORD that
36: 7 wrath pronounced against this **people** by the LORD are great."
36: 9 before the LORD was proclaimed for all the **people** in Jerusalem
36: 9 and **[RPH]** those who had come from the towns of Judah.
36: 10 Baruch read to all the **people** at the LORD's temple the words of
36: 13 everything he had heard Baruch read to the **people** from the scroll,
36: 14 "Bring the scroll from which you have read to the **people**
37: 2 Neither he nor his attendants nor the **people** *of* the land paid any
37: 4 Now Jeremiah was free to come and go among the **people**,
37: 12 Benjamin to get his share of the property among the **people** there.
37: 18 have I committed against you or your officials or this **people**,
38: 1 heard what Jeremiah was telling all the **people** when he said,
38: 4 as well as all the **people**, by the things he is saying to them.
38: 4 This man is not seeking the good of these **people** but their ruin."
39: 8 the houses of the **people** and broke down the walls of Jerusalem.
39: 9 carried into exile to Babylon the **people** who remained in the city,
39: 9 with those who had gone over to him, and the rest of the **people**.
39: 10 the guard left behind in the land of Judah some of the poor **people**,
39: 14 take him back to his home. So he remained among his own **people**.
40: 5 live with him among the **people**, or go anywhere else you please."
40: 6 stayed with him among the **people** who were left behind in the
41: 10 Ishmael made captives of all the rest of the **people** who were in
41: 10 the king's daughters along with all the **others**[s] who were left there,
41: 13 When all the **people** Ishmael had with him saw Johanan son of
41: 14 All the **people** Ishmael had taken captive at Mizpah turned
41: 16 **[RPH]** from Mizpah whom he had recovered from Ishmael son of
42: 1 and all the **people** from the least to the greatest approached
42: 8 were with him and all the **people** from the least to the greatest.
43: 1 When Jeremiah finished telling the **people** all the words of the
43: 4 all the **people** disobeyed the LORD's command to stay in the land
44: 15 all the **people** living in Lower and Upper Egypt, said to Jeremiah,
44: 20 Then Jeremiah said to all the **people**, both men and women,
44: 20 both men and women, **[RPH]** who were answering him,
44: 21 your kings and your officials and the **people** *of* the land?
44: 24 Then Jeremiah said to all the **people**, including the women,
46: 16 'Get up, let us go back to our own **people** and our native lands,
46: 24 will be put to shame, handed over to the **people** *of* the north."
48: 42 Moab will be destroyed as a **nation** because she defied the
48: 46 The **people** *of* Chemosh are destroyed; your sons are taken into
49: 1 taken possession of Gad? Why do his **people** live in its towns?
50: 6 "My **people** have been lost sheep; their shepherds have led them
50: 16 the sword of the oppressor let everyone return to his own **people**,
50: 41 An **army** is coming from the north; a great nation and many kings
51: 45 "Come out of her, my **people**! Run for your lives! Run from the
51: 58 the **peoples** exhaust themselves for nothing, the nations' labor is
52: 6 had become so severe that there was no food for the **people** to eat.
52: 15 **[RPH]** Nebuzaradan the commander of the guard carried into
52: 15 of the guard carried into exile some of the poorest **people**
52: 25 was chief officer in charge of conscripting the **people** *of* the land
52: 25 people of the land and sixty of his **men** who were found in the city.
52: 28 This is the number of the **people** Nebuchadnezzar carried into
La 1: 1 How deserted lies the city, once so full of **people**! How like a
1: 7 When her **people** fell into enemy hands, there was no one to help
1: 11 All her **people** groan as they search for bread; they barter their
1: 18 Listen, all you **peoples**; look upon my suffering. My young
2: 11 out on the ground because my **people** [+1426] are destroyed,
3: 14 I became the laughingstock of all my **people**; they mock me in
3: 45 You have made us scum and refuse among the **nations**.
3: 48 tears flow from my eyes because my **people** [+1426] are destroyed.
4: 3 my **people** [+1426] have become heartless like ostriches in the
4: 6 The punishment of my **people** [+1426] is greater than that of
4: 10 who became their food when my **people** [+1426] were destroyed.
Eze 3: 5 You are not being sent to a **people** *of* obscure speech and difficult
3: 6 not to many **peoples** *of* obscure speech and difficult language,
3: 11 Go now to your **countrymen** [+1201] in exile and speak to them.
7: 27 with despair, and the hands of the **people** *of* the land will tremble.
11: 1 son of Azzur and Pelatiah son of Benaiah, leaders of the **people**.
11: 17 I will gather you from the **nations** and bring you back from the
11: 20 to keep my laws. They will be my **people**, and I will be their God.
12: 19 Say to the **people** *of* the land: 'This is what the Sovereign LORD
13: 9 They will not belong to the council of my **people** or be listed in the
13: 10 " 'Because they lead my **people** astray, saying, "Peace,"
13: 17 set your face against the daughters of your **people** who prophesy
13: 18 Will you ensnare the lives of my **people** but preserve your own?
13: 19 You have profaned me among my **people** for a few handfuls of
13: 19 By lying to my **people**, who listen to lies, you have killed those
13: 21 I will tear off your veils and save my **people** from your hands,
13: 23 I will save my **people** from your hands. And then you will know
14: 8 him an example and a byword. I will cut him off from my **people**.
14: 9 hand against him and destroy him from among my **people** Israel.
14: 11 They will be my **people**, and I will be their God,
17: 9 will not take a strong arm or many **people** to pull it up by the roots.
17: 15 by sending his envoys to Egypt to get horses and a large **army**.
18: 18 robbed his brother and did what was wrong among his **people**.
20: 34 I will bring you from the **nations** and gather you from the
20: 35 I will bring you into the desert of the **nations** and there, face to
20: 41 you as fragrant incense when I bring you out from the **nations**
21: 12 [21:17] Cry out and wail, son of man, for it is against my **people**;
21: 12 [21:17] They are thrown to the sword along with my **people**.
22: 29 The **people** *of* the land practice extortion and commit robbery;
23: 24 with weapons, chariots and wagons and with a throng of **people**;
24: 18 So I spoke to the **people** in the morning, and in the evening my
24: 19 the **people** asked me, "Won't you tell us what these things have to
25: 7 I will cut you off from the **nations** and exterminate you from the
25: 14 I will take vengeance on Edom by the hand of my **people** Israel,
26: 2 The gate to the **nations** is broken, and its doors have swung open
26: 7 and chariots, with horsemen and a great **army** [+2256+7736].
26: 11 he will kill your **people** with the sword, and your strong pillars will
26: 20 down with those who go down to the pit, to the **people** *of* long ago.
27: 3 at the gateway to the sea, merchant of **peoples** on many coasts,
27: 33 merchandise went out on the seas, you satisfied many **nations**;
27: 36 The merchants among the **nations** hiss at you; you have come to a
28: 19 All the **nations** who knew you are appalled at you; you have come
28: 25 When I gather the people of Israel from the **nations** where they
29: 13 gather the Egyptians from the **nations** where they were scattered.
30: 11 He and his **army**—the most ruthless of nations—will be brought in
31: 12 All the **nations** *of* the earth came out from under its shade
32: 3 " 'With a great throng of **people** I will cast my net over you,
32: 9 I will trouble the hearts of many **peoples** when I bring about your
32: 10 I will cause many **peoples** to be appalled at you, and their kings
33: 2 "Son of man, speak to your **countrymen** [+1201] and say to them:
33: 2 the **people** *of* the land choose one of their men and make him their
33: 3 coming against the land and blows the trumpet to warn the **people**,
33: 6 does not blow the trumpet to warn the **people** and the sword comes
33: 12 "Therefore, son of man, say to your **countrymen** [+1201],
33: 17 "Yet your **countrymen** [+1201] say, 'The way of the Lord is not
33: 30 your **countrymen** [+1201] are talking together about you by the
33: 31 My **people** come to you, as they usually do, and sit before you to
33: 31 My people come to you, as **they**[s] usually do, and sit before you to
34: 13 I will bring them out from the **nations** and gather them from the
34: 30 am with them and that they, the house of Israel, are my **people**,
36: 3 the nations and the object of **people's** malicious talk and slander,
36: 8 of Israel, will produce branches and fruit for my **people** Israel,

Eze 36: 12 I will cause people, my **people** Israel, to walk upon you. They will
36: 15 no longer will you suffer the scorn of the **peoples** or cause your
36: 20 for it was said of them, 'These are the LORD's **people**, and yet
36: 28 your forefathers; you will be my **people**, and I will be your God.
37: 12 O my **people**, I am going to open your graves and bring you up
37: 13 you, my **people**, will know that I am the LORD, when I open
37: 18 "When your **countrymen** [+1201] ask you, 'Won't you tell us what
37: 23 will cleanse them. They will be my **people**, and I will be their God.
37: 27 will be with them; I will be their God, and they will be my **people**.
38: 6 from the far north with all its troops—the many **nations** with you.
38: 8 whose people were gathered from many **nations** to the mountains
38: 8 They had been brought out from the **nations**, and now all of them
38: 9 and all your troops and the many **nations** with you will go up,
38: 12 the resettled ruins and the **people** gathered from the nations,
38: 14 In that day, when my **people** Israel are living in safety, will you not
38: 15 you and many **nations** with you, all of them riding on horses,
38: 16 You will advance against my **people** Israel like a cloud that covers
38: 22 sulfur on him and on his troops and on the many **nations** with him.
39: 4 you will fall, you and all your troops and the **nations** with you.
39: 7 " 'I will make known my holy name among my **people** Israel.
39: 13 All the **people** *of* the land will bury them, and the day I am
39: 27 When I have brought them back from the **nations** and have
42: 14 clothes before they go near the places that are for the **people**."
44: 11 sacrifices for the **people** and stand before the people and serve
44: 19 When they go out into the outer court where the **people** are,
44: 19 so that they do not consecrate the **people** by means of their
44: 23 They are to teach my **people** the difference between the holy
45: 8 my princes will no longer oppress my **people** but will allow the
45: 9 Stop dispossessing my **people**, declares the Sovereign LORD.
45: 16 All the **people** *of* the land will participate in this special gift for the
45: 22 bull as a sin offering for himself and for all the **people** *of* the land.
46: 3 New Moons the **people** *of* the land are to worship in the presence
46: 9 " 'When the **people** *of* the land come before the LORD at the
46: 18 The prince must not take any of the inheritance of the **people**,
46: 18 so that none of my **people** will be separated from his property.' "
46: 20 bringing them into the outer court and consecrating the **people**."
46: 24 who minister at the temple will cook the sacrifices of the **people**."
Da 8: 24 he does. He will destroy the mighty men and the holy **people**.
9: 6 our princes and our fathers, and to all the **people** *of* the land.
9: 15 who brought your **people** out of Egypt with a mighty hand
9: 16 and your **people** an object of scorn to all those around us.
9: 19 do not delay, because your city and your **people** bear your Name."
9: 20 confessing my sin and the sin of my **people** Israel and making my
9: 24 "Seventy 'sevens' are decreed for your **people** and your holy city to
9: 26 The **people** *of* the ruler who will come will destroy the city
10: 14 to explain to you what will happen to your **people** in the future,
11: 14 The violent men among your own **people** will rebel in fulfillment
11: 15 to resist; even their best **troops** will not have the strength to stand.
11: 32 but the **people** who know their God will firmly resist him.
11: 33 "**Those**[s] who are wise will instruct many, though for a time they
12: 1 the great prince who protects your **people** [+1201], will arise.
12: 1 at that time your **people**—everyone whose name is found written
12: 7 When the power of the holy **people** has been finally broken,
Hos 1: 9 the LORD said, "Call him Lo-Ammi, for you are not my **people**,
1: 10 [2:1] place where it was said to them, 'You are not my **people**,'
2: 1 [2:3] 'My **people**,' and of your sisters, 'My loved one.'
2: 23 [2:25] I will say to those called 'Not my **people**,' 'You are my
2: 23 [2:25] say to those called 'Not my people,' 'You are my **people**';
4: 4 for your **people** are like those who bring charges against a priest.
4: 6 my **people** are destroyed from lack of knowledge. "Because you
4: 8 They feed on the sins of my **people** and relish their wickedness.
4: 9 it will be: Like **people**, like priests. I will punish both of them for
4: 12 of my **people**. They consult a wooden idol and are answered by a
4: 14 a **people** without understanding will come to ruin!
6: 11 "Whenever I would restore the fortunes of my **people**,
7: 8 "Ephraim mixes with the **nations**; Ephraim is a flat cake not turned
9: 1 Do not rejoice, O Israel; do not be jubilant like the other **nations**.
10: 5 Its **people** will mourn over it, and so will its idolatrous priests,
10: 10 **nations** will be gathered against them to put them in bonds for
10: 14 the roar of battle will rise against your **people**, so that all your
11: 7 My **people** are determined to turn from me. Even if they call to the
Joel 2: 2 spreading across the mountains a large and mighty **army** comes,
2: 5 fire consuming stubble, like a mighty **army** drawn up for battle.
2: 6 At the sight of them, **nations** are in anguish; every face turns pale.
2: 16 Gather the **people**, consecrate the assembly; bring together the
2: 17 and the altar. Let them say, "Spare your **people**, O LORD.
2: 17 Why should they say among the **peoples**, 'Where is their God?' "
2: 18 the LORD will be jealous for his land and take pity on his **people**.
2: 19 The LORD will reply to **them**[s] [+2257]: "I am sending you grain,
2: 26 worked wonders for you; never again will my **people** be shamed.
2: 27 and that there is no other; never again will my **people** be shamed.
3: 2 [4:2] my **people** Israel, for they scattered my people among the
3: 3 [4:3] They cast lots for my **people** and traded boys for prostitutes;
3: 16 [4:16] the LORD will be a refuge for his **people**, a stronghold
Am 1: 5 The **people** *of* Aram will go into exile to Kir," says the LORD.
3: 6 When a trumpet sounds in a city, do not the **people** tremble?
7: 8 "Look, I am setting a plumb line among my **people** Israel;
7: 15 the flock and said to me, 'Go, prophesy to my **people** Israel.'
8: 2 the LORD said to me, "The time is ripe for my **people** Israel;
9: 10 All the sinners among my **people** will die by the sword, all those
9: 14 I will bring back my exiled **people** Israel; they will rebuild the
Ob 1: 13 You should not march through the gates of my **people** in the day of
Jnh 1: 8 come from? What is your country? From what **people** are you?"
Mic 1: 2 Hear, O **peoples**, all of you, listen, O earth and all who are in it,
1: 9 It has reached the very gate of my **people**, even to Jerusalem itself.
2: 4 'We are utterly ruined; my **people's** possession is divided up.
2: 8 Lately my **people** have risen up like an enemy. You strip off the
2: 9 You drive the women of my **people** from their pleasant homes.
2: 11 of wine and beer,' he would be just the prophet for this **people**!
3: 3 who eat my **people's** flesh, strip off their skin and break their
3: 5 "As for the prophets who lead my **people** astray, if one feeds them,
4: 1 it will be raised above the hills, and **peoples** will stream to it.
4: 3 He will judge between many **peoples** and will settle disputes for
4: 5 All the **nations** may walk in the name of their gods; we will walk
4: 13 you hoofs of bronze and you will break to pieces many **nations**."
5: 7 [5:6] The remnant of Jacob will be in the midst of many **peoples**
5: 8 [5:7] in the midst of many **peoples**, like a lion among the beasts
6: 2 For the LORD has a case against his **people**; he is lodging a
6: 3 "My **people**, what have I done to you? How have I burdened you?
6: 5 My **people**, remember what Balak king of Moab counseled
6: 16 your people to derision; you will bear the scorn of the **nations**."
7: 14 Shepherd your **people** with your staff, the flock of your
Na 3: 13 Look at your **troops**—they are all women! The gates of your land
3: 18 Your **people** are scattered on the mountains with no one to gather
Hab 2: 5 gathers to himself all the nations and takes captive all the **peoples**.
2: 8 plundered many nations, the **peoples** who are left will plunder you.
2: 10 You have plotted the ruin of many **peoples**, shaming your own
2: 13 Has not the LORD Almighty determined that the **people's** labor
3: 13 You came out to deliver your **people**, to save your anointed one.
3: 16 for the day of calamity to come on the **nation** invading us.
Zep 1: 11 all your **merchants** [+4047] will be wiped out, all who trade with
2: 8 who insulted my **people** and made threats against their land.
2: 9 The remnant of my **people** will plunder them; the survivors of my
2: 10 for insulting and mocking the **people** *of* the LORD Almighty.
3: 9 "Then will I purify the lips of the **peoples**, that all of them may call
3: 12 I will leave within you **[NIE]** the meek and humble, who trust in
3: 20 praise among all the **peoples** *of* the earth when I restore your
Hag 1: 2 "These **people** say, 'The time has not yet come for the LORD's
1: 12 the whole remnant of the **people** obeyed the voice of the LORD
1: 12 their God had sent him. And the **people** feared the LORD.
1: 13 gave this message of the LORD to the **people**:
1: 14 the high priest, and the spirit of the whole remnant of the **people**.
2: 2 son of Jehozadak, the high priest, and to the remnant of the **people**.
2: 4 Be strong, all you **people** *of* the land,' declares the LORD,
2: 14 Haggai said, " 'So it is with this **people** and this nation in my sight,'
Zec 2: 11 [2:15] with the LORD in that day and will become my **people**.
7: 5 "Ask all the **people** *of* the land and the priests, 'When you fasted
8: 6 "It may seem marvelous to the remnant of this **people** at that time,
8: 7 "I will save my **people** from the countries of the east and the west.
8: 8 they will be my **people**, and I will be faithful and righteous to them
8: 11 now I will not deal with the remnant of this **people** as I did in the
8: 12 give all these things as an inheritance to the remnant of this **people**.
8: 20 "Many **peoples** and the inhabitants of many cities will yet come,
8: 22 many **peoples** and powerful nations will come to Jerusalem to seek
9: 16 their God will save them on that day as the flock of his **people**.
10: 9 Though I scatter them among the **peoples**, yet in distant lands they
11: 10 broke it, revoking the covenant I had made with all the **nations**.
12: 2 Jerusalem a cup that sends all the surrounding **peoples** reeling.
12: 3 I will make Jerusalem an immovable rock for all the **nations**.
12: 4 the house of Judah, but I will blind all the horses of the **nations**.
12: 6 They will consume right and left all the surrounding **peoples**,
13: 9 I will say, 'They are my **people**,' and they will say, 'The LORD is
14: 2 into exile, but the rest of the **people** will not be taken from the city.
14: 12 LORD will strike all the **nations** that fought against Jerusalem:
Mal 1: 4 the Wicked Land, a **people** always under the wrath of the LORD.
2: 9 caused you to be despised and humiliated before all the **people**,

6640 עִם *ʿim*, pp. [1048 / 1049] [→ 6672; cf. 6669; Ar 10554]

See Select Index

with [527], *untranslated* [106], to [63], against [42], and [25], from [+4946] [25], among [24], in [15], for [13], near [12], along with [11], toward [10], together with [8], at [7], before [7], like [7], on [5], sleeps with [+8886] [5], join [4], lie with [+8886] [4], of [+4946] [4], away from [+4946] [3], beside [3], by [3], have [3], help [3], slept with [+8886] [3], accompanied by [2], accompany [2], also [2], around [2], as well as [2], by [+4946] [2], come to bed with [+8886] [2], has sexual relations with [+8886] [2], help [+2118] [2], his [+2257] [2], in company with [2], into [2], lay with [+8886] [2], sleep with [+8886] [2], to [+4946] [2], to belong [2], accompanied by [+2143] [1], accomplice [+2745] [1], allies[s] [+8611] [1], allots to [1], and alike [1], and all [1], as long as [1], aside [1], attitude [1], away [+4946] [1], because of [1], bed with [+8886] [1], before [+4946] [1], belong to [1], besides [1], both and [1], call to account [+2011+4946] [1], concerning [1], convictions [+4222] [1], decided [+2118+4213] [1], demand [1], desire [1], despite [1], done this[s] [+8886] [1], dwell with [1], endued with [1], even as [1], followed [+3655] [1], followed [1], followers [+408+889+2143] [1], from [+4946+7156] [1], from [1], gave strong support [+928+2616] [1], give [1], harbor [+2118+4222] [1], has [+2118] [1], has [1], he[s] [+408+2021+2021+8886] [1], help [+3338] [1], help [+3338+8883] [1], here [1], here[s] [+3276] [1], impartially [+465+465] [1], in mind [1], in spite of [1], in store [1], in the care of [1], in the presence of [1], intend [+4222] [1], join [+2143] [1], leave [+2143+4946] [1], left [+2143+4946] [1], lies with [+8886] [1], manned by [1], my [+3276] [1], of [1], on terms [+4946] [1], present [1], rapes [+2256+2616+8886] [1], rapes [+2256+8886 +9530] [1], share their duties [+465] [1], sided with [+3338] [1], sleeping with [+8886] [1], support [1], supports [+2616] [1], take part [+2143] [1], the LORD's [+3378+4946] [1], took care of [1], treated [+2118] [1], treated [+6913] [1], when [1], where [1], with help [1], with the help of [1], withstand [+3656] [1]

6641 עָמַד *'āmad*, v. [523 / 522] [→ 5096, 5097, 6642, 6643, 6644, 6647]

stood [82], stand [64], standing [53], stopped [19], appointed [10], stationed [8], *untranslated* [7], stands [7], stay [7], stop [7], assigned [6], present [6], serve [+4200+7156] [6], stood still [6], endure [5], stand up [5], stood up [5], arise [4], endures [4], have stand [4], ministering [4], put in place [4], set [4], stayed [4], had stand [3], presented [3], raised [3], remain [3], remains [3], serve [3], set in place [3], stand firm [3], appear [2], appoint [2], came to a halt [2], confirmed [2], delay [2], enables to stand [2], entered service [+4200+7156] [2], last [2], minister [2], perform [2], propped up [2], protect [+6584] [2], remained [2], resist [+4200+7156] [2], rise [2], rose up [2], served [+4200+7156] [2], served [2], serving [+4200+7156] [2], set up [2], stand ground [2], stayed behind [2], take stand [2], took places [2], took stand [2], unchanged [+9393] [2], unchanged [2], upright [2], wait [2], withstand [+4200+7156] [2], withstand [+928+7156] [2], act [1], appeared [1], appointing [1], as did[s] [1], assist [+907] [1], assistant [+4200+7156] [1], assume the responsibility for carrying out [+6584] [1], attend [+4200+7156] [1], attendants [+6584] [1], avoid [1], be presented [1], be [1], broke out [1], built [1], calm [1], can[s] [1], claim [1], come forward [1], come [1], confronted [+6584] [1], crowd [+889+3972] [1], decided [+1821] [1], defend [+5584] [1], do anything that endangers life [+1947+6584] [1], emerge [1], enduring [1], enter service [+4200+7156] [1], entered the service [+4200+7156] [1], establish [1], face [1], fulfillment [1], gets up [1], gives stability [1], gives way [+4202] [1], gone [+928+4202] [1], had pledge [1], had serve [1], halt [1], halted [1], held [1], in charge [+6584] [1], installed [1], joined together [+285+3869] [1], keep on [1], leave alone [+4946] [1], linger [1], live [1], made stand [1], making strong [1], muster [1], occupied [+448] [1], on duty [1], opposed [+6584] [1], performed [1], persists [1], pledged [1], position [1], post [1], posted [1], posting [1], protects [+6584] [1], put in charge [+3338+6584] [1], putting in place [1], raise [1], raised up [1], reach [1], rebuilding [1], rebuilt [1], rely [1], repair [1], replaced [+9393] [1], represent [1], resist [1], resisted [+4200+5584] [1], rise up [1], rises [1], serve [+6584] [1], served [+907+7156] [1], sets up [1], stand the strain [1], stand up [+6584+6642] [1], standing trial [1], stands firm [1], stared with a fixed gaze [+906+2256+7156+8492] [1], staying [1], stays [1], stirred up [1], stood by [1], stood firm [1], stood in places [1], stood waiting [1], succeed [1], succeeded [+4030 +6584] [1], successor [+4030+6584] [1], successor [+9393] [1], surviving [1], to feet [1], tolerated [1], took up [+6584] [1], took [1], uphold [1], was [1], were [1], withstood [+928+7156] [1], worked [1]

Ge 18: 8 [A] before them. While they ate, he **stood** near them under a tree.
18: 22 [A] but Abraham remained **standing** before the LORD.
19: 17 [A] Don't look back, and don't **stop** anywhere in the plain!
19: 27 [A] returned to the place where *he had* **stood** before the LORD.
24: 30 [A] and found *him* **standing** by the camels near the spring.
24: 31 [A] by the LORD," he said. "Why *are you* **standing** out here?
29: 35 [A] So she named him Judah. Then *she* **stopped** having children.
30: 9 [A] When Leah saw that *she had* **stopped** having children, she
41: 1 [A] Pharaoh had a dream: *He was* **standing** by the Nile,
41: 3 [A] up out of the Nile and **stood** beside those on the riverbank.
41: 17 [A] "In my dream I *was* **standing** on the bank of the Nile,
41: 46 [A] **entered the service** [+4200+7156] *of* Pharaoh king of Egypt.
43: 15 [A] hurried down to Egypt and **presented** *themselves* to Joseph.
45: 1 [A] So *there* **was** no one with Joseph when he made himself
45: 9 [A] made me lord of all Egypt. Come down to me; don't **delay**.
47: 7 [G] his father Jacob in and **presented** him before Pharaoh.

Ex 3: 5 [A] for the place where you *are* **standing** is holy ground."
8: 22 [8:18] [A] with the land of Goshen, where my people **live**;
9: 10 [A] So they took soot from a furnace and **stood** before Pharaoh.
9: 11 [A] The magicians could not **stand** before Moses because of the
9: 16 [G] *I have* **raised** you **up** for this very purpose, that I might show
9: 28 [A] I will let you go; *you* don't *have to* **stay** any longer."
14: 19 [A] of cloud also moved from in front and **stood** behind them,
17: 6 [A] I *will* **stand** there before you by the rock at Horeb. Strike the
18: 13 [A] and they **stood** around him from morning till evening.
18: 23 [A] and God so commands, you will be able *to* **stand the strain**,
20: 18 [A] in smoke, they trembled with fear. *They* **stayed** at a distance
20: 21 [A] The people **remained** at a distance, while Moses approached
21: 21 [A] but he is not to be punished if the slave **gets up** after a day
26: 15 [A] "Make **upright** frames of acacia wood for the tabernacle.
32: 26 [A] So he **stood** at the entrance to the camp and said,
33: 9 [A] pillar of cloud would come down and **stay** at the entrance,
33: 10 [A] Whenever the people saw the pillar of cloud **standing** at the
36: 20 [A] They made **upright** frames of acacia wood for the
Lev 9: 5 [A] the entire assembly came near and **stood** before the LORD.
13: 5 [A] if he sees that the sore *is* **unchanged** and has not spread in
13: 23 [A] if the spot *is* **unchanged** [+9393] and has not spread, it is
13: 28 [A] the spot *is* **unchanged** [+9393] and has not spread in the skin
13: 37 [A] in his judgment it *is* **unchanged** and black hair has grown in
14: 11 [G] him clean *shall* **present** both the one to be cleansed and
16: 7 [G] **present** them before the LORD at the entrance to the Tent
16: 10 [H] the goat chosen by lot as the scapegoat *shall* **be presented**
18: 23 [A] A woman *must* not **present** *herself* to an animal to have
19: 16 [A] " '*Do* not **do** [+1947+6584] **anything that endangers** your neighbor's **life**.
27: 8 [G] specified amount, *he is to* **present** the person to the priest,
27: 11 [G] as an offering to the LORD—the animal *must be* **presented**
Nu 1: 5 [A] These are the names of the men who *are to* **assist** [+907]
3: 6 [G] of Levi and **present** them to Aaron the priest to assist him.
5: 16 [G] priest shall bring her and **have** her **stand** before the LORD.
5: 18 [G] After the priest *has* **had** the woman **stand** before the
5: 30 [G] The priest *is to* **have** her **stand** before the LORD and is to
7: 2 [A] tribal leaders **in charge** [+6584] *of* those who were counted,
8: 13 [G] **Have** the Levites **stand** in front of Aaron and his sons and
9: 8 [A] "**Wait** until I find out what the LORD commands
11: 24 [G] seventy of their elders and **had** them **stand** around the Tent.
12: 5 [A] *he* **stood** *at* the entrance to the Tent and summoned Aaron
14: 14 [A] have been seen face to face, that your cloud **stays** over them,
16: 9 [A] and to **stand** before the community and minister to them?
16: 18 [A] **stood** with Moses and Aaron at the entrance to the Tent of
16: 48 [17:13] [A] *He* **stood** between the living and the dead,
22: 24 [A] the angel of the LORD **stood** in a narrow path between two
22: 26 [A] and **stood** in a narrow place where there was no room to turn,
27: 2 [A] the entrance to the Tent of Meeting and **stood** before Moses,
27: 19 [G] **Have** him **stand** before Eleazar the priest and the entire
27: 21 [A] *He is to* **stand** before Eleazar the priest, who will obtain
27: 22 [G] He took Joshua and **had** him **stand** before Eleazar the priest
35: 12 [A] may not die before he **stands** trial before the assembly.
Dt 1: 38 [A] your **assistant** [+4200+7156], Joshua son of Nun, will enter
4: 10 [A] Remember the day *you* **stood** before the LORD your God at
4: 11 [A] **stood** at the foot of the mountain while it blazed with fire to
5: 5 [A] (At that time I **stood** between the LORD and you to declare
5: 31 [A] you **stay** here with me so that I may give you all the
10: 8 [A] to **stand** before the LORD to minister and to pronounce
10: 10 [A] Now I *had* **stayed** on the mountain forty days and nights,
17: 12 [A] or for the priest who **stands** ministering there to the LORD
18: 5 [A] and their descendants out of all your tribes to **stand**
18: 7 [A] Levites who **serve** there in the presence of the LORD.
19: 17 [A] the two men involved in the dispute *must* **stand** in the
24: 11 [A] **Stay** outside and let the man to whom you are making the
25: 8 [A] to him. If *he* **persists** in saying, "I do not want to marry her,"
27: 12 [A] these tribes *shall* **stand** on Mount Gerizim to bless the
27: 13 [A] these tribes *shall* **stand** on Mount Ebal to pronounce curses:
29: 15 [29:14] [A] who are **standing** here with us today in the presence
31: 15 [A] of cloud, and the cloud **stood** over the entrance to the Tent.
Jos 3: 8 [A] the edge of the Jordan's waters, go and **stand** in the river.' "
3: 13 [A] flowing downstream will be cut off and **stand up** in a heap."
3: 16 [A] the water from upstream **stopped** flowing. It piled up in a
3: 17 [A] **stood** firm on dry ground in the middle of the Jordan,
4: 10 [A] Now the priests who carried the ark *remained* **standing** in
5: 13 [A] saw a man **standing** in front of him with a drawn sword in
5: 15 [A] your sandals, for the place where you *are* **standing** is holy."
8: 33 [A] *were* **standing** on both sides of the ark of the covenant of the
10: 8 [A] Not one of them *will be able to* **withstand** [+928+7156]
10: 13 [A] So the sun stood still, and the moon **stopped**, till the nation
10: 13 [A] The sun **stopped** in the middle of the sky and delayed going
10: 19 [A] don't **stop**! Pursue your enemies, attack them from the rear
11: 13 [A] Yet Israel did not burn any of the cities **built** on their
18: 5 [A] Judah *is to* **remain** in its territory on the south and the house
18: 5 [A] and the house of Joseph **[RPH]** in its territory on the north.

Jos 20: 4 [A] *he is to* **stand** *in* the entrance of the city gate and state his
20: 6 [A] He is to stay in that city until he *has* **stood** trial before the
20: 9 [A] not be killed by the avenger of blood prior *to* **standing trial**
21:44 [A] Not one of their enemies **withstood** [+928+7156] them;
23: 9 [A] to this day no one *has been able to* **withstand** [+928+7156]
Jdg 2:14 [A] whom they were no longer able to **resist** [+4200+7156].
3:19 [A] king said, "Quiet!" And all his **attendants** [+6584] left him.
4:20 [A] "**Stand** *in* the doorway of the tent," he told her. "If someone
6:31 [A] Joash replied to the hostile **crowd** [+889+3972] around him,
7:21 [A] While each man **held** his position around the camp, all the
9: 7 [A] he climbed up **[NIE]** on the top of Mount Gerizim
9:35 [A] *was* **standing** *at* the entrance to the city gate just as
9:44 [A] the companies with him rushed forward *to a* **position** at the
16:25 [G] performed for them. When *they* **stood** him among the pillars,
20:28 [A] son of Eleazar, the son of Aaron, **ministering** before it.)
Ru 2: 7 [A] the field and *has* **worked** *steadily* from morning till now,
1Sa 6:14 [A] of Beth Shemesh, and there *it* **stopped** beside a large rock.
6:20 [A] "Who can **stand** in the presence of the LORD, this holy
9:27 [A] "but you **stay** here awhile, so that I may give you a message
14: 9 [A] to you,' *we will* **stay** where we are and not go up to them.
16:21 [A] David came to Saul and **entered** his **service** [+4200+7156].
16:22 [A] saying, "*Allow* David *to* **remain** in my service, for I am
17: 3 [A] The Philistines **occupied** [+448] one hill and the Israelites
17: 3 [A] occupied one hill and the Israelites **[RPH]** another,
17: 8 [A] Goliath **stood** and shouted to the ranks of Israel, "Why do
17:26 [A] David asked the men **standing** near him, "What will be done
17:51 [A] David ran and **stood** over him. He took hold of the
19: 3 [A] go out and **stand** with my father in the field where you are.
19:20 [A] with Samuel **standing** there as their leader, the Spirit of God
20:38 [A] he shouted, "Hurry! Go quickly! Don't **stop**!" The boy
26:13 [A] other side and **stood** on top of the hill some distance away;
30: 9 [A] him came to the Besor Ravine, where some **stayed behind**,
30:10 [A] for two hundred men **[RPH]** were too exhausted to cross the
2Sa 1: 9 [A] "Then he said to me, '**Stand** over me and kill me! I am in the
1:10 [A] "So *I* **stood** over him and killed him, because I knew that
2:23 [A] every man **stopped** when he came to the place where Asahel
2:25 [A] themselves into a group and **took** *their* **stand** on top of a hill.
2:28 [A] So Joab blew the trumpet, and all the men **came to a halt**;
15: 2 [A] and **stand** by the side of the road leading to the city gate.
15:17 [A] and *they* **halted** *at* a place some distance away.
17:17 [A] Jonathan and Ahimaaz *were* **staying** at En Rogel. A servant
18: 4 [A] So the king **stood** beside the gate while all the men marched
18:30 [A] and wait here." So he stepped aside and **stood** there.
20: 4 [A] to come to me within three days, and **be** here yourself."
20:11 [A] One of Joab's men **stood** beside Amasa and said,
20:12 [A] and the man saw that all the troops **came to a halt** there.
20:12 [A] he realized that everyone who came up to Amasa **stopped**,
20:15 [A] up to the city, and *it* **stood** against the outer fortifications.
22:34 [G] like the feet of a deer; *he* **enables** me **to stand** on the heights.
1Ki 1: 2 [A] "Let us look for a young virgin *to* **attend** [+4200+7156] the
1:28 [A] So she came into the king's presence and **stood** before him.
3:15 [A] **stood** before the ark of the Lord's covenant and sacrificed
3:16 [A] Now two prostitutes came to the king and **stood** before him.
7:25 [A] The Sea **stood** on twelve bulls, three facing north, three
8:11 [A] the priests could not **perform** their service because of the
8:14 [A] While the whole assembly of Israel *was* **standing** there,
8:22 [A] Solomon **stood** before the altar of the LORD in front of the
8:55 [A] *He* **stood** and blessed the whole assembly of Israel in a loud
10: 8 [A] who continually **stand** before you and hear your wisdom!
10:19 [A] seat were armrests, with a lion **standing** beside each of them.
10:20 [A] Twelve lions **stood** on the six steps, one at either end of each
12: 6 [A] *had* **served** [+907+7156] his father Solomon during his
12: 8 [A] grown up with him and *were* **serving** [+4200+7156] him.
12:32 [G] at Bethel *he* also **installed** priests at the high places he had
13: 1 [A] as Jeroboam *was* **standing** by the altar to make an offering.
13:24 [A] with both the donkey and the lion **standing** beside it.
13:24 [A] with both the donkey and the lion standing **[RPH]** beside it.
13:25 [A] with the lion **standing** beside the body, and they went
13:28 [A] on the road, with the donkey and the lion **standing** beside it.
15: 4 [G] up a son to succeed him and by **making** Jerusalem **strong**.
17: 1 [A] the God of Israel, lives, whom *I* **serve** [+4200+7156],
18:15 [A] the LORD Almighty lives, whom *I* **serve** [+4200+7156],
19:11 [A] and **stand** on the mountain in the presence of the LORD,
19:13 [A] his face and went out and **stood** at the mouth of the cave.
20:38 [A] the prophet went and **stood** by the road **waiting** for the king.
22:19 [A] with all the host of heaven **standing** around him on his right
22:21 [A] **stood** before the LORD and said, 'I will entice him.'
22:35 [H] the king was **propped up** in his chariot facing the Arameans.
2Ki 2: 7 [A] of the company of the prophets went and **stood** at a distance,
2: 7 [A] the place where Elijah and Elisha *had* **stopped** at the Jordan.
2:13 [A] and went back and **stood** on the bank of the Jordan.
3:14 [A] as the LORD Almighty lives, whom *I* **serve** [+4200+7156],
3:21 [A] could bear arms was called up and **stationed** on the border.
4: 6 [A] "There is not a jar left." Then the oil **stopped** flowing.
4:12 [A] So he called her, and *she* **stood** before him.
4:15 [A] "Call her." So he called her, and *she* **stood** in the doorway.
5: 9 [A] and chariots and **stopped** at the door of Elisha's house.
5:11 [A] and **stand** and call on the name of the LORD his God,
5:15 [A] *He* **stood** before him and said, "Now I know that there is no
5:16 [A] whom *I* **serve** [+4200+7156], I will not accept a thing."
5:25 [A] he went in and **stood** before his master Elisha. "Where have
6:31 [A] if the head of Elisha son of Shaphat **remains** on his shoulders
8: 9 [A] He went in and **stood** before him, and said, "Your son
8:11 [G] He **stared** *at* him **with a fixed** [+906+2256+7156+8492] **gaze**
9:17 [A] When the lookout **standing** on the tower in Jezreel saw
10: 4 [A] and said, "If two kings *could* not **resist** [+4200+7156] him,
10: 4 [A] and said, "If two kings could not resist him, how **can**ˢ we?"
10: 9 [A] *He* **stood** before all the people and said, "You are innocent.
11:11 [A] weapon in his hand, **stationed** *themselves* around the king—
11:14 [A] there was the king, **standing** by the pillar, as the custom was.
13: 6 [A] Also, the Asherah pole *remained* **standing** in Samaria.
13:18 [A] "Strike the ground." He struck it three times and **stopped**.
15:20 [A] king of Assyria withdrew and **stayed** in the land no *longer*.
18:17 [A] to Jerusalem and **stopped** at the aqueduct of the Upper Pool,
18:28 [A] the commander **stood** and called out in Hebrew: "Hear the
23: 3 [A] The king **stood** by the pillar and renewed the covenant in the
23: 3 [A] Then all the people **pledged** *themselves* to the covenant.
1Ch 6:31 [6:16] [G] **put in charge** [+3338+6584] *of* the music in the
6:32 [6:17] [A] *They* **performed** their duties according to the
6:33 [6:18] [A] Here are the *men who* **served**, together with their
6:39 [6:24] [A] associate Asaph, who **served** at his right hand:
15:16 [G] David told the leaders of the Levites to **appoint** their
15:17 [G] So the Levites **appointed** Heman son of Joel; from his
16:17 [G] *He* **confirmed** it to Jacob as a decree, to Israel as an
17:14 [G] *I will* **set** him over my house and my kingdom forever; his
20: 4 [A] course of time, war **broke out** with the Philistines, at Gezer.
21: 1 [A] Satan **rose up** against Israel and incited David to take a
21:15 [A] The angel of the LORD *was* then **standing** at the threshing
21:16 [A] and saw the angel of the LORD **standing** between heaven
22: 2 [G] from among them *he* **appointed** stonecutters to prepare
23:30 [A] They *were* also to **stand** every morning to thank and praise
2Ch 3:13 [A] twenty cubits. They **stood** on their feet, facing the main hall.
4: 4 [A] The Sea **stood** on twelve bulls, three facing north, three
5:12 [A] **stood** on the east side of the altar, dressed in fine linen
5:14 [A] the priests could not **perform** their service because of the
6: 3 [A] While the whole assembly of Israel *was* **standing** there,
6:12 [A] Solomon **stood** before the altar of the LORD in front of the
6:13 [A] *He* **stood** on the platform and then knelt down before the
7: 6 [A] The priests **took** their positions, as did the Levites with the
7: 6 [A] blew their trumpets, and all the Israelites *were* **standing**.
8:14 [G] *he* **appointed** the divisions of the priests for their duties,
9: 7 [A] who continually **stand** before you and hear your wisdom!
9: 8 [G] of your God for Israel and his desire to **uphold** them forever,
9:18 [A] seat were armrests, with a lion **standing** beside each of them.
9:19 [A] Twelve lions **stood** on the six steps, one at either end of each
10: 6 [A] *had* **served** [+4200+7156] his father Solomon during his
10: 8 [A] grown up with him and *were* **serving** [+4200+7156] him.
11:15 [G] *he* **appointed** his own priests for the high places and for the
11:22 [G] Rehoboam **appointed** Abijah son of Maacah to be the chief
18:18 [A] his throne with all the host of heaven **standing** on his right
18:20 [A] **stood** before the LORD and said, 'I will entice him.'
18:34 [G] the king of Israel **propped** *himself* **up** in his chariot facing
19: 5 [G] *He* **appointed** judges in the land, in each of the fortified
19: 8 [G] Jehoshaphat **appointed** some of the Levites, priests
20: 5 [A] Jehoshaphat **stood up** in the assembly of Judah
20: 9 [A] *we will* **stand** in your presence before this temple that bears
20:13 [A] and children and little ones, **stood** there before the LORD.
20:17 [A] **stand firm** and see the deliverance the LORD will give
20:20 [A] Jehoshaphat **stood** and said, "Listen to me, Judah and people
20:21 [G] Jehoshaphat **appointed** men to sing to the LORD and to
20:23 [A] Moab **rose up** against the men from Mount Seir to destroy
23:10 [G] *He* **stationed** all the men, each with his weapon in his hand,
23:13 [A] and there was the king, **standing** by his pillar at the entrance.
23:19 [G] *He* also **stationed** doorkeepers at the gates of the LORD's
24:13 [G] *They* **rebuilt** the temple of God according to its original
24:20 [A] *He* **stood** before the people and said, "This is what God says:
25: 5 [G] **assigned** them according to their families to commanders of
25:14 [G] *He* **set** them **up** as his own gods, bowed down to them
26:18 [A] *They* **confronted** [+6584] him and said, "It is not right for
29:11 [A] for the LORD has chosen you to **stand** before him
29:25 [G] *He* **stationed** the Levites in the temple of the LORD with
29:26 [A] So the Levites **stood** *ready* with David's instruments,
30: 5 [G] *They* **decided** [+1821] to send a proclamation throughout
30:16 [A] *they* **took** [+6584] **up** their regular positions as prescribed in
31: 2 [G] Hezekiah **assigned** the priests and Levites to divisions—each
33: 8 [G] of the Israelites leave the land *I* **assigned** to your forefathers,
33:19 [G] **set up** Asherah poles and idols before he humbled himself—
34:31 [A] The king **stood** by his pillar and renewed the covenant in the

2Ch 34:32 [G] *he* **had** everyone in Jerusalem and Benjamin **pledge** *themselves*
34:33 [G] *he* **had** all who were present in Israel **serve** the LORD their
35: 2 [G] *He* **appointed** the priests to their duties and encouraged them
35: 5 [A] "**Stand** in the holy place with a group of Levites for each
35:10 [A] the priests **stood** in their places with the Levites in their
Ezr 2:63 [A] food until *there was* a priest **ministering** with the Urim
2:68 [G] toward the **rebuilding** *of* the house of God on its site.
3: 8 [G] **appointing** Levites twenty years of age and older to
3: 9 [A] **joined** [+285+3869] **together** in supervising those working
3:10 [G] with cymbals, **took** *their* **places** to praise the LORD,
9: 9 [G] new life to rebuild the house of our God and **repair** its ruins,
9:15 [A] because of it not one of us *can* **stand** in your presence."
10:13 [A] and it is the rainy season; so we cannot **stand** outside.
10:14 [A] *Let* our officials **act** for the whole assembly. Then let
10:15 [A] and Shabbethai the Levite, **opposed** [+6584] this.
Ne 3: 1 [G] They dedicated it and **set** its doors **in place**, building as far as
3: 3 [G] laid its beams and **put** its doors and bolts and bars **in place**.
3: 6 [G] laid its beams and **put** its doors and bolts and bars **in place**.
3:13 [G] They rebuilt it and **put** its doors and bolts and bars **in place**.
3:14 [G] He rebuilt it and **put** its doors and bolts and bars **in place**.
3:15 [G] it over and **putting** its doors and bolts and bars **in place**.
4: 9 [4:3] [G] we prayed to our God and **posted** a guard day
4:13 [4:7] [G] Therefore *I* **stationed** some of the people behind the
4:13 [4:7] [G] **posting** them by families, with their swords, spears
6: 1 [G] though up to that time *I had* not **set** the doors in the gates—
6: 7 [G] *have* even **appointed** prophets to make this proclamation
7: 1 [G] the wall had been rebuilt and *I had* **set** the doors **in place**,
7: 3 [A] While the gatekeepers *are still* **on duty**, have them shut the
7: 3 [G] Also **appoint** residents of Jerusalem as guards, some at their
7:65 [A] food until there should be a priest **ministering** with the Urim
8: 4 [A] Ezra the scribe **stood** on a high wooden platform built for the
8: 4 [A] Beside him on his right **stood** Mattithiah, Shema, Anaiah,
8: 5 [A] above them; and as he opened it, the people all **stood up**.
9: 2 [A] *They* **stood in** *their* **places** and confessed their sins
10:32 [10:33] [G] **assume** [+6584] **the responsibility for carrying out**
12:31 [G] *I* also **assigned** two large choirs to give thanks. One was to
12:39 [A] as the Sheep Gate. At the Gate of the Guard *they* **stopped**.
12:40 [A] that gave thanks then **took** *their* **places** in the house of God;
12:44 [A] for Judah was pleased with the **ministering** priests
13:11 [G] I called them together and **stationed** them at their posts.
13:19 [G] *I* **stationed** some of my own men at the gates so that no load
13:30 [G] and **assigned** them duties, each to his own task.
Est 3: 4 [A] it to see whether Mordecai's behavior *would be* **tolerated**,
4: 5 [G] one of the king's eunuchs **assigned** to attend her,
4:14 [A] and deliverance for the Jews *will* **arise** from another place,
5: 1 [A] on her royal robes and **stood** in the inner court of the palace,
5: 2 [A] When he saw Queen Esther **standing** in the court, he was
6: 5 [A] His attendants answered, "Haman *is* **standing** in the court."
7: 7 [A] his fate, **stayed behind** to beg Queen Esther for his life.
7: 9 [A] "A gallows seventy-five feet high **stands** by Haman's house.
8: 4 [A] gold scepter to Esther and she arose and **stood** before him.
8:11 [A] city the right to assemble and **protect** [+6584] themselves;
9: 2 [A] No one *could* **stand** against them, because the people of all
9:16 [A] provinces also assembled *to* **protect** [+6584] themselves
Job 4:16 [A] *It* **stopped**, but I could not tell what it was. A form stood
8:15 [A] He leans on his web, but *it* **gives** [+4202] **way**; he clings to it,
14: 2 [A] withers away; like a fleeting shadow, *he does* not **endure**.
29: 8 [A] saw me and stepped aside and the old men rose **to** *their* **feet**;
30:20 [A] you do not answer; *I* **stand up**, but you merely look at me.
32:16 [A] that they are silent, now that *they* **stand** there with no reply?
34:24 [G] he shatters the mighty and **sets up** others in their place.
37:14 [A] "Listen to this, Job; **stop** and consider God's wonders.
Ps 1: 1 [A] or **stand** in the way of sinners or sit in the seat of mockers.
10: 1 [A] Why, O LORD, *do you* **stand** far off? Why do you hide
18:33 [18:34] [G] of a deer; *he* **enables** me **to stand** on the heights.
19: 9 [19:10] [A] The fear of the LORD is pure, **enduring** forever.
26:12 [A] My feet **stand** on level ground; in the great assembly I will
30: 7 [30:8] [G] you favored me, *you* **made** my mountain **stand** firm;
31: 8 [31:9] [G] the enemy but *have* **set** my feet in a spacious place.
33: 9 [A] and it came to be; he commanded, and *it* **stood firm**.
33:11 [A] the plans of the LORD **stand firm** forever, the purposes of
38:11 [38:12] [A] My friends and companions **avoid** me because of
38:11 [38:12] [A] of my wounds; my neighbors **stay** far away.
76: 7 [76:8] [A] Who *can* **stand** before you when you are angry?
102:26 [102:27] [A] They will perish, but you **remain**; they will all
104: 6 [A] as with a garment; the waters **stood** above the mountains.
105:10 [G] *He* **confirmed** it to Jacob as a decree, to Israel as an
106:23 [A] *had* not Moses, his chosen one, **stood** in the breach before
106:30 [A] Phinehas **stood up** and intervened, and the plague was
107:25 [G] he spoke and **stirred up** a tempest that lifted high the waves.
109: 6 [A] man to oppose him; *let* an accuser **stand** at his right hand.
109:31 [A] For *he* **stands** at the right hand of the needy one, to save his
111: 3 [A] are his deeds, and his righteousness **endures** forever.
111:10 [A] good understanding. To him belongs eternal praise. **[NIE]**
112: 3 [A] are in his house, and his righteousness **endures** forever.
112: 9 [A] his gifts to the poor, his righteousness **endures** forever;
119:90 [A] all generations; you established the earth, and *it* **endures**.
119:91 [A] Your laws **endure** to this day, for all things serve you.
122: 2 [A] Our feet are **standing** in your gates, O Jerusalem.
130: 3 [A] O LORD, kept a record of sins, O Lord, who *could* **stand**?
134: 1 [A] all you servants of the LORD who **minister** by night in the
135: 2 [A] you who **minister** in the house of the LORD, in the courts
147:17 [A] Who *can* **withstand** [+4200+7156] his icy blast?
148: 6 [G] *He* **set** them **in place** for ever and ever; he gave a decree that
Pr 12: 7 [A] and are no more, but the house of the righteous **stands firm**.
25: 6 [A] king's presence, and *do* not **claim** a place among great men;
27: 4 [A] and fury overwhelming, but who *can* **stand** before jealousy?
29: 4 [G] By justice a king **gives** a country **stability**, but one who is
Ecc 1: 4 [A] and generations go, but the earth **remains** forever.
2: 9 [A] Jerusalem before me. In all this my wisdom **stayed** with me.
4:12 [A] may be overpowered, two *can* **defend** [+5584] *themselves*.
4:15 [A] the sun followed the youth, the king's **successor** [+9393].
8: 3 [A] *Do* not **stand up** for a bad cause, for he will do whatever he
SS 2: 9 [A] There *he* **stands** behind our wall, gazing through the
Isa 3:13 [A] LORD takes his place in court; *he* **rises** to judge the people.
6: 2 [A] Above him **were** seraphs, each with six wings: With two
10:32 [A] This day they *will* **halt** at Nob; they will shake their fist at
11:10 [A] In that day the Root of Jesse *will* **stand** as a banner for the
21: 6 [G] to me: "Go, **post** a lookout and have him report what he sees.
21: 8 [A] "Day after day, my lord, I **stand** on the watchtower;
36: 2 [A] When the commander **stopped** at the aqueduct of the Upper
36:13 [A] the commander **stood** and called out in Hebrew, "Hear the
44:11 [A] Let them all come together and **take** *their* **stand**; they will be
46: 7 [A] and carry it; they set it up in its place, and there *it* **stands**.
47:12 [A] "**Keep on**, then, with your magic spells and with your many
47:13 [A] *Let* your astrologers **come forward**, those stargazers who
48:13 [A] when I summon them, *they all* **stand up** together.
50: 8 [A] *Let us* **face** each other! Who is my accuser? Let him confront
59:14 [A] justice is driven back, and righteousness **stands** at a distance;
61: 5 [A] Aliens **[NIE]** will shepherd your flocks; foreigners will
66:22 [A] and the new earth that I make *will* **endure** before me,"
66:22 [A] the LORD, "so *will* your name and descendants **endure**.
Jer 4: 6 [A] Raise the signal to go to Zion! Flee for safety without **delay**!
6:16 [A] "**Stand** at the crossroads and look; ask for the ancient paths,
7: 2 [A] "**Stand** at the gate of the LORD's house and there proclaim
7:10 [A] then come and **stand** before me in this house, which bears
14: 6 [A] Wild donkeys **stand** on the barren heights and pant like
15: 1 [A] "Even if Moses and Samuel *were to* **stand** before me,
15:19 [A] I will restore you *that you may* **serve** [+4200+7156] me;
17:19 [A] "Go and **stand** at the gate of the people, through which the
18:20 [A] Remember that I **stood** before you and spoke in their behalf
19:14 [A] **stood** in the court of the LORD's temple and said to all the
23:18 [A] which of *them has* **stood** in the council of the LORD to see
23:22 [A] if *they had* **stood** in my council, they would have proclaimed
26: 2 [A] **Stand** in the courtyard of the LORD's house and speak to
28: 5 [A] all the people who *were* **standing** in the house of the
32:14 [A] and put them in a clay jar so *they will* **last** a long time.
35:19 [A] will never fail to have a man *to* **serve** [+4200+7156] me.' "
36:21 [A] read it to the king and all the officials **standing** beside him.
40:10 [A] I myself will stay at Mizpah to **represent** you before the
44:15 [A] to other gods, along with all the women who *were* **present**—
46:15 [A] *They* cannot **stand**, for the LORD will push them down.
46:21 [A] will turn and flee together, *they will* not **stand** *their* **ground**,
48:11 [A] So she tastes **as she did**[s], and her aroma is unchanged.
48:19 [A] **Stand** by the road and watch, you who live in Aroer.
48:45 [A] "In the shadow of Heshbon the fugitives **stand** helpless, for a
49:19 [A] challenge me? And what shepherd *can* **stand** against me?"
50:44 [A] challenge me? And what shepherd *can* **stand** against me?"
51:50 [A] You who have escaped the sword, leave and *do* not **linger**!
52:12 [A] *who* **served** [+4200+7156] the king of Babylon, came to
Eze 1:21 [A] when the creatures **stood still**, they also stood still;
1:21 [A] when the creatures stood still, *they* also **stood still**;
1:24 [A] of an army. When they **stood still**, they lowered their wings.
1:25 [A] expanse over their heads as they **stood** with lowered wings.
2: 1 [A] "Son of man, **stand up** on your feet and I will speak to you."
2: 2 [G] he spoke, the Spirit came into me and **raised** me to my feet,
3:23 [A] the glory of the LORD *was* **standing** there, like the glory I
3:24 [G] the Spirit came into me and **raised** me to my feet. He spoke
8:11 [A] In front of them **stood** seventy elders of the house of Israel,
8:11 [A] and Jaazaniah son of Shaphan *was* **standing** among them.
9: 2 [A] at his side. They came in and **stood** beside the bronze altar.
10: 3 [A] Now the cherubim *were* **standing** on the south side of the
10: 6 [A] the cherubim," the man went in and **stood** beside a wheel.
10:17 [A] When the cherubim **stood still**, they also stood still;
10:17 [A] When the cherubim stood still, *they* also **stood still**;
10:18 [A] the threshold of the temple and **stopped** above the cherubim.
10:19 [A] *They* **stopped** at the entrance to the east gate of the
11:23 [A] within the city and **stopped** above the mountain east of it.

Eze 13: 5 [A] so that *it will* **stand firm** in the battle on the day of the
17: 14 [A] unable to rise again, **surviving** only by keeping his treaty.
21: 21 [21:26] [A] For the king of Babylon *will* **stop** at the fork in the
22: 14 [A] *Will* your courage **endure** or your hands be strong in the day
22: 30 [A] **stand** before me in the gap on behalf of the land so I would
24: 11 [G] **set** the empty pot on the coals till it becomes hot and its
27: 29 [A] the mariners and all the seamen *will* **stand** on the shore.
29: 7 [g] their backs *were* wrenched. [BHS ***caused to stand***; NIV 5048]
31: 14 [A] other trees so well-watered *are ever to* **reach** such a height;
33: 26 [A] *You* **rely** on your sword, you do detestable things, and each
37: 10 [A] they came to life and **stood up** on their feet—a vast army.
40: 3 [A] he *was* **standing** in the gateway with a linen cord and a
43: 6 [A] While the man was **standing** beside me, I heard someone
44: 11 [A] for the people and **stand** before the people and serve them.
44: 15 [A] *they are to* **stand** before me to offer sacrifices of fat
44: 24 [A] the priests *are to* **serve** as judges and decide it according to
46: 2 [A] through the portico of the gateway and **stand** by the gatepost.
47: 10 [A] Fishermen *will* **stand** along the shore; from En Gedi to En
Da 1: 4 [A] to understand, and qualified to **serve** in the king's palace.
1: 5 [A] that *they were to* **enter** the king's **service** [+4200+7156].
1: 19 [A] so *they* **entered** the king's **service** [+4200+7156].
2: 2 [A] had dreamed. When they came in and **stood** before the king,
8: 3 [A] **standing** beside the canal, and the horns were long.
8: 4 [A] No animal *could* **stand** against him, and none could rescue
8: 6 [A] He came toward the two-horned ram I had seen **standing**
8: 7 [A] The ram was powerless to **stand** against him; the goat
8: 15 [A] there before me **stood** one who looked like a man.
8: 18 [G] to the ground. Then he touched me and **raised** me to my feet.
8: 22 [A] The four horns *that* **replaced** [+9393] the one that was
8: 22 [A] off represent four kingdoms *that will* **emerge** from his nation
8: 23 [A] a stern-faced king, a master of intrigue, *will* **arise**.
8: 25 [A] and **take** *his* **stand** against the Prince of princes.
10: 11 [A] **stand** [+6584+6642] **up**, for I have now been sent to you."
10: 11 [A] to you." And when he said this to me, *I* **stood up** trembling.
10: 13 [A] the prince of the Persian kingdom **resisted** [+4200+5584] me
10: 16 [A] I said to the *one* **standing** before me, "I am overcome with
10: 17 [A] My strength *is* **gone** [+928+4202] and I can hardly breathe."
11: 1 [A] the Mede, I **took** my **stand** to support and protect him.)
11: 2 [A] Three more kings *will* **appear** in Persia, and then a fourth,
11: 3 [A] a mighty king *will* **appear**, who will rule with great power
11: 4 [A] After he *has* **appeared**, his empire will be broken up
11: 6 [A] will not retain her power, and *he* and his power *will* not **last**.
11: 7 [A] "*One* from her family line *will* **arise** to take her place. He
11: 8 [A] years he *will* **leave** the king of the North **alone** [+4946].
11: 11 [G] *who will* **raise** a large army, but it will be defeated.
11: 13 [G] For the king of the North *will* **muster** another army,
11: 14 [A] "In those times many *will* **rise** against the king of the South.
11: 14 [G] your own people will rebel in **fulfillment** *of* the vision,
11: 15 [A] The forces of the South will be powerless *to* **resist**;
11: 15 [A] even their best troops will not have the strength to **stand**.
11: 16 [A] do as he pleases; no *one will be able to* **stand** against him.
11: 16 [A] *He will* **establish** *himself* in the Beautiful Land and will
11: 17 [A] the kingdom, but his plans *will* not **succeed** or help him.
11: 20 [A] "His **successor** [+4030+6584] will send out a tax collector to
11: 21 [A] "He *will be* **succeeded** [+4030+6584] *by* a contemptible person
11: 25 [A] *he will* not *be able to* **stand** because of the plots devised
11: 31 [A] "His armed forces *will* **rise up** to desecrate the temple
12: 1 [A] the great prince who **protects** [+6584] your people,
12: 1 [A] the great prince who protects your people, *will* **arise**.
12: 5 [A] Daniel, looked, and there before me **stood** two others,
12: 13 [A] at the end of the days *you will* **rise** to receive your allotted
Hos 10: 9 [A] you have sinned, O Israel, and there *you have* **remained**.
13: 13 [A] time arrives, *he does* not **come** to the opening of the womb.
Am 2: 15 [A] The archer *will* not **stand** *his* **ground**, the fleet-footed soldier
Ob 1: 11 [A] On the day you **stood** aloof while strangers carried off his
1: 14 [A] *You should* not **wait** at the crossroads to cut down their
Jnh 1: 15 [A] and threw him overboard, and the raging sea *grew* **calm**.
Mic 5: 4 [5:3] [A] *He will* **stand** and shepherd his flock in the strength of
Na 1: 6 [A] Who *can* **withstand** [+4200+7156] his indignation?
2: 8 [2:9] [A] "**Stop**! Stop!" they cry, but no one turns back.
2: 8 [2:9] [A] "Stop! **Stop**!" they cry, but no one turns back.
Hab 2: 1 [A] *I will* **stand** at my watch and station myself on the ramparts;
3: 6 [A] *He* **stood**, and shook the earth; he looked, and made the
3: 11 [A] moon **stood still** in the heavens at the glint of your flying
Hag 2: 5 [A] of Egypt. And my Spirit **remains** among you. Do not fear.'
Zec 1: 8 [A] He *was* **standing** among the myrtle trees in a ravine. Behind
1: 10 [A] Then the man **standing** among the myrtle trees explained,
1: 11 [A] who *was* **standing** among the myrtle trees, "We have gone
3: 1 [A] he showed me Joshua the high priest **standing** before the
3: 1 [A] and Satan **standing** at his right side to accuse him.
3: 3 [A] Now Joshua was dressed in filthy clothes as *he* **stood** before
3: 4 [A] The angel said to those *who were* **standing** before him,
3: 5 [A] and clothed him, while the angel of the LORD **stood by**.
3: 7 [A] and I will give you a place among these **standing** here.
4: 14 [A] "These are the two who are anointed *to* **serve** [+6584] the
14: 4 [A] On that day his feet *will* **stand** on the Mount of Olives, east
14: 12 [A] Their flesh will rot while they *are still* **standing** on their feet,
Mal 3: 2 [A] Who *can* **stand** when he appears? For he will be like a

6642 עֹמֶד *'ōmed*, n.[m.]. [9] [√ 6641]

feet [1], pillar [1], place where standing [1], places [1], positions [1], posts [1], stand up [+6584+6641] [1], standing [1], where[s] [+6584] [1]

2Ch 30: 16 they took up their *regular* **positions** as prescribed in the Law of
34: 31 The king stood by his **pillar** and renewed the covenant in the
35: 10 the priests stood in their **places** with the Levites in their divisions
Ne 8: 7 instructed the people in the Law while the people were **standing**
9: 3 They stood **where**[s] [+6584] they were and read from the Book of
13: 11 Then I called them together and stationed them at their **posts**.
Da 8: 17 As he came near the **place where** I was **standing**, I was terrified
8: 18 face to the ground. Then he touched me and raised me to my **feet**.
10: 11 and **stand up** [+6584+6641], for I have now been sent to you."

6643 עִמָּד *'immād*, pp. [45] [√ 6641] See Select Index

with [16], *untranslated* [11], to [6], against [2], in [2], besides [1], for [1], leave [+2143+4946] [1], mine [+3276] [1], oppose [+8189] [1], oppose [1], surround [1], toward [1]

6644 עֶמְדָּה *'emdâ*, n.f. [1] [√ 6641]

protection [1]

Mic 1: 11 Beth Ezel is in mourning; its **protection** is taken from you.

6645 עֻמָּה¹ *'ummâ¹*, n.f. (used as pp.). [32] [√ 6669]

close to [+4200] [5], *untranslated* [2], along with [+4200] [2], as [+4200] [2], beside [+4200] [2], just as [+4200] [2], parallel to [+4200] [2], above [+4200+4946+4946+5087] [1], adjoining [+4200] [1], alike [+4200] [1], alongside [+4200] [1], alongside of [+4200] [1], as [+3972+8611] [1], as well as [+4200] [1], at [+4200] [1], bordering [+4200] [1], length [+4200] [1], like [+4200] [1], opposite [+4200] [1], responding to [+4200] [1], treated the same as [+4200] [1], with [+4200] [1]

Ex 25: 27 The rings are to be **close** [+4200] **to** the rim to hold the poles used
28: 27 of the shoulder pieces on the front of the ephod, **close** [+4200] **to**
37: 14 The rings were put **close** [+4200] **to** the rim to hold the poles used
38: 18 It was twenty cubits long and, **like** [+4200] the curtains of the
39: 20 of the shoulder pieces on the front of the ephod, **close** [+4200] **to**
Lev 3: 9 its fat, the entire fat tail cut off **close** [+4200] **to** the backbone,
2Sa 16: 13 while Shimei was going along the hillside **opposite** [+4200] him,
16: 13 cursing as he went and throwing stones **at** [+4200] him
1Ki 7: 20 **above** [+4200+4946+4946+5087] the bowl-shaped part next to the
1Ch 24: 31 They also cast lots, **just as** [+4200] their brothers the descendants
24: 31 brother were **treated the same as** [+4200] those of the youngest.
25: 8 Young and old **alike** [+4200], teacher as well as student, cast lots
26: 12 duties for ministering in the temple of the LORD, **just as** [+4200]
26: 16 to Shuppim and Hosah. Guard was **alongside** [+4200] **of** guard:
Ne 12: 24 and thanksgiving, one section **responding** [+4200] **to** the other,
Ecc 5: 16 [5:15] This too is a grievous evil: **As** [+3972+8611] a man comes,
7: 14 consider: God has made the one **as** [+4200] **well as** the other.
Eze 1: 20 would go, and the wheels would rise **along with** [+4200] them,
1: 21 rose from the ground, the wheels rose **along with** [+4200] them,
3: 8 I will make you as unyielding and hardened **as** [+4200] they are.
3: 8 I will make you as unyielding and hardened as **[RPH]** they are.
3: 13 each other and the sound of the wheels **beside** [+4200] them,
10: 19 the ground, and as they went, the wheels went **with** [+4200] them.
11: 22 with the wheels **beside** [+4200] them, spread their wings,
40: 18 sides of the gateways and was as wide **as** [+4200] they were long;
42: 7 There was an outer wall **parallel** [+4200] **to** the rooms and the
45: 6 and 25,000 cubits long, **adjoining** [+4200] the sacred portion;
45: 7 to the eastern border **parallel** [+4200] **to** one of the tribal portions.
48: 13 "**Alongside** [+4200] the territory of the priests, the Levites will
48: 18 What remains of the area, **bordering** [+4200] *on* the sacred portion
48: 18 **[RPH]** Its produce will supply food for the workers of the city.
48: 21 Both these areas running the **length** [+4200] *of* the tribal portions

6646 עֻמָּה² *'ummâ²*, n.pr.loc. [1]

Ummah [1]

Jos 19: 30 **Ummah**, Aphek and Rehob. There were twenty-two towns

6647 עַמּוּד *'ammûd*, n.m. [111] [√ 6641]

pillars [38], posts [36], pillar [25], *untranslated* [7], columns [2], colonnade [+395] [1], column [1], one[s] [1]

Ex 13: 21 By day the LORD went ahead of them in a **pillar** *of* cloud to
13: 21 on their way and by night in a **pillar** *of* fire to give them light,
13: 22 Neither the **pillar** *of* cloud by day nor the pillar of fire by night left
13: 22 Neither the pillar of cloud by day nor the **pillar** *of* fire by night left

Ex 14: 19 The **pillar** *of* cloud also moved from in front and stood behind
14: 24 watch of the night the LORD looked down from the **pillar** *of* fire
26: 32 Hang it with gold hooks on four **posts** *of* acacia wood overlaid
26: 37 for this curtain and five **posts** *of* acacia wood overlaid with gold.
27: 10 with twenty **posts** and twenty bronze bases and with silver hooks
27: 10 twenty bronze bases and with silver hooks and bands on the **posts**.
27: 11 with twenty **posts** and twenty bronze bases and with silver hooks
27: 11 twenty bronze bases and with silver hooks and bands on the **posts**.
27: 12 be fifty cubits wide and have curtains, with ten **posts** and ten bases.
27: 14 to be on one side of the entrance, with three **posts** and three bases,
27: 15 long are to be on the other side, with three **posts** and three bases.
27: 16 the work of an embroiderer—with four **posts** and four bases.
27: 17 All the **posts** around the courtyard are to have silver bands
33: 9 the **pillar** *of* cloud would come down and stay at the entrance,
33: 10 Whenever the people saw the **pillar** *of* cloud standing at the
35: 11 and its covering, clasps, frames, crossbars, **posts** and bases;
35: 17 the curtains of the courtyard with its **posts** and bases, and the
36: 36 They made four **posts** *of* acacia wood for it and overlaid them with
36: 38 they made five **posts** with hooks for them. They overlaid the tops
38: 10 with twenty **posts** and twenty bronze bases, and with silver hooks
38: 10 twenty bronze bases, and with silver hooks and bands on the **posts**.
38: 11 hundred cubits long and had twenty **posts** and twenty bronze bases,
38: 11 and twenty bronze bases, with silver hooks and bands on the **posts**.
38: 12 fifty cubits wide and had curtains, with ten **posts** and ten bases,
38: 12 ten posts and ten bases, with silver hooks and bands on the **posts**.
38: 14 were on one side of the entrance, with three **posts** and three bases,
38: 15 of the entrance to the courtyard, with three **posts** and three bases.
38: 17 The bases for the **posts** were bronze. The hooks and bands on the
38: 17 The hooks and bands on the **posts** were silver, and their tops were
38: 17 with silver; so all the **posts** *of* the courtyard had silver bands.
38: 19 with four **posts** and four bronze bases. Their hooks and bands were
38: 28 They used the 1,775 shekels to make the hooks for the **posts**,
39: 33 all its furnishings, its clasps, frames, crossbars, **posts** and bases;
39: 40 the curtains of the courtyard with its **posts** and bases, and the
40: 18 erected the frames, inserted the crossbars and set up the **posts**.
Nu 3: 36 its crossbars, **posts**, bases, all its equipment, and everything related
3: 37 as well as the **posts** *of* the surrounding courtyard with their bases,
4: 31 to carry the frames of the tabernacle, its crossbars, **posts** and bases,
4: 32 as well as the **posts** *of* the surrounding courtyard with their bases,
12: 5 the LORD came down in a **pillar** *of* cloud; he stood at the
14: 14 that you go before them in a **pillar** *of* cloud by day and a pillar of
14: 14 before them in a pillar of cloud by day and a **pillar** *of* fire by night.
Dt 31: 15 Then the LORD appeared at the Tent in a **pillar** *of* cloud,
31: 15 and **[RPH]** the cloud stood over the entrance to the Tent.
Jdg 16: 25 he performed for them. When they stood him among the **pillars**,
16: 26 "Put me where I can feel the **pillars** that support the temple,
16: 29 Samson reached toward the two central **pillars** on which the
20: 40 But when the **column** *of* smoke began to rise from the city,
1Ki 7: 2 with four rows of cedar **columns** supporting trimmed cedar beams.
7: 2 with four rows of cedar columns supporting **[RPH]** trimmed
7: 3 roofed with cedar above the beams that rested on the **columns**—
7: 6 He made a **colonnade** [+395] fifty cubits long and thirty wide.
7: 6 a portico, and in front of that were **pillars** and an overhanging roof.
7: 15 He cast two bronze **pillars**, each eighteen cubits high and twelve
7: 15 each **[RPH]** eighteen cubits high and twelve cubits around,
7: 15 eighteen cubits high and twelve cubits around, by line. **[RPH]**
7: 16 made two capitals of cast bronze to set on the tops of the **pillars**;
7: 17 of interwoven chains festooned the capitals on top of the **pillars**,
7: 18 He made pomegranates [BHS *pillars*; NIV 8232] in two rows
7: 18 network to decorate the capitals on top of the **pillars**. [BHS 8232]
7: 19 The capitals on top of the **pillars** in the portico were in the shape
7: 20 On the capitals of both **pillars**, above the bowl-shaped part next to
7: 21 He erected the **pillars** at the portico of the temple. The pillar to the
7: 21 The **pillar** to the south he named Jakin and the one to the north
7: 21 pillar to the south he named Jakin and the **one**[s] to the north Boaz.
7: 22 The capitals on top **[RPH]** were in the shape of lilies. And
7: 22 the shape of lilies. And so the work on the **pillars** was completed.
7: 41 the two **pillars**; the two bowl-shaped capitals on top of the pillars;
7: 41 the two pillars; the two bowl-shaped capitals on top of the **pillars**;
7: 41 decorating the two bowl-shaped capitals on top of the **pillars**;
7: 42 decorating the bowl-shaped capitals on top of the **pillars**);
2Ki 11: 14 and there was the king, standing by the **pillar**, as the custom was.
23: 3 The king stood by the **pillar** and renewed the covenant in the
25: 13 The Babylonians broke up the bronze **pillars**, the movable stands
25: 16 The bronze from the two **pillars**, the Sea and the movable stands,
25: 17 Each **pillar** was twenty-seven feet high. The bronze capital on top
25: 17 bronze all around. The other **pillar**, with its network, was similar.
1Ch 18: 8 to make the bronze Sea, the **pillars** and various bronze articles.
2Ch 3: 15 In the front of the temple he made two **pillars**, which ˻together˼
3: 16 He made interwoven chains and put them on top of the **pillars**.
3: 17 He erected the **pillars** in the front of the temple, one to the south
4: 12 the two **pillars**; the two bowl-shaped capitals on top of the pillars;
4: 12 the two pillars; the two bowl-shaped capitals on top of the **pillars**;
4: 12 decorating the two bowl-shaped capitals on top of the **pillars**;
4: 13 decorating the bowl-shaped capitals on top of the **pillars**);
23: 13 and there was the king, standing by his **pillar** at the entrance.
Ne 9: 12 By day you led them with a **pillar** *of* cloud, and by night with a
9: 12 by night with a **pillar** *of* fire to give them light on the way they
9: 19 By day the **pillar** *of* cloud did not cease to guide them on their
9: 19 nor the **pillar** *of* fire by night to shine on the way they were to
Est 1: 6 of white linen and purple material to silver rings on marble **pillars**.
Job 9: 6 He shakes the earth from its place and makes its **pillars** tremble.
26: 11 The **pillars** *of* the heavens quake, aghast at his rebuke.
Ps 75: 3 [75:4] and all its people quake, it is I who hold its **pillars** firm.
99: 7 He spoke to them from the **pillar** *of* cloud; they kept his statutes
Pr 9: 1 Wisdom has built her house; she has hewn out its seven **pillars**.
SS 3: 10 Its **posts** he made of silver, its base of gold. Its seat was
5: 15 His legs are **pillars** *of* marble set on bases of pure gold.
Jer 1: 18 an iron **pillar** and a bronze wall to stand against the whole land—
27: 19 For this is what the LORD Almighty says about the **pillars**,
52: 17 The Babylonians broke up the bronze **pillars**, the movable stands
52: 20 The bronze from the two **pillars**, the Sea and the twelve bronze
52: 21 **[RPH]** Each of the pillars was eighteen cubits high and twelve
52: 21 Each of the **pillars** was eighteen cubits high and twelve cubits in
52: 22 all around. The other **pillar**, with its pomegranates, was similar.
Eze 40: 49 a flight of stairs, and there were **pillars** on each side of the jambs.
42: 6 The rooms on the third floor had no **pillars**, as the courts had;
42: 6 rooms on the third floor had no pillars, as **[RPH]** the courts had;

6648 עַמּוֹן ***'ammôn***, n.pr.[loc.]. [106] [→ 2194, 6649; cf. 6639]
Ammonites [+1201] [79], Ammon [+1201] [9], Ammonite [+1201] [8], Ammon [5], *untranslated* [1], Ammonites [1], their[s] [+1201] [1], them[s] [+1201] [1], they[s] [+1201] [1]

Ge 19: 38 he is the father of the **Ammonites** [+1201] of today.
Nu 21: 24 only as far as the **Ammonites** [+1201], because their border was
21: 24 far as the Ammonites, because **their**[s] [+1201] border was fortified.
Dt 2: 19 When you come to the **Ammonites** [+1201], do not harass them
2: 19 you possession of any land belonging to the **Ammonites** [+1201].
2: 37 did not encroach on any of the land of the **Ammonites** [+1201],
3: 11 and six feet wide. It is still in Rabbah of the **Ammonites** [+1201].)
3: 16 the Jabbok River, which is the border of the **Ammonites** [+1201].
Jos 12: 2 the Jabbok River, which is the border of the **Ammonites** [+1201].
13: 10 ruled in Heshbon, out to the border of the **Ammonites** [+1201].
13: 25 of Gilead and half the **Ammonite** [+1201] country as far as Aroer,
Jdg 3: 13 Getting the **Ammonites** [+1201] and Amalekites to join him,
10: 6 the gods of the **Ammonites** [+1201] and the gods of the
10: 7 them into the hands of the Philistines and the **Ammonites** [+1201],
10: 9 The **Ammonites** [+1201] also crossed the Jordan to fight against
10: 11 the Amorites, the **Ammonites** [+1201], the Philistines,
10: 17 When the **Ammonites** [+1201] were called to arms and camped in
10: 18 "Whoever will launch the attack against the **Ammonites** [+1201]
11: 4 time later, when the **Ammonites** [+1201] made war on Israel,
11: 5 the **[RPH]** elders of Gilead went to get Jephthah from the land of
11: 6 "be our commander, so we can fight the **Ammonites** [+1201]."
11: 8 come with us to fight the **Ammonites** [+1201], and you will be our
11: 9 "Suppose you take me back to fight the **Ammonites** [+1201]
11: 12 Jephthah sent messengers to the **Ammonite** [+1201] king with the
11: 13 The king of the **Ammonites** [+1201] answered Jephthah's
11: 14 Jephthah sent back messengers to the **Ammonite** [+1201] king,
11: 15 not take the land of Moab or the land of the **Ammonites** [+1201].
11: 27 this day between the Israelites and the **Ammonites** [+1201]."
11: 28 The king of **Ammon** [+1201], however, paid no attention to the
11: 29 and from there he advanced against the **Ammonites** [+1201].
11: 30 the LORD: "If you give the **Ammonites** [+1201] into my hands,
11: 31 in triumph from the **Ammonites** [+1201] will be the LORD's,
11: 32 Then Jephthah went over to fight the **Ammonites** [+1201],
11: 33 as far as Abel Keramim. Thus Israel subdued **Ammon** [+1201].
11: 36 has avenged you of your enemies, the **Ammonites** [+1201].
12: 1 "Why did you go to fight the **Ammonites** [+1201] without calling
12: 2 were engaged in a great struggle with the **Ammonites** [+1201],
12: 3 life in my hands and crossed over to fight the **Ammonites** [+1201],
1Sa 11: 11 last watch of the night they broke into the camp of the **Ammonites**
12: 12 "But when you saw that Nahash king of the **Ammonites** [+1201]
14: 47 Moab, the **Ammonites** [+1201], Edom, the kings of Zobah,
2Sa 8: 12 Edom and Moab, the **Ammonites** [+1201] and the Philistines,
10: 1 In the course of time, the king of the **Ammonites** [+1201] died,
10: 2 When David's men came to the land of the **Ammonites** [+1201],
10: 3 the **Ammonite** [+1201] nobles said to Hanun their lord, "Do you
10: 6 When the **Ammonites** [+1201] realized that they had become a
10: 6 that they had become a stench in David's nostrils, **they**[s] [+1201]
10: 8 The **Ammonites** [+1201] came out and drew up in battle formation
10: 10 his brother and deployed them against the **Ammonites** [+1201].
10: 11 if the **Ammonites** [+1201] are too strong for you, then I will come
10: 14 When the **Ammonites** [+1201] saw that the Arameans were
10: 14 So Joab returned from fighting the **Ammonites** [+1201] and came
10: 19 So the Arameans were afraid to help the **Ammonites** [+1201]
11: 1 They destroyed the **Ammonites** [+1201] and besieged Rabbah.

2Sa 12: 9 You killed him with the sword of the **Ammonites** [+1201].
12:26 Meanwhile Joab fought against Rabbah of the **Ammonites** [+1201]
12:31 He did this to all the **Ammonite** [+1201] towns. Then David
17:27 Shobi son of Nahash from Rabbah of the **Ammonites** [+1201],
1Ki 11: 7 and for Molech the detestable god of the **Ammonites** [+1201].
11:33 Molech the god of the **Ammonites** [+1201], and have not walked
2Ki 23:13 and for Molech the detestable god of the people of **Ammon**.
24: 2 Aramean, Moabite and **Ammonite** [+1201] raiders against him.
1Ch 18:11 Edom and Moab, the **Ammonites** [+1201] and the Philistines,
19: 1 the course of time, Nahash king of the **Ammonites** [+1201] died,
19: 2 in the land of the **Ammonites** [+1201] to express sympathy to him,
19: 3 the **Ammonite** [+1201] nobles said to Hanun, "Do you think David
19: 6 When the **Ammonites** [+1201] realized that they had become a
19: 6 the **Ammonites** [+1201] sent a thousand talents of silver to hire
19: 7 while the **Ammonites** [+1201] were mustered from their towns
19: 9 The **Ammonites** [+1201] came out and drew up in battle formation
19:11 and they were deployed against the **Ammonites** [+1201].
19:12 if the **Ammonites** [+1201] are too strong for you, then I will rescue
19:15 When the **Ammonites** [+1201] saw that the Arameans were
19:19 So the Arameans were not willing to help the **Ammonites** [+1201]
20: 1 He laid waste the land of the **Ammonites** [+1201] and went to
20: 3 and axes. David did this to all the **Ammonite** [+1201] towns.
2Ch 20: 1 **Ammonites** [+1201] with some of the Meunites came to make war
20:10 "But now here are men from **Ammon**, Moab and Mount Seir,
20:22 the LORD set ambushes against the men of **Ammon** and Moab
20:23 The men of **Ammon** and Moab rose up against the men from
27: 5 Jotham made war on the king of the **Ammonites** [+1201]
27: 5 That year the **Ammonites** [+1201] paid him a hundred talents of
27: 5 The **Ammonites** [+1201] brought him the same amount also in the
Ps 83: 7 [83:8] Gebal, **Ammon** and Amalek, Philistia, with the people of
Isa 11:14 and Moab, and the **Ammonites** [+1201] will be subject to them.
Jer 9:26 [9:25] Edom, **Ammon** [+1201], Moab and all who live in the
25:21 Edom, Moab and **Ammon** [+1201];
27: 3 Moab, **Ammon** [+1201], Tyre and Sidon through the envoys who
40:11 When all the Jews in Moab, **Ammon** [+1201], Edom and all the
40:14 "Don't you know that Baalis king of the **Ammonites** [+1201] has
41:10 them captive and set out to cross over to the **Ammonites** [+1201].
41:15 men escaped from Johanan and fled to the **Ammonites** [+1201].
49: 1 Concerning the **Ammonites** [+1201]: This is what the LORD
49: 2 sound the battle cry against Rabbah of the **Ammonites** [+1201];
49: 6 I will restore the fortunes of the **Ammonites** [+1201],"
Eze 21:20 [21:25] to come against Rabbah of the **Ammonites** [+1201]
21:28 [21:33] Sovereign LORD says about the **Ammonites** [+1201]
25: 2 set your face against the **Ammonites** [+1201] and prophesy against
25: 3 Say to **them**[s] [+1201], 'Hear the word of the Sovereign LORD.
25: 5 for camels and **Ammon** [+1201] into a resting place for sheep.
25:10 I will give Moab along with the **Ammonites** [+1201] to the people
25:10 so that the **Ammonites** [+1201] will not be remembered among the
Da 11:41 the leaders of **Ammon** [+1201] will be delivered from his hand.
Am 1:13 "For three sins of **Ammon** [+1201], even for four, I will not turn
Zep 2: 8 the insults of Moab and the taunts of the **Ammonites** [+1201],
2: 9 will become like Sodom, the **Ammonites** [+1201] like Gomorrah—

6649 עַמּוֹנִי *'ammônî*, a.g. [21 / 20] [√ 6648]

Ammonite [13], Ammonites [6], Ammon [1]

Dt 2:20 used to live there; but the **Ammonites** called them Zamzummites.
23: 3 [23:4] No **Ammonite** or Moabite or any of his descendants may
1Sa 11: 1 Nahash the **Ammonite** went up and besieged Jabesh Gilead.
11: 2 Nahash the **Ammonite** replied, "I will make a treaty with you only
2Sa 23:37 Zelek the **Ammonite**, Naharai the Beerothite, the armor-bearer of
1Ki 11: 1 Moabites, **Ammonites**, Edomites, Sidonians and Hittites.
11: 5 the Sidonians, and Molech the detestable god of the **Ammonites**.
14:21 His mother's name was Naamah; she was an **Ammonite**.
14:31 His mother's name was Naamah; she was an **Ammonite**.
1Ch 11:39 Zelek the **Ammonite**, Naharai the Berothite, the armor-bearer of
2Ch 12:13 His mother's name was Naamah; she was an **Ammonite**.
20: 1 with some of the Meunites [BHS *Ammonites*; NIV 5064] came
24:26 son of Shimeath an **Ammonite** *woman*, and Jehozabad, son of
26: 8 The **Ammonites** brought tribute to Uzziah, and his fame spread as
Ezr 9: 1 Jebusites, **Ammonites**, Moabites, Egyptians and Amorites.
Ne 2:10 the Horonite and Tobiah the **Ammonite** official heard about this,
2:19 Tobiah the **Ammonite** official and Geshem the Arab heard about
4: 3 [3:35] Tobiah the **Ammonite**, who was at his side, said, "What
4: 7 [4:1] the **Ammonites** and the men of Ashdod heard that the
13: 1 there it was found written that no **Ammonite** or Moabite should
13:23 Judah who had married women from Ashdod, **Ammon** and Moab.

6650 עָמוֹס *'āmôs*, n.pr.m. [7] [√ 6673?]

Amos [7]

Am 1: 1 The words of **Amos**, one of the shepherds of Tekoa—what he saw
7: 8 the LORD asked me, "What do you see, **Amos**?" "A plumb line,"
7:10 "**Amos** is raising a conspiracy against you in the very heart of
7:11 For this is what **Amos** is saying: " 'Jeroboam will die by the sword,
7:12 Amaziah said to **Amos**, "Get out, you seer! Go back to the land of
7:14 **Amos** answered Amaziah, "I was neither a prophet nor a prophet's
8: 2 "What do you see, **Amos**?" he asked. "A basket of ripe fruit,"

6651 עָמוֹק *'āmôq*, n.pr.m. [2] [√ 6676]

Amok [1], Amok's [1]

Ne 12: 7 Sallu, **Amok**, Hilkiah and Jedaiah. These were the leaders of the
12:20 of Sallu's, Kallai; of **Amok's**, Eber;

6652 עַמִּי *'ammî*, n.pr.m. Not used in NIV/BHS [→ 4204]

6653 עַמִּיאֵל *'ammî'ēl*, n.pr.m. [6] [√ 6639 + 446]

Ammiel [6]

Nu 13:12 from the tribe of Dan, **Ammiel** son of Gemalli;
2Sa 9: 4 "He is at the house of Makir son of **Ammiel** in Lo Debar."
9: 5 brought from Lo Debar, from the house of Makir son of **Ammiel**.
17:27 Makir son of **Ammiel** from Lo Debar, and Barzillai the Gileadite
1Ch 3: 5 and Solomon. These four were by Bathsheba daughter of **Ammiel**.
26: 5 **Ammiel** the sixth, Issachar the seventh and Peullethai the eighth.

6654 עַמִּיהוּד *'ammîhûd*, n.pr.m. [10] [√ 6639 + 2086]

Ammihud [10]

Nu 1:10 from Ephraim, Elishama son of **Ammihud**; from Manasseh,
2:18 The leader of the people of Ephraim is Elishama son of **Ammihud**.
7:48 On the seventh day Elishama son of **Ammihud**, the leader of the
7:53 This was the offering of Elishama son of **Ammihud**.
10:22 under their standard. Elishama son of **Ammihud** was in command.
34:20 Shemuel son of **Ammihud**, from the tribe of Simeon;
34:28 Pedahel son of **Ammihud**, the leader from the tribe of Naphtali."
2Sa 13:37 Absalom fled and went to Talmai son of **Ammihud**, [K 6656]
1Ch 7:26 Ladan his son, **Ammihud** his son, Elishama his son,
9: 4 Uthai son of **Ammihud**, the son of Omri, the son of Imri,

6655 עַמִּיזָבָד *'ammîzābād*, n.pr.m. [1] [√ 6639 + 2272]

Ammizabad [1]

1Ch 27: 6 over the Thirty. His son **Ammizabad** was in charge of his division.

6656 עַמִּיחוּר *'ammîḥûr*, n.pr.m. [0] [√ 6639 + 2581?]

2Sa 13:37 [fled and went to Talmai son of **Ammihud**, [K; see Q 6654]]

6657 עַמִּינָדָב *'ammînādāb*, n.pr.m. [13] [√ 6639 + 5605]

Amminadab [13]

Ex 6:23 daughter of **Amminadab** and sister of Nahshon, and she bore him
Nu 1: 7 from Judah, Nahshon son of **Amminadab**;
2: 3 The leader of the people of Judah is Nahshon son of **Amminadab**.
7:12 first day was Nahshon son of **Amminadab** of the tribe of Judah.
7:17 This was the offering of Nahshon son of **Amminadab**.
10:14 their standard. Nahshon son of **Amminadab** was in command.
Ru 4:19 Hezron the father of Ram, Ram the father of **Amminadab**,
4:20 **Amminadab** the father of Nahshon, Nahshon the father of Salmon,
1Ch 2:10 Ram was the father of **Amminadab**, and Amminadab the father of
2:10 **Amminadab** the father of Nahshon, the leader of the people of
6:22 [6:7] **Amminadab** his son, Korah his son, Assir his son,
15:10 descendants of Uzziel, **Amminadab** the leader and 112 relatives.
15:11 Asaiah, Joel, Shemaiah, Eliel and **Amminadab** the Levites.

6658 עָמִיר *'āmîr*, n.[m.]. [4] [√ 6682]

sheaves [2], cut grain [1], grain [1]

Jer 9:22 [9:21] like **cut grain** behind the reaper, with no one to gather
Am 2:13 I will crush you as a cart crushes when loaded with **grain**.
Mic 4:12 his plan, he who gathers them like **sheaves** to the threshing floor.
Zec 12: 6 like a firepot in a woodpile, like a flaming torch among **sheaves**.

6659 עַמִּישַׁדָּי *'ammîšadday*, n.pr.m. [5] [√ 6639 + 8724]

Ammishaddai [5]

Nu 1:12 from Dan, Ahiezer son of **Ammishaddai**;
2:25 The leader of the people of Dan is Ahiezer son of **Ammishaddai**.
7:66 On the tenth day Ahiezer son of **Ammishaddai**, the leader of the
7:71 This was the offering of Ahiezer son of **Ammishaddai**.
10:25 their standard. Ahiezer son of **Ammishaddai** was in command.

6660 עָמִית *'āmît*, n.m. [12] [√ 6669]

neighbor [4], another[s] [1], close [1], countryman [1], countrymen [1], him[s] [+2257] [1], him[s] [1], neighbor's [1], other[s] [1]

Lev 6: 2 [5:21] is unfaithful to the LORD by deceiving his **neighbor**
6: 2 [5:21] or left in his care or stolen, or if he cheats **him**[s] [+2257],

Lev 18:20 " 'Do not have sexual relations with your **neighbor's** wife
19:11 " 'Do not steal. " 'Do not lie. " 'Do not deceive one **another**[s].
19:15 or favoritism to the great, but judge your **neighbor** fairly.
19:17 Rebuke your **neighbor** frankly so you will not share in his guilt.
24:19 If anyone injures his **neighbor**, whatever he has done must be done
25:14 " 'If you sell land to one of your **countrymen** or buy any from him,
25:14 you sell land to one of your countrymen or buy any from **him**[s],
25:15 You are to buy from your **countryman** on the basis of the number
25:17 Do not take advantage of each **other**[s], but fear your God. I am the
Zec 13: 7 against my shepherd, against the man who is **close** *to* me!"

6661 עָמַל *ʿāmal*, v. [11] [→ 6662, 6663, 6664, 6665]

labor [3], toils [2], efforts [1], poured effort [1], tend [1], toiled [1], worked [1], works [1]

Ps 127: 1 [A] the LORD builds the house, its builders **labor** in vain.
Pr 16:26 [A] The laborer's appetite **works** for him; his hunger drives him
Ecc 1: 3 [A] What does man gain from all his labor at which *he* **toils**
2:11 [A] all that my hands had done and what *I had* **toiled** to achieve,
2:19 [A] over all the work into which *I have* **poured** *my* **effort**
2:20 [A] So my heart began to despair over all my toilsome **labor**
2:21 [A] he must leave all he owns to someone who *has* not **worked**
5:16 [5:15] [A] and what does he gain, since *he* **toils** for the wind?
5:18 [5:17] [A] to find satisfaction in his toilsome **labor** under the
8:17 [A] Despite *all his* **efforts** to search it out, man cannot discover
Jnh 4:10 [A] about this vine, though *you did* not **tend** it or make it grow.

6662 עָמָל *ʿāmāl¹*, n.m. & f. [55] [√ 6661]

trouble [15], work [8], labor [5], misery [5], toil [5], oppressive [2], toilsome [2], wrong [2], abuse [1], bitter labor [1], burdens [1], distress [1], efforts [1], making trouble [1], miserable [1], suffering [1], things[s] [1], what toiled for [1], what[s] [1]

Ge 41:51 "It is because God has made me forget all my **trouble** and all my
Nu 23:21 "No misfortune is seen in Jacob, no **misery** observed in Israel.
Dt 26: 7 LORD heard our voice and saw our misery, **toil** and oppression.
Jdg 10:16 served the LORD. And he could bear Israel's **misery** no longer.
Job 3:10 for it did not shut the doors of the womb on me to hide **trouble**
4: 8 those who plow evil and those who sow **trouble** reap it.
5: 6 not spring from the soil, nor does **trouble** sprout from the ground.
5: 7 Yet man is born to **trouble** as surely as sparks fly upward.
7: 3 months of futility, and nights of **misery** have been assigned to me.
11:16 You will surely forget your **trouble**, recalling it only as waters
15:35 They conceive **trouble** and give birth to evil; their womb fashions
16: 2 heard many things like these; **miserable** comforters are you all!
Ps 7:14 [7:15] and conceives **trouble** gives birth to disillusionment.
7:16 [7:17] The **trouble** he *causes* recoils on himself; his violence
10: 7 and lies and threats; **trouble** and evil are under his tongue.
10:14 you, O God, do see **trouble** and grief; you consider it to take it in
25:18 Look upon my affliction and my **distress** and take away all my
55:10 [55:11] prowl about on its walls; malice and **abuse** are within it.
73: 5 They are free from the **burdens** *common to* man; they are not
73:16 When I tried to understand all this, it was **oppressive** to me
90:10 yet their span is but **trouble** and sorrow, for they quickly pass,
94:20 be allied with you—one that brings on **misery** by its decrees?
105:44 of the nations, and they fell heir to **what** others had **toiled for**—
107:12 So he subjected them to **bitter labor**; they stumbled, and there was
140: 9 [140:10] me be covered with the **trouble** their lips have *caused*.
Pr 24: 2 their hearts plot violence, and their lips talk about **making trouble**.
31: 7 and forget their poverty and remember their **misery** no more.
Ecc 1: 3 What does man gain from all his **labor** at which he toils under the
2:10 My heart took delight in all my **work**, and this was the reward for
2:10 delight in all my work, and this was the reward for all my **labor**.
2:11 all that my hands had done and **what**[s] I had toiled to achieve,
2:18 I hated all the **things**[s] I had toiled for under the sun, because I must
2:19 Yet he will have control over all the **work** into which I have
2:20 So my heart began to despair over all my **toilsome** labor under the
2:21 For a man may do his **work** with wisdom, knowledge and skill,
2:22 What does a man get for all the **toil** and anxious striving with
2:24 better than to eat and drink and find satisfaction in his **work**.
3:13 everyone may eat and drink, and find satisfaction in all his **toil**—
4: 4 I saw that all **labor** and all achievement spring from man's envy of
4: 6 Better one handful with tranquillity than two handfuls with **toil**
4: 8 There was no end to his **toil**, yet his eyes were not content with his
4: 9 are better than one, because they have a good return for their **work**:
5:15 [5:14] He takes nothing from his **labor** that he can carry in his
5:18 [5:17] to find satisfaction in his **toilsome** labor under the sun
5:19 [5:18] to enjoy them, to accept his lot and be happy in his **work**—
6: 7 All man's **efforts** are for his mouth, yet his appetite is never
8:15 joy will accompany him in his **work** all the days of the life God
9: 9 For this is your lot in life and in your toilsome **labor** under the sun.
10:15 A fool's **work** wearies him; he does not know the way to town.
Isa 10: 1 who make unjust laws, to those who issue **oppressive** decrees,
53:11 After the **suffering** *of* his soul, he will see the light ⌞of life⌟
59: 4 and speak lies; they conceive **trouble** and give birth to evil.
Jer 20:18 Why did I ever come out of the womb to see **trouble** and sorrow
Hab 1: 3 Why do you tolerate **wrong**? Destruction and violence are before
1:13 Your eyes are too pure to look on evil; you cannot tolerate **wrong**.

6663 ²עָמָל *ʿāmāl²*, n.pr.m. [1] [√ 6662; cf. 6661]

Amal [1]

1Ch 7:35 The sons of his brother Helem: Zophah, Imna, Shelesh and **Amal**.

6664 ¹עָמֵל *ʿāmēl¹*, n.m. [4] [√ 6661]

misery [2], laborer's [1], workman's [1]

Jdg 5:26 for the tent peg, her right hand for the **workman's** hammer.
Job 3:20 "Why is light given to *those in* **misery**, and life to the bitter of
20:22 will overtake him; the full force of **misery** will come upon him.
Pr 16:26 The **laborer's** appetite works for him; his hunger drives him on.

6665 ²עָמֵל *ʿāmēl²*, a.vbl. [5] [√ 6661]

labors [1], toil [1], toiled for [1], toiling [1], toilsome [1]

Ecc 2:18 I hated all the things I had **toiled for** under the sun, because I must
2:22 and anxious striving with which he **labors** under the sun?
3: 9 What does the worker gain from his **toil**?
4: 8 "For whom am I **toiling**," he asked, "and why am I depriving
9: 9 For this is your lot in life and in your **toilsome** labor under the sun.

6666 עַמְלָץ *ʿamlāṣ*, n.[m.]. Not used in NIV/BHS [√ 4914]

6667 עֲמָלֵק *ʿᵃmālēq*, n.pr.m. [39] [→ 6668]

Amalekites [25], Amalek [12], Amalekite [1], their[s] [1]

Ge 36:12 also had a concubine named Timna, who bore him **Amalek**.
36:16 Korah, Gatam and **Amalek**. These were the chiefs descended from
Ex 17: 8 The **Amalekites** came and attacked the Israelites at Rephidim.
17: 9 "Choose some of our men and go out to fight the **Amalekites**.
17:10 So Joshua fought the **Amalekites** as Moses had ordered, and
17:11 but whenever he lowered his hands, the **Amalekites** were winning.
17:13 So Joshua overcame the **Amalekite** army with the sword.
17:14 because I will completely blot out the memory of **Amalek** from
17:16 The LORD will be at war against the **Amalekites** from generation
Nu 13:29 The **Amalekites** live in the Negev; the Hittites, Jebusites
24:20 Balaam saw **Amalek** and uttered his oracle: "Amalek was first
24:20 "**Amalek** was first among the nations, but he will come to ruin at
Dt 25:17 Remember what the **Amalekites** did to you along the way when
25:19 you shall blot out the memory of **Amalek** from under heaven.
Jdg 3:13 Getting the Ammonites and **Amalekites** to join him, Eglon came
5:14 Some came from Ephraim, whose roots were in **Amalek**;
6: 3 **Amalekites** and other eastern peoples invaded the country.
6:33 **Amalekites** and other eastern peoples joined forces and crossed
7:12 the **Amalekites** and all the other eastern peoples had settled in the
10:12 the **Amalekites** and the Maonites oppressed you and you cried to
1Sa 14:48 He fought valiantly and defeated the **Amalekites**, delivering Israel
15: 2 'I will punish the **Amalekites** for what they did to Israel when they
15: 3 attack the **Amalekites** and totally destroy everything that belongs
15: 5 Saul went to the city of **Amalek** and set an ambush in the ravine.
15: 6 out of Egypt." So the Kenites moved away from the **Amalekites**.
15: 7 Saul attacked the **Amalekites** all the way from Havilah to Shur,
15: 8 He took Agag king of the **Amalekites** alive, and all his people he
15:18 and completely destroy those wicked people, the **Amalekites**;
15:20 I completely destroyed the **Amalekites** and brought back Agag
15:20 destroyed the Amalekites and brought back Agag **their**[s] king.
15:32 Then Samuel said, "Bring me Agag king of the **Amalekites**."
28:18 the LORD or carry out his fierce wrath against the **Amalekites**,
30:18 David recovered everything the **Amalekites** had taken,
2Sa 1: 1 David returned from defeating the **Amalekites** and stayed in
8:12 and Moab, the Ammonites and the Philistines, and **Amalek**.
1Ch 1:36 Teman, Omar, Zepho, Gatam and Kenaz; by Timna: **Amalek**.
4:43 They killed the remaining **Amalekites** who had escaped, and they
18:11 and Moab, the Ammonites and the Philistines, and **Amalek**.
Ps 83: 7 [83:8] Gebal, Ammon and **Amalek**, Philistia, with the people of

6668 עֲמָלֵקִי *ʿᵃmālēqî*, a.g. [12] [√ 6667]

Amalekites [9], Amalekite [3]

Ge 14: 7 and they conquered the whole territory of the **Amalekites**,
Nu 14:25 Since the **Amalekites** and Canaanites are living in the valleys,
14:43 for the **Amalekites** and Canaanites will face you there.
14:45 the **Amalekites** and Canaanites who lived in that hill country came
Jdg 12:15 at Pirathon in Ephraim, in the hill country of the **Amalekites**.
1Sa 15: 6 leave the **Amalekites** so that I do not destroy you along with them;
15:15 Saul answered, "The soldiers brought them from the **Amalekites**;
27: 8 and raided the Geshurites, the Girzites and the **Amalekites**.
30: 1 Now the **Amalekites** had raided the Negev and Ziklag. They had
30:13 He said, "I am an Egyptian, the slave of an **Amalekite**.

2Sa 1: 8 "He asked me, 'Who are you?' " 'An **Amalekite**,' I answered.
1: 13 you from?" "I am the son of an alien, an **Amalekite**," he answered.

6669 ¹עָמַם ***ʿāmam*[1]**, v. [1] [→ 6640, 6645, 6660]

rival [1]

Eze 31: 8 [A] The cedars in the garden of God *could* not **rival** it, nor could

6670 ²עָמַם ***ʿāmam*[2]**, v. [2]

hidden [1], lost luster [1]

La 4: 1 [H] How the gold *has* **lost** *its* **luster**, the fine gold become dull!
Eze 28: 3 [A] Are you wiser than Daniel? *Is* no secret **hidden** *from* you?

6671 עַמֹּנָה ***ʿammōnâ***, n.pr.loc.[?] [0] [cf. 2194, 4112]

Jos 18: 24 [**Kephar Ammoni**, [Q +2021; see K 4112] Ophni and Geba—]

6672 עִמָּנוּ אֵל ***ʿimmānû ʾēl***, n.pr.m. [2] [√ 6640 + 5646 + 446]

Immanuel [2]

Isa 7: 14 and will give birth to a son, and will call him **Immanuel**.
8: 8 wings will cover the breadth of your land, O **Immanuel**!"

6673 עָמַס ***ʿāmas***, v. [9] [→ 5098, 6650?, 6674]

laid [2], bears burdens [1], burdensome [1], carried [+928+5951] [1], loaded [1], loading [1], move [1], upheld [1]

Ge 44: 13 [A] Then *they* all **loaded** their donkeys and returned to the city.
1Ki 12: 11 [G] My father **laid** on you a heavy yoke; I will make it even
2Ch 10: 11 [G] My father **laid** on you a heavy yoke; I will make it even
Ne 4: 17 [4:11] [A] Those *who* **carried** [+928+5951] materials did their
13: 15 [A] the Sabbath and bringing in grain and **loading** it on donkeys,
Ps 68: 19 [68:20] [A] to God our Savior, *who* daily **bears** our **burdens**.
Isa 46: 1 [B] The images that are carried about *are* **burdensome**, a burden
46: 3 [B] you whom I *have* **upheld** since you were conceived,
Zec 12: 3 [A] all the nations. All *who try to* **move** it will injure themselves.

6674 עֲמַסְיָה ***ʿămasyâ***, n.pr.m. [1] [√ 6673 + 3378]

Amasiah [1]

2Ch 17: 16 next, **Amasiah** son of Zicri, who volunteered himself for the

6675 עַמְעָד ***ʿamʿād***, n.pr.loc. [1]

Amad [1]

Jos 19: 26 Allammelech, **Amad** and Mishal. On the west the boundary

6676 עָמַק ***ʿāmaq***, v. [9] [→ 1097, 2195, 5099, 6651, 6677, 6678, 6679, 6680, 6681]

deep [3], deepest [1], go to great depths [1], greatly [1], made deep [1], profound [1], sunk deep [1]

Ps 92: 5 [92:6] [A] O LORD, how **profound** your thoughts!
Isa 7: 11 [G] whether in the **deepest** depths or in the highest heights."
29: 15 [G] Woe to those *who* **go to great depths** to hide their plans
30: 33 [G] Its fire pit *has been* **made deep** and wide, with an abundance
31: 6 [G] Return to him *you have so* **greatly** revolted against,
Jer 49: 8 [G] Turn and flee, hide in **deep** caves, you who live in Dedan,
49: 30 [G] Stay in **deep** caves, you who live in Hazor,"
Hos 5: 2 [G] The rebels *are* **deep** *in* slaughter. I will discipline all of them.
9: 9 [G] *They have* **sunk deep** *into* corruption, as in the days of

6677 עֵמֶק ***ʿēmeq***, n.m. [68] [→ 1097; cf. 6676]

valley [52], valleys [11], plain [2], fiercely [+928+2021] [1], plain [+824] [1], plains [1]

Ge 14: 3 All these latter kings joined forces in the **Valley** *of* Siddim (the
14: 8 marched out and drew up their battle lines in the **Valley** *of* Siddim
14: 10 Now the **Valley** *of* Siddim was full of tar pits, and when the kings
14: 17 the king of Sodom came out to meet him in the **Valley** *of* Shaveh
14: 17 to meet him in the Valley of Shaveh (that is, the King's **Valley**).
37: 14 back to me." Then he sent him off from the **Valley** *of* Hebron.
Nu 14: 25 Since the Amalekites and Canaanites are living in the **valleys**,
Jos 7: 24 and sheep, his tent and all that he had, to the **Valley** *of* Achor.
7: 26 Therefore that place has been called the **Valley** *of* Achor ever
8: 13 ambush to the west of it. That night Joshua went into the **valley**.
10: 12 stand still over Gibeon, O moon, over the **Valley** *of* Aijalon."
13: 19 Kiriathaim, Sibmah, Zereth Shahar on the hill in the **valley**,
13: 27 in the **valley**, Beth Haram, Beth Nimrah, Succoth and Zaphon with
15: 7 The boundary then went up to Debir from the **Valley** *of* Achor
15: 8 the Hinnom Valley at the northern end of the **Valley** *of* Rephaim.
17: 16 all the Canaanites who live in the **plain** [+824] have iron chariots,
17: 16 Beth Shan and its settlements and those in the **Valley** *of* Jezreel."
18: 16 facing the Valley of Ben Hinnom, north of the **Valley** *of* Rephaim.
Jdg 1: 19 they were unable to drive the people from the **plains**, because they
1: 34 to the hill country, not allowing them to come down into the **plain**.
5: 15 Issachar was with Barak, rushing after him into the **valley**.
6: 33 and crossed over the Jordan and camped in the **Valley** *of* Jezreel.
7: 1 The camp of Midian was north of them in the **valley** near the hill
7: 8 of the others. Now the camp of Midian lay below him in the **valley**.
7: 12 and all the other eastern peoples had settled in the **valley**,
18: 28 The city was in a **valley** near Beth Rehob. The Danites rebuilt the
1Sa 6: 13 people of Beth Shemesh were harvesting their wheat in the **valley**,
17: 2 and the Israelites assembled and camped in the **Valley** *of* Elah
17: 19 They are with Saul and all the men of Israel in the **Valley** *of* Elah,
21: 9 [21:10] whom you killed in the **Valley** *of* Elah, is here;
31: 7 When the Israelites along the **valley** and those across the Jordan
2Sa 5: 18 the Philistines had come and spread out in the **Valley** *of* Rephaim;
5: 22 the Philistines came up and spread out in the **Valley** *of* Rephaim;
18: 18 and erected it in the King's **Valley** as a monument to himself,
23: 13 while a band of Philistines was encamped in the **Valley** *of*
1Ki 20: 28 think the LORD is a god of the hills and not a god of the **valleys**,
1Ch 10: 7 When all the Israelites in the **valley** saw that the army had fled
11: 15 while a band of Philistines was encamped in the **Valley** *of*
12: 15 [12:16] they put to flight everyone living in the **valleys**, to the east
14: 9 Now the Philistines had come and raided the **Valley** *of* Rephaim;
14: 13 Once more the Philistines raided the **valley**;
27: 29 Shaphat son of Adlai was in charge of the herds in the **valleys**.
2Ch 20: 26 On the fourth day they assembled in the **Valley** *of* Beracah,
20: 26 This is why it is called the **Valley** *of* Beracah to this day.
Job 39: 10 to the furrow with a harness? Will he till the **valleys** behind you?
39: 21 He paws **fiercely** [+928+2021], rejoicing in his strength,
Ps 60: 6 [60:8] parcel out Shechem and measure off the **Valley** *of* Succoth.
65: 13 [65:14] with flocks and the **valleys** are mantled with grain;
84: 6 [84:7] As they pass through the **Valley** *of* Baca, they make it a
108: 7 [108:8] out Shechem and measure off the **Valley** *of* Succoth.
SS 2: 1 I am a rose of Sharon, a lily of the **valleys**.
Isa 17: 5 as when a man gleans heads of grain in the **Valley** *of* Rephaim.
22: 7 Your choicest **valleys** are full of chariots, and horsemen are posted
28: 21 Mount Perazim, he will rouse himself as in the **Valley** of Gibeon—
65: 10 the **Valley** *of* Achor a resting place for herds, for my people who
Jer 21: 13 ⌞Jerusalem,⌟ you who live above this **valley** on the rocky plateau,
31: 40 The whole **valley** *where* dead bodies and ashes are thrown,
47: 5 O remnant on the **plain**, how long will you cut yourselves?
48: 8 The **valley** will be ruined and the plateau destroyed,
49: 4 Why do you boast of your **valleys**, boast of your valleys
49: 4 do you boast of your valleys, boast of your **valleys** so fruitful?
Hos 1: 5 In that day I will break Israel's bow in the **Valley** *of* Jezreel."
2: 15 [2:17] and will make the **Valley** *of* Achor a door of hope.
Joel 3: 2 [4:2] and bring them down to the **Valley** *of* Jehoshaphat.
3: 12 [4:12] let them advance into the **Valley** *of* Jehoshaphat, for there I
3: 14 [4:14] Multitudes, multitudes in the **valley** *of* decision!
3: 14 [4:14] For the day of the LORD is near in the **valley** *of* decision.
Mic 1: 4 The mountains melt beneath him and the **valleys** split apart,

6678 עָמֹק ***ʿāmōq***, a. [17] [√ 6676; Ar 10555]

deep [13], most profound [+6678] [2], cunning [1], deeper [1]

Lev 13: 3 has turned white and the sore appears to be more than skin **deep**,
13: 4 on his skin is white but does not appear to be more than skin **deep**
13: 25 in it has turned white, and it appears to be more than skin **deep**,
13: 30 if it appears to be more than skin **deep** and the hair in it is yellow
13: 31 it does not seem to be more than skin **deep** and there is no black
13: 32 yellow hair in it and it does not appear to be more than skin **deep**,
13: 34 not spread in the skin and appears to be no more than skin **deep**,
Job 11: 8 They are **deeper** than the depths of the grave—what can you
12: 22 He reveals the **deep** *things* of darkness and brings deep shadows
Ps 64: 6 [64:7] Surely the mind and heart of man are **cunning**.
Pr 18: 4 The words of a man's mouth are **deep** waters, but the fountain of
20: 5 The purposes of a man's heart are **deep** waters, but a man of
22: 14 The mouth of an adulteress is a **deep** pit; he who is under the
23: 27 for a prostitute is a **deep** pit and a wayward wife is a narrow well.
Ecc 7: 24 wisdom may be, it is far off and **most profound** [+6678]—
7: 24 wisdom may be, it is far off and **most profound** [+6678]—
Eze 23: 32 "You will drink your sister's cup, a cup large and **deep**; it will

6679 עֹמֶק ***ʿōmeq***, n.[m.] [2] [√ 6676]

deep [1], depths [1]

Pr 9: 18 the dead are there, that her guests are in the **depths** *of* the grave.
25: 3 As the heavens are high and the earth is **deep**, so the hearts of

6680 עָמֵק ***ʿāmēq***, a. [3] [√ 6676]

obscure [2], obscure [+4946+9048] [1]

Isa 33: 19 those people of an **obscure** [+4946+9048] speech, with their
Eze 3: 5 You are not being sent to a people of **obscure** speech and difficult
3: 6 not to many peoples of **obscure** speech and difficult language,

6681 עֵמֶק קְצִיץ ʿēmeq qᵉṣîṣ, n.pr.loc. [1] [√ 6676 + 7906]
Emek Keziz [1]
Jos 18: 21 had the following cities: Jericho, Beth Hoglah, **Emek Keziz**,

6682 עָמַר ʿāmar[1], v.den. [1] [→ 6658, 6684, 6685, 6890, 6891; cf. 6890]
gathers [1]
Ps 129: 7 [D] cannot fill his hands, nor the *one who* **gathers** fill his arms.

6683 עָמַר ʿāmar[2], v. [2] [→ 6686, 6688, 6689]
treat as a slave [1], treats as a slave [1]
Dt 21: 14 [F] You must not sell her or **treat** her **as a slave**, since you have
24: 7 [F] of his brother Israelites and **treats** him **as a slave** or sells him,

6684 עֹמֶר ʿōmer[1], n.m. [8] [√ 6682]
sheaf [4], sheaves [3], sheaf of grain [1]
Lev 23: 10 its harvest, bring to the priest a **sheaf of** the first **grain** you harvest.
23: 11 He is to wave the **sheaf** before the LORD so it will be accepted
23: 12 On the day you wave the **sheaf**, you must sacrifice as a burnt
23: 15 the day you brought the **sheaf** *of* the wave offering, count off seven
Dt 24: 19 When you are harvesting in your field and you overlook a **sheaf**,
Ru 2: 7 let me glean and gather among the **sheaves** behind the harvesters.'
2: 15 "Even if she gathers among the **sheaves**, don't embarrass her.
Job 24: 10 they go about naked; they carry the **sheaves**, but still go hungry.

6685 עֹמֶר ʿōmer[2], n.m. [6] [√ 6682]
omer [5], omers [1]
Ex 16: 16 he needs. Take an **omer** for each person you have in your tent.' "
16: 18 when they measured it by the **omer**, he who gathered much did not
16: 22 they gathered twice as much—two **omers** for each person—
16: 32 'Take an **omer** of manna and keep it for the generations to come,
16: 33 Moses said to Aaron, "Take a jar and put an **omer** *of* manna in it.
16: 36 (An **omer** is one tenth of an ephah.)

6686 עֲמֹרָה ᵃmōrâ, n.pr.loc. [19] [√ 6683]
Gomorrah [19]
Ge 10: 19 toward Sodom, **Gomorrah**, Admah and Zeboiim, as far as Lasha.
13: 10 (This was before the LORD destroyed Sodom and **Gomorrah**.)
14: 2 Birsha king of **Gomorrah**, Shinab king of Admah, Shemeber king
14: 8 the king of **Gomorrah**, the king of Admah, the king of Zeboiim
14: 10 when the kings of Sodom and **Gomorrah** fled, some of the men
14: 11 seized all the goods of Sodom and **Gomorrah** and all their food;
18: 20 against Sodom and **Gomorrah** is so great and their sin so grievous
19: 24 LORD rained down burning sulfur on Sodom and **Gomorrah**—
19: 28 He looked down toward Sodom and **Gomorrah**, toward all the
Dt 29: 23 [29:22] It will be like the destruction of Sodom and **Gomorrah**,
32: 32 comes from the vine of Sodom and from the fields of **Gomorrah**.
Isa 1: 9 have become like Sodom, we would have been like **Gomorrah**.
1: 10 of Sodom; listen to the law of our God, you people of **Gomorrah**!
13: 19 will be overthrown by God like Sodom and **Gomorrah**.
Jer 23: 14 like Sodom to me; the people of Jerusalem are like **Gomorrah**."
49: 18 As Sodom and **Gomorrah** were overthrown, along with their
50: 40 and **Gomorrah** along with their neighboring towns,"
Am 4: 11 "I overthrew some of you as I overthrew Sodom and **Gomorrah**.
Zep 2: 9 Moab will become like Sodom, the Ammonites like **Gomorrah**—

6687 עָמְרִי ʿomrî, n.pr.m. [18]
Omri [15], Omri's [2], he[s] [+281+1201] [1]
1Ki 16: 16 plotted against the king and murdered him, they proclaimed **Omri**,
16: 17 **Omri** and all the Israelites with him withdrew from Gibbethon
16: 21 Tibni son of Ginath for king, and the other half supported **Omri**.
16: 22 **Omri's** followers proved stronger than those of Tibni son of
16: 22 of Tibni son of Ginath. So Tibni died and **Omri** became king.
16: 23 **Omri** became king of Israel, and he reigned twelve years,
16: 25 **Omri** did evil in the eyes of the LORD and sinned more than all
16: 27 As for the other events of **Omri's** reign, what he did and the things
16: 28 **Omri** rested with his fathers and was buried in Samaria. And Ahab
16: 29 of Asa king of Judah, Ahab son of **Omri** became king of Israel,
16: 29 **he**[s] [+281+1201] reigned in Samaria over Israel twenty-two years.
16: 30 Ahab son of **Omri** did more evil in the eyes of the LORD than
2Ki 8: 26 name was Athaliah, a granddaughter of **Omri** king of Israel.
1Ch 7: 8 Zemirah, Joash, Eliezer, Elioenai, **Omri**, Jeremoth, Abijah,
9: 4 of Ammihud, the son of **Omri**, the son of Imri, the son of Bani,
27: 18 Elihu, a brother of David; over Issachar: **Omri** son of Michael;
2Ch 22: 2 His mother's name was Athaliah, a granddaughter of **Omri**.
Mic 6: 16 You have observed the statutes of **Omri** and all the practices of

6688 עַמְרָם ʿamrām, n.pr.m. [14] [→ 6689; cf. 6683? *or* 6639? + 8123?]
Amram [13], Amram's [1]
Ex 6: 18 The sons of Kohath were **Amram**, Izhar, Hebron and Uzziel.
6: 20 **Amram** married his father's sister Jochebed, who bore him Aaron
6: 20 who bore him Aaron and Moses. **Amram** lived 137 years.
Nu 3: 19 The Kohathite clans: **Amram**, Izhar, Hebron and Uzziel.
26: 58 the Korahite clan. (Kohath was the forefather of **Amram**;
26: 59 the name of **Amram's** wife was Jochebed, a descendant of Levi,
26: 59 To **Amram** she bore Aaron, Moses and their sister Miriam.
1Ch 6: 2 [5:28] The sons of Kohath: **Amram**, Izhar, Hebron and Uzziel.
6: 3 [5:29] The children of **Amram**: Aaron, Moses and Miriam. The
6: 18 [6:3] The sons of Kohath: **Amram**, Izhar, Hebron and Uzziel.
23: 12 sons of Kohath: **Amram**, Izhar, Hebron and Uzziel—four in all.
23: 13 The sons of **Amram**: Aaron and Moses. Aaron was set apart,
24: 20 from the sons of **Amram**: Shubael; from the sons of Shubael:
Ezr 10: 34 From the descendants of Bani: Maadai, **Amram**, Uel,

6689 עַמְרָמִי ʿamrāmî, a.g. [2] [√ 6688]
Amramites [2]
Nu 3: 27 To Kohath belonged the clans of the **Amramites**, Izharites,
1Ch 26: 23 From the **Amramites**, the Izharites, the Hebronites and the

6690 עֲמָשָׂא ᵃmāśāʾ, n.pr.m. [16] [→ 6691]
Amasa [15], whose[s] [1]
2Sa 17: 25 Absalom had appointed **Amasa** over the army in place of Joab.
17: 25 **Amasa** was the son of a man named Jether, an Israelite who had
19: 13 [19:14] And say to **Amasa**, 'Are you not my own flesh and blood?
20: 4 the king said to **Amasa**, "Summon the men of Judah to come to me
20: 5 when **Amasa** went to summon Judah, he took longer than the time
20: 8 they were at the great rock in Gibeon, **Amasa** came to meet them.
20: 9 Joab said to **Amasa**, "How are you, my brother?" Then Joab took
20: 9 Joab took **Amasa** by the beard with his right hand to kiss him.
20: 10 **Amasa** was not on his guard against the dagger in Joab's hand,
20: 12 **Amasa** lay wallowing in his blood in the middle of the road,
20: 12 When he realized that everyone who came up to **Amasa** stopped,
1Ki 2: 5 of Israel's armies, Abner son of Ner and **Amasa** son of Jether.
2: 32 son of Ner, commander of Israel's army, and **Amasa** son of Jether,
1Ch 2: 17 Abigail was the mother of **Amasa**, whose father was Jether the
2: 17 was the mother of Amasa, **whose**[s] father was Jether the Ishmaelite.
2Ch 28: 12 Jehizkiah son of Shallum, and **Amasa** son of Hadlai—

6691 עֲמָשַׂי ᵃmāśay, n.pr.m. [5] [√ 6690]
Amasai [5]
1Ch 6: 25 [6:10] The descendants of Elkanah: **Amasai**, Ahimoth,
6: 35 [6:20] the son of Elkanah, the son of Mahath, the son of **Amasai**,
12: 18 [12:19] the Spirit came upon **Amasai**, chief of the Thirty, and he
15: 24 Joshaphat, Nethanel, **Amasai**, Zechariah, Benaiah and Eliezer the
2Ch 29: 12 the Kohathites, Mahath son of **Amasai** and Joel son of Azariah;

6692 עֲמַשְׁסַי ᵃmaššay, n.pr.m. [1]
Amashsai [1]
Ne 11: 13 **Amashsai** son of Azarel, the son of Ahzai, the son of

6693 עֲנָב ᵃnāb, n.pr.loc. [2] [√ 6694]
Anab [2]
Jos 11: 21 from Hebron, Debir and **Anab**, from all the hill country of Judah,
15: 50 **Anab**, Eshtemoh, Anim,

6694 עֵנָב ʿēnāb, n.m. [19] [→ 6693]
grapes [12], good grapes [2], grape [2], *untranslated* [1], grapes or raisins [+2256+3313+4300] [1], raisin [1]
Ge 40: 10 as it budded, it blossomed, and its clusters ripened into **grapes**.
40: 11 Pharaoh's cup was in my hand, and I took the **grapes**, squeezed
49: 11 will wash his garments in wine, his robes in the blood of **grapes**.
Lev 25: 5 what grows of itself or harvest the **grapes** *of* your untended vines.
Nu 6: 3 He must not drink **grape** juice or eat grapes or raisins.
6: 3 not drink grape juice or eat **grapes** [+2256+3313+4300] **or raisins**.
13: 20 the fruit of the land." (It was the season for the first ripe **grapes**.)
13: 23 of Eshcol, they cut off a branch bearing a single cluster of **grapes**.
Dt 23: 24 [23:25] you may eat all the **grapes** you want, but do not put any
32: 14 finest kernels of wheat. You drank the foaming blood of the **grape**.
32: 32 Their **grapes** are *filled with* poison, and their clusters with
32: 32 Their grapes are **[RPH]** filled with poison, and their clusters with
Ne 13: 15 together with wine, **grapes**, figs and all other kinds of loads.
Isa 5: 2 he looked for a crop of **good grapes**, but it yielded only bad fruit.
5: 4 When I looked for **good grapes**, why did it yield only bad?
Jer 8: 13 declares the LORD. There will be no **grapes** on the vine.

[A] Qal [B] Qal passive [C] Niphal [D] Piel (poel, polel, pilel, pilal, pealal, pilpel) [E] Pual (poal, polal, poaal, pulal, pualal)

Hos 3: 1 though they turn to other gods and love the sacred **raisin** cakes."
9: 10 "When I found Israel, it was like finding **grapes** in the desert;
Am 9: 13 by the plowman and the planter by the one treading **grapes**.

6695 עָנַג **'ānag**, v. [10] [→ 6696, 6697, 9503]

delight [2], find delight [2], delicate [1], delight yourself [1], enjoy [1], find joy [1], mocking [1], sensitive [1]

Dt 28: 56 [F] so **sensitive** and gentle that she would not venture to touch
Job 22: 26 [F] Surely then *you will* **find delight** in the Almighty and will lift
27: 10 [F] *Will he* **find delight** in the Almighty? Will he call upon God
Ps 37: 4 [F] **Delight yourself** in the LORD and he will give you the
37: 11 [F] But the meek will inherit the land and **enjoy** great peace.
Isa 55: 2 [F] what is good, and your soul *will* **delight** in the richest of fare.
57: 4 [F] Whom *are you* **mocking**? At whom do you sneer and stick
58: 14 [F] *you will* **find** *your* **joy** in the LORD, and I will cause you to
66: 11 [F] will drink deeply and **delight** in her overflowing abundance."
Jer 6: 2 [E] I will destroy the Daughter of Zion, so beautiful and **delicate**.

6696 עֹנֶג **'ōneg**, n.[m.]. [2] [√ 6695]

delight [1], luxurious [1]

Isa 13: 22 will howl in her strongholds, jackals in her **luxurious** palaces.
58: 13 if you call the Sabbath a **delight** and the LORD's holy day

6697 עָנֹג **'ānōg**, a. [3] [√ 6695]

sensitive [2], delicate [1]

Dt 28: 54 **sensitive** man among you will have no compassion on his own
28: 56 The most gentle and **sensitive** *woman* among you—so sensitive
Isa 47: 1 of the Babylonians. No more will you be called tender or **delicate**.

6698 עָנַד **'ānad**, v. [2] [cf. 5051]

fasten [1], put on [1]

Job 31: 36 [A] wear it on my shoulder, *I would* **put** it **on** like a crown.
Pr 6: 21 [A] them upon your heart forever; **fasten** them around your neck.

6699 עָנָה **'ānâ**[1], v. [313] [→ 3614?, 5101, 6717; Ar 10558]

answered [74], answer [73], replied [41], said [29], answers [9], asked [7], respond [7], responded [6], testify [5], reply [4], testifies [4], *untranslated* [3], spoke [3], answering [2], declare [2], give [2], help [2], said in reply [2], spoke up [2], accept [1], accuse [1], answer [+1821] [1], answer given [1], arguing [1], be answered [1], come to relief [1], dispute [1], echo [1], explained [1], gave ruling [1], get response [1], give answer [1], give testimony [1], gives back answer [1], gives [1], giving testimony [1], go unanswered [+4202] [1], had[s] [1], have answer [1], have say [+2750] [1], recite [+606+2256] [1], reported [1], said a word [1], save [1], say [+606+2256] [1], say [1], says [1], shout [1], shouted [1], tell [1], testified [1], testify [+4200+6332] [1], testimony [1], told [1], whoever he may be [+2256+6424] [1]

Ge 18: 27 [A] Abraham **spoke up** again: "Now that I have been so bold as
23: 5 [A] The Hittites **replied** *to* Abraham,
23: 10 [A] he **replied** *to* Abraham in the hearing of all the Hittites who
23: 14 [A] Ephron **answered** Abraham,
24: 50 [A] Laban and Bethuel **answered**, "This is from the LORD;
27: 37 [A] Isaac **answered** Esau, "I have made him lord over you
27: 39 [A] His father Isaac **answered** him, "Your dwelling will be away
30: 33 [A] my honesty *will* **testify** for me in the future, whenever you
31: 14 [A] Rachel and Leah **replied**, "Do we still have any share in the
31: 31 [A] Jacob **answered** Laban, "I was afraid, because I thought you
31: 36 [A] took Laban to task. "What is my crime?" he **asked** Laban.
31: 43 [A] Laban **answered** Jacob, "The women are my daughters,
34: 13 [A] sons **replied** deceitfully as they spoke to Shechem and
35: 3 [A] who **answered** me in the day of my distress and who has
40: 18 [A] "This is what it means," Joseph **said**. "The three baskets are
41: 16 [A] "I cannot do it," Joseph **replied** *to* Pharaoh, "but God will
41: 16 [A] "but God *will* **give** Pharaoh *the* **answer** he desires."
42: 22 [A] Reuben **replied**, "Didn't I tell you not to sin against the boy?
45: 3 [A] his brothers were not able to **answer** him, because they were
Ex 4: 1 [A] Moses **answered**, "What if they do not believe me or listen
19: 8 [A] The people all **responded** together, "We will do everything
19: 19 [A] Then Moses spoke and the voice of God **answered** him.
20: 16 [A] "*You shall* not **give** false testimony against your neighbor.
23: 2 [A] When *you* **give testimony** in a lawsuit, do not pervert justice
24: 3 [A] LORD's words and laws, they **responded** *with* one voice,
Nu 11: 28 [A] **spoke up** and said, "Moses, my lord, stop them!"
22: 18 [A] Balaam **answered** them, "Even if Balak gave me his palace
23: 12 [A] *He* **answered**, "Must I not speak what the LORD puts in
23: 26 [A] Balaam **answered**, "Did I not tell you I must do whatever the
32: 31 [A] The Gadites and Reubenites **answered**, "Your servants will
35: 30 [A] no one is to be put to death *on the* **testimony** *of* only one
Dt 1: 14 [A] *You* **answered** me, "What you propose to do is good."
1: 41 [A] *you* **replied**, "We have sinned against the LORD. We will
5: 20 [A] "*You shall* not **give** false testimony against your neighbor.
19: 16 [A] If a malicious witness takes the stand to **accuse** a man of a
19: 18 [A] to be a liar, **giving** false **testimony** against his brother,
20: 11 [A] If *they* **accept** and open their gates, all the people in it shall
21: 7 [A] and *they shall* **declare**: "Our hands did not shed this blood,
25: 9 [A] take off one of his sandals, spit in his face **[NIE]** and say,
26: 5 [A] *you shall* **declare** before the LORD your God: "My father
27: 14 [A] The Levites *shall* **recite** [+606+2256] to all the people of
27: 15 [A] Then all the people *shall* **say** [+606+2256], "Amen!"
31: 21 [A] upon them, this song *will* **testify** [+4200+6332] against them,
Jos 1: 16 [A] *they* **answered** Joshua, "Whatever you have commanded us
7: 20 [A] Achan **replied**, "It is true! I have sinned against the LORD,
9: 24 [A] *They* **answered** Joshua, "Your servants were clearly told
22: 21 [A] the half-tribe of Manasseh **replied** *to* the heads of the clans
24: 16 [A] the people **answered**, "Far be it from us to forsake the
Jdg 5: 29 [A] The wisest of her ladies **answer** her; indeed, she keeps
7: 14 [A] His friend **responded**, "This can be nothing other than the
8: 8 [A] of them, but they **answered** as the men of Succoth had.
8: 8 [A] of them, but they answered as the men of Succoth **had**[s].
18: 14 [A] the five men who had spied out the land of Laish **[NIE]** said
19: 28 [A] He said to her, "Get up; let's go." But there was no **answer**.
20: 4 [A] **said**, "I and my concubine came to Gibeah in Benjamin to
Ru 2: 6 [A] The foreman **replied**, "She is the Moabitess who came back
2: 11 [A] Boaz **replied**, "I've been told all about what you have done
1Sa 1: 15 [A] "Not so, my lord," Hannah **replied**, "I am a woman who is
1: 17 [A] Eli **answered**, "Go in peace, and may the God of Israel grant
4: 17 [A] The man who brought the news **replied**, "Israel fled before
4: 20 [A] birth to a son." But *she did* not **respond** or pay any attention.
7: 9 [A] LORD on Israel's behalf, and the LORD **answered** him.
8: 18 [A] and the LORD *will* not **answer** you in that day."
9: 8 [A] The servant **answered** him again. "Look," he said, "I have a
9: 12 [A] "He is," *they* **answered**. "He's ahead of you. Hurry now;
9: 17 [A] When Samuel caught sight of Saul, the LORD **said** *to* him,
9: 19 [A] "I am the seer," Samuel **replied**. "Go up ahead of me to the
9: 21 [A] Saul **answered**, "But am I not a Benjamite, from the smallest
10: 12 [A] A man who lived there **answered**, "And who is their father?"
12: 3 [A] **Testify** against me in the presence of the LORD and his
14: 12 [A] The men of the outpost **shouted** *to* Jonathan and his
14: 28 [A] one of the soldiers **told** him, "Your father bound the army
14: 37 [A] into Israel's hand?" But God *did* not **answer** him that day.
14: 39 [A] he must die." But not one of the men **said a word**.
16: 18 [A] One of the servants **answered**, "I have seen a son of Jesse of
20: 10 [A] "Who will tell me if your father **answers** you harshly?"
20: 28 [A] Jonathan **answered**, "David earnestly asked me for
20: 32 [A] put to death? What has he done?" Jonathan **asked** his father.
21: 4 [21:5] [A] the priest **answered** David, "I don't have any
21: 5 [21:6] [A] David **replied**, "Indeed women have been kept from
22: 9 [A] the Edomite, who was standing with Saul's officials, **said**,
22: 14 [A] Ahimelech **answered** the king, "Who of all your servants is
23: 4 [A] and the LORD **answered** him, "Go down to Keilah,
25: 10 [A] Nabal **answered** David's servants, "Who is this David? Who
26: 6 [A] **asked** Ahimelech the Hittite and Abishai son of Zeruiah,
26: 14 [A] Abner son of Ner, "Aren't *you going to* **answer** me, Abner?"
26: 14 [A] Abner **replied**, "Who are you who calls to the king?"
26: 22 [A] "Here is the king's spear," David **answered**. "Let one of
28: 6 [A] the LORD *did* not **answer** him by dreams or Urim
28: 15 [A] *He* no longer **answers** me, either by prophets or by dreams.
29: 9 [A] Achish **answered**, "I know that you have been as pleasing in
30: 22 [A] evil men and troublemakers among David's followers **said**,
2Sa 1: 16 [A] Your own mouth **testified** against you when you said,
4: 9 [A] David **answered** Recab and his brother Baanah, the sons of
13: 32 [A] Jonadab son of Shimeah, David's brother, **said**, "My lord
14: 18 [A] the king **said** to the woman, "Do not keep from me the
14: 19 [A] The woman **answered**, "As surely as you live, my lord the
15: 21 [A] But Ittai **replied** *to* the king, "As surely as the LORD lives,
19: 21 [19:22] [A] Abishai son of Zeruiah **said**, "Shouldn't Shimei be
19: 42 [19:43] [A] All the men of Judah **answered** the men of Israel,
19: 43 [19:44] [A] the men of Israel **answered** the men of Judah, "We
20: 20 [A] Joab **replied**, "Far be it from me to swallow up or destroy!
22: 42 [A] no one to save them—to the LORD, but *he did* not **answer**.
1Ki 1: 28 [A] King David **said**, "Call in Bathsheba." So she came into the
1: 36 [A] Benaiah son of Jehoiada **answered** the king, "Amen!
1: 43 [A] "Not at all!" Jonathan **answered**. "Our lord King David has
2: 22 [A] King Solomon **answered** his mother, "Why do you request
2: 30 [A] reported to the king, "This is how Joab **answered** me."
3: 27 [A] the king **gave** *his* **ruling**: "Give the living baby to the first
12: 7 [A] and serve them and **[NIE]** give them a favorable answer,
12: 13 [A] The king **answered** the people harshly. Rejecting the advice
13: 6 [A] the king **said** to the man of God, "Intercede with the LORD
18: 21 [A] but if Baal is God, follow him." But the people **said** nothing.
18: 24 [A] The god who **answers** by fire—he is God." Then all the
18: 24 [A] is God." Then all the people **said**, "What you say is good."
18: 26 [A] "O Baal, **answer** us!" they shouted. But there was no
18: 26 [A] they shouted. But there was no response; no *one* **answered**.

1Ki 18:29 [A] was no response, no *one* **answered**, no one paid attention.
18:37 [A] **Answer** me, O LORD, answer me, so these people will
18:37 [A] Answer me, O LORD, **answer** me, so these people will
20: 4 [A] The king of Israel **answered**, "Just as you say, my lord the
20:11 [A] The king of Israel **answered**, "Tell him: 'One who puts on
2Ki 1:10 [A] Elijah **answered** the captain, "If I am a man of God, may fire
1:11 [A] The captain **said** to him, "Man of God, this is what the king
1:12 [A] "If I am a man of God," Elijah **replied**, "may fire come down
3:11 [A] An officer of the king of Israel **answered**, "Elisha son of
4:29 [A] do not greet him, and if anyone greets you, *do* not **answer**.
7: 2 [A] The officer on whose arm the king was leaning **said** *to* the
7:13 [A] One of his officers **answered**, "Have some men take five of
7:19 [A] The officer *had* **said** *to* the man of God, "Look, even if the
18:36 [A] But the people remained silent and **said** nothing **in reply**,
18:36 [A] because the king had commanded, "*Do* not **answer** him."
1Ch 12:17 [12:18] [A] David went out to meet them and **said** to them,
21:26 [A] the LORD **answered** him with fire from heaven on the altar
21:28 [A] when David saw that the LORD *had* **answered** him on the
2Ch 10:13 [A] The king **answered** them harshly. Rejecting the advice of the
29:31 [A] Hezekiah **said**, "You have now dedicated yourselves to the
34:15 [A] Hilkiah **said** to Shaphan the secretary, "I have found the
Ezr 10: 2 [A] son of Jehiel, one of the descendants of Elam, **said** to Ezra,
10:12 [A] The whole assembly **responded** with a loud voice: "You are
Ne 8: 6 [A] and all the people lifted their hands and **responded**, "Amen!
Est 5: 7 [A] Esther **replied**, "My petition and my request is this:
7: 3 [A] Queen Esther **answered**, "If I have found favor with you,
Job 1: 7 [A] Satan **answered** the LORD, "From roaming through the
1: 9 [A] "Does Job fear God for nothing?" Satan **replied**.
2: 2 [A] Satan **answered** the LORD, "From roaming through the
2: 4 [A] "Skin for skin!" Satan **replied**. "A man will give all he has
3: 2 [A] He **said**:
4: 1 [A] Then Eliphaz the Temanite **replied**:
5: 1 [A] "Call if you will, but *who will* **answer** you? To which of the
6: 1 [A] Then Job **replied**:
8: 1 [A] Then Bildad the Shuhite **replied**:
9: 1 [A] Then Job **replied**:
9: 3 [A] *he could* not **answer** him one time out of a thousand.
9:14 [A] "How then *can* I **dispute** *with* him? How can I find words to
9:15 [A] Though I were innocent, *I could* not **answer** him; I could
9:16 [A] Even if I summoned him and *he* **responded**, I do not believe
9:32 [A] "He is not a man like me that *I might* **answer** him, that we
11: 1 [A] Then Zophar the Naamathite **replied**:
11: 2 [C] "*Are* all these words *to* **go unanswered** [+4202]? Is this
12: 1 [A] Then Job **replied**:
12: 4 [A] to my friends, though I called upon God and *he* **answered**—
13:22 [A] summon me and I *will* **answer**, or let me speak, and you
14:15 [A] You will call and I *will* **answer** you; you will long for the
15: 1 [A] Then Eliphaz the Temanite **replied**:
15: 2 [A] "*Would* a wise man **answer** *with* empty notions or fill his
15: 6 [A] condemns you, not mine; your own lips **testify** against you.
16: 1 [A] Then Job **replied**:
16: 3 [A] never end? What ails you that *you keep on* **arguing**?
16: 8 [A] a witness; my gauntness rises up and **testifies** against me.
18: 1 [A] Then Bildad the Shuhite **replied**:
19: 1 [A] Then Job **replied**:
19: 7 [C] *I* **get** no **response**; though I call for help, there is no justice.
19:16 [A] I summon my servant, but *he does* not **answer**, though I beg
20: 1 [A] Then Zophar the Naamathite **replied**:
20: 3 [A] dishonors me, and my understanding inspires me *to* **reply**.
21: 1 [A] Then Job **replied**:
22: 1 [A] Then Eliphaz the Temanite **replied**:
23: 1 [A] Then Job **replied**:
23: 5 [A] I would find out what *he would* **answer** me, and consider
25: 1 [A] Then Bildad the Shuhite **replied**:
26: 1 [A] Then Job **replied**:
30:20 [A] "I cry out to you, O God, but *you do* not **answer**; I stand up,
31:35 [A] I sign now my defense—*let* the Almighty **answer** me; let my
32: 1 [A] So these three men stopped **answering** Job, because he was
32: 6 [A] So Elihu son of Barakel the Buzite **said**: "I am young in
32:12 [A] proved Job wrong; none of you *has* **answered** his arguments.
32:15 [A] "They are dismayed and *have* no more *to* **say**; words have
32:16 [A] that they are silent, now that they stand there with no **reply**?
32:17 [A] I too *will* **have** my **say** [+2750]; I too will tell what I know.
32:20 [A] I must speak and find relief; I must open my lips and **reply**.
33:12 [A] "But *I* **tell** you, in this you are not right, for God is greater
33:13 [A] Why do you complain to him that *he* **answers** none of man's
34: 1 [A] Then Elihu **said**:
35: 1 [A] Then Elihu **said**:
35:12 [A] *He does* not **answer** when men cry out because of the
38: 1 [A] Then the LORD **answered** Job out of the storm. He said:
40: 1 [A] The LORD **said** *to* Job:
40: 2 [A] correct him? *Let him* who accuses God **answer** him!"
40: 3 [A] Then Job **answered** the LORD:
40: 5 [A] I spoke once, but *I* **have** no **answer**—twice, but I will say no
40: 6 [A] Then the LORD **spoke** *to* Job out of the storm:
42: 1 [A] Then Job **replied** *to* the LORD:
Ps 3: 4 [3:5] [A] I cry aloud, and *he* **answers** me from his holy hill.
4: 1 [4:2] [A] **Answer** me when I call to you, O my righteous God.
13: 3 [13:4] [A] Look on me and **answer**, O LORD my God.
17: 6 [A] I call on you, O God, for *you will* **answer** me; give ear to me
18:41 [18:42] [A] save them—to the LORD, but *he did* not **answer**.
20: 1 [20:2] [A] *May* the LORD **answer** you when you are in
20: 6 [20:7] [A] *he* **answers** him from his holy heaven with the
20: 9 [20:10] [A] O LORD, save the king! **Answer** us when we call!
22: 2 [22:3] [A] I cry out by day, but *you do* not **answer**, by night,
22:21 [22:22] [A] the lions; **save** me from the horns of the wild oxen.
27: 7 [A] when I call, O LORD; be merciful to me and **answer** me.
34: 4 [34:5] [A] I sought the LORD, and *he* **answered** me; he
38:15 [38:16] [A] O LORD; you *will* **answer**, O Lord my God.
55: 2 [55:3] [A] hear me and **answer** me. My thoughts trouble me
60: 5 [60:7] [A] Save us and **help** us with your right hand, that those
65: 5 [65:6] [A] *You* **answer** us with awesome deeds of
69:13 [69:14] [A] O God, **answer** me with your sure salvation.
69:16 [69:17] [A] **Answer** me, O LORD, out of the goodness of your
69:17 [69:18] [A] **answer** me quickly, for I am in trouble.
81: 7 [81:8] [A] I rescued you, *I* **answered** you out of a thundercloud;
86: 1 [A] Hear, O LORD, and **answer** me, for I am poor and needy.
86: 7 [A] day of my trouble I will call to you, for *you will* **answer** me.
91:15 [A] He will call upon me, and *I will* **answer** him; I will be with
99: 6 [A] his name; they called on the LORD and he **answered** them.
99: 8 [A] O LORD our God, you **answered** them; you were to Israel
102: 2 [102:3] [A] your ear to me; when I call, **answer** me quickly.
108: 6 [108:7] [A] Save us and **help** us with your right hand, that those
118: 5 [A] I cried to the LORD, and he **answered** by setting me free.
118:21 [A] I will give you thanks, for *you* **answered** me; you have
119:26 [A] I recounted my ways and *you* **answered** me; teach me your
119:42 [A] *I will* **answer** [+1821] the one who taunts me, for I trust in
119:145 [A] **answer** me, O LORD, and I will obey your decrees.
120: 1 [A] I call on the LORD in my distress, and *he* **answers** me.
138: 3 [A] When I called, *you* **answered** me; you made me bold
143: 1 [A] in your faithfulness and righteousness **come to** my **relief**.
143: 7 [A] **Answer** me quickly, O LORD; my spirit fails. Do not hide
Pr 1:28 [A] "Then they will call to me but *I will* not **answer**; they will
15:28 [A] The heart of the righteous weighs its **answers**, but the mouth
18:23 [A] poor man pleads for mercy, but a rich man **answers** harshly.
21:13 [C] the cry of the poor, he too will cry out and not **be answered**.
25:18 [A] or a sharp arrow is the man *who* **gives** false testimony against
26: 4 [A] *Do* not **answer** a fool according to his folly, or you will be
26: 5 [A] **Answer** a fool according to his folly, or he will be wise in his
Ecc 10:19 [A] makes life merry, but money *is the* **answer** *for* everything.
SS 2:10 [A] My lover **spoke** and said to me, "Arise, my darling,
5: 6 [A] but did not find him. I called him but *he did* not **answer**.
Isa 3: 9 [A] The look on their faces **testifies** against them; they parade
14:10 [A] They *will* all **respond**, they will say to you, "You also have
14:32 [A] What **answer** *shall be* **given** *to* the envoys of that nation?
21: 9 [A] *he* **gives back** *the* **answer**: 'Babylon has fallen, has fallen!
30:19 [A] you cry for help! As soon as he hears, *he will* **answer** you.
36:21 [A] But the people remained silent and **said** nothing **in reply**,
36:21 [A] because the king had commanded, "*Do* not **answer** him."
41:17 [A] I the LORD *will* **answer** them; I, the God of Israel, will not
46: 7 [A] Though one cries out to it, *it does* not **answer**; it cannot save
49: 8 [A] "In the time of my favor *I will* **answer** you, and in the day of
50: 2 [A] no one? When I called, why was there no *one to* **answer**?
58: 9 [A] you will call, and the LORD *will* **answer**; you will cry for
59:12 [A] are many in your sight, and our sins **testify** against us.
65:12 [A] for I called but *you did* not **answer**, I spoke but you did not
65:24 [A] Before they call I *will* **answer**; while they are still speaking I
66: 4 [A] I called, no *one* **answered**, when I spoke, no one listened.
Jer 7:13 [A] but you did not listen; I called you, but *you did* not **answer**.
7:27 [A] listen to you; when you call to them, *they will* not **answer**.
11: 5 [A] the land you possess today." *I* **answered**, "Amen, LORD."
14: 7 [A] Although our sins **testify** against us, O LORD,
23:35 [A] to his friend or relative: 'What *is* the LORD's **answer**?'
23:37 [A] 'What *is* the LORD's **answer** *to* you?' or 'What has the
25:30 [A] who tread the grapes, **shout** against all who live on the earth.
33: 3 [A] 'Call to me and *I will* **answer** you and tell you great
35:17 [A] did not listen; I called to them, but *they did* not **answer**.' "
42: 4 [A] I will tell you everything the LORD **says** and will keep
44:15 [A] people living in Lower and Upper Egypt, **said** *to* Jeremiah,
44:20 [A] the people, both men and women, who *were* **answering** him,
Eze 14: 4 [C] I the LORD *will* **answer** him myself in keeping with his
14: 7 [C] to inquire of me, I the LORD *will* **answer** him myself.
Hos 2:21 [2:23] [A] "In that day *I will* **respond**," declares the LORD—
2:21 [2:23] [A] "*I will* **respond** *to* the skies, and they will respond to
2:21 [2:23] [A] to the skies, and they *will* **respond** *to* the earth;
2:22 [2:24] [A] the earth *will* **respond** *to* the grain, the new wine and
2:22 [2:24] [A] new wine and oil, and they *will* **respond** *to* Jezreel.
5: 5 [A] Israel's arrogance **testifies** against them; the Israelites,

Hos 7:10 [A] Israel's arrogance **testifies** against him, but despite all this he
14: 8 [14:9] [A] I *will* **answer** him and care for him. I am like a green
Joel 2:19 [A] The LORD *will* **reply** to them: "I am sending you grain,
Am 7:14 [A] Amos **answered** Amaziah, "I was neither a prophet nor a
Jnh 2: 2 [2:3] [A] distress I called to the LORD, and *he* **answered** me.
Mic 3: 4 [A] will cry out to the LORD, but *he will* not **answer** them.
6: 3 [A] have I done to you? How have I burdened you? **Answer** me.
6: 5 [A] of Moab counseled and what Balaam son of Beor **answered**.
Hab 2: 2 [A] the LORD **replied**: "Write down the revelation and make it
2:11 [A] will cry out, and the beams of the woodwork *will* **echo** it.
Hag 2:12 [A] does it become consecrated?' " The priests **answered**, "No."
2:13 [A] "Yes," the priests **replied**, "it becomes defiled."
2:14 [A] Haggai **said**, " 'So it is with this people and this nation in my
Zec 1:10 [A] Then the man standing among the myrtle trees **explained**,
1:11 [A] *they* **reported** to the angel of the LORD, who was standing
1:12 [A] the angel of the LORD **said**, "LORD Almighty, how long
1:13 [A] So the LORD **spoke** kind and comforting words *to* the
3: 4 [A] The angel **said** to those who were standing before him, "Take
4: 4 [A] *I* **asked** the angel who talked with me, "What are these,
4: 5 [A] He **answered**, "Do you not know what these are?" "No,
4: 6 [A] So *he* **said** to me, "This is the word of the LORD to
4:11 [A] *I* **asked** the angel, "What are these two olive trees on the
4:12 [A] Again *I* **asked** him, "What are these two olive branches
6: 4 [A] *I* **asked** the angel who was speaking to me, "What are these,
6: 5 [A] The angel **answered** me, "These are the four spirits of
10: 6 [A] for I am the LORD their God and *I will* **answer** them.
13: 9 [A] They will call on my name and I *will* **answer** them; I will
Mal 2:12 [A] the man who does this, **whoever he may be** [+2256+6424],

6700 [2]עָנָה **ʿānâ[2]**, v. [81] [→ 4361?, 5103, 6703? 6705, 6708, 6709, 6713, 6714, 6715, 9504]

afflicted [12], deny [6], oppress [5], humble [4], oppressed [4], humbled [3], subdue [3], afflict [2], do[s] [+906+6700] [2], humble yourself [2], mistreated [2], raped [2], shared hardships [+889+928+6700] [2], violated [2], *untranslated* [1], be afflicted [1], bring affliction [1], broke [1], bruised [1], deny himself [1], disgraced [1], dishonored [1], disturbed [1], force [1], hardships endured [1], humble ourselves [1], made suffer [1], mistreat [1], oppressors [1], overwhelmed [1], punish [1], raped [+906+2256+8886] [1], ravished [1], stilled [1], stoop down [1], subdued [1], submit [1], suffered affliction [1], suffered [1], take advantage of [1], use [1], violate women [1], violated [+906+2256+8886] [1], violates [1]

Ge 15:13 [D] they will be enslaved and **mistreated** four hundred years.
16: 6 [D] Then Sarai **mistreated** Hagar; so she fled from her.
16: 9 [F] told her, "Go back to your mistress and **submit** to her."
31:50 [D] If *you* **mistreat** my daughters or if you take any wives
34: 2 [D] saw her, he took her and **violated** [+906+2256+8886] her.
Ex 1:11 [D] So they put slave masters over them to **oppress** them with
1:12 [D] But the more they *were* **oppressed**, the more they multiplied
10: 3 [C] 'How long will you refuse to **humble yourself** before me?
22:22 [22:21] [D] "*Do* not **take advantage of** a widow or an orphan.
22:23 [22:22] [D] If *you* **do**[s] [+906+6700] and they cry out to me,
22:23 [22:22] [D] If *you* **do**[s] [+906+6700] and they cry out to me,
Lev 16:29 [D] On the tenth day of the seventh month *you must* **deny**
16:31 [D] It is a sabbath of rest, and *you must* **deny** yourselves; it is a
23:27 [D] Hold a sacred assembly and **deny** yourselves, and present an
23:29 [E] Anyone who *does* not **deny himself** on that day must be cut
23:32 [D] It is a sabbath of rest for you, and *you must* **deny** yourselves.
Nu 24:24 [D] *they will* **subdue** Asshur and Eber, but they too will come to
24:24 [D] they will subdue Asshur and **[RPH]** Eber, but they too will
29: 7 [D] *You must* **deny** yourselves and do no work.
30:13 [30:14] [D] vow she makes or any sworn pledge to **deny** herself.
Dt 8: 2 [D] to **humble** you and to test you in order to know what was in
8: 3 [D] *He* **humbled** you, causing you to hunger and then feeding
8:16 [D] to **humble** and to test you so that in the end it might go well
21:14 [D] or treat her as a slave, since *you have* **dishonored** her.
22:24 [D] and the man because *he* **violated** another man's wife.
22:29 [D] He must marry the girl, for *he has* **violated** her. He can never
26: 6 [D] the Egyptians mistreated us and **made us suffer**, putting us to
Jdg 16: 5 [D] can overpower him so we may tie him up and **subdue** him.
16: 6 [D] great strength and how you can be tied up and **subdued**."
16:19 [D] off the seven braids of his hair, and so began to **subdue** him.
19:24 [D] and *you can* **use** them and do to them whatever you wish.
20: 5 [D] to kill me. *They* **raped** my concubine, and she died.
Ru 1:21 [A] The LORD *has* **afflicted** me; the Almighty has brought
2Sa 7:10 [D] Wicked people *will* not **oppress** them anymore, as they did
13:12 [D] "Don't, my brother!" she said to him. "Don't **force** me. Such
13:14 [D] But he refused to listen to her, and since he was stronger than she, *he* **raped** [+906+2256+8886] her.
13:22 [D] he hated Amnon because *he had* **disgraced** his sister Tamar.
13:32 [D] intention ever since the day Amnon **raped** his sister Tamar.
22:36 [A] me your shield of victory; you **stoop down** to make me great.
1Ki 2:26 [F] and **shared** all my father's **hardships** [+889+928+6700]."
2:26 [F] and **shared** all my father's **hardships** [+889+928+6700]."
8:35 [G] and turn from their sin because *you have* **afflicted** them,
11:39 [D] *I will* **humble** David's descendants because of this, but not
2Ki 17:20 [D] *he* **afflicted** them and gave them into the hands of
2Ch 6:26 [G] and turn from their sin because *you have* **afflicted** them,
Ezr 8:21 [F] so that we *might* **humble ourselves** before our God and ask
Job 30:11 [D] Now that God has unstrung my bow and **afflicted** me, they
37:23 [D] in his justice and great righteousness, *he does* not **oppress**.
Ps 35:13 [D] were ill, I put on sackcloth and **humbled** myself with fasting.
55:19 [55:20] [G] enthroned forever, will hear them and **afflict** them—
88: 7 [88:8] [D] *you have* **overwhelmed** me *with* all your waves.
89:22 [89:23] [D] him to tribute; no wicked man *will* **oppress** him.
90:15 [D] Make us glad for as many days as *you have* **afflicted** us,
94: 5 [D] your people, O LORD; *they* **oppress** your inheritance.
102:23 [102:24] [D] In the course of my life *he* **broke** my strength; he
105:18 [D] *They* **bruised** his feet with shackles, his neck was put in
107:17 [F] and **suffered affliction** because of their iniquities.
116:10 [A] I believed; therefore I said, "I *am* greatly **afflicted**."
119:67 [A] Before *I was* **afflicted** I went astray, but now I obey your
119:71 [E] It was good for me *to* **be afflicted** so that I might learn your
119:75 [D] are righteous, and *in* faithfulness *you have* **afflicted** me.
119:107 [C] *I have* **suffered** much; preserve my life, O LORD,
132: 1 [E] remember David and all the **hardships** he **endured**.
Isa 25: 5 [A] the shadow of a cloud, so the song of the ruthless *is* **stilled**.
31: 4 [A] not frightened by their shouts or **disturbed** by their clamor—
53: 4 [E] him stricken by God, smitten by him, and **afflicted**.
53: 7 [C] He was oppressed and **afflicted**, yet he did not open his
58: 3 [D] Why *have we* **humbled** ourselves, and you have not
58: 5 [D] fast I have chosen, only a day for a man *to* **humble** himself?
58:10 [C] behalf of the hungry and satisfy the needs of the **oppressed**,
60:14 [D] The sons of your **oppressors** will come bowing before you;
64:12 [64:11] [D] you keep silent and **punish** us beyond measure?
La 3:33 [D] For *he does* not willingly **bring affliction** or grief to the
5:11 [D] Women *have been* **ravished** in Zion, and virgins in the
Eze 22:10 [D] in you are *those who* **violate women** during their period,
22:11 [D] and another **violates** his sister, his own father's daughter.
Da 10:12 [F] gain understanding and to **humble yourself** before your God,
Na 1:12 [D] Although *I have* **afflicted** you, ⌞O Judah,⌟ I will afflict you
1:12 [D] I have afflicted you, ⌞O Judah,⌟ *I will* **afflict** you no more.
Zep 3:19 [D] At that time I will deal with all *who* **oppressed** you; I will
Zec 10: 2 [A] Therefore the people wander like sheep **oppressed** for lack

6701 [3]עָנָה **ʿānâ[3]**, v. [3] [→ 3610, 4348, 5100, 5102, 6703?, 6721, 6961, 6964, 6967, 6968]

burden [+6721] [2], keeps occupied [1]

Ecc 1:13 [A] What a heavy **burden** [+6721] God has laid on men!
3:10 [A] I have seen the **burden** [+6721] God has laid on men.
5:20 [5:19] [G] God **keeps** him **occupied** with gladness of heart.

6702 [4]עָנָה **ʿānâ[4]**, v. [15]

sing [6], sang [4], sound [+7754] [2], howl [1], shout in triumph [+2116] [1], singing [1]

Ex 15:21 [A] Miriam **sang** to them: "Sing to the LORD, for he is highly
32:18 [A] "It is not the **sound of** [+7754] victory, it is not the sound of
32:18 [A] the sound of victory, it is not the **sound of** [+7754] defeat;
32:18 [D] not the sound of defeat; it is the sound of **singing** that I hear."
Nu 21:17 [A] Then Israel sang this song: "Spring up, O well! **Sing** about it,
1Sa 18: 7 [A] As they danced, *they* **sang**: "Saul has slain his thousands,
21:11 [21:12] [A] Isn't he the one *they* **sing** about in their dances:
29: 5 [A] Isn't this the David *they* **sang** about in their dances: " 'Saul
Ezr 3:11 [A] With praise and thanksgiving *they* **sang** to the LORD: "He
Ps 119:172 [A] *May* my tongue **sing** *of* your word, for all your commands
147: 7 [A] **Sing** to the LORD with thanksgiving; make music to our
Isa 13:22 [A] Hyenas *will* **howl** in her strongholds, jackals in her luxurious
27: 2 [D] In that day—"**Sing** about a fruitful vineyard:
Jer 51:14 [A] of locusts, and *they will* **shout** [+2116] **in triumph** over you.
Hos 2:15 [2:17] [A] There *she will* **sing** as in the days of her youth, as in

6703 עֹנָה **ʿōnâ**, n.f. [1] [√ 6700? *or* 6701?]

marital rights [1]

Ex 21:10 not deprive the first one of her food, clothing and **marital rights**.

6704 עֲנָה **ʿ*a*nâ**, n.pr.m. [12] [√ 6742]

Anah [12]

Ge 36: 2 Oholibamah daughter of **Anah** and granddaughter of Zibeon the
36:14 The sons of Esau's wife Oholibamah daughter of **Anah**
36:18 chiefs descended from Esau's wife Oholibamah daughter of **Anah**.
36:20 who were living in the region: Lotan, Shobal, Zibeon, **Anah**,
36:24 The sons of Zibeon: Aiah and **Anah**. This is the Anah who
36:24 This is the **Anah** who discovered the hot springs in the desert

Ge 36:25 The children of **Anah**: Dishon and Oholibamah daughter of Anah.
36:25 The children of Anah: Dishon and Oholibamah daughter of **Anah**.
36:29 These were the Horite chiefs: Lotan, Shobal, Zibeon, **Anah**,
1Ch 1:38 of Seir: Lotan, Shobal, Zibeon, **Anah**, Dishon, Ezer and Dishan.
1:40 Ebal, Shepho and Onam. The sons of Zibeon: Aiah and **Anah**.
1:41 The son of **Anah**: Dishon. The sons of Dishon: Hemdan, Eshban,

6705 עָנָו *ʿānāw*, n.m. [21] [→ 6718; cf. 6700; Ar 10559]

humble [7], afflicted [4], poor [4], oppressed [2], helpless [1], meek [1], needy [1], them[s] [1]

Nu 12:3 (Now Moses was a very **humble** man, more humble than anyone
Ps 9:12 [9:13] he does not ignore the cry of the **afflicted**. [K 6714]
9:18 [9:19] [nor the hope of the **afflicted** ever perish. [K; see Q 6714]
10:12 Lift up your hand, O God. Do not forget the **helpless**. [K 6714]
10:17 You hear, O LORD, the desire of the **afflicted**; you encourage
22:26 [22:27] The **poor** will eat and be satisfied; they who seek the
25:9 He guides the **humble** in what is right and teaches them his way.
25:9 He guides the humble in what is right and teaches **them**[s] his way.
34:2 [34:3] will boast in the LORD; let the **afflicted** hear and rejoice.
37:11 But the **meek** will inherit the land and enjoy great peace.
69:32 [69:33] The **poor** will see and be glad—you who seek God, may
76:9 [76:10] rose up to judge, to save all the **afflicted** *of* the land.
147:6 The LORD sustains the **humble** but casts the wicked to the
149:4 takes delight in his people; he crowns the **humble** with salvation.
Pr 3:34 He mocks proud mockers but gives grace to the **humble**. [K 6714]
14:21 neighbor sins, but blessed is he who is kind to the **needy**. [K 6714]
16:19 among the **oppressed** [K 6714] than to share plunder with the
Isa 11:4 with justice he will give decisions for the **poor** *of* the earth.
29:19 Once more the **humble** will rejoice in the LORD; the needy will
32:7 [he makes up evil schemes to destroy the **poor** [K; see Q 6714]]
61:1 the LORD has anointed me to preach good news to the **poor**.
Am 2:7 as upon the dust of the ground and deny justice to the **oppressed**.
8:4 [the needy and do away with the **poor** [K; see Q 6714] *of* the land,]
Zep 2:3 Seek the LORD, all you **humble** *of* the land, you who do what he

6706 עֻנּוֹ *ʿunnô*, n.pr.m. [0] [cf. 6716]

Ne 12:9 [Bakbukiah and Unni, [K; see Q 6716] their associates,]

6707 עָנוּב *ʿānûb*, n.pr.m. [1]

Anub [1]

1Ch 4:8 who was the father of **Anub** and Hazzobebah and of the clans of

6708 עֲנָוָה *ʿanāwâ*, n.f. [6] [√ 6700]

humility [5], stoop down [1]

Ps 18:35 [18:36] hand sustains me; you **stoop down** to make me great.
45:4 [45:5] victoriously in behalf of truth, **humility** and righteousness;
Pr 15:33 LORD teaches a man wisdom, and **humility** comes before honor.
18:12 downfall a man's heart is proud, but **humility** comes before honor.
22:4 **Humility** and the fear of the LORD bring wealth and honor
Zep 2:3 Seek righteousness, seek **humility**; perhaps you will be sheltered

6709 עַנְוָה *ʿanwâ*, n.f. Not used in NIV/BHS [√ 6700]

6710 עֲנוֹק *ʿanôq*, n.pr.[m. *or* loc.]. [1] [→ 6737]

Anak [1]

Jos 21:11 in the hill country of Judah. (Arba was the forefather of **Anak**.)

6711 עֲנוּשִׁים *ʿanûšîm*, n.[m.pl.] *or* v.ptcp. [1] [√ 6740]

fines [1]

Am 2:8 in pledge. In the house of their god they drink wine taken as **fines**.

6712 עֲנוֹת *ʿanôt*, n.pr.m. & loc. Not used in NIV/BHS [√ 6742]

6713 עֱנוּת *ʿenût*, n.f. [1] [√ 6700]

suffering [1]

Ps 22:24 [22:25] or disdained the **suffering** *of* the afflicted one;

6714 עָנִי *ʿānî*, a. [75 / 74] [√ 6700; Ar 10559]

poor [39], afflicted [15], oppressed [5], needy [3], helpless [2], humble [+6639] [2], weak [2], distress [1], gentle [1], humble [1], meek [1], suffer [1], wretched [1]

Ex 22:25 [22:24] money to one of my people among you who is **needy**,
Lev 19:10 Leave them for the **poor** and the alien. I am the LORD your God.
23:22 Leave them for the **poor** and the alien. I am the LORD your
Dt 15:11 toward your brothers and toward the **poor** and needy in your land.
24:12 If the man is **poor**, do not go to sleep with his pledge in your
24:14 Do not take advantage of a hired man who is **poor** and needy,
24:15 each day before sunset, because he is **poor** and is counting on it.
2Sa 22:28 You save the **humble** [+6639], but your eyes are on the haughty to
Job 24:4 needy from the path and force all the **poor** *of* the land into hiding.
24:9 snatched from the breast; the infant of the **poor** is seized for a debt.
24:14 is gone, the murderer rises up and kills the **poor** and needy;
29:12 because I rescued the **poor** who cried for help, and the fatherless
34:28 the poor to come before him, so that he heard the cry of the **needy**.
36:6 does not keep the wicked alive but gives the **afflicted** their rights.
36:15 *those who* **suffer** he delivers in their suffering; he speaks to them
Ps 9:12 [9:13] [he does not ignore the cry of the **afflicted**. [K; see Q 6705]]
9:18 [9:19] nor the hope of the **afflicted** [K 6705] ever perish.
10:2 In his arrogance the wicked man hunts down the **weak**, who are
10:9 he lies in wait to catch the **helpless**; he catches the helpless
10:9 the helpless; he catches the **helpless** and drags them off in his net.
10:12 [Do not forget the **helpless**. [K; see Q 6705]]
12:5 [12:6] "Because of the oppression of the **weak** and the groaning
14:6 You evildoers frustrate the plans of the **poor**, but the LORD is
18:27 [18:28] You save the **humble** [+6639] but bring low those whose
22:24 [22:25] or disdained the suffering of the **afflicted** *one*;
25:16 Turn to me and be gracious to me, for I am lonely and **afflicted**.
34:6 [34:7] This **poor** *man* called, and the LORD heard him; he
35:10 You rescue the **poor** from those too strong for them, the poor
35:10 strong for them, the **poor** and needy from those who rob them."
37:14 the sword and bend the bow to bring down the **poor** and needy,
40:17 [40:18] Yet I am **poor** and needy; may the Lord think of me.
68:10 [68:11] and from your bounty, O God, you provided for the **poor**.
69:29 [69:30] I am in pain and **distress**; may your salvation, O God,
70:5 [70:6] Yet I am **poor** and needy; come quickly to me, O God.
72:2 your people in righteousness, your **afflicted** *ones* with justice.
72:4 He will defend the **afflicted** *among* the people and save the
72:12 the needy who cry out, the **afflicted** who have no one to help.
74:19 do not forget the lives of your **afflicted** *people* forever.
74:21 retreat in disgrace; may the **poor** and needy praise your name.
82:3 and fatherless; maintain the rights of the poor and **oppressed**.
86:1 Hear, O LORD, and answer me, for I am **poor** and needy.
88:15 [88:16] From my youth I have been **afflicted** and close to death;
102:T [102:1] A prayer of an **afflicted** *man*. When he is faint and pours
109:16 hounded to death the **poor** and the needy and the brokenhearted.
109:22 For I am **poor** and needy, and my heart is wounded within me.
140:12 [140:13] I know that the LORD secures justice for the **poor**
Pr 3:34 [proud mockers but gives grace to the **humble**. [K; see Q 6705]]
14:21 [but blessed is he who is kind to the **needy**. [K; see Q 6705]]
15:15 All the days of the **oppressed** are wretched, but the cheerful heart
16:19 [to be lowly in spirit and among the **oppressed** [K; see Q 6705]]
22:22 because they are poor and do not crush the **needy** in court,
30:14 whose jaws are set with knives to devour the **poor** from the earth,
31:9 and judge fairly; defend the rights of the **poor** and needy."
31:20 She opens her arms to the **poor** and extends her hands to the
Ecc 6:8 What does a **poor** *man* gain by knowing how to conduct himself
Isa 3:14 ruined my vineyard; the plunder from the **poor** is in your houses.
3:15 mean by crushing my people and grinding the faces of the **poor**?"
10:2 their rights and withhold justice from the **oppressed** *of* my people,
10:30 O Daughter of Gallim! Listen, O Laishah! **Poor** Anathoth!
14:32 established Zion, and in her his **afflicted** people will find refuge."
26:6 it down—the feet of the **oppressed**, the footsteps of the poor.
32:7 he makes up evil schemes to destroy the **poor** [K 6705] with lies,
41:17 "The **poor** and needy search for water, but there is none;
49:13 his people and will have compassion on his **afflicted** *ones*.
51:21 hear this, you **afflicted** *one*, made drunk, but not with wine.
54:11 "O **afflicted** city, lashed by storms and not comforted, I will build
58:7 with the hungry and to provide the **poor** wanderer with shelter—
66:2 *he who* is **humble** and contrite in spirit, and trembles at my word.
Jer 22:16 He defended the cause of the **poor** and needy, and so all went well.
Eze 16:49 overfed and unconcerned; they did not help the **poor** and needy.
18:12 He oppresses the **poor** and needy. He commits robbery. He does
18:17 He withholds his hand from <u>sin</u> [BHS *the poor*; NIV 6404]
22:29 they oppress the **poor** and needy and mistreat the alien, denying
Am 8:4 the needy and do away with the **poor** [K 6705] *of* the land,
Hab 3:14 gloating as though about to devour the **wretched** who were in
Zep 3:12 I will leave within you the **meek** and humble, who trust in the
Zec 7:10 Do not oppress the widow or the fatherless, the alien or the **poor**.
9:9 **gentle** and riding on a donkey, on a colt, the foal of a donkey.
11:7 flock marked for slaughter, particularly the **oppressed** *of* the flock.
11:11 so the **afflicted** *of* the flock who were watching me knew it was the

6715 עֳנִי *ʿonî*, n.m. [36] [√ 6701]

affliction [14], suffering [9], misery [8], grief [1], hardship [1], oppressed [+1201] [1], persecute [1], taken great pains [+928] [1]

Ge 16:11 shall name him Ishmael, for the LORD has heard of your **misery**.
29:32 for she said, "It is because the LORD has seen my **misery**.
31:42 God has seen my **hardship** and the toil of my hands, and last night
41:52 because God has made me fruitful in the land of my **suffering**."
Ex 3:7 "I have indeed seen the **misery** *of* my people in Egypt.
3:17 I have promised to bring you up out of your **misery** *in* Egypt into

Ex 4:31 the LORD was concerned about them and had seen their **misery**,
Dt 16: 3 the bread of **affliction**, because you left Egypt in haste—
26: 7 the LORD heard our voice and saw our **misery**, toil and
1Sa 1:11 if you will only look upon your servant's **misery** and remember
2Ki 14:26 bitterly everyone in Israel, whether slave or free, was **suffering**;
1Ch 22:14 "I have **taken great pains** [+928] to provide for the temple of the
Ne 9: 9 "You saw the **suffering** *of* our forefathers in Egypt; you heard their
Job 10:15 lift my head, for I am full of shame and drowned in my **affliction**.
30:16 "And now my life ebbs away; days of **suffering** grip me.
30:27 churning inside me never stops; days of **suffering** confront me.
36: 8 But if men are bound in chains, held fast by cords of **affliction**,
36:15 those who suffer he delivers in their **suffering**; he speaks to them
36:21 Beware of turning to evil, which you seem to prefer to **affliction**.
Ps 9:13 [9:14] O LORD, see how my enemies **persecute** me!
25:18 Look upon my **affliction** and my distress and take away all my
31: 7 [31:8] for you saw my **affliction** and knew the anguish of my
44:24 [44:25] you hide your face and forget our **misery** and oppression?
88: 9 [88:10] my eyes are dim with **grief**. I call to you, O LORD,
107:10 and the deepest gloom, prisoners **suffering** in iron chains,
107:41 he lifted the needy out of their **affliction** and increased their
119:50 My comfort in my **suffering** is this: Your promise preserves my
119:92 had not been my delight, I would have perished in my **affliction**.
119:153 Look upon my **suffering** and deliver me, for I have not forgotten
Pr 31: 5 law decrees, and deprive all the **oppressed** [+1201] of their rights.
Isa 48:10 though not as silver; I have tested you in the furnace of **affliction**.
La 1: 3 After **affliction** and harsh labor, Judah has gone into exile.
1: 7 In the days of her **affliction** and wandering Jerusalem remembers
1: 9 "Look, O LORD, on my **affliction**, for the enemy has
3: 1 I am the man who has seen **affliction** by the rod of his wrath.
3:19 I remember my **affliction** and my wandering, the bitterness

6716 עֻנִּי ***ʿunnî***, n.pr.m. [3] [cf. 6706]

Unni [3]

1Ch 15:18 Jehiel, **Unni**, Eliab, Benaiah, Maaseiah, Mattithiah, Eliphelehu,
15:20 Jehiel, **Unni**, Eliab, Maaseiah and Benaiah were to play the lyres
Ne 12: 9 Bakbukiah and **Unni**, [K 6706] their associates, stood opposite

6717 עֲנָיָה ***ʿanāyâ***, n.pr.m. [2] [√ 6699 + 3378]

Anaiah [2]

Ne 8: 4 stood Mattithiah, Shema, **Anaiah**, Uriah, Hilkiah and Maaseiah;
10:22 [10:23] Pelatiah, Hanan, **Anaiah**,

6718 עָנָיו ***ʿānāyw***, n.m. Not used in NIV/BHS [√ 6705; cf. 6701]

6719 עָנִים ***ʿānîm***, n.pr.loc. [1]

Anim [1]

Jos 15:50 Anab, Eshtemoh, **Anim**,

6720 עֵנִים ***ʿēnîm***, n.[m.]. [0] [cf. 3613]

La 4: 3 [but my people have become heartless like **ostriches** [K; see Q 3612]]

6721 עִנְיָן ***ʿinyān***, n.m. [8] [√ 6701]

burden [+6701] [2], business [1], cares [1], labor [1], misfortune [+8273] [1], task [1], work [1]

Ecc 1:13 What a heavy **burden** [+6701] God has laid on men!
2:23 All his days his **work** is pain and grief; even at night his mind does
2:26 to the sinner he gives the **task** of gathering and storing up wealth to
3:10 I have seen the **burden** [+6701] God has laid on men.
4: 8 of enjoyment?" This too is meaningless—a miserable **business**!
5: 3 [5:2] As a dream comes when there are many **cares**, so the speech
5:14 [5:13] or wealth lost through *some* **misfortune** [+8273], so that
8:16 my mind to know wisdom and to observe man's **labor** on earth—

6722 עָנֵם ***ʿānēm***, n.pr.loc. [1]

Anem [1]

1Ch 6:73 [6:58] Ramoth and **Anem**, together with their pasturelands;

6723 עֲנָמִים ***ʿanāmîm***, n.pr.g. [2]

Anamites [2]

Ge 10:13 was the father of the Ludites, **Anamites**, Lehabites, Naphtuhites,
1Ch 1:11 was the father of the Ludites, **Anamites**, Lehabites, Naphtuhites,

6724 עֲנַמֶּלֶךְ ***ʿanammelek***, n.pr.[m.]. [1] [√ 6742 + 4889]

Anammelech [1]

2Ki 17:31 in the fire as sacrifices to Adrammelech and **Anammelech**,

6725 עָנַן[1] ***ʿānan[1]***, v.den. [1] [→ 6727, 6728, 6729, 6730, 6731]

bring clouds [+6727] [1]

Ge 9:14 [D] Whenever I **bring clouds** [+6727] over the earth

6726 עָנַן[2] ***ʿānan[2]***, v. [10] [√ 6701]

practiced sorcery [2], sorcery [2], cast spells [1], mediums [1], practice divination [1], practice sorcery [1], soothsayers [1], sorceress [1]

Lev 19:26 [D] the blood still in it. " 'Do not practice divination or **sorcery**.
Dt 18:10 [D] who practices divination or **sorcery**, interprets omens,
18:14 [D] you will dispossess listen to *those who* **practice sorcery**
Jdg 9:37 [D] a company is coming from the direction of the **soothsayers'**
2Ki 21: 6 [D] **practiced sorcery** and divination, and consulted mediums
2Ch 33: 6 [D] **practiced sorcery**, divination and witchcraft, and consulted
Isa 2: 6 [D] *they* **practice divination** like the Philistines and clasp hands
57: 3 [D] come here, you sons of a **sorceress**, you offspring of
Jer 27: 9 [D] of dreams, your **mediums** or your sorcerers who tell you,
Mic 5:12 [5:11] [D] your witchcraft and you will no longer **cast spells**.

6727 עָנָן[1] ***ʿānān[1]***, n.m. [87] [√ 6729; cf. 6725; Ar 10560]

cloud [63], clouds [17], mist [2], bring clouds [+6725] [1], it[s] [+2021] [1], morning mist [1], smoke [1], them[s] [1]

Ge 9:13 I have set my rainbow in the **clouds**, and it will be the sign of the
9:14 Whenever I **bring clouds** [+6725] over the earth and the rainbow
9:14 I bring clouds over the earth and the rainbow appears in the **clouds**,
9:16 Whenever the rainbow appears in the **clouds**, I will see it
Ex 13:21 By day the LORD went ahead of them in a pillar of **cloud** to
13:22 Neither the pillar of **cloud** by day nor the pillar of fire by night left
14:19 The pillar of **cloud** also moved from in front and stood behind
14:20 Throughout the night the **cloud** brought darkness to the one side
14:24 and **cloud** at the Egyptian army and threw it into confusion.
16:10 and there was the glory of the LORD appearing in the **cloud**.
19: 9 said to Moses, "I am going to come to you in a dense **cloud**,
19:16 was thunder and lightning, with a thick **cloud** over the mountain,
24:15 When Moses went up on the mountain, the **cloud** covered it,
24:16 For six days the **cloud** covered the mountain, and on the seventh
24:16 the seventh day the LORD called to Moses from within the **cloud**.
24:18 Then Moses entered the **cloud** as he went on up the mountain.
33: 9 the pillar of **cloud** would come down and stay at the entrance,
33:10 Whenever the people saw the pillar of **cloud** standing at the
34: 5 the LORD came down in the **cloud** and stood there with him
40:34 the **cloud** covered the Tent of Meeting, and the glory of the
40:35 enter the Tent of Meeting because the **cloud** had settled upon it,
40:36 whenever the **cloud** lifted from above the tabernacle, they would
40:37 if the **cloud** did not lift, they did not set out—until the day it lifted.
40:38 So the **cloud** *of* the LORD was over the tabernacle by day,
Lev 16: 2 will die, because I appear in the **cloud** over the atonement cover.
16:13 the **smoke** *of* the incense will conceal the atonement cover above
Nu 9:15 the Tent of the Testimony, was set up, the **cloud** covered it.
9:16 to be; the **cloud** covered it, and at night it looked like fire.
9:17 Whenever the **cloud** lifted from above the Tent, the Israelites set
9:17 set out; wherever the **cloud** settled, the Israelites encamped.
9:18 As long as the **cloud** stayed over the tabernacle, they remained in
9:19 When the **cloud** remained over the tabernacle a long time,
9:20 Sometimes the **cloud** was over the tabernacle only a few days;
9:21 Sometimes the **cloud** stayed only from evening till morning,
9:21 and when **it**[s] [+2021] lifted in the morning, they set out.
9:21 Whether by day or by night, whenever the **cloud** lifted, they set
9:22 Whether the **cloud** stayed over the tabernacle for two days
10:11 the **cloud** lifted from above the tabernacle of the Testimony.
10:12 traveled from place to place until the **cloud** came to rest in the
10:34 The **cloud** *of* the LORD was over them by day when they set out
11:25 Then the LORD came down in the **cloud** and spoke with him,
12: 5 the LORD came down in a pillar of **cloud**; he stood at the
12:10 When the **cloud** lifted from above the Tent, there stood Miriam—
14:14 have been seen face to face, that your **cloud** stays over them,
14:14 that you go before them in a pillar of **cloud** by day and a pillar of
16:42 [17:7] suddenly the **cloud** covered it and the glory of the LORD
Dt 1:33 in fire by night and in a **cloud** by day, to search out places for you
4:11 with fire to the very heavens, with black **clouds** and deep darkness.
5:22 the mountain from out of the fire, the **cloud** and the deep darkness;
31:15 Then the LORD appeared at the Tent in a pillar of **cloud**,
31:15 a pillar of cloud, and the **cloud** stood over the entrance to the Tent.
1Ki 8:10 from the Holy Place, the **cloud** filled the temple of the LORD.
8:11 the priests could not perform their service because of the **cloud**,
2Ch 5:13 Then the temple of the LORD was filled with a **cloud**,
5:14 the priests could not perform their service because of the **cloud**,
Ne 9:12 By day you led them with a pillar of **cloud**, and by night with a
9:19 By day the pillar of **cloud** did not cease to guide them on their
Job 7: 9 As a **cloud** vanishes and is gone, so he who goes down to the grave
26: 8 waters in his clouds, yet the **clouds** do not burst under their weight.

Job 26: 9 He covers the face of the full moon, spreading his **clouds** over it.
37: 11 the clouds with moisture; he scatters his lightning through **them**[s].
37: 15 Do you know how God controls the **clouds** and makes his
38: 9 when I made the **clouds** its garment and wrapped it in thick
Ps 78: 14 He guided them with the **cloud** by day and with light from the fire
97: 2 **Clouds** and thick darkness surround him; righteousness and justice
99: 7 He spoke to them from the pillar of **cloud**; they kept his statutes
105: 39 He spread out a **cloud** as a covering, and a fire to give light at
Isa 4: 5 and over those who assemble there a **cloud** of smoke by day
44: 22 away your offenses like a cloud, your sins like the **morning mist**.
Jer 4: 13 He advances like the **clouds**, his chariots come like a whirlwind,
La 3: 44 You have covered yourself with a **cloud** so that no prayer can get
Eze 1: 4 an immense **cloud** with flashing lightning and surrounded by
1: 28 Like the appearance of a rainbow in the **clouds** on a rainy day,
8: 11 a censer in his hand, and a fragrant **cloud** *of* incense was rising.
10: 3 temple when the man went in, and a **cloud** filled the inner court.
10: 4 The **cloud** filled the temple, and the court was full of the radiance
30: 3 LORD is near—a day of **clouds**, a time of doom for the nations.
30: 18 She will be covered with **clouds**, and her villages will go into
32: 7 I will cover the sun with a **cloud**, and the moon will not give its
34: 12 from all the places where they were scattered on a day of **clouds**
38: 9 advancing like a storm; you will be like a **cloud** covering the land.
38: 16 You will advance against my people Israel like a **cloud** that covers
Hos 6: 4 Your love is like the morning **mist**, like the early dew that
13: 3 Therefore they will be like the morning **mist**, like the early dew
Joel 2: 2 a day of darkness and gloom, a day of **clouds** and blackness.
Na 1: 3 in the whirlwind and the storm, and **clouds** are the dust of his feet.
Zep 1: 15 a day of darkness and gloom, a day of **clouds** and blackness,

6728 ²עָנָן ʿānān[2], n.pr.m. [1] [√ 6727; cf. 6725]

Anan [1]

Ne 10: 26 [10:27] Ahiah, Hanan, **Anan**,

6729 עֲנָנָה ʿ[a]nānâ, n.f. [1] [√ 6727; cf. 6725]

cloud [1]

Job 3: 5 may a **cloud** settle over it; may blackness overwhelm its light.

6730 עֲנָנִי ʿ[a]nānî, n.pr.m. [1] [√ 6725 + 3378]

Anani [1]

1Ch 3: 24 Hodaviah, Eliashib, Pelaiah, Akkub, Johanan, Delaiah and **Anani**—

6731 ¹עֲנָנְיָה ʿ[a]nān[e]yâ[1], n.pr.m. [1] [√ 6725 + 3378]

Ananiah [1]

Ne 3: 23 and next to them, Azariah son of Maaseiah, the son of **Ananiah**,

6732 ²עֲנָנְיָה ʿ[a]nān[e]yâ[2], n.pr.loc. [1]

Ananiah [1]

Ne 11: 32 in Anathoth, Nob and **Ananiah**,

6733 עָנָף ʿānāp, n.[m.]. [7] [→ 6734; Ar 10561]

branches [6], branch [1]

Lev 23: 40 palm fronds, leafy **branches** and poplars, and rejoice before the
Ps 80: 10 [80:11] with its shade, the mighty cedars with its **branches**.
Eze 17: 8 in good soil by abundant water so that it would produce **branches**,
17: 23 it will produce **branches** and bear fruit and become a splendid
31: 3 in Lebanon, with beautiful **branches** overshadowing the forest;
36: 8 of Israel, will produce **branches** and fruit for my people Israel,
Mal 4: 1 [3:19] "Not a root or a **branch** will be left to them.

6734 עָנֵף ʿānēp, a. [1] [√ 6733]

full of branches [1]

Eze 19: 10 it was fruitful and **full of branches** because of abundant water.

6735 עָנַק ʿānaq, v.den. [3] [√ 6736]

supply liberally [+4200+6735] [2], necklace [1]

Dt 15: 14 [G] **Supply** [+4200+6735] him **liberally** from your flock, your
15: 14 [G] **Supply** him **liberally** [+4200+6735] from your flock, your
Ps 73: 6 [A] Therefore pride is their **necklace**; they clothe themselves

6736 ¹עֲנָק ʿ[a]nāq[1], n.m. [3] [→ 6735]

chain [1], chains [1], jewel [1]

Jdg 8: 26 the kings of Midian or the **chains** that were on their camels' necks.
Pr 1: 9 be a garland to grace your head and a **chain** to adorn your neck.
SS 4: 9 with one glance of your eyes, with one **jewel** of your necklace.

6737 ²עֲנָק ʿ[a]nāq[2], n.[m.] & g. [17] [√ 6710]

Anakites [7], Anak [6], Anakites [+1201] [4]

Nu 13: 22 Sheshai and Talmai, the descendants of **Anak**, lived.
13: 28 and very large. We even saw descendants of **Anak** there.
13: 33 We saw the Nephilim there (the descendants of **Anak** come from
Dt 1: 28 walls up to the sky. We even saw the **Anakites** [+1201] there.' "
2: 10 a people strong and numerous, and as tall as the **Anakites**.
2: 11 Like the **Anakites**, they too were considered Rephaites,
2: 21 were a people strong and numerous, and as tall as the **Anakites**.
9: 2 The people are strong and tall—**Anakites** [+1201]! You know
9: 2 heard it said: "Who can stand up against the **Anakites** [+1201]?"
Jos 11: 21 Joshua went and destroyed the **Anakites** from the hill country:
11: 22 No **Anakites** were left in Israelite territory; only in Gaza, Gath
14: 12 You yourself heard then that the **Anakites** were there and their
14: 15 Arba after Arba, who was the greatest man among the **Anakites**.)
15: 13 Kiriath Arba, that is, Hebron. (Arba was the forefather of **Anak**.)
15: 14 From Hebron Caleb drove out the three **Anakites** [+1201]—
15: 14 Sheshai, Ahiman and Talmai—descendants of **Anak**.
Jdg 1: 20 was given to Caleb, who drove from it the three sons of **Anak**.

6738 ¹עָנֵר ʿānēr[1], n.pr.[m.]. [2]

Aner [2]

Ge 14: 13 a brother of Eshcol and **Aner**, all of whom were allied with
14: 24 to the men who went with me—to **Aner**, Eshcol and Mamre.

6739 ²עָנֵר ʿānēr[2], n.pr.loc. [1]

Aner [1]

1Ch 6: 70 [6:55] from half the tribe of Manasseh the Israelites gave **Aner**

6740 עָנַשׁ ʿānaš, v.den. [8] [→ 6711, 6741; Ar 10562]

must be fined [+6740] [2], suffer [2], fine [1], imposed a levy [1], punish [1], punished [1]

Ex 21: 22 [C] the offender **must be fined** [+6740] whatever the woman's
21: 22 [A] the offender **must be fined** [+6740] whatever the woman's
Dt 22: 19 [A] *They shall* **fine** him a hundred shekels of silver and give
2Ch 36: 3 [A] and **imposed** *on* Judah **a levy** *of* a hundred talents of silver
Pr 17: 26 [A] It is not good *to* **punish** an innocent man, or to flog officials
21: 11 [A] When a mocker *is* **punished**, the simple gain wisdom; when
22: 3 [C] and takes refuge, but the simple keep going and **suffer** for it.
27: 12 [C] and take refuge, but the simple keep going and **suffer** for it.

6741 עֹנֶשׁ ʿōneš, n.[m.]. [2] [√ 6740]

levy [1], penalty [1]

2Ki 23: 33 and he imposed on Judah a **levy** of a hundred talents of silver
Pr 19: 19 A hot-tempered man must pay the **penalty**; if you rescue him,

6742 עֲנָת ʿ[a]nāt, n.pr.m. [2] [→ 1116, 1117, 6704, 6712, 6724, 6743, 6744, 6745]

Anath [2]

Jdg 3: 31 After Ehud came Shamgar son of **Anath**, who struck down six
5: 6 "In the days of Shamgar son of **Anath**, in the days of Jael,

6743 ¹עֲנָתוֹת ʿ[a]nātôt[1], n.pr.loc. [13] [√ 6742]

Anathoth [13]

Jos 21: 18 **Anathoth** and Almon, together with their pasturelands—
1Ki 2: 26 the priest the king said, "Go back to your fields in **Anathoth**.
1Ch 6: 60 [6:45] Geba, Alemeth and **Anathoth**, together with their
Ezr 2: 23 of **Anathoth** 128
Ne 7: 27 of **Anathoth** 128
11: 32 in **Anathoth**, Nob and Ananiah,
Isa 10: 30 O Daughter of Gallim! Listen, O Laishah! Poor **Anathoth**!
Jer 1: 1 one of the priests at **Anathoth** in the territory of Benjamin.
11: 21 LORD says about the men of **Anathoth** who are seeking your life
11: 23 because I will bring disaster on the men of **Anathoth** in the year
32: 7 uncle is going to come to you and say, 'Buy my field at **Anathoth**,
32: 8 and said, 'Buy my field at **Anathoth** in the territory of Benjamin.
32: 9 so I bought the field at **Anathoth** from my cousin Hanamel

6744 ²עֲנָתוֹת ʿ[a]nātôt[2], n.pr.m. [2] [√ 6742]

Anathoth [2]

1Ch 7: 8 Elioenai, Omri, Jeremoth, Abijah, **Anathoth** and Alemeth.
Ne 10: 19 [10:20] Hariph, **Anathoth**, Nebai,

6745 עַנְּתֹתִי ʿann[e]tōtî, a.g. [5] [√ 6742]

from Anathoth [3], Anathothite [2]

2Sa 23: 27 Abiezer **from Anathoth**, Mebunnai the Hushathite,
1Ch 11: 28 Ira son of Ikkesh from Tekoa, Abiezer **from Anathoth**,

1Ch 12: 3 and Pelet the sons of Azmaveth; Beracah, Jehu the **Anathothite**,
27: 12 for the ninth month, was Abiezer the **Anathothite**, a Benjamite.
Jer 29: 27 So why have you not reprimanded Jeremiah **from Anathoth**,

6746 עַנְתֹתִיָּה ***'antōtiyyâ***, n.pr.m. [1]
Anthothijah [1]
1Ch 8: 24 Hananiah, Elam, **Anthothijah**,

6747 עָסִיס ***'āsîs***, n.m. [5] [√ 6748]
new wine [3], nectar [1], wine [1]
SS 8: 2 give you spiced wine to drink, the **nectar** *of* my pomegranates.
Isa 49: 26 own flesh; they will be drunk on their own blood, as with **wine**.
Joel 1: 5 wail because of the **new wine**, for it has been snatched from your
3: 18 [4:18] "In that day the mountains will drip **new wine**, and the hills
Am 9: 13 **New wine** will drip from the mountains and flow from all the hills.

6748 עָסַס ***'āsas***, v. [1] [→ 6747]
trample down [1]
Mal 4: 3 [3:21] [A] *you will* **trample down** the wicked; they will be

6749 עָעַר ***'ā'ar***, v. Not used in NIV/BHS [√ 6424]

6750 עֳפָאִים ***'ºpā'yim***, n.m.pl. Not used in NIV/BHS [→ 6751]

6751 עֳפִי ***'ºpî***, n.[m.]. [1] [√ 6750; Ar 10564]
branches [1]
Ps 104: 12 birds of the air nest by the waters; they sing among the **branches**.

6752 עָפַל[1] ***'āpal***[1], v. [1] [→ 6754, 6755; cf. 6753]
puffed up [1]
Hab 2: 4 [E] "See, *he is* **puffed up**; his desires are not upright—but the

6753 עָפַל[2] ***'āpal***[2], v. [1] [cf. 6752]
presumption [1]
Nu 14: 44 [G] *in their* **presumption** they went up toward the high hill

6754 עֹפֶל[1] ***'ōpel***[1], n.m. [6] [√ 6752]
tumors [6]
Dt 28: 27 will afflict you with the boils of Egypt and with **tumors**, [Q 3224]
1Sa 5: 6 devastation upon them and afflicted them with **tumors**. [Q 3224]
5: 9 both young and old, with an outbreak of **tumors**. [Q 3224]
5: 12 Those who did not die were afflicted with **tumors**, [Q 3224]
6: 4 They replied, "Five gold **tumors** [Q 3224] and five gold rats,
6: 5 Make models of the **tumors** [Q 3224] and of the rats that are

6755 עֹפֶל[2] ***'ōpel***[2], n.[m.]. [8] [√ 6754]
hill of Ophel [4], citadel [1], hill [1], Ophel [1], stronghold [1]
2Ki 5: 24 When Gehazi came to the **hill**, he took the things from the servants
2Ch 27: 3 and did extensive work on the wall at the **hill of Ophel**.
33: 14 as the entrance of the Fish Gate and encircling the **hill of Ophel**;
Ne 3: 26 the temple servants living on the **hill of Ophel** made repairs up to a
3: 27 from the great projecting tower to the wall of **Ophel**.
11: 21 The temple servants lived on the **hill of Ophel**, and Ziha
Isa 32: 14 **citadel** and watchtower will become a wasteland forever,
Mic 4: 8 O watchtower of the flock, O **stronghold** *of* the Daughter of Zion,

6756 עָפְנִי ***'opnî***, n.pr.loc. [1]
Ophni [1]
Jos 18: 24 Kephar Ammoni, **Ophni** and Geba—twelve towns and their

6757 עַפְעַפַּיִם ***'ap'appayim***, n.m. [10] [√ 6415]
eyelids [3], eyes [3], first rays [1], gaze [1], glances [1], rays [1]
Job 3: 9 may it wait for daylight in vain and not see the **first rays** *of* dawn,
16: 16 My face is red with weeping, deep shadows ring my **eyes**;
41: 18 [41:10] out flashes of light; his eyes are like the **rays** *of* dawn.
Ps 11: 4 He observes the sons of men; his **eyes** examine them.
132: 4 I will allow no sleep to my eyes, no slumber to my **eyelids**,
Pr 4: 25 your eyes look straight ahead, fix your **gaze** directly before you.
6: 4 Allow no sleep to your eyes, no slumber to your **eyelids**.
6: 25 in your heart after her beauty or let her captivate you with her **eyes**,
30: 13 whose eyes are ever so haughty, whose **glances** are so disdainful;
Jer 9: 18 [9:17] overflow with tears and water streams from our **eyelids**.

6758 עָפַף ***'āpap***, v. [1]
brandish [1]
Eze 32: 10 [D] because of you when I **brandish** my sword before them.

6759 עָפַר ***'āpar***, v.den. [1] [√ 6760]
showering [1]
2Sa 16: 13 [D] and throwing stones at him and **showering** him with dirt.

6760 עָפָר ***'āpār***, n.m. [110] [→ 6759; cf. 6762]
dust [81], earth [5], rubble [5], soil [4], ground [3], ashes [2], powder [2], clay [1], dirt [1], earthen ramps [1], material [1], plaster [1], sand [1], scabs [+1641] [1], soil [+824] [1]
Ge 2: 7 the LORD God formed the man from the **dust** of the ground
3: 14 crawl on your belly and you will eat **dust** all the days of your life.
3: 19 it you were taken; for **dust** you are and to dust you will return."
3: 19 it you were taken; for dust you are and to **dust** you will return."
13: 16 I will make your offspring like the **dust** *of* the earth, so that if
13: 16 so that if anyone could count the **dust**, then your offspring could be
18: 27 as to speak to the Lord, though I am nothing but **dust** and ashes,
26: 15 the Philistines stopped up, filling them with **earth**.
28: 14 Your descendants will be like the **dust** *of* the earth, and you will
Ex 8: 16 [8:12] 'Stretch out your staff and strike the **dust** *of* the ground,'
8: 17 [8:13] his hand with the staff and struck the **dust** *of* the ground,
8: 17 [8:13] All the **dust** throughout the land of Egypt became gnats.
Lev 14: 41 the **material** that is scraped off dumped into an unclean place
14: 42 stones to replace these and take new **clay** and plaster the house.
14: 45 It must be torn down—its stones, timbers and all the **plaster**—
17: 13 that may be eaten must drain out the blood and cover it with **earth**,
Nu 5: 17 and put some **dust** from the tabernacle floor into the water.
19: 17 put some **ashes** *from* the burned purification offering into a jar
23: 10 Who can count the **dust** *of* Jacob or number the fourth part of
Dt 9: 21 I crushed it and ground it to powder as fine as **dust** and threw the
9: 21 and threw the **dust** into a stream that flowed down the mountain.
28: 24 The LORD will turn the rain of your country into **dust**
32: 24 the fangs of wild beasts, the venom of vipers that glide in the **dust**.
Jos 7: 6 elders of Israel did the same, and sprinkled **dust** on their heads.
1Sa 2: 8 He raises the poor from the **dust** and lifts the needy from the ash
2Sa 16: 13 he went and throwing stones at him and showering him with **dirt**.
22: 43 I beat them as fine as the **dust** *of* the earth; I pounded and trampled
1Ki 16: 2 "I lifted you up from the **dust** and made you leader of my people
18: 38 and burned up the sacrifice, the wood, the stones and the **soil**,
20: 10 if enough **dust** remains *in* Samaria to give each of my men a
2Ki 13: 7 destroyed the rest and made them like the **dust** at threshing time.
23: 4 in the fields of the Kidron Valley and took the **ashes** to Bethel.
23: 6 He ground it to **powder** and scattered the dust over the graves of
23: 6 and scattered the **dust** over the graves of the common people.
23: 12 them to pieces and threw the **rubble** into the Kidron Valley.
23: 15 He burned the high place and ground it to **powder**, and burned the
2Ch 1: 9 king over a people who are as numerous as the **dust** *of* the earth.
Ne 4: 2 [3:34] bring the stones back to life from those heaps of **rubble**—
4: 10 [4:4] there is so much **rubble** that we cannot rebuild the wall."
Job 2: 12 and they tore their robes and sprinkled **dust** on their heads.
4: 19 whose foundations are in the **dust**, who are crushed more readily
5: 6 For hardship does not spring from the **soil**, nor does trouble sprout
7: 5 My body is clothed with worms and **scabs** [+1641], my skin is
7: 21 For I will soon lie down in the **dust**; you will search for me,
8: 19 Surely its life withers away, and from the **soil** other plants grow.
10: 9 that you molded me like clay. Will you now turn me to **dust** again?
14: 8 Its roots may grow old in the ground and its stump die in the **soil**,
14: 19 water wears away stones and torrents wash away the **soil** [+824],
16: 15 sewed sackcloth over my skin and buried my brow in the **dust**.
17: 16 to the gates of death? Will we descend together into the **dust**?"
19: 25 Redeemer lives, and that in the end he will stand upon the **earth**.
20: 11 The youthful vigor that fills his bones will lie with him in the **dust**.
21: 26 Side by side they lie in the **dust**, and worms cover them both.
22: 24 assign your nuggets to the **dust**, your gold of Ophir to the rocks in
27: 16 Though he heaps up silver like **dust** and clothes like piles of clay,
28: 2 Iron is taken from the **earth**, and copper is smelted from ore.
28: 6 come from its rocks, and its **dust** contains nuggets of gold.
30: 6 the dry stream beds, among the rocks and in holes in the **ground**.
30: 19 He throws me into the mud, and I am reduced to **dust** and ashes.
34: 15 mankind would perish together and man would return to the **dust**.
38: 38 when the **dust** becomes hard and the clods of earth stick together?
39: 14 She lays her eggs on the ground and lets them warm in the **sand**,
40: 13 Bury them all in the **dust** together; shroud their faces in the grave.
41: 33 [41:25] Nothing on **earth** is his equal—a creature without fear.
42: 6 Therefore I despise myself and repent in **dust** and ashes."
Ps 7: 5 [7:6] my life to the ground and make me sleep in the **dust**.
18: 42 [18:43] I beat them as fine as **dust** borne on the wind; I poured
22: 15 [22:16] to the roof of my mouth; you lay me in the **dust** *of* death.
22: 29 [22:30] all who go down to the **dust** will kneel before him—
30: 9 [30:10] in my going down into the pit? Will the **dust** praise you?
44: 25 [44:26] We are brought down to the **dust**; our bodies cling to the
72: 9 tribes will bow before him and his enemies will lick the **dust**.
78: 27 He rained meat down on them like **dust**, flying birds like sand on
102: 14 [102:15] dear to your servants; her very **dust** moves them to pity.

Ps 103: 14 for he knows how we are formed, he remembers that we are **dust**.
104: 29 when you take away their breath, they die and return to the **dust**.
113: 7 He raises the poor from the **dust** and lifts the needy from the ash
119: 25 I am laid low in the **dust**; preserve my life according to your word.
Pr 8: 26 he made the earth or its fields or any of the **dust** *of* the world.
Ecc 3: 20 All go to the same place; all come from **dust**, and to dust all return.
3: 20 All go to the same place; all come from dust, and to **dust** all return.
12: 7 the **dust** returns to the ground it came from, and the spirit returns
Isa 2: 10 hide in the **ground** from dread of the LORD and the splendor of
2: 19 to holes in the **ground** from dread of the LORD and the splendor
25: 12 them low; he will bring them down to the ground, to the very **dust**.
26: 5 city low; he levels it to the ground and casts it down to the **dust**.
26: 19 will rise. You who dwell in the **dust**, wake up and shout for joy.
29: 4 speak from the ground; your speech will mumble out of the **dust**.
29: 4 ghostlike from the earth; out of the **dust** your speech will whisper.
34: 7 will be drenched with blood, and the **dust** will be soaked with fat.
34: 9 streams will be turned into pitch, her **dust** into burning sulfur;
40: 12 Who has held the **dust** *of* the earth in a basket, or weighed the
41: 2 He turns them to **dust** with his sword, to windblown chaff with his
47: 1 "Go down, sit in the **dust**, Virgin Daughter of Babylon; sit on the
49: 23 with their faces to the ground; they will lick the **dust** *at* your feet.
52: 2 Shake off your **dust**; rise up, sit enthroned, O Jerusalem.
65: 25 lion will eat straw like the ox, but **dust** will be the serpent's food.
La 2: 10 they have sprinkled **dust** on their heads and put on sackcloth.
3: 29 Let him bury his face in the **dust**—there may yet be hope.
Eze 24: 7 she did not pour it on the ground, where the **dust** would cover it.
26: 4 I will scrape away her **rubble** and make her a bare rock.
26: 12 fine houses and throw your stones, timber and **rubble** into the sea.
27: 30 over you; they will sprinkle **dust** on their heads and roll in ashes.
Da 12: 2 Multitudes who sleep in the **dust** *of* the earth will awake: some to
Am 2: 7 They trample on the heads of the poor as upon the **dust** *of* the
Mic 1: 10 Tell it not in Gath; weep not at all. In Beth Ophrah roll in the **dust**.
7: 17 They will lick **dust** like a snake, like creatures that crawl on the
Hab 1: 10 at all fortified cities; they build **earthen ramps** and capture them.
Zep 1: 17 Their blood will be poured out like **dust** and their entrails like filth.
Zec 9: 3 she has heaped up silver like **dust**, and gold like the dirt of the

6761 עֵ֫פֶר ʿēper, n.pr.m. [4] [→ 6766, 6767, 6768]

Epher [4]

Ge 25: 4 sons of Midian were Ephah, **Epher**, Hanoch, Abida and Eldaah.
1Ch 1: 33 The sons of Midian: Ephah, **Epher**, Hanoch, Abida and Eldaah.
4: 17 The sons of Ezrah: Jether, Mered, **Epher** and Jalon. One of
5: 24 **Epher**, Ishi, Eliel, Azriel, Jeremiah, Hodaviah and Jahdiel.

6762 עֹ֫פֶר ʿōper, n.m. [5] [→ 6763, 6764, 6765; cf. 6760]

young stag [+385] [3], fawns [2]

SS 2: 9 My lover is like a gazelle or a **young stag** [+385]. Look! There he
2: 17 be like a gazelle or like a **young stag** [+385] on the rugged hills.
4: 5 Your two breasts are like two **fawns**, like twin fawns of a gazelle
7: 3 [7:4] Your breasts are like two **fawns**, twins of a gazelle.
8: 14 or like a **young stag** [+385] on the spice-laden mountains.

6763 עָפְרָה¹ ʿoprâ¹, n.pr.m. [1] [→ 6764; cf. 6762]

Ophrah [1]

1Ch 4: 14 Meonothai was the father of **Ophrah**. Seraiah was the father of

6764 עָפְרָה² ʿoprâ², n.pr.loc. [7] [√ 6763; cf. 6762]

Ophrah [7]

Jos 18: 23 Avvim, Parah, **Ophrah**,
Jdg 6: 11 sat down under the oak in **Ophrah** that belonged to Joash the
6: 24 is Peace. To this day it stands in **Ophrah** *of* the Abiezrites.
8: 27 the gold into an ephod, which he placed in **Ophrah**, his town.
8: 32 was buried in the tomb of his father Joash in **Ophrah** *of* the
9: 5 He went to his father's home in **Ophrah** and on one stone
1Sa 13: 17 One turned toward **Ophrah** in the vicinity of Shual,

6765 עַפְרָה ʿaprâ, n.pr.loc. Not used in NIV/BHS [√ 4364; cf. 6762?]

6766 עֶפְרוֹן¹ ʿeprôn¹, n.pr.m. [12] [→ 6767?, 6768; cf. 6761]

Ephron [8], Ephron's [2], he[s] [1], him[s] [1]

Ge 23: 8 listen to me and intercede with **Ephron** son of Zohar on my behalf
23: 10 **Ephron** the Hittite was sitting among his people and he replied to
23: 10 **he**[s] replied to Abraham in the hearing of all the Hittites who had
23: 13 and he said to **Ephron** in their hearing, "Listen to me, if you will.
23: 14 **Ephron** answered Abraham,
23: 16 Abraham agreed to **Ephron's** terms and weighed out for him the
23: 16 weighed out for **him**[s] the price he had named in the hearing of the
23: 17 So **Ephron's** field in Machpelah near Mamre—both the field
25: 9 near Mamre, in the field of **Ephron** son of Zohar the Hittite,
49: 29 Bury me with my fathers in the cave in the field of **Ephron** the
49: 30 which Abraham bought as a burial place from **Ephron** the Hittite,
50: 13 which Abraham had bought as a burial place from **Ephron** the

6767 עֶפְרוֹן² ʿeprôn², n.pr.loc. [2] [√ 6766?; cf. 6761]

Ephron [2]

Jos 15: 9 came out at the towns of Mount **Ephron** and went down toward
2Ch 13: 19 Jeshanah and **Ephron**, [Q 6768] with their surrounding villages.

6768 עֶפְרַ֫יִן ʿeprayin, n.pr.loc. [0] [√ 6766; cf. 6761]

2Ch 13: 19 [took from him the towns of Bethel, Jeshanah and **Ephron**, [Q; see K 6767]]

6769 עֹפֶ֫רֶת ʿōperet, n.m. [9]

lead [9]

Ex 15: 10 the sea covered them. They sank like **lead** in the mighty waters.
Nu 31: 22 Gold, silver, bronze, iron, tin, **lead**
Job 19: 24 that they were inscribed with an iron tool on **lead**, or engraved in
Jer 6: 29 The bellows blow fiercely to burn away the **lead** with fire,
Eze 22: 18 all of them are the copper, tin, iron and **lead** left inside a furnace.
22: 20 iron, **lead** and tin into a furnace to melt it with a fiery blast,
27: 12 they exchanged silver, iron, tin and **lead** for your merchandise.
Zec 5: 7 the cover of **lead** was raised, and there in the basket sat a woman!
5: 8 into the basket and pushed the **lead** cover down over its mouth.

6770 עֵץ ʿēṣ, n.m. [330 / 329] [→ 6785; Ar 10058]

wood [100], trees [69], tree [61], timber [12], *untranslated* [10], wooden [10], gallows [9], logs [9], stick [7], shaft [4], almugwood [+523] [3], carpenters [+3093] [3], stick of wood [3], sticks [3], woodcutters [+2634] [3], algumwood [+454] [2], timbers [2], beams [1], branches [+8457] [1], carpenter [+3093] [1], carpenters [1], firewood [1], it[s] [+2021] [1], loads of wood [1], lumber [1], olive [+9043] [1], paneling [+7596] [1], piece of wood [1], pine [+1360] [1], plant life [1], stalks [1], that[s] [1], them[s] [+780] [1], wooden idol [1], woodpile [1], woodwork [1]

Ge 1: 11 and **trees** on the land that bear fruit with seed in it,
1: 12 and **trees** bearing fruit with seed in it according to their kinds.
1: 29 face of the whole earth and every **tree** that has fruit with seed in it.
1: 29 the whole earth and every tree that has fruit **[RPH]** with seed in it.
2: 9 the LORD God made all kinds of **trees** grow out of the ground—
2: 9 In the middle of the garden were the **tree** *of* life and the tree of the
2: 9 the tree of life and the **tree** *of* the knowledge of good and evil.
2: 16 the man, "You are free to eat from any **tree** *in* the garden;
2: 17 but you must not eat from the **tree** *of* the knowledge of good
3: 1 God really say, 'You must not eat from any **tree** *in* the garden'?"
3: 2 said to the serpent, "We may eat fruit from the **trees** *in* the garden,
3: 3 'You must not eat fruit from the **tree** that is in the middle of the
3: 6 When the woman saw that the fruit of the **tree** was good for food
3: 6 and also desirable **[RPH]** for gaining wisdom, she took some
3: 8 and they hid from the LORD God among the **trees** *of* the garden.
3: 11 Have you eaten from the **tree** that I commanded you not to eat
3: 12 here with me—she gave me some fruit from the **tree**, and I ate it."
3: 17 to your wife and ate from the **tree** about which I commanded you,
3: 22 to reach out his hand and take also from the **tree** *of* life and eat,
3: 24 sword flashing back and forth to guard the way to the **tree** *of* life.
6: 14 So make yourself an ark of cypress **wood**; make rooms in it
18: 4 and then you may all wash your feet and rest under this **tree**.
18: 8 these before them. While they ate, he stood near them under a **tree**.
22: 3 When he had cut *enough* **wood** *for* the burnt offering, he set out
22: 6 Abraham took the **wood** *for* the burnt offering and placed it on his
22: 7 "The fire and **wood** are here," Isaac said, "but where is the lamb
22: 9 Abraham built an altar there and arranged the **wood** on it.
22: 9 bound his son Isaac and laid him on the altar, on top of the **wood**.
23: 17 and the cave in it, and all the **trees** within the borders of the field—
40: 19 three days Pharaoh will lift off your head and hang you on a **tree**.
Ex 7: 19 everywhere in Egypt, even in the **wooden** *buckets* and stone jars."
9: 25 beat down everything growing in the fields and stripped every **tree**.
10: 5 after the hail, including every **tree** that is growing in your fields.
10: 15 everything growing in the fields and the fruit on the **trees**.
10: 15 Nothing green remained on **tree** or plant in all the land of Egypt.
15: 25 out to the LORD, and the LORD showed him a **piece of wood**.
25: 5 ram skins dyed red and hides of sea cows; acacia **wood**;
25: 10 "Have them make a chest of acacia **wood**—two and a half cubits
25: 13 Then make poles of acacia **wood** and overlay them with gold.
25: 23 "Make a table of acacia **wood**—two cubits long, a cubit wide
25: 28 Make the poles of acacia **wood**, overlay them with gold and carry
26: 15 "Make upright frames of acacia **wood** for the tabernacle.
26: 26 "Also make crossbars of acacia **wood**: five for the frames on one
27: 1 "Build an altar of acacia **wood**, three cubits high; it is to be square,
27: 6 Make poles of acacia **wood** for the altar and overlay them with
30: 1 "Make an altar of acacia **wood** for burning incense.

Ex 30: 5 Make the poles of acacia **wood** and overlay them with gold.
31: 5 to cut and set stones, to work in **wood**, and to engage in all kinds of
35: 7 ram skins dyed red and hides of sea cows; acacia **wood**;
35:24 everyone who had acacia **wood** for any part of the work brought it.
35:33 to work in **wood** and to engage in all kinds of artistic
36:20 They made upright frames of acacia **wood** for the tabernacle.
36:31 They also made crossbars of acacia **wood**: five for the frames on
37: 1 Bezalel made the ark of acacia **wood**—two and a half cubits long,
37: 4 Then he made poles of acacia **wood** and overlaid them with gold.
37:10 They made the table of acacia **wood**—two cubits long, a cubit
37:15 The poles for carrying the table were made of acacia **wood**
37:25 They made the altar of incense out of acacia **wood**. It was square,
37:28 They made the poles of acacia **wood** and overlaid them with gold.
38: 1 They built the altar of burnt offering of acacia **wood**, three cubits
38: 6 They made the poles of acacia **wood** and overlaid them with
Lev 1: 7 the priest are to put fire on the altar and arrange **wood** on the fire.
1: 8 the head and the fat, on the burning **wood** that is on the altar.
1:12 the head and the fat, on the burning **wood** that is on the altar.
1:17 the priest shall burn it on the **wood** that is on the fire on the altar.
3: 5 the altar on top of the burnt offering that is on the burning **wood**,
4:12 the ashes are thrown, and burn it in a **wood** fire on the ash heap.
6:12 [6:5] Every morning the priest is to add **firewood** and arrange the
11:32 be unclean, whether it is made of **wood**, cloth, hide or sackcloth.
14: 4 priest shall order that two live clean birds and *some* cedar **wood**,
14: 6 then to take the live bird and dip it, together with the cedar **wood**,
14:45 It must be torn down—its stones, **timbers** and all the plaster—
14:49 To purify the house he is to take two birds and *some* cedar **wood**,
14:51 Then he is to take the cedar **wood**, the hyssop, the scarlet yarn
14:52 the live bird, the cedar **wood**, the hyssop and the scarlet yarn.
15:12 must be broken, and any **wooden** article is to be rinsed with water.
19:23 " 'When you enter the land and plant any kind of fruit **tree**,
23:40 On the first day you are to take choice fruit from the **trees**,
23:40 palm fronds, leafy branches **[RPH]** and poplars, and rejoice
26: 4 the ground will yield its crops and the **trees** *of* the field their fruit.
26:20 not yield its crops, nor will the **trees** *of* the land yield their fruit.
27:30 whether grain from the soil or fruit from the **trees**, belongs to the
Nu 13:20 How is the soil? Is it fertile or poor? Are there **trees** on it or not?
15:32 in the desert, a man was found gathering **wood** on the Sabbath day.
15:33 Those who found him gathering **wood** brought him to Moses
19: 6 The priest is to take *some* cedar **wood**, hyssop and scarlet wool
31:20 garment as well as everything made of leather, goat hair or **wood**."
35:18 Or if anyone has a **wooden** object in his hand that could kill,
Dt 4:28 There you will worship man-made gods of **wood** and stone,
10: 1 and come up to me on the mountain. Also make a **wooden** chest.
10: 3 So I made the ark out of acacia **wood** and chiseled out two stone
12: 2 under every spreading **tree** where the nations you are dispossessing
16:21 Do not set up any **wooden** Asherah pole beside the altar you build
19: 5 a man may go into the forest with his neighbor to cut **wood**,
19: 5 and as he swings his ax to fell a **tree**, the head may fly off
19: 5 the head may fly off **[NIE]** and hit his neighbor and kill him.
20:19 do not destroy its **trees** by putting an ax to them, because you can
20:19 Are the **trees** *of* the field people, that you should besiege them?
20:20 you may cut down **trees** that you know are not fruit trees and use
20:20 you may cut down trees that you know are not fruit **trees** and use
21:22 of a capital offense is put to death and his body is hung on a **tree**,
21:23 you must not leave his body on the **tree** overnight. Be sure to bury
22: 6 either in a **tree** or on the ground, and the mother is sitting on the
28:36 There you will worship other gods, gods of **wood** and stone.
28:42 Swarms of locusts will take over all your **trees** and the crops of
28:64 gods of **wood** and stone, which neither you nor your fathers have
29:11 [29:10] the aliens living in your camps who chop your **wood**
29:17 [29:16] them their detestable images and idols of **wood** and stone,
Jos 2: 6 hidden them under the **stalks** *of* flax she had laid out on the roof.)
8:29 He hung the king of Ai on a **tree** and left him there until evening.
8:29 Joshua ordered them to take his body from the **tree** and throw it
9:21 let them be **woodcutters** [+2634] and water carriers for the entire
9:23 You will never cease to serve as **woodcutters** [+2634] and water
9:27 That day he made the Gibeonites **woodcutters** [+2634] and water
10:26 Joshua struck and killed the kings and hung them on five **trees**,
10:26 on five trees, and they were left hanging on the **trees** until evening.
10:27 Joshua gave the order and they took them down from the **trees**
Jdg 6:26 Using the **wood** *of* the Asherah pole that you cut down, offer the
9: 8 One day the **trees** went out to anoint a king for themselves.
9: 9 both gods and men are honored, to hold sway over the **trees**?'
9:10 "Next, the **trees** said to the fig tree, 'Come and be our king.'
9:11 I give up my fruit, so good and sweet, to hold sway over the **trees**?'
9:12 "Then the **trees** said to the vine, 'Come and be our king.'
9:13 which cheers both gods and men, to hold sway over the **trees**?'
9:14 "Finally all the **trees** said to the thornbush, 'Come and be our king.'
9:15 "The thornbush said to the **trees**, 'If you really want to anoint me
9:48 He took an ax and cut off *some* **branches** [+8457], which he lifted
1Sa 6:14 The people chopped up the **wood** *of* the cart and sacrificed the
17: 7 His spear **shaft** [K 2932] was like a weaver's rod, and its iron
2Sa 5:11 along with cedar **logs** and carpenters and stonemasons, and they
5:11 along with cedar logs and **carpenters** [+3093] and stonemasons,
6: 5 with all their might [BHS *instruments made of pine*; NIV 6437]
21:19 the Gittite, who had a spear with a **shaft** like a weaver's rod.
23: 7 Whoever touches thorns uses a tool of iron or the **shaft** *of* a spear;
24:22 and here are threshing sledges and ox yokes for the **wood**.
1Ki 4:33 [5:13] He described **plant life**, from the cedar of Lebanon to the
5: 6 [5:20] have no one so skilled in felling **timber** as the Sidonians."
5: 8 [5:22] all you want in providing the cedar **[RPH]** and pine logs.
5: 8 [5:22] will do all you want in providing the cedar and pine **logs**.
5:10 [5:24] with all the cedar **[RPH]** and pine logs he wanted,
5:10 [5:24] supplied with all the cedar and pine **logs** he wanted,
5:18 [5:32] and the men of Gebal cut and prepared the **timber**
6:10 and they were attached to the temple by **beams** *of* cedar.
6:15 **paneling** [+7596] them from the floor of the temple to the ceiling,
6:23 In the inner sanctuary he made a pair of cherubim of olive **wood**,
6:31 the entrance of the inner sanctuary he made doors of olive **wood**
6:32 And on the two olive **wood** doors he carved cherubim, palm trees
6:33 In the same way he made four-sided jambs of olive **wood** for the
6:34 He also made two **[RPH]** pine doors, each having two leaves that
9:11 because Hiram had supplied him with **[NIE]** all the cedar
9:11 because Hiram had supplied him with all the **[NIE]** cedar
10:11 and from there they brought great cargoes of **almugwood** [+523]
10:12 The king used the **almugwood** [+523] to make supports for the
10:12 So much **almugwood** [+523] has never been imported or seen
14:23 Asherah poles on every high hill and under every spreading **tree**.
15:22 from Ramah the stones and **timber** Baasha had been using there.
17:10 he came to the town gate, a widow was there gathering **sticks**.
17:12 I am gathering a few **sticks** to take home and make a meal for
18:23 them cut it into pieces and put it on the **wood** but not set fire to it.
18:23 prepare the other bull and put it on the **wood** but not set fire to it.
18:33 He arranged the **wood**, cut the bull into pieces and laid it on the
18:33 arranged the wood, cut the bull into pieces and laid it on the **wood**.
18:33 [18:34] with water and pour it on the offering and on the **wood**."
18:38 and burned up the sacrifice, the **wood**, the stones and the soil,
2Ki 3:19 You will cut down every good **tree**, stop up all the springs,
3:25 They stopped up all the springs and cut down every good **tree**.
6: 4 with them. They went to the Jordan and began to cut down **trees**.
6: 6 Elisha cut a **stick** and threw it there, and made the iron float.
12:11 [12:12] of the LORD—the **carpenters** [+3093] and builders,
12:12 [12:13] They purchased **timber** and dressed stone for the repair of
16: 4 at the high places, on the hilltops and under every spreading **tree**.
17:10 Asherah poles on every high hill and under every spreading **tree**.
19:18 destroyed them, for they were not gods but only **wood** and stone,
22: 6 Also have them purchase **timber** and dressed stone to repair the
1Ch 14: 1 along with cedar **logs**, stonemasons and carpenters to build a
14: 1 stonemasons and **carpenters** [+3093] to build a palace for him.
16:33 the **trees** *of* the forest will sing, they will sing for joy before the
20: 5 the Gittite, who had a spear with a **shaft** like a weaver's rod.
21:23 the threshing sledges for the **wood**, and the wheat for the grain
22: 4 He also provided more cedar **logs** than could be counted,
22: 4 and Tyrians had brought large numbers of **them**[s] [+780] to David.
22:14 of bronze and iron too great to be weighed, and **wood** and stone.
22:15 stonecutters, masons and **carpenters**, as well as men skilled in
29: 2 bronze for the bronze, iron for the iron and **wood** for the wood,
29: 2 bronze for the bronze, iron for the iron and wood for the **wood**,
2Ch 2: 8 [2:7] "Send me also cedar, pine and algum **logs** from Lebanon,
2: 8 [2:7] for I know that your men are skilled in cutting **timber** there.
2: 9 [2:8] to provide me with plenty of **lumber**, because the temple I
2:10 [2:9] I will give your servants, the woodsmen who cut the **timber**,
2:14 [2:13] work in gold and silver, bronze and iron, stone and **wood**,
2:16 [2:15] we will cut all the **logs** from Lebanon that you need
3: 5 He paneled the main hall with **pine** [+1360] and covered it with
9:10 they also brought **algumwood** [+454] and precious stones.
9:11 The king used the **algumwood** [+454] to make steps for the temple
16: 6 away from Ramah the stones and **timber** Baasha had been using.
28: 4 at the high places, on the hilltops and under every spreading **tree**.
34:11 **timber** for joists and beams for the buildings that the kings of
Ezr 3: 7 so that they would bring cedar **logs** by sea from Lebanon to Joppa,
Ne 2: 8 so he will give me **timber** to make beams for the gates of the
8: 4 Ezra the scribe stood on a high **wooden** platform built for the
8:15 and bring back branches from olive and wild olive **trees**,
8:15 and from myrtles, palms and shade **trees**, to make booths"—
9:25 already dug, vineyards, olive groves and fruit **trees** in abundance.
10:34 [10:35] of **wood** to burn on the altar of the LORD our God,
10:35 [10:36] year the firstfruits of our crops and of every fruit **tree**.
10:37 [10:38] of the fruit of all our **trees** and of our new wine and oil.
13:31 I also made provision for contributions of **wood** at designated
Est 2:23 and found to be true, the two officials were hanged on a **gallows**.
5:14 friends said to him, "Have a **gallows** built, seventy-five feet high,
5:14 This suggestion delighted Haman, and he had the **gallows** built.
6: 4 about hanging Mordecai on the **gallows** he had erected for him.
7: 9 "A **gallows** seventy-five feet high stands by Haman's house.
7:10 So they hanged Haman on the **gallows** he had prepared for
8: 7 his estate to Esther, and they have hanged him on the **gallows**.

Est 9:13 tomorrow also, and let Haman's ten sons be hanged on **gallows**."
9:25 and that he and his sons should be hanged on the **gallows**.
Job 14:7 "At least there is hope for a **tree**: If it is cut down, it will sprout
19:10 down on every side till I am gone; he uproots my hope like a **tree**.
24:20 evil men are no longer remembered but are broken like a **tree**.
41:27 [41:19] Iron he treats like straw and bronze like rotten **wood**.
Ps 1:3 He is like a **tree** planted by streams of water, which yields its fruit
74:5 behaved like men wielding axes to cut through a thicket of **trees**.
96:12 in them. Then all the **trees** *of* the forest will sing for joy;
104:16 The **trees** *of* the LORD are well watered, the cedars of Lebanon
105:33 their vines and fig trees and shattered the **trees** *of* their country.
148:9 you mountains and all hills, fruit **trees** and all cedars,
Pr 3:18 She is a **tree** *of* life to those who embrace her; those who lay hold
11:30 The fruit of the righteous is a **tree** *of* life, and he who wins souls is
13:12 makes the heart sick, but a longing fulfilled is a **tree** *of* life.
15:4 The tongue that brings healing is a **tree** *of* life, but a deceitful
26:20 Without **wood** a fire goes out; without gossip a quarrel dies down.
26:21 As charcoal to embers and as **wood** to fire, so is a quarrelsome
Ecc 2:5 and parks and planted all kinds of fruit **trees** in them.
2:6 I made reservoirs to water groves of flourishing **trees**.
10:9 injured by them; whoever splits **logs** may be endangered by them.
11:3 Whether a **tree** falls to the south or to the north, in the place where
11:3 to the south or to the north, in the place where **it**ˢ [+2021] falls,
SS 2:3 Like an apple tree among the **trees** *of* the forest is my lover among
3:9 made for himself the carriage; he made it of **wood** *from* Lebanon.
4:14 with every kind of incense **tree**, with myrrh and aloes and all the
Isa 7:2 were shaken, as the **trees** *of* the forest are shaken by the wind.
10:15 wield him who lifts it up, or a club brandish him who is not **wood**!
10:19 the remaining **trees** *of* his forests will be so few that a child could
30:33 been made deep and wide, with an abundance of fire and **wood**;
37:19 destroyed them, for they were not gods but only **wood** and stone,
40:20 A man too poor to present such an offering selects **wood** that will
41:19 desert the cedar and the acacia, the myrtle and the **olive** [+9043].
44:13 The **carpenter** [+3093] measures with a line and makes an outline
44:14 He let it grow among the **trees** *of* the forest, or planted a pine,
44:19 thing from what is left? Shall I bow down to a block of **wood**?"
44:23 Burst into song, you mountains, you forests and all your **trees**,
45:20 Ignorant are those who carry about idols of **wood**, who pray to
55:12 song before you, and all the **trees** *of* the field will clap their hands.
56:3 And let not any eunuch complain, "I am only a dry **tree**."
57:5 burn with lust among the oaks and under every spreading **tree**;
60:17 Instead of **wood** I will bring you bronze, and iron in place of
65:22 For as the days of a **tree**, so will be the days of my people;
Jer 2:20 and under every spreading **tree** you lay down as a prostitute.
2:27 They say to **wood**, 'You are my father,' and to stone, 'You gave me
3:6 and under every spreading **tree** and has committed adultery there.
3:9 she defiled the land and committed adultery with stone and **wood**.
3:13 scattered your favors to foreign gods under every spreading **tree**,
5:14 words in your mouth a fire and these people the **wood** it consumes.
7:18 The children gather **wood**, the fathers light the fire, and the women
7:20 and beast, on the **trees** *of* the field and on the fruit of the ground,
10:3 they cut a **tree** out of the forest, and a craftsman shapes it with his
10:8 and foolish; they are taught by worthless **wooden** idols.
11:19 plotted against me, saying, "Let us destroy the **tree** and its fruit;
17:2 and Asherah poles beside the spreading **trees** and on the high hills.
17:8 He will be like a **tree** planted by the water that sends out its roots
28:13 You have broken a **wooden** yoke, but in its place you will get a
46:22 will come against her with axes, like men who cut down **trees**.
La 4:8 skin has shriveled on their bones; it has become as dry as a **stick**.
5:4 must buy the water we drink; our **wood** can be had only at a price.
5:13 men toil at the millstones; boys stagger under **loads of wood**.
Eze 6:13 under every spreading **tree** and every leafy oak—
15:2 how is the **wood** *of* a vine better than that of a branch on any of the
15:2 how is the wood of a vine better than **that**ˢ *of* a branch on any of
15:2 a vine better than that of a branch on any of the **trees** *in* the forest?
15:3 Is **wood** ever taken from it to make anything useful? Do they make
15:6 As I have given the **wood** *of* the vine among the trees of the forest
15:6 As I have given the wood of the vine among the **trees** *of* the forest
17:24 All the **trees** *of* the field will know that I the LORD bring down
17:24 of the field will know that I the LORD bring down the tall **tree**
17:24 LORD bring down the tall tree and make the low **tree** grow tall.
17:24 I dry up the green **tree** and make the dry tree flourish.
17:24 I dry up the green tree and make the dry **tree** flourish.
20:28 sworn to give them and they saw any high hill or any leafy **tree**,
20:32 like the peoples of the world, who serve **wood** and stone."
20:47 [21:3] and it will consume all your **trees**, both green and dry.
20:47 [21:3] it will consume all your trees, both green and **[RPH]** dry.
21:10 [21:15] of my son ‹Judah›? The sword despises every such **stick**.
24:10 So heap on the **wood** and kindle the fire. Cook the meat well,
26:12 fine houses and throw your stones, **timber** and rubble into the sea.
31:4 around its base and sent their channels to all the **trees** *of* the field.
31:5 So it towered higher than all the **trees** *of* the field; its boughs
31:8 its branches—no **tree** in the garden of God could match its beauty.
31:9 the envy of all the **trees** *of* Eden in the garden of God.
31:14 Therefore no other **trees** *by* the waters are ever to tower proudly
31:15 Lebanon with gloom, and all the **trees** *of* the field withered away.
31:16 Then all the **trees** *of* Eden, the choicest and best of Lebanon,
31:18 " 'Which of the **trees** *of* Eden can be compared with you in
31:18 will be brought down with the **trees** *of* Eden to the earth below;
34:27 The **trees** *of* the field will yield their fruit and the ground will yield
36:30 I will increase the fruit of the **trees** and the crops of the field,
37:16 "Son of man, take a **stick of wood** and write on it, 'Belonging to
37:16 Then take another **stick of wood**, and write on it, 'Ephraim's stick,
37:16 write on it, 'Ephraim's **stick**, belonging to Joseph and all the house
37:17 Join them together into one **stick** so that they will become one in
37:19 I am going to take the **stick** *of* Joseph—which is in Ephraim's
37:19 and join it to Judah's **stick**, making them a single stick of wood,
37:19 and join it to Judah's stick, making them a single **stick of wood**,
37:20 Hold before their eyes the **sticks** you have written on
39:10 They will not need to gather **wood** from the fields or cut it from the
41:16 and including the threshold was covered with **wood**.
41:22 There was a **wooden** altar three cubits high and two cubits square;
41:22 two cubits square; its corners, its base and its sides were of **wood**.
41:25 and there was a **wooden** overhang on the front of the portico.
47:7 I saw a great number of **trees** on each side of the river.
47:12 Fruit **trees** of all kinds will grow on both banks of the river.
Hos 4:12 They consult a **wooden idol** and are answered by a stick of wood.
Joel 1:12 and the apple tree—all the **trees** *of* the field—are dried up.
1:19 open pastures and flames have burned up all the **trees** *of* the field.
2:22 The **trees** are bearing their fruit; the fig tree and the vine yield their
Hab 2:11 the wall will cry out, and the beams of the **woodwork** will echo it.
2:19 Woe to him who says to **wood**, 'Come to life!' Or to lifeless stone,
Hag 1:8 up into the mountains and bring down **timber** and build the house,
2:19 fig tree, the pomegranate and the olive **tree** have not borne fruit.
Zec 5:4 in his house and destroy it, both its **timbers** and its stones.' "
12:6 day I will make the leaders of Judah like a firepot in a **woodpile**,

6771 ¹עָצַב 'āṣab¹, v. [2] [→ 6773, 6775, 67777]

like image [1], shaped [1]

Job 10:8 [D] "Your hands **shaped** me and made me. Will you now turn
Jer 44:19 [G] husbands know that we were making cakes **like her image**

6772 ²עָצַב 'āṣab², v. [15] [→ 5107, 6774, 6776, 6778, 6779, 6780, Ar 10565]

distressed [2], grieve [2], grieved [2], be grieved [1], be injured [1], filled with grief [1], grieving [1], interfered with [1], pain [1], twist [1], was filled with pain [1], was grieved [1]

Ge 6:6 [F] made man on the earth, and his heart **was filled with pain**.
34:7 [F] They *were* **filled with grief** and fury, because Shechem had
45:5 [C] *do* not *be* **distressed** and do not be angry with yourselves for
1Sa 20:3 [C] 'Jonathan must not know this or *he will* **be grieved**.'
20:34 [C] because *he* **was grieved** at his father's shameful treatment of
2Sa 19:2 [19:3] [C] heard it said, "The king *is* **grieving** for his son."
1Ki 1:6 [A] (His father *had* never **interfered with** him by asking,
1Ch 4:10 [A] and keep me from harm so that I will be free from **pain**."
Ne 8:10 [C] *Do* not **grieve**, for the joy of the LORD is your strength."
8:11 [C] "Be still, for this is a sacred day. *Do* not **grieve**."
Ps 56:5 [56:6] [D] All day long *they* **twist** my words; they are always
78:40 [G] against him in the desert and **grieved** him in the wasteland!
Ecc 10:9 [C] Whoever quarries stones *may* **be injured** by them;
Isa 54:6 [B] back as if you were a wife deserted and **distressed** *in* spirit—
63:10 [D] Yet they rebelled and **grieved** his Holy Spirit. So he turned

6773 עָצָב 'āṣāb, n.[m.]. [17] [√ 6771]

idols [13], images [4]

1Sa 31:9 of the Philistines to proclaim the news in the temple of their **idols**
2Sa 5:21 The Philistines abandoned their **idols** there, and David and his men
1Ch 10:9 the land of the Philistines to proclaim the news among their **idols**
2Ch 24:18 the God of their fathers, and worshiped Asherah poles and **idols**.
Ps 106:36 They worshiped their **idols**, which became a snare to them.
106:38 and daughters, whom they sacrificed to the **idols** *of* Canaan,
115:4 But their **idols** are silver and gold, made by the hands of men.
135:15 The **idols** *of* the nations are silver and gold, made by the hands of
Isa 10:11 and her **images** as I dealt with Samaria and her idols?' "
46:1 Nebo stoops low; their **idols** are borne by beasts of burden.
Jer 50:2 Her **images** will be put to shame and her idols filled with terror.'
Hos 4:17 Ephraim is joined to **idols**; leave him alone!
8:4 and gold they make **idols** for themselves to their own destruction.
13:2 cleverly fashioned **images**, all of them the work of craftsmen.
14:8 [14:9] O Ephraim, what more have I to do with **idols**? I will
Mic 1:7 temple gifts will be burned with fire; I will destroy all her **images**.
Zec 13:2 "On that day, I will banish the names of the **idols** from the land,

6774 עַצָּב 'aṣṣāb, n.[m.]. [1] [√ 6772]

workers [1]

Isa 58: 3 of your fasting, you do as you please and exploit all your **workers**.

6775 ¹עֶצֶב 'eṣeb¹, n.m. [1] [√ 6771]

pot [1]

Jer 22: 28 man Jehoiachin a despised, broken **pot**, an object no one wants?

6776 ²עֶצֶב 'eṣeb², n.[m.]. [6] [√ 6772]

hard work [1], harsh [1], pain [1], toil [1], toiling [1], trouble [1]

Ge 3: 16 pains in childbearing; with **pain** you will give birth to children.
Ps 127: 2 In vain you rise early and stay up late, **toiling** for food to eat—
Pr 5: 10 feast on your wealth and your **toil** enrich another man's house.
10: 22 blessing of the LORD brings wealth, and he adds no **trouble** to it.
14: 23 All **hard work** brings a profit, but mere talk leads only to poverty.
15: 1 A gentle answer turns away wrath, but a **harsh** word stirs up anger.

6777 ¹עֹצֶב 'ōṣeb¹, n.m. [1] [√ 6771]

idols [1]

Isa 48: 5 them to you so that you could not say, 'My **idols** did them;

6778 ²עֹצֶב 'ōṣeb², n.[m.]. [3] [√ 6772]

offensive [1], pain [1], suffering [1]

1Ch 4: 9 had named him Jabez, saying, "I gave birth to him in **pain**."
Ps 139: 24 See if there is any **offensive** way in me, and lead me in the way
Isa 14: 3 On the day the LORD gives you relief from **suffering** and turmoil

6779 עִצָּבוֹן 'iṣṣābôn, n.[m.]. [3] [√ 6772]

painful toil [2], pains [1]

Ge 3: 16 woman he said, "I will greatly increase your **pains** in childbearing;
3: 17 through **painful toil** you will eat of it all the days of your life.
5: 29 **painful toil** *of* our hands caused by the ground the LORD has

6780 עַצֶּבֶת 'aṣṣebet, n.f. [5] [√ 6772]

grief [1], heartache [+4213] [1], sorrows [1], sufferings [1], wounds [1]

Job 9: 28 I still dread all my **sufferings**, for I know you will not hold me
Ps 16: 4 The **sorrows** *of* those will increase who run after other gods.
147: 3 He heals the brokenhearted and binds up their **wounds**.
Pr 10: 10 He who winks maliciously causes **grief**, and a chattering fool
15: 13 makes the face cheerful, but **heartache** [+4213] crushes the spirit.

6781 עָצָה 'āṣâ, v. [1]

winks [1]

Pr 16: 30 [A] *He who* **winks** *with* his eye is plotting perversity; he who

6782 עָצֶה 'āṣeh, n.[m.]. [1]

backbone [1]

Lev 3: 9 its fat, the entire fat tail cut off close to the **backbone**, all the fat

6783 ¹עֵצָה 'ēṣâ¹, n.f. [87] [√ 3619; Ar 10539]

counsel [23], advice [15], plans [9], plan [4], advice gave [+3619] [3], purpose [3], schemes [3], strategy [3], advice given [+3619] [2], planned [+3619] [2], purposes [2], advise [+3619] [1], bent on [+928] [1], consultation [1], counselor [+408] [1], counselors [+408] [1], decision [1], giving advice [+3619] [1], harmony [+8934] [1], planned [1], planning [+3619] [1], plot [1], plots [1], plotted [+3619] [1], predictions [1], sense [1], that[s] [1], thoughts [+928+5883] [1], verdict [1]

Dt 32: 28 They are a nation without **sense**, there is no discernment in them.
Jdg 20: 7 Now, all you Israelites, speak up and give your **verdict**."
2Sa 15: 31 "O LORD, turn Ahithophel's **counsel** into foolishness."
15: 34 then you can help me by frustrating Ahithophel's **advice**.
16: 20 Absalom said to Ahithophel, "Give us your **advice**. What should
16: 23 Now in those days the **advice** Ahithophel **gave** [+3619] was like
16: 23 how both David and Absalom regarded all of Ahithophel's **advice**.
17: 7 "The **advice** Ahithophel *has* **given** [+3619] is not good this time.
17: 14 "The **advice** *of* Hushai the Arkite is better than that of
17: 14 "The advice of Hushai the Arkite is better than **that**[s] *of*
17: 14 For the LORD had determined to frustrate the good **advice** *of*
17: 23 When Ahithophel saw that his **advice** had not been followed,
1Ki 1: 12 *let me* **advise** [+3619] you how you can save your own life
12: 8 But Rehoboam rejected the **advice** the elders **gave** [+3619] him
12: 13 Rejecting the **advice given** [+3619] him by the elders,
12: 14 he followed the **advice** *of* the young men and said, "My father
2Ki 18: 20 You say you have **strategy** and military strength—but you speak
1Ch 12: 19 [12:20] after **consultation**, their rulers sent him away.
2Ch 10: 8 But Rehoboam rejected the **advice** the elders **gave** [+3619] him
10: 13 king answered them harshly. Rejecting the **advice** *of* the elders,
10: 14 he followed the **advice** *of* the young men and said, "My father
22: 5 He also followed their **counsel** when he went with Joram son of
25: 16 because you have done this and have not listened to my **counsel**."
Ezr 4: 5 frustrate their **plans** during the entire reign of Cyrus king of Persia
10: 3 in accordance with the **counsel** *of* my lord and of those who fear
10: 8 in accordance with the **decision** *of* the officials and elders,
Ne 4: 15 [4:9] When our enemies heard that we were aware of their **plot**
Job 5: 13 in their craftiness, and the **schemes** *of* the wily are swept away.
10: 3 of your hands, while you smile on the **schemes** *of* the wicked?
12: 13 God belong wisdom and power; **counsel** and understanding are his.
18: 7 vigor of his step is weakened; his own **schemes** throw him down.
21: 16 their own hands, so I stand aloof from the **counsel** *of* the wicked.
22: 18 with good things, so I stand aloof from the **counsel** *of* the wicked.
29: 21 listened to me expectantly, waiting in silence for my **counsel**.
38: 2 "Who is this that darkens my **counsel** with words without
42: 3 ⌊You asked,⌋ 'Who is this that obscures my **counsel** without
Ps 1: 1 Blessed is the man who does not walk in the **counsel** *of* the wicked
13: 2 [13:3] How long must I wrestle with my **thoughts** [+928+5883]
14: 6 You evildoers frustrate the **plans** *of* the poor, but the LORD is
20: 4 [20:5] the desire of your heart and make all your **plans** succeed.
33: 10 The LORD foils the **plans** *of* the nations; he thwarts the purposes
33: 11 the **plans** *of* the LORD stand firm forever, the purposes of his
73: 24 You guide me with your **counsel**, and afterward you will take me
106: 13 soon forgot what he had done and did not wait for his **counsel**.
106: 43 they were **bent** [+928] **on** rebellion and they wasted away in their
107: 11 the words of God and despised the **counsel** *of* the Most High.
119: 24 Your statutes are my delight; they are my **counselors** [+408].
Pr 1: 25 since you ignored all my **advice** and would not accept my rebuke,
1: 30 since they would not accept my **advice** and spurned my rebuke,
8: 14 **Counsel** and sound judgment are mine; I have understanding
12: 15 way of a fool seems right to him, but a wise man listens to **advice**.
19: 20 Listen to **advice** and accept instruction, and in the end you will be
19: 21 in a man's heart, but it is the LORD's **purpose** that prevails.
20: 5 The **purposes** of a man's heart are deep waters, but a man of
20: 18 Make plans by seeking **advice**; if you wage war, obtain guidance.
21: 30 no insight, no **plan** that can succeed against the LORD.
27: 9 the pleasantness of one's friend springs from his earnest **counsel**.
Isa 5: 19 Let it approach, let the **plan** *of* the Holy One of Israel come,
8: 10 Devise your **strategy**, but it will be thwarted; propose your plan,
11: 2 and of understanding, the Spirit of **counsel** and of power,
14: 26 This is the **plan** determined for the whole world; this is the hand
16: 3 "Give us **counsel**, render a decision. Make your shadow like
19: 3 Egyptians will lose heart, and I will bring their **plans** to nothing;
19: 11 but fools; the wise counselors of Pharaoh give senseless **advice**.
19: 17 because of what the LORD Almighty *is* **planning** [+3619] against
25: 1 you have done marvelous things, *things* **planned** long ago.
28: 29 wonderful in **counsel** and magnificent in wisdom.
29: 15 Woe to those who go to great depths to hide their **plans** from the
30: 1 "to those who carry out **plans** that are not mine, forming an
36: 5 You say you have **strategy** and military strength—but you speak
40: 13 mind of the LORD, or instructed him as his **counselor** [+408]?
44: 26 of his servants and fulfills the **predictions** *of* his messengers,
46: 10 I say: My **purpose** will stand, and I will do all that I please.
46: 11 a bird of prey; from a far-off land, a man to fulfill my **purpose**.
47: 13 All the **counsel** you have *received* has only worn you out!
Jer 18: 18 nor will **counsel** from the wise, nor the word from the prophets.
18: 23 you know, O LORD, all their **plots** to kill me. Do not forgive
19: 7 " 'In this place I will ruin the **plans** *of* Judah and Jerusalem.
32: 19 great are your **purposes** and mighty are your deeds. Your eyes are
49: 7 Has **counsel** perished from the prudent? Has their wisdom
49: 20 hear what the LORD *has* **planned** [+3619] against Edom,
49: 30 "Nebuchadnezzar king of Babylon *has* **plotted** [+3619] against
50: 45 hear what the LORD *has* **planned** [+3619] against Babylon,
Eze 7: 26 the law by the priest will be lost, as will the **counsel** of the elders.
11: 2 are plotting evil and **giving** wicked **advice** [+3619] in this city.
Mic 4: 12 they do not understand his **plan**, he who gathers them like sheaves
Zec 6: 13 his throne. And there will be **harmony** [+8934] between the two.'

6784 ²עֵצָה 'ēṣâ², n.f. Not used in NIV/BHS

6785 ³עֵצָה 'ēṣâ³, n.f.col. [2] [√ 6770]

trees [1], wooden idols [1]

Jer 6: 6 "Cut down the **trees** and build siege ramps against Jerusalem.
Hos 10: 6 will be disgraced; Israel will be ashamed of its **wooden idols**.

6786 עָצוּם 'āṣûm, a. [31] [→ 6802; cf. 6793]

mighty [8], powerful [7], stronger [6], strong [4], great [1], much too numerous [+2256+8041] [1], power [1], strength [1], throngs [1], very [+4394] [1]

Ge 18: 18 Abraham will surely become a great and **powerful** nation,
Ex 1: 9 Israelites have become **much too numerous** [+2256+8041] for us.

Nu 14:12 but I will make you into a nation greater and **stronger** than they."
22: 6 put a curse on these people, because they are too **powerful** for me.
32: 1 and Gadites, who had **very** [+4394] large herds and flocks,
Dt 4:38 to drive out before you nations greater and **stronger** than you
7: 1 and Jebusites, seven nations larger and **stronger** than you—
9: 1 to go in and dispossess nations greater and **stronger** than you,
9:14 I will make you into a nation **stronger** and more numerous than
11:23 and you will dispossess nations larger and **stronger** than you.
26: 5 lived there and became a great nation, **powerful** and numerous.
Jos 23: 9 LORD has driven out before you great and **powerful** nations;
Ps 10:10 His victims are crushed, they collapse; they fall under his **strength**.
35:18 in the great assembly; among **throngs** of people I will praise you.
135:10 He struck down many nations and killed **mighty** kings—
Pr 7:26 the victims she has brought down; her slain are a **mighty** throng.
18:18 Casting the lot settles disputes and keeps **strong** *opponents* apart.
30:26 coneys are creatures of little **power**, yet they make their home in
Isa 8: 7 therefore the Lord is about to bring against them the **mighty**
53:12 he will divide the spoils with the **strong**, because he poured out his
60:22 least of you will become a thousand, the smallest a **mighty** nation.
Da 8:24 he does. He will destroy the **mighty** *men* and the holy people.
11:25 of the South will wage war with a large and very **powerful** army,
Joel 1: 6 A nation has invaded my land, **powerful** and without number;
2: 2 spreading across the mountains a large and **mighty** army comes,
2: 5 fire consuming stubble, like a **mighty** army drawn up for battle.
2:11 are beyond number, and **mighty** are those who obey his command.
Am 5:12 For I know how many are your offenses and how **great** your sins.
Mic 4: 3 and will settle disputes for **strong** nations far and wide.
4: 7 I will make the lame a remnant, those driven away a **strong** nation.
Zec 8:22 **powerful** nations will come to Jerusalem to seek the LORD

6787 עֶצְיוֹן גֶּבֶר *'eṣyôn geber*, n.pr.loc. [7]

Ezion Geber [7]

Nu 33:35 They left Abronah and camped at **Ezion Geber**.
33:36 They left **Ezion Geber** and camped at Kadesh, in the Desert of
Dt 2: 8 the Arabah road, which comes up from Elath and **Ezion Geber**,
1Ki 9:26 King Solomon also built ships at **Ezion Geber**, which is near Elath
22:48 [22:49] they never set sail—they were wrecked at **Ezion Geber**.
2Ch 8:17 Solomon went to **Ezion Geber** and Elath on the coast of Edom.
20:36 a fleet of trading ships. After these were built at **Ezion Geber**,

6788 עָצַל *'āṣal*, v. [1] [→ 6789, 6790, 6791, 6792]

hesitate [1]

Jdg 18: 9 [C] to do something? Don't **hesitate** to go there and take it over.

6789 עָצֵל *'āṣēl*, a. [14] [√ 6788]

sluggard [13], sluggard's [1]

Pr 6: 6 Go to the ant, you **sluggard**; consider its ways and be wise!
6: 9 How long will you lie there, you **sluggard**? When will you get up
10:26 and smoke to the eyes, so is a **sluggard** to those who send him.
13: 4 The **sluggard** craves and gets nothing, but the desires of the
15:19 The way of the **sluggard** is blocked with thorns, but the path of the
19:24 The **sluggard** buries his hand in the dish; he will not even bring it
20: 4 A **sluggard** does not plow in season; so at harvest time he looks
21:25 The **sluggard's** craving will be the death of him, because his hands
22:13 The **sluggard** says, "There is a lion outside!" or, "I will be
24:30 I went past the field of the **sluggard**, past the vineyard of the man
26:13 The **sluggard** says, "There is a lion in the road, a fierce lion
26:14 As a door turns on its hinges, so a **sluggard** turns on his bed.
26:15 The **sluggard** buries his hand in the dish; he is too lazy to bring it
26:16 The **sluggard** is wiser in his own eyes than seven men who answer

6790 עַצְלָה *'aṣlâ*, n.f. [1] [√ 6788]

laziness [1]

Pr 19:15 **Laziness** brings on deep sleep, and the shiftless man goes hungry.

6791 עַצְלוּת *'aṣlût*, n.f. [1] [√ 6788]

idleness [1]

Pr 31:27 the affairs of her household and does not eat the bread of **idleness**.

6792 עֲצַלְתַּיִם *'ᵃṣaltayim*, n.f.du. [1] [√ 6788]

lazy [1]

Ecc 10:18 If a man is **lazy**, the rafters sag; if his hands are idle, the house

6793 [1]עָצַם *'āṣam[1]*, v. [18] [→ 6492, 6786, 6795, 6796, 6797, 6798, 6799, 6800, 6801, 9508]

many [6], numerous [3], crush bones [1], height of power [1], made numerous [1], more [1], power [1], powerful [1], strength [1], vast [1], very strong [+3946] [1]

Ge 26:16 [A] away from us; *you have become* too **powerful** for us."
Ex 1: 7 [A] and multiplied greatly and *became* exceedingly **numerous**,
1:20 [A] and the people increased and *became* even more **numerous**.
Ps 38:19 [38:20] [A] **Many** *are* those who are my vigorous enemies;
40: 5 [40:6] [A] and tell of them, *they would be* too **many** to declare.
40:12 [40:13] [A] *They are* **more** than the hairs of my head, and my
69: 4 [69:5] [A] **many** *are* my enemies without cause, those who seek
105:24 [G] very fruitful; *he* **made** them too **numerous** for their foes,
139:17 [A] me are your thoughts, O God! How **vast** *is* the sum of them!
Isa 31: 1 [A] of their chariots and in the great **strength** of their horsemen,
Jer 5: 6 [A] for their rebellion is great and their backslidings **many**.
15: 8 [A] I *will make* their widows more **numerous** than the sand of
30:14 [A] because your guilt is so great and your sins *so* **many**.
30:15 [A] great guilt and **many** sins I have done these things to you.
50:17 [D] the last *to* **crush** his **bones** was Nebuchadnezzar king of
Da 8: 8 [A] but at the **height of** his **power** his large horn was broken off,
8:24 [A] *He will become* **very strong** [+3946], but not by his own
11:23 [A] and with only a few people he will rise *to* **power**.

6794 [2]עָצַם *'āṣam[2]*, v. [2]

sealed [1], shuts [1]

Isa 29:10 [D] *He has* **sealed** your eyes (the prophets); he has covered your
33:15 [A] of murder and **shuts** his eyes against contemplating evil—

6795 [1]עֶצֶם *'eṣem[1]*, n.f. [126] [→ 6796; cf. 6793]

bones [80], very [11], *untranslated* [8], blood [6], bone [6], body [3], same [3], bodies [2], being [1], frame [1], itself [1], limb [1], those[s] [1], vigor [1], you [+4013] [1]

Ge 2:23 man said, "This is now **bone** of my bones and flesh of my flesh;
2:23 man said, "This is now bone of my **bones** and flesh of my flesh;
7:13 On that **very** day Noah and his sons, Shem, Ham and Japheth,
17:23 On that **very** day Abraham took his son Ishmael and all those born
17:26 and his son Ishmael were both circumcised on that **same** day.
29:14 Then Laban said to him, "You are my own flesh and **blood**."
50:25 to your aid, and then you must carry my **bones** up from this place."
Ex 12:17 because it was on this **very** day that I brought your divisions out of
12:41 At the end of the 430 years, to the **very** day, all the LORD's
12:46 none of the meat outside the house. Do not break any of the **bones**.
12:51 on that **very** day the LORD brought the Israelites out of Egypt by
13:19 Moses took the **bones** *of* Joseph with him because Joseph had
13:19 then you must carry my **bones** up with you from this place."
24:10 like a pavement made of sapphire, clear as the sky **itself**.
Lev 23:14 new grain, until the **very** day you bring this offering to your God.
23:21 On that **same** day you are to proclaim a sacred assembly and do no
23:28 Do no work on **[RPH]** that day, because it is the Day of
23:29 Anyone who does not deny himself on **[RPH]** that day must be
23:30 among his people anyone who does any work on **[RPH]** that day.
Nu 9:12 must not leave any of it till morning or break any of its **bones**.
19:16 or anyone who touches a human **bone** or a grave, will be unclean
19:18 He must also sprinkle anyone who has touched a human **bone**
24: 8 They devour hostile nations and break their **bones** in pieces;
Dt 32:48 On that **same** day the LORD told Moses,
Jos 5:11 The day after the Passover, that **very** day, they ate some of the
10:27 cave they placed large rocks, which are there to this day. **[NIE]**
24:32 Joseph's **bones**, which the Israelites had brought up from Egypt,
Jdg 9: 2 or just one man?' Remember, I am your flesh and **blood**."
19:29 limb by **limb**, into twelve parts and sent them into all the areas of
1Sa 31:13 they took their **bones** and buried them under a tamarisk tree at
2Sa 5: 1 to David at Hebron and said, "We are your own flesh and **blood**.
19:12 [19:13] You are my brothers, my own flesh and **blood**. So why
19:13 [19:14] And say to Amasa, 'Are you not my own flesh and **blood**?
21:12 he went and took the **bones** *of* Saul and his son Jonathan from the
21:12 and **[RPH]** his son Jonathan from the citizens of Jabesh Gilead.
21:13 David brought the **bones** *of* Saul and his son Jonathan from there,
21:13 brought the bones of Saul and **[RPH]** his son Jonathan from there,
21:13 the **bones** *of* those who had been killed and exposed were gathered
21:14 They buried the **bones** *of* Saul and his son Jonathan in the tomb of
1Ki 13: 2 make offerings here, and human **bones** will be burned on you.' "
13:31 where the man of God is buried; lay my **bones** beside his bones.
13:31 where the man of God is buried; lay my bones beside his **bones**.
2Ki 13:21 When the body touched Elisha's **bones**, the man came to life
23:14 down the Asherah poles and covered the sites with human **bones**.
23:16 he had the **bones** removed from them and burned on the altar to
23:18 "Leave it alone," he said. "Don't let anyone disturb his **bones**."
23:18 So they spared his **bones** and those of the prophet who had come
23:18 his bones and **those**[s] *of* the prophet who had come from Samaria.

2Ki 23:20 those high places on the altars and burned human **bones** on them.
1Ch 10:12 Then they buried their **bones** under the great tree in Jabesh,
11: 1 to David at Hebron and said, "We are your own flesh and **blood**.
2Ch 34: 5 He burned the **bones** *of* the priests on their altars, and so he purged
Job 2: 5 stretch out your hand and strike his flesh and **bones**, and he will
4:14 fear and trembling seized me and made all my **bones** shake.
7:15 so that I prefer strangling and death, rather than this **body** *of* mine.
10:11 with skin and flesh and knit me together with **bones** and sinews?
19:20 I am nothing but skin and **bones**; I have escaped with only the skin
20:11 The youthful vigor that fills his **bones** will lie with him in the dust.
21:23 One man dies in full **vigor**, completely secure and at ease,
21:24 his body well nourished, his **bones** rich with marrow.
30:17 Night pierces my **bones**; my gnawing pains never rest.
30:30 My skin grows black and peels; my **body** burns with fever.
33:19 be chastened on a bed of pain with constant distress in his **bones**,
33:21 wastes away to nothing, and his **bones**, once hidden, now stick out.
40:18 His **bones** are tubes of bronze, his limbs like rods of iron.
Ps 6: 2 [6:3] I am faint; O LORD, heal me, for my **bones** are in agony.
22:14 [22:15] poured out like water, and all my **bones** are out of joint.
22:17 [22:18] I can count all my **bones**; people stare and gloat over me.
31:10 [31:11] because of my affliction, and my **bones** grow weak.
32: 3 my **bones** wasted away through my groaning all day long.
34:20 [34:21] he protects all his **bones**, not one of them will be broken.
35:10 My whole **being** will exclaim, "Who is like you, O LORD?
38: 3 [38:4] my body; my **bones** have no soundness because of my sin.
42:10 [42:11] My **bones** suffer mortal agony as my foes taunt me,
51: 8 [51:10] and gladness; let the **bones** you have crushed rejoice.
53: 5 [53:6] God scattered the **bones** *of* those who attacked you;
102: 3 [102:4] vanish like smoke; my **bones** burn like glowing embers.
102: 5 [102:6] of my loud groaning I am reduced to skin and **bones**.
109:18 it entered into his body like water, into his **bones** like oil.
141: 7 so our **bones** have been scattered at the mouth of the grave."
Pr 3: 8 This will bring health to your body and nourishment to your **bones**.
12: 4 husband's crown, but a disgraceful wife is like decay in his **bones**.
14:30 A heart at peace gives life to the body, but envy rots the **bones**.
15:30 brings joy to the heart, and good news gives health to the **bones**.
16:24 are a honeycomb, sweet to the soul and healing to the **bones**.
Ecc 11: 5 path of the wind, or how the **body** is formed in a mother's womb,
Isa 38:13 I waited patiently till dawn, but like a lion he broke all my **bones**;
58:11 your needs in a sun-scorched land and will strengthen your **frame**.
66:14 your heart will rejoice and **you** [+4013] will flourish like grass;
Jer 8: 1 declares the LORD, the **bones** *of* the kings and officials of Judah,
8: 1 the LORD, the bones of the kings and **[RPH]** officials of Judah,
8: 1 and officials of Judah, the **bones** *of* the priests and prophets,
8: 1 officials of Judah, the bones of the priests and **[RPH]** prophets,
8: 1 the **bones** *of* the people of Jerusalem will be removed from their
20: 9 his word is in my heart like a fire, a fire shut up in my **bones**.
23: 9 My heart is broken within me; all my **bones** tremble. I am like a
La 1:13 "From on high he sent fire, sent it down into my **bones**. He spread
3: 4 made my skin and my flesh grow old and has broken my **bones**.
4: 7 and whiter than milk, their **bodies** more ruddy than rubies,
4: 8 Their skin has shriveled on their **bones**; it has become as dry as a
Eze 2: 3 and their fathers have been in revolt against me to this **very** day.
6: 5 of their idols, and I will scatter your **bones** around your altars.
24: 2 "Son of man, record this date, this **very** date, because the king of
24: 2 because the king of Babylon has laid siege to Jerusalem this **very**
24: 4 the leg and the shoulder. Fill it with the best of these **bones**;
24: 5 Pile wood beneath it for the **bones**; bring it to a boil and cook the
24: 5 beneath it for the bones; bring it to a boil and cook the **bones** in it.
24:10 the meat well, mixing in the spices; and let the **bones** be charred.
32:27 The punishment for their sins rested on their **bones**,
37: 1 and set me in the middle of a valley; it was full of **bones**.
37: 3 He asked me, "Son of man, can these **bones** live?" I said,
37: 4 said to me, "Prophesy to these **bones** and say to them, 'Dry bones,
37: 4 said to me, "Prophesy to these bones and say to them, 'Dry **bones**,
37: 5 This is what the Sovereign LORD says to these **bones**: I will
37: 7 a rattling sound, and the **bones** came together, bone to bone.
37: 7 a rattling sound, and the bones came together, **bone** to bone.
37: 7 a rattling sound, and the bones came together, bone to **bone**.
37:11 "Son of man, these **bones** are the whole house of Israel. They say,
37:11 They say, 'Our **bones** are dried up and our hope is gone; we are cut
39:15 As they go through the land and one of them sees a human **bone**,
40: 1 on that **very** day the hand of the LORD was upon me and he took
Am 2: 1 Because he burned, as if to lime, the **bones** *of* Edom's king,
6:10 if a relative who is to burn the **bodies** comes to carry them out of
Mic 3: 2 who tear the skin from my people and the flesh from their **bones**;
3: 3 people's flesh, strip off their skin and break their **bones** in pieces;
Hab 3:16 at the sound; decay crept into my **bones**, and my legs trembled.

6796 ²עֶצֶם ***'eṣem²***, n.pr.loc. [3] [√ 6795; cf. 6793]

Ezem [3]

Jos 15:29 Baalah, Iim, **Ezem**,
19: 3 Hazar Shual, Balah, **Ezem**,
1Ch 4:29 Bilhah, **Ezem**, Tolad,

6797 ¹עֹצֶם ***'ōṣem¹***, n.[m.]. [3] [√ 6793]

strength [2], might [1]

Dt 8:17 and the **strength** *of* my hands have produced this wealth for me."
Job 30:21 turn on me ruthlessly; with the **might** *of* your hand you attack me.
Na 3: 9 Cush and Egypt were her boundless **strength**; Put and Libya were

6798 ²עֹצֶם ***'ōṣem²***, n.[m.]. [1] [√ 6793]

frame [1]

Ps 139:15 My **frame** was not hidden from you when I was made in the secret

6799 עַצְמָה ***'aṣmâ***, n.f. Not used in NIV/BHS [√ 6793]

6800 עָצְמָה ***'oṣmâ***, n.f. [2] [√ 6793]

potent [1], power [1]

Isa 40:29 gives strength to the weary and increases the **power** of the weak.
47: 9 in spite of your many sorceries and all your **potent** spells.

6801 עַצְמוֹן ***'aṣmôn***, n.pr.loc. [3] [√ 6795; cf. 6793]

Azmon [2], where[s] [1]

Nu 34: 4 Then it will go to Hazar Addar and over to **Azmon**,
34: 5 **where**[s] it will turn, join the Wadi of Egypt and end at the Sea.
Jos 15: 4 It then passed along to **Azmon** and joined the Wadi of Egypt,

6802 עֲצֻמוֹת ***ᵃṣumôt***, n.f.[pl.]. [1] [√ 6786]

arguments [1]

Isa 41:21 says the LORD. "Set forth your **arguments**," says Jacob's King.

6803 עֵצֶן ***'ēṣen***, var. Not used in NIV/BHS

6804 עֶצְנִי ***'eṣnî***, n.pr. *or* a.g.?. [1]

spear [1]

2Sa 23: 8 he raised his **spear** against eight hundred men, whom he killed in

6805 עָצַץ ***'āṣaṣ***, v. Not used in NIV/BHS

6806 עָצַר ***'āṣar***, v. [46] [→ 5109, 5110, 6807, 6808, 6809]

slave [5], shut up [4], able [+3946] [2], be stopped [2], closed up [+1237+6806] [2], helpless [+3946+4202] [2], retain [2], stopped [2], was stopped [2], able [1], been kept [1], close up [1], confined [1], detain [1], detained [1], govern [1], holds back [1], keep [1], kept [1], prevail [1], refrained [1], regain [+6388] [1], restricted [1], seized [1], shut [1], slow down [+4200+8206] [1], stay [1], stops [1], was banished [1], was checked [1], was confined [1], was shut in [1]

Ge 16: 2 [A] to Abram, "The LORD *has* **kept** me from having children.
20:18 [A] for the LORD *had* **closed** [+1237+6806] **up** every womb in
20:18 [A] for the LORD *had* **closed up** [+1237+6806] every womb in
Nu 16:48 [17:13] [C] the living and the dead, and the plague **stopped**.
16:50 [17:15] [C] to the Tent of Meeting, for the plague *had* **stopped**.
25: 8 [C] Then the plague against the Israelites **was stopped**;
Dt 11:17 [A] *he will* **shut** the heavens so that it will not rain
32:36 [B] he sees their strength is gone and no one is left, **slave** or free.
Jdg 13:15 [A] "*We would like* you *to* **stay** until we prepare a young goat
13:16 [A] "Even though *you* **detain** me, I will not eat any of your food.
1Sa 9:17 [A] is the man I spoke to you about; he *will* **govern** my people."
21: 5 [21:6] [B] David replied, "Indeed women *have* **been kept** from
21: 7 [21:8] [C] was there that day, **detained** before the LORD;
2Sa 24:21 [C] the LORD, that the plague on the people *may* **be stopped**."
24:25 [C] in behalf of the land, and the plague on Israel **was stopped**.
1Ki 8:35 [C] "When the heavens *are* **shut up** and there is no rain
14:10 [B] off from Jeroboam every last male in Israel—**slave** or free.
18:44 [A] up your chariot and go down before the rain **stops** you.' "
21:21 [B] cut off from Ahab every last male in Israel—**slave** or free.
2Ki 4:24 [A] don't **slow** [+4200+8206] **down** for me unless I tell you."
9: 8 [B] cut off from Ahab every last male in Israel—**slave** or free.
14:26 [B] everyone in Israel, whether **slave** or free, was suffering;
17: 4 [A] Therefore Shalmaneser **seized** him and put him in prison.
1Ch 12: 1 [B] while *he* **was banished** from the presence of Saul son of
21:22 [C] the LORD, that the plague on the people *may* **be stopped**.
29:14 [A] that *we should be* **able** [+3946] to give as generously as this?
2Ch 2: 6 [2:5] [A] who *is* **able** [+3946] to build a temple for him,
6:26 [C] "When the heavens *are* **shut up** and there is no rain
7:13 [A] "When *I* **shut up** the heavens so that there is no rain,
13:20 [A] Jeroboam *did* not **regain** [+6388] power during the time of
14:11 [14:10] [A] are our God; *do* not *let* man **prevail** against you."
20:37 [A] ships were wrecked and *were* not **able** to set sail to trade.
22: 9 [A] house of Ahaziah powerful enough to **retain** the kingdom.

Ne 6:10 [B] the son of Mehetabel, who **was shut in** at his home.
Job 4: 2 [A] will you be impatient? But who can **keep** from speaking?
12:15 [A] If *he* **holds back** the waters, there is drought; if he lets them
29: 9 [A] the chief men **refrained** from speaking and covered their
Ps 106:30 [C] stood up and intervened, and the plague **was checked**.
Isa 66: 9 [A] "*Do I* **close up** the womb when I bring to delivery?"
Jer 20: 9 [B] his word is in my heart like a fire, a fire **shut up** in my bones.
33: 1 [B] While Jeremiah **was** still **confined** in the courtyard of the
36: 5 [B] Jeremiah told Baruch, "I *am* **restricted**; I cannot go to the
39:15 [B] While Jeremiah had been **confined** in the courtyard of the
Da 10: 8 [A] face turned deathly pale and *I was* **helpless** [+3946+4202].
10:16 [A] of the vision, my lord, and *I am* **helpless** [+3946+4202].
11: 6 [A] *she will* not **retain** her power, and he and his power will not

6807 עֶצֶר *'eṣer*, n.[m.]. [1] [√ 6806]

prosperous [+3769] [1]

Jdg 18: 7 since their land lacked nothing, *they were* **prosperous** [+3769].

6808 עֹצֶר *'ōṣer*, n.[m.]. [3] [√ 6806]

oppression [2], barren [1]

Ps 107:39 and they were humbled by **oppression**, calamity and sorrow;
Pr 30:16 the grave, the **barren** womb, land, which is never satisfied with
Isa 53: 8 By **oppression** and judgment he was taken away. And who can

6809 עֲצָרָה *ᵃṣārâ*, n.f. [11] [√ 6806]

assembly [5], assemblies [2], sacred assembly [2], closing assembly [1], crowd [1]

Lev 23:36 the LORD by fire. It is the **closing assembly**; do no regular work.
Nu 29:35 " 'On the eighth day hold an **assembly** and do no regular work.
Dt 16: 8 and on the seventh day hold an **assembly** to the LORD your God
2Ki 10:20 Jehu said, "Call an **assembly** in honor of Baal." So they
2Ch 7: 9 On the eighth day they held an **assembly**, for they had celebrated
Ne 8:18 in accordance with the regulation, there was an **assembly**.
Isa 1:13 Sabbaths and convocations—I cannot bear your evil **assemblies**.
Jer 9: 2 [9:1] for they are all adulterers, a **crowd** *of* unfaithful people.
Joel 1:14 Declare a holy fast; call a **sacred assembly**. Summon the elders
2:15 the trumpet in Zion, declare a holy fast, call a **sacred assembly**.
Am 5:21 I despise your religious feasts; I cannot stand your **assemblies**.

6810 עָקַב *'āqab*, v. [5] [√ 6812; cf. 6811, 6812, 7693]

deceiver [+6810] [2], deceived [1], grasped heel [1], holds back [1]

Ge 27:36 [A] *He has* **deceived** me these two times: He took my birthright,
Job 37: 4 [D] When his voice resounds, *he* **holds** nothing **back**.
Jer 9: 4 [9:3] [A] For every brother *is a* **deceiver** [+6810], and every
9: 4 [9:3] [A] For every brother *is a* **deceiver** [+6810], and every
Hos 12: 3 [12:4] [A] In the womb *he* **grasped** his brother's **heel**; as a man

6811 עָקֵב *'āqēb¹*, n.m. [13] [→ 6813, 6814; cf. 3620, 6810, 6812]

heel [4], heels [2], ambush [1], body [1], footprints [1], hoofs [1], step [1], steps [1], tracks [1]

Ge 3:15 and hers; he will crush your head, and you will strike his **heel**."
25:26 his brother came out, with his hand grasping Esau's **heel**;
49:17 that bites the horse's **heels** so that its rider tumbles backward.
49:19 attacked by a band of raiders, but he will attack them at their **heels**.
Jos 8:13 the camp to the north of the city and the **ambush** to the west of it.
Jdg 5:22 thundered the horses' **hoofs**—galloping, galloping go his mighty
Job 18: 9 A trap seizes him by the **heel**; a snare holds him fast.
Ps 41: 9 [41:10] who shared my bread, has lifted up his **heel** against me.
56: 6 [56:7] They conspire, they lurk, they watch my **steps**, eager to
77:19 [77:20] the mighty waters, though your **footprints** were not seen.
89:51 [89:52] with which they have mocked *every* **step** *of* your
SS 1: 8 follow the **tracks** *of* the sheep and graze your young goats by the
Jer 13:22 sins that your skirts have been torn off and your **body** mistreated.

6812 עָקֵב *'āqēb²*, a.vbl. [1] [→ 6810, 6815, 6816, 6817; cf. 3620, 6810, 6811, 7693]

deceivers [1]

Ps 49: 5 [49:6] evil days come, when wicked **deceivers** surround me—

6813 עֵקֶב *'ēqeb*, n.[m.] (used as adv. & c.). [15] [√ 6811]

because [+889] [3], because [+3954] [2], for [2], at [+6584] [1], because of [+6584] [1], because [1], bring [1], if [1], reward [1], to the end [1], to the very end [+4200+6409] [1]

Ge 22:18 on earth will be blessed, **because** [+889] you have obeyed me."
26: 5 **because** [+889] Abraham obeyed me and kept my requirements,
Nu 14:24 **because** my servant Caleb has a different spirit and follows me
Dt 7:12 **If** you pay attention to these laws and are careful to follow them,
8:20 so you will be destroyed **for** not obeying the LORD your God.
2Sa 12: 6 times over, **because** [+889] he did such a thing and had no pity."
12:10 **because** [+3954] you despised me and took the wife of Uriah the
Ps 19:11 [19:12] servant warned; in keeping them there is great **reward**.
40:15 [40:16] "Aha! Aha!" be appalled **at** [+6584] their own shame.
70: 3 [70:4] "Aha! Aha!" turn back **because** [+6584] **of** their shame.
119:33 to follow your decrees; then I will keep them **to the end**.
119:112 is set on keeping your decrees **to the very end** [+4200+6409].
Pr 22: 4 Humility and the fear of the LORD **bring** wealth and honor
Isa 5:23 who acquit the guilty **for** a bribe, but deny justice to the innocent.
Am 4:12 Israel, and **because** [+3954] I will do this to you, prepare to meet

6814 עָקֹב *'āqōb¹*, a. [1] [√ 6811]

footprints [1]

Hos 6: 8 Gilead is a city of wicked men, *stained with* **footprints** of blood.

6815 עָקֹב *'āqōb²*, a. [2] [√ 6812]

deceitful [1], rough [1]

Isa 40: 4 the **rough** *ground* shall become level, the rugged places a plain.
Jer 17: 9 The heart is **deceitful** above all things and beyond cure. Who can

6816 עֹקֶב *'ōqeb*, n.[m.]. Not used in NIV/BHS [√ 6812]

6817 עָקְבָה *'oqbâ*, n.f. [1] [√ 6812]

deceptively [+928] [1]

2Ki 10:19 Jehu was acting **deceptively** [+928] in order to destroy the

6818 עָקַד *'āqad*, v. [1] [→ 6819, 6820]

bound [1]

Ge 22: 9 [A] *He* **bound** his son Isaac and laid him on the altar, on top of

6819 עָקֹד *'āqōd*, a. [7] [√ 6818]

streaked [7]

Ge 30:35 That same day he removed all the male goats that were **streaked**
30:39 And they bore young that were **streaked** or speckled or spotted.
30:40 made the rest face the **streaked** and dark-colored animals that
31: 8 if he said, 'The **streaked** *ones* will be your wages,' then all the
31: 8 ones will be your wages,' then all the flocks bore **streaked** *young*.
31:10 and saw that the male goats mating with the flock were **streaked**,
31:12 and see that all the male goats mating with the flock are **streaked**,

6820 עֵקֶד *'ēqed*, n.pr.loc. Not used in NIV/BHS [→ 1118; cf. 6818]

6821 עָקָה *'āqâ*, n.f. [1] [√ 6421]

stares [1]

Ps 55: 3 [55:4] at the voice of the enemy, at the **stares** *of* the wicked;

6822 עַקּוּב *'aqqûb*, n.pr.m. [8]

Akkub [8]

1Ch 3:24 Pelaiah, **Akkub**, Johanan, Delaiah and Anani—
9:17 Shallum, **Akkub**, Talmon, Ahiman and their brothers,
Ezr 2:42 of Shallum, Ater, Talmon, **Akkub**, Hatita and Shobai 139
2:45 Lebanah, Hagabah, **Akkub**,
Ne 7:45 of Shallum, Ater, Talmon, **Akkub**, Hatita and Shobai 138
8: 7 Jeshua, Bani, Sherebiah, Jamin, **Akkub**, Shabbethai, Hodiah,
11:19 **Akkub**, Talmon and their associates, who kept watch at the gates—
12:25 **Akkub** were gatekeepers who guarded the storerooms at the gates.

6823 עָקַל *'āqal*, v. [1] [→ 6824, 6825]

perverted [1]

Hab 1: 4 [E] The wicked hem in the righteous, so that justice is **perverted**.

6824 עֲקַלְקַל *ᵃqalqāl*, a.intens. [2] [√ 6823]

crooked ways [1], winding [1]

Jdg 5: 6 the roads were abandoned; travelers took to **winding** paths.
Ps 125: 5 those who turn to **crooked ways** the LORD will banish with the

6825 עֲקַלָּתוֹן *ᵃqallātôn*, a. [1] [√ 6823]

coiling [1]

Isa 27: 1 Leviathan the gliding serpent, Leviathan the **coiling** serpent;

6826 עֲקָן *ᵃqān*, n.pr.m. [1 / 2] [→ 3622?]

Akan [2]

Ge 36:27 The sons of Ezer: Bilhan, Zaavan and **Akan**.

1Ch 1: 42 The sons of Ezer: Bilhan, Zaavan and **Akan**. [BHS 3622]

6827 [1]עָקַר **ʿāqar**[1], v.den. [2] [→ 6829, 6830, 6831; cf. 6828; Ar 10566, 10567]

uproot [1], uprooted [1]

Ecc 3: 2 [A] and a time to die, a time to plant and a time to **uproot**,
Zep 2: 4 [C] At midday Ashdod will be emptied and Ekron **uprooted**.

6828 [2]עָקַר **ʿāqar**[2], v.den. [5] [cf. 6827]

hamstrung [4], hamstring [1]

Ge 49: 6 [D] men in their anger and **hamstrung** oxen as they pleased.
Jos 11: 6 [D] *You are to* **hamstring** their horses and burn their chariots."
11: 9 [D] *He* **hamstrung** their horses and burned their chariots.
2Sa 8: 4 [D] He **hamstrung** all but a hundred of the chariot horses.
1Ch 18: 4 [D] He **hamstrung** all but a hundred of the chariot horses.

6829 עָקָר **ʿāqār**, a. [12] [√ 6827]

barren [8], sterile [2], childless [1], without young [1]

Ge 11: 30 Now Sarai was **barren**; she had no children.
25: 21 to the LORD on behalf of his wife, because she was **barren**.
29: 31 Leah was not loved, he opened her womb, but Rachel was **barren**.
Ex 23: 26 none will miscarry or be **barren** in your land. I will give you a full
Dt 7: 14 none of your men or *women* will be **childless**, nor any of your
7: 14 will be childless, nor any of your livestock **without young**.
Jdg 13: 2 of the Danites, had a wife who was **sterile** and remained childless.
13: 3 LORD appeared to her and said, "You are **sterile** and childless,
1Sa 2: 5 *She who was* **barren** has borne seven children, but she who has
Job 24: 21 They prey on the **barren** and childless woman, and to the widow
Ps 113: 9 He settles the **barren** *woman* in her home as a happy mother of
Isa 54: 1 "Sing, O **barren** *woman*, you who never bore a child; burst into

6830 [1]עֵקֶר **ʿēqer**[1], n.m. [1] [√ 6827]

member [1]

Lev 25: 47 to the alien living among you or to a **member** *of* the alien's clan,

6831 [2]עֵקֶר **ʿēqer**[2], n.pr.m. [1] [√ 6827?]

Eker [1]

1Ch 2: 27 sons of Ram the firstborn of Jerahmeel: Maaz, Jamin and **Eker**.

6832 עַקְרָב **ʿaqrāb**, n.m. [9] [√ 7930]

scorpions [6], scorpion [3]

Nu 34: 4 cross south of **Scorpion** Pass, continue on to Zin and go south of
Dt 8: 15 and waterless land, with its venomous snakes and **scorpions**.
Jos 15: 3 crossed south of **Scorpion** Pass, continued on to Zin and went over
Jdg 1: 36 The boundary of the Amorites was from **Scorpion** Pass to Sela
1Ki 12: 11 scourged you with whips; I will scourge you with **scorpions**.' "
12: 14 scourged you with whips; I will scourge you with **scorpions**."
2Ch 10: 11 scourged you with whips; I will scourge you with **scorpions**.' "
10: 14 scourged you with whips; I will scourge you with **scorpions**."
Eze 2: 6 and thorns are all around you and you live among **scorpions**.

6833 עֶקְרוֹן **ʿeqrôn**, n.pr.loc. [22] [→ 6834]

Ekron [22]

Jos 13: 3 River on the east of Egypt to the territory of **Ekron** on the north,
15: 11 It went to the northern slope of **Ekron**, turned toward Shikkeron,
15: 45 **Ekron**, with its surrounding settlements and villages;
15: 46 west of **Ekron**, all that were in the vicinity of Ashdod,
19: 43 Elon, Timnah, **Ekron**,
Jdg 1: 18 The men of Judah also took Gaza, Ashkelon and **Ekron**—
1Sa 5: 10 So they sent the ark of God to **Ekron**. As the ark of God was
5: 10 As the ark of God was entering **Ekron**, the people of Ekron cried
6: 16 Philistines saw all this and then returned that same day to **Ekron**.
6: 17 one each for Ashdod, Gaza, Ashkelon, Gath and **Ekron**.
7: 14 The towns from **Ekron** to Gath that the Philistines had captured
17: 52 the Philistines to the entrance of Gath and to the gates of **Ekron**.
17: 52 dead were strewn along the Shaaraim road to Gath and **Ekron**.
2Ki 1: 2 saying to them, "Go and consult Baal-Zebub, the god of **Ekron**,
1: 3 that you are going off to consult Baal-Zebub, the god of **Ekron**?'
1: 6 you are sending men to consult Baal-Zebub, the god of **Ekron**?
1: 16 have sent messengers to consult Baal-Zebub, the god of **Ekron**?
Jer 25: 20 (those of Ashkelon, Gaza, **Ekron**, and the people left at Ashdod);
Am 1: 8 I will turn my hand against **Ekron**, till the last of the Philistines is
Zep 2: 4 in ruins. At midday Ashdod will be emptied and **Ekron** uprooted.
Zec 9: 5 will writhe in agony, and **Ekron** too, for her hope will wither.
9: 7 and become leaders in Judah, and **Ekron** will be like the Jebusites.

6834 עֶקְרוֹנִי **ʿeqrônî**, a.g. [2] [√ 6833]

Ekron [1], people of Ekron [1]

Jos 13: 3 Philistine rulers in Gaza, Ashdod, Ashkelon, Gath and **Ekron**—
1Sa 5: 10 the ark of God was entering Ekron, the **people of Ekron** cried out,

6835 עָקַשׁ **ʿāqaš**, v. [5] [→ 5112, 6836, 6837, 6838]

distort [1], perverse [1], pronounce guilty [1], takes crooked [1], turned crooked [1]

Job 9: 20 [G] if I were blameless, *it would* **pronounce** me **guilty**.
Pr 10: 9 [D] but *he who* **takes crooked** paths will be found out.
28: 18 [C] kept safe, but he whose ways *are* **perverse** will suddenly fall.
Isa 59: 8 [D] *They have* **turned** them *into* **crooked** roads; no one who
Mic 3: 9 [D] of Israel, who despise justice and **distort** all that is right;

6836 [1]עִקֵּשׁ **ʿiqqēš**[1], a. [11] [→ 6837; cf. 6835]

perverse [6], crooked [3], warped [1], wicked [1]

Dt 32: 5 are no longer his children, but a **warped** and crooked generation.
2Sa 22: 27 show yourself pure, but to the **crooked** you show yourself shrewd.
Ps 18: 26 [18:27] but to the **crooked** you show yourself shrewd.
101: 4 *Men of* **perverse** heart shall be far from me; I will have nothing to
Pr 2: 15 whose paths are **crooked** and who are devious in their ways.
8: 8 words of my mouth are just; none of them is crooked or **perverse**.
11: 20 The LORD detests *men of* **perverse** heart but he delights in those
17: 20 A *man of* **perverse** heart does not prosper; he whose tongue is
19: 1 man whose walk is blameless than a fool whose lips are **perverse**.
22: 5 In the paths of the **wicked** lie thorns and snares, but he who guards
28: 6 walk is blameless than a rich man whose ways are **perverse**.

6837 [2]עִקֵּשׁ **ʿiqqēš**[2], n.pr.m. [3] [√ 6836; cf. 6835]

Ikkesh [3]

2Sa 23: 26 Helez the Paltite, Ira son of **Ikkesh** from Tekoa,
1Ch 11: 28 Ira son of **Ikkesh** from Tekoa, Abiezer from Anathoth,
27: 9 for the sixth month, was Ira the son of **Ikkesh** the Tekoite.

6838 עִקְּשׁוּת **ʿiqqᵉšût**, n.f. [2] [√ 6835]

corrupt [1], perversity [1]

Pr 4: 24 Put away **perversity** from your mouth; keep corrupt talk far from
6: 12 A scoundrel and villain, who goes about with a **corrupt** mouth,

6839 [1]עָר **ʿār**[1], n.m. [2] [√ 6910?]

adversaries [1], enemy [1]

1Sa 28: 16 the LORD has turned away from you and become your **enemy**?
Ps 139: 20 speak of you with evil intent; your **adversaries** misuse your name.

6840 [2]עָר **ʿār**[2], n.pr.loc. [6] [√ 6551?]

Ar [6]

Nu 21: 15 the slopes of the ravines that lead to the site of **Ar** and lie along the
21: 28 It consumed **Ar** *of* Moab, the citizens of Arnon's heights.
Dt 2: 9 I have given **Ar** to the descendants of Lot as a possession."
2: 18 "Today you are to pass by the region of Moab at **Ar**.
2: 29 who live in Seir, and the Moabites, who live in **Ar**, did for us—
Isa 15: 1 **Ar** *in* Moab is ruined, destroyed in a night! Kir in Moab is ruined,

6841 עֵר **ʿēr**, n.pr.m. [10] [√ 6424; Ar 10541]

Er [9], *untranslated* [1]

Ge 38: 3 she became pregnant and gave birth to a son, who was named **Er**.
38: 6 Judah got a wife for **Er**, his firstborn, and her name was Tamar.
38: 7 But **Er**, Judah's firstborn, was wicked in the LORD's sight;
46: 12 **Er**, Onan, Shelah, Perez and Zerah (but Er and Onan had died in
46: 12 Perez and Zerah (but **Er** and Onan had died in the land of Canaan).
Nu 26: 19 **Er** and Onan were sons of Judah, but they died in Canaan.
26: 19 and Onan were sons of Judah, but **[RPH]** they died in Canaan.
1Ch 2: 3 The sons of Judah: **Er**, Onan and Shelah. These three were born to
2: 3 **Er**, Judah's firstborn, was wicked in the LORD's sight;
4: 21 **Er** the father of Lecah, Laadah the father of Mareshah

6842 [1]עָרַב **ʿārab**[1], v. [17] [→ 5114, 6859, 6860, 9510; cf. 6843?, 6845]

puts up security [4], make a bargain [2], come to aid [1], devote [1], ensure [1], guarantee safety [1], guaranteed safety [1], merchants [+5114] [1], mortgaging [1], pledge [1], put up security [1], puts up security [+6859] [1], trade [1]

Ge 43: 9 [A] *I* myself *will* **guarantee** his **safety**; you can hold me
44: 32 [A] Your servant **guaranteed** the boy's **safety** to my father. I
2Ki 18: 23 [F] " 'Come now, **make a bargain** with my master, the king of
Ne 5: 3 [A] "We *are* **mortgaging** our fields, our vineyards and our
Job 17: 3 [A] "Give me, O God, the **pledge** you demand. Who else will put

Ps 119:122 [A] **Ensure** your servant's well-being; let not the arrogant
Pr 6: 1 [A] My son, if *you have* **put up security** for your neighbor,
11:15 [A] *He who* **puts up security** *for* another will surely suffer, but
17:18 [A] in pledge and **puts up security** [+6859] for his neighbor.
20:16 [A] Take the garment of *one who* **puts up security** *for* a
22:26 [A] who strikes hands in pledge or **puts up security** *for* debts;
27:13 [A] Take the garment of one *who* **puts up security** *for* a
Isa 36: 8 [F] " 'Come now, **make a bargain** with my master, the king of
38:14 [A] to the heavens. I am troubled; O Lord, **come to** my **aid**!"
Jer 30:21 [A] for who is he who *will* **devote** himself to be close to me?'
Eze 27: 9 [A] and their sailors came alongside to **trade** *for* your wares.
27:27 [A] your **merchants** [+5114] and all your soldiers,

6843 ²עָרַב 'ārab², v. [5] [→ 6849, 6850, 6856; cf. 6842?; Ar 10569]

mingled [2], avoid [+4200+4202] [1], join [1], share [1]

Ezr 9: 2 [F] *have* **mingled** the holy race with the peoples around them.
Ps 106:35 [F] but *they* **mingled** with the nations and adopted their customs.
Pr 14:10 [F] knows its own bitterness, and no one else *can* **share** its joy.
20:19 [F] so **avoid** [+4200+4202] a man who talks too much.
24:21 [F] and the king, my son, and *do* not **join** with the rebellious,

6844 ³עָרֵב 'ārab³, v. [8] [→ 6853]

please [2], sweet [2], acceptable [1], found pleasure [1], pleasant [1], pleasing [1]

Ps 104:34 [A] *May* my meditation *be* **pleasing** to him, as I rejoice in the
Pr 3:24 [A] not be afraid; when you lie down, your sleep *will be* **sweet**.
13:19 [A] A longing fulfilled *is* **sweet** to the soul, but fools detest
Jer 6:20 [A] are not acceptable; your sacrifices *do* not **please** me."
31:26 [A] and looked around. My sleep *had been* **pleasant** to me.
Eze 16:37 [A] with whom *you* **found pleasure**, those you loved as well as
Hos 9: 4 [A] offerings to the LORD, nor *will* their sacrifices **please** him.
Mal 3: 4 [A] of Judah and Jerusalem *will be* **acceptable** to the LORD,

6845 ⁴עָרַב 'ārab⁴, v.den. [3] [→ 5115, 6847; cf. 6842]

evening [2], turns to gloom [1]

Jdg 19: 9 [A] the girl's father, said, "Now look, it's almost **evening**.
1Sa 17:16 [G] came forward every morning and **evening** and took his stand.
Isa 24:11 [A] all joy **turns to gloom**, all gaiety is banished from the earth.

6846 ¹עֶרֶב 'ereb¹, n.m. Not used in NIV/BHS [cf. 6850]

6847 ²עֶרֶב 'ereb², n.[m.]. [134] [√ 6845]

evening [110], at twilight [+1068+2021] [11], dusk [2], evening [+928+928+2021+2021+6847] [2], evenings [2], every evening [+928+928+2021+2021+6847] [2], night [2], *untranslated* [1], evening [+2021+6961] [1], fading [1]

Ge 1: 5 And there was **evening**, and there was morning—the first day.
1: 8 And there was **evening**, and there was morning—the second day.
1:13 And there was **evening**, and there was morning—the third day.
1:19 And there was **evening**, and there was morning—the fourth day.
1:23 And there was **evening**, and there was morning—the fifth day.
1:31 And there was **evening**, and there was morning—the sixth day.
8:11 When the dove returned to him in the **evening**, there in its beak
19: 1 The two angels arrived at Sodom in the **evening**, and Lot was
24:11 it was toward **evening**, the time the women go out to draw water.
24:63 He went out to the field one **evening** to meditate, and as he looked
29:23 when **evening** came, he took his daughter Leah and gave her to
30:16 So when Jacob came in from the fields that **evening**, Leah went out
49:27 he devours the prey, in the **evening** he divides the plunder."
Ex 12: 6 of Israel must slaughter them **at twilight** [+1068+2021].
12:18 from the **evening** of the fourteenth day until the evening of the
12:18 from the evening of the fourteenth day until the **evening** *of* the
16: 6 "*In* the **evening** you will know that it was the LORD who
16: 8 it was the LORD when he gives you meat to eat in the **evening**
16:12 Tell them, '**At twilight** [+1068+2021] you will eat meat, and in the
16:13 That **evening** quail came and covered the camp, and in the
18:13 the people, and they stood around him from morning till **evening**.
18:14 all these people stand around you from morning till **evening**?"
27:21 the lamps burning before the LORD from **evening** till morning.
29:39 Offer one in the morning and the other **at twilight** [+1068+2021].
29:41 Sacrifice the other lamb **at twilight** [+1068+2021] with the same
30: 8 incense again when he lights the lamps **at twilight** [+1068+2021]
Lev 6:20 [6:13] half of it in the morning and half in the **evening**.
11:24 whoever touches their carcasses will be unclean till **evening**.
11:25 must wash his clothes, and he will be unclean till **evening**.
11:27 whoever touches their carcasses will be unclean till **evening**.
11:28 must wash his clothes, and he will be unclean till **evening**.
11:31 touches them when they are dead will be unclean till **evening**.
11:32 it in water; it will be unclean till **evening**, and then it will be clean.
11:39 anyone who touches the carcass will be unclean till **evening**.
11:40 carcass must wash his clothes, and he will be unclean till **evening**.
11:40 carcass must wash his clothes, and he will be unclean till **evening**.
14:46 into the house while it is closed up will be unclean till **evening**.
15: 5 and bathe with water, and he will be unclean till **evening**.
15: 6 and bathe with water, and he will be unclean till **evening**.
15: 7 and bathe with water, and he will be unclean till **evening**.
15: 8 and bathe with water, and he will be unclean till **evening**.
15:10 any of the things that were under him will be unclean till **evening**;
15:10 and bathe with water, and he will be unclean till **evening**.
15:11 and bathe with water, and he will be unclean till **evening**.
15:16 his whole body with water, and he will be unclean till **evening**.
15:17 it must be washed with water, and it will be unclean till **evening**.
15:18 both must bathe with water, and they will be unclean till **evening**.
15:19 and anyone who touches her will be unclean till **evening**.
15:21 and bathe with water, and he will be unclean till **evening**.
15:22 and bathe with water, and he will be unclean till **evening**.
15:23 sitting on, when anyone touches it, he will be unclean till **evening**.
15:27 and bathe with water, and he will be unclean till **evening**.
17:15 bathe with water, and he will be ceremonially unclean till **evening**;
22: 6 The one who touches any such thing will be unclean till **evening**.
23: 5 The LORD's Passover begins **at twilight** [+1068+2021] on the
23:32 From the **evening** of the ninth day of the month until the following
23:32 From the evening of the ninth day of the month **[RPH]** until the
23:32 until the following **evening** you are to observe your sabbath."
24: 3 Aaron is to tend the lamps before the LORD from **evening** till
Nu 9: 3 Celebrate it at the appointed time, **at twilight** [+1068+2021] on the
9: 5 so in the Desert of Sinai **at twilight** [+1068+2021] on the
9:11 the fourteenth day of the second month **at twilight** [+1068+2021].
9:15 From **evening** till morning the cloud above the tabernacle looked
9:21 Sometimes the cloud stayed only from **evening** till morning,
19: 7 into the camp, but he will be ceremonially unclean till **evening**.
19: 8 and bathe with water, and he too will be unclean till **evening**.
19:10 must also wash his clothes, and he too will be unclean till **evening**.
19:19 his clothes and bathe with water, and that **evening** he will be clean.
19:21 who touches the water of cleansing will be unclean till **evening**.
19:22 and anyone who touches it becomes unclean till **evening**."
28: 4 one lamb in the morning and the other **at twilight** [+1068+2021],
28: 8 Prepare the second lamb **at twilight** [+1068+2021], along with the
Dt 16: 4 Do not let any of the meat you sacrifice on the **evening** of the first
16: 6 There you must sacrifice the Passover in the **evening**, when the sun
23:11 [23:12] as **evening** approaches he is to wash himself, and at
28:67 In the morning you will say, "If only it were **evening**!" and in the
28:67 in the **evening**, "If only it were morning!"—because of the terror
Jos 5:10 On the **evening** of the fourteenth day of the month, while camped
7: 6 ground before the ark of the LORD, remaining there till **evening**.
8:29 king of Ai on a tree and left him there until **evening** [+2021+6961].
10:26 on five trees, and they were left hanging on the trees until **evening**.
Jdg 19:16 That **evening** an old man from the hill country of Ephraim,
20:23 The Israelites went up and wept before the LORD until **evening**,
20:26 They fasted that day until **evening** and presented burnt offerings
21: 2 where they sat before God until **evening**, raising their voices
Ru 2:17 So Ruth gleaned in the field until **evening**. Then she threshed the
1Sa 14:24 "Cursed be any man who eats food before **evening** comes,
20: 5 and hide in the field until the **evening** of the day after tomorrow.
30:17 David fought them from dusk until the **evening** of the next day,
2Sa 1:12 They mourned and wept and fasted till **evening** for Saul and his
11: 2 One **evening** David got up from his bed and walked around on the
11:13 in the **evening** Uriah went out to sleep on his mat among his
1Ki 17: 6 and meat in the morning and bread and meat in the **evening**,
22:35 wound ran onto the floor of the chariot, and that **evening** he died.
2Ki 16:15 offer the morning burnt offering and the **evening** grain offering,
1Ch 16:40 morning and **evening**, in accordance with everything written in the
23:30 and praise the LORD. They were to do the same in the **evening**
2Ch 2: 4 [2:3] and **evening** and on Sabbaths and New Moons
13:11 Every morning and **evening** [+928+928+2021+2021+6847] they
13:11 Every morning and **evening** [+928+928+2021+2021+6847] they
13:11 the gold lampstand **every evening** [+928+928+2021+2021+6847].
13:11 the gold lampstand **every evening** [+928+928+2021+2021+6847].
18:34 himself up in his chariot facing the Arameans until **evening**.
31: 3 **evening** burnt offerings and for the burnt offerings on the
Ezr 3: 3 on it to the LORD, both the morning and **evening** sacrifices.
9: 4 of the exiles. And I sat there appalled until the **evening** sacrifice.
9: 5 Then, at the **evening** sacrifice, I rose from my self-abasement,
Est 2:14 In the **evening** she would go there and in the morning return to
Job 4:20 Between dawn and **dusk** they are broken to pieces; unnoticed,
7: 4 long before I get up?' The **night** drags on, and I toss till dawn.
Ps 30: 5 [30:6] weeping may remain for a **night**, but rejoicing comes in the
55:17 [55:18] **Evening**, morning and noon I cry out in distress, and he
59: 6 [59:7] They return at **evening**, snarling like dogs, and prowl about
59:14 [59:15] They return at **evening**, snarling like dogs, and prowl
65: 8 [65:9] and **evening** fades you call forth songs of joy.
90: 6 in the morning it springs up new, by **evening** it is dry and withered.
104:23 Then man goes out to his work, to his labor until **evening**.

Ps 141: 2 may the lifting up of my hands be like the **evening** sacrifice.
Pr 7: 9 at twilight, as the day was **fading**, as the dark of night set in.
Ecc 11: 6 seed in the morning, and at **evening** let not your hands be idle,
Isa 17: 14 In the **evening**, sudden terror! Before the morning, they are gone!
Jer 6: 4 the daylight is fading, and the shadows of **evening** grow long.
Eze 12: 4 in the **evening**, while they are watching, go out like those who go
12: 7 Then in the **evening** I dug through the wall with my hands.
24: 18 to the people in the morning, and in the **evening** my wife died.
33: 22 Now the **evening** before the man arrived, the hand of the LORD
46: 2 and then go out, but the gate will not be shut until **evening**.
Da 8: 14 He said to me, "It will take 2,300 **evenings** and mornings;
8: 26 "The vision of the **evenings** and mornings that has been given you
9: 21 came to me in swift flight about the time of the **evening** sacrifice.
Hab 1: 8 Their horses are swifter than leopards, fiercer than wolves at **dusk**.
Zep 2: 7 In the **evening** they will lie down in the houses of Ashkelon.
3: 3 Her officials are roaring lions, her rulers are **evening** wolves,
Zec 14: 7 known to the LORD. When **evening** comes, there will be light.

6848 ³עֶרֶב *ʿereb³*, n.m. [1 / 0] [cf. 6851, 6858]

1Ki 10: 15 and from all the Arabian [BHS *Arabian* ?; NIV 6851] kings

6849 ¹עֶרֶב *ʿereb¹*, n.[m.]. [9] [√ 6843]

knitted material [9]

Lev 13: 48 any woven or **knitted material** of linen or wool, any leather
13: 49 or leather, or woven or **knitted material**, or any leather article,
13: 51 or the woven or **knitted material**, or the leather, whatever its use,
13: 52 up the clothing, or the woven or **knitted material** of wool or linen,
13: 53 or the woven or **knitted material**, or the leather article,
13: 56 of the clothing, or the leather, or the woven or **knitted material**.
13: 57 or in the woven or **knitted material**, or in the leather article,
13: 58 The clothing, or the woven or **knitted material**, or any leather
13: 59 by mildew in woolen or linen clothing, woven or **knitted material**,

6850 ²עֶרֶב *ʿereb²*, n.m. [5] [cf. 6843, 6846]

foreign people [2], foreigners [1], of foreign descent [1], other people [1]

Ex 12: 38 Many **other people** went up with them, as well as large droves of
Ne 13: 3 they excluded from Israel all who were **of foreign descent**.
Jer 25: 20 all the **foreign people** there; all the kings of Uz; all the kings of the
25: 24 and all the kings of the **foreign people** who live in the desert;
50: 37 against her horses and chariots and all the **foreigners** in her ranks!

6851 ¹עֲרָב *ᵃrab¹*, n.pr.loc. & g. [6 / 7] [√ 6858; cf. 6848]

Arabia [6], Arabian [1]

1Ki 10: 15 traders and from all the **Arabian** [BHS 6848] kings
2Ch 9: 14 Also all the kings of **Arabia** and the governors of the land brought
Isa 21: 13 An oracle concerning **Arabia**: You caravans of Dedanites,
21: 13 You caravans of Dedanites, who camp in the thickets of **Arabia**,
Jer 25: 24 all the kings of **Arabia** and all the kings of the foreign people who
Eze 27: 21 " '**Arabia** and all the princes of Kedar were your customers;
30: 5 Lydia and all **Arabia**, Libya and the people of the covenant land

6852 ²עֲרַב *ᵃrab²*, n.[pr.loc.?]. Not used in NIV/BHS [√ 6858]

6853 עָרֵב *ʿārēb*, a. [2] [√ 6844]

sweet [1], tastes sweet [1]

Pr 20: 17 Food gained by fraud **tastes sweet** to a man, but he ends up with a
SS 2: 14 hear your voice; for your voice is **sweet**, and your face is lovely.

6854 ¹עֹרֵב *ʿōrēb¹*, n.m. [10] [→ 6855]

raven [6], ravens [4]

Ge 8: 7 sent out a **raven**, and it kept flying back and forth until the water
Lev 11: 15 any kind of **raven**,
Dt 14: 14 any kind of **raven**,
1Ki 17: 4 from the brook, and I have ordered the **ravens** to feed you there."
17: 6 The **ravens** brought him bread and meat in the morning and bread
Job 38: 41 Who provides food for the **raven** when its young cry out to God
Ps 147: 9 food for the cattle and for the young **ravens** when they call.
Pr 30: 17 will be pecked out by the **ravens** *of* the valley, will be eaten by the
SS 5: 11 His head is purest gold; his hair is wavy and black as a **raven**.
Isa 34: 11 owl will possess it; the great owl and the **raven** will nest there.

6855 ²עֹרֵב *ʿōrēb²*, n.pr.m. [7] [√ 6854]

Oreb [7]

Jdg 7: 25 They also captured two of the Midianite leaders, **Oreb** and Zeeb.
7: 25 They killed **Oreb** at the rock of Oreb, and Zeeb at the winepress of
7: 25 They killed Oreb at the rock of **Oreb**, and Zeeb at the winepress of
7: 25 the Midianites and brought the heads of **Oreb** and Zeeb to Gideon,
8: 3 God gave **Oreb** and Zeeb, the Midianite leaders, into your hands.
Ps 83: 11 [83:12] Make their nobles like **Oreb** and Zeeb, all their princes
Isa 10: 26 with a whip, as when he struck down Midian at the rock of **Oreb**;

6856 עָרֹב *ʿārōb*, n.m. [9] [√ 6843]

swarms of flies [5], flies [4]

Ex 8: 21 [8:17] I will send **swarms of flies** on you and your officials, on
8: 21 [8:17] The houses of the Egyptians will be full of **flies**, and even
8: 22 [8:18] no **swarms of flies** will be there, so that you will know that
8: 24 [8:20] Dense **swarms of flies** poured into Pharaoh's palace
8: 24 [8:20] and throughout Egypt the land was ruined by the **flies**.
8: 29 [8:25] and tomorrow the **flies** will leave Pharaoh and his officials
8: 31 [8:27] The **flies** left Pharaoh and his officials and his people; not a
Ps 78: 45 He sent **swarms of flies** that devoured them, and frogs that
105: 31 He spoke, and there came **swarms of flies**, and gnats throughout

6857 ¹עֲרָבָה *ᵃrābâ¹*, n.[f.]. [5] [→ 6863]

poplars [3], poplar trees [1], poplars [+5707] [1]

Lev 23: 40 palm fronds, leafy branches and **poplars** [+5707], and rejoice
Job 40: 22 him in their shadow; the **poplars** *by* the stream surround him.
Ps 137: 2 There on the **poplars** we hung our harps,
Isa 15: 7 and stored up they carry away over the Ravine of the **Poplars**.
44: 4 up like grass in a meadow, like **poplar trees** by flowing streams.

6858 ²עֲרָבָה *ᵃrābâ²*, n.f. [59 / 57] [→ 6851, 6852, 6861, 6862; cf. 6848]

Arabah [28], plains [17], desert [4], wasteland [3], wastelands [2], wilderness [2], deserts [1]

Nu 22: 1 the Israelites traveled to the **plains** *of* Moab and camped along the
26: 3 So on the **plains** *of* Moab by the Jordan across from Jericho,
26: 63 Eleazar the priest when they counted the Israelites on the **plains** *of*
31: 12 and the Israelite assembly at their camp on the **plains** *of* Moab,
33: 48 camped on the **plains** *of* Moab by the Jordan across from Jericho.
33: 49 There on the **plains** *of* Moab they camped along the Jordan from
33: 50 On the **plains** *of* Moab by the Jordan across from Jericho the
35: 1 On the **plains** *of* Moab by the Jordan across from Jericho,
36: 13 Israelites on the **plains** *of* Moab by the Jordan across from Jericho.
Dt 1: 1 that is, in the **Arabah**—opposite Suph, between Paran and Tophel,
1: 7 go to all the neighboring peoples in the **Arabah**, in the mountains,
2: 8 We turned from the **Arabah** road, which comes up from Elath
3: 17 Its western border was the Jordan in the **Arabah**, from Kinnereth
3: 17 from Kinnereth to the Sea of the **Arabah** (the Salt Sea),
4: 49 included all the **Arabah** east of the Jordan, as far as the Sea of the
4: 49 as far as the Sea of the **Arabah**, below the slopes of Pisgah.
11: 30 in the territory of those Canaanites living in the **Arabah** in the
34: 1 Moses climbed Mount Nebo from the **plains** *of* Moab to the top of
34: 8 The Israelites grieved for Moses in the **plains** *of* Moab thirty days,
Jos 3: 16 while the water flowing down to the Sea of the **Arabah** (the Salt
4: 13 crossed over before the LORD to the **plains** *of* Jericho for war.
5: 10 while camped at Gilgal on the **plains** *of* Jericho, the Israelites
8: 14 to meet Israel in battle at a certain place overlooking the **Arabah**.
11: 2 in the **Arabah** south of Kinnereth, in the western foothills
11: 16 the **Arabah** and the mountains of Israel with their foothills,
12: 1 to Mount Hermon, including all the eastern side of the **Arabah**:
12: 3 He also ruled over the eastern **Arabah** from the Sea of Kinnereth
12: 3 from the Sea of Kinnereth to the Sea of the **Arabah** (the Salt Sea),
12: 8 the **Arabah**, the mountain slopes, the desert and the Negev—
13: 32 is the inheritance Moses had given when he was in the **plains** *of*
18: 18 the northern slope of Beth Arabah and on down into the **Arabah**.
1Sa 23: 24 men were in the Desert of Maon, in the **Arabah** south of Jeshimon.
2Sa 2: 29 All that night Abner and his men marched through the **Arabah**.
4: 7 Taking it with them, they traveled all night by way of the **Arabah**.
15: 28 [I will wait at the **fords** [Q; see K 6302] *in* the desert]
17: 16 spend the night at the fords [BHS *wasteland*; NIV 6302] *in*
2Ki 14: 25 boundaries of Israel from Lebo Hamath to the Sea of the **Arabah**,
25: 4 were surrounding the city. They fled toward the **Arabah**,
25: 5 army pursued the king and overtook him in the **plains** *of* Jericho.
Job 24: 5 of foraging food; the **wasteland** provides food for their children.
39: 6 I gave him the **wasteland** as his home, the salt flats as his habitat.
Ps 68: 4 [68:5] who rides on the clouds—[BHS *deserts*; NIV 6265]
Isa 33: 9 Sharon is like the **Arabah**, and Bashan and Carmel drop their
35: 1 parched land will be glad; the **wilderness** will rejoice and blossom.
35: 6 Water will gush forth in the wilderness and streams in the **desert**.
40: 3 make straight in the **wilderness** a highway for our God.
41: 19 I will set pines in the **wasteland**, the fir and the cypress together,
51: 3 deserts like Eden, her **wastelands** like the garden of the LORD.
Jer 2: 6 through a land of **deserts** and rifts, a land of drought and darkness,
5: 6 forest will attack them, a wolf from the **desert** will ravage them,
17: 6 He will be like a bush in the **wastelands**; he will not see prosperity
39: 4 the gate between the two walls, and headed toward the **Arabah**.
39: 5 army pursued them and overtook Zedekiah in the **plains** *of* Jericho.
50: 12 will be the least of the nations—a wilderness, a dry land, a **desert**.

Jer 51:43 will be desolate, a dry and **desert** land, a land where no one lives,
52: 7 were surrounding the city. They fled toward the **Arabah**,
52: 8 pursued King Zedekiah and overtook him in the **plains** *of* Jericho.
Eze 47: 8 flows toward the eastern region and goes down into the **Arabah**,
Am 6:14 you all the way from Lebo Hamath to the valley of the **Arabah**."
Zec 14:10 to Rimmon, south of Jerusalem, will become like the **Arabah**.

6859 עֲרֻבָּה ᵃrubbâ, n.f. [2] [√ 6842]

assurance [1], puts up security [+6842] [1]

1Sa 17:18 how your brothers are and bring back *some* **assurance** *from* them.
Pr 17:18 hands in pledge and **puts up security** [+6842] for his neighbor.

6860 עֵרָבוֹן 'ērābôn, n.[m.]. [3] [√ 6842]

pledge [3]

Ge 38:17 "Will you give me something as a **pledge** until you send it?"
38:18 He said, "What **pledge** should I give you?" "Your seal and its cord,
38:20 the Adullamite in order to get his **pledge** back from the woman,

6861 עַרְבִי 'arbî, a.g. [7] [√ 6858]

Arabs [5], Arab [2]

2Ch 17:11 and silver as tribute, and the **Arabs** brought him flocks:
21:16 of the Philistines and of the **Arabs** who lived near the Cushites.
22: 1 since the raiders, who came with the **Arabs** into the camp,
26: 7 against the **Arabs** who lived in Gur Baal and against the Meunites.
Ne 2:19 the Ammonite official and Geshem the **Arab** heard about it,
4: 7 [4:1] Tobiah, the **Arabs**, the Ammonites and the men of Ashdod
6: 1 Geshem the **Arab** and the rest of our enemies that I had rebuilt the

6862 עֲרָבִי ᵃrābî, n.g. [2] [√ 6858]

Arab [1], nomad [1]

Isa 13:20 no **Arab** will pitch his tent there, no shepherd will rest his flocks
Jer 3: 2 roadside you sat waiting for lovers, sat like a **nomad** in the desert.

6863 עַרְבָתִי 'arbātî, a.g. [2] [√ 6857]

Arbathite [2]

2Sa 23:31 Abi-Albon the **Arbathite**, Azmaveth the Barhumite,
1Ch 11:32 Hurai from the ravines of Gaash, Abiel the **Arbathite**,

6864 עָרַג 'ārag, v. [3] [√ 6870?]

pants [2], pant [1]

Ps 42: 1 [42:2] [A] As the deer **pants** for streams of water, so my soul
42: 1 [42:2] [A] streams of water, so my soul **pants** for you, O God.
Joel 1:20 [A] Even the wild animals **pant** for you; the streams of water

6865 עֲרָדִי ᵃrād¹, n.pr.m. [1] [√ 6871]

Arad [1]

1Ch 8:15 Zebadiah, **Arad**, Eder,

6866 ²עֲרָד ᵃrād², n.pr.loc. [4] [√ 6871]

Arad [4]

Nu 21: 1 When the Canaanite king of **Arad**, who lived in the Negev,
33:40 The Canaanite king of **Arad**, who lived in the Negev of Canaan,
Jos 12:14 the king of Hormah one the king of **Arad** one
Jdg 1:16 among the people of the Desert of Judah in the Negev near **Arad**.

6867 ¹עָרָה 'ārâ¹, v. [15] [→ 4623, 5118, 5122, 6567, 6872, 6873, 6880, 6895, 9509; cf. 6910, 6423]

exposed [2], tear down [2], dishonor [1], emptied [1], empty [1], flourishing [1], give over to death [1], is poured [1], make bald [1], poured out [1], stripped naked [1], stripped [1], uncovers [1]

Ge 24:20 [D] So she quickly **emptied** her jar into the trough, ran back to
Lev 20:18 [G] *he has* **exposed** the source of her flow, and she has also
20:19 [G] or your father, for *that would* **dishonor** a close relative;
2Ch 24:11 [D] and **empty** the chest and carry it back to its place.
Ps 37:35 [F] ruthless man **flourishing** like a green tree in its native soil,
137: 7 [D] "**Tear it down**," they cried, "tear it down to its foundations!"
137: 7 [D] "Tear it down," they cried, "**tear it down** to its foundations!"
141: 8 [D] in you I take refuge—*do* not **give** me **over to death**.
Isa 3:17 [D] women of Zion; the LORD *will* **make** their scalps **bald**."
22: 6 [D] with her charioteers and horses; Kir **uncovers** the shield.
32:15 [C] till the Spirit **is poured** upon us from on high, and the desert
53:12 [G] because *he* **poured out** his life unto death, and was
La 4:21 [F] cup will be passed; you will be drunk and **stripped naked**.
Hab 3:13 [D] the land of wickedness, *you* **stripped** him from head to foot.
Zep 2:14 [D] will be in the doorways, the beams of cedar *will be* **exposed**.

6868 ²עָרָה 'ārâ², n.f. [1]

plants [1]

Isa 19: 7 also the **plants** along the Nile, at the mouth of the river. Every

6869 ³עָרָה 'ārâ³, n.pr.loc. [0 / 1] [→ 5117?]

Arah [1]

Jos 13: 4 from **Arah** [BHS 5117] of the Sidonians as far as Aphek,

6870 עֲרוּגָה ᵃrûgâ, n.f. [4] [√ 6864?]

beds [2], plot [2]

SS 5:13 His cheeks are like **beds** *of* spice yielding perfume. His lips are
6: 2 to the **beds** *of* spices, to browse in the gardens and to gather lilies.
Eze 17: 7 The vine now sent out its roots toward him from the **plot** *where* it
17:10 the east wind strikes it—wither away in the **plot** *where* it grew?' "

6871 עָרוֹד 'ārôd, n.[m.]. [1] [→ 6563, 6865, 6866; Ar 10570]

his^s [1]

Job 39: 5 "Who let the wild donkey go free? Who untied **his**^s ropes?

6872 עֶרְוָה 'erwâ, n.f. [54] [√ 6867; Ar 10571]

nakedness [11], have sexual relations with [+1655] [10], *untranslated* [5], dishonored [+1655] [4], dishonor [3], have sexual relations [+1655] [3], have relations with [+1655] [2], indecent [2], shame [2], unprotected [2], body [+1414] [1], dishonor bed [+1655] [1], dishonor by having sexual relations with [+1655] [1], dishonor by to have sexual relations [+1655] [1], has sexual relations with [+906+1655] [1], have sexual relations [+906+8011] [1], have sexual relations with [+906+1655] [1], naked [1], shame [+1425] [1], strip [+1655] [1]

Ge 9:22 saw his father's **nakedness** and told his two brothers outside.
9:23 they walked in backward and covered their father's **nakedness**.
9:23 the other way so that they would not see their father's **nakedness**.
42: 9 are spies! You have come to see where our land is **unprotected**."
42:12 to them. "You have come to see where our land is **unprotected**."
Ex 20:26 go up to my altar on steps, lest your **nakedness** be exposed on it.'
28:42 "Make linen undergarments as a covering for the **body** [+1414],
Lev 18: 6 is to approach any close relative to **have sexual relations** [+1655].
18: 7 not **dishonor** your father **by having sexual relations with** [+1655]
18: 7 your father by having sexual relations with **[RPH]** your mother.
18: 7 She is your mother; *do* not **have relations with** [+1655] her.
18: 8 " '*Do* not **have sexual relations with** [+1655] your father's wife;
18: 8 relations with your father's wife; that would **dishonor** your father.
18: 9 " '*Do* not **have sexual relations with** [+1655] your sister,
18: 9 whether she was born in the same home or elsewhere. **[RPH]**
18:10 " '*Do* not **have sexual relations with** [+1655] your son's daughter
18:10 or your daughter's daughter; **[RPH]** that would dishonor you.
18:10 or your daughter's daughter; that would **dishonor** you.
18:11 " '*Do* not **have sexual relations with** [+1655] the daughter of your
18:11 your father's wife, born to your father; she is your sister. **[RPH]**
18:12 " '*Do* not **have sexual relations with** [+1655] your father's sister;
18:13 " '*Do* not **have sexual relations with** [+1655] your mother's sister,
18:14 " '*Do* not **dishonor** your father's brother **by** approaching his wife **to have sexual relations** [+1655];
18:15 " '*Do* not **have sexual relations with** [+1655] your
18:15 She is your son's wife; *do* not **have relations with** [+1655] her.
18:16 " '*Do* not **have sexual relations with** [+1655] your brother's wife;
18:16 with your brother's wife; that would **dishonor** your brother.
18:17 " '*Do* not **have sexual relations with** [+1655] both a woman
18:17 *Do* not **have sexual relations with** [+906+1655] either her son's
18:18 **have sexual relations** [+1655] with her while your wife is living.
18:19 " 'Do not approach a woman to **have sexual relations** [+1655]
20:11 with his father's wife, *he has* **dishonored** [+1655] his father.
20:17 or his mother, and *they* **have sexual relations** [+906+8011],
20:17 his mother, and they have sexual relations, **[RPH]** it is a disgrace.
20:17 *He has* **dishonored** [+1655] his sister and will be held responsible.
20:18 monthly period and **has sexual relations with** [+906+1655] her,
20:19 " '*Do* not **have sexual relations with** [+1655] the sister of either
20:20 a man sleeps with his aunt, *he has* **dishonored** [+1655] his uncle.
20:21 it is an act of impurity; *he has* **dishonored** [+1655] his brother.
Dt 23:14 [23:15] so that he will not see among you anything **indecent**
24: 1 displeasing to him because he finds something **indecent** about her,
1Sa 20:30 own shame and to the **shame of** [+1425] the mother who bore you?
Isa 20: 4 young and old, with buttocks bared—*to* Egypt's **shame**.
47: 3 Your **nakedness** will be exposed and your shame uncovered.
La 1: 8 who honored her despise her, for they have seen her **nakedness**;
Eze 16: 8 the corner of my garment over you and covered your **nakedness**.
16:36 and exposed your **nakedness** in your promiscuity with your lovers,
16:37 you from all around and *will* **strip** [+1655] you in front of them,
16:37 strip you in front of them, and they will see all your **nakedness**.
22:10 In you are *those who* **dishonor** their fathers' **bed** [+1655];
23:10 They stripped her **naked**, took away her sons and daughters

Eze 23:18 she carried on her prostitution openly and exposed her **nakedness**,
23:29 and bare, and the **shame** *of* your prostitution will be exposed.
Hos 2: 9 [2:11] my wool and my linen, intended to cover her **nakedness**.

6873 עָרֹם **'ārôm**, a. [16] [√ 6873]

naked [12], stripped [3], that way[s] [1]

Ge 2:25 The man and his wife were both **naked**, and they felt no shame.
1Sa 19:24 He lay **that way**[s] all that day and night. This is why people say,
Job 1:21 "**Naked** I came from my mother's womb, and naked I will depart.
1:21 "Naked I came from my mother's womb, and **naked** I will depart.
22: 6 no reason; you stripped men of their clothing, leaving them **naked**.
24: 7 Lacking clothes, they spend the night **naked**; they have nothing to
24:10 Lacking clothes, they go about **naked**; they carry the sheaves,
26: 6 Death is **naked** before God; Destruction lies uncovered.
Ecc 5:15 [5:14] **Naked** a man comes from his mother's womb, and as he
Isa 20: 2 your feet." And he did so, going around **stripped** and barefoot.
20: 3 "Just as my servant Isaiah has gone **stripped** and barefoot for three
20: 4 so the king of Assyria will lead away **stripped** and barefoot the
58: 7 when you see the **naked**, to clothe him, and not to turn away from
Hos 2: 3 [2:5] Otherwise I will strip her **naked** and make her as bare as on
Am 2:16 Even the bravest warriors will flee **naked** on that day,"
Mic 1: 8 of this I will weep and wail; I will go about barefoot and **naked**.

6874 עָרוּם **'ārûm**, a. [11] [√ 6891]

prudent [8], crafty [3]

Ge 3: 1 Now the serpent was more **crafty** than any of the wild animals the
Job 5:12 He thwarts the plans of the **crafty**, so that their hands achieve no
15: 5 Your sin prompts your mouth; you adopt the tongue of the **crafty**.
Pr 12:16 his annoyance at once, but a **prudent** *man* overlooks an insult.
12:23 A **prudent** man keeps his knowledge to himself, but the heart of
13:16 Every **prudent** *man* acts out of knowledge, but a fool exposes his
14: 8 The wisdom of the **prudent** is to give thought to their ways,
14:15 believes anything, but a **prudent** *man* gives thought to his steps.
14:18 simple inherit folly, but the **prudent** are crowned with knowledge.
22: 3 A **prudent** *man* sees danger and takes refuge, but the simple keep
27:12 The **prudent** see danger and take refuge, but the simple keep going

6875 עֲרוֹעֵר[1] **'ᵃrô'ēr[1]**, n.[m.]. Not used in NIV/BHS [→ 6876; cf. 6910]

6876 עֲרוֹעֵר[2] **'ᵃrô'ēr[2]**, n.pr.loc. [16] [→ 6901; cf. 6875, 6910]

Aroer [16]

Nu 32:34 The Gadites built up Dibon, Ataroth, **Aroer**,
Dt 2:36 From **Aroer** on the rim of the Arnon Gorge, and from the town in
3:12 and the Gadites the territory north of **Aroer** by the Arnon Gorge,
4:48 This land extended from **Aroer** on the rim of the Arnon Gorge to
Jos 12: 2 He ruled from **Aroer** on the rim of the Arnon Gorge—from the
13: 9 It extended from **Aroer** on the rim of the Arnon Gorge, and from
13:16 The territory from **Aroer** on the rim of the Arnon Gorge, and from
13:25 towns of Gilead and half the Ammonite country as far as **Aroer**,
Jdg 11:26 **Aroer**, [BHS 6898] the surrounding settlements and all the towns
11:33 He devastated twenty towns from **Aroer** to the vicinity of Minnith,
1Sa 30:28 to those in **Aroer**, Siphmoth, Eshtemoa
2Sa 24: 5 After crossing the Jordan, they camped near **Aroer**, south of the
2Ki 10:33 from **Aroer** by the Arnon Gorge through Gilead to Bashan.
1Ch 5: 8 They settled in the area from **Aroer** to Nebo and Baal Meon.
Isa 17: 2 The cities of **Aroer** will be deserted and left to flocks, which will
Jer 48: 6 become like a bush [BHS *Aroer*; NIV 6899] in the desert.
48:19 Stand by the road and watch, you who live in **Aroer**. Ask the man

6877 עָרוּץ **'ārûṣ**, a. [1] [√ 6907]

dry [1]

Job 30: 6 They were forced to live in the **dry** stream beds, among the rocks

6878 עֵרִי[1] **'ērî[1]**, n.pr.m. [2] [→ 6879; cf. 6424]

Eri [2]

Ge 46:16 sons of Gad: Zephon, Haggi, Shuni, Ezbon, **Eri**, Arodi and Areli.
Nu 26:16 through Ozni, the Oznite clan; through **Eri**, the Erite clan;

6879 עֵרִי[2] **'ērî[2]**, a.g. [1] [√ 6878; cf. 6424]

Erite [1]

Nu 26:16 through Ozni, the Oznite clan; through Eri, the **Erite** clan;

6880 עֶרְיָה **'eryâ**, n.f. [6] [√ 6867]

bare [4], nakedness [1], uncovered [+6423] [1]

Eze 16: 7 were formed and your hair grew, you who were naked and **bare**.
16:22 when you were naked and **bare**, kicking about in your blood.
16:39 and take your fine jewelry and leave you naked and **bare**.
23:29 They will leave you naked and **bare**, and the shame of your
Mic 1:11 Pass on in **nakedness** and shame, you who live in Shaphir.
Hab 3: 9 *You* **uncovered** [+6423] your bow, you called for many arrows.

6881 עֲרִיסָה **'ᵃrîsâ**, n.f. [4]

ground meal [4]

Nu 15:20 Present a cake from the first of your **ground meal** and present it as
15:21 this offering to the LORD from the first of your **ground meal**.
Ne 10:37 [10:38] to the priests, the first of our **ground meal**, of our ⌞grain⌟
Eze 44:30 You are to give them the first portion of your **ground meal**

6882 עֲרִיפִים **'ᵃrîpîm**, n.[m.pl.]. [1] [√ 6903]

clouds [1]

Isa 5:30 and distress; even the light will be darkened by the **clouds**.

6883 עָרִיץ **'ārîṣ**, a. [20 / 21] [√ 6907]

ruthless [17], fierce [2], cruel [1], mighty [1]

Job 6:23 hand of the enemy, ransom me from the clutches of the **ruthless**'?
15:20 the **ruthless** through all the years stored up for him.
27:13 the heritage a **ruthless** *man* receives from the Almighty:
Ps 37:35 and **ruthless** *man* flourishing like a green tree in its native soil,
54: 3 [54:5] Strangers are attacking me; **ruthless** *men* seek my life—
86:14 are attacking me, O God; a band of **ruthless** *men* seeks my life—
Pr 11:16 woman gains respect, but **ruthless** *men* gain only wealth.
Isa 13:11 arrogance of the haughty and will humble the pride of the **ruthless**.
25: 3 peoples will honor you; cities of **ruthless** nations will revere you.
25: 4 For the breath of the **ruthless** is like a storm driving against a wall
25: 5 by the shadow of a cloud, so the song of the **ruthless** is stilled.
29: 5 will become like fine dust, the **ruthless** hordes like blown chaff.
29:20 The **ruthless** will vanish, the mockers will disappear, and all who
49:24 from warriors, or captives rescued from the **fierce**? [BHS 7404]
49:25 will be taken from warriors, and plunder retrieved from the **fierce**;
Jer 15:21 hands of the wicked and redeem you from the grasp of the **cruel**."
20:11 the LORD is with me like a **mighty** warrior; so my persecutors
Eze 28: 7 going to bring foreigners against you, the *most* **ruthless** *of* nations;
30:11 He and his army—the *most* **ruthless** *of* nations—will be brought
31:12 and the *most* **ruthless** *of* foreign nations cut it down and left it.
32:12 by the swords of mighty men—the *most* **ruthless** *of* all nations.

6884 עֲרִירִי **'ᵃrîrî**, a. [4] [√ 6910]

childless [4]

Ge 15: 2 what can you give me since I remain **childless** and the one who
Lev 20:20 his uncle. They will be held responsible; they will die **childless**.
20:21 of impurity; he has dishonored his brother. They will be **childless**.
Jer 22:30 "Record this man as if **childless**, a man who will not prosper in his

6885 עָרַךְ **'ārak**, v.[den.]. [75] [→ 6886, 5119, 5120, 5121]

took up positions [5], arrange [4], deployed [4], prepared [4], arranged [3], compare [3], prepare [3], spread [3], drew up line [2], drew up [2], formed battle lines [2], judge quality [2], marshaled [2], set out [2], set [2], take up positions [2], *untranslated* [1], accuse [1], been prepared [1], compare with [1], deployed forces [1], draw up case [1], drawing up [1], drawn up [1], drew up lines [1], formation [1], formed lines [1], handle [1], in formation [1], keep [1], laid out [1], lay out [1], lay [1], line up [1], ready [1], recount [1], set out [+6886] [1], set up [1], set value [1], state [1], stationed [1], sustain [1], taxed [1], tend [1], tended [1], value sets [1]

Ge 14: 8 [A] and **drew up** their battle **lines** in the Valley of Siddim
22: 9 [A] Abraham built an altar there and **arranged** the wood on it.
Ex 27:21 [A] his sons *are to* **keep** the lamps burning before the LORD
40: 4 [A] Bring in the table and **set out** what belongs on it. Then bring
40:23 [A] **set** [+6886] **out** the bread on it before the LORD, as the
Lev 1: 7 [A] are to put fire on the altar and **arrange** wood on the fire.
1: 8 [A] the priests *shall* **arrange** the pieces, including the head and
1:12 [A] the priest *shall* **arrange** them, including the head and the fat,
6:12 [6:5] [A] and **arrange** the burnt offering on the fire
24: 3 [A] Aaron *is to* **tend** the lamps before the LORD from evening
24: 4 [A] the pure gold lampstand before the LORD *must be* **tended**
24: 8 [A] This bread *is to be* **set out** before the LORD regularly,
27: 8 [G] who *will* **set** *the* **value** *for* him according to what the man
27: 8 [G] to what the man making the vow can afford. **[RPH]**
27:12 [G] who *will* **judge** its **quality** as good or bad. Whatever value
27:14 [G] the LORD, the priest *will* **judge** its **quality** as good or bad.
27:14 [G] or bad. Whatever **value** the priest then **sets**, so it will remain.
Nu 23: 4 [A] with him, and Balaam said, "*I have* **prepared** seven altars,
Jos 2: 6 [B] hidden them under the stalks of flax she *had* **laid out** on the
Jdg 20:20 [A] and **took up** battle **positions** against them at Gibeah.
20:22 [A] again **took up** *their* **positions** where they had stationed
20:22 [A] positions where *they had* **stationed** *themselves* the first day.
20:30 [A] **took up positions** against Gibeah as they had done before.

Jdg 20:33 [A] from their places and **took up positions** at Baal Tamar,
1Sa 4: 2 [A] The Philistines **deployed** *their* **forces** to meet Israel, and as
17: 2 [A] of Elah and **drew up** their battle **line** to meet the Philistines.
17: 8 [A] of Israel, "Why do you come out and **line up** *for* battle?
17:21 [A] the Philistines *were* **drawing up** *their* lines facing each
2Sa 10: 8 [A] **drew up** *in* battle formation *at* the entrance to their city gate,
10: 9 [A] troops in Israel and **deployed** them against the Arameans.
10:10 [A] his brother and **deployed** them against the Ammonites.
10:17 [A] The Arameans **formed** *their* **battle lines** to meet David
23: 5 [B] an everlasting covenant, **arranged** and secured in every part?
1Ki 18:33 [A] *He* **arranged** the wood, cut the bull into pieces and laid it on
2Ki 23:35 [G] *he* **taxed** the land and exacted the silver and gold from the
1Ch 12: 8 [12:9] [A] for battle and *able to* **handle** the shield and spear.
12:33 [12:34] [A] experienced soldiers **prepared** *for* battle with every
12:35 [12:36] [A] men of Dan, **ready** *for* battle—28,600;
12:36 [12:37] [A] experienced soldiers **prepared** *for* battle—
19: 9 [A] and **drew up** *in* battle formation *at* the entrance to their city,
19:10 [A] troops in Israel and **deployed** them against the Arameans.
19:11 [A] his brother, and *they were* **deployed** against the Ammonites.
19:17 [A] against them and **formed** *his* **battle lines** opposite them.
19:17 [A] David **formed** *his* **lines** to meet the Arameans in battle,
2Ch 13: 3 [A] Jeroboam **drew up** *a* battle **line** against him with eight
14:10 [14:9] [A] *they* **took up** battle **positions** in the Valley of
Job 6: 4 [A] in their poison; God's terrors *are* **marshaled** *against* me.
13:18 [A] Now that *I have* **prepared** my case, I know I will be
23: 4 [A] *I would* **state** my case before him and fill my mouth with
28:17 [A] Neither gold nor crystal *can* **compare** *with* it, nor can it be
28:19 [A] The topaz of Cush cannot **compare with** it; it cannot be
32:14 [A] Job *has* not **marshaled** his words against me, and I will not
33: 5 [A] me then, if you can; **prepare** *yourself* and confront me.
36:19 [A] your wealth or even all your mighty efforts **sustain** you
37:19 [A] *we* cannot **draw up** our **case** because of our darkness.
Ps 5: 3 [5:4] [A] in the morning *I* **lay** my requests before you and wait
23: 5 [A] *You* **prepare** a table before me in the presence of my
40: 5 [40:6] [A] The things you planned for us no *one can* **recount** to
50:21 [A] like you. But I will rebuke you and **accuse** you to your face.
78:19 [A] against God, saying, "Can God **spread** a table in the desert?
89: 6 [89:7] [A] For who in the skies above *can* **compare** with the
132:17 [A] horn grow for David and **set up** a lamp for my anointed one.
Pr 9: 2 [A] her meat and mixed her wine; *she has* also **set** her table.
Isa 21: 5 [A] They **set** the tables, they spread the rugs, they eat, they drink!
30:33 [B] Topheth *has* long **been prepared**; it has been made ready for
40:18 [A] you compare God? What image *will you* **compare** him to?
44: 7 [A] **lay out** before me what has happened since I established my
65:11 [A] who **spread** a table for Fortune and fill bowls of mixed wine
Jer 6:23 [B] they come like men in battle **formation** to attack you,
46: 3 [A] "**Prepare** your shields, both large and small, and march out
50: 9 [A] *They will* **take up** *their* **positions** against her, and from the
50:14 [A] "**Take up** *your* **positions** around Babylon, all you who draw
50:42 [B] they come like men **in** battle **formation** to attack you,
Eze 23:41 [B] with a table **spread** before it on which you had placed the
Joel 2: 5 [B] consuming stubble, like a mighty army **drawn up** *for* battle.

6886 עֵרֶךְ ʿērek, n.m. [33] [√ 6885]

value [11], proper value [3], set value [3], value [+4084] [2], *untranslated* [1], assessments [1], clothes [+955] [1], equivalent values [1], form [1], like [+3869] [1], personal vows [+5883] [1], price set [1], set out [+6885] [1], specified amount [1], that[s] [1], value [+4831] [1], what belongs [1], worth [1]

Ex 40: 4 Bring in the table and set out **what belongs** *on* it. Then bring in the
40:23 **set out** [+6885] the bread on it before the LORD, as the LORD
Lev 5:15 one without defect and of the **proper value** *in* silver, according to
5:18 a ram from the flock, one without defect and of the **proper value**.
6: 6 [5:25] from the flock, one without defect and of the **proper value**.
27: 2 to dedicate persons to the LORD by giving **equivalent values**,
27: 3 set the **value** *of* a male between the ages of twenty and sixty at
27: 3 the ages of twenty and sixty **[RPH]** at fifty shekels of silver,
27: 4 and if it is a female, set her **value** at thirty shekels.
27: 5 set the **value** *of* a male at twenty shekels and of a female at ten
27: 6 set the **value** *of* a male at five shekels of silver and that of a female
27: 6 shekels of silver and **that**[s] of a female at three shekels of silver.
27: 7 set the **value** *of* a male at fifteen shekels and of a female at ten
27: 8 If anyone making the vow is too poor to pay the **specified amount**,
27:12 Whatever **value** the priest then sets, that is what it will be.
27:13 wishes to redeem the animal, he must add a fifth to its **value**.
27:15 he must add a fifth to its **value** [+4084], and the house will again
27:16 its **value** is to be set according to the amount of seed required for
27:17 during the Year of Jubilee, the **value** that has been set remains.
27:18 until the next Year of Jubilee, and its **set value** will be reduced.
27:19 he must add a fifth to its **value** [+4084], and the field will again
27:23 the priest will determine its **value** [+4831] up to the Year of
27:23 the man must pay its **value** on that day as something holy to the
27:25 Every **value** is to be set according to the sanctuary shekel,
27:27 he may buy it back at its **set value**, adding a fifth of the value to it.
27:27 value to it. If he does not redeem it, it is to be sold at its **set value**.
Nu 18:16 you must redeem them at the redemption **price set** *at* five shekels
Jdg 17:10 ten shekels of silver a year, your **clothes** [+955] and your food."
2Ki 12: 4 [12:5] the money received from **personal vows** [+5883] and the
23:35 gold from the people of the land according to their **assessments**.
Job 28:13 Man does not comprehend its **worth**; it cannot be found in the land
41:12 [41:4] to speak of his limbs, his strength and his graceful **form**.
Ps 55:13 [55:14] it is you, a man **like** [+3869] myself, my companion, my

6887 עָרַל ʿāral, v.den. [2] [√ 6889]

be exposed [1], regard as forbidden [+906+6889] [1]

Lev 19:23 [A] fruit tree, **regard** its fruit **as forbidden** [+906+6889].
Hab 2:16 [C] instead of glory. Now it is your turn! Drink and **be exposed**!

6888 עָרֵל ʿārēl, a. [35] [√ 6889]

uncircumcised [29], *untranslated* [2], faltering [2], closed [1], forbidden [1]

Ge 17:14 Any **uncircumcised** male, who has not been circumcised in the
Ex 6:12 would Pharaoh listen to me, since I speak with **faltering** lips?"
6:30 But Moses said to the LORD, "Since I speak with **faltering** lips,
12:48 like one born in the land. No **uncircumcised** *male* may eat of it.
Lev 19:23 For three years you are to consider it **forbidden**; it must not be
26:41 when their **uncircumcised** hearts are humbled and they pay for
Jos 5: 7 They were still **uncircumcised** because they had not been
Jdg 14: 3 Must you go to the **uncircumcised** Philistines to get a wife?"
15:18 I now die of thirst and fall into the hands of the **uncircumcised**?"
1Sa 14: 6 let's go over to the outpost of those **uncircumcised** *fellows*.
17:26 Who is this **uncircumcised** Philistine that he should defy the
17:36 this **uncircumcised** Philistine will be like one of them, because he
31: 4 or these **uncircumcised** *fellows* will come and run me through
2Sa 1:20 be glad, lest the daughters of the **uncircumcised** rejoice.
1Ch 10: 4 or these **uncircumcised** *fellows* will come and abuse me."
Isa 52: 1 holy city. The **uncircumcised** and defiled will not enter you again.
Jer 6:10 Who will listen to me? Their ears are **closed** so they cannot hear.
9:26 [9:25] For all these nations are really **uncircumcised**, and even
9:26 [9:25] even the whole house of Israel is **uncircumcised** *in* heart."
Eze 28:10 You will die the death of the **uncircumcised** at the hands of
31:18 you will lie among the **uncircumcised**, with those killed by the
32:19 than others? Go down and be laid among the **uncircumcised**.'
32:21 'They have come down and they lie with the **uncircumcised**,
32:24 land of the living went down **uncircumcised** to the earth below.
32:25 her grave. All of them are **uncircumcised**, killed by the sword.
32:26 All of them are **uncircumcised**, killed by the sword because they
32:27 Do they not lie with the other **uncircumcised** warriors who have
32:28 O Pharaoh, will be broken and will lie among the **uncircumcised**,
32:29 They lie with the **uncircumcised**, with those who go down to the
32:30 They lie **uncircumcised** with those killed by the sword and bear
32:32 Pharaoh and all his hordes will be laid among the **uncircumcised**,
44: 7 you brought foreigners **uncircumcised** *in* heart and flesh into my
44: 7 uncircumcised in heart and **[RPH]** flesh into my sanctuary,
44: 9 No foreigner **uncircumcised** *in* heart and flesh is to enter my
44: 9 uncircumcised in heart and **[RPH]** flesh is to enter my sanctuary,

6889 עָרְלָה ʿorlâ, n.f. [15] [→ 1502, 6887, 6888]

foreskins [3], *untranslated* [1], be circumcised [+1414+4576] [1], been circumcised [+906+4576] [1], circumcise [+6073] [1], circumcise [+906+4576] [1], circumcised [+906+1414+4576] [1], flesh [1], foreskin [1], not circumcised [+2257+4200] [1], regard as forbidden [+906+6887] [1], undergo circumcision [+906+1414+4576] [1], was circumcised [+1414+4576] [1]

Ge 17:11 You *are to* **undergo circumcision** [+906+1414+4576], and it will
17:14 who *has* not **been circumcised in** [+906+4576] the flesh,
17:23 and **circumcised** [+906+1414+4576] them, as God told him.
17:24 was ninety-nine years old when he **was circumcised** [+1414+4576],
17:25 and his son Ishmael was thirteen; **[RPH]**
34:14 our sister to a man who is **not circumcised** [+2257+4200].
Ex 4:25 cut off her son's **foreskin** and touched ⌞Moses'⌟ feet with it.
Lev 12: 3 On the eighth day the boy *is to* **be circumcised** [+1414+4576].
19:23 of fruit tree, **regard** its fruit **as forbidden** [+906+6887].
Dt 10:16 **Circumcise** [+906+4576] your hearts, therefore, and do not be
1Sa 18:25 no other price for the bride than a hundred Philistine **foreskins**,
18:27 He brought their **foreskins** and presented the full number to the
2Sa 3:14 to myself for the price of a hundred Philistine **foreskins**."
Jer 4: 4 **circumcise** your hearts, **you** [+6073] men of Judah and people of
9:25 [9:24] I will punish all who are circumcised only in the **flesh**—

6890 עָרַם ʿāram[1], v. [1] [→ 6894; cf. 6682]

piled up [1]

Ex 15: 8 [C] By the blast of your nostrils the waters **piled up**. The surging

6891 ²עָרַם *ʿāram²*, v. [6] [→ 6874, 6892, 6893]

very crafty [+6891] [2], craftiness [1], cunning [1], learn prudence [1], shows prudence [1]

1Sa 23:22 [A] has seen him there. They tell me he *is* **very crafty** [+6891].
23:22 [A] has seen him there. They tell me he *is* **very crafty** [+6891].
Job 5:13 [A] He catches the wise in their **craftiness**, and the schemes of
Ps 83:3 [83:4] [G] *With* **cunning** *they* conspire against your people;
Pr 15:5 [A] but whoever heeds correction **shows prudence**.
19:25 [A] Flog a mocker, and the simple *will* **learn prudence**; rebuke a

6892 עֹרֶם *ʿōrem*, n.[m.]. Not used in NIV/BHS [√ 6891]

6893 עָרְמָה *ʿormâ*, n.f. [5] [√ 6891]

prudence [3], deliberately [+928] [1], ruse [1]

Ex 21:14 But if a man schemes and kills another man **deliberately** [+928],
Jos 9:4 they resorted to a **ruse**: They went as a delegation whose donkeys
Pr 1:4 for giving **prudence** to the simple, knowledge and discretion to the
8:5 You who are simple, gain **prudence**; you who are foolish,
8:12 "I, wisdom, dwell together with **prudence**; I possess knowledge

6894 עֲרֵמָה *ʿarēmâ*, n.f. [11] [√ 6890]

heaps [3], in heaps [+6894] [2], doing this[s] [+2021+3569] [1], grain pile [1], grain [1], heap [1], heaps of grain [1], mound [1]

Ru 3:7 he went over to lie down at the far end of the **grain pile**.
2Ch 31:6 to the LORD their God, and they piled them **in heaps** [+6894].
31:6 to the LORD their God, and they piled them **in heaps** [+6894].
31:7 They began **doing**[s] **this** [+2021+3569] in the third month
31:8 When Hezekiah and his officials came and saw the **heaps**,
31:9 Hezekiah asked the priests and Levites about the **heaps**;
Ne 4:2 [3:34] Can they bring the stones back to life from those **heaps** *of*
13:15 on the Sabbath and bringing in **grain** and loading it on donkeys,
SS 7:2 [7:3] Your waist is a **mound** *of* wheat encircled by lilies.
Jer 50:26 Break open her granaries; pile her up like **heaps of grain**.
Hag 2:16 When anyone came to a **heap** *of* twenty measures, there were only

6895 עֶרְמוֹן *ʿermôn*, n.[m.]. [2] [√ 6867]

plane trees [2]

Ge 30:37 almond and **plane trees** and made white stripes on them by peeling
Eze 31:8 its boughs, nor could the **plane trees** compare with its branches—

6896 עֵרָן *ʿērān*, n.pr.m. [1] [→ 6897]

Eran [1]

Nu 26:36 were the descendants of Shuthelah: through **Eran**, the Eranite clan.

6897 עֵרָנִי *ʿērānî*, a.g. [1] [√ 6896]

Eranite [1]

Nu 26:36 were the descendants of Shuthelah: through Eran, the **Eranite** clan.

6898 עֲרֹעוֹר *ʿarʿôr*, n.pr.loc. [1 / 0] [cf. 6876]

Jdg 11:26 Israel occupied Heshbon, Aroer, [BHS *Aror* ?; NIV 6876]

6899 עַרְעָר *ʿarʿār*, a. [2 / 3] [→ 6900; cf. 6910]

bush [2], destitute [1]

Ps 102:17 [102:18] He will respond to the prayer of the **destitute**; he will
Jer 17:6 He will be like a **bush** in the wastelands; he will not see prosperity
48:6 Run for your lives; become like a **bush** [BHS 6876] in the desert.

6900 עַרְעָרָה *ʿarʿārâ*, n.pr.loc. Not used in NIV/BHS [cf. 6368, 6899]

6901 עֲרֹעֵרִי *ʿarōʿērî*, a.g. [1] [√ 6876; cf. 6910]

Aroerite [1]

1Ch 11:44 the Ashterathite, Shama and Jeiel the sons of Hotham the **Aroerite**,

6902 עֹרֶף *ʿōrep*, n.m. [33] [→ 6905]

backs [7], stiff-necked [+7997] [7], stiff-necked [+906+7996] [7], neck [4], stiff-necked [+7996] [4], back [2], *untranslated* [1], routed [+2200] [1]

Ge 49:8 will praise you; your hand will be on the **neck** *of* your enemies;
Ex 23:27 I will make all your enemies turn their **backs** and run.
32:9 said to Moses, "and they are a **stiff-necked** [+7997] people.
33:3 because you are a **stiff-necked** [+7997] people and I might destroy
33:5 "Tell the Israelites, 'You are a **stiff-necked** [+7997] people.
34:9 Although this is a **stiff-necked** [+7997] people, forgive our
Lev 5:8 He is to wring its head from its **neck**, not severing it completely,
Dt 9:6 good land to possess, for you are a **stiff-necked** [+7997] people.
9:13 this people, and they are a **stiff-necked** [+7997] people indeed!
10:16 therefore, and *do* not *be* **stiff-necked** [+7996] any longer.
31:27 For I know how rebellious and **stiff-necked** [+7997] you are.
Jos 7:8 can I say, now that Israel *has been* **routed** [+2200] by its enemies?
7:12 they turn their **backs** and run because they have been made liable
2Sa 22:41 You made my enemies turn their **backs** in flight, and I destroyed
2Ki 17:14 But they would not listen and *were* as **stiff-necked** [+906+7996] as
17:14 would not listen and were as stiff-necked as **[RPH]** their fathers,
2Ch 29:6 from the LORD's dwelling place and turned their **backs** on him.
30:8 *Do* not *be* **stiff-necked** [+7996], as your fathers were; submit to
36:13 *He became* **stiff-necked** [+906+7996] and hardened his heart and
Ne 9:16 our forefathers, became arrogant and **stiff-necked** [+906+7996],
9:17 *They became* **stiff-necked** [+906+7996] and in their rebellion
9:29 backs on you, *became* **stiff-necked** [+7996] and refused to listen.
Job 16:12 but he shattered me; he seized me by the **neck** and crushed me.
Ps 18:40 [18:41] You made my enemies turn their **backs** in flight, and I
Pr 29:1 A man *who remains* **stiff-necked** [+7996] after many rebukes will
Isa 48:4 the sinews of your **neck** were iron, your forehead was bronze.
Jer 2:27 They have turned their **backs** to me and not their faces; yet when
7:26 *They were* **stiff-necked** [+906+7996] and did more evil than their
17:23 *they were* **stiff-necked** [+906+7996] and would not listen or
18:17 I will show them my **back** and not my face in the day of their
19:15 because *they were* **stiff-necked** [+906+7996] and would not listen
32:33 They turned their **backs** to me and not their faces; though I taught
48:39 she is! How they wail! How Moab turns her **back** in shame!

6903 ¹עָרַף *ʿārap¹*, v. [2] [→ 6882, 6906?; cf. 8319]

drop [1], fall [1]

Dt 32:2 [A] *Let* my teaching **fall** like rain and my words descend like
33:28 [A] a land of grain and new wine, where the heavens **drop** dew.

6904 ²עָרַף *ʿārap²* v.den. [6]

break neck [3], breaks neck [1], demolish [1], neck was broken [1]

Ex 13:13 [A] firstborn donkey, but if you do not redeem it, **break** its **neck**.
34:20 [A] with a lamb, but if you do not redeem it, **break** its **neck**.
Dt 21:4 [A] There in the valley *they are to* **break** the heifer's **neck**.
21:6 [B] hands over the heifer whose **neck was broken** in the valley,
Isa 66:3 [A] whoever offers a lamb, like *one who* **breaks** a dog's **neck**;
Hos 10:2 [A] The LORD *will* **demolish** their altars and destroy their

6905 עָרְפָּה *ʿorpâ*, n.pr.f. [2] [√ 6902]

Orpah [2]

Ru 1:4 married Moabite women, one named **Orpah** and the other Ruth.
1:14 **Orpah** kissed her mother-in-law good-by, but Ruth clung to her.

6906 עֲרָפֶל *ʿarāpel*, n.m. [15] [√ 6903?]

thick darkness [4], blackness [2], dark cloud [2], dark clouds [2], darkness [2], deep darkness [2], deep gloom [1]

Ex 20:21 while Moses approached the **thick darkness** where God was.
Dt 4:11 fire to the very heavens, with black clouds and **deep darkness**.
5:22 mountain from out of the fire, the cloud and the **deep darkness**;
2Sa 22:10 the heavens and came down; **dark clouds** were under his feet.
1Ki 8:12 "The LORD has said that he would dwell in a **dark cloud**;
2Ch 6:1 "The LORD has said that he would dwell in a **dark cloud**;
Job 22:13 'What does God know? Does he judge through such **darkness**?
38:9 I made the clouds its garment and wrapped it in **thick darkness**,
Ps 18:9 [18:10] and came down; **dark clouds** were under his feet.
97:2 Clouds and **thick darkness** surround him; righteousness
Isa 60:2 darkness covers the earth and **thick darkness** is over the peoples,
Jer 13:16 but he will turn it to thick darkness and change it to **deep gloom**.
Eze 34:12 places where they were scattered on a day of clouds and **darkness**.
Joel 2:2 a day of darkness and gloom, a day of clouds and **blackness**.
Zep 1:15 a day of darkness and gloom, a day of clouds and **blackness**,

6907 עָרַץ *ʿāraṣ*, v. [15] [→ 5123, 5124, 6877, 6883]

terrified [4], dread [2], shake [2], cause terror [1], feared [1], give way to panic [1], is feared [1], stand in awe [1], terrify [1], torment [1]

Dt 1:29 [A] I said to you, "*Do* not *be* **terrified**; do not be afraid of them.
7:21 [A] *Do* not *be* **terrified** by them, for the LORD your God,
20:3 [A] do not be terrified or **give way to panic** before them.
31:6 [A] Do not be afraid or **terrified** because of them,
Jos 1:9 [A] *Do* not *be* **terrified**; do not be discouraged, for the LORD
Job 13:25 [A] *Will you* **torment** a windblown leaf? Will you chase after
31:34 [A] because *I* so **feared** the crowd and so dreaded the contempt
Ps 10:18 [A] in order that man, who is of the earth, *may* **terrify** no more.
89:7 [89:8] [C] In the council of the holy ones God is greatly **feared**;
Isa 2:19 [A] the splendor of his majesty, when he rises to **shake** the earth.
2:21 [A] the splendor of his majesty, when he rises to **shake** the earth.
8:12 [G] do not fear what they fear, and *do* not **dread** it.
8:13 [G] he is the one you are to fear, he is the *one* you are to **dread**,

Isa 29:23 [G] One of Jacob, and *will* **stand in awe** *of* the God of Israel.
47:12 [A] Perhaps you will succeed, perhaps *you will* **cause terror**.

6908 עָרַק 'āraq, v. [2]

gnawing pains [1], roamed [1]

Job 30: 3 [A] *they* **roamed** the parched land in desolate wastelands at
30:17 [A] Night pierces my bones; my **gnawing pains** never rest.

6909 עַרְקִי 'arqî, a.g. [2]

Arkites [2]

Ge 10:17 Hivites, **Arkites**, Sinites,
1Ch 1:15 Hivites, **Arkites**, Sinites,

6910 עָרַר 'ārar, v. [4] [→ 6839?, 6875, 6876, 6884, 6899, 6901; cf. 6867]

be leveled [+6910] [2], strip off clothes [+2256+7320] [1], stripped bare [1]

Isa 23:13 [D] *they* **stripped** its fortresses **bare** and turned it into a ruin.
32:11 [A] **Strip off** *your* **clothes** [+2256+7320], put sackcloth around
Jer 51:58 [F] "Babylon's thick wall *will* **be leveled** [+6910] and her high
51:58 [D] "Babylon's thick wall *will* **be leveled** [+6910] and her high

6911 עֶרֶשׂ 'ereś, n.f. [10]

bed [4], couches [2], *untranslated* [1], bed [+3661] [1], couch [1], sickbed [+1867] [1]

Dt 3:11 His **bed** was *made of* iron and was more than thirteen feet long
3:11 **[RPH]** and was more than thirteen feet long and six feet wide.
Job 7:13 When I think my **bed** will comfort me and my couch will ease my
Ps 6: 6 [6:7] flood my bed with weeping and drench my **couch** with tears.
41: 3 [41:4] The LORD will sustain him on his **sickbed** [+1867] and
132: 3 "I will not enter my house or go to my **bed** [+3661]—
Pr 7:16 I have covered my **bed** with colored linens from Egypt.
SS 1:16 you are, my lover! Oh, how charming! And our **bed** is verdant.
Am 3:12 on the edge of their beds and in Damascus on their **couches**."
6: 4 You lie on beds inlaid with ivory and lounge on your **couches**.

6912 עֵשֶׂב 'ēśeb, n.m. [33] [→ Ar 10572]

grass [11], plants [8], growing [4], plant [4], vegetation [2], *untranslated* [1], green thing [1], pasture [1], tender plants [1]

Ge 1:11 seed-bearing **plants** and trees on the land that bear fruit with seed
1:12 **plants** bearing seed according to their kinds and trees bearing fruit
1:29 "I give you every seed-bearing **plant** on the face of the whole earth
1:30 that has the breath of life in it—I give every green **plant** for food."
2: 5 appeared on the earth and no **plant** *of* the field had yet sprung up,
3:18 and thistles for you, and you will eat the **plants** *of* the field.
9: 3 Just as I gave you the green **plants**, I now give you everything.
Ex 9:22 and animals and on everything **growing** in the fields of Egypt."
9:25 it beat down everything **growing** *in* the fields and stripped every
10:12 swarm over the land and devour everything **growing** *in* the fields,
10:15 everything **growing** *in* the fields and the fruit on the trees.
10:15 Nothing green remained on tree or **plant** in all the land of Egypt.
Dt 11:15 I will provide **grass** in the fields for your cattle, and you will eat
29:23 [29:22] nothing sprouting, no **vegetation** growing on it.
32: 2 like showers on new grass, like abundant rain on **tender plants**.
2Ki 19:26 They are like **plants** *in* the field, like tender green shoots,
Job 5:25 will be many, and your descendants like the **grass** *of* the earth.
Ps 72:16 fruit flourish like Lebanon; let it thrive like the **grass** *of* the field.
92: 7 [92:8] that though the wicked spring up like **grass** and all
102: 4 [102:5] My heart is blighted and withered like **grass**; I forget to
102:11 [102:12] are like the evening shadow; I wither away like **grass**.
104:14 makes grass grow for the cattle, and **plants** for man to cultivate—
105:35 they ate up every **green thing** in their land, ate up the produce of
106:20 exchanged their Glory for an image of a bull, which eats **grass**.
Pr 19:12 rage is like the roar of a lion, but his favor is like dew on the **grass**.
27:25 new growth appears and the **grass** *from* the hills is gathered in,
Isa 37:27 They are like **plants** *in* the field, like tender green shoots,
42:15 lay waste the mountains and hills and dry up all their **vegetation**;
Jer 12: 4 will the land lie parched and the **grass** *in* every field be withered?
14: 6 and pant like jackals; their eyesight fails for lack of **pasture**."
Am 7: 2 When they had stripped **[NIE]** the land clean, I cried out,
Mic 5: 7 [5:6] like showers on the **grass**, which do not wait for man
Zec 10: 1 gives showers of rain to men, and **plants** of the field to everyone.

6913 עָשָׂה 'āśâ¹, v. [2626 / 2627] [→ 543, 3632, 3633, 3634, 5126, 5127, 5128, 5129, 6914, 6915, 6918, 6919]

do [405], did [286], made [270], done [263], make [161], *untranslated* [86], doing [61], does [55], follow [39], prepare [30], celebrate [25], deal [24], built [22], obey [22], Maker [21], show [21], carry out [20], be done [18], act [17], sacrifice [16], committed [14], inflict [14], provide [14], celebrated [13], prepared [13], keep [11], acted [10], bring [10], been done [9], gave [9], observe [9], performed [9], shown [9], accomplish [8], makes [8], offer [8], treated [8], work [8], brought [7], making [7], present [7], treat [7], workers [+4856] [7], bear [6], build [6], perform [6], worked [6], commits [5], deal with [5], forbidden [+4202] [5], is done [5], obeys [5], produce [5], showed [5], uphold [5], acquired [4], appointed [4], be made [4], carried out [4], deal [+6913] [4], exploits [4], give [4], grant [4], observed [4], provided [4], put [4], use [4], used [4], working [4], yield [4], achieve [3], acting [3], be granted [3], brought about [3], caused [3], completely destroy [+906+3986] [3], conduct [3], do work [3], engage [3], gain [3], gained [3], held [3], instituted [3], offered [3], performs [3], practice [3], produced [3], sends [3], showing [3], shows [3], supervise [3], used to make [3], waged [3], were carved [3], workmen [+4856] [3], works [3], achieved [2], acts [2], are done [2], bake [2], be fulfilled [2], be prepared [2], been made [2], been observed [2], behaved [2], busy [2], careful to carry out [+906+6913] [2], carrying out [2], carved [2], certainly carry out [+906+6913] [2], certainly do [+906+6913] [2], certainly make [+6913] [2], completely destroy [+928+3986] [2], conformed to [+3869] [2], consulted [2], deals [2], dealt [2], destroy completely [+3986] [2], do [+906+6913] [2], do great things [+6913] [2], done [+5126] [2], dug [2], establishes [2], fight [2], fighting [+4878] [2], follow [+3869] [2], followed the example [+3869+6913] [2], formed [2], fought [2], fulfill [2], fully accomplishes [+2256+7756] [2], get [2], happen [2], happens [2], imitate [+3869] [2], inflicted [2], introduced [2], kept [2], maintain [2], obeyed [2], open [2], ordained [2], pack [2], practices [2], put into practice [2], responsible [2], serve [2], set up [2], shaping [2], surely show [+6640+6913] [2], surely sprout [+4200+6913] [2], undertaken [2], was celebrated [2], worship [2], yielded [2], accomplished [1], accomplishing [1], add [1], adhere to [+3869] [1], administer [1], administrators [+4856] [1], am [1], amassed [1], answer [1], applies [1], apply [1], are [1], artificial [1], assign [1], assigned [1], at war [+4878] [1], at work [1], attack [+4200] [1], attend to [1], avenged [+4200+5935] [1], be carried out [1], be completed [1], be paid back [1], be presented [1], be used [1], be [1], bearing [1], became famous [+9005] [1], been committed [1], been constructed [1], been followed [1], been used [+928+4856] [1], been [1], began [1], behave [1], behaves [1], bring up [1], bulges with flesh [+6584+7089] [1], cancel debts [+9024] [1], carried on [1], carried through [1], carrying on [1], carves [1], cast [1], celebrating [1], celebration [1], comes [1], commit [1], committing [1], construct [1], constructed [1], continue [1], continued [1], cooked [1], copied [1], created [1], creature [1], crop [1], custom [+4027] [1], custom [1], customary [1], deeds [1], defends [1], defiled[s] [1], deserve [1], destroy completely [+907+3986] [1], did[s] so [+906+2021+7175] [1], diligent [1], displayed [1], do something [1], dressed [1], earners [1], earns [1], engaged in [1], erected [1], establish [1], established [1], evildoer [+8288] [1], evildoer [+8402] [1], evildoers [+8402] [1], executed [1], exempt from taxes [+906+2930] [1], exercises [1], express [1], faithfully [+622] [1], fashion [1], fashioned [1], finished [1], fit for [1], follow [+4027] [1], follow lead [+4027] [1], followed [+4027] [1], founded [1], fulfill [+3869+4027+7023] [1], fulfilled [1], fulfills [1], fully obeyed [+2256+3869+9048] [1], gains [1], get ready [1], give over [1], given [1], goes on [1], going [1], got ready [1], granted [1], grow [1], hammer [+906+8393] [1], hammer out [+5251] [1], handle [1], handled [1], harm [+4200+8273] [1], harm [+4200+8288] [1], harm [+6640+8273] [1], harm [+6640+8288] [1], have [1], have[s] [1], help [+4200] [1], help [1], holding [1], honor [+3702] [1], honored [+3883+4200] [1], howl [+5027] [1], in charge [1], is built [1], is carried out [1], is done [+5126] [1], is made [1], judge[s] [1], judges [+5477] [1], keeping [1], keeps [1], make provision [1], make up [1], manage [1], marks off [1], master craftsmen [+4856] [1], may do [1], measured [1], meet [1], merchants [+4856] [1], molded [1], mount [1], mounted [1], mourn [+65+4200] [1], move [1], obey [+906+2256+9068] [1], observance [1], occurs [1], officiate [1], on way [+2006] [1], oppressed [+928+2021+4200+6945] [1], passes through [1], persist [1], persisted in [+3869] [1], pervert [+928+6404] [1], piled [1], presents [1], proclaimed [1], proud [+1452] [1], provides [1], providing [1], punish [+928+5477] [1], put forth [1], put in jeopardy [+928+9214] [1], ready [1], received [1], reduces [1], render [1], rescued [+928+9591] [1], resist [1], resorted [1], rich [1], roughs out [1], sacrificed [1], secures [1], serve [+7372] [1], set [1], shapes [1], sins defiantly [+928+3338+8123] [1], sins unintentionally [+928+8705] [1], still to come [+4202] [1], stir up [1], such[s] [+2021] [1], take action [1], take part [+7928] [1], take place [1], take [1], taken care of [1], taking place [1], these men[s] [+2021+4856] [1], trained [1], treated [+6640] [1], tried [+4027] [1], trim [1], trimmed [1], turns to [1], unlike [+4027+4202] [1], upheld [1], upholds [1], use [+4856] [1], use [+928+4856] [1], use to make [1], useful [1], wage [1], waging [1], was happening [1], was made [1], was spent for making [+4946] [1], well-trained [+4878] [1], went about [1], went on [1], went to war [+906+906+4878] [1], were made [1], were practiced [1], were prepared [1], were[s] [1], won [1], work [+4856] [1], work [+5126] [1], worker [1], workers [1], working [+4856] [1], workmen

[+928+2021+4856] [1], works out [1], wrongdoing [+8400] [1], wrongs [+2633] [1]

Ge 1: 7 [A] So God **made** the expanse and separated the water under the
1: 11 [A] and trees on the land *that* **bear** fruit with seed in it,
1: 12 [A] trees **bearing** fruit with seed in it according to their kinds.
1: 16 [A] **made** two great lights—the greater light to govern the day and
1: 25 [A] God **made** the wild animals according to their kinds, the
1: 26 [A] God said, "*Let us* **make** man in our image, in our likeness,
1: 31 [A] God saw all that *he had* **made**, and it was very good.
2: 2 [A] seventh day God had finished the work *he had been* **doing**;
2: 2 [A] so on the seventh day he rested from all his work. **[RPH]**
2: 3 [A] it he rested from all the work of creating that he *had* **done**.
2: 4 [A] When the LORD God **made** the earth and the heavens—
2: 18 [A] the man to be alone. *I will* **make** a helper suitable for him."
3: 1 [A] than any of the wild animals the LORD God *had* **made**.
3: 7 [A] fig leaves together and **made** coverings for themselves.
3: 13 [A] God said to the woman, "What is this *you have* **done**?"
3: 14 [A] "Because *you have* **done** this, "Cursed are you above all the
3: 21 [A] The LORD God **made** garments of skin for Adam and his
4: 10 [A] The LORD said, "What *have you* **done**? Listen!
5: 1 [A] When God created man, *he* **made** him in the likeness of God.
6: 6 [A] The LORD was grieved that *he had* **made** man on the
6: 7 [A] birds of the air—for I am grieved that *I have* **made** them."
6: 14 [A] So **make** yourself an ark of cypress wood; make rooms in it
6: 14 [A] **make** rooms in it and coat it with pitch inside and out.
6: 15 [A] This is how *you are to* **build** it: The ark is to be 450 feet
6: 16 [A] **Make** a roof for it and finish the ark to within 18 inches of
6: 16 [A] Put a door in the side of the ark and **make** lower, middle
6: 22 [A] Noah **did** everything just as God commanded him.
6: 22 [A] Noah did everything just as God commanded him. **[RPH]**
7: 4 [A] the face of the earth every living creature *I have* **made**."
7: 5 [A] And Noah **did** all that the LORD commanded him.
8: 6 [A] After forty days Noah opened the window *he had* **made** in
8: 21 [A] never again will I destroy all living creatures, as *I have* **done**.
9: 6 [A] blood be shed; for in the image of God *has* God **made** man.
9: 24 [A] and found out what his youngest son *had* **done** to him,
11: 4 [A] so that *we may* **make** a name for ourselves and not be
11: 6 [A] speaking the same language they have begun to **do** this,
11: 6 [A] then nothing they plan to **do** will be impossible for them.
12: 2 [A] "*I will* **make** you into a great nation and I will bless you; I
12: 5 [A] and the people *they had* **acquired** in Haran,
12: 18 [A] summoned Abram. "What *have you* **done** to me?" he said.
13: 4 [A] where *he had* first **built** an altar. There Abram called on the
14: 2 [A] **went to war against** [+906+906+4878] Bera king of Sodom,
16: 6 [A] Abram said. "**Do** with her whatever you think best."
18: 5 [A] your servant." "Very well," they answered, "**do** as you say."
18: 6 [A] three seahs of fine flour and knead it and **bake** some bread."
18: 7 [A] and gave it to a servant, who hurried to **prepare** it.
18: 8 [A] some curds and milk and the calf that *had been* **prepared**,
18: 17 [A] "Shall I hide from Abraham what I *am about to* **do**?
18: 19 [A] him to keep the way of the LORD by **doing** what is right
18: 21 [A] see if *what they have* **done** is as bad as the outcry that has
18: 25 [A] Far be it from you *to* **do** such a thing—to kill the righteous
18: 25 [A] be it from you! *Will* not the Judge of all the earth **do** right?"
18: 29 [A] He said, "For the sake of forty, *I will* not **do** it."
18: 30 [A] He answered, "*I will* not **do** it if I find thirty there."
19: 3 [A] *He* **prepared** a meal for them, baking bread without yeast,
19: 8 [A] them out to you, and *you can* **do** what you like with them.
19: 8 [A] don't **do** anything to these men, for they have come under the
19: 19 [A] and you have **shown** great kindness to me in sparing my life.
19: 22 [A] because I cannot **do** anything until you reach it."
20: 5 [A] *I have* **done** this with a clear conscience and clean hands."
20: 6 [A] I know *you* **did** this with a clear conscience, and so I have
20: 9 [A] called Abraham in and said, "What *have you* **done** to us?
20: 9 [A] *You have* **done** things to me that should not be done."
20: 9 [C] You have done things to me that *should* not **be done**."
20: 10 [A] asked Abraham, "What was your reason for **doing** this?"
20: 13 [A] I said to her, 'This is how *you can* **show** your love to me:
21: 1 [A] and the LORD **did** for Sarah what he had promised.
21: 6 [A] Sarah said, "God *has* **brought** me laughter, and everyone
21: 8 [A] and on the day Isaac was weaned Abraham **held** a great feast.
21: 22 [A] said to Abraham, "God is with you in everything you **do**.
21: 23 [A] **Show** to me and the country where you are living as an alien
21: 23 [A] living as an alien the same kindness *I have* **shown** to you."
21: 26 [A] Abimelech said, "I don't know who *has* **done** this. You did
22: 12 [A] lay a hand on the boy," he said. "*Do* not **do** anything to him.
22: 16 [A] that because *you have* **done** this and have not withheld your
24: 12 [A] success today, and **show** kindness to my master Abraham.
24: 14 [A] By this I will know that *you have* **shown** kindness to my
24: 49 [A] Now if you will **show** kindness and faithfulness to my
24: 66 [A] Then the servant told Isaac all *he had* **done**.
26: 10 [A] Then Abimelech said, "What is this *you have* **done** to us?
26: 29 [A] that *you will* **do** us no harm, just as we did not molest you
26: 29 [A] but always **treated** you well and sent you away in peace.
26: 30 [A] Isaac then **made** a feast for them, and they ate and drank.
27: 4 [A] **Prepare** me the kind of tasty food I like and bring it to me to
27: 7 [A] me some game and **prepare** me some tasty food to eat,
27: 9 [A] so *I can* **prepare** some tasty food for your father, just the
27: 14 [A] she **prepared** some tasty food, just the way his father liked
27: 17 [A] to her son Jacob the tasty food and the bread *she had* **made**.
27: 19 [A] *I have* **done** as you told me. Please sit up and eat some of my
27: 31 [A] He too **prepared** some tasty food and brought it to his father.
27: 37 [A] and new wine. So what *can I possibly* **do** for you, my son?"
27: 45 [A] is no longer angry with you and forgets what *you* **did** to him,
28: 15 [A] I will not leave you until *I have* **done** what I have promised
29: 22 [A] brought together all the people of the place and **gave** a feast.
29: 25 [A] So Jacob said to Laban, "What is this *you have* **done** to me?
29: 26 [C] "*It is* not our **custom** [+4027] here to give the younger
29: 28 [A] Jacob **did** so. He finished the week with Leah, and
30: 30 [A] when *may* I **do** *something* for my own household?"
30: 31 [A] "But if *you will* **do** this one thing for me, I will go on tending
31: 1 [A] *has* **gained** all this wealth from what belonged to our father."
31: 12 [A] for I have seen all that Laban *has been* **doing** to you.
31: 16 [A] to us and our children. So **do** whatever God has told you."
31: 26 [A] Laban said to Jacob, "What *have you* **done**? You've
31: 28 [A] and my daughters good-by. *You have* **done** a foolish thing.
31: 29 [A] I have the power to **harm** [+6640+8273] you; but last night
31: 43 [A] Yet what *can I* **do** today about these daughters of mine,
31: 46 [A] So they took stones and **piled** them *in* a heap, and they ate
32: 10 [32:11] [A] and faithfulness *you have* **shown** your servant.
33: 17 [A] built a place for himself and **made** shelters for his livestock.
34: 7 [A] because Shechem *had* **done** a disgraceful thing in Israel by
34: 7 [C] with Jacob's daughter—a *thing that should* not **be done**.
34: 14 [A] They said to them, "We can't **do** such a thing; we can't give
34: 19 [A] lost no time in **doing** what they said, because he was
34: 31 [A] "*Should he have* **treated** our sister like a prostitute?"
35: 1 [A] up to Bethel and settle there, and **build** an altar there to God,
35: 3 [A] let us go up to Bethel, where *I will* **build** an altar to God,
37: 3 [A] his old age; and *he* **made** a richly ornamented robe for him.
38: 10 [A] What *he* **did** was wicked in the LORD's sight; so he put
39: 3 [A] and that the LORD gave him success in everything he **did**,
39: 9 [A] How then *could I* **do** such a wicked thing and sin against
39: 11 [A] One day he went into the house to **attend to** his duties,
39: 19 [A] saying, "This is how your slave **treated** me," he burned with
39: 22 [A] and he was *made* **responsible** *for* all that was done there.
39: 22 [A] and he was made responsible for all that *was* **done** there.
39: 23 [A] was with Joseph and gave him success in whatever he **did**.
40: 14 [A] all goes well with you, remember me and **show** me kindness;
40: 15 [A] even here *I have* **done** nothing to deserve being put in a
40: 20 [A] Pharaoh's birthday, and *he* **gave** a feast for all his officials.
41: 25 [A] God has revealed to Pharaoh what *he is about to* **do**.
41: 28 [A] to Pharaoh: God has shown Pharaoh what *he is about to* **do**.
41: 32 [A] has been firmly decided by God, and God *will* **do** it soon.
41: 34 [A] **[NIE]** Let Pharaoh appoint commissioners over the land to
41: 47 [A] During the seven years of abundance the land **produced**
41: 55 [A] all the Egyptians, "Go to Joseph and **do** what he tells you."
42: 18 [A] said to them, "**Do** this and you will live, for I fear God:
42: 20 [A] and that you may not die." This *they proceeded to* **do**.
42: 25 [A] provisions for their journey. After this *was* **done** for them,
42: 28 [A] and said, "What is this that God *has* **done** to us?"
43: 11 [A] their father Israel said to them, "If it must be, then **do** this:
43: 17 [A] The man **did** as Joseph told him and took the men to
44: 2 [A] with the silver for his grain." And *he* **did** as Joseph said.
44: 5 [A] for divination? This is a wicked thing *you have* **done**.' "
44: 7 [A] Far be it from your servants *to* **do** anything like that!
44: 15 [A] Joseph said to them, "What is this *you have* **done**? Don't
44: 17 [A] Joseph said, "Far be it from me *to* **do** such a thing!
45: 17 [A] Pharaoh said to Joseph, "Tell your brothers, '**Do** this:
45: 19 [A] "You are also directed to tell them, '**Do** this: Take some carts
45: 21 [A] So the sons of Israel **did** this. Joseph gave them carts,
47: 29 [A] promise that *you will* **show** me kindness and faithfulness.
47: 30 [A] me where they are buried." "I *will* **do** as you say," he said.
50: 10 [A] there Joseph **observed** a seven-day period of mourning for
50: 12 [A] So Jacob's sons **did** as he had commanded them:
50: 20 [A] God intended it for good to **accomplish** what is now being
Ex 1: 17 [A] and *did* not **do** what the king of Egypt had told them to do;
1: 18 [A] the midwives and asked them, "Why *have you* **done** this?
1: 21 [A] midwives feared God, *he* **gave** them families of their own.
2: 4 [C] His sister stood at a distance to see what *would* **happen** to
3: 16 [B] over you and have seen what *has* **been done** to you in Egypt.
3: 20 [A] strike the Egyptians with all the wonders that *I will* **perform**
4: 15 [A] I will help both of you speak and will teach you what *to* **do**.
4: 17 [A] in your hand so *you can* **perform** miraculous signs with it."
4: 21 [A] see that *you* **perform** before Pharaoh all the wonders I have
4: 30 [A] to Moses. *He* also **performed** the signs before the people,
5: 8 [A] require them *to* **make** the same number of bricks as before;
5: 9 [A] so that *they keep* **working** and pay no attention to lies."

Ex 5:15 [A] to Pharaoh: "Why *have you* **treated** your servants this way?
5:16 [A] servants are given no straw, yet we are told, '**Make** bricks!'
6:1 [A] said to Moses, "Now you will see what *I will* **do** to Pharaoh:
7:6 [A] Moses and Aaron **did** just as the LORD commanded them.
7:6 [A] Aaron did just as the LORD commanded them. **[RPH]**
7:10 [A] went to Pharaoh and **did** just as the LORD commanded.
7:11 [A] the Egyptian magicians also **did** the same things by their
7:20 [A] Moses and Aaron **did** just as the LORD had commanded.
7:22 [A] the Egyptian magicians **did** the same things by their secret
8:7 [8:3] [A] the magicians **did** the same things by their secret arts;
8:13 [8:9] [A] the LORD **did** what Moses asked. The frogs died in
8:17 [8:13] [A] *They* **did** this, and when Aaron stretched out his
8:18 [8:14] [A] when the magicians **tried** [+4027] to produce gnats
8:24 [8:20] [A] the LORD **did** this. Dense swarms of flies poured
8:26 [8:22] [A] **[NIE]** The sacrifices we offer the LORD our God
8:31 [8:27] [A] the LORD **did** what Moses asked: The flies left
9:5 [A] and said, "Tomorrow the LORD *will* **do** this in the land."
9:6 [A] the next day the LORD **did** it: All the livestock of the
10:25 [A] and burnt offerings *to* **present** to the LORD our God.
11:10 [A] and Aaron **performed** all these wonders before Pharaoh,
12:12 [A] and *I will* **bring** judgment on all the gods of Egypt.
12:16 [C] **Do** no work at all on these days, except to prepare food for
12:16 [C] to prepare food for everyone to eat—that is all you *may* **do**.
12:28 [A] The Israelites **did** just what the LORD commanded Moses
12:28 [A] what the LORD commanded Moses and Aaron. **[RPH]**
12:35 [A] The Israelites **did** as Moses instructed and asked the
12:39 [A] and did not have time *to* **prepare** food for themselves.
12:47 [A] The whole community of Israel *must* **celebrate** it.
12:48 [A] "An alien living among you *who wants to* **celebrate** the
12:48 [A] then *he may* **take part** [+7928] like one born in the land.
12:50 [A] All the Israelites **did** just what the LORD had commanded
12:50 [A] the LORD had commanded Moses and Aaron. **[RPH]**
13:8 [A] because of what the LORD **did** for me when I came out of
14:4 [A] will know that I am the LORD." So the Israelites **did** this.
14:5 [A] their minds about them and said, "What *have we* **done**?
14:11 [A] What *have you* **done** to us by bringing us out of Egypt?
14:13 [A] you will see the deliverance the LORD *will* **bring** you
14:31 [A] the great power the LORD **displayed** against the Egyptians,
15:11 [A] majestic in holiness, awesome in glory, **working** wonders?
15:26 [A] of the LORD your God and **do** what is right in his eyes,
16:17 [A] The Israelites **did** as they were told; some gathered much,
17:4 [A] out to the LORD, "What *am I to* **do** with these people?
17:6 [A] So Moses **did** this in the sight of the elders of Israel.
17:10 [A] So Joshua **[NIE]** fought the Amalekites as Moses had
18:1 [A] heard of everything God *had* **done** for Moses and for his
18:8 [A] about everything the LORD *had* **done** to Pharaoh
18:9 [A] *had* **done** for Israel in rescuing them from the hand of the
18:14 [A] When his father-in-law saw all that Moses *was* **doing** for the
18:14 [A] he said, "What is this you *are* **doing** for the people?
18:17 [A] father-in-law replied, "What you *are* **doing** is not good.
18:18 [A] The work is too heavy for you; you cannot **handle** it alone.
18:20 [A] them the way to live and the duties *they are to* **perform**.
18:23 [A] If *you* **do** this and God so commands, you will be able to
18:24 [A] listened to his father-in-law and **did** everything he said.
19:4 [A] 'You yourselves have seen what *I* **did** to Egypt, and how I
19:8 [A] "*We will* **do** everything the LORD has said."
20:4 [A] "*You shall* not **make** for yourself an idol in the form of
20:6 [A] **showing** love to a thousand ⌞generations⌟ of those who love
20:9 [A] Six days you shall labor and **do** all your work,
20:10 [A] On it *you shall* not **do** any work, neither you, nor your son
20:11 [A] the LORD **made** the heavens and the earth, the sea, and
20:23 [A] *Do* not **make** any gods to be alongside me; do not make for
20:23 [A] *do* not **make** for yourselves gods of silver or gods of gold.
20:24 [A] " '**Make** an altar of earth for me and sacrifice on it your burnt
20:25 [A] If *you* **make** an altar of stones for me, do not build it with
21:9 [A] her for his son, *he must* **grant** her the rights of a daughter.
21:11 [A] If *he does* not **provide** her *with* these three things, she is to
21:31 [C] This law also **applies** if the bull gores a son or daughter.
22:30 [22:29] [A] **Do** the same with your cattle and your sheep.
23:11 [A] **Do** the same with your vineyard and your olive grove.
23:12 [A] "Six days **do** your work, but on the seventh day do not work,
23:22 [A] If you listen carefully to what he says and **do** all that I say,
23:24 [A] their gods or worship them or **follow** [+3869] their practices.
24:3 [A] one voice, "Everything the LORD has said *we will* **do**."
24:7 [A] "*We will* **do** everything the LORD has said;
25:8 [A] "Then *have them* **make** a sanctuary for me, and I will dwell
25:9 [A] **Make** this tabernacle and all its furnishings exactly like the
25:10 [A] "*Have them* **make** a chest of acacia wood—two and a half
25:11 [A] both inside and out, and **make** a gold molding around it.
25:13 [A] **make** poles of acacia wood and overlay them with gold.
25:17 [A] "**Make** an atonement cover of pure gold—two and a half
25:18 [A] **make** two cherubim *out of* hammered gold at the ends of the
25:18 [A] make two cherubim out of hammered gold **[RPH]** at the
25:19 [A] **Make** one cherub on one end and the second cherub on the
25:19 [A] **make** the cherubim of one piece with the cover, at the two
25:23 [A] "**Make** a table of acacia wood—two cubits long, a cubit wide
25:24 [A] it with pure gold and **make** a gold molding around it.
25:25 [A] Also **make** around it a rim a handbreadth wide and put a gold
25:25 [A] a rim a handbreadth wide and **put** a gold molding on the rim.
25:26 [A] **Make** four gold rings for the table and fasten them to the
25:28 [A] **Make** the poles *of* acacia wood, overlay them with gold
25:29 [A] **make** its plates and dishes *of* pure gold, as well as its pitchers
25:29 [A] and bowls for the pouring out of offerings. **[RPH]**
25:31 [A] "**Make** a lampstand *of* pure gold and hammer it out, base and
25:31 [C] "Make a lampstand of pure gold and **hammer it out** [+5251],
25:37 [A] "Then **make** its seven lamps and set them up on it so that
25:39 [A] A talent of pure gold *is to be* **used** *for* the lampstand and all
25:40 [A] See that *you* **make** them according to the pattern shown you
26:1 [A] "**Make** the tabernacle with ten curtains of finely twisted linen
26:1 [A] cherubim worked into them by a skilled craftsman. **[RPH]**
26:4 [A] **Make** loops of blue material along the edge of the end
26:4 [A] one set, and **do** the same with the end curtain in the other set.
26:5 [A] **Make** fifty loops on one curtain and fifty loops on the end
26:5 [A] and fifty loops **[RPH]** on the end curtain of the other set,
26:6 [A] **make** fifty gold clasps and use them to fasten the curtains
26:7 [A] "**Make** curtains of goat hair for the tent over the tabernacle—
26:7 [A] for the tent over the tabernacle—eleven altogether. **[RPH]**
26:10 [A] **Make** fifty loops along the edge of the end curtain in one set
26:11 [A] **make** fifty bronze clasps and put them in the loops to fasten
26:14 [A] **Make** for the tent a covering of ram skins dyed red, and over
26:15 [A] "**Make** upright frames *of* acacia wood for the tabernacle.
26:17 [A] each other. **Make** all the frames of the tabernacle in this way.
26:18 [A] **Make** twenty frames for the south side of the tabernacle
26:19 [A] **make** forty silver bases to go under them—two bases for
26:22 [A] **Make** six frames for the far end, that is, the west end of the
26:23 [A] and **make** two frames for the corners at the far end.
26:26 [A] "Also **make** crossbars of acacia wood: five for the frames on
26:29 [A] frames with gold and **make** gold rings to hold the crossbars.
26:31 [A] "**Make** a curtain of blue, purple and scarlet yarn and finely
26:31 [A] with cherubim worked into it by a skilled craftsman. **[RPH]**
26:36 [A] "For the entrance to the tent **make** a curtain of blue, purple
26:37 [A] **Make** gold hooks for this curtain and five posts of acacia
27:1 [A] "**Build** an altar of acacia wood, three cubits high; it is to be
27:2 [A] **Make** a horn at each of the four corners, so that the horns
27:3 [A] **Make** all its utensils *of* bronze—its pots to remove the ashes,
27:3 [A] **[RPH]** its pots to remove the ashes, and its shovels,
27:4 [A] **Make** a grating for it, a bronze network, and make a bronze
27:4 [A] **make** a bronze ring at each of the four corners of the
27:6 [A] **Make** poles of acacia wood for the altar and overlay them
27:8 [A] **Make** the altar hollow, *out of* boards. It is to be made just as
27:8 [A] *It is to be* **made** just as you were shown on the mountain.
27:9 [A] "**Make** a courtyard for the tabernacle. The south side shall be
28:2 [A] **Make** sacred garments for your brother Aaron, to give him
28:3 [A] in such matters that *they are to* **make** garments for Aaron,
28:4 [A] These are the garments *they are to* **make**: a breastpiece, an
28:4 [A] *They are to* **make** these sacred garments for your brother
28:6 [A] "**Make** the ephod *of* gold, and *of* blue, purple and scarlet
28:11 [A] a seal. Then **mount** the stones in gold filigree settings
28:13 [A] **Make** gold filigree settings
28:14 [A] like a rope, **[RPH]** and attach the chains to the settings.
28:15 [A] "**Fashion** a breastpiece for making decisions—the work of a
28:15 [A] **Make** it like the ephod: of gold, and of blue, purple
28:15 [A] purple and scarlet yarn, and of finely twisted linen. **[RPH]**
28:22 [A] "For the breastpiece **make** braided chains of pure gold, like a
28:23 [A] **Make** two gold rings for it and fasten them to two corners of
28:26 [A] **Make** two gold rings and attach them to the other two
28:27 [A] **Make** two more gold rings and attach them to the bottom of
28:31 [A] "**Make** the robe of the ephod entirely of blue cloth,
28:33 [A] **Make** pomegranates of blue, purple and scarlet yarn around
28:36 [A] "**Make** a plate of pure gold and engrave on it as on a seal:
28:39 [A] the tunic of fine linen and **make** the turban of fine linen.
28:39 [A] of fine linen. The sash *is to* **be** the work of an embroiderer.
28:40 [A] **Make** tunics, sashes and headbands for Aaron's sons, to give
28:40 [A] **[RPH]** sashes and headbands for Aaron's sons,
28:40 [A] for Aaron's sons, **[RPH]** to give them dignity and honor.
28:42 [A] "**Make** linen undergarments as a covering for the body,
29:1 [A] "This is what *you are to* **do** to consecrate them, so they may
29:2 [A] *from* fine wheat flour, without yeast, **make** bread, and cakes
29:35 [A] "**Do** for Aaron and his sons everything I have commanded
29:36 [A] **Sacrifice** a bull each day as a sin offering to make
29:38 [A] "This is what *you are to* **offer** on the altar regularly each
29:39 [A] **Offer** one in the morning and the other at twilight.
29:39 [A] Offer one in the morning and the other **[RPH]** at twilight.
29:41 [A] **Sacrifice** the other lamb at twilight with the same grain
29:41 [A] **[RPH]** a pleasing aroma, an offering made to the LORD
30:1 [A] "**Make** an altar of acacia wood for burning incense.
30:1 [A] "Make an altar of acacia wood for burning incense. **[RPH]**
30:3 [A] the horns with pure gold, and **make** a gold molding around it.

Ex 30: 4 [A] **Make** two gold rings for the altar below the molding—
30: 4 [A] on opposite sides—**[RPH]** to hold the poles used to carry it.
30: 5 [A] **Make** the poles *of* acacia wood and overlay them with gold.
30: 18 [A] "**Make** a bronze basin, with its bronze stand, for washing.
30: 25 [A] **Make** these *into* a sacred anointing oil, a fragrant blend,
30: 32 [A] and *do* not **make** any oil with the same formula.
30: 35 [A] **make** a fragrant blend of incense, the work of a perfumer.
30: 37 [A] *Do* not **make** any incense with this formula for yourselves;
30: 37 [A] Do not make any incense **[RPH]** with this formula for
30: 38 [A] Whoever **makes** any like it to enjoy its fragrance must be cut
31: 4 [A] to make artistic designs for **work** in gold, silver and bronze,
31: 5 [A] to work in wood, and to **engage** in all kinds of craftsmanship.
31: 6 [A] Also I have given skill to all the craftsmen *to* **make**
31: 11 [A] *They are to* **make** them just as I commanded you."
31: 14 [A] whoever **does** any work on that day must be cut off from his
31: 15 [C] For six days, work *is to* **be done**, but the seventh day is a
31: 15 [A] Whoever **does** any work on the Sabbath day must be put to
31: 16 [A] **celebrating** it for the generations to come as a lasting
31: 17 [A] for in six days the LORD **made** the heavens and the earth,
32: 1 [A] and said, "Come, **make** us gods who will go before us.
32: 4 [A] and **made** it *into* an idol cast in the shape of a calf,
32: 8 [A] and *have* **made** themselves an idol cast in the shape of a calf.
32: 10 [A] may destroy them. Then *I will* **make** you into a great nation."
32: 14 [A] did not **bring** on his people the disaster he had threatened.
32: 20 [A] And he took the calf *they had* **made** and burned it in the fire;
32: 21 [A] He said to Aaron, "What *did* these people **do** to you, that you
32: 23 [A] They said to me, '**Make** us gods who will go before us.
32: 28 [A] The Levites **did** as Moses commanded, and that day about
32: 31 [A] have committed! *They have* **made** themselves gods of gold.
32: 35 [A] because of what *they* **did** *with* the calf Aaron had made.
32: 35 [A] because of what they did with the calf Aaron *had* **made**.
33: 5 [A] off your ornaments and I will decide what *to* **do** with you.' "
33: 17 [A] "*I will* **do** the very thing you have asked, because I am
34: 10 [A] Before all your people *I will* **do** wonders never before done
34: 10 [A] how awesome is the work that I, the LORD, *will* **do** for you.
34: 17 [A] "*Do* not **make** cast idols.
34: 22 [A] "**Celebrate** the Feast of Weeks with the firstfruits of the
35: 1 [A] "These are the things the LORD has commanded you to **do**:
35: 2 [C] For six days, work *is to* **be done**, but the seventh day shall be
35: 2 [A] Whoever **does** any work on it must be put to death.
35: 10 [A] to come and **make** everything the LORD has commanded:
35: 29 [A] the LORD through Moses had commanded them to **do**.
35: 32 [A] to make artistic designs for **work** in gold, silver and bronze,
35: 33 [A] in wood and to **engage** in all kinds of artistic craftsmanship.
35: 35 [A] He has filled them with skill to **do** all kinds of work as
35: 35 [A] all of them **master craftsmen** [+4856] and designers.
36: 1 [A] ability to know how to **carry out** all the work of constructing
36: 1 [A] *are to* **do** *the* **work** just as the LORD has commanded."
36: 2 [A] given ability and who was willing to come and **do** the work.
36: 3 [A] brought to **carry out** the work of constructing the sanctuary.
36: 4 [A] So all the skilled craftsmen who *were* **doing** all the work on
36: 4 [A] doing all the work on the sanctuary left their work **[RPH]**
36: 5 [A] for doing the work the LORD commanded to *be* **done**."
36: 6 [A] or woman *is to* **make** anything else as an offering for the
36: 7 [A] because what they already had was more than enough to **do**
36: 8 [A] All the skilled men among the **workmen** [+4856] made the
36: 8 [A] All the skilled men among the workmen **made** the tabernacle
36: 8 [A] cherubim worked into them by a skilled craftsman. **[RPH]**
36: 11 [A] *they* **made** loops of blue material along the edge of the end
36: 11 [A] and the same *was* **done** with the end curtain in the other set.
36: 12 [A] *They* also **made** fifty loops on one curtain and fifty loops on
36: 12 [A] and **[RPH]** fifty loops on the end curtain of the other set,
36: 13 [A] *they* **made** fifty gold clasps and used them to fasten the two
36: 14 [A] *They* **made** curtains of goat hair for the tent over the
36: 14 [A] for the tent over the tabernacle—eleven altogether. **[RPH]**
36: 17 [A] *they* **made** fifty loops along the edge of the end curtain in
36: 17 [A] also **[RPH]** along the edge of the end curtain in the other
36: 18 [A] *They* **made** fifty bronze clasps to fasten the tent together as a
36: 19 [A] *they* **made** for the tent a covering of ram skins dyed red,
36: 20 [A] *They* **made** upright frames of acacia wood for the tabernacle.
36: 22 [A] *They* **made** all the frames of the tabernacle in this way.
36: 23 [A] *They* **made** twenty frames for the south side of the
36: 24 [A] **made** forty silver bases to go under them—two bases for
36: 25 [A] the north side of the tabernacle, *they* **made** twenty frames
36: 27 [A] *They* **made** six frames for the far end, that is, the west end of
36: 28 [A] two frames *were* **made** for the corners of the tabernacle at
36: 29 [A] to the top and fitted into a single ring; both *were* **made** alike.
36: 31 [A] *They* also **made** crossbars of acacia wood: five for the
36: 33 [A] *They* **made** the center crossbar so that it extended from end
36: 34 [A] frames with gold and **made** gold rings to hold the crossbars.
36: 35 [A] *They* **made** the curtain *of* blue, purple and scarlet yarn and
36: 35 [A] with cherubim worked into **[RPH]** it by a skilled craftsman.
36: 36 [A] *They* **made** four posts of acacia wood for it and overlaid
36: 37 [A] For the entrance to the tent *they* **made** a curtain of blue,
37: 1 [A] Bezalel **made** the ark *of* acacia wood—two and a half cubits
37: 2 [A] both inside and out, and **made** a gold molding around it.
37: 4 [A] *he* **made** poles of acacia wood and overlaid them with gold.
37: 6 [A] *He* **made** the atonement cover *of* pure gold—two and a half
37: 7 [A] *he* **made** two cherubim *out of* hammered gold at the ends of
37: 7 [A] he made two cherubim out of hammered gold **[RPH]** at the
37: 8 [A] at the two ends *he* **made** them of one piece with the cover.
37: 10 [A] *They* **made** the table *of* acacia wood—two cubits long, a
37: 11 [A] it with pure gold and **made** a gold molding around it.
37: 12 [A] *They* also **made** around it a rim a handbreadth wide and put
37: 12 [A] a rim a handbreadth wide and **put** a gold molding on the rim.
37: 15 [A] The poles for carrying the table *were* **made** *of* acacia wood
37: 16 [A] *they* **made** *from* pure gold the articles for the table—its plates
37: 17 [A] *They* **made** the lampstand *of* pure gold and hammered it out,
37: 17 [A] of pure gold and hammered it out, **[RPH]** base and shaft;
37: 23 [A] *They* **made** its seven lamps, as well as its wick trimmers
37: 24 [A] *They* **made** the lampstand and all its accessories from one
37: 25 [A] *They* **made** the altar of incense *out of* acacia wood. It was
37: 26 [A] the horns with pure gold, and **made** a gold molding around it.
37: 27 [A] *They* **made** two gold rings below the molding—two on
37: 28 [A] *They* **made** the poles of acacia wood and overlaid them with
37: 29 [A] *They* also **made** the sacred anointing oil and the pure,
38: 1 [A] *They* **built** the altar of burnt offering of acacia wood, three
38: 2 [A] *They* **made** a horn at each of the four corners, so that the
38: 3 [A] *They* **made** all its utensils of bronze—its pots, shovels,
38: 3 [A] shovels, sprinkling bowls, meat forks and firepans. **[RPH]**
38: 4 [A] *They* **made** a grating for the altar, a bronze network, to be
38: 6 [A] *They* **made** the poles *of* acacia wood and overlaid them with
38: 7 [A] the altar for carrying it. *They* **made** it hollow, out of boards.
38: 8 [A] *They* **made** the bronze basin and its bronze stand from the
38: 9 [A] Next *they* **made** the courtyard. The south side was a hundred
38: 22 [A] of Judah, **made** everything the LORD commanded Moses;
38: 24 [B] The total amount of the gold from the wave offering **used** for
38: 28 [A] *They* **used** the 1,775 shekels **to make** the hooks for the
38: 30 [A] *They* used it *to* **make** the bases for the entrance to the Tent of
39: 1 [A] scarlet yarn *they* **made** woven garments for ministering in
39: 1 [A] *They* also **made** sacred garments for Aaron, as the LORD
39: 2 [A] *They* **made** the ephod *of* gold, and of blue, purple and scarlet
39: 3 [A] sheets of gold and cut strands to *be* **worked** into the blue,
39: 4 [A] *They* **made** shoulder pieces for the ephod, which were
39: 6 [A] *They* **mounted** the onyx stones *in* gold filigree settings
39: 8 [A] *They* **fashioned** the breastpiece—the work of a skilled
39: 9 [A] a span long and a span wide—and folded double. **[RPH]**
39: 15 [A] For the breastpiece *they* **made** braided chains *of* pure gold,
39: 16 [A] *They* **made** two gold filigree settings and two gold rings,
39: 19 [A] *They* **made** two gold rings and attached them to the other
39: 20 [A] *they* **made** two more gold rings and attached them to the
39: 22 [A] *They* **made** the robe of the ephod entirely of blue cloth—
39: 24 [A] *They* **made** pomegranates of blue, purple and scarlet yarn
39: 25 [A] *they* **made** bells of pure gold and attached them around the
39: 27 [A] For Aaron and his sons, *they* **made** tunics of fine linen—
39: 30 [A] *They* **made** the plate, the sacred diadem, *out of* pure gold
39: 32 [A] The Israelites **did** everything just as the LORD commanded
39: 32 [A] everything just as the LORD commanded Moses. **[RPH]**
39: 42 [A] The Israelites *had* **done** all the work just as the LORD had
39: 43 [A] saw that *they had* **done** it just as the LORD had
39: 43 [A] LORD had commanded. **[RPH]** So Moses blessed them.
40: 16 [A] Moses **did** everything just as the LORD commanded him.
40: 16 [A] did everything just as the LORD commanded him. **[RPH]**
Lev 2: 7 [C] is cooked in a pan, *it is to* **be made** *of* fine flour and oil.
2: 8 [C] Bring the grain offering **made** of these things to the LORD;
2: 11 [C] you bring to the LORD *must* **be made** without yeast,
4: 2 [A] **does** what is forbidden in any of the LORD's commands—
4: 2 [C] does what *is* **forbidden** [+4202] in any of the LORD's
4: 13 [A] **does** what is forbidden in any of the LORD's commands,
4: 13 [C] does what *is* **forbidden** [+4202] in any of the LORD's
4: 20 [A] **do** with this bull just as he did with the bull for the sin
4: 20 [A] do with this bull just as *he* **did** with the bull for the sin
4: 20 [A] **[RPH]** In this way the priest will make atonement for them,
4: 22 [A] **does** what is forbidden in any of the commands of the
4: 22 [C] does what *is* **forbidden** [+4202] in any of the commands of
4: 27 [A] **does** what is forbidden in any of the LORD's commands,
4: 27 [C] does what *is* **forbidden** [+4202] in any of the LORD's
5: 10 [A] The priest *shall* then **offer** the other as a burnt offering in the
5: 17 [A] **does** what is forbidden in any of the LORD's commands,
5: 17 [C] does what *is* **forbidden** [+4202] in any of the LORD's
6: 3 [5:22] [A] or if he commits any such sin that people *may* **do**—
6: 7 [5:26] [A] he will be forgiven for any of these things *he* **did** that
6: 21 [6:14] [C] **Prepare** it with oil on a griddle; bring it well-mixed
6: 22 [6:15] [A] is to succeed him as anointed priest *shall* **prepare** it.
7: 9 [C] Every grain offering baked in an oven or **cooked** in a pan
7: 24 [C] or torn by wild animals *may* **be used** for any other purpose,
8: 4 [A] Moses **did** as the LORD commanded him, and the assembly
8: 5 [A] "This is what the LORD has commanded to *be* **done**."

Lev 8:34 [A] What *has been* **done** today was commanded by the LORD
8:34 [A] was commanded by the LORD to **make** atonement for you.
8:36 [A] his sons **did** everything the LORD commanded through
9:6 [A] "This is what the LORD has commanded you *to* **do**,
9:7 [A] and **sacrifice** your sin offering and your burnt offering
9:7 [A] **sacrifice** the offering that is for the people and make
9:16 [A] the burnt offering and **offered** it in the prescribed way.
9:22 [A] And *having* **sacrificed** the sin offering, the burnt offering
10:7 [A] anointing oil is on you." So *they* **did** as Moses said.
11:32 [C] that article, whatever its **use** [+928+4856], will be unclean,
13:51 [C] or knitted material, or the leather, whatever its **use**,
14:19 [A] "Then the priest *is to* **sacrifice** the sin offering and make
14:30 [A] *he shall* **sacrifice** the doves or the young pigeons, which the
15:15 [A] The priest *is to* **sacrifice** them, the one for a sin offering
15:30 [A] The priest *is to* **sacrifice** one for a sin offering and the other
16:9 [A] lot falls to the LORD and **sacrifice** it for a sin offering.
16:15 [A] the curtain and **do** with it as he did with the bull's blood:
16:15 [A] the curtain and do with it as *he* **did** with the bull's blood:
16:16 [A] *He is to* **do** the same for the Tent of Meeting, which is
16:24 [A] **sacrifice** the burnt offering for himself and the burnt offering
16:29 [A] month you must deny yourselves and not **do** any work—
16:34 [A] And *it was* **done**, as the LORD commanded Moses.
17:9 [A] to the Tent of Meeting to **sacrifice** it to the LORD—
18:3 [A] *You must* not **do** as they do in Egypt, where you used to
18:3 [A] and *you must* not **do** as they do in the land of Canaan,
18:4 [A] *You must* **obey** my laws and be careful to follow my
18:5 [A] and laws, for the man who **obeys** them will live by them.
18:26 [A] the aliens living among you *must* not **do** any of these
18:27 [A] for all these things *were* **done** *by* the people who lived in the
18:29 [A] " 'Everyone who **does** any of these detestable things—such
18:29 [A] who does any of these detestable things—**such**[s] [+2021]
18:30 [A] *do* not **follow** any of the detestable customs that were
18:30 [C] the detestable customs that **were practiced** before you came
19:4 [A] not turn to idols or **make** gods of cast metal for yourselves.
19:15 [A] " '*Do* not **pervert** [+928+6404] justice; do not show
19:35 [A] " '*Do* not **use** dishonest standards when measuring length,
19:37 [A] " 'Keep all my decrees and all my laws and **follow** them.
20:8 [A] Keep my decrees and **follow** them. I am the LORD,
20:12 [A] What *they have* **done** is a perversion; their blood will be on
20:13 [A] with a woman, both of them *have* **done** what is detestable.
20:22 [A] " 'Keep all my decrees and laws and **follow** them, so that the
20:23 [A] Because *they* **did** all these things, I abhorred them.
22:23 [A] *You may*, however, **present** as a freewill offering an ox or a
22:24 [A] crushed, torn or cut. *You must* not **do** this in your own land,
22:31 [A] "Keep my commands and **follow** them. I am the LORD.
23:3 [A] " 'There are six days when *you may* **work** [+4856], but the
23:3 [A] *You are* not *to* **do** any work; wherever you live, it is a
23:7 [A] the first day hold a sacred assembly and **do** no regular work.
23:8 [A] day hold a sacred assembly and **do** no regular work.' "
23:12 [A] *you must* **sacrifice** as a burnt offering to the LORD a lamb
23:19 [A] **sacrifice** one male goat for a sin offering and two lambs,
23:21 [A] are to proclaim a sacred assembly and **do** no regular work.
23:25 [A] **Do** no regular work, but present an offering made to the
23:28 [A] **Do** no work on that day, because it is the Day of Atonement,
23:30 [A] I will destroy from among his people anyone who **does** any
23:31 [A] *You shall* **do** no work at all. This is to be a lasting ordinance
23:35 [A] The first day is a sacred assembly; **do** no regular work.
23:36 [A] by fire. It is the closing assembly; **do** no regular work.
24:19 [A] his neighbor, whatever *he has* **done** must be done to him:
24:19 [C] his neighbor, whatever he has done *must* **be done** to him:
24:23 [A] The Israelites **did** as the LORD commanded Moses.
25:18 [A] " '**Follow** my decrees and be careful to obey my laws, and
25:18 [A] " 'Follow my decrees and be careful *to* **obey** my laws, and
25:21 [A] the sixth year that the land *will* **yield** enough for three years.
26:1 [A] " '*Do* not **make** idols or set up an image or a sacred stone for
26:3 [A] follow my decrees and are careful *to* **obey** my commands,
26:14 [A] you will not listen to me and **carry out** all these commands,
26:15 [A] abhor my laws and fail *to* **carry out** all my commands and
26:16 [A] I *will* **do** this to you: I will bring upon you sudden terror,
Nu 1:54 [A] The Israelites **did** all this just as the LORD commanded
1:54 [A] did all this just as the LORD commanded Moses. **[RPH]**
2:34 [A] So the Israelites **did** everything the LORD commanded
4:3 [A] come to **serve in** [+7372] the work in the Tent of Meeting.
4:19 [A] when they come near the most holy things, **do** this for them:
4:26 [C] The Gershonites are to do all that *needs to* **be done** with
5:4 [A] The Israelites **did** this; they sent them outside the camp. They
5:4 [A] the camp. They **did** just as the LORD had instructed Moses.
5:6 [A] a man or woman **wrongs** [+2633] another in any way and
5:7 [A] must confess the sin *he has* **committed**. He must make full
5:30 [A] before the LORD and *is to* **apply** this entire law to her.
6:4 [C] he must not eat anything that **comes** from the grapevine, not
6:11 [A] The priest *is to* **offer** one as a sin offering and the other as a
6:16 [A] the LORD and **make** the sin offering and the burnt offering.
6:17 [A] *is to* **present** the basket of unleavened bread and is to sacrifice
6:17 [A] to present the basket of unleavened bread and *is to* **sacrifice**
6:21 [A] *He must* **fulfill** [+3869+4027+7023] the vow he has made,
8:3 [A] Aaron **did** so; he set up the lamps so that they faced forward
8:4 [A] The lampstand *was* **made** exactly like the pattern the LORD
8:7 [A] To purify them, **do** this: Sprinkle the water of cleansing on
8:12 [A] **use** the one for a sin offering to the LORD and the other for
8:20 [A] the whole Israelite community **did** with the Levites just as
8:20 [A] the Levites just as the LORD commanded Moses. **[RPH]**
8:22 [A] *They* **did** with the Levites just as the LORD commanded
8:26 [A] is how *you are to* **assign** the responsibilities of the Levites."
9:2 [A] "*Have* the Israelites **celebrate** the Passover at the appointed
9:3 [A] **Celebrate** it at the appointed time, at twilight on the
9:3 [A] in accordance with all its rules and regulations." **[RPH]**
9:4 [A] So Moses told the Israelites to **celebrate** the Passover,
9:5 [A] *they* **did**[s] [+906+2021+7175] **so** in the Desert of Sinai at
9:5 [A] The Israelites **did** everything just as the LORD commanded
9:6 [A] some of them could not **celebrate** the Passover on that day
9:10 [A] a journey, *they may still* **celebrate** the LORD's Passover.
9:11 [A] *They are to* **celebrate** it on the fourteenth day of the second
9:12 [A] *When they* **celebrate** the Passover, they must follow all the
9:13 [A] and not on a journey fails to **celebrate** the Passover,
9:14 [A] " 'An alien living among you *who wants to* **celebrate** the
9:14 [A] you who wants to celebrate the LORD's Passover *must* **do**
10:2 [A] "**Make** two trumpets of hammered silver, and use them for
10:2 [A] **use** them for calling the community together and for having
11:8 [A] it in a mortar. They cooked it in a pot or **made** it *into* cakes.
11:15 [A] If this is how you *are going to* **treat** me, put me to death
14:11 [A] in spite of all the miraculous signs *I have* **performed** among
14:12 [A] *I will* **make** you into a nation greater and stronger than they."
14:22 [A] the miraculous signs *I* **performed** in Egypt and in the desert
14:28 [A] the LORD, *I will* **do** to you the very things I heard you say:
14:35 [A] *I will* surely **do** these things to this whole wicked
15:3 [A] *you* **present** to the LORD offerings made by fire, from the
15:3 [A] or the flock, **[RPH]** as an aroma pleasing to the LORD—
15:5 [A] **prepare** a quarter of a hin of wine as a drink offering.
15:6 [A] " 'With a ram **prepare** a grain offering of two-tenths of an
15:8 [A] " 'When *you* **prepare** a young bull as a burnt offering
15:11 [C] or ram, each lamb or young goat, *is to* **be prepared** in this
15:12 [A] **Do** this for each one, for as many as you prepare.
15:12 [A] Do this for each one, for as many as *you* **prepare**.
15:13 [A] " 'Everyone who is native-born *must* **do** these things in this
15:14 [A] or anyone else living among you **presents** an offering made
15:14 [A] aroma pleasing to the LORD, *he must* **do** exactly as you do.
15:14 [A] aroma pleasing to the LORD, he must do exactly as *you* **do**.
15:22 [A] " 'Now if you unintentionally fail *to* **keep** any of these
15:24 [C] if *this is* **done** unintentionally without the community being
15:24 [A] the whole community *is to* **offer** a young bull for a burnt
15:29 [A] everyone *who* **sins unintentionally** [+928+8705], whether he
15:30 [A] " 'But anyone who **sins** [+928+3338+8123] **defiantly**,
15:34 [C] because it was not clear what *should* **be done** to him.
15:38 [A] 'Throughout the generations to come *you are to* **make** tassels
15:39 [A] that *you may* **obey** them and not prostitute yourselves by
15:40 [A] you will remember *to* **obey** all my commands and will be
16:6 [A] *You*, Korah, and all your followers *are to* **do** this:
16:28 [A] is how you will know that the LORD has sent me to **do**
16:38 [17:3] [A] of their lives. **Hammer** the censers **into** [+906+8393]
17:11 [17:26] [A] Moses **did** just as the LORD commanded him.
17:11 [17:26] [A] Moses did just as **[RPH]** the LORD commanded
20:27 [A] Moses **did** as the LORD commanded: They went up Mount
21:8 [A] said to Moses, "**Make** a snake and put it up on a pole;
21:9 [A] So Moses **made** a bronze snake and put it up on a pole.
21:34 [A] **Do** to him what you did to Sihon king of the Amorites,
21:34 [A] Do to him what *you* **did** to Sihon king of the Amorites,
22:2 [A] Now Balak son of Zippor saw all that Israel *had* **done** to the
22:17 [A] I will reward you handsomely and **do** whatever you say.
22:18 [A] I could not **do** anything great or small to go beyond the
22:20 [A] to summon you, go with them, but **do** only what I tell you."
22:28 [A] "What *have I* **done** to you to make you beat me these three
22:30 [A] Have I been in the habit of **doing** this to you?" "No," he said.
23:2 [A] Balak **did** as Balaam said, and the two of them offered a bull
23:11 [A] Balak said to Balaam, "What *have you* **done** to me?
23:19 [A] Does he speak and then not **act**? Does he promise and not
23:26 [A] "Did I not tell you *I must* **do** whatever the LORD says?"
23:30 [A] Balak **did** as Balaam had said, and offered a bull and a ram
24:13 [A] I could not **do** anything of my own accord, good or bad,
24:14 [A] let me warn you of what this people *will* **do** to your people in
24:18 [A] his enemy, will be conquered, but Israel *will* **grow** strong.
27:22 [A] Moses **did** as the LORD commanded him. He took Joshua
28:4 [A] **Prepare** one lamb in the morning and the other at twilight,
28:4 [A] one lamb in the morning and the other at twilight, **[RPH]**
28:6 [B] This is the regular burnt offering **instituted** at Mount Sinai as
28:8 [A] **Prepare** the second lamb at twilight, along with the same
28:8 [A] and drink offering that *you* **prepare** in the morning.
28:15 [C] one male goat *is to* **be presented** to the LORD as a sin

Nu 28:18 [A] the first day hold a sacred assembly and **do** no regular work.
28:20 [A] With each bull **prepare** a grain offering of three-tenths of an
28:21 [A] **[RPH]** and with each of the seven lambs, one-tenth.
28:23 [A] **Prepare** these in addition to the regular morning burnt
28:24 [A] In this way **prepare** the food for the offering made by fire
28:24 [B] *it is to* **be prepared** in addition to the regular burnt offering
28:25 [A] seventh day hold a sacred assembly and **do** no regular work.
28:26 [A] of Weeks, hold a sacred assembly and **do** no regular work.
28:31 [A] **Prepare** these together with their drink offerings, in addition
29: 1 [A] month hold a sacred assembly and **do** no regular work.
29: 2 [A] **prepare** a burnt offering of one young bull, one ram
29: 7 [A] sacred assembly. You must deny yourselves and **do** no work.
29:12 [A] hold a sacred assembly and **do** no regular work.
29:35 [A] the eighth day hold an assembly and **do** no regular work.
29:39 [A] **prepare** these for the LORD at your appointed feasts:
30: 2 [30:3] [A] not break his word but *must* **do** everything he said.
31:31 [A] and Eleazar the priest **did** as the LORD commanded Moses.
32: 8 [A] This is what your fathers **did** when I sent them from Kadesh
32:13 [A] until the whole generation of those *who had* **done** evil in his
32:20 [A] Moses said to them, "If *you will* **do** this—if you will arm
32:23 [A] "But if *you* fail *to* **do** this, you will be sinning against the
32:24 [A] and pens for your flocks, but **do** what you have promised."
32:25 [A] to Moses, "*We* your servants *will* **do** as our lord commands.
32:31 [A] "Your servants *will* **do** what the LORD has said.
33: 4 [A] for the LORD *had* **brought** judgment on their gods.
33:56 [A] And then *I will* **do** to you what I plan to do to them.' "
33:56 [A] And then I will do to you what I plan to **do** to them.' "
36:10 [A] So Zelophehad's daughters **did** as the LORD commanded
Dt 1:14 [A] You answered me, "What you propose to **do** is good."
1:18 [A] And at that time I told you everything *you were to* **do**.
1:30 [A] will fight for you, as *he* **did** for you in Egypt, before your
1:44 [A] they chased you like a **[NIE]** swarm of bees and beat you
2:12 [A] just as Israel **did** in the land the LORD gave them as their
2:22 [A] The LORD *had* **done** the same for the descendants of Esau,
2:29 [A] live in Seir, and the Moabites, who live in Ar, **did** for us—
3: 2 [A] **Do** to him what you did to Sihon king of the Amorites,
3: 2 [A] Do to him what *you* **did** to Sihon king of the Amorites,
3: 6 [A] as *we had* **done** with Sihon king of Heshbon,
3:21 [A] all that the LORD your God *has* **done** to these two kings.
3:21 [A] The LORD *will* **do** the same to all the kingdoms over there
3:24 [A] or on earth who *can* **do** the deeds and mighty works you do?
4: 1 [A] **Follow** them so that you may live and may go in and take
4: 3 [A] You saw with your own eyes what the LORD **did** at Baal
4: 5 [A] so that you *may* **follow** [+4027] them in the land you are
4: 6 [A] **Observe** them carefully, for this will show your wisdom
4:13 [A] which he commanded you to **follow** and then wrote them on
4:14 [A] laws you *are to* **follow** in the land that you are crossing the
4:16 [A] you do not become corrupt and **make** for yourselves an idol,
4:23 [A] *do* not **make** for yourselves an idol in the form of anything
4:25 [A] if you then become corrupt and **make** any kind of idol, doing
4:25 [A] **doing** evil in the eyes of the LORD your God
4:34 [A] like all the things the LORD your God **did** for you in Egypt
5: 1 [A] your hearing today. Learn them and be sure to **follow** them.
5: 8 [A] "*You shall* not **make** for yourself an idol in the form of
5:10 [A] **showing** love to a thousand ⌞generations⌟ of those who love
5:13 [A] Six days you shall labor and **do** all your work,
5:14 [A] On it *you shall* not **do** any work, neither you, nor your son
5:15 [A] your God has commanded you to **observe** the Sabbath day.
5:27 [A] the LORD our God tells you. We will listen and **obey**."
5:31 [A] laws you are to teach them *to* **follow** in the land I am giving
5:32 [A] So be careful to **do** what the LORD your God has
6: 1 [A] **observe** in the land that you are crossing the Jordan to
6: 3 [A] be careful to **obey** so that it may go well with you and that
6:18 [A] **Do** what is right and good in the LORD's sight, so that it
6:24 [A] The LORD commanded us to **obey** all these decrees and to
6:25 [A] if we are careful to **obey** all this law before the LORD our
7: 5 [A] This is what *you are to* **do** to them: Break down their altars,
7:11 [A] take care to **follow** the commands, decrees and laws I give
7:12 [A] pay attention to these laws and are careful *to* **follow** them,
7:18 [A] remember well what the LORD your God **did** to Pharaoh
7:19 [A] The LORD your God *will* **do** the same to all the peoples
8: 1 [A] Be careful to **follow** every command I am giving you today,
8:17 [A] the strength of my hands *have* **produced** this wealth for me."
8:18 [A] for it is he who gives you the ability to **produce** wealth, and
9:12 [A] and *have* **made** a cast idol for themselves."
9:14 [A] *I will* **make** you into a nation stronger and more numerous
9:16 [A] *you had* **made** for yourselves an idol cast in the shape of a
9:18 [A] **doing** what was evil in the LORD's sight and so provoking
9:21 [A] of yours, the calf *you had* **made**, and burned it in the fire.
10: 1 [A] come up to me on the mountain. Also **make** a wooden chest.
10: 3 [A] So *I* **made** the ark *out of* acacia wood and chiseled out two
10: 5 [A] down the mountain and put the tablets in the ark *I had* **made**,
10:18 [A] *He* **defends** the cause of the fatherless and the widow,
10:21 [A] who **performed** for you those great and awesome wonders
11: 3 [A] the signs *he* **performed** and the things he did in the heart of
11: 4 [A] what *he* **did** to the Egyptian army, to its horses and chariots,
11: 5 [A] It was not your children who saw what *he* **did** for you in the
11: 6 [A] what *he* **did** to Dathan and Abiram, sons of Eliab the
11: 7 [A] eyes that saw all these great things the LORD *has* **done**.
11:22 [A] observe all these commands I am giving you to **follow**—
11:32 [A] be sure that *you* **obey** all the decrees and laws I am setting
12: 1 [A] laws you must be careful to **follow** in the land that the
12: 4 [A] *You must* not **worship** the LORD your God in their way.
12: 8 [A] *You are* not *to* **do** as we do here today, everyone as he sees
12: 8 [A] You are not to do as we **do** here today, everyone as he sees
12:14 [A] of your tribes, and there **observe** everything I command you.
12:25 [A] because *you will be* **doing** what is right in the eyes of the
12:27 [A] **Present** your burnt offerings on the altar of the LORD your
12:28 [A] because *you will be* **doing** what is good and right in the eyes
12:30 [A] do these nations serve their gods? We *will* **do** the same."
12:31 [A] *You must* not **worship** the LORD your God in their way,
12:31 [A] because in worshiping their gods, *they* **do** all kinds of
12:32 [13:1] [A] See that *you* **do** all I command you; do not add to it
13:11 [13:12] [A] no one among you *will* **do** such an evil thing again.
13:14 [13:15] [C] that this detestable thing *has* **been done** among you,
13:18 [13:19] [A] you today and **doing** what is right in his eyes.
14:29 [A] God may bless you in all the **work of** [+5126] your hands.
15: 1 [A] the end of every seven years *you must* **cancel debts** [+9024].
15: 5 [A] are careful to **follow** all these commands I am giving you
15:17 [A] your servant for life. **Do** the same for your maidservant.
15:18 [A] the LORD your God will bless you in everything *you* **do**.
16: 1 [A] of Abib and **celebrate** the Passover of the LORD your God,
16: 8 [A] hold an assembly to the LORD your God and **do** no work.
16:10 [A] **celebrate** the Feast of Weeks to the LORD your God by
16:12 [A] you were slaves in Egypt, and **follow** carefully these decrees.
16:13 [A] **Celebrate** the Feast of Tabernacles for seven days after you
16:21 [A] pole beside the altar *you* **build** to the LORD your God,
17: 2 [A] **doing** evil in the eyes of the LORD your God in violation of
17: 4 [C] it has been proved that this detestable thing *has* **been done** in
17: 5 [A] or woman who *has* **done** this evil deed to your city gate
17:10 [A] *You must* **act** according to the decisions they give you at the
17:10 [A] Be careful to **do** everything they direct you to do.
17:11 [A] **Act** according to the law they teach you and the decisions
17:12 [A] The man who **shows** contempt for the judge or for the priest
17:19 [A] **follow** carefully all the words of this law and these decrees
18: 9 [A] do not learn to **imitate** [+3869] the detestable ways of the
18:12 [A] Anyone *who* **does** these things is detestable to the LORD,
19: 9 [A] because you carefully **follow** all these laws I command you
19:19 [A] **do** to him as he intended to do to his brother. You must purge
19:19 [A] do to him as he intended to **do** to his brother. You must purge
19:20 [A] and never again *will* such an evil thing *be* **done** among you.
20:12 [A] If they refuse to make peace and *they* **engage** you in battle,
20:15 [A] This is how *you are to* **treat** all the cities that are at a
20:18 [A] they will teach you to **follow** [+3869] all the detestable things
20:18 [A] all the detestable things *they* **do** in worshiping their gods,
20:20 [A] use them to build siege works until the city **at war** [+4878]
21: 9 [A] since *you have* **done** what is right in the eyes of the LORD.
21:12 [A] into your home and have her shave her head, **trim** her nails
22: 3 [A] **Do** the same if you find your brother's donkey or his cloak
22: 3 [A] brother's donkey or **[RPH]** his cloak or anything he loses.
22: 3 [A] brother's donkey or his cloak or **[RPH]** anything he loses.
22: 5 [A] for the LORD your God detests anyone *who* **does** this.
22: 8 [A] **make** a parapet around your roof so that you may not bring
22:12 [A] **Make** tassels on the four corners of the cloak you wear.
22:21 [A] *She has* **done** a disgraceful thing in Israel by being
22:26 [A] **Do** nothing to the girl; she has committed no sin deserving
23:23 [23:24] [A] Whatever your lips utter you must be sure *to* **do**,
24: 8 [A] In cases of leprous diseases be very careful to **do** exactly as
24: 8 [A] You *must* **follow** carefully what I have commanded them.
24: 9 [A] Remember what the LORD your God **did** to Miriam along
24:18 [A] you from there. That is why I command you to **do** this.
24:22 [A] were slaves in Egypt. That is why I command you to **do** this.
25: 9 [C] "This is what **is done** to the man who will not build up his
25:16 [A] For the LORD your God detests anyone *who* **does** these
25:16 [A] who does these things, anyone *who* **deals** dishonestly.
25:17 [A] Remember what the Amalekites **did** to you along the way
26:14 [A] my God; *I have* **done** everything you commanded me.
26:16 [A] your God commands you this day to **follow** these decrees and
26:16 [A] carefully **observe** them with all your heart and with all your
26:19 [A] fame and honor high above all the nations *he has* **made**
27:10 [A] and **follow** his commands and decrees that I give you today."
27:15 [A] "Cursed is the man who **carves** an image or casts an idol—
27:26 [A] not uphold the words of this law by **carrying** them **out**."
28: 1 [A] and carefully **follow** all his commands I give you today,
28:13 [A] your God that I give you this day and carefully **follow** them,
28:15 [A] *do* not carefully **follow** all his commands and decrees I am
28:20 [A] **[NIE]** until you are destroyed and come to sudden ruin
28:58 [A] If you do not carefully **follow** all the words of this law,

Dt 29: 2 [29:1] [A] Your eyes have seen all that the LORD **did** in Egypt
29: 9 [29:8] [A] Carefully **follow** the terms of this covenant, so that
29: 9 [29:8] [A] so that you may prosper in everything *you* **do**.
29:24 [29:23] [A] "Why *has* the LORD **done** this to this land?
29:29 [29:28] [A] that we *may* **follow** all the words of this law.
30: 8 [A] and **follow** all his commands I am giving you today.
30:12 [A] heaven to get it and proclaim it to us so *we may* **obey** it?"
30:13 [A] the sea to get it and proclaim it to us so *we may* **obey** it?"
30:14 [A] it is in your mouth and in your heart so you *may* **obey** it.
31: 4 [A] the LORD *will* **do** to them what he did to Sihon and Og,
31: 4 [A] the LORD will do to them what *he* **did** to Sihon and Og,
31: 5 [A] and *you must* **do** to them all that I have commanded you.
31:12 [A] your God and **follow** carefully all the words of this law.
31:18 [A] because of all their wickedness **[NIE]** in turning to other
31:21 [A] I know what they are disposed *to* **do**, even before I bring
31:29 [A] upon you because *you will* **do** evil in the sight of the LORD
32: 6 [A] your Father, your Creator, who **made** you and formed you?
32:15 [A] He abandoned the God *who* **made** him and rejected the Rock
32:46 [A] so that you may command your children to **obey** carefully all
33:21 [A] *he* **carried out** the LORD's righteous will, and his
34: 9 [A] to him and **did** what the LORD had commanded Moses.
34:11 [A] and wonders the LORD sent him to **do** in Egypt—
34:12 [A] or performed the awesome deeds that Moses **did** in the sight
Jos 1: 7 [A] Be careful to **obey** all the law my servant Moses gave you;
1: 8 [A] so that you may be careful to **do** everything written in it.
1:16 [A] "Whatever you have commanded us *we will* **do**,
2:10 [A] what *you* **did** to Sihon and Og, the two kings of the Amorites
2:12 [A] please swear to me by the LORD that you *will* **show**
2:12 [A] to my family, because *I have* **shown** kindness to you.
2:14 [A] *we will* **treat** you kindly and faithfully when the LORD
3: 5 [A] for tomorrow the LORD *will* **do** amazing things among
4: 8 [A] So the Israelites **did** as Joshua commanded them. They took
4:23 [A] *he had* **done** to the Red Sea when he dried it up before us
5: 2 [A] "**Make** flint knives and circumcise the Israelites again."
5: 3 [A] So Joshua **made** flint knives and circumcised the Israelites at
5:10 [A] the plains of Jericho, the Israelites **celebrated** the Passover.
5:15 [A] place where you are standing is holy." And Joshua **did** so.
6: 3 [A] the city once with all the armed men. **Do** this for six days.
6:14 [A] and returned to the camp. *They* **did** this for six days.
7: 9 [A] the earth. What then *will you* **do** for your own great name?"
7:15 [A] of the LORD and *has* **done** a disgraceful thing in Israel!' "
7:19 [A] Tell me what *you have* **done**; do not hide it from me."
7:20 [A] the LORD, the God of Israel. This is what *I have* **done**:
8: 2 [A] *You shall* **do** to Ai and its king as you did to Jericho and its
8: 2 [A] shall do to Ai and its king as *you* **did** to Jericho and its king,
8: 8 [A] **Do** what the LORD has commanded. See to it; you have my
9: 3 [A] when the people of Gibeon heard what Joshua *had* **done** to
9: 4 [A] they **resorted** to a ruse: They went as a delegation whose
9: 9 [A] For we have heard reports of him: all that *he* **did** in Egypt,
9:10 [A] all that *he* **did** to the two kings of the Amorites east of the
9:15 [A] Joshua made a treaty **[NIE]** of peace with them to let them
9:20 [A] This is what *we will* **do** to them: We will let them live, so
9:24 [A] for our lives because of you, and that is why *we* **did** this.
9:25 [A] your hands. **Do** to us whatever seems good and right to you."
9:25 [A] Do to us whatever seems good and right to you." **[RPH]**
9:26 [A] So **[RPH]** Joshua saved them from the Israelites, and they
10: 1 [A] **doing** to Ai and its king as he had done to Jericho and its
10: 1 [A] doing to Ai and its king as *he had* **done** to Jericho and its
10:23 [A] So **[NIE]** they brought the five kings out of the cave—
10:25 [A] This is what the LORD *will* **do** to all the enemies you are
10:28 [A] *he* **did** to the king of Makkedah as he had done to the king of
10:28 [A] he did to the king of Makkedah as *he had* **done** to the king of
10:30 [A] And *he* **did** to its king as he had done to the king of Jericho.
10:30 [A] And he did to its king as *he had* **done** to the king of Jericho.
10:32 [A] in it he put to the sword, just as *he had* **done** to Libnah.
10:35 [A] destroyed everyone in it, just as *they had* **done** to Lachish.
10:37 [A] Just as **[RPH]** at Eglon, they totally destroyed it
10:39 [A] *They* **did** to Debir and its king as they had done to Libnah
10:39 [A] its king as *they had* **done** to Libnah and its king and to
10:39 [A] they had done to Libnah and its king and **[RPH]** to Hebron.
11: 9 [A] Joshua **did** to them as the LORD had directed: He
11:15 [A] so Moses commanded Joshua, and Joshua **did** it;
11:18 [A] Joshua **waged** war against all these kings for a long time.
14: 5 [A] just as the LORD had commanded Moses. **[RPH]**
22: 5 [A] be very careful to **keep** the commandment and the law that
22:23 [A] and grain offerings, or to **sacrifice** fellowship offerings on it,
22:24 [A] *We* **did** it for fear that some day your descendants might say
22:26 [A] "That is why we said, '*Let us* **get ready** and build an altar—
22:28 [A] which our fathers **built**, not for burnt offerings and sacrifices,
23: 3 [A] your God *has* **done** to all these nations for your sake;
23: 6 [A] be careful to **obey** all that is written in the Book of the Law
23: 8 [A] to hold fast to the LORD your God, as *you* **have**ˢ until now.
24: 5 [A] and Aaron, and I afflicted the Egyptians by what *I* **did** there,
24: 7 [A] You saw with your own eyes what *I* **did** to the Egyptians.
24:17 [A] of slavery, and **performed** those great signs before our eyes.
24:31 [A] who had experienced everything the LORD *had* **done** for
Jdg 1: 7 [A] Now God has paid me back for what *I* **did** to them." They
1:24 [A] the city and *we will see that* you *are* **treated** [+6640] well."
2: 2 [A] Yet you have disobeyed me. Why *have you* **done** this?
2: 7 [A] who had seen all the great things the LORD *had* **done** for
2:10 [A] who knew neither the LORD nor what *he had* **done** for
2:11 [A] the Israelites **did** evil in the eyes of the LORD and served
2:17 [A] **Unlike** [+4027+4202] their fathers, they quickly turned from
3: 7 [A] The Israelites **did** evil in the eyes of the LORD; they forgot
3:12 [A] Once again the Israelites **did** evil in the eyes of the LORD,
3:12 [A] because *they* **did** this evil the LORD gave Eglon king of
3:16 [A] Now Ehud *had* **made** a double-edged sword about a foot
4: 1 [A] the Israelites once again **did** evil in the eyes of the LORD.
6: 1 [A] Again the Israelites **did** evil in the eyes of the LORD,
6: 2 [A] **prepared** shelters for themselves in mountain clefts, caves and
6:17 [A] your eyes, **give** me a sign that it is really you talking to me.
6:19 [A] Gideon went in, **prepared** a young goat, and from an ephah
6:20 [A] on this rock, and pour out the broth." And Gideon **did** so.
6:27 [A] took ten of his servants and **did** as the LORD told him.
6:27 [A] men of the town, *he* **did** it at night rather than in the daytime.
6:27 [A] he did it at night rather than **[RPH]** in the daytime.
6:29 [A] They asked each other, "Who **did** this?" When they carefully
6:29 [A] they were told, "Gideon son of Joash **did** it."
6:40 [A] That night God **did** so. Only the fleece was dry; all the
7:17 [A] "Watch me," he told them. "**Follow** [+4027] my **lead**. When
7:17 [A] When I get to the edge of the camp, **do** exactly as I do.
7:17 [A] When I get to the edge of the camp, do exactly as *I* **do**.
8: 1 [A] asked Gideon, "Why *have you* **treated** us like this?
8: 2 [A] "What *have I* **accomplished** compared to you?
8: 3 [A] What was I able *to* **do** compared to you?" At this, their
8:27 [A] Gideon **made** the gold into an ephod, which he placed in
8:35 [A] *They* also failed *to* **show** kindness to the family of
8:35 [A] Gideon) for all the good things *he had* **done** for them.
9:16 [A] "Now if *you have* **acted** honorably and in good faith when
9:16 [A] if *you have* **been** fair to Jerub-Baal and his family, and if you
9:16 [A] and his family, and if *you have* **treated** him as he deserves—
9:19 [A] if then *you have* **acted** honorably and in good faith toward
9:27 [A] trodden them, *they* **held** a festival in the temple of their god.
9:33 [A] come out against you, **do** whatever your hand finds to do."
9:48 [A] the men with him, "Quick! **Do** what you have seen me do!"
9:48 [A] the men with him, "Quick! Do what you have seen me **do**!"
9:56 [A] Thus God repaid the wickedness that Abimelech *had* **done** to
10: 6 [A] Again the Israelites **did** evil in the eyes of the LORD. They
10:15 [A] **Do** with us whatever you think best, but please rescue us
11:10 [A] LORD is our witness; *we will* certainly **do** as you say."
11:27 [A] but you *are* **doing** me wrong by waging war against me.
11:36 [A] **Do** to me just as you promised, now that the LORD has
11:36 [A] now that the LORD *has* **avenged** [+4200+5935] you of
11:37 [C] **grant** me this one request," she said. "Give me two months
11:39 [A] she returned to her father and *he* **did** to her as he had vowed.
13: 1 [A] Again the Israelites **did** evil in the eyes of the LORD,
13: 8 [A] to teach us how *to* **bring up** the boy who is to be born."
13:15 [A] "We would like you to stay until *we* **prepare** a young goat
13:16 [A] But if *you* **prepare** a burnt offering, offer it to the LORD."
13:19 [A] the LORD **did** an amazing thing while Manoah and his wife
14: 6 [A] he told neither his father nor his mother what *he had* **done**.
14:10 [A] Samson **made** a feast there, as was customary for
14:10 [A] made a feast there, as *was* **customary** *for* bridegrooms.
15: 3 [A] with the Philistines; I *will* really **harm** [+6640+8288] them."
15: 6 [A] When the Philistines asked, "Who **did** this?" they were told,
15: 7 [A] Samson said to them, "Since *you've* **acted** like this, I won't
15:10 [A] they answered, "to **do** to him as he did to us."
15:10 [A] they answered, "to do to him as *he* **did** to us."
15:11 [A] What *have you* **done** to us?" He answered, "I merely did to
15:11 [A] He answered, "*I* merely **did** to them what they did to me."
15:11 [A] He answered, "I merely did to them what *they* **did** to me."
16:11 [C] with new ropes that *have* never **been used** [+928+4856],
17: 3 [A] my silver to the LORD for my son to **make** a carved image
17: 4 [A] to a silversmith, *who* **made** them *into* the image and the idol.
17: 5 [A] *he* **made** an ephod and some idols and installed one of his
17: 6 [A] In those days Israel had no king; everyone **did** as he saw fit.
17: 8 [A] in search of some other place to stay. **On** his **way** [+2006]
18: 3 [A] What *are* you **doing** in this place? Why are you here?"
18: 4 [A] He told them what Micah *had* **done** for him, and said, "He
18:14 [A] a carved image and a cast idol? Now you know what *to* **do**."
18:18 [A] the cast idol, the priest said to them, "What *are* you **doing**?"
18:24 [A] He replied, "You took the gods *I* **made**, and my priest,
18:27 [A] they took what Micah *had* **made**, and his priest, and went on
18:31 [A] They continued to use the idols Micah *had* **made**,
19:23 [A] Since this man is my guest, don't **do** this disgraceful thing.
19:24 [A] and you can use them and **do** to them whatever you wish.
19:24 [A] you wish. But to this man, don't **do** such a disgraceful thing."
20: 6 [A] because *they* **committed** this lewd and disgraceful act in

Jdg 20: 9 [A] now this is what *we'll* **do** to Gibeah: We'll go up against it as
20: 10 [A] it *can* **give** them what they deserve for all this vileness done
20: 10 [A] it can give them what they deserve for all this vileness **done**
21: 7 [A] "How *can we* **provide** wives for those who are left, since we
21: 11 [A] "This is what *you are to* **do**," they said. "Kill every male
21: 15 [A] because the LORD *had* **made** a gap in the tribes of Israel.
21: 16 [A] how *shall we* **provide** wives for the men who are left?
21: 23 [A] So that is what the Benjamites **did**. While the girls were
21: 25 [A] In those days Israel had no king; everyone **did** as he saw fit.
Ru 1: 8 [A] *May* the LORD **show** kindness to you, as you have shown
1: 8 [A] kindness to you, as *you have* **shown** to your dead and to me.
1: 17 [A] *May* the LORD **deal** with me, be it ever so severely, if
2: 11 [A] "I've been told all about what *you have* **done** *for* your
2: 19 [A] "Where did you glean today? Where *did you* **work**?
2: 19 [A] about the one at whose place *she had been* **working**.
2: 19 [A] "The name of the man *I* **worked** with today is Boaz,"
3: 4 [A] uncover his feet and lie down. He will tell you what *to* **do**."
3: 5 [A] "*I will* **do** whatever you say," Ruth answered.
3: 6 [A] and **did** everything her mother-in-law told her to do.
3: 11 [A] my daughter, don't be afraid. *I will* **do** for you all you ask.
3: 16 [A] Then she told her everything Boaz *had* **done** for her
4: 11 [A] *May you* **have** standing in Ephrathah and be famous in
1Sa 1: 7 [A] This **went on** year after year. Whenever Hannah went up to
1: 23 [A] "**Do** what seems best to you," Elkanah her husband told her.
2: 14 [A] This is how *they* **treated** all the Israelites who came to
2: 19 [A] Each year his mother **made** him a little robe and took it to
2: 22 [A] heard about everything his sons *were* **doing** to all Israel
2: 23 [A] So he said to them, "Why *do you* **do** such things? I hear from
2: 35 [A] *who will* **do** according to what is in my heart and mind.
3: 11 [A] I *am about to* **do** something in Israel that will make the ears
3: 17 [A] *May* God **deal** with you, be it ever so severely, if you hide
3: 18 [A] "He is the LORD; *let him* **do** what is good in his eyes."
5: 8 [A] "What *shall we* **do** with the ark of the god of Israel?"
6: 2 [A] and said, "What *shall we* **do** with the ark of the LORD?
6: 5 [A] **Make** models of the tumors and of the rats that are
6: 7 [A] "Now then, get a new cart **ready**, with two cows that have
6: 9 [A] then the LORD *has* **brought** this great disaster on us.
6: 10 [A] So they **did** this. They took two such cows and hitched them
8: 8 [A] As *they have* **done** from the day I brought them up out of
8: 8 [A] and serving other gods, so they *are* **doing** to you.
8: 12 [A] still others to **make** weapons of war and equipment for his
8: 16 [A] your cattle and donkeys he will take for his own **use** [+4856].
10: 2 [A] about you. He is asking, "What *shall I* **do** about my son?" '
10: 7 [A] **do** whatever your hand finds to do, for God is with you.
10: 8 [A] days until I come to you and tell you what *you are to* **do**."
11: 7 [C] "This is what *will* **be done** to the oxen of anyone who does
11: 10 [A] to you, and *you can* **do** to us whatever seems good to you."
11: 13 [A] for this day the LORD *has* **rescued** [+928+9591] Israel."
12: 6 [A] "It is the LORD who **appointed** Moses and Aaron
12: 7 [A] as to all the righteous acts **performed** *by* the LORD for you
12: 16 [A] see this great thing the LORD *is about to* **do** before your
12: 17 [A] you will realize what an evil thing *you* **did** in the eyes of the
12: 20 [A] "You *have* **done** all this evil; yet do not turn away from the
12: 22 [A] because the LORD was pleased to **make** you his own.
13: 11 [A] "What *have you* **done**?" asked Samuel. Saul replied,
13: 19 [A] "Otherwise the Hebrews *will* **make** swords or spears!"
14: 6 [A] Perhaps the LORD *will* **act** in our behalf. Nothing can
14: 7 [A] "**Do** all that you have in mind," his armor-bearer said. "Go
14: 32 [a] [They **pounced** [K; see Q 6513] on the plunder and, taking]
14: 36 [A] "**Do** whatever seems best to you," they replied. But the priest
14: 40 [A] over here." "**Do** what seems best to you," the men replied.
14: 43 [A] Then Saul said to Jonathan, "Tell me what *you have* **done**."
14: 44 [A] Saul said, "*May* God **deal** with me, be it ever so severely,
14: 45 [A] *he* who *has* **brought about** this great deliverance in Israel?
14: 45 [A] fall to the ground, for *he* **did** this today with God's help."
14: 48 [A] *He* **fought** valiantly and defeated the Amalekites, delivering
15: 2 [A] 'I will punish the Amalekites for what *they* **did** to Israel
15: 6 [A] for you **showed** kindness to all the Israelites when they came
15: 19 [A] on the plunder and **do** evil in the eyes of the LORD?"
16: 3 [A] Invite Jesse to the sacrifice, and I will show you what *to* **do**.
16: 4 [A] Samuel **did** what the LORD said. When he arrived at
17: 25 [A] *will* **exempt** his father's family **from taxes** [+906+2930] in
17: 26 [C] "What *will* **be done** for the man who kills this Philistine
17: 27 [C] "This is what *will* **be done** for the man who kills him."
17: 29 [A] "Now what *have I* **done**?" said David. "Can't I even speak?"
19: 5 [A] The LORD **won** a great victory for all Israel, and you saw it
19: 18 [A] Samuel at Ramah and told him all that Saul *had* **done** to him.
20: 1 [A] and went to Jonathan and asked, "What *have I* **done**?
20: 2 [A] Look, my father doesn't **do** anything, great or small, without
20: 4 [A] to David, "Whatever you want me to do, *I'll* **do** for you."
20: 8 [A] As for *you*, **show** kindness to your servant, for you have
20: 13 [A] *may* the LORD **deal** with me, be it ever so severely, if I do
20: 14 [A] **show** me unfailing kindness like that of the LORD as long
20: 32 [A] put to death? What *has he* **done**?" Jonathan asked his father.
22: 3 [A] and stay with you until I learn what God *will* **do** for me?"
24: 4 [24:5] [A] will give your enemy into your hands *for you to* **deal**
24: 6 [24:7] [A] "The LORD forbid that *I should* **do** such a thing to
24: 18 [24:19] [A] You have just now told me of the good *you* **did** to
24: 19 [24:20] [A] reward you well for the way *you* **treated** me today.
25: 17 [A] Now think it over and see what *you can* **do**, because disaster
25: 18 [B] two skins of wine, five **dressed** sheep, five seahs of roasted
25: 22 [A] *May* God **deal** with David, be it ever so severely, if by
25: 28 [A] for the LORD *will* **certainly make** [+6913] a lasting
25: 28 [A] for the LORD *will* **certainly make** [+6913] a lasting
25: 30 [A] When the LORD *has* **done** for my master every good thing
26: 16 [A] What *you have* **done** is not good. As surely as the LORD
26: 18 [A] What *have I* **done**, and what wrong am I guilty of?
26: 25 [A] *you will* **do** [+6913] **great things** and surely triumph."
26: 25 [A] *you will* **do great things** [+6913] and surely triumph."
27: 11 [A] 'This is what David **did**.' " And such was his practice as long
28: 2 [A] "Then you will see for yourself what your servant *can* **do**."
28: 9 [A] woman said to him, "Surely you know what Saul *has* **done**.
28: 15 [A] or by dreams. So I have called on you to tell me what *to* **do**."
28: 17 [A] The LORD *has* **done** what he predicted through me. The
28: 18 [A] or **carry out** his fierce wrath against the Amalekites,
28: 18 [A] the Amalekites, the LORD *has* **done** this to you today.
29: 7 [A] go in peace; **do** nothing to displease the Philistine rulers."
29: 8 [A] "But what *have I* **done**?" asked David. "What have you
30: 23 [A] *you must* not **do** that with what the LORD has given us.
31: 11 [A] Jabesh Gilead heard of what the Philistines *had* **done** to Saul,
2Sa 2: 5 [A] "The LORD bless you for **showing** this kindness to Saul
2: 6 [A] *May* the LORD now **show** you kindness and faithfulness,
2: 6 [A] I too *will* **show** you the same favor because you have done
2: 6 [A] will show you the same favor because *you have* **done** this.
3: 8 [A] This very day *I* **am** loyal to the house of your father Saul
3: 9 [A] *May* God **deal** with Abner, be it ever so severely, if I do not
3: 9 [A] if *I do* not **do** for David what the LORD promised him on
3: 18 [A] Now **do** *it*! For the LORD promised David, 'By my servant
3: 20 [A] at Hebron, David **prepared** a feast for him and his men.
3: 24 [A] So Joab went to the king and said, "What *have you* **done**?
3: 25 [A] your movements and find out everything you *are* **doing**."
3: 35 [A] saying, "*May* God **deal** with me, be it ever so severely, if I
3: 36 [A] were pleased; indeed, everything the king **did** pleased them.
3: 39 [A] May the LORD repay the **evildoer** [+8288] according to his
5: 25 [A] So David **did** as the LORD commanded him, and he struck
7: 3 [A] in mind, go ahead and **do** it, for the LORD is with you."
7: 9 [A] Now *I will* **make** your name great, like the names of the
7: 11 [A] you that the LORD *himself will* **establish** a house for you:
7: 21 [A] *you have* **done** this great thing and made it known to your
7: 23 [A] to **perform** great and awesome wonders by driving out
7: 25 [A] concerning your servant and his house. **Do** as you promised,
8: 13 [A] David **became famous** [+9005] after he returned from
8: 15 [A] all Israel, **doing** what was just and right for all his people.
9: 1 [A] of Saul to whom *I can* **show** kindness for Jonathan's sake?"
9: 3 [A] of the house of Saul to whom *I can* **show** God's kindness?"
9: 7 [A] "for *I will* **surely show** [+6640+6913] you kindness for the
9: 7 [A] "for *I will* **surely show** [+6640+6913] you kindness for the
9: 11 [A] "Your servant *will* **do** whatever my lord the king commands
10: 2 [A] "*I will* **show** kindness to Hanun son of Nahash,
10: 2 [A] son of Nahash, just as his father **showed** kindness to me."
10: 12 [A] of our God. The LORD *will* **do** what is good in his sight."
11: 11 [A] my wife? As surely as you live, *I will* not **do** such a thing!"
11: 27 [A] a son. But the thing David *had* **done** displeased the LORD.
12: 4 [A] or cattle to **prepare** a meal for the traveler who had come to
12: 4 [A] poor man and **prepared** it for the one who had come to him."
12: 5 [A] as the LORD lives, the man who **did** this deserves to die!
12: 6 [A] times over, because *he* **did** such a thing and had no pity."
12: 9 [A] Why did you despise the word of the LORD by **doing** what
12: 12 [A] You **did** it in secret, but I will do this thing in broad daylight
12: 12 [A] but I *will* **do** this thing in broad daylight before all Israel.' "
12: 18 [A] tell him the child is dead? *He may* **do** something desperate."
12: 21 [A] His servants asked him, "Why *are you* **acting** this way?
12: 31 [A] *He* **did** this to all the Ammonite towns. Then David and his
13: 2 [A] and it seemed impossible for him to **do** anything to her.
13: 5 [A] *Let her* **prepare** the food in my sight so I may watch her and
13: 7 [A] of your brother Amnon and **prepare** some food for him."
13: 10 [A] Tamar took the bread *she had* **prepared** and brought it to her
13: 12 [C] "Don't force me. Such a thing *should* not **be done** in Israel!
13: 12 [A] should not be done in Israel! Don't **do** this wicked thing.
13: 16 [A] be a greater wrong than what *you have already* **done** to me."
13: 29 [A] So Absalom's men **did** to Amnon what Absalom had
14: 15 [A] speak to the king; perhaps he *will* **do** what his servant asks.
14: 20 [A] Your servant Joab **did** this to change the present situation.
14: 21 [A] The king said to Joab, "Very well, *I will* **do** it. Go,
14: 22 [A] because the king *has* **granted** his servant's request."
15: 1 [A] Absalom **provided** himself with a chariot and horses
15: 6 [A] Absalom **behaved** in this way toward all the Israelites who
15: 26 [A] I am ready; *let him* **do** to me whatever seems good to him."

2Sa 16:10 [A] to him, 'Curse David,' who can ask, 'Why *do you* **do** this?' "
16:20 [A] to Ahithophel, "Give us your advice. What *should we* **do**?"
17: 6 [A] *Should we* **do** what he says? If not, give us your opinion."
17:23 [C] When Ahithophel saw that his advice *had* not **been followed**,
18: 4 [A] The king answered, "*I will* **do** whatever seems best to you."
18:13 [A] if *I had* **put** [+928+9214] my life **in jeopardy**—and nothing
19:13 [19:14] [A] *May* God **deal** with me, be it ever so severely, if
19:18 [19:19] [A] household over and to **do** whatever he wished.
19:24 [19:25] [A] *He had* not **taken care of** his feet or trimmed his
19:24 [19:25] [A] not taken care of his feet or **trimmed** his mustache
19:27 [19:28] [A] is like an angel of God; so **do** whatever pleases you.
19:37 [19:38] [A] lord the king. **Do** for him whatever pleases you."
19:38 [19:39] [A] and I *will* **do** for him whatever pleases you.
19:38 [19:39] [A] anything you desire from me *I will* **do** for you."
21: 3 [A] David asked the Gibeonites, "What *shall I* **do** for you? How
21: 4 [A] "What do you want *me to* **do** for you?" David asked.
21:11 [A] what Aiah's daughter Rizpah, Saul's concubine, *had* **done**,
21:14 [A] Zela in Benjamin, and **did** everything the king commanded.
22:51 [A] *he* **shows** unfailing kindness to his anointed, to David and his
23:10 [A] The LORD **brought about** a great victory that day.
23:12 [A] and the LORD **brought about** a great victory.
23:17 [A] "Far be it from me, O LORD, *to* **do** this!" he said. "Is it not
23:17 [A] not drink it. Such *were the* **exploits** of the three mighty men.
23:22 [A] Such *were the* **exploits** *of* Benaiah son of Jehoiada; he too
24:10 [A] to the LORD, "I have sinned greatly in what *I have* **done**.
24:12 [A] Choose one of them *for me to* **carry out** against you.' "
24:17 [A] and done wrong. These are but sheep. What *have they* **done**?
1Ki 1: 5 [A] So *he* **got** chariots and horses **ready**, with fifty men to run
1: 6 [A] with him by asking, "Why *do you* **behave** as you do?"
1:30 [A] *I will* surely **carry out** today what I swore to you by the
2: 3 [A] so that you may prosper in all *you* **do** and wherever you go,
2: 5 [A] "Now you yourself know what Joab son of Zeruiah **did** to
2: 5 [A] what *he* **did** to the two commanders of Israel's armies, Abner
2: 6 [A] **Deal with** him according to your wisdom, but do not let his
2: 7 [A] "But **show** kindness to the sons of Barzillai of Gilead and let
2: 9 [A] You are a man of wisdom; you will know what *to* **do** to him.
2:23 [A] "*May* God **deal** with me, be it ever so severely, if Adonijah
2:24 [A] and *has* **founded** a dynasty for me as he promised—
2:31 [A] the king commanded Benaiah, "**Do** as he says. Strike him
2:38 [A] is good. Your servant *will* **do** as my lord the king has said."
2:44 [A] "You know in your heart all the wrong *you* **did** to my father
3: 6 [A] "You *have* **shown** great kindness to your servant, my father
3:12 [A] *I will* **do** what you have asked. I will give you a wise
3:15 [A] sacrificed burnt offerings and **[RPH]** fellowship offerings.
3:15 [A] fellowship offerings. Then *he* **gave** a feast for all his court.
3:28 [A] saw that he had wisdom from God to **administer** justice.
5: 8 [5:22] [A] *will* **do** all you want in providing the cedar and pine
5: 9 [5:23] [A] you *are to* **grant** my wish by providing food for my
5:16 [5:30] [A] project and directed the **workmen** [+928+2021+4856].
6: 4 [A] *He* **made** narrow clerestory windows in the temple.
6: 5 [A] around the building, in which *there* **were**[s] side rooms.
6:12 [A] **carry out** my regulations and keep all my commands
6:23 [A] In the inner sanctuary *he* **made** a pair of cherubim of olive
6:31 [A] For the entrance of the inner sanctuary *he* **made** doors of
6:33 [A] In the same way *he* **made** four-sided jambs of olive wood for
7: 6 [A] *He* **made** a colonnade fifty cubits long and thirty wide. In
7: 7 [A] *He* **built** the throne hall, the Hall of Justice, where he was to
7: 8 [A] Solomon also **made** a palace like this hall for Pharaoh's
7:14 [A] and experienced in **[NIE]** all kinds of bronze work.
7:14 [A] came to King Solomon and **did** all the work assigned to him.
7:16 [A] *He* also **made** two capitals of cast bronze to set on the tops of
7:18 [A] *He* **made** pomegranates in two rows encircling each network
7:18 [A] on top of the pillars. *He* **did** the same for each capital.
7:23 [A] *He* **made** the Sea of cast metal, circular in shape, measuring
7:27 [A] *He* also **made** ten movable stands of bronze; each was four
7:37 [A] This is the way *he* **made** the ten stands. They were all cast in
7:38 [A] *He* then **made** ten bronze basins, each holding forty baths
7:40 [A] He also **made** the basins and shovels and sprinkling bowls.
7:40 [A] So Huram finished **[RPH]** all the work he had undertaken
7:40 [A] So Huram finished all the work *he had* **undertaken** for King
7:45 [A] All these objects that Huram **made** for King Solomon for the
7:48 [A] **made** all the furnishings that were in the LORD's temple:
7:51 [A] When all the work King Solomon *had* **done** for the temple of
8:32 [A] then hear from heaven and **act**. Judge between your servants,
8:39 [A] Forgive and **act**; deal with each man according to all he does,
8:43 [A] dwelling place, and **do** whatever the foreigner asks of you,
8:45 [A] heaven their prayer and their plea, and **uphold** their cause.
8:49 [A] hear their prayer and their plea, and **uphold** their cause.
8:59 [A] that he *may* **uphold** the cause of his servant and the cause of
8:64 [A] there *he* **offered** burnt offerings, grain offerings and the fat
8:65 [A] So Solomon **observed** the festival at that time, and all Israel
8:66 [A] glad in heart for all the good things the LORD *had* **done** for
9: 1 [A] the royal palace, and had achieved all he had desired to **do**,
9: 4 [A] and **do** all I command and observe my decrees and laws,
9: 8 [A] 'Why *has* the LORD **done** such a thing to this land and to
9:23 [A] 550 officials supervising the men who **did** the work.
9:26 [A] King Solomon also **built** ships at Ezion Geber, which is near
10: 9 [A] has made you king, to **maintain** justice and righteousness."
10:12 [A] The king **used** the almugwood **to make** supports for the
10:16 [A] King Solomon **made** two hundred large shields of hammered
10:18 [A] the king **made** a great throne inlaid with ivory and overlaid
10:20 [C] Nothing like it *had ever* **been made** for any other kingdom.
11: 6 [A] So Solomon **did** evil in the eyes of the LORD; he did not
11: 8 [A] *He* **did** the same for all his foreign wives, who burned
11:12 [A] of David your father, *I will* not **do** it during your lifetime.
11:25 [A] adding to the trouble **caused** [BHS 889] *by* Hadad.
11:28 [A] when Solomon saw how well the young man **did** his work,
11:33 [A] nor **done** what is right in my eyes, nor kept my statutes
11:38 [A] **do** what is right in my eyes by keeping my statutes
11:38 [A] my statutes and commands, as David my servant **did**,
11:41 [A] Solomon's reign—all *he* **did** and the wisdom he displayed—
12:21 [A] a hundred and eighty thousand **fighting** [+4878] men—
12:27 [A] If these people go up to **offer** sacrifices at the temple of the
12:28 [A] After seeking advice, the king **made** two golden calves. He
12:31 [A] Jeroboam **built** shrines on high places and appointed priests
12:31 [A] on high places and **appointed** priests from all sorts of people,
12:32 [A] He **instituted** a festival on the fifteenth day of the eighth
12:32 [A] This *he* **did** in Bethel, sacrificing to the calves he had made.
12:32 [A] This he did in Bethel, sacrificing to the calves *he had* **made**.
12:32 [A] he also installed priests at the high places *he had* **made**.
12:33 [A] he offered sacrifices on the altar *he had* **built** at Bethel.
12:33 [A] So *he* **instituted** the festival for the Israelites and went up to
13:11 [A] told him all that the man of God *had* **done** [+5126] there that
13:33 [A] once more **appointed** priests for the high places from all
14: 4 [A] So Jeroboam's wife **did** what he said and went to Ahijah's
14: 8 [A] me with all his heart, **doing** only what was right in my eyes.
14: 9 [A] You have **done** more evil than all who lived before you. You
14: 9 [A] *You have* **made** for yourself other gods, idols made of metal;
14:15 [A] because they provoked the LORD to anger *by* **making**
14:22 [A] Judah **did** evil in the eyes of the LORD. By the sins they
14:22 [A] stirred up his jealous anger more than their fathers *had* **done**.
14:24 [A] the people **engaged in** all the detestable practices of the
14:26 [A] including all the gold shields Solomon *had* **made**.
14:27 [A] So King Rehoboam **made** bronze shields to replace them
14:29 [A] As for the other events of Rehoboam's reign, and all *he* **did**,
15: 3 [A] He committed all the sins his father *had* **done** before him;
15: 5 [A] For David *had* **done** what was right in the eyes of the
15: 7 [A] As for the other events of Abijah's reign, and all *he* **did**, are
15:11 [A] Asa **did** what was right in the eyes of the LORD, as his
15:12 [A] the land and got rid of all the idols his fathers *had* **made**.
15:13 [A] because *she had* **made** a repulsive Asherah pole.
15:23 [A] all his achievements, all *he* **did** and the cities he built,
15:26 [A] *He* **did** evil in the eyes of the LORD, walking in the ways
15:31 [A] As for the other events of Nadab's reign, and all *he* **did**, are
15:34 [A] *He* **did** evil in the eyes of the LORD, walking in the ways
16: 5 [A] events of Baasha's reign, what *he* **did** and his achievements,
16: 7 [A] because of all the evil *he had* **done** in the eyes of the
16:14 [A] As for the other events of Elah's reign, and all *he* **did**, are
16:19 [A] **doing** evil in the eyes of the LORD and walking in the ways
16:19 [A] in the sin *he had* **committed** and had caused Israel to
16:25 [A] Omri **did** evil in the eyes of the LORD and sinned more
16:27 [A] of Omri's reign, what *he* **did** and the things he achieved,
16:27 [A] of Omri's reign, what he did and the things *he* **achieved**,
16:30 [A] Ahab son of Omri **did** more evil in the eyes of the LORD
16:33 [A] Ahab also **made** an Asherah pole and did more to provoke
16:33 [A] made an Asherah pole and **did** more to provoke the LORD,
17: 5 [A] So *he* **did** what the LORD had told him. He went to the
17:12 [A] sticks to take home and **make** a meal for myself and my son,
17:13 [A] to her, "Don't be afraid. Go home and **do** as you have said.
17:13 [A] first **make** a small cake of bread for me from what you have
17:13 [A] it to me, and then **make** something for yourself and your son.
17:15 [A] She went away and **did** as Elijah had told her. So there was
18:13 [A] what *I* **did** while Jezebel was killing the prophets of the
18:23 [A] I *will* **prepare** the other bull and put it on the wood but not
18:25 [A] "Choose one of the bulls and **prepare** it first, since there are
18:26 [A] So they took the bull given them and **prepared** it. Then they
18:26 [A] And they danced around the altar *they had* **made**.
18:32 [A] *he* **dug** a trench around it large enough to hold two seahs of
18:36 [A] and *have* **done** all these things at your command.
19: 1 [A] Now Ahab told Jezebel everything Elijah *had* **done** and how
19: 2 [A] to say, "*May* the gods **deal with** me, be it ever so severely,
19:20 [A] "Go back," Elijah replied. "What *have I* **done** to you?"
20: 9 [A] 'Your servant *will* **do** all you demanded the first time,
20: 9 [A] this demand I cannot **meet**.' " They left and took the answer
20:10 [A] "*May* the gods **deal** with me, be it ever so severely, if
20:22 [A] "Strengthen your position and see what *must be* **done**,
20:24 [A] **Do** this: Remove all the kings from their commands
20:25 [A] than they." He agreed with them and **acted** accordingly.

1Ki 20:40 [A] While your servant was **busy** here and there, the man
21: 7 [A] his wife said, "Is this how you **act** as king over Israel?
21:11 [A] nobles who lived in Naboth's city **did** as Jezebel directed in
21:20 [A] "because you have sold yourself to **do** evil in the eyes of the
21:25 [A] who sold himself to **do** evil in the eyes of the LORD, urged
21:26 [A] like **[NIE]** the Amorites the LORD drove out before
22:11 [A] Now Zedekiah son of Kenaanah *had* **made** iron horns and he
22:22 [A] will succeed in enticing him,' said the LORD. 'Go and **do** it.'
22:39 [A] including all *he* **did**, the palace he built and inlaid with ivory,
22:43 [A] from them; he **did** what was right in the eyes of the LORD.
22:45 [22:46] [A] the things he **achieved** and his military exploits,
22:48 [22:49] [A] Now Jehoshaphat **built** [K 6925] a fleet of trading
22:52 [22:53] [A] *He* **did** evil in the eyes of the LORD, because he
22:53 [22:54] [A] God of Israel, to anger, just as his father *had* **done**.
2Ki 1:18 [A] for all the other events of Ahaziah's reign, and what *he* **did**,
2: 9 [A] what *can I* **do** for you before I am taken from you?"
3: 2 [A] *He* **did** evil in the eyes of the LORD, but not as his father
3: 2 [A] got rid of the sacred stone of Baal that his father *had* **made**.
3:16 [A] is what the LORD says: **Make** this valley full of ditches.
4: 2 [A] Elisha replied to her, "How *can I* **help** [+4200] you? Tell me,
4:10 [A] *Let's* **make** a small room on the roof and put in it a bed and a
4:13 [A] to all this trouble for us. Now what *can be* **done** for you?
4:14 [A] "What *can be* **done** for her?" Elisha asked. Gehazi said,
5:13 [A] you to do some great thing, *would you* not *have* **done** it?
5:17 [A] for your servant *will* never again **make** burnt offerings
6: 2 [A] can get a pole; and *let us* **build** a place there for us to live."
6:15 [A] the city. "Oh, my lord, what *shall we* **do**?" the servant asked.
6:31 [A] He said, "*May* God **deal** with me, be it ever so severely, if
7: 2 [A] *even if* the LORD *should* **open** the floodgates of the
7: 9 [A] they said to each other, "We're not **doing** right. This is a day
7:12 [A] "I will tell you what the Arameans *have* **done** to us.
7:19 [A] *even if* the LORD *should* **open** the floodgates of the
8: 2 [A] The woman proceeded *to* **do** as the man of God said. She
8: 4 [A] "Tell me about all the great things Elisha *has* **done**."
8:12 [A] "Because I know the harm *you will* **do** to the Israelites,"
8:13 [A] "How *could* your servant, a mere dog, **accomplish** such a
8:18 [A] as the house of Ahab *had* **done**, for he married a daughter of
8:18 [A] a daughter of Ahab. *He* **did** evil in the eyes of the LORD.
8:23 [A] As for the other events of Jehoram's reign, and all *he* **did**,
8:27 [A] of the house of Ahab and **did** evil in the eyes of the LORD,
10: 5 [A] "We are your servants and *we will* **do** anything you say. We
10: 5 [A] not appoint anyone as king; *you* **do** whatever you think best."
10:10 [A] The LORD *has* **done** what he promised through his servant
10:19 [A] Jehu *was* **acting** deceptively in order to destroy the ministers
10:24 [A] So they went in to **make** sacrifices and burnt offerings.
10:25 [A] As soon as Jehu had finished **making** the burnt offering, he
10:30 [A] "Because you have done well in **accomplishing** what is right
10:30 [A] and *have* **done** to the house of Ahab all I had in mind to do,
10:34 [A] events of Jehu's reign, all *he* **did**, and all his achievements,
11: 5 [A] He commanded them, saying, "This is what *you are to* **do**:
11: 9 [A] The commanders of units of a hundred **did** just as Jehoiada
12: 2 [12:3] [A] Joash **did** what was right in the eyes of the LORD
12:11 [12:12] [A] men appointed *to* **supervise** the work on the temple.
12:11 [12:12] [A] With it they paid those *who* **worked** on the temple
12:13 [12:14] [C] **was** not **spent for making** [+4946] silver basins,
12:14 [12:15] [A] it was paid to the **workmen** [+4856], who used it to
12:15 [12:16] [A] they gave the money to pay the **workers** [+4856],
12:15 [12:16] [A] because they **acted** with complete honesty.
12:19 [12:20] [A] other events of the reign of Joash, and all *he* **did**,
13: 2 [A] *He* **did** evil in the eyes of the LORD by following the sins
13: 8 [A] of the reign of Jehoahaz, all *he* **did** and his achievements,
13:11 [A] *He* **did** evil in the eyes of the LORD and did not turn away
13:12 [A] of the reign of Jehoash, all *he* **did** and his achievements,
14: 3 [A] *He* **did** what was right in the eyes of the LORD, but not as
14: 3 [A] In everything *he* **followed** [+3869+6913] **the example** *of* his
14: 3 [A] In everything *he* **followed the example of** [+3869+6913] his
14:15 [A] of the reign of Jehoash, what *he* **did** and his achievements,
14:24 [A] *He* **did** evil in the eyes of the LORD and did not turn away
14:28 [A] Jeroboam's reign, all *he* **did**, and his military achievements,
15: 3 [A] *He* **did** what was right in the eyes of the LORD, just as his
15: 3 [A] the eyes of the LORD, just as his father Amaziah *had* **done**.
15: 6 [A] As for the other events of Azariah's reign, and all *he* **did**, are
15: 9 [A] *He* **did** evil in the eyes of the LORD, as his fathers had
15: 9 [A] did evil in the eyes of the LORD, as his fathers *had* **done**.
15:18 [A] *He* **did** evil in the eyes of the LORD. During his entire
15:21 [A] As for the other events of Menahem's reign, and all *he* **did**,
15:24 [A] Pekahiah **did** evil in the eyes of the LORD. He did not turn
15:26 [A] The other events of Pekahiah's reign, and all *he* **did**, are
15:28 [A] *He* **did** evil in the eyes of the LORD. He did not turn away
15:31 [A] As for the other events of Pekah's reign, and all *he* **did**,
15:34 [A] *He* **did** what was right in the eyes of the LORD, just as his
15:34 [A] the eyes of the LORD, just as his father Uzziah *had* **done**.
15:34 [A] of the LORD, just as his father Uzziah had done. **[RPH]**
15:36 [A] As for the other events of Jotham's reign, and what *he* **did**,
16: 2 [A] *he did* not **do** what was right in the eyes of the LORD his
16:11 [A] from Damascus and **finished** it before King Ahaz returned.
16:16 [A] And Uriah the priest **did** just as King Ahaz had ordered.
16:19 [A] As for the other events of the reign of Ahaz, and what *he* **did**,
17: 2 [A] *He* **did** evil in the eyes of the LORD, but not like the kings
17: 8 [A] well as the practices that the kings of Israel *had* **introduced**.
17:11 [A] *They* **did** wicked things that provoked the LORD to anger.
17:12 [A] though the LORD had said, "*You shall* not **do** this."
17:15 [A] "*Do* not **do** as they do," and they did the things the LORD
17:16 [A] **made** for themselves two idols cast in the shape of calves,
17:16 [A] cast in the shape of calves, and **[RPH]** an Asherah pole.
17:17 [A] and sold themselves to **do** evil in the eyes of the LORD,
17:19 [A] They followed the practices Israel *had* **introduced**.
17:22 [A] sins of Jeroboam **[RPH]** and did not turn away from them
17:29 [A] each national group **made** its own gods in the several towns
17:29 [A] set them up in the shrines the people of Samaria *had* **made** at
17:30 [A] The men from Babylon **made** Succoth Benoth, the men from
17:30 [A] the men from Cuthah **made** Nergal, and the men from
17:30 [A] made Nergal, and the men from Hamath **made** Ashima;
17:31 [A] the Avvites **made** Nibhaz and Tartak, and the Sepharvites
17:32 [A] *they* also **appointed** all sorts of their own people to officiate
17:32 [A] *to* **officiate** for them *as* priests in the shrines at the high
17:34 [A] To this day they **persist** in their former practices.
17:34 [A] They neither worship the LORD nor **adhere** [+3869] **to** the
17:37 [A] You must always be careful to **keep** the decrees and
17:40 [A] however, but **persisted** [+3869] **in** their former practices.
17:41 [A] and grandchildren *continue to* **do** as their fathers did.
17:41 [A] and grandchildren continue to do as their fathers **did**.
18: 3 [A] *He* **did** what was right in the eyes of the LORD, just as his
18: 3 [A] in the eyes of the LORD, just as his father David *had* **done**.
18: 4 [A] He broke into pieces the bronze snake Moses *had* **made**,
18:12 [A] They neither listened to the commands nor **carried** them **out**.
18:31 [A] of Assyria says: **Make** peace with me and come out to me.
19:11 [A] Surely you have heard what the kings of Assyria *have* **done**
19:15 [A] the kingdoms of the earth. You *have* **made** heaven and earth.
19:25 [A] " 'Have you not heard? Long ago *I* **ordained** it. In days of
19:30 [A] the house of Judah will take root below and **bear** fruit above.
19:31 [A] The zeal of the LORD Almighty *will* **accomplish** this.
20: 3 [A] and *have* **done** what is good in your eyes."
20: 9 [A] "This is the LORD's sign to you that the LORD *will* **do**
20:20 [A] how *he* **made** the pool and the tunnel by which he brought
21: 2 [A] *He* **did** evil in the eyes of the LORD,
21: 3 [A] he also erected altars to Baal and **made** an Asherah pole,
21: 3 [A] and made an Asherah pole, as Ahab king of Israel *had* **done**.
21: 6 [A] and divination, and **consulted** mediums and spiritists.
21: 6 [A] He **did** much evil in the eyes of the LORD, provoking him
21: 7 [A] He took the carved Asherah pole *he had* **made** and put it in
21: 8 [A] be careful to **do** everything I commanded them and will keep
21: 9 [A] so that they **did** more evil than the nations the LORD had
21:11 [A] "Manasseh king of Judah *has* **committed** these detestable
21:11 [A] He has done more evil than the Amorites **[NIE]** who
21:15 [A] because *they have* **done** evil in my eyes and have provoked
21:16 [A] to commit, so that they **did** evil in the eyes of the LORD.
21:17 [A] and all *he* **did**, including the sin he committed,
21:20 [A] *He* **did** evil in the eyes of the LORD, as his father
21:20 [A] in the eyes of the LORD, as his father Manasseh *had* **done**.
21:25 [A] As for the other events of Amon's reign, and what *he* **did**,
22: 2 [A] *He* **did** what was right in the eyes of the LORD and walked
22: 5 [A] Have them entrust it to the men appointed *to* **supervise** the
22: 5 [A] have these men pay the **workers** [+4856] who repair the
22: 7 [A] entrusted to them, because they *are* **acting** faithfully."
22: 9 [A] have entrusted it to the **workers** [+4856] and supervisors at
22:13 [A] they *have* not **acted** in accordance with all that is written
23: 4 [B] from the temple of the LORD all the articles **made** for Baal
23:12 [A] He pulled down the altars the kings of Judah *had* **erected** on
23:12 [A] the altars Manasseh *had* **built** in the two courts of the temple
23:15 [A] at Bethel, the high place **made** *by* Jeroboam son of Nebat,
23:17 [A] the altar of Bethel the very things *you have* **done** to it."
23:19 [A] Just as *he had* **done** [+5126] at Bethel, Josiah removed
23:19 [A] **defiled**[s] all the shrines at the high places that the kings of
23:19 [A] *had* **built** in the towns of Samaria that had provoked the
23:21 [A] "**Celebrate** the Passover to the LORD your God, as it is
23:22 [C] the kings of Judah, *had* any such Passover **been observed**.
23:23 [C] this Passover **was celebrated** to the LORD in Jerusalem.
23:28 [A] As for the other events of Josiah's reign, and all *he* **did**, are
23:32 [A] *He* **did** evil in the eyes of the LORD, just as his fathers had
23:32 [A] evil in the eyes of the LORD, just as his fathers *had* **done**.
23:37 [A] *he* **did** evil in the eyes of the LORD, just as his fathers had
23:37 [A] evil in the eyes of the LORD, just as his fathers *had* **done**.
24: 3 [A] because of the sins of Manasseh and all *he had* **done**,
24: 5 [A] As for the other events of Jehoiakim's reign, and all *he* **did**,
24: 9 [A] *He* **did** evil in the eyes of the LORD, just as his father had
24: 9 [A] evil in the eyes of the LORD, just as his father *had* **done**.
24:13 [A] king of Israel *had* **made** for the temple of the LORD.

2Ki 24:16 [A] strong and **fit for** war, and a thousand craftsmen and artisans.
24:19 [A] *He* **did** evil in the eyes of the LORD, just as Jehoiakim had
24:19 [A] evil in the eyes of the LORD, just as Jehoiakim *had* **done**.
25:16 [A] which Solomon *had* **made** for the temple of the LORD,
1Ch 4:10 [A] and **keep** me from harm so that I will be free from pain."
5:10 [A] During Saul's reign *they* **waged** war against the Hagrites,
5:19 [A] *They* **waged** war against the Hagrites, Jetur, Naphish
10:11 [A] Gilead heard of everything the Philistines *had* **done** to Saul,
11:19 [A] "God forbid that I *should* **do** this!" he said. "Should I drink
11:19 [A] not drink it. Such *were the* **exploits** *of* the three mighty men.
11:24 [A] Such *were the* **exploits** *of* Benaiah son of Jehoiada; he too
12:32 [12:33] [A] the times and knew what Israel *should* **do**—
13:4 [A] The whole assembly agreed to **do** this, because it seemed
14:16 [A] So David **did** as God commanded him, and they struck down
15:1 [A] After David *had* **constructed** buildings for himself in the
16:12 [A] Remember the wonders *he has* **done**, his miracles,
16:26 [A] of the nations are idols, but the LORD **made** the heavens.
17:2 [A] "Whatever you have in mind, **do** it, for God is with you."
17:8 [A] Now *I will* **make** your name like the names of the greatest
17:19 [A] *you have* **done** this great thing and made known all these
17:23 [A] and his house be established forever. **Do** as you promised,
18:8 [A] which Solomon used *to* **make** the bronze Sea, the pillars and
18:14 [A] all Israel, **doing** what was just and right for all his people.
19:2 [A] "*I will* **show** kindness to Hanun son of Nahash,
19:2 [A] son of Nahash, because his father **showed** kindness to me."
19:13 [A] of our God. The LORD *will* **do** what is good in his sight."
20:3 [A] and axes. David **did** this to all the Ammonite towns.
21:8 [A] David said to God, "I have sinned greatly *by* **doing** this.
21:10 [A] Choose one of them *for me to* **carry out** against you.' "
21:17 [A] and done wrong. These are but sheep. What *have they* **done**?
21:23 [A] *Let* my lord the king **do** whatever pleases him. Look, I will
21:29 [A] of the LORD, which Moses *had* **made** in the desert,
22:8 [A] 'You have shed much blood and *have* **fought** many wars.
22:13 [A] have success if you are careful to **observe** the decrees and
22:15 [A] You have many **workmen** [+4856]: stonecutters, masons and
22:16 [A] Now begin *the* **work**, and the LORD be with you."
23:5 [A] the musical instruments *I have* **provided** for that purpose."
23:24 [A] the **workers** [+4856] twenty years old or more who served in
27:26 [A] Ezri son of Kelub was in charge of the field **workers** [+4856]
28:7 [A] forever if he is unswerving in **carrying out** my commands
28:10 [A] build a temple as a sanctuary. Be strong and **do** *the* **work**."
28:20 [A] his son, "Be strong and courageous, and **do** *the* **work**.
29:19 [A] to **do** everything to build the palatial structure for which I
2Ch 1:3 [A] which Moses the LORD's servant *had* **made** in the desert.
1:5 [A] *had* **made** was in Gibeon in front of the tabernacle of the
1:8 [A] "You *have* **shown** great kindness to David my father
2:3 [2:2] [A] "Send me cedar logs as *you* **did** for my father David
2:7 [2:6] [A] a man skilled to **work** in gold and silver, bronze
2:12 [2:11] [A] the God of Israel, who **made** heaven and earth!
2:14 [2:13] [A] He is trained to **work** in gold and silver, bronze
2:18 [2:17] [A] *He* **assigned** 70,000 of them to be carriers
3:8 [A] *He* **built** the Most Holy Place, its length corresponding to the
3:10 [A] In the Most Holy Place *he* **made** a pair of sculptured
3:14 [A] *He* **made** the curtain of blue, purple and crimson yarn
3:15 [A] In the front of the temple *he* **made** two pillars,
3:16 [A] *He* **made** interwoven chains and put them on top of the
3:16 [A] *He* also **made** a hundred pomegranates and attached them to
4:1 [A] *He* **made** a bronze altar twenty cubits long, twenty cubits
4:2 [A] *He* **made** the Sea of cast metal, circular in shape, measuring
4:6 [A] *He* then **made** ten basins for washing and placed five on the
4:7 [A] *He* **made** ten gold lampstands according to the specifications
4:8 [A] *He* **made** ten tables and placed them in the temple, five on
4:8 [A] on the north. *He* also **made** a hundred gold sprinkling bowls.
4:9 [A] *He* **made** the courtyard of the priests, and the large court
4:11 [A] He also **made** the pots and shovels and sprinkling bowls.
4:11 [A] So Huram finished **[RPH]** the work he had undertaken for
4:11 [A] So Huram finished the work *he had* **undertaken** for King
4:14 [A] the stands **[RPH]** with their basins;
4:14 [A] the stands with their basins; **[RPH]**
4:16 [A] All the objects that Huram-Abi **made** for King Solomon for
4:18 [A] All these things that Solomon **made** amounted to so much
4:19 [A] also **made** all the furnishings that were in God's temple:
5:1 [A] When all the work Solomon *had* **done** for the temple of the
6:13 [A] Now he *had* **made** a bronze platform, five cubits long, five
6:23 [A] then hear from heaven and **act**. Judge between your servants,
6:33 [A] dwelling place, and **do** whatever the foreigner asks of you,
6:35 [A] heaven their prayer and their plea, and **uphold** their cause.
6:39 [A] hear their prayer and their pleas, and **uphold** their cause.
7:6 [A] which King David *had* **made** for praising the LORD
7:7 [A] there *he* **offered** burnt offerings and the fat of the fellowship
7:7 [A] because the bronze altar he *had* **made** could not hold the
7:8 [A] So Solomon **observed** the festival at that time for seven days,
7:9 [A] On the eighth day *they* **held** an assembly, for they had
7:9 [A] for *they had* **celebrated** the dedication of the altar for seven
7:10 [A] glad in heart for the good things the LORD *had* **done** for
7:11 [A] had succeeded in carrying out all he had in mind to **do** in the
7:17 [A] and **do** all I command, and observe my decrees and laws,
7:21 [A] 'Why *has* the LORD **done** such a thing to this land and to
9:8 [A] you king over them, to **maintain** justice and righteousness."
9:11 [A] The king **used** the algumwood **to make** steps for the temple
9:15 [A] King Solomon **made** two hundred large shields of hammered
9:17 [A] the king **made** a great throne inlaid with ivory and overlaid
9:19 [C] Nothing like it *had ever* **been made** for any other kingdom.
11:1 [A] a hundred and eighty thousand **fighting** [+4878] men—
11:15 [A] the high places and for the goat and calf idols *he had* **made**.
12:9 [A] including the gold shields Solomon *had* **made**.
12:10 [A] So King Rehoboam **made** bronze shields to replace them
12:14 [A] *He* **did** evil because he had not set his heart on seeking the
13:8 [A] you the golden calves that Jeroboam **made** to be your gods.
13:9 [A] **make** priests of your own as the peoples of other lands do?
14:2 [14:1] [A] Asa **did** what was good and right in the eyes of the
14:4 [14:3] [A] of their fathers, and to **obey** his laws and commands.
15:16 [A] because *she had* **made** a repulsive Asherah pole.
18:10 [A] Now Zedekiah son of Kenaanah *had* **made** iron horns,
18:21 [A] will succeed in enticing him,' said the LORD. 'Go and **do** it.'
19:6 [A] He told them, "Consider carefully what you **do**, because you
19:7 [A] **Judge**[s] carefully, for with the LORD our God there is no
19:9 [A] "*You must* **serve** faithfully and wholeheartedly in the fear of
19:10 [A] come on you and your brothers. **Do** this, and you will not sin.
19:11 [A] **Act** with courage, and may the LORD be with those who do
20:12 [A] We do not know what *to* **do**, but our eyes are upon you."
20:32 [A] from them; *he* **did** what was right in the eyes of the LORD.
20:35 [A] king of Israel, who was guilty of wickedness. **[NIE]**
20:36 [A] He agreed with him to **construct** a fleet of trading ships.
20:36 [A] fleet of trading ships. After these *were* **built** at Ezion Geber,
21:6 [A] as the house of Ahab *had* **done**, for he married a daughter of
21:6 [A] a daughter of Ahab. *He* **did** evil in the eyes of the LORD.
21:11 [A] He *had* also **built** high places on the hills of Judah and had
21:19 [A] His people **made** no fire in his honor, as they had for his
22:4 [A] *He* **did** evil in the eyes of the LORD, as the house of Ahab
23:4 [A] Now this is what *you are to* **do**: A third of you priests
23:8 [A] all the men of Judah **did** just as Jehoiada the priest ordered.
24:2 [A] Joash **did** what was right in the eyes of the LORD all the
24:7 [A] of God and *had* **used** even its sacred objects for the Baals.
24:8 [A] the king's command, a chest *was* **made** and placed outside,
24:11 [A] *They* **did** this regularly and collected a great amount of
24:12 [A] Jehoiada gave it to the *men who* **carried out** the work
24:13 [A] The *men* **in charge** *of* the work were diligent, and the repairs
24:13 [A] The men in charge of the work *were* **diligent**, and the repairs
24:14 [A] and *with* it *were* **made** articles for the LORD's temple:
24:16 [A] because of the good *he had* **done** in Israel for God and his
24:22 [A] the kindness Zechariah's father Jehoiada *had* **shown** him
24:24 [A] the God of their fathers, judgment *was* **executed** *on* Joash.
25:2 [A] *He* **did** what was right in the eyes of the LORD, but not
25:8 [A] Even if you go and **fight** courageously in battle, God will
25:9 [A] "But what **[NIE]** about the hundred talents I paid for these
25:16 [A] because *you have* **done** this and have not listened to my
26:4 [A] *He* **did** what was right in the eyes of the LORD, just as his
26:4 [A] the eyes of the LORD, just as his father Amaziah *had* **done**.
26:11 [A] Uzziah had a **well-trained** [+4878] army, ready to go out by
26:13 [A] command was an army of 307,500 *men* **trained** *for* war,
26:15 [A] In Jerusalem *he* **made** machines designed by skillful men for
27:2 [A] *He* **did** what was right in the eyes of the LORD, just as his
27:2 [A] the eyes of the LORD, just as his father Uzziah *had* **done**,
28:1 [A] *he did* not **do** what was right in the eyes of the LORD.
28:2 [A] of Israel and also **made** cast idols for worshiping the Baals.
28:24 [A] and **set up** altars at every street corner in Jerusalem.
28:25 [A] In every town in Judah *he* **built** high places to burn sacrifices
29:2 [A] *He* **did** what was right in the eyes of the LORD, just as his
29:2 [A] in the eyes of the LORD, just as his father David *had* **done**.
29:6 [A] *they* **did** evil in the eyes of the LORD our God and forsook
30:1 [A] in Jerusalem and **celebrate** the Passover to the LORD,
30:2 [A] the whole assembly in Jerusalem decided to **celebrate** the
30:3 [A] They had not been able to **celebrate** it at the regular time
30:5 [A] to Jerusalem and **celebrate** the Passover to the LORD,
30:5 [A] *It had* not *been* **celebrated** in large numbers according to
30:12 [A] people to give them unity of mind to **carry out** what the king
30:13 [A] **celebrate** the Feast of Unleavened Bread in the second
30:21 [A] The Israelites who were present in Jerusalem **celebrated** the
30:23 [A] then agreed to **celebrate** the festival seven more days;
30:23 [A] so for another seven days *they* **celebrated** joyfully.
31:20 [A] This is what Hezekiah **did** throughout Judah, doing what was
31:20 [A] **doing** what was good and right and faithful before the
31:21 [A] he sought his God and **worked** wholeheartedly.
32:5 [A] *He* also **made** large numbers of weapons and shields.
32:13 [A] my fathers *have* **done** to all the peoples of the other lands?
32:27 [A] *he* **made** treasuries for his silver and gold and for his
32:29 [A] *He* **built** villages and acquired great numbers of flocks

2Ch 32:33 [A] the people of Jerusalem **honored** [+3883+4200] him when
33: 2 [A] *He* **did** evil in the eyes of the LORD,
33: 3 [A] he also erected altars to the Baals and **made** Asherah poles.
33: 6 [A] and witchcraft, and **consulted** mediums and spiritists.
33: 6 [A] He **did** much evil in the eyes of the LORD, provoking him
33: 7 [A] He took the carved image *he had* **made** and put it in God's
33: 8 [A] if only they will be careful to **do** everything I commanded
33: 9 [A] so that they **did** more evil than the nations the LORD had
33:22 [A] *He* **did** evil in the eyes of the LORD, as his father
33:22 [A] in the eyes of the LORD, as his father Manasseh *had* **done**.
33:22 [A] and offered sacrifices to all the idols Manasseh *had* **made**.
34: 2 [A] *He* **did** what was right in the eyes of the LORD and walked
34:10 [A] they entrusted it to the men appointed *to* **supervise** the work
34:10 [A] **These men**[s] [+2021+4856] paid the workers who repaired
34:10 [A] These men paid the **workers** who repaired and restored the
34:12 [A] The men **did** the work faithfully. Over them to direct them
34:13 [A] and supervised all the **workers** [+4856] from job to job.
34:16 [A] "Your officials *are* **doing** everything that has been
34:17 [A] have entrusted it to the supervisors and **workers** [+4856]."
34:21 [A] they *have* not **acted** in accordance with all that is written in
34:31 [A] and to **obey** the words of the covenant written in this book.
34:32 [A] the people of Jerusalem **did** this in accordance with the
35: 1 [A] Josiah **celebrated** the Passover to the LORD in Jerusalem,
35: 6 [A] **doing** what the LORD commanded through Moses."
35:16 [A] LORD was carried out for the **celebration** *of* the Passover
35:17 [A] present **celebrated** the Passover at that time and observed
35:18 [C] The Passover *had* not **been observed** like this in Israel since
35:18 [A] none of the kings of Israel *had ever* **celebrated** such a
35:18 [A] of Israel had ever celebrated such a Passover as **did** Josiah,
35:19 [C] This Passover **was celebrated** in the eighteenth year of
36: 5 [A] eleven years. *He* **did** evil in the eyes of the LORD his God.
36: 8 [A] the detestable things *he* **did** and all that was found against
36: 9 [A] and ten days. *He* **did** evil in the eyes of the LORD.
36:12 [A] *He* **did** evil in the eyes of the LORD his God and did not
Ezr 3: 4 [A] *they* **celebrated** the Feast of Tabernacles with the required
3: 9 [A] joined together in supervising *those* **working** *on* the house of
6:19 [A] day of the first month, the exiles **celebrated** the Passover.
6:22 [A] For seven days *they* **celebrated** with joy the Feast of
7:10 [A] to the study and **observance** *of* the Law of the LORD,
10: 3 [C] commands of our God. *Let it* **be done** according to the Law.
10: 4 [A] your hands. We will support you, so take courage and **do** it."
10: 5 [A] and all Israel under oath to **do** what had been suggested.
10:11 [A] to the LORD, the God of your fathers, and **do** his will.
10:12 [A] with a loud voice: "You are right! We *must* **do** as you say.
10:16 [A] So the exiles **did** as was proposed. Ezra the priest selected
Ne 1: 9 [A] you return to me and **obey** [+906+2256+9068] my commands,
2:12 [A] I had not told anyone what my God had put in my heart to **do**
2:16 [A] officials did not know where I had gone or what I *was* **doing**,
2:16 [A] or officials or any others *who would be* **doing** the work.
2:19 [A] and ridiculed us. "What is this you *are* **doing**?" they asked.
3:16 [B] as far as the **artificial** pool and the House of the Heroes.
4: 2 [3:34] [A] he said, "What are those feeble Jews **doing**?
4: 6 [3:38] [A] its height, for the people **worked** with all their heart.
4: 8 [4:2] [A] fight against Jerusalem and **stir up** trouble against it.
4:16 [4:10] [A] From that day on, half of my men **did** the work,
4:17 [4:11] [A] Those who carried materials **did** their work with one
4:21 [4:15] [A] So we **continued** the work with half the men holding
5: 9 [A] So I continued, "What you *are* **doing** is not right. Shouldn't
5:12 [A] *We will* **do** as you say." Then I summoned the priests
5:12 [A] and officials take an oath to **do** what they had promised.
5:13 [A] the LORD. And the people **did** as they had promised.
5:15 [A] But out of reverence for God I *did* not **act** like that.
5:18 [C] **[RPH]** Each day one ox, six choice sheep and some poultry
5:18 [C] six choice sheep and some poultry **were prepared** for me,
5:19 [A] with favor, O my God, for all *I have* **done** for these people.
6: 2 [A] But they were scheming to **harm** [+4200+8288] me;
6: 3 [A] "I *am* **carrying on** a great project and cannot go down. Why
6: 9 [C] get too weak for the work, and *it will* not **be completed**."
6:13 [A] to intimidate me so that I would commit a sin *by* **doing** this,
6:16 [C] because they realized that this work *had* **been done** with the
8: 4 [A] Ezra the scribe stood on a high wooden platform **built** for the
8:12 [A] to send portions of food and to **celebrate** with great joy,
8:15 [A] and from myrtles, palms and shade trees, to **make** booths"—
8:16 [A] and **built** themselves booths on their own roofs,
8:17 [A] The whole company that had returned from exile **built**
8:17 [A] until that day, the Israelites *had* not **celebrated** it like this.
8:18 [A] *They* **celebrated** the feast for seven days, and on the eighth
9: 6 [A] You **made** the heavens, even the highest heavens, and all
9:10 [A] *You* **made** a name for yourself, which remains to this day.
9:17 [A] failed to remember the miracles *you* **performed** among
9:18 [A] even when *they* **cast** for themselves an image of a calf
9:18 [A] out of Egypt,' or when *they* **committed** awful blasphemies.
9:24 [A] the peoples of the land, to **deal** with them as they pleased.
9:26 [A] turn them back to you; *they* **committed** awful blasphemies.
9:28 [A] they were at rest, they again **did** what was evil in your sight.
9:29 [A] your ordinances, by which a man will live if *he* **obeys** them.
9:31 [A] in your great mercy *you did* not **put** an end *to* them
9:33 [A] been just; *you have* **acted** faithfully, while we did wrong.
9:34 [A] our priests and our fathers *did* not **follow** your law;
10:29 [10:30] [A] of God and to **obey** carefully all the commands,
11:12 [A] and their associates, *who* **carried on** work for the temple—
12:27 [A] were brought to Jerusalem to **celebrate** joyfully the
13: 5 [A] *he had* **provided** him *with* a large room formerly used to
13: 7 [A] Here I learned about the evil thing Eliashib *had* **done** in
13: 7 [A] *in* **providing** Tobiah a room in the courts of the house of
13:10 [A] singers **responsible** *for* the service had gone back to their
13:14 [A] do not blot out what I *have* so faithfully **done** for the house
13:17 [A] and said to them, "What is this wicked thing you *are* **doing**—
13:18 [A] Didn't your forefathers **do** the same things, so that our God
13:27 [A] Must we hear now that you too *are* **doing** all this terrible
Est 1: 3 [A] in the third year of his reign *he* **gave** a banquet for all his
1: 5 [A] days were over, the king **gave** a banquet, lasting seven days,
1: 8 [A] for the king instructed all the wine stewards to **serve** each
1: 9 [A] Queen Vashti also **gave** a banquet for the women in the royal
1:15 [A] "According to law, what *must be* **done** to Queen Vashti?"
1:15 [A] "*She has* not **obeyed** the command of King Xerxes that the
1:20 [A] when the king's edict is proclaimed **[NIE]** throughout all his
1:21 [A] with this advice, so the king **did** as Memucan proposed.
2: 1 [A] he remembered Vashti and what *she had* **done** and what he
2: 4 [A] This advice appealed to the king, and *he* **followed** [+4027] it.
2:11 [C] to find out how Esther was and what **was happening** to her.
2:18 [A] the king **gave** a great banquet, Esther's banquet, for all his
2:18 [A] *He* **proclaimed** a holiday throughout the provinces
2:20 [A] for she *continued to* **follow** Mordecai's instructions as she
3: 8 [A] of all other people and who *do* not **obey** the king's laws;
3: 9 [A] the royal treasury for the *men who* **carry out** this business."
3:11 [A] king said to Haman, "and **do** with the people as you please."
4: 1 [C] When Mordecai learned of all that *had* **been done**, he tore
4:17 [A] went away and **carried out** all of Esther's instructions.
5: 4 [A] come today to a banquet *I have* **prepared** for him."
5: 5 [A] the king said, "so that we **may do** what Esther asks."
5: 5 [A] and Haman went to the banquet Esther *had* **prepared**.
5: 6 [C] Even up to half the kingdom, *it will* **be granted**."
5: 8 [A] it pleases the king to grant my petition and **fulfill** my request,
5: 8 [A] Haman come tomorrow to the banquet *I will* **prepare** for
5: 8 [A] prepare for them. Then *I will* **answer** the king's question."
5:12 [A] invited to accompany the king to the banquet *she* **gave**.
5:14 [A] said to him, "*Have* a gallows **built**, seventy-five feet high,
5:14 [A] suggestion delighted Haman, and *he had* the gallows **built**.
6: 3 [C] and recognition *has* Mordecai **received** for this?"
6: 3 [C] "Nothing *has* **been done** for him," his attendants answered.
6: 6 [A] "What *should be* **done** for the man the king delights to
6: 6 [A] "Who is there that the king would rather **honor** [+3702] than
6: 9 [C] 'This is what **is done** for the man the king delights to
6:10 [A] and **do** just as you have suggested for Mordecai the Jew,
6:11 [C] "This is what **is done** for the man the king delights to honor!"
6:14 [A] hurried Haman away to the banquet Esther *had* **prepared**.
7: 2 [C] Even up to half the kingdom, *it will* **be granted**."
7: 5 [A] is he? Where is the man who has dared to **do** such a thing?"
7: 9 [A] He *had* it **made** for Mordecai, who spoke up to help the
9: 1 [C] the edict commanded by the king was to **be carried out**.
9: 3 [A] and the king's **administrators** [+4856] helped the Jews,
9: 5 [A] and *they* **did** what they pleased to those who hated them.
9:12 [A] What *have they* **done** in the rest of the king's provinces?
9:12 [C] be given you. What is your request? *It will* also **be granted**."
9:13 [A] "give the Jews in Susa permission to **carry out** this day's
9:14 [C] So the king commanded that this **be done**. An edict was
9:17 [A] fourteenth they rested and **made** it a day of feasting and joy.
9:18 [A] fifteenth they rested and **made** it a day of feasting and joy.
9:19 [A] **observe** the fourteenth of the month of Adar as a day of joy
9:21 [A] to have them **celebrate** annually the fourteenth and fifteenth
9:22 [A] He wrote them to **observe** the days as days of feasting
9:23 [A] So the Jews agreed to **continue** the celebration they had
9:27 [A] all who join them should without fail **observe** these two days
9:28 [C] and **observed** in every generation by every family,
Job 1: 4 [A] His sons used to take turns **holding** feasts in their homes,
1: 5 [A] cursed God in their hearts." This *was* Job's regular **custom**.
4:17 [A] than God? Can a man be more pure than his **Maker**?
5: 9 [A] *He* **performs** wonders that cannot be fathomed, miracles that
5:12 [A] the plans of the crafty, so that their hands **achieve** no success.
9: 9 [A] *He is* the **Maker** *of* the Bear and Orion, the Pleiades
9:10 [A] *He* **performs** wonders that cannot be fathomed, miracles that
9:12 [A] can stop him? Who can say to him, 'What *are you* **doing**?'
10: 8 [A] "Your hands shaped me and **made** me. Will you now turn
10: 9 [A] Remember that *you* **molded** me like clay. Will you now turn
10:12 [A] *You* gave me life and **showed** me kindness, and in your
12: 9 [A] does not know that the hand of the LORD *has* **done** this?
13:20 [A] "Only **grant** me these two things, O God, and then I will not

Job 14: 5 [A] number of his months and *have* **set** limits he cannot exceed.
14: 9 [A] scent of water it will bud and **put forth** shoots like a plant.
15:27 [A] with fat and his waist **bulges with flesh** [+6584+7089],
21:31 [A] conduct to his face? Who repays him for what *he has* **done**?
23: 9 [A] When he *is* **at work** in the north, I do not see him; when he
23:13 [A] and who can oppose him? *He* **does** whatever he pleases.
25: 2 [A] belong to God; *he* **establishes** order in the heights of heaven.
27:18 [A] is like a moth's cocoon, like a hut **made** *by* a watchman.
28:25 [A] When he **established** the force of the wind and measured out
28:26 [A] when he **made** a decree for the rain and a path for the
31:14 [A] what *will I* **do** when God confronts me? What will I answer
31:15 [A] Did not *he who* **made** me in the womb make them? Did not
31:15 [A] *Did* not he who made me in the womb **make** them? Did not
32:22 [A] skilled in flattery, my **Maker** would soon take me away.
33: 4 [A] The Spirit of God *has* **made** me; the breath of the Almighty
35: 6 [A] affect him? If your sins are many, what *does that* **do** to him?
35:10 [A] no one says, 'Where is God my **Maker**, who gives songs in
37: 5 [A] *he* **does** great things beyond our understanding.
40:15 [A] which *I* **made** along with you and which feeds on grass like
40:19 [A] of God, yet his **Maker** can approach him with his sword.
41:33 [41:25] [B] on earth is his equal—a **creature** without fear.
42: 8 [A] his prayer and not **deal** with you according to your folly.
42: 9 [A] and Zophar the Naamathite **did** what the LORD told them;
Ps 1: 3 [A] and whose leaf does not wither. Whatever *he* **does** prospers.
7: 3 [7:4] [A] if *I have* **done** this and there is guilt on my hands—
9: 4 [9:5] [A] For *you have* **upheld** my right and my cause;
9:15 [9:16] [A] The nations have fallen into the pit *they have* **dug**;
9:16 [9:17] [A] **[NIE]** the wicked are ensnared by the work of their
14: 1 [A] their deeds are vile; there is no *one who* **does** good.
14: 3 [A] there is no *one who* **does** good, not even one.
15: 3 [A] *who* **does** his neighbor no wrong and casts no slur on his
15: 5 [A] the innocent. *He who* **does** these things will never be shaken.
18:50 [18:51] [A] *he* **shows** unfailing kindness to his anointed,
22:31 [22:32] [A] to a people yet unborn—for *he has* **done** it.
31:23 [31:24] [A] but the **proud** [+1452] he pays back in full.
33: 6 [C] By the word of the LORD **were** the heavens **made**, their
34:14 [34:15] [A] Turn from evil and **do** good; seek peace and pursue
34:16 [34:17] [A] the face of the LORD is against *those who* **do** evil,
37: 1 [A] because of evil men or be envious of *those who* **do** wrong;
37: 3 [A] Trust in the LORD and **do** good; dwell in the land
37: 5 [A] your way to the LORD; trust in him and he *will* **do** this:
37: 7 [A] in their ways, when they **carry out** their wicked schemes.
37:27 [A] Turn from evil and **do** good; then you will dwell in the land
39: 9 [39:10] [A] my mouth, for you are the *one who has* **done** this.
40: 5 [40:6] [A] O LORD my God, are the wonders you *have* **done**.
40: 8 [40:9] [A] I desire to **do** your will, O my God; your law is
50:21 [A] These things *you have* **done** and I kept silent; you thought I
51: 4 [51:6] [A] have I sinned and **done** what is evil in your sight,
52: 2 [52:4] [A] it is like a sharpened razor, you *who* **practice** deceit.
52: 9 [52:11] [A] I will praise you forever for *what you have* **done**;
53: 1 [53:2] [A] their ways are vile; there is no *one who* **does** good.
53: 3 [53:4] [A] there is no *one who* **does** good, not even one.
56: 4 [56:5] [A] I will not be afraid. What *can* mortal man **do** to me?
56:11 [56:12] [A] I trust; I will not be afraid. What *can* man **do** to me?
60:12 [60:14] [A] With God *we will* **gain** the victory, and he will
66:15 [A] to you and an offering of rams; *I will* **offer** bulls and goats.
66:16 [A] you who fear God; let me tell you what *he has* **done** for me.
71:19 [A] to the skies, O God, *you* who *have* **done** great things.
72:18 [A] the God of Israel, *who* alone **does** marvelous deeds.
77:14 [77:15] [A] You are the God *who* **performs** miracles;
78: 4 [A] of the LORD, his power, and the wonders *he has* **done**.
78:12 [A] *He* **did** miracles in the sight of their fathers in the land of
83: 9 [83:10] [A] **Do** to them as you did to Midian, as you did to
86: 9 [A] All the nations *you have* **made** will come and worship
86:10 [A] For you are great and **do** marvelous deeds; you alone are
86:17 [A] **Give** me a sign of your goodness, that my enemies may see it
88:10 [88:11] [A] *Do you* **show** your wonders to the dead? Do those
95: 5 [A] The sea is his, for he **made** it, and his hands formed the dry
95: 6 [A] down in worship, let us kneel before the LORD our **Maker**;
96: 5 [A] of the nations are idols, but the LORD **made** the heavens.
98: 1 [A] the LORD a new song, for *he has* **done** marvelous things;
99: 4 [A] in Jacob you *have* **done** what is just and right.
100: 3 [A] It is *he who* **made** us, and we are his; we are his people,
101: 3 [A] The **deeds** *of* faithless men I hate; they will not cling to me.
101: 7 [A] No *one who* **practices** deceit will dwell in my house; no one
103: 6 [A] The LORD **works** righteousness and justice for all the
103:10 [A] *he does* not **treat** us as our sins deserve or repay us
103:18 [A] who keep his covenant and remember to **obey** his precepts.
103:20 [A] you his angels, you mighty ones *who* **do** his bidding,
103:21 [A] all his heavenly hosts, you his servants *who* **do** his will.
104: 4 [A] *He* **makes** winds his messengers, flames of fire his servants.
104:19 [A] The moon **marks off** the seasons, and the sun knows when to
104:24 [A] In wisdom *you* **made** them all; the earth is full of your
105: 5 [A] Remember the wonders *he has* **done**, his miracles,
106: 3 [A] they who maintain justice, *who* constantly **do** what is right.
106:19 [A] At Horeb *they* **made** a calf and worshiped an idol cast from
106:21 [A] God who saved them, *who had* **done** great things in Egypt,
107:23 [A] went out on the sea in ships; *they were* **merchants** [+4856]
107:37 [A] and planted vineyards *that* **yielded** a fruitful harvest;
108:13 [108:14] [A] With God *we will* **gain** the victory, and he will
109:16 [A] For he never thought of **doing** a kindness, but hounded to
109:21 [A] Sovereign LORD, **deal** well with me for your name's sake;
109:27 [A] know that it is your hand, that you, O LORD, *have* **done** it.
111: 4 [A] *He has* **caused** his wonders to be remembered; the LORD
111: 8 [B] for ever and ever, **done** in faithfulness and uprightness.
111:10 [A] all *who* **follow** his precepts have good understanding.
115: 3 [A] Our God is in heaven; *he* **does** whatever pleases him.
115: 8 [A] *Those who* **make** them will be like them, and so will all who
115:15 [A] be blessed by the LORD, the **Maker** *of* heaven and earth.
118: 6 [A] is with me; I will not be afraid. What *can* man **do** to me?
118:15 [A] "The LORD's right hand *has* **done** mighty things!
118:16 [A] the LORD's right hand *has* **done** mighty things!"
118:24 [A] This is the day the LORD *has* **made**; let us rejoice and be
119:65 [A] **Do** good to your servant according to your word, O LORD.
119:73 [A] Your hands **made** me and formed me; give me understanding
119:84 [A] When *will you* **punish** [+928+5477] my persecutors?
119:112 [A] My heart is set on **keeping** your decrees to the very end.
119:121 [A] *I have* **done** what is righteous and just; do not leave me to
119:124 [A] **Deal** with your servant according to your love and teach me
119:126 [A] It is time for you to **act**, O LORD; your law is being broken.
119:166 [A] for your salvation, O LORD, and *I* **follow** your commands.
121: 2 [A] comes from the LORD, the **Maker** *of* heaven and earth.
124: 8 [A] in the name of the LORD, the **Maker** *of* heaven and earth.
126: 2 [A] the nations, "The LORD *has* **done** great things for them."
126: 3 [A] The LORD *has* **done** great things for us, and we are filled
134: 3 [A] May the LORD, the **Maker** *of* heaven and earth, bless you
135: 6 [A] The LORD **does** whatever pleases him, in the heavens
135: 7 [A] *he* **sends** lightning with the rain and brings out the wind from
135:18 [A] *Those who* **make** them will be like them, and so will all who
136: 4 [A] to *him who* alone **does** great wonders, *His love*
136: 5 [A] *who* by his understanding **made** the heavens, *His love*
136: 7 [A] *who* **made** the great lights—*His love endures*
139:15 [E] My frame was not hidden from you when *I* **was made** in the
140:12 [140:13] [A] I know that the LORD **secures** justice for the
143:10 [A] Teach me to **do** your will, for you are my God; may your
145:19 [A] *He* **fulfills** the desires of those who fear him; he hears their
146: 6 [A] the **Maker** *of* heaven and earth, the sea, and everything in
146: 7 [A] *He* **upholds** the cause of the oppressed and gives food to the
147:20 [A] *He has* **done** this for no other nation; they do not know his
148: 8 [A] and hail, snow and clouds, stormy winds *that* **do** his bidding,
149: 2 [A] Let Israel rejoice in their **Maker**; let the people of Zion be
149: 7 [A] to **inflict** vengeance on the nations and punishment on the
149: 9 [A] to **carry out** the sentence written against them. This is the
Pr 2:14 [A] who delight in **doing** wrong and rejoice in the perverseness
3:27 [A] from those who deserve it, when it is in your power to **act**.
6: 3 [A] **do** this, my son, to free yourself, since you have fallen into
6:32 [A] adultery lacks judgment; whoever **does** so destroys himself.
8:26 [A] before *he* **made** the earth or its fields or any of the dust of the
10: 4 [A] Lazy hands **make** a man poor, but diligent hands bring
10:23 [A] A fool finds pleasure in evil **conduct**, but a man of
11:18 [A] The wicked man **earns** deceptive wages, but he who sows
12:22 [A] detests lying lips, but he delights in *men who* **are** truthful.
13:16 [A] Every prudent man **acts** out of knowledge, but a fool exposes
14:17 [A] A quick-tempered man **does** foolish things, and a crafty man
14:31 [A] He who oppresses the poor shows contempt for their **Maker**,
16:12 [A] Kings detest **wrongdoing** [+8400], for a throne is established
17: 5 [A] He who mocks the poor shows contempt for their **Maker**;
20:12 [A] and eyes that see—the LORD *has* **made** them both.
20:18 [A] plans by seeking advice; if *you* **wage** war, obtain guidance.
21: 3 [A] *To* **do** what is right and just is more acceptable to the
21: 7 [A] will drag them away, for they refuse to **do** what is right.
21:15 [A] *When* justice *is* **done**, it brings joy to the righteous but terror
21:24 [A] "Mocker" is his name; *he* **behaves** with overweening pride.
21:25 [A] will be the death of him, because his hands refuse to **work**.
22: 2 [A] have this in common: The LORD *is* the **Maker** *of* them all.
22:28 [A] Do not move an ancient boundary stone **set up** *by* your
23: 5 [A] for *they will* **surely sprout** [+4200+6913] wings and fly off
23: 5 [A] for *they will* **surely sprout** [+4200+6913] wings and fly off
24: 6 [A] for **waging** war you need guidance, and for victory many
24:29 [A] Do not say, "*I'll* **do** to him as he has done to me; I'll pay that
24:29 [A] Do not say, "I'll do to him as *he has* **done** to me; I'll pay that
25: 8 [A] for what *will you* **do** in the end if your neighbor puts you to
26:28 [A] hates those it hurts, and a flattering mouth **works** ruin.
31:13 [A] She selects wool and flax and **works** with eager hands.
31:22 [A] *She* **makes** coverings for her bed; she is clothed in fine linen
31:24 [A] *She* **makes** linen garments and sells them, and supplies the
31:29 [A] "Many women **do** noble things, but you surpass them all."
Ecc 1: 9 [C] been will be again, what *has* **been done** will be done again;

Ecc 1: 9 [C] been will be again, what has been done *will* **be done** *again*;
1:13 [C] and to explore by wisdom all that **is done** under heaven.
1:14 [C] I have seen all the things that **are done** under the sun; all of
2: 2 [A] I said, "is foolish. And what *does* pleasure **accomplish**?"
2: 3 [A] I wanted to see what was worthwhile for men *to* **do** under
2: 5 [A] *I* **made** gardens and parks and planted all kinds of fruit trees
2: 6 [A] *I* **made** reservoirs to water groves of flourishing trees.
2: 8 [A] *I* **acquired** men and women singers, and a harem as well—
2:11 [A] Yet when I surveyed all that my hands *had* **done** and what I
2:11 [A] all that my hands had done and what I had toiled to **achieve**,
2:12 [A] the king's successor do than what *has* already *been* **done**?
2:17 [C] because the work that **is done** under the sun was grievous to
3: 9 [A] What does the **worker** gain from his toil?
3:11 [A] *He has* **made** everything beautiful in its time. He has also set
3:11 [A] yet they cannot fathom what God *has* **done** from beginning
3:12 [A] better for men than to be happy and **do** good while they live.
3:14 [A] I know that everything God **does** will endure forever;
3:14 [A] taken from it. God **does** it so that men will revere him.
4: 1 [A] saw all the oppression that *was* **taking place** under the sun:
4: 3 [C] who has not seen the evil that **is done** [+5126] under the sun.
5: 1 [4:17] [A] of fools, who do not know that they **do** wrong.
6:12 [A] and meaningless days *he* **passes through** like a shadow?
7:14 [A] are bad, consider: God *has* **made** the one as well as the other.
7:20 [A] There is not a righteous man on earth who **does** what is right
7:29 [A] God **made** mankind upright, but men have gone in search of
8: 3 [A] stand up for a bad cause, for *he will* **do** whatever he pleases.
8: 4 [A] is supreme, who can say to him, "What *are you* **doing**?"
8: 9 [C] as I applied my mind to everything **done** under the sun.
8:10 [A] holy place and receive praise in the city where *they* **did** this.
8:11 [C] When the sentence for a crime **is** not quickly **carried out**,
8:11 [A] the hearts of the people are filled with schemes to **do** wrong.
8:12 [A] Although a wicked man **commits** a hundred crimes and still
8:14 [C] There is something else meaningless that **occurs** on earth:
8:16 [C] know wisdom and to observe man's labor **[NIE]** on earth—
8:17 [C] No one can comprehend what **goes on** under the sun.
9: 3 [C] This is the evil in everything that **happens** under the sun: The
9: 6 [C] never again will they have a part in anything that **happens**
9:10 [A] Whatever your hand finds to **do**, do it with all your might,
9:10 [A] **do** it with all your might, for in the grave, where you are
10:19 [A] A feast *is* **made** for laughter, and wine makes life merry,
11: 5 [A] cannot understand the work of God, the **Maker** *of* all things.
12:12 [A] Of **making** many books there is no end, and much study
SS 1:11 [A] *We will* **make** you earrings of gold, studded with silver.
3: 9 [A] King Solomon **made** for himself the carriage; he made it of
3:10 [A] Its posts *he* **made** *of* silver, its base of gold. Its seat was
8: 8 [A] What *shall we* **do** for our sister for the day she is spoken for?
Isa 2: 8 [A] to the work of their hands, to what their fingers *have* **made**.
2:20 [A] of silver and idols of gold, which *they* **made** to worship.
3:11 [C] They *will* **be paid back** *for* what their hands have done.
5: 2 [A] he looked for a **crop** of good grapes, but it yielded only bad
5: 2 [A] for a crop of good grapes, but *it* **yielded** only bad fruit.
5: 4 [A] What more *could have been* **done** for my vineyard than I
5: 4 [A] have been done for my vineyard than *I have* **done** for it?
5: 4 [A] When I looked for **[RPH]** good grapes, why did it yield
5: 4 [A] When I looked for good grapes, why *did it* **yield** only bad?
5: 5 [A] Now I will tell you what I *am going to* **do** to my vineyard:
5:10 [A] A ten-acre vineyard *will* **produce** only a bath of wine, a
5:10 [A] of wine, a homer of seed **[RPH]** only an ephah of grain."
7:22 [A] because of the abundance of the milk *they* **give**, he will have
9: 7 [9:6] [A] zeal of the LORD Almighty *will* **accomplish** this.
10: 3 [A] What *will you* **do** on the day of reckoning, when disaster
10:11 [A] *shall I* not **deal** with Jerusalem and her images as I dealt with
10:11 [A] and her images as *I* **dealt** with Samaria and her idols?' "
10:13 [A] " 'By the strength of my hand *I have* **done** this, and by my
10:23 [A] *will* **carry out** the destruction decreed upon the whole land.
12: 5 [A] Sing to the LORD, for *he has* **done** glorious things; let this
15: 7 [A] So the wealth *they have* **acquired** and stored up they carry
16: 3 [A] "Give us counsel, **render** a decision. Make your shadow like
17: 7 [A] In that day men will look to their **Maker** and turn their eyes
17: 8 [A] and the incense altars their fingers *have* **made**.
19:10 [A] be dejected, and all the wage **earners** will be sick at heart.
19:15 [A] There is nothing Egypt *can* **do**—head or tail, palm branch
20: 2 [A] And *he* **did** so, going around stripped and barefoot.
22:11 [A] *You* **built** a reservoir between the two walls for the water of
22:11 [A] you did not look to the *One who* **made** it, or have regard for
25: 1 [A] for in perfect faithfulness *you have* **done** marvelous things,
25: 6 [A] On this mountain the LORD Almighty *will* **prepare** a feast
26:18 [A] *We have* not **brought** salvation *to* the earth; we have not
27: 5 [A] *let them* **make** peace with me, yes, let them make peace with
27: 5 [A] make peace with me, yes, *let them* **make** peace with me."
27:11 [A] so their **Maker** has no compassion on them, and their Creator
28:15 [A] with death, with the grave *we have* **made** an agreement.
28:21 [A] to **do** his work, his strange work, and perform his task,
29:16 [A] Shall what is formed say to *him who* **formed** it, "He did not
29:16 [A] is formed say to him who formed it, "*He did* not **make** me"?
30: 1 [A] "to those *who* **carry out** plans that are not mine, forming an
31: 7 [A] the idols of silver and gold your sinful hands *have* **made**.
32: 6 [A] For the fool speaks folly, his mind *is* **busy** *with* evil: He
32: 6 [A] He **practices** ungodliness and spreads error concerning the
33:13 [A] You who are far away, hear what *I have* **done**; you who are
36:16 [A] of Assyria says: **Make** peace with me and come out to me.
37:11 [A] Surely you have heard what the kings of Assyria *have* **done**
37:16 [A] the kingdoms of the earth. You *have* **made** heaven and earth.
37:26 [A] "Have you not heard? Long ago *I* **ordained** it. In days of old
37:31 [A] the house of Judah will take root below and **bear** fruit above.
37:32 [A] The zeal of the LORD Almighty *will* **accomplish** this.
38: 3 [A] and *have* **done** what is good in your eyes."
38: 7 [A] " 'This is the LORD's sign to you that the LORD *will* **do**
38:15 [A] I say? He has spoken to me, and *he* himself *has* **done** this.
40:23 [A] to naught and **reduces** the rulers of this world to nothing.
41: 4 [A] Who has done this and **carried** *it* **through**, calling forth the
41:20 [A] and understand, that the hand of the LORD *has* **done** this,
42:16 [A] These are the things *I will* **do**; I will not forsake them.
43: 7 [A] whom I created for my glory, whom I formed and **made**."
43:19 [A] See, I *am* **doing** a new thing! Now it springs up; do you not
44: 2 [A] *he who* **made** you, who formed you in the womb, and who
44:13 [A] *he* **roughs** it **out** with chisels and marks it with compasses.
44:13 [A] *He* **shapes** it in the form of man, of man in all his glory,
44:15 [A] a god and worships it; *he* **makes** an idol and bows down to it.
44:17 [A] *From* the rest *he* **makes** a god, his idol; he bows down to it
44:19 [A] and I ate. *Shall I* **make** a detestable thing *from* what is left?
44:23 [A] Sing for joy, O heavens, for the LORD *has* **done** this;
44:24 [A] I am the LORD, *who has* **made** all things, who alone
45: 7 [A] and create darkness, I **bring** prosperity and create disaster;
45: 7 [A] and create disaster; I, the LORD, **do** all these things.
45: 9 [A] Does the clay say to the potter, 'What *are you* **making**?'
45:12 [A] It is I *who* **made** the earth and created mankind upon it. My
45:18 [A] is God; he who fashioned and **made** the earth, he founded it;
46: 4 [A] I *have* **made** you and I will carry you; I will sustain you
46: 6 [A] they hire a goldsmith *to* **make** it *into* a god, and they bow
46:10 [C] from ancient times, what *is* **still to come** [+4202].
46:10 [A] I say: My purpose will stand, and *I will* **do** all that I please.
46:11 [A] that will I bring about; what I have planned, that *will I* **do**.
48: 3 [A] them known; then suddenly *I* **acted**, and they came to pass.
48: 5 [A] them to you so that you could not say, 'My idols **did** them;
48:11 [A] For my own sake, for my own sake, *I* **do** this. How can I let
48:14 [A] The LORD's chosen ally *will* **carry out** his purpose against
51:13 [A] that you forget the LORD your **Maker**, who stretched out
53: 9 [A] with the rich in his death, though *he had* **done** no violence,
54: 5 [A] For your **Maker** is your husband—the LORD Almighty is
55:11 [A] *will* **accomplish** what I desire and achieve the purpose for
56: 1 [A] "Maintain justice and **do** what is right, for my salvation is
56: 2 [A] Blessed is the man *who* **does** this, the man who holds it fast,
56: 2 [A] desecrating it, and keeps his hand from **doing** any evil."
57:16 [A] grow faint before me—the breath of man that I *have* **created**.
58: 2 [A] as if they were a nation that **does** what is right and has not
58:13 [A] the Sabbath and from **doing** as you please on my holy day,
58:13 [A] if you honor it by not **going** your own way and not doing as
63:12 [A] waters before them, to **gain** for himself everlasting renown,
63:14 [A] This is how you guided your people to **make** for yourself a
64: 3 [64:2] [A] For when you **did** awesome things that we did not
64: 4 [64:3] [A] *who* **acts** on behalf of those who wait for him.
64: 5 [64:4] [A] You come to the help of those who gladly **do** right,
65: 8 [A] is yet some good in it,' so *will I* **do** in behalf of my servants;
65:12 [A] *You* **did** evil in my sight and chose what displeases me."
66: 2 [A] *Has* not my hand **made** all these things, and so they came
66: 4 [A] *They* **did** evil in my sight and chose what displeases me."
66:22 [A] and the new earth that I **make** will endure before me,"
Jer 1:12 [A] for I am watching to *see that* my word *is* **fulfilled**."
2:13 [A] "My people *have* **committed** two sins: They have forsaken
2:17 [A] *Have you* not **brought** this on yourselves by forsaking the
2:23 [A] you behaved in the valley; consider what *you have* **done**.
2:28 [A] Where then are the gods *you* **made** for yourselves? Let them
3: 5 [A] This is how you talk, but *you* **do** all the evil you can."
3: 6 [A] said to me, "Have you seen what faithless Israel *has* **done**?
3: 7 [A] I thought that after she *had* **done** all this she would return to
3:16 [C] it will not be missed, nor *will* another *one* **be made**.
4:18 [A] "Your own conduct and actions *have* **brought** this upon you.
4:27 [A] be ruined, though *I will* not **destroy** it **completely** [+3986].
4:30 [A] What *are* you **doing**, O devastated one? Why dress yourself
5: 1 [A] If you can find but one person *who* **deals** honestly and seeks
5:10 [A] ravage them, but *do* not **destroy** them **completely** [+3986].
5:13 [C] word is not in them; so *let* what they say **be done** to them."
5:18 [A] "*I will* not **destroy** you **completely** [+907+3986].
5:19 [A] 'Why *has* the LORD our God **done** all this to us?'
5:31 [A] my people love it this way. But what *will you* **do** in the end?
6:13 [A] for gain; prophets and priests alike, all **practice** deceit.
6:15 [A] Are they ashamed of *their* loathsome **conduct**? No,

Jer 6: 26 [A] roll in ashes; **mourn** with bitter wailing *as* **for** [+65+4200]
7: 5 [A] and your actions and **deal** [+6913] with each other justly,
7: 5 [A] and your actions and **deal** [+6913] with each other justly,
7: 10 [A] "We are safe"—safe to **do** all these detestable things?
7: 12 [A] see what *I* **did** to it because of the wickedness of my people
7: 13 [A] While you *were* **doing** all these things, declares the LORD,
7: 14 [A] what *I* **did** to Shiloh I will now do to the house that bears my
7: 14 [A] what I did to Shiloh *I will now* **do** to the house that bears my
7: 17 [A] Do you not see what they *are* **doing** in the towns of Judah
7: 18 [A] the dough and **make** cakes of bread for the Queen of Heaven.
7: 30 [A] " 'The people of Judah *have* **done** evil in my eyes,
8: 6 [A] one repents of his wickedness, saying, "What *have I* **done**?"
8: 8 [A] when actually the lying pen of the scribes *has* **handled** it
8: 10 [A] for gain; prophets and priests alike, all **practice** deceit.
8: 12 [A] Are they ashamed of *their* loathsome **conduct**? No,
9: 7 [9:6] [A] what else *can I* **do** because of the sin of my people?
9: 24 [9:23] [A] *who* **exercises** kindness, justice and righteousness on
10: 12 [A] God **made** the earth by his power; he founded the world by
10: 13 [A] *He* **sends** lightning with the rain and brings out the wind
11: 4 [A] I said, 'Obey me and **do** everything I command you, and you
11: 6 [A] 'Listen to the terms of this covenant and **follow** them.
11: 8 [A] the curses of the covenant I had commanded them to **follow**
11: 8 [A] commanded them to follow but that *they did* not **keep**.' "
11: 15 [A] in my temple *as* she **works out** her evil schemes *with* many?
11: 17 [A] the house of Israel and the house of Judah *have* **done** evil
12: 2 [A] and they have taken root; they grow and **bear** fruit.
12: 5 [A] how *will you* **manage** in the thickets by the Jordan?
14: 7 [A] O LORD, **do something** for the sake of your name.
14: 22 [A] our hope is in you, for you are the *one who* **does** all this.
15: 4 [A] Manasseh son of Hezekiah king of Judah **did** in Jerusalem.
16: 12 [A] you *have* **behaved** more wickedly than your fathers. See
16: 20 [A] *Do* men **make** their own gods? Yes, but they are not gods!"
17: 8 [A] no worries in a year of drought and never fails *to* **bear** fruit."
17: 11 [A] it did not lay is the *man who* **gains** riches by unjust means.
17: 22 [A] a load out of your houses or **do** any work on the Sabbath,
17: 24 [A] but keep the Sabbath day holy by not **doing** any work on it,
18: 3 [A] potter's house, and I saw him **working** [+4856] at the wheel.
18: 4 [A] the pot he *was* **shaping** from the clay was marred in his
18: 4 [A] so the potter **formed** it *into* another pot, shaping it as seemed
18: 4 [A] formed it into another pot, **shaping** it as seemed best to him.
18: 6 [A] house of Israel, can I not **do** with you as this potter does?"
18: 8 [A] I will relent and not **inflict** on it the disaster I had planned.
18: 10 [A] if *it* **does** evil in my sight and does not obey me, then I will
18: 12 [A] each of *us will* **follow** the stubbornness of his evil heart.' "
18: 13 [A] A most horrible thing *has been* **done** *by* Virgin Israel.
18: 23 [A] before you; **deal** with them in the time of your anger.
19: 12 [A] This is what *I will* **do** to this place and to those who live
21: 2 [A] Perhaps the LORD *will* **perform** wonders for us as in times
22: 3 [A] This is what the LORD says: **Do** what is just and right.
22: 4 [A] For if *you are* **careful to carry** [+906+6913] **out** these
22: 4 [A] For if *you are* **careful to carry out** [+906+6913] these
22: 8 [A] 'Why *has* the LORD **done** such a thing to this great city?'
22: 15 [A] *He* **did** what was right and just, so all went well with him.
22: 17 [A] innocent blood and on oppression and extortion." **[NIE]**
23: 5 [A] will reign wisely and **do** what is just and right in the land.
23: 20 [A] will not turn back until he **fully accomplishes** [+2256+7756]
26: 3 [A] will relent and not **bring** on them the disaster I was planning
26: 14 [A] **do** with me whatever you think is good and right.
26: 19 [A] We *are about to* **bring** a terrible disaster on ourselves!"
27: 2 [A] "**Make** a yoke out of straps and crossbars and put it on your
27: 5 [A] outstretched arm I **made** the earth and its people and the
28: 6 [A] He said, "Amen! *May* the LORD **do** so! May the LORD
28: 13 [A] a wooden yoke, but in its place *you will* **get** a yoke of iron.
29: 23 [A] For *they have* **done** outrageous things in Israel; they have
29: 32 [A] nor will he see the good things I *will* **do** for my people,
30: 11 [A] 'Though *I* **completely destroy** [+928+3986] all the nations
30: 11 [A] I scatter you, *I will* not **completely destroy** [+906+3986]
30: 15 [A] great guilt and many sins *I have* **done** these things to you.
30: 24 [A] will not turn back until he **fully accomplishes** [+2256+7756]
31: 37 [A] all the descendants of Israel because of all *they have* **done**,"
32: 17 [A] you *have* **made** the heavens and the earth by your great
32: 18 [A] You **show** love to thousands but bring the punishment for the
32: 20 [A] all mankind, and *have* **gained** the renown that is still yours.
32: 23 [A] your law; *they did* not **do** what you commanded them to do.
32: 23 [A] your law; they did not do what you commanded them to **do**.
32: 30 [A] "The people of Israel and Judah *have* **done** nothing but evil
32: 32 [A] Judah have provoked me by all the evil *they have* **done**—
32: 35 [A] that they *should* **do** such a detestable thing and so make
33: 2 [A] *he who* **made** the earth, the LORD who formed it
33: 9 [A] all nations on earth that hear of all the good things I **do** *for* it;
33: 9 [A] tremble at the abundant prosperity and peace I **provide** for it.'
33: 15 [A] David's line; *he will* **do** what is just and right in the land.
33: 18 [A] to burn grain offerings and *to* **present** sacrifices.' "
34: 15 [A] Recently you repented and **did** what is right in my sight:
35: 10 [A] and *have* **fully obeyed** [+2256+3869+9048] everything our
35: 18 [A] all his instructions and *have* **done** everything he ordered.'
36: 3 [A] of Judah hear about every disaster I plan to **inflict** on them,
36: 8 [A] Baruch son of Neriah **did** everything Jeremiah the prophet
37: 15 [A] Jonathan the secretary, which *they had* **made** into a prison.
38: 9 [A] these men have acted wickedly in all *they have* **done** to
38: 12 [A] clothes under your arms to pad the ropes." Jeremiah **did** so,
38: 16 [A] "As surely as the LORD lives, who *has* **given** us breath,
39: 12 [A] and look after him; don't **harm** [+4200+8273] him
39: 12 [A] after him; don't harm him but **do** for him whatever he asks."
40: 3 [A] has brought it about; *he has* **done** just as he said he would.
40: 16 [A] said to Johanan son of Kareah, "Don't **do** such a thing!
41: 9 [A] *had* **made** as part of his defense against Baasha king of
41: 11 [A] all the crimes Ishmael son of Nethaniah *had* **committed**,
42: 3 [A] will tell us where we should go and what *we should* **do**."
42: 5 [A] faithful witness against us if we *do* not **act** in accordance
42: 10 [A] for I am grieved over the disaster *I have* **inflicted** on you.
42: 20 [A] our God for us; tell us everything he says and *we will* **do** it.'
44: 3 [A] because of the evil *they have* **done**. They provoked me to
44: 4 [A] who said, '*Do* not **do** this detestable thing that I hate!'
44: 7 [A] Why **bring** such great disaster on yourselves by cutting off
44: 9 [A] Have you forgotten the wickedness **committed** by your
44: 17 [A] *We will* **certainly do** [+906+6913] everything we said we
44: 17 [A] *We will* **certainly do** [+906+6913] everything we said we
44: 17 [A] our kings and our officials **did** in the towns of Judah and in
44: 19 [A] did not our husbands know that *we were* **making** cakes like
44: 22 [A] your wicked actions and the detestable things *you* **did**,
44: 25 [A] '*We will* **certainly carry** [+906+6913] **out** the vows we
44: 25 [A] '*We will* **certainly carry out** [+906+6913] the vows we
44: 25 [A] "*Go ahead* then, **do** [+906+6913] what you promised!
44: 25 [A] "*Go ahead* then, **do** [+906+6913] what you promised!
46: 19 [A] **Pack** your belongings for exile, you who live in Egypt,
46: 28 [A] "Though *I* **completely destroy** [+928+3986] all the nations
46: 28 [A] I scatter you, *I will* not **completely destroy** [+906+3986]
48: 10 [A] "A curse on *him who is* lax *in* **doing** the LORD's work!
48: 30 [A] declares the LORD, "and her boasts **accomplish** nothing.
48: 36 [A] the men of Kir Hareseth. The wealth *they* **acquired** is gone.
50: 15 [A] take vengeance on her; **do** to her as she has done to others.
50: 15 [A] take vengeance on her; do to her as *she has* **done** to others.
50: 21 [A] the LORD. "**Do** everything I have commanded you.
50: 29 [A] Repay her for her deeds; **do** to her as she has done.
50: 29 [A] Repay her for her deeds; do to her as *she has* **done**.
51: 12 [A] his purpose, **[NIE]** his decree against the people of Babylon.
51: 15 [A] "*He* **made** the earth by his power; he founded the world by
51: 16 [A] *He* **sends** lightning with the rain and brings out the wind
51: 24 [A] all who live in Babylonia for all the wrong *they have* **done**
52: 2 [A] *He* **did** evil in the eyes of the LORD, just as Jehoiakim had
52: 2 [A] evil in the eyes of the LORD, just as Jehoiakim *had* **done**.
52: 20 [A] which King Solomon *had* **made** for the temple of the
La 1: 21 [A] heard of my distress; they rejoice at what you *have* **done**.
2: 17 [A] The LORD *has* **done** what he planned; he has fulfilled his
Eze 3: 20 [A] a righteous man turns from his righteousness and **does** evil,
3: 20 [A] The righteous things *he* **did** will not be remembered, and I
4: 9 [A] in a storage jar and **use** them **to make** bread for yourself.
4: 15 [A] "I will let you **bake** your bread over cow manure instead of
5: 7 [A] and have not followed my decrees or **kept** my laws.
5: 7 [A] *You have* not even **conformed** [+3869] **to** the standards of
5: 8 [A] *I will* **inflict** punishment on you in the sight of the nations.
5: 9 [A] *I will* **do** to you what I have never done before and will never
5: 9 [A] I will do to you what *I have* never **done** *before* and will
5: 9 [A] you what I have never done before and *will* never **do** again.
5: 10 [A] *I will* **inflict** punishment on you and will scatter all your
5: 15 [A] an object of horror to the nations around you when I **inflict**
6: 9 [A] They will loathe themselves for the evil *they have* **done**
6: 10 [A] I did not threaten in vain to **bring** this calamity on them.
7: 20 [A] and used it *to* **make** their detestable idols and vile images.
7: 23 [A] "**Prepare** chains, because the land is full of bloodshed
7: 27 [A] *I will* **deal with** them according to their conduct, and by their
8: 6 [A] said to me, "Son of man, do you see what they *are* **doing**—
8: 6 [A] the utterly detestable things the house of Israel *is* **doing** here,
8: 9 [A] see the wicked and detestable things they *are* **doing** here."
8: 12 [A] the elders of the house of Israel *are* **doing** in the darkness,
8: 13 [A] "You will see them **doing** things that are even more
8: 17 [A] Is it a trivial matter for the house of Judah *to* **do** the
8: 17 [A] of Judah to do the detestable things *they are* **doing** here?
8: 18 [A] Therefore I *will* **deal with** them in anger; I will not look on
9: 4 [C] and lament over all the detestable things that **are done** in it."
9: 11 [A] back word, saying, "*I have* **done** as you commanded."
11: 9 [A] hand you over to foreigners and **inflict** punishment on you.
11: 12 [A] for you have not followed my decrees or **kept** my laws
11: 12 [A] *have* **conformed** [+3869] **to** the standards of the nations
11: 13 [A] *Will* you **completely destroy** [+906+3986] the remnant of
11: 20 [A] they will follow my decrees and be careful *to* **keep** my laws.
12: 3 [A] of man, **pack** your belongings for exile and in the daytime,

Eze 12: 7 [A] So *I* **did** as I was commanded. During the day I brought out
12: 9 [A] that rebellious house of Israel ask you, 'What *are* you **doing**?'
12: 11 [A] a sign to you.' "As *I have* **done**, so it will be done to them.
12: 11 [C] a sign to you.' "As I have done, so *it will* **be done** to them.
12: 25 [C] will speak what I will, and *it shall* **be fulfilled** without delay.
12: 25 [A] your days, you rebellious house, *I will* **fulfill** whatever I say,
12: 28 [C] whatever I say *will* **be fulfilled**, declares the Sovereign
13: 18 [A] **make** veils of various lengths for their heads in order to
14: 23 [A] for you will know that *I have* **done** nothing in it without
14: 23 [A] for you will know that I have done nothing **[RPH]** in it
15: 3 [A] Is wood ever taken from it to **make** anything useful? Do they
15: 5 [C] If *it was* not **useful** for anything when it was whole,
15: 5 [C] how much less *can it* **be made** into something useful when
16: 5 [A] or had compassion enough to **do** any of these things for you.
16: 16 [A] You took some of your garments *to* **make** gaudy high places,
16: 17 [A] *you* **made** for yourself male idols and engaged in prostitution
16: 24 [A] for yourself and **made** a lofty shrine in every public square.
16: 30 [A] when you **do** all these things, acting like a brazen prostitute!
16: 31 [A] and **made** your lofty shrines in every public square,
16: 41 [A] and **inflict** punishment on you in the sight of many women.
16: 43 [A] *Did you* not **add** lewdness to all your other detestable
16: 47 [A] walked in their ways and **copied** their detestable practices,
16: 48 [A] your sister Sodom and her daughters never **did** what you
16: 48 [A] daughters never did what you and your daughters *have* **done**.
16: 50 [A] They were haughty and **did** detestable things before me.
16: 51 [A] sisters seem righteous by all these things *you have* **done**.
16: 54 [A] be ashamed of all *you have* **done** in giving them comfort.
16: 59 [A] *I will* **deal with** you as you deserve, because you have
16: 59 [A] I will deal with you as *you* **deserve**, because you have
16: 63 [A] Then, when I make atonement for you for all *you have* **done**,
17: 6 [A] So it became a vine and **produced** branches and put out leafy
17: 8 [A] soil by abundant water so that *it would* **produce** branches,
17: 15 [A] Will he succeed? Will he who **does** such things escape?
17: 17 [A] and great horde *will be of* no **help** *to* him in war,
17: 18 [A] he had given his hand in pledge and yet **did** all these things,
17: 23 [A] it will produce branches and **bear** fruit and become a
17: 24 [A] tree flourish. " 'I the LORD have spoken, and *I will* **do** it.' "
18: 5 [A] "Suppose there is a righteous man *who* **does** what is just
18: 8 [A] and **judges** [+5477] fairly between man and man.
18: 9 [A] He follows my decrees and **faithfully** [+622] keeps my laws.
18: 10 [A] who sheds blood or **does** any of these other things
18: 11 [A] (though the father *has* **done** none of them): "He eats at the
18: 12 [A] in pledge. He looks to the idols. *He* **does** detestable things.
18: 13 [A] Because *he has* **done** all these detestable things, he will
18: 14 [A] this son has a son who sees all the sins his father **commits**,
18: 14 [A] and though he sees them, *he does* not **do** such things:
18: 17 [A] *He* **keeps** my laws and follows my decrees.
18: 18 [A] his brother and **did** what was wrong among his people.
18: 19 [A] Since the son *has* **done** what is just and right and has been
18: 19 [A] is just and right and has been careful *to* **keep** all my decrees,
18: 21 [A] a wicked man turns away from all the sins *he has* **committed**
18: 21 [A] and keeps all my decrees and **does** what is just and right,
18: 22 [A] None of the offenses *he has* **committed** will be remembered
18: 22 [A] Because of the righteous things *he has* **done**, he will live.
18: 24 [A] righteous man turns from his righteousness and **commits** sin
18: 24 [A] and **does** the same detestable things the wicked man does,
18: 24 [A] and does the same detestable things the wicked man **does**,
18: 24 [A] None of the righteous things *he has* **done** will be
18: 26 [A] righteous man turns from his righteousness and **commits** sin,
18: 26 [A] die for it; because of the sin *he has* **committed** he will die.
18: 27 [A] man turns away from the wickedness *he has* **committed**
18: 27 [A] wickedness he has committed and **does** what is just and right,
18: 28 [A] Because he considers all the offenses *he has* **committed**
18: 31 [A] you have committed, and **get** a new heart and a new spirit.
20: 9 [A] for the sake of my name *I* **did** what would keep it from being
20: 11 [A] my laws, for the man *who* **obeys** them will live by them.
20: 13 [A] although the man who **obeys** them will live by them—
20: 14 [A] for the sake of my name *I* **did** what would keep it from being
20: 17 [A] and did not destroy them or **put** an end *to* them in the desert.
20: 19 [A] follow my decrees and be careful *to* **keep** my laws.
20: 21 [A] follow my decrees, they were not careful to **keep** my laws—
20: 21 [A] although the man who **obeys** them will live by them—
20: 22 [A] for the sake of my name *I* **did** what would keep it from being
20: 24 [A] because *they had* not **obeyed** my laws but had rejected my
20: 43 [A] you will loathe yourselves for all the evil *you have* **done**.
20: 44 [A] when I **deal** with you for my name's sake and not according
21: 15 [21:20] [B] *It* **is made** to flash like lightning, it is grasped for
22: 3 [A] blood in her midst and defiles herself by **making** idols,
22: 4 [A] and have become defiled by the idols *you have* **made**.
22: 7 [A] in you *they have* **oppressed** [+928+2021+4200+6945] the
22: 9 [A] those who eat at the mountain shrines and **commit** lewd acts.
22: 11 [A] In you one man **commits** a detestable offense with his
22: 13 [A] strike my hands together at the unjust gain *you have* **made**
22: 14 [A] or your hands be strong in the day I **deal** with you?
22: 14 [A] I deal with you? I the LORD have spoken, and *I will* **do** it.
23: 10 [A] among women, and punishment *was* **inflicted** on her.
23: 25 [A] anger against you, and *they will* **deal** with you in fury.
23: 29 [A] *They will* **deal** with you in hatred and take away everything
23: 30 [A] *have* **brought** this upon you, because you lusted after the
23: 38 [A] *They have* also **done** this to me: At that same time they
23: 39 [A] and desecrated it. That is what *they* **did** in my house.
23: 48 [A] all women may take warning and not **imitate** [+3869] you.
24: 14 [A] The time has come *for me to* **act**. I will not hold back; I will
24: 17 [A] Groan quietly; **do** not mourn for the dead. Keep your turban
24: 18 [A] wife died. The next morning *I* **did** as I had been commanded.
24: 19 [A] you tell us what these things have to do with us?" **[NIE]**
24: 22 [A] *you will* **do** as I have done. You will not cover the lower part
24: 22 [A] you will do as *I have* **done**. You will not cover the lower part
24: 24 [A] Ezekiel will be a sign to you; *you will* **do** just as he has done.
24: 24 [A] will be a sign to you; you will do just as *he has* **done**.
25: 11 [A] *I will* **inflict** punishment on Moab. Then they will know that
25: 12 [A] 'Because Edom **[NIE]** took revenge on the house of Judah
25: 14 [A] and *they will* **deal** with Edom in accordance with my anger
25: 15 [A] 'Because the Philistines **acted** in vengeance and took revenge
25: 17 [A] *I will* **carry out** great vengeance on them and punish them in
27: 5 [A] they took a cedar from Lebanon to **make** a mast for you.
27: 6 [A] *Of* oaks from Bashan *they* **made** your oars; of cypress wood
27: 6 [A] of cypress wood from the coasts of Cyprus *they* **made** your
28: 4 [A] and understanding *you have* **gained** wealth for yourself
28: 4 [A] for yourself and **amassed** gold and silver in your treasuries.
28: 22 [A] when I **inflict** punishment on her and show myself holy
28: 26 [A] they will live in safety when I **inflict** punishment on all their
29: 3 [A] You say, "The Nile is mine; I **made** it *for* myself."
29: 9 [A] " 'Because you said, "The Nile is mine; I **made** it,"
29: 20 [A] reward for his efforts because *he and his army* **did** it for me,
30: 14 [A] set fire to Zoan and **inflict** punishment on Thebes.
30: 19 [A] So *I will* **inflict** punishment on Egypt, and they will know
31: 9 [A] *I* **made** it beautiful with abundant branches, the envy of all
31: 11 [A] *for him to* **deal** [+6913] with according to its wickedness.
31: 11 [A] *for him to* **deal** [+6913] with according to its wickedness.
33: 13 [A] but then he trusts in his righteousness and **does** evil,
33: 13 [A] will be remembered; he will die for the evil *he has* **done**.
33: 14 [A] then turns away from his sin and **does** what is just and right—
33: 15 [A] decrees that give life, and **does** no evil, he will surely live;
33: 16 [A] *He has* **done** what is just and right; he will surely live.
33: 18 [A] If a righteous man turns from his righteousness and **does** evil,
33: 19 [A] away from his wickedness and **does** what is just and right,
33: 26 [A] You rely on your sword, *you* **do** detestable things, and each
33: 29 [A] because of all the detestable things *they have* **done**.'
33: 31 [A] listen to your words, but *they do* not **put** them **into practice**.
33: 31 [A] With their mouths they **express** devotion, but their hearts are
33: 32 [A] for they hear your words but *do* not **put** them **into practice**.
35: 6 [A] *I will* **give** you **over** to bloodshed and it will pursue you.
35: 11 [A] *I will* **treat** you in accordance with the anger and jealousy
35: 11 [A] the anger and jealousy *you* **showed** in your hatred of them
35: 14 [A] While the whole earth rejoices, *I will* **make** you desolate.
35: 15 [A] house of Israel became desolate, that is how *I will* **treat** you.
36: 22 [A] O house of Israel, that I *am going to* **do** these things,
36: 27 [A] will put my Spirit in you and **move** you to follow my decrees
36: 27 [A] you to follow my decrees and be careful *to* **keep** my laws.
36: 32 [A] I want you to know that I *am* not **doing** this for your sake,
36: 36 [A] was desolate. I the LORD have spoken, and *I will* **do** it.'
36: 37 [A] yield to the plea of the house of Israel and **do** this for them:
37: 14 [A] have spoken, and *I have* **done** it, declares the LORD.' "
37: 19 [A] join it to Judah's stick, **making** them a single stick of wood,
37: 22 [A] *I will* **make** them one nation in the land, on the mountains of
37: 24 [A] They will follow my laws and be careful *to* **keep** my decrees.
38: 12 [A] **rich** *in* livestock and goods, living at the center of the land."
39: 21 [A] all the nations will see the punishment *I* **inflict** and the hand I
39: 24 [A] *I* **dealt** with them according to their uncleanness and their
40: 14 [A] *He* **measured** *along* the faces of the projecting walls all
40: 17 [B] a pavement *that had* **been constructed** all around the court;
41: 18 [B] were **carved** cherubim and palm trees. Palm trees alternated
41: 19 [B] on the other. *They* **were carved** all around the whole temple.
41: 20 [B] palm trees **were carved** on the wall of the outer sanctuary.
41: 25 [B] on the doors of the outer sanctuary **were carved** cherubim
41: 25 [B] and palm trees like *those* **carved** on the walls,
43: 8 [A] **[NIE]** So I destroyed them in my anger.
43: 11 [A] if they are ashamed of all *they have* **done**, make known to
43: 11 [A] may be faithful to its design and **follow** all its regulations.
43: 18 [C] and sprinkling blood upon the altar when it **is built**:
43: 25 [A] "For seven days *you are to* **provide** a male goat daily *for* a
43: 25 [A] *you are* also *to* **provide** a young bull and a ram from the
43: 27 [A] the priests *are to* **present** your burnt offerings and fellowship
44: 13 [A] must bear the shame of their detestable practices. **[NIE]**
44: 14 [C] duties of the temple and all the work that *is to* **be done** in it.
45: 9 [A] your violence and oppression and **do** what is just and right.
45: 17 [A] *will* **provide** the sin offerings, grain offerings, burnt offerings

Eze 45:20 [A] *You are to* **do** the same on the seventh day of the month for
45:22 [A] On that day the prince *is to* **provide** a bull as a sin offering
45:23 [A] the seven days of the Feast *he is to* **provide** seven bulls
45:24 [A] *He is to* **provide** as a grain offering an ephah for each bull
45:25 [A] *he is to* **make** the same **provision** *for* sin offerings, burnt
46: 2 [A] The priests *are to* **sacrifice** his burnt offering and his
46: 7 [A] *He is to* **provide** as a grain offering one ephah with the bull,
46:12 [A] When the prince **provides** a freewill offering to the
46:12 [A] *He shall* **offer** his burnt offering or his fellowship offerings
46:12 [A] or his fellowship offerings as *he* **does** on the Sabbath day.
46:13 [A] " 'Every day *you are to* **provide** a year-old lamb without
46:13 [A] to the LORD; morning by morning *you shall* **provide** it.
46:14 [A] *You are* also *to* **provide** with it morning by morning a grain
46:15 [A] the lamb and the grain offering and the oil *shall be* **provided**
46:23 [B] of stone, with places for fire **built** all around under the ledge.
Da 1:13 [A] and **treat** your servants in accordance with what you see."
8: 4 [A] from his power. *He* **did** as he pleased and became great.
8:12 [A] It prospered in everything *it* **did**, and truth was thrown to the
8:24 [A] astounding devastation and will succeed in whatever *he* **does**.
8:27 [A] Then I got up and **went about** the king's business.
9:12 [C] Under the whole heaven nothing *has ever* **been done** like
9:12 [C] has ever been done like what *has* **been done** to Jerusalem.
9:14 [A] for the LORD our God is righteous in everything *he* **does**;
9:15 [A] and *who* **made** for yourself a name that endures to this day,
9:19 [A] O Lord, listen! O Lord, forgive! O Lord, hear and **act**! For
11: 3 [A] who will rule with great power and **do** as he pleases.
11: 6 [A] South will go to the king of the North to **make** an alliance,
11: 7 [A] his fortress; *he will* **fight** against them and be victorious.
11:16 [A] The invader *will* **do** as he pleases; no one will be able to
11:17 [A] and *will* **make** an alliance with him, the king of the South.
11:23 [A] coming to an agreement with him, *he will* **act** deceitfully,
11:24 [A] *will* **achieve** what neither his fathers nor his forefathers did.
11:24 [A] will achieve what neither his fathers nor his forefathers **did**.
11:28 [A] *He will* **take action** against it and then return to his own
11:30 [A] **[RPH]** He will return and show favor to those who forsake
11:32 [A] but the people who know their God *will* firmly **resist** him.
11:36 [A] "The king *will* **do** as he pleases. He will exalt and magnify
11:36 [C] is completed, for what has been determined *must* **take place**.
11:39 [A] *He will* **attack** [+4200] the mightiest fortresses with the help
Hos 2: 8 [2:10] [A] her the silver and gold—which *they* **used** for Baal.
6: 4 [A] "What *can I* **do** with you, Ephraim? What can I do with you,
6: 4 [A] can I do with you, Ephraim? What *can I* **do** with you, Judah?
6: 9 [A] on the road to Shechem, **committing** shameful crimes.
8: 4 [A] gold *they* **make** idols for themselves to their own
8: 6 [A] This calf—a craftsman *has* **made** it; it is not God.
8: 7 [A] The stalk has no head; *it will* **produce** no flour. Were it to
8: 7 [A] Were it to **yield** grain, foreigners would swallow it up.
8:14 [A] Israel has forgotten his **Maker** and built palaces; Judah has
9: 5 [A] What *will you* **do** on the day of your appointed feasts, on the
9:16 [A] is blighted, their root is withered, *they* **yield** no fruit.
10: 3 [A] But even if we had a king, what *could he* **do** for us?"
10:15 [A] Thus *will it* **happen** to you, O Bethel, because your
11: 9 [A] *I will* not **carry out** my fierce anger, nor will I turn
13: 2 [A] *they* **make** idols for themselves from their silver, cleverly
Joel 2:11 [A] and mighty are *those who* **obey** his command.
2:20 [A] go up; its smell will rise." Surely *he has* **done** great things.
2:21 [A] and rejoice. Surely the LORD *has* **done** great things.
2:26 [A] of the LORD your God, who *has* **worked** wonders for you;
Am 3: 6 [A] disaster comes to a city, *has* not the LORD **caused** it?
3: 7 [A] Surely the Sovereign LORD **does** nothing without revealing
3:10 [A] "They do not know how *to* **do** right," declares the LORD,
4:12 [A] "Therefore this is what *I will* **do** to you, Israel, and because I
4:12 [A] Israel, and because *I will* **do** this to you, prepare to meet your
4:13 [A] reveals his thoughts to man, *he who* **turns** dawn **to** darkness,
5: 8 [A] (*he who* **made** the Pleiades and Orion, who turns blackness
5:26 [A] the star of your god—which *you* **made** for yourselves.
9:12 [A] my name," declares the LORD, *who will* **do** these things.
9:14 [A] drink their wine; *they will* **make** gardens and eat their fruit.
Ob 1:15 [A] As *you have* **done**, it will be done to you; your deeds will
1:15 [C] As you have done, *it will* **be done** to you; your deeds will
Jnh 1: 9 [A] the God of heaven, who **made** the sea and the land."
1:10 [A] This terrified them and they asked, "What *have you* **done**?"
1:11 [A] "What *should we* **do** to you to make the sea calm down for
1:14 [A] for you, O LORD, *have* **done** as you pleased."
3:10 [A] *did* not **bring** upon them the destruction he had threatened.
3:10 [A] bring upon them the destruction he had threatened. **[RPH]**
4: 5 [A] There *he* **made** himself a shelter, sat in its shade and waited
Mic 1: 8 [A] *I will* **howl** [+5027] like a jackal and moan like an owl.
2: 1 [A] At morning's light *they* **carry** it **out** because it is in their
5:15 [5:14] [A] *I will* **take** vengeance in anger and wrath upon the
6: 3 [A] "My people, what *have I* **done** to you? How have I burdened
6: 8 [A] *To* **act** justly and to love mercy and to walk humbly with
7: 9 [A] until he pleads my case and **establishes** my right.
Na 1: 8 [A] with an overwhelming flood *he will* **make** an end of
1: 9 [A] Whatever they plot against the LORD he *will* **bring** to an
Hab 1:14 [A] *You have* **made** men like fish in the sea, like sea creatures
2:18 [A] trusts in his own creation; *he* **makes** idols that cannot speak.
3:17 [A] though the olive crop fails and the fields **produce** no food,
Zep 1:18 [A] for *he will* **make** a sudden end *of* all who live in the earth."
3: 5 [A] The LORD within her is righteous; *he* **does** no wrong.
3:13 [A] The remnant of Israel *will* **do** no wrong; they will speak no
3:19 [A] At that time I *will* **deal** with all who oppressed you; I will
Hag 1:14 [A] and **began** *to* work on the house of the LORD Almighty,
2: 4 [A] all you people of the land,' declares the LORD, 'and **work**.
Zec 1: 6 [A] 'The LORD Almighty *has* **done** to us what our ways
1: 6 [A] and practices deserve, just as he determined to **do**.' "
1:21 [2:4] [A] I asked, "What are these coming to **do**?" He answered,
6:11 [A] Take the silver and gold and **make** a crown, and set it on the
7: 3 [A] fast in the fifth month, as *I have* **done** for so many years?"
7: 9 [A] true justice; **show** mercy and compassion to one another.
8:16 [A] These are the things *you are to* **do**: Speak the truth to each
10: 1 [A] it is the LORD *who* **makes** the storm clouds.
Mal 2:11 [C] A detestable thing *has* **been committed** in Israel and in
2:12 [A] As for the man who **does** this, whoever he may be, may the
2:13 [A] Another thing *you* **do**: You flood the LORD's altar with
2:15 [A] *Has* not ⌞the LORD⌟ **made** them one? In flesh and spirit
2:17 [A] "All *who* **do** evil are good in the eyes of the LORD,
3:15 [A] Certainly the **evildoers** [+8402] prosper, and even those who
3:17 [A] "in the day when I **make up** my treasured possession.
4: 1 [3:19] [A] and every **evildoer** [+8402] will be stubble,
4: 3 [3:21] [A] soles of your feet on the day when I **do** these things,"

6914 ²עָשָׂה ***ʿāśâ***[2], v. [3] [√ 6913]
caressed [3]

Eze 23: 3 [D] their breasts were fondled and their virgin bosoms **caressed**.
23: 8 [D] **caressed** her virgin bosom and poured out their lust upon
23:21 [A] when in Egypt your bosom *was* **caressed** and your young

6915 עֲשָׂהאֵל ***ʿăśāh'ēl***, עֲשָׂה־אֵל ***ʿăśāh-'ēl***, n.pr.m. [18]
[√ 6913 + 446]
Asahel [17], he[s] [1]

2Sa 2:18 The three sons of Zeruiah were there: Joab, Abishai and **Asahel**.
2:18 and Asahel. Now **Asahel** was as fleet-footed as a wild gazelle.
2:19 **He**[s] chased Abner, turning neither to the right nor to the left as he
2:20 Abner looked behind him and asked, "Is that you, **Asahel**?"
2:21 strip him of his weapons." But **Asahel** would not stop chasing him.
2:22 Again Abner warned **Asahel**, "Stop chasing me! Why should I
2:23 every man stopped when he came to the place where **Asahel** had
2:30 Besides **Asahel**, nineteen of David's men were found missing.
2:32 They took **Asahel** and buried him in his father's tomb at
3:27 there, to avenge the blood of his brother **Asahel**, Joab stabbed him
3:30 because he had killed their brother **Asahel** in the battle at Gibeon.)
23:24 **Asahel** the brother of Joab, Elhanan son of Dodo from Bethlehem,
1Ch 2:16 and Abigail. Zeruiah's three sons were Abishai, Joab and **Asahel**.
11:26 **Asahel** the brother of Joab, Elhanan son of Dodo from Bethlehem,
27: 7 The fourth, for the fourth month, was **Asahel** the brother of Joab;
2Ch 17: 8 Shemaiah, Nethaniah, Zebadiah, **Asahel**, Shemiramoth,
31:13 Jehiel, Azaziah, Nahath, **Asahel**, Jerimoth, Jozabad, Eliel,
Ezr 10:15 Only Jonathan son of **Asahel** and Jahzeiah son of Tikvah,

6916 עֵשָׂו ***ʿēśāw***, n.pr.m. [97]
Esau [79], Esau's [14], he[s] [3], *untranslated* [1]

Ge 25:25 his whole body was like a hairy garment; so they named him **Esau**.
25:26 his brother came out, with his hand grasping **Esau's** heel;
25:27 The boys grew up, and **Esau** became a skillful hunter, a man of the
25:28 had a taste for wild game, loved **Esau**, but Rebekah loved Jacob.
25:29 some stew, **Esau** came in from the open country, famished.
25:30 **He**[s] said to Jacob, "Quick, let me have some of that red stew!
25:32 "Look, I am about to die," **Esau** said. "What good is the birthright
25:34 Then Jacob gave **Esau** some bread and some lentil stew. He ate
25:34 and then got up and left. So **Esau** despised his birthright.
26:34 When **Esau** was forty years old, he married Judith daughter of
27: 1 he called for **Esau** his older son and said to him, "My son."
27: 5 Now Rebekah was listening as Isaac spoke to his son **Esau**.
27: 5 When **Esau** left for the open country to hunt game and bring it
27: 6 "Look, I overheard your father say to your brother **Esau**,
27:11 "But my brother **Esau** is a hairy man, and I'm a man with smooth
27:15 Then Rebekah took the best clothes of **Esau** her older son,
27:19 Jacob said to his father, "I am **Esau** your firstborn. I have done as
27:21 my son, to know whether you really are my son **Esau** or not."
27:22 voice is the voice of Jacob, but the hands are the hands of **Esau**."
27:23 for his hands were hairy like those of his brother **Esau**;
27:24 "Are you really my son **Esau**?" he asked. "I am," he replied.
27:30 left his father's presence, his brother **Esau** came in from hunting.
27:32 are you?" "I am your son," he answered, "your firstborn, **Esau**."

Ge 27:34 When **Esau** heard his father's words, he burst out with a loud
27:37 Isaac answered **Esau**, "I have made him lord over you and have
27:38 **Esau** said to his father, "Do you have only one blessing,
27:38 my father? Bless me too, my father!" Then **Esau** wept aloud.
27:41 **Esau** held a grudge against Jacob because of the blessing his father
27:41 **He**[s] said to himself, "The days of mourning for my father are near;
27:42 When Rebekah was told what her older son **Esau** had said,
27:42 "Your brother **Esau** is consoling himself with the thought of
28:5 the brother of Rebekah, who was the mother of Jacob and **Esau**.
28:6 Now **Esau** learned that Isaac had blessed Jacob and had sent him
28:8 **Esau** then realized how displeasing the Canaanite women were to
28:9 so **he**[s] went to Ishmael and married Mahalath, the sister of
32:3 [32:4] Jacob sent messengers ahead of him to his brother **Esau** in
32:4 [32:5] "This is what you are to say to my master **Esau**:
32:6 [32:7] they said, "We went to your brother **Esau**, and now he is
32:8 [32:9] He thought, "If **Esau** comes and attacks one group,
32:11 [32:12] Save me, I pray, from the hand of my brother **Esau**, for I
32:13 [32:14] he had with him he selected a gift for his brother **Esau**:
32:17 [32:18] "When my brother **Esau** meets you and asks, 'To whom
32:18 [32:19] They are a gift sent to my lord **Esau**, and he is coming
32:19 [32:20] "You are to say the same thing to **Esau** when you meet
33:1 Jacob looked up and there was **Esau**, coming with his four hundred
33:4 **Esau** ran to meet Jacob and embraced him; he threw his arms
33:9 **Esau** said, "I already have plenty, my brother. Keep what you have
33:15 **Esau** said, "Then let me leave some of my men with you."
33:16 So that day **Esau** started on his way back to Seir.
35:1 appeared to you when you were fleeing from your brother **Esau**."
35:29 and full of years. And his sons **Esau** and Jacob buried him.
36:1 This is the account of **Esau** (that is, Edom).
36:2 **Esau** took his wives from the women of Canaan: Adah daughter of
36:4 Adah bore Eliphaz to **Esau**, Basemath bore Reuel,
36:5 These were the sons of **Esau**, who were born to him in Canaan.
36:6 **Esau** took his wives and sons and daughters and all the members
36:8 So **Esau** (that is, Edom) settled in the hill country of Seir.
36:8 So Esau (that is, Edom) **[RPH]** settled in the hill country of Seir.
36:9 This is the account of **Esau** the father of the Edomites in the hill
36:10 These are the names of **Esau's** sons: Eliphaz, the son of Esau's
36:10 Eliphaz, the son of **Esau's** wife Adah, and Reuel, the son of Esau's
36:10 of Esau's wife Adah, and Reuel, the son of **Esau's** wife Basemath.
36:12 **Esau's** son Eliphaz also had a concubine named Timna, who bore
36:12 bore him Amalek. These were grandsons of **Esau's** wife Adah.
36:13 and Mizzah. These were grandsons of **Esau's** wife Basemath.
36:14 The sons of **Esau's** wife Oholibamah daughter of Anah
36:14 of Anah and granddaughter of Zibeon, whom she bore to **Esau**:
36:15 These were the chiefs among **Esau's** descendants: The sons of
36:15 The sons of Eliphaz the firstborn of **Esau**: Chiefs Teman,
36:17 The sons of **Esau's** son Reuel: Chiefs Nahath, Zerah, Shammah
36:17 Reuel in Edom; they were grandsons of **Esau's** wife Basemath.
36:18 The sons of **Esau's** wife Oholibamah: Chiefs Jeush, Jalam
36:18 These were the chiefs descended from **Esau's** wife Oholibamah
36:19 These were the sons of **Esau** (that is, Edom), and these were their
36:40 These were the chiefs descended from **Esau**, by name, according
36:43 the land they occupied. This was **Esau** the father of the Edomites.
Dt 2:4 pass through the territory of your brothers the descendants of **Esau**,
2:5 your foot on. I have given **Esau** the hill country of Seir as his own.
2:8 So we went on past our brothers the descendants of **Esau**,
2:12 used to live in Seir, but the descendants of **Esau** drove them out.
2:22 The LORD had done the same for the descendants of **Esau**,
2:29 as the descendants of **Esau**, who live in Seir, and the Moabites,
Jos 24:4 to Isaac I gave Jacob and **Esau**. I assigned the hill country of Seir
24:4 I assigned the hill country of Seir to **Esau**, but Jacob and his sons
1Ch 1:34 was the father of Isaac. The sons of Isaac: **Esau** and Israel.
1:35 The sons of **Esau**: Eliphaz, Reuel, Jeush, Jalam and Korah.
Jer 49:8 in Dedan, for I will bring disaster on **Esau** at the time I punish him.
49:10 But I will strip **Esau** bare; I will uncover his hiding places,
Ob 1:6 But how **Esau** will be ransacked, his hidden treasures pillaged!
1:8 men of Edom, men of understanding in the mountains of **Esau**?
1:9 everyone in **Esau's** mountains will be cut down in the slaughter.
1:18 the house of **Esau** will be stubble, and they will set it on fire
1:18 consume it. There will be no survivors from the house of **Esau**."
1:19 People from the Negev will occupy the mountains of **Esau**,
1:21 will go up on Mount Zion to govern the mountains of **Esau**.
Mal 1:2 "Was not **Esau** Jacob's brother?" the LORD says. "Yet I have
1:3 **Esau** I have hated, and I have turned his mountains into a

6917 עָשׂוֹר ʿāśôr, n.[m.]. [16] [√ 6923]

tenth [12], ten-stringed [3], ten [1]

Ge 24:55 and her mother replied, "Let the girl remain with us **ten** days or so;
Ex 12:3 Tell the whole community of Israel that on the **tenth** day of this
Lev 16:29 On the **tenth** day of the seventh month you must deny yourselves
23:27 "The **tenth** day of this seventh month is the Day of Atonement.
25:9 have the trumpet sounded everywhere on the **tenth** day of the
Nu 29:7 " 'On the **tenth** day of this seventh month hold a sacred assembly.
Jos 4:19 On the **tenth** day of the first month the people went up from the
2Ki 25:1 year of Zedekiah's reign, on the **tenth** day of the tenth month,
Ps 33:2 with the harp; make music to him on the **ten-stringed** lyre.
92:3 [92:4] to the music of the **ten-stringed** lyre and the melody of the
144:9 O God; on the **ten-stringed** lyre I will make music to you,
Jer 52:4 year of Zedekiah's reign, on the **tenth** day of the tenth month,
52:12 On the **tenth** day of the fifth month, in the nineteenth year of
Eze 20:1 In the seventh year, in the fifth month on the **tenth** day, some of
24:1 In the ninth year, in the tenth month on the **tenth** day, the word of
40:1 our exile, at the beginning of the year, on the **tenth** of the month,

6918 עֲשִׂיאֵל ʿaśîʾēl, n.pr.m. [1] [√ 6913 + 446]

Asiel [1]

1Ch 4:35 Jehu son of Joshibiah, the son of Seraiah, the son of **Asiel**,

6919 עֲשָׂיָה ʿaśāyâ, n.pr.m. [8] [√ 6913 + 3378]

Asaiah [8]

2Ki 22:12 of Micaiah, Shaphan the secretary and **Asaiah** the king's attendant:
22:14 Shaphan and **Asaiah** went to speak to the prophetess Huldah,
1Ch 4:36 Jaakobah, Jeshohaiah, **Asaiah**, Adiel, Jesimiel, Benaiah,
6:30 [6:15] Shimea his son, Haggiah his son and **Asaiah** his son.
9:5 Of the Shilonites: **Asaiah** the firstborn and his sons.
15:6 the descendants of Merari, **Asaiah** the leader and 220 relatives;
15:11 Uriel, **Asaiah**, Joel, Shemaiah, Eliel and Amminadab the Levites.
2Ch 34:20 of Micah, Shaphan the secretary and **Asaiah** the king's attendant:

6920 עֲשִׂירִי ʿaśîrî, a.num.ord. [29] [√ 6923]

tenth [29]

Ge 8:5 The waters continued to recede until the **tenth** month, and on the
8:5 on the first day of the **tenth** month the tops of the mountains
Ex 16:36 (An omer is *one* **tenth** *of* an ephah.)
Lev 5:11 he is to bring as an offering for his sin a **tenth** *of* an ephah of fine
6:20 [6:13] a **tenth** *of* an ephah of fine flour as a regular grain offering,
27:32 every **tenth** animal that passes under the shepherd's rod—
Nu 5:15 He must also take an offering of a **tenth** *of* an ephah of barley flour
7:66 On the **tenth** day Ahiezer son of Ammishaddai, the leader of the
28:5 together with a grain offering of a **tenth** *of* an ephah of fine flour
Dt 23:2 [23:3] of the LORD, even down to the **tenth** generation.
23:3 [23:4] of the LORD, even down to the **tenth** generation.
2Ki 25:1 year of Zedekiah's reign, on the tenth day of the **tenth** month,
1Ch 12:13 [12:14] Jeremiah the **tenth** and Macbannai the eleventh.
24:11 the ninth to Jeshua, the **tenth** to Shecaniah,
25:17 the **tenth** to Shimei, his sons and relatives, 12
27:13 The **tenth**, for the tenth month, was Maharai the Netophathite,
27:13 The tenth, for the **tenth** month, was Maharai the Netophathite,
Ezr 10:16 On the first day of the **tenth** month they sat down to investigate the
Est 2:16 She was taken to King Xerxes in the royal residence in the **tenth**
Isa 6:13 And though a **tenth** remains in the land, it will again be laid waste.
Jer 32:1 from the LORD in the **tenth** year of Zedekiah king of Judah,
39:1 In the ninth year of Zedekiah king of Judah, in the **tenth** month,
52:4 year of Zedekiah's reign, on the tenth day of the **tenth** month,
Eze 24:1 In the ninth year, in the **tenth** month on the tenth day, the word of
29:1 In the **tenth** year, in the tenth month on the twelfth day, the word
29:1 In the tenth year, in the **tenth** month on the twelfth day, the word
33:21 In the twelfth year of our exile, in the **tenth** month on the fifth day,
45:11 containing a tenth of a homer and the ephah a **tenth** *of* a homer;
Zec 8:19 seventh and **tenth** months will become joyful and glad occasions

6921 עָשַׂק ʿāśaq, v. [1] [→ 5131]

disputed [1]

Ge 26:20 [F] So he named the well Esek, because *they* **disputed** with him.

6922 עֵשֶׂק ʿēśeq, n.pr.loc. [1]

Esek [1]

Ge 26:20 So he named the well **Esek**, because they disputed with him.

6923 עָשַׂר ʿāśar, v.den. [9] [→ 5130, 6917, 6920, 6924, 6925, 6926, 6927, 6928, 6929, 6930]

be sure to set aside a tenth [+906+6923] [2], give a tenth [+4200+6923] [2], take a tenth [2], collect tithes [1], receive tithes [1], setting aside a tenth [+906+5130] [1]

Ge 28:22 [D] *of* all that you give me *I will* **give** you **a tenth** [+4200+6923]."
28:22 [D] *of* all that you give me *I will* **give** you **a tenth** [+4200+6923]."
Dt 14:22 [D] **Be sure to set aside a tenth** [+906+6923] *of* all that your
14:22 [D] **Be sure to set aside a tenth of** [+906+6923] all that your
26:12 [G] **setting aside a tenth** [+906+5130] *of* all your produce in the
1Sa 8:15 [A] *He will* **take a tenth** *of* your grain and of your vintage
8:17 [A] *He will* **take a tenth** *of* your flocks, and you yourselves will
Ne 10:37 [10:38] [D] for it is the Levites who **collect** *the* **tithes** in all the

[F] Hitpael (hitpoel, hitpoal, hitpolel, hitpolal, hitpalel, hitpalal, hitpalpel, hitpalpal, hotpael, hotpaal) [G] Hiphil (hiphtil) [H] Hophal [I] Hishtaphel

Ne 10:38 [10:39] [G] the Levites when they **receive** *the* **tithes**,

6924 עֶשֶׂר *'eśer*, n.m. & f. [60 / 59] [√ 6923; Ar 10573]

ten [57], 910 [+2256+4395+9596] [1], fifteen feet [+564+928+2021] [1]

Ge 5:14 Kenan lived **910** [+2256+4395+9596] years, and then he died.
16:3 So after Abram had been living in Canaan **ten** years, Sarai his wife
45:23 **ten** female donkeys loaded with grain and bread and other
50:22 with all his father's family. He lived a hundred and **ten** years
50:26 So Joseph died at the age of a hundred and **ten**. And after they
Ex 26:1 "Make the tabernacle with **ten** curtains of finely twisted linen
26:16 Each frame is to be **ten** cubits long and a cubit and a half wide,
27:12 be fifty cubits wide and have curtains, with **ten** posts and **ten** bases.
36:8 made the tabernacle with **ten** curtains of finely twisted linen
36:21 Each frame was **ten** cubits long and a cubit and a half wide,
Lev 26:26 of bread, **ten** women will be able to bake your bread in one oven,
Nu 14:22 and in the desert but who disobeyed me and tested me **ten** times—
Jos 15:57 Kain, Gibeah and Timnah—**ten** towns and their villages.
21:5 The rest of Kohath's descendants were allotted **ten** towns from the
21:26 All these **ten** towns and their pasturelands were given to the rest of
24:29 the servant of the LORD, died at the age of a hundred and **ten**.
Jdg 2:8 the servant of the LORD, died at the age of a hundred and **ten**.
12:11 After him, Elon the Zebulunite led Israel **ten** years.
20:10 We'll take **ten** men out of every hundred from all the tribes of
Ru 1:4 and the other Ruth. After they had lived there about **ten** years,
1Sa 1:8 are you downhearted? Don't I mean more to you than **ten** sons?"
2Sa 15:16 but he left **ten** concubines to take care of the palace.
19:43 [19:44] the men of Judah, "We have **ten** shares in the king;
20:3 he took the **ten** concubines he had left to take care of the palace
1Ki 6:3 and projected **ten** cubits from the front of the temple.
6:23 he made a pair of cherubim of olive wood, each **ten** cubits high.
6:24 the other wing five cubits—**ten** cubits from wing tip to wing tip.
6:25 The second cherub also measured **ten** cubits, for the two cherubim
6:26 The height of each cherub was **ten** cubits.
7:10 stones of good quality, some measuring **ten** cubits and some eight.
7:23 measuring **ten** cubits from rim to rim and five cubits high.
7:24 Below the rim, gourds encircled it—**ten** to a cubit. The gourds
7:27 He also made **ten** movable stands of bronze; each was four cubits
7:37 This is the way he made the **ten** stands. They were all cast in the
7:38 four cubits across, one basin to go on each of the **ten** stands.
7:43 the **ten** stands with their ten basins;
2Ki 5:5 So Naaman left, taking with him **ten** talents of silver, six thousand
5:5 of silver, six thousand shekels of gold and **ten** sets of clothing.
15:17 Gadi became king of Israel, and he reigned in Samaria **ten** years.
20:9 Shall the shadow go forward **ten** steps, or shall it go back ten
20:9 the shadow go forward ten steps, or shall it go back **ten** steps?"
20:10 "It is a simple matter for the shadow to go forward **ten** steps,"
20:10 ten steps," said Hezekiah. "Rather, have it go back **ten** steps."
20:11 the LORD made the shadow go back the **ten** steps it had gone
1Ch 6:61 [6:46] The rest of Kohath's descendants were allotted **ten** towns
2Ch 4:1 altar twenty cubits long, twenty cubits wide and **ten** cubits high.
4:2 measuring **ten** cubits from rim to rim and five cubits high.
4:3 Below the rim, figures of bulls encircled it—**ten** to a cubit.
4:7 He made **ten** gold lampstands according to the specifications for
14:1 [13:23] and in his days the country was at peace for **ten** years.
Ne 4:12 [4:6] Jews who lived near them came and told us **ten** times over,
Job 19:3 **Ten** times now you have reproached me; shamelessly you attack
Isa 38:8 I will make the shadow cast by the sun go back the **ten** steps it has
38:8 Ahaz.' " So the sunlight went back the **ten** steps it had gone down.
Eze 40:11 to the gateway; it was **ten** cubits and its length was thirteen cubits.
41:2 The entrance was **ten** cubits wide, and the projecting walls on each
42:4 In front of the rooms was an inner passageway **ten** cubits wide
45:1 and 20,000 [BHS ***10,000*** +547; NIV 6929] cubits wide;
Da 1:20 he found them **ten** times better than all the magicians
Zec 5:2 thirty feet long and **fifteen feet** [+564+928+2021] wide."

6925 עָשָׂר *'āśār*, n. *or* a.num. [203 / 204] [√ 6923]

twelve [+9109] [51], 12 [+9109] [24], fourteenth [+752] [19], fifteenth [+2822] [15], twelfth [+9109] [15], fourteen [+752] [12], eleventh [+6954] [8], thirteenth [+8993] [8], fifteen [+2822] [6], eighteen [+9046] [4], seventeenth [+8679] [4], sixteen [+9252] [4], eleven [+285] [3], sixteenth [+9252] [3], 112 [+2256+4395+9109] [2], 16,000 [+547+9252] [2], 18 [+9046] [2], 18,000 [+547+9046] [2], eighteenth [+9046] [2], nineteenth [+9596] [2], thirteen [+8993] [2], 1,017 [+547+2256+8679] [1], 1,017 [+547+8679] [1], 112 [+4395+9109] [1], 13 [+8993] [1], 14,700 [+547+752+2256+4395+8679] [1], 16,750 [+547+2256+2822+4395+8679+9252] [1], 17,200 [+547+2256+4395+8679] [1], 2,812 [+547+2256+4395+9046+9109] [1], 2,818 [+547+2256+4395+9046+9046] [1], 212 [+2256+4395+9109] [1], 218 [+2256+4395+9046] [1], 318 [+2256+4395+8993+9046] [1], eleven [+6954] [1], nineteen [+9596] [1]

Ge 7:11 Noah's life, on the **seventeenth** [+8679] day of the second month—
8:4 on the **seventeenth** [+8679] day of the seventh month the ark came
14:14 he called out the **318** [+2256+4395+8993+9046] trained men born
17:20 He will be the father of **twelve** [+9109] rulers, and I will make him
25:16 these are the names of the **twelve** [+9109] tribal rulers according to
32:22 [32:23] his two maidservants and his **eleven** [+285] sons
35:22 and Israel heard of it. Jacob had **twelve** [+9109] sons:
37:9 and moon and **eleven** [+285] stars were bowing down to me."
42:13 But they replied, "Your servants were **twelve** [+9109] brothers,
42:32 We were **twelve** [+9109] brothers, sons of one father. One is no
46:22 sons of Rachel who were born to Jacob—**fourteen** [+752] in all.
49:28 All these are the **twelve** [+9109] tribes of Israel, and this is what
Ex 12:6 Take care of them until the **fourteenth** [+752] day of the month,
12:18 from the evening of the **fourteenth** [+752] day until the evening of
16:1 on the **fifteenth** [+2822] day of the second month after they had
24:4 set up twelve stone pillars representing the **twelve** [+9109] tribes
26:25 So there will be eight frames and **sixteen** [+9252] silver bases—
28:21 like a seal with the name of one of the **twelve** [+9109] tribes.
36:30 So there were eight frames and **sixteen** [+9252] silver bases—
39:14 like a seal with the name of one of the **twelve** [+9109] tribes.
Lev 23:5 LORD's Passover begins at twilight on the **fourteenth** [+752]
23:6 On the **fifteenth** [+2822] day of that month the LORD's Feast of
23:34 'On the **fifteenth** [+2822] day of the seventh month the LORD's
23:39 " 'So beginning with the **fifteenth** [+2822] day of the seventh
27:7 set the value of a male at **fifteen** [+2822] shekels and of a female at
Nu 1:44 by Moses and Aaron and the **twelve** [+9109] leaders of Israel,
7:3 before the LORD six covered carts and **twelve** [+9109] oxen—
7:72 On the **eleventh** [+6954] day Pagiel son of Ocran, the leader of the
7:78 On the **twelfth** [+9109] day Ahira son of Enan, the leader of the
7:84 **twelve** [+9109] silver sprinkling bowls and twelve gold dishes.
7:87 animals for the burnt offering came to **twelve** [+9109] young bulls,
7:87 **twelve** [+9109] rams and twelve male lambs a year old, together
7:87 twelve rams and **twelve** [+9109] male lambs a year old, together
7:87 **Twelve** [+9109] male goats were used for the sin offering.
9:3 at twilight on the **fourteenth** [+752] day of this month,
9:5 so in the Desert of Sinai at twilight on the **fourteenth** [+752] day
9:11 They are to celebrate it on the **fourteenth** [+752] day of the second
16:49 [17:14] But **14,700** [+547+752+2256+4395+8679] people died
17:2 [17:17] to the Israelites and get **twelve** [+9109] staffs from them,
17:6 [17:21] and their leaders gave him **twelve** [+9109] staffs,
28:16 " 'On the **fourteenth** [+752] day of the first month the LORD's
28:17 On the **fifteenth** [+2822] day of this month there is to be a festival;
29:12 " 'On the **fifteenth** [+2822] day of the seventh month, hold a
29:13 a burnt offering of **thirteen** [+8993] young bulls, two rams
29:13 two rams and **fourteen** [+752] male lambs a year old, all without
29:14 With each of the **thirteen** [+8993] bulls prepare a grain offering of
29:15 and with each of the **fourteen** [+752] lambs, one-tenth.
29:17 " 'On the second day prepare **twelve** [+9109] young bulls,
29:17 two rams and **fourteen** [+752] male lambs a year old, all without
29:20 " 'On the third day prepare **eleven** [+6954] bulls, two rams
29:20 two rams and **fourteen** [+752] male lambs a year old, all without
29:23 two rams and **fourteen** [+752] male lambs a year old, all without
29:26 two rams and **fourteen** [+752] male lambs a year old, all without
29:29 two rams and **fourteen** [+752] male lambs a year old, all without
29:32 two rams and **fourteen** [+752] male lambs a year old, all without
31:5 So **twelve** [+9109] thousand men armed for battle, a thousand from
31:40 **16,000** [+547+9252] people, of which the tribute for the LORD
31:46 and **16,000** [+547+9252] people.
31:52 weighed **16,750** [+547+2256+2822+4395+8679+9252] shekels.
33:3 The Israelites set out from Rameses on the **fifteenth** [+2822] day
Dt 1:2 (It takes **eleven** [+285] days to go from Horeb to Kadesh Barnea
1:3 In the fortieth year, on the first day of the **eleventh** [+6954] month,
1:23 so I selected **twelve** [+9109] of you, one man from each tribe.
Jos 3:12 Now then, choose **twelve** [+9109] men from the tribes of Israel,
4:2 "Choose **twelve** [+9109] men from among the people, one from
4:4 So Joshua called together the **twelve** [+9109] men he had
5:10 On the evening of the **fourteenth** [+752] day of the month,
8:25 **Twelve** [+9109] thousand men and women fell that day—
Jdg 8:10 Zalmunna were in Karkor with a force of about **fifteen** [+2822]
19:29 into **twelve** [+9109] parts and sent them into all the areas of Israel.
20:25 they cut down another **eighteen** [+9046] thousand Israelites,
20:44 **Eighteen** [+9046] thousand Benjamites fell, all of them valiant
21:10 So the assembly sent **twelve** [+9109] thousand fighting men with
2Sa 2:15 **twelve** [+9109] men for Benjamin and Ish-Bosheth son of Saul,
2:15 and Ish-Bosheth son of Saul, and **twelve** [+9109] for David.
2:30 **nineteen** [+9596] of David's men were found missing.
8:13 down **eighteen** [+9046] thousand Edomites in the Valley of Salt.
9:10 (Now Ziba had **fifteen** [+2822] sons and twenty servants.)
10:6 a thousand men, and also **twelve** [+9109] thousand men from Tob.
17:1 "I would choose **twelve** [+9109] thousand men and set out tonight
19:17 [19:18] and his **fifteen** [+2822] sons and twenty servants.
1Ki 4:7 Solomon also had **twelve** [+9109] district governors over all Israel,
4:26 [5:6] for chariot horses, and **twelve** [+9109] thousand horses.
7:3 rested on the columns—forty-five beams, **fifteen** [+2822] to a row.
7:25 The Sea stood on **twelve** [+9109] bulls, three facing north,
7:44 the Sea and the **twelve** [+9109] bulls under it;

1Ki 8:65 for seven days and seven days more, **fourteen** [+752] days in all.
10:20 **Twelve** [+9109] lions stood on the six steps, one at either end of
10:26 had fourteen hundred chariots and **twelve** [+9109] thousand horses,
11:30 new cloak he was wearing and tore it into **twelve** [+9109] pieces.
12:32 He instituted a festival on the **fifteenth** [+2822] day of the eighth
12:33 On the **fifteenth** [+2822] day of the eighth month, a month of his
19:19 He was plowing with **twelve** [+9109] yoke of oxen, and he himself
19:19 yoke of oxen, and he himself was driving the **twelfth** [+9109] pair.
22:48 [22:49] [Now Jehoshaphat **built** [K; see Q 6913] a fleet of]
2Ki 25:27 prison on the twenty-seventh day of the **twelfth** [+9109] month.
1Ch 4:27 Shimei had **sixteen** [+9252] sons and six daughters, but his
7:11 There were **17,200** [+547+2256+4395+8679] fighting men ready
9:22 gatekeepers at the thresholds numbered **212** [+2256+4395+9109].
12:13 [12:14] Jeremiah the tenth and Macbannai the **eleventh** [+6954].
12:31 [12:32] to come and make David king—**18,000** [+547+9046];
15:10 Amminadab the leader and **112** [+2256+4395+9109] relatives.
18:12 Abishai son of Zeruiah struck down **eighteen** [+9046] thousand
24:4 **sixteen** [+9252] heads of families from Eleazar's descendants
24:12 the **eleventh** [+6954] to Eliashib, the twelfth to Jakim,
24:12 the eleventh to Eliashib, the **twelfth** [+9109] to Jakim,
24:13 the **thirteenth** [+8993] to Huppah, the fourteenth to Jeshebeab,
24:13 the thirteenth to Huppah, the **fourteenth** [+752] to Jeshebeab,
24:14 the **fifteenth** [+2822] to Bilgah, the sixteenth to Immer,
24:14 the fifteenth to Bilgah, the **sixteenth** [+9252] to Immer,
24:15 the **seventeenth** [+8679] to Hezir, the eighteenth to Happizzez,
24:15 the seventeenth to Hezir, the **eighteenth** [+9046] to Happizzez,
24:16 the **nineteenth** [+9596] to Pethahiah, the twentieth to Jehezkel,
25:5 God gave Heman **fourteen** [+752] sons and three daughters.
25:9 Joseph, his sons and relatives, **12** [+9109] [BHS-]
25:9 the second to Gedaliah, he and his relatives and sons, **12** [+9109]
25:10 the third to Zaccur, his sons and relatives, **12** [+9109]
25:11 the fourth to Izri, his sons and relatives, **12** [+9109]
25:12 the fifth to Nethaniah, his sons and relatives, **12** [+9109]
25:13 the sixth to Bukkiah, his sons and relatives, **12** [+9109]
25:14 the seventh to Jesarelah, his sons and relatives, **12** [+9109]
25:15 the eighth to Jeshaiah, his sons and relatives, **12** [+9109]
25:16 the ninth to Mattaniah, his sons and relatives, **12** [+9109]
25:17 the tenth to Shimei, his sons and relatives, **12** [+9109]
25:18 the **eleventh** [+6954] to Azarel, his sons and relatives, 12
25:18 the eleventh to Azarel, his sons and relatives, **12** [+9109]
25:19 the **twelfth** [+9109] to Hashabiah, his sons and relatives, 12
25:19 the twelfth to Hashabiah, his sons and relatives, **12** [+9109]
25:20 the **thirteenth** [+8993] to Shubael, his sons and relatives,
25:20 the thirteenth to Shubael, his sons and relatives, **12** [+9109]
25:21 the **fourteenth** [+752] to Mattithiah, his sons and relatives,
25:21 the fourteenth to Mattithiah, his sons and relatives, **12** [+9109]
25:22 the **fifteenth** [+2822] to Jerimoth, his sons and relatives, 12
25:22 the fifteenth to Jerimoth, his sons and relatives, **12** [+9109]
25:23 the **sixteenth** [+9252] to Hananiah, his sons and relatives,
25:23 the sixteenth to Hananiah, his sons and relatives, **12** [+9109]
25:24 the **seventeenth** [+8679] to Joshbekashah, his sons and relatives,
25:24 seventeenth to Joshbekashah, his sons and relatives, **12** [+9109]
25:25 the **eighteenth** [+9046] to Hanani, his sons and relatives, 12
25:25 the eighteenth to Hanani, his sons and relatives, **12** [+9109]
25:26 the **nineteenth** [+9596] to Mallothi, his sons and relatives,
25:26 the nineteenth to Mallothi, his sons and relatives, **12** [+9109]
25:27 the twentieth to Eliathah, his sons and relatives, **12** [+9109]
25:28 the twenty-first to Hothir, his sons and relatives, **12** [+9109]
25:29 the twenty-second to Giddalti, his sons and relatives, **12** [+9109]
25:30 the twenty-third to Mahazioth, his sons and relatives, **12** [+9109]
25:31 twenty-fourth to Romamti-Ezer, his sons and relatives, **12** [+9109]
26:9 had sons and relatives, who were able men—**18** [+9046] in all.
26:11 the fourth. The sons and relatives of Hosah were **13** [+8993] in all.
27:14 The **eleventh** [+6954], for the eleventh month, was Benaiah the
27:14 The eleventh, for the **eleventh** [+6954] month, was Benaiah the
27:15 The **twelfth** [+9109], for the twelfth month, was Heldai the
27:15 The twelfth, for the **twelfth** [+9109] month, was Heldai the
2Ch 1:14 had fourteen hundred chariots and **twelve** [+9109] thousand horses,
4:4 The Sea stood on **twelve** [+9109] bulls, three facing north,
4:15 the Sea and the **twelve** [+9109] bulls under it;
9:19 **Twelve** [+9109] lions stood on the six steps, one at either end of
9:25 stalls for horses and chariots, and **twelve** [+9109] thousand horses,
29:17 finishing on the **sixteenth** [+9252] day of the first month.
30:15 They slaughtered the Passover lamb on the **fourteenth** [+752] day
35:1 the Passover lamb was slaughtered on the **fourteenth** [+752] day
Ezr 2:6 the line of Jeshua and Joab) **2,812** [+547+2256+4395+9046+9109]
2:18 of Jorah **112** [+2256+4395+9109]
2:39 of Harim **1,017** [+547+2256+8679]
6:19 On the **fourteenth** [+752] day of the first month, the exiles
8:9 Obadiah son of Jehiel, and with him **218** [+2256+4395+9046] men;
8:18 son of Israel, and Sherebiah's sons and brothers, **18 men** [+9046];
8:24 I set apart **twelve** [+9109] of the leading priests, together with
8:31 On the **twelfth** [+9109] day of the first month we set out from the
8:35 **twelve** [+9109] bulls for all Israel, ninety-six rams,
8:35 male lambs and, as a sin offering, **twelve** [+9109] male goats.
Ne 7:11 the line of Jeshua and Joab) **2,818** [+547+2256+4395+9046+9046]
7:24 of Hariph **112** [+4395+9109]
7:42 of Harim **1,017** [+547+8679]
Est 2:12 she had to complete **twelve** [+9109] months of beauty treatments
3:7 And the lot fell on the **twelfth** [+9109] month, the month of Adar.
3:12 on the **thirteenth** [+8993] day of the first month the royal
3:13 on a single day, the **thirteenth** [+8993] day of the twelfth month,
3:13 on a single day, the thirteenth day of the **twelfth** [+9109] month,
8:12 King Xerxes was the **thirteenth** [+8993] day of the twelfth month,
8:12 King Xerxes was the thirteenth day of the **twelfth** [+9109] month,
9:1 On the **thirteenth** [+8993] day of the twelfth month, the month of
9:1 On the thirteenth day of the **twelfth** [+9109] month, the month of
9:15 The Jews in Susa came together on the **fourteenth** [+752] day of
9:17 This happened on the **thirteenth** [+8993] day of the month of
9:17 on the **fourteenth** [+752] they rested and made it a day of feasting
9:18 had assembled on the **thirteenth** [+8993] and fourteenth, and
9:18 had assembled on the thirteenth and **fourteenth** [+752], and
9:18 then on the **fifteenth** [+2822] they rested and made it a day of
9:19 observe the **fourteenth** [+752] of the month of Adar as a day of
9:21 to have them celebrate annually the **fourteenth** [+752] and
9:21 the fourteenth and **fifteenth** [+2822] days of the month of Adar
Job 42:12 He had **fourteen** [+752] thousand sheep, six thousand camels,
Ps 60:T [60:2] struck down **twelve** [+9109] thousand Edomites in the
Jer 52:20 the Sea and the **twelve** [+9109] bronze bulls under it,
52:31 from prison on the twenty-fifth day of the **twelfth** [+9109] month.
Eze 29:1 In the tenth year, in the tenth month on the **twelfth** [+9109] day,
32:1 In the twelfth year, in the **twelfth** [+9109] month on the first day,
32:17 In the twelfth year, on the **fifteenth** [+2822] day of the month,
45:21 " 'In the first month on the **fourteenth** [+752] day you are to
45:25 which begins in the seventh month on the **fifteenth** [+2822] day,
47:13 land for an inheritance among the **twelve** [+9109] tribes of Israel,
48:35 "The distance all around will be **18,000** [+547+9046] cubits.
Hos 3:2 So I bought her for **fifteen** shekels **of** [+2822] silver and about a
Zec 1:7 On the twenty-fourth day of the **eleventh** [+6954] month,

6926 עֶשְׂרֵה *'eśrēh*, n.f. [134 / 136] [√ 6923]

twelve [+9109] [29], sixteen [+9252] [14], thirteen [+8993] [10], eighteenth [+9046] [9], fifteen [+2822] [8], eighteen [+9046] [7], twelfth [+9109] [7], eleven [+285] [6], fourteen [+752] [6], eleventh [+6954] [5], seventeen [+8679] [5], eleven [+6954] [4], eleventh [+285] [4], fourteenth [+752] [4], thirteenth [+8993] [3], fifteenth [+2822] [2], nineteenth [+9596] [2], seventeenth [+8679] [2], 119 [+2256+4395+9596] [1], 815 [+2256+2822+4395+9046] [1], 912 [+2256+4395+9109+9596] [1], fourteen [1], hundred and twenty thousand [+8052+9109] [1], nineteen [+9596] [1], twelve [+6954] [1], twenty feet [+564+2822] [1], twenty-seven feet [+564+9046] [1]

Ge 5:8 Seth lived **912** [+2256+4395+9109+9596] years, and then he died.
5:10 Enosh lived **815** [+2256+2822+4395+9046] years and had other
7:20 the mountains to a depth of more than **twenty feet** [+564+2822].
11:25 Nahor lived **119** [+2256+4395+9596] years and had other sons and
14:4 For **twelve** [+9109] years they had been subject to Kedorlaomer,
14:4 to Kedorlaomer, but in the **thirteenth** [+8993] year they rebelled.
14:5 In the **fourteenth** [+752] year, Kedorlaomer and the kings allied
17:25 and his son Ishmael was **thirteen** [+8993];
31:41 I worked for you **fourteen** [+752] years for your two daughters
37:2 Joseph, a young man *of* **seventeen** [+8679], was tending the flocks
46:18 Laban had given to his daughter Leah—**sixteen** [+9252] in all.
47:28 Jacob lived in Egypt **seventeen** [+8679] years, and the years of his
Ex 15:27 where there were **twelve** [+9109] springs and seventy palm trees,
24:4 set up **twelve** [+9109] stone pillars representing the twelve tribes
26:7 hair for the tent over the tabernacle—**eleven** [+6954] altogether.
26:8 All **eleven** [+6954] curtains are to be the same size—thirty cubits
27:14 Curtains **fifteen** [+2822] cubits long are to be on one side of the
27:15 and curtains **fifteen** [+2822] cubits long are to be on the other side,
28:21 There are to be **twelve** [+9109] stones, one for each of the names
36:14 hair for the tent over the tabernacle—**eleven** [+6954] altogether.
36:15 All **eleven** [+6954] curtains were the same size—thirty cubits long
38:14 Curtains **fifteen** [+2822] cubits long were on one side of the
38:15 curtains **fifteen** [+2822] cubits long were on the other side of the
39:14 There were **twelve** [+9109] stones, one for each of the names of
Lev 24:5 "Take fine flour and bake **twelve** [+9109] loaves of bread,
Nu 7:84 **twelve** [+9109] silver plates, twelve silver sprinkling bowls
7:84 twelve silver sprinkling bowls and **twelve** [+9109] gold dishes.
7:86 The **twelve** [+9109] gold dishes filled with incense weighed ten
33:9 where there were **twelve** [+9109] springs and seventy palm trees,
Jos 4:3 tell them to take up **twelve** [+9109] stones from the middle of the
4:8 They took **twelve** [+9109] stones from the middle of the Jordan,
4:9 Joshua set up the **twelve** [+9109] stones that had been in the
4:20 Joshua set up at Gilgal the **twelve** [+9109] stones they had taken
15:36 (or Gederothaim)—**fourteen** [+752] towns and their villages.
15:41 and Makkedah—**sixteen** [+9252] towns and their villages.
15:51 Holon and Giloh—**eleven** [+285] towns and their villages.

Jos 18:24 Ophni and Geba—**twelve** [+9109] towns and their villages.
18:28 Gibeah and Kiriath—**fourteen** [+752] towns and their villages.
19: 6 and Sharuhen—**thirteen** [+8993] towns and their villages;
19:15 There were **twelve** [+9109] towns and their villages.
19:22 at the Jordan. There were **sixteen** [+9252] towns and their villages.
19:38 There were **nineteen** [+9596] towns and their villages.
21: 4 were allotted **thirteen** [+8993] towns from the tribes of Judah,
21: 6 The descendants of Gershon were allotted **thirteen** [+8993] towns
21: 7 received **twelve** [+9109] towns from the tribes of Reuben,
21:19 for the priests, the descendants of Aaron, were **thirteen** [+8993],
21:33 All the towns of the Gershonite clans were **thirteen** [+8993],
21:40 who were the rest of the Levites, were **twelve** [+9109].
Jdg 3:14 were subject to Eglon king of Moab for **eighteen** [+9046] years.
10: 8 For **eighteen** [+9046] years they oppressed all the Israelites on the
1Ki 6:38 In the **eleventh** [+285] year in the month of Bul, the eighth month,
7: 1 It took Solomon **thirteen** [+8993] years, however, to complete the
7:15 each **eighteen** [+9046] cubits high and twelve cubits around,
7:15 each eighteen cubits high and **twelve** [+9109] cubits around,
14:21 and he reigned **seventeen** [+8679] years in Jerusalem,
15: 1 In the **eighteenth** [+9046] year of the reign of Jeroboam son of
16:23 and he reigned **twelve** [+9109] years, six of them in Tirzah.
18:31 Elijah took **twelve** [+9109] stones, one for each of the tribes
22:51 [22:52] **seventeenth** [+8679] year of Jehoshaphat king of Judah,
2Ki 3: 1 in the **eighteenth** [+9046] year of Jehoshaphat king of Judah,
3: 1 Jehoshaphat king of Judah, and he reigned **twelve** [+9109] years.
8:25 In the **twelfth** [+9109] year of Joram son of Ahab king of Israel,
9:29 (In the **eleventh** [+285] year of Joram son of Ahab, Ahaziah had
13: 1 king of Israel in Samaria, and he reigned **seventeen** [+8679] years.
13:10 king of Israel in Samaria, and he reigned **sixteen** [+9252] years.
14:17 Amaziah son of Joash king of Judah lived for **fifteen** [+2822] years
14:21 people of Judah took Azariah, who was **sixteen** [+9252] years old,
14:23 In the **fifteenth** [+2822] year of Amaziah son of Joash king of
15: 2 He was **sixteen** [+9252] years old when he became king, and he
15:33 became king, and he reigned in Jerusalem **sixteen** [+9252] years.
16: 1 In the **seventeenth** [+8679] year of Pekah son of Remaliah,
16: 2 became king, and he reigned in Jerusalem **sixteen** [+9252] years.
17: 1 In the **twelfth** [+9109] year of Ahaz king of Judah, Hoshea son of
18:13 In the **fourteenth** [+752] year of King Hezekiah's reign,
20: 6 I will add **fifteen** [+2822] years to your life. And I will deliver you
21: 1 Manasseh was **twelve** [+9109] years old when he became king,
22: 3 In the **eighteenth** [+9046] year of his reign, King Josiah sent the
23:23 in the **eighteenth** [+9046] year of King Josiah, this Passover was
23:36 he became king, and he reigned in Jerusalem **eleven** [+285] years.
24: 8 Jehoiachin was **eighteen** [+9046] years old when he became king,
24:18 he became king, and he reigned in Jerusalem **eleven** [+285] years.
25: 2 The city was kept under siege until the **eleventh** [+6954] year of
25: 8 in the **nineteenth** [+9596] year of Nebuchadnezzar king of
25:17 Each pillar was **twenty-seven feet** [+564+9046] high. The bronze
1Ch 6:60 [6:45] among the Kohathite clans, were **thirteen** [+8993] in all.
6:62 [6:47] were allotted **thirteen** [+8993] towns from the tribes of
6:63 [6:48] were allotted **twelve** [+9109] towns from the tribes of
2Ch 11:21 In all, he had **eighteen** [+9046] wives and sixty concubines,
12:13 and he reigned **seventeen** [+8679] years in Jerusalem,
13: 1 In the **eighteenth** [+9046] year of the reign of Jeroboam, Abijah
13:21 He married **fourteen** [+752] wives and had twenty-two sons
13:21 and had twenty-two sons and **sixteen** [+9252] daughters.
15:10 in the third month of the **fifteenth** [+2822] year of Asa's reign.
25:25 Amaziah son of Joash king of Judah lived for **fifteen** [+2822] years
26: 1 people of Judah took Uzziah, who was **sixteen** [+9252] years old,
26: 3 Uzziah was **sixteen** [+9252] years old when he became king,
27: 1 became king, and he reigned in Jerusalem **sixteen** [+9252] years.
27: 8 became king, and he reigned in Jerusalem **sixteen** [+9252] years.
28: 1 became king, and he reigned in Jerusalem **sixteen** [+9252] years.
33: 1 Manasseh was **twelve** [+9109] years old when he became king,
34: 3 In his **twelfth** [+9109] year he began to purge Judah and Jerusalem
34: 8 In the **eighteenth** [+9046] year of Josiah's reign, to purify the land
35:19 This Passover was celebrated in the **eighteenth** [+9046] year of
36: 5 he became king, and he reigned in Jerusalem **eleven** [+285] years.
36: 9 Jehoiachin was **eighteen** [+9046] [BHS-] years old
36:11 he became king, and he reigned in Jerusalem **eleven** [+285] years.
Ne 5:14 land of Judah, until his thirty-second year—**twelve** [+9109] years—
Est 3: 7 In the **twelfth** [+9109] year of King Xerxes, in the first month,
Isa 36: 1 In the **fourteenth** [+752] year of King Hezekiah's reign,
38: 5 and seen your tears; I will add **fifteen** [+2822] years to your life.
Jer 1: 2 The word of the LORD came to him in the **thirteenth** [+8993]
1: 3 down to the fifth month of the **eleventh** [+6954] year of Zedekiah
25: 3 from the **thirteenth** [+8993] year of Josiah son of Amon king of
32: 1 which was the **eighteenth** [+9046] year of Nebuchadnezzar.
39: 2 day of the fourth month of Zedekiah's **eleventh** [+6954] year,
52: 1 he became king, and he reigned in Jerusalem **eleven** [+285] years.
52: 5 The city was kept under siege until the **eleventh** [+6954] year of
52:12 in the **nineteenth** [+9596] year of Nebuchadnezzar king of
52:21 Each of the pillars was **eighteen** [+9046] cubits high and twelve
52:21 eighteen cubits high and **twelve** [+9109] cubits in circumference;
52:29 in Nebuchadnezzar's **eighteenth** [+9046] year, 832 people from
Eze 26: 1 In the **eleventh** [+6954] year, on the first day of the month,
30:20 In the **eleventh** [+285] year, in the first month on the seventh day,
31: 1 In the **eleventh** [+285] year, in the third month on the first day,
32: 1 In the **twelfth** [+9109] year, in the twelfth month on the first day,
32:17 In the **twelfth** [+9109] year, on the fifteenth day of the month,
33:21 In the **twelfth** [+9109] year of our exile, in the tenth month on the
40: 1 the month, in the **fourteenth** [+752] year after the fall of the city—
40:11 it was ten cubits and its length was **thirteen** [+8993] cubits.
40:48 The width of the entrance was **fourteen** [BHS-] cubits
40:49 twenty cubits wide, and **twelve** [+6954] cubits from front to back.
43:16 is square, **twelve** [+9109] cubits long and twelve cubits wide.
43:16 is square, twelve cubits long and **twelve** [+9109] cubits wide.
43:17 **fourteen** [+752] cubits long and fourteen cubits wide, with a rim
43:17 fourteen cubits long and **fourteen** [+752] cubits wide, with a rim
Jnh 4:11 has more than a **hundred and twenty thousand** [+8052+9109]

6927 עֲשָׂרָה *ʿaśārâ*, n.m. [64] [√ 6923; Ar 10573]

ten [59], 110 [+2256+4395] [1], 410 [+752+2256+4395] [1], *untranslated* [1], fifteen [+2256+2822] [1], seventeen [+2256+8679] [1]

Ge 18:32 What if only **ten** can be found there?" He answered, "For the sake
18:32 He answered, "For the sake of **ten**, I will not destroy it."
24:10 the servant took **ten** of his master's camels and left, taking with
24:22 ring weighing a beka and two gold bracelets weighing **ten** shekels.
32:15 [32:16] forty cows and **ten** bulls, and twenty female donkeys
32:15 [32:16] and twenty female donkeys and **ten** male donkeys.
42: 3 Then **ten** of Joseph's brothers went down to buy grain from Egypt.
45:23 **ten** donkeys loaded with the best things of Egypt, and ten female
Ex 27:12 be fifty cubits wide and have curtains, with **ten** posts and ten bases.
38:12 fifty cubits wide and had curtains, with **ten** posts and ten bases,
38:12 fifty cubits wide and had curtains, with ten posts and **ten** bases,
Lev 27: 7 value of a male at fifteen shekels and of a female at **ten** shekels.
Nu 7:14 one gold dish weighing **ten** shekels, filled with incense;
7:20 one gold dish weighing **ten** shekels, filled with incense;
7:26 one gold dish weighing **ten** shekels, filled with incense;
7:32 one gold dish weighing **ten** shekels, filled with incense;
7:38 one gold dish weighing **ten** shekels, filled with incense;
7:44 one gold dish weighing **ten** shekels, filled with incense;
7:50 one gold dish weighing **ten** shekels, filled with incense;
7:56 one gold dish weighing **ten** shekels, filled with incense;
7:62 one gold dish weighing **ten** shekels, filled with incense;
7:68 one gold dish weighing **ten** shekels, filled with incense;
7:74 one gold dish weighing **ten** shekels, filled with incense;
7:80 one gold dish weighing **ten** shekels, filled with incense;
7:86 The twelve gold dishes filled with incense weighed **ten** shekels
7:86 The twelve gold dishes filled with incense weighed ten **[RPH]**
11:19 not eat it for just one day, or two days, or five, **ten** or twenty days,
11:32 and gathered quail. No one gathered less than **ten** homers.
29:23 " 'On the fourth day prepare **ten** bulls, two rams and fourteen male
Jos 17: 5 Manasseh's share consisted of **ten** tracts of land besides Gilead
22:14 With him they sent **ten** *of* the chief men, one for each of the tribes
Jdg 6:27 So Gideon took **ten** of his servants and did as the LORD told him.
Ru 4: 2 Boaz took **ten** of the elders of the town and said, "Sit here,"
1Sa 17:17 these **ten** loaves of bread for your brothers and hurry to their camp.
25: 5 So he sent **ten** young men and said to them, "Go up to Nabal at
2Sa 18: 3 of us die, they won't care; but you are worth **ten** thousand of us.
18:11 I would have had to give you **ten** shekels of silver and a warrior's
18:15 And **ten** of Joab's armor-bearers surrounded Absalom, struck him
1Ki 4:23 [5:3] **ten** head of stall-fed cattle, twenty of pasture-fed cattle and a
7:38 He then made **ten** bronze basins, each holding forty baths
7:43 the ten stands with their **ten** basins;
11:31 he said to Jeroboam, "Take **ten** pieces for yourself, for this is what
11:31 to tear the kingdom out of Solomon's hand and give you **ten** tribes.
14: 3 Take **ten** loaves of bread with you, some cakes and a jar of honey,
2Ki 13: 7 **ten** chariots and ten thousand foot soldiers, for the king of Aram
24:14 [and artisans—a total of **ten** [K; see Q 6930] thousand.]
25:25 came with **ten** men and assassinated Gedaliah and also the men of
2Ch 4: 6 He then made **ten** basins for washing and placed five on the south
4: 8 He made **ten** tables and placed them in the temple, five on the
Ezr 1:10 gold bowls 30 matching silver bowls **410** [+752+2256+4395]
8:12 Johanan son of Hakkatan, and with him **110** [+2256+4395] men;
8:24 together with Sherebiah, Hashabiah and **ten** of their brothers,
Ne 11: 1 the rest of the people cast lots to bring one out of every **ten** to live
Ecc 7:19 Wisdom makes one wise man more powerful than **ten** rulers in a
Jer 32: 9 weighed out for him **seventeen** [+2256+8679] shekels of silver.
41: 1 came with **ten** men to Gedaliah son of Ahikam at Mizpah.
41: 8 But **ten** of them said to Ishmael, "Don't kill us! We have wheat
Eze 45:12 shekels plus **fifteen** [+2256+2822] shekels equal one mina.
Da 1:12 "Please test your servants for **ten** days: Give us nothing
1:14 So he agreed to this and tested them for **ten** days.
1:15 At the end of the **ten** days they looked healthier and better
Am 5: 3 the town that marches out a hundred strong will have only **ten**
6: 9 If **ten** men are left in one house, they too will die.

Hag 2:16 anyone came to a heap of twenty measures, there were only **ten**.
Zec 8:23 "In those days **ten** men from all languages and nations will take

6928 עִשָּׂרוֹן *'iśśārôn*, n.m. [33] [√ 6923]

two-tenths [+9109] [11], three-tenths [+8993] [8], *untranslated* [5], one-tenth [4], tenth [4], one-tenth [+285] [1]

Ex 29:40 With the first lamb offer a **tenth** *of* an ephah of fine flour mixed
Lev 14:10 along with **three-tenths** [+8993] of an ephah of fine flour mixed
14:21 together with a **tenth** of an ephah of fine flour mixed with oil for a
23:13 together with its grain offering of **two-tenths** [+9109] *of* an ephah
23:17 bring two loaves made of **two-tenths** [+9109] *of* an ephah of fine
24: 5 of bread, using **two-tenths** [+9109] of an ephah for each loaf.
Nu 15: 4 **tenth** *of* an ephah of fine flour mixed with a quarter of a hin of oil.
15: 6 " 'With a ram prepare a grain offering of **two-tenths** [+9109] of an
15: 9 bring with the bull a grain offering of **three-tenths** [+8993] of an
28: 9 a grain offering of **two-tenths** [+9109] of an ephah of fine flour
28:12 of **three-tenths** [+8993] of an ephah of fine flour mixed with oil;
28:12 a grain offering of **two-tenths** [+9109] of an ephah of fine flour
28:13 a grain offering of a **tenth** of an ephah of fine flour mixed with oil.
28:13 a grain offering of a tenth **[RPH]** of an ephah of fine flour mixed
28:20 With each bull prepare a grain offering of **three-tenths** [+8993] of
28:20 of fine flour mixed with oil; with the ram, **two-tenths** [+9109];
28:21 and with each of the seven lambs, **one-tenth**.
28:21 and with each of the seven lambs, one-tenth. **[RPH]**
28:28 of **three-tenths** [+8993] of an ephah of fine flour mixed with oil;
28:28 of fine flour mixed with oil; with the ram, **two-tenths** [+9109];
28:29 and with each of the seven lambs, **one-tenth**.
28:29 and with each of the seven lambs, one-tenth. **[RPH]**
29: 3 With the bull prepare a grain offering of **three-tenths** [+8993] of
29: 3 of fine flour mixed with oil; with the ram, **two-tenths** [+9109];
29: 4 and with each of the seven lambs, **one-tenth** [+285].
29: 9 With the bull prepare a grain offering of **three-tenths** [+8993] of
29: 9 of fine flour mixed with oil; with the ram, **two-tenths** [+9109];
29:10 and with each of the seven lambs, **one-tenth**.
29:10 and with each of the seven lambs, one-tenth. **[RPH]**
29:14 of **three-tenths** [+8993] of an ephah of fine flour mixed with oil;
29:14 mixed with oil; with each of the two rams, **two-tenths** [+9109];
29:15 and with each of the fourteen lambs, **one-tenth**.
29:15 and with each of the fourteen lambs, one-tenth. **[RPH]**

6929 עֶשְׂרִים *'eśrîm*, n.pl.indecl. [315 / 316] [√ 6923; Ar 10574]

twenty [119], twenty-five [+2256+2822] [23], twenty-two [+2256+9109] [15], 24,000 [+547+752+2256] [14], 25,000 [+547+2256+2822] [14], twentieth [9], twenty-fourth [+752+2256] [9], twenty-third [+2256+8993] [7], twenty-seventh [+2256+8679] [6], twenty-three [+2256+8993] [6], 120 [+2256+4395] [5], twenty-four [+752+2256] [5], twenty-nine [+2256+9596] [5], 128 [+2256+4395 +9046] [4], twenty-eight [+2256+9046] [4], twenty-first [+285+2256] [4], twenty-one [+285+2256] [4], 127 [+2256+2256+4395+8679] [3], 29 [+2256+9596] [3], twenty-fifth [+2256+2822] [3], 123 [+2256+4395 +8993] [2], 20 [2], 220 [+2256+4395] [2], 223 [+2256+4395+8993] [2], 320 [+2256+4395+8993] [2], 6,720 [+547+2256+4395+8679 +9252] [2], 621 [+285+2256+4395+9252] [2], *untranslated* [2], twenty-second [+2256+9109] [2], twenty-seven [+2256+8679] [2], 1,222 [+547+2256+4395+9109] [1], 120,000 [+547+2256+4395] [1], 122 [+2256+2256+4395+9109] [1], 122 [+2256+4395+9109] [1], 2,322 [+547+2256+4395+8993+9109] [1], 20,000 [+547] [1], 20,200 [+547+2256+4395] [1], 20,800 [+547+2256+4395+9046] [1], 22 [+2256+9109] [1], 22,000 [+547+2256+9109] [1], 22,034 [+547+752+2256+2256+2256+8993+9109] [1], 22,200 [+547+2256 +2256+4395+9109] [1], 22,273 [+547+2256+2256+2256+4395 +8679+8993+9109] [1], 22,600 [+547+2256+2256+4395+9109 +9252] [1], 23,000 [+547+2256+8993] [1], 25,100 [+547+2256+2256 +2822+4395] [1], 26,000 [+547+2256+9252] [1], 28 [+2256+9046] [1], 28,600 [+547+2256+2256+4395+9046+9252] [1], 3,023 [+547+2256+2256+8993+8993] [1], 323 [+2256+4395+8993+8993] [1], 324 [+752+2256+4395+8993] [1], 328 [+2256+4395+8993 +9046] [1], 420 [+752+2256+4395] [1], 623 [+2256+4395+8993 +9252] [1], 628 [+2256+4395+9046+9252] [1], 721 [+285+2256 +2256+4395+8679] [1], 725 [+2256+2822+4395+8679] [1], 822 [+2256+4395+9046+9109] [1], 928 [+2256+4395+9046+9596] [1], them[s] [+2021+7983] [1], thirty feet [+564+928+2021] [1], twenty-six [+2256+9252] [1], twenty-sixth [+2256+9252] [1]

Ge 6: 3 for he is mortal; his days will be a hundred and **twenty** years."
8:14 By the **twenty-seventh** [+2256+8679] day of the second month the
11:24 When Nahor had lived **29** [+2256+9596] years, he became the
18:31 as to speak to the Lord, what if only **twenty** can be found there?"
18:31 He said, "For the sake of **twenty**, I will not destroy it."
23: 1 Sarah lived to be a hundred and **twenty-seven** [+2256+8679] years
31:38 "I have been with you for **twenty** years now. Your sheep and goats
31:41 It was like this for the **twenty** years I was in your household.
32:14 [32:15] two hundred female goats and **twenty** male goats,
32:14 [32:15] twenty male goats, two hundred ewes and **twenty** rams,
32:15 [32:16] and **twenty** female donkeys and ten male donkeys.
37:28 and sold him for **twenty** shekels *of* silver to the Ishmaelites,
Ex 12:18 until the evening of the **twenty-first** [+285+2256] day.
26: 2 the same size—**twenty-eight** [+2256+9046] cubits long and four
26:18 Make **twenty** frames for the south side of the tabernacle
26:19 and make forty silver bases to go under **them**[s] [+2021+7983]—
26:20 other side, the north side of the tabernacle, make **twenty** frames
27:10 with **twenty** posts and twenty bronze bases and with silver hooks
27:10 with twenty posts and **twenty** bronze bases and with silver hooks
27:11 with **twenty** posts and twenty bronze bases and with silver hooks
27:11 with twenty posts and **twenty** bronze bases and with silver hooks
27:16 provide a curtain **twenty** cubits long, of blue, purple and scarlet
30:13 according to the sanctuary shekel, which weighs **twenty** gerahs.
30:14 All who cross over, those **twenty** years old or more, are to give an
36: 9 the same size—**twenty-eight** [+2256+9046] cubits long and four
36:23 They made **twenty** frames for the south side of the tabernacle
36:24 made forty silver bases to go under **[RPH]** them—two bases for
36:25 the north side of the tabernacle, they made **twenty** frames
38:10 with **twenty** posts and twenty bronze bases, and with silver hooks
38:10 with twenty posts and **twenty** bronze bases, and with silver hooks
38:11 cubits long and had **twenty** posts and twenty bronze bases,
38:11 cubits long and had twenty posts and **twenty** bronze bases,
38:18 It was **twenty** cubits long and, like the curtains of the courtyard,
38:24 used for all the work on the sanctuary was **29** [+2256+9596] talents
38:26 to those counted, **twenty** years old or more, a total of 603,550 men.
Lev 27: 3 set the value of a male between the ages of **twenty** and sixty at
27: 5 If it is a person between the ages of five and **twenty**, set the value
27: 5 set the value of a male at **twenty** shekels and of a female at ten
27:25 set according to the sanctuary shekel, **twenty** gerahs to the shekel.
Nu 1: 3 Aaron are to number by their divisions all the men in Israel **twenty**
1:18 and the men **twenty** years old or more were listed by name,
1:20 All the men **twenty** years old or more who were able to serve in
1:22 All the men **twenty** years old or more who were able to serve in
1:24 All the men **twenty** years old or more who were able to serve in
1:26 All the men **twenty** years old or more who were able to serve in
1:28 All the men **twenty** years old or more who were able to serve in
1:30 All the men **twenty** years old or more who were able to serve in
1:32 All the men **twenty** years old or more who were able to serve in
1:34 All the men **twenty** years old or more who were able to serve in
1:36 All the men **twenty** years old or more who were able to serve in
1:38 All the men **twenty** years old or more who were able to serve in
1:40 All the men **twenty** years old or more who were able to serve in
1:42 All the men **twenty** years old or more who were able to serve in
1:45 All the Israelites **twenty** years old or more who were able to serve
3:39 every male a month old or more, was **22,000** [+547+2256+9109].
3:43 was **22,273** [+547+2256+2256+2256+4395+8679+8993+9109].
3:47 according to the sanctuary shekel, which weighs **twenty** gerahs.
7:86 Altogether, the gold dishes weighed a hundred and **twenty** shekels.
7:88 the fellowship offering came to **twenty-four** [+752+2256] oxen,
8:24 Men **twenty-five** [+2256+2822] years old or more shall come to
10:11 On the **twentieth** day of the second month of the second year,
11:19 not eat it for just one day, or two days, or five, ten or **twenty** days,
14:29 every one of you **twenty** years old or more who was counted in the
18:16 according to the sanctuary shekel, which weighs **twenty** gerahs.
25: 9 those who died in the plague numbered **24,000** [+547+752+2256].
26: 2 all those **twenty** years old or more who are able to serve in the
26: 4 "Take a census of the men **twenty** years old or more, as the
26:14 Simeon; there were **22,200** [+547+2256+2256+4395+9109] men.
26:62 Levites a month old or more numbered **23,000** [+547+2256+8993].
32:11 not one of the men **twenty** years old or more who came up out of
33:39 Aaron was a hundred and **twenty-three** [+2256+8993] years old
Dt 31: 2 "I am now a hundred and **twenty** years old and I am no longer able
34: 7 Moses was a hundred and **twenty** years old when he died,
Jos 15:32 a total of **twenty-nine** [+2256+9596] towns and their villages.
19:30 There were **twenty-two** [+2256+9109] towns and their villages.
Jdg 4: 3 and had cruelly oppressed the Israelites for **twenty** years,
7: 3 So **twenty-two** [+2256+9109] thousand men left,
8:10 a hundred and **twenty** thousand swordsmen had fallen.
10: 2 He led Israel **twenty-three** [+2256+8993] years; then he died, and
10: 3 Jair of Gilead, who led Israel **twenty-two** [+2256+9109] years.
11:33 He devastated **twenty** towns from Aroer to the vicinity of Minnith,
15:20 Samson led Israel for **twenty** years in the days of the Philistines.
16:31 in the tomb of Manoah his father. He had led Israel **twenty** years.
20:15 Benjamites mobilized **twenty-six** [+2256+9252] thousand
20:21 and cut down **twenty-two** [+2256+9109] thousand Israelites on the
20:35 the Israelites struck down **25,100** [+547+2256+2256+2822+4395]
20:46 **twenty-five** [+2256+2822] thousand Benjamite swordsmen fell, all
1Sa 7: 2 It was a long time, **twenty** years in all, that the ark remained at
14:14 his armor-bearer killed some **twenty** men in an area of about half
2Sa 3:20 When Abner, who had **twenty** men with him, came to David at
8: 4 seven thousand charioteers and **twenty** thousand foot soldiers.
8: 5 David struck down **twenty-two** [+2256+9109] thousand of them.

2Sa 9:10 eat at my table." (Now Ziba had fifteen sons and **twenty** servants.)
10: 6 they hired **twenty** thousand Aramean foot soldiers from Beth
18: 7 and the casualties that day were great—**twenty** thousand men.
19:17 [19:18] and his fifteen sons and **twenty** servants.
21:20 hand and six toes on each foot—**twenty-four** [+752+2256] in all.
24: 8 back to Jerusalem at the end of nine months and **twenty** days.
1Ki 4:23 [5:3] **twenty** of pasture-fed cattle and a hundred sheep and goats,
5:11 [5:25] Solomon gave Hiram **twenty** thousand cors of wheat as
5:11 [5:25] in addition to **twenty** thousand baths of pressed olive oil.
6: 2 for the LORD was sixty cubits long, **twenty** wide and thirty high.
6: 3 that is **twenty** cubits, and projected ten cubits from the front of the
6:16 He partitioned off **twenty** cubits at the rear of the temple with
6:20 The inner sanctuary was **twenty** cubits long, twenty wide
6:20 sanctuary was twenty cubits long, **twenty** wide and twenty high.
6:20 sanctuary was twenty cubits long, twenty wide and **twenty** high.
8:63 **twenty-two** [+2256+9109] thousand cattle and a hundred and
8:63 and a hundred and **twenty** thousand sheep and goats.
9:10 At the end of **twenty** years, during which Solomon built these two
9:11 King Solomon gave **twenty** towns in Galilee to Hiram king of
9:14 Now Hiram had sent to the king **120** [+2256+4395] talents of gold.
9:28 and brought back **420** [+752+2256+4395] talents of gold,
10:10 she gave the king **120** [+2256+4395] talents of gold, large
14:20 He reigned for **twenty-two** [+2256+9109] years and then rested
15: 9 In the **twentieth** year of Jeroboam king of Israel, Asa became king
15:33 Israel in Tirzah, and he reigned **twenty-four** [+752+2256] years.
16: 8 In the **twenty-sixth** [+2256+9252] year of Asa king of Judah, Elah
16:10 and killed him in the **twenty-seventh** [+2256+8679] year of Asa
16:15 In the **twenty-seventh** [+2256+8679] year of Asa king of Judah,
16:29 he reigned in Samaria over Israel **twenty-two** [+2256+9109] years.
20:30 wall collapsed on **twenty-seven** [+2256+8679] thousand of them.
22:42 and he reigned in Jerusalem **twenty-five** [+2256+2822] years.
2Ki 4:42 bringing the man of God **twenty** loaves of barley bread baked from
8:26 Ahaziah was **twenty-two** [+2256+9109] years old when he became
10:36 over Israel in Samaria was **twenty-eight** [+2256+9046] years.
12: 6 [12:7] But by the **twenty-third** [+2256+8993] year of King Joash
13: 1 In the **twenty-third** [+2256+8993] year of Joash son of Ahaziah
14: 2 He was **twenty-five** [+2256+2822] years old when he became king,
14: 2 He was twenty-five years old when he became king, and he reigned
15: 1 In the **twenty-seventh** [+2256+8679] year of Jeroboam king of
15:27 became king of Israel in Samaria, and he reigned **twenty** years.
15:30 succeeded him as king in the **twentieth** year of Jotham son of
15:33 He was **twenty-five** [+2256+2822] years old when he became king,
16: 2 Ahaz was **twenty** years old when he became king, and he reigned
18: 2 He was **twenty-five** [+2256+2822] years old when he became king,
18: 2 and he reigned in Jerusalem **twenty-nine** [+2256+9596] years.
21:19 Amon was **twenty-two** [+2256+9109] years old when he became
23:31 Jehoahaz was **twenty-three** [+2256+8993] years old when he
23:36 Jehoiakim was **twenty-five** [+2256+2822] years old when he
24:18 Zedekiah was **twenty-one** [+285+2256] years old when he became
25:27 on the **twenty-seventh** [+2256+8679] day of the twelfth month.
1Ch 2:22 Jair, who controlled **twenty-three** [+2256+8993] towns in Gilead.
7: 2 numbered **22,600** [+547+2256+2256+4395+9109+9252].
7: 7 listed **22,034** [+547+752+2256+2256+2256+8993+9109] fighting
7: 9 the heads of families and **20,200** [+547+2256+4395] fighting men.
7:40 as listed in their genealogy, was **26,000** [+547+2256+9252].
12:28 [12:29] with **22** [+2256+9109] officers from his family;
12:30 [12:31] in their own clans—**20,800** [+547+2256+4395+9046];
12:35 [12:36] for battle—**28,600** [+547+2256+2256+4395+9046+9252];
12:37 [12:38] every type of weapon—**120,000** [+547+2256+4395].
15: 5 of Kohath, Uriel the leader and **120** [+2256+4395] relatives;
15: 6 of Merari, Asaiah the leader and **220** [+2256+4395] relatives;
18: 4 seven thousand charioteers and **twenty** thousand foot soldiers.
18: 5 David struck down **twenty-two** [+2256+9109] thousand of them.
20: 6 hand and six toes on each foot—**twenty-four** [+752+2256] in all.
23: 4 **twenty-four** [+752+2256] thousand are to supervise the work of
23:24 the workers **twenty** years old or more who served in the temple of
23:27 the Levites were counted from those **twenty** years old or more.
24:16 the nineteenth to Pethahiah, the **twentieth** to Jehezkel,
24:17 the **twenty-first** [+285+2256] to Jakin, the twenty-second to
24:17 twenty-first to Jakin, the **twenty-second** [+2256+9109] to Gamul,
24:18 the **twenty-third** [+2256+8993] to Delaiah and the twenty-fourth
24:18 to Delaiah and the **twenty-fourth** [+752+2256] to Maaziah.
25:27 the **twentieth** to Eliathah, his sons and relatives, 12
25:28 the **twenty-first** [+285+2256] to Hothir, his sons and relatives, 12
25:29 the **twenty-second** [+2256+9109] to Giddalti, his sons and
25:30 the **twenty-third** [+2256+8993] to Mahazioth, his sons and
25:31 the **twenty-fourth** [+752+2256] to Romamti-Ezer, his sons and
27: 1 Each division consisted of **24,000** [+547+752+2256] men.
27: 2 There were **24,000** [+547+752+2256] men in his division.
27: 4 There were **24,000** [+547+752+2256] men in his division.
27: 5 and there were **24,000** [+547+752+2256] men in his division.
27: 7 There were **24,000** [+547+752+2256] men in his division.
27: 8 There were **24,000** [+547+752+2256] men in his division.
27: 9 There were **24,000** [+547+752+2256] men in his division.
27:10 There were **24,000** [+547+752+2256] men in his division.
27:11 There were **24,000** [+547+752+2256] men in his division.
27:12 There were **24,000** [+547+752+2256] men in his division.
27:13 There were **24,000** [+547+752+2256] men in his division.
27:14 There were **24,000** [+547+752+2256] men in his division.
27:15 There were **24,000** [+547+752+2256] men in his division.
27:23 David did not take the number of the men **twenty** years old
2Ch 2:10 [2:9] **twenty** thousand cors of ground wheat, twenty thousand
2:10 [2:9] **twenty** thousand cors of barley, twenty thousand baths of
2:10 [2:9] **twenty** thousand baths of wine and twenty thousand baths of
2:10 [2:9] baths of wine and **twenty** thousand baths of olive oil."
3: 3 and **twenty** cubits wide (using the cubit of the old standard).
3: 4 The portico at the front of the temple was **twenty** cubits long
3: 4 long across the width of the building and **twenty** cubits high.
3: 8 width of the temple—**twenty** cubits long and twenty cubits wide.
3: 8 width of the temple—twenty cubits long and **twenty** cubits wide.
3:11 The total wingspan of the cherubim was **twenty** cubits. One wing
3:13 The wings of these cherubim extended **twenty** cubits. They stood
4: 1 He made a bronze altar **twenty** cubits long, twenty cubits wide
4: 1 altar twenty cubits long, **twenty** cubits wide and ten cubits high.
5:12 They were accompanied by **120** [+2256+4395] priests sounding
7: 5 Solomon offered a sacrifice of **twenty-two** [+2256+9109] thousand
7: 5 head of cattle and a hundred and **twenty** thousand sheep and goats.
7:10 On the **twenty-third** [+2256+8993] day of the seventh month he
8: 1 At the end of **twenty** years, during which Solomon built the temple
9: 9 Then she gave the king **120** [+2256+4395] talents of gold,
11:21 concubines, **twenty-eight** [+2256+9046] sons and sixty daughters.
13:21 He married fourteen wives and had **twenty-two** [+2256+9109] sons
20:31 and he reigned in Jerusalem **twenty-five** [+2256+2822] years.
22: 2 Ahaziah was **twenty-two** [+2256+9109] [BHS 752] years old
25: 1 Amaziah was **twenty-five** [+2256+2822] years old when he
25: 1 and he reigned in Jerusalem **twenty-nine** [+2256+9596] years.
25: 5 He then mustered those **twenty** years old or more and found that
27: 1 Jotham was **twenty-five** [+2256+2822] years old when he became
27: 8 He was **twenty-five** [+2256+2822] years old when he became king,
28: 1 Ahaz was **twenty** years old when he became king, and he reigned
28: 6 Remaliah killed a hundred and **twenty** thousand soldiers in Judah—
29: 1 Hezekiah was **twenty-five** [+2256+2822] years old when he
29: 1 and he reigned in Jerusalem **twenty-nine** [+2256+9596] years.
31:17 and likewise to the Levites **twenty** years old or more,
33:21 Amon was **twenty-two** [+2256+9109] years old when he became
36: 2 Jehoahaz was **twenty-three** [+2256+8993] years old when he
36: 5 Jehoiakim was **twenty-five** [+2256+2822] years old when he
36:11 Zedekiah was **twenty-one** [+285+2256] years old when he became
Ezr 1: 9 gold dishes 30 silver dishes 1,000 silver pans **29** [+2256+9596]
2:11 of Bebai **623** [+2256+4395+8993+9252]
2:12 of Azgad **1,222** [+547+2256+4395+9109]
2:17 of Bezai **323** [+2256+4395+8993+8993]
2:19 of Hashum **223** [+2256+4395+8993]
2:21 the men of Bethlehem **123** [+2256+4395+8993]
2:23 of Anathoth **128** [+2256+4395+9046]
2:26 of Ramah and Geba **621** [+285+2256+4395+9252]
2:27 of Micmash **122** [+2256+4395+9109]
2:28 of Bethel and Ai **223** [+2256+4395+8993]
2:32 of Harim **320** [+2256+4395+8993]
2:33 of Lod, Hadid and Ono **725** [+2256+2822+4395+8679]
2:41 The singers: the descendants of Asaph **128** [+2256+4395+9046]
2:67 435 camels and **6,720** [+547+2256+4395+8679+9252] donkeys.
3: 8 appointing Levites **twenty** years of age and older to supervise the
8:11 Zechariah son of Bebai, and with him **28** [+2256+9046] men;
8:19 the descendants of Merari, and his brothers and nephews, **20** *men*.
8:20 They also brought **220** [+2256+4395] of the temple servants—
8:27 **20** bowls of gold valued at 1,000 darics, and two fine articles of
10: 9 on the **twentieth** day of the ninth month, all the people were sitting
Ne 1: 1 In the month of Kislev in the **twentieth** year, while I was in the
2: 1 In the month of Nisan in the **twentieth** year of King Artaxerxes,
5:14 Moreover, from the **twentieth** year of King Artaxerxes, when I
6:15 the wall was completed on the **twenty-fifth** [+2256+2822] of Elul,
7:16 of Bebai **628** [+2256+4395+9046+9252]
7:17 of Azgad **2,322** [+547+2256+4395+8993+9109]
7:22 of Hashum **328** [+2256+4395+8993+9046]
7:23 of Bezai **324** [+752+2256+4395+8993]
7:27 of Anathoth **128** [+2256+4395+9046]
7:30 of Ramah and Geba **621** [+285+2256+4395+9252]
7:31 of Micmash **122** [+2256+2256+4395+9109]
7:32 of Bethel and Ai **123** [+2256+4395+8993]
7:35 of Harim **320** [+2256+4395+8993]
7:37 of Lod, Hadid and Ono **721** [+285+2256+2256+4395+8679]
7:69 [7:68] and **6,720** [+547+2256+4395+8679+9252] donkeys.
9: 1 On the **twenty-fourth** [+752+2256] day of the same month, the
11: 8 followers, Gabbai and Sallai—**928** [+2256+4395+9046+9596] men.
11:12 **822** [+2256+4395+9046+9109] men; Adaiah son of Jeroham, the
11:14 and his associates, who were able men—**128** [+2256+4395+9046].
Est 1: 1 Xerxes who ruled over **127** [+2256+2256+4395+8679] provinces

Est 8: 9 on the **twenty-third** [+2256+8993] day of the third month, the
8: 9 and nobles of the **127** [+2256+2256+4395+8679] provinces
9: 30 all the Jews in the **127** [+2256+2256+4395+8679] provinces of the
Jer 25: 3 *For* **twenty-three** [+2256+8993] years—from the thirteenth year
52: 1 Zedekiah was **twenty-one** [+285+2256] years old when he became
52: 28 the seventh year, **3,023** [+547+2256+2256+8993+8993] Jews;
52: 30 in his **twenty-third** [+2256+8993] year, 745 Jews taken into exile
52: 31 on the **twenty-fifth** [+2256+2822] day of the twelfth month.
Eze 4: 10 Weigh out **twenty** shekels of food to eat each day and eat it at set
8: 16 portico and the altar, were about **twenty-five** [+2256+2822] men.
11: 1 at the entrance to the gate were **twenty-five** [+2256+2822] men,
29: 17 In the **twenty-seventh** [+2256+8679] year, in the first month on
40: 1 In the **twenty-fifth** [+2256+2822] year of our exile, at the
40: 13 the distance was **twenty-five** [+2256+2822] cubits from one
40: 21 It was fifty cubits long and **twenty-five** [+2256+2822] cubits wide.
40: 25 It was fifty cubits long and **twenty-five** [+2256+2822] cubits wide.
40: 29 It was fifty cubits long and **twenty-five** [+2256+2822] cubits wide.
40: 30 were **twenty-five** [+2256+2822] cubits wide and five cubits deep.)
40: 33 It was fifty cubits long and **twenty-five** [+2256+2822] cubits wide.
40: 36 It was fifty cubits long and **twenty-five** [+2256+2822] cubits wide.
40: 49 The portico was **twenty** cubits wide, and twelve cubits from front
41: 2 outer sanctuary; it was forty cubits long and **twenty** cubits wide.
41: 4 it was **twenty** cubits, and its width was twenty cubits across the
41: 4 its width was **twenty** cubits across the end of the outer sanctuary.
41: 10 the ⌊priests'⌋ rooms was **twenty** cubits wide all around the temple.
42: 3 Both in the section **twenty** cubits from the inner court and in the
45: 1 **25,000** [+547+2256+2822] cubits long and 20,000 cubits wide;
45: 1 25,000 cubits long and **20,000** [+547; BHS 6924] cubits wide;
45: 3 measure off a section **25,000** [+547+2256+2822] cubits long and
45: 5 An area **25,000** [+547+2256+2822] cubits long and 10,000 cubits
45: 5 as their possession for towns [BHS *20 rooms*; NIV 6551] to live in.
45: 6 area 5,000 cubits wide and **25,000** [+547+2256+2822] cubits long,
45: 12 The shekel is to consist of **twenty** gerahs. Twenty shekels plus
45: 12 **Twenty** shekels plus twenty-five shekels plus fifteen shekels equal
45: 12 Twenty shekels plus **twenty-five** [+2256+2822] shekels plus
48: 8 It will be **25,000** [+547+2256+2822] cubits wide, and its length
48: 9 to offer to the LORD will be **25,000** [+547+2256+2822] cubits long
48: 10 It will be **25,000** [+547+2256+2822] cubits long on the north side,t
48: 10 and **25,000** [+547+2256+2822] cubits long on the south side.
48: 13 will have an allotment **25,000** [+547+2256+2822] cubits long and
48: 13 Its total length will be **25,000** [+547+2256+2822] cubits and its
48: 15 5,000 cubits wide and **25,000** [+547+2256+2822] cubits long, will
48: 20 a square, **25,000** [+547+2256+2822] cubits on each side.
48: 20 **[RPH]** As a special gift you will set aside the sacred portion,
48: 21 It will extend eastward from the **25,000** [+547+2256+2822] cubits
48: 21 from the **25,000** [+547+2256+2822] cubits to the western border.
Da 10: 4 On the **twenty-fourth** [+752+2256] day of the first month, as I was
10: 13 of the Persian kingdom resisted me **twenty-one** [+285+2256] days.
Hag 1: 15 on the **twenty-fourth** [+752+2256] day of the sixth month in the
2: 1 On the **twenty-first** [+285+2256] day of the seventh month, the
2: 10 On the **twenty-fourth** [+752+2256] day of the ninth month, in the
2: 16 When anyone came to a heap of **twenty** measures, there were only
2: 16 went to a wine vat to draw fifty measures, there were only **twenty**.
2: 18 from this **twenty-fourth** [+752+2256] day of the ninth month, give
2: 20 on the **twenty-fourth** [+752+2256] day of the month:
Zec 1: 7 On the **twenty-fourth** [+752+2256] day of the eleventh month, the
5: 2 "I see a flying scroll, **thirty feet** [+564+928+2021] long and

6930 עֲשֶׂרֶת *ʿᵃśeret*, n.f. [52] [√ 6923]

ten [39], 10,000 [+547] [9], tens [3], ten-acre [+7538] [1]

Ge 31: 7 yet your father has cheated me by changing my wages **ten** times.
31: 41 six years for your flocks, and you changed my wages **ten** times.
Ex 18: 21 them as officials over thousands, hundreds, fifties and **tens**.
18: 25 of the people, officials over thousands, hundreds, fifties and **tens**.
34: 28 the tablets the words of the covenant—the **Ten** Commandments.
Lev 27: 5 value of a male at twenty shekels and of a female at **ten** shekels.
Dt 1: 15 of hundreds, of fifties and of **tens** and as tribal officials.
4: 13 He declared to you his covenant, the **Ten** Commandments,
10: 4 the **Ten** Commandments he had proclaimed to you on the
Jdg 1: 4 into their hands and they struck down **ten** thousand men at Bezek.
3: 29 At that time they struck down about **ten** thousand Moabites,
4: 6 take with you **ten** thousand men of Naphtali and Zebulun and lead
4: 10 **Ten** thousand men followed him, and Deborah also went with him.
4: 14 So Barak went down Mount Tabor, followed by **ten** thousand men.
7: 3 So twenty-two thousand men left, while **ten** thousand remained.
17: 10 my father and priest, and I'll give you **ten** shekels of silver a year,
20: 34 **ten** thousand of Israel's finest men made a frontal attack on
1Sa 15: 4 hundred thousand foot soldiers and **ten** thousand men from Judah.
17: 18 Take along these **ten** cheeses to the commander of their unit.
25: 38 About **ten** days later, the LORD struck Nabal and he died.
1Ki 5: 14 [5:28] He sent them off to Lebanon in shifts of **ten** thousand a
11: 35 will take the kingdom from his son's hands and give you **ten** tribes.
2Ki 13: 7 ten chariots and **ten** thousand foot soldiers, for the king of Aram
14: 7 He was the one who defeated **ten** thousand Edomites in the Valley
24: 14 all the craftsmen and artisans—a total of **ten** [K 6927] thousand.
1Ch 29: 7 and ten thousand darics of gold, **ten** thousand talents of silver,
2Ch 25: 11 to the Valley of Salt, where he killed **ten** thousand men of Seir.
25: 12 The army of Judah also captured **ten** thousand men alive, took
27: 5 **ten** thousand cors of wheat and ten thousand cors of barley.
27: 5 ten thousand cors of wheat and **ten** thousand cors of barley.
30: 24 them with a thousand bulls and **ten** thousand sheep and goats.
36: 9 and he reigned in Jerusalem three months and **ten** days.
Ne 5: 18 and every **ten** days an abundant supply of wine of all kinds.
Est 3: 9 I will put **ten** thousand talents of silver into the royal treasury for
9: 10 the **ten** sons of Haman son of Hammedatha, the enemy of the Jews.
9: 12 five hundred men and the **ten** sons of Haman in the citadel of Susa.
9: 13 tomorrow also, and let Haman's **ten** sons be hanged on gallows."
9: 14 edict was issued in Susa, and they hanged the **ten** sons of Haman.
Isa 5: 10 A **ten-acre** [+7538] vineyard will produce only a bath of wine,
Jer 41: 2 son of Nethaniah and the **ten** men who were with him got up
42: 7 **Ten** days later the word of the LORD came to Jeremiah.
Eze 45: 3 off a section 25,000 cubits long and **10,000** [+547] cubits wide.
45: 5 and **10,000** [+547] cubits wide will belong to the Levites,
45: 14 is a tenth of a bath from each cor (which consists of **ten** baths
45: 14 of ten baths or one homer, for **ten** baths are equivalent to a homer).
48: 9 LORD will be 25,000 cubits long and **10,000** [+547] cubits wide.
48: 10 **10,000** [+547] cubits wide on the west side, 10,000 cubits wide on
48: 10 **10,000** [+547] cubits wide on the east side and 25,000 cubits long
48: 13 an allotment 25,000 cubits long and **10,000** [+547] cubits wide.
48: 13 length will be 25,000 cubits and its width **10,000** [+547] cubits.
48: 18 will be **10,000** [+547] cubits on the east side and 10,000 cubits on
48: 18 cubits on the east side and **10,000** [+547] cubits on the west side.

6931 עָשׁ *ʿāš¹*, n.m. [7] [√ 6949]

moth [4], moths [2], moth's cocoon [1]

Job 4: 19 are in the dust, who are crushed more readily than a **moth**!
13: 28 wastes away like something rotten, like a garment eaten by **moths**.
27: 18 The house he builds is like a **moth's cocoon**, like a hut made by a
Ps 39: 11 [39:12] you consume their wealth like a **moth**—each man is but a
Isa 50: 9 They will all wear out like a garment; the **moths** will eat them up.
51: 8 For the **moth** will eat them up like a garment; the worm will
Hos 5: 12 I am like a **moth** to Ephraim, like rot to the people of Judah.

6932 עָשׁ *ʿāš²*, n.m. Not used in NIV/BHS [√ 6949]

6933 עָשׁ *ʿāš³*, n.[f.]. [1] [√ 6568]

Bear [1]

Job 9: 9 He is the Maker of the **Bear** and Orion, the Pleiades

6934 עָשׁוֹק *ʿāšôq*, n.[m.]. [1] [√ 6943]

oppressor [1]

Jer 22: 3 Rescue from the hand of his **oppressor** the one who has been

6935 עֲשׁוּקִים *ʿᵃšûqîm*, n.pl.abst. [3] [√ 6943]

oppression [3]

Job 35: 9 "Men cry out under a load of **oppression**; they plead for relief
Ecc 4: 1 and saw all the **oppression** that was taking place under the sun:
Am 3: 9 the great unrest within her and the **oppression** among her people."

6936 עָשׁוֹת *ʿāšôt*, a. [1] [√ 6950]

wrought [1]

Eze 27: 19 they exchanged **wrought** iron, cassia and calamus for your wares.

6937 עַשְׁוָת *ʿašwāt*, n.pr.m. [1]

Ashvath [1]

1Ch 7: 33 The sons of Japhlet: Pasach, Bimhal and **Ashvath**. These were

6938 עָשִׁיר *ʿāšîr*, a. (used as n.). [23] [√ 6947]

rich [21], wealth [1], wealthy [1]

Ex 30: 15 The **rich** are not to give more than a half shekel and the poor are
Ru 3: 10 You have not run after the younger men, whether **rich** or poor.
2Sa 12: 1 were two men in a certain town, one **rich** and the other poor.
12: 2 The **rich** *man* had a very large number of sheep and cattle,
12: 4 "Now a traveler came to the **rich** man, but the rich man refrained
Job 27: 19 He lies down **wealthy**, but will do so no more; when he opens his
Ps 45: 12 [45:13] will come with a gift, men of **wealth** will seek your favor.
49: 2 [49:3] both low and high, **rich** and poor alike:
Pr 10: 15 The wealth of the **rich** is their fortified city, but poverty is the ruin
14: 20 shunned even by their neighbors, but the **rich** have many friends.
18: 11 The wealth of the **rich** is their fortified city; they imagine it an
18: 23 A poor man pleads for mercy, but a **rich** *man* answers harshly.
22: 2 **Rich** and poor have this in common: The LORD is the Maker of

Pr 22: 7 The **rich** rule over the poor, and the borrower is servant to the
22: 16 the poor to increase his wealth and he who gives gifts to the **rich**—
28: 6 Better a poor man whose walk is blameless than a **rich** *man* whose
28: 11 A **rich** man may be wise in his own eyes, but a poor man who has
Ecc 5: 12 [5:11] but the abundance of a **rich** *man* permits him no sleep.
10: 6 are put in many high positions, while the **rich** occupy the low ones.
10: 20 the king even in your thoughts, or curse the **rich** in your bedroom,
Isa 53: 9 and with the **rich** in his death, though he had done no violence,
Jer 9: 23 [9:22] boast of his strength or the **rich** *man* boast of his riches,
Mic 6: 12 Her **rich** *men* are violent; her people are liars and their tongues

6939 עָשַׁן 'āšan, v.den. [6] [→ 6940, 6942]

smoke [2], anger smolder [1], burn [1], covered with smoke [1], smolder [1]

Ex 19: 18 [A] Mount Sinai *was* **covered with smoke**, because the LORD
Dt 29: 20 [29:19] [A] his wrath and zeal *will* **burn** against that man.
Ps 74: 1 [A] Why *does* your **anger smolder** against the sheep of your
80: 4 [80:5] [A] how long *will your* **anger smolder** against the
104: 32 [A] and it trembles, who touches the mountains, and *they* **smoke**.
144: 5 [A] and come down; touch the mountains, so that *they* **smoke**.

6940 עָשָׁן 'āšān¹, n.m. [25] [→ 1016; cf. 6939]

smoke [23], cloud of smoke [1], smoking [1]

Ge 15: 17 a **smoking** firepot with a blazing torch appeared and passed
Ex 19: 18 The **smoke** billowed up from it like smoke from a furnace,
19: 18 The smoke billowed up from it like **smoke** *from* a furnace,
Jos 8: 20 looked back and saw the **smoke** *of* the city rising against the sky,
8: 21 had taken the city and that **smoke** was going up from the city,
Jdg 20: 38 that they should send up a great cloud of **smoke** from the city,
20: 40 But when the column of **smoke** began to rise from the city,
2Sa 22: 9 **Smoke** rose from his nostrils; consuming fire came from his
Job 41: 20 [41:12] **Smoke** pours from his nostrils as from a boiling pot over
Ps 18: 8 [18:9] **Smoke** rose from his nostrils; consuming fire came from
37: 20 like the beauty of the fields, they will vanish—vanish like **smoke**.
68: 2 [68:3] As **smoke** is blown away by the wind, may you blow them
102: 3 [102:4] For my days vanish like **smoke**; my bones burn like
Pr 10: 26 As vinegar to the teeth and **smoke** to the eyes, so is a sluggard to
SS 3: 6 Who is this coming up from the desert like a column of **smoke**,
Isa 4: 5 and over those who assemble there a cloud of **smoke** by day
6: 4 and thresholds shook and the temple was filled with **smoke**.
9: 18 [9:17] so that it rolls upward in a column of **smoke**.
14: 31 A **cloud of smoke** comes from the north, and there is not a
34: 10 It will not be quenched night and day; its **smoke** will rise forever.
51: 6 the heavens will vanish like **smoke**, the earth will wear out like a
65: 5 Such people are **smoke** in my nostrils, a fire that keeps burning all
Hos 13: 3 from a threshing floor, like **smoke** escaping through a window.
Joel 2: 30 [3:3] and on the earth, blood and fire and billows of **smoke**.
Na 2: 13 [2:14] "I will burn up your chariots in **smoke**, and the sword will

6941 ²עָשָׁן 'āšān², n.pr.loc. [4] [cf. 1014, 1016]

Ashan [4]

Jos 15: 42 Libnah, Ether, **Ashan**,
19: 7 Ain, Rimmon, Ether and **Ashan**—four towns and their villages—
1Ch 4: 32 villages were Etam, Ain, Rimmon, Token and **Ashan**—
6: 59 [6:44] **Ashan**, Juttah and Beth Shemesh, together with their

6942 עָשֵׁן 'āšēn, a. [2] [√ 6939]

in smoke [1], smoldering [1]

Ex 20: 18 and heard the trumpet and saw the mountain **in smoke**,
Isa 7: 4 not lose heart because of these two **smoldering** stubs of firewood—

6943 עָשַׁק 'āšaq, v. [37] [→ 6934, 6935, 6944, 6945, 6946]

oppress [7], oppressed [7], defraud [4], oppresses [3], cheated [2], oppressor [2], oppressors [2], cheats [1], crushed [1], mistreat [1], oppression [1], practice extortion [+6945] [1], practiced extortion [+6945] [1], rages [1], take advantage [1], taken by extortion [+906+6945] [1], tormented [1]

Lev 6: 2 [5:21] [A] or left in his care or stolen, or if *he* **cheats** him,
6: 4 [5:23] [A] he has stolen or **taken by extortion** [+906+6945],
19: 13 [A] " '*Do* not **defraud** your neighbor or rob him. " 'Do not hold
Dt 24: 14 [A] *Do* not **take advantage** *of* a hired man who is poor
28: 29 [B] day after day you will be **oppressed** and robbed, with no one
28: 33 [B] and you will have nothing but cruel **oppression** all your days.
1Sa 12: 3 [A] Whose donkey have I taken? Whom *have I* **cheated**?
12: 4 [A] "*You have* not **cheated** or oppressed us," they replied. "You
1Ch 16: 21 [A] He allowed no man to **oppress** them; for their sake he
Job 10: 3 [A] Does it please you *to* **oppress** me, to spurn the work of your
40: 23 [A] When the river **rages**, he is not alarmed; he is secure,
Ps 72: 4 [A] save the children of the needy; he will crush the **oppressor**.
103: 6 [B] works righteousness and justice for all the **oppressed**.
105: 14 [A] He allowed no one to **oppress** them; for their sake he
119: 121 [A] is righteous and just; do not leave me to my **oppressors**.
119: 122 [A] your servant's well-being; *let* not the arrogant **oppress** me.
146: 7 [B] He upholds the cause of the **oppressed** and gives food to the
Pr 14: 31 [A] *He who* **oppresses** the poor shows contempt for their Maker,
22: 16 [A] *He who* **oppresses** the poor to increase his wealth and he
28: 3 [A] A ruler *who* **oppresses** the poor is like a driving rain that
28: 17 [B] A man **tormented** by the guilt of murder will be a fugitive
Ecc 4: 1 [B] I saw the tears of the **oppressed**—and they have no
4: 1 [A] power was on the side of their **oppressors**—and they have
Isa 23: 12 [E] of your reveling, O Virgin Daughter of Sidon, *now* **crushed**!
52: 4 [A] down to Egypt to live; lately, Assyria *has* **oppressed** them.
Jer 7: 6 [A] if *you do* not **oppress** the alien, the fatherless or the widow
21: 12 [A] rescue from the hand of his **oppressor** the one who has been
50: 33 [B] "The people of Israel *are* **oppressed**, and the people of Judah
Eze 18: 18 [A] because *he* **practiced extortion** [+6945], robbed his brother
22: 29 [A] The people of the land **practice extortion** [+6945] and
22: 29 [A] they oppress the poor and needy and **mistreat** the alien,
Hos 5: 11 [B] Ephraim *is* **oppressed**, trampled in judgment, intent on
12: 7 [12:8] [A] merchant uses dishonest scales; he loves to **defraud**.
Am 4: 1 [A] you *women who* **oppress** the poor and crush the needy
Mic 2: 2 [A] *They* **defraud** a man *of* his home, a fellowman of his
Zec 7: 10 [A] *Do* not **oppress** the widow or the fatherless, the alien
Mal 3: 5 [A] against *those who* **defraud** laborers *of* their wages,

6944 עֵשֶׁק 'ēšeq, n.pr.m. [1] [√ 6943]

Eshek [1]

1Ch 8: 39 The sons of his brother **Eshek**: Ulam his firstborn,

6945 עֹשֶׁק 'ōšeq, n.m. [15] [√ 6943]

oppression [6], extortion [3], oppressed [+928+2021+4200+6913] [1], oppressed [1], practice extortion [+6943] [1], practiced extortion [+6943] [1], taken by extortion [+906+6943] [1], tyranny [1]

Lev 6: 4 [5:23] what he has stolen or **taken by extortion** [+906+6943],
Ps 62: 10 [62:11] Do not trust in **extortion** or take pride in stolen goods;
73: 8 speak with malice; in their arrogance they threaten **oppression**.
119: 134 Redeem me from the **oppression** *of* men, that I may obey your
Ecc 5: 8 [5:7] If you see the poor **oppressed** in a district, and justice
7: 7 **Extortion** turns a wise man into a fool, and a bribe corrupts the
Isa 30: 12 this message, relied on **oppression** and depended on deceit,
54: 14 **Tyranny** will be far from you; you will have nothing to fear.
59: 13 turning our backs on our God, fomenting **oppression** and revolt,
Jer 6: 6 This city must be punished; it is filled with **oppression**.
22: 17 on shedding innocent blood and on **oppression** and extortion."
Eze 18: 18 because *he* **practiced extortion** [+6943], robbed his brother
22: 7 in you *they have* **oppressed** [+928+2021+4200+6913] the alien and
22: 12 and make unjust gain from your neighbors by **extortion**.
22: 29 The people of the land **practice extortion** [+6943] and commit

6946 עָשְׁקָה 'ošqâ, n.f. [1] [√ 6945; cf. 6943]

troubled [1]

Isa 38: 14 I looked to the heavens. I am **troubled**; O Lord, come to my aid!"

6947 עָשַׁר 'āšar, v. [17] [→ 6938, 6948]

rich [7], bring wealth [1], brings wealth [1], enrich [1], enriched [1], get rich [1], give wealth [+6948] [1], made rich [1], pretends to be rich [1], richer [+6948] [1], wealth [1]

Ge 14: 23 [G] so that you will never be able to say, 'I **made** Abram **rich**.'
1Sa 2: 7 [G] The LORD sends poverty and **wealth**; he humbles and he
17: 25 [G] The king *will* **give** great **wealth** [+6948] *to* the man who kills
Job 15: 29 [A] *He will* no longer *be* **rich** and his wealth will not endure, nor
Ps 49: 16 [49:17] [G] Do not be overawed when a man *grows* **rich**,
65: 9 [65:10] [G] for the land and water it; *you* **enrich** it abundantly.
Pr 10: 4 [G] hands make a man poor, but diligent hands **bring wealth**.
10: 22 [G] The blessing of the LORD **brings wealth**, and he adds no
13: 7 [F] *One man* **pretends to be rich**, yet has nothing; another
21: 17 [G] become poor; whoever loves wine and oil *will* never *be* **rich**.
23: 4 [G] Do not wear yourself out to *get* **rich**; have the wisdom to
28: 20 [G] but one eager to **get rich** will not go unpunished.
Jer 5: 27 [G] are full of deceit; *they have become* **rich** and powerful
Eze 27: 33 [G] and your wares *you* **enriched** the kings of the earth.
Da 11: 2 [G] a fourth, *who will be* far **richer** [+6948] than all the others.
Hos 12: 8 [12:9] [A] Ephraim boasts, "*I am* very **rich**; I have become
Zec 11: 5 [G] Those who sell them say, 'Praise the LORD, *I am* **rich**!'

6948 עֹשֶׁר 'ōšer, n.m. [37] [√ 6947]

wealth [21], riches [14], give wealth [+6947] [1], richer [+6947] [1]

Ge 31: 16 Surely all the **wealth** that God took away from our father belongs
1Sa 17: 25 The king *will* **give** great **wealth to** [+6947] the man who kills him.
1Ki 3: 11 you have asked for this and not for long life or **wealth** for yourself,

1Ki 3:13 give you what you have not asked for—both **riches** and honor—
10:23 King Solomon was greater in **riches** and wisdom than all the other
1Ch 29:12 **Wealth** and honor come from you; you are the ruler of all things.
29:28 died at a good old age, having enjoyed long life, **wealth** and honor.
2Ch 1:11 this is your heart's desire and you have not asked for **wealth**,
1:12 I will also give you **wealth**, riches and honor, such as no king who
9:22 King Solomon was greater in **riches** and wisdom than all the other
17:5 gifts to Jehoshaphat, so that he had great **wealth** and honor.
18:1 Now Jehoshaphat had great **wealth** and honor, and he allied
32:27 Hezekiah had very great **riches** and honor, and he made treasuries
Est 1:4 For a full 180 days he displayed the vast **wealth** *of* his kingdom
5:11 Haman boasted to them about his vast **wealth**, his many sons,
Ps 49:6 [49:7] who trust in their wealth and boast of their great **riches**?
52:7 [52:9] trusted in his great **wealth** and grew strong by destroying
112:3 Wealth and **riches** are in his house, and his righteousness endures
Pr 3:16 Long life is in her right hand; in her left hand are **riches** and honor.
8:18 With me are **riches** and honor, enduring wealth and prosperity.
11:16 woman gains respect, but ruthless men gain only **wealth**.
11:28 Whoever trusts in his **riches** will fall, but the righteous will thrive
13:8 A man's **riches** may ransom his life, but a poor man hears no
14:24 The **wealth** *of* the wise is their crown, but the folly of fools yields
22:1 A good name is more desirable than great **riches**; to be esteemed is
22:4 Humility and the fear of the LORD bring **wealth** and honor
30:8 give me neither poverty nor **riches**, but give me only my daily
Ecc 4:8 no end to his toil, yet his eyes were not content with his **wealth**.
5:13 [5:12] under the sun: **wealth** hoarded to the harm of its owner,
5:14 [5:13] or **wealth** lost through some misfortune, so that when he
5:19 [5:18] when God gives any man **wealth** and possessions,
6:2 God gives a man **wealth**, possessions and honor, so that he lacks
9:11 come to the wise or **wealth** to the brilliant or favor to the learned;
Jer 9:23 [9:22] boast of his strength or the rich man boast of his **riches**,
17:11 eggs it did not lay is the man who gains **riches** by unjust means.
Da 11:2 then a fourth, *who will be* far **richer** [+6947] than all the others.
11:2 When he has gained power by his **wealth**, he will stir up everyone

6949 עָשַׁשׁ *'āšaš*, v. [3] [→ 6931, 6932]

weak [3]

Ps 6:7 [6:8] [A] My eyes *grow* **weak** with sorrow; they fail because of
31:9 [31:10] [A] my eyes *grow* **weak** with sorrow, my soul and my
31:10 [31:11] [A] because of my affliction, and my bones *grow* **weak**.

6950 עָשַׁת *'āšat[1]*, v. [1] [→ 6936, 6952]

sleek [1]

Jer 5:28 [A] and have grown fat and **sleek**. Their evil deeds have no limit;

6951 עָשַׁת *'āšat[2]*, v. [1] [→ 6953, 6955; Ar 10575]

take notice [1]

Jnh 1:6 [F] Maybe he *will* **take notice** of us, and we will not perish."

6952 עֶשֶׁת *'ešet*, n.[m.]. [1] [√ 6950]

polished [1]

SS 5:14 His body is like **polished** ivory decorated with sapphires.

6953 עַשְׁתּוּת *'aštût*, n.f. [1] [√ 6951]

have [1]

Job 12:5 Men at ease **have** contempt for misfortune as the fate of those

6954 עַשְׁתֵּי *'aštê*, n. *or* a.num. [19 / 18]

eleventh [+6925] [8], eleventh [+6926] [5], eleven [+6926] [4], eleven [+6925] [1]

Ex 26:7 hair for the tent over the tabernacle—**eleven** [+6926] altogether.
26:8 All **eleven** [+6926] curtains are to be the same size—thirty cubits
36:14 hair for the tent over the tabernacle—**eleven** [+6926] altogether.
36:15 All **eleven** [+6926] curtains were the same size—thirty cubits long
Nu 7:72 On the **eleventh** [+6925] day Pagiel son of Ocran, the leader of the
29:20 " 'On the third day prepare **eleven** [+6925] bulls, two rams
Dt 1:3 In the fortieth year, on the first day of the **eleventh** [+6925] month,
2Ki 25:2 The city was kept under siege until the **eleventh** [+6926] year of
1Ch 12:13 [12:14] Jeremiah the tenth and Macbannai the **eleventh** [+6925].
24:12 the **eleventh** [+6925] to Eliashib, the twelfth to Jakim,
25:18 the **eleventh** [+6925] to Azarel, his sons and relatives, 12
27:14 The **eleventh** [+6925], for the eleventh month, was Benaiah the
27:14 The eleventh, for the **eleventh** [+6925] month, was Benaiah the
Jer 1:3 down to the fifth month of the **eleventh** [+6926] year of Zedekiah
39:2 day of the fourth month of Zedekiah's **eleventh** [+6926] year,
52:5 The city was kept under siege until the **eleventh** [+6926] year of
Eze 26:1 In the **eleventh** [+6926] year, on the first day of the month,
40:49 and twelve [+6926] [BHS *eleven*; NIV 9109] cubits from front to
Zec 1:7 On the twenty-fourth day of the **eleventh** [+6925] month,

6955 עֶשְׁתֹּנֹת *'eštōnet*, n.f. [1] [√ 6951]

plans [1]

Ps 146:4 return to the ground; on that very day their **plans** come to nothing.

6956 עַשְׁתֹּרֶת *'aštōret*, n.pr.f. [9] [√ 6958]

Ashtoreths [6], Ashtoreth [3]

Jdg 2:13 because they forsook him and served Baal and the **Ashtoreths**.
10:6 They served the Baals and the **Ashtoreths**, and the gods of Aram,
1Sa 7:3 and the **Ashtoreths** and commit yourselves to the LORD
7:4 So the Israelites put away their Baals and **Ashtoreths**, and served
12:10 forsaken the LORD and served the Baals and the **Ashtoreths**.
31:10 They put his armor in the temple of the **Ashtoreths** and fastened
1Ki 11:5 He followed **Ashtoreth** the goddess of the Sidonians, and Molech
11:33 and worshiped **Ashtoreth** the goddess of the Sidonians,
2Ki 23:13 the ones Solomon king of Israel had built for **Ashtoreth** the vile

6957 עַשְׁתְּרֹת *'ašteret*, n.f. [4]

lambs [4]

Dt 7:13 the **lambs** *of* your flocks in the land that he swore to your
28:4 the calves of your herds and the **lambs** *of* your flocks.
28:18 and the calves of your herds and the **lambs** *of* your flocks.
28:51 calves of your herds or **lambs** *of* your flocks until you are ruined.

6958 עַשְׁתָּרֹת *'aštārōt*, n.pr.loc. [6] [→ 1119, 6956, 6959, 6960; cf. 895, 1285?]

Ashtaroth [6]

Dt 1:4 Edrei had defeated Og king of Bashan, who reigned in **Ashtaroth**.
Jos 9:10 of Heshbon, and Og king of Bashan, who reigned in **Ashtaroth**.
12:4 of the last of the Rephaites, who reigned in **Ashtaroth** and Edrei.
13:12 who had reigned in **Ashtaroth** and Edrei and had survived as one
13:31 and **Ashtaroth** and Edrei (the royal cities of Og in Bashan).
1Ch 6:71 [6:56] they received Golan in Bashan and also **Ashtaroth**,

6959 עַשְׁתְּרֹת קַרְנַיִם *'ašt[e]rōt qarnayim*, n.pr.loc. [1] [√ 6958 + 7969]

Ashteroth Karnaim [1]

Ge 14:5 him went out and defeated the Rephaites in **Ashteroth Karnaim**,

6960 עַשְׁתְּרָתִי *'ašt[e]rātî*, a.g. [1] [√ 6958]

Ashterathite [1]

1Ch 11:44 Uzzia the **Ashterathite**, Shama and Jeiel the sons of Hotham the

6961 עֵת *'ēt*, n.f. [296 / 298] [√ 6701]

time [179], times [26], season [12], when [+928] [11], *untranslated* [8], always [+928+3972] [5], at set times [+4946+6330+6961] [4], when [3], as [+928] [2], at [+928] [2], days [2], in [+4200] [2], next year [+2645] [2], now [+2021+3869] [2], now [2], proper time [2], sunset [+995+2021+9087] [2], when [+4200] [2], appointed time [1], as [+3869] [1], as [+4200] [1], as long as [+928+3972] [1], at once [+928+2021+2021+2085] [1], circumstances [1], constantly [+928+3972] [1], doom [1], due time [1], end [1], evening [+2021+6847] [1], future [1], hour [1], mealtime [+431+2021] [1], occasion [1], old [1], past [+8037] [1], punishment [1], ripens [1], seasons [1], spring [+9102+9588] [1], springtime [+4919] [1], then[s] [+2021+2021+2085] [1], till [+6330] [1], time after time [+8041] [1], timely [+928] [1], whenever [+928] [1], whenever [+928+3972] [1], while [+4200] [1], years [+2021+9102] [1]

Ge 8:11 When the dove returned to him in the **[NIE]** evening, there in its
18:10 LORD said, "I will surely return to you about this **time** next year,
18:14 I will return to you at the appointed **time** next year and Sarah will
21:22 At that **time** Abimelech and Phicol the commander of his forces
24:11 it was toward **[RPH]** evening, the time the women go out to draw
24:11 it was toward evening, the **time** the women go out to draw water.
29:7 "the sun is still high; it is not **time** *for* the flocks to be gathered.
31:10 "In breeding **season** I once had a dream in which I looked up
38:1 At that **time**, Judah left his brothers and went down to stay with a
38:27 When the **time** came *for* her to give birth, there were twin boys in
Ex 9:18 at this **time** tomorrow I will send the worst hailstorm that has ever
18:22 Have them serve as judges for the people at all **times**, but have
18:26 They served as judges for the people at all **times**. The difficult
Lev 15:25 " 'When a woman has a discharge of blood for many days at a **time**
16:2 "Tell your brother Aaron not to come **whenever** [+928+3972] he
26:4 I will send you rain in its **season**, and the ground will yield its
Nu 22:4 So Balak son of Zippor, who was king of Moab at that **time**,
23:23 no divination against Israel. It will **now** [+2021+3869] be said of
Dt 1:9 At that **time** I said to you, "You are too heavy a burden for me to
1:16 I charged your judges at that **time**: Hear the disputes between your
1:18 And at that **time** I told you everything you were to do.

Dt 2:34 At that **time** we took all his towns and completely destroyed
3: 4 At that **time** we took all his cities. There was not one of the sixty
3: 8 So at that **time** we took from these two kings of the Amorites the
3:12 Of the land that we took over at that **time**, I gave the Reubenites
3:18 I commanded you at that **time**: "The LORD your God has given
3:21 At that **time** I commanded Joshua: "You have seen with your own
3:23 At that **time** I pleaded with the LORD:
4:14 And the LORD directed me at that **time** to teach you the decrees
5: 5 (At that **time** I stood between the LORD and you to declare to
9:20 with Aaron to destroy him, but at that **time** I prayed for Aaron too.
10: 1 At that **time** the LORD said to me, "Chisel out two stone tablets
10: 8 At that **time** the LORD set apart the tribe of Levi to carry the ark
11:14 then I will send rain on your land in its **season**, both autumn
28:12 to send rain on your land in **season** and to bless all the work of
32:35 In **due time** their foot will slip; their day of disaster is near
Jos 5: 2 At that **time** the LORD said to Joshua, "Make flint knives
6:26 At that **time** Joshua pronounced this solemn oath: "Cursed before
8:29 king of Ai on a tree and left him there until **evening** [+2021+6847].
10:27 At **sunset** [+995+2021+9087] Joshua gave the order and they took
11: 6 because by this **time** tomorrow I will hand all of them over to
11:10 At that **time** Joshua turned back and captured Hazor and put its
11:21 At that **time** Joshua went and destroyed the Anakites from the hill
Jdg 3:29 At that **time** they struck down about ten thousand Moabites,
4: 4 a prophetess, the wife of Lappidoth, was leading Israel at that **time**.
10:14 have chosen. Let them save you **when** [+928] you are in trouble!"
11:26 along the Arnon. Why didn't you retake them during that **time**?
12: 6 Forty-two thousand Ephraimites were killed at that **time**.
13:23 nor shown us all these things or **now** [+2021+3869] told us this."
14: 4 the Philistines; for at that **time** they were ruling over Israel.)
21:14 So the Benjamites returned at that **time** and were given the women
21:22 **[NIE]** you are innocent, since you did not give your daughters to
21:24 At that **time** the Israelites left that place and went home to their
Ru 2:14 At **mealtime** [+431+2021] Boaz said to her, "Come over here.
1Sa 4:20 **As** [+3869] she was dying, the women attending her said,
9:16 "About this **time** tomorrow I will send you a man from the land of
18:19 So when the **time** came *for* Merab, Saul's daughter, to be given to
20:12 I will surely sound out my father by this **time** the day after
2Sa 11: 1 In the spring, at the **time** *when* kings go off to war, David sent
11: 2 **[NIE]** One evening David got up from his bed and walked around
24:15 on Israel from that morning until the end of the **time** designated,
1Ki 8:65 So Solomon observed the festival at that **time**, and all Israel with
11: 4 **As** [+4200] Solomon grew old, his wives turned his heart after
11:29 About that **time** Jeroboam was going out of Jerusalem, and Ahijah
14: 1 At that **time** Abijah son of Jeroboam became ill,
15:23 **In** [+4200] his old age, however, his feet became diseased.
19: 2 if by this **time** tomorrow I do not make your life like that of one of
20: 6 about this **time** tomorrow I am going to send my officials to search
2Ki 4:16 "About this time **next year** [+2645]," Elisha said, "you will hold a
4:17 the **next year** [+2645] about that same time she gave birth to a son,
5:26 Is this the **time** to take money, or to accept clothes, olive groves,
7: 1 About this **time** tomorrow, a seah of flour will sell for a shekel
7:18 "About this **time** tomorrow, a seah of flour will sell for a shekel
8:22 been in rebellion against Judah. Libnah revolted at the same **time**.
10: 6 master's sons and come to me in Jezreel by this **time** tomorrow."
16: 6 At that **time**, Rezin king of Aram recovered Elath for Aram by
18:16 At this **time** Hezekiah king of Judah stripped off the gold with
20:12 At that **time** Merodach-Baladan son of Baladan king of Babylon
24:10 At that **time** the officers of Nebuchadnezzar king of Babylon
1Ch 9:25 Their brothers in their villages had to come from **time** to time
9:25 Their brothers in their villages had to come from time to **time**
12:22 [12:23] **[NIE]** Day after day men came to help David, until he
12:32 [12:33] who understood the **times** and knew what Israel should
20: 1 In the **spring** [+9102+9588], at the time when kings go off to war,
20: 1 In the spring, at the **time** *when* kings go off to war, Joab led out
21:28 At that **time**, when David saw that the LORD had answered him
21:29 the altar of burnt offering were at that **time** on the high place at
29:30 the **circumstances** that surrounded him and Israel and the
2Ch 7: 8 So Solomon observed the festival at that **time** for seven days,
13:18 The men of Israel were subdued on that **occasion**, and the men of
15: 5 In those **days** it was not safe to travel about, for all the inhabitants
16: 7 At that **time** Hanani the seer came to Asa king of Judah and said to
16:10 At the same **time** Asa brutally oppressed some of the people.
18:34 Then at **sunset** [+995+2021+9087] he died.
20:22 **As** [+928] they began to sing and praise, the LORD set ambushes
21:10 Libnah revolted at the same **time**, because Jehoram had forsaken
21:19 at **[NIE]** the end of the second year, his bowels came out
24:11 **Whenever** [+928] the chest was brought in by the Levites to the
25:27 From the **time** that Amaziah turned away from following the
28:16 At that **time** King Ahaz sent to the king of Assyria for help.
28:22 In his **time** *of* trouble King Ahaz became even more unfaithful to
29:27 **As** [+928] the offering began, singing to the LORD began also,
30: 3 They had not been able to celebrate it at the regular **time**
35:17 Israelites who were present celebrated the Passover at that **time**
Ezr 8:34 and weight, and the entire weight was recorded at that **time**.
10:13 But there are many people here and it is the rainy **season**;
10:14 in our towns who has married a foreign woman come at a set **time**,
Ne 4:22 [4:16] At that **time** I also said to the people, "Have every man
6: 1 though up to that **time** I had not set the doors in the gates—
9:27 But **when** [+928] they were oppressed they cried out to you.
9:28 in your compassion you delivered them **time** [+8041] **after time**.
10:34 [10:35] **times** each year a contribution of wood to burn on the
13:21 on you." From that **time** on they no longer came on the Sabbath.
13:31 also made provision for contributions of wood at designated **times**,
Est 1:13 and justice, he spoke with the wise men who understood the **times**
4:14 For if you remain silent at this **time**, relief and deliverance for the
4:14 but that you have come to royal position for such a **time** as this?"
5:13 all this gives me no satisfaction **as long as** [+928+3972] I see that
8: 9 **At once** [+928+2021+2021+2085] the royal secretaries were
Job 5:26 come to the grave in full vigor, like sheaves gathered in **season**.
6:17 that cease to flow in the dry **season**, and in the heat vanish from
22:16 They were carried off before their **time**, their foundations washed
24: 1 "Why does the Almighty not set **times** for judgment? Why must
27:10 find delight in the Almighty? Will he call upon God at all **times**?
38:23 which I reserve for **times** *of* trouble, for days of war and battle?
38:32 Can you bring forth the constellations in their **seasons** or lead out
39: 1 "Do you know **when** the mountain goats give birth? Do you watch
39: 2 the months till they bear? Do you know the **time** they give birth?
39:18 Yet **when** she spreads her feathers to run, she laughs at horse
Ps 1: 3 which yields its fruit in **season** and whose leaf does not wither.
4: 7 [4:8] You have filled my heart with greater joy than **when** their
9: 9 [9:10] a refuge for the oppressed, a stronghold in **times** *of* trouble.
10: 1 you stand far off? Why do you hide yourself in **times** *of* trouble?
10: 5 His ways are **always** [+928+3972] prosperous; he is haughty
21: 9 [21:10] At the **time** *of* your appearing you will make them like a
31:15 [31:16] My **times** are in your hands; deliver me from my enemies
32: 6 Therefore let everyone who is godly pray to you **while** [+4200]
34: 1 [34:2] I will extol the LORD at all **times**; his praise will always
37:19 In **times** *of* disaster they will not wither; in days of famine they
37:39 comes from the LORD; he is their stronghold in **time** *of* trouble.
62: 8 [62:9] Trust in him at all **times**, O people; pour out your hearts to
69:13 [69:14] I pray to you, O LORD, in the **time** *of* your favor;
71: 9 Do not cast me away **when** [+4200] I am old; do not forsake me
81:15 [81:16] before him, and their **punishment** would last forever.
102:13 [102:14] compassion on Zion, for it is **time** to show favor to her;
104:27 These all look to you to give them their food at the **proper time**.
105:19 **till** [+6330] what he foretold came to pass, till the word of the
106: 3 maintain justice, who **constantly** [+928+3972] do what is right.
119:20 My soul is consumed with longing for your laws at all **times**.
119:126 It is **time** for you to act, O LORD; your law is being broken.
145:15 of all look to you, and you give them their food at the **proper time**.
Pr 5:19 may her breasts satisfy you **always** [+928+3972], may you ever be
6:14 deceit in his heart—he **always** [+928+3972] stirs up dissension.
8:30 day after day, rejoicing **always** [+928+3972] in his presence,
15:23 joy in giving an apt reply—and how good is a **timely** [+928] word!
17:17 A friend loves at all **times**, and a brother is born for adversity.
Ecc 3: 1 time for everything, and a **season** for every activity under heaven:
3: 2 a **time** to be born and a time to die, a time to plant and a time to
3: 2 a time to be born and a **time** to die, a time to plant and a time to
3: 2 to be born and a time to die, a **time** to plant and a time to uproot,
3: 2 to be born and a time to die, a time to plant and a **time** to uproot,
3: 3 a **time** to kill and a time to heal, a time to tear down and a time to
3: 3 a time to kill and a **time** to heal, a time to tear down and a time to
3: 3 and a time to heal, a **time** to tear down and a time to build,
3: 3 and a time to heal, a time to tear down and a **time** to build,
3: 4 a **time** to weep and a time to laugh, a time to mourn and a time to
3: 4 a time to weep and a **time** to laugh, a time to mourn and a time to
3: 4 to weep and a time to laugh, a **time** to mourn and a time to dance,
3: 4 to weep and a time to laugh, a time to mourn and a **time** to dance,
3: 5 a **time** to scatter stones and a time to gather them, a time to
3: 5 a time to scatter stones and a **time** to gather them, a time to
3: 5 and a time to gather them, a **time** to embrace and a time to refrain,
3: 5 and a time to gather them, a time to embrace and a **time** to refrain,
3: 6 a **time** to search and a time to give up, a time to keep and a time to
3: 6 a time to search and a **time** to give up, a time to keep and a time to
3: 6 and a time to give up, a **time** to keep and a time to throw away,
3: 6 and a time to give up, a time to keep and a **time** to throw away,
3: 7 a **time** to tear and a time to mend, a time to be silent and a time to
3: 7 a time to tear and a **time** to mend, a time to be silent and a time to
3: 7 and a time to mend, a **time** to be silent and a time to speak,
3: 7 and a time to mend, a time to be silent and a **time** to speak,
3: 8 a **time** to love and a time to hate, a time for war and a time for
3: 8 a time to love and a **time** to hate, a time for war and a time for
3: 8 to love and a time to hate, a **time** *for* war and a time for peace.
3: 8 to love and a time to hate, a time for war and a **time** *for* peace.
3:11 He has made everything beautiful in its **time**. He has also set
3:17 and the wicked, for there will be a **time** for every activity,
7:17 be overwicked, and do not be a fool—why die before your **time**?
8: 5 and the wise heart will know the proper **time** and procedure.

Ecc 8: 6 For there is a proper **time** and procedure for every matter,
8: 9 There is a **time** when a man lords it over others to his own hurt.
9: 8 **Always** [+928+3972] be clothed in white, and always anoint your
9: 11 or favor to the learned; but **time** and chance happen to them all.
9: 12 Moreover, no man knows when his **hour** will come: As fish are
9: 12 so men are trapped by evil **times** that fall unexpectedly upon them.
10: 17 king is of noble birth and whose princes eat at a *proper* **time**—
SS 2: 12 the **season** *of* singing has come, the cooing of doves is heard in our
Isa 9: 1 [8:23] In the **past** [+8037] he humbled the land of Zebulun
13: 22 Her **time** is at hand, and her days will not be prolonged.
17: 14 **In** [+4200] the evening, sudden terror! Before the morning,
18: 7 At that **time** gifts will be brought to the LORD Almighty from a
20: 2 at that **time** the LORD spoke through Isaiah son of Amoz.
33: 2 Be our strength every morning, our salvation in **time** *of* distress.
33: 6 He will be the sure foundation for your **times**, a rich store of
39: 1 At that **time** Merodach-Baladan son of Baladan king of Babylon
48: 16 I have not spoken in secret; at the **time** it happens, I am there."
49: 8 "In the **time** *of* my favor I will answer you, and in the day of
60: 22 mighty nation. I am the LORD; in its **time** I will do this swiftly."
Jer 2: 17 the LORD your God **when** [+928] he led you in the way?
2: 27 yet **when** [+928] they are in trouble, they say, 'Come and save us!'
2: 28 Let them come if they can save you **when** [+928] you are in
3: 17 At that **time** they will call Jerusalem The Throne of the LORD,
4: 11 At that **time** this people and Jerusalem will be told, "A scorching
5: 24 the LORD our God, who gives autumn and spring rains in **season**,
6: 15 they will be brought down **when** [+928] I punish them,"
8: 1 " 'At that **time**, declares the LORD, the bones of the kings
8: 7 the swift and the thrush observe the **time** *of* their migration.
8: 12 they will be brought down **when** [+928] they are punished,
8: 15 no good has come, for a **time** *of* healing but there was only terror.
10: 15 of mockery; **when** [+928] their judgment comes, they will perish.
11: 12 but they will not help them at all **when** [+928] disaster strikes.
11: 14 because I will not listen **when** [+928] they call to me in the time of
11: 14 listen when they call to me in the **time** [BHS-] *of* their distress.
14: 8 O Hope of Israel, its Savior in **times** *of* distress, why are you like a
14: 19 but no good has come, for a **time** *of* healing but there is only terror.
15: 11 surely I will make your enemies plead with you in **times** *of* disaster
15: 11 enemies plead with you in times of disaster and **times** *of* distress.
18: 23 overthrown before you; deal with them in the **time** *of* your anger.
20: 16 May he hear wailing in the morning, a battle cry **at** [+928] noon.
27: 7 and his son and his grandson until the **time** *for* his land comes;
30: 7 It will be a **time** *of* trouble for Jacob, but he will be saved out of it.
31: 1 "At that **time**," declares the LORD, "I will be the God of all the
33: 15 at that **time** I will make a righteous Branch sprout from David's
33: 20 so that day and night no longer come at their **appointed time**,
46: 21 of disaster is coming upon them, the **time** *for* them to be punished.
49: 8 for I will bring disaster on Esau *at* the **time** I punish him.
50: 4 "In those days, at that **time**," declares the LORD, "the people of
50: 16 the sower, and the reaper with his sickle **at** [+928] harvest.
50: 20 In those days, at that **time**," declares the LORD, "search will be
50: 27 For their day has come, the **time** *for* them to be punished.
50: 31 "for your day has come, the **time** *for* you to be punished.
51: 6 It is **time** *for* the LORD's vengeance; he will pay her what she
51: 18 of mockery; **when** [+928] their judgment comes, they will perish.
51: 33 "The Daughter of Babylon is like a threshing floor at the **time** it is
51: 33 at the time it is trampled; the **time** to harvest her will soon come."
Eze 4: 10 food to eat each day and eat it **at set times** [+4946+6330+6961].
4: 10 food to eat each day and eat it **at set times** [+4946+6330+6961].
4: 11 a hin of water and drink it **at set times** [+4946+6330+6961].
4: 11 a hin of water and drink it **at set times** [+4946+6330+6961].
7: 7 The **time** has come, the day is near; there is panic, not joy,
7: 12 The **time** has come, the day has arrived. Let not the buyer rejoice
12: 27 many years from now, and he prophesies about the distant **future**.'
16: 8 when I looked at you and saw that you were **old** *enough for* love,
16: 8 looked at you and saw that you were old enough for **[RPH]** love,
16: 57 you are **now** scorned by the daughters of Edom and all her
21: 25 [21:30] whose **time** *of* punishment has reached its climax,
21: 29 [21:34] whose **time** *of* punishment has reached its climax.
22: 3 O city that brings on herself **doom** by shedding blood in her midst
22: 4 days to a close, and the **end** [BHS 6330] *of* your years has come.
27: 34 **Now** you are shattered by the sea in the depths of the waters;
30: 3 LORD is near—a day of clouds, a **time** *of* doom *for* the nations.
34: 26 I will send down showers in **season**; there will be showers of
35: 5 delivered the Israelites over to the sword at the **time** *of* their
35: 5 of their calamity, the **time** their punishment reached its climax,
Da 8: 17 "understand that the vision concerns the **time** *of* the end."
9: 21 came to me in swift flight about the **time** *of* the evening sacrifice.
9: 25 It will be rebuilt with streets and a trench, but in **times** of trouble.
11: 6 In those **days** she will be handed over, together with her royal
11: 13 after *several* **years** [+2021+9102], he will advance with a huge
11: 14 "In those **times** many will rise against the king of the South.
11: 24 He will plot the overthrow of fortresses—but only for a **time**.
11: 35 be refined, purified and made spotless until the **time** *of* the end,
11: 40 "At the **time** *of* the end the king of the South will engage him in
12: 1 "At that **time** Michael, the great prince who protects your people,
12: 1 There will be a **time** *of* distress such as has not happened from the
12: 1 from the beginning of nations until **then** [+2021+2021+2085].
12: 1 at that **time** your people—everyone whose name is found written
12: 4 close up and seal the words of the scroll until the **time** *of* the end.
12: 9 the words are closed up and sealed until the **time** *of* the end.
12: 11 "From the **time** *that* the daily sacrifice is abolished
Hos 2: 9 [2:11] "Therefore I will take away my grain when it **ripens**,
10: 12 for it is **time** to seek the LORD, until he comes and showers
13: 13 when the **time** arrives, he does not come to the opening of the
Joel 3: 1 [4:1] "In those days and at that **time**, when I restore the fortunes
Am 5: 13 Therefore the prudent man keeps quiet in such **times**, for the times
5: 13 the prudent man keeps quiet in such times, for the **times** are evil.
Mic 2: 3 You will no longer walk proudly, for it will be a **time** *of* calamity.
3: 4 At that **time** he will hide his face from them because of the evil
5: 3 [5:2] Therefore Israel will be abandoned until the **time** when she
Zep 1: 12 At that **time** I will search Jerusalem with lamps and punish those
3: 19 At that **time** I will deal with all who oppressed you; I will rescue
3: 20 At that **time** I will gather you; at that time I will bring you home.
3: 20 At that time I will gather you; at that **time** I will bring you home.
Hag 1: 2 'The **time** has not yet come *for* the LORD's house to be built.' "
1: 2 'The time has not yet come **[RPH]** for the LORD's house to be
1: 4 "Is it a **time** for you yourselves to be living in your paneled houses,
Zec 10: 1 Ask the LORD for rain in the **springtime** [+4919]; it is the
14: 7 to the LORD. **When** [+4200] evening comes, there will be light.

6962 עֵת קָצִין *'ēt qāṣîn*, n.pr.loc. [1] [cf. 7903]

Eth Kazin [1]

Jos 19: 13 Then it continued eastward to Gath Hepher and **Eth Kazin**;

6963 עָתַד *'ātad*, v. [2] [→ 6965, 6966?, 6969]

crumbling [1], get ready [1]

Job 15: 28 [F] and houses where no one lives, houses **crumbling** to rubble.
Pr 24: 27 [D] Finish your outdoor work and **get** your fields **ready**; after

6964 עַתָּה *'attâ*, adv. [433 / 432] [√ 6701] See Select Index

now [317], *untranslated* [63], then [10], come now [+5528] [3], therefore [3], already [2], but [2], longer [2], soon [2], when [2], about to [+4946+7940] [1], although [1], always [1], further [1], furthermore [+2256] [1], furthermore [1], going to [1], if so [+3954] [1], just [+2296] [1], just [+4946] [1], now [+2256] [1], now [+2296] [1], now then [1], on [+6330] [1], right now [1], so [1], surely [+3954] [1], surely [+421] [1], that day [1], that time on [1], then [+2256] [1], this day [1], this time on [1], this [1], yet [+2256] [1], yet [+6330] [1]

6965 עָתוּד *'ātûd*, a. [1] [√ 6963]

treasures [1]

Est 8: 13 [so that the Jews would be **ready** [K; see Q 6969] on that day to]
Isa 10: 13 the boundaries of nations, I plundered their **treasures**; [K 6969]

6966 עַתּוּד *'attûd*, n.m. [29] [√ 6963?]

male goats [15], goats [12], leaders [2]

Ge 31: 10 and saw that the **male goats** mating with the flock were streaked,
31: 12 and see that all the **male goats** mating with the flock are streaked,
Nu 7: 17 five rams, five **male goats** and five male lambs a year old,
7: 23 five rams, five **male goats** and five male lambs a year old,
7: 29 five rams, five **male goats** and five male lambs a year old,
7: 35 five rams, five **male goats** and five male lambs a year old,
7: 41 five rams, five **male goats** and five male lambs a year old,
7: 47 five rams, five **male goats** and five male lambs a year old,
7: 53 five rams, five **male goats** and five male lambs a year old,
7: 59 five rams, five **male goats** and five male lambs a year old,
7: 65 five rams, five **male goats** and five male lambs a year old,
7: 71 five rams, five **male goats** and five male lambs a year old,
7: 77 five rams, five **male goats** and five male lambs a year old,
7: 83 five rams, five **male goats** and five male lambs a year old,
7: 88 sixty rams, sixty **male goats** and sixty male lambs a year old.
Dt 32: 14 and milk from herd and flock and with fattened lambs and **goats**,
Ps 50: 9 I have no need of a bull from your stall or of **goats** from your pens,
50: 13 Do I eat the flesh of bulls or drink the blood of **goats**?
66: 15 animals to you and an offering of rams; I will offer bulls and **goats**.
Pr 27: 26 provide you with clothing, and the **goats** with the price of a field.
Isa 1: 11 I have no pleasure in the blood of bulls and lambs and **goats**.
14: 9 all *those who* were **leaders** *in* the world; it makes them rise from
34: 6 the blood of lambs and **goats**, fat from the kidneys of rams.
Jer 50: 8 land of the Babylonians, and be like the **goats** that lead the flock.
51: 40 bring them down like lambs to the slaughter, like rams and **goats**.
Eze 27: 21 they did business with you in lambs, rams and **goats**.
34: 17 between one sheep and another, and between rams and **goats**.
39: 18 of the earth as if they were rams and lambs, **goats** and bulls—

[F] Hitpael (hitpoel, hitpoal, hitpolel, hitpolal, hitpalel, hitpalal, hitpalpel, hitpalpal, hotpael, hotpaal) [G] Hiphil (hiphtil) [H] Hophal [I] Hishtaphel

Zec 10: 3 anger burns against the shepherds, and I will punish the **leaders**;

6967 עִתִּי 'ittî, a. [1] [√ 6701]

appointed for the task [1]

Lev 16:21 away into the desert in the care of a man **appointed for the task**.

6968 עַתַּי 'attay, n.pr.m. [4] [√ 6701]

Attai [4]

1Ch 2:35 daughter in marriage to his servant Jarha, and she bore him **Attai**.
2:36 **Attai** was the father of Nathan, Nathan the father of Zabad,
12:11 [12:12] **Attai** the sixth, Eliel the seventh,
2Ch 11:20 of Absalom, who bore him Abijah, **Attai**, Ziza and Shelomith.

6969 עָתִיד 'ātîd, a. [5] [√ 6963; Ar 10577]

ready [3], doom [1], poised [1]

Dt 32:35 their day of disaster is near and their **doom** rushes upon them."
Est 3:14 people of every nationality so they would be **ready** for that day.
8:13 so that the Jews would be **ready** [K 6965] on that day to avenge
Job 3: 8 curse days curse that day, those *who are* **ready** to rouse Leviathan.
15:24 him with terror; they overwhelm him, like a king **poised** to attack,
Isa 10:13 [of nations, I plundered their **treasures**; [K; see Q 6965]]

6970 עֲתָיָה ªtāyâ, n.pr.m. [1]

Athaiah [1]

Ne 11: 4 **Athaiah** son of Uzziah, the son of Zechariah, the son of Amariah,

6971 עָתִיק 'ātîq, a. [1] [√ 6980]

fine [1]

Isa 23:18 who live before the LORD, for abundant food and **fine** clothes.

6972 עַתִּיק 'attîq, a. [2] [√ 6980]

from ancient times [1], taken [1]

1Ch 4:22 and Jashubi Lehem. (These records are **from ancient times**.)
Isa 28: 9 weaned from their milk, to *those just* **taken** from the breast?

6973 עֲתָךְ ªtāk, n.pr.loc. [1]

Athach [1]

1Sa 30:30 to those in Hormah, Bor Ashan, **Athach**

6974 עַתְלָי 'atlāy, n.pr.m. & f. [1] [→ 6975, 6976]

Athlai [1]

Ezr 10:28 descendants of Bebai: Jehohanan, Hananiah, Zabbai and **Athlai**.

6975 עֲתַלְיָה ªtalyâ, n.pr.m. & f. [7] [√ 6474]

Athaliah [7]

2Ki 11: 1 When **Athaliah** the mother of Ahaziah saw that her son was dead,
11: 3 temple of the LORD for six years while **Athaliah** ruled the land.
11:13 When **Athaliah** heard the noise made by the guards
11:14 Then **Athaliah** tore her robes and called out, "Treason! Treason!"
1Ch 8:26 Shamsherai, Shehariah, **Athaliah**,
2Ch 22:12 at the temple of God for six years while **Athaliah** ruled the land.
Ezr 8: 7 of Elam, Jeshaiah son of **Athaliah**, and with him 70 men;

6976 עֲתַלְיָהוּ ªtalyāhû, n.pr.m. & f. [10] [√ 6974]

Athaliah [10]

2Ki 8:26 His mother's name was **Athaliah**, a granddaughter of Omri king of
11: 2 put him and his nurse in a bedroom to hide him from **Athaliah**;
11:20 because **Athaliah** had been slain with the sword at the palace.
2Ch 22: 2 His mother's name was **Athaliah**, a granddaughter of Omri.
22:10 When **Athaliah** the mother of Ahaziah saw that her son was dead,
22:11 she hid the child from **Athaliah** so she could not kill him.
23:12 When **Athaliah** heard the noise of the people running and cheering
23:13 Then **Athaliah** tore her robes and shouted, "Treason! Treason!"
23:21 city was quiet, because **Athaliah** had been slain with the sword.
24: 7 Now the sons of that wicked woman **Athaliah** had broken into the

6977 עָתַם 'ātam, v. [1]

be scorched [1]

Isa 9:19 [9:18] [C] of the LORD Almighty the land *will* **be scorched**

6978 עָתְנִי 'otnî, n.pr.m. [1] [→ 6979]

Othni [1]

1Ch 26: 7 **Othni**, Rephael, Obed and Elzabad; his relatives Elihu

6979 עָתְנִיאֵל 'otnî'ēl, n.pr.m. [7] [√ 6978 + 446]

Othniel [7]

Jos 15:17 **Othniel** son of Kenaz, Caleb's brother, took it; so Caleb gave his
Jdg 1:13 **Othniel** son of Kenaz, Caleb's younger brother, took it; so Caleb
3: 9 **Othniel** son of Kenaz, Caleb's younger brother, who saved them.
3:11 the land had peace for forty years, until **Othniel** son of Kenaz died.
1Ch 4:13 The sons of Kenaz: **Othniel** and Seraiah. The sons of Othniel:
4:13 and Seraiah. The sons of **Othniel**: Hathath and Meonothai.
27:15 was Heldai the Netophathite, from the family of **Othniel**.

6980 עָתַק 'ātaq, v. [9] [→ 6971, 6972, 6981, 6982; Ar 10578]

moved [2], copied [1], fail [1], failed [+4946] [1], growing old [1], moved on [1], moves [1], went on [1]

Ge 12: 8 [G] From there *he* **went on** toward the hills east of Bethel and
26:22 [G] *He* **moved on** from there and dug another well, and no one
Job 9: 5 [G] He **moves** mountains without their knowing it and overturns
14:18 [A] and crumbles and as a rock *is* **moved** from its place,
18: 4 [A] for your sake? Or *must* the rocks *be* **moved** from their place?
21: 7 [A] do the wicked live on, **growing old** and increasing in power?
32:15 [G] and have no more to say; words *have* **failed** [+4946] them.
Ps 6: 7 [6:8] [A] weak with sorrow; *they* **fail** because of all my foes.
Pr 25: 1 [G] of Solomon, **copied** *by* the men of Hezekiah king of Judah:

6981 עָתָק 'ātāq, a. [4] [√ 6980]

arrogance [1], arrogant [1], arrogantly [1], outstretched [1]

1Sa 2: 3 keep talking so proudly or let your mouth speak such **arrogance**,
Ps 31:18 [31:19] contempt they speak **arrogantly** against the righteous.
75: 5 [75:6] against heaven; do not speak with **outstretched** neck.' "
94: 4 They pour out **arrogant** words; all the evildoers are full of

6982 עָתֵק 'ātēq, a. [1] [√ 6980]

enduring [1]

Pr 8:18 With me are riches and honor, **enduring** wealth and prosperity.

6983 עָתַר 'ātar[1], v. [20] [→ 6985, 6986, 6987?; cf. 6984?]

pray [7], answered prayer [4], prayed [4], was moved by entreaty [2], answered prayers [1], prays [1], respond to pleas [1]

Ge 25:21 [A] Isaac **prayed** to the LORD on behalf of his wife,
25:21 [C] The LORD **answered** his **prayer**, and his wife Rebekah
Ex 8: 8 [8:4] [G] "**Pray** to the LORD to take the frogs away from me
8: 9 [8:5] [G] the honor of setting the time *for me to* **pray** for you
8:28 [8:24] [G] but you must not go very far. Now **pray** for me."
8:29 [8:25] [G] "As soon as I leave you, *I will* **pray** to the LORD,
8:30 [8:26] [A] Then Moses left Pharaoh and **prayed** to the LORD,
9:28 [G] **Pray** to the LORD, for we have had enough thunder
10:17 [G] **pray** to the LORD your God to take this deadly plague
10:18 [A] Moses then left Pharaoh and **prayed** to the LORD.
Jdg 13: 8 [A] Then Manoah **prayed** to the LORD: "O Lord, I beg you,
2Sa 21:14 [C] After that, God **answered prayer** in behalf of the land.
24:25 [C] Then the LORD **answered prayer** in behalf of the land,
1Ch 5:20 [C] He **answered** their **prayers**, because they trusted in him.
2Ch 33:13 [C] the LORD **was moved by** his **entreaty** and listened to his
33:19 [C] His prayer and how God **was moved by** his **entreaty**, as well
Ezr 8:23 [C] petitioned our God about this, and *he* **answered** our **prayer**.
Job 22:27 [G] *You will* **pray** to him, and he will hear you, and you will
33:26 [A] *He* **prays** to God and finds favor with him, he sees God's
Isa 19:22 [C] and *he will* **respond to** their **pleas** and heal them.

6984 עָתַר 'ātar[2], v. [2] [→ 6988; cf. 6983?]

multiplies [1], without restraint [1]

Pr 27: 6 [C] from a friend can be trusted, but an enemy **multiplies** kisses.
Eze 35:13 [G] boasted against me and spoke against me **without restraint**,

6985 עָתָר 'ātār[1], n.[m.] [1] [√ 6983]

worshipers [1]

Zep 3:10 From beyond the rivers of Cush my **worshipers**, my scattered

6986 עָתָר 'ātār[2], n.[m.] [1] [√ 6983]

fragrant [1]

Eze 8:11 a censer in his hand, and a **fragrant** cloud of incense was rising.

6987 עֶתֶר 'eter, n.pr.loc. [2] [√ 6983?]

Ether [2]

Jos 15:42 Libnah, **Ether**, Ashan,
19: 7 Ain, Rimmon, **Ether** and Ashan—four towns and their villages—

6988 עֲטֶרֶת ***'ateret***, n.f. [1] [√ 6984]

abundant [1]

Jer 33: 6 my people and will let them enjoy **abundant** peace and security.

פ, *p*

6989 פ ***p***, letter. Not used in NIV/BHS [→ Ar 10579]

6990 פָּאָה ***pā'â***, v. [1] [→ 6991?, 6992]

scatter [1]

Dt 32:26 [G] I said *I would* **scatter** them and blot out their memory from

6991 ¹פֵּאָה ***pē'â¹***, n.f. [85] [√ 6990?]

side [33], *untranslated* [27], boundary [4], edges [4], end [4], places [3], corners [2], foreheads [2], border [1], edge [1], front [1], sides [1], southern [+448+5582] [1], started [+4200] [1]

Ex 25:26 four gold rings for the table and fasten them to the four **corners**,
26:18 Make twenty frames for the south **side** of the tabernacle
26:20 For the other side, the north **side** *of* the tabernacle, make twenty
27: 9 The south **side** shall be a hundred cubits long and is to have
27: 9 cubits long **[RPH]** and is to have curtains of finely twisted linen,
27:11 The north **side** shall also be a hundred cubits long and is to have
27:12 "The west **end** *of* the courtyard shall be fifty cubits wide and have
27:13 On the east **end**, toward the sunrise, the courtyard shall also be
36:23 They made twenty frames for the south **side** of the tabernacle
36:25 For the other side, the north **side** *of* the tabernacle, they made
37:13 four gold rings for the table and fastened them to the four **corners**,
38: 9 The south **side** was a hundred cubits long and had curtains of
38:11 The north **side** was also a hundred cubits long and had twenty
38:12 The west **end** was fifty cubits wide and had curtains, with ten posts
38:13 The east **end**, toward the sunrise, was also fifty cubits wide.
Lev 13:41 If he has lost his hair from the **front** *of* his scalp and has a bald
19: 9 do not reap to the very **edges** *of* your field or gather the gleanings
19:27 " 'Do not cut the hair at the **sides** *of* your head or clip off the edges
19:27 hair at the sides of your head or clip off the **edges** *of* your beard.
21: 5 or shave off the **edges** *of* their beards or cut their bodies.
23:22 do not reap to the very **edges** *of* your field or gather the gleanings
Nu 24:17 He will crush the **foreheads** *of* Moab, the skulls of all the sons of
34: 3 " 'Your southern **side** will include some of the Desert of Zin along
35: 5 Outside the town, measure three thousand feet on the east **side**,
35: 5 three thousand on the south **side**, three thousand on the west
35: 5 thousand on the west **[RPH]** and three thousand on the north,
35: 5 three thousand on the north, **[RPH]** with the town in the center.
Jos 15: 5 The northern boundary **started** [+4200] from the bay of the sea at
18:12 On the north **side** their boundary began at the Jordan, passed the
18:14 on the south the boundary turned south along the western **side**
18:14 a town of the people of Judah. This was the western **side**.
18:15 The southern **side** began at the outskirts of Kiriath Jearim on the
18:20 The Jordan formed the boundary on the eastern **side**. These were
Jer 9:26 [9:25] and all who live in the desert in distant **places**.
25:23 Dedan, Tema, Buz and all who are in distant **places**;
48:45 it burns the **foreheads** *of* Moab, the skulls of the noisy boasters.
49:32 I will scatter to the winds those who are in distant **places** and will
Eze 41:12 The building facing the temple courtyard *on* the west **side** was
45: 7 It will extend westward from the west **side** and eastward from the
45: 7 westward from the west side and eastward from the east **side**,
47:15 "On the north **side** it will run from the Great Sea by the Hethlon
47:17 border of Hamath to the north. This will be the north **boundary**.
47:18 "On the east **side** the boundary will run between Hauran
47:18 eastern sea and as far as Tamar. This will be the east **boundary**.
47:19 "On the south **side** it will run from Tamar as far as the waters of
47:19 ˪of Egypt˩ to the Great Sea. This will be the south **boundary**.
47:20 "On the west **side**, the Great Sea will be the boundary to a point
47:20 to a point opposite Lebo Hamath. This will be the west **boundary**.
48: 1 will be part of its **border** *from* the east side to the west side.
48: 2 it will border the territory of Dan from **[RPH]** east to west.
48: 2 it will border the territory of Dan from east to **[RPH]** west.
48: 3 it will border the territory of Asher from **[RPH]** east to west.
48: 3 it will border the territory of Asher from east to **[RPH]** west.
48: 4 it will border the territory of Naphtali from **[RPH]** east to west.
48: 4 it will border the territory of Naphtali from east to **[RPH]** west.
48: 5 it will border the territory of Manasseh from **[RPH]** east to west.
48: 5 it will border the territory of Manasseh from east to **[RPH]** west.
48: 6 it will border the territory of Ephraim from **[RPH]** east to west.
48: 6 it will border the territory of Ephraim from east to **[RPH]** west.
48: 7 it will border the territory of Reuben from **[RPH]** east to west.
48: 7 it will border the territory of Reuben from east to **[RPH]** west.
48: 8 "Bordering the territory of Judah from **[RPH]** east to west will be
48: 8 "Bordering the territory of Judah from east to **[RPH]** west will be
48: 8 its length from **[RPH]** east to west will equal one of the tribal
48: 8 its length from east to **[RPH]** west will equal one of the tribal
48:16 the north **side** 4,500 cubits, the south side 4,500 cubits, the east
48:16 4,500 cubits, the south **side** 4,500 cubits, the east side 4,500 cubits,
48:16 4,500 cubits, the south side 4,500 cubits, the east **side** 4,500 cubits,
48:16 the east side 4,500 cubits, and the west **side** 4,500 cubits.
48:23 have one portion; it will extend from the east **side** to the west side.
48:23 have one portion; it will extend from the east side to the west **side**.
48:24 it will border the territory of Benjamin from **[RPH]** east to west.
48:24 it will border the territory of Benjamin from east to **[RPH]** west.
48:25 it will border the territory of Simeon from **[RPH]** east to west.
48:25 it will border the territory of Simeon from east to **[RPH]** west.
48:26 it will border the territory of Issachar from **[RPH]** east to west.
48:26 it will border the territory of Issachar from east to **[RPH]** west.
48:27 it will border the territory of Zebulun from **[RPH]** east to west.
48:27 it will border the territory of Zebulun from east to **[RPH]** west.
48:28 "The **southern** [+448+5582] boundary of Gad will run south from
48:30 of the city: Beginning on the north **side**, which is 4,500 cubits long,
48:32 "On the east **side**, which is 4,500 cubits long, will be three gates:
48:33 "On the south **side**, which measures 4,500 cubits, will be three
48:34 "On the west **side**, which is 4,500 cubits long, will be three gates:
Am 3:12 those who sit in Samaria on the **edge** *of* their beds and in

6992 ²פֵּאָה ***pē'â²***, n.f. [1] [√ 6990]

remotest frontiers [1]

Ne 9:22 and nations, allotting to them even the **remotest frontiers**.

6993 ³פֵּאָה ***pē'â³***, n.f. Not used in NIV/BHS [cf. 3636]

6994 ¹פָּאַר ***pā'ar¹***, v.den. [1] [√ 6998]

go over the branches a second time [+339] [1]

Dt 24:20 [D] *do* not **go** [+339] **over the branches a second time**.

6995 ²פָּאַר ***pā'ar²***, v. [13] [→ 6996?, 9514]

display splendor [3], adorn [2], endowed with splendor [2], boast [1], bring honor [1], crowns [1], displays glory [1], leave the honor [1], raise itself [1]

Ex 8: 9 [8:5] [F] "**I leave** *to you* **the honor** *of* setting the time for me to
Jdg 7: 2 [F] In order that Israel *may* not **boast** against me that her own
Ezr 7:27 [D] who has put it into the king's heart to **bring honor** *to* the
Ps 149: 4 [D] delight in his people; *he* **crowns** the humble with salvation.
Isa 10:15 [F] *Does* the ax **raise itself** above him who swings it, or the saw
44:23 [F] LORD has redeemed Jacob, *he* **displays** *his* **glory** in Israel.
49: 3 [F] are my servant, Israel, in whom *I will* **display** *my* **splendor**."
55: 5 [D] Holy One of Israel, for *he has* **endowed** you **with splendor**."
60: 7 [D] offerings on my altar, and *I will* **adorn** my glorious temple.
60: 9 [D] Holy One of Israel, for *he has* **endowed** you **with splendor**.
60:13 [D] and the cypress together, to **adorn** the place of my sanctuary;
60:21 [F] the work of my hands, for *the* **display** *of* my **splendor**.
61: 3 [F] a planting of the LORD for *the* **display** *of* his **splendor**.

6996 פְּאֵר ***pe'ēr***, n.m. [7] [√ 6995?]

turbans [2], adorns head [1], crown of beauty [1], headbands [+4457] [1], headdresses [1], turban [1]

Ex 39:28 the linen **headbands** [+4457] and the undergarments of finely
Isa 3:20 the **headdresses** and ankle chains and sashes, the perfume bottles
61: 3 to bestow on them a **crown of beauty** instead of ashes, the oil of
61:10 of righteousness, as a bridegroom **adorns** his **head** like a priest,
Eze 24:17 Keep your **turban** fastened and your sandals on your feet;
24:23 You will keep your **turbans** on your heads and your sandals on
44:18 They are to wear linen **turbans** on their heads and linen

6997 פֹּארָה ***pō'râ***, n.f. [6]

branches [5], leafy boughs [1]

Eze 17: 6 it became a vine and produced branches and put out **leafy boughs**.
31: 5 its boughs increased and its **branches** grew long, spreading
31: 6 its boughs, all the beasts of the field gave birth under its **branches**;
31: 8 its boughs, nor could the plane trees compare with its **branches**—
31:12 the valleys; its **branches** lay broken in all the ravines of the land.
31:13 fallen tree, and all the beasts of the field were among its **branches**.

6998 פֻּארָה ***pu'râ***, n.f.col. [1] [→ 6994]

boughs [1]

Isa 10:33 the LORD Almighty, will lop off the **boughs** with great power.

6999 פָּארוּר ***pā'rûr***, n.[m.]. [2] [√ 7248]

grows pale [+7695] [1], turns pale [+7695] [1]

Joel 2: 6 of them, nations are in anguish; every face **turns pale** [+7695].
Na 2:10 [2:11] give way, bodies tremble, every face **grows pale** [+7695].

7000 פָּארָן *pā'rān*, n.pr.loc. [11 / 10] [→ 386; cf. 7230?]
Paran [10]

Ge 21:21 While he was living in the Desert of **Paran**, his mother got a wife
Nu 10:12 place to place until the cloud came to rest in the Desert of **Paran**.
12:16 the people left Hazeroth and encamped in the Desert of **Paran**.
13: 3 command Moses sent them out from the Desert of **Paran**.
13:26 the whole Israelite community at Kadesh in the Desert of **Paran**.
Dt 1: 1 between **Paran** and Tophel, Laban, Hazeroth and Dizahab.
33: 2 dawned over them from Seir; he shone forth from Mount **Paran**.
1Sa 25: 1 moved down into the Desert of Maon. [BHS ***Paran***; NIV 5063]
1Ki 11:18 They set out from Midian and went to **Paran**. Then taking men
11:18 Then taking men from **Paran** with them, they went to Egypt,
Hab 3: 3 God came from Teman, the Holy One from Mount **Paran**.

7001 פַּג *pag*, n.f. [1]
early fruit [1]

SS 2:13 The fig tree forms its **early fruit**; the blossoming vines spread their

7002 פִּגּוּל *piggûl*, n.m. [4]
impure [2], unclean meat [1], unclean [1]

Lev 7:18 It will not be credited to the one who offered it, for it is **impure**;
19: 7 of it is eaten on the third day, it is **impure** and will not be accepted.
Isa 65: 4 eat the flesh of pigs, and whose pots hold broth of **unclean meat**;
Eze 4:14 by wild animals. No **unclean** meat has ever entered my mouth."

7003 פָּגַע *pāga'*, n.m. [46] [→ 5133, 7004, 7005]
touched [6], strike down [4], struck down [4], meet [2], meets [2], plead [2], strike [2], *untranslated* [1], attack [1], attacked [1], bordered [1], come across [1], come to the help of [1], do[s] [1], extended [1], find [1], found [1], harmed [1], intercede [1], intervene [1], kill [1], laid [1], made intercession [1], make plead [1], met [1], praying [1], reached [1], spare [1], strike mark [1], urge [1], urged [1]

Ge 23: 8 [A] to me and **intercede** with Ephron son of Zohar on my behalf
28:11 [A] When *he* **reached** a certain place, he stopped for the night
32: 1 [32:2] [A] went on his way, and the angels of God **met** him.
Ex 5: 3 [A] or *he may* **strike** us with plagues or with the sword."
5:20 [A] *they* **found** Moses and Aaron waiting to meet them,
23: 4 [A] "If *you* **come across** your enemy's ox or donkey wandering
Nu 35:19 [A] to death; when he **meets** him, he shall put him to death.
35:21 [A] of blood shall put the murderer to death when he **meets** him.
Jos 2:16 [A] to them, "Go to the hills so the pursuers *will* not **find** you.
16: 7 [A] and Naarah, **touched** Jericho and came out at the Jordan.
17:10 [A] and **bordered** Asher on the north and Issachar on the east.
19:11 [A] Going west it ran to Maralah, **touched** Dabbesheth,
19:11 [A] and **extended** to the ravine near Jokneam.
19:22 [A] The boundary **touched** Tabor, Shahazumah and Beth
19:26 [A] On the west the boundary **touched** Carmel and Shihor
19:27 [A] **touched** Zebulun and the Valley of Iphtah El, and went north
19:34 [A] *It* **touched** Zebulun on the south, Asher on the west and the
19:34 [A] Asher **[RPH]** on the west and the Jordan on the east.
Jdg 8:21 [A] Zebah and Zalmunna said, "Come, **do**[s] *it* yourself. 'As is the
15:12 [A] "Swear to me that *you* won't **kill** me yourselves."
18:25 [A] or some hot-tempered men *will* **attack** you, and you and your
Ru 1:16 [A] "Don't **urge** me to leave you or to turn back from you.
2:22 [A] because in someone else's field you *might be* **harmed**."
1Sa 10: 5 [A] *you will* **meet** a procession of prophets coming down from
22:17 [A] the king's officials were not willing to raise a hand to **strike**
22:18 [A] then ordered Doeg, "You turn and **strike down** the priests."
22:18 [A] So Doeg the Edomite turned and **struck** them **down**.
2Sa 1:15 [A] called one of his men and said, "Go, **strike** him **down**!"
1Ki 2:25 [A] son of Jehoiada, and *he* **struck down** Adonijah and he died.
2:29 [A] ordered Benaiah son of Jehoiada, "Go, **strike** him **down**!"
2:31 [A] **Strike** him **down** and bury him, and so clear me and my
2:32 [A] the knowledge of my father David *he* **attacked** two men
2:34 [A] of Jehoiada went up and **struck down** Joab and killed him,
2:46 [A] and he went out and **struck** Shimei **down** and killed him.
Job 21:15 [A] should serve him? What would we gain by **praying** to him?'
36:32 [G] his hands with lightning and commands it *to* **strike** its **mark**.
Isa 47: 3 [A] I will take vengeance; *I will* **spare** no one."
53: 6 [G] and the LORD *has* **laid** on him the iniquity of us all.
53:12 [G] the sin of many, and **made intercession** for the transgressors.
59:16 [G] no one, he was appalled that there was no *one to* **intervene**;
64: 5 [64:4] [A] *You* **come to the help of** those who gladly do right,
Jer 7:16 [A] for them; *do* not **plead** with me, for I will not listen to you.
15:11 [G] surely *I will* **make** your enemies **plead** with you in times of
27:18 [A] *let them* **plead** with the LORD Almighty that the
36:25 [G] Delaiah and Gemariah **urged** the king not to burn the scroll,
Am 5:19 [A] It will be as though a man fled from a lion only *to* **meet** a

7004 פֶּגַע *pega'*, n.m. [2] [√ 7003]
chance [1], disaster [+8273] [1]

1Ki 5: 4 [5:18] every side, and there is no adversary or **disaster** [+8273].
Ecc 9:11 or favor to the learned; but time and **chance** happen to them all.

7005 פַּגְעִיאֵל *pag'î'ēl*, n.pr.m. [5] [√ 7003 + 446]
Pagiel [5]

Nu 1:13 from Asher, **Pagiel** son of Ocran;
2:27 to them. The leader of the people of Asher is **Pagiel** son of Ocran.
7:72 On the eleventh day **Pagiel** son of Ocran, the leader of the people
7:77 a fellowship offering. This was the offering of **Pagiel** son of Ocran.
10:26 **Pagiel** son of Ocran was over the division of the tribe of Asher,

7006 פָּגַר *pāgar*, v. [2] [→ 7007]
exhausted [2]

1Sa 30:10 [D] for two hundred men *were* too **exhausted** to cross the ravine.
30:21 [D] hundred men who *had been* too **exhausted** to follow him

7007 פֶּגֶר *peger*, n.m. [22 / 21] [√ 7006]
bodies [7], dead bodies [7], carcasses [2], lifeless idols [2], corpse [1], dead [1], lifeless forms [1]

Ge 15:11 birds of prey came down on the **carcasses**, but Abram drove them
Lev 26:30 and pile your **dead bodies** on the lifeless forms of your idols,
26:30 and pile your dead bodies on the **lifeless forms** *of* your idols,
Nu 14:29 In this desert your **bodies** will fall—every one of you twenty years
14:32 But you—your **bodies** will fall in this desert.
14:33 your unfaithfulness, until the last of your **bodies** lies in the desert.
1Sa 17:46 Today I will give the **carcasses** *of* the Philistine army to the birds
2Ki 19:35 people got up the next morning—there were all the dead **bodies**!
2Ch 20:24 the vast army, they saw only **dead bodies** lying on the ground;
20:25 a great amount of equipment and clothing [BHS ***corpses***; NIV 955]
Isa 14:19 descend to the stones of the pit. Like a **corpse** trampled underfoot,
34: 3 slain will be thrown out, their **dead bodies** will send up a stench;
37:36 people got up the next morning—there were all the dead **bodies**!
66:24 and look upon the **dead bodies** *of* those who rebelled against me;
Jer 31:40 The whole valley where **dead bodies** and ashes are thrown,
33: 5 'They will be filled with the **dead bodies** *of* the men I will slay in
41: 9 Now the cistern where he threw all the **bodies** *of* the men he had
Eze 6: 5 I will lay the **dead bodies** *of* the Israelites in front of their idols,
43: 7 and the **lifeless idols** *of* their kings at their high places.
43: 9 from me their prostitution and the **lifeless idols** *of* their kings,
Am 8: 3 turn to wailing. Many, many **bodies**—flung everywhere! Silence!"
Na 3: 3 Many casualties, piles of **dead**, bodies without number, people

7008 פָּגַשׁ *pāgaš*, v. [14]
met [6], have in common [2], meet [2], attack [1], comes [1], meet together [1], meets [1]

Ge 32:17 [32:18] [A] "When my brother Esau **meets** you and asks, 'To
33: 8 [A] Esau asked, "What do you mean by all these droves *I* **met**?"
Ex 4:24 [A] the way, the LORD **met** ⌊Moses⌋ and was about to kill him.
4:27 [A] So *he* **met** Moses at the mountain of God and kissed him.
1Sa 25:20 [A] and his men descending toward her, and *she* **met** them.
2Sa 2:13 [A] David's men went out and **met** them at the pool of Gibeon.
Job 5:14 [D] Darkness **comes** *upon* them in the daytime; at noon they
Ps 85:10 [85:11] [C] Love and faithfulness **meet together**; righteousness
Pr 17:12 [A] Better *to* **meet** a bear robbed of her cubs than a fool in his
22: 2 [C] Rich and poor **have** *this* **in common**: The LORD is the
29:13 [C] The poor man and the oppressor **have** *this* **in common**:
Isa 34:14 [A] Desert creatures *will* **meet** with hyenas, and wild goats will
Jer 41: 6 [A] When he **met** them, he said, "Come to Gedaliah son of
Hos 13: 8 [A] robbed of her cubs, *I will* **attack** them and rip them open.

7009 פָּדָה *pādâ*, v. [60] [→ 7012, 7013, 7014, 7017, 7018; *also used with compound proper names*]
redeem [22], redeemed [15], ransom [4], been ransomed [+7009] [2], delivered [2], must redeem [+906+906+7009] [2], ransomed [2], redeem [+7009] [2], *untranslated* [1], be ransomed [1], be redeemed [1], buy back [1], let be redeemed [1], ransoms [1], redeems [1], redemption [1], rescued [1]

Ex 13:13 [A] **Redeem** with a lamb every firstborn donkey, but if you do
13:13 [A] firstborn donkey, but if *you do* not **redeem** it, break its neck.
13:13 [A] break its neck. **Redeem** every firstborn among your sons.
13:15 [A] of every womb and **redeem** each of my firstborn sons.'
21: 8 [G] has selected her for himself, *he must* **let** her **be redeemed**.
34:20 [A] **Redeem** the firstborn donkey with a lamb, but if you do not
34:20 [A] with a lamb, but if *you do* not **redeem** it, break its neck.
34:20 [A] not redeem it, break its neck. **Redeem** all your firstborn sons.
Lev 19:20 [C] *who has* not **been ransomed** [+7009] or given her freedom,
19:20 [H] *who has* not **been ransomed** [+7009] or given her freedom,

Lev 27:27 [A] *he may* **buy** it **back** at its set value, adding a fifth of the
27:29 [C] " 'No person devoted to destruction *may* **be ransomed**;
Nu 3:49 [B] those who exceeded the number **redeemed** *by* the Levites.
18:15 [A] But *you* **must redeem** [+906+906+7009] every firstborn son
18:15 [A] But *you* **must redeem** [+906+906+7009] every firstborn son
18:15 [A] and every firstborn male of unclean animals. **[RPH]**
18:16 [A] *you must* **redeem** them at the redemption price set at five
18:16 [B] you must redeem them at the **redemption** price set at five
18:17 [A] "But *you must* not **redeem** the firstborn of an ox, a sheep
Dt 7:8 [A] a mighty hand and **redeemed** you from the land of slavery,
9:26 [A] your own inheritance that *you* **redeemed** by your great
13:5 [13:6] [A] of Egypt and **redeemed** you from the land of slavery;
15:15 [A] slaves in Egypt and the LORD your God **redeemed** you.
21:8 [A] your people Israel, whom *you have* **redeemed**, O LORD,
24:18 [A] and the LORD your God **redeemed** you from there.
1Sa 14:45 [A] So the men **rescued** Jonathan, and he was not put to death.
2Sa 4:9 [A] as the LORD lives, who *has* **delivered** me out of all trouble,
7:23 [A] the one nation on earth that God went out to **redeem** as a
7:23 [A] from before your people, whom *you* **redeemed** from Egypt?
1Ki 1:29 [A] LORD lives, who *has* **delivered** me out of every trouble,
1Ch 17:21 [A] the one nation on earth whose God went out to **redeem** a
17:21 [A] from before your people, whom *you* **redeemed** from Egypt?
Ne 1:10 [A] whom *you* **redeemed** by your great strength and your mighty
Job 5:20 [A] In famine *he will* **ransom** you from death, and in battle from
6:23 [A] of the enemy, **ransom** me from the clutches of the ruthless'?
33:28 [A] *He* **redeemed** my soul from going down to the pit, and I will
Ps 25:22 [A] **Redeem** Israel, O God, from all their troubles!
26:11 [A] I lead a blameless life; **redeem** me and be merciful to me.
31:5 [31:6] [A] my spirit; **redeem** me, O LORD, the God of truth.
34:22 [34:23] [A] The LORD **redeems** his servants; no one will be
44:26 [44:27] [A] help us; **redeem** us because of your unfailing love.
49:7 [49:8] [A] No man *can* **redeem** [+7009] the life of another
49:7 [49:8] [A] No man *can* **redeem** [+7009] the life of another
49:15 [49:16] [A] God *will* **redeem** my life from the grave; he will
55:18 [55:19] [A] *He* **ransoms** me unharmed from the battle waged
69:18 [69:19] [A] and rescue me; **redeem** me because of my foes.
71:23 [A] joy when I sing praise to you—I, whom *you have* **redeemed**.
78:42 [A] his power—the day *he* **redeemed** them from the oppressor,
119:134 [A] **Redeem** me from the oppression of men, that I may obey
130:8 [A] *He* himself *will* **redeem** Israel from all their sins.
Isa 1:27 [C] Zion *will* **be redeemed** with justice, her penitent ones with
29:22 [A] who **redeemed** Abraham, says to the house of Jacob:
35:10 [B] the **ransomed** *of* the LORD will return. They will enter
51:11 [B] The **ransomed** *of* the LORD will return. They will enter
Jer 15:21 [A] of the wicked and **redeem** you from the grasp of the cruel."
31:11 [A] For the LORD *will* **ransom** Jacob and redeem them from
Hos 7:13 [A] I *long to* **redeem** them but they speak lies against me.
13:14 [A] "*I will* **ransom** them from the power of the grave; I will
Mic 6:4 [A] up out of Egypt and **redeemed** you from the land of slavery.
Zec 10:8 [A] Surely *I will* **redeem** them; they will be as numerous as

7010 פְּדָהאֵל *pᵉdah'ēl*, n.pr.m. [1] [√ 7009 + 446]

Pedahel [1]

Nu 34:28 **Pedahel** son of Ammihud, the leader from the tribe of Naphtali."

7011 פְּדָהצוּר *pᵉdāhṣûr*, פְּדָה־צוּר *pᵉdāh-ṣûr*, n.pr.m. [5] [√ 7009 + 7446]

Pedahzur [5]

Nu 1:10 son of Ammihud; from Manasseh, Gamaliel son of **Pedahzur**;
2:20 leader of the people of Manasseh is Gamaliel son of **Pedahzur**.
7:54 On the eighth day Gamaliel son of **Pedahzur**, the leader of the
7:59 This was the offering of Gamaliel son of **Pedahzur**.
10:23 Gamaliel son of **Pedahzur** was over the division of the tribe of

7012 פְּדוּיִם *pᵉdûyim*, n.[m.]pl.abst. [3] [√ 7009]

redemption [2], redeem [1]

Nu 3:46 *To* **redeem** the 273 firstborn Israelites who exceed the number of
3:48 Give the money for the **redemption** *of* the additional Israelites to
3:51 Moses gave the **redemption** money to Aaron and his sons,

7013 פָּדוֹן *pādôn*, n.pr.m. [2] [√ 7009]

Padon [2]

Ezr 2:44 Keros, Siaha, **Padon**,
Ne 7:47 Keros, Sia, **Padon**,

7014 פְּדוּת *pᵉdût*, n.f. [4 / 3] [√ 7009]

redemption [2], ransom [1]

Ex 8:23 [8:19] I will make a distinction [BHS *deliverance*; NIV 7151]
Ps 111:9 He provided **redemption** for his people; he ordained his covenant
130:7 with the LORD is unfailing love and with him is full **redemption**.

Isa 50:2 there no one to answer? Was my arm too short to **ransom** you?

7015 פְּדָיָה *pᵉdāyâ*, n.pr.m. [7] [√ 7009 + 3378]

Pedaiah [7]

2Ki 23:36 His mother's name was Zebidah daughter of **Pedaiah**; she was
1Ch 3:18 Malkiram, **Pedaiah**, Shenazzar, Jekamiah, Hoshama
3:19 The sons of **Pedaiah**: Zerubbabel and Shimei. The sons of
Ne 3:25 near the court of the guard. Next to him, **Pedaiah** son of Parosh
8:4 and on his left were **Pedaiah**, Mishael, Malkijah, Hashum,
11:7 the son of Joed, the son of **Pedaiah**, the son of Kolaiah, the son of
13:13 a Levite named **Pedaiah** in charge of the storerooms and made

7016 פְּדָיָהוּ *pᵉdāyāhû*, n.pr.m. [1] [√ 7009 + 3378]

Pedaiah [1]

1Ch 27:20 of Azaziah; over half the tribe of Manasseh: Joel son of **Pedaiah**;

7017 פִּדְיוֹם *pidyôm*, n.m. [1] [√ 7009]

redemption [1]

Nu 3:49 So Moses collected the **redemption** money from those who

7018 פִּדְיוֹן *pidyôn*, n.m. [2] [√ 7009]

ransom [1], redeem [1]

Ex 21:30 he may **redeem** his life by paying whatever is demanded.
Ps 49:8 [49:9] the **ransom** *for* a life is costly, no payment is ever

7019 פַּדָּן *paddān*, n.pr.loc. [1] [→ 7020]

Paddan [1]

Ge 48:7 As I was returning from **Paddan**, to my sorrow Rachel died in the

7020 פַּדַּן אֲרָם *paddan 'ᵃrām*, n.pr.loc. [10] [√ 7019 + 806]

Paddan Aram [10]

Ge 25:20 Rebekah daughter of Bethuel the Aramean from **Paddan Aram**
28:2 Go at once to **Paddan Aram**, to the house of your mother's father
28:5 Then Isaac sent Jacob on his way, and he went to **Paddan Aram**,
28:6 and had sent him to **Paddan Aram** to take a wife from there,
28:7 had obeyed his father and mother and had gone to **Paddan Aram**.
31:18 along with all the goods he had accumulated in **Paddan Aram**,
33:18 After Jacob came from **Paddan Aram**, he arrived safely at the city
35:9 After Jacob returned from **Paddan Aram**, God appeared to him
35:26 were the sons of Jacob, who were born to him in **Paddan Aram**.
46:15 These were the sons Leah bore to Jacob in **Paddan Aram**,

7021 פָּדַע *pāda'*, v. [1]

spare [1]

Job 33:24 [A] to him and say, '**Spare** him from going down to the pit;

7022 פֶּדֶר *peder*, n.[m.]. [3]

fat [3]

Lev 1:8 including the head and the **fat**, on the burning wood that is on the
1:12 and the priest shall arrange them, including the head and the **fat**,
8:20 cut the ram into pieces and burned the head, the pieces and the **fat**.

7023 פֶּה *peh*, n.m. [498] [→ 7092; Ar 10588]

mouth [199], mouths [40], command [39], to [+4200] [25], lips [13], *untranslated* [10], opening [8], face [7], with [+4200] [5], word [5], commanded [4], end [4], speech [4], spoken [4], testimony [4], according to [+6584] [3], by [+4200] [3], number [3], according to [+4200] [2], as much as [+4200] [2], commands [2], dictated [+4946] [2], man [2], other[s] [2], promised [+3655+4946] [2], pronounced [2], required [2], said [+3655+4946] [2], said [2], speak [+4946] [2], speak up [+7337] [2], speak [2], what say [+609] [2], when [+4200] [2], words [+609] [2], according to [+3869] [1], accordingly [+3869] [1], amount [1], as much as [+3869] [1], at [+4200] [1], beak [1], because [+889+3869] [1], big talk [1], boast so much [+1540+3870] [1], boasted [+928+1540] [1], by [+4946] [1], by [+6584] [1], collar [+9389] [1], collar [1], consulting [+8626] [1], decide [+2118+6584] [1], demanded [+6584] [1], dictate [+4946] [1], dictated [+906+4946 +7924] [1], dictated [1], dictating [+4946] [1], dictation [+4946] [1], direction [1], don't say a word [+3338+6584+8492] [1], double-edged [+9109] [1], double-edged [1], drank in [+7196] [1], expressed [+6584] [1], fruit [1], fulfill [+3869+4027+6913] [1], gape [+8143] [1], give command [+928+7337] [1], given word [+906+7198] [1], giving an apt reply [+5101] [1], had [+928] [1], have [+928] [1], hunger [1], I [+3276] [1], in accordance with [+4200] [1], in accordance with [+6584] [1], in proportion to [+3869] [1], in the way should go [+2006 +6584] [1], inquire of [+906+8626] [1], instructed [+448+1819] [1], invoke [+928+7924] [1], jaws [1], just like [+3869] [1], keep silent [+3104] [1], killed [+906+2995+4200+5782] [1], leading into [+4200] [1], made a vow [+7198] [1], make spew out [+906+3655+4946] [1], mention [+928+9019] [1], neck [1], offered a kiss of homage [+4200+5975] [1], on [+6584] [1], orders [1], portion [1], promised [+928+1819] [1], requires [1], say [+3655+4946] [1], say [+7337] [1], say [1], sayings [1], share [1], simply [+6584] [1], sing [+928+8492] [1], sneer [+8143] [1], so that [+3869] [1], speak [+928] [1], speaks [+7337] [1], spoke the word [+4946] [1], spoken [+1819] [1], spokesman [+3869] [1], talk [1], taste [1], told [+928+8492] [1], two-thirds [+9109] [1], what said [+609] [1], when [+3954+4200] [1], whenever [+4200] [1], will [+6584] [1], words [+1821] [1], words [+7339] [1]

Ge 4:11 which opened its **mouth** to receive your brother's blood from your
8:11 in the evening, there in its **beak** was a freshly plucked olive leaf!
24:57 Then they said, "Let's call the girl and ask her **[NIE]** about it."
25:28 Isaac, who had a **taste** *for* wild game, loved Esau, but Rebekah
29: 2 from that well. The stone over the **mouth** *of* the well was large.
29: 3 the shepherds would roll the stone away from the well's **mouth**
29: 3 they would return the stone to its place over the **mouth** *of* the well.
29: 8 and the stone has been rolled away from the **mouth** *of* the well.
29:10 he went over and rolled the stone away from the **mouth** *of* the well
34:26 They put Hamor and his son Shechem **to** [+4200] the sword
41:40 of my palace, and all my people are to submit to your **orders**.
42:27 feed for his donkey, and he saw his silver in the **mouth** *of* his sack.
43: 7 have another brother?' We **simply** [+6584] answered his questions.
43:12 for you must return the silver that was put back into the **mouths** *of*
43:21 us found his silver—the exact weight—in the **mouth** *of* his sack.
44: 1 they can carry, and put each man's silver in the **mouth** *of* his sack.
44: 2 my cup, the silver one, in the **mouth** *of* the youngest one's sack,
44: 8 land of Canaan the silver we found inside the **mouths** *of* our sacks.
45:12 that it is really **I** [+3276] who am speaking to you.
45:21 Joseph gave them carts, as Pharaoh had **commanded**, and he also
47:12 household with food, according to the **number** *of* their children.
Ex 4:10 you have spoken to your servant. I am slow of **speech** and tongue."
4:11 The LORD said to him, "Who gave man his **mouth**? Who makes
4:12 Now go; I will help you **speak** and will teach you what to say."
4:15 You shall speak to him and put words in his **mouth**; I will help
4:15 I will help both of you **speak** and will teach you what to do.
4:15 will help both of you speak **[RPH]** and will teach you what to do.
4:16 it will be as if he were your **mouth** and as if you were God to him.
12: 4 needed **in accordance with what** [+4200] each person will eat.
13: 9 on your forehead that the law of the LORD is to be on your **lips**.
16:16 'Each one is to gather **as much** [+4200] **as** he needs.
16:18 have too little. Each one gathered **as much** [+4200] **as** he needed.
16:21 Each morning everyone gathered **as much** [+3869] **as** he needed,
17: 1 traveling from place to place as the LORD **commanded**.
17:13 So Joshua overcame the Amalekite army **with** [+4200] the sword.
23:13 the names of other gods; do not let them be heard on your **lips**.
28:32 with an **opening** *for* the head in its center. There shall be a woven
28:32 There shall be a woven edge like a **collar** [+9389] around this
28:32 There shall be a woven edge like a collar around this **opening**,
34:27 for **in accordance with** [+6584] these words I have made a
38:21 which were recorded at Moses' **command** by the Levites under the
39:23 with an **opening** in the center of the robe like the opening of a
39:23 with an opening in the center of the robe like the **opening** *of* a
39:23 a collar, and a band around this **opening**, so that it would not tear.
Lev 24:12 They put him in custody until the **will** [+6584] *of* the LORD
25:16 **When** [+4200] the years are many, you are to increase the price,
25:16 you are to increase the price, and **when** [+4200] the years are few,
25:51 **[NIE]** he must pay for his redemption a larger share of the price
25:52 to compute that and pay for his redemption **accordingly** [+3869].
27: 8 who will set the value for him **according to** [+6584] what the man
27:16 its value is to be set according to the **amount** *of* seed required for
27:18 the priest will determine the value according to the **number** *of*
Nu 3:16 counted them, as he was commanded by the **word** *of* the LORD.
3:39 The total number of Levites counted at the LORD's **command** *by*
3:51 and his sons, as he was commanded by the **word** *of* the LORD.
4:27 is to be done under the **direction** *of* Aaron and his sons.
4:37 Aaron counted them according to the LORD's **command** through
4:41 and Aaron counted them according to the LORD's **command**.
4:45 Aaron counted them according to the LORD's **command** through
4:49 At the LORD's **command** through Moses, each was assigned his
6:21 *He must* **fulfill** [+3869+4027+6913] the vow he has made,
7: 5 Give them to the Levites as each man's work **requires**."
7: 7 and four oxen to the Gershonites, as their work **required**,
7: 8 four carts and eight oxen to the Merarites, as their work **required**.
9:17 **Whenever** [+4200] the cloud lifted from above the Tent, the
9:18 At the LORD's **command** the Israelites set out, and at his
9:18 the Israelites set out, and at his **command** they encamped.
9:20 at the LORD's **command** they would encamp, and then at his
9:20 they would encamp, and then at his **command** they would set out.
9:23 At the LORD's **command** they encamped, and at the LORD's
9:23 they encamped, and at the LORD's **command** they set out.
9:23 LORD's order, in accordance with his **command** through Moses.
10:13 this first time, at the LORD's **command** through Moses.
12: 8 With him I speak **face** to face, clearly and not in riddles; he sees
12: 8 With him I speak face to **face**, clearly and not in riddles; he sees
13: 3 So at the LORD's **command** Moses sent them out from the
14:41 Moses said, "Why are you disobeying the LORD's **command**?
16:30 the earth opens its **mouth** and swallows them, with everything that
16:32 the earth opened its **mouth** and swallowed them, with their
20:24 because both of you rebelled against my **command** at the waters of
21:24 put him **to** [+4200] the sword and took over his land from the
22:18 or small to go beyond the **command** *of* the LORD my God.
22:28 the LORD opened the donkey's **mouth**, and she said to Balaam,
22:38 say just anything? I must speak only what God puts in my **mouth**."
23: 5 The LORD put a message in Balaam's **mouth** and said, "Go back
23:12 "Must I not speak what the LORD puts in my **mouth**?"
23:16 met with Balaam and put a message in his **mouth** and said,
24:13 good or bad, to go beyond the **command** *of* the LORD—
26:10 The earth opened its **mouth** and swallowed them along with
26:54 each is to receive its inheritance according to the **number** *of* those
26:56 Each inheritance is to be distributed **by** [+6584] lot among the
27:14 both of you disobeyed my **command** to honor me as holy before
27:21 At his **command** he and the entire community of the Israelites will
27:21 the Israelites will go out, and at his **command** they will come in."
30: 2 [30:3] his word but must do everything he **said** [+3655+4946].
32:24 for your flocks, but do what you have **promised** [+3655+4946]."
33: 2 At the LORD's **command** Moses recorded the stages in their
33:38 At the LORD's **command** Aaron the priest went up Mount Hor,
35: 8 to be given **in proportion to** [+3869] the inheritance of each tribe:
35:30 be put to death as a murderer only on the **testimony** *of* witnesses.
36: 5 at the LORD's **command** Moses gave this order to the Israelites:
Dt 1:26 you rebelled against the **command** *of* the LORD your God.
1:43 You rebelled against the LORD's **command** and in your
8: 3 but on every word that comes from the **mouth** *of* the LORD.
9:23 But you rebelled against the **command** *of* the LORD your God.
11: 6 when the earth opened its **mouth** right in the middle of all Israel
13:15 [13:16] you must certainly put **to** [+4200] the sword all who live
13:15 [13:16] it completely, both its people and its livestock. **[RPH]**
17: 6 On the **testimony** *of* two or three witnesses a man shall be put to
17: 6 no one shall be put to death on the **testimony** *of* only one witness.
17:10 You must act **according to** [+6584] the decisions they give you at
17:11 Act **according to** [+6584] the law they teach you and the decisions
18:18 I will put my words in his **mouth**, and he will tell them everything
19:15 A matter must be established by the **testimony** *of* two or three
19:15 be established by the testimony of two or **[RPH]** three witnesses.
20:13 it into your hand, put **to** [+4200] the sword all the men in it.
21: 5 and to **decide** [+2118+6584] all cases of dispute and assault.
21:17 wife as the firstborn by giving him a double **share** of all he has.
23:23 [23:24] freely to the LORD your God with your own **mouth**.
30:14 near you; it is in your **mouth** and in your heart so you may obey it.
31:19 and teach it to the Israelites and *have* them **sing** [+928+8492] it,
31:21 because it will not be forgotten **by** [+4946] their descendants.
32: 1 and I will speak; hear, O earth, the words of my **mouth**.
34: 5 servant of the LORD died there in Moab, as the LORD had **said**.
Jos 1: 8 Do not let this Book of the Law depart from your **mouth**;
1:18 Whoever rebels against your **word** and does not obey your words,
6:10 do not raise your voices, *do* not **say** [+3655+4946] a word until the
6:21 and destroyed **with** [+4200] the sword every living thing in it—
8:24 and when every one of them had been put **to** [+4200] the sword,
8:24 to Ai and **killed** [+906+2995+4200+5782] those who were in it.
9: 2 they came together to make war against Joshua and Israel. **[NIE]**
9:14 their provisions but *did* not **inquire of** [+906+8626] the LORD.
10:18 he said, "Roll large rocks up to the **mouth** *of* the cave, and post
10:22 "Open the **mouth** *of* the cave and bring those five kings out to
10:27 At the **mouth** *of* the cave they placed large rocks, which are there
10:28 He put the city and its king **to** [+4200] the sword and totally
10:30 The city and everyone in it Joshua put **to** [+4200] the sword.
10:32 The city and everyone in it he put **to** [+4200] the sword, just as he
10:35 They captured it that same day and put it **to** [+4200] the sword
10:37 They took the city and put it **to** [+4200] the sword, together with
10:39 its king and its villages, and put them **to** [+4200] the sword.
11:11 Everyone in it they put **to** [+4200] the sword. They totally
11:12 royal cities and their kings and put them **to** [+4200] the sword.
11:14 all the people they put **to** [+4200] the sword until they completely
15:13 In accordance with the LORD's **command** to him, Joshua gave to
17: 4 the brothers of their father, according to the LORD's **command**.
18: 4 a description of it, **according to** [+4200] the inheritance of each.
19:47 took it, put it **to** [+4200] the sword and occupied it.
19:50 as the LORD had **commanded**. They gave him the town he asked
21: 3 So, as the LORD had **commanded**, the Israelites gave the Levites
22: 9 which they had acquired in accordance with the **command** *of* the
Jdg 1: 8 took it. They put the city **to** [+4200] the sword and set it on fire.
1:25 and they put the city **to** [+4200] the sword but spared the man
3:16 Now Ehud had made a **double-edged** [+9109] sword about a foot
4:15 routed Sisera and all his chariots and army **by** [+4200] the sword,
4:16 All the troops of Sisera fell **by** [+4200] the sword; not a man was

Jdg 7: 6 Three hundred men lapped with their hands to their **mouths**.
9:38 Zebul said to him, "Where is your **big talk** now, you who said,
11:35 because I *have* **made a vow** [+7198] to the LORD that I cannot
11:36 "*you have* **given** your **word** [+906+7198] to the LORD.
11:36 Do to me just as you **promised** [+3655+4946], now that the LORD
18:19 answered him, "Be quiet! **Don't say** [+3338+6584+8492] **a word**.
18:27 They attacked them **with** [+4200] the sword and burned down their
20:37 spread out and put the whole city **to** [+4200] the sword.
20:48 went back to Benjamin and put all the towns **to** [+4200] the sword,
21:10 to Jabesh Gilead and put **to** [+4200] the sword those living there,
1Sa 1:12 As she kept on praying to the LORD, Eli observed her **mouth**.
2: 1 My **mouth** boasts over my enemies, for I delight in your
2: 3 keep talking so proudly or let your **mouth** speak such arrogance,
12:14 and serve and obey him and do not rebel against his **commands**,
12:15 if you rebel against his **commands**, his hand will be against you,
14:26 yet no one put his hand to his **mouth**, because they feared the oath.
14:27 He raised his hand to his **mouth**, and his eyes brightened.
15: 8 and all his people he totally destroyed **with** [+4200] the sword.
15:24 I violated the LORD's **command** and your instructions.
17:35 I went after it, struck it and rescued the sheep from its **mouth**.
22:19 He also put **to** [+4200] the sword Nob, the town of the priests,
22:19 its children and infants, and its cattle, donkeys and sheep. **[RPH]**
2Sa 1:16 Your own **mouth** testified against you when you said, 'I killed the
13:32 This has been Absalom's **expressed** [+6584] intention ever since
14: 3 speak these words to him." And Joab put the words in her **mouth**.
14:19 and who put all these words into the **mouth** *of* your servant.
15:14 and bring ruin upon us and put the city **to** [+4200] the sword."
17: 5 also Hushai the Arkite, so we can hear what he has to **say**."
18:25 The king said, "If he is alone, he must **have** [+928] good news."
22: 9 consuming fire came from his **mouth**, burning coals blazed out of
1Ki 7:31 On the inside of the stand there was an **opening** that had a circular
7:31 This **opening** was round, and with its basework it measured a cubit
7:31 a cubit and a half. Around its **opening** there was engraving.
8:15 what he promised with his own **mouth** to my father David.
8:24 with your **mouth** you have promised and with your hand you have
13:21 'You have defied the **word** *of* the LORD and have not kept the
13:26 "It is the man of God who defied the **word** *of* the LORD.
17: 1 dew nor rain in the next few years except **at** [+4200] my word."
17:24 and that the word of the LORD from your **mouth** is the truth."
19:18 bowed down to Baal and all whose **mouths** have not kissed him."
22:13 as one **man** the other prophets are predicting success for the king.
22:22 will go out and be a lying spirit in the **mouths** *of* all his prophets,'
22:23 "So now the LORD has put a lying spirit in the **mouths** *of* all
2Ki 2: 9 "Let me inherit a double **portion** of your spirit," Elisha replied.
4:34 lay upon the boy, **mouth** to mouth, eyes to eyes, hands to hands.
4:34 lay upon the boy, mouth to **mouth**, eyes to eyes, hands to hands.
10:21 crowded into the temple of Baal until it was full from *one* **end**
10:21 into the temple of Baal until it was full from one end to the **other**[s].
10:25 So they cut them down **with** [+4200] the sword. The guards
21:16 so much innocent blood that he filled Jerusalem from **end** to end—
21:16 so much innocent blood that he filled Jerusalem from end to **end**—
23:35 paid Pharaoh Neco the silver and gold he **demanded** [+6584].
24: 3 things happened to Judah according to the LORD's **command**,
1Ch 12:23 [12:24] turn Saul's kingdom over to him, as the LORD had **said**:
12:32 [12:33] 200 chiefs, with all their relatives under their **command**;
16:12 he has done, his miracles, and the judgments he **pronounced**,
2Ch 6: 4 who with his hands has fulfilled what he promised with his **mouth**
6:15 with your **mouth** you have promised and with your hand you have
18:12 as one **man** the other prophets are predicting success for the king.
18:21 " 'I will go and be a lying spirit in the **mouths** *of* all his prophets,'
18:22 "So now the LORD has put a lying spirit in the **mouths** *of* these
31: 2 each of them **according to** [+3869] their duties as priests
35:22 He would not listen to what Neco had said at God's **command**
36:12 the prophet, who **spoke the word** [+4946] *of* the LORD.
36:21 in fulfillment of the word of the LORD **spoken** by Jeremiah.
36:22 in order to fulfill the word of the LORD **spoken** by Jeremiah,
Ezr 1: 1 in order to fulfill the word of the LORD **spoken** by Jeremiah,
8:17 *I* **told** [+928+8492] them what to say to Iddo and his kinsmen,
9:11 they have filled it with their impurity from *one* **end** to the other.
9:11 they have filled it with their impurity from one end to the **other**[s].
Ne 9:20 You did not withhold your manna from their **mouths**, and you
Est 7: 8 As soon as the word left the king's **mouth**, they covered Haman's
Job 1:15 They put the servants **to** [+4200] the sword, and I am the only one
1:17 They put the servants **to** [+4200] the sword, and I am the only one
3: 1 After this, Job opened his **mouth** and cursed the day of his birth.
5:15 He saves the needy from the sword in their **mouth**; he saves them
5:16 So the poor have hope, and injustice shuts its **mouth**.
7:11 "Therefore I *will* not **keep silent** [+3104]; I will speak out in the
8: 2 you say such things? Your **words** [+609] are a blustering wind.
8:21 He will yet fill your **mouth** with laughter and your lips with shouts
9:20 Even if I were innocent, my **mouth** would condemn me; if I were
15: 5 Your sin prompts your **mouth**; you adopt the tongue of the crafty.
15: 6 Your own **mouth** condemns you, not mine; your own lips testify
15:13 your rage against God and pour out such words from your **mouth**?
15:30 his shoots, and the breath of God's **mouth** will carry him away.
16: 5 my **mouth** would encourage you; comfort from my lips would
16:10 Men open their **mouths** to jeer at me; they strike my cheek in scorn
19:16 but he does not answer, though I beg him with my own **mouth**.
20:12 "Though evil is sweet in his **mouth** and he hides it under his
21: 5 Look at me and be astonished; clap your hand over your **mouth**.
22:22 Accept instruction from his **mouth** and lay up his words in your
23: 4 state my case before him and fill my **mouth** with arguments.
23:12 I have treasured the words of his **mouth** more than my daily bread.
29: 9 from speaking and covered their **mouths** with their hands;
29:23 as for showers and **drank in** [+7196] my words as the spring rain.
30:18 like clothing to me; he binds me like the **neck** *of* my garment.
31:27 and my hand **offered** them **a kiss of homage** [+4200+5975],
32: 5 when he saw that the three men **had** [+928] nothing more to say,
33: 2 I am about to open my **mouth**; my words are on the tip of my
33: 6 I am **just like** [+3869] you before God; I too have been taken from
35:16 So Job opens his **mouth** with empty talk; without knowledge he
36:16 "He is wooing you from the **jaws** *of* distress to a spacious place
37: 2 the roar of his voice, to the rumbling that comes from his **mouth**.
39:27 Does the eagle soar at your **command** and build his nest on high?
40: 4 how can I reply to you? I put my hand over my **mouth**.
40:23 he is secure, though the Jordan should surge against his **mouth**.
41:19 [41:11] Firebrands stream from his **mouth**; sparks of fire shoot
41:21 [41:13] breath sets coals ablaze, and flames dart from his **mouth**.
Ps 5: 9 [5:10] Not a word from their **mouth** can be trusted; their heart is
8: 2 [8:3] From the **lips** *of* children and infants you have ordained
10: 7 His **mouth** is full of curses and lies and threats; trouble and evil are
17: 3 you will find nothing; I have resolved that my **mouth** will not sin.
17:10 up their callous hearts, and their **mouths** speak with arrogance.
18: 8 [18:9] consuming fire came from his **mouth**, burning coals blazed
19:14 [19:15] May the words of my **mouth** and the meditation of my
22:13 [22:14] Roaring lions tearing their prey open their **mouths** wide
22:21 [22:22] Rescue me from the **mouth** *of* the lions; save me from the
33: 6 the heavens made, their starry host by the breath of his **mouth**.
34: 1 [34:2] LORD at all times; his praise will always be on my **lips**.
35:21 *They* **gape** [+8143] at me and say, "Aha! Aha! With our own eyes
36: 3 [36:4] The words of his **mouth** are wicked and deceitful; he has
37:30 The **mouth** *of* the righteous man utters wisdom, and his tongue
38:13 [38:14] cannot hear, like a mute, who cannot open his **mouth**;
38:14 [38:15] man who does not hear, whose **mouth** can offer no reply.
39: 1 [39:2] I will put a muzzle on my **mouth** as long as the wicked are
39: 9 [39:10] I would not open my **mouth**, for you are the one who has
40: 3 [40:4] He put a new song in my **mouth**, a hymn of praise to our
49: 3 [49:4] My **mouth** will speak words of wisdom; the utterance from
49:13 [49:14] and of their followers, who approve their **sayings**.
50:16 right have you to recite my laws or take my covenant on your **lips**?
50:19 You use your **mouth** for evil and harness your tongue to deceit.
51:15 [51:17] open my lips, and my **mouth** will declare your praise.
54: 2 [54:4] Hear my prayer, O God; listen to the words of my **mouth**.
55:21 [55:22] His **speech** is smooth as butter, yet war is in his heart;
58: 6 [58:7] Break the teeth in their **mouths**, O God; tear out,
59: 7 [59:8] See what they spew from their **mouths**—they spew out
59:12 [59:13] For the sins of their **mouths**, for the words of their lips,
62: 4 [62:5] With their **mouths** they bless, but in their hearts they curse.
63: 5 [63:6] of foods; with singing lips my **mouth** will praise you.
63:11 [63:12] praise him, while the **mouths** *of* liars will be silenced.
66:14 my lips promised and my **mouth** spoke when I was in trouble.
66:17 I cried out to him with my **mouth**; his praise was on my tongue.
69:15 [69:16] depths swallow me up or the pit close its **mouth** over me.
71: 8 My **mouth** is filled with your praise, declaring your splendor all
71:15 My **mouth** will tell of your righteousness, of your salvation all day
73: 9 Their **mouths** lay claim to heaven, and their tongues take
78: 1 O my people, hear my teaching; listen to the words of my **mouth**.
78: 2 I will open my **mouth** in parables, I will utter hidden things,
78:30 from the food they craved, even while it was still in their **mouths**,
78:36 then they would flatter him with their **mouths**, lying to him with
81:10 [81:11] up out of Egypt. Open wide your **mouth** and I will fill it.
89: 1 [89:2] with my **mouth** I will make your faithfulness known
105: 5 he has done, his miracles, and the judgments he **pronounced**,
107:42 The upright see and rejoice, but all the wicked shut their **mouths**.
109: 2 and deceitful men have opened their **mouths** against me;
109: 2 and deceitful men have opened their mouths **[RPH]** against me;
109:30 With my **mouth** I will greatly extol the LORD; in the great
115: 5 They have **mouths**, but cannot speak, eyes, but they cannot see;
119:13 With my lips I recount all the laws that come from your **mouth**.
119:43 Do not snatch the word of truth from my **mouth**, for I have put my
119:72 The law from your **mouth** is more precious to me than thousands
119:88 according to your love, and I will obey the statutes of your **mouth**.
119:103 are your words to my taste, sweeter than honey to my **mouth**!
119:108 Accept, O LORD, the willing praise of my **mouth**, and teach me
119:131 I open my **mouth** and pant, longing for your commands.
126: 2 Our **mouths** were filled with laughter, our tongues with songs of
133: 2 down on Aaron's beard, down upon the **collar** *of* his robes.
135:16 They have **mouths**, but cannot speak, eyes, but they cannot see;

Ps 135:17 they have ears, but cannot hear, nor is there breath in their **mouths**.
138: 4 praise you, O LORD, when they hear the words of your **mouth**.
141: 3 Set a guard over my **mouth**, O LORD; keep watch over the door
141: 7 so our bones have been scattered at the **mouth** *of* the grave."
144: 8 whose **mouths** are full of lies, whose right hands are deceitful.
144:11 rescue me from the hands of foreigners whose **mouths** are full of
145:21 My **mouth** will speak in praise of the LORD. Let every creature
Pr 2: 6 and from his **mouth** come knowledge and understanding.
4: 5 do not forget my **words** [+609] or swerve from them.
4:24 Put away perversity from your **mouth**; keep corrupt talk far from
5: 4 but in the end she is bitter as gall, sharp as a **double-edged** sword.
5: 7 my sons, listen to me; do not turn aside from **what** I **say** [+609].
6: 2 if you have been trapped by **what** you **said** [+609], ensnared by the
6: 2 trapped by what you said, ensnared by the words of your **mouth**,
6:12 A scoundrel and villain, who goes about with a corrupt **mouth**,
7:24 my sons, listen to me; pay attention to **what** I **say** [+609].
8: 3 beside the gates **leading into** [+4200] the city, at the entrances,
8: 8 All the words of my **mouth** are just; none of them is crooked
8:13 I hate pride and arrogance, evil behavior and perverse **speech**.
8:29 sea its boundary so the waters would not overstep his **command**,
10: 6 the righteous, but violence overwhelms the **mouth** *of* the wicked.
10:11 The **mouth** *of* the righteous is a fountain of life, but violence
10:11 fountain of life, but violence overwhelms the **mouth** *of* the wicked.
10:14 men store up knowledge, but the **mouth** *of* a fool invites ruin.
10:31 The **mouth** *of* the righteous brings forth wisdom, but a perverse
10:32 what is fitting, but the **mouth** *of* the wicked only what is perverse.
11: 9 With his **mouth** the godless destroys his neighbor, but through
11:11 a city is exalted, but by the **mouth** *of* the wicked it is destroyed.
12: 6 lie in wait for blood, but the **speech** *of* the upright rescues them.
12: 8 A man is praised **according to** [+4200] his wisdom, but men with
12:14 From the fruit of his **lips** a man is filled with good things as surely
13: 2 From the fruit of his **lips** a man enjoys good things,
13: 3 He who guards his **lips** guards his life, but he who speaks rashly
14: 3 A fool's **talk** brings a rod to his back, but the lips of the wise
15: 2 commends knowledge, but the **mouth** *of* the fool gushes folly.
15:14 seeks knowledge, but the **mouth** [K 7156] *of* a fool feeds on folly.
15:23 A man finds joy in **giving an apt reply** [+5101]—and how good is
15:28 weighs its answers, but the **mouth** *of* the wicked gushes evil.
16:10 a king speak as an oracle, and his **mouth** should not betray justice.
16:23 A wise man's heart guides his **mouth**, and his lips promote
16:26 The laborer's appetite works for him; his **hunger** drives him on.
18: 4 The words of a man's **mouth** are deep waters, but the fountain of
18: 6 A fool's lips bring him strife, and his **mouth** invites a beating.
18: 7 A fool's **mouth** is his undoing, and his lips are a snare to his soul.
18:20 From the fruit of his **mouth** a man's stomach is filled;
19:24 his hand in the dish; he will not even bring it back to his **mouth**!
19:28 mocks at justice, and the **mouth** *of* the wicked gulps down evil.
20:17 tastes sweet to a man, but he ends up with a **mouth** full of gravel.
21:23 He who guards his **mouth** and his tongue keeps himself from
22: 6 Train a child **in the way** he **should go** [+2006+6584], and when he
22:14 The **mouth** *of* an adulteress is a deep pit; he who is under the
24: 7 in the assembly at the gate he *has* nothing *to* **say** [+7337].
26: 7 Like a lame man's legs that hang limp is a proverb in the **mouth** *of*
26: 9 Like a thornbush in a drunkard's hand is a proverb in the **mouth** *of*
26:15 his hand in the dish; he is too lazy to bring it back to his **mouth**.
26:28 tongue hates those it hurts, and a flattering **mouth** works ruin.
27: 2 Let another praise you, and not your own **mouth**; someone else,
27:21 for gold, but man is tested **by** [+4200] the praise he receives.
30:20 She eats and wipes her **mouth** and says, 'I've done nothing wrong.'
30:32 or if you have planned evil, clap your hand over your **mouth**!
31: 8 "**Speak** [+7337] **up** for those who cannot speak for themselves,
31: 9 **Speak** [+7337] **up** and judge fairly; defend the rights of the poor
31:26 She **speaks** [+7337] with wisdom, and faithful instruction is on her
Ecc 5: 2 [5:1] Do not be quick with your **mouth**, do not be hasty in your
5: 6 [5:5] Do not let your **mouth** lead you into sin. And do not protest
6: 7 All man's efforts are for his **mouth**, yet his appetite is never
8: 2 Obey the king's **command**, I say, because you took an oath before
10:12 Words from a wise man's **mouth** are gracious, but a fool is
10:13 At the beginning his **words** [+1821] are folly; at the end they are
10:13 his words are folly; at the end **[RPH]** they are wicked madness—
SS 1: 2 Let him kiss me with the kisses of his **mouth**—for your love is
Isa 1:20 devoured by the sword." For the **mouth** *of* the LORD has spoken.
5:14 the grave enlarges its appetite and opens its **mouth** without limit;
6: 7 With it he touched my **mouth** and said, "See, this has touched your
9:12 [9:11] from the west have devoured Israel with open **mouth**.
9:17 [9:16] is ungodly and wicked, every **mouth** speaks vileness.
10:14 not one flapped a wing, or opened its **mouth** to chirp.' "
11: 4 He will strike the earth with the rod of his **mouth**; with the breath
19: 7 also the plants along the Nile, at the **mouth** *of* the river. Every
29:13 "These people come near to me with their **mouth** and honor me
30: 2 who go down to Egypt without **consulting** [+8626] me; who look
34:16 For it is his **mouth** that has given the order, and his Spirit will
40: 5 together will see it. For the **mouth** *of* the LORD has spoken."
45:23 my **mouth** has uttered in all integrity a word that will not be
48: 3 long ago, my **mouth** announced them and I made them known;
49: 2 He made my **mouth** like a sharpened sword, in the shadow of his
51:16 I have put my words in your **mouth** and covered you with the
52:15 many nations, and kings will shut their **mouths** because of him.
53: 7 He was oppressed and afflicted, yet he did not open his **mouth**;
53: 7 a sheep before her shearers is silent, so he did not open his **mouth**.
53: 9 though he had done no violence, nor was any deceit in his **mouth**.
55:11 so is my word that goes out from my **mouth**: It will not return to
57: 4 At whom *do you* **sneer** [+8143] and stick out your tongue?
58:14 of your father Jacob." The **mouth** *of* the LORD has spoken.
59:21 my words that I have put in your **mouth** will not depart from your
59:21 that I have put in your mouth will not depart from your **mouth**,
59:21 or from the **mouths** *of* your children, or from the mouths of their
59:21 or from the **mouths** *of* their descendants from this time on
62: 2 you will be called by a new name that the **mouth** *of* the LORD
Jer 1: 9 reached out his hand and touched my **mouth** and said to me,
1: 9 and said to me, "Now, I have put my words in your **mouth**.
5:14 I will make my words in your **mouth** a fire and these people the
7:28 to correction. Truth has perished; it has vanished from their **lips**.
9: 8 [9:7] With his **mouth** each speaks cordially to his neighbor, but in
9:12 [9:11] Who *has been* **instructed by** [+448+1819] the LORD
9:20 [9:19] of the LORD; open your ears to the words of his **mouth**.
12: 2 bear fruit. You are always on their **lips** but far from their hearts.
15:19 not worthless, words, you will be my **spokesman** [+3869].
21: 7 He will put them **to** [+4200] the sword; he will show them no
23:16 visions from their own minds, not from the **mouth** *of* the LORD.
29:10 "**When** [+3954+4200] seventy years are completed for Babylon,
32: 4 will speak with him **face** to face and see him with his own eyes.
32: 4 will speak with him face to **face** and see him with his own eyes.
34: 3 with your own eyes, and he will speak with you **face** to face.
34: 3 with your own eyes, and he will speak with you face to **face**.
36: 4 while Jeremiah **dictated** [+4946] all the words the LORD had
36: 6 the words of the LORD that you wrote as I **dictated** [+4946].
36:17 did you come to write all this? Did Jeremiah **dictate** [+4946] it?"
36:18 Baruch replied, "he **dictated** [+906+4946+7924] all these words to
36:27 the words that Baruch had written *at* Jeremiah's **dictation** [+4946],
36:32 it to the scribe Baruch son of Neriah, and as Jeremiah **dictated**,
44:17 We will certainly do everything we **said** [+3655+4946] we would:
44:25 by your actions what you **promised** [+928+1819] when you said,
44:26 anywhere in Egypt *will* ever again **invoke** [+928+7924] my name
45: 1 written on a scroll the words Jeremiah was then **dictating** [+4946]:
48:28 in Moab. Be like a dove that makes its nest at the **mouth** *of* a cave.
51:44 **make** him **spew out** [+906+3655+4946] what he has swallowed.
La 1:18 "The LORD is righteous, yet I rebelled against his **command**.
2:16 All your enemies open their **mouths** wide against you; they scoff
3:29 Let him bury his **face** in the dust—there may yet be hope.
3:38 Is it not from the **mouth** *of* the Most High that both calamities
3:46 "All our enemies have opened their **mouths** wide against us.
Eze 2: 8 that rebellious house; open your **mouth** and eat what I give you."
3: 2 So I opened my **mouth**, and he gave me the scroll to eat.
3: 3 with it." So I ate it, and it tasted as sweet as honey in my **mouth**.
3:17 so hear the word I **speak** [+4946] and give them warning from me.
3:27 I speak to you, I will open your **mouth** and you shall say to them,
4:14 by wild animals. No unclean meat has ever entered my **mouth**."
16:56 You would not even **mention** [+928+9019] your sister Sodom in
16:63 will remember and be ashamed and never again open your **mouth**
21:22 [21:27] to **give** *the* **command** [+928+7337] to slaughter, to sound
24:27 At that time your **mouth** will be opened; you will speak with him
29:21 for the house of Israel, and I will open your **mouth** among them.
33: 7 so hear the word I **speak** [+4946] and give them warning from me.
33:22 he opened my **mouth** before the man came to me in the morning.
33:22 the morning. So my **mouth** was opened and I was no longer silent.
33:31 With their **mouths** they express devotion, but their hearts are
34:10 I will rescue my flock from their **mouths**, and it will no longer be
35:13 You **boasted** [+928+1540] against me and spoke against me
Da 10: 3 I ate no choice food; no meat or wine touched my **lips**; and I used
10:16 man touched my lips, and I opened my **mouth** and began to speak.
Hos 2:17 [2:19] I will remove the names of the Baals from her **lips**; no
6: 5 pieces with my prophets, I killed you with the words of my **mouth**;
10:12 Sow for yourselves righteousness, reap the **fruit** *of* unfailing love,
Joel 1: 5 because of the new wine, for it has been snatched from your **lips**.
Am 3:12 "As a shepherd saves from the lion's **mouth** only two leg bones
6: 5 You strum away **on** [+6584] your harps like David and improvise
Ob 1:12 nor **boast so much** [+1540+3870] in the day of their trouble.
Mic 3: 5 if he does not, **[RPH]** they prepare to wage war against him.
4: 4 make them afraid, for the LORD Almighty *has* **spoken** [+1819].
6:12 her people are liars and their tongues **speak** [+928] deceitfully.
7: 5 her who lies in your embrace be careful of your **words** [+7339].
7:16 They will lay their hands on their **mouths** and their ears will
Na 3:12 when they are shaken, the figs fall into the **mouth** *of* the eater.
Zep 3:13 they will speak no lies, nor will deceit be found in their **mouths**.
Zec 1:21 [2:4] scattered Judah **so that** [+3869] no one could raise his head,
5: 8 into the basket and pushed the lead cover down over its **mouth**.
8: 9 "You who now hear these words **spoken** by the prophets who were

Zec 9: 7 I will take the blood from their **mouths**, the forbidden food from
13: 8 declares the LORD, "**two-thirds** [+9109] will be struck down
14: 12 will rot in their sockets, and their tongues will rot in their **mouths**.
Mal 2: 6 True instruction was in his **mouth** and nothing false was found on
2: 7 and from his **mouth** men should seek instruction—
2: 9 **because** [+889+3869] you have not followed my ways but have

7024 פֹּה ***pōh***, adv.loc. [82] [→ 407, 686?]
here [43], on each side [+2256+4946+4946+7024] [20], on either side [+2256+4946+4946+7024] [8], *untranslated* [3], other[s] [2], side [2], square [+2256+4946+4946+7024] [2], arrives [+995] [1], this far [+6330] [1]

Ge 19: 12 The two men said to Lot, "Do you have anyone else **here**—
22: 5 "Stay **here** with the donkey while I and the boy go over there.
40: 15 even **here** I have done nothing to deserve being put in a dungeon."
Nu 22: 8 "Spend the night **here**," Balaam said to them, "and I will bring you
32: 6 "Shall your countrymen go to war while you sit **here**?
32: 16 "We would like to build pens **here** for our livestock and cities for
Dt 5: 3 this covenant, but with us, with all of us who are alive **here** today.
5: 31 you stay **here** with me so that I may give you all the commands,
12: 8 You are not to do as we do **here** today, everyone as he sees fit,
29: 15 [29:14] who are standing **here** with us today in the presence of
29: 15 [29:14] our God but also with those who are not **here** today.
Jos 18: 6 I will cast lots for you **[NIE]** in the presence of the LORD our
18: 8 I will cast lots for you **here** at Shiloh in the presence of the
Jdg 4: 20 "If someone comes by and asks you, 'Is anyone **here**?' say 'No.' "
18: 3 you here? What are you doing in this place? Why are you **here**?"
19: 9 Spend the night **here**; the day is nearly over. Stay and enjoy
Ru 4: 1 Boaz said, "Come over **here**, my friend, and sit down."
4: 2 Boaz took ten of the elders of the town and said, "Sit **here**,"
1Sa 16: 11 "Send for him; we will not sit down until he **arrives** [+995]."
21: 8 [21:9] "Don't you have a spear or a sword **here**?
23: 3 But David's men said to him, "**Here** in Judah we are afraid.
2Sa 20: 4 of Judah to come to me within three days, and be **here** yourself."
1Ki 2: 30 king says, 'Come out!' " But he answered, "No, I will die **here**."
19: 9 of the LORD came to him: "What are you doing **here**, Elijah?"
19: 13 Then a voice said to him, "What are you doing **here**, Elijah?"
22: 7 "Is there not a prophet of the LORD **here** whom we can inquire
2Ki 2: 2 Elijah said to Elisha, "Stay **here**; the LORD has sent me to
2: 4 Elijah said to him, "Stay **here**, Elisha; the LORD has sent me to
2: 6 Elijah said to him, "Stay **here**; the LORD has sent me to the
3: 11 But Jehoshaphat asked, "Is there no prophet of the LORD **here**,
3: 11 of the king of Israel answered, "Elisha son of Shaphat is **here**.
7: 3 the city gate. They said to each other, "Why stay **here** until we die?
7: 4 famine is there, and we will die. And if we stay **here**, we will die.
10: 23 and see that no servants of the LORD are **here** with you—
1Ch 29: 17 now I have seen with joy how willingly your people who are **here**
2Ch 18: 6 "Is there not a prophet of the LORD **here** whom we can inquire
Ezr 4: 2 the time of Esarhaddon king of Assyria, who brought us **here**."
Job 38: 11 when I said, '**This far** [+6330] you may come and no farther;
38: 11 may come and no farther; **here** is where your proud waves halt'?
Ps 132: 14 for ever and ever; **here** I will sit enthroned, for I have desired it—
Isa 22: 16 What are you doing **here** and who gave you permission to cut out a
22: 16 who gave you permission **[RPH]** to cut out a grave for yourself
22: 16 and who gave you permission to cut out a grave for yourself **here**,
52: 5 "And now what do I have **here**?" declares the LORD. "For my
Eze 8: 6 the utterly detestable things the house of Israel is doing **here**,
8: 9 and see the wicked and detestable things they are doing **here**."
8: 17 the house of Judah to do the detestable things they are doing **here**?
40: 10 gate were three alcoves **on each side** [+2256+4946+4946+7024];
40: 10 gate were three alcoves **on each side** [+2256+4946+4946+7024];
40: 10 the projecting walls **on each side** [+2256+4946+4946+7024] had
40: 10 the projecting walls **on each side** [+2256+4946+4946+7024] had
40: 12 one cubit high, **[RPH]** and the alcoves were six cubits square.
40: 12 the alcoves were six cubits **square** [+2256+4946+4946+7024].
40: 12 the alcoves were six cubits **square** [+2256+4946+4946+7024].
40: 21 Its alcoves—three **on each side** [+2256+4946+4946+7024]—its
40: 21 Its alcoves—three **on each side** [+2256+4946+4946+7024]—its
40: 26 of the projecting walls **on each side** [+2256+4946+4946+7024].
40: 26 of the projecting walls **on each side** [+2256+4946+4946+7024].
40: 34 decorated the jambs **on either side** [+2256+4946+4946+7024],
40: 34 decorated the jambs **on either side** [+2256+4946+4946+7024],
40: 37 decorated the jambs **on either side** [+2256+4946+4946+7024],
40: 37 decorated the jambs **on either side** [+2256+4946+4946+7024],
40: 39 gateway were two tables **on each side** [+2256+4946+4946+7024],
40: 39 gateway were two tables **on each side** [+2256+4946+4946+7024],
40: 41 So there were four tables on *one* **side** of the gateway and four on
40: 41 four tables on one side of the gateway and four on the **other**[s]—
40: 48 were five cubits wide **on either side** [+2256+4946+4946+7024].
40: 48 were five cubits wide **on either side** [+2256+4946+4946+7024].
40: 48 were three cubits wide **on either side** [+2256+4946+4946+7024].
40: 48 were three cubits wide **on either side** [+2256+4946+4946+7024].
40: 49 were pillars **on each side** [+2256+4946+4946+7024] of the jambs.
40: 49 were pillars **on each side** [+2256+4946+4946+7024] of the jambs.
41: 1 the jambs was six cubits **on each side** [+2256+4946+4946+7024].
41: 1 the jambs was six cubits **on each side** [+2256+4946+4946+7024].
41: 2 and the projecting walls **on each side** [+2256+4946+4946+7024]
41: 2 and the projecting walls **on each side** [+2256+4946+4946+7024]
41: 15 including its galleries **on each side** [+2256+4946+4946+7024];
41: 15 including its galleries **on each side** [+2256+4946+4946+7024];
41: 19 the face of a man toward the palm tree on one **side** and the face of
41: 19 one side and the face of a lion toward the palm tree on the **other**[s].
41: 26 with palm trees carved **on each side** [+2256+4946+4946+7024].
41: 26 with palm trees carved **on each side** [+2256+4946+4946+7024].

7025 פּוּאָה ***pû'â***, n.pr.m. [2 / 4] [→ 7026, 7027, 7030; cf. 7043]
Puah [4]

Ge 46: 13 sons of Issachar: Tola, **Puah**, [BHS 7030] Jashub and Shimron.
Nu 26: 23 the Tolaite clan; through **Puah**, [BHS 7026] the Puite clan;
Jdg 10: 1 of Issachar, Tola son of **Puah**, the son of Dodo, rose to save Israel.
1Ch 7: 1 sons of Issachar: Tola, **Puah**, Jashub and Shimron—four in all.

7026 פֻּוָּה ***puû'â***, n.pr.m. [1 / 0] [√ 7025]

Nu 26: 23 through Puah, [BHS ***Puvah***; NIV 7025] the Puite clan;

7027 פּוּאִי ***pû'î***, a.g. [0 / 1] [√ 7025]
Puite [1]

Nu 26: 23 the Tolaite clan; through Puah, the **Puite** [BHS 7043] clan;

7028 פּוּג ***pûg***, v. [4] [→ 2198, 7029]
feeble [1], paralyzed [1], stunned [+4213] [1], untiring [+4202] [1]

Ge 45: 26 [A] Jacob *was* **stunned** [+4213]; he did not believe them.
Ps 38: 8 [38:9] [C] *I am* **feeble** and utterly crushed; I groan in anguish of
77: 2 [77:3] [A] at night I stretched out **untiring** [+4202] hands
Hab 1: 4 [A] Therefore the law *is* **paralyzed**, and justice never prevails.

7029 פּוּגָה ***pûgâ***, n.f. [1] [√ 7028]
relief [1]

La 2: 18 a river day and night; give yourself no **relief**, your eyes no rest.

7030 פֻּוָּה ***puwwâ***, n.pr.m. [1 / 0] [√ 7025]

Ge 46: 13 The sons of Issachar: Tola, Puah, [BHS ***Puvah***; NIV 7025] Jashub

7031 פּוּחַ¹ ***pûaḥ***[1], v. [3] [→ 7086; cf. 5870, 7032]
breaks [2], blow [1]

SS 2: 17 [A] Until the day **breaks** and the shadows flee, turn, my lover,
4: 6 [A] Until the day **breaks** and the shadows flee, I will go to the
4: 16 [G] **Blow** *on* my garden, that its fragrance may spread abroad.

7032 פּוּחַ² ***pûaḥ***[2], v. [11] [cf. 3640, 7031?]
pours out [4], breathe out [1], gives [1], malign [1], sneers [1], speaks [1], stir up [1], witness [1]

Ps 10: 5 [G] and your laws are far from him; *he* **sneers** at all his enemies.
12: 5 [12:6] [G] "I will protect them from *those who* **malign** them."
Pr 6: 19 [G] a false witness *who* **pours out** lies and a man who stirs up
12: 17 [G] A truthful witness **gives** honest testimony, but a false witness
14: 5 [G] witness does not deceive, but a false witness **pours out** lies.
14: 25 [G] A truthful witness saves lives, but a false **witness** is deceitful.
19: 5 [G] go unpunished, and *he who* **pours out** lies will not go free.
19: 9 [G] not go unpunished, and *he who* **pours out** lies will perish.
29: 8 [G] Mockers **stir up** a city, but wise men turn away anger.
Eze 21: 31 [21:36] [G] and **breathe out** my fiery anger against you;
Hab 2: 3 [G] appointed time; *it* **speaks** of the end and will not prove false.

7033 פּוּט ***pûṭ***, n.pr.g. [7 / 8]
Put [7], Libyans [1]

Ge 10: 6 The sons of Ham: Cush, Mizraim, **Put** and Canaan.
1Ch 1: 8 The sons of Ham: Cush, Mizraim, **Put** and Canaan.
Isa 66: 19 to the **Libyans** [BHS 7039] and Lydians (famous as archers),
Jer 46: 9 men of Cush and **Put** who carry shields, men of Lydia who draw
Eze 27: 10 " 'Men of Persia, Lydia and **Put** served as soldiers in your army.
30: 5 Cush and **Put**, Lydia and all Arabia, Libya and the people of the
38: 5 Persia, Cush and **Put** will be with them, all with shields
Na 3: 9 were her boundless strength; **Put** and Libya were among her allies.

7034 פּוּטִיאֵל ***pûṭî'ēl***, n.pr.m. [1] [√ 446]
Putiel [1]

Ex 6: 25 Eleazar son of Aaron married one of the daughters of **Putiel**,

7035 פּוֹטִיפַר *pôṭîpar*, n.pr.m. [2] [cf. 7036]

Potiphar [2]

Ge 37:36 Meanwhile, the Midianites sold Joseph in Egypt to **Potiphar**,
39: 1 **Potiphar**, an Egyptian who was one of Pharaoh's officials,

7036 פּוֹטִי פֶרַע *pôṭî pera'*, n.pr.m. [3] [cf. 7280]

Potiphera [3]

Ge 41:45 and gave him Asenath daughter of **Potiphera**,
41:50 two sons were born to Joseph by Asenath daughter of **Potiphera**,
46:20 Ephraim were born to Joseph by Asenath daughter of **Potiphera**,

7037 פּוּךְ *pûk*, n.[m.]. [4]

turquoise [2], paint [1], painted [+928+2021+8531] [1]

2Ki 9:30 Jezebel heard about it, *she* **painted** [+928+2021+8531] her eyes,
1Ch 29: 2 **turquoise**, stones of various colors, and all kinds of fine stone
Isa 54:11 and not comforted, I will build you with stones of **turquoise**,
Jer 4:30 and put on jewels of gold? Why shade your eyes with **paint**?

7038 פּוֹל *pôl*, n.[m.]col. [2]

beans [2]

2Sa 17:28 and barley, flour and roasted grain, **beans** and lentils,
Eze 4: 9 "Take wheat and barley, **beans** and lentils, millet and spelt;

7039 פּוּל¹ *pûl¹*, n.pr.loc.?. [1 / 0]

Isa 66:19 to Tarshish, to the Libyans [BHS ***Pul***; NIV 7033] and Lydians

7040 פּוּל² *pûl²*, n.pr.m. [3] [√ 7189; cf. 7188]

Pul [2], him[s] [1]

2Ki 15:19 **Pul** king of Assyria invaded the land, and Menahem gave him a
15:19 Menahem gave **him**[s] a thousand talents of silver to gain his
1Ch 5:26 So the God of Israel stirred up the spirit of **Pul** king of Assyria

7041 פּוּן *pûn*, v. [1] [→ 687]

in despair [1]

Ps 88:15 [88:16] [A] I have suffered your terrors and *am* **in despair**.

7042 פּוֹנֶה *pôneh*, n.f. [1 / 0] [cf. 7157]

2Ch 25:23 the Ephraim Gate to the Corner [BHS ***Facing*** ?; NIV 7157] Gate—

7043 פּוּנִי *pûnî*, a.g. [1 / 0] [cf. 7025]

Nu 26:23 through Puah, the Puite [BHS ***Punite***; NIV 7027] clan;

7044 פּוּנֹן *pûnōn*, n.pr.loc. [2] [cf. 7091]

Punon [2]

Nu 33:42 They left Zalmonah and camped at **Punon**.
33:43 They left **Punon** and camped at Oboth.

7045 פּוּעָה *pû'â*, n.pr.f. [1]

Puah [1]

Ex 1:15 to the Hebrew midwives, whose names were Shiphrah and **Puah**,

7046 פּוּץ¹ *pûṣ¹*, v. [65] [→ 5138, 9518; cf. 5879, 7207, 7047]

scattered [21], scatter [11], disperse [7], were scattered [5], been scattered [4], dispersed [2], overflow [2], attacker [1], be scattered [1], blow away [1], dog [1], driven [1], go out [1], is scattered [1], scattering [1], scatters [1], separated [1], sow [1], spread out [1], unleash [1]

Ge 10:18 [C] and Hamathites. Later the Canaanite clans **scattered**
11: 4 [A] and not *be* **scattered** over the face of the whole earth."
11: 8 [G] So the LORD **scattered** them from there over all the earth,
11: 9 [G] From there the LORD **scattered** them over the face of the
49: 7 [G] I will scatter them in Jacob and **disperse** them in Israel.
Ex 5:12 [G] So the people **scattered** all over Egypt to gather stubble to
Nu 10:35 [A] *May* your enemies *be* **scattered**; may your foes flee before
Dt 4:27 [G] The LORD *will* **scatter** you among the peoples, and only a
28:64 [G] the LORD *will* **scatter** you among all nations, from one end
30: 3 [G] gather you again from all the nations where he **scattered**
1Sa 11:11 [A] Those who survived *were* **scattered**, so that no two of them
13: 8 [G] did not come to Gilgal, and Saul's men *began to* **scatter**.
14:34 [A] he said, "**Go out** among the men and tell them, 'Each of you
2Sa 18: 8 [C] The battle **spread out** over the whole countryside,
20:22 [A] his men **dispersed** from the city, each returning to his home.
22:15 [G] He shot arrows and **scattered** ⌞the enemies⌟, bolts of
1Ki 22:17 [C] "I saw all Israel **scattered** on the hills like sheep without a
2Ki 25: 5 [C] All his soldiers **were** separated from him and **scattered**,
2Ch 18:16 [C] "I saw all Israel **scattered** on the hills like sheep without a
Ne 1: 8 [G] 'If you are unfaithful, I *will* **scatter** you among the nations,
Job 18:11 [G] Terrors startle him on every side and **dog** his every step.
37:11 [G] with moisture; *he* **scatters** his lightning *through* them.
38:24 [G] or the place where the east winds *are* **scattered** over the
40:11 [G] **Unleash** the fury of your wrath, look at every proud man
Ps 18:14 [18:15] [G] He shot his arrows and **scattered** ⌞the enemies⌟,
68: 1 [68:2] [A] May God arise, *may* his enemies *be* **scattered**; may
144: 6 [G] Send forth lightning and **scatter** ⌞the enemies⌟; shoot your
Pr 5:16 [A] *Should* your springs **overflow** in the streets, your streams of
Isa 11:12 [C] he will assemble the **scattered** *people of* Judah from the four
24: 1 [G] devastate it; he will ruin its face and **scatter** its inhabitants—
28:25 [G] the surface, *does he* not **sow** caraway and scatter cummin?
41:16 [G] the wind will pick them up, and a gale *will* **blow** them **away**.
Jer 9:16 [9:15] [G] *I will* **scatter** them among nations that neither they
10:21 [C] so they do not prosper and all their flock **is scattered.**
13:24 [G] "*I will* **scatter** you like chaff driven by the desert wind.
18:17 [G] wind from the east, *I will* **scatter** them before their enemies;
23: 1 [G] who are destroying and **scattering** the sheep of my pasture!"
23: 2 [G] "Because you *have* **scattered** my flock and driven them
30:11 [G] destroy all the nations among which *I* **scatter** you,
40:15 [C] *cause* all the Jews who are gathered around you *to* **be scattered**
52: 8 [C] All his soldiers **were** separated from him and **scattered**,
Eze 11:16 [G] among the nations and **scattered** them among the countries,
11:17 [C] you back from the countries where *you have* **been scattered**,
12:15 [G] when I **disperse** them among the nations and scatter them
20:23 [G] in the desert that I *would* **disperse** them among the nations
20:34 [C] you from the countries where *you have* **been scattered**—
20:41 [C] you from the countries where *you have* **been scattered**,
22:15 [G] *I will* **disperse** you among the nations and scatter you
28:25 [C] of Israel from the nations where *they have* **been scattered**,
29:12 [G] *I will* **disperse** the Egyptians among the nations and scatter
29:13 [C] the Egyptians from the nations where *they* **were scattered**.
30:23 [G] *I will* **disperse** the Egyptians among the nations and scatter
30:26 [G] *I will* **disperse** the Egyptians among the nations and scatter
34: 5 [A] So *they were* **scattered** because there was no shepherd,
34: 5 [A] when *they were* **scattered** they became food for all the wild
34: 6 [C] They **were scattered** over the whole earth, and no one
34:12 [C] all the places where *they* **were scattered** on a day of clouds
34:21 [G] sheep with your horns until *you have* **driven** them away,
36:19 [G] *I* **dispersed** them among the nations, and they were scattered
46:18 [A] so that none of my people *will be* **separated** from his
Na 2: 1 [2:2] [G] An **attacker** advances against you, ⌞Nineveh⌟.
Hab 3:14 [G] pierced his head when his warriors stormed out to **scatter** us,
Zep 3:10 [B] my worshipers, my **scattered** people, will bring me offerings.
Zec 1:17 [A] 'My towns *will* again **overflow** with prosperity,
13: 7 [A] "Strike the shepherd, and the sheep *will be* **scattered**, and I

7047 פּוּץ² *pûṣ²*, v. Not used in NIV/BHS [cf. 7046]

7048 פּוּק¹ *pûq¹*, v. [2] [→ 7050,; cf. 7049, 7211]

stumble [1], totter [1]

Isa 28: 7 [A] seeing visions, *they* **stumble** when rendering decisions.
Jer 10: 4 [G] they fasten it with hammer and nails so *it will* not **totter**.

7049 פּוּק² *pûq²*, v. [7] [cf. 7048]

receives [2], gains [1], let succeed [1], obtains [1], provision [1], spend [1]

Ps 140: 8 [140:9] [G] *do* not **let** their plans **succeed**, or they will become
144:13 [G] Our barns will be filled with every kind of **provision**.
Pr 3:13 [G] man who finds wisdom, the man *who* **gains** understanding,
8:35 [G] finds me finds life and **receives** favor from the LORD.
12: 2 [G] A good man **obtains** favor from the LORD, but the LORD
18:22 [G] wife finds what is good and **receives** favor from the LORD.
Isa 58:10 [G] if *you* **spend** yourselves in behalf of the hungry and satisfy

7050 פּוּקָה *pûqâ*, n.f. [1] [√ 7048]

staggering burden [+2256+4842] [1]

1Sa 25:31 have on his conscience the **staggering** [+2256+4842] **burden** of

7051 פּוּר¹ *pûr¹*, v. Not used in NIV/BHS [cf. 7296]

7052 פּוּר² *pûr²*, n.m. [8]

Purim [5], pur [3]

Est 3: 7 the month of Nisan, they cast the ***pur*** (that is, the lot)
9:24 against the Jews to destroy them and had cast the ***pur*** (that is,
9:26 (Therefore these days were called **Purim**, from the word *pur*.)
9:26 (Therefore these days were called Purim, from the word ***pur***.)
9:28 these days of **Purim** should never cease to be celebrated by the
9:29 with full authority to confirm this second letter concerning **Purim**.
9:31 to establish these days of **Purim** at their designated times,
9:32 Esther's decree confirmed these regulations about **Purim**,

7053 פּוּרָה **pûrâ**, n.f. [2]

measures [1], winepress [1]

Isa 63: 3 "I have trodden the **winepress** alone; from the nations no one was
Hag 2: 16 When anyone went to a wine vat to draw fifty **measures**, there

7054 פּוֹרָתָא **pôrātā'**, n.pr.m. [1]

Poratha [1]

Est 9: 8 **Poratha**, Adalia, Aridatha,

7055 ¹פּוּשׁ **pûš¹**, v. [3]

frolic [1], gallops headlong [1], leap [1]

Jer 50: 11 [A] because *you* **frolic** like a heifer threshing grain and neigh
Hab 1: 8 [A] Their cavalry **gallops headlong**; their horsemen come from
Mal 4: 2 [3:20] [A] go out and **leap** like calves released from the stall.

7056 ²פּוּשׁ **pûš²**, v. [1]

scattered [1]

Na 3: 18 [C] Your people *are* **scattered** on the mountains with no one to

7057 פּוּתִי **pûtî**, a.g. [1]

Puthites [1]

1Ch 2: 53 Kiriath Jearim: the Ithrites, **Puthites**, Shumathites and Mishraites.

7058 פַּז **paz**, n.m. [9] [→ 502, 7059]

pure gold [5], gold [2], fine gold [1], purest gold [+4188] [1]

Job 28: 17 crystal can compare with it, nor can it be had for jewels of **gold**.
Ps 19: 10 [19:11] They are more precious than gold, than much **pure gold**;
21: 3 [21:4] and placed a crown of **pure gold** on his head.
119: 127 I love your commands more than gold, more than **pure gold**,
Pr 8: 19 My fruit is better than **fine gold**; what I yield surpasses choice
SS 5: 11 His head is **purest gold** [+4188]; his hair is wavy and black as a
5: 15 His legs are pillars of marble set on bases of **pure gold**.
Isa 13: 12 I will make man scarcer than **pure gold**, more rare than the gold of
La 4: 2 How the precious sons of Zion, once worth their weight in **gold**,

7059 ¹פָּזַז **pāzaz¹**, v. [1] [√ 7058]

fine [1]

1Ki 10: 18 [H] a great throne inlaid with ivory and overlaid with **fine** gold.

7060 ²פָּזַז **pāzaz²**, v. [2]

leaping [1], limber [1]

Ge 49: 24 [A] But his bow remained steady, his strong arms *stayed* **limber**,
2Sa 6: 16 [D] when she saw King David **leaping** and dancing before the

7061 פָּזַר **pāzar**, v. [10] [cf. 1029]

scattered [5], been scattered [1], dispersed [1], gives freely [1], scattered abroad [1], scatters [1]

Est 3: 8 [E] "There is a certain people **dispersed** and scattered among the
Ps 53: 5 [53:6] [D] God **scattered** the bones of those who attacked you;
89: 10 [89:11] [D] with your strong arm *you* **scattered** your enemies.
112: 9 [D] *He has* **scattered abroad** his gifts to the poor,
141: 7 [C] so our bones *have* **been scattered** at the mouth of the grave."
147: 16 [D] spreads the snow like wool and **scatters** the frost like ashes.
Pr 11: 24 [D] *One man* **gives freely**, yet gains even more; another
Jer 3: 13 [D] *you have* **scattered** your favors to foreign gods under every
50: 17 [B] "Israel is a **scattered** flock that lions have chased away.
Joel 3: 2 [4:2] [D] for *they* **scattered** my people among the nations

7062 ¹פַּח **paḥ¹**, n.m. [25 / 24] [→ 7072]

snare [14], snares [5], trap [4], snares [+3687] [1]

Jos 23: 13 Instead, they will become **snares** and traps for you, whips on your
Job 18: 9 A **trap** seizes him by the heel; a snare holds him fast.
22: 10 That is why **snares** are all around you, why sudden peril terrifies
Ps 11: 6 On the wicked he will rain fiery coals [BHS *snares*; NIV 7073]
69: 22 [69:23] May the table set before them become a **snare**; may it
91: 3 Surely he will save you from the fowler's **snare** and from the
119: 110 The wicked have set a **snare** for me, but I have not strayed from
124: 7 We have escaped like a bird out of the fowler's **snare**; the snare
124: 7 fowler's snare; the **snare** has been broken, and we have escaped.
140: 5 [140:6] Proud men have hidden a **snare** for me; they have spread
141: 9 Keep me from the **snares** they have laid for me, from the traps set
142: 3 [142:4] In the path where I walk men have hidden a **snare** for me.
Pr 7: 23 till an arrow pierces his liver, like a bird darting into a **snare**,
22: 5 In the paths of the wicked lie thorns and **snares**, but he who guards
Ecc 9: 12 As fish are caught in a cruel net, or birds are taken in a **snare**,
Isa 8: 14 And for the people of Jerusalem he will be a **trap** and a snare.
24: 17 Terror and pit and **snare** await you, O people of the earth.
24: 18 into a pit; whoever climbs out of the pit will be caught in a **snare**.
Jer 18: 22 have dug a pit to capture me and have hidden **snares** for my feet.
48: 43 Terror and pit and **snare** await you, O people of Moab,"
48: 44 into a pit, whoever climbs out of the pit will be caught in a **snare**;
Hos 5: 1 You have been a **snare** at Mizpah, a net spread out on Tabor.
9: 8 over Ephraim, yet **snares** [+3687] await him on all his paths,
Am 3: 5 Does a bird fall into a **trap** *on* the ground where no snare has been
3: 5 Does a **trap** spring up from the earth when there is nothing to

7063 ²פַּח **paḥ²**, n.[m.] [2]

sheets [1], thin sheets [1]

Ex 39: 3 They hammered out **thin sheets** *of* gold and cut strands to be
Nu 16: 38 [17:3] Hammer the censers into **sheets** to overlay the altar,

7064 פָּחַד **pāḥad**, v. [25] [→ 7065, 7067]

afraid [3], fear [2], overwhelmed with dread [+7065] [2], terrified [2], brought down to terror [1], come trembling [1], feared [1], fears [1], fill [1], filled with dread [1], in awe [1], live in terror [1], looked in fear [1], made shake [1], showed fear [1], throb [1], tremble [1], trembles [1], turn in fear [1], unafraid [+4202] [1]

Dt 28: 66 [A] **filled with dread** both night and day, never sure of your life.
28: 67 [A] because of the terror that *will* **fill** your hearts and the sights
Job 3: 25 [A] What *I* **feared** has come upon me; what I dreaded has
4: 14 [G] fear and trembling seized me and **made** all my bones **shake**.
23: 15 [A] I am terrified before him; when I think of all this, *I* **fear** him.
Ps 14: 5 [A] There they are, **overwhelmed with dread** [+7065], for God
27: 1 [A] is the stronghold of my life—of whom *shall I be* **afraid**?
53: 5 [53:6] [A] There they were, **overwhelmed with dread** [+7065],
78: 53 [A] He guided them safely, so *they were* **unafraid** [+4202];
119: 161 [A] me without cause, but my heart **trembles** at your word.
Pr 3: 24 [A] when you lie down, *you will* not *be* **afraid**; when you lie
28: 14 [D] Blessed is the man *who* always **fears** the LORD, but he
Isa 12: 2 [A] Surely God is my salvation; I will trust and not *be* **afraid**.
19: 16 [A] They will shudder *with* **fear** at the uplifted hand that the
19: 17 [A] everyone to whom Judah is mentioned *will be* **terrified**,
33: 14 [A] The sinners in Zion *are* **terrified**; trembling grips the
44: 8 [A] *Do* not **tremble**, do not be afraid. Did I not proclaim this and
44: 11 [A] *they will be* **brought down to terror** and infamy.
51: 13 [D] that *you* **live in** constant **terror** every day because of the
60: 5 [A] and be radiant, your heart *will* **throb** and swell with joy;
Jer 33: 9 [A] *they will be* **in awe** and will tremble at the abundant
36: 16 [A] *they* **looked** at each other **in fear** and said to Baruch,
36: 24 [A] all his attendants who heard all these words **showed** no **fear**,
Hos 3: 5 [A] *They will* **come trembling** to the LORD and to his
Mic 7: 17 [A] *they will* **turn in fear** to the LORD our God and will be

7065 ¹פַּחַד **paḥad¹**, n.m. [49] [√ 7064; cf. 7524]

fear [14], terror [13], dread [8], calamity [2], overwhelmed with dread [+7064] [2], afraid [+5877+6584] [1], awe [1], cares [1], disaster [1], dreaded [1], peril [1], terrifying [1], terrors [1], threat [1], what[s] [1]

Ge 31: 42 the God of Abraham and the **Fear** *of* Isaac, had not been with me,
31: 53 So Jacob took an oath in the name of the **Fear** *of* his father Isaac.
Ex 15: 16 terror and **dread** will fall upon them. By the power of your arm
Dt 2: 25 This very day I will begin to put the **terror** and fear of you on all
11: 25 will put the **terror** and fear of you on the whole land,
28: 67 because of the **terror** that will fill your hearts and the sights that
1Sa 11: 7 the **terror** *of* the LORD fell on the people, and they turned out as
1Ch 14: 17 every land, and the LORD made all the nations **fear** him.
2Ch 14: 14 [14:13] for the **terror** *of* the LORD had fallen upon them.
17: 10 The **fear** *of* the LORD fell on all the kingdoms of the lands
19: 7 Now let the **fear** *of* the LORD be upon you. Judge carefully,
20: 29 The **fear** *of* God came upon all the kingdoms of the countries when
Est 8: 17 became Jews because **fear** *of* the Jews had seized them.
9: 2 of all the other nationalities *were* **afraid** [+5877+6584] *of* them.
9: 3 helped the Jews, because **fear** *of* Mordecai had seized them.
Job 3: 25 **What**[s] I feared has come upon me; what I dreaded has happened to
4: 14 **fear** and trembling seized me and made all my bones shake.
13: 11 his splendor terrify you? Would not the **dread** *of* him fall on you?
15: 21 **Terrifying** sounds fill his ears; when all seems well,
21: 9 Their homes are safe and free from **fear**; the rod of God is not
22: 10 is why snares are all around you, why sudden **peril** terrifies you,
25: 2 "Dominion and **awe** belong to God; he establishes order in the
31: 23 For I **dreaded** destruction from God, and for fear of his splendor I
39: 16 as if they were not hers; she **cares** not that her labor was in vain,
39: 22 He laughs at **fear**, afraid of nothing; he does not shy away from the
Ps 14: 5 There they are, **overwhelmed with dread** [+7064], for God is
31: 11 [31:12] contempt of my neighbors; I am a **dread** to my friends—
36: 1 [36:2] of the wicked: There is no **fear** *of* God before his eyes.
53: 5 [53:6] There they were, **overwhelmed with dread** [+7064],
53: 5 [53:6] with dread, where there was nothing to **dread**.

[F] Hitpael (hitpoel, hitpoal, hitpolel, hitpolal, hitpalel, hitpalal, hitpalpel, hitpalpal, hotpael, hotpaal) [G] Hiphil (hiphtil) [H] Hophal [I] Hishtaphel

Ps 64: 1 [64:2] protect my life from the **threat** *of* the enemy.
91: 5 You will not fear the **terror** *of* night, nor the arrow that flies by
105: 38 glad when they left, because **dread** *of* Israel had fallen on them.
119: 120 My flesh trembles in **fear** *of* you; I stand in awe of your laws.
Pr 1: 26 laugh at your disaster; I will mock when **calamity** overtakes you—
1: 27 when **calamity** overtakes you like a storm, when disaster sweeps
1: 33 to me will live in safety and be at ease, without **fear** *of* harm."
3: 25 Have no fear of sudden **disaster** or of the ruin that overtakes the
SS 3: 8 with his sword at his side, prepared for the **terrors** of the night.
Isa 2: 10 hide in the ground from **dread** *of* the LORD and the splendor of
2: 19 to holes in the ground from **dread** *of* the LORD and the splendor
2: 21 to the overhanging crags from **dread** *of* the LORD and the
24: 17 **Terror** and pit and snare await you, O people of the earth.
24: 18 Whoever flees at the sound of **terror** will fall into a pit; whoever
Jer 30: 5 the LORD says: " 'Cries of fear are heard—**terror**, not peace.
48: 43 **Terror** and pit and snare await you, O people of Moab,"
48: 44 "Whoever flees from the **terror** will fall into a pit, whoever climbs
49: 5 I will bring **terror** on you from all those around you,"
La 3: 47 We have suffered **terror** and pitfalls, ruin and destruction."

7066 ²פַּחַד ***paḥad²***, n.[m.]. [1]

thighs [1]

Job 40: 17 His tail sways like a cedar; the sinews of his **thighs** are close-knit.

7067 פַּחְדָּה ***paḥdâ***, n.f. [1] [√ 7064]

awe [1]

Jer 2: 19 when you forsake the LORD your God and have no **awe** *of* me,"

7068 פֶּחָה ***peḥâ***, n.m. [28] [→ 7075?; Ar 10580]

governors [15], governor [10], officer [2], officers [1]

1Ki 10: 15 and from all the Arabian kings and the **governors** *of* the land.
20: 24 kings from their commands and replace them with *other* **officers**.
2Ki 18: 24 How can you repulse one **officer** *of* the least of my master's
2Ch 9: 14 and the **governors** *of* the land brought gold and silver to Solomon.
Ezr 8: 36 to the royal satraps and to the **governors** *of* Trans-Euphrates,
Ne 2: 7 the king, may I have letters to the **governors** *of* Trans-Euphrates,
2: 9 So I went to the **governors** *of* Trans-Euphrates and gave them the
3: 7 places under the authority of the **governor** *of* Trans-Euphrates.
5: 14 when I was appointed to be their **governor** in the land of Judah,
5: 14 neither I nor my brothers ate the food allotted to the **governor**.
5: 15 the earlier **governors**—those preceding me—placed a heavy
5: 18 of all this, I never demanded the food allotted to the **governor**,
12: 26 and in the days of Nehemiah the **governor** and of Ezra the priest
Est 3: 12 the **governors** of the various provinces and the nobles of the
8: 9 **governors** and nobles of the 127 provinces stretching from India to
9: 3 the **governors** and the king's administrators helped the Jews,
Isa 36: 9 can you repulse one **officer** *of* the least *of* my master's officials,
Jer 51: 23 shatter farmer and oxen, with you I shatter **governors** and officials.
51: 28 the kings of the Medes, their **governors** and all their officials,
51: 57 and wise men drunk, her **governors**, officers and warriors as well;
Eze 23: 6 clothed in blue, **governors** and commanders, all of them handsome
23: 12 **governors** and commanders, warriors in full dress,
23: 23 all of them **governors** and commanders, chariot officers and men
Hag 1: 1 **governor** *of* Judah, and to Joshua son of Jehozadak, the high
1: 14 **governor** *of* Judah, and the spirit of Joshua son of Jehozadak,
2: 2 **governor** *of* Judah, to Joshua son of Jehozadak, the high priest,
2: 21 "Tell Zerubbabel **governor** *of* Judah that I will shake the heavens
Mal 1: 8 is that not wrong? Try offering them to your **governor**!

7069 פָּחַז ***pāḥaz***, v. [2] [→ 7070, 7071]

adventurers [1], arrogant [1]

Jdg 9: 4 [A] Abimelech used it to hire reckless **adventurers**, who became
Zep 3: 4 [A] Her prophets *are* **arrogant**; they are treacherous men.

7070 פַּחַז ***paḥaz***, n.[m.]. [1] [√ 7069]

turbulent [1]

Ge 49: 4 **Turbulent** as the waters, you will no longer excel, for you went up

7071 פַּחֲזוּת ***paḥᵃzût***, n.f. [1] [√ 7069]

reckless [1]

Jer 23: 32 "They tell them and lead my people astray with their **reckless** lies,

7072 פָּחַח ***pāḥaḥ***, v.den. [1] [√ 7062]

trapped [1]

Isa 42: 22 [H] all of them **trapped** in pits or hidden away in prisons.

7073 פֶּחָם ***peḥām***, n.[m.]. [3 / 4]

coals [3], charcoal [1]

Ps 11: 6 On the wicked he will rain fiery **coals** [BHS 7062] and burning
Pr 26: 21 As **charcoal** to embers and as wood to fire, so is a quarrelsome
Isa 44: 12 The blacksmith takes a tool and works with it in the **coals**;
54: 16 it is I who created the blacksmith who fans the **coals** into flame

7074 פַּחַת ***paḥat***, n.m. [10] [→ 7076]

pit [7], cave [2], pitfalls [1]

2Sa 17: 9 Even now, he is hidden in a **cave** or some other place. If he should
18: 17 threw him into a big **pit** in the forest and piled up a large heap of
Isa 24: 17 Terror and **pit** and snare await you, O people of the earth.
24: 18 Whoever flees at the sound of terror will fall into a **pit**; whoever
24: 18 into a pit; whoever climbs out of the **pit** will be caught in a snare.
Jer 48: 28 in Moab. Be like a dove that makes its nest at the mouth of a **cave**.
48: 43 Terror and **pit** and snare await you, O people of Moab,"
48: 44 "Whoever flees from the terror will fall into a **pit**, whoever climbs
48: 44 into a pit, whoever climbs out of the **pit** will be caught in a snare;
La 3: 47 We have suffered terror and **pitfalls**, ruin and destruction."

7075 פַּחַת מוֹאָב ***paḥat mô'āb***, n.pr.m. [6] [√ 7068? + 4565]

Pahath-Moab [6]

Ezr 2: 6 of **Pahath-Moab** (through the line of Jeshua and Joab) 2,812
8: 4 of the descendants of **Pahath-Moab**, Eliehoenai son of Zerahiah,
10: 30 From the descendants of **Pahath-Moab**: Adna, Kelal, Benaiah,
Ne 3: 11 and Hasshub son of **Pahath-Moab** repaired another section
7: 11 of **Pahath-Moab** (through the line of Jeshua and Joab) 2,818
10: 14 [10:15] of the people: Parosh, **Pahath-Moab**, Elam, Zattu, Bani,

7076 פְּחֶתֶת ***pᵉḥetet***, n.m. [1] [√ 7074]

mildew [1]

Lev 13: 55 it with fire, whether the **mildew** has affected one side or the other.

7077 פִּטְדָה ***piṭdâ***, n.f. [*or* m.?]. [4]

topaz [4]

Ex 28: 17 on it. In the first row there shall be a ruby, a **topaz** and a beryl;
39: 10 stones on it. In the first row there was a ruby, a **topaz** and a beryl;
Job 28: 19 The **topaz** *of* Cush cannot compare with it; it cannot be bought
Eze 28: 13 ruby, **topaz** and emerald, chrysolite, onyx and jasper, sapphire,

7078 פְּטִירִים ***pᵉṭîrîm***, var. [0] [√ 7080]

1Ch 9: 33 [b] [and **were exempt** [K; see Q 7080] **from** *other* **duties**]

7079 פַּטִּישׁ ***paṭṭîš***, n.m. [3]

hammer [3]

Isa 41: 7 he who smooths with the **hammer** spurs on him who strikes the
Jer 23: 29 the LORD, "and like a **hammer** that breaks a rock in pieces?
50: 23 How broken and shattered is the **hammer** *of* the whole earth!

7080 פָּטַר ***pāṭar***, v. [9] [→ 7078, 7081, 7082]

open [4], breaching [1], eluded [1], hurl insults [+928+8557] [1], released [1], were exempt from duties [1]

1Sa 19: 10 [A] but David **eluded** him as Saul drove the spear into the wall.
1Ki 6: 18 [B] the temple was cedar, carved with gourds and **open** flowers.
6: 29 [B] he carved cherubim, palm trees and **open** flowers.
6: 32 [B] palm trees and **open** flowers, and overlaid the cherubim
6: 35 [B] palm trees and **open** flowers on them and overlaid them with
1Ch 9: 33 [B] of the temple and **were exempt** [K 7078] **from** *other* **duties**
2Ch 23: 8 [A] for Jehoiada the priest *had* not **released** any of the divisions.
Ps 22: 7 [22:8] [G] see me mock me; *they* **hurl insults** [+928+8557],
Pr 17: 14 [A] Starting a quarrel is like **breaching** a dam; so drop the matter

7081 פֶּטֶר ***peṭer***, n.[m.]. [11] [→ 7082; cf. 7080]

first offspring [5], firstborn [3], first male offspring [+1147+8167] [1], firstborn [+8167] [1], firstborn [+8715] [1]

Ex 13: 2 The **first offspring** *of* every womb among the Israelites belongs to
13: 12 you are to give over to the LORD the **first offspring** *of* every
13: 12 All the **firstborn** [+8715] males *of* your livestock belong to the
13: 13 Redeem with a lamb every **firstborn** donkey, but if you do not
13: 15 This is why I sacrifice to the LORD the **first** male **offspring** *of*
34: 19 "The **first offspring** *of* every womb belongs to me, including all
34: 19 including all the **firstborn** males *of* your livestock, whether *from*
34: 20 Redeem the **firstborn** donkey with a lamb, but if you do not
Nu 3: 12 the **first male offspring** [+1147+8167] of every Israelite woman.
18: 15 The **first offspring** *of* every womb, both man and animal,
Eze 20: 26 the sacrifice of every **firstborn** [+8167]—that I might fill them

7082 פִּטְרָה *piṭrâ*, n.f. [1] [√ 7081; cf. 7080]

firstborn [1]

Nu 8: 16 I have taken them as my own in place of the **firstborn**, the first

7083 פִּי־בֶסֶת *pî-beset*, n.pr.loc. [1]

Bubastis [1]

Eze 30: 17 The young men of Heliopolis and **Bubastis** will fall by the sword,

7084 פִּי הַחִירֹת *pî haḥîrôt*, n.pr.loc. [3 / 4] [√ 2672]

Pi Hahiroth [4]

Ex 14: 2 "Tell the Israelites to turn back and encamp near **Pi Hahiroth**,
14: 9 and overtook them as they camped by the sea near **Pi Hahiroth**,
Nu 33: 7 They left Etham, turned back to **Pi Hahiroth**, to the east of Baal
33: 8 They left **Pi** [BHS 7156] **Hahiroth** and passed through the sea

7085 פִּיד *pîd*, n.[m.]. [4]

misfortune [2], calamities [1], distress [1]

Job 12: 5 Men at ease have contempt for **misfortune** as the fate of those
30: 24 lays a hand on a broken man when he cries for help in his **distress**.
31: 29 "If I have rejoiced at my enemy's **misfortune** or gloated over the
Pr 24: 22 upon them, and who knows what **calamities** they can bring?

7086 פִּיחַ *pîaḥ*, n.[m.]. [2] [√ 7031]

soot [2]

Ex 9: 8 "Take handfuls of **soot** *from* a furnace and have Moses toss it into
9: 10 So they took **soot** *from* a furnace and stood before Pharaoh.

7087 פִּיכֹל *pîkōl*, n.pr.m. [3]

Phicol [3]

Ge 21: 22 and **Phicol** the commander of his forces said to Abraham,
21: 32 **Phicol** the commander of his forces returned to the land of the
26: 26 his personal adviser and **Phicol** the commander of his forces.

7088 פִּים *pîm*, n.[m.]. [1]

two thirds of a shekel [1]

1Sa 13: 21 The price was **two thirds of a shekel** for sharpening plowshares

7089 פִּימָה *pîmâ*, n.f. [1]

bulges with flesh [+6584+6913] [1]

Job 15: 27 is covered with fat and his waist **bulges** [+6584+6913] **with flesh**,

7090 פִּינְחָס *pîneḥās*, n.pr.m. [25] [cf. 9387]

Phinehas [25]

Ex 6: 25 married one of the daughters of Putiel, and she bore him **Phinehas**.
Nu 25: 7 When **Phinehas** son of Eleazar, the son of Aaron, the priest,
25: 11 "**Phinehas** son of Eleazar, the son of Aaron, the priest, has turned
31: 6 from each tribe, along with **Phinehas** son of Eleazar, the priest,
Jos 22: 13 So the Israelites sent **Phinehas** son of Eleazar, the priest,
22: 30 When **Phinehas** the priest and the leaders of the community—
22: 31 And **Phinehas** son of Eleazar, the priest, said to Reuben, Gad
22: 32 **Phinehas** son of Eleazar, the priest, and the leaders returned to
24: 33 which had been allotted to his son **Phinehas** in the hill country of
Jdg 20: 28 with **Phinehas** son of Eleazar, the son of Aaron, ministering before
1Sa 1: 3 where Hophni and **Phinehas**, the two sons of Eli, were priests of
2: 34 to your two sons, Hophni and **Phinehas**, will be a sign to you—
4: 4 Eli's two sons, Hophni and **Phinehas**, were there with the ark of
4: 11 God was captured, and Eli's two sons, Hophni and **Phinehas**, died.
4: 17 Also your two sons, Hophni and **Phinehas**, are dead, and the ark of
4: 19 the wife of **Phinehas**, was pregnant and near the time of delivery.
14: 3 He was a son of Ichabod's brother Ahitub son of **Phinehas**,
1Ch 6: 4 [5:30] Eleazar was the father of **Phinehas**, Phinehas the father of
6: 4 [5:30] the father of Phinehas, **Phinehas** the father of Abishua,
6: 50 [6:35] Eleazar his son, **Phinehas** his son, Abishua his son,
9: 20 In earlier times **Phinehas** son of Eleazar was in charge of the
Ezr 7: 5 the son of Abishua, the son of **Phinehas**, the son of Eleazar,
8: 2 of the descendants of **Phinehas**, Gershom; of the descendants of
8: 33 Eleazar son of **Phinehas** was with him, and so were the Levites
Ps 106: 30 **Phinehas** stood up and intervened, and the plague was checked.

7091 פִּינֹן *pînōn*, n.pr.m. [2] [cf. 7044]

Pinon [2]

Ge 36: 41 Oholibamah, Elah, **Pinon**,
1Ch 1: 52 Oholibamah, Elah, **Pinon**,

7092 פִּיפִיּוֹת *pîpiyyôt*, n.[f.pl.?]. [2] [√ 7023]

double-edged [1], many teeth [1]

Ps 149: 6 God be in their mouths and a **double-edged** sword in their hands,
Isa 41: 15 make you into a threshing sledge, new and sharp, with **many teeth**.

7093 פִּישׁוֹן *pîšôn*, n.pr.loc. [1]

Pishon [1]

Ge 2: 11 The name of the first is the **Pishon**; it winds through the entire land

7094 פִּיתוֹן *pîtôn*, n.pr.m. [2]

Pithon [2]

1Ch 8: 35 The sons of Micah: **Pithon**, Melech, Tarea and Ahaz.
9: 41 The sons of Micah: **Pithon**, Melech, Tahrea and Ahaz.

7095 פַּךְ *pak*, n.m. [3] [→ 7096]

flask [3]

1Sa 10: 1 Then Samuel took a **flask** *of* oil and poured it on Saul's head
2Ki 9: 1 your belt, take this **flask** *of* oil with you and go to Ramoth Gilead.
9: 3 Then take the **flask** and pour the oil on his head and declare,

7096 פָּכָה *pākâ*, v. [1] [√ 7095]

flowing [1]

Eze 47: 2 [D] facing east, and the water *was* **flowing** from the south side.

7097 פֹּכֶרֶת הַצְּבָיִים *pōkeret haṣṣebāyîm*, n.pr.m. [2] [cf. 2207]

Pokereth-Hazzebaim [2]

Ezr 2: 57 Shephatiah, Hattil, **Pokereth-Hazzebaim** and Ami
Ne 7: 59 Shephatiah, Hattil, **Pokereth-Hazzebaim** and Amon

7098 פָּלָא *pālā'*, v.den. [73] [→ 504?, 5140, 7098, 7099, 7100, 7101, 7102, 7112; cf. 7111]

wonders [17], wonderful [15], marvelous [10], miracles [5], amazing [3], hard [3], difficult [2], am wonderfully made [1], are wonderful [1], astound [1], astounding [1], display awesome power [1], fulfill a special vow [+5624] [1], greatly [1], impossible [1], magnificent [1], make a special vow [+5623] [1], makes a special vow [+5624] [1], send fearful [1], show wonder [1], showed wonderful [1], special vow [+5624] [1], special vows [+5624] [1], unheard-of [1], wonder [1]

Ge 18: 14 [C] *Is* anything too **hard** for the LORD? I will return to you at
Ex 3: 20 [C] strike the Egyptians with all the **wonders** that I will perform
34: 10 [C] Before all your people I will do **wonders** never before done
Lev 22: 21 [D] offering to the LORD to **fulfill a special vow** [+5624]
27: 2 [G] 'If anyone **makes a special vow** [+5624] to dedicate persons
Nu 6: 2 [G] 'If a man or woman *wants* to **make a special vow** [+5623],
15: 3 [D] for **special vows** [+5624] or freewill offerings or festival
15: 8 [D] for a **special vow** [+5624] or a fellowship offering to the
Dt 17: 8 [C] If cases come before your courts *that are* too **difficult** for
28: 59 [G] the LORD *will* **send fearful** plagues on you and your
30: 11 [C] Now what I am commanding you today *is* not too **difficult**
Jos 3: 5 [C] for tomorrow the LORD will do **amazing** *things* among
Jdg 6: 13 [C] Where are all his **wonders** that our fathers told us about
13: 19 [G] the LORD did an **amazing** *thing* while Manoah and his
2Sa 1: 26 [C] Your love for me *was* **wonderful**, more wonderful than that
13: 2 [C] and it seemed **impossible** *for* him to do anything to her.
1Ch 16: 9 [C] Sing to him, sing praise to him; tell of all his **wonderful** *acts*.
16: 12 [C] Remember the **wonders** he has done, his miracles,
16: 24 [C] among the nations, his **marvelous** *deeds* among all peoples.
2Ch 2: 9 [2:8] [G] the temple I build *must be* large and **magnificent**.
26: 15 [G] for he was **greatly** helped until he became powerful.
Ne 9: 17 [C] failed to remember the **miracles** you performed among them.
Job 5: 9 [C] that cannot be fathomed, **miracles** that cannot be counted.
9: 10 [C] that cannot be fathomed, **miracles** that cannot be counted.
10: 16 [F] a lion and again **display** *your* **awesome power** against me.
37: 5 [C] God's voice thunders *in* **marvelous** *ways*; he does great
37: 14 [C] "Listen to this, Job; stop and consider God's **wonders**.
42: 3 [C] I did not understand, *things* too **wonderful** for me to know.
Ps 9: 1 [9:2] [C] with all my heart; I will tell of all your **wonders**.
17: 7 [G] **Show** *the* **wonder** *of* your great love, you who save by your
26: 7 [C] aloud your praise and telling of all your **wonderful** *deeds*.
31: 21 [31:22] [G] for *he* **showed** his **wonderful** love to me when I
40: 5 [40:6] [C] O LORD my God, are the **wonders** you have done.
71: 17 [C] taught me, and to this day I declare your **marvelous** *deeds*.
72: 18 [C] the God of Israel, who alone does **marvelous** *deeds*.
75: 1 [75:2] [C] Name is near; men tell of your **wonderful** *deeds*.
78: 4 [C] of the LORD, his power, and the **wonders** he has done.
78: 11 [C] forgot what he had done, the **wonders** he had shown them.
78: 32 [C] kept on sinning; in spite of his **wonders**, they did not believe.

Ps 86:10 [C] For you are great and do **marvelous** *deeds*; you alone are
96: 3 [C] among the nations, his **marvelous** *deeds* among all peoples.
98: 1 [C] the LORD a new song, for he has done **marvelous** *things*;
105: 2 [C] Sing to him, sing praise to him; tell of all his **wonderful** *acts*.
105: 5 [C] Remember the **wonders** he has done, his miracles,
106: 7 [C] fathers were in Egypt, they gave no thought to your **miracles**;
106:22 [C] **miracles** in the land of Ham and awesome deeds by the Red
107: 8 [C] for his unfailing love and his **wonderful** *deeds* for men,
107:15 [C] for his unfailing love and his **wonderful** *deeds* for men,
107:21 [C] for his unfailing love and his **wonderful** *deeds* for men.
107:24 [C] the works of the LORD, his **wonderful** *deeds* in the deep.
107:31 [C] for his unfailing love and his **wonderful** *deeds* for men.
111: 4 [C] He has caused his **wonders** to be remembered; the LORD is
118:23 [C] the LORD has done this, and it *is* **marvelous** in our eyes.
119:18 [C] Open my eyes that I may see **wonderful** *things* in your law.
119:27 [C] of your precepts; then I will meditate on your **wonders**.
131: 1 [C] myself with great matters or *things* too **wonderful** for me.
136: 4 [C] to him who alone does great **wonders**, *His love*
139:14 [C] I praise you because *I* **am** fearfully and **wonderfully made**;
139:14 [C] your works **are wonderful**, I know that full well.
145: 5 [C] your majesty, and I will meditate on your **wonderful** *works*.
Pr 30:18 [C] "There are three things *that are* too **amazing** for me, four
Isa 28:29 [G] **wonderful** *in* counsel and magnificent in wisdom.
29:14 [G] Therefore once more I *will* **astound** these people with
29:14 [G] more I will astound these people with **wonder** upon wonder;
Jer 21: 2 [C] Perhaps the LORD will perform **wonders** for us as in times
32:17 [C] and outstretched arm. Nothing *is* too **hard** for you.
32:27 [C] the God of all mankind. *Is* anything too **hard** for me?
Da 8:24 [C] He will cause **astounding** devastation and will succeed in
11:36 [C] and will say **unheard-of** *things* against the God of gods.
Joel 2:26 [G] of the LORD your God, who has worked **wonders** for you;
Mic 7:15 [C] you came out of Egypt, I will show them my **wonders**."
Zec 8: 6 [C] "*It may* seem **marvelous** to the remnant of this people at that
8: 6 [C] this people at that time, but *will it* seem **marvelous** to me?"

7099 פֶּלֶא *pele'*, n.m. [13] [√ 7098]

wonders [4], miracles [3], wonderful [2], astonishing things [1], astounding [1], marvelous things [1], wonder [1]

Ex 15:11 majestic in holiness, awesome in glory, working **wonders**?
Ps 77:11 [77:12] yes, I will remember your **miracles** of long ago.
77:14 [77:15] You are the God who performs **miracles**; you display
78:12 He did **miracles** in the sight of their fathers in the land of Egypt,
88:10 [88:11] Do you show your **wonders** to the dead? Do those who
88:12 [88:13] Are your **wonders** known in the place of darkness,
89: 5 [89:6] The heavens praise your **wonders**, O LORD,
119:129 Your statutes are **wonderful**; therefore I obey them.
Isa 9: 6 [9:5] And he will be called **Wonderful** Counselor, Mighty God,
25: 1 for in perfect faithfulness you have done **marvelous things**,
29:14 once more I will astound these people with wonder upon **wonder**;
La 1: 9 Her fall was **astounding**; there was none to comfort her. "Look,
Da 12: 6 "How long will it be before these **astonishing things** are

7100 פִּלְאִי *pil'î*, a. [2] [√ 7098]

beyond understanding [1], wonderful [1]

Jdg 13:18 "Why do you ask my name? It is **beyond understanding**."
Ps 139: 6 Such knowledge is too **wonderful** for me, too lofty for me to

7101 פַּלֻּאִי *pallu'î*, a.g. [1] [√ 7112; cf. 7098]

Palluite [1]

Nu 26: 5 the Hanochite clan; through Pallu, the **Palluite** clan;

7102 פְּלָאיָה *p^{e}lā'yâ*, n.pr.m. [2] [√ 7098 + 3378]

Pelaiah [2]

Ne 8: 7 Maaseiah, Kelita, Azariah, Jozabad, Hanan and **Pelaiah**—
10:10 [10:11] Shebaniah, Hodiah, Kelita, **Pelaiah**, Hanan,

7103 פָּלַג *pālag*, v. [4] [→ 5141, 7104, 7106, 7107; cf. 7135; Ar 10583, 10584]

was divided [2], confound [1], cuts [1]

Ge 10:25 [C] was named Peleg, because in his time the earth **was divided**;
1Ch 1:19 [C] was named Peleg, because in his time the earth **was divided**;
Job 38:25 [D] Who **cuts** a channel for the torrents of rain, and a path for the
Ps 55: 9 [55:10] [D] O Lord, **confound** their speech, for I see violence

7104 פֶּלֶג *peleg^1*, n.m. [10] [√ 7103]

streams [9], watercourse [+4784] [1]

Job 29: 6 with cream and the rock poured out for me **streams** *of* olive oil.
Ps 1: 3 He is like a tree planted by **streams** *of* water, which yields its fruit
46: 4 [46:5] There is a river whose **streams** make glad the city of God,
65: 9 [65:10] The **streams** *of* God are filled with water to provide the
119:136 **Streams** *of* tears flow from my eyes, for your law is not obeyed.
Pr 5:16 in the streets, your **streams** *of* water in the public squares?
21: 1 he directs it like a **watercourse** [+4784] wherever he pleases.
Isa 30:25 **streams** *of* water will flow on every high mountain and every lofty
32: 2 like **streams** *of* water in the desert and the shadow of a great rock
La 3:48 **Streams** *of* tears flow from my eyes because my people are

7105 ^{2}פֶּלֶג *peleg^2*, n.pr.m. [7]

Peleg [7]

Ge 10:25 One was named **Peleg**, because in his time the earth was divided;
11:16 When Eber had lived 34 years, he became the father of **Peleg**.
11:17 And after he became the father of **Peleg**, Eber lived 430 years
11:18 When **Peleg** had lived 30 years, he became the father of Reu.
11:19 of Reu, **Peleg** lived 209 years and had other sons and daughters.
1Ch 1:19 One was named **Peleg**, because in his time the earth was divided;
1:25 Eber, **Peleg**, Reu,

7106 פְּלַגָּה *p^{e}laggâ*, n.f. [3] [√ 7103]

districts [2], streams [1]

Jdg 5:15 In the **districts** *of* Reuben there was much searching of heart.
5:16 In the **districts** *of* Reuben there was much searching of heart.
Job 20:17 He will not enjoy the **streams**, the rivers flowing with honey

7107 פְּלֻגָּה *p^{e}luggâ*, n.f. [1] [√ 7103; Ar 10585]

subdivision [1]

2Ch 35: 5 for *each* **subdivision** *of* the families of your fellow countrymen,

7108 פִּלֶגֶשׁ *pileges̆*, n.f. [37]

concubine [21], concubines [14], lovers [1], she^s [+2257] [1]

Ge 22:24 His **concubine**, whose name was Reumah, also had sons: Tebah,
25: 6 he gave gifts to the sons of his **concubines** and sent them away
35:22 Reuben went in and slept with his father's **concubine** Bilhah,
36:12 Esau's son Eliphaz also had a **concubine** named Timna, who bore
Jdg 8:31 His **concubine**, who lived in Shechem, also bore him a son,
19: 1 country of Ephraim took a **concubine** from Bethlehem in Judah.
19: 2 **she**^{s} [+2257] was unfaithful to him. She left him and went back to
19: 9 with his **concubine** and his servant, got up to leave, his
19:10 Jerusalem), with his two saddled donkeys and his **concubine**.
19:24 Look, here is my virgin daughter, and his **concubine**. I will bring
19:25 So the man took his **concubine** and sent her outside to them,
19:27 there lay his **concubine**, fallen in the doorway of the house,
19:29 he took a knife and cut up his **concubine**, limb by limb, into twelve
20: 4 and my **concubine** came to Gibeah in Benjamin to spend the night.
20: 5 intending to kill me. They raped my **concubine**, and she died.
20: 6 I took my **concubine**, cut her into pieces and sent one piece to each
2Sa 3: 7 Now Saul had had a **concubine** named Rizpah daughter of Aiah.
3: 7 said to Abner, "Why did you sleep with my father's **concubine**?"
5:13 David took more **concubines** and wives in Jerusalem, and more
15:16 but he left ten **concubines** to take care of the palace.
16:21 "Lie with your father's **concubines** whom he left to take care of
16:22 and he lay with his father's **concubines** in the sight of all Israel.
19: 5 [19:6] and daughters and the lives of your wives and **concubines**.
20: 3 he took the ten **concubines** he had left to take care of the palace
21:11 told what Aiah's daughter Rizpah, Saul's **concubine**, had done,
1Ki 11: 3 seven hundred wives of royal birth and three hundred **concubines**,
1Ch 1:32 The sons born to Keturah, Abraham's **concubine**: Zimran,
2:46 Caleb's **concubine** Ephah was the mother of Haran, Moza
2:48 Caleb's **concubine** Maacah was the mother of Sheber
3: 9 these were the sons of David, besides his sons by his **concubines**.
7:14 Asriel was his descendant through his Aramean **concubine**.
2Ch 11:21 of Absalom more than any of his other wives and **concubines**.
11:21 In all, he had eighteen wives and sixty **concubines**, twenty-eight
Est 2:14 the king's eunuch who was in charge of the **concubines**.
SS 6: 8 Sixty queens there may be, and eighty **concubines**, and virgins
6: 9 and called her blessed; the queens and **concubines** praised her.
Eze 23:20 There she lusted after her **lovers**, whose genitals were like those of

7109 פִּלְדָּשׁ *pildās̆*, n.pr.m. [1]

Pildash [1]

Ge 22:22 Kesed, Hazo, **Pildash**, Jidlaph and Bethuel."

7110 פְּלָדֹת *p^{e}lādōt*, n.f. [1]

metal [1]

Na 2: 3 [2:4] The **metal** *on* the chariots flashes on the day they are made

7111 פָּלָה pālâ, v. [5] [→ 7113, 7126, 7141, 7151; cf. 7098]

deal differently [1], distinguish [1], make a distinction [1], makes a distinction [1], set apart [1]

Ex 8:22 [8:18] [G] " 'But on that day *I will* **deal differently** *with* the
9: 4 [G] the LORD *will* **make a distinction** between the livestock of
11: 7 [G] you will know that the LORD **makes a distinction** between
33:16 [C] What else *will* **distinguish** me and your people from all the
Ps 4: 3 [4:4] [G] Know that the LORD *has* **set apart** the godly for

7112 פַּלּוּא pallû', n.pr.m. [5] [→ 7101; cf. 7098]

Pallu [5]

Ge 46: 9 The sons of Reuben: Hanoch, **Pallu**, Hezron and Carmi.
Ex 6:14 sons of Reuben the firstborn son of Israel were Hanoch and **Pallu**,
Nu 26: 5 the Hanochite clan; through **Pallu**, the Palluite clan;
26: 8 The son of **Pallu** was Eliab,
1Ch 5: 3 Reuben the firstborn of Israel: Hanoch, **Pallu**, Hezron and Carmi.

7113 פְּלוֹנִי pelônî, a.g. [3] [√ 7111]

Pelonite [3]

1Ch 11:27 Shammoth the Harorite, Helez the **Pelonite**,
11:36 Hepher the Mekerathite, Ahijah the **Pelonite**,
27:10 for the seventh month, was Helez the **Pelonite**, an Ephraimite.

7114 פָּלַח pālaḥ, v. [5] [→ 7115, 7116; Ar 10586]

pierces [2], bring forth [1], cut up [1], plows [1]

2Ki 4:39 [D] When he returned, *he* **cut** them **up** into the pot of stew,
Job 16:13 [D] *he* **pierces** my kidneys and spills my gall on the ground.
39: 3 [D] They crouch down and **bring forth** their young; their labor
Ps 141: 7 [A] ˻They will say,˼ "As *one* **plows** and breaks up the earth,
Pr 7:23 [D] till an arrow **pierces** his liver, like a bird darting into a snare,

7115 פֶּלַח pelaḥ, n.f. [6] [√ 7114]

millstone [3], halves [2], part [1]

Jdg 9:53 a woman dropped an upper **millstone** on his head and cracked his
1Sa 30:12 **part** *of* a cake of pressed figs and two cakes of raisins. He ate
2Sa 11:21 Didn't a woman throw an upper **millstone** on him from the wall,
Job 41:24 [41:16] His chest is hard as rock, hard as a lower **millstone**.
SS 4: 3 Your temples behind your veil are like the **halves** *of* a
6: 7 Your temples behind your veil are like the **halves** *of* a

7116 פִּלְחָא pilḥā', n.pr.m. [1] [√ 7114]

Pilha [1]

Ne 10:24 [10:25] Hallohesh, **Pilha**, Shobek,

7117 פָּלַט pālaṭ, v. [26] [→ 3646, 3647, 5144, 7118, 7119, 7122, 7123, 7124, 7125, 7127, 7128, 7129; cf. 4880]

deliverer [5], rescue [5], delivered [4], deliver [3], delivers [2], save [2], calve [1], carry off [1], let escape [1], saves [1], survive [1]

2Sa 22: 2 [D] "The LORD is my rock, my fortress and my **deliverer**;
22:44 [D] "*You have* **delivered** me from the attacks of my people;
Job 21:10 [D] never fail to breed; their cows **calve** and do not miscarry.
23: 7 [D] and *I would be* **delivered** forever from my judge.
Ps 17:13 [D] bring them down; **rescue** me from the wicked by your sword.
18: 2 [18:3] [D] LORD is my rock, my fortress and my **deliverer**;
18:43 [18:44] [D] *You have* **delivered** me from the attacks of the
18:48 [18:49] [D] *who* **saves** me from my enemies. You exalted me
22: 4 [22:5] [D] put their trust; they trusted and *you* **delivered** them.
22: 8 [22:9] [D] "He trusts in the LORD; *let* the LORD **rescue** him.
31: 1 [31:2] [D] be put to shame; **deliver** me in your righteousness.
37:40 [D] The LORD helps them and **delivers** them; he delivers them
37:40 [D] *he* **delivers** them from the wicked and saves them,
40:17 [40:18] [D] You are my help and my **deliverer**; O my God,
43: 1 [D] ungodly nation; **rescue** me from deceitful and wicked men.
56: 7 [56:8] [D] On no account **let** them **escape**; in your anger,
70: 5 [70:6] [D] You are my help and my **deliverer**; O LORD,
71: 2 [D] Rescue me and **deliver** me in your righteousness; turn your
71: 4 [D] **Deliver** me, O my God, from the hand of the wicked,
82: 4 [D] **Rescue** the weak and needy; deliver them from the hand of
91:14 [D] "Because he loves me," says the LORD, "*I will* **rescue** him;
144: 2 [D] and my fortress, my stronghold and my **deliverer**, my shield,
Isa 5:29 [G] they seize their prey and **carry** it **off** with no one to rescue.
Eze 7:16 [A] All *who* **survive** and escape will be in the mountains,
Mic 6:14 [G] You will store up but **save** nothing, because what you save I
6:14 [D] save nothing, because what *you* **save** I will give to the sword.

7118 פֶּלֶט peleṭ, n.pr.m. [2] [→ 7121; cf. 7117; *also used with compound proper names*]

Pelet [2]

1Ch 2:47 sons of Jahdai: Regem, Jotham, Geshan, **Pelet**, Ephah and Shaaph.
12: 3 Jeziel and **Pelet** the sons of Azmaveth; Beracah, Jehu the

7119 פַּלֵּט palleṭ, n.[m.]. [1] [√ 7117]

deliverance [1]

Ps 32: 7 me from trouble and surround me with songs of **deliverance**.

7120 פַּלְטִי palṭî[1], n.pr.m. [2] [√ 7123]

Palti [1], Paltiel [1]

Nu 13: 9 from the tribe of Benjamin, **Palti** son of Raphu;
1Sa 25:44 David's wife, to **Paltiel** son of Laish, who was from Gallim.

7121 פַּלְטִי palṭî[2], a.g. [1] [√ 7118]

Paltite [1]

2Sa 23:26 Helez the **Paltite**, Ira son of Ikkesh from Tekoa,

7122 פִּלְטָי pilṭāy, n.pr.m. [1] [√ 7117]

Piltai [1]

Ne 12:17 of Abijah's, Zicri; of Miniamin's and of Moadiah's, **Piltai**;

7123 פַּלְטִיאֵל palṭî'ēl, n.pr.m. [2] [→ 7120; cf. 7117 + 446]

Paltiel [2]

Nu 34:26 **Paltiel** son of Azzan, the leader from the tribe of Issachar;
2Sa 3:15 and had her taken away from her husband **Paltiel** son of Laish.

7124 פְּלַטְיָה pelaṭyâ, n.pr.m. [3] [√ 7117 + 3378]

Pelatiah [3]

1Ch 3:21 **Pelatiah** and Jeshaiah, and the sons of Rephaiah, of Arnan,
4:42 led by **Pelatiah**, Neariah, Rephaiah and Uzziel, the sons of Ishi,
Ne 10:22 [10:23] **Pelatiah**, Hanan, Anaiah,

7125 פְּלַטְיָהוּ pelaṭyāhû, n.pr.m. [2] [√ 7117 + 3378]

Pelatiah [2]

Eze 11: 1 among them Jaazaniah son of Azzur and **Pelatiah** son of Benaiah,
11:13 Now as I was prophesying, **Pelatiah** son of Benaiah died.

7126 פְּלָיָה pelāyâ, n.pr.m. [1] [√ 7111 + 3378]

Pelaiah [1]

1Ch 3:24 **Pelaiah**, Akkub, Johanan, Delaiah and Anani—

7127 פָּלִיט pālîṭ, n.m. [19] [√ 7117]

escape [6], fugitives [3], escaped [2], anyone[s] [1], escape [+4880] [1], fugitive [1], him[s] [+2021] [1], man who escaped [1], man[s] [1], renegades [1], survivor [1]

Ge 14:13 One who *had* **escaped** came and reported this to Abram the
Jos 8:22 Israel cut them down, leaving them neither survivors nor **fugitives**.
Jdg 12: 4 "You Gileadites are **renegades** from Ephraim and Manasseh."
12: 5 and whenever a **survivor** *of* Ephraim said, "Let me cross over,"
2Ki 9:15 don't let **anyone**[s] slip out of the city to go and tell the news in
Isa 45:20 and come; assemble, you **fugitives** *from* the nations.
Jer 42:17 of them will survive or **escape** the disaster I will bring on them.'
44:14 the remnant of Judah who have gone to live in Egypt will **escape**
44:28 *Those who* **escape** the sword and return to the land of Judah from
La 2:22 In the day of the LORD's anger no one **escaped** or survived;
Eze 6: 8 for some of you will **escape** the sword when you are scattered
6: 9 have been carried captive, *those who* **escape** will remember me—
7:16 All who survive and **escape** will be in the mountains, moaning like
24:26 on that day a **fugitive** will come to tell you the news.
24:27 you will speak with **him**[s] [+2021] and will no longer be silent.
33:21 a **man who** *had* **escaped** from Jerusalem came to me and said,
33:22 Now the evening before the **man**[s] arrived, the hand of the LORD
Am 9: 1 with the sword. Not one will get away, none *will* **escape** [+4880].
Ob 1:14 You should not wait at the crossroads to cut down their **fugitives**,

7128 פָּלֵיט pālêṭ, n.m. [5] [√ 7117]

fugitives [2], escaped [1], refugees [1], survive [1]

Nu 21:29 He has given up his sons as **fugitives** and his daughters as captives
Isa 66:19 and I will send some of those *who* **survive** to the nations—
Jer 44:14 long to return and live; none will return except a *few* **fugitives**."
50:28 **refugees** from Babylon declaring in Zion how the LORD our God
51:50 You *who* have **escaped** the sword, leave and do not linger!

7129 פְּלֵיטָה *pᵉlêṭâ*, n.f. [28] [√ 7117]

remnant [6], deliverance [4], escape [4], survivors [4], escaped [3], band of survivors [2], escapes [+2118+4200] [1], fugitives [1], little left [+3856+8636] [1], place to escape [1], survivor [1]

Ge 32: 8 [32:9] and attacks one group, the group that is left may **escape**."
45: 7 a remnant on earth and to save your lives by a great **deliverance**.
Ex 10: 5 They will devour what **little** you have **left** [+3856+8636] after the
Jdg 21: 17 The Benjamite **survivors** must have heirs," they said, "so that a
2Sa 15: 14 "Come! We must flee, or none of us will **escape** from Absalom.
2Ki 19: 30 Once more a **remnant** *of* the house of Judah will take root below
19: 31 will come a remnant, and out of Mount Zion a **band of survivors**.
1Ch 4: 43 They killed the remaining Amalekites who had **escaped**, and they
2Ch 12: 7 I will not destroy them but will soon give them **deliverance**.
20: 24 saw only dead bodies lying on the ground; no one had **escaped**.
30: 6 are left, who have **escaped** from the hand of the kings of Assyria.
Ezr 9: 8 the LORD our God has been gracious in leaving us a **remnant**
9: 13 than our sins have deserved and have given us a **remnant** like this.
9: 14 enough with us to destroy us, leaving us no remnant or **survivor**?
9: 15 of Israel, you are righteous! We are left this day as a **remnant**.
Ne 1: 2 I questioned them about the Jewish **remnant** that survived the
Isa 4: 2 of the land will be the pride and glory of the **survivors** *in* Israel.
10: 20 that day the remnant of Israel, the **survivors** *of* the house of Jacob,
15: 9 a lion upon the **fugitives** *of* Moab and upon those who remain in
37: 31 Once more a **remnant** *of* the house of Judah will take root below
37: 32 will come a remnant, and out of Mount Zion a **band of survivors**.
Jer 25: 35 have nowhere to flee, the leaders of the flock no **place to escape**.
50: 29 Encamp all around her; let no *one* **escape**. Repay her for her deeds;
Eze 14: 22 Yet there will be some **survivors**—sons and daughters who will be
Da 11: 42 will extend his power over many countries; Egypt will not **escape**.
Joel 2: 3 a desert waste—nothing **escapes** [+2118+4200] them.
2: 32 [3:5] on Mount Zion and in Jerusalem there will be **deliverance**,
Ob 1: 17 on Mount Zion will be **deliverance**; it will be holy, and the house

7130 פָּלִיל *pālîl*, n.m. [2] [√ 7136]

concede [1], court [1]

Ex 21: 22 whatever the woman's husband demands and the **court** allows.
Dt 32: 31 For their rock is not like our Rock, as even our enemies **concede**.

7131 פְּלִילָה *pᵉlîlâ*, n.f. [1] [√ 7136]

decision [1]

Isa 16: 3 "Give us counsel, render a **decision**. Make your shadow like

7132 פְּלִילִי *pᵉlîlî*, a. [2] [√ 7136]

to be judged [2]

Job 31: 11 For that would have been shameful, a sin **to be judged**.
31: 28 these also would be sins **to be judged**, for I would have been

7133 פְּלִילִיָּה *pᵉlîliyyâ*, n.f. [1] [√ 7136]

rendering decisions [1]

Isa 28: 7 when seeing visions, they stumble when **rendering decisions**.

7134 ¹פֶּלֶךְ *pelek¹*, n.[m.] [2]

crutch [1], spindle [1]

2Sa 3: 29 or leprosy or who leans on a **crutch** or who falls by the sword
Pr 31: 19 hand she holds the distaff and grasps the **spindle** with her fingers.

7135 ²פֶּלֶךְ *pelek²*, n.[m.] [8] [cf. 7103]

district [4], half-district [+2942] [4]

Ne 3: 9 Rephaiah son of Hur, ruler of a **half-district of** [+2942] Jerusalem,
3: 12 son of Hallohesh, ruler of a **half-district of** [+2942] Jerusalem,
3: 14 by Malkijah son of Recab, ruler of the **district** *of* Beth Hakkerem.
3: 15 by Shallun son of Col-Hozeh, ruler of the **district** *of* Mizpah.
3: 16 son of Azbuk, ruler of a **half-district of** [+2942] Beth Zur,
3: 17 Beside him, Hashabiah, ruler of half the **district** *of* Keilah,
3: 17 of half the district of Keilah, carried out repairs for his **district**.
3: 18 son of Henadad, ruler of the other **half-district of** [+2942] Keilah.

7136 ¹פָּלַל *pālal¹*, v. [4] [→ 697, 7130, 7131, 7132, 7133, 7138, 7139; *also used with compound proper names*]

expected [1], furnished justification [1], intervened [1], mediate [1]

Ge 48: 11 [D] said to Joseph, "*I* never **expected** to see your face again,
1Sa 2: 25 [D] a man sins against another man, God *may* **mediate** *for* him;
Ps 106: 30 [D] Phinehas stood up and **intervened**, and the plague was
Eze 16: 52 [D] for *you have* **furnished** *some* **justification** for your sisters.

7137 ²פָּלַל *pālal²*, v. [80] [→ 9525]

pray [30], prayed [28], praying [10], prays [5], intercede [2], prayer [2], *untranslated* [1], offer prayer [+448+906+9525] [1], plead [1]

Ge 20: 7 [F] he is a prophet, and *he will* **pray** for you and you will live.
20: 17 [F] Then Abraham **prayed** to God, and God healed Abimelech,
Nu 11: 2 [F] to Moses, he **prayed** to the LORD and the fire died down.
21: 7 [F] **Pray** that the LORD will take the snakes away from us."
21: 7 [F] the snakes away from us." So Moses **prayed** for the people.
Dt 9: 20 [F] to destroy him, but at that time *I* **prayed** for Aaron too.
9: 26 [F] *I* **prayed** to the LORD and said, "O Sovereign LORD,
1Sa 1: 10 [F] of soul Hannah wept much and **prayed** to the LORD.
1: 12 [F] As she kept on **praying** to the LORD, Eli observed her
1: 26 [F] I am the woman who stood here beside you **praying** to the
1: 27 [F] *I* **prayed** for this child, and the LORD has granted me what
2: 1 [F] Hannah **prayed** and said: "My heart rejoices in the LORD;
2: 25 [F] a man sins against the LORD, who *will* **intercede** for him?"
7: 5 [F] at Mizpah and *I will* **intercede** with the LORD for you."
8: 6 [F] this displeased Samuel; so he **prayed** to the LORD.
12: 19 [F] "**Pray** to the LORD your God for your servants so that we
12: 23 [F] I should sin against the LORD by failing to **pray** for you.
2Sa 7: 27 [F] has found courage to **offer** you this **prayer** [+448+906+9525].
1Ki 8: 28 [F] the prayer that your servant *is* **praying** in your presence this
8: 29 [F] so that you will hear the prayer your servant **prays** toward
8: 30 [F] and of your people Israel when *they* **pray** toward this place.
8: 33 [F] **praying** and making supplication to you in this temple,
8: 35 [F] and when *they* **pray** toward this place and confess your name
8: 42 [F] when he comes and **prays** toward this temple,
8: 44 [F] when *they* **pray** to the LORD toward the city you have
8: 48 [F] **pray** to you toward the land you gave their fathers,
8: 54 [F] When Solomon had finished **[RPH]** all these prayers
13: 6 [F] your God and **pray** for me that my hand may be restored."
2Ki 4: 33 [F] shut the door on the two of them and **prayed** to the LORD.
6: 17 [F] Elisha **prayed**, "O LORD, open his eyes so he may see."
6: 18 [F] Elisha **prayed** to the LORD, "Strike these people with
19: 15 [F] Hezekiah **prayed** to the LORD: "O LORD, God of Israel,
19: 20 [F] I have heard *your* **prayer** concerning Sennacherib king of
20: 2 [F] turned his face to the wall and **prayed** to the LORD,
1Ch 17: 25 [F] for him. So your servant has found courage to **pray** to you.
2Ch 6: 19 [F] and the prayer that your servant *is* **praying** in your presence.
6: 20 [F] May you hear the prayer your servant **prays** toward this
6: 21 [F] and of your people Israel when *they* **pray** toward this place.
6: 24 [F] **praying** and making supplication before you in this temple,
6: 26 [F] and when *they* **pray** toward this place and confess your name
6: 32 [F] when he comes and **prays** toward this temple,
6: 34 [F] and when *they* **pray** to you toward this city you have chosen
6: 38 [F] **pray** toward the land you gave their fathers, toward the city
7: 1 [F] When Solomon finished **praying**, fire came down from
7: 14 [F] will humble themselves and **pray** and seek my face and turn
30: 18 [F] But Hezekiah **prayed** for them, saying, "May the LORD,
32: 20 [F] the prophet Isaiah son of Amoz cried out *in* **prayer** *to* heaven
32: 24 [F] *He* **prayed** to the LORD, who answered him and gave him a
33: 13 [F] when *he* **prayed** to him, the LORD was moved by his
Ezr 10: 1 [F] While Ezra *was* **praying** and confessing, weeping
Ne 1: 4 [F] I mourned and fasted and **prayed** before the God of heaven.
1: 6 [F] your eyes open to hear the prayer your servant *is* **praying**
2: 4 [F] "What is it you want?" Then *I* **prayed** to the God of heaven,
4: 9 [4:3] [F] *we* **prayed** to our God and posted a guard day
Job 42: 8 [F] My servant Job *will* **pray** for you, and I will accept his prayer
42: 10 [F] After Job *had* **prayed** for his friends, the LORD made him
Ps 5: 2 [5:3] [F] cry for help, my King and my God, for to you *I* **pray**.
32: 6 [F] Therefore *let* everyone who is godly **pray** to you while you
72: 15 [F] *May people* ever **pray** for him and bless him all day long.
Isa 16: 12 [F] when she goes to her shrine to **pray**, it is to no avail.
37: 15 [F] And Hezekiah **prayed** to the LORD:
37: 21 [F] Because *you have* **prayed** to me concerning Sennacherib
38: 2 [F] turned his face to the wall and **prayed** to the LORD,
44: 17 [F] *He* **prays** to it and says, "Save me; you are my god."
45: 14 [F] They will bow down before you and **plead** with you, saying,
45: 20 [F] about idols of wood, *who* **pray** to gods that cannot save.
Jer 7: 16 [F] "So *do* not **pray** for this people nor offer any plea or petition
11: 14 [F] "*Do* not **pray** for this people nor offer any plea or petition for
14: 11 [F] said to me, "*Do* not **pray** for the well-being of this people.
29: 7 [F] **Pray** to the LORD for it, because if it prospers, you too will
29: 12 [F] you will call upon me and come and **pray** to me, and I will
32: 16 [F] purchase to Baruch son of Neriah, *I* **prayed** to the LORD:
37: 3 [F] this message: "Please **pray** to the LORD our God for us."
42: 2 [F] and **pray** to the LORD your God for this entire remnant.
42: 4 [F] "I *will* certainly **pray** to the LORD your God as you have
42: 20 [F] your God and said, '**Pray** to the LORD our God for us;
Da 9: 4 [F] *I* **prayed** to the LORD my God and confessed: "O Lord,
9: 20 [F] While I was speaking and **praying**, confessing my sin
Jnh 2: 1 [2:2] [F] From inside the fish Jonah **prayed** to the LORD his
4: 2 [F] *He* **prayed** to the LORD, "O LORD, is this not what I said

7138 פָּלָל pālāl, n.pr.m. [1] [√ 7136]

Palal [1]

Ne 3: 25 **Palal** son of Uzai worked opposite the angle and the tower

7139 פְּלַלְיָה p^elalyâ, n.pr.m. [1] [√ 7136 + 3378]

Pelaliah [1]

Ne 11: 12 the son of **Pelaliah**, the son of Amzi, the son of Zechariah,

7140 פַּלְמֹנִי palmōnî, p. [1] [cf. 532, 7141]

him[s] [+2021] [1]

Da 8: 13 a holy one speaking, and another holy one said to **him**[s] [+2021],

7141 פְּלֹנִי p^elōnî, p. [3] [√ 7111; cf. 532, 7140]

certain [+532] [1], friend [+532] [1], such and such [+532] [1]

Ru 4: 1 Boaz said, "Come over here, my **friend** [+532], and sit down."
1Sa 21: 2 [21:3] I have told them to meet me at a **certain** [+532] place.
2Ki 6: 8 "I will set up my camp in **such** [+532] **and such** a place."

7142 פָּלַס pālas[1], v.den. [4]

make level [1], make smooth [1], mete out [1], prepared [1]

Ps 58: 2 [58:3] [D] and your hands **mete out** violence on the earth.
78: 50 [D] *He* **prepared** a path for his anger; he did not spare them
Pr 4: 26 [D] **Make level** paths for your feet and take only ways that are
Isa 26: 7 [D] O upright One, *you* **make** the way of the righteous **smooth**.

7143 פָּלַס pālas[2], v.den. [2] [→ 7144]

examines [1], gives thought [1]

Pr 5: 6 [D] *She* **gives** no **thought** *to* the way of life; her paths are
5: 21 [D] in full view of the LORD, and *he* **examines** all his paths.

7144 פֶּלֶס peles, n.[m.]. [2] [√ 7143]

balances [1], scales [1]

Pr 16: 11 Honest scales and **balances** are from the LORD; all the weights
Isa 40: 12 or weighed the mountains on the **scales** and the hills in a balance?

7145 פָּלַץ pālaṣ, v. [1] [→ 5145, 7146, 9526]

makes tremble [1]

Job 9: 6 [F] shakes the earth from its place and **makes** its pillars **tremble**.

7146 פַּלָּצוּת pallāṣût, n.f. [4] [√ 7145]

fear [1], horror [1], terror [1], trembling [1]

Job 21: 6 When I think about this, I am terrified; **trembling** seizes my body.
Ps 55: 5 [55:6] trembling have beset me; **horror** has overwhelmed me.
Isa 21: 4 My heart falters, **fear** makes me tremble; the twilight I longed for
Eze 7: 18 They will put on sackcloth and be clothed with **terror**. Their faces

7147 פָּלַשׁ pālaš, v. [4]

roll [4]

Jer 6: 26 [F] O my people, put on sackcloth and **roll** in ashes; mourn with
25: 34 [F] you shepherds; **roll** in the dust, *you* leaders of the flock.
Eze 27: 30 [F] they will sprinkle dust on their heads and **roll** in ashes.
Mic 1: 10 [F] it not in Gath; weep not at all. In Beth Ophrah **roll** in the dust.

7148 פְּלֶשֶׁת p^elešet, n.pr.loc. [9] [→ 7149]

Philistia [7], Philistines [2]

Ex 15: 14 will hear and tremble; anguish will grip the people of **Philistia**.
Ps 60: 8 [60:10] Edom I toss my sandal; over **Philistia** I shout in triumph."
83: 7 [83:8] Gebal, Ammon and Amalek, **Philistia**, with the people of
87: 4 **Philistia** too, and Tyre, along with Cush—and will say, 'This one
108: 9 [108:10] I toss my sandal; over **Philistia** I shout in triumph."
Isa 14: 29 Do not rejoice, all you **Philistines**, that the rod that struck you is
14: 31 Wail, O gate! Howl, O city! Melt away, all you **Philistines**!
Joel 3: 4 [4:4] O Tyre and Sidon and all you regions of **Philistia**?
Am 6: 2 from there to great Hamath, and then go down to Gath in **Philistia**.

7149 פְּלִשְׁתִּי p^elištî, a.g. [287] [√ 7148]

Philistines [200], Philistine [62], they[s] [8], Philistine's [4], he[s] [+2021] [3], them[s] [3], *untranslated* [2], him[s] [+2021] [1], his[s] [1], Philistia [1], Philistines [+824] [1], their[s] [1]

Ge 10: 14 Pathrusites, Casluhites (from whom the **Philistines** came)
21: 32 the commander of his forces returned to the land of the **Philistines**.
21: 34 And Abraham stayed in the land of the **Philistines** for a long time.
26: 1 and Isaac went to Abimelech king of the **Philistines** in Gerar.
26: 8 Abimelech king of the **Philistines** looked down from a window
26: 14 and herds and servants that the **Philistines** envied him.
26: 15 father Abraham, the **Philistines** stopped up, filling them with earth.
26: 18 which the **Philistines** had stopped up after Abraham died,
Ex 13: 17 God did not lead them on the road through the **Philistine** country,
23: 31 your borders from the Red Sea to the Sea of the **Philistines**,
Jos 13: 2 land that remains: all the regions of the **Philistines** and Geshurites:
13: 3 all of it counted as Canaanite (the territory of the five **Philistine**
Jdg 3: 3 the five rulers of the **Philistines**, all the Canaanites, the Sidonians,
3: 31 who struck down six hundred **Philistines** with an oxgoad.
10: 6 the gods of the Ammonites and the gods of the **Philistines**.
10: 7 He sold them into the hands of the **Philistines** and the Ammonites,
10: 11 the Egyptians, the Amorites, the Ammonites, the **Philistines**,
13: 1 so the LORD delivered them into the hands of the **Philistines** for
13: 5 begin the deliverance of Israel from the hands of the **Philistines**."
14: 1 went down to Timnah and saw there a young **Philistine** woman.
14: 2 his father and mother, "I have seen a **Philistine** woman in Timnah;
14: 3 Must you go to the uncircumcised **Philistines** to get a wife?"
14: 4 who was seeking an occasion to confront the **Philistines**;
14: 4 the Philistines; for at that time **they**[s] were ruling over Israel.)
15: 3 to them, "This time I have a right to get even with the **Philistines**;
15: 5 and let the foxes loose in the standing grain of the **Philistines**.
15: 6 When the **Philistines** asked, "Who did this?" they were told,
15: 6 So the **Philistines** went up and burned her and her father to death.
15: 9 The **Philistines** went up and camped in Judah, spreading out near
15: 11 "Don't you realize that the **Philistines** are rulers over us?
15: 12 "We've come to tie you up and hand you over to the **Philistines**."
15: 14 As he approached Lehi, the **Philistines** came toward him shouting.
15: 20 Samson led Israel for twenty years in the days of the **Philistines**.
16: 5 The rulers of the **Philistines** went to her and said, "See if you can
16: 8 the rulers of the **Philistines** brought her seven fresh thongs that had
16: 9 she called to him, "Samson, the **Philistines** are upon you!"
16: 12 she called to him, "Samson, the **Philistines** are upon you!"
16: 14 Again she called to him, "Samson, the **Philistines** are upon you!"
16: 18 she sent word to the rulers of the **Philistines**, "Come back once
16: 18 So the rulers of the **Philistines** returned with the silver in their
16: 20 Then she called, "Samson, the **Philistines** are upon you!"
16: 21 the **Philistines** seized him, gouged out his eyes and took him down
16: 23 Now the rulers of the **Philistines** assembled to offer a great
16: 27 all the rulers of the **Philistines** were there, and on the roof were
16: 28 let me with one blow get revenge on the **Philistines** for my two
16: 30 Samson said, "Let me die with the **Philistines**!" Then he pushed
1Sa 4: 1 Now the Israelites went out to fight against the **Philistines**.
4: 1 The Israelites camped at Ebenezer, and the **Philistines** at Aphek.
4: 2 The **Philistines** deployed their forces to meet Israel, and as the
4: 2 and as the battle spread, Israel was defeated by the **Philistines**,
4: 3 did the LORD bring defeat upon us today before the **Philistines**?
4: 6 Hearing the uproar, the **Philistines** asked, "What's all this shouting
4: 7 the **Philistines** were afraid. "A god has come into the camp,"
4: 9 Be strong, **Philistines**! Be men, or you will be subject to the
4: 10 So the **Philistines** fought, and the Israelites were defeated
4: 17 "Israel fled before the **Philistines**, and the army has suffered heavy
5: 1 After the **Philistines** had captured the ark of God, they took it from
5: 2 **they**[s] carried the ark into Dagon's temple and set it beside Dagon.
5: 8 So they called together all the rulers of the **Philistines** and asked
5: 11 So they called together all the rulers of the **Philistines** and said,
6: 1 When the ark of the LORD had been in **Philistine** territory seven
6: 2 the **Philistines** called for the priests and the diviners and said,
6: 4 and five gold rats, according to the number of the **Philistine** rulers,
6: 12 The rulers of the **Philistines** followed them as far as the border of
6: 16 The five rulers of the **Philistines** saw all this and then returned that
6: 17 These are the gold tumors the **Philistines** sent as a guilt offering to
6: 18 to the number of **Philistine** towns belonging to the five rulers—
6: 21 saying, "The **Philistines** have returned the ark of the LORD.
7: 3 and he will deliver you out of the hand of the **Philistines**."
7: 7 When the **Philistines** heard that Israel had assembled at Mizpah,
7: 7 at Mizpah, the rulers of the **Philistines** came up to attack them.
7: 7 Israelites heard of it, they were afraid because of the **Philistines**.
7: 8 for us, that he may rescue us from the hand of the **Philistines**."
7: 10 burnt offering, the **Philistines** drew near to engage Israel in battle.
7: 10 the LORD thundered with loud thunder against the **Philistines**
7: 11 men of Israel rushed out of Mizpah and pursued the **Philistines**,
7: 13 So the **Philistines** were subdued and did not invade Israelite
7: 13 the hand of the LORD was against the **Philistines**.
7: 14 The towns from Ekron to Gath that the **Philistines** had captured
7: 14 the neighboring territory from the power of the **Philistines**.
9: 16 he will deliver my people from the hand of the **Philistines**.
10: 5 you will go to Gibeah of God, where there is a **Philistine** outpost.
12: 9 and into the hands of the **Philistines** and the king of Moab,
13: 3 Jonathan attacked the **Philistine** outpost at Geba,
13: 3 the Philistine outpost at Geba, and the **Philistines** heard about it.
13: 4 "Saul has attacked the **Philistine** outpost, and now Israel has
13: 4 and now Israel has become a stench to the **Philistines**."
13: 5 The **Philistines** assembled to fight Israel, with three thousand
13: 11 the set time, and that the **Philistines** were assembling at Micmash,
13: 12 'Now the **Philistines** will come down against me at Gilgal,

1Sa 13:16 in Gibeah in Benjamin, while the **Philistines** camped at Micmash.
13:17 Raiding parties went out from the **Philistine** camp in three
13:19 because the **Philistines** had said, "Otherwise the Hebrews will
13:20 So all Israel went down to the **Philistines** to have their plowshares,
13:23 Now a detachment of **Philistines** had gone out to the pass at
14: 1 "Come, let's go over to the **Philistine** outpost on the other side."
14: 4 intended to cross to reach the **Philistine** outpost was a cliff;
14:11 So both of them showed themselves to the **Philistine** outpost.
14:11 themselves to the Philistine outpost. "Look!" said the **Philistines**.
14:19 the tumult in the **Philistine** camp increased more and more.
14:21 Those Hebrews who had previously been with the **Philistines**
14:22 hill country of Ephraim heard that the **Philistines** were on the run,
14:30 Would not the slaughter of the **Philistines** have been even
14:31 after the Israelites had struck down the **Philistines** from Micmash
14:36 "Let us go down after the **Philistines** by night and plunder them till
14:37 So Saul asked God, "Shall I go down after the **Philistines**?
14:46 Saul stopped pursuing the **Philistines**, and they withdrew to their
14:46 pursuing the Philistines, and **they**[s] withdrew to their own land.
14:47 the Ammonites, Edom, the kings of Zobah, and the **Philistines**.
14:52 All the days of Saul there was bitter war with the **Philistines**,
17: 1 Now the **Philistines** gathered their forces for war and assembled at
17: 2 Valley of Elah and drew up their battle line to meet the **Philistines**.
17: 3 The **Philistines** occupied one hill and the Israelites another,
17: 4 who was from Gath, came out of the **Philistine** camp.
17: 8 Am I not a **Philistine**, and are you not the servants of Saul?
17:10 Then the **Philistine** said, "This day I defy the ranks of Israel!
17:11 On hearing the **Philistine's** words, Saul and all the Israelites were
17:16 For forty days the **Philistine** came forward every morning
17:19 of Israel in the Valley of Elah, fighting against the **Philistines**."
17:21 and the **Philistines** were drawing up their lines facing each other.
17:23 Goliath, the **Philistine** champion from Gath, stepped out from his
17:23 stepped out from **his**[s] lines and shouted his usual defiance,
17:26 "What will be done for the man who kills this **Philistine**
17:26 Who is this uncircumcised **Philistine** that he should defy the
17:32 said to Saul, "Let no one lose heart on account of this **Philistine**;
17:33 "You are not able to go out against this **Philistine** and fight him;
17:36 this uncircumcised **Philistine** will be like one of them, because he
17:37 paw of the bear will deliver me from the hand of this **Philistine**."
17:40 bag and, with his sling in his hand, approached the **Philistine**.
17:41 Meanwhile, the **Philistine**, with his shield bearer in front of him,
17:42 **He**[s] [+2021] looked David over and saw that he was only a boy,
17:43 **He**[s] [+2021] said to David, "Am I a dog, that you come at me with
17:43 at me with sticks?" And the **Philistine** cursed David by his gods.
17:44 "Come here," **he**[s] [+2021] said, "and I'll give your flesh to the
17:45 David said to the **Philistine**, "You come against me with sword
17:46 Today I will give the carcasses of the **Philistine** army to the birds
17:48 As the **Philistine** moved closer to attack him, David ran quickly
17:48 David ran quickly toward the battle line to meet **him**[s] [+2021].
17:49 out a stone, he slung it and struck the **Philistine** on the forehead.
17:50 So David triumphed over the **Philistine** with a sling and a stone;
17:50 without a sword in his hand he struck down the **Philistine**
17:51 He took hold of the **Philistine's** sword and drew it from the
17:51 When the **Philistines** saw that their hero was dead, they turned
17:52 pursued the **Philistines** to the entrance of Gath and to the gates of
17:52 **Their**[s] dead were strewn along the Shaaraim road to Gath
17:53 When the Israelites returned from chasing the **Philistines**,
17:54 David took the **Philistine's** head and brought it to Jerusalem,
17:55 As Saul watched David going out to meet the **Philistine**, he said to
17:57 As soon as David returned from killing the **Philistine**, Abner took
17:57 him before Saul, with David still holding the **Philistine's** head.
18: 6 the men were returning home after David had killed the **Philistine**,
18:17 "I will not raise a hand against him. Let the **Philistines** do that!"
18:21 and so that the hand of the **Philistines** may be against him."
18:25 no other price for the bride than a hundred **Philistine** foreskins,
18:25 Saul's plan was to have David fall by the hands of the **Philistines**.
18:27 David and his men went out and killed two hundred **Philistines**.
18:30 The **Philistine** commanders continued to go out to battle, and as
19: 5 He took his life in his hands when he killed the **Philistine**.
19: 8 war broke out, and David went out and fought the **Philistines**.
21: 9 [21:10] The priest replied, "The sword of Goliath the **Philistine**,
22:10 also gave him provisions and the sword of Goliath the **Philistine**."
23: 1 the **Philistines** are fighting against Keilah and are looting the
23: 2 of the LORD, saying, "Shall I go and attack these **Philistines**?"
23: 2 answered him, "Go, attack the **Philistines** and save Keilah."
23: 3 much more, then, if we go to Keilah against the **Philistine** forces!"
23: 4 to Keilah, for I am going to give the **Philistines** into your hand."
23: 5 to Keilah, fought the **Philistines** and carried off their livestock.
23:27 saying, "Come quickly! The **Philistines** are raiding the land."
23:28 broke off his pursuit of David and went to meet the **Philistines**.
24: 1 [24:2] After Saul returned from pursuing the **Philistines**, he was
27: 1 The best thing I can do is to escape to the land of the **Philistines**.
27: 7 David lived in **Philistine** territory a year and four months.
27:11 such was his practice as long as he lived in **Philistine** territory.
28: 1 In those days the **Philistines** gathered their forces to fight against
28: 4 The **Philistines** assembled and came and set up camp at Shunem,
28: 5 When Saul saw the **Philistine** army, he was afraid; terror filled his
28:15 "The **Philistines** are fighting against me, and God has turned away
28:19 The LORD will hand over both Israel and you to the **Philistines**,
28:19 LORD will also hand over the army of Israel to the **Philistines**."
29: 1 The **Philistines** gathered all their forces at Aphek, and Israel
29: 2 As the **Philistine** rulers marched with their units of hundreds
29: 3 The commanders of the **Philistines** asked, "What about these
29: 3 Achish replied, **[RPH]** "Is this not David, who was an officer of
29: 4 But the **Philistine** commanders were angry with him and said,
29: 4 were angry with him and said, **[RPH]** "Send the man back,
29: 7 and go in peace; do nothing to displease the **Philistine** rulers."
29: 9 nevertheless, the **Philistine** commanders have said, 'He must not
29:11 up early in the morning to go back to the land of the **Philistines**,
29:11 to the land of the Philistines, and the **Philistines** went up to Jezreel.
30:16 amount of plunder they had taken from the land of the **Philistines**
31: 1 Now the **Philistines** fought against Israel; the Israelites fled before
31: 1 the Israelites fled before **them**[s], and many fell slain on Mount
31: 2 The **Philistines** pressed hard after Saul and his sons, and they
31: 2 and **they**[s] killed his sons Jonathan, Abinadab and Malki-Shua.
31: 7 their towns and fled. And the **Philistines** came and occupied them.
31: 8 The next day, when the **Philistines** came to strip the dead,
31: 9 they sent messengers throughout the land of the **Philistines** to
31:11 When the people of Jabesh Gilead heard of what the **Philistines**
2Sa 1:20 streets of Ashkelon, lest the daughters of the **Philistines** be glad,
3:14 whom I betrothed to myself for the price of a hundred **Philistine**
3:18 I will rescue my people Israel from the hand of the **Philistines**
5:17 When the **Philistines** heard that David had been anointed king over
5:17 **they**[s] went up in full force to search for him, but David heard
5:18 Now the **Philistines** had come and spread out in the Valley of
5:19 inquired of the LORD, "Shall I go and attack the **Philistines**?
5:19 "Go, for I will surely hand the **Philistines** over to you."
5:22 Once more the **Philistines** came up and spread out in the Valley of
5:24 LORD has gone out in front of you to strike the **Philistine** army."
5:25 he struck down the **Philistines** all the way from Gibeon to Gezer.
8: 1 course of time, David defeated the **Philistines** and subdued them,
8: 1 and he took Metheg Ammah from the control of the **Philistines**.
8:12 Edom and Moab, the Ammonites and the **Philistines**, and Amalek.
19: 9 [19:10] the one who rescued us from the hand of the **Philistines**.
21:12 [where **the** [Q; see K 2021] Philistines had hung them after they]
21:12 where the **Philistines** [no Q] had hung them after they struck Saul
21:12 where the Philistines had hung them after **they**[s] struck Saul down
21:15 Once again there was a battle between the **Philistines** and Israel.
21:15 David went down with his men to fight against the **Philistines**,
21:17 to David's rescue; he struck the **Philistine** down and killed him.
21:18 of time, there was another battle with the **Philistines**, at Gob.
21:19 In another battle with the **Philistines** at Gob, Elhanan son of
23: 9 he was with David when they taunted the **Philistines** gathered ⌞at
23:10 struck down the **Philistines** till his hand grew tired and froze to the
23:11 When the **Philistines** banded together at a place where there was a
23:11 there was a field full of lentils, Israel's troops fled from **them**[s].
23:12 He defended it and struck the **Philistines** down, and the LORD
23:13 while a band of **Philistines** was encamped in the Valley of
23:14 in the stronghold, and the **Philistine** garrison was at Bethlehem.
23:16 So the three mighty men broke through the **Philistine** lines,
1Ki 4:21 [5:1] the kingdoms from the River to the land of the **Philistines**,
15:27 a **Philistine** town, while Nadab and all Israel were besieging it.
16:15 The army was encamped near Gibbethon, a **Philistine** town.
2Ki 8: 2 went away and stayed in the land of the **Philistines** seven years.
8: 3 of the seven years she came back from the land of the **Philistines**
18: 8 he defeated the **Philistines**, as far as Gaza and its territory.
1Ch 1:12 Pathrusites, Casluhites (from whom the **Philistines** came)
10: 1 Now the **Philistines** fought against Israel; the Israelites fled before
10: 1 the Israelites fled before **them**[s], and many fell slain on Mount
10: 2 The **Philistines** pressed hard after Saul and his sons, and they
10: 2 and **they**[s] killed his sons Jonathan, Abinadab and Malki-Shua.
10: 7 their towns and fled. And the **Philistines** came and occupied them.
10: 8 The next day, when the **Philistines** came to strip the dead,
10: 9 sent messengers throughout the land of the **Philistines** to proclaim
10:11 Jabesh Gilead heard of everything the **Philistines** had done to Saul,
11:13 He was with David at Pas Dammim when the **Philistines** gathered
11:13 there was a field full of barley, the troops fled from the **Philistines**.
11:14 They defended it and struck the **Philistines** down, and the LORD
11:15 while a band of **Philistines** was encamped in the Valley of
11:16 in the stronghold, and the **Philistine** garrison was at Bethlehem.
11:18 So the Three broke through the **Philistine** lines, drew water from
12:19 [12:20] when he went with the **Philistines** to fight against Saul.
12:19 [12:20] (He and his men did not help the **Philistines** because,
14: 8 When the **Philistines** heard that David had been anointed king over
14: 8 **they**[s] went up in full force to search for him, but David heard
14: 9 Now the **Philistines** had come and raided the Valley of Rephaim;
14:10 so David inquired of God: "Shall I go and attack the **Philistines**?
14:13 Once more the **Philistines** raided the valley;
14:15 God has gone out in front of you to strike the **Philistine** army."

1Ch 14:16 they struck down the **Philistine** army, all the way from Gibeon to
18: 1 David defeated the **Philistines** and subdued them, and he took
18: 1 and its surrounding villages from the control of the **Philistines**.
18:11 Edom and Moab, the Ammonites and the **Philistines**, and Amalek.
20: 4 In the course of time, war broke out with the **Philistines**, at Gezer.
20: 5 In another battle with the **Philistines**, Elhanan son of Jair killed
2Ch 9:26 over all the kings from the River to the land of the **Philistines**,
17:11 Some **Philistines** brought Jehoshaphat gifts and silver as tribute,
21:16 LORD aroused against Jehoram the hostility of the **Philistines**
26: 6 He went to war against the **Philistines** and broke down the walls of
26: 6 rebuilt towns near Ashdod and elsewhere among the **Philistines**.
26: 7 God helped him against the **Philistines** and against the Arabs who
28:18 while the **Philistines** had raided towns in the foothills and in the
Ps 56: T [56:1] A *miktam*. When the **Philistines** had seized him in Gath.
Isa 2: 6 they practice divination like the **Philistines** and clasp hands with
9:12 [9:11] **Philistines** from the west have devoured Israel with open
11:14 They will swoop down on the slopes of **Philistia** to the west;
Jer 25:20 all the kings of the **Philistines** [+824] (those of Ashkelon,
47: 1 prophet concerning the **Philistines** before Pharaoh attacked Gaza:
47: 4 For the day has come to destroy all the **Philistines** and to cut off all
47: 4 The LORD is about to destroy the **Philistines**, the remnant from
Eze 16:27 the daughters of the **Philistines**, who were shocked by your lewd
16:57 and all her neighbors and the daughters of the **Philistines**—
25:15 'Because the **Philistines** acted in vengeance and took revenge with
25:16 I am about to stretch out my hand against the **Philistines**, and I will
Am 1: 8 till the last of the **Philistines** is dead," says the Sovereign LORD.
9: 7 the **Philistines** from Caphtor and the Arameans from Kir?
Ob 1:19 people from the foothills will possess the land of the **Philistines**.
Zep 2: 5 of the LORD is against you, O Canaan, land of the **Philistines**.
Zec 9: 6 will occupy Ashdod, and I will cut off the pride of the **Philistines**.

7150 פֶּלֶת *pelet*, n.pr.m. [2]

Peleth [2]

Nu 16: 1 Dathan and Abiram, sons of Eliab, and On son of **Peleth**—
1Ch 2:33 The sons of Jonathan: **Peleth** and Zaza. These were the

7151 פְּלֻת *pᵉlut*, n.f. [0 / 1] [√ 7111]

distinction [1]

Ex 8:23 [8:19] I will make a **distinction** [BHS 7014] between my people

7152 פְּלֵתִי *pᵉlētî*, a.g. [7] [cf. 4165?]

Pelethites [7]

2Sa 8:18 Benaiah son of Jehoiada was over the Kerethites and **Pelethites**;
15:18 marched past him, along with all the Kerethites and **Pelethites**;
20: 7 So Joab's men and the Kerethites and **Pelethites** and all the mighty
20:23 Benaiah son of Jehoiada was over the Kerethites and **Pelethites**;
1Ki 1:38 the Kerethites and the **Pelethites** went down and put Solomon on
1:44 Benaiah son of Jehoiada, the Kerethites and the **Pelethites**,
1Ch 18:17 Benaiah son of Jehoiada was over the Kerethites and **Pelethites**;

7153 פֶּן *pen*, c. [133] [√ 7155?]

or [49], not [16], *untranslated* [9], otherwise [9], lest [8], so that not [6], if [4], might [4], no [3], and [2], because [2], for [2], so not [2], that no [2], that not [2], can't [1], for if [1], in order that not [1], may [1], not be allowed [1], or else [1], perhaps [1], so cannot [1], so that no [1], that [1], too [1], won't [1], would [1]

Ge 3: 3 middle of the garden, and you must not touch it, **or** you will die.' "
3:22 He must **not be allowed** to reach out his hand and take also from
11: 4 and **not** be scattered over the face of the whole earth."
19:15 are here, **or** you will be swept away when the city is punished."
19:17 in the plain! Flee to the mountains **or** you will be swept away!"
19:19 the mountains; **[NIE]** this disaster will overtake me, and I'll die.
24: 6 "Make sure that you do **not** take my son back there," Abraham
26: 7 "The men of this place **might** kill me on account of Rebekah,
26: 9 "Because I thought I **might** lose my life on account of her."
31:24 "Be careful **not** to say anything to Jacob, either good or bad."
31:31 because I thought you **would** take your daughters away from me
32:11 [32:12] for I am afraid he **[NIE]** will come and attack me,
38:11 For he thought, "He **may** die too, just like his brothers." So Tamar
38:23 "Let her keep what she has, **or** we will become a laughingstock.
42: 4 the others, because he was afraid **that** harm might come to him.
44:34 Do **not** let me see the misery that would come upon my father."
45:11 **Otherwise** you and your household and all who belong to you will
Ex 1:10 shrewdly with them **or** they will become even more numerous and,
5: 3 our God, **or** he may strike us with plagues or with the sword."
13:17 they face war, they **might** change their minds and return to Egypt."
19:21 **so** they do **not** force their way through to see the LORD
19:22 **or** the LORD will break out against them."
19:24 to come up to the LORD, **or** he will break out against them."
20:19 we will listen. But do not have God speak to us **or** we will die."
23:29 **because** the land would become desolate and the wild animals too
23:33 let them live in your land, **or** they will cause you to sin against me,
33: 3 you are a stiff-necked people **and** I might destroy you on the way."
34:12 Be careful **not** to make a treaty with those who live in the land
34:12 the land where you are going, **or** they will be a snare among you.
34:15 "Be careful **not** to make a treaty with those who live in the land;
Lev 10: 7 Do not leave the entrance to the Tent of Meeting **or** you will die,
Nu 16:26 to them, **or** you will be swept away because of all their sins."
16:34 them fled, shouting, "The earth is going to swallow us **too**!"
20:18 **if** you try, we will march out and attack you with the sword."
Dt 4: 9 **so that** you do **not** forget the things your eyes have seen
4: 9 or **[RPH]** let them slip from your heart as long as you live.
4:16 **so that** you do **not** become corrupt and make for yourselves an
4:19 do **not** be enticed into bowing down to them and worshiping things
4:23 Be careful **not** to forget the covenant of the LORD your God that
6:12 be careful **that** you do **not** forget the LORD, who brought you out
6:15 is a jealous God **[RPH]** and his anger will burn against you,
7:22 them all at once, **or** the wild animals will multiply around you.
7:25 and do not take it for yourselves, **or** you will be ensnared by it,
8:11 Be careful **that** you do **not** forget the LORD your God, failing to
8:12 **Otherwise**, when you eat and are satisfied, when you build fine
9:28 **Otherwise**, the country from which you brought us will say,
11:16 **or** you will be enticed to turn away and worship other gods
12:13 Be careful **not** to sacrifice your burnt offerings anywhere you
12:19 Be careful **not** to neglect the Levites as long as you live in your
12:30 be careful **not** to be ensnared by inquiring about their gods,
12:30 be careful not to be ensnared **[RPH]** by inquiring about their
15: 9 Be careful **not** to harbor this wicked thought: "The seventh year,
19: 6 **Otherwise**, the avenger of blood might pursue him in a rage,
20: 5 **or** he may die in battle and someone else may dedicate it.
20: 6 him go home, **or** he may die in battle and someone else enjoy it.
20: 7 him go home, **or** he may die in battle and someone else marry her."
22: 9 **if** you do, not only the crops you plant but also the fruit of the
25: 3 **If** he is flogged more than that, your brother will be degraded in
29:18 [29:17] Make sure there is **no** man or woman, clan or tribe among
29:18 [29:17] make sure there is **no** root among you that produces such
32:27 **lest** the adversary misunderstand and say, 'Our hand has
32:27 lest the adversary misunderstand and **[RPH]** say, 'Our hand has
Jos 2:16 had said to them, "Go to the hills **so** the pursuers will **not** find you.
6:18 **so that** you will **not** bring about your own destruction by taking
24:27 It will be a witness against you **if** you are untrue to your God."
Jdg 7: 2 **In order that** Israel may **not** boast against me that her own
9:54 "Draw your sword and kill me, so that they **can't** say,
14:15 **or** we will burn you and your father's household to death.
15:12 Samson said, "Swear to me that you **won't** kill me yourselves."
18:25 **or** some hot-tempered men will attack you, and you and your
Ru 4: 6 "Then I cannot redeem it **because** I might endanger my own estate.
1Sa 4: 9 Be men, **or** you will be subject to the Hebrews, as they have been
9: 5 **or** my father will stop thinking about the donkeys and start
13:19 had said, "**Otherwise** the Hebrews will make swords or spears!"
15: 6 leave the Amalekites **so that** I do **not** destroy you along with them;
20: 3 to himself, 'Jonathan must not know this **or** he will be grieved.'
27:11 to Gath, for he thought, "They **might** inform on us and say,
31: 4 **or** these uncircumcised fellows will come and run me through
2Sa 1:20 streets of Ashkelon, **lest** the daughters of the Philistines be glad,
1:20 Philistines be glad, **lest** the daughters of the uncircumcised rejoice.
12:28 **Otherwise** I will take the city, and it will be named after me."
15:14 **or** he will move quickly to overtake us and bring ruin upon us
17:16 **or** the king and all the people with him will be swallowed up.' "
20: 6 and pursue him, **or** he will find fortified cities and escape from us."
2Ki 2:16 **Perhaps** the Spirit of the LORD has picked him up and set him
10:23 and see **that no** servants of the LORD are here with you—
1Ch 10: 4 **or** these uncircumcised fellows will come and abuse me."
Job 32:13 Do **not** say, 'We have found wisdom; let God refute him, not man.'
36:18 Be careful **that no** one entices you by riches; do not let a large
Ps 2:12 Kiss the Son, **lest** he be angry and you be destroyed in your way,
7: 2 [7:3] **or** they will tear me like a lion and rip me to pieces with no
13: 3 [13:4] my God. Give light to my eyes, **or** I will sleep in death;
13: 4 [13:5] **[RPH]** my enemy will say, "I have overcome him,"
28: 1 **For if** you remain silent, I will be like those who have gone down
38:16 [38:17] "Do **not** let them gloat or exalt themselves over me when
50:22 who forget God, **or** I will tear you to pieces, with none to rescue:
59:11 [59:12] not kill them, O Lord our shield, **or** my people will forget.
91:12 in their hands, **so that** you will **not** strike your foot against a stone.
Pr 5: 6 She gives **no** thought to the way of life; her paths are crooked,
5: 9 **lest** you give your best strength to others and your years to one
5:10 **lest** strangers feast on your wealth and your toil enrich another
9: 8 Do not rebuke a mocker **or** he will hate you; rebuke a wise man
20:13 Do not love sleep **or** you will grow poor; stay awake and you will
22:25 **or** you may learn his ways and get yourself ensnared.
24:18 **or** the LORD will see and disapprove and turn his wrath away
25: 8 **for** what will you do in the end if your neighbor puts you to
25:10 **or** he who hears it may shame you and you will never lose your
25:16 eat just enough—**[NIE]** too much of it, and you will vomit.
25:17 neighbor's house—**[NIE]** too much of you, and he will hate you.

Pr 26: 4 a fool according to his folly, **or** you will be like him yourself.
26: 5 a fool according to his folly, **or** he will be wise in his own eyes.
30: 6 not add to his words, **or** he will rebuke you and prove you a liar.
30: 9 **Otherwise**, I may have too much and disown you and say,
30: 9 **Or** I may become poor and steal, and so dishonor the name of my
30: 10 servant to his master, **or** he will curse you, and you will pay for it.
31: 5 **lest** they drink and forget what the law decrees, and deprive all the
Isa 6: 10 **Otherwise** they might see with their eyes, hear with their ears,
27: 3 it continually. I guard it day and night **so that no** one may harm it.
28: 22 Now stop your mocking, **or** your chains will become heavier;
36: 18 "Do **not** let Hezekiah mislead you when he says, 'The LORD will
48: 5 they happened I announced them to you **so that** you could **not** say,
48: 7 of them before today. **So** you **cannot** say, 'Yes, I knew of them.'
Jer 1: 17 Do not be terrified by them, **or** I will terrify you before them.
4: 4 **or** my wrath will break out and burn like fire because of the evil
6: 8 **or** I will turn away from you and make your land desolate
6: 8 from you **and** make your land desolate so no one can live in it."
10: 24 with justice—not in your anger, **lest** you reduce me to nothing.
21: 12 **or** my wrath will break out and burn like fire because of the evil
38: 19 **for** the Babylonians may hand me over to them and they will
51: 46 Do **not** lose heart or be afraid when rumors are heard in the land;
Hos 2: 3 [2:5] **Otherwise** I will strip her naked and make her as bare as on
Am 5: 6 and live, **or** he will sweep through the house of Joseph like a fire;
Mal 4: 6 [3:24] **or else** I will come and strike the land with a curse."

7154 פַּנַּג *pannag*, n.[m.]. [1]

confections [1]

Eze 27: 17 they exchanged wheat from Minnith and **confections**, honey,

7155 פָּנָה *pānâ*, v. [134] [→ 3648, 4367, 4368, 7153?, 7156, 7157, 7158, 7159, 7160, 7161, 7163, 7164]

turned [27], turn [18], facing [14], *untranslated* [5], looked [4], prepare [4], look [3], return [3], turning [3], turns [3], faces [2], give attention [2], left [2], look with favor [2], turned back [2], turns away [2], accept [1], approaches [1], back [+339] [1], back [1], break camp [1], break of day [+1332] [1], cleared ground [1], daybreak [+1332] [1], daybreak [+1332+2021] [1], emptied [1], expected [1], face [1], faced [1], fading [1], fled [1], glancing [1], go [1], goes [1], looked around [1], looking back [1], looking [1], notice [1], overlook [+440 +448+448+448] [1], pass away [1], pays attention [1], prepared [1], respond [1], return [+2143+2256] [1], showed concern for [+448] [1], surveyed [1], tied [1], turn around [1], turn back [1], turn to help [1], turned [+8900] [1], turned around [1], turned away [1], turns back [1]

Ge 18: 22 [A] The men **turned** away and went toward Sodom,
24: 31 [D] I *have* **prepared** the house and a place for the camels."
24: 49 [A] and if not, tell me, so *I may know* which way *to* **turn**."
24: 63 [A] He went out to the field **[NIE]** one evening to meditate,
Ex 2: 12 [A] **Glancing** this way and that and seeing no one, he killed the
7: 23 [A] Instead, he **turned** and went into his palace, and did not take
10: 6 [A] day they settled in this land till now.' " Then Moses **turned**
14: 27 [A] and at **daybreak** [+1332] the sea went back to its place.
16: 10 [A] whole Israelite community, *they* **looked** toward the desert,
32: 15 [A] Moses **turned** and went down the mountain with the two
Lev 14: 36 [D] The priest is to order the house *to be* **emptied** before he goes
19: 4 [A] " '*Do* not **turn** to idols or make gods of cast metal for
19: 31 [A] " '*Do* not **turn** to mediums or seek out spiritists, for you will
20: 6 [A] " 'I will set my face against the person who **turns** to
26: 9 [A] " '*I will* **look** on you **with favor** and make you fruitful and
Nu 12: 10 [A] Aaron **turned** toward her and saw that she had leprosy;
14: 25 [A] **turn back** tomorrow and set out toward the desert along the
16: 15 [A] and said to the LORD, "*Do* not **accept** their offering.
16: 42 [17:7] [A] and Aaron and **turned** toward the Tent of Meeting,
21: 33 [A] *they* **turned** and went up along the road toward Bashan,
Dt 1: 7 [A] **Break camp** and advance into the hill country of the
1: 24 [A] *They* **left** and went up into the hill country, and came to the
1: 40 [A] **turn around** and set out toward the desert along the route to
2: 1 [A] *we* **turned back** and set out toward the desert along the route
2: 3 [A] way around this hill country long enough; now **turn** north.
2: 8 [A] *We* **turned** from the Arabah road, which comes up from
3: 1 [A] Next *we* **turned** and went up along the road toward Bashan,
9: 15 [A] So *I* **turned** and went down from the mountain while it was
9: 27 [A] Isaac and Jacob. **Overlook** [+440+448+448+448] the stubbornness of this people, their wickedness and their sin.
10: 5 [A] *I came* **back** down the mountain and put the tablets in the
16: 7 [A] Then in the morning **return** [+2143+2256] to your tents.
23: 11 [23:12] [A] as evening **approaches** he is to wash himself, and at
29: 18 [29:17] [A] or tribe among you today whose heart **turns away**
30: 17 [A] if your heart **turns away** and you are not obedient, and if you
31: 18 [A] because of all their wickedness *in* **turning** to other gods.
31: 20 [A] and thrive, *they will* **turn** to other gods and worship them,
Jos 7: 12 [A] *they* **turn** their backs and run because they have been made
8: 20 [A] The men of Ai looked **back** [+339] and saw the smoke of the
15: 2 [A] Their southern boundary started from the bay at the **[NIE]**
15: 7 [A] Debir from the Valley of Achor and **turned** north to Gilgal,
22: 4 [A] **return** to your homes in the land that Moses the servant of
Jdg 6: 14 [A] The LORD **turned** to him and said, "Go in the strength you
15: 4 [G] caught three hundred foxes and **tied** them tail to tail in pairs.
18: 21 [A] possessions in front of them, *they* **turned away** and left.
18: 26 [A] too strong for him, **turned around** and went back home.
19: 26 [A] At **daybreak** [+1332+2021] the woman went back to the house
20: 40 [A] the Benjamites **turned** and saw the smoke of the whole city
20: 42 [A] So *they* **fled** before the Israelites in the direction of the
20: 45 [A] As *they* **turned** and fled toward the desert to the rock of
20: 47 [A] six hundred men **turned** and fled into the desert to the rock
1Sa 10: 9 [G] As Saul **turned** [+8900] to leave Samuel, God changed
13: 17 [A] One **turned** toward Ophrah in the vicinity of Shual,
13: 18 [A] another **[RPH]** toward Beth Horon, and the third toward the
13: 18 [A] the third **[RPH]** toward the borderland overlooking the
14: 47 [A] Wherever *he* **turned**, he inflicted punishment on them.
2Sa 1: 7 [A] When *he* **turned** around and saw me, he called out to me,
2: 20 [A] Abner **looked** behind him and asked, "Is that you, Asahel?"
9: 8 [A] is your servant, that *you should* **notice** a dead dog like me?"
1Ki 2: 3 [A] so that you may prosper in all you do and wherever *you* **go**,
7: 25 [A] three **facing** north, three facing west, three facing south and
7: 25 [A] three **facing** west, three facing south and three facing east.
7: 25 [A] three facing west, three **facing** south and three facing east.
7: 25 [A] three facing west, three facing south and three **facing** east.
8: 28 [A] Yet **give attention** to your servant's prayer and his plea for
10: 13 [A] *she* **left** and returned with her retinue to her own country.
17: 3 [A] "Leave here, **turn** eastward and hide in the Kerith Ravine,
2Ki 2: 24 [A] *He* **turned** around, looked at them and called down a curse
5: 12 [A] and be cleansed?" So *he* **turned** and went off in a rage.
13: 23 [A] and had compassion and **showed concern** [+448] **for** them
23: 16 [A] Josiah **looked around**, and when he saw the tombs that were
2Ch 4: 4 [A] three **facing** north, three facing west, three facing south and
4: 4 [A] three **facing** west, three facing south and three facing east.
4: 4 [A] three facing west, three **facing** south and three facing east.
4: 4 [A] three facing west, three facing south and three **facing** east.
6: 19 [A] Yet **give attention** to your servant's prayer and his plea for
13: 14 [A] Judah **turned** and saw that they were being attacked at both
20: 24 [A] that overlooks the desert and **looked** toward the vast army,
26: 20 [A] the chief priest and all the other priests **looked** at him,
Job 5: 1 [A] will answer you? To which of the holy ones *will you* **turn**?
6: 28 [A] "But now be so kind as *to* **look** at me. Would I lie to your
21: 5 [A] **Look** at me and be astonished; clap your hand over your
24: 18 [A] of the land is cursed, so that no *one* **goes** to the vineyards.
36: 21 [A] Beware of **turning** to evil, which you seem to prefer to
Ps 25: 16 [A] **Turn** to me and be gracious to me, for I am lonely
40: 4 [40:5] [A] *who does* not **look** to the proud, to those who turn
46: 5 [46:6] [A] not fall; God will help her at **break of day** [+1332].
69: 16 [69:17] [A] of your love; in your great mercy **turn** to me.
80: 9 [80:10] [D] *You* **cleared** *the* **ground** for it, and it took root and
86: 16 [A] **Turn** to me and have mercy on me; grant your strength to
90: 9 [A] All our days **pass away** under your wrath; we finish our
102: 17 [102:18] [A] *He will* **respond** to the prayer of the destitute; he
119: 132 [A] **Turn** to me and have mercy on me, as you always do to
Pr 17: 8 [A] to the one who gives it; wherever *he* **turns**, he succeeds.
Ecc 2: 11 [A] Yet *when* I **surveyed** all that my hands had done and what I
2: 12 [A] I **turned** my thoughts to consider wisdom, and also madness
SS 6: 1 [A] Which way *did* your lover **turn**, that we may look for him
Isa 8: 21 [A] **looking** upward, will curse their king and their God.
13: 14 [A] without a shepherd, each *will* **return** to his own people,
40: 3 [D] "In the desert **prepare** the way for the LORD;
45: 22 [A] "**Turn** to me and be saved, all you ends of the earth; for I am
53: 6 [A] have gone astray, each of *us has* **turned** to his own way;
56: 11 [A] they all **turn** to their own way, each seeks his own gain.
57: 14 [D] And it will be said: "Build up, build up, **prepare** the road!
62: 10 [D] **Prepare** the way for the people. Build up, build up the
Jer 2: 27 [A] *They have* **turned** their backs to me and not their faces;
6: 4 [A] But, alas, the daylight *is* **fading**, and the shadows of evening
32: 33 [A] *They* **turned** their backs to me and not their faces; though I
46: 5 [G] They flee in haste without **looking back**, and there is terror
46: 21 [G] They too *will* **turn** and flee together, they will not stand their
47: 3 [G] Fathers *will* not **turn to help** their children; their hands will
48: 39 [G] she is! How they wail! How Moab **turns** *her* back in shame!
49: 8 [H] **Turn** and flee, hide in deep caves, you who live in Dedan,
49: 24 [G] *she has* **turned** to flee and panic has gripped her;
50: 16 [A] Because of the sword of the oppressor *let* everyone **return** to
Eze 8: 3 [A] to the entrance to the **[NIE]** north gate of the inner court,
9: 2 [H] which **faces** north, each with a deadly weapon in his hand.
10: 11 [A] The cherubim went in whatever direction the head **faced**,
11: 1 [A] brought me to the gate of the house of the LORD that **faces**
17: 6 [A] Its branches **turned** toward him, but its roots remained under
29: 16 [A] but will be a reminder of their sin in **turning** to her for help.
36: 9 [A] I am concerned for you and *will* **look** on you **with favor**; you
43: 1 [A] Then the man brought me to the gate **facing** east,

Eze 43:17 [A] a gutter of a cubit all around. The steps of the altar **face** east."
44: 1 [A] gate of the sanctuary, the *one* **facing** east, and it was shut.
46: 1 [A] The gate of the inner court **facing** east is to be shut on the six
46:12 [A] the gate **facing** east is to be opened for him.
46:19 [A] at the side of the gate to the sacred rooms **facing** north,
47: 2 [A] and led me around the outside to the outer gate **facing** east,
Hos 3: 1 [A] though they **turn** to other gods and love the sacred raisin
Na 2: 8 [2:9] [G] "Stop! Stop!" they cry, but no *one* **turns back**.
Zep 3:15 [D] away your punishment, *he has* **turned back** your enemy.
Hag 1: 9 [A] "*You* **expected** much, but see, it turned out to be little. What
Mal 2:13 [A] because *he* no longer **pays attention** to your offerings
3: 1 [D] send my messenger, *who will* **prepare** the way before me.

7156 פָּנֶה *pāneh*, n.m. & f. [2127 / 2126] [→ 2209, 7163; cf. 7155]

before [+4200] [542], face [211], *untranslated* [120], presence [108], before [+4946] [82], in front of [+4200] [66], because of [+4946] [54], to [+4200] [50], ahead [+4200] [45], from [+4946] [45], faces [35], front [25], before [+4200+4946] [24], by [+4200] [21], before [19], presence [+4200] [19], of [+4946] [17], sight [17], facedown [+6584] [15], against [+4200] [13], on [+6584] [13], from [+4200+4946] [11], for [+4200] [10], over [+6584] [10], surface [10], before [+907] [9], facing [9], because [+4946] [8], from [+4200] [8], near [+6584] [8], open [8], by [+4946] [7], formerly [+4200] [7], meet [+4200] [7], with [+4200] [7], in [+6584] [6], in front of [+6584] [6], near [+4200] [6], serve [+4200+6641] [6], against [+928] [5], before [+6584] [5], east [+6584] [5], used to [+4200] [5], at [+4946] [4], in front of [+448] [4], show partiality [+5795] [4], show partiality [+5951] [4], upon [+6584] [4], accept [+5951] [3], against [+4946] [3], east [3], entreat [+906+2704] [3], escape [+4946] [3], face [+4200] [3], face [+6425] [3], facedown [+448] [3], faces [+6584] [3], facing [+448] [3], facing [+6584] [3], leading [+4200] [3], me [+3276] [3], opposite [+4200] [3], sight [+4200] [3], sought the favor of [+906+2704] [3], straight ahead [+448+6298] [3], toward [+6584] [3], accompanies [+4200] [2], across [+6584] [2], across from [+6584] [2], advisers [+8011] [2], as long as [+4200] [2], at [+4200] [2], at table[s] [+4200] [2], attitude [2], audience [2], before [+5584] [2], beside [+4200] [2], covered with [+4200] [2], entered service [+4200+6641] [2], face to face [2], faced [+448] [2], faced each other [+8011] [2], faced [2], floor [2], from [+4946+6584] [2], from [+6584] [2], in front of [+907] [2], in front of [2], in way [+4200] [2], inside [+4200] [2], leader [+2143+4200] [2], led in campaigns [+995+2256+3655+4200] [2], looking [2], lying on [+6584] [2], of [+4200] [2], of [+4200+4946] [2], preceded [+2118+4200] [2], preceded [+4200] [2], prostrate [+6584] [2], reflects a face [+2021+2021+4200+7156] [2], reject [+8740] [2], repulse [+906+8740] [2], resist [+4200+6641] [2], see [+4200] [2], seems to [+4200] [2], served [+4200+6641] [2], serving [+4200 +6641] [2], shows partiality [+5951] [2], top [2], under [+4200] [2], withstand [+4200+6641] [2], withstand [+928+6641] [2], won [+4200+5951] [2], you [+3871] [2], yourselves [+4013] [2], above [+6584] [1], accept [+4946+5951] [1], accepted [+906+5951] [1], adjoining [+448] [1], advance [+2025] [1], against [+6584] [1], ahead [+4200+4946] [1], ahead [+6584] [1], all [1], appear before [+8011] [1], appearance [1], appearing [1], approach [1], are shown respect [+2075] [1], assistant [+4200+6641] [1], at [+6584] [1], at advance [+4200] [1], at sanctuary[s] [+4200] [1], at the head of [+4200] [1], attend [+4200] [1], attend [+4200+6641] [1], attending [+4200] [1], attention [+4200] [1], attention [1], awaits [+4200] [1], away from [+4946] [1], because of [+3954+4946] [1], before [+448] [1], before eyes [+4200] [1], before time [+4200+4946] [1], beforehand [+4200+4946] [1], beginning [1], bent on [+5584] [1], beside [+6584] [1], blade [1], blindfolds [+4059] [1], border [1], borne on [+6584] [1], bowed down [+5877+6584] [1], bowed down to the ground [+5877 +6584] [1], check [+995+4200] [1], come across [+4200+7925] [1], come into presence [+906+8011] [1], condition [1], confronting [+4946] [1], consult [+4200] [1], corresponding to [+6584] [1], countenance [1], court favor [+2704] [1], cover [+4848] [1], crossing [+6584] [1], curry favor with [+2704] [1], defense against [+4946] [1], determine [+8492] [1], determined [+4200+8492] [1], determined [+8492] [1], determined [+8492+8492] [1], determined [+906+8492] [1], determined [+928+4200+4200+8492] [1], directly opposite [+4200+5790] [1], disgrace [+1425] [1], earlier times [1], east [+6584+7710] [1], edge [1], eluded [+4946+6015] [1], end [1], enter service [+4200+6641] [1], entered the service [+4200+6641] [1], ever [+4200] [1], expression [1], extended [+6584] [1], face [+4946] [1], faced [+4200] [1], faced forward [+448+4578] [1], favoritism [+2075] [1], field [1], fierce-looking [+6434] [1], for [+4946] [1], for fear of [+4946] [1], for relief from [+4200+4946] [1], for sake [+4946] [1], for [1], forward [+4200] [1], found [+906+4200+8011] [1], from [+448] [1], from [+4946+6640] [1], front columns [1], frown [+5877] [1], give [+4200] [1], grant [+4200+5951] [1], granted request [+5951] [1], ground [1], had been [+4200] [1], had special access to [+8011] [1], head [1], headed for [+906+8492] [1], hear [+4200+5877] [1], here [+4200] [1], highly regarded [+5951] [1], honored [+5951] [1], humiliation [+1425] [1], implore [+2704] [1], in [+4200] [1], in deference to [+4946] [1], in earlier times [+4200] [1], in eyes [+4200] [1], in front of [+448+4578] [1], in front of [+4946] [1], in front [1], in hostility toward [+6584] [1], in path [+4200] [1], in preference to [+6584] [1], in service [+4200] [1], in sight [+907] [1], in the eyes of [+4200] [1], in the front line [+448+4578] [1], in the presence of [+5790] [1], in view [+907] [1], in [1], inner [+4200] [1], instead of [+4200] [1], intended [1], intercede with [+906+2704] [1], interceded with [+906+2704] [1], lead [+2143+4200] [1], lead [+4200] [1], lead [+995+2256+3655+4200] [1], lead across [+4200+6296] [1], lead [1], led [+4200] [1], led out [+3655+4200] [1], lifetime [1], lived in hostility toward [+5877+6584] [1], look in the face [+448+5951] [1], look with favor [+239] [1], look with favor [+5564] [1], looked [+8492] [1], looked [1], looks [1], made face [+448+5989] [1], make room for [+4946] [1], man of rank [+5951] [1], meet [+448] [1], meet [+4946] [1], meet with [+8011] [1], more quickly than [+4200] [1], more readily than [+4200] [1], mouth [1], my [+3276] [1], my [+3276+4200] [1], nearest [+6584] [1], never [+4200+4202] [1], obstinate [+7997] [1], on both sides [+294+2256] [1], open [+4200] [1], open before [+5790] [1], opening [1], opposite [+448] [1], ours [+4200+5646] [1], out [+4946] [1], out of [+4946] [1], out of way [+4200+4946] [1], outer [1], over [+4200] [1], overlooking [+4200] [1], pacify [+4105] [1], parallel [+928] [1], partial [+5951] [1], partiality [+5365] [1], preceding [+4200] [1], predecessor [+889+2118+4200] [1], present [+4200] [1], present [+4200+5877] [1], present [1], previous [+4200] [1], prominent [+5951] [1], protection from [+4946] [1], put [+995+4200] [1], puts up a bold front [+928+6451] [1], receive [+5951] [1], regard [+2118+4200] [1], regarded in the sight of [+4200] [1], regards [+4200+5162] [1], region [1], reject [+906+4946 +6584+8938] [1], reject [+906+4946+6584+8959] [1], renounce [+4946+6584+8740] [1], resist [1], resolved [+906+5989] [1], respect [+5951] [1], scalp [1], see [+8011] [1], seek an audience with [+1335] [1], seek favor [+2704] [1], seek favor [+906+2704] [1], seen for myself [+906+8011] [1], serve [+2118+4200] [1], serve [+4200] [1], served [+2118+4200] [1], served [+907+6641] [1], show [+4200] [1], showed partiality [+5951] [1], shown honor [+5951] [1], shown partiality [+5951] [1], some distance from [+4946] [1], sought favor [+2704] [1], sought favor [+906+2704] [1], spared from [+4946] [1], stared with a fixed gaze [+906+2256+6641+8492] [1], stern-faced [+6434] [1], sulking [+906+6015] [1], table[s] [1], take for [+906+4200 +5989] [1], taken from [+4200+4946] [1], that[s] [1], the LORD himself [+3378] [1], their own [+2157] [1], themselves [+2157] [1], those[s] [+2021] [1], throughout [+3972+6584] [1], tilting away from [+4946] [1], to [+4200+6584] [1], to [+4946] [1], to [+907] [1], toward [+2006 +6584] [1], toward [+448] [1], toward [1], turn away [+6015] [1], turned [+6015] [1], turned [+8492] [1], turned [+906+5989] [1], under [+4946] [1], under [+907] [1], under blessing [+4200] [1], under direction [+4200] [1], under supervision [+4200] [1], unless [+561 +3954+4200] [1], unyielding [+2617] [1], upside down [+6584] [1], watched [+4200] [1], way [1], where[s] [+4200] [1], while still alive [+6584] [1], with [+6584] [1], with [+907] [1], within sight of [+907] [1], withstood [+928+6641] [1], worship [+4200] [1], you [+4013] [1], you yourself [+3870] [1]

Ge 1: 2 and empty, darkness was over the **surface** *of* the deep,
1: 2 and the Spirit of God was hovering **over** [+6584] the waters.
1:20 let birds fly above the earth **across** [+6584] the expanse of the
1:29 "I give you every seed-bearing plant on the **face** *of* the whole earth
2: 6 up from the earth and watered the whole **surface** *of* the ground—
3: 8 they hid **from** [+4946] the LORD God among the trees of the
4: 5 with favor. So Cain was very angry, and his **face** was downcast.
4: 6 said to Cain, "Why are you angry? Why is your **face** downcast?
4:14 Today you are driving me **from** [+4946+6584] the land, and I will
4:14 driving me from the land, and I will be hidden from your **presence**;
4:16 So Cain went out from the LORD's **presence** [+4200] and lived
6: 1 When men began to increase in number **on** [+6584] the earth
6: 7 wipe mankind, whom I have created, from the **face** *of* the earth—
6:11 Now the earth was corrupt in God's **sight** and was full of violence.
6:13 So God said to Noah, "I *am going to* **put** [+995+4200] an end to
6:13 for the earth is filled with violence **because of** [+4946] them.
7: 1 I *have* **found** [+906+4200+8011] you righteous in this generation.
7: 3 keep their various kinds alive **throughout** [+3972+6584] the earth.
7: 4 I will wipe from the **face** *of* the earth every living creature I have
7: 7 his sons' wives entered the ark *to* **escape** [+4946] the waters of the
7:18 on the earth, and the ark floated on the **surface** *of* the water.
7:23 Every living thing on the **face** *of* the earth was wiped out;
8: 8 to see if the water had receded from the **surface** *of* the ground.
8: 9 its feet because there was water over all the **surface** *of* the earth;
8:13 from the ark and saw that the **surface** *of* the ground was dry.
9:23 Their **faces** were turned the other way so that they would not see
10: 9 He was a mighty hunter **before** [+4200] the LORD; that is why it
10: 9 "Like Nimrod, a mighty hunter **before** [+4200] the LORD."
11: 4 and not be scattered over the **face** *of* the whole earth."

Ge 11: 8 So the LORD scattered them from there **over** [+6584] all the
11: 9 From there the LORD scattered them over the **face** *of* the whole
11:28 **While** his father Terah was **still alive** [+6584], Haran died in Ur of
13: 9 Is not the whole land **before** [+4200] you? Let's part company.
13:10 (This was **before** [+4200] the LORD destroyed Sodom
16: 6 Then Sarai mistreated Hagar; so she fled **from** [+4946] her.
16: 8 "I'm running away **from** [+4946] my mistress Sarai,"
16:12 and he will live **in hostility toward** [+6584] all his brothers."
17: 1 "I am God Almighty; walk **before** [+4200] me and be blameless.
17: 3 Abram fell **facedown** [+6584], and God said to him,
17:17 Abraham fell **facedown** [+6584]; he laughed and said to himself,
17:18 "If only Ishmael might live **under** your **blessing** [+4200]!"
18: 8 the calf that had been prepared, and set these **before** [+4200] them.
18:16 men got up to leave, they looked down **toward** [+6584] Sodom,
18:22 but Abraham remained standing **before** [+4200] the LORD.
19:13 The outcry **to** [+907] the LORD against its people is so great that
19:21 to him, "Very well, *I will* **grant** [+4200+5951] this request too;
19:27 returned to the place where he had stood **before** [+907] the
19:28 He looked down **toward** [+6584] Sodom and Gomorrah, toward
19:28 and Gomorrah, **toward** [+6584] all the land of the plain,
20:15 Abimelech said, "My land is **before** [+4200] you; live wherever
23: 3 Abraham rose from **beside** [+6584] his dead wife and spoke to the
23: 4 property for a burial site here so I can bury my dead." **[OBJ]**
23: 8 **[OBJ]** then listen to me and intercede with Ephron son of Zohar
23:12 Again Abraham bowed down **before** [+4200] the people of the
23:17 So Ephron's field in Machpelah **near** [+4200] Mamre—
23:19 the field of Machpelah **near** [+6584] Mamre (which is at Hebron)
24: 7 he will send his angel **before** [+4200] you so that you can get a
24:12 God of my master Abraham, give me success **[OBJ]** today,
24:33 food was set **before** [+4200] him, but he said, "I will not eat until I
24:40 "He replied, 'The LORD, **before** [+4200] whom I have walked,
24:51 Here **[NIE]** is Rebekah; take her and go, and let her become the
25: 9 Ishmael buried him in the cave of Machpelah **near** [+6584]
25:18 to Shur, near the **border** *of* Egypt, as you go toward Asshur.
25:18 *they* **lived in hostility toward** [+5877+6584] all their brothers.
27: 7 so that I may give you my blessing in the **presence** *of* the LORD
27: 7 my blessing in the presence of the LORD **before** [+4200] I die.'
27:10 so that he may give you his blessing **before** [+4200] he dies."
27:20 "The LORD your God gave me success," **[OBJ]** he replied.
27:30 blessing him and Jacob had scarcely left his father's **presence**,
27:46 disgusted with living **because of** [+4946] these Hittite women.
29:26 the younger daughter in marriage **before** [+4200] the older one.
30:30 The little you had **before** [+4200] I came has increased greatly,
30:33 whenever *you* **check** [+995+4200] on the wages you have paid me.
30:40 **made** the rest **face** [+448+5989] the streaked and dark-colored
31: 2 Jacob noticed that Laban's **attitude** toward him was not what it
31: 5 "I see that your father's **attitude** toward me is not what it was
31:21 the River, he **headed for** [+906+8492] the hill country of Gilead.
31:35 "Don't be angry, my lord, that I cannot stand up in your **presence**;
32: 3 [32:4] Jacob sent messengers **ahead** [+4200] *of* him to his brother
32:16 [32:17] and said to his servants, "Go **ahead** [+4200] *of* me,
32:17 [32:18] and who owns all these animals **in front** [+4200] **of** you?'
32:20 [32:21] "*I will* **pacify** [+4105] him with these gifts I am sending
32:20 [32:21] him with these gifts I am sending on **ahead** [+4200];
32:20 [32:21] later, when *I* **see** [+8011] him, perhaps he will receive
32:20 [32:21] when I see him, perhaps *he will* **receive** [+5951] me."
32:21 [32:22] So Jacob's gifts went on **ahead of** [+6584] him, but he
32:30 [32:31] saying, "It is because I saw God **face** to face, and yet my
32:30 [32:31] saying, "It is because I saw God face to **face**, and yet my
33: 3 He himself went on **ahead** [+4200] and bowed down to the ground
33:10 For to see your **face** is like seeing the face of God, now that you
33:10 For to see your face is like seeing the **face** *of* God, now that you
33:14 So let my lord go on **ahead** [+4200] *of* his servant, while I move
33:14 I move along slowly at the pace of the droves **before** [+4200] me
33:18 of Shechem in Canaan and camped **within sight** [+907] **of** the city.
34:10 You can settle among us; the land is **open** [+4200] *to* you.
34:21 and trade in it; the land has plenty of room **for** [+4200] them.
35: 1 who appeared to you when you were fleeing **from** [+4946] your
35: 7 himself to him when he was fleeing **from** [+4946] his brother.
36: 6 moved to a land **some distance from** [+4946] his brother Jacob.
36: 7 could not support them both **because of** [+4946] their livestock.
36:31 These were the kings who reigned in Edom **before** [+4200] any
38:15 he thought she was a prostitute, for she had covered her **face**.
40: 7 him in his master's house, "Why are your **faces** so sad today?"
40: 9 He said to him, "In my dream I saw a vine **in front** [+4200] **of** me,
41:31 **because** [+4946] the famine that follows it will be so severe.
41:43 and men shouted **before** [+4200] him, "Make way!"
41:46 he **entered the service of** [+4200+6641] Pharaoh king of Egypt.
41:46 Joseph went out from Pharaoh's **presence** [+4200] and traveled
41:56 When the famine had spread **over** [+6584] the whole country,
43: 3 'You will not see my **face** again unless your brother is with you.'
43: 5 'You will not see my **face** again unless your brother is with you.' "
43: 9 do not bring him back to you and set him here **before** [+4200] you,
43:14 And may God Almighty grant you mercy **before** [+4200] the man
43:15 down to Egypt and presented themselves **to** [+4200] Joseph.
43:31 After he had washed his **face**, he came out and,
43:33 The men had been seated **before** [+4200] him in the order of their
43:34 When portions were served to them from Joseph's **table**ˢ,
44:14 and they threw themselves to the ground **before** [+4200] him.
44:23 brother comes down with you, you will not see my **face** again.'
44:26 We cannot see the man's **face** unless our youngest brother is with
44:29 If you take this one **from** [+4946+6640] me too and harm comes to
45: 3 not able to answer him, because they were terrified at his **presence**.
45: 5 because it was to save lives that God sent me **ahead** [+4200] *of*
45: 7 God sent me **ahead** [+4200] *of* you to preserve for you a remnant
46:28 Now Jacob sent Judah **ahead** [+4200] *of* him to Joseph to get
46:28 Judah ahead of him to Joseph to get directions **[RPH]** to Goshen.
46:30 since *I have* **seen for myself** [+906+8011] that you are still alive."
47: 2 five of his brothers and presented them **before** [+4200] Pharaoh.
47: 6 and the land of Egypt is **before** [+4200] you; settle your father
47: 7 his father Jacob in and presented him **before** [+4200] Pharaoh.
47:10 Jacob blessed Pharaoh and went out from his **presence** [+4200].
47:13 and Canaan wasted away **because of** [+4946] the famine.
47:18 there is nothing left **for** [+4200] our lord except our bodies
48:11 Israel said to Joseph, "I never expected to see your **face** again,
48:15 "May the God **before** [+4200] whom my fathers Abraham
48:20 and Manasseh.' " So he put Ephraim **ahead** [+4200] *of* Manasseh.
49:30 cave in the field of Machpelah, **near** [+6584] Mamre in Canaan,
50: 1 Joseph threw himself **upon** [+6584] his father and wept over him
50:13 him in the cave in the field of Machpelah, **near** [+6584] Mamre,
50:16 "Your father left these instructions **before** [+4200] he died:
50:18 then came and threw themselves down **before** [+4200] him.
Ex 1:12 and spread; so the Egyptians came to dread **[OBJ]** the Israelites
2:15 but Moses fled **from** [+4946] Pharaoh and went to live in Midian,
3: 6 At this, Moses hid his **face**, because he was afraid to look at God.
3: 7 have heard them crying out **because of** [+4946] their slave drivers,
4: 3 it on the ground and it became a snake, and he ran **from** [+4946] it.
4:21 see that you perform **before** [+4200] Pharaoh all the wonders I
6:12 Moses said **to** [+4200] the LORD, "If the Israelites will not listen
6:30 Moses said **to** [+4200] the LORD, "Since I speak with faltering
7: 9 'Take your staff and throw it down **before** [+4200] Pharaoh,'
7:10 Aaron threw his staff down **in front** [+4200] **of** Pharaoh and his
7:10 threw his staff down in front of Pharaoh and **[RPH]** his officials,
8:20 [8:16] confront **[OBJ]** Pharaoh as he goes to the water and say to
8:24 [8:20] throughout Egypt the land was ruined **by** [+4946] the flies.
9:10 they took soot from a furnace and stood **before** [+4200] Pharaoh.
9:11 The magicians could not stand **before** [+4200] Moses because of
9:11 **because of** [+4946] the boils that were on them and on all the
9:13 confront **[OBJ]** Pharaoh and say to him, 'This is what the
9:30 and your officials still do not fear **[OBJ]** the LORD God."
10: 3 'How long will you refuse to humble yourself **before** [+4946] me?
10:10 your women and children! Clearly you are **bent on** [+5584] evil.
10:11 Then Moses and Aaron were driven out of Pharaoh's **presence**.
10:14 Never **before** [+4200] had there been such a plague of locusts,
10:28 out of my sight! Make sure you do not appear **before** me again!
10:28 appear before me again! The day you see my **face** you will die."
10:29 you say," Moses replied, "I will never appear **before** you again."
11:10 and Aaron performed all these wonders **before** [+4200] Pharaoh,
13:21 By day the LORD went **ahead** [+4200] *of* them in a pillar of
13:22 pillar of fire by night left its place **in front** [+4200] **of** the people.
14: 2 the Israelites to turn back and encamp **near** [+4200] Pi Hahiroth,
14: 2 encamp by the sea, **directly opposite** [+4200+5790] Baal Zephon.
14: 9 by the sea near Pi Hahiroth, **opposite** [+4200] Baal Zephon.
14:19 who had been traveling **in front** [+4200] **of** Israel's army,
14:19 The pillar of cloud also moved from **in front** and stood behind
14:25 the Egyptians said, "Let's get away **from** [+4946] the Israelites!
16: 9 'Come **before** [+4200] the LORD, for he has heard your
16:14 thin flakes like frost on the ground appeared on the desert **floor**.
16:33 place it **before** [+4200] the LORD to be kept for the generations
16:34 Aaron put the manna **in front** [+4200] **of** the Testimony, that it
17: 5 LORD answered Moses, "Walk on **ahead** [+4200] *of* the people.
17: 6 I will stand there **before** [+4200] you by the rock at Horeb.
18:12 to eat bread with Moses' father-in-law in the **presence** *of* God.
19: 7 set **before** [+4200] them all the words the LORD had commanded
19:18 with smoke, **because** [+4946] the LORD descended on it in fire.
20: 3 "You shall have no other gods **before** [+6584] me.
20:20 so that the fear of God will be **with** [+6584] you to keep you from
21: 1 "These are the laws you are to set **before** [+4200] them:
23:15 came out of Egypt. "No one is to appear **before** me empty-handed.
23:17 "Three times a year all the men are to appear **before** [+448] the
23:20 I am sending an angel **ahead** [+4200] *of* you to guard you along
23:21 Pay attention **to** [+4946] him and listen to what he says. Do not
23:23 My angel will go **ahead** [+4200] *of* you and bring you into the land
23:27 "I will send my terror **ahead** [+4200] *of* you and throw into
23:28 I will send the hornet **ahead** [+4200] *of* you to drive the Hivites,
23:28 Canaanites and Hittites **out of** your **way** [+4200+4946].
23:29 I will not drive them **out** [+4946] in a single year, because the land
23:30 Little by little I will drive them out **before** you, until you have

Ex 23:31 who live in the land and you will drive them out **before** you.
25:20 The cherubim are to **face** each other, looking toward the cover.
25:20 The cherubim are to face each other, **looking** toward the cover.
25:30 Put the bread of the **Presence** on this table to be before me at all
25:30 Put the bread of the Presence on this table to be **before** [+4200] me
25:37 and set them up on it so that they light the space **in front of** it.
26: 9 another set. Fold the sixth curtain double at the **front** *of* the tent.
27:21 his sons are to keep the lamps burning **before** [+4200] the LORD
28:12 names on his shoulders as a memorial **before** [+4200] the LORD.
28:25 attaching them to the shoulder pieces of the ephod at the **front**.
28:27 attach them to the bottom of the shoulder pieces on the **front** *of* the
28:29 of decision as a continuing memorial **before** [+4200] the LORD.
28:30 heart whenever he enters the **presence** [+4200] *of* the LORD.
28:30 for the Israelites over his heart **before** [+4200] the LORD.
28:35 heard when he enters the Holy Place **before** [+4200] the LORD
28:37 to it to attach it to the turban; it is to be on the **front** *of* the turban.
28:38 so that they will be acceptable **to** [+4200] the LORD.
29:10 "Bring the bull to the **front** *of* the Tent of Meeting, and Aaron
29:11 Slaughter it in the LORD's **presence** at the entrance to the Tent
29:23 which is **before** [+4200] the LORD, take a loaf, and a cake made
29:24 and wave them **before** [+4200] the LORD as a wave offering.
29:25 the burnt offering for a pleasing aroma **to** [+4200] the LORD,
29:26 wave it **before** [+4200] the LORD as a wave offering, and it will
29:42 at the entrance to the Tent of Meeting **before** [+4200] the LORD.
30: 6 Put the altar **in front** [+4200] **of** the curtain that is before the ark of
30: 6 the curtain that is before the ark of the Testimony—**before** [+4200]
30: 8 so incense will burn regularly **before** [+4200] the LORD for the
30:16 It will be a memorial for the Israelites **before** [+4200] the LORD,
30:36 place it **in front** [+4200] **of** the Testimony in the Tent of Meeting,
32: 1 and said, "Come, make us gods who will go **before** [+4200] us.
32: 5 he built an altar **in front** [+4200] **of** the calf and announced,
32:11 But Moses **sought the favor of** [+906+2704] the LORD his God.
32:12 them in the mountains and to wipe them off the **face** *of* the earth'?
32:20 scattered it **on** [+6584] the water and made the Israelites drink it.
32:23 They said to me, 'Make us gods who will go **before** [+4200] us.
32:34 to the place I spoke of, and my angel will go **before** [+4200] you.
33: 2 I will send an angel **before** [+4200] you and drive out the
33:11 The LORD would speak to Moses **face** to face, as a man speaks
33:11 The LORD would speak to Moses face to **face**, as a man speaks
33:14 The LORD replied, "My **Presence** will go with you, and I will
33:15 Then Moses said to him, "If your **Presence** does not go with us,
33:16 and your people from all the other people on the **face** *of* the earth?"
33:19 "I will cause all my goodness to pass **in front** [+6584] **of** you,
33:19 and I will proclaim my name, the LORD, in your **presence**.
33:20 But," he said, "you cannot see my **face**, for no one may see me
33:23 and you will see my back; but my **face** must not be seen."
34: 6 he passed **in front** [+6584] **of** Moses, proclaiming, "The LORD,
34:11 I will drive out **before** [+4946] you the Amorites, Canaanites,
34:20 your firstborn sons. "No one is to appear **before** me empty-handed.
34:23 Three times a year all your men are to appear **before** [+907] the
34:24 I will drive out nations **before** [+4946] you and enlarge your
34:24 times each year to appear **before** [+907] the LORD your God.
34:29 he was not aware that his **face** [+6425] was radiant because he had
34:30 and all the Israelites saw Moses, his **face** [+6425] was radiant,
34:33 When Moses finished speaking to them, he put a veil over his **face**.
34:34 whenever he entered the LORD's **presence** [+4200] to speak with
34:35 they saw that his **face** [+6425] was radiant. Then Moses would put
34:35 **[RPH]** Then Moses would put the veil back over his face until he
34:35 Moses would put the veil back over his **face** until he went in to
35:13 with its poles and all its articles and the bread of the **Presence**;
35:20 Israelite community withdrew from Moses' **presence** [+4200],
36: 3 They received **from** [+4200+4946] Moses all the offerings the
37: 9 The cherubim **faced** each other, looking toward the cover.
37: 9 The cherubim faced each other, **looking** toward the cover.
39:18 attaching them to the shoulder pieces of the ephod at the **front**.
39:20 attached them to the bottom of the shoulder pieces on the **front** *of*
39:36 the table with all its articles and the bread of the **Presence**;
40: 5 Place the gold altar of incense **in front** [+4200] **of** the ark of the
40: 6 "Place the altar of burnt offering **in front** [+4200] **of** the entrance
40:23 set out the bread on it **before** [+4200] the LORD, as the LORD
40:25 set up the lamps **before** [+4200] the LORD, as the LORD
40:26 gold altar in the Tent of Meeting **in front** [+4200] **of** the curtain
Lev 1: 3 of Meeting so that it will be acceptable **to** [+4200] the LORD.
1: 5 He is to slaughter the young bull **before** [+4200] the LORD,
1:11 He is to slaughter it at the north side of the altar **before** [+4200] the
3: 1 he is to present **before** [+4200] the LORD an animal without
3: 7 If he offers a lamb, he is to present it **before** [+4200] the LORD.
3: 8 and slaughter it **in front** [+4200] **of** the Tent of Meeting.
3:12 offering is a goat, he is to present it **before** [+4200] the LORD.
3:13 its head and slaughter it **in front** [+4200] **of** the Tent of Meeting.
4: 4 at the entrance to the Tent of Meeting **before** [+4200] the LORD.
4: 4 his hand on its head and slaughter it **before** [+4200] the LORD.
4: 6 and sprinkle some of it seven times **before** [+4200] the LORD,
4: 6 some of it seven times before the LORD, **in front** [+907] **of**
4: 7 incense that is **before** [+4200] the LORD in the Tent of Meeting.
4:14 as a sin offering and present it **before** [+4200] the Tent of Meeting.
4:15 to lay their hands on the bull's head **before** [+4200] the LORD,
4:15 and the bull shall be slaughtered **before** [+4200] the LORD.
4:17 sprinkle it **before** [+4200] the LORD seven times in front of the
4:17 sprinkle it before the LORD seven times **in front** [+907] **of** the
4:18 the altar that is **before** [+4200] the LORD in the Tent of Meeting.
4:24 the burnt offering is slaughtered **before** [+4200] the LORD.
6: 7 [5:26] will make atonement for him **before** [+4200] the LORD,
6:14 [6:7] Aaron's sons are to bring it **before** [+4200] the LORD, in
6:14 [6:7] sons are to bring it before the LORD, **in front** [+448] **of**
6:25 [6:18] The sin offering is to be slaughtered **before** [+4200] the
7:30 wave the breast **before** [+4200] the LORD as a wave offering.
8: 9 and set the gold plate, the sacred diadem, on the **front** *of* it,
8:26 which was **before** [+4200] the LORD, he took a cake of bread,
8:27 and waved them **before** [+4200] the LORD as a wave offering.
8:29 and waved it **before** [+4200] the LORD as a wave offering,
9: 2 both without defect, and present them **before** [+4200] the LORD.
9: 4 a ram for a fellowship offering to sacrifice **before** [+4200] the
9: 5 They took the things Moses commanded to the **front** *of* the Tent of
9: 5 entire assembly came near and stood **before** [+4200] the LORD.
9:21 and the right thigh **before** [+4200] the LORD as a wave offering,
9:24 Fire came out from the **presence** [+4200] *of* the LORD
9:24 the people saw it, they shouted for joy and fell **facedown** [+6584].
10: 1 and they offered unauthorized fire **before** [+4200] the LORD,
10: 2 So fire came out from the **presence** [+4200] *of* the LORD
10: 2 and consumed them, and they died **before** [+4200] the LORD.
10: 3 in the **sight** *of* all the people I will be honored.' " Aaron remained
10: 4 cousins outside the camp, away from the **front** *of* the sanctuary."
10:15 to be waved **before** [+4200] the LORD as a wave offering.
10:17 by making atonement for them **before** [+4200] the LORD.
10:19 sin offering and their burnt offering **before** [+4200] the LORD,
12: 7 He shall offer them **before** [+4200] the LORD to make atonement
13:41 If he has lost his hair from the front of his **scalp** and has a bald
14: 7 him clean. Then he is to release the live bird in the **open** fields.
14:11 his offerings **before** [+4200] the LORD at the entrance to the
14:12 he shall wave them **before** [+4200] the LORD as a wave offering.
14:16 with his finger sprinkle some of it **before** [+4200] the LORD
14:18 and make atonement for him **before** [+4200] the LORD.
14:23 to the priest at the entrance to the Tent of Meeting, **before** [+4200]
14:24 and wave them **before** [+4200] the LORD as a wave offering.
14:27 of the oil from his palm seven times **before** [+4200] the LORD.
14:29 to make atonement for him **before** [+4200] the LORD.
14:31 In this way the priest will make atonement **before** [+4200] the
14:53 he is to release the live bird in the **open** fields outside the town.
15:14 come **before** [+4200] the LORD to the entrance to the Tent of
15:15 In this way he will make atonement **before** [+4200] the LORD
15:30 In this way he will make atonement for her **before** [+4200] the
16: 1 of Aaron who died when they approached **[OBJ]** the LORD.
16: 2 the curtain **in front** [+448] **of** the atonement cover on the ark,
16: 7 present them **before** [+4200] the LORD at the entrance to the
16:10 **before** [+4200] the LORD to be used for making atonement by
16:12 of burning coals from the altar **before** [+4200+4946] the LORD
16:13 He is to put the incense on the fire **before** [+4200] the LORD,
16:14 and with his finger sprinkle it on the **front** *of* the atonement cover;
16:14 it with his finger seven times **before** [+4200] the atonement cover.
16:15 shall sprinkle it on the atonement cover and **in front** [+4200] **of** it.
16:18 "Then he shall come out to the altar that is **before** [+4200] the
16:30 Then, **before** [+4200] the LORD, you will be clean from all your
17: 4 to the LORD **in front** [+4200] **of** the tabernacle of the LORD—
17: 5 the LORD the sacrifices they are now making in the **open** fields.
17:10 I will set my **face** against that person who eats blood and will cut
18:23 A woman must not present herself **to** [+4200] an animal to have
18:24 that I am going to drive out **before** [+4946] you became defiled.
18:27 were done by the people who lived in the land **before** [+4200] you,
18:28 you out as it vomited out the nations that were **before** [+4200] you.
18:30 detestable customs that were practiced **before** [+4200] you came
19:14 the deaf or put a stumbling block **in front** [+4200] **of** the blind,
19:15 *do* not **show partiality to** [+5951] the poor or favoritism to the
19:15 not show partiality to the poor or **favoritism to** [+2075] the great,
19:22 for him **before** [+4200] the LORD for the sin he has committed,
19:32 " 'Rise in the **presence** *of* the aged, show respect for the elderly
19:32 of the aged, show respect **for** the elderly and revere your God.
20: 3 I will set my **face** against that man and I will cut him off from his
20: 5 I will set my **face** against that man and his family and will cut off
20: 6 " 'I will set my **face** against the person who turns to mediums
20:23 customs of the nations I am going to drive out **before** [+4946] you.
22: 3 that person must be cut off from my **presence** [+4200].
23:11 He is to wave the sheaf **before** [+4200] the LORD so it will be
23:20 The priest is to wave the two lambs **before** [+4200] the LORD as
23:28 when atonement is made for you **before** the LORD your God.
23:40 and rejoice **before** [+4200] the LORD your God for seven days.
24: 3 Aaron is to tend the lamps **before** [+4200] the LORD from
24: 4 The lamps on the pure gold lampstand **before** [+4200] the LORD

Lev 24: 6 in each row, on the table of pure gold **before** [+4200] the LORD.
24: 8 This bread is to be set out **before** [+4200] the LORD regularly,
26: 7 your enemies, and they will fall by the sword **before** [+4200] you.
26: 8 and your enemies will fall by the sword **before** [+4200] you.
26: 10 you will have to move it out to **make room** [+4946] **for** the new.
26: 17 I will set my **face** against you so that you will be defeated by your
26: 17 against you so that you will be defeated **by** [+4200] your enemies;
26: 37 over one another as though fleeing **from** [+4946] the sword,
26: 37 So you will not be able to stand **before** [+4200] your enemies.
27: 8 specified amount, he is to present the person **to** [+4200] the priest,
27: 11 the LORD—the animal must be presented **to** [+4200] the priest,
Nu 3: 4 fell dead **before** [+4200] the LORD when they made an offering
3: 4 with unauthorized fire **before** [+4200] him in the Desert of Sinai.
3: 4 Ithamar served as priests during the **lifetime** *of* their father Aaron.
3: 6 and present them **to** [+4200] Aaron the priest to assist him.
3: 7 for the whole community **at** [+4200] the Tent of Meeting by doing
3: 38 and his sons were to camp to the east of **[RPH]** the tabernacle,
3: 38 toward the sunrise, **in front** [+4200] **of** the Tent of Meeting.
4: 7 "Over the table of the **Presence** they are to spread a blue cloth
5: 16 shall bring her and have her stand **before** [+4200] the LORD.
5: 18 After the priest has had the woman stand **before** [+4200] the
5: 25 wave it **before** [+4200] the LORD and bring it to the altar.
5: 30 The priest is to have her stand **before** [+4200] the LORD
6: 16 " 'The priest is to present them **before** [+4200] the LORD
6: 20 then wave them **before** [+4200] the LORD as a wave offering;
6: 25 the LORD make his **face** shine upon you and be gracious to you;
6: 26 the LORD turn his **face** toward you and give you peace." '
7: 3 They brought as their gifts **before** [+4200] the LORD six covered
7: 3 every two. These they presented **before** [+4200] the tabernacle.
7: 10 for its dedication and presented them **before** [+4200] the altar.
8: 2 they are to light the area **in front** [+448+4578] **of** the
8: 3 so that they **faced** [+448+4578] **forward** *on* the lampstand,
8: 9 Bring the Levites to the **front** *of* the Tent of Meeting and assemble
8: 10 You are to bring the Levites **before** [+4200] the LORD,
8: 11 Aaron is to present the Levites **before** [+4200] the LORD as a
8: 13 Have the Levites stand **in front** [+4200] **of** Aaron and his sons
8: 13 Have the Levites stand in front of Aaron and **[RPH]** his sons and
8: 21 Aaron presented them as a wave offering **before** [+4200] the
8: 22 at the Tent of Meeting **under** the **supervision** [+4200] *of* Aaron
8: 22 of Meeting under the supervision of Aaron and **[RPH]** his sons.
9: 6 So they came **to** [+4200] Moses and Aaron that same day
9: 6 So they came to Moses and **[RPH]** Aaron that same day
10: 9 Then you will be remembered **by** [+4200] the LORD your God
10: 10 and they will be a memorial for you **before** [+4200] your God.
10: 33 The ark of the covenant of the LORD went **before** [+4200] them
10: 35 enemies be scattered; may your foes flee **before** [+4946] you."
11: 20 who is among you, and have wailed **before** [+4200] him, saying,
11: 31 all around the camp to about three feet **above** [+6584] the ground,
12: 3 more humble than anyone else on the **face** *of* the earth.)
12: 14 The LORD replied to Moses, "If her father had spit in her **face**,
13: 22 (Hebron had been built seven years **before** [+4200] Zoan in
14: 5 Aaron fell **facedown** [+6584] in front of the whole Israelite
14: 5 Aaron fell facedown **in front** [+4200] **of** the whole Israelite
14: 14 and that you go **before** [+4200] them in a pillar of cloud by day
14: 37 struck down and died of a plague **before** [+4200] the LORD.
14: 42 is not with you. You will be defeated **by** [+4200] your enemies,
14: 43 for the Amalekites and Canaanites will **face** [+4200] you there.
15: 15 and the alien shall be the same **before** [+4200] the LORD:
15: 25 they have brought **to** [+4200] the LORD for their wrong an
15: 28 The priest is to make atonement **before** [+4200] the LORD for
16: 2 rose up **against** [+4200] Moses. With them were 250 Israelite men,
16: 4 When Moses heard this, he fell **facedown** [+6584].
16: 7 tomorrow put fire and incense in them **before** [+4200] the LORD.
16: 9 and to stand **before** [+4200] the community and minister to them?
16: 16 all your followers are to appear **before** [+4200] the LORD
16: 17 250 censers in all—and present it **before** [+4200] the LORD.
16: 22 But Moses and Aaron fell **facedown** [+6584] and cried out,
16: 38 [17:3] for they were presented **before** [+4200] the LORD
16: 40 [17:5] should come to burn incense **before** [+4200] the LORD,
16: 43 [17:8] and Aaron went to the **front** *of* the Tent of Meeting,
16: 45 [17:10] an end to them at once." And they fell **facedown** [+6584].
16: 46 [17:11] Wrath has come out **from** [+4200+4946] the LORD;
17: 4 [17:19] Place them in the Tent of Meeting **in front** [+4200] **of** the
17: 7 [17:22] Moses placed the staffs **before** [+4200] the LORD in the
17: 9 [17:24] from the LORD's **presence** [+4200] to all the Israelites.
17: 10 [17:25] "Put back Aaron's staff **in front** [+4200] **of** the
18: 2 and your sons minister **before** [+4200] the Tent of the Testimony.
18: 19 It is an everlasting covenant of salt **before** [+4200] the LORD for
19: 3 it is to be taken outside the camp and slaughtered in his **presence**.
19: 4 sprinkle it seven times toward the **front** *of* the Tent of Meeting.
19: 16 "Anyone out **in** [+6584] the open who touches someone who has
20: 3 "If only we had died when our brothers fell dead **before** [+4200]
20: 6 Aaron went **from** [+4946] the assembly to the entrance to the Tent
20: 6 to the entrance to the Tent of Meeting and fell **facedown** [+6584],
20: 9 So Moses took the staff from the LORD's **presence** [+4200],
20: 10 Aaron gathered the assembly together **in front** [+448] **of** the rock
21: 11 in the desert that **faces** [+6584] Moab toward the sunrise.
21: 20 in Moab where the top of Pisgah overlooks **[OBJ]** the wasteland.
22: 3 Moab was terrified **because** [+4946] there were so many people.
22: 3 Moab was filled with dread **because of** [+4946] the Israelites.
22: 33 saw me and turned away **from** [+4200] me these three times.
22: 33 turned away, **[RPH]** I would certainly have killed you by now,
23: 28 took Balaam to the top of Peor, overlooking **[OBJ]** the wasteland.
24: 1 to sorcery as at other times, but turned his **face** toward the desert.
26: 61 Abihu died when they made an offering **before** [+4200] the
27: 2 entrance to the Tent of Meeting and stood **before** [+4200] Moses,
27: 2 **[RPH]** Eleazar the priest, the leaders and the whole assembly,
27: 2 the priest, **[RPH]** the leaders and the whole assembly, and said,
27: 5 So Moses brought their case **before** [+4200] the LORD
27: 17 to go out **[RPH]** and come in before them, one who will lead
27: 17 to go out and come in **before** [+4200] them, one who will lead
27: 19 Have him stand **before** [+4200] Eleazar the priest and the entire
27: 19 **[RPH]** the entire assembly and commission him in their presence.
27: 21 He is to stand **before** [+4200] Eleazar the priest, who will obtain
27: 21 for him by inquiring of the Urim **before** [+4200] the LORD.
27: 22 took Joshua and had him stand **before** [+4200] Eleazar the priest
27: 22 stand before Eleazar the priest and **[RPH]** the whole assembly.
31: 50 to make atonement for ourselves **before** [+4200] the LORD."
31: 54 as a memorial for the Israelites **before** [+4200] the LORD.
32: 4 the land the LORD subdued **before** [+4200] the people of Israel—
32: 17 go **ahead** [+4200] *of* the Israelites until we have brought them to
32: 17 for **protection from** [+4946] the inhabitants of the land.
32: 20 if you will arm yourselves **before** [+4200] the LORD for battle,
32: 21 if all of you will go armed over the Jordan **before** [+4200] the
32: 21 LORD until he has driven his enemies out **before** [+4946] him—
32: 22 then when the land is subdued **before** [+4200] the LORD,
32: 22 And this land will be your possession **before** [+4200] the LORD.
32: 27 will cross over to fight **before** [+4200] the LORD, just as our lord
32: 29 cross over the Jordan with you **before** [+4200] the LORD,
32: 29 when the land is subdued **before** [+4200] you, give them the land
32: 32 We will cross over **before** [+4200] the LORD into Canaan armed,
33: 7 Pi Hahiroth, to the **east** *of* Baal Zephon, and camped near Migdol.
33: 7 to the east of Baal Zephon, and camped **near** [+4200] Migdol.
33: 8 They left <u>Pi</u> **Hahiroth** [BHS *from before Hahiroth*; NIV 7084]
33: 47 and camped in the mountains of Abarim, **near** [+4200] Nebo.
33: 52 drive out all the inhabitants of the land **before** [+4946] you.
33: 55 **[OBJ]** those you allow to remain will become barbs in your eyes
35: 12 may not die before he stands trial **before** [+4200] the assembly.
36: 1 came and spoke **before** [+4200] Moses and the leaders, the heads
36: 1 came and spoke before Moses and **[RPH]** the leaders, the heads
Dt 1: 8 See, I have given **[OBJ]** you this land. Go in and take possession
1: 17 *Do* not **show partiality** [+5795] in judging; hear both small
1: 17 Do not be afraid **of** [+4946] any man, for judgment belongs to
1: 21 See, the LORD your God has given **[OBJ]** you the land.
1: 22 "Let us send men **ahead** [+4200] to spy out the land for us
1: 30 your God, who is going **before** [+4200] you, will fight for you,
1: 33 who went **ahead** [+4200] *of* you on your journey, in fire by night
1: 38 But your **assistant** [+4200+6641], Joshua son of Nun, will enter it.
1: 42 not be with you. You will be defeated **by** [+4200] your enemies.' "
1: 45 You came back and wept **before** [+4200] the LORD, but he paid
2: 10 (The Emites **used** [+4200] **to** live there—a people strong
2: 12 Horites **used** [+4200] **to** live in Seir, but the descendants of Esau
2: 12 They destroyed the Horites from **before** them and settled in their
2: 20 considered a land of the Rephaites, who **used** [+4200] **to** live there;
2: 21 The LORD destroyed them from **before** the Ammonites,
2: 22 lived in Seir, when he destroyed the Horites from **before** them.
2: 25 the terror and fear of you **on** [+6584] all the nations under heaven.
2: 25 and will tremble and be in anguish **because of** [+4946] you."
2: 31 I have begun to deliver Sihon and his country over **to** [+4200] you.
2: 33 the LORD our God delivered him over **to** [+4200] us and we
2: 36 strong for us. The LORD our God gave **[OBJ]** us all of them.
3: 18 must cross over **ahead** [+4200] *of* your brother Israelites.
3: 28 for he *will* **lead** this people **across** [+4200+6296] and will cause
4: 8 laws as this body of laws I am setting **before** [+4200] you today?
4: 10 Remember the day you stood **before** [+4200] the LORD your
4: 32 Ask now about the former days, long **before** [+4200] your time,
4: 37 he brought you out of Egypt by his **Presence** and his great
4: 38 to drive out **before** [+4946] you nations greater and stronger than
4: 44 This is the law Moses set **before** [+4200] the Israelites.
5: 4 The LORD spoke to you **face** to face out of the fire on the
5: 4 The LORD spoke to you face to **face** out of the fire on the
5: 5 because you were afraid **of** [+4946] the fire and did not go up the
5: 7 "You shall have no other gods **before** [+6584] me.
6: 15 burn against you, and he will destroy you from the **face** *of* the land.
6: 19 thrusting out all your enemies **before** [+4946] you, as the LORD
6: 25 if we are careful to obey all this law **before** [+4200] the LORD
7: 1 to possess and drives out **before** [+4946] you many nations—
7: 2 when the LORD your God has delivered them over **to** [+4200]

Dt 7: 6 you out of all the peoples on the **face** *of* the earth to be his people,
7: 10 But those who hate him he will repay to their **face** by destruction;
7: 10 he will not be slow to repay to their **face** those who hate him.
7: 19 your God will do the same to all the peoples you now fear. **[OBJ]**
7: 20 until even the survivors who hide **from** [+4946] you have perished.
7: 21 Do not be terrified **by** [+4946] them, for the LORD your God,
7: 22 The LORD your God will drive out those nations **before** [+4946]
7: 23 But the LORD your God will deliver them over **to** [+4200] you,
7: 24 No one will be able to stand up **against** [+928] you; you will
8: 20 Like the nations the LORD destroyed **before** [+4946] you,
9: 2 heard it said: "Who can stand up **against** [+4200] the Anakites?"
9: 3 one who goes across **ahead** [+4200] *of* you like a devouring fire.
9: 3 He will destroy them; he will subdue them **before** [+4200] you.
9: 4 LORD your God has driven them out **before** [+4200+4946] you,
9: 4 that the LORD is going to drive them out **before** [+4946] you.
9: 5 the LORD your God will drive them out **before** [+4946] you,
9: 18 once again I fell prostrate **before** [+4200] the LORD for forty
9: 19 I feared **[OBJ]** the anger and wrath of the LORD, for he was
9: 25 I lay prostrate **before** [+4200] the LORD those forty days
10: 8 to stand **before** [+4200] the LORD to minister and to pronounce
10: 11 "and **lead** [+2143+4200] the people on their way, so that they may
10: 17 who **shows** no **partiality** [+5951] and accepts no bribes.
11: 4 how he overwhelmed **[OBJ]** them with the waters of the Red Sea
11: 23 the LORD will drive out all these nations **before** [+4200+4946]
11: 25 No man will be able to stand **against** [+928] you. The LORD
11: 25 will put the terror and fear of you **on** [+6584] the whole land,
11: 26 I am setting **before** [+4200] you today a blessing and a curse—
11: 32 all the decrees and laws I am setting **before** [+4200] you today.
12: 7 in the **presence** *of* the LORD your God, you and your families
12: 12 And there rejoice **before** [+4200] the LORD your God, you,
12: 18 you are to eat them in the **presence** *of* the LORD your God at the
12: 18 you are to rejoice **before** [+4200] the LORD your God in
12: 29 The LORD your God will cut off **before** [+4946] you the nations
12: 30 after they have been destroyed **before** [+4946] you, be careful not
14: 2 Out of all the peoples on the **face** *of* the earth, the LORD has
14: 23 flocks in the **presence** *of* the LORD your God at the place he will
14: 26 your household shall eat there in the **presence** *of* the LORD your
15: 20 your family are to eat them in the **presence** *of* the LORD your
16: 11 rejoice **before** [+4200] the LORD your God at the place he will
16: 16 Three times a year all your men must appear **before** [+907] the
16: 16 No man should appear **before** [+907] the LORD empty-handed:
16: 19 Do not pervert justice or **show partiality** [+5795]. Do not accept a
17: 18 **taken from** [+4200+4946] that of the priests, who are Levites.
18: 7 his fellow Levites who serve there in the **presence** *of* the LORD.
18: 12 LORD your God will drive out those nations **before** [+4946] you.
19: 17 the two men involved in the dispute must stand in the **presence** *of*
19: 17 stand in the presence of the LORD **before** [+4200] the priests
20: 3 do not be terrified or give way to panic **before** [+4946] them.
20: 19 the trees of the field people, that you should besiege **[OBJ]** them?
21: 16 of the wife he loves **in preference** [+6584] **to** his actual firstborn,
22: 6 If you **come across** [+4200+7925] a bird's nest beside the road,
22: 17 her parents shall display the cloth **before** [+4200] the elders of the
23: 14 [23:15] protect you and to deliver your enemies **to** [+4200] you.
24: 4 That would be detestable **in the eyes** [+4200] **of** the LORD.
24: 13 it will be **regarded** as a righteous act **in the sight** [+4200] **of** the
25: 2 have him flogged in his **presence** with the number of lashes his
25: 9 of the elders, take off one of his sandals, spit in his **face** and say,
26: 4 set it down **in front** [+4200] **of** the altar of the LORD your God.
26: 5 Then you shall declare **before** [+4200] the LORD your God:
26: 10 Place the basket **before** [+4200] the LORD your God and bow
26: 10 before the LORD your God and bow down **before** [+4200] him.
26: 13 say **to** [+4200] the LORD your God: "I have removed from my
27: 7 eating them and rejoicing in the **presence** *of* the LORD your God.
28: 7 who rise up against you will be defeated **before** [+4200] you.
28: 7 at you from one direction but flee **from** [+4200] you in seven.
28: 20 **because of** [+4946] the evil you have done in forsaking him.
28: 25 The LORD will cause you to be defeated **before** [+4200] your
28: 25 at them from one direction but flee **from** [+4200] them in seven,
28: 31 Your donkey will be forcibly taken **from** [+4200+4946] you
28: 50 a **fierce-looking** [+6434] nation without respect for the old
28: 50 a fierce-looking nation without **respect** [+5951] for the old
28: 60 of Egypt that you dreaded, **[OBJ]** and they will cling to you.
29: 10 [29:9] All of you are standing today in the **presence** *of* the
29: 15 [29:14] who are standing here with us today in the **presence** *of*
30: 1 and curses I have set **before** [+4200] you come upon you
30: 15 See, I set **before** [+4200] you today life and prosperity, death
30: 19 earth as witnesses against you that I have set **before** [+4200] you
31: 3 The LORD your God himself will cross over **ahead** [+4200] *of*
31: 3 He will destroy these nations **before** [+4200+4946] you, and you
31: 3 Joshua also will cross over **ahead** [+4200] *of* you, as the LORD
31: 5 The LORD will deliver them **to** [+4200] you, and you must do to
31: 6 Do not be afraid or terrified **because of** [+4946] them,
31: 8 The LORD himself goes **before** [+4200] you and will be with
31: 11 when all Israel comes to appear **before** [+907] the LORD your
31: 17 I will hide my **face** from them, and they will be destroyed.
31: 18 I will certainly hide my **face** on that day because of all their
31: 21 come upon them, this song will testify **against** [+4200] them,
32: 20 "I will hide my **face** from them," he said, "and see what their end
32: 49 Nebo in Moab, **across from** [+6584] Jericho, and view Canaan,
33: 1 man of God pronounced on the Israelites **before** [+4200] his death.
33: 27 He will drive out your enemy **before** [+4946] you, saying,
34: 1 plains of Moab to the top of Pisgah, **across from** [+6584] Jericho.
34: 10 risen in Israel like Moses, whom the LORD knew **face** to face,
34: 10 risen in Israel like Moses, whom the LORD knew face to **face**,
Jos 1: 5 No one will be able to stand up **against** [+4200] you all the days of
1: 14 fully armed, must cross over **ahead** [+4200] *of* your brothers.
2: 9 live in this country are melting in fear **because of** [+4946] you.
2: 10 of the Red Sea **for** [+4946] you when you came out of Egypt,
2: 11 and everyone's courage failed **because of** [+4946] you,
2: 24 all the people are melting in fear **because of** [+4946] us."
3: 6 the ark of the covenant and pass on **ahead** [+4200] *of* the people."
3: 6 of the people." So they took it up and went **ahead** [+4200] *of* them.
3: 10 that he will certainly drive out **before** [+4946] you the Canaanites,
3: 11 Lord of all the earth will go into the Jordan **ahead** [+4200] *of* you.
3: 14 the priests carrying the ark of the covenant went **ahead** [+4200] *of*
4: 5 "Go over **before** [+4200] the ark of the LORD your God into the
4: 7 tell them that the flow of the Jordan was cut off **before** [+4946] the
4: 11 priests came to the other side while the people **watched** [+4200].
4: 12 armed, **in front** [+4200] **of** the Israelites, as Moses had directed
4: 13 About forty thousand armed for battle crossed over **before** [+4200]
4: 23 For the LORD your God dried up the Jordan **before** [+4946] you
4: 23 when he dried it up **before** [+4946] us until we had crossed over.
5: 1 the Jordan **before** [+4946] the Israelites until we had crossed over,
5: 1 and they no longer had the courage to **face** [+4946] the Israelites.
5: 14 Then Joshua fell **facedown** [+448] to the ground in reverence,
6: 1 Now Jericho was tightly shut up **because of** [+4946] the Israelites.
6: 4 priests carry trumpets of rams' horns **in front** [+4200] **of** the ark.
6: 6 and have seven priests carry trumpets **in front** [+4200] **of** it."
6: 7 with the armed guard going **ahead** [+4200] *of* the ark of the
6: 8 the seven priests carrying the seven trumpets **before** [+4200] the
6: 9 The armed guard marched **ahead** [+4200] *of* the priests who blew
6: 13 marching **before** [+4200] the ark of the LORD and blowing the
6: 13 The armed men went **ahead** [+4200] *of* them and the rear guard
6: 26 "Cursed **before** [+4200] the LORD is the man who undertakes to
7: 4 men went up; but they were routed **by** [+4200] the men of Ai,
7: 5 They chased the Israelites **from** [+4200] the city gate as far as the
7: 6 fell **facedown** [+6584] to the ground before the ark of the LORD,
7: 6 fell facedown to the ground **before** [+4200] the ark of the LORD,
7: 8 can I say, now that Israel has been routed **by** [+4200] its enemies?
7: 10 said to Joshua, "Stand up! What are you doing down on your **face**?
7: 12 That is why the Israelites cannot stand **against** [+4200] their
7: 12 **[RPH]** because they have been made liable to destruction.
7: 13 You cannot stand **against** [+4200] your enemies until you remove
7: 23 all the Israelites and spread them out **before** [+4200] the LORD.
8: 5 out against us, as they did before, we will flee **from** [+4200] them.
8: 6 'They are running away **from** [+4200] us as they did before.'
8: 6 from us as they did before.' So when we flee **from** [+4200] them,
8: 10 and the leaders of Israel marched **before** [+4200] them to Ai.
8: 14 Israel in battle at a certain place **overlooking** [+4200] the Arabah.
8: 15 and all Israel let themselves be driven back **before** [+4200] them,
8: 32 There, in the **presence** *of* the Israelites, Joshua copied on stones
9: 24 the whole land and to wipe out all its inhabitants from **before** you.
9: 24 So we feared for our lives **because of** [+4946] you, and that is why
10: 8 Not one of them *will be able to* **withstand** [+928+6641] you."
10: 10 The LORD threw them into confusion **before** [+4200] Israel,
10: 11 As they fled **before** [+4946] Israel on the road down from Beth
10: 12 On the day the LORD gave the Amorites over **to** [+4200] Israel,
10: 14 There has never been a day like it **before** [+4200] or since,
11: 6 The LORD said to Joshua, "Do not be afraid **of** [+4946] them,
11: 6 this time tomorrow I will hand all of them over **to** [+4200] Israel,
11: 10 (Hazor **had been** [+4200] the head of all these kingdoms.)
13: 3 from the Shihor River on the **east** *of* Egypt to the territory of Ekron
13: 6 I myself will drive them out **before** [+4946] the Israelites.
13: 25 half the Ammonite country as far as Aroer, **near** [+6584] Rabbah;
14: 15 (Hebron **used** [+4200] **to** be called Kiriath Arba after Arba,
15: 8 From there it climbed to the top of the hill west of **[NIE]** the
15: 15 people living in Debir (**formerly** [+4200] called Kiriath Sepher).
17: 4 They went **to** [+4200] Eleazar the priest, Joshua son of Nun,
17: 4 the priest, **[RPH]** Joshua son of Nun, and the leaders and said,
17: 4 the priest, Joshua son of Nun, and **[RPH]** the leaders and said,
17: 7 extended from Asher to Micmethath **east** [+6584] *of* Shechem.
18: 1 The country was brought under their control, **[OBJ]**
18: 6 and I will cast lots for you in the **presence** *of* the LORD our God.
18: 8 I will cast lots for you here at Shiloh in the **presence** *of* the
18: 10 then cast lots for them in Shiloh in the **presence** *of* the LORD,
18: 14 From the hill **facing** [+6584] Beth Horon on the south the
18: 16 The boundary went down to the foot of the hill **facing** [+6584] the
19: 11 and extended to the ravine **near** [+6584] Jokneam.

Jos 19:51 the **presence** *of* the LORD at the entrance to the Tent of Meeting.
20: 6 He is to stay in that city until he has stood trial **before** [+4200] the
20: 9 of blood prior to standing trial **before** [+4200] the assembly.
21:44 Not one of their enemies **withstood** [+928+6641] them;
22:27 that we will worship the LORD **at** his **sanctuary**[s] [+4200] with
22:29 of the LORD our God that stands **before** [+4200] his tabernacle."
23: 3 your God has done to all these nations **for** your **sake** [+4946];
23: 5 The LORD your God himself will drive them out of your **way**.
23: 5 He will push them out **before** [+4200+4946] you, and you will
23: 9 "The LORD has driven out **before** [+4946] you great
23: 9 to this day no one *has been able to* **withstand** [+928+6641] you.
23:13 will no longer drive out these nations **before** [+4200+4946] you.
24: 1 of Israel, and they presented themselves **before** [+4200] God.
24: 8 I destroyed them from **before** you, and you took possession of
24:12 I sent the hornet **ahead** [+4200] *of* you, which drove them out
24:12 hornet ahead of you, which drove them out **before** [+4946] you—
24:18 And the LORD drove out **before** [+4946] us all the nations,
Jdg 1:10 living in Hebron (**formerly** [+4200] called Kiriath Arba)
1:11 people living in Debir (**formerly** [+4200] called Kiriath Sepher).
1:23 When they sent men to spy out Bethel (**formerly** [+4200] called
2: 3 therefore I tell you that I will not drive them out **before** [+4946]
2:14 all around, whom they were no longer able to **resist** [+4200+6641].
2:18 on them as they groaned **under** [+4946] those who oppressed
2:21 I will no longer drive out **before** [+4946] them any of the nations
3: 2 the Israelites who had not had **previous** [+4200] battle experience):
3:27 down with him from the hills, with him **leading** [+4200] them.
4:14 Has not the LORD gone **ahead** [+4200] *of* you?" So Barak went
4:15 **At** Barak's **advance** [+4200], the LORD routed Sisera and all his
4:23 subdued Jabin, the Canaanite king, **before** [+4200] the Israelites.
5: 5 The mountains quaked **before** [+4946] the LORD, the One of
5: 5 the One of Sinai, **before** [+4946] the LORD, the God of Israel.
6: 2 **Because** [+4946] the power of Midian was so oppressive,
6: 6 so impoverished the Israelites **[NIE]** that they cried out to the
6: 9 I drove them from **before** you and gave you their land.
6:11 wheat in a winepress to keep it **from** [+4946] the Midianites.
6:18 I come back and bring my offering and set it **before** [+4200] you."
6:22 I have seen the angel of the LORD **face** to face!"
6:22 I have seen the angel of the LORD face to **face**!"
8:28 Thus Midian was subdued **before** [+4200] the Israelites and did
9:21 he lived there **because** [+4946] he was afraid **of** his brother
9:39 So Gaal **led out** [+3655+4200] the citizens of Shechem and fought
9:40 in the flight—**[OBJ]** all the way to the entrance to the gate.
11: 3 So Jephthah fled **from** [+4946] his brothers and settled in the land
11: 9 fight the Ammonites and the LORD gives them **to** [+4200] me—
11:11 he repeated all his words **before** [+4200] the LORD in Mizpah.
11:23 has driven the Amorites out **before** [+4946] his people Israel,
11:24 Likewise, whatever the LORD our God has given **[OBJ]** us,
11:33 as far as Abel Keramim. Thus Israel subdued Ammon. **[OBJ]**
13:15 like you to stay until we prepare a young goat **for** [+4200] you."
13:20 Manoah and his wife fell with their **faces** to the ground.
16: 3 and carried them to the top of the hill that **faces** [+6584] Hebron.
16:25 Samson out of the prison, and he performed **for** [+4200] them.
18:21 their livestock and their possessions **in front** [+4200] **of** them,
18:23 shouted after them, the Danites **turned** [+6015] and said to Micah,
20:23 went up and wept **before** [+4200] the LORD until evening,
20:26 to Bethel, and there they sat weeping **before** [+4200] the LORD.
20:26 burnt offerings and fellowship offerings **to** [+4200] the LORD.
20:28 son of Eleazar, the son of Aaron, ministering **before** [+4200] it.)
20:32 "We are defeating **[OBJ]** them as before," the Israelites were
20:35 The LORD defeated Benjamin **before** [+4200] Israel, and on that
20:39 they said, "We are defeating them **[OBJ]** as in the first battle."
20:42 So they fled **before** [+4200] the Israelites in the direction of the
21: 2 where they sat **before** [+4200] God until evening, raising their
Ru 2:10 At this, she bowed down with her **face** to the ground. She
4: 7 (Now in **earlier times** in Israel, for the redemption and transfer of
1Sa 1:12 As she kept on praying **to** [+4200] the LORD, Eli observed her
1:15 or beer; I was pouring out my soul **to** [+4200] the LORD.
1:16 *Do* not **take** your servant **for** [+906+4200+5989] a wicked woman;
1:18 her way and ate something, and her **face** was no longer downcast.
1:19 morning they arose and worshiped **before** [+4200] the LORD and
1:22 I will take him and present him **before** [+907] the LORD,
2:11 the boy ministered before the LORD **under** [+907] Eli the priest.
2:17 sin of the young men was very great **in** the LORD's **sight** [+907],
2:18 Samuel was ministering **before** [+907] the LORD—a boy
2:28 to my altar, to burn incense, and to wear an ephod in my **presence**.
2:30 your father's house would minister **before** [+4200] me forever.'
2:35 and he will minister **before** [+4200] my anointed one always.
3: 1 The boy Samuel ministered before the LORD **under** [+4200] Eli.
4: 2 as the battle spread, Israel was defeated **by** [+4200] the Philistines,
4: 3 "Why did the LORD bring defeat upon us today **before** [+4200]
4:17 "Israel fled **before** [+4200] the Philistines, and the army has
5: 3 fallen on his **face** on the ground before the ark of the LORD!
5: 3 fallen on his face on the ground **before** [+4200] the ark of the
5: 4 fallen on his **face** on the ground before the ark of the LORD!
5: 4 fallen on his face on the ground **before** [+4200] the ark of the
6:20 "Who can stand in the **presence** *of* the LORD, this holy God?
7: 6 they drew water and poured it out **before** [+4200] the LORD.
7: 7 heard of it, they were afraid **because of** [+4946] the Philistines.
7:10 threw them into such a panic that they were routed **before** [+4200]
8:11 and horses, and they will run **in front** [+4200] **of** his chariots.
8:18 you will cry out **for relief** [+4200+4946] **from** the king you have
8:20 with a king to lead us and to go out **before** [+4200] us and fight
9: 9 (**Formerly** [+4200] in Israel, if a man went to inquire of God,
9: 9 because the prophet of today **used** [+4200] **to** be called a seer.)
9:12 "He's **ahead** [+4200] *of* you. Hurry now; he has just come to our
9:15 Now the day **before** [+4200] Saul came, the LORD had revealed
9:19 "Go up **ahead** [+4200] *of* me to the high place, for today you are to
9:24 up the leg with what was on it and set it **in front** [+4200] **of** Saul.
9:24 Samuel said, "Here is what has been kept **for** [+4200] you.
9:27 said to Saul, "Tell the servant to go on **ahead** [+4200] *of* us"—
10: 5 tambourines, flutes and harps being played **before** [+4200] them,
10: 8 "Go down **ahead** [+4200] *of* me to Gilgal. I will surely come down
10:19 So now present yourselves **before** [+4200] the LORD by your
10:25 down on a scroll and deposited it **before** [+4200] the LORD.
11:15 and confirmed Saul as king in the **presence** *of* the LORD.
11:15 There they sacrificed fellowship offerings **before** [+4200] the
12: 2 Now you have a king *as* your **leader** [+2143+4200]. As for me,
12: 2 I *have been* your **leader** [+2143+4200] from my youth until this
12: 7 because I am going to confront you with evidence **before** [+4200]
13:12 me at Gilgal, and *I have* not **sought** the LORD's **favor** [+2704].'
14:13 The Philistines fell **before** [+4200] Jonathan, and his armor-bearer
14:25 entered the woods, and there was honey **on** [+6584] the ground.
15: 7 Amalekites all the way from Havilah to Shur, to the **east** *of* Egypt.
15:33 Samuel put Agag to death **before** [+4200] the LORD at Gilgal.
16: 8 called Abinadab and had him pass **in front** [+4200] **of** Samuel.
16:10 Jesse had seven of his sons pass **before** [+4200] Samuel,
16:16 Let our lord command his servants **here** [+4200] to search for
16:21 David came to Saul and **entered** his **service** [+4200+6641].
16:22 saying, "Allow David to remain **in** my **service** [+4200], for I am
17: 7 six hundred shekels. His shield bearer went **ahead** [+4200] *of* him.
17:24 Israelites saw the man, they all ran **from** [+4946] him in great fear.
17:31 What David said was overheard and reported **to** [+4200] Saul,
17:41 the Philistine, with his shield bearer **in front** [+4200] **of** him,
17:49 into his forehead, and he fell **facedown** [+6584] on the ground.
17:57 Abner took him and brought him **before** [+4200] Saul, with David
18:11 David to the wall." But David **eluded** [+4946+6015] him twice.
18:12 Saul was afraid **of** [+4200+4946] David, because the LORD was
18:13 David **led** the troops **in** their **campaigns** [+995+2256+3655+4200].
18:15 Saul saw how successful he was, he was afraid **of** [+4946] him.
18:16 because he **led** them **in** their **campaigns** [+995+2256+3655+4200].
18:29 Saul became still more afraid **of** [+4946] him, and he remained his
19: 7 brought him to Saul, and David was **with** [+4200] Saul as before.
19: 8 He struck them with such force that they fled **before** [+4946] him.
19:10 but David eluded **[OBJ]** him as Saul drove the spear into the wall.
19:24 stripped off his robes and also prophesied in Samuel's **presence**.
20: 1 from Naioth at Ramah and went **to** [+4200] Jonathan and asked,
20: 1 How have I wronged **[OBJ]** your father, that he is trying to take
20:15 cut off every one of David's enemies from the **face** *of* the earth."
21: 6 [21:7] **Presence** that had been removed from before the LORD
21: 6 [21:7] that had been removed from **before** [+4200] the LORD
21: 7 [21:8] was there that day, detained **before** [+4200] the LORD;
21:10 [21:11] That day David fled **from** [+4946] Saul and went to
21:12 [21:13] was very much afraid **of** [+4946] Achish king of Gath.
22: 4 So he left them **with** [+907] the king of Moab, and they stayed
23:18 The two of them made a covenant **before** [+4200] the LORD.
23:24 So they set out and went to Ziph **ahead** [+4200] *of* Saul.
23:26 were on the other side, hurrying to get away **from** [+4946] Saul.
24: 2 [24:3] and his men **near** [+6584] the Crags of the Wild Goats.
25:10 Many servants are breaking away **from** [+4946] their masters these
25:19 she told her servants, "Go on **ahead** [+4200]; I'll follow you."
25:23 and bowed down before David with her **face** to the ground.
25:35 I have heard your words and **granted** your **request** [+5951]."
26: 1 hiding on the hill of Hakilah, which **faces** [+6584] Jeshimon?"
26: 3 beside the road on the hill of Hakilah **facing** [+6584] Jeshimon,
26:19 men have done it, may they be cursed **before** [+4200] the LORD!
26:20 my blood fall to the ground far from the **presence** *of* the LORD.
28:22 and let me give **[OBJ]** you some food so you may eat
28:25 Then she set it **before** [+4200] Saul and his men, and they ate.
28:25 Then she set it before Saul and **[RPH]** his men, and they ate.
29: 8 your servant from the day I came **to** [+4200] you until now?
30:16 scattered **over** [+6584] the countryside, eating, drinking
30:20 and his men drove them **ahead** [+4200] *of* the other livestock,
31: 1 the Israelites fled **before** [+4946] them, and many fell slain on
2Sa 2:14 young men get up and fight hand to hand **in front** [+4200] **of** us."
2:17 and the men of Israel were defeated **by** [+4200] David's men.
2:22 How *could I* **look** your brother Joab **in the face** [+448+5951]?"
2:24 **near** [+6584] Giah on the way to the wasteland of Gibeon.
3:13 one thing of you: *Do* not **come into** my **presence** [+906+8011]

2Sa 3:13 Do not come into my presence **unless** [+561+3954+4200] you
3:13 bring Michal daughter of Saul when you come to see **me** [+3276]."
3:31 on sackcloth and walk in mourning **in front** [+4200] **of** Abner."
3:34 not fettered. You fell as one falls **before** [+4200] wicked men."
3:35 if I taste bread or anything else **before** [+4200] the sun sets!"
5: 3 the king made a compact with them at Hebron **before** [+4200] the
5:20 the LORD has broken out against my enemies **before** [+4200]
5:24 has gone out **in front** [+4200] **of** you to strike the Philistine army."
6: 4 the ark of God on it, and Ahio was walking **in front** [+4200] **of** it.
6: 5 were celebrating with all their might **before** [+4200] the LORD,
6:14 linen ephod, danced **before** [+4200] the LORD with all his might,
6:16 saw King David leaping and dancing **before** [+4200] the LORD,
6:17 and fellowship offerings **before** [+4200] the LORD.
6:21 David said to Michal, "It was **before** [+4200] the LORD,
6:21 people Israel—I will celebrate **before** [+4200] the LORD.
7: 9 have gone, and I have cut off all your enemies from **before** you.
7:15 it away from Saul, whom I removed from **before** [+4200] you.
7:16 and your kingdom will endure forever **before** [+4200] me;
7:18 Then King David went in and sat **before** [+4200] the LORD,
7:23 by driving out nations and their gods from **before** your people,
7:26 the house of your servant David will be established **before** [+4200]
7:29 house of your servant, that it may continue forever in your **sight**;
9: 6 came to David, *he* **bowed down** [+5877+6584] to pay him honor.
10: 9 Joab saw that there were battle lines **in front** [+4946] **of** him
10: 9 that there were battle lines in front of him **[RPH]** and behind him;
10:13 advanced to fight the Arameans, and they fled **before** [+4946] him.
10:14 they fled **before** [+4946] Abishai and went inside the city.
10:15 After the Arameans saw that they had been routed **by** [+4200]
10:16 the commander of Hadadezer's army **leading** [+4200] them.
10:18 they fled **before** [+4946] Israel, and David killed seven hundred of
10:19 of Hadadezer saw that they had been defeated **by** [+4200] Israel,
11:11 my master Joab and my lord's men are camped in the **open** fields.
11:13 At David's invitation, he ate and drank **with** [+4200] him,
11:15 "Put Uriah **in the front** [+448+4578] **line** where the fighting is
13: 9 she took the pan and served **[OBJ]** him the bread, but he refused
14: 7 leaving my husband neither name nor descendant on the **face** *of* the
14:20 Your servant Joab did this to change the **present** situation.
14:22 Joab fell with his **face** to the ground to pay him honor, and he
14:24 "He must go to his own house; he must not see my **face**."
14:24 went to his own house and did not see the **face** *of* the king.
14:28 lived two years in Jerusalem without seeing the king's **face**.
14:32 I want to see the king's **face**, and if I am guilty of anything,
14:33 bowed down with his face to the ground **before** [+4200] the king.
15: 1 and horses and with fifty men to run **ahead** [+4200] *of* him.
15:14 We must flee, or none of us will escape **from** [+4946] Absalom.
15:18 accompanied him from Gath marched **before** [+6584] the king.
15:23 and all the people moved on **toward** [+2006+6584] the desert.
16:19 whom should I serve? Should I not **serve** [+4200] the son?
16:19 the son? Just as I served **[OBJ]** your father, so I will serve you."
16:19 Just as I served your father, so *I will* **serve** [+2118+4200] you."
17:11 to you, with **you yourself** [+3870] leading them into battle.
17:19 wife took a covering and spread it out over the **opening** *of* the well
18: 7 There the army of Israel was defeated **by** [+4200] David's men,
18: 8 The battle spread out **over** [+6584] the whole countryside,
18: 9 Now Absalom happened to **meet** [+4200] David's men. He was
18:14 Joab said, "I'm not going to wait like this **for** [+4200] you."
19: 4 [19:5] The king covered his **face** and cried aloud, "O my son
19: 5 [19:6] **[OBJ]** who have just saved your life and the lives of your
19: 8 [19:9] sitting in the gateway," they all came **before** [+4200] him.
19:13 [19:14] of **my** [+3276+4200] army in place of Joab.' "
19:17 [19:18] They rushed to the Jordan, **where**ˢ [+4200] the king was.
19:18 [19:19] the Jordan, he fell prostrate **before** [+4200] the king
20: 8 at the great rock in Gibeon, Amasa came to **meet** [+4200] them.
21: 1 for three successive years; so David sought the **face** *of* the LORD.
21: 9 who killed and exposed them on a hill **before** [+4200] the LORD.
23:11 was a field full of lentils, Israel's troops fled **from** [+4946] them.
24: 4 so they left the **presence** [+4200] *of* the king to enroll the fighting
24:13 Or three months of fleeing **from** [+4200] your enemies while they
1Ki 1: 2 "Let us look for a young virgin *to* **attend** [+4200+6641] the king
1: 5 and horses ready, with fifty men to run **ahead** [+4200] *of* him.
1:23 So he went **before** [+4200] the king and bowed with his face to the
1:25 now they are eating and drinking **with** [+4200] him and saying,
1:28 So she came *into* the king's **presence** [+4200] and stood before
1:28 she came into the king's presence and stood **before** [+4200] him.
1:32 son of Jehoiada." When they came **before** [+4200] the king,
1:50 in fear **of** [+4946] Solomon, went and took hold of the horns of the
2: 4 and if they walk faithfully **before** [+4200] me with all their heart
2: 7 They stood by me when I fled **from** [+4946] your brother
2:15 All Israel **looked** [+8492] to me as their king. But things changed,
2:16 Do not refuse **me** [+3276]." "You may make it," she said.
2:17 "Please ask King Solomon—he will not refuse **you** [+3871]—
2:20 request to make of you," she said. "Do not refuse **me** [+3276]."
2:20 king replied, "Make it, my mother; I will not refuse **you** [+3871]."
2:26 the ark of the Sovereign LORD **before** [+4200] my father David
2:45 David's throne will remain secure **before** [+4200] the LORD
3: 6 because he was faithful **to** [+4200] you and righteous and upright
3:12 so that there will **never** [+4200+4202] have been anyone like you,
3:15 stood **before** [+4200] the ark of the Lord's covenant and sacrificed
3:16 two prostitutes came to the king and stood **before** [+4200] him.
3:22 living one is mine." And so they argued **before** [+4200] the king.
3:24 me a sword." So they brought a sword **for** [+4200] the king.
3:28 **[OBJ]** because they saw that he had wisdom from God to
5: 3 [5:17] **because of** [+4946] the wars waged against my father
6: 3 The portico at the **front** *of* the main hall of the temple extended the
6: 3 main hall of the temple **extended** [+6584] the width of the temple,
6: 3 and projected ten cubits from the **front** *of* the temple.
6:17 The main hall **in front** [+4200] **of** this room was forty cubits long.
6:20 He overlaid the **inside** [+4200] with pure gold, and he also overlaid
6:21 he extended gold chains across the **front** *of* the inner sanctuary,
6:29 in both the **inner** [+4200] and outer rooms, he carved cherubim,
7: 6 cubits long and thirty wide. **In front** [+6584] **of** it was a portico,
7: 6 and **in front** [+6584] **of** that were pillars and an overhanging roof.
7:42 decorating the bowl-shaped capitals on **top** *of* the pillars);
7:48 the golden table on which was the bread of the **Presence**;
7:49 and five on the left, **in front** [+4200] **of** the inner sanctuary);
8: 5 of Israel that had gathered about him were **before** [+4200] the ark,
8: 8 seen from the Holy Place **in front** [+6584] **of** the inner sanctuary,
8:11 could not perform their service **because of** [+4946] the cloud,
8:14 standing there, the king turned around **[NIE]** and blessed them.
8:22 Solomon stood **before** [+4200] the altar of the LORD in front of
8:23 your servants who continue wholeheartedly **in your way** [+4200].
8:25 'You shall never fail to have a man to sit **before** [+4200+4946] me
8:25 if only your sons are careful in all they do to walk **before** [+4200]
8:25 in all they do to walk before me as you have done.' **[RPH]**
8:28 the prayer that your servant is praying in your **presence** this day.
8:31 and swears the oath **before** [+4200] your altar in this temple,
8:33 "When your people Israel have been defeated **by** [+4200] an
8:40 so that they will fear you all the time they live **in** [+6584] the land
8:46 angry with them and give them over **to** [+4200] the enemy,
8:50 and cause **[OBJ]** their conquerors to show them mercy;
8:54 the LORD, he rose from **before** [+4200] the altar of the LORD,
8:59 words of mine, which I have prayed **before** [+4200] the LORD,
8:62 all Israel with him offered sacrifices **before** [+4200] the LORD.
8:64 part of the courtyard **in front** [+4200] **of** the temple of the LORD,
8:64 because the bronze altar **before** [+4200] the LORD was too small
8:65 They celebrated it **before** [+4200] the LORD our God for seven
9: 3 have heard the prayer and plea you have made **before** [+4200] me;
9: 4 if you walk **before** [+4200] me in integrity of heart
9: 6 decrees I have given **[OBJ]** you and go off to serve other gods
9: 7 I will cut off Israel **from** [+4946+6584] the land I have given them
9: 7 and *will* **reject** [+906+4946+6584+8938] this temple I have
9:25 burning incense **before** [+4200] the LORD along with them,
10: 8 who continually stand **before** [+4200] you and hear your wisdom!
10:24 The whole world sought **audience** *with* Solomon to hear the
11: 7 On a hill **east** [+6584] *of* Jerusalem, Solomon built a high place for
11:36 so that David my servant may always have a lamp **before** [+4200]
12: 2 where he had fled **from** [+4946] King Solomon), he returned from
12: 6 Rehoboam consulted the elders who *had* **served** [+907+6641]
12: 8 who had grown up with him and *were* **serving** [+4200+6641] him.
12:30 the people went even as far as Dan to **worship** [+4200] the one
13: 6 "**Intercede with** [+906+2704] the LORD your God and pray for
13: 6 So the man of God **interceded with** [+906+2704] the LORD,
13:34 led to its downfall and to its destruction from the **face** *of* the earth.
14: 9 You have done more evil than all who lived **before** [+4200] you.
14:24 nations the LORD had driven out **before** [+4946] the Israelites.
15: 3 He committed all the sins his father had done **before** [+4200] him;
16:25 of the LORD and sinned more than all those **before** [+4200] him.
16:30 in the eyes of the LORD than any of those **before** [+4200] him.
16:33 to anger than did all the kings of Israel **before** [+4200] him.
17: 1 the LORD, the God of Israel, lives, whom *I* **serve** [+4200+6641],
17: 3 and hide in the Kerith Ravine, **east** [+6584] *of* the Jordan.
17: 5 He went to the Kerith Ravine, **east** [+6584] *of* the Jordan,
17:14 run dry until the day the LORD gives rain **on** [+6584] the land.' "
18: 1 present yourself to Ahab, and I will send rain **on** [+6584] the land."
18: 7 **bowed down to the ground** [+5877+6584], and said, "Is it really
18:15 "As the LORD Almighty lives, whom *I* **serve** [+4200+6641],
18:39 saw this, they fell **prostrate** [+6584] and cried, "The LORD—
18:42 bent down to the ground and put his **face** between his knees.
18:46 into his belt, he ran **ahead** [+4200] *of* Ahab all the way to Jezreel.
19:11 and stand on the mountain in the **presence** *of* the LORD,
19:11 and shattered the rocks **before** [+4200] the LORD,
19:13 he pulled his cloak over his **face** and went out and stood at the
19:19 yoke of oxen, **[NIE]** and he himself was driving the twelfth pair.
21: 4 He lay on his bed **sulking** [+906+6015] and refused to eat.
21:26 like the Amorites the LORD drove out **before** [+4946] Israel.)
21:29 noticed how Ahab has humbled himself **before** [+4200+4946] me?
21:29 humbled himself, **[RPH]** I will not bring this disaster in his day,
22:10 with all the prophets prophesying **before** [+4200] them.

1Ki 22:21 stood **before** [+4200] the LORD and said, 'I will entice him.'
2Ki 1:15 to Elijah, "Go down with him; do not be afraid **of** [+4946] him."
3:14 as the LORD Almighty lives, whom *I* **serve** [+4200+6641],
3:14 if I did not have respect for the **presence** *of* Jehoshaphat king of
3:24 **[OBJ]** And the Israelites invaded the land and slaughtered the
4:12 So he called her, and she stood **before** [+4200] him.
4:29 anyone greets you, do not answer. Lay my staff on the boy's **face**."
4:31 Gehazi went on **ahead** [+4200] and laid the staff on the boy's face,
4:31 Gehazi went on ahead and laid the staff on the boy's **face**,
4:38 While the company of the prophets was meeting **with** [+4200] him,
4:43 "How can I set this **before** [+4200] a hundred men?" his servant
4:44 he set it **before** [+4200] them, and they ate and had some left over,
5:1 He was a great man in the **sight** *of* his master and highly regarded,
5:1 great man in the sight of his master and **highly regarded** [+5951],
5:2 girl from Israel, and *she* **served** [+2118+4200] Naaman's wife.
5:3 "If only my master would **see** [+4200] the prophet who is in
5:15 He stood **before** [+4200] him and said, "Now I know that there is
5:16 whom *I* **serve** [+4200+6641], I will not accept a thing."
5:23 of his servants, and they carried them **ahead** [+4200] *of* Gehazi.
5:27 Gehazi went from Elisha's **presence** [+4200] and he was leprous,
6:1 the place where we meet **with** [+4200] you is too small for us.
6:22 Set food and water **before** [+4200] them so that they may eat
6:32 The king sent a messenger **ahead** [+4200+4946], but before he
8:9 He went in and stood **before** [+4200] him, and said, "Your son
8:11 He **stared** *at* him **with a fixed gaze** [+906+2256+6641+8492] until
8:15 soaked it in water and spread it over the king's **face**, so that he
9:14 all Israel had been defending Ramoth Gilead **against** [+4946]
9:32 He **looked** up at the window and called out, "Who is on my side?
9:37 Jezebel's body will be like refuse **on** [+6584] the ground in the plot
10:4 and said, "If two kings *could* not **resist** [+4200+6641] him,
11:2 and his nurse in a bedroom to hide him **from** [+4946] Athaliah;
11:18 and killed Mattan the priest of Baal **in front** [+4200] **of** the altars.
12:17 [12:18] captured it. Then he **turned** [+8492] to attack Jerusalem.
13:4 Then Jehoahaz **sought** the LORD's **favor** [+906+2704],
13:14 king of Israel went down to see him and wept **over** [+6584] him.
13:23 been unwilling to destroy them or banish them from his **presence**.
14:8 king of Israel, with the challenge: "Come, meet me **face to face**."
14:11 Amaziah king of Judah **faced** [+8011] **each other** at Beth Shemesh
14:12 Judah was routed **by** [+4200] Israel, and every man fled to his
16:3 nations the LORD had driven out **before** [+4946] the Israelites.
16:14 The bronze altar that stood **before** [+4200] the LORD he brought
16:14 stood before the LORD he brought from the **front** *of* the temple—
16:18 of the LORD, **in deference to** [+4946] the king of Assyria.
17:2 but not like the kings of Israel who **preceded** [+2118+4200] him.
17:8 of the nations the LORD had driven out **before** [+4946] them,
17:11 as the nations whom the LORD had driven out **before** [+4946] them,
17:18 was very angry with Israel and removed them from his **presence**.
17:20 the hands of plunderers, until he thrust them from his **presence**.
17:23 until the LORD removed them from his **presence**, as he had
18:5 all the kings of Judah, either **before** [+4200] him or after him.
18:22 "You must worship **before** [+4200] this altar in Jerusalem"?
18:24 How *can you* **repulse** [+906+8740] one officer of the least of my
19:6 Do not be afraid **of** [+4946] what you have heard—those words
19:14 of the LORD and spread it out **before** [+4200] the LORD.
19:15 And Hezekiah prayed **to** [+4200] the LORD: "O LORD,
19:26 grass sprouting on the roof, scorched **before** [+4200] it grows up.
20:2 Hezekiah turned his **face** to the wall and prayed to the LORD,
20:3 how I have walked **before** [+4200] you faithfully and with
21:2 nations the LORD had driven out **before** [+4946] the Israelites.
21:9 nations the LORD had destroyed **before** [+4946] the Israelites.
21:11 He has done more evil than the Amorites who **preceded** [+4200]
21:13 as one wipes a dish, wiping it and turning it **upside** [+6584] **down**.
22:10 me a book." And Shaphan read from it in the **presence** *of* the king.
22:19 you humbled yourself **before** [+4946] the LORD when you heard
22:19 and because you tore your robes and wept in my **presence**,
23:3 and renewed the covenant in the **presence** *of* the LORD—
23:13 The king also desecrated the high places that were **east** [+6584] *of*
23:25 Neither **before** [+4200] nor after Josiah was there a king like him
23:27 "I will remove Judah also from my **presence** as I removed Israel,
24:3 in order to remove them from his **presence** because of the sins of
24:20 and Judah, and in the end he thrust them from his **presence**.
25:19 in charge of the fighting men and five royal **advisers** [+8011].
25:26 army officers, fled to Egypt for fear **of** [+4946] the Babylonians.
25:29 for the rest of his life ate regularly **at** the king's **table**ᵃ [+4200].
1Ch 1:43 These were the kings who reigned in Edom **before** [+4200] any
4:40 and quiet. Some Hamites had lived there **formerly** [+4200].
5:10 of the Hagrites throughout the entire **region** east of Gilead.
5:25 of the land, whom God had destroyed **before** [+4946] them.
6:32 [6:17] They ministered with music **before** [+4200] the tabernacle,
9:20 **In earlier** [+4200] **times** Phinehas son of Eleazar was in charge of
10:1 the Israelites fled **before** [+4946] them, and many fell slain on
11:3 he made a compact with them at Hebron **before** [+4200] the
11:13 a field full of barley, the troops fled **from** [+4946] the Philistines.
12:1 while he was banished from the **presence** *of* Saul son of Kish (they
12:8 [12:9] Their **faces** were the faces of lions, and they were as swift
12:8 [12:9] Their faces were the **faces** *of* lions, and they were as swift
12:17 [12:18] David went out to **meet** [+4200] them and said to them,
13:8 were celebrating with all their might **before** [+4200] God,
13:10 had put his hand on the ark. So he died there **before** [+4200] God.
14:8 but David heard about it and went out to **meet** [+4200] them.
14:15 because that will mean God has gone out **in front** [+4200] **of** you
15:24 Eliezer the priests were to blow trumpets **before** [+4200] the ark of
16:1 burnt offerings and fellowship offerings **before** [+4200] God.
16:4 He appointed some of the Levites to minister **before** [+4200] the
16:6 trumpets regularly **before** [+4200] the ark of the covenant of God.
16:11 Look to the LORD and his strength; seek his **face** always.
16:27 Splendor and majesty are **before** [+4200] him; strength and joy in
16:29 Bring an offering and come **before** [+4200] him; worship the
16:30 Tremble **before** [+4200+4946] him, all the earth! The world is
16:33 they will sing for joy **before** [+4200+4946] the LORD, for he
16:37 his associates **before** [+4200] the ark of the covenant of the
16:37 of the covenant of the LORD to minister there **[RPH]** regularly,
16:39 his fellow priests **before** [+4200] the tabernacle of the LORD at
17:8 have gone, and I have cut off all your enemies from **before** you.
17:13 as I took it away from your **predecessor** [+889+2118+4200].
17:16 Then King David went in and sat **before** [+4200] the LORD,
17:21 awesome wonders by driving out nations from **before** your people,
17:24 the house of your servant David will be established **before** [+4200]
17:25 So your servant has found courage to pray **to** [+4200] you.
17:27 house of your servant, that it may continue forever in your **sight**;
19:7 with his troops, who came and camped **near** [+4200] Medeba,
19:10 Joab saw that there were **[RPH]** battle lines in front of him
19:10 Joab saw that there were battle lines **in front of** him and behind
19:14 and the troops with him advanced to fight **[OBJ]** the Arameans,
19:14 advanced to fight the Arameans, and they fled **before** [+4946] him.
19:15 they too fled **before** [+4946] his brother Abishai and went inside
19:16 After the Arameans saw that they had been routed **by** [+4200]
19:16 the commander of Hadadezer's army **leading** [+4200] them.
19:18 they fled **before** [+4200+4946] Israel, and David killed seven
19:19 of Hadadezer saw that they had been defeated **by** [+4200] Israel,
21:12 three months of being swept away **before** [+4946] your enemies,
21:16 and the elders, clothed in sackcloth, fell **facedown** [+6584].
21:30 But David could not go **before** [+4200] it to inquire of God,
21:30 because he was afraid **of** [+4946] the sword of the angel of the
22:5 So David made extensive preparations **before** [+4200] his death.
22:8 because you have shed much blood on the earth in my **sight**.
22:18 and the land is subject **to** [+4200] the LORD and to his people.
22:18 and the land is subject to the LORD and **to** [+4200] his people.
23:13 to offer sacrifices **before** [+4200] the LORD, to minister before
23:31 They were to serve **before** [+4200] the LORD regularly in the
24:2 But Nadab and Abihu died **before** [+4200] their father did,
24:6 recorded their names in the **presence** *of* the king and of the
24:31 in the **presence** *of* King David and of Zadok, Ahimelech,
29:12 Wealth and honor come **from** [+4200+4946] you; you are the ruler
29:15 We are aliens and strangers in your **sight**, as were all our
29:22 and drank with great joy in the **presence** *of* the LORD that day.
29:25 splendor such as no king over Israel ever had **before** [+4200].
2Ch 1:5 had made was in Gibeon **in front** [+4200] **of** the tabernacle of the
1:6 Solomon went up to the bronze altar **before** [+4200] the LORD in
1:10 that *I may* **lead** [+995+2256+3655+4200] this people, for who is
1:12 such as no king who was **before** [+4200] you ever had and none
1:13 high place at Gibeon, from **before** [+4200] the Tent of Meeting.
2:4 [2:3] it to him for burning fragrant incense **before** [+4200] him,
2:6 [2:5] except as a place to burn sacrifices **before** [+4200] him?
3:4 The portico at the **front** *of* the temple was twenty cubits long
3:4 was twenty cubits long **across** [+6584] the width of the building
3:8 its length **corresponding to** [+6584] the width of the temple—
3:13 twenty cubits. They stood on their feet, **facing** the main hall.
3:15 **In the front** [+4200] **of** the temple he made two pillars,
3:17 He erected the pillars in the **front** *of* the temple, one to the south
4:13 decorating the bowl-shaped capitals on **top** *of* the pillars);
4:19 golden altar; the tables on which was the bread of the **Presence**;
4:20 to burn **in front** [+4200] **of** the inner sanctuary as prescribed;
5:6 of Israel that had gathered about him were **before** [+4200] the ark,
5:9 could be seen from **in front** [+6584] **of** the inner sanctuary,
5:14 could not perform their service **because of** [+4946] the cloud,
6:3 standing there, the king turned around **[NIE]** and blessed them.
6:12 Solomon stood **before** [+4200] the altar of the LORD in front of
6:14 your servants who continue wholeheartedly **in** your **way** [+4200].
6:16 'You shall never fail to have a man to sit **before** [+4200+4946] me
6:16 if only your sons are careful in all they do to walk **before** [+4200]
6:19 and the prayer that your servant is praying in your **presence**.
6:22 and swears the oath **before** [+4200] your altar in this temple,
6:24 "When your people Israel have been defeated **by** [+4200] an
6:24 and making supplication **before** [+4200] you in this temple,
6:31 walk in your ways all the time they live **in** [+6584] the land you
6:36 angry with them and give them over **to** [+4200] the enemy,
6:42 O LORD God, *do* not **reject** [+8740] your anointed one.

2Ch 7: 4 and all the people offered sacrifices **before** [+4200] the LORD.
7: 7 part of the courtyard **in front** [+4200] **of** the temple of the LORD,
7: 14 will humble themselves and pray and seek my **face** and turn from
7: 17 for you, if you walk **before** [+4200] me as David your father did,
7: 19 and forsake the decrees and commands I have given **[OBJ]** you
7: 20 and *will* **reject** [+906+4946+6584+8959] this temple I have
8: 12 On the altar of the LORD that he had built **in front** [+4200] **of** the
9: 7 who continually stand **before** [+4200] you and hear your wisdom!
9: 11 Nothing like them had **ever** [+4200] been seen in Judah.)
9: 23 All the kings of the earth sought **audience** *with* Solomon to hear
10: 2 where he had fled **from** [+4946] King Solomon), he returned from
10: 6 *had* **served** [+4200+6641] his father Solomon during his lifetime.
10: 8 who had grown up with him and *were* **serving** [+4200+6641] him.
12: 5 who had assembled in Jerusalem **for fear** [+4946] **of** Shishak,
13: 7 he was young and indecisive and not strong enough to **resist** them.
13: 8 "And now you plan to resist **[OBJ]** the kingdom of the LORD,
13: 13 so that while he was **in front** [+4200] **of** Judah the ambush was
13: 14 and saw that they were being attacked at both **front** and rear.
13: 15 routed Jeroboam and all Israel **before** [+4200] Abijah and Judah.
13: 16 The Israelites fled **before** [+4946] Judah, and God delivered them
14: 5 [14:4] and the kingdom was at peace **under** [+4200] him.
14: 7 [14:6] The land is still **ours** [+4200+5646], because we have
14: 10 [14:9] Asa went out to **meet** [+4200] him, and they took up battle
14: 12 [14:11] The LORD struck down the Cushites **before** [+4200]
14: 12 [14:11] struck down the Cushites before Asa and **[RPH]** Judah.
14: 13 [14:12] they were crushed **before** [+4200] the LORD and his
14: 13 [14:12] were crushed before the LORD and **[RPH]** his forces.
15: 2 He went out to **meet** [+4200] Asa and said to him, "Listen to me,
15: 8 He repaired the altar of the LORD that was **in front** [+4200] **of**
18: 9 with all the prophets prophesying **before** [+4200] them.
18: 20 stood **before** [+4200] the LORD and said, 'I will entice him.'
19: 2 son of Hanani, went out to **meet** [+448] him and said to the king,
19: 2 of this, the wrath **of** [+4200+4946] the LORD is upon you.
19: 7 our God there is no injustice or **partiality** [+5365] or bribery."
19: 11 and the Levites will serve as officials **before** [+4200] you.
20: 3 Jehoshaphat **resolved** [+906+5989] to inquire of the LORD,
20: 5 Jerusalem at the temple of the LORD **in** the **front** [+4200] **of** the
20: 7 inhabitants of this land **before** [+4200+4946] your people Israel
20: 9 we will stand in your **presence** before this temple that bears your
20: 9 we will stand in your presence **before** [+4200] this temple that
20: 12 For we have no power to **face** [+4200] this vast army that is
20: 13 and little ones, stood there **before** [+4200] the LORD.
20: 15 not be afraid or discouraged **because of** [+4946] this vast army.
20: 16 you will find them at the end of the gorge **in** the Desert of Jeruel.
20: 17 Go out to **face** [+4200] them tomorrow, and the LORD will be
20: 18 and Jerusalem fell down in worship **before** [+4200] the LORD.
20: 21 of his holiness as they went out **at the head** [+4200] **of** the army,
22: 11 she hid the child **from** [+4946] Athaliah so she could not kill him.
23: 17 and killed Mattan the priest of Baal **in front** [+4200] **of** the altars.
24: 14 they brought the rest of the money **to** [+4200] the king
25: 8 God will overthrow you **before** [+4200] the enemy, for God has
25: 14 bowed down **to** [+4200] them and burned sacrifices to them.
25: 17 the son of Jehu, king of Israel: "Come, meet me **face to face**."
25: 21 Amaziah king of Judah **faced** [+8011] **each other** at Beth Shemesh
25: 22 Judah was routed **by** [+4200] Israel, and every man fled to his
26: 19 While he was raging at the priests in their **presence** before the
27: 6 because he walked steadfastly **before** [+4200] the LORD his
28: 3 nations the LORD had driven out **before** [+4946] the Israelites.
28: 9 he went out to **meet** [+4200] the army when it returned to Samaria.
28: 14 and plunder in the **presence** *of* the officials and all the assembly.
29: 6 They turned their **faces** away from the LORD's dwelling place
29: 11 for the LORD has chosen you to stand **before** [+4200] him
29: 19 was king. They are now **in front** [+4200] **of** the LORD's altar."
29: 23 The goats for the sin offering were brought **before** [+4200] the
30: 9 your children will be shown compassion **by** [+4200] their captors
30: 9 He will not turn his **face** from you if you return to him."
31: 20 and right and faithful **before** [+4200] the LORD his God.
32: 2 had come and that he **intended** to make war on Jerusalem,
32: 7 be afraid or discouraged **because of** [+4946] the king of Assyria
32: 7 because of the king of Assyria and **[RPH]** the vast army with him,
32: 12 'You must worship **before** [+4200] one altar and burn sacrifices on
32: 21 So he withdrew to his own land in **disgrace** [+1425]. And when he
33: 2 nations the LORD had driven out **before** [+4946] the Israelites.
33: 9 nations the LORD had destroyed **before** [+4946] the Israelites.
33: 12 In his distress *he* **sought the favor of** [+906+2704] the LORD his
33: 12 humbled himself greatly **before** [+4200+4946] the God of his
33: 19 up Asherah poles and idols **before** [+4200] he humbled himself—
33: 23 he did not humble himself **before** [+4200+4946] the LORD;
34: 4 **Under** his **direction** [+4200] the altars of the Baals were torn
34: 4 scattered **over** [+6584] the graves of those who had sacrificed to
34: 18 me a book." And Shaphan read from it in the **presence** *of* the king.
34: 24 in the book that has been read in the **presence** *of* the king of Judah.
34: 27 you humbled yourself **before** [+4200+4946] God when you heard
34: 27 because you humbled yourself **before** [+4200] me and tore your
34: 27 yourself before me and tore your robes and wept in my **presence**,
34: 31 and renewed the covenant in the **presence** *of* the LORD—
35: 22 Josiah, however, *would* not **turn away** [+6015] from him,
36: 12 did not humble himself **before** [+4200+4946] Jeremiah the
Ezr 7: 28 who has extended his good favor to me **before** [+4200] the king
8: 21 so that we might humble ourselves **before** [+4200] our God
8: 29 of the LORD in Jerusalem **before** [+4200] the leading priests
9: 6 I am too ashamed and disgraced to lift up my **face** to you,
9: 7 to pillage and **humiliation** [+1425] at the hand of foreign kings,
9: 9 He has shown us kindness in the **sight** *of* the kings of Persia:
9: 15 Here we are **before** [+4200] you in our guilt, though because of it
9: 15 though because of it not one of us can stand in your **presence**."
10: 1 and throwing himself down **before** [+4200] the house of God,
10: 6 Then Ezra withdrew from **before** [+4200] the house of God
Ne 1: 4 and fasted and prayed **before** [+4200] the God of heaven.
1: 6 to hear the prayer your servant is praying **before** [+4200] you day
1: 11 success today by granting him favor in the **presence** *of* this man."
2: 1 when wine was brought **for** [+4200] him, I took the wine and gave
2: 1 and gave it to the king. I had not been sad in his **presence** before;
2: 2 asked me, "Why does your **face** look so sad when you are not ill?
2: 3 Why should my **face** not look sad when the city where my fathers
2: 5 it pleases the king and if your servant has found favor in his **sight**,
2: 6 get back?" It pleased **[OBJ]** the king to send me; so I set a time.
2: 13 By night I went out through the Valley Gate **toward** [+448] the
4: 2 [3:34] in the **presence** *of* his associates and the army of Samaria,
4: 5 [3:37] up their guilt or blot out their sins from your **sight** [+4200],
4: 9 [4:3] posted a guard day and night to **meet** [+4946] this threat.
4: 14 [4:8] and the rest of the people, "Don't be afraid **of** [+4946] them.
5: 15 But the earlier governors—those **preceding** [+4200] me—
5: 15 But **out of** [+4946] reverence for God I did not act like that.
6: 19 they kept reporting **to** [+4200] me his good deeds and then telling
8: 1 all the people assembled as one man in the square **before** [+4200]
8: 2 Ezra the priest brought the Law **before** [+4200] the assembly,
8: 3 He read it aloud from daybreak till noon as he **faced** [+4200] the
8: 3 square **before** [+4200] the Water Gate in the presence of the men,
9: 8 You found his heart faithful **to** [+4200] you, and you made a
9: 11 You divided the sea **before** [+4200] them, so that they passed
9: 24 You subdued **before** [+4200] them the Canaanites, who lived in
9: 28 as they were at rest, they again did what was evil in your **sight**.
9: 32 do not let all this hardship seem trifling **in** your **eyes** [+4200]—
9: 35 to them in the spacious and fertile land you gave **[OBJ]** them,
12: 36 David the man of God. Ezra the scribe **led** [+4200] the procession.
13: 4 **Before** [+4200] this, Eliashib the priest had been put in charge of
13: 5 he had provided him with a large room **formerly** [+4200] used to
13: 19 shadows fell on the gates of Jerusalem **before** [+4200] the Sabbath,
Est 1: 3 the princes, and the nobles of the provinces were **present** [+4200].
1: 10 he commanded the seven eunuchs who served **[OBJ]** him—
1: 11 to bring **before** [+4200] him Queen Vashti, wearing her royal
1: 13 Since it was customary for the king to **consult** [+4200] experts in
1: 14 of Persia and Media *who* **had special access to** [+8011] the king
1: 16 Then Memucan replied in the **presence** *of* the king and the nobles,
1: 17 commanded Queen Vashti to be brought **before** [+4200] him,
1: 19 **[OBJ]** and let it be written in the laws of Persia and Media,
1: 19 that Vashti is never again to enter the **presence** [+4200] *of* King
2: 9 The girl pleased him and **won** [+4200+5951] his favor.
2: 11 forth **near** [+4200] the courtyard of the harem to find out how
2: 17 *she* **won** [+4200+5951] his favor and approval more than any of
2: 23 All this was recorded in the book of the annals in the **presence** *of*
3: 7 the lot) in the **presence** *of* Haman to select a day and month.
4: 2 he went only as far as **[NIE]** the king's gate, because no one
4: 5 one of the king's eunuchs assigned to **attend** [+4200] her,
4: 6 in the open square of the city **in front** [+4200] **of** the king's gate.
4: 8 to beg for mercy and plead with **[OBJ]** him for her people.
5: 14 This suggestion delighted **[OBJ]** Haman, and he had the gallows
6: 1 the record of his reign, to be brought in and read **to** [+4200] him.
6: 9 the horse through the city streets, proclaiming **before** [+4200] him,
6: 11 through the city streets, proclaiming **before** [+4200] him,
6: 13 "Since Mordecai, **before** [+4200] whom your downfall has started,
6: 13 cannot stand against him—you will surely come to ruin!" **[RPH]**
7: 6 Haman was terrified **before** [+4200+4946] the king and queen.
7: 8 as the word left the king's mouth, they covered Haman's **face**.
7: 9 one of the eunuchs **attending** [+4200] the king, said,
8: 1 Mordecai came into the **presence** *of* the king, for Esther had told
8: 3 Esther again pleaded **with** [+4200] the king, falling at his feet
8: 3 pleaded with the king, falling **at** [+4200] his feet and weeping.
8: 4 gold scepter to Esther and she arose and stood **before** [+4200] him.
8: 5 "and if he **regards** *me* **with** [+4200+5162] favor and thinks it the
8: 5 he regards me with favor and thinks it the right thing **[OBJ]** to do,
8: 15 Mordecai left the king's **presence** [+4200] wearing royal garments
9: 2 No one could stand **against** [+4200] them, because the people of
9: 11 the citadel of Susa was reported **to** [+4200] the king that same day.
9: 25 when the plot came to the king's **attention** [+4200], he issued
Job 1: 11 everything he has, and he will surely curse you to your **face**."
1: 12 a finger." Then Satan went out from the **presence** *of* the LORD.

Job 2: 5 his flesh and bones, and he will surely curse you to your **face**."
2: 7 So Satan went out from the **presence** *of* the LORD and afflicted
3: 24 For sighing comes to me **instead** [+4200] **of** food; my groans pour
4: 15 A spirit glided past my **face**, and the hair on my body stood on end.
4: 19 in the dust, who are crushed **more readily than** [+4200] a moth!
5: 10 He bestows rain **on** [+6584] the earth; he sends water upon the
5: 10 rain on the earth; he sends water **upon** [+6584] the countryside.
6: 28 "But now be so kind as to look at me. Would I lie to your **face**?
8: 12 and uncut, they wither **more quickly than** [+4200] grass.
8: 16 He is like a well-watered plant **in** [+4200] the sunshine, spreading
9: 24 into the hands of the wicked, *he* **blindfolds** [+4059] its judges.
9: 27 will forget my complaint, I will change my **expression**, and smile,'
11: 15 then you will lift up your **face** without shame; you will stand firm
11: 19 one to make you afraid, and many *will* **court** your **favor** [+2704].
13: 8 *Will you* **show** him **partiality** [+5951]? Will you argue the case
13: 10 surely rebuke you if *you* secretly **showed partiality** [+5951].
13: 15 yet will I hope in him; I will surely defend my ways to his **face**.
13: 16 for no godless man would dare come **before** [+4200] him!
13: 20 two things, O God, and then I will not hide **from** [+4946] you:
13: 24 Why do you hide your **face** and consider me your enemy?
14: 20 and he is gone; you change his **countenance** and send him away.
15: 4 you even undermine piety and hinder devotion **to** [+4200] God.
15: 7 man ever born? Were you brought forth **before** [+4200] the hills?
15: 27 "Though his **face** is covered with fat and his waist bulges with
16: 8 a witness; my gauntness rises up and testifies **against** [+928] me.
16: 14 Again and again he bursts **upon** [+6584] me; he rushes at me like a
16: 16 My **face** is red with weeping, deep shadows ring my eyes;
17: 6 made me a byword to everyone, a man in whose **face** people spit.
17: 12 turn night into day; in the **face** *of* darkness they say, 'Light is near.'
18: 17 him perishes from the earth; he has no name **in** [+6584] the land.
19: 29 you should fear **[OBJ]** the sword yourselves; for wrath will bring
21: 8 They **see** [+4200] their children established around them, their
21: 18 How often are they like straw **before** [+4200] the wind, like chaff
21: 31 Who denounces his conduct to his **face**? Who repays him for what
21: 33 follow after him, and a countless throng goes **before** [+4200] him.
22: 8 owning land—an **honored man** [+5951], living on it.
22: 26 will find delight in the Almighty and will lift up your **face** to God.
23: 4 I would state my case **before** [+4200] him and fill my mouth with
23: 15 That is why I am terrified **before** [+4946] him; when I think of all
23: 17 Yet I am not silenced **by** [+4946] the darkness, by the thick
23: 17 by the darkness, by the thick darkness that covers my **face**.
24: 15 he thinks, 'No eye will see me,' and he keeps his **face** concealed.
24: 18 "Yet they are foam on the **surface** *of* the water; their portion of the
26: 9 He covers the **face** *of* the full moon, spreading his clouds over it.
26: 10 He marks out the horizon on the **face** *of* the waters for a boundary
29: 24 scarcely believed it; the light of my **face** was precious to them.
30: 10 and keep their distance; they do not hesitate to spit in my **face**.
30: 11 and afflicted me, they throw off restraint in my **presence**.
32: 21 *I will* **show partiality to** [+5951] no one, nor will I flatter any
33: 5 me then, if you can; prepare yourself and confront **[OBJ]** me.
33: 26 and finds favor with him, he sees God's **face** and shouts for joy;
34: 19 who **shows** no **partiality to** [+5951] princes and does not favor the
34: 19 to princes and does not favor the rich **over** [+4200] the poor,
34: 29 If he hides his **face**, who can see him? Yet he is over man
35: 12 when men cry out **because of** [+4946] the arrogance of the wicked.
35: 14 that your case is **before** [+4200] him and you must wait for him,
37: 12 At his direction they swirl around over the **face** *of* the whole earth
37: 19 we cannot draw up our case **because of** [+4946] our darkness.
38: 30 become hard as stone, when the **surface** *of* the deep is frozen?
39: 22 afraid of nothing; he does not shy away **from** [+4946] the sword.
40: 13 Bury them all in the dust together; shroud their **faces** in the grave.
41: 10 [41:2] rouse him. Who then is able to stand **against** [+4200] me?
41: 13 [41:5] Who can strip off his **outer** coat? Who would approach
41: 14 [41:6] Who dares open the doors of his **mouth**, ringed about with
41: 22 [41:14] resides in his neck; dismay goes **before** [+4200] him.
42: 8 *I will* **accept** [+5951] his prayer and not deal with you according to
42: 9 told them; and the LORD **accepted** [+906+5951] Job's prayer.
42: 11 and everyone who had known him **before** [+4200] came
Ps 3: T [3:1] of David. When he fled **from** [+4946] his son Absalom.
4: 6 [4:7] Let the light of your **face** shine upon us, O LORD.
5: 8 [5:9] my enemies—make straight your way **before** [+4200] me.
9: 3 [9:4] turn back; they stumble and perish **before** [+4946] you.
9: 19 [9:20] man triumph; let the nations be judged in your **presence**.
10: 11 to himself, "God has forgotten; he covers his **face** and never sees."
11: 7 is righteous, he loves justice; upright men will see his **face**.
13: 1 [13:2] me forever? How long will you hide your **face** from me?
16: 11 you will fill me with joy in your **presence**, with eternal pleasures at
17: 2 May my vindication come **from** [+4200+4946] you; may your eyes
17: 9 **from** [+4946] the wicked who assail me, from my mortal enemies
17: 13 Rise up, O LORD, confront **[OBJ]** them, bring them down;
17: 15 And I—in righteousness I will see your **face**; when I awake,
18: 6 [18:7] my voice; my cry came **before** [+4200] him, into his ears.
18: 42 [18:43] I beat them as fine as dust **borne on** [+6584] the wind;
19: 14 [19:15] and the meditation of my heart be pleasing in your **sight**,
21: 6 [21:7] and made him glad with the joy of your **presence**.
21: 9 [21:10] At the time of your **appearing** you will make them like a
21: 12 [21:13] backs when you aim **at** [+6584] them with drawn bow.
22: 24 [22:25] he has not hidden his **face** from him but has listened to his
22: 27 [22:28] of the nations will bow down **before** [+4200] him,
22: 29 [22:30] all who go down to the dust will kneel **before** [+4200]
23: 5 You prepare a table **before** [+4200] me in the presence of my
24: 6 of those who seek him, who seek your **face**, O God of Jacob.
27: 8 My heart says of you, "Seek his **face**!" Your face, LORD,
27: 8 heart says of you, "Seek his face!" Your **face**, LORD, I will seek.
27: 9 Do not hide your **face** from me, do not turn your servant away in
30: 7 [30:8] stand firm; but when you hid your **face**, I was dismayed.
31: 16 [31:17] Let your **face** shine on your servant; save me in your
31: 20 [31:21] In the shelter of your **presence** you hide them from the
34: T [34:1] When he pretended to be insane **before** [+4200]
34: 5 [34:6] him are radiant; their **faces** are never covered with shame.
34: 16 [34:17] the **face** *of* the LORD is against those who do evil, to cut
35: 5 May they be like chaff **before** [+4200] the wind, with the angel of
38: 3 [38:4] **Because of** [+4946] your wrath there is no health in my
38: 3 [38:4] my bones have no soundness **because of** [+4946] my sin.
38: 5 [38:6] and are loathsome **because of** [+4946] my sinful folly.
41: 12 [41:13] you uphold me and set me in your **presence** forever.
42: 2 [42:3] living God. When can I go and **meet with** [+8011] God?
42: 5 [42:6] in God, for I will yet praise him, **my** [+3276] Savior and
42: 11 [42:12] for I will yet praise him, **[NIE]** my Savior and my God.
43: 5 in God, for I will yet praise him, **[NIE]** my Savior and my God.
44: 3 [44:4] your arm, and the light of your **face**, for you loved them.
44: 15 [44:16] me all day long, and my **face** is covered with shame
44: 16 [44:17] and revile me, **because of** [+4946] the enemy,
44: 24 [44:25] Why do you hide your **face** and forget our misery
45: 12 [45:13] with a gift, men of wealth *will* **seek** your **favor** [+2704].
50: 3 a fire devours **before** [+4200] him, and around him a tempest
51: 9 [51:11] Hide your **face** from my sins and blot out all my iniquity.
51: 11 [51:13] Do not cast me from your **presence** [+4200] or take your
55: 3 [55:4] the voice of the enemy, **at** [+4946] the stares of the wicked;
56: 13 [56:14] that I may walk **before** [+4200] God in the light of life.
57: T [57:1] When he had fled **from** [+4946] Saul into the cave.
57: 6 [57:7] They dug a pit **in** my **path** [+4200]—but they have fallen
60: 4 [60:6] you have raised a banner to be unfurled **against** [+4946]
61: 3 [61:4] been my refuge, a strong tower **against** [+4946] the foe.
61: 7 [61:8] May he be enthroned in God's **presence** forever;
62: 8 [62:9] pour out your hearts **to** [+4200] him, for God is our refuge.
67: 1 [67:2] to us and bless us and make his **face** shine upon us,
68: 1 [68:2] be scattered; may his foes flee **before** [+4946] him.
68: 2 [68:3] as wax melts **before** [+4946] the fire, may the wicked
68: 2 [68:3] before the fire, may the wicked perish **before** [+4946] God.
68: 3 [68:4] may the righteous be glad and rejoice **before** [+4200] God;
68: 4 [68:5] his name is the LORD—and rejoice **before** [+4200] him.
68: 7 [68:8] When you went out **before** [+4200] your people, O God,
68: 8 [68:9] the heavens poured down rain, **before** [+4946] God,
68: 8 [68:9] before God, the One of Sinai, **before** [+4946] God,
69: 7 [69:8] I endure scorn for your sake, and shame covers my **face**.
69: 17 [69:18] Do not hide your **face** from your servant; answer me
69: 22 [69:23] May the table set **before** [+4200] them become a snare;
72: 5 He will endure as long as the sun, **as** [+4200] **long as** the moon,
72: 9 The desert tribes will bow **before** [+4200] him and his enemies
72: 17 name endure forever; may it continue **as** [+4200] **long as** the sun.
76: 7 [76:8] Who can stand **before** [+4200] you when you are angry?
78: 55 He drove out nations **before** [+4946] them and allotted their lands
79: 11 May the groans of the prisoners come **before** [+4200] you;
80: 2 [80:3] **before** [+4200] Ephraim, Benjamin and Manasseh.
80: 3 [80:4] make your **face** shine upon us, that we may be saved.
80: 7 [80:8] make your **face** shine upon us, that we may be saved.
80: 9 [80:10] You cleared the ground **for** [+4200] it, and it took root
80: 16 [80:17] with fire; at **[NIE]** your rebuke your people perish.
80: 19 [80:20] make your **face** shine upon us, that we may be saved.
82: 2 you defend the unjust and **show partiality to** [+5951] the wicked?
83: 13 [83:14] O my God, like chaff **before** [+4200] the wind.
83: 16 [83:17] Cover their **faces** with shame so that men will seek your
84: 9 [84:10] O God; **look with favor on** [+5564] your anointed one.
85: 13 [85:14] Righteousness goes **before** [+4200] him and prepares the
86: 9 nations you have made will come and worship **before** [+4200] you,
88: 2 [88:3] May my prayer come **before** [+4200] you; turn your ear to
88: 14 [88:15] O LORD, do you reject me and hide your **face** from me?
89: 14 [89:15] of your throne; love and faithfulness go **before** you.
89: 15 [89:16] who walk in the light of your **presence**, O LORD.
89: 23 [89:24] I will crush his foes **before** [+4946] him and strike down
90: 8 iniquities before you, our secret sins in the light of your **presence**.
95: 2 Let us come **before** him with thanksgiving and extol him with
95: 6 in worship, let us kneel **before** [+4200] the LORD our Maker;
96: 6 Splendor and majesty are **before** [+4200] him; strength and glory
96: 9 splendor of his holiness; tremble **before** [+4946] him, all the earth.
96: 13 they will sing **before** [+4200] the LORD, for he comes, he comes
97: 3 Fire goes **before** [+4200] him and consumes his foes on every side.

Ps 97: 5 The mountains melt like wax **before** [+4200+4946] the LORD,
97: 5 mountains melt like wax before the LORD, **before** [+4200+4946]
98: 6 ram's horn—shout for joy **before** [+4200] the LORD, the King.
98: 9 let them sing **before** [+4200] the LORD, for he comes to judge
100: 2 with gladness; come **before** [+4200] him with joyful songs.
102: T [102:1] and pours out his lament **before** [+4200] the LORD.
102: 2 [102:3] Do not hide your **face** from me when I am in distress.
102: 10 [102:11] **because of** [+4946] your great wrath, for you have taken
102: 25 [102:26] In the **beginning** you laid the foundations of the earth,
102: 28 [102:29] their descendants will be established **before** [+4200]
104: 15 oil to make his **face** shine, and bread that sustains his heart.
104: 29 When you hide your **face**, they are terrified; when you take away
104: 30 your Spirit, they are created, and you renew the **face** *of* the earth.
105: 4 Look to the LORD and his strength; seek his **face** always.
105: 17 and he sent a man **before** [+4200] them—Joseph, sold as a slave.
106: 23 stood in the breach **before** [+4200] him to keep his wrath from
106: 46 He caused them to be pitied **by** [+4200] all who held them captive.
114: 7 Tremble, O earth, at the **presence** [+4200] *of* the Lord,
114: 7 presence of the Lord, at the **presence** [+4200] *of* the God of Jacob,
116: 9 that I may walk **before** [+4200] the LORD in the land of the
119: 58 I have sought your **face** with all my heart; be gracious to me
119: 135 Make your **face** shine upon your servant and teach me your
119: 169 May my cry come **before** [+4200] you, O LORD; give me
119: 170 May my supplication come **before** [+4200] you; deliver me
132: 10 of David your servant, *do* not **reject** [+8740] your anointed one.
139: 7 can I go from your Spirit? Where can I flee from your **presence**?
140: 13 [140:14] your name and the upright will live **before** [+907] you.
141: 2 May my prayer be set **before** [+4200] you like incense;
142: 2 [142:3] I pour out my complaint **before** [+4200] him; before him
142: 2 [142:3] I pour out my complaint before him; **before** [+4200] him
143: 2 into judgment, for no one living is righteous **before** [+4200] you.
143: 7 Do not hide your **face** from me or I will be like those who go down
147: 17 Who *can* **withstand** [+4200+6641] his icy blast?
Pr 4: 3 still tender, and an only child **of** [+4200] my mother,
6: 35 *He will* not **accept** [+5951] any compensation; he will refuse the
7: 13 took hold of him and kissed him and with a brazen **face** she said:
7: 15 out to meet you; I looked for **[NIE]** you and have found you!
8: 25 before the mountains were settled in place, **before** [+4200] the
8: 27 in place, when he marked out the horizon on the **face** *of* the deep,
8: 30 filled with delight day after day, rejoicing always in his **presence**,
14: 12 There is a way that **seems** right **to** [+4200] a man, but in the end it
14: 19 Evil men will bow down in the **presence** *of* the good,
15: 13 A happy heart makes the **face** cheerful, but heartache crushes the
15: 14 [but the **mouth** [K; see Q 7023] *of* a fool feeds on folly.]
15: 33 teaches a man wisdom, and humility comes **before** [+4200] honor.
16: 15 When a king's **face** brightens, it means life; his favor is like a rain
16: 18 Pride goes **before** [+4200] destruction, a haughty spirit before a
16: 18 goes before destruction, a haughty spirit **before** [+4200] a fall.
16: 25 There is a way that **seems** right **to** [+4200] a man, but in the end it
17: 14 a dam; so drop the matter **before** [+4200] a dispute breaks out.
17: 18 hands in pledge and puts up security **for** [+4200] his neighbor.
17: 24 A discerning man keeps wisdom **in view** [+907], but a fool's eyes
18: 5 It is not good *to be* **partial to** [+5951] the wicked or to deprive the
18: 12 **Before** [+4200] his downfall a man's heart is proud, but humility
18: 12 a man's heart is proud, but humility comes **before** [+4200] honor.
18: 16 the way for the giver and ushers him into the **presence** *of* the great.
19: 6 Many **curry favor with** [+2704] a ruler, and everyone is the friend
21: 29 A wicked man **puts up a bold front** [+928+6451], but an upright
22: 29 He will serve **before** [+4200] kings; he will not serve before
22: 29 serve before kings; he will not serve **before** [+4200] obscure men.
23: 1 you sit to dine with a ruler, note well what is **before** [+4200] you,
24: 23 of the wise: *To* **show partiality** [+5795] in judging is not good:
24: 31 the **ground** was covered with weeds, and the stone wall was in
25: 5 remove the wicked from the king's **presence**, and his throne will
25: 6 Do not exalt yourself in the king's **presence**, and do not claim a
25: 7 than for him to humiliate you **before** [+4200] a nobleman.
25: 23 As a north wind brings rain, so a sly tongue brings angry **looks**.
25: 26 or a polluted well is a righteous man who gives way **to** [+4200] the
27: 4 fury overwhelming, but who can stand **before** [+4200] jealousy?
27: 17 As iron sharpens iron, so one man sharpens **[OBJ]** another.
27: 19 As water **reflects a face** [+2021+2021+4200+7156], so a man's
27: 19 As water **reflects a face** [+2021+2021+4200+7156], so a man's
27: 23 Be sure you know the **condition** *of* your flocks, give careful
28: 21 *To* **show partiality** [+5795] is not good—yet a man will do wrong
29: 26 Many **seek an audience with** [+1335] a ruler, but it is from the
30: 30 mighty among beasts, who retreats **before** [+4946] nothing;
Ecc 1: 10 here already, long ago; it was here **before** [+4200+4946] our **time**.
1: 16 than anyone who has ruled over Jerusalem **before** [+4200] me;
2: 7 and flocks than anyone in Jerusalem **before** [+4200] me.
2: 9 I became greater by far than anyone in Jerusalem **before** [+4200]
2: 26 To the man who pleases **[OBJ]** him, God gives wisdom,
2: 26 storing up wealth to hand it over to the one who pleases **[OBJ]**
3: 14 taken from it. God does it so that men will revere **[OBJ]** him.
4: 16 There was no end to all the people who were **before** [+4200] them.
5: 2 [5:1] be hasty in your heart to utter anything **before** [+4200] God.
5: 6 [5:5] do not protest **to** [+4200] the ⌞temple⌟ messenger, "My vow
7: 3 is better than laughter, because a sad **face** is good for the heart.
7: 26 The man who pleases **[OBJ]** God will escape her, but the sinner
8: 1 Wisdom brightens a man's **face** and changes its hard appearance.
8: 1 Wisdom brightens a man's face and changes its hard **appearance**.
8: 3 Do not be in a hurry to leave the king's **presence**. Do not stand up
8: 12 God-fearing men, who are reverent **before** [+4200+4946] God.
8: 13 Yet because the wicked do not fear **[OBJ]** God, it will not go well
9: 1 but no man knows whether love or hate **awaits** [+4200] him.
10: 5 the sun, the sort of error that arises **from** [+4200+4946] a ruler:
10: 10 If the ax is dull and its **edge** unsharpened, more strength is needed
11: 1 Cast your bread **upon** [+6584] the waters, for after many days you
SS 7: 4 [7:5] Your nose is like the tower of Lebanon looking **toward**
8: 12 my own vineyard is mine to **give** [+4200]; the thousand shekels are
Isa 1: 12 When you come to **appear before** [+8011] me, who has asked this
2: 10 hide in the ground **from** [+4946] dread of the LORD and the
2: 19 and to holes in the ground **from** [+4946] dread of the LORD
2: 21 and to the overhanging crags **from** [+4946] dread of the LORD
3: 3 the captain of fifty and **man of rank** [+5951], the counselor,
3: 9 The look on their **faces** testifies against them; they parade their sin
3: 15 mean by crushing my people and grinding the **faces** *of* the poor?"
5: 21 those who are wise in their own eyes and clever in their own **sight**.
6: 2 With two wings they covered their **faces**, with two they covered
7: 2 as the trees of the forest are shaken **by** [+4946] the wind.
7: 16 the land of **[NIE]** the two kings you dread will be laid waste.
8: 4 the plunder of Samaria will be carried off **by** [+4200] the king of
8: 17 for the LORD, who is hiding his **face** from the house of Jacob.
9: 3 [9:2] they rejoice **before** [+4200] you as people rejoice at the
9: 15 [9:14] the elders and **prominent men** [+5951] are the head,
10: 27 the yoke will be broken **because** [+4946] you have grown so fat.
13: 8 in labor. They will look aghast at each other, their **faces** aflame.
13: 8 They will look aghast at each other, their faces **[RPH]** aflame.
14: 21 to inherit the land and **cover** the earth **with** [+4848] their cities.
16: 4 stay with you; be their shelter **from** [+4946] the destroyer."
17: 9 strong cities, which they left **because of** [+4946] the Israelites,
17: 13 driven **before** [+4200] the wind like chaff on the hills, like
17: 13 like chaff on the hills, like tumbleweed **before** [+4200] a gale.
18: 2 which sends envoys by sea in papyrus boats **over** [+6584] the
18: 5 For, **before** [+4200] the harvest, when the blossom is gone
19: 1 The idols of Egypt tremble **before** [+4946] him, and the hearts of
19: 8 those who throw nets **on** [+6584] the water will pine away.
19: 16 They will shudder with fear **at** [+4946] the uplifted hand that the
19: 17 **because of** [+4946] what the LORD Almighty is planning against
19: 20 they cry out to the LORD **because of** [+4946] their oppressors,
20: 6 fled to for help and deliverance **from** [+4946] the king of Assyria!
21: 15 They flee **from** [+4946] the sword, from the drawn sword,
21: 15 **from** [+4946] the drawn sword, from the bent bow and from the
21: 15 **from** [+4946] the bent bow and from the heat of battle.
21: 15 from the bent bow and **from** [+4946] the heat of battle.
23: 17 will ply her trade with all the kingdoms on the **face** *of* the earth.
23: 18 Her profits will go to those who live **before** [+4200] the LORD,
24: 1 and devastate it; he will ruin its **face** and scatter its inhabitants—
25: 7 On this mountain he will destroy **[OBJ]** the shroud that enfolds
25: 8 The Sovereign LORD will wipe away the tears from all **faces**;
26: 17 and cries out in her pain, so were we in your **presence**, O LORD.
27: 6 Israel will bud and blossom and fill **all** the world with fruit.
28: 25 When he has leveled the **surface**, does he not sow caraway
29: 22 longer will Jacob be ashamed; no longer will their **faces** grow pale.
30: 11 and stop **confronting** [+4946] us *with* the Holy One of Israel!"
30: 17 A thousand will flee **at** [+4946] the threat of one; at the threat of
30: 17 **at** [+4946] the threat of five you will all flee away, till you are left
31: 8 They will flee **before** [+4946] the sword and their young men will
36: 7 and Jerusalem, "You must worship **before** [+4200] this altar"?
36: 9 *can you* **repulse** [+906+8740] one officer of the least of my
37: 6 Do not be afraid **of** [+4946] what you have heard—those words
37: 14 of the LORD and spread it out **before** [+4200] the LORD.
37: 27 grass sprouting on the roof, scorched **before** [+4200] it grows up.
38: 2 Hezekiah turned his **face** to the wall and prayed to the LORD,
38: 3 how I have walked **before** [+4200] you faithfully and with
40: 10 is with him, and his recompense **accompanies** [+4200] him.
41: 2 hands nations over to him and subdues kings **before** [+4200] him.
41: 26 or **beforehand** [+4200+4946], so we could say, 'He was right'?
42: 16 I will turn the darkness into light **before** [+4200] them and make
43: 10 understand that I am he. **Before** [+4200] me no god was formed,
45: 1 whose right hand I take hold of to subdue nations **before** [+4200]
45: 1 to open doors **before** [+4200] him so that gates will not be shut:
45: 2 I will go **before** [+4200] you and will level the mountains;
48: 7 not long ago; you have not heard of them **before** [+4200] today.
48: 19 would never be cut off nor destroyed from **before** [+4200] me."
50: 6 out my beard; I did not hide my **face** from mocking and spitting.
50: 7 Therefore have I set my **face** like flint, and I know I will not be put
51: 13 terror every day **because of** [+4946] the wrath of the oppressor,
52: 12 for the LORD will go **before** [+4200] you, the God of Israel will

Isa 53: 2 He grew up **before** [+4200] him like a tender shoot, and like a root
53: 3 Like one from whom men hide their **faces** he was despised,
53: 7 as a sheep **before** [+4200] her shearers is silent, so he did not open
54: 8 In a surge of anger I hid my **face** from you for a moment, but with
55: 12 the mountains and hills will burst into song **before** [+4200] you,
57: 1 that the righteous are taken away to be **spared from** [+4946] evil.
57: 16 then the spirit of man would grow faint **before** [+4200+4946] me—
58: 8 your righteousness will go **before** [+4200] you, and the glory of
59: 2 your sins have hidden his **face** from you, so that he will not hear.
62: 11 is with him, and his recompense **accompanies** [+4200] him.' "
63: 9 he too was distressed, and the angel of his **presence** saved them.
63: 12 who divided the waters **before** [+4200] them, to gain for himself
64: 1 [63:19] that the mountains would tremble **before** [+4946] you!
64: 2 [64:1] and cause the nations to quake **before** [+4946] you!
64: 3 [64:2] and the mountains trembled **before** [+4946] you.
64: 7 [64:6] for you have hidden your **face** from us and made us waste
65: 3 a people who continually provoke me to my very **face**,
65: 6 "See, it stands written **before** [+4200] me: I will not keep silent
66: 22 and the new earth that I make will endure **before** [+4200] me,"
66: 23 all mankind will come and bow down **before** [+4200] me,"
Jer 1: 8 Do not be afraid **of** [+4946] them, for I am with you and will
1: 13 see a boiling pot, **[RPH]** tilting away from the north," I answered.
1: 13 a boiling pot, **tilting away from** [+4946] the north," I answered.
1: 17 Do not be terrified **by** [+4946] them, or I will terrify you before
1: 17 not be terrified by them, or I will terrify you **before** [+4200] them.
2: 22 of soap, the stain of your guilt is still **before** [+4200] me,"
2: 27 They have turned their backs to me and not their **faces**; yet when
3: 12 '*I will* **frown** [+5877] on you no longer, for I am merciful,'
4: 1 "If you put your detestable idols out of my **sight** and no longer go
4: 4 and burn like fire **because of** [+4946] the evil you have done—
4: 26 all its towns lay in ruins **before** [+4946] the LORD, before his
4: 26 all its towns lay in ruins before the LORD, **before** [+4946] his
5: 3 They made their **faces** harder than stone and refused to repent.
5: 22 declares the LORD. "Should you not tremble in my **presence**?
6: 7 in her; her sickness and wounds are ever **before** [+6584] me.
7: 10 and then come and stand **before** [+4200] me in this house,
7: 12 I did to it **because of** [+4946] the wickedness of my people Israel.
7: 15 I will thrust you from my **presence**, just as I did all your brothers,
7: 19 they not rather harming themselves, to **their own** [+2157] shame?
7: 24 of their evil hearts. They went backward and not **forward** [+4200].
8: 2 or buried, but will be like refuse **lying on** [+6584] the ground.
9: 7 [9:6] what else can I do **because of** [+4946] the sin of my people?
9: 13 [9:12] have forsaken my law, which I set **before** [+4200] them;
9: 22 [9:21] " 'The dead bodies of men will lie like refuse on the **open**
13: 17 do not listen, I will weep in secret **because of** [+4946] your pride;
13: 26 I will pull up your skirts over your **face** that your shame may be
14: 16 the streets of Jerusalem **because of** [+4946] the famine and sword.
15: 1 "Even if Moses and Samuel were to stand **before** [+4200] me,
15: 1 to this people. Send them away from my **presence**! Let them go!
15: 9 I will put the survivors to the sword **before** [+4200] their
15: 17 I sat alone **because** [+4946] your hand was on me and you had
15: 19 I will restore you *that you may* **serve** [+4200+6641] me;
16: 4 or buried but will be like refuse lying **on** [+6584] the ground.
16: 17 they are not hidden **from** [+4200+4946] me, nor is their sin
17: 16 day of despair. What passes my lips is **open before** [+5790] you.
18: 17 from the east, I will scatter them **before** [+4200] their enemies;
18: 17 show them my back and not my **face** in the day of their disaster."
18: 20 Remember that I stood **before** [+4200] you and spoke in their
18: 23 forgive their crimes or blot out their sins from your **sight** [+4200].
18: 23 Let them be overthrown **before** [+4200] you; deal with them in the
19: 7 I will make them fall by the sword **before** [+4200] their enemies,
21: 8 I am setting **before** [+4200] you the way of life and the way of
21: 10 *I have* **determined** [+928+4200+4200+8492] to do this city harm
21: 12 and burn like fire **because of** [+4946] the evil you have done—
22: 25 **[OBJ]** to Nebuchadnezzar king of Babylon and to the
23: 9 by wine, **because of** [+4946] the LORD and his holy words.
23: 9 by wine, because of the LORD and **[RPH]** his holy words.
23: 10 **because of** [+3954+4946] the curse the land lies parched
23: 39 and cast you out of my **presence** along with the city I gave to you
24: 1 of figs placed **in front** [+4200] **of** the temple of the LORD.
25: 16 go mad **because of** [+4946] the sword I will send among them."
25: 26 one after the other—all the kingdoms on the **face** *of* the earth.
25: 27 rise no more **because of** [+4946] the sword I will send among you.'
25: 33 or buried, but will be like refuse **lying on** [+6584] the ground.
25: 37 be laid waste **because of** [+4946] the fierce anger of the LORD.
25: 38 **because of** [+4946] the sword of the oppressor and
25: 38 the oppressor and **because of** [+4946] the LORD's fierce anger.
26: 3 I was planning **because of** [+4946] the evil they have done.
26: 4 and follow my law, which I have set **before** [+4200] you,
26: 19 not Hezekiah fear the LORD and **seek** his **favor** [+906+2704]?
27: 5 the earth and its people and the animals that are **on** [+6584] it,
28: 8 From early times the prophets who **preceded** [+4200] you
28: 8 prophets who preceded you and **[RPH]** me have prophesied war,
28: 16 LORD says: 'I am about to remove you from the **face** *of* the earth.
30: 6 his stomach like a woman in labor, every **face** turned deathly pale?
30: 20 and their community will be established **before** [+4200] me;
31: 36 "Only if these decrees vanish from my **sight** [+4200],"
31: 36 of Israel ever cease to be a nation **before** [+4200] me."
32: 24 the siege ramps are built up to take the city. **Because** [+4946] **of**
32: 31 aroused my anger and wrath that I must remove it from my **sight**.
32: 33 They turned their backs to me and not their **faces**; though I taught
33: 5 I will hide my **face** from this city because of all its wickedness.
33: 18 ever fail to have a man to stand **before** [+4200+4946] me
33: 24 my people and no longer **regard** [+2118+4200] them *as* a nation.
34: 5 the former kings who **preceded** [+2118+4200] you, so they will
34: 15 You even made a covenant **before** [+4200] me in the house that
34: 18 fulfilled the terms of the covenant they made **before** [+4200] me,
35: 5 and some cups **before** [+4200] the men of the Recabite family
35: 7 you will live a long time **in** [+6584] the land where you are
35: 11 we must go to Jerusalem to **escape** [+4946] the Babylonian
35: 11 Jerusalem to escape the Babylonian and **[RPH]** Aramean armies.'
35: 19 Recab will never fail to have a man *to* **serve** [+4200+6641] me.' "
36: 7 Perhaps they will bring their petition **before** [+4200] the LORD,
36: 9 a time of fasting **before** [+4200] the LORD was proclaimed for
36: 22 with a fire burning in the firepot **in front** [+4200] **of** him.
37: 11 withdrawn from Jerusalem **because of** [+4946] Pharaoh's army,
37: 20 please listen. Let me bring my petition **before** [+4200] you:
38: 9 where he will starve to death **[NIE]** when there is no longer any
38: 26 'I was pleading **with** [+4200] the king not to send me back to
39: 16 At that time they will be fulfilled **before** your **eyes** [+4200].
39: 17 you will not be handed over to those you fear. **[OBJ]**
40: 4 Look, the whole country lies **before** [+4200] you; go wherever you
40: 10 I myself will stay at Mizpah to represent you **before** [+4200] the
41: 9 made as part of his **defense against** [+4946] Baasha king of Israel.
41: 15 eight of his men escaped **from** [+4946] Johanan and fled to the
41: 18 to **escape** [+4946] the Babylonians. They were afraid of them
41: 18 They were afraid **of** [+4946] them because Ishmael son of
42: 2 "Please **hear** [+4200+5877] our petition and pray to the LORD
42: 9 to whom you sent me to **present** [+4200+5877] your petition,
42: 11 Do not be afraid **of** [+4946] the king of Babylon, whom you now
42: 11 **[OBJ]** Do not be afraid of him, declares the LORD, for I am
42: 15 'If you *are* **determined** [+8492+8492] to go to Egypt and you do
42: 17 Indeed, all who *are* **determined** [+906+8492] to go to Egypt to
42: 17 will survive or escape **[OBJ]** the disaster I will bring on them.'
44: 3 **because of** [+4946] the evil they have done. They provoked me to
44: 10 and the decrees I set **before** [+4200] you and your fathers.
44: 10 and the decrees I set before you and **[RPH]** your fathers.
44: 11 I *am* **determined** [+4200+8492] to bring disaster on you and to
44: 12 take away the remnant of Judah who *were* **determined** [+8492]
44: 22 When the LORD could no longer endure **[OBJ]** your wicked
44: 22 your wicked actions **[OBJ]** and the detestable things you did,
44: 23 **Because** [+4946] you have burned incense and have sinned against
46: 16 our native lands, **away from** [+4946] the sword of the oppressor.'
48: 44 "Whoever flees **from** [+4946] the terror will fall into a pit,
49: 5 will be driven away, **[OBJ]** and no one will gather the fugitives.
49: 19 challenge me? And what shepherd can stand **against** [+4200] me?"
49: 37 I will shatter Elam **before** [+4200] their foes, before those who
49: 37 I will shatter Elam before their foes, **before** [+4200] those who
50: 5 They will ask the way to Zion and turn their **faces** toward it.
50: 8 the Babylonians, and be like the goats that **lead** [+4200] the flock.
50: 16 **Because of** [+4946] the sword of the oppressor let everyone return
50: 44 challenge me? And what shepherd can stand **against** [+4200] me?"
51: 51 for we have been insulted and shame covers our **faces**,
51: 64 rise no more **because of** [+4946] the disaster I will bring upon her.
52: 3 and Judah, and in the end he thrust them from his **presence**.
52: 12 *who* **served** [+4200+6641] the king of Babylon, came to
52: 25 in charge of the fighting men, and seven royal **advisers** [+8011].
52: 33 for the rest of his life ate regularly **at** the king's **table**[s] [+4200].
La 1: 5 Her children have gone into exile, captive **before** [+4200] the foe.
1: 6 no pasture; in weakness they have fled **before** [+4200] the pursuer.
1: 22 "Let all their wickedness come **before** [+4200] you; deal with
2: 3 He has withdrawn his right hand at the **approach** *of* the enemy.
2: 19 pour out your heart like water **in the presence** [+5790] **of** the Lord.
3: 35 to deny a man his rights **before** [+5584] the Most High,
4: 16 **The LORD himself** [+3378] has scattered them; he no longer
4: 16 The priests *are* **shown** no **honor** [+5951], the elders no favor.
5: 9 at the risk of our lives **because of** [+4946] the sword in the desert.
5: 10 Our skin is hot as an oven, feverish **from** [+4946] hunger.
5: 12 hung up by their hands; elders **are shown** no **respect** [+2075].
Eze 1: 6 but each of them had four **faces** and four wings.
1: 8 they had the hands of a man. All four of them had **faces** and wings,
1: 9 Each one went **straight ahead** [+448+6298]; they did not turn as
1: 10 Their **faces** looked like this: Each of the four had the face of a man,
1: 10 Each of the four had the **face** *of* a man, and on the right side each
1: 10 on the right side each had the **face** *of* a lion, and on the left the face
1: 10 side each had the face of a lion, and on the left the **face** *of* an ox;
1: 10 and on the left the face of an ox; each also had the **face** *of* an eagle.
1: 11 Such were their **faces**. Their wings were spread out upward;

Eze 1:12 Each one went **straight ahead** [+448+6298]. Wherever the spirit
1:15 saw a wheel on the ground beside each creature with its four **faces**.
1:28 When I saw it, I fell **facedown** [+6584], and I heard the voice of
2:4 The people to whom I am sending you are **obstinate** [+7997]
2:6 Do not be afraid of what they say or terrified **by** [+4946] them,
2:10 which he unrolled **before** [+4200] me. On both sides of it were
2:10 **On both sides** [+294+2256] of it were written words of lament
3:8 I will make you as **unyielding** [+2617] and hardened as they are.
3:8 I will make you as unyielding and hardened as **[RPH]** they are.
3:9 Do not be afraid of them or terrified **by** [+4946] them, though they
3:20 and I put a stumbling block **before** [+4200] him, he will die.
3:23 glory I had seen by the Kebar River, and I fell **facedown** [+6584].
4:1 put it **in front** [+4200] **of** you and draw the city of Jerusalem on it.
4:3 an iron wall between you and the city and turn your **face** toward it.
4:7 Turn your **face** toward the siege of Jerusalem and with bared arm
6:2 "Son of man, set your **face** against the mountains of Israel;
6:4 and I will slay your people **in front** [+4200] **of** your idols.
6:5 I will lay the dead bodies of the Israelites **in front** [+4200] **of** their
6:9 They will loathe **themselves** [+2157] for the evil they have done
7:18 Their **faces** will be covered with shame and their heads will be
7:22 I will turn my **face** away from them, and they will desecrate my
8:1 my house and the elders of Judah were sitting **before** [+4200] me,
8:11 **In front** [+4200] **of** them stood seventy elders of the house of
8:16 toward the temple of the LORD and their **faces** toward the east,
9:6 So they began with the elders who were **in front** [+4200] **of** the
9:8 I fell **facedown** [+6584], crying out, "Ah, Sovereign LORD!
10:14 Each of the cherubim had four **faces**: One face was that of a
10:14 One **face** was that of a cherub, the second the face of a man,
10:14 One face was **that**ˢ *of* a cherub, the second the face of a man,
10:14 the second **[RPH]** the face of a man, the third the face of a lion,
10:14 a cherub, the second the **face** *of* a man, the third the face of a lion,
10:14 a cherub, the second the face of a man, the third the **face** *of* a lion,
10:14 the third the face of a lion, and the fourth the **face** *of* an eagle.
10:21 Each had four **faces** and four wings, and under their wings was
10:22 Their **faces** had the same appearance as those I had seen by the
10:22 Their faces had the same appearance as **those**ˢ [+2021] I had seen
10:22 by the Kebar River. Each one went **straight ahead** [+448+6298].
11:13 Then I fell **facedown** [+6584] and cried out in a loud voice,
12:6 Cover your **face** so that you cannot see the land, for I have made
12:12 to go through. He will cover his **face** so that he cannot see the land.
13:17 set your **face** against the daughters of your people who prophesy
14:1 elders of Israel came to me and sat down **in front** [+4200] **of** me.
14:3 in their hearts and put wicked stumbling blocks before their **faces**.
14:4 puts a wicked stumbling block before his **face** and then goes to a
14:6 and **renounce** [+4946+6584+8740] all your detestable practices!
14:7 in his heart and puts a wicked stumbling block before his **face** and
14:8 I will set my **face** against that man and make him an example
14:15 so that no one can pass through it **because of** [+4946] the beasts,
15:7 I will set my **face** against them. Although they have come out of
15:7 when I set my **face** against them, you will know that I am the
16:5 Rather, you were thrown out into the **open** field, for on the day you
16:18 and you offered my oil and incense **before** [+4200] them.
16:19 you to eat—you offered as fragrant incense **before** [+4200] them.
16:50 They were haughty and did detestable things **before** [+4200] me.
16:63 again open your mouth **because of** [+4946] your humiliation,
20:1 inquire of the LORD, and they sat down **in front** [+4200] **of** me.
20:35 will bring you into the desert of the nations and there, **face** to face,
20:35 will bring you into the desert of the nations and there, face to **face**,
20:43 you will loathe **yourselves** [+4013] for all the evil you have done.
20:46 [21:2] "Son of man, set your **face** toward the south; preach
20:47 [21:3] and every **face** from south to north will be scorched by it.
21:2 [21:7] set your **face** against Jerusalem and preach against the
21:16 [21:21] the right, then to the left, wherever your **blade** is turned.
22:30 and stand **before** [+4200] me in the gap on behalf of the land
23:24 I will turn you over **to** [+4200] them for punishment, and they will
23:41 with a table spread **before** [+4200] it on which you had placed the
25:2 set your **face** against the Ammonites and prophesy against them.
27:35 kings shudder with horror and their **faces** are distorted with fear.
28:9 then say, "I am a god," in the **presence** *of* those who kill you?
28:17 you to the earth; I made a spectacle of you **before** [+4200] kings.
28:21 "Son of man, set your **face** against Sidon; prophesy against her
29:2 set your **face** against Pharaoh king of Egypt and prophesy against
29:5 You will fall on the **open** field and not be gathered or picked up.
30:9 " 'On that day messengers will go out **from** [+4200+4946] me in
30:24 he will groan **before** [+4200] him like a mortally wounded man.
32:4 I will throw you on the land and hurl you on the **open** field.
32:10 because of you when I brandish my sword **before** [+6584] them.
33:22 Now the evening **before** [+4200] the man arrived, the hand of the
33:27 those out **in** [+6584] the country I will give to the wild animals to
33:31 they usually do, and sit **before** [+4200] you to listen to your words,
34:6 They were scattered **over** [+6584] the whole earth, and no one
35:2 "Son of man, set your **face** against Mount Seir; prophesy against it
36:17 conduct was like a woman's monthly uncleanness in my **sight**.
36:31 you will loathe **yourselves** [+4013] for your sins and detestable
37:2 and I saw a great many bones on the **floor** *of* the valley,
38:2 "Son of man, set your **face** against Gog, of the land of Magog,
38:20 all the people on the **face** *of* the earth will tremble at my presence.
38:20 all the people on the face of the earth will tremble at my **presence**.
39:5 You will fall in the open **field**, for I have spoken,
39:14 others will bury those that remain **on** [+6584] the ground.
39:23 So I hid my **face** from them and handed them over to their
39:24 their uncleanness and their offenses, and I hid my **face** from them.
39:29 I will no longer hide my **face** from them, for I will pour out my
40:6 Then he went to the gate **facing** east. He climbed its steps
40:12 **In front** [+4200] **of** each alcove was a wall one cubit high,
40:15 The distance **from** [+6584] the entrance of the gateway to the far
40:15 The distance from the entrance of the gateway **to** [+4200+6584]
40:19 he measured the distance from the **inside** [+4200] *of* the lower
40:19 of the lower gateway **to** [+4200] the outside of the inner court;
40:20 Then he measured the length and width of the gate **facing** north,
40:22 had the same measurements as those of the gate **facing** east.
40:22 Seven steps led up to it, with its portico **opposite** [+4200] them.
40:26 Seven steps led up to it, with its portico **opposite** [+4200] them;
40:44 were two rooms, one at the side of the north gate and **facing** south,
40:44 and another at the side of the south gate and **facing** north.
40:45 "The room **facing** south is for the priests who have charge of the
40:46 the room **facing** north is for the priests who have charge of the
40:47 cubits wide. And the altar was **in front** [+4200] **of** the temple.
41:4 its width was twenty cubits across the **end** *of* the outer sanctuary.
41:12 The building **facing** [+448] the temple courtyard on the west side
41:14 the east, including the **front** *of* the temple, was a hundred cubits.
41:15 he measured the length of the building **facing** [+448] the courtyard
41:18 Palm trees alternated with cherubim. Each cherub had two **faces**:
41:19 the **face** *of* a man toward the palm tree on one side and the face of
41:19 one side and the **face** *of* a lion toward the palm tree on the other.
41:21 and the one at the **front** *of* the Most Holy Place was similar.
41:22 said to me, "This is the table that is **before** [+4200] the LORD."
41:25 and there was a wooden overhang on the **front** *of* the portico.
42:2 The building whose door **faced** [+448] north was a hundred cubits
42:3 of the outer court, gallery **faced** [+448] gallery at the three levels.
42:4 **In front** [+4200] **of** the rooms was an inner passageway ten cubits
42:7 it extended **in front** [+448] **of** the rooms for fifty cubits.
42:8 the row on the side **nearest** [+6584] the sanctuary was a hundred
42:10 along the length of the wall of the outer court, **adjoining** [+448]
42:10 adjoining the temple courtyard and **opposite** [+448] the outer wall,
42:11 with a passageway **in front** [+4200] **of** them. These were like the
42:12 was **parallel** [+928] *to* the corresponding wall extending eastward,
42:13 south rooms **facing** [+448] the temple courtyard are the priests'
42:15 me out by the east gate **[NIE]** and measured the area all around:
43:3 visions I had seen by the Kebar River, and I fell **facedown** [+448].
43:4 glory of the LORD entered the temple through the gate **facing**
43:24 You are to offer them **before** [+4200] the LORD, and the priests
44:3 may sit inside the gateway to eat in the **presence** *of* the LORD.
44:4 the man brought me by way of the north gate to the **front** *of* the
44:4 filling the temple of the LORD, and I fell **facedown** [+448].
44:11 for the people and stand **before** [+4200] the people and serve them.
44:12 But because they served them in the **presence** *of* their idols
44:15 they are to stand **before** [+4200] me to offer sacrifices of fat
45:7 **[NIE]** It will extend westward from the west side and eastward
45:7 **[NIE]** It will extend westward from the west side and eastward
46:3 Moons the people of the land are to worship in the **presence** *of*
46:9 " 'When the people of the land come **before** [+4200] the LORD at
47:1 threshold of the temple toward the east (for the temple **faced** east).
48:15 remaining area, 5,000 cubits wide and **[NIE]** 25,000 cubits long,
48:21 It will extend eastward **from** [+448] the 25,000 cubits of the sacred
48:21 westward **from** [+6584] the 25,000 cubits to the western border.
Da 1:5 and after that *they were to* **enter** the king's **service** [+4200+6641].
1:9 Now God had caused the official to **show** [+4200] favor
1:10 Why should he see **you** [+4013] looking worse than the other
1:13 compare **[OBJ]** our appearance with that of the young men who
1:18 the chief official presented them **to** [+4200] Nebuchadnezzar.
1:19 and Azariah; so *they* **entered** the king's **service** [+4200+6641].
2:2 When they came in and stood **before** [+4200] the king,
8:3 standing **beside** [+4200] the canal, and the horns were long.
8:4 No animal could stand **against** [+4200] him, and none could rescue
8:5 **crossing** [+6584] the whole earth without touching the ground.
8:6 the two-horned ram I had seen standing **beside** [+4200] the canal
8:7 The ram was powerless to stand **against** [+4200] him; the goat
8:17 where I was standing, I was terrified and fell **prostrate** [+6584].
8:18 speaking to me, I was in a deep sleep, with my **face** to the ground.
8:23 a **stern-faced** [+6434] king, a master of intrigue, will arise.
9:3 So *I* **turned** [+906+5989] to the Lord God and pleaded with him in
9:7 are righteous, but this day we are **covered with** [+4200] shame—
9:8 our princes and our fathers are **covered with** [+4200] shame
9:10 or kept the laws he gave **[OBJ]** us through his servants the
9:13 yet *we have* not **sought the favor of** [+906+2704] the LORD our
9:17 O Lord, **look** [+239] **with favor** on your desolate sanctuary.
9:18 We do not make requests **of** [+4200] you because we are righteous,

Da 9:20 making my request **to** [+4200] the LORD my God for his holy
10: 6 His body was like chrysolite, his **face** like lightning, his eyes like
10: 9 to him, I fell into a deep sleep, **[RPH]** my face to the ground.
10: 9 as I listened to him, I fell into a deep sleep, my **face** to the ground.
10:12 and to humble yourself **before** [+4200] your God,
10:15 I bowed with my **face** toward the ground and was speechless.
11:16 do as he pleases; no one will be able to stand **against** [+4200] him.
11:17 *He will* **determine** [+8492] to come with the might of his entire
11:18 he will turn his **attention** to the coastlands and will take many of
11:19 he will turn back **[RPH]** toward the fortresses of his own country
11:22 an overwhelming army will be swept away **before** [+4200+4946]
Hos 2: 2 [2:4] Let her remove the adulterous look from her **face**
5: 5 Israel's arrogance testifies **against** [+928] them; the Israelites,
5:15 they will seek my **face**; in their misery they will earnestly seek
6: 2 the third day he will restore us, that we may live in his **presence**.
7: 2 Their sins engulf them; they are always **before** [+5584] me.
7:10 Israel's arrogance testifies **against** [+928] him, but despite all this
10: 7 its king will float away like a twig on the **surface** *of* the waters.
10:15 to you, O Bethel, **because** [+4946] your wickedness is great.
11: 2 the more I called Israel, the further they went **from** [+4946] me.
Joel 2: 3 **Before** [+4200] them fire devours, behind them a flame blazes.
2: 3 behind them a flame blazes. **Before** [+4200] them the land is like
2: 6 At the **sight** *of* them, nations are in anguish; every face turns pale.
2: 6 At the sight of them, nations are in anguish; every **face** turns pale.
2:10 **Before** [+4200] them the earth shakes, the sky trembles, the sun
2:11 The LORD thunders at the **head** *of* his army; his forces are
2:20 with its **front columns** going into the eastern sea and those in the
2:31 [3:4] the moon to blood **before** [+4200] the coming of the great
Am 1: 1 what he saw concerning Israel two years **before** [+4200] the
2: 9 "I destroyed the Amorite **before** [+4946] them, though he was tall
5: 8 the waters of the sea and pours them out over the **face** *of* the land—
5:19 It will be as though a man fled **from** [+4946] a lion only to meet a
9: 4 Though they are driven into exile **by** [+4200] their enemies,
9: 6 the waters of the sea and pours them out over the **face** *of* the land—
9: 8 I will destroy it from the **face** *of* the earth—yet I will not totally
Jnh 1: 2 because its wickedness has come up **before** [+4200] me."
1: 3 Jonah ran away **from** [+4200+4946] the LORD and headed for
1: 3 and sailed for Tarshish to flee **from** [+4200+4946] the LORD.
1:10 (They knew he was running away **from** [+4200+4946] the
Mic 1: 4 and the valleys split apart, like wax **before** [+4946] the fire,
2:13 One who breaks open the way will go up **before** [+4200] them;
2:13 Their king will pass through **before** [+4200] them, the LORD at
3: 4 At that time he will hide his **face** from them because of the evil
6: 4 land of slavery. I sent Moses to **lead** you, also Aaron and Miriam.
Na 1: 5 The earth trembles at his **presence**, the world and all who live in it.
1: 6 Who *can* **withstand** [+4200+6641] his indignation?
2: 1 [2:2] An attacker advances **against** [+6584] you, ⌞Nineveh⌟.
2:10 [2:11] knees give way, bodies tremble, every **face** grows pale.
3: 5 the LORD Almighty. "I will lift your skirts over your **face**.
Hab 1: 9 Their hordes **advance** [+2025] like a desert wind and gather
2:20 in his holy temple; let all the earth be silent **before** [+4946] him."
3: 5 Plague went **before** [+4200] him; pestilence followed his steps.
Zep 1: 2 "I will sweep away everything from the **face** *of* the earth,"
1: 3 heaps of rubble when I cut off man from the **face** *of* the earth,"
1: 7 Be silent **before** [+4946] the Sovereign LORD, for the day of the
Hag 1:12 their God had sent him. And the people feared **[OBJ]** the LORD.
2:14 Haggai said, " 'So it is with this people and this nation in my **sight**,'
Zec 2:13 [2:17] Be still **before** [+4946] the LORD, all mankind,
3: 1 he showed me Joshua the high priest standing **before** [+4200] the
3: 3 was dressed in filthy clothes as he stood **before** [+4200] the angel.
3: 4 The angel said to those who were standing **before** [+4200] him,
3: 8 high priest Joshua and your associates seated **before** [+4200] you,
3: 9 See, the stone I have set **in front** [+4200] **of** Joshua! There are
4: 7 **Before** [+4200] Zerubbabel you will become level ground.
5: 3 "This is the curse that is going out **over** [+6584] the whole land;
7: 2 together with their men, to **entreat** [+906+2704] the LORD
8:10 **Before** [+4200] that time there were no wages for man or beast.
8:21 'Let us go at once to **entreat** [+906+2704] the LORD and seek the
8:22 to seek the LORD Almighty and to **entreat** [+906+2704] him."
12: 8 like the Angel of the LORD going **before** [+4200] them.
14: 4 day his feet will stand on the Mount of Olives, **east** [+6584+7710]
14: 5 You will flee as you fled **from** [+4946] the earthquake in the days
14:20 house will be like the sacred bowls **in front** [+4200] **of** the altar.
Mal 1: 8 *Would he* **accept** [+5951] you?" says the LORD Almighty.
1: 9 "Now **implore** [+2704] God to be gracious to us. With such
1: 9 offerings from your hands, *will he* **accept** [+4946+5951] you?"—
2: 3 I will spread on your **faces** the offal from your festival sacrifices,
2: 5 and he revered me and stood in awe **of** [+4946] my name.
2: 9 but *have* **shown partiality** [+5951] in matters of the law."
3: 1 send my messenger, who will prepare the way **before** [+4200] me.
3:14 going about like mourners **before** [+4946] the LORD Almighty?
3:16 A scroll of remembrance was written in his **presence** concerning
4: 5 [3:23] I will send you the prophet Elijah **before** [+4200] that great
and dreadful day of the LORD comes.

7157 פִּנָּה **pinnâ**, n.f. [30 / 31] [√ 7155]

corner [15], corners [5], cornerstone [3], leaders [2], capstone [+8031] [1], corner defenses [1], cornerstone [+74] [1], cornerstones [1], street corner [1], strongholds [1]

Ex 27: 2 Make a horn at each of the four **corners**, so that the horns
38: 2 They made a horn at each of the four **corners**, so that the horns
Jdg 20: 2 The **leaders** *of* all the people of the tribes of Israel took their places
1Sa 14:38 therefore said, "Come here, all you who are **leaders** *of* the army,
1Ki 7:34 had four handles, one on each **corner**, projecting from the stand.
2Ki 14:13 the wall of Jerusalem from the Ephraim Gate to the **Corner** Gate—
2Ch 25:23 from the Ephraim Gate to the **Corner** [BHS 7042] Gate—
26: 9 Uzziah built towers in Jerusalem at the **Corner** Gate, at the Valley
26:15 and on the **corner defenses** to shoot arrows and hurl large stones.
28:24 and set up altars at every **street corner** in Jerusalem.
Ne 3:24 another section, from Azariah's house to the angle and the **corner**,
3:31 the Inspection Gate, and as far as the room above the **corner**;
3:32 between the room above the **corner** and the Sheep Gate the
Job 1:19 swept in from the desert and struck the four **corners** *of* the house.
38: 6 On what were its footings set, or who laid its **cornerstone** [+74]—
Ps 118:22 The stone the builders rejected has become the **capstone** [+8031];
Pr 7: 8 He was going down the street near her **corner**, walking along in
7:12 now in the street, now in the squares, at every **corner** she lurks.)
21: 9 Better to live on a **corner** *of* the roof than share a house with a
25:24 Better to live on a **corner** *of* the roof than share a house with a
Isa 19:13 the **cornerstones** *of* her peoples have led Egypt astray.
28:16 a tested stone, a precious **cornerstone** *for* a sure foundation;
Jer 31:38 be rebuilt for me from the Tower of Hananel to the **Corner** Gate.
31:40 Kidron Valley on the east as far as the **corner** *of* the Horse Gate,
51:26 No rock will be taken from you for a **cornerstone**, nor any stone
Eze 43:20 and on the four **corners** *of* the upper ledge and all around the rim,
45:19 on the four **corners** *of* the upper ledge of the altar and on the
Zep 1:16 battle cry against the fortified cities and against the **corner** towers.
3: 6 "I have cut off nations; their **strongholds** are demolished.
Zec 10: 4 From Judah will come the **cornerstone**, from him the tent peg,
14:10 the Benjamin Gate to the site of the First Gate, to the **Corner** Gate,

7158 [1]פְּנוּאֵל p^{e}**nû'ēl**[1], n.pr.m. [2] [√ 7159; cf. 7155 + 446]

Penuel [2]

1Ch 4: 4 **Penuel** was the father of Gedor, and Ezer the father of Hushah.
8:25 Iphdeiah and **Penuel** [K 7160] were the sons of Shashak.

7159 [2]פְּנוּאֵל p^{e}**nû'ēl**[2], n.pr.loc. [6] [√ 7158; cf. 7155 + 446]

Peniel [5], they[s] [+408] [1]

Ge 32:31 [32:32] The sun rose above him as he passed **Peniel**, and he was
Jdg 8: 8 From there he went up to **Peniel** and made the same request of
8: 8 of them, but **they**[s] [+408] answered as the men of Succoth had.
8: 9 So he said to the men of **Peniel**, "When I return in triumph,
8:17 He also pulled down the tower of **Peniel** and killed the men of the
1Ki 12:25 and lived there. From there he went out and built up **Peniel**.

7160 [1]פְּנִיאֵל p^{e}**nî'ēl**[1], n.pr.m. [0] [√ 7161; cf. 7155 + 446]

1Ch 8:25 [Iphdeiah and **Penuel** [K; see Q 7158] were the sons of Shashak.]

7161 [2]פְּנִיאֵל p^{e}**nî'ēl**[2], n.pr.loc. [1] [√ 7160; cf. 7155 + 446]

Peniel [1]

Ge 32:30 [32:31] So Jacob called the place **Peniel**, saying, "It is because I

7162 פְּנִיִּים p^{e}**nîyyim**, var. Not used in NIV/BHS [√ 7165]

7163 פְּנִימָה p^{e}**nîmâ**, adv. *or* pp. [13] [→ 7164; cf. 7156, 7155]

inside [2], within [2], *untranslated* [1], in [1], inner [+4200] [1], inner sanctuary [1], inside [+4200] [1], inside [+4946] [1], into [+4200] [1], into [+448] [1], inward [1]

Lev 10:18 Since its blood was not taken **into** [+448] the Holy Place,
1Ki 6:18 The **inside** of the temple was cedar, carved with gourds and open
6:19 He prepared the inner sanctuary within the temple **[RPH]** to set
6:21 Solomon covered the **inside** [+4946] *of* the temple with pure gold,
6:30 He also covered the floors of both the **inner** [+4200] and outer
2Ki 7:11 shouted the news, and it was reported **within** the palace.
2Ch 3: 4 and twenty cubits high. He overlaid the **inside** with pure gold.
29:16 The priests went **into** [+4200] the sanctuary of the LORD to
29:18 they went **in** to King Hezekiah and reported: "We have purified the
Ps 45:13 [45:14] All glorious is the princess **within** ⌞her chamber⌟;
Eze 40:16 the projecting walls **inside** [+4200] the gateway were surmounted
40:16 as was the portico; the openings all around faced **inward**.
41: 3 he went into the **inner sanctuary** and measured the jambs of the

7164 פנימי פְּנִימִי ***p[e]nîmî***, a. [31] [√ 7163]

inner [25], inner sanctuary [2], innermost [2], far end [1], inside [1]

1Ki 6:27 He placed the cherubim inside the **innermost** *room* of the temple,
6:36 And he built the **inner** courtyard of three courses of dressed stone
7:12 as was the **inner** courtyard of the temple of the LORD with its
7:50 and the gold sockets for the doors of the **innermost** room,
1Ch 28:11 its upper parts, its **inner** rooms and the place of atonement.
2Ch 4:22 the **inner** doors to the Most Holy Place and the doors of the main
Est 4:11 or woman who approaches the king in the **inner** court without
5:1 put on her royal robes and stood in the **inner** court of the palace,
Eze 8:3 to the entrance to the north gate of the **inner** court, where the idol
8:16 then brought me into the **inner** court of the house of the LORD,
10:3 temple when the man went in, and a cloud filled the **inner** court.
40:15 The distance from the entrance of the gateway to the **far end** of its
40:19 the inside of the lower gateway to the outside of the **inner** court;
40:23 There was a gate to the **inner** court facing the north gate, just as
40:27 The **inner** court also had a gate facing south, and he measured
40:28 Then he brought me into the **inner** court through the south gate,
40:32 he brought me to the **inner** court on the east side, and he measured
40:44 Outside the **inner** gate, within the inner court, were two rooms,
41:15 the **inner sanctuary** and the portico facing the court,
41:17 In the space above the outside of the entrance to the **inner**
41:17 walls at regular intervals all around the **inner** and outer **sanctuary**
42:3 Both in the section twenty cubits from the **inner** court and in the
42:4 In front of the rooms was an **inner** passageway ten cubits wide
42:15 When he had finished measuring what was **inside** the temple area,
43:5 Then the Spirit lifted me up and brought me into the **inner** court,
44:17 " 'When they enter the gates of the **inner** court, they are to wear
44:17 woolen garment while ministering at the gates of the **inner** court
44:21 No priest is to drink wine when he enters the **inner** court.
44:27 On the day he goes into the **inner** court of the sanctuary to minister
45:19 the upper ledge of the altar and on the gateposts of the **inner** court.
46:1 The gate of the **inner** court facing east is to be shut on the six

7165 פנינים פְּנִינִים ***p[e]nînîm***, n.[f.]pl. [6] [→ 7162, 7166]

rubies [6]

Job 28:18 are not worthy of mention; the price of wisdom is beyond **rubies**.
Pr 3:15 She is more precious than **rubies**; nothing you desire can compare
8:11 for wisdom is more precious than **rubies**, and nothing you desire
20:15 Gold there is, and **rubies** in abundance, but lips that speak
31:10 noble character who can find? She is worth far more than **rubies**.
La 4:7 and whiter than milk, their bodies more ruddy than **rubies**,

7166 פננה פְּנִנָּה ***p[e]ninnâ***, n.pr.f. [3] [√ 7165]

Peninnah [3]

1Sa 1:2 He had two wives; one was called Hannah and the other **Peninnah**.
1:2 the other Peninnah. **Peninnah** had children, but Hannah had none.
1:4 he would give portions of the meat to his wife **Peninnah** and to all

7167 פנק פָּנַק ***pānaq***, v. [1]

pampers [1]

Pr 29:21 [D] If a *man* **pampers** his servant from youth, he will bring grief

7168 פס פַּס ***pas***, n.[m.]. [5] [→ 7169; cf. 701; Ar 10589]

richly ornamented [3], ornamented [2]

Ge 37:3 in his old age; and he made a **richly ornamented** robe for him.
37:23 him of his robe—the **richly ornamented** robe he was wearing—
37:32 They took the **ornamented** robe back to their father and said,
2Sa 13:18 She was wearing a **richly ornamented** robe, for this was the kind
13:19 ashes on her head and tore the **ornamented** robe she was wearing.

7169 פס דמים פַּס דַּמִּים ***pas dammîm***, n.pr.loc. [1] [√ 7168 + 1956]

Pas Dammim [1]

1Ch 11:13 He was with David at **Pas Dammim** when the Philistines gathered

7170 פסג פָּסַג ***pāsag***, v. [1]

view [1]

Ps 48:13 [48:14] [D] consider well her ramparts, **view** her citadels, that

7171 פסגה פִּסְגָּה ***pisgâ***, n.pr.loc. [8] [→ 849]

Pisgah [8]

Nu 21:20 from Bamoth to the valley in Moab where the top of **Pisgah**
23:14 So he took him to the field of Zophim on the top of **Pisgah**,
Dt 3:17 to the Sea of the Arabah (the Salt Sea), below the slopes of **Pisgah**.
3:27 Go up to the top of **Pisgah** and look west and north and south
4:49 as far as the Sea of the Arabah, below the slopes of **Pisgah**.
34:1 climbed Mount Nebo from the plains of Moab to the top of **Pisgah**,
Jos 12:3 to Beth Jeshimoth, and then southward below the slopes of **Pisgah**.
13:20 Beth Peor, the slopes of **Pisgah**, and Beth Jeshimoth

7172 פסה פִּסָּה ***pissâ***, n.f. [1]

abound [+2118] [1]

Ps 72:16 *Let* grain **abound** [+2118] throughout the land; on the tops of the

7173 פסח ¹פָּסַח ***pāsaḥ[1]***, v. [4] [→ 7175, 9527; cf. 7174]

pass over [3], passed over [1]

Ex 12:13 [A] you are; and when I see the blood, *I will* **pass over** you.
12:23 [A] and sides of the doorframe and *will* **pass over** that doorway,
12:27 [A] who **passed over** the houses of the Israelites in Egypt
Isa 31:5 [A] and deliver it, *he will* '**pass over**' it and will rescue it."

7174 פסח ²פָּסַח ***pāsaḥ[2]***, v. [3] [→ 7176, 7177; cf. 7173]

became crippled [1], danced [1], waver [1]

2Sa 4:4 [C] but as she hurried to leave, he fell and **became crippled**.
1Ki 18:21 [A] and said, "How long *will* you **waver** between two opinions?
18:26 [D] And *they* **danced** around the altar they had made.

7175 פסח פֶּסַח ***pesaḥ***, n.m. [49] [√ 7173]

Passover [36], Passover lamb [4], Passover lambs [3], Passover offerings [3], did so[s] [+906+2021+6913] [1], its[s] [+2021] [1], Passover animals [1]

Ex 12:11 staff in your hand. Eat it in haste; it is the LORD's **Passover**.
12:21 the animals for your families and slaughter the **Passover lamb**.
12:27 then tell them, 'It is the **Passover** sacrifice to the LORD,
12:43 to Moses and Aaron, "These are the regulations for the **Passover**:
12:48 **Passover** must have all the males in his household circumcised;
34:25 do not let any of the sacrifice from the **Passover** Feast remain until
Lev 23:5 The LORD's **Passover** begins at twilight on the fourteenth day of
Nu 9:2 "Have the Israelites celebrate the **Passover** at the appointed time.
9:4 So Moses told the Israelites to celebrate the **Passover**,
9:5 *they* **did**[s] **so** [+906+2021+6913] in the Desert of Sinai at twilight
9:6 But some of them could not celebrate the **Passover** on that day
9:10 on a journey, they may still celebrate the LORD's **Passover**.
9:12 When they celebrate the **Passover**, they must follow all the
9:13 and not on a journey fails to celebrate the **Passover**,
9:14 you who wants to celebrate the LORD's **Passover** must do
9:14 must do so in accordance with **its**[s] [+2021] rules and regulations.
28:16 " 'On the fourteenth day of the first month the LORD's **Passover**
33:3 on the fifteenth day of the first month, the day after the **Passover**.
Dt 16:1 of Abib and celebrate the **Passover** of the LORD your God,
16:2 Sacrifice as the **Passover** to the LORD your God an animal from
16:5 You must not sacrifice the **Passover** in any town the LORD your
16:6 There you must sacrifice the **Passover** in the evening,
Jos 5:10 on the plains of Jericho, the Israelites celebrated the **Passover**.
5:11 The day after the **Passover**, that very day, they ate some of the
2Ki 23:21 "Celebrate the **Passover** to the LORD your God, as it is written in
23:22 and the kings of Judah, had any such **Passover** been observed.
23:23 this **Passover** was celebrated to the LORD in Jerusalem.
2Ch 30:1 LORD in Jerusalem and celebrate the **Passover** to the LORD,
30:2 the whole assembly in Jerusalem decided to celebrate the **Passover**
30:5 to come to Jerusalem and celebrate the **Passover** to the LORD,
30:15 They slaughtered the **Passover lamb** on the fourteenth day of the
30:17 the Levites had to kill the **Passover lambs** for all those who were
30:18 yet they ate the **Passover**, contrary to what was written.
35:1 Josiah celebrated the **Passover** to the LORD in Jerusalem,
35:1 the **Passover lamb** was slaughtered on the fourteenth day of the
35:6 Slaughter the **Passover lambs**, consecrate yourselves and prepare
35:7 total of thirty thousand sheep and goats for the **Passover offerings**,
35:8 gave the priests twenty-six hundred **Passover offerings** and three
35:9 provided five thousand **Passover offerings** and five hundred head
35:11 The **Passover lambs** were slaughtered, and the priests sprinkled
35:13 They roasted the **Passover animals** over the fire as prescribed,
35:16 of the LORD was carried out for the celebration of the **Passover**
35:17 The Israelites who were present celebrated the **Passover** at that
35:18 The **Passover** had not been observed like this in Israel since the
35:18 none of the kings of Israel had ever celebrated such a **Passover** as
35:19 This **Passover** was celebrated in the eighteenth year of Josiah's
Ezr 6:19 day of the first month, the exiles celebrated the **Passover**.
6:20 The Levites slaughtered the **Passover lamb** for all the exiles,
Eze 45:21 first month on the fourteenth day you are to observe the **Passover**,

7176 פסח פָּסֵחַ ***pāsēaḥ***, n.pr.m. [4] [√ 7174]

Paseah [4]

1Ch 4:12 of Beth Rapha, **Paseah** and Tehinnah the father of Ir Nahash.
Ezr 2:49 Uzza, **Paseah**, Besai,
Ne 3:6 The Jeshanah Gate was repaired by Joiada son of **Paseah**
7:51 Gazzam, Uzza, **Paseah**,

7177 פִּסֵּחַ pisséaḥ, a. [14] [√ 7174]

lame [11], crippled [3]

Lev 21:18 come near: no man who is blind or **lame**, disfigured or deformed;
Dt 15:21 If an animal has a defect, is **lame** or blind, or has any serious flaw,
2Sa 5: 6 will not get in here; even the blind and the **lame** can ward you off."
5: 8 the Jebusites will have to use the water shaft to reach those '**lame**
5: 8 is why they say, "The 'blind and **lame**' will not enter the palace."
9:13 he always ate at the king's table, and he was **crippled** *in* both feet.
19:26 [19:27] "My lord the king, since I your servant am **lame**, I said,
Job 29:15 I was eyes to the blind and feet to the **lame**.
Pr 26: 7 Like a **lame** *man's* legs that hang limp is a proverb in the mouth of
Isa 33:23 of spoils will be divided and even the **lame** will carry off plunder.
35: 6 will the **lame** leap like a deer, and the mute tongue shout for joy.
Jer 31: 8 Among them will be the blind and the **lame**, expectant mothers
Mal 1: 8 When you sacrifice **crippled** or diseased animals, is that not
1:13 **crippled** or diseased animals and offer them as sacrifices,

7178 פְּסִיל pāsîl, n.m. [23] [√ 7180]

idols [16], images [5], carved idols [1], carved images [1]

Dt 7: 5 cut down their Asherah poles and burn their **idols** in the fire.
7:25 The **images** *of* their gods you are to burn in the fire. Do not covet
12: 3 cut down the **idols** *of* their gods and wipe out their names from
Jdg 3:19 At the **idols** near Gilgal he himself turned back and said, "I have a
3:26 Ehud got away. He passed by the **idols** and escaped to Seirah.
2Ki 17:41 people were worshiping the LORD, they were serving their **idols**.
2Ch 33:19 and set up Asherah poles and **idols** before he humbled himself—
33:22 and offered sacrifices to all the **idols** Manasseh had made.
34: 3 of high places, Asherah poles, **carved idols** and cast images.
34: 4 and smashed the Asherah poles, the **idols** and the images.
34: 7 the altars and the Asherah poles and crushed the **idols** to powder
Ps 78:58 with their high places; they aroused his jealousy with their **idols**.
Isa 10:10 kingdoms whose **images** excelled those of Jerusalem
21: 9 All the **images** *of* its gods lie shattered on the ground!' "
30:22 you will defile your **idols** overlaid with silver and your images
42: 8 my name! I will not give my glory to another or my praise to **idols**.
Jer 8:19 "Why have they provoked me to anger with their **images**,
50:38 For it is a land of **idols**, idols that will go mad with terror.
51:47 For the time will surely come when I will punish the **idols** *of*
51:52 are coming," declares the LORD, "when I will punish her **idols**,
Hos 11: 2 They sacrificed to the Baals and they burned incense to **images**.
Mic 1: 7 All her **idols** will be broken to pieces; all her temple gifts will be
5:13 [5:12] I will destroy your **carved images** and your sacred stones

7179 פָּסַךְ pāsak, n.pr.m. [1]

Pasach [1]

1Ch 7:33 The sons of Japhlet: **Pasach**, Bimhal and Ashvath. These were

7180 פָּסַל pāsal, v. [6] [→ 7178, 7181]

chisel out [2], chiseled out [2], carved [1], cut [1]

Ex 34: 1 [A] to Moses, "**Chisel out** two stone tablets like the first ones,
34: 4 [A] So Moses **chiseled out** two stone tablets like the first ones
Dt 10: 1 [A] "**Chisel out** two stone tablets like the first ones and come up
10: 3 [A] and **chiseled out** two stone tablets like the first ones,
1Ki 5:18 [5:32] [A] Hiram and the men of Gebal **cut** and prepared the
Hab 2:18 [A] "Of what value is an idol, since a man *has* **carved** it? Or an

7181 פֶּסֶל pesel, n.m. [31] [√ 7180]

idol [11], idols [7], carved image [5], image [4], carved [2], carved images [1], images [1]

Ex 20: 4 "You shall not make for yourself an **idol** in the form of anything in
Lev 26: 1 " 'Do not make idols or set up an **image** or a sacred stone for
Dt 4:16 so that you do not become corrupt and make for yourselves an **idol**,
4:23 do not make for yourselves an **idol** *in* the form of anything the
4:25 if you then become corrupt and make any kind of **idol**, doing evil
5: 8 "You shall not make for yourself an **idol** in the form *of* anything in
27:15 "Cursed is the man who carves an **image** or casts an idol—
Jdg 17: 3 my silver to the LORD for my son to make a **carved image**
17: 4 them to a silversmith, who made them into the **image** and the idol.
18:14 an ephod, other household gods, a **carved image** and a cast idol?
18:17 who had spied out the land went inside and took the **carved image**,
18:18 these men went into Micah's house and took the **carved image**,
18:20 the other household gods and the **carved image** and went along
18:30 There the Danites set up for themselves the **idols**, and Jonathan son
18:31 They continued to use the **idols** Micah had made, all the time the
2Ki 21: 7 He took the **carved** Asherah pole he had made and put it in the
2Ch 33: 7 He took the **carved** image he had made and put it in God's temple,
Ps 97: 7 All who worship **images** are put to shame, those who boast in
Isa 40:19 As for an **idol**, a craftsman casts it, and a goldsmith overlays it
40:20 He looks for a skilled craftsman to set up an **idol** that will not
42:17 But those who trust in **idols**, who say to images, 'You are our gods,'
44: 9 All who make **idols** are nothing, and the things they treasure are
44:10 Who shapes a god and casts an **idol**, which can profit him nothing?
44:15 a god and worships it; he makes an **idol** and bows down to it.
44:17 From the rest he makes a god, his **idol**; he bows down to it
45:20 Ignorant are those who carry about **idols** *of* wood, who pray to
48: 5 idols did them; my wooden **image** and metal god ordained them.'
Jer 10:14 and without knowledge; every goldsmith is shamed by his **idols**.
51:17 and without knowledge; every goldsmith is shamed by his **idols**.
Na 1:14 I will destroy the **carved images** and cast idols that are in the
Hab 2:18 "Of what value is an **idol**, since a man has carved it? Or an image

7182 פָּסַס pāsas, v. [1]

vanished [1]

Ps 12: 1 [12:2] [A] the faithful *have* **vanished** from among men.

7183 פִּסְפָּה pispâ, n.pr.m. [1]

Pispah [1]

1Ch 7:38 The sons of Jether: Jephunneh, **Pispah** and Ara.

7184 פָּעָה pā'â, v. [1] [√ 704?]

cry out [1]

Isa 42:14 [A] like a woman in childbirth, *I* **cry out**, I gasp and pant.

7185 פָּעוּ pā'û, n.pr.loc. [1 / 2] [cf. 7187]

Pau [2]

Ge 36:39 His city was named **Pau**, and his wife's name was Mehetabel
1Ch 1:50 His city was named **Pau**, [BHS 7187] and his wife's name was

7186 פְּעוֹר p^e'ôr, n.pr.loc. [9] [→ 1121, 1261; cf. 7196?]

Peor [9]

Nu 23:28 Balak took Balaam to the top of **Peor**, overlooking the wasteland.
25: 3 So Israel joined in worshiping the Baal of **Peor**. And the LORD's
25: 5 of your men who have joined in worshiping the Baal of **Peor**."
25:18 you as enemies when they deceived you in the affair of **Peor**
25:18 woman who was killed when the plague came as a result of **Peor**."
31:16 the Israelites away from the LORD in what happened at **Peor**,
Dt 4: 3 from among you everyone who followed the Baal of **Peor**,
Jos 22:17 Was not the sin of **Peor** enough for us? Up to this very day we
Ps 106:28 They yoked themselves to the Baal of **Peor** and ate sacrifices

7187 פָּעִי pā'î, n.pr.loc. [1 / 0] [cf. 7185]

1Ch 1:50 His city was named Pau, [BHS *Pai*; NIV 7185] and his wife's

7188 פָּעַל pā'al, v. [57] [→ 551, 5148, 5149, 7040, 7189, 7190, 7191]

evildoers [+224] [16], do [12], done [9], does [2], made [2], act [1], affect [1], bestow [1], bring [1], devise [1], did [1], evildoer [+224] [1], fashions [1], forges [1], Maker [1], makes ready [1], plot [1], practice [1], wicked men [+224] [1], works out [1], works [1]

Ex 15:17 [A] the place, O LORD, *you* **made** for your dwelling,
Nu 23:23 [A] now be said of Jacob and of Israel, 'See what God *has* **done**!'
Dt 32:27 [A] hand has triumphed; the LORD *has* not **done** all this.' "
Job 7:20 [A] If I have sinned, what *have I* **done** to you, O watcher of
11: 8 [A] They are higher than the heavens—what *can you* **do**?
22:17 [A] to God, 'Leave us alone! What *can* the Almighty **do** to us?'
31: 3 [A] it not ruin for the wicked, disaster for *those who* **do** wrong?
33:29 [A] "God **does** all these things to a man—twice, even three
34: 8 [A] He keeps company with **evildoers** [+224]; he associates with
34:22 [A] no deep shadow, where **evildoers** [+224] can hide.
34:32 [A] I cannot see; if *I have* **done** wrong, I will not do so again.'
35: 6 [A] If you sin, how *does that* **affect** him? If your sins are many,
36: 3 [A] my knowledge from afar; I will ascribe justice to my **Maker**.
36:23 [A] his ways for him, or said to him, '*You have* **done** wrong'?
37:12 [A] face of the whole earth to **do** whatever he commands them.
Ps 5: 5 [5:6] [A] stand in your presence; you hate all *who* **do** wrong.
6: 8 [6:9] [A] Away from me, all you *who* **do** evil, for the LORD
7:13 [7:14] [A] *he* **makes ready** his flaming arrows.
7:15 [7:16] [A] and scoops it out falls into the pit *he has* **made**.
11: 3 [A] foundations are being destroyed, what *can* the righteous **do**?"
14: 4 [A] Will **evildoers** [+224] never learn—those who devour my
15: 2 [A] He whose walk is blameless and *who* **does** what is righteous,
28: 3 [A] not drag me away with the wicked, with *those who* **do** evil,
31:19 [31:20] [A] which *you* **bestow** in the sight of men on those who
36:12 [36:13] [A] See how the **evildoers** [+224] lie fallen—
44: 1 [44:2] [A] our fathers have told us what *you* **did** in their days,
53: 4 [53:5] [A] Will the **evildoers** [+224] never learn—those who
58: 2 [58:3] [A] No, in your heart *you* **devise** injustice, and your
59: 2 [59:3] [A] Deliver me from **evildoers** [+224] and save me from
64: 2 [64:3] [A] from that noisy crowd of **evildoers** [+224].

Ps 68:28 [68:29] [A] us your strength, O God, as *you have* **done** before.
74:12 [A] are my king from of old; *you* **bring** salvation upon the earth.
92:7 [92:8] [A] spring up like grass and all **evildoers** [+224] flourish,
92:9 [92:10] [A] will perish; all **evildoers** [+224] will be scattered.
94:4 [A] arrogant words; all the **evildoers** [+224] are full of boasting.
94:16 [A] Who will take a stand for me against **evildoers** [+224]?
101:8 [A] I will cut off every **evildoer** [+224] from the city of the
119:3 [A] *They* **do** nothing wrong; they walk in his ways.
125:5 [A] ways the LORD will banish with the **evildoers** [+224].
141:4 [A] part in wicked deeds with men *who are* **evildoers** [+224];
141:9 [A] they have laid for me, from the traps set by **evildoers** [+224].
Pr 10:29 [A] for the righteous, but it is the ruin of *those who* **do** evil.
16:4 [A] The LORD **works out** everything for his own ends—even
21:15 [A] it brings joy to the righteous but terror to **evildoers** [+224].
30:20 [A] and wipes her mouth and says, '*I've* **done** nothing wrong.'
Isa 26:12 [A] for us; all that we have accomplished *you have* **done** for us.
31:2 [A] of the wicked, against those who help **evildoers** [+224].
41:4 [A] Who *has* **done** this and carried it through, calling forth the
43:13 [A] can deliver out of my hand. *When I* **act**, who can reverse it?"
44:12 [A] The blacksmith takes a tool and **works** with it in the coals;
44:12 [A] an idol with hammers, *he* **forges** it with the might of his arm.
44:15 [A] But *he* also **fashions** a god and worships it; he makes an idol
Hos 6:8 [A] Gilead is a city of **wicked men** [+224], stained with
7:1 [A] *They* **practice** deceit, thieves break into houses, bandits rob
Mic 2:1 [A] those who plan iniquity, to *those who* **plot** evil on their beds!
Hab 1:5 [A] For *I am going to* **do** something in your days that you would
Zep 2:3 [A] all you humble of the land, *you who* **do** what he commands.

7189 פֹּעַל **pō'al**, n.m. [37] [→ 7040; cf. 7188]

deeds [8], work [7], works [5], what done [4], conduct [2], labor [2], acts [1], did [1], exploits [1], made [1], performed exploits [1], something [1], wages [1], what did [1], what[s] [1]

Dt 32:4 He is the Rock, his **works** are perfect, and all his ways are just.
33:11 his skills, O LORD, and be pleased with the **work** *of* his hands.
Ru 2:12 May the LORD repay you for **what** you have **done**. May you be
2Sa 23:20 was a valiant fighter from Kabzeel, who performed great **exploits**.
1Ch 11:22 was a valiant fighter from Kabzeel, who **performed** great **exploits**.
Job 7:2 the evening shadows, or a hired man waiting eagerly for his **wages**,
24:5 in the desert, the poor go about their **labor** of foraging food;
34:11 He repays a man for **what** he has **done**; he brings upon him what
36:9 he tells them **what** they have **done**—that they have sinned
36:24 Remember to extol his **work**, which men have praised in song.
Ps 9:16 [9:17] the wicked are ensnared by the **work** *of* their hands.
28:4 Repay them for their **deeds** and for their evil work; repay them for
44:1 [44:2] our fathers have told us **what**[s] you did in their days,
64:9 [64:10] they will proclaim the **works** *of* God and ponder what he
77:12 [77:13] I will meditate on all your **works** and consider all your
90:16 May your **deeds** be shown to your servants, your splendor to their
92:4 [92:5] For you make me glad by your **deeds**, O LORD; I sing for
95:9 your fathers tested and tried me, though they had seen **what I did**.
104:23 Then man goes out to his **work**, to his labor until evening.
111:3 Glorious and majestic are his **deeds**, and his righteousness endures
143:5 I meditate on all your **works** and consider what your hands have
Pr 20:11 is known by his actions, by whether his **conduct** is pure and right.
21:6 A fortune **made** by a lying tongue is a fleeting vapor and a deadly
21:8 of the guilty is devious, but the **conduct** *of* the innocent is upright.
24:12 Will he not repay each person according to **what** he has **done**?
24:29 him as he has done to me; I'll pay that man back for what he **did**."
Isa 1:31 The mighty man will become tinder and his **work** a spark;
5:12 and wine, but they have no regard for the **deeds** *of* the LORD,
41:24 But you are less than nothing and your **works** are utterly worthless;
45:9 'What are you making?' Does your **work** say, 'He has no hands'?
45:11 about my children, or give me orders about the **work** *of* my hands?
59:6 Their deeds are evil deeds, and **acts** *of* violence are in their hands.
Jer 22:13 his countrymen work for nothing, not paying them for their **labor**.
25:14 I will repay them according to their **deeds** and the work of their
50:29 no one escape. Repay her for her **deeds**; do to her as she has done.
Hab 1:5 For I am going to do **something** in your days that you would not
3:2 have heard of your fame; I stand in awe of your **deeds**, O LORD.

7190 פְּעֻלָּה p^{e}**'ullâ**, n.f. [14] [→ 7191; cf. 7188]

wages [3], deeds [2], recompense [2], reward [2], work [2], payment [1], reward [+5989] [1], works [1]

Lev 19:13 rob him. " 'Do not hold back the **wages** *of* a hired man overnight.
2Ch 15:7 be strong and do not give up, for your **work** will be rewarded."
Ps 17:4 As for the **deeds** *of* men—by the word of your lips I have kept
28:5 Since they show no regard for the **works** *of* the LORD and what
109:20 May this be the LORD's **payment** *to* my accusers, *to* those who
Pr 10:16 The **wages** *of* the righteous bring them life, but the income of the
11:18 The wicked man earns deceptive **wages**, but he who sows
Isa 40:10 his reward is with him, and his **recompense** accompanies him.
49:4 due me is in the LORD's hand, and my **reward** is with my God."
61:8 In my faithfulness *I will* **reward** [+5989] them and make an
62:11 his reward is with him, and his **recompense** accompanies him.' "
65:7 measure into their laps the full payment for their former **deeds**."
Jer 31:16 from tears, for your **work** will be rewarded," declares the LORD.
Eze 29:20 I have given him Egypt as a **reward** for his efforts because he

7191 פְּעֻלְּתַי p^{e}**'ull**^{e}**tay**, n.pr.m. [1] [√ 7190; cf. 7188]

Peullethai [1]

1Ch 26:5 Ammiel the sixth, Issachar the seventh and **Peullethai** the eighth.

7192 פָּעַם **pā'am**, v. [5] [→ 7193, 7194]

troubled [3], stir [1], troubles [1]

Ge 41:8 [C] In the morning his mind *was* **troubled**, so he sent for all the
Jdg 13:25 [A] the Spirit of the LORD began to **stir** him while he was in
Ps 77:4 [77:5] [C] my eyes from closing; *I was* too **troubled** to speak.
Da 2:1 [F] had dreams; his mind *was* **troubled** and he could not sleep.
2:3 [C] "I have had a dream *that* **troubles** me and I want to know

7193 פַּעַם **pa'am**, n.f. [118] [→ 7194; cf. 7192]

times [44], time [14], feet [10], twice [5], as before [+928+3869+7193] [4], now [3], once [+285] [3], once more [3], as done before [+928+3869+7193] [2], at other times [+928+7193] [2], customary [+928+3869+7193] [2], encounter [2], footsteps [2], one more [2], steps [2], *untranslated* [1], again [+928+1685+2021+2021+2085] [1], annual [+928+2021+9102] [1], anvil [1], at last [+2021] [1], campaign [1], clatter [1], forms [1], level [1], moment [1], now [+2021] [1], once more [+421+2021] [1], once [1], other[s] [1], sets [1], supports [+4190] [1], thrust [1], twice over [1]

Ge 2:23 man said, "This is **now** bone of my bones and flesh of my flesh;
18:32 "May the Lord not be angry, but let me speak just **once more**.
27:36 He has deceived me these *two* **times**: He took my birthright,
29:34 "Now **at last** [+2021] my husband will become attached to me,
29:35 gave birth to a son she said, "This **time** I will praise the LORD."
30:20 This **time** my husband will treat me with honor, because I have
33:3 bowed down to the ground seven **times** as he approached his
41:32 The reason the dream was given to Pharaoh *in two* **forms** is that
43:10 if we had not delayed, we could have gone and returned **twice**."
46:30 Israel said to Joseph, "**Now** [+2021] I am ready to die, since I have
Ex 8:32 [8:28] this **time** also Pharaoh hardened his heart and would not let
9:14 or this **time** I will send the full force of my plagues against you
9:27 and Aaron. "This **time** I have sinned," he said to them.
10:17 Now forgive my sin **once** [+421+2021] **more** and pray to the
23:17 "Three **times** a year all the men are to appear before the Sovereign
25:12 Cast four gold rings for it and fasten them to its four **feet**, with two
34:23 Three **times** a year all your men are to appear before the Sovereign
34:24 no one will covet your land when you go up three **times** each year
37:3 He cast four gold rings for it and fastened them to its four **feet**,
Lev 4:6 the blood and sprinkle some of it seven **times** before the LORD,
4:17 sprinkle it before the LORD seven **times** in front of the curtain.
8:11 He sprinkled some of the oil on the altar seven **times**, anointing the
14:7 Seven **times** he shall sprinkle the one to be cleansed of the
14:16 with his finger sprinkle some of it before the LORD seven **times**.
14:27 some of the oil from his palm seven **times** before the LORD.
14:51 dead bird and the fresh water, and sprinkle the house seven **times**.
16:14 he shall sprinkle some of it with his finger seven **times** before the
16:19 some of the blood on it with his finger seven **times** to cleanse it
25:8 " 'Count off seven sabbaths of years—seven **times** seven years—
Nu 14:22 and in the desert but who disobeyed me and tested me ten **times**—
19:4 and sprinkle it seven **times** toward the front of the Tent of Meeting.
20:11 Then Moses raised his arm and struck the rock **twice** with his staff.
24:1 he did not resort to sorcery as **at other times** [+928+7193],
24:1 he did not resort to sorcery as **at other times** [+928+7193],
24:10 to curse my enemies, but you have blessed them these three **times**.
Dt 1:11 increase you a thousand **times** and bless you as he has promised!
9:19 But **again** [+928+1685+2021+2021+2085] the LORD listened to
10:10 I did the first time, and the LORD listened to me at this **time** also.
16:16 Three **times** a year all your men must appear before the LORD
Jos 6:3 March around the city **once** [+285] with all the armed men.
6:4 On the seventh day, march around the city seven **times**,
6:11 ark of the LORD carried around the city, circling it **once** [+285].
6:14 So on the second day they marched around the city **once** [+285]
6:15 and marched around the city seven **times** in the same manner,
6:15 except that on that day they circled the city seven **times**.
6:16 The seventh **time** around, when the priests sounded the trumpet
10:42 All these kings and their lands Joshua conquered in one **campaign**,
Jdg 5:28 so long in coming? Why is the **clatter** *of* his chariots delayed?'
6:39 "Do not be angry with me. Let me make just **one more** request.
6:39 Allow me **one more** test with the fleece. This time make the fleece
15:3 to them, "This **time** I have a right to get even with the Philistines;
16:15 This is the third **time** you have made a fool of me and haven't told
16:18 sent word to the rulers of the Philistines, "Come back **once more**;

Jdg 16: 20 "I'll go out **as before** [+928+3869+7193] and shake myself free."
16: 20 "I'll go out **as before** [+928+3869+7193] and shake myself free."
16: 28 O God, please strengthen me just **once more**, and let me with one
20: 30 against Gibeah **as** they had **done before** [+928+3869+7193].
20: 30 against Gibeah **as** they had **done before** [+928+3869+7193].
20: 31 to inflict casualties on the Israelites **as before** [+928+3869+7193],
20: 31 to inflict casualties on the Israelites **as before** [+928+3869+7193],
1Sa 3: 10 and stood there, calling as at the **other**ˢ times, "Samuel!
3: 10 and stood there, calling as at the other **times**, "Samuel!
18: 11 "I'll pin David to the wall." But David eluded him **twice**.
20: 25 He sat in his **customary** [+928+3869+7193] place by the wall,
20: 25 He sat in his **customary** [+928+3869+7193] place by the wall,
20: 41 side ˪of the stone˩ and bowed down before Jonathan three **times**,
26: 8 Now let me pin him to the ground with one **thrust** of my spear;
2Sa 17: 7 "The advice Ahithophel has given is not good this **time**.
23: 8 against eight hundred men, whom he killed in one **encounter**.
24: 3 the LORD your God multiply the troops a hundred **times** *over*,
1Ki 7: 4 were placed high in sets of three, facing each other. **[NIE]**
7: 5 they were in the front part in **sets** of three, facing each other.
7: 30 each had a basin resting on four **supports** [+4190], cast with
9: 25 Three **times** a year Solomon sacrificed burnt offerings
11: 9 the LORD, the God of Israel, who had appeared to him **twice**.
17: 21 he stretched himself out on the boy three **times** and cried to the
18: 43 is nothing there," he said. Seven **times** Elijah said, "Go back."
22: 16 "How many **times** must I make you swear to tell me nothing
2Ki 4: 35 him once more. The boy sneezed seven **times** and opened his eyes.
5: 10 "Go, wash yourself seven **times** in the Jordan, and your flesh will
5: 14 So he went down and dipped himself in the Jordan seven **times**,
13: 18 "Strike the ground." He struck it three **times** and stopped.
13: 19 and said, "You should have struck the ground five or six **times**;
13: 19 destroyed it. But now you will defeat it only three **times**."
13: 25 Three **times** Jehoash defeated him, and so he recovered the
19: 24 With the soles of my **feet** I have dried up all the streams of Egypt."
1Ch 11: 11 against three hundred men, whom he killed in one **encounter**.
21: 3 "May the LORD multiply his troops a hundred **times** *over*.
2Ch 8: 13 New Moons and the three **annual** [+928+2021+9102] feasts—
18: 15 "How many **times** must I make you swear to tell me nothing
Ne 4: 12 [4:6] Jews who lived near them came and told us ten **times** *over*,
6: 4 Four **times** they sent me the same message, and each time I gave
6: 5 Then, the fifth **time**, Sanballat sent his aide to me with the same
13: 20 **Once** or twice the merchants and sellers of all kinds of goods spent
Job 19: 3 Ten **times** now you have reproached me; shamelessly you attack
33: 29 "God does all these things to a man—**twice**, even three times—
Ps 17: 5 My steps have held to your paths; my **feet** have not slipped.
57: 6 [57:7] They spread a net for my **feet**—I was bowed down in
58: 10 [58:11] when they bathe their **feet** in the blood of the wicked.
74: 3 Turn your **steps** toward these everlasting ruins, all this destruction
85: 13 [85:14] goes before him and prepares the way for his **steps**.
106: 43 Many **times** he delivered them, but they were bent on rebellion
119: 133 Direct my **footsteps** according to your word; let no sin rule over
140: 4 [140:5] protect me from men of violence who plan to trip my **feet**.
Pr 7: 12 **now** in the street, now in the squares, at every corner she lurks.)
7: 12 now in the street, **now** in the squares, at every corner she lurks.)
29: 5 Whoever flatters his neighbor is spreading a net for his **feet**.
Ecc 6: 6 even if he lives a thousand years **twice over** but fails to enjoy his
7: 22 for you know in your heart that many **times** you yourself have
SS 7: 1 [7:2] How beautiful your sandaled **feet**, O prince's daughter!
Isa 26: 6 it down—the feet of the oppressed, the **footsteps** *of* the poor.
37: 25 With the soles of my **feet** I have dried up all the streams of Egypt.'
41: 7 who smooths with the hammer spurs on him who strikes the **anvil**.
66: 8 country be born in a day or a nation be brought forth in a **moment**?
Jer 10: 18 "At this **time** I will hurl out those who live in this land; I will bring
16: 21 will teach them—this **time** I will teach them my power and might.
Eze 41: 6 were on three levels, one above another, thirty on *each* **level**.
Na 1: 9 he will bring to an end; trouble will not come a *second* **time**.

7194 פַּעֲמוֹן pa'ᵃmôn, n.[m.]. [7] [√ 7193; cf. 7192]

bells [4], alternateˢ [+2256+2298+8232] [1], alternatedˢ [+2256+8232] [1], themˢ [+2021] [1]

Ex 28: 33 yarn around the hem of the robe, with gold **bells** between them.
28: 34 The gold **bells** and the pomegranates are to alternate around the
28: 34 and the pomegranates *are to* **alternate**ˢ [+2256+2298+8232]
39: 25 they made **bells** *of* pure gold and attached them around the hem
39: 25 attached **them**ˢ [+2021] around the hem between the
39: 26 The **bells** and pomegranates alternated around the hem of the robe
39: 26 The bells and pomegranates **alternated**ˢ [+2256+8232] around the

7195 פַּעְנֵחַ pa'nēaḥ, n.pr.m. Not used in NIV/BHS [√ 7624]

7196 פָּעַר pā'ar, v. [4] [cf. 7186?, 7197?]

open [2], drank in [+7023] [1], opens [1]

Job 16: 10 [A] *Men* **open** their mouths to jeer at me; they strike my cheek in
29: 23 [A] and **drank** [+7023] **in** my words as the spring rain.
Ps 119: 131 [A] *I* **open** my mouth and pant, longing for your commands.
Isa 5: 14 [A] grave enlarges its appetite and **opens** its mouth without limit;

7197 פַּעֲרַי pa'ᵃray, n.pr.m. [1] [cf. 7196?]

Paarai [1]

2Sa 23: 35 Hezro the Carmelite, **Paarai** the Arbite,

7198 פָּצָה pāṣâ, v. [15]

opened [3], deliver [2], open wide [2], opens [2], delivers [1], given word [+906+7023] [1], made a vow [+7023] [1], open [1], opened wide [1], promised [1]

Ge 4: 11 [A] which **opened** its mouth to receive your brother's blood from
Nu 16: 30 [A] the earth **opens** its mouth and swallows them,
Dt 11: 6 [A] when the earth **opened** its mouth right in the middle of all
Jdg 11: 35 [A] because I *have* **made a vow** [+7023] to the LORD that I
11: 36 [A] "*you have* **given** your **word** [+906+7023] to the LORD.
Job 35: 16 [A] So Job **opens** his mouth *with* empty talk; without knowledge
Ps 22: 13 [22:14] [A] their prey **open** their mouths **wide** against me.
66: 14 [A] vows my lips **promised** and my mouth spoke when I was in
144: 7 [A] **deliver** me and rescue me from the mighty waters,
144: 10 [A] who **delivers** his servant David from the deadly sword.
144: 11 [A] **Deliver** me and rescue me from the hands of foreigners
Isa 10: 14 [A] not one flapped a wing, or **opened** its mouth to chirp.' "
La 2: 16 [A] All your enemies **open** their mouths **wide** against you;
3: 46 [A] "All our enemies *have* **opened** their mouths **wide** against us.
Eze 2: 8 [A] rebellious house; **open** your mouth and eat what I give you."

7199 פָּצַח¹ pāṣaḥ¹, v. Not used in NIV/BHS

7200 פָּצַח² pāṣaḥ², v. [8]

burst [6], break in pieces [1], break [1]

Ps 98: 4 [A] all the earth, **burst** *into* jubilant song with music;
Isa 14: 7 [A] the lands are at rest and at peace; *they* **break** *into* singing.
44: 23 [A] **Burst** *into* song, *you* mountains, you forests and all your
49: 13 [A] O heavens; rejoice, O earth; **burst** *into* song, O mountains!
52: 9 [A] **Burst** *into* songs of joy together, you ruins of Jerusalem,
54: 1 [A] **burst** *into* song, shout for joy, you who were never in labor;
55: 12 [A] the mountains and hills *will* **burst** *into* song before you,
Mic 3: 3 [D] strip off their skin and **break** their bones **in pieces**;

7201 פְּצִירָה pᵉṣîrâ, n.f. [1]

sharpening [1]

1Sa 13: 21 The price was two thirds of a shekel for **sharpening** plowshares

7202 פָּצַל pāṣal, v. [2] [→ 7203]

peeled [1], peeling [1]

Ge 30: 37 [D] and *made* white stripes on them *by* **peeling** *the bark*
30: 38 [D] he placed the **peeled** branches in all the watering troughs,

7203 פְּצָלוֹת pᵉṣālôt, n.f.pl. [1] [√ 7202]

stripes [1]

Ge 30: 37 plane trees and made white **stripes** on them by peeling the bark

7204 פָּצַם pāṣam, v. [1]

torn open [1]

Ps 60: 2 [60:4] [A] You have shaken the land and **torn** it **open**; mend its

7205 פָּצַע pāṣa', v. [3] [→ 7206]

been emasculated [1], bruised [1], wounded [1]

Dt 23: 1 [23:2] [B] No *one who has* **been emasculated** *by* crushing
1Ki 20: 37 [A] please." So the man struck him and **wounded** him.
SS 5: 7 [A] They beat me, *they* **bruised** me; they took away my cloak,

7206 פֶּצַע peṣa', n.m. [8] [√ 7205]

wounds [4], wound [2], bruises [1], wounding [1]

Ge 4: 23 I have killed a man for **wounding** me, a young man for injuring
Ex 21: 25 burn for burn, **wound** for wound, bruise for bruise.
21: 25 burn for burn, wound for **wound**, bruise for bruise.
Job 9: 17 crush me with a storm and multiply my **wounds** for no reason.
Pr 20: 30 Blows and **wounds** cleanse away evil, and beatings purge the
23: 29 Who has strife? Who has complaints? Who has needless **bruises**?
27: 6 **Wounds** *from* a friend can be trusted, but an enemy multiplies
Isa 1: 6 only **wounds** and welts and open sores, not cleansed or bandaged

7207 פָּצַץ *pāṣaṣ*, v. [3] [→ 1122, 2204, 7209; cf. 5879, 7046]
breaks in pieces [1], crumbled [1], crushed [1]

Job 16:12 [D] he shattered me; he seized me by the neck and **crushed** me.
Jer 23:29 [D] "and like a hammer *that* **breaks** a rock **in pieces**?
Hab 3: 6 [F] The ancient mountains **crumbled** and the age-old hills

7208 פַּצֵּץ *paṣṣēṣ*, n.pr.loc. Not used in NIV/BHS [√ 7207]

7209 פִּצֵּץ *piṣṣēṣ*, n.pr.m. Not used in NIV/BHS [√ 7207]

7210 פָּצַר *pāṣar*, v. [7] [cf. 7287]
insisted [2], arrogance [1], kept bringing pressure [+4394] [1], persisted [1], persuaded [1], urged [1]

Ge 19: 3 [A] *he* **insisted** so strongly that they did go with him and entered
19: 9 [A] *They* **kept bringing pressure** [+4394] on Lot and moved
33:11 [A] all I need." And because Jacob **insisted**, Esau accepted it.
Jdg 19: 7 [A] his father-in-law **persuaded** him, so he stayed there that
1Sa 15:23 [G] the sin of divination, and **arrogance** like the evil of idolatry.
2Ki 2:17 [A] *they* **persisted** until he was too ashamed to refuse. So he
5:16 [A] a thing." And even though Naaman **urged** him, he refused.

7211 פִּק *piq*, n.[m.]. [1] [cf. 7048]
give way [1]

Na 2:10 [2:11] Hearts melt, knees **give way**, bodies tremble, every face

7212 פָּקַד *pāqad*, v. [302] [→ 5152, 7213, 7214, 7215, 7216, 7217, 7218, 7224]
punish [45], counted [23], number [19], numbered [13], numbers [12], appoint [11], were counted [11], appointed [9], assigned [9], count [8], mustered [8], care for [6], missing [6], put in charge [6], surely come to aid [+906+7212] [6], *untranslated* [5], appointed as governor [5], punished [5], come [3], empty [3], punishes [3], assign [2], be punished [2], counted [+7212] [2], deal [2], enroll [2], examine [2], gracious [2], misses at all [+7212] [2], missing [+7212] [2], mobilized [2], officers [2], punishing [2], supervisors [2], total [2], watched over and seen [+906+906+7212] [2], were appointed [2], accuse [+6584] [1], assembled [1], be called to arms [1], be missed [1], be missing [1], be robbed [1], bestow punishment [1], bestowed care on [1], bring punishment [1], bring [1], called to account [1], came [1], come to aid [1], come to the aid of [1], commit [1], concerned about [1], destroy [1], did[s] [1], experience [1], fails to come [1], harm [1], in charge of [1], in charge [1], lack [1], listed [1], longed for [1], missed [1], muster forces [1], mustering [1], numbering [1], placed [1], post [1], posted [1], prescribed [1], punishments come [1], put away [1], put [1], see [1], send [1], sets [1], store [1], summoned [1], take care of [1], take stock of [1], total [+3972] [1], untouched [+1153] [1], visit [1], was counted [1], was entrusted [+906+7214] [1], watch over [1], were counted in the census [1], were found missing [1], were recorded [1], were registered [1]

Ge 21: 1 [A] Now the LORD *was* **gracious** *to* Sarah as he had said,
39: 4 [G] Potiphar **put** him **in charge** of his household, and he
39: 5 [G] From the time *he* **put** him **in charge** of his household and of
40: 4 [A] The captain of the guard **assigned** them *to* Joseph, and he
41:34 [G] *Let* Pharaoh **appoint** commissioners over the land to take a
50:24 [A] God *will* **surely come** [+906+7212] **to** your **aid** and take you
50:24 [A] God *will* **surely come to** your **aid** [+906+7212] and take you
50:25 [A] "God *will* **surely come** [+906+7212] **to** your **aid**, and
50:25 [A] "God *will* **surely come to** your **aid** [+906+7212], and
Ex 3:16 [A] appeared to me and said: *I have* **watched** [+906+906+7212] **over** you **and** *have* **seen** what has been done to you in Egypt.
3:16 [A] *I have* **watched over** you **and** *have* **seen** [+906+906+7212]
4:31 [A] when they heard that the LORD *was* **concerned about**
13:19 [A] "God *will* **surely come** [+906+7212] **to** your **aid**, and
13:19 [A] "God *will* **surely come to** your **aid** [+906+7212], and
20: 5 [A] **punishing** the children *for* the sin of the fathers to the third
30:12 [B] "When you take a census of the Israelites to **count** them,
30:12 [A] the LORD a ransom for his life at the time he *is* **counted**.
30:12 [A] Then no plague will come on them when *you* **number** them.
30:13 [B] Each one who crosses over to those *already* **counted** is to
30:14 [B] All who cross over, **[RPH]** those twenty years old or more,
32:34 [A] However, when the time comes for me *to* **punish**, I will
32:34 [A] comes for me to punish, *I will* **punish** them *for* their sin."
34: 7 [A] *he* **punishes** the children and their children *for* the sin of the
38:21 [E] which **were recorded** at Moses' command by the Levites
38:25 [B] *those of* the community *who* **were counted in the census**
38:26 [B] from everyone who had crossed over to those **counted**,
Lev 6: 4 [5:23] [H] or what **was entrusted** [+906+7214] to him,
18:25 [A] so *I* **punished** it *for* its sin, and the land vomited out its
26:16 [G] *I will* **bring** upon you sudden terror, wasting diseases and
Nu 1: 3 [A] Aaron *are to* **number** by their divisions all the men in Israel
1:19 [A] And so *he* **counted** them in the Desert of Sinai:
1:21 [B] The **number** from the tribe of Reuben was 46,500.
1:22 [B] or more who were able to serve in the army **were counted**
1:23 [B] The **number** from the tribe of Simeon was 59,300.
1:25 [B] The **number** from the tribe of Gad was 45,650.
1:27 [B] The **number** from the tribe of Judah was 74,600.
1:29 [B] The **number** from the tribe of Issachar was 54,400.
1:31 [B] The **number** from the tribe of Zebulun was 57,400.
1:33 [B] The **number** from the tribe of Ephraim was 40,500.
1:35 [B] The **number** from the tribe of Manasseh was 32,200.
1:37 [B] The **number** from the tribe of Benjamin was 35,400.
1:39 [B] The **number** from the tribe of Dan was 62,700.
1:41 [B] The **number** from the tribe of Asher was 41,500.
1:43 [B] The **number** from the tribe of Naphtali was 53,400.
1:44 [B] These were the *men* **counted** [+7212] by Moses and Aaron
1:44 [A] These were the *men* **counted** [+7212] by Moses and Aaron
1:45 [B] in Israel's army were **counted** according to their families.
1:46 [B] The total **number** was 603,550.
1:47 [F] of Levi, however, **were** not **counted** along with the others.
1:49 [A] "*You must* not **count** the tribe of Levi or include them in the
1:50 [G] **appoint** the Levites to be in charge of the tabernacle of the
2: 4 [B] His division **numbers** 74,600.
2: 6 [B] His division **numbers** 54,400.
2: 8 [B] His division **numbers** 57,400.
2: 9 [B] All the *men* **assigned** to the camp of Judah, according to
2:11 [B] His division **numbers** 46,500.
2:13 [B] His division **numbers** 59,300.
2:15 [B] His division **numbers** 45,650.
2:16 [B] All the *men* **assigned** to the camp of Reuben, according to
2:19 [B] His division **numbers** 40,500.
2:21 [B] His division **numbers** 32,200.
2:23 [B] His division **numbers** 35,400.
2:24 [B] All the *men* **assigned** to the camp of Ephraim, according to
2:26 [B] His division **numbers** 62,700.
2:28 [B] His division **numbers** 41,500.
2:30 [B] His division **numbers** 53,400.
2:31 [B] All the *men* **assigned** to the camp of Dan number 157,600.
2:32 [B] These are the Israelites, **counted** according to their families.
2:32 [B] All those in the camps, by their divisions, **number** 603,550.
2:33 [F] however, **were** not **counted** along with the other Israelites,
3:10 [A] **Appoint** Aaron and his sons to serve as priests; anyone else
3:15 [A] "**Count** the Levites by their families and clans. Count every
3:15 [A] and clans. **Count** every male a month old or more."
3:16 [A] So Moses **counted** them, as he was commanded by the word
3:22 [B] the males a month old or more who **were counted** was 7,500.
3:22 [B] a month old or more who were counted was 7,500. **[RPH]**
3:34 [B] the males a month old or more who **were counted** was 6,200.
3:39 [B] The total **number** *of* Levites counted at the LORD's
3:39 [A] The total number of Levites **counted** at the LORD's
3:40 [A] "**Count** all the firstborn Israelite males who are a month old
3:42 [A] So Moses **counted** all the firstborn of the Israelites, as the
3:43 [B] The total **number** *of* firstborn males a month old or more,
4:23 [A] **Count** all the men from thirty to fifty years of age who come
4:27 [A] *You shall* **assign** to them as their responsibility all they are
4:29 [A] "**Count** the Merarites by their clans and families.
4:30 [A] **Count** all the men from thirty to fifty years of age who come
4:32 [A] **Assign** to each man the specific things he is to carry.
4:34 [A] the leaders of the community **counted** the Kohathites by their
4:36 [B] **counted** by clans, were 2,750.
4:37 [B] This was the **total** *of* all those in the Kohathite clans who
4:37 [A] Aaron **counted** them according to the LORD's command
4:38 [B] The Gershonites **were counted** by their clans and families.
4:40 [B] **counted** by their clans and families, were 2,630.
4:41 [B] This was the **total** *of those* **in** [+3972] the Gershonite clans
4:41 [A] Aaron **counted** them according to the LORD's command.
4:42 [B] The Merarites **were counted** by their clans and families.
4:44 [B] **counted** by their clans, were 3,200.
4:45 [B] This was the **total** *of those in* the Merarite clans. Moses
4:45 [A] Aaron **counted** them according to the LORD's command
4:46 [A] the leaders of Israel **counted** all the Levites by their clans
4:46 [B] the leaders of Israel counted all **[RPH]** the Levites by their
4:48 [B] **numbered** 8,580.
4:49 [A] each *was* **assigned** his work and told what to carry.
4:49 [B] Thus they **were counted**, as the LORD commanded Moses.
7: 2 [B] were the tribal leaders in charge of those *who* **were counted**,
14:18 [A] *he* **punishes** the children *for* the sin of the fathers to the third
14:29 [B] you twenty years old or more *who* **was counted** in the census
16:29 [C] and **experience** only what usually happens to men,
26: 7 [B] were the clans of Reuben; those **numbered** were 43,730.
26:18 [B] These were the clans of Gad; those **numbered** were 40,500.
26:22 [B] These were the clans of Judah; those **numbered** were 76,500.
26:25 [B] were the clans of Issachar; those **numbered** were 64,300.
26:27 [B] were the clans of Zebulun; those **numbered** were 60,500.
26:34 [B] were the clans of Manasseh; those **numbered** were 52,700.

Nu 26:37 [B] were the clans of Ephraim; those **numbered** were 32,500.
26:41 [B] were the clans of Benjamin; those **numbered** were 45,600.
26:43 [B] were Shuhamite clans; and those **numbered** were 64,400.
26:47 [B] were the clans of Asher; those **numbered** were 53,400.
26:50 [B] were the clans of Naphtali; those **numbered** were 45,400.
26:51 [B] The total **number** *of* the men of Israel was 601,730.
26:54 [B] its inheritance according to the number of those **listed**.
26:57 [B] These were the Levites *who* **were counted** by their clans:
26:62 [B] All the male Levites a month old or more **numbered** 23,000.
26:62 [F] *They* **were** not **counted** along with the other Israelites
26:63 [B] These are the *ones* **counted** *by* Moses and Eleazar the priest
26:63 [A] Eleazar the priest when *they* **counted** the Israelites on the
26:64 [B] Not one of them was among *those* **counted** *by* Moses
26:64 [A] Aaron the priest when *they* **counted** the Israelites in the
27:16 [A] "*May* the LORD, the God of the spirits of all mankind, **appoint**
31:14 [B] Moses was angry with the **officers** *of* the army—
31:48 [B] the **officers** who were over the units of the army—
31:49 [C] the soldiers under our command, and not one *is* **missing**.
Dt 5: 9 [A] **punishing** the children *for* the sin of the fathers to the third
20: 9 [A] to the army, *they shall* **appoint** commanders over it.
Jos 8:10 [A] Early the next morning Joshua **mustered** his men, and he
10:18 [G] the mouth of the cave, and **post** some men there to guard it.
Jdg 15: 1 [A] Samson took a young goat and *went to* **visit** his wife.
20:15 [F] At once the Benjamites **mobilized** twenty-six thousand
20:15 [F] in addition to seven hundred chosen men **[RPH]** from those
20:17 [F] **mustered** four hundred thousand swordsmen,
21: 3 [C] Why *should* one tribe *be* **missing** from Israel today?"
21: 9 [F] For when *they* **counted** the people, they found that none of
Ru 1: 6 [A] *had* **come to the aid of** his people by providing food for
1Sa 2:21 [A] And the LORD *was* **gracious** *to* Hannah; she conceived
11: 8 [A] When Saul **mustered** them at Bezek, the men of Israel
13:15 [A] in Benjamin, and Saul **counted** the men who were with him.
14:17 [A] were with him, "**Muster** *the* **forces** and see who has left us."
14:17 [A] When *they* **did**ᵎ, it was Jonathan and his armor-bearer who
15: 2 [A] '*I will* **punish** the Amalekites *for* what they did to Israel
15: 4 [A] **mustered** them at Telaim—two hundred thousand foot soldiers
17:18 [A] **See** how your brothers are and bring back some assurance
20: 6 [A] If your father **misses** [+7212] me **at all**, tell him,
20: 6 [A] If your father **misses** me **at all** [+7212], tell him,
20:18 [C] *You will* **be missed**, because your seat will be empty.
20:18 [C] You will be missed, because your seat *will be* **empty**.
20:25 [C] and Abner sat next to Saul, but David's place *was* **empty**.
20:27 [C] second day of the month, David's place *was* **empty** again.
25: 7 [C] time they were at Carmel nothing of theirs *was* **missing**.
25:15 [A] we were out in the fields near them nothing *was* **missing**.
25:21 [C] property in the desert so that nothing of his *was* **missing**.
29: 4 [G] man back, that he may return to the place *you* **assigned** him.
2Sa 2:30 [C] nineteen of David's men **were found missing**.
3: 8 [A] Yet now *you* **accuse** [+6584] me *of* an offense involving this
18: 1 [A] David **mustered** the men who were with him and appointed
24: 2 [A] of Israel from Dan to Beersheba and **enroll** the fighting men,
24: 4 [A] the presence of the king to **enroll** the fighting men of Israel.
1Ki 11:28 [G] *he* **put** him **in charge** of the whole labor force of the house
14:27 [G] **assigned** these to the commanders of the guard on duty at the
20:15 [A] So Ahab **summoned** the young officers of the provincial
20:15 [A] Then *he* **assembled** the rest of the Israelites, 7,000 in all.
20:26 [A] The next spring Ben-Hadad **mustered** the Arameans
20:27 [F] When the Israelites *were* also **mustered** and given
20:39 [C] If *he is* **missing** [+7212], it will be your life for his life,
20:39 [C] If *he is* **missing** [+7212], it will be your life for his life,
2Ki 3: 6 [A] King Joram set out from Samaria and **mobilized** all Israel.
5:24 [A] the things from the servants and **put** them **away** in the house.
7:17 [G] *had* **put** the officer on whose arm he leaned **in charge** of the
9:34 [A] "**Take care of** that cursed woman," he said, "and bury her,
10:19 [C] See that no one *is* **missing**, because I am going to hold a
10:19 [C] for Baal. Anyone who **fails to come** will no longer live."
11:15 [B] of units of a hundred, *who were* **in charge** *of* the troops:
12:11 [12:12] [H] they gave the money to the *men* **appointed** to
22: 5 [H] Have them entrust it to the *men* **appointed** to supervise the
22: 9 [H] entrusted it to the workers and **supervisors** at the temple."
25:22 [G] Nebuchadnezzar king of Babylon **appointed** Gedaliah son of
25:23 [G] the king of Babylon *had* **appointed** Gedaliah **as governor**,
1Ch 21: 6 [A] Joab *did* not include Levi and Benjamin *in the* **numbering**,
23:24 [B] the heads of families as they **were registered** under their
26:32 [G] King David **put** them **in charge** of the Reubenites,
2Ch 12:10 [G] **assigned** these to the commanders of the guard on duty at the
23:14 [B] *who were* **in charge of** the troops, and said to them:
25: 5 [A] *He* then **mustered** those twenty years old or more and found
34:10 [H] they entrusted it to the *men* **appointed** to supervise the work
34:12 [H] **[RPH]** The Levites—all who were skilled in playing
34:17 [H] and have entrusted it to the **supervisors** and workers."
36:23 [A] he *has* **appointed** me to build a temple for him at Jerusalem
Ezr 1: 2 [A] he *has* **appointed** me to build a temple for him at Jerusalem
Ne 7: 1 [C] and the singers and the Levites **were appointed**.
12:44 [C] At that time men **were appointed** to be in charge of the
Est 2: 3 [G] *Let* the king **appoint** commissioners in every province of his
Job 5:24 [A] *you will* **take stock of** your property and find nothing
7:18 [A] that *you* **examine** him every morning and test him every
31:14 [A] confronts me? What will I answer when **called to account**?
34:13 [A] Who **appointed** him over the earth? Who put him in charge
35:15 [A] that his anger never **punishes** and he does not take the least
36:23 [A] Who *has* **prescribed** his ways for him, or said to him,
Ps 8: 4 [8:5] [A] mindful of him, the son of man that *you* **care for** him?
17: 3 [A] Though you probe my heart and **examine** me at night,
31: 5 [31:6] [G] Into your hands *I* **commit** my spirit; redeem me,
59: 5 [59:6] [A] of Israel, rouse yourself to **punish** all the nations;
65: 9 [65:10] [A] *You* **care for** the land and water it; you enrich it
80:14 [80:15] [A] down from heaven and see! **Watch over** this vine,
89:32 [89:33] [A] *I will* **punish** their sin with the rod, their iniquity
106: 4 [A] favor to your people, **come to** my **aid** when you save them,
109: 6 [G] **Appoint** an evil man to oppose him; let an accuser stand at
Pr 19:23 [C] Then one rests content, **untouched** [+1153] *by* trouble.
Isa 10:12 [A] "*I will* **punish** the king of Assyria for the willful pride of his
10:28 [G] they pass through Migron; *they* **store** supplies at Micmash.
13: 4 [D] The LORD Almighty *is* **mustering** an army for war.
13:11 [A] *I will* **punish** the world *for* its evil, the wicked *for* their sins.
23:17 [A] At the end of seventy years, the LORD *will* **deal** *with* Tyre.
24:21 [A] the LORD *will* **punish** the powers in the heavens above and
24:22 [C] will be shut up in prison and **be punished** after many days.
26:14 [A] *You* **punished** them and brought them to ruin; you wiped out
26:16 [A] LORD, *they* **came** *to* you in their distress; when you
26:21 [A] his dwelling to **punish** the people of the earth *for* their sins.
27: 1 [A] *will* **punish** with his sword, his fierce, great and powerful
27: 3 [A] I guard it day and night so that no *one may* **harm** it.
29: 6 [C] the LORD Almighty *will* **come** with thunder and earthquake
34:16 [A] None of these will be missing, not one *will* **lack** her mate.
38:10 [E] the gates of death and **be robbed** *of* the rest of my years?"
62: 6 [G] *I have* **posted** watchmen on your walls, O Jerusalem;
Jer 1:10 [G] today *I* **appoint** you over nations and kingdoms to uproot
3:16 [A] *it will* not be **missed**, nor will another one be made.
5: 9 [A] *Should I* not **punish** them for this?" declares the LORD.
5:29 [A] *Should I* not **punish** them for this?" declares the LORD.
6: 6 [H] This city *must* **be punished**; it is filled with oppression.
6:15 [A] they will be brought down when *I* **punish** them,"
9: 9 [9:8] [A] *Should I* not **punish** them for this?"
9:25 [9:24] [A] "when *I will* **punish** all who are circumcised only in
11:22 [A] 'I *will* **punish** them. Their young men will die by the sword,
13:21 [A] What will you say when ⌞the LORD⌟ **sets** over you those
14:10 [A] remember their wickedness and **punish** them *for* their sins."
15: 3 [A] "*I will* **send** four kinds of destroyers against them," declares the
15:15 [A] You understand, O LORD; remember me and **care for** me.
21:14 [A] *I will* **punish** you as your deeds deserve,
23: 2 [A] and driven them away and *have* not **bestowed care on** them,
23: 2 [A] I *will* **bestow punishment** on you *for* the evil you have
23: 4 [C] no longer be afraid or terrified, nor *will any* **be missing**,"
23:34 [A] of the LORD,' *I will* **punish** that man and his household.
25:12 [A] *I will* **punish** the king of Babylon and his nation, the land of
27: 8 [A] *I will* **punish** that nation with the sword, famine and plague,
27:22 [A] and there they will remain until the day I **come** *for* them,'
29:10 [A] *I will* **come** *to* you and fulfill my gracious promise to bring
29:32 [A] I *will* surely **punish** Shemaiah the Nehelamite and his
30:20 [A] established before me; *I will* **punish** all who oppress them.
32: 5 [A] where he will remain until I **deal** *with* him,
36:20 [G] After *they* **put** the scroll in the room of Elishama the
36:31 [A] *I will* **punish** him and his children and his attendants *for*
37:21 [G] gave orders for Jeremiah *to be* **placed** in the courtyard of the
40: 5 [G] whom the king of Babylon *has* **appointed** over the towns of
40: 7 [G] *had* **appointed** Gedaliah son of Ahikam **as governor** over
40: 7 [G] *had* **put** him **in charge** *of* the men, women and children who
40:11 [G] *had* **appointed** Gedaliah son of Ahikam, … **as governor**
41: 2 [G] king of Babylon *had* **appointed as governor** over the land.
41:10 [G] Nebuzaradan commander of the imperial guard *had* **appointed**
41:18 [G] whom the king of Babylon *had* **appointed as governor** over
44:13 [A] *I will* **punish** those who live in Egypt with the sword, famine
44:13 [A] with the sword, famine and plague, as *I* **punished** Jerusalem.
44:29 [A] " 'This will be the sign to you that I *will* **punish** you in this
46:25 [A] "I *am about to* **bring punishment** on Amon god of Thebes,
49: 8 [A] for I will bring disaster on Esau at the time *I* **punish** him.
49:19 [A] Who is the chosen one *I will* **appoint** for this? Who is like
50:18 [A] "I *will* **punish** the king of Babylon and his land as I punished
50:18 [A] of Babylon and his land as *I* **punished** the king of Assyria.
50:31 [A] "for your day has come, the time for you *to be* **punished**.
50:44 [A] Who is the chosen one *I will* **appoint** for this? Who is like
51:27 [A] **Appoint** a commander against her; send up horses like a
51:44 [A] *I will* **punish** Bel in Babylon and make him spew out what
51:47 [A] For the time will surely come when *I will* **punish** the idols of
51:52 [A] declares the LORD, "when *I will* **punish** her idols,
La 4:22 [A] *he will* **punish** your sin and expose your wickedness.

Eze 23:21 [A] So *you* **longed for** the lewdness of your youth, when in
38: 8 [C] After many days *you will* **be called to arms.** In future years
Hos 1: 4 [A] because *I will* soon **punish** the house of Jehu *for* the
2:13 [2:15] [A] *I will* **punish** her *for* the days she burned incense to
4: 9 [A] *I will* **punish** both of them *for* their ways and repay them for
4:14 [A] "*I will* not **punish** your daughters when they turn to
8:13 [A] he will remember their wickedness and **punish** their sins:
9: 9 [A] remember their wickedness and **punish** them *for* their sins.
12: 2 [12:3] [A] *he will* **punish** Jacob according to his ways
Am 3: 2 [A] of the earth; therefore *I will* **punish** you *for* all your sins."
3:14 [A] "On the day I **punish** Israel for her sins, I will destroy the
3:14 [A] I punish Israel for her sins, *I will* **destroy** the altars of Bethel;
Zep 1: 8 [A] sacrifice *I will* **punish** the princes and the king's sons and
1: 9 [A] On that day *I will* **punish** all who avoid stepping on the
1:12 [A] Jerusalem with lamps and **punish** those who are complacent,
2: 7 [A] The LORD their God *will* **care for** them; he will restore
3: 7 [A] not be cut off, nor all *my* **punishments come** upon her.
Zec 10: 3 [A] burns against the shepherds, and *I will* **punish** the leaders;
10: 3 [A] for the LORD Almighty *will* **care for** his flock, the house
11:16 [A] up a shepherd over the land *who will* not **care for** the lost,

7213 פְּקֻדָּה *pᵉquddâ*, n.f. [32] [√ 7212]

punished [4], punishment [3], appointed order [2], appointed [2], guards [2], judgment [2], assignment [1], charge [1], enrollment [1], governor [1], having charge [1], in charge [1], mustered [1], officials [1], oversight [1], place of leadership [1], prison [+1074+2021] [1], providence [1], reckoning [1], responsible [1], stored up [1], visits [1], what usually happens [1]

Nu 3:32 He was **appointed** *over* those who were responsible for the care of
3:36 The Merarites were **appointed** *to* take care of the frames of the
4:16 the priest, is to have **charge** *of* the oil for the light, the fragrant
4:16 He is to be **in charge** *of* the entire tabernacle and everything in it,
16:29 a natural death and experience only **what usually happens** *to* men,
2Ki 11:18 Jehoiada the priest posted **guards** at the temple of the LORD.
1Ch 23:11 so they were counted as one family with one **assignment**.
24: 3 David separated them into divisions for their **appointed order** of
24:19 This was their **appointed order** of ministering when they entered
26:30 were **responsible** in Israel west of the Jordan for all the work of
2Ch 17:14 Their **enrollment** by families was as follows: From Judah,
23:18 Jehoiada placed the **oversight** *of* the temple of the LORD in the
24:11 the chest was brought in by the Levites to the king's **officials**
26:11 to go out by divisions according to their numbers as **mustered**
Job 10:12 me kindness, and in your **providence** watched over my spirit.
Ps 109: 8 May his days be few; may another take his **place of leadership**.
Isa 10: 3 What will you do on the day of **reckoning**, when disaster comes
15: 7 and **stored up** they carry away over the Ravine of the Poplars.
60:17 I will make peace your **governor** and righteousness your ruler.
Jer 8:12 they will be brought down when they are **punished**,
10:15 objects of mockery; when their **judgment** comes, they will perish.
11:23 on the men of Anathoth in the year of their **punishment**.' "
23:12 I will bring disaster on them in the year they are **punished**,"
46:21 of disaster is coming upon them, the time for them to be **punished**.
48:44 for I will bring upon Moab the year of her **punishment**,"
50:27 For their day has come, the time for them to be **punished**.
51:18 objects of mockery; when their **judgment** comes, they will perish.
52:11 where he put him in **prison** [+1074+2021] till the day of his death.
Eze 9: 1 "Bring the **guards** *of* the city here, each with a weapon in his
44:11 **having charge** of the gates of the temple and serving in it;
Hos 9: 7 The days of **punishment** are coming, the days of reckoning are at
Mic 7: 4 The day of your watchmen has come, the day God **visits** you.

7214 פִּקָּדוֹן *piqqādôn*, n.m. [3] [√ 7212]

held in reserve [1], something entrusted [1], was entrusted [+906+7212] [1]

Ge 41:36 This food should be **held in reserve** for the country, to be used
Lev 6: 2 [5:21] deceiving his neighbor about **something entrusted** to him
6: 4 [5:23] by extortion, or what **was entrusted** [+906+7212] to him,

7215 פְּקִדֻת *pᵉqidut*, n.f. [1] [√ 7212]

guard [1]

Jer 37:13 But when he reached the Benjamin Gate, the captain of the **guard**,

7216 פְּקוֹד *pᵉqôd*, n.pr.loc. [2] [√ 7212]

Pekod [2]

Jer 50:21 "Attack the land of Merathaim and those who live in **Pekod**.
Eze 23:23 and all the Chaldeans, the men of **Pekod** and Shoa and Koa,

7217 פְּקוּדִים *pᵉqûdîm*, n.pl.[m.]. [1] [√ 7212]

amounts [1]

Ex 38:21 These are the **amounts** *of* the materials used for the tabernacle,

7218 פִּקּוּדִים *piqqûdîm*, n.m.[pl.]. [24] [√ 7212]

precepts [24]

Ps 19: 8 [19:9] The **precepts** *of* the LORD are right, giving joy to the
103:18 those who keep his covenant and remember to obey his **precepts**.
111: 7 of his hands are faithful and just; all his **precepts** are trustworthy.
119: 4 You have laid down **precepts** that are to be fully obeyed.
119:15 I meditate on your **precepts** and consider your ways.
119:27 Let me understand the teaching of your **precepts**; then I will
119:40 How I long for your **precepts**! Preserve my life in your
119:45 I will walk about in freedom, for I have sought out your **precepts**.
119:56 This has been my practice: I obey your **precepts**.
119:63 I am a friend to all who fear you, to all who follow your **precepts**.
119:69 have smeared me with lies, I keep your **precepts** with all my heart.
119:78 wronging me without cause; but I will meditate on your **precepts**.
119:87 wiped me from the earth, but I have not forsaken your **precepts**.
119:93 I will never forget your **precepts**, for by them you have preserved
119:94 Save me, for I am yours; I have sought out your **precepts**.
119:100 have more understanding than the elders, for I obey your **precepts**.
119:104 I gain understanding from your **precepts**; therefore I hate every
119:110 have set a snare for me, but I have not strayed from your **precepts**.
119:128 because I consider all your **precepts** right, I hate every wrong path.
119:134 me from the oppression of men, that I may obey your **precepts**.
119:141 Though I am lowly and despised, I do not forget your **precepts**.
119:159 See how I love your **precepts**; preserve my life, O LORD,
119:168 I obey your **precepts** and your statutes, for all my ways are known
119:173 your hand be ready to help me, for I have chosen your **precepts**.

7219 פָּקַח *pāqaḥ*, v. [19] [→ 7220?, 7221, 7222, 7223]

open [7], opened [4], be opened [2], fix [1], gives sight [1], keep watchful [1], opens [1], stay awake [+6524] [1], were opened [1]

Ge 3: 5 [C] God knows that when you eat of it your eyes *will* **be opened**,
3: 7 [C] the eyes of both of them **were opened**, and they realized they
21:19 [A] God **opened** her eyes and she saw a well of water. So she
2Ki 4:35 [A] The boy sneezed seven times and **opened** his eyes.
6:17 [A] Then the LORD **opened** the servant's eyes, and he looked
6:20 [A] "LORD, **open** the eyes of these men so they can see."
6:20 [A] the LORD **opened** their eyes and they looked, and there
19:16 [A] O LORD, and hear; **open** your eyes, O LORD, and see;
Job 14: 3 [A] *Do you* **fix** your eye on such a one? Will you bring him
27:19 [A] but will do so no more; *when he* **opens** his eyes, all is gone.
Ps 146: 8 [A] the LORD **gives sight** *to* the blind, the LORD lifts up
Pr 20:13 [A] **stay awake** [+6524] and you will have food to spare.
Isa 35: 5 [C] *will* the eyes of the blind **be opened** and the ears of the deaf
37:17 [A] O LORD, and hear; **open** your eyes, O LORD, and see;
42: 7 [A] to **open** eyes that are blind, to free captives from prison
42:20 [A] paid no attention; your ears *are* **open**, but you hear nothing."
Jer 32:19 [B] Your eyes *are* **open** to all the ways of men; you reward
Da 9:18 [A] **open** your eyes and see the desolation of the city that bears
Zec 12: 4 [A] "*I will* **keep** a **watchful** eye over the house of Judah, but I

7220 פֶּקַח *peqaḥ*, n.pr.m. [11] [√ 7219?]

Pekah [10], Pekah's [1]

2Ki 15:25 his chief officers, **Pekah** son of Remaliah, conspired against him.
15:27 **Pekah** son of Remaliah became king of Israel in Samaria,
15:29 In the time of **Pekah** king of Israel, Tiglath-Pileser king of Assyria
15:30 Hoshea son of Elah conspired against **Pekah** son of Remaliah.
15:31 As for the other events of **Pekah's** reign, and all he did, are they
15:32 In the second year of **Pekah** son of Remaliah king of Israel,
15:37 Rezin king of Aram and **Pekah** son of Remaliah against Judah.)
16: 1 In the seventeenth year of **Pekah** son of Remaliah, Ahaz son of
16: 5 **Pekah** son of Remaliah king of Israel marched up to fight against
2Ch 28: 6 In one day **Pekah** son of Remaliah killed a hundred and twenty
Isa 7: 1 **Pekah** son of Remaliah king of Israel marched up to fight against

7221 פִּקֵּחַ *piqqēaḥ*, a. [2] [√ 7219]

see [1], sight [1]

Ex 4:11 him deaf or mute? Who gives him **sight** or makes him blind?
23: 8 for a bribe blinds *those who* **see** and twists the words of the

7222 פְּקַחְיָה *pᵉqaḥyâ*, n.pr.m. [3] [√ 7219 + 3378]

Pekahiah [2], Pekahiah's [1]

2Ki 15:22 with his fathers. And **Pekahiah** his son succeeded him as king.
15:23 **Pekahiah** son of Menahem became king of Israel in Samaria,
15:26 The other events of **Pekahiah's** reign, and all he did, are written in

7223 פְּקַח־קוֹחַ *pᵉqaḥ-qôaḥ*, n.[m.]. [0 / 1] [√ 7219; cf. 7751]

release from darkness [1]

Isa 61: 1 the captives and **release from darkness** for the prisoners,

7224 פָּקִיד pāqîd, n.m. [13] [√ 7212]

chief officer [3], in charge [3], commissioners [2], officer [2], deputy [1], direction [1], supervisors [1]

Ge 41:34 Let Pharaoh appoint **commissioners** over the land to take a fifth of
Jdg 9:28 Isn't he Jerub-Baal's son, and isn't Zebul his **deputy**? Serve the
2Ki 25:19 he took the officer **in charge** of the fighting men and five royal
2Ch 24:11 the royal secretary and the **officer** *of* the chief priest would come
31:13 Mahath and Benaiah were **supervisors** under Conaniah and Shimei
Ne 11:9 Joel son of Zicri was their **chief officer**, and Judah son of
11:14 128. Their **chief officer** was Zabdiel son of Haggedolim.
11:22 The **chief officer** *of* the Levites in Jerusalem was Uzzi son of Bani,
12:42 and Ezer. The choirs sang under the **direction** of Jezrahiah.
Est 2:3 Let the king appoint **commissioners** in every province of his realm
Jer 20:1 son of Immer, the chief **officer** in the temple of the LORD,
29:26 in place of Jehoiada to be **in charge** *of* the house of the LORD;
52:25 still in the city, he took the officer **in charge** of the fighting men,

7225 פְּקָעִים pᵉqāʿîm, n.m.pl. [3] [→ 7226]

gourds [3]

1Ki 6:18 of the temple was cedar, carved with **gourds** and open flowers.
7:24 Below the rim, **gourds** encircled it—ten to a cubit. The gourds
7:24 The **gourds** were cast in two rows in one piece with the Sea.

7226 פַּקֻּעֹת paqquʿōt, n.[f.]pl. [1] [√ 7225]

gourds [1]

2Ki 4:39 He gathered some of its **gourds** and filled the fold of his cloak.

7227 פֶּקֶר peqer, n.m. Not used in NIV/BHS

7228 פַּר par, n.m. [133 / 132] [→ 7239]

bull [47], bulls [30], bull [+1330] [27], bull's [9], bulls [+1330] [5], *untranslated* [3], young bulls [3], it[s] [+2021] [2], its[s] [+2021] [2], bull calves [1], its[s] [1], one[s] [1], oxen [1]

Ge 32:15 [32:16] forty cows and ten **bulls**, and twenty female donkeys
Ex 24:5 and sacrificed **young bulls** as fellowship offerings to the LORD.
29:1 as priests: Take a young **bull** [+1330] and two rams without defect.
29:3 and present them in it—along with the **bull** and the two rams.
29:10 "Bring the **bull** to the front of the Tent of Meeting, and Aaron
29:10 and Aaron and his sons shall lay their hands on **its**[s] [+2021] head.
29:11 Slaughter **it**[s] [+2021] in the LORD's presence at the entrance to
29:12 Take some of the **bull's** blood and put it on the horns of the altar
29:14 But burn the **bull's** flesh and its hide and its offal outside the camp.
29:36 Sacrifice a **bull** each day as a sin offering to make atonement.
Lev 4:3 he must bring to the LORD a young **bull** [+1330] without defect
4:4 He is to present the **bull** at the entrance to the Tent of Meeting
4:4 He is to lay his hand on **its**[s] [+2021] head and slaughter it before
4:4 his hand on its head and slaughter **it**[s] [+2021] before the LORD.
4:5 Then the anointed priest shall take some of the **bull's** blood
4:7 The rest of the **bull's** blood he shall pour out at the base of the altar
4:8 He shall remove all the fat from the **bull** *of* the sin offering—
4:11 But the hide of the **bull** and all its flesh, as well as the head
4:12 that is, all the rest of the **bull**—he must take outside the camp to a
4:14 the assembly must bring a young **bull** [+1330] as a sin offering
4:15 The elders of the community are to lay their hands on the **bull's**
4:15 the LORD, and the **bull** shall be slaughtered before the LORD.
4:16 the anointed priest is to take some of the **bull's** blood into the Tent
4:20 do with this **bull** just as he did with the bull for the sin offering.
4:20 do with this bull just as he did with the **bull** *for* the sin offering.
4:21 he shall take the **bull** outside the camp and burn it as he burned the
4:21 the bull outside the camp and burn it as he burned the first **bull**.
8:2 the **bull** *for* the sin offering, the two rams and the basket
8:14 He then presented the **bull** *for* the sin offering, and Aaron
8:14 sin offering, and Aaron and his sons laid their hands on **its**[s] head.
8:17 the **bull** with its hide and its flesh and its offal he burned up
16:3 with a young **bull** [+1330] for a sin offering and a ram for a burnt
16:6 "Aaron is to offer the **bull** for his own sin offering to make
16:11 "Aaron shall bring the **bull** for his own sin offering to make
16:11 and he is to slaughter the **bull** for his own sin offering.
16:14 He is to take some of the **bull's** blood and with his finger sprinkle
16:15 behind the curtain and do with it as he did with the **bull's** blood:
16:18 He shall take some of the **bull's** blood and some of the goat's
16:27 The **bull** and the goat for the sin offerings, whose blood was
23:18 and without defect, one young **bull** [+1330] and two rams.
Nu 7:15 one young **bull** [+1330], one ram and one male lamb a year old,
7:21 one young **bull** [+1330], one ram and one male lamb a year old,
7:27 one young **bull** [+1330], one ram and one male lamb a year old,
7:33 one young **bull** [+1330], one ram and one male lamb a year old,
7:39 one young **bull** [+1330], one ram and one male lamb a year old,
7:45 one young **bull** [+1330], one ram and one male lamb a year old,
7:51 one young **bull** [+1330], one ram and one male lamb a year old,
7:57 one young **bull** [+1330], one ram and one male lamb a year old,
7:63 one young **bull** [+1330], one ram and one male lamb a year old,
7:69 one young **bull** [+1330], one ram and one male lamb a year old,
7:75 one young **bull** [+1330], one ram and one male lamb a year old,
7:81 one young **bull** [+1330], one ram and one male lamb a year old,
7:87 of animals for the burnt offering came to twelve **young bulls**,
7:88 the sacrifice of the fellowship offering came to twenty-four **oxen**,
8:8 Have them take a young **bull** [+1330] with its grain offering of fine
8:8 then you are to take a second young **bull** [+1330] for a sin offering.
8:12 "After the Levites lay their hands on the heads of the **bulls**,
15:24 the whole community is to offer a young **bull** [+1330] for a burnt
23:1 seven altars here, and prepare seven **bulls** and seven rams for me."
23:2 and the two of them offered a **bull** and a ram on each altar.
23:4 seven altars, and on each altar I have offered a **bull** and a ram."
23:14 he built seven altars and offered a **bull** and a ram on each altar.
23:29 seven altars here, and prepare seven **bulls** and seven rams for me."
23:30 did as Balaam had said, and offered a **bull** and a ram on each altar.
28:11 present to the LORD a burnt offering of two young **bulls** [+1330],
28:12 With each **bull** there is to be a grain offering of three-tenths of an
28:14 With each **bull** there is to be a drink offering of half a hin of wine;
28:19 a burnt offering of two young **bulls** [+1330], one ram and seven
28:20 With each **bull** prepare a grain offering of three-tenths of an ephah
28:27 Present a burnt offering of two young **bulls** [+1330], one ram
28:28 With each **bull** there is to be a grain offering of three-tenths of an
29:2 prepare a burnt offering of one young **bull** [+1330], one ram an
29:3 With the **bull** prepare a grain offering of three-tenths of an ephah
29:8 pleasing to the LORD a burnt offering of one young **bull** [+1330],
29:9 With the **bull** prepare a grain offering of three-tenths of an ephah
29:13 a burnt offering of thirteen young **bulls** [+1330], two rams
29:14 With each of the thirteen **bulls** prepare a grain offering of
29:14 With each of the thirteen bulls **[RPH]** prepare a grain offering of
29:17 " 'On the second day prepare twelve young **bulls** [+1330],
29:18 With the **bulls**, rams and lambs, prepare their grain offerings
29:20 " 'On the third day prepare eleven **bulls**, two rams and fourteen
29:21 With the **bulls**, rams and lambs, prepare their grain offerings
29:23 " 'On the fourth day prepare ten **bulls**, two rams and fourteen male
29:24 With the **bulls**, rams and lambs, prepare their grain offerings
29:26 " 'On the fifth day prepare nine **bulls**, two rams and fourteen male
29:27 With the **bulls**, rams and lambs, prepare their grain offerings
29:29 " 'On the sixth day prepare eight **bulls**, two rams and fourteen male
29:30 With the **bulls**, rams and lambs, prepare their grain offerings
29:32 " 'On the seventh day prepare seven **bulls**, two rams and fourteen
29:33 With the **bulls**, rams and lambs, prepare their grain offerings
29:36 a burnt offering of one **bull**, one ram and seven male lambs a year
29:37 With the **bull**, the ram and the lambs, prepare their grain offerings
Jdg 6:25 "Take the second **bull** from your father's herd, the one seven years
6:25 the second bull from your father's herd, the **one**[s] seven years old.
6:26 pole that you cut down, offer the second **bull** as a burnt offering."
6:28 it cut down and the second **bull** sacrificed on the newly built altar!
1Sa 1:24 young as he was, along with a three-year-old **bull**, an ephah of
1:25 When they had slaughtered the **bull**, they brought the boy to Eli,
1Ki 18:23 Get two **bulls** for us. Let them choose one for themselves,
18:23 Let them choose one **[RPH]** for themselves, and let them cut it
18:23 I will prepare the other **bull** and put it on the wood but not set fire
18:25 "Choose one of the **bulls** and prepare it first, since there are
18:26 So they took the **bull** given them and prepared it. Then they called
18:33 arranged the wood, cut the **bull** into pieces and laid it on the wood.
1Ch 15:26 of the LORD, seven **bulls** and seven rams were sacrificed.
29:21 a thousand **bulls**, a thousand rams and a thousand male lambs,
2Ch 13:9 Whoever comes to consecrate himself with a **[RPH]** young bull
29:21 They brought seven **bulls**, seven rams, seven male lambs
30:24 Hezekiah king of Judah provided a thousand **bulls** and seven
30:24 the officials provided them with a thousand **bulls** and ten thousand
Ezr 8:35 twelve **bulls** for all Israel, ninety-six rams, seventy-seven male
Job 42:8 So now take seven **bulls** and seven rams and go to my servant Job
Ps 22:12 [22:13] Many **bulls** surround me; strong bulls of Bashan encircle
50:9 I have no need of a **bull** from your stall or of goats from your pens,
51:19 [51:21] to delight you; then **bulls** will be offered on your altar.
69:31 [69:32] than an ox, more than a **bull** with its horns and hoofs.
Isa 1:11 I have no pleasure in the blood of **bulls** and lambs and goats.
34:7 wild oxen will fall with them, the **bull calves** and the great bulls.
Jer 50:27 Kill all her **young bulls**; let them go down to the slaughter!
Eze 39:18 of the earth as if they were rams and lambs, goats and **bulls**—
43:19 You are to give a young **bull** [+1330] as a sin offering to the
43:21 You are to take the **bull** *for* the sin offering and burn it in the
43:22 and the altar is to be purified as it was purified with the **bull**.
43:23 you are to offer a young **bull** [+1330] and a ram from the flock,
43:25 you are also to provide a young **bull** [+1330] and a ram from the
45:18 on the first day you are to take a young **bull** [+1330] without defect
45:22 On that day the prince is to provide a **bull** as a sin offering for
45:23 day during the seven days of the Feast he is to provide seven **bulls**
45:24 He is to provide as a grain offering an ephah for each **bull**
46:6 On the day of the New Moon he is to offer a young **bull** [+1330],
46:7 He is to provide as a grain offering one ephah with the **bull**,

Eze 46: 11 the grain offering is to be an ephah with a **bull**, an ephah with a
Hos 14: 2 [14:3] offer the fruit [BHS *bulls*; NIV 7262] *of* our lips.

7229 פָּרָא pārā', v. [1] [cf. 7238]

thrives [1]

Hos 13: 15 [G] even though he **thrives** among his brothers. An east wind

7230 פֶּרֶא pere', n.m. *or* f. [9] [→ 7000?, 7231; cf. 7241]

wild donkey [4], wild donkeys [3], donkeys [1], wild donkey's [1]

Ge 16: 12 He will be a **wild donkey** of a man; his hand will be against
Job 6: 5 Does a **wild donkey** bray when it has grass, or an ox bellow when
11: 12 a witless man can no more become wise than a **wild donkey's** colt
24: 5 Like **wild donkeys** in the desert, the poor go about their labor of
39: 5 "Who let the **wild donkey** go free? Who untied his ropes?
Ps 104: 11 to all the beasts of the field; the **wild donkeys** quench their thirst.
Isa 32: 14 a wasteland forever, the delight of **donkeys**, a pasture for flocks,
Jer 14: 6 **Wild donkeys** stand on the barren heights and pant like jackals;
Hos 8: 9 For they have gone up to Assyria like a **wild donkey** wandering

7231 פִּרְאָם pir'ām, n.pr.m. [1] [√ 7230]

Piram [1]

Jos 10: 3 **Piram** king of Jarmuth, Japhia king of Lachish and Debir king of

7232 פַּרְבָּר parbār, n.[m.]. [2] [cf. 7247]

court [2]

1Ch 26: 18 As for the **court** to the west, there were four at the road and two at
26: 18 to the west, there were four at the road and two at the **court** itself.

7233 פָּרַד pārad, v. [26] [→ 7234, 7235, 7237]

separates [3], spread out [3], are scattered [1], be parted [1], be scattered [1], be separated [1], consort [1], deserts [1], divided [1], keeps apart [1], left [1], out of joint [1], part company [1], parted company [1], parted [1], scattered [1], separated [+1068] [1], separated [1], set apart by themselves [1], unfriendly [1], was separated [1], were parted [1]

Ge 2: 10 [C] from there *it* **was separated** into four headwaters.
10: 5 [C] (From these the maritime peoples **spread out** into their
10: 32 [C] From these the nations **spread out** over the earth after the
13: 9 [C] *Let's* **part company**. If you go to the left, I'll go to the right;
13: 11 [C] and set out toward the east. The two men **parted company**:
13: 14 [C] The LORD said to Abram after Lot *had* **parted** from him,
25: 23 [C] and two peoples from within you *will* **be separated**;
30: 40 [G] Jacob **set apart** the young of the flock **by themselves**,
Dt 32: 8 [G] the nations their inheritance, when he **divided** all mankind,
Jdg 4: 11 [C] Now Heber the Kenite *had* **left** the other Kenites,
Ru 1: 17 [G] so severely, if anything but death **separates** you and me."
2Sa 1: 23 [C] were loved and gracious, and in death they **were** not **parted**.
2Ki 2: 11 [G] of fire appeared and **separated** [+1068] the two of them,
Ne 4: 19 [4:13] [C] we *are* widely **separated** from each other along the
Est 3: 8 [E] **scattered** among the peoples in all the provinces of your
Job 4: 11 [F] for lack of prey, and the cubs of the lioness **are scattered**.
41: 17 [41:9] [F] they cling together and cannot **be parted**.
Ps 22: 14 [22:15] [F] out like water, and all my bones *are* **out of joint**.
92: 9 [92:10] [F] enemies will perish; all evildoers *will* **be scattered**.
Pr 16: 28 [G] man stirs up dissension, and a gossip **separates** close friends.
17: 9 [G] but whoever repeats the matter **separates** close friends.
18: 1 [C] An **unfriendly** *man* pursues selfish ends; he defies all sound
18: 18 [G] the lot settles disputes and **keeps** strong opponents **apart**.
19: 4 [C] brings many friends, but a poor man's friend **deserts** him.
Eze 1: 11 [B] Their wings *were* **spread out** upward; each had two wings,
Hos 4: 14 [D] because the men themselves **consort** with harlots

7234 פֶּרֶד pered, n.m. [14 / 15] [→ 7235; cf. 7233]

mules [11], mule [4]

2Sa 13: 29 Then all the king's sons got up, mounted their **mules** and fled.
18: 9 He was riding his **mule**, and as the mule went under the thick
18: 9 and as the **mule** went under the thick branches of a large oak,
18: 9 left hanging in midair, while the **mule** he was riding kept on going.
1Ki 10: 25 and gold, robes, weapons and spices, and horses and **mules**.
18: 5 and **mules** alive so we will not have to kill any of our animals."
2Ki 5: 17 your servant, be given as much earth as a pair of **mules** can carry,
1Ch 12: 40 [12:41] came bringing food on donkeys, camels, **mules** and oxen.
2Ch 9: 24 and gold, and robes, weapons and spices, and horses and **mules**.
Ezr 2: 66 They had 736 horses, 245 **mules**,
Ne 7: 68 [7:67] There were 736 horses, 245 **mules**, [BHS-]
Ps 32: 9 Do not be like the horse or the **mule**, which have no understanding
Isa 66: 20 on horses, in chariots and wagons, and on **mules** and camels,"
Eze 27: 14 work horses, war horses and **mules** for your merchandise.
Zec 14: 15 A similar plague will strike the horses and **mules**, the camels

7235 פִּרְדָּה pirdâ, n.f. [3] [√ 7234]

mule [3]

1Ki 1: 33 set Solomon my son on my own **mule** and take him down to
1: 38 put Solomon on King David's **mule** and escorted him to Gihon.
1: 44 and the Pelethites, and they have put him on the king's **mule**,

7236 פַּרְדֵּס pardēs, n.[m.]. [3]

forest [1], orchard [1], parks [1]

Ne 2: 8 And may I have a letter to Asaph, keeper of the king's **forest**,
Ecc 2: 5 I made gardens and **parks** and planted all kinds of fruit trees in
SS 4: 13 Your plants are an **orchard** *of* pomegranates with choice fruits,

7237 פְּרֻדֹת p^e^rudōt, n.f. [1] [√ 7233]

seeds [1]

Joel 1: 17 The **seeds** are shriveled beneath the clods. The storehouses are in

7238 פָּרָה pārâ¹, v. [29] [→ 713?, 7242, 7262, 7311; cf. 7229]

fruitful [14], make fruitful [5], fruitful vine [+1201] [2], made fruitful [2], bear fruit [1], flourish [1], increased [1], numbers increased greatly [+2256+8049] [1], produces [1], spring up [1]

Ge 1: 22 [A] "*Be* **fruitful** and increase in number and fill the water in the
1: 28 [A] and said to them, "*Be* **fruitful** and increase in number;
8: 17 [A] on the earth and *be* **fruitful** and increase in number upon it."
9: 1 [A] "*Be* **fruitful** and increase in number and fill the earth.
9: 7 [A] As for you, *be* **fruitful** and increase in number; multiply on
17: 6 [G] *I will* **make** you very **fruitful**; I will make nations of you,
17: 20 [G] *I will* **make** him **fruitful** and will greatly increase his
26: 22 [A] LORD has given us room and *we will* **flourish** in the land."
28: 3 [G] May God Almighty bless you and **make** you **fruitful**
35: 11 [A] "I am God Almighty; *be* **fruitful** and increase in number.
41: 52 [G] because God *has* **made** me **fruitful** in the land of my
47: 27 [A] They acquired property there and *were* **fruitful**
48: 4 [G] 'I *am going to* **make** you **fruitful** and will increase your
49: 22 [A] "Joseph is a **fruitful** [+1201] **vine**, a fruitful vine near a
49: 22 [A] is a fruitful vine, a **fruitful** [+1201] **vine** near a spring,
Ex 1: 7 [A] the Israelites *were* **fruitful** and multiplied greatly
23: 30 [A] until *you have* **increased** *enough* to take possession of the
Lev 26: 9 [G] and **make** you **fruitful** and increase your numbers,
Dt 29: 18 [29:17] [A] sure there is no root among you *that* **produces**
Ps 105: 24 [G] The LORD **made** his people very **fruitful**; he made them
128: 3 [A] Your wife *will be* like a **fruitful** vine within your house;
Isa 11: 1 [A] the stump of Jesse; from his roots a Branch *will* **bear fruit**.
17: 6 [A] four or five on the **fruitful** boughs," declares the LORD,
32: 12 [A] your breasts for the pleasant fields, for the **fruitful** vines
45: 8 [A] Let the earth open wide, *let* salvation **spring up**, let
Jer 3: 16 [A] when *your* **numbers** *have* **increased greatly** [+2256+8049]
23: 3 [A] where *they will be* **fruitful** and increase in number.
Eze 19: 10 [A] it was **fruitful** and full of branches because of abundant
36: 11 [A] upon you, and *they will be* **fruitful** and become numerous.

7239 ²פָּרָה pārâ², n.f. [26] [√ 7228]

cows [18], heifer [6], cow [1], those[s] [+2021] [1]

Ge 32: 15 [32:16] forty **cows** and ten bulls, and twenty female donkeys
41: 2 when out of the river there came up seven **cows**, sleek and fat,
41: 3 After them, seven other **cows**, ugly and gaunt, came up out of the
41: 3 out of the Nile and stood beside **those**[s] [+2021] on the riverbank.
41: 4 And the **cows** that were ugly and gaunt ate up the seven sleek,
41: 4 the cows that were ugly and gaunt ate up the seven sleek, fat **cows**.
41: 18 when out of the river there came up seven **cows**, fat and sleek,
41: 19 After them, seven other **cows** came up—scrawny and very ugly
41: 20 The lean, ugly **cows** ate up the seven fat cows that came up first.
41: 20 The lean, ugly cows ate up the seven fat **cows** that came up first.
41: 26 The seven good **cows** are seven years, and the seven good heads of
41: 27 ugly **cows** that came up afterward are seven years, and so are the
Nu 19: 2 Tell the Israelites to bring you a red **heifer** without defect
19: 5 While he watches, the **heifer** is to be burned—its hide, flesh,
19: 6 hyssop and scarlet wool and throw them onto the burning **heifer**.
19: 9 "A man who is clean shall gather up the ashes of the **heifer**
19: 10 The man who gathers up the ashes of the **heifer** must also wash his
1Sa 6: 7 with two **cows** that have calved and have never been yoked.
6: 7 Hitch the **cows** to the cart, but take their calves away and pen them
6: 10 They took two such **cows** and hitched them to the cart and penned
6: 12 the **cows** went straight up toward Beth Shemesh, keeping on the
6: 14 and sacrificed the **cows** as a burnt offering to the LORD.
Job 21: 10 bulls never fail to breed; their **cows** calve and do not miscarry.
Isa 11: 7 The **cow** will feed with the bear, their young will lie down
Hos 4: 16 The Israelites are stubborn, like a stubborn **heifer**. How then can
Am 4: 1 Hear this word, you **cows** *of* Bashan on Mount Samaria,

7240 ³פָּרָה **pārâ³**, n.pr.loc. [1]

Parah [1]

Jos 18:23 Avvim, **Parah**, Ophrah,

7241 פֶּרֶה **pereh**, n.m. [1] [cf. 7230]

wild donkey [1]

Jer 2:24 a **wild donkey** accustomed to the desert, sniffing the wind in her

7242 פֻּרָה **purâ**, n.pr.m. [2] [√ 7238]

Purah [2]

Jdg 7:10 are afraid to attack, go down to the camp with your servant **Purah**
7:11 and **Purah** his servant went down to the outposts of the camp.

7243 פְּרוּדָא **perûdā'**, n.pr.m. [1] [cf. 7263]

Peruda [1]

Ezr 2:55 of Solomon: the descendants of Sotai, Hassophereth, **Peruda**,

7244 פְּרוֹזִים **perôzîm**, n.[m.]. [0] [√ 7253; cf. 7252]

Est 9:19 [That is why **rural** [K; see Q 7253] Jews—those living in]

7245 פָּרוּחַ **pārûaḥ**, n.pr.m. [1] [√ 7255]

Paruah [1]

1Ki 4:17 Jehoshaphat son of **Paruah**—in Issachar;

7246 פַּרְוַיִם **parwayim**, n.pr.loc. [1]

Parvaim [1]

2Ch 3:6 with precious stones. And the gold he used was gold of **Parvaim**.

7247 פַּרְוָר **parwār**, n.[m.]. [1] [cf. 7232]

court [1]

2Ki 23:11 They were in the **court** near the room of an official named

7248 פָּרוּר **pārûr**, n.[m.]. [3] [→ 6999]

pot [3]

Nu 11:8 it in a mortar. They cooked it in a **pot** or made it into cakes.
Jdg 6:19 Putting the meat in a basket and its broth in a **pot**, he brought them
1Sa 2:14 He would plunge it into the pan or kettle or caldron or **pot**,

7249 פֵּרוֹת **pērôt**, n.f. [1 / 0] [√ 2916]

Isa 2:20 throw away to the rodents [BHS ***rodents*** ?; NIV 2923] and bats

7250 פָּרָז **pārāz**, n.[m.]. [1]

warriors [1]

Hab 3:14 With his own spear you pierced his head when his **warriors**

7251 פְּרָזוֹן **perāzôn**, n.[m.]. [2] [√ 7252]

village life [1], warriors [1]

Jdg 5:7 **Village life** in Israel ceased, ceased until I, Deborah, arose,
5:11 acts of the LORD, the righteous acts of his **warriors** in Israel.

7252 פְּרָזוֹת **perāzôt**, n.f.[pl.]. [3] [→ 7244, 7251, 7253, 7254]

city without walls [1], unwalled villages [1], villages [+6551] [1]

Est 9:19 That is why rural Jews—those living in **villages** [+6551]—
Eze 38:11 You will say, "I will invade a land of **unwalled villages**; I will
Zec 2:4 [2:8] 'Jerusalem will be a **city without walls** because of the great

7253 פְּרָזִי **perāzî**, n.[m.]. [3] [√ 7244; cf. 7252]

country [1], rural [1], unwalled [1]

Dt 3:5 and bars, and there were also a great many **unwalled** villages.
1Sa 6:18 to the five rulers—the fortified towns with their **country** villages.
Est 9:19 That is why **rural** [K 7244] Jews—those living in villages—

7254 פְּרִזִּי **perizzî**, a.g. [23] [√ 7252]

Perizzites [23]

Ge 13:7 and **Perizzites** were also living in the land at that time.
15:20 Hittites, **Perizzites**, Rephaites,
34:30 on me by making me a stench to the Canaanites and **Perizzites**,
Ex 3:8 Hittites, Amorites, **Perizzites**, Hivites and Jebusites.
3:17 Hittites, Amorites, **Perizzites**, Hivites and Jebusites—
23:23 Hittites, **Perizzites**, Canaanites, Hivites and Jebusites, and I will
33:2 Amorites, Hittites, **Perizzites**, Hivites and Jebusites.
34:11 Canaanites, Hittites, **Perizzites**, Hivites and Jebusites.
Dt 7:1 Canaanites, **Perizzites**, Hivites and Jebusites,
20:17 Amorites, Canaanites, **Perizzites**, Hivites and Jebusites—
Jos 3:10 Hittites, Hivites, **Perizzites**, Girgashites, Amorites and Jebusites.
9:1 Amorites, Canaanites, **Perizzites**, Hivites and Jebusites)—
11:3 the Amorites, Hittites, **Perizzites** and Jebusites in the hill country;
12:8 Amorites, Canaanites, **Perizzites**, Hivites and Jebusites):
17:15 and clear land for yourselves there in the land of the **Perizzites**
24:11 **Perizzites**, Canaanites, Hittites, Girgashites, Hivites and Jebusites,
Jdg 1:4 the LORD gave the Canaanites and **Perizzites** into their hands
1:5 fought against him, putting to rout the Canaanites and **Perizzites**.
3:5 Hittites, Amorites, **Perizzites**, Hivites and Jebusites.
1Ki 9:20 **Perizzites**, Hivites and Jebusites (these peoples were not
2Ch 8:7 **Perizzites**, Hivites and Jebusites (these peoples were not
Ezr 9:1 Hittites, **Perizzites**, Jebusites, Ammonites, Moabites, Egyptians
Ne 9:8 Amorites, **Perizzites**, Jebusites and Girgashites.

7255 ¹פָּרַח **pāraḥ¹**, v. [34] [→ 7245, 7258, 7259?; cf. 7257]

flourish [5], blossom [4], broken out [3], budded [3], breaks out all over [+928+7255] [2], bud [2], burst into bloom [+7255] [2], spring up [2], blossomed [1], break out [1], breaking out [1], bring to bud [1], broke out [1], make flourish [1], reappears [+2256+8740] [1], spreading [1], sprout [1], sprouted [1], thrive [1]

Ge 40:10 [A] As soon as it **budded**, it blossomed, and its clusters ripened
Ex 9:9 [A] festering boils will **break out** on men and animals
9:10 [A] the air, and festering boils **broke out** on men and animals.
Lev 13:12 [A] "If the disease **breaks** [+928+7255] **out all over** his skin
13:12 [A] "If the disease **breaks out all over** [+928+7255] his skin
13:20 [A] It is an infectious skin disease *that has* **broken out** where
13:25 [A] it is an infectious disease *that has* **broken out** in the burn.
13:39 [A] it is a harmless rash *that has* **broken out** on the skin;
13:42 [A] it is an infectious disease **breaking out** on his head
13:57 [A] or knitted material, or in the leather article, it *is* **spreading**,
14:43 [A] "If the mildew **reappears** [+2256+8740] in the house after the
Nu 17:5 [17:20] [A] The staff belonging to the man I choose *will* **sprout**,
17:8 [17:23] [A] *had* not only **sprouted** but had budded, blossomed
Job 14:9 [G] yet at the scent of water *it will* **bud** and put forth shoots like
Ps 72:7 [A] In his days the righteous *will* **flourish**; prosperity will
92:7 [92:8] [A] that though the wicked **spring up** like grass and all
92:12 [92:13] [A] The righteous *will* **flourish** like a palm tree,
92:13 [92:14] [G] *they will* **flourish** in the courts of our God.
Pr 11:28 [A] riches will fall, but the righteous *will* **thrive** like a green leaf.
14:11 [G] will be destroyed, but the tent of the upright *will* **flourish**.
SS 6:11 [A] to see if the vines *had* **budded** or the pomegranates were in
7:12 [7:13] [A] to the vineyards to see if the vines *have* **budded**,
Isa 17:11 [G] the morning when you plant them, *you* **bring** them **to bud**,
27:6 [A] Israel will bud and **blossom** and fill all the world with fruit.
35:1 [A] land will be glad; the wilderness will rejoice and **blossom**.
35:2 [A] *it will* **burst into bloom** [+7255]; it will rejoice greatly and
35:2 [A] *it will* **burst into bloom** [+7255]; it will rejoice greatly and
66:14 [A] your heart will rejoice and you *will* **flourish** like grass;
Eze 7:10 [A] burst forth, the rod has budded, arrogance *has* **blossomed**!
17:24 [G] I dry up the green tree and **make** the dry tree **flourish**.
Hos 10:4 [A] therefore lawsuits **spring up** like poisonous weeds in a
14:5 [14:6] [A] be like the dew to Israel; *he will* **blossom** like a lily.
14:7 [14:8] [A] *He will* **blossom** like a vine, and his fame will be like
Hab 3:17 [A] Though the fig tree *does* not **bud** and there are no grapes on

7256 ²פָּרַח **pāraḥ²**, v. [2] [→ 711]

birds [2]

Eze 13:20 [A] your magic charms with which you ensnare people like **birds**
13:20 [A] I will set free the people that you ensnare like **birds**.

7257 ³פָּרַח **pāraḥ³**, v. Not used in NIV/BHS [cf. 7255]

7258 פֶּרַח **peraḥ**, n.m. [17] [√ 7255]

blossoms [8], blossom [3], *untranslated* [2], floral work [2], budded [+3655] [1], flowers [1]

Ex 25:31 flowerlike cups, buds and **blossoms** shall be of one piece with it.
25:33 almond flowers with buds and **blossoms** are to be on one branch,
25:33 **[RPH]** and the same for all six branches extending from the
25:34 be four cups shaped like almond flowers with buds and **blossoms**.
37:17 its flowerlike cups, buds and **blossoms** were of one piece with it.
37:19 like almond flowers with buds and **blossoms** were on one branch,
37:19 three **[RPH]** on the next branch and the same for all six branches
37:20 four cups shaped like almond flowers with buds and **blossoms**.
Nu 8:4 It was made of hammered gold—from its base to its **blossoms**.
17:8 [17:23] had not only sprouted but *had* **budded** [+3655],
1Ki 7:26 and its rim was like the rim of a cup, like a lily **blossom**.
7:49 of the inner sanctuary); the gold **floral work** and lamps and tongs;
2Ch 4:5 and its rim was like the rim of a cup, like a lily **blossom**.
4:21 the gold **floral work** and lamps and tongs (they were solid gold);
Isa 5:24 so their roots will decay and their **flowers** blow away like dust;
18:5 when the **blossom** is gone and the flower becomes a ripening

Na 1: 4 Bashan and Carmel wither and the **blossoms** *of* Lebanon fade.

7259 פִּרְחָה *pirḥaḥ*, n.m.col. [1] [√ 7255?]

tribe [1]

Job 30: 12 On my right the **tribe** attacks; they lay snares for my feet,

7260 פָּרַט *pāraṭ*, v. [1] [→ 7261?]

strum away [1]

Am 6: 5 [A] *You* **strum away** on your harps like David and improvise on

7261 פֶּרֶט *pereṭ*, n.[m.]col. [1] [√ 7260?]

grapes that have fallen [1]

Lev 19: 10 vineyard a second time or pick up the **grapes that have fallen**.

7262 פְּרִי *p[e]rî*, n.m. [119 / 120] [√ 7238]

fruit [80], crops [7], produce [4], young [4], fruits [3], deserve [2], firstfruits [+8040] [2], fruitful [2], *untranslated* [1], children [+1061] [1], children [+1061+2021] [1], crops [+141+2021] [1], descendants [+1061] [1], descendants [1], earnings [+4090] [1], fruitage [1], fruitfulness [1], infants [+1061] [1], offspring [1], result [1], reward earned [+3338] [1], rewarded [1], what deserve [1], willful pride [+1542] [1]

Ge 1: 11 and trees **[RPH]** on the land that bear fruit with seed in it,
1: 11 and trees on the land that bear **fruit** with seed in it,
1: 12 and trees bearing **fruit** with seed in it according to their kinds.
1: 29 face of the whole earth and every tree that has **fruit** with seed in it.
3: 2 said to the serpent, "We may eat **fruit** from the trees in the garden,
3: 3 'You must not eat **fruit** from the tree that is in the middle of the
3: 6 When the woman saw that the **fruit** of the tree was good for food
4: 3 In the course of time Cain brought some of the **fruits** *of* the soil as
30: 2 place of God, who has kept you from *having* **children** [+1061]?"
Ex 10: 15 everything growing in the fields and the **fruit** *on* the trees.
Lev 19: 23 and plant any kind of fruit tree, regard its **fruit** as forbidden.
19: 24 In the fourth year all its **fruit** will be holy, an offering of praise to
19: 25 in the fifth year you may eat its **fruit**. In this way your harvest will
23: 40 On the first day you are to take choice **fruit** *from* the trees,
25: 19 Then the land will yield its **fruit**, and you will eat your fill
26: 4 the ground will yield its crops and the trees of the field their **fruit**.
26: 20 not yield its crops, nor will the trees of the land yield their **fruit**.
27: 30 whether grain from the soil or **fruit** *from* the trees, belongs to the
Nu 13: 20 Do your best to bring back some of the **fruit** *of* the land."
13: 26 and to the whole assembly and showed them the **fruit** *of* the land.
13: 27 you sent us, and it does flow with milk and honey! Here is its **fruit**.
Dt 1: 25 Taking with them some of the **fruit** *of* the land, they brought it
7: 13 He will bless the **fruit** *of* your womb, the crops of your land—
7: 13 He will bless the fruit of your womb, the **crops** *of* your land—
26: 2 take some of the **firstfruits of** [+8040] all that you produce from
26: 10 and now I bring the **firstfruits of** [+8040] the soil that you,
28: 4 The **fruit** *of* your womb will be blessed, and the crops of your land
28: 4 and the **crops** *of* your land and the young of your livestock—
28: 4 and the crops of your land and the **young** *of* your livestock—
28: 11 in the **fruit** *of* your womb, the young of your livestock and the
28: 11 the **young** *of* your livestock and the crops of your ground—
28: 11 the young of your livestock and the **crops** *of* your ground—
28: 18 The **fruit** *of* your womb will be cursed, and the crops of your land,
28: 18 the **crops** *of* your land, and the calves of your herds and the lambs
28: 33 that you do not know will eat what your land and labor **produce**,
28: 42 of locusts will take over all your trees and the **crops** *of* your land.
28: 51 They will devour the **young** *of* your livestock and the crops of your
28: 51 your livestock and the **crops** *of* your land until you are destroyed.
28: 53 you will eat the **fruit** *of* the womb, the flesh of the sons
30: 9 in all the work of your hands and in the **fruit** *of* your womb,
30: 9 the **young** *of* your livestock and the crops of your land.
30: 9 the young of your livestock and the **crops** *of* your land.
2Ki 19: 29 in the third year sow and reap, plant vineyards and eat their **fruit**.
19: 30 of the house of Judah will take root below and bear **fruit** above.
Ne 9: 36 so they could eat its **fruit** and the other good things it produces.
10: 35 [10:36] year the firstfruits of our crops and of every **fruit** tree.
10: 37 [10:38] of the **fruit** *of* all our trees and of our new wine and oil.
Ps 1: 3 which yields its **fruit** in season and whose leaf does not wither.
21: 10 [21:11] You will destroy their **descendants** from the earth, their
58: 11 [58:12] men will say, "Surely the righteous still are **rewarded**;
72: 16 Let its **fruit** flourish like Lebanon; let it thrive like the grass of the
104: 13 his upper chambers; the earth is satisfied by the **fruit** *of* his work.
105: 35 up every green thing in their land, ate up the **produce** *of* their soil.
107: 34 **fruitful** land into a salt waste, because of the wickedness of those
107: 37 sowed fields and planted vineyards that yielded a **fruitful** harvest;
127: 3 from the LORD, **children** [+1061+2021] a reward from him.
132: 11 "One of your own **descendants** [+1061] I will place on your
148: 9 you mountains and all hills, **fruit** trees and all cedars,
Pr 1: 31 they will eat the **fruit** *of* their ways and be filled with the fruit of
8: 19 My **fruit** is better than fine gold; what I yield surpasses choice
11: 30 The **fruit** *of* the righteous is a tree of life, and he who wins souls is
12: 14 From the **fruit** *of* his lips a man is filled with good things as surely
13: 2 From the **fruit** *of* his lips a man enjoys good things,
18: 20 From the **fruit** *of* his mouth a man's stomach is filled;
18: 21 the power of life and death, and those who love it will eat its **fruit**.
27: 18 He who tends a fig tree will eat its **fruit**, and he who looks after his
31: 16 and buys it; out of her **earnings** [+4090] she plants a vineyard.
31: 31 Give her the **reward** [+3338] she has **earned**, and let her works
Ecc 2: 5 and parks and planted all kinds of **fruit** trees in them.
SS 2: 3 I delight to sit in his shade, and his **fruit** is sweet to my taste.
4: 13 Your plants are an orchard of pomegranates with choice **fruits**,
4: 16 Let my lover come into his garden and taste its choice **fruits**.
8: 11 Each was to bring for its **fruit** a thousand shekels of silver.
8: 12 O Solomon, and two hundred are for those who tend its **fruit**.
Isa 3: 10 will be well with them, for they will enjoy the **fruit** *of* their deeds.
4: 2 the **fruit** *of* the land will be the pride and glory of the survivors in
10: 12 "I will punish the king of Assyria for the **willful pride of** [+1542]
13: 18 they will have no mercy on **infants** [+1061] nor will they look with
14: 29 will spring up a viper, its **fruit** will be a darting, venomous serpent.
27: 9 and this will be the full **fruitage** *of* the removal of his sin:
37: 30 in the third year sow and reap, plant vineyards and eat their **fruit**.
37: 31 of the house of Judah will take root below and bear **fruit** above.
65: 21 and dwell in them; they will plant vineyards and eat their **fruit**.
Jer 2: 7 I brought you into a fertile land to eat its **fruit** and rich produce.
6: 19 I am bringing disaster on this people, the **fruit** *of* their schemes,
7: 20 and beast, on the trees of the field and on the **fruit** *of* the ground,
11: 16 The LORD called you a thriving olive tree with **fruit** beautiful in
12: 2 planted them, and they have taken root; they grow and bear **fruit**.
17: 8 It has no worries in a year of drought and never fails to bear **fruit**."
17: 10 according to his conduct, according to **what** his deeds **deserve**."
21: 14 I will punish you as your deeds **deserve**, declares the LORD.
29: 5 and settle down; plant gardens and eat *what* they **produce**.
29: 28 and settle down; plant gardens and eat *what* they **produce**.' "
32: 19 everyone according to his conduct and as his deeds **deserve**.
La 2: 20 Should women eat their **offspring**, the children they have cared
Eze 17: 8 it would produce branches, bear **fruit** and become a splendid vine.'
17: 9 Will it not be uprooted and stripped of its **fruit** so that it withers?
17: 23 it will produce branches and bear **fruit** and become a splendid
19: 12 The east wind made it shrivel, it was stripped of its **fruit**; its strong
19: 14 Fire spread from one of its main branches and consumed its **fruit**.
25: 4 their tents among you; they will eat your **fruit** and drink your milk.
34: 27 The trees of the field will yield their **fruit** and the ground will yield
36: 8 of Israel, will produce branches and **fruit** for my people Israel,
36: 30 I will increase the **fruit** *of* the trees and the crops of the field,
47: 12 Their leaves will not wither, nor will their **fruit** fail. Every month
47: 12 Their **fruit** will serve for food and their leaves for healing."
Hos 9: 16 Ephraim is blighted, their root is withered, they yield no **fruit**.
10: 1 Israel was a spreading vine; he brought forth **fruit** for himself.
10: As his **fruit** increased, he built more altars; as his land prospered,
10: 13 you have reaped evil, you have eaten the **fruit** *of* deception.
14: 2 [14:3] that we may offer the **fruit** [BHS 7228] *of* our lips.
14: 8 [14:9] like a green pine tree; your **fruitfulness** comes from me."
Joel 2: 22 The trees are bearing their **fruit**; the fig tree and the vine yield their
Am 2: 9 strong as the oaks. I destroyed his **fruit** above and his roots below.
6: 12 justice into poison and the **fruit** *of* righteousness into bitterness—
9: 14 and drink their wine; they will make gardens and eat their **fruit**.
Mic 6: 7 for my transgression, the **fruit** *of* my body for the sin of my soul?
7: 13 because of its inhabitants, as the **result** *of* their deeds.
Zec 8: 12 "The seed will grow well, the vine will yield its **fruit**, the ground
Mal 3: 11 I will prevent pests from devouring your **crops** [+141+2021],

7263 פְּרִידָא *p[e]rîdā'*, n.pr.m. [1] [cf. 7243]

Perida [1]

Ne 7: 57 servants of Solomon: the descendants of Sotai, Sophereth, **Perida**,

7264 ¹פָּרִיץ *pāriṣ[1]*, n.m. [1] [√ 7287]

ferocious [1]

Isa 35: 9 No lion will be there, nor will any **ferocious** beast get up on it;

7265 ²פָּרִיץ *pāriṣ[2]*, n.m. [5] [√ 7287]

violent [3], robbers [2]

Ps 17: 4 word of your lips I have kept myself from the ways of the **violent**.
Jer 7: 11 which bears my Name, become a den of **robbers** to you?
Eze 7: 22 desecrate my treasured place; **robbers** will enter it and desecrate it.
18: 10 "Suppose he has a **violent** son, who sheds blood or does any of
Da 11: 14 The **violent** men *among* your own people will rebel in fulfillment

7266 פֶּרֶךְ *perek*, n.[m.]. [6]

ruthlessly [+928] [5], brutally [+928] [1]

Ex 1: 13 and worked them **ruthlessly** [+928].

Ex 1:14 in all their hard labor the Egyptians used them **ruthlessly** [+928].
Lev 25:43 Do not rule over them **ruthlessly** [+928], but fear your God.
25:46 but you must not rule over your fellow Israelites **ruthlessly** [+928].
25:53 see to it that his owner does not rule over him **ruthlessly** [+928].
Eze 34: 4 for the lost. You have ruled them harshly and **brutally** [+928].

7267 פָּרֹכֶת *pārōket*, n.f. [25]

curtain [25]

Ex 26:31 "Make a **curtain** *of* blue, purple and scarlet yarn and finely twisted
26:33 Hang the **curtain** from the clasps and place the ark of the
26:33 the clasps and place the ark of the Testimony behind the **curtain**.
26:33 The **curtain** will separate the Holy Place from the Most Holy
26:35 Place the table outside the **curtain** on the north side of the
27:21 outside the **curtain** that is in front of the Testimony, Aaron
30: 6 Put the altar in front of the **curtain** that is before the ark of the
35:12 its poles and the atonement cover and the **curtain** that shields it;
36:35 They made the **curtain** of blue, purple and scarlet yarn and finely
38:27 were used to cast the bases for the sanctuary and for the **curtain**—
39:34 the covering of hides of sea cows and the shielding **curtain**;
40: 3 the ark of the Testimony in it and shield the ark with the **curtain**.
40:21 hung the shielding **curtain** and shielded the ark of the Testimony,
40:22 of Meeting on the north side of the tabernacle outside the **curtain**
40:26 placed the gold altar in the Tent of Meeting in front of the **curtain**
Lev 4: 6 times before the LORD, in front of the **curtain** *of* the sanctuary.
4:17 sprinkle it before the LORD seven times in front of the **curtain**.
16: 2 behind the **curtain** in front of the atonement cover on the ark,
16:12 finely ground fragrant incense and take them behind the **curtain**.
16:15 take its blood behind the **curtain** and do with it as he did with the
21:23 he must not go near the **curtain** or approach the altar, and
24: 3 Outside the **curtain** *of* the Testimony in the Tent of Meeting,
Nu 4: 5 and his sons are to go in and take down the shielding **curtain**
18: 7 in connection with everything at the altar and inside the **curtain**.
2Ch 3:14 He made the **curtain** *of* blue, purple and crimson yarn and fine

7268 פָּרַם *pāram*, v. [3]

tear [2], torn [1]

Lev 10: 6 [A] *do* not **tear** your clothes, or you will die and the LORD will
13:45 [B] "The person with such an infectious disease must wear **torn**
21:10 [A] must not let his hair become unkempt or **tear** his clothes.

7269 פַּרְמַשְׁתָּא *parmaštā'*, n.pr.m. [1]

Parmashta [1]

Est 9: 9 **Parmashta**, Arisai, Aridai and Vaizatha,

7270 פַּרְנָךְ *parnāk*, n.pr.m. [1]

Parnach [1]

Nu 34:25 Elizaphan son of **Parnach**, the leader from the tribe of Zebulun;

7271 פָּרַס *pāras[1]*, v. [14] [→ 7272?, 7274; Ar 10592]

split [11], hoofs [1], offer food [1], share [1]

Lev 11: 3 [G] You may eat any animal *that has a* **split** hoof completely
11: 4 [G] are some that only chew the cud or only *have* a **split** hoof,
11: 4 [G] though it chews the cud, *does* not *have* a **split** hoof;
11: 5 [G] though it chews the cud, *does* not *have* a **split** hoof;
11: 6 [G] though it chews the cud, *does* not *have* a **split** hoof;
11: 7 [G] And the pig, though it *has* a **split** hoof completely divided,
11:26 [G] " 'Every animal that *has* a **split** hoof not completely divided
Dt 14: 6 [G] You may eat any animal that *has a* **split** hoof divided in two
14: 7 [G] or *that have* a **split** hoof completely divided you may not eat
14: 7 [G] Although they chew the cud, *they do* not *have a* **split** hoof;
14: 8 [G] although it *has a* **split** hoof, it does not chew the cud.
Ps 69:31 [69:32] [G] an ox, more than a bull with its horns and **hoofs**.
Isa 58: 7 [A] Is it not *to* **share** your food with the hungry and to provide
Jer 16: 7 [A] No *one will* **offer food** to comfort those who mourn for the

7272 פֶּרֶס *peres*, n.[m.]. [2] [√ 7271?]

vulture [2]

Lev 11:13 they are detestable: the eagle, the **vulture**, the black vulture,
Dt 14:12 these you may not eat: the eagle, the **vulture**, the black vulture,

7273 פָּרַס *pāras[2]*, n.pr.loc. [28] [→ 7275; Ar 10594, 10595]

Persia [26], Persian [2]

2Ch 36:20 to him and his sons until the kingdom of **Persia** came to power.
36:22 In the first year of Cyrus king of **Persia**, in order to fulfill the word
36:22 the LORD moved the heart of Cyrus king of **Persia** to make a
36:23 "This is what Cyrus king of **Persia** says: " 'The LORD, the God
Ezr 1: 1 In the first year of Cyrus king of **Persia**, in order to fulfill the word
1: 1 the LORD moved the heart of Cyrus king of **Persia** to make a
1: 2 "This is what Cyrus king of **Persia** says: " 'The LORD, the God
1: 8 Cyrus king of **Persia** had them brought by Mithredath the
3: 7 sea from Lebanon to Joppa, as authorized by Cyrus king of **Persia**.
4: 3 God of Israel, as King Cyrus, the king of **Persia**, commanded us."
4: 5 frustrate their plans during the entire reign of Cyrus king of **Persia**
4: 5 king of Persia and down to the reign of Darius king of **Persia**.
4: 7 in the days of Artaxerxes king of **Persia**, Bishlam, Mithredath,
7: 1 After these things, during the reign of Artaxerxes king of **Persia**,
9: 9 He has shown us kindness in the sight of the kings of **Persia**:
Est 1: 3 The military leaders of **Persia** and Media, the princes,
1:14 the seven nobles of **Persia** and Media who had special access to
1:18 This very day the **Persian** and Median women of the nobility who
1:19 a royal decree and let it be written in the laws of **Persia** and Media,
10: 2 written in the book of the annals of the kings of Media and **Persia**?
Eze 27:10 " 'Men of **Persia**, Lydia and Put served as soldiers in your army.
38: 5 **Persia**, Cush and Put will be with them, all with shields
Da 8:20 ram that you saw represents the kings of Media and **Persia**.
10: 1 In the third year of Cyrus king of **Persia**, a revelation was given to
10:13 the prince of the **Persian** kingdom resisted me twenty-one days.
10:13 to help me, because I was detained there with the king of **Persia**.
10:20 Soon I will return to fight against the prince of **Persia**, and when I
11: 2 Three more kings will appear in **Persia**, and then a fourth,

7274 פַּרְסָה *parsâ*, n.f. [21] [√ 7271]

hoof [12], hoofs [6], *untranslated* [3]

Ex 10:26 Our livestock too must go with us; not a **hoof** is to be left behind.
Lev 11: 3 You may eat any animal that has a split **hoof** completely divided
11: 3 a split hoof completely divided **[RPH]** and that chews the cud.
11: 4 " 'There are some that only chew the cud or only have a split **hoof**,
11: 4 The camel, though it chews the cud, does not have a split **hoof**;
11: 5 The coney, though it chews the cud, does not have a split **hoof**;
11: 6 The rabbit, though it chews the cud, does not have a split **hoof**;
11: 7 And the pig, though it has a split **hoof** completely divided,
11: 7 a split hoof completely divided, **[RPH]** does not chew the cud;
11:26 " 'Every animal that has a split **hoof** not completely divided
Dt 14: 6 You may eat any animal that has a split **hoof** divided in two
14: 6 that has a split hoof divided in two **[RPH]** and that chews the cud.
14: 7 or that have a split **hoof** completely divided you may not eat the
14: 7 Although they chew the cud, they do not have a split **hoof**;
14: 8 also unclean; although it has a split **hoof**, it does not chew the cud.
Isa 5:28 their horses' **hoofs** seem like flint, their chariot wheels like a
Jer 47: 3 at the sound of the **hoofs** *of* galloping steeds, at the noise of enemy
Eze 26:11 The **hoofs** *of* his horses will trample all your streets; he will kill
32:13 to be stirred by the foot of man or muddied by the **hoofs** *of* cattle.
Mic 4:13 I will give you **hoofs** *of* bronze and you will break to pieces many
Zec 11:16 but will eat the meat of the choice sheep, tearing off their **hoofs**.

7275 פַּרְסִי *pārsî*, a.g. [1] [√ 7273; Ar 10595]

Persian [1]

Ne 12:22 of the priests, were recorded in the reign of Darius the **Persian**.

7276 פָּרַע *pāra'[1]*, v.den. [1] [→ 7278; cf. 7277]

take the lead [1]

Jdg 5: 2 [A] "When the princes in Israel **take the lead**, when the people

7277 פָּרַע *pāra'[2]*, v. [15] [cf. 7276]

unkempt [3], ignores [2], avoid [1], cast off restraint [1], get out of control [1], hold back [1], ignore [1], ignored [1], loosen [1], promoted wickedness [1], running wild [1], taking away [1]

Ex 5: 4 [G] why *are you* **taking** the people **away** from their labor?
32:25 [B] Moses saw that the people *were* **running wild** and that
32:25 [A] that Aaron *had let* them **get out of control** and so become a
Lev 10: 6 [A] and Ithamar, "*Do* not *let* your hair *become* **unkempt**,
13:45 [B] let his hair be **unkempt**, cover the lower part of his face
21:10 [A] *must* not *let* his hair *become* **unkempt** or tear his clothes.
Nu 5:18 [A] *he shall* **loosen** her hair and place in her hands the reminder
2Ch 28:19 [G] for *he had* **promoted wickedness** in Judah and had been
Pr 1:25 [A] since *you* **ignored** all my advice and would not accept my
4:15 [A] **Avoid** it, do not travel on it; turn from it and go on your way.
8:33 [A] Listen to my instruction and be wise; *do* not **ignore** it.
13:18 [A] *He who* **ignores** discipline comes to poverty and shame,
15:32 [A] *He who* **ignores** discipline despises himself, but whoever
29:18 [C] Where there is no revelation, the people **cast off restraint**;
Eze 24:14 [A] *I will* not **hold back**; I will not have pity, nor will I relent.

7278 פֶּרַע *pera'[1]*, n.[m.]. [2] [√ 7276; cf. 7279?]

leaders [1], princes [1]

Dt 32:42 of the slain and the captives, the heads of the enemy **leaders**."
Jdg 5: 2 "When the **princes** in Israel take the lead, when the people

7279 [2]פֶּרַע ***pera'***[2], n.[m.]. [2] [cf. 7278?]
hair [+8552] [1], hair long [1]

Nu 6: 5 is over; he must let the **hair of** [+8552] his head grow long.
Eze 44: 20 " 'They must not shave their heads or let their **hair** grow **long**,

7280 [3]פֶּרַע ***pera'***[3], n.pr.m. Not used in NIV/BHS [cf. 7036]

7281 פַּרְעֹה ***par'ōh***, n.m. [274]
Pharaoh [206], Pharaoh's [51], his[s] [5], he[s] [4], him[s] [2], Pharaoh's [+4200] [2], *untranslated* [1], royal [1], she[s] [+1426] [1], there[s] [+1074] [1]

Ge 12: 15 when **Pharaoh's** officials saw her, they praised her to Pharaoh,
12: 15 they praised her to **Pharaoh**, and she was taken into his palace.
12: 15 they praised her to Pharaoh, and she was taken into **his**[s] palace.
12: 17 the LORD inflicted serious diseases on **Pharaoh** and his
12: 18 So **Pharaoh** summoned Abram. "What have you done to me?"
12: 20 **Pharaoh** gave orders about Abram to his men, and they sent him
37: 36 to Potiphar, one of **Pharaoh's** officials, the captain of the guard.
39: 1 Potiphar, an Egyptian who was one of **Pharaoh's** officials,
40: 2 **Pharaoh** was angry with his two officials, the chief cupbearer
40: 7 So he asked **Pharaoh's** officials who were in custody with him in
40: 11 **Pharaoh's** cup was in my hand, and I took the grapes, squeezed
40: 11 squeezed them into **Pharaoh's** cup and put the cup in his hand."
40: 11 squeezed them into Pharaoh's cup and put the cup in **his**[s] hand."
40: 13 Within three days **Pharaoh** will lift up your head and restore you
40: 13 you to your position, and you will put **Pharaoh's** cup in his hand,
40: 14 mention me to **Pharaoh** and get me out of this prison.
40: 17 In the top basket were all kinds of baked goods for **Pharaoh**,
40: 19 Within three days **Pharaoh** will lift off your head and hang you on
40: 20 Now the third day was **Pharaoh's** birthday, and he gave a feast for
40: 21 so that he once again put the cup into **Pharaoh's** hand,
41: 1 When two full years had passed, **Pharaoh** had a dream: He was
41: 4 gaunt ate up the seven sleek, fat cows. Then **Pharaoh** woke up.
41: 7 full heads. Then **Pharaoh** woke up; it had been a dream.
41: 8 **Pharaoh** told them his dreams, but no one could interpret them for
41: 8 told them his dreams, but no one could interpret them for **him**[s].
41: 9 the chief cupbearer said to **Pharaoh**, "Today I am reminded of my
41: 10 **Pharaoh** was once angry with his servants, and he imprisoned me
41: 14 So **Pharaoh** sent for Joseph, and he was quickly brought from the
41: 14 he had shaved and changed his clothes, he came before **Pharaoh**.
41: 15 **Pharaoh** said to Joseph, "I had a dream, and no one can interpret
41: 16 "I cannot do it," Joseph replied to **Pharaoh**, "but God will give
41: 16 to Pharaoh, "but God will give **Pharaoh** the answer he desires."
41: 17 **Pharaoh** said to Joseph, "In my dream I was standing on the bank
41: 25 Then Joseph said to **Pharaoh**, "The dreams of Pharaoh are one
41: 25 said to Pharaoh, "The dreams of **Pharaoh** are one and the same.
41: 25 and the same. God has revealed to **Pharaoh** what he is about to do.
41: 28 "It is just as I said to **Pharaoh**: God has shown Pharaoh what he is
41: 28 I said to Pharaoh: God has shown **Pharaoh** what he is about to do.
41: 32 The reason the dream was given to **Pharaoh** in two forms is that
41: 33 "And now let **Pharaoh** look for a discerning and wise man
41: 34 Let **Pharaoh** appoint commissioners over the land to take a fifth of
41: 35 are coming and store up the grain under the authority of **Pharaoh**,
41: 37 The plan seemed good to **Pharaoh** and to all his officials.
41: 38 So **Pharaoh** asked them, "Can we find anyone like this man,
41: 39 **Pharaoh** said to Joseph, "Since God has made all this known to
41: 41 So **Pharaoh** said to Joseph, "I hereby put you in charge of the
41: 42 **Pharaoh** took his signet ring from his finger and put it on Joseph's
41: 44 **Pharaoh** said to Joseph, "I am Pharaoh, but without your word no
41: 44 Pharaoh said to Joseph, "I am **Pharaoh**, but without your word no
41: 45 **Pharaoh** gave Joseph the name Zaphenath-Paneah and gave him
41: 46 years old when he entered the service of **Pharaoh** king of Egypt.
41: 46 Joseph went out from **Pharaoh's** presence and traveled throughout
41: 55 began to feel the famine, the people cried to **Pharaoh** for food.
41: 55 **Pharaoh** told all the Egyptians, "Go to Joseph and do what he tells
42: 15 As surely as **Pharaoh** lives, you will not leave this place unless
42: 16 If you are not, then as surely as **Pharaoh** lives, you are spies!"
44: 18 angry with your servant, though you are equal to **Pharaoh** *himself.*
45: 2 the Egyptians heard him, and **Pharaoh's** household heard about it.
45: 8 He made me father to **Pharaoh**, lord of his entire household
45: 16 When the news reached **Pharaoh's** palace that Joseph's brothers
45: 16 brothers had come, **Pharaoh** and all his officials were pleased.
45: 17 **Pharaoh** said to Joseph, "Tell your brothers, 'Do this: Load your
45: 21 Joseph gave them carts, as **Pharaoh** had commanded, and he also
46: 5 and their wives in the carts that **Pharaoh** had sent to transport him.
46: 31 "I will go up and speak to **Pharaoh** and will say to him,
46: 33 When **Pharaoh** calls you in and asks, 'What is your occupation?'
47: 1 Joseph went and told **Pharaoh**, "My father and brothers, with their
47: 2 He chose five of his brothers and presented them before **Pharaoh**.
47: 3 **Pharaoh** asked the brothers, "What is your occupation?" "Your
47: 3 are shepherds," they replied to **Pharaoh**, "just as our fathers were."
47: 4 They also said to **him**[s], "We have come to live here awhile,
47: 5 **Pharaoh** said to Joseph, "Your father and your brothers have come
47: 7 brought his father Jacob in and presented him before **Pharaoh**.
47: 7 and presented him before Pharaoh. After Jacob blessed **Pharaoh**,
47: 8 **Pharaoh** asked him, "How old are you?"
47: 9 Jacob said to **Pharaoh**, "The years of my pilgrimage are a hundred
47: 10 Then Jacob blessed **Pharaoh** and went out from his presence.
47: 10 Then Jacob blessed Pharaoh and went out from **his**[s] presence.
47: 11 best part of the land, the district of Rameses, as **Pharaoh** directed.
47: 14 the grain they were buying, and he brought it to **Pharaoh's** palace.
47: 19 for food, and we with our land will be in bondage to **Pharaoh**.
47: 20 So Joseph bought all the land in Egypt for **Pharaoh**. The
47: 20 was too severe for them. The land became **Pharaoh's** [+4200],
47: 22 because they received a regular allotment from **Pharaoh** and had
47: 22 and had food enough from the allotment **Pharaoh** gave them.
47: 23 "Now that I have bought you and your land today for **Pharaoh**,
47: 24 But when the crop comes in, give a fifth of it to **Pharaoh**.
47: 25 favor in the eyes of our lord; we will be in bondage to **Pharaoh**."
47: 26 in force today—that a fifth of the produce belongs to **Pharaoh**.
47: 26 the land of the priests that did not become **Pharaoh's** [+4200].
50: 4 Joseph said to **Pharaoh's** court, "If I have found favor in your
50: 4 "If I have found favor in your eyes, speak to **Pharaoh** for me.
50: 6 **Pharaoh** said, "Go up and bury your father, as he made you swear
50: 7 All **Pharaoh's** officials accompanied him—the dignitaries of his
Ex 1: 11 and they built Pithom and Rameses as store cities for **Pharaoh**.
1: 19 The midwives answered **Pharaoh**, "Hebrew women are not like
1: 22 **Pharaoh** gave this order to all his people: "Every boy that is born
2: 5 Then **Pharaoh's** daughter went down to the Nile to bathe,
2: 7 his sister asked **Pharaoh's** daughter, "Shall I go and get one of the
2: 8 "Yes, go," **she**[s] [+1426] answered. And the girl went and got the
2: 9 **Pharaoh's** daughter said to her, "Take this baby and nurse him for
2: 10 she took him to **Pharaoh's** daughter and he became her son.
2: 15 When **Pharaoh** heard of this, he tried to kill Moses, but Moses fled
2: 15 but Moses fled from **Pharaoh** and went to live in Midian,
3: 10 I am sending you to **Pharaoh** to bring my people the Israelites out
3: 11 that I should go to **Pharaoh** and bring the Israelites out of Egypt?"
4: 21 see that you perform before **Pharaoh** all the wonders I have given
4: 22 say to **Pharaoh**, 'This is what the LORD says: Israel is my
5: 1 Afterward Moses and Aaron went to **Pharaoh** and said, "This is
5: 2 **Pharaoh** said, "Who is the LORD, that I should obey him
5: 5 **Pharaoh** said, "Look, the people of the land are now numerous,
5: 6 That same day **Pharaoh** gave this order to the slave drivers
5: 10 went out and said to the people, "This is what **Pharaoh** says:
5: 14 The Israelite foremen appointed by **Pharaoh's** slave drivers were
5: 15 Then the Israelite foremen went and appealed to **Pharaoh**:
5: 20 When they left **Pharaoh**, they found Moses and Aaron waiting to
5: 21 You have made us a stench to **Pharaoh** and his officials and have
5: 23 Ever since I went to **Pharaoh** to speak in your name, he has
6: 1 said to Moses, "Now you will see what I will do to **Pharaoh**:
6: 11 tell **Pharaoh** king of Egypt to let the Israelites go out of his
6: 12 why would **Pharaoh** listen to me, since I speak with faltering
6: 13 and Aaron about the Israelites and **Pharaoh** king of Egypt,
6: 27 They were the ones who spoke to **Pharaoh** king of Egypt about
6: 29 am the LORD. Tell **Pharaoh** king of Egypt everything I tell you."
6: 30 I speak with faltering lips, why would **Pharaoh** listen to me?"
7: 1 said to Moses, "See, I have made you like God to **Pharaoh**,
7: 2 your brother Aaron is to tell **Pharaoh** to let the Israelites go out of
7: 3 I will harden **Pharaoh's** heart, and though I multiply my
7: 4 **he**[s] will not listen to you. Then I will lay my hand on Egypt
7: 7 years old and Aaron eighty-three when they spoke to **Pharaoh**.
7: 9 "When **Pharaoh** says to you, 'Perform a miracle,' then say to
7: 9 say to Aaron, 'Take your staff and throw it down before **Pharaoh**,'
7: 10 So Moses and Aaron went to **Pharaoh** and did just as the LORD
7: 10 Aaron threw his staff down in front of **Pharaoh** and his officials,
7: 11 **Pharaoh** then summoned wise men and sorcerers,
7: 13 Yet **Pharaoh's** heart became hard and he would not listen to them,
7: 14 Then the LORD said to Moses, "**Pharaoh's** heart is unyielding;
7: 15 Go to **Pharaoh** in the morning as he goes out to the water.
7: 20 He raised his staff in the presence of **Pharaoh** and his officials
7: 22 same things by their secret arts, and **Pharaoh's** heart became hard;
7: 23 Instead, **he**[s] turned and went into his palace, and did not take even
8: 1 [7:26] "Go to **Pharaoh** and say to him, 'This is what the LORD
8: 8 [8:4] **Pharaoh** summoned Moses and Aaron and said, "Pray to
8: 9 [8:5] Moses said to **Pharaoh**, "I leave to you the honor of setting
8: 12 [8:8] After Moses and Aaron left **Pharaoh**, Moses cried out to the
8: 12 [8:8] to the LORD about the frogs he had brought on **Pharaoh**.
8: 15 [8:11] when **Pharaoh** saw that there was relief, he hardened his
8: 19 [8:15] The magicians said to **Pharaoh**, "This is the finger of
8: 19 [8:15] **Pharaoh's** heart was hard and he would not listen, just as
8: 20 [8:16] confront **Pharaoh** as he goes to the water and say to him,
8: 24 [8:20] Dense swarms of flies poured into **Pharaoh's** palace
8: 25 [8:21] Then **Pharaoh** summoned Moses and Aaron and said, "Go,
8: 28 [8:24] **Pharaoh** said, "I will let you go to offer sacrifices to the
8: 29 [8:25] and tomorrow the flies will leave **Pharaoh** and his officials
8: 29 [8:25] Only be sure that **Pharaoh** does not act deceitfully again
8: 30 [8:26] Then Moses left **Pharaoh** and prayed to the LORD,

Ex 8:31 [8:27] The flies left **Pharaoh** and his officials and his people;
8:32 [8:28] this time also **Pharaoh** hardened his heart and would not
9: 1 "Go to **Pharaoh** and say to him, 'This is what the LORD,
9: 7 **Pharaoh** sent men to investigate and found that not even one of
9: 7 Yet **his**ˢ heart was unyielding and he would not let the people go.
9: 8 and have Moses toss it into the air in the presence of **Pharaoh**.
9:10 So they took soot from a furnace and stood before **Pharaoh**.
9:12 the LORD hardened **Pharaoh's** heart and he would not listen to
9:13 confront **Pharaoh** and say to him, 'This is what the LORD,
9:20 Those officials of **Pharaoh** who feared the word of the LORD
9:27 **Pharaoh** summoned Moses and Aaron. "This time I have sinned,"
9:33 Moses left **Pharaoh** and went out of the city. He spread out his
9:34 When **Pharaoh** saw that the rain and hail and thunder had stopped,
9:35 So **Pharaoh's** heart was hard and he would not let the Israelites go,
10: 1 "Go to **Pharaoh**, for I have hardened his heart and the hearts of his
10: 3 So Moses and Aaron went to **Pharaoh** and said to him, "This is
10: 6 in this land till now.' " Then Moses turned and left **Pharaoh**.
10: 7 **Pharaoh's** officials said to him, "How long will this man be a
10: 8 Then Moses and Aaron were brought back to **Pharaoh**. "Go,
10:11 Then Moses and Aaron were driven out of **Pharaoh's** presence.
10:16 **Pharaoh** quickly summoned Moses and Aaron and said, "I have
10:18 Moses then left **Pharaoh** and prayed to the LORD.
10:20 the LORD hardened **Pharaoh's** heart, and he would not let the
10:24 **Pharaoh** summoned Moses and said, "Go, worship the LORD.
10:27 the LORD hardened **Pharaoh's** heart, and he was not willing to
10:28 **Pharaoh** said to Moses, "Get out of my sight! Make sure you do
11: 1 to Moses, "I will bring one more plague on **Pharaoh** and on Egypt.
11: 3 Moses himself was highly regarded in Egypt by **Pharaoh's**
11: 5 from the firstborn son of **Pharaoh**, who sits on the throne,
11: 8 After that I will leave." Then Moses, hot with anger, left **Pharaoh**.
11: 9 LORD had said to Moses, "**Pharaoh** will refuse to listen to you—
11:10 Moses and Aaron performed all these wonders before **Pharaoh**,
11:10 the LORD hardened **Pharaoh's** heart, and he would not let the
12:29 from the firstborn of **Pharaoh**, who sat on the throne,
12:30 **Pharaoh** and all his officials and all the Egyptians got up during
13:15 When **Pharaoh** stubbornly refused to let us go, the LORD killed
13:17 When **Pharaoh** let the people go, God did not lead them on the
14: 3 **Pharaoh** will think, 'The Israelites are wandering around the land
14: 4 And I will harden **Pharaoh's** heart, and he will pursue them.
14: 4 But I will gain glory for myself through **Pharaoh** and all his army,
14: 5 **Pharaoh** and his officials changed their minds about them
14: 8 The LORD hardened the heart of **Pharaoh** king of Egypt,
14: 9 all **Pharaoh's** horses and chariots, horsemen and troops—
14:10 As **Pharaoh** approached, the Israelites looked up, and there were
14:17 I will gain glory through **Pharaoh** and all his army, through his
14:18 know that I am the LORD when I gain glory through **Pharaoh**,
14:23 all **Pharaoh's** horses and chariots and horsemen followed them
14:28 the entire army of **Pharaoh** that had followed the Israelites into the
15: 4 **Pharaoh's** chariots and his army he has hurled into the sea.
15:19 When **Pharaoh's** horses, chariots and horsemen went into the sea,
18: 4 God was my helper; he saved me from the sword of **Pharaoh**."
18: 8 father-in-law about everything the LORD had done to **Pharaoh**
18:10 who rescued you from the hand of the Egyptians and of **Pharaoh**,
Dt 6:21 "We were slaves of **Pharaoh** in Egypt, but the LORD brought us
6:22 and terrible—upon Egypt and **Pharaoh** and his whole household.
7: 8 the land of slavery, from the power of **Pharaoh** king of Egypt.
7:18 remember well what the LORD your God did to **Pharaoh**
11: 3 of Egypt, both to **Pharaoh** king of Egypt and to his whole country;
29: 2 [29:1] have seen all that the LORD did in Egypt to **Pharaoh**,
34:11 to **Pharaoh** and to all his officials and to his whole land.
1Sa 2:27 to your father's house when they were in Egypt under **Pharaoh**?
6: 6 Why do you harden your hearts as the Egyptians and **Pharaoh** did?
1Ki 3: 1 Solomon made an alliance with **Pharaoh** king of Egypt
3: 1 an alliance with Pharaoh king of Egypt and married **his**ˢ daughter.
7: 8 Solomon also made a palace like this hall for **Pharaoh's** daughter,
9:16 (**Pharaoh** king of Egypt had attacked and captured Gezer.
9:24 After **Pharaoh's** daughter had come up from the City of David to
11: 1 loved many foreign women besides **Pharaoh's** daughter—
11:18 they went to Egypt, to **Pharaoh** king of Egypt, who gave Hadad a
11:19 **Pharaoh** was so pleased with Hadad that he gave him a sister of
11:20 named Genubath, whom Tahpenes brought up in the **royal** palace.
11:20 **There**ˢ [+1074] Genubath lived with Pharaoh's own children.
11:20 royal palace. There Genubath lived with **Pharaoh's** *own* children.
11:21 Hadad said to **Pharaoh**, "Let me go, that I may return to my own
11:22 **Pharaoh** asked. "Nothing," Hadad replied, "but do let me go!"
2Ki 17: 7 up out of Egypt from under the power of **Pharaoh** king of Egypt.
18:21 Such is **Pharaoh** king of Egypt to all who depend on him.
23:29 **Pharaoh** Neco king of Egypt went up to the Euphrates River to
23:33 **Pharaoh** Neco put him in chains at Riblah in the land of Hamath
23:34 **Pharaoh** Neco made Eliakim son of Josiah king in place of his
23:35 Jehoiakim paid **Pharaoh** Neco the silver and gold he demanded.
23:35 Jehoiakim paid Pharaoh Neco the silver and gold **he**ˢ demanded.
23:35 the people of the land according to their assessments. **[RPH]**
1Ch 4:18 These were the children of **Pharaoh's** daughter Bithiah,
2Ch 8:11 Solomon brought **Pharaoh's** daughter up from the City of David
Ne 9:10 You sent miraculous signs and wonders against **Pharaoh**,
Ps 135: 9 into your midst, O Egypt, against **Pharaoh** and all his servants.
136:15 swept **Pharaoh** and his army into the Red Sea; *His love*
SS 1: 9 my darling, to a mare harnessed to one of the chariots of **Pharaoh**.
Isa 19:11 but fools; the wise counselors of **Pharaoh** give senseless advice.
19:11 How can you say to **Pharaoh**, "I am one of the wise men,
30: 2 who look for help to **Pharaoh's** protection, to Egypt's shade for
30: 3 **Pharaoh's** protection will be to your shame, Egypt's shade will
36: 6 Such is **Pharaoh** king of Egypt to all who depend on him.
Jer 25:19 **Pharaoh** king of Egypt, his attendants, his officials and all his
37: 5 **Pharaoh's** army had marched out of Egypt, and when the
37: 7 the king of Judah, who sent you to inquire of me, '**Pharaoh's** army,
37:11 army had withdrawn from Jerusalem because of **Pharaoh's** army,
43: 9 brick pavement at the entrance to **Pharaoh's** palace in Tahpanhes.
44:30 'I am going to hand **Pharaoh** Hophra king of Egypt over to his
46: 2 This is the message against the army of **Pharaoh** Neco king of
46:17 they will exclaim, '**Pharaoh** king of Egypt is only a loud noise;
46:25 on **Pharaoh**, on Egypt and her gods and her kings, and on those
46:25 and her gods and her kings, and on those who rely on **Pharaoh**.
47: 1 prophet concerning the Philistines before **Pharaoh** attacked Gaza:
Eze 17:17 **Pharaoh** with his mighty army and great horde will be of no help
29: 2 set your face against **Pharaoh** king of Egypt and prophesy against
29: 3 " 'I am against you, **Pharaoh** king of Egypt, you great monster
30:21 "Son of man, I have broken the arm of **Pharaoh** king of Egypt.
30:22 I am against **Pharaoh** king of Egypt. I will break both his arms,
30:24 put my sword in his hand, but I will break the arms of **Pharaoh**,
30:25 of the king of Babylon, but the arms of **Pharaoh** will fall limp.
31: 2 "Son of man, say to **Pharaoh** king of Egypt and to his hordes:
31:18 " 'This is **Pharaoh** and all his hordes, declares the Sovereign
32: 2 take up a lament concerning **Pharaoh** king of Egypt and say to
32:31 "**Pharaoh**—he and all his army—will see them and he will be
32:31 "Pharaoh—**he**ˢ and all his army—will see them and he will be
32:32 **Pharaoh** and all his hordes will be laid among the uncircumcised,

7282 ¹פַּרְעֹשׁ *par'ōš¹*, n.m. [2] [→ 7283]

flea [2]

1Sa 24:14 [24:15] come out? Whom are you pursuing? A dead dog? A **flea**?
26:20 The king of Israel has come out to look for a **flea**—as one hunts a

7283 ²פַּרְעֹשׁ *par'ōš²*, n.pr.m. [6] [√ 7282]

Parosh [6]

Ezr 2: 3 the descendants of **Parosh** 2,172
8: 3 of the descendants of **Parosh**, Zechariah, and with him were
10:25 From the descendants of **Parosh**: Ramiah, Izziah, Malkijah,
Ne 3:25 near the court of the guard. Next to him, Pedaiah son of **Parosh**
7: 8 the descendants of **Parosh** 2,172
10:14 [10:15] of the people: **Parosh**, Pahath-Moab, Elam, Zattu, Bani,

7284 פִּרְעָתוֹן *pir'ātôn*, n.pr.loc. [1] [→ 7285]

Pirathon [1]

Jdg 12:15 Abdon son of Hillel died, and was buried at **Pirathon** in Ephraim,

7285 פִּרְעָתוֹנִי *pir'ātônî*, a.g. [5] [√ 7284]

Pirathonite [3], *untranslated* [1], from Pirathon [1]

Jdg 12:13 After him, Abdon son of Hillel, **from Pirathon**, led Israel.
12:15 Abdon son of Hillel **[RPH]** died, and was buried at Pirathon in
2Sa 23:30 Benaiah the **Pirathonite**, Hiddai from the ravines of Gaash,
1Ch 11:31 son of Ribai from Gibeah in Benjamin, Benaiah the **Pirathonite**,
27:14 the eleventh month, was Benaiah the **Pirathonite**, an Ephraimite.

7286 פַּרְפַּר *parpar*, n.pr.loc. [1]

Pharpar [1]

2Ki 5:12 Are not Abana and **Pharpar**, the rivers of Damascus, better than

7287 פָּרַץ *pāraṣ*, v. [49] [→ 1262, 5153, 7264, 7265, 7288, 7289, 7290, 7291, 7292; cf. 7210]

broken out [4], broke down [3], broken down [3], urged [3], break down [2], break out [2], increased [2], spread out [2], spread [2], again and again bursts [+7288+7288] [1], are broken down [1], break all bounds [1], break [1], breaking away [1], breaks open [1], breaks through [1], brim over [1], broke out in anger [1], broke out [1], broken into [1], broken out [+6584+7288] [1], broken through [1], broken [1], burst forth [1], cuts [1], destroy [1], dispersing [1], far and wide [1], gaps [1], increase [1], many [1], prosperous [1], tear down [1], urging [1], went out [1]

Ge 28:14 [A] *you will* **spread out** to the west and to the east, to the north
30:30 [A] The little you had before I came *has* **increased** greatly, and
30:43 [A] In this way the man *grew* exceedingly **prosperous** and came

Ge 38:29 [A] "So this is how *you have* **broken** [+6584+7288] **out**!"
Ex 1:12 [A] they were oppressed, the more they multiplied and **spread**;
19:22 [A] or the LORD *will* **break out** against them."
19:24 [A] come up to the LORD, or *he will* **break out** against them."
1Sa 3:1 [C] word of the LORD was rare; there were not **many** visions.
25:10 [F] Many servants *are* **breaking away** from their masters these
28:23 [A] his men joined the woman *in* **urging** him, and he listened to
2Sa 5:20 [A] the LORD *has* **broken out** *against* my enemies before me."
6:8 [A] because the LORD's wrath *had* **broken out** against Uzzah,
13:25 [A] Although Absalom **urged** him, he still refused to go,
13:27 [A] Absalom **urged** him, so he sent with him Amnon and the rest
2Ki 5:23 [A] *He* **urged** Gehazi to accept them, and then tied up the two
14:13 [A] **broke down** the wall of Jerusalem from the Ephraim Gate to
1Ch 4:38 [A] were leaders of their clans. Their families **increased** greatly,
13:2 [A] let us send word **far and wide** to the rest of our brothers
13:11 [A] because the LORD's wrath *had* **broken out** against Uzzah,
14:11 [A] God *has* **broken out** *against* my enemies by my hand."
15:13 [A] time that the LORD our God **broke out in anger** against us.
2Ch 11:23 [A] **dispersing** some of his sons throughout the districts of Judah
20:37 [A] the LORD *will* **destroy** what you have made."
24:7 [A] wicked woman Athaliah *had* **broken into** the temple of God
25:23 [A] **broke down** the wall of Jerusalem from the Ephraim Gate to
26:6 [A] and **broke down** the walls of Gath, Jabneh and Ashdod.
31:5 [A] As soon as the order **went out**, the Israelites generously gave
32:5 [B] he worked hard repairing all the **broken** *sections* of the wall
Ne 1:3 [E] The wall of Jerusalem *is* **broken down**, and its gates have
2:13 [B] which *had been* **broken down**, and its gates, which had been
4:3 [3:35] [A] up on it, *he would* **break down** their wall of stones!"
4:7 [4:1] [B] had gone ahead and that the **gaps** were being closed,
Job 1:10 [A] so that his flocks and herds *are* **spread** throughout the land.
16:14 [A] **Again and again** *he* **bursts** [+7288+7288] upon me;
28:4 [A] Far from where people dwell *he* **cuts** a shaft, in places
Ps 60:1 [60:3] [A] You have rejected us, O God, and **burst forth** *upon*
80:12 [80:13] [A] Why *have you* **broken down** its walls so that all
89:40 [89:41] [A] *You have* **broken through** all his walls
106:29 [A] by their wicked deeds, and a plague **broke out** among them.
Pr 3:10 [A] to overflowing, and your vats *will* **brim over** *with* new wine.
25:28 [B] Like a city whose walls **are broken down** is a man who
Ecc 3:3 [A] and a time to heal, a time to **tear down** and a time to build,
10:8 [A] *whoever* **breaks through** a wall may be bitten by a snake.
Isa 5:5 [A] I *will* **break down** its wall, and it will be trampled.
54:3 [A] For *you will* **spread out** *to* the right and *to* the left; your
Hos 4:2 [A] *they* **break all bounds**, and bloodshed follows bloodshed.
4:10 [A] they will engage in prostitution but not **increase**,
Mic 2:13 [A] One *who* **breaks open** the way will go up before them;
2:13 [A] up before them; *they will* **break** through the gate and go out.

7288 [1]פֶּרֶץ *pereṣ*[1], n.m. [19] [→ 1262, 8236; cf. 7287]

gap [3], again and again bursts [+7287+7288] [2], breach [2], break out [2], wrath [2], breaching of walls [1], breaks in the wall [1], breaks [1], broken out [+6584+7287] [1], broken places [1], broken [1], cracked [+5877] [1], gap in the wall [1]

Ge 38:29 she said, "So this is how *you have* **broken out** [+6584+7287]!"
Jdg 21:15 because the LORD had made a **gap** in the tribes of Israel.
2Sa 5:20 He said, "As waters **break out**, the LORD has broken out against
6:8 because the LORD's **wrath** had broken out against Uzzah,
1Ki 11:27 and had filled in the **gap in the wall** *of* the city of David his father.
1Ch 13:11 because the LORD's **wrath** had broken out against Uzzah,
14:11 He said, "As waters **break out**, God has broken out against my
Ne 6:1 our enemies that I had rebuilt the wall and not a **gap** was left in it—
Job 16:14 **Again and again** *he* **bursts** [+7287+7288] upon me; he rushes at
16:14 **Again and again** *he* **bursts** [+7287+7288] upon me; he rushes at
30:14 They advance as through a gaping **breach**; amid the ruins they
Ps 106:23 stood in the **breach** before him to keep his wrath from destroying
144:14 There will be no **breaching of walls**, no going into captivity,
Isa 30:13 **cracked** [+5877] and bulging, that collapses suddenly, in an
58:12 you will be called Repairer of **Broken** Walls, Restorer of Streets
Eze 13:5 You have not gone up to the **breaks** in the wall to repair it for the
22:30 stand before me in the **gap** on behalf of the land so I would not
Am 4:3 You will each go straight out through **breaks in the wall**,
9:11 I will repair its **broken places**, restore its ruins, and build it as it

7289 [2]פֶּרֶץ *pereṣ*[2], n.pr.m. [15] [→ 7291; cf. 7287]

Perez [15]

Ge 38:29 "So this is how you have broken out!" And he was named **Perez**.
46:12 **Perez** and Zerah (but Er and Onan had died in the land of Canaan).
46:12 in the land of Canaan). The sons of **Perez**: Hezron and Hamul.
Nu 26:20 through **Perez**, the Perezite clan; through Zerah, the Zerahite clan.
26:21 The descendants of **Perez** were: through Hezron, the Hezronite
Ru 4:12 may your family be like that of **Perez**, whom Tamar bore to
4:18 This, then, is the family line of **Perez**: Perez was the father of
4:18 is the family line of Perez: **Perez** was the father of Hezron,
1Ch 2:4 Tamar, Judah's daughter-in-law, bore him **Perez** and Zerah.
2:5 The sons of **Perez**: Hezron and Hamul.
4:1 The descendants of Judah: **Perez**, Hezron, Carmi, Hur and Shobal.
9:4 son of Imri, the son of Bani, a descendant of **Perez** son of Judah.
27:3 He was a descendant of **Perez** and chief of all the army officers for
Ne 11:4 the son of Shephatiah, the son of Mahalalel, a descendant of **Perez**;
11:6 The descendants of **Perez** who lived in Jerusalem totaled 468 able

7290 פֶּרֶץ עֻזָּא *pereṣ 'uzzā'*, פֶּרֶץ עֻזָּה *pereṣ 'uzzâ*, n.pr.loc. [2] [√ 7288 + 6446]

Perez Uzzah [2]

2Sa 6:8 out against Uzzah, and to this day that place is called **Perez Uzzah**.
1Ch 13:11 out against Uzzah, and to this day that place is called **Perez Uzzah**.

7291 פַּרְצִי *parṣî*, a.g. [1] [√ 7289; cf. 7287]

Perezite [1]

Nu 26:20 through Perez, the **Perezite** clan; through Zerah, the Zerahite clan.

7292 פְּרָצִים *p^erāṣîm*, n.pr.loc. [1] [√ 7288; cf. 7287]

Perazim [1]

Isa 28:21 The LORD will rise up as he did at Mount **Perazim**, he will rouse

7293 פָּרַק *pāraq*, v. [10] [→ 5154, 7294, 7295; Ar 10596]

take off [2], free [1], freed [1], rip to pieces [1], tearing off [1], throw off [1], took off [1], tore apart [1], was stripped [1]

Ge 27:40 [A] grow restless, *you will* **throw** his yoke from **off** your neck."
Ex 32:2 [D] "**Take off** the gold earrings that your wives, your sons
32:3 [F] So all the people **took off** their earrings and brought them to
32:24 [F] So I told them, 'Whoever has any gold jewelry, **take** it **off**.'
1Ki 19:11 [D] Then a great and powerful wind **tore** the mountains **apart**
Ps 7:2 [7:3] [A] a lion and **rip** me **to pieces** with no one to rescue me.
136:24 [A] **freed** us from our enemies, *His love endures*
La 5:8 [A] rule over us, and there is none *to* **free** us from their hands.
Eze 19:12 [F] The east wind made it shrivel, *it* **was stripped** *of* its fruit;
Zec 11:16 [D] will eat the meat of the choice sheep, **tearing off** their hoofs.

7294 פֶּרֶק *pereq*, n.[m.]. [2] [√ 7293]

crossroads [1], plunder [1]

Ob 1:14 You should not wait at the **crossroads** to cut down their fugitives,
Na 3:1 city of blood, full of lies, full of **plunder**, never without victims!

7295 פָּרָק *pārāq*, n.[m.]. [0] [√ 7293]

Isa 65:4 [and whose pots hold **broth** [K; see Q 5348] *of* unclean meat;]

7296 [1]פָּרַר *pārar*[1], v. [49] [cf. 7051]

break [8], broken [6], breaking [5], broke [4], nullifies [+906+7296] [4], foils [2], frustrate [2], be broken [1], be thwarted [1], discredit [1], fail [1], frustrated [1], frustrating [1], no longer stirred [1], nullified [1], nullifies [1], nullify [1], put away [1], revoking [1], take [1], thwart [1], thwarts [1], undermine [1], violate [1], was revoked [1]

Ge 17:14 [G] be cut off from his people; he *has* **broken** my covenant."
Lev 26:15 [G] to carry out all my commands and so **violate** my covenant,
26:44 [G] destroy them completely, **breaking** my covenant with them.
Nu 15:31 [G] has despised the LORD's word and **broken** his commands,
30:8 [30:9] [G] *he* **nullifies** the vow that obligates her or the rash
30:12 [30:13] [G] if her husband **nullifies** [+906+7296] them when he
30:12 [30:13] [G] if her husband **nullifies** [+906+7296] them when he
30:12 [30:13] [G] Her husband *has* **nullified** them, and the LORD
30:13 [30:14] [G] Her husband may confirm or **nullify** any vow she
30:15 [30:16] [G] *he* **nullifies** [+906+7296] them some time after he
30:15 [30:16] [G] *he* **nullifies** [+906+7296] them some time after he
Dt 31:16 [G] will forsake me and **break** the covenant I made with them.
31:20 [G] and worship them, rejecting me and **breaking** my covenant.
Jdg 2:1 [G] I said, '*I will* never **break** my covenant with you,
2Sa 15:34 [G] then *you can* help me *by* **frustrating** Ahithophel's advice.
17:14 [G] For the LORD had determined to **frustrate** the good advice
1Ki 15:19 [G] Now **break** your treaty with Baasha king of Israel so he will
2Ch 16:3 [G] Now **break** your treaty with Baasha king of Israel so he will
Ezr 4:5 [G] **frustrate** their plans during the entire reign of Cyrus king of
9:14 [G] Shall we again **break** your commands and intermarry with
Ne 4:15 [4:9] [G] aware of their plot and that God *had* **frustrated** it,
Job 5:12 [G] *He* **thwarts** the plans of the crafty, so that their hands
15:4 [G] But you even **undermine** piety and hinder devotion to God.
40:8 [G] "*Would you* **discredit** my justice? Would you condemn me
Ps 33:10 [G] The LORD **foils** the plans of the nations; he thwarts the
85:4 [85:5] [G] our Savior, and **put away** your displeasure toward us.
89:33 [89:34] [G] *I will* not **take** my love from him, nor will I ever
119:126 [G] is time for you to act, O LORD; your law *is being* **broken**.
Pr 15:22 [G] Plans **fail** for lack of counsel, but with many advisers they

Ecc 12: 5 [G] drags himself along and desire **no longer** *is* **stirred**.
Isa 8: 10 [H] Devise your strategy, but *it will* **be thwarted**; propose your
14: 27 [G] LORD Almighty has purposed, and who *can* **thwart** him?
24: 5 [G] violated the statutes and **broken** the everlasting covenant.
33: 8 [G] The treaty *is* **broken**, its witnesses are despised, no one is
44: 25 [G] *who* **foils** the signs of false prophets and makes fools of
Jer 11: 10 [G] the house of Judah *have* **broken** the covenant I made with
14: 21 [G] Remember your covenant with us and *do* not **break** it.
31: 32 [G] because they **broke** my covenant, though I was a husband to
33: 20 [G] 'If *you can* **break** my covenant with the day and my
33: 21 [H] *can* **be broken** and David will no longer have a descendant
Eze 16: 59 [G] because you have despised my oath by **breaking** the
17: 15 [G] such things escape? *Will he* **break** the treaty and yet escape?
17: 16 [G] whose oath he despised and whose treaty *he* **broke**.
17: 18 [G] He despised the oath by **breaking** the covenant. Because he
17: 19 [G] my oath that he despised and my covenant that *he* **broke**.
44: 7 [G] offered me food, fat and blood, and *you* **broke** my covenant.
Zec 11: 10 [G] **revoking** the covenant I had made with all the nations.
11: 11 [H] *It* **was revoked** on that day, and so the afflicted of the flock
11: 14 [G] **breaking** the brotherhood between Judah and Israel.

7297 ²פָּרַר pārar², v. [4]

is split asunder [+7297] [2], shattered [1], split open [1]

Job 16: 12 [D] All was well with me, but *he* **shattered** me; he seized me by
Ps 74: 13 [D] It was you *who* **split open** the sea by your power; you broke
Isa 24: 19 [F] The earth is broken up, the earth **is split** [+7297] **asunder**,
24: 19 [A] The earth is broken up, the earth **is split asunder** [+7297],

7298 פָּרַשׂ pāraś, v. [67 / 69] [→ 5155; cf. 7299]

spread [21], spread out [19], spreading [5], scattered [3], spreading out [2], throw [2], be scattered [1], cast [1], chop up [1], display [1], exposes [1], extended [1], gives [1], held out [1], laid [1], opens [1], scatters [1], spreads out [1], spreads [1], stretch out [1], stretches out [1], stretching out [1], unrolled [1]

Ex 9: 29 [A] the city, *I will* **spread out** my hands in prayer to the LORD.
9: 33 [A] *He* **spread out** his hands toward the LORD; the thunder
25: 20 [A] The cherubim are to have their wings **spread** upward,
37: 9 [A] The cherubim had their wings **spread** upward,
40: 19 [A] *he* **spread** the tent over the tabernacle and put the covering
Nu 4: 6 [A] **spread** a cloth of solid blue over that and put the poles in
4: 7 [A] "Over the table of the Presence *they are to* **spread** a blue
4: 8 [A] Over these *they are to* **spread** a scarlet cloth, cover that with
4: 11 [A] "Over the gold altar *they are to* **spread** a blue cloth
4: 13 [A] ashes from the bronze altar and **spread** a purple cloth over it.
4: 14 [A] Over it *they are to* **spread** a covering of hides of sea cows
Dt 22: 17 [A] her parents *shall* **display** the cloth before the elders of the
32: 11 [A] *that* **spreads** its wings to catch them and carries them on its
Jdg 8: 25 [A] So *they* **spread out** a garment, and each man threw a ring
Ru 3: 9 [A] "**Spread** the corner of your garment over me, since you are a
2Sa 17: 19 [A] a covering and **spread** it **out** over the opening of the well
1Ki 6: 27 [A] innermost room of the temple, with their wings **spread out**.
8: 7 [A] The cherubim **spread** their wings over the place of the ark
8: 22 [A] assembly of Israel, **spread out** his hands *toward* heaven
8: 38 [A] own heart, and **spreading out** his hands toward this temple—
8: 54 [B] had been kneeling with his hands **spread out** *toward* heaven.
2Ki 8: 15 [A] soaked it in water and **spread** it over the king's face, so that
19: 14 [A] temple of the LORD and **spread** it **out** before the LORD.
1Ch 28: 18 [A] the cherubim of gold *that* **spread** their wings and shelter the
2Ch 3: 13 [A] The wings of these cherubim **extended** twenty cubits. They
5: 8 [A] The cherubim **spread** their wings over the place of the ark
6: 12 [A] of the whole assembly of Israel and **spread out** his hands.
6: 13 [A] assembly of Israel and **spread out** his hands toward heaven.
6: 29 [A] and pains, and **spreading out** his hands toward this temple—
Ezr 9: 5 [A] fell on my knees with my hands **spread out** to the LORD
Job 11: 13 [A] devote your heart to him and **stretch out** your hands to him,
26: 9 [a] of the full moon, **spreading** [BHS 7299] his clouds over it.
36: 30 [A] See how *he* **scatters** his lightning about him, bathing the
39: 26 [A] by your wisdom and **spread** his wings toward the south?
Ps 44: 20 [44:21] [A] our God or **spread out** our hands to a foreign god,
68: 14 [68:15] [D] When the Almighty **scattered** the kings in the land,
105: 39 [A] *He* **spread out** a cloud as a covering, and a fire to give light
140: 5 [140:6] [A] *they have* **spread out** the cords of their net
143: 6 [D] *I* **spread out** my hands to you; my soul thirsts for you like a
Pr 13: 16 [A] man acts out of knowledge, but a fool **exposes** his folly.
29: 5 [A] Whoever flatters his neighbor *is* **spreading** a net for his feet.
31: 20 [A] *She* **opens** her arms to the poor and extends her hands to the
Isa 1: 15 [D] When you **spread out** your hands in prayer, I will hide my
19: 8 [A] the Nile; *those who* **throw** nets on the water will pine away.
25: 11 [D] *They will* **spread out** their hands in it, as a swimmer spreads
25: 11 [D] hands in it, as a swimmer **spreads out** his hands to swim.
33: 23 [A] The mast is not held secure, the sail *is* not **spread**.
37: 14 [A] temple of the LORD and **spread** it **out** before the LORD.
65: 2 [D] All day long *I have* **held out** my hands to an obstinate
Jer 4: 31 [D] for breath, **stretching out** her hands and saying, "Alas!
48: 40 [A] An eagle is swooping down, **spreading** its wings over Moab.
49: 22 [A] will soar and swoop down, **spreading** its wings over Bozrah.
La 1: 10 [A] The enemy **laid** hands on all her treasures; she saw pagan
1: 13 [A] *He* **spread** a net for my feet and turned me back. He made
1: 17 [D] Zion **stretches out** her hands, but there is no one to comfort
4: 4 [A] the children beg for bread, but no *one* **gives** it to them.
Eze 2: 10 [A] which *he* **unrolled** before me. On both sides of it were
12: 13 [A] *I will* **spread** my net for him, and he will be caught in my
16: 8 [A] *I* **spread** the corner of my garment over you and covered
17: 20 [A] *I will* **spread** my net for him, and he will be caught in my
17: 21 [C] the sword, and the survivors *will* **be scattered** to the winds.
19: 8 [A] *They* **spread** their net for him, and he was trapped in their
32: 3 [A] " 'With a great throng of people *I will* **cast** my net over you,
34: 12 [c] As a shepherd looks after his **scattered** [BHS 7300] flock
Hos 5: 1 [B] You have been a snare at Mizpah, a net **spread out** on Tabor.
7: 12 [A] When they go, *I will* **throw** my net over them; I will pull
Joel 2: 2 [B] Like dawn **spreading** across the mountains a large
Mic 3: 3 [A] *who* **chop** them **up** like meat for the pan, like flesh for the
Zec 2: 6 [2:10] [D] "for *I have* **scattered** you to the four winds of

7299 פַּרְשֵׁז parśēz, a.vbl. *or* v. [1 / 0] [cf. 7298]

Job 26: 9 [d] spreading [BHS *spreading*; NIV 7298] his clouds over it.

7300 ¹פָּרַשׁ pāraš¹, v. [4 / 3] [→ 7304, 7305, 7308; cf. 7301; Ar 10597]

clear [1], made clear [1], making clear [1]

Lev 24: 12 [A] until the will of the LORD *should be* **made clear** to them.
Nu 15: 34 [E] because *it was* not **clear** what should be done to him.
Ne 8: 8 [E] **making** it **clear** and giving the meaning so that the people
Eze 34: 12 [c] looks after his scattered [BHS *distinct* ?; NIV 7298] flock

7301 ²פָּרַשׁ pāraš², v. [1] [cf. 7300, 7302]

poisons [1]

Pr 23: 32 [G] In the end it bites like a snake and **poisons** like a viper.

7302 ¹פֶּרֶשׁ pereš¹, n.[m.]. [7] [→ 7303; cf. 7301]

offal [6], *untranslated* [1]

Ex 29: 14 But burn the bull's flesh and its hide and its **offal** outside the camp.
Lev 4: 11 all its flesh, as well as the head and legs, the inner parts and **offal**—
8: 17 its hide and its flesh and its **offal** he burned up outside the camp,
16: 27 outside the camp; their hides, flesh and **offal** are to be burned up.
Nu 19: 5 the heifer is to be burned—its hide, flesh, blood and **offal**.
Mal 2: 3 I will spread on your faces the **offal** *from* your festival sacrifices,
2: 3 I will spread on your faces the offal from **[RPH]** your festival

7303 ²פֶּרֶשׁ pereš², n.pr.m. [1] [√ 7302]

Peresh [1]

1Ch 7: 16 Makir's wife Maacah gave birth to a son and named him **Peresh**.

7304 ¹פָּרָשׁ pārāš¹, n.[m.]. [18] [√ 7300]

horses [14], war horses [2], riders [+1251] [1], steeds [1]

1Sa 8: 11 take your sons and make them serve with his chariots and **horses**,
2Sa 1: 6 his spear, with the chariots and **riders** [+1251] almost upon him.
1Ki 1: 5 So he got chariots and **horses** ready, with fifty men to run ahead of
4: 26 [5:6] stalls for chariot horses, and twelve thousand **horses**.
9: 19 his store cities and the towns for his chariots and for his **horses**—
10: 26 Solomon accumulated chariots and **horses**; he had fourteen
10: 26 he had fourteen hundred chariots and twelve thousand **horses**,
2Ch 1: 14 Solomon accumulated chariots and **horses**; he had fourteen
1: 14 he had fourteen hundred chariots and twelve thousand **horses**,
8: 6 store cities, and all the cities for his chariots and for his **horses**—
9: 25 stalls for horses and chariots, and twelve thousand **horses**,
Isa 21: 7 When he sees chariots with teams of **horses**, riders on donkeys
21: 9 Look, here comes a man in a chariot with a team of **horses**.
22: 6 Elam takes up the quiver, with her charioteers and **horses**;
28: 28 the wheels of his threshing cart over it, his **horses** do not grind it.
Jer 46: 4 Harness the horses, mount the **steeds**! Take your positions with
Eze 26: 10 Your walls will tremble at the noise of the **war horses**, wagons
27: 14 work horses, **war horses** and mules for your merchandise.

7305 ²פָּרָשׁ pārāš², n.m. [39 / 38] [√ 7300]

horsemen [27], charioteers [6], cavalry [5]

Ge 50: 9 Chariots and **horsemen** also went up with him. It was a very large
Ex 14: 9 all Pharaoh's horses and chariots, **horsemen** and troops—
14: 17 and all his army, through his chariots and his **horsemen**.
14: 18 I gain glory through Pharaoh, his chariots and his **horsemen**."
14: 23 and chariots and **horsemen** followed them into the sea.

Ex 14:26 flow back over the Egyptians and their chariots and **horsemen.**"
14:28 The water flowed back and covered the chariots and **horsemen**—
15:19 When Pharaoh's horses, chariots and **horsemen** went into the sea,
Jos 24:6 pursued them with chariots and **horsemen** as far as the Red Sea.
1Sa 13:5 fight Israel, with three thousand chariots, six thousand **charioteers**,
2Sa 8:4 seven thousand **charioteers** and twenty thousand foot soldiers.
10:18 forty thousand of their foot soldiers. [BHS ***horsemen***; NIV 8081]
1Ki 9:22 his captains, and the commanders of his chariots and **charioteers**.
20:20 king of Aram escaped on horseback with *some* of his **horsemen**.
2Ki 2:12 "My father! My father! The chariots and **horsemen** *of* Israel!"
13:7 had been left of the army of Jehoahaz except fifty **horsemen**,
13:14 My father!" he cried. "The chariots and **horsemen** *of* Israel!"
18:24 though you are depending on Egypt for chariots and **horsemen**?
1Ch 18:4 seven thousand **charioteers** and twenty thousand foot soldiers.
19:6 of silver to hire chariots and **charioteers** from Aram Naharaim,
2Ch 8:9 of his captains, and commanders of his chariots and **charioteers**.
12:3 With twelve hundred chariots and sixty thousand **horsemen**
16:8 a mighty army with great numbers of chariots and **horsemen**?
Ezr 8:22 for soldiers and **horsemen** to protect us from enemies on the road,
Ne 2:9 The king had also sent army officers and **cavalry** with me.
Isa 22:7 are full of chariots, and **horsemen** are posted at the city gates;
31:1 of their chariots and in the great strength of their **horsemen**,
36:9 though you are depending on Egypt for chariots and **horsemen**?
Jer 4:29 At the sound of **horsemen** and archers every town takes to flight.
Eze 23:6 all of them handsome young men, and mounted **horsemen**.
23:12 and commanders, warriors in full dress, mounted **horsemen**,
26:7 with horses and chariots, with **horsemen** and a great army.
38:4 your horses, your **horsemen** fully armed, and a great horde with
Da 11:40 out against him with chariots and **cavalry** and a great fleet of ships.
Hos 1:7 not by bow, sword or battle, or by horses and **horsemen**, but by the
Joel 2:4 have the appearance of horses; they gallop along like **cavalry**.
Na 3:3 Charging **cavalry**, flashing swords and glittering spears! Many
Hab 1:8 Their **cavalry** gallops headlong; their horsemen come from afar.
1:8 Their cavalry gallops headlong; their **horsemen** come from afar.

7306 פַּרְשֶׁגֶן *paršegen*, n.m. [1] [cf. 7358; Ar 10598]

copy [1]

Ezr 7:11 This is a **copy** *of* the letter King Artaxerxes had given to Ezra the

7307 פַּרְשְׁדֹן *paršᵉdōn*, n.[m.]. [1]

back [1]

Jdg 3:22 Even the handle sank in after the blade, which came out his **back**.

7308 פָּרָשָׁה *pārāšâ*, n.f. [2] [√ 7300]

exact amount [1], full account [1]

Est 4:7 including the **exact amount** *of* money Haman had promised to pay
10:2 together with a **full account** *of* the greatness of Mordecai to which

7309 פַּרְשַׁנְדָּתָא *paršandātā'*, n.pr.m. [1]

Parshandatha [1]

Est 9:7 They also killed **Parshandatha**, Dalphon, Aspatha,

7310 פְּרָת *pᵉrāt*, n.pr.loc. [19]

Euphrates [15], Perath [4]

Ge 2:14 the east side of Asshur. And the fourth river is the **Euphrates**.
15:18 from the river of Egypt to the great river, the **Euphrates**—
Dt 1:7 and to Lebanon, as far as the great river, the **Euphrates**.
11:24 to Lebanon, and from the **Euphrates** River to the western sea.
Jos 1:4 the desert to Lebanon, and from the great river, the **Euphrates**—
2Sa 8:3 when he went to restore his control along the **Euphrates** [no K]
2Ki 23:29 Pharaoh Neco king of Egypt went up to the **Euphrates** River to
24:7 all his territory, from the Wadi of Egypt to the **Euphrates** River.
1Ch 5:9 up to the edge of the desert that extends to the **Euphrates** River,
18:3 when he went to establish his control along the **Euphrates** River.
2Ch 35:20 king of Egypt went up to fight at Carchemish on the **Euphrates**,
Jer 13:4 and go now to **Perath** and hide it there in a crevice in the rocks."
13:5 So I went and hid it at **Perath**, as the LORD told me.
13:6 "Go now to **Perath** and get the belt I told you to hide there."
13:7 So I went to **Perath** and dug up the belt and took it from the place
46:2 which was defeated at Carchemish on the **Euphrates** River by
46:6 In the north by the River **Euphrates** they stumble and fall.
46:10 will offer sacrifice in the land of the north by the River **Euphrates**.
51:63 reading this scroll, tie a stone to it and throw it into the **Euphrates**.

7311 פֹּרָת *pōrāt*, var. Not used in NIV/BHS [√ 7238]

7312 פַּרְתְּמִים *partᵉmîm*, n.m.pl. [3]

most noble [1], nobility [1], princes [1]

Est 1:3 The military leaders of Persia and Media, the **princes**,
6:9 and horse be entrusted to one of the king's **most noble** princes.
Da 1:3 in some of the Israelites from the royal family and the **nobility**—

7313 פָּשָׂה *pāśâ*, v. [22]

spread [14], spread [+7313] [4], spreading [+7313] [4]

Lev 13:5 [A] that the sore is unchanged and *has* not **spread** in the skin,
13:6 [A] if the sore has faded and *has* not **spread** in the skin,
13:7 [A] if the rash *does* **spread** [+7313] in his skin after he has
13:7 [A] if the rash *does* **spread** [+7313] in his skin after he has
13:8 [A] is to examine him, and if the rash *has* **spread** in the skin,
13:22 [A] If *it is* **spreading** [+7313] in the skin, the priest shall
13:22 [A] If *it is* **spreading** [+7313] in the skin, the priest shall
13:23 [A] if the spot is unchanged and *has* not **spread**, it is only a scar
13:27 [A] if *it is* **spreading** [+7313] in the skin, the priest shall
13:27 [A] if *it is* **spreading** [+7313] in the skin, the priest shall
13:28 [A] is unchanged and *has* not **spread** in the skin but has faded,
13:32 [A] and if the itch *has* not **spread** and there is no yellow hair in it
13:34 [A] if it *has* not **spread** in the skin and appears to be no more
13:35 [A] if the itch *does* **spread** [+7313] in the skin after he is
13:35 [A] if the itch *does* **spread** [+7313] in the skin after he is
13:36 [A] is to examine him, and if the itch *has* **spread** in the skin,
13:51 [A] and if the mildew *has* **spread** in the clothing, or the woven
13:53 [A] the mildew *has* not **spread** in the clothing, or the woven
13:55 [A] its appearance, even though it *has* not **spread**, it is unclean.
14:39 [A] to inspect the house. If the mildew *has* **spread** on the walls,
14:44 [A] and examine it and, if the mildew *has* **spread** in the house,
14:48 [A] the mildew *has* not **spread** after the house has been

7314 פָּשַׂע *pāśa'*, v. [1] [→ 7315; cf. 5156]

march [1]

Isa 27:4 [A] *I would* **march** against them in battle; I would set them all

7315 פֶּשַׂע *peśa'*, n.[m.]. [1] [√ 7314]

step [1]

1Sa 20:3 and as you live, there is only a **step** between me and death."

7316 פָּשַׂק *pāśaq*, v. [2]

offering body [+906+8079] [1], speaks rashly [+8557] [1]

Pr 13:3 [A] his life, but he *who* **speaks rashly** [+8557] will come to ruin.
Eze 16:25 [D] **offering** [+906+8079] your **body** with increasing

7317 פַּשׂ *paś*, n.[m.]. [1]

wickedness [1]

Job 35:15 never punishes and he does not take the least notice of **wickedness**.

7318 פָּשַׁח *pāšaḥ*, v. [1]

mangled [1]

La 3:11 [D] me from the path and **mangled** me and left me without help.

7319 פַּשְׁחוּר *pašḥûr*, n.pr.m. [14]

Pashhur [13], he[s] [1]

1Ch 9:12 Adaiah son of Jeroham, the son of **Pashhur**, the son of Malkijah;
Ezr 2:38 of **Pashhur** 1,247
10:22 From the descendants of **Pashhur**: Elioenai, Maaseiah, Ishmael,
Ne 7:41 of **Pashhur** 1,247
10:3 [10:4] **Pashhur**, Amariah, Malkijah,
11:12 the son of Zechariah, the son of **Pashhur**, the son of Malkijah,
Jer 20:1 When the priest **Pashhur** son of Immer, the chief officer in the
20:2 **he**[s] had Jeremiah the prophet beaten and put in the stocks at the
20:3 The next day, when **Pashhur** released him from the stocks,
20:3 "The LORD's name for you is not **Pashhur**, but Magor-Missabib.
20:6 you, **Pashhur**, and all who live in your house will go into exile to
21:1 LORD when King Zedekiah sent to him **Pashhur** son of Malkijah
38:1 of Mattan, Gedaliah son of **Pashhur**, Jehucal son of Shelemiah,
38:1 **Pashhur** son of Malkijah heard what Jeremiah was telling all the

7320 פָּשַׁט *pāšaṭ*, v. [43]

raided [7], strip [7], stripped [4], take off [4], skin [2], stripped off [2], took off [2], advance [1], go raiding [1], made a dash [1], raiding [1], remove [1], removed [1], rob [1], rushed forward [1], rushed [1], skinned [1], strip off clothes [+2256+6910] [1], strip off [1], strip the dead [1], swept down [1], taken off [1]

Ge 37:23 [G] Joseph came to his brothers, *they* **stripped** him *of* his robe—
Lev 1:6 [G] *He is to* **skin** the burnt offering and cut it into pieces.
6:11 [6:4] [A] *he is to* **take off** these clothes and put on others, and
16:23 [A] **take off** the linen garments he put on before he entered the
Nu 20:26 [G] **Remove** Aaron's garments and put them on his son Eleazar,
20:28 [G] Moses **removed** Aaron's garments and put them on his son

Jdg 9:33 [A] In the morning at sunrise, **advance** against the city.
9:44 [A] the companies with him **rushed forward** to a position at the
9:44 [A] two companies **rushed** upon those in the fields and struck
20:37 [A] The men who had been in ambush **made a** sudden **dash** into
1Sa 18:4 [F] Jonathan **took off** the robe he was wearing and gave it to
19:24 [A] He **stripped off** his robes and also prophesied in Samuel's
23:27 [A] "Come quickly! The Philistines *are* **raiding** the land."
27:8 [A] Now David and his men went up and **raided** the Geshurites,
27:10 [A] When Achish asked, "Where *did you* **go raiding** today?"
30:1 [A] Now the Amalekites *had* **raided** the Negev and Ziklag. They
30:14 [A] **raided** the Negev of the Kerethites and the territory belonging
31:8 [D] The next day, when the Philistines came to **strip** the dead,
31:9 [G] They cut off his head and **stripped off** his armor, and they
2Sa 23:10 [D] The troops returned to Eleazar, but only to **strip the dead**.
1Ch 10:8 [D] The next day, when the Philistines came to **strip** the dead,
10:9 [G] *They* **stripped** him and took his head and his armor, and sent
14:9 [A] the Philistines had come and **raided** the Valley of Rephaim;
14:13 [A] Once more the Philistines **raided** the valley;
2Ch 25:13 [A] had not allowed to take part in the war **raided** Judean towns
28:18 [A] while the Philistines *had* **raided** towns in the foothills and in
29:34 [G] however, were too few to **skin** all the burnt offerings;
35:11 [G] handed to them, while the Levites **skinned** the animals.
Ne 4:23 [4:17] [A] my men nor the guards with me **took off** our clothes;
Job 1:17 [A] and **swept down** on your camels and carried them off.
19:9 [G] *He has* **stripped** me *of* my honor and removed the crown
22:6 [G] *you* **stripped** men *of* their clothing, leaving them naked.
SS 5:3 [A] *I have* **taken off** my robe—must I put it on again? I have
Isa 32:11 [A] **Strip** [+2256+6910] **off** *your* **clothes**, put sackcloth around
Eze 16:39 [G] *They will* **strip** you *of* your clothes and take your fine
23:26 [G] *They will* also **strip** you *of* your clothes and take your fine
26:16 [A] aside their robes and **take off** their embroidered garments.
44:19 [A] *they are to* **take off** the clothes they have been ministering in
Hos 2:3 [2:5] [G] Otherwise *I will* **strip** her naked and make her as bare
7:1 [A] thieves break into houses, bandits **rob** in the streets;
Mic 2:8 [G] *You* **strip** off the rich robe from those who pass by without a
3:3 [G] **strip off** their skin and break their bones in pieces;
Na 3:16 [A] but like locusts *they* **strip** the land and then fly away.

7321 פָּשַׁע *pāšaʿ*, v. [41] [→ 7322]

rebelled [13], in rebellion [4], rebels [3], transgressors [3], committed [2], rebel [2], rebellion [2], revolted [2], sin [2], sinned [2], do wrong [1], in revolt [1], offended [1], rebellious [1], sinners [1], wrongs [1]

1Ki 8:50 [A] forgive all the offenses *they have* **committed** against you,
12:19 [A] So Israel *has been* **in rebellion** against the house of David to
2Ki 1:1 [A] After Ahab's death, Moab **rebelled** against Israel.
3:5 [A] the king of Moab **rebelled** against the king of Israel.
3:7 [A] "The king of Moab *has* **rebelled** against me. Will you go
8:20 [A] Edom **rebelled** against Judah and set up its own king.
8:22 [A] To this day Edom *has been* **in rebellion** against Judah.
8:22 [A] in rebellion against Judah. Libnah **revolted** at the same time.
2Ch 10:19 [A] So Israel *has been* **in rebellion** against the house of David to
21:8 [A] Edom **rebelled** against Judah and set up its own king.
21:10 [A] To this day Edom *has been* **in rebellion** against Judah.
21:10 [A] Libnah **revolted** at the same time, because Jehoram had
Ezr 10:13 [A] in a day or two, because we have **sinned** greatly in this thing.
Ps 37:38 [A] all **sinners** will be destroyed; the future of the wicked will be
51:13 [51:15] [A] I will teach **transgressors** your ways, and sinners
Pr 18:19 [C] An **offended** brother is more unyielding than a fortified city,
28:21 [A] is not good—yet a man *will* **do wrong** for a piece of bread.
Isa 1:2 [A] and brought them up, but they *have* **rebelled** against me.
1:28 [A] **rebels** and sinners will both be broken, and those who
43:27 [A] first father sinned; your spokesmen **rebelled** against me.
46:8 [A] "Remember this, fix it in mind, take it to heart, you **rebels**.
48:8 [A] how treacherous you are; you were called a **rebel** from birth.
53:12 [A] life unto death, and was numbered with the **transgressors**.
53:12 [A] the sin of many, and made intercession for the **transgressors**.
59:13 [A] **rebellion** and treachery against the LORD, turning our
66:24 [A] look upon the dead bodies of those who **rebelled** against me;
Jer 2:8 [A] the law did not know me; the leaders **rebelled** against me.
2:29 [A] You *have* all **rebelled** against me," declares the LORD.
3:13 [A] *you have* **rebelled** against the LORD your God, you have
33:8 [A] and will forgive all their sins of **rebellion** against me.
La 3:42 [A] "We *have* **sinned** and rebelled and you have not forgiven.
Eze 2:3 [A] their fathers *have been* **in revolt** against me to this very day.
18:31 [A] Rid yourselves of all the offenses *you have* **committed**, and
20:38 [A] I will purge you of those who revolt and **rebel** against me.
Da 8:23 [A] when **rebels** have become completely wicked, a stern-faced
Hos 7:13 [A] Destruction to them, because *they have* **rebelled** against me!
8:1 [A] have broken my covenant and **rebelled** against my law.
14:9 [14:10] [A] walk in them, but the **rebellious** stumble in them.
Am 4:4 [A] "Go to Bethel and **sin**; go to Gilgal and sin yet more. Bring
4:4 [A] "Go to Bethel and sin; go to Gilgal and **sin** yet more. Bring
Zep 3:11 [A] not be put to shame for all the **wrongs** you *have* done to me,

7322 פֶּשַׁע *pešaʿ*, n.m. [93] [√ 7321]

sins [20], offenses [14], rebellion [13], transgressions [11], transgression [8], sin [7], offense [5], rebellious [3], crime [1], disobeys [1], guilt of rebellion [1], guiltless [+1172] [1], illegal possession [1], penalty of sin [1], rebels [1], sinful [1], sinfulness [1], sinned [1], wrong [1], wrongs [1]

Ge 31:36 and took Laban to task. "What is my **crime**?" he asked Laban.
50:17 I ask you to forgive your brothers the **sins** and the wrongs they
50:17 Now please forgive the **sins** *of* the servants of the God of your
Ex 22:9 [22:8] In all cases of **illegal possession** of an ox, a donkey, a
23:21 he will not forgive your **rebellion**, since my Name is in him.
34:7 love to thousands, and forgiving wickedness, **rebellion** and sin.
Lev 16:16 because of the uncleanness and **rebellion** *of* the Israelites,
16:21 confess over it all the wickedness and **rebellion** *of* the Israelites—
Nu 14:18 slow to anger, abounding in love and forgiving sin and **rebellion**.
Jos 24:19 is a jealous God. He will not forgive your **rebellion** and your sins.
1Sa 24:11 [24:12] recognize that I am not guilty of wrongdoing or **rebellion**.
25:28 Please forgive your servant's **offense**, for the LORD will
1Ki 8:50 forgive all the **offenses** they have committed against you,
Job 7:21 Why do you not pardon my **offenses** and forgive my sins?
8:4 sinned against him, he gave them over to the **penalty of** their **sin**.
13:23 and sins have I committed? Show me my **offense** and my sin.
14:17 My **offenses** will be sealed up in a bag; you will cover over my sin.
31:33 if I have concealed my **sin** as men do, by hiding my guilt in my
33:9 'I am pure and without **sin**; I am clean and free from guilt.
34:6 although I am **guiltless** [+1172], his arrow inflicts an incurable
34:37 To his sin he adds **rebellion**; scornfully he claps his hands among
35:6 that affect him? If your **sins** are many, what does that do to him?
36:9 tells them what they have done—that they have **sinned** arrogantly.
Ps 5:10 [5:11] Banish them for their many **sins**, for they have rebelled
19:13 [19:14] Then will I be blameless, innocent of great **transgression**.
25:7 Remember not the sins of my youth and my **rebellious** *ways*;
32:1 Blessed is he whose **transgressions** are forgiven, whose sins are
32:5 I said, "I will confess my **transgressions** to the LORD"—
36:1 [36:2] An oracle is within my heart concerning the **sinfulness** of
39:8 [39:9] Save me from all my **transgressions**; do not make me the
51:1 [51:3] to your great compassion blot out my **transgressions**.
51:3 [51:5] For I know my **transgressions**, and my sin is always
59:3 [59:4] Fierce men conspire against me *for* no **offense** or sin of
65:3 [65:4] overwhelmed by sins, you forgave our **transgressions**.
89:32 [89:33] I will punish their **sin** with the rod, their iniquity with
103:12 from the west, so far has he removed our **transgressions** from us.
107:17 Some became fools through their **rebellious** ways and suffered
Pr 10:12 Hatred stirs up dissension, but love covers over all **wrongs**.
10:19 When words are many, **sin** is not absent, but he who holds his
12:13 An evil man is trapped by his **sinful** talk, but a righteous man
17:9 He who covers over an **offense** promotes love, but whoever repeats
17:19 He who loves a quarrel loves **sin**; he who builds a high gate invites
19:11 gives him patience; it is to his glory to overlook an **offense**.
28:2 When a country is **rebellious**, it has many rulers, but a man of
28:13 He who conceals his **sins** does not prosper, but whoever confesses
28:24 He who robs his father or mother and says, "It's not **wrong**"—
29:6 An evil man is snared by his own **sin**, but a righteous one can sing
29:16 When the wicked thrive, so does **sin**, but the righteous will see
29:22 stirs up dissension, and a hot-tempered one commits many **sins**.
Isa 24:20 so heavy upon it is the **guilt of** its **rebellion** that it falls—never to
43:25 "I, even I, am he who blots out your **transgressions**, for my own
44:22 I have swept away your **offenses** like a cloud, your sins like the
50:1 because of your **transgressions** your mother was sent away.
53:5 he was pierced for our **transgressions**, he was crushed for our
53:8 of the living; for the **transgression** *of* my people he was stricken.
57:4 your tongue? Are you not a brood of **rebels**, the offspring of liars?
58:1 Declare to my people their **rebellion** and to the house of Jacob
59:12 For our **offenses** are many in your sight, and our sins testify against
59:12 Our **offenses** are ever with us, and we acknowledge our iniquities:
59:20 to those in Jacob who repent of their **sins**," declares the LORD.
Jer 5:6 for their **rebellion** is great and their backslidings many.
La 1:5 The LORD has brought her grief because of her many **sins**.
1:14 "My **sins** have been bound into a yoke; by his hands they were
1:22 deal with them as you have dealt with me because of all my **sins**.
Eze 14:11 nor will they defile themselves anymore with all their **sins**.
18:22 None of the **offenses** he has committed will be remembered against
18:28 Because he considers all the **offenses** he has committed and turns
18:30 Turn away from all your **offenses**; then sin will not be your
18:31 Rid yourselves of all the **offenses** you have committed, and get a
21:24 [21:29] have brought to mind your guilt by your open **rebellion**,
33:10 "Our **offenses** and sins weigh us down, and we are wasting away
33:12 of the righteous man will not save him when he **disobeys**,
37:23 with their idols and vile images or with any of their **offenses**,
39:24 I dealt with them according to their uncleanness and their **offenses**,
Da 8:12 Because of **rebellion**, the host ⌊of the saints⌋ and the daily sacrifice
8:13 the **rebellion** that causes desolation, and the surrender of the
9:24 decreed for your people and your holy city to finish **transgression**,

Am 1: 3 "For three **sins** *of* Damascus, even for four, I will not turn back
1: 6 "For three **sins** *of* Gaza, even for four, I will not turn back ⌊my
1: 9 "For three **sins** *of* Tyre, even for four, I will not turn back ⌊my
1: 11 "For three **sins** *of* Edom, even for four, I will not turn back ⌊my
1: 13 "For three **sins** *of* Ammon, even for four, I will not turn back ⌊my
2: 1 "For three **sins** *of* Moab, even for four, I will not turn back ⌊my
2: 4 "For three **sins** *of* Judah, even for four, I will not turn back ⌊my
2: 6 "For three **sins** *of* Israel, even for four, I will not turn back ⌊my
3: 14 "On the day I punish Israel for her **sins**, I will destroy the altars of
5: 12 For I know how many are your **offenses** and how great your sins.
Mic 1: 5 All this is because of Jacob's **transgression**, because of the sins of
1: 5 What is Jacob's **transgression**? Is it not Samaria? What is Judah's
1: 13 of Zion, for the **transgressions** *of* Israel were found in you.
3: 8 and with justice and might, to declare to Jacob his **transgression**,
6: 7 Shall I offer my firstborn for my **transgression**, the fruit of my
7: 18 and forgives the **transgression** of the remnant of his inheritance?

7323 פֵּשֶׁר **pēšer**, n.[m.]. [1] [→ Ar 10599, 10600]

explanation [1]

Ecc 8: 1 Who is like the wise man? Who knows the **explanation** *of* things?

7324 פֵּשֶׁת **pēšet**, n.[m.]. [16] [→ 7325]

linen [12], flax [4]

Lev 13: 47 is contaminated with mildew—any woolen or **linen** clothing,
13: 48 any woven or knitted material of **linen** or wool, any leather
13: 52 up the clothing, or the woven or knitted material of wool or **linen**,
13: 59 concerning contamination by mildew in woolen or **linen** clothing,
Dt 22: 11 Do not wear clothes of wool and **linen** woven together.
Jos 2: 6 hidden them under the stalks of **flax** she had laid out on the roof.)
Jdg 15: 14 The ropes on his arms became like charred **flax**, and the bindings
Pr 31: 13 She selects wool and **flax** and works with eager hands.
Isa 19: 9 Those who work with combed **flax** will despair, the weavers of
Jer 13: 1 "Go and buy a **linen** belt and put it around your waist, but do not
Eze 40: 3 he was standing in the gateway with a **linen** cord and a measuring
44: 17 enter the gates of the inner court, they are to wear **linen** clothes;
44: 18 They are to wear **linen** turbans on their heads and linen
44: 18 on their heads and **linen** undergarments around their waists.
Hos 2: 5 [2:7] and my water, my wool and my **linen**, my oil and my drink.'
2: 9 [2:11] I will take back my wool and my **linen**, intended to cover

7325 פִּשְׁתָּה **pištâ**, n.f. [4] [√ 7324]

flax [2], wick [2]

Ex 9: 31 (The **flax** and barley were destroyed, since the barley had headed
9: 31 since the barley had headed and the **flax** was in bloom.
Isa 42: 3 reed he will not break, and a smoldering **wick** he will not snuff out.
43: 17 lay there, never to rise again, extinguished, snuffed out like a **wick**:

7326 פַּת **pat**, n.f. [14] [→ 7329; cf. 7359]

piece [2], something to eat [+4312] [2], bread [1], crumble [+906+7359] [1], crust [1], food [+4312] [1], food [1], it[s] [1], little [1], pebbles [1], pieces [1], some [1]

Ge 18: 5 Let me get you **something to eat** [+4312], so you can be refreshed
Lev 2: 6 **Crumble** [+906+7359] it and pour oil on it; it is a grain offering.
6: 21 [6:14] present the grain offering broken in **pieces** as an aroma
Jdg 19: 5 his son-in-law, "Refresh yourself with **something to eat** [+4312];
Ru 2: 14 over here. Have some bread and dip **it**[s] in the wine vinegar."
1Sa 2: 36 me to some priestly office so I can have **food** [+4312] to eat." '"
28: 22 to your servant and let me give you **some** food so you may eat
2Sa 12: 3 It shared his **food**, drank from his cup and even slept in his arms.
1Ki 17: 11 going to get it, he called, "And bring me, please, a **piece** *of* bread."
Job 31: 17 if I have kept my **bread** to myself, not sharing it with the
Ps 147: 17 He hurls down his hail like **pebbles**. Who can withstand his icy
Pr 17: 1 Better a dry **crust** with peace and quiet than a house full of
23: 8 You will vomit up the **little** you have eaten and will have wasted
28: 21 is not good—yet a man will do wrong for a **piece** *of* bread.

7327 פֹּת **pōt**, n.[f.]. [2] [cf. 5159]

scalps [1], sockets [1]

1Ki 7: 50 and the gold **sockets** for the doors of the innermost room,
Isa 3: 17 of the women of Zion; the LORD will make their **scalps** bald."

7328 פִּתְאֹם **pitʾōm**, subst. (used as adv.). [25] [√ 7353]

suddenly [13], sudden [4], in an instant [2], all at once [1], at once [1], by surprise [1], so quickly [+928] [1], suddenly [+928+7353] [1], unexpectedly [1]

Nu 6: 9 " 'If someone dies **suddenly** [+928+7353] in his presence,
12: 4 **At once** the LORD said to Moses, Aaron and Miriam, "Come out
Jos 10: 9 an all-night march from Gilgal, Joshua took them **by surprise**.
11: 7 his whole army came against them **suddenly** at the Waters of
2Ch 29: 36 about for his people, because it was done **so quickly** [+928].
Job 5: 3 have seen a fool taking root, but **suddenly** his house was cursed.
9: 23 When a scourge brings **sudden** death, he mocks the despair of the
22: 10 is why snares are all around you, why **sudden** peril terrifies you,
Ps 64: 4 [64:5] innocent man; they shoot at him **suddenly**, without fear.
64: 7 [64:8] them with arrows; **suddenly** they will be struck down.
Pr 3: 25 Have no fear of **sudden** disaster or of the ruin that overtakes the
6: 15 Therefore disaster will overtake him **in an instant**; he will
7: 22 **All at once** he followed her like an ox going to the slaughter,
24: 22 for those two will send **sudden** destruction upon them, and who
Ecc 9: 12 so men are trapped by evil times that fall **unexpectedly** upon them.
Isa 29: 5 the ruthless hordes like blown chaff. **Suddenly**, in an instant,
30: 13 cracked and bulging, that collapses **suddenly**, in an instant.
47: 11 a catastrophe you cannot foresee will **suddenly** come upon you.
48: 3 I made them known; then **suddenly** I acted, and they came to pass.
Jer 4: 20 **In an instant** my tents are destroyed, my shelter in a moment.
6: 26 as for an only son, for **suddenly** the destroyer will come upon us.
15: 8 **suddenly** I will bring down on them anguish and terror.
18: 22 Let a cry be heard from their houses when you **suddenly** bring
51: 8 Babylon will **suddenly** fall and be broken. Wail over her!
Mal 3: 1 Then **suddenly** the Lord you are seeking will come to his temple;

7329 פַּת־בַּג **pat-bag**, n.[m.]. [6] [√ 7326 + 952 [?]]

food [4], choice food [1], provisions [1]

Da 1: 5 The king assigned them a daily amount of **food** and wine *from* the
1: 8 But Daniel resolved not to defile himself with the royal **food**
1: 13 our appearance with that of the young men who eat the royal **food**,
1: 15 better nourished than any of the young men who ate the royal **food**.
1: 16 So the guard took away their **choice food** and the wine they were
11: 26 Those who eat from the king's **provisions** will try to destroy him;

7330 פִּתְגָם **pitgām**, n.m. [2] [→ Ar 10601]

edict [1], sentence [1]

Est 1: 20 when the king's **edict** is proclaimed throughout all his vast realm,
Ecc 8: 11 When the **sentence** for a crime is not quickly carried out, the hearts

7331 [1]פָּתָה **pātâ[1]**, v.den. [27] [→ 7343, 7344, 7346]

entice [5], deceive [2], enticed [2], enticing [2], allure [1], be deceived [1], be persuaded [1], been enticed [1], coax [1], deceived [1], easily deceived [1], enticed [+4222] [1], entices [1], flatter [1], is enticed [1], lure [1], seduces [1], simple [1], talks too much [+8557] [1], was deceived [1]

Ex 22: 16 [22:15] [D] "If a man **seduces** a virgin who is not pledged to be
Dt 11: 16 [A] or you *will be* **enticed** [+4222] to turn away and worship
Jdg 14: 15 [D] "**Coax** your husband *into* explaining the riddle for us, or we
16: 5 [D] "*See if you can* **lure** him *into* showing you the secret of his
2Sa 3: 25 [D] he came to **deceive** you and observe your movements
1Ki 22: 20 [D] 'Who *will* **entice** Ahab *into* attacking Ramoth Gilead and
22: 21 [D] stood before the LORD and said, 'I *will* **entice** him.'
22: 22 [D] " 'You will succeed *in* **enticing** him,' said the LORD. 'Go
2Ch 18: 19 [D] 'Who *will* **entice** Ahab king of Israel *into* attacking Ramoth
18: 20 [D] stood before the LORD and said, 'I *will* **entice** him.'
18: 21 [D] " 'You will succeed *in* **enticing** him,' said the LORD. 'Go
Job 5: 2 [A] Resentment kills a fool, and envy slays the **simple**.
31: 9 [C] "If my heart *has* **been enticed** by a woman, or if I have
31: 27 [A] so that my heart *was* secretly **enticed** and my hand offered
Ps 78: 36 [D] then *they would* **flatter** him with their mouths, lying to him
Pr 1: 10 [D] My son, if sinners **entice** you, do not give in to them.
16: 29 [D] A violent man **entices** his neighbor and leads him down a
20: 19 [A] a confidence; so avoid a *man who* **talks too much** [+8557].
24: 28 [D] your neighbor without cause, or use your lips *to* **deceive**.
25: 15 [E] Through patience a ruler *can* **be persuaded**, and a gentle
Jer 20: 7 [D] O LORD, *you* **deceived** me, and I was deceived;
20: 7 [C] O LORD, you deceived me, and *I* **was deceived**;
20: 10 [E] waiting for me to slip, saying, "Perhaps *he will* **be deceived**;
Eze 14: 9 [E] " 'And if the prophet **is enticed** to utter a prophecy,
14: 9 [D] I the LORD *have* **enticed** that prophet, and I will stretch out
Hos 2: 14 [2:16] [D] "Therefore I *am* now *going to* **allure** her; I will lead
7: 11 [A] "Ephraim is like a dove, **easily deceived** and senseless—

7332 [2]פָּתָה **pātâ[2]**, v. [1] [→ 3651; Ar 10603]

extend the territory [1]

Ge 9: 27 [G] *May* God **extend the territory** of Japheth; may Japheth live

7333 פְּתוּאֵל **p^{e}tûʾēl**, n.pr.m. [1] [√ 7343 + 446]

Pethuel [1]

Joel 1: 1 The word of the LORD that came to Joel son of **Pethuel**.

[F] Hitpael (hitpoel, hitpoal, hitpolel, hitpolal, hitpalel, hitpalal, hitpalpel, hitpalpal, hotpael, hotpaal) [G] Hiphil (hiphtil) [H] Hophal [I] Hishtaphel

7334 פִּתּוּחַ *pittûaḥ*, n.m. [11] [√ 7338]

engraved [2], *untranslated* [1], art of engraving [+7338] [1], carved paneling [1], engrave [+7338] [1], engraved [+7338] [1], engraves [1], experienced in engraving [+7338] [1], inscription [+4844] [1], inscription [1]

Ex 28: 11 of Israel on the two stones the way a gem cutter **engraves** a seal.
28: 21 each **engraved** *like* a seal with the name of one of the twelve
28: 36 "Make a plate of pure gold and **engrave** [+7338] on it as on a seal:
39: 6 **engraved** them **like** [+7338] a seal with the names of the sons of
39: 14 each **engraved** *like* a seal with the name of one of the twelve
39: 30 and engraved on it, like an **inscription** [+4844] *on* a seal:
1Ki 6: 29 he carved cherubim, **[NIE]** palm trees and open flowers.
2Ch 2: 7 [2:6] blue yarn, and experienced in the **art of engraving** [+7338],
2: 14 [2:13] He *is* **experienced in** all kinds of **engraving** [+7338] and
Ps 74: 6 They smashed all the **carved paneling** with their axes
Zec 3: 9 I will engrave an **inscription** *on* it,' says the LORD Almighty,

7335 פְּתוֹר *pᵉtôr*, n.pr.loc. [2]

Pethor [2]

Nu 22: 5 son of Beor, who was at **Pethor**, near the River, in his native land.
Dt 23: 4 [23:5] they hired Balaam son of Beor from **Pethor** *in* Aram

7336 פְּתוֹת *pᵉtôt*, n.[m.]. [1] [√ 7359]

scraps [1]

Eze 13: 19 among my people for a few handfuls of barley and **scraps** *of* bread.

7337 פָּתַח *pātaḥ*[1], v. [136] [→ 3652, 3653, 3654, 5157, 5158, 7339, 7340, 7341, 7342, 7347; Ar 10602]

open [44], opened [33], be opened [4], loose [2], openhanded [+906+3338+4200+7337] [2], openhanded [+906+3338+7337] [2], speak up [+7023] [2], takes off [2], were opened [2], wide open [+7337] [2], *untranslated* [1], are opened [1], be poured out [1], be released [1], be set free [1], bottled-up [+4202] [1], break open [1], breaking up [1], draw [1], drawn [1], expose [1], expound [1], free yourself [1], freed [1], freeing [1], give command [+928+7023] [1], go [1], loosened [1], make flow [1], market [1], open wide [1], opened up [1], opens [1], reach [1], release [1], removed [1], say [+7023] [1], set free [1], speaks [+7023] [1], strip [1], take off [1], throw open [1], thrown open [1], uncovers [1], unloaded [1], unlocked [1], unsealed [1], unstopped [1], unstrung [1], untied [1], was opened [1]

Ge 7: 11 [C] burst forth, and the floodgates of the heavens **were opened**.
8: 6 [A] After forty days Noah **opened** the window he had made in
24: 32 [D] the man went to the house, and the camels *were* **unloaded**.
29: 31 [A] was not loved, *he* **opened** her womb, but Rachel was barren.
30: 22 [A] he listened to her and **opened** her womb.
41: 56 [A] Joseph **opened** the storehouses and sold grain to the
42: 27 [A] night one of them **opened** his sack to get feed for his donkey,
43: 21 [A] at the place where we stopped for the night *we* **opened** our
44: 11 [A] them quickly lowered his sack to the ground and **opened** it.
Ex 2: 6 [A] *She* **opened** it and saw the baby. He was crying, and she felt
21: 33 [A] "If a man **uncovers** a pit or digs one and fails to cover it
Nu 16: 32 [A] the earth **opened** its mouth and swallowed them, with their
19: 15 [B] every **open** container without a lid fastened on it will be
22: 28 [A] the LORD **opened** the donkey's mouth, and she said to
26: 10 [A] The earth **opened** its mouth and swallowed them along with
Dt 15: 8 [A] Rather *be* **openhanded** [+906+3338+4200+7337] and freely
15: 8 [A] Rather *be* **openhanded** [+906+3338+4200+7337] and freely
15: 11 [A] I command you *to be* **openhanded** [+906+3338+7337] toward
15: 11 [A] I command you *to be* **openhanded** [+906+3338+7337] toward
20: 11 [A] If they accept and **open** their gates, all the people in it shall
28: 12 [A] The LORD *will* **open** the heavens, the storehouse of his
Jos 8: 17 [B] They left the city **open** and went in pursuit of Israel.
10: 22 [A] "**Open** the mouth of the cave and bring those five kings out
Jdg 3: 25 [A] when he *did* not **open** the doors of the room, they took a key
3: 25 [A] the doors of the room, they took a key and **unlocked** them.
4: 19 [A] *She* **opened** a skin of milk, gave him a drink, and covered
19: 27 [A] got up in the morning and **opened** the door of the house
1Sa 3: 15 [A] and then **opened** the doors of the house of the LORD.
1Ki 8: 29 [B] May your eyes be **open** toward this temple night and day,
8: 52 [B] "May your eyes be **open** to your servant's plea and to the
20: 11 [D] on his armor should not boast like *one who* **takes** *it* **off**.' "
2Ki 6: 17 [A] Elisha prayed, "O LORD, **open** his eyes so he may see."
9: 3 [A] king over Israel.' Then **open** the door and run; don't delay!"
9: 10 [A] no one will bury her.' " Then *he* **opened** the door and ran.
13: 17 [A] "**Open** the east window," he said, and he opened it. "Shoot!"
13: 17 [A] "Open the east window," he said, and *he* **opened** it. "Shoot!"
15: 16 [A] and its vicinity, because *they* refused *to* **open** their gates.
2Ch 6: 20 [B] May your eyes be **open** toward this temple day and night,
6: 40 [B] may your eyes be **open** and your ears attentive to the prayers
7: 15 [B] Now my eyes will be **open** and my ears attentive to the
29: 3 [A] he **opened** the doors of the temple of the LORD
Ne 1: 6 [B] your eyes **open** to hear the prayer your servant is praying
6: 5 [B] the same message, and in his hand was an **unsealed** letter
7: 3 [C] "The gates of Jerusalem *are* not *to* **be opened** until the sun is
8: 5 [A] Ezra **opened** the book. All the people could see him
8: 5 [A] above them; and as *he* **opened** it, the people all stood up.
13: 19 [A] doors to be shut and not **opened** until the Sabbath was over.
Job 3: 1 [A] Job **opened** his mouth and cursed the day of his birth.
11: 5 [A] God would speak, that *he would* **open** his lips against you
12: 14 [C] cannot be rebuilt; the man he imprisons cannot **be released**.
12: 18 [D] *He* **takes off** the shackles put on by kings and ties a loincloth
29: 19 [B] My roots *will* **reach** to the water, and the dew will lie all
30: 11 [D] Now that God *has* **unstrung** my bow and afflicted me, they
31: 32 [A] in the street, for my door *was always* **open** to the traveler—
32: 19 [C] inside I am like **bottled-up** [+4202] wine, like new wineskins
32: 20 [A] I must speak and find relief; *I must* **open** my lips and reply.
33: 2 [A] *I am about to* **open** my mouth; my words are on the tip of
38: 31 [D] the beautiful Pleiades? *Can you* **loose** the cords of Orion?
39: 5 [D] "Who let the wild donkey go free? Who **untied** his ropes?
41: 14 [41:6] [D] Who *dares* **open** the doors of his mouth,
Ps 5: 9 [5:10] [B] Their throat is an **open** grave; with their tongue they
30: 11 [30:12] [D] *you* **removed** my sackcloth and clothed me with
37: 14 [A] The wicked **draw** the sword and bend the bow to bring down
38: 13 [38:14] [A] like a mute, *who* cannot **open** his mouth;
39: 9 [39:10] [A] *I would* not **open** my mouth, for you are the one
49: 4 [49:5] [A] to a proverb; with the harp *I will* **expound** my riddle:
51: 15 [51:17] [A] O Lord, **open** my lips, and my mouth will declare
78: 2 [A] *I will* **open** my mouth in parables, I will utter hidden things,
78: 23 [A] to the skies above and **opened** the doors of the heavens;
102: 20 [102:21] [D] and **release** those condemned to death."
104: 28 [A] *when you* **open** your hand, they are satisfied with good
105: 20 [D] king sent and released him, the ruler of peoples **set** him **free**.
105: 41 [A] *He* **opened** the rock, and water gushed out; like a river it
106: 17 [A] The earth **opened up** and swallowed Dathan; it buried the
109: 2 [A] and deceitful men *have* **opened** their mouths against me;
116: 16 [D] of your maidservant; *you have* **freed** me from my chains.
118: 19 [A] **Open** for me the gates of righteousness; I will enter and give
145: 16 [A] You **open** your hand and satisfy the desires of every living
Pr 24: 7 [A] in the assembly at the gate he *has* nothing *to* **say** [+7023].
31: 8 [A] "**Speak up** [+7023] for those who cannot speak for
31: 9 [A] **Speak up** [+7023] and judge fairly; defend the rights of the
31: 26 [A] She **speaks** [+7023] with wisdom, and faithful instruction is
SS 5: 2 [A] "**Open** to me, my sister, my darling, my dove, my flawless
5: 5 [A] I arose to **open** for my lover, and my hands dripped with
5: 6 [A] I **opened** for my lover, but my lover had left; he was gone.
7: 12 [7:13] [D] if their blossoms *have* **opened**, and if the
Isa 5: 27 [C] not a belt *is* **loosened** at the waist, not a sandal thong is
14: 17 [A] overthrew its cities and *would* not *let* his captives **go** home?"
20: 2 [D] "**Take off** the sackcloth from your body and the sandals from
22: 22 [A] what *he* **opens** no one can shut, and what he shuts no one can
22: 22 [A] opens no one can shut, and what he shuts no *one can* **open**.
24: 18 [C] The floodgates of the heavens **are opened**, the foundations of
26: 2 [A] **Open** the gates that the righteous nation may enter,
28: 24 [D] *Does he keep on* **breaking up** and harrowing the soil?
35: 5 [C] of the blind be opened and the ears of the deaf **unstopped**.
41: 18 [A] *I will* **make** rivers **flow** on barren heights, and springs within
45: 1 [D] subdue nations before him and *to* **strip** kings *of* their armor,
45: 1 [A] to **open** doors before him so that gates will not be shut:
45: 8 [A] *Let* the earth **open wide**, let salvation spring up, let
48: 8 [D] nor understood; from of old your ear *has* not *been* **open**.
50: 5 [A] The Sovereign LORD *has* **opened** my ears, and I have not
51: 14 [C] The cowering prisoners *will* soon **be set free**; they will not
52: 2 [F] **Free yourself** *from* the chains on your neck, O captive
53: 7 [A] was oppressed and afflicted, yet *he did* not **open** his mouth;
53: 7 [A] before her shearers is silent, so *he did* not **open** his mouth.
58: 6 [D] *to* **loose** the chains of injustice and untie the cords of the
60: 11 [D] Your gates *will* always *stand* **open**, they will never be shut,
Jer 1: 14 [C] "From the north disaster *will* **be poured out** on all who live
5: 16 [B] Their quivers are like an **open** grave; all of them are mighty
13: 19 [A] will be shut up, and there will be no *one to* **open** them.
40: 4 [D] But today *I am* **freeing** you from the chains on your wrists.
50: 25 [A] The LORD *has* **opened** his arsenal and brought out the
50: 26 [A] **Break open** her granaries; pile her up like heaps of grain.
Eze 1: 1 [C] the heavens **were opened** and I saw visions of God.
3: 2 [A] So *I* **opened** my mouth, and he gave me the scroll to eat.
3: 27 [A] to you, *I will* **open** your mouth and you shall say to them,
21: 22 [21:27] [A] to **give** *the* **command** [+928+7023] to slaughter,
21: 28 [21:33] [B] " 'A sword, a sword, **drawn** for the slaughter,
24: 27 [C] At that time your mouth *will* **be opened**; you will speak with
25: 9 [A] therefore I *will* **expose** the flank of Moab, beginning at its
33: 22 [A] *he* **opened** my mouth before the man came to me in the
33: 22 [C] So my mouth **was opened** and I was no longer silent.
37: 12 [A] I *am going to* **open** your graves and bring you up from them;
37: 13 [A] when I **open** your graves and bring you up from them.

Eze 44: 2 [C] *It must* not **be opened**; no one may enter through it. It is to
46: 1 [C] and on the day of the New Moon *it is to* **be opened**.
46: 1 [C] and on the day of the New Moon it is to be opened. **[RPH]**
46: 12 [A] the gate facing east *is to be* **opened** for him.
Da 10: 16 [A] my lips, and *I* **opened** my mouth and began to speak.
Am 8: 5 [A] and the Sabbath be ended that *we may* **market** wheat?"—
Na 2: 6 [2:7] [C] The river gates *are* **thrown open** and the palace
3: 13 [C] The gates of your land *are* **wide open** [+7337] to your
3: 13 [A] The gates of your land *are* **wide open** [+7337] to your
Zec 11: 1 [A] **Open** your doors, O Lebanon, so that fire may devour your
13: 1 [C] "On that day a fountain will be **opened** to the house of David
Mal 3: 10 [A] "and see if *I will* not **throw open** the floodgates of heaven

7338 פָּתַח[2] *pātaḥ*[2], v. [9] [→ 7334]

engrave [3], art of engraving [+7334] [1], carved [1], engrave [+7334] [1], engraved [+7334] [1], engraved [1], experienced in engraving [+7334] [1]

Ex 28: 9 [D] and **engrave** on them the names of the sons of Israel
28: 11 [D] **Engrave** the names of the sons of Israel *on* the two stones
28: 36 [D] a plate of pure gold and **engrave** [+7334] on it as on a seal:
39: 6 [E] **engraved** [+7334] them *like* a seal with the names of the
1Ki 7: 36 [D] *He* **engraved** cherubim, lions and palm trees on the surfaces
2Ch 2: 7 [2:6] [D] and experienced in the **art of engraving** [+7334],
2: 14 [2:13] [D] He *is* **experienced in** all kinds of **engraving** [+7334]
3: 7 [D] the temple with gold, and *he* **carved** cherubim on the walls.
Zec 3: 9 [D] I *will* **engrave** an inscription on it,' says the LORD

7339 פֶּתַח *petaḥ*, n.m. [164 / 163] [√ 7337]

entrance [110], door [15], doorway [9], doors [5], entrances [3], *untranslated* [2], doorways [2], gate [2], gates [2], it[s] [+2021] [2], doorway [+4647] [1], doorways [+4647] [1], entrance [+9133] [1], entrances [+4427] [1], gateways [+9133] [1], mouth [1], one[s] [1], outside [+2025] [1], outside [1], parapet opening [1], words [+7023] [1]

Ge 4: 7 But if you do not do what is right, sin is crouching at your **door**;
6: 16 Put a **door** in the side of the ark and make lower, middle and upper
18: 1 he was sitting at the **entrance** *to* his tent in the heat of the day.
18: 2 he hurried from the **entrance** *of* his tent to meet them and bowed
18: 10 Now Sarah was listening at the **entrance** *to* the tent, which was
19: 6 Lot went **outside** [+2025] to meet them and shut the door behind
19: 11 Then they struck the men who were at the **door** *of* the house,
19: 11 and old, with blindness so that they could not find the **door**.
38: 14 then sat down at the **entrance** *to* Enaim, which is on the road to
43: 19 to Joseph's steward and spoke to him at the **entrance** *to* the house.
Ex 12: 22 Not one of you shall go out the **door** *of* his house until morning.
12: 23 and sides of the doorframe and will pass over that **doorway**,
26: 36 "For the **entrance** *to* the tent make a curtain of blue, purple
29: 4 bring Aaron and his sons to the **entrance** *to* the Tent of Meeting
29: 11 Slaughter it in the LORD's presence at the **entrance** *to* the Tent
29: 32 At the **entrance** *to* the Tent of Meeting, Aaron and his sons are to
29: 42 at the **entrance** *to* the Tent of Meeting before the LORD.
33: 8 all the people rose and stood at the **entrances** *to* their tents,
33: 9 the pillar of cloud would come down and stay at the **entrance**,
33: 10 people saw the pillar of cloud standing at the **entrance** *to* the tent,
33: 10 they all stood and worshiped, each at the **entrance** *to* his tent.
35: 15 the curtain for the **doorway** at the entrance to the tabernacle;
35: 15 the curtain for the doorway at the **entrance** *to* the tabernacle;
36: 37 For the **entrance** *to* the tent they made a curtain of blue, purple
38: 8 of the women who served at the **entrance** *to* the Tent of Meeting.
38: 30 They used it to make the bases for the **entrance** *to* the Tent of
39: 38 the fragrant incense, and the curtain for the **entrance** *to* the tent;
40: 5 the Testimony and put the curtain at the **entrance** to the tabernacle.
40: 6 "Place the altar of burnt offering in front of the **entrance** *to* the
40: 12 "Bring Aaron and his sons to the **entrance** *to* the Tent of Meeting
40: 28 Then he put up the curtain at the **entrance** to the tabernacle.
40: 29 He set the altar of burnt offering near the **entrance** *to* the
Lev 1: 3 He must present it at the **entrance** *to* the Tent of Meeting
1: 5 sprinkle it against the altar on all sides at the **entrance** *to* the Tent
3: 2 his offering and slaughter it at the **entrance** *to* the Tent of Meeting.
4: 4 He is to present the bull at the **entrance** *to* the Tent of Meeting
4: 7 the altar of burnt offering at the **entrance** *to* the Tent of Meeting.
4: 18 the altar of burnt offering at the **entrance** *to* the Tent of Meeting.
8: 3 gather the entire assembly at the **entrance** *to* the Tent of Meeting."
8: 4 and the assembly gathered at the **entrance** *to* the Tent of Meeting.
8: 31 "Cook the meat at the **entrance** *to* the Tent of Meeting and eat it
8: 33 Do not leave the **entrance** *to* the Tent of Meeting for seven days,
8: 35 You must stay at the **entrance** *to* the Tent of Meeting day
10: 7 Do not leave the **entrance** *to* the Tent of Meeting or you will die,
12: 6 she is to bring to the priest at the **entrance** *to* the Tent of Meeting a
14: 11 his offerings before the LORD at the **entrance** *to* the Tent of
14: 23 his cleansing to the priest at the **entrance** *to* the Tent of Meeting,
14: 38 the priest shall go out the **doorway** *of* the house and close it up for
15: 14 come before the LORD to the **entrance** *to* the Tent of Meeting
15: 29 and bring them to the priest at the **entrance** *to* the Tent of Meeting.
16: 7 present them before the LORD at the **entrance** *to* the Tent of
17: 4 instead of bringing it to the **entrance** *to* the Tent of Meeting to
17: 5 at the **entrance** *to* the Tent of Meeting and sacrifice them as
17: 6 the altar of the LORD at the **entrance** *to* the Tent of Meeting
17: 9 does not bring it to the **entrance** *to* the Tent of Meeting to sacrifice
19: 21 must bring a ram to the **entrance** *to* the Tent of Meeting for a guilt
Nu 3: 25 its coverings, the curtain at the **entrance** *to* the Tent of Meeting,
3: 26 the curtain at the **entrance** *to* the courtyard surrounding the
4: 25 of sea cows, the curtains for the **entrance** *to* the Tent of Meeting,
4: 26 the curtain for the **entrance** [+9133], the ropes and all the
6: 10 or two young pigeons to the priest at the **entrance** *to* the Tent of
6: 13 He is to be brought to the **entrance** *to* the Tent of Meeting.
6: 18 " 'Then at the **entrance** *to* the Tent of Meeting, the Nazirite must
10: 3 the whole community is to assemble before you at the **entrance** *to*
11: 10 people of every family wailing, each at the **entrance** *to* his tent.
12: 5 he stood at the **entrance** *to* the Tent and summoned Aaron
16: 18 with Moses and Aaron at the **entrance** *to* the Tent of Meeting.
16: 19 in opposition to them at the **entrance** *to* the Tent of Meeting,
16: 27 their wives, children and little ones at the **entrances** *to* their tents.
16: 50 [17:15] Aaron returned to Moses at the **entrance** *to* the Tent of
20: 6 Aaron went from the assembly to the **entrance** *to* the Tent of
25: 6 while they were weeping at the **entrance** *to* the Tent of Meeting.
27: 2 the **entrance** *to* the Tent of Meeting and stood before Moses,
Dt 22: 21 she shall be brought to the **door** *of* her father's house and there the
31: 15 a pillar of cloud, and the cloud stood over the **entrance** *to* the Tent.
Jos 8: 29 from the tree and throw it down at the **entrance** *of* the city gate.
19: 51 the presence of the LORD at the **entrance** *to* the Tent of Meeting.
20: 4 he is to stand in the **entrance** *of* the city gate and state his case
Jdg 4: 20 "Stand in the **doorway** *of* the tent," he told her. "If someone comes
9: 35 and was standing at the **entrance** *to* the city gate just as Abimelech
9: 40 fell wounded in the flight—all the way to the **entrance** *to* the gate.
9: 44 him rushed forward to a position at the **entrance** *to* the city gate.
9: 52 But as he approached the **entrance** *to* the tower to set it on fire,
18: 16 armed for battle, stood at the **entrance** *to* the gate.
18: 17 and the six hundred armed men stood at the **entrance** *to* the gate.
19: 26 was staying, fell down at the **door** and lay there until daylight.
19: 27 there lay his concubine, fallen in the **doorway** *of* the house,
1Sa 2: 22 how they slept with the women who served at the **entrance** *to* the
2Sa 10: 8 and drew up in battle formation at the **entrance** *to* their city gate,
11: 9 Uriah slept at the **entrance** *to* the palace with all his master's
11: 23 the open, but we drove them back to the **entrance** *to* the city gate.
1Ki 6: 8 The **entrance** *to* the lowest floor was on the south side of the
6: 31 For the **entrance** *of* the inner sanctuary he made doors of olive
6: 33 four-sided jambs of olive wood for the **entrance** *to* the main hall.
7: 5 All the **doorways** [+4647] had rectangular frames; they were in the
14: 6 So when Ahijah heard the sound of her footsteps at the **door**,
14: 27 of the guard on duty at the **entrance** *to* the royal palace.
17: 10 When he came to the town **gate**, a widow was there gathering
19: 13 over his face and went out and stood at the **mouth** *of* the cave.
22: 10 at the threshing floor by the **entrance** *of* the gate of Samaria,
2Ki 4: 15 "Call her." So he called her, and she stood in the **doorway**.
5: 9 his horses and chariots and stopped at the **door** of Elisha's house.
7: 3 Now there were four men with leprosy at the **entrance** *of* the city
10: 8 "Put them in two piles at the **entrance** *of* the city gate until
23: 8 at the **entrance** *to* the Gate of Joshua, the city governor, which is
1Ch 9: 21 Zechariah son of Meshelemiah was the gatekeeper at the **entrance**
19: 9 and drew up in battle formation at the **entrance** *to* their city,
2Ch 4: 22 dishes and censers; and the gold **doors** *of* the temple:
12: 10 of the guard on duty at the **entrance** *to* the royal palace.
18: 9 at the threshing floor by the **entrance** *to* the gate of Samaria,
Ne 3: 20 from the angle to the **entrance** *of* the house of Eliashib the high
3: 21 from the **entrance** *of* Eliashib's house to the end of it.
Est 5: 1 was sitting on his royal throne in the hall, facing the **entrance**.
Job 31: 9 enticed by a woman, or if I have lurked at my neighbor's **door**,
31: 34 contempt of the clans that I kept silent and would not go **outside**
Ps 24: 7 be lifted up, you ancient **doors**, that the King of glory may come
24: 9 lift them up, you ancient **doors**, that the King of glory may come
Pr 1: 21 in the **gateways** [+9133] of the city she makes her speech:
5: 8 Keep to a path far from her, do not go near the **door** *of* her house,
8: 3 leading into the city, at the **entrances** [+4427], she cries aloud:
8: 34 watching daily at my doors, waiting at my **doorway** [+4647].
9: 14 She sits at the **door** *of* her house, on a seat at the highest point of
17: 19 a quarrel loves sin; he who builds a high **gate** invites destruction.
SS 7: 13 [7:14] at our **door** is every delicacy, both new and old, that I have
Isa 3: 26 The **gates** *of* Zion will lament and mourn; destitute, she will sit on
13: 2 shout to them; beckon to them to enter the **gates** *of* the nobles.
Jer 1: 15 and set up their thrones in the **entrance** *of* the gates of Jerusalem;
19: 2 the Valley of Ben Hinnom, near the **entrance** *of* the Potsherd Gate.
26: 10 took their places at the **entrance** *of* the New Gate of the LORD's
36: 10 which was in the upper courtyard at the **entrance** *of* the New Gate
43: 9 bury them in clay in the brick pavement at the **entrance** *to*
Eze 8: 3 to the **entrance** *to* the north gate of the inner court, where the idol
8: 7 Then he brought me to the **entrance** *to* the court. I looked,

Eze 8: 8 dig into the wall." So I dug into the wall and saw a **doorway** there.
8: 14 he brought me to the **entrance** to the north gate of the house of the
8: 16 and there at the **entrance** *to* the temple, between the portico
10: 19 They stopped at the **entrance** *to* the east gate of the LORD's
11: 1 There at the **entrance** *to* the gate were twenty-five men, and I saw
33: 30 together about you by the walls and at the **doors** *of* the houses,
40: 11 Then he measured the width of the **entrance** *to* the gateway;
40: 13 the distance was twenty-five cubits from *one* **parapet opening** to
40: 13 twenty-five cubits from one parapet opening to the opposite **one**[s].
40: 38 A room with a **doorway** was by the portico in each of the inner
40: 40 near the steps at the **entrance** *to* the north gateway were two
41: 2 The **entrance** was ten cubits wide, and the projecting walls on
41: 2 the projecting walls on each side of **it**[s] [+2021] were five cubits
41: 3 into the inner sanctuary and measured the jambs of the **entrance**;
41: 3 The **entrance** was six cubits wide, and the projecting walls on each
41: 3 the projecting walls on each side of **it**[s] [+2021] were seven cubits
41: 11 There were **entrances** *to* the side rooms from the open area,
41: 11 the open area, **[RPH]** one on the north and another on the south;
41: 11 the open area, one on the north and **[RPH]** another on the south;
41: 17 In the space above the outside of the **entrance** to the inner
41: 20 From the floor to the area above the **entrance**, cherubim and palm
42: 2 The building whose **door** faced north was a hundred cubits long
42: 4 and a hundred cubits long. Their **doors** were on the north.
42: 11 and dimensions. Similar to the **doorways** on the north
42: 12 were the **doorways** *of* the rooms on the south. There was a
42: 12 There was a **doorway** at the beginning of the passageway that was
46: 3 in the presence of the LORD at the **entrance** *to* that gateway.
47: 1 The man brought me back to the **entrance** *of* the temple, and I saw
Hos 2: 15 [2:17] and will make the Valley of Achor a **door** *of* hope.
Mic 5: 6 [5:5] land of Nimrod with drawn **sword**. [BHS *its gates*; NIV 7347]
7: 5 her who lies in your embrace be careful of your **words** [+7023].

7340 פֶּתַח pēṯaḥ, n.m. [1] [√ 7337]

unfolding [1]

Ps 119:130 The **unfolding** *of* your words gives light; it gives understanding to

7341 פִּתָּחוֹן pittāḥôn, n.[m.]. [2] [√ 7337]

open [+5989] [1], open [1]

Eze 16: 63 will remember and be ashamed and never again **open** your mouth
29: 21 house of Israel, and *I will* **open** [+5989] your mouth among them.

7342 פְּתַחְיָה pᵉtaḥyâ, n.pr.m. [4] [√ 7337 + 3378]

Pethahiah [4]

1Ch 24: 16 the nineteenth to **Pethahiah**, the twentieth to Jehezkel,
Ezr 10: 23 Shimei, Kelaiah (that is, Kelita), **Pethahiah**, Judah and Eliezer.
Ne 9: 5 Hashabneiah, Sherebiah, Hodiah, Shebaniah and **Pethahiah**—
11: 24 **Pethahiah** son of Meshezabel, one of the descendants of Zerah son

7343 פְּתִי petî[1], a. [16] [√ 7331, 7333]

simple [15], simplehearted [1]

Ps 19: 7 [19:8] of the LORD are trustworthy, making wise the **simple**.
116: 6 The LORD protects the **simplehearted**; when I was in great need,
119:130 of your words gives light; it gives understanding to the **simple**.
Pr 1: 4 for giving prudence to the **simple**, knowledge and discretion to the
1: 22 "How long will you **simple** *ones* love your simple ways? How
1: 32 For the waywardness of the **simple** will kill them,
7: 7 I saw among the **simple**, I noticed among the young men,
8: 5 You who are **simple**, gain prudence; you who are foolish,
9: 4 "Let all who are **simple** come in here!" she says to those who lack
9: 16 "Let all who are **simple** come in here!" she says to those who lack
14: 15 A **simple** *man* believes anything, but a prudent man gives thought
14: 18 The **simple** inherit folly, but the prudent are crowned with
19: 25 Flog a mocker, and the **simple** will learn prudence; rebuke a
21: 11 When a mocker is punished, the **simple** gain wisdom; when a wise
22: 3 and takes refuge, but the **simple** keep going and suffer for it.
27: 12 and take refuge, but the **simple** keep going and suffer for it.

7344 פְּתִי petî[2], n.f. [3] [√ 7331]

simple ways [2], ignorance [1]

Pr 1: 22 "How long will you simple ones love your **simple ways**? How
9: 6 Leave your **simple ways** and you will live; walk in the way of
Eze 45: 20 month for anyone who sins unintentionally or through **ignorance**;

7345 פְּתִיגִיל pᵉtîgîl, n.[m.]. [1]

fine clothing [1]

Isa 3: 24 of well-dressed hair, baldness; instead of **fine clothing**, sackcloth;

7346 פְּתַיּוּת pᵉtayyût, n.f. [1] [√ 7331]

undisciplined [1]

Pr 9: 13 woman Folly is loud; she is **undisciplined** and without knowledge.

7347 פְּתִיחָה pᵉtîḥâ, n.[f.]. [1 / 2] [√ 7337]

drawn sword [1], drawn swords [1]

Ps 55: 21 [55:22] are more soothing than oil, yet they are **drawn swords**.
Mic 5: 6 [5:5] the land of Nimrod with **drawn** [BHS 7339] **sword**.

7348 פָּתִיל pāṯîl, n.m. [11] [√ 7349]

cord [8], fastened [1], piece of string [+5861] [1], strands [1]

Ge 38: 18 "Your seal and its **cord**, and the staff in your hand," she answered.
38: 25 "See if you recognize whose seal and **cord** and staff these are."
Ex 28: 28 breastpiece are to be tied to the rings of the ephod with blue **cord**,
28: 37 Fasten a blue **cord** to it to attach it to the turban; it is to be on the
39: 3 out thin sheets of gold and cut **strands** to be worked into the blue,
39: 21 rings of the breastpiece to the rings of the ephod with blue **cord**,
39: 31 Then they fastened a blue **cord** to it to attach it to the turban,
Nu 15: 38 on the corners of your garments, with a blue **cord** on each tassel.
19: 15 every open container without a lid **fastened** on it will be unclean.
Jdg 16: 9 he snapped the thongs as easily as a **piece of string** [+5861] snaps
Eze 40: 3 he was standing in the gateway with a linen **cord** and a measuring

7349 פָּתַל pāṯal, v. [4 / 5] [→ 5887, 5889?, 7348, 7350]

show yourself shrewd [2], crooked [1], had a struggle [+5887] [1], wily [1]

Ge 30: 8 [C] "*I have* **had a** great **struggle** [+5887] with my sister, and I
2Sa 22: 27 [f] but to the crooked *you* **show yourself shrewd**. [BHS 9520]
Job 5: 13 [C] their craftiness, and the schemes of the **wily** are swept away.
Ps 18: 26 [18:27] [F] but to the crooked *you* **show yourself shrewd**.
Pr 8: 8 [C] of my mouth are just; none of them *is* **crooked** or perverse.

7350 פְּתַלְתֹּל pᵉtaltōl, a. [1] [√ 7349]

crooked [1]

Dt 32: 5 are no longer his children, but a warped and **crooked** generation.

7351 פִּתֹם pitōm, n.pr.loc. [1]

Pithom [1]

Ex 1: 11 and they built **Pithom** and Rameses as store cities for Pharaoh.

7352 פֶּתֶן peten, n.m. [6]

cobra [3], serpents [2], cobras [1]

Dt 32: 33 Their wine is the venom of serpents, the deadly poison of **cobras**.
Job 20: 14 in his stomach; it will become the venom of **serpents** within him.
20: 16 He will suck the poison of **serpents**; the fangs of an adder will kill
Ps 58: 4 [58:5] of a snake, like that of a **cobra** that has stopped its ears,
91: 13 You will tread upon the lion and the **cobra**; you will trample the
Isa 11: 8 The infant will play near the hole of the **cobra**, and the young child

7353 פֶּתַע petaʿ, subst. (used as adv.). [7] [→ 7328]

suddenly [3], instant [2], suddenly [+928] [1], suddenly [+928+7328] [1]

Nu 6: 9 " 'If someone dies **suddenly** [+928+7328] in his presence,
35: 22 " 'But if without hostility someone **suddenly** [+928] shoves
Pr 6: 15 him in an instant; he will **suddenly** be destroyed—without remedy.
29: 1 A man who remains stiff-necked after many rebukes will **suddenly**
Isa 29: 5 the ruthless hordes like blown chaff. Suddenly, in an **instant**,
30: 13 cracked and bulging, that collapses suddenly, in an **instant**.
Hab 2: 7 Will not your debtors **suddenly** arise? Will they not wake up

7354 פָּתַר pāṯar, v. [9] [→ 7355; Ar 10599, 10600]

interpret [4], interpreted [2], given interpretation [1], giving interpretation [1], said in interpretation [1]

Ge 40: 8 [A] they answered, "but there is no *one to* **interpret** them."
40: 16 [A] baker saw that Joseph *had* **given** *a* favorable **interpretation**,
40: 22 [A] just as Joseph *had* **said** to them **in** *his* **interpretation**.
41: 8 [A] them his dreams, but no *one could* **interpret** them for him.
41: 12 [A] We told him our dreams, and *he* **interpreted** them for us,
41: 12 [A] for us, **giving** each man *the* **interpretation** *of* his dream.
41: 13 [A] And things turned out exactly as *he* **interpreted** them to us:
41: 15 [A] said to Joseph, "I had a dream, and no *one can* **interpret** it.
41: 15 [A] of you that when you hear a dream *you can* **interpret** it."

7355 פִּתְרוֹן pittārôn, n.m. [5] [√ 7354]

meaning [2], means [2], interpretations [1]

Ge 40: 5 a dream the same night, and each dream had a **meaning** *of* its own.
40: 8 Then Joseph said to them, "Do not **interpretations** belong to God?
40: 12 "This is *what* it **means**," Joseph said to him. "The three branches

Ge 40:18 "This is *what* it **means**," Joseph said. "The three baskets are three
41:11 a dream the same night, and each dream had a **meaning** *of* its own.

7356 פַּתְרוֹס *patrôs*, n.pr.loc. [5] [→ 7357]

Upper Egypt [3], Upper Egypt [+824] [2]

Isa 11:11 from **Upper Egypt**, from Cush, from Elam, from Babylonia,
Jer 44:1 in Migdol, Tahpanhes and Memphis—and in **Upper Egypt** [+824]:
44:15 all the people living in Lower and **Upper Egypt**, said to Jeremiah,
Eze 29:14 them back from captivity and return them to **Upper Egypt** [+824],
30:14 I will lay waste **Upper Egypt**, set fire to Zoan and inflict

7357 פַּתְרֻסִים *patrusîm*, a.g.pl. [2] [√ 7356]

Pathrusites [2]

Ge 10:14 **Pathrusites**, Casluhites (from whom the Philistines came)
1Ch 1:12 **Pathrusites**, Casluhites (from whom the Philistines came)

7358 פַּתְשֶׁגֶן *patšegen*, n.m. [3] [cf. 7306; Ar 10598]

copy [3]

Est 3:14 A **copy** *of* the text of the edict was to be issued as law in every
4:8 He also gave him a **copy** *of* the text of the edict for their
8:13 A **copy** *of* the text of the edict was to be issued as law in every

7359 פָּתַת *pātat*, v. [1] [→ 7326, 7336]

crumble [+906+7326] [1]

Lev 2:6 [A] **Crumble** [+906+7326] it and pour oil on it; it is a grain

---

צ, ṣ

7360 צ *ṣ*, letter. Not used in NIV/BHS [→ Ar 10604]

7361 צֵא *ṣē'*, n.[m.]. Not used in NIV/BHS [→ 7362, 7363, 7364]

7362 צֵאָה *ṣē'â*, n.f. [2] [√ 7361]

excrement [+1645] [1], excrement [1]

Dt 23:13 [23:14] relieve yourself, dig a hole and cover up your **excrement**.
Eze 4:12 the sight of the people, using human **excrement** [+1645] for fuel."

7363 צֹאָה *ṣō'â*, n.f. [3] [√ 7361]

filth [3]

2Ki 18:27 [will have to eat their own **filth** [Q; see K 2989] and drink their]
Pr 30:12 are pure in their own eyes and yet are not cleansed of their **filth**;
Isa 4:4 The Lord will wash away the **filth** *of* the women of Zion; he will
28:8 tables are covered with vomit and there is not a spot without **filth**.
36:12 [will have to eat their own **filth** [Q; see K 2989] and drink their]

7364 צֹאִי *ṣō'î*, a. [2] [√ 7361]

filthy [2]

Zec 3:3 Now Joshua was dressed in **filthy** clothes as he stood before the
3:4 those who were standing before him, "Take off his **filthy** clothes."

7365 צֶאֱלִים *ṣe'ĕlîm*, n.m.pl. [2]

lotus plants [1], lotuses [1]

Job 40:21 Under the **lotus plants** he lies, hidden among the reeds in the
40:22 The **lotuses** conceal him in their shadow; the poplars by the stream

7366 צֹאן *ṣō'n*, n.col.f. *or* m. [275] [→ 7555, 7556; cf. 3655]

sheep [97], flocks [69], flock [66], sheep and goats [11], animals [6], *untranslated* [3], shepherds [+8286] [3], lambs [+1201] [2], they[s] [+2021] [2], animal from flock [1], breeding [+2021+3501] [1], choice lambs [+4119+4946] [1], ewes [1], flocks [+5238] [1], goats [1], pens [+1556] [1], rest[s] [1], sheep [+3897] [1], sheep and goats [+5238] [1], sheep goats or [1], sheep or goats [1], them[s] [+2257] [1], they[s] [+3276] [1], which[s] [+2021] [1], which[s] [+2257] [1]

Ge 4:2 his brother Abel. Now Abel kept **flocks**, and Cain worked the soil.
4:4 Abel brought fat portions from some of the firstborn of his **flock**.
12:16 and Abram acquired **sheep** and cattle, male and female donkeys,
13:5 moving about with Abram, also had **flocks** and herds and tents.
20:14 Abimelech brought **sheep** and cattle and male and female slaves
21:27 So Abraham brought **sheep** and cattle and gave them to
21:28 Abraham set apart seven ewe lambs from the **flock**,
24:35 He has given him **sheep** and cattle, silver and gold, menservants
26:14 He had so many **flocks** [+5238] and herds and servants that the
27:9 Go out to the **flock** and bring me two choice young goats,
29:2 with three flocks of **sheep** lying near it because the flocks were
29:3 roll the stone away from the well's mouth and water the **sheep**.
29:6 they said, "and here comes his daughter Rachel with the **sheep**."
29:7 to be gathered. Water the **sheep** and take them back to pasture."
29:8 away from the mouth of the well. Then we will water the **sheep**."
29:9 Rachel came with her father's **sheep**, for she was a shepherdess.
29:10 Laban's **sheep**, he went over and rolled the stone away from the
29:10 away from the mouth of the well and watered his uncle's **sheep**.
30:31 for me, I will go on tending your **flocks** and watching over them:
30:32 Let me go through all your **flocks** today and remove from them
30:36 while Jacob continued to tend the rest of Laban's **flocks**.
30:38 so that they would be directly in front of the **flocks** when they
30:38 came to drink. When the **flocks** were in heat and came to drink,
30:39 **they**[s] [+2021] mated in front of the branches. And they bore young
30:39 And **they**[s] [+2021] bore young that were streaked or speckled
30:40 made the **rest**[s] face the streaked and dark-colored animals that
30:40 the streaked and dark-colored **animals** *that belonged to* Laban.
30:40 flocks for himself and did not put them with Laban's **animals**.
30:41 Whenever the stronger females **[RPH]** were in heat, Jacob would
30:41 would place the branches in the troughs in front of the **animals**
30:42 but if the **animals** were weak, he would not place them there.
30:43 man grew exceedingly prosperous and came to own large **flocks**,
31:4 to Rachel and Leah to come out to the fields where his **flocks** were.
31:8 be your wages,' then all the **flocks** gave birth to speckled young;
31:8 ones will be your wages,' then all the **flocks** bore streaked young.
31:10 "In **breeding** [+2021+3501] season I once had a dream in which I
31:10 and saw that the male goats mating with the **flock** were streaked,
31:12 and see that all the male goats mating with the **flock** are streaked,
31:19 When Laban had gone to shear his **sheep**, Rachel stole her father's
31:38 goats have not miscarried, nor have I eaten rams from your **flocks**.
31:41 years for your two daughters and six years for your **flocks**,
31:43 the children are my children, and the **flocks** are my flocks.
31:43 the children are my children, and the flocks are my **flocks**.
32:5 [32:6] **sheep and goats**, menservants and maidservants.
32:7 [32:8] two groups, and the **flocks** and herds and camels as well.
33:13 that I must care for the **ewes** and cows that are nursing their young.
33:13 If they are driven hard just one day, all the **animals** will die.
34:28 They seized their **flocks** and herds and donkeys and everything
37:2 was tending the **flocks** with his brothers, the sons of Bilhah
37:12 Now his brothers had gone to graze their father's **flocks** near
37:14 and see if all is well with your brothers and with the **flocks**,
38:12 he went up to Timnah, to the men who were shearing his **sheep**,
38:13 "Your father-in-law is on his way to Timnah to shear his **sheep**,"
38:17 "I'll send you a young goat from my **flock**," he said. "Will you
45:10 and grandchildren, your **flocks** and herds, and all you have.
46:32 The men *are* **shepherds** [+8286]; they tend livestock, and they
46:32 they have brought along their **flocks** and herds and everything they
46:34 for all **shepherds** [+8286] are detestable to the Egyptians."
47:1 and brothers, with their **flocks** and herds and everything they own,
47:3 "Your servants are **shepherds** [+8286]," they replied to Pharaoh,
47:4 is severe in Canaan and your servants' **flocks** have no pasture.
47:17 their **sheep** [+5238] **and goats**, their cattle and donkeys.
50:8 Only their children and their **flocks** and herds were left in Goshen.
Ex 2:16 to draw water and fill the troughs to water their father's **flock**.
2:17 but Moses got up and came to their rescue and watered their **flock**.
2:19 the shepherds. He even drew water for us and watered the **flock**."
3:1 Now Moses was tending the **flock** *of* Jethro his father-in-law,
3:1 and he led the **flock** to the far side of the desert and came to Horeb,
9:3 and donkeys and camels and on your cattle and **sheep and goats**.
10:9 with our sons and daughters, and with our **flocks** and herds,
10:24 may go with you; only leave your **flocks** and herds behind."
12:21 "Go at once and select the **animals** for your families and slaughter
12:32 Take your **flocks** and herds, as you have said, and go. And also
12:38 as well as large droves of livestock, both **flocks** and herds.
20:24 and fellowship offerings, your **sheep and goats** and your cattle.
22:1 [21:37] five head of cattle for the ox and four **sheep** for the sheep.
22:30 [22:29] Do the same with your cattle and your **sheep**. Let them
34:3 not even the **flocks** and herds may graze in front of the mountain."
Lev 1:2 bring as your offering an animal from either the herd or the **flock**.
1:10 " 'If the offering is a burnt offering from the **flock**, from either the
3:6 " 'If he offers an animal from the **flock** as a fellowship offering to
5:6 the LORD a female lamb or goat from the **flock** as a sin offering;
5:15 he is to bring to the LORD as a penalty a ram from the **flock**,
5:18 He is to bring to the priest as a guilt offering a ram from the **flock**,
6:6 [5:25] to the LORD, his guilt offering, a ram from the **flock**,
22:21 or **flock** a fellowship offering to the LORD to fulfill a special
27:32 The entire tithe of the herd and **flock**—every tenth animal that
Nu 11:22 Would they have enough if **flocks** and herds were slaughtered for
15:3 from the herd or the **flock**, as an aroma pleasing to the LORD—
22:40 Balak sacrificed cattle and **sheep**, and gave some to Balaam
27:17 so the LORD's people will not be like **sheep** without a shepherd."
31:28 five hundred, whether persons, cattle, donkeys, **sheep or goats**.
31:30 whether persons, cattle, donkeys, **sheep**, **goats or** other animals.
31:32 from the spoils that the soldiers took was 675,000 **sheep**,

Nu 31:36 half share of those who fought in the battle was: 337,500 **sheep**,
31:37 of **which**[s] [+2021] the tribute for the LORD was 675;
31:43 the community's half—was 337,500 **sheep**,
32:16 "We would like to build **pens** [+1556] here for our livestock
32:24 Build cities for your women and children, and pens for your **flocks**,
32:36 and Beth Haran as fortified cities, and built pens for their **flocks**.
Dt 7:13 the lambs of your **flocks** in the land that he swore to your
8:13 your herds and **flocks** grow large and your silver and gold increase
12:6 your freewill offerings, and the firstborn of your herds and **flocks**.
12:17 and new wine and oil, or the firstborn of your herds and **flocks**,
12:21 animals from the herds and **flocks** the LORD has given you,
14:23 **flocks** in the presence of the LORD your God at the place he will
14:26 cattle, **sheep**, wine or other fermented drink, or anything you wish.
15:14 Supply him liberally from your **flock**, your threshing floor
15:19 LORD your God every firstborn male of your herds and **flocks**.
15:19 of your oxen to work, and do not shear the firstborn of your **sheep**.
16:2 the Passover to the LORD your God an **animal from** your **flock**
18:4 and oil, and the first wool from the shearing of your **sheep**,
28:4 the calves of your herds and the lambs of your **flocks**.
28:18 and the calves of your herds and the lambs of your **flocks**.
28:31 Your **sheep** will be given to your enemies, and no one will rescue
28:51 calves of your herds or lambs of your **flocks** until you are ruined.
32:14 with curds and milk from herd and **flock** and with fattened lambs
Jos 7:24 his cattle, donkeys and **sheep**, his tent and all that he had,
1Sa 8:17 He will take a tenth of your **flocks**, and you yourselves will
14:32 They pounced on the plunder and, taking **sheep**, cattle and calves,
15:9 and the army spared Agag and the best of the **sheep** and cattle,
15:14 But Samuel said, "What then is this bleating of **sheep** in my ears?
15:15 they spared the best of the **sheep** and cattle to sacrifice to the
15:21 The soldiers took **sheep** and cattle from the plunder, the best of
16:11 still the youngest," Jesse answered, "but he is tending the **sheep**."
16:19 and said, "Send me your son David, who is with the **sheep**."
17:15 and forth from Saul to tend his father's **sheep** at Bethlehem.
17:20 Early in the morning David left the **flock** with a shepherd,
17:28 And with whom did you leave those few **sheep** in the desert?
17:34 said to Saul, "Your servant has been keeping his father's **sheep**.
24:3 [24:4] He came to the **sheep** pens along the way; a cave was
25:2 He had a thousand goats and three thousand **sheep**, which he was
25:2 three thousand sheep, **which**[s] [+2257] he was shearing in Carmel.
25:4 David was in the desert, he heard that Nabal was shearing **sheep**.
25:16 a wall around us all the time we were herding our **sheep** near them.
25:18 two skins of wine, five dressed **sheep**, five seahs of roasted grain,
27:9 but took **sheep** and cattle, donkeys and camels, and clothes.
30:20 He took all the **flocks** and herds, and his men drove them ahead of
2Sa 7:8 and from following the **flock** to be ruler over my people Israel.
12:2 The rich man had a very large number of **sheep** and cattle,
12:4 but the rich man refrained from taking one of his own **sheep**
17:29 honey and curds, **sheep**, and cheese from cows' milk for David
24:17 am the one who has sinned and done wrong. These are but **sheep**.
1Ki 1:9 Adonijah then sacrificed **sheep**, cattle and fattened calves at the
1:19 fattened calves, and **sheep**, and has invited all the king's sons,
1:25 and sacrificed great numbers of cattle, fattened calves, and **sheep**.
4:23 [5:3] twenty of pasture-fed cattle and a hundred **sheep and goats**,
8:5 sacrificing so many **sheep** and cattle that they could not be
8:63 and a hundred and twenty thousand **sheep and goats**.
22:17 "I saw all Israel scattered on the hills like **sheep** without a
2Ki 5:26 olive groves, vineyards, **flocks**, herds, or menservants
1Ch 4:39 Gedor to the east of the valley in search of pasture for their **flocks**.
4:41 settled in their place, because there was pasture for their **flocks**.
5:21 two hundred fifty thousand **sheep** and two thousand donkeys.
12:40 [12:41] fig cakes, raisin cakes, wine, oil, cattle and **sheep**,
17:7 I took you from the pasture and from following the **flock**,
21:17 I am the one who has sinned and done wrong. These are but **sheep**.
27:31 Jaziz the Hagrite was in charge of the **flocks**. All these were the
2Ch 5:6 sacrificing so many **sheep** and cattle that they could not be
7:5 of cattle and a hundred and twenty thousand **sheep and goats**.
14:15 [14:14] and carried off droves of **sheep and goats** and camels.
15:11 seven thousand **sheep and goats** from the plunder they had
17:11 and silver as tribute, and the Arabs brought him **flocks**:
18:2 Ahab slaughtered many **sheep** and cattle for him and the people
18:16 "I saw all Israel scattered on the hills like **sheep** without a
29:33 to six hundred bulls and three thousand **sheep and goats**.
30:24 and seven thousand **sheep and goats** for the assembly,
30:24 them with a thousand bulls and ten thousand **sheep and goats**.
31:6 **flocks** and a tithe of the holy things dedicated to the LORD their
32:29 He built villages and acquired great numbers of **flocks** and herds,
35:7 lay people who were there a total of thirty thousand **sheep** [+3897]
Ezr 10:19 for their guilt they each presented a ram from the **flock** as a guilt
Ne 3:1 and his fellow priests went to work and rebuilt the **Sheep** Gate.
3:32 and the **Sheep** Gate the goldsmiths and merchants made repairs.
5:18 one ox, six choice **sheep** and some poultry were prepared for me,
10:36 [10:37] of our herds and of our **flocks** to the house of our God,
12:39 and the Tower of the Hundred, as far as the **Sheep** Gate.
Job 1:3 and he owned seven thousand **sheep**, three thousand camels,
1:16 of God fell from the sky and burned up the **sheep** and the servants,
21:11 They send forth their children as a **flock**; their little ones dance
30:1 whose fathers I would have disdained to put with my **sheep** dogs.
42:12 He had fourteen thousand **sheep**, six thousand camels, a thousand
Ps 44:11 [44:12] You gave us up to be devoured like **sheep** and have
44:22 [44:23] day long; we are considered as **sheep** to be slaughtered.
49:14 [49:15] Like **sheep** they are destined for the grave, and death will
65:13 [65:14] The meadows are covered with **flocks** and the valleys are
74:1 Why does your anger smolder against the **sheep** *of* your pasture?
77:20 [77:21] You led your people like a **flock** by the hand of Moses
78:52 he brought his people out like a **flock**; he led them like sheep
78:70 He chose David his servant and took him from the **sheep** pens;
79:13 we your people, the **sheep** *of* your pasture, will praise you forever;
80:1 [80:2] O Shepherd of Israel, you who lead Joseph like a **flock**;
95:7 and we are the people of his pasture, the **flock** under his care.
100:3 and we are his; we are his people, the **sheep** *of* his pasture.
107:41 needy out of their affliction and increased their families like **flocks**.
114:4 the mountains skipped like rams, the hills like **lambs** [+1201].
114:6 that you skipped like rams, you hills, like **lambs** [+1201]?
144:13 Our **sheep** will increase by thousands, by tens of thousands in our
Pr 27:23 Be sure you know the condition of your **flocks**, give careful
Ecc 2:7 owned more herds and **flocks** than anyone in Jerusalem before me.
SS 1:8 follow the tracks of the **sheep** and graze your young goats by the
Isa 7:21 In that day, a man will keep alive a young cow and two **goats**.
13:14 Like a hunted gazelle, like **sheep** without a shepherd, each will
22:13 there is joy and revelry, slaughtering of cattle and killing of **sheep**,
53:6 We all, like **sheep**, have gone astray, each of us has turned to his
60:7 All Kedar's **flocks** will be gathered to you, the rams of Nebaioth
61:5 Aliens will shepherd your **flocks**; foreigners will work your fields
63:11 who brought them through the sea, with the shepherd of his **flock**?
65:10 Sharon will become a pasture for **flocks**, and the Valley of Achor a
Jer 3:24 our fathers' labor—their **flocks** and herds, their sons and daughters.
5:17 they will devour your **flocks** and herds, devour your vines
12:3 my thoughts about you. Drag them off like **sheep** to be butchered!
13:20 flock that was entrusted to you, the **sheep** *of* which you boasted?
23:1 who are destroying and scattering the **sheep** *of* my pasture!"
23:2 "Because you have scattered my **flock** and driven them away
23:3 "I myself will gather the remnant of my **flock** out of all the
25:34 and wail, you shepherds; roll in the dust, you leaders of the **flock**.
25:35 have nowhere to flee, the leaders of the **flock** no place to escape.
25:36 the cry of the shepherds, the wailing of the leaders of the **flock**,
31:12 the new wine and the oil, the young of the **flocks** and herds.
33:12 there will again be pastures for shepherds to rest their **flocks**.
33:13 **flocks** will again pass under the hand of the one who counts them,'
49:20 The young of the **flock** will be dragged away; he will completely
49:29 Their tents and their **flocks** will be taken; their shelters will be
50:6 "My people have been lost **sheep**; their shepherds have led them
50:8 land of the Babylonians, and be like the goats that lead the **flock**.
50:45 The young of the **flock** will be dragged away; he will completely
Eze 24:5 take the pick of the **flock**. Pile wood beneath it for the bones;
25:5 a pasture for camels and Ammon into a resting place for **sheep**.
34:2 care of themselves! Should not shepherds take care of the **flock**?
34:3 slaughter the choice animals, but you do not take care of the **flock**.
34:6 My **sheep** wandered over all the mountains and on every high hill.
34:6 **They**[s] [+3276] were scattered over the whole earth, and no one
34:8 because my **flock** lacks a shepherd and so has been plundered
34:8 and has become food **[RPH]** for all the wild animals,
34:8 because my shepherds did not search for my **flock** but cared for
34:8 for my flock but cared for themselves rather than for my **flock**,
34:10 against the shepherds and will hold them accountable for my **flock**.
34:10 I will remove them from tending the **flock** so that the shepherds
34:10 I will rescue my **flock** from their mouths, and it will no longer be
34:11 I myself will search for my **sheep** and look after them.
34:12 looks after his scattered flock when he is with **them**[s] [+2257],
34:12 scattered flock when he is with them, so will I look after my **sheep**.
34:15 I myself will tend my **sheep** and have them lie down,
34:17 " 'As for you, my **flock**, this is what the Sovereign LORD says:
34:19 Must my **flock** feed on what you have trampled and drink what
34:22 I will save my **flock**, and they will no longer be plundered.
34:31 You my **sheep**, the sheep of my pasture, are people, and I am your
34:31 You my sheep, the **sheep** *of* my pasture, are people, and I am your
36:37 do this for them: I will make their people as numerous as **sheep**,
36:38 as numerous as the **flocks** *for* offerings at Jerusalem during her
36:38 as numerous as the flocks for offerings **[RPH]** at Jerusalem
36:38 So will the ruined cities be filled with **flocks** *of* people. Then they
43:23 you are to offer a young bull and a ram from the **flock**,
43:25 you are also to provide a young bull and a ram from the **flock**,
45:15 Also one sheep is to be taken from every **flock** of two hundred
Hos 5:6 When they go with their **flocks** and herds to seek the LORD,
Joel 1:18 they have no pasture; even the flocks of **sheep** are suffering.
Am 6:4 You dine on **choice lambs** [+4119+4946] and fattened calves.
7:15 But the LORD took me from tending the **flock** and said to me,
Jnh 3:7 Do not let any man or beast, herd or **flock**, taste anything;
Mic 2:12 I will bring them together like **sheep** *in* a pen, like a flock in its

Mic 5: 8 [5:7] like a young lion among flocks of **sheep**, which mauls
7: 14 the **flock** *of* your inheritance, which lives by itself in a forest,
Hab 3: 17 though there are no **sheep** in the pen and no cattle in the stalls,
Zep 2: 6 the Kerethites dwell, will be a place for shepherds and **sheep** pens.
Zec 9: 16 The LORD their God will save them on that day as the **flock** *of*
10: 2 Therefore the people wander like **sheep** oppressed for lack of a
11: 4 LORD my God says: "Pasture the **flock** *marked for* slaughter.
11: 7 So I pastured the **flock** *marked for* slaughter, particularly the
11: 7 flock marked for slaughter, particularly the oppressed of the **flock**.
11: 7 and called one Favor and the other Union, and I pastured the **flock**.
11: 11 so the afflicted of the **flock** who were watching me knew it was the
11: 17 "Woe to the worthless shepherd, who deserts the **flock**!
13: 7 "Strike the shepherd, and the **sheep** will be scattered, and I will

7367 צַאֲנָן ṣaʾănān, n.pr.loc. [1] [cf. 7569?]

Zaanan [1]

Mic 1: 11 who live in Shaphir. Those who live in **Zaanan** will not come out.

7368 צֶאֱצָאִים ṣeʾĕṣāʾîm, n.m.[pl.]. [11] [√ 3655]

offspring [4], descendants [3], all that comes out [1], children [+5055] [1], crops [1], that comes out [1]

Job 5: 25 will be many, and your **descendants** like the grass of the earth.
21: 8 children established around them, their **offspring** before their eyes.
27: 14 their fate is the sword; his **offspring** will never have enough to eat.
31: 8 may others eat what I have sown, and may my **crops** be uprooted.
Isa 22: 24 its **offspring** and offshoots—all its lesser vessels, from the bowls
34: 1 and all that is in it, the world, and all **that comes out** *of* it!
42: 5 them out, who spread out the earth and **all that comes out** *of* it,
44: 3 my Spirit on your offspring, and my blessing on your **descendants**.
48: 19 like the sand, your **children** [+5055] like its numberless grains;
61: 9 known among the nations and their **offspring** among the peoples.
65: 23 blessed by the LORD, they and their **descendants** with them.

7369 ¹צָב ṣāb[1], n.[m.]. [2] [→ 7376]

covered [1], wagons [1]

Nu 7: 3 They brought as their gifts before the LORD six **covered** carts
Isa 66: 20 on horses, in chariots and **wagons**, and on mules and camels,"

7370 ²צָב ṣāb[2], n.[m.]. [1] [√ 7377?]

great lizard [1]

Lev 11: 29 are unclean for you: the weasel, the rat, any kind of **great lizard**,

7371 ¹צָבָא ṣābāʾ[1], v. [14] [→ 7372]

conscripting [2], fight [2], fought [2], served [+7371] [2], attack [1], do battle [1], fighting [1], serve [+7372] [1], served [1], take part [+7372] [1]

Ex 38: 8 [A] *women* who **served** [+7371] at the entrance to the Tent of
38: 8 [A] *women* who **served** [+7371] at the entrance to the Tent of
Nu 4: 23 [A] come to **serve** [+7372] in the work at the Tent of Meeting.
8: 24 [A] or more shall come to **take part** [+7372] in the work at the
31: 7 [A] *They* **fought** against Midian, as the LORD commanded
31: 42 [A] which Moses set apart from that of the **fighting** men—
1Sa 2: 22 [A] how they slept with the women who **served** *at* the entrance
2Ki 25: 19 [G] chief officer in charge of **conscripting** the people of the land
Isa 29: 7 [A] Then the hordes of all the nations that **fight** against Ariel,
29: 7 [A] *that* **attack** her and her fortress and besiege her, will be as it
29: 8 [A] So will it be with the hordes of all the nations that **fight**
31: 4 [A] so the LORD Almighty will come down to **do battle** on
Jer 52: 25 [G] chief officer in charge of **conscripting** the people of the land
Zec 14: 12 [A] will strike all the nations that **fought** against Jerusalem:

7372 ²צָבָא ṣābāʾ[2], n.m. & f. [485 / 486] [√ 7371]

Almighty [285], army [59], divisions [21], division [20], battle [12], host [8], hosts [8], armies [6], war [6], forces [5], in command [+6584] [4], serve [4], starry host [4], stars [4], hard service [3], *untranslated* [2], chief officer [+2021+8569] [2], experienced soldiers [+3655] [2], heavenly hosts [2], ready for military service [+3655] [2], ready to go out [+3655] [2], troops [2], armed forces [+2657] [1], army [+2657] [1], array [1], battle [+4878] [1], commander in chief [+2021+6584] [1], commanders [+8569] [1], company [1], men ready for battle [+1522+4878] [1], multitudes [1], powers [1], ready for battle [+408+2021+4200+4878] [1], ready for battle [+928+2021+4878] [1], regular service [+6275] [1], serve [+6913] [1], serve [+7371] [1], soldier [+408] [1], soldiers [+408] [1], soldiers [+6639] [1], soldiers [1], starry hosts [1], take part [+7371] [1], vast array [1], weapon [+3998+4878] [1]

Ge 2: 1 the heavens and the earth were completed in all their **vast array**.
21: 22 and Phicol the commander of his **forces** said to Abraham,
21: 32 Phicol the commander of his **forces** returned to the land of the
26: 26 his personal adviser and Phicol the commander of his **forces**.
Ex 6: 26 LORD said, "Bring the Israelites out of Egypt by their **divisions**."
7: 4 and with mighty acts of judgment I will bring out my **divisions**,
12: 17 because it was on this very day that I brought your **divisions** out of
12: 41 430 years, to the very day, all the LORD's **divisions** left Egypt.
12: 51 the LORD brought the Israelites out of Egypt by their **divisions**.
Nu 1: 3 Aaron are to number by their **divisions** all the men in Israel twenty
1: 3 Israel twenty years old or more who are able to serve in the **army**.
1: 20 or more who were able to serve in the **army** were listed by name,
1: 22 or more who were able to serve in the **army** were counted
1: 24 or more who were able to serve in the **army** were listed by name,
1: 26 or more who were able to serve in the **army** were listed by name,
1: 28 or more who were able to serve in the **army** were listed by name,
1: 30 or more who were able to serve in the **army** were listed by name,
1: 32 or more who were able to serve in the **army** were listed by name,
1: 34 or more who were able to serve in the **army** were listed by name,
1: 36 or more who were able to serve in the **army** were listed by name,
1: 38 or more who were able to serve in the **army** were listed by name,
1: 40 or more who were able to serve in the **army** were listed by name,
1: 42 or more who were able to serve in the **army** were listed by name,
1: 45 or more who were able to serve in Israel's **army** were counted
1: 52 The Israelites are to set up their tents by **divisions**, each man in his
2: 3 the **divisions** *of* the camp of Judah are to encamp under their
2: 4 His **division** numbers 74,600.
2: 6 His **division** numbers 54,400.
2: 8 His **division** numbers 57,400.
2: 9 the camp of Judah, according to their **divisions**, number 186,400.
2: 10 On the south will be the **divisions** *of* the camp of Reuben under
2: 11 His **division** numbers 46,500.
2: 13 His **division** numbers 59,300.
2: 15 His **division** numbers 45,650.
2: 16 the camp of Reuben, according to their **divisions**, number 151,450.
2: 18 On the west will be the **divisions** *of* the camp of Ephraim under
2: 19 His **division** numbers 40,500.
2: 21 His **division** numbers 32,200.
2: 23 His **division** numbers 35,400.
2: 24 camp of Ephraim, according to their **divisions**, number 108,100.
2: 25 On the north will be the **divisions** *of* the camp of Dan, under their
2: 26 His **division** numbers 62,700.
2: 28 His **division** numbers 41,500.
2: 30 His **division** numbers 53,400.
2: 32 All those in the camps, by their **divisions**, number 603,550.
4: 3 who come to **serve** [+6913] *in* the work in the Tent of Meeting.
4: 23 age who come to **serve** [+7371] in the work at the Tent of Meeting.
4: 30 all the men from thirty to fifty years of age who come to **serve**
4: 35 All the men from thirty to fifty years of age who came to **serve** in
4: 39 All the men from thirty to fifty years of age who came to **serve** in
4: 43 All the men from thirty to fifty years of age who came to **serve** in
8: 24 or more shall come to **take part** [+7371] in the work at the Tent of
8: 25 they must retire from their **regular service** [+6275] and work no
10: 14 The **divisions** *of* the camp of Judah went first, under their standard.
10: 14 Nahshon son of Amminadab was **in command** [+6584].
10: 15 Nethanel son of Zuar was over the **division** *of* the tribe of Issachar,
10: 16 Eliab son of Helon was over the **division** *of* the tribe of Zebulun.
10: 18 The **divisions** *of* the camp of Reuben went next, under their
10: 18 their standard. Elizur son of Shedeur was **in command** [+6584].
10: 19 Shelumiel son of Zurishaddai was over the **division** *of* the tribe of
10: 20 Eliasaph son of Deuel was over the **division** *of* the tribe of Gad.
10: 22 The **divisions** *of* the camp of Ephraim went next, under their
10: 22 Elishama son of Ammihud was **in command** [+6584].
10: 23 Gamaliel son of Pedahzur was over the **division** *of* the tribe of
10: 24 Abidan son of Gideoni was over the **division** *of* the tribe of
10: 25 the **divisions** *of* the camp of Dan set out, under their standard.
10: 25 Ahiezer son of Ammishaddai was **in command** [+6584].
10: 26 Pagiel son of Ocran was over the **division** *of* the tribe of Asher,
10: 27 Ahira son of Enan was over the **division** *of* the tribe of Naphtali.
10: 28 This was the order of march for the Israelite **divisions** as they set
26: 2 years old or more who are able to serve in the **army** of Israel."
31: 3 "Arm some of your men to go to **war** against the Midianites
31: 4 Send into **battle** a thousand men from each of the tribes of Israel."
31: 5 So twelve thousand men armed for **battle**, a thousand from each
31: 6 Moses sent them into **battle**, a thousand from each tribe,
31: 6 **[RPH]** who took with him articles from the sanctuary
31: 14 commanders of hundreds—who returned from the **battle** [+4878].
31: 21 Eleazar the priest said to the **soldiers** [+408] who had gone into
31: 27 Divide the spoils between the soldiers who took part in the **battle**
31: 28 From the soldiers who fought in the **battle**, set apart as tribute for
31: 32 The plunder remaining from the spoils that the **soldiers** [+6639]
31: 36 The half share of those who fought in the **battle** was:
31: 48 the officers who were over the units of the **army**—
31: 53 Each **soldier** [+408] had taken plunder for himself.
32: 27 your servants, every man armed for **battle**, will cross over to fight
33: 1 they came out of Egypt by **divisions** under the leadership of Moses
Dt 4: 19 and see the sun, the moon and the stars—all the heavenly **array**—

Dt 17: 3 down to them or to the sun or the moon or the **stars** *of* the sky,
20: 9 to the army, they shall appoint **commanders** [+8569] over it.
24: 5 he must not be sent to **war** or have any other duty laid on him.
Jos 4: 13 About forty thousand armed for **battle** crossed over before the
5: 14 "but as commander of the **army** *of* the LORD I have now come."
5: 15 The commander of the LORD's **army** replied, "Take off your
22: 12 the whole assembly of Israel gathered at Shiloh to go to **war**
22: 33 they talked no more about going to **war** against them to devastate
Jdg 4: 2 The commander of his **army** was Sisera, who lived in Harosheth
4: 7 the commander of Jabin's **army**, with his chariots and his troops to
8: 6 in your possession? Why should we give bread to your **troops**?"
9: 29 I would say to Abimelech, 'Call out your whole **army**!' "
1Sa 1: 3 town to worship and sacrifice to the LORD **Almighty** at Shiloh,
1: 11 she made a vow, saying, "O LORD **Almighty**, if you will only
4: 4 brought back the ark of the covenant of the LORD **Almighty**,
12: 9 the commander of the **army** *of* Hazor, and into the hands of the
14: 50 The name of the commander of Saul's **army** was Abner son of
15: 2 This is what the LORD **Almighty** says: 'I will punish the
17: 45 but I come against you in the name of the LORD **Almighty**,
17: 55 he said to Abner, commander of the **army**, "Abner, whose son is
26: 5 and Abner son of Ner, the commander of the **army**, had lain down.
28: 1 In those days the Philistines gathered their forces **[NIE]** to fight
2Sa 2: 8 Meanwhile, Abner son of Ner, the commander of Saul's **army**,
3: 23 When Joab and all the **soldiers** with him arrived, he was told that
5: 10 more powerful, because the LORD God **Almighty** was with him.
6: 2 which is called by the Name, the name of the LORD **Almighty**,
6: 18 he blessed the people in the name of the LORD **Almighty**.
7: 8 tell my servant David, 'This is what the LORD **Almighty** says:
7: 26 Then men will say, 'The LORD **Almighty** is God over Israel!'
7: 27 "O LORD **Almighty**, God of Israel, you have revealed this to
8: 16 Joab son of Zeruiah was over the **army**; Jehoshaphat son of Ahilud
10: 7 David sent Joab out with the entire **army** of fighting men.
10: 16 with Shobach the commander of Hadadezer's **army** leading them.
10: 18 He also struck down Shobach the commander of their **army**,
17: 25 Absalom had appointed Amasa over the **army** in place of Joab.
19: 13 [19:14] if from now on you are not the commander of my **army**
20: 23 Joab was over Israel's entire **army**; Benaiah son of Jehoiada was
1Ki 1: 19 Abiathar the priest and Joab the commander of the **army**,
1: 25 king's sons, the commanders of the **army** and Abiathar the priest.
2: 5 what he did to the two commanders of Israel's **armies**, Abner son
2: 32 Abner son of Ner, commander of Israel's **army**, and Amasa son of
2: 32 and Amasa son of Jether, commander of Judah's **army**—
2: 35 The king put Benaiah son of Jehoiada over the **army** in Joab's
4: 4 **commander in chief** [+2021+6584]; Zadok and Abiathar—
11: 15 Joab the commander of the **army**, who had gone up to bury the
11: 21 and that Joab the commander of the **army** was also dead.
16: 16 murdered him, they proclaimed Omri, the commander of the **army**,
18: 15 Elijah said, "As the LORD **Almighty** lives, whom I serve,
19: 10 "I have been very zealous for the LORD God **Almighty**.
19: 14 "I have been very zealous for the LORD God **Almighty**.
22: 19 I saw the LORD sitting on his throne with all the **host** *of* heaven
2Ki 3: 14 Elisha said, "As surely as the LORD **Almighty** lives, whom I
4: 13 behalf to the king or the commander of the **army**?' " She replied,
5: 1 Now Naaman was commander of the **army** *of* the king of Aram.
17: 16 They bowed down to all the starry **hosts**, and they worshiped Baal.
19: 31 The zeal of the LORD **Almighty** [no K] will accomplish this.
21: 3 He bowed down to all the starry **hosts** and worshiped them.
21: 5 of the temple of the LORD, he built altars to all the starry **hosts**.
23: 4 all the articles made for Baal and Asherah and all the starry **hosts**.
23: 5 and moon, to the constellations and to all the starry **hosts**.
25: 19 He also took the secretary who was **chief officer** [+2021+8569] in
1Ch 5: 18 Manasseh had 44,760 men **ready for military** [+3655] **service**—
7: 4 they had 36,000 **men ready for battle** [+1522+4878], for they had
7: 11 There were 17,200 fighting men **ready to go out** [+3655] to war.
7: 40 The number of men **ready for battle** [+928+2021+4878], as listed
11: 9 and more powerful, because the LORD **Almighty** was with him.
12: 8 [12:9] brave warriors, **ready for battle** [+408+2021+4200+4878]
12: 14 [12:15] These Gadites were **army** commanders; the least was a
12: 21 [12:22] brave warriors, and they were commanders in his **army**.
12: 23 [12:24] These are the numbers of the men armed for **battle** who
12: 24 [12:25] carrying shield and spear—6,800 armed for **battle**;
12: 25 [12:26] men of Simeon, warriors ready for **battle**—7,100;
12: 33 [12:34] men of Zebulun, **experienced soldiers** [+3655] prepared
12: 36 [12:37] men of Asher, **experienced soldiers** [+3655] prepared for
12: 37 [12:38] armed with every type of **weapon** [+3998+4878]—
17: 7 tell my servant David, 'This is what the LORD **Almighty** says:
17: 24 Then men will say, 'The LORD **Almighty**, the God over Israel,
18: 15 Joab son of Zeruiah was over the **army**; Jehoshaphat son of Ahilud
19: 8 David sent Joab out with the entire **army** *of* fighting men.
19: 16 with Shophach the commander of Hadadezer's **army** leading them.
19: 18 He also killed Shophach the commander of their **army**.
20: 1 when kings go off to war, Joab led out the **armed** [+2657] **forces**.
25: 1 David, together with the commanders of the **army**, set apart some
26: 26 and commanders of hundreds, and by the other **army** commanders.
27: 3 of Perez and chief of all the **army** officers for the first month.
27: 5 The third **army** commander, for the third month, was Benaiah son
27: 34 and by Abiathar. Joab was the commander of the royal **army**.
2Ch 17: 18 next, Jehozabad, with 180,000 men armed for **battle**.
18: 18 I saw the LORD sitting on his throne with all the **host** *of* heaven
25: 5 three hundred thousand men **ready for military** [+3655] **service**,
25: 7 "O king, these **troops** *from* Israel must not march with you,
26: 11 **ready to go out** [+3655] by divisions according to their numbers
26: 13 Under their command was an **army** [+2657] of 307,500 men
26: 14 helmets, coats of armor, bows and slingstones for the entire **army**.
28: 9 and he went out to meet the **army** when it returned to Samaria.
28: 12 son of Hadlai—confronted those who were arriving from the **war**.
33: 3 He bowed down to all the starry **hosts** and worshiped them.
33: 5 of the temple of the LORD, he built altars to all the starry **hosts**.
33: 11 So the LORD brought against them the **army** commanders of the
Ne 9: 6 and all their **starry host**, the earth and all that is on it, the seas
9: 6 give life to everything, and the **multitudes** *of* heaven worship you.
Job 7: 1 "Does not man have **hard service** on earth? Are not his days like
10: 17 anger toward me; your **forces** come against me wave upon wave.
14: 14 All the days of my **hard service** I will wait for my renewal to
Ps 24: 10 The LORD **Almighty**—he is the King of glory. *Selah*
33: 6 the heavens made, their **starry host** by the breath of his mouth.
44: 9 [44:10] and humbled us; you no longer go out with our **armies**.
46: 7 [46:8] The LORD **Almighty** is with us; the God of Jacob is our
46: 11 [46:12] The LORD **Almighty** is with us; the God of Jacob is our
48: 8 [48:9] so have we seen in the city of the LORD **Almighty**,
59: 5 [59:6] O LORD God **Almighty**, the God of Israel, rouse yourself
60: 10 [60:12] have rejected us and no longer go out with our **armies**?
68: 11 [68:12] and great was the **company** of those who proclaimed it:
68: 12 [68:13] "Kings and **armies** flee in haste; in the camps men divide
69: 6 [69:7] because of me, O Lord, the LORD **Almighty**;
80: 4 [80:5] O LORD God **Almighty**, how long will your anger
80: 7 [80:8] Restore us, O God **Almighty**; make your face shine upon
80: 14 [80:15] Return to us, O God **Almighty**! Look down from heaven
80: 19 [80:20] Restore us, O LORD God **Almighty**; make your face
84: 1 [84:2] How lovely is your dwelling place, O LORD **Almighty**!
84: 3 [84:4] your altar, O LORD **Almighty**, my King and my God.
84: 8 [84:9] Hear my prayer, O LORD God **Almighty**; listen to me,
84: 12 [84:13] O LORD **Almighty**, blessed is the man who trusts in
89: 8 [89:9] O LORD God **Almighty**, who is like you? You are
103: 21 Praise the LORD, all his **heavenly hosts**, you his servants who do
108: 11 [108:12] have rejected us and no longer go out with our **armies**?
148: 2 Praise him, all his angels, praise him, all his **heavenly hosts**.
Isa 1: 9 Unless the LORD **Almighty** had left us some survivors,
1: 24 Therefore the Lord, the LORD **Almighty**, the Mighty One of
2: 12 The LORD **Almighty** has a day in store for all the proud
3: 1 See now, the Lord, the LORD **Almighty**, is about to take from
3: 15 the faces of the poor?" declares the Lord, the LORD **Almighty**.
5: 7 The vineyard of the LORD **Almighty** is the house of Israel,
5: 9 The LORD **Almighty** has declared in my hearing: "Surely the
5: 16 the LORD **Almighty** will be exalted by his justice, and the holy
5: 24 for they have rejected the law of the LORD **Almighty**
6: 3 "Holy, holy, holy is the LORD **Almighty**; the whole earth is full
6: 5 and my eyes have seen the King, the LORD **Almighty**."
8: 13 The LORD **Almighty** is the one you are to regard as holy,
8: 18 We are signs and symbols in Israel from the LORD **Almighty**,
9: 7 [9:6] The zeal of the LORD **Almighty** will accomplish this.
9: 13 [9:12] struck them, nor have they sought the LORD **Almighty**.
9: 19 [9:18] By the wrath of the LORD **Almighty** the land will be
10: 16 Therefore, the Lord, the LORD **Almighty**, will send a wasting
10: 23 The Lord, the LORD **Almighty**, will carry out the destruction
10: 24 Therefore, this is what the Lord, the LORD **Almighty**, says:
10: 26 The LORD **Almighty** will lash them with a whip, as when he
10: 33 See, the Lord, the LORD **Almighty**, will lop off the boughs with
13: 4 The LORD **Almighty** is mustering an army for war.
13: 4 The LORD Almighty is mustering an **army** *for* war.
13: 13 will shake from its place at the wrath of the LORD **Almighty**,
14: 22 "I will rise up against them," declares the LORD **Almighty**.
14: 23 with the broom of destruction," declares the LORD **Almighty**.
14: 24 The LORD **Almighty** has sworn, "Surely, as I have planned,
14: 27 For the LORD **Almighty** has purposed, and who can thwart him?
17: 3 be like the glory of the Israelites," declares the LORD **Almighty**.
18: 7 At that time gifts will be brought to the LORD **Almighty** from a
18: 7 to Mount Zion, the place of the Name of the LORD **Almighty**.
19: 4 will rule over them," declares the Lord, the LORD **Almighty**.
19: 12 make known what the LORD **Almighty** has planned against
19: 16 at the uplifted hand that the LORD **Almighty** raises against them.
19: 17 because of what the LORD **Almighty** is planning against them.
19: 18 language of Canaan and swear allegiance to the LORD **Almighty**.
19: 20 and witness to the LORD **Almighty** in the land of Egypt.
19: 25 The LORD **Almighty** will bless them, saying, "Blessed be Egypt
21: 10 I tell you what I have heard from the LORD **Almighty**,
22: 5 The Lord, the LORD **Almighty**, has a day of tumult
22: 12 The Lord, the LORD **Almighty**, called you on that day to weep

Isa 22: 14 The LORD **Almighty** has revealed this in my hearing: "Till your
22: 14 sin will not be atoned for," says the Lord, the LORD **Almighty**.
22: 15 This is what the Lord, the LORD **Almighty**, says: "Go, say to this
22: 25 "In that day," declares the LORD **Almighty**, "the peg driven into
23: 9 The LORD **Almighty** planned it, to bring low the pride of all
24: 21 In that day the LORD will punish the **powers** *in* the heavens
24: 23 for the LORD **Almighty** will reign on Mount Zion and in
25: 6 On this mountain the LORD **Almighty** will prepare a feast of rich
28: 5 In that day the LORD **Almighty** will be a glorious crown,
28: 22 the Lord, the LORD **Almighty**, has told me of the destruction
28: 29 All this also comes from the LORD **Almighty**, wonderful in
29: 6 the LORD **Almighty** will come with thunder and earthquake
31: 4 so the LORD **Almighty** will come down to do battle on Mount
31: 5 hovering overhead, the LORD **Almighty** will shield Jerusalem;
34: 2 is angry with all nations; his wrath is upon all their **armies**.
34: 4 All the **stars** *of* the heavens will be dissolved and the sky rolled up
34: 4 all the **starry host** will fall like withered leaves from the vine,
37: 16 "O LORD **Almighty**, God of Israel, enthroned between the
37: 32 The zeal of the LORD **Almighty** will accomplish this.
39: 5 Isaiah said to Hezekiah, "Hear the word of the LORD **Almighty**:
40: 2 and proclaim to her that her **hard service** has been completed,
40: 26 He who brings out the **starry host** one by one, and calls them each
44: 6 Israel's King and Redeemer, the LORD **Almighty**:
45: 12 hands stretched out the heavens; I marshaled their **starry hosts**.
45: 13 but not for a price or reward, says the LORD **Almighty**."
47: 4 Our Redeemer—the LORD **Almighty** is his name—is the Holy
48: 2 and rely on the God of Israel—the LORD **Almighty** is his name:
51: 15 so that its waves roar—the LORD **Almighty** is his name.
54: 5 your Maker is your husband—the LORD **Almighty** is his name—
Jer 2: 19 and have no awe of me," declares the Lord, the LORD **Almighty**.
5: 14 Therefore this is what the LORD God **Almighty** says:
6: 6 This is what the LORD **Almighty** says: "Cut down the trees
6: 9 This is what the LORD **Almighty** says: "Let them glean the
7: 3 This is what the LORD **Almighty**, the God of Israel, says:
7: 21 " 'This is what the LORD **Almighty**, the God of Israel, says:
8: 2 exposed to the sun and the moon and all the **stars** *of* the heavens,
8: 3 nation will prefer death to life, declares the LORD **Almighty**.'
9: 7 [9:6] Therefore this is what the LORD **Almighty** says: "See,
9: 15 [9:14] Therefore, this is what the LORD **Almighty**, the God of
9: 17 [9:16] This is what the LORD **Almighty** says: "Consider now!
10: 16 the tribe of his inheritance—the LORD **Almighty** is his name.
11: 17 The LORD **Almighty**, who planted you, has decreed disaster for
11: 20 But, O LORD **Almighty**, you who judge righteously and test the
11: 22 therefore this is what the LORD **Almighty** says: 'I will punish
15: 16 heart's delight, for I bear your name, O LORD God **Almighty**.
16: 9 For this is what the LORD **Almighty**, the God of Israel, says:
19: 3 This is what the LORD **Almighty**, the God of Israel, says:
19: 11 and say to them, 'This is what the LORD **Almighty** says:
19: 13 where they burned incense on the roofs to all the starry **hosts**
19: 15 "This is what the LORD **Almighty**, the God of Israel, says:
20: 12 O LORD **Almighty**, you who examine the righteous and probe
23: 15 this is what the LORD **Almighty** says concerning the prophets:
23: 16 This is what the LORD **Almighty** says: "Do not listen to what the
23: 36 the words of the living God, the LORD **Almighty**, our God.
25: 8 Therefore the LORD **Almighty** says this: "Because you have not
25: 27 "Then tell them, 'This is what the LORD **Almighty**, the God of
25: 28 and drink, tell them, 'This is what the LORD **Almighty** says:
25: 29 upon all who live on the earth, declares the LORD **Almighty**.'
25: 32 This is what the LORD **Almighty** says: "Look! Disaster is
26: 18 all the people of Judah, 'This is what the LORD **Almighty** says:
27: 4 for their masters and say, 'This is what the LORD **Almighty**,
27: 18 let them plead with the LORD **Almighty** that the furnishings
27: 19 For this is what the LORD **Almighty** says about the pillars,
27: 21 yes, this is what the LORD **Almighty**, the God of Israel,
28: 2 "This is what the LORD **Almighty**, the God of Israel, says:
28: 14 This is what the LORD **Almighty**, the God of Israel, says:
29: 4 This is what the LORD **Almighty**, the God of Israel, says to all
29: 8 Yes, this is what the LORD **Almighty**, the God of Israel,
29: 17 yes, this is what the LORD **Almighty** says: "I will send the
29: 21 This is what the LORD **Almighty**, the God of Israel, says about
29: 25 "This is what the LORD **Almighty**, the God of Israel, says:
30: 8 " 'In that day,' declares the LORD **Almighty**, 'I will break the
31: 23 This is what the LORD **Almighty**, the God of Israel, says:
31: 35 so that its waves roar—the LORD **Almighty** is his name:
32: 14 'This is what the LORD **Almighty**, the God of Israel, says:
32: 15 For this is what the LORD **Almighty**, the God of Israel, says:
32: 18 and powerful God, whose name is the LORD **Almighty**,
33: 11 saying, "Give thanks to the LORD **Almighty**, for the LORD is
33: 12 "This is what the LORD **Almighty** says: 'In this place, desolate
33: 22 the Levites who minister before me as countless as the **stars** *of* the
35: 13 "This is what the LORD **Almighty**, the God of Israel, says:
35: 17 "Therefore, this is what the LORD God **Almighty**, the God of
35: 18 "This is what the LORD **Almighty**, the God of Israel, says:
35: 19 Therefore, this is what the LORD **Almighty**, the God of Israel,
38: 17 "This is what the LORD God **Almighty**, the God of Israel,
39: 16 'This is what the LORD **Almighty**, the God of Israel, says:
42: 15 This is what the LORD **Almighty**, the God of Israel, says:
42: 18 This is what the LORD **Almighty**, the God of Israel, says:
43: 10 'This is what the LORD **Almighty**, the God of Israel, says:
44: 2 "This is what the LORD **Almighty**, the God of Israel, says:
44: 7 "Now this is what the LORD God **Almighty**, the God of Israel,
44: 11 "Therefore, this is what the LORD **Almighty**, the God of Israel,
44: 25 This is what the LORD **Almighty**, the God of Israel, says:
46: 10 But that day belongs to the Lord, the LORD **Almighty**—
46: 10 For the Lord, the LORD **Almighty**, will offer sacrifice in the land
46: 18 as I live," declares the King, whose name is the LORD **Almighty**,
46: 25 The LORD **Almighty**, the God of Israel, says: "I am about to
48: 1 This is what the LORD **Almighty**, the God of Israel, says:
48: 15 declares the King, whose name is the LORD **Almighty**.
49: 5 all those around you," declares the Lord, the LORD **Almighty**.
49: 7 Concerning Edom: This is what the LORD **Almighty** says:
49: 26 will be silenced in that day," declares the LORD **Almighty**.
49: 35 This is what the LORD **Almighty** says: "See, I will break the bow
50: 18 Therefore this is what the LORD **Almighty**, the God of Israel,
50: 25 for the Sovereign LORD **Almighty** has work to do in the land of
50: 31 O arrogant one," declares the Lord, the LORD **Almighty**,
50: 33 This is what the LORD **Almighty** says: "The people of Israel are
50: 34 Yet their Redeemer is strong; the LORD **Almighty** is his name.
51: 3 Do not spare her young men; completely destroy her **army**.
51: 5 Judah have not been forsaken by their God, the LORD **Almighty**,
51: 14 The LORD **Almighty** has sworn by himself: I will surely fill you
51: 19 the tribe of his inheritance—the LORD **Almighty** is his name.
51: 33 This is what the LORD **Almighty**, the God of Israel, says:
51: 57 declares the King, whose name is the LORD **Almighty**.
51: 58 This is what the LORD **Almighty** says: "Babylon's thick wall
52: 25 He also took the secretary who was **chief officer** [+2021+8569] in
Da 8: 10 It grew until it reached the **host** *of* the heavens, and it threw some
8: 10 it threw some of the starry **host** down to the earth and trampled on
8: 11 It set itself up to be as great as the Prince of the **host**; it took away
8: 12 the **host** ⌞of the saints⌟ and the daily sacrifice were given over to it.
8: 13 of the sanctuary and of the **host** that will be trampled underfoot?"
10: 1 Its message was true and it concerned a great **war**. The
Hos 12: 5 [12:6] the LORD God **Almighty**, the LORD is his name of
Am 3: 13 the house of Jacob," declares the Lord, the LORD God **Almighty**.
4: 13 high places of the earth—the LORD God **Almighty** is his name.
5: 14 the LORD God **Almighty** will be with you, just as you say he is.
5: 15 Perhaps the LORD God **Almighty** will have mercy on the
5: 16 Therefore this is what the Lord, the LORD God **Almighty**, says:
5: 27 says the LORD, whose name is God **Almighty**.
6: 8 has sworn by himself—the LORD God **Almighty** declares:
6: 14 For the LORD God **Almighty** declares, "I will stir up a nation
9: 5 The Lord, the LORD **Almighty**, he who touches the earth
Mic 4: 4 one will make them afraid, for the LORD **Almighty** has spoken.
Na 2: 13 [2:14] "I am against you," declares the LORD **Almighty**. "I will
3: 5 "I am against you," declares the LORD **Almighty**. "I will lift
Hab 2: 13 Has not the LORD **Almighty** determined that the people's labor
Zep 1: 5 those who bow down on the roofs to worship the starry **host**,
2: 9 surely as I live," declares the LORD **Almighty**, the God of Israel,
2: 10 for insulting and mocking the people of the LORD **Almighty**.
Hag 1: 2 This is what the LORD **Almighty** says: "These people say,
1: 5 Now this is what the LORD **Almighty** says: "Give careful
1: 7 This is what the LORD **Almighty** says: "Give careful thought to
1: 9 I blew away. Why?" declares the LORD **Almighty**.
1: 14 and began to work on the house of the LORD **Almighty**,
2: 4 'and work. For I am with you,' declares the LORD **Almighty**.
2: 6 "This is what the LORD **Almighty** says: 'In a little while I will
2: 7 and I will fill this house with glory,' says the LORD **Almighty**.
2: 8 is mine and the gold is mine,' declares the LORD **Almighty**.
2: 9 than the glory of the former house,' says the LORD **Almighty**.
2: 9 in this place I will grant peace,' declares the LORD **Almighty**."
2: 11 "This is what the LORD **Almighty** says: 'Ask the priests what the
2: 23 " 'On that day,' declares the LORD **Almighty**, 'I will take you,
2: 23 for I have chosen you,' declares the LORD **Almighty**."
Zec 1: 3 This is what the LORD **Almighty** says: 'Return to me,'
1: 3 'Return to me,' declares the LORD **Almighty**, 'and I will return to
1: 3 'and I will return to you,' says the LORD **Almighty**.
1: 4 This is what the LORD **Almighty** says: 'Turn from your evil ways
1: 6 'The LORD **Almighty** has done to us what our ways and practices
1: 12 the angel of the LORD said, "LORD **Almighty**, how long will
1: 14 "Proclaim this word: This is what the LORD **Almighty** says:
1: 16 be stretched out over Jerusalem,' declares the LORD **Almighty**.
1: 17 "Proclaim further: This is what the LORD **Almighty** says:
2: 8 [2:12] For this is what the LORD **Almighty** says: "After he has
2: 9 [2:13] you will know that the LORD **Almighty** has sent me.
2: 11 [2:15] you will know that the LORD **Almighty** has sent me to
3: 7 "This is what the LORD **Almighty** says: 'If you will walk in my
3: 9 and I will engrave an inscription on it,' says the LORD **Almighty**,
3: 10 to sit under his vine and fig tree,' declares the LORD **Almighty**."

Zec 4: 6 might nor by power, but by my Spirit,' says the LORD **Almighty**.
4: 9 Then you will know that the LORD **Almighty** has sent me to you.
5: 4 The LORD **Almighty** declares, 'I will send it out, and it will enter
6: 12 Tell him this is what the LORD **Almighty** says: 'Here is the man
6: 15 and you will know that the LORD **Almighty** has sent me to you.
7: 3 by asking the priests of the house of the LORD **Almighty**
7: 4 Then the word of the LORD **Almighty** came to me:
7: 9 "This is what the LORD **Almighty** says: 'Administer true justice;
7: 12 or to the words that the LORD **Almighty** had sent by his Spirit
7: 12 the earlier prophets. So the LORD **Almighty** was very angry.
7: 13 when they called, I would not listen,' says the LORD **Almighty**.
8: 1 Again the word of the LORD **Almighty** came to me.
8: 2 This is what the LORD **Almighty** says: "I am very jealous for
8: 3 the mountain of the LORD **Almighty** will be called the Holy
8: 4 This is what the LORD **Almighty** says: "Once again men
8: 6 This is what the LORD **Almighty** says: "It may seem marvelous
8: 6 but will it seem marvelous to me?" declares the LORD **Almighty**.
8: 7 This is what the LORD **Almighty** says: "I will save my people
8: 9 This is what the LORD **Almighty** says: "You who now hear these
8: 9 the foundation was laid for the house of the LORD **Almighty**,
8: 11 of this people as I did in the past," declares the LORD **Almighty**.
8: 14 This is what the LORD **Almighty** says: "Just as I had determined
8: 14 pity when your fathers angered me," says the LORD **Almighty**,
8: 18 Again the word of the LORD **Almighty** came to me.
8: 19 This is what the LORD **Almighty** says: "The fasts of the fourth,
8: 20 This is what the LORD **Almighty** says: "Many peoples
8: 21 go at once to entreat the LORD and seek the LORD **Almighty**.
8: 22 nations will come to Jerusalem to seek the LORD **Almighty**
8: 23 This is what the LORD **Almighty** says: "In those days ten men
9: 8 But I will defend my house against marauding **forces**. [BHS 5166]
9: 15 and the LORD **Almighty** will shield them. They will destroy
10: 3 for the LORD **Almighty** will care for his flock, the house of
12: 5 Jerusalem are strong, because the LORD **Almighty** is their God.'
13: 2 will be remembered no more," declares the LORD **Almighty**.
13: 7 declares the LORD **Almighty**. "Strike the shepherd,
14: 16 the LORD **Almighty**, and to celebrate the Feast of Tabernacles.
14: 17 to worship the King, the LORD **Almighty**, they will have no rain.
14: 21 pot in Jerusalem and Judah will be holy to the LORD **Almighty**,
14: 21 no longer be a Canaanite in the house of the LORD **Almighty**.
Mal 1: 4 But this is what the LORD **Almighty** says: "They may build,
1: 6 says the LORD **Almighty**. "It is you, O priests, who show
1: 8 with you? Would he accept you?" says the LORD **Almighty**.
1: 9 your hands, will he accept you?"—says the LORD **Almighty**.
1: 10 I am not pleased with you," says the LORD **Almighty**, "and I will
1: 11 will be great among the nations," says the LORD **Almighty**.
1: 13 and you sniff at it contemptuously," says the LORD **Almighty**.
1: 14 For I am a great king," says the LORD **Almighty**, "and my name
2: 2 says the LORD **Almighty**, "I will send a curse upon you,
2: 4 my covenant with Levi may continue," says the LORD **Almighty**.
2: 7 because he is the messenger of the LORD **Almighty**.
2: 8 have violated the covenant with Levi," says the LORD **Almighty**.
2: 12 even though he brings offerings to the LORD **Almighty**.
2: 16 violence as well as with his garment," says the LORD **Almighty**.
3: 1 whom you desire, will come," says the LORD **Almighty**.
3: 5 aliens of justice, but do not fear me," says the LORD **Almighty**.
3: 7 to me, and I will return to you," says the LORD **Almighty**.
3: 10 Test me in this," says the LORD **Almighty**, "and see if I will not
3: 11 in your fields will not cast their fruit," says the LORD **Almighty**.
3: 12 for yours will be a delightful land," says the LORD **Almighty**.
3: 14 and going about like mourners before the LORD **Almighty**?
3: 17 "They will be mine," says the LORD **Almighty**, "in the day when
4: 1 [3:19] coming will set them on fire," says the LORD **Almighty**.
4: 3 [3:21] day when I do these things," says the LORD **Almighty**.

7373 [3]צָבָא ṣābāʾ[3], n.m. [1] [→ 7374; cf. 7475, 7383]

gazelles [1]

1Ch 12: 8 [12:9] and they were as swift as **gazelles** in the mountains.

7374 צְבָאָה ṣᵉbāʾâ, n.f. [2] [√ 7373]

gazelles [2]

SS 2: 7 I charge you by the **gazelles** and by the does of the field:
3: 5 I charge you by the **gazelles** and by the does of the field:

7375 צְבֹאִים ṣᵉbōʾîm, n.pr.loc. [5] [cf. 7373, 7387]

Zeboiim [5]

Ge 10: 19 toward Sodom, Gomorrah, Admah and **Zeboiim**, as far as Lasha.
14: 2 Shinab king of Admah, Shemeber king of **Zeboiim**, [K 7387]
14: 8 the king of **Zeboiim** [K 7387] and the king of Bela (that is,
Dt 29: 23 [29:22] of Sodom and Gomorrah, Admah and **Zeboiim**, [Q 7387]
Hos 11: 8 How can I make you like **Zeboiim**? My heart is changed within

7376 צֹבֵבָה ṣōbēbâ, n.pr.m. Not used in NIV/BHS [→ 2206, 7369]

7377 צָבָה ṣābâ, v. [2] [→ 7370?, 7379]

swell [1], swells [1]

Nu 5: 22 [G] so that your abdomen **swells** and your thigh wastes away."
5: 27 [A] her abdomen *will* **swell** and her thigh waste away, and she

7378 צֹבֶה ṣōbeh, var. Not used in NIV/BHS

7379 צָבֶה ṣābeh, a. [1] [√ 7377]

swell [1]

Nu 5: 21 he causes your thigh to waste away and your abdomen to **swell**.

7380 צָבוּעַ ṣābûaʿ, a. [1] [√ 7388]

speckled [1]

Jer 12: 9 Has not my inheritance become to me like a **speckled** bird of prey

7381 צָבַט ṣābaṭ, v. [1] [cf. 7395]

offered [1]

Ru 2: 14 [A] down with the harvesters, *he* **offered** her some roasted grain.

7382 [1]צְבִי ṣᵉbî[1], n.m. [19 / 18] [→ Ar 10605]

beautiful [6], glory [4], beauty [2], most beautiful [+7382] [2], most beautiful [2], beautiful jewelry [+6344] [1], jewel [1]

2Sa 1: 19 "Your **glory**, O Israel, lies slain on your heights. How the mighty
Isa 4: 2 In that day the Branch of the LORD will be **beautiful**
13: 19 Babylon, the **jewel** *of* kingdoms, the glory of the Babylonians'
23: 9 to bring low the pride of all **glory** and to humble all who are
24: 16 "**Glory** to the Righteous One." But I said, "I waste away, I waste
28: 1 of Ephraim's drunkards, to the fading flower, his glorious **beauty**,
28: 4 That fading flower, his glorious **beauty**, set on the head of a fertile
28: 5 a glorious crown, a **beautiful** wreath for the remnant of his people.
Jer 3: 19 the **most beautiful** [+7382] inheritance of any nation.'
3: 19 the **most beautiful** [+7382] inheritance of any nation.'
Eze 7: 20 They were proud of their **beautiful jewelry** [+6344] and used it to
20: 6 land flowing with milk and honey, the **most beautiful** of all lands.
20: 15 a land flowing with milk and honey, **most beautiful** of all lands—
25: 9 Baal Meon and Kiriathaim—the **glory** *of* that land.
26: 20 or take your place [*I will give* ***glory***] in the land of the living.
Da 8: 9 power to the south and to the east and toward the **Beautiful** Land.
11: 16 He will establish himself in the **Beautiful** Land and will have the
11: 41 He will also invade the **Beautiful** Land. Many countries will fall,
11: 45 He will pitch his royal tents between the seas at the **beautiful** holy

7383 [2]צְבִי ṣᵉbî[2], n.m. [11] [→ 7384, 7385, 7386; cf. 7373, 7387]

gazelle [10], gazelles [1]

Dt 12: 15 eat as much of the meat as you want, as if it were **gazelle** or deer,
12: 22 Eat them as you would **gazelle** or deer. Both the ceremonially
14: 5 the deer, the **gazelle**, the roe deer, the wild goat, the ibex,
15: 22 and the clean may eat it, as if it were **gazelle** or deer.
2Sa 2: 18 and Asahel. Now Asahel was as fleet-footed as a wild **gazelle**.
1Ki 4: 23 [5:3] as well as deer, **gazelles**, roebucks and choice fowl.
Pr 6: 5 Free yourself, like a **gazelle** from the hand of the hunter, like a bird
SS 2: 9 My lover is like a **gazelle** or a young stag. Look! There he stands
2: 17 and be like a **gazelle** or like a young stag on the rugged hills.
8: 14 be like a **gazelle** or like a young stag on the spice-laden mountains.
Isa 13: 14 Like a hunted **gazelle**, like sheep without a shepherd, each will

7384 צִבְיָא ṣibyāʾ, n.pr.m. [1] [√ 7383]

Zibia [1]

1Ch 8: 9 By his wife Hodesh he had Jobab, **Zibia**, Mesha, Malcam,

7385 צִבְיָה ṣibyâ, n.pr.f. [2] [√ 7383]

Zibiah [2]

2Ki 12: 1 [12:2] His mother's name was **Zibiah**; she was from Beersheba.
2Ch 24: 1 His mother's name was **Zibiah**; she was from Beersheba.

7386 צְבִיָּה ṣᵉbiyyâ, n.f. [2] [√ 7383]

gazelle [2]

SS 4: 5 like twin fawns of a **gazelle** that browse among the lilies.
7: 3 [7:4] Your breasts are like two fawns, twins of a **gazelle**.

7387 צְבֹיִים ṣᵉbōyim, n.pr.loc. [0] [cf. 7375, 7383]

Ge 14: 2 [king of Admah, Shemeber king of **Zeboiim**, [K; see Q 7375]]

[A] Qal [B] Qal passive [C] Niphal [D] Piel (poel, polel, pilel, pilal, pealal, pilpel) [E] Pual (poal, polal, poalal, pulal, pualal)

Ge 14: 8 [the king of Admah, the king of **Zeboiim** [K; see Q 7375]]
Dt 29:23 [29:22] [and **Zeboiim**, [Q; see K 7375] which the LORD overthrew]

7388 צָבַע ***ṣaba'***, v. Not used in NIV/BHS [→ 7380, 7389; 7390, 7391; Ar 10607]

7389 צֶבַע ***ṣeba'***, n.[m.]. [3] [√ 7388; Ar 10607]

colorful garments [2], garments [1]

Jdg 5:30 or two for each man, **colorful garments** as plunder for Sisera,
5:30 garments as plunder for Sisera, **colorful garments** embroidered,
5:30 highly embroidered **garments** for my neck—

7390 צִבְעוֹן ***ṣib'ôn***, n.pr.m. [8] [cf. 7388, 7391]

Zibeon [8]

Ge 36: 2 daughter of Anah and granddaughter of **Zibeon** the Hivite—
36:14 wife Oholibamah daughter of Anah and granddaughter of **Zibeon**,
36:20 who were living in the region: Lotan, Shobal, **Zibeon**, Anah,
36:24 The sons of **Zibeon**: Aiah and Anah. This is the Anah who
36:24 the desert while he was grazing the donkeys of his father **Zibeon**.
36:29 These were the Horite chiefs: Lotan, Shobal, **Zibeon**, Anah,
1Ch 1:38 of Seir: Lotan, Shobal, **Zibeon**, Anah, Dishon, Ezer and Dishan.
1:40 Ebal, Shepho and Onam. The sons of **Zibeon**: Aiah and Anah.

7391 צְבֹעִים ***ṣ^e bō'îm***, n.pr.loc. [2] [cf. 7388, 7390]

Zeboim [2]

1Sa 13:18 the third toward the borderland overlooking the Valley of **Zeboim**
Ne 11:34 in Hadid, **Zeboim** and Neballat,

7392 צָבַר ***ṣābar***, v. [7] [→ 7393, 7394]

build [1], heaped up [1], heaps up wealth [1], heaps up [1], piled [1], store up [1], stored up [1]

Ge 41:35 [A] and **store up** the grain under the authority of Pharaoh,
41:49 [A] Joseph **stored up** huge quantities of grain, like the sand of
Ex 8:14 [8:10] [A] They *were* **piled** *into* heaps, and the land reeked of
Job 27:16 [A] Though *he* **heaps up** silver like dust and clothes like piles of
Ps 39: 6 [39:7] [A] *he* **heaps up wealth**, not knowing who will get it.
Hab 1:10 [A] fortified cities; *they* **build** earthen ramps and capture them.
Zec 9: 3 [A] *she has* **heaped up** silver like dust, and gold like the dirt of

7393 צִבֻּר ***ṣibbur***, n.m. [1] [√ 7392]

piles [1]

2Ki 10: 8 "Put them in two **piles** at the entrance of the city gate until

7394 צִבָּרוֹן ***ṣibbārôn***, n.m. Not used in NIV/BHS [√ 7392]

7395 צֶבֶת ***ṣebet***, n.[m.]pl. [1] [cf. 7381]

bundles [1]

Ru 2:16 pull out some stalks for her from the **bundles** and leave them for

7396 [1]צַד ***ṣad[1]***, n.m. [33 / 34] [→ 7398; Ar 10608]

side [14], sides [5], *untranslated* [2], arm [2], beside [+4946] [2], opposite sides [+7521] [2], backs [1], flank [1], near [+4946] [1], next to [+4946] [1], other[s] [1], vicinity [1], with [+4946] [1]

Ge 6:16 Put a door in the **side** *of* the ark and make lower, middle and upper
Ex 25:32 Six branches are to extend from the **sides** *of* the lampstand—
25:32 sides of the lampstand—three on one **side** and three on the other.
25:32 the lampstand—three on one side and three on the other. **[RPH]**
26:13 what is left will hang over the **sides** *of* the tabernacle so as to cover
30: 4 two on **opposite sides** [+7521]—to hold the poles used to carry it.
37:18 Six branches extended from the **sides** *of* the lampstand—three on
37:18 sides of the lampstand—three on one **side** and three on the other.
37:18 the lampstand—three on one side and three on the other. **[RPH]**
37:27 two on **opposite sides** [+7521]—to hold the poles used to carry it.
Nu 33:55 to remain will become barbs in your eyes and thorns in your **sides**.
Dt 31:26 place it **beside** [+4946] the ark of the covenant of the LORD your
Jos 3:16 distance away, at a town called Adam in the **vicinity** *of* Zarethan,
12: 9 the king of Jericho one the king of Ai (**near** [+4946] Bethel)
23:13 and traps for you, whips on your **backs** and thorns in your eyes,
Jdg 2: 3 they will be ⌊thorns⌋ in your **sides** and their gods will be a snare to
Ru 2:14 When she sat down **with** [+4946] the harvesters, he offered her
1Sa 6: 8 in a chest **beside** [+4946] it put the gold objects you are sending
20:20 I will shoot three arrows to the **side** *of* it, as though I were shooting
20:25 opposite Jonathan, and Abner sat **next** [+4946] **to** Saul,
23:26 Saul was going along one **side** *of* the mountain, and David
23:26 David and his men were on the other **side**, hurrying to get away
2Sa 2:16 by the head and thrust his dagger into his opponent's **side**,
13:34 people on the road west of him, coming down the **side** *of* the hill.
13:34 men in the direction of Horonaim, on the **side** [BHS-] *of* the hill."

Ps 91: 7 A thousand may fall at your **side**, ten thousand at your right hand,
Isa 60: 4 sons come from afar, and your daughters are carried on the **arm**.
66:12 you will nurse and be carried on her **arm** and dandled on her
Eze 4: 4 "Then lie on your left **side** and put the sin of the house of Israel
4: 6 you have finished this, lie down again, this time on your right **side**,
4: 8 so that you cannot turn from one **side** to the other until you have
4: 8 so that you cannot turn from one side to the **other**[s] until you have
4: 9 You are to eat it during the 390 days you lie on your **side**.
34:21 Because you shove with **flank** and shoulder, butting all the weak

7397 [2]צַד ***ṣad[2]***, n.m. Not used in NIV/BHS [cf. 7403]

7398 צְדָד ***ṣādād***, n.pr.loc. [2] [√ 7396]

Zedad [2]

Nu 34: 8 Mount Hor to Lebo Hamath. Then the boundary will go to **Zedad**,
Eze 47:15 the Great Sea by the Hethlon road past Lebo Hamath to **Zedad**,

7399 [1]צָדָה ***ṣādâ[1]***, v. [2] [→ 7402]

do intentionally [1], hunting down [1]

Ex 21:13 [A] However, if he *does* not **do** it **intentionally**, but God lets it
1Sa 24:11 [24:12] [A] but you *are* **hunting** me **down** to take my life.

7400 [2]צָדָה ***ṣādâ[2]***, v. [1]

are destroyed [1]

Zep 3: 6 [C] Their cities **are destroyed**; no one will be left—no one at all.

7401 צָדוֹק ***ṣādôq***, n.pr.m. [53] [√ 7405]

Zadok [51], them[s] [+59+2256] [1], Zadokites [+1201] [1]

2Sa 8:17 **Zadok** son of Ahitub and Ahimelech son of Abiathar were priests;
15:24 **Zadok** was there, too, and all the Levites who were with him were
15:25 the king said to **Zadok**, "Take the ark of God back into the city.
15:27 The king also said to **Zadok** the priest, "Aren't you a seer?
15:29 So **Zadok** and Abiathar took the ark of God back to Jerusalem
15:35 Won't the priests **Zadok** and Abiathar be there with you?
15:35 Tell **them**[s] [+59+2256] anything you hear in the king's palace.
15:36 two sons, Ahimaaz son of **Zadok** and Jonathan son of Abiathar,
17:15 Hushai told **Zadok** and Abiathar, the priests, "Ahithophel has
18:19 Now Ahimaaz son of **Zadok** said, "Let me run and take the news
18:22 Ahimaaz son of **Zadok** again said to Joab, "Come what may,
18:27 seems to me that the first one runs like Ahimaaz son of **Zadok**."
19:11 [19:12] King David sent this message to **Zadok** and Abiathar,
20:25 Sheva was secretary; **Zadok** and Abiathar were priests;
1Ki 1: 8 **Zadok** the priest, Benaiah son of Jehoiada, Nathan the prophet,
1:26 me your servant, and **Zadok** the priest, and Benaiah son of
1:32 King David said, "Call in **Zadok** the priest, Nathan the prophet
1:34 There have **Zadok** the priest and Nathan the prophet anoint him
1:38 So **Zadok** the priest, Nathan the prophet, Benaiah son of Jehoiada,
1:39 **Zadok** the priest took the horn of oil from the sacred tent
1:44 The king has sent with him **Zadok** the priest, Nathan the prophet,
1:45 **Zadok** the priest and Nathan the prophet have anointed him king at
2:35 in Joab's position and replaced Abiathar with **Zadok** the priest.
4: 2 these were his chief officials: Azariah son of **Zadok**—the priest;
4: 4 of Jehoiada—commander in chief; **Zadok** and Abiathar—priests;
2Ki 15:33 sixteen years. His mother's name was Jerusha daughter of **Zadok**.
1Ch 6: 8 [5:34] Ahitub the father of **Zadok**, Zadok the father of Ahimaaz,
6: 8 [5:34] Ahitub the father of Zadok, **Zadok** the father of Ahimaaz,
6:12 [5:38] Ahitub the father of **Zadok**, Zadok the father of Shallum,
6:12 [5:38] Ahitub the father of Zadok, **Zadok** the father of Shallum,
6:53 [6:38] **Zadok** his son and Ahimaaz his son.
9:11 the son of **Zadok**, the son of Meraioth, the son of Ahitub,
12:28 [12:29] **Zadok**, a brave young warrior, with 22 officers from his
15:11 Then David summoned **Zadok** and Abiathar the priests, and Uriel,
16:39 David left **Zadok** the priest and his fellow priests before the
18:16 **Zadok** son of Ahitub and Ahimelech son of Abiathar were priests;
24: 3 With the help of **Zadok** a descendant of Eleazar and Ahimelech a
24: 6 **Zadok** the priest, Ahimelech son of Abiathar and the heads of
24:31 in the presence of King David and of **Zadok**, Ahimelech,
27:17 over Levi: Hashabiah son of Kemuel; over Aaron: **Zadok**;
29:22 him before the LORD to be ruler and **Zadok** to be priest.
2Ch 27: 1 sixteen years. His mother's name was Jerusha daughter of **Zadok**.
31:10 and Azariah the chief priest, from the family of **Zadok**, answered,
Ezr 7: 2 the son of Shallum, the son of **Zadok**, the son of Ahitub,
Ne 3: 4 and next to him **Zadok** son of Baana also made repairs.
3:29 to them, **Zadok** son of Immer made repairs opposite his house.
10:21 [10:22] Meshezabel, **Zadok**, Jaddua,
11:11 the son of **Zadok**, the son of Meraioth, the son of Ahitub,
13:13 I put Shelemiah the priest, **Zadok** the scribe, and a Levite named
Eze 40:46 These are the sons of **Zadok**, who are the only Levites who may
43:19 who are Levites, of the family of **Zadok**, who come near to
44:15 who are Levites and descendants of **Zadok** and who faithfully
48:11 the **Zadokites** [+1201], who were faithful in serving me and did

7402 צְדִיָּה ṣᵉdiyyâ, n.f. [2] [√ 7399; Ar 10216, 10609]
intentionally [+928] [1], unintentionally [+928+4202] [1]

Nu 35:20 or throws something at him **intentionally** [+928] so that he dies
35:22 or throws something at him **unintentionally** [+928+4202]

7403 צִדִּים ṣiddîm, n.pr.loc. [1] [cf. 7397]
Ziddim [1]

Jos 19:35 The fortified cities were **Ziddim**, Zer, Hammath, Rakkath,

7404 צַדִּיק ṣaddîq, a. [206 / 205] [√ 7405]
righteous [178], innocent [12], just [3], right [2], Righteous One [2], upright [2], *untranslated* [1], honest [1], in the right [1], overrighteous [+2221] [1], righteous [+2446] [1], righteousness [1]

Ge 6: 9 Noah was a **righteous** man, blameless among the people of his
7: 1 because I have found you **righteous** in this generation.
18:23 and said: "Will you sweep away the **righteous** with the wicked?
18:24 What if there are fifty **righteous** *people* in the city? Will you really
18:24 not spare the place for the sake of the fifty **righteous** *people* in it?
18:25 to kill the **righteous** with the wicked, treating the righteous
18:25 with the wicked, treating the **righteous** and the wicked alike.
18:26 "If I find fifty **righteous** *people* in the city of Sodom,
18:28 what if the number of the **righteous** is five less than fifty?
20: 4 near her, so he said, "Lord, will you destroy an **innocent** nation?
Ex 9:27 "The LORD is **in the right**, and I and my people are in the
23: 7 false charge and do not put an innocent or **honest** *person* to death,
23: 8 a bribe blinds those who see and twists the words of the **righteous**.
Dt 4: 8 what other nation is so great as to have such **righteous** decrees
16:19 blinds the eyes of the wise and twists the words of the **righteous**.
25: 1 the case, acquitting the **innocent** and condemning the guilty.
32: 4 A faithful God who does no wrong, **upright** and just is he.
1Sa 24:17 [24:18] "You are more **righteous** than I," he said. "You have
2Sa 4:11 when wicked men have killed an **innocent** man in his own house
23: 3 'When one rules over men in **righteousness**, when he rules in the
1Ki 2:32 of Judah's army—were better men and more **upright** than he.
8:32 Declare the **innocent** not guilty, and so establish his innocence.
2Ki 10: 9 He stood before all the people and said, "You are **innocent**.
2Ch 6:23 Declare the **innocent** not guilty and so establish his innocence.
12: 6 and the king humbled themselves and said, "The LORD is **just**."
Ezr 9:15 O LORD, God of Israel, you are **righteous**! We are left this day
Ne 9: 8 You have kept your promise because you are **righteous**.
9:33 In all that has happened to us, you have been **just**; you have acted
Job 12: 4 a mere laughingstock, though **righteous** and blameless!
17: 9 Nevertheless, the **righteous** will hold to their ways, and those with
22:19 "The **righteous** see their ruin and rejoice; the innocent mock them,
27:17 what he lays up the **righteous** will wear, and the innocent will
32: 1 stopped answering Job, because he was **righteous** in his own eyes.
34:17 hates justice govern? Will you condemn the **just** and mighty One?
36: 7 He does not take his eyes off the **righteous**; he enthrones them
Ps 1: 5 in the judgment, nor sinners in the assembly of the **righteous**.
1: 6 For the LORD watches over the way of the **righteous**,
5:12 [5:13] For surely, O LORD, you bless the **righteous**;
7: 9 [7:10] O **righteous** God, who searches minds and hearts, bring to
7: 9 [7:10] the violence of the wicked and make the **righteous** secure.
7:11 [7:12] God is a **righteous** judge, a God who expresses his wrath
11: 3 the foundations are being destroyed, what can the **righteous** do?"
11: 5 The LORD examines the **righteous**, but the wicked and those
11: 7 For the LORD is **righteous**, he loves justice; upright men will see
14: 5 with dread, for God is present in the company of the **righteous**.
31:18 [31:19] and contempt they speak arrogantly against the **righteous**.
32:11 Rejoice in the LORD and be glad, you **righteous**; sing, all you
33: 1 Sing joyfully to the LORD, you **righteous**; it is fitting for the
34:15 [34:16] The eyes of the LORD are on the **righteous** and his ears
34:19 [34:20] A **righteous** *man* may have many troubles,
34:21 [34:22] the wicked; the foes of the **righteous** will be condemned.
37:12 The wicked plot against the **righteous** and gnash their teeth at
37:16 Better the little that the **righteous** have than the wealth of many
37:17 the wicked will be broken, but the LORD upholds the **righteous**.
37:21 and do not repay, but the **righteous** give generously;
37:25 yet I have never seen the **righteous** forsaken or their children
37:29 the **righteous** will inherit the land and dwell in it forever.
37:30 The mouth of the **righteous** *man* utters wisdom, and his tongue
37:32 The wicked lie in wait for the **righteous**, seeking their very lives;
37:39 The salvation of the **righteous** comes from the LORD; he is their
52: 6 [52:8] The **righteous** will see and fear; they will laugh at him,
55:22 [55:23] he will sustain you; he will never let the **righteous** fall.
58:10 [58:11] The **righteous** will be glad when they are avenged,
58:11 [58:12] men will say, "Surely the **righteous** still are rewarded;
64:10 [64:11] Let the **righteous** rejoice in the LORD and take refuge
68: 3 [68:4] may the **righteous** be glad and rejoice before God; may
69:28 [69:29] of the book of life and not be listed with the **righteous**.
72: 7 In his days the **righteous** will flourish; prosperity will abound till
75:10 [75:11] but the horns of the **righteous** will be lifted up.
92:12 [92:13] The **righteous** will flourish like a palm tree, they will
94:21 They band together against the **righteous** and condemn the
97:11 Light is shed upon the **righteous** and joy on the upright in heart.
97:12 Rejoice in the LORD, you *who* are **righteous**, and praise his holy
112: 4 for the gracious and compassionate and **righteous** *man*.
112: 6 never be shaken; a **righteous** *man* will be remembered forever.
116: 5 The LORD is gracious and **righteous**; our God is full of
118:15 Shouts of joy and victory resound in the tents of the **righteous**:
118:20 This is the gate of the LORD through which the **righteous** may
119:137 **Righteous** are you, O LORD, and your laws are right.
125: 3 the wicked will not remain over the land allotted to the **righteous**,
125: 3 for then the **righteous** might use their hands to do evil.
129: 4 the LORD is **righteous**; he has cut me free from the cords of the
140:13 [140:14] Surely the **righteous** will praise your name
141: 5 Let a **righteous** *man* strike me—it is a kindness; let him rebuke
142: 7 [142:8] the **righteous** will gather about me because of your
145:17 The LORD is **righteous** in all his ways and loving toward all he
146: 8 up those who are bowed down, the LORD loves the **righteous**.
Pr 2:20 in the ways of good men and keep to the paths of the **righteous**.
3:33 the house of the wicked, but he blesses the home of the **righteous**.
4:18 The path of the **righteous** is like the first gleam of dawn, shining
9: 9 wiser still; teach a **righteous** *man* and he will add to his learning.
10: 3 The LORD does not let the **righteous** go hungry but he thwarts
10: 6 Blessings crown the head of the **righteous**, but violence
10: 7 The memory of the **righteous** will be a blessing, but the name of
10:11 The mouth of the **righteous** is a fountain of life, but violence
10:16 The wages of the **righteous** bring them life, but the income of the
10:20 The tongue of the **righteous** is choice silver, but the heart of the
10:21 The lips of the **righteous** nourish many, but fools die for lack of
10:24 will overtake him; what the **righteous** desire will be granted.
10:25 the wicked are gone, but the **righteous** stand firm forever.
10:28 The prospect of the **righteous** is joy, but the hopes of the wicked
10:30 The **righteous** will never be uprooted, but the wicked will not
10:31 The mouth of the **righteous** brings forth wisdom, but a perverse
10:32 The lips of the **righteous** know what is fitting, but the mouth of the
11: 8 The **righteous** *man* is rescued from trouble, and it comes on the
11: 9 his neighbor, but through knowledge the **righteous** escape.
11:10 When the **righteous** prosper, the city rejoices; when the wicked
11:21 go unpunished, but *those who* are **righteous** [+2446] will go free.
11:23 The desire of the **righteous** ends only in good, but the hope of the
11:28 in his riches will fall, but the **righteous** will thrive like a green leaf.
11:30 The fruit of the **righteous** is a tree of life, and he who wins souls is
11:31 If the **righteous** receive their due on earth, how much more the
12: 3 through wickedness, but the **righteous** cannot be uprooted.
12: 5 The plans of the **righteous** are just, but the advice of the wicked is
12: 7 and are no more, but the house of the **righteous** stands firm.
12:10 A **righteous** *man* cares for the needs of his animal, but the kindest
12:12 the plunder of evil men, but the root of the **righteous** flourishes.
12:13 is trapped by his sinful talk, but a **righteous** *man* escapes trouble.
12:21 No harm befalls the **righteous**, but the wicked have their fill of
12:26 A **righteous** *man* is cautious in friendship, but the way of the
13: 5 The **righteous** hate what is false, but the wicked bring shame
13: 9 The light of the **righteous** shines brightly, but the lamp of the
13:21 pursues the sinner, but prosperity is the reward of the **righteous**.
13:22 but a sinner's wealth is stored up for the **righteous**.
13:25 The **righteous** eat to their hearts' content, but the stomach of the
14:19 presence of the good, and the wicked at the gates of the **righteous**.
14:32 are brought down, but even in death the **righteous** have a refuge.
15: 6 The house of the **righteous** contains great treasure, but the income
15:28 The heart of the **righteous** weighs its answers, but the mouth of the
15:29 is far from the wicked but he hears the prayer of the **righteous**.
17:15 Acquitting the guilty and condemning the **innocent**—the LORD
17:26 It is not good to punish an **innocent** *man*, or to flog officials for
18: 5 to be partial to the wicked or to deprive the **innocent** of justice.
18:10 the LORD is a strong tower; the **righteous** run to it and are safe.
18:17 The first to present his case seems **right**, till another comes
20: 7 The **righteous** *man* leads a blameless life; blessed are his children
21:12 The **Righteous One** takes note of the house of the wicked
21:15 justice is done, it brings joy to the **righteous** but terror to evildoers.
21:18 The wicked become a ransom for the **righteous**, and the unfaithful
21:26 long he craves for more, but the **righteous** give without sparing.
23:24 The father of a **righteous** *man* has great joy; he who has a wise
24:15 Do not lie in wait like an outlaw against a **righteous** *man's* house,
24:16 for though a **righteous** *man* falls seven times, he rises again,
24:24 Whoever says to the guilty, "You are **innocent**"—peoples will
25:26 or a polluted well is a **righteous** *man* who gives way to the
28: 1 though no one pursues, but the **righteous** are as bold as a lion.
28:12 When the **righteous** triumph, there is great elation; but when the
28:28 go into hiding; but when the wicked perish, the **righteous** thrive.
29: 2 When the **righteous** thrive, the people rejoice; when the wicked
29: 6 is snared by his own sin, but a **righteous** *one* can sing and be glad.
29: 7 The **righteous** care about justice for the poor, but the wicked have
29:16 so does sin, but the **righteous** will see their downfall.

Pr 29:27 The **righteous** detest the dishonest; the wicked detest the upright.
Ecc 3:17 "God will bring to judgment both the **righteous** and the wicked,
7:15 a **righteous** *man* perishing in his righteousness, and a wicked man
7:16 Do not be **overrighteous** [+2221], neither be overwise—why
7:20 There is not a **righteous** man on earth who does what is right
8:14 **righteous** *men* who get what the wicked deserve, and wicked men
8:14 and wicked men who get what the **righteous** deserve.
9:1 reflected on all this and concluded that the **righteous** and the wise
9:2 the **righteous** and the wicked, the good and the bad, the clean
Isa 3:10 Tell the **righteous** it will be well with them, for they will enjoy the
5:23 who acquit the guilty for a bribe, but deny justice to the **innocent**.
24:16 "Glory to the **Righteous One**." But I said, "I waste away,
26:2 Open the gates that the **righteous** nation may enter, the nation that
26:7 The path of the **righteous** is level; O upright One, you make the
26:7 O upright One, you make the way of the **righteous** smooth.
29:21 in court and with false testimony deprive the **innocent** of justice.
41:26 so we could know, or beforehand, so we could say, 'He was **right**'?
45:21 And there is no God apart from me, a **righteous** God and a Savior;
49:24 or captives rescued from the fierce? [BHS ***righteous***; NIV 6883]
53:11 by his knowledge my **righteous** servant will justify many,
57:1 The **righteous** perish, and no one ponders it in his heart; devout
57:1 no one understands that the **righteous** are taken away to be spared
60:21 will all your people be **righteous** and they will possess the land
Jer 12:1 You are always **righteous**, O LORD, when I bring a case before
20:12 you who examine the **righteous** and probe the heart and mind,
23:5 the LORD, "when I will raise up to David a **righteous** Branch,
La 1:18 "The LORD is **righteous**, yet I rebelled against his command.
4:13 of her priests, who shed within her the blood of the **righteous**.
Eze 3:20 when a **righteous** *man* turns from his righteousness and does evil,
3:21 if you do warn the **righteous** *man* not to sin and he does not sin,
3:21 do warn the righteous man not to sin **[RPH]** and he does not sin,
13:22 Because you disheartened the **righteous** with your lies, when I had
18:5 "Suppose there is a **righteous** man who does what is just and right.
18:9 That man is **righteous**; he will surely live, declares the Sovereign
18:20 The righteousness of the **righteous** *man* will be credited to him,
18:24 "But if a **righteous** *man* turns from his righteousness and commits
18:26 If a **righteous** *man* turns from his righteousness and commits sin,
21:3 [21:8] and cut off from you both the **righteous** and the wicked.
21:4 [21:9] Because I am going to cut off the **righteous**
23:45 **righteous** men will sentence them to the punishment of women
33:12 'The righteousness of the **righteous** *man* will not save him when
33:12 The **righteous** *man*, if he sins, will not be allowed to live
33:13 If I tell the **righteous** *man* that he will surely live, but then he
33:18 If a **righteous** *man* turns from his righteousness and does evil,
Da 9:14 for the LORD our God is **righteous** in everything he does;
Hos 14:9 [14:10] the **righteous** walk in them, but the rebellious stumble in
Am 2:6 They sell the **righteous** for silver, and the needy for a pair of
5:12 You oppress the **righteous** and take bribes and you deprive the
Hab 1:4 The wicked hem in the **righteous**, so that justice is perverted.
1:13 the wicked swallow up *those* more **righteous** than themselves?
2:4 desires are not upright—but the **righteous** will live by his faith—
Zep 3:5 The LORD within her is **righteous**; he does no wrong. Morning
Zec 9:9 **righteous** and having salvation, gentle and riding on a donkey,
Mal 3:18 And you will again see the distinction between the **righteous**

7405 צָדַק *ṣādaq*, v.den. [41] [→ 3392, 3449, 7401, 7404, 7406, 7407, 7408, 7409]

righteous [11], innocent [4], acquit [2], acquitting [2], declare not guilty [2], justify [2], vindicated [2], admit in the right [1], appear righteous [1], be reconsecrated [1], cleared [1], innocence [1], justifying [1], lead to righteousness [1], made appear righteous [1], made seem righteous [1], maintain rights [1], prove innocence [1], prove right [1], proved right [1], right [1], see that gets justice [1], vindicates [1]

Ge 38:26 [A] recognized them and said, "*She is* more **righteous** than I,
44:16 [F] "What can we say? How *can we* **prove** *our* **innocence**?
Ex 23:7 [G] or honest person to death, for *I will* not **acquit** the guilty.
Dt 25:1 [G] the case, **acquitting** the innocent and condemning the guilty.
2Sa 15:4 [G] case could come to me and *I would* **see that** he **gets justice**."
1Ki 8:32 [G] **Declare** the innocent **not guilty**, and so establish his
2Ch 6:23 [G] **Declare** the innocent **not guilty** and so establish his
Job 4:17 [A] '*Can* a mortal *be* more **righteous** than God? Can a man be
9:2 [A] this is true. But how *can* a mortal *be* **righteous** before God?
9:15 [A] Though *I were* **innocent**, I could not answer him; I could
9:20 [A] Even if *I were* **innocent**, my mouth would condemn me; if I
10:15 [A] Even if *I am* **innocent**, I cannot lift my head, for I am full of
11:2 [A] words to go unanswered? *Is* this talker *to be* **vindicated**?
13:18 [A] that I have prepared my case, I know I *will be* **vindicated**.
15:14 [A] be pure, or one born of woman, that *he could be* **righteous**?
22:3 [A] pleasure would it give the Almighty if *you were* **righteous**?
25:4 [A] How then *can* a man *be* **righteous** before God? How can one
27:5 [G] I will never **admit** you are **in the right**; till I die, I will not
32:2 [D] became very angry with Job for **justifying** himself rather
33:12 [A] "But I tell you, in this *you are* not **right**, for God is greater
33:32 [D] to say, answer me; speak up, for I want you *to be* **cleared**.
34:5 "Job says, '*I am* **innocent**, but God denies me justice.
35:7 [A] If *you are* **righteous**, what do you give to him, or what does
40:8 [A] my justice? Would you condemn me to **justify** *yourself*?
Ps 19:9 [19:10] [A] of the LORD are sure and altogether **righteous**.
51:4 [51:6] [A] so that *you are* **proved right** when you speak
82:3 [G] **maintain** *the* **rights** *of* the poor and oppressed.
143:2 [A] into judgment, for no one living *is* **righteous** before you.
Pr 17:15 [G] **Acquitting** the guilty and condemning the innocent—
Isa 5:23 [G] *who* **acquit** the guilty for a bribe, but deny justice to the
43:9 [A] Let them bring in their witnesses *to* **prove** *they were* **right**,
43:26 [A] argue the matter together; state the *case for* your **innocence**.
45:25 [A] LORD all the descendants of Israel *will be found* **righteous**
50:8 [G] *He who* **vindicates** me is near. Who then will bring charges
53:11 [G] by his knowledge my righteous servant *will* **justify** many,
Jer 3:11 [D] "Faithless Israel *is* more **righteous** than unfaithful Judah.
Eze 16:51 [D] *have* **made** your sisters **seem righteous** by all these things
16:52 [A] more vile than theirs, *they* **appear** more **righteous** than you.
16:52 [D] for you *have* **made** your sisters **appear righteous**.
Da 8:14 [C] and mornings; then the sanctuary *will* **be reconsecrated**."
12:3 [G] *those who* **lead** many **to righteousness**, like the stars for

7406 צֶדֶק *ṣedeq*, n.m. [119 / 118] [→ 155, 4900, 7408, 7409; cf. 7405]

righteousness [58], righteous [16], honest [8], right [7], justice [5], accurate [3], fairly [3], just [3], *untranslated* [2], righteously [2], truth [2], cleared [1], fairly [+928] [1], integrity [1], justly [1], rightful [1], rights [1], true [1], unrighteousness [+4202] [1], vindication [1]

Lev 19:15 or favoritism to the great, but judge your neighbor **fairly** [+928].
19:36 Use **honest** scales and honest weights, an honest ephah and an
19:36 Use honest scales and **honest** weights, an honest ephah and an
19:36 and honest weights, an **honest** ephah and an honest hin.
19:36 and honest weights, an honest ephah and an **honest** hin.
Dt 1:16 Hear the disputes between your brothers and judge **fairly**,
16:18 your God is giving you, and they shall judge the people **fairly**.
16:20 Follow **justice** and justice alone, so that you may live and possess
16:20 Follow justice and **justice** *alone*, so that you may live and possess
25:15 You must have accurate and **honest** weights and measures,
25:15 **[RPH]** so that you may live long in the land the LORD your
33:19 to the mountain and there offer sacrifices of **righteousness**;
Job 6:29 Relent, do not be unjust; reconsider, for my **integrity** is at stake.
8:3 God pervert justice? Does the Almighty pervert *what* is **right**?
8:6 himself on your behalf and restore you to your **rightful** place.
29:14 I put on **righteousness** as my clothing; justice was my robe
31:6 let God weigh me in **honest** scales and he will know that I am
35:2 "Do you think this is just? You say, 'I will be **cleared** by God.'
36:3 I get my knowledge from afar; I will ascribe **justice** to my Maker.
Ps 4:1 [4:2] Answer me when I call to you, O my **righteous** God.
4:5 [4:6] Offer **right** sacrifices and trust in the LORD.
7:8 [7:9] Judge me, O LORD, according to my **righteousness**,
7:17 [7:18] give thanks to the LORD because of his **righteousness**
9:4 [9:5] my cause; you have sat on your throne, judging **righteously**.
9:8 [9:9] He will judge the world in **righteousness**; he will govern the
15:2 He whose walk is blameless and who does *what* is **righteous**,
17:1 Hear, O LORD, my **righteous** plea; listen to my cry. Give ear to
17:15 And I—in **righteousness** I will see your face; when I awake,
18:20 [18:21] has dealt with me according to my **righteousness**;
18:24 [18:25] LORD has rewarded me according to my **righteousness**,
23:3 He guides me in paths of **righteousness** for his name's sake.
35:24 Vindicate me in your **righteousness**, O LORD my God; do not let
35:27 May those who delight in my **vindication** shout for joy
35:28 My tongue will speak of your **righteousness** and of your praises all
37:6 He will make your **righteousness** shine like the dawn, the justice
40:9 [40:10] I proclaim **righteousness** in the great assembly; I do not
45:4 [45:5] victoriously in behalf of truth, humility and **righteousness**;
45:7 [45:8] You love **righteousness** and hate wickedness; therefore
48:10 [48:11] of the earth; your right hand is filled with **righteousness**.
50:6 the heavens proclaim his **righteousness**, for God himself is judge.
51:19 [51:21] there will be **righteous** sacrifices, whole burnt offerings
52:3 [52:5] rather than good, falsehood rather than speaking the **truth**.
58:1 [58:2] Do you rulers indeed speak **justly**? Do you judge uprightly
65:5 [65:6] You answer us with awesome deeds of **righteousness**,
72:2 He will judge your people in **righteousness**, your afflicted ones
85:10 [85:11] meet together; **righteousness** and peace kiss each other.
85:11 [85:12] the earth, and **righteousness** looks down from heaven.
85:13 [85:14] **Righteousness** goes before him and prepares the way for
89:14 [89:15] **Righteousness** and justice are the foundation of your
94:15 Judgment will again be founded on **righteousness**, and all the
96:13 He will judge the world in **righteousness** and the peoples in his
97:2 **righteousness** and justice are the foundation of his throne.
97:6 The heavens proclaim his **righteousness**, and all the peoples see
98:9 He will judge the world in **righteousness** and the peoples with

Ps 118:19 Open for me the gates of **righteousness**; I will enter and give
119: 7 I will praise you with an upright heart as I learn your **righteous**
119:62 At midnight I rise to give you thanks for your **righteous** laws.
119:75 I know, O LORD, that your laws are **righteous**, and in
119:106 an oath and confirmed it, that I will follow your **righteous** laws.
119:121 I have done *what* is **righteous** and just; do not leave me to my
119:123 looking for your salvation, looking for your **righteous** promise.
119:138 The statutes you have laid down are **righteous**; they are fully
119:142 Your righteousness is **[RPH]** everlasting and your law is true.
119:144 Your statutes are forever **right**; give me understanding that I may
119:160 All your words are true; all your **righteous** laws are eternal.
119:164 Seven times a day I praise you for your **righteous** laws.
119:172 tongue sing of your word, for all your commands are **righteous**.
132: 9 May your priests be clothed with **righteousness**; may your saints
Pr 1: 3 and prudent life, *doing what* is **right** and just and fair;
2: 9 Then you will understand *what* is **right** and just and fair—
8: 8 All the words of my mouth are **just**; none of them is crooked
8:15 By me kings reign and rulers make laws *that* are **just**;
8:16 all nobles who rule on earth. [BHS *righteous rulers*; NIV 824]
12:17 A truthful witness gives **honest** testimony, but a false witness tells
16:13 Kings take pleasure in **honest** lips; they value a man who speaks
25: 5 and his throne will be established through **righteousness**.
31: 9 Speak up and judge **fairly**; defend the rights of the poor
Ecc 3:16 wickedness was there, in the place of **justice**—wickedness was
5: 8 [5:7] justice and **rights** denied, do not be surprised at such things;
7:15 a righteous man perishing in his **righteousness**, and a wicked man
Isa 1:21 of justice; **righteousness** used to dwell in her—but now murderers!
1:26 Afterward you will be called the City of **Righteousness**,
11: 4 with **righteousness** he will judge the needy, with justice he will
11: 5 **Righteousness** will be his belt and faithfulness the sash around his
16: 5 in judging seeks justice and speeds the cause of **righteousness**.
26: 9 come upon the earth, the people of the world learn **righteousness**.
26:10 grace is shown to the wicked, they do not learn **righteousness**;
32: 1 a king will reign in **righteousness** and rulers will rule with justice.
41: 2 up one from the east, calling him *in* **righteousness** to his service?
41:10 and help you; I will uphold you with my **righteous** right hand.
42: 6 "I, the LORD, have called you in **righteousness**; I will take hold
42:21 It pleased the LORD for the sake of his **righteousness** to make
45: 8 "You heavens above, rain down **righteousness**; let the clouds
45:13 I will raise up Cyrus in my **righteousness**: I will make all his ways
45:19 me in vain.' I, the LORD, speak the **truth**; I declare what is right.
51: 1 you who pursue **righteousness** and who seek the LORD:
51: 5 My **righteousness** draws near speedily, my salvation is on the
51: 7 "Hear me, you who know *what* is **right**, you people who have my
58: 2 They ask me for **just** decisions and seem eager for God to come
58: 8 your **righteousness** will go before you, and the glory of the
59: 4 No one calls for **justice**; no one pleads his case with integrity.
61: 3 They will be called oaks of **righteousness**, a planting of the
62: 1 till her **righteousness** shines out like the dawn, her salvation like a
62: 2 The nations will see your **righteousness**, and all kings your glory;
64: 5 [64:4] You come to the help of those who gladly do **right**,
Jer 11:20 you who judge **righteously** and test the heart and mind,
22:13 "Woe to him who builds his palace by **unrighteousness** [+4202],
23: 6 name by which he will be called: The LORD Our **Righteousness**.
31:23 'The LORD bless you, O **righteous** dwelling, O sacred mountain.'
33:16 name by which it will be called: The LORD Our **Righteousness**.'
50: 7 their **true** pasture, the LORD, the hope of their fathers.'
Eze 3:20 when a righteous man turns from his **righteousness** and does evil,
45:10 You are to use **accurate** scales, an accurate ephah and an accurate
45:10 are to use accurate scales, an **accurate** ephah and an accurate bath.
45:10 are to use accurate scales, an accurate ephah and an **accurate** bath.
Da 9:24 to bring in everlasting **righteousness**, to seal up vision
Hos 2:19 [2:21] I will betroth you in **righteousness** and justice, in love
10:12 the LORD, until he comes and showers **righteousness** on you.
Zep 2: 3 Seek **righteousness**, seek humility; perhaps you will be sheltered

7407 צְדָקָה ṣᵉdāqâ, n.f. [157] [√ 7405; Ar 10610]

righteousness [98], right [20], righteous [9], righteous acts [7], righteous things [4], innocence [2], justice [2], prosperity [2], vindication [2], claim [1], honesty [1], integrity [1], just [1], righteous act [1], righteous deeds [1], righteous state [1], righteous will [1], righteously [1], salvation [1], vindicated [+906+3655] [1]

Ge 15: 6 believed the LORD, and he credited it to him as **righteousness**.
18:19 after him to keep the way of the LORD by doing *what* is **right**
30:33 my **honesty** will testify for me in the future, whenever you check
Dt 6:25 as he has commanded us, that will be our **righteousness**."
9: 4 here to take possession of this land because of my **righteousness**."
9: 5 It is not because of your **righteousness** or your integrity that you
9: 6 because of your **righteousness** that the LORD your God is giving
24:13 it will be regarded as a **righteous act** in the sight of the LORD
33:21 he carried out the LORD's **righteous will**, and his judgments
Jdg 5:11 They recite the **righteous acts** *of* the LORD, the righteous acts of
5:11 acts of the LORD, the **righteous acts** *of* his warriors in Israel.
1Sa 12: 7 as to all the **righteous acts** performed by the LORD for you
26:23 The LORD rewards every man for his **righteousness**
2Sa 8:15 over all Israel, doing what was just and **right** for all his people.
19:28 [19:29] So what **right** do I have to make any more appeals to the
22:21 "The LORD has dealt with me according to my **righteousness**;
22:25 The LORD has rewarded me according to my **righteousness**,
1Ki 3: 6 because he was faithful to you and **righteous** and upright in heart.
8:32 Declare the innocent not guilty, and so establish his **innocence**.
10: 9 he has made you king, to maintain justice and **righteousness**."
1Ch 18:14 over all Israel, doing what was just and **right** for all his people.
2Ch 6:23 Declare the innocent not guilty and so establish his **innocence**.
9: 8 made you king over them, to maintain justice and **righteousness**."
Ne 2:20 you have no share in Jerusalem or any **claim** or historic right to it."
Job 27: 6 I will maintain my **righteousness** and never let go of it;
33:26 and shouts for joy; he is restored by God to his **righteous state**.
35: 8 a man like yourself, and your **righteousness** only the sons of men.
37:23 in his justice and great **righteousness**, he does not oppress.
Ps 5: 8 [5:9] O LORD, in your **righteousness** because of my enemies—
11: 7 For the LORD is righteous, he loves **justice**; upright men will see
22:31 [22:32] They will proclaim his **righteousness** to a people yet
24: 5 blessing from the LORD and **vindication** from God his Savior.
31: 1 [31:2] never be put to shame; deliver me in your **righteousness**.
33: 5 The LORD loves **righteousness** and justice; the earth is full of his
36: 6 [36:7] Your **righteousness** is like the mighty mountains,
36:10 [36:11] know you, your **righteousness** to the upright in heart.
40:10 [40:11] I do not hide your **righteousness** in my heart; I speak of
51:14 [51:16] saves me, and my tongue will sing of your **righteousness**.
69:27 [69:28] upon crime; do not let them share in your **salvation**.
71: 2 Rescue me and deliver me in your **righteousness**; turn your ear to
71:15 My mouth will tell of your **righteousness**, of your salvation all day
71:16 I will proclaim your **righteousness**, yours alone.
71:19 Your **righteousness** reaches to the skies, O God, you who have
71:24 My tongue will tell of your **righteous acts** all day long, for those
72: 1 with your justice, O God, the royal son with your **righteousness**.
72: 3 bring prosperity to the people, the hills the fruit of **righteousness**.
88:12 [88:13] or your **righteous deeds** in the land of oblivion?
89:16 [89:17] your name all day long; they exult in your **righteousness**.
98: 2 his salvation known and revealed his **righteousness** to the nations.
99: 4 established equity; in Jacob you have done what is just and **right**.
103: 6 The LORD works **righteousness** and justice for all the oppressed.
103:17 fear him, and his **righteousness** with their children's children—
106: 3 are they who maintain justice, who constantly do *what* is **right**.
106:31 This was credited to him as **righteousness** for endless generations
111: 3 and majestic are his deeds, and his **righteousness** endures forever.
112: 3 and riches are in his house, and his **righteousness** endures forever.
112: 9 abroad his gifts to the poor, his **righteousness** endures forever;
119:40 I long for your precepts! Preserve my life in your **righteousness**.
119:142 Your **righteousness** is everlasting and your law is true.
143: 1 in your faithfulness and **righteousness** come to my relief.
143:11 preserve my life; in your **righteousness**, bring me out of trouble.
145: 7 your abundant goodness and joyfully sing of your **righteousness**.
Pr 8:18 With me are riches and honor, enduring wealth and **prosperity**.
8:20 I walk in the way of **righteousness**, along the paths of justice,
10: 2 treasures are of no value, but **righteousness** delivers from death.
11: 4 in the day of wrath, but **righteousness** delivers from death.
11: 5 The **righteousness** *of* the blameless makes a straight way for them,
11: 6 The **righteousness** *of* the upright delivers them, but the unfaithful
11:18 but he who sows **righteousness** reaps a sure reward.
11:19 The truly **righteous** *man* attains life, but he who pursues evil goes
12:28 In the way of **righteousness** there is life; along that path is
13: 6 **Righteousness** guards the man of integrity, but wickedness
14:34 **Righteousness** exalts a nation, but sin is a disgrace to any people.
15: 9 way of the wicked but he loves those who pursue **righteousness**.
16: 8 Better a little with **righteousness** than much gain with injustice.
16:12 for a throne is established through **righteousness**.
16:31 Gray hair is a crown of splendor; it is attained by a **righteous** life.
21: 3 To do *what* is **right** and just is more acceptable to the LORD than
21:21 He who pursues **righteousness** and love finds life, prosperity
21:21 pursues righteousness and love finds life, **prosperity** and honor.
Isa 1:27 be redeemed with justice, her penitent ones with **righteousness**.
5: 7 but saw bloodshed; for **righteousness**, but heard cries of distress.
5:16 and the holy God will show himself holy by his **righteousness**.
5:23 who acquit the guilty for a bribe, but deny **justice** *to* the innocent.
9: 7 [9:6] and **righteousness** from that time on and forever.
10:22 Destruction has been decreed, overwhelming and **righteous**.
28:17 make justice the measuring line and **righteousness** the plumb line;
32:16 will dwell in the desert and **righteousness** live in the fertile field.
32:17 The fruit of **righteousness** will be peace; the effect of
32:17 the effect of **righteousness** will be quietness and confidence
33: 5 he dwells on high; he will fill Zion with justice and **righteousness**.
33:15 He who walks **righteously** and speaks what is right, who rejects
45: 8 open wide, let salvation spring up, let **righteousness** grow with it;
45:23 my mouth has uttered *in all* **integrity** a word that will not be
45:24 'In the LORD alone are **righteousness** and strength.' " All who

Isa 46:12 you stubborn-hearted, you who are far from **righteousness**.
46:13 I am bringing my **righteousness** near, it is not far away; and my
48: 1 and invoke the God of Israel—but not in truth or **righteousness**—
48:18 been like a river, your **righteousness** like the waves of the sea.
51: 6 my salvation will last forever, my **righteousness** will never fail.
51: 8 my **righteousness** will last forever, my salvation through all
54:14 In **righteousness** you will be established: Tyranny will be far from
54:17 and this is their **vindication** from me," declares the LORD.
56: 1 "Maintain justice and do *what* is **right**, for my salvation is close at
56: 1 is close at hand and my **righteousness** will soon be revealed.
57:12 I will expose your **righteousness** and your works, and they will not
58: 2 as if they were a nation that does *what* is **right** and has not
59: 9 So justice is far from us, and **righteousness** does not reach us.
59:14 So justice is driven back, and **righteousness** stands at a distance;
59:16 salvation for him, and his own **righteousness** sustained him.
59:17 He put on **righteousness** as his breastplate, and the helmet of
60:17 I will make peace your governor and **righteousness** your ruler.
61:10 garments of salvation and arrayed me in a robe of **righteousness**,
61:11 so the Sovereign LORD will make **righteousness** and praise
63: 1 his strength? "It is I, speaking in **righteousness**, mighty to save."
64: 6 [64:5] is unclean, and all our **righteous acts** are like filthy rags;
Jer 4: 2 if in a truthful, just and **righteous** *way* you swear, 'As surely as the
9:24 [9:23] justice and **righteousness** on earth, for in these I delight,"
22: 3 This is what the LORD says: Do what is just and **right**. Rescue
22:15 He did what was right and **just**, so all went well with him.
23: 5 who will reign wisely and do what is just and **right** in the land.
33:15 at that time I will make a **righteous** Branch sprout from David's
33:15 from David's line; he will do what is just and **right** in the land.
51:10 " 'The LORD *has* **vindicated** [+906+3655] us; come, let us tell in
Eze 3:20 The **righteous things** he did will not be remembered, and I will
14:14 were in it, they could save only themselves by their **righteousness**,
14:20 They would save only themselves by their **righteousness**.
18: 5 "Suppose there is a righteous man who does what is just and **right**.
18:19 Since the son has done what is just and **right** and has been careful
18:20 The **righteousness** *of* the righteous man will be credited to him,
18:21 and keeps all my decrees and does what is just and **right**,
18:22 Because of the **righteous things** he has done, he will live.
18:24 "But if a righteous man turns from his **righteousness** and commits
18:24 None of the **righteous things** he has done will be remembered.
18:26 If a righteous man turns from his **righteousness** and commits sin,
18:27 the wickedness he has committed and does what is just and **right**,
33:12 'The **righteousness** *of* the righteous man will not save him when he
33:13 surely live, but then he trusts in his **righteousness** and does evil,
33:13 none of the **righteous things** he has done will be remembered;
33:14 then turns away from his sin and does what is just and **right**—
33:16 against him. He has done what is just and **right**; he will surely live.
33:18 If a righteous man turns from his **righteousness** and does evil,
33:19 turns away from his wickedness and does what is just and **right**,
45: 9 up your violence and oppression and do what is just and **right**.
Da 9: 7 "Lord, you are **righteous**, but this day we are covered with
9:16 O Lord, in keeping with all your **righteous acts**, turn away your
9:18 We do not make requests of you because we are **righteous**,
Hos 10:12 Sow for yourselves **righteousness**, reap the fruit of unfailing love,
Joel 2:23 your God, for he has given you the autumn rains in **righteousness**.
Am 5: 7 turn justice into bitterness and cast **righteousness** to the ground
5:24 roll on like a river, **righteousness** like a never-failing stream!
6:12 justice into poison and the fruit of **righteousness** into bitterness—
Mic 6: 5 to Gilgal, that you may know the **righteous acts** *of* the LORD."
7: 9 He will bring me out into the light; I will see his **righteousness**.
Zec 8: 8 and I will be faithful and **righteous** to them as their God."
Mal 3: 3 LORD will have men who will bring offerings in **righteousness**,
4: 2 [3:20] the sun of **righteousness** will rise with healing in its wings.

7408 צִדְקִיָּה ṣidqiyyâ, n.pr.m. [7] [√ 7406 + 3378]

Zedekiah [7]

1Ki 22:11 Now **Zedekiah** son of Kenaanah had made iron horns and he
1Ch 3:16 The successors of Jehoiakim: Jehoiachin his son, and **Zedekiah**.
Ne 10: 1 [10:2] Nehemiah the governor, the son of Hacaliah. **Zedekiah**,
Jer 27:12 I gave the same message to **Zedekiah** king of Judah. I said,
28: 1 the fourth year, early in the reign of **Zedekiah** king of Judah,
29: 3 whom **Zedekiah** king of Judah sent to King Nebuchadnezzar in
49:34 concerning Elam, early in the reign of **Zedekiah** king of Judah:

7409 צִדְקִיָּהוּ ṣidqiyyāhû, n.pr.m. [56 / 57] [√ 7406 + 3378]

Zedekiah [53], Zedekiah's [2], his[s] [1], Zedekiah's [+4200] [1]

1Ki 22:24 **Zedekiah** son of Kenaanah went up and slapped Micaiah in the
2Ki 24:17 king in his place and changed his name to **Zedekiah**.
24:18 **Zedekiah** was twenty-one years old when he became king,
24:20 his presence. Now **Zedekiah** rebelled against the king of Babylon.
25: 2 was kept under siege until the eleventh year of King **Zedekiah**.
25: 7 They killed the sons of **Zedekiah** before his eyes. Then they put
25: 7 Then they put out **his**[s] eyes, bound him with bronze shackles
1Ch 3:15 Jehoiakim the second son, **Zedekiah** the third, Shallum the fourth.
2Ch 18:10 Now **Zedekiah** son of Kenaanah had made iron horns, and he
18:23 **Zedekiah** son of Kenaanah went up and slapped Micaiah in the
36:10 Jehoiachin's uncle, **Zedekiah**, king over Judah and Jerusalem.
36:11 **Zedekiah** was twenty-one years old when he became king,
Jer 1: 3 down to the fifth month of the eleventh year of **Zedekiah** son of
21: 1 word came to Jeremiah from the LORD when King **Zedekiah**
21: 3 But Jeremiah answered them, "Tell **Zedekiah**,
21: 7 I will hand over **Zedekiah** king of Judah, his officials
24: 8 'so will I deal with **Zedekiah** king of Judah, his officials and the
27: 1 Early in the reign of **Zedekiah** [BHS 3383] son of Josiah king of
27: 3 envoys who have come to Jerusalem to **Zedekiah** king of Judah.
29:21 says about Ahab son of Kolaiah and **Zedekiah** son of Maaseiah,
29:22 'The LORD treat you like **Zedekiah** and Ahab, whom the king of
32: 1 from the LORD in the tenth year of **Zedekiah** king of Judah,
32: 3 Now **Zedekiah** king of Judah had imprisoned him there, saying,
32: 4 **Zedekiah** king of Judah will not escape out of the hands of the
32: 5 He will take **Zedekiah** to Babylon, where he will remain until I
34: 2 Go to **Zedekiah** king of Judah and tell him, 'This is what the
34: 4 " 'Yet hear the promise of the LORD, O **Zedekiah** king of Judah.
34: 6 Then Jeremiah the prophet told all this to **Zedekiah** king of Judah,
34: 8 The word came to Jeremiah from the LORD after King **Zedekiah**
34:21 "I will hand **Zedekiah** king of Judah and his officials over to their
36:12 of Shaphan, **Zedekiah** son of Hananiah, and all the other officials.
37: 1 **Zedekiah** son of Josiah was made king of Judah by
37: 3 King **Zedekiah**, however, sent Jehucal son of Shelemiah with the
37:17 King **Zedekiah** sent for him and had him brought to the palace,
37:18 Jeremiah said to King **Zedekiah**, "What crime have I committed
37:21 King **Zedekiah** then gave orders for Jeremiah to be placed in the
38: 5 "He is in your hands," King **Zedekiah** answered. "The king can do
38:14 King **Zedekiah** sent for Jeremiah the prophet and had him brought
38:15 Jeremiah said to **Zedekiah**, "If I give you an answer, will you not
38:16 King **Zedekiah** swore this oath secretly to Jeremiah: "As surely as
38:17 Jeremiah said to **Zedekiah**, "This is what the LORD God
38:19 King **Zedekiah** said to Jeremiah, "I am afraid of the Jews who
38:24 **Zedekiah** said to Jeremiah, "Do not let anyone know about this
39: 1 In the ninth year of **Zedekiah** king of Judah, in the tenth month,
39: 2 on the ninth day of the fourth month of **Zedekiah's** [+4200]
39: 4 When **Zedekiah** king of Judah and all the soldiers saw them,
39: 5 pursued them and overtook **Zedekiah** in the plains of Jericho.
39: 6 king of Babylon slaughtered the sons of **Zedekiah** before his eyes
39: 7 he put out **Zedekiah's** eyes and bound him with bronze shackles to
44:30 just as I handed **Zedekiah** king of Judah over to Nebuchadnezzar
51:59 when he went to Babylon with **Zedekiah** king of Judah in the
52: 1 **Zedekiah** was twenty-one years old when he became king,
52: 3 his presence. Now **Zedekiah** rebelled against the king of Babylon.
52: 5 was kept under siege until the eleventh year of King **Zedekiah**.
52: 8 the Babylonian army pursued King **Zedekiah** and overtook him in
52:10 king of Babylon slaughtered the sons of **Zedekiah** before his eyes;
52:11 Then he put out **Zedekiah's** eyes, bound him with bronze shackles

7410 צָהַב ṣāhab, v. [1] [→ 5176, 7411, 7419, 7420; cf. 2298]

polished [1]

Ezr 8:27 [H] and two fine articles of **polished** bronze, as precious as gold.

7411 צָהֹב ṣāhōb, a. [3] [√ 7410]

yellow [3]

Lev 13:30 to be more than skin deep and the hair in it is **yellow** and thin,
13:32 and if the itch has not spread and there is no **yellow** hair in it
13:36 spread in the skin, the priest does not need to look for **yellow** hair;

7412 צָהַל¹ ṣāhal¹, v. [8] [→ 5177]

acclaim [1], cry out [+7754] [1], held a celebration [1], neigh [1], neighing [1], shout aloud [1], shout for joy [1], shout [1]

Est 8:15 [A] of fine linen. And the city of Susa **held a** joyous **celebration**.
Isa 10:30 [D] **Cry** [+7754] **out**, O Daughter of Gallim! Listen, O Laishah!
12: 6 [A] **Shout aloud** and sing for joy, people of Zion, for great is the
24:14 [A] for joy; from the west *they* **acclaim** the LORD's majesty.
54: 1 [A] burst into song, **shout for joy**, *you* who were never in labor;
Jer 5: 8 [A] lusty stallions, each **neighing** for another man's wife.
31: 7 [A] with joy for Jacob; **shout** for the foremost of the nations.
50:11 [A] frolic like a heifer threshing grain and **neigh** like stallions,

7413 צָהַל² ṣāhal², v. [1] [cf. 2301, 7414]

make shine [1]

Ps 104:15 [G] oil to **make** his face **shine**, and bread that sustains his heart.

7414 צָהַר ***ṣāhar***, v.den. [1] [→ 3658, 3659, 3660, 7415, 7416; cf. 2301, 7413]

crush olives [1]

Job 24: 11 [G] *They* **crush olives** among the terraces; they tread the

7415 צֹהַר ***ṣōhar***, n.f. [1] [√ 7414]

roof [1]

Ge 6: 16 Make a **roof** for it and finish the ark to within 18 inches of the top.

7416 צָהֳרַיִם ***ṣohᵒrayim***, n.[m.]. [23] [√ 7414]

noon [11], midday [7], noonday [3], high noon [1], noonday sun [1]

Ge 43: 16 an animal and prepare dinner; they are to eat with me at **noon**."
43: 25 They prepared their gifts for Joseph's arrival at **noon**, because they
Dt 28: 29 At **midday** you will grope about like a blind man in the dark.
2Sa 4: 5 there in the heat of the day while he was taking his **noonday** rest.
1Ki 18: 26 Then they called on the name of Baal from morning till **noon**.
18: 27 At **noon** Elijah began to taunt them. "Shout louder!" he said.
18: 29 **Midday** passed, and they continued their frantic prophesying until
20: 16 They set out at **noon** while Ben-Hadad and the 32 kings allied with
2Ki 4: 20 to his mother, the boy sat on her lap until **noon**, and then he died.
Job 5: 14 upon them in the daytime; at **noon** they grope as in the night.
11: 17 Life will be brighter than **noonday**, and darkness will become like
Ps 37: 6 like the dawn, the justice of your cause like the **noonday sun**.
55: 17 [55:18] Evening, morning and **noon** I cry out in distress, and he
91: 6 that stalks in the darkness, nor the plague that destroys *at* **midday**.
SS 1: 7 you graze your flock and where you rest your sheep at **midday**.
Isa 16: 3 render a decision. Make your shadow like night—at **high noon**.
58: 10 rise in the darkness, and your night will become like the **noonday**.
59: 10 At **midday** we stumble as if it were twilight; among the strong,
Jer 6: 4 Arise, let us attack at **noon**! But, alas, the daylight is fading,
15: 8 At **midday** I will bring a destroyer against the mothers of their
20: 16 May he hear wailing in the morning, a battle cry at **noon**.
Am 8: 9 "I will make the sun go down at **noon** and darken the earth in
Zep 2: 4 in ruins. At **midday** Ashdod will be emptied and Ekron uprooted.

7417 צַו ***ṣaw***, n.[m.]. [1] [√ 8736? *or* 7422?]

idols [1]

Hos 5: 11 is oppressed, trampled in judgment, intent on pursuing **idols**.

7418 צַוָּאר ***ṣawwā'r***, n.m. [41] [→ 7454; Ar 10611]

neck [25], necks [7], threw arms around [+5877+6584] [2], *untranslated* [1], at heels [+6584] [1], defiantly [+928] [1], embraced [+6584] [1], head [1], shoulders [1], yourselves [+4013] [1]

Ge 27: 16 his hands and the smooth part of his **neck** with the goatskins.
27: 40 you grow restless, you will throw his yoke from off your **neck**."
33: 4 embraced him; he threw his arms around his **neck** and kissed him.
41: 42 him in robes of fine linen and put a gold chain around his **neck**.
45: 14 *he* **threw** *his* **arms around** [+5877+6584] his brother Benjamin
45: 14 and wept, and Benjamin **embraced** [+6584] him, weeping.
46: 29 *he* **threw** *his* **arms around** [+5877+6584] his father and wept for a
46: 29 threw his arms around his father and wept **[RPH]** for a long time.
Dt 28: 48 He will put an iron yoke on your **neck** until he has destroyed you.
Jos 10: 24 "Come here and put your feet on the **necks** *of* these kings."
10: 24 So they came forward and placed their feet on their **necks**.
Jdg 5: 30 highly embroidered garments for my **neck**—
8: 21 and killed them, and took the ornaments off their camels' **necks**.
8: 26 the kings of Midian or the chains that were on their camels' **necks**.
Ne 3: 5 their nobles would not put their **shoulders** to the work under their
Job 15: 26 **defiantly** [+928] charging against him with a thick, strong shield.
39: 19 give the horse his strength or clothe his **neck** with a flowing mane?
41: 22 [41:14] Strength resides in his **neck**; dismay goes before him.
Ps 75: 5 [75:6] against heaven; do not speak with outstretched **neck**.' "
SS 1: 10 are beautiful with earrings, your **neck** with strings of jewels.
4: 4 Your **neck** is like the tower of David, built with elegance;
7: 4 [7:5] Your **neck** is like an ivory tower. Your eyes are the pools of
Isa 8: 8 swirling over it, passing through it and reaching up to the **neck**.
10: 27 will be lifted from your shoulders, their yoke from your **neck**;
30: 28 His breath is like a rushing torrent, rising up to the **neck**. He shakes
52: 2 Free yourself from the chains on your **neck**, O captive Daughter of
Jer 27: 2 "Make a yoke out of straps and crossbars and put it on your **neck**.
27: 8 Nebuchadnezzar king of Babylon or bow its **neck** under his yoke,
27: 11 if any nation will bow its **neck** under the yoke of the king of
27: 12 I said, "Bow your **neck** under the yoke of the king of Babylon;
28: 10 the prophet Hananiah took the yoke off the **neck** *of* the prophet
28: 11 Babylon off the **neck** *of* all the nations within two years.' " At this,
28: 12 had broken the yoke off the **neck** *of* the prophet Jeremiah,
28: 14 I will put an iron yoke on the **necks** *of* all these nations to make
30: 8 'I will break the yoke off their **necks** and will tear off their bonds;
La 1: 14 They have come upon my **neck** and the Lord has sapped my
5: 5 Those who pursue us are **at** our **heels** [+6584]; we are weary
Eze 21: 29 [21:34] it will be laid on the **necks** *of* the wicked who are to be
Hos 10: 11 heifer that loves to thresh; so I will put a yoke on her fair **neck**.
Mic 2: 3 this people, from which you cannot save **yourselves** [+4013].
Hab 3: 13 of the land of wickedness, you stripped him from **head** to foot.

7419 צוֹבָא ***ṣôbā'***, n.pr.loc. [2] [cf. 7420]

Zobah [2]

2Sa 10: 6 thousand Aramean foot soldiers from Beth Rehob and **Zobah**,
10: 8 while the Arameans of **Zobah** and Rehob and the men of Tob

7420 צוֹבָה ***ṣôbâ***, n.pr.loc. [10] [→ 809, 2832; cf. 7410, 7419]

Zobah [10]

1Sa 14: 47 Moab, the Ammonites, Edom, the kings of **Zobah**, and the
2Sa 8: 3 Moreover, David fought Hadadezer son of Rehob, king of **Zobah**,
8: 5 Arameans of Damascus came to help Hadadezer king of **Zobah**,
8: 12 the plunder taken from Hadadezer son of Rehob, king of **Zobah**.
23: 36 Igal son of Nathan from **Zobah**, the son of Hagri,
1Ki 11: 23 who had fled from his master, Hadadezer king of **Zobah**.
1Ch 18: 3 Moreover, David fought Hadadezer king of **Zobah**, as far as
18: 5 Arameans of Damascus came to help Hadadezer king of **Zobah**,
18: 9 David had defeated the entire army of Hadadezer king of **Zobah**,
19: 6 and charioteers from Aram Naharaim, Aram Maacah and **Zobah**.

7421 צוּד ***ṣûd***, v. [17] [→ 5171, 5178, 5179, 5180, 5181?, 5182, 5183, 7473, 7475]

ensnare [4], hunt [3], hunted [+7421] [2], hunts [2], hunt down [+4200 +4511] [1], hunt down [1], hunted [1], preys upon [1], stalk [1], stalked [1]

Ge 27: 3 [A] go out to the open country *to* **hunt** some wild game for me.
27: 5 [A] When Esau left for the open country to **hunt** game and bring
27: 33 [A] "Who was it, then, that **hunted** game and brought it to me?
Lev 17: 13 [A] or any alien living among you who **hunts** any animal
Job 10: 16 [A] *you* **stalk** me like a lion and again display your awesome
38: 39 [A] "*Do you* **hunt** the prey for the lioness and satisfy the hunger
Ps 140: 11 [140:12] [A] *may* disaster **hunt** [+4200+4511] **down** men of
Pr 6: 26 [A] a loaf of bread, and the adulteress **preys upon** your very life.
Jer 16: 16 [A] and *they will* **hunt** them **down** on every mountain and hill
La 3: 52 [A] Those who were my enemies without cause **hunted** [+7421]
3: 52 [A] Those who were my enemies without cause **hunted** [+7421]
4: 18 [A] *Men* **stalked** us *at* every step, so we could not walk in our
Eze 13: 18 [D] of various lengths for their heads in order to **ensnare** people.
13: 18 [D] *Will you* **ensnare** the lives of my people but preserve your
13: 20 [D] I am against your magic charms with which you **ensnare**
13: 20 [D] I will set free the people that you **ensnare** like birds.
Mic 7: 2 [A] lie in wait to shed blood; each **hunts** his brother with a net.

7422 צָוָה ***ṣāwâ***, v. [502] [→ 5184, 7417?]

commanded [210], command [45], gave [25], ordered [22], commands [13], giving [13], gave orders [10], give [10], instructed [9], appointed [8], do [8], told [8], gave order [7], directed [6], gave command [5], order [5], tell [5], been commanded [4], give command [4], given [4], orders [4], charged [3], commission [3], decreed [3], gave instructions [3], give orders [3], instructions [3], laid down [3], put in order [3], was commanded [3], given order [2], given orders [2], giving orders [2], ordained [2], send [2], appoint [1], are directed [1], bestows [1], commanded [+5184] [1], commanded [+906+5184] [1], commander [1], commanding [1], commissioned [1], decree [1], decrees [1], determined [1], direct [1], directs [1], dispatch [1], forbidden [+4202] [1], forbidden [+4202+6584] [1], forbidden [+448+1194+6584] [1], forbidden [1], gave a charge [1], gave an order [1], gave commands [1], gave the order [1], give a message [1], give commands [1], give the order [1], given a command [1], given an order [1], given the command [1], giving instructions [1], issue an order [1], left instructions [1], marshaled [1], prescribed [1], put in charge [1], puts in command [1], say [1], sent word [1], sent [1], summon [1], urge [1]

Ge 2: 16 [D] the LORD God **commanded** the man, "You are free to eat
3: 11 [D] Have you eaten from the tree that *I* **commanded** you not to
3: 17 [D] and ate from the tree *about* which *I* **commanded** you,
6: 22 [D] Noah did everything just as God **commanded** him.
7: 5 [D] And Noah did all that the LORD **commanded** him.
7: 9 [D] to Noah and entered the ark, as God *had* **commanded** Noah.
7: 16 [D] female of every living thing, as God *had* **commanded** Noah.
12: 20 [D] Pharaoh **gave orders** about Abram *to* his men, and they sent
18: 19 [D] so that *he will* **direct** his children and his household after
21: 4 [D] Abraham circumcised him, as God **commanded** him.
26: 11 [D] So Abimelech **gave orders** *to* all the people: "Anyone who
27: 8 [D] Now, my son, listen carefully and do what I **tell** you:
28: 1 [D] Isaac called for Jacob and blessed him and **commanded** him:
28: 6 [D] that when he blessed him *he* **commanded** him, "Do not
32: 4 [32:5] [D] *He* **instructed** them: "This is what you are to say to
32: 17 [32:18] [D] *He* **instructed** the one in the lead: "When my

Ge 32:19 [32:20] [D] *He* also **instructed** the second, the third and all the
42:25 [D] Joseph **gave orders** to fill their bags with grain, to put each
44:1 [D] Now Joseph **gave** *these* **instructions** *to* the steward of his
45:19 [E] "You **are** also **directed** to tell them, 'Do this: Take some
47:11 [D] part of the land, the district of Rameses, as Pharaoh **directed**.
49:29 [D] *he* **gave** them *these* **instructions**: "I am about to be gathered
49:33 [D] When Jacob had finished **giving instructions** *to* his sons,
50:2 [D] Joseph **directed** the physicians in his service to embalm his
50:12 [D] So Jacob's sons did as *he had* **commanded** them:
50:16 [D] So *they* **sent word** to Joseph, saying, "Your father left these
50:16 [D] saying, "Your father **left** *these* **instructions** before he died:
Ex 1:22 [D] Pharaoh **gave** *this* **order** to all his people: "Every boy that is
4:28 [D] also about all the miraculous signs *he had* **commanded** him
5:6 [D] same day Pharaoh **gave** *this* **order** *to* the slave drivers and
6:13 [D] and *he* **commanded** them to bring the Israelites out of Egypt.
7:2 [D] You are to say everything *I* **command** you, and your brother
7:6 [D] Moses and Aaron did just as the LORD **commanded** them.
7:10 [D] went to Pharaoh and did just as the LORD **commanded**.
7:20 [D] Moses and Aaron did just as the LORD *had* **commanded**.
12:28 [D] The Israelites did just what the LORD **commanded** Moses
12:50 [D] did just what the LORD *had* **commanded** Moses and
16:16 [D] This is what the LORD *has* **commanded**: 'Each one is to
16:24 [D] as Moses **commanded**, and it did not stink or get maggots in
16:32 [D] Moses said, "This is what the LORD *has* **commanded**:
16:34 [D] As the LORD **commanded** Moses, Aaron put the manna in
18:23 [D] If you do this and God so **commands**, you will be able to
19:7 [D] set before them all the words the LORD *had* **commanded**
23:15 [D] days eat bread made without yeast, as *I* **commanded** you.
25:22 [D] with you and give you all *my* **commands** for the Israelites.
27:20 [D] "**Command** the Israelites to bring you clear oil of pressed
29:35 [D] for Aaron and his sons everything *I have* **commanded** you,
31:6 [D] the craftsmen to make everything *I have* **commanded** you:
31:11 [D] They are to make them just as *I* **commanded** you."
32:8 [D] They have been quick to turn away from what *I* **commanded**
34:4 [D] early in the morning, as the LORD *had* **commanded** him;
34:11 [D] Obey what I **command** you today. I will drive out before you
34:18 [D] days eat bread made without yeast, as *I* **commanded** you.
34:32 [D] *he* **gave** them all *the* **commands** the LORD had given him
34:34 [E] and told the Israelites what *he had* **been commanded**,
35:1 [D] "These are the things the LORD *has* **commanded** you to
35:4 [D] "This is what the LORD *has* **commanded**:
35:10 [D] to come and make everything the LORD *has* **commanded**:
35:29 [D] the LORD through Moses *had* **commanded** them to do.
36:1 [D] are to do the work just as the LORD *has* **commanded**."
36:5 [D] for doing the work the LORD **commanded** to be done."
36:6 [D] Moses **gave an order** and they sent this word throughout the
38:22 [D] of Judah, made everything the LORD **commanded** Moses;
39:1 [D] garments for Aaron, as the LORD **commanded** Moses.
39:5 [D] with finely twisted linen, as the LORD **commanded** Moses.
39:7 [D] for the sons of Israel, as the LORD **commanded** Moses.
39:21 [D] out from the ephod—as the LORD **commanded** Moses.
39:26 [D] be worn for ministering, as the LORD **commanded** Moses.
39:29 [D] of an embroiderer—as the LORD **commanded** Moses.
39:31 [D] to attach it to the turban, as the LORD **commanded** Moses.
39:32 [D] The Israelites did everything just as the LORD **commanded**
39:42 [D] all the work just as the LORD *had* **commanded** Moses.
39:43 [D] that they had done it just as the LORD *had* **commanded**.
40:16 [D] Moses did everything just as the LORD **commanded** him.
40:19 [D] the covering over the tent, as the LORD **commanded** him.
40:21 [D] the ark of the Testimony, as the LORD **commanded** him.
40:23 [D] on it before the LORD, as the LORD **commanded** him.
40:25 [D] lamps before the LORD, as the LORD **commanded** him.
40:27 [D] fragrant incense on it, as the LORD **commanded** him.
40:29 [D] and grain offerings, as the LORD **commanded** him.
40:32 [D] or approached the altar, as the LORD **commanded** Moses.
Lev 6:9 [6:2] [D] "**Give** Aaron and his sons *this* **command**: 'These are
7:36 [D] the LORD **commanded** that the Israelites give this to them
7:38 [D] which the LORD **gave** Moses on Mount Sinai on the day he
7:38 [D] **commanded** the Israelites to bring their offerings to the
8:4 [D] Moses did as the LORD **commanded** him,
8:5 [D] "This is what the LORD *has* **commanded** to be done."
8:9 [D] on the front of it, as the LORD **commanded** Moses.
8:13 [D] put headbands on them, as the LORD **commanded** Moses.
8:17 [D] up outside the camp, as the LORD **commanded** Moses.
8:21 [D] to the LORD by fire, as the LORD **commanded** Moses.
8:29 [D] as a wave offering, as the LORD **commanded** Moses.
8:31 [D] as *I* **commanded**, saying, 'Aaron and his sons are to eat it.'
8:34 [D] What has been done today *was* **commanded** by the LORD
8:35 [E] you will not die; for that is what *I have* **been commanded**."
8:36 [D] his sons did everything the LORD **commanded** through
9:5 [D] They took the things Moses **commanded** to the front of the
9:6 [D] "This is what the LORD *has* **commanded** you to do,
9:7 [D] make atonement for them, as the LORD *has* **commanded**."
9:10 [D] from the sin offering, as the LORD **commanded** Moses;
9:21 [D] the LORD as a wave offering, as Moses **commanded**.
10:1 [D] fire before the LORD, contrary to *his* **command**.
10:13 [E] made to the LORD by fire; for so *I have* **been commanded**.
10:15 [D] for you and your children, as the LORD *has* **commanded**."
10:18 [D] have eaten the goat in the sanctuary area, as *I* **commanded**."
13:54 [D] he *shall* **order** that the contaminated article be washed. Then
14:4 [D] the priest *shall* **order** that two live clean birds and some
14:5 [D] the priest *shall* **order** that one of the birds be killed over
14:36 [D] The priest *is to* **order** the house to be emptied before he goes
14:40 [D] he *is to* **order** that the contaminated stones be torn out and
16:34 [D] And it was done, as the LORD **commanded** Moses.
17:2 [D] and say to them: 'This is what the LORD *has* **commanded**:
24:2 [D] "**Command** the Israelites to bring you clear oil of pressed
24:23 [D] The Israelites did as the LORD **commanded** Moses.
25:21 [D] *I will* **send** you such a blessing in the sixth year that the land
27:34 [D] These are the commands the LORD **gave** Moses on Mount
Nu 1:19 [D] as the LORD **commanded** Moses. And so he counted them
1:54 [D] The Israelites did all this just as the LORD **commanded**
2:33 [D] with the other Israelites, as the LORD **commanded** Moses.
2:34 [D] So the Israelites did everything the LORD **commanded**
3:16 [E] as *he* **was commanded** by the word of the LORD.
3:42 [D] firstborn of the Israelites, as the LORD **commanded** him.
3:51 [D] his sons, as he *was* **commanded** by the word of the LORD.
4:49 [D] Thus they were counted, as the LORD **commanded** Moses.
5:2 [D] "**Command** the Israelites to send away from the camp
8:3 [D] on the lampstand, just as the LORD **commanded** Moses.
8:20 [D] did with the Levites just as the LORD **commanded** Moses.
8:22 [D] They did with the Levites just as the LORD **commanded**
9:5 [D] The Israelites did everything just as the LORD **commanded**
9:8 [D] "Wait until I find out what the LORD **commands**
15:23 [D] any of the LORD's **commands** to you through him,
15:23 [D] from the day the LORD **gave** them and continuing through
15:36 [D] and stoned him to death, as the LORD **commanded** Moses.
17:11 [17:26] [D] Moses did just as the LORD **commanded** him.
19:2 [D] a requirement of the law that the LORD *has* **commanded**:
20:9 [D] from the LORD's presence, just as *he* **commanded** him.
20:27 [D] Moses did as the LORD **commanded**: They went up Mount
26:4 [D] years old or more, as the LORD **commanded** Moses."
27:11 [D] for the Israelites, as the LORD **commanded** Moses.' "
27:19 [D] the entire assembly and **commission** him in their presence.
27:22 [D] Moses did as the LORD **commanded** him. He took Joshua
27:23 [D] he laid his hands on him and **commissioned** him, as the
28:2 [D] "**Give** *this* **command** *to* the Israelites and say to them:
29:40 [30:1] [D] the Israelites all that the LORD **commanded** him.
30:1 [30:2] [D] of Israel: "This is what the LORD **commands**:
30:16 [30:17] [D] These are the regulations the LORD **gave** Moses
31:7 [D] as the LORD **commanded** Moses, and killed every man.
31:21 [D] "This is the requirement of the law that the LORD **gave**
31:31 [D] Eleazar the priest did as the LORD **commanded** Moses.
31:41 [D] as the LORD's part, as the LORD **commanded** Moses.
31:47 [D] fifty persons and animals, as the LORD **commanded** him,
32:25 [D] to Moses, "We your servants will do as our lord **commands**.
32:28 [D] **gave orders** about them *to* Eleazar the priest and Joshua son of
34:2 [D] "**Command** the Israelites and say to them: 'When you enter
34:13 [D] Moses **commanded** the Israelites: "Assign this land by lot as
34:13 [D] The LORD *has* **ordered** that it be given to the nine and a
34:29 [D] These are the men the LORD **commanded** to assign the
35:2 [D] "**Command** the Israelites to give the Levites towns to live in
36:2 [D] "When the LORD **commanded** my lord to give the land as
36:2 [E] he **ordered** you to give the inheritance of our brother
36:5 [D] at the LORD's command Moses **gave** *this* **order** *to* the
36:6 [D] This is what the LORD **commands** for Zelophehad's
36:10 [D] So Zelophehad's daughters did as the LORD **commanded**
36:13 [D] regulations the LORD **gave** through Moses to the Israelites
Dt 1:3 [D] all that the LORD *had* **commanded** him concerning them.
1:16 [D] *I* **charged** your judges at that time: Hear the disputes
1:18 [D] And at that time *I* **told** you everything you were to do.
1:19 [D] Then, as the LORD our God **commanded** us, we set out
1:41 [D] go up and fight, as the LORD our God **commanded** us."
2:4 [D] **Give** the people *these* **orders**: 'You are about to pass through
2:37 [D] in accordance with the **command** *of* the LORD our God,
3:18 [D] *I* **commanded** you at that time: "The LORD your God has
3:21 [D] At that time *I* **commanded** Joshua: "You have seen with
3:28 [D] But **commission** Joshua, and encourage and strengthen him,
4:2 [D] Do not add to what I **command** you and do not subtract from
4:2 [D] keep the commands of the LORD your God that I **give** you.
4:5 [D] and laws as the LORD my God **commanded** me,
4:13 [D] which *he* **commanded** you to follow and then wrote them on
4:14 [D] the LORD **directed** me at that time to teach you the decrees
4:23 [D] in the form of anything the LORD your God *has* **forbidden**.
4:40 [D] his decrees and commands, which I *am* **giving** you today,
5:12 [D] it holy, as the LORD your God *has* **commanded** you.
5:15 [D] Therefore the LORD your God *has* **commanded** you to
5:16 [D] your mother, as the LORD your God *has* **commanded** you,

Dt 5:32 [D] to do what the LORD your God *has* **commanded** you;
5:33 [D] all the way that the LORD your God *has* **commanded** you,
6:1 [D] laws the LORD your God **directed** me to teach you to
6:2 [D] live by keeping all his decrees and commands that I **give** you,
6:6 [D] These commandments that I **give** you today are to be upon
6:17 [D] your God and the stipulations and decrees *he has* **given** you.
6:20 [D] and laws the LORD our God *has* **commanded** you?"
6:24 [D] The LORD **commanded** us to obey all these decrees and to
6:25 [D] as *he has* **commanded** us, that will be our righteousness."
7:11 [D] to follow the commands, decrees and laws I **give** you today.
8:1 [D] Be careful to follow every command I *am* **giving** you today,
8:11 [D] his laws and his decrees that I *am* **giving** you this day.
9:12 [D] They have turned away quickly from what *I* **commanded**
9:16 [D] quickly from the way that the LORD *had* **commanded** you.
10:5 [D] as the LORD **commanded** me, and they are there now.
10:13 [D] and decrees that I *am* **giving** you today for your own good?
11:8 [D] Observe therefore all the commands I *am* **giving** you today,
11:13 [D] So if you faithfully obey the commands I *am* **giving** you
11:22 [D] If you carefully observe all these commands I *am* **giving** you
11:27 [D] of the LORD your God that I *am* **giving** you today;
11:28 [D] turn from the way that I **command** you today by following
12:11 [D] there you are to bring everything I **command** you:
12:14 [D] of your tribes, and there observe everything I **command** you.
12:21 [D] the LORD has given you, as *I have* **commanded** you,
12:28 [D] Be careful to obey all these regulations I *am* **giving** you, so
12:32 [13:1] [D] See that you do all I **command** you; do not add to it
13:5 [13:6] [D] the LORD your God **commanded** you to follow.
13:18 [13:19] [D] keeping all his commands that I *am* **giving** you
15:5 [D] are careful to follow all these commands I *am* **giving** you
15:11 [D] Therefore I **command** you to be openhanded toward your
15:15 [D] redeemed you. That is why I **give** you this command today.
17:3 [D] contrary to *my* **command** has worshiped other gods, bowing
18:18 [D] his mouth, and he will tell them everything *I* **command** him.
18:20 [D] in my name anything *I have* not **commanded** him to say,
19:7 [D] This is why I **command** you to set aside for yourselves three
19:9 [D] because you carefully follow all these laws I **command** you
20:17 [D] as the LORD your God *has* **commanded** you.
24:8 [D] You must follow carefully what *I have* **commanded** them.
24:18 [D] you from there. That is why I **command** you to do this.
24:22 [D] were slaves in Egypt. That is why I **command** you to do this.
26:13 [D] and the widow, according to all you **commanded** [+5184].
26:14 [D] my God; I have done everything *you* **commanded** me.
26:16 [D] The LORD your God **commands** you this day to follow
27:1 [D] Moses and the elders of Israel **commanded** the people:
27:1 [D] the people: "Keep all these commands that I **give** you today.
27:4 [D] as I **command** you today, and coat them with plaster.
27:10 [D] and follow his commands and decrees that I **give** you today."
27:11 [D] On the same day Moses **commanded** the people:
28:1 [D] and carefully follow all his commands I **give** you today,
28:8 [D] The LORD *will* **send** a blessing on your barns and on
28:13 [D] commands of the LORD your God that I **give** you this day
28:14 [D] Do not turn aside from any of the commands I **give** you
28:15 [D] follow all his commands and decrees I *am* **giving** you today,
28:45 [D] and observe the commands and decrees *he* **gave** you.
29:1 [28:69] [D] **commanded** Moses to make with the Israelites in
30:2 [D] with all your soul according to everything I **command** you
30:8 [D] and follow all his commands I *am* **giving** you today.
30:11 [D] Now what I *am* **commanding** you today is not too difficult
30:16 [D] For I **command** you today to love the LORD your God,
31:5 [D] must do to them all that *I have* **commanded** [+906+5184] you.
31:10 [D] Moses **commanded** them: "At the end of every seven years,
31:14 [D] at the Tent of Meeting, where *I will* **commission** him."
31:23 [D] The LORD **gave** *this* **command** *to* Joshua son of Nun: "Be
31:25 [D] he **gave** *this* **command** *to* the Levites who carried the ark of
31:29 [D] and to turn from the way *I have* **commanded** you.
32:46 [D] so that *you may* **command** your children to obey carefully
33:4 [D] the law that Moses **gave** us, the possession of the assembly
34:9 [D] to him and did what the LORD *had* **commanded** Moses.
Jos 1:7 [D] Be careful to obey all the law my servant Moses **gave** you;
1:9 [D] *Have I* not **commanded** you? Be strong and courageous.
1:10 [D] So Joshua **ordered** the officers of the people:
1:11 [D] "Go through the camp and **tell** the people, 'Get your supplies
1:13 [D] command that Moses the servant of the LORD **gave** you:
1:16 [D] "Whatever *you have* **commanded** us we will do,
1:18 [D] whatever *you may* **command** them, will be put to death.
3:3 [D] **giving orders** *to* the people: "When you see the ark of the
3:8 [D] **Tell** the priests who carry the ark of the covenant: 'When you
4:3 [D] **tell** them to take up twelve stones from the middle of the
4:8 [D] So the Israelites did as Joshua **commanded** them. They took
4:10 [D] LORD *had* **commanded** Joshua was done by the people,
4:10 [D] was done by the people, just as Moses *had* **directed** Joshua.
4:16 [D] "**Command** the priests carrying the ark of the Testimony to
4:17 [D] So Joshua **commanded** the priests, "Come up out of the
6:10 [D] Joshua *had* **commanded** the people, "Do not give a war cry,
7:11 [D] violated my covenant, which *I* **commanded** them to keep.
8:4 [D] with these **orders**: "Listen carefully. You are to set an
8:8 [D] LORD has commanded. See to it; you *have my* **orders**."
8:27 [D] plunder of this city, as the LORD *had* **instructed** Joshua.
8:29 [D] Joshua **ordered** them to take his body from the tree
8:31 [D] as Moses the servant of the LORD *had* **commanded** the
8:33 [D] *had* formerly **commanded** when he gave instructions to
8:35 [D] There was not a word of all that Moses *had* **commanded** that
9:24 [D] *had* **commanded** his servant Moses to give you the whole
10:27 [D] At sunset Joshua **gave** *the* **order** and they took them down
10:40 [D] just as the LORD, the God of Israel, *had* **commanded**.
11:12 [D] as Moses the servant of the LORD *had* **commanded**.
11:15 [D] As the LORD **commanded** his servant Moses, so Moses
11:15 [D] so Moses **commanded** Joshua, and Joshua did it;
11:15 [D] he left nothing undone of all that the LORD **commanded**
11:20 [D] without mercy, as the LORD *had* **commanded** Moses.
13:6 [D] land to Israel for an inheritance, as *I have* **instructed** you,
14:2 [D] as the LORD *had* **commanded** through Moses.
14:5 [D] the land, just as the LORD *had* **commanded** Moses.
17:4 [D] "The LORD **commanded** Moses to give us an inheritance
18:8 [D] Joshua **instructed** them, "Go and make a survey of the land
21:2 [D] "The LORD **commanded** through Moses that you give us
21:8 [D] as the LORD *had* **commanded** through Moses.
22:2 [D] done all that Moses the servant of the LORD **commanded**,
22:2 [D] and you have obeyed me in everything *I* **commanded**.
22:5 [D] and the law that Moses the servant of the LORD **gave** you:
23:16 [D] which *he* **commanded** you, and go and serve other gods
Jdg 2:20 [D] violated the covenant that *I* **laid down** *for* their forefathers
3:4 [D] which *he had* **given** their forefathers through Moses.
4:6 [D] to him, "The LORD, the God of Israel, **commands** you:
13:14 [D] She must do everything *I have* **commanded** her."
21:10 [D] fighting men with **instructions** to go to Jabesh Gilead
21:20 [D] So *they* **instructed** the Benjamites, saying, "Go and hide in
Ru 2:9 [D] *I have* **told** the men not to touch you. And whenever you are
2:15 [D] As she got up to glean, Boaz **gave orders** *to* his men, "Even
3:6 [D] and did everything her mother-in-law **told** her to do.
1Sa 2:29 [D] my sacrifice and offering that *I* **prescribed** for my dwelling?
13:13 [D] "You have not kept the command the LORD your God **gave**
13:14 [D] after his own heart and **appointed** him leader of his people,
13:14 [D] because you have not kept the LORD's **command**."
17:20 [D] a shepherd, loaded up and set out, as Jesse *had* **directed**.
18:22 [D] Then Saul **ordered** his attendants: "Speak to David privately
20:29 [D] in the town and my brother *has* **ordered** me to be there.
21:2 [21:3] [D] "The king **charged** me *with* a certain matter and said
21:2 [21:3] [D] anything about your mission and your **instructions**.'
25:30 [D] concerning him and *has* **appointed** him leader over Israel,
2Sa 4:12 [D] So David **gave** *an* **order** *to* his men, and they killed them.
5:25 [D] So David did as the LORD **commanded** him, and he struck
6:21 [D] or anyone from his house when he **appointed** me ruler over
7:7 [D] rulers whom *I* **commanded** to shepherd my people Israel,
7:11 [D] have done ever since the time *I* **appointed** leaders over my
9:11 [D] "Your servant will do whatever my lord the king **commands**
11:19 [D] *He* **instructed** the messenger: "When you have finished
13:28 [D] Absalom **ordered** his men, "Listen! When Amnon is in high
13:28 [D] *Have* not I **given** you *this* **order**? Be strong and brave."
13:29 [D] Absalom's men did to Amnon what Absalom *had* **ordered**.
14:8 [D] "Go home, and I *will* **issue an order** in your behalf."
14:19 [D] it was your servant Joab *who* **instructed** me to do this
17:14 [D] For the LORD *had* **determined** to frustrate the good advice
17:23 [D] *He* **put** his house **in order** and then hanged himself. So he
18:5 [D] The king **commanded** Joab, Abishai and Ittai, "Be gentle
18:5 [D] **giving orders** concerning Absalom *to* each of the
18:12 [D] In our hearing the king **commanded** you and Abishai and
21:14 [D] Zela in Benjamin, and did everything the king **commanded**.
24:19 [D] went up, as the LORD *had* **commanded** through Gad.
1Ki 1:35 [D] *I have* **appointed** him ruler over Israel and Judah."
2:1 [D] near for David to die, *he* **gave a charge** *to* Solomon his son.
2:43 [D] oath to the LORD and obey the command *I* **gave** you?"
2:46 [D] Then the king **gave the order** *to* Benaiah son of Jehoiada,
5:6 [5:20] [D] "So **give orders** that cedars of Lebanon be cut for
5:17 [5:31] [D] *At* the king's **command** they removed from the
8:58 [D] the commands, decrees and regulations *he* **gave** our fathers.
9:4 [D] and do all *I* **command** and observe my decrees and laws,
11:10 [D] Although *he had* **forbidden** [+448+1194+6584] Solomon to
11:10 [D] other gods, Solomon did not keep the LORD's **command**.
11:11 [D] kept my covenant and my decrees, which *I* **commanded** you,
11:38 [D] If you do whatever *I* **command** you and walk in my ways
13:9 [D] For I *was* **commanded** by the word of the LORD: 'You
13:21 [D] have not kept the command the LORD your God **gave** you.
15:5 [D] had not failed to keep any of the LORD's **commands** all the
17:4 [D] the brook, and *I have* **ordered** the ravens to feed you there."
17:9 [D] *I have* **commanded** a widow in that place to supply you with
22:31 [D] Now the king of Aram *had* **ordered** his thirty-two chariot
2Ki 11:5 [D] *He* **commanded** them, saying, "This is what you are to do:

2Ki 11: 9 [D] of units of a hundred did just as Jehoiada the priest **ordered**.
11: 15 [D] Jehoiada the priest **ordered** the commanders of units of a
14: 6 [D] Book of the Law of Moses where the LORD **commanded**:
16: 16 [D] And Uriah the priest did just as King Ahaz *had* **ordered**.
16: 25 [D] King Ahaz then **gave** these **orders** to Uriah the priest:
17: 13 [D] in accordance with the entire Law that *I* **commanded** your
17: 15 [D] around them although the LORD *had* **ordered** them,
17: 27 [D] the king of Assyria **gave** *this* **order**: "Have one of the priests
17: 34 [D] commands that the LORD **gave** the descendants of Jacob,
17: 35 [D] made a covenant with the Israelites, *he* **commanded** them:
18: 6 [D] he kept the commands the LORD *had* **given** Moses.
18: 12 [D] all that Moses the servant of the LORD **commanded**.
20: 1 [D] **Put** your house **in order**, because you are going to die; you
21: 8 [D] if only they will be careful to do everything *I* **commanded**
21: 8 [D] will keep the whole Law that my servant Moses **gave** them."
22: 12 [D] **gave** *these* **orders** *to* Hilkiah the priest, Ahikam son of
23: 4 [D] **ordered** Hilkiah the high priest, the priests next in rank and
23: 21 [D] The king **gave** *this* **order** *to* all the people: "Celebrate the
1Ch 6: 49 [6:34] [D] all that Moses the servant of God *had* **commanded**.
14: 16 [D] So David did as God **commanded** him, and they struck down
15: 15 [D] as Moses *had* **commanded** in accordance with the word of
16: 15 [D] the word *he* **commanded**, for a thousand generations,
16: 40 [D] written in the Law of the LORD, which *he had* **given** Israel.
17: 6 [D] did I ever say to any of their leaders whom *I* **commanded** to
17: 10 [D] have done ever since the time *I* **appointed** leaders over my
22: 6 [D] and **charged** him to build a house for the LORD,
22: 12 [D] understanding when *he* **puts** you **in command** over Israel,
22: 13 [D] the decrees and laws that the LORD **gave** Moses for Israel.
22: 17 [D] David **ordered** all the leaders of Israel to help his son
24: 19 [D] as the LORD, the God of Israel, *had* **commanded** him.
2Ch 7: 13 [D] or **command** locusts to devour the land or send a plague
7: 17 [D] and do all *I* **command**, and observe my decrees and laws,
18: 30 [D] Now the king of Aram *had* **ordered** his chariot commanders,
19: 9 [D] *He* **gave** them *these* **orders**: "You must serve faithfully and
23: 8 [D] all the men of Judah did just as Jehoiada the priest **ordered**.
25: 4 [D] in the Book of Moses, where the LORD **commanded**:
33: 8 [D] if only they will be careful to do everything *I* **commanded**
34: 20 [D] He **gave** *these* **orders** *to* Hilkiah, Ahikam son of Shaphan,
Ezr 4: 3 [D] of Israel, as King Cyrus, the king of Persia, **commanded** us."
8: 17 [D] *I* **sent** [K 3655] them to Iddo, the leader in Casiphia. I told
9: 11 [D] *you* **gave** through your servants the prophets when you said:
Ne 1: 7 [D] decrees and laws *you* **gave** your servant Moses.
1: 8 [D] "Remember the instruction *you* **gave** your servant Moses,
5: 14 [D] when I *was* **appointed** to be their governor in the land of
7: 2 [D] *I* **put in charge** of Jerusalem my brother Hanani, along with
8: 1 [D] of Moses, which the LORD *had* **commanded** *for* Israel.
8: 14 [D] which the LORD *had* **commanded** through Moses,
9: 14 [D] known to them your holy Sabbath and **gave** them commands,
Est 2: 10 [D] because Mordecai *had* **forbidden** [+4202+6584] her to do so.
2: 20 [D] and nationality just as Mordecai *had* **told** her to do,
3: 2 [D] for the king *had* **commanded** this concerning him.
3: 12 [D] in the language of each people all Haman's **orders** to the
4: 5 [D] and **ordered** him to find out what was troubling Mordecai
4: 8 [D] he told him to **urge** her to go into the king's presence to beg
4: 10 [D] Then she instructed him *to* **say** to Mordecai,
4: 17 [D] went away and carried out all of Esther's **instructions**.
8: 9 [D] They wrote out all Mordecai's **orders** to the Jews, and to the
Job 36: 32 [D] his hands with lightning and **commands** it to strike its mark.
37: 12 [D] face of the whole earth to do whatever *he* **commands** them.
38: 12 [D] "*Have you* ever **given orders** *to* the morning, or shown the
Ps 7: 6 [7:7] [D] rage of my enemies. Awake, my God; **decree** justice.
33: 9 [D] and it came to be; he **commanded**, and it stood firm.
42: 8 [42:9] [D] By day the LORD **directs** his love, at night his song
44: 4 [44:5] [D] and my God, *who* **decrees** victories for Jacob.
68: 28 [68:29] [D] **Summon** your power, O God; show us your
71: 3 [D] **give** *the* **command** to save me, for you are my rock and my
78: 5 [D] which *he* **commanded** our forefathers to teach their children,
78: 23 [D] Yet *he* **gave** *a* **command** *to* the skies above and opened the
91: 11 [D] For *he will* **command** his angels concerning you to guard
105: 8 [D] the word *he* **commanded**, for a thousand generations,
111: 9 [D] *he* **ordained** his covenant forever—holy and awesome is his
119: 4 [D] You *have* **laid down** precepts that are to be fully obeyed.
119: 138 [D] The statutes *you have* **laid down** are righteous; they are fully
133: 3 [D] For there the LORD **bestows** his blessing, even life
148: 5 [D] of the LORD, for he **commanded** and they were created.
Isa 5: 6 [D] grow there. *I will* **command** the clouds not to rain on it."
10: 6 [D] *I* **dispatch** him against a people who anger me, to seize loot
13: 3 [D] I *have* **commanded** my holy ones; I have summoned my
23: 11 [D] *He has* **given an order** concerning Phoenicia that her
28: 10 [D] **Do** and do, do and do, rule on rule, rule on rule; a little here,
28: 10 [D] Do and **do**, do and do, rule on rule, rule on rule; a little here,
28: 10 [D] Do and do, **do** and do, rule on rule, rule on rule; a little here,
28: 10 [D] Do and do, do and **do**, rule on rule, rule on rule; a little here,
28: 13 [D] **Do** and do, do and do, rule on rule, rule on rule; a little here,
28: 13 [D] Do and **do**, do and do, rule on rule, rule on rule; a little here,
28: 13 [D] Do and do, **do** and do, rule on rule, rule on rule; a little here,
28: 13 [D] Do and do, do and **do**, rule on rule, rule on rule; a little here,
34: 16 [D] For it is his mouth that *has* **given** *the* **order**, and his Spirit
38: 1 [D] **Put** your house **in order**, because you are going to die; you
45: 11 [D] my children, or **give** me **orders** about the work of my hands?
45: 12 [D] stretched out the heavens; *I* **marshaled** their starry hosts.
48: 5 [D] did them; my wooden image and metal god **ordained** them.'
55: 4 [D] to the peoples, a leader and **commander** *of* the peoples.
Jer 1: 7 [D] to everyone I send you to and say whatever *I* **command** you.
1: 17 [D] Stand up and say to them whatever I **command** you.
7: 22 [D] *I did* not *just* **give** them **commands** about burnt offerings
7: 23 [D] *I* **gave** them this **command**: Obey me, and I will be your
7: 23 [D] Walk in all the ways *I* **command** you, that it may go well
7: 31 [D] something *I did* not **command**, nor did it enter my mind.
11: 4 [D] the terms *I* **commanded** your forefathers when I brought
11: 4 [D] I said, 'Obey me and do everything *I* **command** you, and you
11: 8 [D] the curses of the covenant *I had* **commanded** them to follow
13: 5 [D] So I went and hid it at Perath, as the LORD **told** me.
13: 6 [D] "Go now to Perath and get the belt *I* **told** you to hide there."
14: 14 [D] I have not sent them or **appointed** them or spoken to them.
17: 22 [D] the Sabbath day holy, as *I* **commanded** your forefathers.
19: 5 [D] something *I did* not **command** or mention, nor did it enter
23: 32 [D] with their reckless lies, yet I did not send or **appoint** them.
26: 2 [D] Tell them everything *I* **command** you; do not omit a word.
26: 8 [D] people everything the LORD *had* **commanded** him to say,
27: 4 [D] **Give** them **a message** for their masters and say, 'This is what
29: 23 [D] in my name have spoken lies, which *I did* not **tell** them to do.
32: 13 [D] "In their presence *I* **gave** Baruch *these* **instructions**:
32: 23 [D] your law; they did not do what *you* **commanded** them to do.
32: 35 [D] though *I* never **commanded**, nor did it enter my mind,
34: 22 [D] I *am going to* **give the order**, declares the LORD, and I
35: 6 [D] our forefather Jonadab son of Recab **gave** us *this* **command**:
35: 8 [D] our forefather Jonadab son of Recab **commanded** us.
35: 10 [D] obeyed everything our forefather Jonadab **commanded** us.
35: 14 [D] 'Jonadab son of Recab **ordered** his sons not to drink wine
35: 16 [D] have carried out the command their forefather **gave** them,
35: 18 [D] all his instructions and have done everything *he* **ordered**.'
36: 5 [D] Jeremiah **told** Baruch, "I am restricted; I cannot go to the
36: 8 [D] Neriah did everything Jeremiah the prophet **told** him to do;
36: 26 [D] **commanded** Jerahmeel, a son of the king, Seraiah son of
37: 21 [D] **gave orders** *for* Jeremiah to be placed in the courtyard of the
38: 10 [D] the king **commanded** Ebed-Melech the Cushite, "Take thirty
38: 27 [D] he told them everything the king *had* **ordered** him to say.
39: 11 [D] *had* **given** *these* **orders** about Jeremiah through
47: 7 [D] But how can it rest when the LORD *has* **commanded** it,
50: 21 [D] the LORD. "Do everything *I have* **commanded** you.
51: 59 [D] This is the message Jeremiah **gave** *to* the staff officer Seraiah
La 1: 10 [D] those *you had* **forbidden** [+4202] to enter your assembly.
1: 17 [D] The LORD *has* **decreed** for Jacob that his neighbors
2: 17 [D] he has fulfilled his word, which *he* **decreed** long ago.
3: 37 [D] can speak and have it happen if the Lord *has* not **decreed** it?
Eze 9: 11 [D] back word, saying, "I have done as *you* **commanded**."
10: 6 [D] When the LORD **commanded** the man in linen, "Take fire
12: 7 [E] So I did as *I* **was commanded**. During the day I brought out
24: 18 [E] The next morning I did as *I had* **been commanded**.
37: 7 [E] So I prophesied as *I* **was commanded**. And as I was
37: 10 [D] So I prophesied as *he* **commanded** me, and breath entered
Am 2: 12 [D] drink wine and **commanded** the prophets not to prophesy.
6: 11 [D] For the LORD *has* **given the command**, and he will smash
9: 3 [D] of the sea, there *I will* **command** the serpent to bite them.
9: 4 [D] their enemies, there *I will* **command** the sword to slay them.
9: 9 [D] "For I *will* **give** *the* **command**, and I will shake the house of
Na 1: 14 [D] The LORD *has* **given a command** concerning you,
Zec 1: 6 [D] my decrees, which *I* **commanded** my servants the prophets,
Mal 4: 4 [3:22] [D] and laws *I* **gave** him at Horeb for all Israel.

7423 צָוַח *ṣāwaḥ*, v. [1] [→ 7424]

shout [1]

Isa 42: 11 [A] of Sela sing for joy; *let them* **shout** from the mountaintops.

7424 צְוָחָה *ṣᵉwāḥâ*, n.f. [4] [√ 7423]

cries [1], cry of distress [1], cry out [1], cry [1]

Ps 144: 14 of walls, no going into captivity, no **cry of distress** in our streets.
Isa 24: 11 In the streets they **cry out** for wine; all joy turns to gloom,
Jer 14: 2 they wail for the land, and a **cry** goes up *from* Jerusalem.
46: 12 The nations will hear of your shame; your **cries** will fill the earth.

7425 צוּלָה *ṣûlâ*, n.f. [1] [→ 5185, 5198; cf. 7510]

watery deep [1]

Isa 44: 27 who says to the **watery deep**, 'Be dry, and I will dry up your

7426 צוּם ṣûm, v. [21] [→ 7427]
fasted [12], fast [5], fasted [+7426] [2], fasted [+7427] [1], fasting [1]

Jdg 20:26 [A] *They* **fasted** that day until evening and presented burnt
1Sa 7: 6 [A] On that day *they* **fasted** and there they confessed, "We have
31:13 [A] under a tamarisk tree at Jabesh, and *they* **fasted** seven days.
2Sa 1:12 [A] They mourned and wept and **fasted** till evening for Saul
12:16 [A] He **fasted** [+7427] and went into his house and spent the
12:21 [A] While the child was alive, *you* **fasted** and wept, but now that
12:22 [A] "While the child was still alive, *I* **fasted** and wept.
12:23 [A] now that he is dead, why *should* I **fast**? Can I bring him back
1Ki 21:27 [A] these words, he tore his clothes, put on sackcloth and **fasted**.
1Ch 10:12 [A] under the great tree in Jabesh, and *they* **fasted** seven days.
Ezr 8:23 [A] So *we* **fasted** and petitioned our God about this, and he
Ne 1: 4 [A] For some days I mourned and **fasted** and prayed before the
Est 4:16 [A] gather together all the Jews who are in Susa, and **fast** for me.
4:16 [A] three days, night or day. I and my maids *will* **fast** as you do.
Isa 58: 3 [A] 'Why *have we* **fasted**,' they say, 'and you have not seen it?
58: 4 [A] *Your* **fasting** ends in quarreling and strife, and in striking
58: 4 [A] *You* cannot **fast** as you do today and expect your voice to be
Jer 14:12 [A] Although *they* **fast**, I will not listen to their cry; though they
Zec 7: 5 [A] 'When *you* **fasted** and mourned in the fifth and seventh
7: 5 [A] seventy years, was it really *for* me that *you* **fasted** [+7426]?
7: 5 [A] seventy years, was it really *for* me that *you* **fasted** [+7426]?

7427 צוֹם ṣôm, n.m. [26] [√ 7426]
fasting [10], fast [9], *untranslated* [3], day of fasting [1], fasted [+7426] [1], fasts [1], time of fasting [1]

2Sa 12:16 He **fasted** [+7426] and went into his house and spent the nights
1Ki 21: 9 "Proclaim a **day of fasting** and seat Naboth in a prominent place
21:12 They proclaimed a **fast** and seated Naboth in a prominent place
2Ch 20: 3 to inquire of the LORD, and he proclaimed a **fast** for all Judah.
Ezr 8:21 There, by the Ahava Canal, I proclaimed a **fast**, so that we might
Ne 9: 1 **fasting** and wearing sackcloth and having dust on their heads.
Est 4: 3 mourning among the Jews, with **fasting**, weeping and wailing.
9:31 their descendants in regard to their times of **fasting**
Ps 35:13 they were ill, I put on sackcloth and humbled myself with **fasting**.
69:10 [69:11] When I weep and **fast**, I must endure scorn;
109:24 My knees give way from **fasting**; my body is thin and gaunt.
Isa 58: 3 "Yet on the day of your **fasting**, you do as you please and exploit
58: 5 Is this the kind of **fast** I have chosen, only a day for a man to
58: 5 Is that what you call a **fast**, a day acceptable to the LORD?
58: 6 "Is not this the kind of **fasting** I have chosen: to loose the chains of
Jer 36: 6 So you go to the house of the LORD on a day of **fasting**
36: 9 a **time of fasting** before the LORD was proclaimed for all the
Da 9: 3 Lord God and pleaded with him in prayer and petition, in **fasting**,
Joel 1:14 Declare a holy **fast**; call a sacred assembly. Summon the elders
2:12 me with all your heart, with **fasting** and weeping and mourning."
2:15 the trumpet in Zion, declare a holy **fast**, call a sacred assembly.
Jnh 3: 5 They declared a **fast**, and all of them, from the greatest to the least,
Zec 8:19 "The **fasts** *of* the fourth, fifth, seventh and tenth months will
8:19 **[RPH]** fifth, seventh and tenth months will become joyful
8:19 **[RPH]** seventh and tenth months will become joyful and glad
8:19 seventh and **[RPH]** tenth months will become joyful and glad

7428 צוּעָר ṣûʿār, n.pr.m. [5] [√ 7592]
Zuar [5]

Nu 1: 8 from Issachar, Nethanel son of **Zuar**;
2: 5 The leader of the people of Issachar is Nethanel son of **Zuar**.
7:18 On the second day Nethanel son of **Zuar**, the leader of Issachar,
7:23 This was the offering of Nethanel son of **Zuar**.
10:15 Nethanel son of **Zuar** was over the division of the tribe of Issachar,

7429 [1]צוּף ṣûp[1], v. [3] [→ 7430, 7431?, 7433, 7487, 7597?]
closed [1], made float [1], overwhelmed [1]

Dt 11: 4 [G] how *he* **overwhelmed** them *with* the waters of the Red Sea
2Ki 6: 6 [G] Elisha cut a stick and threw it there, and **made** the iron **float**.
La 3:54 [A] the waters **closed** over my head, and I thought I was about to

7430 [2]צוּף ṣûp[2], n.m. [2] [√ 7429]
comb [1], honeycomb [+1831] [1]

Ps 19:10 [19:11] they are sweeter than honey, than honey from the **comb**.
Pr 16:24 Pleasant words are a **honeycomb** [+1831], sweet to the soul

7431 [3]צוּף ṣûp[3], n.pr.m.[loc.?]. [3] [√ 7429?]
Zuph [3]

1Sa 1: 1 the son of Elihu, the son of Tohu, the son of **Zuph**, an Ephraimite.
9: 5 When they reached the district of **Zuph**, Saul said to the servant
1Ch 6:35 [6:20] the son of **Zuph**, [K 7487] the son of Elkanah, the son of

7432 צוֹפַח ṣôpaḥ, n.pr.m. [2] [√ 7613]
Zophah [2]

1Ch 7:35 The sons of his brother Helem: **Zophah**, Imna, Shelesh and Amal.
7:36 The sons of **Zophah**: Suah, Harnepher, Shual, Beri, Imrah,

7433 צוֹפַי ṣôpay, n.pr.m. [1] [√ 7429; cf. 7434]
Zophai [1]

1Ch 6:26 [6:11] Elkanah his son, **Zophai** his son, Nahath his son,

7434 צוּפִי ṣûpî, a.g. [0 / 1] [cf. 7433]
Zuphite [1]

1Sa 1: 1 a **Zuphite** [BHS 7435] from the hill country of Ephraim,

7435 צוֹפִים ṣôpîm, a.g. [1 / 0] [cf. 7434, 7614]

1Sa 1: 1 Ramathaim, a Zuphite [BHS *from Ramathaim* ***Zuphim***; NIV 7434]

7436 צוֹפַר ṣôpar, n.pr.m. [4] [√ 7606?]
Zophar [4]

Job 2:11 the Temanite, Bildad the Shuhite and **Zophar** the Naamathite,
11: 1 Then **Zophar** the Naamathite replied:
20: 1 Then **Zophar** the Naamathite replied:
42: 9 and **Zophar** the Naamathite did what the LORD told them;

7437 [1]צוּץ ṣûṣ[1], v. [8] [→ 7488, 7490, 7491, 7492]
flourish [2], blossomed [+7488] [1], bud [1], budded [1], flourishes [1], resplendent [1], springs up [1]

Nu 17: 8 [17:23] [G] **blossomed** [+7488] and produced almonds.
Ps 72:16 [G] *Let* its fruit **flourish** like Lebanon; let it thrive like the grass
90: 6 [G] though in the morning *it* **springs up** new, by evening it is dry
92: 7 [92:8] [G] spring up like grass and all evildoers **flourish**,
103:15 [G] days are like grass, *he* **flourishes** like a flower of the field;
132:18 [G] with shame, but the crown on his head *will be* **resplendent**."
Isa 27: 6 [G] Israel *will* **bud** and blossom and fill all the world with fruit.
Eze 7:10 [A] Doom has burst forth, the rod *has* **budded**, arrogance has

7438 [2]צוּץ ṣûṣ[2], v. [1]
peering [1]

SS 2: 9 [G] gazing through the windows, **peering** through the lattice.

7439 [1]צוּק ṣûq[1], v. [11] [→ 4608, 5186, 5188, 7441, 7442; cf. 7636]
inflict [3], besiege [2], oppressor [2], compels [1], imposed [1], nagging [1], press [1]

Dt 28:53 [G] Because of the suffering that your enemy *will* **inflict** on you
28:55 [G] Because of the suffering your enemy *will* **inflict** on you
28:57 [G] in the distress that your enemy *will* **inflict** on you in your
Jdg 14:17 [G] day he finally told her, because *she continued to* **press** him.
16:16 [G] With such **nagging** she prodded him day after day until he
Job 32:18 [G] For I am full of words, and the spirit within me **compels** me;
Isa 29: 2 [G] Yet *I will* **besiege** Ariel; she will mourn and lament, she will
29: 7 [G] that attack her and her fortress and **besiege** her, will be as it
51:13 [G] terror every day because of the wrath of the **oppressor**,
51:13 [G] on destruction? For where is the wrath of the **oppressor**?
Jer 19: 9 [G] siege **imposed** on them *by* the enemies who seek their lives.'

7440 [2]צוּק ṣûq[2], v. [1] [√ 3668?]
barely whisper a prayer [+4318] [1]

Isa 26:16 [A] *they could* **barely whisper a prayer** [+4318].

7441 צוֹק ṣôq, n.[m.]. [1] [√ 7439]
trouble [1]

Da 9:25 It will be rebuilt with streets and a trench, but in times of **trouble**.

7442 צוּקָה ṣûqâ, n.f. [3] [√ 7439]
distress [1], fearful [1], trouble [1]

Pr 1:27 you like a whirlwind, when distress and **trouble** overwhelm you.
Isa 8:22 the earth and see only distress and darkness and **fearful** gloom,
30: 6 Through a land of hardship and **distress**, of lions and lionesses,

7443 [1]צוּר ṣûr[1], v. [34 / 35] [→ 5189, 5190, 5192, 5193; cf. 7493, 7674]
besieging [7], besieged [6], laid siege [5], besiege [3], lay siege [3], besieges [1], encircle [+6584] [1], enclose [1], hem in [1], put into

bags [1], siege [1], stirring up [1], take [1], tied up [1], tuck away [1], under siege [1]

Dt 14:25 [A] **take** the silver with you and go to the place the LORD your
20:12 [A] and they engage you in battle, **lay siege** to that city.
20:19 [A] When *you* **lay siege** to a city for a long time, fighting against
Jdg 9:31 [A] come to Shechem and *are* **stirring up** the city against you.
1Sa 23:8 [A] to go down to Keilah to **besiege** David and his men.
2Sa 11:1 [A] They destroyed the Ammonites and **besieged** Rabbah.
20:15 [A] with Joab came and **besieged** Sheba in Abel Beth Maacah.
1Ki 8:37 [A] or when an enemy **besieges** them in any of their cities,
15:27 [A] Philistine town, while Nadab and all Israel *were* **besieging** it.
16:17 [A] with him withdrew from Gibbethon and **laid siege** to Tirzah.
20:1 [A] he went up and **besieged** Samaria and attacked it.
2Ki 5:23 [A] then **tied up** the two talents of silver in two bags, with two
6:24 [A] his entire army and marched up and **laid siege** to Samaria.
6:25 [A] *the* **siege** lasted so long that a donkey's head sold for eighty
12:10 [12:11] [A] into the temple of the LORD and **put** it **into bags**.
16:5 [A] marched up to fight against Jerusalem and **besieged** Ahaz,
17:5 [A] marched against Samaria and **laid siege** to it for three years.
18:9 [A] king of Assyria marched against Samaria and **laid siege** to it.
24:11 [A] came up to the city while his officers *were* **besieging** it.
1Ch 20:1 [A] land of the Ammonites and went to Rabbah and **besieged** it,
2Ch 6:28 [A] or when enemies **besiege** them in any of their cities,
Ps 139:5 [A] *You* **hem** me **in**—behind and before; you have laid your
SS 8:9 [A] If she is a door, *we will* **enclose** her *with* panels of cedar.
Isa 1:8 [C] like a hut in a field of melons, like a city **under siege**.
21:2 [A] the looter takes loot. Elam, attack! Media, **lay siege**!
29:3 [A] *I will* **encircle** [+6584] you *with* towers and set up my siege
Jer 4:16 [a] 'A **besieging** [BHS 5915] *army* is coming from a distant
21:4 [A] and the Babylonians who *are* outside the wall **besieging** you.
21:9 [A] surrenders to the Babylonians who *are* **besieging** you will
32:2 [A] The army of the king of Babylon *was* then **besieging**
37:5 [A] when the Babylonians who *were* **besieging** Jerusalem heard
39:1 [A] against Jerusalem with his whole army and **laid siege** to it.
Eze 4:3 [A] toward it. It will be under siege, and *you shall* **besiege** it.
5:3 [A] of hair and **tuck** them **away** in the folds of your garment.
Da 1:1 [A] king of Babylon came to Jerusalem and **besieged** it.

7444 צוּר[2] **ṣûr[2]**, v. [4] [√ 7496?]

harass [2], attack [1], oppose [1]

Ex 23:22 [A] to your enemies and *will* **oppose** those who oppose you.
Dt 2:9 [A] to me, "*Do* not **harass** the Moabites or provoke them to war,
2:19 [A] the Ammonites, *do* not **harass** them or provoke them to war,
Est 8:11 [A] or province that *might* **attack** them and their women

7445 צוּר[3] **ṣûr[3]**, v. [2] [→ 7451, 7497?]

cast [1], fashioning [1]

Ex 32:4 [A] an idol cast in the shape of a calf, **fashioning** it with a tool.
1Ki 7:15 [A] *He* **cast** two bronze pillars, each eighteen cubits high

7446 צוּר[4] **ṣûr[4]**, n.m. [74] [→ 506, 1123, 7011, 7448, 7449?, 7452, 7453; Ar 10296]

rock [60], rocks [8], rocky [3], crag [1], crags [1], strength [1]

Ex 17:6 I will stand there before you by the **rock** at Horeb. Strike the rock,
17:6 Strike the **rock**, and water will come out of it for the people to
33:21 "There is a place near me where you may stand on a **rock**.
33:22 I will put you in a cleft in the **rock** and cover you with my hand
Nu 23:9 From the **rocky** peaks I see them, from the heights I view them.
Dt 8:15 and scorpions. He brought you water out of hard **rock**.
32:4 He is the **Rock**, his works are perfect, and all his ways are just.
32:13 him with honey from the rock, and with oil from the flinty **crag**,
32:15 the God who made him and rejected the **Rock** his Savior.
32:18 You deserted the **Rock**, who fathered you; you forgot the God who
32:30 or two put ten thousand to flight, unless their **Rock** had sold them,
32:31 For their **rock** is not like our Rock, as even our enemies concede.
32:31 For their rock is not like our **Rock**, as even our enemies concede.
32:37 will say: "Now where are their gods, the **rock** they took refuge in,
Jdg 6:21 Fire flared from the **rock**, consuming the meat and the bread.
7:25 They killed Oreb at the **rock** *of* Oreb, and Zeeb at the winepress of
13:19 with the grain offering, and sacrificed it on a **rock** to the LORD.
1Sa 2:2 there is no one besides you; there is no **Rock** like our God.
24:2 [24:3] for David and his men near the **Crags** *of* the Wild Goats.
2Sa 21:10 of Aiah took sackcloth and spread it out for herself on a **rock**.
22:3 my God is my **rock**, in whom I take refuge, my shield and the horn
22:32 is God besides the LORD? And who is the **Rock** except our God?
22:47 Praise be to my **Rock**! Exalted be God, the Rock, my Savior!
22:47 Praise be to my Rock! Exalted be God, the **Rock**, my Savior!
23:3 The God of Israel spoke, the **Rock** *of* Israel said to me: 'When one
1Ch 11:15 Three of the thirty chiefs came down to David to the **rock** at the
Job 14:18 and crumbles and as a **rock** is moved from its place,
18:4 for your sake? Or must the **rocks** be moved from their place?
19:24 inscribed with an iron tool on lead, or engraved in **rock** forever!
22:24 nuggets to the dust, your gold of Ophir to the **rocks** *in* the ravines,
24:8 drenched by mountain rains and hug the **rocks** for lack of shelter.
28:10 He tunnels through the **rock**; his eyes see all its treasures.
29:6 with cream and the **rock** poured out for me streams of olive oil.
Ps 18:2 [18:3] my deliverer; my God is my **rock**, in whom I take refuge.
18:31 [18:32] the LORD? And who is the **Rock** except our God?
18:46 [18:47] The LORD lives! Praise be to my **Rock**! Exalted be God
19:14 [19:15] in your sight, O LORD, my **Rock** and my Redeemer.
27:5 me in the shelter of his tabernacle and set me high upon a **rock**.
28:1 To you I call, O LORD my **Rock**; do not turn a deaf ear to me.
31:2 [31:3] be my **rock** *of* refuge, a strong fortress to save me.
61:2 [61:3] heart grows faint; lead me to the **rock** that is higher than I.
62:2 [62:3] He alone is my **rock** and my salvation; he is my fortress,
62:6 [62:7] He alone is my **rock** and my salvation; he is my fortress,
62:7 [62:8] honor depend on God; he is my mighty **rock**, my refuge.
71:3 Be my **rock** *of* refuge, to which I can always go; give the
73:26 but God is the **strength** *of* my heart and my portion forever.
78:15 He split the **rocks** in the desert and gave them water as abundant as
78:20 When he struck the **rock**, water gushed out, and streams flowed
78:35 They remembered that God was their **Rock**, that God Most High
81:16 [81:17] of wheat; with honey from the **rock** I would satisfy you."
89:26 [89:27] to me, 'You are my Father, my God, the **Rock** my Savior.'
92:15 [92:16] he is my **Rock**, and there is no wickedness in him."
94:22 become my fortress, and my God the **rock** *in whom* I take refuge.
95:1 joy to the LORD; let us shout aloud to the **Rock** *of* our salvation.
105:41 He opened the **rock**, and water gushed out; like a river it flowed in
114:8 who turned the **rock** into a pool, the hard rock into springs of
144:1 Praise be to the LORD my **Rock**, who trains my hands for war,
Pr 30:19 the way of an eagle in the sky, the way of a snake on a **rock**,
Isa 2:10 Go into the **rocks**, hide in the ground from dread of the LORD
2:19 Men will flee to caves in the **rocks** and to holes in the ground from
2:21 They will flee to caverns in the **rocks** and to the overhanging crags
8:14 stone that causes men to stumble and a **rock** *that* makes them fall.
10:26 with a whip, as when he struck down Midian at the **rock** *of* Oreb;
17:10 your Savior; you have not remembered the **Rock**, your fortress.
26:4 LORD forever, for the LORD, the LORD, is the **Rock** eternal.
30:29 with flutes to the mountain of the LORD, to the **Rock** *of* Israel.
44:8 any God besides me? No, there is no other **Rock**; I know not one."
48:21 he made water flow for them from the **rock**; he split the rock
48:21 for them from the rock; he split the **rock** and water gushed out.
51:1 Look to the **rock** *from which* you were cut and to the quarry from
Jer 18:14 Does the snow of Lebanon ever vanish from its **rocky** slopes?
21:13 ⌞Jerusalem,⌟ you who live above this valley on the **rocky** plateau,
Na 1:6 wrath is poured out like fire; the **rocks** are shattered before him.
Hab 1:12 to execute judgment; O **Rock**, you have ordained them to punish.

7447 צוּר[5] **ṣûr[5]**, n.m. Not used in NIV/BHS [√ 7644]

7448 צוּר[6] **ṣûr[6]**, n.pr.m. [5] [√ 7446]

Zur [5]

Nu 25:15 woman who was put to death was Cozbi daughter of **Zur**,
31:8 Among their victims were Evi, Rekem, **Zur**, Hur and Reba—
Jos 13:21 and the Midianite chiefs, Evi, Rekem, **Zur**, Hur and Reba—
1Ch 8:30 son was Abdon, followed by **Zur**, Kish, Baal, Ner, Nadab,
9:36 son was Abdon, followed by **Zur**, Kish, Baal, Ner, Nadab,

7449 צוּר[7] **ṣûr[7]**, n.pr.loc. Not used in NIV/BHS [√ 7446?]

7450 צֹר **ṣôr**, n.pr.loc. [42] [√ 7645; cf. 7644]

Tyre [42]

Jos 19:29 turned back toward Ramah and went to the fortified city of **Tyre**,
2Sa 5:11 Now Hiram king of **Tyre** sent messengers to David, along with
24:7 they went toward the fortress of **Tyre** and all the towns of the
1Ki 5:1 [5:15] When Hiram king of **Tyre** heard that Solomon had been
7:13 King Solomon sent to **Tyre** and brought Huram,
9:11 Solomon gave twenty towns in Galilee to Hiram king of **Tyre**,
9:12 when Hiram went from **Tyre** to see the towns that Solomon had
1Ch 14:1 Now Hiram king of **Tyre** sent messengers to David, along with
2Ch 2:3 [2:2] Solomon sent this message to Hiram king of **Tyre**:
2:11 [2:10] Hiram king of **Tyre** replied by letter to Solomon:
Ps 45:12 [45:13] The Daughter of **Tyre** will come with a gift, men of
83:7 [83:8] and Amalek, Philistia, with the people of **Tyre**.
87:4 Philistia too, and **Tyre**, along with Cush—and will say, 'This one
Isa 23:1 An oracle concerning **Tyre**: Wail, O ships of Tarshish! For Tyre is
23:5 comes to Egypt, they will be in anguish at the report from **Tyre**.
23:8 Who planned this against **Tyre**, the bestower of crowns,
23:15 At that time **Tyre** will be forgotten for seventy years, the span of a
23:15 it will happen to **Tyre** as in the song of the prostitute:
23:17 At the end of seventy years, the LORD will deal with **Tyre**.
Jer 25:22 all the kings of **Tyre** and Sidon; the kings of the coastlands across
27:3 **Tyre** and Sidon through the envoys who have come to Jerusalem

Jer 47: 4 and to cut off all survivors who could help **Tyre** and Sidon.
Eze 26: 2 "Son of man, because **Tyre** has said of Jerusalem, 'Aha! The gate
26: 3 I am against you, O **Tyre**, and I will bring many nations against
26: 4 They will destroy the walls of **Tyre** and pull down her towers;
26: 7 From the north I am going to bring against **Tyre** Nebuchadnezzar
26: 15 "This is what the Sovereign LORD says to **Tyre**: Will not the
27: 2 "Son of man, take up a lament concerning **Tyre**.
27: 3 Say to **Tyre**, situated at the gateway to the sea, merchant of
27: 3 LORD says: " 'You say, O **Tyre**, "I am perfect in beauty."
27: 8 your skilled men, O **Tyre**, were aboard as your seamen.
27: 32 "Who was ever silenced like **Tyre**, surrounded by the sea?"
28: 2 "Son of man, say to the ruler of **Tyre**, 'This is what the Sovereign
28: 12 take up a lament concerning the king of **Tyre** and say to him:
29: 18 king of Babylon drove his army in a hard campaign against **Tyre**;
29: 18 his army got no reward from the campaign he led against **Tyre**.
Hos 9: 13 I have seen Ephraim, like **Tyre**, planted in a pleasant place.
Joel 3: 4 [4:4] O **Tyre** and Sidon and all you regions of Philistia?
Am 1: 9 "For three sins of **Tyre**, even for four, I will not turn back ⌞my
1: 10 I will send fire upon the walls of **Tyre** that will consume her
Zec 9: 2 upon Hamath too, which borders on it, and upon **Tyre** and Sidon,
9: 3 **Tyre** has built herself a stronghold; she has heaped up silver like

7451 צוּרָה *ṣûrâ*, n.f. [4 / 3] [√ 7445]

design [3]

Ps 49: 14 [49:15] [their **forms** [Q; see K 7497] will decay in the grave,]
Eze 43: 11 all they have done, make known to them the **design** *of* the temple—
43: 11 and entrances—its whole **design** and all its regulations and laws.
43: 11 its whole design and all its regulations and [BHS+ *its whole design*]
43: 11 so that they may be faithful to its **design** and follow all its

7452 צוּרִיאֵל *ṣûrî'ēl*, n.pr.m. [1] [√ 7446 + 446]

Zuriel [1]

Nu 3: 35 The leader of the families of the Merarite clans was **Zuriel** son of

7453 צוּרִישַׁדָּי *ṣûrîšadday*, צוּרִי־שַׁדָּי *ṣûrî-šadday*, n.pr.m. [5] [√ 7446 + 8724]

Zurishaddai [5]

Nu 1: 6 from Simeon, Shelumiel son of **Zurishaddai**;
2: 12 leader of the people of Simeon is Shelumiel son of **Zurishaddai**.
7: 36 On the fifth day Shelumiel son of **Zurishaddai**, the leader of the
7: 41 This was the offering of Shelumiel son of **Zurishaddai**.
10: 19 Shelumiel son of **Zurishaddai** was over the division of the tribe of

7454 צַוְּרֹנִים *ṣawwᵉrōnîm*, n.[m.]pl. [1] [√ 7418]

necklace [1]

SS 4: 9 with one glance of your eyes, with one jewel of your **necklace**.

7455 צוּת *ṣût*, v. [1] [cf. 3675]

set on fire [1]

Isa 27: 4 [G] march against them in battle; *I would* **set** them all **on fire**.

7456 צַח *ṣaḥ*, a. [4] [√ 7458]

clear [1], radiant [1], scorching [1], shimmering [1]

SS 5: 10 My lover is **radiant** and ruddy, outstanding among ten thousand.
Isa 18: 4 on from my dwelling place, like **shimmering** heat in the sunshine,
32: 4 and the stammering tongue will be fluent and **clear**.
Jer 4: 11 "A **scorching** wind from the barren heights in the desert blows

7457 צִחֶה *ṣiḥeh*, a. [1] [cf. 7458]

parched [1]

Isa 5: 13 will die of hunger and their masses will be **parched** *with* thirst.

7458 צָחַח *ṣāḥaḥ*, v. [1] [→ 5195?, 5196?, 7456, 7460, 7461, 7463; cf. 7457, 7459]

whiter [1]

La 4: 7 [A] Their princes were brighter than snow and **whiter** than milk,

7459 צְחִיחִי *ṣᵉḥîḥî*, n.[m.]. [0] [cf. 7458, 7460]

Ne 4: 13 [4:7] [lowest points of the wall at the **exposed** [K; see Q 7460] **places**.]

7460 צָחִיחַ *ṣāḥîaḥ*, n.[m.]. [5] [√ 7458; cf. 7459]

bare [4], exposed places [1]

Ne 4: 13 [4:7] lowest points of the wall at the **exposed** [K 7459] **places**,
Eze 24: 7 She poured it on the **bare** rock; she did not pour it on the ground,
24: 8 To stir up wrath and take revenge I put her blood on the **bare** rock,
26: 4 I will scrape away her rubble and make her a **bare** rock.
26: 14 I will make you a **bare** rock, and you will become a place to spread

7461 צְחִיחָה *ṣᵉḥîḥâ*, n.f. [1] [√ 7458]

sun-scorched land [1]

Ps 68: 6 [68:7] but the rebellious live in a **sun-scorched land**.

7462 צַחֲנָה *ṣaḥᵃnâ*, n.f. [1]

smell [1]

Joel 2: 20 its stench will go up; its **smell** will rise." Surely he has done great

7463 צַחְצָחוֹת *ṣaḥṣāḥôt*, n.[f.pl.]. [1] [√ 7458]

sun-scorched land [1]

Isa 58: 11 he will satisfy your needs in a **sun-scorched land** and will

7464 צָחַק *ṣāḥaq*, v. [13] [→ 3663, 7465; cf. 8471]

laugh [4], laughed [2], make sport [2], caressing [1], indulge in revelry [1], joking [1], mocking [1], performed [1]

Ge 17: 17 [A] *he* **laughed** and said to himself, "Will a son be born to a man
18: 12 [A] So Sarah **laughed** to herself as she thought, "After I am worn
18: 13 [A] "Why *did* Sarah **laugh** and say, 'Will I really have a child,
18: 15 [A] Sarah was afraid, so she lied and said, "*I did* not **laugh**."
18: 15 [A] "I did not laugh." But he said, "Yes, *you did* **laugh**."
19: 14 [D] destroy the city!" But his sons-in-law thought he was **joking**.
21: 6 [A] and everyone who hears about this *will* **laugh** with me."
21: 9 [D] Hagar the Egyptian had borne to Abraham *was* **mocking**,
26: 8 [D] from a window and saw Isaac **caressing** his wife Rebekah.
39: 14 [D] "this Hebrew has been brought to us to **make sport** of us!
39: 17 [D] slave you brought us came to me to **make sport** of me.
Ex 32: 6 [D] sat down to eat and drink and got up to **indulge in revelry**.
Jdg 16: 25 [D] called Samson out of the prison, and *he* **performed** for them.

7465 צְחֹק *ṣᵉḥōq*, n.[m.]. [2] [√ 7464]

laughter [1], scorn [1]

Ge 21: 6 Sarah said, "God has brought me **laughter**, and everyone who
Eze 23: 32 and deep; it will bring **scorn** and derision, for it holds so much.

7466 צַחַר *ṣāḥar*, n.[m.]. [1] [√ 7467]

Zahar [1]

Eze 27: 18 did business with you in wine from Helbon and wool from **Zahar**.

7467 צָחֹר *ṣāḥōr*, a. [1] [→ 7466, 7468]

white [1]

Jdg 5: 10 "You who ride on **white** donkeys, sitting on your saddle blankets,

7468 צֹחַר *ṣōḥar*, n.pr.m. [5] [√ 7467; cf. 3664]

Zohar [5]

Ge 23: 8 listen to me and intercede with Ephron son of **Zohar** on my behalf
25: 9 near Mamre, in the field of Ephron son of **Zohar** the Hittite,
46: 10 Ohad, Jakin, **Zohar** and Shaul the son of a Canaanite woman.
Ex 6: 15 Ohad, Jakin, **Zohar** and Shaul the son of a Canaanite woman.
1Ch 4: 7 The sons of Helah: Zereth, **Zohar**, [K 3664] Ethnan,

7469 צִי[1] *ṣî[1]*, n.m. [4]

ships [3], ship [1]

Nu 24: 24 **Ships** will come from the shores of Kittim; they will subdue
Isa 33: 21 No galley with oars will ride them, no mighty **ship** will sail them.
Eze 30: 9 " 'On that day messengers will go out from me in **ships** to frighten
Da 11: 30 **Ships** *of* the western coastlands will oppose him, and he will lose

7470 צִי[2] *ṣî[2]*, n.m. [6] [√ 7480]

desert creatures [4], creatures of the desert [1], desert tribes [1]

Ps 72: 9 The **desert tribes** will bow before him and his enemies will lick
74: 14 of Leviathan and gave him as food to the **creatures of the desert**.
Isa 13: 21 But **desert creatures** will lie there, jackals will fill her houses;
23: 13 The Assyrians have made it a place for **desert creatures**;
34: 14 **Desert creatures** will meet with hyenas, and wild goats will bleat
Jer 50: 39 "So **desert creatures** and hyenas will live there, and there the owl

7471 צִיבָא *ṣîbā'*, n.pr.m. [16]

Ziba [15], Ziba's [1]

2Sa 9: 2 Now there was a servant of Saul's household named **Ziba**.
9: 2 to appear before David, and the king said to him, "Are you **Ziba**?"
9: 3 **Ziba** answered the king, "There is still a son of Jonathan; he is
9: 4 **Ziba** answered, "He is at the house of Makir son of Ammiel in Lo
9: 9 Then the king summoned **Ziba**, Saul's servant, and said to him,

2Sa 9:10 eat at my table." (Now **Ziba** had fifteen sons and twenty servants.)
9:11 **Ziba** said to the king, "Your servant will do whatever my lord the
9:12 all the members of **Ziba's** household were servants of
16: 1 there was **Ziba**, the steward of Mephibosheth, waiting to meet him.
16: 2 The king asked **Ziba**, "Why have you brought these?" Ziba
16: 2 **Ziba** answered, "The donkeys are for the king's household to ride
16: 3 **Ziba** said to him, "He is staying in Jerusalem, because he thinks,
16: 4 the king said to **Ziba**, "All that belonged to Mephibosheth is now
16: 4 "I humbly bow," **Ziba** said. "May I find favor in your eyes,
19:17 [19:18] along with **Ziba**, the steward of Saul's household, and his
19:29 [19:30] say more? I order you and **Ziba** to divide the fields."

7472 צִיד ṣîd, v.den. [1] [→ 7474, 7476]

packed [1]

Jos 9:12 [F] This bread of ours was warm *when we* **packed** it at home on

7473 צַיִד ṣayid[1], n.m. [14] [√ 7421]

game [7], hunter [2], wild game [2], animal [+2651] [1], hunter [+408] [1], hunting [1]

Ge 10: 9 He was a mighty **hunter** before the LORD; that is why it is said,
10: 9 it is said, "Like Nimrod, a mighty **hunter** before the LORD."
25:27 The boys grew up, and Esau became a skillful **hunter** [+408],
25:28 Isaac, who had a taste for **wild game**, loved Esau, but Rebekah
27: 3 go out to the open country to hunt *some* **wild game** [K 7476] for
27: 5 When Esau left for the open country to hunt **game** and bring it
27: 7 'Bring me *some* **game** and prepare me some tasty food to eat,
27:19 Please sit up and eat some of my **game** so that you may give me
27:25 Then he said, "My son, bring me some of your **game** to eat,
27:30 left his father's presence, his brother Esau came in from **hunting**.
27:31 Then he said to him, "My father, sit up and eat some of my **game**,
27:33 "Who was it, then, that hunted **game** and brought it to me?
Lev 17:13 or any alien living among you who hunts any **animal** [+2651]
Pr 12:27 The lazy man does not roast his **game**, but the diligent man prizes

7474 צַיִד ṣayid[2], n.[m.]. [5] [√ 7472]

food [2], provisions [2], food supply [1]

Jos 9: 5 old clothes. All the bread of their **food supply** was dry and moldy.
9:14 The men of Israel sampled their **provisions** but did not inquire of
Ne 13:15 Therefore I warned them against selling **food** on that day.
Job 38:41 Who provides **food** for the raven when its young cry out to God
Ps 132:15 I will bless her with abundant **provisions**; her poor will I satisfy

7475 צַיָּד ṣayyād, n.m. [1] [√ 7421]

hunters [1]

Jer 16:16 After that I will send for many **hunters**, and they will hunt them

7476 צֵידָה ṣêdâ, n.f. [9] [√ 7472]

provisions [6], food [2], supplies [1]

Ge 27: 3 [the open country to hunt *some* **wild game** [K; see Q 7473] for me.]
42:25 back in his sack, and to give them **provisions** for their journey.
45:21 and he also gave them **provisions** for their journey.
Ex 12:39 out of Egypt and did not have time to prepare **food** for themselves.
Jos 1:11 through the camp and tell the people, 'Get your **supplies** ready.
9:11 living in our country said to us, 'Take **provisions** for your journey;
Jdg 7: 8 who took over the **provisions** and trumpets of the others.
20:10 and a thousand from ten thousand, to get **provisions** for the army.
1Sa 22:10 he also gave him **provisions** and the sword of Goliath the
Ps 78:25 ate the bread of angels; he sent them all the **food** they could eat.

7477 צִידוֹן ṣîdôn, n.pr.loc. [20] [→ 7478, 7479]

Sidon [20]

Ge 10:15 Canaan was the father of **Sidon** his firstborn, and of the Hittites,
10:19 the borders of Canaan reached from **Sidon** toward Gerar as far as
49:13 become a haven for ships; his border will extend toward **Sidon**.
Jdg 1:31 or **Sidon** or Ahlab or Aczib or Helbah or Aphek or Rehob,
10: 6 and the gods of Aram, the gods of **Sidon**, the gods of Moab,
18:28 no one to rescue them because they lived a long way from **Sidon**
2Sa 24: 6 of Tahtim Hodshi, and on to Dan Jaan and around toward **Sidon**.
1Ki 17: 9 "Go at once to Zarephath of **Sidon** and stay there. I have
1Ch 1:13 Canaan was the father of **Sidon** his firstborn, and of the Hittites,
Isa 23: 2 Be silent, you people of the island and you merchants of **Sidon**,
23: 4 Be ashamed, O **Sidon**, and you, O fortress of the sea, for the sea
23:12 more of your reveling, O Virgin Daughter of **Sidon**, now crushed!
Jer 25:22 all the kings of Tyre and **Sidon**; the kings of the coastlands across
27: 3 **Sidon** through the envoys who have come to Jerusalem to
47: 4 and to cut off all survivors who could help Tyre and **Sidon**.
Eze 27: 8 Men of **Sidon** and Arvad were your oarsmen; your skilled men,
28:21 "Son of man, set your face against **Sidon**; prophesy against her
28:22 " 'I am against you, O **Sidon**, and I will gain glory within you.
Joel 3: 4 [4:4] O Tyre and **Sidon** and all you regions of Philistia?
Zec 9: 2 upon Hamath too, which borders on it, and upon Tyre and **Sidon**,

7478 צִידוֹן רַבָּה ṣîdôn rabbâ, n.pr.loc. [2] [√ 7477 + 8045]

Greater Sidon [2]

Jos 11: 8 defeated them and pursued them all the way to **Greater Sidon**,
19:28 to Abdon, Rehob, Hammon and Kanah, as far as **Greater Sidon**.

7479 צִידֹנִי ṣîdōnî, a.g. [16] [√ 7477]

Sidonians [15], people of Sidon [1]

Dt 3: 9 (Hermon is called Sirion by the **Sidonians**; the Amorites call it
Jos 13: 4 from Arah of the **Sidonians** as far as Aphek, the region of the
13: 6 that is, all the **Sidonians**, I myself will drive them out before the
Jdg 3: 3 the five rulers of the Philistines, all the Canaanites, the **Sidonians**,
10:12 the **Sidonians**, the Amalekites and the Maonites oppressed you
18: 7 were living in safety, like the **Sidonians**, unsuspecting and secure.
18: 7 they lived a long way from the **Sidonians** and had no relationship
1Ki 5: 6 [5:20] have no one so skilled in felling timber as the **Sidonians**."
11: 1 Moabites, Ammonites, Edomites, **Sidonians** and Hittites.
11: 5 He followed Ashtoreth the goddess of the **Sidonians**, and Molech
11:33 and worshiped Ashtoreth the goddess of the **Sidonians**,
16:31 he also married Jezebel daughter of Ethbaal king of the **Sidonians**,
2Ki 23:13 of Israel had built for Ashtoreth the vile goddess of the **Sidonians**,
1Ch 22: 4 for the **Sidonians** and Tyrians had brought large numbers of them
Ezr 3: 7 and gave food and drink and oil to the **people of Sidon** and Tyre,
Eze 32:30 "All the princes of the north and all the **Sidonians** are there;

7480 צִיָּה ṣiyyâ, n.f. [16] [→ 7470, 7481]

dry [5], parched [4], desert [2], drought [2], parched land [2], dry land [1]

Job 24:19 As heat and **drought** snatch away the melted snow, so the grave
30: 3 they roamed the **parched land** in desolate wastelands at night.
Ps 63: 1 [63:2] for you, in a **dry** and weary land where there is no water.
78:17 to sin against him, rebelling in the **desert** against the Most High.
105:41 the rock, and water gushed out; like a river it flowed in the **desert**.
107:35 into pools of water and the **parched** ground into flowing springs;
Isa 35: 1 The desert and the **parched land** will be glad; the wilderness will
41:18 desert into pools of water, and the **parched** ground into springs.
53: 2 before him like a tender shoot, and like a root out of **dry** ground.
Jer 2: 6 through a land of deserts and rifts, a land of **drought** and darkness,
50:12 will be the least of the nations—a wilderness, a **dry land**, a desert.
51:43 will be desolate, a **dry** and desert land, a land where no one lives,
Eze 19:13 Now it is planted in the desert, in a **dry** and thirsty land.
Hos 2: 3 [2:5] turn her into a **parched** land, and slay her with thirst.
Joel 2:20 army far from you, pushing it into a **parched** and barren land,
Zep 2:13 leaving Nineveh utterly desolate and **dry** as the desert.

7481 צָיוֹן ṣāyôn, n.[m.]. [2] [√ 7480]

desert [2]

Isa 25: 5 like the heat of the **desert**. You silence the uproar of foreigners;
32: 2 like streams of water in the **desert** and the shadow of a great rock

7482 צִיּוֹן ṣiyyôn, n.pr.loc. [154]

Zion [152], Zion's [2]

2Sa 5: 7 Nevertheless, David captured the fortress of **Zion**, the City of
1Ki 8: 1 to bring up the ark of the LORD's covenant from **Zion**, the City
2Ki 19:21 " 'The Virgin Daughter of **Zion** despises you and mocks you.
19:31 will come a remnant, and out of Mount **Zion** a band of survivors.
1Ch 11: 5 Nevertheless, David captured the fortress of **Zion**, the City of
2Ch 5: 2 to bring up the ark of the LORD's covenant from **Zion**, the City
Ps 2: 6 "I have installed my King on **Zion**, my holy hill."
9:11 [9:12] Sing praises to the LORD, enthroned in **Zion**;
9:14 [9:15] declare your praises in the gates of the Daughter of **Zion**
14: 7 Oh, that salvation for Israel would come out of **Zion**!
20: 2 [20:3] help from the sanctuary and grant you support from **Zion**.
48: 2 [48:3] Like the utmost heights of Zaphon is Mount **Zion**, the city
48:11 [48:12] Mount **Zion** rejoices, the villages of Judah are glad
48:12 [48:13] Walk about **Zion**, go around her, count her towers,
50: 2 From **Zion**, perfect in beauty, God shines forth.
51:18 [51:20] In your good pleasure make **Zion** prosper; build up the
53: 6 [53:7] Oh, that salvation for Israel would come out of **Zion**!
65: 1 [65:2] Praise awaits you, O God, in **Zion**; to you our vows will be
69:35 [69:36] for God will save **Zion** and rebuild the cities of Judah.
74: 2 whom you redeemed—Mount **Zion**, where you dwelt.
76: 2 [76:3] His tent is in Salem, his dwelling place in **Zion**.
78:68 but he chose the tribe of Judah, Mount **Zion**, which he loved.
84: 7 [84:8] strength to strength, till each appears before God in **Zion**.
87: 2 the LORD loves the gates of **Zion** more than all the dwellings of
87: 5 Indeed, of **Zion** it will be said, "This one and that one were born in
97: 8 **Zion** hears and rejoices and the villages of Judah are glad
99: 2 Great is the LORD in **Zion**; he is exalted over all the nations.

Ps 102: 13 [102:14] You will arise and have compassion on **Zion**, for it is
102: 16 [102:17] For the LORD will rebuild **Zion** and appear in his
102: 21 [102:22] So the name of the LORD will be declared in **Zion**
110: 2 The LORD will extend your mighty scepter from **Zion**; you will
125: 1 Those who trust in the LORD are like Mount **Zion**, which cannot
126: 1 When the LORD brought back the captives to **Zion**, we were like
128: 5 May the LORD bless you from **Zion** all the days of your life;
129: 5 May all who hate **Zion** be turned back in shame.
132: 13 For the LORD has chosen **Zion**, he has desired it for his dwelling:
133: 3 It is as if the dew of Hermon were falling on Mount **Zion**.
134: 3 the LORD, the Maker of heaven and earth, bless you from **Zion**.
135: 21 Praise be to the LORD from **Zion**, to him who dwells in
137: 1 the rivers of Babylon we sat and wept when we remembered **Zion**.
137: 3 songs of joy; they said, "Sing us one of the songs of **Zion**!"
146: 10 The LORD reigns forever, your God, O **Zion**, for all generations.
147: 12 Extol the LORD, O Jerusalem; praise your God, O **Zion**,
149: 2 rejoice in their Maker; let the people of **Zion** be glad in their King.
SS 3: 11 Come out, you daughters of **Zion**, and look at King Solomon
Isa 1: 8 The Daughter of **Zion** is left like a shelter in a vineyard, like a hut
1: 27 **Zion** will be redeemed with justice, her penitent ones with
2: 3 The law will go out from **Zion**, the word of the LORD from
3: 16 The LORD says, "The women of **Zion** are haughty, walking
3: 17 the Lord will bring sores on the heads of the women of **Zion**;
4: 3 Those who are left in **Zion**, who remain in Jerusalem, will be
4: 4 The Lord will wash away the filth of the women of **Zion**; he will
4: 5 the LORD will create over all of Mount **Zion** and over those who
8: 18 in Israel from the LORD Almighty, who dwells on Mount **Zion**.
10: 12 When the Lord has finished all his work against Mount **Zion**
10: 24 "O my people who live in **Zion**, do not be afraid of the Assyrians,
10: 32 they will shake their fist at the mount of the Daughter of **Zion**,
12: 6 Shout aloud and sing for joy, people of **Zion**, for great is the Holy
14: 32 "The LORD has established **Zion**, and in her his afflicted people
16: 1 from Sela, across the desert, to the mount of the Daughter of **Zion**.
18: 7 the gifts will be brought to Mount **Zion**, the place of the Name of
24: 23 for the LORD Almighty will reign on Mount **Zion** and in
28: 16 "See, I lay a stone in **Zion**, a tested stone, a precious cornerstone
29: 8 be with the hordes of all the nations that fight against Mount **Zion**.
30: 19 O people of **Zion**, who live in Jerusalem, you will weep no more.
31: 4 the LORD Almighty will come down to do battle on Mount **Zion**
31: 9 declares the LORD, whose fire is in **Zion**, whose furnace is in
33: 5 he dwells on high; he will fill **Zion** with justice and righteousness.
33: 14 The sinners in **Zion** are terrified; trembling grips the godless:
33: 20 Look upon **Zion**, the city of our festivals; your eyes will see
34: 8 a day of vengeance, a year of retribution, to uphold **Zion's** cause.
35: 10 They will enter **Zion** with singing; everlasting joy will crown their
37: 22 "The Virgin Daughter of **Zion** despises and mocks you.
37: 32 will come a remnant, and out of Mount **Zion** a band of survivors.
40: 9 You who bring good tidings to **Zion**, go up on a high mountain.
41: 27 I was the first to tell **Zion**, 'Look, here they are!' I gave to
46: 13 be delayed. I will grant salvation to **Zion**, my splendor to Israel.
49: 14 **Zion** said, "The LORD has forsaken me, the Lord has forgotten
51: 3 The LORD will surely comfort **Zion** and will look with
51: 11 They will enter **Zion** with singing; everlasting joy will crown their
51: 16 of the earth, and who say to **Zion**, 'You are my people.' "
52: 1 Awake, awake, O **Zion**, clothe yourself with strength. Put on your
52: 2 from the chains on your neck, O captive Daughter of **Zion**.
52: 7 who proclaim salvation, who say to **Zion**, "Your God reigns!"
52: 8 When the LORD returns to **Zion**, they will see it with their own
59: 20 "The Redeemer will come to **Zion**, to those in Jacob who repent of
60: 14 call you the City of the LORD, **Zion** *of* the Holy One of Israel.
61: 3 provide for those who grieve in **Zion**—to bestow on them a crown
62: 1 For **Zion's** sake I will not keep silent, for Jerusalem's sake I will
62: 11 "Say to the Daughter of **Zion**, 'See, your Savior comes! See,
64: 10 [64:9] a desert; even **Zion** is a desert, Jerusalem a desolation.
66: 8 Yet no sooner is **Zion** in labor than she gives birth to her children.
Jer 3: 14 one from a town and two from a clan—and bring you to **Zion**.
4: 6 Raise the signal to go to **Zion**! Flee for safety without delay!
4: 31 the cry of the Daughter of **Zion** gasping for breath, stretching out
6: 2 I will destroy the Daughter of **Zion**, so beautiful and delicate.
6: 23 like men in battle formation to attack you, O Daughter of **Zion**."
8: 19 "Is the LORD not in **Zion**? Is her King no longer there?"
9: 19 [9:18] The sound of wailing is heard from **Zion**: 'How ruined we
14: 19 Do you despise **Zion**? Why have you afflicted us so that we cannot
26: 18 " '**Zion** will be plowed like a field, Jerusalem will become a heap
30: 17 'because you are called an outcast, **Zion** for whom no one cares.'
31: 6 'Come, let us go up to **Zion**, to the LORD our God.' "
31: 12 They will come and shout for joy on the heights of **Zion**; they will
50: 5 They will ask the way to **Zion** and turn their faces toward it.
50: 28 refugees from Babylon declaring in **Zion** how the LORD our God
51: 10 come, let us tell in **Zion** what the LORD our God has done.'
51: 24 who live in Babylonia for all the wrong they have done in **Zion**,"
51: 35 done to our flesh be upon Babylon," say the inhabitants of **Zion**.
La 1: 4 The roads to **Zion** mourn, for no one comes to her appointed
1: 6 All the splendor has departed from the Daughter of **Zion**.
1: 17 **Zion** stretches out her hands, but there is no one to comfort her.
2: 1 How the Lord has covered the Daughter of **Zion** with the cloud of
2: 4 poured out his wrath like fire on the tent of the Daughter of **Zion**.
2: 6 The LORD has made **Zion** forget her appointed feasts and her
2: 8 determined to tear down the wall around the Daughter of **Zion**.
2: 10 The elders of the Daughter of **Zion** sit on the ground in silence;
2: 13 I liken you, that I may comfort you, O Virgin Daughter of **Zion**?
2: 18 O wall of the Daughter of **Zion**, let your tears flow like a river day
4: 2 How the precious sons of **Zion**, once worth their weight in gold,
4: 11 He kindled a fire in **Zion** that consumed her foundations.
4: 22 O Daughter of **Zion**, your punishment will end; he will not prolong
5: 11 Women have been ravished in **Zion**, and virgins in the towns of
5: 18 for Mount **Zion**, which lies desolate, with jackals prowling over it.
Joel 2: 1 Blow the trumpet in **Zion**; sound the alarm on my holy hill.
2: 15 Blow the trumpet in **Zion**, declare a holy fast, call a sacred
2: 23 Be glad, O people of **Zion**, rejoice in the LORD your God,
2: 32 [3:5] for on Mount **Zion** and in Jerusalem there will be
3: 16 [4:16] The LORD will roar from **Zion** and thunder from
3: 17 [4:17] that I, the LORD your God, dwell in **Zion**, my holy hill.
3: 21 [4:21] not pardoned, I will pardon." The LORD dwells in **Zion**!
Am 1: 2 "The LORD roars from **Zion** and thunders from Jerusalem;
6: 1 Woe to you who are complacent in **Zion**, and to you who feel
Ob 1: 17 on Mount **Zion** will be deliverance; it will be holy, and the house
1: 21 Deliverers will go up on Mount **Zion** to govern the mountains of
Mic 1: 13 You were the beginning of sin to the Daughter of **Zion**,
3: 10 who build **Zion** with bloodshed, and Jerusalem with wickedness.
3: 12 Therefore because of you, **Zion** will be plowed like a field,
4: 2 The law will go out from **Zion**, the word of the LORD from
4: 7 The LORD will rule over them in Mount **Zion** from that day
4: 8 O watchtower of the flock, O stronghold of the Daughter of **Zion**,
4: 10 Writhe in agony, O Daughter of **Zion**, like a woman in labor,
4: 11 They say, "Let her be defiled, let our eyes gloat over **Zion**!"
4: 13 "Rise and thresh, O Daughter of **Zion**, for I will give you horns of
Zep 3: 14 Sing, O Daughter of **Zion**; shout aloud, O Israel! Be glad
3: 16 On that day they will say to Jerusalem, "Do not fear, O **Zion**;
Zec 1: 14 LORD Almighty says: 'I am very jealous for Jerusalem and **Zion**,
1: 17 and the LORD will again comfort **Zion** and choose Jerusalem.' "
2: 7 [2:11] "Come, O **Zion**! Escape, you who live in the Daughter of
2: 10 [2:14] "Shout and be glad, O Daughter of **Zion**. For I am coming,
8: 2 "I am very jealous for **Zion**; I am burning with jealousy for her."
8: 3 the LORD says: "I will return to **Zion** and dwell in Jerusalem.
9: 9 Rejoice greatly, O Daughter of **Zion**! Shout, Daughter of
9: 13 I will rouse your sons, O **Zion**, against your sons, O Greece,

7483 צִיּוּן ṣiyyûn, n.m. [3]

marker [1], road signs [1], tombstone [1]

2Ki 23: 17 The king asked, "What is that **tombstone** I see?" The men of the
Jer 31: 21 "Set up **road signs**; put up guideposts. Take note of the highway,
Eze 39: 15 he will set up a **marker** beside it until the gravediggers have

7484 צִיחָא ṣîḥā', n.pr.m. [3]

Ziha [3]

Ezr 2: 43 The temple servants: the descendants of **Ziha**, Hasupha, Tabbaoth,
Ne 7: 46 The temple servants: the descendants of **Ziha**, Hasupha, Tabbaoth,
11: 21 on the hill of Ophel, and **Ziha** and Gishpa were in charge of them.

7485 צִינֹק ṣînōq, n.[m.]. [1]

neck-irons [1]

Jer 29: 26 madman who acts like a prophet into the stocks and **neck-irons**.

7486 צִיעֹר ṣî'ōr, n.pr.loc. [1] [√ 7592]

Zior [1]

Jos 15: 54 Humtah, Kiriath Arba (that is, Hebron) and **Zior**—nine towns

7487 צִיף ṣîp, n.pr.m. [0] [√ 7430; cf. 7431]

1Ch 6: 35 [[6:20] the son of Zuph, [K; see Q 7431] the son of Elkanah,]

7488 צִיץ ṣîṣ[1], n.m. [14] [→ 7491, 7492; cf. 7437]

flowers [7], flower [3], plate [3], blossomed [+7437] [1]

Ex 28: 36 "Make a **plate** *of* pure gold and engrave on it as on a seal:
39: 30 They made the **plate**, the sacred diadem, out of pure gold
Lev 8: 9 Then he placed the turban on Aaron's head and set the gold **plate**,
Nu 17: 8 [17:23] had budded, **blossomed** [+7437] and produced almonds.
1Ki 6: 18 of the temple was cedar, carved with gourds and open **flowers**.
6: 29 and outer rooms, he carved cherubim, palm trees and open **flowers**.
6: 32 palm trees and open **flowers**, and overlaid the cherubim and palm
6: 35 palm trees and open **flowers** on them and overlaid them with gold
Job 14: 2 He springs up like a **flower** and withers away; like a fleeting
Ps 103: 15 his days are like grass, he flourishes like a **flower** *of* the field;
Isa 28: 1 of Ephraim's drunkards, to the fading **flower**, his glorious beauty,

Isa 40: 6 are like grass, and all their glory is like the **flowers** *of* the field.
40: 7 The grass withers and the **flowers** fall, because the breath of the
40: 8 The grass withers and the **flowers** fall, but the word of our God

7489 [2]צִיץ ***ṣîṣ***[2], n.pr.loc. [1]

Ziz [1]

2Ch 20: 16 They will be climbing up by the Pass of **Ziz**, and you will find

7490 [3]צִיץ ***ṣîṣ***[3], n.[m.]. [1] [√ 7437]

salt [1]

Jer 48: 9 Put **salt** on Moab, for she will be laid waste; her towns will

7491 צִיצָה ***ṣîṣâ***, n.f. [1] [√ 7488; cf. 7437]

flower [1]

Isa 28: 4 That fading **flower**, his glorious beauty, set on the head of a fertile

7492 צִיצִת ***ṣîṣit***, n.f. [4] [√ 7488; cf. 7437]

tassels [2], hair [1], tassel [1]

Nu 15: 38 'Throughout the generations to come you are to make **tassels** on the
15: 38 on the corners of your garments, with a blue cord on each **tassel**.
15: 39 You will have these **tassels** to look at and so you will remember all
Eze 8: 3 out what looked like a hand and took me by the **hair** *of* my head.

7493 [1]צִיר ***ṣîr***[1], v.den. [1] [cf. 7443]

delegation [1]

Jos 9: 4 [F] They went *as a* **delegation** whose donkeys were loaded with

7494 [2]צִיר ***ṣîr***[2], n.[m.]. [1]

hinges [1]

Pr 26: 14 As a door turns on its **hinges**, so a sluggard turns on his bed.

7495 [3]צִיר ***ṣîr***[3], n.m. [6]

envoy [3], ambassadors [1], envoys [1], messenger [1]

Pr 13: 17 falls into trouble, but a trustworthy **envoy** brings healing.
25: 13 at harvest time is a trustworthy **messenger** to those who send him;
Isa 18: 2 which sends **envoys** by sea in papyrus boats over the water.
57: 9 You sent your **ambassadors** far away; you descended to the grave
Jer 49: 14 An **envoy** was sent to the nations to say, "Assemble yourselves to
Ob 1: 1 An **envoy** was sent to the nations to say, "Rise, and let us go

7496 [4]צִיר ***ṣîr***[4], n.[m.]. [5] [√ 7444?]

anguish [1], labor pains [1], pain [1], pangs [1], those[s] [1]

1Sa 4: 19 into labor and gave birth, but was overcome by her **labor pains**.
Isa 13: 8 Terror will seize them, **pain** and anguish will grip them; they will
21: 3 racked with pain, **pangs** seize me, like those of a woman in labor;
21: 3 racked with pain, pangs seize me, like **those**[s] *of* a woman in labor;
Da 10: 16 "I am overcome with **anguish** because of the vision, my lord,

7497 [5]צִיר ***ṣîr***[5], n.m. [2] [√ 7445?]

forms [1], idols [1]

Ps 49: 14 [49:15] their **forms** [Q 7451] will decay in the grave, far from
Isa 45: 16 All the makers of **idols** will be put to shame and disgraced;

7498 צֵל ***ṣēl***, n.m. [53] [→ 1295, 7500, 7516, 7524; cf. 7511]

shadow [27], shade [16], shadows [4], protection [2], shelter [2], evening shadows [1], it[s] [+2021] [1]

Ge 19: 8 these men, for they have come under the **protection** *of* my roof."
Nu 14: 9 Their **protection** is gone, but the LORD is with us. Do not be
Jdg 9: 15 to anoint me king over you, come and take refuge in my **shade**;
9: 36 "You mistake the **shadows** *of* the mountains for men."
2Ki 20: 9 Shall the **shadow** go forward ten steps, or shall it go back ten
20: 10 "It is a simple matter for the **shadow** to go forward ten steps,"
20: 10 said Hezekiah. "Rather, have **it**[s] [+2021] go back ten steps."
20: 11 the LORD made the **shadow** go back the ten steps it had gone
1Ch 29: 15 our forefathers. Our days on earth are like a **shadow**, without hope.
Job 7: 2 Like a slave longing for the **evening shadows**, or a hired man
8: 9 and know nothing, and our days on earth are but a **shadow**.
14: 2 and withers away; like a fleeting **shadow**, he does not endure.
17: 7 eyes have grown dim with grief; my whole frame is but a **shadow**.
40: 22 The lotuses conceal him in their **shadow**; the poplars by the stream
Ps 17: 8 me as the apple of your eye; hide me in the **shadow** *of* your wings
36: 7 [36:8] low among men find refuge in the **shadow** *of* your wings.
57: 1 [57:2] I will take refuge in the **shadow** *of* your wings until the
63: 7 [63:8] you are my help, I sing in the **shadow** *of* your wings.
80: 10 [80:11] The mountains were covered with its **shade**, the mighty
91: 1 shelter of the Most High will rest in the **shadow** *of* the Almighty.
102: 11 [102:12] My days are like the evening **shadow**; I wither away like
109: 23 I fade away like an evening **shadow**; I am shaken off like a locust.
121: 5 watches over you—the LORD is your **shade** at your right hand;
144: 4 Man is like a breath; his days are like a fleeting **shadow**.
Ecc 6: 12 the few and meaningless days he passes through like a **shadow**?
7: 12 Wisdom is a **shelter** as money is a shelter, but the advantage of
7: 12 Wisdom is a shelter as money is a **shelter**, but the advantage of
8: 13 go well with them, and their days will not lengthen like a **shadow**.
SS 2: 3 I delight to sit in his **shade**, and his fruit is sweet to my taste.
2: 17 Until the day breaks and the **shadows** flee, turn, my lover,
4: 6 Until the day breaks and the **shadows** flee, I will go to the
Isa 4: 6 It will be a shelter and **shade** from the heat of the day, and a refuge
16: 3 render a decision. Make your **shadow** like night—at high noon.
25: 4 in his distress, a shelter from the storm and a **shade** from the heat.
25: 5 as heat is reduced by the **shadow** *of* a cloud, so the song of the
30: 2 look for help to Pharaoh's protection, to Egypt's **shade** for refuge.
30: 3 will be to your shame, Egypt's **shade** will bring you disgrace.
32: 2 water in the desert and the **shadow** *of* a great rock in a thirsty land.
34: 15 hatch them, and care for her young under the **shadow** *of* her wings;
38: 8 I will make the **shadow** cast by the sun go back the ten steps it has
49: 2 like a sharpened sword, in the **shadow** *of* his hand he hid me;
51: 16 in your mouth and covered you with the **shadow** *of* my hand—
Jer 6: 4 the daylight is fading, and the **shadows** *of* evening grow long.
48: 45 "In the **shadow** *of* Heshbon the fugitives stand helpless, for a fire
La 4: 20 We thought that under his **shadow** we would live among the
Eze 17: 23 will nest in it; they will find shelter in the **shade** *of* its branches.
31: 6 birth under its branches; all the great nations lived in its **shade**.
31: 12 All the nations of the earth came out from under its **shade**
31: 17 Those who lived in its **shade**, its allies among the nations,
Hos 4: 13 under oak, poplar and terebinth, where the **shade** is pleasant.
14: 7 [14:8] Men will dwell again in his **shade**. He will flourish like the
Jnh 4: 5 sat in its **shade** and waited to see what would happen to the city.
4: 6 made it grow up over Jonah to give **shade** for his head to ease his

7499 צָלָה ***ṣālâ***, v. [3] [→ 7507]

roast [1], roasted [1], roasts [1]

1Sa 2: 15 [A] who was sacrificing, "Give the priest some meat to **roast**;
Isa 44: 16 [A] it he prepares his meal, *he* **roasts** his meat and eats his fill.
44: 19 [A] I even baked bread over its coals, *I* **roasted** meat and I ate.

7500 צִלָּה ***ṣillâ***, n.pr.f. [3] [√ 7498; cf. 5511]

Zillah [3]

Ge 4: 19 married two women, one named Adah and the other **Zillah**.
4: 22 **Zillah** also had a son, Tubal-Cain, who forged all kinds of tools
4: 23 Lamech said to his wives, "Adah and **Zillah**, listen to me;

7501 צְלוּל ***ṣ[e]lûl***, n.m. [1] [cf. 7508]

round loaf [1]

Jdg 7: 13 "A **round** [Q 7508] **loaf** *of* barley bread came tumbling into the

7502 [1]צָלַח ***ṣālaḥ***[1], v. [10]

came in power [6], came forcefully [1], come in power [1], rushed [1], sweep through [1]

Jdg 14: 6 [A] The Spirit of the LORD **came** upon him **in power** so that he
14: 19 [A] the Spirit of the LORD **came** upon him **in power**. He went
15: 14 [A] The Spirit of the LORD **came** upon him **in power**.
1Sa 10: 6 [A] The Spirit of the LORD *will* **come** upon you **in power**,
10: 10 [A] the Spirit of God **came** upon him **in power**, and he joined in
11: 6 [A] the Spirit of God **came** upon him **in power**, and he burned
16: 13 [A] day on the Spirit of the LORD **came** upon David **in power**.
18: 10 [A] The next day an evil spirit from God **came forcefully** upon
2Sa 19: 17 [19:18] [A] *They* **rushed** *to* the Jordan, where the king was.
Am 5: 6 [A] or *he will* **sweep through** the house of Joseph like a fire;

7503 [2]צָלַח ***ṣālaḥ***[2], v. [55] [→ Ar 10613]

prosper [7], succeed [7], prospered [5], victorious [4], gave success [3], successful [3], give success [2], grant success [2], have success [2], thrive [2], useless [+4202] [2], achieve purpose [1], avail [1], granted success [1], helped [1], made successful [1], make success [1], prevail [1], prosperous [1], prospers [1], rose [1], succeeded in carrying out [1], succeeded [1], unsuccessful [+906+4202] [1], useful [1], victoriously [1], win [1]

Ge 24: 21 [G] or not the LORD *had* **made** his journey **successful**.
24: 40 [G] send his angel with you and **make** your journey a **success**,
24: 42 [G] please **grant success** *to* the journey on which I have come.
24: 56 [G] now that the LORD *has* **granted success** *to* my journey.
39: 2 [G] The LORD was with Joseph and he **prospered**, and he lived
39: 3 [G] and that the LORD **gave** him **success** *in* everything he did,
39: 23 [G] was with Joseph and **gave** him **success** *in* whatever he did.
Nu 14: 41 [A] disobeying the LORD's command? This *will* not **succeed**!
Dt 28: 29 [G] *You will be* **unsuccessful** [+906+4202] *in* everything you do;

[F] Hitpael (hitpoel, hitpoal, hitpolel, hitpolal, hitpalel, hitpalal, hitpalpel, hitpalpal, hotpael, hotpaal) [G] Hiphil (hiphtil) [H] Hophal [I] Hishtaphel

Jos 1: 8 [G] written in it. Then you *will be* **prosperous** and successful.
Jdg 18: 5 [G] of God to learn whether our journey *will be* **successful.**"
1Ki 22: 12 [G] "Attack Ramoth Gilead and *be* **victorious**," they said,
22: 15 [G] "Attack and *be* **victorious**," he answered, "for the LORD
1Ch 22: 11 [G] *may you* **have success** and build the house of the LORD
22: 13 [G] *you will* **have success** if you are careful to observe the
29: 23 [G] of his father David. *He* **prospered** and all Israel obeyed him.
2Ch 7: 11 [G] *had* **succeeded in carrying out** all he had in mind to do in
13: 12 [G] the God of your fathers, for *you will* not **succeed.**"
14: 7 [14:6] [G] us rest on every side." So they built and **prospered**.
18: 11 [G] "Attack Ramoth Gilead and *be* **victorious**," they said,
18: 14 [G] "Attack and *be* **victorious**," he answered, "for they will be
20: 20 [G] have faith in his prophets and *you will be* **successful.**"
24: 20 [G] *You will* not **prosper**. Because you have forsaken the
26: 5 [G] As long as he sought the LORD, God **gave** him **success**.
31: 21 [G] his God and worked wholeheartedly. And so *he* **prospered**.
32: 30 [G] the City of David. He **succeeded** in everything he undertook.
Ne 1: 11 [G] **Give** your servant **success** today by granting him favor in the
2: 20 [G] them by saying, "The God of heaven *will* **give** us **success**.
Ps 1: 3 [G] and whose leaf does not wither. Whatever he does **prospers**.
37: 7 [G] do not fret when men **succeed** *in* their ways, when they carry
45: 4 [45:5] [A] In your majesty ride forth **victoriously** in behalf of
118: 25 [G] O LORD, save us; O LORD, **grant** us **success**.
Pr 28: 13 [G] He who conceals his sins *does* not **prosper**, but whoever
Isa 48: 15 [G] I will bring him, and *he will* **succeed** *in* his mission.
53: 10 [A] and the will of the LORD *will* **prosper** in his hand.
54: 17 [A] no weapon forged against you *will* **prevail**, and you will
55: 11 [G] what I desire and **achieve** *the* **purpose** for which I sent it.
Jer 2: 37 [G] has rejected those you trust; *you will* not *be* **helped** by them.
5: 28 [G] they do not plead the case of the fatherless *to* **win** it, they do
12: 1 [A] Why *does* the way of the wicked **prosper**? Why do all the
13: 7 [A] but now it was ruined and completely **useless** [+4202].
13: 10 [A] will be like this belt—completely **useless** [+4202]!
22: 30 [A] as if childless, a man *who will* not **prosper** in his lifetime,
22: 30 [A] for none of his offspring *will* **prosper**, none will sit on the
32: 5 [G] If you fight against the Babylonians, *you will* not **succeed**.' "
Eze 15: 4 [A] and chars the middle, *is it* then **useful** for anything?
16: 13 [A] olive oil. You became very beautiful and **rose** to be a queen.
17: 9 [A] *Will it* **thrive**? Will it not be uprooted and stripped of its
17: 10 [A] Even if it is transplanted, *will it* **thrive**? Will it not wither
17: 15 [A] to Egypt to get horses and a large army. *Will he* **succeed**?
Da 8: 12 [G] *It* **prospered** in everything it did, and truth was thrown to the
8: 24 [G] astounding devastation and *will* **succeed** in whatever he does.
8: 25 [G] He *will* cause deceit *to* **prosper**, and he will consider himself
11: 27 [A] sit at the same table and lie to each other, but *to* no **avail**,
11: 36 [G] *He will be* **successful** until the time of wrath is completed,

7504 צְלֹחִית *ṣᵉlōḥît*, n.f. [1] [√ 7505]

bowl [1]

2Ki 2: 20 "Bring me a new **bowl**," he said, "and put salt in it." So they

7505 צַלַּחַת *ṣallaḥat*, n.[f.]. [4] [→ 7504, 7506]

dish [3], pans [1]

2Ki 21: 13 I will wipe out Jerusalem as one wipes a **dish**, wiping it
2Ch 35: 13 caldrons and **pans** and served them quickly to all the people.
Pr 19: 24 The sluggard buries his hand in the **dish**; he will not even bring it
26: 15 The sluggard buries his hand in the **dish**; he is too lazy to bring it

7506 צֵלָחַת *ṣēlaḥat*, n.[f.]. Not used in NIV/BHS [√ 7505]

7507 צָלִי *ṣālî*, a. [3] [√ 7499]

meat [1], roast [1], roasted [1]

Ex 12: 8 That same night they are to eat the meat **roasted** *over* the fire,
12: 9 not eat the meat raw or cooked in water, but **roast** it *over* the fire—
Isa 44: 16 over it he prepares his meal, he roasts his **meat** and eats his fill.

7508 צְלִיל *ṣᵉlîl*, n.m. [0] [cf. 7501]

Jdg 7: 13 ["A **round** [Q; see K 7501] **loaf** *of* barley bread came tumbling]

7509 ¹צָלַל *ṣālal¹*, v. [4] [→ 5197, 5199, 7526, 7527, 7528?, 7529]

tingle [2], make tingle [1], quivered [1]

1Sa 3: 11 [A] that *will make* the ears of everyone who hears of it **tingle**.
2Ki 21: 12 [A] Judah that the ears of everyone who hears of it *will* **tingle**.
Jer 19: 3 [A] that *will* **make** the ears of everyone who hears of it **tingle**.
Hab 3: 16 [A] and my heart pounded, my lips **quivered** at the sound;

7510 ²צָלַל *ṣālal²*, v. [1] [cf. 7425]

sank [1]

Ex 15: 10 [A] sea covered them. *They* **sank** like lead in the mighty waters.

7511 ³צָלַל *ṣālal³*, v. [2] [→ 1295, 2209, 7498, 7500, 7516, 7524; cf. 3233; Ar 10300]

evening shadows fell [1], overshadowing [1]

Ne 13: 19 [A] When **evening shadows fell** *on* the gates of Jerusalem before
Eze 31: 3 [G] with beautiful branches **overshadowing** the forest;

7512 ¹צֶלֶם *ṣelem¹*, n.m. [15] [→ 7513, 7514?; Ar 10614]

idols [6], image [5], models [2], *untranslated* [1], figures [1]

Ge 1: 26 Then God said, "Let us make man in our **image**, in our likeness,
1: 27 So God created man in his own **image**, in the image of God he
1: 27 created man in his own image, in the **image** *of* God he created him;
5: 3 130 years, he had a son in his own likeness, in his own **image**;
9: 6 his blood be shed; for in the **image** *of* God has God made man.
Nu 33: 52 Destroy all their carved images and their cast **idols**, and demolish
1Sa 6: 5 Make **models** *of* the tumors and of the rats that are destroying the
6: 5 the tumors and **[RPH]** of the rats that are destroying the country,
6: 11 it the chest containing the gold rats and the **models** *of* the tumors.
2Ki 11: 18 They smashed the altars and **idols** to pieces and killed Mattan the
2Ch 23: 17 They smashed the altars and **idols** and killed Mattan the priest of
Eze 7: 20 and used it to make their detestable **idols** and vile images.
16: 17 you made for yourself male **idols** and engaged in prostitution with
23: 14 men portrayed on a wall, **figures** *of* Chaldeans portrayed in red,
Am 5: 26 of your king, the pedestal of your **idols**, the star of your god—

7513 ²צֶלֶם *ṣelem²*, n.m. [2] [√ 7512]

fantasies [1], phantom [1]

Ps 39: 6 [39:7] Man is a mere **phantom** as he goes to and fro: He bustles
73: 20 so when you arise, O Lord, you will despise them as **fantasies**.

7514 ¹צַלְמוֹן *ṣalmôn¹*, n.pr.m. [1] [√ 7512?]

Zalmon [1]

2Sa 23: 28 **Zalmon** the Ahohite, Maharai the Netophathite,

7515 ²צַלְמוֹן *ṣalmôn²*, n.pr.loc. [2]

Zalmon [2]

Jdg 9: 48 he and all his men went up Mount **Zalmon**. He took an ax
Ps 68: 14 [68:15] the kings in the land, it was like snow fallen on **Zalmon**.

7516 צַלְמָוֶת *ṣalmāwet*, n.[m.]. [18] [√ 7498 + 4637]

deep shadow [4], shadow of death [3], darkness [2], deep darkness [2], deep shadows [2], deepest gloom [2], blackest [1], blackness [1], thick darkness [1]

Job 3: 5 May darkness and **deep shadow** claim it once more; may a cloud
10: 21 to the place of no return, to the land of gloom and **deep shadow**,
10: 22 to the land of deepest night, of **deep shadow** and disorder,
12: 22 deep things of darkness and brings **deep shadows** into the light.
16: 16 My face is red with weeping, **deep shadows** ring my eyes;
24: 17 For all of them, **deep darkness** is their morning; they make friends
24: 17 is their morning; they make friends with the terrors of **darkness**.
28: 3 he searches the farthest recesses for ore in the **blackest** darkness.
34: 22 There is no dark place, no **deep shadow**, where evildoers can hide.
38: 17 shown to you? Have you seen the gates of the **shadow of death**?
Ps 23: 4 Even though I walk through the valley of the **shadow of death**,
44: 19 [44:20] for jackals and covered us over with **deep darkness**.
107: 10 Some sat in darkness and the **deepest gloom**, prisoners suffering in
107: 14 of darkness and the **deepest gloom** and broke away their chains.
Isa 9: 2 [9:1] on those living in the land of the **shadow of death** a light
Jer 2: 6 through a land of deserts and rifts, a land of drought and **darkness**,
13: 16 but he will turn it to **thick darkness** and change it to deep gloom.
Am 5: 8 who turns **blackness** into dawn and darkens day into night,

7517 צַלְמֹנָה *ṣalmōnâ*, n.pr.loc. [2]

Zalmonah [2]

Nu 33: 41 They left Mount Hor and camped at **Zalmonah**.
33: 42 They left **Zalmonah** and camped at Punon.

7518 צַלְמֻנָּע *ṣalmunnā'*, n.pr.m. [12]

Zalmunna [10], them[s] [+2256+2286] [2]

Jdg 8: 5 they are worn out, and I am still pursuing Zebah and **Zalmunna**,
8: 6 have the hands of Zebah and **Zalmunna** in your possession?
8: 7 when the LORD has given Zebah and **Zalmunna** into my hand,
8: 10 **Zalmunna** were in Karkor with a force of about fifteen thousand
8: 12 Zebah and **Zalmunna**, the two kings of Midian, fled, but he

Jdg 8:12 fled, but he pursued them and captured **them**[s] [+2256+2286],
8:15 and said to the men of Succoth, "Here are Zebah and **Zalmunna**,
8:15 have the hands of Zebah and **Zalmunna** in your possession?
8:18 he asked Zebah and **Zalmunna**, "What kind of men did you kill at
8:21 Zebah and **Zalmunna** said, "Come, do it yourself. 'As is the man,
8:21 So Gideon stepped forward and killed **them**[s] [+2256+2286],
Ps 83:11 [83:12] and Zeeb, all their princes like Zebah and **Zalmunna**,

7519 צָלַע ṣāla', v. [4] [→ 7520]

lame [3], limping [1]

Ge 32:31 [32:32] [A] and he *was* **limping** because of his hip.
Mic 4:6 [A] "In that day," declares the LORD, "I will gather the **lame**;
4:7 [A] I will make the **lame** a remnant, those driven away a strong
Zep 3:19 [A] I will rescue the **lame** and gather those who have been

7520 צֶלַע ṣela', n.[m.]. [4] [√ 7519]

fall [1], falls [1], slip [1], stumbled [1]

Job 18:12 Calamity is hungry for him; disaster is ready for him when he **falls**.
Ps 35:15 when I **stumbled**, they gathered in glee; attackers gathered against
38:17 [38:18] For I am about to **fall**, and my pain is ever with me.
Jer 20:10 All my friends are waiting for me to **slip**, saying, "Perhaps he will

7521 צֵלָע¹ ṣēlā'¹, n.f. & m. [40 / 41] [→ 7522; Ar 10552]

side [10], side rooms [9], *untranslated* [4], sides [4], boards [2], opposite sides [+7396] [2], another[s] [1], beams [1], floor [1], hillside [+2215] [1], leaves [1], one[s] [1], planks [1], rib [1], ribs [1], side room [1]

Ge 2:21 he took one of the man's **ribs** and closed up the place with flesh.
2:22 the LORD God made a woman from the **rib** he had taken out of
Ex 25:12 its four feet, with two rings on one **side** and two rings on the other.
25:12 with two rings on one side and two rings on the other. **[RPH]**
25:14 Insert the poles into the rings on the **sides** *of* the chest to carry it.
26:20 For the other **side**, the north side of the tabernacle, make twenty
26:26 of acacia wood: five for the frames on one **side** *of* the tabernacle,
26:27 five for those on the other **side**, and five for the frames on the west,
26:27 five for the frames **[RPH]** on the west, at the far end of the
26:35 Place the table outside the curtain on the north **side** *of* the
26:35 the tabernacle and put the lampstand opposite it on the south **side**.
27:7 so they will be on two **sides** *of* the altar when it is carried.
30:4 two on **opposite sides** [+7396]—to hold the poles used to carry it.
36:25 For the other **side**, the north side of the tabernacle, they made
36:31 of acacia wood: five for the frames on one **side** *of* the tabernacle,
36:32 five for those on the other **side**, and five for the frames on the west,
37:3 its four feet, with two rings on one **side** and two rings on the other.
37:3 with two rings on one side and two rings on the other. **[RPH]**
37:5 he inserted the poles into the rings on the **sides** *of* the ark to carry
37:27 two on **opposite sides** [+7396]—to hold the poles used to carry it.
38:7 the rings so they would be on the **sides** *of* the altar for carrying it.
2Sa 16:13 while Shimei was going along the **hillside** [+2215] opposite him,
1Ki 6:5 a structure around the building, in which there were **side rooms**.
6:8 The entrance to the lowest **floor** was on the south side of the
6:15 He lined its interior walls with cedar **boards**, paneling them from
6:15 and covered the floor of the temple with **planks** *of* pine.
6:16 **boards** from floor to ceiling to form within the temple an inner
6:34 two pine doors, each having two **leaves** that turned in sockets.
6:34 each having two leaves that turned in sockets. [RPH; BHS 7846]
7:3 It was roofed with cedar above the **beams** that rested on the
Eze 41:5 and each **side room** around the temple was four cubits wide.
41:6 The **side rooms** were on three levels, one above another, thirty on
41:6 were on three levels, **one**[s] above another, thirty on each level.
41:6 were on three levels, one above **another**[s], thirty on each level.
41:6 the wall of the temple to serve as supports for the **side rooms**,
41:7 The **side rooms** all around the temple were wider at each
41:8 raised base all around it, forming the foundation of the **side rooms**.
41:9 The outer wall of the **side rooms** was five cubits thick. The open
41:9 cubits thick. The open area between the **side rooms** of the temple
41:11 There were entrances to the **side rooms** from the open area,
41:26 on each side. The **side rooms** *of* the temple also had overhangs.

7522 ²צֵלָע ṣēlā'², n.pr.loc. [2] [√ 7521]

Zela [1], Zelah [1]

Jos 18:28 **Zelah**, Haeleph, the Jebusite city (that is, Jerusalem), Gibeah
2Sa 21:14 at **Zela** in Benjamin, and did everything the king commanded.

7523 צָלָף ṣālāp, n.pr.m. [1]

Zalaph [1]

Ne 3:30 and Hanun, the sixth son of **Zalaph**, repaired another section.

7524 צְלָפְחָד ṣᵉlopḥād, n.pr.m. [11] [√ 7498 + 7065]

Zelophehad [5], Zelophehad's [4], who[s] [1], whose[s] [+1426] [1]

Nu 26:33 (**Zelophehad** son of Hepher had no sons; he had only daughters,
26:33 **whose**[s] [+1426] names were Mahlah, Noah, Hoglah, Milcah
27:1 The daughters of **Zelophehad** son of Hepher, the son of Gilead,
27:7 "What **Zelophehad's** daughters are saying is right. You must
36:2 he ordered you to give the inheritance of our brother **Zelophehad**
36:6 This is what the LORD commands for **Zelophehad's** daughters:
36:10 So **Zelophehad's** daughters did as the LORD commanded Moses.
36:11 **Zelophehad's** daughters—Mahlah, Tirzah, Hoglah, Milcah
Jos 17:3 Now **Zelophehad** son of Hepher, the son of Gilead, the son of
1Ch 7:15 Another descendant was named **Zelophehad**, who had only
7:15 descendant was named Zelophehad, **who**[s] had only daughters.

7525 צֶלְצַח ṣelṣaḥ, n.pr.loc. [1]

Zelzah [1]

1Sa 10:2 two men near Rachel's tomb, at **Zelzah** on the border of Benjamin.

7526 צְלָצַל ṣᵉlāṣal, n.m. [1] [√ 7509]

swarms of locusts [1]

Dt 28:42 **Swarms of locusts** will take over all your trees and the crops of

7527 צִלְצַל¹ ṣilṣāl¹, n.[m.]. [1] [√ 7509]

whirring [1]

Isa 18:1 Woe to the land of **whirring** wings along the rivers of Cush,

7528 ²צִלְצַל ṣilṣāl², n.[m.]. [1] [√ 7509?]

spears [1]

Job 41:7 [40:31] his hide with harpoons or his head with fishing **spears**?

7529 צֶלְצְלִים ṣelṣelîm, n.m.pl. [3] [√ 7509]

cymbals [3]

2Sa 6:5 and with harps, lyres, tambourines, sistrums and **cymbals**.
Ps 150:5 praise him with the clash of **cymbals**, praise him with resounding
150:5 with the clash of cymbals, praise him with resounding **cymbals**.

7530 צֶלֶק ṣeleq, n.pr.m. [2]

Zelek [2]

2Sa 23:37 **Zelek** the Ammonite, Naharai the Beerothite, the armor-bearer of
1Ch 11:39 **Zelek** the Ammonite, Naharai the Berothite, the armor-bearer of

7531 צִלְּתַי ṣillᵉtay, n.pr.m. [2]

Zillethai [2]

1Ch 8:20 Elienai, **Zillethai**, Eliel,
12:20 [12:21] Jediael, Michael, Jozabad, Elihu and **Zillethai**,

7532 צָמֵא¹ ṣāmē'¹, v. [10] [→ 7533, 7534, 7535, 7536]

thirsty [5], thirst [2], thirsts [2], suffer thirst [1]

Ex 17:3 [A] the people *were* **thirsty** for water there, and they grumbled
Jdg 4:19 [A] "*I'm* **thirsty**," he said. "Please give me some water." She
15:18 [A] Because *he was* very **thirsty**, he cried out to the LORD,
Ru 2:9 [A] *whenever you are* **thirsty**, go and get a drink from the water
Job 24:11 [A] the terraces; they tread the winepresses, yet **suffer thirst**.
Ps 42:2 [42:3] [A] My soul **thirsts** for God, for the living God.
63:1 [63:2] [A] my soul **thirsts** for you, my body longs for you, in a
Isa 48:21 [A] *They did* not **thirst** when he led them through the deserts;
49:10 [A] They will neither hunger nor **thirst**, nor will the desert heat
65:13 [A] go hungry; my servants will drink, but you *will go* **thirsty**;

7533 צָמָא ṣāmā', n.[m.]. [17] [√ 7532]

thirst [15], parched ground [1], thirsty [1]

Ex 17:3 of Egypt to make us and our children and livestock die of **thirst**?"
Dt 28:48 therefore in hunger and **thirst**, in nakedness and dire poverty,
Jdg 15:18 Must I now die of **thirst** and fall into the hands of the
2Ch 32:11 he is misleading you, to let you die of hunger and **thirst**.
Ne 9:15 and in their **thirst** you brought them water from the rock;
9:20 manna from their mouths, and you gave them water for their **thirst**.
Ps 69:21 [69:22] put gall in my food and gave me vinegar for my **thirst**.
104:11 to all the beasts of the field; the wild donkeys quench their **thirst**.
Isa 5:13 will die of hunger and their masses will be parched with **thirst**.
41:17 for water, but there is none; their tongues are parched with **thirst**.
50:2 rivers into a desert; their fish rot for lack of water and die of **thirst**.
Jer 48:18 "Come down from your glory and sit on the **parched ground**,
La 4:4 Because of **thirst** the infant's tongue sticks to the roof of its
Eze 19:13 Now it is planted in the desert, in a dry and **thirsty** land.
Hos 2:3 [2:5] turn her into a parched land, and slay her with **thirst**.

Am 8:11 not a famine of food or a **thirst** for water, but a famine of hearing
8:13 young women and strong young men will faint because of **thirst**.

7534 ²צָמֵא ṣāmēʾ², a. [10] [√ 7532]
thirsty [9], dry [1]

Dt 29:19 [29:18] will bring disaster on the watered land as well as the **dry**.
2Sa 17:29 people have become hungry and tired and **thirsty** in the desert."
Job 5:5 it even from among thorns, and the **thirsty** pant after his wealth.
Ps 107:5 They were hungry and **thirsty**, and their lives ebbed away.
Pr 25:21 give him food to eat; if he is **thirsty**, give him water to drink.
Isa 21:14 bring water for the **thirsty**; you who live in Tema, bring food for
29:8 as when a **thirsty** *man* dreams that he is drinking, but he awakens
32:6 hungry he leaves empty and from the **thirsty** he withholds water.
44:3 For I will pour water on the **thirsty** land, and streams on the dry
55:1 "Come, all you *who* are **thirsty**, come to the waters; and you who

7535 צִמְאָה ṣimʾâ, n.f. [1] [√ 7532]
dry [1]

Jer 2:25 Do not run until your feet are bare and your throat is **dry**. But you

7536 צִמָּאוֹן ṣimmāʾôn, n.[m.]. [3] [√ 7532]
thirsty ground [2], thirsty [1]

Dt 8:15 the vast and dreadful desert, that **thirsty** and waterless land,
Ps 107:33 He turned rivers into a desert, flowing springs into **thirsty ground**,
Isa 35:7 sand will become a pool, the **thirsty ground** bubbling springs.

7537 צָמַד ṣāmad, v. [5] [→ 7538, 7543, 7544]
joined in worshiping [2], harness [1], strapped [1], yoked themselves [1]

Nu 25:3 [C] So Israel **joined in worshiping** the Baal of Peor.
25:5 [C] *those of* your men who *have* **joined in worshiping** the Baal
2Sa 20:8 [E] **strapped** over it at his waist was a belt with a dagger in its
Ps 50:19 [G] use your mouth for evil and **harness** your tongue to deceit.
106:28 [C] *They* **yoked themselves** to the Baal of Peor and ate sacrifices

7538 צֶמֶד ṣemed, n.m. [15] [√ 7537]
yoke [3], pair [2], two [2], acre [+5103] [1], oxen [1], string [1], team [1], teams [1], ten-acre [+6930] [1], together [1], yoke of oxen [1]

Jdg 19:3 He had with him his servant and **two** donkeys. She took him into
19:10 Jerusalem), with his **two** saddled donkeys and his concubine.
1Sa 11:7 He took a **pair** *of* oxen, cut them into pieces, and sent the pieces by
14:14 killed some twenty men in an area of about half an **acre** [+5103].
2Sa 16:1 He had a **string** *of* donkeys saddled and loaded with two hundred
1Ki 19:19 He was plowing with twelve **yoke of oxen**, and he himself was
19:21 and went back. He took his **yoke** *of* oxen and slaughtered them.
2Ki 5:17 your servant, be given as much earth as a **pair** *of* mules can carry,
9:25 I were riding **together** in chariots behind Ahab his father when the
Job 1:3 five hundred **yoke** *of* oxen and five hundred donkeys,
42:12 a thousand **yoke** *of* oxen and a thousand donkeys.
Isa 5:10 A **ten-acre** [+6930] vineyard will produce only a bath of wine,
21:7 When he sees chariots with **teams** *of* horses, riders on donkeys
21:9 Look, here comes a man in a chariot with a **team** *of* horses.
Jer 51:23 I shatter shepherd and flock, with you I shatter farmer and **oxen**,

7539 צַמָּה ṣammâ, n.f. [4]
veil [4]

SS 4:1 Oh, how beautiful! Your eyes behind your **veil** are doves.
4:3 Your temples behind your **veil** are like the halves of a
6:7 Your temples behind your **veil** are like the halves of a
Isa 47:2 Take millstones and grind flour; take off your **veil**. Lift up your

7540 צִמּוּקִים ṣimmûqîm, n.m.[pl.]. [4] [√ 7546]
cakes of raisins [3], raisin cakes [1]

1Sa 25:18 a hundred **cakes of raisins** and two hundred cakes of pressed figs,
30:12 part of a cake of pressed figs and two **cakes of raisins**. He ate
2Sa 16:1 a hundred **cakes of raisins**, a hundred cakes of figs and a skin of
1Ch 12:40 [12:41] fig cakes, **raisin cakes**, wine, oil, cattle and sheep,

7541 צָמַח ṣāmaḥ, v. [33] [→ 7542]
grow [3], grown [3], sprouted [3], make grow [2], make sprout [2], makes grow [2], appear [1], branch out [1], bring to fruition [1], causes to grow [1], flourish [1], flourishing [1], grew [1], growing [1], made grow [1], make spring up [1], produce [1], spring into being [1], spring up [1], springs forth [1], springs up [1], sprout [1], sprouting [1], sprung up [1]

Ge 2:5 [A] on the earth and no plant of the field *had* yet **sprung up**,
2:9 [G] the LORD God **made** all kinds of trees **grow** out of the
3:18 [G] *It will* **produce** thorns and thistles for you, and you will eat
41:6 [A] After them, seven other heads of grain **sprouted**—thin
41:23 [A] After them, seven other heads **sprouted**—withered and thin
Ex 10:5 [A] the hail, including every tree that *is* **growing** in your fields.
Lev 13:37 [A] his judgment it is unchanged and black hair *has* **grown** in it,
Dt 29:23 [29:22] [G] nothing planted, nothing **sprouting**, no vegetation
Jdg 16:22 [D] the hair on his head began to **grow** again after it had been
2Sa 10:5 [D] "Stay at Jericho till your beards *have* **grown**, and then come
23:5 [G] *Will he* not **bring to fruition** my salvation and grant me my
1Ch 19:5 [D] "Stay at Jericho till your beards *have* **grown**, and then come
Job 5:6 [A] from the soil, nor *does* trouble **sprout** from the ground.
8:19 [A] its life withers away, and from the soil other plants **grow**.
38:27 [G] satisfy a desolate wasteland and **make it sprout** *with* grass?
Ps 85:11 [85:12] [A] Faithfulness **springs forth** from the earth,
104:14 [G] *He* **makes** grass **grow** for the cattle, and plants for man to
132:17 [G] "Here *I will* **make** a horn **grow** for David and set up a lamp
147:8 [G] the earth with rain and **makes** grass **grow** *on* the hills.
Ecc 2:6 [A] I made reservoirs to water groves of **flourishing** trees.
Isa 42:9 [A] before *they* **spring into being** I announce them to you."
43:19 [A] a new thing! Now *it* **springs up**; do you not perceive it?
44:4 [A] *They will* **spring up** like grass in a meadow, like poplar trees
45:8 [G] let salvation spring up, *let* righteousness **grow** with it;
55:10 [G] it without watering the earth and making it bud and **flourish**,
58:8 [A] forth like the dawn, and your healing *will* quickly **appear**;
61:11 [G] the sprout come up and a garden **causes** seeds **to grow**,
61:11 [G] LORD *will* **make** righteousness and praise **spring up**
Jer 33:15 [G] at that time *I will* **make** a righteous Branch **sprout** from
Eze 16:7 [D] Your breasts were formed and your hair **grew**, you who were
17:6 [A] *it* **sprouted** and became a low, spreading vine. Its branches
29:21 [G] "On that day *I will* **make** a horn **grow** for the house of Israel,
Zec 6:12 [A] *he will* **branch out** from his place and build the temple of

7542 צֶמַח ṣemaḥ, n.m. [12] [√ 7541]
branch [5], crops [1], grew [1], growth [1], head [1], plant [1], sprout [1], vegetation [1]

Ge 19:25 all those living in the cities—and also the **vegetation** *in* the land.
Ps 65:10 [65:11] its ridges; you soften it with showers and bless its **crops**.
Isa 4:2 In that day the **Branch** *of* the LORD will be beautiful
61:11 For as the soil makes the **sprout** come up and a garden causes
Jer 23:5 the LORD, "when I will raise up to David a righteous **Branch**,
33:15 at that time I will make a righteous **Branch** sprout from David's
Eze 16:7 I made you grow like a **plant** *of* the field. You grew up
17:9 of its fruit so that it withers? All its new **growth** will wither.
17:10 the east wind strikes it—wither away in the plot where it **grew**?' "
Hos 8:7 The stalk has no **head**; it will produce no flour. Were it to yield
Zec 3:8 of things to come: I am going to bring my servant, the **Branch**.
6:12 'Here is the man whose name is the **Branch**, and he will branch out

7543 ¹צָמִיד ṣāmîd¹, n.m. [6] [√ 7537]
bracelets [5], bracelets [+3338+6584] [1]

Ge 24:22 and two gold **bracelets** [+3338+6584] weighing ten shekels.
24:30 as he had seen the nose ring, and the **bracelets** on his sister's arms,
24:47 "Then I put the ring in her nose and the **bracelets** on her arms,
Nu 31:50 armlets, **bracelets**, signet rings, earrings and necklaces—to make
Eze 16:11 I put **bracelets** on your arms and a necklace around your neck,
23:42 and they put **bracelets** on the arms of the woman and her sister

7544 ²צָמִיד ṣāmîd², n.[m.]. [1] [√ 7537]
lid [1]

Nu 19:15 every open container without a **lid** fastened on it will be unclean.

7545 צַמִּים ṣammîm, n.m. [1]
snare [1]

Job 18:9 A trap seizes him by the heel; a **snare** holds him fast.

7546 צָמַק ṣāmaq, v. [1] [→ 7540]
dry [1]

Hos 9:14 [A] Give them wombs that miscarry and breasts *that are* **dry**.

7547 צֶמֶר ṣemer, n.m. [16] [→ 7549, 7550; Ar 10556]
wool [13], woolen [2], woolen garment [1]

Lev 13:47 is contaminated with mildew—any **woolen** or linen clothing,
13:48 any woven or knitted material of linen or **wool**, any leather
13:52 up the clothing, or the woven or knitted material of **wool** or linen,
13:59 are the regulations concerning contamination by mildew in **woolen**
Dt 22:11 Do not wear clothes of **wool** and linen woven together.
Jdg 6:37 look, I will place a **wool** fleece on the threshing floor. If there is
2Ki 3:4 thousand lambs and with the **wool** of a hundred thousand rams.
Ps 147:16 He spreads the snow like **wool** and scatters the frost like ashes.
Pr 31:13 She selects **wool** and flax and works with eager hands.

Isa 1:18 as snow; though they are red as crimson, they shall be like **wool**.
51: 8 eat them up like a garment; the worm will devour them like **wool**.
Eze 27:18 did business with you in wine from Helbon and **wool** *from* Zahar.
34: 3 clothe yourselves with the **wool** and slaughter the choice animals,
44:17 they must not wear any **woolen garment** while ministering at the
Hos 2: 5 [2:7] and my water, my **wool** and my linen, my oil and my drink.'
2: 9 [2:11] I will take back my **wool** and my linen, intended to cover

7548 צְמָרִי ṣ^emārî, a.g. [2]

Zemarites [2]

Ge 10:18 Arvadites, **Zemarites** and Hamathites. Later the Canaanite clans
1Ch 1:16 Arvadites, **Zemarites** and Hamathites.

7549 צְמָרַיִם ṣ^emārayim, n.pr.loc. [2] [√ 7547]

Zemaraim [2]

Jos 18:22 Beth Arabah, **Zemaraim**, Bethel,
2Ch 13: 4 Abijah stood on Mount **Zemaraim**, in the hill country of Ephraim,

7550 צַמֶּרֶת ṣammeret, n.f. [5] [√ 7547]

top [3], shoot [1], tops [1]

Eze 17: 3 varied colors came to Lebanon. Taking hold of the **top** *of* a cedar,
17:22 I myself will take a **shoot** from the very top *of* a cedar and plant it;
31: 3 the forest; it towered on high, its **top** above the thick foliage.
31:10 lifting its **top** above the thick foliage, and because it was proud of
31:14 to tower proudly on high, lifting their **tops** above the thick foliage.

7551 צָמַת ṣāmat, v. [15] [→ 7552]

destroy [4], destroyed [3], put to silence [2], cease to flow [1], end [1], seek to destroy [1], silence [1], silenced [1], wears out [1]

2Sa 22:41 [G] enemies turn their backs in flight, and *I* **destroyed** my foes.
Job 6:17 [C] that **cease to flow** in the dry season, and in the heat vanish
23:17 [C] Yet *I am* not **silenced** by the darkness, by the thick darkness
Ps 18:40 [18:41] [G] turn their backs in flight, and *I* **destroyed** my foes.
54: 5 [54:7] [G] who slander me; in your faithfulness **destroy** them.
69: 4 [69:5] [G] without cause, *those who* **seek to destroy** me.
73:27 [G] you will perish; *you* **destroy** all who are unfaithful to you.
88:16 [88:17] [D] has swept over me; your terrors *have* **destroyed** me.
94:23 [G] for their sins and **destroy** them for their wickedness;
94:23 [G] for their wickedness; the LORD our God *will* **destroy** them.
101: 5 [G] slanders his neighbor in secret, him *will I* **put to silence**;
101: 8 [G] Every morning *I will* **put to silence** all the wicked in the
119:139 [D] My zeal **wears** me **out**, for my enemies ignore your words.
143:12 [G] In your unfailing love, **silence** my enemies; destroy all my
La 3:53 [A] *They tried to* **end** my life in a pit and threw stones at me;

7552 צְמִתֻת ṣ^emitut, n.f. [2] [√ 7551]

permanently [+2021+4200] [1], permanently [+4200] [1]

Lev 25:23 " 'The land must not be sold **permanently** [+4200],
25:30 shall belong **permanently** [+2021+4200] to the buyer and his

7553 צֵן ṣēn, n.[m.]. [3] [→ 7559, 7564]

thorns [2], hooks [1]

Job 5: 5 hungry consume his harvest, taking it even from among **thorns**,
Pr 22: 5 In the paths of the wicked lie **thorns** and snares, but he who guards
Am 4: 2 time will surely come when you will be taken away with **hooks**,

7554 צִן ṣin, n.pr.loc. [10]

Zin [10]

Nu 13:21 and explored the land from the Desert of **Zin** as far as Rehob,
20: 1 month the whole Israelite community arrived at the Desert of **Zin**,
27:14 when the community rebelled at the waters in the Desert of **Zin**,
27:14 (These were the waters of Meribah Kadesh, in the Desert of **Zin**.)
33:36 They left Ezion Geber and camped at Kadesh, in the Desert of **Zin**.
34: 3 " 'Your southern side will include some of the Desert of **Zin** along
34: 4 Scorpion Pass, continue on to **Zin** and go south of Kadesh Barnea.
Dt 32:51 the Israelites at the waters of Meribah Kadesh in the Desert of **Zin**
Jos 15: 1 to the territory of Edom, to the Desert of **Zin** in the extreme south.
15: 3 continued on to **Zin** and went over to the south of Kadesh Barnea.

7555 צֹנֶא ṣōnāʾ, [n.m.]. Not used in NIV/BHS [√ 7366]

7556 צֹנֶה ṣōneh, [n.m.]. [1] [√ 7366; cf. 3655]

flocks [1]

Ps 8: 7 [8:8] all **flocks** and herds, and the beasts of the field,

7557 צִנָּה ṣinnâ¹, n.f. [1]

coolness [1]

Pr 25:13 Like the **coolness** *of* snow at harvest time is a trustworthy

7558 צִנָּה ṣinnâ², n.f. [20]

shield [9], large shields [7], shields [3], buckler [1]

1Sa 17: 7 weighed six hundred shekels. His **shield** bearer went ahead of him.
17:41 Meanwhile, the Philistine, with his **shield** bearer in front of him,
1Ki 10:16 King Solomon made two hundred **large shields** of hammered gold;
10:16 hammered gold; six hundred bekas of gold went into each **shield**.
1Ch 12: 8 [12:9] ready for battle and able to handle the **shield** and spear.
12:24 [12:25] men of Judah, carrying **shield** and spear—6,800 armed
12:34 [12:35] together with 37,000 men carrying **shields** and spears;
2Ch 9:15 King Solomon made two hundred **large shields** of hammered gold;
9:15 six hundred bekas of hammered gold went into each **shield**.
11:12 He put **shields** and spears in all the cities, and made them very
14: 8 [14:7] equipped with **large shields** and with spears, and two
25: 5 men ready for military service, able to handle the spear and **shield**.
Ps 5:12 [5:13] you surround them with your favor as with a **shield**.
35: 2 Take up shield and **buckler**; arise and come to my aid.
91: 4 will find refuge; his faithfulness will be your **shield** and rampart.
Jer 46: 3 "Prepare your **shields**, both **large** and small, and march out for
Eze 23:24 positions against you on every side with **large** and small **shields**
26: 8 build a ramp up to your walls and raise his **shields** against you.
38: 4 fully armed, and a great horde with **large** and small **shields**,
39: 9 the small and **large shields**, the bows and arrows, the war clubs

7559 צִנָּה ṣinnâ³, n.f. Not used in NIV/BHS [√ 7553]

7560 צָנוּעַ ṣānûaʿ, a. [1] [√ 7570]

humility [1]

Pr 11: 2 then comes disgrace, but with **humility** comes wisdom.

7561 צָנוּף ṣānûp, n.m. Not used in NIV/BHS [√ 7571; cf. 7565]

7562 צִנּוֹר ṣinnôr, n.m. [2] [→ 7574]

water shaft [1], waterfalls [1]

2Sa 5: 8 the Jebusites will have to use the **water shaft** to reach those 'lame
Ps 42: 7 [42:8] Deep calls to deep in the roar of your **waterfalls**; all your

7563 צָנַח ṣānaḥ, v. [3]

got off [+4946+6584] [2], *untranslated* [1]

Jos 15:18 [A] When *she* **got off** [+4946+6584] her donkey, Caleb asked
Jdg 1:14 [A] When *she* **got off** [+4946+6584] her donkey, Caleb asked
4:21 [A] She drove the peg through his temple **[RPH]** into the

7564 צְנִינִים ṣ^eninîm, n.[m.pl.]. [2] [√ 7553]

thorns [2]

Nu 33:55 to remain will become barbs in your eyes and **thorns** in your sides.
Jos 23:13 and traps for you, whips on your backs and **thorns** in your eyes,

7565 צָנִיף ṣānîp, n.m. [4] [→ 7566; cf. 7561, 7571]

turban [3], diadem [1]

Job 29:14 righteousness as my clothing; justice was my robe and my **turban**.
Isa 62: 3 in the LORD's hand, a royal **diadem** in the hand of your God.
Zec 3: 5 I said, "Put a clean **turban** on his head." So they put a clean turban
3: 5 So they put a clean **turban** on his head and clothed him,

7566 צְנִיפָה ṣ^enîpâ, n.m. [1] [√ 7565; cf. 7571]

tiaras [1]

Isa 3:23 and mirrors, and the linen garments and **tiaras** and shawls.

7567 צָנַם ṣānam, v. Not used in NIV/BHS [→ 7568]

7568 צָנֻם ṣānum, a. *or* v.ptcp. [1] [√ 7567]

withered [1]

Ge 41:23 heads sprouted—**withered** and thin and scorched by the east wind.

7569 צְנָן ṣ^enān, n.pr.loc. [1] [cf. 7367?]

Zenan [1]

Jos 15:37 **Zenan**, Hadashah, Migdal Gad,

7570 צָנַע ṣānaʿ, v. [1] [→ 5760]

humbly [1]

Mic 6: 8 [G] and to love mercy and to walk **humbly** with your God.

7571 צָנַף *ṣānap*, v. [3] [→ 5200, 7561, 7565, 7566, 7572]
roll up tightly [+7571+7572] [2], put on [1]

Lev 16: 4 [A] to tie the linen sash around him and **put on** the linen turban.
Isa 22: 18 [A] *He will* **roll** [+7571+7572] you **up tightly** like a ball
22: 18 [A] *He will* **roll** you **up tightly** [+7571+7572] like a ball

7572 צְנֵפָה *ṣ^{e}nēpâ*, n.f. [1] [√ 7571]
roll up tightly [+7571+7571] [1]

Isa 22: 18 *He will* **roll** you **up tightly** [+7571+7571] like a ball and throw

7573 צִנְצֶנֶת *ṣinṣenet*, n.f. [1]
jar [1]

Ex 16: 33 Moses said to Aaron, "Take a **jar** and put an omer of manna in it.

7574 צַנְתָּרוֹת *ṣantārôt*, n.m.pl. [1] [√ 7562]
pipes [1]

Zec 4: 12 "What are these two olive branches beside the two gold **pipes** that

7575 צָעַד *ṣāʿad*, v. [8] [→ 731, 5202, 7576, 7577, 7578]
marched [2], climb [1], marched off [1], strode through [1], taken steps [+7576] [1], walk [1], walking along [1]

Ge 49: 22 [A] fruitful vine near a spring, whose branches **climb** over a wall.
Jdg 5: 4 [A] when you **marched** from the land of Edom, the earth shook,
2Sa 6: 13 [A] carrying the ark of the LORD *had* **taken** six **steps** [+7576],
Job 18: 14 [G] security of his tent and **marched off** to the king of terrors.
Ps 68: 7 [68:8] [A] O God, when you **marched** through the wasteland,
Pr 7: 8 [A] near her corner, **walking along** *in* the direction of her house
Jer 10: 5 [A] they must be carried because *they* cannot **walk**.
Hab 3: 12 [A] In wrath *you* **strode through** the earth and in anger you

7576 צַעַד *ṣaʿad*, n.m. [14] [√ 7575]
step [5], steps [5], path [2], stride [1], taken steps [+7575] [1]

2Sa 6: 13 were carrying the ark of the LORD *had* **taken** six **steps** [+7575],
22: 37 You broaden the **path** beneath me, so that my ankles do not turn.
Job 14: 16 Surely then you will count my **steps** but not keep track of my sin.
18: 7 The vigor of his **step** is weakened; his own schemes throw him
31: 4 Does he not see my ways and count my every **step**?
31: 37 I would give him an account of my *every* **step**; like a prince I
34: 21 "His eyes are on the ways of men; he sees their every **step**.
Ps 18: 36 [18:37] You broaden the **path** beneath me, so that my ankles do
Pr 4: 12 When you walk, your **steps** will not be hampered; when you run,
5: 5 Her feet go down to death; her **steps** lead straight to the grave.
16: 9 heart a man plans his course, but the LORD determines his **steps**.
30: 29 "There are three things that are stately in their **stride**, four that
Jer 10: 23 that a man's life is not his own; it is not for man to direct his **steps**.
La 4: 18 Men stalked us at *every* **step**, so we could not walk in our streets.

7577 צְעָדָה *ṣ^{e}ʿādâ^{1}*, n.f. [2] [√ 7575]
marching [2]

2Sa 5: 24 As soon as you hear the sound of **marching** in the tops of the
1Ch 14: 15 As soon as you hear the sound of **marching** in the tops of the

7578 צְעָדָה *ṣ^{e}ʿādâ^{2}*, n.f. [1] [√ 7575]
ankle chains [1]

Isa 3: 20 the headdresses and **ankle chains** and sashes, the perfume bottles

7579 צָעָה *ṣāʿâ*, v. [5]
cowering prisoners [1], lay down [1], pour out [1], pour [1], striding forward [1]

Isa 51: 14 [A] The **cowering prisoners** will soon be set free; they will not
63: 1 [A] **striding forward** in the greatness of his strength?
Jer 2: 20 [A] and under every spreading tree you **lay down** as a prostitute.
48: 12 [A] the LORD, "when I will send *men who* **pour** from jars,
48: 12 [A] send men who pour from jars, and *they will* **pour** her **out**;

7580 צָעוֹר *ṣāʿôr*, a. [0] [√ 7592]

Jer 14: 3 [The nobles send their **servants** [K; see Q 7582] for water;]
48: 4 [Moab will be broken; her **little** [K; see Q 7582] *ones* will cry out.]

7581 צָעִיף *ṣāʿîp*, n.[m.]. [3]
veil [3]

Ge 24: 65 the servant answered. So she took her **veil** and covered herself.
38: 14 covered herself with a **veil** to disguise herself, and then sat down at
38: 19 she took off her **veil** and put on her widow's clothes again.

7582 צָעִיר *ṣāʿîr^{1}*, a. [23] [√ 7592; cf. 7580, 7584]
younger [7], young [3], youngest [3], least [2], little [2], small [2], lowly [1], servants [1], smallest [1], younger [+3427+4200] [1]

Ge 19: 31 One day the older daughter said to the **younger**, "Our father is old,
19: 34 The next day the older daughter said to the **younger**, "Last night I
19: 35 that night also, and the **younger** *daughter* went and lay with him.
19: 38 The **younger** *daughter* also had a son, and she named him
25: 23 be stronger than the other, and the older will serve the **younger**."
29: 26 "It is not our custom here to give the **younger** *daughter* in
43: 33 him in the order of their ages, from the firstborn to the **youngest**;
48: 14 though he was the **younger**, and crossing his arms,
Jos 6: 26 its foundations; at the cost of his **youngest** will he set up its gates."
Jdg 6: 15 clan is the weakest in Manasseh, and I am the **least** in my family."
1Sa 9: 21 is not my clan the **least** of all the clans of the tribe of Benjamin?
1Ki 16: 34 and he set up its gates at the cost of his **youngest** *son* Segub,
Job 30: 1 "But now they mock me, *men* **younger** [+3427+4200] than I,
32: 6 "I am **young** in years, and you are old; that is why I was fearful,
Ps 68: 27 [68:28] There is the **little** tribe of Benjamin, leading them,
119: 141 Though I am **lowly** and despised, I do not forget your precepts.
Isa 60: 22 least of you will become a thousand, the **smallest** a mighty nation.
Jer 14: 3 The nobles send their **servants** [K 7580] for water; they go to the
48: 4 Moab will be broken; her **little** [K 7580] *ones* will cry out.
49: 20 The **young** *of* the flock will be dragged away; he will completely
50: 45 The **young** *of* the flock will be dragged away; he will completely
Da 8: 9 which started **small** but grew in power to the south and to the east
Mic 5: 2 [5:1] though you are **small** among the clans of Judah,

7583 צָעִיר *ṣāʿîr^{2}*, n.pr.loc. [1]
Zair [1]

2Ki 8: 21 So Jehoram went to **Zair** with all his chariots. The Edomites

7584 צְעִירָה *ṣ^{e}ʿîrâ*, n.f. [1] [cf. 7582]
ages [+1148] [1]

Ge 43: 33 men had been seated before him in the order of their **ages** [+1148],

7585 צָעַן *ṣāʿan*, v. [1]
moved [1]

Isa 33: 20 [A] a peaceful abode, a tent *that will* not *be* **moved**;

7586 צֹעַן *ṣōʿan*, n.pr.loc. [7]
Zoan [7]

Nu 13: 22 (Hebron had been built seven years before **Zoan** *in* Egypt.)
Ps 78: 12 sight of their fathers in the land of Egypt, in the region of **Zoan**.
78: 43 his miraculous signs in Egypt, his wonders in the region of **Zoan**.
Isa 19: 11 The officials of **Zoan** are nothing but fools; the wise counselors of
19: 13 The officials of **Zoan** have become fools, the leaders of Memphis
30: 4 Though they have officials in **Zoan** and their envoys have arrived
Eze 30: 14 Upper Egypt, set fire to **Zoan** and inflict punishment on Thebes.

7587 צְעַנִּים *ṣ^{e}ʿannîm*, n.pr.loc. [0] [cf. 7588]

Jdg 4: 11 [pitched his tent by the great tree in **Zaanannim** [K; see Q 7588]]

7588 צַעֲנַנִּים *ṣaʿanannîm*, n.pr.loc. [2] [cf. 1300, 7587]
Zaanannim [2]

Jos 19: 33 boundary went from Heleph and the large tree in **Zaanannim**,
Jdg 4: 11 pitched his tent by the great tree in **Zaanannim** [K 7587] near

7589 צַעֲצֻעִים *ṣaʿaṣuʿîm*, n.[m.]pl. [1]
sculptured [+5126] [1]

2Ch 3: 10 In the Most Holy Place he made a pair of **sculptured** [+5126]

7590 צָעַק *ṣāʿaq*, v. [55] [→ 7591; cf. 2410; Ar 10237]
cried out [16], cry out [9], cried for help [3], cries out [3], beg [2], called out [2], cried [2], cry out [+7590] [2], crying out [2], were called out [2], appealed [1], burst out [1], cried out for help [+7754] [1], cry aloud [1], cry [1], scream for help [1], screamed [1], shout [1], summoned [1], was called up [1], were called to arms [1], were summoned [1]

Ge 4: 10 [A] Your brother's blood **cries out** to me from the ground.
27: 34 [A] *he* **burst out** *with* a loud and bitter cry and said to his father,
41: 55 [A] to feel the famine, the people **cried** to Pharaoh for food.
Ex 5: 8 [A] that is why they *are* **crying out**, 'Let us go and sacrifice to
5: 15 [A] Then the Israelite foremen went and **appealed** to Pharaoh:
8: 12 [8:8] [A] Moses **cried out** to the LORD about the frogs he had
14: 10 [A] after them. They were terrified and **cried out** to the LORD.
14: 15 [A] the LORD said to Moses, "Why *are you* **crying out** to me?
15: 25 [A] Moses **cried out** to the LORD, and the LORD showed him

Ex 17: 4 [A] Moses **cried out** to the LORD, "What am I to do with these
22: 23 [22:22] [A] If you do and *they* **cry** [+7590] **out** to me, I will
22: 23 [22:22] [A] If you do and *they* **cry out** [+7590] to me, I will
22: 27 [22:26] [A] When *he* **cries out** to me, I will hear, for I am
Nu 11: 2 [A] When the people **cried out** to Moses, he prayed to the
12: 13 [A] So Moses **cried out** to the LORD, "O God, please heal
20: 16 [A] when *we* **cried out** to the LORD, he heard our cry and sent
Dt 22: 24 [A] because she was in a town and *did* not **scream for help**,
22: 27 [A] though the betrothed girl **screamed**, there was no one to
26: 7 [A] Then *we* **cried out** to the LORD, the God of our fathers,
Jos 24: 7 [A] *they* **cried** to the LORD **for help**, and he put darkness
Jdg 4: 3 [A] for twenty years, they **cried** to the LORD **for help**.
7: 23 [C] from Naphtali, Asher and all Manasseh **were called out**,
7: 24 [C] So all the men of Ephraim **were called out** and they took the
10: 12 [A] the Maonites oppressed you and *you* **cried** to me **for help**,
10: 17 [C] When the Ammonites **were called to arms** and camped in
12: 1 [C] The men of Ephraim **called out** their forces, crossed over to
1Sa 10: 17 [G] Samuel **summoned** the people of Israel to the LORD at
13: 4 [C] And the people **were summoned** to join Saul at Gilgal.
1Ki 20: 39 [A] As the king passed by, the prophet **called out** to him, "Your
2Ki 2: 12 [D] Elisha saw this and **cried out**, "My father! My father!
3: 21 [C] who could bear arms **was called up** and stationed on the
4: 1 [A] a man from the company of the prophets **cried out** to Elisha,
4: 40 [A] they **cried out**, "O man of God, there is death in the pot!"
6: 5 [A] the water. "Oh, my lord," *he* **cried out**, "it was borrowed!"
6: 26 [A] a woman **cried** to him, "Help me, my lord the king!"
8: 3 [A] and went to the king to **beg** for her house and land.
8: 5 [A] had brought back to life came *to* **beg** the king for her house
2Ch 13: 14 [A] at both front and rear. Then *they* **cried out** to the LORD.
Ne 9: 27 [A] But when they were oppressed *they* **cried out** to you.
Job 19: 7 [A] "Though *I* **cry**, 'I've been wronged!' I get no response;
35: 12 [A] He does not answer when *men* **cry out** because of the
Ps 34: 17 [34:18] [A] The righteous **cry out**, and the LORD hears them;
77: 1 [77:2] [A] *I* **cried** [+7754] **out** to God **for help**; I cried out to
88: [88:2] [A] who saves me, day and night *I* **cry out** before you.
107: 6 [A] *they* **cried out** to the LORD in their trouble, and he
107: 28 [A] *they* **cried out** to the LORD in their trouble, and he brought
Isa 19: 20 [A] When *they* **cry out** to the LORD because of their
33: 7 [A] Look, their brave men **cry aloud** in the streets; the envoys of
42: 2 [A] *He will* not **shout** or cry out, or raise his voice in the streets.
46: 7 [A] Though *one* **cries out** to it, it does not answer; it cannot save
65: 14 [A] you *will* **cry out** from anguish of heart and wail in
Jer 22: 20 [A] "Go up to Lebanon and **cry out**, let your voice be heard in
22: 20 [A] **cry out** from Abarim, for all your allies are crushed.
49: 3 [A] **Cry out**, O inhabitants of Rabbah! Put on sackcloth
La 2: 18 [A] The hearts of the people **cry out** to the Lord. O wall of the

7591 צְעָקָה ṣᵉʿāqâ, n.f. [21] [√ 7590]

cry [9], outcry [3], cries [2], cry [+7754] [2], wailing [2], cries of distress [1], crying out [1], outcry [+7754] [1]

Ge 18: 21 see if what they have done is as bad as the **outcry** that has reached
19: 13 The **outcry** to the LORD *against* its people is so great that he has
27: 34 he burst out with a loud and bitter **cry** and said to his father,
Ex 3: 7 I have heard them **crying out** because of their slave drivers,
3: 9 now the **cry** *of* the Israelites has reached me, and I have seen the
11: 6 There will be loud **wailing** throughout Egypt—worse than there
12: 30 got up during the night, and there was loud **wailing** in Egypt,
22: 23 [22:22] and they cry out to me, I will certainly hear their **cry**.
1Sa 4: 14 Eli heard the **outcry** [+7754] and asked, "What is the meaning of
9: 16 I have looked upon my people, for their **cry** has reached me."
Ne 5: 1 and their wives raised a great **outcry** against their Jewish brothers.
Job 27: 9 Does God listen to his **cry** when distress comes upon him?
34: 28 They caused the **cry** *of* the poor to come before him, so that he
34: 28 the poor to come before him, so that he heard the **cry** *of* the needy.
Ps 9: 12 [9:13] he does not ignore the **cry** *of* the afflicted.
Isa 5: 7 but saw bloodshed; for righteousness, but heard **cries of distress**.
Jer 25: 36 Hear the **cry** *of* the shepherds, the wailing of the leaders of the
48: 3 Listen to the **cries** from Horonaim, cries of great havoc
48: 5 on the road down to Horonaim anguished **cries** *over* the
49: 21 earth will tremble; their **cry** [+7754] will resound to the Red Sea.
Zep 1: 10 the LORD, "a **cry** [+7754] will go up from the Fish Gate,

7592 צָעַר ṣāʿar, v. [3] [→ 5203, 5204, 7428, 7486, 7580, 7582, 7593; cf. 2402]

brought low [1], disdained [1], little ones [1]

Job 14: 21 [A] does not know it; if *they are* **brought low**, he does not see it.
Jer 30: 19 [A] I will bring them honor, and *they will* not *be* **disdained**.
Zec 13: 7 [A] be scattered, and I will turn my hand against the **little ones**.

7593 צֹעַר ṣōʿar, n.pr.loc. [10] [√ 7592]

Zoar [10]

Ge 13: 10 like the garden of the LORD, like the land of Egypt, toward **Zoar**.
14: 2 Shemeber king of Zeboiim, and the king of Bela (that is, **Zoar**).
14: 8 of Admah, the king of Zeboiim and the king of Bela (that is, **Zoar**)
19: 22 until you reach it." (That is why the town was called **Zoar**.)
19: 23 By the time Lot reached **Zoar**, the sun had risen over the land.
19: 30 Lot and his two daughters left **Zoar** and settled in the mountains,
19: 30 and settled in the mountains, for he was afraid to stay in **Zoar**.
Dt 34: 3 from the Valley of Jericho, the City of Palms, as far as **Zoar**.
Isa 15: 5 her fugitives flee as far as **Zoar**, as far as Eglath Shelishiyah.
Jer 48: 34 and Jahaz, from **Zoar** as far as Horonaim and Eglath Shelishiyah,

7594 צָפַד ṣāpad, v. [1]

shriveled [1]

La 4: 8 [A] Their skin *has* **shriveled** on their bones; it has become as dry

7595 ¹צָפָה ṣāpâ¹, v. [35 / 36] [→ 2174, 5205, 5206, 5207, 7600, 7601, 7603, 7610, 7611?]

watchman [11], lookout [4], watchmen [4], watch [3], he^s [+2021] [1], keep watch [1], keeping watch [1], lie in wait [1], look [1], looking [1], lookouts [1], marked [1], standing watch [1], wait in expectation [1], watch in hope [1], watched [1], watches over [1], watching [1]

Ge 31: 49 [A] "*May* the LORD **keep watch** between you and me when
1Sa 4: 13 [D] **watching**, because his heart feared for the ark of God.
14: 16 [A] Saul's **lookouts** at Gibeah in Benjamin saw the army melting
2Sa 13: 34 [A] Now the man **standing watch** looked up and saw many
13: 34 [A] The **watchman** [BHS-] went and told the king, "I see men
18: 24 [A] the **watchman** went up to the roof of the gateway by the
18: 25 [A] The **watchman** called out to the king and reported it. The
18: 26 [A] the **watchman** saw another man running, and he called down
18: 26 [A] **he**^s [+2021] called down to the gatekeeper, "Look,
18: 27 [A] The **watchman** said, "It seems to me that the first one runs
2Ki 9: 17 [A] When the **lookout** standing on the tower in Jezreel saw
9: 18 [A] The **lookout** reported, "The messenger has reached them,
9: 20 [A] The **lookout** reported, "He has reached them, but he isn't
Job 15: 22 [B] of escaping the darkness; he *is* **marked** for the sword.
Ps 5: 3 [5:4] [D] I lay my requests before you and **wait in expectation**.
37: 32 [A] The wicked **lie in wait** for the righteous, seeking their very
66: 7 [A] He rules forever by his power, his eyes **watch** the nations—
Pr 15: 3 [A] are everywhere, **keeping watch** *on* the wicked and the good.
31: 27 [A] *She* **watches over** the affairs of her household and does not
SS 7: 4 [7:5] [A] Your nose is like the tower of Lebanon **looking**
Isa 21: 6 [D] to me: "Go, post a **lookout** and have him report what he sees.
52: 8 [A] Your **watchmen** lift up their voices; together they shout for
56: 10 [A] Israel's **watchmen** are blind, they all lack knowledge;
Jer 6: 17 [A] I appointed **watchmen** over you and said, 'Listen to the
48: 19 [D] Stand by the road and **watch**, you who live in Aroer.
La 4: 17 [D] from our towers *we* **watched** for a nation that could not save
Eze 3: 17 [A] of man, I have made you a **watchman** for the house of Israel;
33: 2 [A] land choose one of their men and make him their **watchman**,
33: 6 [A] if the **watchman** sees the sword coming and does not blow
33: 6 [A] but I will hold the **watchman** accountable for his blood.'
33: 7 [A] of man, I have made you a **watchman** for the house of Israel;
Hos 9: 8 [A] along with my God, *is* the **watchman** *over* Ephraim,
Mic 7: 4 [D] The day of your **watchmen** has come, the day God visits
7: 7 [D] as for me, *I* **watch in hope** for the LORD, I wait for God
Na 2: 1 [2:2] [D] Guard the fortress, **watch** the road, brace yourselves,
Hab 2: 1 [D] *I will* **look** to see what he will say to me, and what answer I

7596 ²צָפָה ṣāpâ², v. [47] [→ 7599, 7620, 7633, 7634?]

overlaid [27], overlay [11], covered [4], *untranslated* [1], adorned [+906+4200+9514] [1], coating [1], paneling [+6770] [1], spread [1]

Ex 25: 11 [D] **Overlay** it *with* pure gold, both inside and out, and make a
25: 11 [D] and out, **[RPH]** and make a gold molding around it.
25: 13 [D] make poles of acacia wood and **overlay** them *with* gold.
25: 24 [D] **Overlay** it *with* pure gold and make a gold molding around
25: 28 [D] **overlay** them *with* gold and carry the table with them.
26: 29 [D] **Overlay** the frames *with* gold and make gold rings to hold
26: 29 [D] to hold the crossbars. Also **overlay** the crossbars *with* gold.
26: 32 [E] gold hooks on four posts of acacia wood **overlaid** *with* gold
26: 37 [D] and five posts of acacia wood **overlaid** *with* gold.
27: 2 [D] the altar are of one piece, and **overlay** the altar *with* bronze.
27: 6 [D] of acacia wood for the altar and **overlay** them *with* bronze.
30: 3 [D] **Overlay** the top and all the sides and the horns with pure
30: 5 [D] Make the poles of acacia wood and **overlay** them *with* gold.
36: 34 [D] *They* **overlaid** the frames *with* gold and made gold rings to
36: 34 [D] the crossbars. *They* also **overlaid** the crossbars *with* gold.
36: 36 [D] four posts of acacia wood for it and **overlaid** them *with* gold.
36: 38 [D] *They* **overlaid** the tops of the posts and their bands *with* gold

Ex 37: 2 [D] *He* **overlaid** it *with* pure gold, both inside and out, and made
37: 4 [D] he made poles of acacia wood and **overlaid** them *with* gold.
37: 11 [D] *they* **overlaid** it *with* pure gold and made a gold molding
37: 15 [D] were made of acacia wood and *were* **overlaid** *with* gold.
37: 26 [D] *They* **overlaid** the top and all the sides and the horns with
37: 28 [D] made the poles of acacia wood and **overlaid** them *with* gold.
38: 2 [D] were of one piece, and *they* **overlaid** the altar *with* bronze.
38: 6 [D] the poles of acacia wood and **overlaid** them *with* bronze.
38: 28 [D] *to* **overlay** the tops of the posts, and to make their bands.
1Ki 6: 15 [D] **paneling** [+6770] them from the floor of the temple to the
6: 15 [D] and **covered** the floor of the temple with planks of pine.
6: 20 [D] *He* **overlaid** the inside with pure gold, and he also overlaid
6: 20 [D] inside with pure gold, and *he* also **overlaid** the altar of cedar.
6: 21 [D] Solomon **covered** the inside of the temple with pure gold,
6: 21 [D] front of the inner sanctuary, which *was* **overlaid** *with* gold.
6: 22 [D] So *he* **overlaid** the whole interior *with* gold. He also overlaid
6: 22 [D] *He* also **overlaid** *with* gold the altar that belonged to the
6: 28 [D] *He* **overlaid** the cherubim *with* gold.
6: 30 [D] *He* also **covered** the floors of both the inner and outer rooms of
6: 32 [D] and **overlaid** the cherubim and palm trees *with* beaten gold.
6: 35 [D] **overlaid** them *with* gold hammered evenly over the carvings.
10: 18 [D] a great throne inlaid with ivory and **overlaid** *with* fine gold.
2Ki 18: 16 [D] stripped off the gold with which he *had* **covered** the doors
2Ch 3: 4 [D] twenty cubits high. *He* **overlaid** the inside *with* pure gold.
3: 6 [D] *He* **adorned** [+906+4200+9514] the temple *with* precious
3: 10 [D] a pair of sculptured cherubim and **overlaid** them *with* gold.
4: 9 [D] the doors for the court, and **overlaid** the doors *with* bronze.
9: 17 [D] a great throne inlaid with ivory and **overlaid** with pure gold.
Pr 26: 23 [E] Like a **coating** *of* glaze over earthenware are fervent lips with
Isa 21: 5 [A] set the tables, they **spread** the rugs, they eat, they drink!

7597 צָפָה³ ṣāpâ³, n.f. [1] [√ 7429?]

flowing [1]

Eze 32: 6 I will drench the land with your **flowing** blood all the way to the

7598 צְפוֹ ṣᵉpô, n.pr.m. [2 / 3] [cf. 7609]

Zepho [3]

Ge 36: 11 The sons of Eliphaz: Teman, Omar, **Zepho**, Gatam and Kenaz.
36: 15 Eliphaz the firstborn of Esau: Chiefs Teman, Omar, **Zepho**, Kenaz,
1Ch 1: 36 Teman, Omar, **Zepho**, [BHS 7609] Gatam and Kenaz; by Timna:

7599 צִפּוּי ṣippûy, n.[m.]. [5] [√ 7596]

overlaid [3], overlay [2]

Ex 38: 17 on the posts were silver, and their tops were **overlaid** *with* silver;
38: 19 and bands were silver, and their tops were **overlaid** *with* silver.
Nu 16: 38 [17:3] Hammer the censers into sheets to **overlay** the altar,
16: 39 [17:4] and he had them hammered out to **overlay** the altar,
Isa 30: 22 you will defile your idols **overlaid** *with* silver and your images

7600 צָפוֹן¹ ṣāpôn¹, n.f. [151] [→ 1263, 7601, 7603; cf. 7595]

north [97], north [+2025] [26], northern [+2025] [9], north [+4946] [7], northern [4], northern [+4946] [3], *untranslated* [1], north wind [1], northern [+2025+4946] [1], northward [+2006+2021] [1], sacred mountain [1]

Ge 13: 14 your eyes from where you are and look **north** [+2025] and south,
28: 14 spread out to the west and to the east, to the **north** and to the south.
Ex 26: 20 For the other side, the **north** side of the tabernacle, make twenty
26: 35 Place the table outside the curtain on the **north** side of the
27: 11 The **north** side shall also be a hundred cubits long and is to have
36: 25 For the other side, the **north** side of the tabernacle, they made
38: 11 The **north** side was also a hundred cubits long and had twenty
40: 22 placed the table in the Tent of Meeting on the **north** [+2025]
Lev 1: 11 He is to slaughter it at the **north** [+2025] side of the altar before
Nu 2: 25 On the **north** will be the divisions of the camp of Dan, under their
3: 35 they were to camp on the **north** [+2025] side of the tabernacle.
34: 7 " 'For your **northern** boundary, run a line from the Great Sea to
34: 9 and end at Hazar Enan. This will be your boundary on the **north**.
35: 5 three thousand on the west and three thousand on the **north**,
Dt 2: 3 way around this hill country long enough; now turn **north** [+2025].
3: 27 top of Pisgah and look west and **north** [+2025] and south and east.
Jos 8: 11 They set up camp **north** of Ai, with the valley between them
8: 13 all those in the camp to the **north** of the city and the ambush to the
11: 2 and to the **northern** [+4946] kings who were in the mountains,
13: 3 River on the east of Egypt to the territory of Ekron on the **north**,
15: 5 The **northern** [+2025] boundary started from the bay of the sea at
15: 6 continued **north** [+4946] of Beth Arabah to the Stone of Bohan
15: 7 from the Valley of Achor and turned **north** [+2025] to Gilgal,
15: 8 Valley at the **northern** [+2025] end of the Valley of Rephaim.
15: 10 ran along the **northern** [+2025+4946] slope of Mount Jearim (that
15: 11 It went to the **northern** [+2025] slope of Ekron, turned toward
16: 6 From Micmethath on the **north** it curved eastward to Taanath
17: 9 the boundary of Manasseh was the **northern** [+4946] *side* of the
17: 10 the south the land belonged to Ephraim, on the **north** to Manasseh.
17: 10 and bordered Asher on the **north** and Issachar on the east.
18: 5 on the south and the house of Joseph in its territory on the **north**.
18: 12 On the **north** side their boundary began at the Jordan, passed the
18: 12 passed the **northern** [+4946] slope of Jericho and headed west into
18: 16 Valley of Ben Hinnom, **north** [+2025] of the Valley of Rephaim.
18: 17 It then curved **north** [+4946], went to En Shemesh, continued to
18: 18 It continued to the **northern** [+2025] slope of Beth Arabah
18: 19 It then went to the **northern** [+2025] slope of Beth Hoglah
18: 19 and came out at the **northern** [+2025] bay of the Salt Sea,
19: 14 There the boundary went around on the **north** to Hannathon
19: 27 went **north** [+2025] to Beth Emek and Neiel, passing Cabul on the
24: 30 at Timnath Serah in the hill country of Ephraim, **north** [+4946] of
Jdg 2: 9 at Timnath Heres in the hill country of Ephraim, **north** [+4946] of
7: 1 The camp of Midian was **north** [+4946] of them in the valley near
21: 19 festival of the LORD in Shiloh, to the **north** [+4946] of Bethel,
1Sa 14: 5 One cliff stood to the **north** toward Micmash, the other to the
1Ki 7: 25 three facing **north** [+2025], three facing west, three facing south
2Ki 16: 14 the LORD—and put it on the **north** [+2025] side of the new altar.
1Ch 9: 24 were on the four sides: east, west, **north** [+2025] and south.
26: 14 a wise counselor, and the lot for the **North** Gate fell to him.
26: 17 four a day on the **north** [+2025], four a day on the south and two at
2Ch 4: 4 three facing **north** [+2025], three facing west, three facing south
Job 26: 7 He spreads out the **northern** ⌞skies⌟ over empty space; he suspends
37: 22 Out of the **north** he comes in golden splendor; God comes in
Ps 89: 12 [89:13] You created the **north** and the south; Tabor and Hermon
107: 3 gathered from the lands, from east and west, from **north** and south.
Pr 25: 23 As a **north** wind brings rain, so a sly tongue brings angry looks.
Ecc 1: 6 The wind blows to the south and turns to the **north**; round
11: 3 Whether a tree falls to the south or to the **north**, in the place where
SS 4: 16 Awake, **north wind**, and come, south wind! Blow on my garden,
Isa 14: 13 mount of assembly, on the utmost heights of the **sacred mountain**.
14: 31 A cloud of smoke comes from the **north**, and there is not a
41: 25 "I have stirred up one from the **north**, and he comes—one from the
43: 6 I will say to the **north**, 'Give them up!' and to the south, 'Do not
49: 12 some from the **north**, some from the west, some from the region of
Jer 1: 13 a boiling pot, tilting away from the **north** [+2025]," I answered.
1: 14 "From the **north** disaster will be poured out on all who live in the
1: 15 I am about to summon all the peoples of the **northern** [+2025]
3: 12 Go, proclaim this message toward the **north**: " 'Return,
3: 18 together they will come from a **northern** land to the land I gave
4: 6 For I am bringing disaster from the **north**, even terrible
6: 1 For disaster looms out of the **north**, even terrible destruction.
6: 22 "Look, an army is coming from the land of the **north**; a great
10: 22 report is coming—a great commotion from the land of the **north**!
13: 20 Lift up your eyes and see those who are coming from the **north**.
15: 12 "Can a man break iron—iron from the **north**—or bronze?
16: 15 who brought the Israelites up out of the land of the **north** and out
23: 8 the descendants of Israel up out of the land of the **north** [+2025]
25: 9 I will summon all the peoples of the **north** and my servant
25: 26 and all the kings of the **north**, near and far, one after the other—
31: 8 I will bring them from the land of the **north** and gather them from
46: 6 In the **north** by the River Euphrates they stumble and fall.
46: 10 will offer sacrifice in the land of the **north** by the River Euphrates.
46: 20 beautiful heifer, but a gadfly is coming against her from the **north**.
46: 24 will be put to shame, handed over to the people of the **north**."
47: 2 "See how the waters are rising in the **north**; they will become an
50: 3 A nation from the **north** will attack her and lay waste her land.
50: 9 Babylon an alliance of great nations from the land of the **north**.
50: 41 An army is coming from the **north**; a great nation and many kings
51: 48 for out of the **north** destroyers will attack her,"
Eze 1: 4 I looked, and I saw a windstorm coming out of the **north**—
8: 3 to the entrance to the **north** [+2025] gate of the inner court,
8: 5 Then he said to me, "Son of man, look toward the **north** [+2025]."
8: 5 **[RPH]** and in the entrance north of the gate of the altar I saw this
8: 5 in the entrance **north** [+4946] of the gate of the altar I saw this idol
8: 14 he brought me to the entrance to the **north** [+2025] gate of the
9: 2 which faces **north** [+2025], each with a deadly weapon in his
20: 47 [21:3] and every face from south to **north** will be scorched by it.
21: 4 [21:9] will be unsheathed against everyone from south to **north**.
26: 7 From the **north** I am going to bring against Tyre Nebuchadnezzar
32: 30 "All the princes of the **north** and all the Sidonians are there;
38: 6 and Beth Togarmah from the far **north** with all its troops—
38: 15 You will come from your place in the far **north**, you and many
39: 2 I will bring you from the far **north** and send you against the
40: 19 it was a hundred cubits on the east side as well as on the **north**.
40: 20 Then he measured the length and width of the gate facing **north**,
40: 23 There was a gate to the inner court facing the **north** gate, just as
40: 35 he brought me to the **north** gate and measured it. It had the same
40: 40 near the steps at the entrance to the **north** [+2025] gateway were
40: 44 were two rooms, one at the side of the **north** gate and facing south,
40: 44 and another at the side of the south gate and facing **north**.
40: 46 the room facing **north** is for the priests who have charge of the

Eze 41:11 from the open area, one on the **north** and another on the south;
42: 1 Then the man led me **northward** [+2006+2021] into the outer
42: 1 the temple courtyard and opposite the outer wall on the **north** *side.*
42: 2 The building whose door faced **north** was a hundred cubits long
42: 4 and a hundred cubits long. Their doors were on the **north**.
42:11 These were like the rooms on the **north**; they had the same length
42:13 "The **north** and south rooms facing the temple courtyard are the
42:17 He measured the **north** side; it was five hundred cubits by the
44: 4 the man brought me by way of the **north** gate to the front of the
46: 9 whoever enters by the **north** gate to worship is to go out the south
46: 9 whoever enters by the south gate is to go out the **north** [+2025]
46:19 at the side of the gate to the sacred rooms facing **north** [+2025],
47: 2 He then brought me out through the **north** [+2025] gate and led me
47:15 "On the **north** [+2025] side it will run from the Great Sea by the
47:17 along the **northern** border of Damascus, with the border of
47:17 border of Damascus, with the border of Hamath to the **north**.
47:17 border of Hamath to the north. This will be the **north** boundary.
48: 1 At the **northern** [+2025] frontier, Dan will have one portion;
48: 1 the **northern** [+2025] border of Damascus next to Hamath will be
48:10 It will be 25,000 cubits long on the **north** *side*, 10,000 cubits wide
48:16 the **north** side 4,500 cubits, the south side 4,500 cubits, the east
48:17 The pastureland for the city will be 250 cubits on the **north**,
48:30 the city: Beginning on the **north** side, which is 4,500 cubits long,
48:31 The three gates on the **north** *side* will be the gate of Reuben,
Da 8: 4 the ram as he charged toward the west and the **north** and the south.
11: 6 of the South will go to the king of the **North** to make an alliance,
11: 7 He will attack the forces of the king of the **North** and enter his
11: 8 For some years he will leave the king of the **North** alone.
11:11 will march out in a rage and fight against the king of the **North**,
11:13 For the king of the **North** will muster another army, larger than the
11:15 Then the king of the **North** will come and build up siege ramps
11:40 and the king of the **North** will storm out against him with chariots
11:44 reports from the east and the **north** will alarm him, and he will set
Am 8:12 Men will stagger from sea to sea and wander from **north** to east,
Zep 2:13 He will stretch out his hand against the **north** and destroy Assyria,
Zec 2: 6 [2:10] Flee from the land of the **north**," declares the LORD,
6: 6 The one with the black horses is going toward the **north** country,
6: 8 those going toward the **north** country have given my Spirit rest in
6: 8 north country have given my Spirit rest in the land of the **north**."
14: 4 with half of the mountain moving **north** [+2025] and half moving

7601 [2]צָפוֹן **ṣāpôn[2]**, n.pr.loc. [3] [√ 7600; cf. 7595]

Zaphon [3]

Jos 13:27 **Zaphon** with the rest of the realm of Sihon king of Heshbon (the
Jdg 12: 1 out their forces, crossed over to **Zaphon** and said to Jephthah,
Ps 48: 2 [48:3] Like the utmost heights of **Zaphon** is Mount Zion, the city

7602 צְפוֹן **ṣ[e]pôn**, n.pr.m. [1 / 2] [→ 7604; cf. 7611]

Zephon [2]

Ge 46:16 **Zephon**, [BHS 7611] Haggi, Shuni, Ezbon, Eri, Arodi and Areli.
Nu 26:15 through **Zephon**, the Zephonite clan; through Haggi, the Haggite

7603 [1]צְפוֹנִי **ṣ[e]pônî[1]**, a. [1] [√ 7600; cf. 7595]

northern [1]

Joel 2:20 "I will drive the **northern** *army* far from you, pushing it into a

7604 [2]צְפוֹנִי **ṣ[e]pônî[2]**, a.g. [1] [√ 7602]

Zephonite [1]

Nu 26:15 through Zephon, the **Zephonite** clan; through Haggi, the Haggite

7605 צָפוּעַ **ṣāpûaʻ**, n.[m.]. [0] [cf. 7616]

Eze 4:15 [over cow **manure** [K; see Q 7616] instead of human excrement."]

7606 [1]צִפּוֹר **ṣippôr[1]**, n.f. & m. [40] [→ 7436?, 7607, 7631]

bird [18], birds [12], bird's [2], sparrow [2], *untranslated* [1], bird [+4053] [1], birds [+4053] [1], carrion birds [+6514] [1], it[s] [+2021+2021+2645] [1], poultry [1]

Ge 7:14 every bird according to its kind, **[RPH]** everything with wings.
15:10 opposite each other; the **birds**, however, he did not cut in half.
Lev 14: 4 the priest shall order that two live clean **birds** and some cedar
14: 5 the priest shall order that one of the **birds** be killed over fresh
14: 6 He is then to take the live **bird** and dip it, together with the cedar
14: 6 then to take the live bird and dip **it**[s] [+2021+2021+2645],
14: 6 into the blood of the **bird** that was killed over the fresh water.
14: 7 him clean. Then he is to release the live **bird** in the open fields.
14:49 To purify the house he is to take two **birds** and some cedar wood,
14:50 He shall kill one of the **birds** over fresh water in a clay pot.
14:51 take the cedar wood, the hyssop, the scarlet yarn and the live **bird**,
14:51 dip them into the blood of the dead **bird** and the fresh water,
14:52 He shall purify the house with the **bird's** blood, the fresh water,
14:52 the fresh water, the live **bird**, the cedar wood, the hyssop and the
14:53 he is to release the live **bird** in the open fields outside the town.
Dt 4:17 or like any animal on earth or any **bird** [+4053] that flies in the air,
14:11 You may eat any clean **bird**.
22: 6 If you come across a **bird's** nest beside the road, either in a tree
Ne 5:18 six choice sheep and *some* **poultry** were prepared for me,
Job 41: 5 [40:29] Can you make a pet of him like a **bird** or put him on a
Ps 8: 8 [8:9] the **birds** *of* the air, and the fish of the sea, all that swim the
11: 1 then can you say to me: "Flee like a **bird** to your mountain.
84: 3 [84:4] Even the **sparrow** has found a home, and the swallow a
102: 7 [102:8] I lie awake; I have become like a **bird** alone on a roof.
104:17 There the **birds** make their nests; the stork has its home in the pine
124: 7 We have escaped like a **bird** out of the fowler's snare; the snare
148:10 wild animals and all cattle, small creatures and flying **birds**,
Pr 6: 5 the hand of the hunter, like a **bird** from the snare of the fowler.
7:23 till an arrow pierces his liver, like a **bird** darting into a snare,
26: 2 Like a fluttering **sparrow** or a darting swallow, an undeserved
27: 8 Like a **bird** that strays from its nest is a man who strays from his
Ecc 9:12 As fish are caught in a cruel net, or **birds** are taken in a snare,
12: 4 when men rise up at the sound of **birds**, but all their songs grow
Isa 31: 5 Like **birds** hovering overhead, the LORD Almighty will shield
La 3:52 Those who were my enemies without cause hunted me like a **bird**.
Eze 17:23 **Birds** [+4053] of every kind will nest in it; they will find shelter in
39: 4 I will give you as food to all kinds of **carrion birds** [+6514]
39:17 Call out to every kind of **bird** and all the wild animals: 'Assemble
Hos 11:11 They will come trembling like **birds** from Egypt, like doves from
Am 3: 5 Does a **bird** fall into a trap on the ground where no snare has been

7607 [2]צִפּוֹר **ṣippôr[2]**, n.pr.m. [7] [√ 7606; Ar 10616]

Zippor [7]

Nu 22: 2 Now Balak son of **Zippor** saw all that Israel had done to the
22: 4 So Balak son of **Zippor**, who was king of Moab at that time,
22:10 Balaam said to God, "Balak son of **Zippor**, king of Moab,
22:16 came to Balaam and said: "This is what Balak son of **Zippor** says:
23:18 his oracle: "Arise, Balak, and listen; hear me, son of **Zippor**.
Jos 24: 9 When Balak son of **Zippor**, the king of Moab, prepared to fight
Jdg 11:25 Are you better than Balak son of **Zippor**, king of Moab? Did he

7608 צַפַּחַת **ṣappaḥat**, n.f. [7] [√ 7613]

jug [6], jar [1]

1Sa 26:11 Now get the spear and water **jug** that are near his head, and let's
26:12 So David took the spear and water **jug** near Saul's head, and they
26:16 Where are the king's spear and water **jug** that were near his head?"
1Ki 17:12 any bread—only a handful of flour in a jar and a little oil in a **jug**.
17:14 the **jug** *of* oil will not run dry until the day the LORD gives rain
17:16 the jar of flour was not used up and the **jug** *of* oil did not run dry,
19: 6 head was a cake of bread baked over hot coals, and a **jar** *of* water.

7609 צְפִי **ṣ[e]pî**, n.pr.m. [1 / 0] [cf. 7598]

1Ch 1:36 sons of Eliphaz: Teman, Omar, Zepho, [BHS *Zephi*; NIV 7598]

7610 צְפִיָּה **ṣippiyyâ**, n.f. [1] [√ 7595]

towers [1]

La 4:17 from our **towers** we watched for a nation that could not save us.

7611 צִפְיוֹן **ṣipyôn**, n.pr.m. [1 / 0] [→ 7612; cf. 7595?, 7602]

Ge 46:16 The sons of Gad: Zephon, [BHS *Ziphion*; NIV 7602] Haggi, Shuni,

7612 צִפְיוֹנִי **ṣipyônî**, a.g. Not used in NIV/BHS [√ 7611]

7613 צַפִּיחִת **ṣappîḥit**, n.f. [1] [→ 7432, 7608]

wafers [1]

Ex 16:31 white like coriander seed and tasted like **wafers** made with honey.

7614 צֹפִים **ṣōpîm**, n.pr.[loc.?]. [1] [cf. 7435]

Zophim [1]

Nu 23:14 So he took him to the field of **Zophim** on the top of Pisgah,

7615 צָפִין **ṣāpîn**, n.[m.]. [0] [√ 7621]

Ps 17:14 [b] [You still the hunger of those you **cherish**; [K; see Q 7621]]

7616 צָפִיעַ **ṣāpîaʻ**, n.[m.]. [1] [cf. 7605]

manure [1]

Eze 4:15 "I will let you bake your bread over cow **manure** [K 7605] instead

7617 צְפִיעָה ṣᵉpî'â, n.f. [1]

offshoots [1]

Isa 22:24 its offspring and **offshoots**—all its lesser vessels, from the bowls to

7618 צָפִיר ṣāpîr, n.m. [6] [→ Ar 10615]

goat [+6436] [2], *untranslated* [1], goat [1], male goats [+6436] [1], male goats [1]

2Ch 29:21 and seven **male goats** [+6436] as a sin offering for the kingdom,
Ezr 8:35 male lambs and, as a sin offering, twelve **male goats**.
Da 8:5 suddenly a **goat** [+6436] with a prominent horn between his eyes
8:5 suddenly a goat **[RPH]** with a prominent horn between his eyes
8:8 The **goat** [+6436] became very great, but at the height of his power
8:21 The shaggy **goat** is the king of Greece, and the large horn between

7619 צְפִירָה ṣᵉpîrâ, n.f. [3]

doom [2], crown [1]

Isa 28:5 In that day the LORD Almighty will be a glorious **crown**,
Eze 7:7 **Doom** has come upon you—you who dwell in the land. The time
7:10 **Doom** has burst forth, the rod has budded, arrogance has

7620 צָפִית ṣāpît, n.f. [1] [√ 7596]

rugs [1]

Isa 21:5 They set the tables, they spread the **rugs**, they eat, they drink!

7621 צָפַן ṣāpan, v. [32] [→ 5208, 7615; *also used with compound proper names*]

store up [3], stored up [3], cherish [2], hidden [2], hide [2], keep safe [2], restraining [2], waylay [2], closed [1], concealed [1], hid [1], holds in store [1], is concealed [1], is stored up [1], kept on record [1], lurk [1], secret [1], set [1], stores up [1], treasured place [1], treasured [1], treasures [1]

Ex 2:2 [A] saw that he was a fine child, *she* **hid** him for three months.
2:3 [G] when she could **hide** him no longer, she got a papyrus basket
Jos 2:4 [A] The woman had taken the two men and **hidden** them. She
Job 10:13 [A] "But this is what *you* **concealed** in your heart, and I know
14:13 [G] "If only *you would* **hide** me in the grave and conceal me till
15:20 [C] the ruthless through all the years **stored up** for him.
17:4 [A] *You have* **closed** their minds to understanding; therefore you
20:26 [B] total darkness lies in wait for his **treasures**. A fire unfanned
21:19 [A] ⌞It is said,⌟ 'God **stores up** a man's punishment for his sons.'
23:12 [A] *I have* **treasured** the words of his mouth more than my daily
24:1 [C] "Why *does* the Almighty not **set** times for judgment? Why
Ps 10:8 [A] he murders the innocent, watching *in* **secret** for his victims.
17:14 [B] You still the hunger of those you **cherish**; [K 7615] their
27:5 [A] For in the day of trouble *he will* **keep** me **safe** in his
31:19 [31:20] [A] which *you have* **stored up** for those who fear you,
31:20 [31:21] [A] in your dwelling *you* **keep** them **safe** from accusing
56:6 [56:7] [A] They conspire, they **lurk**, they watch my steps, eager
83:3 [83:4] [B] your people; they plot against *those* you **cherish**.
119:11 [A] *I have* **hidden** your word in my heart that I might not sin
Pr 1:11 [A] wait for someone's blood, *let's* **waylay** some harmless soul;
1:18 [A] lie in wait for their own blood; *they* **waylay** only themselves!
2:1 [A] accept my words and **store up** my commands within you,
2:7 [A] *He* **holds** victory **in store** for the upright, he is a shield to
7:1 [A] keep my words and **store up** my commands within you.
10:14 [A] Wise men **store up** knowledge, but the mouth of a fool
13:22 [B] but a sinner's wealth **is stored up** for the righteous.
27:16 [A] **restraining** her is like restraining the wind or grasping oil
27:16 [A] restraining her is like **restraining** the wind or grasping oil
SS 7:13 [7:14] [A] both new and old, that *I have* **stored up** for you,
Jer 16:17 [C] not hidden from me, nor **is** their sin **concealed** from my eyes.
Eze 7:22 [B] from them, and they will desecrate my **treasured place**;
Hos 13:12 [B] guilt of Ephraim is stored up, his sins *are* **kept on record**.

7622 צְפַנְיָה ṣᵉpanyâ, n.pr.m. [8] [√ 7621 + 3378]

Zephaniah [8]

1Ch 6:36 [6:21] the son of Joel, the son of Azariah, the son of **Zephaniah**,
Jer 21:1 son of Malkijah and the priest **Zephaniah** son of Maaseiah.
29:25 to **Zephaniah** son of Maaseiah the priest, and to all the other
29:29 **Zephaniah** the priest, however, read the letter to Jeremiah the
52:24 **Zephaniah** the priest next in rank and the three doorkeepers.
Zep 1:1 The word of the LORD that came to **Zephaniah** son of Cushi,
Zec 6:10 Go the same day to the house of Josiah son of **Zephaniah**.
6:14 Hen son of **Zephaniah** as a memorial in the temple of the LORD.

7623 צְפַנְיָהוּ ṣᵉpanyāhû, n.pr.m. [2] [√ 7621 + 3378]

Zephaniah [2]

2Ki 25:18 **Zephaniah** the priest next in rank and the three doorkeepers.
Jer 37:3 sent Jehucal son of Shelemiah with the priest **Zephaniah** son of

7624 צָפְנַת פַּעְנֵחַ ṣāpᵉnat pa'nēaḥ, n.pr.m. [1] [√ 7195]

Zaphenath-Paneah [1]

Ge 41:45 Pharaoh gave Joseph the name **Zaphenath-Paneah** and gave him

7625 צֶפַע ṣepa', n.m. [1] [→ 7626]

viper [1]

Isa 14:29 from the root of that snake will spring up a **viper**, its fruit will be a

7626 צִפְעֹנִי ṣip'ōnî, n.m. [4] [√ 7625]

vipers [2], viper [1], viper's [1]

Pr 23:32 In the end it bites like a snake and poisons like a **viper**.
Isa 11:8 of the cobra, and the young child put his hand into the **viper's** nest.
59:5 They hatch the eggs of **vipers** and spin a spider's web.
Jer 8:17 **vipers** that cannot be charmed, and they will bite you,"

7627 צָפַף ṣāpap, v. [4] [→ 7628]

whisper [2], chirp [1], cried [1]

Isa 8:19 [D] to consult mediums and spiritists, who **whisper** and mutter,
10:14 [D] not one flapped a wing, or opened its mouth *to* **chirp**.' "
29:4 [D] from the earth; out of the dust your speech *will* **whisper**.
38:14 [D] *I* **cried** like a swift or thrush, I moaned like a mourning dove.

7628 צַפְצָפָה ṣapṣāpâ, n.f. [1] [√ 7627]

willow [1]

Eze 17:5 put it in fertile soil. He planted it like a **willow** by abundant water,

7629 צָפַר ṣāpar, v. [1]

leave [1]

Jdg 7:3 [A] and **leave** Mount Gilead.' " So twenty-two thousand men left,

7630 צְפַרְדֵּעַ ṣᵉpardēa', n.f. [13]

frogs [13]

Ex 8:2 [7:27] to let them go, I will plague your whole country with **frogs**.
8:3 [7:28] The Nile will teem with **frogs**. They will come up into your
8:4 [7:29] The **frogs** will go up on you and your people and all your
8:5 [8:1] and ponds, and make **frogs** come up on the land of Egypt.' "
8:6 [8:2] of Egypt, and the **frogs** came up and covered the land.
8:7 [8:3] they also made **frogs** come up on the land of Egypt.
8:8 [8:4] "Pray to the LORD to take the **frogs** away from me and my
8:9 [8:5] people that you and your houses may be rid of the **frogs**,
8:11 [8:7] The **frogs** will leave you and your houses, your officials
8:12 [8:8] Moses cried out to the LORD about the **frogs** he had
8:13 [8:9] The **frogs** died in the houses, in the courtyards and in the
Ps 78:45 of flies that devoured them, and **frogs** that devastated them.
105:30 Their land teemed with **frogs**, which went up into the bedrooms of

7631 צִפֹּרָה ṣippōrâ, n.pr.f. [3] [√ 7606]

Zipporah [3]

Ex 2:21 the man, who gave his daughter **Zipporah** to Moses in marriage.
4:25 But **Zipporah** took a flint knife, cut off her son's foreskin
18:2 After Moses had sent away his wife **Zipporah**, his father-in-law

7632 צִפֹּרֶן ṣippōren, n.[m.] [2] [→ Ar 10303]

nails [1], point [1]

Dt 21:12 her into your home and have her shave her head, trim her **nails**
Jer 17:1 inscribed with a flint **point**, on the tablets of their hearts and on the

7633 צֶפֶת ṣepet, n.f. [1] [√ 7596]

capital [1]

2Ch 3:15 cubits long, each with a **capital** on top measuring five cubits.

7634 צְפַת ṣᵉpat, n.pr.loc. [1] [√ 7596?]

Zephath [1]

Jdg 1:17 their brothers and attacked the Canaanites living in **Zephath**,

7635 צְפָתָה ṣᵉpatâ, n.pr.loc. [1]

Zephathah [1]

2Ch 14:10 [14:9] they took up battle positions in the Valley of **Zephathah**

7636 צָקוּן ṣāqûn, var. Not used in NIV/BHS [cf. 7439]

7637 צִקְלַג ṣiqlag, n.pr.loc. [15]

Ziklag [14], it^s [1]

Jos 15:31 **Ziklag**, Madmannah, Sansannah,
19:5 **Ziklag**, Beth Marcaboth, Hazar Susah,
1Sa 27:6 So on that day Achish gave him **Ziklag**, and it has belonged to the
27:6 him Ziklag, and **it**^s has belonged to the kings of Judah ever since.
30:1 David and his men reached **Ziklag** on the third day.
30:1 Now the Amalekites had raided the Negev and **Ziklag**. They had
30:1 the Negev and Ziklag. They had attacked **Ziklag** and burned it,
30:14 to Judah and the Negev of Caleb. And we burned **Ziklag**."
30:26 When David arrived in **Ziklag**, he sent some of the plunder to the
2Sa 1:1 from defeating the Amalekites and stayed in **Ziklag** two days.
4:10 bringing good news, I seized him and put him to death in **Ziklag**.
1Ch 4:30 Bethuel, Hormah, **Ziklag**,
12:1 These were the men who came to David at **Ziklag**, while he was
12:20 [12:21] When David went to **Ziklag**, these were the men of
Ne 11:28 in **Ziklag**, in Meconah and its settlements,

7638 צִקְלֹן ṣiqqālôn, n.[m.]. [1 / 0]

2Ki 4:42 with some heads of new grain. [BHS+ *in his sack*]

7639 צַר¹ ṣar¹, a. & n.m. [47] [√ 7674]

distress [20], trouble [11], narrow [3], small [3], distressed [2], adversity [1], anguish [1], anguished [1], critical [1], grieve [1], misery [1], pent-up [1], tightly [1]

Nu 22:26 and stood in a **narrow** place where there was no room to turn,
Dt 4:30 When you are in **distress** and all these things have happened to
Jdg 11:7 Why do you come to me now, when you're *in* **trouble**?"
1Sa 2:32 you will see **distress** *in* my dwelling. Although good will be done
13:6 When the men of Israel saw that their situation was **critical**
28:15 "I am in great **distress**," Saul said. "The Philistines are fighting
2Sa 1:26 I **grieve** for you, Jonathan my brother; you were very dear to me.
22:7 In my **distress** I called to the LORD; I called out to my God.
24:14 David said to Gad, "I am in deep **distress**. Let us fall into the
2Ki 6:1 "Look, the place where we meet with you is too **small** for us.
1Ch 21:13 David said to Gad, "I am in deep **distress**. Let me fall into the
2Ch 15:4 But in their **distress** they turned to the LORD, the God of Israel,
Est 7:4 because no such **distress** would justify disturbing the king."
Job 7:11 I will speak out in the **anguish** *of* my spirit, I will complain in the
15:24 **Distress** and anguish fill him with terror; they overwhelm him,
36:16 "He is wooing you from the jaws of **distress** to a spacious place
36:19 your mighty efforts sustain you so you would not be in **distress**?
38:23 which I reserve for times of **trouble**, for days of war and battle?
41:15 [41:7] His back has rows of shields **tightly** sealed together;
Ps 4:1 [4:2] Give me relief from my **distress**; be merciful to me and hear
18:6 [18:7] In my **distress** I called to the LORD; I cried to my God
31:9 [31:10] Be merciful to me, O LORD, for I am in **distress**; my
32:7 you will protect me from **trouble** and surround me with songs of
59:16 [59:17] for you are my fortress, my refuge in times of **trouble**.
66:14 my lips promised and my mouth spoke when I was in **trouble**.
69:17 [69:18] your servant; answer me quickly, for I am in **trouble**.
102:2 [102:3] Do not hide your face from me when I am *in* **distress**.
106:44 But he took note of their **distress** when he heard their cry;
107:6 they cried out to the LORD in their **trouble**, and he delivered
107:13 they cried to the LORD in their **trouble**, and he saved them from
107:19 they cried to the LORD in their **trouble**, and he saved them from
107:28 they cried out to the LORD in their **trouble**, and he brought them
119:143 **Trouble** and distress have come upon me, but your commands are
Pr 23:27 for a prostitute is a deep pit and a wayward wife is a **narrow** well.
24:10 If you falter in times of trouble, how **small** is your strength!
Isa 5:30 And if one looks at the land, he will see darkness and **distress**;
25:4 a refuge for the needy in his **distress**, a shelter from the storm
26:16 LORD, they came to you in their **distress**; when you disciplined
28:20 short to stretch out on, the blanket *too* **narrow** to wrap around you.
30:20 Although the Lord gives you the bread of **adversity** and the water
49:20 will yet say in your hearing, 'This place is too **small** for us;
59:19 For he will come like a **pent-up** flood that the breath of the
63:9 In all their distress he too was **distressed**, and the angel of his
Jer 48:5 on the road down to Horonaim **anguished** cries over the
La 1:20 "See, O LORD, how **distressed** I am! I am in torment within,
Eze 30:16 will be taken by storm; Memphis will be *in* constant **distress**.
Hos 5:15 will seek my face; in their **misery** they will earnestly seek me."

7640 צַר² ṣar², n.f. [68] [√ 7675; Ar 10568]

enemies [28], foes [19], enemy [11], foe [3], adversaries [2], adversary [2], hostile [1], opponent [1], oppressor [1]

Ge 14:20 be God Most High, who delivered your **enemies** into your hand."
Nu 10:9 When you go into battle in your own land against an **enemy** who is
24:8 They devour **hostile** nations and break their bones in pieces;
Dt 32:27 lest the **adversary** misunderstand and say, 'Our hand has
32:41 I will take vengeance on my **adversaries** and repay those who hate
32:43 he will take vengeance on his **enemies** and make atonement for his
33:7 own hands he defends his cause. Oh, be his help against his **foes**!"
Jos 5:13 went up to him and asked, "Are you for us or for our **enemies**?"
2Sa 24:13 Or three months of fleeing from your **enemies** while they pursue
1Ch 12:17 [12:18] if you have come to betray me to my **enemies** when my
21:12 of famine, three months of being swept away before your **enemies**,
Ezr 4:1 When the **enemies** *of* Judah and Benjamin heard that the exiles
Ne 4:11 [4:5] Also our **enemies** said, "Before they know it or see us, we
9:27 So you handed them over to their **enemies**, who oppressed them.
9:27 them deliverers, who rescued them from the hand of their **enemies**.
Est 7:6 Esther said, "The **adversary** and enemy is this vile Haman."
Job 6:23 deliver me from the hand of the **enemy**, ransom me from the
16:9 his teeth at me; my **opponent** fastens on me his piercing eyes.
19:11 His anger burns against me; he counts me among his **enemies**.
Ps 3:1 [3:2] O LORD, how many are my **foes**! How many rise up
13:4 [13:5] have overcome him," and my **foes** will rejoice when I fall.
27:2 when my **enemies** and my foes attack me, they will stumble
27:12 Do not turn me over to the desire of my **foes**, for false witnesses
44:5 [44:6] Through you we push back our **enemies**; through your
44:7 [44:8] you give us victory over our **enemies**, you put our
44:10 [44:11] You made us retreat before the **enemy**, and our
60:11 [60:13] Give us aid against the **enemy**, for the help of man is
60:12 [60:14] gain the victory, and he will trample down our **enemies**.
74:10 How long will the **enemy** mock you, O God? Will the foe revile
78:42 his power—the day he redeemed them from the **oppressor**,
78:61 his might into captivity, his splendor into the hands of the **enemy**.
78:66 He beat back his **enemies**; he put them to everlasting shame.
81:14 [81:15] subdue their enemies and turn my hand against their **foes**!
89:23 [89:24] I will crush his **foes** before him and strike down his
89:42 [89:43] You have exalted the right hand of his **foes**; you have
97:3 Fire goes before him and consumes his **foes** on every side.
105:24 his people very fruitful; he made them too numerous for their **foes**,
106:11 The waters covered their **adversaries**; not one of them survived.
107:2 the LORD say this—those he redeemed from the hand of the **foe**,
108:12 [108:13] Give us aid against the **enemy**, for the help of man is
108:13 [108:14] gain the victory, and he will trample down our **enemies**.
112:8 he will have no fear; in the end he will look in triumph on his **foes**.
119:139 My zeal wears me out, for my **enemies** ignore your words.
119:157 Many are the **foes** who persecute me, but I have not turned from
136:24 and freed us from our **enemies**, *His love endures forever.*
Isa 1:24 I will get relief from my **foes** and avenge myself on my enemies.
9:11 [9:10] But the LORD has strengthened Rezin's **foes** against them
26:11 put to shame; let the fire reserved for your **enemies** consume them.
59:18 so will he repay wrath to his **enemies** and retribution to his foes;
63:18 but now our **enemies** have trampled down your sanctuary.
64:2 [64:1] come down to make your name known to your **enemies**
Jer 30:16 devour you will be devoured; all your **enemies** will go into exile.
46:10 LORD Almighty—a day of vengeance, for vengeance on his **foes**.
50:7 their **enemies** said, 'We are not guilty, for they sinned against the
La 1:5 Her **foes** have become her masters; her enemies are at ease.
1:5 Her children have gone into exile, captive before the **foe**.
1:7 When her people fell into **enemy** hands, there was no one to help
1:7 Her **enemies** looked at her and laughed at her destruction.
1:10 The **enemy** laid hands on all her treasures; she saw pagan nations
1:17 LORD has decreed for Jacob that his neighbors become his **foes**;
2:4 Like a **foe** he has slain all who were pleasing to the eye; he has
2:17 let the enemy gloat over you, he has exalted the horn of your **foes**.
4:12 that enemies and **foes** could enter the gates of Jerusalem.
Eze 39:23 I hid my face from them and handed them over to their **enemies**,
Am 3:11 "An **enemy** will overrun the land; he will pull down your
Mic 5:9 [5:8] Your hand will be lifted up in triumph over your **enemies**,
Na 1:2 The LORD takes vengeance on his **foes** and maintains his wrath
Zec 8:10 No one could go about his business safely because of his **enemy**,

7641 צַר³ ṣar³, a. *or* n.[m.]. [1] [√ 7644]

flint [1]

Isa 5:28 their horses' hoofs seem like **flint**, their chariot wheels like a

7642 צַר⁴ ṣar⁴, n.m. *or* a. Not used in NIV/BHS

7643 צֵר ṣēr, n.pr.loc. [1]

Zer [1]

Jos 19:35 fortified cities were Ziddim, **Zer**, Hammath, Rakkath, Kinnereth,

7644 צֹר¹ ṣōr¹, n.[m.]. [5] [→ 7447, 7450, 7641, 7645, 7656, 7660]

flint [3], edge [1], flint knife [1]

Ex 4:25 But Zipporah took a **flint knife**, cut off her son's foreskin
Jos 5:2 to Joshua, "Make **flint** knives and circumcise the Israelites again."
5:3 So Joshua made **flint** knives and circumcised the Israelites at
Ps 89:43 [89:44] You have turned back the **edge** *of* his sword and have not

Eze 3: 9 I will make your forehead like the hardest stone, harder than **flint**.

7645 ²צֹר **ṣōr²**, n.pr.loc. Not used in NIV/BHS [→ 7450, 7660; cf. 7644]

7646 צָרַב **ṣārab**, v. [1] [→ 7647, 7648]
be scorched [1]

Eze 20:47 [21:3] [C] every face from south to north *will* **be scorched** by it.

7647 צָרָב **ṣārāb**, a. [1] [√ 7646]
scorching [1]

Pr 16:27 A scoundrel plots evil, and his speech is like a **scorching** fire.

7648 צָרֶבֶת **ṣārebet**, n.f. [2] [√ 7646]
scar [2]

Lev 13:23 is unchanged and has not spread, it is only a **scar** *from* the boil,
13:28 priest shall pronounce him clean; it is only a **scar** *from* the burn.

7649 צְרֵדָה **ṣ**ᵉ**rēdâ**, n.pr.loc. [2 / 1]
Zeredah [1]

1Ki 11:26 He was one of Solomon's officials, an Ephraimite from **Zeredah**,
2Ch 4:17 Jordan between Succoth and Zarethan. [BHS *Zeredatha*; NIV 7681]

7650 ¹צָרָה **ṣārâ¹**, n.f. [70] [√ 7639; cf. 7674]
trouble [24], distress [22], troubles [8], anguish [4], calamity [2], difficulties [2], adversity [1], calamities [1], distressed [1], distresses [1], groan [1], hardship [1], hostility [1], oppressed [1]

Ge 35: 3 who answered me in the day of my **distress** and who has been with
42:21 We saw *how* **distressed** he was when he pleaded with us for his
42:21 we would not listen; that's why this **distress** has come upon us."
Dt 31:17 Many disasters and **difficulties** will come upon them, and on that
31:21 And when many disasters and **difficulties** come upon them,
Jdg 10:14 you have chosen. Let them save you when you are in **trouble**!"
1Sa 10:19 your God, who saves you out of all your calamities and **distresses**.
26:24 so may the LORD value my life and deliver me from all **trouble**."
2Sa 4: 9 as the LORD lives, who has delivered me out of all **trouble**,
1Ki 1:29 as the LORD lives, who has delivered me out of every **trouble**,
2Ki 19: 3 This day is a day of **distress** and rebuke and disgrace, as when
2Ch 15: 6 because God was troubling them with every kind of **distress**.
20: 9 that bears your Name and will cry out to you in our **distress**,
Ne 9:27 But when they were **oppressed** they cried out to you.
9:37 our bodies and our cattle as they please. We are in great **distress**.
Job 5:19 From six **calamities** he will rescue you; in seven no harm will
27: 9 Does God listen to his cry when **distress** comes upon him?
Ps 20: 1 [20:2] May the LORD answer you when you are in **distress**;
22:11 [22:12] from me, for **trouble** is near and there is no one to help.
25:17 The **troubles** *of* my heart have multiplied; free me from my
25:22 Redeem Israel, O God, from all their **troubles**!
31: 7 [31:8] you saw my affliction and knew the **anguish** *of* my soul.
34: 6 [34:7] LORD heard him; he saved him out of all his **troubles**.
34:17 [34:18] hears them; he delivers them from all their **troubles**.
37:39 comes from the LORD; he is their stronghold in time of **trouble**.
46: 1 [46:2] is our refuge and strength, an ever-present help in **trouble**.
50:15 and call upon me in the day of **trouble**; I will deliver you,
54: 7 [54:9] For he has delivered me from all my **troubles**, and my eyes
71:20 Though you have made me see **troubles**, many and bitter,
77: 2 [77:3] When I was *in* **distress**, I sought the Lord; at night I
78:49 against them his hot anger, his wrath, indignation and **hostility**—
81: 7 [81:8] In your **distress** you called and I rescued you, I answered
86: 7 In the day of my **trouble** I will call to you, for you will answer me.
91:15 I will be with him in **trouble**, I will deliver him and honor him.
116: 3 the grave came upon me; I was overcome by **trouble** and sorrow.
120: 1 I call on the LORD in my **distress**, and he answers me.
138: 7 Though I walk in the midst of **trouble**, you preserve my life;
142: 2 [142:3] my complaint before him; before him I tell my **trouble**.
143:11 preserve my life; in your righteousness, bring me out of **trouble**.
Pr 1:27 you like a whirlwind, when **distress** and trouble overwhelm you.
11: 8 The righteous man is rescued from **trouble**, and it comes on the
12:13 is trapped by his sinful talk, but a righteous man escapes **trouble**.
17:17 A friend loves at all times, and a brother is born for **adversity**.
21:23 guards his mouth and his tongue keeps himself from **calamity**.
24:10 If you falter in times of **trouble**, how small is your strength!
25:19 or a lame foot is reliance on the unfaithful in times of **trouble**.
Isa 8:22 the earth and see only **distress** and darkness and fearful gloom,
30: 6 Through a land of **hardship** and distress, of lions and lionesses,
33: 2 Be our strength every morning, our salvation in time of **distress**.
37: 3 This day is a day of **distress** and rebuke and disgrace, as when
46: 7 out to it, it does not answer; it cannot save him from his **troubles**.
63: 9 In all their **distress** he too was distressed, and the angel of his
65:16 For the past **troubles** will be forgotten and hidden from my eyes.
Jer 4:31 as of a woman in labor, a **groan** as of one bearing her first child—
6:24 **Anguish** has gripped us, pain like that of a woman in labor.
14: 8 O Hope of Israel, its Savior in times of **distress**, why are you like a
15:11 enemies plead with you in times of disaster and times of **distress**.
16:19 my strength and my fortress, my refuge in time of **distress**,
30: 7 It will be a time of **trouble** for Jacob, but he will be saved out of it.
49:24 **anguish** and pain have seized her, pain like that of a woman in
50:43 **Anguish** has gripped him, pain like that of a woman in labor.
Da 12: 1 There will be a time of **distress** such as has not happened from the
Ob 1:12 of their destruction, nor boast so much in the day of their **trouble**.
1:14 nor hand over their survivors in the day of their **trouble**.
Jnh 2: 2 [2:3] "In my **distress** I called to the LORD, and he answered me.
Na 1: 7 The LORD is good, a refuge in times of **trouble**. He cares for
1: 9 he will bring to an end; **trouble** will not come a second time.
Hab 3:16 Yet I will wait patiently for the day of **calamity** to come on the
Zep 1:15 a day of **distress** and anguish, a day of trouble and ruin, a day of
Zec 10:11 They will pass through the sea of **trouble**; the surging sea will be

7651 ²צָרָה **ṣārâ²**, n.f. [1] [√ 7675]
rival [1]

1Sa 1: 6 her womb, her **rival** kept provoking her in order to irritate her.

7652 צִרָה **ṣirâ**, n.f. Not used in NIV/BHS [cf. 3227]

7653 צְרוּיָה **ṣ**ᵉ**rûyâ**, n.pr.f. [26]
Zeruiah [25], Zeruiah's [1]

1Sa 26: 6 then asked Ahimelech the Hittite and Abishai son of **Zeruiah**,
2Sa 2:13 Joab son of **Zeruiah** and David's men went out and met them at
2:18 The three sons of **Zeruiah** were there: Joab, Abishai and Asahel.
3:39 I am weak, and these sons of **Zeruiah** are too strong for me.
8:16 Joab son of **Zeruiah** was over the army; Jehoshaphat son of Ahilud
14: 1 Joab son of **Zeruiah** knew that the king's heart longed for
16: 9 Abishai son of **Zeruiah** said to the king, "Why should this dead
16:10 "What do you and I have in common, you sons of **Zeruiah**?
17:25 the daughter of Nahash and sister of **Zeruiah** the mother of Joab.
18: 2 a third under Joab's brother Abishai son of **Zeruiah**, and a third
19:21 [19:22] Abishai son of **Zeruiah** said, "Shouldn't Shimei be put to
19:22 [19:23] do you and I have in common, you sons of **Zeruiah**?
21:17 Abishai son of **Zeruiah** came to David's rescue; he struck the
23:18 Abishai the brother of Joab son of **Zeruiah** was chief of the Three.
23:37 Naharai the Beerothite, the armor-bearer of Joab son of **Zeruiah**,
1Ki 1: 7 Adonijah conferred with Joab son of **Zeruiah** and with Abiathar
2: 5 "Now you yourself know what Joab son of **Zeruiah** did to me—
2:22 for him and for Abiathar the priest and Joab son of **Zeruiah**!"
1Ch 2:16 Their sisters were **Zeruiah** and Abigail. Zeruiah's three sons were
2:16 and Abigail. **Zeruiah's** three sons were Abishai, Joab and Asahel.
11: 6 Joab son of **Zeruiah** went up first, and so he received the
11:39 Naharai the Berothite, the armor-bearer of Joab son of **Zeruiah**,
18:12 Abishai son of **Zeruiah** struck down eighteen thousand Edomites
18:15 Joab son of **Zeruiah** was over the army; Jehoshaphat son of Ahilud
26:28 by Saul son of Kish, Abner son of Ner and Joab son of **Zeruiah**,
27:24 Joab son of **Zeruiah** began to count the men but did not finish.

7654 צְרוּעָה **ṣ**ᵉ**rûʿâ**, n.pr.loc. [1] [√ 7665]
Zeruah [1]

1Ki 11:26 from Zeredah, and his mother was a widow named **Zeruah**.

7655 ¹צְרוֹר **ṣ**ᵉ**rōr¹**, n.m. [7] [→ 7657?; cf. 7674]
purse [2], bag [1], bundle [1], pouch [1], pouches [1], sachet [1]

Ge 42:35 their sacks, there in each man's sack was his **pouch** *of* silver!
42:35 When they and their father saw the money **pouches**, they were
1Sa 25:29 the life of my master will be bound securely in the **bundle** *of* the
Job 14:17 My offenses will be sealed up in a **bag**; you will cover over my sin.
Pr 7:20 He took his **purse** *filled with* money and will not be home till full
SS 1:13 My lover is to me a **sachet** *of* myrrh resting between my breasts.
Hag 1: 6 You earn wages, only to put them in a **purse** with holes in it."

7656 ²צְרוֹר **ṣ**ᵉ**rôr²**, n.m. [2] [→ 7657?; cf. 7644]
pebble [1], piece [1]

2Sa 17:13 we will drag it down to the valley until not even a **piece** of it can
Am 9: 9 grain is shaken in a sieve, and not a **pebble** will reach the ground.

7657 ³צְרוֹר **ṣ**ᵉ**rôr³**, n.pr.m. [1] [√ 7656? *or* 7655?]
Zeror [1]

1Sa 9: 1 the son of **Zeror**, the son of Becorath, the son of Aphiah of

7658 צָרַח **ṣāraḥ**, v. [2] [→ 7659]
raise the battle cry [1], shouting [1]

Isa 42:13 [G] with a shout *he will* **raise the battle cry** and will triumph

Zep 1: 14 [A] the LORD will be bitter, the **shouting** *of* the warrior there.

7659 צֶרַח ṣeraḥ, n.[m.]. Not used in NIV/BHS [√ 7658]

7660 צֹרִי ṣōrî, a.g. [5] [√ 7645]

from Tyre [1], men from Tyre [1], of Tyre [1], Tyre [1], Tyrians [1]

1Ki 7: 14 and whose father was a man **of Tyre** and a craftsman in bronze.
1Ch 22: 4 and **Tyrians** had brought large numbers of them to David.
2Ch 2: 14 [2:13] mother was from Dan and whose father was **from Tyre**.
Ezr 3: 7 and gave food and drink and oil to the people of Sidon and **Tyre**,
Ne 13: 16 **Men from Tyre** who lived in Jerusalem were bringing in fish

7661 צֳרִי ṣᵒrî, n.[m.]. [6] [→ 7662]

balm [6]

Ge 37: 25 Their camels were loaded with spices, **balm** and myrrh, and they
43: 11 a little **balm** and a little honey, some spices and myrrh,
Jer 8: 22 Is there no **balm** in Gilead? Is there no physician there? Why
46: 11 "Go up to Gilead and get **balm**, O Virgin Daughter of Egypt.
51: 8 Wail over her! Get **balm** for her pain; perhaps she can be healed.
Eze 27: 17 from Minnith and confections, honey, oil and **balm** for your wares.

7662 צְרִי ṣᵉrî, n.pr.m. [1] [√ 7661]

Zeri [1]

1Ch 25: 3 Gedaliah, **Zeri**, Jeshaiah, Shimei, Hashabiah and Mattithiah,

7663 צְרִיחַ ṣᵉrîaḥ, n.[m.]. [4]

stronghold [2], it[s] [+2021] [1], pits [1]

Jdg 9: 46 the citizens in the tower of Shechem went into the **stronghold** *of*
9: 49 They piled them against the **stronghold** and set it on fire over the
9: 49 the stronghold and set **it**[s] [+2021] on fire over the people inside.
1Sa 13: 6 hid in caves and thickets, among the rocks, and in **pits** and cisterns.

7664 צֹרֶךְ ṣōrek, n.[m.]. [1]

need [1]

2Ch 2: 16 [2:15] we will cut all the logs from Lebanon that you **need**

7665 צָרַע ṣāraʿ, v.den. [20] [→ 7654, 7665?, 7669]

had leprosy [6], leprosy [4], leprous [4], diseased [2], disease [1], has an infectious skin disease [1], infectious skin disease [1], person[s] [1]

Ex 4: 6 [E] his cloak, and when he took it out, it *was* **leprous**, like snow.
Lev 13: 44 [B] the man *is* **diseased** and is unclean. The priest shall
13: 45 [B] "The *person with* such an infectious **disease** must wear torn
14: 2 [E] "These are the regulations for the **diseased** *person* at the time
14: 3 [B] If the **person**[s] has been healed of his infectious skin disease,
22: 4 [B] " 'If a descendant of Aaron *has an* **infectious skin disease**
Nu 5: 2 [B] from the camp anyone *who* **has an infectious skin disease**
12: 10 [E] above the Tent, there stood Miriam—**leprous**, like snow.
12: 10 [E] Aaron turned toward her and saw that *she* **had leprosy**;
2Sa 3: 29 [E] or **leprosy** or who leans on a crutch or who falls by the sword
2Ki 5: 1 [E] to Aram. He was a valiant soldier, but *he* **had leprosy**.
5: 11 [E] wave his hand over the spot and cure me of my **leprosy**.
5: 27 [E] Gehazi went from Elisha's presence and *he was* **leprous**,
7: 3 [E] Now there were four men *with* **leprosy** at the entrance of the
7: 8 [E] The *men who* **had leprosy** reached the edge of the camp
15: 5 [E] The LORD afflicted the king with **leprosy** until the day he
2Ch 26: 20 [E] they saw that he **had leprosy** on his forehead, so they hurried
26: 21 [E] King Uzziah **had leprosy** until the day he died. He lived in a
26: 21 [E] **leprous**, and excluded from the temple of the LORD.
26: 23 [E] that belonged to the kings, for people said, "He **had leprosy**."

7666 צָרְעָה ṣorʿâ, n.pr.loc. [10] [→ 7668, 7670]

Zorah [10]

Jos 15: 33 In the western foothills: Eshtaol, **Zorah**, Ashnah,
19: 41 territory of their inheritance included: **Zorah**, Eshtaol, Ir Shemesh,
Jdg 13: 2 A certain man of **Zorah**, named Manoah, from the clan of the
13: 25 him while he was in Mahaneh Dan, between **Zorah** and Eshtaol.
16: 31 They brought him back and buried him between **Zorah**
18: 2 So the Danites sent five warriors from **Zorah** and Eshtaol to spy
18: 8 When they returned to **Zorah** and Eshtaol, their brothers asked
18: 11 of the Danites, armed for battle, set out from **Zorah** and Eshtaol.
2Ch 11: 10 **Zorah**, Aijalon and Hebron. These were fortified cities in Judah
Ne 11: 29 in En Rimmon, in **Zorah**, in Jarmuth,

7667 צִרְעָה ṣirʿâ, n.f.col. [3] [√ 7665?]

hornet [3]

Ex 23: 28 I will send the **hornet** ahead of you to drive the Hivites, Canaanites
Dt 7: 20 the LORD your God will send the **hornet** among them until even
Jos 24: 12 I sent the **hornet** ahead of you, which drove them out before you—

7668 צָרְעִי ṣorʿî, a.g. [1] [√ 7666]

Zorites [1]

1Ch 2: 54 Atroth Beth Joab, half the Manahathites, the **Zorites**,

7669 צָרַעַת ṣāraʿat, n.f. [35] [√ 7665]

skin disease [10], infectious disease [7], mildew [6], leprosy [5], disease [2], infectious skin diseases and mildew [1], it[s] [1], leprous [1], spreading mildew [+5596] [1], spreading mildew [1]

Lev 13: 2 bright spot on his skin that may become an infectious **skin disease**,
13: 3 appears to be more than skin deep, it is an infectious **skin disease**.
13: 8 he shall pronounce him unclean; it is an **infectious disease**.
13: 9 "When anyone has an infectious **skin disease**, he must be brought
13: 11 it is a chronic **skin disease** and the priest shall pronounce him
13: 12 "If the **disease** breaks out all over his skin and, so far as the priest
13: 12 **it**[s] covers all the skin of the infected person from head to foot,
13: 13 is to examine him, and if the **disease** has covered his whole body,
13: 15 The raw flesh is unclean; he has an **infectious disease**.
13: 20 It is an infectious **skin disease** that has broken out where the boil
13: 25 it is an **infectious disease** that has broken out in the burn.
13: 25 priest shall pronounce him unclean; it is an infectious **skin disease**.
13: 27 priest shall pronounce him unclean; it is an infectious **skin disease**.
13: 30 it is an itch, an **infectious disease** *of* the head or chin.
13: 42 it is an **infectious disease** breaking out on his head or forehead.
13: 43 or forehead is reddish-white like an **infectious** skin **disease**,
13: 47 "If any clothing is contaminated with **mildew**—any woolen
13: 49 it is a **spreading mildew** and must be shown to the priest.
13: 51 or the leather, whatever its use, it is a destructive **mildew**;
13: 52 that has the contamination in it, because the **mildew** is destructive;
13: 59 These are the regulations concerning contamination by **mildew** in
14: 3 If the person has been healed of his infectious **skin disease**,
14: 7 he shall sprinkle the one to be cleansed of the **infectious disease**
14: 32 are the regulations for anyone who has an infectious **skin disease**
14: 34 and I put a **spreading mildew** [+5596] in a house in that land,
14: 44 if the mildew has spread in the house, it is a destructive **mildew**;
14: 54 These are the regulations for any infectious **skin disease**, for an
14: 55 for **mildew** *in* clothing or in a house,
14: 57 These are the regulations for **infectious skin diseases and mildew**.
Dt 24: 8 In cases of **leprous** diseases be very careful to do exactly as the
2Ki 5: 3 the prophet who is in Samaria! He would cure him of his **leprosy**."
5: 6 servant Naaman to you so that you may cure him of his **leprosy**."
5: 7 does this fellow send someone to me to be cured of his **leprosy**?
5: 27 Naaman's **leprosy** will cling to you and to your descendants
2Ch 26: 19 altar in the LORD's temple, **leprosy** broke out on his forehead.

7670 צָרְעָתִי ṣārᵉʿātî, a.g. [2] [√ 7666]

Zorathites [2]

1Ch 2: 53 From these descended the **Zorathites** and Eshtaolites.
4: 2 of Ahumai and Lahad. These were the clans of the **Zorathites**.

7671 צָרַף ṣārap, v. [33] [→ 5214, 7672]

goldsmith [6], refined [5], flawless [3], *untranslated* [2], goldsmiths [2], refine [2], refining goes on [+7671] [2], silversmith [2], been tested [1], examine [1], fashions [1], proved true [1], refiner [1], refiner's [1], sift [1], test [1], thoroughly purge away [+1342+2021+3869] [1]

Jdg 7: 4 [A] them down to the water, and *I will* **sift** them for you there.
17: 4 [A] hundred shekels of silver and gave them to a **silversmith**,
2Sa 22: 31 [B] his way is perfect; the word of the LORD *is* **flawless**.
Ne 3: 8 [A] Uzziel son of Harhaiah, one of the **goldsmiths**,
3: 32 [A] the Sheep Gate the **goldsmiths** and merchants made repairs.
Ps 12: 6 [12:7] [B] like silver **refined** in a furnace of clay, purified seven
17: 3 [A] me at night, though *you* **test** me, you will find nothing;
18: 30 [18:31] [B] way is perfect; the word of the LORD *is* **flawless**.
26: 2 [A] O LORD, and try me, **examine** my heart and my mind;
66: 10 [A] For you, O God, tested us; *you* **refined** us like silver.
66: 10 [A] For you, O God, tested us; you refined us like **[RPH]** silver.
105: 19 [A] came to pass, till the word of the LORD **proved** him **true**.
119: 140 [B] Your promises *have* **been** thoroughly **tested**, and your
Pr 25: 4 [A] from the silver, and out comes material for the **silversmith**;
30: 5 [B] "Every word of God *is* **flawless**; he is a shield to those who
Isa 1: 25 [A] *I will* **thoroughly purge** [+1342+2021+3869] **away** your dross
40: 19 [A] a **goldsmith** overlays it with gold and fashions silver chains
40: 19 [A] overlays it with gold and **fashions** silver chains for it.
41: 7 [A] The craftsman encourages the **goldsmith**, and he who
46: 6 [A] they hire a **goldsmith** to make it into a god, and they bow
48: 10 [A] See, *I have* **refined** you, though not as silver; I have tested
Jer 6: 29 [A] the lead with fire, but *the* **refining** [+7671] **goes on** in vain;
6: 29 [A] the lead with fire, but *the* **refining goes on** [+7671] in vain;
9: 7 [9:6] [A] "See, I *will* **refine** and test them, for what else can I do
10: 9 [A] What the craftsman and **goldsmith** have made is then dressed
10: 14 [A] without knowledge; every **goldsmith** is shamed by his idols.
51: 17 [A] without knowledge; every **goldsmith** is shamed by his idols.

Da 11:35 [A] so that they *may be* **refined**, purified and made spotless until
12:10 [C] Many will be purified, made spotless and **refined**,
Zec 13: 9 [A] the fire; *I will* **refine** them like silver and test them like gold.
13: 9 [A] I will refine them like **[RPH]** silver and test them like gold.
Mal 3: 2 [D] For he will be like a **refiner's** fire or a launderer's soap.
3: 3 [D] He will sit as a **refiner** and purifier of silver; he will purify

7672 צֹרְפִי **ṣōrᵉpî**, n.[m.]col. [1] [√ 7671]

goldsmiths [1]

Ne 3:31 Next to him, Malkijah, one of the **goldsmiths**, made repairs as far

7673 צָרְפַת **ṣārᵉpat**, n.pr.loc. [3]

Zarephath [3]

1Ki 17: 9 "Go at once to **Zarephath** of Sidon and stay there. I have
17:10 So he went to **Zarephath**. When he came to the town gate,
Ob 1:20 who are in Canaan will possess ˻the land˼ as far as **Zarephath**;

7674 ¹צָרַר **ṣārar¹**, v. [30] [→ 5210, 7639, 7650, 7655, 7676; cf. 7443, 7675]

distress [3], bring distress [2], in distress [2], in labor [2], besiege [1], bind up [1], bound securely [1], distressed [1], frustrated [1], gave trouble [1], hampered [1], kept in confinement [1], lay siege [1], mended [1], oppress [1], oppressed [1], small [1], stored up [1], sweep away [+906+928+4053] [1], trouble [1], tying [1], weakened [1], wrapped up [1], wrapped [1], wraps up [1]

Ge 32: 7 [32:8] [A] **distress** Jacob divided the people who were with him
Ex 12:34 [B] carried it on their shoulders in kneading troughs **wrapped** in
Dt 28:52 [G] *They will* **lay siege** to all the cities throughout your land until
28:52 [G] *They will* **besiege** all the cities throughout the land the
Jos 9: 4 [E] with worn-out sacks and old wineskins, cracked and **mended**.
Jdg 2:15 [A] just as he had sworn to them. They *were* **in** great **distress**.
10: 9 [A] and the house of Ephraim; and Israel *was* **in** great **distress**.
1Sa 25:29 [B] the life of my master will be **bound securely** in the bundle of
30: 6 [A] David *was* greatly **distressed** because the men were talking
2Sa 13: 2 [A] Amnon *became* **frustrated** to the point of illness on account
20: 3 [B] They were **kept in confinement** till the day of their death,
2Ch 28:20 [G] came to him, but *he* **gave** him **trouble** instead of help.
28:22 [G] In his time of **trouble** King Ahaz became even more
33:12 [G] In his **distress** he sought the favor of the LORD his God
Ne 9:27 [G] handed them over to their enemies, *who* **oppressed** them.
Job 18: 7 [A] The vigor of his step *is* **weakened**; his own schemes throw
20:22 [A] In the midst of his plenty, **distress** *will* overtake him; the full
26: 8 [A] *He* **wraps up** the waters in his clouds, yet the clouds do not
Pr 4:12 [A] When you walk, your steps *will* not *be* **hampered**; when you
26: 8 [A] Like **tying** a stone in a sling is the giving of honor to a fool.
30: 4 [A] Who *has* **wrapped up** the waters in his cloak? Who has
Isa 8:16 [A] **Bind up** the testimony and seal up the law among my
49:19 [A] land laid waste, now *you will be* too **small** for your people,
Jer 10:18 [G] *I will* **bring distress** on them so that they may be captured."
48:41 [G] Moab's warriors will be like the heart of a woman **in labor**.
49:22 [G] Edom's warriors will be like the heart of a woman **in labor**.
Hos 4:19 [A] A whirlwind *will* **sweep** [+906+928+4053] them **away**, and
13:12 [B] The guilt of Ephraim *is* **stored up**, his sins are kept on
Am 5:12 [A] *You* **oppress** the righteous and take bribes and you deprive
Zep 1:17 [G] *I will* **bring distress** on the people and they will walk like

7675 ²צָרַר **ṣārar²**, v. [26] [→ 7640, 7651, 7677; cf. 7674]

enemies [7], enemy [4], foes [4], oppressed [2], adversaries [1], foe [1], give trouble [1], hostile [1], oppose [1], oppressing [1], rival wife [1], treat as enemies [1], treated as enemies [1]

Ex 23:22 [A] to your enemies and will oppose *those who* **oppose** you.
Lev 18:18 [A] " 'Do not take your wife's sister as a **rival wife** and have
Nu 10: 9 [A] in your own land against an enemy who *is* **oppressing** you,
25:17 [A] "**Treat** the Midianites **as enemies** and kill them,
25:18 [A] because they **treated** you **as enemies** when they deceived
33:55 [A] *They will* **give** you **trouble** in the land where you will live.
Est 3:10 [A] son of Hammedatha, the Agagite, the **enemy** *of* the Jews.
8: 1 [A] Queen Esther the estate of Haman, the **enemy** *of* the Jews.
9:10 [A] sons of Haman son of Hammedatha, the **enemy** *of* the Jews.
9:24 [A] son of Hammedatha, the Agagite, the **enemy** *of* all the Jews,
Ps 6: 7 [6:8] [A] weak with sorrow; they fail because of all my **foes**.
7: 4 [7:5] [A] peace with me or without cause have robbed my **foe**—
7: 6 [7:7] [A] in your anger; rise up against the rage of my **enemies**.
8: 2 [8:3] [A] you have ordained praise because of your **enemies**,
10: 5 [A] and your laws are far from him; he sneers at all his **enemies**.
23: 5 [A] prepare a table before me in the presence of my **enemies**.
31:11 [31:12] [A] Because of all my **enemies**, I am the utter contempt
42:10 [42:11] [A] My bones suffer mortal agony as my **foes** taunt me,
69:19 [69:20] [A] and shamed; all my **enemies** are before you.
74: 4 [A] Your **foes** roared in the place where you met with us; they set
74:23 [A] Do not ignore the clamor of your **adversaries**, the uproar of
129: 1 [A] *They have* greatly **oppressed** me from my youth—let Israel
129: 2 [A] *they have* greatly **oppressed** me from my youth, but they
143:12 [A] my enemies; destroy all my **foes**, for I am your servant.
Isa 11:13 [A] jealousy will vanish, and Judah's **enemies** will be cut off;
11:13 [A] not be jealous of Judah, nor Judah **hostile** *toward* Ephraim.

7676 ³צָרַר **ṣārar³**, v.den. Not used in NIV/BHS [√ 7674]

7677 ⁴צָרַר **ṣārar⁴**, v.den. Not used in NIV/BHS [√ 7675]

7678 צְרֵרָה **ṣᵉrērâ**, n.p.loc. [1]

Zererah [1]

Jdg 7:22 The army fled to Beth Shittah toward **Zererah** as far as the border

7679 צֶרֶת **ṣeret**, n.pr.m. [1] [→ 7680]

Zereth [1]

1Ch 4: 7 The sons of Helah: **Zereth**, Zohar, Ethnan,

7680 צֶרֶת הַשַּׁחַר **ṣeret haššaḥar**, n.pr.loc. [1] [√ 7679 + 2241]

Zereth Shahar [1]

Jos 13:19 Kiriathaim, Sibmah, **Zereth Shahar** on the hill in the valley,

7681 צָרְתָן **ṣārᵉtān**, n.pr.loc. [3 / 4]

Zarethan [4]

Jos 3:16 distance away, at a town called Adam in the vicinity of **Zarethan**,
1Ki 4:12 and in all of Beth Shan next to **Zarethan** below Jezreel,
7:46 molds in the plain of the Jordan between Succoth and **Zarethan**.
2Ch 4:17 plain of the Jordan between Succoth and **Zarethan**. [BHS 7649]

ק, q

7682 ק **q**, letter. Not used in NIV/BHS [→ Ar 10617]

7683 קֵא **qē'**, n.[m.]. [1] [√ 7794]

vomit [1]

Pr 26:11 As a dog returns to its **vomit**, so a fool repeats his folly.

7684 קָאַת **qā'at**, n.[f.]. [5]

desert owl [4], owl [1]

Lev 11:18 the white owl, the **desert owl**, the osprey,
Dt 14:17 the **desert owl**, the osprey, the cormorant,
Ps 102: 6 [102:7] I am like a desert **owl**, like an owl among the ruins.
Isa 34:11 The **desert owl** and screech owl will possess it; the great owl
Zep 2:14 The **desert owl** and the screech owl will roost on her columns.

7685 קַב **qab**, n.[m.]. [1] [→ 7688]

cab [1]

2Ki 6:25 of silver, and a quarter of a **cab** *of* seed pods for five shekels.

7686 קָבַב **qābab**, v. [14] [cf. 5918, 5919]

curse [8], curse at all [+7686] [2], cursed [2], put a curse on [2]

Nu 22:11 [A] Now come and **put a curse on** them for me. Perhaps then I
22:17 [A] you say. Come and **put a curse on** these people for me."
23: 8 [A] How *can I* **curse** those whom God has not cursed? How can
23: 8 [A] How can I curse those whom God *has* not **cursed**? How can
23:11 [A] I brought you to **curse** my enemies, but you have done
23:13 [A] but not all of them. And from there, **curse** them for me."
23:25 [A] "Neither **curse** [+7686] them **at all** nor bless them at all!"
23:25 [A] "Neither **curse** them **at all** [+7686] nor bless them at all!"
23:27 [A] Perhaps it will please God *to let you* **curse** them for me from
24:10 [A] and said to him, "I summoned you to **curse** my enemies,
Job 3: 8 [A] *May* those who curse days **curse** that day, those who are
5: 3 [A] seen a fool taking root, but suddenly his house *was* **cursed**.
Pr 11:26 [A] People **curse** the man who hoards grain, but blessing crowns
24:24 [A] peoples *will* **curse** him and nations denounce him.

7687 קֵבָה **qēbâ**, n.f. [2]

body [1], inner parts [1]

Nu 25: 8 both of them—through the Israelite and into the woman's **body**.
Dt 18: 3 a bull or a sheep: the shoulder, the jowls and the **inner parts**.

7688 קֻבָּה qubbâ, n.f. [1] [√ 7685]

tent [1]

Nu 25: 8 followed the Israelite into the **tent**. He drove the spear through

7689 קִבּוּץ qibbûṣ, n.m. [1] [√ 7695]

collection [1]

Isa 57: 13 When you cry out for help, let your **collection** ⸤of idols⸥ save you!

7690 קְבוּרָה qᵉbûrâ, n.f. [14] [√ 7699]

tomb [5], grave [4], burial [2], buried [1], have burial [+7699] [1], proper burial [1]

Ge 35: 20 Over her **tomb** Jacob set up a pillar, and to this day that pillar
35: 20 set up a pillar, and to this day that pillar marks Rachel's **tomb**.
47: 30 carry me out of Egypt and bury me where they are **buried**."
Dt 34: 6 Beth Peor, but to this day no one knows where his **grave** is.
1Sa 10: 2 you leave me today, you will meet two men near Rachel's **tomb**,
2Ki 9: 28 and buried him with his fathers in his **tomb** in the City of David.
21: 26 He was buried in his **grave** in the garden of Uzza. And Josiah his
23: 30 from Megiddo to Jerusalem and buried him in his own **tomb**.
2Ch 26: 23 was buried near them in a field for **burial** that belonged to the
Ecc 6: 3 he cannot enjoy his prosperity and does not receive **proper burial**,
Isa 14: 20 you will not join them in **burial**, for you have destroyed your land
Jer 22: 19 *He will* **have** *the* **burial of** [+7699] a donkey—dragged away
Eze 32: 23 are in the depths of the pit and her army lies around her **grave**.
32: 24 "Elam is there, with all her hordes around her **grave**. All of them

7691 קָבַל qābal, v. [13] [→ 7692; Ar 10618]

accept [3], took [3], opposite [2], received [2], *untranslated* [1], agreed [1], take choice [1]

Ex 26: 5 [G] curtain of the other set, with the loops **opposite** each other.
36: 12 [G] curtain of the other set, with the loops **opposite** each other.
1Ch 12: 18 [12:19] [D] So David **received** them and made them leaders of
21: 11 [D] to him, "This is what the LORD says: '**Take** your **choice**:
2Ch 29: 16 [D] The Levites **took** it and carried it out to the Kidron Valley.
29: 22 [D] and the priests **took** the blood and sprinkled it on the altar;
Ezr 8: 30 [D] the priests and Levites **received** the silver and gold
Est 4: 4 [D] on instead of his sackcloth, but *he would* not **accept** them.
9: 23 [D] **agreed** to continue the celebration they had begun, doing
9: 27 [D] the Jews **took** it upon themselves to establish the custom that
Job 2: 10 [D] *Shall we* **accept** good from God, and not trouble?" In all this,
2: 10 [D] Shall we accept good from God, and **[RPH]** not trouble?"
Pr 19: 20 [D] Listen to advice and **accept** instruction, and in the end you

7692 קְבֹל qᵉbōl, n.[m.]. [2] [√ 7691]

battering rams [1], in front of [1]

2Ki 15: 10 He attacked him **in front of** the people, assassinated him
Eze 26: 9 He will direct the blows of his **battering rams** against your walls

7693 קָבַע qābaʿ, v. [6] [cf. 6810, 6812]

rob [3], plunder [+906+5883] [1], plunder [1], robbing [1]

Pr 22: 23 [A] and *will* **plunder** [+906+5883] those who plunder them.
22: 23 [A] take up their case and will plunder *those who* **plunder** them.
Mal 3: 8 [A] "*Will* a man **rob** God? Yet you rob me. "But you ask, 'How
3: 8 [A] Yet you **rob** me. "But you ask, 'How do we rob you?'
3: 8 [A] "But you ask, 'How *do we* **rob** you?' "In tithes and offerings.
3: 9 [A] the whole nation of you—because you *are* **robbing** me.

7694 קֻבַּעַת qubbaʿat, n.f. [2]

goblet [+3926] [2]

Isa 51: 17 you who have drained to its dregs the **goblet** [+3926] that makes
51: 22 from that cup, the **goblet** [+3926] *of* my wrath, you will never

7695 קָבַץ qābaṣ, v. [127] [→ 7689, 7697, 7698; *also used with compound proper names*]

gather [38], gathered [15], assembled [12], assemble [10], gathers [5], called together [4], brought together [3], gather together [3], bring [2], came together [2], collect [2], come together [2], surely bring together [+7695] [2], were assembled [2], amasses [1], assemble [+3481] [1], assemble yourselves [1], be gathered [1], be reunited [+3481] [1], bring back [1], bring together [1], came together [+3481] [1], collected [1], come and join [1], gather in [1], gathered together [1], grows pale [+6999] [1], join [1], joined forces [1], mobilized [1], mustered [1], picked up [1], rallied [1], shepherd [1], stored up [1], takes captive [1], turns pale [+6999] [1], were brought [1], were gathered [1]

Ge 41: 35 [A] *They should* **collect** all the food of these good years that are
41: 48 [A] Joseph **collected** all the food produced in those seven years
49: 2 [C] "**Assemble** and listen, sons of Jacob; listen to your father
Dt 13: 16 [13:17] [A] **Gather** all the plunder of the town into the middle
30: 3 [D] **gather** you again from all the nations where he scattered you.
30: 4 [D] from there the LORD your God *will* **gather** you and bring
Jos 9: 2 [F] *they* **came together** [+3481] to make war against Joshua
10: 6 [C] kings from the hill country *have* **joined forces** against us."
Jdg 9: 47 [F] When Abimelech heard that they *had* **assembled** there,
12: 4 [A] Jephthah then **called together** the men of Gilead and fought
1Sa 7: 5 [A] "**Assemble** all Israel at Mizpah and I will intercede with the
7: 6 [C] When *they had* **assembled** at Mizpah, they drew water
7: 7 [F] When the Philistines heard that Israel *had* **assembled** at
8: 4 [F] So all the elders of Israel **gathered together** and came to
22: 2 [F] in distress or in debt or discontented **gathered** around him,
25: 1 [C] Samuel died, and all Israel **assembled** and mourned for him;
28: 1 [A] In those days the Philistines **gathered** their forces to fight
28: 4 [C] The Philistines **assembled** and came and set up camp at
28: 4 [A] while Saul **gathered** all the Israelites and set up camp at
29: 1 [A] The Philistines **gathered** all their forces at Aphek, and Israel
2Sa 2: 25 [F] the men of Benjamin **rallied** behind Abner. They formed
2: 30 [A] returned from pursuing Abner and **assembled** all his men.
3: 21 [A] me go at once and **assemble** all Israel for my lord the king,
1Ki 11: 24 [A] *He* **gathered** men around him and became the leader of a
18: 19 [A] **bring** the four hundred and fifty prophets of Baal
18: 20 [A] all Israel and **assembled** the prophets on Mount Carmel.
20: 1 [A] Now Ben-Hadad king of Aram **mustered** his entire army.
22: 6 [A] So the king of Israel **brought together** the prophets—
2Ki 6: 24 [A] Ben-Hadad king of Aram **mobilized** his entire army
10: 18 [A] Then Jehu **brought** all the people **together** and said to them,
1Ch 11: 1 [C] All Israel **came together** to David at Hebron and said, "We
13: 2 [C] them in their towns and pasturelands, *to* **come and join** us.
16: 35 [D] **gather** us and deliver us from the nations, that we may give
2Ch 13: 7 [C] Some worthless scoundrels **gathered** around him
15: 9 [A] *he* **assembled** all Judah and Benjamin and the people from
15: 10 [C] *They* **assembled** *at* Jerusalem in the third month of the
18: 5 [A] So the king of Israel **brought together** the prophets—
20: 4 [C] The people of Judah **came together** to seek help from the
23: 2 [A] They went throughout Judah and **gathered** the Levites
24: 5 [A] *He* **called together** the priests and Levites and said to them,
24: 5 [A] of Judah and **collect** the money due annually from all Israel,
25: 5 [A] Amaziah **called** the people of Judah **together** and assigned
32: 4 [C] A large force of men **assembled**, and they blocked all the
32: 6 [A] and **assembled** them before him in the square at the city gate
Ezr 7: 28 [A] and **gathered** leading men from Israel to go up with me.
8: 15 [A] *I* **assembled** them at the canal that flows toward Ahava,
10: 1 [C] men, women and children—**gathered** around him.
10: 7 [C] and Jerusalem for all the exiles to **assemble** *in* Jerusalem.
10: 9 [C] the men of Judah and Benjamin *had* **gathered** *in* Jerusalem.
Ne 1: 9 [D] *I will* **gather** them from there and bring them to the place I
4: 20 [4:14] [C] you hear the sound of the trumpet, **join** us there.
5: 16 [B] All my men **were assembled** there for the work; we did not
7: 5 [A] put it into my heart *to* **assemble** the nobles, the officials and
13: 11 [A] *I* **called** them **together** and stationed them at their posts.
Est 2: 3 [A] *to* **bring** all these beautiful girls into the harem at the citadel
2: 8 [C] many girls **were brought** to the citadel of Susa and put under
2: 19 [C] When the virgins **were assembled** a second time, Mordecai
Ps 41: 6 [41:7] [A] he speaks falsely, *while* his heart **gathers** slander;
102: 22 [102:23] [C] the kingdoms **assemble** [+3481] to worship the
106: 47 [D] Save us, O LORD our God, and **gather** us from the nations,
107: 3 [D] those *he* **gathered** from the lands, from east and west,
Pr 13: 11 [A] but *he who* **gathers** money little by little makes it grow.
28: 8 [A] He who increases his wealth by exorbitant interest **amasses** it
Isa 11: 12 [D] *he will* **assemble** the scattered people of Judah from the four
13: 14 [D] Like a hunted gazelle, like sheep without a **shepherd**,
22: 9 [D] in its defenses; *you* **stored up** water in the Lower Pool.
34: 15 [C] there also the falcons *will* **gather**, each with its mate.
34: 16 [D] has given the order, and his Spirit *will* **gather** them **together**.
40: 11 [D] *He* **gathers** the lambs in his arms and carries them close to
43: 5 [D] your children from the east and **gather** you from the west.
43: 9 [C] All the nations **gather** together and the peoples assemble.
44: 11 [F] *Let* them all **come together** and take their stand; they will be
45: 20 [C] "**Gather together** and come; assemble, you fugitives from
48: 14 [C] "**Come together**, all of you, and listen: Which of ⸤the idols⸥
49: 18 [C] and look around; all your sons **gather** and come to you.
54: 7 [D] but with deep compassion *I will* **bring** you **back**.
56: 8 [D] LORD declares—*he who* **gathers** the exiles of Israel:
56: 8 [D] "*I will* **gather** still others to them besides those already
56: 8 [C] gather still others to them besides *those already* **gathered**."
60: 4 [C] All **assemble** and come to you; your sons come from afar,
60: 7 [C] All Kedar's flocks *will* **be gathered** to you, the rams of
62: 9 [D] *those who* **gather** the grapes will drink it in the courts of my
66: 18 [D] am about to come and **gather** all nations and tongues,
Jer 23: 3 [D] "*I myself will* **gather** the remnant of my flock out of all the
29: 14 [D] *I will* **gather** you from all the nations and places where I
31: 8 [D] land of the north and **gather** them from the ends of the earth.

Jer 31:10 [D] 'He who scattered Israel *will* **gather** them and will watch
32:37 [D] I *will* surely **gather** them from all the lands where I banish
40:15 [C] cause all the Jews who *are* **gathered** around you to be
49:5 [D] will be driven away, and no *one will* **gather** the fugitives.
49:14 [F] sent to the nations to say, "**Assemble yourselves** to attack it!
Eze 11:17 [D] *I will* **gather** you from the nations and bring you back from
16:37 [D] therefore I *am going to* **gather** all your lovers, with whom
16:37 [D] *I will* **gather** them against you from all around and will strip
20:34 [D] **gather** you from the countries where you have been
20:41 [D] **gather** you from the countries where you have been
22:19 [A] you have all become dross, I *will* **gather** you into Jerusalem.
22:20 [A] so *will I* **gather** you in my anger and my wrath and put you
28:25 [D] When I **gather** the people of Israel from the nations where
29:5 [C] will fall on the open field and not be gathered or **picked up**.
29:13 [D] At the end of forty years *I will* **gather** the Egyptians from the
34:13 [D] out from the nations and **gather** them from the countries,
36:24 [D] *I will* **gather** you from all the countries and bring you back
37:21 [D] *I will* **gather** them from all around and bring them back into
38:8 [E] whose *people* **were gathered** from many nations to the
39:17 [C] '**Assemble** and come together from all around to the sacrifice
39:27 [D] and *have* **gathered** them from the countries of their enemies,
Hos 1:11 [2:2] [C] and the people of Israel *will* **be reunited** [+3481],
8:10 [D] among the nations, *I will* now **gather** them **together**.
9:6 [D] Egypt *will* **gather** them, and Memphis will bury them.
Joel 2:6 [D] nations are in anguish; every face **turns pale** [+6999].
2:16 [A] **bring together** the elders, gather the children, those nursing
3:2 [4:2] [D] *I will* **gather** all nations and bring them down to the
3:11 [4:11] [C] all you nations from every side, and **assemble** there.
Mic 1:7 [D] Since *she* **gathered** her gifts from the wages of prostitutes,
2:12 [D] *I will* **surely bring together** [+7695] the remnant of Israel.
2:12 [D] *I will* **surely bring together** [+7695] the remnant of Israel.
4:6 [D] *I will* **assemble** the exiles and those I have brought to grief.
4:12 [D] *he who* **gathers** them like sheaves to the threshing floor.
Na 2:10 [2:11] [D] bodies tremble, every face **grows pale** [+6999].
3:18 [D] are scattered on the mountains with no *one to* **gather** them.
Hab 2:5 [A] to himself all the nations and **takes captive** all the peoples.
Zep 3:8 [A] to **gather** the kingdoms and to pour out my wrath on them—
3:19 [D] rescue the lame and **gather** those who have been scattered.
3:20 [D] At that time I *will* **gather** you; at that time I will bring you
Zec 10:8 [D] I will signal for them and **gather** them **in**. Surely I will
10:10 [D] bring them back from Egypt and **gather** them from Assyria.

7696 קַבְצְאֵל *qabṣᵉʾēl*, n.pr.loc. [3] [√ 7695 + 446]

Kabzeel [3]

Jos 15:21 Negev toward the boundary of Edom were: **Kabzeel**, Eder, Jagur,
2Sa 23:20 Benaiah son of Jehoiada was a valiant fighter from **Kabzeel**,
1Ch 11:22 Benaiah son of Jehoiada was a valiant fighter from **Kabzeel**,

7697 קְבֻצָה *qᵉbuṣâ*, n.f. [1] [√ 7695]

gather [1]

Eze 22:20 As men **gather** silver, copper, iron, lead and tin into a furnace to

7698 קִבְצַיִם *qibṣayim*, n.pr.loc. [1] [√ 7695]

Kibzaim [1]

Jos 21:22 **Kibzaim** and Beth Horon, together with their pasturelands—

7699 קָבַר *qābar*, v. [133] [→ 7690, 7700, 7701]

buried [54], was buried [31], bury [30], burying [7], be buried [4], *untranslated* [2], be sure to bury [+7699] [2], gravediggers [1], have burial [+7690] [1], is buried [1]

Ge 15:15 [C] go to your fathers in peace and **be buried** at a good old age.
23:4 [A] some property for a burial site here so *I can* **bury** my dead."
23:6 [A] among us. **Bury** your dead in the choicest of our tombs.
23:6 [A] None of us will refuse you his tomb for **burying** your dead."
23:8 [A] He said to them, "If you are willing to *let* me **bury** my dead,
23:11 [A] give it to you in the presence of my people. **Bury** your dead."
23:13 [A] of the field. Accept it from me so *I can* **bury** my dead there."
23:15 [A] but what is that between me and you? **Bury** your dead."
23:19 [A] Afterward Abraham **buried** his wife Sarah in the cave in the
25:9 [A] Ishmael **buried** him in the cave of Machpelah near Mamre,
25:10 [E] the Hittites. There Abraham **was buried** with his wife Sarah.
35:8 [C] died and **was buried** under the oak below Bethel.
35:19 [C] Rachel died and **was buried** on the way to Ephrath (that is,
35:29 [A] and full of years. And his sons Esau and Jacob **buried** him.
47:29 [A] me kindness and faithfulness. *Do* not **bury** me in Egypt,
47:30 [A] carry me out of Egypt and **bury** me where they are buried."
48:7 [A] So *I* **buried** her there beside the road to Ephrath" (that is,
49:29 [A] **Bury** me with my fathers in the cave in the field of Ephron
49:31 [A] There Abraham and his wife Sarah *were* **buried**, there Isaac
49:31 [A] there Isaac and his wife Rebekah *were* **buried**, and there I
49:31 [A] and his wife Rebekah were buried, and there *I* **buried** Leah.
50:5 [A] **bury** me in the tomb I dug for myself in the land of Canaan."
50:5 [A] Now let me go up and **bury** my father; then I will return.' "
50:6 [A] Pharaoh said, "Go up and **bury** your father, as he made you
50:7 [A] So Joseph went up to **bury** his father. All Pharaoh's officials
50:13 [A] and **buried** him in the cave in the field of Machpelah,
50:14 [A] After **burying** his father, Joseph returned to Egypt, together
50:14 [A] and all the others who had gone with him to **bury** his father.
Nu 11:34 [A] because there *they* **buried** the people who had craved other
20:1 [C] they stayed at Kadesh. There Miriam died and **was buried**.
33:4 [D] who *were* **burying** all their firstborn, whom the LORD had
Dt 10:6 [C] There Aaron died and **was buried**, and Eleazar his son
21:23 [A] **Be sure to bury** [+7699] him that same day, because anyone
21:23 [A] **Be sure to bury** [+7699] him that same day, because anyone
34:6 [A] *He* **buried** him in Moab, in the valley opposite Beth Peor,
Jos 24:30 [A] *they* **buried** him in the land of his inheritance, at Timnath
24:32 [A] which the Israelites had brought up from Egypt, *were* **buried**
24:33 [A] And Eleazar son of Aaron died and *was* **buried** at Gibeah,
Jdg 2:9 [A] *they* **buried** him in the land of his inheritance, at Timnath
8:32 [C] **was buried** in the tomb of his father Joash in Ophrah of the
10:2 [C] twenty-three years; then he died, and **was buried** in Shamir.
10:5 [C] When Jair died, *he* **was buried** in Kamon.
12:7 [C] the Gileadite died, and **was buried** in a town in Gilead.
12:10 [C] Then Ibzan died, and **was buried** in Bethlehem.
12:12 [C] Elon died, and **was buried** in Aijalon in the land of Zebulun.
12:15 [C] son of Hillel died, and **was buried** at Pirathon in Ephraim,
16:31 [A] They brought him back and **buried** him between Zorah
Ru 1:17 [C] Where you die I will die, and there *I will* **be buried**. May the
1Sa 25:1 [A] for him; and *they* **buried** him at his home in Ramah.
28:3 [A] mourned for him and **buried** him in his own town of Ramah.
31:13 [A] their bones and **buried** them under a tamarisk tree at Jabesh,
2Sa 2:4 [A] that it was the men of Jabesh Gilead who *had* **buried** Saul,
2:5 [A] showing this kindness to Saul your master *by* **burying** him.
2:32 [A] and **buried** him in his father's tomb at Bethlehem.
3:32 [A] *They* **buried** Abner in Hebron, and the king wept aloud at
4:12 [A] of Ish-Bosheth and **buried** it in Abner's tomb at Hebron.
17:23 [C] So he died and **was buried** in his father's tomb.
21:14 [A] *They* **buried** the bones of Saul and his son Jonathan in the
1Ki 2:10 [C] rested with his fathers and **was buried** in the City of David.
2:31 [A] Strike him down and **bury** him, and so clear me and my
2:34 [C] killed him, and *he* **was buried** on his own land in the desert.
11:15 [D] commander of the army, who had gone up to **bury** the dead,
11:43 [C] his fathers and **was buried** in the city of David his father.
13:29 [A] it back to his own city to mourn for him and **bury** him.
13:31 [A] After **burying** him, he said to his sons, "When I die, bury me
13:31 [A] I die, **bury** me in the grave where the man of God is buried;
13:31 [B] I die, bury me in the grave where the man of God **is buried**;
14:13 [A] All Israel will mourn for him and **bury** him. He is the only
14:18 [A] *They* **buried** him, and all Israel mourned for him,
14:31 [C] his fathers and **was buried** with them in the City of David.
15:8 [A] rested with his fathers and *was* **buried** in the City of David.
15:24 [C] and **was buried** with them in the city of his father David.
16:6 [C] Baasha rested with his fathers and **was buried** in Tirzah.
16:28 [C] Omri rested with his fathers and **was buried** in Samaria.
22:37 [A] and was brought to Samaria, and *they* **buried** him there.
22:50 [22:51] [C] **was buried** with them in the city of David his
2Ki 8:24 [C] his fathers and **was buried** with them in the City of David.
9:10 [A] no *one will* **bury** her.' " Then he opened the door and ran.
9:28 [A] **buried** him with his fathers in his tomb in the City of David.
9:34 [A] he said, "and **bury** her, for she was a king's daughter."
9:35 [A] when they went out to **bury** her, they found nothing except
10:35 [A] Jehu rested with his fathers and *was* **buried** in Samaria.
12:21 [12:22] [A] *was* **buried** with his fathers in the City of David.
13:9 [A] Jehoahaz rested with his fathers and *was* **buried** in Samaria.
13:13 [C] Jehoash **was buried** in Samaria with the kings of Israel.
13:20 [A] Elisha died and *was* **buried**. Now Moabite raiders used to
13:21 [A] Once *while* some Israelites *were* **burying** a man, suddenly
14:16 [C] and **was buried** in Samaria with the kings of Israel.
14:20 [C] back by horse and **was buried** in Jerusalem with his fathers,
15:7 [A] his fathers and *was* **buried** near them in the City of David.
15:38 [C] his fathers and **was buried** with them in the City of David,
16:20 [C] his fathers and **was buried** with them in the City of David.
21:18 [C] rested with his fathers and **was buried** in his palace garden,
21:26 [A] He *was* **buried** in his grave in the garden of Uzza.
23:30 [A] from Megiddo to Jerusalem and **buried** him in his own tomb.
1Ch 10:12 [A] Then *they* **buried** their bones under the great tree in Jabesh,
2Ch 9:31 [A] his fathers and *was* **buried** in the city of David his father.
12:16 [C] rested with his fathers and **was buried** in the City of David.
14:1 [13:23] [A] his fathers and *was* **buried** in the City of David.
16:14 [A] *They* **buried** him in the tomb that he had cut out for himself
21:1 [C] his fathers and **was buried** with them in the City of David.
21:20 [A] to no one's regret, and *was* **buried** in the City of David,
22:9 [A] *They* **buried** him, for they said, "He was a son of
24:16 [A] He *was* **buried** with the kings in the City of David,
24:25 [A] So he died and *was* **buried** in the City of David, but not in

2Ch 24:25 [A] the City of David, but not **[RPH]** in the tombs of the kings.
25:28 [A] and *was* **buried** with his fathers in the City of Judah.
26:23 [A] *was* **buried** near them in a field for burial that belonged to
27: 9 [A] rested with his fathers and *was* **buried** in the City of David.
28:27 [A] with his fathers and *was* **buried** in the city of Jerusalem,
32:33 [A] *was* **buried** on the hill where the tombs of David's
33:20 [A] rested with his fathers and *was* **buried** in his palace.
35:24 [C] *He* **was buried** in the tombs of his fathers, and all Judah
Job 27:15 [C] The plague *will* **bury** those who survive him, and their
Ps 79: 3 [A] all around Jerusalem, and there is no *one to* **bury** the dead.
Ecc 8:10 [B] Then too, I saw the wicked **buried**—those who used to come
Jer 7:32 [A] for *they will* **bury** the dead in Topheth until there is no more
8: 2 [C] They will not be gathered up or **buried**, but will be like
14:16 [D] There will be no *one to* **bury** them or their wives, their sons
16: 4 [C] They will not be mourned or **buried** but will be like refuse
16: 6 [C] *They will* not **be buried** or mourned, and no one will cut
19:11 [A] *They will* **bury** the dead in Topheth until there is no more
19:11 [A] the dead in Topheth until there is no more room. **[RPH]**
20: 6 [C] There you will die and **be buried**, you and all your friends to
22:19 [C] *He will* **have** *the* **burial** [+7690] *of* a donkey—dragged away
25:33 [C] They will not be mourned or gathered up or **buried**, but will
Eze 39:11 [A] because Gog and all his hordes *will be* **buried** there.
39:12 [A] " 'For seven months the house of Israel *will be* **burying** them
39:13 [A] All the people of the land *will* **bury** them, and the day I am
39:14 [D] to them, *others will* **bury** those that remain on the ground.
39:15 [D] he will set up a marker beside it until the **gravediggers** have
39:15 [A] the gravediggers *have* **buried** it in the Valley of Hamon Gog.
Hos 9: 6 [D] Egypt will gather them, and Memphis *will* **bury** them.

7700 קֶבֶר **qeber**, n.m. [67 / 68] [→ 7701]

grave [18], tomb [16], graves [10], tombs [9], burial [5], be buried [+448+665] [2], buried [2], them[s] [+4013] [2], burial place [1], burial site [1], buried [+448+995] [1], them[s] [+2021] [1]

Ge 23: 4 Sell me some property for a **burial site** here so I can bury my
23: 6 prince among us. Bury your dead in the choicest of our **tombs**.
23: 6 None of us will refuse you his **tomb** for burying your dead."
23: 9 Ask him to sell it to me for the full price as a **burial** site among
23:20 the cave in it were deeded to Abraham by the Hittites as a **burial**
49:30 which Abraham bought as a **burial** place from Ephron the Hittite,
50: 5 bury me in the **tomb** I dug for myself in the land of Canaan."
50:13 which Abraham had bought as a **burial** place from Ephron the
Ex 14:11 because there were no **graves** in Egypt that you brought us to the
Nu 19:16 or anyone who touches a human bone or a **grave**, will be unclean
19:18 or a **grave** or someone who has been killed or someone who has
Jdg 8:32 was buried in the **tomb** *of* his father Joash in Ophrah of the
16:31 him between Zorah and Eshtaol in the **tomb** *of* Manoah his father.
2Sa 2:32 took Asahel and buried him in his father's **tomb** at Bethlehem.
3:32 buried Abner in Hebron, and the king wept aloud at Abner's **tomb**.
4:12 the head of Ish-Bosheth and buried it in Abner's **tomb** at Hebron.
17:23 hanged himself. So he died and was buried in his father's **tomb**.
19:37 [19:38] that I may die in my own town near the **tomb** *of* my
21:14 of Saul and his son Jonathan in the **tomb** *of* Saul's father Kish,
1Ki 13:22 Therefore your body will not be buried in the **tomb** *of* your
13:30 he laid the body in his own **tomb**, and they mourned over him
13:31 "When I die, bury me in the **grave** where the man of God is buried;
14:13 only one belonging to Jeroboam *who will be* **buried** [+448+995],
2Ki 13:21 a band of raiders; so they threw the man's body into Elisha's **tomb**.
22:20 you to your fathers, and *you will* **be buried** [+448+665] in peace.
23: 6 and scattered the dust over the **graves** *of* the common people.
23:16 and when he saw the **tombs** that were there on the hillside,
23:16 he had the bones removed from **them**[s] [+2021] and burned on the
23:17 "It marks the **tomb** *of* the man of God who came from Judah
2Ch 16:14 They buried him in the **tomb** that he had cut out for himself in the
21:20 was buried in the City of David, but not in the **tombs** *of* the kings.
24:25 was buried in the City of David, but not in the **tombs** *of* the kings.
28:27 but he was not placed in the **tombs** *of* the kings of Israel.
32:33 was buried on the hill where the **tombs** *of* David's descendants are.
34: 4 and scattered over the **graves** of those who had sacrificed to them.
34:28 you to your fathers, and *you will* **be buried** [+448+665] in peace.
35:24 He was buried in the **tombs** *of* his fathers, and all Judah
Ne 2: 3 look sad when the city where my fathers are **buried** lies in ruins,
2: 5 let him send me to the city in Judah where my fathers are **buried**
3:16 made repairs up to a point opposite the **tombs** *of* David, as far as
Job 3:22 are filled with gladness and rejoice when they reach the **grave**?
5:26 You will come to the **grave** in full vigor, like sheaves gathered in
10:19 or had been carried straight from the womb to the **grave**!
17: 1 My spirit is broken, my days are cut short, the **grave** awaits me.
21:32 He is carried to the **grave**, and watch is kept over his tomb.
Ps 5: 9 [5:10] Their throat is an open **grave**; with their tongue they speak
49:11 [49:12] Their **tombs** [BHS 7931] will remain their houses
88: 5 [88:6] set apart with the dead, like the slain who lie in the **grave**,
88:11 [88:12] Is your love declared in the **grave**, your faithfulness in
Isa 14:19 you are cast out of your **tomb** like a rejected branch; you are
22:16 and who gave you permission to cut out a **grave** for yourself here,
22:16 hewing your **grave** on the height and chiseling your resting place
53: 9 He was assigned a **grave** with the wicked, and with the rich in his
65: 4 who sit among the **graves** and spend their nights keeping secret
Jer 5:16 Their quivers are like an open **grave**; all of them are mighty
8: 1 of the people of Jerusalem will be removed from their **graves**.
20:17 with my mother as my **grave**, her womb enlarged forever.
26:23 and his body thrown into the **burial place** *of* the common people.)
Eze 32:22 she is surrounded by the **graves** *of* all her slain, all who have fallen
32:23 Their **graves** are in the depths of the pit and her army lies around
32:25 for her among the slain, with all her hordes around her **grave**.
32:26 and Tubal are there, with all their hordes around their **graves**.
37:12 I am going to open your **graves** and bring you up from them;
37:12 going to open your graves and bring you up from **them**[s] [+4013];
37:13 the LORD, when I open your **graves** and bring you up from them.
37:13 when I open your graves and bring you up from **them**[s] [+4013].
39:11 " 'On that day I will give Gog a **burial** place in Israel, in the valley
Na 1:14 temple of your gods. I will prepare your **grave**, for you are vile."

7701 קִבְרוֹת הַתַּאֲוָה **qibrôt hatta'ᵃwâ**, n.pr.loc. [5] [√ 7700 + 2246]

Kibroth Hattaavah [5]

Nu 11:34 Therefore the place was named **Kibroth Hattaavah**, because there
11:35 From **Kibroth Hattaavah** the people traveled to Hazeroth
33:16 They left the Desert of Sinai and camped at **Kibroth Hattaavah**.
33:17 They left **Kibroth Hattaavah** and camped at Hazeroth.
Dt 9:22 LORD angry at Taberah, at Massah and at **Kibroth Hattaavah**.

7702 קָדַד **qādad**, v. [15] [√ 7721?]

bowed down [7], bowed low [5], bowed [2], bowed heads [1]

Ge 24:26 [A] Then the man **bowed down** and worshiped the LORD,
24:48 [A] *I* **bowed down** and worshiped the LORD. I praised the
43:28 [A] still alive and well." And *they* **bowed low** to pay him honor.
Ex 4:31 [A] and had seen their misery, *they* **bowed down** and worshiped.
12:27 [A] struck down the Egyptians.' " Then the people **bowed down**
34: 8 [A] Moses **bowed** to the ground at once and worshiped.
Nu 22:31 [A] with his sword drawn. So *he* **bowed low** and fell facedown.
1Sa 24: 8 [24:9] [A] David **bowed down** and prostrated himself with his
28:14 [A] *he* **bowed down** and prostrated himself with his face to the
1Ki 1:16 [A] Bathsheba **bowed low** and knelt before the king. "What is it
1:31 [A] Then Bathsheba **bowed low** with her face to the ground and,
1Ch 29:20 [A] *they* **bowed low** and fell prostrate before the LORD and the
2Ch 20:18 [A] Jehoshaphat **bowed** with his face to the ground, and all the
29:30 [A] praises with gladness and **bowed** *their* **heads** and worshiped.
Ne 8: 6 [A] *they* **bowed down** and worshiped the LORD with their

7703 קִדָּה **qiddâ**, n.f. [2]

cassia [2]

Ex 30:24 500 shekels of **cassia**—all according to the sanctuary shekel—
Eze 27:19 they exchanged wrought iron, **cassia** and calamus for your wares.

7704 קְדוּמִים **qᵉdûmîm**, n.[m.pl.]. [1] [√ 7709]

age-old [1]

Jdg 5:21 river Kishon swept them away, the **age-old** river, the river Kishon.

7705 קָדוֹשׁ **qādôš**, a. [115] [√ 7727; Ar 10620]

holy [62], Holy One [43], consecrated [4], sacred [4], saints [2]

Ex 19: 6 you will be for me a kingdom of priests and a **holy** nation.'
29:31 the ram for the ordination and cook the meat in a **sacred** place.
Lev 6:16 [6:9] rest of it, but it is to be eaten without yeast in a **holy** place;
6:26 [6:19] it is to be eaten in a **holy** place, in the courtyard of the Tent
6:27 [6:20] is spattered on a garment, you must wash it in a **holy** place.
7: 6 in a priest's family may eat it, but it must be eaten in a **holy** place;
10:13 Eat it in a **holy** place, because it is your share and your sons' share
11:44 your God; consecrate yourselves and be **holy**, because I am holy.
11:44 your God; consecrate yourselves and be holy, because I am **holy**.
11:45 out of Egypt to be your God; therefore be **holy**, because I am holy.
11:45 out of Egypt to be your God; therefore be holy, because I am **holy**.
16:24 He shall bathe himself with water in a **holy** place and put on his
19: 2 say to them: 'Be **holy** because I, the LORD your God, am holy.
19: 2 say to them: 'Be holy because I, the LORD your God, am **holy**.
20: 7 " 'Consecrate yourselves and be **holy**, because I am the LORD
20:26 You are to be **holy** to me because I, the LORD, am holy,
20:26 You are to be holy to me because I, the LORD, am **holy**,
21: 6 They must be **holy** to their God and must not profane the name of
21: 7 from their husbands, because priests are **holy** to their God.
21: 8 Consider them **holy**, because I the LORD am holy—I who make
21: 8 Consider them holy, because I the LORD am **holy**—I who make
24: 9 It belongs to Aaron and his sons, who are to eat it in a **holy** place,
Nu 5:17 he shall take some **holy** water in a clay jar and put some dust from

Nu 6: 5 He must be **holy** until the period of his separation to the LORD is
6: 8 Throughout the period of his separation he is **consecrated** to the
15:40 to obey all my commands and will be **consecrated** to your God.
16: 3 The whole community is **holy**, every one of them, and the LORD
16: 5 the LORD will show who belongs to him and who is **holy**,
16: 7 The man the LORD chooses will be the one who is **holy**.
Dt 7: 6 For you are a people **holy** to the LORD your God. The LORD
14: 2 for you are a people **holy** to the LORD your God. Out of all the
14:21 to a foreigner. But you are a people **holy** to the LORD your God.
23:14 [23:15] Your camp must be **holy**, so that he will not see among
26:19 and that you will be a people **holy** to the LORD your God,
28: 9 The LORD will establish you as his **holy** people, as he promised
33: 3 it is you who love the people; all the **holy** *ones* are in your hand.
Jos 24:19 He is a **holy** God; he is a jealous God. He will not forgive your
1Sa 2: 2 "There is no *one* **holy** like the LORD; there is no one besides
6:20 "Who can stand in the presence of the LORD, this **holy** God?
2Ki 4: 9 "I know that this man who often comes our way is a **holy** man of
19:22 and lifted your eyes in pride? Against the **Holy** *One of* Israel!
2Ch 35: 3 instructed all Israel and who had been **consecrated** to the LORD:
Ne 8: 9 said to them all, "This day is **sacred** to the LORD your God.
8:10 This day is **sacred** to our Lord. Do not grieve, for the joy of the
8:11 calmed all the people, saying, "Be still, for this is a **sacred** day.
Job 5: 1 but who will answer you? To which of the **holy** *ones* will you turn?
6:10 that I had not denied the words of the **Holy One**.
15:15 If God places no trust in his **holy** *ones*, if even the heavens are not
Ps 16: 3 As for the **saints** who are in the land, they are the glorious ones in
22: 3 [22:4] Yet you are enthroned as the **Holy One**; you are the praise
34: 9 [34:10] Fear the LORD, you his **saints**, for those who fear him
46: 4 [46:5] city of God, the **holy** *place* where the Most High dwells.
65: 4 [65:5] with the good things of your house, of your **holy** temple.
71:22 I will sing praise to you with the lyre, O **Holy One** *of* Israel.
78:41 again they put God to the test; they vexed the **Holy One** *of* Israel.
89: 5 [89:6] your faithfulness too, in the assembly of the **holy** *ones*.
89: 7 [89:8] In the council of the **holy** *ones* God is greatly feared; he is
89:18 [89:19] to the LORD, our king to the **Holy One** *of* Israel.
99: 3 Let them praise your great and awesome name—he is **holy**.
99: 5 Exalt the LORD our God and worship at his footstool; he is **holy**.
99: 9 and worship at his holy mountain, for the LORD our God is **holy**.
106:16 of Moses and of Aaron, who was **consecrated** *to* the LORD.
111: 9 he ordained his covenant forever—**holy** and awesome is his name.
Pr 9:10 of wisdom, and knowledge of the **Holy One** is understanding.
30: 3 I have not learned wisdom, nor have I knowledge of the **Holy One**.
Ecc 8:10 those who used to come and go from the **holy** place and receive
Isa 1: 4 they have spurned the **Holy One** *of* Israel and turned their backs on
4: 3 who are left in Zion, who remain in Jerusalem, will be called **holy**,
5:16 and the **holy** God will show himself holy by his righteousness.
5:19 Let it approach, let the plan of the **Holy One** *of* Israel come,
5:24 LORD Almighty and spurned the word of the **Holy One** *of* Israel.
6: 3 "**Holy**, holy, holy is the LORD Almighty; the whole earth is full
6: 3 "Holy, **holy**, holy is the LORD Almighty; the whole earth is full
6: 3 "Holy, holy, **holy** is the LORD Almighty; the whole earth is full
10:17 The Light of Israel will become a fire, their **Holy One** a flame;
10:20 but will truly rely on the LORD, the **Holy One** *of* Israel.
12: 6 people of Zion, for great is the **Holy One** *of* Israel among you."
17: 7 look to their Maker and turn their eyes to the **Holy One** *of* Israel.
29:19 in the LORD; the needy will rejoice in the **Holy One** *of* Israel.
29:23 they will acknowledge the holiness of the **Holy One** *of* Jacob,
30:11 off this path, and stop confronting us with the **Holy One** *of* Israel!"
30:12 Therefore, this is what the **Holy One** *of* Israel says: "Because you
30:15 This is what the Sovereign LORD, the **Holy One** *of* Israel, says:
31: 1 do not look to the **Holy One** *of* Israel, or seek help from the
37:23 and lifted your eyes in pride? Against the **Holy One** *of* Israel!
40:25 will you compare me? Or who is my equal?" says the **Holy One**.
41:14 declares the LORD, your Redeemer, the **Holy One** *of* Israel.
41:16 you will rejoice in the LORD and glory in the **Holy One** *of* Israel.
41:20 LORD has done this, that the **Holy One** *of* Israel has created it.
43: 3 I am the LORD, your God, the **Holy One** *of* Israel, your Savior;
43:14 is what the LORD says—your Redeemer, the **Holy One** *of* Israel:
43:15 I am the LORD, your **Holy One**, Israel's Creator, your King."
45:11 is what the LORD says—the **Holy One** *of* Israel, and its Maker:
47: 4 the LORD Almighty is his name—is the **Holy One** *of* Israel.
48:17 is what the LORD says—your Redeemer, the **Holy One** *of* Israel:
49: 7 the Redeemer and **Holy One** *of* Israel—to him who was despised
54: 5 the **Holy One** *of* Israel is your Redeemer; he is called the God of
55: 5 because of the LORD your God, the **Holy One** *of* Israel,
57:15 and lofty One says—he who lives forever, whose name is **holy**:
57:15 "I live in a high and **holy** *place*, but also with him who is contrite
58:13 call the Sabbath a delight and the LORD's **holy** day honorable,
60: 9 to the honor of the LORD your God, the **Holy One** *of* Israel,
60:14 call you the City of the LORD, Zion of the **Holy One** *of* Israel.
Jer 50:29 has done. For she has defied the LORD, the **Holy One** *of* Israel.
51: 5 though their land is full of guilt before the **Holy One** *of* Israel.
Eze 39: 7 the nations will know that I the LORD am the **Holy One** in Israel.
42:13 the sin offerings and the guilt offerings—for the place is **holy**.
Da 8:13 I heard a **holy** *one* speaking, and another holy one said to him,
8:13 I heard a holy one speaking, and another **holy** *one* said to him,
8:24 he does. He will destroy the mighty men and the **holy** people.
Hos 11: 9 For I am God, and not man—the **Holy One** among you.
11:12 [12:1] is unruly against God, even against the faithful **Holy One**.
Hab 1:12 My God, my **Holy One**, we will not die. O LORD, you have
3: 3 God came from Teman, the **Holy One** from Mount Paran.
Zec 14: 5 the LORD my God will come, and all the **holy** *ones* with him.

7706 קָדַח *qādaḥ*, v. [5] [→ 734, 7707]

kindle [1], kindled [+836+928] [1], kindled [1], light [1], sets ablaze [1]

Dt 32:22 [A] For a fire *has been* **kindled** by my wrath, one that burns to
Isa 50:11 [A] all you *who* **light** fires and provide yourselves with flaming
64: 2 [64:1] [A] As *when* fire **sets** twigs **ablaze** and causes water to
Jer 15:14 [A] for my anger *will* **kindle** a fire that will burn against you."
17: 4 [A] for *you have* **kindled** [+836+928] my anger, and it will burn

7707 קַדַּחַת *qaddaḥat*, n.f. [2] [√ 7706]

fever [2]

Lev 26:16 wasting diseases and **fever** that will destroy your sight and drain
Dt 28:22 with **fever** and inflammation, with scorching heat and drought,

7708 קָדִים *qādîm*, n.m. [69 / 67] [√ 7709]

east [38], east [+2025] [13], east wind [7], eastward [2], *untranslated* [1], desert wind [1], east winds [1], eastern [+2025] [1], eastward [+2025] [1], extend eastward [+2025] [1], hot east wind [1]

Ge 41: 6 other heads of grain sprouted—thin and scorched by the **east wind**.
41:23 heads sprouted—withered and thin and scorched by the **east wind**.
41:27 are the seven worthless heads of grain scorched by the **east wind**:
Ex 10:13 the LORD made an **east** wind blow across the land all that day
10:13 that night. By morning the wind **[RPH]** had brought the locusts;
14:21 all that night the LORD drove the sea back with a strong **east**
Job 15: 2 answer with empty notions or fill his belly with the **hot east wind**?
27:21 The **east wind** carries him off, and he is gone; it sweeps him out of
38:24 or the place where the **east winds** are scattered over the earth?
Ps 48: 7 [48:8] them like ships of Tarshish shattered by an **east** wind.
78:26 He let loose the **east wind** from the heavens and led forth the south
Isa 27: 8 his fierce blast he drives her out, as on a day the **east wind** blows.
Jer 18:17 Like a wind from the **east**, I will scatter them before their enemies;
Eze 11: 1 me to the gate of the house of the LORD that faces **east** [+2025].
17:10 Will it not wither completely when the **east** wind strikes it—
19:12 The **east** wind made it shrivel, it was stripped of its fruit; its strong
27:26 But the **east** wind will break you to pieces in the heart of the sea.
40: 6 Then he went to the gate facing **east** [+2025]. He climbed its steps
40:10 Inside the **east** gate were three alcoves on each side; the three had
40:19 it was a hundred cubits on the **east** *side* as well as on the north.
40:22 had the same measurements as those of the gate facing **east**.
40:23 the inner court facing the north gate, just as there was on the **east**.
40:32 he brought me to the inner court on the **east** side, and he measured
40:44 another at the side of the south [BHS *east*; NIV 1999] gate
41:14 The width of the temple courtyard on the **east**, including the front
42: 9 The lower rooms had an entrance on the **east** *side* as one enters
42:10 On the south [BHS *east*; NIV 1999] side along the length
42:12 that was parallel to the corresponding wall extending **eastward**,
42:15 he led me out by the **east** gate and measured the area all around:
42:16 He measured the **east** side with the measuring rod; it was five
43: 1 Then the man brought me to the gate facing **east**,
43: 2 and I saw the glory of the God of Israel coming from the **east**.
43: 4 of the LORD entered the temple through the gate facing **east**.
43:17 and a gutter of a cubit all around. The steps of the altar face **east**."
44: 1 the outer gate of the sanctuary, the one facing **east**, and it was shut.
45: 7 from the west side and **eastward** [+2025] from the east side,
45: 7 running lengthwise from the western to the **eastern** [+2025] border
46: 1 The gate of the inner court facing **east** is to be shut on the six
46:12 fellowship offerings—the gate facing **east** is to be opened for him.
47: 1 threshold of the temple toward the **east** (for the temple faced east).
47: 1 threshold of the temple toward the east (for the temple faced **east**).
47: 2 and led me around the outside to the outer gate facing **east**,
47: 3 As the man went **eastward** with a measuring line in his hand,
47:18 "On the **east** side the boundary will run between Hauran
47:18 and as far as Tamar. This will be the **east** [+2025] boundary.
48: 1 will be part of its border from the **east** *side* to the west side.
48: 2 one portion; it will border the territory of Dan from **east** to west.
48: 3 it will border the territory of Asher from **east** [+2025] to west.
48: 4 it will border the territory of Naphtali from **east** [+2025] to west.
48: 5 it will border the territory of Manasseh from **east** [+2025] to west.
48: 6 it will border the territory of Ephraim from **east** to west.
48: 7 it will border the territory of Reuben from **east** to west.
48: 8 "Bordering the territory of Judah from **east** to west will be the
48: 8 its length from **east** [+2025] to west will equal one of the tribal
48:10 10,000 cubits wide on the **east** *side* and 25,000 cubits long on the

Eze 48:16 4,500 cubits, the south side 4,500 cubits, the **east** side 4,500 cubits,
48:17 250 cubits on the south, 250 cubits on the **east**, and 250 cubits on
48:18 will be 10,000 cubits on the **east** *side* and 10,000 cubits on the
48:21 It will **extend eastward** [+2025] from the 25,000 cubits of the
48:23 it will extend from the **east** [+2025] side to the west side.
48:24 it will border the territory of Benjamin from **east** [+2025] to west.
48:25 it will border the territory of Simeon from **east** [+2025] to west.
48:26 it will border the territory of Issachar from **east** [+2025] to west.
48:27 it will border the territory of Zebulun from **east** [+2025] to west.
48:32 "On the **east** [+2025] side, which is 4,500 cubits long, will be three
Hos 12:1 [12:2] he pursues the **east wind** all day and multiplies lies
13:15 An **east** wind from the LORD will come, blowing in from the
Jnh 4:8 When the sun rose, God provided a scorching **east** wind,
Hab 1:9 Their hordes advance like a **desert wind** and gather prisoners like

7709 קָדַם qādam, v.den. [26 / 27] [→ 7704, 7708, 7710, 7711, 7712, 7713, 7714, 7715, 7716, 7717, 7718, 7719, 7720; Ar 10621, 10623]

come before [4], confronted [4], come to meet [2], confront [2], bring [1], come [1], comes before [1], go before [1], go [1], has a claim against [1], in front [1], meet [1], met [1], opposite [1], quick [1], receive [1], rise [1], stay open [1], welcomed [1]

Dt 23:4 [23:5] [D] For *they did* not **come to meet** you with bread
1Sa 20:25 [d] **opposite** [BHS 7756] Jonathan, and Abner sat next to Saul,
2Sa 22:6 [D] grave coiled around me; the snares of death **confronted** me.
22:19 [D] *They* **confronted** me in the day of my disaster,
2Ki 19:32 [D] *He will* not **come before** it with shield or build a siege ramp
Ne 13:2 [D] because *they had* not **met** the Israelites with food and water
Job 3:12 [D] Why were there knees *to* **receive** me and breasts that I might
30:27 [D] inside me never stops; days of suffering **confront** me.
41:11 [41:3] [G] Who **has a claim against** me that I must pay?
Ps 17:13 [D] Rise up, O LORD, **confront** them, bring them down;
18:5 [18:6] [D] around me; the snares of death **confronted** me.
18:18 [18:19] [D] *They* **confronted** me in the day of my disaster,
21:3 [21:4] [D] *You* **welcomed** him *with* rich blessings and placed a
59:10 [59:11] [D] God *will* **go before** me and will let me gloat over
68:25 [68:26] [D] **In front** *are* the singers, after them the musicians;
79:8 [D] *may* your mercy **come** quickly **to meet** us, for we are in
88:13 [88:14] [D] in the morning my prayer **comes before** you.
89:14 [89:15] [D] of your throne; love and faithfulness **go** before you.
95:2 [D] *Let us* **come** before him with thanksgiving and extol him
119:147 [D] *I* **rise** before dawn and cry for help; I have put my hope in
119:148 [D] My eyes **stay open** *through* the watches of the night, that I
Isa 21:14 [D] you who live in Tema, **bring** food for the fugitives.
37:33 [D] *He will* not **come before** it with shield or build a siege ramp
Am 9:10 [G] all those who say, 'Disaster will not overtake or **meet** us.'
Jnh 4:2 [D] That is why *I was so* **quick** to flee to Tarshish. I knew that
Mic 6:6 [D] With what *shall I* **come before** the LORD and bow down
6:6 [D] *Shall I* **come before** him with burnt offerings, with calves a

7710 קֶדֶם qedem, n.[m.]. [61] [√ 7709]

east [17], of old [8], eastern [7], long ago [5], ancient [3], east [+4946] [3], before [2], gone by [2], long ago [+4946] [2], ancient times [1], before began [1], days of old [1], east [+6584+7156] [1], eastward [+4946] [1], eternal [1], everlasting [1], forever [1], former [+4946] [1], long ago [+3427+4946] [1], old [+3427+4946] [1], past [1]

Ge 2:8 Now the LORD God had planted a garden in the **east**, in Eden;
3:24 he placed on the **east** *side* of the Garden of Eden cherubim
10:30 stretched from Mesha toward Sephar, in the **eastern** hill country.
11:2 As men moved **eastward** [+4946], they found a plain in Shinar
12:8 From there he went on toward the hills **east** [+4946] of Bethel
12:8 and pitched his tent, with Bethel on the west and Ai on the **east**.
13:11 himself the whole plain of the Jordan and set out toward the **east**.
25:6 and sent them away from his son Isaac to the land of the **east**.
29:1 on his journey and came to the land of the **eastern** peoples.
Nu 23:7 me from Aram, the king of Moab from the **eastern** mountains.
34:11 will go down from Shepham to Riblah on the **east** *side* of Ain
Dt 33:15 with the choicest gifts of the **ancient** mountains and the
33:27 The **eternal** God is your refuge, and underneath are the everlasting
Jos 7:2 which is near Beth Aven to the **east** of Bethel, and told them,
Jdg 6:3 Amalekites and other **eastern** peoples invaded the country.
6:33 Amalekites and other **eastern** peoples joined forces and crossed
7:12 and all the other **eastern** peoples had settled in the valley,
8:10 all that were left of the armies of the **eastern** peoples;
8:11 Gideon went up by the route of the nomads **east** [+4946] of Nobah
1Ki 4:30 [5:10] was greater than the wisdom of all the men of the **East**,
2Ki 19:25 In days **of old** I planned it; now I have brought it to pass, that you
Ne 12:46 For **long** [+4946] **ago**, in the days of David and Asaph, there had
Job 1:3 He was the greatest man among all the people of the **East**.
23:8 "But if I go to the **east**, he is not there; if I go to the west, I do not
29:2 "How I long for the months **gone by**, for the days when God
Ps 44:1 [44:2] have told us what you did in their days, in days **long ago**.
55:19 [55:20] God, who is enthroned **forever**, will hear them and afflict
68:33 [68:34] to him who rides the **ancient** skies above, who thunders
74:2 Remember the people you purchased **of old**, the tribe of your
74:12 you, O God, are my king from **of old**; you bring salvation upon the
77:5 [77:6] I thought about the **former** [+4946] days, the years of long
77:11 [77:12] yes, I will remember your miracles of **long ago**.
78:2 mouth in parables, I will utter hidden things, things from **of old**—
119:152 **Long ago** I learned from your statutes that you established them to
139:5 You hem me in—behind and **before**; you have laid your hand upon
143:5 I remember the days of **long ago**; I meditate on all your works
Pr 8:22 brought me forth as the first of his works, **before** his deeds of old;
8:23 from eternity, from the beginning, **before** the world **began**.
Isa 2:6 They are full of superstitions from the **East**; they practice
9:12 [9:11] Arameans from the **east** and Philistines from the west have
11:14 to the west; together they will plunder the people to the **east**.
19:11 "I am one of the wise men, a disciple of the **ancient** kings"?
23:7 Is this your city of revelry, the **old** [+3427+4946], old city,
37:26 In days **of old** I planned it; now I have brought it to pass, that you
45:21 Who foretold this **long** [+4946] **ago**, who declared it from the
46:10 end from the beginning, from **ancient times**, what is still to come.
51:9 of the LORD; awake, as in days **gone by**, as in generations of old.
Jer 30:20 Their children will be as in **days of old**, and their community will
46:26 Later, however, Egypt will be inhabited as in times **past**,"
49:28 "Arise, and attack Kedar and destroy the people of the **East**.
La 1:7 remembers all the treasures that were hers in days **of old**.
2:17 has fulfilled his word, which he decreed **long** [+3427+4946] **ago**.
5:21 O LORD, that we may return; renew our days as **of old**
Eze 11:23 within the city and stopped above the mountain **east** [+4946] of it.
25:4 therefore I am going to give you to the people of the **East** as a
25:10 with the Ammonites to the people of the **East** as a possession,
Jnh 4:5 Jonah went out and sat down at a place **east** of the city. There he
Mic 5:2 [5:1] whose origins are from **of old**, from ancient times."
7:20 as you pledged on oath to our fathers in days **long ago**.
Hab 1:12 O LORD, are you not from **everlasting**? My God, my Holy One,
Zec 14:4 day his feet will stand on the Mount of Olives, **east** [+6584+7156]

7711 קֵדֶם qēdem, adv. [26] [→ 7714; cf. 7709]

east [10], east [+2025] [7], eastern [+2025] [3], *untranslated* [2], eastward [+2025] [1], eastward [+2025+2025+4667] [1], southeast [+2025+2025+5582] [1], southeast [+2025+5582] [1]

Ge 13:14 where you are and look north and south, **east** [+2025] and west.
25:6 sent them away from his son Isaac **[RPH]** to the land of the east.
28:14 and you will spread out to the west and to the **east**, to the north
Ex 27:13 On the **east** [+2025] end, toward the sunrise, the courtyard shall
38:13 The **east** [+2025] end, toward the sunrise, was also fifty cubits
Lev 1:16 the crop with its contents and throw it to the **east** side of the altar,
16:14 **[RPH]** then he shall sprinkle some of it with his finger seven
Nu 2:3 On the **east**, toward the sunrise, the divisions of the camp of Judah
3:38 and Aaron and his sons were to camp to the **east** *of* the tabernacle,
10:5 blast is sounded, the tribes camping on the **east** are to set out.
34:3 On the **east**, your southern boundary will start from the end of the
34:10 " 'For your **eastern** [+2025] boundary, run a line from Hazar Enan
34:11 continue along the slopes **east** [+2025] of the Sea of Kinnereth.
34:15 a half tribes have received their inheritance on the **east** side of the
35:5 Outside the town, measure three thousand feet on the **east** side,
Jos 15:5 The **eastern** [+2025] boundary is the Salt Sea as far as the mouth
18:20 The Jordan formed the boundary on the **eastern** [+2025] side.
19:12 It turned **east** [+2025] from Sarid toward the sunrise to the territory
19:13 Then it continued **eastward** [+2025+2025+4667] to Gath Hepher
1Ki 7:39 the south side, at the **southeast** [+2025+5582] corner of the temple.
17:3 "Leave here, turn **eastward** [+2025] and hide in the Kerith Ravine,
2Ki 13:17 "Open the **east** [+2025] window," he said, and he opened it.
2Ch 4:10 on the south side, at the **southeast** [+2025+2025+5582] corner.
Eze 8:16 toward the temple of the LORD and their faces toward the **east**,
8:16 toward the east, they were bowing down to the sun in the **east**.
45:7 from the west side and eastward from the **east** [+2025] side,

7712 קַדְמָה qadmâ, n.f. [6] [√ 7709; Ar 10622]

before [3], *untranslated* [1], old [1], past [1]

Ps 129:6 they be like grass on the roof, which withers **before** it can grow;
Isa 23:7 Is this your city of revelry, the old, **old** city, whose feet have taken
Eze 16:55 Samaria with her daughters, will return to *what* they were **before**;
16:55 **[RPH]** and you and your daughters will return to what you were
16:55 and you and your daughters will return to *what* you were **before**.
36:11 I will settle people on you as *in* the **past** and will make you prosper

7713 קִדְמָה qidmâ, n.f. [4] [√ 7709]

east [4]

Ge 2:14 of the third river is the Tigris; it runs along the **east** *side of* Asshur.
4:16 the LORD's presence and lived in the land of Nod, **east** *of* Eden.

1Sa 13: 5 They went up and camped at Micmash, **east** *of* Beth Aven.
Eze 39: 11 in Israel, in the valley of those who travel **east** *toward* the Sea.

7714 קֵדְמָה[1] **qēdᵉmâ[1]**, adv. Not used in NIV/BHS [√ 7711; cf. 7709]

7715 קֵדְמָה[2] **qēdᵉmâ[2]**, n.pr.m. [2] [√ 7709]

Kedemah [2]

Ge 25: 15 Hadad, Tema, Jetur, Naphish and **Kedemah**.
1Ch 1: 31 Jetur, Naphish and **Kedemah**. These were the sons of Ishmael.

7716 קַדְמוֹן **qadmôn**, a. [1] [→ 7719, 7720; cf. 7709]

eastern [1]

Eze 47: 8 "This water flows toward the **eastern** region and goes down into

7717 קְדֵמוֹת **qᵉdēmôt**, n.pr.loc. [4] [√ 7709]

Kedemoth [4]

Dt 2: 26 From the desert of **Kedemoth** I sent messengers to Sihon king of
Jos 13: 18 Jahaz, **Kedemoth**, Mephaath,
21: 37 **Kedemoth** and Mephaath, together with their pasturelands—
1Ch 6: 79 [6:64] **Kedemoth** and Mephaath, together with their pasturelands;

7718 קַדְמִיאֵל **qadmî'ēl**, n.pr.m. [8] [√ 7709 + 446]

Kadmiel [8]

Ezr 2: 40 descendants of Jeshua and **Kadmiel** (through the line of Hodaviah)
3: 9 Jeshua and his sons and brothers and **Kadmiel** and his sons
Ne 7: 43 the descendants of Jeshua (through **Kadmiel** through the line of
9: 4 Jeshua, Bani, **Kadmiel**, Shebaniah, Bunni, Sherebiah, Bani
9: 5 Jeshua, **Kadmiel**, Bani, Hashabneiah, Sherebiah, Hodiah,
10: 9 [10:10] son of Azaniah, Binnui of the sons of Henadad, **Kadmiel**,
12: 8 Binnui, **Kadmiel**, Sherebiah, Judah, and also Mattaniah, who,
12: 24 Sherebiah, Jeshua son of **Kadmiel**, and their associates, who stood

7719 קַדְמֹנִי[1] **qadmōnî[1]**, a. [10] [√ 7716; cf. 7709]

eastern [3], east [2], former [2], *untranslated* [1], old [1], past [1]

1Sa 24: 13 [24:14] As the **old** saying goes, 'From evildoers come evil deeds,'
Job 18: 20 are appalled at his fate; *men of the* **east** are seized with horror.
Isa 43: 18 "Forget the former things; do not dwell on the **past**.
Eze 10: 19 They stopped at the entrance to the **east** gate of the LORD's
11: 1 **[RPH]** There at the entrance to the gate were twenty-five men,
38: 17 Are you not the one I spoke of in **former** days by my servants the
47: 18 and the land of Israel, to the **eastern** sea and as far as Tamar.
Joel 2: 20 with its front columns going into the **eastern** sea and those in the
Zec 14: 8 half to the **eastern** sea and half to the western sea, in summer
Mal 3: 4 acceptable to the LORD, as in days gone by, as in **former** years.

7720 קַדְמֹנִי[2] **qadmōnî[2]**, a.g. [1] [√ 7716; cf. 7709]

Kadmonites [1]

Ge 15: 19 the land of the Kenites, Kenizzites, **Kadmonites**,

7721 קָדְקֹד **qodqōd**, n.[m.]. [11 / 12] [√ 7702?]

top of head [3], brow [2], head [2], skulls [2], crown of head [1], crowns [1], heads [1]

Ge 49: 26 the head of Joseph, on the **brow** *of* the prince among his brothers.
Nu 24: 17 foreheads of Moab, the **skulls** [BHS 7979] *of* all the sons of Sheth.
Dt 28: 35 spreading from the soles of your feet to the **top of** your **head**.
33: 16 the head of Joseph, on the **brow** *of* the prince among his brothers.
33: 20 Gad's domain! Gad lives there like a lion, tearing at arm or **head**.
2Sa 14: 25 From the **top of** his **head** to the sole of his foot there was no
Job 2: 7 with painful sores from the soles of his feet to the **top of** his **head**.
Ps 7: 16 [7:17] on himself; his violence comes down on his own **head**.
68: 21 [68:22] the hairy **crowns** *of* those who go on in their sins.
Isa 3: 17 Therefore the Lord will bring sores on the **heads** *of* the women of
Jer 2: 16 of Memphis and Tahpanhes have shaved the **crown** of your **head**.
48: 45 it burns the foreheads of Moab, the **skulls** *of* the noisy boasters.

7722 קָדַר **qādar**, v. [17] [→ 7723, 7724, 7725, 7726]

darkened [3], mourning [3], darken [2], mourn [2], black [1], blackened [1], clothed with gloom [1], dark [1], go dark [1], grief [1], wail [1]

1Ki 18: 45 [F] Meanwhile, the sky *grew* **black** *with* clouds, the wind rose,
Job 5: 11 [A] he sets on high, and *those who* **mourn** are lifted to safety.
6: 16 [A] *when* **darkened** by thawing ice and swollen with melting
30: 28 [A] I go about **blackened**, but not by the sun; I stand up in the
Ps 35: 14 [A] I bowed my head *in* **grief** as though weeping for my mother.
38: 6 [38:7] [A] brought very low; all day long I go about **mourning**.
42: 9 [42:10] [A] Why must I go about **mourning**, oppressed by the
43: 2 [A] Why must I go about **mourning**, oppressed by the enemy?
Jer 4: 28 [A] the earth will mourn and the heavens above *grow* **dark**,
8: 21 [A] are crushed, I am crushed; *I* **mourn**, and horror grips me.
14: 2 [A] *they* **wail** for the land, and a cry goes up from Jerusalem.
Eze 31: 15 [G] Because of it *I* **clothed** Lebanon **with gloom**, and all the
32: 7 [G] you out, I will cover the heavens and **darken** their stars;
32: 8 [G] All the shining lights in the heavens *I will* **darken** over you;
Joel 2: 10 [A] the sky trembles, the sun and moon *are* **darkened**,
3: 15 [4:15] [A] The sun and moon *will be* **darkened**, and the stars no
Mic 3: 6 [A] will set for the prophets, and the day *will* **go dark** for them.

7723 קֵדָר **qēdār**, n.pr.g. [12] [√ 7722]

Kedar [10], Kedar [+1201] [1], Kedar's [1]

Ge 25: 13 Nebaioth the firstborn of Ishmael, **Kedar**, Adbeel, Mibsam,
1Ch 1: 29 Nebaioth the firstborn of Ishmael, **Kedar**, Adbeel, Mibsam,
Ps 120: 5 me that I dwell in Meshech, that I live among the tents of **Kedar**!
SS 1: 5 yet lovely, O daughters of Jerusalem, dark like the tents of **Kedar**,
Isa 21: 16 would count it, all the pomp of **Kedar** will come to an end.
21: 17 of the bowmen, the warriors of **Kedar** [+1201], will be few."
42: 11 raise their voices; let the settlements where **Kedar** lives rejoice.
60: 7 All **Kedar's** flocks will be gathered to you, the rams of Nebaioth
Jer 2: 10 the coasts of Kittim and look, send to **Kedar** and observe closely;
49: 28 Concerning **Kedar** and the kingdoms of Hazor,
49: 28 "Arise, and attack **Kedar** and destroy the people of the East.
Eze 27: 21 " 'Arabia and all the princes of **Kedar** were your customers;

7724 קִדְרוֹן **qidrôn**, n.pr.loc. [11] [√ 7722]

Kidron [10], there[s] [+928+5707] [1]

2Sa 15: 23 The king also crossed the **Kidron** Valley, and all the people moved
1Ki 2: 37 The day you leave and cross the **Kidron** Valley, you can be sure
15: 13 Asa cut the pole down and burned it in the **Kidron** Valley.
2Ki 23: 4 He burned them outside Jerusalem in the fields of the **Kidron**
23: 6 the temple of the LORD to the **Kidron** Valley outside Jerusalem
23: 6 Valley outside Jerusalem and burned it **there**[s] [+928+5707].
23: 12 them to pieces and threw the rubble into the **Kidron** Valley.
2Ch 15: 16 cut the pole down, broke it up and burned it in the **Kidron** Valley.
29: 16 The Levites took it and carried it out to the **Kidron** Valley.
30: 14 away the incense altars and threw them into the **Kidron** Valley.
Jer 31: 40 all the terraces out to the **Kidron** Valley on the east as far as the

7725 קַדְרוּת **qadrût**, n.f. [1] [√ 7722]

darkness [1]

Isa 50: 3 I clothe the sky with **darkness** and make sackcloth its covering."

7726 קְדֹרַנִּית **qᵉdōrannît**, adv. [1] [√ 7722]

mourners [1]

Mal 3: 14 and going about like **mourners** before the LORD Almighty?

7727 קָדַשׁ **qādaš**, v.den. [171] [→ 5219, 7705, 7728, 7729, 7730, 7731, 7732]

consecrate [30], consecrated [22], dedicated [10], consecrate yourselves [9], consecrated themselves [7], dedicates [7], holy [7], keep holy [7], makes holy [7], show myself holy [7], set apart [6], prepare [5], consecration [3], made holy [3], been consecrated [2], declare holy [2], dedicate [2], honor as holy [2], keeping holy [2], make holy [2], regard as holy [2], sacred [2], set aside [2], solemnly consecrate [+906+4946+7727] [2], *untranslated* [1], acknowledge holiness [1], be acknowledged as holy [1], be consecrated [1], call in honor of [+4200] [1], celebrate holy [1], consecrate themselves [1], consecrating themselves [+7731] [1], consecrating themselves [1], consecrating [1], defiled [1], done[s] [1], have purified [1], holiness [1], purified herself [1], send [1], set apart as holy [1], show himself holy [1], show holiness [1], showed himself holy [1], uphold holiness [1]

Ge 2: 3 [D] God blessed the seventh day and **made it holy**, because on it
Ex 13: 2 [D] "**Consecrate** to me every firstborn male. The first offspring
19: 10 [D] "Go to the people and **consecrate** them today and tomorrow.
19: 14 [D] *he* **consecrated** them, and they washed their clothes.
19: 22 [F] who approach the LORD, *must* **consecrate themselves**,
19: 23 [D] 'Put limits around the mountain and **set it apart as holy**.' "
20: 8 [D] "Remember the Sabbath day by **keeping** it **holy**.
20: 11 [D] the LORD blessed the Sabbath day and **made** it **holy**.
28: 3 [D] for his **consecration**, so he may serve me as priest.
28: 38 [G] guilt involved in the sacred gifts the Israelites **consecrate**,
28: 41 [D] **Consecrate** them so they may serve me as priests.
29: 1 [D] "This is what you are to do to **consecrate** them, so they may
29: 21 [A] Then he and his sons and their garments *will be* **consecrated**.
29: 27 [D] "**Consecrate** those parts of the ordination ram that belong to
29: 33 [D] atonement was made for their ordination and **consecration**.
29: 36 [D] by making atonement for it, and anoint it to **consecrate** it.
29: 37 [D] seven days make atonement for the altar and **consecrate** it.

Ex 29:37 [A] altar will be most holy, and whatever touches it *will be* **holy**.
29:43 [C] the Israelites, and the place *will* **be consecrated** by my glory.
29:44 [D] "So *I will* **consecrate** the Tent of Meeting and the altar
29:44 [D] *will* **consecrate** Aaron and his sons to serve me as priests.
30:29 [D] *You shall* **consecrate** them so they will be most holy, and
30:29 [A] will be most holy, and whatever touches them *will be* **holy**.
30:30 [D] "Anoint Aaron and his sons and **consecrate** them so they
31:13 [D] you may know that I am the LORD, *who* **makes** you **holy**.
40: 9 [D] in it; **consecrate** it and all its furnishings, and it will be holy.
40:10 [D] all its utensils; **consecrate** the altar, and it will be most holy.
40:11 [D] Anoint the basin and its stand and **consecrate** them.
40:13 [D] anoint him and **consecrate** him so he may serve me as priest.
Lev 6:18 [6:11] [A] Whatever touches them *will become* **holy**.' "
6:27 [6:20] [A] Whatever touches any of the flesh *will become* **holy**,
8:10 [D] the tabernacle and everything in it, and so **consecrated** them.
8:11 [D] its utensils and the basin with its stand, to **consecrate** them.
8:12 [D] oil on Aaron's head and anointed him to **consecrate** him.
8:15 [D] of the altar. So *he* **consecrated** it to make atonement for it.
8:30 [D] So *he* **consecrated** Aaron and his garments and his sons and
10: 3 [C] " 'Among those who approach me *I will* **show myself holy**;
11:44 [F] **consecrate yourselves** and be holy, because I am holy.
16:19 [D] and *to* **consecrate** it from the uncleanness of the Israelites.
20: 7 [F] " '**Consecrate yourselves** and be holy, because I am the
20: 8 [D] and follow them. I am the LORD, *who* **makes** you **holy**.
21: 8 [D] **Regard** them **as holy**, because they offer up the food of your
21: 8 [D] because I the LORD am holy—I *who* **make** you **holy**.
21:15 [D] his people. I am the LORD, *who* **makes** him **holy**.' "
21:23 [D] my sanctuary. I am the LORD, *who* **makes** them **holy**.' "
22: 2 [G] respect the sacred offerings the Israelites **consecrate** to me,
22: 3 [G] sacred offerings that the Israelites **consecrate** to the LORD,
22: 9 [D] with contempt. I am the LORD, *who* **makes** them **holy**.
22:16 [D] I am the LORD, *who* **makes** them **holy**.' "
22:32 [C] *I must* **be acknowledged as holy** by the Israelites. I am the
22:32 [D] by the Israelites. I am the LORD, *who* **makes** you **holy**
25:10 [D] **Consecrate** the fiftieth year and proclaim liberty throughout
27:14 [G] " 'If a man **dedicates** his house as something holy to the
27:15 [G] If the *man who* **dedicates** his house redeems it, he must add
27:16 [G] " 'If a man **dedicates** to the LORD part of his family land,
27:17 [G] If *he* **dedicates** his field during the Year of Jubilee, the value
27:18 [G] if *he* **dedicates** his field after the Jubilee, the priest will
27:19 [G] If the *man who* **dedicates** the field wishes to redeem it, he
27:22 [G] " 'If a *man* **dedicates** to the LORD a field he has bought,
27:26 [G] *may* **dedicate** the firstborn of an animal, since the firstborn
Nu 3:13 [G] *I* **set apart** for myself every firstborn in Israel, whether man
6:11 [D] the dead body. That same day *he is to* **consecrate** his head.
7: 1 [D] he anointed it and **consecrated** it and all its furnishings.
7: 1 [D] also anointed and **consecrated** the altar and all its utensils.
8:17 [G] down all the firstborn in Egypt, *I* **set** them **apart** for myself.
11:18 [F] '**Consecrate yourselves** in preparation for tomorrow,
16:37 [17:2] [A] coals some distance away, for the censers *are* **holy**—
16:38 [17:3] [A] presented before the LORD and *have become* **holy**.
20:12 [G] you did not trust in me enough to **honor** me **as holy**
20:13 [C] the LORD and where *he* **showed himself holy** among them.
27:14 [G] both of you disobeyed my command to **honor** me **as holy**
Dt 5:12 [D] "Observe the Sabbath day by **keeping** it **holy**, as the LORD
15:19 [G] **Set apart** for the LORD your God every firstborn male of
22: 9 [A] you plant but also the fruit of the vineyard *will be* **defiled**.
32:51 [D] because *you did* not **uphold** my **holiness** among the
Jos 3: 5 [F] Joshua told the people, "**Consecrate yourselves**,
7:13 [D] "Go, **consecrate** the people. Tell them,
7:13 [F] '**Consecrate yourselves** in preparation for tomorrow;
20: 7 [G] So *they* **set apart** Kedesh in Galilee in the hill country of
Jdg 17: 3 [G] "*I* **solemnly consecrate** [+906+4946+7727] my silver to the
17: 3 [G] "*I* **solemnly consecrate** [+906+4946+7727] my silver to the
1Sa 7: 1 [D] **consecrated** Eleazar his son to guard the ark of the LORD.
16: 5 [F] **Consecrate yourselves** and come to the sacrifice with me."
16: 5 [D] *he* **consecrated** Jesse and his sons and invited them to the
21: 5 [21:6] [A] are not holy. How much more so today!" **[RPH]**
2Sa 8:11 [G] King David **dedicated** these articles to the LORD, as he had
8:11 [G] as *he had* **done**[s] with the silver and gold from all the nations
11: 4 [F] (She *had* **purified herself** from her uncleanness.) Then she
1Ki 8:64 [D] On that same day the king **consecrated** the middle part of the
9: 3 [G] *I have* **consecrated** this temple, which you have built,
9: 7 [G] and will reject this temple *I have* **consecrated** for my Name.
2Ki 10:20 [D] Jehu said, "**Call** an assembly **in honor** [+4200] **of** Baal."
12:18 [12:19] [G] all the sacred objects **dedicated** *by* his fathers—
1Ch 15:12 [F] you and your fellow Levites *are to* **consecrate yourselves**
15:14 [F] Levites **consecrated themselves** in order to bring up the ark
18:11 [G] King David **dedicated** these articles to the LORD, as he had
23:13 [G] his descendants forever, to **consecrate** the most holy things,
26:26 [G] of all the treasuries for the things **dedicated** *by* King David,
26:27 [G] Some of the plunder taken in battle *they* **dedicated** for the
26:28 [G] everything **dedicated** *by* Samuel the seer and by Saul son of
26:28 [G] all the other **dedicated** *things* were in the care of Shelomith
2Ch 2: 4 [2:3] [G] to **dedicate** it to him for burning fragrant incense
5:11 [F] All the priests who were there *had* **consecrated themselves**,
7: 7 [D] Solomon **consecrated** the middle part of the courtyard in
7:16 [G] I have chosen and **consecrated** this temple so that my Name
7:20 [G] and will reject this temple *I have* **consecrated** for my Name.
26:18 [E] of Aaron, who *have* **been consecrated** to burn incense.
29: 5 [F] **Consecrate yourselves** now and consecrate the temple of the
29: 5 [D] yourselves now and **consecrate** the temple of the LORD,
29:15 [F] had assembled their brothers and **consecrated themselves**,
29:17 [D] They began the **consecration** on the first day of the first
29:17 [D] For eight more days *they* **consecrated** the temple of the
29:19 [G] **consecrated** all the articles that King Ahaz removed in his
29:34 [F] was finished and until other priests *had* **been consecrated**,
29:34 [F] **in consecrating themselves** than the priests had been.
30: 3 [F] because not enough priests *had* **consecrated themselves**
30: 8 [G] Come to the sanctuary, which *he has* **consecrated** forever.
30:15 [F] and the Levites were ashamed and **consecrated themselves**
30:17 [F] Since many in the crowd *had* not **consecrated themselves**,
30:17 [G] and *could* not **consecrate** ⌊their lambs⌋ to the LORD.
30:24 [F] A great number of priests **consecrated themselves**.
31: 6 [E] a tithe of the holy things **dedicated** to the LORD their God,
31:18 [F] For they *were* faithful in **consecrating** [+7731] **themselves**.
35: 6 [F] **consecrate yourselves** and prepare ⌊the lambs⌋ for your
36:14 [G] of the LORD, which *he had* **consecrated** in Jerusalem.
Ezr 3: 5 [E] the sacrifices for all the appointed **sacred** feasts of the
Ne 3: 1 [D] They **dedicated** it and set its doors in place, building as far as
3: 1 [D] which *they* **dedicated**, and as far as the Tower of Hananel.
12:47 [G] *They* also **set aside** the portion for the other Levites,
12:47 [G] the Levites **set aside** the portion for the descendants of
13:22 [D] and guard the gates in order to **keep** the Sabbath day **holy**.
Job 1: 5 [D] had run its course, Job would send and **have** them **purified**.
Isa 5:16 [C] the holy God *will* **show himself holy** by his righteousness.
8:13 [G] The LORD Almighty is the one *you are to* **regard as holy**,
13: 3 [E] I have commanded my **holy** *ones*; I have summoned my
29:23 [G] the work of my hands, *they will* **keep** my name **holy**;
29:23 [G] *they will* **acknowledge** *the* **holiness** *of* the Holy One of
30:29 [F] you will sing as on the night you **celebrate** a **holy** festival;
65: 5 [A] don't come near me, for *I am too* **sacred** *for* you!'
66:17 [F] "Those *who* **consecrate** and purify themselves to go into the
Jer 1: 5 [G] the womb I knew you, before you were born *I* **set** you **apart**;
6: 4 [D] "**Prepare** *for* battle against her! Arise, let us attack at noon!
12: 3 [G] to be butchered! **Set** them **apart** for the day of slaughter!
17:22 [D] do any work on the Sabbath, but **keep** the Sabbath day **holy**,
17:24 [D] but **keep** the Sabbath day **holy** by not doing any work on it,
17:27 [D] if you do not obey me to **keep** the Sabbath day **holy** by not
22: 7 [D] *I will* **send** destroyers against you, each man with his
51:27 [D] **Prepare** the nations for battle against her; summon against
51:28 [D] **Prepare** the nations for battle against her—the kings of the
Eze 20:12 [D] so they would know that I the LORD **made** them **holy**.
20:20 [D] **Keep** my Sabbaths **holy**, that they may be a sign between us.
20:41 [C] *I will* **show myself holy** among you in the sight of the
28:22 [C] I inflict punishment on her and **show myself holy** within her.
28:25 [C] *I will* **show myself holy** among them in the sight of the
36:23 [D] *I will* **show** *the* **holiness** *of* my great name, which has been
36:23 [C] when I **show myself holy** through you before their eyes.
37:28 [D] the nations will know that I the LORD **make** Israel **holy**,
38:16 [C] so that the nations may know me when I **show myself holy**
38:23 [F] so I will show my greatness and *my* **holiness**, and I will make
39:27 [C] *I will* **show myself holy** through them in the sight of many
44:19 [D] so that *they do* not **consecrate** the people by means of their
44:24 [D] appointed feasts, and *they are to* **keep** my Sabbaths **holy**.
46:20 [D] them into the outer court and **consecrating** the people."
48:11 [E] This will be for the **consecrated** priests, the Zadokites,
Joel 1:14 [D] **Declare** *a* **holy** fast; call a sacred assembly.
2:15 [D] trumpet in Zion, **declare** a **holy** fast, call a sacred assembly.
2:16 [D] Gather the people, **consecrate** the assembly; bring together
3: 9 [4:9] [D] the nations: **Prepare** *for* war! Rouse the warriors!
Mic 3: 5 [D] if he does not, *they* **prepare** to wage war against him.
Zep 1: 7 [G] a sacrifice; *he has* **consecrated** those he has invited.
Hag 2:12 [A] *does it become* **consecrated**?' " The priests answered, "No."

7728 קָדֵשׁ *qādēš*[1], n.m. [11] [√ 7727]

shrine prostitutes [5], shrine prostitute [4], *untranslated* [1], prostitutes of the shrines [1]

Ge 38:21 "Where is the **shrine prostitute** who was beside the road at
38:21 "There hasn't been any **shrine prostitute** here," they said.
38:22 lived there said, 'There hasn't been any **shrine prostitute** here.' "
Dt 23:17 [23:18] Israelite man or woman is to become a **shrine prostitute**.
23:17 [23:18] or woman is to become a shrine prostitute. **[RPH]**
1Ki 14:24 There were even *male* **shrine prostitutes** in the land; the people
15:12 He expelled the *male* **shrine prostitutes** from the land and got rid
22:46 [22:47] He rid the land of the rest of the *male* **shrine prostitutes**
2Ki 23: 7 He also tore down the quarters of the *male* **shrine prostitutes**,

[F] Hitpael (hitpoel, hitpoal, hitpolel, hitpolal, hitpalel, hitpalal, hitpalpel, hitpalpal, hotpael, hotpaal) [G] Hiphil (hiphtil) [H] Hophal [I] Hishtaphel

Job 36: 14 They die in their youth, among *male* **prostitutes of the shrines**.
Hos 4: 14 consort with harlots and sacrifice with **shrine prostitutes**—

7729 ²קָדֵשׁ qādēš[2], n.pr.loc. [14] [→ 5315; cf. 7727]
Kadesh [14]

Ge 14: 7 Then they turned back and went to En Mishpat (that is, **Kadesh**),
16: 14 called Beer Lahai Roi; it is still there, between **Kadesh** and Bered.
20: 1 into the region of the Negev and lived between **Kadesh** and Shur.
Nu 13: 26 the whole Israelite community at **Kadesh** in the Desert of Paran.
20: 1 arrived at the Desert of Zin, and they stayed at **Kadesh**.
20: 14 Moses sent messengers from **Kadesh** to the king of Edom,
20: 16 "Now we are here at **Kadesh**, a town on the edge of your territory.
20: 22 The whole Israelite community set out from **Kadesh** and came to
33: 36 They left Ezion Geber and camped at **Kadesh**, in the Desert of Zin.
33: 37 They left **Kadesh** and camped at Mount Hor, on the border of
Dt 1: 46 so you stayed in **Kadesh** many days—all the time you spent there.
Jdg 11: 16 Israel went through the desert to the Red Sea and on to **Kadesh**.
11: 17 to the king of Moab, and he refused. So Israel stayed at **Kadesh**.
Ps 29: 8 shakes the desert; the LORD shakes the Desert of **Kadesh**.

7730 קֶדֶשׁ qedeš, n.pr.loc. [12] [√ 7727]
Kedesh [11], where[s] [+2025] [1]

Jos 12: 22 the king of **Kedesh** one the king of Jokneam in Carmel one
15: 23 **Kedesh**, Hazor, Ithnan,
19: 37 **Kedesh**, Edrei, En Hazor,
20: 7 So they set apart **Kedesh** in Galilee in the hill country of Naphtali,
21: 32 **Kedesh** in Galilee (a city of refuge for one accused of murder),
Jdg 4: 6 She sent for Barak son of Abinoam from **Kedesh** *in* Naphtali
4: 9 Sisera over to a woman." So Deborah went with Barak to **Kedesh**,
4: 10 **where**[s] [+2025] he summoned Zebulun and Naphtali. Ten
4: 11 and pitched his tent by the great tree in Zaanannim near **Kedesh**.
2Ki 15: 29 and took Ijon, Abel Beth Maacah, Janoah, **Kedesh** and Hazor.
1Ch 6: 72 [6:57] from the tribe of Issachar they received **Kedesh**, Daberath,
6: 76 [6:61] from the tribe of Naphtali they received **Kedesh** in Galilee,

7731 קֹדֶשׁ qōdeš, n.m. [470] [√ 7727]
holy [136], sanctuary [72], sacred [65], most holy [+7731] [46], Most Holy Place [+7731] [22], holy place [14], holy things [10], most holy offerings [+7731] [10], holiness [9], Most Holy Place [8], sacred offerings [8], consecrated [7], *untranslated* [6], most holy things [+7731] [6], holy offerings [5], sacred offering [3], consecrated gifts [+7731] [2], dedicated things [2], dedicated [2], holy furnishings [2], most sacred [+7731] [2], most sacred food [+7731] [2], sacred gifts [2], sacred objects [2], something holy [2], things dedicated [2], another[s] [+5246] [1], consecrated things [1], consecrating themselves [+7727] [1], dedicate [1], dedicated gifts [1], gifts dedicated [1], Holy One [1], holy ones [1], holy precincts [1], it[s] [1], Most Holy Place [+1808] [1], Most Holy Place [+5219] [1], offering [1], offerings [1], priests rooms [+4384] [1], sacred portion [1], sacred things [1], sanctuary [+5226] [1], sanctuary area [1], set apart [1], temple [1], things[s] [1], what holy [1]

Ex 3: 5 your sandals, for the place where you are standing is **holy** ground."
12: 16 On the first day hold a **sacred** assembly, and another one on the
12: 16 a sacred assembly, and **another**[s] **one** [+5246] on the seventh day.
15: 11 majestic in **holiness**, awesome in glory, working wonders?
15: 13 In your strength you will guide them to your **holy** dwelling.
16: 23 'Tomorrow is to be a day of rest, a **holy** Sabbath to the LORD.
22: 31 [22:30] "You are to be my **holy** people. So do not eat the meat of
26: 33 The curtain will separate the **Holy Place** from the Most Holy
26: 33 will separate the Holy Place from the **Most Holy** [+7731] **Place**.
26: 33 will separate the Holy Place from the **Most Holy Place** [+7731].
26: 34 cover on the ark of the Testimony in the **Most Holy** [+7731] **Place**.
26: 34 cover on the ark of the Testimony in the **Most Holy Place** [+7731].
28: 2 Make **sacred** garments for your brother Aaron, to give him dignity
28: 4 They are to make these **sacred** garments for your brother Aaron
28: 29 "Whenever Aaron enters the **Holy Place**, he will bear the names of
28: 35 The sound of the bells will be heard when he enters the **Holy Place**
28: 36 pure gold and engrave on it as on a seal: **HOLY** TO THE LORD.
28: 38 he will bear the guilt involved in the **sacred gifts** the Israelites
28: 38 gifts the Israelites consecrate, whatever their gifts **[RPH]** may be.
28: 43 of Meeting or approach the altar to minister in the **Holy Place**,
29: 6 the turban on his head and attach the **sacred** diadem to the turban.
29: 29 "Aaron's **sacred** garments will belong to his descendants so that
29: 30 comes to the Tent of Meeting to minister in the **Holy Place** is to
29: 33 But no one else may eat them, because they are **sacred**.
29: 34 till morning, burn it up. It must not be eaten, because it is **sacred**.
29: 37 the altar will be **most holy** [+7731], and whatever touches it will
29: 37 the altar will be **most holy** [+7731], and whatever touches it will
30: 10 the generations to come. It is **most holy** [+7731] to the LORD."
30: 10 the generations to come. It is **most holy** [+7731] to the LORD."
30: 13 according to the **sanctuary** shekel, which weighs twenty gerahs.
30: 24 all according to the **sanctuary** shekel—and a hin of olive oil.
30: 25 Make these into a **sacred** anointing oil, a fragrant blend, the work
30: 25 the work of a perfumer. It will be the **sacred** anointing oil.
30: 29 You shall consecrate them so they will be **most holy** [+7731],
30: 29 You shall consecrate them so they will be **most holy** [+7731],
30: 31 'This is to be my **sacred** anointing oil for the generations to come.
30: 32 the same formula. It is **sacred**, and you are to consider it sacred.
30: 32 the same formula. It is sacred, and you are to consider it **sacred**.
30: 35 the work of a perfumer. It is to be salted and pure and **sacred**.
30: 36 where I will meet with you. It shall be **most holy** [+7731] to you.
30: 36 where I will meet with you. It shall be **most holy** [+7731] to you.
30: 37 with this formula for yourselves; consider it **holy** to the LORD.
31: 10 both the **sacred** garments for Aaron the priest and the garments for
31: 11 and the anointing oil and fragrant incense for the **Holy Place**.
31: 14 " 'Observe the Sabbath, because it is **holy** to you. Anyone who
31: 15 but the seventh day is a Sabbath of rest, **holy** to the LORD.
35: 2 work is to be done, but the seventh day shall be your **holy** day,
35: 19 the woven garments worn for ministering in the **sanctuary**—
35: 19 both the **sacred** garments for Aaron the priest and the garments for
35: 21 Tent of Meeting, for all its service, and for the **sacred** garments.
36: 1 **sanctuary** are to do the work just as the LORD has commanded."
36: 3 had brought to carry out the work of constructing the **sanctuary**.
36: 4 who were doing all the work on the **sanctuary** left their work
36: 6 woman is to make anything else as an offering for the **sanctuary**."
37: 29 They also made the **sacred** anointing oil and the pure,
38: 24 offering used for all the work on the **sanctuary** was 29 talents
38: 24 was 29 talents and 730 shekels, according to the **sanctuary** shekel.
38: 25 100 talents and 1,775 shekels, according to the **sanctuary** shekel—
38: 26 that is, half a shekel, according to the **sanctuary** shekel,
38: 27 100 talents of silver were used to cast the bases for the **sanctuary**
39: 1 yarn they made woven garments for ministering in the **sanctuary**.
39: 1 They also made **sacred** garments for Aaron, as the LORD
39: 30 the plate, the **sacred** diadem, out of pure gold and engraved on it,
39: 30 on it, like an inscription on a seal: **HOLY** TO THE LORD.
39: 41 and the woven garments worn for ministering in the **sanctuary**,
39: 41 both the **sacred** garments for Aaron the priest and the garments for
40: 9 in it; consecrate it and all its furnishings, and it will be **holy**.
40: 10 its utensils; consecrate the altar, and it will be **most holy** [+7731].
40: 10 its utensils; consecrate the altar, and it will be **most holy** [+7731].
40: 13 dress Aaron in the **sacred** garments, anoint him and consecrate him
Lev 2: 3 it is a **most holy** [+7731] *part* of the offerings made to the LORD
2: 3 it is a **most holy part** [+7731] of the offerings made to the LORD
2: 10 it is a **most holy** [+7731] *part* of the offerings made to the LORD
2: 10 it is a **most holy part** [+7731] of the offerings made to the LORD
4: 6 times before the LORD, in front of the curtain of the **sanctuary**.
5: 15 sins unintentionally in regard to any of the LORD's **holy things**,
5: 15 of the proper value in silver, according to the **sanctuary** shekel.
5: 16 restitution for what he has failed to do in regard to the **holy things**,
6: 17 [6:10] sin offering and the guilt offering, it is **most holy** [+7731].
6: 17 [6:10] sin offering and the guilt offering, it is **most holy** [+7731].
6: 25 [6:18] the burnt offering is slaughtered; it is **most holy** [+7731].
6: 25 [6:18] the burnt offering is slaughtered; it is **most holy** [+7731].
6: 29 [6:22] in a priest's family may eat it; it is **most holy** [+7731].
6: 29 [6:22] in a priest's family may eat it; it is **most holy** [+7731].
6: 30 [6:23] to make atonement in the **Holy Place** must not be eaten;
7: 1 the regulations for the guilt offering, which is **most holy** [+7731]:
7: 1 the regulations for the guilt offering, which is **most holy** [+7731]:
7: 6 but it must be eaten in a holy place; it is **most holy** [+7731].
7: 6 but it must be eaten in a holy place; it is **most holy** [+7731].
8: 9 and set the gold plate, the **sacred** diadem, on the front of it,
10: 4 cousins outside the camp, away from the front of the **sanctuary**."
10: 10 You must distinguish between the **holy** and the common, between
10: 12 prepared without yeast beside the altar, for it is **most holy** [+7731].
10: 12 prepared without yeast beside the altar, for it is **most holy** [+7731].
10: 17 "Why didn't you eat the sin offering in the **sanctuary** area?
10: 17 It is **most holy** [+7731]; it was given to you to take away the guilt
10: 17 It is **most holy** [+7731]; it was given to you to take away the guilt
10: 18 Since its blood was not taken into the **Holy Place**, you should have
10: 18 you should have eaten the goat in the **sanctuary** area, as I
12: 4 She must not touch anything **sacred** or go to the sanctuary until the
14: 13 He is to slaughter the lamb in the **holy** place where the sin offering
14: 13 the guilt offering belongs to the priest; it is **most holy** [+7731].
14: 13 the guilt offering belongs to the priest; it is **most holy** [+7731].
16: 2 **Most Holy Place** behind the curtain in front of the atonement
16: 3 "This is how Aaron is to enter the **sanctuary area**: with a young
16: 4 He is to put on the **sacred** linen tunic, with linen undergarments
16: 4 These are **sacred** garments; so he must bathe himself with water
16: 16 In this way he will make atonement for the **Most Holy Place**
16: 17 in to make atonement in the **Most Holy Place** until he comes out,
16: 20 Aaron has finished making atonement for the **Most Holy Place**,
16: 23 linen garments he put on before he entered the **Most Holy Place**,
16: 27 whose blood was brought into the **Most Holy Place** to make
16: 32 is to make atonement. He is to put on the **sacred** linen garments
16: 33 make atonement for the **Most Holy** [+5219] **Place**, for the Tent of

Lev 19: 8 because he has desecrated **what is holy** *to* the LORD;
19:24 In the fourth year all its fruit will be **holy**, an offering of praise to
20: 3 he has defiled my sanctuary and profaned my **holy** name.
21: 6 to the LORD by fire, the food of their God, they are to be **holy**.
21:22 He may eat the **most holy** [+7731] food of his God, as well as the
21:22 He may eat the **most holy** [+7731] food of his God, as well as the
21:22 may eat the most holy food of his God, as well as the **holy** food;
22: 2 his sons to treat with respect the **sacred offerings** the Israelites
22: 2 Israelites consecrate to me, so they will not profane my **holy** name.
22: 3 yet comes near the **sacred offerings** that the Israelites consecrate
22: 4 he may not eat the **sacred offerings** until he is cleansed.
22: 6 He must not eat any of the **sacred offerings** unless he has bathed
22: 7 he will be clean, and after that he may eat the **sacred offerings**,
22:10 " 'No one outside a priest's family may eat the **sacred offering**,
22:10 nor may the guest of a priest or his hired worker eat **it**ˢ.
22:12 other than a priest, she may not eat any of the **sacred** contributions.
22:14 " 'If anyone eats a **sacred offering** by mistake, he must make
22:14 he must make restitution to the priest for the **offering** and add a
22:15 The priests must not desecrate the **sacred offerings** the Israelites
22:16 by allowing them to eat the **sacred offerings** and so bring upon
22:32 Do not profane my **holy** name. I must be acknowledged as holy by
23: 2 of the LORD, which you are to proclaim as **sacred** assemblies.
23: 3 but the seventh day is a Sabbath of rest, a day of **sacred** assembly.
23: 4 the **sacred** assemblies you are to proclaim at their appointed times:
23: 7 On the first day hold a **sacred** assembly and do no regular work.
23: 8 on the seventh day hold a **sacred** assembly and do no regular
23:20 They are a **sacred offering** to the LORD for the priest.
23:21 On that same day you are to proclaim a **sacred** assembly and do no
23:24 day of rest, a **sacred** assembly commemorated with trumpet blasts.
23:27 Hold a **sacred** assembly and deny yourselves, and present an
23:35 The first day is a **sacred** assembly; do no regular work.
23:36 on the eighth day hold a **sacred** assembly and present an offering
23:37 which you are to proclaim as **sacred** assemblies for bringing
24: 9 because it is a **most holy** [+7731] part of their regular share of the
24: 9 because it is a **most holy** [+7731] part of their regular share of the
25:12 For it is a jubilee and is to be **holy** for you; eat only what is taken
27: 3 sixty at fifty shekels of silver, according to the **sanctuary** shekel;
27: 9 to the LORD, such an animal given to the LORD becomes **holy**.
27:10 one animal for another, both it and the substitute become **holy**.
27:14 " 'If a man dedicates his house as **something holy** to the LORD,
27:21 it will become **holy**, like a field devoted to the LORD;
27:23 the man must pay its value on that day as **something holy** to the
27:25 Every value is to be set according to the **sanctuary** shekel,
27:28 everything so devoted is **most holy** [+7731] to the LORD.
27:28 everything so devoted is **most holy** [+7731] to the LORD.
27:30 from the trees, belongs to the LORD; it is **holy** to the LORD.
27:32 that passes under the shepherd's rod—will be **holy** to the LORD.
27:33 both the animal and its substitute become **holy** and cannot be
Nu 3:28 The Kohathites were responsible for the care of the **sanctuary**.
3:31 the altars, the articles of the **sanctuary** used in ministering,
3:32 over those who were responsible for the care of the **sanctuary**.
3:47 according to the **sanctuary** shekel, which weighs twenty gerahs.
3:50 silver weighing 1,365 shekels, according to the **sanctuary** shekel.
4: 4 in the Tent of Meeting: the care of the **most holy** [+7731] **things**.
4: 4 in the Tent of Meeting: the care of the **most holy things** [+7731].
4:12 are to take all the articles used for ministering in the **sanctuary**,
4:15 and his sons have finished covering the **holy furnishings**
4:15 finished covering the holy furnishings and all the **holy** articles,
4:15 But they must not touch the **holy things** or they will die.
4:16 and everything in it, including its **holy furnishings** and articles."
4:19 and not die when they come near the **most holy** [+7731] **things**,
4:19 and not die when they come near the **most holy things** [+7731],
4:20 But the Kohathites must not go in to look at the **holy things**,
5: 9 All the **sacred** contributions the Israelites bring to a priest will
5:10 Each man's **sacred gifts** are his own, but what he gives to the
6:20 they are **holy** and belong to the priest, together with the breast that
7: 9 because they were to carry on their shoulders the **holy things**,
7:13 weighing seventy shekels, both according to the **sanctuary** shekel,
7:19 weighing seventy shekels, both according to the **sanctuary** shekel,
7:25 weighing seventy shekels, both according to the **sanctuary** shekel,
7:31 weighing seventy shekels, both according to the **sanctuary** shekel,
7:37 weighing seventy shekels, both according to the **sanctuary** shekel,
7:43 weighing seventy shekels, both according to the **sanctuary** shekel,
7:49 weighing seventy shekels, both according to the **sanctuary** shekel,
7:55 weighing seventy shekels, both according to the **sanctuary** shekel,
7:61 weighing seventy shekels, both according to the **sanctuary** shekel,
7:67 weighing seventy shekels, both according to the **sanctuary** shekel,
7:73 weighing seventy shekels, both according to the **sanctuary** shekel,
7:79 weighing seventy shekels, both according to the **sanctuary** shekel,
7:85 thousand four hundred shekels, according to the **sanctuary** shekel.
7:86 weighed ten shekels each, according to the **sanctuary** shekel.
8:19 plague will strike the Israelites when they go near the **sanctuary**."
18: 3 but they must not go near the furnishings of the **sanctuary**
18: 5 "You are to be responsible for the care of the **sanctuary** and the
18: 8 all the **holy offerings** the Israelites give me I give to you and your
18: 9 You are to have the part of the **most holy offerings** [+7731] that is
18: 9 You are to have the part of the **most holy** [+7731] **offerings** that is
18: 9 From all the gifts they bring me as **most holy offerings** [+7731],
18: 9 From all the gifts they bring me as **most holy** [+7731] **offerings**,
18:10 Eat it as something **most holy** [+7731]; every male shall eat it.
18:10 Eat it as something **most holy** [+7731]; every male shall eat it.
18:10 most holy; every male shall eat it. You must regard it as **holy**.
18:16 according to the **sanctuary** shekel, which weighs twenty gerahs.
18:17 not redeem the firstborn of an ox, a sheep or a goat; they are **holy**.
18:19 Whatever is set aside from the **holy offerings** the Israelites present
18:32 then you will not defile the **holy offerings** *of* the Israelites,
28: 7 Pour out the drink offering to the LORD at the **sanctuary**.
28:18 On the first day hold a **sacred** assembly and do no regular work.
28:25 On the seventh day hold a **sacred** assembly and do no regular
28:26 Feast of Weeks, hold a **sacred** assembly and do no regular work.
29: 1 " 'On the first day of the seventh month hold a **sacred** assembly
29: 7 " 'On the tenth day of this seventh month hold a **sacred** assembly.
29:12 seventh month, hold a **sacred** assembly and do no regular work.
31: 6 who took with him articles from the **sanctuary** and the trumpets
35:25 the death of the high priest, who was anointed with the **holy** oil.
Dt 12:26 take your **consecrated things** and whatever you have vowed to
26:13 "I have removed from my house the **sacred portion** and have
26:15 Look down from heaven, your **holy** dwelling place, and bless your
33: 2 He came with myriads of **holy ones** from the south, from his
Jos 5:15 off your sandals, for the place where you are standing is **holy**."
6:19 and the articles of bronze and iron are **sacred** to the LORD
1Sa 21: 4 [21:5] on hand; however, there is some **consecrated** bread here—
21: 5 [21:6] The men's things are **holy** even on missions that are not
21: 6 [21:7] So the priest gave him the **consecrated** bread, since there
1Ki 6:16 the temple an inner sanctuary, the **Most Holy** [+7731] **Place**.
6:16 the temple an inner sanctuary, the **Most Holy Place** [+7731].
7:50 the **Most Holy Place** [+7731], and also for the doors of the main
7:50 the **Most Holy** [+7731] **Place**, and also for the doors of the main
7:51 he brought in the **things** his father David had **dedicated**—
8: 4 and the Tent of Meeting and all the **sacred** furnishings in it.
8: 6 the **Most Holy Place** [+7731], and put it beneath the wings of the
8: 6 the **Most Holy** [+7731] **Place**, and put it beneath the wings of the
8: 8 so long that their ends could be seen from the **Holy Place** in front
8:10 When the priests withdrew from the **Holy Place**, the cloud filled
15:15 and gold and the articles that he and his father had **dedicated**.
15:15 and the articles that he and his father had dedicated. **[RPH]**
2Ki 12: 4 [12:5] "Collect all the money that is brought as **sacred offerings**
12:18 [12:19] Joash king of Judah took all the **sacred objects** dedicated
12:18 [12:19] the **gifts** he himself had **dedicated** and all the gold found
1Ch 6:49 [6:34] with all that was done in the **Most Holy Place** [+7731],
6:49 [6:34] with all that was done in the **Most Holy** [+7731] **Place**,
9:29 care of the furnishings and all the other articles of the **sanctuary**,
16:10 Glory in his **holy** name; let the hearts of those who seek the
16:29 before him; worship the LORD in the splendor of his **holiness**.
16:35 us from the nations, that we may give thanks to your **holy** name,
22:19 the **sacred** articles belonging to God into the temple that will be
23:13 descendants forever, to consecrate the **most holy things** [+7731],
23:13 descendants forever, to consecrate the **most holy** [+7731] **things**,
23:28 the purification of all **sacred things** and the performance of other
23:32 for the **Holy Place** and, under their brothers the descendants of
24: 5 for there were officials of the **sanctuary** and officials of God
26:20 of the house of God and the treasuries for the **dedicated things**.
26:26 his relatives were in charge of all the treasuries for the **things**ˢ
28:12 the temple of God and for the treasuries for the **dedicated things**.
29: 3 and above everything I have provided for this **holy** temple:
29:16 we have provided for building you a temple for your **Holy** Name,
2Ch 3: 8 He built the **Most Holy Place** [+7731], its length corresponding to
3: 8 He built the **Most Holy** [+7731] **Place**, its length corresponding to
3:10 In the **Most Holy** [+7731] Place he made a pair of sculptured
3:10 In the **Most Holy** [+7731] Place he made a pair of sculptured
4:22 the inner doors to the **Most Holy Place** [+7731] and the doors of
4:22 the inner doors to the **Most Holy** [+7731] **Place** and the doors of
5: 1 he brought in the **things** his father David had **dedicated**—
5: 5 and the Tent of Meeting and all the **sacred** furnishings in it.
5: 7 the **Most Holy Place** [+7731], and put it beneath the wings of the
5: 7 the **Most Holy** [+7731] **Place**, and put it beneath the wings of the
5:11 The priests then withdrew from the **Holy Place**. All the priests who
8:11 because the places the ark of the LORD has entered are **holy**."
15:18 and gold and the articles that he and his father had **dedicated**.
15:18 and the articles that he and his father had dedicated. **[RPH]**
20:21 to praise him for the splendor of his **holiness** as they went out at
23: 6 they may enter because they are **consecrated**, but all the other men
24: 7 temple of God and had used even its **sacred objects** for the Baals.
29: 5 God of your fathers. Remove all defilement from the **sanctuary**.
29: 7 or present any burnt offerings at the **sanctuary** to the God of
29:33 The *animals* **consecrated** as sacrifices amounted to six hundred
30:19 even if he is not clean according to the rules of the **sanctuary**."
30:27 for their prayer reached heaven, his **holy** dwelling place.

2Ch 31: 6 and a tithe of the **holy things** dedicated to the LORD their God,
31: 12 faithfully brought in the contributions, tithes and **dedicated gifts**.
31: 14 made to the LORD and also the **consecrated gifts** [+7731].
31: 14 made to the LORD and also the **consecrated** [+7731] **gifts**.
31: 18 For they *were* faithful in **consecrating themselves** [+7727].
35: 3 "Put the **sacred** ark in the temple that Solomon son of David king
35: 5 "Stand in the **holy place** with a group of Levites for each
35: 13 boiled the **holy offerings** in pots, caldrons and pans and served
Ezr 2: 63 **most sacred food** [+7731] until there was a priest ministering with
2: 63 **most sacred** [+7731] *food* until there was a priest ministering with
8: 28 "You as well as these articles are **consecrated** to the LORD.
8: 28 **[RPH]** The silver and gold are a freewill offering to the LORD,
9: 2 and have mingled the **holy** race with the peoples around them.
9: 8 us a remnant and giving us a firm place in his **sanctuary** [+5226],
Ne 7: 65 ordered them not to eat any of the **most sacred food** [+7731] until
7: 65 ordered them not to eat any of the **most sacred** [+7731] **food** until
9: 14 You made known to them your **holy** Sabbath and gave them
10: 31 [10:32] not buy from them on the Sabbath or on any **holy** day.
10: 33 [10:34] and appointed feasts; for the **holy offerings**;
11: 1 the **holy** city, while the remaining nine were to stay in their own
11: 18 The Levites in the **holy** city totaled 284.
Ps 2: 6 "I have installed my King on Zion, my **holy** hill."
3: 4 [3:5] LORD I cry aloud, and he answers me from his **holy** hill.
5: 7 [5:8] in reverence will I bow down toward your **holy** temple.
11: 4 The LORD is in his **holy** temple; the LORD is on his heavenly
15: 1 may dwell in your sanctuary? Who may live on your **holy** hill?
20: 2 [20:3] May he send you help from the **sanctuary** and grant you
20: 6 [20:7] he answers him from his **holy** heaven with the saving
24: 3 ascend the hill of the LORD? Who may stand in his **holy** place?
28: 2 as I lift up my hands toward your **Most Holy** [+1808] **Place**.
29: 2 due his name; worship the LORD in the splendor of his **holiness**.
30: 4 [30:5] to the LORD, you saints of his; praise his **holy** name.
33: 21 In him our hearts rejoice, for we trust in his **holy** name.
43: 3 let them bring me to your **holy** mountain, to the place where you
47: 8 [47:9] reigns over the nations; God is seated on his **holy** throne.
48: 1 [48:2] worthy of praise, in the city of our God, his **holy** mountain.
51: 11 [51:13] me from your presence or take your **Holy** Spirit from me.
60: 6 [60:8] God has spoken from his **sanctuary**: "In triumph I will
63: 2 [63:3] I have seen you in the **sanctuary** and beheld your power
68: 5 [68:6] a defender of widows, is God in his **holy** dwelling.
68: 17 [68:18] the Lord ⌊has come⌋ from Sinai into his **sanctuary**.
68: 24 [68:25] the procession of my God and King into the **sanctuary**.
74: 3 all this destruction the enemy has brought on the **sanctuary**.
77: 13 [77:14] Your ways, O God, are **holy**. What god is so great as our
78: 54 Thus he brought them to the border of his **holy** land, to the hill
79: 1 they have defiled your **holy** temple, they have reduced Jerusalem
87: 1 He has set his foundation on the **holy** mountain;
89: 20 [89:21] my servant; with my **sacred** oil I have anointed him.
89: 35 [89:36] Once for all, I have sworn by my **holiness**—and I will not
93: 5 **holiness** adorns your house for endless days, O LORD.
96: 9 Worship the LORD in the splendor of his **holiness**;
97: 12 in the LORD, you who are righteous, and praise his **holy** name.
98: 1 his right hand and his **holy** arm have worked salvation for him.
99: 9 Exalt the LORD our God and worship at his **holy** mountain,
102: 19 [102:20] "The LORD looked down from his **sanctuary** on high,
103: 1 the LORD, O my soul; all my inmost being, praise his **holy** name.
105: 3 Glory in his **holy** name; let the hearts of those who seek the
105: 42 For he remembered his **holy** promise given to his servant
106: 47 that we may give thanks to your **holy** name and glory in your
108: 7 [108:8] God has spoken from his **sanctuary**: "In triumph I will
110: 3 Arrayed in **holy** majesty, from the womb of the dawn you will
114: 2 Judah became God's **sanctuary**, Israel his dominion.
134: 2 Lift up your hands in the **sanctuary** and praise the LORD.
138: 2 I will bow down toward your **holy** temple and will praise your
145: 21 Let every creature praise his **holy** name for ever and ever.
150: 1 Praise God in his **sanctuary**; praise him in his mighty heavens.
Pr 20: 25 It is a trap for a man to **dedicate** something rashly and only later to
Isa 6: 13 they are cut down, so the **holy** seed will be the stump in the land."
11: 9 They will neither harm nor destroy on all my **holy** mountain,
23: 18 Yet her profit and her earnings will be **set apart** for the LORD;
27: 13 and worship the LORD on the **holy** mountain in Jerusalem.
35: 8 And a highway will be there; it will be called the Way of **Holiness**.
43: 28 So I will disgrace the dignitaries of your **temple**, and I will consign
48: 2 you who call yourselves citizens of the **holy** city and rely on the
49: 7 who is faithful, the **Holy One** *of* Israel, who has chosen you."
52: 1 Put on your garments of splendor, O Jerusalem, the **holy** city.
52: 10 The LORD will lay bare his **holy** arm in the sight of all the
56: 7 these I will bring to my **holy** mountain and give them joy in my
57: 13 me his refuge will inherit the land and possess my **holy** mountain."
58: 13 the Sabbath and from doing as you please on my **holy** day,
62: 9 who gather the grapes will drink it in the courts of my **sanctuary**."
62: 12 They will be called the **Holy** People, the Redeemed of the LORD;
63: 10 Yet they rebelled and grieved his **Holy** Spirit. So he turned
63: 11 of his flock? Where is he who set his **Holy** Spirit among them,
63: 15 from heaven and see from your lofty throne, **holy** and glorious.
63: 18 For a little while your people possessed your **holy place**, but now
64: 10 [64:9] Your **sacred** cities have become a desert; even Zion is a
64: 11 [64:10] Our **holy** and glorious temple, where our fathers praised
65: 11 as for you who forsake the LORD and forget my **holy** mountain,
65: 25 They will neither harm nor destroy on all my **holy** mountain,"
66: 20 to my **holy** mountain in Jerusalem as an offering to the LORD—
Jer 2: 3 Israel was **holy** to the LORD, the firstfruits of his harvest;
11: 15 Can **consecrated** meat avert ⌊your punishment⌋? When you engage
23: 9 overcome by wine, because of the LORD and his **holy** words.
25: 30 he will thunder from his **holy** dwelling and roar mightily against
31: 23 'The LORD bless you, O righteous dwelling, O **sacred** mountain.'
31: 40 as far as the corner of the Horse Gate, will be **holy** to the LORD.
La 4: 1 The **sacred** gems are scattered at the head of every street.
Eze 20: 39 and no longer profane my **holy** name with your gifts and idols.
20: 40 For on my **holy** mountain, the high mountain of Israel,
20: 40 and your choice gifts, along with all your **holy** sacrifices.
22: 8 You have despised my **holy things** and desecrated my Sabbaths.
22: 26 Her priests do violence to my law and profane my **holy things**;
22: 26 they do not distinguish between the **holy** and the common;
28: 14 You were on the **holy** mount of God; you walked among the fiery
36: 20 wherever they went among the nations they profaned my **holy**
36: 21 I had concern for my **holy** name, which the house of Israel
36: 22 I am going to do these things, but for the sake of my **holy** name,
36: 38 as numerous as the flocks for **offerings** at Jerusalem during her
39: 7 " 'I will make known my **holy** name among my people Israel.
39: 7 I will no longer let my **holy** name be profaned, and the nations will
39: 25 on all the people of Israel, and I will be zealous for my **holy** name.
41: 4 He said to me, "This is the **Most Holy** [+7731] **Place**."
41: 4 He said to me, "This is the **Most Holy Place** [+7731]."
41: 21 and the one at the front of the **Most Holy Place** was similar.
41: 23 the outer sanctuary and the **Most Holy Place** had double doors.
42: 13 rooms facing the temple courtyard are the **priests' rooms** [+4384],
42: 13 approach the LORD will eat the **most holy** [+7731] **offerings**.
42: 13 approach the LORD will eat the **most holy offerings** [+7731].
42: 13 There they will put the **most holy** [+7731] **offerings**—the grain
42: 13 There they will put the **most holy offerings** [+7731]—the grain
42: 14 Once the priests enter the **holy precincts**, they are not to go into
42: 14 behind the garments in which they minister, for these are **holy**.
42: 20 five hundred cubits wide, to separate the **holy** from the common.
43: 7 The house of Israel will never again defile my **holy** name—
43: 8 and them, they defiled my **holy** name by their detestable practices.
43: 12 area on top of the mountain will be **most holy** [+7731].
43: 12 area on top of the mountain will be **most holy** [+7731].
44: 8 Instead of carrying out your duty in regard to my **holy things**,
44: 13 or come near any of my **holy things** or my most holy offerings;
44: 13 near any of my holy things or my **most holy** [+7731] **offerings**;
44: 13 near any of my holy things or my **most holy offerings** [+7731];
44: 19 been ministering in and are to leave them in the **sacred** rooms,
44: 23 They are to teach my people the difference between the **holy**
44: 27 On the day he goes into the inner court of the **sanctuary** to
44: 27 into the inner court of the sanctuary to minister in the **sanctuary**,
45: 1 to present to the LORD a portion of the land as a **sacred** *district*,
45: 1 cubits long and 20,000 cubits wide; the entire area will be **holy**.
45: 2 Of this, a section 500 cubits square is to be for the **sanctuary**,
45: 3 In it will be the sanctuary, the **Most Holy** [+7731] **Place**.
45: 3 In it will be the sanctuary, the **Most Holy Place** [+7731].
45: 4 It will be the **sacred** portion of the land for the priests,
45: 6 cubits wide and 25,000 cubits long, adjoining the **sacred** portion;
45: 7 land bordering each side of the area formed by the **sacred** district
45: 7 **[RPH]** It will extend westward from the west side and eastward
46: 19 entrance at the side of the gate to the **sacred** rooms facing north,
48: 10 This will be the **sacred** portion for the priests. It will be 25,000
48: 12 a **most holy** [+7731] portion, bordering the territory of the Levites.
48: 12 a **most holy** [+7731] portion, bordering the territory of the Levites.
48: 14 must not pass into other hands, because it is **holy** to the LORD.
48: 18 bordering on the **sacred** portion and running the length of it,
48: 18 **[RPH]** Its produce will supply food for the workers of the city.
48: 20 As a special gift you will set aside the **sacred** portion, along with
48: 21 "What remains on both sides of the area formed by the **sacred**
48: 21 the **sacred** portion with the temple sanctuary will be in the center
Da 8: 13 the surrender of the **sanctuary** and of the host that will be trampled
8: 14 and mornings; then the **sanctuary** will be reconsecrated."
9: 16 and your wrath from Jerusalem, your city, your **holy** hill.
9: 20 and making my request to the LORD my God for his **holy** hill—
9: 24 decreed for your people and your **holy** city to finish transgression,
9: 24 seal up vision and prophecy and to anoint the **most holy** [+7731].
9: 24 seal up vision and prophecy and to anoint the **most holy** [+7731].
9: 26 of the ruler who will come will destroy the city and the **sanctuary**.
11: 28 great wealth, but his heart will be set against the **holy** covenant.
11: 30 Then he will turn back and vent his fury against the **holy** covenant.
11: 30 will return and show favor to those who forsake the **holy** covenant.
11: 45 He will pitch his royal tents between the seas at the beautiful **holy**
12: 7 When the power of the **holy** people has been finally broken,

Joel 2: 1 Blow the trumpet in Zion; sound the alarm on my **holy** hill.
3: 17 [4:17] that I, the LORD your God, dwell in Zion, my **holy** hill.
3: 17 [4:17] Jerusalem will be **holy**; never again will foreigners invade
Am 2: 7 Father and son use the same girl and so profane my **holy** name.
4: 2 The Sovereign LORD has sworn by his **holiness**: "The time will
Ob 1: 16 Just as you drank on my **holy** hill, so all the nations will drink
1: 17 it will be **holy**, and the house of Jacob will possess its inheritance.
Jnh 2: 4 [2:5] your sight; yet I will look again toward your **holy** temple.'
2: 7 [2:8] LORD, and my prayer rose to you, to your **holy** temple.
Mic 1: 2 LORD may witness against you, the Lord from his **holy** temple.
Hab 2: 20 the LORD is in his **holy** temple; let all the earth be silent before
Zep 3: 4 Her priests profane the **sanctuary** and do violence to the law.
3: 11 in their pride. Never again will you be haughty on my **holy** hill.
Hag 2: 12 If a person carries **consecrated** meat in the fold of his garment,
Zec 2: 12 [2:16] The LORD will inherit Judah as his portion in the **holy**
2: 13 [2:17] because he has roused himself from his **holy** dwelling."
8: 3 the mountain of the LORD Almighty will be called the **Holy**
14: 20 On that day **HOLY TO THE LORD** will be inscribed on the bells
14: 21 pot in Jerusalem and Judah will be **holy** to the LORD Almighty,
Mal 2: 11 Judah has desecrated the **sanctuary** the LORD loves, by

7732 קָדֵשׁ בַּרְנֵעַ **qādēš barnēaʿ**, n.pr.loc. [10] [√ 7727 + 1395]

Kadesh Barnea [10]

Nu 32: 8 did when I sent them from **Kadesh Barnea** to look over the land.
34: 4 Scorpion Pass, continue on to Zin and go south of **Kadesh Barnea**.
Dt 1: 2 (It takes eleven days to go from Horeb to **Kadesh Barnea** by the
1: 19 desert that you have seen, and so we reached **Kadesh Barnea**.
2: 14 Thirty-eight years passed from the time we left **Kadesh Barnea**
9: 23 And when the LORD sent you out from **Kadesh Barnea**,
Jos 10: 41 Joshua subdued them from **Kadesh Barnea** to Gaza and from the
14: 6 said to Moses the man of God at **Kadesh Barnea** about you
14: 7 of the LORD sent me from **Kadesh Barnea** to explore the land.
15: 3 continued on to Zin and went over to the south of **Kadesh Barnea**.

7733 קָהָה **qāhâ**, v. [4] [→ 7734]

set on edge [3], dull [1]

Ecc 10: 10 [D] If the ax *is* **dull** and its edge unsharpened, more strength is
Jer 31: 29 [A] eaten sour grapes, and the children's teeth *are* **set on edge**.'
31: 30 [A] whoever eats sour grapes—his own teeth *will be* **set on edge**.
Eze 18: 2 [A] eat sour grapes, and the children's teeth *are* **set on edge**'?

7734 קֵהָיוֹן **qēhāyôn**, n.[m.]. Not used in NIV/BHS [√ 7733]

7735 קָהַל **qāhal**, v.den. [39] [√ 7736]

gathered [9], assembled [8], assemble [5], came together [3], gather [2], gathered together [2], mustered [2], summoned [2], called together [1], came as a group [1], convenes a court [1], crowded [1], gather together [1], summoned to assemble [1]

Ex 32: 1 [C] they **gathered** around Aaron and said, "Come, make us gods
35: 1 [G] Moses **assembled** the whole Israelite community and said to
Lev 8: 3 [G] **gather** the entire assembly at the entrance to the Tent of
8: 4 [C] the assembly **gathered** at the entrance to the Tent of
Nu 1: 18 [G] *they* **called** the whole community **together** on the first day
8: 9 [G] of Meeting and **assemble** the whole Israelite community.
10: 7 [G] *To* **gather** the assembly, blow the trumpets, but not with the
16: 3 [C] *They* **came as a group** to oppose Moses and Aaron and said
16: 19 [G] When Korah *had* **gathered** all his followers in opposition to
16: 42 [17:7] [C] when the assembly **gathered** in opposition to Moses
20: 2 [C] and the people **gathered** in opposition to Moses and Aaron.
20: 8 [G] and your brother Aaron **gather** the assembly **together**.
20: 10 [G] Aaron **gathered** the assembly **together** in front of the rock
Dt 4: 10 [G] "**Assemble** the people before me to hear my words so that
31: 12 [G] **Assemble** the people—men, women and children,
31: 28 [G] **Assemble** before me all the elders of your tribes and all your
Jos 18: 1 [C] The whole assembly of the Israelites **gathered** *at* Shiloh
22: 12 [C] the whole assembly of Israel **gathered** at Shiloh to go to war
Jdg 20: 1 [C] out as one man and **assembled** before the LORD in Mizpah.
2Sa 20: 14 [C] *who* **gathered** [K 7827] **together** and followed him.
1Ki 8: 1 [G] King Solomon **summoned** into his presence at Jerusalem the
8: 2 [C] All the men of Israel **came together** to King Solomon at the
12: 21 [G] *he* **mustered** the whole house of Judah and the tribe of
1Ch 13: 5 [G] So David **assembled** all the Israelites, from the Shihor River
15: 3 [G] David **assembled** all Israel in Jerusalem to bring up the ark
28: 1 [G] David **summoned** all the officials of Israel **to assemble** at
2Ch 5: 2 [G] Then Solomon **summoned** to Jerusalem the elders of Israel,
5: 3 [C] all the men of Israel **came together** to the king at the time of
11: 1 [G] *he* **mustered** the house of Judah and Benjamin—
20: 26 [C] On the fourth day *they* **assembled** in the Valley of Beracah,
Est 8: 11 [C] edict granted the Jews in every city the right to **assemble**
9: 2 [C] The Jews **assembled** in their cities in all the provinces of
9: 15 [C] The Jews in Susa **came together** on the fourteenth day of the
9: 16 [C] in the king's provinces also **assembled** to protect themselves
9: 18 [C] *had* **assembled** on the thirteenth and fourteenth, and then on
Job 11: 10 [G] and confines you in prison and **convenes a court**,
Jer 26: 9 [C] all the people **crowded** around Jeremiah in the house of the
Eze 38: 7 [C] be prepared, you and all the hordes **gathered** about you,
38: 13 [G] *Have you* **gathered** your hordes to loot, to carry off silver

7736 קָהָל **qāhāl**, n.m. [123] [→ 5220, 5221, 7735, 7736, 7737, 7738, 7739, 7827; cf. 7754]

assembly [72], community [13], company [5], horde [4], crowd [3], mob [3], throng [3], *untranslated* [2], army [2], gathered [2], hordes [2], them [+3776+3972] [2], alliance [1], army [+2256+6639] [1], assemble [+928+2021+6590] [1], assembled [+995] [1], congregation [1], everyone else [+3972] [1], people [1], them[s] [+2021] [1], they[s] [+2021] [1], whole assembly [+2256+6337] [1]

Ge 28: 3 increase your numbers until you become a **community** *of* peoples.
35: 11 A nation and a **community** *of* nations will come from you,
48: 4 I will make you a **community** *of* peoples, and I will give this land
49: 6 Let me not enter their council, let me not join their **assembly**,
Ex 12: 6 when all the **people** *of* the community of Israel must slaughter
16: 3 us out into this desert to starve this entire **assembly** to death."
Lev 4: 13 even though the **community** is unaware of the matter, they are
4: 14 the **assembly** must bring a young bull as a sin offering and present
4: 21 he burned the first bull. This is the sin offering for the **community**.
16: 17 for himself, his household and the whole **community** *of* Israel.
16: 33 the altar, and for the priests and all the people of the **community**.
Nu 10: 7 To gather the **assembly**, blow the trumpets, but not with the same
14: 5 facedown in front of the whole Israelite assembly **gathered** there.
15: 15 The **community** is to have the same rules for you and for the alien
16: 3 then do you set yourselves above the LORD's **assembly**?"
16: 33 over them, and they perished and were gone from the **community**.
16: 47 [17:12] did as Moses said, and ran into the midst of the **assembly**.
19: 20 he must be cut off from the **community**, because he has defiled the
20: 4 Why did you bring the LORD's **community** into this desert,
20: 6 Aaron went from the **assembly** to the entrance to the Tent of
20: 10 and Aaron gathered the **assembly** together in front of the rock
20: 12 you will not bring this **community** into the land I give them."
22: 4 "This **horde** is going to lick up everything around us, as an ox
Dt 5: 22 to your whole **assembly** there on the mountain from out of the fire,
9: 10 to you on the mountain out of the fire, on the day of the **assembly**.
10: 4 to you on the mountain, out of the fire, on the day of the **assembly**.
18: 16 your God at Horeb on the day of the **assembly** when you said,
23: 1 [23:2] or cutting may enter the **assembly** *of* the LORD.
23: 2 [23:3] of his descendants may enter the **assembly** *of* the LORD,
23: 2 [23:3] of the LORD, **[RPH]** even down to the tenth generation.
23: 3 [23:4] or any of his descendants may enter the **assembly** *of* the
23: 3 [23:4] of the LORD, **[RPH]** even down to the tenth generation.
23: 8 [23:9] born to them may enter the **assembly** *of* the LORD.
31: 30 beginning to end in the hearing of the whole **assembly** *of* Israel:
Jos 8: 35 that Joshua did not read to the whole **assembly** *of* Israel,
Jdg 20: 2 of Israel took their places in the **assembly** *of* the people of God,
21: 5 *has* failed *to* **assemble** [+928+2021+6590] before the LORD?"
21: 8 no one from Jabesh Gilead had come to the camp for the **assembly**.
1Sa 17: 47 All those **gathered** here will know that it is not by sword or spear
1Ki 8: 14 While the whole **assembly** *of* Israel was standing there, the king
8: 14 the king turned around and blessed **them**[s] [+3776+3972].
8: 22 the altar of the LORD in front of the whole **assembly** *of* Israel,
8: 55 He stood and blessed the whole **assembly** *of* Israel in a loud voice,
8: 65 a vast **assembly**, people from Lebo Hamath to the Wadi of Egypt.
12: 3 and he and the whole **assembly** *of* Israel went to Rehoboam
1Ch 13: 2 He then said to the whole **assembly** *of* Israel, "If it seems good to
13: 4 The whole **assembly** agreed to do this, because it seemed right to
28: 8 you in the sight of all Israel and of the **assembly** *of* the LORD,
29: 1 Then King David said to the whole **assembly**: "My son Solomon,
29: 10 David praised the LORD in the presence of the whole **assembly**,
29: 20 David said to the whole **assembly**, "Praise the LORD your God."
29: 20 So **they**[s] [+2021] all praised the LORD, the God of their fathers;
2Ch 1: 3 and the whole **assembly** went to the high place at Gibeon,
1: 5 the LORD; so Solomon and the **assembly** inquired of him there.
6: 3 While the whole **assembly** *of* Israel was standing there, the king
6: 3 the king turned around and blessed **them**[s] [+3776+3972].
6: 12 the altar of the LORD in front of the whole **assembly** *of* Israel
6: 13 and then knelt down before the whole **assembly** *of* Israel
7: 8 a vast **assembly**, people from Lebo Hamath to the Wadi of Egypt.
20: 5 Jehoshaphat stood up in the **assembly** *of* Judah and Jerusalem at
20: 14 a Levite and descendant of Asaph, as he stood in the **assembly**.
23: 3 the whole **assembly** made a covenant with the king at the temple
24: 6 and by the **assembly** of Israel for the Tent of the Testimony?"
28: 14 and plunder in the presence of the officials and all the **assembly**.
29: 23 for the sin offering were brought before the king and the **assembly**,
29: 28 The whole **assembly** bowed in worship, while the singers sang
29: 31 So the **assembly** brought sacrifices and thank offerings, and all

2Ch 29: 32 The number of burnt offerings the **assembly** brought was seventy
30: 2 the whole **assembly** in Jerusalem decided to celebrate the Passover
30: 4 The plan seemed right both to the king and to the whole **assembly**.
30: 13 A very large **crowd** of people assembled in Jerusalem to celebrate
30: 17 Since many in the **crowd** had not consecrated themselves,
30: 23 The whole **assembly** then agreed to celebrate the festival seven
30: 24 and seven thousand sheep and goats for the **assembly**,
30: 24 and the officials provided **them**[s] [+2021] with a thousand bulls
30: 25 The entire **assembly** *of* Judah rejoiced, along with the priests
30: 25 and Levites and all who *had* **assembled** [+995] from Israel,
31: 18 daughters of the whole **community** listed in these genealogical
Ezr 2: 64 The whole **company** numbered 42,360,
10: 1 down before the house of God, a large **crowd** of Israelites—
10: 8 and would himself be expelled from the **assembly** *of* the exiles.
10: 12 The whole **assembly** responded with a loud voice: "You are right!
10: 14 Let our officials act for the whole **assembly**. Then let everyone in
Ne 5: 13 At this the whole **assembly** said, "Amen," and praised the LORD.
7: 66 The whole **company** numbered 42,360,
8: 2 month Ezra the priest brought the Law before the **assembly**,
8: 17 The whole **company** that had returned from exile built booths
13: 1 or Moabite should ever be admitted into the **assembly** *of* God,
Job 30: 28 but not by the sun; I stand up in the **assembly** and cry for help.
Ps 22: 22 [22:23] to my brothers; in the **congregation** I will praise you.
22: 25 [22:26] you comes the theme of my praise in the great **assembly**;
26: 5 I abhor the **assembly** *of* evildoers and refuse to sit with the wicked.
35: 18 I will give you thanks in the great **assembly**; among throngs of
40: 9 [40:10] I proclaim righteousness in the great **assembly**; I do not
40: 10 [40:11] conceal your love and your truth from the great **assembly**.
89: 5 [89:6] your faithfulness too, in the **assembly** *of* the holy ones.
107: 32 Let them exalt him in the **assembly** *of* the people and praise him in
149: 1 to the LORD a new song, his praise in the **assembly** *of* the saints.
Pr 5: 14 utter ruin in the midst of the **whole assembly** [+2256+6337]."
21: 16 path of understanding comes to rest in the **company** *of* the dead.
26: 26 by deception, but his wickedness will be exposed in the **assembly**.
Jer 26: 17 the land stepped forward and said to the entire **assembly** *of* people,
31: 8 expectant mothers and women in labor; a great **throng** will return.
44: 15 a large **assembly**—and all the people living in Lower and Upper
50: 9 bring against Babylon an **alliance** *of* great nations from the land of
La 1: 10 her sanctuary—those you had forbidden to enter your **assembly**.
Eze 16: 40 They will bring a **mob** against you, who will stone you and hack
17: 17 his mighty army and great **horde** will be of no help to him in war,
23: 24 with weapons, chariots and wagons and with a **throng** *of* people;
23: 46 Bring a **mob** against them and give them over to terror
23: 47 The **mob** will stone them and cut them down with their swords;
26: 7 and chariots, with horsemen and a great **army** [+2256+6639].
27: 27 **everyone else** [+3972] on board will sink into the heart of the sea
27: 34 your wares and all your **company** have gone down with you.
32: 3 " 'With a great **throng** *of* people I will cast my net over you,
32: 22 "Assyria is there with her whole **army**; she is surrounded by the
32: 23 are in the depths of the pit and her **army** lies around her grave.
38: 4 fully armed, and a great **horde** with large and small shields,
38: 7 be prepared, you and all the **hordes** gathered about you, and take
38: 13 Have you gathered your **hordes** to loot, to carry off silver
38: 15 all of them riding on horses, a great **horde**, a mighty army.
Joel 2: 16 Gather the people, consecrate the **assembly**; bring together the
Mic 2: 5 Therefore you will have no one in the **assembly** *of* the LORD to

7737 קְהִלָּה q^ehillâ, n.f. [2] [√ 7736]

assembly [1], meeting [1]

Dt 33: 4 law that Moses gave us, the possession of the **assembly** *of* Jacob.
Ne 5: 7 So I called together a large **meeting** to deal with them

7738 קֹהֶלֶת qōhelet, n.m. [7] [√ 7736]

Teacher [7]

Ecc 1: 1 The words of the **Teacher**, son of David, king in Jerusalem:
1: 2 "Meaningless! Meaningless!" says the **Teacher**. "Utterly
1: 12 I, the **Teacher**, was king over Israel in Jerusalem.
7: 27 "Look," says the **Teacher**, "this is what I have discovered:
12: 8 "Meaningless! Meaningless!" says the **Teacher**. "Everything is
12: 9 Not only was the **Teacher** wise, but also he imparted knowledge to
12: 10 The **Teacher** searched to find just the right words, and what he

7739 קְהֵלָתָה q^ehēlātâ, n.pr.loc. [2] [√ 7736]

Kehelathah [2]

Nu 33: 22 They left Rissah and camped at **Kehelathah**.
33: 23 They left **Kehelathah** and camped at Mount Shepher.

7740 קְהָת q^ehāt, n.pr.m. [32] [→ 7741]

Kohath [18], Kohathite [+1201] [7], Kohathites [+1201] [4], Kohath's [2], *untranslated* [1]

Ge 46: 11 The sons of Levi: Gershon, **Kohath** and Merari.
Ex 6: 16 their records: Gershon, **Kohath** and Merari. Levi lived 137 years.
6: 18 The sons of **Kohath** were Amram, Izhar, Hebron and Uzziel.
6: 18 were Amram, Izhar, Hebron and Uzziel. **Kohath** lived 133 years.
Nu 3: 17 were the names of the sons of Levi: Gershon, **Kohath** and Merari.
3: 19 The **Kohathite** [+1201] clans: Amram, Izhar, Hebron and Uzziel.
3: 27 To **Kohath** belonged the clans of the Amramites, Izharites,
3: 29 The **Kohathite** [+1201] clans were to camp on the south side of
4: 2 "Take a census of the **Kohathite** [+1201] branch of the Levites by
4: 4 "This is the work of the **Kohathites** [+1201] in the Tent of
4: 15 to move, the **Kohathites** [+1201] are to come to do the carrying.
4: 15 The **Kohathites** [+1201] are to carry those things that are in the
7: 9 Moses did not give any to the **Kohathites** [+1201], because they
16: 1 Korah son of Izhar, the son of **Kohath**, the son of Levi, and certain
26: 57 through **Kohath**, the Kohathite clan; through Merari, the Merarite
26: 58 the Korahite clan. (**Kohath** was the forefather of Amram;
Jos 21: 5 The rest of **Kohath's** descendants were allotted ten towns from the
21: 20 The rest of the **Kohathite** [+1201] clans of the Levites were
21: 20 The rest of the Kohathite clans **[RPH]** of the Levites were allotted
21: 26 their pasturelands were given to the rest of the **Kohathite** [+1201]
1Ch 6: 1 [5:27] The sons of Levi: Gershon, **Kohath** and Merari.
6: 2 [5:28] The sons of **Kohath**: Amram, Izhar, Hebron and Uzziel.
6: 16 [6:1] The sons of Levi: Gershon, **Kohath** and Merari.
6: 18 [6:3] The sons of **Kohath**: Amram, Izhar, Hebron and Uzziel.
6: 22 [6:7] The descendants of **Kohath**: Amminadab his son, Korah his
6: 38 [6:23] the son of Izhar, the son of **Kohath**, the son of Levi,
6: 61 [6:46] The rest of **Kohath's** descendants were allotted ten towns
6: 66 [6:51] Some of the **Kohathite** [+1201] clans were given as their
6: 70 [6:55] to the rest of the **Kohathite** [+1201] clans.
15: 5 From the descendants of **Kohath**, Uriel the leader and 120
23: 6 corresponding to the sons of Levi: Gershon, **Kohath** and Merari.
23: 12 The sons of **Kohath**: Amram, Izhar, Hebron and Uzziel—

7741 קְהָתִי q^ehātî, a.g. [15] [√ 7740]

Kohathite [7], Kohathites [+1201] [3], Kohathites [3], Kohath [1], Kohathite [+1201] [1]

Nu 3: 27 Hebronites and Uzzielites; these were the **Kohathite** clans.
3: 30 The leader of the families of the **Kohathite** clans was Elizaphan
4: 18 "See that the **Kohathite** tribal clans are not cut off from the
4: 34 the leaders of the community counted the **Kohathites** [+1201] by
4: 37 This was the total of all those in the **Kohathite** clans who served in
10: 21 the **Kohathites** set out, carrying the holy things. The tabernacle
26: 57 through Kohath, the **Kohathite** clan; through Merari, the Merarite
Jos 21: 4 The first lot came out for the **Kohathites**, clan by clan. The Levites
21: 10 of Aaron who were from the **Kohathite** clans of the Levites,
1Ch 6: 33 [6:18] From the **Kohathites**: Heman, the musician, the son of
6: 54 [6:39] descendants of Aaron who were from the **Kohathite** clan,
9: 32 Some of their **Kohathite** [+1201] brothers were in charge of
2Ch 20: 19 some Levites from the **Kohathites** [+1201] and Korahites stood up
29: 12 from the **Kohathites** [+1201], Mahath son of Amasai and Joel son
34: 12 and Zechariah and Meshullam, descended from **Kohath**.

7742 קַו qāw[1], n.m. [21 / 20] [√ 7747?; cf. 7749]

rule [8], measuring line [7], line [4], measure [1]

1Ki 7: 23 It took a **line** [K 7749] of thirty cubits to measure around it.
2Ki 21: 13 I will stretch out over Jerusalem the **measuring line** *used against*
2Ch 4: 2 five cubits high. It took a **line** of thirty cubits to measure around it.
Job 38: 5 Surely you know! Who stretched a **measuring line** across it?
Ps 19: 4 [19:5] Their voice [BHS *line*; NIV 7754] goes out into all the earth,
Isa 28: 10 Do and do, do and do, **rule** on rule, rule on rule; a little here,
28: 10 Do and do, do and do, rule on **rule**, rule on rule; a little here,
28: 10 Do and do, do and do, rule on rule, **rule** on rule; a little here,
28: 10 Do and do, do and do, rule on rule, rule on **rule**; a little here,
28: 13 Do and do, do and do, **rule** on rule, rule on rule; a little here,
28: 13 Do and do, do and do, rule on **rule**, rule on rule; a little here,
28: 13 Do and do, do and do, rule on rule, **rule** on rule; a little here,
28: 13 Do and do, do and do, rule on rule, rule on **rule**; a little here,
28: 17 I will make justice the **measuring line** and righteousness the
34: 11 God will stretch out over Edom the **measuring line** *of* chaos
34: 17 He allots their portions; his hand distributes them by **measure**.
44: 13 The carpenter measures with a **line** and makes an outline with a
Jer 31: 39 The measuring **line** [K 7749] will stretch from there straight to the
La 2: 8 He stretched out a **measuring line** and did not withhold his hand
Eze 47: 3 As the man went eastward with a **measuring line** in his hand,
Zec 1: 16 the **measuring line** [K 7749] will be stretched out over Jerusalem,'

7743 קַו qāw[2], n.m. [4] [√ 7744?; cf. 7768]

strange speech [+7743] [4]

Isa 18: 2 and wide, an aggressive nation of **strange speech** [+7743],
18: 2 and wide, an aggressive nation of **strange speech** [+7743],
18: 7 and wide, an aggressive nation of **strange speech** [+7743],
18: 7 and wide, an aggressive nation of **strange speech** [+7743],

7744 ³קָו **qāw³**, n.m. Not used in NIV/BHS [√ 7743?]

7745 קְוֵא **qᵉwēʼ**, n.pr.loc. [2] [cf. 7750]

Kue [2]

2Ch 1:16 Solomon's horses were imported from Egypt and from **Kue**—
1:16 and from Kue—the royal merchants purchased them from **Kue**.

7746 קוֹבַע **qôbaʻ**, n.[m.]. [2] [cf. 3916]

helmet [1], helmets [1]

1Sa 17:38 He put a coat of armor on him and a bronze **helmet** on his head.
Eze 23:24 you on every side with large and small shields and with **helmets**.

7747 ¹קָוָה **qāwâ¹**, v. [47] [→ 5223, 7742?, 9535, 9536, 9537]

hope in [7], wait [7], look [5], looked for [4], hope [3], hoped [2], trusted [2], wait for [2], waited patiently for [+7747] [2], eager [1], expect [1], hope for [1], hoped for [1], in hope [1], long for [1], look for [1], look in hope [1], put trust [1], waited for [1], waiting eagerly [1], waiting [1], waits [1]

Ge 49:18 [D] "*I* **look** for your deliverance, O LORD.
Job 3:9 [D] *may it* **wait** for daylight in vain and not see the first rays of
6:19 [D] for water, the traveling merchants of Sheba **look in hope**.
7:2 [D] or a hired man **waiting eagerly** *for* his wages,
17:13 [D] If the only home *I* **hope for** is the grave, if I spread out my
30:26 [D] Yet *when I* **hoped for** good, evil came; when I looked for
Ps 25:3 [A] No one *whose* **hope** *is* **in** you will ever be put to shame,
25:5 [D] you are God my Savior, and *my* **hope** *is* **in** you all day long.
25:21 [D] and uprightness protect me, because *my* **hope** *is* **in** you.
27:14 [D] **Wait** for the LORD; be strong and take heart and wait for
27:14 [D] be strong and take heart and **wait** for the LORD.
37:9 [A] but *those who* **hope in** the LORD will inherit the land.
37:34 [D] **Wait** for the LORD and keep his way. He will exalt you to
39:7 [39:8] [D] "But now, Lord, what *do I* **look for**? My hope is in
40:1 [40:2] [D] *I* **waited** [+7747] **patiently for** the LORD; he
40:1 [40:2] [D] *I* **waited patiently for** [+7747] the LORD; he
52:9 [52:11] [D] **in** your name *I will* **hope**, for your name is good.
56:6 [56:7] [D] they lurk, they watch my steps, **eager** to take my life.
69:6 [69:7] [A] May *those who* **hope in** you not be disgraced
69:20 [69:21] [D] *I* **looked for** sympathy, but there was none, for
119:95 [D] The wicked *are* **waiting** to destroy me, but I will ponder
130:5 [D] *I* **wait for** the LORD, my soul waits, and in his word I put
130:5 [D] I wait for the LORD, my soul **waits**, and in his word I put
Pr 20:22 [D] this wrong!" **Wait** for the LORD, and he will deliver you.
Isa 5:2 [D] *he* **looked for** a crop of good grapes, but it yielded only bad
5:4 [D] *When I* **looked for** good grapes, why did it yield only bad?
5:7 [D] *he* **looked for** justice, but saw bloodshed; for righteousness,
8:17 [D] his face from the house of Jacob. *I will* **put** *my* **trust** in him.
25:9 [D] "Surely this is our God; *we* **trusted** in him, and he saved us.
25:9 [D] This is the LORD, *we* **trusted** in him; let us rejoice and be
26:8 [D] LORD, walking in the way of your laws, *we* **wait for** you;
33:2 [D] O LORD, be gracious to us; *we* **long for** you. Be our
40:31 [A] but *those who* **hope in** the LORD will renew their strength.
49:23 [A] those *who* **hope in** me will not be disappointed."
51:5 [D] The islands *will* **look** to me and wait in hope for my arm.
59:9 [D] *We* **look** for light, but all is darkness; for brightness, but we
59:11 [D] *We* **look** for justice, but find none; for deliverance, but it is
60:9 [D] Surely the islands **look** to me; in the lead are the ships of
64:3 [64:2] [D] you did awesome things that *we did* not **expect**,
Jer 8:15 [D] We **hoped** for peace but no good has come, for a time of
13:16 [D] *You* **hope** for light, but he will turn it to thick darkness
14:19 [D] We **hoped** for peace but no good has come, for a time of
14:22 [D] Therefore *our* **hope** *is* in you, for you are the one who does
La 2:16 [D] This is the day *we have* **waited for**; we have lived to see it."
3:25 [A] The LORD is good to *those whose* **hope** *is in* him,
Hos 12:6 [12:7] [D] and justice, and **wait** for your God always.
Mic 5:7 [5:6] [D] which *do* not **wait** for man or linger for mankind.

7748 ²קָוָה **qāwâ²**, v. [2] [→ 5224, 5225]

be gathered [1], gather [1]

Ge 1:9 [C] "*Let* the water under the sky **be gathered** to one place,
Jer 3:17 [C] all nations *will* **gather** in Jerusalem to honor the name of the

7749 קָוֶה **qāweh**, n.m. [0] [cf. 7742]

1Ki 7:23 [It took a **line** [K; see Q 7742] of thirty cubits to measure around it.]
Jer 31:39 [The measuring **line** [K; see Q 7742] will stretch from there]
Zec 1:16 [the **measuring line** [K; see Q 7742] will be stretched out over]

7750 קְוֵה **qᵉwēh**, n.pr.loc. [2] [cf. 7745]

Kue [2]

1Ki 10:28 Solomon's horses were imported from Egypt and from **Kue**—
10:28 and from Kue—the royal merchants purchased them from **Kue**.

7751 קוֹחַ **qôaḥ**, n.[m.]. Not used in NIV/BHS [cf. 7223]

7752 קוּט **qûṭ**, v. [7] [cf. 7762, 9210]

loathe [4], abhor [1], angry [1], loathing [1]

Job 10:1 [C] "I **loathe** my very life; therefore I will give free rein to my
Ps 95:10 [A] For forty years *I was* **angry** with that generation; I said,
119:158 [F] I look on the faithless *with* **loathing**, for they do not obey
139:21 [F] O LORD, and **abhor** those who rise up against you?
Eze 6:9 [C] *They will* **loathe** themselves for the evil they have done
20:43 [C] and *you will* **loathe** yourselves for all the evil you have done.
36:31 [C] *you will* **loathe** yourselves for your sins and detestable

7753 קוֹט **qôṭ**, v. *or* n.m. Not used in NIV/BHS [cf. 3684]

7754 קוֹל **qôl**, n.m. [505 / 506] [→ 7755?, 7826; cf. 7736; Ar 10631]

voice [101], sound [62], obey [+928+9048] [36], *untranslated* [23], obeyed [+928+9048] [17], voices [17], to [+928] [15], listen [12], thunder [12], noise [11], to [+4200] [9], cry [8], cry for mercy [+9384] [6], sounds [6], aloud [+906+5951] [5], proclamation [5], roar [5], aloud [+5951] [4], thunders [+5989] [4], blast [3], called out [+928+1524+7924] [3], cries [3], plea [3], word [3], aloud [+1524] [2], aloud [2], crackling [2], cry [+7591] [2], crying [2], disobeyed [+928+4202+9048] [2], fully obey [+928+9048+9048] [2], hear [2], heard [+928+9048] [2], heard [2], lowing [2], response [2], shout [2], shouts of joy [+8262] [2], sound [+6702] [2], sounding [2], speech [2], thunder [+5989] [2], thunderstorm [+2613] [2], what say [2], what says [2], words [2], acclamation [1], agreed with [+4200+9048] [1], aloud [+928] [1], aloud [+928+1524] [1], argue [+9048] [1], began [+906+5951] [1], blast [+8795] [1], bleating [1], calling [+7924] [1], calls [1], clamor [1], clatter [+8323] [1], command [1], cooing [1], crack [1], cried out for help [+7590] [1], cried out [1], cry aloud [+5989] [1], cry for help [+2410] [1], cry for help [+8776] [1], cry out [+2411] [1], cry out [+7412] [1], diligently obey [+928+9048+9048] [1], disobedience [+928+4202+9048] [1], disobey [+928+1194+9048] [1], gave in [+928+9048] [1], give a hearing [+263] [1], growl [+5989] [1], growl [1], growled [+5989] [1], hears [+9048] [1], hears [+906+9048+9048] [1], hiss [1], it^s [+3276] [1], listen [+9048] [1], listen carefully [+928+4200+9048] [1], loud [1], loudly [+5951] [1], loudly [+928+1524] [1], music [1], neighing [+5177] [1], news [1], noise [+2159] [1], noisy din [+1524] [1], obey [+4200+9048] [1], obey fully [+928+9048+9048] [1], obeyed [+928+4200+9048] [1], obeying [+928+9048] [1], obeys [+928+9048] [1], outcry [+7591] [1], rebuke [1], resound [1], roared [+5989] [1], roaring [+8614] [1], roars [+928+5989] [1], say [1], scream for help [+2256+7924+8123] [1], screamed [+928+1524+7924] [1], screamed for help [+2256+7924+8123] [1], shout [+1524+7924] [1], shout [+8123] [1], shout [+928+7924] [1], shouted [+2256+5951+7924] [1], shouted [+928+7924] [1], shouted [+928+8123+9558] [1], shouting [+9558] [1], shouts [1], sing [+5989] [1], sing songs [+928+4200+8123+9048] [1], song [1], sound [+928+8123] [1], speaking [+1821] [1], taunts [1], thunders [+928+5989] [1], tumult [+2167] [1], tune [1], uproar [+2162] [1], uproar [+9558] [1], very [1], war cry [1], weeping [1], wept so loudly [+906+928+1140+5989] [1], what^s [+1821] [1], what have to say [1], what said [+1821] [1], what said [1], what saying [1], what^s [1], whisper [+1960] [1]

Ge 3:8 his wife heard the **sound** *of* the LORD God as he was walking in
3:10 He answered, "I heard **[RPH]** you in the garden, and I was afraid
3:17 "Because you listened **to** [+4200] your wife and ate from the tree
4:10 The LORD said, "What have you done? **Listen**! Your brother's
4:23 Lamech said to his wives, "Adah and Zillah, listen to **[NIE]** me;
16:2 can build a family through her." Abram agreed to **what** Sarai **said**.
21:12 Listen **to** [+928] whatever Sarah tells you, because it is through
21:16 And as she sat there nearby, *she* **began** [+906+5951] to sob.
21:17 God heard the boy **crying**, and the angel of God called to Hagar
21:17 Do not be afraid; God has heard the boy **crying** as he lies there.
22:18 earth will be blessed, because *you have* **obeyed** [+928+9048] me."
26:5 because Abraham **obeyed** [+928+9048] me and kept my
27:8 Now, my son, **listen carefully** [+928+4200+9048] and do what I
27:13 the curse fall on me. Just do what I **say**; go and get them for me."
27:22 who touched him and said, "The **voice** is the voice of Jacob,
27:22 who touched him and said, "The voice is the **voice** *of* Jacob,
27:38 Bless me too, my father!" Then Esau wept **aloud** [+5951].
27:43 Now then, my son, do **what** I **say**: Flee at once to my brother
29:11 Then Jacob kissed Rachel and began to weep **aloud** [+906+5951].
30:6 has vindicated me; he has listened to my **plea** and given me a son."
39:14 came in here to sleep with me, but *I* **screamed** [+928+1524+7924].
39:15 When he heard me **scream for help** [+2256+7924+8123], he left
39:18 But as soon as I **screamed for help** [+2256+7924+8123], he left
45:2 And he **wept so loudly** [+906+928+1140+5989] that the Egyptians

Ge 45:16 When the **news** reached Pharaoh's palace that Joseph's brothers
Ex 3:18 "The elders of Israel will listen **to** [+4200] you. Then you
4: 1 "What if they do not believe me or listen **to** [+928] me and say,
4: 8 believe you or pay attention **to** [+4200] the first miraculous sign,
4: 8 to the first miraculous sign, they may believe **[RPH]** the second.
4: 9 But if they do not believe these two signs or listen **to** [+4200] you,
5: 2 that *I should* **obey** [+928+9048] him and let Israel go?
9:23 the LORD sent **thunder** and hail, and lightning flashed down to
9:28 Pray to the LORD, for we have had enough **thunder** and hail.
9:29 The **thunder** will stop and there will be no more hail, so you may
9:33 the **thunder** and hail stopped, and the rain no longer poured down
9:34 When Pharaoh saw that the rain and hail and **thunder** had stopped,
15:26 "If you listen carefully to the **voice** *of* the LORD your God
18:19 Listen now **to** [+928] me and I will give you some advice,
18:24 Moses listened **to** [+4200] his father-in-law and did everything he
19: 5 if *you* **obey** me **fully** [+928+9048+9048] and keep my covenant,
19:16 On the morning of the third day there was **thunder** and lightning,
19:16 a thick cloud over the mountain, and a very loud trumpet **blast**.
19:19 the **sound** *of* the trumpet grew louder and louder. Then Moses
19:19 and louder. Then Moses spoke and the **voice** of God answered him.
20:18 When the people saw the **thunder** and lightning and heard the
20:18 lightning and **heard** the trumpet and saw the mountain in smoke,
23:21 Pay attention to him and listen to **what** he **says**. Do not rebel
23:22 If you listen carefully to **what** he **says** and do all that I say,
24: 3 all the LORD's words and laws, they responded with one **voice**,
28:35 The **sound** *of* the bells will be heard when he enters the Holy Place
32:17 When Joshua heard the **noise** *of* the people shouting, he said to
32:17 he said to Moses, "There is the **sound** *of* war in the camp."
32:18 "It is not the **sound** [+6702] *of* victory, it is not the sound of
32:18 is not the sound of victory, it is not the **sound** [+6702] *of* defeat;
32:18 it is not the sound of defeat; it is the **sound** *of* singing that I hear."
36: 6 Moses gave an order and they sent this **word** throughout the camp:
Lev 5: 1 because he does not speak up when *he* **hears** [+9048] a public
26:36 so fearful in the lands of their enemies that the **sound** *of* a
Nu 7:89 he heard the **voice** speaking to him from between the two cherubim
14: 1 That night all the people of the community raised their **voices**
14:22 *who* **disobeyed** [+928+4202+9048] me and tested me ten times—
16:34 At their **cries**, all the Israelites around them fled, shouting,
20:16 he heard our **cry** and sent an angel and brought us out of Egypt.
21: 3 The LORD listened to Israel's **plea** and gave the Canaanites over
Dt 1:34 When the LORD heard **what** you **said** [+1821], he was angry
1:45 he paid no attention to your **weeping** and turned a deaf ear to you.
4:12 You heard the **sound** *of* words but saw no form; there was only a
4:12 heard the sound of words but saw no form; there was only a **voice**.
4:30 will return to the LORD your God and **obey** [+928+9048] him.
4:33 Has any other people heard the **voice** *of* God speaking out of fire,
4:36 From heaven he made you hear his **voice** to discipline you.
5:22 **voice** to your whole assembly there on the mountain from out of
5:23 When you heard the **voice** out of the darkness, while the mountain
5:24 and his majesty, and we have heard his **voice** from the fire.
5:25 we will die if we hear the **voice** *of* the LORD our God any longer.
5:26 For what mortal man has ever heard the **voice** *of* the living God
5:28 The LORD heard **[RPH]** you when you spoke to me
5:28 said to me, "I have heard **what**[s] [+1821] this people said to you.
8:20 so you will be destroyed for not **obeying** [+928+9048] the LORD
9:23 your God. You did not trust him or **obey** [+928+9048] him.
13: 4 [13:5] Keep his commands and **obey** [+928+9048] him; serve him
13:18 [13:19] because *you* **obey** [+928+9048] the LORD your God,
15: 5 if only *you* **fully obey** [+928+9048+9048] the LORD your God and
18:16 "Let us not hear the **voice** *of* the LORD our God nor see this great
21:18 and rebellious son who *does* not **obey** [+928+9048] his father
21:18 rebellious son who does not obey his father and **[RPH]** mother
21:20 ours is stubborn and rebellious. He *will* not **obey** [+928+9048] us.
26: 7 the LORD heard our **voice** and saw our misery, toil and
26:14 *I have* **obeyed** [+928+9048] the LORD my God; I have done
26:17 commands and laws, and that you *will* **obey** [+928+9048] him.
27:10 **Obey** [+928+9048] the LORD your God and follow his
27:14 The Levites shall recite to all the people of Israel in a loud **voice**:
28: 1 If *you* **fully obey** [+928+9048+9048] the LORD your God and
28: 2 accompany you if *you* **obey** [+928+9048] the LORD your God:
28:15 if *you do* not **obey** [+928+9048] the LORD your God and do not
28:45 because *you did* not **obey** [+928+9048] the LORD your God
28:62 because *you did* not **obey** [+928+9048] the LORD your God.
30: 2 LORD your God and **obey** [+928+9048] him with all your heart
30: 8 You *will* again **obey** [+928+9048] the LORD and follow all his
30:10 if *you* **obey** [+928+9048] the LORD your God and keep his
30:20 love the LORD your God, listen to his **voice**, and hold fast to him.
33: 7 "Hear, O LORD, the **cry** *of* Judah; bring him to his people.
Jos 5: 6 had died, since *they had* not **obeyed** [+928+9048] the LORD.
6: 5 When you hear them sound a long **blast** [+8795] on the trumpets,
6:10 the people, "Do not give a war cry, do not raise your **voices**,
6:20 the people shouted, and at the **sound** *of* the trumpet,
10:14 or since, a day when the LORD listened **to** [+928] a man.
22: 2 *you have* **obeyed** [+928+9048] me in everything I commanded.
24:24 "We will serve the LORD our God and **obey** [+928+9048] him."
Jdg 2: 2 Yet *you have* **disobeyed** [+928+4202+9048] me. Why have you
2: 4 things to all the Israelites, the people wept **aloud** [+906+5951],
2:20 laid down for their forefathers and has not listened **to** [+4200] me,
5:11 the **voice** *of* the singers at the watering places. They recite the
6:10 in whose land you live.' But you have not listened **to** [+928] me."
9: 7 top of Mount Gerizim and **shouted** [+2256+5951+7924] to them,
13: 9 God **heard** [+928+9048] Manoah, and the angel of God came
18: 3 near Micah's house, they recognized the **voice** *of* the young Levite;
18:25 The Danites answered, "Don't **argue** [+9048] with us, or some
20:13 the Benjamites would not listen **to** [+928] their fellow Israelites.
21: 2 before God until evening, raising their **voices** and weeping bitterly.
Ru 1: 9 Then she kissed them and they wept **aloud** [+5951]
1:14 At this **[RPH]** they wept again. Then Orpah kissed her
1Sa 1:13 in her heart, and her lips were moving but her **voice** was not heard.
2:25 His sons, however, did not listen to their father's **rebuke**,
4: 6 Hearing the **uproar** [+9558], the Philistines asked, "What's all this
4: 6 "What's all this **shouting** [+9558] in the Hebrew camp?"
4:14 Eli heard the **outcry** [+7591] and asked, "What is the meaning of
4:14 and asked, "What is the meaning of this **uproar** [+2162]?"
7:10 that day the LORD thundered with loud **thunder** against the
8: 7 "Listen **to** [+928] all that the people are saying to you; it is not you
8: 9 Now listen **to** [+928] them; but warn them solemnly and let them
8:19 But the people refused to listen **to** [+928] Samuel. "No!" they said.
8:22 LORD answered, "Listen **to** [+928] them and give them a king."
11: 4 these terms to the people, they all wept **aloud** [+906+5951].
12: 1 "I have listened **to** [+928] everything you said to me and have set a
12:14 If you fear the LORD and serve and **obey** [+928+9048] him
12:15 if *you do* not **obey** [+928+9048] the LORD, and if you rebel
12:17 I will call upon the LORD to send **thunder** and rain.
12:18 the LORD, and that same day the LORD sent **thunder** and rain.
15: 1 so listen now **to** [+4200] the message from the LORD.
15:14 But Samuel said, "What then is this **bleating** *of* sheep in my ears?
15:14 of sheep in my ears? What is this **lowing** *of* cattle that I hear?"
15:19 Why *did you* not **obey** [+928+9048] the LORD? Why did you
15:20 "But *I did* **obey** [+928+9048] the LORD," Saul said. "I went on
15:22 and sacrifices as much as in obeying the **voice** *of* the LORD?
15:24 I was afraid of the people and so *I* **gave in to** [+928+9048] them.
19: 6 Saul listened **to** [+928] Jonathan and took this oath: "As surely as
24:16 [24:17] Saul asked, "Is that your **voice**, David my son?"
24:16 [24:17] your voice, David my son?" And he wept **aloud** [+5951].
25:35 home in peace. I have heard your **words** and granted your request."
26:17 Saul recognized David's **voice** and said, "Is that your voice,
26:17 Saul recognized David's voice and said, "Is that your **voice**,
26:17 my son?" David replied, "Yes **it**[s] [+3276] is, my lord the king."
28:12 she cried out at the top of her **voice** and said to Saul, "Why have
28:18 Because *you did* not **obey** [+928+9048] the LORD or carry out
28:21 she said, "Look, your maidservant *has* **obeyed** [+928+9048] you.
28:22 Now please listen **to** [+928] your servant and let me give you some
28:23 joined the woman in urging him, and he listened **to** [+4200] them.
30: 4 his men wept **aloud** [+906+5951] until they had no strength left to
2Sa 3:32 in Hebron, and the king wept **aloud** [+906+5951] at Abner's tomb.
5:24 As soon as you hear the **sound** *of* marching in the tops of the
6:15 up the ark of the LORD with shouts and the **sound** *of* trumpets.
12:18 still living, we spoke to David but he would not listen **to** [+928] us.
13:14 he refused to listen **to** [+928] her, and since he was stronger than
13:36 the king's sons came in, wailing **loudly** [+5951].
15:10 "As soon as you hear the **sound** *of* the trumpets, then say,
15:23 The whole countryside wept **aloud** [+1524] as all the people
19: 4 [19:5] The king covered his face and cried **aloud** [+1524], "O my
19:35 [19:36] Can I still hear the **voices** *of* men and women singers?
22: 7 From his temple he heard my **voice**; my cry came to his ears.
22:14 thundered from heaven; the **voice** *of* the Most High resounded.
1Ki 1:40 and rejoicing greatly, so that the ground shook with the **sound**.
1:41 On hearing the **sound** *of* the trumpet, Joab asked, "What's the
1:41 "What's the meaning of all the **noise** [+2159] *in* the city?"
1:45 and the city resounds with it. That's the **noise** you hear.
8:55 He stood and blessed the whole assembly of Israel in a loud **voice**,
14: 6 So when Ahijah heard the **sound** *of* her footsteps at the door,
17:22 The LORD heard Elijah's **cry**, and the boy's life returned to him,
18:26 they shouted. But there was no **response**; no one answered.
18:27 "**Shout** [+928+7924] louder!" he said. "Surely he is a god!
18:28 So *they* **shouted** [+928+7924] louder and slashed themselves with
18:29 there was no **response**, no one answered, no one paid attention.
18:41 "Go, eat and drink, for there is the **sound** *of* a heavy rain."
19:12 not in the fire. And after the fire came a gentle **whisper** [+1960].
19:13 Then a **voice** said to him, "What are you doing here, Elijah?"
20:25 *He* **agreed with** [+4200+9048] them and acted accordingly.
20:36 "Because *you have* not **obeyed** [+928+9048] the LORD,
2Ki 4:31 the staff on the boy's face, but there was no **sound** or response.
6:32 Is not the **sound** *of* his master's footsteps behind him?"
7: 6 for the Lord had caused the Arameans to hear the **sound** *of*
7: 6 to hear the sound of chariots and **[RPH]** horses and a great army,
7: 6 to hear the sound of chariots and horses and **[RPH]** a great army,

2Ki 7:10 not a **sound** *of* anyone—only tethered horses and donkeys,
10: 6 saying, "If you are on my side and *will* **obey** [+4200+9048] me,
11:13 When Athaliah heard the **noise** *made by* the guards
18:12 because *they had* not **obeyed** [+928+9048] the LORD their God,
18:28 commander stood and **called out** [+928+1524+7924] in Hebrew:
19:22 Against whom have you raised your **voice** and lifted your eyes in
1Ch 14:15 As soon as you hear the **sound** *of* marching in the tops of the
15:16 brothers as singers *to* **sing** joyful **songs** [+928+4200+8123+9048],
15:28 with the **sounding** *of* rams' horns and trumpets, and of cymbals,
2Ch 5:13 as with one **voice**, to give praise and thanks to the LORD.
5:13 they raised their **voices** in praise to the LORD and sang:
15:14 They took an oath to the LORD with loud **acclamation**, with
20:19 and praised the LORD, the God of Israel, with very loud **voice**.
23:12 When Athaliah heard the **noise** *of* the people running and cheering
24: 9 A **proclamation** was then issued in Judah and Jerusalem that they
30: 5 They decided to send a **proclamation** throughout Israel,
30:27 God **heard** [+928+9048] them, for their prayer reached heaven,
32:18 *they* **called out** [+928+1524+7924] in Hebrew to the people of
36:22 Cyrus king of Persia to make a **proclamation** throughout his realm
Ezr 1: 1 Cyrus king of Persia to make a **proclamation** throughout his realm
3:12 wept **aloud** [+928+1524] when they saw the foundation of this
3:12 while many others **shouted** [+928+8123+9558] for joy.
3:13 No one could distinguish the **sound** *of* the shouts of joy from the
3:13 the sound of the shouts of joy from the **sound** *of* weeping,
3:13 people made so much noise. And the **sound** was heard far away.
10: 7 A **proclamation** was then issued throughout Judah and Jerusalem
10:12 The whole assembly responded with a loud **voice**: "You are right!
Ne 4:20 [4:14] Wherever you hear the **sound** *of* the trumpet, join us there.
8:15 that they should proclaim this **word** and spread it throughout their
9: 4 who called with loud **voices** to the LORD their God.
Job 2:12 they began to weep **aloud** [+5951], and they tore their robes
3:18 also enjoy their ease; they no longer hear the slave driver's **shout**.
4:10 The lions may roar and **growl**, yet the teeth of the great lions are
4:16 A form stood before my eyes, and I heard a hushed **voice**:
9:16 I do not believe *he would* **give** me **a hearing** [+263].
15:21 Terrifying **sounds** fill his ears; when all seems well,
21:12 of tambourine and harp; they make merry to the **sound** *of* the flute.
28:26 a decree for the rain and a path for the **thunderstorm** [+2613],
29:10 the **voices** *of* the nobles were hushed, and their tongues stuck to the
30:31 harp is tuned to mourning, and my flute to the **sound** *of* wailing.
33: 8 "But you have said in my hearing—I heard the **very** words—
34:16 "If you have understanding, hear this; listen to **what**ˢ I say.
37: 2 Listen to the roar of his **voice**, to the rumbling that comes from his
37: 4 After that comes the **sound** of his roar; he thunders with his
37: 4 comes the sound of his roar; he thunders with his majestic **voice**.
37: 4 majestic voice. When his **voice** resounds, he holds nothing back.
37: 5 God's **voice** thunders in marvelous ways; he does great things
38:25 for the torrents of rain, and a path for the **thunderstorm** [+2613],
38:34 "Can you raise your **voice** to the clouds and cover yourself with a
39:24 eats up the ground; he cannot stand still when the trumpet **sounds**.
40: 9 you have an arm like God's, and can your **voice** thunder like his?
Ps 3: 4 [3:5] To the LORD I cry **aloud**, and he answers me from his
5: 2 [5:3] Listen to my **cry for help** [+8776], my King and my God,
5: 3 [5:4] In the morning, O LORD, you hear my **voice**;
6: 8 [6:9] who do evil, for the LORD has heard **[RPH]** my weeping.
18: 6 [18:7] From his temple he heard my **voice**; my cry came before
18:13 [18:14] from heaven; the **voice** *of* the Most High resounded.
19: 3 [19:4] is no speech or language where their **voice** is not heard.
19: 4 [19:5] Their **voice** [BHS 7742] goes out into all the earth, their
26: 7 proclaiming **aloud** [+928] your praise and telling of all your
27: 7 Hear my **voice** when I call, O LORD; be merciful to me
28: 2 Hear my **cry for mercy** [+9384] as I call to you for help, as I lift
28: 6 be to the LORD, for he has heard my **cry for mercy** [+9384].
29: 3 The **voice** *of* the LORD is over the waters; the God of glory
29: 4 The **voice** *of* the LORD is powerful; the voice of the LORD is
29: 4 of the LORD is powerful; the **voice** *of* the LORD is majestic.
29: 5 The **voice** *of* the LORD breaks the cedars; the LORD breaks in
29: 7 The **voice** *of* the LORD strikes with flashes of lightning.
29: 8 The **voice** *of* the LORD shakes the desert; the LORD shakes the
29: 9 The **voice** *of* the LORD twists the oaks and strips the forests bare.
31:22 [31:23] Yet you heard my **cry for mercy** [+9384] when I called
42: 4 [42:5] with **shouts of joy** [+8262] and thanksgiving among the
42: 7 [42:8] Deep calls to deep in the **roar** *of* your waterfalls; all your
44:16 [44:17] at the **taunts** *of* those who reproach and revile me,
46: 6 [46:7] in uproar, kingdoms fall; he lifts his **voice**, the earth melts.
47: 1 [47:2] your hands, all you nations; shout to God with **cries** *of* joy.
47: 5 [47:6] shouts of joy, the LORD amid the **sounding** *of* trumpets.
55: 3 [55:4] at the **voice** *of* the enemy, at the stares of the wicked;
55:17 [55:18] and noon I cry out in distress, and he hears my **voice**.
58: 5 [58:6] that will not heed the **tune** *of* the charmer, however skillful
64: 1 [64:2] Hear me, O God, as I **voice** my complaint; protect my life
66: 8 Praise our God, O peoples, let the **sound** *of* his praise be heard;
66:19 but God has surely listened and heard my **voice** *in* prayer.
68:33 [68:34] the ancient skies above, *who* **thunders** [+928+5989] *with*
68:33 [68:34] the ancient skies above, who thunders with mighty **voice**.
74:23 Do not ignore the **clamor** *of* your adversaries, the uproar of your
77: 1 [77:2] *I* **cried out** to God **for help** [+7590]; I cried out to God to
77: 1 [77:2] I cried out to God for help; I **cried out** to God to hear me.
77:17 [77:18] poured down water, the skies resounded with **thunder**;
77:18 [77:19] Your thunder was **heard** in the whirlwind, your lightning
81:11 [81:12] "But my people would not listen **to** [+4200] me; Israel
86: 6 Hear my prayer, O LORD; listen to my **cry for mercy** [+9384].
93: 3 seas have lifted up, O LORD, the seas have lifted up their **voice**;
93: 4 Mightier than the **thunder** *of* the great waters, mightier than the
95: 7 his pasture, the flock under his care. Today, if you hear his **voice**,
98: 5 the LORD with the harp, with the harp and the **sound** *of* singing,
98: 6 with trumpets and the **blast** *of* the ram's horn—shout for joy
102: 5 [102:6] Because of my **loud** groaning I am reduced to skin and
103:20 mighty ones who do his bidding, *who* **obey** [+928+9048] his word.
104: 7 the waters fled, at the **sound** *of* your thunder they took to flight;
104:12 The birds of the air nest by the waters; *they* **sing** [+5989] among
106:25 grumbled in their tents and *did* not **obey** [+928+9048] the LORD.
116: 1 I love the LORD, for he heard my **voice**; he heard my cry for
118:15 Shouts of joy and victory **resound** in the tents of the righteous:
119:149 Hear my **voice** in accordance with your love; preserve my life,
130: 2 O Lord, hear my **voice**. Let your ears be attentive to my cry for
130: 2 my voice. Let your ears be attentive to my **cry for mercy** [+9384].
140: 6 [140:7] my God." Hear, O LORD, my **cry for mercy** [+9384].
141: 1 call to you; come quickly to me. Hear my **voice** when I call to you.
142: 1 [142:2] I cry **aloud** to the LORD; I lift up my voice to the
142: 1 [142:2] the LORD; I lift up my **voice** to the LORD for mercy.
Pr 1:20 calls aloud in the street, she raises her **voice** in the public squares;
2: 3 if you call out for insight and **cry** [+5989] **aloud** for understanding,
5:13 *I would* not **obey** [+928+9048] my teachers or listen to my
8: 1 Does not wisdom call out? Does not understanding raise her **voice**?
8: 4 "To you, O men, I call out; I raise my **voice** to all mankind.
26:25 Though his **speech** is charming, do not believe him, for seven
27:14 If a man **loudly** [+928+1524] blesses his neighbor early in the
Ecc 5: 3 [5:2] so the **speech** *of* a fool when there are many words.
5: 6 [5:5] Why should God be angry at **what** you **say** and destroy the
7: 6 Like the **crackling** *of* thorns under the pot, so is the laughter of
10:20 in your bedroom, because a bird of the air may carry your **words**,
12: 4 the doors to the street are closed and the **sound** *of* grinding fades;
12: 4 when men rise up at the **sound** *of* birds, but all their songs grow
SS 2: 8 **Listen**! My lover! Look! Here he comes, leaping across the
2:12 of singing has come, the **cooing** *of* doves is heard in our land.
2:14 on the mountainside, show me your face, let me hear your **voice**;
2:14 hear your voice; for your **voice** is sweet, and your face is lovely.
5: 2 **Listen**! My lover is knocking: "Open to me, my sister, my darling,
8:13 in the gardens with friends in attendance, let me hear your **voice**!
Isa 6: 4 At the **sound** *of* their voices the doorposts and thresholds shook
6: 8 Then I heard the **voice** *of* the Lord saying, "Whom shall I send?
10:30 **Cry out** [+7412], O Daughter of Gallim! Listen, O Laishah!
13: 2 Raise a banner on a bare hilltop, **shout** [+8123] to them; beckon to
13: 4 **Listen**, a noise on the mountains, like that of a great multitude!
13: 4 **Listen**, an uproar among the kingdoms, like nations massing
15: 4 and Elealeh cry out, their **voices** are heard all the way to Jahaz.
24:14 They raise their **voices**, they shout for joy; from the west they
24:18 Whoever flees at the **sound** *of* terror will fall into a pit; whoever
28:23 Listen and hear my **voice**; pay attention and hear what I say.
29: 4 Your **voice** will come ghostlike from the earth; out of the dust your
29: 6 Almighty will come with thunder and earthquake and great **noise**,
30:19 How gracious he will be when you **cry for help** [+2410]!
30:30 The LORD will cause men to hear his majestic **voice** and will
30:31 The **voice** *of* the LORD will shatter Assyria; with his scepter he
31: 4 he is not frightened by their **shouts** or disturbed by their clamor—
32: 9 and **listen** *to* me; **you** [+9048] daughters who feel secure,
33: 3 At the thunder of your **voice**, the peoples flee; when you rise up,
36:13 commander stood and **called out** [+928+1524+7924] in Hebrew,
37:23 Against whom have you raised your **voice** and lifted your eyes in
40: 3 A **voice** *of* one calling: "In the desert prepare the way for the
40: 6 A **voice** says, "Cry out." And I said, "What shall I cry?" "All men
40: 9 lift up your **voice** with a shout, lift it up, do not be afraid;
42: 2 He will not shout or cry out, or raise his **voice** in the streets.
48:20 Announce this with **shouts of joy** [+8262] and proclaim it.
50:10 among you fears the LORD and obeys the **word** *of* his servant?
51: 3 will be found in her, thanksgiving and the **sound** *of* singing.
52: 8 **Listen**! Your watchmen lift up their voices; together they shout for
52: 8 Your watchmen lift up their **voices**; together they shout for joy.
58: 1 "Shout it aloud, do not hold back. Raise your **voice** like a trumpet.
58: 4 fast as you do today and expect your **voice** to be heard on high.
65:19 the **sound** *of* weeping and of crying will be heard in it no more.
65:19 of weeping and **[RPH]** of crying will be heard in it no more.
66: 6 **Hear** that uproar from the city, hear that noise from the temple!
66: 6 Hear that uproar from the city, hear that **noise** from the temple!
66: 6 It is the **sound** *of* the LORD repaying his enemies all they
Jer 2:15 Lions have roared; *they have* **growled** [+5989] at him. They have
3:13 and *have* not **obeyed** [+928+9048] me,' " declares the LORD.

Jer 3:21 A **cry** is heard on the barren heights, the weeping and pleading of
3:25 from our youth till this day *we have* not **obeyed** [+928+9048] the
4:15 A **voice** is announcing from Dan, proclaiming disaster from the
4:16 from a distant land, raising a **war cry** against the cities of Judah.
4:19 For I have heard the **sound** *of* the trumpet; I have heard the battle
4:21 must I see the battle standard and hear the **sound** *of* the trumpet?
4:29 At the **sound** *of* horsemen and archers every town takes to flight.
4:31 I hear a **cry** as of a woman in labor, a groan as of one bearing her
4:31 the **cry** *of* the Daughter of Zion gasping for breath, stretching out
6:17 watchmen over you and said, 'Listen to the **sound** *of* the trumpet!'
6:23 They **sound** like the roaring sea as they ride on their horses;
7:23 **Obey** [+928+9048] me, and I will be your God and you will be my
7:28 'This is the nation that *has* not **obeyed** [+928+9048] the LORD its
7:34 I will bring an end to the **sounds** *of* joy and gladness and to the
7:34 **[RPH]** gladness and to the voices of bride and bridegroom in the
7:34 gladness and to the **voices** *of* bride and bridegroom in the towns of
7:34 gladness and to the voices of **[RPH]** bride and bridegroom in the
8:16 at the **neighing of** [+5177] their stallions the whole land trembles.
8:19 **Listen** *to* the cry of my people from a land far away: "Is the
9:10 [9:9] and untraveled, and the **lowing** *of* cattle is not heard.
9:13 [9:12] *they have* not **obeyed** [+928+9048] me or followed my
9:19 [9:18] The **sound** *of* wailing is heard from Zion: 'How ruined we
10:13 When he **thunders** [+5989], the waters in the heavens roar;
10:22 **Listen**! The report is coming—a great commotion from the land of
11:4 '**Obey** [+928+9048] me and do everything I command you,
11:7 I warned them again and again, saying, "**Obey** [+928+9048] me."
11:16 with the **roar** *of* a mighty storm he will set it on fire, and its
12:8 has become to me like a lion in the forest. *She* **roars** [+928+5989]
16:9 in your days I will bring an end to the **sounds** *of* joy and gladness
16:9 **[RPH]** gladness and to the voices of bride and bridegroom in this
16:9 gladness and to the **voices** *of* bride and bridegroom in this place.
16:9 gladness and to the voices of **[RPH]** bride and bridegroom in this
18:10 and if it does evil in my sight and *does* not **obey** [+928+9048] me,
18:19 Listen to me, O LORD; hear **what** my accusers are **saying**!
22:20 "Go up to Lebanon and cry out, let your **voice** be heard in Bashan,
22:21 your way from your youth; *you have* not **obeyed** [+928+9048] me.
25:10 I will banish from them the **sounds** *of* joy and gladness, the voices
25:10 I will banish from them the sounds of joy and **[RPH]** gladness,
25:10 the sounds of joy and gladness, the **voices** *of* bride and bridegroom,
25:10 and gladness, the voices of **[RPH]** bride and bridegroom,
25:10 and bridegroom, the **sound** *of* millstones and the light of the lamp.
25:30 " 'The LORD will roar from on high; *he will* **thunder** [+5989]
25:36 **Hear** the cry of the shepherds, the wailing of the leaders of the
26:13 and your actions and **obey** [+928+9048] the LORD your God.
30:5 the LORD says: " '**Cries** *of* fear are heard—terror, not peace.
30:19 them will come songs of thanksgiving and the **sound** *of* rejoicing.
31:15 "A **voice** is heard in Ramah, mourning and great weeping,
31:16 "Restrain your **voice** from weeping and your eyes from tears,
32:23 but *they did* not **obey** [+928+9048] you or follow your law;
33:11 the **sounds** *of* joy and gladness, the voices of bride
33:11 the sounds of joy and **[RPH]** gladness, the voices of bride
33:11 the sounds of joy and gladness, the **voices** *of* bride and bridegroom,
33:11 and gladness, the voices of bride and **[RPH]** bridegroom,
33:11 the **voices** *of* those who bring thank offerings to the house of the
35:8 *We have* **obeyed** [+928+4200+9048] everything our forefather
38:20 "**Obey** [+928+9048] the LORD by doing what I tell you.
40:3 sinned against the LORD and *did* not **obey** [+928+9048] him.
42:6 or unfavorable, *we will* **obey** [+928+9048] the LORD our God,
42:6 well with us, for *we will* **obey** [+928+9048] the LORD our God."
42:13 and so **disobey** [+928+1194+9048] the LORD your God,
42:14 not see war or hear **[NIE]** the trumpet or be hungry for bread,'
42:21 *you still have* not **obeyed** [+928+9048] the LORD your God in
43:4 all the people disobeyed the LORD's **command** to stay in the
43:7 So they entered Egypt *in* **disobedience to** [+928+4202+9048] the
44:23 and *have* not **obeyed** [+928+9048] him or followed his law
46:22 Egypt will **hiss** like a fleeing serpent as the enemy advances in
47:3 at the **sound** *of* the hoofs of galloping steeds, at the noise of enemy
48:3 **Listen** *to* the cries from Horonaim, cries of great havoc
48:34 "The **sound** *of* their cry rises from Heshbon to Elealeh and Jahaz,
49:21 At the **sound** *of* their fall the earth will tremble; their cry will
49:21 earth will tremble; their **cry** [+7591] will resound to the Red Sea.
50:22 The **noise** *of* battle is in the land, the noise of great destruction!
50:28 **Listen** *to* the fugitives and refugees from Babylon declaring in
50:42 They **sound** like the roaring sea as they ride on their horses;
50:46 At the **sound** *of* Babylon's capture the earth will tremble;
51:16 When he **thunders** [+5989], the waters in the heavens roar;
51:54 "The **sound** *of* a cry comes from Babylon, the sound of great
51:55 will destroy Babylon; he will silence her **noisy din** [+1524].
51:55 will rage like great waters; the roar of their **voices** will resound.
La 2:7 they have raised a **shout** in the house of the LORD as on the day
3:56 You heard my **plea**: "Do not close your ears to my cry for relief."
Eze 1:24 When the creatures moved, I heard the **sound** *of* their wings,
1:24 like the **roar** *of* rushing waters, like the voice of the Almighty,
1:24 like the **voice** *of* the Almighty, like the tumult of an army.
1:24 like the voice of the Almighty, like the **tumult** [+2167] of an army.
1:24 like the voice of the Almighty, like the tumult of an **[RPH]** army.
1:25 there came a **voice** from above the expanse over their heads as they
1:28 I saw it, I fell facedown, and I heard the **voice** *of* one speaking.
3:12 Spirit lifted me up, and I heard behind me a loud rumbling **sound**—
3:13 the **sound** *of* the wings of the living creatures brushing against
3:13 against each other and the **sound** *of* the wheels beside them,
3:13 and the sound of the wheels beside them, a loud rumbling **sound**.
8:18 Although *they* **shout** [+1524+7924] in my ears, I will not listen to
9:1 I heard him call out in a loud **voice**, "Bring the guards of the city
10:5 The **sound** *of* the wings of the cherubim could be heard as far
10:5 as the outer court, like the **voice** *of* God Almighty when he speaks.
11:13 I fell facedown and cried out in a loud **voice**, "Ah,
19:7 and all who were in it were terrified by his **roaring** [+8614].
19:9 so his **roar** was heard no longer on the mountains of Israel.
21:22 [21:27] to slaughter, to **sound** [+928+8123] the battle cry,
23:42 "The **noise** *of* a carefree crowd was around her; Sabeans were
26:10 Your walls will tremble at the **noise** *of* the war horses, wagons
26:13 noisy songs, and the **music** *of* your harps will be heard no more.
26:15 Will not the coastlands tremble at the **sound** *of* your fall, when the
27:28 The shorelands will quake when your seamen **cry out** [+2411].
27:30 They will raise their **voice** and cry bitterly over you; they will
31:16 I made the nations tremble at the **sound** *of* its fall when I brought it
33:4 if *anyone* **hears** [+906+9048+9048] the trumpet but does not take
33:5 Since he heard the **sound** *of* the trumpet but did not take warning,
33:32 nothing more than one who sings love songs with a beautiful **voice**
37:7 And as I was prophesying, there was a **noise**, a rattling sound,
43:2 His **voice** was like the roar of rushing waters, and the land was
43:2 His voice was like the **roar** *of* rushing waters, and the land was
Da 8:16 And I heard a man's **voice** from the Ulai calling, "Gabriel,
9:10 *we have* not **obeyed** [+928+9048] the LORD our God or kept the
9:11 your law and turned away, refusing *to* **obey** [+928+9048] you.
9:14 in everything he does; yet *we have* not **obeyed** [+928+9048] him.
10:6 and his **[RPH]** voice like the sound of a multitude.
10:6 of burnished bronze, and his voice like the **sound** *of* a multitude.
10:9 Then I heard him **speaking** [+1821], and as I listened to him,
10:9 as I listened to **[RPH]** him, I fell into a deep sleep, my face to the
Joel 2:5 With a **noise** like that of chariots they leap over the mountaintops,
2:5 like a **crackling** fire consuming stubble, like a mighty army drawn
2:11 The LORD **thunders** [+5989] at the head of his army; his forces
3:16 [4:16] will roar from Zion and **thunder** [+5989] from Jerusalem;
Am 1:2 LORD roars from Zion and **thunders** [+5989] from Jerusalem;
2:2 down in great tumult amid war cries and the **blast** *of* the trumpet.
3:4 *Does* he **growl** [+5989] in his den when he has caught nothing?
Jnh 2:2 [2:3] of the grave I called for help, and you listened to my **cry**.
2:9 [2:10] I, with a **song** *of* thanksgiving, will sacrifice to you. What I
Mic 6:1 case before the mountains; let the hills hear **what** you **have to say**.
6:9 Listen! The LORD *is* **calling** [+7924] to the city—and to fear
Na 2:7 [2:8] Its slave girls moan like **[RPH]** doves and beat upon their
2:13 [2:14] The **voices** *of* your messengers will no longer be heard."
3:2 The **crack** *of* whips, the clatter of wheels, galloping horses
3:2 the **clatter of** [+8323] wheels, galloping horses and jolting
Hab 3:10 swept by; the deep **roared** [+5989] and lifted its waves on high.
3:16 I heard and my heart pounded, my lips quivered at the **sound**;
Zep 1:10 the LORD, "a **cry** [+7591] will go up from the Fish Gate,
1:14 The **cry** *on* the day of the LORD will be bitter, the shouting of the
2:14 Their **calls** will echo through the windows, rubble will be in the
3:2 *She* **obeys** [+928+9048] no one, she accepts no correction.
Hag 1:12 the whole remnant of the people obeyed the **voice** *of* the LORD
Zec 6:15 if *you* **diligently obey** [+928+9048+9048] the LORD your God."
11:3 **Listen** *to* the wail of the shepherds; their rich pastures are
11:3 **Listen** *to* the roar of the lions; the lush thicket of the Jordan is

7755 קוֹלָיָה qôlāyâ, n.pr.m. [2] [√ 7754?]

Kolaiah [2]

Ne 11:7 the son of Joed, the son of Pedaiah, the son of **Kolaiah**, the son of
Jer 29:21 says about Ahab son of **Kolaiah** and Zedekiah son of Maaseiah,

7756 קוּם qûm, v. [627] [→ 3685, 3691, 5226, 7757, 7758, 7799, 7800, 7850, 9538, 9539; Ar 10624; *also used with compound proper names*]

untranslated [64], got up [50], rise up [28], rise [28], get up [24], arise [22], set up [17], rose [16], stand [16], establish [13], raise up [11], set out [11], fulfill [10], come [9], go [9], raised up [9], at once [8], established [8], stood up [8], restore [7], rose up [7], stand up [7], foes [5], stood [5], arose [4], confirm [4], erected [4], keep [4], prepared [4], adversaries [3], attacking [+6584] [3], carried out [3], confirms [3], endure [3], enemies [3], fulfilled [3], help up [3], kept [3], left [+4946] [3], now [3], proceeded [3], rises up [3], rises [3], set [3], standing [3], up [3], begin [2], build [2], came [2], changed [+906+7756] [2], confirmed [2], decreed [2], deeded [2], fully accomplishes [+2256+6913] [2], get it to its feet [+7756] [2], get ready [2], gets up [2], got ready [2], hurry [2], keep [+906+7756] [2], maintain [2], place [2], raise [2], raises [2], raising up [2], rise to power [2], risen up [2], rouse [2], stands [2], start [2], stepped forward [2], succeeded [+9393] [2], supported [2], surely stand [+7756] [2], survive [2], went [2], accomplish [1], accuses [+907+2021+4200+5477] [1], all right do[s] it [1], appear [1], appears [1], appointed [1], arise and come [1], assaults [+6584] [1], attack [+448] [1], attack [1], attacked [+448] [1], attacked [+6584] [1], attacks [+6584] [1], attacks [1], be [1], become [1], been kept [1], began [1], belong [1], binding [1], break out [1], brighter [1], bring [1], came out [1], came to power [1], carries out [1], carry on [+6584] [1], carry on [1], carry out [1], come forward [1], come on [1], come out [1], confirming [1], confronted [+6584] [1], confronts [1], convict [1], crept up [1], do[s] [1], done [1], erect [1], establish the custom [1], exalted [1], failed [+4202+6388] [1], final [1], follow [+339] [1], follow [+339+4946] [1], followed [+339] [1], gave [1], get away [1], go up [1], gone [1], grew up [1], grown [1], has effect [1], have [1], heaped up [1], hold [1], hurried [1], in turn [1], incited [1], leave [+4946] [1], left [+4946+9348] [1], left [1], lift up [1], made [1], make good [1], makes rise [1], moved out [1], moved [1], obeyed [+3869] [1], opposed [1], piled up [1], prevails [1], produce [1], provide [1], raised [1], rebelled [1], remain [1], remains [1], revolted [1], risen [1], send [1], set to work [1], setting up [1], sit up [1], soon [1], started [1], station [1], stilled [1], stir up [1], stood ground [1], strengthen [1], succeed [1], surged forward [1], take place [1], takes the stand [+928] [1], turned [1], undertakes [1], uphold [1], was set up [1], went out [1], went to work [1], withdrew [1], withstand [1]

Ge 4: 8 [A] Cain **attacked** [+448] his brother Abel and killed him.
6: 18 [G] *I will* **establish** my covenant with you, and you will enter the
9: 9 [G] "I now **establish** my covenant with you and with your
9: 11 [G] *I* **establish** my covenant with you: Never again will all life
9: 17 [G] "This is the sign of the covenant *I have* **established** between
13: 17 [A] **Go**, walk through the length and breadth of the land, for I am
17: 7 [G] *I will* **establish** my covenant as an everlasting covenant
17: 19 [G] *I will* **establish** my covenant with him as an everlasting
17: 21 [G] my covenant *I will* **establish** with Isaac, whom Sarah will
18: 16 [A] When the men **got up** to leave, they looked down toward
19: 1 [A] *he* **got up** to meet them and bowed down with his face to the
19: 14 [A] He said, "**Hurry** and get out of this place,
19: 15 [A] the coming of dawn, the angels urged Lot, saying, "**Hurry**!
19: 33 [A] was not aware of it when she lay down or when she **got up**.
19: 35 [A] night also, and the younger daughter **went** and lay with him.
19: 35 [A] was not aware of it when she lay down or when she **got up**.
21: 18 [A] **[NIE]** Lift the boy up and take him by the hand, for I will
21: 32 [A] **[NIE]** Abimelech and Phicol the commander of his forces
22: 3 [A] **[NIE]** he set out for the place God had told him about.
22: 19 [A] his servants, and **[NIE]** they set off together for Beersheba.
23: 3 [A] Abraham **rose** from beside his dead wife and spoke to the
23: 7 [A] Abraham **rose** and bowed down before the people of the
23: 17 [A] and all the trees within the borders of the field—*was* **deeded**
23: 20 [A] the cave in it *were* **deeded** to Abraham by the Hittites as a
24: 10 [A] *He* **set out** for Aram Naharaim and made his way to the town
24: 54 [A] When *they* **got up** the next morning, he said, "Send me on
24: 61 [A] Rebekah and her maids **got ready** and mounted their camels
25: 34 [A] some lentil stew. He ate and drank, and then **got up** and left.
26: 3 [G] and *will* **confirm** the oath I swore to your father Abraham.
27: 19 [A] Please sit **up** and eat some of my game so that you may give
27: 31 [A] he said to him, "My father, **sit up** and eat some of my game,
27: 43 [A] do what I say: Flee **at once** to my brother Laban in Haran.
28: 2 [A] Go **at once** to Paddan Aram, to the house of your mother's
31: 13 [A] Now leave this land **at once** and go back to your native
31: 17 [A] Then **[NIE]** Jacob put his children and his wives on camels,
31: 21 [A] So he fled with all he had, and **[NIE]** crossing the River,
31: 35 [A] be angry, my lord, that I cannot **stand up** in your presence;
32: 22 [32:23] [A] That night Jacob **got up** and took his two wives, his
35: 1 [A] Then God said to Jacob, "**Go** up to Bethel and settle there,
35: 3 [A] **come**, let us go up to Bethel, where I will build an altar to
37: 7 [A] of grain out in the field when suddenly my sheaf **rose**
37: 35 [A] All his sons and daughters **came** to comfort him, but he
38: 8 [G] fulfill your duty to her as a brother-in-law *to* **produce**
38: 19 [A] **[NIE]** After she left, she took off her veil and put on her
41: 30 [A] seven years of famine *will* **follow** [+339] them. Then all the
43: 8 [A] "Send the boy along with me and we will go **at once**, so that
43: 13 [A] Take your brother also and go back to the man **at once**.
43: 15 [A] *They* **hurried** down to Egypt and presented themselves to
44: 4 [A] "Go after those men **at once**, and when you catch up with
46: 5 [A] Jacob **left** [+4946] Beersheba, and Israel's sons took their
49: 9 [G] and lies down, like a lioness—who *dares to* **rouse** him?
Ex 1: 8 [A] who did not know about Joseph, **came to power** in Egypt.
2: 17 [A] Moses **got up** and came to their rescue and watered their
6: 4 [G] *I* also **established** my covenant with them to give them the
10: 23 [A] see anyone else or **leave** [+4946] his place for three days.
12: 30 [A] all his officials and all the Egyptians **got up** during the night,
12: 31 [A] night Pharaoh summoned Moses and Aaron and said, "**Up**!
15: 7 [A] of your majesty you threw down *those who* **opposed** you.
21: 19 [A] the blow will not be held responsible if the other **gets up**
24: 13 [A] Moses **set out** with Joshua his aide, and Moses went up on
26: 30 [G] "**Set up** the tabernacle according to the plan shown you on
32: 1 [A] they gathered around Aaron and said, "**Come**, make us gods
32: 6 [A] sat down to eat and drink and **got up** to indulge in revelry.
32: 25 [A] of control and so become a laughingstock to their **enemies**.
33: 8 [A] all the people **rose** and stood at the entrances to their tents,
33: 10 [A] they all **stood** and worshiped, each at the entrance to his tent.
40: 2 [G] "**Set up** the tabernacle, the Tent of Meeting, on the first day
40: 17 [H] So the tabernacle **was set up** on the first day of the first
40: 18 [G] When Moses **set up** the tabernacle, he put the bases in place,
40: 18 [G] the frames, inserted the crossbars and **set up** the posts.
40: 33 [G] Moses **set up** the courtyard around the tabernacle and altar
Lev 19: 32 [A] " '**Rise** in the presence of the aged, show respect for the
25: 30 [A] the house in the walled city *shall* **belong** permanently to the
26: 1 [G] " 'Do not make idols or **set up** an image or a sacred stone for
26: 9 [G] your numbers, and *I will* **keep** my covenant with you.
27: 14 [A] or bad. Whatever value the priest then sets, so *it will* **remain**.
27: 17 [A] the Year of Jubilee, the value that has been set **remains**.
27: 19 [A] add a fifth to its value, and the field *will again* **become** his.
Nu 1: 51 [G] the tabernacle is to be set up, the Levites *shall* **do[s]** it.
7: 1 [G] When Moses finished **setting up** the tabernacle, he anointed
9: 15 [G] the Tent of the Testimony, *was* **set up**, the cloud covered it.
10: 21 [G] The tabernacle *was to be* **set up** before they arrived.
10: 35 [A] Whenever the ark set out, Moses said, "**Rise up**, O LORD!
11: 32 [A] that day and night and all the next day the people **went out**
16: 2 [A] **rose up** against Moses. With them were 250 Israelite men,
16: 25 [A] Moses **got up** and went to Dathan and Abiram, and the elders
22: 13 [A] The next morning Balaam **got up** and said to Balak's princes,
22: 14 [A] So the Moabite princes **[NIE]** returned to Balak and said,
22: 20 [A] **[NIE]** go with them, but do only what I tell you."
22: 21 [A] Balaam **got up** in the morning, saddled his donkey and went
23: 18 [A] his oracle: "**Arise**, Balak, and listen; hear me, son of Zippor.
23: 19 [G] he speak and then not act? Does he promise and not **fulfill**?
23: 24 [A] The people **rise** like a lioness; they rouse themselves like a
24: 9 [G] and lie down, like a lioness—who *dares to* **rouse** them?
24: 17 [A] star will come out of Jacob; a scepter *will* **rise** out of Israel.
24: 25 [A] Balaam **got up** and returned home and Balak went his own
25: 7 [A] the priest, saw this, *he* **left** [+4946+9348] the assembly,
30: 4 [30:5] [A] pledge by which she obligated herself *will* **stand**.
30: 4 [30:5] [A] by which she obligated herself will stand. **[RPH]**
30: 5 [30:6] [A] pledges by which she obligated herself *will* **stand**;
30: 7 [30:8] [A] pledges by which she obligated herself *will* **stand**.
30: 7 [30:8] [A] by which she obligated herself will stand. **[RPH]**
30: 9 [30:10] [A] a widow or divorced woman *will be* **binding** on her.
30: 11 [30:12] [A] pledges by which she obligated herself *will* **stand**.
30: 11 [30:12] [A] by which she obligated herself will stand. **[RPH]**
30: 12 [30:13] [A] or pledges that came from her lips *will* **stand**.
30: 13 [30:14] [G] Her husband *may* **confirm** or nullify any vow she
30: 14 [30:15] [G] *he* **confirms** all her vows or the pledges binding on
30: 14 [30:15] [G] *He* **confirms** them by saying nothing to her when
32: 14 [A] **standing** in the place of your fathers and making the LORD
Dt 2: 13 [A] the LORD said, "Now **get up** and cross the Zered Valley."
2: 24 [A] "Set out **now** and cross the Arnon Gorge. See, I have given
6: 7 [A] along the road, when you lie down and when you **get up**.
8: 18 [G] so **confirms** his covenant, which he swore to your
9: 5 [G] to **accomplish** what he swore to your fathers, to Abraham,
9: 12 [A] the LORD told me, **[NIE]** "Go down from here at once,
10: 11 [A] "**Go**," the LORD said to me, "and lead the people on their
11: 19 [A] along the road, when you lie down and when you **get up**.
13: 1 [13:2] [A] **appears** among you and announces to you a
16: 22 [G] *do* not **erect** a sacred stone, for these the LORD your God
17: 8 [A] **[NIE]** take them to the place the LORD your God will
18: 15 [G] The LORD your God *will* **raise up** for you a prophet like
18: 18 [G] *I will* **raise up** for them a prophet like you from among their
19: 11 [A] **assaults** [+6584] and kills him, and then flees to one of these
19: 15 [A] One witness *is* not *enough to* **convict** a man accused of any
19: 15 [A] A matter *must be* **established** by the testimony of two or
19: 16 [A] If a malicious witness **takes the stand** [+928] to accuse a
22: 4 [G] the road, do not ignore it. Help him **get it to its feet** [+7756].
22: 4 [G] the road, do not ignore it. Help him **get it to its feet** [+7756].
22: 26 [A] This case is like that of someone *who* **attacks** [+6584] and
25: 6 [A] The first son she bears *shall* **carry** [+6584] **on** the name of
25: 7 [G] "My husband's brother refuses to **carry on** his brother's
27: 2 [G] **set up** some large stones and coat them with plaster.
27: 4 [G] **set up** these stones on Mount Ebal, as I command you today,
27: 26 [G] "Cursed is the man who *does* not **uphold** the words of this
28: 7 [A] The LORD will grant that the enemies who **rise up** against
28: 9 [G] The LORD *will* **establish** you as his holy people, as he
28: 36 [G] and the king *you* **set** over you to a nation unknown to you
29: 13 [29:12] [G] to **confirm** you this day as his people, that he may
29: 22 [29:21] [A] Your children who **follow** [+339+4946] you in later
31: 16 [A] these people will **soon** prostitute themselves to the foreign
32: 38 [A] *Let them* **rise up** to help you! Let them give you shelter!

Dt 33:11 [A] Smite the loins of *those who* **rise up** *against* him; strike his
33:11 [A] rise up against him; strike his foes till *they* **rise** no more."
34:10 [A] Since then, no prophet *has* **risen** in Israel like Moses,
Jos 1:2 [A] **get ready** to cross the Jordan River into the land I am about
2:11 [A] and everyone's courage **failed** [+4202+6388] because of you,
3:16 [A] *It* **piled up** in a heap a great distance away, at a town called
4:9 [G] Joshua **set up** the twelve stones that had been in the middle
4:20 [G] Joshua **set up** at Gilgal the twelve stones they had taken out
5:7 [G] So *he* **raised up** their sons in their place, and these were the
6:26 [A] "Cursed before the LORD is the man who **undertakes** to
7:10 [A] The LORD said to Joshua, "**Stand up**! What are you doing
7:12 [A] That is why the Israelites cannot **stand** against their enemies;
7:13 [A] "**Go**, consecrate the people. Tell them,
7:13 [A] You cannot **stand** against your enemies until you remove it.
7:26 [G] Over Achan *they* **heaped up** a large pile of rocks,
8:1 [A] Take the whole army with you, and **go up** and attack Ai.
8:3 [A] So Joshua and the whole army **moved out** to attack Ai. He
8:7 [A] you *are to* **rise up** from ambush and take the city. The
8:19 [A] the men in the ambush **rose** quickly from their position
8:29 [G] *they* **raised** a large pile of rocks over it, which remains to
18:4 [A] I will send them out **[NIE]** to make a survey of the land
18:8 [A] *As* the men **started** on their way to map out the land, Joshua
24:9 [A] of Zippor, the king of Moab, **prepared** to fight against Israel,
24:26 [G] **set** it **up** there under the oak near the holy place of the
Jdg 2:10 [A] been gathered to their fathers, another generation **grew up**,
2:16 [G] the LORD **raised up** judges, who saved them out of the
2:18 [G] Whenever the LORD **raised up** a judge for them, he was
3:9 [G] he **raised up** for them a deliverer, Othniel son of Kenaz,
3:15 [G] cried out to the LORD, and he **gave** them a deliverer—
3:20 [A] a message from God for you." As the king **rose** from his seat,
4:9 [A] a woman." So **[NIE]** Deborah went with Barak to Kedesh,
4:14 [A] Deborah said to Barak, "**Go**! This is the day the LORD has
5:7 [A] ceased until *I*, Deborah, **arose**, arose a mother in Israel.
5:7 [A] ceased until I, Deborah, arose, **arose** a mother in Israel.
5:12 [A] Wake up, wake up, break out in song! **Arise**, O Barak!
7:9 [A] LORD said to Gideon, "**Get up**, go down against the camp,
7:15 [A] He returned to the camp of Israel and called out, "**Get up**!
7:19 [G] just after *they had* **changed** [+906+7756] the guard.
7:19 [G] just after *they had* **changed** [+906+7756] the guard.
8:20 [A] to Jether, his oldest son, he said, **[NIE]** "Kill them!"
8:21 [A] Zebah and Zalmunna said, "**Come**, do it yourself. 'As is the
8:21 [A] so is his strength.' " So Gideon **stepped forward** and killed
9:18 [A] (but today you *have* **revolted** against my father's family,
9:32 [A] during the night you and your men *should* **come** and lie in
9:34 [A] So Abimelech and all his troops **set out** by night and took up
9:35 [A] and his soldiers **came out** from their hiding place.
9:43 [A] the people coming out of the city, *he* **rose** to attack them.
10:1 [A] Tola son of Puah, the son of Dodo, **rose** to save Israel.
10:3 [A] He *was* **followed** [+339] by Jair of Gilead, who led Israel
13:11 [A] Manoah **got up** and followed his wife. When he came to the
16:3 [A] Then *he* **got up** and took hold of the doors of the city gate,
18:9 [A] They answered, "**Come on**, let's attack them! We have seen
18:30 [G] There the Danites **set up** for themselves the idols,
19:3 [A] **[NIE]** her husband went to her to persuade her to return.
19:5 [A] the fourth day they got up early and *he* **prepared** to leave,
19:7 [A] when the man **got up** to go, his father-in-law persuaded him,
19:9 [A] with his concubine and his servant, **got up** to leave, his
19:10 [A] the man **[NIE]** left and went toward Jebus (that is,
19:27 [A] When her master **got up** in the morning and opened the door
19:28 [A] He said to her, "**Get up**; let's go." But there was no answer.
19:28 [A] the man put her on his donkey **[NIE]** and set out for home.
20:5 [A] During the night the men of Gibeah **came** after me
20:8 [A] All the people **rose** as one man, saying, "None of us will go
20:18 [A] The Israelites **[NIE]** went up to Bethel and inquired of God.
20:19 [A] The next morning the Israelites **got up** and pitched camp
20:33 [A] All the men of Israel **moved** from their places and took up
Ru 1:6 [A] her daughters-in-law **prepared** to return home from there.
2:15 [A] As *she* **got up** to glean, Boaz gave orders to his men, "Even
3:14 [A] but **got up** before anyone could be recognized;
4:5 [G] in order to **maintain** the name of the dead with his property."
4:7 [D] for the redemption and transfer of property to *become* **final**,
4:10 [G] in order to **maintain** the name of the dead with his property,
1Sa 1:9 [A] had finished eating and drinking in Shiloh, Hannah **stood up**.
1:23 [G] weaned him; only *may* the LORD **make good** his word."
2:8 [G] *He* **raises** the poor from the dust and lifts the needy from the
2:35 [G] *I will* **raise up** for myself a faithful priest, who will do
3:6 [A] And Samuel **got up** and went to Eli and said, "Here I am;
3:8 [A] and Samuel **got up** and went to Eli and said, "Here I am;
3:12 [G] At that time *I will* **carry out** against Eli everything I spoke
4:15 [A] years old and whose eyes *were* **set** so that he could not see.
9:3 [A] servants with you and **[NIE]** go and look for the donkeys."
9:26 [A] on the roof, "**Get ready**, and I will send you on your way."
9:26 [A] When Saul **got ready**, he and Samuel went outside together.
13:14 [A] now your kingdom *will* not **endure**; the LORD has sought
13:15 [A] Samuel **left** [+4946] Gilgal and went up to Gibeah in
15:11 [G] away from me and *has* not **carried out** my instructions."
15:13 [G] bless you! *I have* **carried out** the LORD's instructions."
16:12 [A] Then the LORD said, "**Rise** and anoint him; he is the one."
16:13 [A] upon David in power. **[NIE]** Samuel then went to Ramah.
17:35 [A] When *it* **turned** on me, I seized it by its hair, struck it
17:48 [A] As the Philistine **[NIE]** moved closer to attack him, David
17:52 [A] the men of Israel and Judah **surged forward** with a shout
18:27 [A] David and his men **[NIE]** went out and killed two hundred
20:25 [a] opposite [BHS ***he arose***; NIV 7709] Jonathan, and Abner sat
20:34 [A] Jonathan **got up** from the table in fierce anger; on that second
20:41 [A] David **got up** from the south side ⌊of the stone⌋ and bowed
20:42 [21:1] [A] my descendants forever.' " Then David **[NIE]** left,
21:10 [21:11] [A] **[NIE]** That day David fled from Saul and went to
22:8 [G] or tells me that my son *has* **incited** my servant to lie in wait
22:13 [A] so that he *has* **rebelled** against me and lies in wait for me,
23:4 [A] and the LORD answered him, **[NIE]** "Go down to Keilah,
23:13 [A] So David **[NIE]** and his men, about six hundred in number,
23:16 [A] And **[NIE]** Saul's son Jonathan went to David at Horesh
23:24 [A] So *they* **set out** and went to Ziph ahead of Saul. Now David
24:4 [24:5] [A] with as you wish.' " Then David **crept up** unnoticed
24:7 [24:8] [A] and did not allow them to **attack** [+448] Saul.
24:7 [24:8] [A] And Saul **left** [+4946] the cave and went his way.
24:8 [24:9] [A] **[NIE]** Then David went out of the cave and called
24:20 [24:21] [A] that the kingdom of Israel *will be* **established** in
25:1 [A] Then David **[NIE]** moved down into the Desert of Maon.
25:29 [A] Even though **[NIE]** someone is pursuing you to take your
25:41 [A] **[NIE]** She bowed down with her face to the ground
25:42 [A] Abigail quickly **[NIE]** got on a donkey and, attended by her
26:2 [A] So **[NIE]** Saul went down to the Desert of Ziph, with his
26:5 [A] David **set out** and went to the place where Saul had camped.
27:2 [A] So David and the six hundred men with him **left** and went
28:23 [A] to them. *He* **got up** from the ground and sat on the couch.
28:25 [A] his men, and they ate. That same night *they* **got up** and left.
31:12 [A] **[NIE]** all their valiant men journeyed through the night to
2Sa 2:14 [A] "*Let's have* some of the young men **get up** and fight hand to
2:14 [A] hand in front of us." "**All right**, *let them* **do**[s] **it**," Joab said.
2:15 [A] So *they* **stood up** and were counted off—twelve men for
3:10 [G] **establish** David's throne over Israel and Judah from Dan to
3:21 [A] "Let me go **at once** and assemble all Israel for my lord the
6:2 [A] all his men **[NIE]** set out from Baalah of Judah to bring up
7:12 [G] your fathers, *I will* **raise up** your offspring to succeed you,
7:25 [G] **keep** forever the promise you have made concerning your
11:2 [A] One evening David **got up** from his bed and walked around
12:11 [G] 'Out of your own household I *am going to* **bring** calamity
12:17 [A] The elders of his household **stood** beside him to get him up
12:17 [G] The elders of his household stood beside him to **get** him **up**
12:20 [A] Then David **got up** from the ground. After he had washed,
12:21 [A] but now that the child is dead, *you* **get up** and eat!"
13:15 [A] he had loved her. Amnon said to her, "**Get up** and get out!"
13:29 [A] all the king's sons **got up**, mounted their mules and fled.
13:31 [A] The king **stood up**, tore his clothes and lay down on the
14:7 [A] Now the whole clan *has* **risen up** against your servant; they
14:23 [A] Joab **[NIE]** went to Geshur and brought Absalom back to
14:31 [A] Joab **[NIE]** did go to Absalom's house and he said to him,
15:9 [A] said to him, "Go in peace." So **[NIE]** he went to Hebron.
15:14 [A] to all his officials who were with him in Jerusalem, "**Come**!
17:1 [A] twelve thousand men and **set out** tonight in pursuit of David.
17:21 [A] They said to him, "**Set out** and cross the river at once;
17:22 [A] So David and all the people with him **set out** and crossed the
17:23 [A] his donkey and **[NIE]** set out for his house in his hometown.
18:31 [A] The LORD has delivered you today from all who **rose up**
18:32 [A] and all who **rise up** to harm you be like that young man."
19:7 [19:8] [A] Now **go** out and encourage your men. I swear by the
19:8 [19:9] [A] So the king **got up** and took his seat in the gateway.
22:39 [A] I crushed them completely, and *they could* not **rise**; they fell
22:40 [A] strength for battle; you made my **adversaries** bow at my feet.
22:49 [A] You exalted me above my **foes**; from violent men you
23:1 [H] son of Jesse, the oracle of the man **exalted** *by* the Most High,
23:10 [A] he **stood** *his* **ground** and struck down the Philistines till his
24:11 [A] Before David **got up** the next morning, the word of the
24:18 [G] **build** an altar to the LORD on the threshing floor of
1Ki 1:49 [A] At this, all Adonijah's guests **rose** in alarm and dispersed.
1:50 [A] **[RPH]** went and took hold of the horns of the altar.
2:4 [G] that the LORD *may* **keep** his promise to me: 'If your
2:19 [A] the king **stood up** to meet her, bowed down to her and sat
2:40 [A] **[NIE]** he saddled his donkey and went to Achish at Gath in
3:12 [A] will never have been anyone like you, nor *will there* ever **be**.
3:20 [A] So *she* **got up** in the middle of the night and took my son
3:21 [A] The next morning, *I* **got up** to nurse my son—and he was
6:12 [G] *I will* **fulfill** through you the promise I gave to David your
7:21 [G] *He* **erected** the pillars at the portico of the temple. The pillar
7:21 [G] **[RPH]** The pillar to the south he named Jakin and the one to
7:21 [G] south he named Jakin and **[RPH]** the one to the north Boaz.

1Ki 8:20 [G] "The LORD *has* **kept** the promise he made: I have
8:20 [A] *I have* **succeeded** [+9393] David my father and now I sit on
8:54 [A] to the LORD, *he* **rose** from before the altar of the LORD,
9:5 [G] *I will* **establish** your royal throne over Israel forever, as I
11:14 [G] Then the LORD **raised up** against Solomon an adversary,
11:18 [A] *They* **set out** from Midian and went to Paran. Then taking
11:23 [G] God **raised up** against Solomon another adversary, Rezon
11:40 [A] but **[NIE]** Jeroboam fled to Egypt, to Shishak the king,
12:15 [G] to **fulfill** the word the LORD had spoken to Jeroboam son
14:2 [A] Jeroboam said to his wife, "**Go**, disguise yourself, so you
14:2 [A] what he said and **[NIE]** went to Ahijah's house in Shiloh.
14:4 [A] Ahijah could not see; his sight *was* **gone** because of his age.
14:12 [A] "As for you, **[NIE]** go back home. When you set foot in
14:14 [G] "The LORD *will* **raise up** for himself a king over Israel
14:17 [A] Then Jeroboam's wife **got up** and left and went to Tirzah.
15:4 [G] him a lamp in Jerusalem by **raising up** a son to succeed him
16:32 [G] *He* **set up** an altar for Baal in the temple of Baal that he built
17:9 [A] "Go **at once** to Zarephath of Sidon and stay there. I have
17:10 [A] So **[NIE]** he went to Zarephath. When he came to the town
19:3 [A] Elijah was afraid and **[NIE]** ran for his life. When he came
19:5 [A] All at once an angel touched him and said, "**Get up** and eat."
19:7 [A] a second time and touched him and said, "**Get up** and eat,
19:8 [A] So *he* **got up** and ate and drank. Strengthened by that food,
19:21 [A] Then *he* **set out** to follow Elijah and became his attendant.
21:7 [A] how you act as king over Israel? **Get up** and eat! Cheer up.
21:15 [A] "**Get up** and take possession of the vineyard of Naboth the
21:16 [A] he **got up** and went down to take possession of Naboth's
21:18 [A] "**Go** down to meet Ahab king of Israel, who rules in Samaria.
2Ki 1:3 [A] **[NIE]** "Go up and meet the messengers of the king of
1:15 [A] So Elijah **got up** and went down with him to the king.
3:24 [A] the Israelites **rose up** and fought them until they fled.
4:30 [A] I will not leave you." So *he* **got up** and followed her.
6:15 [A] When the servant of the man of God **got up** and went out
7:5 [A] At dusk *they* **got up** and went to the camp of the Arameans.
7:7 [A] So *they* **got up** and fled in the dusk and abandoned their
7:12 [A] The king **got up** in the night and said to his officers, "I will
8:1 [A] **[NIE]** "Go away with your family and stay for a while
8:2 [A] The woman **proceeded** to do as the man of God said. She
8:21 [A] but he **rose up** and broke through by night;
9:2 [G] **get** him **away** from his companions and take him into an
9:6 [A] Jehu **got up** and went into the house. Then the prophet
10:12 [A] Jehu then **[NIE]** set out and went toward Samaria. At Beth
11:1 [A] was dead, *she* **proceeded** to destroy the whole royal family.
12:20 [12:21] [A] **[NIE]** His officials conspired against him
13:21 [A] the man came to life and **stood up** on his feet.
16:7 [A] and of the king of Israel, who *are* **attacking** [+6584] me."
21:3 [G] *he* also **erected** altars to Baal and made an Asherah pole,
23:3 [G] thus **confirming** the words of the covenant written in this
23:24 [G] This he did to **fulfill** the requirements of the law written in
23:25 [A] Neither before nor after Josiah **[NIE]** was there a king like
25:26 [A] At this, **[NIE]** all the people from the least to the greatest,
1Ch 10:12 [A] all their valiant men **went** and took the bodies of Saul and his
17:11 [G] *I will* **raise up** your offspring to succeed you, one of your
21:18 [G] **build** an altar to the LORD on the threshing floor of
22:16 [A] Now **begin** the work, and the LORD be with you."
22:19 [A] **Begin** to build the sanctuary of the LORD God, so that you
28:2 [A] King David **rose** to his feet and said: "Listen to me,
2Ch 3:17 [G] *He* **erected** the pillars in the front of the temple, one to the
6:10 [G] "The LORD *has* **kept** the promise he made. I have
6:10 [G] *I have* **succeeded** [+9393] David my father and now I sit on
6:41 [A] "Now **arise**, O LORD God, and come to your resting place,
7:18 [G] *I will* **establish** your royal throne, as I covenanted with
10:15 [G] to **fulfill** the word the LORD had spoken to Jeroboam son
13:4 [A] Abijah **stood** on Mount Zemaraim, in the hill country of
13:6 [A] of Solomon son of David, **[NIE]** rebelled against his master.
20:19 [A] and Korahites **stood up** and praised the LORD,
21:4 [A] When Jehoram **established** *himself* firmly over his father's
21:9 [A] but *he* **rose up** and broke through by night.
22:10 [A] *she* **proceeded** to destroy the whole royal family of the
28:12 [A] **confronted** [+6584] those who were arriving from the war.
28:15 [A] **[NIE]** The men designated by name took the prisoners,
29:12 [A] these Levites **set to work**: from the Kohathites, Mahath son
30:14 [A] **[NIE]** They removed the altars in Jerusalem and cleared
30:27 [A] The priests and the Levites **stood** to bless the people,
33:3 [G] *he* also **erected** altars to the Baals and made Asherah poles.
Ezr 1:5 [A] **prepared** to go up and build the house of the LORD in
3:2 [A] his associates **began** to build the altar of the God of Israel to
9:5 [A] *I* **rose** from my self-abasement, with my tunic and cloak torn,
10:4 [A] **Rise up**; this matter is in your hands. We will support you,
10:5 [A] So Ezra **rose up** and put the leading priests and Levites
10:6 [A] Ezra **withdrew** from before the house of God and went to the
10:10 [A] Ezra the priest **stood up** and said to them, "You have been
Ne 2:12 [A] I **set out** during the night with a few men. I had not told
2:18 [A] They replied, "*Let us* **start** rebuilding." So they began this
2:20 [A] We his servants *will* **start** rebuilding, but as for you,
3:1 [A] Eliashib the high priest and his fellow priests **went to work**
4:14 [4:8] [A] *I* **stood up** and said to the nobles, the officials and the
5:13 [G] and possessions every man who *does* not **keep** this promise.
9:3 [A] *They* **stood** where they were and read from the Book of the
9:4 [A] **Standing** on the stairs were the Levites—Jeshua, Bani,
9:5 [A] "**Stand up** and praise the LORD your God, who is from
9:8 [G] *You have* **kept** your promise because you are righteous.
Est 5:9 [A] observed that *he* neither **rose** nor showed fear in his
7:7 [A] The king **got up** in a rage, left his wine and went out into the
8:4 [A] gold scepter to Esther and she **arose** and stood before him.
9:21 [D] to **have** them celebrate annually the fourteenth and fifteenth
9:27 [D] the Jews took it upon themselves *to* **establish the custom**
9:29 [D] wrote with full authority to **confirm** this second letter
9:31 [D] to **establish** these days of Purim at their designated times,
9:31 [D] Mordecai the Jew and Queen Esther *had* **decreed** for them,
9:31 [D] as *they had* **established** for themselves and their
9:32 [D] Esther's decree **confirmed** these regulations about Purim,
Job 1:20 [A] At this, Job **got up** and tore his robe and shaved his head.
4:4 [G] Your words *have* **supported** those who stumbled; you have
7:4 [A] When I lie down I think, 'How long before *I* **get up**?' The
8:15 [A] his web, but it gives way; he clings to it, but *it does* not **hold**.
11:17 [A] Life *will be* **brighter** than noonday, and darkness will
14:12 [A] so man lies down and *does* not **rise**; till the heavens are no
15:29 [A] He will no longer be rich and his wealth *will* not **endure**, nor
16:8 [A] a witness; my gauntness **rises up** and testifies against me.
16:12 [G] me by the neck and crushed me. *He has* **made** me his target;
19:18 [A] the little boys scorn me; *when I* **appear**, they ridicule me.
19:25 [A] and that in the end *he will* **stand** upon the earth.
20:27 [F] will expose his guilt; the earth *will* **rise up** against him.
22:28 [A] What you decide on *will be* **done**, and light will shine on
24:14 [A] is gone, the murderer **rises up** and kills the poor and needy;
24:22 [A] though *they become* **established**, they have no assurance of
25:3 [A] his forces be numbered? Upon whom *does* his light not **rise**?
27:7 [F] enemies be like the wicked, my **adversaries** like the unjust!
29:8 [A] saw me and stepped aside and the old men **rose** to their feet;
30:12 [A] On my right the tribe **attacks**; they lay snares for my feet,
30:28 [A] not by the sun; *I* **stand up** in the assembly and cry for help.
31:14 [A] what will I do when God **confronts** me? What will I answer
41:26 [41:18] [A] The sword that reaches him **has** no **effect**, nor does
Ps 1:5 [A] Therefore the wicked *will* not **stand** in the judgment,
3:1 [3:2] [A] many are my foes! How many **rise up** against me!
3:7 [3:8] [A] **Arise**, O LORD! Deliver me, O my God! Strike all
7:6 [7:7] [A] **Arise**, O LORD, in your anger; rise up against the
9:19 [9:20] [A] **Arise**, O LORD, let not man triumph; let the nations
10:12 [A] **Arise**, LORD! Lift up your hand, O God. Do not forget the
12:5 [12:6] [A] of the needy, *I will* now **arise**," says the LORD.
17:7 [F] your right hand those who take refuge in you from their **foes**.
17:13 [A] **Rise up**, O LORD, confront them, bring them down;
18:38 [18:39] [A] I crushed them so that they could not **rise**; they fell
18:39 [18:40] [A] you made my **adversaries** bow at my feet.
18:48 [18:49] [A] You exalted me above my **foes**; from violent men
20:8 [20:9] [A] to their knees and fall, but we **rise up** and stand firm.
24:3 [A] the hill of the LORD? Who *may* **stand** in his holy place?
27:3 [A] though war **break out** against me, even then will I be
27:12 [A] for false witnesses **rise up** against me, breathing out
35:2 [A] Take up shield and buckler; **arise and come** to my aid.
35:11 [A] Ruthless witnesses **come forward**; they question me on
36:12 [36:13] [A] evildoers lie fallen—thrown down, not able *to* **rise**!
40:2 [40:3] [G] *he* **set** my feet on a rock and gave me a firm place to
41:8 [41:9] [A] *he will* never **get up** *from* the place where he lies."
41:10 [41:11] [G] mercy on me; **raise** me **up**, that I may repay them.
44:5 [44:6] [A] our enemies; through your name we trample our **foes**.
44:26 [44:27] [A] **Rise up** and help us; redeem us because of your
54:3 [54:5] [A] Strangers *are* **attacking** [+6584] me; ruthless men
59:1 [59:2] [F] protect me from *those who* **rise up** *against* me.
68:1 [68:2] [A] *May* God **arise**, may his enemies be scattered; may
74:22 [A] **Rise up**, O God, and defend your cause; remember how fools
74:23 [A] the uproar of your **enemies**, which rises continually.
76:9 [76:10] [A] when you, O God, **rose up** to judge, to save all the
78:5 [G] *He* **decreed** statutes for Jacob and established the law in
78:6 [A] yet to be born, and they **in turn** would tell their children.
82:8 [A] **Rise up**, O God, judge the earth, for all the nations are your
86:14 [A] The arrogant are **attacking** [+6584] me, O God; a band of
88:10 [88:11] [A] *Do* those who are dead **rise up** and praise you?
89:43 [89:44] [G] of his sword and *have* not **supported** him in battle.
92:11 [92:12] [A] my ears have heard the rout of my wicked **foes**.
94:16 [A] Who *will* **rise up** for me against the wicked? Who will take a
102:13 [102:14] [A] You *will* **arise** and have compassion on Zion, for it
107:29 [G] *He* **stilled** the storm to a whisper; the waves of the sea were
109:28 [A] *when they* **attack** they will be put to shame, but your servant
113:7 [G] *He* **raises** the poor from the dust and lifts the needy from the
119:28 [D] weary with sorrow; **strengthen** me according to your word.
119:38 [G] **Fulfill** your promise to your servant, so that you may be

[F] Hitpael (hitpoel, hitpoal, hitpolel, hitpolal, hitpalel, hitpalal, hitpalpel, hitpalpal, hotpael, hotpaal) [G] Hiphil (hiphtil) [H] Hophal [I] Hishtaphel

Ps 119:62 [A] At midnight *I* **rise** to give you thanks for your righteous
119:106 [D] I have taken an oath and **confirmed** it, that I will follow your
124: 2 [A] had not been on our side when men **attacked** [+6584] us,
127: 2 [A] In vain you **rise** early and stay up late, toiling for food to
132: 8 [A] **arise**, O LORD, and come to your resting place, you
139: 2 [A] You know when I sit and *when* I **rise**; you perceive my
139:21 [f] and abhor *those who* **rise** [BHS 9539] **up** *against* you?
140:10 [140:11] [A] thrown into the fire, into miry pits, never *to* **rise**.
Pr 6: 9 [A] you sluggard? When *will you* **get up** from your sleep?
15:22 [A] for lack of counsel, but with many advisers *they* **succeed**.
19:21 [A] a man's heart, but it is the LORD's purpose *that* **prevails**.
24:16 [A] for though a righteous man falls seven times, *he* **rises** again,
24:22 [A] for those two *will* **send** sudden destruction *upon* them,
28:12 [A] but when the wicked **rise to power**, men go into hiding.
28:28 [A] When the wicked **rise to power**, people go into hiding;
30: 4 [G] Who *has* **established** all the ends of the earth? What is his
31:15 [A] *She* **gets up** while it is still dark; she provides food for her
31:28 [A] Her children **arise** and call her blessed; her husband also,
Ecc 4:10 [G] If one falls down, his friend *can* **help** him **up**. But pity the
4:10 [G] But pity the man who falls and has no one to **help** him **up**!
12: 4 [A] when *men* **rise up** at the sound of birds, but all their songs
SS 2:10 [A] My lover spoke and said to me, "**Arise**, my darling,
2:13 [A] **Arise**, come, my darling; my beautiful one, come with me."
3: 2 [A] *I will* **get up** now and go about the city, through its streets
5: 5 [A] I **arose** to open for my lover, and my hands dripped with
Isa 2:19 [A] the splendor of his majesty, when he **rises** to shake the earth.
2:21 [A] the splendor of his majesty, when he **rises** to shake the earth.
7: 7 [A] LORD says: " '*It will* not **take place**, it will not happen,
8:10 [A] propose your plan, but *it will* not **stand**, for God is with us.
14: 9 [G] leaders in the world; *it* **makes** them **rise** from their thrones—
14:21 [A] *they are* not *to* **rise** to inherit the land and cover the earth
14:22 [A] "*I will* **rise up** against them," declares the LORD Almighty.
14:24 [A] so it will be, and as I have purposed, so it *will* **stand**.
21: 5 [A] they eat, they drink! **Get up**, *you* officers, oil the shields!
23:12 [A] "**Up**, cross over to Cyprus; even there you will find no rest."
23:13 [G] *they* **raised up** their siege towers, they stripped its fortresses
24:20 [A] it is the guilt of its rebellion that it falls—never *to* **rise** again.
26:14 [A] they live no more; those departed spirits *do* not **rise**.
26:19 [A] your dead will live; their bodies *will* **rise**. You who dwell in
27: 9 [A] no Asherah poles or incense altars *will be left* **standing**.
28:18 [A] be annulled; your agreement with the grave *will* not **stand**.
28:21 [A] The LORD *will* **rise up** as he did at Mount Perazim, he will
29: 3 [G] you with towers and **set up** my siege works against you.
31: 2 [A] *He will* **rise up** against the house of the wicked, against
32: 8 [A] noble man makes noble plans, and by noble deeds he **stands**.
32: 9 [A] You women who are so complacent, **rise up** and listen to me;
33:10 [A] "Now *will I* **arise**," says the LORD. "Now will I be exalted;
40: 8 [A] the flowers fall, but the word of our God **stands** forever."
43:17 [A] they lay there, never *to* **rise** *again*, extinguished, snuffed out
44:26 [G] *who* **carries out** the words of his servants and fulfills the
44:26 [D] 'They shall be built,' and of their ruins, '*I will* **restore** them,'
46:10 [A] I say: My purpose *will* **stand**, and I will do all that I please.
49: 6 [G] "It is too small a thing for you to be my servant to **restore**
49: 7 [A] "Kings will see you and **rise up**, princes will see and bow
49: 8 [G] to **restore** the land and to reassign its desolate inheritances,
51:17 [A] **Rise up**, O Jerusalem, you who have drunk from the hand of
52: 2 [A] Shake off your dust; **rise up**, sit enthroned, O Jerusalem.
54:17 [A] every tongue *that* **accuses** [+907+2021+4200+5477] you.
58:12 [D] the ancient ruins and *will* **raise up** the age-old foundations;
60: 1 [A] "**Arise**, shine, for your light has come, and the glory of the
61: 4 [D] the ancient ruins and **restore** the places long devastated;
Jer 1:17 [A] **Stand up** and say to them whatever I command you.
2:27 [A] yet when they are in trouble, they say, '**Come** and save us!'
2:28 [A] *Let them* **come** if they can save you when you are in trouble!
6: 4 [A] **Arise**, let us attack at noon! But, alas, the daylight is fading,
6: 5 [A] So **arise**, let us attack at night and destroy her fortresses!"
6:17 [G] *I* **appointed** watchmen over you and said, 'Listen to the
8: 4 [A] " 'When men fall down, *do they* not **get up**? When a man
10:20 [G] no one is left now to pitch my tent or *to* **set up** my shelter.
11: 5 [G] *I will* **fulfill** the oath I swore to your forefathers, to give them
13: 4 [A] go **now** to Perath and hide it there in a crevice in the rocks."
13: 6 [A] "Go **now** to Perath and get the belt I told you to hide there."
18: 2 [A] **[NIE]** "Go down to the potter's house, and there I will give
23: 4 [G] *I will* **place** shepherds over them who will tend them,
23: 5 [G] "when *I will* **raise up** to David a righteous Branch,
23:20 [G] he **fully accomplishes** [+2256+6913] the purposes of his heart.
25:27 [A] fall *to* **rise** no more because of the sword I will send among
26:17 [A] Some of the elders of the land **stepped forward** and said to
28: 6 [G] *May* the LORD **fulfill** the words you have prophesied by
29:10 [G] **fulfill** my gracious promise to bring you back to this place.
29:15 [G] "The LORD *has* **raised up** prophets for us in Babylon,"
30: 9 [G] and David their king, whom *I will* **raise up** for them.
30:24 [G] he **fully accomplishes** [+2256+6913] the purposes of his heart.
31: 6 [A] '**Come**, let us go up to Zion, to the LORD our God.' "
33:14 [G] 'when *I will* **fulfill** the gracious promise I made to the house
34:18 [G] *have* not **fulfilled** the terms of the covenant they made before
35:14 [H] his sons not to drink wine and this command *has* **been kept**.
35:16 [G] The descendants of Jonadab son of Recab *have* **carried out**
37:10 [A] in their tents, *they would* **come out** and burn this city down."
41: 2 [A] son of Nethaniah and the ten men who were with him **got up**
44:25 [G] do what you promised! **Keep** [+906+7756] your vows!
44:25 [G] do what you promised! **Keep** [+906+7756] your vows!
44:28 [A] came to live in Egypt will know whose word *will* **stand**—
44:29 [A] my threats of harm against you *will* **surely stand** [+7756].'
44:29 [A] my threats of harm against you *will* **surely stand** [+7756].'
46:16 [A] They will say, '**Get up**, let us go back to our own people
49:14 [A] to say, "Assemble yourselves to attack it! **Rise up** for battle!"
49:28 [A] "**Arise**, and attack Kedar and destroy the people of the East.
49:31 [A] "**Arise** and attack a nation at ease, which lives in
50:32 [G] one will stumble and fall and no *one will* **help** her **up**;
51:12 [G] the guard, **station** the watchmen, prepare an ambush!
51:29 [A] for the LORD's purposes against Babylon **stand**—
51:64 [A] 'So will Babylon sink *to* **rise** no more because of the disaster
La 1:14 [A] He has handed me over to those I cannot **withstand**.
2:19 [A] **Arise**, cry out in the night, as the watches of the night begin;
3:62 [A] what my **enemies** whisper and mutter against me all day
Eze 3:22 [A] he said to me, "**Get up** and go out to the plain, and there I
3:23 [A] So *I* **got up** and went out to the plain. And the glory of the
7:11 [A] Violence *has* **grown** into a rod to punish wickedness;
13: 6 [D] has not sent them; yet they expect their words to *be* **fulfilled**.
16:60 [G] and *I will* **establish** an everlasting covenant with you.
16:62 [G] So I *will* **establish** my covenant with you, and you will know
26: 8 [G] a ramp up to your walls and **raise** his shields against you.
34:23 [G] *I will* **place** over them one shepherd, my servant David,
34:29 [G] *I will* **provide** for them a land renowned for its crops,
Da 8:27 [A] Then *I* **got up** and went about the king's business.
9:12 [G] *You have* **fulfilled** the words spoken against us and against
Hos 6: 2 [G] on the third day *he will* **restore** us, that we may live in his
10:14 [A] the roar of battle *will* **rise** against your people, so that all
Am 2:11 [G] *I* also **raised up** prophets from among your sons and
5: 2 [A] "Fallen is Virgin Israel, never *to* **rise** again, deserted in her
5: 2 [G] deserted in her own land, with no *one to* **lift** her **up**."
6:14 [G] "I *will* **stir up** a nation against you, O house of Israel,
7: 2 [A] forgive! How *can* Jacob **survive**? He is so small!"
7: 5 [A] I beg you, stop! How *can* Jacob **survive**?
7: 9 [A] with my sword *I will* **rise** against the house of Jeroboam."
8:14 [A] god of Beersheba lives'—they will fall, never *to* **rise** again."
9:11 [G] "In that day *I will* **restore** David's fallen tent. I will repair its
9:11 [G] broken places, **restore** its ruins, and build it as it used to be,
Ob 1: 1 [A] nations to say, "**Rise**, and let us go against her for battle"—
1: 1 [A] nations to say, "Rise, and *let us* **go** against her for battle"—
Jnh 1: 2 [A] **[NIE]** "Go to the great city of Nineveh and preach against
1: 3 [A] **[NIE]** Jonah ran away from the LORD and headed for
1: 6 [A] and said, "How can you sleep? **Get up** and call on your god!
3: 2 [A] **[NIE]** "Go to the great city of Nineveh and proclaim to it
3: 3 [A] Jonah **obeyed** [+3869] the word of the LORD and went to
3: 6 [A] *he* **rose** from his throne, took off his royal robes, covered
Mic 2: 8 [D] Lately my people *have* **risen up** like an enemy. You strip off
2:10 [A] **Get up**, go away! For this is not your resting place, because
4:13 [A] "**Rise** and thresh, O Daughter of Zion, for I will give you
5: 5 [5:4] [G] *we will* **raise** against him seven shepherds, even eight
6: 1 [A] "**Stand up**, plead your case before the mountains; let the hills
7: 6 [A] dishonors his father, a daughter **rises up** against her mother,
7: 8 [A] gloat over me, my enemy! Though I have fallen, *I will* **rise**.
Na 1: 6 [A] Who *can* **endure** his fierce anger? His wrath is poured out
1: 9 [A] he will bring to an end; trouble *will* not **come** a second time.
Hab 1: 6 [G] I *am* **raising up** the Babylonians, that ruthless and impetuous
2: 7 [A] *Will* not your debtors suddenly **arise**? Will they not wake up
Zep 3: 8 [A] declares the LORD, "for the day I *will* **stand up** to testify.
Zec 11:16 [G] For I *am going to* **raise up** a shepherd over the land who will

7757 קוֹמָה qômâ, n.f. [45] [√ 7756]

high [28], height [2], on high [+928] [2], tallest [2], *untranslated* [1], deep [1], diameter [1], height [+1469] [1], higher [1], length [1], lengths [1], lofty trees [+8123] [1], low [+9166] [1], on high [1], stature [1]

Ge 6:15 The ark is to be 450 feet long, 75 feet wide and 45 feet **high**.
Ex 25:10 cubits long, a cubit and a half wide, and a cubit and a half **high**.
25:23 two cubits long, a cubit wide and a cubit and a half **high**.
27: 1 "Build an altar of acacia wood, three cubits **high**; it is to be square,
27:18 cubits wide, with curtains of finely twisted linen five cubits **high**,
30: 2 is to be square, a cubit long and a cubit wide, and two cubits **high**—
37: 1 cubits long, a cubit and a half wide, and a cubit and a half **high**.
37:10 two cubits long, a cubit wide, and a cubit and a half **high**.
37:25 It was square, a cubit long and a cubit wide, and two cubits **high**—
38: 1 built the altar of burnt offering of acacia wood, three cubits **high**;
38:18 cubits long and, like the curtains of the courtyard, five cubits **high**,
1Sa 16: 7 "Do not consider his appearance or his **height** [+1469], for I have

1Sa 28:20 Immediately Saul fell full **length** on the ground, filled with fear
1Ki 6: 2 for the LORD was sixty cubits long, twenty wide and thirty **high**.
6:10 The **height** *of* each was five cubits, and they were attached to the
6:20 sanctuary was twenty cubits long, twenty wide and twenty **high**.
6:23 he made a pair of cherubim of olive wood, each ten cubits **high**.
6:26 The **height** *of* each cherub was ten cubits.
7: 2 fifty wide and thirty **high**, with four rows of cedar columns
7:15 each eighteen cubits **high** and twelve cubits around, by line.
7:16 to set on the tops of the pillars; each capital was five cubits **high**.
7:16 the tops of the pillars; each capital was five cubits high. **[RPH]**
7:23 measuring ten cubits from rim to rim and five cubits **high**.
7:27 of bronze; each was four cubits long, four wide and three **high**.
7:32 to the stand. The **diameter** *of* each wheel was a cubit and a half.
7:35 At the top of the stand there was a circular band half a cubit **deep**.
2Ki 19:23 I have cut down its **tallest** cedars, the choicest of its pines.
25:17 Each pillar was twenty-seven feet **high**. The bronze capital on top
25:17 a half feet **high** and was decorated with a network
2Ch 4: 1 altar twenty cubits long, twenty cubits wide and ten cubits **high**.
4: 2 measuring ten cubits from rim to rim and five cubits **high**.
6:13 five cubits long, five cubits wide and three cubits **high**,
SS 7: 7 [7:8] Your **stature** is like that of the palm, and your breasts like
Isa 10:33 The **lofty** [+8123] **trees** will be felled, the tall ones will be brought
37:24 I have cut down its **tallest** cedars, the choicest of its pines.
Jer 52:21 Each of the pillars was eighteen cubits **high** and twelve cubits in
52:22 The bronze capital on top of the one pillar was five cubits **high**
Eze 13:18 make veils of various **lengths** for their heads in order to ensnare
17: 6 and it sprouted and became a **low** [+9166], spreading vine.
19:11 It towered **high** above the thick foliage, conspicuous for its height
31: 3 the forest; it towered **on high**, its top above the thick foliage.
31: 5 So it towered **higher** than all the trees of the field; its boughs
31:10 Because it towered **on high** [+928], lifting its top above the thick
31:14 other trees by the waters are ever to tower proudly **on high** [+928],
40: 5 the wall; it was one measuring rod thick and one rod **high**.

7758 קוֹמְמִיּוּת ***qômᵉmiyyût***, n.f. [1] [√ 7756]

with heads held high [1]

Lev 26:13 bars of your yoke and enabled you to walk **with heads held high**.

7759 קוֹנֵן ***qônēn***, var. Not used in NIV/BHS [cf. 7801]

7760 קוֹעַ ***qôaʿ***, n.pr.g. [1] [cf. 8778]

Koa [1]

Eze 23:23 and all the Chaldeans, the men of Pekod and Shoa and **Koa**,

7761 קוֹף ***qôp***, n.[m.]. [2]

apes [2]

1Ki 10:22 it returned, carrying gold, silver and ivory, and **apes** and baboons.
2Ch 9:21 it returned, carrying gold, silver and ivory, and **apes** and baboons.

7762 ¹קוּץ ***qûṣ¹***, v. [8] [→ 7764?; cf. 7752, 9210]

dread [2], abhorred [1], detest [1], disgusted [1], filled with dread [1], hostile [1], resent [1]

Ge 27:46 [A] "*I'm* **disgusted** with living because of these Hittite women.
Ex 1:12 [A] and spread; so the Egyptians *came to* **dread** the Israelites
Lev 20:23 [A] Because they did all these things, *I* **abhorred** them.
Nu 21: 5 [A] There is no water! And we **detest** this miserable food!"
22: 3 [A] Moab *was* **filled with dread** because of the Israelites.
1Ki 11:25 [A] So Rezon ruled in Aram and *was* **hostile** toward Israel.
Pr 3:11 [A] the LORD's discipline and *do* not **resent** his rebuke,
Isa 7:16 [A] the land of the two kings you **dread** will be laid waste.

7763 ²קוּץ ***qûṣ²***, v. [1]

tear apart [1]

Isa 7: 6 [G] *let us* **tear** it **apart** and divide it among ourselves, and make

7764 ¹קוֹץ ***qôṣ¹***, n.m. [12] [→ 2212?, 7766?; cf. 7762?]

thorns [10], thornbushes [2]

Ge 3:18 It will produce **thorns** and thistles for you, and you will eat the
Ex 22: 6 [22:5] "If a fire breaks out and spreads into **thornbushes** so that it
Jdg 8: 7 into my hand, I will tear your flesh with desert **thorns** and briers."
8:16 the men of Succoth a lesson by punishing them with desert **thorns**
2Sa 23: 6 evil men are all to be cast aside like **thorns**, which are not gathered
Ps 118:12 me like bees, but they died out as quickly as burning **thorns**;
Isa 32:13 the land of my people, a land overgrown with **thorns** and briers—
33:12 burned as if to lime; like cut **thornbushes** they will be set ablaze."
Jer 4: 3 "Break up your unplowed ground and do not sow among **thorns**.
12:13 They will sow wheat but reap **thorns**; they will wear themselves
Eze 28:24 have malicious neighbors who are painful briers and sharp **thorns**.
Hos 10: 8 of Israel. **Thorns** and thistles will grow up and cover their altars.

7765 ²קוֹץ ***qôṣ²***, n.pr.m. Not used in NIV/BHS [√ 7916; cf. 7891]

7766 ³קוֹץ ***qôṣ³***, n.pr.m. [1] [√ 7764?]

Koz [1]

1Ch 4: 8 **Koz**, who was the father of Anub and Hazzobebah and of the clans

7767 קְוֻצּוֹת ***qᵉwuṣṣôt***, n.f.pl. [2]

hair [2]

SS 5: 2 is drenched with dew, my **hair** with the dampness of the night."
5:11 His head is purest gold; his **hair** is wavy and black as a raven.

7768 קַוְקָו ***qawqāw***, n.[m.]. Not used in NIV/BHS [cf. 7743]

7769 ¹קוּר ***qûr¹***, v. [2] [→ 5227, 7981?]

dug wells [2]

2Ki 19:24 [A] I *have* **dug wells** in foreign lands and drunk the water there.
Isa 37:25 [A] I *have* **dug wells** in foreign lands and drunk the water there.

7770 ²קוּר ***qûr²***, n.m. [2]

cobwebs [1], web [1]

Isa 59: 5 They hatch the eggs of vipers and spin a spider's **web**.
59: 6 Their **cobwebs** are useless for clothing; they cannot cover

7771 קוֹרָה ***qôrâ***, n.f. [5] [√ 7939]

beams [1], ceiling beams [1], pole [1], roof [1], tree [1]

Ge 19: 8 to these men, for they have come under the protection of my **roof**."
2Ki 6: 2 Let us go to the Jordan, where each of us can get a **pole**; and let us
6: 5 As one of them was cutting down a **tree**, the iron axhead fell into
2Ch 3: 7 He overlaid the **ceiling beams**, doorframes, walls and doors of the
SS 1:17 The **beams** *of* our house are cedars; our rafters are firs.

7772 קוּשׁ ***qûš***, v. [1] [cf. 3704, 5943]

ensnare [1]

Isa 29:21 [A] *who* **ensnare** the defender in court and with false testimony

7773 קוּשָׁיָהוּ ***qûšāyāhû***, n.pr.m. [1] [cf. 7823]

Kushaiah [1]

1Ch 15:17 and from their brothers the Merarites, Ethan son of **Kushaiah**;

7774 קָח ***qāḥ***, n.[m.] Not used in NIV/BHS

7775 קָט ***qāṭ***, pt. [1]

soon [+3869+5071] [1]

Eze 16:47 in all your ways you **soon** [+3869+5071] became more depraved

7776 קֶטֶב ***qeṭeb***, n.m. [4]

plague [2], destruction [1], destructive [1]

Dt 32:24 famine against them, consuming pestilence and deadly **plague**;
Ps 91: 6 that stalks in the darkness, nor the **plague** that destroys at midday.
Isa 28: 2 Like a hailstorm and a **destructive** wind, like a driving rain
Hos 13:14 O death, are your plagues? Where, O grave, is your **destruction**?

7777 קְטוֹרָה ***qᵉṭôrâ***, n.m. [1] [√ 7787]

incense [1]

Dt 33:10 He offers **incense** before you and whole burnt offerings on your

7778 קְטוּרָה ***qᵉṭûrâ***, n.pr.f. [4] [√ 7787]

Keturah [4]

Ge 25: 1 Abraham took another wife, whose name was **Keturah**.
25: 4 Abida and Eldaah. All these were descendants of **Keturah**.
1Ch 1:32 The sons born to **Keturah**, Abraham's concubine: Zimran,
1:33 Abida and Eldaah. All these were descendants of **Keturah**.

7779 קָטַל ***qāṭal***, v. [3] [→ 7780; Ar 10625]

slay [2], kills [1]

Job 13:15 [A] Though *he* **slay** me, yet will I hope in him; I will surely
24:14 [A] is gone, the murderer rises up and **kills** the poor and needy;
Ps 139:19 [A] If only *you would* **slay** the wicked, O God! Away from me,

7780 קֶטֶל ***qeṭel***, n.[m.]. [1] [√ 7779]

slaughter [1]

Ob 1: 9 everyone in Esau's mountains will be cut down in the **slaughter**.

7781 [1]קָטֹן ***qāṭōn[1]***, v. [4] [→ 7782, 7783, 7784, 7785]

not enough [+6388] [1], not enough [1], skimping [1], unworthy [1]

Ge 32: 10 [32:11] [A] *I am* **unworthy** of all the kindness and faithfulness
2Sa 7: 19 [A] as if this *were* **not enough** [+6388] in your sight,
1Ch 17: 17 [A] as if this *were* **not enough** in your sight, O God, you have
Am 8: 5 [G] **skimping** the measure, boosting the price and cheating with

7782 קֹטֶן ***qōṭen***, n.m. [2] [√ 7781]

little finger [2]

1Ki 12: 10 tell them, 'My **little finger** is thicker than my father's waist.
2Ch 10: 10 tell them, 'My **little finger** is thicker than my father's waist.

7783 [1]קָטָן ***qāṭān[1]***, a. [47] [→ 2214, 7784; cf. 7781]

small [12], least [9], younger [8], young [5], youngest [4], little [2], boy [+5853] [1], lesser [1], light [1], low [1], smaller [1], smallest [1], youths [+5853] [1]

Ge 9: 24 his wine and found out what his **youngest** son had done to him,
27: 15 she had in the house, and put them on her **younger** son Jacob.
27: 42 Esau had said, she sent for her **younger** son Jacob and said to him,
29: 16 of the older was Leah, and the name of the **younger** was Rachel.
29: 18 "I'll work for you seven years in return for your **younger** daughter
44: 20 an aged father, and there is a **young** son born to him in his old age.
Nu 22: 18 or **small** to go beyond the command of the LORD my God.
Dt 25: 13 not have two differing weights in your bag—one heavy, one **light**.
25: 14 have two differing measures in your house—one large, one **small**.
Jdg 15: 2 Isn't her **younger** sister more attractive? Take her instead."
1Sa 9: 21 "But am I not a Benjamite, from the **smallest** tribe of Israel,
14: 49 his older daughter was Merab, and that of the **younger** was Michal.
16: 11 "There is still the **youngest**," Jesse answered, "but he is tending the
17: 14 David was the **youngest**. The three oldest followed Saul,
2Sa 9: 12 Mephibosheth had a **young** son named Mica, and all the members
12: 3 the poor man had nothing except one **little** ewe lamb he had
1Ki 2: 20 "I have one **small** request to make of you," she said. "Do not
11: 17 Hadad, still only a **boy** [+5853], fled to Egypt with some Edomite
17: 13 But first make a **small** cake of bread for me from what you have
18: 44 "A cloud as **small** as a man's hand is rising from the sea."
2Ki 2: 23 *some* **youths** [+5853] came out of the town and jeered at him.
4: 10 Let's make a **small** room on the roof and put in it a bed and a table,
5: 2 Aram had gone out and had taken captive a **young** girl from Israel,
18: 24 How can you repulse one officer of the **least** of my master's
1Ch 12: 14 [12:15] the **least** was a match for a hundred, and the greatest for a
24: 31 the oldest brother were treated the same as those of the **youngest**.
2Ch 31: 15 fellow priests according to their divisions, old and **young** alike.
34: 30 and the Levites—all the people from the **least** to the greatest.
36: 18 both large and **small**, and the treasures of the LORD's temple
Est 1: 5 for all the people from the **least** to the greatest, who were in the
1: 20 women will respect their husbands, from the **least** to the greatest."
Ps 104: 25 with creatures beyond number—living things both large and **small**.
115: 13 he will bless those who fear the LORD—**small** and great alike.
Pr 30: 24 "Four things on earth are **small**, yet they are extremely wise:
Ecc 9: 14 There was once a **small** city with only a few people in it. And a
SS 2: 15 Catch for us the foxes, the **little** foxes that ruin the vineyards,
8: 8 We have a **young** sister, and her breasts are not yet grown.
Isa 22: 24 and offshoots—all its **lesser** vessels, from the bowls to all the jars.
36: 9 can you repulse one officer of the **least** of my master's officials,
Jer 6: 13 "From the **least** to the greatest, all are greedy for gain; prophets
16: 6 "Both high and **low** will die in this land. They will not be buried
31: 34 from the **least** *of* them to the greatest," declares the LORD.
Eze 16: 46 your **younger** sister, who lived to the south of you with her
16: 61 both those who are older than you and those *who* are **younger**.
43: 14 from the **smaller** ledge up to the larger ledge it is four cubits high
Jnh 3: 5 and all of them, from the greatest to the **least**, put on sackcloth.
Zec 4: 10 "Who despises the day of **small** *things*? Men will rejoice when

7784 [2]קָטָן ***qāṭān[2]***, n.pr.m. Not used in NIV/BHS [√ 7783; cf. 7781]

7785 [2]קָטֹן ***qāṭōn[2]***, a. [54] [√ 7781]

small [14], youngest [14], least [7], young [7], little [3], younger [3], simple [2], at all [+196+1524] [1], brief [1], lesser [1], nothing [+1524+1821+2256+4202] [1]

Ge 1: 16 light to govern the day and the **lesser** light to govern the night.
19: 11 **young** and old, with blindness so that they could not find the door.
42: 13 The **youngest** is now with our father, and one is no more."
42: 15 you will not leave this place unless your **youngest** brother comes
42: 20 you must bring your **youngest** brother to me, so that your words
42: 32 is no more, and the **youngest** is now with our father in Canaan.'
42: 34 bring your **youngest** brother to me so I will know that you are not
43: 29 his own mother's son, he asked, "Is this your **youngest** brother,
44: 2 my cup, the silver one, in the mouth of the **youngest** *one's* sack,
44: 12 to search, beginning with the oldest and ending with the **youngest**.
44: 23 'Unless your **youngest** brother comes down with you,
44: 26 go down. Only if our **youngest** brother is with us will we go.
44: 26 We cannot see the man's face unless our **youngest** brother is with
48: 19 Nevertheless, his **younger** brother will be greater than he,
Ex 18: 22 difficult case to you; the **simple** cases they can decide themselves.
18: 26 brought to Moses, but the **simple** ones they decided themselves.
Dt 1: 17 Do not show partiality in judging; hear both **small** and great alike.
Jdg 1: 13 Othniel son of Kenaz, Caleb's **younger** brother, took it; so Caleb
3: 9 Othniel son of Kenaz, Caleb's **younger** brother, who saved them.
9: 5 But Jotham, the **youngest** son of Jerub-Baal, escaped by hiding.
1Sa 2: 19 Each year his mother made him a **little** robe and took it to him
5: 9 people of the city, both **young** and old, with an outbreak of tumors.
15: 17 Samuel said, "Although you were once **small** in your own eyes,
20: 2 father doesn't do anything, great or **small**, without confiding in me.
20: 35 the field for his meeting with David. He had a **small** boy with him,
22: 15 for your servant knows nothing **at all** [+196+1524] about this
25: 36 So she told him **nothing** [+1524+1821+2256+4202] until daybreak.
30: 2 captive the women and all who were in it, both **young** and old.
30: 19 **young** or old, boy or girl, plunder or anything else they had taken.
1Ki 3: 7 I am only a **little** child and do not know how to carry out my
8: 64 because the bronze altar before the LORD was too **small** to hold
22: 31 not fight with anyone, **small** or great, except the king of Israel."
2Ki 5: 14 his flesh was restored and became clean like that of a **young** boy.
23: 2 and the prophets—all the people from the **least** to the greatest.
25: 26 At this, all the people from the **least** to the greatest, together with
1Ch 25: 8 **Young** and old alike, teacher as well as student, cast lots for their
26: 13 cast for each gate, according to their families, **young** and old alike.
2Ch 15: 13 were to be put to death, whether **small** or great, man or woman.
18: 30 not fight with anyone, **small** or great, except the king of Israel."
21: 17 and wives. Not a son was left to him except Ahaziah, the **youngest**.
22: 1 Jehoram's **youngest** son, king in his place, since the raiders,
Job 3: 19 The **small** and the great are there, and the slave is freed from his
Isa 11: 6 and the yearling together; and a **little** child will lead them.
54: 7 "For a **brief** moment I abandoned you, but with deep compassion I
60: 22 The **least** of you will become a thousand, the smallest a mighty
Jer 8: 10 From the **least** to the greatest, all are greedy for gain; prophets
42: 1 and all the people from the **least** to the greatest approached
42: 8 were with him and all the people from the **least** to the greatest.
44: 12 From the **least** to the greatest, they will die by sword or famine.
49: 15 "Now I will make you **small** among the nations, despised among
Am 6: 11 smash the great house into pieces and the **small** house into bits.
7: 2 forgive! How can Jacob survive? He is so **small**!"
7: 5 I beg you, stop! How can Jacob survive? He is so **small**!"
Ob 1: 2 "See, I will make you **small** among the nations; you will be utterly

7786 קָטַף ***qāṭap***, v. [5]

break off [1], broke off [1], gathered [1], pick [1], uncut [+4202] [1]

Dt 23: 25 [23:26] [A] *you may* **pick** kernels with your hands,
Job 8: 12 [C] While still growing and **uncut** [+4202], they wither more
30: 4 [A] In the brush *they* **gathered** salt herbs, and their food was the
Eze 17: 4 [A] *he* **broke off** its topmost shoot and carried it away to a land
17: 22 [A] *I will* **break off** a tender sprig from its topmost shoots

7787 [1]קָטַר ***qāṭar[1]***, v.den. [114] [→ 5230, 5231, 5232, 5233, 7777, 7778, 7789, 7790, 7792, 7798]

burn [35], burn incense [18], burned incense [14], burned [12], burning incense [11], burned sacrifices [4], burn sacrifices [3], burned up [+7787] [2], make offerings [2], *untranslated* [1], be burned [1], burn offerings [1], burning [1], burns incense [1], make offering [1], offer sacrifices [1], offer [1], offered up [1], perfumed [1], present [1], presented offerings [1], presenting [1]

Ex 29: 13 [G] kidneys with the fat on them, and **burn** them on the altar.
29: 18 [G] **burn** the entire ram on the altar. It is a burnt offering to the
29: 25 [G] **burn** them on the altar along with the burnt offering for a
30: 7 [G] "Aaron *must* **burn** fragrant incense on the altar every
30: 7 [G] on the altar every morning when he tends the lamps. **[RPH]**
30: 8 [G] *He must* **burn** incense again when he lights the lamps at
30: 20 [G] when they approach the altar to minister by **presenting** an
40: 27 [G] **burned** fragrant incense on it, as the LORD commanded
Lev 1: 9 [G] legs with water, and the priest *is to* **burn** all of it on the altar.
1: 13 [G] and the priest is to bring all of it and **burn** it on the altar.
1: 15 [G] it to the altar, wring off the head and **burn** it on the altar;
1: 17 [G] the priest *shall* **burn** it on the wood that is on the fire on the
2: 2 [G] **burn** this as a memorial portion on the altar, an offering
2: 9 [G] and **burn** it on the altar as an offering made by fire,
2: 11 [G] for *you are* not *to* **burn** any yeast or honey in an offering
2: 16 [G] The priest *shall* **burn** the memorial portion of the crushed
3: 5 [G] Aaron's sons *are to* **burn** it on the altar on top of the burnt
3: 11 [G] The priest *shall* **burn** them on the altar as food, an offering
3: 16 [G] The priest *shall* **burn** them on the altar as food, an offering
4: 10 [G] the priest *shall* **burn** them on the altar of burnt offering.

Lev 4:19 [G] He shall remove all the fat from it and **burn** it on the altar,
4:26 [G] *He shall* **burn** all the fat on the altar as he burned the fat of
4:31 [G] the priest *shall* **burn** it on the altar as an aroma pleasing to
4:35 [G] the priest *shall* **burn** it on the altar on top of the offerings
5:12 [G] **burn** it on the altar on top of the offerings made to the
6:12 [6:5] [G] and **burn** the fat of the fellowship offerings on it.
6:15 [6:8] [G] **burn** the memorial portion on the altar as an aroma
6:22 [6:15] [H] regular share and *is to* **be burned** completely.
7:5 [G] The priest *shall* **burn** them on the altar as an offering made
7:31 [G] The priest *shall* **burn** the fat on the altar, but the breast
8:16 [G] and both kidneys and their fat, and **burned** it on the altar.
8:20 [G] ram into pieces and **burned** the head, the pieces and the fat.
8:21 [G] and **burned** the whole ram on the altar as a burnt offering,
8:28 [G] **burned** them on the altar on top of the burnt offering as an
9:10 [G] On the altar *he* **burned** the fat, the kidneys and the covering
9:13 [G] including the head, and *he* **burned** them on the altar.
9:14 [G] and **burned** them on top of the burnt offering on the altar.
9:17 [G] **burned** it on the altar in addition to the morning's burnt
9:20 [G] on the breasts, and then Aaron **burned** the fat on the altar.
16:25 [G] *He shall* also **burn** the fat of the sin offering on the altar.
17:6 [G] and **burn** the fat as an aroma pleasing to the LORD.
Nu 5:26 [G] offering as a memorial offering and **burn** it on the altar;
16:40 [17:5] [G] should come to **burn** incense before the LORD,
18:17 [G] on the altar and **burn** their fat as an offering made by fire,
1Sa 2:15 [G] even before the fat *was* **burned**, the servant of the priest
2:16 [G] "*Let* the fat *be* **burned** [+7787] **up** first, and then take
2:16 [D] "*Let* the fat *be* **burned up** [+7787] first, and then take
2:28 [G] to go up to my altar, to **burn** incense, and to wear an ephod
1Ki 3:3 [G] he offered sacrifices and **burned incense** on the high places.
9:25 [G] **burning incense** before the LORD along with them, and
11:8 [G] *who* **burned incense** and offered sacrifices to their gods.
12:33 [G] for the Israelites and went up to the altar to **make offerings**.
13:1 [G] as Jeroboam was standing by the altar to **make** *an* **offering**.
13:2 [G] the priests of the high places who now **make offerings** here,
22:43 [22:44] [D] to offer sacrifices and **burn incense** there.
2Ki 12:3 [12:4] [D] continued to offer sacrifices and **burn incense** there.
14:4 [D] people continued to offer sacrifices and **burn incense** there.
15:4 [D] people continued to offer sacrifices and **burn incense** there.
15:35 [D] people continued to offer sacrifices and **burn incense** there.
16:4 [D] He offered sacrifices and **burned incense** at the high places,
16:13 [G] *He* **offered up** his burnt offering and grain offering, poured
16:15 [G] **offer** the morning burnt offering and the evening grain
17:11 [D] At every high place *they* **burned incense**, as the nations
18:4 [D] for up to that time the Israelites had been **burning incense** to
22:17 [D] they have forsaken me and **burned incense** to other gods
23:5 [D] *to* **burn incense** on the high places of the towns of Judah
23:5 [D] those *who* **burned incense** to Baal, to the sun and moon, to
23:8 [D] Geba to Beersheba, where the priests *had* **burned incense**.
1Ch 6:49 [6:34] [G] *ones who* **presented offerings** on the altar of burnt
23:13 [G] to **offer sacrifices** before the LORD, to minister before him
2Ch 2:4 [2:3] [G] to dedicate it to him for **burning** fragrant incense
2:6 [2:5] [G] except as a place to **burn sacrifices** before him?
13:11 [G] Every morning and evening *they* **present** burnt offerings
25:14 [D] bowed down to them and **burned sacrifices** to them.
26:16 [G] entered the temple of the LORD to **burn incense** on the
26:18 [G] is not right for you, Uzziah, to **burn incense** to the LORD.
26:18 [G] of Aaron, who have been consecrated to **burn incense**.
26:19 [G] Uzziah, who had a censer in his hand *ready* to **burn incense**,
28:3 [G] He **burned sacrifices** in the Valley of Ben Hinnom and
28:4 [D] He offered sacrifices and **burned incense** at the high places,
28:25 [D] in Judah he built high places to **burn sacrifices** to other gods
29:7 [G] *They did* not **burn** incense or present any burnt offerings at
29:11 [G] and serve him, to minister before him and *to* **burn incense**."
32:12 [G] must worship before one altar and **burn sacrifices** on it'?
34:25 [D] they have forsaken me and **burned incense** to other gods
SS 3:6 [E] **perfumed** *with* myrrh and incense made from all the spices
Isa 65:3 [D] sacrifices in gardens and **burning incense** on altars of brick;
65:7 [D] "Because *they* **burned sacrifices** on the mountains
Jer 1:16 [D] *in* **burning incense** to other gods and in worshiping what
7:9 [D] **burn incense** to Baal and follow other gods you have not
11:12 [D] will go and cry out to the gods to whom they **burn incense**,
11:13 [D] the altars you have set up to **burn incense** to that shameful
11:17 [D] and provoked me to anger by **burning incense** to Baal.
18:15 [D] *they* **burn incense** to worthless idols, which made them
19:4 [D] *they have* **burned sacrifices** in it to gods that neither they
19:13 [D] all the houses where *they* **burned incense** on the roofs to all
32:29 [D] me to anger by **burning incense** on the roofs to Baal
33:18 [G] *to* **burn** grain offerings and to present sacrifices.' "
44:3 [D] They provoked me to anger by **burning incense** and by
44:5 [D] from their wickedness or stop **burning incense** to other gods.
44:8 [D] **burning incense** to other gods in Egypt, where you have
44:15 [D] all the men who knew that their wives *were* **burning incense**
44:17 [D] We *will* **burn incense** to the Queen of Heaven and will pour
44:18 [D] ever since we stopped **burning incense** to the Queen of
44:19 [D] "When we **burned incense** to the Queen of Heaven
44:21 [D] and think about the incense **burned** in the towns of Judah
44:23 [D] Because *you have* **burned incense** and have sinned against
44:25 [D] will certainly carry out the vows we made to **burn incense**
48:35 [G] offerings on the high places and **burn incense** to their gods,"
Hos 2:13 [2:15] [G] I will punish her for the days *she* **burned incense** to
4:13 [D] on the mountaintops and **burn offerings** on the hills,
11:2 [D] sacrificed to the Baals and *they* **burned incense** to images.
Am 4:5 [D] **Burn** leavened bread as a thank offering and brag about your
Hab 1:16 [D] he sacrifices to his net and **burns incense** to his dragnet,

7788 ²קָטַר **qāṭar²**, v. [1] [√ 7791]

enclosed [1]

Eze 46:22 [B] In the four corners of the outer court were **enclosed** courts,

7789 קִטֵּר **qiṭṭēr**, n.f. [1] [√ 7787]

incense [1]

Jer 44:21 and think about the **incense** burned in the towns of Judah

7790 קִטְרוֹן **qiṭrôn**, n.pr.loc. [1] [√ 7787]

Kitron [1]

Jdg 1:30 Neither did Zebulun drive out the Canaanites living in **Kitron**

7791 קְטֻרוֹת **qᵉṭurôt**, n.[f.pl.] Not used in NIV/BHS [√ 7788]

7792 קְטֹרֶת **qᵉṭōret**, n.f. [60] [√ 7787]

incense [59], offering [1]

Ex 25:6 the light; spices for the anointing oil and for the fragrant **incense**;
30:1 "Make an altar of acacia wood for burning **incense**.
30:7 "Aaron must burn fragrant **incense** on the altar every morning
30:8 so **incense** will burn regularly before the LORD for the
30:9 Do not offer on this altar any other **incense** or any burnt offering
30:27 its articles, the lampstand and its accessories, the altar of **incense**,
30:35 and make a fragrant blend of **incense**, the work of a perfumer.
30:37 Do not make any **incense** with this formula for yourselves;
31:8 the pure gold lampstand and all its accessories, the altar of **incense**,
31:11 and the anointing oil and fragrant **incense** for the Holy Place.
35:8 the light; spices for the anointing oil and for the fragrant **incense**;
35:15 the altar of **incense** with its poles, the anointing oil and the fragrant
35:15 of incense with its poles, the anointing oil and the fragrant **incense**;
35:28 for the light and for the anointing oil and for the fragrant **incense**.
37:25 They made the altar of **incense** out of acacia wood. It was square,
37:29 also made the sacred anointing oil and the pure, fragrant **incense**—
39:38 the gold altar, the anointing oil, the fragrant **incense**, and the
40:5 Place the gold altar of **incense** in front of the ark of the Testimony
40:27 and burned fragrant **incense** on it, as the LORD commanded him.
Lev 4:7 put some of the blood on the horns of the altar of fragrant **incense**
10:1 and Abihu took their censers, put fire in them and added **incense**;
16:12 two handfuls of finely ground fragrant **incense** and take them
16:13 He is to put the **incense** on the fire before the LORD,
16:13 the smoke of the **incense** will conceal the atonement cover above
Nu 4:16 the fragrant **incense**, the regular grain offering and the anointing
7:14 one gold dish weighing ten shekels, filled with **incense**;
7:20 one gold dish weighing ten shekels, filled with **incense**;
7:26 one gold dish weighing ten shekels, filled with **incense**;
7:32 one gold dish weighing ten shekels, filled with **incense**;
7:38 one gold dish weighing ten shekels, filled with **incense**;
7:44 one gold dish weighing ten shekels, filled with **incense**;
7:50 one gold dish weighing ten shekels, filled with **incense**;
7:56 one gold dish weighing ten shekels, filled with **incense**;
7:62 one gold dish weighing ten shekels, filled with **incense**;
7:68 one gold dish weighing ten shekels, filled with **incense**;
7:74 one gold dish weighing ten shekels, filled with **incense**;
7:80 one gold dish weighing ten shekels, filled with **incense**;
7:86 The twelve gold dishes filled with **incense** weighed ten shekels
16:7 and tomorrow put fire and **incense** in them before the LORD.
16:17 Each man is to take his censer and put **incense** in it—250 censers
16:18 put fire and **incense** in it, and stood with Moses and Aaron at the
16:35 and consumed the 250 men who were offering the **incense**.
16:40 [17:5] of Aaron should come to burn **incense** before the LORD,
16:46 [17:11] said to Aaron, "Take your censer and put **incense** in it,
16:47 [17:12] Aaron offered the **incense** and made atonement for them.
1Sa 2:28 to go up to my altar, to burn **incense**, and to wear an ephod in my
1Ch 6:49 [6:34] on the altar of **incense** in connection with all that was done
28:18 and the weight of the refined gold for the altar of **incense**.
2Ch 2:4 [2:3] to dedicate it to him for burning fragrant **incense** before
13:11 they present burnt offerings and fragrant **incense** to the LORD.
26:16 the temple of the LORD to burn incense on the altar of **incense**.
26:19 in their presence before the **incense** altar in the LORD's temple,
29:7 They did not burn **incense** or present any burnt offerings at the
Ps 66:15 I will sacrifice fat animals to you and an **offering** *of* rams;

Ps 141: 2 May my prayer be set before you like **incense**; may the lifting up
Pr 27: 9 Perfume and **incense** bring joy to the heart, and the pleasantness of
Isa 1: 13 Your **incense** is detestable to me. New Moons, Sabbaths
Eze 8: 11 a censer in his hand, and a fragrant cloud of **incense** was rising.
16: 18 to put on them, and you offered my oil and **incense** before them.
23: 41 with a table spread before it on which you had placed the **incense**

7793 קַטָּת qaṭṭāt, n.pr.loc. [1]

Kattath [1]

Jos 19: 15 Included were **Kattath**, Nahalal, Shimron, Idalah and Bethlehem.

7794 ¹קִיא qî¹, v. [9] [→ 7683, 7795; cf. 7796]

vomit out [2], vomit [2], vomited out [2], spit out [1], vomit up [1], vomited [1]

Lev 18: 25 [G] it for its sin, and the land **vomited out** its inhabitants.
18: 28 [G] it *will* **vomit** you **out** as it vomited out the nations that were
18: 28 [A] it will vomit you out as *it* **vomited out** the nations that were
20: 22 [G] land where I am bringing you to live *may* not **vomit** you **out**.
Job 20: 15 [G] *He will* **spit out** the riches he swallowed; God will make his
Pr 23: 8 [G] *You will* **vomit up** the little you have eaten and will have
25: 16 [G] eat just enough—too much of it, and *you will* **vomit**.
Jer 25: 27 [A] Drink, get drunk and **vomit**, and fall to rise no more
Jnh 2: 10 [2:11] [G] the fish, and *it* **vomited** Jonah onto dry land.

7795 ²קִיא qî², n.m. [3] [√ 7794]

vomit [3]

Isa 19: 14 in all that she does, as a drunkard staggers around in his **vomit**.
28: 8 All the tables are covered with **vomit** and there is not a spot
Jer 48: 26 Let Moab wallow in her **vomit**; let her be an object of ridicule.

7796 קָיָה qāyâ, v. Not used in NIV/BHS [cf. 7794]

7797 קַיִט qayiṭ, n.m. [1] [cf. 7811; Ar 10627]

summer [1]

Da 2: 35 and became like chaff on a threshing floor in the **summer**.

7798 קִיטוֹר qîṭôr, n.m. [4] [√ 7787]

smoke [2], clouds [1], dense smoke [1]

Ge 19: 28 he saw **dense smoke** rising *from* the land, like smoke from a
19: 28 saw dense smoke rising from the land, like **smoke** *from* a furnace.
Ps 119: 83 Though I am like a wineskin in the **smoke**, I do not forget your
148: 8 lightning and hail, snow and **clouds**, stormy winds that do his

7799 קִים qîm, n.m. [1] [√ 7756]

foes [1]

Job 22: 20 'Surely our **foes** are destroyed, and fire devours their wealth.'

7800 קִימָה qîmâ, n.f. [1] [√ 7756]

standing [1]

La 3: 63 Look at them! Sitting or **standing**, they mock me in their songs.

7801 קִין qîn, v.den. [8] [→ 7806; cf. 7759]

chant [3], composed laments [1], sang lament [1], take up a lament [1], took up lament [+906+7806] [1], wailing [1]

2Sa 1: 17 [D] David **took up** this **lament** [+906+7806] concerning Saul
3: 33 [D] The king **sang** *this* **lament** for Abner: "Should Abner have
2Ch 35: 25 [D] Jeremiah **composed laments** for Josiah, and to this day all
Jer 9: 17 [9:16] [D] Call for the **wailing** *women* to come; send for the
Eze 27: 32 [D] mourn over you, *they will* **take up a lament** concerning you:
32: 16 [D] "This is the lament *they will* **chant** *for* her. The daughters of
32: 16 [D] The daughters of the nations *will* **chant** it; for Egypt and all
32: 16 [D] for Egypt and all her hordes *they will* **chant** it,

7802 ¹קַיִן qayin¹, n.[m.]. [1]

spearhead [1]

2Sa 21: 16 whose bronze **spearhead** weighed three hundred shekels and who

7803 ²קַיִן qayin², n.pr.m. [16] [→ 7804?, 7808, 7809, 9340; cf. 7864, 7865]

Cain [16]

Ge 4: 1 his wife Eve, and she became pregnant and gave birth to **Cain**.
4: 2 his brother Abel. Now Abel kept flocks, and **Cain** worked the soil.
4: 3 In the course of time **Cain** brought some of the fruits of the soil as
4: 5 on **Cain** and his offering he did not look with favor. So Cain was
4: 5 with favor. So **Cain** was very angry, and his face was downcast.
4: 6 the LORD said to **Cain**, "Why are you angry? Why is your face
4: 8 Now **Cain** said to his brother Abel, "Let's go out to the field."
4: 8 were in the field, **Cain** attacked his brother Abel and killed him.
4: 9 Then the LORD said to **Cain**, "Where is your brother Abel?"
4: 13 **Cain** said to the LORD, "My punishment is more than I can bear.
4: 15 if anyone kills **Cain**, he will suffer vengeance seven times over."
4: 15 the LORD put a mark on **Cain** so that no one who found him
4: 16 So **Cain** went out from the LORD's presence and lived in the
4: 17 **Cain** lay with his wife, and she became pregnant and gave birth to
4: 24 If **Cain** is avenged seven times, then Lamech seventy-seven
4: 25 granted me another child in place of Abel, since **Cain** killed him."

7804 ³קַיִן qayin³, n.pr.g. [2] [→ 7808, 7803?]

Kenites [2]

Nu 24: 22 yet you **Kenites** will be destroyed when Asshur takes you captive."
Jdg 4: 11 Now Heber the Kenite had left the other **Kenites**, the descendants

7805 ⁴קַיִן qayin⁴, n.pr.loc. [1] [√ 7803]

Kain [1]

Jos 15: 57 **Kain**, Gibeah and Timnah—ten towns and their villages.

7806 ¹קִינָה qînâ¹, n.f. [18] [√ 7801]

lament [13], laments [2], mourn [+5951] [1], took up lament [+906+7801] [1], weeping [1]

2Sa 1: 17 David **took up** this **lament** [+906+7801] concerning Saul
2Ch 35: 25 the men and women singers commemorate Josiah in the **laments**.
35: 25 These became a tradition in Israel and are written in the **Laments**.
Jer 7: 29 take up a **lament** on the barren heights, for the LORD has
9: 10 [9:9] and take up a **lament** concerning the desert pastures.
9: 20 [9:19] your daughters how to wail; teach one another a **lament**.
Eze 2: 10 On both sides of it were written words of **lament** and mourning
19: "Take up a **lament** concerning the princes of Israel
19: 14 a ruler's scepter.' This is a **lament** and is to be used as a lament."
19: 14 a ruler's scepter.' This is a lament and is to be used as a **lament**."
26: 17 Then they will take up a **lament** concerning you and say to you:
27: 2 "Son of man, take up a **lament** concerning Tyre.
27: 32 As they wail and **mourn** [+5951] over you, they will take up a
28: 12 take up a **lament** concerning the king of Tyre and say to him:
32: 2 take up a **lament** concerning Pharaoh king of Egypt and say to
32: 16 "This is the **lament** they will chant for her. The daughters of the
Am 5: 1 this word, O house of Israel, this **lament** I take up concerning you:
8: 10 religious feasts into mourning and all your singing into **weeping**.

7807 ²קִינָה qînâ², n.pr.loc. [1]

Kinah [1]

Jos 15: 22 **Kinah**, Dimonah, Adadah,

7808 קֵינִי qênî, a.g. [12] [√ 7804; cf. 7803]

Kenites [7], Kenite [5]

Ge 15: 19 the land of the **Kenites**, Kenizzites, Kadmonites,
Nu 24: 21 he saw the **Kenites** and uttered his oracle: "Your dwelling place is
Jdg 1: 16 The descendants of Moses' father-in-law, the **Kenite**, went up from
4: 11 Now Heber the **Kenite** had left the other Kenites, the descendants
4: 17 fled on foot to the tent of Jael, the wife of Heber the **Kenite**,
4: 17 between Jabin king of Hazor and the clan of Heber the **Kenite**.
5: 24 "Most blessed of women be Jael, the wife of Heber the **Kenite**,
1Sa 15: 6 Then he said to the **Kenites**, "Go away, leave the Amalekites
15: 6 out of Egypt." So the **Kenites** moved away from the Amalekites.
27: 10 the Negev of Jerahmeel" or "Against the Negev of the **Kenites**."
30: 29 to those in the towns of the Jerahmeelites and the **Kenites**;
1Ch 2: 55 These are the **Kenites** who came from Hammath, the father of the

7809 קֵינָן qênān, n.pr.m. [6] [√ 7803]

Kenan [6]

Ge 5: 9 When Enosh had lived 90 years, he became the father of **Kenan**.
5: 10 And after he became the father of **Kenan**, Enosh lived 815 years
5: 12 When **Kenan** had lived 70 years, he became the father of
5: 13 **Kenan** lived 840 years and had other sons and daughters.
5: 14 Altogether, **Kenan** lived 910 years, and then he died.
1Ch 1: 2 **Kenan**, Mahalalel, Jared,

7810 קִיץ qîṣ, v. [23] [→ 7811; cf. 3699]

awake [7], wake up [4], awakens [2], rouse [2], all summer [1], awakened [1], awakes [1], awoke [1], come to life [1], rise [1], roused [1], wake [1]

1Sa 26: 12 [G] No one saw or knew about it, nor *did anyone* **wake up**.
2Ki 4: 31 [G] to meet Elisha and told him, "The boy *has* not **awakened**."
Job 14: 12 [G] no more, men *will* not **awake** or be roused from their sleep.
Ps 3: 5 [3:6] [G] *I* **wake** again, because the LORD sustains me.
17: 15 [G] when I **awake**, I will be satisfied with seeing your likeness.

Ps 35: 23 [G] Awake, and **rise** to my defense! Contend for me, my God
44: 23 [44:24] [G] O Lord! Why do you sleep? **Rouse** *yourself*!
59: 5 [59:6] [G] of Israel, **rouse** yourself to punish all the nations;
73: 20 [G] As a dream when *one* **awakes**, so when you arise, O Lord,
139: 18 [G] the grains of sand. *When I* **awake**, I am still with you.
Pr 6: 22 [G] watch over you; when *you* **awake**, they will speak to you.
23: 35 [G] feel it! When *will I* **wake up** so I can find another drink?"
Isa 18: 6 [A] the birds *will* feed on them **all summer**, the wild animals all
26: 19 [G] You who dwell in the dust, **wake up** and shout for joy.
29: 8 [G] that he is eating, but *he* **awakens**, and his hunger remains;
29: 8 [G] is drinking, but *he* **awakens** faint, with his thirst unquenched.
Jer 31: 26 [G] At this *I* **awoke** and looked around. My sleep had been
51: 39 [G] then sleep forever and not **awake**," declares the LORD.
51: 57 [G] they will sleep forever and not **awake**," declares the King,
Eze 7: 6 [G] end has come! *It has* **roused** *itself* against you. It has come!
Da 12: 2 [G] Multitudes who sleep in the dust of the earth *will* **awake**:
Joel 1: 5 [G] **Wake up**, you drunkards, and weep! Wail, all you drinkers
Hab 2: 19 [G] Woe to him who says to wood, '**Come to life**!' Or to lifeless

7811 קַ֫יִץ *qayiṣ*, n.m. [20] [√ 7810; cf. 7797; Ar 10627]

summer [10], summer fruit [3], ripe fruit [2], ripened fruit [2], cakes of figs [1], fruit [1], harvest [1]

Ge 8: 22 and heat, **summer** and winter, day and night will never cease."
2Sa 16: 1 cakes of raisins, a hundred **cakes of figs** and a skin of wine.
16: 2 household to ride on, the bread and **fruit** are for the men to eat,
Ps 32: 4 heavy upon me; my strength was sapped as in the heat of **summer**.
74: 17 all the boundaries of the earth; you made both **summer** and winter.
Pr 6: 8 yet it stores its provisions in **summer** and gathers its food at
10: 5 He who gathers crops in **summer** is a wise son, but he who sleeps
26: 1 Like snow in **summer** or rain in harvest, honor is not fitting for a
30: 25 of little strength, yet they store up their food in the **summer**;
Isa 16: 9 The shouts of joy over your **ripened fruit** and over your harvests
28: 4 the head of a fertile valley, will be like a fig ripe before **harvest**—
Jer 8: 20 "The harvest is past, the **summer** has ended, and we are not
40: 10 you are to harvest the wine, **summer fruit** and oil, and put them in
40: 12 And they harvested an abundance of wine and **summer fruit**.
48: 32 The destroyer has fallen on your **ripened fruit** and grapes.
Am 3: 15 I will tear down the winter house along with the **summer** house;
8: 1 is what the Sovereign LORD showed me: a basket of **ripe fruit**.
8: 2 you see, Amos?" he asked. "A basket of **ripe fruit**," I answered.
Mic 7: 1 I am like one who gathers **summer fruit** at the gleaning of the
Zec 14: 8 eastern sea and half to the western sea, in **summer** and in winter.

7812 קִיצוֹן *qîṣôn*, a. [4] [√ 7891]

end [4]

Ex 26: 4 in one set, and do the same with the **end** curtain in the other set.
26: 10 Make fifty loops along the edge of the **end** curtain in one set
36: 11 and the same was done with the **end** curtain in the other set.
36: 17 they made fifty loops along the edge of the **end** curtain in one set

7813 קִיקָיוֹן *qîqāyôn*, n.m. [5]

vine [5]

Jnh 4: 6 the LORD God provided a **vine** and made it grow up over Jonah
4: 6 to ease his discomfort, and Jonah was very happy about the **vine**.
4: 7 God provided a worm, which chewed the **vine** so that it withered.
4: 9 said to Jonah, "Do you have a right to be angry about the **vine**?"
4: 10 But the LORD said, "You have been concerned about this **vine**,

7814 קִיקָלוֹן *qîqālôn*, n.[m.]. [1] [√ 7837]

disgrace [1]

Hab 2: 16 hand is coming around to you, and **disgrace** will cover your glory.

7815 קִיר¹ *qîr*¹, n.m. [74 / 75] [→ 7816, 7817; cf. 7984; *also used with compound proper names*]

wall [38], walls [16], every last male [+928+8874] [3], male [+928+8874] [3], sides [3], *untranslated* [2], ceiling [2], side [2], agony [1], city [1], it[s] [+2021] [1], roof [1], stonemasons [+3093] [1], stonemasons [+74+3093] [1]

Ex 30: 3 Overlay the top and all the **sides** and the horns with pure gold,
37: 26 They overlaid the top and all the **sides** and the horns with pure
Lev 1: 15 it on the altar; its blood shall be drained out on the **side** *of* the altar.
5: 9 some of the blood of the sin offering against the **side** *of* the altar;
14: 37 He is to examine the mildew on the **walls**, and if it has greenish
14: 37 depressions that appear to be deeper than the surface of the **wall**,
14: 39 return to inspect the house. If the mildew has spread on the **walls**,
Nu 22: 25 she pressed close to the **wall**, crushing Balaam's foot against it.
22: 25 close to the wall, crushing Balaam's foot against **it**[s] [+2021].
35: 4 the Levites will extend out fifteen hundred feet from the town **wall**.
Jos 2: 15 the window, for the house she lived in was part of the **city** wall.
1Sa 18: 11 and he hurled it, saying to himself, "I'll pin David to the **wall**."
19: 10 Saul tried to pin him to the **wall** with his spear, but David eluded
19: 10 but David eluded him as Saul drove the spear into the **wall**.
20: 25 He sat in his customary place by the **wall**, opposite Jonathan,
25: 22 if by morning I leave alive *one* **male** [+928+8874] of all who
25: 34 not *one* **male** [+928+8874] belonging to Nabal would have been
2Sa 5: 11 with cedar logs and carpenters and **stonemasons** [+74+3093],
1Ki 4: 33 [5:13] the cedar of Lebanon to the hyssop that grows out of **walls**.
6: 5 Against the **walls** of the main hall and inner sanctuary he built a
6: 5 inner sanctuary he built a structure around **[RPH]** the building,
6: 6 the temple so that nothing would be inserted into the temple **walls**.
6: 15 He lined its interior **walls** with cedar boards, paneling them from
6: 15 paneling them from the floor of the temple to **[RPH]** the ceiling,
6: 16 from floor to **ceiling** to form within the temple an inner sanctuary,
6: 27 The wing of one cherub touched one **wall**, while the wing of the
6: 27 one wall, while the wing of the other touched the other **wall**,
6: 29 On the **walls** all around the temple, in both the inner and outer
7: 7 and he covered it with cedar from floor to **ceiling**. [BHS 7977]
14: 10 I will cut off from Jeroboam **every last male** [+928+8874] in
16: 11 He did not spare a *single* **male** [+928+8874], whether relative
21: 21 and cut off from Ahab **every last male** [+928+8874] in Israel—
2Ki 4: 10 Let's make a small room on the **roof** and put in it a bed and a table,
9: 8 I will cut off from Ahab **every last male** [+928+8874] in Israel—
9: 33 some of her blood spattered the **wall** and the horses as they
20: 2 Hezekiah turned his face to the **wall** and prayed to the LORD,
1Ch 14: 1 **stonemasons** [+3093] and carpenters to build a palace for him.
29: 4 of refined silver, for the overlaying of the **walls** *of* the buildings,
2Ch 3: 7 doorframes, **walls** and doors of the temple with gold,
3: 7 of the temple with gold, and he carved cherubim on the **walls**.
3: 11 the first cherub was five cubits long and touched the temple **wall**,
3: 12 cherub was five cubits long and touched the other temple **wall**,
Ps 62: 3 [62:4] throw him down—this leaning **wall**, this tottering fence?
Isa 22: 5 a day of battering down **walls** and of crying out to the mountains.
25: 4 For the breath of the ruthless is like a storm driving against a **wall**
38: 2 Hezekiah turned his face to the **wall** and prayed to the LORD,
59: 10 Like the blind we grope along the **wall**, feeling our way like men
Jer 4: 19 my anguish! I writhe in pain. Oh, the **agony** *of* my heart!
Eze 4: 3 place it as an iron **wall** between you and the city and turn your face
8: 7 to the entrance to the court. I looked, and I saw a hole in the **wall**.
8: 8 He said to me, "Son of man, now dig into the **wall**." So I dug into
8: 8 dig into the wall." So I dug into the **wall** and saw a doorway there.
8: 10 and I saw portrayed all over the **walls** all kinds of crawling things
12: 5 dig through the **wall** and take your belongings out through it.
12: 7 Then in the evening I dug through the **wall** with my hands.
12: 12 and leave, and a hole will be dug in the **wall** for him to go through.
13: 12 When the **wall** collapses, will people not ask you, "Where is the
13: 14 I will tear down the **wall** you have covered with whitewash
13: 15 So I will spend my wrath against the **wall** and against those who
13: 15 say to you, "The **wall** is gone and so are those who whitewashed it,
23: 14 She saw men portrayed on a **wall**, figures of Chaldeans portrayed
33: 30 your countrymen are talking together about you by the **walls**
41: 5 Then he measured the **wall** *of* the temple; it was six cubits thick,
41: 6 There were ledges all around the **wall** of the temple to serve as
41: 6 so that the supports were not inserted into the **wall** *of* the temple.
41: 9 The outer **wall** of the side rooms was five cubits thick. The open
41: 12 The **wall** *of* the building was five cubits thick all around, and its
41: 13 and the building with its **walls** were also a hundred cubits long.
41: 17 on the **walls** at regular intervals all around the inner and outer
41: 20 and palm trees were carved on the **wall** *of* the outer sanctuary.
41: 22 two cubits square; its corners, its base and its **sides** were of wood.
41: 25 carved cherubim and palm trees like those carved on the **walls**,
43: 8 beside my doorposts, with only a **wall** between me and them,
Am 5: 19 and rested his hand on the **wall** only to have a snake bite him.
Hab 2: 11 The stones of the **wall** will cry out, and the beams of the

7816 קִיר² *qîr*², n.pr.loc. [1] [√ 7815]

Kir [1]

Isa 15: 1 destroyed in a night! **Kir** *in* Moab is ruined, destroyed in a night!

7817 קִיר³ *qîr*³, n.pr.loc. [4] [√ 7815]

Kir [4]

2Ki 16: 9 He deported its inhabitants to **Kir** and put Rezin to death.
Isa 22: 6 with her charioteers and horses; **Kir** uncovers the shield.
Am 1: 5 The people of Aram will go into exile to **Kir**," says the LORD.
9: 7 the Philistines from Caphtor and the Arameans from **Kir**?

7818 קִיר־חֶ֫רֶשׂ *qîr-ḥereś*, n.pr.loc. [3] [√ 7815 + 3084]

Kir Hareseth [3]

Isa 16: 11 laments for Moab like a harp, my inmost being for **Kir Hareseth**.
Jer 48: 31 for all Moab I cry out, I moan for the men of **Kir Hareseth**.
48: 36 like a flute; it laments like a flute for the men of **Kir Hareseth**.

7819 קִיר חֲרֶשֶׂת qîr ḥ^a reśet, n.pr.loc. [2] [√ 7815 + 3084]

Kir Hareseth [2]

2Ki 3:25 Only **Kir Hareseth** was left with its stones in place, but men
Isa 16: 7 for Moab. Lament and grieve for the men of **Kir Hareseth**.

7820 קֵרֹס qêrōs, n.pr.m. [2]

Keros [2]

Ezr 2:44 **Keros**, Siaha, Padon,
Ne 7:47 **Keros**, Sia, Padon,

7821 קִישׁ qîš, n.pr.m. [21]

Kish [21]

1Sa 9: 1 of standing, whose name was **Kish** son of Abiel, the son of Zeror,
9: 3 Now the donkeys belonging to Saul's father **Kish** were lost,
9: 3 and **Kish** said to his son Saul, "Take one of the servants with you
10:11 each other, "What is this that has happened to the son of **Kish**?
10:21 and Matri's clan was chosen. Finally Saul son of **Kish** was chosen.
14:51 Saul's father **Kish** and Abner's father Ner were sons of Abiel.
2Sa 21:14 of Saul and his son Jonathan in the tomb of Saul's father **Kish**,
1Ch 8:30 son was Abdon, followed by Zur, **Kish**, Baal, Ner, Nadab,
8:33 Ner was the father of **Kish**, Kish the father of Saul, and Saul the
8:33 Ner was the father of Kish, **Kish** the father of Saul, and Saul the
9:36 son was Abdon, followed by Zur, **Kish**, Baal, Ner, Nadab,
9:39 Ner was the father of **Kish**, Kish the father of Saul, and Saul the
9:39 Ner was the father of Kish, **Kish** the father of Saul, and Saul the
12: 1 while he was banished from the presence of Saul son of **Kish** (they
23:21 of Merari: Mahli and Mushi. The sons of Mahli: Eleazar and **Kish**.
23:22 had only daughters. Their cousins, the sons of **Kish**, married them.
24:29 From **Kish**: the son of Kish: Jerahmeel.
24:29 From Kish: the son of **Kish**: Jerahmeel.
26:28 everything dedicated by Samuel the seer and by Saul son of **Kish**,
2Ch 29:12 the Merarites, **Kish** son of Abdi and Azariah son of Jehallelel;
Est 2: 5 named Mordecai son of Jair, the son of Shimei, the son of **Kish**,

7822 קִישׁוֹן qîšôn, n.pr.loc. [6]

Kishon [6]

Jdg 4: 7 with his chariots and his troops to the **Kishon** River and give him
4:13 the men with him, from Harosheth Haggoyim to the **Kishon** River.
5:21 The river **Kishon** swept them away, the age-old river, the river
5:21 river Kishon swept them away, the age-old river, the river **Kishon**.
1Ki 18:40 Elijah had them brought down to the **Kishon** Valley
Ps 83: 9 [83:10] as you did to Sisera and Jabin at the river **Kishon**,

7823 קִישִׁי qîšî, n.pr.m. [1] [cf. 7773]

Kishi [1]

1Ch 6:44 [6:29] Ethan son of **Kishi**, the son of Abdi, the son of Malluch,

7824 קַל qal, a. [13] [√ 7837]

swift [7], fleet-footed [+928+8079] [2], foam [1], speedily [1], swifter [1], swiftly [1]

2Sa 2:18 Now Asahel was as **fleet-footed** [+928+8079] as a wild gazelle.
Job 24:18 "Yet they are **foam** on the surface of the water; their portion of the
Ecc 9:11 The race is not to the **swift** or the battle to the strong, nor does food
Isa 5:26 at the ends of the earth. Here they come, swiftly and **speedily**!
18: 2 Go, **swift** messengers, to a people tall and smooth-skinned,
19: 1 the LORD rides on a **swift** cloud and is coming to Egypt.
30:16 you will flee! You said, 'We will ride off on **swift** horses.'
Jer 2:23 you have done. You are a **swift** she-camel running here and there,
46: 6 "The **swift** cannot flee nor the strong escape. In the north by the
La 4:19 Our pursuers were **swifter** than eagles in the sky; they chased us
Joel 3: 4 [4:4] I will **swiftly** and speedily return on your own heads what
Am 2:14 The **swift** will not escape, the strong will not muster their strength,
2:15 the **fleet-footed** [+928+8079] soldier will not get away, and the

7825 קֹלִי qōl¹, n.[m.]. [1] [√ 7837]

little [1]

Jer 3: 9 Because Israel's immorality mattered so **little** to her, she defiled

7826 ²קֹל qōl², n.m. Not used in NIV/BHS [√ 7754]

7827 קָלָה qālah, v.den. [0] [√ 7736]

2Sa 20:14 [c] [the Berites, *who* **gathered** [K; see Q 7735] **together** and followed him.]

7828 ¹קָלָה qālâ¹, v. [4] [→ 7833]

burned [1], roasted grain [1], roasted [1], searing pain [1]

Lev 2:14 [B] offer crushed heads of new grain **roasted** in the fire.
Jos 5:11 [B] the produce of the land: unleavened bread and **roasted grain**.
Ps 38: 7 [38:8] [C] My back is filled with **searing pain**; there is no
Jer 29:22 [A] and Ahab, whom the king of Babylon **burned** in the fire.'

7829 ²קָלָה qālâ², v. [7] [→ 7830; cf. 7837]

base [1], be a nobody [1], be degraded [1], be despised [1], dishonors [1], little known [1], small [1]

Dt 25: 3 [C] more than that, your brother *will* **be degraded** in your eyes.
27:16 [G] "Cursed is the man *who* **dishonors** his father or his mother."
1Sa 18:23 [C] "*Do* you think *it is a* **small** *matter* to become the king's
18:23 [C] king's son-in-law? I'm only a poor man and **little known**."
Pr 12: 9 [C] Better *to* **be a nobody** and yet have a servant than pretend to
Isa 3: 5 [C] will rise up against the old, the **base** against the honorable.
16:14 [C] Moab's splendor and all her many people *will* **be despised**,

7830 קָלוֹן qālôn, n.m. [17] [√ 7829]

shame [9], disgrace [3], insult [2], disgraceful [1], insults [1], shameful ways [1]

Job 10:15 lift my head, for I am full of **shame** and drowned in my affliction.
Ps 83:16 [83:17] Cover their faces with **shame** so that men will seek your
Pr 3:35 The wise inherit honor, but fools he holds up to **shame**.
6:33 Blows and **disgrace** are his lot, and his shame will never be wiped
9: 7 "Whoever corrects a mocker invites **insult**; whoever rebukes a
11: 2 When pride comes, then comes **disgrace**, but with humility comes
12:16 his annoyance at once, but a prudent man overlooks an **insult**.
13:18 He who ignores discipline comes to poverty and **shame**,
18: 3 so does contempt, and with **shame** comes disgrace.
22:10 out the mocker, and out goes strife; quarrels and **insults** are ended.
Isa 22:18 chariots will remain—you **disgrace** *to* your master's house!
Jer 13:26 I will pull up your skirts over your face that your **shame** may be
46:12 The nations will hear of your **shame**; your cries will fill the earth.
Hos 4: 7 against me; they exchanged their Glory for *something* **disgraceful**.
4:18 continue their prostitution; their rulers dearly love **shameful ways**.
Na 3: 5 show the nations your nakedness and the kingdoms your **shame**.
Hab 2:16 You will be filled with **shame** instead of glory. Now it is your

7831 קַלַּחַת qallaḥat, n.f. [2]

caldron [1], pot [1]

1Sa 2:14 He would plunge it into the pan or kettle or **caldron** or pot,
Mic 3: 3 who chop them up like meat for the pan, like flesh for the **pot**?"

7832 קָלַט qālaṭ, v. [1] [→ 5236, 7836]

stunted [1]

Lev 22:23 [B] offering an ox or a sheep that is deformed or **stunted**,

7833 קָלִי qālî, n.m. [6 / 5] [√ 7828]

roasted grain [4], roasted [1]

Lev 23:14 You must not eat any bread, or **roasted** or new grain, until the very
Ru 2:14 sat down with the harvesters, he offered her *some* **roasted grain**.
1Sa 17:17 "Take this ephah of **roasted grain** and these ten loaves of bread
25:18 two skins of wine, five dressed sheep, five seahs of **roasted grain**,
2Sa 17:28 and barley, flour and **roasted grain**, beans and lentils,
17:28 and roasted grain, beans and lentils, [BHS+ *and roasted grain*]

7834 קַלַּי qallay, n.pr.m. [1]

Kallai [1]

Ne 12:20 of Sallu's, **Kallai**; of Amok's, Eber;

7835 קֵלָיָה qēlāyâ, n.pr.m. [1]

Kelaiah [1]

Ezr 10:23 Jozabad, Shimei, **Kelaiah** (that is, Kelita), Pethahiah, Judah

7836 קְלִיטָא q^e lîṭā', n.pr.m. [3] [√ 7832]

Kelita [3]

Ezr 10:23 Shimei, Kelaiah (that is, **Kelita**), Pethahiah, Judah and Eliezer.
Ne 8: 7 Maaseiah, **Kelita**, Azariah, Jozabad, Hanan and Pelaiah—
10:10 [10:11] Shebaniah, Hodiah, **Kelita**, Pelaiah, Hanan,

7837 קָלַל qālal, v. [81] [→ 7814, 7824, 7825, 7838, 7839, 7848; cf. 7829]

curse [12], cursed [8], curses [7], lighten [5], swifter [5], cursing [3], make lighter [3], blasphemer [2], not serious [2], receded [2], be considered accursed [1], become undignified [1], blaspheme [1], call a curse down [1], called curses down [1], called down a curse [1], called down curses [+7839] [1], cast lots [1], comes easily [1], considered trivial [1], despise [+928+6524] [1], despises [+928+6524] [1], disdained [1], easy [1], humble [1], humbled [1], is cursed [1], lift [1], made contemptible [1], pronounce a curse on [1], put a curse on [1], revile [1], simple [1], small [1], swaying [1], swift [1], treat with contempt [1], treated with contempt [1], trivial [1], unsharpened [+4202] [1], unworthy [1], vile [1]

Ge 8: 8 [A] he sent out a dove to see if the water *had* **receded** from the
8: 11 [A] Then Noah knew that the water *had* **receded** from the earth.
8: 21 [D] "Never again *will I* **curse** the ground because of man,
12: 3 [D] those who bless you, and *whoever* **curses** you I will curse;
16: 4 [A] *she began to* **despise** [+928+6524] her mistress.
16: 5 [A] she knows she is pregnant, she **despises** [+928+6524] *me*.
Ex 18: 22 [G] *That will* **make** your load **lighter**, because they will share it
21: 17 [D] "*Anyone who* **curses** his father or mother must be put to
22: 28 [22:27] [D] "*Do* not **blaspheme** God or curse the ruler of your
Lev 19: 14 [D] " '*Do* not **curse** the deaf or put a stumbling block in front of
20: 9 [D] " 'If anyone **curses** his father or mother, he must be put to
20: 9 [D] *He has* **cursed** his father or his mother, and his blood will be
24: 11 [D] of the Israelite woman blasphemed the Name with a **curse**;
24: 14 [D] "Take the **blasphemer** outside the camp. All those who
24: 15 [D] 'If anyone **curses** his God, he will be held responsible;
24: 23 [D] they took the **blasphemer** outside the camp and stoned him.
Dt 23: 4 [23:5] [D] in Aram Naharaim to **pronounce a curse on** you.
Jos 24: 9 [D] he sent for Balaam son of Beor to **put a curse on** you.
Jdg 9: 27 [D] they were eating and drinking, *they* **cursed** Abimelech.
1Sa 2: 30 [A] me I will honor, but those who despise me *will be* **disdained**.
3: 13 [D] his sons **made** themselves **contemptible**, and he failed to
6: 5 [G] Perhaps *he will* **lift** his hand from you and your gods
17: 43 [D] with sticks?" And the Philistine **cursed** David by his gods.
2Sa 1: 23 [A] *They were* **swifter** than eagles, they were stronger than
6: 22 [C] *I will* **become** even more **undignified** than this, and I will be
16: 5 [D] name was Shimei son of Gera, and *he* **cursed** as he came out.
16: 7 [D] As he **cursed**, Shimei said, "Get out, get out, you man of
16: 9 [D] the king, "Why *should* this dead dog **curse** my lord the king?
16: 10 [D] If *he is* **cursing** because the LORD said to him,
16: 10 [D] to him, '**Curse** David,' who can ask, 'Why do you do this?' "
16: 11 [D] him alone; *let* him **curse**, for the LORD has told him to.
16: 13 [D] **cursing** as he went and throwing stones at him
19: 21 [19:22] [D] death for this? *He* **cursed** the LORD's anointed."
19: 43 [19:44] [G] you have. So why *do you* **treat** us **with contempt**?
1Ki 2: 8 [D] who **called down** bitter **curses** [+7839] *on* me the day I went
12: 4 [G] now **lighten** the harsh labor and the heavy yoke he put on us,
12: 9 [G] who say to me, '**Lighten** the yoke your father put on us'?"
12: 10 [G] father put a heavy yoke on us, but **make** our yoke **lighter**'—
16: 31 [C] He not only **considered** *it* **trivial** to commit the sins of
2Ki 2: 24 [D] **called down a curse** *on* them in the name of the LORD.
3: 18 [C] This *is an* **easy** *thing* in the eyes of the LORD; he will also
20: 10 [C] "*It is a* **simple** *matter* for the shadow to go forward ten
2Ch 10: 4 [G] now **lighten** the harsh labor and the heavy yoke he put on us,
10: 9 [G] who say to me, '**Lighten** the yoke your father put on us'?"
10: 10 [G] father put a heavy yoke on us, but **make** our yoke **lighter**'—
Ne 13: 2 [D] but had hired Balaam to **call a curse down** *on* them.
13: 25 [D] I rebuked them and **called curses down** *on* them. I beat some
Job 3: 1 [D] Job opened his mouth and **cursed** the day of his birth.
7: 6 [A] "My days *are* **swifter** than a weaver's shuttle, and they come
9: 25 [A] "My days *are* **swifter** than a runner; they fly away without a
24: 18 [E] their portion of the land **is cursed**, so that no one goes to the
40: 4 [A] "*I am* **unworthy**—how can I reply to you? I put my hand
Ps 37: 22 [E] will inherit the land, but *those* he **curses** will be cut off.
62: 4 [62:5] [D] mouths they bless, but in their hearts *they* **curse**.
109: 28 [D] They *may* **curse**, but you will bless; when they attack they
Pr 14: 6 [C] finds none, but knowledge **comes easily** to the discerning.
20: 20 [D] If a *man* **curses** his father or mother, his lamp will be
30: 10 [D] to his master, or *he will* **curse** you, and you will pay for it.
30: 11 [D] "There are those *who* **curse** their fathers and do not bless
Ecc 7: 21 [D] people say, or you may hear your servant **cursing** you—
7: 22 [D] your heart that many times *you* yourself *have* **cursed** others.
10: 10 [D] If the ax is dull and its edge **unsharpened** [+4202], more
10: 20 [D] *Do* not **revile** the king even in your thoughts, or curse the
10: 20 [D] even in your thoughts, or **curse** the rich in your bedroom,
Isa 8: 21 [D] looking upward, *will* **curse** their king and their God.
9: 1 [8:23] [G] In the past *he* **humbled** the land of Zebulun and the
23: 9 [G] all glory and to **humble** all who are renowned on the earth.
30: 16 [C] off on swift horses.' Therefore your pursuers *will be* **swift**!
49: 6 [C] "*It is* too **small** *a thing for* you to be my servant to restore
65: 20 [E] he who fails to reach a hundred *will* **be considered accursed**.
Jer 4: 13 [A] come like a whirlwind, his horses *are* **swifter** than eagles.
4: 24 [F] and they were quaking; all the hills *were* **swaying**.
6: 14 [C] dress the wound of my people as though *it were* **not serious**.
8: 11 [C] dress the wound of my people as though *it were* **not serious**.
15: 10 [D] I have neither lent nor borrowed, yet everyone **curses** me.
Eze 8: 17 [C] *Is it a* **trivial** *matter* for the house of Judah to do the
21: 21 [21:26] [D] *He will* **cast lots** with arrows, he will consult his
22: 7 [G] In you *they have* **treated** father and mother **with contempt**;
Jnh 1: 5 [G] they threw the cargo into the sea to **lighten** the ship. But
Na 1: 14 [A] of your gods. I will prepare your grave, for *you are* **vile**."
Hab 1: 8 [A] Their horses *are* **swifter** than leopards, fiercer than wolves at

7838 קָלָל qālāl, a. [2] [√ 7837]

burnished [2]

Eze 1: 7 feet were like those of a calf and gleamed like **burnished** bronze.
Da 10: 6 his arms and legs like the gleam of **burnished** bronze,

7839 קְלָלָה qᵉlālâ, n.f. [33] [√ 7837]

curse [12], curses [7], cursing [5], object of cursing [4], condemnation [2], accursed [1], called down curses [+7837] [1], pronounce curses [1]

Ge 27: 12 and would bring down a **curse** on myself rather than a blessing."
27: 13 His mother said to him, "My son, let the **curse** fall on me.
Dt 11: 26 See, I am setting before you today a blessing and a **curse**—
11: 28 the **curse** if you disobey the commands of the LORD your God
11: 29 on Mount Gerizim the blessings, and on Mount Ebal the **curses**.
21: 23 because anyone who is hung on a tree is *under* God's **curse**.
23: 5 [23:6] to Balaam but turned the **curse** into a blessing for you,
27: 13 And these tribes shall stand on Mount Ebal to **pronounce curses**:
28: 15 you today, all these **curses** will come upon you and overtake you:
28: 45 All these **curses** will come upon you. They will pursue you
29: 27 [29:26] so that he brought on it all the **curses** written in this book.
30: 1 all these blessings and **curses** I have set before you come upon you
30: 19 you that I have set before you life and death, blessings and **curses**.
Jos 8: 34 read all the words of the law—the blessings and the **curses**—
Jdg 9: 57 The **curse** *of* Jotham son of Jerub-Baal came on them.
2Sa 16: 12 and repay me with good for the **cursing** I am receiving today."
1Ki 2: 8 who **called down** bitter **curses on** [+7837] me the day I went to
2Ki 22: 19 that they would become **accursed** and laid waste, and because you
Ne 13: 2 on them. (Our God, however, turned the **curse** into a blessing.)
Ps 109: 17 He loved to pronounce a **curse**—may it come on him; he found no
109: 18 He wore **cursing** as his garment; it entered into his body like
Pr 26: 2 or a darting swallow, an undeserved **curse** does not come to rest.
27: 14 his neighbor early in the morning, it will be taken as a **curse**.
Jer 24: 9 a reproach and a byword, an object of ridicule and **cursing**,
25: 18 to make them a ruin and an object of horror and scorn and **cursing**,
26: 6 this city an **object of cursing** among all the nations of the earth.' "
29: 22 all the exiles from Judah who are in Babylon will use this **curse**:
42: 18 be an object of cursing and horror, of **condemnation** and reproach;
44: 8 will destroy yourselves and make yourselves an **object of cursing**
44: 12 an object of cursing and horror, of **condemnation** and reproach.
44: 22 your land became an **object of cursing** and a desolate waste
49: 13 become a ruin and an object of horror, of reproach and of **cursing**;
Zec 8: 13 As you have been an **object of cursing** among the nations,

7840 קָלַס qālas, v. [4] [→ 7841, 7842]

deride [1], jeered [1], mock [1], scorned [1]

2Ki 2: 23 [F] some youths came out of the town and **jeered** at him.
Eze 16: 31 [D] you were unlike a prostitute, because you **scorned** payment.
22: 5 [F] who are near and those who are far away *will* **mock** you,
Hab 1: 10 [F] They **deride** kings and scoff at rulers. They laugh at all

7841 קֶלֶס qeles, n.[m.]. [3] [√ 7840]

derision [2], reproach [1]

Ps 44: 13 [44:14] our neighbors, the scorn and **derision** of those around us.
79: 4 to our neighbors, of scorn and **derision** to those around us.
Jer 20: 8 of the LORD has brought me insult and **reproach** all day long.

7842 קַלָּסָה qallāsâ, n.f. [1] [√ 7840]

laughingstock [1]

Eze 22: 4 of scorn to the nations and a **laughingstock** to all the countries.

7843 קָלַע qālaʿ[1], v. [4] [√ 7845]

hurl away [1], hurl out [1], sling [1], slung [1]

Jdg 20: 16 [A] each of whom *could* **sling** a stone at a hair and not miss.
1Sa 17: 49 [D] a stone, *he* **slung** it and struck the Philistine on the forehead.
25: 29 [D] the lives of your enemies *he will* **hurl away** as from the
Jer 10: 18 [A] "At this time I *will* **hurl out** those who live in this land; I

7844 קָלַע qālaʿ[2], v. [3] [→ 5237, 7846]

carved [+5237] [1], carved [+906+5237] [1], carved [1]

1Ki 6: 29 [A] *he* **carved** [+906+5237] cherubim, palm trees and open
6: 32 [A] on the two olive wood doors *he* **carved** [+5237] cherubim,
6: 35 [A] *He* **carved** cherubim, palm trees and open flowers on them

7845 קֶלַע qelaʿ[1], n.[m.]. [6] [→ 7843, 7847]

sling [3], slingstones [+74] [3]

1Sa 17: 40 bag and, with his **sling** in his hand, approached the Philistine.

1Sa 17:50 So David triumphed over the Philistine with a **sling** and a stone;
25:29 of your enemies he will hurl away as from the pocket of a **sling**.
2Ch 26:14 coats of armor, bows and **slingstones** [+74] for the entire army.
Job 41:28 [41:20] make him flee; **slingstones** [+74] are like chaff to him.
Zec 9:15 They will destroy and overcome with **slingstones** [+74]. They will

7846 קֶלַע² qela'², n.[m.]. [16 / 15] [√ 7844]

curtains [15]

Ex 27:9 hundred cubits long and is to have **curtains** of finely twisted linen,
27:11 side shall also be a hundred cubits long and is to have **curtains**,
27:12 end of the courtyard shall be fifty cubits wide and have **curtains**,
27:14 **Curtains** fifteen cubits long are to be on one side of the entrance,
27:15 and **curtains** fifteen cubits long are to be on the other side,
35:17 the **curtains** *of* the courtyard with its posts and bases, and the
38:9 was a hundred cubits long and had **curtains** *of* finely twisted linen,
38:12 The west end was fifty cubits wide and had **curtains**, with ten
38:14 **Curtains** fifteen cubits long were on one side of the entrance,
38:15 **curtains** fifteen cubits long were on the other side of the entrance
38:16 All the **curtains** around the courtyard were of finely twisted linen.
38:18 cubits long and, like the **curtains** *of* the courtyard, five cubits high,
39:40 the **curtains** *of* the courtyard with its posts and bases, and the
Nu 3:26 the **curtains** *of* the courtyard, the curtain at the entrance to the
4:26 the **curtains** *of* the courtyard surrounding the tabernacle and altar,
1Ki 6:34 two leaves that turned in sockets. [BHS ***curtains***; NIV RPH 7521]

7847 קַלָּע qallā', n.m. [1] [√ 7845]

men armed with slings [1]

2Ki 3:25 but **men armed with slings** surrounded it and attacked it as well.

7848 קְלֹקֵל qᵉlōqēl, a. [1] [√ 7837]

miserable [1]

Nu 21:5 no bread! There is no water! And we detest this **miserable** food!"

7849 קִלְּשׁוֹן qillᵉšôn, n.[m.]. [1]

forks [1]

1Sa 13:21 a third of a shekel for sharpening **forks** and axes and for repointing

7850 קָמָה qāmâ, n.f. [10] [√ 7756]

standing grain [6], grows up [2], grainfield [1], stalk [1]

Ex 22:6 [22:5] burns shocks of grain or **standing grain** or the whole field,
Dt 16:9 from the time you begin to put the sickle to the **standing grain**.
23:25 [23:26] If you enter your neighbor's **grainfield**, you may pick
23:25 [23:26] but you must not put a sickle to his **standing grain**.
Jdg 15:5 and let the foxes loose in the **standing grain** *of* the Philistines.
15:5 He burned up the shocks and **standing grain**, together with the
2Ki 19:26 like grass sprouting on the roof, scorched before it **grows up**.
Isa 17:5 It will be as when a reaper gathers the **standing grain** and harvests
37:27 like grass sprouting on the roof, scorched before it **grows up**.
Hos 8:7 The **stalk** has no head; it will produce no flour. Were it to yield

7851 קְמוּאֵל qᵉmû'ēl, n.pr.m. [3] [√ 7756 + 446]

Kemuel [3]

Ge 22:21 Uz the firstborn, Buz his brother, **Kemuel** (the father of Aram),
Nu 34:24 **Kemuel** son of Shiphtan, the leader from the tribe of Ephraim son
1Ch 27:17 over Levi: Hashabiah son of **Kemuel**; over Aaron: Zadok;

7852 קָמוֹן qāmôn, n.pr.loc. [1]

Kamon [1]

Jdg 10:5 When Jair died, he was buried in **Kamon**.

7853 קִמּוֹשׂ qimmôś, n.m. [3]

briers [1], nettles [1], thorns [1]

Pr 24:31 **thorns** had come up everywhere, the ground was covered with
Isa 34:13 will overrun her citadels, **nettles** and brambles her strongholds.
Hos 9:6 Their treasures of silver will be taken over by **briers**, and thorns

7854 קֶמַח qemaḥ, n.[m.]. [14]

flour [13], meal [1]

Ge 18:6 "get three seahs of fine **flour** and knead it and bake some bread."
Nu 5:15 He must also take an offering of a tenth of an ephah of barley **flour**
Jdg 6:19 and from an ephah of **flour** he made bread without yeast.
1Sa 1:24 with a three-year-old bull, an ephah of **flour** and a skin of wine,
28:24 She took *some* **flour**, kneaded it and baked bread without yeast
2Sa 17:28 and barley, **flour** and roasted grain, beans and lentils,
1Ki 4:22 [5:2] were thirty cors of fine flour and sixty cors of **meal**,
17:12 any bread—only a handful of **flour** in a jar and a little oil in a jug.
17:14 'The jar of **flour** will not be used up and the jug of oil will not run
17:16 For the jar of **flour** was not used up and the jug of oil did not run
2Ki 4:41 Elisha said, "Get *some* **flour**." He put it into the pot and said,
1Ch 12:40 [12:41] There were plentiful supplies of **flour**, fig cakes, raisin
Isa 47:2 Take millstones and grind **flour**; take off your veil. Lift up your
Hos 8:7 The stalk has no head; it will produce no **flour**. Were it to yield

7855 קָמַט qāmaṭ, v. [2]

bound [1], were carried off [1]

Job 16:8 [A] *You have* **bound** me—and it has become a witness; my
22:16 [E] They **were carried off** before their time, their foundations

7856 קָמַי qāmāy, n.pr.loc. Not used in NIV/BHS [→ 4214]

7857 קָמַל qāmal, v. [2]

wither [1], withers [1]

Isa 19:6 [A] will dwindle and dry up. The reeds and rushes *will* **wither**,
33:9 [A] and wastes away, Lebanon is ashamed and **withers**;

7858 קָמַץ qāmaṣ, v. [3] [→ 7859]

take a handful [+4850+7859] [1], take a handful [+906+4850+7859] [1], take a handful [1]

Lev 2:2 [A] The priest *shall* **take a handful** [+4850+7859] of the fine
5:12 [A] who *shall* **take a handful** [+906+4850+7859] of it as a
Nu 5:26 [A] The priest *is* then *to* **take a handful** of the grain offering as a

7859 קֹמֶץ qōmeṣ, n.[m.]. [4] [√ 7858]

handful [1], plentifully [+4200] [1], take a handful [+4850+7858] [1], take a handful [+906+4850+7858] [1]

Ge 41:47 seven years of abundance the land produced **plentifully** [+4200].
Lev 2:2 The priest *shall* **take a handful** [+4850+7858] of the fine flour
5:12 who *shall* **take a handful** [+906+4850+7858] of it as a memorial
6:15 [6:8] The priest is to take a **handful** of fine flour and oil, together

7860 קֵן qēn, n.m. [13] [√ 7873]

nest [11], house [1], rooms [1]

Ge 6:14 make **rooms** in it and coat it with pitch inside and out.
Nu 24:21 "Your dwelling place is secure, your **nest** is set in a rock;
Dt 22:6 If you come across a bird's **nest** beside the road, either in a tree
32:11 like an eagle that stirs up its **nest** and hovers over its young,
Job 29:18 "I thought, 'I will die in my own **house**, my days as numerous as
39:27 Does the eagle soar at your command and build his **nest** on high?
Ps 84:3 [84:4] the swallow a **nest** for herself, where she may have her
Pr 27:8 Like a bird that strays from its **nest** is a man who strays from his
Isa 10:14 As one reaches into a **nest**, so my hand reached for the wealth of
16:2 Like fluttering birds pushed from the **nest**, so are the women of
Jer 49:16 Though you build your **nest** as high as the eagle's, from there I
Ob 1:4 you soar like the eagle and make your **nest** among the stars,
Hab 2:9 "Woe to him who builds his realm by unjust gain to set his **nest** on

7861 קָנָא qānā', v.den. [34] [→ 7862, 7863, 7868]

jealous [5], envy [4], very zealous [+7861] [4], envious [3], suspects [3], envied [2], jealous [+7863] [2], made jealous [2], zealous [2], aroused jealousy [1], jealousy [1], make envious [1], provokes to jealousy [1], stirred up jealous anger [1], zeal [1], zealous [+7863] [1]

Ge 26:14 [D] and herds and servants that the Philistines **envied** him.
30:1 [D] bearing Jacob any children, she *became* **jealous** of her sister.
37:11 [D] His brothers *were* **jealous** of him, but his father kept the
Nu 5:14 [D] her husband and *he* **suspects** his wife and she is impure—
5:14 [D] is jealous and **suspects** her even though she is not impure—
5:30 [D] of jealousy come over a man because *he* **suspects** his wife.
11:29 [D] Moses replied, "*Are* you **jealous** for my sake? I wish that all
25:11 [D] for he *was* as **zealous** [+7863] as I am for my honor among
25:13 [D] because *he was* **zealous** for the honor of his God and made
Dt 32:16 [G] *They* **made** him **jealous** with their foreign gods and angered
32:21 [D] They **made** me **jealous** by what is no god and angered me
32:21 [G] I *will* **make** them **envious** by those who are not a people;
2Sa 21:2 [D] Saul in his **zeal** for Israel and Judah had tried to annihilate
1Ki 14:22 [D] the sins they committed *they* **stirred up** his **jealous anger**
19:10 [D] "*I have been* **very zealous** [+7861] for the LORD God
19:10 [D] "*I have been* **very zealous** [+7861] for the LORD God
19:14 [D] "*I have been* **very zealous** [+7861] for the LORD God
19:14 [D] "*I have been* **very zealous** [+7861] for the LORD God
Ps 37:1 [D] because of evil men or *be* **envious** of those who do wrong;
73:3 [D] For *I* **envied** the arrogant when I saw the prosperity of the
78:58 [G] their high places; *they* **aroused** his **jealousy** with their idols.
106:16 [D] In the camp *they grew* **envious** of Moses and of Aaron,
Pr 3:31 [D] *Do* not **envy** a violent man or choose any of his ways,
23:17 [D] *Do* not *let* your heart **envy** sinners, but always be zealous for
24:1 [D] *Do* not **envy** wicked men, do not desire their company;

Pr 24: 19 [D] Do not fret because of evil men or *be* **envious** of the wicked,
Isa 11: 13 [D] Ephraim *will* not *be* **jealous** *of* Judah, nor Judah hostile
Eze 8: 3 [G] inner court, where the idol that **provokes to jealousy** stood.
31: 9 [D] *the* **envy** *of* all the trees of Eden in the garden of God.
39: 25 [D] the people of Israel, and *I will be* **zealous** for my holy name.
Joel 2: 18 [D] the LORD *will be* **jealous** for his land and take pity on his
Zec 1: 14 [D] '*I am* very **jealous** [+7863] for Jerusalem and Zion,
8: 2 [D] "*I am* very **jealous** [+7863] for Zion; I am burning with
8: 2 [D] very jealous for Zion; *I am* burning with **jealousy** for her."

7862 קַנָּא *qannā'*, a. [6] [→ 7868; cf. 7861]

jealous [6]

Ex 20: 5 for I, the LORD your God, am a **jealous** God, punishing the
34: 14 for the LORD, whose name is **Jealous**, is a jealous God.
34: 14 for the LORD, whose name is Jealous, is a **jealous** God.
Dt 4: 24 For the LORD your God is a consuming fire, a **jealous** God.
5: 9 for I, the LORD your God, am a **jealous** God, punishing the
6: 15 is among you, is a **jealous** God and his anger will burn against you,

7863 קִנְאָה *qin'â*, n.f. [43] [√ 7861]

jealousy [15], zeal [15], jealous anger [4], envy [3], jealous [+7861] [2], *untranslated* [1], jealous [+6296+6584+8120] [1], jealous [1], zealous [+7861] [1]

Nu 5: 14 if feelings of **jealousy** come over her husband and he suspects his
5: 14 or if he *is* **jealous** [+6296+6584+8120] and suspects her even
5: 15 or put incense on it, because it is a grain offering for **jealousy**,
5: 18 in her hands the reminder offering, the grain offering for **jealousy**,
5: 25 The priest is to take from her hands the grain offering for **jealousy**,
5: 29 is the law of **jealousy** when a woman goes astray and defiles
5: 30 or when feelings of **jealousy** come over a man because he suspects
25: 11 for he *was* as **zealous** [+7861] as I am for my honor among them,
25: 11 honor among them, so that in my **zeal** I did not put an end to them.
Dt 29: 20 [29:19] his wrath and **zeal** will burn against that man.
2Ki 10: 16 Jehu said, "Come with me and see my **zeal** for the LORD."
19: 31 The **zeal** *of* the LORD Almighty will accomplish this.
Job 5: 2 Resentment kills a fool, and **envy** slays the simple.
Ps 69: 9 [69:10] for **zeal** *for* your house consumes me, and the insults of
79: 5 you be angry forever? How long will your **jealousy** burn like fire?
119:139 My **zeal** wears me out, for my enemies ignore your words.
Pr 6: 34 for **jealousy** arouses a husband's fury, and he will show no mercy
14: 30 A heart at peace gives life to the body, but **envy** rots the bones.
27: 4 and fury overwhelming, but who can stand before **jealousy**?
Ecc 4: 4 and all achievement spring from man's **envy** of his neighbor.
9: 6 Their love, their hate and their **jealousy** have long since vanished;
SS 8: 6 for love is as strong as death, its **jealousy** unyielding as the grave.
Isa 9: 7 [9:6] The **zeal** *of* the LORD Almighty will accomplish this.
11: 13 Ephraim's **jealousy** will vanish, and Judah's enemies will be cut
26: 11 Let them see your **zeal** *for* your people and be put to shame;
37: 32 The **zeal** *of* the LORD Almighty will accomplish this.
42: 13 march out like a mighty man, like a warrior he will stir up his **zeal**;
59: 17 garments of vengeance and wrapped himself in **zeal** as in a cloak.
63: 15 holy and glorious. Where are your **zeal** and your might?
Eze 5: 13 they will know that I the LORD have spoken in my **zeal**.
8: 3 inner court, where the idol **[RPH]** that provokes to jealousy stood.
8: 5 entrance north of the gate of the altar I saw this idol of **jealousy**.
16: 38 upon you the blood vengeance of my wrath and **jealous anger**.
16: 42 you will subside and my **jealous anger** will turn away from you;
23: 25 I will direct my **jealous anger** against you, and they will deal with
35: 11 with the anger and **jealousy** you showed in your hatred of them
36: 5 In my burning **zeal** I have spoken against the rest of the nations,
36: 6 I speak in my **jealous** wrath because you have suffered the scorn of
38: 19 In my **zeal** and fiery wrath I declare that at that time there shall be
Zep 1: 18 In the fire of his **jealousy** the whole world will be consumed,
3: 8 whole world will be consumed by the fire of my **jealous anger**.
Zec 1: 14 Almighty says: '*I am* very **jealous** [+7861] for Jerusalem and Zion,
8: 2 "*I am* very **jealous** [+7861] for Zion; I am burning with jealousy

7864 קָנָה¹ *qānâ¹*, v. [78 / 77] [→ 5238, 5239, 5240, 7871; cf. 7803, 7865; Ar 10632]

buy [20], bought [19], get [7], buyer [6], acquire [2], be bought [2], insist on paying [+928+7864] [2], insist on paying for [+907+928+4697+4946+7864] [2], purchase [2], purchased [2], acquired [1], acquires [1], bought [+928+2021+4084] [1], bought back [1], buyers [1], buying [1], buys [+7871] [1], choose [+1047] [1], gains [1], gets [1], master [1], reclaim [1], taken [1]

Ge 25: 10 [A] the field Abraham *had* **bought** from the Hittites.
33: 19 [A] *he* **bought** from the sons of Hamor, the father of Shechem, the
39: 1 [A] **bought** him from the Ishmaelites who had taken him there.
47: 19 [A] **Buy** us and our land in exchange for food, and we with our
47: 20 [A] So Joseph **bought** all the land in Egypt for Pharaoh. The
47: 22 [A] However, *he did* not **buy** the land of the priests, because they
47: 23 [A] "Now that *I have* **bought** you and your land today for
49: 30 [A] which Abraham **bought** as a burial place from Ephron the
50: 13 [A] which Abraham *had* **bought** as a burial place from Ephron
Ex 15: 16 [A] pass by, O LORD, until the people *you* **bought** pass by.
21: 2 [A] "If *you* **buy** a Hebrew servant, he is to serve you for six
Lev 22: 11 [A] if a priest **buys** [+7871] a slave *with* money, or if a slave is
25: 14 [A] sell land to one of your countrymen or **buy** any from him,
25: 15 [A] *You are to* **buy** from your countryman on the basis of the
25: 28 [A] what he sold will remain in the possession of the **buyer** until
25: 30 [A] in the walled city shall belong permanently to the **buyer**
25: 44 [A] the nations around you; from them *you may* **buy** slaves.
25: 45 [A] *You may* also **buy** some of the temporary residents living
25: 50 [A] his **buyer** are to count the time from the year he sold himself
27: 24 [A] the field will revert to the person from whom *he* **bought** it,
Dt 28: 68 [A] enemies as male and female slaves, but no *one will* **buy** you.
Jos 24: 32 [A] buried at Shechem in the tract of land that Jacob **bought**
Ru 4: 4 [A] suggest that *you* **buy** it in the presence of these seated here
4: 5 [A] "On the day you **buy** the land from Naomi and from Ruth the
4: 5 [A] Ruth the Moabitess, *you* **acquire** the dead man's widow,
4: 8 [A] So the kinsman-redeemer said to Boaz, "**Buy** it yourself."
4: 9 [A] "Today you are witnesses that *I have* **bought** from Naomi all
4: 10 [A] *I have* also **acquired** Ruth the Moabitess, Mahlon's widow,
2Sa 12: 3 [A] man had nothing except one little ewe lamb *he had* **bought**.
24: 21 [A] "To **buy** your threshing floor," David answered, "so I can
24: 24 [A] ***I* insist on paying** [+907+928+4697+4946+7864] you **for** it.
24: 24 [A] ***I* insist on paying** you **for** [+907+928+4697+4946+7864] it.
24: 24 [A] So David **bought** the threshing floor and the oxen and paid
1Ki 16: 24 [A] *He* **bought** the hill of Samaria from Shemer for two talents
2Ki 12: 12 [12:13] [A] They **purchased** timber and dressed stone for the
22: 6 [A] Also *have* them **purchase** timber and dressed stone to repair
1Ch 21: 24 [A] "No, *I* **insist on paying** [+928+7864] the full price.
21: 24 [A] "No, *I* **insist on paying** [+928+7864] the full price.
2Ch 34: 11 [A] to the carpenters and builders to **purchase** dressed stone,
Ne 5: 8 [A] we *have* **bought back** our Jewish brothers who were sold to
5: 16 [A] assembled there for the work; *we did* not **acquire** any land.
Ps 74: 2 [A] Remember the people *you* **purchased** of old, the tribe of
78: 54 [A] of his holy land, to the hill country his right hand *had* **taken**.
Pr 1: 5 [A] add to their learning, and *let* the discerning **get** guidance—
4: 5 [A] **Get** wisdom, get understanding; do not forget my words or
4: 5 [A] Get wisdom, **get** understanding; do not forget my words or
4: 7 [A] Wisdom is supreme; therefore **get** wisdom. Though it cost all
4: 7 [A] get wisdom. Though it cost all you have, **get** understanding.
15: 32 [A] but whoever heeds correction **gains** understanding.
16: 16 [A] How much better *to* **get** wisdom than gold, to choose
16: 16 [A] much better to get wisdom than gold, *to* **choose** [+1047]
17: 16 [A] in the hand of a fool, since he has no desire to **get** wisdom?
18: 15 [A] The heart of the discerning **acquires** knowledge; the ears of
19: 8 [A] *He who* **gets** wisdom loves his own soul; he who cherishes
20: 14 [A] says the **buyer**; then off he goes and boasts about his
23: 23 [A] **Buy** the truth and do not sell it; get wisdom, discipline
Ecc 2: 7 [A] *I* **bought** male and female slaves and had other slaves who
Isa 1: 3 [A] The ox knows his **master**, the donkey his owner's manger,
11: 11 [A] to **reclaim** the remnant that is left of his people from Assyria,
24: 2 [A] for servant, for mistress as for maid, for seller as for **buyer**,
43: 24 [A] *You have* not **bought** [+928+2021+4084] any fragrant calamus
Jer 13: 1 [A] "Go and **buy** a linen belt and put it around your waist, but do
13: 2 [A] So *I* **bought** a belt, as the LORD directed, and put it around
13: 4 [A] "Take the belt *you* **bought** and are wearing around your
19: 1 [A] what the LORD says: "Go and **buy** a clay jar from a potter.
32: 7 [A] is going to come to you and say, '**Buy** my field at Anathoth,
32: 7 [A] because as nearest relative it is your right and duty to **buy** it.'
32: 8 [A] '**Buy** my field at Anathoth in the territory of Benjamin.
32: 8 [A] is your right to redeem it and possess it, **buy** it for yourself.'
32: 9 [A] so *I* **bought** the field at Anathoth from my cousin Hanamel
32: 15 [C] and vineyards *will* again **be bought** in this land.'
32: 25 [A] '**Buy** the field with silver and have the transaction
32: 43 [C] Once more fields *will* **be bought** in this land of which you
32: 44 [A] Fields *will be* **bought** for silver, and deeds will be signed,
Eze 7: 12 [A] Let not the **buyer** rejoice nor the seller grieve, for wrath is
Am 8: 6 [A] **buying** the poor with silver and the needy for a pair of
Zec 11: 5 [A] Their **buyers** slaughter them and go unpunished.
13: 5 [g] land has been my livelihood [BHS *a man sold me*; NIV 7871]

7865 ²קָנָה *qānâ²*, v. [6] [→ 555; cf. 7803, 7864]

Creator [3], brought forth [2], created [1]

Ge 4: 1 [A] "With the help of the LORD *I have* **brought forth** a man."
14: 19 [A] be Abram by God Most High, **Creator** *of* heaven and earth.
14: 22 [A] God Most High, **Creator** *of* heaven and earth, and have
Dt 32: 6 [A] your Father, your **Creator**, who made you and formed you?
Ps 139: 13 [A] For you **created** my inmost being; you knit me together in
Pr 8: 22 [A] "The LORD **brought** me **forth** as the first of his works,

7866 קָנֶה qāneh, n.m. [62 / 56] [→ 7867]

rod [12], branches [10], *untranslated* [9], reed [5], branch [4], reeds [4], calamus [3], shaft [2], stalk [2], cane [1], fragrant calamus [1], joint [1], measuring rod [1], scales [1]

Ge 41: 5 heads of grain, healthy and good, were growing on a single **stalk**.
41: 22 saw seven heads of grain, full and good, growing on a single **stalk**.
Ex 25: 31 a lampstand of pure gold and hammer it out, base and **shaft**;
25: 32 Six **branches** are to extend from the sides of the lampstand—
25: 32 the lampstand—three **[RPH]** on one side and three on the other.
25: 32 the lampstand—three on one side and three **[RPH]** on the other.
25: 33 almond flowers with buds and blossoms are to be on one **branch**,
25: 33 and blossoms are to be on one branch, three on the next **branch**,
25: 33 and the same for all six **branches** extending from the lampstand.
25: 35 One bud shall be under the first pair of **branches** extending from
25: 35 the second pair, **[RPH]** and a third bud under the third pair—
25: 35 and a third bud under the third pair—**[RPH]** six branches in all.
25: 35 and a third bud under the third pair—six **branches** in all.
25: 36 and **branches** shall all be of one piece with the lampstand,
30: 23 250 shekels) of fragrant cinnamon, 250 shekels of fragrant **cane**,
37: 17 the lampstand of pure gold and hammered it out, base and **shaft**;
37: 18 Six **branches** extended from the sides of the lampstand—three on
37: 18 the lampstand—three **[RPH]** on one side and three on the other.
37: 18 the lampstand—three on one side and three **[RPH]** on the other.
37: 19 like almond flowers with buds and blossoms were on one **branch**,
37: 19 three on the next **branch** and the same for all six branches
37: 19 and the same for all six **branches** extending from the lampstand.
37: 21 One bud was under the first pair of **branches** extending from the
37: 21 the second pair, **[RPH]** and a third bud under the third pair—
37: 21 and a third bud under the third pair—**[RPR]** six branches in all.
37: 21 and a third bud under the third pair—six **branches** in all.
37: 22 and the **branches** were all of one piece with the lampstand,
1Ki 14: 15 will strike Israel, so that it will be like a **reed** swaying in the water.
2Ki 18: 21 that splintered **reed** of a staff, which pierces a man's hand
Job 31: 22 let my arm fall from the shoulder, let it be broken off at the **joint**.
40: 21 the lotus plants he lies, hidden among the **reeds** in the marsh.
Ps 68: 30 [68:31] Rebuke the beast among the **reeds**, the herd of bulls
SS 4: 14 nard and saffron, **calamus** and cinnamon, with every kind of
Isa 19: 6 Egypt will dwindle and dry up. The **reeds** and rushes will wither,
35: 7 where jackals once lay, grass and **reeds** and papyrus will grow.
36: 6 that splintered **reed** of a staff, which pierces a man's hand
42: 3 A bruised **reed** he will not break, and a smoldering wick he will
43: 24 You have not bought *any* **fragrant calamus** for me, or lavished on
46: 6 pour out gold from their bags and weigh out silver on the **scales**;
Jer 6: 20 about incense from Sheba or sweet **calamus** from a distant land?
Eze 27: 19 they exchanged wrought iron, cassia and **calamus** for your wares.
29: 6 " 'You have been a staff of **reed** for the house of Israel.
40: 3 in the gateway with a linen cord and a measuring **rod** in his hand.
40: 5 The length of the measuring **rod** in the man's hand was six long
40: 5 the wall; it was one **measuring rod** thick and one rod high.
40: 5 the wall; it was one measuring rod thick and one **rod** high.
40: 6 and measured the threshold of the gate; it was one **rod** deep.
40: 6 it was one rod deep. [BHS+ *threshold, one rod deep*]
40: 7 The alcoves for the guards were one **rod** long and one rod wide,
40: 7 The alcoves for the guards were one rod long and one **rod** wide,
40: 7 of the gate next to the portico facing the temple was one **rod** deep.
40: 8 the portico of the gateway; [BHS+ *one rod deep*]
41: 8 of the side rooms. It was the length of the **rod**, six long cubits.
42: 16 He measured the east side with the measuring **rod**; it was five
42: 16 the measuring rod; it was five hundred <u>cubits</u>. [BHS *rods*; NIV 564]
42: 16 side with the measuring rod; it was five hundred cubits. **[RPH]**
42: 17 five hundred <u>cubits</u> [BHS ***rods***; NIV 564] by the measuring rod.
42: 17 the north side; it was five hundred cubits by the measuring **rod**.
42: 18 five hundred <u>cubits</u> [BHS ***rods***; NIV 564] by the measuring rod.
42: 18 the south side; it was five hundred cubits by the measuring **rod**.
42: 19 five hundred <u>cubits</u> [BHS ***rods***; NIV 564] by the measuring rod.
42: 19 and measured; it was five hundred cubits by the measuring **rod**.

7867 קָנָה qānâ[3], n.pr.loc. [3] [√ 7866]

Kanah [3]

Jos 16: 8 From Tappuah the border went west to the **Kanah** Ravine
17: 9 Then the boundary continued south to the **Kanah** Ravine.
19: 28 It went to Abdon, Rehob, Hammon and **Kanah**, as far as Greater

7868 קַנּוֹא qannô', a. [2] [√ 7862; cf. 7861]

jealous [2]

Jos 24: 19 He is a holy God; he is a **jealous** God. He will not forgive your
Na 1: 2 The LORD is a **jealous** and avenging God; the LORD takes

7869 קְנַז q^{e}naz, n.pr.m. [11] [→ 7870]

Kenaz [11]

Ge 36: 11 The sons of Eliphaz: Teman, Omar, Zepho, Gatam and **Kenaz**.
36: 15 Eliphaz the firstborn of Esau: Chiefs Teman, Omar, Zepho, **Kenaz**,
36: 42 **Kenaz**, Teman, Mibzar,
Jos 15: 17 Othniel son of **Kenaz**, Caleb's brother, took it; so Caleb gave his
Jdg 1: 13 Othniel son of **Kenaz**, Caleb's younger brother, took it; so Caleb
3: 9 Othniel son of **Kenaz**, Caleb's younger brother, who saved them.
3: 11 the land had peace for forty years, until Othniel son of **Kenaz** died.
1Ch 1: 36 Teman, Omar, Zepho, Gatam and **Kenaz**; by Timna: Amalek.
1: 53 **Kenaz**, Teman, Mibzar,
4: 13 The sons of **Kenaz**: Othniel and Seraiah. The sons of Othniel:
4: 15 son of Jephunneh: Iru, Elah and Naam. The son of Elah: **Kenaz**.

7870 קְנִזִּי q^{e}nizzî, a.g. [4] [√ 7869]

Kenizzite [3], Kenizzites [1]

Ge 15: 19 the land of the Kenites, **Kenizzites**, Kadmonites,
Nu 32: 12 not one except Caleb son of Jephunneh the **Kenizzite** and Joshua
Jos 14: 6 at Gilgal, and Caleb son of Jephunneh the **Kenizzite** said to him,
14: 14 So Hebron has belonged to Caleb son of Jephunneh the **Kenizzite**

7871 קִנְיָן qinyān, n.[m.]. [10 / 11] [√ 7864]

goods [3], *untranslated* [1], buys [+7864] [1], creatures [1], have [1], herds [1], livelihood [1], possessed [1], property [1]

Ge 31: 18 along with all the goods **[NIE]** he had accumulated in Paddan
34: 23 their **property** and all their other animals become ours?
36: 6 all his other animals and all the **goods** he had acquired in Canaan,
Lev 22: 11 if a priest **buys** a slave **with** [+7864] money, or if a slave is born in
Jos 14: 4 only towns to live in, with pasturelands for their flocks and **herds**.
Ps 104: 24 In wisdom you made them all; the earth is full of your **creatures**.
105: 21 He made him master of his household, ruler over all he **possessed**,
Pr 4: 7 get wisdom. Though it cost all you **have**, get understanding.
Eze 38: 12 rich in livestock and **goods**, living at the center of the land."
38: 13 to take away livestock and **goods** and to seize much plunder?" '
Zec 13: 5 the land has been my **livelihood** [BHS 7864] since my youth.'

7872 קִנָּמוֹן qinnāmôn, n.m. [3]

cinnamon [3]

Ex 30: 23 250 shekels) of fragrant **cinnamon**, 250 shekels of fragrant cane,
Pr 7: 17 I have perfumed my bed with myrrh, aloes and **cinnamon**.
SS 4: 14 nard and saffron, calamus and **cinnamon**, with every kind of

7873 קָנַן qānan, v.den. [5] [→ 7860]

make nests [1], makes nest [1], nest [1], nested [1], nestled [1]

Ps 104: 17 [D] There the birds **make** *their* **nests**; the stork has its home in
Isa 34: 15 [D] The owl *will* **nest** there and lay eggs, she will hatch them,
Jer 22: 23 [E] who live in 'Lebanon,' *who are* **nestled** in cedar buildings,
48: 28 [D] Be like a dove *that* **makes** *its* **nest** at the mouth of a cave.
Eze 31: 6 [D] All the birds of the air **nested** in its boughs, all the beasts of

7874 קֵנֶץ qeneṣ, n.[m.]. [1] [cf. 7891]

end [+4200+8492] [1]

Job 18: 2 "When *will you* **end** [+4200+8492] these speeches? Be sensible,

7875 קְנָת q^{e}nāt, n.pr.loc. [2]

Kenath [2]

Nu 32: 42 And Nobah captured **Kenath** and its surrounding settlements
1Ch 2: 23 Havvoth Jair, as well as **Kenath** with its surrounding settlements—

7876 קָסַם qāsam, v.den. [20] [→ 5241, 7877]

diviners [6], divination [2], divinations [2], consult [1], omen [1], practice divination [+7877] [1], practiced divination [+7877] [1], practiced divination [1], practices divination [+7877] [1], seek an omen [+7877] [1], soothsayer [1], tell fortunes [1], utter divinations [1]

Dt 18: 10 [A] *who* **practices divination** [+7877] or sorcery, interprets
18: 14 [A] dispossess listen to those who practice sorcery or **divination**.
Jos 13: 22 [A] to the sword Balaam son of Beor, who **practiced divination**.
1Sa 6: 2 [A] the Philistines called for the priests and the **diviners** and said,
28: 8 [A] "**Consult** a spirit for me," he said, "and bring up for me the
2Ki 17: 17 [A] *They* **practiced divination** [+7877] and sorcery and sold
Isa 3: 2 [A] and warrior, the judge and prophet, the **soothsayer** and elder,
44: 25 [A] foils the signs of false prophets and makes fools of **diviners**,
Jer 27: 9 [A] your **diviners**, your interpreters of dreams, your mediums
29: 8 [A] not let the prophets and **diviners** among you deceive you.
Eze 13: 9 [A] prophets who see false visions and **utter** lying **divinations**.
13: 23 [A] no longer see false visions or **practice divination** [+7877].
21: 21 [21:26] [A] junction of the two roads, to **seek an omen** [+7877]:
21: 23 [21:28] [A] It will seem like a false **omen** to those who have
21: 29 [21:34] [A] concerning you and lying **divinations** about you,
22: 28 [A] these deeds for them by false visions and lying **divinations**.
Mic 3: 6 [A] over you, without visions, and darkness, without **divination**.
3: 7 [A] The seers will be ashamed and the **diviners** disgraced. They

[A] Qal [B] Qal passive [C] Niphal [D] Piel (poel, polel, pilel, pilal, pealal, pilpel) [E] Pual (poal, polal, poalal, pulal, pualal)

Mic 3: 11 [A] teach for a price, and her prophets **tell fortunes** for money.
Zec 10: 2 [A] The idols speak deceit, **diviners** see visions that lie; they tell

7877 קֶסֶם *qesem*, n.[m.]. [11] [√ 7876]

divination [2], divinations [2], fee for divination [1], lot [1], oracle [1], practice divination [+7876] [1], practiced divination [+7876] [1], practices divination [+7876] [1], seek an omen [+7876] [1]

Nu 22: 7 of Moab and Midian left, taking with them the **fee for divination**.
23: 23 There is no sorcery against Jacob, no **divination** against Israel.
Dt 18: 10 *who* **practices divination** [+7876] or sorcery, interprets omens,
1Sa 15: 23 For rebellion is like the sin of **divination**, and arrogance like the
2Ki 17: 17 *They* **practiced divination** [+7876] and sorcery and sold
Pr 16: 10 The lips of a king speak as an **oracle**, and his mouth should not
Jer 14: 14 **divinations**, idolatries and the delusions of their own minds.
Eze 13: 6 Their visions are false and their **divinations** a lie. They say,
13: 23 will no longer see false visions or **practice divination** [+7876].
21: 21 [21:26] the junction of the two roads, to **seek an omen** [+7876]:
21: 22 [21:27] Into his right hand will come the **lot** *for* Jerusalem,

7878 קָסַס *qāsas*, v. [1] [cf. 7989]

stripped [1]

Eze 17: 9 [D] it not be uprooted and **stripped** *of* its fruit so that it withers?

7879 קֶסֶת *qeset*, n.[f.]. [3]

kit [2], writing kit [1]

Eze 9: 2 With them was a man clothed in linen who had a writing **kit** at his
9: 3 to the man clothed in linen who had the writing **kit** at his side
9: 11 the man in linen with the **writing kit** at his side brought back

7880 קָעָה *qā'â*, v. Not used in NIV/BHS [cf. 1716]

7881 קְעִילָה *qᵉ'îlâ*, n.pr.loc. [18]

Keilah [18]

Jos 15: 44 **Keilah**, Aczib and Mareshah—nine towns and their villages.
1Sa 23: 1 the Philistines are fighting against **Keilah** and are looting the
23: 2 answered him, "Go, attack the Philistines and save **Keilah**."
23: 3 much more, then, if we go to **Keilah** against the Philistine forces!"
23: 4 the LORD, and the LORD answered him, "Go down to **Keilah**,
23: 5 So David and his men went to **Keilah**, fought the Philistines
23: 5 heavy losses on the Philistines and saved the people of **Keilah**.
23: 6 the ephod down with him when he fled to David at **Keilah**.)
23: 7 Saul was told that David had gone to **Keilah**, and he said,
23: 8 for battle, to go down to **Keilah** to besiege David and his men.
23: 10 your servant has heard definitely that Saul plans to come to **Keilah**
23: 11 Will the citizens of **Keilah** surrender me to him? Will Saul come
23: 12 "Will the citizens of **Keilah** surrender me and my men to Saul?"
23: 13 in number, left **Keilah** and kept moving from place to place.
23: 13 When Saul was told that David had escaped from **Keilah**,
1Ch 4: 19 the father of **Keilah** the Garmite, and Eshtemoa the Maacathite.
Ne 3: 17 Beside him, Hashabiah, ruler of half the district of **Keilah**,
3: 18 Binnui son of Henadad, ruler of the other half-district of **Keilah**.

7882 קַעֲקַע *qa'ᵃqa'*, n.[m.]. [1]

tattoo [1]

Lev 19: 28 not cut your bodies for the dead or put **tattoo** marks on yourselves.

7883 קְעָרָה *qᵉ'ārâ*, n.f. [17] [√ 9206]

plate [13], plates [4]

Ex 25: 29 And make its **plates** and dishes of pure gold, as well as its pitchers
37: 16 its **plates** and dishes and bowls and its pitchers for the pouring out
Nu 4: 7 the Presence they are to spread a blue cloth and put on it the **plates**,
7: 13 His offering was one silver **plate** weighing a hundred and thirty
7: 19 The offering he brought was one silver **plate** weighing a hundred
7: 25 His offering was one silver **plate** weighing a hundred and thirty
7: 31 His offering was one silver **plate** weighing a hundred and thirty
7: 37 His offering was one silver **plate** weighing a hundred and thirty
7: 43 His offering was one silver **plate** weighing a hundred and thirty
7: 49 His offering was one silver **plate** weighing a hundred and thirty
7: 55 His offering was one silver **plate** weighing a hundred and thirty
7: 61 His offering was one silver **plate** weighing a hundred and thirty
7: 67 His offering was one silver **plate** weighing a hundred and thirty
7: 73 His offering was one silver **plate** weighing a hundred and thirty
7: 79 His offering was one silver **plate** weighing a hundred and thirty
7: 84 twelve silver **plates**, twelve silver sprinkling bowls and twelve
7: 85 Each silver **plate** weighed a hundred and thirty shekels, and each

7884 קָפָא *qāpā'*, v. [3] [→ 3698, 7885]

complacent [1], congealed [1], curdle [1]

Ex 15: 8 [A] like a wall; the deep waters **congealed** in the heart of the sea.
Job 10: 10 [G] you not pour me out like milk and **curdle** me like cheese,
Zep 1: 12 [A] Jerusalem with lamps and punish those who *are* **complacent**,
Zec 14: 6 [that day there will be no light, no cold or **frost**. [K; see Q 7885]]

7885 קִפָּאוֹן *qippā'ôn*, n.[m.]. [1] [√ 7884]

frost [1]

Zec 14: 6 On that day there will be no light, no cold or **frost**. [K 7884]

7886 קָפַד *qāpad*, v. [1] [→ 7887, 7888; cf. 7889]

rolled up [1]

Isa 38: 12 [D] Like a weaver *I have* **rolled up** my life, and he has cut me

7887 קִפֹּד *qippōd*, n.[m.]. [3] [√ 7886]

screech owl [2], owls [1]

Isa 14: 23 "I will turn her into a place for **owls** and into swampland; I will
34: 11 The desert owl and **screech owl** will possess it; the great owl
Zep 2: 14 The desert owl and the **screech owl** will roost on her columns.

7888 קְפָדָה *qᵉpādâ*, n.[f.]. [1] [√ 7886]

terror [1]

Eze 7: 25 When **terror** comes, they will seek peace, but there will be none.

7889 קִפּוֹז *qippôz*, n.f. [1] [cf. 7886, 7890]

owl [1]

Isa 34: 15 The **owl** will nest there and lay eggs, she will hatch them,

7890 קָפַץ *qāpaṣ*, v. [7] [cf. 7889]

shut [2], bounding [1], gathered up [1], shuts [1], tightfisted [+906+3338] [1], withheld [1]

Dt 15: 7 [A] or **tightfisted** [+906+3338] toward your poor brother.
Job 5: 16 [A] So the poor have hope, and injustice **shuts** its mouth.
24: 24 [C] they are brought low and **gathered up** like all others;
Ps 77: 9 [77:10] [A] *Has he* in anger **withheld** his compassion?"
107: 42 [A] upright see and rejoice, but all the wicked **shut** their mouths.
SS 2: 8 [D] leaping across the mountains, **bounding** over the hills.
Isa 52: 15 [A] and kings *will* **shut** their mouths because of him.

7891 קֵץ *qēṣ*, n.m. [67] [→ 7812, 7916; cf. 7874, 7915]

end [40], later [+4946] [4], after [+4946] [3], climax [3], after [+4200] [2], remotest [2], afar [1], complete [+2118+4200+4946] [1], course [1], endless [+401+4200] [1], every [+4946] [1], from [+4946] [1], fulfilled [1], later [+4200] [1], limit [1], passed [1], prospects [1], some years later [+4200+9102] [1], time is ripe [+995] [1]

Ge 4: 3 In the **course** *of* time Cain brought some of the fruits of the soil as
6: 13 So God said to Noah, "I am going to put an **end** *to* all people,
8: 6 **After** [+4946] forty days Noah opened the window he had made
16: 3 So **after** [+4946] Abram had been living in Canaan ten years,
41: 1 When two full years had **passed**, Pharaoh had a dream: He was
Ex 12: 41 At the **end** *of* the 430 years, to the very day, all the LORD's
Nu 13: 25 At the **end** *of* forty days they returned from exploring the land.
Dt 9: 11 At the **end** *of* the forty days and forty nights, the LORD gave me
15: 1 At the **end** *of* every seven years you must cancel debts.
31: 10 "At the **end** *of* every seven years, in the year for canceling debts,
Jdg 11: 39 **After** [+4946] the two months, she returned to her father and he
2Sa 14: 26 he used to cut his hair **from** [+4946] time to time when it became
15: 7 At the **end** *of* four years, Absalom said to the king, "Let me go to
1Ki 2: 39 three years **later** [+4946], two of Shimei's slaves ran off to Achish
17: 7 Some time **later** [+4946] the brook dried up because there had
2Ki 19: 23 its pines. I have reached its **remotest** parts, the finest of its forests.
2Ch 8: 1 At the **end** *of* twenty years, during which Solomon built the temple
18: 2 **Some years later** [+4200+9102] he went down to visit Ahab in
21: 19 at the **end** of the second year, his bowels came out because of the
Ne 13: 6 to the king. Some time **later** [+4200] I asked his permission
Est 2: 12 she *had to* **complete** [+2118+4200+4946] twelve months of beauty
Job 6: 11 that I should still hope? What **prospects**, that I should be patient?
16: 3 Will your long-winded speeches never **end**? What ails you that you
22: 5 your wickedness great? Are not your sins **endless** [+401+4200]?
28: 3 Man puts an **end** to the darkness; he searches the farthest recesses
Ps 39: 4 [39:5] O LORD, my life's **end** and the number of my days;
119: 96 To all perfection I see a **limit**; but your commands are boundless.
Ecc 4: 8 There was no **end** to his toil, yet his eyes were not content with his
4: 16 There was no **end** to all the people who were before them.
12: 12 Of making many books there is no **end**, and much study wearies
Isa 9: 7 [9:6] increase of his government and peace there will be no **end**.
23: 15 at the **end** *of* these seventy years, it will happen to Tyre as in the
23: 17 At the **end** *of* seventy years, the LORD will deal with Tyre.
37: 24 I have reached its **remotest** heights, the finest of its forests.
Jer 13: 6 Many days **later** [+4946] the LORD said to me, "Go now to
34: 14 '**Every** [+4946] seventh year each of you must free any fellow

Jer 42: 7 Ten days **later** [+4946] the word of the LORD came to Jeremiah.
50: 26 Come against her from **afar**. Break open her granaries; pile her up
51: 13 live by many waters and are rich in treasures, your **end** has come,
La 4: 18 Our **end** was near, our days were numbered, for our end had come.
4: 18 Our end was near, our days were numbered, for our **end** had come.
Eze 7: 2 The **end**! The end has come upon the four corners of the land.
7: 2 The end! The **end** has come upon the four corners of the land.
7: 3 The **end** is now upon you and I will unleash my anger against you.
7: 6 The **end** has come! The end has come! It has roused itself against
7: 6 The end has come! The **end** has come! It has roused itself against
21: 25 [21:30] whose time of punishment has reached its **climax**,
21: 29 [21:34] whose time of punishment has reached its **climax**.
29: 13 At the **end** *of* forty years I will gather the Egyptians from the
35: 5 of their calamity, the time their punishment reached its **climax**,
Da 8: 17 "understand that the vision concerns the time of the **end**."
8: 19 because the vision concerns the appointed time of the **end**.
9: 26 destroy the city and the sanctuary. The **end** will come like a flood:
9: 26 War will continue until the **end**, and desolations have been
11: 6 **After** [+4200] some years, they will become allies. The daughter
11: 13 **after** [+4200] several years, he will advance with a huge army
11: 27 to no avail, because an **end** will still come at the appointed time.
11: 35 be refined, purified and made spotless until the time of the **end**,
11: 40 "At the time of the **end** the king of the South will engage him in
11: 45 Yet he will come to his **end**, and no one will help him.
12: 4 close up and seal the words of the scroll until the time of the **end**.
12: 6 "How long will it be before these astonishing things are **fulfilled**?"
12: 9 the words are closed up and sealed until the time of the **end**.
12: 13 "As for you, go your way till the **end**. You will rest, and then at the
12: 13 at the **end** *of* the days you will rise to receive your allotted
Am 8: 2 LORD said to me, "The **time is ripe** [+995] for my people Israel;
Hab 2: 3 an appointed time; it speaks of the **end** and will not prove false.

7892 קָצַב *qāṣab*, v. [2] [→ 7893]

cut [1], sheep just shorn [1]

2Ki 6: 6 [A] Elisha **cut** a stick and threw it there, and made the iron float.
SS 4: 2 [B] Your teeth are like a flock of **sheep just shorn**, coming up

7893 קֶצֶב *qeṣeb*, n.m. [3] [√ 7892]

shape [2], roots [1]

1Ki 6: 25 ten cubits, for the two cherubim were identical in size and **shape**.
7: 37 all cast in the same molds and were identical in size and **shape**.
Jnh 2: 6 [2:7] To the **roots** *of* the mountains I sank down; the earth

7894 קָצָה *qāṣâ*[1], v. [4] [→ 7895, 7896, 7897, 7898, 7899?, 7901, 7921; cf. 7915]

cutting off [1], reduce size [1], scraped off [1], scraped [1]

Lev 14: 41 [G] the material that *is* **scraped off** dumped into an unclean place
14: 43 [G] have been torn out and the house **scraped** and plastered,
2Ki 10: 32 [D] In those days the LORD began to **reduce** *the* **size** of Israel.
Pr 26: 6 [D] Like **cutting off** one's feet or drinking violence is the

7895 קָצֶה *qāṣeh*, n.[m.]. [93] [√ 7894]

end [28], ends [16], edge [11], other[s] [4], *untranslated* [3], border [3], mouth [3], outskirts [3], foot [2], frontier [2], part [2], the other[s] [+824+2021] [2], after [+4946] [1], distant [1], end [+1473] [1], entire [+4946] [1], every part [1], extreme [1], far end [1], farthest [1], most distant land [1], of [+4946] [1], other[s] [+9028] [1], outposts [+2821] [1], southernmost [+4946] [1], tip [1]

Ge 8: 3 At the **end** *of* the hundred and fifty days the water had gone down,
19: 4 gone to bed, all the men from **every part** of the city of Sodom—
23: 9 of Machpelah, which belongs to him and is at the **end** *of* his field.
47: 2 He chose five **of** [+4946] his brothers and presented them before
47: 21 people to servitude, from *one* **end** [+1473] *of* Egypt to the other.
47: 21 the people to servitude, from one end of Egypt to the **other**[s].
Ex 13: 20 After leaving Succoth they camped at Etham on the **edge** *of* the
16: 35 they ate manna until they reached the **border** *of* Canaan.
19: 12 careful that you do not go up the mountain or touch the **foot** *of* it.
26: 5 on one curtain and fifty loops on the **end** curtain of the other set,
26: 28 The center crossbar is to extend from **end** to end at the middle of
26: 28 The center crossbar is to extend from end to **end** at the middle of
36: 12 on one curtain and fifty loops on the **end** curtain of the other set,
36: 33 so that it extended from **end** to end at the middle of the frames.
36: 33 so that it extended from end to **end** at the middle of the frames.
Nu 11: 1 among them and consumed some of the **outskirts** *of* the camp.
20: 16 "Now we are here at Kadesh, a town on the **edge** *of* your territory.
22: 36 the Moabite town on the Arnon border, at the **edge** *of* his territory.
22: 41 up to Bamoth Baal, and from there he saw **part** *of* the people.
23: 13 you can see them; you will see only a **part** but not all of them.
33: 6 They left Succoth and camped at Etham, on the **edge** *of* the desert.
33: 37 left Kadesh and camped at Mount Hor, on the **border** *of* Edom.
34: 3 your southern boundary will start from the **end** *of* the Salt Sea,
Dt 4: 32 man on the earth; ask from *one* **end** *of* the heavens to the other.
4: 32 the earth; ask from one end of the heavens to the **other**[s] [+9028].
13: 7 [13:8] whether near or far, from one **end** *of* the land to the other),
13: 7 [13:8] from one end of the land to **the other**[s] [+824+2021]),
14: 28 At the **end** *of* every three years, bring all the tithes of that year's
28: 49 from the **ends** *of* the earth, like an eagle swooping down, a nation
28: 64 you among all nations, from one **end** *of* the earth to the other.
28: 64 you among all nations, from one end of the earth to the **other**[s].
30: 4 Even if you have been banished to the **most distant land** *under*
Jos 3: 2 **After** [+4946] three days the officers went throughout the camp,
3: 8 'When you reach the **edge** *of* the Jordan's waters, go and stand in
3: 15 the ark reached the Jordan and their feet touched the water's **edge**,
4: 19 the Jordan and camped at Gilgal on the eastern **border** *of* Jericho.
9: 16 **[NIE]** Three days after they made the treaty with the Gibeonites,
13: 27 of the Jordan, the territory up to the **end** *of* the Sea of Kinnereth).
15: 1 to the territory of Edom, to the Desert of Zin in the **extreme** south.
15: 2 boundary started from the bay at the southern **end** *of* the Salt Sea,
15: 5 The eastern boundary is the Salt Sea as far as the **mouth** *of* the
15: 5 started from the bay of the sea at the **mouth** *of* the Jordan,
15: 8 the Hinnom Valley at the northern **end** *of* the Valley of Rephaim.
15: 21 The **southernmost** [+4946] towns of the tribe of Judah in the
18: 15 The southern side began at the **outskirts** *of* Kiriath Jearim on the
18: 16 The boundary went down to the **foot** *of* the hill facing the Valley of
18: 19 bay of the Salt Sea, at the **mouth** *of* the Jordan in the south.
Jdg 6: 21 With the **tip** *of* the staff that was in his hand, the angel of the
7: 11 Purah his servant went down to the **outposts** [+2821] of the camp.
7: 17 my lead. When I get to the **edge** *of* the camp, do exactly as I do.
7: 19 the hundred men with him reached the **edge** *of* the camp at the
Ru 3: 7 he went over to lie down at the **far end** *of* the grain pile.
1Sa 9: 27 As they were going down to the **edge** *of* the town, Samuel said to
14: 2 Saul was staying on the **outskirts** *of* Gibeah under a pomegranate
14: 27 so he reached out the **end** *of* the staff that was in his hand
14: 43 told him, "I merely tasted a little honey with the **end** *of* my staff.
2Sa 24: 8 they came back to Jerusalem at the **end** *of* nine months and twenty
1Ki 9: 10 At the **end** *of* twenty years, during which Solomon built these two
2Ki 7: 5 When they reached the **edge** *of* the camp, not a man was there,
7: 8 The men who had leprosy reached the **edge** *of* the camp
8: 3 At the **end** *of* the seven years she came back from the land of the
18: 10 At the **end** *of* three years the Assyrians took it. So Samaria was
Ne 1: 9 then even if your exiled people are at the **farthest** horizon,
Ps 19: 4 [19:5] out into all the earth, their words to the **ends** *of* the world.
19: 6 [19:7] It rises at *one* **end** *of* the heavens and makes its circuit to
19: 6 [19:7] one end of the heavens and makes its circuit to the **other**[s];
46: 9 [46:10] He makes wars cease to the **ends** *of* the earth; he breaks
61: 2 [61:3] From the **ends** *of* the earth I call to you, I call as my heart
135: 7 He makes clouds rise from the **ends** *of* the earth; he sends lightning
Pr 17: 24 wisdom in view, but a fool's eyes wander to the **ends** *of* the earth.
Isa 5: 26 the distant nations, he whistles for those at the **ends** *of* the earth.
7: 3 to meet Ahaz at the **end** *of* the aqueduct of the Upper Pool,
7: 18 In that day the LORD will whistle for flies from the **distant**
13: 5 They come from faraway lands, from the **ends** *of* the heavens—
42: 10 his praise from the **ends** *of* the earth, you who go down to the sea,
43: 6 my sons from afar and my daughters from the **ends** *of* the earth—
48: 20 Send it out to the **ends** *of* the earth; say, "The LORD has
49: 6 that you may bring my salvation to the **ends** *of* the earth."
56: 11 they all turn to their own way, each seeks his own gain. **[NIE]**
62: 11 The LORD has made proclamation to the **ends** *of* the earth:
Jer 10: 13 the heavens roar; he makes clouds rise from the **ends** *of* the earth.
12: 12 for the sword of the LORD will devour from *one* **end** *of* the land
12: 12 of the LORD will devour from one end of the land to the **other**[s];
25: 31 The tumult will resound to the **ends** *of* the earth, for the LORD
25: 33 will be everywhere—from *one* **end** *of* the earth to the other.
25: 33 from one end of the earth to **the other**[s] [+824+2021].
51: 16 the heavens roar; he makes clouds rise from the **ends** *of* the earth.
51: 31 to the king of Babylon that his **entire** [+4946] city is captured,
Eze 3: 16 At the **end** *of* seven days the word of the LORD came to me:
25: 9 I will expose the flank of Moab, beginning at its **frontier** towns—
33: 2 choose one of their men **[NIE]** and make him their watchman,
39: 14 At the **end** *of* the seven months they will begin their search.
48: 1 At the northern **frontier**, Dan will have one portion; it will follow

7896 קָצָה[2] *qāṣâ*[2], n.f. & m.[pl.]. [35] [√ 7894]

ends [11], corners [9], end [4], all sorts [2], tip [2], *untranslated* [1], all sorts [+4946] [1], all [1], other[s] [1], outer fringe [1], quarters [1], ruin [1]

Ex 25: 18 make two cherubim out of hammered gold at the **ends** *of* the cover.
25: 19 Make one cherub on one **end** and the second cherub on the other;
25: 19 Make one cherub on one end and the second cherub on the **other**[s];
25: 19 make the cherubim of one piece with the cover, at the two **ends**.
26: 4 Make loops of blue material along the edge of the **end** curtain in
27: 4 and make a bronze ring at each of the four **corners** *of* the network.
28: 7 It is to have two shoulder pieces attached to two of its **corners**,
28: 23 gold rings for it and fasten them to two **corners** *of* the breastpiece.

Ex 28:24 Fasten the two gold chains to the rings at the **corners** *of* the
28:25 the other **ends** *of* the chains to the two settings, attaching them to
28:26 attach them to the other two **corners** *of* the breastpiece on the
36:11 they made loops of blue material along the edge of the **end** curtain
37: 7 he made two cherubim out of hammered gold at the **ends** *of* the
37: 8 He made one cherub on one **end** and the second cherub on the
37: 8 **[RPH]** at the two ends he made them of one piece with the cover.
37: 8 at the two **ends** [K 7921] he made them of one piece with the
39: 4 which were attached to two of its **corners**, [K 7921] so it could be
39:16 and fastened the rings to two of the **corners** *of* the breastpiece.
39:17 They fastened the two gold chains to the rings at the **corners** *of* the
39:18 the other **ends** *of* the chains to the two settings, attaching them to
39:19 attached them to the other two **corners** *of* the breastpiece on the
Jdg 18: 2 out the land and explore it. These men represented **all** their clans.
1Ki 6:24 the other wing five cubits—ten cubits from wing **tip** to wing tip.
6:24 the other wing five cubits—ten cubits from wing tip to wing **tip**.
12:31 on high places and appointed priests from **all sorts** *of* people,
13:33 once more appointed priests for the high places from **all sorts** *of*
2Ki 17:32 they also appointed **all sorts** [+4946] *of* their own *people* to
Job 26:14 these are but the **outer fringe** *of* his works; how faint the whisper
28:24 for he views the **ends** *of* the earth and sees everything under the
Isa 40:28 LORD is the everlasting God, the Creator of the **ends** *of* the earth.
41: 5 The islands have seen it and fear; the **ends** *of* the earth tremble.
41: 9 I took you from the **ends** *of* the earth, from its farthest corners I
Jer 49:36 I will bring against Elam the four winds from the four **quarters** *of*
Eze 15: 4 the fire as fuel and the fire burns both **ends** and chars the middle,
Hab 2:10 You have plotted the **ruin** *of* many peoples, shaming your own

7897 קֵצֶה qēṣeh, n.[m.]. [5] [√ 7894]

end [2], boundless [+401] [1], endless [+401] [1], number [1]

Isa 2: 7 land is full of silver and gold; there is no **end** to their treasures.
2: 7 Their land is full of horses; there is no **end** to their chariots.
Na 2: 9 [2:10] The supply is **endless** [+401], the wealth from all its
3: 3 Many casualties, piles of dead, bodies without **number**, people
3: 9 Cush and Egypt were her **boundless** [+401] strength; Put

7898 קָצוּ qāṣû, n.[m.]. [3] [√ 7894]

ends [2], borders [1]

Ps 48:10 [48:11] O God, your praise reaches to the **ends** *of* the earth;
65: 5 [65:6] the hope of all the **ends** *of* the earth and of the farthest seas,
Isa 26:15 glory for yourself; you have extended all the **borders** *of* the land.

7899 קָצוּץ qāṣûṣ, n. *or* v.ptcp. Not used in NIV/BHS [√ 7916 *or* 7894]

7900 קָצוּר qāṣûr, a. *or* v.ptcp. [1] [√ 7918]

narrower [1]

Eze 42: 5 Now the upper rooms were **narrower**, for the galleries took more

7901 קְצוֹת q^{e}ṣôt, n.[m.]. Not used in NIV/BHS [√ 7894]

7902 קֶצַח qeṣaḥ, n.m. [3]

caraway [3]

Isa 28:25 leveled the surface, does he not sow **caraway** and scatter cummin?
28:27 **Caraway** is not threshed with a sledge, nor is a cartwheel rolled
28:27 **caraway** is beaten out with a rod, and cummin with a stick.

7903 קָצִין qāṣîn, n.m. [12] [→ 6962]

commander [4], rulers [3], leader [2], commanders [1], leaders [1], ruler [1]

Jos 10:24 and said to the army **commanders** who had come with him,
Jdg 11: 6 "Come," they said, "be our **commander**, so we can fight the
11:11 and the people made him head and **commander** over them.
Pr 6: 7 It has no **commander**, no overseer or ruler,
25:15 Through patience a **ruler** can be persuaded, and a gentle tongue
Isa 1:10 Hear the word of the LORD, you **rulers** *of* Sodom; listen to the
3: 6 his father's home, and say, "You have a cloak, you be our **leader**;
3: 7 or clothing in my house; do not make me the **leader** *of* the people."
22: 3 All your **leaders** have fled together; they have been captured
Da 11:18 a **commander** will put an end to his insolence and will turn his
Mic 3: 1 "Listen, you leaders of Jacob, you **rulers** *of* the house of Israel.
3: 9 you **rulers** *of* the house of Israel, who despise justice and distort all

7904 ¹קְצִיעָה q^{e}ṣîʿâ¹, n.f. [1] [√ 7905; cf. 7909]

cassia [1]

Ps 45: 8 [45:9] your robes are fragrant with myrrh and aloes and **cassia**;

7905 ²קְצִיעָה q^{e}ṣîʿâ², n.pr.f. [1] [√ 7904; cf. 7909]

Keziah [1]

Job 42:14 named Jemimah, the second **Keziah** and the third Keren-Happuch.

7906 קְצִיץ q^{e}ṣîṣ, n.pr.loc. Not used in NIV/BHS [√ 6681; cf. 7916, 7891]

7907 ¹קָצִיר qāṣîr¹, n.m. [49] [√ 7917]

harvest [37], harvests [3], harvest time [2], harvesting [+7917] [2], *untranslated* [1], harvesting grain [1], reap [+906+7917] [1], reaper [1], reaping [1]

Ge 8:22 seedtime and **harvest**, cold and heat, summer and winter, day
30:14 During wheat **harvest**, Reuben went out into the fields and found
45: 6 and for the next five years there will not be plowing and **reaping**.
Ex 23:16 "Celebrate the Feast of **Harvest** with the firstfruits of the crops you
34:21 even during the plowing season and **harvest** you must rest.
34:22 the Feast of Weeks with the firstfruits of the wheat **harvest**,
Lev 19: 9 " 'When you reap the **harvest** *of* your land, do not reap to the very
19: 9 very edges of your field or gather the gleanings of your **harvest**.
23:10 you enter the land I am going to give you and you reap its **harvest**,
23:10 its harvest, bring to the priest a sheaf of the first grain you **harvest**.
23:22 " 'When you reap the **harvest** *of* your land, do not reap to the very
23:22 very edges of your field or gather the gleanings of your **harvest**.
25: 5 *Do* not **reap** [+906+7917] what grows of itself or harvest the
Dt 24:19 When you *are* **harvesting** [+7917] in your field and you overlook
Jos 3:15 Now the Jordan is at flood stage all during **harvest**. Yet as soon as
Jdg 15: 1 Later on, at the time of wheat **harvest**, Samson took a young goat
Ru 1:22 arriving in Bethlehem as the barley **harvest** was beginning.
2:21 'Stay with my workers until they finish **harvesting** all my **grain**.' "
2:23 of Boaz to glean until the barley and wheat **harvests** were finished.
2:23 to glean until the barley and wheat harvests **[RPH]** were finished.
1Sa 6:13 Now the people of Beth Shemesh *were* **harvesting** [+7917] their
8:12 of fifties, and others to plow his ground and reap his **harvest**,
12:17 Is it not wheat **harvest** now? I will call upon the LORD to send
2Sa 21: 9 they were put to death during the first days of the **harvest**,
21: 9 first days of the harvest, just as the barley **harvest** was beginning.
21:10 From the beginning of the **harvest** till the rain poured down from
23:13 During **harvest time**, three of the thirty chief men came down to
Job 5: 5 The hungry consume his **harvest**, taking it even from among
Pr 6: 8 it stores its provisions in summer and gathers its food at **harvest**.
10: 5 a wise son, but he who sleeps during **harvest** is a disgraceful son.
20: 4 not plow in season; so at **harvest time** he looks but finds nothing.
25:13 Like the coolness of snow at **harvest** time is a trustworthy
26: 1 Like snow in summer or rain in **harvest**, honor is not fitting for a
Isa 9: 3 [9:2] they rejoice before you as people rejoice at the **harvest**,
16: 9 over your ripened fruit and over your **harvests** have been stilled.
17: 5 It will be as when a **reaper** gathers the standing grain and harvests
17:11 yet the **harvest** will be as nothing in the day of disease and
18: 4 heat in the sunshine, like a cloud of dew in the heat of **harvest**."
18: 5 For, before the **harvest**, when the blossom is gone and the flower
23: 3 the **harvest** *of* the Nile was the revenue of Tyre, and she became
Jer 5:17 They will devour your **harvests** and food, devour your sons
5:24 rains in season, who assures us of the regular weeks of **harvest**.'
8:20 "The **harvest** is past, the summer has ended, and we are not
50:16 from Babylon the sower, and the reaper with his sickle at **harvest**.
51:33 at the time it is trampled; the time to **harvest** her will soon come."
Hos 6:11 "Also for you, Judah, a **harvest** is appointed. "Whenever I would
Joel 1:11 and the barley, because the **harvest** *of* the field is destroyed.
3:13 [4:13] Swing the sickle, for the **harvest** is ripe. Come,
Am 4: 7 "I also withheld rain from you when the **harvest** was still three

7908 ²קָצִיר qāṣîr², n.m. [5] [√ 7918?]

branches [2], boughs [1], shoots [1], twigs [1]

Job 14: 9 at the scent of water it will bud and put forth **shoots** like a plant.
18:16 His roots dry up below and his **branches** wither above.
29:19 reach to the water, and the dew will lie all night on my **branches**.
Ps 80:11 [80:12] It sent out its **boughs** to the Sea, its shoots as far as the
Isa 27:11 When its **twigs** are dry, they are broken off and women come

7909 ¹קָצַע qāṣa'¹, v. [1] [→ 5244, 7904, 7905]

have scraped [1]

Lev 14:41 [G] *He must* **have** all the inside walls of the house **scraped** and

7910 ²קָצַע qāṣa'², v.den. [3] [→ 4553, 5243]

corners [3]

Ex 26:23 [E] and make two frames for the **corners** at the far end.
36:28 [E] two frames were made for the **corners** *of* the tabernacle at the
Eze 46:22 [H] each of the courts in the four **corners** was the same size.

7911 קָצַף ***qāṣap***, v. [34] [→ 7912; Ar 10633]

angry [23], angered [2], enraged [2], anger [1], angry [+7912] [1], aroused wrath [1], furious [+4394] [1], made angry [+906+2118] [1], provoked to anger [1], very angry [+7912] [1]

Ge 40: 2 [A] Pharaoh *was* **angry** with his two officials, the chief
41: 10 [A] Pharaoh *was once* **angry** with his servants, and he
Ex 16: 20 [A] and began to smell. So Moses *was* **angry** with them.
Lev 10: 6 [A] and the LORD *will be* **angry** with the whole community.
10: 16 [A] *he was* **angry** with Eleazar and Ithamar, Aaron's remaining
Nu 16: 22 [A] *will you be* **angry** with the entire assembly when only one
31: 14 [A] Moses *was* **angry** with the officers of the army—
Dt 1: 34 [A] heard what you said, *he was* **angry** and solemnly swore:
9: 7 [G] *you* **provoked** the LORD your God **to anger** in the desert.
9: 8 [G] At Horeb *you* **aroused** the LORD's **wrath** so that he was
9: 19 [A] for *he was* **angry** *enough* with you to destroy you.
9: 22 [G] *You* also **made** the LORD **angry** [+906+2118] at Taberah,
Jos 22: 18 [A] tomorrow *he will be* **angry** with the whole community of
1Sa 29: 4 [A] the Philistine commanders *were* **angry** with him and said,
2Ki 5: 11 [A] Naaman went away **angry** and said, "I thought that he would
13: 19 [A] The man of God *was* **angry** with him and said, "You should
Est 1: 12 [A] the king *became* **furious** [+4394] and burned with anger.
2: 21 [A] *became* **angry** and conspired to assassinate King Xerxes.
Ps 106: 32 [G] By the waters of Meribah *they* **angered** the LORD,
Ecc 5: 6 [5:5] [A] Why *should* God *be* **angry** at what you say
Isa 8: 21 [F] *they will become* **enraged** and, looking upward, will curse
47: 6 [A] *I was* **angry** with my people and desecrated my inheritance;
54: 9 [A] So now I have sworn not *to be* **angry** with you, never to
57: 16 [A] nor *will I* always *be* **angry**, for then the spirit of man would
57: 17 [A] *I was* **enraged** by his sinful greed; I punished him, and hid
57: 17 [A] I punished him, and hid my face *in* **anger**, yet he kept on in
64: 5 [64:4] [A] we continued to sin against them, you *were* **angry**.
64: 9 [64:8] [A] *Do* not *be* **angry** beyond measure, O LORD; do not
Jer 37: 15 [A] They *were* **angry** with Jeremiah and had him beaten and
La 5: 22 [A] utterly rejected us and *are* **angry** with us beyond measure.
Zec 1: 2 [A] "The LORD *was* **very angry** [+7912] with your forefathers.
1: 15 [A] I *am* very **angry** [+7912] with the nations that feel secure.
1: 15 [A] I *was* only a little **angry**, but they added to the calamity.'
8: 14 [G] and showed no pity when your fathers **angered** me,"

7912 ¹קֶצֶף ***qeṣep¹***, n.m. [28] [√ 7911; Ar 10634]

wrath [13], anger [7], angry [3], angry [+7911] [1], discord [1], fury [1], great wrath [+2256+2405] [1], very angry [+7911] [1]

Nu 1: 53 so that **wrath** will not fall on the Israelite community.
16: 46 [17:11] **Wrath** has come out from the LORD; the plague has
18: 5 and the altar, so that **wrath** will not fall on the Israelites again.
Dt 29: 28 [29:27] in great **wrath** the LORD uprooted them from their land
Jos 9: 20 so that **wrath** will not fall on us for breaking the oath we swore to
22: 20 did not **wrath** come upon the whole community of Israel?
2Ki 3: 27 The **fury** against Israel was great; they withdrew and returned to
1Ch 27: 24 **Wrath** came on Israel on account of this numbering,
2Ch 19: 2 Because of this, the **wrath** of the LORD is upon you.
19: 10 otherwise his **wrath** will come on you and your brothers.
24: 18 of their guilt, God's **anger** came upon Judah and Jerusalem.
29: 8 the **anger** *of* the LORD has fallen on Judah and Jerusalem;
32: 25 therefore the LORD's **wrath** was on him and on Judah
32: 26 therefore the LORD's **wrath** did not come upon them during the
Est 1: 18 in the same way. There will be no end of disrespect and **discord**.
Ps 38: 1 [38:2] do not rebuke me in your **anger** or discipline me in your
102: 10 [102:11] because of your **great wrath** [+2256+2405], for you
Ecc 5: 17 [5:16] in darkness, with great frustration, affliction and **anger**.
Isa 34: 2 The LORD **is angry** with all nations; his wrath is upon all their
54: 8 In a surge of **anger** I hid my face from you for a moment,
60: 10 Though in **anger** I struck you, in favor I will show you
Jer 10: 10 When he is **angry**, the earth trembles; the nations cannot endure
21: 5 and a mighty arm in anger and fury and great **wrath**.
32: 37 lands where I banish them in my furious anger and great **wrath**;
50: 13 Because of the LORD's **anger** she will not be inhabited but will
Zec 1: 2 "The LORD *was* **very angry** [+7911] with your forefathers.
1: 15 but I *am* very **angry** [+7911] with the nations that feel secure.
7: 12 the earlier prophets. So the LORD Almighty was very **angry**.

7913 ²קֶצֶף ***qeṣep²***, n.[m.]. [1] [→ 7914]

twig [1]

Hos 10: 7 and its king will float away like a **twig** on the surface of the waters.

7914 קְצָפָה ***qᵉṣāpâ***, n.f. [1] [√ 7913]

ruined [+4200] [1]

Joel 1: 7 It has laid waste my vines and **ruined** [+4200] my fig trees.

7915 ¹קָצַץ ***qāṣaṣ¹***, v. [11] [cf. 7891, 7894]

cut off [4], took away [3], cut free [1], cut [1], shatters [1], stripped off [1]

Ex 39: 3 [D] thin sheets of gold and **cut** strands to be worked into the blue,
Dt 25: 12 [A] *you shall* **cut off** her hand. Show her no pity.
Jdg 1: 6 [D] and caught him, and **cut off** his thumbs and big toes.
1: 7 [E] and big toes **cut off** have picked up scraps under my table.
2Sa 4: 12 [D] *They* **cut off** their hands and feet and hung the bodies by the
2Ki 16: 17 [D] King Ahaz **took away** the side panels and removed the
18: 16 [D] At this time Hezekiah king of Judah **stripped off** the gold
24: 13 [D] **took away** all the gold articles that Solomon king of Israel
2Ch 28: 24 [D] the furnishings from the temple of God and **took** them **away**.
Ps 46: 9 [46:10] [D] he breaks the bow and **shatters** the spear, he burns
129: 4 [D] *he has* **cut** me **free** *from* the cords of the wicked.

7916 ²קָצַץ ***qāṣaṣ²***, v. [3] [→ 7765, 7899?, 7906; cf. 7891]

distant [3]

Jer 9: 26 [9:25] [B] and all who live in the desert in **distant** places.
25: 23 [B] Dedan, Tema, Buz and all who are in **distant** places;
49: 32 [B] I will scatter to the winds those who are in **distant** places

7917 ¹קָצַר ***qāṣar¹***, v. [34] [→ 7907]

reap [15], harvesters [5], reaper [3], harvesting [+7907] [2], *untranslated* [1], gather [1], harvest [1], harvesting [1], harvests [1], reap [+906+7907] [1], reaped [1], reapers [1], reaps [1]

Lev 19: 9 [A] " 'When you **reap** the harvest of your land, do not reap to the
19: 9 [A] *do* not **reap** *to* the very edges of your field or gather the
23: 10 [A] the land I am going to give you and *you* **reap** its harvest,
23: 22 [A] " 'When you **reap** the harvest of your land, do not reap to the
23: 22 [A] *do* not **reap** *to* the very edges of your field or gather the
25: 5 [A] *Do* not **reap** [+906+7907] what grows of itself or harvest the
25: 11 [A] do not sow and *do* not **reap** what grows of itself or harvest
Dt 24: 19 [A] When you *are* **harvesting** [+7907] in your field and you
Ru 2: 3 [A] and began to glean in the fields behind the **harvesters**.
2: 4 [A] Boaz arrived from Bethlehem and greeted the **harvesters**,
2: 5 [A] Boaz asked the foreman of his **harvesters**, "Whose young
2: 6 [A] The foreman **[RPH]** replied, "She is the Moabitess who
2: 7 [A] and gather among the sheaves behind the **harvesters**.'
2: 9 [A] Watch the field where *the men are* **harvesting**, and follow
2: 14 [A] When she sat down with the **harvesters**, he offered her some
1Sa 6: 13 [A] Now the people of Beth Shemesh *were* **harvesting** [+7907]
8: 12 [A] of fifties, and others to plow his ground and **reap** his harvest,
2Ki 4: 18 [A] one day he went out to his father, who was with the **reapers**.
19: 29 [A] in the third year sow and **reap**, plant vineyards and eat their
Job 4: 8 [A] those who plow evil and those who sow trouble **reap** it.
24: 6 [A] *They* **gather** fodder in the fields and glean in the vineyards
Ps 126: 5 [A] Those who sow in tears *will* **reap** with songs of joy.
129: 7 [A] with it the **reaper** cannot fill his hands, nor the one who
Pr 22: 8 [A] He who sows wickedness **reaps** trouble, and the rod of his
Ecc 11: 4 [A] will not plant; whoever looks at the clouds *will* not **reap**.
Isa 17: 5 [A] the standing grain and **harvests** the grain *with* his arm—
37: 30 [A] in the third year sow and **reap**, plant vineyards and eat their
Jer 9: 22 [9:21] [A] like cut grain behind the **reaper**, with no one to
12: 13 [A] They will sow wheat but **reap** thorns; they will wear
Hos 8: 7 [A] "They sow the wind and **reap** the whirlwind. The stalk has
10: 12 [A] for yourselves righteousness, **reap** the fruit of unfailing love,
10: 13 [A] you have planted wickedness, *you have* **reaped** evil,
Am 9: 13 [A] "when the **reaper** will be overtaken by the plowman
Mic 6: 15 [A] You will plant but not **harvest**; you will press olives but not

7918 ²קָצַר ***qāṣar²***, v. [14] [→ 7900, 7908?, 7919, 7920]

cut short [3], short [+7918] [2], short [2], angry [1], bear no longer [1], grew weary [1], impatient [+5883] [1], impatient [1], tired [1], too short [1]

Nu 11: 23 [A] LORD answered Moses, "*Is* the LORD's arm **too short**?
21: 4 [A] But the people *grew* **impatient** [+5883] on the way;
Jdg 10: 16 [A] the LORD. And he *could* **bear** Israel's misery **no longer**.
16: 16 [A] she prodded him day after day until he *was* **tired** to death.
Job 21: 4 [A] complaint directed to man? Why *should* I not *be* **impatient**?
Ps 89: 45 [89:46] [G] *You have* **cut short** the days of his youth; you have
102: 23 [102:24] [D] life he broke my strength; *he* **cut short** my days.
Pr 10: 27 [A] adds length to life, but the years of the wicked *are* **cut short**.
Isa 28: 20 [A] The bed *is* too **short** to stretch out on, the blanket too narrow
50: 2 [A] to answer? *Was* my arm too **short** [+7918] to ransom you?
50: 2 [A] to answer? *Was* my arm too **short** [+7918] to ransom you?
59: 1 [A] Surely the arm of the LORD *is* not too **short** to save, nor his
Mic 2: 7 [A] O house of Jacob: "*Is* the Spirit of the LORD **angry**?
Zec 11: 8 [A] The flock detested me, and I **grew weary** of them

7919 קֹצֶר ***qōṣer***, n.[m.]. [1] [√ 7918]

discouragement [+8120] [1]

Ex 6: 9 did not listen to him because of their **discouragement** [+8120] and

7920 קָצֵר ***qāṣēr***, a. [5] [√ 7918]

drained [2], few [1], quick-tempered [+678] [1], quick-tempered [+8120] [1]

2Ki 19:26 Their people, **drained** *of* power, are dismayed and put to shame.
Job 14: 1 "Man born of woman is of **few** days and full of trouble.
Pr 14:17 A **quick-tempered** [+678] *man* does foolish things, and a crafty
14:29 but a **quick-tempered** [+8120] *man* displays folly.
Isa 37:27 Their people, **drained** *of* power, are dismayed and put to shame.

7921 קְצָת ***qᵉṣāt***, n.f. [7] [√ 7894; Ar 10636]

end [2], some [+4946] [2], after [+4946] [1], corners [1], far away [1]

Ex 37: 8 [at the two **ends** [K; see Q 7896] he made them of one piece with]
38: 5 They cast bronze rings to hold the poles for the four **corners** of the
39: 4 [which were attached to two of its **corners**, [K; see Q 7896]]
Ne 7:70 [7:69] **Some of** [+4946] the heads of the families contributed to
Ps 65: 8 [65:9] Those living **far away** fear your wonders; where morning
Da 1: 2 along with **some** [+4946] *of* the articles from the temple of God.
1: 5 and **after** [+4946] that they were to enter the king's service.
1:15 At the **end** *of* the ten days they looked healthier and better
1:18 At the **end** *of* the time set by the king to bring them in, the chief

7922 קַר ***qar***, a. [3] [√ 7981]

cold [1], cool [1], even-tempered [+8120] [1]

Pr 17:27 a man of understanding is **even-tempered** [+8120]. [Q 3701]
25:25 Like **cold** water to a weary soul is good news from a distant land.
Jer 18:14 Do its **cool** waters from distant sources ever cease to flow?

7923 קֹר ***qōr***, n.[m.]. [1] [√ 7981]

cold [1]

Ge 8:22 **cold** and heat, summer and winter, day and night will never cease."

7924 קָרָאי ***qārā'¹***, v. [733] [→ 5246, 7926, 7927, 7951, 7952; Ar 10637]

called [139], call [81], summoned [45], read [33], named [+9005] [28], named [+906+9005] [23], proclaim [23], called [+9005] [21], summon [18], calls [15], be called [14], invited [12], proclaimed [12], called out [11], calling [11], bears [+6584] [10], cried out [9], call out [7], cry out [7], gave [7], invite [7], called [+906+9005] [6], cry [6], sent for [+2256+4200+8938] [6], shouted [6], is called [5], *untranslated* [4], bear [+6584] [4], call [+9005] [4], call upon [4], called together [4], proclaiming [4], summons [4], are called [3], call on [3], called out [+928+1524+7754] [3], cried [3], guests [3], name [+9005] [3], named [3], was called [3], announced [2], asks [2], be reckoned [2], call [+906+9005] [2], call in [2], chosen [+928+9005] [2], declared [2], famous [+9005] [2], gave name [2], given [2], named [+4200+9005] [2], read aloud [2], say [2], were summoned [2], announce [1], appeal [1], be called [+9005] [1], be called [+906+9005] [1], be known as [+9005] [1], be known as [1], be mentioned [1], be named [+9005] [1], been called [1], been invited as guests [1], been named [+9005] [1], being called [1], being summoned [1], bleat [1], blurts out [1], brag [1], bring out [1], call back [1], call for help [1], call yourselves [1], called down [1], called in [1], calling [+7754] [1], calling [+906+9005] [1], calling down [1], calling for help [1], calling forth [1], calling out [1], calls in [1], claims [1], convocations [+5246] [1], cries out [1], decreed [1], dictated [+906+4946+7023] [1], did[s] [1], exclaim [1], foretold [1], get [1], give [1], got [1], grasping [1], herald [1], invitation [1], invite [+2256+4200+8938] [1], invites [1], invoke [+928+7023] [1], is called [+9005] [1], is called together [1], known as [1], make an offer [1], make proclamation [1], men of high rank [1], name [+906+9005] [1], name [1], named [+6584+9005] [1], named [+906+906+9005] [1], named [+906+928+9005] [1], offer [1], pray [1], prayed [1], preach [1], proclaim [+928] [1], proclaimed [+928] [1], pronounced [1], raised a cry [1], reading [1], scream for help [+2256+7754+8123] [1], screamed [+928+1524+7754] [1], screamed for help [+2256+7754+8123] [1], sent for [+906+2256+8938] [1], sent for [+906+906+2256+8938] [1], sent for [+906+906+4200+8938] [1], sent word [+2256+8938] [1], shout [+1524+7754] [1], shout [+928+7754] [1], shout aloud [+928+1744] [1], shout [1], shouted [+2256+5951+7754] [1], shouted [+928+7754] [1], shouted the news [1], summoned [+2256+4200+4200+8938] [1], summoned [+2256+4200+8938] [1], summoned [+4200+4200+4200+8938] [1], voices [1], was called [+9005] [1], was read aloud [1], were appointed [1], were called [1], were counted [1], were invited [1], word [1]

Ge 1: 5 [A] God **called** the light "day," and the darkness he called
1: 5 [A] called the light "day," and the darkness *he* **called** "night."
1: 8 [A] God **called** the expanse "sky." And there was evening,
1:10 [A] God **called** the dry ground "land," and the gathered waters he
1:10 [A] dry ground "land," and the gathered waters *he* **called** "seas."
2:19 [A] He brought them to the man to see what *he would* **name**
2:19 [A] whatever the man **called** each living creature, that was its
2:20 [A] So the man **gave** names to all the livestock, the birds of the
2:23 [C] my bones and flesh of my flesh; she *shall* **be called** 'woman,'
3: 9 [A] But the LORD God **called** to the man, "Where are you?"
3:20 [A] Adam **named** [+9005] his wife Eve, because she would
4:17 [A] building a city, and *he* **named** [+9005] it after his son Enoch.
4:25 [A] she gave birth to a son and **named** [+906+9005] him Seth,
4:26 [A] Seth also had a son, and *he* **named** [+906+9005] him Enosh.
4:26 [A] At that time men began to **call** on the name of the LORD.
5: 2 [A] when they were created, *he* **called** [+906+9005] them "man."
5: 3 [A] in his own image; and *he* **named** [+906+9005] him Seth.
5:29 [A] *He* **named** [+906+9005] him Noah and said, "He will
11: 9 [A] That is why it *was* **called** [+9005] Babel—because there the
12: 8 [A] altar to the LORD and **called** on the name of the LORD.
12:18 [A] So Pharaoh **summoned** Abram. "What have you done to
13: 4 [A] an altar. There Abram **called** on the name of the LORD.
16:11 [A] *You shall* **name** [+9005] him Ishmael, for the LORD has
16:13 [A] *She* **gave** this name *to* the LORD who spoke to her:
16:14 [A] That is why the well *was* **called** Beer Lahai Roi; it is still
16:15 [A] and Abram **gave** the name Ishmael to the son she had borne.
17: 5 [C] No longer *will* you **be called** [+906+9005] Abram; your
17:15 [A] your wife, *you are* no longer *to* **call** [+906+9005] her Sarai;
17:19 [A] bear you a son, and *you will* **call** [+906+9005] him Isaac.
19: 5 [A] *They* **called** to Lot, "Where are the men who came to you
19:22 [A] reach it." (That is why the town *was* **called** [+9005] Zoar.)
19:37 [A] older daughter had a son, and *she* **named** [+9005] him Moab;
19:38 [A] also had a son, and *she* **named** [+9005] him Ben-Ammi;
20: 8 [A] Early the next morning Abimelech **summoned** all his
20: 9 [A] Abimelech **called** Abraham **in** and said, "What have you
21: 3 [A] Abraham **gave** the name Isaac *to* the son Sarah bore him.
21:12 [C] it is through Isaac that your offspring *will* **be reckoned**.
21:17 [A] the angel of God **called** to Hagar from heaven and said to
21:31 [A] So that place *was* **called** Beersheba, because the two men
21:33 [A] there *he* **called** upon the name of the LORD, the Eternal
22:11 [A] But the angel of the LORD **called out** to him from heaven,
22:14 [A] So Abraham **called** [+9005] that place The LORD Will
22:15 [A] The angel of the LORD **called** to Abraham from heaven a
24:57 [A] Then they said, "*Let's* **call** the girl and ask her about it."
24:58 [A] So *they* **called** Rebekah and asked her, "Will you go with
25:25 [A] was like a hairy garment; so *they* **named** [+9005] him Esau.
25:26 [A] hand grasping Esau's heel; so he *was* **named** [+9005] Jacob.
25:30 [A] (That is why he *was* also **called** [+9005] Edom.)
26: 9 [A] So Abimelech **summoned** Isaac and said, "She is really your
26:18 [A] and *he* **gave** them the same names his father had given them.
26:18 [A] and he gave them the same names his father *had* **given** them.
26:20 [A] So *he* **named** [+9005] the well Esek, because they disputed
26:21 [A] quarreled over that one also; so *he* **named** [+9005] it Sitnah.
26:22 [A] *He* **named** [+9005] it Rehoboth, saying, "Now the LORD
26:25 [A] built an altar there and **called** on the name of the LORD.
26:33 [A] *He* **called** it Shibah, and to this day the name of the town has
27: 1 [A] *he* **called** *for* Esau his older son and said to him, "My son."
27:36 [A] Esau said, "*Isn't* he rightly **named** [+9005] Jacob? He has
27:42 [A] *she* **sent for** [+2256+4200+8938] her younger son Jacob
28: 1 [A] So Isaac **called** for Jacob and blessed him and commanded
28:19 [A] *He* **called** [+906+9005] that place Bethel, though the city
29:32 [A] *She* **named** [+9005] him Reuben, for she said, "It is
29:33 [A] gave me this one too." So *she* **named** [+9005] him Simeon.
29:34 [A] have borne him three sons." So he *was* **named** [+9005] Levi.
29:35 [A] So *she* **named** [+9005] him Judah. Then she stopped having
30: 6 [A] me a son." Because of this *she* **named** [+9005] him Dan.
30: 8 [A] and I have won." So *she* **named** [+9005] him Naphtali.
30:11 [A] "What good fortune!" So *she* **named** [+906+9005] him Gad.
30:13 [A] will call me happy." So *she* **named** [+906+9005] him Asher.
30:18 [A] to my husband." So *she* **named** [+9005] him Issachar.
30:20 [A] him six sons." So *she* **named** [+906+9005] him Zebulun.
30:21 [A] gave birth to a daughter and **named** [+906+9005] her Dinah.
30:24 [A] *She* **named** [+906+9005] him Joseph, and said,
31: 4 [A] So Jacob **sent word** [+2256+8938] to Rachel and Leah to
31:47 [A] Laban **called** it Jegar Sahadutha, and Jacob called it Galeed.
31:47 [A] Laban called it Jegar Sahadutha, and Jacob **called** it Galeed.
31:48 [A] and me today." That is why it *was* **called** [+9005] Galeed.
31:54 [A] there in the hill country and **invited** his relatives to a meal.
32: 2 [32:3] [A] So *he* **named** [+9005] that place Mahanaim.
32:30 [32:31] [A] So Jacob **called** [+9005] the place Peniel, saying,
33:17 [A] That is why the place *is* **called** [+9005] Succoth.
33:20 [A] There he set up an altar and **called** it El Elohe Israel.
35: 7 [A] There he built an altar, and *he* **called** the place El Bethel,
35: 8 [A] oak below Bethel. So it *was* **named** [+9005] Allon Bacuth.
35:10 [C] is Jacob, but you *will* no longer **be called** [+9005] Jacob;

Ge 35:10 [A] name will be Israel." So *he* **named** [+906+9005] him Israel.
35:15 [A] Jacob **called** [+906+9005] the place where God had talked
35:18 [A] for she was dying—*she* **named** [+9005] her son Ben-Oni.
35:18 [A] her son Ben-Oni. But his father **named** him Benjamin.
38: 3 [A] and gave birth to a son, who *was* **named** [+906+9005] Er.
38: 4 [A] and gave birth to a son and **named** [+906+9005] him Onan.
38: 5 [A] to still another son and **named** [+906+9005] him Shelah.
38:29 [A] you have broken out!" And he *was* **named** [+9005] Perez.
38:30 [A] on his wrist, came out and he *was* **given** the name Zerah.
39:14 [A] *she* **called** her household servants. "Look," she said to them,
39:14 [A] in here to sleep with me, but *I* **screamed** [+928+1524+7754].
39:15 [A] When he heard me **scream** [+2256+7754+8123] **for help**, he
39:18 [A] But as soon as I **screamed** [+2256+7754+8123] **for help**, he
41: 8 [A] so *he* **sent for** [+906+906+2256+8938] all the magicians and
41:14 [A] So Pharaoh **sent for** [+906+2256+8938] Joseph, and he was
41:43 [A] and *men* **shouted** before him, "Make way!"
41:45 [A] Pharaoh **gave** Joseph the name Zaphenath-Paneah and gave
41:51 [A] Joseph **named** [+906+9005] his firstborn Manasseh and said,
41:52 [A] The second son *he* **named** [+906+9005] Ephraim and said,
45: 1 [A] and *he* **cried out**, "Have everyone leave my presence!"
46:33 [A] When Pharaoh **calls** you **in** and asks, 'What is your
47:29 [A] *he* **called** for his son Joseph and said to him, "If I have found
48: 6 [C] in the territory they inherit *they will* **be reckoned** under the
48:16 [C] *May* they **be called** by my name and the names of my fathers
49: 1 [A] Jacob **called** for his sons and said: "Gather around so I can
50:11 [A] That is why that place near the Jordan *is* **called** [+9005] Abel
Ex 1:18 [A] the king of Egypt **summoned** the midwives and asked them,
2: 7 [A] **get** one of the Hebrew women to nurse the baby for you?"
2: 8 [A] she answered. And the girl went and **got** the baby's mother.
2:10 [A] *She* **named** [+9005] him Moses, saying, "I drew him out of
2:20 [A] did you leave him? **Invite** him to have something to eat."
2:22 [A] a son, and Moses **named** [+906+9005] him Gershom, saying,
3: 4 [A] to look, God **called** to him from within the bush, "Moses!
7:11 [A] Pharaoh then **summoned** wise men and sorcerers,
8: 8 [8:4] [A] Pharaoh **summoned** Moses and Aaron and said,
8:25 [8:21] [A] Pharaoh **summoned** Moses and Aaron and said, "Go,
9:27 [A] Pharaoh **summoned** [+2256+4200+4200+8938] Moses and
10:16 [A] Pharaoh quickly **summoned** Moses and Aaron and said,
10:24 [A] Pharaoh **summoned** Moses and said, "Go, worship the
12:21 [A] Moses **summoned** all the elders of Israel and said to them,
12:31 [A] During the night Pharaoh **summoned** Moses and Aaron
15:23 [A] it was bitter. (That is why the place *is* **called** [+9005] Marah.)
16:31 [A] The people of Israel **called** [+906+9005] the bread manna.
17: 7 [A] *he* **called** [+9005] the place Massah and Meribah
17:15 [A] an altar and **called** [+9005] it The LORD is my Banner.
19: 3 [A] and the LORD **called** to him from the mountain and said,
19: 7 [A] So Moses went back and **summoned** the elders of the people
19:20 [A] of Mount Sinai and **called** Moses to the top of the mountain.
24: 7 [A] he took the Book of the Covenant and **read** it to the people.
24:16 [A] on the seventh day the LORD **called** to Moses from within
31: 2 [A] "See, *I have* **chosen** [+928+9005] Bezalel son of Uri, the son
32: 5 [A] saw this, he built an altar in front of the calf and **announced**,
33: 7 [A] camp some distance away, **calling** it the "tent of meeting."
33:19 [A] *I will* **proclaim** [+928] my name, the LORD, in your
34: 5 [A] and stood there with him and **proclaimed** [+928] his name,
34: 6 [A] **proclaiming**, "The LORD, the LORD, the compassionate
34:15 [A] to them, *they will* **invite** you and you will eat their sacrifices.
34:31 [A] Moses **called** to them; so Aaron and all the leaders of the
35:30 [A] the LORD *has* **chosen** [+928+9005] Bezalel son of Uri,
36: 2 [A] Moses **summoned** Bezalel and Oholiab and every skilled
Lev 1: 1 [A] The LORD **called** to Moses and spoke to him from the Tent
9: 1 [A] On the eighth day Moses **summoned** Aaron and his sons and
10: 4 [A] Moses **summoned** Mishael and Elzaphan, sons of Aaron's
13:45 [A] cover the lower part of his face and **cry out**, 'Unclean!
23: 2 [A] which *you are to* **proclaim** as sacred assemblies.
23: 4 [A] the sacred assemblies *you are to* **proclaim** at their appointed
23:21 [A] On that same day *you are to* **proclaim** a sacred assembly
23:37 [A] which *you are to* **proclaim** as sacred assemblies for bringing
25:10 [A] **proclaim** liberty throughout the land to all its inhabitants.
Nu 1:16 [B] These **were** the *men* **appointed** [K 7951] *from* the
11: 3 [A] So that place *was* **called** [+9005] Taberah, because fire from
11:34 [A] Therefore the place *was* **named** [+906+9005] Kibroth
12: 5 [A] the entrance to the Tent and **summoned** Aaron and Miriam.
13:16 [A] the land. (Moses **gave** Hoshea son of Nun *the* **name** Joshua.)
13:24 [A] That place *was* **called** the Valley of Eshcol because of the
16:12 [A] Then Moses **summoned** [+4200+4200+4200+8938] Dathan
21: 3 [A] and their towns; so the place *was* **named** [+9005] Hormah.
22: 5 [A] sent messengers to **summon** Balaam son of Beor, who was at
22:20 [A] and said, "Since these men have come to **summon** you,
22:37 [A] said to Balaam, "Did I not send you an urgent **summons**?
24:10 [A] and said to him, "*I* **summoned** you to curse my enemies,
25: 2 [A] *who* **invited** them to the sacrifices to their gods. The people
26: 9 [b] [and Abiram were the community **officials** [K; see Q 7951]]
32:38 [A] and Sibmah. *They* **gave** names *to* the cities they rebuilt.
32:41 [A] captured their settlements and **called** them Havvoth Jair.
32:42 [A] its surrounding settlements and **called** it Nobah after himself.
Dt 2:11 [A] considered Rephaites, but the Moabites **called** them Emites.
2:20 [A] to live there; but the Ammonites **called** them Zamzummites.
3: 9 [A] (Hermon *is* **called** Sirion by the Sidonians; the Amorites call
3: 9 [A] is called Sirion by the Sidonians; the Amorites **call** it Senir.)
3:13 [C] (The whole region of Argob in Bashan *used to* **be known as**
3:14 [A] the Maacathites; it *was* **named** [+906+906+9005] after him,
4: 7 [A] the LORD our God is near us whenever we **pray** to him?
5: 1 [A] Moses **summoned** all Israel and said: Hear, O Israel,
15: 2 [A] the LORD's time for canceling debts *has been* **proclaimed.**
15: 9 [A] *He may* then **appeal** to the LORD against you, and you will
17:19 [A] *he is to* **read** it all the days of his life so that he may learn to
20:10 [A] march up to attack a city, **make** its people **an offer** of peace.
24:15 [A] Otherwise *he may* **cry** to the LORD against you, and you
25: 8 [A] the elders of his town *shall* **summon** him and talk to him.
25:10 [C] That man's line *shall* **be known** [+9005] in Israel **as** The
28:10 [C] all the peoples on earth will see that you *are* **called** *by* the
29: 2 [29:1] [A] Moses **summoned** all the Israelites and said to them:
31: 7 [A] Moses **summoned** Joshua and said to him in the presence of
31:11 [A] *you shall* **read** this law before them in their hearing.
31:14 [A] **Call** Joshua and present yourselves at the Tent of Meeting,
32: 3 [A] *I will* **proclaim** the name of the LORD. Oh,
33:19 [A] *They will* **summon** peoples *to* the mountain and there offer
Jos 4: 4 [A] So Joshua **called together** the twelve men he had appointed
5: 9 [A] So the place *has been* **called** [+9005] Gilgal to this day.
6: 6 [A] So Joshua son of Nun **called** the priests and said to them,
7:26 [A] Therefore that place *has been* **called** [+9005] the Valley of
8:34 [A] Afterward, Joshua **read** all the words of the law—
8:35 [A] that Joshua *did* not **read** to the whole assembly of Israel,
9:22 [A] Joshua **summoned** the Gibeonites and said, "Why did you
10:24 [A] he **summoned** all the men of Israel and said to the army
19:47 [A] settled in Leshem and **named** it Dan after their forefather.)
21: 9 [A] Simeon they allotted the following towns **[NIE]** by name
22: 1 [A] Joshua **summoned** the Reubenites, the Gadites and the
22:34 [A] the Reubenites and the Gadites **gave** the altar *this* **name**:
23: 2 [A] **summoned** all Israel—their elders, leaders, judges and
24: 1 [A] *He* **summoned** the elders, leaders, judges and officials of
24: 9 [A] *he* **sent for** [+2256+4200+8938] Balaam son of Beor to put a
Jdg 1:17 [A] the city. Therefore it *was* **called** [+906+9005] Hormah.
1:26 [A] where he built a city and **called** [+9005] it Luz, which is its
2: 5 [A] *they* **called** [+9005] that place Bokim. There they offered
4: 6 [A] *She* **sent for** [+2256+4200+8938] Barak son of Abinoam
6:24 [A] altar to the LORD there and **called** it The LORD is Peace.
6:32 [A] So that day *they* **called** Gideon "Jerub-Baal," saying,
7: 3 [A] **announce** now to the people, 'Anyone who trembles with
7:20 [A] *they* **shouted**, "A sword for the LORD and for Gideon!"
8: 1 [A] Why didn't *you* **call** us when you went to fight Midian?'
9: 7 [A] Mount Gerizim and **shouted** [+2256+5951+7754] to them,
9:54 [A] Hurriedly *he* **called** to his armor-bearer, "Draw your sword
10: 4 [A] towns in Gilead, which to this day *are* **called** Havvoth Jair.
12: 1 [A] "Why did you go to fight the Ammonites without **calling** us
13:24 [A] gave birth to a boy and **named** [+906+9005] him Samson.
14:15 [A] household to death. *Did you* **invite** us here to rob us?"
15:17 [A] away the jawbone; and the place *was* **called** Ramath Lehi.
15:18 [A] Because he was very thirsty, *he* **cried out** to the LORD,
15:19 [A] So the spring *was* **called** [+9005] En Hakkore, and it is still
16:18 [A] she sent **word** to the rulers of the Philistines, "Come back
16:19 [A] *she* **called** a man to shave off the seven braids of his hair,
16:25 [A] they shouted, "**Bring out** Samson to entertain us."
16:25 [A] So *they* **called** Samson out of the prison, and he performed
16:28 [A] Then Samson **prayed** to the LORD, "O Sovereign LORD,
18:12 [A] This is why the place west of Kiriath Jearim *is* **called**
18:23 [A] As *they* **shouted** after them, the Danites turned and said to
18:29 [A] *They* **named** [+9005] it Dan after their forefather Dan,
21:13 [A] the whole assembly sent an **offer** *of* peace to the Benjamites
Ru 1:20 [A] "Don't **call** me Naomi," she told them. "Call me Mara,
1:20 [A] "**Call** me Mara, because the Almighty has made my life very
1:21 [A] Why **call** me Naomi? The LORD has afflicted me;
4:11 [A] standing in Ephrathah and *be* **famous** [+9005] in Bethlehem.
4:14 [C] a kinsman-redeemer. *May* he *become* **famous** [+9005]
4:17 [A] has a son." And *they* **named** [+4200+9005] him Obed.
4:17 [A] **[RPH]** He was the father of Jesse, the father of David.
1Sa 1:20 [A] *She* **named** [+906+9005] him Samuel, saying, "Because I
3: 4 [A] the LORD **called** Samuel. Samuel answered, "Here I am."
3: 5 [A] he ran to Eli and said, "Here I am; *you* **called** me." But Eli
3: 5 [A] Eli said, "*I did* not **call**; go back and lie down." So he went
3: 6 [A] Again the LORD **called**, "Samuel!" And Samuel got up
3: 6 [A] got up and went to Eli and said, "Here I am; *you* **called** me."
3: 6 [A] "My son," Eli said, "*I did* not **call**; go back and lie down."
3: 8 [A] The LORD **called** Samuel a third time, and Samuel got up
3: 8 [A] got up and went to Eli and said, "Here I am; *you* **called** me."
3: 8 [A] Then Eli realized that the LORD *was* **calling** the boy.
3: 9 [A] "Go and lie down, and if *he* **calls** you, say, 'Speak, LORD,

1Sa 3:10 [A] and stood there, **calling** as at the other times, "Samuel!
3:16 [A] Eli **called** him and said, "Samuel, my son." Samuel
4:21 [A] *She* **named** the boy Ichabod, saying, "The glory has departed
6:2 [A] the Philistines **called** for the priests and the diviners and said,
7:12 [A] and Shen. *He* **named** [+906+9005] it Ebenezer,
9:9 [C] because the prophet of today used to **be called** a seer.)
9:13 [B] bless the sacrifice; afterward, those *who are* **invited** will eat.
9:22 [B] and seated them at the head of those *who* **were invited**—
9:24 [A] '*I have* **invited** guests.' " And Saul dined with Samuel that
9:26 [A] rose about daybreak and Samuel **called** to Saul on the roof,
12:17 [A] *I will* **call** upon the LORD to send thunder and rain.
12:18 [A] Samuel **called** upon the LORD, and that same day the
16:3 [A] **Invite** Jesse to the sacrifice, and I will show you what to do.
16:5 [A] and his sons and **invited** them to the sacrifice.
16:8 [A] Jesse **called** Abinadab and had him pass in front of Samuel.
17:8 [A] Goliath stood and **shouted** to the ranks of Israel, "Why do
19:7 [A] So Jonathan **called** David and told him the whole
20:37 [A] Jonathan **called out** after him, "Isn't the arrow beyond you?"
20:38 [A] he **shouted**, "Hurry! Go quickly! Don't stop!" The boy
22:11 [A] king **sent for** [+906+906+4200+8938] the priest Ahimelech
23:28 [A] That is why *they* **call** this place Sela Hammahlekoth.
24:8 [24:9] [A] David went out of the cave and **called out** to Saul,
26:14 [A] He **called out** to the army and to Abner son of Ner, "Aren't
26:14 [A] Abner replied, "Who are you *who* **calls** to the king?"
28:15 [A] or by dreams. So *I have* **called** on you to tell me what to do."
29:6 [A] So Achish **called** David and said to him, "As surely as the
2Sa 1:7 [A] turned around and saw me, *he* **called out** to me, and I said,
1:15 [A] David **called** one of his men and said, "Go, strike him
2:16 [A] So that place in Gibeon *was* **called** Helkath Hazzurim.
2:26 [A] Abner **called out** to Joab, "Must the sword devour forever?
5:9 [A] up residence in the fortress and **called** it the City of David.
5:20 [A] before me." So that place *was* **called** [+9005] Baal Perazim.
6:2 [C] which **is called** *by* the Name, the name of the LORD
6:8 [A] and to this day that place *is* **called** Perez Uzzah.
9:2 [A] *They* **called** him to appear before David, and the king said to
9:9 [A] the king **summoned** Ziba, Saul's servant, and said to him,
11:13 [A] *At* David's **invitation**, he ate and drank with him, and David
12:24 [A] birth to a son, and *they* **named** [+906+9005] him Solomon.
12:25 [A] Nathan the prophet *to* **name** [+906+9005] him Jedidiah.
12:28 [C] I will take the city, and it *will* **be named** [+9005] after me."
13:17 [A] *He* **called** his personal servant and said, "Get this woman out
13:23 [A] of Ephraim, he **invited** all the king's sons to come there.
14:33 [A] the king **summoned** Absalom, and he came in and bowed
15:2 [A] Absalom *would* **call out** to him, "What town are you from?"
15:11 [B] *They had* **been invited as guests** and went quite innocently,
17:5 [A] Absalom said, "**Summon** also Hushai the Arkite, so we can
18:18 [A] on the memory of my name." *He* **named** [+4200+9005]
18:18 [C] and it **is called** Absalom's Monument to this day.
18:25 [A] The watchman **called out** to the king and reported it. The
18:26 [A] he **called** down to the gatekeeper, "Look, another man
18:28 [A] Ahimaaz **called out** to the king, "All is well!" He bowed
20:16 [A] a wise woman **called** from the city, "Listen! Listen! Tell Joab
21:2 [A] The king **summoned** the Gibeonites and spoke to them.
22:4 [A] *I* **call** *to* the LORD, who is worthy of praise, and I am saved
22:7 [A] In my distress *I* **called** *to* the LORD; I called out to my
22:7 [A] my distress I called to the LORD; *I* **called out** to my God.
1Ki 1:9 [A] *He* **invited** all his brothers, the king's sons, and all the men
1:10 [A] *he did* not **invite** Nathan the prophet or Benaiah or the special
1:19 [A] *has* **invited** all the king's sons, Abiathar the priest and Joab
1:19 [A] of the army, but *he has* not **invited** Solomon your servant.
1:25 [A] *He has* **invited** all the king's sons, the commanders of the
1:26 [A] son of Jehoiada, and your servant Solomon *he did* not **invite**.
1:28 [A] King David said, "**Call in** Bathsheba." So she came into the
1:32 [A] "**Call in** Zadok the priest, Nathan the prophet and Benaiah
1:41 [B] all the **guests** who were with him heard it as they were
1:49 [B] At this, all Adonijah's **guests** rose in alarm and dispersed.
2:36 [A] the king **sent for** [+2256+4200+8938] Shimei and said to
2:42 [A] the king **summoned** [+2256+4200+8938] Shimei and said to
7:21 [A] The pillar to the south *he* **named** [+906+9005] Jakin and the
7:21 [A] south he named Jakin and the one to the north **[RPH]** Boaz.
8:43 [A] dwelling place, and do whatever the foreigner **asks** of you,
8:43 [C] may know that this house I have built **bears** [+6584] your
8:52 [A] and may you listen to them whenever they **cry out** to you.
9:13 [A] *he* **called** them the Land of Cabul, a name they have to this
12:3 [A] So *they* **sent for** [+2256+4200+8938] Jeroboam, and he
12:20 [A] they sent and **called** him to the assembly and made him king
13:2 [A] *He* **cried out** against the altar by the word of the LORD:
13:4 [A] When King Jeroboam heard what the man of God **cried out**
13:21 [A] *He* **cried out** to the man of God who had come from Judah,
13:32 [A] For the message *he* **declared** by the word of the LORD
16:24 [A] on the hill, **calling** [+906+9005] it Samaria, after Shemer,
17:10 [A] *He* **called** to her and asked, "Would you bring me a little
17:11 [A] to get it, *he* **called**, "And bring me, please, a piece of bread."
17:20 [A] *he* **cried out** to the LORD, "O LORD my God, have you
17:21 [A] himself out on the boy three times and **cried** to the LORD,
18:3 [A] Ahab *had* **summoned** Obadiah, who was in charge of his
18:24 [A] *you* **call** on the name of your god, and I will call on the name
18:24 [A] name of your god, and I *will* **call** on the name of the LORD.
18:25 [A] **Call** on the name of your god, but do not light the fire."
18:26 [A] *they* **called** on the name of Baal from morning till noon.
18:27 [A] "**Shout** [+928+7754] louder!" he said. "Surely he is a god!
18:28 [A] So *they* **shouted** [+928+7754] louder and slashed themselves
20:7 [A] The king of Israel **summoned** all the elders of the land
21:9 [A] "**Proclaim** a day of fasting and seat Naboth in a prominent
21:12 [A] *They* **proclaimed** a fast and seated Naboth in a prominent
22:9 [A] So the king of Israel **called** one of his officials and said,
22:13 [A] The messenger who had gone to **summon** Micaiah said to
2Ki 3:10 [A] "*Has* the LORD **called** us three kings **together** only to hand
3:13 [A] it was the LORD *who* **called** us three kings **together**
4:12 [A] He said to his servant Gehazi, "**Call** the Shunammite." So he
4:12 [A] So *he* **called** her, and she stood before him.
4:15 [A] Elisha said, "**Call** her." So he called her, and she stood in the
4:15 [A] "Call her." So *he* **called** her, and she stood in the doorway.
4:22 [A] *She* **called** her husband and said, "Please send me one of the
4:36 [A] Elisha **summoned** Gehazi and said, "Call the Shunammite."
4:36 [A] Elisha summoned Gehazi and said, "**Call** the Shunammite."
4:36 [A] And *he* **did**[s]. When she came, he said, "Take your son."
5:7 [A] As soon as the king of Israel **read** the letter, he tore his robes
5:11 [A] to me and stand and **call** on the name of the LORD his God,
6:11 [A] *He* **summoned** his officers and demanded of them, "Will
7:10 [A] So they went and **called out** to the city gatekeepers and told
7:11 [A] The gatekeepers **shouted the news**, and it was reported
8:1 [A] because the LORD *has* **decreed** a famine in the land that
9:1 [A] The prophet Elisha **summoned** a man from the company of
10:19 [A] Now **summon** all the prophets of Baal, all his ministers
10:20 [A] "Call an assembly in honor of Baal." So *they* **proclaimed** it.
11:14 [A] Athaliah tore her robes and **called out**, "Treason! Treason!"
12:7 [12:8] [A] King Joash **summoned** Jehoiada the priest and
14:7 [A] Sela in battle, **calling** it Joktheel, the name it has to this day.
18:4 [A] had been burning incense to it. (It *was* **called** Nehushtan.)
18:18 [A] *They* **called** for the king; and Eliakim son of Hilkiah the
18:28 [A] stood and **called** [+928+1524+7754] **out** in Hebrew: "Hear the
19:14 [A] Hezekiah received the letter from the messengers and **read** it.
20:11 [A] the prophet Isaiah **called** upon the LORD, and the LORD
22:8 [A] temple of the LORD." He gave it to Shaphan, *who* **read** it.
22:10 [A] And Shaphan **read** *from* it in the presence of the king.
22:16 [A] to everything written in the book the king of Judah *has* **read**.
23:2 [A] *He* **read** in their hearing all the words of the Book of the
23:16 [A] in accordance with the word of the LORD **proclaimed** *by*
23:16 [A] proclaimed by the man of God who **foretold** these things.
23:17 [A] **pronounced** against the altar of Bethel the very things you
1Ch 4:9 [A] His mother *had* **named** [+9005] him Jabez, saying, "I gave
4:10 [A] Jabez **cried out** to the God of Israel, "Oh, that you would
6:65 [6:50] [A] allotted the *previously* **named** [+906+928+9005] towns.
7:16 [A] Maacah gave birth to a son and **named** [+9005] him Peresh.
7:23 [A] and gave birth to a son. *He* **named** [+906+9005] him Beriah,
11:7 [A] in the fortress, and so it *was* **called** the City of David.
13:6 [C] between the cherubim—the ark that **is called** *by* the Name.
13:11 [A] and to this day that place *is* **called** Perez Uzzah.
14:11 [A] my hand." So that place *was* **called** [+9005] Baal Perazim.
15:11 [A] David **summoned** Zadok and Abiathar the priests, and Uriel,
16:8 [A] Give thanks to the LORD, **call** on his name; make known
21:26 [A] *He* **called** on the LORD, and the LORD answered him
22:6 [A] *he* **called** for his son Solomon and charged him to build a
23:14 [C] The sons of Moses the man of God **were counted** as part of
2Ch 3:17 [A] The one to the south *he* **named** [+9005] Jakin and the one to
6:33 [A] dwelling place, and do whatever the foreigner **asks** of you,
6:33 [C] may know that this house I have built **bears** [+6584] your
7:14 [C] if my people, who **are called** *by* my name, will humble
10:3 [A] So *they* **sent for** [+2256+4200+8938] Jeroboam, and he
14:11 [14:10] [A] Asa **called** to the LORD his God and said,
18:8 [A] So the king of Israel **called** one of his officials and said,
18:12 [A] The messenger who had gone to **summon** Micaiah said to
20:3 [A] of the LORD, and *he* **proclaimed** a fast for all Judah.
20:26 [A] This is why it *is* **called** [+906+9005] the Valley of Beracah
24:6 [A] Therefore the king **summoned** Jehoiada the chief priest
32:18 [A] *they* **called** [+928+1524+7754] **out** in Hebrew to the people of
34:18 [A] And Shaphan **read** from it in the presence of the king.
34:24 [A] all the curses written in the book that *has been* **read** in the
34:30 [A] *He* **read** in their hearing all the words of the Book of the
Ezr 2:61 [C] of Barzillai the Gileadite and **was called** by that name).
8:21 [A] There, by the Ahava Canal, *I* **proclaimed** a fast, so that we
Ne 5:12 [A] *I* **summoned** the priests and made the nobles and officials
6:7 [A] have even appointed prophets to **make** *this* **proclamation**
7:63 [C] of Barzillai the Gileadite and **was called** by that name).
8:3 [A] *He* **read** it **aloud** from daybreak till noon as he faced the
8:8 [A] *They* **read** from the Book of the Law of God, making it clear
8:18 [A] day to the last, Ezra **read** from the Book of the Law of God.

Ne 9: 3 [A] **read** from the Book of the Law of the LORD their God for
13: 1 [C] On that day the Book of Moses **was read aloud** in the
Est 2: 14 [C] unless he was pleased with her and **summoned** *her* by name.
3: 12 [C] day of the first month the royal secretaries **were summoned**.
4: 5 [A] Esther **summoned** Hathach, one of the king's eunuchs
4: 11 [C] in the inner court without **being summoned** the king has
4: 11 [C] thirty days have passed since I **was called** to go to the king."
5: 12 [B] And she *has* **invited** me along with the king tomorrow.
6: 1 [C] the record of his reign, to be brought in and **read** to him.
6: 9 [A] the horse through the city streets, **proclaiming** before him,
6: 11 [A] horseback through the city streets, **proclaiming** before him,
8: 9 [C] At once the royal secretaries **were summoned**—
9: 26 [A] (Therefore these days *were* **called** Purim, from the word
Job 1: 4 [A] and *they would* **invite** [+2256+4200+8938] their three sisters to
5: 1 [A] "**Call** if you will, but who will answer you? To which of the
9: 16 [A] Even if *I* **summoned** him and he responded, I do not believe
12: 4 [A] to my friends, though *I* **called** upon God and he answered—
13: 22 [A] **summon** me and I will answer, or let me speak, and you
14: 15 [A] *You will* **call** and I will answer you; you will long for the
17: 14 [A] if *I* **say** to corruption, 'You are my father,' and to the worm,
19: 16 [A] *I* **summon** my servant, but he does not answer, though I beg
27: 10 [A] delight in the Almighty? *Will he* **call upon** God at all times?
42: 14 [A] The first daughter *he* **named** [+9005] Jemimah, the second
Ps 3: 4 [3:5] [A] To the LORD *I* **cry** aloud, and he answers me from
4: 1 [4:2] [A] Answer me when I **call** to you, O my righteous God.
4: 3 [4:4] [A] for himself; the LORD will hear when I **call** to him.
14: 4 [A] people as men eat bread and *who do* not **call on** the LORD?
17: 6 [A] I **call on** you, O God, for you will answer me; give ear to me
18: 3 [18:4] [A] *I* **call** *to* the LORD, who is worthy of praise, and I
18: 6 [18:7] [A] In my distress *I* **called** *to* the LORD; I cried to my
20: 9 [20:10] [A] O LORD, save the king! Answer us when we **call**!
22: 2 [22:3] [A] O my God, *I* **cry out** by day, but you do not answer,
27: 7 [A] Hear my voice *when I* **call**, O LORD; be merciful to me
28: 1 [A] To you *I* **call**, O LORD my Rock; do not turn a deaf ear to
30: 8 [30:9] [A] To you, O LORD, *I* **called**; to the Lord I cried for
31: 17 [31:18] [A] to shame, O LORD, for *I have* **cried out** *to* you;
34: 6 [34:7] [A] This poor man **called**, and the LORD heard him; he
42: 7 [42:8] [A] Deep **calls** to deep in the roar of your waterfalls;
49: 11 [49:12] [A] though *they had* **named** [+6584+9005] lands after
50: 1 [A] **summons** the earth from the rising of the sun to the place
50: 4 [A] *He* **summons** the heavens above, and the earth, that he may
50: 15 [A] and **call upon** me in the day of trouble; I will deliver you,
53: 4 [53:5] [A] as men eat bread and *who do* not **call on** God?
55: 16 [55:17] [A] But I **call** to God, and the LORD saves me.
56: 9 [56:10] [A] my enemies will turn back when *I* **call for help**.
57: 2 [57:3] [A] *I* **cry out** to God Most High, to God, who fulfills his
61: 2 [61:3] [A] From the ends of the earth *I* **call** to you, I call as my
66: 17 [A] *I* **cried out** to him *with* my mouth; his praise was on my
69: 3 [69:4] [A] I am worn out **calling for help**; my throat is parched.
79: 6 [A] on the kingdoms that *do* not **call** on your name;
80: 18 [80:19] [A] from you; revive us, and *we will* **call** on your name.
81: 7 [81:8] [A] In your distress *you* **called** and I rescued you,
86: 3 [A] Have mercy on me, O Lord, for *I* **call** to you all day long.
86: 5 [A] and good, O Lord, abounding in love to all *who* **call** *to* you.
86: 7 [A] In the day of my trouble *I will* **call** to you, for you will
88: 9 [88:10] [A] *I* **call** *to* you, O LORD, every day; I spread out my
89: 26 [89:27] [A] He *will* **call out** *to* me, 'You are my Father,
91: 15 [A] *He will* **call upon** me, and I will answer him; I will be with
99: 6 [A] Samuel was among *those who* **called** *on* his name;
99: 6 [A] his name; *they* **called** on the LORD and he answered them.
102: 2 [102:3] [A] your ear to me; when *I* **call**, answer me quickly.
105: 1 [A] Give thanks to the LORD, **call** on his name; make known
105: 16 [A] *He* **called down** famine on the land and destroyed all their
116: 2 [A] he turned his ear to me, *I will* **call** *on* him as long as I live.
116: 4 [A] *I* **called** on the name of the LORD: "O LORD, save me!"
116: 13 [A] up the cup of salvation and **call** on the name of the LORD.
116: 17 [A] a thank offering to you and **call** on the name of the LORD.
118: 5 [A] In my anguish *I* **cried** *to* the LORD, and he answered by
119: 145 [A] *I* **call** with all my heart; answer me, O LORD, and I will
119: 146 [A] *I* **call out** *to* you; save me and I will keep your statutes.
120: 1 [A] *I* **call** on the LORD in my distress, and he answers me.
130: 1 [A] Out of the depths *I* **cry** *to* you, O LORD;
138: 3 [A] When *I* **called**, you answered me; you made me bold
141: 1 [A] O LORD, *I* **call** *to* you; come quickly to me. Hear my voice
141: 1 [A] come quickly to me. Hear my voice when I **call** to you.
145: 18 [A] The LORD is near to all *who* **call** *on* him, to all who call on
145: 18 [A] is near to all who call on him, to all who **call** *on* him in truth.
147: 4 [A] the number of the stars and **calls** them each by name.
147: 9 [A] food for the cattle and for the young ravens when *they* **call**.
Pr 1: 21 [A] at the head of the noisy streets *she* **cries out**, in the gateways
1: 24 [A] since you rejected me *when I* **called** and no one gave heed
1: 28 [A] "Then *they will* **call** *to* me but I will not answer; they will
2: 3 [A] if *you* **call out** for insight and cry aloud for understanding,
7: 4 [A] "You are my sister," and **call** understanding your kinsman;
8: 1 [A] *Does* not wisdom **call out**? Does not understanding raise her
8: 4 [A] "To you, O men, *I* **call out**; I raise my voice to all mankind.
9: 3 [A] her maids, and *she* **calls** from the highest point of the city.
9: 15 [A] **calling out** to those who pass by, who go straight on their
9: 18 [B] dead are there, that her **guests** are in the depths of the grave.
12: 23 [A] knowledge to himself, but the heart of fools **blurts out** folly.
16: 21 [C] The wise in heart **are called** discerning, and pleasant words
18: 6 [A] fool's lips bring him strife, and his mouth **invites** a beating.
20: 6 [A] Many a man **claims** to have unfailing love, but a faithful man
21: 13 [A] the cry of the poor, he too *will* **cry out** and not be answered.
24: 8 [A] He who plots evil *will be* **known as** a schemer.
27: 16 [A] her is like restraining the wind or **grasping** oil *with* the hand.
Ecc 6: 10 [C] Whatever exists *has* already **been named** [+9005], and what
SS 5: 6 [A] but did not find him. *I* **called** him but he did not answer.
Isa 1: 13 [A] New Moons, Sabbaths and **convocations** [+5246]—I cannot
1: 26 [C] Afterward you *will* **be called** the City of Righteousness,
4: 1 [C] provide our own clothes; only *let* us **be called** *by* your name.
6: 3 [A] *they were* **calling** to one another: "Holy, holy, holy is the
6: 4 [A] At the sound of their **voices** the doorposts and thresholds
7: 14 [A] will give birth to a son, and *will* **call** [+9005] him Immanuel.
8: 3 [A] the LORD said to me, "**Name** [+9005] him
8: 4 [A] Before the boy knows how *to* **say** 'My father' or 'My mother,'
9: 6 [9:5] [A] he *will be* **called** [+9005] Wonderful Counselor,
12: 4 [A] "Give thanks to the LORD, **call** on his name; make known
13: 3 [A] *I have* **summoned** my warriors to carry out my wrath—
14: 20 [C] The offspring of the wicked *will* never **be mentioned** again.
21: 8 [A] the lookout **shouted**, "Day after day, my lord, I stand on the
21: 11 [A] *Someone* **calls** to me from Seir, "Watchman, what is left of
22: 12 [A] **called** you on that day to weep and to wail, to tear out your
22: 20 [A] "In that day *I will* **summon** my servant, Eliakim son of
29: 11 [A] and say to him, "**Read** this, please," he will answer, "I can't;
29: 12 [A] say, "**Read** this, please," he will answer, "I don't know how
30: 7 [A] is utterly useless. Therefore *I* **call** her Rahab the Do-Nothing.
31: 4 [C] though a whole band of shepherds **is called together** against
32: 5 [C] No longer *will* the fool **be called** noble nor the scoundrel be
34: 12 [A] Her nobles will have nothing there *to be* **called** a kingdom,
34: 14 [A] meet with hyenas, and wild goats *will* **bleat** to each other;
34: 16 [A] Look in the scroll of the LORD and **read**: None of these
35: 8 [C] highway will be there; it *will* **be called** the Way of Holiness.
36: 13 [A] stood and **called** [+928+1524+7754] **out** in Hebrew, "Hear the
37: 14 [A] Hezekiah received the letter from the messengers and **read** it.
40: 2 [A] **proclaim** to her that her hard service has been completed,
40: 3 [A] A voice of *one* **calling**: "In the desert prepare the way for the
40: 6 [A] A voice says, "**Cry out**." And I said, "What shall I cry?"
40: 6 [A] A voice says, "Cry out." And I said, "What *shall I* **cry**?"
40: 26 [A] out the starry host one by one, and **calls** them each by name.
41: 2 [A] from the east, **calling** him in righteousness to his service?
41: 4 [A] it through, **calling forth** the generations from the beginning?
41: 9 [A] the ends of the earth, from its farthest corners *I* **called** you.
41: 25 [A] he comes—one from the rising sun *who* **calls** on my name.
42: 6 [A] "I, the LORD, *have* **called** you in righteousness; I will take
43: 1 [A] *I have* **summoned** you by name; you are mine.
43: 7 [C] everyone who **is called** by my name, whom I created for my
43: 22 [A] "Yet *you have* not **called** *upon* me, O Jacob, you have not
44: 5 [A] the LORD'; another *will* **call** *himself* by the name of Jacob;
44: 7 [A] *Let him* **proclaim** it. Let him declare and lay out before me
45: 3 [A] the LORD, the God of Israel, who **summons** you by name.
45: 4 [A] *I* **summon** you by name and bestow on you a title of honor,
46: 11 [A] From the east I **summon** a bird of prey; from a far-off land,
47: 1 [A] No more *will* you *be* **called** tender or delicate.
47: 5 [A] no more *will* you *be* **called** queen of kingdoms.
48: 1 [C] you who **are called** by the name of Israel and come from the
48: 2 [C] *you who* **call yourselves** citizens of the holy city and rely on
48: 8 [E] how treacherous you are; you **were called** a rebel from birth.
48: 12 [E] "Listen to me, O Jacob, Israel, *whom* I *have* **called**: I am he;
48: 13 [A] *when* I **summon** them, they all stand up together.
48: 15 [A] I, even I, have spoken; yes, *I have* **called** him. I will bring
49: 1 [A] Before I was born the LORD **called** me; from my birth he
50: 2 [A] no one? *When I* **called**, why was there no one to answer?
51: 2 [A] When *I* **called** him he was but one, and I blessed him
54: 5 [C] Israel is your Redeemer; *he* **is called** the God of all the earth.
54: 6 [A] The LORD *will* **call** you **back** as if you were a wife
55: 5 [A] Surely *you will* **summon** nations you know not, and nations
55: 6 [A] LORD while he may be found; **call** *on* him while he is near.
56: 7 [C] for my house *will* **be called** a house of prayer for all nations."
58: 1 [A] "**Shout** [+928+1744] it **aloud**, do not hold back. Raise your
58: 5 [A] Is that what *you* **call** a fast, a day acceptable to the LORD?
58: 9 [A] *you will* **call**, and the LORD will answer; you will cry for
58: 12 [A] you *will be* **called** Repairer of Broken Walls, Restorer of
58: 13 [A] if *you* **call** the Sabbath a delight and the LORD's holy day
59: 4 [A] No *one* **calls** for justice; no one pleads his case with
60: 14 [A] down at your feet and *will* **call** you the City of the LORD,
60: 18 [A] but *you will* **call** your walls Salvation and your gates Praise.
61: 1 [A] to **proclaim** freedom for the captives and release from

[A] Qal [B] Qal passive [C] Niphal [D] Piel (poel, polel, pilel, pilal, pealal, pilpel) [E] Pual (poal, polal, poalal, pulal, pualal)

Isa 61: 2 [A] to **proclaim** the year of the LORD's favor and the day of
61: 3 [E] They *will* **be called** oaks of righteousness, a planting of the
61: 6 [C] you *will* **be called** priests of the LORD, you will be named
62: 2 [E] you *will* **be called** *by* a new name that the mouth of the
62: 4 [C] you *will* **be called** Hephzibah, and your land Beulah;
62: 12 [A] They *will be* **called** the Holy People, the Redeemed of the
62: 12 [C] you *will* **be called** Sought After, the City No Longer
63: 19 [C] ruled over them, they *have* not **been called** *by* your name.
64: 7 [64:6] [A] No *one* **calls** on your name or strives to lay hold of
65: 1 [A] To a nation *that did* not **call** on my name, I said, 'Here am I,
65: 12 [A] for *I* **called** but you did not answer, I spoke but you did not
65: 15 [A] you to death, but to his servants *he will* **give** another name.
65: 24 [A] Before *they* **call** I will answer; while they are still speaking I
66: 4 [A] For *when I* **called**, no one answered, when I spoke, no one
Jer 1: 15 [A] I *am about to* **summon** all the peoples of the northern
2: 2 [A] "Go and **proclaim** in the hearing of Jerusalem: " 'I remember
3: 4 [A] *Have you* not just **called** to me: 'My Father, my friend from
3: 12 [A] Go, **proclaim** this message toward the north: " 'Return,
3: 17 [A] At that time *they will* **call** Jerusalem The Throne of the
3: 19 [A] I thought *you would* **call** me 'Father' and not turn away from
4: 5 [A] **Cry** aloud and say: 'Gather together! Let us flee to the
6: 30 [A] They *are* **called** rejected silver, because the LORD has
7: 2 [A] gate of the LORD's house and there **proclaim** this message:
7: 10 [C] which **bears** [+6584] my Name, and say, "We are safe"—
7: 11 [C] Has this house, which **bears** [+6584] my Name, become a
7: 13 [A] but you did not listen; *I* **called** you, but you did not answer.
7: 14 [C] I will now do to the house that **bears** [+6584] my Name,
7: 27 [A] listen to you; when *you* **call** to them, they will not answer.
7: 30 [C] detestable idols in the house that **bears** [+6584] my Name
9: 17 [9:16] [A] **Call** for the wailing women to come; send for the
10: 25 [A] on the peoples who *do* not **call** on your name.
11: 6 [A] "**Proclaim** all these words in the towns of Judah and in the
11: 14 [A] because I will not listen when they **call** to me in the time of
11: 16 [A] The LORD **called** [+9005] you a thriving olive tree with
12: 6 [A] have betrayed you; they *have* **raised** a loud **cry** against you.
14: 9 [C] are among us, O LORD, and we **bear** [+6584] your name;
15: 16 [C] my joy and my heart's delight, for I **bear** [+6584] your name,
19: 2 [A] of the Potsherd Gate. There **proclaim** the words I tell you,
19: 6 [C] when *people will* no longer **call** this place Topheth
20: 3 [A] "The LORD's **name for** [+9005] you is not Pashhur,
20: 8 [A] I speak, I cry out **proclaiming** violence and destruction.
23: 6 [A] live in safety. This is the name by which he *will be* **called**:
25: 29 [C] to bring disaster on the city that **bears** [+6584] my Name,
25: 29 [A] for I *am* **calling down** a sword upon all who live on the
29: 12 [A] *you will* **call upon** me and come and pray to me, and I will
29: 29 [A] the priest, however, **read** the letter to Jeremiah the prophet.
30: 17 [A] declares the LORD, 'because you *are* **called** an outcast,
31: 6 [A] There will be a day *when* watchmen **cry out** on the hills of
32: 34 [C] abominable idols in the house that **bears** [+6584] my Name
33: 3 [A] '**Call** to me and I will answer you and tell you great
33: 16 [A] live in safety. This is the name by which it *will be* **called**:
34: 8 [A] the people in Jerusalem to **proclaim** freedom for the slaves.
34: 15 [A] Each of you **proclaimed** freedom to his countrymen.
34: 15 [C] before me in the house that **bears** [+6584] my Name.
34: 17 [A] you *have* not **proclaimed** freedom for your fellow
34: 17 [A] So I now **proclaim** 'freedom' for you, declares the LORD—
35: 17 [A] did not listen; *I* **called** to them, but they did not answer.' "
36: 4 [A] So Jeremiah **called** Baruch son of Neriah, and while
36: 6 [A] **read** to the people from the scroll the words of the LORD
36: 6 [A] **Read** them to all the people of Judah who come in from their
36: 8 [A] at the LORD's temple *he* **read** the words of the LORD
36: 9 [A] a time of fasting before the LORD *was* **proclaimed** *for* all
36: 10 [A] Baruch **read** to all the people at the LORD's temple the
36: 13 [A] Micaiah told them everything he had heard Baruch **read**
36: 14 [A] "Bring the scroll from which *you have* **read** to the people
36: 15 [A] They said to him, "Sit down, please, and **read** it to us."
36: 15 [A] please, and read it to us." So Baruch **read** it to them.
36: 18 [A] Baruch replied, "he **dictated** [+906+4946+7023] all these
36: 21 [A] **read** it to the king and all the officials standing beside him.
36: 23 [A] Whenever Jehudi *had* **read** three or four columns of the
42: 8 [A] So *he* **called together** Johanan son of Kareah and all the
44: 26 [C] in Egypt *will* ever again **invoke** [+928+7023] my name
46: 17 [A] There *they will* **exclaim**, 'Pharaoh king of Egypt is only a
49: 29 [A] and camels. *Men will* **shout** to them, 'Terror on every side!'
51: 61 [A] you get to Babylon, see that *you* **read** all these words **aloud**.
51: 63 [A] When you finish **reading** this scroll, tie a stone to it
La 1: 15 [A] *he has* **summoned** an army against me to crush my young
1: 19 [A] "*I* **called** to my allies but they betrayed me. My priests
1: 21 [A] May you bring the day *you have* **announced** so they may
2: 22 [A] "As *you* **summon** *to* a feast day, so you summoned against
3: 55 [A] *I* **called** *on* your name, O LORD, from the depths of the pit.
3: 57 [A] You came near when *I* **called** you, and you said, "Do not
4: 15 [A] *men* **cry** to them. "Away! Away! Don't touch us!"
Eze 8: 18 [A] Although *they* **shout** [+1524+7754] in my ears, I will not
9: 1 [A] I heard *him* **call out** *in* a loud voice, "Bring the guards of the
9: 3 [A] the LORD **called** to the man clothed in linen who had the
10: 13 [E] I heard the wheels **being called** "the whirling wheels."
20: 29 [C] What is this high place you go to?' " (It **is called** [+9005]
23: 23 [B] and commanders, chariot officers and **men of high rank**,
36: 29 [A] *I will* **call** for the grain and make it plentiful and will not
38: 21 [A] *I will* **summon** a sword against Gog on all my mountains,
39: 11 [A] buried there. So *it will be* **called** the Valley of Hamon Gog.
Da 2: 2 [A] the king **summoned** the magicians, enchanters, sorcerers and
8: 16 [A] And I heard a man's voice from the Ulai **calling**, "Gabriel,
9: 18 [C] see the desolation of the city that **bears** [+6584] your Name.
9: 19 [C] your city and your people **bear** [+6584] your Name."
10: 1 [C] a revelation was given to Daniel (who **was called** [+9005]
Hos 1: 4 [A] Then the LORD said to Hosea, "**Call** [+9005] him Jezreel,
1: 6 [A] the LORD said to Hosea, "**Call** [+9005] her Lo-Ruhamah,
1: 9 [A] the LORD said, "**Call** [+9005] him Lo-Ammi, for you are
2: 16 [2:18] [A] declares the LORD, "*you will* **call** me 'my husband';
2: 16 [2:18] [A] 'my husband'; *you will* no longer **call** me 'my master.'
7: 7 [A] All their kings fall, and none of them **calls** on me.
7: 11 [A] now **calling** *to* Egypt, now turning to Assyria.
11: 1 [A] was a child, I loved him, and out of Egypt *I* **called** my son.
11: 2 [A] But the more *I* **called** Israel, the further they went from me.
11: 7 [A] Even *if they* **call** to the Most High, he will by no means exalt
Joel 1: 14 [A] Declare a holy fast; **call** a sacred assembly.
1: 19 [A] To you, O LORD, *I* **call**, for fire has devoured the open
2: 15 [A] trumpet in Zion, declare a holy fast, **call** a sacred assembly.
2: 32 [3:5] [A] everyone who **calls** on the name of the LORD will be
2: 32 [3:5] [A] has said, among the survivors whom the LORD **calls**.
3: 9 [4:9] [A] **Proclaim** this among the nations: Prepare for war!
Am 4: 5 [A] as a thank offering and **brag** *about* your freewill offerings—
5: 8 [A] who **calls** for the waters of the sea and pours them out over
5: 16 [A] The farmers *will be* **summoned** to weep and the mourners to
7: 4 [A] The Sovereign LORD *was* **calling** for judgment by fire; it
9: 6 [A] who **calls** for the waters of the sea and pours them out over
9: 12 [C] of Edom and all the nations that **bear** [+6584] my name,"
Jnh 1: 2 [A] "Go to the great city of Nineveh and **preach** against it,
1: 6 [A] and said, "How can you sleep? Get up and **call** on your god!
1: 14 [A] *they* **cried** to the LORD, "O LORD, please do not let us
2: 2 [2:3] [A] "In my distress *I* **called** to the LORD, and he
3: 2 [A] city of Nineveh and **proclaim** to it the message I give you."
3: 4 [A] *He* **proclaimed**: "Forty more days and Nineveh will be
3: 5 [A] *They* **declared** a fast, and all of them, from the greatest to
3: 8 [A] *Let everyone* **call** urgently on God. Let them give up their
Mic 3: 5 [A] my people astray, if one feeds them, *they* **proclaim** 'peace';
6: 9 [A] Listen! The LORD *is* **calling** [+7754] to the city—and to
Hab 2: 2 [A] and make it plain on tablets so that a **herald** may run with it.
Zep 1: 7 [B] prepared a sacrifice; he has consecrated *those* he *has* **invited**.
3: 9 [A] that all of them *may* **call** on the name of the LORD
Hag 1: 11 [A] *I* **called** *for* a drought on the fields and the mountains, on the
Zec 1: 4 [A] your forefathers, to whom the earlier prophets **proclaimed**:
1: 14 [A] the angel who was speaking to me said, "**Proclaim** this word:
1: 17 [A] "**Proclaim** further: This is what the LORD Almighty says:
3: 10 [A] " 'In that day each of you *will* **invite** his neighbor to sit under
7: 7 [A] Are these not the words the LORD **proclaimed** through the
7: 13 [A] " 'When *I* **called**, they did not listen; so when they called,
7: 13 [A] so *when they* **called**, I would not listen,' says the LORD
8: 3 [C] Jerusalem *will* **be called** the City of Truth, and the mountain
11: 7 [A] I took two staffs and **called** one Favor and the other Union,
11: 7 [A] two staffs and called one Favor and **[RPH]** the other Union,
13: 9 [A] They *will* **call** on my name and I will answer them; I will
Mal 1: 4 [A] but I will demolish. They *will be* **called** the Wicked Land,

7925 ²קָרָא *qārā²*, v. [138] [cf. 7936]

meet [78], against [13], met [5], happened [4], toward [3], *untranslated* [2], attack [2], came toward [2], come upon [2], follows [2], meet in battle [2], oppose [2], breaks out [1], brought upon [1], come across [+4200+7156] [1], come [1], comes [1], facing each other [+5120] [1], fall upon [1], fight [1], follows [+6584] [1], greet [+1385] [1], happen [1], happened to be [+7936] [1], help [1], into [1], opposite [1], out came to meet [1], resort to [+2143+4200] [1], seized [1], wage [1], welcomed [1], went to meet [1]

Ge 14: 17 [A] the king of Sodom came out to **meet** him in the Valley of
15: 10 [A] cut them in two and arranged the halves **opposite** each other;
18: 2 [A] he hurried from the entrance of his tent to **meet** them
19: 1 [A] he got up to **meet** them and bowed down with his face to the
24: 17 [A] The servant hurried to **meet** her and said, "Please give me a
24: 65 [A] "Who is that man in the field coming to **meet** us?"
29: 13 [A] news about Jacob, his sister's son, he hurried to **meet** him.
30: 16 [A] in from the fields that evening, Leah went out to **meet** him.
32: 6 [32:7] [A] brother Esau, and now he is coming to **meet** you,
33: 4 [A] Esau ran to **meet** Jacob and embraced him; he threw his arms
42: 4 [A] because he was afraid that harm *might* **come** to him.
42: 38 [A] If harm **comes** *to* him on the journey you are taking, you will

Ge 46:29 [A] made ready and went to Goshen to **meet** his father Israel.
49: 1 [A] so I can tell you what *will* **happen** *to* you in days to come.
Ex 1:10 [A] if war **breaks out**, will join our enemies, fight against us
4:14 [A] He is already on his way to **meet** you, and his heart will be
4:27 [A] LORD said to Aaron, "Go into the desert to **meet** Moses."
5: 3 [C] Then they said, "The God of the Hebrews *has* **met** with us.
5:20 [A] they found Moses and Aaron waiting to **meet** them,
7:15 [A] Wait on the bank of the Nile to **meet** him, and take in your
14:27 [A] The Egyptians were fleeing **toward** it, and the LORD swept
18: 7 [A] So Moses went out to **meet** his father-in-law and bowed
19:17 [A] Moses led the people out of the camp to **meet** *with* God,
Lev 10:19 [A] the LORD, but such things as this *have* **happened** *to* me.
Nu 20:18 [A] you try, we will march out and **attack** you with the sword."
20:20 [A] Edom came out **against** them with a large and powerful
21:23 [A] entire army and marched out into the desert **against** Israel.
21:33 [A] his whole army marched out to **meet** them in battle at Edrei.
22:34 [A] I did not realize you were standing in the road to **oppose** me.
22:36 [A] he went out to **meet** him at the Moabite town on the Arnon
23: 3 [A] Perhaps the LORD will come to **meet** *with* me. Whatever
24: 1 [A] *he did* not **resort to** [+2143+4200] sorcery as at other times,
31:13 [A] all the leaders of the community went to **meet** them outside
Dt 1:44 [A] The Amorites who lived in those hills came out **against** you;
2:32 [A] and all his army came out to **meet** us in battle at Jahaz,
3: 1 [A] Og king of Bashan with his whole army marched out to **meet**
22: 6 [C] If you **come** [+4200+7156] **across** a bird's nest beside the
29: 7 [29:6] [A] and Og king of Bashan came out to fight **against** us,
31:29 [A] disaster *will* **fall upon** you because you will do evil in the
Jos 8: 5 [A] and when the men come out **against** us, as they did before,
8:14 [A] the men of the city hurried out early in the morning to **meet**
8:22 [A] The men of the ambush also came out of the city **against**
9:11 [A] go and **meet** them and say to them, "We are your servants;
11:20 [A] who hardened their hearts to **wage** war *against* Israel,
Jdg 4:18 [A] Jael went out to **meet** Sisera and said to him, "Come,
4:22 [A] came by in pursuit of Sisera, and Jael went out to **meet** him.
6:35 [A] Zebulun and Naphtali, so that they too went up to **meet** them.
7:24 [A] "Come down **against** the Midianites and seize the waters of
11:31 [A] whatever comes out of the door of my house to **meet** me
11:34 [A] who should come out to **meet** him but his daughter, dancing
14: 5 [A] of Timnah, suddenly a young lion **came** roaring **toward** him.
15:14 [A] approached Lehi, the Philistines **came toward** him shouting.
19: 3 [A] and when her father saw him, he gladly **welcomed** him.
20:25 [A] when the Benjamites came out from Gibeah to **oppose** them,
20:31 [A] The Benjamites came out to **meet** them and were drawn
1Sa 4: 1 [A] Now the Israelites went out to fight **against** the Philistines.
4: 2 [A] The Philistines deployed their forces to **meet** Israel, and as
9:14 [A] coming **toward** them on his way up to the high place.
10:10 [A] they arrived at Gibeah, a procession of prophets **met** him;
13:10 [A] Samuel arrived, and Saul went out to **greet** [+1385] him.
15:12 [A] Early in the morning Samuel got up and **went to meet** Saul,
16: 4 [A] the elders of the town trembled when *they* **met** him.
17: 2 [A] of Elah and drew up their battle line to **meet** the Philistines.
17:21 [A] were drawing up their lines **facing** [+5120] **each other**.
17:48 [A] As the Philistine moved closer to **attack** him, David ran
17:48 [A] David ran quickly toward the battle line to **meet** him.
17:55 [A] As Saul watched David going out to **meet** the Philistine,
18: 6 [A] the women came out from all the towns of Israel to **meet**
21: 1 [21:2] [A] Ahimelech trembled when *he* **met** him, and asked,
23:28 [A] off his pursuit of David and went to **meet** the Philistines.
25:20 [A] there were David and his men descending **toward** her,
25:32 [A] the God of Israel, who has sent you today to **meet** me.
25:34 [A] from harming you, if you had not come quickly to **meet** me,
30:21 [A] They came out to **meet** David and the people with him.
30:21 [A] came out to meet David and **[RPH]** the people with him.
2Sa 1: 6 [C] "*I* **happened to be** [+7936] on Mount Gilboa," the young
6:20 [A] Michal daughter of Saul came out to **meet** him and said,
10: 5 [A] was told about this, he sent messengers to **meet** the men,
10: 9 [A] troops in Israel and deployed them **against** the Arameans.
10:10 [A] his brother and deployed them **against** the Ammonites.
10:17 [A] The Arameans formed their battle lines to **meet** David
15:32 [A] Hushai the Arkite was there to **meet** him, his robe torn
16: 1 [A] was Ziba, the steward of Mephibosheth, waiting to **meet** him.
18: 6 [A] The army marched into the field to **fight** Israel, and the battle
18: 9 [C] Now Absalom **happened** to meet David's men. He was
19:15 [19:16] [A] and **meet** the king and bring him across the Jordan.
19:16 [19:17] [A] hurried down with the men of Judah to **meet** King
19:20 [19:21] [A] Joseph to come down and **meet** my lord the king."
19:24 [19:25] [A] Saul's grandson, also went down to **meet** the king.
19:25 [19:26] [A] When he came from Jerusalem to **meet** the king,
20: 1 [C] Sheba son of Bicri, a Benjamite, **happened** *to be* there.
1Ki 2: 8 [A] When he came down to **meet** me *at* the Jordan, I swore to
2:19 [A] the king stood up to **meet** her, bowed down to her and sat
18: 7 [A] As Obadiah was walking along, Elijah **met** him. Obadiah
18:16 [A] So Obadiah went to **meet** Ahab and told him, and Ahab went
18:16 [A] to meet Ahab and told him, and Ahab went to **meet** Elijah.
20:27 [A] and given provisions, they marched out to **meet** them.
21:18 [A] "Go down to **meet** Ahab king of Israel, who rules in Samaria.
2Ki 1: 3 [A] "Go up and **meet** the messengers of the king of Samaria
1: 6 [A] "A man came to **meet** us," they replied. "And he said to us,
1: 7 [A] "What kind of man was it who came to **meet** you and told
2:15 [A] they went to **meet** him and bowed to the ground before him.
4:26 [A] Run to **meet** her and ask her, 'Are you all right? Is your
4:31 [A] So Gehazi went back to **meet** Elisha and told him, "The boy
5:21 [A] toward him, he got down from the chariot to **meet** him.
5:26 [A] you when the man got down from his chariot to **meet** you?
8: 8 [A] "Take a gift with you and go to **meet** the man of God.
8: 9 [A] Hazael went to **meet** Elisha, taking with him as a gift forty
9:17 [A] "Send him to **meet** them and ask, 'Do you come in peace?' "
9:18 [A] The horseman rode off to **meet** Jehu and said, "This is what
9:21 [A] king of Judah rode out, each in his own chariot, to **meet** Jehu.
10:15 [A] Jehonadab son of Recab, who *was on his way* to **meet** him.
16:10 [A] King Ahaz went to Damascus to **meet** Tiglath-Pileser king of
23:29 [A] King Josiah marched out to **meet** him **in battle**, but Neco
1Ch 19: 5 [A] told David about the men, he sent messengers to **meet** them,
19:10 [A] troops in Israel and deployed them **against** the Arameans.
19:11 [A] his brother, and they were deployed **against** the Ammonites.
19:17 [A] David formed his lines to **meet** the Arameans in battle,
2Ch 35:20 [A] the Euphrates, and Josiah marched out to **meet him in battle**.
Job 4:14 [A] fear and trembling **seized** me and made all my bones shake.
39:21 [A] rejoicing in his strength, and charges **into** the fray.
Ps 35: 3 [A] Brandish spear and javelin **against** those who pursue me.
59: 4 [59:5] [A] to attack me. Arise to **help** me; look on my plight!
Pr 7:10 [A] **out came** a woman **to meet** him, dressed like a prostitute
7:15 [A] So I came out to **meet** you; I looked for you and have found
Isa 7: 3 [A] to **meet** Ahaz at the end of the aqueduct of the Upper Pool,
14: 9 [A] The grave below is all astir to **meet** you at your coming;
21:14 [A] bring water for **[NIE]** the thirsty; you who live in Tema,
51:19 [A] These double calamities *have* **come upon** you—who can
Jer 4:20 [C] Disaster **follows** [+6584] disaster; the whole land lies in
13:22 [A] And if you ask yourself, "Why *has* this **happened** *to* me?"—
32:23 [G] them to do. So *you* **brought** all this disaster **upon** them.
41: 6 [A] Ishmael son of Nethaniah went out from Mizpah to **meet**
44:23 [A] this disaster *has* **come upon** you, as you now see."
51:31 [A] One courier **follows** another and messenger follows
51:31 [A] messenger **follows** messenger to announce to the king of
Am 4:12 [A] I will do this to you, prepare to **meet** your God, O Israel."
Zec 2: 3 [2:7] [A] to me left, and another angel came to **meet** him

7926 קֹרֵא¹ ***qōrē¹***, n.m. [2] [→ 7927; cf. 7924]
partridge [2]

1Sa 26:20 out to look for a flea—as one hunts a **partridge** in the mountains."
Jer 17:11 Like a **partridge** that hatches eggs it did not lay is the man who

7927 קֹרֵא² ***qōrē²***, n.pr.m. [3] [√ 7926; cf. 7924]
Kore [3]

1Ch 9:19 Shallum son of **Kore**, the son of Ebiasaph, the son of Korah,
26: 1 Meshelemiah son of **Kore**, one of the sons of Asaph.
2Ch 31:14 **Kore** son of Imnah the Levite, keeper of the East Gate, was in

7928 קָרַב ***qārab***, v. [280] [→ 6832, 7929, 7930, 7932, 7933, 7934, 7940; Ar 10638]
bring [36], present [36], offer [22], brought [16], come near [11], approached [9], come [9], presented [9], brings [7], go near [7], offers [7], approach [6], came [6], near [6], offered [5], went [5], brought forward [4], brought near [3], came near [3], come forward [3], drew near [3], had come forward [3], *untranslated* [2], about [2], acceptable [2], advance [2], bring near [2], came forward [2], come here [2], join [2], made an offering [2], offering [2], sacrificed [2], add [1], appear [1], approaches [1], approaching [1], bring forward [1], bring here [1], bringing near [1], bringing [1], brought offering [1], brought to a close [1], came together [1], cause to come near [1], closer [1], come closer [1], comes near [1], comes [1], draw near [1], draws near [1], encroach [1], go [1], gone near [1], have come near [1], inquire of [+448] [1], joined [1], keep away [+448+3870] [1], lie with [+448] [1], made offerings [1], made [1], make [1], march up [1], meet [1], offer sacrifices [1], offer up [1], present yourselves [1], presenting [1], presents [1], reach [1], reached [1], soon [1], stood [1], take part [+6913] [1], went near [1]

Ge 12:11 [G] As *he was* **about** to enter Egypt, he said to his wife Sarai,
20: 4 [A] Now Abimelech *had* not **gone near** her, so he said, "Lord,
27:41 [A] to himself, "The days of mourning for my father *are* **near**;
37:18 [A] and before *he* **reached** them, they plotted to kill him.
47:29 [A] When the time **drew near** for Israel to die, he called for his
Ex 3: 5 [A] "*Do* not **come** *any* **closer**," God said. "Take off your sandals,
12:48 [A] then *he may* **take part** [+6913] like one born in the land.
14:10 [G] As Pharaoh **approached**, the Israelites looked up, and there

Ex 14:20 [A] the other side; so neither **went near** the other all night long.
16: 9 [A] '**Come** before the LORD, for he has heard your
22: 8 [22:7] [C] the owner of the house *must* **appear** before the
28: 1 [G] Aaron your brother **brought** to you from among the Israelites,
29: 3 [G] **present** them in it—along with the bull and the two rams.
29: 4 [G] **bring** Aaron and his sons to the entrance to the Tent of
29: 8 [G] **Bring** his sons and dress them in tunics
29:10 [G] "**Bring** the bull to the front of the Tent of Meeting,
32:19 [A] When Moses **approached** the camp and saw the calf
36: 2 [A] given ability and who was willing to **come** and do the work.
40:12 [G] "**Bring** Aaron and his sons to the entrance to the Tent of
40:14 [G] **Bring** his sons and dress them in tunics.
40:32 [A] they entered the Tent of Meeting or **approached** the altar,
Lev 1: 2 [G] 'When any of you **brings** an offering to the LORD, bring as
1: 2 [G] **bring** as your offering an animal from either the herd or the
1: 3 [G] offering from the herd, *he is to* **offer** a male without defect.
1: 3 [G] *He must* **present** it at the entrance to the Tent of Meeting
1: 5 [G] then Aaron's sons the priests *shall* **bring** the blood
1:10 [G] the sheep or the goats, *he is to* **offer** a male without defect.
1:13 [G] and the priest *is to* **bring** all of it and burn it on the altar.
1:14 [G] offering of birds, *he is to* **offer** a dove or a young pigeon.
1:15 [G] The priest *shall* **bring** it to the altar, wring off the head
2: 1 [G] " 'When someone **brings** a grain offering to the LORD,
2: 4 [G] " 'If *you* **bring** a grain offering baked in an oven, it is to
2: 8 [G] **present** it to the priest, who shall take it to the altar.
2:11 [G] " 'Every grain offering *you* **bring** to the LORD must be
2:12 [G] *You may* **bring** them to the LORD as an offering of the
2:13 [G] out of your grain offerings; **add** salt to all your offerings.
2:14 [G] " 'If *you* **bring** a grain offering of firstfruits to the LORD,
2:14 [G] **offer** crushed heads of new grain roasted in the fire.
3: 1 [G] he **offers** an animal from the herd, whether male or female,
3: 1 [G] *he is to* **present** before the LORD an animal without defect.
3: 3 [G] *he is to* **bring** a sacrifice made to the LORD by fire: all the fat
3: 6 [G] the LORD, *he is to* **offer** a male or female without defect.
3: 7 [G] If he **offers** a lamb, he is to present it before the LORD.
3: 7 [G] If he offers a lamb, *he is to* **present** it before the LORD.
3: 9 [G] From the fellowship offering *he is to* **bring** a sacrifice made
3:12 [G] his offering is a goat, *he is to* **present** it before the LORD.
3:14 [G] *he is to* **make** this offering to the LORD by fire: all the fat that
4: 3 [G] *he must* **bring** to the LORD a young bull without defect as
4:14 [G] the assembly *must* **bring** a young bull as a sin offering
5: 8 [G] to the priest, who *shall* first **offer** the one for the sin offering.
6:14 [6:7] [G] Aaron's sons *are to* **bring** it before the LORD, in
6:20 [6:13] [G] his sons *are to* **bring** to the LORD on the day he is
6:21 [6:14] [G] **present** the grain offering broken in pieces as an
7: 3 [G] All its fat *shall be* **offered**: the fat tail and the fat that covers
7: 8 [G] The priest who **offers** a burnt offering for anyone may keep
7: 8 [G] offering for anyone may keep its hide for himself. **[RPH]**
7: 9 [G] in a pan or on a griddle belongs to the priest who **offers** it,
7:11 [G] the fellowship offering a person *may* **present** to the LORD:
7:12 [G] " 'If *he* **offers** it as an expression of thankfulness, then along
7:12 [G] along with this thank offering *he is to* **offer** cakes of bread
7:13 [G] *he is to* **present** an offering with cakes of bread made with
7:14 [G] *He is to* **bring** one of each kind as an offering, a contribution
7:16 [G] the sacrifice shall be eaten on the day *he* **offers** it,
7:18 [G] It will not be credited to the *one who* **offered** it, for it is
7:25 [G] *may be* **made** to the LORD must be cut off from his people.
7:29 [G] 'Anyone *who* **brings** a fellowship offering to the LORD is
7:33 [G] The son of Aaron who **offers** the blood and the fat of the
7:35 [G] his sons on the day they *were* **presented** to serve the LORD
7:38 [G] the Israelites to **bring** their offerings to the LORD,
8: 6 [G] Moses **brought** Aaron and his sons **forward** and washed
8:13 [G] Then he **brought** Aaron's sons **forward**, put tunics on them,
8:18 [G] *He* then **presented** the ram for the burnt offering, and Aaron
8:22 [G] *He* then **presented** the other ram, the ram for the ordination,
8:24 [G] Moses also **brought** Aaron's sons **forward** and put some of
9: 2 [G] both without defect, and **present** them before the LORD.
9: 5 [A] the entire assembly **came near** and stood before the LORD.
9: 7 [A] "**Come** to the altar and sacrifice your sin offering and your
9: 8 [A] So Aaron **came** to the altar and slaughtered the calf as a sin
9: 9 [G] His sons **brought** the blood to him, and he dipped his finger
9:15 [G] Aaron then **brought** the offering that was for the people. He
9:16 [G] *He* **brought** the burnt offering and offered it in the
9:17 [G] *He* also **brought** the grain offering, took a handful of it
10: 1 [G] *they* **offered** unauthorized fire before the LORD, contrary
10: 4 [A] sons of Aaron's uncle Uzziel, and said to them, "**Come here**;
10: 5 [A] So *they* **came** and carried them, still in their tunics, outside
10:19 [G] "Today *they* **sacrificed** their sin offering and their burnt
12: 7 [G] *He shall* **offer** them before the LORD to make atonement
14:12 [G] and **offer** it as a guilt offering, along with the log of oil;
16: 1 [A] sons of Aaron who died when they **approached** the LORD.
16: 6 [G] "Aaron *is to* **offer** the bull for his own sin offering to make
16: 9 [G] Aaron *shall* **bring** the goat whose lot falls to the LORD
16:11 [G] "Aaron *shall* **bring** the bull for his own sin offering to make
16:20 [G] and the altar, *he shall* **bring forward** the live goat.
17: 4 [G] **present** it as an offering to the LORD in front of the
18: 6 [A] " 'No one *is to* **approach** any close relative to have sexual
18:14 [A] " 'Do not dishonor your father's brother by **approaching** his
18:19 [A] " '*Do* not **approach** a woman to have sexual relations during
20:16 [A] " 'If a woman **approaches** an animal to have sexual relations
21: 6 [G] Because they **present** the offerings made to the LORD by
21: 8 [G] them as holy, because they **offer up** the food of your God.
21:17 [A] has a defect *may* **come near** to offer the food of his God.
21:17 [G] who has a defect may come near to **offer** the food of his God.
21:18 [A] No man who has any defect *may* **come near**: no man who is
21:21 [G] near to **present** the offerings made to the LORD by fire.
21:21 [G] a defect; he must not come near to **offer** the food of his God.
22: 3 [A] yet **comes near** the sacred offerings that the Israelites
22:18 [G] **presents** a gift for a burnt offering to the LORD, either to
22:18 [G] either to fulfill a vow or as a freewill offering, **[RPH]**
22:20 [G] *Do* not **bring** anything with a defect, because it will not be
22:21 [G] When anyone **brings** from the herd or flock a fellowship
22:22 [G] *Do* not **offer** to the LORD the blind, the injured or the
22:24 [G] *You must* not **offer** to the LORD an animal whose testicles
22:25 [G] hand of a foreigner and **offer** them as the food of your God.
23: 8 [G] For seven days **present** an offering made to the LORD by
23:16 [G] and then **present** an offering of new grain to the LORD.
23:18 [G] **Present** with this bread seven male lambs, each a year old
23:25 [G] but **present** an offering made to the LORD by fire.' "
23:27 [G] and **present** an offering made to the LORD by fire.
23:36 [G] For seven days **present** offerings made to the LORD by
23:36 [G] and **present** an offering made to the LORD by fire.
23:37 [G] which you are to proclaim as sacred assemblies for **bringing**
27: 9 [G] " 'If what he vowed is an animal that *is* **acceptable** as an
27:11 [G] is a ceremonially unclean animal—one that *is* not **acceptable**
Nu 3: 4 [G] **made an offering** *with* unauthorized fire before him in the
3: 6 [G] "**Bring** the tribe of Levi and present them to Aaron the priest
5: 9 [G] All the sacred contributions the Israelites **bring** to a priest
5:16 [G] " 'The priest *shall* **bring** her and have her stand before the
5:25 [G] wave it before the LORD and **bring** it to the altar.
6:14 [G] There *he is to* **present** his offerings to the LORD:
6:16 [G] " 'The priest *is to* **present** them before the LORD and make
7: 2 [G] in charge of those who were counted, **made offerings.**
7: 3 [G] a cart from every two. These *they* **presented** before the
7:10 [G] the leaders **brought** their offerings for its dedication
7:10 [G] for its dedication and **presented** them before the altar.
7:11 [G] "Each day one leader *is to* **bring** his offering for the
7:12 [G] The *one who* **brought** his offering on the first day was
7:18 [G] son of Zuar, the leader of Issachar, **brought** his **offering.**
7:19 [G] The offering *he* **brought** was one silver plate weighing a
8: 9 [G] **Bring** the Levites to the front of the Tent of Meeting
8:10 [G] *You are to* **bring** the Levites before the LORD,
9: 6 [A] dead body. So *they* **came** to Moses and Aaron that same day
9: 7 [G] why should we be kept from **presenting** the LORD's
9:13 [G] because *he did* not **present** the LORD's offering at the
15: 4 [G] the *one who* **brings** his offering shall present to the LORD
15: 4 [G] the one who brings his offering *shall* **present** to the LORD
15: 7 [G] drink offering. **Offer** it as an aroma pleasing to the LORD.
15: 9 [G] **bring** with the bull a grain offering of three-tenths of an
15:10 [G] Also **bring** half a hin of wine as a drink offering. It will be an
15:13 [G] *he* **brings** an offering made by fire as an aroma pleasing to
15:27 [G] *he must* **bring** a year-old female goat for a sin offering.
15:33 [G] Those who found him gathering wood **brought** him to Moses
16: 5 [G] who is holy, and *he will* **have** that person **come near** him.
16: 5 [G] The man he chooses *he will* **cause to come near** him.
16: 9 [G] **brought** you **near** himself to do the work at the LORD's
16:10 [G] *He has* **brought** you and all your fellow Levites **near**
16:17 [G] in it—250 censers in all—and **present** it before the LORD.
16:35 [G] and consumed the 250 men *who were* **offering** the incense.
16:38 [17:3] [G] for they *were* **presented** before the LORD and have
16:39 [17:4] [G] censers **brought** *by* those who had been burned up,
16:40 [17:5] [A] *should* **come** to burn incense before the LORD,
18: 2 [G] **Bring** your fellow Levites from your ancestral tribe to join
18: 3 [A] *they must* not **go near** the furnishings of the sanctuary or the
18: 4 [A] at the Tent—and no *one* else *may* **come near** where you are.
18:15 [G] both man and animal, that *is* **offered** to the LORD is yours.
18:22 [A] From now on the Israelites *must* not **go near** the Tent of
25: 6 [G] an Israelite man **brought** to his family a Midianite woman
26:61 [G] **made an offering** before the LORD *with* unauthorized
27: 1 [A] Noah, Hoglah, Milcah and Tirzah. *They* **approached**
27: 5 [G] So Moses **brought** their case before the LORD
28: 2 [G] 'See that *you* **present** to me at the appointed time the food
28: 3 [G] 'This is the offering made by fire that *you are to* **present** to
28:11 [G] **present** to the LORD a burnt offering of two young bulls,
28:19 [G] **Present** to the LORD an offering made by fire, a burnt
28:26 [G] when you **present** to the LORD an offering of new grain
28:27 [G] **Present** a burnt offering of two young bulls, one ram
29: 8 [G] **Present** as an aroma pleasing to the LORD a burnt offering

Nu 29:13 [G] **Present** an offering made by fire as an aroma pleasing to the
29:36 [G] **Present** an offering made by fire as an aroma pleasing to the
31:48 [A] of thousands and commanders of hundreds—**went** to Moses
31:50 [G] So *we have* **brought** as an offering to the LORD the gold
36: 1 [A] **came** and spoke before Moses and the leaders, the heads of
Dt 1:17 [G] **Bring** me any case too hard for you, and I will hear it.
1:22 [A] all of you **came** to me and said, "Let us send men ahead to
2:19 [A] When *you* **come** to the Ammonites, do not harass them
2:37 [A] *you did* not **encroach** on any of the land of the Ammonites,
4:11 [A] *You* **came near** and stood at the foot of the mountain while
5:23 [A] the leading men of your tribes and your elders **came** to me.
5:27 [A] **Go near** and listen to all that the LORD our God says.
15: 9 [A] "The seventh year, the year for canceling debts, *is* **near**,"
20: 2 [A] When you *are about to* **go** into battle, the priest shall come
20:10 [A] When *you* **march up** to attack a city, make its people an
22:14 [A] saying, "I married this woman, but when *I* **approached** her,
25:11 [A] the wife of one of them **comes** to rescue her husband from
31:14 [A] LORD said to Moses, "Now the day of your death *is* **near**.
Jos 3: 4 [A] thousand yards between you and the ark; *do* not **go near** it."
7:14 [C] " 'In the morning, **present yourselves** tribe by tribe. The tribe
7:14 [A] The tribe that the LORD takes *shall* **come forward** clan by
7:14 [A] the clan that the LORD takes *shall* **come forward** family
7:14 [A] the family that the LORD takes *shall* **come forward** man
7:16 [G] Early the next morning Joshua **had** Israel **come forward** by
7:17 [G] The clans of Judah **came forward**, and he took the Zerahites.
7:17 [G] *He* **had** the clan of the Zerahites **come forward** by families,
7:18 [G] Joshua **had** his family **come forward** man by man,
8: 5 [A] I and all those with me *will* **advance** on the city, and when
8:23 [G] they took the king of Ai alive and **brought** him to Joshua.
10:24 [A] "**Come here** and put your feet on the necks of these kings."
10:24 [A] So *they* **came forward** and placed their feet on their necks.
17: 4 [A] *They* **went** to Eleazar the priest, Joshua son of Nun, and the
Jdg 3:17 [G] *He* **presented** the tribute to Eglon king of Moab, who was a
3:18 [G] After Ehud *had* **presented** the tribute, he sent on their way
5:25 [G] in a bowl fit for nobles *she* **brought** him curdled milk.
19:13 [A] *let's try to* **reach** Gibeah or Ramah and spend the night in
20:24 [A] Then the Israelites **drew near** to Benjamin the second day.
1Sa 10:20 [G] When Samuel **brought** all the tribes of Israel **near**, the tribe
10:21 [G] *he* **brought forward** the tribe of Benjamin, clan by clan,
14:36 [A] But the priest said, "*Let us* **inquire** [+448] **of** God here."
17:48 [A] As the Philistine moved **closer** to attack him, David ran
2Sa 15: 5 [A] whenever anyone **approached** him to bow down before him,
20:16 [A] Listen! Tell Joab *to* **come** here so I can speak to him."
20:17 [A] *He* **went** toward her, and she asked, "Are you Joab?" "I am,"
1Ki 2: 1 [A] When the time **drew near** for David to die, he gave a charge
2: 7 [A] *They* **stood** by me when I fled from your brother Absalom.
20:29 [A] each other, and on the seventh day the battle *was* **joined**.
2Ki 16:12 [A] saw the altar, he **approached** it and presented offerings on it.
16:14 [G] The bronze altar that stood before the LORD *he* **brought**
1Ch 16: 1 [G] *they* **presented** burnt offerings and fellowship offerings
2Ch 35:12 [G] of the families of the people to **offer** to the LORD,
Ezr 8:35 [G] the exiles who had returned from captivity **sacrificed** burnt
Est 5: 2 [A] So Esther **approached** and touched the tip of the scepter.
Job 31:37 [D] of my every step; like a prince *I would* **approach** him.)—
33:22 [A] His soul **draws near** to the pit, and his life to the messengers
Ps 27: 2 [A] When evil men **advance** against me to devour my flesh,
32: 9 [A] be controlled by bit and bridle or they *will* not **come** to you.
65: 4 [65:5] [D] you choose and **bring near** to live in your courts!
69:18 [69:19] [A] **Come near** and rescue me; redeem me because of
72:10 [G] to him; the kings of Sheba and Seba *will* **present** him gifts.
91:10 [A] harm will befall you, no disaster *will* **come near** your tent.
119:150 [A] Those who devise wicked schemes *are* **near**, but they are far
119:169 [A] *May* my cry **come** before you, O LORD; give me
Pr 5: 8 [A] to a path far from her, *do* not **go near** the door of her house,
Ecc 5: 1 [4:17] [A] **Go near** to listen rather than to offer the sacrifice of
Isa 5: 8 [G] **join** field to field till no space is left and you live alone in the
5:19 [A] *Let it* **approach**, let the plan of the Holy One of Israel come,
8: 3 [A] *I* **went** to the prophetess, and she conceived and gave birth to
26:17 [G] As a woman with child and **about** to give birth writhes
34: 1 [A] **Come near**, you nations, and listen; pay attention,
41: 1 [A] and speak; *let us* **meet** together at the place of judgment.
41: 5 [A] of the earth tremble. *They* **approach** and come forward;
41:21 [A] "**Present** your case," says the LORD. "Set forth your
46:13 [D] *I am* **bringing** my righteousness **near**, it is not far away;
48:16 [A] "**Come near** me and listen to this: "From the first
54:14 [A] Terror will be far removed; *it will* not **come near** you.
57: 3 [A] **come** here, *you* sons of a sorceress, you offspring of
65: 5 [A] who say, '**Keep away** [+448+3870]; don't come near me,
Jer 30:21 [G] *I will* **bring** him **near** and he will come close to me, for who
La 3:57 [A] *You* **came near** when I called you, and you said, "Do not
4:18 [A] Our end *was* **near**, our days were numbered, for our end had
Eze 9: 1 [A] "**Bring** the guards of the city **here**, each with a weapon in his
12:23 [A] 'The days *are* **near** when every vision will be fulfilled.
18: 6 [A] or **lie** [+448] **with** a woman during her period.
22: 4 [G] *You have* **brought** your days **to a close**, and the end of your
36: 8 [D] and fruit for my people Israel, for they will **soon** come home.
37: 7 [A] a rattling sound, and the bones **came together**, bone to bone.
37:17 [A] **Join** them together into one stick so that they will become
42:14 [A] They are to put on other clothes before *they* **go near** the
43:22 [G] "On the second day *you are to* **offer** a male goat without
43:23 [G] *you are to* **offer** a young bull and a ram from the flock,
43:24 [G] *You are to* **offer** them before the LORD, and the priests are
44: 7 [G] desecrating my temple while you **offered** me food, fat
44:15 [A] astray from me, *are to* **come near** to minister before me;
44:15 [G] they are to stand before me to **offer sacrifices** *of* fat
44:16 [A] they alone *are to* **come near** my table to minister before me
44:27 [G] *he is to* **offer** a sin offering *for* himself,
46: 4 [G] The burnt offering the prince **brings** to the LORD on the
Hos 7: 6 [D] hearts are like an oven; *they* **approach** him with intrigue.
Jnh 1: 6 [A] The captain **went** to him and said, "How can you sleep?
Zep 3: 2 [A] not trust in the LORD, *she does* not **draw near** to her God.
Hag 2:14 [G] 'Whatever they do and whatever *they* **offer** there is defiled.
Mal 1: 8 [G] is that not wrong? *Try* **offering** them to your governor!
3: 5 [A] "So *I will* **come near** to you for judgment. I will be quick to

7929 קָרֵב *qārēb*, a.v. [12] [√ 7928]

draw near [2], even comes near [+448+7929] [2], approached [1], approaches [1], came [1], closer and closer [+2143+2256] [1], closer [1], comes near [1], goes near [1], going [1]

Nu 1:51 shall do it. Anyone else who **goes near** it shall be put to death.
3:10 anyone else who **approaches** the sanctuary must be put to death."
3:38 Anyone else who **approached** the sanctuary was to be put to
17:13 [17:28] Anyone who **even comes near** [+448+7929] the
17:13 [17:28] Anyone who **even comes near** [+448+7929] the
18: 7 Anyone else who **comes near** the sanctuary must be put to death."
Dt 20: 3 O Israel, today you are **going** into battle against your enemies.
1Sa 17:41 with his shield bearer in front of him, kept coming **closer** to David.
2Sa 18:25 good news." And the man came **closer** [+2143+2256] **and closer**.
1Ki 4:27 [5:7] for King Solomon and all who **came** to the king's table.
Eze 40:46 who are the only Levites who may **draw near** to the LORD to
45: 4 the sanctuary and who **draw near** to minister before the LORD.

7930 קְרָב *qᵉrāb*, n.[m.]. [9] [→ 6832; cf. 7928; Ar 10639]

war [5], battle [4]

2Sa 17:11 be gathered to you, with you yourself leading them into **battle**.
Job 38:23 which I reserve for times of trouble, for days of **war** and battle?
Ps 55:18 [55:19] He ransoms me unharmed from the **battle** waged against
55:21 [55:22] His speech is smooth as butter, yet **war** is *in* his heart;
68:30 [68:31] bars of silver. Scatter the nations who delight in **war**.
78: 9 though armed with bows, turned back on the day of **battle**;
144: 1 my Rock, who trains my hands for **war**, my fingers for battle.
Ecc 9:18 Wisdom is better than weapons of **war**, but one sinner destroys
Zec 14: 3 and fight against those nations, as he fights in the day of **battle**.

7931 קֶרֶב *qereb*, n.[m.]. [227 / 225]

among [+928] [52], in [+928] [24], within [+928] [20], among [18], from [+4946] [16], inner parts [16], with [+928] [11], *untranslated* [7], midst [6], heart [5], among [+4946] [4], near [+928] [4], them[s] [+2021] [4], through [+928] [3], upon [+928] [3], inmost being [2], on [+928] [2], to [+6584] [2], along with [+928] [1], at [+928] [1], ate [+448+995] [1], body [1], done so [+448+995] [1], entering [+928+995] [1], filled with [+928] [1], folds [1], had [+928] [1], harbor [+928+4328] [1], hearts [1], herself [+2023] [1], in [+4946] [1], inside [+928] [1], into [+928] [1], lose heart [+928+1327+8120] [1], middle [1], mind [1], minds [1], out of [+4946] [1], presence [1], ranks [1], stomach [1], there[s] [+928+2257] [1], thick [1], throughout [+928] [1]

Ge 18:12 So Sarah laughed to **herself** [+2023] as she thought, "After I am
18:24 the place for the sake of the fifty righteous people **in** [+928] it?
24: 3 the daughters of the Canaanites, **among** [+928] whom I am living,
25:22 The babies jostled each other **within** [+928] her, and she said,
41:21 even after they **ate them** [+448+995], no one could tell that they
41:21 ate them, no one could tell that they *had* **done**[s] **so** [+448+995];
45: 6 For two years now there has been famine **in** [+928] the land,
48:16 and Isaac, and may they increase greatly **upon** [+928] the earth."
Ex 3:20 with all the wonders that I will perform **among** [+928] them.
8:22 [8:18] you will know that I, the LORD, am **in** [+928] this land.
10: 1 I may perform these miraculous signs of mine **among** [+928] them
12: 9 in water, but roast it over the fire—head, legs and **inner parts**.
17: 7 the LORD saying, "Is the LORD **among** [+928] us or not?"
23:21 will not forgive your rebellion, since my Name is **in** [+928] him.
23:25 your food and water. I will take away sickness from **among** you,
29:13 take all the fat around the **inner parts**, the covering of the liver,
29:17 Cut the ram into pieces and wash the **inner parts** and the legs,
29:22 the fat tail, the fat around the **inner parts**, the covering of the liver,
31:14 whoever does any work on that day must be cut off **from** [+4946]

Ex 33: 3 I will not go **with** [+928] you, because you are a stiff-necked
33: 5 If I were to go **with** [+928] you even for a moment, I might destroy
34: 9 favor in your eyes," he said, "then let the Lord go **with** [+928] us.
34: 10 The people you live **among** [+928] will see how awesome is the
34: 12 where you are going, or they will be a snare **among** [+928] you.
Lev 1: 9 He is to wash the **inner parts** and the legs with water,
1: 13 He is to wash the **inner parts** and the legs with water,
3: 3 all the fat that covers the **inner parts** or is connected to them,
3: 3 the fat that covers the inner parts or is connected to **them**[s] [+2021],
3: 9 all the fat that covers the **inner parts** or is connected to them,
3: 9 the fat that covers the inner parts or is connected to **them**[s] [+2021],
3: 14 all the fat that covers the **inner parts** or is connected to them,
3: 14 the fat that covers the inner parts or is connected to **them**[s] [+2021],
4: 8 the fat that covers the **inner parts** or is connected to them,
4: 8 the fat that covers the inner parts or is connected to **them**[s] [+2021],
4: 11 its flesh, as well as the head and legs, the **inner parts** and offal—
7: 3 shall be offered: the fat tail and the fat that covers the **inner parts**,
8: 16 Moses also took all the fat around the **inner parts**, the covering of
8: 21 He washed the **inner parts** and the legs with water and burned the
8: 25 He took the fat, the fat tail, all the fat around the **inner parts**,
9: 14 He washed the **inner parts** and the legs and burned them on top of
17: 4 he has shed blood and must be cut off **from** [+4946] his people.
17: 10 who eats blood and will cut him off **from** [+4946] his people.
18: 29 such persons must be cut off **from** [+4946] their people.
20: 3 against that man and I will cut him off **from** [+4946] his people;
20: 5 and his family and will cut off **from** [+4946] their people both him
20: 6 by following them, and I will cut him off **from** [+4946] his people.
20: 18 Both of them must be cut off **from** [+4946] their people.
23: 30 I will destroy from **among** his people anyone who does any work
Nu 5: 27 and she will become accursed **among** [+928] her people.
11: 4 The rabble **with** [+928] them began to crave other food, and again
11: 20 who is **among** [+928] you, and have wailed before him, saying,
11: 21 "Here I am **among** [+928] six hundred thousand men on foot,
14: 11 in spite of all the miraculous signs I have performed **among** [+928]
14: 13 By your power you brought these people up from **among** them.
14: 14 O LORD, are **with** [+928] these people and that you, O LORD,
14: 42 Do not go up, because the LORD is not **with** [+928] you.
14: 44 the ark of the LORD's covenant moved **from** [+4946] the camp.
15: 30 and that person must be cut off **from** [+4946] his people.
Dt 1: 42 'Do not go up and fight, because I will not be **with** [+928] you.
2: 14 that entire generation of fighting men had perished **from** [+4946]
2: 15 until he had completely eliminated them **from** [+4946] the camp.
2: 16 Now when the last of these fighting men **among** [+4946] the
4: 3 The LORD your God destroyed from **among** you everyone who
4: 5 so that you may follow them **in** [+928] the land you are entering to
4: 34 tried to take for himself one nation **out of** [+4946] another nation,
6: 15 who is **among** [+928] you, is a jealous God and his anger will burn
7: 21 your God, who is **among** [+928] you, is a great and awesome God.
11: 6 when the earth opened its mouth right in the **middle** *of* all Israel
13: 1 [13:2] appears **among** [+928] you and announces to you a
13: 5 [13:6] you to follow. You must purge the evil from **among** you.
13: 11 [13:12] no one **among** [+928] you will do such an evil thing
13: 13 [13:14] that wicked men have arisen **among** [+4946] you
13: 14 [13:15] this detestable thing has been done **among** [+928] you,
15: 11 There will always be poor people **in** [+4946] the land. Therefore I
16: 11 the aliens, the fatherless and the widows living **among** [+928] you.
17: 2 or woman living **among** [+928] you in one of the towns the
17: 7 hands of all the people. You must purge the evil from **among** you.
17: 15 He must be from **among** your own brothers. Do not place a
17: 20 his descendants will reign a long time over his kingdom **in** [+928]
18: 2 They shall have no inheritance **among** [+928] their brothers;
18: 15 raise up for you a prophet like me from **among** your own brothers.
18: 18 I will raise up for them a prophet like you from **among** their
19: 10 so that innocent blood will not be shed **in** [+928] your land,
19: 19 to do to his brother. You must purge the evil from **among** you.
19: 20 and never again will such an evil thing be done **among** [+928] you.
21: 8 do not hold **[OBJ]** your people guilty of the blood of an innocent
21: 9 So you will purge **from** [+4946] yourselves the guilt of shedding
21: 21 You must purge the evil from **among** you. All Israel will hear of it
22: 21 in her father's house. You must purge the evil from **among** you.
22: 24 another man's wife. You must purge the evil from **among** you.
23: 14 [23:15] For the LORD your God moves about **in** [+928] your
23: 16 [23:17] Let him live **among** [+928] you wherever he likes and in
24: 7 the kidnapper must die. You must purge the evil from **among** you.
26: 11 the aliens **among** [+928] you shall rejoice in all the good things the
28: 43 The alien who lives **among** [+928] you will rise above you higher
29: 11 [29:10] the aliens living **in** [+928] your camps who chop your
29: 16 [29:15] how we passed **through** [+928] the countries on the way
31: 16 to the foreign gods of the land they *are* **entering** [+928+995].
31: 17 disasters come upon us because our God is not **with** [+928] us?'
Jos 1: 11 "Go **through** [+928] the camp and tell the people, 'Get your
3: 2 After three days the officers went **throughout** [+928] the camp,
3: 5 for tomorrow the LORD will do amazing things **among** [+928]
3: 10 This is how you will know that the living God is **among** [+928]
4: 6 to serve as a sign **among** [+928] you. In the future, when your
6: 25 to Jericho—and she lives **among** [+928] the Israelites to this day.
7: 12 destroy whatever **among** [+4946] you is devoted to destruction.
7: 13 says: That which is devoted is **among** [+928] you, O Israel.
7: 13 cannot stand against your enemies until you remove it. **[OBJ]**
8: 35 and children, and the aliens who lived **among** [+928] them.
9: 7 of Israel said to the Hivites, "But perhaps you live **near** [+928] us.
9: 16 Israelites heard that they were neighbors, living **near** [+928] them.
9: 22 live a long way from you,' while actually you live **near** [+928] us?
10: 1 a treaty of peace with Israel and were living **near** [+928] them.
13: 13 so they continue to live **among** [+928] the Israelites to this day.
16: 10 to this day the Canaanites live **among** [+928] the people of
18: 7 The Levites, however, do not get a portion **among** [+928] you,
24: 5 and I afflicted the Egyptians by what I did **there**[s] [+928+2257],
24: 17 and among all the nations **through** [+928] which we traveled.
24: 23 "throw away the foreign gods that are **among** [+928] you and yield
Jdg 1: 29 but the Canaanites continued to live there **among** [+928] them.
1: 30 living in Kitron or Nahalol, who remained **among** [+928] them;
1: 32 because of this the people of Asher lived **among** [+928] the
1: 33 the Naphtalites too lived **among** [+928] the Canaanite inhabitants
3: 5 The Israelites lived **among** [+928] the Canaanites, Hittites,
10: 16 Then they got rid of the foreign gods **among** [+4946] them
18: 7 where they saw that the people **[NIE]** were living in safety,
18: 20 and the carved image and went **along with** [+928] the people.
1Sa 4: 3 so that it may go **with** [+928] us and save us from the hand of our
16: 13 the horn of oil and anointed him in the **presence** *of* his brothers,
25: 37 and his heart failed **[OBJ]** him and he became like a stone.
1Ki 3: 28 because they saw that he **had** [+928] wisdom from God to
17: 21 "O LORD my God, let this boy's life return **to** [+6584] him!"
17: 22 and the boy's life returned **to** [+6584] him, and he lived.
20: 39 called out to him, "Your servant went into the **thick** *of* the battle,
Job 20: 14 it will become the venom of serpents **within** [+928] him.
Ps 5: 9 [5:10] mouth can be trusted; their **heart** is filled with destruction.
36: 1 [36:2] An oracle is **within** [+928] my heart concerning the
39: 3 [39:4] My heart grew hot **within** [+928] me, and as I meditated,
46: 5 [46:6] God is **within** [+928] her, she will not fall; God will help
48: 9 [48:10] **Within** [+928] your temple, O God, we meditate on your
49: 11 [49:12] Their tombs [BHS ***thoughts***; NIV 7700] will remain their
51: 10 [51:12] O God, and renew a steadfast spirit **within** [+928] me.
55: 4 [55:5] My heart is in anguish **within** [+928] me; the terrors of
55: 10 [55:11] about on its walls; malice and abuse are **within** [+928] it.
55: 11 [55:12] Destructive forces are at work **in** [+928] the city; threats
55: 15 [55:16] to the grave, for evil finds lodging **among** [+928] them.
62: 4 [62:5] With their mouths they bless, but in their **hearts** they curse.
64: 6 [64:7] Surely the **mind** and heart *of* man are cunning.
74: 4 Your foes roared **in** [+928] the place where you met with us;
74: 11 Take it from the **folds** *of* your garment and destroy them!
74: 12 my king from of old; you bring salvation **upon** [+928] the earth.
78: 28 He made them come down **inside** [+928] their camp, all around
82: 1 the great assembly; he gives judgment **among** [+928] the "gods":
94: 19 When anxiety was great **within** [+928] me, your consolation
101: 2 come to me? I will walk **in** [+928] my house with blameless heart.
101: 7 No one who practices deceit will dwell **in** [+928] my house;
103: 1 O my soul; all my **inmost being**, praise his holy name.
109: 18 it entered into his **body** like water, into his bones like oil.
109: 22 I am poor and needy, and my heart is wounded **within** [+928] me.
110: 2 scepter from Zion; you will rule in the **midst** *of* your enemies.
138: 7 Though I walk in the **midst** *of* trouble, you preserve my life;
147: 13 the bars of your gates and blesses your people **within** [+928] you.
Pr 14: 33 and even **among** [+928] fools she lets herself be known.
15: 31 to a life-giving rebuke will be at home **among** [+928] the wise.
26: 24 disguises himself with his lips, but in his **heart** he harbors deceit.
Isa 4: 4 he will cleanse the bloodstains **from** [+4946] Jerusalem by a spirit
5: 8 to field till no space is left and you live alone **in** [+928] the land.
5: 25 and the dead bodies are like refuse **in** [+928] the streets.
6: 12 sent everyone far away and the land is utterly forsaken. **[NIE]**
7: 22 All who remain **in** [+928] the land will eat curds and honey.
10: 23 will carry out the destruction decreed **upon** [+928] the whole land.
12: 6 of Zion, for great is the Holy One of Israel **among** [+928] you."
16: 11 laments for Moab like a harp, my **inmost being** for Kir Hareseth.
19: 1 and the hearts of the Egyptians melt **within** [+928] them.
19: 3 The Egyptians *will* **lose heart** [+928+1327+8120], and I will bring
19: 14 The LORD has poured **into** [+928] them a spirit of dizziness;
19: 24 along with Egypt and Assyria, a blessing **on** [+928] the earth.
24: 13 So will it be **on** [+928] the earth and among the nations, as when
25: 11 They will spread out their hands **in** [+928] it, as a swimmer spreads
26: 9 in the morning [BHS ***within me***; NIV 1332] my spirit longs for you.
29: 23 When they see **among** [+928] them their children, the work of my
63: 11 his flock? Where is he who set his Holy Spirit **among** [+928] them,
Jer 4: 14 How long *will you* **harbor** [+928+4328] wicked thoughts?
6: 1 for safety, people of Benjamin! Flee **from** [+4946] Jerusalem!
6: 6 This city must be punished; it is **filled with** [+928] oppression.
9: 8 [9:7] to his neighbor, but in his **heart** he sets a trap for him.
14: 9 You are **among** [+928] us, O LORD, and we bear your name;

Jer 23: 9 My heart is broken **within** [+928] me; all my bones tremble.
29: 8 not let the prophets and diviners **among** [+928] you deceive you.
30: 21 will be one of their own; their ruler will arise from **among** them.
31: 33 "I will put my law in their **minds** and write it on their hearts.
46: 21 The mercenaries in her **ranks** are like fattened calves. They too
La 1: 15 "The Lord has rejected all the warriors in my **midst**; he has
1: 20 I am in torment **within** [+928], and in my heart I am disturbed,
3: 45 You have made us scum and refuse **among** [+928] the nations.
4: 13 her priests, who shed **within** [+928] her the blood of the righteous.
Eze 11: 19 give them an undivided heart and put a new spirit **in** [+928] them;
22: 27 Her officials **within** [+928] her are like wolves tearing their prey;
36: 26 I will give you a new heart and put a new spirit **in** [+928] you;
36: 27 I will put my Spirit **in** [+928] you and move you to follow my
Hos 5: 4 A spirit of prostitution is in their **heart**; they do not acknowledge
11: 9 For I am God, and not man—the Holy One **among** [+928] you.
Joel 2: 27 you will know that I am **in** [+928] Israel, that I am the LORD
Am 2: 3 I will destroy her ruler **[NIE]** and kill all her officials with him,"
3: 9 unrest within her and the oppression **among** [+928] her people."
5: 17 for I will pass through your **midst**," says the LORD.
7: 8 I am setting a plumb line **among** [+928] my people Israel;
7: 10 "Amos is raising a conspiracy against you in the very **heart** *of*
Mic 3: 11 upon the LORD and say, "Is not the LORD **among** [+928] us?
5: 7 [5:6] The remnant of Jacob will be in the **midst** *of* many peoples
5: 8 [5:7] in the **midst** *of* many peoples, like a lion among the beasts
5: 10 [5:9] "I will destroy your horses from **among** you and demolish
5: 13 [5:12] carved images and your sacred stones from **among** you;
5: 14 [5:13] I will uproot from **among** you your Asherah poles
6: 14 You will eat but not be satisfied; your **stomach** will still be empty.
Na 3: 13 Look **at** [+928] your troops—they are all women! The gates of
Hab 2: 19 It is covered with gold and silver; there is no breath **in** [+928] it.
3: 2 Renew them **in** [+928] our day, in our time make them known;
3: 2 Renew them in our day, **in** [+928] our time make them known;
Zep 3: 3 Her officials **[NIE]** are roaring lions, her rulers are evening
3: 5 The LORD **within** [+928] her is righteous; he does no wrong.
3: 11 because I will remove **from** [+4946] this city those who rejoice in
3: 12 I will leave **within** [+928] you the meek and humble, who trust in
3: 15 The LORD, the King of Israel, is **with** [+928] you; never again
3: 17 The LORD your God is **with** [+928] you, he is mighty to save.
Zec 12: 1 and who forms the spirit of man **within** [+928] him, declares:
14: 1 is coming when your plunder will be divided **among** [+928] you.

7932 קִרְבָה *qirbâ*, n.f. [2] [√ 7928]

come near [1], near [1]

Ps 73: 28 as for me, it is good to be **near** God. I have made the Sovereign
Isa 58: 2 me for just decisions and seem eager for God to **come near** them.

7933 קָרְבָּן *qorbān*, n.m. [80] [√ 7928]

offering [58], *untranslated* [7], offerings [7], gifts [2], offers [2], gift [1], offered [1], offering made by fire [+852] [1], sacrifice [1]

Lev 1: 2 'When any of you brings an **offering** to the LORD, bring as your
1: 2 bring as your **offering** an animal from either the herd or the flock.
1: 3 " 'If the **offering** is a burnt offering from the herd, he is to offer a
1: 10 " 'If the **offering** is a burnt offering from the flock, from either the
1: 14 " 'If the **offering** to the LORD is a burnt offering of birds,
1: 14 offering of birds, he is to offer a dove or a young pigeon. **[RPH]**
2: 1 " 'When someone brings **[RPH]** a grain offering to the LORD,
2: 1 a grain offering to the LORD, his **offering** is to be of fine flour.
2: 4 " 'If you bring **[RPH]** a grain offering baked in an oven, it is to
2: 5 If your grain offering **[RPH]** is prepared on a griddle, it is to be
2: 7 If your grain offering **[RPH]** is cooked in a pan, it is to be made
2: 12 You may bring them to the LORD as an **offering** *of* the firstfruits,
2: 13 Season all your grain offerings **[RPH]** with salt. Do not leave the
2: 13 your God out of your grain offerings; add salt to all your **offerings**.
3: 1 " 'If someone's **offering** is a fellowship offering, and he offers an
3: 2 He is to lay his hand on the head of his **offering** and slaughter it at
3: 6 " 'If he **offers** an animal from the flock as a fellowship offering to
3: 7 If he offers a lamb, **[RPH]** he is to present it before the LORD.
3: 8 He is to lay his hand on the head of his **offering** and slaughter it in
3: 12 " 'If his **offering** is a goat, he is to present it before the LORD.
3: 14 From what he **offers** he is to make this offering to the LORD by
4: 23 he must bring as his **offering** a male goat without defect.
4: 28 he must bring as his **offering** for the sin he committed a female
4: 32 " 'If he brings a lamb as his sin **offering**, he is to bring a female
5: 11 he is to bring as an **offering** for his sin a tenth of an ephah of fine
6: 20 [6:13] "This is the **offering** Aaron and his sons are to bring to the
7: 13 he is to present an **offering** with cakes of bread made with yeast.
7: 14 He is to bring one of each kind as an **offering**, a contribution to the
7: 15 offering of thanksgiving must be eaten on the day it is **offered**;
7: 16 his **offering** is the result of a vow or is a freewill offering,
7: 29 to the LORD is to bring part of it as his **sacrifice** to the LORD.
7: 38 commanded the Israelites to bring their **offerings** to the LORD,
9: 7 sacrifice the **offering** that is *for* the people and make atonement for
9: 15 Aaron then brought the **offering** *that* was *for* the people. He took
17: 4 **offering** to the LORD in front of the tabernacle of the LORD—
22: 18 presents a **gift** for a burnt offering to the LORD, either to fulfill a
22: 27 be acceptable as an **offering made** to the LORD **by fire** [+852].
23: 14 new grain, until the very day you bring this **offering** *to* your God.
27: 9 " 'If what he vowed is an animal that is acceptable as an **offering** to
27: 11 one that is not acceptable as an **offering** to the LORD—the
Nu 5: 15 He must also take an **offering** *of* a tenth of an ephah of barley flour
6: 14 There he is to present his **offerings** to the LORD: a year-old male
6: 21 " 'This is the law of the Nazirite who vows his **offering** to the
7: 3 They brought as their **gifts** before the LORD six covered carts
7: 10 the leaders brought their **offerings** *for* its dedication and presented
7: 11 "Each day one leader is to bring his **offering** for the dedication of
7: 12 The one who brought his **offering** on the first day was Nahshon
7: 13 His **offering** was one silver plate weighing a hundred and thirty
7: 17 This was the **offering** *of* Nahshon son of Amminadab.
7: 19 The **offering** he brought was one silver plate weighing a hundred
7: 23 fellowship offering. This was the **offering** *of* Nethanel son of Zuar.
7: 25 His **offering** was one silver plate weighing a hundred and thirty
7: 29 a fellowship offering. This was the **offering** *of* Eliab son of Helon.
7: 31 His **offering** was one silver plate weighing a hundred and thirty
7: 35 This was the **offering** *of* Elizur son of Shedeur.
7: 37 His **offering** was one silver plate weighing a hundred and thirty
7: 41 This was the **offering** *of* Shelumiel son of Zurishaddai.
7: 43 His **offering** was one silver plate weighing a hundred and thirty
7: 47 This was the **offering** *of* Eliasaph son of Deuel.
7: 49 His **offering** was one silver plate weighing a hundred and thirty
7: 53 This was the **offering** *of* Elishama son of Ammihud.
7: 55 His **offering** was one silver plate weighing a hundred and thirty
7: 59 This was the **offering** *of* Gamaliel son of Pedahzur.
7: 61 His **offering** was one silver plate weighing a hundred and thirty
7: 65 This was the **offering** *of* Abidan son of Gideoni.
7: 67 His **offering** was one silver plate weighing a hundred and thirty
7: 71 This was the **offering** *of* Ahiezer son of Ammishaddai.
7: 73 His **offering** was one silver plate weighing a hundred and thirty
7: 77 fellowship offering. This was the **offering** *of* Pagiel son of Ocran.
7: 79 His **offering** was one silver plate weighing a hundred and thirty
7: 83 a fellowship offering. This was the **offering** *of* Ahira son of Enan.
9: 7 why should we be kept from presenting the LORD's **offering**
9: 13 because he did not present the LORD's **offering** at the appointed
15: 4 the one who brings his **offering** shall present to the LORD a grain
15: 25 they have brought to the LORD for their wrong an **offering** made
18: 9 From all the **gifts** they bring me as most holy offerings,
28: 2 to me at the appointed time the food for my **offerings** made by fire,
31: 50 So we have brought as an **offering** *to* the LORD the gold articles
Eze 20: 28 made **offerings** that provoked me to anger, presented their fragrant
40: 43 the wall all around. The tables were for the flesh of the **offerings**.

7934 קֻרְבָּן *qurbān*, n.[m.]. [2] [√ 7928]

contribution [1], contributions [1]

Ne 10: 34 [10:35] **contribution** *of* wood to burn on the altar of the LORD
13: 31 I also made provision for **contributions** *of* wood at designated

7935 קַרְדֹּם *qardōm*, n.[m.]. [5]

axes [4], ax [1]

Jdg 9: 48 He took an **ax** and cut off some branches, which he lifted to his
1Sa 13: 20 to have their plowshares, mattocks, **axes** and sickles sharpened.
13: 21 of a shekel for sharpening forks and **axes** and for repointing goads.
Ps 74: 5 They behaved like men wielding **axes** to cut through a thicket of
Jer 46: 22 they will come against her with **axes**, like men who cut down trees.

7936 קָרָה[1] *qārâ*[1], v. [27] [→ 3703, 5247, 7937, 7950; cf. 7925]

met [4], happen [3], happened [3], laid beams [2], as it turned out [+5247] [1], beams [1], come true [1], come [1], comes [1], gave success [1], give success [1], happened to be [+7925] [1], lays beams [1], make beams [1], meet [1], overtake [1], overtakes [1], punished [+6411] [1], select [1]

Ge 24: 12 [G] God of my master Abraham, **give me success** today,
27: 20 [G] "The LORD your God **gave me success**," he replied.
42: 29 [A] of Canaan, they told him all that *had* **happened** *to* them.
44: 29 [A] If you take this one from me too and harm **comes** *to* him, you
Ex 3: 18 [C] 'The LORD, the God of the Hebrews, *has* **met** with us.
Nu 11: 23 [A] now see whether or not what I say *will* **come true** *for* you."
23: 3 [C] Perhaps the LORD *will* **come** to meet with me. Whatever he
23: 4 [C] God **met** with him, and Balaam said, "I have prepared seven
23: 15 [C] "Stay here beside your offering while I **meet** *with* him over
23: 16 [C] The LORD **met** with Balaam and put a message in his
35: 11 [G] **select** some towns to be your cities of refuge, to which a
Dt 25: 18 [A] *they* **met** you on your journey and cut off all who were
Ru 2: 3 [A] **As it turned** [+5247] **out**, she found herself working in a
1Sa 28: 10 [A] LORD lives, you *will* not *be* **punished** [+6411] for this."

2Sa 1: 6 [C] "*I* **happened** [+7925] **to be** on Mount Gilboa," the young
2Ch 34: 11 [D] **beams** *for* the buildings that the kings of Judah had allowed
Ne 2: 8 [D] so he will give me timber to **make beams** *for* the gates of the
3: 3 [D] They **laid** its **beams** and put its doors and bolts and bars in
3: 6 [D] They **laid** its **beams** and put its doors and bolts and bars in
Est 4: 7 [A] Mordecai told him everything that *had* **happened** *to* him,
6: 13 [A] and all his friends everything that *had* **happened** *to* him.
Ps 104: 3 [D] and **lays** *the* **beams** *of* his upper chambers on their waters.
Ecc 2: 14 [A] but I came to realize that the same fate **overtakes** them both.
2: 15 [A] in my heart, "The fate of the fool *will* **overtake** me also.
9: 11 [A] favor to the learned; but time and chance **happen** *to* them all.
Isa 41: 22 [A] "Bring in ⌞your idols⌟ to tell us what *is going to* **happen**.
Da 10: 14 [A] Now I have come to explain to you what *will* **happen** to your

7937 קָרֶה *qāreh*, n.[m.]. [1] [√ 7936]

emission [1]

Dt 23: 10 [23:11] of your men is unclean because of a nocturnal **emission**,

7938 ²קָרָה *qārâ²*, n.f. [5 / 6] [√ 7981]

cold [5], icy blast [1]

Job 24: 7 the night naked; they have nothing to cover themselves in the **cold**.
37: 9 comes out from its chamber, the **cold** from the driving winds.
Ps 147: 17 hurls down his hail like pebbles. Who can withstand his **icy blast**?
Pr 25: 20 Like one who takes away a garment on a **cold** day, or like vinegar
Na 3: 17 like swarms of locusts that settle in the walls on a **cold** day—
Zec 14: 6 On that day there will be no light, no **cold** [BHS 3701] or frost.

7939 ³קָרָה *qārâ³*, v.den. Not used in NIV/BHS [→ 5248, 7771]

7940 קָרוֹב *qārôb*, a. [77] [√ 7928]

near [38], nearest [5], neighbors [3], approach [2], close [2], warriors [2], about to [+4946+6964] [1], always [1], at hand [+995] [1], at hand [+995+4200] [1], brief [+4946] [1], close at hand [1], close relative [+8638] [1], close relative [1], close to [+725] [1], close to heart [1], closely associated [1], closely related [1], closest [1], come near [1], dependent [1], fellowman [1], invites [1], kinsmen [1], nearby [+4946] [1], nearby [1], nearer [1], neighbor [1], recently [+2543+4946] [1], shorter [1], soon [+928] [1]

Ge 19: 20 Look, here is a town near *enough* to run to, and it is small.
45: 10 You shall live in the region of Goshen and be **near** me—you,
Ex 12: 4 for a whole lamb, they must share one with their **nearest** neighbor,
13: 17 the road through the Philistine country, though that was **shorter**.
32: 27 to the other, each killing his brother and friend and **neighbor**.' "
Lev 10: 3 " 'Among *those who* **approach** me I will show myself holy;
21: 2 except for a **close relative** [+8638], such as his mother or father,
21: 3 or an unmarried sister who is **dependent** on him since she has no
25: 25 his **nearest** relative is to come and redeem what his countryman
Nu 24: 17 "I see him, but not now; I behold him, but not **near**. A star will
27: 11 give his inheritance to the **nearest** relative in his clan, that he may
Dt 4: 7 so great as to have their gods **near** them the way the LORD our
13: 7 [13:8] gods of the peoples around you, whether **near** or far, from
21: 3 the elders of the town **nearest** the body shall take a heifer that has
21: 6 all the elders of the town **nearest** the body shall wash their hands
22: 2 If the brother does not live **near** you or if you do not know who he
30: 14 No, the word is very **near** you; it is in your mouth and in your
32: 17 they had not known, gods that **recently** [+2543+4946] appeared,
32: 35 their day of disaster is **near** and their doom rushes upon them."
Jos 9: 16 the Israelites heard that they were **neighbors**, living near them.
Ru 2: 20 She added, "That man is our **close relative**; he is one of our
3: 12 that I am near of kin, there is a kinsman-redeemer **nearer** than I.
2Sa 19: 42 [19:43] "We did this because the king is **closely related** to us.
1Ki 8: 46 who takes them captive to his own land, far away or **near**;
8: 59 before the LORD, be **near** to the LORD our God day and night,
21: 2 to use for a vegetable garden, since it is **close** [+725] **to** my palace.
1Ch 12: 40 [12:41] Also, their **neighbors** from as far away as Issachar,
2Ch 6: 36 to the enemy, who takes them captive to a land far away or **near**;
Ne 13: 4 of the house of our God. He was **closely associated** with Tobiah,
Est 1: 14 and were **closest** to the king—Carshena, Shethar, Admatha,
9: 20 the Jews throughout the provinces of King Xerxes, **near** and far,
Job 17: 12 turn night into day; in the face of darkness they say, 'Light is **near**.'
19: 14 My **kinsmen** have gone away; my friends have forgotten me.
20: 5 that the mirth of the wicked is **brief** [+4946], the joy of the godless
Ps 15: 3 does his neighbor no wrong and casts no slur on his **fellowman**,
22: 11 [22:12] from me, for trouble is **near** and there is no one to help.
34: 18 [34:19] The LORD is **close** to the brokenhearted and saves those
38: 11 [38:12] because of my wounds; my **neighbors** stay far away.
75: 1 [75:2] to you, O God, we give thanks, for your Name is **near**;
85: 9 [85:10] Surely his salvation is **near** those who fear him, that his
119: 151 Yet you are **near**, O LORD, and all your commands are true.
145: 18 The LORD is **near** to all who call on him, to all who call on him
148: 14 the praise of all his saints, of Israel, the people **close to** his **heart**.
Pr 10: 14 Wise men store up knowledge, but the mouth of a fool **invites** ruin.
27: 10 strikes you—better a neighbor **nearby** than a brother far away.
Isa 13: 6 Wail, for the day of the LORD is **near**; it will come like
13: 22 Her time *is* **at hand** [+995+4200], and her days will not be
33: 13 hear what I have done; you *who* are **near**, acknowledge my power!
50: 8 He who vindicates me is **near**. Who then will bring charges against
51: 5 My righteousness *draws* **near** speedily, my salvation is on the
55: 6 the LORD while he may be found; call on him while he is **near**.
56: 1 for my salvation is **close** at hand and my righteousness will soon be
57: 19 Peace, peace, to those far and **near**," says the LORD. "And I will
Jer 12: 2 bear fruit. You are **always** on their lips but far from their hearts.
23: 23 "Am I only a God **nearby** [+4946]," declares the LORD,
25: 26 and all the kings of the north, **near** and far, one after the other—
48: 16 "The fall of Moab *is* **at hand** [+995]; her calamity will come
48: 24 to Kerioth and Bozrah—to all the towns of Moab, far and **near**.
Eze 6: 12 and he *that* is **near** will fall by the sword, and he that survives
7: 7 The time has come, the day is **near**; there is panic, not joy,
7: 8 I am **about to** [+4946+6964] pour out my wrath on you and spend
11: 3 They say, 'Will it not **soon** [+928] be time to build houses?
22: 5 Those who are **near** and those who are far away will mock you,
23: 5 and she lusted after her lovers, the Assyrians—**warriors**
23: 12 governors and commanders, **warriors** in full dress,
30: 3 For the day is **near**, the day of the LORD is near—a day of
30: 3 For the day is near, the day of the LORD is **near**—a day of
42: 13 where the priests who **approach** the LORD will eat the most holy
43: 19 of the family of Zadok, who **come near** to minister before me,
Da 9: 7 of Judah and people of Jerusalem and all Israel, both **near** and far,
Joel 1: 15 For the day of the LORD is **near**; it will come like destruction
2: 1 for the day of the LORD is coming. It is **close at hand**—
3: 14 [4:14] For the day of the LORD is **near** in the valley of decision.
Ob 1: 15 "The day of the LORD is **near** for all nations. As you have done,
Zep 1: 7 before the Sovereign LORD, for the day of the LORD is **near**.
1: 14 "The great day of the LORD is **near**—near and coming quickly.
1: 14 "The great day of the LORD is near—**near** and coming quickly.

7941 קָרוּת *qārût*, n.f. Not used in NIV/BHS [√ 7981]

7942 קָרַח *qāraḥ*, v. [5] [→ 7944, 7945, 7946, 7947, 7948, 7949]

must shave [+928+7947] [1], shave head [1], shave heads [+1605] [1], shave heads [+7947] [1], was rubbed bare [1]

Lev 21: 5 [A] " 'Priests **must** not **shave** [+928+7947] their heads or shave
Jer 16: 6 [C] and no one will cut himself or **shave** *his* **head** for them.
Eze 27: 31 [G] *They will* **shave** [+7947] *their* **heads** because of you
29: 18 [H] every head **was rubbed bare** and every shoulder made raw.
Mic 1: 16 [A] **Shave** [+1605] *your* **heads** in mourning for the children in

7943 קֶרַח *qeraḥ*, n.m. [7]

ice [4], cold [1], frost [1], hail [1]

Ge 31: 40 The heat consumed me in the daytime and the **cold** at night,
Job 6: 16 when darkened by thawing **ice** and swollen with melting snow,
37: 10 The breath of God produces **ice**, and the broad waters become
38: 29 From whose womb comes the **ice**? Who gives birth to the frost
Ps 147: 17 He hurls down his **hail** like pebbles. Who can withstand his icy
Jer 36: 30 thrown out and exposed to the heat by day and the **frost** by night.
Eze 1: 22 was what looked like an expanse, sparkling like **ice**, and awesome.

7944 קֵרֵחַ *qērēaḥ*, a. [3] [√ 7942]

baldhead [2], bald [1]

Lev 13: 40 "When a man has lost his hair and is **bald**, he is clean.
2Ki 2: 23 "Go on up, you **baldhead**!" they said. "Go on up, you baldhead!"
2: 23 "Go on up, you baldhead!" they said. "Go on up, you **baldhead**!"

7945 קָרֵחַ *qārēaḥ*, n.pr.m. [14] [√ 7942]

Kareah [14]

2Ki 25: 23 Ishmael son of Nethaniah, Johanan son of **Kareah**, Seraiah son of
Jer 40: 8 son of Nethaniah, Johanan and Jonathan the sons of **Kareah**,
40: 13 Johanan son of **Kareah** and all the army officers still in the open
40: 15 Then Johanan son of **Kareah** said privately to Gedaliah in Mizpah,
40: 16 But Gedaliah son of Ahikam said to Johanan son of **Kareah**,
41: 11 When Johanan son of **Kareah** and all the army officers who were
41: 13 all the people Ishmael had with him saw Johanan son of **Kareah**
41: 14 captive at Mizpah turned and went over to Johanan son of **Kareah**.
41: 16 Johanan son of **Kareah** and all the army officers who were with
42: 1 including Johanan son of **Kareah** and Jezaniah son of Hoshaiah,
42: 8 So he called together Johanan son of **Kareah** and all the army
43: 2 Azariah son of Hoshaiah and Johanan son of **Kareah** and all the
43: 4 So Johanan son of **Kareah** and all the army officers and all the
43: 5 Johanan son of **Kareah** and all the army officers led away all the

7946 קֹרַח ***qōraḥ***, n.pr.m. [37] [→ 7948; cf. 7942]
Korah [34], Korah's [2], Korah's [+4200] [1]

Ge 36: 5 Oholibamah bore Jeush, Jalam and **Korah**. These were the sons of
36: 14 of Zibeon, whom she bore to Esau: Jeush, Jalam and **Korah**.
36: 16 **Korah**, Gatam and Amalek. These were the chiefs descended from
36: 18 sons of Esau's wife Oholibamah: Chiefs Jeush, Jalam and **Korah**.
Ex 6: 21 The sons of Izhar were **Korah**, Nepheg and Zicri.
6: 24 The sons of **Korah** were Assir, Elkanah and Abiasaph. These were
Nu 16: 1 **Korah** son of Izhar, the son of Kohath, the son of Levi, and certain
16: 5 he said to **Korah** and all his followers: "In the morning the
16: 6 You, **Korah**, and all your followers are to do this: Take censers
16: 8 Moses also said to **Korah**, "Now listen, you Levites!
16: 16 Moses said to **Korah**, "You and all your followers are to appear
16: 19 When **Korah** had gathered all his followers in opposition to them
16: 24 'Move away from the tents of **Korah**, Dathan and Abiram.' "
16: 27 So they moved away from the tents of **Korah**, Dathan and Abiram.
16: 32 with their households and all **Korah's** [+4200] men and all their
16: 40 [17:5] or he would become like **Korah** and his followers.
16: 49 [17:14] in addition to those who had died because of **Korah**.
26: 9 were among **Korah's** followers when they rebelled against the
26: 10 earth opened its mouth and swallowed them along with **Korah**,
26: 11 The line of **Korah**, however, did not die out.
27: 3 He was not among **Korah's** followers, who banded together
1Ch 1: 35 The sons of Esau: Eliphaz, Reuel, Jeush, Jalam and **Korah**.
2: 43 The sons of Hebron: **Korah**, Tappuah, Rekem and Shema.
6: 22 [6:7] Amminadab his son, **Korah** his son, Assir his son,
6: 37 [6:22] the son of Assir, the son of Ebiasaph, the son of **Korah**,
9: 19 Shallum son of Kore, the son of Ebiasaph, the son of **Korah**,
Ps 42: T [42:1] the director of music. A *maskil* of the Sons of **Korah**.
44: T [44:1] the director of music. Of the Sons of **Korah**. A *maskil*.
45: T [45:1] Of the Sons of **Korah**. A *maskil*. A wedding song.
46: T [46:1] Of the Sons of **Korah**. According to *alamoth*. A song.
47: T [47:1] For the director of music. Of the Sons of **Korah**. A psalm.
48: T [48:1] A song. A psalm of the Sons of **Korah**.
49: T [49:1] For the director of music. Of the Sons of **Korah**. A psalm.
84: T [84:1] According to *gittith*. Of the Sons of **Korah**. A psalm.
85: T [85:1] For the director of music. Of the Sons of **Korah**. A psalm.
87: T [87:1] Of the Sons of **Korah**. A psalm. A song.
88: T [88:1] A song. A psalm of the Sons of **Korah**. For the director of

7947 קָרְחָה ***qorḥâ***, n.f. [11] [√ 7942]
shaved [3], baldness [1], make bald [+8143] [1], must shave [+928+7942] [1], shave [+6584] [1], shave [+8492] [1], shave head in mourning [+448+995] [1], shave heads [+7942] [1], tear out hair [1]

Lev 21: 5 " 'Priests **must** not **shave** [+928+7942] their heads or shave off the
Dt 14: 1 or **shave** [+8492] the front of your heads for the dead,
Isa 3: 24 instead of a sash, a rope; instead of well-dressed hair, **baldness**;
15: 2 and Medeba. Every head is **shaved** and every beard cut off.
22: 12 to weep and to wail, to **tear out** your **hair** and put on sackcloth.
Jer 47: 5 Gaza *will* **shave** [+448+995] *her* **head in mourning**; Ashkelon
48: 37 Every head is **shaved** and every beard cut off; every hand is
Eze 7: 18 faces will be covered with shame and their heads will be **shaved**.
27: 31 *They will* **shave** *their* **heads** [+7942] because of you and will put
Am 8: 10 will make all of you wear sackcloth and **shave** [+6584] your heads.
Mic 1: 16 **make** yourselves as **bald** [+8143] as the vulture, for they will go

7948 קָרְחִי ***qorḥî***, a.g. [8] [√ 7946; cf. 7942]
Korahite [3], Korahites [3], Korah [1], Korahites [+1201] [1]

Ex 6: 24 were Assir, Elkanah and Abiasaph. These were the **Korahite** clans.
Nu 26: 58 the Mahlite clan, the Mushite clan, the **Korahite** clan.
1Ch 9: 19 and his fellow gatekeepers from his family (the **Korahites**)
9: 31 named Mattithiah, the firstborn son of Shallum the **Korahite**,
12: 6 [12:7] Azarel, Joezer and Jashobeam the **Korahites**;
26: 1 From the **Korahites**: Meshelemiah son of Kore, one of the sons of
26: 19 the divisions of the gatekeepers who were descendants of **Korah**
2Ch 20: 19 and **Korahites** [+1201] stood up and praised the LORD,

7949 קָרַחַת ***qāraḥat***, n.f. [4] [√ 7942]
head [2], bald head [1], side[s] [1]

Lev 13: 42 But if he has a reddish-white sore on his **bald head** or forehead,
13: 42 it is an infectious disease breaking out on his **head** or forehead.
13: 43 if the swollen sore on his **head** or forehead is reddish-white like an
13: 55 it with fire, whether the mildew has affected one **side**[s] or the other.

7950 קֶרִי ***qerî***, n.[m.]. [7] [√ 7936]
hostile [6], hostility [1]

Lev 26: 21 " 'If you remain **hostile** toward me and refuse to listen to me,
26: 23 do not accept my correction but continue to be **hostile** toward me,
26: 24 I myself will be **hostile** toward you and will afflict you for your
26: 27 you still do not listen to me but continue to be **hostile** toward me,
26: 28 in my anger I will be **hostile** toward you, and I myself will punish
26: 40 their treachery against me and their **hostility** toward me,
26: 41 which made me **hostile** toward them so that I sent them into the

7951 קָרִיא ***qārîʾ***, a. [2] [√ 7924]
appointed [1], officials [1]

Nu 1: 16 [These **were** the *men* **appointed** [K; see Q 7924]]
16: 2 leaders *who* had been **appointed** *members of* the council.
26: 9 Abiram were the community **officials** [K 7924] who rebelled

7952 קְרִיאָה ***qerîʾâ***, n.f. [1] [√ 7924]
message [1]

Jnh 3: 2 great city of Nineveh and proclaim to it the **message** I give you."

7953 קִרְיָה ***qiryâ***, n.f. [29] [√ 7984; Ar 10640]
city [20], town [5], cities [3], one[s] [1]

Nu 21: 28 "Fire went out from Heshbon, a blaze from the **city** *of* Sihon.
Dt 2: 36 even as far as Gilead, not one **town** was too strong for us.
3: 4 There was not **one**[s] of the sixty cities that we did not take from
1Ki 1: 41 Joab asked, "What's the meaning of all the noise in the **city**?"
1: 45 there they have gone up cheering, and the **city** resounds with it.
Job 39: 7 He laughs at the commotion in the **town**; he does not hear a
Ps 48: 2 [48:3] of Zaphon is Mount Zion, the **city** *of* the Great King.
Pr 10: 15 The wealth of the rich is their fortified **city**, but poverty is the ruin
11: 10 When the righteous prosper, the **city** rejoices; when the wicked
18: 11 The wealth of the rich is their fortified **city**; they imagine it an
18: 19 An offended brother is more unyielding than a fortified **city**,
29: 8 Mockers stir up a **city**, but wise men turn away anger.
Isa 1: 21 See how the faithful **city** has become a harlot! She once was full of
1: 26 you will be called the City of Righteousness, the Faithful **City**."
22: 2 O town full of commotion, O **city** *of* tumult and revelry?
24: 10 The ruined **city** lies desolate; the entrance to every house is barred.
25: 2 You have made the city a heap of rubble, the fortified **town** a ruin,
25: 3 peoples will honor you; **cities** *of* ruthless nations will revere you.
26: 5 He humbles those who dwell on high, he lays the lofty **city** low;
29: 1 Woe to you, Ariel, Ariel, the **city** *where* David settled! Add year to
32: 13 mourn for all houses of merriment and for this **city** *of* revelry.
33: 20 Look upon Zion, the **city** *of* our festivals; your eyes will see
Jer 49: 25 city of renown not been abandoned, the **town** *in which* I delight?
La 2: 11 because children and infants faint in the streets of the **city**.
Hos 6: 8 Gilead is a **city** *of* wicked men, stained with footprints of blood.
Mic 4: 10 for now you must leave the **city** to camp in the open field.
Hab 2: 8 you have destroyed lands and **cities** and everyone in them.
2: 12 who builds a city with bloodshed and establishes a **town** by crime!
2: 17 you have destroyed lands and **cities** and everyone in them.

7954 קְרִיּוֹת ***qeriyyôt***, n.pr.loc. [3] [√ 7984]
Kerioth [3]

Jer 48: 24 to **Kerioth** and Bozrah—to all the towns of Moab, far and near.
48: 41 **Kerioth** will be captured and the strongholds taken. In that day the
Am 2: 2 send fire upon Moab that will consume the fortresses of **Kerioth**.

7955 קְרִיּוֹת חֶצְרוֹן ***qeriyyôt ḥeṣrôn***, n.pr.loc. [1] [√ 7984 + 2970]
Kerioth Hezron [1]

Jos 15: 25 Hazor Hadattah, **Kerioth Hezron** (that is, Hazor),

7956 קִרְיַת ***qiryat***, n.f. [1] [√ 7984]
Kiriath [1]

Jos 18: 28 the Jebusite city (that is, Jerusalem), Gibeah and **Kiriath**—

7957 קִרְיַת אַרְבַּע ***qiryat ʾarbaʿ***, n.pr.loc. [7] [√ 7984 + 752]
Kiriath Arba [7]

Ge 23: 2 She died at **Kiriath Arba** (that is, Hebron) in the land of Canaan,
Jos 14: 15 (Hebron used to be called **Kiriath Arba** after Arba, who was the
15: 13 of Jephunneh a portion in Judah—**Kiriath Arba**, that is, Hebron.
15: 54 Humtah, **Kiriath Arba** (that is, Hebron) and Zior—nine towns
20: 7 in the hill country of Ephraim, and **Kiriath Arba** (that is, Hebron)
21: 11 They gave them **Kiriath Arba** (that is, Hebron), with its
Jdg 1: 10 the Canaanites living in Hebron (formerly called **Kiriath Arba**)

7958 קִרְיַת־בַּעַל ***qiryat-baʿal***, n.pr.loc. [2] [√ 7984 + 1251]
Kiriath Baal [2]

Jos 15: 60 **Kiriath Baal** (that is, Kiriath Jearim) and Rabbah—two towns
18: 14 south along the western side and came out at **Kiriath Baal** (that is,

7959 קִרְיַת הָאַרְבַּע ***qiryat hā'arba'***, n.pr.loc. [2] [√ 7984 + 752]

Kiriath Arba [2]

Ge 35:27 near **Kiriath Arba** (that is, Hebron), where Abraham and Isaac
Ne 11:25 some of the people of Judah lived in **Kiriath Arba** and its

7960 קִרְיַת חֻצוֹת ***qiryat ḥuṣôt***, n.pr.loc. [1] [√ 7984 + 2941]

Kiriath Huzoth [1]

Nu 22:39 Then Balaam went with Balak to **Kiriath Huzoth**.

7961 קִרְיַת יְעָרִים ***qiryat yᵉʿārîm***, n.pr.loc. [19] [√ 7984 + 3630]

Kiriath Jearim [19]

Jos 9:17 to their cities: Gibeon, Kephirah, Beeroth and **Kiriath Jearim**.
15:9 and went down toward Baalah (that is, **Kiriath Jearim**).
15:60 Kiriath Baal (that is, **Kiriath Jearim**) and Rabbah—two towns
18:14 Baal (that is, **Kiriath Jearim**), a town of the people of Judah.
18:15 The southern side began at the outskirts of **Kiriath Jearim** on the
Jdg 18:12 On their way they set up camp near **Kiriath Jearim** in Judah.
18:12 This is why the place west of **Kiriath Jearim** is called Mahaneh
1Sa 6:21 Then they sent messengers to the people of **Kiriath Jearim**,
7:1 So the men of **Kiriath Jearim** came and took up the ark of the
7:2 twenty years in all, that the ark remained at **Kiriath Jearim**,
1Ch 2:50 the firstborn of Ephrathah: Shobal the father of **Kiriath Jearim**,
2:52 The descendants of Shobal the father of **Kiriath Jearim** were:
2:53 and the clans of **Kiriath Jearim**: the Ithrites, Puthites, Shumathites
13:5 to Lebo Hamath, to bring the ark of God from **Kiriath Jearim**.
13:6 the Israelites with him went to Baalah of Judah (**Kiriath Jearim**)
2Ch 1:4 Now David had brought up the ark of God from **Kiriath Jearim** to
Ezr 2:25 of **Kiriath Jearim**, Kephirah and Beeroth 743
Ne 7:29 of **Kiriath Jearim**, Kephirah and Beeroth 743
Jer 26:20 (Now Uriah son of Shemaiah from **Kiriath Jearim** was another

7962 קִרְיַת־סַנָּה ***qiryat-sannâ***, n.pr.loc. [1] [√ 7984 + 6173]

Kiriath Sannah [1]

Jos 15:49 Dannah, **Kiriath Sannah** (that is, Debir),

7963 קִרְיַת־סֵפֶר ***qiryat-sēper***, n.pr.loc. [4] [√ 7984 + 6219]

Kiriath Sepher [4]

Jos 15:15 the people living in Debir (formerly called **Kiriath Sepher**).
15:16 in marriage to the man who attacks and captures **Kiriath Sepher**."
Jdg 1:11 the people living in Debir (formerly called **Kiriath Sepher**).
1:12 in marriage to the man who attacks and captures **Kiriath Sepher**."

7964 קִרְיָתַיִם ***qiryātayim***, n.pr.loc. [6] [√ 7984]

Kiriathaim [6]

Nu 32:37 And the Reubenites rebuilt Heshbon, Elealeh and **Kiriathaim**,
Jos 13:19 **Kiriathaim**, Sibmah, Zereth Shahar on the hill in the valley,
1Ch 6:76 [6:61] Hammon and **Kiriathaim**, together with their pasturelands.
Jer 48:1 **Kiriathaim** will be disgraced and captured; the stronghold will be
48:23 to **Kiriathaim**, Beth Gamul and Beth Meon,
Eze 25:9 Beth Jeshimoth, Baal Meon and **Kiriathaim**—the glory of that

7965 קָרַם ***qāram***, v. [2]

cover [1], covered [1]

Eze 37:6 [A] and make flesh come upon you and **cover** you *with* skin;
37:8 [A] and flesh appeared on them and skin **covered** them,

7966 קָרַן ***qāran***, v.den. [4] [√ 7967]

radiant [3], horns [1]

Ex 34:29 [A] he was not aware that his face *was* **radiant** because he had
34:30 [A] and all the Israelites saw Moses, his face *was* **radiant**,
34:35 [A] they saw that his face *was* **radiant**. Then Moses would put
Ps 69:31 [69:32] [G] an ox, more than a bull *with its* **horns** and hoofs.

7967 קֶרֶן ***qeren***, n.f. [75] [→ 7966, 7968, 7969; Ar 10641]

horns [44], horn [23], two-horned [+1251+2021] [2], brow [1], hillside [1], him[s] [1], rays [1], trumpets [+3413] [1], tusks [1]

Ge 22:13 looked up and there in a thicket he saw a ram caught by its **horns**.
Ex 27:2 Make a **horn** at each of the four corners, so that the horns
27:2 so that the **horns** and the altar are of one piece, and overlay the
29:12 bull's blood and put it on the **horns** *of* the altar with your finger,
30:2 a cubit wide, and two cubits high—its **horns** of one piece with it.
30:3 Overlay the top and all the sides and the **horns** with pure gold,
30:10 Once a year Aaron shall make atonement on its **horns**. This annual
37:25 a cubit wide, and two cubits high—its **horns** of one piece with it.
37:26 overlaid the top and all the sides and the **horns** with pure gold,
38:2 They made a **horn** at each of the four corners, so that the horns
38:2 so that the **horns** and the altar were of one piece, and they overlaid
Lev 4:7 put some of the blood on the **horns** *of* the altar of fragrant incense
4:18 He is to put some of the blood on the **horns** *of* the altar that is
4:25 put it on the **horns** *of* the altar of burnt offering and pour out the
4:30 put it on the **horns** *of* the altar of burnt offering and pour out the
4:34 put it on the **horns** *of* the altar of burnt offering and pour out the
8:15 with his finger he put it on all the **horns** *of* the altar to purify the
9:9 dipped his finger into the blood and put it on the **horns** *of* the altar;
16:18 some of the goat's blood and put it on all the **horns** *of* the altar.
Dt 33:17 he is like a firstborn bull; his **horns** are the horns of a wild ox.
33:17 he is like a firstborn bull; his horns are the **horns** *of* a wild ox.
Jos 6:5 When you hear them sound a long blast on the **trumpets** [+3413],
1Sa 2:1 heart rejoices in the LORD; in the LORD my **horn** is lifted high.
2:10 will give strength to his king and exalt the **horn** *of* his anointed."
16:1 Fill your **horn** with oil and be on your way; I am sending you to
16:13 So Samuel took the **horn** *of* oil and anointed him in the presence of
2Sa 22:3 in whom I take refuge, my shield and the **horn** *of* my salvation.
1Ki 1:39 Zadok the priest took the **horn** *of* oil from the sacred tent
1:50 in fear of Solomon, went and took hold of the **horns** *of* the altar.
1:51 is afraid of King Solomon and is clinging to the **horns** *of* the altar.
2:28 to the tent of the LORD and took hold of the **horns** *of* the altar.
22:11 Now Zedekiah son of Kenaanah had made iron **horns** and he
1Ch 25:5 They were given him through the promises of God to exalt **him**[s].
2Ch 18:10 Now Zedekiah son of Kenaanah had made iron **horns**, and he
Job 16:15 sewed sackcloth over my skin and buried my **brow** in the dust.
Ps 18:2 [18:3] He is my shield and the **horn** *of* my salvation,
22:21 [22:22] of the lions; save me from the **horns** *of* the wild oxen.
75:4 [75:5] no more,' and to the wicked, 'Do not lift up your **horns**.
75:5 [75:6] Do not lift your **horns** against heaven; do not speak with
75:10 [75:11] I will cut off the **horns** *of* all the wicked, but the horns of
75:10 [75:11] but the **horns** *of* the righteous will be lifted up.
89:17 [89:18] and strength, and by your favor you exalt our **horn**.
89:24 [89:25] with him, and through my name his **horn** will be exalted.
92:10 [92:11] You have exalted my **horn** like that of a wild ox; fine oils
112:9 endures forever; his **horn** will be lifted high in honor.
118:27 in hand, join in the festal procession up to the **horns** *of* the altar.
132:17 "Here I will make a **horn** grow for David and set up a lamp for my
148:14 He has raised up for his people a **horn**, the praise of all his saints,
Isa 5:1 his vineyard: My loved one had a vineyard on a fertile **hillside**.
Jer 17:1 on the tablets of their hearts and on the **horns** *of* their altars.
48:25 Moab's **horn** is cut off; her arm is broken," declares the LORD.
La 2:3 In fierce anger he has cut off every **horn** *of* Israel. He has
2:17 let the enemy gloat over you, he has exalted the **horn** *of* your foes.
Eze 27:15 were your customers; they paid you with ivory **tusks** and ebony.
29:21 "On that day I will make a **horn** grow for the house of Israel,
34:21 butting all the weak sheep with your **horns** until you have driven
43:15 is four cubits high, and four **horns** project upward from the hearth.
43:20 to take some of its blood and put it on the four **horns** *of* the altar
Da 8:3 I looked up, and there before me was a ram with *two* **horns**,
8:3 two horns, standing beside the canal, and the **horns** were long.
8:5 suddenly a goat with a prominent **horn** between his eyes came
8:6 He came toward the **two-horned** [+1251+2021] ram I had seen
8:7 the ram furiously, striking the ram and shattering his two **horns**.
8:8 but at the height of his power his large **horn** was broken off,
8:9 Out of one of them came another **horn**, which started small
8:20 The **two-horned** [+1251+2021] ram that you saw represents the
8:21 of Greece, and the large **horn** between his eyes is the first king.
Am 3:14 the **horns** *of* the altar will be cut off and fall to the ground.
Mic 4:13 and thresh, O Daughter of Zion, for I will give you **horns** *of* iron;
Hab 3:4 **rays** flashed from his hand, where his power was hidden.
Zec 1:18 [2:1] Then I looked up—and there before me were four **horns**!
1:19 [2:2] "These are the **horns** that scattered Judah, Israel
1:21 [2:4] "These are the **horns** that scattered Judah so that no one
1:21 [2:4] throw down these **horns** *of* the nations who lifted up their
1:21 [2:4] their **horns** against the land of Judah to scatter its people."

7968 קֶרֶן הַפּוּךְ ***qeren happûk***, n.pr.f. [1] [√ 7967 + 2199]

Keren-Happuch [1]

Job 42:14 the second Keziah and the third **Keren-Happuch**.

7969 קַרְנַיִם ***qarnayim***, n.pr.loc. [1] [→ 6959; cf. 7967]

Karnaim [1]

Am 6:13 and say, "Did we not take **Karnaim** by our own strength?"

7970 קָרַס ***qāras***, v. [2] [→ 7971, 7972]

stoop [1], stoops low [1]

Isa 46:1 [A] Bel bows down, Nebo **stoops low**; their idols are borne by
46:2 [A] *They* **stoop** and bow down together; unable to rescue the

7971 קֶרֶס *qeres*, n.[m.]. [10] [√ 7970]

clasps [7], them[s] [+2021] [3]

Ex 26: 6 make fifty gold **clasps** and use them to fasten the curtains together
26: 6 gold clasps and use **them**[s] [+2021] to fasten the curtains together
26: 11 make fifty bronze **clasps** and put them in the loops to fasten the
26: 11 put **them**[s] [+2021] in the loops to fasten the tent together as a unit.
26: 33 Hang the curtain from the **clasps** and place the ark of the
35: 11 and its covering, **clasps**, frames, crossbars, posts and bases;
36: 13 they made fifty gold **clasps** and used them to fasten the two sets of
36: 13 and used **them**[s] [+2021] to fasten the two sets of curtains together
36: 18 They made fifty bronze **clasps** to fasten the tent together as a unit.
39: 33 all its furnishings, its **clasps**, frames, crossbars, posts and bases;

7972 קַרְסֹל *qarsōl*, n.[f.]. [2] [√ 7970]

ankles [2]

2Sa 22: 37 You broaden the path beneath me, so that my **ankles** do not turn.
Ps 18: 36 [18:37] the path beneath me, so that my **ankles** do not turn.

7973 קָרַע *qāra'*, v. [63] [→ 7974]

tore [26], torn [12], tear [10], most certainly tear away [+906+7973] [2], rend [2], tore away [2], be split apart [1], cut off [1], makes large [1], rip open [+4213+6033] [1], shade [1], slandered [1], tear off [1], tore apart [+4200+7974+9109] [1], was split apart [1]

Ge 37: 29 [A] and saw that Joseph was not there, *he* **tore** his clothes.
37: 34 [A] Jacob **tore** his clothes, put on sackcloth and mourned for his
44: 13 [A] At this, *they* **tore** their clothes. Then they all loaded their
Ex 28: 32 [C] edge like a collar around this opening, so that it *will* not **tear**.
39: 23 [C] and a band around this opening, so that *it would* not **tear**.
Lev 13: 56 [A] *he is to* **tear** the contaminated part out of the clothing, or the
Nu 14: 6 [A] among those who had explored the land, **tore** their clothes
Jos 7: 6 [A] Joshua **tore** his clothes and fell facedown to the ground
Jdg 11: 35 [A] When he saw her, *he* **tore** his clothes and cried, "Oh!
1Sa 4: 12 [B] and went to Shiloh, his clothes **torn** and dust on his head.
15: 27 [C] to leave, Saul caught hold of the hem of his robe, and *it* **tore**.
15: 28 [A] "The LORD *has* **torn** the kingdom of Israel from you today
28: 17 [A] The LORD *has* **torn** the kingdom out of your hands
2Sa 1: 2 [B] Saul's camp, with his clothes **torn** and with dust on his head.
1: 11 [A] the men with him took hold of their clothes and **tore** them.
3: 31 [A] "**Tear** your clothes and put on sackcloth and walk in
13: 19 [A] on her head and **tore** the ornamented robe she was wearing.
13: 31 [A] king stood up, **tore** his clothes and lay down on the ground;
13: 31 [B] and all his servants stood by with their clothes **torn**.
15: 32 [B] was there to meet him, his robe **torn** and dust on his head.
1Ki 11: 11 [A] *I will* **most certainly tear** [+906+7973] the kingdom **away**
11: 11 [A] *I will* **most certainly tear** the kingdom **away** [+906+7973]
11: 12 [A] your lifetime. *I will* **tear** it out of the hand of your son.
11: 13 [A] Yet *I will* not **tear** the whole kingdom from him, but will
11: 30 [A] the new cloak he was wearing and **tore** it *into* twelve pieces.
11: 31 [A] I *am going to* **tear** the kingdom out of Solomon's hand
13: 3 [C] The altar *will* **be split apart** and the ashes on it will be
13: 5 [C] the altar **was split apart** and its ashes poured out according
14: 8 [A] *I* **tore** the kingdom **away** from the house of David and gave
21: 27 [A] these words, *he* **tore** his clothes, put on sackcloth and fasted.
2Ki 2: 12 [A] his own clothes and **tore** [+4200+7974+9109] them **apart**.
5: 7 [A] Israel read the letter, *he* **tore** his robes and said, "Am I God?
5: 8 [A] man of God heard that the king of Israel *had* **torn** his robes,
5: 8 [A] he sent him this message: "Why *have you* **torn** your robes?
6: 30 [A] When the king heard the woman's words, *he* **tore** his robes.
11: 14 [A] Athaliah **tore** her robes and called out, "Treason! Treason!"
17: 21 [A] When *he* **tore** Israel **away** from the house of David, they
18: 37 [B] with their clothes **torn**, and told him what the field
19: 1 [A] *he* **tore** his clothes and put on sackcloth and went into the
22: 11 [A] heard the words of the Book of the Law, *he* **tore** his robes.
22: 19 [A] and because *you* **tore** your robes and wept in my presence,
2Ch 23: 13 [A] Athaliah **tore** her robes and shouted, "Treason! Treason!"
34: 19 [A] When the king heard the words of the Law, *he* **tore** his robes.
34: 27 [A] before me and **tore** your robes and wept in my presence,
Ezr 9: 3 [A] When I heard this, *I* **tore** my tunic and cloak, pulled hair
9: 5 [A] rose from my self-abasement, with my tunic and cloak **torn**,
Est 4: 1 [A] he **tore** his clothes, put on sackcloth and ashes, and went out
Job 1: 20 [A] At this, Job got up and **tore** his robe and shaved his head.
2: 12 [A] and *they* **tore** their robes and sprinkled dust on their heads.
Ps 35: 15 [A] when I was unaware. *They* **slandered** me without ceasing.
Ecc 3: 7 [A] a time to **tear** and a time to mend, a time to be silent and a
Isa 36: 22 [B] with their clothes **torn**, and told him what the field
37: 1 [A] *he* **tore** his clothes and put on sackcloth and went into the
64: 1 [63:19] [A] Oh, that *you would* **rend** the heavens and come
Jer 4: 30 [A] and put on jewels of gold? Why **shade** your eyes with paint?
22: 14 [A] So *he* **makes large** windows in it, panels it with cedar
36: 23 [A] the king **cut** them **off** with a scribe's knife and threw them
36: 24 [A] these words showed no fear, nor *did they* **tear** their clothes.
41: 5 [B] **torn** their clothes and cut themselves came from Shechem,
Eze 13: 20 [A] people like birds and *I will* **tear** them from your arms;
13: 21 [A] *I will* **tear off** your veils and save my people from your
Hos 13: 8 [A] I will attack them and **rip** [+4213+6033] them **open**.
Joel 2: 13 [A] **Rend** your heart and not your garments. Return to the

7974 קְרָעִים *qᵉrā'îm*, n.m.[pl.]. [4] [√ 7973]

pieces [2], rags [1], tore apart [+4200+7973+9109] [1]

1Ki 11: 30 of the new cloak he was wearing and tore it into twelve **pieces**.
11: 31 he said to Jeroboam, "Take ten **pieces** for yourself, for this is what
2Ki 2: 12 hold of his own clothes and **tore** them **apart** [+4200+7973+9109].
Pr 23: 21 and gluttons become poor, and drowsiness clothes them in **rags**.

7975 קָרַץ *qāraṣ*, v. [5] [→ 7976; Ar 10642]

been taken [1], maliciously wink [1], purses [1], winks maliciously [+6524] [1], winks [1]

Job 33: 6 [E] just like you before God; I too *have* **been taken** from clay.
Ps 35: 19 [A] *let* not those who hate me without reason **maliciously wink**
Pr 6: 13 [A] *who* **winks** with his eye, signals with his feet and motions
10: 10 [A] *He who* **winks** [+6524] **maliciously** causes grief, and a
16: 30 [A] is plotting perversity; *he who* **purses** his lips is bent on evil.

7976 קֶרֶץ *qereṣ*, n.m. [1] [√ 7975]

gadfly [1]

Jer 46: 20 beautiful heifer, but a **gadfly** is coming against her from the north.

7977 ¹קַרְקַע *qarqa'¹*, n.[m.]. [8 / 7] [→ 7978, 7980]

floor [5], bottom [1], floors [1]

Nu 5: 17 and put some dust from the tabernacle **floor** into the water.
1Ki 6: 15 paneling them from the **floor** *of* the temple to the ceiling,
6: 15 and covered the **floor** *of* the temple with planks of pine.
6: 16 from **floor** to ceiling to form within the temple an inner sanctuary,
6: 30 He also covered the **floors** *of* both the inner and outer rooms of the
7: 7 he was to judge, and he covered it with cedar from **floor** to ceiling.
7: 7 covered it with cedar from floor to ceiling. [BHS *floor*; NIV 7815]
Am 9: 3 Though they hide from me at the **bottom** *of* the sea, there I will

7978 ²קַרְקַע *qarqa'²*, n.pr.loc. [1] [√ 7977]

Karka [1]

Jos 15: 3 Then it ran past Hezron up to Addar and curved around to **Karka**.

7979 קַרְקַר *qarqar*, var. [1 / 0]

Nu 24: 17 the skulls [BHS *destroy* ?; NIV 7721] *of* all the sons of Sheth.

7980 קַרְקֹר *qarqōr*, n.pr.loc. [1] [√ 7977]

Karkor [1]

Jdg 8: 10 Zalmunna were in **Karkor** with a force of about fifteen thousand

7981 ¹קָרַר *qārar¹*, v. [2] [√ 7769 *or* →r √ 5249, 7922, 7923, 7938, 7941; cf. 7982]

pours out [2]

Jer 6: 7 [G] As a well **pours out** its water, so she pours out her
6: 7 [G] a well pours out its water, so *she* **pours out** her wickedness.

7982 ²קָרַר *qārar²*, v. [1] [cf. 7981]

battering down [1]

Isa 22: 5 [D] a day of **battering down** walls and of crying out to the

7983 קֶרֶשׁ *qereš*, n.m. [51]

frames [27], *untranslated* [11], frame [8], those[s] [2], deck [1], them[s] [+2021] [1], them[s] [+2021+6929] [1]

Ex 26: 15 "Make upright **frames** of acacia wood for the tabernacle.
26: 16 Each **frame** is to be ten cubits long and a cubit and a half wide,
26: 16 frame is to be ten cubits long **[RPH]** and a cubit and a half wide,
26: 17 with two projections **[RPH]** set parallel to each other. Make all
26: 17 to each other. Make all the **frames** *of* the tabernacle in this way.
26: 18 Make twenty **frames** for the south side of the tabernacle
26: 18 Make twenty frames **[RPH]** for the south side of the tabernacle
26: 19 and make forty silver bases to go under **them**[s] [+2021+6929]—
26: 19 under them—two bases for each **frame**, one under each projection.
26: 19 two bases for each frame, one under each projection. **[RPH]**
26: 20 other side, the north side of the tabernacle, make twenty **frames**
26: 21 and forty silver bases—two under each **frame**.
26: 21 and forty silver bases—two under each frame. **[RPH]**
26: 22 Make six **frames** for the far end, that is, the west end of the
26: 23 and make two **frames** for the corners at the far end.
26: 25 So there will be eight **frames** and sixteen silver bases—two under

Ex 26:25 be eight frames and sixteen silver bases—two under each **frame**.
26:25 and sixteen silver bases—two under each frame. **[RPH]**
26:26 of acacia wood: five for the **frames** *on* one side of the tabernacle,
26:27 five for **those**[s] *on* the other side, and five for the frames on the
26:27 five for the **frames** on the west, at the far end of the tabernacle.
26:28 crossbar is to extend from end to end at the middle of the **frames**.
26:29 Overlay the **frames** with gold and make gold rings to hold the
35:11 and its covering, clasps, **frames**, crossbars, posts and bases;
36:20 They made upright **frames** of acacia wood for the tabernacle.
36:21 Each **frame** was ten cubits long and a cubit and a half wide,
36:21 Each frame **[RPH]** was ten cubits long and a cubit and a half
36:22 **[RPH]** They made all the frames of the tabernacle in this way.
36:22 each other. They made all the **frames** *of* the tabernacle in this way.
36:23 They made **[RPH]** twenty frames for the south side of the
36:23 They made twenty **frames** for the south side of the tabernacle
36:24 made forty silver bases to go under **them**[s] [+2021]—two bases for
36:24 under them—two bases for each **frame**, one under each projection.
36:24 two bases for each frame, one under each projection. **[RPH]**
36:25 the north side of the tabernacle, they made twenty **frames**
36:26 and forty silver bases—two under each **frame**.
36:26 and forty silver bases—two under each frame. **[RPH]**
36:27 They made six **frames** for the far end, that is, the west end of the
36:28 two **frames** were made for the corners of the tabernacle at the far
36:30 So there were eight **frames** and sixteen silver bases—two under
36:30 were eight frames and sixteen silver bases—two under each **frame**.
36:31 of acacia wood: five for the **frames** *on* one side of the tabernacle,
36:32 five for **those**[s] *on* the other side, and five for the frames on the
36:32 five for the **frames** on the west, at the far end of the tabernacle.
36:33 so that it extended from end to end at the middle of the **frames**.
36:34 They overlaid the **frames** with gold and made gold rings to hold
39:33 all its furnishings, its clasps, **frames**, crossbars, posts and bases;
40:18 erected the **frames**, inserted the crossbars and set up the posts.
Nu 3:36 The Merarites were appointed to take care of the **frames** *of* the
4:31 to carry the **frames** *of* the tabernacle, its crossbars, posts and bases,
Eze 27:6 of cypress wood from the coasts of Cyprus they made your **deck**,

7984 קֶרֶת *qeret*, n.f. [5] [→ 7953, 7954, 7956, 7964, 7985, 7986; cf. 7815; *also used with compound proper names*]

city [5]

Job 29:7 "When I went to the gate of the **city** and took my seat in the public
Pr 8:3 beside the gates leading into the **city**, at the entrances, she cries
9:3 sent out her maids, and she calls from the highest point of the **city**.
9:14 at the door of her house, on a seat at the highest point of the **city**,
11:11 Through the blessing of the upright a **city** is exalted, but by the

7985 קַרְתָּה *qartâ*, n.pr.loc. [1 / 2] [√ 7984]

Kartah [2]

Jos 21:34 were given: from the tribe of Zebulun, Jokneam, **Kartah**,
1Ch 6:77 [6:62] **Kartah**, [BHS-] Rimmono and Tabor, together with their

7986 קַרְתָּן *qartān*, n.pr.loc. [1] [√ 7984]

Kartan [1]

Jos 21:32 Hammoth Dor and **Kartan**, together with their pasturelands—

7987 קַשְׂוָה *qaśwâ*, n.f. [4]

pitchers [3], jars [1]

Ex 25:29 as well as its **pitchers** and bowls for the pouring out of offerings.
37:16 and bowls and its **pitchers** for the pouring out of drink offerings.
Nu 4:7 on it the plates, dishes and bowls, and the **jars** *for* drink offerings;
1Ch 28:17 weight of pure gold for the forks, sprinkling bowls and **pitchers**;

7988 קְשִׂיטָה *qᵉśîṭâ*, n.f. [3]

pieces of silver [2], piece of silver [1]

Ge 33:19 For a hundred **pieces of silver**, he bought from the sons of Hamor,
Jos 24:32 bought for a hundred **pieces of silver** from the sons of Hamor,
Job 42:11 upon him, and each one gave him a **piece of silver** and a gold ring.

7989 קַשְׂקֶשֶׂת *qaśqeśet*, n.f. [8] [cf. 7878]

scales [7], coat of scale armor [+9234] [1]

Lev 11:9 and the streams, you may eat any that have fins and **scales**.
11:10 creatures in the seas or streams that do not have fins and **scales**—
11:12 water that does not have fins and **scales** is to be detestable to you.
Dt 14:9 living in the water, you may eat any that has fins and **scales**.
14:10 But anything that does not have fins and **scales** you may not eat;
1Sa 17:5 wore a **coat of scale armor of** [+9234] bronze weighing five
Eze 29:4 in your jaws and make the fish of your streams stick to your **scales**.
29:4 from among your streams, with all the fish sticking to your **scales**.

7990 קַשׁ *qaš*, n.m. [16] [√ 8006]

stubble [7], chaff [6], straw [2], piece of straw [1]

Ex 5:12 So the people scattered all over Egypt to gather **stubble** to use for
15:7 You unleashed your burning anger; it consumed them like **stubble**.
Job 13:25 you torment a windblown leaf? Will you chase after dry **chaff**?
41:28 [41:20] do not make him flee; slingstones are like **chaff** to him.
41:29 [41:21] A club seems to him but a **piece of straw**; he laughs at the
Ps 83:13 [83:14] like tumbleweed, O my God, like **chaff** before the wind.
Isa 5:24 as tongues of fire lick up **straw** and as dry grass sinks down in the
33:11 You conceive chaff, you give birth to **straw**; your breath is a fire
40:24 and they wither, and a whirlwind sweeps them away like **chaff**.
41:2 them to dust with his sword, to windblown **chaff** with his bow.
47:14 Surely they are like **stubble**; the fire will burn them up.
Jer 13:24 "I will scatter you like **chaff** driven by the desert wind.
Joel 2:5 like a crackling fire consuming **stubble**, like a mighty army drawn
Ob 1:18 the house of Esau will be **stubble**, and they will set it on fire
Na 1:10 and drunk from their wine; they will be consumed like dry **stubble**.
Mal 4:1 [3:19] All the arrogant and every evildoer will be **stubble**,

7991 קִשֻּׁאָה *qiššu'â*, n.f. [1] [√ 5252]

cucumbers [1]

Nu 11:5 at no cost—also the **cucumbers**, melons, leeks, onions and garlic.

7992 קָשַׁב *qāšab*, v. [46] [→ 7993, 7994, 7995]

listen [14], pay attention [12], hear [4], listened [3], listens [2], paid attention [2], alert [+7993] [1], attendance [1], attentively [1], gave heed [1], heard [1], heed [1], listen [+265] [1], pay close attention [+2256+9048] [1], turning [1]

1Sa 15:22 [G] than sacrifice, and to **heed** is better than the fat of rams.
2Ch 20:15 [G] "**Listen**, King Jehoshaphat and all who live in Judah
33:10 [G] to Manasseh and his people, but *they* **paid** no **attention**.
Ne 9:34 [G] *they did* not **pay attention** to your commands or the
Job 13:6 [G] Hear now my argument; **listen** *to* the plea of my lips.
33:31 [G] "**Pay attention**, Job, and listen to me; be silent, and I will
Ps 5:2 [5:3] [G] **Listen** to my cry for help, my King and my God, for to
10:17 [G] you encourage them, and *you* **listen** [+265] to their cry,
17:1 [G] Hear, O LORD, my righteous plea; **listen** *to* my cry.
55:2 [55:3] [G] **hear** me and answer me. My thoughts trouble me
61:1 [61:2] [G] Hear my cry, O God; **listen** *to* my prayer.
66:19 [G] but God has surely listened and **heard** my voice in prayer.
86:6 [G] Hear my prayer, O LORD; **listen** to my cry for mercy.
142:6 [142:7] [G] **Listen** to my cry, for I am in desperate need;
Pr 1:24 [G] I called and no *one* **gave heed** when I stretched out my hand,
2:2 [G] **turning** your ear to wisdom and applying your heart to
4:1 [G] a father's instruction; **pay attention** and gain understanding.
4:20 [G] My son, **pay attention** to what I say; listen closely to my
5:1 [G] My son, **pay attention** to my wisdom, listen well to my
7:24 [G] Now then, my sons, listen to me; **pay attention** to what I say.
17:4 [G] A wicked man **listens** to evil lips; a liar pays attention to a
29:12 [G] If a ruler **listens** to lies, all his officials become wicked.
SS 8:13 [G] You who dwell in the gardens with friends *in* **attendance**,
Isa 10:30 [G] O Daughter of Gallim! **Listen**, O Laishah! Poor Anathoth!
21:7 [G] or riders on camels, *let him be* **alert** [+7993], fully alert."
28:23 [G] Listen and hear my voice; **pay attention** and hear what I say.
32:3 [A] longer be closed, and the ears of those who hear *will* **listen**.
34:1 [G] you nations, and listen; **pay attention**, *you* peoples!
42:23 [G] or **pay close attention** [+2256+9048] in time to come?
48:18 [G] If only *you had* **paid attention** to my commands, your peace
49:1 [G] Listen to me, you islands; **hear** this, *you* distant nations:
51:4 [G] "**Listen** to me, my people; hear me, my nation: The law will
Jer 6:10 [G] will listen to me? Their ears are closed so they cannot **hear**.
6:17 [G] over you and said, '**Listen** to the sound of the trumpet!'
6:17 [G] the sound of the trumpet!' But you said, '*We will* not **listen**.'
6:19 [G] because *they have* not **listened** to my words and have
8:6 [G] I have listened **attentively**, but they do not say what is right.
18:18 [G] with our tongues and **pay** no **attention** to anything he says."
18:19 [G] **Listen** to me, O LORD; hear what my accusers are saying!
23:18 [G] or to hear his word? Who *has* **listened** and heard his word?
Da 9:19 [G] O Lord, listen! O Lord, forgive! O Lord, **hear** and act! For
Hos 5:1 [G] **Pay attention**, *you* Israelites! Listen, O royal house!
Mic 1:2 [G] O peoples, all of you, **listen**, O earth and all who are in it,
Zec 1:4 [G] they would not listen or **pay attention** to me,
7:11 [G] "But they refused to **pay attention**; stubbornly they turned
Mal 3:16 [G] talked with each other, and the LORD **listened** and heard.

7993 קֶשֶׁב *qešeb*, n.m. [4] [√ 7992]

alert [+7992] [1], alert [1], paid attention [1], response [1]

1Ki 18:29 there was no response, no one answered, no one **paid attention**.
2Ki 4:31 the staff on the boy's face, but there was no sound or **response**.
Isa 21:7 or riders on camels, *let him be* **alert** [+7992], fully alert."
21:7 riders on donkeys or riders on camels, let him be alert, fully **alert**."

7994 קַשָּׁב qaššāb, a. [2] [√ 7992]

attentive [2]

Ne 1: 6 let your ear be **attentive** and your eyes open to hear the prayer
1: 11 let your ear be **attentive** to the prayer of this your servant

7995 קַשֻּׁב qaššub, a. [3] [√ 7992]

attentive [3]

2Ch 6: 40 and your ears **attentive** to the prayers offered in this place.
7: 15 be open and my ears **attentive** to the prayers offered in this place.
Ps 130: 2 hear my voice. Let your ears be **attentive** to my cry for mercy.

7996 קָשָׁה qāšâ, v. [28] [→ 7997, 8001]

stiff-necked [+906+6902] [7], stiff-necked [+6902] [4], harden [2], put heavy [2], cruel [1], difficult [1], distressed [1], great difficulty [1], hard [1], hardens [1], hardship [1], harshly [1], having great difficulty [1], heavy [1], made stubborn [1], resisted [1], stubbornly refused [1]

Ge 35: 16 [D] Rachel began to give birth and *had* **great difficulty**.
35: 17 [G] as she *was* **having great difficulty** in childbirth, the midwife
49: 7 [A] Cursed be their anger, so fierce, and their fury, so **cruel**!
Ex 7: 3 [G] I *will* **harden** Pharaoh's heart, and though I multiply my
13: 15 [G] When Pharaoh **stubbornly refused** to let us go, the LORD
Dt 1: 17 [A] Bring me any case too **hard** for you, and I will hear it.
2: 30 [G] For the LORD your God *had* **made** his spirit **stubborn** and
10: 16 [G] therefore, and *do* not *be* **stiff-necked** [+6902] any longer.
15: 18 [A] Do not consider it a **hardship** to set your servant free,
1Sa 5: 7 [A] because his hand *is* **heavy** upon us and upon Dagon our
2Sa 19: 43 [19:44] [A] the men of Judah responded even more **harshly**
1Ki 12: 4 [G] "Your father **put** *a* **heavy** yoke on us, but now lighten the
2Ki 2: 10 [G] "You have asked a **difficult** *thing*," Elijah said, "yet if you
17: 14 [G] and *were* as **stiff-necked** [+906+6902] as their fathers, who did
2Ch 10: 4 [G] "Your father **put** *a* **heavy** yoke on us, but now lighten the
30: 8 [G] *Do* not *be* **stiff-necked** [+6902], as your fathers were;
36: 13 [G] *He became* **stiff-necked** [+906+6902] and hardened his heart
Ne 9: 16 [G] forefathers, became arrogant and **stiff-necked** [+906+6902],
9: 17 [G] *They became* **stiff-necked** [+906+6902] and in their rebellion
9: 29 [G] on you, *became* **stiff-necked** [+6902] and refused to listen.
Job 9: 4 [G] is vast. Who *has* **resisted** him and come out unscathed?
Ps 95: 8 [G] *do* not **harden** your hearts as you did at Meribah, as you did
Pr 28: 14 [G] the LORD, but *he who* **hardens** his heart falls into trouble.
29: [G] A man *who remains* **stiff-necked** [+6902] after many
Isa 8: 21 [C] **Distressed** and hungry, they will roam through the land;
Jer 7: 26 [G] *They were* **stiff-necked** [+906+6902] and did more evil than
17: 23 [G] *they were* **stiff-necked** [+906+6902] and would not listen or
19: 15 [G] because *they were* **stiff-necked** [+906+6902] and would not

7997 קָשֶׁה qāšeh, a. [36] [√ 7996]

stiff-necked [+6902] [7], harshly [5], cruel [3], fierce [3], hard [2], harsh [2], stubborn [2], bad news [1], deeply troubled [+8120] [1], desperate times [1], difficult [1], dire [1], grew stronger and stronger [+2143+2256] [1], in trouble [+3427] [1], obstinate [+4213] [1], obstinate [+7156] [1], strong [1], surly [1], unyielding [1]

Ge 42: 7 but he pretended to be a stranger and spoke **harshly** to them.
42: 30 "The man who is lord over the land spoke **harshly** to us
Ex 1: 14 They made their lives bitter with **hard** labor in brick and mortar
6: 9 listen to him because of their discouragement and **cruel** bondage.
18: 26 The **difficult** cases they brought to Moses, but the simple ones they
32: 9 said to Moses, "and they are a **stiff-necked** [+6902] people.
33: 3 because you are a **stiff-necked** [+6902] people and I might destroy
33: 5 "Tell the Israelites, 'You are a **stiff-necked** [+6902] people.
34: 9 Although this is a **stiff-necked** [+6902] people, forgive our
Dt 9: 6 good land to possess, for you are a **stiff-necked** [+6902] people.
9: 13 this people, and they are a **stiff-necked** [+6902] people indeed!
26: 6 mistreated us and made us suffer, putting us to **hard** labor.
31: 27 For I know how rebellious and **stiff-necked** [+6902] you are.
Jdg 2: 19 They refused to give up their evil practices and **stubborn** ways.
4: 24 hand of the Israelites **grew stronger** [+2143+2256] **and stronger**
1Sa 1: 15 Hannah replied, "I am a woman who is **deeply troubled** [+8120].
20: 10 "Who will tell me if your father answers you **harshly**?"
25: 3 but her husband, a Calebite, was **surly** and mean in his dealings.
2Sa 2: 17 The battle that day was very **fierce**, and Abner and the men of
3: 39 I am weak, and these sons of Zeruiah are too **strong** for me.
1Ki 12: 4 but now lighten the **harsh** labor and the heavy yoke he put on us,
12: 13 The king answered the people **harshly**. Rejecting the advice given
14: 6 Why this pretense? I have been sent to you with **bad news**.
2Ch 10: 4 but now lighten the **harsh** labor and the heavy yoke he put on us,
10: 13 The king answered them **harshly**. Rejecting the advice of the
Job 30: 25 Have I not wept for *those* **in trouble** [+3427]? Has not my soul
Ps 60: 3 [60:5] You have shown your people **desperate times**; you have
SS 8: 6 for love is as strong as death, its jealousy **unyielding** as the grave.
Isa 14: 3 gives you relief from suffering and turmoil and **cruel** bondage,
19: 4 I will hand the Egyptians over to the power of a **cruel** master,
21: 2 A **dire** vision has been shown to me: The traitor betrays, the looter
27: 1 his **fierce**, great and powerful sword, Leviathan the gliding serpent,
27: 8 with his **fierce** blast he drives her out, as on a day the east wind
48: 4 For I knew how **stubborn** you were; the sinews of your neck were
Eze 2: 4 The people to whom I am sending you are **obstinate** [+7156]
3: 7 for the whole house of Israel is hardened and **obstinate** [+4213].

7998 קָשַׁח qāšaḥ, v. [2]

harden [1], treats harshly [1]

Job 39: 16 [G] *She* **treats** her young **harshly**, as if they were not hers;
Isa 63: 17 [G] your ways and **harden** our hearts so we do not revere you?

7999 קֹשְׁט qōšṭ, n.m. [1] [→ Ar 10643]

true [1]

Pr 22: 21 teaching you **true** and reliable words, so that you can give sound

8000 קֹשֶׁט qōšeṭ, n.[m.?]. [1] [cf. 8008]

bow [1]

Ps 60: 4 [60:6] you have raised a banner to be unfurled against the **bow**.

8001 קְשִׁי qᵉšî, n.[m.]. [1] [√ 7996]

stubbornness [1]

Dt 9: 27 Overlook the **stubbornness** *of* this people, their wickedness

8002 קִשְׁיוֹן qišyôn, n.pr.loc. [2]

Kishion [2]

Jos 19: 20 Rabbith, **Kishion**, Ebez,
21: 28 from the tribe of Issachar, **Kishion**, Daberath,

8003 קָשַׁר qāšar, v. [44] [→ 8004, 8005]

conspired [10], plotted [7], bind [4], conspired [+8004] [4], tie [3], tied [3], became one with [1], carried out [1], closely bound up [1], conspiracy led [+8004] [1], conspirators [1], hold [1], is bound up [1], put on a leash [1], put on [1], raising a conspiracy [1], reached height [+6330] [1], strong [1], stronger [1]

Ge 30: 41 [E] Whenever the **stronger** *females* were in heat, Jacob would
30: 42 [B] weak animals went to Laban and the **strong** *ones* to Jacob.
38: 28 [A] took a scarlet thread and **tied** it on his wrist and said,
44: 30 [B] my father, whose life *is* **closely bound up** with the boy's life,
Dt 6: 8 [A] **Tie** them as symbols on your hands and bind them on your
11: 18 [A] **tie** them as symbols on your hands and bind them on your
Jos 2: 18 [A] *you have* **tied** this scarlet cord in the window through which
2: 21 [A] they departed. And *she* **tied** the scarlet cord in the window.
1Sa 18: 1 [C] Jonathan **became one** in spirit **with** David, and he loved him
22: 8 [A] Is that why you *have* all **conspired** against me? No one tells
22: 13 [A] "Why *have you* **conspired** against me, you and the son of
2Sa 15: 31 [A] "Ahithophel is among the **conspirators** with Absalom."
1Ki 15: 27 [A] Baasha son of Ahijah of the house of Issachar **plotted** against
16: 9 [A] who had command of half his chariots, **plotted** against him.
16: 16 [A] in the camp heard that Zimri *had* **plotted** *against* the king
16: 20 [A] events of Zimri's reign, and the rebellion *he* **carried out**,
2Ki 9: 14 [F] of Jehoshaphat, the son of Nimshi, **conspired** against Joram.
10: 9 [A] It was I *who* **conspired** against my master and killed him,
12: 20 [12:21] [A] His officials **conspired** [+8004] *against* him
14: 19 [A] *They* **conspired** [+8004] against him in Jerusalem, and he
15: 10 [A] Shallum son of Jabesh **conspired** against Zechariah. He
15: 15 [A] of Shallum's reign, and the **conspiracy** he **led** [+8004],
15: 25 [A] Pekah son of Remaliah, **conspired** against him.
15: 30 [A] Hoshea son of Elah **conspired** [+8004] against Pekah son of
21: 23 [A] Amon's officials **conspired** against him and assassinated the
21: 24 [A] the people of the land killed all who *had* **plotted** against
2Ch 24: 21 [A] *they* **plotted** against him, and by order of the king they
24: 25 [F] His officials **conspired** against him for murdering the son of
24: 26 [F] Those *who* **conspired** against him were Zabad, son of
25: 27 [A] *they* **conspired** [+8004] against him in Jerusalem and he fled
33: 24 [A] Amon's officials **conspired** against him and assassinated him
33: 25 [A] the people of the land killed all who *had* **plotted** against
Ne 4: 6 [3:38] [C] the wall till all of it **reached** [+6330] half its **height**,
4: 8 [4:2] [A] They all **plotted** together to come and fight against
Job 38: 31 [D] "*Can you* **bind** the beautiful Pleiades? Can you loose the
39: 10 [A] *Can you* **hold** him to the furrow with a harness? Will he till
41: 5 [40:29] [A] him like a bird or **put** him **on a leash** for your girls?
Pr 3: 3 [A] **bind** them around your neck, write them on the tablet of your
6: 21 [A] **Bind** them upon your heart forever; fasten them around your
7: 3 [A] **Bind** them on your fingers; write them on the tablet of your
22: 15 [B] Folly **is bound up** in the heart of a child, but the rod of
Isa 49: 18 [D] them all as ornaments; *you will* **put** them **on**, like a bride.
Jer 51: 63 [A] this scroll, **tie** a stone to it and throw it into the Euphrates.
Am 7: 10 [A] "Amos *is* **raising a conspiracy** against you in the very heart

8004 קֶשֶׁר ***qešer***, n.m. [16] [√ 8003]

conspiracy [5], conspired [+8003] [4], treason [4], conspiracy led [+8003] [1], rebellion [1], traitor [1]

2Sa 15:12 so the **conspiracy** gained strength, and Absalom's following kept
1Ki 16:20 the other events of Zimri's reign, and the **rebellion** he carried out,
2Ki 11:14 Then Athaliah tore her robes and called out, "**Treason**! Treason!"
11:14 Then Athaliah tore her robes and called out, "Treason! **Treason**!"
12:20 [12:21] His officials **conspired against** [+8003] him
14:19 *They* **conspired** [+8003] against him in Jerusalem, and he fled to
15:15 events of Shallum's reign, and the **conspiracy** [+8003] he **led**,
15:30 Hoshea son of Elah **conspired** [+8003] against Pekah son of
17:4 But the king of Assyria discovered that Hoshea was a **traitor**,
2Ch 23:13 Then Athaliah tore her robes and shouted, "**Treason**! Treason!"
23:13 Then Athaliah tore her robes and shouted, "Treason! **Treason**!"
25:27 *they* **conspired** [+8003] against him in Jerusalem and he fled to
Isa 8:12 "Do not call **conspiracy** everything that these people call
8:12 not call conspiracy everything that these people call **conspiracy**;
Jer 11:9 "There is a **conspiracy** among the people of Judah and those who
Eze 22:25 There is a **conspiracy** *of* her princes within her like a roaring lion

8005 קִשֻּׁרִים ***qiššurîm***, n.[m.]pl. [2] [√ 8003]

sashes [1], wedding ornaments [1]

Isa 3:20 the headdresses and ankle chains and **sashes**, the perfume bottles
Jer 2:32 a maiden forget her jewelry, a bride her **wedding ornaments**?

8006 קָשַׁשׁ¹ ***qāšaš¹***, v.den. [8] [→ 7990; cf. 8007]

gathering [4], gather together [2], gather [2]

Ex 5:7 [D] for making bricks; let them go and **gather** their own straw.
5:12 [D] So the people scattered all over Egypt to **gather** stubble to
Nu 15:32 [D] a man was found **gathering** wood on the Sabbath day.
15:33 [D] Those who found him **gathering** wood brought him to Moses
1Ki 17:10 [D] came to the town gate, a widow was there **gathering** sticks.
17:12 [D] I *am* **gathering** a few sticks to take home and make a meal
Zep 2:1 [F] **Gather together**, gather together, O shameful nation,
2:1 [A] Gather together, **gather together**, O shameful nation,

8007 קָשַׁשׁ² ***qāšaš²***, v. Not used in NIV/BHS [cf. 8006]

8008 קֶשֶׁת ***qešet***, n.f. [& m.?]. [76] [→ 8009; cf. 8000]

bow [45], bows [14], rainbow [4], archer [+9530] [1], archers [+408+928+2021+4619] [1], archers [+5432] [1], archers [+8227] [1], archers [+928+2021+4619] [1], arrow [1], arrows [+1201] [1], arrows [1], bowmen [+5031] [1], bowshot [+3217] [1], did so[s] [+448+2256+2932+4374] [1], shoot [+928+2021] [1], with bows [+2005] [1]

Ge 9:13 I have set my **rainbow** in the clouds, and it will be the sign of the
9:14 bring clouds over the earth and the **rainbow** appears in the clouds,
9:16 Whenever the **rainbow** appears in the clouds, I will see it
21:16 sat down nearby, about a **bowshot** [+3217] away, for she thought,
27:3 Now then, get your weapons—your quiver and **bow**—and go out
48:22 of land I took from the Amorites with my sword and my **bow**."
49:24 But his **bow** remained steady, his strong arms stayed limber,
Jos 24:12 Amorite kings. You did not do it with your own sword and **bow**.
1Sa 2:4 "The **bows** *of* the warriors are broken, but those who stumbled are
18:4 along with his tunic, and even his sword, his **bow** and his belt.
31:3 and when the **archers** [+408+928+2021+4619] overtook him, they
2Sa 1:18 ordered that the men of Judah be taught this lament of the **bow** (it
1:22 the flesh of the mighty, the **bow** *of* Jonathan did not turn back,
22:35 He trains my hands for battle; my arms can bend a **bow** *of* bronze.
1Ki 22:34 someone drew his **bow** at random and hit the king of Israel
2Ki 6:22 you kill men you have captured with your own sword or **bow**?
9:24 Then Jehu drew his **bow** and shot Joram between the shoulders.
13:15 Elisha said, "Get a **bow** and some arrows," and he did so.
13:15 a bow and some arrows," and *he* **did**[s] **so** [+448+2256+2932+4374].
13:16 "Take the **bow** in your hands," he said to the king of Israel.
1Ch 5:18 men who could handle shield and sword, who could use a **bow**,
8:40 The sons of Ulam were brave warriors who could handle the **bow**.
10:3 The fighting grew fierce around Saul, and when the **archers** [+928+2021+4619] overtook him, they wounded him.
12:2 they were armed with **bows** and were able to shoot arrows
12:2 were armed with bows and were able to **shoot** [+928+2021] arrows
2Ch 14:8 [14:7] armed with small shields and **with bows** [+2005].
17:17 a valiant soldier, with 200,000 men armed with **bows** and shields;
18:33 someone drew his **bow** at random and hit the king of Israel
26:14 helmets, coats of armor, **bows** and slingstones for the entire army.
Ne 4:13 [4:7] them by families, with their swords, spears and **bows**.
4:16 [4:10] half were equipped with spears, shields, **bows** and armor.
Job 20:24 he flees from an iron weapon, a bronze-tipped **arrow** pierces him.
29:20 My glory will remain fresh in me, the **bow** ever new in my hand.'
41:28 [41:20] **Arrows** [+1201] do not make him flee; slingstones are
Ps 7:12 [7:13] he will sharpen his sword; he will bend and string his **bow**.
11:2 For look, the wicked bend their **bows**; they set their arrows against
18:34 [18:35] my hands for battle; my arms can bend a **bow** *of* bronze.
37:14 the sword and bend the **bow** to bring down the poor and needy,
37:15 swords will pierce their own hearts, and their **bows** will be broken.
44:6 [44:7] I do not trust in my **bow**, my sword does not bring me
46:9 [46:10] he breaks the **bow** and shatters the spear, he burns the
76:3 [76:4] There he broke the flashing **arrows**, the shields
78:9 The men of Ephraim, though armed with **bows**, turned back on the
78:57 they were disloyal and faithless, as unreliable as a faulty **bow**.
Isa 5:28 Their arrows are sharp, all their **bows** are strung; their horses'
7:24 Men will go there with **bow** and arrow, for the land will be covered
13:18 Their **bows** will strike down the young men; they will have no
21:15 the drawn sword, from the bent **bow** and from the heat of battle.
21:17 The survivors of the **bowmen** [+5031], the warriors of Kedar,
22:3 have fled together; they have been captured without using the **bow**.
41:2 them to dust with his sword, to windblown chaff with his **bow**.
66:19 to the Libyans and Lydians (famous as **archers** [+5432]),
Jer 4:29 sound of horsemen and **archers** [+8227] every town takes to flight.
6:23 They are armed with **bow** and spear; they are cruel and show no
9:3 [9:2] "They make ready their tongue like a **bow**, to shoot lies; it is
46:9 and Put who carry shields, men of Lydia who draw the **bow**.
49:35 "See, I will break the **bow** *of* Elam, the mainstay of their might.
50:14 up your positions around Babylon, all you who draw the **bow**.
50:29 "Summon archers against Babylon, all those who draw the **bow**.
50:42 They are armed with **bows** and spears; they are cruel and without
51:3 Let not the archer string his **bow**, nor let him put on his armor.
51:56 her warriors will be captured, and their **bows** will be broken.
La 2:4 Like an enemy he has strung his **bow**; his right hand is ready.
3:12 He drew his **bow** and made me the target for his arrows.
Eze 1:28 Like the appearance of a **rainbow** in the clouds on a rainy day,
39:3 I will strike your **bow** from your left hand and make your arrows
39:9 and large shields, the **bows** and arrows, the war clubs and spears.
Hos 1:5 In that day I will break Israel's **bow** in the Valley of Jezreel."
1:7 not by **bow**, sword or battle, or by horses and horsemen, but by the
2:18 [2:20] **Bow** and sword and battle I will abolish from the land,
7:16 They do not turn to the Most High; they are like a faulty **bow**.
Am 2:15 The **archer** [+9530] will not stand his ground, the fleet-footed
Hab 3:9 You uncovered your **bow**, you called for many arrows.
Zec 9:10 the war-horses from Jerusalem, and the battle **bow** will be broken.
9:13 I will bend Judah as I bend my **bow** and fill it with Ephraim.
10:4 him the tent peg, from him the battle **bow**, from him every ruler.

8009 קַשָּׁת ***qaššāt***, n.m. [1] [√ 8008]

archer [+8050] [1]

Ge 21:20 he grew up. He lived in the desert and became an **archer** [+8050].

ר, r

8010 ר ***r***, letter. Not used in NIV/BHS [→ Ar 10645]

8011 רָאָה¹ ***rā'â¹***, v. [1296 / 1294] [→ 2218, 4307, 5260, 5261, 5262, 8012?, 8013, 8014, 8015, 8016, 8019, 8021, 8022, 8023, 8024, 8026; *also used with compound proper names*]

see [342], saw [306], seen [102], look [52], looked [37], appeared [33], *untranslated* [27], sees [27], examine [25], show [23], appear [20], showed [17], shown [12], consider [10], be seen [9], realized [9], find out [8], seeing [8], appears [7], watching [7], examines [6], enjoy [5], looks [5], watch [5], find [4], have regard for [4], learned [4], noticed [4], watched [4], been seen [3], observe [3], remember [3], advisers [+7156] [2], be shown [2], decide [2], ever seeing [+8011] [2], face [2], faced each other [+7156] [2], find out [+2256+3359] [2], had[s] [2], here [2], indeed seen [+906+8011] [2], inspect [2], knows [2], let see [2], look after [2], look around [2], look down on [2], look for [2], look over [2], looking [2], meet [2], notice [2], observed [2], only look [+8011] [2], present himself [2], provide [2], revealed [2], saw clearly [+8011] [2], see [+2256+3359] [2], view [2], were exposed [2], ah [1], allowed to see [1], appear before [+7156] [1], appearing [1], are given [1], attract [1], be found [1], be provided [1], bear in mind [1], beheld [1], being seen [1], blind [+1153] [1], catch glimpse [1], caught sight of [1], cherished [1], choose [1], chose [1], chosen [1], clearly [+3954] [1], come into presence [+906+7156] [1], come into view [1], compare [1], consider carefully [1], considers [1], conspicuous [1], contemplating [1], display [1], displayed [1], experienced [1], faced [1], find out [+906+2256+3359] [1], found [+906+4200+7156] [1], found [1], gaze [1], gazing [1], glimpse [1], gloat [1], had a vision [1], had special access to [+7156] [1], have sexual relations [+906+6872] [1], hidden [+4202] [1], inspected [1], keeping watch [+928+6524] [1], knew [1], knowing [1], let gloat [1], listen carefully [1], listen [1], look carefully [+928+6524] [1], looked

[+5260] [1], looked things over [1], looking at each other [1], lookout [1], looks down on [1], made see [1], make look [1], make see [1], meet with [+7156] [1], met [1], mistake for [+906+3869] [1], paid attention [1], please [1], present myself [1], present yourself [1], present [1], probe [1], realize [+2256+3359] [1], realize [1], realized [+2256+3359] [1], realizing [1], reappears [+6388] [1], reason [1], recognize [1], regard [1], regarded [1], respect [1], revealing [1], reveals [1], see [+7156] [1], see [+906+2021+4200+6524] [1], see [+906+2256+3359] [1], see [+906+6524] [1], see for yourselves [+4013+6524] [1], see visions [1], seems [1], seen for myself [+906+7156] [1], selected [1], show himself [1], showing [1], sight [1], someone[s] [+2021] [1], stare [1], suffered [1], took note [1], turn [1], uncovered [1], understand [1], very well [1], viewed [1], visible [1], visit [1], was seen [1], were shown [1]

Ge 1: 4 [A] God **saw** that the light was good, and he separated the light
1: 9 [C] the sky be gathered to one place, and *let* dry ground **appear**."
1: 10 [A] waters he called "seas." And God **saw** that it was good.
1: 12 [A] in it according to their kinds. And God **saw** that it was good.
1: 18 [A] separate light from darkness. And God **saw** that it was good.
1: 21 [A] bird according to its kind. And God **saw** that it was good.
1: 25 [A] according to their kinds. And God **saw** that it was good.
1: 31 [A] God **saw** all that he had made, and it was very good.
2: 19 [A] He brought them to the man to **see** what he would name
3: 6 [A] When the woman **saw** that the fruit of the tree was good for
6: 2 [A] the sons of God **saw** that the daughters of men were
6: 5 [A] The LORD **saw** how great man's wickedness on the earth
6: 12 [A] God **saw** how corrupt the earth had become, for all the
7: 1 [A] because I *have* **found** [+906+4200+7156] you righteous in this
8: 5 [C] of the tenth month the tops of the mountains *became* **visible**.
8: 8 [A] he sent out a dove to **see** if the water had receded from the
8: 13 [A] from the ark and **saw** that the surface of the ground was dry.
9: 14 [C] clouds over the earth and the rainbow **appears** in the clouds,
9: 16 [A] *I will* **see** it and remember the everlasting covenant between
9: 22 [A] **saw** his father's nakedness and told his two brothers outside.
9: 23 [A] so that *they would* not **see** their father's nakedness.
11: 5 [A] the LORD came down to **see** the city and the tower that the
12: 1 [G] your father's household and go to the land *I will* **show** you.
12: 7 [C] The LORD **appeared** to Abram and said, "To your
12: 7 [C] built an altar there to the LORD, who *had* **appeared** to him.
12: 12 [A] When the Egyptians **see** you, they will say, 'This is his wife.'
12: 14 [A] the Egyptians **saw** that she was a very beautiful woman.
12: 15 [A] when Pharaoh's officials **saw** her, they praised her to
13: 10 [A] and **saw** that the whole plain of the Jordan was well watered,
13: 14 [A] up your eyes from where you are and **look** north and south,
13: 15 [A] All the land that you **see** I will give to you and your offspring
16: 4 [A] When *she* **knew** she was pregnant, she began to despise her
16: 5 [A] and now that *she* **knows** she is pregnant, she despises me.
16: 13 [A] for she said, "*I have* now **seen** the One who sees me."
16: 13 [A] for she said, "I have now seen the *One who* **sees** me."
17: 1 [C] the LORD **appeared** to him and said, "I am God Almighty;
18: 1 [C] The LORD **appeared** to Abraham near the great trees of
18: 2 [A] Abraham looked up and **saw** three men standing nearby.
18: 2 [A] When *he* **saw** them, he hurried from the entrance of his tent
18: 21 [A] **see** if what they have done is as bad as the outcry that has
19: 1 [A] When he **saw** them, he got up to meet them and bowed down
19: 28 [A] *he* **saw** dense smoke rising from the land, like smoke from a
20: 10 [A] asked Abraham, "What *was your* **reason** for doing this?"
21: 9 [A] Sarah **saw** that the son whom Hagar the Egyptian had borne
21: 16 [A] for she thought, "*I* cannot **watch** the boy die."
21: 19 [A] God opened her eyes and *she* **saw** a well of water. So she
22: 4 [A] day Abraham looked up and **saw** the place in the distance.
22: 8 [A] "God himself *will* **provide** the lamb for the burnt offering,
22: 13 [A] and there in a thicket *he* **saw** a ram caught by its horns.
22: 14 [A] So Abraham called that place The LORD *Will* **Provide**.
22: 14 [C] "On the mountain of the LORD *it will* **be provided**."
24: 30 [A] As soon as *he had* **seen** the nose ring, and the bracelets on
24: 63 [A] and as he looked up, *he* **saw** camels approaching.
24: 64 [A] Rebekah also looked up and **saw** Isaac. She got down from
26: 2 [C] The LORD **appeared** to Isaac and said, "Do not go down to
26: 8 [A] from a window and **saw** Isaac caressing his wife Rebekah.
26: 24 [C] That night the LORD **appeared** to him and said, "I am the
26: 28 [A] "*We* **saw** [+8011] **clearly** that the LORD was with you;
26: 28 [A] "*We* **saw clearly** [+8011] that the LORD was with you;
27: 1 [A] and his eyes were so weak that *he could* no longer **see**,
27: 27 [A] caught the smell of his clothes, he blessed him and said, "**Ah**,
28: 6 [A] Now Esau **learned** that Isaac had blessed Jacob and had sent
28: 8 [A] **realized** how displeasing the Canaanite women were to his
29: 2 [A] There *he* **saw** a well in the field, with three flocks of sheep
29: 10 [A] **saw** Rachel daughter of Laban, his mother's brother, and
29: 31 [A] When the LORD **saw** that Leah was not loved, he opened
29: 32 [A] for she said, "It is because the LORD *has* **seen** my misery.
30: 1 [A] When Rachel **saw** that she was not bearing Jacob any
30: 9 [A] When Leah **saw** that she had stopped having children, she
31: 2 [A] Jacob **noticed** *that* Laban's attitude toward him was not what
31: 5 [A] "I **see** that your father's attitude toward me is not what it was
31: 10 [A] "In breeding season *I once* **had**[s] a dream in which I looked
31: 12 [A] **see** that all the male goats mating with the flock are streaked,
31: 12 [A] for *I have* **seen** all that Laban has been doing to you.
31: 42 [A] God *has* **seen** my hardship and the toil of my hands, and last
31: 43 [A] and the flocks are my flocks. All you **see** is mine.
31: 50 [A] **remember** *that* God is a witness between you and me."
32: 2 [32:3] [A] When Jacob **saw** them, he said, "This is the camp of
32: 20 [32:21] [A] later, when *I* **see** [+7156] him, perhaps he will
32: 25 [32:26] [A] When the man **saw** that he could not overpower
32: 30 [32:31] [A] saying, "It is because *I* **saw** God face to face,
33: 1 [A] Jacob looked up **[NIE]** and there was Esau, coming with his
33: 5 [A] Esau looked up and **saw** the women and children. "Who are
33: 10 [A] For *to* **see** your face is like seeing the face of God, now that
33: 10 [A] For to see your face is like **seeing** the face of God, now that
34: 1 [A] had borne to Jacob, went out to **visit** the women of the land.
34: 2 [A] the ruler of that area, **saw** her, he took her and violated her.
35: 1 [C] who **appeared** to you when you were fleeing from your
35: 9 [C] Paddan Aram, God **appeared** to him again and blessed him.
37: 4 [A] When his brothers **saw** that their father loved him more than
37: 14 [A] and **see** if all is well with your brothers and with the flocks,
37: 18 [A] *they* **saw** him in the distance, and before he reached them,
37: 20 [A] devoured him. Then *we'll* **see** what comes of his dreams."
37: 25 [A] and **saw** a caravan of Ishmaelites coming from Gilead.
38: 2 [A] There Judah **met** the daughter of a Canaanite man named
38: 14 [A] For *she* **saw** that, though Shelah had now grown up, she had
38: 15 [A] When Judah **saw** her, he thought she was a prostitute, for she
39: 3 [A] When his master **saw** that the LORD was with him and that
39: 13 [A] When she **saw** that he had left his cloak in her hand and had
39: 14 [A] "**Look**," she said to them, "this Hebrew has been brought to
39: 23 [A] The warden **paid** no **attention** *to* anything under Joseph's
40: 6 [A] to them the next morning, *he* **saw** that they were dejected.
40: 16 [A] When the chief baker **saw** that Joseph had given a favorable
41: 19 [A] *I had* never **seen** such ugly cows in all the land of Egypt.
41: 22 [A] "In my dreams *I* also **saw** seven heads of grain, full
41: 28 [G] to Pharaoh: God *has* **shown** Pharaoh what he is about to do.
41: 33 [A] "And now *let* Pharaoh **look for** a discerning and wise man
41: 41 [A] **[NIE]** "I hereby put you in charge of the whole land of
42: 1 [A] When Jacob **learned** that there was grain in Egypt, he said to
42: 1 [F] to his sons, "Why *do you just keep* **looking at each other**?"
42: 7 [A] As soon as Joseph **saw** his brothers, he recognized them,
42: 9 [A] You have come to **see** where our land is unprotected."
42: 12 [A] "You have come to **see** where our land is unprotected."
42: 21 [A] *We* **saw** how distressed he was when he pleaded with us for
42: 27 [A] his donkey, and *he* **saw** his silver in the mouth of his sack.
42: 35 [A] When they and their father **saw** the money pouches, they
43: 3 [A] '*You will* not **see** my face again unless your brother is with
43: 5 [A] '*You will* not **see** my face again unless your brother is with
43: 16 [A] When Joseph **saw** Benjamin with them, he said to the
43: 29 [A] As he looked about and **saw** his brother Benjamin, his own
44: 23 [A] comes down with you, *you will* not **see** my face again.'
44: 26 [A] We cannot **see** the man's face unless our youngest brother is
44: 28 [A] surely been torn to pieces." And *I have* not **seen** him since.
44: 31 [A] **sees** that the boy isn't there, he will die. Your servants will
44: 34 [A] *Do* not *let me* **see** the misery that would come upon my
45: 12 [A] "*You can* **see** [+4013+6524] **for yourselves**, and so can my
45: 13 [A] accorded me in Egypt and about everything *you have* **seen**.
45: 27 [A] and when *he* **saw** the carts Joseph had sent to carry him back,
45: 28 [A] son Joseph is still alive. I will go and **see** him before I die."
46: 29 [C] As soon as Joseph **appeared** before him, he threw his arms
46: 30 [A] since *I have* **seen** [+906+7156] **for myself** that you are still
48: 3 [C] "God Almighty **appeared** to me at Luz in the land of
48: 8 [A] When Israel **saw** the sons of Joseph, he asked, "Who are
48: 10 [A] eyes were failing because of old age, and he could hardly **see**.
48: 11 [A] said to Joseph, "I never expected *to* **see** your face again,
48: 11 [G] and now God *has* **allowed** me **to see** your children too."
48: 17 [A] When Joseph **saw** his father placing his right hand on
49: 15 [A] When *he* **sees** how good is his resting place and how pleasant
50: 11 [A] When the Canaanites who lived there **saw** the mourning at
50: 15 [A] When Joseph's brothers **saw** that their father was dead, they
50: 23 [A] **saw** the third generation of Ephraim's children.
Ex 1: 16 [A] women in childbirth and **observe** them on the delivery stool,
2: 2 [A] When *she* **saw** that he was a fine child, she hid him for three
2: 5 [A] *She* **saw** the basket among the reeds and sent her slave girl to
2: 6 [A] She opened it and **saw** the baby. He was crying, and she felt
2: 11 [A] his own people were and **watched** them at their hard labor.
2: 11 [A] *He* **saw** an Egyptian beating a Hebrew, one of his own
2: 12 [A] Glancing this way and that and **seeing** no one, he killed the
2: 25 [A] So God **looked** *on* the Israelites and was concerned about
3: 2 [C] There the angel of the LORD **appeared** to him in flames of
3: 2 [A] Moses **saw** that though the bush was on fire it did not burn
3: 3 [A] So Moses thought, "I will go over and **see** this strange sight—
3: 4 [A] When the LORD **saw** that he had gone over to look, God

Ex 3: 4 [A] When the LORD saw that he had gone over to **look**, God
3: 7 [A] "*I have* **indeed seen** [+906+8011] the misery of my people
3: 7 [A] "*I have* **indeed seen** [+906+8011] the misery of my people
3: 9 [A] and *I have* **seen** the way the Egyptians are oppressing them.
3: 16 [C] of Abraham, Isaac and Jacob—**appeared** to me and said:
4: 1 [C] listen to me and say, 'The LORD *did* not **appear** to you'?"
4: 5 [C] God of Isaac and the God of Jacob—*has* **appeared** to you."
4: 14 [A] to meet you, and his heart will be glad when *he* **sees** you.
4: 18 [A] "Let me go back to my own people in Egypt *to* **see** if any of
4: 21 [A] **see** that you perform before Pharaoh all the wonders I have
4: 31 [A] was concerned about them and *had* **seen** their misery,
5: 19 [A] The Israelite foremen **realized** they were in trouble when
5: 21 [A] they said, "*May* the LORD **look** upon you and judge you!
6: 1 [A] said to Moses, "Now *you will* **see** what I will do to Pharaoh:
6: 3 [C] *I* **appeared** to Abraham, to Isaac and to Jacob as God
7: 1 [A] the LORD said to Moses, "**See**, I have made you like God
8: 15 [8:11] [A] when Pharaoh **saw** that there was relief, he hardened
9: 16 [G] that *I might* **show** you my power and that my name might be
9: 34 [A] When Pharaoh **saw** that the rain and hail and thunder had
10: 5 [A] will cover the face of the ground so that it cannot *be* **seen**.
10: 6 [A] *have ever* **seen** from the day they settled in this land till
10: 10 [A] and children! **Clearly** [+3954] you are bent on evil.
10: 23 [A] No one *could* **see** anyone else or leave his place for three
10: 28 [A] of my sight! Make sure *you do* not **appear** before me again!
10: 28 [A] before me again! The day you **see** my face you will die."
10: 29 [A] Moses replied, "*I will* never **appear** before you again."
12: 13 [A] you are; and when *I* **see** the blood, I will pass over you.
12: 23 [A] *he will* **see** the blood on the top and sides of the doorframe
13: 7 [C] nothing with yeast in it *is to* **be seen** among you, nor shall
13: 7 [C] nor *shall* any yeast **be seen** anywhere within your borders.
13: 17 [A] For God said, "If they **face** war, they might change their
14: 13 [A] *you will* **see** the deliverance the LORD will bring you
14: 13 [A] The Egyptians *you* **see** today you will never see again.
14: 13 [A] The Egyptians you see today *you will* never **see** again.
14: 30 [A] and Israel **saw** the Egyptians lying dead on the shore.
14: 31 [A] when the Israelites **saw** the great power the LORD
16: 7 [A] in the morning *you will* **see** the glory of the LORD,
16: 10 [C] there was the glory of the LORD **appearing** in the cloud.
16: 15 [A] When the Israelites **saw** it, they said to each other, "What is
16: 29 [A] **Bear in mind** that the LORD has given you the Sabbath;
16: 32 [A] so *they can* **see** the bread I gave you to eat in the desert
18: 14 [A] When his father-in-law **saw** all that Moses was doing for the
19: 4 [A] '*You* yourselves *have* **seen** what I did to Egypt, and how I
19: 21 [A] so they do not force their way through to **see** the LORD
20: 18 [A] **saw** the thunder and lightning and heard the trumpet and
20: 18 [a] they trembled *with* fear. [BHS *they saw*; NIV 3707]
20: 22 [A] '*You have* **seen** for yourselves that I have spoken to you
22: 10 [22:9] [A] is injured or is taken away *while* no *one is* **looking**,
23: 5 [A] If *you* **see** the donkey of someone who hates you fallen down
23: 15 [C] out of Egypt. "No *one is to* **appear** before me empty-handed.
23: 17 [C] "Three times a year all the men *are to* **appear** before the
24: 10 [A] **saw** the God of Israel. Under his feet was something like a
25: 9 [G] all its furnishings exactly like the pattern I *will* **show** you.
25: 40 [A] **See** that you make them according to the pattern shown you
25: 40 [H] See that you make them according to the pattern **shown** you
26: 30 [H] "Set up the tabernacle according to the plan **shown** *you* on
27: 8 [G] It is to be made just as you *were* **shown** on the mountain.
31: 2 [A] "**See**, I have chosen Bezalel son of Uri, the son of Hur,
32: 1 [A] When the people **saw** that Moses was so long in coming
32: 5 [A] When Aaron **saw** this, he built an altar in front of the calf
32: 9 [A] "*I have* **seen** these people," the LORD said to Moses,
32: 19 [A] approached the camp and **saw** the calf and the dancing,
32: 25 [A] Moses **saw** that the people were running wild and that Aaron
33: 10 [A] Whenever the people **saw** the pillar of cloud standing at the
33: 12 [A] **[NIE]** "You have been telling me, 'Lead these people,'
33: 13 [A] favor with you. **Remember** that this nation is your people."
33: 18 [G] Then Moses said, "Now **show** me your glory."
33: 20 [A] But," he said, "you cannot **see** my face, for no one may see
33: 20 [A] "you cannot see my face, for no one *may* **see** me and live."
33: 23 [A] I will remove my hand and *you will* **see** my back; but my
33: 23 [C] and you will see my back; but my face *must* not **be seen**."
34: 3 [C] is to come with you or **be seen** anywhere on the mountain;
34: 10 [A] The people you live among *will* **see** how awesome is the
34: 20 [C] "No *one is to* **appear** before me empty-handed.
34: 23 [C] Three times a year all your men *are to* **appear** before the
34: 24 [C] times each year to **appear** before the LORD your God.
34: 30 [A] When Aaron and all the Israelites **saw** Moses, his face was
34: 35 [A] they **saw** that his face was radiant. Then Moses would put the
35: 30 [A] Moses said to the Israelites, "**See**, the LORD has chosen
39: 43 [A] Moses **inspected** the work and saw that they had done it just
Lev 5: 1 [A] a public charge to testify regarding something *he has* **seen**
9: 4 [C] mixed with oil. For today the LORD *will* **appear** to you.' "
9: 6 [C] to do, so that the glory of the LORD *may* **appear** to you."
9: 23 [C] and the glory of the LORD **appeared** to all the people.
9: 24 [A] when all the people **saw** it, they shouted for joy and fell
13: 3 [A] The priest *is to* **examine** the sore on his skin, and if the hair
13: 3 [A] When the priest **examines** him, he shall pronounce him
13: 5 [A] On the seventh day the priest *is to* **examine** him, and if he
13: 6 [A] On the seventh day the priest *is to* **examine** him again, and if
13: 7 [C] if the rash does spread in his skin after *he has* **shown** himself
13: 7 [C] pronounced clean, *he must* **appear** before the priest again.
13: 8 [A] The priest *is to* **examine** him, and if the rash has spread in
13: 10 [A] The priest *is to* **examine** him, and if there is a white swelling
13: 13 [A] the priest *is to* **examine** him, and if the disease has covered
13: 14 [C] But whenever raw flesh **appears** on him, he will be unclean.
13: 15 [A] When the priest **sees** the raw flesh, he shall pronounce him
13: 17 [A] The priest *is to* **examine** him, and if the sores have turned
13: 19 [C] spot appears, *he must* **present himself** to the priest.
13: 20 [A] The priest *is to* **examine** it, and if it appears to be more than
13: 21 [A] But if, when the priest **examines** it, there is no white hair in it
13: 25 [A] the priest *is to* **examine** the spot, and if the hair in it has
13: 26 [A] if the priest **examines** it and there is no white hair in the spot
13: 27 [A] On the seventh day the priest *is to* **examine** him, and if it is
13: 30 [A] the priest *is to* **examine** the sore, and if it appears to be more
13: 31 [A] if, when the priest **examines** this kind of sore, it does not
13: 32 [A] On the seventh day the priest *is to* **examine** the sore, and if
13: 34 [A] On the seventh day the priest *is to* **examine** the itch, and if it
13: 36 [A] the priest *is to* **examine** him, and if the itch has spread in the
13: 39 [A] the priest *is to* **examine** them, and if the spots are dull white,
13: 43 [A] The priest *is to* **examine** him, and if the swollen sore on his
13: 49 [H] it is a spreading mildew and *must* **be shown** *to* the priest.
13: 50 [A] The priest *is to* **examine** the mildew and isolate the affected
13: 51 [A] On the seventh day *he is to* **examine** it, and if the mildew has
13: 53 [A] "But if, when the priest **examines** it, the mildew has not
13: 55 [A] affected article has been washed, the priest *is to* **examine** it,
13: 56 [A] If, when the priest **examines** it, the mildew has faded after
13: 57 [C] But if *it* **reappears** [+6388] in the clothing, or in the woven
14: 3 [A] The priest is to go outside the camp and **examine** him. If the
14: 35 [C] 'I *have* **seen** something that looks like mildew in my house.'
14: 36 [A] to be emptied before he goes in to **examine** the mildew,
14: 36 [A] After this the priest is to go in and **inspect** the house.
14: 37 [A] *He is to* **examine** the mildew on the walls, and if it has
14: 39 [A] On the seventh day the priest shall return *to* **inspect** the
14: 44 [A] the priest is to go and **examine** it and, if the mildew has
14: 48 [A] "But if the priest comes *to* **examine** it and the mildew has
16: 2 [C] because *I* **appear** in the cloud over the atonement cover.
20: 17 [A] or his mother, and *they* **have sexual** [+906+6872] **relations**,
20: 17 [A] and they have sexual relations, **[RPH]** it is a disgrace.
Nu 4: 20 [A] But the Kohathites must not go in to **look** *at* the holy things,
8: 4 [G] made exactly like the pattern the LORD *had* **shown** Moses.
11: 15 [A] favor in your eyes—and *do* not *let me* **face** my own ruin."
11: 23 [A] *You will* now **see** whether or not what I say will come true
13: 18 [A] **See** what the land is like and whether the people who live
13: 26 [G] to the whole assembly and **showed** them the fruit of the land.
13: 28 [A] and very large. *We* even **saw** descendants of Anak there.
13: 32 [A] living in it. All the people *we* **saw** there are of great size.
13: 33 [A] *We* **saw** the Nephilim there (the descendants of Anak come
14: 10 [C] the glory of the LORD **appeared** at the Tent of Meeting to
14: 14 [C] and that you, O LORD, *have* **been seen** face to face,
14: 22 [A] not one of the men who **saw** my glory and the miraculous
14: 23 [A] not *one* of them *will ever* **see** the land I promised on oath to
14: 23 [A] No one who has treated me with contempt *will ever* **see** it.
15: 39 [A] You will have these tassels *to* **look** *at* and so you will
16: 19 [C] the glory of the LORD **appeared** to the entire assembly.
16: 42 [17:7] [C] covered it and the glory of the LORD **appeared**.
17: 9 [17:24] [A] *They* **looked** *at* them, and each man took his own
20: 6 [C] and the glory of the LORD **appeared** to them.
20: 29 [A] when the whole community **learned** that Aaron had died,
21: 8 [A] it up on a pole; anyone who is bitten *can* **look** *at* it and live."
22: 2 [A] Now Balak son of Zippor **saw** all that Israel had done to the
22: 23 [A] When the donkey **saw** the angel of the LORD standing in
22: 25 [A] When the donkey **saw** the angel of the LORD, she pressed
22: 27 [A] When the donkey **saw** the angel of the LORD, she lay down
22: 31 [A] *he* **saw** the angel of the LORD standing in the road with his
22: 33 [A] The donkey **saw** me and turned away from me these three
22: 41 [A] up to Bamoth Baal, and from there *he* **saw** part of the people.
23: 3 [G] Whatever *he* **reveals** *to* me I will tell you." Then he went off
23: 9 [A] From the rocky peaks *I* **see** them, from the heights I view
23: 13 [A] "Come with me to another place where *you can* **see** them;
23: 13 [A] can see them; *you will* **see** only a part but not all of them.
23: 13 [A] not all of them. **[RPH]** And from there, curse them for me."
23: 21 [A] misfortune is seen in Jacob, no misery **observed** in Israel.
24: 1 [A] Now when Balaam **saw** that it pleased the LORD to bless
24: 2 [A] Balaam looked out and **saw** Israel encamped tribe by tribe,
24: 17 [A] "*I* **see** him, but not now; I behold him, but not near. A star
24: 20 [A] Balaam **saw** Amalek and uttered his oracle: "Amalek was
24: 21 [A] *he* **saw** the Kenites and uttered his oracle: "Your dwelling
25: 7 [A] the son of Aaron, the priest, **saw** this, he left the assembly,

Nu 27:12 [A] the Abarim range and **see** the land I have given the Israelites.
27:13 [A] After *you have* **seen** it, you too will be gathered to your
32:1 [A] **saw** that the lands of Jazer and Gilead were suitable for
32:8 [A] when I sent them from Kadesh Barnea to **look over** the land.
32:9 [A] they went up to the Valley of Eshcol and **viewed** the land,
32:11 [A] or more who came up out of Egypt *will* **see** the land I
35:23 [A] or, without **seeing** him, drops a stone on him that could kill
Dt 1:8 [A] **See**, I have given you this land. Go in and take possession of
1:19 [A] through all that vast and dreadful desert that *you have* **seen**,
1:21 [A] **See**, the LORD your God has given you the land. Go up
1:28 [A] with walls up to the sky. *We* even **saw** the Anakites there.' "
1:31 [A] There *you* **saw** how the LORD your God carried you, as a
1:33 [G] for you to camp and to **show** you the way you should go.
1:35 [A] "Not a man of this evil generation *shall* **see** the good land I
1:36 [A] He *will* **see** it, and I will give him and his descendants the
2:24 [A] **See**, I have given into your hand Sihon the Amorite, king of
2:31 [A] The LORD said to me, "**See**, I have begun to deliver Sihon
3:21 [A] "You *have* **seen** *with* your own eyes all that the LORD
3:24 [G] you have begun to **show** *to* your servant your greatness and
3:25 [A] Let me go over and **see** the good land beyond the Jordan—
3:27 [A] **Look** at the land with your own eyes, since you are not going
3:28 [A] and will cause them to inherit the land that *you will* **see**."
4:3 [A] You **saw** with your own eyes what the LORD did at Baal
4:5 [A] **See**, I have taught you decrees and laws as the LORD my
4:9 [A] so that you do not forget the things your eyes *have* **seen**
4:12 [A] You heard the sound of words but **saw** no form; there was
4:15 [A] *You* **saw** no form of any kind the day the LORD spoke to
4:19 [A] look up to the sky and **see** the sun, the moon and the stars—
4:28 [A] of wood and stone, which cannot **see** or hear or eat or smell.
4:35 [H] You **were shown** these things so that you might know that
4:36 [G] On earth *he* **showed** you his great fire, and you heard his
5:24 [G] "The LORD our God *has* **shown** us his glory and his
5:24 [A] Today *we have* **seen** that a man can live even if God speaks
7:19 [A] *You* **saw** with your own eyes the great trials, the miraculous
9:13 [A] the LORD said to me, "*I have* **seen** this people, and they
9:16 [A] When *I* **looked**, I saw that you had sinned against the
10:21 [A] and awesome wonders you **saw** with your own eyes.
11:2 [A] today that your children *were* not *the ones* who **saw**
11:7 [A] it was your own eyes that **saw** all these great things the
11:26 [A] **See**, I am setting before you today a blessing and a curse—
12:13 [A] not to sacrifice your burnt offerings anywhere *you* **please**.
16:4 [C] *Let* no yeast **be found** in your possession in all your land for
16:16 [C] Three times a year all your men *must* **appear** before the
16:16 [C] No man *should* **appear** before the LORD empty-handed:
18:16 [A] "Let us not hear the voice of the LORD our God nor **see** this
20:1 [A] and **see** horses and chariots and an army greater than yours,
21:7 [A] hands did not shed this blood, nor *did* our eyes **see** it done.
21:11 [A] if *you* **notice** among the captives a beautiful woman and are
22:1 [A] If *you* **see** your brother's ox or sheep straying, do not ignore
22:4 [A] If *you* **see** your brother's donkey or his ox fallen on the road,
23:14 [23:15] [A] so that *he will* not **see** among you anything indecent
26:7 [A] heard our voice and **saw** our misery, toil and oppression.
28:10 [A] all the peoples on earth *will* **see** that you are called by the
28:32 [A] you will wear out your eyes **watching** for them day after day,
28:34 [A] The sights *you* **see** will drive you mad.
28:67 [A] that will fill your hearts and the sights that your eyes *will* **see**.
28:68 [A] **[NIE]** There you will offer yourselves for sale to your
29:2 [29:1] [A] Your eyes *have* **seen** all that the LORD did in Egypt
29:3 [29:2] [A] With your own eyes *you* **saw** those great trials, those
29:4 [29:3] [A] that understands or eyes that **see** or ears that hear.
29:17 [29:16] [A] *You* **saw** among them their detestable images and
29:22 [29:21] [A] *will* **see** the calamities that have fallen on the land and
30:15 [A] **See**, I set before you today life and prosperity, death
31:11 [C] when all Israel comes to **appear** before the LORD your
31:15 [C] Then the LORD **appeared** at the Tent in a pillar of cloud,
32:19 [A] The LORD **saw** this and rejected them because he was
32:20 [A] my face from them," he said, "and **see** what their end will be;
32:36 [A] have compassion on his servants when *he* **sees** their strength
32:39 [A] "**See** now that I myself am He! There is no god besides me.
32:49 [A] Mount Nebo in Moab, across from Jericho, and **view** Canaan,
32:52 [A] Therefore, *you will* **see** the land only from a distance; you
33:9 [A] said of his father and mother, '*I* **have** no **regard for** them.'
33:21 [A] *He* **chose** the best land for himself; the leader's portion was
34:1 [G] There the LORD **showed** him the whole land—from Gilead
34:4 [G] *I have* **let** you **see** it with your eyes, but you will not cross
Jos 2:1 [A] "Go, **look over** the land," he said, "especially Jericho."
3:3 [A] "When you **see** the ark of the covenant of the LORD your
5:6 [G] For the LORD had sworn to them that they *would* not **see**
5:13 [A] **saw** a man standing in front of him with a drawn sword in his
6:2 [A] the LORD said to Joshua, "**See**, I have delivered Jericho
7:21 [A] When *I* **saw** in the plunder a beautiful robe from Babylonia,
8:1 [A] For **[NIE]** I have delivered into your hands the king of Ai,
8:4 [A] with these orders: "**Listen carefully**. You are to set an
8:8 [A] the LORD has commanded. **See** *to* it; you have my orders."
8:14 [A] When the king of Ai **saw** this, he and all the men of the city
8:20 [A] The men of Ai **looked** back and saw the smoke of the city
8:21 [A] and all Israel **saw** that the ambush had taken the city
22:28 [A] **Look** *at* the replica of the LORD's altar, which our fathers
23:3 [A] *You* yourselves *have* **seen** everything the LORD your God
23:4 [A] **Remember** how I have allotted as an inheritance for your
24:7 [A] *You* **saw** with your own eyes what I did to the Egyptians.
Jdg 1:24 [A] the spies **saw** a man coming out of the city and they said to
1:24 [G] "**Show** us how to get into the city and we will see that you
1:25 [G] So *he* **showed** them, and they put the city to the sword
2:7 [A] who *had* **seen** all the great things the LORD had done for
3:24 [A] servants came and **found** the doors of the upper room locked.
4:22 [G] she said, "*I will* **show** you the man you're looking for."
5:8 [C] a shield or spear **was seen** among forty thousand in Israel.
6:12 [C] When the angel of the LORD **appeared** to Gideon, he said,
6:22 [A] When Gideon **realized** that it was the angel of the LORD,
6:22 [A] *I have* **seen** the angel of the LORD face to face!"
7:17 [A] "**Watch** me," he told them. "Follow my lead. When I get to
9:36 [A] When Gaal **saw** them, he said to Zebul, "Look, people are
9:36 [A] **mistake** [+906+3869] the shadows of the mountains **for**
9:43 [A] When *he* **saw** the people coming out of the city, he rose to
9:48 [A] the men with him, "Quick! Do what *you have* **seen** me do!"
9:55 [A] When the Israelites **saw** that Abimelech was dead, they went
11:35 [A] When he **saw** her, he tore his clothes and cried, "Oh!
12:3 [A] When *I* **saw** that you wouldn't help, I took my life in my
13:3 [C] The angel of the LORD **appeared** to her and said, "You are
13:10 [C] "He's here! The man who **appeared** to me the other day!"
13:19 [A] did an amazing thing while Manoah and his wife **watched**:
13:20 [A] **Seeing** this, Manoah and his wife fell with their faces to the
13:21 [C] When the angel of the LORD did not **show himself** again to
13:22 [A] doomed to die!" he said to his wife. "*We have* **seen** God!"
13:23 [G] our hands, nor **shown** us all these things or now told us this."
14:1 [A] down to Timnah and **saw** there a young Philistine woman.
14:2 [A] and mother, "*I have* **seen** a Philistine woman in Timnah;
14:8 [A] to marry her, he turned aside to **look** *at* the lion's carcass.
14:11 [A] When he **appeared**, he was given thirty companions.
16:1 [A] One day Samson went to Gaza, where *he* **saw** a prostitute.
16:5 [A] "See if you can lure him into **showing** *you* the secret of his
16:18 [A] When Delilah **saw** that he had told her everything, she sent
16:24 [A] When the people **saw** him, they praised their god, saying,
16:27 [A] three thousand men and women **watching** Samson perform.
18:7 [A] where *they* **saw** that the people were living in safety, like the
18:9 [A] let's attack them! *We have* **seen** that the land is very good.
18:26 [A] Micah, **seeing** that they were too strong for him, turned
19:3 [A] and when her father **saw** him, he gladly welcomed him.
19:17 [A] When he looked and **saw** the traveler in the city square,
19:30 [A] Everyone who **saw** it said, "Such a thing has never been seen
19:30 [C] who saw it said, "Such a thing *has* never **been seen** or done,
20:36 [A] the Benjamites **saw** that they were beaten. Now the men of
20:41 [A] because *they* **realized** that disaster had come upon them.
21:21 [A] **watch**. When the girls of Shiloh come out to join in the
Ru 1:18 [A] When Naomi **realized** that Ruth was determined to go with
2:18 [A] and her mother-in-law **saw** how much she had gathered.
1Sa 1:11 [A] if *you will* **only look** [+8011] upon your servant's misery
1:11 [A] if *you will* **only look** [+8011] upon your servant's misery
1:22 [C] I will take him and **present** him before the LORD,
3:2 [A] whose eyes were becoming so weak that he could barely **see**,
3:21 [C] The LORD continued to **appear** at Shiloh, and there he
4:15 [A] years old and whose eyes were set so that he could not **see**.
5:7 [A] When the men of Ashdod **saw** what was happening, they
6:9 [A] *keep* **watching** it. If it goes up to its own territory,
6:13 [A] when they looked up and **saw** the ark, they rejoiced at the
6:13 [A] they looked up and saw the ark, they rejoiced at the **sight**.
6:16 [A] The five rulers of the Philistines **saw** all this and
6:19 [A] because *they had* **looked** into the ark of the LORD.
9:16 [A] *I have* **looked** *upon* my people, for their cry has reached
9:17 [A] When Samuel **caught sight of** Saul, the LORD said to him,
10:11 [A] When all those who had formerly known him **saw** him
10:14 [A] "But when *we* **saw** they were not to be found, we went to
10:24 [A] all the people, "*Do you* **see** the man the LORD has chosen?
12:12 [A] "But when *you* **saw** that Nahash king of the Ammonites was
12:16 [A] **see** this great thing the LORD is about to do before your
12:17 [A] *you will* **realize** [+2256+3359] what an evil thing you did in
12:24 [A] your heart; **consider** what great things he has done for you.
13:6 [A] When the men of Israel **saw** that their situation was critical
13:11 [A] Saul replied, "When *I* **saw** that the men were scattering, and
14:16 [A] Saul's lookouts at Gibeah in Benjamin **saw** the army melting
14:17 [A] were with him, "Muster the forces and **see** who has left us."
14:27 [a] [his hand to his mouth, and his eyes **brightened**. [K; see Q 239]]
14:29 [A] **See** how my eyes brightened when I tasted a little of this
14:38 [A] *let us* **find out** [+2256+3359] what sin has been committed
14:52 [A] whenever Saul **saw** a mighty or brave man, he took him into
15:35 [A] Until the day Samuel died, *he did* not go to **see** Saul again,
16:1 [A] of Bethlehem. *I have* **chosen** one of his sons to be king."

1Sa 16: 6 [A] When they arrived, Samuel **saw** Eliab and thought,
16: 7 [A] The LORD does not look at the things man **looks** *at*.
16: 7 [A] Man **looks** at the outward appearance, but the LORD looks
16: 7 [A] the outward appearance, but the LORD **looks** at the heart."
16:17 [A] "**Find** someone who plays well and bring him to me."
16:18 [A] "*I have* **seen** a son of Jesse of Bethlehem who knows how to
17:24 [A] When the Israelites **saw** the man, they all ran from him in
17:25 [A] been saying, "*Do you* **see** how this man keeps coming out?
17:28 [A] your heart is; you came down only to **watch** the battle."
17:42 [A] He looked David over and **saw** that he was only a boy, ruddy
17:51 [A] When the Philistines **saw** that their hero was dead, they
17:55 [A] As Saul **watched** David going out to meet the Philistine,
18:15 [A] When Saul **saw** how successful he was, he was afraid of him.
18:28 [A] When Saul **realized** [+2256+3359] that the LORD was with
19: 3 [A] speak to him about you and will tell you what *I* **find out**."
19: 5 [A] a great victory for all Israel, and *you* **saw** it and were glad.
19:15 [A] Saul sent the men back to **see** David and told them,
19:20 [A] when *they* **saw** a group of prophets prophesying,
20:29 [A] favor in your eyes, let me get away *to* **see** my brothers.'
21:14 [21:15] [A] Achish said to his servants, "**Look** *at* the man! He is
22: 9 [A] "*I* **saw** the son of Jesse come to Ahimelech son of Ahitub at
23:15 [A] of Ziph, he **learned** that Saul had come out to take his life.
23:22 [A] **Find out** [+906+2256+3359] where David usually goes and
23:22 [A] out where David usually goes and who *has* **seen** him there.
23:23 [A] **Find** [+2256+3359] **out** about all the hiding places he uses
24:10 [24:11] [A] This day *you have* **seen** with your own eyes how
24:11 [24:12] [A] **See**, my father, look at this piece of your robe in my
24:11 [24:12] [A] **look** *at* this piece of your robe in my hand!
24:11 [24:12] [A] **recognize** that I am not guilty of wrongdoing
24:15 [24:16] [A] *May he* **consider** my cause and uphold it; may he
25:17 [A] Now think it over and **see** what you can do, because disaster
25:23 [A] When Abigail **saw** David, she quickly got off her donkey
25:25 [A] for me, your servant, *I did* not **see** the men my master sent.
25:35 [A] **[NIE]** I have heard your words and granted your request."
26: 3 [A] in the desert. When *he* **saw** that Saul had followed him there,
26: 5 [A] He **saw** where Saul and Abner son of Ner, the commander of
26:12 [A] No *one* **saw** or knew about it, nor did anyone wake up.
26:16 [A] your master, the LORD's anointed. **Look around** you.
28: 5 [A] When Saul **saw** the Philistine army, he was afraid; terror
28:12 [A] When the woman **saw** Samuel, she cried out at the top of her
28:13 [A] The king said to her, "Don't be afraid. What *do you* **see**?"
28:13 [A] woman said, "*I* **see** a spirit coming up out of the ground."
28:21 [A] the woman came to Saul and **saw** that he was greatly shaken,
31: 5 [A] When the armor-bearer **saw** that Saul was dead, he too fell
31: 7 [A] those across the Jordan **saw** that the Israelite army had fled
2Sa 1: 7 [A] When he turned around and **saw** me, he called out to me,
3:13 [A] thing of you: *Do* not **come into** my **presence** [+906+7156]
3:13 [A] bring Michal daughter of Saul when you come to **see** me."
6:16 [A] when *she* **saw** King David leaping and dancing before the
7: 2 [A] Nathan the prophet, "**Here** I am, living in a palace of cedar,
10: 6 [A] When the Ammonites **realized** that they had become a stench
10: 9 [A] Joab **saw** that there were battle lines in front of him and
10:14 [A] When the Ammonites **saw** that the Arameans were fleeing,
10:15 [A] After the Arameans **saw** that they had been routed by Israel,
10:19 [A] When all the kings who were vassals of Hadadezer **saw** that
11: 2 [A] From the roof *he* **saw** a woman bathing. The woman was
12:19 [A] David **noticed** that his servants were whispering among
13: 5 [A] "When your father comes to **see** you, say to him, 'I would
13: 5 [A] so *I may* **watch** her and then eat it from her hand.' "
13: 6 [A] When the king came to **see** him, Amnon said to him,
13:28 [A] Absalom ordered his men, "**Listen**! When Amnon is in high
13:34 [A] looked up and **saw** many people on the road west of him,
13:34 [a] the king, "*I* **see** [BHS-] men in the direction of Horonaim,
14:24 [A] "He must go to his own house; *he must* not **see** my face."
14:24 [A] went to his own house and *did* not **see** the face of the king.
14:28 [A] Absalom lived two years in Jerusalem without **seeing** the
14:30 [A] "**Look**, Joab's field is next to mine, and he has barley there.
14:32 [A] *I want to* **see** the king's face, and if I am guilty of anything,
15: 3 [A] would say to him, "**Look**, your claims are valid and proper,
15:25 [G] bring me back and **let** me **see** it and his dwelling place again.
15:28 [A] **[NIE]** I will wait at the fords in the desert until word comes
16:12 [A] It may be that the LORD *will* **see** my distress and repay me
17:17 [C] for they could not risk **being seen** entering the city.
17:18 [A] a young man **saw** them and told Absalom. So the two of
17:23 [A] When Ahithophel **saw** that his advice had not been followed,
18:10 [A] When one of the men **saw** this, he told Joab, "I just saw
18:10 [A] he told Joab, "*I* just **saw** Absalom hanging in an oak tree."
18:11 [A] said to the man who had told him this, "What! *You* **saw** him?
18:21 [A] said to a Cushite, "Go, tell the king what *you have* **seen**."
18:24 [A] by the wall. As he looked out, *he* **saw** a man running alone.
18:26 [A] the watchman **saw** another man running, and he called down
18:27 [A] "*It* **seems** *to* me that the first one runs like Ahimaaz son of
18:29 [A] "*I* **saw** great confusion just as Joab was about to send the
20:12 [A] and the man **saw** that all the troops came to a halt there.
20:12 [A] When *he* **realized** that everyone who came up to Amasa
22:11 [c] *he* soared [BHS *appeared*; NIV 1797] on the wings of the wind.
22:16 [C] The valleys of the sea **were exposed** and the foundations of
24: 3 [A] times over, and *may* the eyes of my lord the king **see** it.
24:13 [A] and **decide** how I should answer the one who sent me."
24:17 [A] When David **saw** the angel who was striking down the
24:20 [A] and **saw** the king and his men coming toward him,
24:22 [A] **Here** are oxen for the burnt offering, and here are threshing
1Ki 1:48 [A] who has allowed my eyes *to* **see** a successor on my throne
3: 5 [C] At Gibeon the LORD **appeared** to Solomon during the
3:28 [A] because *they* **saw** that he had wisdom from God to
6:18 [C] Everything was cedar; no stone *was to* **be seen**.
8: 8 [C] so long that their ends *could* **be seen** from the Holy Place in
8: 8 [C] inner sanctuary, but not **[RPH]** from outside the Holy Place;
9: 2 [C] the LORD **appeared** to him a second time, as he had
9: 2 [C] to him a second time, as *he had* **appeared** to him at Gibeon.
9:12 [A] when Hiram went from Tyre to **see** the towns that Solomon
10: 4 [A] When the queen of Sheba **saw** all the wisdom of Solomon
10: 7 [A] believe these things until I came and **saw** *with* my own eyes.
10:12 [C] almugwood has never been imported or **seen** since that day.)
11: 9 [C] the God of Israel, who *had* **appeared** to him twice.
11:28 [A] when Solomon **saw** how well the young man did his work,
12:16 [A] When all Israel **saw** that the king refused to listen to them,
12:16 [A] your tents, O Israel! **Look after** your own house, O David!"
13:12 [G] his sons **showed** him which road the man of God from Judah
13:25 [A] people who passed by **saw** the body thrown down there, with
14: 4 [A] Now Ahijah could not **see**; his sight was gone because of his
16:18 [A] When Zimri **saw** that the city was taken, he went into the
17:23 [A] He gave him to his mother and said, "**Look**, your son is
18: 1 [C] "Go and **present yourself** to Ahab, and I will send rain on
18: 2 [C] So Elijah went to **present himself** to Ahab. Now the famine
18:15 [C] whom I serve, *I will* surely **present myself** to Ahab today."
18:17 [A] When he **saw** Elijah, he said to him, "Is that you,
18:39 [A] When all the people **saw** this, they fell prostrate and cried,
19: 3 [a] Elijah *was* afraid [BHS *saw*; NIV 3707] and ran for his life.
20: 7 [A] "**See** [+2256+3359] how this man is looking for trouble!
20:13 [A] "This is what the LORD says: '*Do you* **see** this vast army?
20:22 [A] your position and **see** [+906+2256+3359] what must be done,
21:29 [A] "*Have you* **noticed** how Ahab has humbled himself before
22:17 [A] "*I* **saw** all Israel scattered on the hills like sheep without a
22:19 [A] *I* **saw** the LORD sitting on his throne with all the host of
22:25 [A] "You *will* **find out** on the day you go to hide in an inner
22:32 [A] When the chariot commanders **saw** Jehoshaphat, they
22:33 [A] the chariot commanders **saw** that he was not the king of
2Ki 2:10 [A] Elijah said, "yet if *you* **see** me when I am taken from you,
2:12 [A] Elisha **saw** this and cried out, "My father! My father!
2:12 [A] and horsemen of Israel!" And Elisha **saw** him no more.
2:15 [A] who *were* **watching**, said, "The spirit of Elijah is resting on
2:19 [A] as you *can* **see**, but the water is bad and the land is
2:24 [A] **looked** *at* them and called down a curse on them in the name
3:14 [A] king of Judah, I would not look at you or even **notice** you.
3:17 [A] *You will* **see** neither wind nor rain, yet this valley will be
3:17 [A] You will see neither wind nor **[RPH]** rain, yet this valley
3:22 [A] To the Moabites across the way, the water **looked** red—
3:26 [A] When the king of Moab **saw** that the battle had gone against
4:25 [A] When he **saw** her in the distance, the man of God said to his
5: 7 [A] someone to me to be cured of his leprosy? **See** [+2256+3359]
5:21 [A] When Naaman **saw** him running toward him, he got down
6: 6 [G] When *he* **showed** him the place, Elisha cut a stick and threw
6:13 [A] "Go, **find out** where he is," the king ordered, "so I can send
6:17 [A] Elisha prayed, "O LORD, open his eyes so *he may* **see**."
6:17 [A] *he* **looked** and saw the hills full of horses and chariots of fire
6:20 [A] "LORD, open the eyes of these men so *they can* **see**."
6:20 [A] the LORD opened their eyes and *they* **looked**, and there
6:21 [A] When the king of Israel **saw** them, he asked Elisha, "Shall I
6:30 [A] along the wall, the people **looked**, and there, underneath,
6:32 [A] "Don't *you* **see** how this murderer is sending someone to cut
6:32 [A] **Look**, when the messenger comes, shut the door and hold it
7: 2 [A] "You *will* **see** it with your own eyes," answered Elisha,
7:13 [A] are doomed. So let us send them *to* **find out** what happened."
7:14 [A] the drivers, "Go and **find out** what has happened."
7:19 [A] man of God had replied, "You *will* **see** it with your own eyes,
8:10 [G] but the LORD *has* **revealed** *to* me that he will in fact die."
8:13 [G] "The LORD *has* **shown** me that you will become king of
8:29 [A] of Judah went down to Jezreel to **see** Joram son of Ahab,
9: 2 [A] **look for** Jehu son of Jehoshaphat, the son of Nimshi.
9:16 [A] and Ahaziah king of Judah had gone down to **see** him.
9:17 [A] When the lookout standing on the tower in Jezreel **saw**
9:17 [A] he called out, "I **see** some troops coming."
9:22 [A] When Joram **saw** Jehu he asked, "Have you come in peace,
9:26 [A] 'Yesterday *I* **saw** the blood of Naboth and the blood of his
9:27 [A] When Ahaziah king of Judah **saw** what had happened, he
10: 3 [A] **choose** the best and most worthy of your master's sons
10:16 [A] Jehu said, "Come with me and **see** my zeal for the LORD."

2Ki 10:23 [A] and **see** that no servants of the LORD are here with you—
11: 1 [A] When Athaliah the mother of Ahaziah **saw** that her son was
11: 4 [G] temple of the LORD. Then *he* **showed** them the king's son.
11:14 [A] *She* **looked** and there was the king, standing by the pillar,
12:10 [12:11] [A] Whenever they **saw** that there was a large amount of
13: 4 [A] for *he* **saw** how severely the king of Aram was oppressing
13:21 [A] were burying a man, suddenly *they* **saw** a band of raiders;
14: 8 [F] of Israel, with the challenge: "Come, **meet** *me* face to face."
14:11 [F] Amaziah king of Judah **faced each other** [+7156] at Beth
14:26 [A] The LORD *had* **seen** how bitterly everyone in Israel,
16:10 [A] *He* **saw** an altar in Damascus and sent to Uriah the priest a
16:12 [A] When the king came back from Damascus and **saw** the altar,
19:16 [A] O LORD, and hear; open your eyes, O LORD, and **see**;
20: 5 [A] I have heard your prayer and **seen** your tears; I will heal you.
20:13 [G] and **showed** them all that was in his storehouses—
20:13 [G] or in all his kingdom that Hezekiah *did* not **show** them.
20:15 [A] The prophet asked, "What *did they* **see** in your palace?"
20:15 [A] "*They* **saw** everything in my palace," Hezekiah said.
20:15 [G] "There is nothing among my treasures that *I did* not **show**
22:20 [A] Your eyes *will* not **see** all the disaster I am going to bring on
23:16 [A] and when *he* **saw** the tombs that were there on the hillside,
23:17 [A] The king asked, "What is that tombstone I **see**?" The men of
23:24 [C] the idols and all the other detestable things **seen** in Judah
23:29 [A] him in battle, but Neco **faced** him and killed him at Megiddo.
25:19 [A] charge of the fighting men and five royal **advisers** [+7156].
1Ch 10: 5 [A] When the armor-bearer **saw** that Saul was dead, he too fell
10: 7 [A] When all the Israelites in the valley **saw** that the army had
12:17 [12:18] [A] *may* the God of our fathers **see** it and judge you."
15:29 [A] when *she* **saw** King David dancing and celebrating, she
17:17 [A] *You have* **looked** *on* me as though I were the most exalted of
19: 6 [A] When the Ammonites **realized** that they had become a stench
19:10 [A] Joab **saw** that there were battle lines in front of him
19:15 [A] When the Ammonites **saw** that the Arameans were fleeing,
19:16 [A] After the Arameans **saw** that they had been routed by Israel,
19:19 [A] When the vassals of Hadadezer **saw** that they had been
21:12 [A] **decide** how I should answer the one who sent me."
21:15 [A] the LORD **saw** it and was grieved because of the calamity
21:16 [A] and **saw** the angel of the LORD standing between heaven
21:20 [A] Araunah was threshing wheat, he turned and **saw** the angel;
21:21 [A] David approached, and when Araunah looked and **saw** him,
21:23 [A] **Look**, I will give the oxen for the burnt offerings,
21:28 [A] when David **saw** that the LORD had answered him on the
28:10 [A] **Consider** now, for the LORD has chosen you to build a
29:17 [A] now *I have* **seen** with joy how willingly your people who are
2Ch 1: 7 [C] That night God **appeared** to Solomon and said to him,
3: 1 [C] where the LORD *had* **appeared** to his father David.
5: 9 [C] the ark, *could* **be seen** *from* in front of the inner sanctuary,
5: 9 [C] inner sanctuary, but not **[RPH]** from outside the Holy Place;
7: 3 [A] When all the Israelites **saw** the fire coming down
7:12 [C] the LORD **appeared** to him at night and said: "I have heard
9: 3 [A] When the queen of Sheba **saw** the wisdom of Solomon,
9: 6 [A] what they said until I came and **saw** *with* my own eyes.
9:11 [C] Nothing like them *had* ever **been seen** in Judah.)
10:16 [a] When all Israel **saw** [BHS-] that the king refused to listen to
10:16 [A] your tents, O Israel! **Look after** your own house, O David!"
12: 7 [A] When the LORD **saw** that they humbled themselves,
15: 9 [A] Israel when they **saw** that the LORD his God was with him.
18:16 [A] "*I* **saw** all Israel scattered on the hills like sheep without a
18:18 [A] *I* **saw** the LORD sitting on his throne with all the host of
18:24 [A] "You *will* **find out** on the day you go to hide in an inner
18:31 [A] When the chariot commanders **saw** Jehoshaphat, they
18:32 [A] for when the chariot commanders **saw** that he was not the
19: 6 [A] He told them, "**Consider carefully** what you do, because you
20:17 [A] stand firm and **see** the deliverance the LORD will give you,
22: 6 [A] king of Judah went down to Jezreel to **see** Joram son of Ahab
22:10 [A] When Athaliah the mother of Ahaziah **saw** that her son was
23:13 [A] *She* **looked**, and there was the king, standing by his pillar at
24:11 [A] and they **saw** that there was a large amount of money,
24:22 [A] "*May* the LORD **see** this and call you to account."
25:17 [F] the son of Jehu, king of Israel: "Come, **meet** *me* face to face."
25:21 [F] Amaziah king of Judah **faced each other** [+7156] at Beth
26: 5 [a] who instructed him in the fear [BHS *visions*; NIV 3711] *of* God.
29: 8 [A] and horror and scorn, as you *can* **see** with your own eyes.
30: 7 [A] so that he made them an object of horror, as you **see**.
31: 8 [A] When Hezekiah and his officials came and **saw** the heaps,
32: 2 [A] When Hezekiah **saw** that Sennacherib had come and that he
34:28 [A] Your eyes *will* not **see** all the disaster I am going to bring on
Ezr 3:12 [A] and family heads, who *had* **seen** the former temple,
Ne 2:17 [A] I said to them, "You **see** the trouble we are in: Jerusalem lies
4:11 [4:5] [A] Also our enemies said, "Before they know it or **see** us,
4:14 [4:8] [A] After *I* **looked things over**, I stood up and said to the
9: 9 [A] "*You* **saw** the suffering of our forefathers in Egypt; you
13:15 [A] In those days *I* **saw** men in Judah treading winepresses on the
13:23 [A] in those days *I* **saw** men of Judah who had married women
Est 1: 4 [G] 180 days he **displayed** the vast wealth of his kingdom and
1:11 [G] in order to **display** her beauty to the people and nobles,
1:14 [A] and Media *who* **had special access** [+7156] **to** the king
2: 9 [B] He assigned to her seven maids **selected** from the king's
2:15 [A] And Esther won the favor of everyone *who* **saw** her.
3: 4 [A] Therefore they told Haman about it to **see** whether
3: 5 [A] When Haman **saw** that Mordecai would not kneel down
4: 8 [G] published in Susa, to **show** *to* Esther and explain it to her,
5: 2 [A] When he **saw** Queen Esther standing in the court, he was
5: 9 [A] when he **saw** Mordecai at the king's gate and observed that
5:13 [A] all this gives me no satisfaction as long as I **see** that Jew
7: 7 [A] **realizing** that the king had already decided his fate,
8: 6 [A] For how can I bear *to* **see** disaster fall on my people? How
8: 6 [A] How can I bear *to* **see** the destruction of my family?"
9:26 [A] because of what *they had* **seen** and what had happened to
Job 2:13 [A] word to him, because *they* **saw** how great his suffering was.
3: 9 [A] it wait for daylight in vain and not **see** the first rays of dawn,
3:16 [A] stillborn child, like an infant *who* never **saw** the light of day?
4: 8 [A] As *I have* **observed**, those who plow evil and those who sow
5: 3 [A] *I* myself *have* **seen** a fool taking root, but suddenly his house
6:21 [A] to be of no help; *you* **see** something dreadful and are afraid.
7: 7 [A] life is but a breath; my eyes *will* never **see** happiness again.
7: 8 [A] The eye *that now* **sees** me will see me no longer; you will
8:18 [A] its spot, that place disowns it and says, '*I* never **saw** you.'
9:11 [A] When he passes me, *I* cannot **see** him; when he goes by, I
9:25 [A] swifter than a runner; they fly away without a **glimpse** *of* joy.
10: 4 [A] Do you have eyes of flesh? *Do you* **see** as a mortal sees?
10: 4 [A] Do you have eyes of flesh? Do you see as a mortal **sees**?
10:18 [A] out of the womb? I wish I had died before any eye **saw** me.
11:11 [A] deceitful men; and when *he* **sees** evil, does he not take note?
13: 1 [A] "My eyes *have* **seen** all this, my ears have heard
19:27 [A] I myself will see him **[RPH]** with my own eyes—I, and not
20: 7 [A] own dung; *those who have* **seen** him will say, 'Where is he?'
20:17 [A] *He will* not **enjoy** the streams, the rivers flowing with honey
21:20 [A] *Let* his own eyes **see** his destruction; let him drink of the
22:11 [A] why it is so dark *you* cannot **see**, and why a flood of water
22:12 [A] heights of heaven? And **see** how lofty are the highest stars!
22:14 [A] so *he does* not **see** us as he goes about in the vaulted
22:19 [A] "The righteous **see** their ruin and rejoice; the innocent mock
23: 9 [A] when he turns to the south, *I* **catch** no **glimpse** of him.
28:10 [A] He tunnels through the rock; his eyes **see** all its treasures.
28:24 [A] the ends of the earth and **sees** everything under the heavens.
28:27 [A] then *he* **looked** *at* wisdom and appraised it; he confirmed it
29: 8 [A] the young men **saw** me and stepped aside and the old men
29:11 [A] spoke well of me, and those *who* **saw** me commended me,
31: 4 [A] *Does* he not **see** my ways and count my every step?
31:19 [A] if *I have* **seen** anyone perishing for lack of clothing, or a
31:21 [A] against the fatherless, **knowing** that I had influence in court,
31:26 [A] if *I have* **regarded** the sun in its radiance or the moon
32: 5 [A] But when he **saw** that the three men had nothing more to say,
33:21 [E] and his bones, *once* **hidden** [+4202], now stick out.
33:26 [A] finds favor with him, *he* **sees** God's face and shouts for joy;
33:28 [A] from going down to the pit, and I will live *to* **enjoy** the light.'
34:21 [A] "His eyes are on the ways of men; *he* **sees** their every step.
34:26 [A] them for their wickedness where *everyone can* **see** them,
35: 5 [A] Look up at the heavens and **see**; gaze at the clouds so high
37:21 [A] Now no *one can* **look** *at* the sun, bright as it is in the skies
37:24 [A] for *does he* not **have regard for** all the wise in heart?"
38:17 [A] to you? *Have you* **seen** the gates of the shadow of death?
38:22 [A] storehouses of the snow or **seen** the storehouses of the hail,
40:11 [A] of your wrath, **look** *at* every proud man and bring him low,
40:12 [A] **look** *at* every proud man and humble him, crush the wicked
41:34 [41:26] [A] *He* **looks down on** all that are haughty; he is king
42: 5 [A] My ears had heard of you but now my eyes *have* **seen** you.
42:16 [A] *he* **saw** his children and their children to the fourth
Ps 4: 6 [4:7] [G] Many are asking, "Who *can* **show** us any good?"
8: 3 [8:4] [A] When *I* **consider** your heavens, the work of your
9:13 [9:14] [A] O LORD, **see** how my enemies persecute me!
10:11 [A] "God has forgotten; he covers his face and never **sees**."
10:14 [A] you, O God, *do* **see** trouble and grief; you consider it to take
14: 2 [A] on the sons of men to **see** if there are any who understand,
16:10 [A] me to the grave, nor will you let your Holy One **see** decay.
18:15 [18:16] [C] The valleys of the sea **were exposed**
22: 7 [22:8] [A] All *who* **see** me mock me; they hurl insults,
22:17 [22:18] [A] count all my bones; people stare and **gloat** over me.
25:18 [A] **Look** *upon* my affliction and my distress and take away all
25:19 [A] **See** how my enemies have increased and how fiercely they
27:13 [A] I *will* **see** the goodness of the LORD in the land of the
31: 7 [31:8] [A] for *you* **saw** my affliction and knew the anguish of
31:11 [31:12] [A] *those who* **see** me on the street flee from me.
33:13 [A] From heaven the LORD looks down and **sees** all mankind;
34: 8 [34:9] [A] Taste and **see** that the LORD is good; blessed is the
34:12 [34:13] [A] of you loves life and desires to **see** many good days,
35:17 [A] O Lord, how long *will you* **look** *on*? Rescue my life from

Ps 35:21 [A] and say, "Aha! Aha! *With* our own eyes *we have* **seen** it."
35:22 [A] O LORD, *you have* **seen** this; be not silent. Do not be far
36: 9 [36:10] [A] you is the fountain of life; in your light *we* **see** light.
37:13 [A] Lord laughs at the wicked, for *he* **knows** their day is coming.
37:25 [A] yet *I have* never **seen** the righteous forsaken or their children
37:34 [A] inherit the land; when the wicked are cut off, *you will* **see** it.
37:35 [A] *I have* **seen** a wicked and ruthless man flourishing like a
37:37 [A] Consider the blameless, **observe** the upright; there is a future
40: 3 [40:4] [A] *will* **see** and fear and put their trust in the LORD.
40:12 [40:13] [A] my sins have overtaken me, and I cannot **see**.
41: 6 [41:7] [A] Whenever one comes to **see** me, he speaks falsely,
42: 2 [42:3] [C] When can I go and **meet** [+7156] **with** God?
45:10 [45:11] [A] Listen, O daughter, **consider** and give ear: Forget
48: 5 [48:6] [A] they **saw** ⌞her⌟ and were astounded; they fled in
48: 8 [48:9] [A] so *have we* **seen** in the city of the LORD Almighty,
49: 9 [49:10] [A] that he should live on forever and not **see** decay.
49:10 [49:11] [A] For *all can* **see** that wise men die; the foolish
49:19 [49:20] [A] of his fathers, *who will* never **see** the light ⌞of life⌟.
50:18 [A] When *you* **see** a thief, you join with him; you throw in your
50:23 [G] the way so that *I may* **show** him the salvation of God."
52: 6 [52:8] [A] The righteous *will* **see** and fear; they will laugh at
53: 2 [53:3] [A] sons of men to **see** if there are any who understand,
54: 7 [54:9] [A] and my eyes *have* **looked** in triumph on my foes.
55: 9 [55:10] [A] their speech, for *I* **see** violence and strife in the city.
59: 4 [59:5] [A] to attack me. Arise to help me; **look** *on* my plight!
59:10 [59:11] [G] and *will* **let** me **gloat** over those who slander me.
60: 3 [60:5] [G] *You have* **shown** your people desperate times;
63: 2 [63:3] [A] the sanctuary and **beheld** your power and your glory.
64: 5 [64:6] [A] hiding their snares; they say, "Who *will* **see** them?"
64: 8 [64:9] [A] all *who* **see** them will shake their heads in scorn.
66: 5 [A] Come and **see** what God has done, how awesome his works
66:18 [A] If *I had* **cherished** sin in my heart, the Lord would not have
68:24 [68:25] [A] Your procession *has* **come into view**, O God,
69:23 [69:24] [A] May their eyes be darkened so they cannot **see**,
69:32 [69:33] [A] The poor *will* **see** and be glad—you who seek God,
71:20 [G] Though *you have* **made** me **see** troubles, many and bitter,
73: 3 [A] For I envied the arrogant *when I* **saw** the prosperity of the
74: 9 [A] *We* **are given** no miraculous signs; no prophets are left,
77:16 [77:17] [A] The waters **saw** you, O God, the waters saw you
77:16 [77:17] [A] saw you, O God, the waters **saw** you and writhed;
78:11 [G] forgot what he had done, the wonders *he had* **shown** them.
80:14 [80:15] [A] O God Almighty! Look down from heaven and **see**!
84: 7 [84:8] [C] to strength, till *each* **appears** before God in Zion.
84: 9 [84:10] [A] **Look** *upon* our shield, O God; look with favor on
85: 7 [85:8] [G] **Show** us your unfailing love, O LORD, and grant us
86:17 [A] that my enemies *may* **see** it and be put to shame, for you,
89:48 [89:49] [A] What man can live and not **see** death, or save
90:15 [A] have afflicted us, for as many years as *we have* **seen** trouble.
90:16 [C] *May* your deeds **be shown** to your servants, your splendor to
91: 8 [A] with your eyes and **see** the punishment of the wicked.
91:16 [G] With long life will I satisfy him and **show** him my salvation."
94: 7 [A] They say, "The LORD *does* not **see**; the God of Jacob pays
95: 9 [A] fathers tested and tried me, though *they had* **seen** what I did.
97: 4 [A] His lightning lights up the world; the earth **sees** and trembles.
97: 6 [A] proclaim his righteousness, and all the peoples **see** his glory.
98: 3 [A] all the ends of the earth *have* **seen** the salvation of our God.
102:16 [102:17] [C] LORD will rebuild Zion and **appear** in his glory.
106: 5 [A] that I *may* **enjoy** the prosperity of your chosen ones, that I
106:44 [A] But *he* **took note** of their distress when he heard their cry;
107:24 [A] They **saw** the works of the LORD, his wonderful deeds in
107:42 [A] The upright **see** and rejoice, but all the wicked shut their
109:25 [A] to my accusers; *when they* **see** me, they shake their heads.
112: 8 [A] have no fear; in the end *he will* **look** in triumph on his foes.
112:10 [A] The wicked man *will* **see** and be vexed, he will gnash his
113: 6 [A] who stoops down to **look** on the heavens and the earth?
114: 3 [A] The sea **looked** and fled, the Jordan turned back;
115: 5 [A] have mouths, but cannot speak, eyes, but *they* cannot **see**;
118: 7 [A] he is my helper. I *will* **look** in triumph on my enemies.
119:37 [A] Turn my eyes away from **[NIE]** worthless things;
119:74 [A] May those who fear you rejoice *when they* **see** me, for I have
119:96 [A] To all perfection *I* **see** a limit; but your commands are
119:153 [A] **Look** *upon* my suffering and deliver me, for I have not
119:158 [A] *I* **look** *on* the faithless with loathing, for they do not obey
119:159 [A] **See** how I love your precepts; preserve my life, O LORD,
128: 5 [A] days of your life; *may you* **see** the prosperity of Jerusalem,
128: 6 [A] *may you* live to **see** your children's children. Peace be upon
135:16 [A] have mouths, but cannot speak, eyes, but *they* cannot **see**;
138: 6 [A] Though the LORD is on high, *he* **looks** *upon* the lowly,
139:16 [A] your eyes **saw** my unformed body. All the days ordained for
139:24 [A] **See** if there is any offensive way in me, and lead me in the
142: 4 [142:5] [A] Look to my right and **see**; no one is concerned for
Pr 6: 6 [A] Go to the ant, you sluggard; **consider** its ways and be wise!
7: 7 [A] *I* **saw** among the simple, I noticed among the young men,
20:12 [A] Ears that hear and eyes *that* **see**—the LORD has made them
22: 3 [A] A prudent man **sees** danger and takes refuge, but the simple
23:31 [A] *Do* not **gaze** *at* wine when it is red, when it sparkles in the
23:33 [A] Your eyes *will* **see** strange *sights* and your mind imagine
24:18 [A] or the LORD *will* **see** and disapprove and turn his wrath
24:32 [A] to what I observed and learned a lesson from what *I* **saw**:
25: 7 [A] you before a nobleman. What *you have* **seen** *with* your eyes
26:12 [A] *Do you* **see** a man wise in his own eyes? There is more hope
27:12 [A] The prudent **see** danger and take refuge, but the simple keep
27:25 [C] When the hay is removed and new growth **appears**
29:16 [A] so does sin, but the righteous *will* **see** their downfall.
Ecc 1: 8 [A] The eye never has enough of **seeing**, nor the ear its fill of
1:10 [A] Is there anything of which one can say, "**Look**! This is
1:14 [A] *I have* **seen** all the things that are done under the sun; all of
1:16 [A] I *have* **experienced** much of wisdom and knowledge."
2: 1 [A] I will test you with pleasure *to* **find out** what is good."
2: 3 [A] *I wanted to* **see** what was worthwhile for men to do under
2:12 [A] I turned my thoughts to **consider** wisdom, and also madness
2:13 [A] I **saw** that wisdom is better than folly, just as light is better
2:24 [G] better than to eat and drink and **find** satisfaction in his work.
2:24 [A] in his work. This too, I **see**, is from the hand of God,
3:10 [A] *I have* **seen** the burden God has laid on men.
3:13 [A] may eat and drink, and **find** satisfaction in all his toil—
3:16 [A] *I* **saw** something else under the sun: In the place of
3:18 [A] tests them so that they *may* **see** that they are like the animals.
3:22 [A] So *I* **saw** that there is nothing better for a man than to enjoy
3:22 [A] For who can bring him to **see** what will happen after him?
4: 1 [A] **saw** all the oppression that was taking place under the sun:
4: 3 [A] who *has* not **seen** the evil that is done under the sun.
4: 4 [A] I **saw** that all labor and all achievement spring from man's
4: 7 [A] Again I **saw** something meaningless under the sun:
4:15 [A] *I* **saw** that all who lived and walked under the sun followed
5: 8 [5:7] [A] If *you* **see** the poor oppressed in a district, and justice
5:13 [5:12] [A] *I have* **seen** a grievous evil under the sun:
5:18 [5:17] [A] I **realized** that it is good and proper for a man to eat
5:18 [5:17] [A] to **find** satisfaction in his toilsome labor under the
6: 1 [A] *I have* **seen** another evil under the sun, and it weighs heavily
6: 5 [A] Though *it* never **saw** the sun or knew anything, it has more
6: 6 [A] a thousand years twice over but fails *to* **enjoy** his prosperity.
7:11 [A] is a good thing and benefits *those who* **see** the sun.
7:13 [A] **Consider** what God has done: Who can straighten what he
7:14 [A] times are good, be happy; but when times are bad, **consider**:
7:15 [A] In this meaningless life of mine *I have* **seen** both of these:
7:27 [A] "**Look**," says the Teacher, "this is what I have discovered:
7:29 [A] **[RPH]** God made mankind upright, but men have gone in
8: 9 [A] All this *I* **saw**, as I applied my mind to everything done under
8:10 [A] Then too, *I* **saw** the wicked buried—those who used to come
8:16 [A] mind to know wisdom and to **observe** man's labor on earth—
8:16 [A] labor on earth—his eyes not **seeing** sleep day or night—
8:17 [A] *I* **saw** all that God has done. No one can comprehend what
9: 9 [A] **Enjoy** life with your wife, whom you love, all the days of
9:11 [A] *I have* **seen** something else under the sun: The race is not to
9:13 [A] *I* also **saw** under the sun this example of wisdom that greatly
10: 5 [A] There is an evil *I have* **seen** under the sun, the sort of error
10: 7 [A] *I have* **seen** slaves on horseback, while princes go on foot
11: 4 [A] will not plant; *whoever* **looks** at the clouds will not reap.
11: 7 [A] Light is sweet, and it pleases the eyes to **see** the sun.
12: 3 [A] are few, and those **looking** through the windows grow dim;
SS 1: 6 [A] *Do* not **stare** *at* me because I am dark, because I am
2:12 [C] Flowers **appear** on the earth; the season of singing has come,
2:14 [G] **show** me your face, let me hear your voice;
3: 3 [A] rounds in the city. "*Have you* **seen** the one my heart loves?"
3:11 [A] of Zion, and **look** at King Solomon wearing the crown,
6: 9 [A] The maidens **saw** her and called her blessed; the queens
6:11 [A] I went down to the grove of nut trees to **look** at the new
6:11 [A] to **see** if the vines had budded or the pomegranates were in
7:12 [7:13] [A] Let us go early to the vineyards *to* **see** if the vines
Isa 1:12 [A] When you come to **appear** [+7156] **before** me, who has
5:12 [A] deeds of the LORD, no **respect** *for* the work of his hands.
5:19 [A] "Let God hurry, let him hasten his work so *we may* **see** it.
6: 1 [A] *I* **saw** the Lord seated on a throne, high and exalted,
6: 5 [A] and my eyes *have* **seen** the King, the LORD Almighty."
6: 9 [A] *be* **ever seeing** [+8011], but never perceiving.'
6: 9 [A] *be* **ever seeing** [+8011], but never perceiving.'
6:10 [A] Otherwise *they might* **see** with their eyes, hear with their
9: 2 [9:1] [A] The people walking in darkness *have* **seen** a great
14:16 [A] *Those who* **see** you stare at you, they ponder your fate: "Is
16:12 [C] When Moab **appears** at her high place, she only wears
17: 7 [A] to their Maker and **turn** their eyes to the Holy One of Israel.
17: 8 [A] *they will* **have** no **regard for** the Asherah poles
18: 3 [A] *you will* **see** it, and when a trumpet sounds, you will hear it.
21: 3 [A] am staggered by what I hear, I am bewildered by *what* I **see**.
21: 6 [A] to me: "Go, post a lookout and have him report what *he* **sees**.
21: 7 [A] When *he* **sees** chariots with teams of horses, riders on
21: 8 [a] the **lookout** [BHS 793] shouted, "Day after day, my lord,

Isa 22: 9 [A] *you* **saw** that the City of David had many breaches in its
22:11 [A] or **have regard for** the One who planned it long ago.
26:10 [A] go on doing evil and **regard** not the majesty of the LORD.
28: 4 [A] as soon as **someone**° [+2021] sees it and takes it in his hand,
28: 4 [A] as soon as someone **sees** it and takes it in his hand,
29:15 [A] who do their work in darkness and think, "Who **sees** us?
29:18 [A] and out of gloom and darkness the eyes of the blind *will* **see**.
29:23 [A] When they **see** among them their children, the work of my
30:10 [A] They say to the seers, "**See** no *more* **visions**!" and to the
30:20 [A] be hidden no more; *with* your own eyes you *will* **see** them.
30:30 [G] *will* **make** them **see** his arm coming down with raging anger
32: 3 [A] the eyes of *those who* **see** will no longer be closed, and the
33:15 [A] of murder and shuts his eyes against **contemplating** evil—
33:17 [A] see the king in his beauty and **view** a land that stretches afar.
33:19 [A] *You will* **see** those arrogant people no more, those people of
33:20 [A] your eyes *will* **see** Jerusalem, a peaceful abode, a tent that
35: 2 [A] they *will* **see** the glory of the LORD, the splendor of our
37:17 [A] O LORD, and hear; open your eyes, O LORD, and **see**;
38: 5 [A] I have heard your prayer and **seen** your tears; I will add
38:11 [A] I said, "*I will* not again **see** the LORD, the LORD,
39: 2 [G] and **showed** them what was in his storehouses—
39: 2 [G] or in all his kingdom that Hezekiah *did* not **show** them.
39: 4 [A] The prophet asked, "What *did they* **see** in your palace?"
39: 4 [A] "*They* **saw** everything in my palace," Hezekiah said.
39: 4 [G] "There is nothing among my treasures that *I did* not **show**
40: 5 [A] will be revealed, and all mankind together *will* **see** it.
40:26 [A] Lift your eyes and **look** *to* the heavens: Who created all
41: 5 [A] The islands *have* **seen** it and fear; the ends of the earth
41:20 [A] so that people *may* **see** and know, may consider
41:23 [a] [we will be dismayed and *filled with* **fear**. [Q; see K 3707]]
41:28 [A] *I* **look** but there is no one—no one among them to give
42:18 [A] "Hear, you deaf; look, you blind, and **see**!
42:20 [A] *You have* **seen** many things, but have paid no attention;
44: 9 [A] Those who would speak up for them *are* **blind** [+1153]; they
44:16 [A] warms himself and says, "Ah! I am warm; *I* **see** the fire."
44:18 [A] their eyes are plastered over so they cannot **see**, and their
47: 3 [C] Your nakedness will be exposed and your shame **uncovered**.
47:10 [A] trusted in your wickedness and have said, 'No *one* **sees** me.'
49: 7 [A] "Kings *will* **see** you and rise up, princes will see and bow
49:18 [A] Lift up your eyes and **look** around; all your sons gather
52: 8 [A] LORD returns to Zion, *they will* **see** it with their own eyes.
52:10 [A] and all the ends of the earth *will* **see** the salvation of our God.
52:15 [A] For what they were not told, *they will* **see**, and what they
53: 2 [A] He had no beauty or majesty *to* **attract** *us to* him, nothing in
53:10 [A] *he will* **see** his offspring and prolong his days, and the will of
53:11 [A] of his soul, *he will* **see** the light ⌞of life⌟ and be satisfied;
57:18 [A] *I have* **seen** his ways, but I will heal him; I will guide him
58: 3 [A] 'Why have we fasted,' they say, 'and *you have* not **seen** it?
58: 7 [A] when *you* **see** the naked, to clothe him, and not to turn away
59:15 [A] The LORD **looked** and was displeased that there was no
59:16 [A] *He* **saw** that there was no one, he was appalled that there was
60: 2 [C] the LORD rises upon you and his glory **appears** over you.
60: 4 [A] "Lift up your eyes and **look** about you: All assemble
60: 5 [A] *you will* **look** and be radiant, your heart will throb and swell
61: 9 [A] All *who* **see** them will acknowledge that they are a people the
62: 2 [A] The nations *will* **see** your righteousness, and all kings your
63:15 [A] Look down from heaven and **see** from your lofty throne, holy
64: 4 [64:3] [A] has perceived, no eye *has* **seen** any God besides you,
66: 5 [A] 'Let the LORD be glorified, that *we may* **see** your joy!'
66: 8 [A] Who *has ever* **seen** such things? Can a country be born in a
66:14 [A] When *you* **see** this, your heart will rejoice and you will
66:18 [A] all nations and tongues, and they will come and **see** my glory.
66:19 [A] islands that have not heard of my fame or **seen** my glory.
66:24 [A] **look** upon the dead bodies of those who rebelled against me;
Jer 1:10 [A] **See**, today I appoint you over nations and kingdoms to uproot
1:11 [A] "What *do* you **see**, Jeremiah?" "I see the branch of an
1:11 [A] Jeremiah?" "I **see** the branch of an almond tree," I replied.
1:12 [A] The LORD said to me, "You have **seen** correctly, for I am
1:13 [A] "What *do* you **see**?" "I see a boiling pot, tilting away from
1:13 [A] "I **see** a boiling pot, tilting away from the north," I answered.
2:10 [A] Cross over to the coasts of Kittim and **look**, send to Kedar
2:10 [A] observe closely; **see** if there has ever been anything like this:
2:19 [A] Consider then and **realize** how evil and bitter it is for you
2:23 [A] **See** how you behaved in the valley; consider what you have
2:31 [A] "You of this generation, **consider** the word of the LORD:
3: 2 [A] "Look up to the barren heights and **see**. Is there any place
3: 6 [A] said to me, "*Have you* **seen** what faithless Israel has done?
3: 7 [A] to me but she did not, and her unfaithful sister Judah **saw** it.
3: 8 [A] Yet *I* **saw** that her unfaithful sister Judah had no fear; she
4:21 [A] How long *must I* **see** the battle standard and hear the sound
4:23 [A] *I* **looked** *at* the earth, and it was formless and empty; and at
4:24 [A] *I* **looked** *at* the mountains, and they were quaking; all the
4:25 [A] *I* **looked**, and there were no people; every bird in the sky had
4:26 [A] *I* **looked**, and the fruitful land was a desert; all its towns lay
5: 1 [A] **look around** and consider, search through her squares.
5:12 [A] No harm will come to us; *we will* never **see** sword or famine.
5:21 [A] who have eyes but *do* not **see**, who have ears but do not hear:
6:16 [A] "Stand at the crossroads and **look**; ask for the ancient paths,
7:11 [A] to you? But I *have been* **watching**! declares the LORD.
7:12 [A] **see** what I did to it because of the wickedness of my people
7:17 [A] *Do* you not **see** what they are doing in the towns of Judah
11:18 [G] knew it, for at that time *he* **showed** me what they were doing.
11:20 [A] the heart and mind, *let me* **see** your vengeance upon them,
12: 3 [A] O LORD; *you* **see** me and test my thoughts about you.
12: 4 [A] the people are saying, "*He will* not **see** what happens to us."
13:20 [A] up your eyes and **see** those who are coming from the north.
13:26 [C] up your skirts over your face that your shame *may* **be seen**—
13:27 [A] *I have* **seen** your detestable acts on the hills and in the fields.
14:13 [A] telling them, '*You will* not **see** the sword or suffer famine.
17: 6 [A] in the wastelands; *he will* not **see** prosperity when it comes.
17: 8 [a] [*It does* not **fear** [Q; see K 3707] when heat comes;]
18:17 [G] *I will* **show** them my back and not my face in the day of their
20: 4 [A] with your own eyes you *will* **see** them fall by the sword of
20:12 [A] who examine the righteous and **probe** the heart and mind,
20:12 [A] the heart and mind, *let me* **see** your vengeance upon them,
20:18 [A] Why did I ever come out of the womb to **see** trouble
22:10 [A] because he will never return nor **see** his native land again.
22:12 [A] they have led him captive; *he will* not **see** this land again."
23:13 [A] "Among the prophets of Samaria *I* **saw** this repulsive thing:
23:14 [A] among the prophets of Jerusalem *I have* **seen** something
23:18 [A] which of them has stood in the council of the LORD *to* **see**
23:24 [A] Can anyone hide in secret places so that I cannot **see** him?"
24: 1 [G] the LORD **showed** me two baskets of figs placed in front of
24: 3 [A] Then the LORD asked me, "What *do* you **see**, Jeremiah?"
29:32 [A] nor *will he* **see** the good things I will do for my people,
30: 6 [A] Ask and **see**: Can a man bear children? Then why do I see
30: 6 [A] why *do I* **see** every strong man with his hands on his stomach
31: 3 [C] The LORD **appeared** to us in the past, saying: "I have
31:26 [A] At this I awoke and **looked** *around*. My sleep had been
32: 4 [A] speak with him face to face and **see** him with his own eyes.
32:24 [A] attacking it. What you said has happened, as you now **see**.
33:24 [A] "*Have you* not **noticed** that these people are saying, 'The
34: 3 [A] You *will* **see** the king of Babylon *with* your own eyes, and he
38:21 [G] to surrender, this is what the LORD *has* **revealed** *to* me:
39: 4 [A] When Zedekiah king of Judah and all the soldiers **saw** them,
40: 4 [A] **Look**, the whole country lies before you; go wherever you
41:13 [A] people Ishmael had with him **saw** Johanan son of Kareah and
42: 2 [A] For as you now **see** [+906+6524], though we were once
42:14 [A] where *we will* not **see** war or hear the trumpet or be hungry
42:18 [A] and reproach; *you will* never **see** this place again.'
44: 2 [A] You **saw** the great disaster I brought on Jerusalem and on all
44:17 [A] had plenty of food and were well off and **suffered** no harm.
46: 5 [A] What *do I* **see**? They are terrified, they are retreating, their
51:61 [A] you get to Babylon, **see** that you read all these words aloud.
52:25 [A] of the fighting men, and seven royal **advisers** [+7156].
La 1: 7 [A] Her enemies **looked** *at* her and laughed at her destruction.
1: 8 [A] honored her despise her, for *they have* **seen** her nakedness;
1: 9 [A] "**Look**, O LORD, *on* my affliction, for the enemy has
1:10 [A] all her treasures; *she* **saw** pagan nations enter her sanctuary—
1:11 [A] "**Look**, O LORD, and consider, for I am despised."
1:12 [A] it nothing to you, all you who pass by? Look around and **see**.
1:18 [A] Listen, all you peoples; **look** *upon* my suffering. My young
1:20 [A] "**See**, O LORD, how distressed I am! I am in torment
2:16 [A] This is the day we have waited for; we have lived *to* **see** it."
2:20 [A] "**Look**, O LORD, and consider: Whom have you ever
3: 1 [A] I am the man *who has* **seen** affliction by the rod of his wrath.
3:36 [A] a man of justice—*would* not the Lord **see** such things?
3:50 [A] until the LORD looks down from heaven and **sees**.
3:59 [A] *You have* **seen**, O LORD, the wrong done to me.
3:60 [A] *You have* **seen** the depth of their vengeance, all their plots
5: 1 [A] what has happened to us; look, and **see** our disgrace.
Eze 1: 1 [A] the heavens were opened and *I* **saw** visions of God.
1: 4 [A] *I* **looked**, and I saw a windstorm coming out of the north—
1:15 [A] As *I* **looked** *at* the living creatures, I saw a wheel on the
1:27 [A] *I* **saw** that from what appeared to be his waist up he looked
1:27 [A] of fire, and that from there down **[RPH]** he looked like fire;
1:28 [A] When *I* **saw** it, I fell facedown, and I heard the voice of one
2: 9 [A] *I* **looked**, and I saw a hand stretched out to me. In it was a
3:23 [A] like the glory *I had* **seen** by the Kebar River, and I fell
4:15 [A] "**Very well**," he said, "I will let you bake your bread over
8: 2 [A] *I* **looked**, and I saw a figure like that of a man. From what
8: 4 [A] of the God of Israel, as in the vision *I had* **seen** in the plain.
8: 6 [A] he said to me, "Son of man, *do* you **see** what they are doing—
8: 6 [A] But *you will* **see** things that are even more detestable."
8: 7 [A] entrance to the court. *I* **looked**, and I saw a hole in the wall.
8: 9 [A] "Go in and **see** the wicked and detestable things they are
8:10 [A] So I went in and **looked**, and I saw portrayed all over the
8:12 [A] *have you* **seen** what the elders of the house of Israel are

Eze 8:12 [A] They say, 'The LORD *does* not **see** us; the LORD has
8:13 [A] "*You will* **see** them doing things that are even more
8:15 [A] He said to me, "*Do you* **see** this, son of man? You will see
8:15 [A] *You will* **see** things that are even more detestable than this."
8:17 [A] He said to me, "*Have you* **seen** this, son of man? Is it a
9:9 [A] LORD has forsaken the land; the LORD *does* not **see**.'
10:1 [A] *I* **looked**, and I saw the likeness of a throne of sapphire above
10:1 [C] the expanse that was over the heads of the cherubim. **[NIE]**
10:8 [C] (Under the wings of the cherubim *could* **be seen** what looked
10:9 [A] *I* **looked**, and I saw beside the cherubim four wheels,
10:15 [A] These were the living creatures *I had* **seen** by the Kebar
10:20 [A] These were the living creatures *I had* **seen** beneath the God
10:22 [A] Their faces had the same appearance as those *I had* **seen** by
11:1 [A] *I* **saw** among them Jaazaniah son of Azzur and Pelatiah son
11:24 [A] Spirit of God. Then the vision *I had* **seen** went up from me,
11:25 [G] and I told the exiles everything the LORD *had* **shown** me.
12:2 [A] They have eyes to **see** but do not see and ears to hear but do
12:2 [A] eyes to see but *do* not **see** and ears to hear but do not hear,
12:3 [A] Perhaps *they will* **understand**, though they are a rebellious
12:6 [A] Cover your face so that *you* cannot **see** the land, for I have
12:12 [A] so that *he* cannot **see** [+906+2021+4200+6524] the land.
12:13 [A] of the Chaldeans, but *he will* not **see** it, and there he will die.
13:3 [A] prophets who follow their own spirit and *have* **seen** nothing!
14:22 [A] to you, and when *you* **see** their conduct and their actions,
14:23 [A] You will be consoled when *you* **see** their conduct and their
16:6 [A] " 'Then I passed by and **saw** you kicking about in your blood,
16:8 [A] when *I* **looked** *at* you and saw that you were old enough for
16:37 [A] you in front of them, and *they will* **see** all your nakedness.
16:50 [A] before me. Therefore I did away with them as *you have* **seen**.
18:14 [A] "But suppose this son has a son *who* **sees** all the sins his
18:14 [A] and though *he* **sees** them, he does not do such things:
18:28 [A] Because *he* **considers** all the offenses he has committed
19:5 [A] " 'When *she* **saw** her hope unfulfilled, her expectation gone,
19:11 [C] **conspicuous** for its height and for its many branches.
20:28 [A] to give them and *they* **saw** any high hill or any leafy tree,
20:48 [21:4] [A] Everyone *will* **see** that I the LORD have kindled it;
21:21 [21:26] [A] he will consult his idols, *he will* **examine** the liver.
21:24 [21:29] [C] **revealing** your sins in all that you do—
23:11 [A] "Her sister Oholibah **saw** this, yet in her lust and prostitution
23:13 [A] *I* **saw** that she too defiled herself; both of them went the
23:14 [A] *She* **saw** men portrayed on a wall, figures of Chaldeans
28:18 [A] ashes on the ground in the sight of all *who were* **watching**.
32:31 [A] *will* **see** them and he will be consoled for all his hordes that
33:3 [A] *he* **sees** the sword coming against the land and blows the
33:6 [A] if the watchman **sees** the sword coming and does not blow
37:8 [A] *I* **looked**, and tendons and flesh appeared on them and skin
39:15 [A] go through the land and *one of them* **sees** a human bone,
39:21 [A] all the nations *will* **see** the punishment I inflict and the hand I
40:4 [A] **look** with your eyes and hear with your ears and pay
40:4 [G] and pay attention to everything I *am going to* **show** you,
40:4 [G] for that is why **[RPH]** you have been brought here.
40:4 [A] brought here. Tell the house of Israel everything you **see**."
41:8 [A] *I* **saw** that the temple had a raised base all around it,
43:3 [A] The vision *I* **saw** was like the vision I had seen when he
43:3 [A] The vision I saw was like the vision *I had* **seen** when he
43:3 [A] the city and like the visions *I had* **seen** by the Kebar River,
44:4 [A] *I* **looked** and saw the glory of the LORD filling the temple
44:5 [A] **look** [+928+6524] **carefully**, listen closely and give attention
47:6 [A] He asked me, "Son of man, *do you* **see** this?" Then he led me
Da 1:10 [A] Why *should he* **see** you looking worse than the other young
1:13 [C] **compare** our appearance with that of the young men who eat
1:13 [A] and treat your servants in accordance with what *you* **see**."
1:15 [C] At the end of the ten days they **looked** [+5260] healthier
8:1 [C] year of King Belshazzar's reign, I, Daniel, **had**[s] a vision,
8:1 [C] had a vision, after the *one that had* already **appeared** to me.
8:2 [A] In my vision *I* **saw** myself in the citadel of Susa in the
8:2 [A] In my vision I saw **[RPH]** myself in the citadel of Susa in
8:2 [A] of Elam; **[RPH]** in the vision I was beside the Ulai Canal.
8:3 [A] **[RPH]** and there before me was a ram with two horns,
8:4 [A] *I* **watched** the ram as he charged toward the west
8:6 [A] He came toward the two-horned ram *I had* **seen** standing
8:7 [A] *I* **saw** him attack the ram furiously, striking the ram
8:15 [A] Daniel, *was* **watching** the vision and trying to understand it,
8:20 [A] The two-horned ram that *you* **saw** represents the kings of
9:18 [A] and **see** the desolation of the city that bears your Name.
9:21 [A] in prayer, Gabriel, the man *I had* **seen** in the earlier vision,
10:5 [A] **[NIE]** and there before me was a man dressed in linen,
10:7 [A] I, Daniel, was the only one *who* **saw** the vision; the men with
10:7 [A] the men with me *did* not **see** it, but such terror overwhelmed
10:8 [A] So I was left alone, **gazing** *at* this great vision; I had no
12:5 [A] I, Daniel, **looked**, and there before me stood two others,
Hos 5:13 [A] "When Ephraim **saw** his sickness, and Judah his sores,
6:10 [A] *I have* **seen** a horrible thing in the house of Israel.
9:10 [A] when *I* **saw** your fathers, it was like seeing the early fruit on
9:13 [A] *I have* **seen** Ephraim, like Tyre, planted in a pleasant place.
Joel 2:28 [3:1] [A] will dream dreams, your young men *will* **see** visions.
Am 3:9 [A] **see** the great unrest within her and the oppression among her
6:2 [A] Go to Calneh and **look** *at* it; go from there to great Hamath,
7:1 [G] This is what the Sovereign LORD **showed** me: He was
7:4 [G] This is what the Sovereign LORD **showed** me: The
7:7 [G] This is what *he* **showed** me: The Lord was standing by a wall
7:8 [A] the LORD asked me, "What *do* you **see**, Amos?" "A plumb
8:1 [G] This is what the Sovereign LORD **showed** me: a basket of
8:2 [A] "What *do* you **see**, Amos?" he asked. "A basket of ripe
9:1 [A] *I* **saw** the Lord standing by the altar, and he said:
Ob 1:12 [A] *You should* not **look down on** your brother in the day of his
1:13 [A] nor **look down on** them in their calamity in the day of their
Jnh 3:10 [A] When God **saw** what they did and how they turned from their
4:5 [A] in its shade and waited *to* **see** what would happen to the city.
Mic 6:9 [a] *to* fear [BHS *see*; NIV 3707] your name is wisdom—
7:9 [A] will bring me out into the light; *I will* **see** his righteousness.
7:10 [A] Then my enemy *will* **see** it and will be covered with shame,
7:10 [A] My eyes *will* **see** her downfall; even now she will be
7:15 [G] you came out of Egypt, *I will* **show** them my wonders."
7:16 [A] Nations *will* **see** and be ashamed, deprived of all their power.
Na 3:5 [G] *I will* **show** the nations your nakedness and the kingdoms
3:7 [A] All *who* **see** you will flee from you and say, 'Nineveh is in
Hab 1:3 [G] Why *do you* **make** me **look** *at* injustice? Why do you
1:5 [A] "**Look** at the nations and watch—and be utterly amazed. For
1:13 [A] Your eyes are too pure *to* **look** *on* evil; you cannot tolerate
2:1 [A] I will look to **see** what he will say to me, and what answer I
3:6 [A] shook the earth; *he* **looked**, and made the nations tremble.
3:7 [A] *I* **saw** the tents of Cushan in distress, the dwellings of Midian
3:10 [A] the mountains **saw** you and writhed. Torrents of water swept
Hag 2:3 [A] 'Who of you is left who **saw** this house in its former glory?
2:3 [A] How *does* it **look** to you now? Does it not seem to you like
Zec 1:8 [A] During the night *I* **had a vision**—and there before me was a
1:9 [G] talking with me answered, "I *will* **show** you what they are."
1:18 [2:1] [A] **[NIE]** and there before me were four horns!
1:20 [2:3] [G] Then the LORD **showed** me four craftsmen.
2:1 [2:5] [A] **[NIE]** and there before me was a man with a
2:2 [2:6] [A] to **find out** how wide and how long it is."
3:1 [G] *he* **showed** me Joshua the high priest standing before the
3:4 [A] Then he said to Joshua, "**See**, I have taken away your sin,
4:2 [A] He asked me, "What *do* you **see**?" I answered, "I see a solid
4:2 [A] "*I* **see** a solid gold lampstand with a bowl at the top
4:10 [A] Men will rejoice when *they* **see** the plumb line in the hand of
5:1 [A] **[NIE]** and there before me was a flying scroll!
5:2 [A] He asked me, "What *do* you **see**?" I answered, "I see a flying
5:2 [A] I answered, "I **see** a flying scroll, thirty feet long and fifteen
5:5 [A] said to me, "Look up and **see** what this is that is appearing."
5:9 [A] **[NIE]** and there before me were two women, with the wind
6:1 [A] **[NIE]** and there before me were four chariots coming out
6:8 [A] he called to me, "**Look**, those going toward the north country
9:5 [A] Ashkelon *will* **see** it and fear; Gaza will writhe in agony, and
9:8 [A] my people, for now I *am* **keeping watch** [+928+6524].
9:14 [C] the LORD *will* **appear** over them; his arrow will flash like
10:7 [A] Their children *will* **see** it and be joyful; their hearts will
Mal 1:5 [A] *You will* **see** it with your own eyes and say, 'Great is the
3:2 [C] Who can stand when he **appears**? For he will be like a
3:18 [A] And *you will* again **see** the distinction between the righteous

8012 רָאָה² *rā'â²*, n.f. [1] [√ 8011?]

red kite [1]

Dt 14:13 the **red kite**, the black kite, any kind of falcon,

8013 רָאֶה *rā'eh*, a. [1 / 0] [√ 8011]

Job 10:15 and drowned [BHS *aware of*; NIV 8116] *in* my affliction.

8014 רֹאֶה¹ *rō'eh¹*, n.[m.]. [12] [√ 8011]

seer [10], seer's [1], seers [1]

1Sa 9:9 to inquire of God, he would say, "Come, let us go to the **seer**,"
9:9 to the seer," because the prophet of today used to be called a **seer**.)
9:11 coming out to draw water, and they asked them, "Is the **seer** here?"
9:18 and asked, "Would you please tell me where the **seer's** house is?"
9:19 "I am the **seer**," Samuel replied. "Go up ahead of me to the high
2Sa 15:27 The king also said to Zadok the priest, "Aren't you a **seer**?
1Ch 9:22 assigned to their positions of trust by David and Samuel the **seer**.
26:28 everything dedicated by Samuel the **seer** and by Saul son of Kish,
29:29 to end, they are written in the records of Samuel the **seer**,
2Ch 16:7 At that time Hanani the **seer** came to Asa king of Judah and said to
16:10 Asa was angry with the **seer** because of this; he was so enraged
Isa 30:10 They say to the **seers**, "See no more visions!" and to the prophets,

8015 ²רֹאֶה ***rō'eh²***, n.[m.]. [1] [√ 8011]
seeing visions [1]

Isa 28: 7 they reel from beer, they stagger when **seeing visions**,

8016 ³רֹאֶה ***rō'eh³***, n.pr.m. Not used in NIV/BHS [√ 8011; cf. 2218]

8017 רְאוּבֵן ***r^e'ûbēn***, n.pr.m. [72] [→ 8018; cf. 8011 + 1201]
Reuben [45], Reubenites [+1201] [17], Reuben [+1201] [6], *untranslated* [2], Reubenite [+1201] [1], they[s] [+1201+1201+1514+2256] [1]

Ge 29:32 She named him **Reuben**, for she said, "It is because the LORD
30:14 **Reuben** went out into the fields and found some mandrake plants,
35:22 **Reuben** went in and slept with his father's concubine Bilhah,
35:23 **Reuben** the firstborn of Jacob, Simeon, Levi, Judah, Issachar
37:21 When **Reuben** heard this, he tried to rescue him from their hands.
37:22 **Reuben** said this to rescue him from them and take him back to his
37:29 When **Reuben** returned to the cistern and saw that Joseph was not
42:22 **Reuben** replied, "Didn't I tell you not to sin against the boy?
42:37 **Reuben** said to his father, "You may put both of my sons to death
46: 8 who went to Egypt: **Reuben** the firstborn of Jacob.
46: 9 The sons of **Reuben**: Hanoch, Pallu, Hezron and Carmi.
48: 5 and Manasseh will be mine, just as **Reuben** and Simeon are mine.
49: 3 "**Reuben**, you are my firstborn, my might, the first sign of my
Ex 1: 2 **Reuben**, Simeon, Levi and Judah;
6:14 The sons of **Reuben** the firstborn son of Israel were Hanoch
6:14 and Pallu, Hezron and Carmi. These were the clans of **Reuben**.
Nu 1: 5 men who are to assist you: from **Reuben**, Elizur son of Shedeur;
1:20 From the descendants of **Reuben** the firstborn son of Israel:
1:21 The number from the tribe of **Reuben** was 46,500.
2:10 On the south will be the divisions of the camp of **Reuben** under
2:10 The leader of the people of **Reuben** is Elizur son of Shedeur.
2:16 All the men assigned to the camp of **Reuben**, according to their
7:30 the leader of the people of **Reuben**, brought his offering.
10:18 The divisions of the camp of **Reuben** went next, under their
13: 4 their names: from the tribe of **Reuben**, Shammua son of Zaccur;
16: 1 son of Kohath, the son of Levi, and certain **Reubenites** [+1201]—
26: 5 The descendants of **Reuben**, the firstborn son of Israel, were:
26: 5 descendants of Reuben, **[RPH]** the firstborn son of Israel, were:
32: 1 The **Reubenites** [+1201] and Gadites, who had very large herds
32: 2 So **they**[s] [+1201+1201+1514+2256] came to Moses and Eleazar
32: 6 Moses said to the Gadites and **Reubenites** [+1201], "Shall your
32:25 The Gadites and **Reubenites** [+1201] said to Moses, "We your
32:29 He said to them, "If the Gadites and **Reubenites** [+1201],
32:31 The Gadites and **Reubenites** [+1201] answered, "Your servants
32:33 the **Reubenites** [+1201] and the half-tribe of Manasseh son of
32:37 the **Reubenites** [+1201] rebuilt Heshbon, Elealeh and Kiriathaim,
Dt 11: 6 did to Dathan and Abiram, sons of Eliab the **Reubenite** [+1201],
27:13 **Reuben**, Gad, Asher, Zebulun, Dan and Naphtali.
33: 6 "Let **Reuben** live and not die, nor his men be few."
Jos 4:12 The men of **Reuben**, Gad and the half-tribe of Manasseh crossed
13:15 This is what Moses had given to the tribe of **Reuben** [+1201],
13:23 The boundary of the **Reubenites** [+1201] was the bank of the
13:23 and their villages were the inheritance of the **Reubenites** [+1201],
15: 6 north of Beth Arabah to the Stone of Bohan son of **Reuben**.
18: 7 **Reuben** and the half-tribe of Manasseh have already received their
18:17 of Adummim, and ran down to the Stone of Bohan son of **Reuben**.
20: 8 Bezer in the desert on the plateau in the tribe of **Reuben**,
21: 7 received twelve towns from the tribes of **Reuben**, Gad
21:36 from the tribe of **Reuben**, Bezer, Jahaz,
22: 9 So the **Reubenites** [+1201], the Gadites and the half-tribe of
22:10 the **Reubenites** [+1201], the Gadites and the half-tribe of
22:11 of Canaan at Geliloth **[RPH]** near the Jordan on the Israelite side,
22:13 to **Reuben** [+1201], Gad and the half-tribe of Manasseh.
22:15 to **Reuben** [+1201], Gad and the half-tribe of Manasseh—
22:21 **Reuben** [+1201], Gad and the half-tribe of Manasseh replied to the
22:25 between us and you—you **Reubenites** [+1201] and Gadites!
22:30 heard what **Reuben** [+1201], Gad and Manasseh had to say,
22:31 of Eleazar, the priest, said to **Reuben** [+1201], Gad and Manasseh,
22:32 to Canaan from their meeting with the **Reubenites** [+1201]
22:33 them to devastate the country where the **Reubenites** [+1201]
22:34 the **Reubenites** [+1201] and the Gadites gave the altar this name:
Jdg 5:15 In the districts of **Reuben** there was much searching of heart.
5:16 In the districts of **Reuben** there was much searching of heart.
1Ch 2: 1 sons of Israel: **Reuben**, Simeon, Levi, Judah, Issachar, Zebulun,
5: 1 The sons of **Reuben** the firstborn of Israel (he was the firstborn,
5: 3 the sons of **Reuben** the firstborn of Israel: Hanoch, Pallu,
5:18 The **Reubenites** [+1201], the Gadites and the half-tribe of
6:63 [6:48] were allotted twelve towns from the tribes of **Reuben**, Gad
6:78 [6:63] from the tribe of **Reuben** across the Jordan east of Jericho
Eze 48: 6 "**Reuben** will have one portion; it will border the territory of
48: 7 it will border the territory of **Reuben** from east to west.
48:31 The three gates on the north side will be the gate of **Reuben**,

8018 רְאוּבֵנִי ***r^e'ûbēnî***, a.g. [18] [√ 8017]
Reubenites [13], Reuben [2], men of Reuben [1], Reuben [+1201] [1], Reubenite [1]

Nu 26: 7 These were the clans of **Reuben**; those numbered were 43,730.
34:14 because the families of the tribe of **Reuben** [+1201], the tribe of
Dt 3:12 I gave the **Reubenites** and the Gadites the territory north of Aroer
3:16 to the **Reubenites** and the Gadites I gave the territory extending
4:43 Bezer in the desert plateau, for the **Reubenites**; Ramoth in Gilead,
29: 8 [29:7] their land and gave it as an inheritance to the **Reubenites**,
Jos 1:12 But to the **Reubenites**, the Gadites and the half-tribe of Manasseh,
12: 6 the servant of the LORD gave their land to the **Reubenites**,
13: 8 the **Reubenites** and the Gadites had received the inheritance that
22: 1 Joshua summoned the **Reubenites**, the Gadites and the half-tribe
2Ki 10:33 **Reuben** and Manasseh), from Aroer by the Arnon Gorge through
1Ch 5: 6 of Assyria took into exile. Beerah was a leader of the **Reubenites**.
5:26 who took the **Reubenites**, the Gadites and the half-tribe of
11:42 Adina son of Shiza the **Reubenite**, who was chief of the
11:42 who was chief of the **Reubenites**, and the thirty with him,
12:37 [12:38] **men of Reuben**, Gad and the half-tribe of Manasseh,
26:32 and King David put them in charge of the **Reubenites**, the Gadites
27:16 over the **Reubenites**: Eliezer son of Zicri; over the Simeonites:

8019 רַאֲוָה ***ra^awâ***, n.f. [1] [√ 8011]
spectacle [1]

Eze 28:17 So I threw you to the earth; I made a **spectacle** of you before kings.

8020 רְאוּמָה ***r^e'ûmâ***, n.pr.f. [1] [√ 8163? *or* 8028?]
Reumah [1]

Ge 22:24 His concubine, whose name was **Reumah**, also had sons:

8021 רְאוּת ***r^e'ût***, n.f. [1] [√ 8011]
feast on [1]

Ecc 5:11 [5:10] to the owner except to **feast** [K 8026] his eyes **on** them?

8022 רֹאִי ***rō'î***, n.pr.loc. Not used in NIV/BHS [√ 8011; cf. 936]

8023 רְאִי ***r^e'î***, n.m. [1] [√ 8011]
mirror [1]

Job 37:18 him in spreading out the skies, hard as a **mirror** *of* cast bronze?

8024 רֳאִי ***r^o'î***, n.[m.]. [4] [√ 8011; Ar 10657]
features [1], sees [1], spectacle [1], to nothing [+4946] [1]

Ge 16:13 "You are the God *who* **sees** me," for she said, "I have now seen the
1Sa 16:12 He was ruddy, with a fine appearance and handsome **features**.
Job 33:21 His flesh wastes away **to nothing** [+4946], and his bones,
Na 3: 6 with filth, I will treat you with contempt and make you a **spectacle**.

8025 רְאָיָה ***r^e'āyâ***, n.pr.m. [4] [√ 8011 + 3378]
Reaiah [4]

1Ch 4: 2 **Reaiah** son of Shobal was the father of Jahath, and Jahath the
5: 5 Micah his son, **Reaiah** his son, Baal his son,
Ezr 2:47 Giddel, Gahar, **Reaiah**,
Ne 7:50 **Reaiah**, Rezin, Nekoda,

8026 רְאִית ***r^e'ît***, n.f. [0] [√ 8011]

Ecc 5:11 [5:10] [except to **feast** [K; see Q 8021] his eyes **on** them?]

8027 רָאַם ***rā'am***, v. [1] [→ 8030; cf. 8123]
raised up [1]

Zec 14:10 [A] Jerusalem *will be* **raised up** and remain in its place, from the

8028 רְאֵם ***r^e'ēm***, n.m. [9] [√ 8020?]
wild ox [6], wild oxen [2], him[s] [1]

Nu 23:22 brought them out of Egypt; they have the strength of a **wild ox**.
24: 8 brought them out of Egypt; they have the strength of a **wild ox**.
Dt 33:17 he is like a firstborn bull; his horns are the horns of a **wild ox**.
Job 39: 9 "Will the **wild ox** consent to serve you? Will he stay by your
39:10 Can you hold **him**[s] to the furrow with a harness? Will he till the
Ps 22:21 [22:22] of the lions; save me from the horns of the **wild oxen**.
29: 6 He makes Lebanon skip like a calf, Sirion like a young **wild ox**.
92:10 [92:11] You have exalted my horn like that of a **wild ox**; fine oils
Isa 34: 7 the **wild oxen** will fall with them, the bull calves and the great

8029 רָאמוֹת[1] ***rā'môt***[1], n.[f.pl.]. [2]

coral [2]

Job 28:18 **Coral** and jasper are not worthy of mention; the price of wisdom is
Eze 27:16 fine linen, **coral** and rubies for your merchandise.

8030 רָאמוֹת[2] ***rā'môt***[2], n.pr.loc. [5] [√ 8027; cf. 8123]

Ramoth [5]

Dt 4:43 for the Reubenites; **Ramoth** in Gilead, for the Gadites;
Jos 20: 8 **Ramoth** in Gilead in the tribe of Gad, and Golan in Bashan in the
21:38 **Ramoth** in Gilead (a city of refuge for one accused of murder),
1Ch 6:73 [6:58] **Ramoth** and Anem, together with their pasturelands;
6:80 [6:65] and from the tribe of Gad they received **Ramoth** in Gilead,

8031 רֹאשׁ[1] ***rō'š***[1], n.m. [599 / 602] [→ 8033, 8035, 8034?, 8036, 8037, 8038, 8040, 8396; Ar 10646]

head [217], heads [124], top [45], chief [33], leaders [19], first [16], *untranslated* [10], tops [10], beginning [8], hair [8], chiefs [6], companies [6], leader [6], take a census [+906+5951] [5], mountaintops [+2215] [4], summit [3], topmost [3], ends [2], finest [2], helmet [+5057] [2], high [2], leading [2], led by [+928] [2], lost hair [+5307] [2], over [+928] [2], prominent place [2], released [+906+5951] [2], all [1], any [1], authority [1], begin [1], bodyguard [+4200+9068] [1], branches off [1], capstone [+7157] [1], choicest gifts [1], command [1], commander-in-chief [+2256+8569] [1], commanders [1], company [1], count [+906+928+928+5951] [1], counted [+906+5951] [1], crest [1], crowns [+4200] [1], detachments [1], director [1], directors [1], divisions [1], down [+4946] [1], each [1], fine [1], foremost [1], full [1], hair [+1929] [1], headwaters [1], heights [+5294] [1], highest [+6584] [1], highest [1], hilltop [+2215] [1], hilltops [+2215] [1], himself [+2257] [1], include in the census [+906+5951] [1], it[s] [+8552] [1], it[s] [+2257] [1], junction [1], leaders [+408] [1], leaders [+6639] [1], leading men [1], made pay for [+906+928+8740] [1], make full restitution [+906+928+8740] [1], masters [1], men [1], mountaintop [+2215] [1], New Moon festivals [+2544] [1], oldest [1], outstanding [1], overwhelmed [+6296] [1], peaks [1], raiding parties [1], reaches [1], repay [+906+6584+8740] [1], repay [+906+928+8740] [1], ruler [+1505] [1], rulers [1], special [1], sum [1], tip [1]

Ge 2:10 from Eden; from there it was separated into four **headwaters**.
3:15 and hers; he will crush your **head**, and you will strike his heel."
8: 5 on the first day of the tenth month the **tops** *of* the mountains
11: 4 us build ourselves a city, with a tower that **reaches** to the heavens,
28:12 with its **top** reaching to heaven, and the angels of God were
28:18 under his head and set it up as a pillar and poured oil on **top** *of* it.
40:13 Within three days Pharaoh will lift up your **head** and restore you to
40:16 "I too had a dream: On my **head** were three baskets of bread.
40:17 but the birds were eating them out of the basket on my **head**."
40:19 Within three days Pharaoh will lift off your **head** and hang you on
40:20 He lifted up the **heads** *of* the chief cupbearer and the chief baker in
40:20 and **[RPH]** the chief baker in the presence of his officials:
47:31 to him, and Israel worshiped as he leaned on the **top** *of* his staff.
48:14 But Israel reached out his right hand and put it on Ephraim's **head**,
48:14 and crossing his arms, he put his left hand on Manasseh's **head**,
48:17 father placing his right hand on Ephraim's **head** he was displeased;
48:17 father's hand to move it from Ephraim's **head** to Manasseh's head.
48:17 father's hand to move it from Ephraim's head to Manasseh's **head**.
48:18 this one is the firstborn; put your right hand on his **head**."
49:26 Let all these rest on the **head** *of* Joseph, on the brow of the prince
Ex 6:14 These were the **heads** *of* their families: The sons of Reuben the
6:25 These were the **heads** *of* the Levite families, clan by clan.
12: 2 "This month is to be for you the **first** month, the first month of
12: 9 in water, but roast it over the fire—**head**, legs and inner parts.
17: 9 Tomorrow I will stand on **top** *of* the hill with the staff of God in
17:10 had ordered, and Moses, Aaron and Hur went to the **top** *of* the hill.
18:25 capable men from all Israel and made them **leaders** of the people,
19:20 The LORD descended to the **top** *of* Mount Sinai and called
19:20 top of Mount Sinai and called Moses to the **top** *of* the mountain.
24:17 the LORD looked like a consuming fire on **top** *of* the mountain.
26:24 they must be double from the bottom all the way to the **top**,
28:32 with an opening for the **head** in its center. There shall be a woven
29: 6 Put the turban on his **head** and attach the sacred diadem to the
29: 7 Take the anointing oil and anoint him by pouring it on his **head**.
29:10 and Aaron and his sons shall lay their hands on its **head**.
29:15 the rams, and Aaron and his sons shall lay their hands on its **head**.
29:17 and the legs, putting them with the **head** and the other pieces.
29:19 other ram, and Aaron and his sons shall lay their hands on its **head**.
30:12 "When *you* **take a census of** [+906+5951] the Israelites to count
30:23 "Take the following **fine** spices: 500 shekels of liquid myrrh,
34: 2 Mount Sinai. Present yourself to me there on **top** *of* the mountain.
36:29 the frames were double from the bottom all the way to the **top**
36:38 They overlaid the **tops** *of* the posts and their bands with gold
38:17 on the posts were silver, and their **tops** were overlaid with silver;
38:19 and bands were silver, and their **tops** were overlaid with silver.
38:28 the posts, to overlay the **tops** *of* the posts, and to make their bands.
Lev 1: 4 He is to lay his hand on the **head** *of* the burnt offering, and it will
1: 8 including the **head** and the fat, on the burning wood that is on the
1:12 and the priest shall arrange them, including the **head** and the fat,
1:15 bring it to the altar, wring off the **head** and burn it on the altar;
3: 2 He is to lay his hand on the **head** *of* his offering and slaughter it at
3: 8 He is to lay his hand on the **head** *of* his offering and slaughter it in
3:13 He is to lay his hand on its **head** and slaughter it in front of the
4: 4 He is to lay his hand on its **head** and slaughter it before the
4:11 all its flesh, as well as the **head** and legs, the inner parts and offal—
4:15 are to lay their hands on the bull's **head** before the LORD,
4:24 He is to lay his hand on the goat's **head** and slaughter it at the
4:29 He is to lay his hand on the **head** *of* the sin offering and slaughter
4:33 He is to lay his hand on its **head** and slaughter it for a sin offering
5: 8 He is to wring its **head** from its neck, not severing it completely,
6: 5 [5:24] He must make restitution in **full**, add a fifth of the value to
8: 9 Then he placed the turban on Aaron's **head** and set the gold plate,
8:12 He poured some of the anointing oil on Aaron's **head** and anointed
8:14 sin offering, and Aaron and his sons laid their hands on its **head**.
8:18 burnt offering, and Aaron and his sons laid their hands on its **head**.
8:20 He cut the ram into pieces and burned the **head**, the pieces
8:22 the ordination, and Aaron and his sons laid their hands on its **head**.
9:13 by piece, including the **head**, and he burned them on the altar.
10: 6 sons Eleazar and Ithamar, "Do not let your **hair** become unkempt,
13:12 it covers all the skin of the infected person from **head** to foot,
13:29 "If a man or woman has a sore on the **head** or on the chin,
13:30 it is an itch, an infectious disease of the **head** or chin.
13:40 "When a man *has* **lost** his **hair** [+5307] and is bald, he is clean.
13:41 If *he has* **lost** his **hair** [+5307] from the front of his scalp and has a
13:44 shall pronounce him unclean because of the sore on his **head**.
13:45 let his **hair** be unkempt, cover the lower part of his face and cry
14: 9 he must shave his **head**, his beard, his eyebrows and the rest of his
14:18 The rest of the oil in his palm the priest shall put on the **head** *of* the
14:29 The rest of the oil in his palm the priest shall put on the **head** *of* the
16:21 He is to lay both hands on the **head** *of* the live goat and confess
16:21 of the Israelites—all their sins—and put them on the goat's **head**.
19:27 " 'Do not cut the hair at the sides of your **head** or clip off the edges
21: 5 " 'Priests must not shave their **heads** or shave off the edges of their
21:10 his brothers who has had the anointing oil poured on his **head**
21:10 must not let his **hair** become unkempt or tear his clothes.
24:14 All those who heard him are to lay their hands on his **head**,
Nu 1: 2 "**Take a census of** [+906+5951] the whole Israelite community by
1: 4 man from each tribe, each the **head** of his family, is to help you.
1:16 of their ancestral tribes. They were the **heads** *of* the clans of Israel.
1:49 or **include** them **in the census** [+906+5951] of the other Israelites.
4: 2 "**Take a census of** [+906+5951] the Kohathite branch of the
4:22 "**Take a census** also **of** [+906+5951] the Gershonites by their
5: 7 *He must* **make full restitution for** [+906+928+8740] his wrong,
5:18 he shall loosen her **hair** and place in her hands the reminder
6: 5 period of his vow of separation no razor may be used on his **head**.
6: 5 to the LORD is over; he must let the hair of his **head** grow long.
6: 7 because the symbol of his separation to God is on his **head**.
6: 9 suddenly in his presence, thus defiling the **hair** he has dedicated,
6: 9 has dedicated, he must shave his **head** on the day of his cleansing—
6:11 of the dead body. That same day he is to consecrate his **head**.
6:18 of Meeting, the Nazirite must shave off the **hair** *that* he dedicated.
6:18 **[RPH]** and put it in the fire that is under the sacrifice of the
7: 2 the **heads** *of* families who were the tribal leaders in charge of those
8:12 "After the Levites lay their hands on the **heads** *of* the bulls,
10: 4 only one is sounded, the leaders—the **heads** *of* the clans of Israel—
10:10 your appointed feasts and **New Moon festivals** [+2544]—
13: 3 Desert of Paran. All of them were **leaders** [+408] *of* the Israelites.
14: 4 to each other, "We should choose a **leader** and go back to Egypt."
14:40 Early the next morning they went up toward the **high** hill country.
14:44 in their presumption they went up toward the **high** hill country,
17: 3 [17:18] for there must be one staff for the **head** *of* each ancestral
20:28 And Aaron died there on **top** *of* the mountain. Then Moses
21:20 from Bamoth to the valley in Moab where the **top** *of* Pisgah
23: 9 From the rocky **peaks** I see them, from the heights I view them.
23:14 So he took him to the field of Zophim on the **top** *of* Pisgah,
23:28 Balak took Balaam to the **top** *of* Peor, overlooking the wasteland.
25: 4 "Take all the **leaders** *of* these people, kill them and expose them in
25:15 was Cozbi daughter of Zur, a tribal **chief** of a Midianite family.
26: 2 "**Take a census of** [+906+5951] the whole Israelite community by
28:11 " 'On the **first** *of* every month, present to the LORD a burnt
30: 1 [30:2] Moses said to the **heads** *of* the tribes of Israel: "This is
31:26 and the family **heads** *of* the community are to count all the people
31:26 heads of the community *are to* **count** [+906+928+928+5951] all
31:49 "Your servants *have* **counted** [+906+5951] the soldiers under our
32:28 Joshua son of Nun and to the family **heads** of the Israelite tribes.
36: 1 The family **heads** of the clan of Gilead son of Makir, the son of
36: 1 before Moses and the leaders, the **heads** of the Israelite families.
Dt 1:13 from each of your tribes, and I will set them **over** [+928] you."

Dt 1:15 So I took the **leading** *men of* your tribes, wise and respected men,
1:15 respected men, and appointed them to have **authority** over you—
3:27 Go up to the **top** *of* Pisgah and look west and north and south
5:23 all the **leading men** *of* your tribes and your elders came to me.
20:9 to the army, they shall appoint commanders **over** [+928] it.
21:12 Bring her into your home and have her shave her **head**, trim her
28:13 The LORD will make you the **head**, not the tail. If you pay
28:23 The sky over your **head** will be bronze, the ground beneath you
28:44 will not lend to him. He will be the **head**, but you will be the tail.
29:10 [29:9] your **leaders** and chief men, your elders and officials, and
32:42 of the slain and the captives, the **heads** *of* the enemy leaders."
33:5 He was king over Jeshurun when the **leaders** *of* the people
33:15 with the **choicest gifts** *of* the ancient mountains and the
33:16 Let all these rest on the **head** *of* Joseph, on the brow of the prince
33:21 When the **heads** *of* the people assembled, he carried out the
34:1 Moses climbed Mount Nebo from the plains of Moab to the **top** *of*
Jos 2:19 your house into the street, his blood will be on his own **head**;
2:19 with you, his blood will be on our **head** if a hand is laid on him.
7:6 elders of Israel did the same, and sprinkled dust on their **heads**.
11:10 to the sword. (Hazor had been the **head** *of* all these kingdoms.)
14:1 and the **heads** *of* the tribal clans of Israel allotted to them.
15:8 From there it climbed to the **top** *of* the hill west of the Hinnom
15:9 From the **hilltop** [+2215] the boundary headed toward the spring
19:51 the **heads** *of* the tribal clans of Israel assigned by lot at Shiloh in
21:1 Now the family **heads** *of* the Levites approached Eleazar the priest,
21:1 son of Nun, and the **heads** *of* the other tribal families of Israel
22:14 each the **head** *of* a family division among the Israelite clans.
22:21 the half-tribe of Manasseh replied to the **heads** *of* the clans of
22:30 the **heads** *of* the clans of the Israelites—heard what Reuben,
23:2 their elders, **leaders**, judges and officials—and said to them:
24:1 He summoned the elders, **leaders**, judges and officials of Israel,
Jdg 5:26 she crushed his **head**, she shattered and pierced his temple.
5:30 a girl or two for **each** man, colorful garments as plunder for Sisera,
6:26 build a proper kind of altar to the LORD your God on the **top** *of*
7:16 Dividing the three hundred men into three **companies**, he placed
7:19 the edge of the camp at the **beginning** *of* the middle watch,
7:20 The three **companies** blew the trumpets and smashed the jars.
7:25 the Midianites and brought the **heads** *of* Oreb and Zeeb to Gideon,
8:28 was subdued before the Israelites and did not raise its **head** again.
9:7 he climbed up on the **top** *of* Mount Gerizim and shouted to them,
9:25 citizens of Shechem set men on the **hilltops** [+2215] to ambush
9:34 and took up concealed positions near Shechem in four **companies**.
9:36 people are coming down from the **tops** *of* the mountains!"
9:37 a **company** is coming from the direction of the soothsayers' tree."
9:43 divided them into three **companies** and set an ambush in the fields.
9:44 the **companies** with him rushed forward to a position at the
9:44 two **companies** rushed upon those in the fields and struck them
9:53 a woman dropped an upper millstone on his **head** and cracked his
9:57 God also **made** the men of Shechem **pay for** [+906+928+8740] all
10:18 the Ammonites will be the **head** of all those living in Gilead."
11:8 and you will be our **head** over all who live in Gilead."
11:9 and the LORD gives them to me—will I really be your **head**?"
11:11 and the people made him **head** and commander over them.
13:5 No razor may be used on his **head**, because the boy is to be a
16:3 and carried them to the **top** *of* the hill that faces Hebron.
16:13 "If you weave the seven braids of my **head** into the fabric ⌊on the
16:13 was sleeping, Delilah took the seven braids of his **head**, [BHS-]
16:17 "No razor has ever been used on my **head**," he said, "because I
16:19 she called a man to shave off the seven braids of his **hair**,
16:22 the hair on his **head** began to grow again after it had been shaved.
1Sa 1:11 all the days of his life, and no razor will ever be used on his **head**."
4:12 and went to Shiloh, his clothes torn and dust on his **head**.
5:4 His **head** and hands had been broken off and were lying on the
9:22 the hall and seated them at the **head** *of* those who were invited—
10:1 took a flask of oil and poured it on Saul's **head** and kissed him,
11:11 The next day Saul separated his men into three **divisions**; during
13:17 parties went out from the Philistine camp in three **detachments**.
13:17 **[RPH]** One turned toward Ophrah in the vicinity of Shual,
13:18 **[RPH]** another toward Beth Horon, and the third toward the
13:18 the **[RPH]** third toward the borderland overlooking the Valley of
14:45 as the LORD lives, not a hair of his **head** will fall to the ground,
15:17 own eyes, did you not become the **head** *of* the tribes of Israel?
17:5 He had a bronze helmet on his **head** and wore a coat of scale armor
17:38 He put a coat of armor on him and a bronze helmet on his **head**.
17:46 you over to me, and I'll strike you down and cut off your **head**.
17:51 After he killed him, he cut off his **head** with the sword.
17:54 David took the Philistine's **head** and brought it to Jerusalem,
17:57 him before Saul, with David still holding the Philistine's **head**.
25:39 and has brought Nabal's wrongdoing down on his own **head**."
26:13 to the other side and stood on **top** *of* the hill some distance away;
28:2 "Very well, I will make you my **bodyguard** [+4200+9068] for life."
29:4 his master's favor than by taking the **heads** *of* our own men?
31:9 They cut off his **head** and stripped off his armor, and they sent
2Sa 1:2 from Saul's camp, with his clothes torn and with dust on his **head**.
1:10 And I took the crown that was on his **head** and the band on his arm
1:16 For David had said to him, "Your blood be on your own **head**.
2:16 each man grabbed his opponent by the **head** and thrust his dagger
2:25 themselves into a group and took their stand on **top** *of* a hill.
3:8 of what Ish-Bosheth said and he answered, "Am I a dog's **head**—
3:29 May his blood fall upon the **head** *of* Joab and upon all his father's
4:7 After they stabbed and killed him, they cut off his **head**. Taking it
4:7 Taking **it**[s] [+2257] with them, they traveled all night by way of the
4:8 They brought the **head** *of* Ish-Bosheth to David at Hebron
4:8 "Here is the **head** *of* Ish-Bosheth son of Saul, your enemy,
4:12 they took the **head** *of* Ish-Bosheth and buried it in Abner's tomb at
5:24 As soon as you hear the sound of marching in the **tops** *of* the
12:30 He took the crown from the **head** *of* their king—its weight was a
12:30 was set with precious stones—and it was placed on David's **head**.
13:19 Tamar put ashes on her **head** and tore the ornamented robe she was
13:19 She put her hand on her **head** and went away, weeping aloud as
14:26 Whenever he cut the hair of his **head**—he used to cut his hair from
14:26 he would weigh **it**[s] [+8552], and its weight was two hundred
15:30 weeping as he went; his **head** was covered and he was barefoot.
15:30 All the people with him covered their **heads** too and were weeping
15:32 When David arrived at the **summit**, where people used to worship
15:32 Arkite was there to meet him, his robe torn and dust on his **head**.
16:1 When David had gone a short distance beyond the **summit**,
16:9 dog curse my lord the king? Let me go over and cut off his **head**."
18:9 branches of a large oak, Absalom's **head** got caught in the tree.
20:21 said to Joab, "His **head** will be thrown to you from the wall."
20:22 they cut off the **head** *of* Sheba son of Bicri and threw it to Joab.
22:44 of my people; you have preserved me as the **head** *of* nations.
23:8 Josheb-Basshebeth, a Tahkemonite, was **chief** *of* the Three;
23:13 three of the thirty **chief** *men* came down to David at the cave of
23:18 Abishai the brother of Joab son of Zeruiah was **chief** *of* the Three.
1Ki 2:32 The LORD *will* **repay** him **for** [+906+6584+8740] the blood he
2:33 May the guilt of their blood rest on the **head** *of* Joab and his
2:33 rest on the head of Joab and **[RPH]** his descendants forever.
2:37 can be sure you will die; your blood will be on your own **head**."
2:44 Now the LORD *will* **repay** you **for** [+906+928+8740] your
7:16 He also made two capitals of cast bronze to set on the **tops** *of* the
7:17 A network of interwoven chains festooned the capitals on **top** *of*
7:18 each network to decorate the capitals on **top** *of* the pillars.
7:19 The capitals on **top** *of* the pillars in the portico were in the shape of
7:22 The capitals on **top** were in the shape of lilies. And so the work on
7:35 At the **top** *of* the stand there was a circular band half a cubit deep.
7:35 The supports and panels were attached to the **top** *of* the stand.
7:41 the two pillars; the two bowl-shaped capitals on **top** *of* the pillars;
7:41 decorating the two bowl-shaped capitals on **top** *of* the pillars;
8:1 all the **heads** *of* the tribes and the chiefs of the Israelite families,
8:8 so long that their **ends** could be seen from the Holy Place in front
8:32 the guilty and bringing down on his own **head** what he has done.
10:19 The throne had six steps, and its back had a rounded **top**. On both
18:42 went off to eat and drink, but Elijah climbed to the **top** *of* Carmel,
20:31 with sackcloth around our waists and ropes around our **heads**.
20:32 sackcloth around their waists and ropes around their **heads**,
21:9 and seat Naboth in a **prominent place** *among* the people.
21:12 and seated Naboth in a **prominent place** *among* the people.
2Ki 1:9 who was sitting on the **top** *of* a hill, and said to him, "Man of God,
2:3 the LORD is going to take your master from **[NIE]** you today?"
2:5 the LORD is going to take your master from **[NIE]** you today?"
4:19 "My **head**! My head!" he said to his father. His father told a
4:19 "My head! My **head**!" he said to his father. His father told a
6:25 so long that a donkey's **head** sold for eighty shekels of silver,
6:31 if the **head** *of* Elisha son of Shaphat remains on his shoulders
6:32 you see how this murderer is sending someone to cut off my **head**?
9:3 Then take the flask and pour the oil on his **head** and declare,
9:6 Then the prophet poured the oil on Jehu's **head** and declared,
9:30 painted her eyes, arranged her **hair** and looked out of a window.
10:6 take the **heads** *of* your master's sons and come to me in Jezreel by
10:7 They put their **heads** in baskets and sent them to Jehu in Jezreel.
10:8 he told Jehu, "They have brought the **heads** *of* the princes."
19:21 mocks you. The Daughter of Jerusalem tosses her **head** as you flee.
25:18 The commander of the guard took as prisoners Seraiah the **chief**
25:27 *he* **released** [+906+5951] Jehoiachin from prison on the
1Ch 4:42 And five hundred of these Simeonites, **led** [+928] **by** Pelatiah,
5:7 according to their genealogical records: Jeiel the **chief**, Zechariah,
5:12 Joel was the **chief**, Shapham the second, then Janai and Shaphat,
5:15 Ahi son of Abdiel, the son of Guni, was **head** of their family.
5:24 These were the **heads** *of* their families: Epher, Ishi, Eliel, Azriel,
5:24 were brave warriors, famous men, and **heads** of their families.
7:2 Jeriel, Jahmai, Ibsam and Samuel—**heads** of their families.
7:3 Michael, Obadiah, Joel and Isshiah. All five of them were **chiefs**.
7:7 Ezbon, Uzzi, Uzziel, Jerimoth and Iri, **heads** *of* families—
7:9 Their genealogical record listed the **heads** *of* families and 20,200
7:11 All these sons of Jediael were **heads** *of* families. There were
7:40 **heads** *of* families, choice men, brave warriors and outstanding
7:40 of families, choice men, brave warriors and **outstanding** leaders.

1Ch 8: 6 who were **heads** *of* families of those living in Geba and were
8:10 Sakia and Mirmah. These were his sons, **heads** *of* families.
8:13 who were **heads** *of* families of those living in Aijalon and who
8:28 All these were **heads** *of* families, chiefs as listed in their
8:28 **chiefs** as listed in their genealogy, and they lived in Jerusalem.
9: 9 numbered 956. All these men were **heads** of their families.
9:13 The priests, who were **heads** of families, numbered 1,760.
9:17 Akkub, Talmon, Ahiman and their brothers, Shallum their **chief**
9:33 Those who were musicians, **heads** of Levite families, stayed in the
9:34 All these were **heads** of Levite families, chiefs as listed in their
9:34 **chiefs** as listed in their genealogy, and they lived in Jerusalem.
10: 9 They stripped him and took his **head** and his armor, and sent
11: 6 will become **commander-in-chief** [+2256+8569]."
11: 6 son of Zeruiah went up first, and so he received the **command**.
11:10 These were the **chiefs** *of* David's mighty men—they, together with
11:11 Jashobeam, a Hacmonite, was **chief** *of* the officers; he raised his
11:15 Three of the thirty **chiefs** came down to David to the rock at the
11:20 Abishai the brother of Joab was **chief** *of* the Three. He raised his
11:42 who was **chief** of the Reubenites, and the thirty with him,
12: 3 Ahiezer their **chief** and Joash the sons of Shemaah the Gibeathite;
12: 9 [12:10] Ezer was the **chief**, Obadiah the second in command,
12:14 [12:15] These Gadites were army **commanders**; the least was a
12:18 [12:19] Spirit came upon Amasai, **chief** *of* the Thirty, and he said:
12:18 [12:19] and made them **leaders** *of* his raiding bands.
12:19 [12:20] "It will cost us our **heads** if he deserts to his master
12:20 [12:21] and Zillethai, **leaders** *of* units of a thousand in Manasseh.
12:23 [12:24] These are the numbers of the **men** armed for battle who
12:32 [12:33] 200 **chiefs**, with all their relatives under their command;
14:15 As soon as you hear the sound of marching in the **tops** *of* the
15:12 He said to them, "You are the **heads** of the Levitical families;
16: 5 Asaph was the **chief**, Zechariah second, then Jeiel, Shemiramoth,
16: 7 That day David **first** committed to Asaph and his associates this
20: 2 David took the crown from the **head** *of* their king—its weight was
20: 2 was set with precious stones—and it was placed on David's **head**.
23: 8 The sons of Ladan: Jehiel the **first**, Zetham and Joel—three in all.
23: 9 three in all. These were the **heads** *of* the families of Ladan.
23:11 Jahath was the **first** and Ziza the second, but Jeush and Beriah did
23:16 The descendants of Gershom: Shubael was the **first**.
23:17 Rehabiah was the **first**. Eliezer had no other sons, but the sons of
23:18 The sons of Izhar: Shelomith was the **first**.
23:19 Jeriah the **first**, Amariah the second, Jahaziel the third
23:20 The sons of Uzziel: Micah the **first** and Isshiah the second.
23:24 the **heads** *of* families as they were registered under their names
24: 4 A larger number of **leaders** were found among Eleazar's
24: 4 sixteen **heads** of families from Eleazar's descendants and eight
24: 6 and the **heads** *of* families of the priests and of the Levites—
24:21 As for Rehabiah, from his sons: Isshiah was the **first**.
24:23 Jeriah the **first**, [BHS-] Amariah the second, Jahaziel the third
24:31 and the **heads** *of* families of the priests and of the Levites.
24:31 The families of the **oldest** brother were treated the same as those of
26:10 Shimri the **first** (although he was not the firstborn, his father had
26:10 he was not the firstborn, his father had appointed him the **first**),
26:12 These divisions of the gatekeepers, through their **chief** men,
26:21 who were **heads** *of* families belonging to Ladan the Gershonite,
26:26 by the **heads** *of* families who were the commanders of thousands
26:31 Jeriah was their **chief** according to the genealogical records of their
26:32 hundred relatives, who were able men and **heads** *of* families,
27: 1 **heads** *of* families, commanders of thousands and commanders of
27: 3 of Perez and **chief** of all the army officers for the first month.
27: 5 the priest. He was **chief** and there were 24,000 men in his division.
29:11 O LORD, is the kingdom; you are exalted as **head** over all.
2Ch 1: 2 to the judges and to all the leaders in Israel, the **heads** *of* families—
3:15 cubits long, each with a capital on **top** measuring five cubits.
3:16 He made interwoven chains and put them on **top** *of* the pillars.
4:12 the two pillars; the two bowl-shaped capitals on **top** *of* the pillars;
4:12 decorating the two bowl-shaped capitals on **top** *of* the pillars;
5: 2 all the **heads** *of* the tribes and the chiefs of the Israelite families,
5: 9 These poles were so long that their **ends**, extending from the ark,
6:23 repaying the guilty by bringing down on his own **head** what he has
11:22 Rehoboam appointed Abijah son of Maacah to be the **chief** prince
13:12 God is with us; he is our **leader**. His priests with their trumpets
19: 8 and **heads** of Israelite families to administer the law of the LORD
19:11 "Amariah the **chief** priest will be over you in any matter
20:27 Then, **led** [+928] **by** Jehoshaphat, all the men of Judah
23: 2 the Levites and the **heads** of Israelite families from all the towns.
24: 6 Therefore the king summoned Jehoiada the **chief** priest and said to
24:11 the royal secretary and the officer of the **chief** priest would come
25:12 took them to the **top** *of* a cliff and threw them down so that all
25:12 took them to the top of a cliff and threw them **down** [+4946]
26:12 The total number of family **leaders** over the fighting men was
26:20 When Azariah the **chief** priest and all the other priests looked at
28:12 Then some of the **leaders** *in* Ephraim—Azariah son of Jehohanan,
31:10 and Azariah the **chief** priest, from the family of Zadok, answered,
Ezr 1: 5 Then the family **heads** of Judah and Benjamin, and the priests
2:68 some of the **heads** *of* the families gave freewill offerings toward
3:12 But many of the older priests and Levites and family **heads**,
4: 2 they came to Zerubbabel and to the **heads** *of* the families and said,
4: 3 and the rest of the **heads** *of* the families of Israel answered,
7: 5 of Phinehas, the son of Eleazar, the son of Aaron the **chief** priest—
7:28 and gathered **leading** *men* from Israel to go up with me.
8: 1 These are the family **heads** and those registered with them who
8:16 and Meshullam, *who* were **leaders**, and Joiarib and Elnathan,
8:17 I sent them to Iddo, the **leader** in Casiphia. I told them what to say
9: 3 pulled hair from my **head** and beard and sat down appalled.
9: 6 because our sins are higher than our **heads** and our guilt has
10:16 Ezra the priest selected men who were family **heads**, one from
Ne 4: 4 [3:36] are despised. Turn their insults back on their own **heads**.
7:70 [7:69] Some of the **heads** *of* the families contributed to the work.
7:71 [7:70] Some of the **heads** *of* the families gave to the treasury for
8:13 the **heads** of all the families, along with the priests and the Levites,
9:17 in their rebellion appointed a **leader** in order to return to their
10:14 [10:15] The **leaders** *of* the people: Parosh, Pahath-Moab, Elam,
11: 3 These are the provincial **leaders** who settled in Jerusalem (now
11:13 and his associates, who were **heads** of families—242 men;
11:16 Shabbethai and Jozabad, two of the **heads** *of* the Levites, who had
11:17 the son of Asaph, the **director** who led in thanksgiving and prayer;
12: 7 These were the **leaders** *of* the priests and their associates in the
12:12 the days of Joiakim, these were the **heads** *of* the priestly families:
12:22 The family **heads** of the Levites in the days of Eliashib, Joiada,
12:23 The family **heads** among the descendants of Levi up to the time of
12:24 And the **leaders** *of* the Levites were Hashabiah, Sherebiah,
12:46 there had been **directors** *for* the singers and for the songs of praise
Est 2:17 So he set a royal crown on her **head** and made her queen instead of
5: 2 his hand. So Esther approached and touched the **tip** *of* the scepter.
6: 8 horse the king has ridden, one with a royal crest placed on its **head**.
6:12 But Haman rushed home, with his **head** covered in grief,
9:25 had devised against the Jews should come back onto his own **head**,
Job 1:17 "The Chaldeans formed three **raiding parties** and swept down on
1:20 At this, Job got up and tore his robe and shaved his **head**.
2:12 and they tore their robes and sprinkled dust on their **heads**.
10:15 I cannot lift my **head**, for I am full of shame and drowned in my
12:24 He deprives the **leaders** [+6639] *of* the earth of their reason;
16: 4 I could make fine speeches against you and shake my **head** at you.
19: 9 stripped me of my honor and removed the crown from my **head**.
20: 6 his pride reaches to the heavens and his **head** touches the clouds,
22:12 in the heights of heaven? And see how lofty are the **highest** stars!
24:24 and gathered up like all others; they are cut off like **heads** *of* grain.
29: 3 when his lamp shone upon my **head** and by his light I walked
29:25 I chose the way for them and sat as their **chief**; I dwelt as a king
41: 7 [40:31] his hide with harpoons or his **head** with fishing spears?
Ps 3: 3 [3:4] O LORD; you bestow glory on me and lift up my **head**.
7:16 [7:17] The trouble he causes recoils on **himself** [+2257]; his
18:43 [18:44] you have made me the **head** *of* nations; people I did not
21: 3 [21:4] rich blessings and placed a crown of pure gold on his **head**.
22: 7 [22:8] see me mock me; they hurl insults, shaking their **heads**:
23: 5 of my enemies. You anoint my **head** with oil; my cup overflows.
24: 7 Lift up your **heads**, O you gates; be lifted up, you ancient doors,
24: 9 Lift up your **heads**, O you gates; lift them up, you ancient doors,
27: 6 my **head** will be exalted above the enemies who surround me;
38: 4 [38:5] My guilt *has* **overwhelmed** [+6296] me like a burden too
40:12 [40:13] They are more than the hairs of my **head**, and my heart
44:14 [44:15] among the nations; the peoples shake their **heads** at us.
60: 7 [60:9] is mine; Ephraim is my **helmet** [+5057], Judah my scepter.
66:12 You let men ride over our **heads**; we went through fire and water,
68:21 [68:22] Surely God will crush the **heads** *of* his enemies, the hairy
69: 4 [69:5] hate me without reason outnumber the hairs of my **head**;
72:16 abound throughout the land; on the **tops** *of* the hills may it sway.
74:13 by your power; you broke the **heads** *of* the monster in the waters.
74:14 It was you who crushed the **heads** *of* Leviathan and gave him as
83: 2 [83:3] how your enemies are astir, how your foes rear their **heads**.
108: 8 [108:9] Ephraim is my **helmet** [+5057], Judah my scepter.
109:25 of scorn to my accusers; when they see me, they shake their **heads**.
110: 6 heaping up the dead and crushing the **rulers** of the whole earth.
110: 7 from a brook beside the way; therefore he will lift up his **head**.
118:22 The stone the builders rejected has become the **capstone** [+7157];
119:160 **All** your words are true; all your righteous laws are eternal.
133: 2 It is like precious oil poured on the **head**, running down on the
137: 6 if I do not consider Jerusalem my **highest** [+6584] joy.
139:17 to me are your thoughts, O God! How vast is the **sum** *of* them!
140: 7 [140:8] who shields my **head** in the day of battle—
140: 9 [140:10] Let the **heads** *of* those who surround me be covered with
141: 5 it is a kindness; let him rebuke me—it is oil on my **head**.
141: 5 him rebuke me—it is oil on my head. My **head** will not refuse it.
Pr 1: 9 They will be a garland to grace your **head** and a chain to adorn
1:21 at the **head** *of* the noisy streets she cries out, in the gateways of the
4: 9 She will set a garland of grace on your **head** and present you with
8: 2 On the **heights** [+5294] along the way, where the paths meet,
8:23 from eternity, from the **beginning**, before the world began.

Pr 8:26 he made the earth or its fields or **any** *of* the dust of the world.
10: 6 Blessings crown the **head** *of* the righteous, but violence
11:26 but blessing **crowns** [+4200] him who is willing to sell.
23:34 be like one sleeping on the high seas, lying on **top** *of* the rigging.
25:22 In doing this, you will heap burning coals on his **head**,
28: 3 A **ruler** [+1505] [BHS 8133] who oppresses the poor is like a
Ecc 2:14 The wise man has eyes in his **head**, while the fool walks in the
3:11 yet they cannot fathom what God has done from **beginning** to end.
9: 8 Always be clothed in white, and always anoint your **head** with oil.
SS 2: 6 His left arm is under my **head**, and his right arm embraces me.
4: 8 Descend from the **crest** *of* Amana, from the top of Senir,
4: 8 from the **top** *of* Senir, the summit of Hermon, from the lions' dens
4:14 kind of incense tree, with myrrh and aloes and all the **finest** spices.
5: 2 My **head** is drenched with dew, my hair with the dampness of the
5:11 His **head** is purest gold; his hair is wavy and black as a raven.
7: 5 [7:6] Your **head** crowns you like Mount Carmel. Your hair is like
7: 5 [7:6] Your **hair** [+1929] is like royal tapestry; the king is held
8: 3 His left arm is under my **head** and his right arm embraces me.
Isa 1: 5 Your whole **head** is injured, your whole heart afflicted.
1: 6 From the sole of your foot to the *top of* your **head** there is no
2: 2 temple will be established as **chief** *among* the mountains;
7: 8 for the **head** *of* Aram is Damascus, and the head of Damascus is
7: 8 of Aram is Damascus, and the **head** *of* Damascus is only Rezin.
7: 9 The **head** *of* Ephraim is Samaria, and the head of Samaria is only
7: 9 is Samaria, and the **head** *of* Samaria is only Remaliah's son.
7:20 to shave your **head** and the hair of your legs, and to take off your
9:14 [9:13] So the LORD will cut off from Israel both **head** and tail,
9:15 [9:14] the elders and prominent men are the **head**, the prophets
15: 2 and Medeba. Every **head** is shaved and every beard cut off.
17: 6 leaving two or three olives on the **topmost** branches, four
19:15 There is nothing Egypt can do—**head** or tail, palm branch or reed.
28: 1 his glorious beauty, set on the **head** *of* a fertile valley—
28: 4 his glorious beauty, set on the **head** *of* a fertile valley,
29:10 your eyes (the prophets); he has covered your **heads** (the seers).
30:17 till you are left like a flagstaff on a **mountaintop** [+2215],
35:10 enter Zion with singing; everlasting joy will crown their **heads**.
37:22 mocks you. The Daughter of Jerusalem tosses her **head** as you flee.
40:21 Have you not heard? Has it not been told you from the **beginning**?
41: 4 it through, calling forth the generations from the **beginning**?
41:26 Who told of this from the **beginning**, so we could know,
42:11 Sela sing for joy; let them shout from the **mountaintops** [+2215].
48:16 "From the **first** announcement I have not spoken in secret;
51:11 enter Zion with singing; everlasting joy will crown their **heads**.
51:20 they lie at the **head** *of* every street, like antelope caught in a net.
58: 5 Is it only for bowing one's **head** like a reed and for lying on
59:17 as his breastplate, and the helmet of salvation on his **head**;
Jer 2:37 You will also leave that place with your hands on your **head**,
9: 1 [8:23] that my **head** were a spring of water and my eyes a
13:21 LORD⌋ sets over you those you cultivated as your **special** allies?
14: 3 jars unfilled; dismayed and despairing, they cover their **heads**.
14: 4 rain in the land; the farmers are dismayed and cover their **heads**.
18:16 all who pass by will be appalled and will shake their **heads**.
22: 6 "Though you are like Gilead to me, like the **summit** *of* Lebanon,
23:19 in wrath, a whirlwind swirling down on the **heads** *of* the wicked.
30:23 a driving wind swirling down on the **heads** *of* the wicked.
31: 7 "Sing with joy for Jacob; shout for the **foremost** *of* the nations.
48:37 Every **head** is shaved and every beard cut off; every hand is
52:24 The commander of the guard took as prisoners Seraiah the **chief**
52:31 *he* **released** [+906+5951] Jehoiachin king of Judah and freed him
La 1: 5 Her foes have become her **masters**; her enemies are at ease.
2:10 they have sprinkled dust on their **heads** and put on sackcloth.
2:10 The young women of Jerusalem have bowed their **heads** to the
2:15 they scoff and shake their **heads** at the Daughter of Jerusalem:
2:19 Arise, cry out in the night, as the watches of the night **begin**;
2:19 of your children, who faint from hunger at the **head** *of* every street.
3:54 the waters closed over my **head**, and I thought I was about to be
4: 1 The sacred gems are scattered at the **head** *of* every street.
5:16 The crown has fallen from our **head**. Woe to us, for we have
Eze 1:22 Spread out above the **heads** *of* the living creatures was what
1:22 looked like an expanse, sparkling like ice, and awesome. **[RPH]**
1:25 there came a voice from above the expanse over their **heads** as
1:26 Above the expanse over their **heads** was what looked like a throne
5: 1 and use it as a barber's razor to shave your **head** and your beard.
6:13 on every high hill and on all the **mountaintops** [+2215], under
7:18 faces will be covered with shame and their **heads** will be shaved.
8: 3 out what looked like a hand and took me by the hair of my **head**.
9:10 but I will bring down on their own **heads** what they have done."
10: 1 above the expanse that was over the **heads** *of* the cherubim.
10:11 The cherubim went in whatever direction the **head** faced,
11:21 I will bring down on their own **heads** what they have done,
13:18 make veils of various lengths for their **heads** in order to ensnare
16:12 earrings on your ears and a beautiful crown on your **head**.
16:25 At the **head** *of* every street you built your lofty shrines
16:31 When you built your mounds at the **head** *of* every street and made
16:43 I will surely bring down on your **head** what you have done,
17: 4 he broke off its **topmost** shoot and carried it away to a land of
17:19 I will bring down on his **head** my oath that he despised and my
17:22 I will break off a tender sprig from its **topmost** shoots and plant it
21:19 [21:24] Make a signpost where the road **branches off** *to* the city.
21:21 [21:26] at the **junction** *of* the two roads, to seek an omen:
22:31 bringing down on their own **heads** all they have done,
23:15 with belts around their waists and flowing turbans on their **heads**;
23:42 of the woman and her sister and beautiful crowns on their **heads**.
24:23 You will keep your turbans on your **heads** and your sandals on
27:22 for your merchandise they exchanged the **finest** *of* all kinds of
27:30 over you; they will sprinkle dust on their **heads** and roll in ashes.
29:18 every **head** was rubbed bare and every shoulder made raw.
32:27 weapons of war, whose swords were placed under their **heads**?
33: 4 sword comes and takes his life, his blood will be on his own **head**.
38: 2 of the land of Magog, the **chief** prince of Meshech and Tubal;
38: 3 I am against you, O Gog, **chief** prince of Meshech and Tubal.
39: 1 I am against you, O Gog, **chief** prince of Meshech and Tubal.
40: 1 our exile, at the **beginning** *of* the year, on the tenth of the month,
42:12 There was a doorway at the **beginning** *of* the passageway that was
43:12 All the surrounding area on **top** *of* the mountain will be most holy.
44:18 They are to wear linen turbans on their **heads** and linen
44:20 " 'They must not shave their **heads** or let their hair grow long,
44:20 grow long, but they are to keep the hair of their **heads** trimmed.
Da 1:10 your age? The king would then have my **head** because of you."
Hos 1:11 [2:2] they will appoint one **leader** and will come up out of the
4:13 They sacrifice on the **mountaintops** [+2215] and burn offerings on
Joel 2: 5 like that of chariots they leap over the **mountaintops** [+2215],
3: 4 [4:4] and speedily return on your own **heads** what you have done.
3: 7 [4:7] and I will return on your own **heads** what you have done.
Am 1: 2 pastures of the shepherds dry up, and the **top** *of* Carmel withers."
2: 7 They trample on the **heads** *of* the poor as upon the dust of the
6: 7 Therefore you will be among the **first** to go into exile; your
8:10 I will make all of you wear sackcloth and shave your **heads**.
9: 1 Bring them down on the **heads** *of* all the people; those who are left
9: 3 Though they hide themselves on the **top** *of* Carmel, there I will
Ob 1:15 it will be done to you; your deeds will return upon your own **head**.
Jnh 2: 5 [2:6] surrounded me; seaweed was wrapped around my **head**.
4: 6 made it grow up over Jonah to give shade for his **head** to ease his
4: 8 and the sun blazed on Jonah's **head** so that he grew faint.
Mic 2:13 king will pass through before them, the LORD at their **head**."
3: 1 I said, "Listen, you **leaders** *of* Jacob, you rulers of the house of
3: 9 Hear this, you **leaders** *of* the house of Jacob, you rulers of the
3:11 Her **leaders** judge for a bribe, her priests teach for a price,
4: 1 temple will be established as **chief** *among* the mountains;
Na 3:10 Her infants were dashed to pieces at the **head** *of* every street.
Hab 3:13 You crushed the **leader** of the land of wickedness, you stripped
3:14 With his own spear you pierced his **head** when his warriors
Zec 1:21 [2:4] that scattered Judah so that no one could raise his **head**,
3: 5 I said, "Put a clean turban on his **head**." So they put a clean turban
3: 5 So they put a clean turban on his **head** and clothed him,
4: 2 "I see a solid gold lampstand with a bowl at the **top** and seven
4: 2 and seven lights on it, with seven channels to the lights. **[RPH]**
6:11 and make a crown, and set it on the **head** *of* the high priest,

8032 ²ראשׁ *rō'š²*, n.m. [12]

poison [5], poisoned [3], bitterness [2], gall [1], poisonous weeds [1]

Dt 29:18 [29:17] is no root among you that produces such bitter **poison**.
32:32 Their grapes are filled with **poison**, and their clusters with
32:33 Their wine is the venom of serpents, the deadly **poison** *of* cobras.
Job 20:16 He will suck the **poison** *of* serpents; the fangs of an adder will kill
Ps 69:21 [69:22] They put **gall** in my food and gave me vinegar for my
Jer 8:14 has doomed us to perish and given us **poisoned** water to drink,
9:15 [9:14] make this people eat bitter food and drink **poisoned** water.
23:15 "I will make them eat bitter food and drink **poisoned** water,
La 3: 5 has besieged me and surrounded me with **bitterness** and hardship.
3:19 my affliction and my wandering, the **bitterness** and the gall.
Hos 10: 4 therefore lawsuits spring up like **poisonous weeds** in a plowed
Am 6:12 you have turned justice into **poison** and the fruit of righteousness

8033 ³ראשׁ *rō'š³*, n.pr.m. [1] [√ 8031]

Rosh [1]

Ge 46:21 Bela, Beker, Ashbel, Gera, Naaman, Ehi, **Rosh**, Muppim,

8034 ⁴ראשׁ *rō'š⁴*, n.pr.g. Not used in NIV/BHS [√ 8031?]

8035 ראשׁה *ri'šâ*, n.f. [1] [√ 8031]

before [1]

Eze 36:11 on you as in the past and will make you prosper more than **before**.

8036 רֹאשָׁה *rō'šâ*, n.f. [1] [√ 8031]

capstone [+74] [1]

Zec 4: 7 he will bring out the **capstone** [+74] to shouts of 'God bless it!

8037 רִאשׁוֹן *ri'šôn*, a. [182] [→ 8038; cf. 8031]

first [100], former [19], beginning [13], before [+928+2021] [6], earlier [6], before [4], *untranslated* [3], first [+928+2021] [2], old [2], used to [+2021+4200] [2], ancestors [1], chief officials [1], chief [1], days of old [1], early [1], fathers [1], forefathers [+3] [1], formerly [+928+2021] [1], front [1], highest [1], lead [1], leads [+928+2021] [1], led the way [+2118+3338] [1], long ago [+928+2021] [1], long [1], of old [1], older [1], once again [+2021+3869] [1], one in the lead [1], past [+3427] [1], past [+6961] [1], past [1], predecessors [1], previous [1], used to [1]

Ge 8: 13 By the first day of the **first** month of Noah's six hundred and first
13: 4 where he had **first** built an altar. There Abram called on the name
25: 25 The **first** to come out was red, and his whole body was like a hairy
26: 1 in the land—besides the **earlier** famine of Abraham's time—
28: 19 place Bethel, though the city **used** [+2021+4200] **to** be called Luz.
32: 17 [32:18] He instructed the **one in the lead**: "When my brother
33: 2 He put the maidservants and their children *in* **front**, Leah
38: 28 and tied it on his wrist and said, "This one came out **first**."
40: 13 in his hand, just as you **used to** do when you were his cupbearer.
41: 20 The lean, ugly cows ate up the seven fat cows that came up **first**.
Ex 4: 8 do not believe you or pay attention to the **first** miraculous sign,
12: 2 month is to be for you the first month, the **first** month of your year.
12: 15 On the **first** day remove the yeast from your houses, for whoever
12: 15 for whoever eats anything with yeast in it from the **first** day
12: 16 On the **first** day hold a sacred assembly, and another one on the
12: 18 In the **first** month you are to eat bread made without yeast,
34: 1 said to Moses, "Chisel out two stone tablets like the **first** *ones*,
34: 1 and I will write on them the words that were on the **first** tablets,
34: 4 So Moses chiseled out two stone tablets like the **first** *ones*
40: 2 the Tent of Meeting, on the first day of the **first** month.
40: 17 So the tabernacle was set up on the first day of the **first** month in
Lev 4: 21 the bull outside the camp and burn it as he burned the **first** bull.
5: 8 them to the priest, who shall **first** offer the one for the sin offering.
9: 15 and offered it for a sin offering as he did with the **first** *one*.
23: 5 begins at twilight on the fourteenth day of the **first** month.
23: 7 On the **first** day hold a sacred assembly and do no regular work.
23: 35 The **first** day is a sacred assembly; do no regular work.
23: 39 the **first** day is a day of rest, and the eighth day also is a day of
23: 40 On the **first** day you are to take choice fruit from the trees,
26: 45 for their sake I will remember the covenant with their **ancestors**
Nu 2: 9 to their divisions, number 186,400. They will set out **first**.
6: 12 The **previous** days do not count, because he became defiled during
7: 12 The one who brought his offering on the **first** day was Nahshon
9: 1 The LORD spoke to Moses in the Desert of Sinai in the **first**
9: 5 in the Desert of Sinai at twilight on the fourteenth day of the **first**
10: 13 They set out, this **first** *time*, at the LORD's command through
10: 14 The divisions of the camp of Judah went **first**, under their standard.
20: 1 In the **first** month the whole Israelite community arrived at the
21: 26 who had fought against the **former** king of Moab and had taken
28: 16 " 'On the fourteenth day of the **first** month the LORD's Passover
28: 18 On the **first** day hold a sacred assembly and do no regular work.
33: 3 The Israelites set out from Rameses on the fifteenth day of the **first**
33: 3 fifteenth day of the first month, **[RPH]** the day after the Passover.
Dt 4: 32 Ask now about the **former** days, long before your time, from the
9: 18 **once** [+2021+3869] **again** I fell prostrate before the LORD for
10: 1 "Chisel out two stone tablets like the **first** *ones* and come up to me
10: 2 I will write on the tablets the words that were on the **first** tablets,
10: 3 acacia wood and chiseled out two stone tablets like the **first** *ones*,
10: 4 The LORD wrote on these tablets what he had written **before**,
10: 10 on the mountain forty days and nights, as I did the **first** time,
13: 9 [13:10] Your hand must be the **first** in putting him to death, and
16: 4 Do not let any of the meat you sacrifice on the evening of the **first**
17: 7 The hands of the witnesses must be the **first** in putting him to
19: 14 **predecessors** in the inheritance you receive in the land the LORD
24: 4 her **first** husband, who divorced her, is not allowed to marry her
Jos 4: 19 On the tenth day of the **first** month the people went up from the
8: 5 as they did **before** [+928+2021], we will flee from them.
8: 6 'They are running away from us as they did **before** [+928+2021].'
8: 33 as Moses the servant of the LORD had **formerly** [+928+2021]
21: 10 Kohathite clans of the Levites, because the **first** lot fell to them):
Jdg 18: 29 to Israel—though the city **used** [+2021+4200] **to** be called Laish.
20: 22 their positions where they had stationed themselves the **first** day.
20: 32 "We are defeating them as **before** [+928+2021]," the Israelites
20: 39 and they said, "We are defeating them as in the **first** battle."
Ru 3: 10 "This kindness is greater than that which you showed **earlier**:
1Sa 14: 14 In that **first** attack Jonathan and his armor-bearer killed some
17: 30 brought up the same matter, and the men answered him as **before**.
2Sa 7: 10 will not oppress them anymore, as they did at the **beginning**
18: 27 "It seems to me that the **first** *one* runs like Ahimaaz son of
19: 20 [19:21] today I have come here as the **first** of the whole house of
19: 43 [19:44] Were we not the **first** to speak of bringing back our
20: 18 She continued, "**Long ago** [+928+2021] they used to say,
21: 9 they were put to death during the **first** days of the harvest,
1Ki 13: 6 hand was restored and became as it was **before** [+928+2021].
17: 13 **first** [+928+2021] make a small cake of bread for me from what
18: 25 "Choose one of the bulls and prepare it **first**, since there are
20: 9 the king, 'Your servant will do all you demanded the **first** *time*,
20: 17 The young officers of the provincial commanders went out **first**.
2Ki 1: 14 and consumed the **first** two captains and all their men.
17: 34 To this day they persist in their **former** practices. They neither
17: 40 would not listen, however, but persisted in their **former** practices.
1Ch 9: 2 Now the **first** to resettle on their own property in their own towns
11: 6 "Whoever **leads** [+928+2021] the attack on the Jebusites will
11: 6 Joab son of Zeruiah went up **first**, and so he received the
12: 15 [12:16] It was they who crossed the Jordan in the **first** month
15: 13 did not bring it up the **first** *time* that the LORD our God broke
17: 9 will not oppress them anymore, as they did at the **beginning**
18: 17 and David's sons were **chief officials** at the king's side.
24: 7 The **first** lot fell to Jehoiarib, the second to Jedaiah,
25: 9 The **first** lot, which was for Asaph, fell to Joseph, his sons
27: 2 In charge of the **first** division, for the first month, was Jashobeam
27: 2 In charge of the first division, for the **first** month, was Jashobeam
27: 3 of Perez and chief of all the army officers for the **first** month.
29: 29 As for the events of King David's reign, from **beginning** to end,
2Ch 3: 3 and twenty cubits wide (using the cubit of the **old** standard).
9: 29 As for the other events of Solomon's reign, from **beginning** to end,
12: 15 As for the events of Rehoboam's reign, from **beginning** to end,
16: 11 The events of Asa's reign, from **beginning** to end, are written in
17: 3 because in his **early** years he walked in the ways his father David
20: 34 The other events of Jehoshaphat's reign, from **beginning** to end,
22: 1 came with the Arabs into the camp, had killed all the **older** sons.
25: 26 As for the other events of Amaziah's reign, from **beginning** to end,
26: 22 The other events of Uzziah's reign, from **beginning** to end,
28: 26 other events of his reign and all his ways, from **beginning** to end,
29: 3 In the **first** month of the first year of his reign, he opened the doors
29: 3 In the first month of the **first** year of his reign, he opened the doors
29: 17 They began the consecration on the first day of the **first** month,
29: 17 the LORD itself, finishing on the sixteenth day of the **first** month.
35: 1 lamb was slaughtered on the fourteenth day of the **first** month.
35: 27 all the events, from **beginning** to end, are written in the book of the
Ezr 3: 12 and Levites and family heads, who had seen the **former** temple,
6: 19 On the fourteenth day of the **first** month, the exiles celebrated the
7: 9 He had begun his journey from Babylon on the first day of the **first**
8: 31 On the twelfth day of the **first** month we set out from the Ahava
9: 2 officials *have* **led** [+2118+3338] **the way** in this unfaithfulness."
10: 17 by the first day of the **first** month they finished dealing with all the
Ne 5: 15 the **earlier** governors—those preceding me—placed a heavy
7: 5 I found the genealogical record of those who had been the **first** to
8: 18 Day after day, from the **first** day to the last, Ezra read from the
Est 1: 14 had special access to the king and were **highest** in the kingdom.
3: 7 in the **first** month, the month of Nisan, they cast the *pur* (that is,
3: 12 on the thirteenth day of the **first** month the royal secretaries were
Job 8: 8 "Ask the **former** generations and find out what their fathers
15: 7 "Are you the **first** man *ever* born? Were you brought forth before
Ps 79: 8 Do not hold against us the sins of the **fathers**; may your mercy
89: 49 [89:50] O Lord, where is your **former** great love, which in your
Pr 18: 17 The **first** to present his case seems right, till another comes
20: 21 An inheritance quickly gained at the **beginning** will not be blessed
Ecc 1: 11 There is no remembrance of *men* **of old**, and even those who are
7: 10 Do not say, "Why were the **old** days better than these?" For it is
Isa 1: 26 I will restore your judges as in **days of old**, your counselors as at
9: 1 [8:23] In the **past** [+6961] he humbled the land of Zebulun
41: 4 the LORD—with the **first** of them and with the last—I am he."
41: 22 Tell us what the **former** *things* were, so that we may consider
41: 27 I was the **first** to tell Zion, 'Look, here they are!' I gave to
42: 9 See, the **former** *things* have taken place, and new things I declare;
43: 9 of them foretold this and proclaimed to us the **former** *things*?
43: 18 "Forget the **former** *things*; do not dwell on the past.
43: 27 Your **first** father sinned; your spokesmen rebelled against me.
44: 6 I am the **first** and I am the last; apart from me there is no God.
46: 9 Remember the **former** *things*, those of long ago; I am God,
48: 3 I foretold the **former** *things* long ago, my mouth announced them
48: 12 whom I have called: I am he; I am the **first** and I am the last.
52: 4 "At **first** my people went down to Egypt to live; lately, Assyria has
60: 9 in the **lead** are the ships of Tarshish, bringing your sons from afar,
61: 4 rebuild the ancient ruins and restore the places **long** devastated;
65: 7 I will measure into their laps the full payment for their **former**
65: 16 For the **past** troubles will be forgotten and hidden from my eyes.
65: 17 The **former** *things* will not be remembered, nor will they come to
Jer 7: 12 " 'Go now to the place in Shiloh where I **first** [+928+2021] made a
11: 10 They have returned to the sins of their **forefathers** [+3], who
16: 18 I will repay them **[NIE]** double for their wickedness and their sin,
17: 12 A glorious throne, exalted from the **beginning**, is the place of our

Jer 33: 7 and will rebuild them as they were **before** [+928+2021].
33: 11 restore the fortunes of the land as they were **before** [+928+2021],'
34: 5 the **former** kings who preceded you, so they will make a fire in
36: 28 and write on it all the words **[RPH]** that were on the first scroll,
36: 28 and write on it all the words that were on the **first** scroll,
50: 17 The **first** to devour him was the king of Assyria; the last to crush
Eze 29: 17 In the twenty-seventh year, in the **first** month on the first day,
30: 20 In the eleventh year, in the **first** month on the seventh day,
40: 21 its portico had the same measurements as those of the **first**
45: 18 In the **first** month on the first day you are to take a young bull
45: 21 " 'In the **first** month on the fourteenth day you are to observe the
Da 8: 21 of Greece, and the large horn between his eyes is the **first** king.
10: 4 On the twenty-fourth day of the **first** month, as I was standing on
10: 12 Since the **first** day that you set your mind to gain understanding
10: 13 Michael, one of the **chief** princes, came to help me, because I was
11: 13 king of the North will muster another army, larger than the **first**;
11: 29 this time the outcome will be different from what it was **before**.
Hos 2: 7 [2:9] 'I will go back to my husband as at **first**, for then I was
Joel 2: 23 you abundant showers, both autumn and spring rains, as **before**.
Mic 4: 8 the Daughter of Zion, the **former** dominion will be restored to you;
Hag 2: 3 'Who of you is left who saw this house in its **former** glory?
2: 9 present house will be greater than the glory of the **former** house,'
Zec 1: 4 be like your forefathers, to whom the **earlier** prophets proclaimed:
6: 2 The **first** chariot had red horses, the second black,
7: 7 LORD proclaimed through the **earlier** prophets when Jerusalem
7: 12 Almighty had sent by his Spirit through the **earlier** prophets.
8: 11 deal with the remnant of this people as I did in the **past** [+3427],"
12: 7 "The LORD will save the dwellings of Judah **first**, so that the
14: 10 from the Benjamin Gate to the site of the **First** Gate, to the Corner

8038 ראשׁוֹנִי *ri'šônî*, a. [1] [√ 8037; cf. 8031]

first [1]

Jer 25: 1 which was the **first** year of Nebuchadnezzar king of Babylon.

8039 רַאֲשׁוֹת *ra'ašôt*, n.[f.]pl.den. Not used in NIV/BHS [√ 8031; cf. 5265]

8040 רֵאשִׁית *rē'šît*, n.f. [51] [√ 8031]

first [13], firstfruits [8], beginning [7], best [6], early [+928] [3], firstfruits [+7262] [2], beginnings [1], choice parts [1], choice [1], early [1], finest [1], firstfruits of harvest [1], foremost [1], leaders [1], mainstay [1], starting [1], supreme [1], when [+928] [1]

Ge 1: 1 In the **beginning** God created the heavens and the earth.
10: 10 The **first** *centers of* his kingdom were Babylon, Erech, Akkad
49: 3 my might, the **first** *sign of* my strength, excelling in honor,
Ex 23: 19 "Bring the **best** *of* the firstfruits of your soil to the house of the
34: 26 "Bring the **best** *of* the firstfruits of your soil to the house of the
Lev 2: 12 may bring them to the LORD as an offering of the **firstfruits**,
23: 10 its harvest, bring to the priest a sheaf of the **first** grain you harvest.
Nu 15: 20 Present a cake from the **first** *of* your ground meal and present it as
15: 21 this offering to the LORD from the **first** *of* your ground meal.
18: 12 and grain they give the LORD as the **firstfruits of** their **harvest**.
24: 20 "Amalek was **first** *among* the nations, but he will come to ruin at
Dt 11: 12 God are continually on it from the **beginning** *of* the year to its end.
18: 4 You are to give them the **firstfruits** *of* your grain, new wine
18: 4 and oil, and the **first** wool from the shearing of your sheep,
21: 17 That son is the **first** sign of his father's strength. The right of the
26: 2 take some of the **firstfruits** [+7262] *of* all that you produce from
26: 10 and now I bring the **firstfruits** [+7262] *of* the soil that you,
33: 21 He chose the **best** land for himself; the leader's portion was kept
1Sa 2: 29 on the **choice parts** *of* every offering made by my people Israel?'
15: 21 and cattle from the plunder, the **best** *of* what was devoted to God,
2Ch 31: 5 the Israelites generously gave the **firstfruits** *of* their grain,
Ne 10: 37 [10:38] to the priests, the **first** *of* our ground meal, of our ⌊grain⌋
12: 44 of the storerooms for the contributions, **firstfruits** and tithes.
Job 8: 7 Your **beginnings** will seem humble, so prosperous will your future
40: 19 He ranks **first** *among* the works of God, yet his Maker can
42: 12 The LORD blessed the latter part of Job's life more than the **first**.
Ps 78: 51 firstborn of Egypt, the **firstfruits** *of* manhood in the tents of Ham.
105: 36 all the firstborn in their land, the **firstfruits** of all their manhood.
111: 10 The fear of the LORD is the **beginning** *of* wisdom; all who
Pr 1: 7 The fear of the LORD is the **beginning** *of* knowledge, but fools
3: 9 the LORD with your wealth, with the **firstfruits** *of* all your crops;
4: 7 Wisdom is **supreme**; therefore get wisdom. Though it cost all you
8: 22 "The LORD brought me forth as the **first** *of* his works, before his
17: 14 **Starting** a quarrel is like breaching a dam; so drop the matter
Ecc 7: 8 The end of a matter is better than its **beginning**, and patience is
Isa 46: 10 I make known the end from the **beginning**, from ancient times,
Jer 2: 3 Israel was holy to the LORD, the **firstfruits** *of* his harvest;
26: 1 **Early** [+928] *in* the reign of Jehoiakim son of Josiah king of
27: 1 **Early** [+928] *in* the reign of Zedekiah son of Josiah king of Judah,
28: 1 the fourth year, **early** [+928] *in* the reign of Zedekiah king of
49: 34 concerning Elam, **early** in the reign of Zedekiah king of Judah:
49: 35 I will break the bow of Elam, the **mainstay** *of* their might.
Eze 20: 40 There I will require your offerings and your **choice** gifts,
44: 30 The **best** *of* all the firstfruits and of all your special gifts will
44: 30 You are to give them the **first** *portion of* your ground meal
48: 14 This is the **best** *of* the land and must not pass into other hands,
Da 11: 41 and the **leaders** *of* Ammon will be delivered from his hand.
Hos 9: 10 "**When** [+928] I found Israel, it was like finding grapes in the
Am 6: 1 you notable men of the **foremost** nation, to whom the people of
6: 6 You drink wine by the bowlful and use the **finest** lotions, but you
Mic 1: 13 You were the **beginning** *of* sin to the Daughter of Zion,

8041 רַב *rab*[1], a. [424 / 423] [→ 8051; cf. 8045; Ar 10647]

many [162], great [73], long [18], numerous [13], abundant [12], mighty [10], much [10], abounding [8], large [8], enough [6], larger [6], vast [6], full [4], more [4], greatly [3], number [3], plenty [3], crowd [2], deep [2], fully [2], gone too far [2], great deal [2], heavy [2], large [+4394] [2], large amount [2], long enough [2], rushing [2], so great [2], so many [2], weighs heavily [2], abundantly [1], all abound [1], beyond number [+4394] [1], chief [1], convinced [1], distant future [+3427] [1], distant [1], floodwaters [+4784] [1], gone far enough [1], great quantities [1], greater power [1], greater [1], gushed out [+3655] [1], high [1], huge [1], increased more and more [+2143+2143+2256] [1], increasing [1], larger number [1], mansions [+1074] [1], many [+4394] [1], more [+3578] [1], most [1], much too numerous [+2256+6786] [1], multitude [1], multitudes [1], never [+4202] [1], numbers [1], old [1], older [1], powerful [1], quantities [1], quantity [1], rich [1], richly [1], severe [+4394] [1], severely [1], so many [+5031] [1], so much [1], so [1], stronger [1], surging [1], time after time [+6961] [1], too long [1], tyrannical [+5131] [1], very [1], what [1], whole [1], wide [1]

Ge 6: 5 The LORD saw how **great** man's wickedness on the earth had
7: 11 on that day all the springs of the **great** deep burst forth,
13: 6 possessions were **so great** that they were not able to stay together.
21: 34 And Abraham stayed in the land of the Philistines for a **long** time.
24: 25 she added, "We have **plenty** *of* straw and fodder, as well as room
25: 23 be stronger than the other, and the **older** will serve the younger."
26: 14 He had **so many** flocks and herds and servants that the Philistines
30: 43 man grew exceedingly prosperous and came to own **large** flocks,
33: 9 Esau said, "I already have **plenty**, my brother. Keep what you have
36: 7 Their possessions were too **great** for them to remain together;
37: 34 his clothes, put on sackcloth and mourned for his son **many** days.
45: 28 And Israel said, "I'm **convinced**! My son Joseph is still alive.
50: 20 to accomplish what is now being done, the saving of **many** lives.
Ex 1: 9 Israelites have become **much too numerous** [+2256+6786] for us.
2: 23 During that **long** period, the king of Egypt died. The Israelites
5: 5 Pharaoh said, "Look, the people of the land are now **numerous**,
9: 28 Pray to the LORD, for we have had **enough** thunder and hail.
12: 38 **Many** other people went up with them, as well as large droves of
19: 21 their way through to see the LORD and **many** of them perish.
23: 2 "Do not follow the **crowd** in doing wrong. When you give
23: 2 in a lawsuit, do not pervert justice by siding with the **crowd**,
34: 6 gracious God, slow to anger, **abounding** *in* love and faithfulness,
Lev 15: 25 " 'When a woman has a discharge of blood for **many** days at a time
25: 51 If **many** years remain, he must pay for his redemption a larger
Nu 9: 19 When the cloud remained over the tabernacle a **long** time,
11: 33 the people, and he struck them with a **severe** [+4394] plague.
13: 18 the people who live there are strong or weak, few or **many**.
14: 18 slow to anger, **abounding** *in* love and forgiving sin and rebellion.
16: 3 and Aaron and said to them, "You have **gone too far**!
16: 7 will be the one who is holy. You Levites have **gone too far**!"
20: 11 Water **gushed out** [+3655], and the community and their livestock
20: 15 forefathers went down into Egypt, and we lived there **many** years.
21: 6 snakes among them; they bit the people and **many** Israelites died.
22: 3 and Moab was terrified because there were so **many** people.
22: 15 more **numerous** and more distinguished than the first.
24: 7 will flow from their buckets; their seed will have **abundant** water.
26: 54 To a **larger** *group* give a larger inheritance, and to a smaller group
26: 56 Each inheritance is to be distributed by lot among the **larger**
32: 1 The Reubenites and Gadites, who had very **large** herds and flocks,
33: 54 To a **larger** *group* give a larger inheritance, and to a smaller group
35: 8 Take many towns from a tribe that has **many**, but few from one
Dt 1: 6 our God said to us at Horeb, "You have stayed **long enough**
1: 46 so you stayed in Kadesh **many** days—all the time you spent there.
2: 1 For a **long** time we made our way around the hill country of Seir.
2: 3 "You have made your way around this hill country **long enough**;
2: 10 a people strong and **numerous**, and as tall as the Anakites.
2: 21 They were a people strong and **numerous**, and as tall as the
3: 19 and your livestock (I know you have **much** livestock)
3: 26 and would not listen to me. "That is **enough**," the LORD said.
7: 1 are entering to possess and drives out before you **many** nations—
7: 1 and Jebusites, seven nations **larger** and stronger than you—
7: 17 may say to yourselves, "These nations are **stronger** than we are.

Dt 9:14 make you into a nation stronger and more **numerous** than they."
15:6 and you will lend to **many** nations but will borrow from none.
15:6 You will rule over **many** nations but none will rule over you.
20:1 and see horses and chariots and an army **greater** than yours,
20:19 When you lay siege to a city for a **long** time, fighting against it to
25:3 If he is flogged **more** [+3578] than that, your brother will be
26:5 lived there and became a great nation, powerful and **numerous**.
28:12 You will lend to **many** nations but will borrow from none.
28:38 You will sow **much** seed in the field but you will harvest little,
31:17 **Many** disasters and difficulties will come upon them, and on that
31:21 And when **many** disasters and difficulties come upon them,
Jos 10:11 **more** of them died from the hailstones than were killed by the
11:4 with all their troops and a large **number** of horses and chariots—
11:4 a **huge** army, as numerous as the sand on the seashore.
11:18 Joshua waged war against all these kings for a **long** time.
17:14 We are a **numerous** people and the LORD has blessed us
17:15 "If you are so **numerous**," Joshua answered, "and if the hill
17:17 and Manasseh—"You are **numerous** and very powerful.
19:9 of Judah, because Judah's portion was **more** than they needed.
22:3 For a **long** time now—to this very day—you have not deserted
22:8 saying, "Return to your homes with your **great** wealth—with large
22:8 with **large** [+4394] herds of livestock, with silver, gold, bronze
23:1 After a **long** time had passed and the LORD had given Israel rest
24:7 I did to the Egyptians. Then you lived in the desert for a **long** time.
Jdg 7:2 "You have too **many** men for me to deliver Midian into their
7:4 But the LORD said to Gideon, "There are still too **many** men.
8:30 He had seventy sons of his own, for he had **many** wives.
9:40 Abimelech chased him, and **many** fell wounded in the flight—
16:30 Thus he killed **many** more when he died than while he lived.
1Sa 2:5 borne seven children, but *she who has had* **many** sons pines away.
12:17 you will realize **what** an evil thing you did in the eyes of the
14:6 can hinder the LORD from saving, whether by **many** or by few."
14:19 Philistine camp **increased more and more** [+2143+2143+2256].
26:13 the hill some distance away; there was a **wide** space between them.
2Sa 3:22 from a raid and brought with them a **great deal** of plunder.
13:34 watch looked up and saw **many** people on the road west of him,
14:2 Act like a woman who has spent **many** days grieving for the dead.
15:12 gained strength, and Absalom's following kept on **increasing**.
22:17 from on high and took hold of me; he drew me out of **deep** waters.
23:20 was a valiant fighter from Kabzeel, who performed **great** exploits.
24:14 Let us fall into the hands of the LORD, for his mercy is **great**;
24:16 and said to the angel who was afflicting the people, "**Enough**!
1Ki 2:38 the king has said." And Shimei stayed in Jerusalem for a **long** time.
3:8 have chosen, a **great** people, too numerous to count or number.
3:11 you have asked for this and not for **long** life or wealth for yourself,
4:20 and Israel were as **numerous** as the sand on the seashore;
5:7 [5:21] for he has given David a wise son to rule over this **great**
10:2 carrying spices, large **quantities** *of* gold, and precious stones—
11:1 loved **many** foreign women besides Pharaoh's daughter—
12:28 said to the people, "It is too **much** for you to go up to Jerusalem.
18:1 After a **long** time, in the third year, the word of the LORD came
18:25 one of the bulls and prepare it first, since there are **so many** of you.
19:4 "I have had **enough**, LORD," he said. "Take my life; I am no
19:7 and said, "Get up and eat, for the journey is too **much** for you."
2Ki 6:16 "Those who are with us are **more** than those who are with them."
9:22 as **all** the idolatry and witchcraft of your mother Jezebel **abound**?"
12:10 [12:11] Whenever they saw that there was a **large amount** *of*
1Ch 4:27 and six daughters, but his brothers did not have **many** children;
5:22 and **many** *others* fell slain, because the battle was God's.
7:22 Their father Ephraim mourned for them **many** days, and his
11:22 was a valiant fighter from Kabzeel, who performed **great** exploits.
18:8 belonged to Hadadezer, David took a great **quantity** of bronze,
21:13 me fall into the hands of the LORD, for his mercy is very **great**;
21:15 and said to the angel who was destroying the people, "**Enough**!
22:8 because you have shed **much** blood on the earth in my sight.
24:4 A **larger number** of leaders were found among Eleazar's
28:5 Of all my sons—and the LORD has given me **many**—he has
2Ch 1:9 for you have made me king over a people who are as **numerous** as
1:11 and since you have not asked for a **long** life but for wisdom
13:8 You are indeed a **vast** army and have with you the golden calves
13:17 Abijah and his men inflicted **heavy** losses on them, so that there
14:11 [14:10] no one like you to help the powerless against the **mighty**.
14:14 [14:13] all these villages, since there was **much** booty there.
15:3 For a **long** time Israel was without the true God, without a priest to
15:5 for all the inhabitants of the lands were in **great** turmoil.
17:13 had **large** supplies in the towns of Judah. He also kept experienced
20:2 told Jehoshaphat, "A **vast** army is coming against you from Edom,
20:12 For we have no power to face this **vast** army that is attacking us.
20:15 'Do not be afraid or discouraged because of this **vast** army.
20:25 There was **so much** plunder that it took three days to collect it.
21:3 Their father had given them **many** gifts of silver and gold
21:15 You yourself will be **very** ill with a lingering disease of the
24:11 and they saw that there was a **large amount** *of* money,
24:25 When the Arameans withdrew, they left Joash **severely** wounded.
25:13 three thousand people and carried off **great quantities** of plunder.
26:10 He also built towers in the desert and dug **many** cisterns,
26:10 because he had **much** livestock in the foothills and in the plain.
28:8 They also took a **great deal** of plunder, which they carried back to
28:13 For our guilt is already **great**, and his fierce anger rests on Israel."
30:13 A very **large** crowd of people assembled in Jerusalem to celebrate
30:17 Since **many** in the crowd had not consecrated themselves,
30:18 Although most of the **many** people who came from Ephraim,
32:4 A **large** force of men assembled, and they blocked all the springs
32:4 "Why should the kings of Assyria come and find **plenty** of water?"
32:7 army with him, for there is a **greater power** with us than with him.
32:23 **Many** brought offerings to Jerusalem for the LORD and valuable
32:29 of flocks and herds, for God had given him very **great** riches.
Ezr 3:12 But **many** of the older priests and Levites and family heads,
3:12 of this temple being laid, while **many** *others* shouted for joy.
10:1 before the house of God, a **large** [+4394] crowd of Israelites—
10:13 But there are **many** people here and it is the rainy season;
Ne 5:2 were saying, "We and our sons and daughters are **numerous**;
6:18 For **many** in Judah were under oath to him, since he was
7:2 he was a man of integrity and feared God more than **most** *men* do.
9:17 and compassionate, slow to anger and **abounding** *in* love.
9:19 "Because of your **great** compassion you did not abandon them in
9:27 and in your **great** compassion you gave them deliverers,
9:28 in your compassion you delivered them **time after time** [+6961].
9:30 For **many** years you were patient with them. By your Spirit you
9:31 in your **great** mercy you did not put an end to them or abandon
9:35 enjoying your **great** goodness to them in the spacious and fertile
13:26 Among the **many** nations there was no king like him. He was
Est 1:4 For a **full** 180 days he displayed the vast wealth of his kingdom
1:7 one different from the other, and the royal wine was **abundant**,
1:20 when the king's edict is proclaimed throughout all his **vast** realm,
2:8 **many** girls were brought to the citadel of Susa and put under the
4:3 weeping and wailing. **Many** lay in sackcloth and ashes.
8:17 **many** *people* of other nationalities became Jews because fear of
Job 1:3 and five hundred donkeys, and had a large **number** of servants.
4:3 Think how you have instructed **many**, how you have strengthened
5:25 You will know that your children will be **many**, and your
11:19 with no one to make you afraid, and **many** will court your favor.
16:2 "I have heard **many** *things* like these; miserable comforters are
22:5 Is not your wickedness **great**? Are not your sins endless?
23:14 his decree against me, and **many** such plans he still has in store.
31:25 if I have rejoiced over my **great** wealth, the fortune my hands had
31:34 because I **so** feared the crowd and so dreaded the contempt of the
32:9 It is not only the **old** who are wise, not only the aged who
35:9 of oppression; they plead for relief from the arm of the **powerful**.
36:28 pour down their moisture and **abundant** showers fall on mankind.
38:21 for you were already born! You have lived **so many** [+5031] years!
39:11 Will you rely on him for his **great** strength? Will you leave your
Ps 3:1 [3:2] how many are my foes! How **many** rise up against me!
3:2 [3:3] **Many** are saying of me, "God will not deliver him."
4:6 [4:7] **Many** are asking, "Who can show us any good?"
18:14 [18:15] ⌞the enemies⌟, **great** bolts of lightning and routed them.
18:16 [18:17] and took hold of me; he drew me out of **deep** waters.
19:10 [19:11] They are more precious than gold, than **much** pure gold;
19:11 [19:12] servant warned; in keeping them there is **great** reward.
19:13 [19:14] Then will I be blameless, innocent of **great** transgression.
22:12 [22:13] **Many** bulls surround me; strong bulls of Bashan encircle
22:25 [22:26] From you comes the theme of my praise in the **great**
25:11 of your name, O LORD, forgive my iniquity, though it is **great**.
29:3 of glory thunders, the LORD thunders over the **mighty** waters.
31:13 [31:14] For I hear the slander of **many**; there is terror on every
31:19 [31:20] How **great** is your goodness, which you have stored up
32:6 surely when the **mighty** waters rise, they will not reach him.
32:10 **Many** are the woes of the wicked, but the LORD's unfailing love
34:19 [34:20] A righteous man may have **many** troubles,
35:18 I will give you thanks in the **great** assembly; among throngs of
36:6 [36:7] like the mighty mountains, your justice like the **great** deep.
37:16 Better the little that the righteous have than the wealth of **many**
40:3 [40:4] **Many** will see and fear and put their trust in the LORD.
40:5 [40:6] **Many**, O LORD my God, are the wonders you have done.
40:9 [40:10] I proclaim righteousness in the **great** assembly; I do not
40:10 [40:11] conceal your love and your truth from the **great** assembly.
48:2 [48:3] of Zaphon is Mount Zion, the city of the **Great** King.
55:18 [55:19] battle waged against me, even though **many** oppose me.
56:2 [56:3] me all day long; **many** are attacking me in their pride.
62:2 [62:3] he is my fortress, I will **never** [+4202] be shaken.
65:9 [65:10] care for the land and water it; you enrich it **abundantly**.
68:11 [68:12] and **great** was the company of those who proclaimed it:
69:13 [69:14] in your **great** love, O God, answer me with your sure
71:7 I have become like a portent to **many**, but you are my strong
71:20 me see troubles, **many** and bitter, you will restore my life again;
77:19 [77:20] led through the sea, your way through the **mighty** waters,
78:15 rocks in the desert and gave them water as **abundant** as the seas;
86:5 and good, O Lord, **abounding** *in* love to all who call to you.

Ps 86:15 gracious God, slow to anger, **abounding** *in* love and faithfulness.
89: 7 [89:8] In the council of the holy ones God is **greatly** feared; he is
89:50 [89:51] the taunts [BHS *many*; NIV 8190] *of* all the nations,
93: 4 Mightier than the thunder of the **great** waters, mightier than the
97: 1 LORD reigns, let the earth be glad; let the **distant** shores rejoice.
103: 8 is compassionate and gracious, slow to anger, **abounding** *in* love.
106:43 **Many** times he delivered them, but they were bent on rebellion
107:23 out on the sea in ships; they were merchants on the **mighty** waters.
109:30 greatly extol the LORD; in the **great** *throng* I will praise him.
110: 6 heaping up the dead and crushing the rulers of the **whole** earth.
119:156 Your compassion is **great**, O LORD; preserve my life according
119:157 **Many** are the foes who persecute me, but I have not turned from
119:162 I rejoice in your promise like one who finds **great** spoil.
119:165 **Great** peace have they who love your law, and nothing can make
120: 6 **Too long** have I lived among those who hate peace.
123: 3 have mercy on us, for we have endured **much** contempt.
123: 4 We have endured **much** ridicule from the proud, much contempt
129: 1 They have **greatly** oppressed me from my youth—let Israel say—
129: 2 they have **greatly** oppressed me from my youth, but they have not
135:10 He struck down **many** nations and killed mighty kings—
144: 7 deliver me and rescue me from the **mighty** waters, from the hands
145: 7 They will celebrate your **abundant** goodness and joyfully sing of
147: 5 Great is our Lord and **mighty** *in* power; his understanding has no
Pr 7:26 **Many** are the victims she has brought down; her slain are a mighty
10:21 The lips of the righteous nourish **many**, but fools die for lack of
13: 7 yet has nothing; another pretends to be poor, yet has **great** wealth.
14:20 shunned even by their neighbors, but the rich have **many** friends.
14:29 A patient man has **great** understanding, but a quick-tempered man
15: 6 The house of the righteous contains **great** treasure, but the income
15:16 Better a little with the fear of the LORD than **great** wealth with
19: 4 Wealth brings **many** friends, but a poor man's friend deserts him.
19: 6 **Many** curry favor with a ruler, and everyone is the friend of a man
19:21 **Many** are the plans in a man's heart, but it is the LORD's
22: 1 A good name is more desirable than **great** riches; to be esteemed is
28: 2 it has **many** rulers, but a man of understanding and knowledge
28:12 When the righteous triumph, there is **great** elation; but when the
28:16 A **tyrannical** [+5131] ruler lacks judgment, but he who hates
28:20 A faithful man will be **richly** blessed, but one eager to get rich will
28:27 but he who closes his eyes to them receives **many** curses.
29:22 stirs up dissension, and a hot-tempered one commits **many** sins.
29:26 **Many** seek an audience with a ruler, but it is from the LORD that
31:29 "**Many** women do noble things, but you surpass them all."
Ecc 2:21 not worked for it. This too is meaningless and a **great** misfortune.
6: 1 seen another evil under the sun, and it **weighs heavily** on men:
6: 3 A man may have a hundred children and live **many** years;
6: 3 yet no matter how **long** he lives, if he cannot enjoy his prosperity
7:22 for you know in your heart that **many** times you yourself have
7:29 mankind upright, but men have gone in search of **many** schemes."
8: 6 for every matter, though a man's misery **weighs heavily** upon him.
10: 6 Fools are put in **many** high positions, while the rich occupy the
SS 8: 7 **Many** waters cannot quench love; rivers cannot wash it away.
Isa 2: 3 **Many** peoples will come and say, "Come, let us go up to the
2: 4 between the nations and will settle disputes for **many** peoples.
5: 9 "Surely the **great** houses will become desolate, the fine mansions
8: 7 bring against them the mighty **floodwaters of** [+4784] the River—
8:15 **Many** of them will stumble; they will fall and be broken, they will
13: 4 Listen, a noise on the mountains, like that of a **great** multitude!
16:14 Moab's splendor and all her **many** people will be despised,
17:12 Oh, the raging of **many** nations—they rage like the raging sea!
17:13 Although the peoples roar like the roar of **surging** waters,
21: 7 riders on donkeys or riders on camels, let him be alert, **fully** alert."
23: 3 On the **great** waters came the grain of the Shihor; the harvest of
30:25 In the day of **great** slaughter, when the towers fall, streams of
31: 1 who trust in the **multitude** *of* their chariots and in the great
42:20 You have seen **many** *things*, but have paid no attention; your ears
51:10 Was it not you who dried up the sea, the waters of the **great** deep,
52:14 Just as there were **many** who were appalled at him—
52:15 so will he sprinkle **many** nations, and kings will shut their mouths
53:11 by his knowledge my righteous servant will justify **many**,
53:12 Therefore I will give him a portion among the **great**, and he will
53:12 For he bore the sin of **many**, and made intercession for the
54: 1 because **more** are the children of the desolate woman than of her
54:13 be taught by the LORD, and **great** will be your children's peace.
63: 1 of his strength? "It is I, speaking in righteousness, **mighty** to save."
63: 7 the **many** good things he has done for the house of Israel,
Jer 3: 1 you have lived as a prostitute with **many** lovers—would you now
11:15 doing in my temple as she works out her evil schemes with **many**?
12:10 **Many** shepherds will ruin my vineyard and trample down my
13: 6 **Many** days later the LORD said to me, "Go now to Perath
13: 9 way I will ruin the pride of Judah and the **great** pride of Jerusalem.
16:16 "But now I will send for **many** fishermen," declares the LORD,
16:16 After that I will send for **many** hunters, and they will hunt them
20:10 I hear **many** whispering, "Terror on every side! Report him!
22: 8 "People from **many** nations will pass by this city and will ask one
25:14 They themselves will be enslaved by **many** nations and great
27: 7 land comes; then **many** nations and great kings will subjugate him.
28: 8 disaster and plague against **many** countries and great kingdoms.
32:14 of purchase, and put them in a clay jar so they will last a **long** time.
32:19 great are your purposes and **mighty** are your deeds. Your eyes are
35: 7 Then you will live a **long** time in the land where you are nomads.'
36:32 burned in the fire. And **many** similar words were added to them.
37:16 into a vaulted cell in a dungeon, where he remained a **long** time.
41:12 They caught up with him near the **great** pool in Gibeon.
50:41 and **many** kings are being stirred up from the ends of the earth.
51:13 You who live by **many** waters and are rich in treasures, your end
51:13 You who live by many waters and are **rich** *in* treasures, your end
51:55 Waves ⌊of enemies⌋ will rage like **great** waters; the roar of their
La 1: 1 How deserted lies the city, once *so* **full** *of* people! How like a
1: 1 How like a widow is she, who once was **great** among the nations!
1:22 because of all my sins. My groans are **many** and my heart is faint."
3:23 They are new every morning; **great** is your faithfulness.
Eze 1:24 like the roar of **rushing** waters, like the voice of the Almighty,
3: 6 not to **many** peoples of obscure speech and difficult language,
12:27 of Israel is saying, 'The vision he sees is for **many** years from now,
16:41 and inflict punishment on you in the sight of **many** women.
17: 5 put it in fertile soil. He planted it like a willow by **abundant** water,
17: 7 was another great eagle with powerful wings and **full** plumage.
17: 8 It had been planted in good soil by **abundant** water so that it
17: 9 will not take a strong arm or **many** people to pull it up by the roots.
17:15 him by sending his envoys to Egypt to get horses and a **large** army.
17:17 his mighty army and **great** horde will be of no help to him in war,
17:17 ramps are built and siege works erected to destroy **many** lives.
19:10 it was fruitful and full of branches because of **abundant** water.
22: 5 who are far away will mock you, O infamous city, **full** *of* turmoil.
24:12 its **heavy** deposit has not been removed, not even by fire.
26: 3 am against you, O Tyre, and I will bring **many** nations against you,
26: 7 with horses and chariots, with horsemen and a **great** army.
26:19 I bring the ocean depths over you and its **vast** waters cover you,
27: 3 at the gateway to the sea, merchant of peoples on **many** coasts,
27:15 traded with you, and **many** coastlands were your customers;
27:26 Your oarsmen take you out to the **high** seas. But the east wind will
27:33 merchandise went out on the seas, you satisfied **many** nations;
31: 5 its branches grew long, spreading because of **abundant** waters.
31: 6 birth under its branches; all the **great** nations lived in its shade.
31: 7 its spreading boughs, for its roots went down to **abundant** waters.
31:15 I held back its streams, and its **abundant** waters were restrained.
32: 3 " 'With a **great** throng of people I will cast my net over you,
32: 9 I will trouble the hearts of **many** peoples when I bring about your
32:10 I will cause **many** peoples to be appalled at you, and their kings
32:13 I will destroy all her cattle from beside **abundant** waters no longer
33:24 we are **many**; surely the land has been given to us as our
37: 2 and I saw a great **many** bones on the floor of the valley,
38: 4 fully armed, and a **great** horde with large and small shields,
38: 6 from the far north with all its troops—the **many** nations with you.
38: 8 After **many** days you will be called to arms. In future years you
38: 8 whose people were gathered from **many** nations to the mountains
38: 9 and all your troops and the **many** nations with you will go up,
38:15 you and **many** nations with you, all of them riding on horses,
38:15 all of them riding on horses, a great horde, a **mighty** army.
38:22 sulfur on him and on his troops and on the **many** nations with him.
38:23 and I will make myself known in the sight of **many** nations.
39:27 I will show myself holy through them in the sight of **many** nations.
43: 2 His voice was like the roar of **rushing** waters, and the land was
44: 6 **Enough** of your detestable practices, O house of Israel!
45: 9 You have **gone far enough**, O princes of Israel! Give up your
47: 7 I saw a great **number** of trees on each side of the river.
47: 9 There will be large **numbers** *of* fish, because this water flows there
47:10 The fish will be of **many** [+4394] kinds—like the fish of the Great
Da 1: 3 Then the king ordered Ashpenaz, **chief** *of* his court officials,
8:25 he will destroy **many** and take his stand against the Prince of
8:26 but seal up the vision, for it concerns the **distant future** [+3427]."
9:18 because we are righteous, but because of your **great** mercy.
9:27 He will confirm a covenant with **many** for one 'seven.' In the
11: 3 will appear, who will rule with **great** power and do as he pleases.
11: 5 stronger than he and will rule his own kingdom with **great** power.
11:10 His sons will prepare for war and assemble a **great** army, which
11:11 of the North, who will raise a **large** army, but it will be defeated.
11:13 king of the North will muster another army, **larger** than the first;
11:13 several years, he will advance with a huge army **fully** equipped.
11:14 "In those times **many** will rise against the king of the South.
11:18 turn his attention to the coastlands and will take **many** of them,
11:26 his army will be swept away, and **many** will fall in battle.
11:33 "Those who are wise will instruct **many**, though for a time they
11:34 receive a little help, and **many** who are not sincere will join them.
11:39 He will make them rulers over **many** *people* and will distribute the
11:40 out against him with chariots and cavalry and a **great** fleet of ships.
11:41 **Many** *countries* will fall, but Edom, Moab and the leaders of
11:44 and he will set out in a great rage to destroy and annihilate **many**.

Da 12: 2 **Multitudes** who sleep in the dust of the earth will awake:
12: 3 and those who lead **many** to righteousness, like the stars for ever
12: 4 of the end. **Many** will go here and there to increase knowledge."
12: 10 **Many** will be purified, made spotless and refined, but the wicked
Hos 3: 3 I told her, "You are to live with me **many** days; you must not be a
3: 4 For the Israelites will live **many** days without king or prince,
9: 7 Because your sins are so many and your hostility **so great**,
Joel 2: 2 Like dawn spreading across the mountains a **large** and mighty
2: 11 his forces are **beyond number** [+4394], and mighty are those who
2: 13 and compassionate, slow to anger and **abounding** *in* love,
3: 13 [4:13] and the vats overflow—so **great** is their wickedness!"
Am 3: 9 see the **great** unrest within her and the oppression among her
3: 15 will be destroyed and the **mansions** [+1074] will be demolished,"
5: 12 For I know how **many** are your offenses and how great your sins.
6: 2 go from there to **great** Hamath, and then go down to Gath in
6: 2 better off than your two kingdoms? Is their land **larger** than yours?
7: 4 judgment by fire; it dried up the **great** deep and devoured the land.
8: 3 turn to wailing. **Many**, many bodies—flung everywhere! Silence!"
Jnh 4: 2 and compassionate God, slow to anger and **abounding** *in* love,
4: 11 cannot tell their right hand from their left, and **many** cattle as well.
Mic 4: 2 **Many** nations will come and say, "Come, let us go up to the
4: 3 He will judge between **many** peoples and will settle disputes for
4: 11 But now **many** nations are gathered against you. They say,
4: 13 you hoofs of bronze and you will break to pieces **many** nations."
5: 7 [5:6] The remnant of Jacob will be in the midst of **many** peoples
5: 8 [5:7] in the midst of **many** peoples, like a lion among the beasts
Na 1: 12 "Although they have allies and are **numerous**, they will be cut off
Hab 2: 8 Because you have plundered **many** nations, the peoples who are
2: 10 You have plotted the ruin of **many** peoples, shaming your own
3: 15 You trampled the sea with your horses, churning the **great** waters.
Zec 2: 11 [2:15] "**Many** nations will be joined with the LORD in that day
8: 20 "Many peoples and the inhabitants of **many** cities will yet come,
8: 22 **many** peoples and powerful nations will come to Jerusalem to seek
14: 13 On that day men will be *stricken* by the LORD *with* **great** panic.
Mal 2: 6 with me in peace and uprightness, and turned **many** from sin.
2: 8 from the way and by your teaching have caused **many** to stumble;

8042 ²רַב ***rab²***, n.m. [33] [→ 8059, 8060, 8072; Ar 10652]

commander [23], chief [3], high [2], officers [2], *untranslated* [1], captain [+2021+2480] [1], wine stewards [+1074] [1]

2Ki 18: 17 his **chief** officer and his field commander with a large army,
25: 8 Nebuzaradan **commander** *of* the imperial guard, an official of the
25: 10 Babylonian army, under the **commander** *of* the imperial guard,
25: 11 Nebuzaradan the **commander** *of* the guard carried into exile the
25: 12 the **commander** left behind some of the poorest people of the land
25: 15 The **commander** *of* the imperial guard took away the censers
25: 18 The **commander** *of* the guard took as prisoners Seraiah the chief
25: 20 Nebuzaradan the **commander** took them all and brought them to
Est 1: 8 for the king instructed all the **wine stewards** [+1074] to serve each
Jer 39: 3 Nergal-Sharezer of Samgar, Nebo-Sarsekim a **chief** officer,
39: 3 Nergal-Sharezer a **high** official and all the other officials of the
39: 9 Nebuzaradan **commander** *of* the imperial guard carried into exile
39: 10 Nebuzaradan the **commander** *of* the guard left behind in the land
39: 11 Jeremiah through Nebuzaradan **commander** *of* the imperial guard:
39: 13 So Nebuzaradan the **commander** *of* the guard, Nebushazban a
39: 13 Nebushazban a **chief** officer, Nergal-Sharezer a high official
39: 13 Nergal-Sharezer a **high** official and all the other officers of the
39: 13 a high official and all the other **officers** *of* the king of Babylon
40: 1 **commander** *of* the imperial guard had released him at Ramah.
40: 2 When the **commander** *of* the guard found Jeremiah, he said to
40: 5 the **commander** gave him provisions and a present and let him go.
41: 1 who was of royal blood and had been one of the king's **officers**,
41: 10 over whom Nebuzaradan **commander** *of* the imperial guard had
43: 6 the king's daughters whom Nebuzaradan **commander** *of* the
52: 12 Nebuzaradan **commander** *of* the imperial guard, who served the
52: 14 The whole Babylonian army under the **commander** *of* the imperial
52: 15 Nebuzaradan the **commander** *of* the guard carried into exile some
52: 16 Nebuzaradan **[RPH]** left behind the rest of the poorest people of
52: 19 The **commander** *of* the imperial guard took away the basins,
52: 24 The **commander** *of* the guard took as prisoners Seraiah the chief
52: 26 Nebuzaradan the **commander** took them all and brought them to
52: 30 745 Jews taken into exile by Nebuzaradan the **commander** *of* the
Jnh 1: 6 The **captain** [+2021+2480] went to him and said, "How can you

8043 ³רַב ***rab³***, n.m. [3] [√ 8046]

archers [2], archer [1]

Job 16: 13 his **archers** surround me. Without pity, he pierces my kidneys
Pr 26: 10 Like an **archer** who wounds at random is he who hires a fool
Jer 50: 29 "Summon **archers** against Babylon, all those who draw the bow.

8044 רֹב ***rōb***, n.m. [151] [√ 8045]

many [31], great [24], *untranslated* [6], numerous [6], all [5], great [+4200] [4], much [4], plentiful [+4200] [4], abundant [3], great amount [+4200] [3], greatly [+4200] [3], in abundance [+4200] [3], large numbers [+4200] [3], abundance [2], extensive [+4200] [2], great [+3972] [2], great numbers [2], greatness [2], large quantities [+4200] [2], large [2], many [+4200] [2], much [+4200] [2], plenty [+4200] [2], so many [+4946] [2], abound [1], abundant [+4200] [1], advanced [1], age [+3427] [1], droves [+4200] [1], great number [+4200] [1], great number [1], great numbers [+4200] [1], great quantities [+4200+4394] [1], harsh [1], in abundance [1], in large numbers [+4200] [1], increased [1], large amount [+4200] [1], larger [+4200] [1], load [1], long [1], mighty [+4200] [1], more [+4200] [1], multitude [1], numerous [+4200] [1], prosperity [+3972] [1], quantities [+4200] [1], rabble [+132] [1], size [1], so many [+4200] [1], so many [1], surpassing [1], thick [1], widespread [1]

Ge 16: 10 so increase your descendants that they will be too **numerous** to
27: 28 and of earth's richness—an **abundance** *of* grain and new wine.
30: 30 The little you had before I came has increased **greatly** [+4200],
32: 12 [32:13] the sand of the sea, which cannot be counted.' " **[NIE]**
48: 16 and Isaac, and may they increase **greatly** [+4200] upon the earth."
Ex 15: 7 In the **greatness** *of* your majesty you threw down those who
Lev 25: 16 When the years are **many**, you are to increase the price, and when
Dt 1: 10 your numbers so that today you are as **many** as the stars in the sky.
10: 22 now the LORD your God has made you as **numerous** as the stars
28: 47 your God joyfully and gladly in the time of **prosperity** [+3972],
28: 62 You who were as **numerous** [+4200] as the stars in the sky will be
Jos 9: 13 our clothes and sandals are worn out by the very **long** journey."
11: 4 a huge army, as **numerous** as the sand on the seashore.
Jdg 6: 5 **[NIE]** It was impossible to count the men and their camels;
7: 12 the other eastern peoples had settled in the valley, **thick** as locusts.
7: 12 could no more be counted than the sand on the seashore. **[RPH]**
1Sa 1: 16 I have been praying here out of my **great** anguish and grief."
13: 5 and soldiers as **numerous** as the sand on the seashore.
2Sa 17: 11 as **numerous** as the sand on the seashore—be gathered to you,
1Ki 1: 19 He has sacrificed **great numbers** of cattle, fattened calves,
1: 25 Today he has gone down and sacrificed **great numbers** of cattle,
3: 8 have chosen, a great people, too **numerous** to count or number.
4: 20 on the seashore; **[RPH]** they ate, they drank and they were happy.
7: 47 left all these things unweighed, because there were so **many**;
8: 5 sacrificing **so many** [+4946] sheep and cattle that they could not be
10: 10 Never again were **so many** [+4200] spices brought in as those the
10: 27 cedar as **plentiful** [+4200] as sycamore-fig trees in the foothills.
2Ki 19: 23 "With my **many** [K 8207] chariots I have ascended the heights of
1Ch 4: 38 leaders of their clans. Their families increased **greatly** [+4200],
12: 40 [12:41] There were **plentiful** [+4200] supplies of flour, fig cakes,
22: 3 He provided a **large** [+4200] **amount** of iron to make nails for the
22: 3 for the fittings, and **more** [+4200] bronze than could be weighed.
22: 4 and Tyrians had brought **large** [+4200] **numbers** of them to David.
22: 5 So David made **extensive** [+4200] preparations before his death.
22: 8 'You have shed **much** [+4200] blood and have fought many wars.
22: 14 quantities of bronze and iron too **great** [+4200] to be weighed,
22: 15 You have **many** [+4200] workmen: stonecutters, masons and
29: 2 of fine stone and marble—all of these *in* **large** [+4200] **quantities**.
29: 21 and other sacrifices **in abundance** [+4200] for all Israel.
2Ch 1: 15 cedar as **plentiful** [+4200] as sycamore-fig trees in the foothills.
2: 9 [2:8] to provide me with **plenty** [+4200] of lumber,
4: 18 so **much** [+4200] that the weight of the bronze was not
5: 6 sacrificing **so many** [+4946] sheep and cattle that they could not be
9: 1 with camels carrying spices, **large** [+4200] **quantities** of gold,
9: 9 of gold, large **quantities** [+4200] of spices, and precious stones.
9: 27 cedar as **plentiful** [+4200] as sycamore-fig trees in the foothills.
11: 23 He gave them **abundant** [+4200] provisions and took many wives
14: 15 [14:14] carried off **droves** [+4200] of sheep and goats and camels.
15: 9 for **large** [+4200] **numbers** had come over to him from Israel
16: 8 Libyans a **mighty** [+4200] army with great numbers of chariots
17: 5 to Jehoshaphat, so that he had **great** [+4200] wealth and honor.
18: 1 Now Jehoshaphat had **great** [+4200] wealth and honor, and he
18: 2 Ahab slaughtered **many** [+4200] sheep and cattle for him
20: 25 and they found among them a **great** [+4200] **amount** of equipment
24: 11 did this regularly and collected a **great** [+4200] **amount** of money.
24: 24 the LORD delivered into their hands a much **larger** [+4200]
24: 27 The account of his sons, the **many** [Q 8049] prophecies about him,
27: 3 and did **extensive** [+4200] work on the wall at the hill of Ophel.
29: 35 There were burnt offerings **in abundance** [+4200], together with
30: 5 It had not been celebrated **in large** [+4200] **numbers** according to
30: 13 A very large **[RPH]** crowd of people assembled in Jerusalem to
30: 24 A **great** [+4200] **number** of priests consecrated themselves.
31: 5 They brought a **great** [+4200] **amount**, a tithe of everything.
31: 10 we have had enough to eat and **plenty** [+4200] to spare, because
32: 5 He also made **large** [+4200] **numbers** of weapons and shields.
32: 29 and acquired **great** [+4200] **numbers** of flocks and herds,
Ne 9: 25 vineyards, olive groves and fruit trees **in abundance** [+4200].

Ne 13:22 O my God, and show mercy to me according to your **great** love.
Est 5:11 his **many** sons, and all the ways the king had honored him
10: 3 among the Jews, and held in high esteem by his **many** fellow Jews,
Job 4:14 fear and trembling seized me and made **all** my bones shake.
11: 2 "Are **all** these words to go unanswered? Is this talker to be
23: 6 Would he oppose me with **great** power? No, he would not press
26: 3 And what **great** [+4200] insight you have displayed!
30:18 In his **great** power ⌞God⌟ becomes like clothing to me; he binds me
32: 7 'Age should speak; **advanced** years should teach wisdom.'
33:19 [a bed of pain with constant **distress** [Q; see K 8190] *in* his bones,]
35: 9 "Men cry out under a **load** *of* oppression; they plead for relief from
36:18 one entices you by riches; do not let a **large** bribe turn you aside.
37:23 in his justice and **great** righteousness, he does not oppress.
Ps 5: 7 [5:8] I, by your **great** mercy, will come into your house;
5:10 [5:11] Banish them for their **many** sins, for they have rebelled
33:16 No king is saved by the **size** *of* his army; no warrior escapes by his
33:16 by the size of his army; no warrior escapes by his **great** strength.
33:17 hope for deliverance; despite *all* its **great** strength it cannot save.
37:11 But the meek will inherit the land and enjoy **great** peace.
49: 6 [49:7] who trust in their wealth and boast of their **great** riches?
51: 1 [51:3] according to your **great** compassion blot out my
52: 7 [52:9] trusted in his **great** wealth and grew strong by destroying
66: 3 *So* **great** is your power that your enemies cringe before you.
69:16 [69:17] goodness of your love; in your **great** mercy turn to me.
72: 7 will flourish; prosperity will **abound** till the moon is no more.
94:19 When anxiety was **great** within me, your consolation brought joy
106: 7 they did not remember your **many** kindnesses, and they rebelled by
106:45 he remembered his covenant and out of his **great** love he relented.
150: 2 him for his acts of power; praise him for his **surpassing** greatness.
Pr 5:23 He will die for lack of discipline, led astray by his own **great** folly.
7:21 With **[NIE]** persuasive words she led him astray; she seduced him
10:19 When words are **many**, sin is not absent, but he who holds his
11:14 of guidance a nation falls, but **many** advisers make victory sure.
13:23 A poor man's field may produce **abundant** food, but injustice
14: 4 but from the strength of an ox comes an **abundant** harvest.
14:28 A **large** population is a king's glory, but without subjects a prince
15:22 fail for lack of counsel, but with **many** advisers they succeed.
16: 8 Better a little with righteousness than **much** gain with injustice.
20: 6 **Many** a man claims to have unfailing love, but a faithful man who
20:15 Gold there is, and rubies **in abundance**, but lips that speak
24: 6 for waging war you need guidance, and for victory **many** advisers.
Ecc 1:18 For with **much** wisdom comes much sorrow; the more knowledge,
1:18 For with much wisdom comes **much** sorrow; the more knowledge,
5: 3 [5:2] As a dream comes when there are **many** cares, so the speech
5: 3 [5:2] so the speech of a fool when there are **many** words.
5: 7 [5:6] **Much** dreaming and many words are meaningless.
11: 1 bread upon the waters, for after **many** days you will find it again.
Isa 1:11 "The **multitude** *of* your sacrifices—what are they to me?"
7:22 because of the **abundance** of the milk they give, he will have curds
24:22 they will be shut up in prison and be punished after **many** days.
37:24 'With my **many** chariots I have ascended the heights of the
40:26 Because of his **great** power and mighty strength, not one of them is
47: 9 in spite of your **many** sorceries and all your potent spells.
47:12 then, with your magic spells and with your **many** sorceries,
47:13 **All** the counsel you have received has only worn you out!
57:10 You were wearied by **all** your ways, but you would not say,
63: 1 in splendor, striding forward in the **greatness** *of* his strength?
63: 7 house of Israel, according to his compassion and **many** kindnesses.
Jer 13:22 because of your **many** sins that your skirts have been torn off
30:14 the cruel, because your guilt is *so* **great** and your sins so many.
30:15 Because of your **great** guilt and many sins I have done these things
La 1: 3 After affliction and **harsh** labor, Judah has gone into exile.
1: 5 The LORD has brought her grief because of her **many** sins.
3:32 he will show compassion, so **great** is his unfailing love.
Eze 14: 4 I the LORD will answer him myself in keeping with his **great**
19:11 thick foliage, conspicuous for its height and for its **many** branches.
23:42 brought from the desert along with men from the **rabble** [+132],
27:12 business with you because of your **great** [+3972] wealth of goods;
27:16 " 'Aram did business with you because of your **many** products;
27:18 because of your **many** products and great wealth of goods,
27:18 because of your many products and **great** [+3972] wealth of goods,
27:33 with your **great** wealth and your wares you enriched the kings of
28: 5 By your **great** skill in trading you have increased your wealth,
28:16 Through your **widespread** trade you were filled with violence,
28:18 By your **many** sins and dishonest trade you have desecrated your
31: 9 I made it beautiful with **abundant** branches, the envy of all the
Hos 8:12 I wrote for them the **many** [K 8052] *things of* my law, but they
9: 7 Because your sins are **so many** and your hostility so great,
10: 1 As his fruit **increased**, he built more altars; as his land prospered,
10:13 have depended on your own strength and on your **many** warriors,
Na 3: 3 **Many** casualties, piles of dead, bodies without number, people
3: 4 **all** because of the wanton lust of a harlot, alluring, the mistress of
Zec 2: 4 [2:8] because of the **great number** *of* men and livestock in it.
8: 4 of Jerusalem, each with cane in hand because of his **age** [+3427].
14:14 nations will be collected—**great** [+4200+4394] **quantities** *of*

8045 ¹רָבַב ***rābab¹***, v. [22] [→ 3714, 3715, 3716, 3717, 5266, 7478, 8041, 8044, 8047, 8051, 8052, 8053, 8056; cf. 8049]
many [7], numerous [4], great [3], increased [2], abound [1], do[s] [1], increase in number [1], outnumber [+4946] [1], tens of thousands [1], utterly [1]

Ge 6: 1 [A] When men began to **increase in number** on the earth
18:20 [A] and Gomorrah *is* so **great** and their sin so grievous
Ex 23:29 [A] become desolate and the wild animals too **numerous** for you.
Dt 7: 7 [A] because you *were* more **numerous** than other peoples,
1Sa 25:10 [A] **Many** servants are breaking away from their masters these
Job 35: 6 [A] affect him? If your sins *are* **many**, what does that do to him?
Ps 3: 1 [3:2] [A] O LORD, how **many** *are* my foes! How many rise
4: 7 [4:8] [A] joy than when their grain and new wine **abound**.
25:19 [A] See how my enemies *have* **increased** and how fiercely they
38:19 [38:20] [A] those who hate me without reason *are* **numerous**.
69: 4 [69:5] [A] reason **outnumber** [+4946] the hairs of my head;
104:24 [A] How **many** *are* your works, O LORD! In wisdom you made
144:13 [E] increase by thousands, *by* **tens of thousands** in our fields;
Ecc 5:11 [5:10] [A] As goods increase, so **do**[s] those who consume them.
Isa 6:12 [A] has sent everyone far away and the land is **utterly** forsaken.
22: 9 [A] you saw that the City of David *had* **many** breaches in its
59:12 [A] For our offenses *are* **many** in your sight, and our sins testify
66:16 [A] upon all men, and **many** *will be* those slain by the LORD.
Jer 5: 6 [A] for their rebellion *is* **great** and their backslidings many.
14: 7 [A] For our backsliding *is* **great**; we have sinned against you.
46:23 [A] *They are* more **numerous** than locusts, they cannot be
Hos 4: 7 [A] The more the priests **increased**, the more they sinned against

8046 ²רָבַב ***rābab²***, v. [1] [→ 8043; cf. 8050]
shot [1]

Ge 49:23 [A] archers attacked him; *they* **shot** *at* him with hostility.

8047 רְבָבָה ***rᵉbābâ***, n.f. [16] [√ 8045]
ten thousand [6], tens of thousands [5], countless [1], grow [1], myriads [1], ten thousands [1], thousands [1]

Ge 24:60 "Our sister, may you increase to thousands upon **thousands**;
Lev 26: 8 chase a hundred, and a hundred of you will chase **ten thousand**,
Nu 10:36 "Return, O LORD, to the **countless** thousands of Israel."
Dt 32:30 or two put **ten thousand** to flight, unless their Rock had sold them,
33: 2 He came with **myriads** *of* holy ones from the south, from his
33:17 Such are the **ten thousands** *of* Ephraim; such are the thousands of
Jdg 20:10 and a thousand from **ten thousand**, to get provisions for the army.
1Sa 18: 7 "Saul has slain his thousands, and David his **tens of thousands**."
18: 8 "They have credited David with **tens of thousands**," he thought,
21:11 [21:12] slain his thousands, and David his **tens of thousands**'?"
29: 5 " 'Saul has slain his thousands, and David his **tens of thousands**'?"
Ps 3: 6 [3:7] I will not fear the **tens of thousands** drawn up against me on
91: 7 **ten thousand** at your right hand, but it will not come near you.
SS 5:10 My lover is radiant and ruddy, outstanding among **ten thousand**.
Eze 16: 7 I made you **grow** like a plant of the field. You grew up
Mic 6: 7 pleased with thousands of rams, with **ten thousand** rivers of oil?

8048 רָבַד ***rābad***, v. [1] [→ 5267, 8054]
covered [+5267] [1]

Pr 7:16 [A] *I have* **covered** [+5267] my bed *with* colored linens from

8049 ¹רָבָה ***rābâ¹***, v. [174] [→ 746?, 1442, 2220, 2221, 5268, 5269, 5270, 9551, 9552; 8045; Ar 10648]
increase [14], many [11], increase in number [9], increased [9], increase numbers [8], numerous [8], multiplied [5], make numerous [4], multiply [4], thrive [4], great [3], greater [3], greatly [3], increases [3], much [3], multiplies [3], gave many [2], give larger [2], greatly increase [+8049] [2], had many [2], increase the number [2], increasing [2], keep [2], long [2], make great [2], make numerous [+906+8049] [2], more [2], reared [2], so increase [+906+8049] [2], take many [2], abundant [1], accumulate large amounts [+4200+4394] [1], acquire great numbers [1], add to numbers [1], adding [1], as much as [+4946] [1], before[s] [1], built many [1], built more [1], distant [+2006+2021] [1], done more [1], enlarge [1], enlarged [1], freely [1], gaining [1], gathered much [1], generously gave [1], get more [1], give more [1], grew up [1], grow large [1], have many [1], heap [1], higher than [+2025+4200+5087] [1], increased in number [1], increased number [1], increased numbers [1], kept on [1], lavished [1], less meaning [+2039] [1], made many [1], made numerous [1], make as great as you like [+4394+6584] [1], make countless [+889+906+906+4202+6218] [1], make many [1], make plentiful [1], makes grow [1], many times [1], more and more unfaithful [+5085+5086] [1], more and more [1], multiply the number [1],

numbers increased greatly [+2256+7238] [1], numbers increased [1], offer many [1], outnumber [+4946] [1], piles up [1], repeatedly [1], so does[s] [1], time after time [1], too much [1], use an abundance [1], whole [1], yet more [1]

Ge 1:22 [A] "Be fruitful and **increase in number** and fill the water in the
1:22 [A] the water in the seas, and *let* the birds **increase** on the earth."
1:28 [A] and said to them, "Be fruitful and **increase in number**;
3:16 [G] "*I will* **greatly increase** [+8049] your pains in childbearing;
3:16 [G] "*I will* **greatly increase** [+8049] your pains in childbearing;
7:17 [A] *as* the waters **increased** they lifted the ark high above the
7:18 [A] The waters rose and **increased** greatly on the earth,
8:17 [A] on the earth and be fruitful and **increase in number** upon it."
9:1 [A] "Be fruitful and **increase in number** and fill the earth.
9:7 [A] As for you, be fruitful and **increase in number**; multiply on
9:7 [A] in number; multiply on the earth and **increase** upon it."
16:10 [G] "*I will* **so increase** [+906+8049] your descendants that they
16:10 [G] "*I will* **so increase** [+906+8049] your descendants that they
17:2 [G] and you and *will* greatly **increase** your **numbers**."
17:20 [G] make him fruitful and *will* greatly **increase** his **numbers**.
22:17 [G] **make** your descendants as **numerous** [+906+8049] as the
22:17 [G] **make** your descendants as **numerous** [+906+8049] as the
26:4 [G] *I will* **make** your descendants as **numerous** as the stars in the
26:24 [G] *will* **increase the number** *of* your descendants for the sake
28:3 [G] **increase** your **numbers** until you become a community of
34:12 [G] **Make** the price for the bride and the gift I am to bring **as great** [+4394+6584] **as you like**,
35:11 [A] "I am God Almighty; be fruitful and **increase in number**.
38:12 [A] After a **long** time Judah's wife, the daughter of Shua, died.
43:34 [A] Benjamin's portion *was* five times **as much** [+4946] **as**
47:27 [A] and were fruitful and **increased** greatly **in number**.
48:4 [G] going to make you fruitful and *will* **increase** your **numbers**.
Ex 1:7 [A] the Israelites were fruitful and multiplied **greatly** and became
1:10 [A] with them or *they will become even more* **numerous** and,
1:12 [A] they were oppressed, the more *they* **multiplied** and spread;
1:20 [A] So God was kind to the midwives and the people **increased**
7:3 [G] though *I* **multiply** my miraculous signs and wonders in
11:9 [A] to you—so that my wonders *may be* **multiplied** in Egypt."
16:17 [G] did as they were told; some gathered **much**, some little.
16:18 [G] by the omer, he *who* **gathered much** did not have too much,
30:15 [G] The rich *are* not *to* **give more** than a half shekel and the poor
32:13 [G] '*I will* **make** your descendants as **numerous** as the stars in
36:5 [G] "The people are bringing **more** than enough for doing the
Lev 11:42 [G] it moves on its belly or walks on all fours or on **many** feet;
25:16 [G] When the years are many, *you are to* **increase** the price,
26:9 [G] and make you fruitful and **increase** your **numbers**,
Nu 26:54 [G] To a larger group **give** a **larger** inheritance, and to a smaller
33:54 [G] To a larger group **give** a **larger** inheritance, and to a smaller
35:8 [G] **Take many** towns from a tribe that has many, but few from
Dt 1:10 [G] The LORD your God *has* **increased** your **numbers** so that
6:3 [A] that *you may* **increase** greatly in a land flowing with milk
7:13 [G] He will love you and bless you and **increase** your **numbers**.
7:22 [A] all at once, or the wild animals *will* **multiply** around you.
8:1 [A] so that you may live and **increase** and may enter and possess
8:13 [A] and flocks **grow large** and your silver and gold increase
8:13 [A] and flocks grow large and your silver and gold **increase**
8:13 [A] your silver and gold increase and all you have *is* **multiplied**,
11:21 [A] the days of your children *may be* **many** in the land that the
13:17 [13:18] [G] compassion on you, and **increase** your **numbers**,
14:24 [A] if that place *is* too **distant** [+2006+2021] and you have been
17:16 [G] *must* not **acquire great numbers** *of* horses for himself
17:16 [G] or make the people return to Egypt to **get more** *of* them,
17:17 [G] *He must* not **take many** wives, or his heart will be led
17:17 [G] *He must* not **accumulate large** [+4200+4394] **amounts** *of*
19:6 [A] him in a rage, overtake him if the distance *is too* **great**,
28:63 [G] the LORD to make you prosper and **increase in number**,
30:5 [G] make you more prosperous and **numerous** than your fathers.
30:16 [A] you will live and **increase**, and the LORD your God will
Jos 24:3 [G] led him throughout Canaan and **gave** him **many** descendants.
Jdg 9:29 [D] I would say to Abimelech, 'Call out your **whole** army!' "
16:24 [G] the one who laid waste our land and **multiplied** our slain."
20:38 [G] they should send up a **great** cloud of smoke from the city,
1Sa 1:12 [G] As *she* **kept on** praying to the LORD, Eli observed her
2:3 [G] "*Do* not **keep** talking so proudly or let your mouth speak
7:2 [A] It was a **long** time, twenty years in all, that the ark remained
14:30 [A] not the slaughter of the Philistines *have been* even **greater**?"
2Sa 14:11 [G] prevent the avenger of blood from **adding** to the destruction,
18:8 [G] and the forest claimed **more** lives that day than the sword.
22:36 [G] your shield of victory; you stoop down *to* **make** me **great**.
1Ki 4:30 [5:10] [A] Solomon's wisdom *was* **greater** than the wisdom of
2Ki 21:6 [G] *He* did **much** evil in the eyes of the LORD, provoking him
1Ch 4:10 [G] that you would bless me and **enlarge** my territory!
4:27 [G] so their entire clan *did* not *become* as **numerous** as the
5:9 [A] because their livestock *had* **increased** in Gilead.
5:23 [A] The people of the half-tribe of Manasseh *were* **numerous**;
7:4 [G] men ready for battle, for *they* **had many** wives and children.
8:40 [G] *They* **had many** sons and grandsons—150 in all. All these
23:11 [G] the second, but Jeush and Beriah *did* not **have many** sons;
23:17 [A] other sons, but the sons of Rehabiah *were* very **numerous**.
27:23 [G] promised to **make** Israel as **numerous** as the stars in the sky.
2Ch 24:27 [a] [his sons, the **many** [Q; see K 8044] prophecies about him,]
31:5 [G] the Israelites **generously gave** the firstfruits of their grain,
33:6 [G] He did **much** evil in the eyes of the LORD, provoking him
33:23 [G] himself before the LORD; Amon **increased** his guilt.
36:14 [G] the people *became* **more and more unfaithful** [+5085+5086],
Ezr 9:6 [A] because our sins *are* **higher** [+2025+4200+5087] **than** our
10:13 [G] a day or two, because *we have* sinned **greatly** in this thing.
Ne 6:17 [G] in those days the nobles of Judah *were* sending **many** letters
9:23 [G] *You* **made** their sons as **numerous** as the stars in the sky,
9:37 [G] its **abundant** harvest goes to the kings you have placed over
Job 9:17 [G] me with a storm and **multiply** my wounds for no reason.
10:17 [G] witnesses against me and **increase** your anger toward me;
27:14 [A] However **many** his children, their fate is the sword; his
29:18 [G] my own house, my days as **numerous** as the grains of sand.
33:12 [A] in this you are not right, for God *is* **greater** than man.
34:37 [G] his hands among us and **multiplies** his words against God."
39:4 [A] Their young **thrive** and grow strong in the wilds; they leave
41:3 [40:27] [G] *Will he* **keep** begging you for mercy? Will he speak
Ps 16:4 [A] The sorrows of those *will* **increase** who run after other gods.
18:35 [18:36] [G] sustains me; you stoop down *to* **make** me **great**.
44:12 [44:13] [D] for a pittance, **gaining** nothing from their sale.
49:16 [49:17] [A] when the splendor of his house **increases**;
51:2 [51:4] [Wash away **all** [Q; see K 2221] my iniquity and cleanse]
71:21 [G] *You will* **increase** my honor and comfort me once again.
78:38 [G] **Time after time** he restrained his anger and did not stir up
107:38 [A] he blessed them, and *their* **numbers** greatly **increased**,
139:18 [A] *they would* **outnumber** [+4946] the grains of sand.
Pr 4:10 [A] accept what I say, and the years of your life *will be* **many**.
6:35 [G] he will refuse the bribe, however **great** it is.
9:11 [A] For through me your days *will be* **many**, and years will be
13:11 [G] but he who gathers money little by little **makes** it **grow**.
22:16 [G] He who oppresses the poor to **increase** his wealth and he
25:27 [G] It is not good to eat **too much** honey, nor is it honorable to
28:8 [G] *He who* **increases** his wealth by exorbitant interest amasses
28:28 [A] into hiding; but when the wicked perish, the righteous **thrive**.
29:2 [A] When the righteous **thrive**, the people rejoice; when the
29:16 [A] When the wicked **thrive**, so does sin, but the righteous will
29:16 [A] When the wicked thrive, **so does**[s] sin, but the righteous will
Ecc 5:11 [5:10] [A] As goods **increase**, so do those who consume them.
6:11 [G] The more the words, the **less** the **meaning** [+2039], and how
10:14 [G] the fool **multiplies** words. No one knows what is coming—
Isa 1:15 [G] from you; even if *you* **offer many** prayers, I will not listen.
9:3 [9:2] [G] *You have* **enlarged** the nation and increased their joy;
23:16 [G] play the harp well, sing **many** a song, so that you will be
40:29 [G] strength to the weary and **increases** the power of the weak.
51:2 [G] him he was but one, and I blessed him and **made** him **many**.
55:7 [G] mercy on him, and to our God, for *he will* **freely** pardon.
57:9 [G] went to Molech with olive oil and **increased** your perfumes.
Jer 2:22 [G] you wash yourself with soda and **use an abundance** *of* soap,
3:16 [A] when *your* **numbers** *have* **increased** [+2256+7238] **greatly** in
23:3 [A] where they will be fruitful and **increase in number**.
29:6 [A] and daughters. **Increase in number** there; do not decrease.
30:19 [G] *I will* **add to** their **numbers**, and they will not be decreased;
33:22 [G] *I will* **make** ... as **countless** [+889+906+906+4202+6218]
46:11 [G] you **multiply** remedies in vain; there is no healing for you.
46:16 [G] *They will* stumble **repeatedly**; they will fall over each other.
La 2:5 [G] *He has* **multiplied** mourning and lamentation for the
2:22 [D] those I cared for and **reared**, my enemy has destroyed."
Eze 11:6 [G] *You have* killed **many** people in this city and filled its streets
16:7 [A] *You* **grew up** and developed and became the most beautiful
16:25 [G] offering your body *with* **increasing** promiscuity to anyone
16:26 [G] and provoked me to anger with your **increasing** promiscuity.
16:29 [G] Then *you* **increased** your promiscuity to include Babylonia,
16:51 [G] *You have* **done more** detestable things than they, and have
19:2 [D] She lay down among the young lions and **reared** her cubs.
21:15 [21:20] [G] So that hearts may melt and the fallen *be* **many**,
22:25 [G] and precious things and **make many** widows within her.
23:19 [G] Yet *she became* **more and more** promiscuous as she
24:10 [G] So **heap** *on* the wood and kindle the fire. Cook the meat
28:5 [G] By your great skill in trading *you have* **increased** your
31:5 [A] its boughs **increased** and its branches grew long, spreading
36:10 [G] *I will* **multiply the number** *of* people upon you,
36:11 [G] *I will* **increase the number** *of* men and animals upon you,
36:11 [A] upon you, and they will be fruitful and *become* **numerous**.
36:29 [G] I will call for the grain and **make** it **plentiful** and will not
36:30 [G] *I will* **increase** the fruit of the trees and the crops of the field,
36:37 [G] for them: *I will* **make** their people as **numerous** as sheep,
37:26 [G] I will establish them and **increase** their **numbers**, and I will

Da 11: 39 [G] and *will* **greatly** honor those who acknowledge him.
12: 4 [A] Many will go here and there *to* **increase** knowledge."
Hos 2: 8 [2:10] [G] and oil, *who* **lavished** on her the silver and gold—
8: 11 [G] "Though Ephraim **built many** altars for sin offerings,
8: 14 [G] his Maker and built palaces; Judah *has* fortified **many** towns.
10: 1 [G] As his fruit increased, *he* **built more** altars; as his land
12: 1 [12:2] [G] east wind all day and **multiplies** lies and violence.
12: 10 [12:11] [G] **gave** them **many** visions and told parables through
Am 4: 4 [G] "Go to Bethel and sin; go to Gilgal and sin **yet more**. Bring
4: 9 [G] "**Many times** I struck your gardens and vineyards, I struck
Na 3: 16 [G] *You have* **increased** *the* **number** *of* your merchants till they
Hab 2: 6 [G] " 'Woe to him *who* **piles up** stolen goods and makes himself
Zec 10: 8 [A] I will redeem them; *they will be* as **numerous** as before.
10: 8 [A] I will redeem them; they will be as numerous as **before**^s.

8050 ²רָבָה ***rābâ²***, v. [1] [cf. 8046]

archer [+8009] [1]

Ge 21: 20 [A] He lived in the desert and became an **archer** [+8009].

8051 רַבָּה ***rabbâ***, n.pr.loc. [15] [√ 8041; cf. 8045]

Rabbah [15]

Dt 3: 11 and six feet wide. It is still in **Rabbah** *of* the Ammonites.)
Jos 13: 25 and half the Ammonite country as far as Aroer, near **Rabbah**;
15: 60 Kiriath Jearim) and **Rabbah**—two towns and their villages.
2Sa 11: 1 They destroyed the Ammonites and besieged **Rabbah**.
12: 26 Meanwhile Joab fought against **Rabbah** *of* the Ammonites
12: 27 "I have fought against **Rabbah** and taken its water supply.
12: 29 So David mustered the entire army and went to **Rabbah**,
17: 27 Shobi son of Nahash from **Rabbah** *of* the Ammonites,
1Ch 20: 1 the land of the Ammonites and went to **Rabbah** and besieged it,
20: 1 remained in Jerusalem. Joab attacked **Rabbah** and left it in ruins.
Jer 49: 2 "when I will sound the battle cry against **Rabbah** *of* the
49: 3 Cry out, O inhabitants of **Rabbah**! Put on sackcloth and mourn;
Eze 21: 20 [21:25] for the sword to come against **Rabbah** *of* the Ammonites
25: 5 I will turn **Rabbah** into a pasture for camels and Ammon into a
Am 1: 14 I will set fire to the walls of **Rabbah** that will consume her

8052 רִבּוֹא ***ribbô'***, n.f. [10] [√ 8045; Ar 10649]

20,000 [+9109] [2], 42,360 [+547+752+2256+4395+8993+9252] [1], 42,360 [+547+752+4395+8993+9252] [1], 61,000 [+547+2256+9252] [1], eighteen thousand [+547+2256+9046] [1], hundred and twenty thousand [+6926+9109] [1], many thousands [1], ten thousand [1], tens of thousands [1]

1Ch 29: 7 of God five thousand talents and **ten thousand** darics of gold,
29: 7 of silver, **eighteen thousand** [+547+2256+9046] talents of bronze
Ezr 2: 64 company numbered **42,360** [+547+752+4395+8993+9252],
2: 69 **61,000** [+547+2256+9252] drachmas of gold, 5,000 minas of silver
Ne 7: 66 company numbered **42,360** [+547+752+2256+4395+8993+9252],
7: 71 [7:70] the treasury for the work **20,000** [+9109] drachmas of gold
7: 72 [7:71] rest of the people was **20,000** [+9109] drachmas of gold,
Ps 68: 17 [68:18] The chariots of God are **tens of thousands** and thousands
Da 11: 12 South will be filled with pride and will slaughter **many thousands**,
Hos 8: 12 [I wrote for them the **many** [K; see Q 8044] *things of* my law,]
Jnh 4: 11 has more than a **hundred and twenty thousand** [+6926+9109]

8053 רְבִיבִים ***r^ebîbîm***, n.m. [6] [√ 8045]

showers [5], abundant rain [1]

Dt 32: 2 like showers on new grass, like **abundant rain** on tender plants.
Ps 65: 10 [65:11] its ridges; you soften it with **showers** and bless its crops.
72: 6 like rain falling on a mown field, like **showers** watering the earth.
Jer 3: 3 Therefore the **showers** have been withheld, and no spring rains
14: 22 Do the skies themselves send down **showers**? No, it is you,
Mic 5: 7 [5:6] like **showers** on the grass, which do not wait for man

8054 רָבִיד ***rābîd***, n.[m.]. [2 / 3] [√ 8048]

chain [1], interwoven [+928+2021] [1], necklace [1]

Ge 41: 42 him in robes of fine linen and put a gold **chain** around his neck.
2Ch 3: 16 He made **interwoven** [+928+2021] [BHS 1808] chains and put them
Eze 16: 11 I put bracelets on your arms and a **necklace** around your neck,

8055 רְבִיעִי ***r^ebî'î***, a.num.ord. [56 / 57] [√ 752; Ar 10651]

fourth [44], quarter [9], fourth generation [2], four-sided [1], square [1]

Ge 1: 19 And there was evening, and there was morning—the **fourth** day.
2: 14 the east side of Asshur. And the **fourth** river is the Euphrates.
15: 16 *In* the **fourth** generation your descendants will come back here,
Ex 28: 20 in the **fourth** row a chrysolite, an onyx and a jasper. Mount them
29: 40 pressed olives, and a **quarter** *of* a hin of wine as a drink offering.
39: 13 in the **fourth** row a chrysolite, an onyx and a jasper. They were
Lev 19: 24 In the **fourth** year all its fruit will be holy, an offering of praise to
23: 13 and its drink offering of a **quarter** *of* a hin of wine.
Nu 7: 30 On the **fourth** day Elizur son of Shedeur, the leader of the people
15: 4 tenth of an ephah of fine flour mixed with a **quarter** *of* a hin of oil.
15: 5 the sacrifice, prepare a **quarter** *of* a hin of wine as a drink offering.
28: 5 fine flour mixed with a **quarter** *of* a hin of oil from pressed olives.
28: 7 The accompanying drink offering is to be a **quarter** *of* a hin of
28: 14 the ram, a third of a hin; and with each lamb, a **quarter** *of* a hin.
29: 23 " 'On the **fourth** day prepare ten bulls, two rams and fourteen male
Jos 19: 17 The **fourth** lot came out for Issachar, clan by clan.
Jdg 14: 15 On the **fourth** [BHS 8668] day, they said to Samson's wife,
19: 5 On the **fourth** day they got up early and he prepared to leave,
2Sa 3: 4 the **fourth**, Adonijah the son of Haggith; the fifth,
1Ki 6: 1 in the **fourth** year of Solomon's reign over Israel, in the month of
6: 33 In the same way he made **four-sided** jambs of olive wood for the
6: 37 The foundation of the temple of the LORD was laid in the **fourth**
2Ki 10: 30 will sit on the throne of Israel to the **fourth generation**."
15: 12 will sit on the throne of Israel to the **fourth generation**."
18: 9 In King Hezekiah's **fourth** year, which was the seventh year of
1Ch 2: 14 the **fourth** Nethanel, the fifth Raddai,
3: 2 Talmai king of Geshur; the **fourth**, Adonijah the son of Haggith;
3: 15 Jehoiakim the second son, Zedekiah the third, Shallum the **fourth**.
8: 2 Nohah the **fourth** and Rapha the fifth.
12: 10 [12:11] Mishmannah the **fourth**, Jeremiah the fifth,
23: 19 Amariah the second, Jahaziel the third and Jekameam the **fourth**.
24: 8 the third to Harim, the **fourth** to Seorim,
24: 23 Amariah the second, Jahaziel the third and Jekameam the **fourth**.
25: 11 the **fourth** to Izri, his sons and relatives, 12
26: 2 Jediael the second, Zebadiah the third, Jathniel the **fourth**,
26: 4 the second, Joah the third, Sacar the **fourth**, Nethanel the fifth,
26: 11 Hilkiah the second, Tabaliah the third and Zechariah the **fourth**.
27: 7 The **fourth**, for the fourth month, was Asahel the brother of Joab;
27: 7 The fourth, for the **fourth** month, was Asahel the brother of Joab;
2Ch 20: 26 On the **fourth** day they assembled in the Valley of Beracah,
Ezr 8: 33 On the **fourth** day, in the house of our God, we weighed out the
Ne 9: 3 Book of the Law of the LORD their God for a **quarter** *of* the day,
9: 3 spent another **quarter** in confession and in worshiping the LORD
Jer 25: 1 Judah in the **fourth** year of Jehoiakim son of Josiah king of Judah,
28: 1 In the fifth month of that same year, the **fourth** year, early in the
36: 1 In the **fourth** year of Jehoiakim son of Josiah king of Judah,
39: 2 on the ninth day of the **fourth** month of Zedekiah's eleventh year,
45: 1 Neriah in the **fourth** year of Jehoiakim son of Josiah king of Judah,
46: 2 in the **fourth** year of Jehoiakim son of Josiah king of Judah:
51: 59 with Zedekiah king of Judah in the **fourth** year of his reign.
52: 6 By the ninth day of the **fourth** month the famine in the city had
Eze 1: 1 In the thirtieth year, in the **fourth** month on the fifth day, while I
10: 14 the third the face of a lion, and the **fourth** the face of an eagle.
48: 20 The entire portion will be a **square**, 25,000 cubits on each side.
Da 11: 2 Three more kings will appear in Persia, and then a **fourth**,
Zec 6: 3 the third white, and the **fourth** dappled—all of them powerful.
8: 19 "The fasts of the **fourth**, fifth, seventh and tenth months will

8056 רַבִּית ***rabbît***, n.pr.loc. [1] [√ 8045]

Rabbith [1]

Jos 19: 20 **Rabbith**, Kishion, Ebez,

8057 רָבַךְ ***rābak***, v. [3]

mixing [1], well-kneaded [1], well-mixed [1]

Lev 6: 21 [6:14] [H] bring it **well-mixed** and present the grain offering
7: 12 [H] and cakes of fine flour **well-kneaded** and mixed with oil.
1Ch 23: 29 [H] the unleavened wafers, the baking and the **mixing**,

8058 רִבְלָה ***riblâ***, n.pr.loc. [11]

Riblah [11]

Nu 34: 11 The boundary will go down from Shepham to **Riblah** on the east
2Ki 23: 33 Pharaoh Neco put him in chains at **Riblah** in the land of Hamath
25: 6 He was taken to the king of Babylon at **Riblah**, where sentence
25: 20 took them all and brought them to the king of Babylon at **Riblah**.
25: 21 There at **Riblah**, in the land of Hamath, the king had them
Jer 39: 5 took him to Nebuchadnezzar king of Babylon at **Riblah** in the land
39: 6 There at **Riblah** the king of Babylon slaughtered the sons of
52: 9 He was taken to the king of Babylon at **Riblah** in the land of
52: 10 There at **Riblah** the king of Babylon slaughtered the sons of
52: 26 took them all and brought them to the king of Babylon at **Riblah**.
52: 27 There at **Riblah**, in the land of Hamath, the king had them

8059 רַב מָג ***rab māg***, n.m. Not used in NIV/BHS [√ 8042 + 4454]

8060 רַב־סָרִיס ***rab-sārîs***, n.m. Not used in NIV/BHS [√ 8042 + 6247]

8061 ¹רָבַע ***rāba'¹***, v.den. [4] [cf. 8069]

have sexual relations with [2], lying down [1], mate [1]

Lev 18:23 [A] present herself to an animal to **have sexual relations with** it;
19:19 [G] my decrees. " '*Do* not **mate** different kinds of animals.
20:16 [A] approaches an animal to **have sexual relations with** it,
Ps 139:3 [A] You discern my going out and my **lying down**; you are

8062 ²רָבַע ***rāba'²***, v.den. [12] [√ 752]

square [9], rectangular [2], square [+448+752+8063] [1]

Ex 27:1 [B] it is to be **square**, five cubits long and five cubits wide.
28:16 [B] It is to be **square**—a span long and a span wide—and folded
30:2 [B] It is to be **square**, a cubit long and a cubit wide, and two
37:25 [B] *It was* **square**, a cubit long and a cubit wide, and two cubits
38:1 [B] *it was* **square**, five cubits long and five cubits wide.
39:9 [B] It was **square**—a span long and a span wide—and folded
1Ki 7:5 [B] All the doorways had **rectangular** frames; they were in the
7:31 [E] The panels of the stands *were* **square**, not round.
Eze 40:47 [E] *It was* **square**—a hundred cubits long and a hundred cubits
41:21 [B] The outer sanctuary had a **rectangular** doorframe,
43:16 [B] The altar hearth *is* **square** [+448+752+8063], twelve cubits
45:2 [E] Of this, a section 500 cubits **square** is to be for the sanctuary,

8063 ¹רֶבַע ***reba'¹***, n.m. [7] [→ 8064?; cf. 752?]

directions [2], quarter [2], sides [1], square [+448+752] [1], square [+448+752+8062] [1]

Ex 29:40 fine flour mixed with a **quarter** *of* a hin of oil from pressed olives,
1Sa 9:8 "Look," he said, "I have a **quarter** *of* a shekel of silver. I will give
Eze 1:8 Under their wings on their four **sides** they had the hands of a man.
1:17 they would go in any one of the four **directions** the creatures
10:11 they would go in any one of the four **directions** the cherubim
43:16 The altar hearth *is* **square** [+448+752+8062], twelve cubits long
43:17 The upper ledge also is **square** [+448+752], fourteen cubits long

8064 ²רֶבַע ***reba'²***, n.m. [2] [√ 8063?; cf. 752?]

Reba [2]

Nu 31:8 Among their victims were Evi, Rekem, Zur, Hur and **Reba**—
Jos 13:21 and the Midianite chiefs, Evi, Rekem, Zur, Hur and **Reba**—

8065 ¹רֹבַע ***rōba'¹***, n.[m.]. [2] [√ 752]

fourth part [1], quarter [1]

Nu 23:10 can count the dust of Jacob or number the **fourth part** *of* Israel?
2Ki 6:25 of silver, and a **quarter** *of* a cab of seed pods for five shekels.

8066 ²רֹבַע ***rōba'²***, n.[m.]. Not used in NIV/BHS

8067 רִבֵּעַ ***ribbēa'***, a. [4] [√ 752]

fourth generation [4]

Ex 20:5 fathers to the third and **fourth generation** of those who hate me,
34:7 for the sin of the fathers to the third and **fourth generation**."
Nu 14:18 for the sin of the fathers to the third and **fourth generation**.'
Dt 5:9 fathers to the third and **fourth generation** of those who hate me,

8068 רְבַעַת ***rᵉbu'at***, var. Not used in NIV/BHS [√ 752]

8069 רָבַץ ***rābaṣ***, v. [30] [→ 5271, 8070; cf. 8061]

lie down [11], lay down [2], lie [2], lying [2], rest [2], build [1], crouching [1], fall [1], fallen down [1], have lie down [1], lies down [1], lies [1], lying down [1], makes lie down [1], rest flocks [1], sitting [1]

Ge 4:7 [A] if you do not do what is right, sin *is* **crouching** at your door;
29:2 [A] with three flocks of sheep **lying** near it because the flocks
49:9 [A] Like a lion he crouches and **lies down**, like a lioness—
49:14 [A] "Issachar is a rawboned donkey **lying down** between two
49:25 [A] blessings of the deep *that* **lies** below, blessings of the breast
Ex 23:5 [A] of someone who hates you **fallen down** under its load,
Nu 22:27 [A] *she* **lay down** under Balaam, and he was angry and beat her
Dt 22:6 [A] and the mother *is* **sitting** on the young or on the eggs,
29:20 [29:19] [A] All the curses written in this book *will* **fall** upon
33:13 [A] from heaven above and with the deep waters *that* **lie** below;
Job 11:19 [A] *You will* **lie down**, with no one to make you afraid,
Ps 23:2 [G] *He* **makes** me **lie down** in green pastures, he leads me beside
104:22 [A] and they steal away; they return and **lie down** in their dens.
SS 1:7 [G] graze your flock and where *you* **rest** your sheep at midday.
Isa 11:6 [A] the leopard *will* **lie down** with the goat, the calf and the lion
11:7 [A] will feed with the bear, their young *will* **lie down** together,
13:20 [G] pitch his tent there, no shepherd *will* **rest** *his* **flocks** there.
13:21 [A] But desert creatures *will* **lie** there, jackals will fill her houses;
14:30 [A] poor will find pasture, and the needy *will* **lie down** in safety.
17:2 [A] will be deserted and left to flocks, *which will* **lie down**,
27:10 [A] like the desert; there the calves graze, there *they* **lie down**;
54:11 [G] and not comforted, I *will* **build** you with stones of turquoise,
Jer 33:12 [G] there will again be pastures for shepherds *to* **rest** their flocks.
Eze 19:2 [A] *She* **lay down** among the young lions and reared her cubs.
29:3 [A] king of Egypt, you great monster **lying** among your streams.
34:14 [A] There *they will* **lie down** in good grazing land, and there
34:15 [G] I myself will tend my sheep and **have** them **lie down**,
Zep 2:7 [A] In the evening *they will* **lie down** in the houses of Ashkelon.
2:14 [A] Flocks and herds *will* **lie down** there, creatures of every kind.
3:13 [A] They will eat and **lie down** and no one will make them

8070 רֵבֶץ ***rēbeṣ***, n.[m.]. [4] [√ 8069]

resting place [2], dwelling place [1], where lay [1]

Pr 24:15 against a righteous man's house, do not raid his **dwelling place**;
Isa 35:7 In the haunts **where** jackals once **lay**, grass and reeds and papyrus
65:10 the Valley of Achor a **resting place** *for* herds, for my people who
Jer 50:6 over mountain and hill and forgot their own **resting place**.

8071 רִבְקָה ***ribqâ***, n.pr.f. [30]

Rebekah [29], Rebekah's [1]

Ge 22:23 Bethuel became the father of **Rebekah**. Milcah bore these eight
24:15 finished praying, **Rebekah** came out with her jar on her shoulder.
24:29 Now **Rebekah** had a brother named Laban, and he hurried out to
24:30 had heard **Rebekah** tell what the man said to her, he went out to
24:45 in my heart, **Rebekah** came out, with her jar on her shoulder.
24:51 Here is **Rebekah**; take her and go, and let her become the wife of
24:53 silver jewelry and articles of clothing and gave them to **Rebekah**;
24:58 So they called **Rebekah** and asked her, "Will you go with this
24:59 So they sent their sister **Rebekah** on her way, along with her nurse
24:60 they blessed **Rebekah** and said to her, "Our sister, may you
24:61 Then **Rebekah** and her maids got ready and mounted their camels
24:61 and went back with the man. So the servant took **Rebekah** and left.
24:64 **Rebekah** also looked up and saw Isaac. She got down from her
24:67 her into the tent of his mother Sarah, and he married **Rebekah**.
25:20 Isaac was forty years old when he married **Rebekah** daughter of
25:21 answered his prayer, and his wife **Rebekah** became pregnant.
25:28 had a taste for wild game, loved Esau, but **Rebekah** loved Jacob.
26:7 "The men of this place might kill me on account of **Rebekah**,
26:8 down from a window and saw Isaac caressing his wife **Rebekah**.
26:35 They were a source of grief to Isaac and **Rebekah**.
27:5 Now **Rebekah** was listening as Isaac spoke to his son Esau.
27:6 **Rebekah** said to her son Jacob, "Look, I overheard your father say
27:11 Jacob said to **Rebekah** his mother, "But my brother Esau is a hairy
27:15 Then **Rebekah** took the best clothes of Esau her older son,
27:42 When **Rebekah** was told what her older son Esau had said,
27:46 **Rebekah** said to Isaac, "I'm disgusted with living because of these
28:5 the brother of **Rebekah**, who was the mother of Jacob and Esau.
29:12 Rachel that he was a relative of her father and a son of **Rebekah**.
35:8 **Rebekah's** nurse, died and was buried under the oak below Bethel.
49:31 there Isaac and his wife **Rebekah** were buried, and there I buried

8072 רַב־שָׁקֵה ***rab-šāqēh***, n.m. [16] [√ 8042 + 9197]

field commander [12], commander [4]

2Ki 18:17 his chief officer and his **field commander** with a large army,
18:19 The **field commander** said to them, "Tell Hezekiah: " 'This is
18:26 son of Hilkiah, and Shebna and Joah said to the **field commander**,
18:27 the **commander** replied, "Was it only to your master and you that
18:28 the **commander** stood and called out in Hebrew: "Hear the word
18:37 clothes torn, and told him what the **field commander** had said.
19:4 LORD your God will hear all the words of the **field commander**,
19:8 When the **field commander** heard that the king of Assyria had left
Isa 36:2 the king of Assyria sent his **field commander** with a large army
36:4 The **field commander** said to them, "Tell Hezekiah, " 'This is
36:11 Then Eliakim, Shebna and Joah said to the **field commander**,
36:12 the **commander** replied, "Was it only to your master and you that
36:13 the **commander** stood and called out in Hebrew, "Hear the words
36:22 clothes torn, and told him what the **field commander** had said.
37:4 the LORD your God will hear the words of the **field commander**,
37:8 When the **field commander** heard that the king of Assyria had left

8073 רֶגֶב ***regeb***, n.m. [2] [→ 757, 758, 759]

clods of earth [1], soil [1]

Job 21:33 The **soil** *in* the valley is sweet to him; all men follow after him,
38:38 when the dust becomes hard and the **clods of earth** stick together?

8074 רָגַז *rāgaz*, v. [41] [→ 761, 8075, 8076, 8077; Ar 10653]
tremble [7], rage [4], shook [4], disturbed [3], shakes [2], trembled [2], all astir [1], anger [1], come trembling [1], convulsed [1], enraged [1], in anguish [1], made tremble [1], make tremble [1], pounded [1], provoke [1], quake [1], quarrel [1], rages [1], rouse [1], shake [1], shaken [1], shudder [1], trembles [1], unrest [1]

Ge 45:24 [A] were leaving he said to them, "Don't **quarrel** on the way!"
Ex 15:14 [A] The nations will hear and **tremble**; anguish will grip the
Dt 2:25 [A] of you and *will* **tremble** and be in anguish because of you."
1Sa 14:15 [A] in the outposts and raiding parties—and the ground **shook**.
28:15 [G] to Saul, "Why *have you* **disturbed** me by bringing me up?"
2Sa 7:10 [A] can have a home of their own and no longer *be* **disturbed**.
18:33 [19:1] [A] The king *was* **shaken**. He went up to the room over
22:8 [A] and quaked, the foundations of the heavens **shook**;
2Ki 19:27 [F] and when you come and go and *how* you **rage** against me.
19:28 [F] Because you **rage** against me and your insolence has reached
1Ch 17:9 [A] can have a home of their own and no longer *be* **disturbed**.
Job 9:6 [G] He **shakes** the earth from its place and makes its pillars
12:6 [G] are undisturbed, and *those who* **provoke** God are secure—
Ps 4:4 [4:5] [A] *In your* **anger** do not sin; when you are on your beds,
18:7 [18:8] [A] and the foundations of the mountains **shook**;
77:16 [77:17] [A] and writhed; the very depths *were* **convulsed**.
77:18 [77:19] [A] lit up the world; the earth **trembled** and quaked.
99:1 [A] The LORD reigns, *let* the nations **tremble**; he sits
Pr 29:9 [A] with a fool, the fool **rages** and scoffs, and there is no peace.
30:21 [A] "Under three things the earth **trembles**, under four it cannot
Isa 5:25 [A] The mountains **shake**, and the dead bodies are like refuse in
13:13 [G] Therefore *I will* **make** the heavens **tremble**; and the earth
14:9 [A] The grave below *is* **all astir** to meet you at your coming;
14:16 [G] "Is this the man *who* **shook** the earth and made kingdoms
23:11 [G] out his hand over the sea and **made** its kingdoms **tremble**.
28:21 [A] *he will* **rouse** *himself* as in the Valley of Gibeon—
32:10 [A] In little more than a year you who feel secure *will* **tremble**;
32:11 [A] **shudder**, *you* daughters who feel secure!
37:28 [F] and when you come and go and *how* you **rage** against me.
37:29 [F] Because you **rage** against me and because your insolence has
64:2 [64:1] [A] and *cause* the nations *to* **quake** before you!
Jer 33:9 [A] will be in awe and *will* **tremble** at the abundant prosperity
50:34 [G] rest to their land, but **unrest** to those who live in Babylon.
Eze 16:43 [A] the days of your youth but **enraged** me with all these things,
Joel 2:1 [A] *Let* all who live in the land **tremble**, for the day of the
2:10 [A] Before them the earth **shakes**, the sky trembles, the sun
Am 8:8 [A] "*Will* not the land **tremble** for this, and all who live in it
Mic 7:17 [A] *They will* **come trembling** out of their dens; they will turn in
Hab 3:7 [A] of Cushan in distress, the dwellings of Midian **in anguish**.
3:16 [A] I heard and my heart **pounded**, my lips quivered at the
3:16 [A] the sound; decay crept into my bones, and my legs **trembled**.

8075 רֹגֶז *rōgez*, n.m. [7] [√ 8074; Ar 10654]
turmoil [3], excitement [1], roar [1], trouble [1], wrath [1]

Job 3:17 There the wicked cease from **turmoil**, and there the weary are at
3:26 I have no peace, no quietness; I have no rest, but only **turmoil**."
14:1 "Man born of woman is of few days and full of **trouble**.
37:2 Listen to the **roar** *of* his voice, to the rumbling that comes from his
39:24 In frenzied **excitement** he eats up the ground; he cannot stand still
Isa 14:3 gives you relief from suffering and **turmoil** and cruel bondage,
Hab 3:2 in our time make them known; in **wrath** remember mercy.

8076 רַגָּז *raggāz*, a. [1] [√ 8074]
anxious [1]

Dt 28:65 There the LORD will give you an **anxious** mind, eyes weary with

8077 רָגְזָה *rogzâ*, n.f. [1] [√ 8074]
shudder [1]

Eze 12:18 as you eat your food, and **shudder** in fear as you drink your water.

8078 רָגַל *rāgal*, v.den. [26] [√ 8079]
spies [8], spied out [4], spy out [4], spying [2], explore [1], explored [1], scouts [1], secret messengers [1], slander [1], slandered [1], spies [+408] [1], taught to walk [1]

Ge 42:9 [D] his dreams about them and said to them, "You *are* **spies**!
42:11 [D] sons of one man. Your servants are honest men, not **spies**."
42:14 [D] Joseph said to them, "It is just as I told you: You *are* **spies**!
42:16 [D] you are not, then as surely as Pharaoh lives, you are **spies**!"
42:30 [D] to us and treated us as though we *were* **spying** *on* the land.
42:31 [D] But we said to him, 'We are honest men; we are not **spies**.
42:34 [D] to me so I will know that you *are* not **spies** but honest men.
Nu 21:32 [D] After Moses had sent **spies** to Jazer, the Israelites captured its
Dt 1:24 [D] and came to the Valley of Eshcol and **explored** it.
Jos 2:1 [D] Joshua son of Nun secretly sent two **spies** [+408] from
6:22 [D] Joshua said to the two men who *had* **spied out** the land,
6:23 [D] So the young men who *had done the* **spying** went in
6:25 [D] because she hid the men Joshua had sent as **spies** to Jericho—
7:2 [D] of Bethel, and told them, "Go up and **spy out** the region."
7:2 [D] spy out the region." So the men went up and **spied out** Ai.
14:7 [D] the LORD sent me from Kadesh Barnea to **explore** the land.
Jdg 18:2 [D] from Zorah and Eshtaol to **spy out** the land and explore it.
18:14 [D] the five men who *had* **spied out** the land of Laish said to
18:17 [D] The five men who *had* **spied out** the land went inside and
1Sa 26:4 [D] he sent out **scouts** and learned that Saul had definitely
2Sa 10:3 [D] to you to explore the city and **spy** it **out** and overthrow it?"
15:10 [D] Absalom sent **secret messengers** throughout the tribes of
19:27 [19:28] [D] *he has* **slandered** your servant to my lord the king.
1Ch 19:3 [D] to you to explore and **spy out** the country and overthrow it?"
Ps 15:3 [A] *has* no **slander** on his tongue, who does his neighbor no
Hos 11:3 [G] It was I *who* **taught** Ephraim **to walk**, taking them by the

8079 רֶגֶל *regel*, n.f. [245] [→ 5274, 8078, 8081; Ar 10655]
feet [131], foot [42], *untranslated* [6], legs [6], feet [+4090] [5], footstool [+2071] [5], foot [+4090] [4], times [4], steps [3], big toes [2], fleet-footed [+928+7824] [2], following [+928] [2], footsteps [2], my [+928+3276] [2], accompanied [+995] [1], after [+928] [1], ankles [1], attended by [+2143+4200] [1], belonged to [+928] [1], continued on journey [+5951] [1], follow [+928] [1], follow [+928+2143] [1], followed [+928+6590] [1], goes [+2118] [1], hasty [+237+928] [1], jointed [+4200+4946+5087] [1], letting range free [+8938] [1], offering body [+906+7316] [1], pace [1], relieve himself [+906+2257+6114] [1], relieving himself [+906+2257+6114] [1], service [1], step [1], stood [+3922+5163] [1], stood [+5163] [1], that[s] [+4200] [1], those[s] [+4090] [1], underfoot [+928] [1], underfoot [+9393] [1], what trampled [+5330] [1], wherever [+4200] [1], with [+928] [1], womb [+1068] [1]

Ge 8:9 the dove could find no place to set its **feet** [+4090] because there
18:4 and then you may all wash your **feet** and rest under this tree.
19:2 You can wash your **feet** and spend the night and then go on your
24:32 and water for him **[RPH]** and his men to wash their feet.
24:32 for the camels, and water for him and his men to wash their **feet**.
29:1 Jacob **continued on** his **journey** [+5951] and came to the land of
30:30 and the LORD has blessed you **wherever** [+4200] I have been.
33:14 while I move along slowly at the **pace** *of* the droves before me
33:14 the pace of the droves before me and **that**[s] [+4200] *of* the children,
41:44 but without your word no one will lift hand or **foot** in all Egypt."
43:24 gave them water to wash their **feet** and provided fodder for their
49:10 nor the ruler's staff from between his **feet**, until he comes to whom
49:33 he drew his **feet** up into the bed, breathed his last and was gathered
Ex 3:5 **[NIE]** for the place where you are standing is holy ground."
4:25 cut off her son's foreskin and touched ⌞Moses'⌟ **feet** with it.
11:8 and saying, 'Go, you and all the people who **follow** [+928] you!'
12:11 your belt, your sandals on your **feet** and your staff in your hand.
21:24 eye for eye, tooth for tooth, hand for hand, **foot** for foot,
21:24 eye for eye, tooth for tooth, hand for hand, foot for **foot**,
23:14 "Three **times** a year you are to celebrate a festival to me.
24:10 Under his **feet** was something like a pavement made of sapphire,
25:26 and fasten them to the four corners, where the four **legs** are.
29:20 thumbs of their right hands, and on the big toes of their right **feet**.
30:19 and his sons are to wash their hands and **feet** with water from it.
30:21 they shall wash their hands and **feet** so that they will not die.
37:13 and fastened them to the four corners, where the four **legs** were.
40:31 and Aaron and his sons used it to wash their hands and **feet**.
Lev 8:23 on the thumb of his right hand and on the big toe of his right **foot**.
8:24 thumbs of their right hands and on the big toes of their right **feet**.
11:21 have **jointed** [+4200+4946+5087] legs for hopping on the ground.
11:23 But all other winged creatures that have four **legs** you are to detest.
11:42 whether it moves on its belly or walks on all fours or on many **feet**;
13:12 it covers all the skin of the infected person from head to **foot**,
14:14 on the thumb of his right hand and on the big toe of his right **foot**.
14:17 on the thumb of his right hand and on the big toe of his right **foot**,
14:25 on the thumb of his right hand and on the big toe of his right **foot**.
14:28 on the thumb of his right hand and on the big toe of his right **foot**.
21:19 no man with a crippled **foot** or hand,
Nu 20:19 pay for it. We only want to pass through on **foot**—nothing else."
22:25 she pressed close to the wall, crushing Balaam's **foot** against it.
22:28 "What have I done to you to make you beat me these three **times**?"
22:32 asked him, "Why have you beaten your donkey these three **times**?
22:33 The donkey saw me and turned away from me these three **times**.
Dt 2:5 you any of their land, not even enough to put your **foot** [+4090] on.
2:28 to drink for their price in silver. Only let us pass through on **foot**—
8:4 not wear out and your **feet** did not swell during these forty years.
11:6 their tents and every living thing that **belonged to** [+928] them.
11:10 planted your seed and irrigated it by **foot** as in a vegetable garden.
11:24 Every place where you set your **foot** [+4090] will be yours:
19:21 for life, eye for eye, tooth for tooth, hand for hand, **foot** for foot.
19:21 for life, eye for eye, tooth for tooth, hand for hand, foot for **foot**.

Dt 25: 9 take off one of his sandals, **[NIE]** spit in his face and say,
28:35 spreading from the soles of your **feet** to the top of your head.
28:56 would not venture to touch the ground with the sole of her **foot**—
28:57 the afterbirth from her **womb** [+1068] and the children she bears.
28:65 you will find no repose, no resting place for the sole of your **foot**.
29: 5 [29:4] clothes did not wear out, nor did the sandals on your **feet**.
32:35 In due time their **foot** will slip; their day of disaster is near
33: 3 At your **feet** they all bow down, and from you receive instruction,
33:24 let him be favored by his brothers, and let him bathe his **feet** in oil.
Jos 1: 3 I will give you every place where you set your **foot** [+4090],
3:13 set **foot** [+4090] in the Jordan, its waters flowing downstream will
3:15 the ark reached the Jordan and their **feet** touched the water's edge,
4: 3 of the Jordan from right where the priests **stood** [+3922+5163]
4: 9 the priests who carried the ark of the covenant had **stood** [+5163].
4:18 No sooner had they set their **feet** [+4090] on the dry ground than
5:15 your sandals, **[NIE]** for the place where you are standing is holy."
9: 5 The men put worn and patched sandals on their **feet** and wore old
10:24 "Come here and put your **feet** on the necks of these kings."
10:24 So they came forward and placed their **feet** on their necks.
14: 9 'The land on which your **feet** have walked will be your inheritance
Jdg 1: 6 chased him and caught him, and cut off his thumbs and **big toes**.
1: 7 and **big toes** cut off have picked up scraps under my table.
3:24 "He *must be* **relieving himself** [+906+2257+6114] in the inner
4:10 Ten thousand men **followed** [+928+6590] him, and Deborah also
4:15 by the sword, and Sisera abandoned his chariot and fled on **foot**.
4:17 Sisera, however, fled on **foot** to the tent of Jael, the wife of Heber
5:15 Issachar was with Barak, rushing **after** [+928] him into the valley.
5:27 At her **feet** he sank, he fell; there he lay. At her feet he sank,
5:27 At her **feet** he sank, he fell; where he sank, there he fell—dead.
8: 5 to the men of Succoth, "Give **my** [+928+3276] troops some bread;
19:21 After they had washed their **feet**, they had something to eat
1Sa 2: 9 He will guard the **feet** *of* his saints, but the wicked will be silenced
14:13 Jonathan climbed up, using his hands and **feet**, with his
17: 6 on his **legs** he wore bronze greaves, and a bronze javelin was slung
23:22 Find out where David *usually* **goes** [+2118] and who has seen him
24: 3 [24:4] and Saul went in to **relieve himself** [+906+2257+6114].
25:24 She fell at his **feet** and said: "My lord, let the blame be on me
25:27 to my master, be given to the men who **follow** [+928+2143] you.
25:41 ready to serve you and wash the **feet** *of* my master's servants."
25:42 **attended by** [+2143+4200] her five maids, went with David's
2Sa 2:18 Now Asahel was as **fleet-footed** [+928+7824] as a wild gazelle.
3:34 Your hands were not bound, your **feet** were not fettered. You fell
4: 4 (Jonathan son of Saul had a son who was lame in *both* **feet**.
4:12 They cut off their hands and **feet** and hung the bodies by the pool
9: 3 "There is still a son of Jonathan; he is crippled in *both* **feet**."
9:13 he always ate at the king's table, and he was crippled in both **feet**.
11: 8 David said to Uriah, "Go down to your house and wash your **feet**."
14:25 From the top of his head to the sole of his **foot** there was no
15:16 The king set out, with his entire household **following** [+928] him;
15:17 So the king set out, with all the people **following** [+928] him,
15:18 all the six hundred Gittites who *had* **accompanied** [+995] him
19:24 [19:25] He had not taken care of his **feet** or trimmed his mustache
21:20 huge man with six fingers on each hand and six toes on each **foot**—
22:10 the heavens and came down; dark clouds were under his **feet**.
22:34 He makes my **feet** like the feet of a deer; he enables me to stand on
22:39 and they could not rise; they fell beneath my **feet**.
1Ki 2: 5 blood stained the belt around his waist and the sandals on his **feet**.
5: 3 [5:17] until the LORD put his enemies under his **feet** [+4090].
14: 6 So when Ahijah heard the sound of her **footsteps** at the door,
14:12 go back home. When you set **foot** in your city, the boy will die.
15:23 kings of Judah? In his old age, however, his **feet** became diseased.
20:10 if enough dust remains in Samaria to give each of **my** [+928+3276]
2Ki 3: 9 no more water for themselves or for the animals **with** [+928] them.
4:27 reached the man of God at the mountain, she took hold of his **feet**.
4:37 She came in, fell at his **feet** and bowed to the ground. Then she
6:32 Is not the sound of his master's **footsteps** behind him?"
9:35 they found nothing except her skull, her **feet** and her hands.
13:21 Elisha's bones, the man came to life and stood up on his **feet**.
18:27 [and drink their own **urine**?" [Q +4784; see K 8875]]
21: 8 I will not again make the **feet** *of* the Israelites wander from the land
1Ch 28: 2 King David rose to his **feet** and said: "Listen to me, my brothers
28: 2 for the **footstool of** [+2071] our God, and I made plans to build it.
2Ch 3:13 twenty cubits. They stood on their **feet**, facing the main hall.
16:12 year of his reign Asa was afflicted with a disease in his **feet**.
33: 8 I will not again make the **feet** *of* the Israelites leave the land I
Ne 9:21 their clothes did not wear out nor did their **feet** become swollen.
Est 8: 3 Esther again pleaded with the king, falling at his **feet** and weeping.
Job 2: 7 afflicted Job with painful sores from the soles of his **feet** to the top
12: 5 for misfortune as the fate of those whose **feet** are slipping.
13:27 You fasten my **feet** in shackles; you keep close watch on all my
13:27 watch on all my paths by putting marks on the soles of my **feet**.
18: 8 His **feet** thrust him into a net and he wanders into its mesh.
18:11 Terrors startle him on every side and dog his *every* **step**.
23:11 My **feet** have closely followed his steps; I have kept to his way
28: 4 people dwell he cuts a shaft, in places forgotten by the **foot** of man;
29:15 I was eyes to the blind and **feet** to the lame.
30:12 they lay snares for my **feet**, they build their siege ramps against
31: 5 "If I have walked in falsehood or my **foot** has hurried after deceit—
33:11 He fastens my **feet** in shackles; he keeps close watch on all my
39:15 unmindful that a **foot** may crush them, that some wild animal may
Ps 8: 6 [8:7] the works of your hands; you put everything under his **feet**:
9:15 [9:16] have dug; their **feet** are caught in the net they have hidden.
18: 9 [18:10] and came down; dark clouds were under his **feet**.
18:33 [18:34] He makes my **feet** like the feet of a deer; he enables me to
18:38 [18:39] so that they could not rise; they fell beneath my **feet**.
22:16 [22:17] encircled me, they have pierced my hands and my **feet**.
25:15 on the LORD, for only he will release my **feet** from the snare.
26:12 My **feet** stand on level ground; in the great assembly I will praise
31: 8 [31:9] over to the enemy but have set my **feet** in a spacious place.
36:11 [36:12] May the **foot** *of* the proud not come against me, nor the
38:16 [38:17] or exalt themselves over me when my **foot** slips."
40: 2 [40:3] he set my **feet** on a rock and gave me a firm place to stand.
47: 3 [47:4] He subdued nations under us, peoples under our **feet**.
56:13 [56:14] delivered me from death and my **feet** from stumbling,
66: 6 the sea into dry land, they passed through the waters on **foot**—
66: 9 he has preserved our lives and kept our **feet** from slipping.
68:23 [68:24] that you may plunge your **feet** in the blood of your foes,
73: 2 as for me, my **feet** had almost slipped; I had nearly lost my
91:12 in their hands, so that you will not strike your **foot** against a stone.
94:18 When I said, "My **foot** is slipping," your love, O LORD,
99: 5 Exalt the LORD our God and worship at his **footstool** [+2071];
105:18 They bruised his **feet** with shackles, his neck was put in irons,
110: 1 my right hand until I make your enemies a footstool for your **feet**."
115: 7 they have hands, but cannot feel, **feet**, but they cannot walk;
116: 8 my soul from death, my eyes from tears, my **feet** from stumbling,
119:59 considered my ways and have turned my **steps** to your statutes.
119:101 I have kept my **feet** from every evil path so that I might obey your
119:105 Your word is a lamp to my **feet** and a light for my path.
121: 3 He will not let your **foot** slip—he who watches over you will not
122: 2 Our **feet** are standing in your gates, O Jerusalem.
132: 7 go to his dwelling place; let us worship at his **footstool** [+2071]—
Pr 1:15 my son, do not go along with them, do not set **foot** on their paths;
1:16 for their **feet** rush into sin, they are swift to shed blood.
3:23 you will go on your way in safety, and your **foot** will not stumble;
3:26 will be your confidence and will keep your **foot** from being snared.
4:26 Make level paths for your **feet** and take only ways that are firm.
4:27 Do not swerve to the right or the left; keep your **foot** from evil.
5: 5 Her **feet** go down to death; her steps lead straight to the grave.
6:13 with his eye, signals with his **feet** and motions with his fingers,
6:18 that devises wicked schemes, **feet** that are quick to rush into evil,
6:28 Can a man walk on hot coals without his **feet** being scorched?
7:11 (She is loud and defiant, her **feet** never stay at home;
19: 2 without knowledge, nor *to be* **hasty** [+237+928] and miss the way.
25:17 Seldom set **foot** in your neighbor's house—too much of you,
25:19 or a lame **foot** is reliance on the unfaithful in times of trouble.
26: 6 Like cutting off one's **feet** or drinking violence is the sending of a
Ecc 5: 1 [4:17] Guard your **steps** when you go to the house of God. Go
SS 5: 3 I put it on again? I have washed my **feet**—must I soil them again?
Isa 1: 6 From the sole of your **foot** to the top of your head there is no
3:16 along with mincing steps, with ornaments jingling on their **ankles**.
6: 2 with two they covered their **feet**, and with two they were flying.
7:20 to shave your head and the hair of your **legs**, and to take off your
20: 2 off the sackcloth from your body and the sandals from your **feet**."
23: 7 old city, whose **feet** have taken her to settle in far-off lands?
26: 6 **Feet** trample it down—the feet of the oppressed, the footsteps of
26: 6 it down—the **feet** *of* the oppressed, the footsteps of the poor.
28: 3 pride of Ephraim's drunkards, will be trampled **underfoot** [+928].
32:20 and **letting** your cattle and donkeys **range free** [+8938].
36:12 [filth and drink their own **urine**?" [Q +4784; see K 8875]]
41: 2 up one from the east, calling him in righteousness to his **service**?
41: 3 moves on unscathed, by a path his **feet** have not traveled before.
49:23 with their faces to the ground; they will lick the dust at your **feet**.
52: 7 How beautiful on the mountains are the **feet** *of* those who bring
58:13 "If you keep your **feet** from breaking the Sabbath and from doing
59: 7 Their **feet** rush into sin; they are swift to shed innocent blood.
60:13 the place of my sanctuary; and I will glorify the place of my **feet**.
60:14 all who despise you will bow down at your **feet** [+4090] and will
66: 1 "Heaven is my throne, and the earth is my **footstool** [+2071].
Jer 2:25 Do not run until your **feet** are bare and your throat is dry. But you
13:16 the darkness, before your **feet** stumble on the darkening hills.
14:10 "They greatly love to wander; they do not restrain their **feet**.
18:22 have dug a pit to capture me and have hidden snares for my **feet**.
38:22 Your **feet** are sunk in the mud; your friends have deserted you.'
La 1:13 He spread a net for my **feet** and turned me back. He made me
2: 1 he has not remembered his **footstool** [+2071] in the day of his
3:34 To crush **underfoot** [+9393] all prisoners in the land,
Eze 1: 7 Their **legs** were straight; their feet were like those of a calf
1: 7 Their legs **[RPH]** were straight; their feet were like those of a calf

Eze 1: 7 their **feet** [+4090] were like those of a calf and gleamed like
1: 7 their feet were like **those**[s] [+4090] *of* a calf and gleamed like
2: 1 "Son of man, stand up on your **feet** and I will speak to you."
2: 2 As he spoke, the Spirit came into me and raised me to my **feet**,
3: 24 the Spirit came into me and raised me to my **feet**. He spoke to me
6: 11 Strike your hands together and stamp your **feet** and cry out "Alas!"
16: 25 **offering** your **body** [+906+7316] with increasing promiscuity to
24: 17 Keep your turban fastened and your sandals on your **feet**; do not
24: 23 keep your turbans on your heads and your sandals on your **feet**.
25: 6 Because you have clapped your hands and stamped your **feet**,
29: 11 No **foot** *of* man or animal will pass through it; no one will live
29: 11 No foot of man or **[RPH]** animal will pass through it; no one will
32: 2 churning the water with your **feet** and muddying the streams.
32: 13 beside abundant waters no longer to be stirred by the **foot** *of* man
34: 18 Must you also trample the rest of your pasture with your **feet**?
34: 18 to drink clear water? Must you also muddy the rest with your **feet**?
34: 19 Must my flock feed on **what** you have **trampled** [+5330]
34: 19 have trampled and drink what you have muddied with your **feet**?
37: 10 they came to life and stood up on their **feet**—a vast army.
43: 7 this is the place of my throne and the place for the soles of my **feet**.
Am 2: 15 the **fleet-footed** [+928+7824] soldier will not get away, and the
Na 1: 3 in the whirlwind and the storm, and clouds are the dust of his **feet**.
1: 15 [2:1] the **feet** *of* one who brings good news, who proclaims peace!
Hab 3: 5 Plague went before him; pestilence followed his **steps**.
3: 19 he makes my **feet** like the feet of a deer, he enables me to go on the
Zec 14: 4 On that day his **feet** will stand on the Mount of Olives, east of
14: 12 Their flesh will rot while they are still standing on their **feet**,
Mal 4: 3 [3:21] they will be ashes under the soles of your **feet** on the day

8080 רֹגֵל rōgēl, n.pr.loc. Not used in NIV/BHS [√ 6537]

8081 רַגְלִי raglî, a. [12 / 13] [√ 8079]

foot soldiers [6], foot soldiers [+408] [3], on foot [2], men on foot [1], soldiers [+408] [1]

Ex 12: 37 There were about six hundred thousand men **on foot**, besides
Nu 11: 21 "Here I am among six hundred thousand men **on foot**, and you say,
Jdg 20: 2 four hundred thousand **soldiers** [+408] armed with swords.
1Sa 4: 10 slaughter was very great; Israel lost thirty thousand **foot soldiers**.
15: 4 two hundred thousand **foot soldiers** and ten thousand men from
2Sa 8: 4 thousand charioteers and twenty thousand **foot** [+408] **soldiers**.
10: 6 they hired twenty thousand Aramean **foot soldiers** from Beth
10: 18 and forty thousand of their **foot** [BHS 7305] **soldiers**.
1Ki 20: 29 thousand casualties on the Aramean **foot soldiers** in one day.
2Ki 13: 7 ten chariots and ten thousand **foot soldiers**, for the king of Aram
1Ch 18: 4 thousand charioteers and twenty thousand **foot** [+408] **soldiers**.
19: 18 their charioteers and forty thousand of their **foot** [+408] **soldiers**.
Jer 12: 5 "If you have raced with **men on foot** and they have worn you out,

8082 רֹגְלִים rōgᵉlîm, n.pr.loc. [2]

Rogelim [2]

2Sa 17: 27 Ammiel from Lo Debar, and Barzillai the Gileadite from **Rogelim**
19: 31 [19:32] Barzillai the Gileadite also came down from **Rogelim** to

8083 רָגַם rāgam, v. [16] [→ 5275, 8086]

stone [+74+906+928+2021] [3], must stone [+928+8083] [2], stone [+74+928+2021] [2], stoned [+74+906] [2], stoned [+74+928] [2], stone [+74+6584] [1], stone [1], stoned [+74+906+928+2021] [1], stoned to death [+74] [1], stoning [+74+906+928+2021] [1]

Lev 20: 2 [A] The people of the community *are to* **stone** [+74+928+2021]
20: 27 [A] *You are to* **stone** [+74+906+928+2021] them; their blood will
24: 14 [A] hands on his head, and the entire assembly *is to* **stone** him.
24: 16 [A] The entire assembly **must stone** [+928+8083] him.
24: 16 [A] The entire assembly **must stone** [+928+8083] him.
24: 23 [A] the blasphemer outside the camp and **stoned** [+74+906] him.
Nu 14: 10 [A] assembly talked about **stoning** [+74+906+928+2021] them.
15: 35 [A] The whole assembly *must* **stone** [+74+906+928+2021] him
15: 36 [A] the camp and **stoned** [+74+906+928+2021] him to death,
Dt 21: 21 [A] all the men of his town *shall* **stone** [+74+928+2021] him to
Jos 7: 25 [A] all Israel **stoned** [+74+906] him, and after they had stoned
1Ki 12: 18 [A] of forced labor, but all Israel **stoned** [+74+928] him to death.
2Ch 10: 18 [A] but the Israelites **stoned** [+74+928] him to death.
24: 21 [A] by order of the king *they* **stoned** [+74] him **to death** in the
Eze 16: 40 [A] a mob against you, *who will* **stone** [+74+906+928+2021] you
23: 47 [A] The mob *will* **stone** [+74+6584] them and cut them down

8084 רֶגֶם regem, n.pr.m. [1] [→ 8085; cf. 9553]

Regem [1]

1Ch 2: 47 sons of Jahdai: **Regem**, Jotham, Geshan, Pelet, Ephah and Shaaph.

8085 רֶגֶם מֶלֶךְ regem melek, n.pr.m. [1] [√ 8084 + 4889]

Regem-Melech [1]

Zec 7: 2 The people of Bethel had sent Sharezer and **Regem-Melech**,

8086 רִגְמָה rigmâ, n.f. [1] [√ 8083]

great throng [1]

Ps 68: 27 [68:28] leading them, there the **great throng** *of* Judah's princes,

8087 רָגַן rāgan, v. [7]

gossip [4], grumbled [2], complain [1]

Dt 1: 27 [C] *You* **grumbled** in your tents and said, "The LORD hates us;
Ps 106: 25 [C] *They* **grumbled** in their tents and did not obey the LORD.
Pr 16: 28 [C] man stirs up dissension, and a **gossip** separates close friends.
18: 8 [C] The words of a **gossip** are like choice morsels; they go down
26: 20 [C] wood a fire goes out; without **gossip** a quarrel dies down.
26: 22 [C] The words of a **gossip** are like choice morsels; they go down
Isa 29: 24 [A] *those who* **complain** will accept instruction."

8088 רָגַע¹ rāga[1], v. [7] [cf. 8089]

churned up [1], churns up [1], in an instant [1], instant [1], moment [1], speedily [1], stirs up [1]

Job 26: 12 [A] By his power *he* **churned up** the sea; by his wisdom he cut
Pr 12: 19 [G] lips endure forever, but a lying tongue lasts *only a* **moment**.
Isa 51: 5 [51:4] [G] My righteousness draws near **speedily**, my salvation
51: 15 [A] your God, *who* **churns up** the sea so that its waves roar—
Jer 31: 35 [A] shine by night, *who* **stirs up** the sea so that its waves roar—
49: 19 [G] I will chase Edom from its land *in an* **instant**.
50: 44 [G] I will chase Babylon from its land **in an instant**.

8089 רָגַע² rāga[2], v. [5] [→ 5273, 5276, 8091, 8092; cf. 8088, 8090]

bring rest [1], cease [1], find repose [1], give rest [1], repose [1]

Dt 28: 65 [G] Among those nations *you will* **find** no **repose**, no resting
Isa 34: 14 [G] there the night creatures *will* also **repose** and find for
Jer 31: 2 [G] find favor in the desert; I will come to **give rest** *to* Israel."
47: 6 [C] long till you rest? Return to your scabbard; **cease** and be still.'
50: 34 [G] defend their cause so that *he may* **bring rest** *to* their land,

8090 רָגַע³ rāga[3], v. [1] [cf. 8089]

broken [1]

Job 7: 5 [A] with worms and scabs, my skin *is* **broken** and festering.

8091 רָגֵעַ rāgēaʿ, a. [1] [√ 8089]

live quietly [1]

Ps 35: 20 devise false accusations against *those who* **live quietly** *in* the land.

8092 רֶגַע regaʿ, n.m. [22] [√ 8089]

moment [9], at once [+3869] [2], in a moment [2], at another time [1], at any time [1], continually [+4200] [1], in a moment [+4017] [1], in an instant [1], little while [+5071] [1], peace [1], sudden [1], suddenly [+3869] [1]

Ex 33: 5 If I were to go with you even for a **moment**, I might destroy you.
Nu 16: 21 from this assembly so I can put an end to them **at once** [+3869]."
16: 45 [17:10] so I can put an end to them **at once** [+3869]."
Ezr 9: 8 "But now, for a brief **moment**, the LORD our God has been
Job 7: 18 that you examine him every morning and test him every **moment**?
20: 5 of the wicked is brief, the joy of the godless lasts but a **moment**.
21: 13 spend their years in prosperity and go down to the grave in **peace**.
34: 20 They die **in an instant**, in the middle of the night; the people are
Ps 6: 10 [6:11] and dismayed; they will turn back in **sudden** disgrace.
30: 5 [30:6] For his anger lasts only a **moment**, but his favor lasts a
73: 19 How **suddenly** [+3869] are they destroyed, completely swept away
Isa 26: 20 hide yourselves for a **little while** [+5071] until his wrath has
27: 3 the LORD, watch over it; I water it **continually** [+4200].
47: 9 Both of these will overtake you **in a moment**, on a single day:
54: 7 "For a brief **moment** I abandoned you, but with deep compassion I
54: 8 In a surge of anger I hid my face from you *for a* **moment**,
Jer 4: 20 In an instant my tents are destroyed, my shelter **in a moment**.
18: 7 If **at any time** I announce that a nation or kingdom is to be
18: 9 if **at another time** I announce that a nation or kingdom is to be
La 4: 6 which was overthrown **in a moment** [+4017] without a hand
Eze 26: 16 will sit on the ground, trembling every **moment**, appalled at you.
32: 10 downfall each of them will tremble every **moment** for his life.

8093 רָגַשׁ rāgaš, v. [1] [→ 8094, 8095; Ar 10656]

conspire [1]

Ps 2: 1 [A] Why *do* the nations **conspire** and the peoples plot in vain?

8094 רֶגֶשׁ *regeš*, n.[m.]. [1] [√ 8093]

throng [1]

Ps 55:14 [55:15] as we walked with the **throng** at the house of God.

8095 רִגְשָׁה *rigšâ*, n.f. [1] [√ 8093]

noisy crowd [1]

Ps 64:2 [64:3] of the wicked, from that **noisy crowd** *of* evildoers.

8096 רָדַד *rādad*, v. [3] [→ 8100]

beaten [1], subdue [1], subdues [1]

1Ki 6:32 [G] and overlaid the cherubim and palm trees with **beaten** gold.
Ps 144:2 [A] in whom I take refuge, who **subdues** peoples under me.
Isa 45:1 [A] whose right hand I take hold of to **subdue** nations before him

8097 רָדָה[1] *rādâ¹*, v. [23] [→ 8099]

rule [11], ruled [3], officials [2], directed [1], leading [1], rule over [1], ruler [1], subdued [1], subdues [1], trample the grapes [1]

Ge 1:26 [A] *let them* **rule** over the fish of the sea and the birds of the air,
1:28 [A] **Rule** over the fish of the sea and the birds of the air and over
Lev 25:43 [A] *Do* not **rule** over them ruthlessly, but fear your God.
25:46 [A] but *you must* not **rule** over your fellow Israelites ruthlessly.
25:53 [A] you must see to it that his owner *does* not **rule over** him
26:17 [A] those who hate you *will* **rule** over you, and you will flee even
Nu 24:19 [A] A **ruler** will come out of Jacob and destroy the survivors of
1Ki 4:24 [5:4] [A] For he **ruled** over all the kingdoms west of the River,
5:16 [5:30] [A] supervised the project and **directed** the workmen.
9:23 [A] 550 **officials** supervising the men who did the work.
2Ch 8:10 [A] two hundred and fifty **officials** supervising the men.
Ne 9:28 [A] to the hand of their enemies so that *they* **ruled** over them.
Ps 49:14 [49:15] [A] The upright *will* **rule** over them in the morning;
68:27 [68:28] [A] There is the little tribe of Benjamin, **leading** them,
72:8 [A] *He will* **rule** from sea to sea and from the River to the ends
110:2 [A] from Zion; *you will* **rule** in the midst of your enemies.
Isa 14:2 [A] make captives of their captors and **rule** over their oppressors.
14:6 [A] and in fury **subdued** nations with relentless aggression.
41:2 [G] He hands nations over to him and **subdues** kings before him.
Jer 5:31 [A] prophesy lies, the priests **rule** by their own authority,
Eze 29:15 [A] make it so weak that it *will* never again **rule** over the nations.
34:4 [A] for the lost. *You have* **ruled** them harshly and brutally.
Joel 3:13 [4:13] [A] Come, **trample the grapes**, for the winepress is full

8098 רָדָה[2] *rādâ²*, v. [2]

scooped out [1], taken [1]

Jdg 14:9 [A] which *he* **scooped out** with his hands and ate as he went
14:9 [A] he did not tell them that *he had* **taken** the honey from the

8099 רַדַּי *radday*, n.pr.m. [1] [√ 8097]

Raddai [1]

1Ch 2:14 the fourth Nethanel, the fifth **Raddai**,

8100 רְדִיד *rᵉdîd*, n.[m.]. [2] [√ 8096]

cloak [1], shawls [1]

SS 5:7 they took away my **cloak**, those watchmen of the walls!
Isa 3:23 and mirrors, and the linen garments and tiaras and **shawls**.

8101 רָדַם *rādam*, v. [7] [→ 9554]

fell into a deep sleep [2], in a deep sleep [1], lay fast asleep [1], lie still [1], sleep [1], sleeps [1]

Jdg 4:21 [C] a hammer and went quietly to him while he **lay fast asleep**,
Ps 76:6 [76:7] [C] O God of Jacob, both horse and chariot **lie still**.
Pr 10:5 [C] but *he who* **sleeps** during harvest is a disgraceful son.
Da 8:18 [C] to me, *I was* **in a deep sleep**, with my face to the ground.
10:9 [C] to him, I **fell into a deep sleep**, my face to the ground.
Jnh 1:5 [C] below deck, where he lay down and **fell into a deep sleep**.
1:6 [C] The captain went to him and said, "How *can* you **sleep**?

8102 רֹדָן *rōdān*, n.pr.loc. *or* g. [1 / 3] [→ 8114; cf. 1849]

Rodanim [2], Rhodes [1]

Ge 10:4 Elishah, Tarshish, the Kittim and the **Rodanim**. [BHS 1849]
1Ch 1:7 The sons of Javan: Elishah, Tarshish, the Kittim and the **Rodanim**.
Eze 27:15 " 'The men of **Rhodes** [BHS 1847] traded with you, and many

8103 רָדַף *rādap*, v. [143] [→ 5284]

pursue [33], pursued [27], pursuing [11], pursues [9], chased [8], pursuers [7], persecute [5], chase [4], persecutors [4], follow [3], pursuit [3], went in pursuit [3], chase after [2], chases [2], go [2], in pursuit [2], *untranslated* [1], came by in pursuit [1], devise [1], driven away [1], driven [1], hound [1], hounded [1], hunts [1], hurried [1], past [1], plague [1], press on [1], pursuer [1], put to flight [1], routs [1], run after [1], set out in pursuit [1], they[s] [+2021] [1]

Ge 14:14 [A] born in his household and **went in pursuit** as far as Dan.
14:15 [A] **pursuing** them as far as Hobah, north of Damascus.
31:23 [A] *he* **pursued** Jacob *for* seven days and caught up with him in
35:5 [A] the towns all around them so that no *one* **pursued** them.
44:4 [A] "**Go** after those men at once, and when you catch up with
Ex 14:4 [A] And I will harden Pharaoh's heart, and *he will* **pursue** them.
14:8 [A] so that *he* **pursued** the Israelites, who were marching out
14:9 [A] **pursued** the Israelites and overtook them as they camped by
14:23 [A] The Egyptians **pursued** them, and all Pharaoh's horses
15:9 [A] "The enemy boasted, '*I will* **pursue**, I will overtake them.
Lev 26:7 [A] *You will* **pursue** your enemies, and they will fall by the
26:8 [A] Five of you *will* **chase** a hundred, and a hundred of you will
26:8 [A] a hundred, and a hundred of you *will* **chase** ten thousand,
26:17 [A] and you will flee even when no *one is* **pursuing** you.
26:36 [A] that the sound of a windblown leaf *will* **put** them **to flight**.
26:36 [A] and they will fall, even though no *one is* **pursuing** them.
26:37 [A] from the sword, even though no *one is* **pursuing** them.
Dt 1:44 [A] *they* **chased** you like a swarm of bees and beat you down
11:4 [A] with the waters of the Red Sea as they *were* **pursuing** you,
16:20 [A] **Follow** justice and justice alone, so that you may live
19:6 [A] Otherwise, the avenger of blood *might* **pursue** him in a rage,
28:22 [A] and mildew, *which will* **plague** you until you perish.
28:45 [A] *They will* **pursue** you and overtake you until you are
30:7 [A] these curses on your enemies who hate and **persecute** you.
32:30 [A] How *could* one man **chase** a thousand, or two put ten
Jos 2:5 [A] **Go** after them quickly. You may catch up with them."
2:7 [A] So the men **set out in pursuit** of the spies *on* the road that
2:7 [A] and as soon as the **pursuers** had gone out, the gate was shut.
2:16 [A] to them, "Go to the hills so the **pursuers** will not find you.
2:16 [A] Hide yourselves there three days until **they**[s] [+2021] return,
2:22 [A] until the **pursuers** had searched all along the road
2:22 [A] all along the road and returned **[RPH]** without finding them.
7:5 [A] *They* **chased** the Israelites from the city gate as far as the
8:16 [A] All the men of Ai were called to **pursue** them, and they
8:16 [A] and *they* **pursued** Joshua and were lured away from the city.
8:17 [A] They left the city open and **went in pursuit** *of* Israel.
8:20 [A] toward the desert had turned back against their **pursuers**.
8:24 [A] in the fields and in the desert where *they had* **chased** them,
10:10 [A] Israel **pursued** them *along* the road going up to Beth Horon
10:19 [A] **Pursue** your enemies, attack them from the rear and don't let
11:8 [A] and **pursued** them all the way to Greater Sidon,
20:5 [A] If the avenger of blood **pursues** him, they must not surrender
23:10 [A] One of you **routs** a thousand, because the LORD your God
24:6 [A] the Egyptians **pursued** them with chariots and horsemen as
Jdg 1:6 [A] Adoni-Bezek fled, but *they* **chased** him and caught him,
3:28 [A] "**Follow** me," he ordered, "for the LORD has given Moab,
4:16 [A] Barak **pursued** the chariots and army as far as Harosheth
4:22 [A] Barak **came by in pursuit** *of* Sisera, and Jael went out to
7:23 [A] Manasseh were called out, and *they* **pursued** the Midianites.
7:25 [A] *They* **pursued** the Midianites and brought the heads of Oreb
8:4 [A] exhausted yet *keeping up the* **pursuit**, came to the Jordan
8:5 [A] are worn out, and I *am still* **pursuing** Zebah and Zalmunna,
8:12 [A] of Midian, fled, but *he* **pursued** them and captured them,
9:40 [A] Abimelech **chased** him, and many fell wounded in the
20:43 [G] **chased** them and easily overran them in the vicinity of
1Sa 7:11 [A] of Israel rushed out of Mizpah and **pursued** the Philistines,
17:52 [A] **pursued** the Philistines to the entrance of Gath and to the
23:25 [A] *he* **went** *into* the Desert of Maon **in pursuit** of David.
23:28 [A] Saul broke off his **pursuit** of David and went to meet the
24:14 [24:15] [A] Whom *are* you **pursuing**? A dead dog? A flea?
25:29 [A] Even though someone *is* **pursuing** you to take your life,
26:18 [A] he added, "Why is my lord **pursuing** his servant? What have
26:20 [A] look for a flea—as *one* **hunts** a partridge in the mountains."
30:8 [A] inquired of the LORD, "*Shall I* **pursue** this raiding party?
30:8 [A] Will I overtake them?" "**Pursue** them," he answered.
30:10 [A] But David and four hundred men *continued the* **pursuit**.
2Sa 2:19 [A] He **chased** Abner, turning neither to the right nor to the left
2:24 [A] Joab and Abishai **pursued** Abner, and as the sun was setting,
2:28 [A] they no longer **pursued** Israel, nor did they fight anymore.
17:1 [A] twelve thousand men and set out tonight **in pursuit** of David.
18:16 [A] and the troops stopped **pursuing** Israel, for Joab halted them.
20:6 [A] Take your master's men and **pursue** him, or he will find
20:7 [A] They marched out from Jerusalem to **pursue** Sheba son of
20:10 [A] and his brother Abishai **pursued** Sheba son of Bicri.
20:13 [A] all the men went on with Joab to **pursue** Sheba son of Bicri.
22:38 [A] "*I* **pursued** my enemies and crushed them; I did not turn
24:13 [A] months of fleeing from your enemies while they **pursue** you?
1Ki 20:20 [A] At that, the Arameans fled, with the Israelites **in pursuit**.
2Ki 5:21 [A] So Gehazi **hurried** after Naaman. When Naaman saw him
9:27 [A] to Beth Haggan. Jehu **chased** him, shouting, "Kill him too!"

2Ki 25: 5 [A] the Babylonian army **pursued** the king and overtook him in
2Ch 13: 19 [A] Abijah **pursued** Jeroboam and took from him the towns of
14: 13 [14:12] [A] Asa and his army **pursued** them as far as Gerar.
Ne 9: 11 [A] you hurled their **pursuers** into the depths, like a stone into
Job 13: 25 [A] torment a windblown leaf? *Will you* **chase** *after* dry chaff?
19: 22 [A] Why *do you* **pursue** me as God does? Will you never get
19: 28 [A] "If you say, 'How *we will* **hound** him, since the root of the
30: 15 [A] my dignity *is* **driven away** as *by* the wind, my safety
Ps 7: 1 [7:2] [A] in you; save and deliver me from all *who* **pursue** me,
7: 5 [7:6] [A] *let* my enemy **pursue** and overtake me; let him
18: 37 [18:38] [A] *I* **pursued** my enemies and overtook them; I did not
23: 6 [A] and love *will* **follow** me all the days of my life,
31: 15 [31:16] [A] from my enemies and from *those who* **pursue** me.
34: 14 [34:15] [A] from evil and do good; seek peace and **pursue** it.
35: 3 [A] Brandish spear and javelin against *those who* **pursue** me.
35: 6 [A] and slippery, with the angel of the LORD **pursuing** them.
38: 20 [38:21] [A] with evil slander me when I **pursue** what is good.
69: 26 [69:27] [A] For *they* **persecute** those you wound and talk about
71: 11 [A] **pursue** him and seize him, for no one will rescue him."
83: 15 [83:16] [A] so **pursue** them with your tempest and terrify them
109: 16 [A] **hounded** to death the poor and the needy
119: 84 [A] your servant wait? When will you punish my **persecutors**?
119: 86 [A] help me, for *men* **persecute** me without cause.
119: 150 [A] *Those who* **devise** wicked schemes are near, but they are far
119: 157 [A] Many are the foes *who* **persecute** me, but I have not turned
119: 161 [A] Rulers **persecute** me without cause, but my heart trembles at
142: 6 [142:7] [A] rescue me from *those who* **pursue** me, for they are
143: 3 [A] The enemy **pursues** me, he crushes me to the ground;
Pr 11: 19 [D] man attains life, but *he who* **pursues** evil goes to his death.
12: 11 [D] abundant food, but *he who* **chases** fantasies lacks judgment.
13: 21 [D] Misfortune **pursues** the sinner, but prosperity is the reward
15: 9 [D] of the wicked but he loves *those who* **pursue** righteousness.
19: 7 [D] Though *he* **pursues** them with pleading, they are nowhere to
21: 21 [A] *He who* **pursues** righteousness and love finds life, prosperity
28: 1 [A] The wicked man flees though no *one* **pursues**,
28: 19 [D] but the *one who* **chases** fantasies will have his fill of poverty.
Ecc 3: 15 [C] he has been before; and God will call the **past** to account.
Isa 1: 23 [A] of thieves; they all love bribes and **chase after** gifts.
5: 11 [A] Woe to those who rise early in the morning *to* **run after** their
17: 13 [E] **driven** before the wind like chaff on the hills, like
30: 16 [A] off on swift horses.' Therefore your **pursuers** will be swift!
41: 3 [A] *He* **pursues** them and moves on unscathed, by a path his feet
51: 1 [A] *you who* **pursue** righteousness and who seek the LORD:
Jer 15: 15 [A] and care for me. Avenge me on my **persecutors**.
17: 18 [A] Let my **persecutors** be put to shame, but keep me from
20: 11 [A] so my **persecutors** will stumble and not prevail.
29: 18 [A] *I will* **pursue** them with the sword, famine and plague
39: 5 [A] the Babylonian army **pursued** them and overtook Zedekiah
52: 8 [A] the Babylonian army **pursued** King Zedekiah and overtook
La 1: 3 [A] All *who* **pursue** her have overtaken her in the midst of her
1: 6 [A] no pasture; in weakness they have fled before the **pursuer**.
3: 43 [A] "You have covered yourself with anger and **pursued** us;
3: 66 [A] **Pursue** them in anger and destroy them from under the
4: 19 [A] Our **pursuers** were swifter than eagles in the sky;
5: 5 [C] *Those who* **pursue** *us* are at our heels; we are weary and find
Eze 35: 6 [A] I will give you over to bloodshed and it *will* **pursue** you.
35: 6 [A] you did not hate bloodshed, bloodshed *will* **pursue** you.
Hos 2: 7 [2:9] [D] *She will* **chase after** her lovers but not catch them; she
6: 3 [A] the LORD; *let us* **press on** to acknowledge him.
8: 3 [A] Israel has rejected what is good; an enemy *will* **pursue** him.
12: 1 [12:2] [A] *he* **pursues** the east wind all day and multiplies lies
Am 1: 11 [A] Because he **pursued** his brother with a sword, stifling all
Na 1: 8 [D] an end of ⌊Nineveh⌋; *he will* **pursue** his foes into darkness.

8104 רָהַב *rāhab*, v. [4] [→ 5290, 8105, 8106, 8107; cf. 4502]
made bold [1], overwhelm [1], press plea [1], rise up [1]

Ps 138: 3 [G] you answered me; *you* **made** me **bold** and stouthearted.
Pr 6: 3 [A] and humble yourself; **press** *your* **plea** *with* your neighbor!
SS 6: 5 [G] Turn your eyes from me; they **overwhelm** me. Your hair is
Isa 3: 5 [A] The young *will* **rise up** against the old, the base against the

8105 רַהַב *rahab*, n.pr. [6] [√ 8104]
Rahab [6]

Job 9: 13 restrain his anger; even the cohorts of **Rahab** cowered at his feet.
26: 12 he churned up the sea; by his wisdom he cut **Rahab** to pieces.
Ps 87: 4 "I will record **Rahab** and Babylon among those who acknowledge
89: 10 [89:11] You crushed **Rahab** like one of the slain; with your
Isa 30: 7 help is utterly useless. Therefore I call her **Rahab** the Do-Nothing.
51: 9 Was it not you who cut **Rahab** to pieces, who pierced that monster

8106 רֹהַב *rōhab*, n.[m.]. [1 / 0] [√ 8104]

Ps 90: 10 their span [BHS *best*; NIV 8145] is but trouble and sorrow,

8107 רָהָב *rāhāb*, a. [1] [√ 8104]
proud [1]

Ps 40: 4 [40:5] who does not look to the **proud**, to those who turn aside to

8108 רָהְגָּה *rohgâ*, n.pr.m. [1] [→ 8117]
Rohgah [1]

1Ch 7: 34 The sons of Shomer: Ahi, **Rohgah**, [K 8117] Hubbah and Aram.

8109 רָהָה *rāhâ*, v. Not used in NIV/BHS [cf. 3724]

8110 רַהַט[1] *rahaṭ[1]*, n.[m.]. [3] [cf. 8111]
troughs [2], troughs [+9216] [1]

Ge 30: 38 he placed the peeled branches in all the watering **troughs** [+9216],
30: 41 Jacob would place the branches in the **troughs** in front of the
Ex 2: 16 to draw water and fill the **troughs** to water their father's flock.

8111 רַהַט[2] *rahaṭ[2]*, n.[m.]. [1] [→ 8112; cf. 8110]
tresses [1]

SS 7: 5 [7:6] is like royal tapestry; the king is held captive by its **tresses**.

8112 רָהִיט *rāhîṭ*, n.m.col. [1] [√ 8111]
rafters [1]

SS 1: 17 The beams of our house are cedars; our **rafters** [K 8159] are firs.

8113 רוּד *rûd*, v. [4] [→ 5291]
restless [1], roam [1], trouble [1], unruly [1]

Ge 27: 40 [G] when *you grow* **restless**, you will throw his yoke from off
Ps 55: 2 [55:3] [G] My thoughts **trouble** *me* and I am distraught
Jer 2: 31 [A] Why do my people say, '*We are free to* **roam**; we will come
Hos 11: 12 [12:1] [A] Judah *is* **unruly** against God, even against the

8114 רוֹדָנִים *rôdānîm*, n.pr.g.pl. Not used in NIV/BHS [√ 8102]

8115 רָוָה *rāwâ*, v. [14] [→ 3453, 8116, 8122, 8188]
drench [2], satisfy [2], drenched [1], drink deep [1], drunk its fill [1], feast [1], lavished on [1], quenched its thirst [1], refresh [1], refreshes [1], sated [1], watering [1]

Ps 36: 8 [36:9] [A] *They* **feast** on the abundance of your house; you give
65: 10 [65:11] [D] You **drench** its furrows and level its ridges;
Pr 5: 19 [D] *may* her breasts **satisfy** you always, may you ever be
7: 18 [A] Come, *let's* **drink deep** *of* love till morning; let's enjoy
11: 25 [G] *he who* **refreshes** others will himself be refreshed.
Isa 16: 9 [D] of Sibmah. O Heshbon, O Elealeh, *I* **drench** you *with* tears!
34: 5 [D] My sword *has* **drunk its fill** in the heavens; see, it descends
34: 7 [D] Their land *will be* **drenched** with blood, and the dust will be
43: 24 [G] calamus for me, or **lavished on** me the fat of your sacrifices.
55: 10 [G] do not return to it without **watering** the earth and making it
Jer 31: 14 [D] *I will* **satisfy** the priests *with* abundance, and my people will
31: 25 [G] *I will* **refresh** the weary and satisfy the faint."
46: 10 [A] till it is satisfied, till *it has* **quenched its thirst** with blood.
La 3: 15 [G] He has filled me with bitter herbs and **sated** me *with* gall.

8116 רָוֶה *rāweh*, a. [3 / 4] [√ 8115]
well-watered [2], drowned [1], watered land [1]

Dt 29: 19 [29:18] This will bring disaster on the **watered land** as well as
Job 10: 15 for I am full of shame and **drowned** [BHS 8013] *in* my affliction.
Isa 58: 11 You will be like a **well-watered** garden, like a spring whose waters
Jer 31: 12 They will be like a **well-watered** garden, and they will sorrow no

8117 רוֹהֲגָה *rôhᵃgâ*, n.pr.m. [0] [√ 8108]

1Ch 7: 34 [The sons of Shomer: Ahi, **Rohgah**, [K; see Q 8108] Hubbah and Aram.]

8118 רָוַח *rāwaḥ*, v. [3] [→ 8119, 8120, 8121, 8193, 8194]
find relief [1], relief come [1], spacious [1]

1Sa 16: 23 [A] **relief** *would* **come** to Saul; he would feel better, and the evil
Job 32: 20 [A] I must speak and **find relief**; I must open my lips and reply.
Jer 22: 14 [E] 'I will build myself a great palace with **spacious** upper

8119 רֶוַח *rewaḥ*, n.m. [2] [√ 8118]
relief [1], space [1]

Ge 32: 16 [32:17] ahead of me, and keep *some* **space** between the herds."
Est 4: 14 **relief** and deliverance for the Jews will arise from another place,

8120 רוּחַ rûaḥ, n.f. [378 / 379] [√ 8118; Ar 10658]

spirit [176], wind [79], breath [31], winds [13], mind [5], *untranslated* [4], heart [4], side [4], spirits [4], blast [3], sides [3], anger [2], courage [2], feelings [2], it[s] [+2021] [2], overwhelmed [+928+2118 +4202+6388] [2], air [1], breath [+5972] [1], breeze [1], breezes [1], cool [1], deep sleep [+9554] [1], deeply troubled [+7997] [1], discouragement [+7919] [1], empty [1], even-tempered [+7922] [1], hostility [1], I [+3276] [1], inspired [1], inspires [1], jealous [+6296+6584+7863] [1], liar [+3941] [1], life breath [+678] [1], life [1], long-winded [1], lose heart [+928+1327+7931] [1], me [+3276] [1], motives [1], pant [+8634] [1], patience [+800] [1], pride [+1468] [1], quick-tempered [+7920] [1], rage [1], resentment [1], revived [+448+8740] [1], self-control [+4200+5110] [1], source of grief [+5289] [1], strength [1], temper [1], tempest [+6185] [1], tempest [+6194] [1], trustworthy [+586] [1], violent wind [+6194] [1], violent winds [+6194] [1], whirlwind [1], willing [+906+5605] [1], windstorm [+6194] [1], wisdom [+2683] [1], you [+3870] [1]

Ge 1: 2 of the deep, and the **Spirit** *of* God was hovering over the waters.
3: 8 God as he was walking in the garden in the **cool** *of* the day,
6: 3 "My **Spirit** will not contend with man forever, for he is mortal;
6: 17 under the heavens, every creature that has the **breath** *of* life in it.
7: 15 Pairs of all creatures that have the **breath** *of* life in them came to
7: 22 Everything on dry land that had the **breath of** [+5972] life in its
8: 1 and he sent a **wind** over the earth, and the waters receded.
26: 35 They were a **source of grief** [+5289] to Isaac and Rebekah.
41: 8 In the morning his **mind** was troubled, so he sent for all the
41: 38 we find anyone like this man, one in whom is the **spirit** *of* God?"
45: 27 had sent to carry him back, the **spirit** *of* their father Jacob revived.
Ex 6: 9 because of their **discouragement** [+7919] and cruel bondage.
10: 13 the LORD made an east **wind** blow across the land all that day
10: 13 and all that night. By morning the **wind** had brought the locusts;
10: 19 And the LORD changed the wind to a very strong west **wind**,
14: 21 that night the LORD drove the sea back with a strong east **wind**
15: 8 By the **blast** *of* your nostrils the waters piled up. The surging
15: 10 But you blew with your **breath**, and the sea covered them.
28: 3 Tell all the skilled men to whom I have given **wisdom** [+2683] in
31: 3 and I have filled him with the **Spirit** *of* God, with skill, ability
35: 21 everyone who *was* **willing** [+906+5605] and whose heart moved
35: 31 and he has filled him with the **Spirit** *of* God, with skill, ability
Nu 5: 14 if **feelings** *of* jealousy come over her husband and he suspects his
5: 14 or if he *is* **jealous** [+6296+6584+7863] and suspects her even
5: 30 or when **feelings** *of* jealousy come over a man because he suspects
11: 17 I will take of the **Spirit** that is on you and put the Spirit on them.
11: 25 he took of the **Spirit** that was on him and put the Spirit on the
11: 25 When the **Spirit** rested on them, they prophesied, but they did not
11: 26 Yet the **Spirit** also rested on them, and they prophesied in the
11: 29 were prophets and that the LORD would put his **Spirit** on them!"
11: 31 Now a **wind** went out from the LORD and drove quail in from the
14: 24 because my servant Caleb has a different **spirit** and follows me
16: 22 and cried out, "O God, God of the **spirits** of all mankind,
24: 2 Israel encamped tribe by tribe, the **Spirit** *of* God came upon him
27: 16 "May the LORD, the God of the **spirits** of all mankind, appoint a
27: 18 "Take Joshua son of Nun, a man in whom is the **spirit**, and lay
Dt 2: 30 For the LORD your God had made his **spirit** stubborn and his
34: 9 Now Joshua son of Nun was filled with the **spirit** *of* wisdom
Jos 2: 11 our hearts melted and everyone's **courage** failed because of you,
5: 1 and they no longer had the **courage** to face the Israelites.
Jdg 3: 10 The **Spirit** *of* the LORD came upon him, so that he became
6: 34 the **Spirit** *of* the LORD came upon Gideon, and he blew a
8: 3 compared to you?" At this, their **resentment** against him subsided.
9: 23 God sent an evil **spirit** between Abimelech and the citizens of
11: 29 the **Spirit** *of* the LORD came upon Jephthah. He crossed Gilead
13: 25 the **Spirit** *of* the LORD began to stir him while he was in
14: 6 The **Spirit** *of* the LORD came upon him in power so that he tore
14: 19 the **Spirit** *of* the LORD came upon him in power. He went down
15: 14 him shouting. The **Spirit** *of* the LORD came upon him in power.
15: 19 When Samson drank, his **strength** returned and he revived.
1Sa 1: 15 Hannah replied, "I am a woman who is **deeply troubled** [+7997].
10: 6 The **Spirit** *of* the LORD will come upon you in power, and you
10: 10 the **Spirit** *of* God came upon him in power, and he joined in their
11: 6 the **Spirit** *of* God came upon him in power, and he burned with
16: 13 from that day on the **Spirit** *of* the LORD came upon David in
16: 14 Now the **Spirit** *of* the LORD had departed from Saul, and an evil
16: 14 from Saul, and an evil **spirit** from the LORD tormented him.
16: 15 said to him, "See, an evil **spirit** *from* God is tormenting you.
16: 16 He will play when the evil **spirit** *from* God comes upon you,
16: 23 Whenever the **spirit** *from* God came upon Saul, David would take
16: 23 to Saul; he would feel better, and the evil **spirit** would leave him.
18: 10 The next day an evil **spirit** *from* God came forcefully upon Saul.
19: 9 an evil **spirit** *from* the LORD came upon Saul as he was sitting in
19: 20 the **Spirit** *of* God came upon Saul's men and they also prophesied.
19: 23 the **Spirit** *of* God came even upon him, and he walked along
30: 12 He ate and *was* **revived** [+448+8740], for he had not eaten any
2Sa 13: 39 And the **spirit** [BHS-] *of* the king longed to go to Absalom,
22: 11 the cherubim and flew; he soared on the wings of the **wind**.
22: 16 the rebuke of the LORD, at the blast of **breath** *from* his nostrils.
23: 2 "The **Spirit** *of* the LORD spoke through me; his word was on my
1Ki 10: 5 of the LORD, she *was* **overwhelmed** [+928+2118+4202+6388].
18: 12 I don't know where the **Spirit** *of* the LORD may carry you when
18: 45 the **wind** rose, a heavy rain came on and Ahab rode off to Jezreel.
19: 11 a great and powerful **wind** tore the mountains apart and shattered
19: 11 the rocks before the LORD, but the LORD was not in the **wind**.
19: 11 After the **wind** there was an earthquake, but the LORD was not in
21: 5 Jezebel came in and asked him, "Why are **you** [+3870] so sullen?
22: 21 Finally, a **spirit** came forward, stood before the LORD and said,
22: 22 will go out and be a lying **spirit** in the mouths of all his prophets,'
22: 23 "So now the LORD has put a lying **spirit** in the mouths of all
22: 24 "Which way did the **spirit** *from* the LORD go when he went
2Ki 2: 9 "Let me inherit a double portion of your **spirit**," Elisha replied.
2: 15 were watching, said, "The **spirit** *of* Elijah is resting on Elisha."
2: 16 Perhaps the **Spirit** *of* the LORD has picked him up and set him
3: 17 You will see neither **wind** nor rain, yet this valley will be filled
19: 7 I am going to put such a **spirit** in him that when he hears a certain
1Ch 5: 26 So the God of Israel stirred up the **spirit** *of* Pul king of Assyria
5: 26 **[RPH]** who took the Reubenites, the Gadites and the half-tribe of
9: 24 The gatekeepers were on the four **sides**: east, west, north and
12: 18 [12:19] the **Spirit** came upon Amasai, chief of the Thirty, and he
28: 12 He gave him the plans of all that the **Spirit** had put in his mind for
2Ch 9: 4 of the LORD, she *was* **overwhelmed** [+928+2118+4202+6388].
15: 1 The **Spirit** *of* God came upon Azariah son of Oded.
18: 20 Finally, a **spirit** came forward, stood before the LORD and said,
18: 21 " 'I will go and be a lying **spirit** in the mouths of all his prophets,'
18: 22 "So now the LORD has put a lying **spirit** in the mouths of these
18: 23 "Which way did the **spirit** *from* the LORD go when he went
20: 14 the **Spirit** *of* the LORD came upon Jahaziel son of Zechariah,
21: 16 The LORD aroused against Jehoram the **hostility** *of* the
24: 20 the **Spirit** *of* God came upon Zechariah son of Jehoiada the priest.
36: 22 the LORD moved the **heart** *of* Cyrus king of Persia to make a
Ezr 1: 1 the LORD moved the **heart** *of* Cyrus king of Persia to make a
1: 5 the priests and Levites—everyone whose **heart** God had moved—
Ne 9: 20 You gave your good **Spirit** to instruct them. You did not withhold
9: 30 By your **Spirit** you admonished them through your prophets.
Job 1: 19 when suddenly a mighty **wind** swept in from the desert and struck
4: 9 of God they are destroyed; at the **blast** *of* his anger they perish.
4: 15 A **spirit** glided past my face, and the hair on my body stood on
6: 4 arrows of the Almighty are in me, my **spirit** drinks in their poison;
6: 26 what I say, and treat the words of a despairing man as **wind**?
7: 7 Remember, O God, that my life is but a **breath**; my eyes will never
7: 11 I will speak out in the anguish of my **spirit**, I will complain in the
8: 2 long will you say such things? Your words are a blustering **wind**.
9: 18 He would not let me regain my **breath** but would overwhelm me
10: 12 me kindness, and in your providence watched over my **spirit**.
12: 10 his hand is the life of every creature and the **breath** *of* all mankind.
15: 2 "Would a wise man answer with **empty** notions or fill his belly
15: 13 so that you vent your **rage** against God and pour out such words
15: 30 his shoots, and the **breath** *of* God's mouth will carry him away.
16: 3 Will your **long-winded** speeches never end? What ails you that
17: 1 My **spirit** is broken, my days are cut short, the grave awaits me.
19: 17 My **breath** is offensive to my wife; I am loathsome to my own
20: 3 that dishonors me, and my understanding **inspires** me to reply.
21: 4 directed to man? Why should **I** [+3276] not be impatient?
21: 18 How often are they like straw before the **wind**, like chaff swept
26: 13 By his **breath** the skies became fair; his hand pierced the gliding
27: 3 as long as I have life within me, the **breath** *of* God in my nostrils,
28: 25 When he established the force of the **wind** and measured out the
30: 15 my dignity is driven away as by the **wind**, my safety vanishes like
30: 22 You snatch me up and drive me before the **wind**; you toss me
32: 8 it is the **spirit** in a man, the breath of the Almighty, that gives him
32: 18 For I am full of words, and the **spirit** within me compels me;
33: 4 The **Spirit** *of* God has made me; the breath of the Almighty gives
34: 14 If it were his intention and he withdrew his **spirit** and breath,
37: 21 bright as it is in the skies after the **wind** has swept them clean.
41: 16 [41:8] each is so close to the next that no **air** can pass between.
Ps 1: 4 so the wicked! They are like chaff that the **wind** blows away.
11: 6 fiery coals and burning sulfur; a scorching **wind** will be their lot.
18: 10 [18:11] and flew; he soared on the wings of the **wind**.
18: 15 [18:16] O LORD, at the blast of **breath** *from* your nostrils.
18: 42 [18:43] I beat them as fine as dust borne on the **wind**; I poured
31: 5 [31:6] Into your hands I commit my **spirit**; redeem me,
32: 2 does not count against him and in whose **spirit** is no deceit.
33: 6 the heavens made, their starry host by the **breath** *of* his mouth.
34: 18 [34:19] and saves those who are crushed in **spirit**.
35: 5 May they be like chaff before the **wind**, with the angel of the
48: 7 [48:8] them like ships of Tarshish shattered by an east **wind**.
51: 10 [51:12] pure heart, O God, and renew a steadfast **spirit** within me.
51: 11 [51:13] me from your presence or take your Holy **Spirit** from me.
51: 12 [51:14] me the joy of your salvation and grant me a willing **spirit**,

Ps 51:17 [51:19] The sacrifices of God are a broken **spirit**; a broken
55: 8 [55:9] place of shelter, far from the **tempest** [+6185] and storm."
76:12 [76:13] He breaks the **spirit** *of* rulers; he is feared by the kings of
77: 3 [77:4] O God, and I groaned; I mused, and my **spirit** grew faint.
77: 6 [77:7] songs in the night. My heart mused and my **spirit** inquired:
78: 8 were not loyal to God, whose **spirits** were not faithful to him.
78:39 that they were but flesh, a passing **breeze** that does not return.
83:13 [83:14] like tumbleweed, O my God, like chaff before the **wind**.
103:16 the **wind** blows over it and it is gone, and its place remembers it no
104: 3 makes the clouds his chariot and rides on the wings of the **wind**.
104: 4 He makes **winds** his messengers, flames of fire his servants.
104:29 when you take away their **breath**, they die and return to the dust.
104:30 When you send your **Spirit**, they are created, and you renew the
106:33 for they rebelled against the **Spirit** *of* God, and rash words came
107:25 and stirred up a **tempest** [+6194] that lifted high the waves.
135: 7 with the rain and brings out the **wind** from his storehouses.
135:17 they have ears, but cannot hear, nor is there **breath** in their mouths.
139: 7 Where can I go from your **Spirit**? Where can I flee from your
142: 3 [142:4] When my **spirit** grows faint within me, it is you who
143: 4 So my **spirit** grows faint within me; my heart within me is
143: 7 Answer me quickly, O LORD; my **spirit** fails. Do not hide your
143:10 you are my God; may your good **Spirit** lead me on level ground.
146: 4 When their **spirit** departs, they return to the ground; on that very
147:18 and melts them; he stirs up his **breezes**, and the waters flow.
148: 8 and hail, snow and clouds, stormy **winds** that do his bidding,
Pr 1:23 I would have poured out my **heart** to you and made my thoughts
11:13 a confidence, but a **trustworthy man** [+586] keeps a secret.
11:29 He who brings trouble on his family will inherit only **wind**,
14:29 but a **quick-tempered man** [+7920] displays folly.
15: 4 healing is a tree of life, but a deceitful tongue crushes the **spirit**.
15:13 heart makes the face cheerful, but heartache crushes the **spirit**.
16: 2 seem innocent to him, but **motives** are weighed by the LORD.
16:18 Pride goes before destruction, a haughty **spirit** before a fall.
16:19 Better to be lowly in **spirit** and among the oppressed than to share
16:32 a man who controls his **temper** than one who takes a city.
17:22 heart is good medicine, but a crushed **spirit** dries up the bones.
17:27 and a man of understanding is **even-tempered** [+7922].
18:14 A man's **spirit** sustains him in sickness, but a crushed spirit who
18:14 spirit sustains him in sickness, but a crushed **spirit** who can bear?
25:14 **wind** without rain is a man who boasts of gifts he does not give.
25:23 As a north **wind** brings rain, so a sly tongue brings angry looks.
25:28 broken down is a man who lacks **self-control** [+4200+5110].
27:16 restraining her is like restraining the **wind** or grasping oil with the
29:11 A fool gives full vent to his **anger**, but a wise man keeps himself
29:23 man's pride brings him low, but a man of lowly **spirit** gains honor.
30: 4 Who has gathered up the **wind** in the hollow of his hands?
Ecc 1: 6 The **wind** blows to the south and turns to the north; round
1: 6 round and round it goes, ever returning on its course. **[RPH]**
1:14 the sun; all of them are meaningless, a chasing after the **wind**.
1:17 and folly, but I learned that this, too, is a chasing after the **wind**.
2:11 to achieve, everything was meaningless, a chasing after the **wind**;
2:17 grievous to me. All of it is meaningless, a chasing after the **wind**.
2:26 pleases God. This too is meaningless, a chasing after the **wind**.
3:19 All have the same **breath**; man has no advantage over the animal.
3:21 Who knows if the **spirit** *of* man rises upward and if the spirit of the
3:21 and if the **spirit** *of* the animal goes down into the earth?"
4: 4 of his neighbor. This too is meaningless, a chasing after the **wind**.
4: 6 tranquillity than two handfuls with toil and chasing after the **wind**.
4:16 the successor. This too is meaningless, a chasing after the **wind**.
5:16 [5:15] and what does he gain, since he toils for the **wind**?
6: 9 of the appetite. This too is meaningless, a chasing after the **wind**.
7: 8 better than its beginning, and **patience** [+800] is better than pride.
7: 8 better than its beginning, and patience is better than **pride** [+1468].
7: 9 Do not be quickly provoked in your **spirit**, for anger resides in the
8: 8 No man has power over the **wind** to contain it; so no one has
8: 8 No man has power over the wind to contain **it**[s] [+2021]; so no one
10: 4 If a ruler's **anger** rises against you, do not leave your post;
11: 4 Whoever watches the **wind** will not plant; whoever looks at the
11: 5 As you do not know the path of the **wind**, or how the body is
12: 7 the ground it came from, and the **spirit** returns to God who gave it.
Isa 4: 4 he will cleanse the bloodstains from Jerusalem by a **spirit** *of*
4: 4 from Jerusalem by a spirit of judgment and a **spirit** *of* fire.
7: 2 were shaken, as the trees of the forest are shaken by the **wind**.
11: 2 The **Spirit** *of* the LORD will rest on him—the Spirit of wisdom
11: 2 the **Spirit** *of* wisdom and *of* understanding, the Spirit of counsel
11: 2 and of understanding, the **Spirit** *of* counsel and *of* power,
11: 2 of power, the **Spirit** *of* knowledge and *of* the fear of the LORD—
11: 4 of his mouth; with the **breath** *of* his lips he will slay the wicked.
11:15 with a scorching **wind** he will sweep his hand over the Euphrates
17:13 driven before the **wind** like chaff on the hills, like tumbleweed
19: 3 The Egyptians *will* **lose heart** [+928+1327+7931], and I will bring
19:14 The LORD has poured into them a **spirit** *of* dizziness; they make
25: 4 For the **breath** *of* the ruthless is like a storm driving against a wall
26: 9 yearns for you in the night; in the morning my **spirit** longs for you.
26:18 We were with child, we writhed in pain, but we gave birth to **wind**.
27: 8 with his fierce **blast** he drives her out, as on a day the east wind
28: 6 He will be a **spirit** *of* justice to him who sits in judgment,
29:10 The LORD has brought over you a **deep sleep** [+9554]: He has
29:24 Those who are wayward in **spirit** will gain understanding;
30: 1 forming an alliance, but not by my **Spirit**, heaping sin upon sin;
30:28 His **breath** is like a rushing torrent, rising up to the neck.
31: 3 are men and not God; their horses are flesh and not **spirit**.
32: 2 Each man will be like a shelter from the **wind** and a refuge from
32:15 till the **Spirit** is poured upon us from on high, and the desert
33:11 you give birth to straw; your **breath** is a fire that consumes you.
34:16 that has given the order, and his **Spirit** will gather them together.
37: 7 I am going to put a **spirit** in him so that when he hears a certain
38:16 by such things men live; and my **spirit** finds life in them too.
40: 7 the flowers fall, because the **breath** *of* the LORD blows on them.
40:13 Who has understood the **mind** *of* the LORD, or instructed him as
41:16 You will winnow them, the **wind** will pick them up, and a gale will
41:29 deeds amount to nothing; their images are but **wind** and confusion.
42: 1 I will put my **Spirit** on him and he will bring justice to the nations.
42: 5 who gives breath to its people, and **life** to those who walk on it:
44: 3 I will pour out my **Spirit** on your offspring, and my blessing on
48:16 And now the Sovereign LORD has sent me, with his **Spirit**.
54: 6 you back as if you were a wife deserted and distressed in **spirit**—
57:13 The **wind** will carry all of them off, a mere breath will blow them
57:15 holy place, but also with him who is contrite and lowly in **spirit**,
57:15 to revive the **spirit** *of* the lowly and to revive the heart of the
57:16 be angry, for then the **spirit** of man would grow faint before me—
59:19 For he will come like a pent-up flood that the **breath** *of* the
59:21 "My **Spirit**, who is on you, and my words that I have put in your
61: 1 The **Spirit** *of* the Sovereign LORD is on me, because the LORD
61: 3 of mourning, and a garment of praise instead of a **spirit** *of* despair.
63:10 Yet they rebelled and grieved his Holy **Spirit**. So he turned
63:11 of his flock? Where is he who set his Holy **Spirit** among them,
63:14 to the plain, they were given rest by the **Spirit** *of* the LORD.
64: 6 [64:5] up like a leaf, and like the **wind** our sins sweep us away.
65:14 will cry out from anguish of heart and wail in brokenness of **spirit**.
66: 2 he who is humble and contrite in **spirit**, and trembles at my word.
Jer 2:24 accustomed to the desert, sniffing the **wind** in her craving—
4:11 "A scorching **wind** *from* the barren heights in the desert blows
4:12 a **wind** too strong for that comes from me. Now I pronounce my
5:13 The prophets are but **wind** and the word is not in them; so let what
10:13 with the rain and brings out the **wind** from his storehouses.
10:14 by his idols. His images are a fraud; they have no **breath** in them.
13:24 "I will scatter you like chaff driven by the desert **wind**.
14: 6 donkeys stand on the barren heights and **pant** [+8634] like jackals;
18:17 Like a **wind** *from* the east, I will scatter them before their enemies;
22:22 The **wind** will drive all your shepherds away, and your allies will
49:32 I will scatter to the **winds** those who are in distant places and will
49:36 I will bring against Elam the four **winds** from the four quarters of
49:36 I will scatter them to the four **winds**, and there will not be a nation
51: 1 I will stir up the **spirit** *of* a destroyer against Babylon and the
51:11 The LORD has stirred up **[NIE]** the kings of the Medes,
51:16 with the rain and brings out the **wind** from his storehouses.
51:17 by his idols. His images are a fraud; they have no **breath** in them.
52:23 There were ninety-six pomegranates on the **sides**; the total number
La 4:20 The LORD's anointed, our very **life breath** [+678], was caught in
Eze 1: 4 and I saw a **windstorm** [+6194] coming out of the north—
1:12 Wherever the **spirit** would go, they would go, without turning as
1:20 Wherever the **spirit** would go, they would go, and the wheels
1:20 would go, **[RPH]** and the wheels would rise along with them,
1:20 because the **spirit** *of* the living creatures was in the wheels.
1:21 because the **spirit** *of* the living creatures was in the wheels.
2: 2 As he spoke, the **Spirit** came into me and raised me to my feet,
3:12 the **Spirit** lifted me up, and I heard behind me a loud rumbling
3:14 The **Spirit** then lifted me up and took me away, and I went in
3:14 me away, and I went in bitterness and in the anger of my **spirit**,
3:24 the **Spirit** came into me and raised me to my feet. He spoke to me
5: 2 scatter a third to the **wind**. For I will pursue them with drawn
5:10 punishment on you and will scatter all your survivors to the **winds**.
5:12 a third I will scatter to the **winds** and pursue with drawn sword.
8: 3 The **Spirit** lifted me up between earth and heaven and in visions of
10:17 with them, because the **spirit** *of* the living creatures was in them.
11: 1 the **Spirit** lifted me up and brought me to the gate of the house of
11: 5 the **Spirit** *of* the LORD came upon me, and he told me to say:
11: 5 O house of Israel, but I know what is going through your **mind**.
11:19 I will give them an undivided heart and put a new **spirit** in them;
11:24 The **Spirit** lifted me up and brought me to the exiles in Babylonia
11:24 to the exiles in Babylonia in the vision given by the **Spirit** *of* God.
12:14 I will scatter to the **winds** all those around him—his staff and all
13: 3 Woe to the foolish prophets who follow their own **spirit** and have
13:11 hurtling down, and **violent winds** [+6194] will burst forth.
13:13 In my wrath I will unleash a **violent wind** [+6194], and in my
17:10 Will it not wither completely when the east **wind** strikes it—
17:21 fall by the sword, and the survivors will be scattered to the **winds**.

Eze 18:31 you have committed, and get a new heart and a new **spirit**.
19:12 The east **wind** made it shrivel, it was stripped of its fruit; its strong
20:32 and stone." But what you have in **mind** will never happen.
21: 7 [21:12] every **spirit** will become faint and every knee become as
27:26 But the east **wind** will break you to pieces in the heart of the sea.
36:26 I will give you a new heart and put a new **spirit** in you; I will
36:27 I will put my **Spirit** in you and move you to follow my decrees
37: 1 he brought me out by the **Spirit** *of* the LORD and set me in the
37: 5 I will make **breath** enter you, and you will come to life.
37: 6 you with skin; I will put **breath** in you, and you will come to life.
37: 8 on them and skin covered them, but there was no **breath** in them.
37: 9 he said to me, "Prophesy to the **breath**; prophesy, son of man,
37: 9 prophesy, son of man, and say to **it*** [+2021], 'This is what the
37: 9 Come from the four **winds**, O breath, and breathe into these slain,
37: 9 Come from the four winds, O **breath**, and breathe into these slain,
37:10 So I prophesied as he commanded me, and **breath** entered them;
37:14 I will put my **Spirit** in you and you will live, and I will settle you
39:29 for I will pour out my **Spirit** on the house of Israel,
42:16 He measured the east **side** with the measuring rod; it was five
42:17 He measured the north **side**; it was five hundred cubits by the
42:18 He measured the south **side**; it was five hundred cubits by the
42:19 he turned to the west **side** and measured; it was five hundred cubits
42:20 So he measured the area on all four **sides**. It had a wall around it,
43: 5 Then the **Spirit** lifted me up and brought me into the inner court,
Da 2: 1 had dreams; his **mind** was troubled and he could not sleep.
2: 3 "I have had a dream that troubles **me** [+3276] and I want to know
8: 8 in its place four prominent horns grew up toward the four **winds** *of*
11: 4 be broken up and parceled out toward the four **winds** *of* heaven.
Hos 4:12 A **spirit** *of* prostitution leads them astray; they are unfaithful to
4:19 A **whirlwind** will sweep them away, and their sacrifices will bring
5: 4 A **spirit** *of* prostitution is in their heart; they do not acknowledge
8: 7 "They sow the **wind** and reap the whirlwind. The stalk has no
9: 7 the prophet is considered a fool, the **inspired** man a maniac.
12: 1 [12:2] Ephraim feeds on the **wind**; he pursues the east wind all
13:15 An east **wind** *from* the LORD will come, blowing in from the
Joel 2:28 [3:1] "And afterward, I will pour out my **Spirit** on all people.
2:29 [3:2] and women, I will pour out my **Spirit** in those days.
Am 4:13 He who forms the mountains, creates the **wind**, and reveals his
Jnh 1: 4 the LORD sent a great **wind** on the sea, and such a violent storm
4: 8 When the sun rose, God provided a scorching east **wind**,
Mic 2: 7 it be said, O house of Jacob: "Is the **Spirit** *of* the LORD angry?
2:11 If a **liar** [+3941] and deceiver comes and says, 'I will prophesy for
3: 8 with the **Spirit** *of* the LORD, and with justice and might,
Hab 1:11 Then they sweep past like the **wind** and go on—guilty men,
2:19 It is covered with gold and silver; there is no **breath** in it.
Hag 1:14 So the LORD stirred up the **spirit** *of* Zerubbabel son of Shealtiel,
1:14 and the **spirit** *of* Joshua son of Jehozadak, the high priest,
1:14 the high priest, and the **spirit** *of* the whole remnant of the people.
2: 5 out of Egypt. And my **Spirit** remains among you. Do not fear.'
Zec 2: 6 [2:10] "for I have scattered you to the four **winds** *of* heaven,"
4: 6 might nor by power, but by my **Spirit**,' says the LORD Almighty.
5: 9 there before me were two women, with the **wind** in their wings!
6: 5 The angel answered me, "These are the four **spirits** *of* heaven,
6: 8 those going toward the north country have given my **Spirit** rest in
7:12 or to the words that the LORD Almighty had sent by his **Spirit**
12: 1 of the earth, and who forms the **spirit** *of* man within him, declares:
12:10 and the inhabitants of Jerusalem a **spirit** *of* grace and supplication.
13: 2 remove both the prophets and the **spirit** *of* impurity from the land.
Mal 2:15 made them one? In flesh and **spirit** they are his. And why one?
2:15 So guard yourself in your **spirit**, and do not break faith with the
2:16 So guard yourself in your **spirit**, and do not break faith.

8121 רְוָחָה *r^ewāḥâ*, n.f. [2] [√ 8118]

relief [2]

Ex 8:15 [8:11] when Pharaoh saw that there was **relief**, he hardened his
La 3:56 You heard my plea: "Do not close your ears to my cry for **relief**."

8122 רְוָיָה *r^ewāyâ*, n.f. [2] [√ 8115]

overflows [1], place of abundance [1]

Ps 23: 5 of my enemies. You anoint my head with oil; my cup **overflows**.
66:12 and water, but you brought us to a **place of abundance**.

8123 רוּם *rûm[1]*, v. [190] [→ 5294, 5295, 8027, 8124, 8125, 8126, 8127, 8128, 8129, 8225, 8226, 9556, 9557; cf. 3727, 3753, 8229, 8250; Ar 10659; *also used with compound proper names*]

exalted [20], exalt [16], present [10], high [9], lift up [8], raised [6], haughty [5], lifted high [5], raise [5], remove [5], provided [4], tall [4], exalts [3], raised up [3], be exalted [2], boldly [+928+3338] [2], brought up [2], lift [2], lifted up [2], lifted [2], lifts [2], lofty [2], offer [2], presenting [2], proud [2], rebelled [+3338] [2], rose [2], take [2], as a special gift set aside [1], be lifted up [1], brandish [1], build on high [1], consider better [+4222] [1], contributed [1], displays [1], donated [1], exalt himself [1], exult [1], filled with pride [+4222] [1], greater [1], heights [1], held up [1], higher [1], highest [1], holds up [1], honored [1], is removed [1], let triumph [1], lift out [1], lifts up [1], lofty trees [+7757] [1], loud [1], made grow tall [1], picked up [1], present [+9556] [1], present a portion [1], presented [1], proud [+4213] [1], proud [+4222] [1], raised and taken an oath [1], rebuild [1], rise up [1], rise [1], rises [1], scream for help [+2256+7754+7924] [1], screamed for help [+2256+7754+7924] [1], set apart [1], set high [1], set up [1], shout [+7754] [1], shouted [+928+7754+9558] [1], sing songs [+928+4200+7754+9048] [1], sins defiantly [+928+3338+6913] [1], sound [+928+7754] [1], stop [1], take out [1], take up [1], taller [1], took away [1], took up [1], towering [1], triumph [1], triumphed [1], turn [1], upraised [1], very top [1], was presented [+9556] [1]

Ge 7:17 [A] as the waters increased they lifted the ark **high** above the
14:22 [G] "*I have* **raised** my hand … **and** *have* **taken an oath**
31:45 [G] So Jacob took a stone and **set it up** as a pillar.
39:15 [G] When he heard me **scream for help** [+2256+7754+7924], he
39:18 [G] But as soon as I **screamed for help** [+2256+7754+7924], he
41:44 [G] without your word no one *will* **lift** hand or foot in all Egypt."
Ex 7:20 [G] *He* **raised** his staff in the presence of Pharaoh and his
14: 8 [A] the Israelites, who were marching out **boldly** [+928+3338].
14:16 [G] **Raise** your staff and stretch out your hand over the sea to
15: 2 [D] and I will praise him, my father's God, and *I will* **exalt** him.
17:11 [G] As long as Moses **held up** his hands, the Israelites were
29:27 [H] that was waved and the thigh that **was presented** [+9556].
35:24 [G] Those **presenting** an offering of silver or bronze brought it
Lev 2: 9 [G] He *shall* **take out** the memorial portion from the grain
4: 8 [G] *He shall* **remove** all the fat from the bull of the sin offering
4:10 [H] just as the fat **is removed** from the ox sacrificed as a
4:19 [G] *He shall* **remove** all the fat from it and burn it on the altar,
6:10 [6:3] [G] *shall* **remove** the ashes of the burnt offering that the
6:15 [6:8] [G] *is to* **take** a handful of fine flour and oil, together with
22:15 [G] the sacred offerings the Israelites **present** to the LORD
Nu 15:19 [G] of the land, **present a portion** as an offering to the LORD.
15:20 [G] **Present** [+9556] a cake from the first of your ground meal
15:20 [G] and **present** it as an offering from the threshing floor.
15:30 [A] " 'But anyone who **sins defiantly** [+928+3338+6913], whether
16:37 [17:2] [G] *to* **take** the censers out of the smoldering remains
18:19 [G] offerings the Israelites **present** to the LORD I give to you
18:24 [G] tithes that the Israelites **present** as an offering to the LORD.
18:26 [G] *you must* **present** a tenth of that tithe as the LORD's
18:28 [G] In this way you also *will* **present** an offering to the LORD
18:29 [G] *You must* **present** as the LORD's portion the best and
18:30 [G] 'When you **present** the best part, it will be reckoned to you as
18:32 [G] By **presenting** the best part of it you will not be guilty in this
20:11 [G] Moses **raised** his arm and struck the rock twice with his
24: 7 [A] "Their king *will be* **greater** than Agag; their kingdom will be
31:28 [G] **set apart** as tribute for the LORD one out of every five
31:52 [G] Eleazar **presented** as a gift to the LORD weighed 16,750
33: 3 [A] They marched out **boldly** [+928+3338] in full view of all the
Dt 1:28 [A] They say, 'The people are stronger and **taller** than we are;
2:10 [A] a people strong and numerous, and as **tall** as the Anakites.
2:21 [A] a people strong and numerous, and as **tall** as the Anakites.
8:14 [A] your heart *will become* **proud** and you will forget the
9: 2 [A] The people *are* strong and **tall**—Anakites! You know about
12: 2 [A] Destroy completely all the places on the **high** mountains
17:20 [A] and not **consider** himself **better** [+4222] than his brothers
27:14 [A] The Levites shall recite to all the people of Israel in a **loud**
32:27 [A] adversary misunderstand and say, 'Our hand *has* **triumphed**;
Jos 4: 5 [G] Each of you *is to* **take up** a stone on his shoulder,
1Sa 2: 1 [A] in the LORD; in the LORD my horn *is* **lifted high**.
2: 7 [D] LORD sends poverty and wealth; he humbles and *he* **exalts**.
2: 8 [G] the poor from the dust and **lifts** the needy from the ash heap;
2:10 [G] give strength to his king and **exalt** the horn of his anointed."
9:24 [G] So the cook **took up** the leg with what was on it and set it in
2Sa 22:28 [A] but your eyes are on the **haughty** to bring them low.
22:47 [A] Praise be to my Rock! **Exalted** *be* God, the Rock, my Savior!
22:49 [D] *You* **exalted** me above my foes; from violent men you
1Ki 11:26 [G] Jeroboam son of Nebat **rebelled** [+3338] against the king.
11:27 [G] Here is the account of how *he* **rebelled** [+3338] against the
14: 7 [G] '*I* **raised** you **up** from among the people and made you a
16: 2 [G] "*I* **lifted** you **up** from the dust and made you leader of my
2Ki 2:13 [G] *He* **picked up** the cloak that had fallen from Elijah and went
6: 7 [G] "**Lift it out**," he said. Then the man reached out his hand
19:22 [G] Against whom *have you* **raised** your voice and lifted your
1Ch 15:16 [G] as singers *to* **sing** joyful **songs** [+928+4200+7754+9048],
25: 5 [G] They were given him through the promises of God to **exalt**
2Ch 5:13 [G] they **raised** their voices in praise to the LORD and sang:
30:24 [G] Hezekiah king of Judah **provided** a thousand bulls and seven
30:24 [G] the officials **provided** them *with* a thousand bulls and ten
35: 7 [G] Josiah **provided** for all the lay people who were there a total

2Ch 35: 8 [G] His officials also **contributed** voluntarily to the people
35: 9 [G] **provided** five thousand Passover offerings and five hundred
Ezr 3: 12 [G] while many others **shouted** [+928+7754+9558] for joy.
8: 25 [G] all Israel present there *had* **donated** *for* the house of our
9: 6 [G] I am too ashamed and disgraced to **lift up** my face to you,
9: 9 [D] He has granted us new life to **rebuild** the house of our God
Ne 9: 5 [E] and *may it* **be exalted** above all blessing and praise.
Job 17: 4 [D] to understanding; therefore *you will* not **let** them **triumph**.
21: 22 [A] teach knowledge to God, since he judges even the **highest**?
22: 12 [A] heights of heaven? And see how **lofty** *are* the highest stars!
38: 15 [A] are denied their light, and their **upraised** arm is broken.
38: 34 [G] "*Can you* **raise** your voice to the clouds and cover yourself
39: 27 [G] the eagle soar at your command and **build** his nest **on high**?
Ps 3: 3 [3:4] [G] you bestow glory on me and **lift up** my head.
9: 13 [9:14] [D] Have mercy and **lift** me **up** from the gates of death,
12: 8 [12:9] [A] strut about when what is vile *is* **honored** among men.
13: 2 [13:3] [A] How long *will* my enemy **triumph** over me?
18: 27 [18:28] [A] but bring low *those* whose eyes *are* **haughty**.
18: 46 [18:47] [A] Praise be to my Rock! **Exalted** *be* God my Savior!
18: 48 [18:49] [D] *You* **exalted** me above my foes; from violent men
21: 13 [21:14] [A] *Be* **exalted**, O LORD, in your strength; we will
27: 5 [D] in the shelter of his tabernacle and **set** me **high** upon a rock.
27: 6 [A] my head *will be* **exalted** above the enemies who surround
30: 1 [30:2] [D] *I will* **exalt** you, O LORD, for you lifted me out of
34: 3 [34:4] [D] the LORD with me; *let us* **exalt** his name together.
37: 34 [D] *He will* **exalt** you to inherit the land; when the wicked are cut
46: 10 [46:11] [A] *I will be* **exalted** among the nations, I will be
46: 10 [46:11] [A] among the nations, *I will be* **exalted** in the earth."
57: 5 [57:6] [A] *Be* **exalted**, O God, above the heavens; let your glory
57: 11 [57:12] [A] *Be* **exalted**, O God, above the heavens; let your
61: 2 [61:3] [A] grows faint; lead me to the rock *that is* **higher** than I.
66: 7 [A] watch the nations—*let* not the rebellious **rise up** against him.
74: 3 [G] **Turn** your steps toward these everlasting ruins, all this
75: 4 [75:5] [G] and to the wicked, '*Do* not **lift up** your horns.
75: 5 [75:6] [G] *Do* not **lift** your horns against heaven; do not speak
75: 6 [75:7] [G] or the west or from the desert *can* **exalt** a man.
75: 7 [75:8] [G] who judges: He brings one down, *he* **exalts** another.
75: 10 [75:11] [E] but the horns of the righteous *will* **be lifted up**.
78: 69 [A] He built his sanctuary like the **heights**, like the earth that he
89: 13 [89:14] [A] your hand is strong, your right hand **exalted**.
89: 16 [89:17] [A] name all day long; *they* **exult** in your righteousness.
89: 17 [89:18] [G] and strength, and by your favor *you* **exalt** our horn.
89: 19 [89:20] [G] *I have* **exalted** a young man from among the
89: 24 [89:25] [A] and through my name his horn *will be* **exalted**.
89: 42 [89:43] [G] *You have* **exalted** the right hand of his foes;
92: 10 [92:11] [G] *You have* **exalted** my horn like that of a wild ox;
99: 2 [A] is the LORD in Zion; he *is* **exalted** over all the nations.
99: 5 [D] **Exalt** the LORD our God and worship at his footstool; he is
99: 9 [D] **Exalt** the LORD our God and worship at his holy mountain,
107: 25 [D] he spoke and stirred up a tempest *that* **lifted high** the waves.
107: 32 [D] *Let them* **exalt** him in the assembly of the people and praise
108: 5 [108:6] [A] *Be* **exalted**, O God, above the heavens, and let your
110: 7 [G] a brook beside the way; therefore *he will* **lift up** his head.
112: 9 [A] endures forever; his horn *will be* **lifted high** in honor.
113: 4 [A] The LORD *is* **exalted** over all the nations, his glory above
113: 7 [G] the poor from the dust and **lifts** the needy from the ash heap;
118: 16 [D] The LORD's right hand *is* **lifted high**; the LORD's right
118: 28 [D] I will give you thanks; you are my God, and *I will* **exalt** you.
131: 1 [A] My heart is not proud, O LORD, my eyes are not **haughty**;
138: 6 [A] Though the LORD *is on* **high**, he looks upon the lowly,
140: 8 [140:9] [A] let their plans succeed, or *they will become* **proud**.
145: 1 [D] *I will* **exalt** you, my God the King; I will praise your name
148: 14 [G] *He has* **raised up** for his people a horn, the praise of all his
Pr 3: 35 [G] The wise inherit honor, but fools *he* **holds up** *to* shame.
4: 8 [D] Esteem her, and *she will* **exalt** you; embrace her, and she will
6: 17 [A] **haughty** eyes, a lying tongue, hands that shed innocent
11: 11 [A] Through the blessing of the upright a city *is* **exalted**, but by
14: 29 [G] but a quick-tempered man **displays** folly.
14: 34 [D] Righteousness **exalts** a nation, but sin is a disgrace to any
24: 7 [A] Wisdom *is too* **high** for a fool; in the assembly at the gate he
30: 13 [A] those whose eyes *are* ever so **haughty**, whose glances are
Isa 1: 2 [D] "I reared children and **brought** them **up**, but they have
2: 12 [A] Almighty has a day in store for all the proud and **lofty**,
2: 13 [A] cedars of Lebanon, **tall** and lofty, and all the oaks of Bashan,
2: 14 [A] for all the **towering** mountains and all the high hills,
6: 1 [A] I saw the Lord seated on a throne, **high** and exalted,
10: 15 [G] As if a rod were to wield *him who* **lifts** it **up**, or a club
10: 15 [G] him who lifts it up, or a club **brandish** him who is not wood!
10: 33 [A] The **lofty trees** [+7757] will be felled, the tall ones will be
13: 2 [G] Raise a banner on a bare hilltop, **shout** [+7754] to them;
14: 13 [G] to heaven; *I will* **raise** my throne above the stars of God;
23: 4 [D] I have neither reared sons nor **brought up** daughters."
25: 1 [D] *I will* **exalt** you and praise your name, for in perfect
26: 11 [A] O LORD, your hand *is* **lifted high**, but they do not see it.
30: 18 [A] to be gracious to you; *he* **rises** to show you compassion.
33: 10 [F] the LORD. "Now *will I* **be exalted**; now will I be lifted up.
37: 23 [G] Against whom *have you* **raised** your voice and lifted your
40: 9 [G] **lift up** your voice with a shout, lift it up, do not be afraid;
40: 9 [G] lift up your voice with a shout, **lift** it **up**, do not be afraid;
49: 11 [A] mountains into roads, and my highways *will be* **raised up**.
49: 22 [G] to the Gentiles, *I will* **lift up** my banner to the peoples;
52: 13 [A] act wisely; *he will be* **raised** and lifted up and highly exalted.
57: 14 [G] **Remove** the obstacles out of the way of my people."
57: 15 [A] For this is what the **high** and lofty One says—he who lives
58: 1 [G] it aloud, do not hold back. **Raise** your voice like a trumpet.
62: 10 [G] Remove the stones. **Raise** a banner for the nations.
La 2: 17 [G] enemy gloat over you, *he has* **exalted** the horn of your foes.
Eze 6: 13 [A] on every **high** hill and on all the mountaintops, under every
10: 4 [A] Then the glory of the LORD **rose** from above the cherubim
10: 16 [A] when the cherubim spread their wings to **rise** from the
10: 17 [A] when the cherubim **rose**, they rose with them,
17: 22 [A] I myself will take a shoot from the **very top** of a cedar
20: 28 [A] to give them and they saw any **high** hill or any leafy tree,
21: 22 [21:27] [G] to slaughter, to **sound** [+928+7754] the battle cry,
21: 26 [21:31] [G] Take off the turban, **remove** the crown. It will not
31: 4 [D] The waters nourished it, deep springs **made** it **grow tall**;
31: 10 [A] and because *it was* **proud** [+4222] of its height,
34: 6 [A] wandered over all the mountains and on every **high** hill.
45: 1 [G] *you are to* **present** to the LORD a portion of the land as a
45: 9 [G] **Stop** dispossessing my people, declares the Sovereign
45: 13 [G] " 'This is the special gift *you are to* **offer**: a sixth of an ephah
48: 8 [G] west will be the portion *you are to* **present** as a special gift.
48: 9 [G] "The special portion *you are to* **offer** to the LORD will be
48: 20 [G] **As a special gift** *you will* **set aside** the sacred portion,
Da 8: 11 [H] *it* **took away** the daily sacrifice from him, and the place of
11: 12 [A] the king of the South *will be* **filled with pride** [+4222] and
11: 36 [F] *He will* **exalt** and magnify **himself** above every god and will
12: 7 [G] **lifted** his right hand and his left hand toward heaven,
Hos 11: 4 [G] I **lifted** the yoke from their neck and bent down to feed them.
11: 7 [D] they call to the Most High, *he will* by no means **exalt** them.
13: 6 [A] when they were satisfied, they *became* **proud** [+4213];
Mic 5: 9 [5:8] [A] Your hand *will be* **lifted up** in triumph over your

8124 ²רוּם ***rûm²***, n.[m.]. [6] [√ 8123; Ar 10660]

haughty [2], pride [2], haughtiness [1], high [1]

Pr 21: 4 **Haughty** eyes and a proud heart, the lamp of the wicked, are sin!
25: 3 As the heavens are **high** and the earth is deep, so the hearts of
Isa 2: 11 arrogant man will be humbled and the **pride** *of* men brought low;
2: 17 of man will be brought low and the **pride** *of* men humbled;
10: 12 for the willful pride of his heart and the **haughty** look in his eyes.
Jer 48: 29 her pride and arrogance and the **haughtiness** *of* her heart.

8125 רוֹם ***rôm***, adv. [1] [√ 8123]

on high [1]

Hab 3: 10 of water swept by; the deep roared and lifted its waves **on high**.

8126 רוּמָה ***rûmâ***, n.pr.loc. [2 / 1] [√ 8123; cf. 777]

Rumah [1]

Jos 15: 52 Arab, Dumah, [BHS ***Rumah***; NIV 1873] Eshan,
2Ki 23: 36 name was Zebidah daughter of Pedaiah; she was from **Rumah**.

8127 רוֹמָה ***rômâ***, adv. [1] [√ 8123]

proudly [1]

Mic 2: 3 You will no longer walk **proudly**, for it will be a time of calamity.

8128 רוֹמָם ***rômām***, n.[m.]. [2] [√ 8123]

praise [2]

Ps 66: 17 I cried out to him with my mouth; his **praise** was on my tongue.
149: 6 May the **praise** *of* God be in their mouths and a double-edged

8129 רוֹמֵמֻת ***rômēmut***, n.f. [1] [√ 8123]

rise up [1]

Isa 33: 3 your voice, the peoples flee; when you **rise up**, the nations scatter.

8130 רוּן ***rûn***, v. [1]

wakes from stupor [1]

Ps 78: 65 [F] as from sleep, as a man **wakes from** *the* **stupor** of wine.

8131 רוּעַ ***rûa'***, v. [45] [→ 8275, 9558]

shout [8], shout aloud [4], shout for joy [4], shouted [3], gave a shout [+9558] [2], shout in triumph [2], shouting [2], cry aloud [+8275] [1], cry out [1], crying out [1], extol [1], give a shout [+9558] [1], give a war cry [1], made noise [+9558] [1], raise the battle cry [1], raise the war cry [1], raised a shout [+9558] [1], raised the battle cry [1], shout with joy [1], shouted for joy [1], shouts [1], signal [1], sound a blast [1], sound alarm [1], sound of battle cry [1], sound [1], triumph [1]

Nu 10: 7 [G] blow the trumpets, but not *with the same* **signal**.
10: 9 [G] who is oppressing you, **sound a blast** on the trumpets.
Jos 6: 5 [G] the trumpets, *have* all the people **give a** loud **shout** [+9558];
6: 10 [G] the people, "*Do* not **give a war cry**, do not raise your voices,
6: 10 [G] do not say a word until the day I tell you *to* **shout**.
6: 10 [G] not say a word until the day I tell you to shout. Then **shout**!"
6: 16 [G] the trumpet blast, Joshua commanded the people, "**Shout**!
6: 20 [G] When the trumpets sounded, the people **shouted**, and at the
6: 20 [G] when the people **gave a** loud **shout** [+9558], the wall
Jdg 7: 21 [G] the camp, all the Midianites ran, **crying out** as they fled.
15: 14 [G] approached Lehi, the Philistines came toward him **shouting**.
1Sa 4: 5 [G] all Israel **raised** such **a** great **shout** [+9558] that the ground
10: 24 [G] the people." Then the people **shouted**, "Long live the king!"
17: 20 [G] was going out to its battle positions, **shouting** the war cry.
17: 52 [G] the men of Israel and Judah surged forward with a **shout**
2Ch 13: 12 [G] His priests with their trumpets *will* **sound** the battle cry
13: 15 [G] the men of Judah **raised the battle cry**. At the sound of their
13: 15 [G] At the **sound of** their **battle cry**, God routed Jeroboam
Ezr 3: 11 [G] all the people **gave a** great **shout** [+9558] of praise to the
3: 13 [G] because the people **made** so much **noise** [+9558].
Job 30: 5 [G] from their fellow men, **shouted** at as if they were thieves.
38: 7 [G] stars sang together and all the angels **shouted for joy**?
Ps 41: 11 [41:12] [G] with me, for my enemy *does* not **triumph** over me.
47: 1 [47:2] [G] all you nations; **shout** to God with cries of joy.
60: 8 [60:10] [F] I toss my sandal; over Philistia *I* **shout in triumph**."
65: 13 [65:14] [F] are mantled with grain; *they* **shout for joy** and sing.
66: 1 [G] **Shout with joy** to God, all the earth!
81: 1 [81:2] [G] God our strength; **shout aloud** to the God of Jacob!
95: 1 [G] the LORD; *let us* **shout aloud** to the Rock of our salvation.
95: 2 [G] him with thanksgiving and **extol** him with music and song.
98: 4 [G] **Shout for joy** to the LORD, all the earth, burst into jubilant
98: 6 [G] the ram's horn—**shout for joy** before the LORD, the King.
100: 1 [G] **Shout for joy** to the LORD, all the earth.
108: 9 [108:10] [F] toss my sandal; over Philistia *I* **shout in triumph**."
Isa 8: 9 [A] **Raise the war cry**, *you* nations, and be shattered! Listen,
15: 4 [G] Therefore the armed men of Moab **cry out**, and their hearts
16: 10 [D] no one sings or **shouts** in the vineyards; no one treads out
42: 13 [G] *with a* **shout** he will raise the battle cry and will triumph
44: 23 [G] for the LORD has done this; **shout aloud**, O earth beneath.
Jer 50: 15 [G] **Shout** against her on every side! She surrenders, her towers
Hos 5: 8 [G] **Raise the battle cry** in Beth Aven; lead on, O Benjamin.
Joel 2: 1 [G] Blow the trumpet in Zion; **sound** *the* **alarm** on my holy hill.
Mic 4: 9 [G] Why *do you* now **cry** [+8275] **aloud**—have you no king?
Zep 3: 14 [G] Sing, O Daughter of Zion; **shout aloud**, O Israel! Be glad
Zec 9: 9 [G] **Shout**, Daughter of Jerusalem! See, your king comes to you,

8132 רוּץ ***rûṣ***, v. [102 / 103] [→ 5296, 5297, 8350; cf. 8351?]

run [20], ran [19], guards [10], couriers [6], running [5], hurried [4], guard [3], hurry [3], rush [3], *untranslated* [2], advance [2], chase [2], guardroom [+9288] [2], another[s] [1], attack [1], busy [1], charge [1], charged [1], charging [1], courier [1], dart about [1], gallop along [1], go quickly [1], go [1], hasten [1], quickly brought [1], raced [1], ran off [1], runner [1], runs [1], rushed forward [1], rushes [1], served quickly [1], submit [+3338] [1], throw down [1]

Ge 18: 2 [A] *he* **hurried** from the entrance of his tent to meet them
18: 7 [A] Then he **ran** to the herd and selected a choice, tender calf
24: 17 [A] The servant **hurried** to meet her and said, "Please give me a
24: 20 [A] **ran** back to the well to draw more water, and drew enough
24: 28 [A] The girl **ran** and told her mother's household about these
24: 29 [A] named Laban, and he **hurried** out to the man at the spring.
29: 12 [A] and a son of Rebekah. So *she* **ran** and told her father.
29: 13 [A] news about Jacob, his sister's son, *he* **hurried** to meet him.
33: 4 [A] Esau **ran** to meet Jacob and embraced him; he threw his arms
41: 14 [G] for Joseph, and he *was* **quickly brought** from the dungeon.
Nu 11: 27 [A] A young man **ran** and told Moses, "Eldad and Medad are
16: 47 [17:12] [A] Moses said, and **ran** into the midst of the assembly.
Jos 7: 22 [A] and *they* **ran** to the tent, and there it was, hidden in his tent,
8: 19 [A] rose quickly from their position and **rushed forward**.
Jdg 7: 21 [A] the camp, all the Midianites **ran**, crying out as they fled.
13: 10 [A] The woman hurried **[NIE]** to tell her husband, "He's here!
1Sa 3: 5 [A] *he* **ran** to Eli and said, "Here I am; you called me." But Eli
4: 12 [A] That same day a Benjamite **ran** from the battle line and went
8: 11 [A] and horses, and *they will* **run** in front of his chariots.
10: 23 [A] *They* **ran** and brought him out, and as he stood among the
17: 17 [G] loaves of bread for your brothers and **hurry** to their camp.
17: 22 [A] of supplies, **ran** *to* the battle lines and greeted his brothers.
17: 48 [A] David **ran** quickly *toward* the battle line to meet him.
17: 51 [A] David **ran** and stood over him. He took hold of the
20: 6 [A] 'David earnestly asked my permission to **hurry** *to*
20: 36 [A] and he said to the boy, "**Run** and find the arrows I shoot."
20: 36 [A] I shoot." *As* the boy **ran**, he shot an arrow beyond him.
22: 17 [A] the king ordered the **guards** at his side: "Turn and kill the
2Sa 15: 1 [A] a chariot and horses and with fifty men *to* **run** ahead of him.
18: 19 [A] "*Let me* **run** and take the news to the king that the LORD
18: 21 [A] The Cushite bowed down before Joab and **ran off**.
18: 22 [A] "Come what may, please *let* me **run** behind the Cushite."
18: 22 [A] But Joab replied, "My son, why *do* you *want to* **go**?
18: 23 [A] He said, "Come what may, *I want to* **run**." So Joab said,
18: 23 [A] "Come what may, I want to run." So Joab said, "**Run**!"
18: 23 [A] Ahimaaz **ran** by way of the plain and outran the Cushite.
18: 24 [A] by the wall. As he looked out, he saw a man **running** alone.
18: 26 [A] the watchman saw another man **running**, and he called down
18: 26 [A] to the gatekeeper, "Look, another man **running** alone!"
22: 30 [A] With your help *I can* **advance** *against* a troop; with my God
1Ki 1: 5 [A] and horses ready, with fifty men *to* **run** ahead of him.
14: 27 [A] assigned these to the commanders of the **guard** on duty at the
14: 28 [A] went to the LORD's temple, the **guards** bore the shields,
14: 28 [A] and afterward they returned them to the **guardroom** [+9288].
18: 46 [A] into his belt, *he* **ran** ahead of Ahab all the way to Jezreel.
19: 20 [A] Elisha then left his oxen and **ran** after Elijah. "Let me kiss
2Ki 4: 22 [A] a donkey so *I can* **go** to the man of God **quickly** and return."
4: 26 [A] **Run** to meet her and ask her, 'Are you all right? Is your
5: 20 [A] *I will* **run** after him and get something from him."
5: 21 [A] When Naaman saw him **running** toward him, he got down
10: 25 [A] the burnt offering, he ordered the **guards** and officers:
10: 25 [A] The **guards** and officers threw the bodies out and
11: 4 [A] the Carites and the **guards** and had them brought to him at
11: 6 [A] at the Sur Gate, and a third at the gate behind the **guard**,
11: 11 [A] The **guards**, each with his weapon in his hand,
11: 13 [A] When Athaliah heard the noise made by the **guards**
11: 19 [A] the Carites, the **guards** and all the people of the land,
11: 19 [A] into the palace, entering by way of the gate of the **guards**.
2Ch 12: 10 [A] assigned these to the commanders of the **guard** on duty at the
12: 11 [A] the **guards** went with him, bearing the shields,
12: 11 [A] and afterward they returned them to the **guardroom** [+9288].
23: 12 [A] When Athaliah heard the noise of the people **running**
30: 6 [A] **couriers** went throughout Israel and Judah with letters from
30: 10 [A] The **couriers** went from town to town in Ephraim
35: 13 [G] caldrons and pans and **served** them **quickly** to all the people.
Est 3: 13 [A] Dispatches were sent by **couriers** to all the king's provinces
3: 15 [A] Spurred on by the king's command, the **couriers** went out,
8: 10 [A] the king's signet ring, and sent them by mounted **couriers**,
8: 14 [A] The **couriers**, riding the royal horses, raced out, spurred on
Job 9: 25 [A] "My days are swifter than a **runner**; they fly away without a
15: 26 [A] defiantly **charging** against him with a thick, strong shield.
16: 14 [A] and again he bursts upon me; *he* **rushes** at me like a warrior.
Ps 18: 29 [18:30] [A] With your help *I can* **advance** *against* a troop; with
19: 5 [19:6] [A] like a champion rejoicing to **run** his course.
59: 4 [59:5] [A] I have done no wrong, yet they are ready *to* **attack**
62: 3 [62:4] [a] *Would* all of you **throw** [BHS 8357] him **down**—
68: 31 [68:32] [G] Cush *will* **submit** [+3338] herself to God.
119: 32 [A] *I* **run** *in* the path of your commands, for you have set my
147: 15 [A] He sends his command to the earth; his word **runs** swiftly.
Pr 1: 16 [A] for their feet **rush** into sin, they are swift to shed blood.
4: 12 [A] will not be hampered; when *you* **run**, you will not stumble.
6: 18 [A] devises wicked schemes, feet that are quick to **rush** into evil,
18: 10 [A] is a strong tower; the righteous **run** to it and are safe.
SS 1: 4 [A] Take me away with you—*let us* **hurry**! Let the king bring
Isa 40: 31 [A] *they will* **run** and not grow weary, they will walk and not be
55: 5 [A] nations that do not know you *will* **hasten** to you, because of
59: 7 [A] Their feet **rush** into sin; they are swift to shed innocent
Jer 12: 5 [A] "If *you have* **raced** with men on foot and they have worn
23: 21 [A] send these prophets, yet they *have* **run** with their message;
49: 19 [G] *I will* **chase** Edom from its land in an instant.
50: 44 [G] *I will* **chase** Babylon from its land in an instant.
51: 31 [A] *One* **courier** follows another and messenger follows
51: 31 [A] One courier follows **another**[s] and messenger follows
51: 31 [A] **[RPH]** and messenger follows messenger to announce to
Da 8: 6 [A] standing beside the canal and **charged** at him in great rage.
Joel 2: 4 [A] the appearance of horses; *they* **gallop along** like cavalry.
2: 7 [A] *They* **charge** like warriors; they scale walls like soldiers.
2: 9 [A] They rush upon the city; *they* **run** along the wall. They climb
Am 6: 12 [A] *Do* horses **run** on the rocky crags? Does one plow there with
Na 2: 4 [2:5] [D] like flaming torches; *they* **dart about** like lightning.
Hab 2: 2 [A] and make it plain on tablets so that a herald *may* **run** with it.
Hag 1: 9 [A] a ruin, while each of you *is* **busy** with his own house.
Zec 2: 4 [2:8] [A] "**Run**, tell that young man, 'Jerusalem will be a city

8133 רוּשׁ ***rûš***, v. [24 / 23] [→ 8203; cf. 3769]

poor [20], poverty [1], pretends to be poor [1], weak [1]

1Sa 18: 23 [A] king's son-in-law? I'm only a **poor** man and little known."
2Sa 12: 1 [A] were two men in a certain town, one rich and the other **poor**.

2Sa 12: 3 [A] the **poor** *man* had nothing except one little ewe lamb he had
12: 4 [A] he took the ewe lamb that belonged to the **poor** man
Ps 34: 10 [34:11] [A] The lions *may grow* **weak** and hungry, but those
82: 3 [A] and fatherless; maintain the rights of the **poor** and oppressed.
Pr 10: 4 [A] Lazy hands make *a man* **poor**, but diligent hands bring
13: 7 [F] *another* **pretends to be poor**, yet has great wealth.
13: 8 [A] riches may ransom his life, but a **poor** *man* hears no threat.
13: 23 [A] A **poor** *man's* field may produce abundant food,
14: 20 [A] The **poor** are shunned even by their neighbors, but the rich
17: 5 [A] He who mocks the **poor** shows contempt for their Maker;
18: 23 [A] A **poor** *man* pleads for mercy, but a rich man answers
19: 1 [A] Better a **poor** *man* whose walk is blameless than a fool
19: 7 [A] A **poor** *man* is shunned by all his relatives—how much more
19: 22 [A] a man desires is unfailing love; better *to be* **poor** than a liar.
22: 2 [A] Rich and **poor** have this in common: The LORD is the
22: 7 [A] The rich rule over the **poor**, and the borrower is servant to
28: 3 [a] A ruler [+1505] [BHS *poor man*; NIV 8031] who oppresses the
28: 6 [A] Better a **poor** *man* whose walk is blameless than a rich man
28: 27 [A] He who gives to the **poor** will lack nothing, but he who
29: 13 [A] The **poor** *man* and the oppressor have this in common:
Ecc 4: 14 [A] or he may have been born in **poverty** within his kingdom.
5: 8 [5:7] [A] If you see the **poor** oppressed in a district, and justice

8134 רוּת rût, n.pr.f. [12] [√ 8287?]

Ruth [12]

Ru 1: 4 married Moabite women, one named Orpah and the other **Ruth**.
1: 14 Orpah kissed her mother-in-law good-by, but **Ruth** clung to her.
1: 16 **Ruth** replied, "Don't urge me to leave you or to turn back from
1: 22 So Naomi returned from Moab accompanied by **Ruth** the
2: 2 And **Ruth** the Moabitess said to Naomi, "Let me go to the fields
2: 8 So Boaz said to **Ruth**, "My daughter, listen to me. Don't go
2: 21 **Ruth** the Moabitess said, "He even said to me, 'Stay with my
2: 22 Naomi said to **Ruth** her daughter-in-law, "It will be good for you,
3: 9 "Who are you?" he asked. "I am your servant **Ruth**," she said.
4: 5 day you buy the land from Naomi and from **Ruth** the Moabitess,
4: 10 I have also acquired **Ruth** the Moabitess, Mahlon's widow,
4: 13 So Boaz took **Ruth** and she became his wife. Then he went to her,

8135 רָזָה rāzâ, v. [2] [→ 8136, 8137, 8140]

destroys [1], waste away [1]

Isa 17: 4 [C] glory of Jacob will fade; the fat of his body *will* **waste away**.
Zep 2: 11 [A] The LORD will be awesome to them when *he* **destroys** all

8136 רָזֶה rāzeh, a. [2] [√ 8135]

lean [1], poor [1]

Nu 13: 20 How is the soil? Is it fertile or **poor**? Are there trees on it or not?
Eze 34: 20 I myself will judge between the fat sheep and the **lean** sheep.

8137 ¹רָזוֹן rāzôn[1], n.[m.]. [3] [√ 8135]

wasting disease [2], short [1]

Ps 106: 15 them what they asked for, but sent a **wasting disease** upon them.
Isa 10: 16 will send a **wasting disease** upon his sturdy warriors;
Mic 6: 10 O wicked house, your ill-gotten treasures and the **short** ephah,

8138 ²רָזוֹן rāzôn[2], n.m. [1] [√ 8142]

prince [1]

Pr 14: 28 is a king's glory, but without subjects a **prince** is ruined.

8139 רְזוֹן rᵉzôn, n.pr.m. [1] [√ 8142]

Rezon [1]

1Ki 11: 23 **Rezon** son of Eliada, who had fled from his master,

8140 רָזִי rāzî, n.[m.]. [2] [√ 8135]

waste away [2]

Isa 24: 16 I said, "**I waste away**, I waste away! Woe to me! The treacherous
24: 16 I said, "I waste away, I **waste away**! Woe to me! The treacherous

8141 רָזַם rāzam, v. [1]

flash [1]

Job 15: 12 [A] Has your heart carried you away, and why *do* your eyes **flash**,

8142 רָזַן rāzan, v. [6] [→ 8138, 8139]

rulers [5], princes [1]

Jdg 5: 3 [A] "Hear this, you kings! Listen, you **rulers**! I will sing to the
Ps 2: 2 [A] the **rulers** gather together against the LORD and against his
Pr 8: 15 [A] By me kings reign and **rulers** make laws that are just;
31: 4 [A] not for kings to drink wine, not for **rulers** to crave beer,
Isa 40: 23 [A] He brings **princes** to naught and reduces the rulers of this
Hab 1: 10 [A] They deride kings and scoff at **rulers**. They laugh at all

8143 רָחַב rāḥab, v. [25] [→ 5303, 5304, 8144, 8145, 8146, 8147, 8148, 8152, 8153, 8154]

enlarges [3], broaden [2], enlarge [2], boasts [1], broad [1], enlarged [1], extend [1], gape [+7023] [1], give relief [1], given room [1], greedy [1], make bald [+7947] [1], multiplied [1], open wide [1], opened wide [1], opens the way [1], set free [1], sneer [+7023] [1], swell with joy [1], wide [1], wider [1]

Ge 26: 22 [G] "Now the LORD *has* **given** us **room** and we will flourish in
Ex 34: 24 [G] I will drive out nations before you and **enlarge** your territory,
Dt 12: 20 [G] When the LORD your God *has* **enlarged** your territory as
19: 8 [G] If the LORD your God **enlarges** your territory, as he
33: 20 [G] Gad he said: "Blessed is *he who* **enlarges** Gad's domain!
1Sa 2: 1 [A] My mouth **boasts** over my enemies, for I delight in your
2Sa 22: 37 [G] *You* **broaden** the path beneath me, so that my ankles do not
Ps 4: 1 [4:2] [G] **Give** me **relief** from my distress; be merciful to me
18: 36 [18:37] [G] *You* **broaden** the path beneath me, so that my
25: 17 [G] The troubles of my heart *have* **multiplied**; free me from my
35: 21 [G] *They* **gape** [+7023] at me and say, "Aha! Aha! With our own
81: 10 [81:11] [G] of Egypt. **Open wide** your mouth and I will fill it.
119: 32 [G] the path of your commands, for *you have* **set** my heart **free**.
Pr 18: 16 [G] A gift **opens the way** for the giver and ushers him into the
Isa 5: 14 [G] Therefore the grave **enlarges** its appetite and opens its mouth
30: 23 [C] In that day your cattle will graze in **broad** meadows.
30: 33 [G] Its fire pit has been made deep and **wide**, with an abundance
54: 2 [G] "**Enlarge** the place of your tent, stretch your tent curtains
57: 4 [G] At whom *do you* **sneer** [+7023] and stick out your tongue?
57: 8 [G] uncovered your bed, you climbed into it and **opened** it **wide**;
60: 5 [A] and be radiant, your heart will throb and **swell with joy**;
Eze 41: 7 [A] The side rooms all around the temple *were* **wider** at each
Am 1: 13 [G] the pregnant women of Gilead in order to **extend** his borders,
Mic 1: 16 [G] **make** yourselves as **bald** [+7947] as the vulture, for they will
Hab 2: 5 [G] Because he *is* as **greedy** as the grave and like death is never

8144 רַחַב raḥab, n.[m.]. [2] [√ 8143]

spacious place [1], vast expanses [1]

Job 36: 16 "He is wooing you from the jaws of distress to a **spacious place**
38: 18 Have you comprehended the **vast expanses** *of* the earth? Tell me,

8145 רֹחַב rōḥab, n.[m.]. [101] [√ 8143]

wide [69], width [11], *untranslated* [4], breadth [3], thick [3], deep [2], distance [2], broad [1], from front to back [1], length [1], projected [1], span [1], square [+802] [1], widened [1]

Ge 6: 15 The ark is to be 450 feet long, 75 feet **wide** and 45 feet high.
13: 17 Go, walk through the length and **breadth** of the land, for I am
Ex 25: 10 cubits long, a cubit and a half **wide**, and a cubit and a half high.
25: 17 pure gold—two and a half cubits long and a cubit and a half **wide**.
25: 23 two cubits long, a cubit **wide** and a cubit and a half high.
26: 2 to be the same size—twenty-eight cubits long and four cubits **wide**.
26: 8 are to be the same size—thirty cubits long and four cubits **wide**.
26: 16 Each frame is to be ten cubits long and a cubit and a half **wide**,
27: 1 cubits high; it is to be square, five cubits long and five cubits **wide**.
27: 12 "The west end of the courtyard shall be fifty cubits **wide** and have
27: 13 toward the sunrise, the courtyard shall also be fifty cubits **wide**.
27: 18 The courtyard shall be a hundred cubits long and fifty cubits **wide**,
28: 16 It is to be square—a span long and a span **wide**—and folded
30: 2 It is to be square, a cubit long and a cubit **wide**, and two cubits
36: 9 were the same size—twenty-eight cubits long and four cubits **wide**.
36: 15 were the same size—thirty cubits long and four cubits **wide**.
36: 21 Each frame was ten cubits long and a cubit and a half **wide**,
37: 1 cubits long, a cubit and a half **wide**, and a cubit and a half high.
37: 6 pure gold—two and a half cubits long and a cubit and a half **wide**.
37: 10 two cubits long, a cubit **wide**, and a cubit and a half high.
37: 25 It was square, a cubit long and a cubit **wide**, and two cubits high—
38: 1 cubits high; it was square, five cubits long and five cubits **wide**.
38: 18 like the curtains of the courtyard, five cubits high, **[NIE]**
39: 9 It was square—a span long and a span **wide**—and folded double.
Dt 3: 11 of iron and was more than thirteen feet long and six feet **wide**.
1Ki 4: 29 [5:9] a **breadth** *of* understanding as measureless as the sand on
6: 2 for the LORD was sixty cubits long, twenty **wide** and thirty high.
6: 3 of the main hall of the temple extended the **width** *of* the temple,
6: 3 and **projected** ten cubits from the front of the temple.
6: 6 The lowest floor was five cubits **wide**, the middle floor six cubits
6: 6 the middle floor six cubits **[RPH]** and the third floor seven.
6: 6 **[RPH]** He made offset ledges around the outside of the temple
6: 20 sanctuary was twenty cubits long, twenty **wide** and twenty high.
7: 2 fifty **wide** and thirty high, with four rows of cedar columns
7: 6 He made a colonnade fifty cubits long and thirty **wide**. In front of
7: 27 of bronze; each was four cubits long, four **wide** and three high.

2Ch 3: 3 and twenty cubits **wide** (using the cubit of the old standard).
3: 4 the temple was twenty cubits long across the **width** *of* the building
3: 8 Holy Place, its length corresponding to the **width** *of* the temple—
3: 8 width of the temple—twenty cubits long and twenty cubits **wide**.
4: 1 altar twenty cubits long, twenty cubits **wide** and ten cubits high.
6: 13 five cubits long, five cubits **wide** and three cubits high,
Job 37: 10 breath of God produces ice, and the **broad** waters become frozen.
Ps 90: 10 yet their **span** [BHS 8106] is but trouble and sorrow, for they
Isa 8: 8 Its outspread wings will cover the **breadth** *of* your land,
Eze 40: 5 the wall; it was one measuring rod **thick** and one rod high.
40: 6 and measured the threshold of the gate; it was one rod **deep**.
40: 6 it was one rod deep. [BHS+ *threshold, one rod **deep***]
40: 7 The alcoves for the guards were one rod long and one rod **wide**,
40: 11 Then he measured the **width** *of* the entrance to the gateway;
40: 13 the **distance** was twenty-five cubits from one parapet opening to
40: 19 he measured the **distance** from the inside of the lower gateway to
40: 20 Then he measured the length and **width** *of* the gate facing north,
40: 21 first gateway. It was fifty cubits long and twenty-five cubits **wide**.
40: 25 of the others. It was fifty cubits long and twenty-five cubits **wide**.
40: 29 all around. It was fifty cubits long and twenty-five cubits **wide**.
40: 30 the inner court were twenty-five cubits wide and five cubits **deep**.)
40: 33 all around. It was fifty cubits long and twenty-five cubits **wide**.
40: 36 all around. It was fifty cubits long and twenty-five cubits **wide**.
40: 42 a cubit and a half long, a cubit and a half **wide** and a cubit high.
40: 47 It was square—a hundred cubits long and a hundred cubits **wide**.
40: 48 The **width** *of* the entrance was fourteen cubits and its projecting
40: 49 was twenty cubits wide, and twelve cubits **from front to back**.
41: 1 the jambs; the **width** *of* the jambs was six cubits on each side.
41: 1 the width of the jambs was six cubits on each side. **[RPH]**
41: 1 six cubits on each side. [BHS+ *the **width** of the tent*]
41: 2 The entrance was ten cubits **wide**, and the projecting walls on each
41: 2 outer sanctuary; it was forty cubits long and twenty cubits **wide**.
41: 3 and the projecting walls on each side of it were seven cubits **wide**.
41: 4 its **width** was twenty cubits across the end of the outer sanctuary.
41: 5 and each side room around the temple was four cubits **wide**.
41: 7 ascending stages, so that the rooms **widened** as one went upward.
41: 9 The outer wall of the side rooms was five cubits **thick**. The open
41: 10 the ⌊priests'⌋ rooms was twenty cubits **wide** all around the temple.
41: 11 the base adjoining the open area was five cubits **wide** all around.
41: 12 the temple courtyard on the west side was seventy cubits **wide**.
41: 12 The wall of the building was five cubits **thick** all around, and its
41: 14 The **width** *of* the temple courtyard on the east, including the front
41: 22 a wooden altar three cubits high and two cubits **square** [+802];
42: 2 door faced north was a hundred cubits long and fifty cubits **wide**.
42: 4 In front of the rooms was an inner passageway ten cubits **wide**
42: 10 On the south side along the **length** *of* the wall of the outer court,
42: 11 they had the same length and **width**, with similar exits and
42: 20 around it, five hundred cubits long and five hundred cubits **wide**,
43: 13 Its gutter is a cubit deep and a cubit **wide**, with a rim of one span
43: 14 ground up to the lower ledge it is two cubits high and a cubit **wide**,
43: 14 ledge up to the larger ledge it is four cubits high and a cubit **wide**.
43: 16 altar hearth is square, twelve cubits long and twelve cubits **wide**.
43: 17 fourteen cubits long and fourteen cubits **wide**, with a rim of half a
45: 1 as a sacred district, 25,000 cubits long and 20,000 cubits **wide**;
45: 3 measure off a section 25,000 cubits long and 10,000 cubits **wide**.
45: 5 cubits long and 10,000 cubits **wide** will belong to the Levites,
45: 6 " 'You are to give the city as its property an area 5,000 cubits **wide**
46: 22 were enclosed courts, forty cubits long and thirty cubits **wide**;
48: 8 It will be 25,000 cubits **wide**, and its length from east to west will
48: 9 to the LORD will be 25,000 cubits long and 10,000 cubits **wide**.
48: 10 10,000 cubits **wide** on the west side, 10,000 cubits wide on the east
48: 10 10,000 cubits **wide** on the east side and 25,000 cubits long on the
48: 13 will have an allotment 25,000 cubits long and 10,000 cubits **wide**.
48: 13 Its total length will be 25,000 cubits and its **width** 10,000 cubits.
48: 15 "The remaining area, 5,000 cubits **wide** and 25,000 cubits long,
Zec 2: 2 [2:6] to find out how **wide** and how long it is."
5: 2 "I see a flying scroll, thirty feet long and fifteen feet **wide**."

8146 ¹רָחָב *rāḥāb¹*, a. [21] [→ 8147?; cf. 8143]

spacious [+3338] [4], broad [2], proud [2], spacious [2], boundless [+4394] [1], broad [+3338] [1], freedom [1], gaping [1], greedy man [+5883] [1], large [+3338] [1], large [1], plenty of room [+3338] [1], spread out [1], thick [1], wider [1]

Ge 34: 21 and trade in it; the land has **plenty of room** [+3338] for them.
Ex 3: 8 to bring them up out of that land into a good and **spacious** land,
Jdg 18: 10 and a **spacious** [+3338] land that God has put into your hands,
1Ch 4: 40 and the land was **spacious** [+3338], peaceful and quiet.
Ne 3: 8 next to that. They restored Jerusalem as far as the **Broad** Wall.
4: 19 [4:13] rest of the people, "The work is extensive and **spread out**,
7: 4 Now the city was large and **spacious** [+3338], but there were few
9: 35 enjoying your great goodness to them in the **spacious** and fertile
12: 38 half the people—past the Tower of the Ovens to the **Broad** Wall,
Job 11: 9 Their measure is longer than the earth and **wider** than the sea.
30: 14 They advance as through a **gaping** breach; amid the ruins they
Ps 101: 5 whoever has haughty eyes and a **proud** heart, him will I not
104: 25 There is the sea, vast and **spacious** [+3338], teeming with creatures
119: 45 I will walk about in **freedom**, for I have sought out your precepts.
119: 96 I see a limit; but your commands are **boundless** [+4394].
Pr 21: 4 Haughty eyes and a **proud** heart, the lamp of the wicked, are sin!
28: 25 A **greedy** [+5883] **man** stirs up dissension, but he who trusts in the
Isa 22: 18 up tightly like a ball and throw you into a **large** [+3338] country.
33: 21 It will be like a place of **broad** [+3338] rivers and streams.
Jer 51: 58 "Babylon's **thick** wall will be leveled and her high gates set on
Eze 23: 32 "You will drink your sister's cup, a cup **large** and deep; it will

8147 ²רָחָב *rāḥāb²*, n.pr.f. [5] [√ 8146?; cf. 8143]

Rahab [5]

Jos 2: 1 So they went and entered the house of a prostitute named **Rahab**
2: 3 So the king of Jericho sent this message to **Rahab**: "Bring out the
6: 17 Only **Rahab** the prostitute and all who are with her in her house
6: 23 men who had done the spying went in and brought out **Rahab**,
6: 25 Joshua spared **Rahab** the prostitute, with her family and all who

8148 ¹רְחֹב *rᵉḥōb¹*, n.f. [43] [→ 1124, 8149, 8150?, 8151, 8155; cf. 8143]

streets [15], square [10], public square [6], public squares [5], squares [4], one[s] [1], open square [1], there[s] [+928+2023] [1]

Ge 19: 2 "No," they answered, "we will spend the night in the **square**."
Dt 13: 16 [13:17] plunder of the town into the middle of the **public square**
Jdg 19: 15 They went and sat in the city **square**, but no one took them into his
19: 17 When he looked and saw the traveler in the city **square**, the old
19: 20 whatever you need. Only don't spend the night in the **square**."
2Sa 21: 12 (They had taken them secretly from the **public square** *at* Beth
2Ch 29: 4 and the Levites, assembled them in the **square** *on* the east side
32: 6 and assembled them before him in the **square** *at* the city gate
Ezr 10: 9 all the people were sitting in the **square** *before* the house of God,
Ne 8: 1 all the people assembled as one man in the **square** before the
8: 3 He read it aloud from daybreak till noon as he faced the **square**
8: 16 courts of the house of God and in the **square** *by* the Water Gate
8: 16 the square by the Water Gate and the **one**[s] *by* the Gate of Ephraim.
Est 4: 6 So Hathach went out to Mordecai in the **open square** *of* the city in
6: 9 lead him on the horse through the city **streets**, proclaiming before
6: 11 robed Mordecai, and led him on horseback through the city **streets**,
Job 29: 7 went to the gate of the city and took my seat in the **public square**,
Ps 55: 11 [55:12] at work in the city; threats and lies never leave its **streets**.
144: 14 of walls, no going into captivity, no cry of distress in our **streets**.
Pr 1: 20 calls aloud in the street, she raises her voice in the **public squares**;
5: 16 in the streets, your streams of water in the **public squares**?
7: 12 now in the street, now in the **squares**, at every corner she lurks.)
22: 13 "There is a lion outside!" or, "I will be murdered in the **streets**!"
26: 13 "There is a lion in the road, a fierce lion roaming the **streets**!"
SS 3: 2 get up now and go about the city, through its streets and **squares**;
Isa 15: 3 on the roofs and in the **public squares** they all wail, prostrate with
59: 14 a distance; truth has stumbled in the **streets**, honesty cannot enter.
Jer 5: 1 look around and consider, search through her **squares**.
9: 21 [9:20] the streets and the young men from the **public squares**.
48: 38 in Moab and in the **public squares** there is nothing but mourning,
49: 26 Surely, her young men will fall in the **streets**; all her soldiers will
50: 30 Therefore, her young men will fall in the **streets**; all her soldiers
La 2: 11 because children and infants faint in the **streets** *of* the city.
2: 12 as they faint like wounded men in the **streets** *of* the city, as their
4: 18 Men stalked us at every step, so we could not walk in our **streets**.
Eze 16: 24 for yourself and made a lofty shrine in every **public square**.
16: 31 of every street and made your lofty shrines in every **public square**,
Da 9: 25 It will be rebuilt with **streets** and a trench, but in times of trouble.
Am 5: 16 in all the streets and cries of anguish in every **public square**.
Na 2: 4 [2:5] the streets, rushing back and forth through the **squares**.
Zec 8: 4 and women of ripe old age will sit in the **streets** *of* Jerusalem,
8: 5 The city **streets** will be filled with boys and girls playing there."
8: 5 will be filled with boys and girls playing **there**[s] [+928+2023]."

8149 ²רְחֹב *rᵉḥōb²*, n.pr.loc. [7] [√ 8148]

Rehob [7]

Nu 13: 21 and explored the land from the Desert of Zin as far as **Rehob**,
Jos 19: 28 It went to Abdon, **Rehob**, Hammon and Kanah, as far as Greater
19: 30 Ummah, Aphek and **Rehob**. There were twenty-two towns
21: 31 Helkath and **Rehob**, together with their pasturelands—four towns;
Jdg 1: 31 or Sidon or Ahlab or Aczib or Helbah or Aphek or **Rehob**,
2Sa 10: 8 while the Arameans of Zobah and **Rehob** and the men of Tob
1Ch 6: 75 [6:60] Hukok and **Rehob**, together with their pasturelands;

8150 רְחֹב[3] *rᵉḥōb*[3], n.pr.m. [3] [√ 8148?]
Rehob [3]

2Sa 8: 3 Moreover, David fought Hadadezer son of **Rehob**, king of Zobah,
8: 12 He also dedicated the plunder taken from Hadadezer son of **Rehob**,
Ne 10: 11 [10:12] Mica, **Rehob**, Hashabiah,

8151 רְחֹבוֹת *rᵉḥōbôt*, n.pr.loc. [3] [√ 8148]
Rehoboth [3]

Ge 26: 22 He named it **Rehoboth**, saying, "Now the LORD has given us
36: 37 Shaul from **Rehoboth** *on* the river succeeded him as king.
1Ch 1: 48 Shaul from **Rehoboth** *on* the river succeeded him as king.

8152 רְחַבְיָה *rᵉḥabyâ*, n.pr.m. [2] [√ 8143 + 3378]
Rehabiah [2]

1Ch 23: 17 **Rehabiah** was the first. Eliezer had no other sons, but the sons of
23: 17 had no other sons, but the sons of **Rehabiah** were very numerous.

8153 רְחַבְיָהוּ *rᵉḥabyāhû*, n.pr.m. [3] [√ 8143 + 3378]
Rehabiah [2], his[s] [1]

1Ch 24: 21 As for **Rehabiah**, from his sons: Isshiah was the first.
24: 21 As for Rehabiah, from **his**[s] sons: Isshiah was the first.
26: 25 **Rehabiah** his son, Jeshaiah his son, Joram his son, Zicri his son

8154 רְחַבְעָם *rᵉḥab'ām*, n.pr.m. [50] [√ 8143 + 6639]
Rehoboam [43], he[s] [3], Rehoboam's [3], *untranslated* [1]

1Ki 11: 43 David his father. And **Rehoboam** his son succeeded him as king.
12: 1 **Rehoboam** went to Shechem, for all the Israelites had gone there
12: 3 and he and the whole assembly of Israel went to **Rehoboam**
12: 6 King **Rehoboam** consulted the elders who had served his father
12: 12 days later Jeroboam and all the people returned to **Rehoboam**,
12: 17 were living in the towns of Judah, **Rehoboam** still ruled over them.
12: 18 King **Rehoboam** sent out Adoniram, who was in charge of forced
12: 18 King **Rehoboam**, however, managed to get into his chariot
12: 21 When **Rehoboam** arrived in Jerusalem, he mustered the whole
12: 21 and to regain the kingdom for **Rehoboam** son of Solomon.
12: 23 "Say to **Rehoboam** son of Solomon king of Judah, to the whole
12: 27 again give their allegiance to their lord, **Rehoboam** king of Judah.
12: 27 king of Judah. They will kill me and return to King **Rehoboam**."
14: 21 **Rehoboam** son of Solomon was king in Judah. He was forty-one
14: 21 **He**[s] was forty-one years old when he became king, and he reigned
14: 25 In the fifth year of King **Rehoboam**, Shishak king of Egypt
14: 27 So King **Rehoboam** made bronze shields to replace them
14: 29 As for the other events of **Rehoboam's** reign, and all he did,
14: 30 There was continual warfare between **Rehoboam** and Jeroboam.
14: 31 **Rehoboam** rested with his fathers and was buried with them in the
15: 6 There was war between **Rehoboam** and Jeroboam throughout
1Ch 3: 10 Solomon's son was **Rehoboam**, Abijah his son, Asa his son,
2Ch 9: 31 David his father. And **Rehoboam** his son succeeded him as king.
10: 1 **Rehoboam** went to Shechem, for all the Israelites had gone there
10: 3 and he and all Israel went to **Rehoboam** and said to him:
10: 6 King **Rehoboam** consulted the elders who had served his father
10: 12 days later Jeroboam and all the people returned to **Rehoboam**,
10: 13 answered them harshly. Rejecting **[RPH]** the advice of the elders,
10: 17 were living in the towns of Judah, **Rehoboam** still ruled over them.
10: 18 King **Rehoboam** sent out Adoniram, who was in charge of forced
10: 18 King **Rehoboam**, however, managed to get into his chariot
11: 1 When **Rehoboam** arrived in Jerusalem, he mustered the house of
11: 1 make war against Israel and to regain the kingdom for **Rehoboam**.
11: 3 "Say to **Rehoboam** son of Solomon king of Judah and to all the
11: 5 **Rehoboam** lived in Jerusalem and built up towns for defense in
11: 17 of Judah and supported **Rehoboam** son of Solomon three years,
11: 18 **Rehoboam** married Mahalath, who was the daughter of David's
11: 21 **Rehoboam** loved Maacah daughter of Absalom more than any of
11: 22 **Rehoboam** appointed Abijah son of Maacah to be the chief prince
12: 1 After **Rehoboam's** position as king was established and he had
12: 2 of Egypt attacked Jerusalem in the fifth year of King **Rehoboam**.
12: 5 the prophet Shemaiah came to **Rehoboam** and to the leaders of
12: 10 So King **Rehoboam** made bronze shields to replace them
12: 13 King **Rehoboam** established himself firmly in Jerusalem
12: 13 **He**[s] was forty-one years old when he became king, and he reigned
12: 15 As for the events of **Rehoboam's** reign, from beginning to end,
12: 15 There was continual warfare between **Rehoboam** and Jeroboam.
12: 16 **Rehoboam** rested with his fathers and was buried in the City of
13: 7 and opposed **Rehoboam** son of Solomon when he was young
13: 7 and opposed Rehoboam son of Solomon when **he**[s] was young

8155 רְחֹבֹת עִיר *rᵉḥōbōt 'îr*, n.pr.loc. [1] [√ 8148 + 6551]
Rehoboth Ir [1]

Ge 10: 11 he went to Assyria, where he built Nineveh, **Rehoboth Ir**, Calah

8156 רְחוּם *rᵉḥûm*, n.pr.m. [4] [√ 8163; cf. 5700; Ar 10662]
Rehum [4]

Ezr 2: 2 Mordecai, Bilshan, Mispar, Bigvai, **Rehum** and Baanah):
Ne 3: 17 the repairs were made by the Levites under **Rehum** son of Bani.
10: 25 [10:26] **Rehum**, Hashabnah, Maaseiah,
12: 3 Shecaniah, **Rehum**, Meremoth,

8157 רַחוּם *raḥûm*, a. [13] [√ 8163]
compassionate [10], merciful [3]

Ex 34: 6 the LORD, the **compassionate** and gracious God, slow to anger,
Dt 4: 31 For the LORD your God is a **merciful** God; he will not abandon
2Ch 30: 9 for the LORD your God is gracious and **compassionate**.
Ne 9: 17 gracious and **compassionate**, slow to anger and abounding in love.
9: 31 or abandon them, for you are a gracious and **merciful** God.
Ps 78: 38 Yet he was **merciful**; he forgave their iniquities and did not
86: 15 But you, O Lord, are a **compassionate** and gracious God,
103: 8 The LORD is **compassionate** and gracious, slow to anger,
111: 4 to be remembered; the LORD is gracious and **compassionate**.
112: 4 for the gracious and **compassionate** and righteous man.
145: 8 The LORD is gracious and **compassionate**, slow to anger
Joel 2: 13 for he is gracious and **compassionate**, slow to anger
Jnh 4: 2 I knew that you are a gracious and **compassionate** God, slow to

8158 רָחוֹק *rāḥôq*, a. (used as noun). [85] [√ 8178; Ar 10663]
far [12], distant [11], afar [10], distance [10], far away [9], far away [+4946] [5], distant [+4946] [2], distant place [2], future [+4946] [2], long ago [+4200+4946] [2], long ago [+4946] [2], long way [2], at a distance [+4394] [1], away [1], beyond reach [1], beyond [1], far and wide [+4200+4946+6330] [1], far and wide [+6330] [1], far away [+4200+4946+6330] [1], far off [+928] [1], far off [1], far-off [1], farthest [1], long [+4946] [1], long way [+4394] [1], past [1], some distance away [+4946] [1], widely [1]

Ge 22: 4 third day Abraham looked up and saw the place in the **distance**.
37: 18 But they saw him in the **distance**, and before he reached them,
Ex 2: 4 His sister stood at a **distance** to see what would happen to him.
20: 18 in smoke, they trembled with fear. They stayed at a **distance**
20: 21 The people remained at a **distance**, while Moses approached the
24: 1 seventy of the elders of Israel. You are to worship at a **distance**,
Nu 9: 10 are unclean because of a dead body or are **away** on a journey,
Dt 13: 7 [13:8] gods of the peoples around you, whether near or **far**, from
20: 15 are to treat all the cities that are **at a distance** [+4394] from you
28: 49 The LORD will bring a nation against you from **far away**,
29: 22 [29:21] foreigners who come from **distant** lands will see the
30: 11 you today is not too difficult for you or **beyond** your **reach**.
Jos 3: 4 But keep a **distance** of about a thousand yards between you
9: 6 and the men of Israel, "We have come from a **distant** country;
9: 9 "Your servants have come from a very **distant** country because of
9: 22 'We live a **long** [+4394] **way** from you,' while actually you live
Jdg 18: 7 they lived a **long way** from the Sidonians and had no relationship
18: 28 no one to rescue them because they lived a **long way** from Sidon
1Sa 26: 13 and stood on top of the hill **some distance** [+4946] **away**;
2Sa 7: 19 you have also spoken about the **future** [+4946] of the house of
1Ki 8: 41 but has come from a **distant** land because of your name—
8: 46 who takes them captive to his own land, **far away** or near;
2Ki 2: 7 men of the company of the prophets went and stood at a **distance**,
19: 25 " 'Have you not heard? **Long** [+4200+4946] **ago** I ordained it.
20: 14 "From a **distant** land," Hezekiah replied. "They came from
1Ch 17: 17 you have spoken about the **future** [+4946] of the house of your
2Ch 6: 32 but has come from a **distant** land because of your great name
6: 36 to the enemy, who takes them captive to a land **far away** or near;
26: 15 His fame spread **far** [+4200+4946+6330] **and wide**, for he was
Ezr 3: 13 And the sound was heard **far** [+4200+4946+6330] **away**.
Ne 4: 19 [4:13] we are **widely** separated from each other along the wall.
12: 43 sound of rejoicing in Jerusalem could be heard **far** [+4946] **away**.
Est 9: 20 all the Jews throughout the provinces of King Xerxes, near and **far**,
Job 2: 12 When they saw him from a **distance**, they could hardly recognize
36: 3 I get my knowledge from **afar**; I will ascribe justice to my Maker.
36: 25 All mankind has seen it; men gaze on it from **afar**.
39: 25 He catches the scent of battle from **afar**, the shout of commanders
39: 29 From there he seeks out his food; his eyes detect it from **afar**.
Ps 10: 1 Why, O LORD, do you stand **far** [+928] **off**? Why do you hide
22: 1 [22:2] Why are you *so* **far** from saving me, so far from the words
38: 11 [38:12] of my wounds; my neighbors stay **far** [+4946] **away**.
56: T [56:1] To ˻the tune of˼ "A Dove on **Distant** Oaks." Of David.
65: 5 [65:6] hope of all the ends of the earth and of the **farthest** seas,
119: 155 Salvation is **far** from the wicked, for they do not seek out your
139: 2 when I sit and when I rise; you perceive my thoughts from **afar**.
Pr 7: 19 husband is not at home; he has gone on a **long** [+4946] journey.
15: 29 The LORD is **far** from the wicked but he hears the prayer of the
27: 10 strikes you—better a neighbor nearby than a brother **far away**.
31: 10 noble character who can find? She is worth **far** more than rubies.

Ecc 7: 23 and I said, "I am determined to be wise"—but this was **beyond** me.
7: 24 Whatever wisdom may be, it is **far off** and most profound—
Isa 5: 26 He lifts up a banner for the **distant** [+4946] nations, he whistles for
22: 3 having fled while the enemy was still **far** [+4946] **away**.
22: 11 or have regard for the One who planned it **long** [+4946] **ago**.
23: 7 old city, whose feet have taken her to settle in **far-off** lands?
25: 1 you have done marvelous things, things planned **long** [+4946] **ago**.
33: 13 You *who* are **far away**, hear what I have done; you who are near,
37: 26 "Have you not heard? **Long** [+4200+4946] **ago** I ordained it.
39: 3 did they come from?" "From a **distant** land," Hezekiah replied.
43: 6 Bring my sons from **afar** and my daughters from the ends of the
46: 12 you stubborn-hearted, you who are **far** from righteousness.
49: 1 Listen to me, you islands; hear this, you **distant** [+4946] nations:
49: 12 See, they will come from **afar**—some from the north, some from
57: 9 You sent your ambassadors **far** [+4946] **away**; you descended to
57: 19 Peace, peace, to those **far** and near," says the LORD. "And I will
59: 14 So justice is driven back, and righteousness stands at a **distance**;
60: 4 your sons come from **afar**, and your daughters are carried on the
60: 9 bringing your sons from **afar**, with their silver and gold,
66: 19 to the **distant** islands that have not heard of my fame or seen my
Jer 12: 2 bear fruit. You are always on their lips but **far** from their hearts.
23: 23 declares the LORD, "and not a God **far** [+4946] **away**?
25: 26 and all the kings of the north, near and **far**, one after the other—
30: 10 'I will surely save you out of a **distant place**, your descendants
31: 3 The LORD appeared to us in the **past**, saying: "I have loved you
46: 27 I will surely save you out of a **distant place**, your descendants
48: 24 to Kerioth and Bozrah—to all the towns of Moab, **far** and near.
51: 50 Remember the LORD in a **distant** *land*, and think on Jerusalem."
Eze 6: 12 He *that* is **far away** will die of the plague, and he that is near will
12: 27 many years from now, and he prophesies about the **distant** future.'
22: 5 Those who are near and those *who* are **far away** will mock you,
Da 9: 7 of Judah and people of Jerusalem and all Israel, both near and **far**,
Joel 3: 8 [4:8] and they will sell them to the Sabeans, a nation **far away**."
Mic 4: 3 and will settle disputes for strong nations **far** [+6330] **and wide**.
Hab 1: 8 Their cavalry gallops headlong; their horsemen come from **afar**.
Zec 6: 15 *Those who are* **far away** will come and help to build the temple of

8159 רָחִיט ***rāḥîṭ***, n.m. [0] [cf. 8112]

SS 1: 17 [of our house are cedars; our **rafters** [K; see Q 8112] are firs.]

8160 רֵחַיִם ***rēḥayim***, n.[m.]. [5]

millstones [2], hand mill [1], handmill [1], pair of millstones [1]

Ex 11: 5 to the firstborn son of the slave girl, who is at her **hand mill**,
Nu 11: 8 and then ground it in a **handmill** or crushed it in a mortar.
Dt 24: 6 Do not take a **pair of millstones**—not even the upper one—
Isa 47: 2 Take **millstones** and grind flour; take off your veil. Lift up your
Jer 25: 10 and bridegroom, the sound of **millstones** and the light of the lamp.

8161 רָחֵל ***rāḥēl¹***, n.f. [4] [→ 8162]

sheep [3], ewes [1]

Ge 31: 38 Your **sheep** and goats have not miscarried, nor have I eaten rams
32: 14 [32:15] twenty male goats, two hundred **ewes** and twenty rams,
SS 6: 6 Your teeth are like a flock of **sheep** coming up from the washing.
Isa 53: 7 as a **sheep** before her shearers is silent, so he did not open his

8162 רָחֵל ***rāḥēl²***, n.pr.f. [47] [√ 8161]

Rachel [40], Rachel's [5], her[s] [1], she[s] [1]

Ge 29: 6 they said, "and here comes his daughter **Rachel** with the sheep."
29: 9 **Rachel** came with her father's sheep, for she was a shepherdess.
29: 10 When Jacob saw **Rachel** daughter of Laban, his mother's brother,
29: 11 Then Jacob kissed **Rachel** and began to weep aloud.
29: 12 He had told **Rachel** that he was a relative of her father and a son of
29: 16 of the older was Leah, and the name of the younger was **Rachel**.
29: 17 Leah had weak eyes, but **Rachel** was lovely in form, and beautiful.
29: 18 Jacob was in love with **Rachel** and said, "I'll work for you seven
29: 18 for you seven years in return for your younger daughter **Rachel**."
29: 20 So Jacob served seven years to get **Rachel**, but they seemed like
29: 25 I served you for **Rachel**, didn't I? Why have you deceived me?"
29: 28 and then Laban gave him his daughter **Rachel** to be his wife.
29: 29 Laban gave his servant girl Bilhah to his daughter **Rachel** as her
29: 30 Jacob lay with **Rachel** also, and he loved Rachel more than Leah.
29: 30 Jacob lay with Rachel also, and he loved **Rachel** more than Leah.
29: 31 Leah was not loved, he opened her womb, but **Rachel** was barren.
30: 1 When **Rachel** saw that she was not bearing Jacob any children,
30: 1 not bearing Jacob any children, **she**[s] became jealous of her sister.
30: 2 Jacob became angry with **her**[s] and said, "Am I in the place of God,
30: 6 **Rachel** said, "God has vindicated me; he has listened to my plea
30: 7 **Rachel's** servant Bilhah conceived again and bore Jacob a second
30: 8 Then **Rachel** said, "I have had a great struggle with my sister,
30: 14 **Rachel** said to Leah, "Please give me some of your son's
30: 15 "Very well," **Rachel** said, "he can sleep with you tonight in return
30: 22 God remembered **Rachel**; he listened to her and opened her womb.
30: 25 After **Rachel** gave birth to Joseph, Jacob said to Laban, "Send me
31: 4 So Jacob sent word to **Rachel** and Leah to come out to the fields
31: 14 **Rachel** and Leah replied, "Do we still have any share in the
31: 19 gone to shear his sheep, **Rachel** stole her father's household gods.
31: 32 Now Jacob did not know that **Rachel** had stolen the gods.
31: 33 After he came out of Leah's tent, he entered **Rachel's** tent.
31: 34 Now **Rachel** had taken the household gods and put them inside her
33: 1 the children among Leah, **Rachel** and the two maidservants.
33: 2 Leah and her children next, and **Rachel** and Joseph in the rear.
33: 7 Last of all came Joseph and **Rachel**, and they too bowed down.
35: 16 from Ephrath, **Rachel** began to give birth and had great difficulty.
35: 19 So **Rachel** died and was buried on the way to Ephrath (that is,
35: 20 set up a pillar, and to this day that pillar marks **Rachel's** tomb.
35: 24 The sons of **Rachel**: Joseph and Benjamin.
35: 25 The sons of **Rachel's** maidservant Bilhah: Dan and Naphtali.
46: 19 The sons of Jacob's wife **Rachel**: Joseph and Benjamin.
46: 22 These were the sons of **Rachel** who were born to Jacob—fourteen
46: 25 Jacob by Bilhah, whom Laban had given to his daughter **Rachel**—
48: 7 to my sorrow **Rachel** died in the land of Canaan while we were
Ru 4: 11 make the woman who is coming into your home like **Rachel**
1Sa 10: 2 you leave me today, you will meet two men near **Rachel's** tomb,
Jer 31: 15 **Rachel** weeping for her children and refusing to be comforted,

8163 רָחַם ***rāḥam***, v.den. [47] [→ 3736, 3737, 3738, 8020?, 8156, 8157, 8172; cf. 8167]

have compassion [15], compassion [4], has compassion [4], show love [4], mercy [3], show compassion [3], have great compassion [+8163] [2], have mercy [2], loved [2], show mercy [2], find compassion [1], finds mercy [1], full of compassion [1], had compassion [1], love [1], pity [1]

Ex 33: 19 [D] *I will* **have compassion** *on* whom I will have compassion.
33: 19 [D] I will have compassion on whom *I will* **have compassion**.
Dt 13: 17 [13:18] [D] he will show you mercy, **have compassion** *on* you,
30: 3 [D] God will restore your fortunes and **have compassion** *on* you
1Ki 8: 50 [D] and cause their conquerors *to* **show** them **mercy**;
2Ki 13: 23 [D] to them and **had compassion** and showed concern for them
Ps 18: 1 [18:2] [A] *I* **love** you, O LORD, my strength.
102: 13 [102:14] [D] You will arise and **have compassion** *on* Zion,
103: 13 [D] As a father **has compassion** on his children, so the LORD
103: 13 [D] so the LORD **has compassion** on those who fear him;
116: 5 [D] is gracious and righteous; our God *is* **full of compassion**.
Pr 28: 13 [E] but whoever confesses and renounces them **finds mercy**.
Isa 9: 17 [9:16] [D] nor *will he* **pity** the fatherless and widows, for
13: 18 [D] *they will* **have** no **mercy** *on* infants nor will they look with
14: 1 [D] The LORD *will* **have compassion** *on* Jacob; once again he
27: 11 [D] so their Maker *has* no **compassion** *on* them, and their
30: 18 [D] to be gracious to you; he rises to **show** you **compassion**.
49: 10 [D] *He who* **has compassion** *on* them will guide them and lead
49: 13 [D] his people and *will have* **compassion** *on* his afflicted ones.
49: 15 [D] and **have** no **compassion** *on* the child she has borne?
54: 8 [D] with everlasting kindness *I will* **have compassion** *on* you,"
54: 10 [D] says the LORD, *who* **has compassion** *on* you.
55: 7 [D] *he will* **have mercy** *on* him, and to our God, for he will
60: 10 [D] in anger I struck you, in favor *I will* **show** you **compassion**.
Jer 6: 23 [D] with bow and spear; they are cruel and **show** no **mercy**.
12: 15 [D] I will again **have compassion** and will bring each of them
13: 14 [D] or **compassion** to keep me from destroying them.' "
21: 7 [D] he will show them no mercy or pity or **compassion**.'
30: 18 [D] of Jacob's tents and **have compassion** *on* his dwellings;
31: 20 [D] *I* **have great compassion** [+8163] *for* him,"
31: 20 [D] *I* **have great compassion for** [+8163] him,"
33: 26 [D] will restore their fortunes and **have compassion** *on* them.' "
42: 12 [D] you compassion so that *he will* **have compassion** *on* you
50: 42 [D] with bows and spears; they are cruel and without **mercy**.
La 3: 32 [D] Though he brings grief, *he will* **show compassion**, so great is
Eze 39: 25 [D] and *will* **have compassion** *on* all the people of Israel,
Hos 1: 6 [D] for *I will* no longer **show love** *to* the house of Israel,
1: 7 [D] Yet *I will* **show love** *to* the house of Judah; and I will save
2: 1 [2:3] [E] 'My people,' and of your sisters, 'My **loved** *one*.'
2: 4 [2:6] [D] *I will* not **show** *my* **love** to her children, because they
2: 23 [2:25] [D] *I will* **show** *my* **love** to the one I called 'Not my loved
2: 23 [2:25] [E] show my love to the one I called 'Not my **loved** *one*.'
14: 3 [14:4] [E] for in you the fatherless **find compassion**."
Mic 7: 19 [D] You will again **have compassion** *on* us; you will tread our
Hab 3: 2 [D] in our time make them known; in wrath remember **mercy**.
Zec 1: 12 [D] how long *will* you withhold **mercy** *from* Jerusalem and *from*
10: 6 [D] I will restore them because *I* **have compassion** *on* them.

8164 רָחָם ***rāḥām***, n.[m.]. [1] [→ 8165, 8168]

osprey [1]

Lev 11: 18 the white owl, the desert owl, the **osprey**,

8165 ¹רַחַם *raḥam*^{1}, n.pr.m. [1] [√ 8164]
Raham [1]
1Ch 2: 44 Shema was the father of **Raham**, and Raham the father of

8166 ²רַחַם *raḥam*^{2}, n.m. Not used in NIV/BHS [√ 8167]

8167 רֶחֶם *reḥem*, n.m. [31] [→ 8166, 8169, 8171; cf. 8163]
womb [20], birth [4], born [+3655+4946] [1], first male offspring [+1147+7081] [1], firstborn [+7081] [1], girl [1], mothers [1], woman [1], wombs [1]
Ge 20: 18 for the LORD had closed up every **womb** in Abimelech's
29: 31 Leah was not loved, he opened her **womb**, but Rachel was barren.
30: 22 God remembered Rachel; he listened to her and opened her **womb**.
49: 25 of the deep that lies below, blessings of the breast and **womb**.
Ex 13: 2 The first offspring of every **womb** among the Israelites belongs to
13: 12 are to give over to the LORD the first offspring of every **womb**.
13: 15 I sacrifice to the LORD the first male offspring of every **womb**
34: 19 "The first offspring of every **womb** belongs to me, including all
Nu 3: 12 the **first male offspring** [+1147+7081] of every Israelite woman.
8: 16 the firstborn, the first male offspring from every Israelite **woman**.
12: 12 coming from its mother's **womb** with its flesh half eaten away."
18: 15 The first offspring of every **womb**, both man and animal, that is
Jdg 5: 30 a **girl** or two for each man, colorful garments as plunder for Sisera,
1Sa 1: 5 because he loved her, and the LORD had closed her **womb**.
1: 6 because the LORD had closed her **womb**, her rival kept
Job 3: 11 "Why did I not perish at **birth**, and die as I came from the womb?
10: 18 "Why then did you bring me out of the **womb**? I wish I had died
24: 20 The **womb** forgets them, the worm feasts on them; evil men are no
31: 15 Did not the same one form us both within our **mothers**?
38: 8 shut up the sea behind doors when it burst forth from the **womb**,
Ps 22: 10 [22:11] From **birth** I was cast upon you; from my mother's womb
58: 3 [58:4] Even from **birth** the wicked go astray; from the womb they
110: 3 from the **womb** *of* the dawn you will receive the dew of your
Pr 30: 16 the grave, the barren **womb**, land, which is never satisfied with
Isa 46: 3 since you were conceived, and have carried since your **birth**.
Jer 1: 5 I knew you, before *you were* **born** [+3655+4946] I set you apart;
20: 17 For he did not kill me in the **womb**, with my mother as my grave,
20: 17 with my mother as my grave, her **womb** enlarged forever.
20: 18 Why did I ever come out of the **womb** to see trouble and sorrow
Eze 20: 26 the sacrifice of every **firstborn** [+7081]—that I might fill them
Hos 9: 14 Give them **wombs** that miscarry and breasts that are dry.

8168 רָחָמָה *rāḥāmâ*, n.[m.]. [1] [√ 8164]
osprey [1]
Dt 14: 17 the desert owl, the **osprey**, the cormorant,

8169 רַחֲמָה *raḥ^{a}mâ*, n.f. [1] [√ 8167]
two^{s} [1]
Jdg 5: 30 a girl or **two**^{s} for each man, colorful garments as plunder for

8170 רֻחָמָה *ruḥāmâ*, n.pr.f. Not used in NIV/BHS [→ 4205]

8171 רַחֲמִים *raḥ^{a}mîm*, n.m.pl.abst. [39] [√ 8167; Ar 10664]
compassion [18], mercy [11], *untranslated* [1], compassions [1], deeply moved [+4023] [1], favor [1], great mercy [1], kindest acts [1], merciful [1], pitied [1], pity [1], sympathy [1]
Ge 43: 14 may God Almighty grant you **mercy** before the man so that he will
43: 30 **Deeply moved** [+4023] at the sight of his brother, Joseph hurried
Dt 13: 17 [13:18] he will show you **mercy**, have compassion on you,
2Sa 24: 14 Let us fall into the hands of the LORD, for his **mercy** is great;
1Ki 3: 26 The woman whose son was alive was filled with **compassion** for
8: 50 and cause **[RPH]** their conquerors to show them mercy;
1Ch 21: 13 me fall into the hands of the LORD, for his **mercy** is very great;
2Ch 30: 9 and your children will be shown **compassion** by their captors
Ne 1: 11 Give your servant success today by granting him **favor** in the
9: 19 "Because of your great **compassion** you did not abandon them in
9: 27 and in your great **compassion** you gave them deliverers,
9: 28 and in your **compassion** you delivered them time after time.
9: 31 in your great **mercy** you did not put an end to them or abandon
Ps 25: 6 Remember, O LORD, your **great mercy** and love, for they are
40: 11 [40:12] Do not withhold your **mercy** from me, O LORD;
51: 1 [51:3] according to your great **compassion** blot out my
69: 16 [69:17] goodness of your love; in your great **mercy** turn to me.
77: 9 [77:10] Has he in anger withheld his **compassion**?" *Selah*
79: 8 may your **mercy** come quickly to meet us, for we are in desperate
103: 4 your life from the pit and crowns you with love and **compassion**,
106: 46 He caused them to be **pitied** by all who held them captive.
119: 77 Let your **compassion** come to me that I may live, for your law is
119: 156 Your **compassion** is great, O LORD; preserve my life according
145: 9 The LORD is good to all; he has **compassion** on all he has made.
Pr 12: 10 needs of his animal, but the **kindest acts** *of* the wicked are cruel.
Isa 47: 6 I gave them into your hand, and you showed them no **mercy**.
54: 7 I abandoned you, but with deep **compassion** I will bring you back.
63: 7 house of Israel, according to his **compassion** and many kindnesses.
63: 15 Your tenderness and **compassion** are withheld from us.
Jer 16: 5 my love and my **pity** from this people," declares the LORD.
42: 12 I will show you **compassion** so that he will have compassion on
La 3: 22 great love we are not consumed, for his **compassions** never fail.
Da 1: 9 had caused the official to show favor and **sympathy** to Daniel,
9: 9 The Lord our God is **merciful** and forgiving, even though we have
9: 18 because we are righteous, but because of your great **mercy**.
Hos 2: 19 [2:21] you in righteousness and justice, in love and **compassion**.
Am 1: 11 stifling *all* **compassion**, because his anger raged continually
Zec 1: 16 'I will return to Jerusalem with **mercy**, and there my house will be
7: 9 true justice; show mercy and **compassion** to one another.

8172 רַחֲמָנִי *raḥ^{a}mānî*, a. [1] [√ 8163]
compassionate [1]
La 4: 10 With their own hands **compassionate** women have cooked their

8173 ¹רָחַף *rāḥap*^{1}, v. [3]
hovering [1], hovers [1], tremble [1]
Ge 1: 2 [D] and the Spirit of God *was* **hovering** over the waters.
Dt 32: 11 [D] like an eagle that stirs up its nest and **hovers** over its young,
Jer 23: 9 [A] My heart is broken within me; all my bones **tremble**. I am

8174 ²רָחַף *rāḥap*^{2}, v. Not used in NIV/BHS

8175 רָחַץ *rāḥaṣ*, v. [72 / 73] [→ 8176, 8177]
bathe [25], wash [23], washed [10], bathed [4], washing [4], are cleansed [1], bathing [1], drenched [1], plunge [1], wash away [1], washed myself [1], were washed [1]
Ge 18: 4 [A] and then *you may all* **wash** your feet and rest under this tree.
19: 2 [A] *You can* **wash** your feet and spend the night and then go on
24: 32 [A] the camels, and water for him and his men to **wash** their feet.
43: 24 [A] gave them water *to* **wash** their feet and provided fodder for
43: 31 [A] After *he had* **washed** his face, he came out and,
Ex 2: 5 [A] Then Pharaoh's daughter went down to the Nile to **bathe**,
29: 4 [A] entrance to the Tent of Meeting and **wash** them with water.
29: 17 [A] Cut the ram into pieces and **wash** the inner parts and the legs,
30: 18 [A] "Make a bronze basin, with its bronze stand, for **washing**.
30: 19 [A] his sons *are to* **wash** their hands and feet with water from it.
30: 20 [A] *they shall* **wash** *with* water so that they will not die.
30: 21 [A] *they shall* **wash** their hands and feet so that they will not die.
40: 12 [A] entrance to the Tent of Meeting and **wash** them with water.
40: 30 [A] Tent of Meeting and the altar and put water in it for **washing**,
40: 31 [A] and Aaron and his sons used it *to* **wash** their hands and feet.
40: 32 [A] *They* **washed** whenever they entered the Tent of Meeting
Lev 1: 9 [A] *He is to* **wash** the inner parts and the legs with water,
1: 13 [A] *He is to* **wash** the inner parts and the legs with water,
8: 6 [A] and his sons forward and **washed** them with water.
8: 21 [A] *He* **washed** the inner parts and the legs with water
9: 14 [A] *He* **washed** the inner parts and the legs and burned them on
14: 8 [A] wash his clothes, shave off all his hair and **bathe** with water;
14: 9 [A] He must wash his clothes and **bathe** himself with water,
15: 5 [A] touches his bed must wash his clothes and **bathe** with water,
15: 6 [A] discharge sat on must wash his clothes and **bathe** with water,
15: 7 [A] has a discharge must wash his clothes and **bathe** with water,
15: 8 [A] that person must wash his clothes and **bathe** with water,
15: 10 [A] up those things must wash his clothes and **bathe** with water,
15: 11 [A] with water must wash his clothes and **bathe** with water,
15: 13 [A] he must wash his clothes and **bathe** himself with fresh water,
15: 16 [A] *he must* **bathe** his whole body with water, and he will be
15: 18 [A] there is an emission of semen, *both must* **bathe** with water,
15: 21 [A] touches her bed must wash his clothes and **bathe** with water,
15: 22 [A] she sits on must wash his clothes and **bathe** with water,
15: 27 [A] he must wash his clothes and **bathe** with water, and he will
16: 4 [A] so *he must* **bathe** himself with water before he puts them on.
16: 24 [A] *He shall* **bathe** himself with water in a holy place and put on
16: 26 [A] must wash his clothes and **bathe** himself with water;
16: 28 [A] them must wash his clothes and **bathe** himself with water;
17: 15 [A] by wild animals must wash his clothes and **bathe** with water,
17: 16 [A] if he does not wash his clothes and **bathe** himself, he will be
22: 6 [A] sacred offerings unless *he has* **bathed** himself with water.
Nu 19: 7 [A] priest must wash his clothes and **bathe** himself with water.
19: 8 [A] burns it must also wash his clothes and **bathe** with water,
19: 19 [A] being cleansed must wash his clothes and **bathe** with water,
Dt 21: 6 [A] all the elders of the town nearest the body *shall* **wash** their
23: 11 [23:12] [A] as evening approaches *he is to* **wash** *himself*, and at
Jdg 19: 21 [A] After *they had* **washed** their feet, they had something to eat
Ru 3: 3 [A] **Wash** and perfume yourself, and put on your best clothes.

[A] Qal [B] Qal passive [C] Niphal [D] Piel (poel, polel, pilel, pilal, pealal, pilpel) [E] Pual (poal, polal, poalal, pulal, pualal)

1Sa 25:41 [A] to serve you and **wash** the feet of my master's servants."
2Sa 11: 2 [A] From the roof he saw a woman **bathing**. The woman was
11: 8 [A] said to Uriah, "Go down to your house and **wash** your feet."
12:20 [A] After *he had* **washed**, put on lotions and changed his clothes,
1Ki 22:38 [A] chariot at a pool in Samaria (where the prostitutes **bathed**),
2Ki 5:10 [A] "Go, **wash** *yourself* seven times in the Jordan, and your flesh
5:12 [A] Couldn't *I* **wash** in them and be cleansed?" So he turned
5:13 [A] then, when he tells you, '**Wash** and be cleansed'!"
2Ch 4: 6 [A] He then made ten basins for **washing** and placed five on the
4: 6 [A] but the Sea was to be used by the priests for **washing**.
Job 9:30 [F] Even if *I* **washed myself** with soap and my hands with
29: 6 [A] when my path *was* **drenched** with cream and the rock
Ps 26: 6 [A] *I* **wash** my hands in innocence, and go about your altar,
58:10 [58:11] [A] *they* **bathe** their feet in the blood of the wicked.
68:23 [68:24] [a] that *you may* **plunge** [BHS 4730] your feet in the
73:13 [A] heart pure; in vain *have I* **washed** my hands in innocence.
Pr 30:12 [E] pure in their own eyes and yet **are** not **cleansed** of their filth;
SS 5: 3 [A] it on again? *I have* **washed** my feet—must I soil them again?
5:12 [A] by the water streams, **washed** in milk, mounted like jewels.
Isa 1:16 [A] **wash** and make yourselves clean. Take your evil deeds out of
4: 4 [A] The Lord *will* **wash away** the filth of the women of Zion;
Eze 16: 4 [E] nor **were** *you* **washed** with water to make you clean, nor
16: 9 [A] " '*I* **bathed** you with water and washed the blood from you
23:40 [A] when they arrived *you* **bathed** *yourself* for them,

8176 רַחַץ *raḥaṣ*, n.[m.]. [2] [√ 8175]

washbasin [+6105] [2]

Ps 60: 8 [60:10] Moab is my **washbasin** [+6105], upon Edom I toss my
108: 9 [108:10] Moab is my **washbasin** [+6105], upon Edom I toss my

8177 רַחְצָה *raḥṣâ*, n.f. [2] [√ 8175]

washing [2]

SS 4: 2 are like a flock of sheep just shorn, coming up from the **washing**.
6: 6 Your teeth are like a flock of sheep coming up from the **washing**.

8178 רָחַק *rāḥaq*, v. [58] [→ 1092, 3439, 5305, 8158, 8179]

far [12], far away [7], drive far [3], keep far [3], must very far [+8178] [2], put away [2], remove far [2], sent far away [2], stand aloof [2], taken [2], alienated [1], avoid [1], away [1], distance away [1], extended [1], extending [1], far off [1], far removed [1], go far [1], gone some distance [1], have nothing to do [1], is severed [1], keep distance [1], no near [1], refrain [1], send far [1], some distance away [+4946] [1], stays far [1], strayed far [1], went far [1], withdraw far [1]

Ge 21:16 [G] and sat down nearby, about a bowshot **away**, for she thought,
44: 4 [G] They had not gone **far** from the city when Joseph said to his
Ex 8:28 [8:24] [G] in the desert, but *you* **must** not go **very far** [+8178].
8:28 [8:24] [G] in the desert, but *you* **must** not go **very far** [+8178].
23: 7 [A] **Have nothing to do** with a false charge and do not put an
33: 7 [G] and pitch it outside the camp **some distance** [+4946] **away**,
Dt 12:21 [A] your God chooses to put his Name *is too* **far away** from you,
14:24 [A] the LORD will choose to put his Name *is so* **far away**),
Jos 3:16 [G] It piled up in a heap a great **distance away**, at a town called
8: 4 [G] the city. Don't **go** very **far** from it. All of you be on the alert.
Jdg 18:22 [G] When they *had* **gone some distance** from Micah's house,
Job 5: 4 [A] His children *are* **far** from safety, crushed in court without a
11:14 [G] if *you* **put away** the sin that is in your hand and allow no evil
13:21 [G] **Withdraw** your hand **far** from me, and stop frightening me
19:13 [G] "*He has* **alienated** my brothers from me; my acquaintances
21:16 [A] own hands, so I **stand aloof** from the counsel of the wicked.
22:18 [A] good things, so I **stand aloof** from the counsel of the wicked.
22:23 [G] be restored: If *you* **remove** wickedness **far** from your tent
30:10 [A] They detest me and **keep** *their* **distance**; they do not hesitate
Ps 22:11 [22:12] [A] *Do* not *be* **far** from me, for trouble is near and there
22:19 [22:20] [A] you, O LORD, *be* not **far off**; O my Strength,
35:22 [A] have seen this; be not silent. *Do* not *be* **far** from me, O Lord.
38:21 [38:22] [A] do not forsake me; *be* not **far** from me, O my God.
55: 7 [55:8] [G] *I would* flee **far away** and stay in the desert;
71:12 [A] *Be* not **far** from me, O God; come quickly, O my God,
88: 8 [88:9] [G] *You have* **taken** from me my closest friends
88:18 [88:19] [G] *You have* **taken** my companions and loved ones
103:12 [A] as **far** as the east *is* from the west, so far has he removed our
103:12 [G] the west, *so* **far** *has he* **removed** our transgressions from us.
109:17 [A] He found no pleasure in blessing—*may it be* **far** from him.
119:150 [A] wicked schemes are near, but *they are* **far** from your law.
Pr 4:24 [G] from your mouth; **keep** corrupt talk **far** from your lips.
5: 8 [G] **Keep** *to* a path **far** from her, do not go near the door of her
19: 7 [A] all his relatives—how much more *do* his friends **avoid** him!
22: 5 [A] and snares, but he who guards his soul **stays far** from them.
22:15 [G] of a child, but the rod of discipline *will* **drive** it **far** from him.
30: 8 [G] **Keep** falsehood and lies **far** from me; give me neither
Ecc 3: 5 [A] time to gather them, a time to embrace and a time to **refrain**,
12: 6 [C] before the silver cord **is severed**, [Q 8415] or the golden
Isa 6:12 [D] until the LORD *has* **sent** everyone **far away** and the land is
26:15 [D] for yourself; *you have* **extended** all the borders of the land.
29:13 [D] honor me with their lips, but their hearts *are* **far** from me.
46:13 [A] I am bringing my righteousness near, *it is* not **far away**;
49:19 [A] your people, and those who devoured you *will be* **far away**.
54:14 [A] Tyranny *will be* **far** from *you*; you will have nothing to fear.
59: 9 [A] So justice *is* **far** from us, and righteousness does not reach
59:11 [A] for justice, but find none; for deliverance, but *it is* **far away**.
Jer 2: 5 [A] your fathers find in me, that *they* **strayed** *so* **far** from me?
27:10 [G] you that *will only serve to* **remove** you **far** from your lands;
La 1:16 [A] **No** *one is* **near** to comfort me, no one to restore my spirit.
Eze 8: 6 [A] doing here, things that *will* **drive** me **far** from my sanctuary?
11:15 [A] Jerusalem have said, '*They are* **far away** from the LORD;
11:16 [G] Although *I* **sent** them **far away** among the nations
43: 9 [D] Now *let them* **put away** from me their prostitution
44:10 [A] " 'The Levites who **went far** from me when Israel went
Joel 2:20 [G] "*I will* **drive** the northern army **far** from you, pushing it into
3: 6 [4:6] [G] that *you might* **send** them **far** from their homeland.
Mic 7:11 [A] walls will come, the day *for* **extending** your boundaries.

8179 רָחֵק *rāḥēq*, a.vbl. [1] [√ 8178]

far [1]

Ps 73:27 *Those who* are **far** *from* you will perish; you destroy all who are

8180 רָחַשׁ *rāḥaš*, v. [1] [→ 5306]

stirred [1]

Ps 45: 1 [45:2] [A] My heart *is* **stirred** *by* a noble theme as I recite my

8181 רַחַת *raḥat*, n.f. [1]

fork [1]

Isa 30:24 the soil will eat fodder and mash, spread out with **fork** and shovel.

8182 רָטַב *rāṭab*, v. [1] [→ 8183]

drenched [1]

Job 24: 8 [A] *They are* **drenched** by mountain rains and hug the rocks for

8183 רָטֹב *rāṭōb*, a. [1] [√ 8182]

well-watered plant [1]

Job 8:16 He is like a **well-watered plant** in the sunshine, spreading its

8184 רָטָה *rāṭâ*, v. Not used in NIV/BHS

8185 רֶטֶט *reṭeṭ*, n.[m.]. [1] [cf. 8417]

panic [1]

Jer 49:24 become feeble, she has turned to flee and **panic** has gripped her;

8186 רֻטֲפַשׁ *ruṭᵃpaš*, v. [1]

is renewed [1]

Job 33:25 [B] his flesh **is renewed** like a child's; it is restored as in the days

8187 רָטַשׁ *rāṭaš*, v. [6]

be dashed to pieces [1], be dashed to the ground [1], dash to the ground [1], strike down [1], were dashed to pieces [1], were dashed to the ground [1]

2Ki 8:12 [D] men with the sword, **dash** their little children **to the ground**,
Isa 13:16 [E] Their infants *will* **be dashed to pieces** before their eyes;
13:18 [D] Their bows *will* **strike down** the young men; they will have
Hos 10:14 [E] when mothers **were dashed to the ground** with their
13:16 [14:1] [E] their little ones *will* **be dashed to the ground**, their
Na 3:10 [E] Her infants **were dashed to pieces** at the head of every street.

8188 רִי *rî*, n.[m.]. [1] [√ 8115]

moisture [1]

Job 37:11 He loads the clouds with **moisture**; he scatters his lightning

8189 רִיב¹ *rîb¹*, v. [68] [→ 3384, 3424, 3742, 5310, 5311, 5312, 5313, 5315, 8190, 8191]

quarreled [7], bring charges [6], contend [4], defend [4], accuse [3], rebuked [3], complain [2], quarrel [+8189] [2], quarrel [2], rebuke [2], take up [2], vigorously defend [+906+8189] [2], accused [1], argue the case [1], argue [1], bring a case [1], bring a charge [1], charges [1], contended [1], contends [1], criticized [1], defender [1], defends cause [1], defends [1], dispute [1], fights [1], in court [1], judgment [1], oppose [+6643] [1], oppose [1], plead case [1], plead cause [1], plead the case [1], plead [1], pleads [1], quarrels [1], took to task [1], took up [1], upheld [1], uphold cause [1], uphold [1]

Ge 26:20 [A] But the herdsmen of Gerar **quarreled** with Isaac's herdsmen
26:21 [A] they dug another well, but *they* **quarreled** over that one also;
26:22 [A] and dug another well, and no *one* **quarreled** over it.
31:36 [A] Jacob was angry and **took** Laban **to task**. "What is my
Ex 17:2 [A] So they **quarreled** with Moses and said, "Give us water to
17:2 [A] to drink." Moses replied, "Why *do you* **quarrel** with me?
17:7 [A] and Meribah because the Israelites **quarreled** and
21:18 [A] "If men **quarrel** and one hits the other with a stone or with
Nu 20:3 [A] They **quarreled** with Moses and said, "If only we had died
20:13 [A] where the Israelites **quarreled** with the LORD and where
Dt 33:7 [A] With his own hands *he* **defends** his **cause**. Oh, be his help
33:8 [A] *you* **contended** *with* him at the waters of Meribah.
Jdg 6:31 [A] crowd around him, "*Are* you *going to* **plead** Baal's **cause**?
6:31 [A] Whoever **fights** for him shall be put to death by morning!
6:31 [A] *he can* **defend** himself when someone breaks down his
6:32 [A] saying, "*Let* Baal **contend** with him," because he broke
8:1 [A] you went to fight Midian?" And *they* **criticized** him sharply.
11:25 [A] *Did he ever* **quarrel** [+8189] with Israel or fight with them?
11:25 [A] *Did he ever* **quarrel** [+8189] with Israel or fight with them?
21:22 [A] When their fathers or brothers **complain** to us, we will say to
1Sa 2:10 [G] *those who* **oppose** the LORD will be shattered. He will
24:15 [24:16] [A] May he consider my cause and **uphold** it; may he
25:39 [A] who *has* **upheld** my cause against Nabal for treating me with
Ne 5:7 [A] them in my mind and then **accused** the nobles and officials.
13:11 [A] So *I* **rebuked** the officials and asked them, "Why is the
13:17 [A] *I* **rebuked** the nobles of Judah and said to them, "What is
13:25 [A] *I* **rebuked** them and called curses down on them. I beat some
Job 9:3 [A] Though one wished to **dispute** with him, he could not answer
10:2 [A] but tell me what **charges** *you have against* me.
13:8 [A] you show him partiality? *Will you* **argue the case** for God?
13:19 [A] *Can* anyone **bring charges** against me? If so, I will be silent
23:6 [A] *Would he* **oppose** [+6643] me with great power? No, he
33:13 [A] Why *do you* **complain** to him that he answers none of man's
40:2 [A] "*Will* the *one who* **contends** with the Almighty correct him?
Ps 35:1 [A] **Contend**, O LORD, with those who contend with me;
43:1 [A] O God, and **plead** my cause against an ungodly nation;
74:22 [A] Rise up, O God, and **defend** your cause; remember how fools
103:9 [A] *He will* not always **accuse**, nor will he harbor his anger
119:154 [A] **Defend** my cause and redeem me; preserve my life according
Pr 3:30 [A] *Do* not **accuse** a man for no reason—when he has done you
22:23 [A] for the LORD *will* **take up** their case and will plunder those
23:11 [A] Defender is strong; he *will* **take up** their case against you.
25:9 [A] If you **argue** your case with a neighbor, do not betray
Isa 1:17 [A] the cause of the fatherless, **plead the case** *of* the widow.
3:13 [A] The LORD takes his place **in court**; he rises to judge the
19:20 [A] he will send them a savior and **defender**, and he will rescue
27:8 [A] By warfare and exile *you* **contend** *with* her—with his fierce
34:8 [A] of vengeance, a year of retribution, to **uphold** Zion's **cause**.
45:9 [A] "Woe to *him who* **quarrels** with his Maker, to him who is
49:25 [A] I *will* **contend** with those who contend with you, and your
50:8 [A] Who then *will* **bring charges** against me? Let us face each
51:22 [A] Sovereign LORD says, your God, *who* **defends** his people:
57:16 [A] *I will* not **accuse** forever, nor will I always be angry, for
Jer 2:9 [A] "Therefore *I* **bring charges** against you again,"
2:9 [A] "And *I will* **bring charges** against your children's children.
2:29 [A] "Why *do you* **bring charges** against me? You have all
12:1 [A] O LORD, when *I* **bring a case** before you.
50:34 [A] *He will* **vigorously defend** [+906+8189] their cause so that
50:34 [A] *He will* **vigorously defend** [+906+8189] their cause so that
51:36 [A] "See, I *will* **defend** your cause and avenge you; I will dry up
La 3:58 [A] O Lord, *you* **took up** my case; you redeemed my life.
Hos 2:2 [2:4] [A] "**Rebuke** your mother, rebuke her, for she is not my
2:2 [2:4] [A] "Rebuke your mother, **rebuke** her, for she is not my
4:4 [A] "But *let* no man **bring a charge**, let no man accuse another,
4:4 [G] for your people are like *those who* **bring charges** *against* a
Am 7:4 [A] The Sovereign LORD was calling for **judgment** by fire;
Mic 6:1 [A] "Stand up, **plead** *your* **case** *before* the mountains; let the
7:9 [A] until *he* **pleads** my case and establishes my right.

8190 ²רִיב *rîb²*, n.m. [59 / 60] [√ 8189]

case [11], cause [9], strife [7], dispute [4], attacks [2], charge [2], complaint [2], disputes [2], lawsuit [2], quarrel [2], quarreling [2], accusation [1], accuser [+408] [1], accusing [1], cases of dispute [1], charges [1], contend [1], court [1], distress [1], grievance [1], justice [1], lawsuits [1], oppose [1], strives [1], struggle [1], taunts [1]

Ge 13:7 **quarreling** arose between Abram's herdsmen and the herdsmen of
Ex 23:2 When you give testimony in a **lawsuit**, do not pervert justice by
23:3 and do not show favoritism to a poor man in his **lawsuit**.
23:6 "Do not deny justice to your poor people in their **lawsuits**.
Dt 1:12 your problems and your burdens and your **disputes** all by myself?
19:17 the two men involved in the **dispute** must stand in the presence of
21:5 name of the LORD and to decide all **cases of dispute** and assault.
25:1 When men have a **dispute**, they are to take it to court
Jdg 12:2 my people were engaged in a great **struggle** with the Ammonites,
1Sa 24:15 [24:16] May he consider my **cause** and uphold it; may he
25:39 who has upheld my **cause** against Nabal for treating me with
2Sa 15:2 Whenever anyone came with a **complaint** to be placed before the
15:4 Then everyone who has a **complaint** or case could come to me
22:44 "You have delivered me from the **attacks** *of* my people; you have
2Ch 19:8 families to administer the law of the LORD and to settle **disputes**.
19:10 In every **case** that comes before you from your fellow countrymen
Job 29:16 I was a father to the needy; I took up the **case** of the stranger.
31:13 and maidservants when they had a **grievance** against me,
31:35 let the Almighty answer me; let my **accuser** [+408] put his
33:19 on a bed of pain with constant **distress** [Q 8044] *in* his bones,
Ps 18:43 [18:44] You have delivered me from the **attacks** *of* the people;
31:20 [31:21] in your dwelling you keep them safe from **accusing**
35:23 and rise to my defense! **Contend** *for* me, my God and Lord.
43:1 O God, and plead my **cause** against an ungodly nation;
55:9 [55:10] their speech, for I see violence and **strife** in the city.
74:22 Rise up, O God, and defend your **cause**; remember how fools
89:50 [89:51] how I bear in my heart the **taunts** [BHS 8041] *of* all the
119:154 Defend my **cause** and redeem me; preserve my life according to
Pr 15:18 man stirs up dissension, but a patient man calms a **quarrel**.
17:1 crust with peace and quiet than a house full of feasting, with **strife**.
17:14 breaching a dam; so drop the matter before a **dispute** breaks out.
18:6 A fool's lips bring him **strife**, and his mouth invites a beating.
18:17 The first to present his **case** seems right, till another comes forward
20:3 It is to a man's honor to avoid **strife**, but every fool is quick to
22:23 for the LORD will take up their **case** and will plunder those who
23:11 for their Defender is strong; he will take up their **case** against you.
25:8 do not bring hastily to **court**, for what will you do in the end if
25:9 If you argue your **case** with a neighbor, do not betray another
26:17 by the ears is a passer-by who meddles in a **quarrel** not his own.
26:21 and as wood to fire, so is a quarrelsome man for kindling **strife**.
30:33 the nose produces blood, so stirring up anger produces **strife**."
Isa 1:23 of the fatherless; the widow's **case** does not come before them.
41:11 those who **oppose** you will be as nothing and perish.
41:21 "Present your **case**," says the LORD. "Set forth your arguments,"
58:4 Your fasting ends in **quarreling** and strife, and in striking each
Jer 11:20 your vengeance upon them, for to you I have committed my **cause**.
15:10 me birth, a man with whom the whole land **strives** and contends!
20:12 your vengeance upon them, for to you I have committed my **cause**.
25:31 of the earth, for the LORD will bring **charges** against the nations;
50:34 He will vigorously defend their **cause** so that he may bring rest to
51:36 "See, I will defend your **cause** and avenge you; I will dry up her
La 3:36 to deprive a man of **justice**—would not the Lord see such things?
3:58 O Lord, you took up my **case**; you redeemed my life.
Eze 44:24 " 'In any **dispute**, the priests are to serve as judges and decide it
Hos 4:1 because the LORD has a **charge** to bring against you who live in
12:2 [12:3] The LORD has a **charge** to bring against Judah; he will
Mic 6:2 Hear, O mountains, the LORD's **accusation**; listen,
6:2 For the LORD has a **case** against his people; he is lodging a
7:9 LORD's wrath, until he pleads my **case** and establishes my right.
Hab 1:3 and violence are before me; there is **strife**, and conflict abounds.

8191 רִיבָה *rîbâ*, n.m. [2] [√ 8189]

cases [+1821] [1], plea [1]

Dt 17:8 If **cases** [+1821] come before your courts that are too difficult for
Job 13:6 Hear now my argument; listen to the **plea** *of* my lips.

8192 רִיבַי *rîbay*, n.pr.m. [2] [√ 3744?]

Ribai [2]

2Sa 23:29 the Netophathite, Ithai son of **Ribai** from Gibeah in Benjamin,
1Ch 11:31 Ithai son of **Ribai** from Gibeah in Benjamin,

8193 רִיחַ *rîaḥ*, v. [11] [→ 8194; cf. 8118]

smell [2], accept [1], catches the scent [1], caught the smell [+906+8194] [1], comes close [1], delight [1], enjoy fragrance [1], smelled [1], stand [1], take delight [1]

Ge 8:21 [G] The LORD **smelled** the pleasing aroma and said in his
27:27 [G] When Isaac **caught the smell** [+906+8194] *of* his clothes,
Ex 30:38 [G] Whoever makes any like it to **enjoy** its **fragrance** must be
Lev 26:31 [G] *I will* **take** no **delight** in the pleasing aroma of your
Dt 4:28 [G] of wood and stone, which cannot see or hear or eat or **smell**.
Jdg 16:9 [G] as a piece of string snaps when it **comes close** *to* a flame.
1Sa 26:19 [G] has incited you against me, then *may he* **accept** an offering.
Job 39:25 [G] *He* **catches the scent** *of* battle from afar, the shout of
Ps 115:6 [G] they have ears, but cannot hear, noses, but *they* cannot **smell**;
Isa 11:3 [G] he *will* **delight** in the fear of the LORD. He will not judge
Am 5:21 [G] despise your religious feasts; *I* cannot **stand** your assemblies.

8194 רֵיחַ **rêaḥ**, n.m. [58] [√ 8193; cf. 8118; Ar 10666]

aroma [40], fragrance [8], fragrant incense [+5767] [4], smell [2], caught the smell [+906+8193] [1], made stench [+906+944] [1], scent [1], that[s] [1]

Ge 8:21 The LORD smelled the pleasing **aroma** and said in his heart:
27:27 When Isaac **caught the smell of** [+906+8193] his clothes,
27:27 the **smell** *of* my son is like the smell of a field that the LORD has
27:27 the smell of my son is like the **smell** *of* a field that the LORD has
Ex 5:21 *You have* **made** us a **stench** [+906+944] to Pharaoh and his
29:18 It is a burnt offering to the LORD, a pleasing **aroma**, an offering
29:25 along with the burnt offering for a pleasing **aroma** to the LORD,
29:41 a pleasing **aroma**, an offering made to the LORD by fire.
Lev 1:9 an offering made by fire, an **aroma** pleasing to the LORD.
1:13 an offering made by fire, an **aroma** pleasing to the LORD.
1:17 an offering made by fire, an **aroma** pleasing to the LORD.
2:2 an offering made by fire, an **aroma** pleasing to the LORD.
2:9 as an offering made by fire, an **aroma** pleasing to the LORD.
2:12 but they are not to be offered on the altar as a pleasing **aroma**.
3:5 as an offering made by fire, an **aroma** pleasing to the LORD.
3:16 on the altar as food, an offering made by fire, a pleasing **aroma**.
4:31 the priest shall burn it on the altar as an **aroma** pleasing to the
6:15 [6:8] burn the memorial portion on the altar as an **aroma** pleasing
6:21 [6:14] present the grain offering broken in pieces as an **aroma**
8:21 a pleasing **aroma**, an offering made to the LORD by fire,
8:28 a pleasing **aroma**, an offering made to the LORD by fire.
17:6 of Meeting and burn the fat as an **aroma** pleasing to the LORD.
23:13 an offering made to the LORD by fire, a pleasing **aroma**—
23:18 an offering made by fire, an **aroma** pleasing to the LORD.
26:31 and I will take no delight in the pleasing **aroma** *of* your offerings.
Nu 15:3 from the herd or the flock, as an **aroma** pleasing to the LORD—
15:7 as a drink offering. Offer it as an **aroma** pleasing to the LORD.
15:10 will be an offering made by fire, an **aroma** pleasing to the LORD.
15:13 an offering made by fire as an **aroma** pleasing to the LORD.
15:14 an offering made by fire as an **aroma** pleasing to the LORD,
15:24 bull for a burnt offering as an **aroma** pleasing to the LORD,
18:17 fat as an offering made by fire, an **aroma** pleasing to the LORD.
28:2 food for my offerings made by fire, as an **aroma** pleasing to me.'
28:6 burnt offering instituted at Mount Sinai as a pleasing **aroma**,
28:8 This is an offering made by fire, an **aroma** pleasing to the LORD.
28:13 This is for a burnt offering, a pleasing **aroma**, an offering made to
28:24 fire every day for seven days as an **aroma** pleasing to the LORD;
28:27 seven male lambs a year old as an **aroma** pleasing to the LORD.
29:2 As an **aroma** pleasing to the LORD, prepare a burnt offering of
29:6 They are offerings made to the LORD by fire—a pleasing **aroma**.
29:8 Present as an **aroma** pleasing to the LORD a burnt offering of
29:13 Present an offering made by fire as an **aroma** pleasing to the
29:36 Present an offering made by fire as an **aroma** pleasing to the
Job 14:9 yet at the **scent** *of* water it will bud and put forth shoots like a
SS 1:3 Pleasing is the **fragrance** *of* your perfumes; your name is like
1:12 While the king was at his table, my perfume spread its **fragrance**.
2:13 forms its early fruit; the blossoming vines spread their **fragrance**.
4:10 love than wine, and the **fragrance** *of* your perfume than any spice!
4:11 The **fragrance** *of* your garments is like that of Lebanon.
4:11 The fragrance of your garments is like **that**[s] *of* Lebanon.
7:8 [7:9] of the vine, the **fragrance** *of* your breath like apples,
7:13 [7:14] The mandrakes send out their **fragrance**, and at our door is
Jer 48:11 into exile. So she tastes as she did, and her **aroma** is unchanged.
Eze 6:13 places where they offered **fragrant** [+5767] **incense** to all their
16:19 you to eat—you offered as **fragrant** [+5767] **incense** before them.
20:28 presented their **fragrant** [+5767] **incense** and poured out their
20:41 I will accept you as **fragrant** [+5767] **incense** when I bring you
Hos 14:6 [14:7] like an olive tree, his **fragrance** like a cedar of Lebanon.

8195 רִיפוֹת **rîpôt**, n.[f.]. [2]

grain [2]

2Sa 17:19 it out over the opening of the well and scattered **grain** over it.
Pr 27:22 you grind a fool in a mortar, grinding him like **grain** with a pestle,

8196 רִיפַת **rîpat**, n.pr.g. [1 / 2] [cf. 1910]

Riphath [2]

Ge 10:3 The sons of Gomer: Ashkenaz, **Riphath** and Togarmah.
1Ch 1:6 sons of Gomer: Ashkenaz, **Riphath** [BHS 1910] and Togarmah.

8197 ¹רִיק **rîq¹**, v. [19] [→ 8198, 8199, 8200]

draw [3], drawn [3], emptying [2], pour out [2], poured out [2], brandish [1], called out [1], draw out [1], empty [1], leaves empty [1], pour [1], poured [1]

Ge 14:14 [G] *he* **called out** the 318 trained men born in his household
42:35 [G] As they were **emptying** their sacks, there in each man's sack
Ex 15:9 [G] *I will* **draw** my sword and my hand will destroy them.'
Lev 26:33 [G] the nations and *will* **draw out** my sword and pursue you.
Ps 18:42 [18:43] [G] the wind; *I* **poured** them **out** like mud in the streets.
35:3 [G] **Brandish** spear and javelin against those who pursue me.
Ecc 11:3 [G] If clouds are full of water, *they* **pour** rain upon the earth.
SS 1:3 [H] of your perfumes; your name is like perfume **poured out**.
Isa 32:6 [G] the hungry he **leaves empty** and from the thirsty he
Jer 48:11 [H] wine left on its dregs, not **poured** from one jar to another—
48:12 [G] pour her out; *they will* **empty** her jars and smash her jugs.
Eze 5:2 [G] third to the wind. For *I will* pursue them *with* **drawn** sword.
5:12 [G] I will scatter to the winds and pursue *with* **drawn** sword.
12:14 [G] all his troops—and *I will* pursue them *with* **drawn** sword.
28:7 [G] *they will* **draw** their swords against your beauty and wisdom
30:11 [G] *They will* **draw** their swords against Egypt and fill the land
Hab 1:17 [G] *Is he to* keep on **emptying** his net, destroying nations
Zec 4:12 [G] beside the two gold pipes that **pour out** golden oil?"
Mal 3:10 [G] I will not throw open the floodgates of heaven and **pour out**

8198 ²רִיק **rîq²**, n.[m.]. [12] [√ 8197]

in vain [+4200] [4], for nothing [+928+1896] [2], in vain [2], delusions [1], empty [1], no purpose [1], utterly useless [+2039+2256] [1]

Lev 26:16 You will plant seed **in vain** [+4200], because your enemies will eat
26:20 Your strength will be spent **in vain** [+4200], because your soil will
Job 39:16 were not hers; she cares not that her labor was **in vain** [+4200],
Ps 2:1 Why do the nations conspire and the peoples plot **in vain**?
4:2 [4:3] How long will you love **delusions** and seek false gods?
73:13 Surely **in vain** have I kept my heart pure; in vain have I washed
Isa 30:7 to Egypt, whose help is **utterly useless** [+2039+2256]. Therefore I
49:4 I said, "I have labored to **no purpose**; I have spent my strength in
65:23 They will not toil **in vain** [+4200] or bear children doomed to
Jer 51:34 he has thrown us into confusion, he has made us an **empty** jar.
51:58 the peoples exhaust themselves **for nothing** [+928+1896],
Hab 2:13 that the nations exhaust themselves **for nothing** [+928+1896]?

8199 רֵק **rêq**, a. [14] [√ 8197]

empty [4], fantasies [2], worthless [2], adventurers [1], emptied [1], hunger [+5883] [1], idle [1], reckless [1], vulgar [1]

Ge 37:24 the cistern. Now the cistern was **empty**; there was no water in it.
41:27 so are the seven **worthless** heads of grain scorched by the east
Dt 32:47 They are not just **idle** words for you—they are your life. By them
Jdg 7:16 he placed trumpets and **empty** jars in the hands of all of them,
9:4 Abimelech used it to hire **reckless** adventurers, who became his
11:3 where a group of **adventurers** gathered around him and followed
2Sa 6:20 sight of the slave girls of his servants as any **vulgar** *fellow* would!"
2Ki 4:3 Elisha said, "Go around and ask all your neighbors for **empty** jars.
2Ch 13:7 Some **worthless** scoundrels gathered around him and opposed
Ne 5:13 So may such a man be shaken out and **emptied**!" At this the whole
Pr 12:11 have abundant food, but he who chases **fantasies** lacks judgment.
28:19 but the one who chases **fantasies** will have his fill of poverty.
Isa 29:8 that he is eating, but he awakens, and his **hunger** [+5883] remains;
Eze 24:11 set the **empty** pot on the coals till it becomes hot and its copper

8200 רֵיקָם **rêqām**, adv. [16] [√ 8197]

empty-handed [9], empty [3], unfilled [1], unsatisfied [1], without cause [1], without excuse [1]

Ge 31:42 with me, you would surely have sent me away **empty-handed**.
Ex 3:21 this people, so that when you leave you will not go **empty-handed**.
23:15 came out of Egypt. "No one is to appear before me **empty-handed**.
34:20 firstborn sons. "No one is to appear before me **empty-handed**.
Dt 15:13 And when you release him, do not send him away **empty-handed**.
16:16 No man should appear before the LORD **empty-handed**:
Ru 1:21 I went away full, but the LORD has brought me back **empty**.
3:17 saying, 'Don't go back to your mother-in-law **empty-handed**.' "
1Sa 6:3 you return the ark of the god of Israel, do not send it away **empty**,
2Sa 1:22 did not turn back, the sword of Saul did not return **unsatisfied**.
Job 22:9 you sent widows away **empty-handed** and broke the strength of
Ps 7:4 [7:5] is at peace with me or **without cause** have robbed my foe—
25:3 but they will be put to shame who are treacherous **without excuse**.
Isa 55:11 It will not return to me **empty**, but will accomplish what I desire
Jer 14:3 They return with their jars **unfilled**; dismayed and despairing,
50:9 will be like skilled warriors who do not return **empty-handed**.

8201 ¹רִיר **rîr¹**, v. [1] [→ 8202]

flowing [1]

Lev 15:3 [A] Whether it *continues* **flowing** *from* his body or is blocked,

8202 ²רִיר **rîr²**, n.m. [2] [√ 8201]

saliva [1], white [1]

1Sa 21:13 [21:14] doors of the gate and letting **saliva** run down his beard.
Job 6:6 food eaten without salt, or is there flavor in the **white** *of* an egg?

8203 רֵישׁ ***rêš***, n.m. [7] [√ 8133]
poverty [7]

Pr 6:11 **poverty** will come on you like a bandit and scarcity like an armed
10:15 of the rich is their fortified city, but **poverty** is the ruin of the poor.
13:18 He who ignores discipline comes to **poverty** and shame,
24:34 **poverty** will come on you like a bandit and scarcity like an armed
28:19 but the one who chases fantasies will have his fill of **poverty**.
30: 8 give me neither **poverty** nor riches, but give me only my daily
31: 7 let them drink and forget their **poverty** and remember their misery

8204 רֹךְ ***rōk***, n.[m.]. [1] [√ 8216]
gentle [1]

Dt 28:56 **gentle** that she would not venture to touch the ground with the sole

8205 רַךְ ***rak***, a. [16] [√ 8216]
gentle [5], tender [5], inexperienced [2], weak [2], fainthearted [+4222] [1], indecisive [+4222] [1]

Ge 18: 7 and selected a choice, **tender** calf and gave it to a servant,
29:17 Leah had **weak** eyes, but Rachel was lovely in form, and beautiful.
33:13 "My lord knows that the children are **tender** and that I must care
Dt 20: 8 the officers shall add, "Is any man afraid or **fainthearted** [+4222]?
28:54 Even the most **gentle** and sensitive man among you will have no
28:56 The most **gentle** and sensitive woman among you—so sensitive
2Sa 3:39 today, though I am the anointed king, I am **weak**, and these sons of
1Ch 22: 5 David said, "My son Solomon is young and **inexperienced**,
29: 1 the one whom God has chosen, is young and **inexperienced**.
2Ch 13: 7 and **indecisive** [+4222] and not strong enough to resist them.
Job 41: 3 [40:27] you for mercy? Will he speak to you with **gentle** words?
Pr 4: 3 in my father's house, still **tender**, and an only child of my mother,
15: 1 A **gentle** answer turns away wrath, but a harsh word stirs up anger.
25:15 a ruler can be persuaded, and a **gentle** tongue can break a bone.
Isa 47: 1 of the Babylonians. No more will you be called **tender** or delicate.
Eze 17:22 I will break off a **tender** *sprig* from its topmost shoots and plant it

8206 רָכַב ***rākab***, v. [78] [→ 5323, 5324, 8207, 8208, 8209, 8210, 8211, 8213]
riding [10], mounted [6], rider [6], put [4], rode [4], horseman [+6061] [3], ride [3], riders [3], rides [3], drive [2], mounted [+6061] [2], ridden [2], ride on [2], rode off [2], set [2], came riding [1], cause to ride [1], driver [1], drivers [1], got into chariot [1], got on [1], had ride along [1], had ride [1], horsemen [+6061] [1], in a chariot [1], lead [1], led on horseback [1], let ride [1], made ride [1], mount [1], moved [1], ride forth [1], ride off [1], rides on [1], riding in chariots [1], slow down [+4200+6806] [1], take [1], taken [1], took by chariot [1]

Ge 24:61 [A] and her maids got ready and **mounted** their camels
41:43 [G] *He* **had** him **ride** in a chariot as his second-in-command,
49:17 [A] bites the horse's heels so that its **rider** tumbles backward.
Ex 4:20 [G] and sons, **put** them on a donkey and started back to Egypt.
15: 1 [A] The horse and its **rider** he has hurled into the sea.
15:21 [A] The horse and its **rider** he has hurled into the sea."
Lev 15: 9 [A] " 'Everything the man sits on when **riding** will be unclean,
Nu 22:22 [A] Balaam *was* **riding** on his donkey, and his two servants were
22:30 [A] own donkey, which *you have* always **ridden**, to this day?
Dt 32:13 [G] *He* **made** him **ride** on the heights of the land and fed him
33:26 [A] *who* **rides on** the heavens to help you and on the clouds in
Jdg 5:10 [A] "*You who* **ride on** white donkeys, sitting on your saddle
10: 4 [A] He had thirty sons, *who* **rode** thirty donkeys. They controlled
12:14 [A] and thirty grandsons, *who* **rode** on seventy donkeys.
1Sa 25:20 [A] As she **came riding** her donkey into a mountain ravine, there
25:42 [A] Abigail quickly **got on** a donkey and, attended by her five
30:17 [A] except four hundred young men who **rode off** on camels
2Sa 6: 3 [G] *They* **set** the ark of God on a new cart and brought it from
13:29 [A] all the king's sons got up, **mounted** their mules and fled.
16: 2 [A] "The donkeys are for the king's household to **ride on**, the
18: 9 [A] He *was* **riding** his mule, and as the mule went under the
19:26 [19:27] [A] I said, 'I will have my donkey saddled and *will* **ride**
22:11 [A] *He* **mounted** the cherubim and flew; he soared on the wings
1Ki 1:33 [G] **set** Solomon my son on my own mule and take him down to
1:38 [G] **put** Solomon on King David's mule and escorted him to
1:44 [G] the Pelethites, and *they have* **put** him on the king's mule,
13:13 [A] when they had saddled the donkey for him, *he* **mounted** it
18:45 [A] a heavy rain came on and Ahab **rode off** to Jezreel.
2Ki 4:24 [A] don't **slow down** [+4200+6806] for me unless I tell you."
9:16 [A] he **got into** *his* **chariot** and rode to Jezreel, because Joram
9:18 [A] The **horseman** [+6061] rode off to meet Jehu and said,
9:19 [A] So the king sent out a second **horseman** [+6061]. When he
9:25 [A] I *were* **riding** together **in chariots** behind Ahab his father
9:28 [G] His servants **took** him **by chariot** to Jerusalem and buried
10:16 [G] for the LORD." Then *he* **had** him **ride along** in his chariot.
13:16 [G] "**Take** the bow in your hands," he said to the king of Israel.
13:16 [G] When *he had* **taken** it, Elisha put his hands on the king's
18:23 [A] you two thousand horses—if you can put **riders** on them!
23:30 [G] Josiah's servants brought his body **in a chariot** from
1Ch 13: 7 [G] *They* **moved** the ark of God from Abinadab's house on a
2Ch 35:24 [G] **put** him in the other chariot he had and brought him to
Ne 2:12 [A] There were no mounts with me except the one I *was* **riding**
Est 6: 8 [A] robe the king has worn and a horse the king *has* **ridden**,
6: 9 [G] **lead** him on the horse through the city streets, proclaiming
6:11 [G] and **led** him **on horseback** through the city streets,
8:10 [A] *who* **rode** fast horses especially bred for the king.
8:14 [A] The couriers, **riding** the royal horses, raced out, spurred on
Job 30:22 [G] You snatch me up and **drive** me before the wind; you toss
39:18 [A] she spreads her feathers to run, she laughs at horse and **rider**.
Ps 18:10 [18:11] [A] *He* **mounted** the cherubim and flew; he soared on
45: 4 [45:5] [A] In your majesty **ride forth** victoriously in behalf of
66:12 [G] *You* **let** men **ride** over our heads; we went through fire
68: 4 [68:5] [A] to his name, extol him *who* **rides** on the clouds—
68:33 [68:34] [A] to him *who* **rides** the ancient skies above, who
Isa 19: 1 [A] the LORD **rides** on a swift cloud and is coming to Egypt.
30:16 [A] you will flee! You said, '*We will* **ride off** on swift horses.'
36: 8 [A] you two thousand horses—if you can put **riders** on them!
58:14 [G] *I will* **cause** you **to ride** on the heights of the land and to
Jer 6:23 [A] They sound like the roaring sea as *they* **ride** on their horses;
17:25 [A] They and their officials *will* come **riding** in chariots and on
22: 4 [A] **riding** in chariots and on horses, accompanied by their
50:42 [A] They sound like the roaring sea as *they* **ride** on their horses;
51:21 [A] with you I shatter horse and **rider**, with you I shatter chariot
51:21 [A] shatter horse and rider, with you I shatter chariot and **driver**,
Eze 23: 6 [A] handsome young men, and **mounted** [+6061] horsemen.
23:12 [A] warriors in full dress, **mounted** [+6061] horsemen,
23:23 [A] and men of high rank, all **mounted** *on* horses.
38:15 [A] all of them **riding** *on* horses, a great horde, a mighty army.
Hos 10:11 [G] *I will* **drive** Ephraim, Judah must plow, and Jacob must
14: 3 [14:4] [A] Assyria cannot save us; *we will* not **mount**
Am 2:15 [A] get away, and the **horseman** [+6061] will not save his life.
Hab 3: 8 [A] Did you rage against the sea when *you* **rode** with your horses
Hag 2:22 [A] I will overthrow chariots and their **drivers**; horses and their
2:22 [A] horses and their **riders** will fall, each by the sword of his
Zec 1: 8 [A] a vision—and there before me was a man **riding** a red horse!
9: 9 [A] gentle and **riding** on a donkey, on a colt, the foal of a
10: 5 [A] they will fight and overthrow the **horsemen** [+6061].
12: 4 [A] strike every horse with panic and its **rider** with madness,"

8207 רֶכֶב ***rekeb***, n.m. [119 / 120] [√ 8206]
chariots [78], chariot [26], *untranslated* [3], charioteers [3], riders [3], chariot horses [2], upper [2], charioteers [+132] [1], chariots and charioteers [1], upper one [1]

Ge 50: 9 **Chariots** and horsemen also went up with him. It was a very large
Ex 14: 6 So he had his **chariot** made ready and took his army with him.
14: 7 He took six hundred of the best **chariots**, along with all the other
14: 7 along with all the other **chariots** *of* Egypt, with officers over all of
14: 9 all Pharaoh's horses and **chariots**, horsemen and troops—
14:17 and all his army, through his **chariots** and his horsemen.
14:18 I gain glory through Pharaoh, his **chariots** and his horsemen."
14:23 all Pharaoh's horses and **chariots** and horsemen followed them
14:26 flow back over the Egyptians and their **chariots** and horsemen."
14:28 The water flowed back and covered the **chariots** and horsemen—
15:19 When Pharaoh's horses, **chariots** and horsemen went into the sea,
Dt 11: 4 what he did to the Egyptian army, to its horses and **chariots**,
20: 1 and see horses and **chariots** and an army greater than yours,
24: 6 not even the **upper one**—as security for a debt, because that would
Jos 11: 4 with all their troops and a large number of horses and **chariots**—
17:16 and all the Canaanites who live in the plain have iron **chariots**,
17:18 though the Canaanites have iron **chariots** and though they are
24: 6 the Egyptians pursued them with **chariots** and horsemen as far as
Jdg 1:19 to drive the people from the plains, because they had iron **chariots**.
4: 3 Because he had nine hundred iron **chariots** and had cruelly
4: 7 with his **chariots** and his troops to the Kishon River and give him
4:13 Sisera gathered together his nine hundred iron **chariots** and all the
4:13 his nine hundred iron chariots **[RPH]** and all the men with him,
4:15 LORD routed Sisera and all his **chariots** and army by the sword,
4:16 Barak pursued the **chariots** and army as far as Harosheth
5:28 the lattice she cried out, 'Why is his **chariot** so long in coming?
9:53 a woman dropped an **upper** millstone on his head and cracked his
1Sa 8:12 others to make weapons of war and equipment for his **chariots**.
13: 5 fight Israel, with three thousand **chariots**, six thousand charioteers,
2Sa 1: 6 leaning on his spear, with the **chariots** and riders almost upon him.
8: 4 David captured a thousand of his **chariots**, [BHS-] seven
8: 4 He hamstrung all but a hundred of the **chariot horses**.
8: 4 He hamstrung all but a hundred of the chariot horses. **[RPH]**
10:18 David killed seven hundred of their **charioteers** and forty thousand
11:21 Didn't a woman throw an **upper** millstone on him from the wall,
1Ki 1: 5 So he got **chariots** and horses ready, with fifty men to run ahead of

1Ki 9:19 his store cities and the towns for his **chariots** and for his horses—
9:22 his captains, and the commanders of his **chariots** and charioteers.
10:26 Solomon accumulated **chariots** and horses; he had fourteen
10:26 he had fourteen hundred **chariots** and twelve thousand horses,
10:26 which he kept in the **chariot** cities and also with him in Jerusalem.
16: 9 one of his officials, who had command of half his **chariots**,
20: 1 Accompanied by thirty-two kings with their horses and **chariots**,
20:21 king of Israel advanced and overpowered the horses and **chariots**
20:25 horse for horse and **chariot** for chariot—so we can fight Israel on
20:25 horse for horse and chariot for **chariot**—so we can fight Israel on
22:31 Now the king of Aram had ordered his thirty-two **chariot**
22:32 When the **chariot** commanders saw Jehoshaphat, they thought,
22:33 the **chariot** commanders saw that he was not the king of Israel
22:35 The blood from his wound ran onto the floor of the **chariot**,
22:38 They washed the **chariot** at a pool in Samaria (where the
2Ki 2:11 suddenly a **chariot** *of* fire and horses of fire appeared
2:12 "My father! My father! The **chariots** and horsemen of Israel!"
5: 9 So Naaman went with his horses and **chariots** and stopped at the
6:14 Then he sent horses and **chariots** and a strong force there.
6:15 an army with horses and **chariots** had surrounded the city.
6:17 saw the hills full of horses and **chariots** *of* fire all around Elisha.
7: 6 the Lord had caused the Arameans to hear the sound of **chariots**
7:14 So they selected two **chariots** *with* their horses, and the king sent
8:21 So Jehoram went to Zair with all his **chariots**. The Edomites
8:21 The Edomites surrounded him and his **chariot** commanders,
9:21 "Hitch up my **chariot**," Joram ordered. And when it was hitched
9:21 king of Judah rode out, each in his own **chariot**, to meet Jehu.
9:24 The arrow pierced his heart and he slumped down in his **chariot**.
10: 2 your master's sons are with you and you have **chariots** and horses,
10:16 zeal for the LORD." Then he had him ride along in his **chariot**.
13: 7 ten **chariots** and ten thousand foot soldiers, for the king of Aram
13:14 My father!" he cried. "The **chariots** and horsemen of Israel!"
18:24 even though you are depending on Egypt for **chariots**
19:23 ["With my **many** [K; see Q 8044] chariots I have ascended the]
19:23 "With my many **chariots** I have ascended the heights of the
1Ch 18: 4 David captured a thousand of his **chariots**, seven thousand
18: 4 He hamstrung all but a hundred **[RPH]** of the chariot horses.
18: 4 He hamstrung all but a hundred of the **chariot horses**.
19: 6 the Ammonites sent a thousand talents of silver to hire **chariots**
19: 7 They hired thirty-two thousand **chariots and charioteers**,
19:18 David killed seven thousand of their **charioteers** and forty
2Ch 1:14 Solomon accumulated **chariots** and horses; he had fourteen
1:14 he had fourteen hundred **chariots** and twelve thousand horses,
1:14 which he kept in the **chariot** cities and also with him in Jerusalem.
8: 6 store cities, and all the cities for his **chariots** and for his horses—
8: 9 of his captains, and commanders of his **chariots** and charioteers.
9:25 which he kept in the **chariot** cities and also with him in Jerusalem.
12: 3 With twelve hundred **chariots** and sixty thousand horsemen
16: 8 and Libyans a mighty army with great numbers of **chariots**
18:30 Now the king of Aram had ordered his **chariot** commanders,
18:31 When the **chariot** commanders saw Jehoshaphat, they thought,
18:32 for when the **chariot** commanders saw that he was not the king of
21: 9 So Jehoram went there with his officers and all his **chariots**.
21: 9 The Edomites surrounded him and his **chariot** commanders,
35:24 put him in the other **chariot** he had and brought him to Jerusalem,
Ps 20: 7 [20:8] Some trust in **chariots** and some in horses, but we trust in
68:17 [68:18] The **chariots** *of* God are tens of thousands and thousands
76: 6 [76:7] O God of Jacob, both horse and **chariot** lie still.
SS 1: 9 my darling, to a mare harnessed to one of the **chariots** *of* Pharaoh.
Isa 21: 7 When he sees **chariots** *with* teams of horses, riders on donkeys
21: 7 **riders** *on* donkeys or riders on camels, let him be alert, fully alert."
21: 7 riders on donkeys or **riders** *on* camels, let him be alert, fully alert."
21: 9 Look, here comes a man in a **chariot** with a team of horses.
22: 6 Elam takes up the quiver, with her **charioteers** [+132] and horses;
22: 7 Your choicest valleys are full of **chariots**, and horsemen are posted
31: 1 who trust in the multitude of their **chariots** and in the great
36: 9 even though you are depending on Egypt for **chariots**
37:24 'With my many **chariots** I have ascended the heights of the
43:17 who drew out the **chariots** and horses, the army
66:20 on horses, in **chariots** and wagons, and on mules and camels,"
Jer 17:25 They and their officials will come riding in **chariots** and on horses,
22: 4 riding in **chariots** and on horses, accompanied by their officials
46: 9 Charge, O horses! Drive furiously, O **charioteers**! March on,
47: 3 at the noise of enemy **chariots** and the rumble of their wheels.
50:37 A sword against her horses and **chariots** and all the foreigners in
51:21 you I shatter horse and rider, with you I shatter **chariot** and driver,
Eze 23:24 with weapons, **chariots** and wagons and with a throng of people;
26: 7 king of kings, with horses and **chariots**, with horsemen and a great
26:10 **chariots** when he enters your gates as men enter a city whose walls
39:20 At my table you will eat your fill of horses and **riders**, mighty men
Da 11:40 and the king of the North will storm out against him with **chariots**
Na 2: 3 [2:4] The metal on the **chariots** flashes on the day they are made
2: 4 [2:5] The **chariots** storm through the streets, rushing back
2:13 [2:14] "I will burn up your **chariots** in smoke, and the sword will
Zec 9:10 I will take away the **chariots** from Ephraim and the war-horses

8208 רַכָּב *rakkāb*, n.m. [3] [√ 8206]

chariot driver [2], horseman [1]

1Ki 22:34 The king told his **chariot driver**, "Wheel around and get me out of
2Ki 9:17 "Get a **horseman**," Joram ordered. "Send him to meet them
2Ch 18:33 The king told the **chariot driver**, "Wheel around and get me out of

8209 רֵכָב *rēkāb*, n.pr.m. [13] [→ 8211; cf. 8206]

Recab [13]

2Sa 4: 2 One was named Baanah and the other **Recab**; they were sons of
4: 5 Now **Recab** and Baanah, the sons of Rimmon the Beerothite,
4: 6 in the stomach. Then **Recab** and his brother Baanah slipped away.
4: 9 David answered **Recab** and his brother Baanah, the sons of
2Ki 10:15 After he left there, he came upon Jehonadab son of **Recab**,
10:23 and Jehonadab son of **Recab** went into the temple of Baal.
1Ch 2:55 who came from Hammath, the father of the house of **Recab**.
Ne 3:14 The Dung Gate was repaired by Malkijah son of **Recab**, ruler of
Jer 35: 6 because our forefather Jonadab son of **Recab** gave us this
35: 8 We have obeyed everything our forefather Jonadab son of **Recab**
35:14 'Jonadab son of **Recab** ordered his sons not to drink wine and this
35:16 The descendants of Jonadab son of **Recab** have carried out the
35:19 'Jonadab son of **Recab** will never fail to have a man to serve

8210 רִכְבָּה *rikbâ*, n.f. [1] [√ 8206]

saddle [1]

Eze 27:20 " 'Dedan traded in **saddle** blankets with you.

8211 רֵכָבִי *rēkābî*, a.g. [4] [√ 8209; cf. 8206]

Recabite [2], Recabites [2]

Jer 35: 2 "Go to the **Recabite** family and invite them to come to one of the
35: 3 his brothers and all his sons—the whole family of the **Recabites**.
35: 5 some cups before the men of the **Recabite** family and said to them,
35:18 Jeremiah said to the family of the **Recabites**, "This is what the

8212 רֵכָה *rēkâ*, n.pr.loc. [1]

Recah [1]

1Ch 4:12 Tehinnah the father of Ir Nahash. These were the men of **Recah**.

8213 רְכוּב *rᵉkûb*, n.[m.]. [1] [√ 8206]

chariot [1]

Ps 104: 3 He makes the clouds his **chariot** and rides on the wings of the

8214 רְכוּשׁ *rᵉkûš*, n.m. [28] [√ 8223]

possessions [11], goods [7], property [3], wealth [2], equipment [1], equipped [1], everything [+3972] [1], flocks [1], riches [1]

Ge 12: 5 all the **possessions** they had accumulated and the people they had
13: 6 for their **possessions** were so great that they were not able to stay
14:11 The four kings seized all the **goods** *of* Sodom and Gomorrah
14:12 They also carried off Abram's nephew Lot and his **possessions**,
14:16 He recovered all the **goods** and brought back his relative Lot
14:16 all the goods and brought back his relative Lot and his **possessions**,
14:21 to Abram, "Give me the people and keep the **goods** for yourself."
15:14 as slaves, and afterward they will come out with great **possessions**.
31:18 along with all the **goods** he had accumulated in Paddan Aram,
36: 7 Their **possessions** were too great for them to remain together;
46: 6 their livestock and the **possessions** they had acquired in Canaan,
Nu 16:32 their households and all Korah's men and all their **possessions**.
35: 3 pasturelands for their cattle, **flocks** and all their other livestock.
1Ch 27:31 All these were the officials in charge of King David's **property**.
28: 1 the officials in charge of all the **property** and livestock belonging
2Ch 20:25 and they found among them a great amount of **equipment**
21:14 your sons, your wives and **everything that** [+3972] is yours,
21:17 invaded it and carried off all the **goods** found in the king's palace,
31: 3 The king contributed from his own **possessions** for the morning
32:29 of flocks and herds, for God had given him very great **riches**.
35: 7 also three thousand cattle—all from the king's own **possessions**.
Ezr 1: 4 are to provide him with silver and gold, with **goods** and livestock,
1: 6 them with articles of silver and gold, with **goods** and livestock,
8:21 for a safe journey for us and our children, with all our **possessions**.
10: 8 failed to appear within three days would forfeit all his **property**,
Da 11:13 several years, he will advance with a huge army fully **equipped**.
11:24 He will distribute plunder, loot and **wealth** among his followers.
11:28 king of the North will return to his own country with great **wealth**,

8215 רָכִיל rākîl, n.[m.]. [6] [√ 8217?]
gossip [+2143] [2], slander [1], slanderer [+2143] [1], slanderous [1], spreading slander [1]

Lev 19: 16 " 'Do not go about **spreading slander** among your people.
Pr 11: 13 A **gossip** [+2143] betrays a confidence, but a trustworthy man
20: 19 A **gossip** [+2143] betrays a confidence; so avoid a man who talks
Jer 6: 28 They are all hardened rebels, going about to **slander**. They are
9: 4 [9:3] brother is a deceiver, and every friend a **slanderer** [+2143].
Eze 22: 9 In you are **slanderous** men bent on shedding blood; in you are

8216 רָכַךְ rākak, v. [8] [→ 5322, 8204, 8205]
lose [2], responsive [2], fainthearted [+4222] [1], made faint [1], soothed [1], soothing [1]

Dt 20: 3 [A] *Do* not *be* **fainthearted** [+4222] or afraid; do not be terrified
2Ki 22: 19 [A] Because your heart *was* **responsive** and you humbled
2Ch 34: 27 [A] Because your heart was **responsive** and you humbled
Job 23: 16 [G] God *has* **made** my heart **faint**; the Almighty has terrified me.
Ps 55: 21 [55:22] [A] his words *are* more **soothing** than oil, yet they are
Isa 1: 6 [E] and open sores, not cleansed or bandaged or **soothed** with oil.
7: 4 [A] *Do* not **lose** heart because of these two smoldering stubs of
Jer 51: 46 [A] *Do* not **lose** heart or be afraid when rumors are heard in the

8217 רָכַל rākal, v. [17] [→ 5326, 8215?, 8218?, 8219]
merchants [6], traded [6], merchant [2], traders [2], traded with [1]

1Ki 10: 15 [A] **traders** and from all the Arabian kings and the governors of
Ne 3: 31 [A] as far as the house of the temple servants and the **merchants**,
3: 32 [A] the Sheep Gate the goldsmiths and **merchants** made repairs.
13: 20 [A] Once or twice the **merchants** and sellers of all kinds of
SS 3: 6 [A] and incense made from all the spices of the **merchant**?
Eze 17: 4 [A] a land of merchants, where he planted it in a city of **traders**.
27: 3 [A] the gateway to the sea, **merchant** *of* peoples on many coasts,
27: 13 [A] " 'Greece, Tubal and Meshech **traded** *with* you;
27: 15 [A] " 'The men of Rhodes **traded** *with* you, and many coastlands
27: 17 [A] " 'Judah and Israel **traded with** you; they exchanged wheat
27: 20 [A] " 'Dedan **traded** in saddle blankets *with* you.
27: 22 [A] " 'The **merchants** *of* Sheba and Raamah traded with you;
27: 22 [A] " 'The merchants of Sheba and Raamah **traded** *with* you;
27: 23 [A] Canneh and Eden and **merchants** *of* Sheba, Asshur
27: 23 [A] merchants of Sheba, Asshur and Kilmad **traded** *with* you.
27: 24 [A] **traded** *with* you beautiful garments, blue fabric, embroidered
Na 3: 16 [A] You have increased the number of your **merchants** till they

8218 רָכָל rākāl, n.pr.loc. [1] [√ 8217?]
Racal [1]

1Sa 30: 29 **Racal**; to those in the towns of the Jerahmeelites and the Kenites;

8219 רְכֻלָּה rᵉkullâ, n.f. [4] [√ 8217]
trade [2], merchandise [1], trading [1]

Eze 26: 12 They will plunder your wealth and loot your **merchandise**;
28: 5 By your great skill in **trading** you have increased your wealth,
28: 16 Through your widespread **trade** you were filled with violence,
28: 18 and dishonest **trade** you have desecrated your sanctuaries.

8220 רָכַס rākas, v. [2] [→ 8221, 8222?; cf. 8224]
tied [2]

Ex 28: 28 [A] The rings of the breastpiece *are to be* **tied** to the rings of the
39: 21 [A] *They* **tied** the rings of the breastpiece to the rings of the

8221 רֶכֶס rekes, n.[m.]. [1] [√ 8220]
rugged places [1]

Isa 40: 4 the rough ground shall become level, the **rugged places** a plain.

8222 רֹכֶס rōkes, n.[m.]. [1] [√ 8220?]
intrigues [1]

Ps 31: 20 [31:21] your presence you hide them from the **intrigues** *of* men;

8223 רָכַשׁ rākaš, v. [5] [→ 8214]
accumulated [2], acquired [2], *untranslated* [1]

Ge 12: 5 [A] all the possessions *they had* **accumulated** and the people
31: 18 [A] along with all the goods **[RPH]** he had accumulated in
31: 18 [A] along with all the goods *he had* **accumulated** in Paddan
36: 6 [A] other animals and all the goods *he had* **acquired** in Canaan,
46: 6 [A] and the possessions *they had* **acquired** in Canaan,

8224 רֶכֶשׁ rekeš, n.m.col. [4] [cf. 8220]
chariot horses [1], fast horses [1], horses [1], team [1]

1Ki 4: 28 [5:8] and straw for the **chariot horses** and the other horses.
Est 8: 10 who rode **fast horses** especially bred for the king.
8: 14 The couriers, riding the royal **horses**, raced out, spurred on by the
Mic 1: 13 You who live in Lachish, harness the **team** to the chariot.

8225 ¹רָם rām¹, a.vbl. *or* v.ptcp. Not used in NIV/BHS [√ 8123]

8226 ²רָם rām², n.pr.m. [7] [√ 8123]
Ram [7]

Ru 4: 19 Hezron the father of **Ram**, Ram the father of Amminadab,
4: 19 Hezron the father of Ram, **Ram** the father of Amminadab,
1Ch 2: 9 The sons born to Hezron were: Jerahmeel, **Ram** and Caleb.
2: 10 **Ram** was the father of Amminadab, and Amminadab the father of
2: 25 of Hezron: **Ram** his firstborn, Bunah, Oren, Ozem and Ahijah.
2: 27 The sons of **Ram** the firstborn of Jerahmeel: Maaz, Jamin
Job 32: 2 But Elihu son of Barakel the Buzite, of the family of **Ram**,

8227 ¹רָמָה rāmâ¹, v. [4] [→ 810, 8239, 3758, 3759; Ar 10667]
hurled [2], archers [+8008] [1], armed [+5976] [1]

Ex 15: 1 [A] The horse and its rider *he has* **hurled** into the sea.
15: 21 [A] The horse and its rider *he has* **hurled** into the sea."
Ps 78: 9 [A] The men of Ephraim, though **armed with** [+5976] bows,
Jer 4: 29 [A] of horsemen and **archers** [+8008] every town takes to flight.

8228 ²רָמָה rāmâ², v. [8] [→ 5327, 5328, 8244, 8245, 9564, 9566, 9567; cf. 8332?]
betrayed [2], deceive [2], deceived [2], betray [1], deceives [1]

Ge 29: 25 [D] you for Rachel, didn't I? Why *have you* **deceived** me?"
Jos 9: 22 [D] the Gibeonites and said, "Why *did you* **deceive** us by saying,
1Sa 19: 17 [D] "Why *did you* **deceive** me like this and send my enemy away
28: 12 [D] of her voice and said to Saul, "Why *have you* **deceived** me?
2Sa 19: 26 [19:27] [D] with the king.' But Ziba my servant **betrayed** me.
1Ch 12: 17 [12:18] [D] if you have come to **betray** me to my enemies when
Pr 26: 19 [D] is a man *who* **deceives** his neighbor and says, "I was only
La 1: 19 [D] "I called to my allies but they **betrayed** me. My priests

8229 ³רָמָה rāmâ³, n.f. [5] [→ 8230, 8238, 8240, 8241, 8255, 8256, 8257, 8258, 8259; cf. 8123]
lofty shrines [3], hill [1], lofty shrine [1]

1Sa 22: 6 in hand, was seated under the tamarisk tree on the **hill** at Gibeah,
Eze 16: 24 mound for yourself and made a **lofty shrine** in every public square.
16: 25 At the head of every street you built your **lofty shrines**
16: 31 of every street and made your **lofty shrines** in every public square,
16: 39 they will tear down your mounds and destroy your **lofty shrines**.

8230 ⁴רָמָה rāmâ⁴, n.pr.loc. [36] [√ 8229]
Ramah [33], Ramoth [2], *untranslated* [1]

Jos 18: 25 Gibeon, **Ramah**, Beeroth,
19: 8 around these towns as far as Baalath Beer (**Ramah** *in* the Negev).
19: 29 The boundary then turned back toward **Ramah** and went to the
19: 36 Adamah, **Ramah**, Hazor,
Jdg 4: 5 She held court under the Palm of Deborah between **Ramah**
19: 13 let's try to reach Gibeah or **Ramah** and spend the night in one of
1Sa 1: 19 before the LORD and then went back to their home at **Ramah**.
2: 11 Elkanah went home to **Ramah**, but the boy ministered before the
7: 17 But he always went back to **Ramah**, where his home was,
8: 4 elders of Israel gathered together and came to Samuel at **Ramah**.
15: 34 Samuel left for **Ramah**, but Saul went up to his home in Gibeah of
16: 13 LORD came upon David in power. Samuel then went to **Ramah**.
19: 18 he went to Samuel at **Ramah** and told him all that Saul had done to
19: 19 Word came to Saul: "David is in Naioth at **Ramah**";
19: 22 he himself left for **Ramah** and went to the great cistern at Secu.
19: 22 are Samuel and David?" "Over in Naioth at **Ramah**," they said.
19: 23 So Saul went to Naioth at **Ramah**. But the Spirit of God came
19: 23 he walked along prophesying until he came to Naioth. **[RPH]**
20: 1 Then David fled from Naioth at **Ramah** and went to Jonathan
25: 1 and mourned for him; and they buried him at his home in **Ramah**.
28: 3 had mourned for him and buried him in his own town of **Ramah**.
1Ki 15: 17 against Judah and fortified **Ramah** to prevent anyone from leaving
15: 21 heard this, he stopped building **Ramah** and withdrew to Tirzah.
15: 22 they carried away from **Ramah** the stones and timber Baasha had
2Ki 8: 29 inflicted on him at **Ramoth** in his battle with Hazael king of Aram.
2Ch 16: 1 fortified **Ramah** to prevent anyone from leaving or entering the
16: 5 heard this, he stopped building **Ramah** and abandoned his work.
16: 6 they carried away from **Ramah** the stones and timber Baasha had
22: 6 inflicted on him at **Ramoth** in his battle with Hazael king of Aram.

Ezr 2:26 of **Ramah** and Geba 621
Ne 7:30 of **Ramah** and Geba 621
11:33 in Hazor, **Ramah** and Gittaim,
Isa 10:29 camp overnight at Geba." **Ramah** trembles; Gibeah of Saul flees.
Jer 31:15 "A voice is heard in **Ramah**, mourning and great weeping,
40: 1 commander of the imperial guard had released him at **Ramah**.
Hos 5: 8 "Sound the trumpet in Gibeah, the horn in **Ramah**. Raise the battle

8231 רִמָּה *rimmâ*, n.f. [7] [√ 8249]

maggots [2], worm [2], worms [2], maggot [1]

Ex 16:24 as Moses commanded, and it did not stink or get **maggots** in it.
Job 7: 5 My body is clothed with **worms** and scabs, my skin is broken
17:14 'You are my father,' and to the **worm**, 'My mother' or 'My sister,'
21:26 Side by side they lie in the dust, and **worms** cover them both.
24:20 The womb forgets them, the **worm** feasts on them; evil men are no
25: 6 how much less man, who is but a **maggot**—a son of man,
Isa 14:11 **maggots** are spread out beneath you and worms cover you.

8232 ¹רִמּוֹן *rimmôn*[1], n.m. [32] [→ 1784, 8233, 8234, 8236, 8237]

pomegranates [24], pomegranate [4], *untranslated* [1], alternate[s] [+2256+2298+7194] [1], alternated[s] [+2256+7194] [1], pomegranate tree [1]

Ex 28:33 Make **pomegranates** *of* blue, purple and scarlet yarn around the
28:34 and the **pomegranates** are to alternate around the hem of the robe.
28:34 bells and the pomegranates *are to* **alternate**[s] [+2256+2298+7194]
39:24 They made **pomegranates** *of* blue, purple and scarlet yarn
39:25 and attached them around the hem between the **pomegranates**.
39:25 attached them around the hem between the pomegranates. **[RPH]**
39:26 **pomegranates** alternated around the hem of the robe to be worn
39:26 The bells and pomegranates **alternated**[s] [+2256+7194] around the
Nu 13:23 on a pole between them, along with some **pomegranates** and figs.
20: 5 It has no grain or figs, grapevines or **pomegranates**. And there is
Dt 8: 8 and barley, vines and fig trees, **pomegranates**, olive oil and honey;
1Sa 14: 2 on the outskirts of Gibeah under a **pomegranate tree** in Migron.
1Ki 7:18 He made **pomegranates** [BHS 6647] in two rows encircling each
7:18 the capitals on top of the pillars. [BHS *pomegranates*; NIV 6647]
7:20 were the two hundred **pomegranates** in rows all around.
7:42 the four hundred **pomegranates** for the two sets of network (two
7:42 two sets of network (two rows of **pomegranates** for each network,
2Ki 25:17 decorated with a network and **pomegranates** of bronze all around.
2Ch 3:16 He also made a hundred **pomegranates** and attached them to the
4:13 the four hundred **pomegranates** for the two sets of network (two
4:13 two sets of network (two rows of **pomegranates** for each network,
SS 4: 3 temples behind your veil are like the halves of a **pomegranate**.
4:13 Your plants are an orchard of **pomegranates** with choice fruits,
6: 7 temples behind your veil are like the halves of a **pomegranate**.
6:11 to see if the vines had budded or the **pomegranates** were in bloom.
7:12 [7:13] have opened, and if the **pomegranates** are in bloom—
8: 2 give you spiced wine to drink, the nectar of my **pomegranates**.
Jer 52:22 decorated with a network and **pomegranates** of bronze all around.
52:22 all around. The other pillar, with its **pomegranates**, was similar.
52:23 There were ninety-six **pomegranates** on the sides; the total
52:23 the total number of **pomegranates** above the surrounding network
Joel 1:12 the **pomegranate**, the palm and the apple tree—all the trees of the
Hag 2:19 fig tree, the **pomegranate** and the olive tree have not borne fruit.

8233 ²רִמּוֹן *rimmôn*[2], n.pr.m. [3] [√ 8232 *or* 8235]

Rimmon [3]

2Sa 4: 2 they were sons of **Rimmon** the Beerothite from the tribe of
4: 5 Now Recab and Baanah, the sons of **Rimmon** the Beerothite,
4: 9 and his brother Baanah, the sons of **Rimmon** the Beerothite,

8234 ³רִמּוֹן *rimmôn*[3], n.pr.loc. [9] [√ 8232 *or* 8235]

Rimmon [8], where[s] [+928+6152] [1]

Jos 15:32 Lebaoth, Shilhim, Ain and **Rimmon**—a total of twenty-nine towns
19: 7 Ain, **Rimmon**, Ether and Ashan—four towns and their villages—
19:13 and Eth Kazin; it came out at **Rimmon** and turned toward Neah.
Jdg 20:45 As they turned and fled toward the desert to the rock of **Rimmon**,
20:47 men turned and fled into the desert to the rock of **Rimmon**,
20:47 fled into the desert to the rock of Rimmon, **where**[s] [+928+6152]
21:13 sent an offer of peace to the Benjamites at the rock of **Rimmon**.
1Ch 4:32 villages were Etam, Ain, **Rimmon**, Token and Ashan—
Zec 14:10 The whole land, from Geba to **Rimmon**, south of Jerusalem,

8235 ⁴רִמּוֹן *rimmôn*[4], n.pr.m. [3] [→ 2062, 3193, 6538; cf. 8233, 8234]

Rimmon [2], there[s] [+1074] [1]

2Ki 5:18 When my master enters the temple of **Rimmon** to bow down
5:18 and he is leaning on my arm and I bow **there**[s] [+1074] also—
5:18 when I bow down in the temple of **Rimmon**, may the LORD

8236 רִמּוֹן פֶּרֶץ *rimmôn pereṣ*, n.pr.loc. [2] [√ 8232 + 7288]

Rimmon Perez [2]

Nu 33:19 They left Rithmah and camped at **Rimmon Perez**.
33:20 They left **Rimmon Perez** and camped at Libnah.

8237 רִמּוֹנוֹ *rimmônô*, n.pr.loc. [1] [√ 8234]

Rimmono [1]

1Ch 6:77 [6:62] Kartah, **Rimmono** and Tabor, together with their

8238 רָמוֹת *rāmôt*, n.pr.loc. [0] [√ 8229]

Ezr 10:29 [Adaiah, Jashub, Sheal and **Jeremoth**. [Q +2256; see K 3756]]

8239 רָמוּת *rāmût*, n.f. [1] [√ 8227]

remains [1]

Eze 32: 5 your flesh on the mountains and fill the valleys with your **remains**.

8240 רָמוֹת גִּלְעָד *rāmôt gil'ād*, n.pr.loc. [20] [√ 8229 + 1680]

Ramoth Gilead [20]

1Ki 4:13 in **Ramoth Gilead** (the settlements of Jair son of Manasseh in
22: 3 "Don't you know that **Ramoth Gilead** belongs to us and yet we
22: 4 "Will you go with me to fight against **Ramoth Gilead**?"
22: 6 and asked them, "Shall I go to war against **Ramoth Gilead**,
22:12 "Attack **Ramoth Gilead** and be victorious," they said,
22:15 "Micaiah, shall we go to war against **Ramoth Gilead**, or shall I
22:20 'Who will entice Ahab into attacking **Ramoth Gilead** and going to
22:29 and Jehoshaphat king of Judah went up to **Ramoth Gilead**.
2Ki 8:28 of Ahab to war against Hazael king of Aram at **Ramoth Gilead**.
9: 1 your belt, take this flask of oil with you and go to **Ramoth Gilead**.
9: 4 So the young man, the prophet, went to **Ramoth Gilead**.
9:14 all Israel had been defending **Ramoth Gilead** against Hazael king
2Ch 18: 2 and the people with him and urged him to attack **Ramoth Gilead**.
18: 3 king of Judah, "Will you go with me against **Ramoth Gilead**?"
18: 5 and asked them, "Shall we go to war against **Ramoth Gilead**,
18:11 "Attack **Ramoth Gilead** and be victorious," they said,
18:14 "Micaiah, shall we go to war against **Ramoth Gilead**, or shall I
18:19 will entice Ahab king of Israel into attacking **Ramoth Gilead**
18:28 and Jehoshaphat king of Judah went up to **Ramoth Gilead**.
22: 5 of Israel to war against Hazael king of Aram at **Ramoth Gilead**.

8241 רָמוֹת־נֶגֶב *rāmôt-negeb*, n.pr.loc. [1] [√ 8241 + 5582]

Ramoth Negev [1]

1Sa 30:27 He sent it to those who were in Bethel, **Ramoth Negev** and Jattir;

8242 רֹמַח *rōmaḥ*, n.[m.]. [15]

spears [10], spear [5]

Nu 25: 7 the priest, saw this, he left the assembly, took a **spear** in his hand
Jdg 5: 8 and not a shield or **spear** was seen among forty thousand in Israel.
1Ki 18:28 shouted louder and slashed themselves with swords and **spears**,
1Ch 12: 8 [12:9] ready for battle and able to handle the shield and **spear**.
12:24 [12:25] men of Judah, carrying shield and **spear**—6,800 armed
2Ch 11:12 He put shields and **spears** in all the cities, and made them very
14: 8 [14:7] equipped with large shields and with **spears**, and two
25: 5 men ready for military service, able to handle the **spear** and shield.
26:14 **spears**, helmets, coats of armor, bows and slingstones for the entire
Ne 4:13 [4:7] them by families, with their swords, **spears** and bows.
4:16 [4:10] while the other half were equipped with **spears**, shields,
4:21 [4:15] we continued the work with half the men holding **spears**,
Jer 46: 4 positions with helmets on! Polish your **spears**, put on your armor!
Eze 39: 9 and large shields, the bows and arrows, the war clubs and **spears**.
Joel 3:10 [4:10] into swords and your pruning hooks into **spears**.

8243 רַמְיָה *ramyâ*, n.pr.m. [1] [√ 8123? + 3378?]

Ramiah [1]

Ezr 10:25 **Ramiah**, Izziah, Malkijah, Mijamin, Eleazar, Malkijah

8244 ¹רְמִיָּה *rᵉmiyyâ*[1], n.f. [7] [√ 8228]

faulty [2], lazy [2], lax [1], laziness [1], shiftless [1]

Ps 78:57 they were disloyal and faithless, as unreliable as a **faulty** bow.
Pr 10: 4 **Lazy** hands make a man poor, but diligent hands bring wealth.
12:24 Diligent hands will rule, but **laziness** ends in slave labor.
12:27 The **lazy** *man* does not roast his game, but the diligent man prizes
19:15 Laziness brings on deep sleep, and the **shiftless** man goes hungry.
Jer 48:10 "A curse on him who is **lax** in doing the LORD's work! A curse

Hos 7: 16 They do not turn to the Most High; they are like a **faulty** bow.

8245 ²רְמִיָּה ***r[e]miyyâ[2]***, n.f. [8] [√ 8228]

deceit [4], deceitful [2], deceitfully [2]

Job 13: 7 wickedly on God's behalf? Will you speak **deceitfully** for him?
27: 4 lips will not speak wickedness, and my tongue will utter no **deceit**.
Ps 32: 2 does not count against him and in whose spirit is no **deceit**.
52: 2 [52:4] it is like a sharpened razor, you who practice **deceit**.
101: 7 No one who practices **deceit** will dwell in my house; no one who
120: 2 Save me, O LORD, from lying lips and from **deceitful** tongues.
120: 3 will he do to you, and what more besides, O **deceitful** tongue?
Mic 6: 12 are violent; her people are liars and their tongues speak **deceitfully**.

8246 רַמִּים ***rammîm***, n.pr. [1 / 0]

2Ch 22: 5 The Arameans [BHS *Ramites* ?; NIV 812] wounded Joram;

8247 רַמָּכָה ***rammākâ***, n.[f.]. [1]

especially bred [+1201+2021] [1]

Est 8: 10 who rode fast horses **especially bred** [+1201+2021] for the king.

8248 רְמַלְיָהוּ ***r[e]malyāhû***, n.pr.m. [13] [√ 3378]

Remaliah [11], Remaliah's [2]

2Ki 15: 25 his chief officers, Pekah son of **Remaliah**, conspired against him.
15: 27 Pekah son of **Remaliah** became king of Israel in Samaria,
15: 30 Hoshea son of Elah conspired against Pekah son of **Remaliah**.
15: 32 In the second year of Pekah son of **Remaliah** king of Israel,
15: 37 Rezin king of Aram and Pekah son of **Remaliah** against Judah.)
16: 1 In the seventeenth year of Pekah son of **Remaliah**, Ahaz son of
16: 5 Pekah son of **Remaliah** king of Israel marched up to fight against
2Ch 28: 6 In one day Pekah son of **Remaliah** killed a hundred and twenty
Isa 7: 1 Pekah son of **Remaliah** king of Israel marched up to fight against
7: 4 of the fierce anger of Rezin and Aram and of the son of **Remaliah**.
7: 5 Aram, Ephraim and **Remaliah's** son have plotted your ruin,
7: 9 is Samaria, and the head of Samaria is only **Remaliah's** son.
8: 6 of Shiloah and rejoices over Rezin and the son of **Remaliah**,

8249 ¹רָמַם ***rāmam[1]***, v.den. [1] [→ 8231]

full [1]

Ex 16: 20 of it until morning, but *it was* **full** *of* maggots and began to smell.

8250 ²רָמַם ***rāmam[2]***, v. [5] [cf. 8123]

rose [2], exalted [1], get away [1], rose upward [1]

Nu 16: 45 [17:10] [C] "**Get away** from this assembly so I can put an end
Job 24: 24 [A] For a little while *they are* **exalted**, and then they are gone;
Eze 10: 15 [C] the cherubim **rose upward**. These were the living creatures I
10: 17 [C] when the cherubim rose, *they* **rose** with them,
10: 19 [C] the cherubim spread their wings and **rose** from the ground,

8251 רֹמַמְתִּי עֶזֶר ***rōmamtî 'ezer***, n.pr.m. [2] [√ 8123 + 6469]

Romamti-Ezer [2]

1Ch 25: 4 Hananiah, Hanani, Eliathah, Giddalti and **Romamti-Ezer**;
25: 31 the twenty-fourth to **Romamti-Ezer**, his sons and relatives,

8252 רָמַס ***rāmas***, v. [19] [→ 5330]

trample [4], trampled [4], trampled underfoot [3], aggressor [1], be trampled [1], mauls [1], trample down [1], trampling [1], tread [1], treading [1], trod down [1]

2Ki 7: 17 [A] and the people **trampled** him in the gateway, and he died,
7: 20 [A] for the people **trampled** him in the gateway, and he died.
9: 33 [A] the wall and the horses as *they* **trampled** her **underfoot**.
14: 9 [A] in Lebanon came along and **trampled** the thistle **underfoot**.
2Ch 25: 18 [A] in Lebanon came along and **trampled** the thistle **underfoot**.
Ps 7: 5 [7:6] [A] *let him* **trample** my life to the ground and make me
91: 13 [A] the cobra; *you will* **trample** the great lion and the serpent.
Isa 1: 12 [A] who has asked this of you, this **trampling** *of* my courts?
16: 4 [A] will cease; the **aggressor** will vanish from the land.
26: 6 [A] Feet **trample** it **down**—the feet of the oppressed,
28: 3 [C] pride of Ephraim's drunkards, *will* **be trampled** underfoot.
41: 25 [A] if they were mortar, as if *he were* a potter **treading** the clay.
63: 3 [A] them in my anger and **trod** them **down** in my wrath;
Eze 26: 11 [A] The hoofs of his horses *will* **trample** all your streets; he will
34: 18 [A] *Must you* also **trample** the rest of your pasture with your
Da 8: 7 [A] the goat knocked him to the ground and **trampled** *on* him,
8: 10 [A] of the starry host down to the earth and **trampled** *on* them.
Mic 5: 8 [5:7] [A] which **mauls** and mangles as it goes, and no one can
Na 3: 14 [A] Work the clay, **tread** the mortar, repair the brickwork!

8253 רָמַשׂ ***rāmaś***, v. [17] [→ 8254]

moves [5], move [4], moves along [2], creature that moves [1], creatures that move [1], moved [1], moves about [1], moving [1], prowl [1]

Ge 1: 21 [A] every living and **moving** thing with which the water teems,
1: 26 [A] and over all the creatures that **move** along the ground."
1: 28 [A] and over every living creature that **moves** on the ground."
1: 30 [A] of the air and all the **creatures that move** on the ground—
7: 8 [A] of birds and of all creatures *that* **move** along the ground,
7: 14 [A] every creature that **moves** along the ground according to its
7: 21 [A] Every living thing that **moved** on the earth perished—birds,
8: 17 [A] and all the creatures that **move** along the ground—
8: 19 [A] and all the birds—everything *that* **moves** on the earth—
9: 2 [A] of the air, upon every creature *that* **moves along** the ground,
Lev 11: 44 [A] unclean by any creature that **moves about** on the ground.
11: 46 [A] every living thing that **moves** in the water and every creature
20: 25 [A] or bird or anything that **moves along** the ground—
Dt 4: 18 [A] or like any **creature that moves** along the ground or any fish
Ps 69: 34 [69:35] [A] earth praise him, the seas and all *that* **move** in them,
104: 20 [A] it becomes night, and all the beasts of the forest **prowl**.
Eze 38: 20 [A] of the field, every creature that **moves** along the ground,

8254 רֶמֶשׂ ***remeś***, n.m. [17] [√ 8253]

creatures that move [5], creature [2], creatures [2], crawling things [1], creature that moves [1], creatures that move along the ground [1], moves [1], reptiles [1], sea creatures [1], small creatures [1], teeming creatures [1]

Ge 1: 24 livestock, **creatures that move** along the ground, and wild
1: 25 all the **creatures that move** *along* the ground according to their
1: 26 the earth, and over all the **creatures** that move along the ground."
6: 7 and animals, and **creatures that move along the ground**,
6: 20 of every kind of **creature that moves** *along* the ground will come
7: 14 every **creature** that moves along the ground according to its kind
7: 23 and animals and the **creatures that move** along the ground
8: 17 the animals, and all the **creatures** that move along the ground—
8: 19 All the animals and all the **creatures that move** along the ground
9: 3 Everything that lives and **moves** will be food for you. Just as I
1Ki 4: 33 [5:13] He also taught about animals and birds, **reptiles** and fish.
Ps 104: 25 vast and spacious, **teeming** with **creatures** beyond number—
148: 10 wild animals and all cattle, **small creatures** and flying birds,
Eze 8: 10 and I saw portrayed all over the walls all kinds of **crawling things**
38: 20 the beasts of the field, every **creature** that moves along the ground,
Hos 2: 18 [2:20] of the air and the **creatures that move** *along* the ground.
Hab 1: 14 made men like fish in the sea, like **sea creatures** that have no ruler.

8255 רֶמֶת ***remet***, n.pr.loc. [1] [√ 8229]

Remeth [1]

Jos 19: 21 **Remeth**, En Gannim, En Haddah and Beth Pazzez.

8256 רָמַת הַמִּצְפֶּה ***rāmat hammiṣpeh***, n.pr.loc. [1] [√ 8229 + 2174]

Ramath Mizpah [1]

Jos 13: 26 from Heshbon to **Ramath Mizpah** and Betonim, and from

8257 רָמַת לְחִי ***rāmat l[e]ḥî***, n.pr.loc. [1] [√ 8229 + 4305?]

Ramath Lehi [1]

Jdg 15: 17 threw away the jawbone; and the place was called **Ramath Lehi**.

8258 רָמָתִי ***rāmātî***, a.g. [1] [√ 8229]

Ramathite [1]

1Ch 27: 27 Shimei the **Ramathite** was in charge of the vineyards. Zabdi the

8259 רָמָתַיִם ***rāmātayim***, n.pr.loc. [1] [√ 8229]

Ramathaim [1]

1Sa 1: 1 There was a certain man from **Ramathaim**, a Zuphite from the hill

8260 רֹן ***rōn***, n.[m.]. [1] [√ 8264]

songs [1]

Ps 32: 7 me from trouble and surround me with **songs** *of* deliverance.

8261 רָנָה ***rānâ***, v. [1] [→ 8262, 8263; cf. 8264]

rattles [1]

Job 39: 23 [A] The quiver **rattles** against his side, along with the flashing

8262 רִנָּה[1] ***rinnâ*[1]**, n.f. [33] [→ 8263; cf. 8261, 8264]

cry [10], singing [4], song [4], songs of joy [4], shouts of joy [3], plea [2], shouts of joy [+7754] [2], joy [1], pride [1], rejoicing [1], sing [1]

1Ki 8:28 Hear the **cry** and the prayer that your servant is praying in your
22:36 As the sun was setting, a **cry** spread through the army: "Every man
2Ch 6:19 Hear the **cry** and the prayer that your servant is praying in your
20:22 As they began to **sing** and praise, the LORD set ambushes against
Ps 17: 1 Hear, O LORD, my righteous plea; listen to my **cry**. Give ear to
30: 5 [30:6] remain for a night, but **rejoicing** comes in the morning.
42: 4 [42:5] with **shouts** [+7754] **of joy** and thanksgiving among the
47: 1 [47:2] your hands, all you nations; shout to God with cries of **joy**.
61: 1 [61:2] Hear my **cry**, O God; listen to my prayer.
88: 2 [88:3] May my prayer come before you; turn your ear to my **cry**.
105:43 out his people with rejoicing, his chosen ones with **shouts of joy**;
106:44 But he took note of their distress when he heard their **cry**;
107:22 sacrifice thank offerings and tell of his works with **songs of joy**.
118:15 **Shouts of joy** and victory resound in the tents of the righteous:
119:169 May my **cry** come before you, O LORD; give me understanding
126: 2 mouths were filled with laughter, our tongues with **songs of joy**.
126: 5 Those who sow in tears will reap with **songs of joy**.
126: 6 out weeping, carrying seed to sow, will return with **songs of joy**,
142: 6 [142:7] Listen to my **cry**, for I am in desperate need; rescue me
Pr 11:10 the city rejoices; when the wicked perish, there are **shouts of joy**.
Isa 14: 7 All the lands are at rest and at peace; they break into **singing**.
35:10 They will enter Zion with **singing**; everlasting joy will crown their
43:14 fugitives all the Babylonians, in the ships in which they took **pride**.
44:23 Burst into **song**, you mountains, you forests and all your trees,
48:20 Announce this with **shouts** [+7754] **of joy** and proclaim it.
49:13 O heavens; rejoice, O earth; burst into **song**, O mountains!
51:11 They will enter Zion with **singing**; everlasting joy will crown their
54: 1 burst into **song**, shout for joy, you who were never in labor;
55:12 the mountains and hills will burst into **song** before you, and all the
Jer 7:16 "So do not pray for this people nor offer any **plea** or petition for
11:14 "Do not pray for this people nor offer any **plea** or petition for
14:12 Although they fast, I will not listen to their **cry**; though they offer
Zep 3:17 will quiet you with his love, he will rejoice over you with **singing**."

8263 רִנָּה[2] ***rinnâ*[2]**, n.pr.m. [1] [√ 8262; cf. 8261]

Rinnah [1]

1Ch 4:20 The sons of Shimon: Amnon, **Rinnah**, Ben-Hanan and Tilon.

8264 רָנַן ***rānan***, v. [53] [→ 8260, 8265, 8266; cf. 8261, 8262]

sing for joy [15], shout for joy [11], sing [9], cry out [2], ever sing for joy [+8264] [2], rejoice [2], call forth songs of joy [1], calls aloud [1], cries aloud [1], joyfully sing [1], jubilant song [1], made sing [1], sang [1], shout [1], shouted for joy [1], sing joyfully [1], sings [1], songs of joy [1]

Lev 9:24 [A] all the people saw it, *they* **shouted for joy** and fell facedown.
Dt 32:43 [G] **Rejoice**, O nations, with his people, for he will avenge the
1Ch 16:33 [D] *they will* **sing for joy** before the LORD, for he comes to
Job 29:13 [G] who was dying blessed me; *I* **made** the widow's heart **sing**.
38: 7 [A] while the morning stars **sang** together and all the angels
Ps 5:11 [5:12] [D] refuge in you be glad; *let them* ever **sing for joy**.
20: 5 [20:6] [D] *We will* **shout for joy** when you are victorious
32:11 [G] be glad, you righteous; **sing**, all *you* who are upright in heart!
33: 1 [D] **Sing joyfully** to the LORD, *you* righteous; it is fitting for
35:27 [A] *May* those who delight in my vindication **shout for joy**
51:14 [51:16] [D] and my tongue *will* **sing** *of* your righteousness.
59:16 [59:17] [D] in the morning *I will* **sing** *of* your love;
63: 7 [63:8] [D] you are my help, *I* **sing** in the shadow of your wings.
65: 8 [65:9] [G] and evening fades *you* **call forth songs of joy**.
67: 4 [67:5] [D] May the nations be glad and **sing for joy**, for you
71:23 [D] My lips *will* **shout for joy** when I sing praise to you—I,
81: 1 [81:2] [G] **Sing for joy** to God our strength; shout aloud to the
84: 2 [84:3] [D] my heart and my flesh **cry out** for the living God.
89:12 [89:13] [D] Tabor and Hermon **sing for joy** at your name.
90:14 [D] that *we may* **sing for joy** and be glad all our days.
92: 4 [92:5] [D] O LORD; *I* **sing for joy** at the works of your hands.
95: 1 [D] Come, *let us* **sing for joy** to the LORD; let us shout aloud
96:12 [D] in them. Then all the trees of the forest *will* **sing for joy**;
98: 4 [D] all the earth, burst into **jubilant song** with music;
98: 8 [D] clap their hands, *let* the mountains **sing** together **for joy**;
132: 9 [D] be clothed with righteousness; *may* your saints **sing for joy**."
132:16 [D] with salvation, and her saints *will* **ever sing** [+8264] **for joy**.
132:16 [D] with salvation, and her saints *will* **ever sing for joy** [+8264].
145: 7 [D] abundant goodness and **joyfully sing** *of* your righteousness.
149: 5 [D] the saints rejoice in this honor and **sing for joy** on their beds.
Pr 1:20 [A] Wisdom **calls aloud** in the street, she raises her voice in the
8: 3 [A] gates leading into the city, at the entrances, *she* **cries aloud**:
29: 6 [A] by his own sin, but a righteous one *can* **sing** and be glad.
Isa 12: 6 [A] Shout aloud and **sing for joy**, people of Zion, for great is the
16:10 [E] no *one* **sings** or shouts in the vineyards; no one treads out
24:14 [A] They raise their voices, *they* **shout for joy**; from the west
26:19 [D] You who dwell in the dust, wake up and **shout for joy**.
35: 2 [D] burst into bloom; it will rejoice greatly and **shout for joy**.
35: 6 [A] the lame leap like a deer, and the mute tongue **shout for joy**.
42:11 [A] *Let* the people of Sela **sing for joy**; let them shout from the
44:23 [A] **Sing for joy**, O heavens, for the LORD has done this;
49:13 [A] **Shout for joy**, O heavens; rejoice, O earth; burst into song,
52: 8 [D] watchmen lift up their voices; together *they* **shout for joy**.
52: 9 [D] Burst into **songs of joy** together, you ruins of Jerusalem,
54: 1 [A] "**Sing**, O barren woman, you who never bore a child;
61: 7 [A] and instead of disgrace *they will* **rejoice** *in* their inheritance;
65:14 [A] My servants *will* **sing** out of the joy of their hearts, but you
Jer 31: 7 [A] "**Sing** *with* joy for Jacob; shout for the foremost of the
31:12 [D] They will come and **shout for joy** on the heights of Zion;
51:48 [D] and all that is in them *will* **shout for joy** over Babylon,
La 2:19 [A] Arise, **cry out** in the night, as the watches of the night begin;
Zep 3:14 [A] **Sing**, O Daughter of Zion; shout aloud, O Israel! Be glad
Zec 2:10 [2:14] [A] "**Shout** and be glad, O Daughter of Zion. For I am

8265 רְנָנָה ***r*^e^*nānâ***, n.f. [4] [√ 8264]

joyful songs [1], mirth [1], shout of joy [1], singing [1]

Job 3: 7 May that night be barren; may no **shout of joy** be heard in it.
20: 5 that the **mirth** *of* the wicked is brief, the joy of the godless lasts
Ps 63: 5 [63:6] of foods; with **singing** lips my mouth will praise you.
100: 2 the LORD with gladness; come before him with **joyful songs**.

8266 רְנָנִים ***r*^e^*nānîm***, n.[m.]pl. [1] [√ 8264]

ostrich [1]

Job 39:13 "The wings of the **ostrich** flap joyfully, but they cannot compare

8267 רִסָּה ***rissâ***, n.pr.loc. [2] [√ 8272?]

Rissah [2]

Nu 33:21 They left Libnah and camped at **Rissah**.
33:22 They left **Rissah** and camped at Kehelathah.

8268 רָסִיס[1] ***rāsîs*[1]**, n.[m.]. [1] [√ 8272]

dampness [1]

SS 5: 2 is drenched with dew, my hair with the **dampness** *of* the night."

8269 רָסִיס[2] ***rāsîs*[2]**, n.[m.]. [1]

pieces [1]

Am 6:11 he will smash the great house into **pieces** and the small house into

8270 רֶסֶן[1] ***resen*[1]**, n.m. [4]

bit [1], bridle [+4101] [1], bridle [+6344] [1], restraint [1]

Job 30:11 and afflicted me, they throw off **restraint** in my presence.
41:13 [41:5] Who would approach him with a **bridle** [+4101]?
Ps 32: 9 must be controlled by bit and **bridle** [+6344] or they will not come
Isa 30:28 he places in the jaws of the peoples a **bit** that leads them astray.

8271 רֶסֶן[2] ***resen*[2]**, n.pr.loc. [1]

Resen [1]

Ge 10:12 **Resen**, which is between Nineveh and Calah; that is the great city.

8272 רסס ***rāsas***, v. [1] [→ 8267?, 8268]

moisten [1]

Eze 46:14 [A] of an ephah with a third of a hin of oil to **moisten** the flour.

8273 רַע[1] ***ra'*[1]**, a. [350 / 351] [→ 8274, 8288; cf. 8317]

evil [190], wicked [24], bad [23], wrong [10], harm [8], trouble [8], disaster [5], wild [4], poor [3], ugly [3], deadly [2], ferocious [2], grievous [2], heavy [2], malice [2], no good [2], painful [2], ruin [2], sad [2], sin [2], terrible [2], ugly [+5260] [2], *untranslated* [1], bitter [1], brings to ruin [+2021+4200+6156] [1], crimes [1], cruel [1], destroying [1], destruction [1], difficult [1], disaster [+7004] [1], displease [+928+6524] [1], displeasing [+928+6524] [1], distressing [1], dreadful [1], flaw [+1821] [1], great [1], hardships [1], harm [+1821] [1], harm [+4200+6913] [1], harm [+6640+6913] [1], harmful [1], horrible [1], hurt [1], immoral [1], impure [1], look sad [1], mean [1], miserable [1], misery [1], misfortune [+6721] [1], not want [+928+6524] [1], not[s] [1], one[s] way [1], savage [1], serious [1], severe [1], stern [1], stingy [+6524] [1], stingy man [+6524] [1], surely suffer [+8317] [1], troubled [+928+6524] [1], ugly [+9307] [1], undesirable [1], unfavorable [1], unjust [1], vile [1], violence [1], worse [1], worst [1], wretched [1]

Ge 2: 9 were the tree of life and the tree of the knowledge of good and **evil**.

Ge 2:17 you must not eat from the tree of the knowledge of good and **evil**,
3:5 will be opened, and you will be like God, knowing good and **evil**."
3:22 "The man has now become like one of us, knowing good and **evil**.
6:5 that every inclination of the thoughts of his heart was only **evil** all
8:21 even though every inclination of his heart is **evil** from childhood.
13:13 Now the men of Sodom were **wicked** and were sinning greatly
24:50 the LORD; we can say nothing to you **one**[s] **way** or the other.
28:8 Esau then realized how **displeasing** [+928+6524] the Canaanite
31:24 "Be careful not to say anything to Jacob, either good or **bad**."
31:29 I have the power to **harm** [+6640+6913] you; but last night the
31:29 'Be careful not to say anything to Jacob, either good or **bad**.'
37:2 father's wives, and he brought their father a **bad** report about them.
37:20 one of these cisterns and say that a **ferocious** animal devoured him.
37:33 "It is my son's robe! Some **ferocious** animal has devoured him.
38:7 But Er, Judah's firstborn, was **wicked** in the LORD's sight;
40:7 him in his master's house, "Why are your faces *so* **sad** today?"
41:3 After them, seven other cows, **ugly** [+5260] and gaunt, came up
41:4 the cows that were **ugly** [+5260] and gaunt ate up the seven sleek,
41:19 other cows came up—scrawny and very **ugly** [+9307] and lean.
41:20 The lean, **ugly** cows ate up the seven fat cows that came up first.
41:21 could tell that they had done so; they looked just as **ugly** as before.
41:27 **ugly** cows that came up afterward are seven years, and so are the
44:34 Do not let me see the **misery** that would come upon my father."
47:9 My years have been few and **difficult**, and they do not equal the
48:16 the Angel who has delivered me from all **harm**—may he bless
Ex 5:19 The Israelite foremen realized they were in **trouble** when they
32:22 Aaron answered. "You know how prone these people are to **evil**.
33:4 When the people heard these **distressing** words, they began to
Lev 26:6 I will remove **savage** beasts from the land, and the sword will not
27:10 He must not exchange it or substitute a good one for a **bad** *one*,
27:10 or substitute a good one for a bad one, or a **bad** *one* for a good one;
27:12 who will judge its quality as good or **bad**. Whatever value the
27:14 holy to the LORD, the priest will judge its quality as good or **bad**.
27:33 He must not pick out the good from the **bad** or make any
Nu 11:1 Now the people complained about their **hardships** in the hearing
11:10 became exceedingly angry, and Moses was **troubled** [+928+6524].
13:19 What kind of land do they live in? Is it good or **bad**? What kind of
14:27 "How long will this **wicked** community grumble against me?
14:35 and I will surely do these things to this whole **wicked** community,
14:37 these men responsible for spreading the **bad** report about the land
20:5 Why did you bring us up out of Egypt to this **terrible** place?
32:13 until the whole generation of those who had done **evil** in his sight
Dt 1:35 "Not a man of this **evil** generation shall see the good land I swore
1:39 taken captive, your children who do not yet know good from **bad**—
4:25 doing **evil** in the eyes of the LORD your God and provoking him
6:22 great and **terrible**—upon Egypt and Pharaoh and his whole
7:15 He will not inflict on you the **horrible** diseases you knew in Egypt,
9:18 doing what was **evil** in the LORD's sight and so provoking him to
13:5 [13:6] you to follow. You must purge the **evil** from among you.
13:11 [13:12] and no one among you will do such an **evil** thing again.
15:21 If an animal has a defect, is lame or blind, or has any **serious** flaw,
17:1 your God an ox or a sheep that has any defect or **flaw** [+1821] in it,
17:2 **evil** in the eyes of the LORD your God in violation of his
17:5 the man or woman who has done this **evil** deed to your city gate
17:7 hands of all the people. You must purge the **evil** from among you.
17:12 God must be put to death. You must purge the **evil** from Israel.
19:19 to do to his brother. You must purge the **evil** from among you.
19:20 and never again will such an **evil** thing be done among you.
21:21 You must purge the **evil** from among you. All Israel will hear of it
22:14 slanders her and gives her a **bad** name, saying, "I married this
22:19 because this man has given an Israelite virgin a **bad** name.
22:21 in her father's house. You must purge the **evil** from among you.
22:22 and the woman must die. You must purge the **evil** from Israel.
22:24 another man's wife. You must purge the **evil** from among you.
23:9 [23:10] your enemies, keep away from everything **impure**.
24:7 the kidnapper must die. You must purge the **evil** from among you.
28:35 afflict your knees and legs with **painful** boils that cannot be cured,
28:59 and prolonged disasters, and **severe** and lingering illnesses.
30:15 I set before you today life and prosperity, death and **destruction**.
31:29 fall upon you because you will do **evil** in the sight of the LORD
Jos 23:15 so the LORD will bring on you all the **evil** he has threatened,
24:15 if serving the LORD seems **undesirable** to you, then choose for
Jdg 2:11 the Israelites did **evil** in the eyes of the LORD and served the
3:7 The Israelites did **evil** in the eyes of the LORD; they forgot the
3:12 Once again the Israelites did **evil** in the eyes of the LORD,
3:12 because they did this **evil** the LORD gave Eglon king of Moab
4:1 the Israelites once again did **evil** in the eyes of the LORD.
6:1 Again the Israelites did **evil** in the eyes of the LORD, and for
9:23 God sent an **evil** spirit between Abimelech and the citizens of
10:6 Again the Israelites did **evil** in the eyes of the LORD. They served
13:1 Again the Israelites did **evil** in the eyes of the LORD,
1Sa 2:23 I hear from all the people about these **wicked** deeds of yours.
15:19 you pounce on the plunder and do **evil** in the eyes of the LORD?"
16:14 from Saul, and an **evil** spirit from the LORD tormented him.
16:15 said to him, "See, an **evil** spirit from God is tormenting you.
16:16 He will play when the **evil** spirit from God comes upon you,
16:23 to Saul; he would feel better, and the **evil** spirit would leave him.
18:10 The next day an **evil** spirit from God came forcefully upon Saul.
19:9 an **evil** spirit from the LORD came upon Saul as he was sitting in
25:3 but her husband, a Calebite, was surly and **mean** in his dealings.
29:7 do nothing to **displease** [+928+6524] the Philistine rulers."
30:22 all the **evil** men and troublemakers among David's followers said,
2Sa 12:9 Why did you despise the word of the LORD by doing what is **evil**
13:22 Absalom never said a word to Amnon, either good or **bad**;
14:17 lord the king is like an angel of God in discerning good and **evil**.
19:7 [19:8] This will be **worse** for you than all the calamities that have
19:35 [19:36] tell the difference between what is good and what is **not**[s]?
1Ki 3:9 to govern your people and to distinguish between right and **wrong**.
5:4 [5:18] every side, and there is no adversary or **disaster** [+7004].
11:6 So Solomon did **evil** in the eyes of the LORD; he did not follow
13:33 Even after this, Jeroboam did not change his **evil** ways, but once
14:22 Judah did **evil** in the eyes of the LORD. By the sins they
15:26 He did **evil** in the eyes of the LORD, walking in the ways of his
15:34 He did **evil** in the eyes of the LORD, walking in the ways of
16:19 doing **evil** in the eyes of the LORD and walking in the ways of
16:25 Omri did **evil** in the eyes of the LORD and sinned more than all
16:30 Ahab son of Omri did more **evil** in the eyes of the LORD than
21:20 "because you have sold yourself to do **evil** in the eyes of the
21:25 who sold himself to do **evil** in the eyes of the LORD, urged on by
22:8 he never prophesies anything good about me, but always **bad**.
22:18 that he never prophesies anything good about me, but only **bad**?"
22:52 [22:53] He did **evil** in the eyes of the LORD, because he walked
2Ki 2:19 as you can see, but the water is **bad** and the land is unproductive."
3:2 He did **evil** in the eyes of the LORD, but not as his father
4:41 it to the people to eat." And there was nothing **harmful** in the pot.
8:18 married a daughter of Ahab. He did **evil** in the eyes of the LORD.
8:27 ways of the house of Ahab and did **evil** in the eyes of the LORD,
13:2 He did **evil** in the eyes of the LORD by following the sins of
13:11 He did **evil** in the eyes of the LORD and did not turn away from
14:24 He did **evil** in the eyes of the LORD and did not turn away from
15:9 He did **evil** in the eyes of the LORD, as his fathers had done.
15:18 He did **evil** in the eyes of the LORD. During his entire reign he
15:24 Pekahiah did **evil** in the eyes of the LORD. He did not turn away
15:28 He did **evil** in the eyes of the LORD. He did not turn away from
17:2 He did **evil** in the eyes of the LORD, but not like the kings of
17:11 They did **wicked** things that provoked the LORD to anger.
17:13 through all his prophets and seers: "Turn from your **evil** ways.
17:17 and sold themselves to do **evil** in the eyes of the LORD,
21:2 He did **evil** in the eyes of the LORD, following the detestable
21:6 He did much **evil** in the eyes of the LORD, provoking him to
21:9 so that they did more **evil** than the nations the LORD had
21:15 because they have done **evil** in my eyes and have provoked me to
21:16 Judah to commit, so that they did **evil** in the eyes of the LORD.
21:20 He did **evil** in the eyes of the LORD, as his father Manasseh had
23:32 He did **evil** in the eyes of the LORD, just as his fathers had done.
23:37 he did **evil** in the eyes of the LORD, just as his fathers had done.
24:9 He did **evil** in the eyes of the LORD, just as his father had done.
24:19 He did **evil** in the eyes of the LORD, just as Jehoiakim had done.
1Ch 2:3 Er, Judah's firstborn, was **wicked** in the LORD's sight;
2Ch 7:14 and pray and seek my face and turn from their **wicked** ways,
12:14 He did **evil** because he had not set his heart on seeking the
18:17 that he never prophesies anything good about me, but only **bad**?"
21:6 married a daughter of Ahab. He did **evil** in the eyes of the LORD.
21:19 bowels came out because of the disease, and he died in **great** pain.
22:4 He did **evil** in the eyes of the LORD, as the house of Ahab had
29:6 they did **evil** in the eyes of the LORD our God and forsook him.
33:2 He did **evil** in the eyes of the LORD, following the detestable
33:6 He did much **evil** in the eyes of the LORD, provoking him to
33:9 so that they did more **evil** than the nations the LORD had
33:22 He did **evil** in the eyes of the LORD, as his father Manasseh had
36:5 eleven years. He did **evil** in the eyes of the LORD his God.
36:9 three months and ten days. He did **evil** in the eyes of the LORD.
36:12 He did **evil** in the eyes of the LORD his God and did not humble
Ezr 9:13 "What has happened to us is a result of our **evil** deeds and our great
Ne 2:1 and gave it to the king. I had not been **sad** in his presence before;
2:2 asked me, "Why does your face **look** *so* **sad** when you are not ill?
6:13 and then they would give me a **bad** name to discredit me.
9:28 as they were at rest, they again did what was **evil** in your sight.
9:35 you gave them, they did not serve you or turn from their **evil** ways.
13:17 and said to them, "What is this **wicked** thing you are doing—
Est 7:6 Esther said, "The adversary and enemy is this **vile** Haman."
Job 1:1 man was blameless and upright; he feared God and shunned **evil**.
1:8 he is blameless and upright, a man who fears God and shuns **evil**."
2:3 he is blameless and upright, a man who fears God and shuns **evil**.
2:7 afflicted Job with **painful** sores from the soles of his feet to the top
2:10 Shall we accept good from God, and not **trouble**?" In all this,
5:19 six calamities he will rescue you; in seven no **harm** will befall you.
21:30 that the **evil** *man* is spared from the day of calamity, that he is

Job 28:28 of the Lord—that is wisdom, and to shun **evil** is understanding.' "
30:26 Yet when I hoped for good, **evil** came; when I looked for light,
31:29 enemy's misfortune or gloated over the **trouble** that came to him—
35:12 answer when men cry out because of the arrogance of the **wicked**.
Ps 5:4 [5:5] takes pleasure in evil; with you the **wicked** cannot dwell.
7:4 [7:5] if I have done **evil** to him who is at peace with me or without
7:9 [7:10] bring to an end the **violence** *of* the wicked and make the
10:6 will shake me; I'll always be happy and never have **trouble**."
10:15 Break the arm of the wicked and **evil** *man*; call him to account for
23:4 of the shadow of death, I will fear no **evil**, for you are with me;
34:13 [34:14] keep your tongue from **evil** and your lips from speaking
34:14 [34:15] Turn from **evil** and do good; seek peace and pursue it.
34:16 [34:17] the face of the LORD is against those who do **evil**, to cut
36:4 [36:5] to a sinful course and does not reject *what* is **wrong**.
37:27 Turn from **evil** and do good; then you will dwell in the land
41:5 [41:6] My enemies say of me *in* **malice**, "When will he die
49:5 [49:6] Why should I fear when **evil** days come, when wicked
51:4 [51:6] you only, have I sinned and done what is **evil** in your sight,
52:3 [52:5] You love **evil** rather than good, falsehood rather than
54:5 [54:7] Let **evil** recoil on those who slander me; in your
56:5 [56:6] they twist my words; they are always plotting to **harm** me.
64:5 [64:6] They encourage each other in **evil** plans, they talk about
71:20 me see troubles, many and **bitter**, you will restore my life again;
73:8 They scoff, and speak with **malice**; in their arrogance they threaten
78:49 his wrath, indignation and hostility—a band of **destroying** angels.
94:13 you grant him relief from days of **trouble**, till a pit is dug for the
97:10 Let those who love the LORD hate **evil**, for he guards the lives of
101:4 heart shall be far from me; I will have nothing to do with **evil**.
109:20 LORD's payment to my accusers, to those who speak **evil** of me.
112:7 He will have no fear of **bad** news; his heart is steadfast, trusting in
119:101 I have kept my feet from every **evil** path so that I might obey your
121:7 The LORD will keep you from all **harm**—he will watch over
140:1 [140:2] Rescue me, O LORD, from **evil** men; protect me from
140:2 [140:3] who devise **evil** plans in their hearts and stir up war every
140:11 [140:12] in the land; may **disaster** hunt down men of violence.
141:4 Let not my heart be drawn to what is **evil**, to take part in wicked
144:10 to kings, who delivers his servant David from the **deadly** sword.
Pr 1:16 for their feet rush into **sin**, they are swift to shed blood.
2:12 Wisdom will save you from the ways of **wicked** *men*, from men
2:14 who delight in doing **wrong** and rejoice in the perverseness of evil,
2:14 who delight in doing wrong and rejoice in the perverseness of **evil**,
3:7 Do not be wise in your own eyes; fear the LORD and shun **evil**.
4:14 set foot on the path of the wicked or walk in the way of **evil** *men*.
4:27 Do not swerve to the right or the left; keep your foot from **evil**.
5:14 I have come to the brink of utter **ruin** in the midst of the whole
6:14 who plots **evil** with deceit in his heart—he always stirs up
6:24 keeping you from the **immoral** woman, from the smooth tongue of
8:13 To fear the LORD is to hate **evil**; I hate pride and arrogance,
8:13 I hate pride and arrogance, **evil** behavior and perverse speech.
11:15 He who puts up security for another *will* **surely suffer** [+8317],
11:21 The **wicked** will not go unpunished, but those who are righteous
12:12 The wicked desire the plunder of **evil** *men*, but the root of the
12:13 An **evil** *man* is trapped by his sinful talk, but a righteous man
12:20 There is deceit in the hearts of those who plot **evil**, but joy for
12:21 befalls the righteous, but the wicked have their fill of **trouble**.
13:17 A wicked messenger falls into **trouble**, but a trustworthy envoy
13:19 fulfilled is sweet to the soul, but fools detest turning from **evil**.
14:16 A wise man fears the LORD and shuns **evil**, but a fool is
14:19 **Evil** *men* will bow down in the presence of the good,
14:22 Do not those who plot **evil** go astray? But those who plan what is
15:3 are everywhere, keeping watch on the **wicked** and the good.
15:10 **Stern** discipline awaits him who leaves the path; he who hates
15:15 All the days of the oppressed are **wretched**, but the cheerful heart
15:26 The LORD detests the thoughts of the **wicked**, but those of the
16:6 sin is atoned for; through the fear of the LORD a man avoids **evil**.
16:17 The highway of the upright avoids **evil**; he who guards his way
17:11 An **evil** *man* is bent only on rebellion; a merciless official will be
19:23 leads to life: Then one rests content, untouched by **trouble**.
20:8 sits on his throne to judge, he winnows out all **evil** with his eyes.
20:14 "It's **no good**, it's no good!" says the buyer; then off he goes
20:14 "It's no good, it's **no good**!" says the buyer; then off he goes
20:22 Do not say, "I'll pay you back for this **wrong**!" Wait for the
20:30 Blows and wounds cleanse away **evil**, and beatings purge the
21:10 The wicked man craves **evil**; his neighbor gets no mercy from him.
21:12 of the wicked and **brings** the wicked **to ruin** [+2021+4200+6156].
23:6 Do not eat the food of a **stingy** [+6524] **man**, do not crave his
24:20 for the **evil** *man* has no future hope, and the lamp of the wicked
25:20 vinegar poured on soda, is one who sings songs to a **heavy** heart.
26:23 of glaze over earthenware are fervent lips with an **evil** heart.
28:5 **Evil** men do not understand justice, but those who seek the
28:10 He who leads the upright along an **evil** path will fall into his own
28:22 A **stingy** [+6524] man is eager to get rich and is unaware that
29:6 An **evil** man is snared by his own sin, but a righteous one can sing
31:12 She brings him good, not **harm**, all the days of her life.
Ecc 1:13 is done under heaven. What a **heavy** burden God has laid on men!
2:17 because the work that is done under the sun was **grievous** to me.
4:3 not yet been, who has not seen the **evil** that is done under the sun.
4:8 of enjoyment?" This too is meaningless—a **miserable** business!
5:1 [4:17] the sacrifice of fools, who do not know that they do **wrong**.
5:14 [5:13] or wealth lost through *some* **misfortune** [+6721], so that
6:2 stranger enjoys them instead. This is meaningless, a **grievous** evil.
8:3 Do not stand up for a **bad** cause, for he will do whatever he
8:5 Whoever obeys his command will come to no **harm** [+1821],
8:9 There is a time when a man lords it over others to his own **hurt**.
8:11 the hearts of the people are filled with schemes to do **wrong**.
8:12 Although a wicked man commits a hundred **crimes** and still lives a
9:2 the good and the **bad**, [BHS-] the clean and the unclean,
9:3 This is the **evil** in everything that happens under the sun: The same
9:3 are full of **evil** and there is madness in their hearts while they live,
9:12 As fish are caught in a **cruel** net, or birds are taken in a snare,
10:13 his words are folly; at the end they are **wicked** madness—
12:14 including every hidden thing, whether it is good or **evil**.
Isa 3:11 Woe to the wicked! **Disaster** is upon them! They will be paid back
5:20 Woe to those who call **evil** good and good evil, who put darkness
5:20 Woe to those who call evil good and good **evil**, who put darkness
7:15 eat curds and honey when he knows enough to reject the **wrong**
7:16 before the boy knows enough to reject the **wrong** and choose the
31:2 Yet he too is wise and can bring **disaster**; he does not take back his
32:7 The scoundrel's methods are **wicked**, he makes up evil schemes to
33:15 plots of murder and shuts his eyes against contemplating **evil**—
45:7 and create darkness, I bring prosperity and create **disaster**;
56:2 without desecrating it, and keeps his hand from doing any **evil**."
59:7 Their feet rush into **sin**; they are swift to shed innocent blood.
59:15 is nowhere to be found, and whoever shuns **evil** becomes a prey.
65:12 not listen. You did **evil** in my sight and chose what displeases me."
66:4 They did **evil** in my sight and chose what displeases me."
Jer 2:19 Consider then and realize how **evil** and bitter it is for you when you
2:33 Even the **worst** *of women* can learn from your ways.
3:5 This is how you talk, but you do *all* the **evil** you can."
3:17 No longer will they follow the stubbornness of their **evil** hearts.
5:28 Their **evil** deeds have no limit; they do not plead the case of the
6:29 but the refining goes on in vain; the **wicked** are not purged out.
7:6 this place, and if you do not follow other gods to your own **harm**,
7:24 they followed the stubborn inclinations of their **evil** hearts.
7:30 " 'The people of Judah have done **evil** in my eyes,
8:3 all the survivors of this **evil** nation will prefer death to life,
11:8 instead, they followed the stubbornness of their **evil** hearts.
12:14 "As for all my **wicked** neighbors who seize the inheritance I gave
13:10 These **wicked** people, who refuse to listen to my words,
15:21 "I will save you from the hands of the **wicked** and redeem you
16:12 See how each of you is following the stubbornness of his **evil** heart
18:10 and if it does **evil** [K 8288] in my sight and does not obey me,
18:11 So turn from your **evil** ways, each one of you, and reform your
18:12 each of us will follow the stubbornness of his **evil** heart.' "
23:22 would have turned them from their **evil** ways and from their evil
24:2 the other basket had very **poor** figs, so bad they could not be eaten.
24:3 are very good, but the **poor** *ones* are so bad they cannot be eaten."
24:3 but the poor ones **[RPH]** are so bad they cannot be eaten."
24:8 " 'But like the **poor** figs, which are so bad they cannot be eaten,'
25:5 each of you, from your **evil** ways and your evil practices,
25:7 your hands have made, and you have brought **harm** to yourselves."
26:3 Perhaps they will listen and each will turn from his **evil** way.
32:30 and Judah have done nothing but **evil** in my sight from their youth;
39:12 "Take him and look after him; don't **harm** [+4200+6913] him
40:4 but if you do **not want** [+928+6524] to, then don't come.
42:6 Whether it is favorable or **unfavorable**, we will obey the LORD
49:23 "Hamath and Arpad are dismayed, for they have heard **bad** news.
52:2 He did **evil** in the eyes of the LORD, just as Jehoiakim had done.
Eze 5:16 When I shoot at you with my **deadly** and destructive arrows of
5:17 I will send famine and **wild** beasts against you, and they will leave
7:24 I will bring the *most* **wicked** *of* the nations to take possession of
8:9 "Go in and see the **wicked** and detestable things they are doing
11:2 men who are plotting evil and giving **wicked** advice in this city.
13:22 because you encouraged the wicked not to turn from their **evil**
14:15 "Or if I send **wild** beasts through that country and they leave it
14:21 it be when I send against Jerusalem my four **dreadful** judgments—
14:21 sword and famine and **wild** beasts and plague—to kill its men
30:12 I will dry up the streams of the Nile and sell the land to **evil** *men*;
33:11 turn from their ways and live. Turn! Turn from your **evil** ways!
34:25 and rid the land of **wild** beasts so that they may live in the desert
36:31 Then you will remember your **evil** ways and wicked deeds,
38:10 will come into your mind and you will devise an **evil** scheme.
Hos 7:15 I trained them and strengthened them, but they plot **evil** against me.
Am 5:13 the prudent man keeps quiet in such times, for the times are **evil**.
5:14 Seek good, not **evil**, that you may live. Then the LORD God
5:15 Hate **evil**, love good; maintain justice in the courts.
6:3 You put off the **evil** day and bring near a reign of terror.
Jnh 3:8 on God. Let them give up their **evil** ways and their violence.

Jnh 3: 10 God saw what they did and how they turned from their **evil** ways,
Mic 1: 12 waiting for relief, because **disaster** has come from the LORD,
2: 1 to those who plan iniquity, to those who plot **evil** on their beds!
3: 2 you who hate good and love **evil**; [K 8288] who tear the skin from
7: 3 Both hands are skilled in doing **evil**; the ruler demands gifts,
Hab 1: 13 Your eyes are too pure to look on **evil**; you cannot tolerate wrong.
2: 9 "Woe to him who builds his realm by **unjust** gain to set his nest on
2: 9 unjust gain to set his nest on high, to escape the clutches of **ruin**!
Zep 3: 15 the King of Israel, is with you; never again will you fear any **harm**.
Zec 1: 4 'Turn from your **evil** ways and your evil practices.' But they would
1: 4 'Turn from your evil ways and your **evil** practices.' But they would
Mal 1: 8 When you bring blind animals for sacrifice, is that not **wrong**?
1: 8 you sacrifice crippled or diseased animals, is that not **wrong**?
2: 17 By saying, "All who do **evil** are good in the eyes of the LORD,

8274 ²רַע *ra'²*, n.m. Not used in NIV/BHS [√ 8273; cf. 8317]

8275 ¹רֵעַ *rēa'¹*, n.m.vbl. [3] [√ 8131]

cry aloud [+8131] [1], shouting [1], thunder [1]

Ex 32: 17 When Joshua heard the noise of the people **shouting**, he said to
Job 36: 33 His **thunder** announces the coming storm; even the cattle make
Mic 4: 9 Why *do you* now **cry aloud** [+8131]—have you no king?

8276 ²רֵעַ *rēa'²*, n.m. [186] [√ 8287]

neighbor [52], other[s] [29], friend [26], neighbor's [18], friends [15], another[s] [12], neighbors [8], companions [3], countrymen [3], another man's [2], companion [2], fellow Israelite [2], *untranslated* [1], another's[s] [1], associates [1], closest friend [+889+3869+3870+5883] [1], each other[s] [1], fellow [1], friendship [1], his[s] [+3870] [1], husband [1], lovers [1], opponent [1], opponent's [1], the parties [+408+2084+2256] [1], together [+408+907+2084] [1]

Ge 11: 3 They said to each **other**[s], "Come, let's make bricks and bake them
11: 7 confuse their language so they will not understand each **other**[s]."
15: 10 cut them in two and arranged the halves opposite each **other**[s];
31: 49 watch between you and me when we are away from each **other**[s].
38: 12 his sheep, and his **friend** Hirah the Adullamite went with him.
38: 20 Meanwhile Judah sent the young goat by his **friend** the Adullamite
43: 33 to the youngest; and they looked at each **other**[s] in astonishment.
Ex 2: 13 the one in the wrong, "Why are you hitting your **fellow** Hebrew?"
11: 2 and women alike are to ask their **neighbors** for articles of silver
18: 7 kissed him. They greeted each **other**[s] and then went into the tent.
18: 16 and I decide between **the parties** [+408+2084+2256] and inform
20: 16 "You shall not give false testimony against your **neighbor**.
20: 17 "You shall not covet your **neighbor's** house. You shall not covet
20: 17 You shall not covet your **neighbor's** wife, or his manservant
20: 17 his ox or donkey, or anything that belongs to your **neighbor**."
21: 14 But if a man schemes and kills **another**[s] *man* deliberately,
21: 18 "If men quarrel and one hits the **other**[s] with a stone or with his fist
21: 35 "If a man's bull injures the bull of **another**[s] and it dies, they are to
22: 7 [22:6] "If a man gives his **neighbor** silver or goods for
22: 8 [22:7] he has laid his hands on the **other**[s] *man's* property.
22: 9 [22:8] declare guilty must pay back double to his **neighbor**.
22: 10 [22:9] or any other animal to his **neighbor** for safekeeping
22: 11 [22:10] did not lay hands on the **other**[s] *person's* property.
22: 14 [22:13] "If a man borrows an animal from his **neighbor** and it is
22: 26 [22:25] If you take your **neighbor's** cloak as a pledge, return it to
32: 27 to the other, each killing his brother and **friend** and neighbor.' "
33: 11 speak to Moses face to face, as a man speaks with his **friend**.
Lev 19: 13 " 'Do not defraud your **neighbor** or rob him. " 'Do not hold back
19: 16 " 'Do not do anything that endangers your **neighbor's** life.
19: 18 against one of your people, but love your **neighbor** as yourself.
20: 10 with the wife of his **neighbor**—both the adulterer
Dt 4: 42 unintentionally killed his **neighbor** without malice aforethought.
5: 20 "You shall not give false testimony against your **neighbor**.
5: 21 "You shall not covet your **neighbor's** wife. You shall not set your
5: 21 You shall not set your desire on your **neighbor's** house or land,
5: 21 his ox or donkey, or anything that belongs to your **neighbor**."
13: 6 [13:7] or your **closest friend** [+889+3869+3870+5883] secretly
15: 2 creditor shall cancel the loan he has made to his **fellow Israelite**.
15: 2 He shall not require payment from his **fellow Israelite** or brother,
19: 4 one who kills his **neighbor** unintentionally, without malice
19: 5 a man may go into the forest with his **neighbor** to cut wood,
19: 5 fell a tree, the head may fly off and hit his **neighbor** and kill him.
19: 11 But if a man hates his **neighbor** and lies in wait for him, assaults
19: 14 Do not move your **neighbor's** boundary stone set up by your
22: 24 for help, and the man because he violated **another man's** wife.
22: 26 case is like that of someone who attacks and murders his **neighbor**,
23: 24 [23:25] If you enter your **neighbor's** vineyard, you may eat all
23: 25 [23:26] If you enter your **neighbor's** grainfield, you may pick
23: 25 [23:26] you must not put a sickle to **his**[s] [+3870] standing grain.
24: 10 When you make a loan of any kind to your **neighbor**, do not go
27: 17 "Cursed is the man who moves his **neighbor's** boundary stone."
27: 24 "Cursed is the man who kills his **neighbor** secretly." Then all the
Jos 20: 5 because he killed his **neighbor** unintentionally and without malice
Jdg 6: 29 They asked each **other**[s], "Who did this?" When they carefully
7: 13 Gideon arrived just as a man was telling a **friend** his dream.
7: 14 His **friend** responded, "This can be nothing other than the sword of
7: 22 men throughout the camp to turn on each **other**[s] with their swords.
10: 18 The leaders of the people of Gilead said to each **other**[s], "Whoever
Ru 3: 14 **[NIE]** and he said, "Don't let it be known that a woman came to
4: 7 one party took off his sandal and gave it to the **other**[s].
1Sa 10: 11 they asked each **other**[s], "What is this that has happened to the son
14: 20 in total confusion, striking each **other**[s] with their swords.
15: 28 Israel from you today and has given it to one of your **neighbors**—
20: 41 they kissed each **other**[s] and wept together—but David wept the
20: 41 Then they kissed each other and wept **together** [+408+907+2084]
28: 17 kingdom out of your hands and given it to one of your **neighbors**—
30: 26 of the plunder to the elders of Judah, who were his **friends**, saying,
2Sa 2: 16 each man grabbed his **opponent** by the head and thrust his dagger
2: 16 by the head and thrust his dagger into his **opponent's** side,
13: 3 Now Amnon had a **friend** named Jonadab son of Shimeah,
16: 17 Absalom asked Hushai, "Is this the love you show your **friend**?
16: 17 love you show your friend? Why didn't you go with your **friend**?"
1Ki 8: 31 "When a man wrongs his **neighbor** and is required to take an oath
16: 11 He did not spare a single male, whether relative or **friend**.
20: 35 the LORD one of the sons of the prophets said to his **companion**,
2Ki 3: 23 "Those kings must have fought and slaughtered each **other**[s].
7: 3 city gate. They said to each **other**[s], "Why stay here until we die?
7: 9 they said to each **other**[s], "We're not doing right. This is a day of
1Ch 27: 33 was the king's counselor. Hushai the Arkite was the king's **friend**.
2Ch 6: 22 "When a man wrongs his **neighbor** and is required to take an oath
20: 23 the men from Seir, they helped to destroy one **another**[s].
Est 9: 19 a day of joy and feasting, a day for giving presents to each **other**[s].
9: 22 joy and giving presents of food to one **another**[s] and gifts to the
Job 2: 11 When Job's three **friends**, Eliphaz the Temanite, Bildad the
6: 27 would even cast lots for the fatherless and barter away your **friend**.
12: 4 "I have become a laughingstock to my **friends**, though I called
16: 20 My intercessor is my **friend** as my eyes pour out tears to God;
16: 21 behalf of a man he pleads with God as a man pleads for his **friend**.
17: 5 If a man denounces his **friends** for reward, the eyes of his children
19: 21 "Have pity on me, my **friends**, have pity, for the hand of God has
30: 29 I have become a brother of jackals, a **companion** of owls.
31: 9 enticed by a woman, or if I have lurked at my **neighbor's** door,
32: 3 He was also angry with the three **friends**, because they had found
35: 4 "I would like to reply to you and to your **friends** with you.
42: 7 Eliphaz the Temanite, "I am angry with you and your two **friends**,
42: 10 After Job had prayed for his **friends**, the LORD made him
Ps 12: 2 [12:3] Everyone lies to his **neighbor**; their flattering lips speak
15: 3 who does his **neighbor** no wrong and casts no slur on his
28: 3 who speak cordially with their **neighbors** but harbor malice in
35: 14 I went about mourning as though for my **friend** or brother.
38: 11 [38:12] My friends and **companions** avoid me because of my
88: 18 [88:19] You have taken my **companions** and loved ones from me;
101: 5 Whoever slanders his **neighbor** in secret, him will I put to silence;
122: 8 For the sake of my brothers and **friends**, I will say, "Peace be
Pr 3: 28 Do not say to your **neighbor**, "Come back later; I'll give it
3: 29 Do not plot harm against your **neighbor**, who lives trustfully near
6: 1 My son, if you have put up security for your **neighbor**, if you have
6: 3 to free yourself, since you have fallen into your **neighbor's** hands:
6: 3 and humble yourself; press your plea with your **neighbor**!
6: 29 So is he who sleeps with **another man's** wife; no one who touches
11: 9 With his mouth the godless destroys his **neighbor**, but through
11: 12 A man who lacks judgment derides his **neighbor**, but a man of
12: 26 A righteous man is cautious in **friendship**, but the way of the
14: 20 The poor are shunned even by their **neighbors**, but the rich have
14: 21 He who despises his **neighbor** sins, but blessed is he who is kind
16: 29 A violent man entices his **neighbor** and leads him down a path that
17: 17 A **friend** loves at all times, and a brother is born for adversity.
17: 18 strikes hands in pledge and puts up security for his **neighbor**.
18: 17 case seems right, till **another**[s] comes forward and questions him.
18: 24 A man of *many* **companions** may come to ruin, but there is a
19: 4 Wealth brings many **friends**, but a poor man's friend deserts him.
19: 4 Wealth brings many friends, but a poor man's **friend** deserts him.
19: 6 with a ruler, and everyone is the **friend** of a man who gives gifts.
21: 10 wicked man craves evil; his **neighbor** gets no mercy from him.
22: 11 and whose speech is gracious will have the king for his **friend**.
24: 28 Do not testify against your **neighbor** without cause, or use your
25: 8 for what will you do in the end if your **neighbor** puts you to
25: 9 If you argue your case with a **neighbor**, do not betray another
25: 17 Seldom set foot in your **neighbor's** house—too much of you,
25: 18 arrow is the man who gives false testimony against his **neighbor**.
26: 19 is a man who deceives his **neighbor** and says, "I was only joking!"
27: 9 the pleasantness of one's **friend** springs from his earnest counsel.
27: 10 Do not forsake your **friend** and the friend of your father, and do
27: 10 Do not forsake your friend and the **friend** [K 8291] *of* your father,
27: 14 If a man loudly blesses his **neighbor** early in the morning,

Pr 27:17 As iron sharpens iron, so one man sharpens **another**[s].
29: 5 Whoever flatters his **neighbor** is spreading a net for his feet.
Ecc 4: 4 and all achievement spring from man's envy of his **neighbor**.
SS 5: 1 and my milk. Eat, O **friends**, and drink; drink your fill, O lovers.
5:16 This is my lover, this my **friend**, O daughters of Jerusalem.
Isa 3: 5 oppress each other—man against man, neighbor against **neighbor**.
13: 8 in labor. They will look aghast at each **other**[s], their faces aflame.
19: 2 neighbor against **neighbor**, city against city, kingdom against
34:14 will meet with hyenas, and wild goats will bleat to **each other**[s];
41: 6 each helps the **other**[s] and says to his brother, "Be strong!"
Jer 3: 1 you have lived as a prostitute with many **lovers**—would you now
3:20 like a woman unfaithful to her **husband**, so you have been
5: 8 lusty stallions, each neighing for **another**[s] *man's* wife.
6:21 alike will stumble over them; neighbors and **friends** will perish."
7: 5 your ways and your actions and deal with each **other**[s] justly,
9: 4 [9:3] "Beware of your **friends**; do not trust your brothers.
9: 4 [9:3] For every brother is a deceiver, and every **friend** a slanderer.
9: 5 [9:4] Friend deceives **friend**, and no one speaks the truth.
9: 8 [9:7] With his mouth each speaks cordially to his **neighbor**, but in
19: 9 they will eat one **another's**[s] flesh during the stress of the siege
22: 8 from many nations will pass by this city and will ask one **another**[s],
22:13 rooms by injustice, making his **countrymen** work for nothing,
23:27 They think the dreams they tell one **another**[s] will make my people
23:30 "I am against the prophets who steal from one **another**[s] words
23:35 This is what each of you keeps on saying to his **friend** or relative:
29:23 they have committed adultery with their **neighbors'** wives
31:34 No longer will a man teach his **neighbor**, or a man his brother,
34:15 in my sight: Each of you proclaimed freedom to his **countrymen**.
34:17 you have not proclaimed freedom for your fellow **countrymen**.
36:16 these words, they looked at each **other**[s] in fear and said to Baruch,
46:16 They will stumble repeatedly; they will fall over each **other**[s].
La 1: 2 All her **friends** have betrayed her; they have become her enemies.
Eze 18: 6 He does not defile his **neighbor's** wife or lie with a woman during
18:11 "He eats at the mountain shrines. He defiles his **neighbor's** wife.
18:15 idols of the house of Israel. He does not defile his **neighbor's** wife.
22:11 In you one man commits a detestable offense with his **neighbor's**
22:12 and make unjust gain from your **neighbors** by extortion.
33:26 do detestable things, and each of you defiles his **neighbor's** wife.
Hos 3: 1 wife again, though she is loved by **another**[s] and is an adulteress.
Jnh 1: 7 the sailors said to each **other**[s], "Come, let us cast lots to find out
Mic 7: 5 Do not trust a **neighbor**; put no confidence in a friend. Even with
Hab 2:15 "Woe to him who gives drink to his **neighbors**, pouring it from the
Zec 3: 8 O high priest Joshua and your **associates** seated before you,
3:10 " 'In that day each of you will invite his **neighbor** to sit under his
8:10 of his enemy, for I had turned every man against his **neighbor**.
8:16 Speak the truth to each **other**[s], and render true and sound judgment
8:17 do not plot evil against your **neighbor**, and do not love to swear
11: 6 "I will hand everyone over to his **neighbor** and his king.
14:13 Each man will seize the hand of **another**[s], and they will attack
14:13 will seize the hand of another, and they will attack each **other**[s].
Mal 3:16 Then those who feared the LORD talked with each **other**[s],

8277 [3]רֵעַ *rēaʿ*[3], n.[m.] [2] [√ 8290]

thoughts [2]

Ps 139: 2 when I sit and when I rise; you perceive my **thoughts** from afar.
139:17 How precious to me are your **thoughts**, O God! How vast is the

8278 רֹעַ *rōaʿ*, n.[m.]. [19] [√ 8317]

evil [9], bad [4], wicked [2], sad [1], sadness [1], sinful [1], ugly [1]

Ge 41:19 and lean. I had never seen such **ugly** cows in all the land of Egypt.
Dt 28:20 to sudden ruin because of the **evil** you have done in forsaking him.
1Sa 17:28 I know how conceited you are and how **wicked** your heart is;
Ne 2: 2 This can be nothing but **sadness** *of* heart." I was very much afraid,
Ps 28: 4 Repay them for their deeds and for their **evil** work; repay them for
Ecc 7: 3 is better than laughter, because a **sad** face is good for the heart.
Isa 1:16 Take your **evil** deeds out of my sight! Stop doing wrong,
Jer 4: 4 break out and burn like fire because of the **evil** you have done—
21:12 break out and burn like fire because of the **evil** you have done—
23: 2 I will bestow punishment on you for the **evil** you have done,"
23:22 have turned them from their evil ways and from their **evil** deeds.
24: 2 the other basket had very poor figs, so **bad** they could not be eaten.
24: 3 are very good, but the poor ones are so **bad** they cannot be eaten."
24: 8 poor figs, which are so **bad** they cannot be eaten,' says the LORD,
25: 5 each of you, from your evil ways and your **evil** practices,
26: 3 the disaster I was planning because of the **evil** they have done.
29:17 will make them like poor figs that are so **bad** they cannot be eaten.
44:22 When the LORD could no longer endure your **wicked** actions
Hos 9:15 Because of their **sinful** deeds, I will drive them out of my house.

8279 [1]רָעֵב *rāʿēb*[1], v. [13] [→ 8280, 8281, 8282]

hungry [6], causing to hunger [1], famished [1], feel the famine [1], goes hungry [1], hunger [1], let go hungry [1], starving [1]

Ge 41:55 [A] When all Egypt *began to* **feel the famine**, the people cried to
Dt 8: 3 [G] **causing** you **to hunger** and then feeding you with manna,
Ps 34:10 [34:11] [A] The lions may grow weak and **hungry**, but those
50:12 [A] If *I were* **hungry** I would not tell you, for the world is mine,
Pr 6:30 [A] a thief if he steals to satisfy his hunger when *he is* **starving**.
10: 3 [G] The LORD *does* not **let** the righteous **go hungry** but he
19:15 [A] brings on deep sleep, and the shiftless man **goes hungry**.
Isa 8:21 [A] when *they are* **famished**, they will become enraged and,
9:20 [9:19] [A] On the right they will devour, but *still be* **hungry**; on
44:12 [A] *He gets* **hungry** and loses his strength; he drinks no water
49:10 [A] *They will* neither **hunger** nor thirst, nor will the desert heat
65:13 [A] "My servants will eat, but you *will go* **hungry**; my servants
Jer 42:14 [A] will not see war or hear the trumpet or *be* **hungry** for bread,'

8280 רָעָב *rāʿāb*, n.m. [101] [√ 8279]

famine [91], hunger [6], starvation [2], starve [2]

Ge 12:10 Now there was a **famine** in the land, and Abram went down to
12:10 to Egypt to live there for a while because the **famine** was severe.
26: 1 Now there was a **famine** in the land—besides the earlier famine of
26: 1 in the land—besides the earlier **famine** of Abraham's time—
41:27 grain scorched by the east wind: They are seven years of **famine**.
41:30 seven years of **famine** will follow them. Then all the abundance in
41:30 in Egypt will be forgotten, and the **famine** will ravage the land.
41:31 because the **famine** that follows it will be so severe.
41:36 to be used during the seven years of **famine** that will come upon
41:36 upon Egypt, so that the country may not be ruined by the **famine**."
41:50 Before the years of **famine** came, two sons were born to Joseph by
41:54 and the seven years of **famine** began, just as Joseph had said.
41:54 There was **famine** in all the other lands, but in the whole land of
41:56 When the **famine** had spread over the whole country, Joseph
41:56 to the Egyptians, for the **famine** was severe throughout Egypt.
41:57 grain from Joseph, because the **famine** was severe in all the world.
42: 5 went to buy grain, for the **famine** was in the land of Canaan also.
43: 1 Now the **famine** was still severe in the land.
45: 6 For two years now there has been **famine** in the land, and for the
45:11 for you there, because five years of **famine** are still to come.
47: 4 because the **famine** is severe in Canaan and your servants' flocks
47:13 however, in the whole region because the **famine** was severe;
47:13 both Egypt and Canaan wasted away because of the **famine**.
47:20 sold their fields, because the **famine** was too severe for them.
Ex 16: 3 you have brought us out into this desert to **starve** this entire
Dt 28:48 therefore in **hunger** and thirst, in nakedness and dire poverty,
32:24 I will send wasting **famine** against them, consuming pestilence
Ru 1: 1 In the days when the judges ruled, there was a **famine** in the land,
2Sa 21: 1 the reign of David, there was a **famine** for three successive years;
24:13 "Shall there come upon you three years of **famine** in your land?
1Ki 8:37 "When **famine** or plague comes to the land, or blight or mildew,
18: 2 present himself to Ahab. Now the **famine** was severe in Samaria,
2Ki 4:38 Elisha returned to Gilgal and there was a **famine** in that region.
6:25 There was a great **famine** in the city; the siege lasted so long that a
7: 4 'We'll go into the city'—the **famine** is there, and we will die.
8: 1 because the LORD has decreed a **famine** in the land that will last
25: 3 By the ninth day of the ⌊fourth⌋ month the **famine** in the city had
1Ch 21:12 three years of **famine**, three months of being swept away before
2Ch 6:28 "When **famine** or plague comes to the land, or blight or mildew,
20: 9 upon us, whether the sword of judgment, or plague or **famine**,
32:11 he is misleading you, to let you die of **hunger** and thirst.
Ne 5: 3 our vineyards and our homes to get grain during the **famine**."
9:15 In their **hunger** you gave them bread from heaven and in their
Job 5:20 In **famine** he will ransom you from death, and in battle from the
Ps 33:19 to deliver them from death and keep them alive in **famine**.
105:16 He called down **famine** on the land and destroyed all their supplies
Isa 5:13 their men of rank will die of **hunger** and their masses will be
14:30 But your root I will destroy by **famine**; it will slay your survivors.
51:19 ruin and destruction, **famine** and sword—who can console you?
Jer 5:12 No harm will come to us; we will never see sword or **famine**.
11:22 men will die by the sword, their sons and daughters by **famine**.
14:12 Instead, I will destroy them with the sword, **famine** and plague."
14:13 keep telling them, 'You will not see the sword or suffer **famine**.
14:15 yet they are saying, 'No sword or **famine** will touch this land.'
14:15 this land.' Those same prophets will perish by sword and **famine**.
14:16 out into the streets of Jerusalem because of the **famine** and sword.
14:18 slain by the sword; if I go into the city, I see the ravages of **famine**.
15: 2 for the sword, to the sword; those for **starvation**, to starvation;
15: 2 for the sword, to the sword; those for starvation, to **starvation**;
16: 4 They will perish by sword and **famine**, and their dead bodies will
18:21 So give their children over to **famine**; hand them over to the power
21: 7 sword and **famine**, to Nebuchadnezzar king of Babylon and to
21: 9 Whoever stays in this city will die by the sword, **famine** or plague.

Jer 24: 10 **famine** and plague against them until they are destroyed from the
27: 8 **famine** and plague, declares the LORD, until I destroy it by his
27: 13 **famine** and plague with which the LORD has threatened any
29: 17 **famine** and plague against them and I will make them like poor
29: 18 **famine** and plague and will make them abhorrent to all the
32: 24 Because of the sword, **famine** and plague, the city will be handed
32: 36 **famine** and plague it will be handed over to the king of Babylon';
34: 17 the LORD—'freedom' to fall by the sword, plague and **famine**.
38: 2 'Whoever stays in this city will die by the sword, **famine** or plague,
38: 9 where he will **starve** to death when there is no longer any bread in
42: 16 the **famine** you dread will follow you into Egypt, and there you
42: 17 to Egypt to settle there will die by the sword, **famine** and plague;
42: 22 **famine** and plague in the place where you want to go to settle."
44: 12 all perish in Egypt; they will fall by the sword or die from **famine**.
44: 12 From the least to the greatest, they will die by sword or **famine**.
44: 13 Egypt with the sword, **famine** and plague, as I punished Jerusalem.
44: 18 have had nothing and have been perishing by sword and **famine**."
44: 27 Egypt will perish by sword and **famine** until they are all destroyed.
52: 6 By the ninth day of the fourth month the **famine** in the city had
La 2: 19 your children, who faint from **hunger** at the head of every street.
4: 9 killed by the sword are better off than those who die of **famine**;
5: 10 Our skin is hot as an oven, feverish from **hunger**.
Eze 5: 12 your people will die of the plague or perish by **famine** inside you;
5: 16 I shoot at you with my deadly and destructive arrows of **famine**,
5: 16 I will bring more and more **famine** upon you and cut off your
5: 17 I will send **famine** and wild beasts against you, and they will leave
6: 11 house of Israel, for they will fall by the sword, **famine** and plague.
6: 12 by the sword, and he that survives and is spared will die of **famine**.
7: 15 "Outside is the sword, inside are plague and **famine**; those in the
7: 15 and those in the city will be devoured by **famine** and plague.
12: 16 But I will spare a few of them from the sword, **famine** and plague,
14: 13 and send **famine** upon it and kill its men and their animals,
14: 21 sword and **famine** and wild beasts and plague—to kill its men
34: 29 they will no longer be victims of **famine** in the land or bear the
36: 29 and make it plentiful and will not bring **famine** upon you.
36: 30 no longer suffer disgrace among the nations because of **famine**.
Am 8: 11 Sovereign LORD, "when I will send a **famine** through the land—
8: 11 not a **famine** of food or a thirst for water, but a famine of hearing

8281 ²רָעֵב ***rā'ēb²***, a. [20] [√ 8279]

hungry [17], hungry [+5883] [2], starving [1]

1Sa 2: 5 out for food, but *those who were* **hungry** hunger no more.
2Sa 17: 29 "The people have become **hungry** and tired and thirsty in the
2Ki 7: 12 They know we are **starving**; so they have left the camp to hide in
Job 5: 5 The **hungry** consume his harvest, taking it even from among
18: 12 Calamity is **hungry** *for* him; disaster is ready for him when he
22: 7 no water to the weary and you withheld food from the **hungry**,
24: 10 they go about naked; they carry the sheaves, but still go **hungry**.
Ps 107: 5 *They* were **hungry** and thirsty, and their lives ebbed away.
107: 9 satisfies the thirsty and fills the **hungry** [+5883] with good things.
107: 36 there he brought the **hungry** to live, and they founded a city where
146: 7 upholds the cause of the oppressed and gives food to the **hungry**.
Pr 25: 21 If your enemy is **hungry**, give him food to eat; if he is thirsty,
27: 7 loathes honey, but to the **hungry** even what is bitter tastes sweet.
Isa 8: 21 Distressed and **hungry**, they will roam through the land; when they
29: 8 as when a **hungry** *man* dreams that he is eating, but he awakens,
32: 6 the **hungry** [+5883] he leaves empty and from the thirsty he
58: 7 Is it not to share your food with the **hungry** and to provide the
58: 10 if you spend yourselves in behalf of the **hungry** and satisfy the
Eze 18: 7 He does not commit robbery but gives his food to the **hungry**
18: 16 He does not commit robbery but gives his food to the **hungry**

8282 רְעָבוֹן ***r^e'ābôn***, n.[m.]. [3] [√ 8279]

starving [2], famine [1]

Ge 42: 19 rest of you go and take grain back for your **starving** households.
42: 33 here with me, and take food for your **starving** households and go.
Ps 37: 19 they will not wither; in days of **famine** they will enjoy plenty.

8283 רָעַד ***rā'ad***, v. [3] [→ 8284, 8285]

greatly distressed [1], trembles [1], trembling [1]

Ezr 10: 9 [G] **greatly distressed** by the occasion and because of the rain.
Ps 104: 32 [A] he who looks at the earth, and *it* **trembles**, who touches the
Da 10: 11 [G] to you." And when he said this to me, I stood up **trembling**.

8284 רַעַד ***ra'ad***, n.m. [2] [√ 8283]

trembling [2]

Ex 15: 15 be terrified, the leaders of Moab will be seized with **trembling**,
Ps 55: 5 [55:6] Fear and **trembling** have beset me; horror has

8285 רְעָדָה ***r^e'ādâ***, n.f. [4] [√ 8283]

trembling [4]

Job 4: 14 fear and **trembling** seized me and made all my bones shake.
Ps 2: 11 Serve the LORD with fear and rejoice with **trembling**.
48: 6 [48:7] **Trembling** seized them there, pain like that of a woman in
Isa 33: 14 The sinners in Zion are terrified; **trembling** grips the godless:

8286 ¹רָעָה ***rā'â¹***, v. [171 / 172] [→ 5337, 5338, 8297]

shepherd [42], shepherds [37], tend [8], feed [7], graze [7], tending [6], pasture [5], *untranslated* [4], feed on [4], feeds on [3], grazing [3], herdsmen [3], shepherds [+7366] [3], take care of [3], browse [2], browses [2], eat [2], find pasture [2], grazed [2], herdsmen [+5238] [2], pastured [2], rule [2], shepherd's [2], cared for [1], devour [1], drive away [1], enjoy pasture [1], graze flock [1], grazing flocks [1], grazing the flocks [1], herding [1], keeping [1], kept [1], lead [1], leaders [1], nourish [1], prey on [1], shaved [1], shepherd flock [1], shepherded [1], shepherdess [1], tends [1]

Ge 4: 2 [A] Now Abel **kept** flocks, and Cain worked the soil.
13: 7 [A] And quarreling arose between Abram's **herdsmen** [+5238]
13: 7 [A] Abram's herdsmen and the **herdsmen** [+5238] *of* Lot.
13: 8 [A] between you and me, or between your **herdsmen** and mine,
13: 8 [A] your herdsmen and mine, **[RPH]** for we are brothers.
26: 20 [A] But the **herdsmen** *of* Gerar quarreled with Isaac's herdsmen
26: 20 [A] But the herdsmen of Gerar quarreled with Isaac's **herdsmen**
29: 7 [A] Water the sheep and take them back to **pasture**."
29: 9 [A] came with her father's sheep, for she *was a* **shepherdess**.
30: 31 [A] I will go on **tending** your flocks and watching over them:
30: 36 [A] while Jacob *continued to* **tend** the rest of Laban's flocks.
36: 24 [A] while he *was* **grazing** the donkeys of his father Zibeon.
37: 2 [A] was **tending** the flocks with his brothers, the sons of Bilhah
37: 12 [A] Now his brothers had gone to **graze** their father's flocks near
37: 13 [A] your brothers *are* **grazing the flocks** near Shechem.
37: 16 [A] Can you tell me where they *are* **grazing** *their* **flocks**?"
41: 2 [A] seven cows, sleek and fat, and *they* **grazed** among the reeds.
41: 18 [A] seven cows, fat and sleek, and *they* **grazed** among the reeds.
46: 32 [A] The men *are* **shepherds** [+7366]; they tend livestock, and
46: 34 [A] for all **shepherds** [+7366] are detestable to the Egyptians."
47: 3 [A] "Your servants are **shepherds** [+7366]," they replied to
48: 15 [A] the God who *has been* my **shepherd** all my life to this day,
49: 24 [A] One of Jacob, because of the **Shepherd**, the Rock of Israel,
Ex 2: 17 [A] Some **shepherds** came along and drove them away,
2: 19 [A] "An Egyptian rescued us from the **shepherds**.
3: 1 [A] Now Moses was **tending** the flock of Jethro his
34: 3 [A] the flocks and herds *may* **graze** in front of the mountain."
Nu 14: 33 [A] Your children will be **shepherds** here for forty years,
27: 17 [A] LORD's people will not be like sheep without a **shepherd**."
1Sa 16: 11 [A] the youngest," Jesse answered, "but *he is* **tending** the sheep."
17: 15 [A] and forth from Saul to **tend** his father's sheep at Bethlehem.
17: 34 [A] to Saul, "Your servant has been **keeping** his father's sheep.
17: 40 [A] put them in the pouch of his **shepherd's** bag and, with his
21: 7 [21:8] [A] he was Doeg the Edomite, Saul's head **shepherd**.
25: 7 [A] When your **shepherds** were with us, we did not mistreat
25: 16 [A] day they were a wall around us all the time we were **herding**
2Sa 5: 2 [A] LORD said to you, 'You *will* **shepherd** my people Israel,
7: 7 [A] rulers whom I commanded to **shepherd** my people Israel,
1Ki 22: 17 [A] all Israel scattered on the hills like sheep without a **shepherd**,
2Ki 10: 12 [A] and went toward Samaria. At Beth Eked of the **Shepherds**,
1Ch 11: 2 [A] 'You *will* **shepherd** my people Israel, and you will become
17: 6 [A] of their leaders whom I commanded to **shepherd** my people,
27: 29 [A] Shitrai the Sharonite was in charge of the herds **grazing** in
2Ch 18: 16 [A] all Israel scattered on the hills like sheep without a **shepherd**,
Job 1: 14 [A] oxen were plowing and the donkeys *were* **grazing** nearby,
20: 26 [A] will consume him and **devour** what is left in his tent.
24: 2 [A] move boundary stones; *they* **pasture** flocks they have stolen.
24: 21 [A] *They* **prey on** the barren and childless woman, and to the
Ps 2: 9 [a] *You will* **rule** [BHS 8318] them with an iron scepter;
23: 1 [A] The LORD *is* my **shepherd**, I shall not be in want.
28: 9 [A] your inheritance; *be* their **shepherd** and carry them forever.
37: 3 [A] and do good; dwell in the land and **enjoy** safe **pasture**.
49: 14 [49:15] [A] destined for the grave, and death *will* **feed on** them.
78: 71 [A] from tending the sheep he brought him to *be* the **shepherd** of
78: 72 [A] David **shepherded** them with integrity of heart; with skillful
80: 1 [80:2] [A] Hear us, O **Shepherd** *of* Israel, you who lead Joseph
80: 13 [80:14] [A] ravage it and the creatures of the field **feed on** it.
Pr 10: 21 [A] The lips of the righteous **nourish** many, but fools die for lack
15: 14 [A] seeks knowledge, but the mouth of a fool **feeds on** folly.
Ecc 12: 11 [A] like firmly embedded nails—given by one **Shepherd**.
SS 1: 7 [A] where *you* **graze** *your* **flock** and where you rest your sheep
1: 8 [A] and **graze** your young goats by the tents of the shepherds.
1: 8 [A] and graze your young goats by the tents of the **shepherds**.
2: 16 [A] My lover is mine and I am his; he **browses** among the lilies.
4: 5 [A] like twin fawns of a gazelle that **browse** among the lilies.

SS 6: 2 [A] beds of spices, to **browse** in the gardens and to gather lilies.
6: 3 [A] and my lover is mine; he **browses** among the lilies.
Isa 5: 17 [A] sheep *will* **graze** as in their own pasture; lambs will feed
11: 7 [A] The cow *will* **feed** with the bear, their young will lie down
13: 20 [A] pitch his tent there, no **shepherd** will rest his flocks there.
14: 30 [A] The poorest of the poor *will* **find pasture**, and the needy will
27: 10 [A] like the desert; there the calves **graze**, there they lie down;
30: 23 [A] In that day your cattle *will* **graze** *in* broad meadows.
31: 4 [A] though a whole band of **shepherds** is called together against
38: 12 [A] Like a **shepherd's** tent my house has been pulled down
40: 11 [A] *He* **tends** his flock like a shepherd: He gathers the lambs in
40: 11 [A] He tends his flock like a **shepherd**: He gathers the lambs in
44: 20 [A] *He* **feeds on** ashes, a deluded heart misleads him; he cannot
44: 28 [A] 'He is my **shepherd** and will accomplish all that I please;
49: 9 [A] "*They will* **feed** beside the roads and find pasture on every
56: 11 [A] They *are* **shepherds** who lack understanding; they all turn to
61: 5 [A] Aliens *will* **shepherd** your flocks; foreigners will work your
63: 11 [A] them through the sea, with the **shepherd** *of* his flock?
65: 25 [A] The wolf and the lamb *will* **feed** together, and the lion will
Jer 2: 8 [A] the law did not know me; the **leaders** rebelled against me.
2: 16 [A] and Tahpanhes *have* **shaved** the crown of your head.
3: 15 [A] I will give you **shepherds** after my own heart, who will lead
3: 15 [A] *who will* **lead** you *with* knowledge and understanding.
6: 3 [A] **Shepherds** with their flocks will come against her; they will
6: 3 [A] pitch their tents around her, each **tending** his own portion."
10: 21 [A] The **shepherds** are senseless and do not inquire of the
12: 10 [A] Many **shepherds** will ruin my vineyard and trample down
17: 16 [A] I have not run away from *being* your **shepherd**; you know I
22: 22 [A] The wind *will* **drive** all your shepherds **away**, and your allies
22: 22 [A] The wind will drive all your **shepherds** away, and your allies
23: 1 [A] "Woe to the **shepherds** who are destroying and scattering the
23: 2 [A] God of Israel, says to the **shepherds** who tend my people:
23: 2 [A] the God of Israel, says to the shepherds who **tend** my people:
23: 4 [A] I will place **shepherds** over them who will tend them,
23: 4 [A] I will place shepherds over them *who will* **tend** them,
25: 34 [A] Weep and wail, you **shepherds**; roll in the dust, you leaders
25: 35 [A] The **shepherds** will have nowhere to flee, the leaders of the
25: 36 [A] Hear the cry of the **shepherds**, the wailing of the leaders of
31: 10 [A] gather them and will watch over his flock like a **shepherd**.'
33: 12 [A] in all its towns there will again be pastures for **shepherds** to
43: 12 [A] As a **shepherd** wraps his garment around him, so will he
49: 19 [A] challenge me? And what **shepherd** can stand against me?"
50: 6 [A] their **shepherds** have led them astray and caused them to
50: 19 [A] to his own pasture and *he will* **graze** *on* Carmel and Bashan;
50: 44 [A] challenge me? And what **shepherd** can stand against me?"
51: 23 [A] with you I shatter **shepherd** and flock, with you I shatter
Eze 34: 2 [A] "Son of man, prophesy against the **shepherds** *of* Israel;
34: 2 [A] to them: **[RPH]** 'This is what the Sovereign LORD says:
34: 2 [A] Woe to the **shepherds** *of* Israel who only take care of
34: 2 [A] Woe to the shepherds of Israel who *only* **take care of**
34: 2 [A] of themselves! Should not **shepherds** take care of the flock?
34: 2 [A] of themselves! *Should* not shepherds **take care of** the flock?
34: 3 [A] the choice animals, but *you do* not **take care of** the flock.
34: 5 [A] So they were scattered because *there was* no **shepherd**,
34: 7 [A] " 'Therefore, you **shepherds**, hear the word of the LORD:
34: 8 [A] because my flock lacks a **shepherd** and so has been
34: 8 [A] because my **shepherds** did not search for my flock but cared
34: 8 [A] my flock but **cared for** themselves rather than for my flock,
34: 8 [A] but cared for themselves **[RPH]** rather than for my flock,
34: 8 [A] but cared for themselves rather than for **[RPH]** my flock,
34: 9 [A] therefore, O **shepherds**, hear the word of the LORD:
34: 10 [A] I am against the **shepherds** and will hold them accountable
34: 10 [A] I will remove them from **tending** the flock so that the
34: 10 [A] so that the **shepherds** can no longer feed themselves.
34: 10 [A] so that the shepherds *can* no longer **feed** themselves.
34: 12 [A] As a **shepherd** looks after his scattered flock when he is with
34: 13 [A] *I will* **pasture** them on the mountains of Israel, in the ravines
34: 14 [A] *I will* **tend** them in a good pasture, and the mountain heights
34: 14 [A] there *they will* **feed** *in* a rich pasture on the mountains of
34: 15 [A] *I* myself *will* **tend** my sheep and have them lie down,
34: 16 [A] strong I will destroy. *I will* **shepherd** the flock with justice.
34: 18 [A] Is it not enough for you *to* **feed on** the good pasture?
34: 19 [A] *Must* my flock **feed on** what you have trampled and drink
34: 23 [A] I will place over them one **shepherd**, my servant David,
34: 23 [A] one shepherd, my servant David, and *he will* **tend** them;
34: 23 [A] he will tend them; he *will* **tend** them and be their shepherd.
34: 23 [A] he will tend them; he will tend them and be their **shepherd**.
37: 24 [A] will be king over them, and they will all have one **shepherd**.
Hos 4: 16 [A] then *can* the LORD **pasture** them like lambs in a meadow?
9: 2 [A] Threshing floors and winepresses *will* not **feed** the people;
12: 1 [12:2] [A] Ephraim **feeds on** the wind; he pursues the east wind
Am 1: 2 [A] the pastures of the **shepherds** dry up, and the top of Carmel
3: 12 [A] "As a **shepherd** saves from the lion's mouth only two leg
Jnh 3: 7 [A] herd or flock, taste anything; *do* not *let them* **eat** or drink.
Mic 5: 4 [5:3] [A] and **shepherd** *his* **flock** in the strength of the LORD,
5: 5 [5:4] [A] we will raise against him seven **shepherds**, even eight
5: 6 [5:5] [A] *They will* **rule** the land of Assyria with the sword, the
7: 14 [A] **Shepherd** your people with your staff, the flock of your
7: 14 [A] *Let them* **feed** in Bashan and Gilead as in days long ago.
Na 3: 18 [A] O king of Assyria, your **shepherds** slumber; your nobles lie
Zep 2: 6 [A] will be a place for **shepherds** and sheep pens.
2: 7 [A] remnant of the house of Judah; there *they will* **find pasture**.
3: 13 [A] They *will* **eat** and lie down and no one will make them
Zec 10: 2 [A] people wander like sheep oppressed for lack of a **shepherd**.
10: 3 [A] "My anger burns against the **shepherds**, and I will punish the
11: 3 [A] Listen to the wail of the **shepherds**; their rich pastures are
11: 4 [A] my God says: "**Pasture** the flock marked for slaughter.
11: 5 [A] I am rich!' Their own **shepherds** do not spare them.
11: 7 [A] So *I* **pastured** the flock marked for slaughter, particularly the
11: 7 [A] one Favor and the other Union, and *I* **pastured** the flock.
11: 8 [A] In one month I got rid of the three **shepherds**. The flock
11: 9 [A] and said, "*I will* not *be* your **shepherd**. Let the dying die,
11: 15 [A] said to me, "Take again the equipment of a foolish **shepherd**.
11: 16 [A] For I am going to raise up a **shepherd** over the land who will
11: 17 [A] "Woe to the worthless **shepherd**, who deserts the flock!
13: 7 [A] "Awake, O sword, against my **shepherd**, against the man
13: 7 [A] "Strike the **shepherd**, and the sheep will be scattered, and I

8287 [2]רָעָה ***rā'â*[2]**, v. [5] [→ 5335, 8134?, 8276, 8291, 8292, 8293, 8294, 8295, 8296, 8298, 8299, 8300; cf. 8289]

companion [3], attended at wedding [1], make friends [1]

Jdg 14: 20 [D] given to the friend who *had* **attended** him **at** his **wedding**.
Pr 13: 20 [A] the wise grows wise, but a **companion** *of* fools suffers harm.
22: 24 [F] *Do* not **make friends** with a hot-tempered man, do not
28: 7 [A] but a **companion** *of* gluttons disgraces his father.
29: 3 [A] but a **companion** *of* prostitutes squanders his wealth.

8288 [3]רָעָה ***rā'â*[3]**, n.f. [316] [√ 8273; cf. 8317]

disaster [79], evil [48], wickedness [32], harm [26], calamity [18], trouble [17], ruin [8], wrong [8], wicked [6], calamities [4], disasters [4], troubles [4], wrongdoing [4], *untranslated* [3], bad [3], distress [3], misfortune [3], badly [2], crimes [2], danger [2], destruction [2], evil deeds [2], evil thing [2], misery [2], wickedness is great [+8288] [2], another[s] [1], awful crime [1], awful thing [1], crime [+5126] [1], cruelty [1], deeds of evildoers [1], defeat [1], discomfort [1], displeased [+448+8317] [1], downfall [1], evil intent [1], evildoer [+6913] [1], fate [1], fault [1], harm [+4200+6913] [1], harm [+6640+6913] [1], harming [1], it[s] [+2021] [1], malice [1], offense [1], peril [1], plotting [+2021+3086] [1], punishment [1], sin [1], sins [1], something desperate [1], very disturbed [+4200+8317] [1], wicked thing [1], worst [1], wrongs [1]

Ge 6: 5 The LORD saw how great man's **wickedness** on the earth had
19: 19 flee to the mountains; this **disaster** will overtake me, and I'll die.
26: 29 that you will do us no **harm**, just as we did not molest you
31: 52 you will not go past this heap and pillar to my side to **harm** me.
39: 9 How then could I do such a **wicked thing** and sin against God?"
44: 4 up with them, say to them, 'Why have you repaid good with **evil**?
44: 29 you will bring my gray head down to the grave in **misery**.'
50: 15 against us and pays us back for all the **wrongs** we did to him?"
50: 17 the sins and the wrongs they committed in treating you *so* **badly**.'
50: 20 You intended to **harm** me, but God intended it for good to
Ex 10: 10 along with your women and children! Clearly you are bent on **evil**.
23: 2 "Do not follow the crowd in *doing* **wrong**. When you give
32: 12 'It was with **evil intent** that he brought them out, to kill them in the
32: 12 your fierce anger; relent and do not bring **disaster** on your people.
32: 14 and did not bring on his people the **disaster** he had threatened.
Nu 11: 15 found favor in your eyes—and do not let me face my own **ruin**."
24: 13 and gold, I could not do anything of my own accord, good or **bad**,
35: 23 since he was not his enemy and he did not intend to **harm** him,
Dt 29: 21 [29:20] single him out from all the tribes of Israel for **disaster**,
31: 17 Many **disasters** and difficulties will come upon them, and on that
31: 17 'Have not these **disasters** come upon us because our God is not
31: 18 that day because of all their **wickedness** in turning to other gods.
31: 21 And when many **disasters** and difficulties come upon them,
31: 29 **disaster** will fall upon you because you will do evil in the sight of
32: 23 "I will heap **calamities** upon them and spend my arrows against
Jdg 2: 15 the hand of the LORD was against them to **defeat** them, just as he
9: 56 Thus God repaid the **wickedness** that Abimelech had done to his
9: 57 God also made the men of Shechem pay for all their **wickedness**.
11: 27 but you are doing me **wrong** by waging war against me.
15: 3 even with the Philistines; I *will* really **harm** [+6640+6913] them."
20: 3 Then the Israelites said, "Tell us how this **awful thing** happened."
20: 12 "What about this **awful crime** that was committed among you?
20: 13 so that we may put them to death and purge the **evil** from Israel."
20: 34 so heavy that the Benjamites did not realize how near **disaster**
20: 41 because they realized that **disaster** had come upon them.

1Sa 6: 9 then the LORD has brought this great **disaster** on us.
10: 19 your God, who saves you out of all your **calamities** and distresses.
12: 17 you will realize what an **evil thing** you did in the eyes of the
12: 19 for we have added to all our other sins the **evil** of asking for a
12: 20 "You have done all this **evil**; yet do not turn away from the
20: 7 his temper, you can be sure that he is determined to **harm** me.
20: 9 "If I had the least inkling that my father was determined to **harm**
20: 13 if my father is inclined to **harm** you, may the LORD deal with
23: 9 When David learned that Saul *was* **plotting** [+2021+3086] against
24: 9 [24:10] listen when men say, 'David is bent on **harming** you'?
24: 11 [24:12] recognize that I am not guilty of **wrongdoing** or rebellion.
24: 17 [24:18] "You have treated me well, but I have treated you **badly**.
25: 17 because **disaster** is hanging over our master and his whole
25: 21 that nothing of his was missing. He has paid me back **evil** for good.
25: 26 your enemies and all who intend to **harm** my master be like Nabal.
25: 28 Let no **wrongdoing** be found in you as long as you live.
25: 39 He has kept his servant from doing **wrong** and has brought Nabal's
25: 39 and has brought Nabal's **wrongdoing** down on his own head."
26: 18 his servant? What have I done, and what **wrong** am I guilty of?
29: 6 I have found no **fault** in you, but the rulers don't approve of you.
2Sa 3: 39 May the LORD repay the **evildoer** [+6913] according to his evil
3: 39 May the LORD repay the evildoer according to his **evil deeds**!"
12: 11 'Out of your own household I am going to bring **calamity** upon
12: 18 we tell him the child is dead? He may do **something desperate**."
13: 16 "Sending me away would be a greater **wrong** than what you have
15: 14 overtake us and bring **ruin** upon us and put the city to the sword."
16: 8 You have come to **ruin** because you are a man of blood!"
17: 14 good advice of Ahithophel in order to bring **disaster** on Absalom.
18: 32 and all who rise up to **harm** you be like that young man."
19: 7 [19:8] This will be worse for you than all the **calamities** that have
24: 16 the LORD was grieved because of the **calamity** and said to the
1Ki 1: 52 head will fall to the ground; but if **evil** is found in him, he will die."
2: 44 "You know in your heart all the **wrong** you did to my father
2: 44 Now the LORD will repay you for your **wrongdoing**.
9: 9 that is why the LORD brought all this **disaster** on them.' "
11: 25 as long as Solomon lived, adding to the **trouble** caused by Hadad.
14: 10 of this, I am going to bring **disaster** on the house of Jeroboam.
16: 7 because of all the **evil** he had done in the eyes of the LORD,
20: 7 and said to them, "See how this man is looking for **trouble**!
21: 21 'I am going to bring **disaster** on you. I will consume your
21: 29 he has humbled himself, I will not bring this **disaster** in his day,
21: 29 but I will bring **it**° [+2021] on his house in the days of his son."
22: 23 prophets of yours. The LORD has decreed **disaster** for you."
2Ki 6: 33 to him. And ⌊the king⌋ said, "This **disaster** is from the LORD.
8: 12 "Because I know the **harm** you will do to the Israelites,"
14: 10 Why ask for **trouble** and cause your own downfall and that of
21: 12 I am going to bring such **disaster** on Jerusalem and Judah that the
22: 16 I am going to bring **disaster** on this place and its people,
22: 20 Your eyes will not see all the **disaster** I am going to bring on this
1Ch 4: 10 with me, and keep me from **harm** so that I will be free from pain."
7: 23 him Beriah, because there had been **misfortune** in his family.
21: 15 the LORD saw it and was grieved because of the **calamity**
2Ch 7: 22 serving them—that is why he brought all this **disaster** on them.' "
18: 7 he never prophesies anything good about me, but always **bad**.
18: 22 prophets of yours. The LORD has decreed **disaster** for you."
20: 9 'If **calamity** comes upon us, whether the sword of judgment,
25: 19 Why ask for **trouble** and cause your own downfall and that of
34: 24 I am going to bring **disaster** on this place and its people—
34: 28 Your eyes will not see all the **disaster** I am going to bring on this
Ne 1: 3 and are back in the province are in great **trouble** and disgrace.
2: 10 they *were* **very** much **disturbed** [+4200+8317] that someone had
2: 17 I said to them, "You see the **trouble** we are in: Jerusalem lies in
6: 2 of Ono." But they were scheming to **harm** [+4200+6913] me;
13: 7 Here I learned about the **evil thing** Eliashib had done in providing
13: 18 so that our God brought all this **calamity** upon us and upon this
13: 27 we hear now that you too are doing all this terrible **wickedness**
Est 7: 7 But Haman, realizing that the king had already decided his **fate**,
8: 3 She begged him to put an end to the **evil** plan of Haman the
8: 6 For how can I bear to see **disaster** fall on my people? How can I
9: 2 of King Xerxes to attack those seeking their **destruction**.
9: 25 he issued written orders that the **evil** scheme Haman had devised
Job 2: 11 heard about all the **troubles** that had come upon him,
20: 12 "Though **evil** is sweet in his mouth and he hides it under his
22: 5 Is not your **wickedness** great? Are not your sins endless?
42: 11 consoled him over all the **trouble** the LORD had brought upon
Ps 15: 3 who does his neighbor no **wrong** and casts no slur on his
21: 11 [21:12] Though they plot **evil** against you and devise wicked
27: 5 For in the day of **trouble** he will keep me safe in his dwelling;
28: 3 cordially with their neighbors but harbor **malice** in their hearts.
34: 19 [34:20] A righteous man may have many **troubles**,
34: 21 [34:22] **Evil** will slay the wicked; the foes of the righteous will be
35: 4 to shame; may those who plot my **ruin** be turned back in dismay.
35: 12 They repay me **evil** for good and leave my soul forlorn.
35: 26 May all who gloat over my **distress** be put to shame
37: 19 In times of **disaster** they will not wither; in days of famine they
38: 12 [38:13] set their traps, those who would **harm** me talk of my ruin;
38: 20 [38:21] Those who repay my good with **evil** slander me when I
40: 12 [40:13] For **troubles** without number surround me; my sins have
40: 14 [40:15] may all who desire my **ruin** be turned back in disgrace.
41: 1 [41:2] for the weak; the LORD delivers him in times of **trouble**.
41: 7 [41:8] against me; they imagine the **worst** for me, saying,
50: 19 You use your mouth for **evil** and harness your tongue to deceit.
52: 1 [52:3] Why do you boast of **evil**, you mighty man? Why do you
55: 15 [55:16] alive to the grave, for **evil** finds lodging among them.
70: 2 [70:3] may all who desire my **ruin** be turned back in disgrace.
71: 13 may those who want to **harm** me be covered with scorn
71: 24 for those who wanted to **harm** me have been put to shame
88: 3 [88:4] For my soul is full of **trouble** and my life draws near the
90: 15 you have afflicted us, for as many years as we have seen **trouble**.
91: 10 then no **harm** will befall you, no disaster will come near your tent.
94: 23 repay them for their sins and destroy them for their **wickedness**;
107: 26 went down to the depths; in their **peril** their courage melted away.
107: 34 a salt waste, because of the **wickedness** *of* those who lived there.
107: 39 and they were humbled by oppression, **calamity** and sorrow;
109: 5 They repay me **evil** for good, and hatred for my friendship.
141: 5 not refuse it. Yet my prayer is ever against the **deeds of evildoers**;
Pr 1: 33 to me will live in safety and be at ease, without fear of **harm**."
3: 29 Do not plot **harm** against your neighbor, who lives trustfully near
3: 30 not accuse a man for no reason—when he has done you no **harm**.
6: 18 that devises wicked schemes, feet that are quick to rush into **evil**,
11: 19 man attains life, but he who pursues **evil** goes to his death.
11: 27 good finds goodwill, but **evil** comes to him who searches for it.
13: 21 **Misfortune** pursues the sinner, but prosperity is the reward of the
14: 32 When **calamity** comes, the wicked are brought down, but even in
15: 28 weighs its answers, but the mouth of the wicked gushes **evil**.
16: 4 for his own ends—even the wicked for a day of **disaster**.
16: 27 A scoundrel plots **evil**, and his speech is like a scorching fire.
16: 30 his eye is plotting perversity; he who purses his lips is bent on **evil**.
17: 13 If a man pays back **evil** for good, evil will never leave his house.
17: 13 If a man pays back evil for good, **evil** will never leave his house.
17: 20 does not prosper; he whose tongue is deceitful falls into **trouble**.
22: 3 A prudent man sees **danger** and takes refuge, but the simple keep
24: 1 Do not envy **wicked** men, do not desire their company;
24: 16 he rises again, but the wicked are brought down by **calamity**.
26: 26 by deception, but his **wickedness** will be exposed in the assembly.
27: 12 The prudent see **danger** and take refuge, but the simple keep going
28: 14 fears the LORD, but he who hardens his heart falls into **trouble**.
Ecc 2: 21 not worked for it. This too is meaningless and a great **misfortune**.
5: 13 [5:12] I have seen a grievous **evil** under the sun: wealth hoarded
5: 13 [5:12] under the sun: wealth hoarded to the **harm** *of* its owner,
5: 16 [5:15] This too is a grievous **evil**: As a man comes, so he departs,
6: 1 I have seen another **evil** under the sun, and it weighs heavily on
7: 14 When times are good, be happy; but when times are **bad**, consider:
7: 15 his righteousness, and a wicked man living long in his **wickedness**.
8: 6 for every matter, though a man's **misery** weighs heavily upon him.
8: 11 When the sentence for a **crime** [+5126] is not quickly carried out,
9: 12 so men are trapped by **evil** times that fall unexpectedly upon them.
10: 5 There is an **evil** I have seen under the sun, the sort of error that
11: 2 for you do not know what **disaster** may come upon the land.
11: 10 anxiety from your heart and cast off the **troubles** of your body,
12: 1 before the days of **trouble** come and the years approach when you
Isa 3: 9 Woe to them! They have brought **disaster** upon themselves.
7: 5 Aram, Ephraim and Remaliah's son have plotted your **ruin**,
13: 11 I will punish the world for its **evil**, the wicked for their sins.
47: 10 You have trusted in your **wickedness** and have said, 'No one sees
47: 11 **Disaster** will come upon you, and you will not know how to
57: 1 that the righteous are taken away to be spared from **evil**.
Jer 1: 14 "From the north **disaster** will be poured out on all who live in the
1: 16 on my people because of their **wickedness** in forsaking me,
2: 3 held guilty, and **disaster** overtook them,' " declares the LORD.
2: 13 "My people have committed two **sins**: They have forsaken me,
2: 19 Your **wickedness** will punish you; your backsliding will rebuke
2: 27 yet when they are in **trouble**, they say, 'Come and save us!'
2: 28 Let them come if they can save you when you are in **trouble**!
3: 2 You have defiled the land with your prostitution and **wickedness**.
4: 6 For I am bringing **disaster** from the north, even terrible
4: 14 O Jerusalem, wash the **evil** from your heart and be saved. How
4: 18 This is your **punishment**. How bitter it is! How it pierces to the
5: 12 No **harm** will come to us; we will never see sword or famine.
6: 1 For **disaster** looms out of the north, even terrible destruction.
6: 7 As a well pours out its water, so she pours out her **wickedness**.
6: 19 I am bringing **disaster** on this people, the fruit of their schemes,
7: 12 see what I did to it because of the **wickedness** *of* my people Israel.
8: 6 No one repents of his **wickedness**, saying, "What have I done?"
9: 3 [9:2] They go from *one* **sin** to another; they do not acknowledge
9: 3 [9:2] They go from one sin to **another**°; they do not acknowledge
11: 11 'I will bring on them a **disaster** they cannot escape. Although they
11: 12 but they will not help them at all when **disaster** strikes.

[A] Qal [B] Qal passive [C] Niphal [D] Piel (poel, polel, pilel, pilal, pealal, pilpel) [E] Pual (poal, polal, poalal, pulal, pualal)

Jer 11: 14 I will not listen when they call to me in the time of their **distress**.
11: 15 When you engage in your **wickedness**, then you rejoice."
11: 17 LORD Almighty, who planted you, has decreed **disaster** for you,
11: 17 because the house of Israel and the house of Judah have done **evil**
11: 23 because I will bring **disaster** on the men of Anathoth in the year
12: 4 Because those who live in it are **wicked**, the animals and birds
14: 16 their daughters. I will pour out on them the **calamity** they *deserve*.
15: 11 I will make your enemies plead with you in times of **disaster**
16: 10 'Why has the LORD decreed such a great **disaster** against us?
17: 17 Do not be a terror to me; you are my refuge in the day of **disaster**.
17: 18 Bring on them the day of **disaster**; destroy them with double
18: 8 and if that nation I warned repents of its **evil**, then I will relent
18: 8 then I will relent and not inflict on it the **disaster** I had planned.
18: 10 [if it does **evil** [K; see Q 8273] in my sight and does not obey me,]
18: 11 I am preparing a **disaster** for you and devising a plan against you.
18: 20 Should good be repaid with **evil**? Yet they have dug a pit for me.
19: 3 I am going to bring a **disaster** on this place that will make the ears
19: 15 the villages around it every **disaster** I pronounced against them,
21: 10 I have determined to do this city **harm** and not good,
22: 22 will be ashamed and disgraced because of all your **wickedness**.
23: 10 The ⌞prophets⌟ follow an **evil** course and use their power unjustly.
23: 11 even in my temple I find their **wickedness**," declares the LORD.
23: 12 I will bring **disaster** on them in the year they are punished,"
23: 14 the hands of evildoers, so that no one turns from his **wickedness**.
23: 17 stubbornness of their hearts they say, 'No **harm** will come to you.'
24: 9 them abhorrent and an **offense** to all the kingdoms of the earth,
25: 32 **Disaster** is spreading from nation to nation; a mighty storm is
26: 3 I will relent and not bring on them the **disaster** I was planning
26: 13 and not bring the **disaster** he has pronounced against you.
26: 19 so that he did not bring the **disaster** he pronounced against them?
26: 19 We are about to bring a terrible **disaster** on ourselves!"
28: 8 **disaster** and plague against many countries and great kingdoms.
29: 11 declares the LORD, "plans to prosper you and not to **harm** you,
32: 23 them to do. So you brought all this **disaster** upon them.
32: 32 and Judah have provoked me by all the **evil** they have done—
32: 42 As I have brought all this great **calamity** on this people, so I will
33: 5 I will hide my face from this city because of all its **wickedness**.
35: 15 "Each of you must turn from your **wicked** ways and reform your
35: 17 on everyone living in Jerusalem every **disaster** I pronounced
36: 3 Perhaps when the people of Judah hear about every **disaster** I plan
36: 3 to inflict on them, each of them will turn from his **wicked** way;
36: 7 each will turn from his **wicked** ways, for the anger and wrath
36: 31 and the people of Judah every **disaster** I pronounced against them,
38: 4 This man is not seeking the good of these people but their **ruin**."
39: 16 I am about to fulfill my words against this city through **disaster**,
40: 2 "The LORD your God decreed this **disaster** for this place.
41: 11 all the army officers who were with him heard about all the **crimes**
42: 10 for I am grieved over the **disaster** I have inflicted on you.
42: 17 of them will survive or escape the **disaster** I will bring on them.'
44: 2 You saw the great **disaster** I brought on Jerusalem and on all the
44: 3 because of the **evil** they have done. They provoked me to anger by
44: 5 they did not turn from their **wickedness** or stop burning incense to
44: 7 Why bring such great **disaster** on yourselves by cutting off from
44: 9 Have you forgotten the **wickedness** committed *by* your fathers
44: 9 **[RPH]** by the kings and queens of Judah and the wickedness
44: 9 queens of Judah **[RPH]** and the wickedness committed by you
44: 9 and queens of Judah and the **wickedness** committed *by* you
44: 9 **[RPH]** your wives in the land of Judah and the streets of
44: 11 I am determined to bring **disaster** on you and to destroy all Judah.
44: 17 we had plenty of food and were well off and suffered no **harm**.
44: 23 his stipulations, this **disaster** has come upon you, as you now see."
44: 27 For I am watching over them for **harm**, not for good; the Jews in
44: 29 'so that you will know that my threats of **harm** against you will
45: 5 For I will bring **disaster** on all people, declares the LORD,
48: 2 will be praised no more; in Heshbon men will plot her **downfall**:
48: 16 "The fall of Moab is at hand; her **calamity** will come quickly.
49: 37 I will bring **disaster** upon them, even my fierce anger,"
51: 2 they will oppose her on every side in the day of her **disaster**.
51: 24 all who live in Babylonia for all the **wrong** they have done in
51: 60 Jeremiah had written on a scroll about all the **disasters** that would
51: 64 sink to rise no more because of the **disaster** I will bring upon her.
La 1: 21 All my enemies have heard of my **distress**; they rejoice at what
1: 22 "Let all their **wickedness** come before you; deal with them as you
3: 38 Is it not from the mouth of the Most High that both **calamities**
Eze 6: 9 They will loathe themselves for the **evil** they have done and for all
6: 10 I did not threaten in vain to bring this **calamity** on them.
6: 11 because of all the **wicked** and detestable practices of the house of
7: 5 LORD says: **Disaster**! An unheard-of disaster is coming.
7: 5 LORD says: Disaster! An unheard-of **disaster** is coming.
14: 22 you will be consoled regarding the **disaster** I have brought upon
16: 23 the Sovereign LORD. In addition to all your other **wickedness**,
16: 57 before your **wickedness** was uncovered. Even so, you are now
20: 43 and you will loathe yourselves for all the **evil** you have done.
20: 44 and not according to your **evil** ways and your corrupt practices,
Da 9: 12 and against our rulers by bringing upon us great **disaster**.
9: 13 is written in the Law of Moses, all this **disaster** has come upon us,
9: 14 The LORD did not hesitate to bring the **disaster** upon us,
Hos 7: 1 sins of Ephraim are exposed and the **crimes** *of* Samaria revealed.
7: 2 but they do not realize that I remember all their **evil deeds**.
7: 3 "They delight the king with their **wickedness**, the princes with
9: 15 "Because of all their **wickedness** in Gilgal, I hated them there.
10: 15 to you, O Bethel, because your **wickedness** [+8288] **is great**.
10: 15 to you, O Bethel, because your **wickedness is great** [+8288].
Joel 2: 13 and abounding in love, and he relents from sending **calamity**.
3: 13 [4:13] and the vats overflow—so great is their **wickedness**!"
Am 3: 6 When **disaster** comes to a city, has not the LORD caused it?
9: 4 slay them. I will fix my eyes upon them for **evil** and not for good."
9: 10 all those who say, '**Disaster** will not overtake or meet us.'
Ob 1: 13 nor look down on them in their **calamity** in the day of their
Jnh 1: 2 preach against it, because its **wickedness** has come up before me."
1: 7 let us cast lots to find out who is responsible for this **calamity**."
1: 8 "Tell us, who is responsible for making all this **trouble** for us?
3: 10 and did not bring upon them the **destruction** he had threatened.
4: 1 But Jonah *was* greatly **displeased** [+448+8317] and became angry.
4: 2 and abounding in love, a God who relents from sending **calamity**.
4: 6 up over Jonah to give shade for his head to ease his **discomfort**,
Mic 2: 3 "I am planning **disaster** against this people, from which you
2: 3 You will no longer walk proudly, for it will be a time of **calamity**.
3: 2 [you who hate good and love **evil**; [K; see Q 8273] who tear the]
3: 11 "Is not the LORD among us? No **disaster** will come upon us."
Na 1: 11 ⌞O Nineveh,⌟ has one come forth who plots **evil** against the
3: 19 his hands at your fall, for who has not felt your endless **cruelty**?
Zec 1: 15 I was only a little angry, but they added to the **calamity**.'
7: 10 or the poor. In your hearts do not think **evil** *of* each other.'
8: 17 do not plot **evil** against your neighbor, and do not love to swear

8289 [4]רָעָה **rā'â[4]**, v.den. Not used in NIV/BHS [cf. 8287]

8290 [5]רָעָה **rā'â[5]**, v. Not used in NIV/BHS

8291 רֵעֶה **rē'eh**, n.m. [4] [√ 8287]

friend [2], one who is close [1], personal adviser [1]

2Sa 12: 11 I will take your wives and give them to **one who is close** *to* you,
15: 37 So David's **friend** Hushai arrived at Jerusalem as Absalom was
16: 16 David's **friend**, went to Absalom and said to him, "Long live the
1Ki 4: 5 Zabud son of Nathan—a priest and **personal adviser** *to* the king;
Pr 27: 10 [forsake your friend and the **friend** [K; see Q 8276] *of* your father,]

8292 רֵעָה **rē'â**, n.f. [3] [√ 8287]

companions [1], friends [1], girls [1]

Jdg 11: 37 "Give me two months to roam the hills and weep with my **friends**,
11: 38 She and the **girls** went into the hills and wept because she would
Ps 45: 14 [45:15] her virgin **companions** follow her and are brought to you.

8293 רְעוּ **rᵉ'û**, n.pr.m. [5] [√ 8287; cf. 8298]

Reu [5]

Ge 11: 18 When Peleg had lived 30 years, he became the father of **Reu**.
11: 19 And after he became the father of **Reu**, Peleg lived 209 years
11: 20 When **Reu** had lived 32 years, he became the father of Serug.
11: 21 of Serug, **Reu** lived 207 years and had other sons and daughters.
1Ch 1: 25 Eber, Peleg, **Reu**,

8294 רְעוּאֵל **rᵉ'û'ēl**, n.pr.m. [11 / 10] [√ 8287 + 446]

Reuel [10]

Ge 36: 4 Adah bore Eliphaz to Esau, Basemath bore **Reuel**,
36: 10 Eliphaz, the son of Esau's wife Adah, and **Reuel**, the son of Esau's
36: 13 The sons of **Reuel**: Nahath, Zerah, Shammah and Mizzah.
36: 17 The sons of Esau's son **Reuel**: Chiefs Nahath, Zerah, Shammah
36: 17 These were the chiefs descended from **Reuel** in Edom; they were
Ex 2: 18 When the girls returned to **Reuel** their father, he asked them,
Nu 2: 14 of Gad is Eliasaph son of Deuel. [BHS ***Reuel***; NIV 1979]
10: 29 Now Moses said to Hobab son of **Reuel** the Midianite,
1Ch 1: 35 The sons of Esau: Eliphaz, **Reuel**, Jeush, Jalam and Korah.
1: 37 The sons of **Reuel**: Nahath, Zerah, Shammah and Mizzah.
9: 8 Meshullam son of Shephatiah, the son of **Reuel**, the son of Ibnijah.

8295 רְעוּת **rᵉ'ût[1]**, n.f. [6] [√ 8287]

mate [2], *untranslated* [1], another's[s] [1], another[s] [1], someone else [1]

Ex 11: 2 women alike are to ask their neighbors for **[RPH]** articles of
Est 1: 19 Also let the king give her royal position to **someone else** who is
Isa 34: 15 of her wings; there also the falcons will gather, each with its **mate**.
34: 16 None of these will be missing, not one will lack her **mate**.
Jer 9: 20 [9:19] your daughters how to wail; teach one **another**[s] a lament.
Zec 11: 9 perishing perish. Let those who are left eat one **another's**[s] flesh."

8296 רְעוּת ***r*e*'ût*[2]**, n.f. [7] [√ 8290; Ar 10668]
chasing after [7]

Ecc 1: 14 the sun; all of them are meaningless, a **chasing after** the wind.
2: 11 to achieve, everything was meaningless, a **chasing after** the wind;
2: 17 grievous to me. All of it is meaningless, a **chasing after** the wind.
2: 26 pleases God. This too is meaningless, a **chasing after** the wind.
4: 4 of his neighbor. This too is meaningless, a **chasing after** the wind.
4: 6 tranquillity than two handfuls with toil and **chasing after** the wind.
6: 9 of the appetite. This too is meaningless, a **chasing after** the wind.

8297 רְעִי ***r*e*'î***, n.[m.]. [1] [√ 8286]
pasture-fed [1]

1Ki 4: 23 [5:3] twenty of **pasture-fed** cattle and a hundred sheep and goats,

8298 רֵעִי ***rē'î***, n.pr.m. [1] [√ 8287; cf. 8293]
Rei [1]

1Ki 1: 8 Shimei and **Rei** and David's special guard did not join Adonijah.

8299 רַעְיָה ***ra'yâ***, n.f. [9] [√ 8287]
darling [9]

SS 1: 9 I liken you, my **darling**, to a mare harnessed to one of the chariots
1: 15 How beautiful you are, my **darling**! Oh, how beautiful! Your eyes
2: 2 Like a lily among thorns is my **darling** among the maidens.
2: 10 My lover spoke and said to me, "Arise, my **darling**, my beautiful
2: 13 Arise, come, my **darling**; my beautiful one, come with me."
4: 1 How beautiful you are, my **darling**! Oh, how beautiful! Your eyes
4: 7 All beautiful you are, my **darling**; there is no flaw in you.
5: 2 "Open to me, my sister, my **darling**, my dove, my flawless one.
6: 4 You are beautiful, my **darling**, as Tirzah, lovely as Jerusalem,

8300 רֵעְיָה ***rē'yâ***, n.f. Not used in NIV/BHS [√ 8287]

8301 רַעְיוֹן ***ra'yôn***, n.[m.]. [3] [√ 8290]
chasing after [2], anxious striving [+4213] [1]

Ecc 1: 17 and folly, but I learned that this, too, is a **chasing after** the wind.
2: 22 and **anxious striving** [+4213] with which he labors under the sun?
4: 16 the successor. This too is meaningless, a **chasing after** the wind.

8302 רָעַל ***rā'al***, v. [1] [→ 5339, 8303, 8304, 9570]
brandished [1]

Na 2: 3 [2:4] [H] are made ready; the spears of pine *are* **brandished**.

8303 רַעַל ***ra'al***, n.[m.]. [1] [√ 8302]
reeling [1]

Zec 12: 2 Jerusalem a cup that sends all the surrounding peoples **reeling**.

8304 רְעָלָה ***r*e*'ālâ***, n.[f.]. [1] [√ 8302]
veils [1]

Isa 3: 19 the earrings and bracelets and **veils**,

8305 רְעֵלָיָה ***r*e*'ēlāyâ***, n.pr.m. [1] [cf. 8313]
Reelaiah [1]

Ezr 2: 2 Seraiah, **Reelaiah**, Mordecai, Bilshan, Mispar, Bigvai, Rehum

8306 רָעַם ***rā'am*[1]**, v.den. [11] [→ 8308, 8312, 8313]
resound [3], thundered [3], thunders [3], thunder [2]

1Sa 2: 10 [G] *He will* **thunder** against them from heaven; the LORD will
7: 10 [G] that day the LORD **thundered** with loud thunder against
2Sa 22: 14 [G] The LORD **thundered** from heaven; the voice of the Most
1Ch 16: 32 [A] *Let* the sea **resound**, and all that is in it; let the fields be
Job 37: 4 [G] the sound of his roar; *he* **thunders** with his majestic voice.
37: 5 [G] God's voice **thunders** in marvelous ways; he does great
40: 9 [G] an arm like God's, and *can* your voice **thunder** like his?
Ps 18: 13 [18:14] [G] The LORD **thundered** from heaven; the voice of
29: 3 [G] the God of glory **thunders**, the LORD thunders over the
96: 11 [A] let the earth be glad; *let* the sea **resound**, and all that is in it;
98: 7 [A] *Let* the sea **resound**, and everything in it, the world, and all

8307 רָעַם ***rā'am*[2]**, v.den. [2]
distorted with fear [1], irritate [1]

1Sa 1: 6 [G] her rival kept provoking her in order to **irritate** her.
Eze 27: 35 [A] shudder with horror and their faces *are* **distorted with fear**.

8308 רַעַם ***ra'am***, n.[m.]. [6] [√ 8306]
thunder [4], shout [1], thundercloud [+6260] [1]

Job 26: 14 hear of him! Who then can understand the **thunder** *of* his power?"
39: 25 of battle from afar, the **shout** *of* commanders and the battle cry.
Ps 77: 18 [77:19] Your **thunder** was heard in the whirlwind, your lightning
81: 7 [81:8] I answered you out of a **thundercloud** [+6260];
104: 7 the waters fled, at the sound of your **thunder** they took to flight;
Isa 29: 6 the LORD Almighty will come with **thunder** and earthquake

8309 רַעְמָא ***ra'mā'***, n.pr.m. [2] [cf. 8311]
Raamah [2]

1Ch 1: 9 The sons of Cush: Seba, Havilah, Sabta, **Raamah** and Sabteca.
1: 9 Raamah and Sabteca. The sons of **Raamah**: Sheba and Dedan.

8310 רַעְמָה[1] ***ra'mâ*[1]**, n.f. [1]
flowing mane [1]

Job 39: 19 give the horse his strength or clothe his neck with a **flowing mane**?

8311 רַעְמָה[2] ***ra'mâ*[2]**, n.pr.m. [3] [cf. 8309]
Raamah [3]

Ge 10: 7 The sons of Cush: Seba, Havilah, Sabtah, **Raamah** and Sabteca.
10: 7 Raamah and Sabteca. The sons of **Raamah**: Sheba and Dedan.
Eze 27: 22 " 'The merchants of Sheba and **Raamah** traded with you; for your

8312 רַעְמָה[3] ***ra'mâ*[3]**, n.f. Not used in NIV/BHS [√ 8306]

8313 רַעַמְיָה ***ra'amyâ***, n.pr.m. [1] [√ 8306 + 3378; cf. 8305]
Raamiah [1]

Ne 7: 7 Azariah, **Raamiah**, Nahamani, Mordecai, Bilshan, Mispereth,

8314 רַעְמְסֵס ***ra'm*e*sēs***, n.pr.loc. [5]
Rameses [5]

Ge 47: 11 best part of the land, the district of **Rameses**, as Pharaoh directed.
Ex 1: 11 and they built Pithom and **Rameses** as store cities for Pharaoh.
12: 37 The Israelites journeyed from **Rameses** to Succoth. There were
Nu 33: 3 The Israelites set out from **Rameses** on the fifteenth day of the first
33: 5 The Israelites left **Rameses** and camped at Succoth.

8315 רָעַן ***rā'an***, v. [1] [→ 8316]
flourish [1]

Job 15: 32 [D] he will be paid in full, and his branches *will* not **flourish**.

8316 רַעֲנָן ***ra'anān***, a. [19] [√ 8315; Ar 10670]
spreading [11], green [3], fine [1], flourishing [1], green tree [1], thriving [1], verdant [1]

Dt 12: 2 under every **spreading** tree where the nations you are
1Ki 14: 23 Asherah poles on every high hill and under every **spreading** tree.
2Ki 16: 4 at the high places, on the hilltops and under every **spreading** tree.
17: 10 Asherah poles on every high hill and under every **spreading** tree.
2Ch 28: 4 at the high places, on the hilltops and under every **spreading** tree.
Ps 37: 35 and ruthless man flourishing like a **green tree** in its native soil,
52: 8 [52:10] I am like an olive tree **flourishing** in the house of God;
92: 10 [92:11] that of a wild ox; **fine** oils have been poured upon me.
92: 14 [92:15] still bear fruit in old age, they will stay fresh and **green**,
SS 1: 16 you are, my lover! Oh, how charming! And our bed is **verdant**.
Isa 57: 5 burn with lust among the oaks and under every **spreading** tree;
Jer 2: 20 and under every **spreading** tree you lay down as a prostitute.
3: 6 and under every **spreading** tree and has committed adultery there.
3: 13 scattered your favors to foreign gods under every **spreading** tree,
11: 16 The LORD called you a **thriving** olive tree with fruit beautiful in
17: 2 and Asherah poles beside the **spreading** trees and on the high hills.
17: 8 It does not fear when heat comes; its leaves are always **green**.
Eze 6: 13 under every **spreading** tree and every leafy oak—
Hos 14: 8 [14:9] I am like a **green** pine tree; your fruitfulness comes from

8317 רָעַע ***rā'a'*[1]**, v.den. [95] [→ 5334, 5336, 8273, 8274, 8278, 8288]
evil [10], wicked [10], harm [6], displeased [+928+6524] [5], evildoers [5], bring disaster [4], bad [3], brought trouble [3], do harm [3], distressed [+928+6524] [2], doing evil [2], done wrong [+8317] [2], mistreated [2], persist in doing evil [+8317] [2], acted wickedly [1], begrudge [+928+928+928+6524] [1], bring trouble [1], brought misfortune [1], brought to grief [1], brought tragedy [1], crushed [1], destruction brought [1], did evil [1], disapprove [+928+6524] [1], displeased [+448+8288] [1], displeased [1], do evil [1], do wicked thing [1], doing wrong [1], done evil [1], downhearted [+4222] [1], galled [+928+6524] [1], grudging [1], harming [1], have no

compassion [+6524] [1], hurts [1], leads to evil [1], look sad [1], not please [+928+6524] [1], show ill will [+6524] [1], sinned [1], suffers harm [1], surely suffer [+8273] [1], treat worse [1], trouble came [1], upset [+906+928+6524] [1], very disturbed [+4200+8288] [1], vile [1], wickedly [1], wronged [1]

Ge 19: 7 [G] and said, "No, my friends. Don't **do** *this* **wicked thing**.
19: 9 [G] *We'll* **treat** you **worse** than them." They kept bringing
21: 11 [A] The matter **distressed** [+928+6524] Abraham greatly
21: 12 [A] "*Do* not *be so* **distressed** [+928+6524] about the boy
31: 7 [G] ten times. However, God has not allowed him to **harm** me.
38: 10 [A] What he did *was* **wicked** in the LORD's sight; so he put
43: 6 [G] "Why *did you* **bring** *this* **trouble** on me by telling the man
44: 5 [G] for divination? *This is a* **wicked** *thing* you have done.' "
48: 17 [A] right hand on Ephraim's head he *was* **displeased** [+928+6524];
Ex 5: 22 [G] "O Lord, why *have you* **brought trouble** upon this people?
5: 23 [G] *he has* **brought trouble** upon this people, and you have not
21: 8 [A] If *she does* **not please** [+928+6524] the master who has
Lev 5: 4 [G] takes an oath to do anything, whether good or **evil**—
Nu 11: 11 [G] "Why *have you* **brought** *this* **trouble** on your servant?
16: 15 [G] as a donkey from them, nor *have I* **wronged** any of them."
20: 15 [G] many years. The Egyptians **mistreated** us and our fathers,
22: 34 [A] Now if you *are* **displeased** [+928+6524], I will go back."
Dt 15: 9 [A] so that you *do* not **show ill** [+6524] **will** toward your needy
15: 10 [A] Give generously to him and do so without a **grudging** heart;
26: 6 [G] the Egyptians **mistreated** us and made us suffer, putting us
28: 54 [A] sensitive man among you *will* **have no compassion** [+6524]
28: 56 [A] *will* **begrudge** [+928+928+928+6524] the husband she loves
Jos 24: 20 [G] he will turn and **bring disaster** on you and make an end of
Jdg 19: 23 [G] and said to them, "No, my friends, don't *be so* **vile**.
Ru 1: 21 [G] the Almighty *has* **brought misfortune** upon me."
1Sa 1: 8 [A] Why don't you eat? Why *are* you **downhearted** [+4222]?
8: 6 [A] us a king to lead us," this **displeased** [+928+6524] Samuel;
12: 25 [G] Yet if *you* **persist in doing evil** [+8317], both you and your
12: 25 [G] Yet if *you* **persist in doing evil** [+8317], both you and your
18: 8 [A] Saul was very angry; this refrain **galled** [+928+6524] him.
25: 34 [G] the God of Israel, lives, who has kept me from **harming** you,
26: 21 [G] my life precious today, *I will* not *try to* **harm** you again.
2Sa 11: 25 [A] 'Don't *let* this **upset** [+906+928+6524] you; the sword
11: 27 [A] the thing David had done **displeased** [+928+6524] the
20: 6 [A] "Now Sheba son of Bicri *will* **do** us more **harm** than
1Ki 14: 9 [G] *You have* done more **evil** than all who lived before you. You
16: 25 [G] of the LORD and **sinned** more than all those before him.
17: 20 [G] *have you* **brought tragedy** also upon this widow I am
2Ki 21: 11 [G] *He has* **done** more **evil** than the Amorites who preceded him
1Ch 16: 22 [G] "Do not touch my anointed ones; *do* my prophets no **harm**."
21: 7 [A] This command *was* also **evil** in the sight of God; so he
21: 17 [G] I am the one who has sinned and **done wrong** [+8317].
21: 17 [G] I am the one who has sinned and **done wrong** [+8317].
Ne 2: 3 [A] Why *should* my face not **look sad** when the city where my
2: 10 [A] they *were* **very** much **disturbed** [+4200+8288] that someone
13: 8 [A] I *was* greatly **displeased** and threw all Tobiah's household
Job 8: 20 [G] reject a blameless man or strengthen the hands of **evildoers**.
Ps 15: 4 [G] fear the LORD, who keeps his oath even when *it* **hurts**,
22: 16 [22:17] [G] a band of **evil** *men* has encircled me, they have
26: 5 [G] I abhor the assembly of **evildoers** and refuse to sit with the
27: 2 [G] When **evil** *men* advance against me to devour my flesh,
37: 1 [G] Do not fret because of **evil** *men* or be envious of those who
37: 8 [G] and turn from wrath; do not fret—it **leads** only **to evil**.
37: 9 [G] For **evil** *men* will be cut off, but those who hope in the
44: 2 [44:3] [G] *you* **crushed** the peoples and made our fathers
64: 2 [64:3] [G] Hide me from the conspiracy of the **wicked**,
74: 3 [G] all *this* **destruction** the enemy *has* **brought** on the
92: 11 [92:12] [G] my ears have heard the rout of my **wicked** foes.
94: 16 [G] Who will rise up for me against the **wicked**? Who will take a
105: 15 [G] "Do not touch my anointed ones; **do** my prophets no **harm**."
106: 32 [A] the LORD, and **trouble came** to Moses because of them;
119: 115 [G] Away from me, you **evildoers**, that I may keep the
Pr 4: 16 [G] For they cannot sleep till *they* **do evil**; they are robbed of
11: 15 [C] who puts up security for another *will* **surely suffer** [+8273],
13: 20 [C] the wise grows wise, but a companion of fools **suffers harm**.
17: 4 [G] A **wicked** *man* listens to evil lips; a liar pays attention to a
24: 8 [G] He who plots **evil** will be known as a schemer.
24: 18 [A] or the LORD will see and **disapprove** [+928+6524] and turn
24: 19 [G] Do not fret because of **evil** *men* or be envious of the wicked,
25: 19 [A] Like a **bad** tooth or a lame foot is reliance on the unfaithful
Isa 1: 4 [G] a people loaded with guilt, a brood of **evildoers**,
1: 16 [G] Take your evil deeds out of my sight! Stop **doing wrong**,
9: 17 [9:16] [G] and widows, for everyone is ungodly and **wicked**,
11: 9 [G] *They will* neither **harm** nor destroy on all my holy mountain,
14: 20 [G] The offspring of the **wicked** will never be mentioned again.
31: 2 [G] He will rise up against the house of the **wicked**, against those
41: 23 [G] Do something, whether good or **bad**, so that we will be
59: 15 [A] and *was* **displeased** [+928+6524] that there was no justice.
65: 25 [G] *They will* neither **harm** nor destroy on all my holy
Jer 4: 22 [G] They are skilled in **doing evil**; they know not how to do
7: 26 [G] were stiff-necked and **did** more **evil** than their forefathers.'
10: 5 [G] fear them; *they can* **do** no **harm** nor can they do any good."
13: 23 [G] Neither can you do good who are accustomed to **doing evil**.
16: 12 [G] you have behaved more **wickedly** than your fathers. See how
20: 13 [G] rescues the life of the needy from the hands of the **wicked**.
23: 14 [G] They strengthen the hands of **evildoers**, so that no one turns
25: 6 [G] what your hands have made. Then *I will* not **harm** you."
25: 29 [G] I am beginning to **bring disaster** on the city that bears my
31: 28 [G] and tear down, and to overthrow, destroy and **bring disaster**,
38: 9 [G] these men *have* **acted wickedly** in all they have done to
Jnh 4: 1 [A] Jonah *was* greatly **displeased** [+448+8288] and became
Mic 3: 4 [G] hide his face from them because of the **evil** they have done.
4: 6 [G] I will assemble the exiles and those *I have* **brought to grief**.
Zep 1: 12 [G] who think, 'The LORD will do nothing, either good or **bad**.'
Zec 8: 14 [G] "Just as I had determined to **bring disaster** upon you

8318 ²רָעַע rā'a², v. [7 / 6] [cf. 8320, 8368]

is broken up [+8318] [2], break [1], broken [1], come to ruin [1], shatters [1]

Job 34: 24 [A] Without inquiry *he* **shatters** the mighty and sets up others in
Ps 2: 9 [a] *You will* rule [BHS ***break***; NIV 8286] them with an iron scepter;
Pr 18: 24 [F] A man of many companions *may* **come to ruin**, but there is a
Isa 24: 19 [F] The earth **is broken** [+8318] **up**, the earth is split asunder,
24: 19 [A] The earth **is broken up** [+8318], the earth is split asunder,
Jer 11: 16 [A] storm he will set it on fire, and its branches *will be* **broken**.
15: 12 [A] "*Can a man* **break** iron—iron from the north—or bronze?

8319 רָעַף rā'ap, v. [5] [cf. 6903]

overflow [2], let drop [1], rain down [1], showers fall [1]

Job 36: 28 [A] down their moisture and abundant **showers fall** on mankind.
Ps 65: 11 [65:12] [A] and your carts **overflow** *with* abundance.
65: 12 [65:13] [A] The grasslands of the desert **overflow**; the hills are
Pr 3: 20 [A] the deeps were divided, and the clouds **let drop** the dew.
Isa 45: 8 [G] "*You* heavens above, **rain down** righteousness; let the

8320 רָעַץ rā'aṣ, v. [2] [cf. 8318, 8368]

shattered [2]

Ex 15: 6 [A] in power. Your right hand, O LORD, **shattered** the enemy.
Jdg 10: 8 [A] *who* that year **shattered** and crushed them. For eighteen

8321 ¹רָעַשׁ rā'aš¹, v. [30] [→ 8323]

shake [6], tremble [6], trembles [4], quake [3], quaked [3], made tremble [2], shook [2], make leap [1], quaking [1], shaken [1], sway [1]

Jdg 5: 4 [A] the earth **shook**, the heavens poured, the clouds poured down
2Sa 22: 8 [A] "The earth trembled and **quaked**, the foundations of the
Job 39: 20 [G] *Do you* **make** him **leap** like a locust, striking terror with his
Ps 18: 7 [18:8] [A] The earth trembled and **quaked**, and the foundations
46: 3 [46:4] [A] and the mountains **quake** with their surging.
60: 2 [60:4] [G] *You have* **shaken** the land and torn it open; mend its
68: 8 [68:9] [A] the earth **shook**, the heavens poured down rain,
72: 16 [A] throughout the land; on the tops of the hills *may it* **sway**.
77: 18 [77:19] [A] lit up the world; the earth trembled and **quaked**.
Isa 13: 13 [A] the earth *will* **shake** from its place at the wrath of the
14: 16 [G] the man who shook the earth and **made** kingdoms **tremble**,
24: 18 [A] the heavens are opened, the foundations of the earth **shake**.
Jer 4: 24 [A] I looked at the mountains, and *they were* **quaking**; all the
8: 16 [A] at the neighing of their stallions the whole land **trembles**.
10: 10 [A] When he is angry, the earth **trembles**; the nations cannot
49: 21 [A] At the sound of their fall the earth *will* **tremble**; their cry will
50: 46 [C] At the sound of Babylon's capture the earth *will* **tremble**;
51: 29 [A] The land **trembles** and writhes, for the LORD's purposes
Eze 26: 10 [A] Your walls *will* **tremble** at the noise of the war horses,
26: 15 [A] *Will* not the coastlands **tremble** at the sound of your fall,
27: 28 [A] The shorelands *will* **quake** when your seamen cry out.
31: 16 [G] *I* **made** the nations **tremble** at the sound of its fall when I
38: 20 [A] all the people on the face of the earth *will* **tremble** at my
Joel 2: 10 [A] the sky **trembles**, the sun and moon are darkened,
3: 16 [4:16] [A] from Jerusalem; the earth and the sky *will* **tremble**.
Am 9: 1 [A] "Strike the tops of the pillars so that the thresholds **shake**.
Na 1: 5 [A] The mountains **quake** before him and the hills melt away.
Hag 2: 6 [G] I *will* once more **shake** the heavens and the earth, the sea and
2: 7 [G] *I will* **shake** all nations, and the desired of all nations will
2: 21 [G] governor of Judah that I *will* **shake** the heavens and

8322 ²רַעַשׁ rā'aš², v. Not used in NIV/BHS

8323 רַעַשׁ *ra'aš*, n.m. [17] [√ 8321]
earthquake [7], rumbling [2], battle [1], clatter [+7754] [1], commotion [1], frenzied [1], noise [1], rattling sound [1], rattling [1], tremble [1]

1Ki 19: 11 After the wind there was an **earthquake**, but the LORD was not
19: 11 was an earthquake, but the LORD was not in the **earthquake**.
19: 12 After the **earthquake** came a fire, but the LORD was not in the
Job 39: 24 In **frenzied** excitement he eats up the ground; he cannot stand still
41: 29 [41:21] but a piece of straw; he laughs at the **rattling** *of* the lance.
Isa 9: 5 [9:4] Every warrior's boot used in **battle** and every garment
29: 6 Almighty will come with thunder and **earthquake** and great noise,
Jer 10: 22 report is coming—a great **commotion** from the land of the north!
47: 3 at the **noise** of enemy chariots and the rumble of their wheels.
Eze 3: 12 lifted me up, and I heard behind me a loud **rumbling** sound—
3: 13 and the sound of the wheels beside them, a loud **rumbling** sound.
12: 18 "Son of man, **tremble** as you eat your food, and shudder in fear as
37: 7 And as I was prophesying, there was a noise, a **rattling sound**,
38: 19 at that time there shall be a great **earthquake** in the land of Israel.
Am 1: 1 what he saw concerning Israel two years before the **earthquake**,
Na 3: 2 the **clatter** [+7754] *of* wheels, galloping horses and jolting
Zec 14: 5 You will flee as you fled from the **earthquake** in the days of

8324 ¹רָפָא *rāpā'*[1], v. [67] [→ 5340, 5342, 8325, 8326, 8334?, 8335?, 8336, 8337, 9559; *also used with compound proper names*]
heal [21], healed [10], heals [5], be healed [4], physicians [4], recover [3], be cured [2], cure [2], dress [2], fresh [2], see that is completely healed [+8324] [2], are healed [1], be repaired [1], been healed [1], gone [1], incurable [+4412] [1], makes fresh [1], mend [1], physician [1], repaired [1], wholesome [1]

Ge 20: 17 [A] God **healed** Abimelech, his wife and his slave girls so they
50: 2 [A] Joseph directed the **physicians** in his service to embalm his
50: 2 [A] embalm his father Israel. So the **physicians** embalmed him,
Ex 15: 26 [A] on the Egyptians, for I am the LORD, *who* **heals** you."
21: 19 [D] of his time and **see that** *he* **is completely healed** [+8324].
21: 19 [D] of his time and **see that** *he* **is completely healed** [+8324].
Lev 13: 18 [C] "When someone has a boil on his skin and *it* **heals**,
13: 37 [C] and black hair has grown in it, the itch *is* **healed**.
14: 3 [C] If the person *has* **been healed** of his infectious skin disease,
14: 48 [C] shall pronounce the house clean, because the mildew *is* **gone**.
Nu 12: 13 [A] So Moses cried out to the LORD, "O God, please **heal** her!"
Dt 28: 27 [C] festering sores and the itch, from which you cannot **be cured**.
28: 35 [C] your knees and legs with painful boils that cannot **be cured**,
32: 39 [A] to death and I bring to life, I have wounded and I *will* **heal**,
1Sa 6: 3 [C] *you will* **be healed**, and you will know why his hand has not
1Ki 18: 30 [D] They came to him, and *he* **repaired** the altar of the LORD,
2Ki 2: 21 [D] '*I have* **healed** this water. Never again will it cause death
2: 22 [C] the water *has remained* **wholesome** to this day, according to
8: 29 [F] so King Joram returned to Jezreel to **recover** from the
9: 15 [F] King Joram had returned to Jezreel to **recover** from the
20: 5 [A] I have heard your prayer and seen your tears; I *will* **heal** you.
20: 8 [A] "What will be the sign that the LORD *will* **heal** me and that
2Ch 7: 14 [A] and will forgive their sin and *will* **heal** their land.
16: 12 [A] seek help from the LORD, but only from the **physicians**.
22: 6 [F] so he returned to Jezreel to **recover** *from* the wounds they
30: 20 [A] And the LORD heard Hezekiah and **healed** the people.
Job 5: 18 [A] but he also binds up; he injures, but his hands also **heal**.
13: 4 [A] smear me with lies; you *are* worthless **physicians**, all of you!
Ps 6: 2 [6:3] [A] O LORD, **heal** me, for my bones are in agony.
30: 2 [30:3] [A] my God, I called to you for help and *you* **healed** me.
41: 4 [41:5] [A] on me; **heal** me, for I have sinned against you."
60: 2 [60:4] [A] and torn it open; **mend** its fractures, for it is quaking.
103: 3 [A] who forgives all your sins and **heals** all your diseases,
107: 20 [A] He sent forth his word and **healed** them; he rescued them
147: 3 [A] He **heals** the brokenhearted and binds up their wounds.
Ecc 3: 3 [A] a time to kill and a time to **heal**, a time to tear down and a
Isa 6: 10 [A] understand with their hearts, and turn and *be* **healed**."
19: 22 [A] Egypt with a plague; he will strike them and **heal** them.
19: 22 [A] the LORD, and he will respond to their pleas and **heal** them.
30: 26 [A] the bruises of his people and **heals** the wounds he inflicted.
53: 5 [C] us peace was upon him, and by his wounds we **are healed**.
57: 18 [A] I have seen his ways, but *I will* **heal** him; I will guide him
57: 19 [A] and near," says the LORD. "And *I will* **heal** them."
Jer 3: 22 [A] "Return, faithless people; *I will* **cure** you *of* backsliding."
6: 14 [D] *They* **dress** the wound of my people as though it were not
8: 11 [D] *They* **dress** the wound of my people as though it were not
8: 22 [A] Is there no **physician** there? Why then is there no healing for
15: 18 [C] and my wound grievous and **incurable** [+4412]?
17: 14 [A] **Heal** me, O LORD, and I will be healed; save me and I will
17: 14 [C] Heal me, O LORD, and *I will* **be healed**; save me and I will
19: 11 [C] just as this potter's jar is smashed and cannot **be repaired**.
30: 17 [A] I will restore you to health and **heal** your wounds,' declares
33: 6 [A] *I will* **heal** my people and will let them enjoy abundant peace
51: 8 [C] over her! Get balm for her pain; perhaps *she can* **be healed**.
51: 9 [D] " '*We would have* **healed** Babylon, but she cannot be
51: 9 [C] " 'We would have healed Babylon, but *she* cannot **be healed**;
La 2: 13 [A] Your wound is as deep as the sea. Who *can* **heal** you?
Eze 34: 4 [D] the weak or **healed** the sick or bound up the injured.
47: 8 [C] When it empties into the Sea, the water there *becomes* **fresh**.
47: 9 [C] this water flows there and **makes** the salt water **fresh**;
47: 11 [C] the swamps and marshes *will* not *become* **fresh**; they will be
Hos 5: 13 [A] But he is not able to **cure** you, not able to heal your sores.
6: 1 [A] He has torn us to pieces but *he will* **heal** us; he has injured us
7: 1 [A] whenever I *would* **heal** Israel, the sins of Ephraim are
11: 3 [A] the arms; but they did not realize *it was I who* **healed** them.
14: 4 [14:5] [A] "*I will* **heal** their waywardness and love them freely,
Zec 11: 16 [D] or seek the young, or **heal** the injured, or feed the healthy,

8325 ²רָפָא *rāpā'*[2], n.pr.m. [3] [√ 8324; cf. 8330]
Rapha [3]

1Ch 8: 2 Nohah the fourth and **Rapha** the fifth.
20: 6 each foot—twenty-four in all. He also was descended from **Rapha**.
20: 8 These were descendants of **Rapha** in Gath, and they fell at the

8326 רִפְאוּת *rip'ût*, n.f. [1] [√ 8324]
health [1]

Pr 3: 8 This will bring **health** to your body and nourishment to your

8327 ¹רְפָאִים *rᵉpā'îm*[1], n.m. [8] [cf. 8332?]
dead [5], departed spirits [1], spirits of the dead [1], spirits of the departed [1]

Job 26: 5 "The **dead** are in deep anguish, those beneath the waters and all
Ps 88: 10 [88:11] Do *those who* are **dead** rise up and praise you? *Selah*
Pr 2: 18 house leads down to death and her paths to the **spirits of the dead**.
9: 18 little do they know that the **dead** are there, that her guests are in the
21: 16 path of understanding comes to rest in the company of the **dead**.
Isa 14: 9 it rouses the **spirits of the departed** to greet you—all those who
26: 14 now dead, they live no more; *those* **departed spirits** do not rise.
26: 19 is like the dew of the morning; the earth will give birth to her **dead**.

8328 ²רְפָאִים *rᵉpā'îm*[2], n.pr.g. [11] [cf. 8332?]
Rephaites [10], who[s] [1]

Ge 14: 5 him went out and defeated the **Rephaites** in Ashteroth Karnaim,
15: 20 Hittites, Perizzites, **Rephaites**,
Dt 2: 11 Like the Anakites, they too were considered **Rephaites**,
2: 20 (That too was considered a land of the **Rephaites**, who used to live
2: 20 was considered a land of the Rephaites, **who**[s] used to live there;
3: 11 (Only Og king of Bashan was left of the remnant of the **Rephaites**.
3: 13 of Argob in Bashan used to be known as a land of the **Rephaites**.
Jos 12: 4 one of the last of the **Rephaites**, who reigned in Ashtaroth
13: 12 and Edrei and had survived as one of the last of the **Rephaites**.
17: 15 for yourselves there in the land of the Perizzites and **Rephaites**."
1Ch 20: 4 one of the descendants of the **Rephaites**, and the Philistines were

8329 ³רְפָאִים *rᵉpā'îm*[3], n.pr.g. [8] [cf. 8332?]
Rephaim [8]

Jos 15: 8 the Hinnom Valley at the northern end of the Valley of **Rephaim**.
18: 16 facing the Valley of Ben Hinnom, north of the Valley of **Rephaim**.
2Sa 5: 18 the Philistines had come and spread out in the Valley of **Rephaim**;
5: 22 the Philistines came up and spread out in the Valley of **Rephaim**;
23: 13 a band of Philistines was encamped in the Valley of **Rephaim**.
1Ch 11: 15 a band of Philistines was encamped in the Valley of **Rephaim**.
14: 9 Now the Philistines had come and raided the Valley of **Rephaim**;
Isa 17: 5 as when a man gleans heads of grain in the Valley of **Rephaim**.

8330 רְפָאֵל *rᵉpā'ēl*, n.pr.m. [1] [√ 8324 + 446; cf. 8325]
Rephael [1]

1Ch 26: 7 Othni, **Rephael**, Obed and Elzabad; his relatives Elihu

8331 רָפַד *rāpad*, v. [3] [→ 8339, 8340]
leaving a trail [1], refresh [1], spread out [1]

Job 17: 13 [D] I hope for is the grave, if *I* **spread out** my bed in darkness,
41: 30 [41:22] [A] **leaving a trail** in the mud like a threshing sledge.
SS 2: 5 [D] with raisins, **refresh** me with apples, for I am faint with love.

8332 ¹רָפָה *rāpâ*[1], v. [46] [→ 5341, 8333, 8342; cf. 8228?, 8327?, 8328?, 8329?]
leave [4], go limp [3], hang limp [3], lazy [3], let alone [3], let go [3], abandon [2], give [2], lowered [2], withdraw [2], abandon [+3338+4946] [1], almost [1], disarms [+4653] [1], discourage

[+3338] [1], discouraging [+906+906+3338] [1], fail [1], falter [1], feeble [1], give up [+3338] [1], leave alone [1], lost courage [+3338] [1], refrain [1], sinks down [1], slack [1], still [1], stop [1], subsided [1], wait [1], weak [1]

Ex 4: 26 [A] So the LORD **let** him **alone**. (At that time she said
5: 8 [C] They *are* **lazy**; that is why they are crying out, 'Let us go
5: 17 [C] Pharaoh said, "**Lazy**, that's what you are—lazy! That is why
5: 17 [C] Pharaoh said, "Lazy, that's what you are—**lazy**! That is why
Dt 4: 31 [G] *he will* not **abandon** or destroy you or forget the covenant
9: 14 [G] **Let** me **alone**, so that I may destroy them and blot out their
31: 6 [G] goes with you; *he will* never **leave** you nor forsake you."
31: 8 [G] will be with you; *he will* never **leave** you nor forsake you.
Jos 1: 5 [G] so I will be with you; *I will* never **leave** you nor forsake you.
10: 6 [G] "*Do* not **abandon** [+3338+4946] your servants. Come up to
18: 3 [F] "How long *will* you **wait** before you begin to take possession
Jdg 8: 3 [A] to you?" At this, their resentment against him **subsided**.
11: 37 [G] "**Give** me two months to roam the hills and weep with my
19: 9 [A] the girl's father, said, "Now look, it's **almost** evening.
1Sa 11: 3 [G] "**Give** us seven days so we can send messengers throughout
15: 16 [G] "**Stop**!" Samuel said to Saul. "Let me tell you what the
2Sa 4: 1 [A] he **lost** [+3338] **courage**, and all Israel became alarmed.
24: 16 [G] was afflicting the people, "Enough! **Withdraw** your hand."
2Ki 4: 27 [G] push her away, but the man of God said, "**Leave** her **alone**!
1Ch 21: 15 [G] was destroying the people, "Enough! **Withdraw** your hand."
28: 20 [G] *He will* not **fail** you or forsake you until all the work for the
2Ch 15: 7 [A] as for you, be strong and *do* not **give** [+3338] **up**, for your
Ezr 4: 4 [D] the peoples around them *set out to* **discourage** [+3338] the
Ne 6: 3 [G] Why should the work stop while *I* **leave** it and go down to
6: 9 [A] thinking, "Their hands *will get* too **weak** for the work, and it
Job 7: 19 [G] look away from me, or **let** me **alone** even for an instant?
12: 21 [D] pours contempt on nobles and **disarms** [+4653] the mighty.
27: 6 [G] I will maintain my righteousness and never **let go** *of* it;
Ps 37: 8 [G] **Refrain** from anger and turn from wrath; do not fret—
46: 10 [46:11] [G] "*Be* **still**, and know that I am God; I will be exalted
138: 8 [G] endures forever—*do* not **abandon** the works of your hands.
Pr 4: 13 [G] Hold on to instruction, *do* not **let** it **go**; guard it well, for it is
18: 9 [F] *One who is* **slack** in his work is brother to one who destroys.
24: 10 [F] If *you* **falter** in times of trouble, how small is your strength!
SS 3: 4 [G] *would* not **let** him **go** till I had brought him to my mother's
Isa 5: 24 [A] fire lick up straw and as dry grass **sinks down** *in* the flames,
13: 7 [A] Because of this, all hands *will* **go limp**, every man's heart
Jer 6: 24 [A] We have heard reports about them, and our hands **hang limp**.
38: 4 [D] He *is* **discouraging** [+906+906+3338] the soldiers who are left
49: 24 [A] Damascus *has become* **feeble**, she has turned to flee
50: 43 [A] has heard reports about them, and his hands **hang limp**.
Eze 1: 24 [D] of an army. When they stood still, *they* **lowered** their wings.
1: 25 [D] expanse over their heads as they stood with **lowered** wings.
7: 17 [A] Every hand *will* **go limp**, and every knee will become as
21: 7 [21:12] [A] Every heart will melt and every hand **go limp**; every
Zep 3: 16 [A] "Do not fear, O Zion; *do* not *let* your hands **hang limp**.

8333 רָפֶה **rāpeh**, a. [4] [√ 8332]

feeble [2], weak [+3338] [1], weak [1]

Nu 13: 18 and whether the people who live there are strong or **weak**,
2Sa 17: 2 I would attack him while he is weary and **weak** [+3338]. I would
Job 4: 3 have instructed many, how you have strengthened **feeble** hands.
Isa 35: 3 Strengthen the **feeble** hands, steady the knees that give way;

8334 [2]רָפָה **rāpâ[2]**, n.pr.m. [1] [√ 8324?]

Raphah [1]

1Ch 8: 37 of Binea; **Raphah** was his son, Eleasah his son and Azel his son.

8335 [3]רָפָה **rāpâ[3]**, n.pr.m. [4] [√ 8324?]

Rapha [4]

2Sa 21: 16 Ishbi-Benob, one of the descendants of **Rapha**, whose bronze
21: 18 the Hushathite killed Saph, one of the descendants of **Rapha**.
21: 20 each foot—twenty-four in all. He also was descended from **Rapha**.
21: 22 These four were descendants of **Rapha** in Gath, and they fell at the

8336 רָפוּא **rāpû'**, n.pr.m. [1] [√ 8324]

Raphu [1]

Nu 13: 9 from the tribe of Benjamin, Palti son of **Raphu**;

8337 רְפוּאָה **r[e]pû'â**, n.f. [3] [√ 8324]

healing [+5989] [1], remedies [1], remedy [1]

Jer 30: 13 to plead your cause, no **remedy** for your sore, no healing for you.
46: 11 But you multiply **remedies** in vain; there is no healing for you.
Eze 30: 21 It has not been bound up for **healing** [+5989] or put in a splint

8338 רֶפַח **repaḥ**, n.pr.m. [1]

Rephah [1]

1Ch 7: 25 **Rephah** was his son, Resheph his son, Telah his son, Tahan his

8339 רְפִידָה **r[e]pîdâ**, n.f. [1] [√ 8331]

base [1]

SS 3: 10 Its posts he made of silver, its **base** *of* gold. Its seat was

8340 רְפִידִים **r[e]pîdîm**, n.pr.loc. [5] [√ 8331]

Rephidim [5]

Ex 17: 1 They camped at **Rephidim**, but there was no water for the people
17: 8 The Amalekites came and attacked the Israelites at **Rephidim**.
19: 2 After they set out from **Rephidim**, they entered the Desert of Sinai,
Nu 33: 14 They left Alush and camped at **Rephidim**, where there was no
33: 15 They left **Rephidim** and camped in the Desert of Sinai.

8341 רְפָיָה **r[e]pāyâ**, n.pr.m. [5] [cf. 8334?]

Rephaiah [5]

1Ch 3: 21 and the sons of **Rephaiah**, of Arnan, of Obadiah and of Shecaniah.
4: 42 led by Pelatiah, Neariah, **Rephaiah** and Uzziel, the sons of Ishi,
7: 2 Uzzi, **Rephaiah**, Jeriel, Jahmai, Ibsam and Samuel—heads of their
9: 43 of Binea; **Rephaiah** was his son, Eleasah his son and Azel his son.
Ne 3: 9 **Rephaiah** son of Hur, ruler of a half-district of Jerusalem,

8342 רִפָּיוֹן **rippāyôn**, n.[m.]. [1] [√ 8332]

hang limp [1]

Jer 47: 3 will not turn to help their children; their hands will **hang limp**.

8343 רַפְסֹדוֹת **rapsōdôt**, n.[f.pl.]. [1]

rafts [1]

2Ch 2: 16 [2:15] you need and will float them in **rafts** by sea down to Joppa.

8344 רָפַף **rāpap**, v. [1]

quake [1]

Job 26: 11 [D] The pillars of the heavens **quake**, aghast at his rebuke.

8345 רָפַק **rāpaq**, v. [1]

leaning [1]

SS 8: 5 [F] Who is this coming up from the desert **leaning** on her lover?

8346 רָפַשׂ **rāpaś**, v. [5] [→ 5343; Ar 10672]

humble yourself [1], humbled [1], muddied [1], muddy [1], muddying [1]

Ps 68: 30 [68:31] [F] **Humbled**, may it bring bars of silver.
Pr 6: 3 [F] Go and **humble yourself**; press your plea with your
25: 26 [C] Like a **muddied** spring or a polluted well is a righteous man
Eze 32: 2 [A] churning the water with your feet and **muddying** the streams.
34: 18 [A] clear water? *Must you* also **muddy** the rest with your feet?

8347 רֶפֶשׁ **repeš**, n.[m.]. [1]

mire [1]

Isa 57: 20 tossing sea, which cannot rest, whose waves cast up **mire** and mud.

8348 רֶפֶת **repet**, n.[m.]. [1]

stalls [1]

Hab 3: 17 though there are no sheep in the pen and no cattle in the **stalls**,

8349 רַץ **raṣ**, n.[m.]. [1]

bars [1]

Ps 68: 30 [68:31] Humbled, may it bring **bars** *of* silver. Scatter the nations

8350 רָץ **rāṣ**, v. Not used in NIV/BHS [√ 8132]

8351 [1]רָצָא **rāṣā'[1]**, v. [1] [cf. 8132?]

sped forth [1]

Eze 1: 14 [A] The creatures **sped** back and **forth** like flashes of lightning.

8352 [2]רָצָא **rāṣā'[2]**, n.m. *or* v.ptcp. Not used in NIV/BHS [√ 8354]

8353 רָצַד **rāṣad**, v. [1]

gaze in envy [1]

Ps 68: 16 [68:17] [D] Why **gaze in envy**, O rugged mountains,

8354 רָצָה¹ rāṣâ[1], v. [52] [→ 8352, 8356, 8359?, 8360?, 9573, 9574]

accept [10], be accepted [5], pleased with [4], enjoy [3], pleased [3], delights in [2], please [2], approve [1], be acceptable [1], dear to [1], delight [1], devotion [1], enjoyed [1], favored [1], favors [1], finds favor with [1], held in high esteem [1], in delight [1], join [1], loved [1], pleasing [1], put in [1], received favorably [1], regain favor [1], show favor [1], showed favor [1], take delight in [1], take pleasure in [1], take pleasure [1], takes delight [1]

Ge 33:10 [A] the face of God, now that *you have* **received** me **favorably**.
Lev 1:4 [C] *it will* **be accepted** on his behalf to make atonement for him.
7:18 [C] offering is eaten on the third day, *it will* not **be accepted**.
19:7 [C] eaten on the third day, it is impure and *will* not **be accepted**.
22:23 [C] or stunted, but *it will* not **be accepted** in fulfillment of a vow.
22:25 [C] *They will* not **be accepted** on your behalf, because they are
22:27 [C] *it will* **be acceptable** as an offering made to the LORD by
26:34 [A] the land *will* **enjoy** its sabbath years all the time that it lies
26:34 [G] your enemies; then the land will rest and **enjoy** its sabbaths.
26:43 [A] *will* **enjoy** its sabbaths while it lies desolate without them.
Dt 33:11 [A] O LORD, and *be* **pleased with** the work of his hands.
33:24 [B] let him be **favored** *by* his brothers, and let him bathe his feet
1Sa 29:4 [F] How better *could* he **regain** his master's **favor** than by taking
2Sa 24:23 [A] also said to him, "*May* the LORD your God **accept** you."
1Ch 28:4 [A] from my father's sons *he was* **pleased** to make me king over
29:3 [A] in my **devotion** to the temple of my God I now give my
29:17 [A] that you test the heart and *are* **pleased with** integrity.
2Ch 10:7 [A] and **please** them and give them a favorable answer,
36:21 [A] The land **enjoyed** its sabbath rests; all the time of its
Est 10:3 [B] the Jews, and **held in high esteem** by his many fellow Jews,
Job 14:6 [A] and let him alone, till *he has* **put in** his time like a hired man.
33:26 [A] He prays to God and **finds favor with** him, he sees God's
34:9 [A] 'It profits a man nothing when he *tries to* **please** God.'
Ps 40:13 [40:14] [A] *Be* **pleased**, O LORD, to save me; O LORD,
44:3 [44:4] [A] and the light of your face, for *you* **loved** them.
49:13 [49:14] [A] and of their followers, *who* **approve** their sayings.
50:18 [A] When you see a thief, *you* **join** with him; you throw in your
51:16 [51:18] [A] *you do* not **take pleasure in** burnt offerings.
62:4 [62:5] [A] him from his lofty place; *they* **take delight in** lies.
77:7 [77:8] [A] reject forever? *Will* he never **show** his **favor** again?
85:1 [85:2] [A] *You* **showed favor** *to* your land, O LORD;
102:14 [102:15] [A] For her stones *are* **dear to** your servants; her very
119:108 [A] **Accept**, O LORD, the willing praise of my mouth,
147:10 [A] the strength of the horse, nor *his* **delight** in the legs of a man;
147:11 [A] the LORD **delights in** those who fear him, who put their
149:4 [A] For the LORD **takes delight** in his people; he crowns the
Pr 3:12 [A] disciplines those he loves, as a father the son *he* **delights in**.
16:7 [A] When a man's ways *are* **pleasing** *to* the LORD, he makes
23:26 [a] [and *let* your eyes **keep** [K; see Q 5915] *to* my ways,]
Ecc 9:7 [A] a joyful heart, for it is now that God **favors** what you do.
Isa 42:1 [A] whom I uphold, my chosen one **in** whom I **delight**;
Jer 14:10 [A] So the LORD *does* not **accept** them; he will now remember
14:12 [A] burnt offerings and grain offerings, I *will* not **accept** them.
Eze 20:40 [A] house of Israel will serve me, and there *I will* **accept** them.
20:41 [A] *I will* **accept** you as fragrant incense when I bring you out
43:27 [A] Then *I will* **accept** you, declares the Sovereign LORD."
Hos 8:13 [A] they eat the meat, but the LORD *is* not **pleased with** them.
Am 5:22 [A] burnt offerings and grain offerings, *I will* not **accept** them.
Mic 6:7 [A] *Will* the LORD *be* **pleased** with thousands of rams,
Hag 1:8 [A] so that *I may* **take pleasure** in it and be honored," says the
Mal 1:8 [A] *Would he be* **pleased with** you? Would he accept you?"
1:10 [A] "and *I will* **accept** no offering from your hands.
1:13 [A] them as sacrifices, *should I* **accept** them from your hands?"

8355 רָצָה² rāṣâ[2], v. [4]

pay for [2], been paid for [1], make amends [1]

Lev 26:41 [A] uncircumcised hearts are humbled and *they* **pay for** their sin,
26:43 [A] They *will* **pay for** their sins because they rejected my laws
Job 20:10 [D] His children *must* **make amends** *to* the poor; his own hands
Isa 40:2 [C] service has been completed, that her sin *has* **been paid for**,

8356 רָצוֹן rāṣôn, n.[m.]. [56] [√ 8354]

favor [15], accepted [7], acceptable [5], pleased [4], pleases [4], will [4], delights [3], desires [2], goodwill [2], pleasure [2], delight [1], eagerly [+928+3972] [1], favored [1], fitting [1], good pleasure [1], please [1], pleasing [1], wished [1]

Ge 49:6 killed men in their anger and hamstrung oxen as they **pleased**.
Ex 28:38 so that they will be **acceptable** to the LORD.
Lev 1:3 to the Tent of Meeting so that it will be **acceptable** to the LORD.
19:5 sacrifice it in such a way that it will be **accepted** *on* your *behalf*.
22:19 sheep or goats in order that it may be **accepted** *on* your *behalf*.
22:20 with a defect, because it will not be **accepted** on your behalf.
22:21 it must be without defect or blemish to be **acceptable**.
22:29 sacrifice it in such a way that it will be **accepted** *on* your *behalf*.
23:11 the sheaf before the LORD so it will be **accepted** *on* your *behalf*;
Dt 33:16 its fullness and the **favor** *of* him who dwelt in the burning bush.
33:23 "Naphtali is abounding with the **favor** of the LORD and is full of
2Ch 15:15 They sought God **eagerly** [+928+3972], and he was found by
Ezr 10:11 confession to the LORD, the God of your fathers, and do his **will**.
Ne 9:24 and the peoples of the land, to deal with them as they **pleased**.
9:37 They rule over our bodies and our cattle as they **please**. We are in
Est 1:8 instructed all the wine stewards to serve each man what he **wished**.
9:5 and they did what they **pleased** to those who hated them.
Ps 5:12 [5:13] you surround them with your **favor** as with a shield.
19:14 [19:15] and the meditation of my heart be **pleasing** in your sight,
30:5 [30:6] anger lasts only a moment, but his **favor** lasts a lifetime;
30:7 [30:8] O LORD, when you **favored** me, you made my mountain
40:8 [40:9] I desire to do your **will**, O my God; your law is within my
51:18 [51:20] In your **good pleasure** make Zion prosper; build up the
69:13 [69:14] I pray to you, O LORD, in the time of your **favor**;
89:17 [89:18] and strength, and by your **favor** you exalt our horn.
103:21 all his heavenly hosts, you his servants who do his **will**.
106:4 Remember me, O LORD, when you show **favor** *to* your people,
143:10 Teach me to do your **will**, for you are my God; may your good
145:16 You open your hand and satisfy the **desires** of every living thing.
145:19 He fulfills the **desires** *of* those who fear him; he hears their cry
Pr 8:35 whoever finds me finds life and receives **favor** from the LORD.
10:32 The lips of the righteous know *what* is **fitting**, but the mouth of the
11:1 abhors dishonest scales, but accurate weights are his **delight**.
11:20 perverse heart but he **delights** *in* those whose ways are blameless.
11:27 He who seeks good finds **goodwill**, but evil comes to him who
12:2 A good man obtains **favor** from the LORD, but the LORD
12:22 LORD detests lying lips, but he **delights** *in* men who are truthful.
14:9 making amends for sin, but **goodwill** is found among the upright.
14:35 A king **delights** in a wise servant, but a shameful servant incurs his
15:8 sacrifice of the wicked, but the prayer of the upright **pleases** him.
16:13 Kings take **pleasure** *in* honest lips; they value a man who speaks
16:15 face brightens, it means life; his **favor** is like a rain cloud in spring.
18:22 a wife finds what is good and receives **favor** from the LORD.
19:12 rage is like the roar of a lion, but his **favor** is like dew on the grass.
Isa 49:8 "In the time of my **favor** I will answer you, and in the day of
56:7 Their burnt offerings and sacrifices *will be* **accepted** on my altar;
58:5 Is that what you call a fast, a day **acceptable** to the LORD?
60:7 they will be **accepted** as offerings on my altar, and I will adorn my
60:10 in anger I struck you, in **favor** I will show you compassion.
61:2 to proclaim the year of the LORD's **favor** and the day of
Jer 6:20 Your burnt offerings are not **acceptable**; your sacrifices do not
Da 8:4 rescue from his power. He did as he **pleased** and became great.
11:3 will appear, who will rule with great power and do as he **pleases**.
11:16 The invader will do as he **pleases**; no one will be able to stand
11:36 "The king will do as he **pleases**. He will exalt and magnify himself
Mal 2:13 to your offerings or accepts them *with* **pleasure** from your hands.

8357 רָצַח rāṣaḥ, v. [47 / 46] [→ 8358]

murderer [12], accused of murder [7], murder [6], accused [3], he[S] [+2021] [2], killed [2], murdered [2], anyone[S] [1], be murdered [1], him[S] [+2021] [1], kill [1], killed [+5782] [1], killed a person [1], kills a man [1], kills another [1], murderer [+1201] [1], murderers [1], murders [+5883] [1], put to death [1]

Ex 20:13 [A] "*You shall* not **murder**.
Nu 35:6 [A] to which a *person who has* **killed** someone may flee.
35:11 [A] to which *a person who has* **killed** [+5782] someone
35:12 [A] so that a *person* **accused of murder** may not die before he
35:16 [A] with an iron object so that he dies, he *is a* **murderer**;
35:16 [A] he dies, he is a murderer; the **murderer** shall be put to death.
35:17 [A] and he strikes someone so that he dies, he *is a* **murderer**;
35:17 [A] he dies, he is a murderer; the **murderer** shall be put to death.
35:18 [A] and he hits someone so that he dies, he *is a* **murderer**;
35:18 [A] he dies, he is a murderer; the **murderer** shall be put to death.
35:19 [A] The avenger of blood shall put the **murderer** to death; when
35:21 [A] he dies, that person shall be put to death; he *is a* **murderer**.
35:21 [A] The avenger of blood shall put the **murderer** to death when
35:25 [A] The assembly must protect the *one* **accused of murder** from
35:26 [A] " 'But if the **accused** ever goes outside the limits of the city
35:27 [A] the avenger of blood *may* **kill** the accused without being
35:27 [A] the avenger of blood may kill the **accused** without being
35:28 [A] only after the death of the high priest may **he**[S] [+2021] return
35:30 [A] " 'Anyone who kills a person *is to be* **put to death** as a
35:30 [A] to death as a **murderer** only on the testimony of witnesses.
35:31 [A] " 'Do not accept a ransom for the life of a **murderer**,
Dt 4:42 [A] to which *anyone* who *had* **killed a person** could flee if he
4:42 [A] **killed** his neighbor without malice aforethought.
5:17 [A] "*You shall* not **murder**.
19:3 [A] so that anyone *who* **kills a man** may flee there.
19:4 [A] This is the rule concerning the *man who* **kills another**

Dt 19: 6 [A] the avenger of blood might pursue **him**[s] [+2021] in a rage,
22: 26 [A] of someone who attacks and **murders** [+5883] his neighbor,
Jos 20: 3 [A] so that **anyone**[s] who kills a person accidentally
20: 5 [A] blood pursues him, they must not surrender the *one* **accused**,
20: 6 [A] **he**[s] [+2021] may go back to his own home in the town from
21: 13 [A] gave Hebron (a city of refuge for *one* **accused of murder**),
21: 21 [A] given Shechem (a city of refuge for *one* **accused of murder**)
21: 27 [A] in Bashan (a city of refuge for *one* **accused of murder**)
21: 32 [A] in Galilee (a city of refuge for *one* **accused of murder**),
21: 38 [A] in Gilead (a city of refuge for *one* **accused of murder**),
Jdg 20: 4 [C] the husband of the **murdered** woman, said, "I and my
1Ki 21: 19 [A] *Have you* not **murdered** a man and seized his property?"
2Ki 6: 32 [D] "Don't you see how this **murderer** [+1201] is sending
Job 24: 14 [A] is gone, the **murderer** rises up and kills the poor and needy;
Ps 62: 3 [62:4] [d] all of you throw [BHS ***murder***; NIV 8132] him down
94: 6 [D] slay the widow and the alien; *they* **murder** the fatherless.
Pr 22: 13 [C] is a lion outside!" or, "*I will* **be murdered** in the streets!"
Isa 1: 21 [D] righteousness used to dwell in her—but now **murderers**!
Jer 7: 9 [A] " 'Will you steal and **murder**, commit adultery and perjury,
Hos 4: 2 [A] is only cursing, lying and **murder**, stealing and adultery;
6: 9 [D] *they* **murder** on the road to Shechem, committing shameful

8358 רֶצַח *reṣaḥ*, n.[m.]. [2] [√ 8357]

mortal agony [1], slaughter [1]

Ps 42: 10 [42:11] My bones suffer **mortal agony** as my foes taunt me,
Eze 21: 22 [21:27] to give the command to **slaughter**, to sound the battle cry,

8359 רִצְיָא *riṣyā'*, n.pr.m. [1] [√ 8354?]

Rizia [1]

1Ch 7: 39 The sons of Ulla: Arah, Hanniel and **Rizia**.

8360 רְצִין *r*[e]*ṣîn*, n.pr.m. [11] [√ 8354?]

Rezin [10], Rezin's [1]

2Ki 15: 37 (In those days the LORD began to send **Rezin** king of Aram
16: 5 **Rezin** king of Aram and Pekah son of Remaliah king of Israel
16: 6 **Rezin** king of Aram recovered Elath for Aram by driving out the
16: 9 He deported its inhabitants to Kir and put **Rezin** to death.
Ezr 2: 48 **Rezin**, Nekoda, Gazzam,
Ne 7: 50 Reaiah, **Rezin**, Nekoda,
Isa 7: 1 King **Rezin** of Aram and Pekah son of Remaliah king of Israel
7: 4 because of the fierce anger of **Rezin** and Aram and of the son of
7: 8 of Aram is Damascus, and the head of Damascus is only **Rezin**.
8: 6 waters of Shiloah and rejoices over **Rezin** and the son of Remaliah,
9: 11 [9:10] the LORD has strengthened **Rezin's** foes against them

8361 רָצַע *rāṣa'*, v. [1] [→ 5345]

pierce [1]

Ex 21: 6 [A] to the door or the doorpost and **pierce** his ear with an awl.

8362 רָצַף *rāṣap*, v. [1] [→ 5346, 8367]

inlaid [1]

SS 3: 10 [B] its interior lovingly **inlaid** by the daughters of Jerusalem.

8363 [1]רֶצֶף *reṣep*[1], n.f. [1] [→ 8364, 8365, 8366]

baked over hot coals [1]

1Ki 19: 6 and there by his head was a cake of bread **baked over hot coals**,

8364 [2]רֶצֶף *reṣep*[2], n.pr.loc. [2] [√ 8363]

Rezeph [2]

2Ki 19: 12 Haran, **Rezeph** and the people of Eden who were in Tel Assar?
Isa 37: 12 Haran, **Rezeph** and the people of Eden who were in Tel Assar?

8365 [1]רִצְפָּה *riṣpâ*[1], n.f. [1] [√ 8363]

live coal [1]

Isa 6: 6 Then one of the seraphs flew to me with a **live coal** in his hand,

8366 [2]רִצְפָּה *riṣpâ*[2], n.pr.f. [4] [√ 8363]

Rizpah [4]

2Sa 3: 7 Now Saul had had a concubine named **Rizpah** daughter of Aiah.
21: 8 and Mephibosheth, the two sons of Aiah's daughter **Rizpah**,
21: 10 **Rizpah** daughter of Aiah took sackcloth and spread it out for
21: 11 When David was told what Aiah's daughter **Rizpah**,

8367 רִצְפָה *riṣ*[e]*pâ*, n.f. [7] [√ 8362]

pavement [5], it[s] [+2021] [1], mosaic pavement [1]

2Ch 7: 3 they knelt on the **pavement** with their faces to the ground,
Est 1: 6 couches of gold and silver on a **mosaic pavement** *of* porphyry,
Eze 40: 17 and a **pavement** that had been constructed all around the court;
40: 17 all around the court; there were thirty rooms along the **pavement**.
40: 18 **It**[s] [+2021] abutted the sides of the gateways and was as wide as
40: 18 and was as wide as they were long; this was the lower **pavement**.
42: 3 and in the section opposite the **pavement** of the outer court,

8368 רָצַץ *rāṣaṣ*, v. [19 / 20] [→ 5298; cf. 8318, 8320; Ar 10671]

oppressed [4], splintered [3], broken [2], crushed [2], bruised [1], brutally oppressed [1], cracked [1], cruel [1], crush [1], discouraged [1], jostled each other [1], smashed to pieces [1], trampled [1]

Ge 25: 22 [F] The babies **jostled each other** within her, and she said, "Why
Dt 28: 33 [B] and you will have nothing but **cruel** oppression all your days.
Jdg 9: 53 [G] an upper millstone on his head and **cracked** his skull.
10: 8 [D] **crushed** them. For eighteen years they oppressed all the
1Sa 12: 3 [A] I taken? Whom have I cheated? Whom *have I* **oppressed**?
12: 4 [A] "You have not cheated or **oppressed** us," they replied. "You
2Ki 18: 21 [B] that **splintered** reed of a staff, which pierces a man's hand
23: 12 [A] **smashed** them **to pieces** and threw the rubble into the Kidron
2Ch 16: 10 [D] At the same time Asa **brutally oppressed** some of the
Job 20: 19 [D] For *he has* **oppressed** the poor and left them destitute; he has
Ps 74: 14 [D] It was you *who* **crushed** the heads of Leviathan and gave
Ecc 12: 6 [A] the silver cord is severed, or the golden bowl *is* **broken**;
12: 6 [C] is shattered at the spring, or the wheel **broken** at the well,
Isa 36: 6 [B] that **splintered** reed of a staff, which pierces a man's hand
42: 3 [B] A **bruised** reed he will not break, and a smoldering wick he
42: 4 [A] he will not falter or *be* **discouraged** till he establishes justice
58: 6 [B] of the yoke, to set the **oppressed** free and break every yoke?
Eze 29: 7 [C] *you* **splintered** and you tore open their shoulders;
Hos 5: 11 [B] Ephraim is oppressed, **trampled** *in* judgment, intent on
Am 4: 1 [A] the poor and **crush** the needy and say to your husbands,

8369 [1]רַק *raq*[1], a. [3] [→ 8370, 8377, 8378, 8386, 8395]

lean [2], lean [+1414] [1]

Ge 41: 19 other cows came up—scrawny and very ugly and **lean** [+1414].
41: 20 The **lean**, ugly cows ate up the seven fat cows that came up first.
41: 27 The seven **lean**, ugly cows that came up afterward are seven years,

8370 [2]רַק *raq*[2], adv. [109] [√ 8369] See Select Index

only [30], but [22], however [13], *untranslated* [12], except [5], nevertheless [4], surely [3], yet [3], always [2], except that [2], although [1], and [1], as for [1], be sure [1], but [+2256] [1], but also [1], but only [1], moreover [1], nothing but [1], only [+4202] [1], only [+421] [1], really [1], sheer [1]

8371 רֹק *rōq*, n.[m.]. [3] [√ 8394]

for an instant [+1180+6330] [1], spit [1], spitting [1]

Job 7: 19 away from me, or let me alone even **for an instant** [+1180+6330]?
30: 10 and keep their distance; they do not hesitate to **spit** in my face.
Isa 50: 6 out my beard; I did not hide my face from mocking and **spitting**.

8372 רָקַב *rāqab*, v. [2] [→ 8373, 8374, 8375]

rot [2]

Pr 10: 7 [A] will be a blessing, but the name of the wicked *will* **rot**.
Isa 40: 20 [A] to present such an offering selects wood *that will* not **rot**.

8373 רָקָב *rāqāb*, n.[m.]. [5] [√ 8372]

decay [2], rot [1], rots [1], something rotten [1]

Job 13: 28 "So man wastes away like **something rotten**, like a garment eaten
Pr 12: 4 husband's crown, but a disgraceful wife is like **decay** in his bones.
14: 30 A heart at peace gives life to the body, but envy **rots** the bones.
Hos 5: 12 I am like a moth to Ephraim, like **rot** to the people of Judah.
Hab 3: 16 at the sound; **decay** crept into my bones, and my legs trembled.

8374 רֹקֶב *rōqeb*, n.[m.]. Not used in NIV/BHS [√ 8372]

8375 רִקָּבוֹן *riqqābôn*, n.[m.]. [1] [√ 8372]

rotten [1]

Job 41: 27 [41:19] Iron he treats like straw and bronze like **rotten** wood.

8376 רָקַד *rāqad*, v. [9]

skipped [2], dance about [1], dance [1], dancing [1], jolting [1], leap about [1], leap [1], makes skip [1]

1Ch 15: 29 [D] when she saw King David **dancing** and celebrating, she
Job 21: 11 [D] forth their children as a flock; their little ones **dance about**.
Ps 29: 6 [G] *He* **makes** Lebanon **skip** like a calf, Sirion like a young wild
114: 4 [A] the mountains **skipped** like rams, the hills like lambs.
114: 6 [A] that *you* **skipped** like rams, you hills, like lambs?

[F] Hitpael (hitpoel, hitpoal, hitpolel, hitpolal, hitpalel, hitpalal, hitpalpel, hitpalpal, hotpael, hotpaal) [G] Hiphil (hiphtil) [H] Hophal [I] Hishtaphel

Ecc 3: 4 [A] and a time to laugh, a time to mourn and a time *to* **dance**,
Isa 13:21 [D] the owls will dwell, and there the wild goats *will* **leap about**.
Joel 2: 5 [D] With a noise like that of chariots *they* **leap** over the
Na 3: 2 [D] the clatter of wheels, galloping horses and **jolting** chariots!

8377 רַקָּה *raqqâ*, n.f. [5] [√ 8369]

temple [3], temples [2]

Jdg 4:21 She drove the peg through his **temple** into the ground, and he died.
4:22 and there lay Sisera with the tent peg through his **temple**—
5:26 she crushed his head, she shattered and pierced his **temple**.
SS 4: 3 Your **temples** behind your veil are like the halves of a
6: 7 Your **temples** behind your veil are like the halves of a

8378 רַקּוֹן *raqqôn*, n.pr.loc. [1] [√ 8369]

Rakkon [1]

Jos 19:46 Me Jarkon and **Rakkon**, with the area facing Joppa.

8379 רָקַח *rāqaḥ*, v. [8] [→ 5349, 5350, 5351, 8380, 8381, 8382, 8383, 8384]

perfumer [3], blended [1], makes perfume [1], mixing in [1], perfume [+9043] [1], took care of mixing [+4200+5351] [1]

Ex 30:25 [A] anointing oil, a fragrant blend, the work of a **perfumer**.
30:33 [A] Whoever **makes perfume** like it and whoever puts it on
30:35 [A] make a fragrant blend of incense, the work of a **perfumer**.
37:29 [A] and the pure, fragrant incense—the work of a **perfumer**.
1Ch 9:30 [A] some of the priests **took care of mixing** [+4200+5351] the
2Ch 16:14 [E] on a bier covered with spices and various **blended** perfumes,
Ecc 10: 1 [A] As dead flies give **perfume** [+9043] a bad smell, so a little
Eze 24:10 [G] Cook the meat well, **mixing in** the spices; and let the bones

8380 רֶקַח *reqaḥ*, n.[m.]. [1] [→ 8381; cf. 8379]

spiced [1]

SS 8: 2 I would give you **spiced** wine to drink, the nectar of my

8381 רֹקַח *rōqaḥ*, n.[m.]. [2] [√ 8380; cf. 8379]

blend [1], fragrant blend [1]

Ex 30:25 a sacred anointing oil, a fragrant **blend**, the work of a perfumer.
30:35 and make a **fragrant blend** *of* incense, the work of a perfumer.

8382 רַקָּח *raqqāḥ*, n.m. [1] [√ 8379]

perfume-makers [1]

Ne 3: 8 Hananiah, one of the **perfume-makers**, made repairs next to that.

8383 רִקֻּחַ *riqquaḥ*, n.[m.]. [1] [√ 8379]

perfumes [1]

Isa 57: 9 You went to Molech with olive oil and increased your **perfumes**.

8384 רַקָּחָה *raqqāḥâ*, n.f. [1] [√ 8379]

perfumers [1]

1Sa 8:13 He will take your daughters to be **perfumers** and cooks

8385 רָקִיעַ *rāqîaʿ*, n.m. [17] [√ 8392]

expanse [13], heavens [2], it[s] [+2021] [1], skies [1]

Ge 1: 6 "Let there be an **expanse** between the waters to separate water
1: 7 So God made the **expanse** and separated the water under the
1: 7 and separated the water under the **expanse** from the water above it.
1: 7 the water under the expanse from the water above **it**[s] [+2021].
1: 8 God called the **expanse** "sky." And there was evening, and there
1:14 "Let there be lights in the **expanse** *of* the sky to separate the day
1:15 let them be lights in the **expanse** *of* the sky to give light on the
1:17 God set them in the **expanse** *of* the sky to give light on the earth,
1:20 and let birds fly above the earth across the **expanse** *of* the sky."
Ps 19: 1 [19:2] the glory of God; the **skies** proclaim the work of his hands.
150: 1 Praise God in his sanctuary; praise him in his mighty **heavens**.
Eze 1:22 the heads of the living creatures was what looked like an **expanse**,
1:23 Under the **expanse** their wings were stretched out one toward the
1:25 there came a voice from above the **expanse** over their heads as
1:26 Above the **expanse** over their heads was what looked like a throne
10: 1 I saw the likeness of a throne of sapphire above the **expanse** that
Da 12: 3 Those who are wise will shine like the brightness of the **heavens**,

8386 רָקִיק *rāqîq*, n.m. [8] [√ 8369]

wafers [5], wafer [3]

Ex 29: 2 make bread, and cakes mixed with oil, and **wafers** spread with oil.
29:23 the LORD, take a loaf, and a cake made with oil, and a **wafer**.
Lev 2: 4 mixed with oil, or **wafers** *made* without yeast and spread with oil.
7:12 and mixed with oil, **wafers** made without yeast and spread with oil,
8:26 he took a cake of bread, and one made with oil, and a **wafer**;
Nu 6:15 made of fine flour mixed with oil, and **wafers** spread with oil.
6:19 and a cake and a **wafer** from the basket, both made without yeast.
1Ch 23:29 grain offerings, the unleavened **wafers**, the baking and the mixing,

8387 רָקַם *rāqam*, v. [9] [→ 8388?, 8389?, 8390?, 8391]

embroiderer [7], embroiderers [1], was woven together [1]

Ex 26:36 [A] and finely twisted linen—the work of an **embroiderer**.
27:16 [A] the work of an **embroiderer**—with four posts and four
28:39 [A] of fine linen. The sash is to be the work of an **embroiderer**.
35:35 [A] **embroiderers** in blue, purple and scarlet yarn and fine linen,
36:37 [A] and finely twisted linen—the work of an **embroiderer**;
38:18 [A] and finely twisted linen—the work of an **embroiderer**.
38:23 [A] an **embroiderer** in blue, purple and scarlet yarn and fine
39:29 [A] purple and scarlet yarn—the work of an **embroiderer**—
Ps 139:15 [E] *When I* **was woven together** in the depths of the earth,

8388 רָקֶם *rāqem*, n.pr.m. [1] [√ 8387?]

Rakem [1]

1Ch 7:16 brother was named Sheresh, and his sons were Ulam and **Rakem**.

8389 רֶקֶם¹ *reqem¹*, n.pr.loc. [1] [√ 8387?]

Rekem [1]

Jos 18:27 **Rekem**, Irpeel, Taralah,

8390 רֶקֶם² *reqem²*, n.pr.m. [4] [√ 8387?]

Rekem [4]

Nu 31: 8 Among their victims were Evi, **Rekem**, Zur, Hur and Reba—
Jos 13:21 and the Midianite chiefs, Evi, **Rekem**, Zur, Hur and Reba—
1Ch 2:43 The sons of Hebron: Korah, Tappuah, **Rekem** and Shema.
2:44 Raham the father of Jorkeam. **Rekem** was the father of Shammai.

8391 רִקְמָה *riqmâ*, n.f. [12] [√ 8387]

embroidered [4], embroidered work [2], embroidered cloth [1], embroidered dress [1], embroidered garments [1], highly embroidered [1], varied colors [1], various colors [1]

Jdg 5:30 garments as plunder for Sisera, colorful garments **embroidered**,
5:30 **highly embroidered** garments for my neck—
1Ch 29: 2 turquoise, stones of **various colors**, and all kinds of fine stone
Ps 45:14 [45:15] In **embroidered garments** she is led to the king;
Eze 16:10 I clothed you with an **embroidered dress** and put leather sandals
16:13 were of fine linen and costly fabric and **embroidered cloth**.
16:18 you took your **embroidered** clothes to put on them, and you
17: 3 long feathers and full plumage *of* **varied colors** came to Lebanon.
26:16 and lay aside their robes and take off their **embroidered** garments.
27: 7 Fine **embroidered** linen from Egypt was your sail and served as
27:16 **embroidered work**, fine linen, coral and rubies for your
27:24 **embroidered work** and multicolored rugs with cords twisted

8392 רָקַע *rāqaʿ*, v. [11] [→ 3767, 8385, 8393]

spread out [3], hammered out [2], hammered [1], overlays [1], spreading out [1], stamp [1], stamped [1], trampled [1]

Ex 39: 3 [D] *They* **hammered out** thin sheets of gold and cut strands to
Nu 16:39 [17:4] [D] and *he had* them **hammered out** to overlay the altar,
2Sa 22:43 [A] I pounded and **trampled** them like mud in the streets.
Job 37:18 [G] *can you* join him in **spreading out** the skies, hard as a mirror
Ps 136: 6 [A] *who* **spread out** the earth upon the waters, *His love*
Isa 40:19 [D] a goldsmith **overlays** it with gold and fashions silver chains
42: 5 [A] *who* **spread out** the earth and all that comes out of it,
44:24 [A] out the heavens, *who* **spread out** the earth by myself,
Jer 10: 9 [E] **Hammered** silver is brought from Tarshish and gold from
Eze 6:11 [A] your hands together and **stamp** your feet and cry out "Alas!"
25: 6 [A] you have clapped your hands and **stamped** your feet,

8393 רִקֻּעַ *riqquaʿ*, n.[m.]. [1] [√ 8392]

hammer [+906+6913] [1]

Nu 16:38 [17:3] cost of their lives. **Hammer** [+906+6913] the censers *into*

8394 רָקַק *rāqaq*, v. [1] [→ 8371; cf. 3762]

spits [1]

Lev 15: 8 [A] " 'If the man with the discharge **spits** on someone who is

8395 רַקַּת *raqqat*, n.pr.loc. [1] [√ 8369]

Rakkath [1]

Jos 19:35 fortified cities were Ziddim, Zer, Hammath, **Rakkath**, Kinnereth,

8396 רֹשׁ ***rōš***, n.pr.loc. & g. Not used in NIV/BHS [√ 8031; cf. 8034]

8397 רִשְׁיוֹן ***rišyôn***, n.[m.]. [1] [√ 3769]

authorized [1]

Ezr 3: 7 sea from Lebanon to Joppa, as **authorized** *by* Cyrus king of Persia.

8398 רָשַׁם ***rāšam***, v. [1] [→ Ar 10673]

written [1]

Da 10: 21 [B] but first I will tell you what *is* **written** in the Book of Truth.

8399 רָשַׁע ***rāša'***, v.den. [34] [→ 5360, 8400, 8401, 8402]

condemn [7], acted wickedly [3], condemning [3], guilty [3], condemns [2], done evil [2], wicked [2], condemned [1], declare guilty [1], did wrong [1], do wrong [1], doing wrong [1], done wrong [1], guilty of wickedness [1], inflicted punishment [1], let be condemned [1], overwicked [+2221] [1], refute [1], violated [1]

Ex 22: 9 [22:8] [G] The one whom the judges **declare guilty** must pay
Dt 25: 1 [G] the case, acquitting the innocent and **condemning** the guilty.
1Sa 14: 47 [G] Wherever he turned, *he* **inflicted punishment** on them.
2Sa 22: 22 [A] the LORD; *I have* not **done evil** by turning from my God.
1Ki 8: 32 [G] **condemning** the guilty and bringing down on his own head
8: 47 [A] have sinned, we have done wrong, *we have* **acted wickedly**';
2Ch 6: 37 [A] 'We have sinned, we have done wrong and **acted wickedly**';
20: 35 [G] with Ahaziah king of Israel, who *was* **guilty of wickedness**.
22: 3 [G] of Ahab, for his mother encouraged him in **doing wrong**.
Ne 9: 33 [G] been just; you have acted faithfully, while we **did wrong**.
Job 9: 20 [G] Even if I were innocent, my mouth *would* **condemn** me; if I
9: 29 [A] Since I *am already found* **guilty**, why should I struggle in
10: 2 [G] *Do* not **condemn** me, but tell me what charges you have
10: 7 [A] though you know that *I am* not **guilty** and that no one can
10: 15 [A] If *I am* **guilty**—woe to me! Even if I am innocent, I cannot
15: 6 [G] Your own mouth **condemns** you, not mine; your own lips
32: 3 [G] found no way to refute Job, and yet *had* **condemned** him.
34: 12 [G] It is unthinkable that God *would* **do wrong**,
34: 17 [G] justice govern? *Will you* **condemn** the just and mighty One?
34: 29 [G] if he remains silent, who *can* **condemn** him? If he hides his
40: 8 [G] my justice? *Would you* **condemn** me to justify yourself?
Ps 18: 21 [18:22] [A] *I have* not **done evil** by turning from my God.
37: 33 [G] their power or **let** them **be condemned** when brought to trial.
94: 21 [G] against the righteous and **condemn** the innocent *to* death.
106: 6 [G] as our fathers did; we have done wrong and **acted wickedly**.
Pr 12: 2 [G] from the LORD, but the LORD **condemns** a crafty man.
17: 15 [G] Acquitting the guilty and **condemning** the innocent—
Ecc 7: 17 [A] *Do* not *be* **overwicked** [+2221], and do not be a fool—why
Isa 50: 9 [G] Who is he *that will* **condemn** me? They will all wear out
54: 17 [G] and *you will* **refute** every tongue that accuses you.
Da 9: 5 [G] *We have been* **wicked** and have rebelled; we have turned
9: 15 [A] endures to this day, we have sinned, *we have* **done wrong**.
11: 32 [G] With flattery he will corrupt *those who have* **violated** the
12: 10 [G] and refined, but the wicked *will continue to be* **wicked**.

8400 רֶשַׁע ***reša'***, n.m. [30] [√ 8399]

wickedness [16], wicked [5], evil [2], ill-gotten [2], dishonest [1], evil deeds [1], injustice [1], it[s] [1], wrongdoing [+6913] [1]

Dt 9: 27 the stubbornness of this people, their **wickedness** and their sin.
1Sa 24: 13 [24:14] As the old saying goes, 'From evildoers come **evil deeds**,'
Job 34: 8 He keeps company with evildoers; he associates with **wicked** men.
34: 10 Far be it from God to do **evil**, from the Almighty to do wrong.
35: 8 Your **wickedness** affects only a man like yourself, and your
Ps 5: 4 [5:5] You are not a God who takes pleasure in **evil**; with you the
10: 15 call him to account for his **wickedness** that would not be found
45: 7 [45:8] You love righteousness and hate **wickedness**; therefore
84: 10 [84:11] house of my God than dwell in the tents of the **wicked**.
125: 3 The scepter of the **wicked** will not remain over the land allotted to
141: 4 is evil, to take part in **wicked** deeds with men who are evildoers;
Pr 4: 17 They eat the bread of **wickedness** and drink the wine of violence.
8: 7 My mouth speaks what is true, for my lips detest **wickedness**.
10: 2 **Ill-gotten** treasures are of no value, but righteousness delivers
12: 3 A man cannot be established through **wickedness**,
16: 12 Kings detest **wrongdoing** [+6913], for a throne is established
Ecc 3: 16 **wickedness** was there, in the place of justice—wickedness was
3: 16 was there, in the place of justice—**wickedness** was there.
7: 25 the scheme of things and to understand the stupidity of **wickedness**
8: 8 time of war, so **wickedness** will not release those who practice it.
Isa 58: 4 and strife, and in striking each other with **wicked** fists.
58: 6 to loose the chains of **injustice** and untie the cords of the yoke,
Jer 14: 20 we acknowledge our **wickedness** and the guilt of our fathers;
Eze 3: 19 and he does not turn from his **wickedness** or from his evil ways,
7: 11 Violence has grown into a rod to punish **wickedness**; none of the
31: 11 of the nations, for him to deal with according to its **wickedness**.
33: 12 the wicked man will not cause him to fall when he turns from **it**[s].
Hos 10: 13 you have planted **wickedness**, you have reaped evil, you have
Mic 6: 10 O wicked house, your **ill-gotten** treasures and the short ephah,
6: 11 Shall I acquit a man with **dishonest** scales, with a bag of false

8401 רָשָׁע ***rāšā'***, a. [263] [√ 8399]

wicked [237], guilty [9], evil [3], wickedness [3], he[s] [2], him[s] [2], deserves [1], evildoers [1], in the wrong [1], one in the wrong [1], outlaw [1], they[s] [1], ungodly [1]

Ge 18: 23 and said: "Will you sweep away the righteous with the **wicked**?
18: 25 to kill the righteous with the **wicked**, treating the righteous
18: 25 with the wicked, treating the righteous and the **wicked** alike.
Ex 2: 13 He asked the **one in the wrong**, "Why are you hitting your fellow
9: 27 LORD is in the right, and I and my people are **in the wrong**.
23: 1 Do not help a **wicked** *man* by being a malicious witness.
23: 7 or honest person to death, for I will not acquit the **guilty**.
Nu 16: 26 the assembly, "Move back from the tents of these **wicked** men!
35: 31 not accept a ransom for the life of a murderer, who **deserves** to die.
Dt 25: 1 decide the case, acquitting the innocent and condemning the **guilty**.
25: 2 If the **guilty** *man* deserves to be beaten, the judge shall make him
1Sa 2: 9 the feet of his saints, but the **wicked** will be silenced in darkness.
24: 13 [24:14] As the old saying goes, 'From **evildoers** come evil deeds,'
2Sa 4: 11 when **wicked** men have killed an innocent man in his own house
1Ki 8: 32 condemning the **guilty** and bringing down on his own head what
2Ch 6: 23 repaying the **guilty** by bringing down on his own head what he has
19: 2 "Should you help the **wicked** and love those who hate the LORD?
Job 3: 17 There the **wicked** cease from turmoil, and there the weary are at
8: 22 be clothed in shame, and the tents of the **wicked** will be no more."
9: 22 that is why I say, 'He destroys both the blameless and the **wicked**.'
9: 24 When a land falls into the hands of the **wicked**, he blindfolds its
10: 3 of your hands, while you smile on the schemes of the **wicked**?
11: 20 But the eyes of the **wicked** will fail, and escape will elude them;
15: 20 All his days the **wicked** *man* suffers torment, the ruthless through
16: 11 over to evil men and thrown me into the clutches of the **wicked**.
18: 5 "The lamp of the **wicked** is snuffed out; the flame of his fire stops
20: 5 that the mirth of the **wicked** is brief, the joy of the godless lasts
20: 29 Such is the fate God allots the **wicked**, the heritage appointed for
21: 7 Why do the **wicked** live on, growing old and increasing in power?
21: 16 their own hands, so I stand aloof from the counsel of the **wicked**.
21: 17 "Yet how often is the lamp of the **wicked** snuffed out? How often
21: 28 now is the great man's house, the tents where **wicked** *men* lived?'
22: 18 with good things, so I stand aloof from the counsel of the **wicked**.
24: 6 fodder in the fields and glean in the vineyards of the **wicked**.
27: 7 "May my enemies be like the **wicked**, my adversaries like the
27: 13 "Here is the fate God allots to the **wicked**, the heritage a ruthless
34: 18 says to kings, 'You are worthless,' and to nobles, 'You are **wicked**,'
34: 26 He punishes them for their **wickedness** where everyone can see
36: 6 He does not keep the **wicked** alive but gives the afflicted their
36: 17 But now you are laden with the judgment due the **wicked**;
38: 13 it might take the earth by the edges and shake the **wicked** out of it?
38: 15 The **wicked** are denied their light, and their upraised arm is broken.
40: 12 proud man and humble him, crush the **wicked** where they stand.
Ps 1: 1 Blessed is the man who does not walk in the counsel of the **wicked**
1: 4 Not so the **wicked**! They are like chaff that the wind blows away.
1: 5 Therefore the **wicked** will not stand in the judgment, nor sinners in
1: 6 the way of the righteous, but the way of the **wicked** will perish.
3: 7 [3:8] all my enemies on the jaw; break the teeth of the **wicked**.
7: 9 [7:10] bring to an end the violence of the **wicked** and make the
9: 5 [9:6] You have rebuked the nations and destroyed the **wicked**;
9: 16 [9:17] the **wicked** are ensnared by the work of their hands.
9: 17 [9:18] The **wicked** return to the grave, all the nations that forget
10: 2 In his arrogance the **wicked** *man* hunts down the weak, who are
10: 3 **He**[s] boasts of the cravings of his heart; he blesses the greedy
10: 4 In his pride the **wicked** does not seek him; in all his thoughts there
10: 13 Why does the **wicked** *man* revile God? Why does he say to
10: 15 Break the arm of the **wicked** and evil man; call him to account for
11: 2 For look, the **wicked** bend their bows; they set their arrows against
11: 5 but the **wicked** and those who love violence his soul hates.
11: 6 On the **wicked** he will rain fiery coals and burning sulfur;
12: 8 [12:9] The **wicked** freely strut about when what is vile is honored
17: 9 from the **wicked** who assail me, from my mortal enemies who
17: 13 bring them down; rescue me from the **wicked** by your sword.
26: 5 I abhor the assembly of evildoers and refuse to sit with the **wicked**.
28: 3 Do not drag me away with the **wicked**, with those who do evil,
31: 17 [31:18] let the **wicked** be put to shame and lie silent in the grave.
32: 10 Many are the woes of the **wicked**, but the LORD's unfailing love
34: 21 [34:22] Evil will slay the **wicked**; the foes of the righteous will be
36: 1 [36:2] is within my heart concerning the sinfulness of the **wicked**:
36: 11 [36:12] against me, nor the hand of the **wicked** drive me away.
37: 10 A little while, and the **wicked** will be no more; though you look for
37: 12 The **wicked** plot against the righteous and gnash their teeth at
37: 14 The **wicked** draw the sword and bend the bow to bring down the

Ps 37:16 the little that the righteous have than the wealth of many **wicked**;
37:17 for the power of the **wicked** will be broken, but the LORD
37:20 the **wicked** will perish: The LORD's enemies will be like the
37:21 The **wicked** borrow and do not repay, but the righteous give
37:28 protected forever, but the offspring of the **wicked** will be cut off;
37:32 The **wicked** lie in wait for the righteous, seeking their very lives;
37:34 you to inherit the land; when the **wicked** are cut off, you will see it.
37:35 I have seen a **wicked** and ruthless man flourishing like a green tree
37:38 sinners will be destroyed; the future of the **wicked** will be cut off.
37:40 he delivers them from the **wicked** and saves them, because they
39: 1 [39:2] I will put a muzzle on my mouth as long as the **wicked** are
50:16 to the **wicked**, God says: "What right have you to recite my laws
55: 3 [55:4] at the voice of the enemy, at the stares of the **wicked**;
58: 3 [58:4] Even from birth the **wicked** go astray; from the womb they
58:10 [58:11] when they bathe their feet in the blood of the **wicked**.
68: 2 [68:3] melts before the fire, may the **wicked** perish before God.
71: 4 Deliver me, O my God, from the hand of the **wicked**,
73: 3 For I envied the arrogant when I saw the prosperity of the **wicked**.
73:12 This is what the **wicked** are like—always carefree, they increase in
75: 4 [75:5] To the arrogant I say, 'Boast no more,' and to the **wicked**,
75: 8 [75:9] all the **wicked** *of* the earth drink it down to its very dregs.
75:10 [75:11] I will cut off the horns of all the **wicked**, but the horns of
82: 2 long will you defend the unjust and show partiality to the **wicked**?
82: 4 the weak and needy; deliver them from the hand of the **wicked**.
91: 8 only observe with your eyes and see the punishment of the **wicked**.
92: 7 [92:8] that though the **wicked** spring up like grass and all
94: 3 How long will the **wicked**, O LORD, how long will the wicked
94: 3 will the wicked, O LORD, how long will the **wicked** be jubilant?
94:13 him relief from days of trouble, till a pit is dug for the **wicked**.
97:10 of his faithful ones and delivers them from the hand of the **wicked**.
101: 8 Every morning I will put to silence all the **wicked** *in* the land;
104:35 But may sinners vanish from the earth and the **wicked** be no more.
106:18 Fire blazed among their followers; a flame consumed the **wicked**.
109: 2 for **wicked** and deceitful men have opened their mouths against
109: 6 Appoint an **evil** *man* to oppose him; let an accuser stand at his
109: 7 When he is tried, let him be found **guilty**, and may his prayers
112:10 The **wicked** *man* will see and be vexed, he will gnash his teeth
112:10 and waste away; the longings of the **wicked** will come to nothing.
119:53 Indignation grips me because of the **wicked**, who have forsaken
119:61 Though the **wicked** bind me with ropes, I will not forget your law.
119:95 The **wicked** are waiting to destroy me, but I will ponder your
119:110 The **wicked** have set a snare for me, but I have not strayed from
119:119 All the **wicked** *of* the earth you discard like dross; therefore I love
119:155 Salvation is far from the **wicked**, for they do not seek out your
129: 4 is righteous; he has cut me free from the cords of the **wicked**.
139:19 If only you would slay the **wicked**, O God! Away from me,
140: 4 [140:5] Keep me, O LORD, from the hands of the **wicked**;
140: 8 [140:9] do not grant the **wicked** their desires, O LORD; do not
141:10 Let the **wicked** fall into their own nets, while I pass by in safety.
145:20 watches over all who love him, but all the **wicked** he will destroy.
146: 9 and the widow, but he frustrates the ways of the **wicked**.
147: 6 LORD sustains the humble but casts the **wicked** to the ground.
Pr 2:22 the **wicked** will be cut off from the land, and the unfaithful will be
3:25 no fear of sudden disaster or of the ruin that overtakes the **wicked**,
3:33 The LORD's curse is on the house of the **wicked**, but he blesses
4:14 Do not set foot on the path of the **wicked** or walk in the way of evil
4:19 the way of the **wicked** is like deep darkness; they do not know
5:22 The evil deeds of a **wicked** *man* ensnare him; the cords of his sin
9: 7 invites insult; whoever rebukes a **wicked** *man* incurs abuse.
10: 3 the righteous go hungry but he thwarts the craving of the **wicked**.
10: 6 the righteous, but violence overwhelms the mouth of the **wicked**.
10: 7 righteous will be a blessing, but the name of the **wicked** will rot.
10:11 fountain of life, but violence overwhelms the mouth of the **wicked**.
10:16 them life, but the income of the **wicked** brings them punishment.
10:20 is choice silver, but the heart of the **wicked** is of little value.
10:24 What the **wicked** dreads will overtake him; what the righteous
10:25 When the storm has swept by, the **wicked** are gone,
10:27 adds length to life, but the years of the **wicked** are cut short.
10:28 the righteous is joy, but the hopes of the **wicked** come to nothing.
10:30 will never be uprooted, but the **wicked** will not remain in the land.
10:32 what is fitting, but the mouth of the **wicked** only what is perverse.
11: 5 but the **wicked** are brought down by their own wickedness.
11: 7 When a **wicked** man dies, his hope perishes; all he expected from
11: 8 man is rescued from trouble, and it comes on the **wicked** instead.
11:10 the city rejoices; when the **wicked** perish, there are shouts of joy.
11:11 a city is exalted, but by the mouth of the **wicked** it is destroyed.
11:18 The **wicked** *man* earns deceptive wages, but he who sows
11:23 ends only in good, but the hope of the **wicked** only in wrath.
11:31 their due on earth, how much more the **ungodly** and the sinner!
12: 5 of the righteous are just, but the advice of the **wicked** is deceitful.
12: 6 The words of the **wicked** lie in wait for blood, but the speech of the
12: 7 **Wicked** *men* are overthrown and are no more, but the house of the
12:10 needs of his animal, but the kindest acts of the **wicked** are cruel.
12:12 The **wicked** desire the plunder of evil men, but the root of the
12:21 harm befalls the righteous, but the **wicked** have their fill of trouble.
12:26 in friendship, but the way of the **wicked** leads them astray.
13: 5 hate what is false, but the **wicked** bring shame and disgrace.
13: 9 shines brightly, but the lamp of the **wicked** is snuffed out.
13:17 A **wicked** messenger falls into trouble, but a trustworthy envoy
13:25 to their hearts' content, but the stomach of the **wicked** goes hungry.
14:11 The house of the **wicked** will be destroyed, but the tent of the
14:19 presence of the good, and the **wicked** at the gates of the righteous.
14:32 When calamity comes, the **wicked** are brought down, but even in
15: 6 great treasure, but the income of the **wicked** brings them trouble.
15: 8 The LORD detests the sacrifice of the **wicked**, but the prayer of
15: 9 The LORD detests the way of the **wicked** but he loves those who
15:28 weighs its answers, but the mouth of the **wicked** gushes evil.
15:29 The LORD is far from the **wicked** but he hears the prayer of the
16: 4 for his own ends—even the **wicked** for a day of disaster.
17:15 Acquitting the **guilty** and condemning the innocent—the LORD
17:23 A **wicked** *man* accepts a bribe in secret to pervert the course of
18: 3 When **wickedness** comes, so does contempt, and with shame
18: 5 It is not good to be partial to the **wicked** or to deprive the innocent
19:28 mocks at justice, and the mouth of the **wicked** gulps down evil.
20:26 A wise king winnows out the **wicked**; he drives the threshing
21: 4 Haughty eyes and a proud heart, the lamp of the **wicked**, are sin!
21: 7 The violence of the **wicked** will drag them away, for they refuse to
21:10 The **wicked** man craves evil; his neighbor gets no mercy from him.
21:12 The Righteous One takes note of the house of the **wicked**
21:12 note of the house of the wicked and brings the **wicked** to ruin.
21:18 The **wicked** become a ransom for the righteous, and the unfaithful
21:27 The sacrifice of the **wicked** is detestable—how much more
21:29 A **wicked** man puts up a bold front, but an upright man gives
24:15 Do not lie in wait like an **outlaw** against a righteous man's house,
24:16 he rises again, but the **wicked** are brought down by calamity.
24:19 Do not fret because of evil men or be envious of the **wicked**,
24:20 has no future hope, and the lamp of the **wicked** will be snuffed out.
24:24 Whoever says to the **guilty**, "You are innocent"—peoples will
25: 5 remove the **wicked** from the king's presence, and his throne will
25:26 or a polluted well is a righteous man who gives way to the **wicked**.
28: 1 The **wicked** *man* flees though no one pursues, but the righteous
28: 4 Those who forsake the law praise the **wicked**, but those who keep
28:12 but when the **wicked** rise to power, men go into hiding.
28:15 or a charging bear is a **wicked** *man* ruling over a helpless people.
28:28 When the **wicked** rise to power, people go into hiding; but when
29: 2 the people rejoice; when the **wicked** rule, the people groan.
29: 7 about justice for the poor, but the **wicked** have no such concern.
29:12 If a ruler listens to lies, all his officials become **wicked**.
29:16 When the **wicked** thrive, so does sin, but the righteous will see
29:27 The righteous detest the dishonest; the **wicked** detest the upright.
Ecc 3:17 "God will bring to judgment both the righteous and the **wicked**,
7:15 and a **wicked** *man* living long in his wickedness.
8:10 Then too, I saw the **wicked** buried—those who used to come
8:13 Yet because the **wicked** do not fear God, it will not go well with
8:14 righteous men who get what the **wicked** deserve, and wicked men
8:14 and **wicked** *men* who get what the righteous deserve.
9: 2 the righteous and the **wicked**, the good and the bad, the clean
Isa 3:11 Woe to the **wicked**! Disaster is upon them! They will be paid back
5:23 who acquit the **guilty** for a bribe, but deny justice to the innocent.
11: 4 of his mouth; with the breath of his lips he will slay the **wicked**.
13:11 I will punish the world for its evil, the **wicked** for their sins.
14: 5 The LORD has broken the rod of the **wicked**, the scepter of the
26:10 Though grace is shown to the **wicked**, they do not learn
48:22 "There is no peace," says the LORD, "for the **wicked**."
53: 9 He was assigned a grave with the **wicked**, and with the rich in his
55: 7 Let the **wicked** forsake his way and the evil man his thoughts.
57:20 But the **wicked** are like the tossing sea, which cannot rest,
57:21 "There is no peace," says my God, "for the **wicked**."
Jer 5:26 "Among my people are **wicked** *men* who lie in wait like men who
12: 1 Why does the way of the **wicked** prosper? Why do all the faithless
23:19 in wrath, a whirlwind swirling down on the heads of the **wicked**.
25:31 and put the **wicked** to the sword,' " declares the LORD.
30:23 a driving wind swirling down on the heads of the **wicked**.
Eze 3:18 When I say to a **wicked** *man*, 'You will surely die,' and you do not
3:18 or speak out to dissuade **him**[s] from his evil ways in order to save
3:18 or speak out to dissuade him from his **evil** ways in order to save his
3:18 that **wicked** *man* will die for his sin, and I will hold you
3:19 if you do warn the **wicked** *man* and he does not turn from his
3:19 and he does not turn from his wickedness or from his **evil** ways,
7:21 over as plunder to foreigners and as loot to the **wicked** *of* the earth,
13:22 because you encouraged the **wicked** not to turn from their evil
18:20 and the wickedness of the **wicked** will be charged against him.
18:21 "But if a **wicked** *man* turns away from all the sins he has
18:23 Do I take any pleasure in the death of the **wicked**?
18:24 and does the same detestable things the **wicked** *man* does,
18:27 if a **wicked** *man* turns away from the wickedness he has
21: 3 [21:8] and cut off from you both the righteous and the **wicked**.
21: 4 [21:9] I am going to cut off the righteous and the **wicked**,

Eze 21:25 [21:30] " 'O profane and **wicked** prince of Israel, whose day has
21:29 [21:34] it will be laid on the necks of the **wicked** who are to be
33: 8 When I say to the **wicked**, 'O wicked man, you will surely die,'
33: 8 When I say to the wicked, 'O **wicked** *man*, you will surely die,'
33: 8 and you do not speak out to dissuade **him**ˢ from his ways,
33: 8 that **wicked** *man* will die for his sin, and I will hold you
33: 9 But if you do warn the **wicked** *man* to turn from his ways
33:11 Sovereign LORD, I take no pleasure in the death of the **wicked**,
33:11 of the wicked, but rather that **they**ˢ turn from their ways and live.
33:12 the wickedness of the **wicked** *man* will not cause him to fall when
33:14 And if I say to the **wicked** *man*, 'You will surely die,' but he
33:15 if **he**ˢ gives back what he took in pledge for a loan, returns what he
33:19 if a **wicked** *man* turns away from his wickedness and does what is
Da 12:10 and refined, but the **wicked** will continue to be wicked.
12:10 None of the **wicked** will understand, but those who are wise will
Mic 6:10 Am I still to forget, O **wicked** house, your ill-gotten treasures
Hab 1: 4 The **wicked** hem in the righteous, so that justice is perverted.
1:13 Why are you silent while the **wicked** swallow up those more
3:13 You crushed the leader of the land of **wickedness**, you stripped
Zep 1: 3 The **wicked** will have only heaps of rubble when I cut off man
Mal 3:18 again see the distinction between the righteous and the **wicked**,
4: 3 [3:21] you will trample down the **wicked**; they will be ashes

8402 רִשְׁעָה ***riš'â***, n.f. [15] [√ 8399]

wickedness [11], crime [1], evildoer [+6913] [1], evildoers [+6913] [1], wicked [1]

Dt 9: 4 it is on account of the **wickedness** *of* these nations that the LORD
9: 5 on account of the **wickedness** *of* these nations, the LORD your
25: 2 in his presence with the number of lashes his **crime** deserves,
Pr 11: 5 but the wicked are brought down by their own **wickedness**.
13: 6 guards the man of integrity, but **wickedness** overthrows the sinner.
Isa 9:18 [9:17] Surely **wickedness** burns like a fire; it consumes briers
Eze 5: 6 Yet in her **wickedness** she has rebelled against my laws
18:20 and the **wickedness** *of* the wicked will be charged against him.
18:27 if a wicked man turns away from the **wickedness** he has committed
33:12 the **wickedness** *of* the wicked man will not cause him to fall when
33:19 if a wicked man turns away from his **wickedness** and does what is
Zec 5: 8 He said, "This is **wickedness**," and he pushed her back into the
Mal 1: 4 They will be called the **Wicked** Land, a people always under the
3:15 Certainly the **evildoers** [+6913] prosper, and even those who
4: 1 [3:19] the arrogant and every **evildoer** [+6913] will be stubble,

8403 רִשְׁעָתַיִם ***riš'ātayim***, n.pr.m. Not used in NIV/BHS [→ 3937]

8404 ¹רֶשֶׁף ***rešep¹***, n.m. [7] [→ 8405]

pestilence [2], blazing [1], bolts of lightning [1], burns [1], flashing [1], sparks [+1201] [1]

Dt 32:24 famine against them, consuming **pestilence** and deadly plague;
Job 5: 7 Yet man is born to trouble as surely as **sparks** [+1201] fly upward.
Ps 76: 3 [76:4] There he broke the **flashing** arrows, the shields
78:48 over their cattle to the hail, their livestock to **bolts of lightning**.
SS 8: 6 as the grave. It **burns** like blazing fire, like a mighty flame.
8: 6 as the grave. It burns like **blazing** fire, like a mighty flame.
Hab 3: 5 Plague went before him; **pestilence** followed his steps.

8405 ²רֶשֶׁף ***rešep²***, n.pr.m. [1] [√ 8404]

Resheph [1]

1Ch 7:25 was his son, **Resheph** his son, Telah his son, Tahan his son,

8406 רָשַׁשׁ ***rāšaš***, v. [2] [→ 9576?, 9577?, 9578?]

been crushed [1], destroy [1]

Jer 5:17 [D] With the sword *they will* **destroy** the fortified cities in which
Mal 1: 4 [E] Edom may say, *"Though we have* **been crushed**, we will

8407 רֶשֶׁת ***rešet***, n.f. [22] [√ 3769]

net [16], network [+5126] [2], itˢ [+2021] [1], network [1], snare [1], trap [1]

Ex 27: 4 Make a grating for it, a bronze **network** [+5126], and make a
27: 4 and make a bronze ring at each of the four corners of the **network**.
27: 5 the ledge of the altar so that **it**ˢ [+2021] is halfway up the altar.
38: 4 a bronze **network** [+5126], to be under its ledge, halfway up the
Job 18: 8 His feet thrust him into a **net** and he wanders into its mesh.
Ps 9:15 [9:16] have dug; their feet are caught in the **net** they have hidden.
10: 9 the helpless; he catches the helpless and drags them off in his **net**.
25:15 on the LORD, for only he will release my feet from the **snare**.
31: 4 [31:5] Free me from the **trap** that is set for me, for you are my
35: 7 Since they hid their **net** for me without cause and without cause
35: 8 may the **net** they hid entangle them, may they fall into the pit,
57: 6 [57:7] They spread a **net** for my feet—I was bowed down in
140: 5 [140:6] they have spread out the cords of their **net** and have set
Pr 1:17 How useless to spread a **net** in full view of all the birds!
29: 5 Whoever flatters his neighbor is spreading a **net** for his feet.
La 1:13 He spread a **net** for my feet and turned me back. He made me
Eze 12:13 I will spread my **net** for him, and he will be caught in my snare;
17:20 I will spread my **net** for him, and he will be caught in my snare.
19: 8 They spread their **net** for him, and he was trapped in their pit.
32: 3 " 'With a great throng of people I will cast my **net** over you,
Hos 5: 1 You have been a snare at Mizpah, a **net** spread out on Tabor.
7:12 When they go, I will throw my **net** over them; I will pull them

8408 רַתּוֹק ***rattôq***, n.[m.]. [1] [√ 8415]

chains [1]

1Ki 6:21 [he extended gold **chains** [Q; see K 8411] across the front of the]
Eze 7:23 "Prepare **chains**, because the land is full of bloodshed and the city

8409 רָתַח ***rātaḥ***, v. [3] [→ 8410]

bring to a boil [+8410] [1], churning [1], makes churn [1]

Job 30:27 [E] The **churning** inside me never stops; days of suffering
41:31 [41:23] [G] *He* **makes** the depths **churn** like a boiling caldron
Eze 24: 5 [D] the bones; **bring it to a boil** [+8410] and cook the bones in it.

8410 רֶתַח ***retaḥ***, n.[m.]. [1] [√ 8409]

bring to a boil [+8409] [1]

Eze 24: 5 it for the bones; **bring it to a boil** [+8409] and cook the bones in it.

8411 רַתִּיקָה ***rattîqâ***, n.[m.]. [1] [√ 8415]

chains [1]

1Ki 6:21 he extended gold **chains** [Q 8408] across the front of the inner

8412 רָתַם ***rātam***, v. [1] [→ 8413, 8414?]

harness [1]

Mic 1:13 [A] You who live in Lachish, **harness** the team to the chariot.

8413 רֹתֶם ***rōtem***, n.m. [4] [→ 8414; cf. 8412?]

broom tree [3], tree [1]

1Ki 19: 4 He came to a **broom tree**, sat down under it and prayed that he
19: 5 he lay down under the **tree** and fell asleep. All at once an angel
Job 30: 4 gathered salt herbs, and their food was the root of the **broom tree**.
Ps 120: 4 a warrior's sharp arrows, with burning coals of the **broom tree**.

8414 רִתְמָה ***ritmâ***, n.pr.loc. [2] [√ 8413; cf. 8412?]

Rithmah [2]

Nu 33:18 They left Hazeroth and camped at **Rithmah**.
33:19 They left **Rithmah** and camped at Rimmon Perez.

8415 רָתַק ***rātaq***, v. [1] [→ 8408, 8411, 8416]

were put in chains [+928+2414] [1]

Ecc 12: 6 [c] [before the silver cord **is severed**, [Q; see K 8178]]
Na 3:10 [E] and all her great men **were put in chains** [+928+2414].

8416 רְתֻקוֹת ***rᵉtuqôt***, n.[f.pl.]. [1] [√ 8415]

chains [1]

Isa 40:19 a goldsmith overlays it with gold and fashions silver **chains** for it.

8417 רְתֵת ***rᵉtēt***, n.[m.]. [1] [cf. 8185]

trembled [1]

Hos 13: 1 When Ephraim spoke, men **trembled**; he was exalted in Israel.

שׂ, *ś*

8418 שׂ ***ś***, letter. Not used in NIV/BHS [→ Ar 10674]

8419 שְׂאֹר ***śᵉʾōr***, n.m. [5] [→ 5389, 5400]

yeast [5]

Ex 12:15 On the first day remove the **yeast** from your houses, for whoever
12:19 For seven days no **yeast** is to be found in your houses. And
13: 7 nor shall *any* **yeast** be seen anywhere within your borders.
Lev 2:11 for you are not to burn any **yeast** or honey in an offering made to
Dt 16: 4 Let no **yeast** be found in your possession in all your land for seven

8420 ¹שְׂאֵת **śᵉ'ēt[1]**, n.f. [7] [→ 8480?, 8481?; cf. 5951]

honor [2], splendor [2], accepted [1], lofty place [1], rises up [1]

Ge 4: 7 If you do what is right, will you not be **accepted**? But if you do not
49: 3 first sign of my strength, excelling in **honor**, excelling in power.
Job 13: 11 Would not his **splendor** terrify you? Would not the dread of him
31: 23 from God, and for fear of his **splendor** I could not do such things.
41: 25 [41:17] When he **rises up**, the mighty are terrified; they retreat
Ps 62: 4 [62:5] They fully intend to topple him from his **lofty place**;
Hab 1: 7 they are a law to themselves and promote their own **honor**.

8421 ²שְׂאֵת **śᵉ'ēt[2]**, n.f. [7] [√ 5951]

swelling [6], swollen [1]

Lev 13: 2 "When anyone has a **swelling** or a rash or a bright spot on his skin
13: 10 if there is a white **swelling** in the skin that has turned the hair white
13: 10 has turned the hair white and if there is raw flesh in the **swelling**,
13: 19 where the boil was, a white **swelling** or reddish-white spot appears,
13: 28 not spread in the skin but has faded, it is a **swelling** *from* the burn,
13: 43 if the **swollen** sore on his head or forehead is reddish-white like an
14: 56 and for a **swelling**, a rash or a bright spot,

8422 שְׂבָכָה **śᵉbākâ**, n.f. [16] [√ 8449; Ar 10676]

network [12], network [+5126+8422] [2], lattice [1], mesh [1]

1Ki 7: 17 A **network** [+5126+8422] of interwoven chains festooned the
7: 17 A **network** [+5126+8422] of interwoven chains festooned the
7: 18 He made pomegranates in two rows encircling each **network** to
7: 20 of both pillars, above the bowl-shaped part next to the **network**,
7: 41 the two sets of **network** decorating the two bowl-shaped capitals
7: 42 the four hundred pomegranates for the two sets of **network** (two
7: 42 two sets of network (two rows of pomegranates for each **network**,
2Ki 1: 2 Now Ahaziah had fallen through the **lattice** of his upper room in
25: 17 a half feet high and was decorated with a **network**
25: 17 bronze all around. The other pillar, with its **network**, was similar.
2Ch 4: 12 the two sets of **network** decorating the two bowl-shaped capitals
4: 13 the four hundred pomegranates for the two sets of **network** (two
4: 13 two sets of network (two rows of pomegranates for each **network**,
Job 18: 8 His feet thrust him into a net and he wanders into its **mesh**.
Jer 52: 22 was decorated with a **network** and pomegranates of bronze all
52: 23 the total number of pomegranates above the surrounding **network**

8423 שְׂבָם **śᵉbām**, n.pr.loc. [1] [→ 8424]

Sebam [1]

Nu 32: 3 Jazer, Nimrah, Heshbon, Elealeh, **Sebam**, Nebo and Beon—

8424 שִׂבְמָה **śibmâ**, n.pr.loc. [5] [√ 8423]

Sibmah [5]

Nu 32: 38 and Baal Meon (these names were changed) and **Sibmah**.
Jos 13: 19 Kiriathaim, **Sibmah**, Zereth Shahar on the hill in the valley,
Isa 16: 8 The fields of Heshbon wither, the vines of **Sibmah** also. The rulers
16: 9 So I weep, as Jazer weeps, for the vines of **Sibmah**. O Heshbon,
Jer 48: 32 I weep for you, as Jazer weeps, O vines of **Sibmah**. Your branches

8425 שָׂבַע **śāba'**, v. [98] [→ 8426, 8427, 8428, 8429, 8430]

satisfied [30], filled [9], satisfy [9], full [6], get enough [3], have enough [3], satisfies [3], endured [2], fill [2], had enough [2], has enough [2], have abundant [2], too much [2], *untranslated* [1], all want [1], all wanted [1], content [1], eat fill [1], eats fill [1], enjoy plenty [1], enjoy [1], feast on [1], fully repaid [1], gorge [1], had fill [1], had plenty [1], have fill [1], have more than enough [1], have plenty [1], have to spare [1], have too much [1], overwhelm [1], satisfy fully [1], supplied all needs [1], toss [+5611] [1], well watered [1]

Ex 16: 8 [A] eat in the evening and **all** the bread you **want** in the morning,
16: 12 [A] eat meat, and in the morning *you will be* **filled** *with* bread.
Lev 26: 26 [A] bread by weight. You will eat, but *you will* not *be* **satisfied**.
Dt 6: 11 [A] you did not plant—then when you eat and *are* **satisfied**,
8: 10 [A] When you have eaten and *are* **satisfied**, praise the LORD
8: 12 [A] Otherwise, when you eat and *are* **satisfied**, when you build
11: 15 [A] in the fields for your cattle, and you will eat and *be* **satisfied**.
14: 29 [A] who live in your towns may come and eat and *be* **satisfied**,
26: 12 [A] so that they may eat in your towns and *be* **satisfied**.
31: 20 [A] when they eat *their* **fill** and thrive, they will turn to other
Ru 2: 14 [A] roasted grain. She ate **all** *she* **wanted** and had some left over.
1Ch 23: 1 [A] When David was old and **full** *of* years, he made his son
2Ch 24: 15 [A] Now Jehoiada was old and **full** *of* years, and he died at the
31: 10 [A] we *have* **had enough** to eat and plenty to spare, because the
Ne 9: 25 [A] They ate *to the* **full** and were well-nourished; they reveled in
Job 7: 4 [A] I get up?' The night drags on, and *I* **toss** [+5611] till dawn.
9: 18 [G] me regain my breath but *would* **overwhelm** me *with* misery.
19: 22 [A] me as God does? *Will you* never **get enough** of my flesh?
27: 14 [A] is the sword; his offspring *will* never **have enough** to eat.
31: 31 [C] have never said, 'Who *has* not **had** *his* **fill** of Job's meat?'—
38: 27 [G] to **satisfy** a desolate wasteland and make it sprout with grass?
Ps 17: 14 [A] their sons **have plenty**, and they store up wealth for their
17: 15 [A] when I awake, *I will be* **satisfied** *with* seeing your likeness.
22: 26 [22:27] [A] The poor will eat and *be* **satisfied**; they who seek
37: 19 [A] will not wither; in days of famine *they will* **enjoy plenty**.
59: 15 [59:16] [A] wander about for food and howl if not **satisfied**.
63: 5 [63:6] [A] My soul *will be* **satisfied** as *with* the richest of foods;
65: 4 [65:5] [A] *We are* **filled** with the good things of your house,
78: 29 [A] They ate till *they* **had** more than **enough**, for he had given
81: 16 [81:17] [G] with honey from the rock *I would* **satisfy** you."
88: 3 [88:4] [A] For my soul *is* **full** of trouble and my life draws near
90: 14 [D] **Satisfy** us in the morning *with* your unfailing love, that we
91: 16 [G] *With* long life *will I* **satisfy** him and show him my
103: 5 [G] who **satisfies** your desires with good things so that your
104: 13 [A] the earth *is* **satisfied** by the fruit of his work.
104: 16 [A] The trees of the LORD *are* **well watered**, the cedars of
104: 28 [A] you open your hand, *they are* **satisfied** *with* good things.
105: 40 [G] them quail and **satisfied** them *with* the bread of heaven.
107: 9 [G] for *he* **satisfies** the thirsty and fills the hungry with good
123: 3 [A] have mercy on us, for *we have* **endured** much contempt.
123: 4 [A] We *have* **endured** much ridicule from the proud, much
132: 15 [G] with abundant provisions; her poor *will I* **satisfy** *with* food.
145: 16 [G] open your hand and **satisfy** the desires of every living thing.
147: 14 [G] to your borders and **satisfies** you *with* the finest of wheat.
Pr 1: 31 [A] of their ways and *be* **filled** with the fruit of their schemes.
5: 10 [A] lest strangers **feast on** your wealth and your toil enrich
12: 11 [A] He who works his land *will* **have abundant** food, but he who
12: 14 [A] From the fruit of his lips a man *is* **filled** *with* good things as
14: 14 [A] The faithless *will be* **fully repaid** for their ways,
18: 20 [A] From the fruit of his mouth a man's stomach *is* **filled**;
18: 20 [A] is filled; *with* the harvest from his lips *he is* **satisfied**.
20: 13 [A] will grow poor; stay awake and *you will* **have** food **to spare**.
25: 16 [A] eat just enough—**too much** *of* it, and you will vomit.
25: 17 [A] neighbor's house—**too much** *of* you, and he will hate you.
27: 20 [A] Death and Destruction *are* never **satisfied**, and neither are
27: 20 [A] are never satisfied, and neither are **[RPH]** the eyes of man.
28: 19 [A] He who works his land *will* **have abundant** food, but the one
28: 19 [A] but the one who chases fantasies *will* **have** *his* **fill** *of* poverty.
30: 9 [A] Otherwise, *I may* **have too much** and disown you and say,
30: 15 [A] "There are three things *that are* never **satisfied**, four that
30: 16 [A] land, *which is* never **satisfied** *with* water, and fire,
30: 22 [A] a servant who becomes king, a fool *who is* **full** *of* food,
Ecc 1: 8 [A] The eye never **has enough** *of* seeing, nor the ear its fill of
4: 8 [A] end to his toil, yet his eyes *were* not **content** *with* his wealth.
5: 10 [5:9] [A] Whoever loves money never **has** money **enough**;
6: 3 [A] if he cannot **enjoy** his prosperity and does not receive proper
Isa 1: 11 [A] "*I* **have more than enough** *of* burnt offerings, of rams
9: 20 [9:19] [A] on the left they will eat, but not *be* **satisfied**.
44: 16 [A] it he prepares his meal, he roasts his meat and **eats** *his* **fill**.
53: 11 [A] of his soul, he will see the light ⌞of life⌟ and *be* **satisfied**;
58: 10 [G] behalf of the hungry and **satisfy** the needs of the oppressed,
58: 11 [G] *he will* **satisfy** your needs in a sun-scorched land and will
66: 11 [A] For you will nurse and *be* **satisfied** at her comforting breasts;
Jer 5: 7 [G] *I* **supplied all** their **needs**, yet they committed adultery
31: 14 [A] my people *will be* **filled** *with* my bounty,"
44: 17 [A] At that time *we* **had plenty** *of* food and were well off
46: 10 [A] The sword will devour till *it is* **satisfied**, till it has quenched
50: 10 [A] all who plunder her *will have their* **fill**,"
50: 19 [A] his appetite *will be* **satisfied** on the hills of Ephraim
La 3: 15 [G] *He has* **filled** me with bitter herbs and sated me with gall.
3: 30 [A] who would strike him, and *let him be* **filled** with disgrace.
5: 6 [A] We submitted to Egypt and Assyria to **get enough** bread.
Eze 7: 19 [D] *They will* not **satisfy** their hunger or fill their stomachs with
16: 28 [A] and even after that, *you* still *were* not **satisfied**.
16: 29 [A] land of merchants, but even with this *you were* not **satisfied**.
27: 33 [G] went out on the seas, *you* **satisfied** many nations;
32: 4 [G] and all the beasts of the earth **gorge** *themselves* on you.
39: 20 [A] At my table *you will* **eat** *your* **fill** *of* horses and riders,
Hos 4: 10 [A] "They will eat but not **have enough**; they will engage in
13: 6 [A] When I fed them, *they were* **satisfied**; when they were
13: 6 [A] *when they were* **satisfied**, they became proud;
Joel 2: 19 [A] you grain, new wine and oil, *enough to* **satisfy** you **fully**;
2: 26 [A] You will have plenty to eat, until *you are* **full**, and you will
Am 4: 8 [A] from town to town for water but *did* not **get enough** to drink,
Mic 6: 14 [A] You will eat but not *be* **satisfied**; your stomach will still be
Hab 2: 5 [A] he is as greedy as the grave and like death is never **satisfied**,
2: 16 [A] *You will be* **filled** *with* shame instead of glory. Now it is
Hag 1: 6 [A] You eat, but never **have enough**. You drink, but never have

8426 שָׂבָע **śābā'**, n.m. [8] [√ 8425]

abundance [7], overflowing [1]

Ge 41: 29 Seven years of great **abundance** are coming throughout the land of

Ge 41:30 all the **abundance** in Egypt will be forgotten, and the famine will
41:31 The **abundance** in the land will not be remembered, because the
41:34 fifth of the harvest of Egypt during the seven years of **abundance**.
41:47 During the seven years of **abundance** the land produced
41:53 The seven years of **abundance** in Egypt came to an end,
Pr 3:10 your barns will be filled *to* **overflowing**, and your vats will brim
Ecc 5:12 [5:11] but the **abundance** of a rich man permits him no sleep.

8427 שֹׂבַע ***śōba'***, n.[m.]. [8] [√ 8425]

all want [2], fill [2], all could eat [1], all wanted [1], content [1], eaten enough [1]

Ex 16: 3 There we sat around pots of meat and ate **all** the food we **wanted**,
Lev 25:19 will yield its fruit, and you will eat your **fill** and live there in safety.
26: 5 you will eat **all** the food you **want** and live in safety in your land.
Dt 23:24 [23:25] you may eat **all** the grapes you **want**, but do not put any
Ru 2:18 and gave her what she had left over after she had **eaten enough**.
Ps 16:11 you will **fill** me *with* joy in your presence, with eternal pleasures at
78:25 ate the bread of angels; he sent them **all** the food they **could eat**.
Pr 13:25 The righteous eat to their hearts' **content**, but the stomach of the

8428 שָׂבֵעַ ***śābēa'***, a. [10] [√ 8425]

full [7], abounding [1], content [1], enjoyed long life [+3427] [1]

Ge 25: 8 his last and died at a good old age, an old man and **full** of years;
35:29 and died and was gathered to his people, old and **full** *of* years.
Dt 33:23 "Naphtali is **abounding** *with* the favor of the LORD and is full of
1Sa 2: 5 *Those who were* **full** hire themselves out for food, but those who
1Ch 29:28 good old age, having **enjoyed long** [+3427] **life**, wealth and honor.
Job 10:15 lift my head, for I am **full** *of* shame and drowned in my affliction.
14: 1 "Man born of woman is of few days and **full** *of* trouble.
42:17 And so he died, old and **full** *of* years.
Pr 19:23 leads to life: Then one rests **content**, untouched by trouble.
27: 7 He who is **full** loathes honey, but to the hungry even what is bitter

8429 שָׂבְעָה ***śob'â***, n.f. [5] [√ 8425]

abundant [1], enough [1], glutted [1], insatiable [+1194] [1], satisfy [1]

Isa 23:18 who live before the LORD, for **abundant** food and fine clothes.
55: 2 on what is not bread, and your labor on *what* does not **satisfy**?
56:11 They are dogs with mighty appetites; they never have **enough**.
Eze 16:28 with the Assyrians too, because you *were* **insatiable** [+1194];
39:19 you will eat fat till you are **glutted** and drink blood till you are

8430 שִׂבְעָה ***śib'â***, n.f. [1] [√ 8425]

overfed [+4312] [1]

Eze 16:49 her daughters were arrogant, **overfed** [+4312] and unconcerned;

8431 [1]שָׂבַר ***śābar***[1], v. [2] [→ Ar 10503]

examining [2]

Ne 2:13 [A] and the Dung Gate, **examining** the walls of Jerusalem,
2:15 [A] so I went up the valley by night, **examining** the wall. Finally,

8432 [2]שָׂבַר ***śābar***[2], v. [6] [→ 8433]

look [2], wait [2], hope [1], hoped [1]

Ru 1:13 [D] *would you* **wait** until they grew up? Would you remain
Est 9: 1 [D] On this day the enemies of the Jews *had* **hoped** to overpower
Ps 104:27 [D] These all **look** to you to give them their food at the proper
119:166 [D] *I* **wait** for your salvation, O LORD, and I follow your
145:15 [D] The eyes of all **look** to you, and you give them their food at
Isa 38:18 [D] those who go down to the pit cannot **hope** for your

8433 שֵׂבֶר ***śēber***, n.m. [2] [√ 8432]

hope [1], hopes [1]

Ps 119:116 to your promise, and I will live; do not let my **hopes** be dashed.
146: 5 help is the God of Jacob, whose **hope** is in the LORD his God,

8434 שָׂגָא ***śāgā'***, v. [2] [√ 8438; cf. 8436; Ar 10677]

extol [1], makes great [1]

Job 12:23 [G] *He* **makes** nations **great**, and destroys them; he enlarges
36:24 [G] Remember *to* **extol** his work, which men have praised in

8435 שָׂגַב ***śāgab***, v. [20] [→ 5369, 5370, 8437]

protect [4], be exalted [2], exalted [2], is exalted [2], lifted [2], lofty [2], high [1], is kept safe [1], safe [1], strengthened [1], strong [1], unscalable [1]

Dt 2:36 [A] even as far as Gilead, not one town was too **strong** for us.
Job 5:11 [A] he sets on high, and those who mourn *are* **lifted** *to* safety.
36:22 [G] "God *is* **exalted** in his power. Who is a teacher like him?
Ps 20: 1 [20:2] [D] *may* the name of the God of Jacob **protect** you.
59: 1 [59:2] [D] **protect** me from those who rise up against me.
69:29 [69:30] [D] *may* your salvation, O God, **protect** me.
91:14 [D] *I will* **protect** him, for he acknowledges my name.
107:41 [D] *he* **lifted** the needy out of their affliction and increased their
139: 6 [C] knowledge is too wonderful for me, too **lofty** for me to attain.
148:13 [C] praise the name of the LORD, for his name alone **is exalted**;
Pr 18:10 [C] LORD is a strong tower; the righteous run to it and *are* **safe**.
18:11 [C] rich is their fortified city; they imagine it an **unscalable** wall.
29:25 [E] to be a snare, but whoever trusts in the LORD **is kept safe**.
Isa 2:11 [C] brought low; the LORD alone *will* **be exalted** in that day.
2:17 [C] men humbled; the LORD alone *will* **be exalted** in that day,
9:11 [9:10] [D] the LORD *has* **strengthened** Rezin's foes against
12: 4 [C] what he has done, and proclaim that his name *is* **exalted**.
26: 5 [C] humbles those who dwell on high, he lays the **lofty** city low;
30:13 [C] this sin will become for you like a **high** wall, cracked and
33: 5 [C] The LORD **is exalted**, for he dwells on high; he will fill

8436 שָׂגָה ***śāgâ***, v. [4] [cf. 8434]

grow [1], increase [1], prosperous [1], thrive [1]

Job 8: 7 [A] will seem humble, so **prosperous** will your future be.
8:11 [A] where there is no marsh? *Can* reeds **thrive** without water?
Ps 73:12 [G] wicked are like—always carefree, *they* **increase** *in* wealth.
92:12 [92:13] [A] a palm tree, *they will* **grow** like a cedar of Lebanon;

8437 שְׂגוּב ***śᵉgûb***, n.pr.m. [3] [√ 8435; cf. 8439]

Segub [3]

1Ki 16:34 he set up its gates at the cost of his youngest son **Segub**, [K 8439]
1Ch 2:21 married her when he was sixty years old), and she bore him **Segub**.
2:22 **Segub** was the father of Jair, who controlled twenty-three towns in

8438 שַׂגִּיא ***śaggî'***, a. [2] [√ 8434; Ar 10678]

exalted [1], great [1]

Job 36:26 *How* **great** is God—beyond our understanding! The number of his
37:23 The Almighty is beyond our reach and **exalted** *in* power; in his

8439 שְׂגִיב ***śᵉgîb***, n.pr.m. [0] [cf. 8437]

1Ki 16:34 [its gates at the cost of his youngest son **Segub**, [K; see Q 8437]]

8440 שָׂדַד ***śādad***, v. [3] [→ 8443; cf. 6040, 8444]

break up the ground [1], harrowing [1], till [1]

Job 39:10 [D] furrow with a harness? *Will he* **till** the valleys behind you?
Isa 28:24 [D] Does he keep on breaking up and **harrowing** the soil?
Hos 10:11 [D] Judah must plow, and Jacob *must* **break up the ground**.

8441 שָׂדֶה ***śādeh***, n.m. [320 / 321] [→ 8442]

field [128], fields [76], wild [24], country [17], land [11], open country [8], Moab [+4566] [7], *untranslated* [6], field [+2754] [4], ground [4], open [4], territory [4], family land [+299] [3], region [3], wild [+928+2021] [3], area [2], countryside [2], mainland [2], open field [2], soil [2], battlefield [+5120] [1], it[s] [+2021] [1], lands [1], outlying districts [1], pastureland [+4494] [1], place [1], southland [+5582] [1], there[s] [+4566] [1], there[s] [+2021] [1]

Ge 2: 5 no shrub of the **field** had yet appeared on the earth and no plant of
2: 5 appeared on the earth and no plant of the **field** had yet sprung up,
2:19 God had formed out of the ground all the beasts of the **field**
2:20 all the livestock, the birds of the air and all the beasts of the **field**.
3: 1 Now the serpent was more crafty than any of the **wild** animals the
3:14 "Cursed are you above all the livestock and all the **wild** animals!
3:18 and thistles for you, and you will eat the plants of the **field**.
4: 8 Cain said to his brother Abel, "Let's go out to the **field**." [BHS-]
4: 8 And while they were in the **field**, Cain attacked his brother Abel
14: 7 and they conquered the whole **territory** *of* the Amalekites,
23: 9 of Machpelah, which belongs to him and is at the end of his **field**.
23:11 to me; I give you the **field**, and I give you the cave that is in it.
23:13 "Listen to me, if you will. I will pay the price of the **field**.
23:17 So Ephron's **field** in Machpelah near Mamre—both the field
23:17 both the **field** and the cave in it, and all the trees within the borders
23:17 and the cave in it, and all the trees within the borders of the **field**—
23:19 Abraham buried his wife Sarah in the cave in the **field** *of*
23:20 So the **field** and the cave in it were deeded to Abraham by the
24:63 He went out to the **field** one evening to meditate, and as he looked
24:65 the servant, "Who is that man in the **field** coming to meet us?"
25: 9 near Mamre, in the **field** *of* Ephron son of Zohar the Hittite,
25:10 the **field** Abraham had bought from the Hittites. There Abraham
25:27 a man of the **open country**, while Jacob was a quiet man,
25:29 some stew, Esau came in from the **open country**, famished.
27: 3 and go out to the **open country** to hunt some wild game for me.
27: 5 When Esau left for the **open country** to hunt game and bring it
27:27 the smell of my son is like the smell of a **field** that the LORD has
29: 2 There he saw a well in the **field**, with three flocks of sheep lying

Ge 30:14 Reuben went out into the **fields** and found some mandrake plants,
30:16 So when Jacob came in from the **fields** that evening, Leah went out
31: 4 to Rachel and Leah to come out to the **fields** where his flocks were.
32: 3 [32:4] his brother Esau in the land of Seir, the **country** *of* Edom.
33:19 father of Shechem, the plot of **ground** where he pitched his tent.
34: 5 had been defiled, his sons were in the **fields** with his livestock;
34: 7 Now Jacob's sons had come in from the **fields** as soon as they
34:28 and everything else of theirs in the city and out in the **fields**.
36:35 son of Bedad, who defeated Midian in the **country** *of* Moab,
37: 7 We were binding sheaves of grain out in the **field** when suddenly
37:15 a man found him wandering around in the **fields** and asked him,
39: 5 was on everything Potiphar had, both in the house and in the **field**.
41:48 In each city he put the food grown in the **fields** surrounding it.
47:20 The Egyptians, one and all, sold their **fields**, because the famine
47:24 The other four-fifths you may keep as seed for the **fields** and as
49:29 Bury me with my fathers in the cave in the **field** *of* Ephron the
49:30 the cave in the **field** *of* Machpelah, near Mamre in Canaan,
49:30 which Abraham bought **[RPH]** as a burial place from Ephron the
49:32 The **field** and the cave in it were bought from the Hittites."
50:13 of Canaan and buried him in the cave in the **field** *of* Machpelah,
50:13 as a burial place from Ephron the Hittite, along with the **field**.
Ex 1:14 labor in brick and mortar and with all kinds of work in the **fields**;
8:13 [8:9] frogs died in the houses, in the courtyards and in the **fields**.
9: 3 LORD will bring a terrible plague on your livestock in the **field**—
9:19 and everything you have in the **field** to a place of shelter,
9:19 and animal that has not been brought in and is still out in the **field**,
9:21 the word of the LORD left their slaves and livestock in the **field**.
9:22 and animals and on everything growing in the **fields** *of* Egypt."
9:25 Throughout Egypt hail struck everything in the **fields**—both men
9:25 it beat down everything growing in the **fields** and stripped every
9:25 everything growing in the fields and stripped every tree. **[RPH]**
10: 5 after the hail, including every tree that is growing in your **fields**.
10:15 green remained on tree or plant **[RPH]** in all the land of Egypt.
16:25 to the LORD. You will not find any of it on the **ground** today.
22: 5 [22:4] "If a man grazes his livestock in a **field** or vineyard and lets
22: 5 [22:4] and lets them stray and they graze in another man's **field**,
22: 5 [22:4] he must make restitution from the best of his own **field**
22: 6 [22:5] burns shocks of grain or standing grain or the *whole* **field**,
22:31 [22:30] the meat of an animal torn by **wild** [+928+2021] beasts;
23:11 get food from it, and the **wild** animals may eat what they leave.
23:16 of Harvest with the firstfruits of the crops you sow in your **field**.
23:16 the end of the year, when you gather in your crops from the **field**.
23:29 become desolate and the **wild** animals too numerous for you.
Lev 14: 7 him clean. Then he is to release the live bird in the open **fields**.
14:53 he is to release the live bird in the open **fields** outside the town.
17: 5 the LORD the sacrifices they are now making in the open **fields**.
19: 9 do not reap to the very edges of your **field** or gather the gleanings
19:19 kinds of animals. " 'Do not plant your **field** with two kinds of seed.
23:22 do not reap to the very edges of your **field** or gather the gleanings
25: 3 For six years sow your **fields**, and for six years prune your
25: 4 to the LORD. Do not sow your **fields** or prune your vineyards.
25:12 to be holy for you; eat only what is taken directly from the **fields**.
25:31 without walls around them are to be considered as **open** country.
25:34 the **pastureland** *belonging* **to** [+4494] their towns must not be
26: 4 the ground will yield its crops and the trees of the **field** their fruit.
26:22 I will send **wild** animals against you, and they will rob you of your
27:16 " 'If a man dedicates to the LORD part of his **family land** [+299],
27:17 If he dedicates his **field** during the Year of Jubilee, the value that
27:18 if he dedicates his **field** after the Jubilee, the priest will determine
27:19 If the man who dedicates the **field** wishes to redeem it, he must add
27:20 If, however, he does not redeem the **field**, or if he has sold it to
27:20 or if he has sold **it**[s] [+2021] to someone else, it can never be
27:21 When the **field** is released in the Jubilee, it will become holy,
27:21 it will become holy, like a **field** devoted to the LORD;
27:22 " 'If a man dedicates to the LORD a **field** he has bought,
27:22 a field he has bought, which is not part of his **family land** [+299],
27:24 In the Year of Jubilee the **field** will revert to the person from whom
27:28 whether man or animal or **family land** [+299]—may be sold
Nu 16:14 and honey or given us an inheritance of **fields** and vineyards.
19:16 "Anyone out in the **open** who touches someone who has been
20:17 We will not go through any **field** or vineyard, or drink water from
21:20 from Bamoth to the valley in **Moab** [+4566] where the top of
21:22 We will not turn aside into any **field** or vineyard, or drink water
22: 4 up everything around us, as an ox licks up the grass of the **field**."
22:23 with a drawn sword in his hand, she turned off the road into a **field**.
23:14 So he took him to the **field** *of* Zophim on the top of Pisgah,
Dt 5:21 You shall not set your desire on your neighbor's house or **land**,
7:22 them all at once, or the **wild** animals will multiply around you.
11:15 I will provide grass in the **fields** for your cattle, and you will eat
14:22 Be sure to set aside a tenth of all that your **fields** produce each
20:19 Are the trees of the **field** people, that you should besiege them?
21: 1 lying in a **field** in the land the LORD your God is giving you to
22:25 if out in the **country** a man happens to meet a girl pledged to be
22:27 for the man found the girl out in the **country**, and though the
24:19 When you are harvesting in your **field** and you overlook a sheaf,
24:19 and you overlook a sheaf, **[RPH]** do not go back to get it.
28: 3 You will be blessed in the city and blessed in the **country**.
28:16 You will be cursed in the city and cursed in the **country**.
28:38 You will sow much seed in the **field** but you will harvest little,
Jos 8:24 When Israel had finished killing all the men of Ai in the **fields**
15:18 she came to Othniel, she urged him to ask her father for a **field**.
21:12 the **fields** and villages around the city they had given to Caleb son
24:32 were buried at Shechem in the tract of **land** that Jacob bought for a
Jdg 1:14 she came to Othniel, she urged him to ask her father for a **field**.
5: 4 when you marched from the **land** *of* Edom, the earth shook,
5:18 risked their very lives; so did Naphtali on the heights of the **field**.
9:27 After they had gone out into the **fields** and gathered the grapes
9:32 night you and your men should come and lie in wait in the **fields**.
9:42 The next day the people of Shechem went out to the **fields**,
9:43 divided them into three companies and set an ambush in the **fields**.
9:44 two companies rushed upon those in the **fields** and struck them
13: 9 of God came again to the woman while she was out in the **field**;
19:16 of the place were Benjamites), came in from his work in the **fields**.
20: 6 and sent one piece to each **region** *of* Israel's inheritance,
20:31 so that about thirty men fell in the **open field** and on the roads—
Ru 1: 1 and two sons, went to live for a while in the **country** *of* Moab.
1: 2 And they went to **Moab** [+4566] and lived there.
1: 6 When she heard in **Moab** [+4566] that the LORD had come to the
1: 6 her daughters-in-law prepared to return home from **there**[s] [+4566].
1:22 So Naomi returned from **Moab** [+4566] accompanied by Ruth the
2: 2 "Let me go to the **fields** and pick up the leftover grain behind
2: 3 she went out and began to glean in the **fields** behind the harvesters.
2: 3 she found herself working in a **field** [+2754] belonging to Boaz,
2: 6 "She is the Moabitess who came back from **Moab** [+4566] with
2: 8 Don't go and glean in another **field** and don't go away from here.
2: 9 Watch the **field** where the men are harvesting, and follow along
2:17 So Ruth gleaned in the **field** until evening. Then she threshed the
2:22 his girls, because in someone else's **field** you might be harmed."
4: 3 "Naomi, who has come back from **Moab** [+4566],
4: 3 is selling the piece of **land** that belonged to our brother Elimelech.
4: 5 "On the day you buy the **land** from Naomi and from Ruth the
1Sa 4: 2 who killed about four thousand of them on the **battlefield** [+5120].
6: 1 When the ark of the LORD had been in Philistine **territory** seven
6:14 The cart came to the **field** *of* Joshua of Beth Shemesh, and there it
6:18 is a witness to this day in the **field** *of* Joshua of Beth Shemesh.
8:14 He will take the best of your **fields** and vineyards and olive groves
11: 5 Just then Saul was returning from the **fields**, behind his oxen,
14:14 his armor-bearer killed some twenty men in an **area** of about half
14:15 those in the camp and **field**, and those in the outposts and raiding
14:25 army entered the woods, and there was honey on the **ground**.
17:44 give your flesh to the birds of the air and the beasts of the **field**!"
19: 3 I will go out and stand with my father in the **field** where you are.
20: 5 and hide in the **field** until the evening of the day after tomorrow.
20:11 "Come," Jonathan said, "let's go out into the **field**." So they went
20:11 "let's go out into the field." So they went **there**[s] [+2021] together.
20:24 So David hid in the **field**, and when the New Moon festival came,
20:35 In the morning Jonathan went out to the **field** for his meeting with
22: 7 Will the son of Jesse give all of you **fields** and vineyards?
25:15 the whole time we were out in the **fields** near them nothing was
27: 5 let a place be assigned to me in one of the **country** towns,
27: 7 David lived in Philistine **territory** a year and four months.
27:11 such was his practice as long as he lived in Philistine **territory**.
30:11 They found an Egyptian in a **field** and brought him to David.
2Sa 1:21 have neither dew nor rain, nor **fields** *that yield* offerings ⌞of grain⌟.
2:18 Now Asahel was as fleet-footed as a **wild** [+928+2021] gazelle.
9: 7 I will restore to you all the **land** *that belonged to* your grandfather
10: 8 men of Tob and Maacah were by themselves in the **open country**.
11:11 my master Joab and my lord's men are camped in the open **fields**.
11:23 "The men overpowered us and came out against us in the **open**,
14: 6 They got into a fight with each other in the **field**, and no one was
17: 8 and as fierce as a **wild** [+928+2021] bear robbed of her cubs.
18: 6 The army marched into the **field** to fight Israel, and the battle took
19:29 [19:30] say more? I order you and Ziba to divide the **fields**."
20:12 he dragged him from the road into a **field** and threw a garment over
21:10 the birds of the air touch them by day or the **wild** animals by night.
23:11 together at a place where there was a **field** [+2754] full of lentils,
1Ki 2:26 the priest the king said, "Go back to your **fields** in Anathoth.
11:29 a new cloak. The two of them were alone out in the **country**,
14:11 and the birds of the air will feed on those who die in the **country**.
16: 4 and the birds of the air will feed on those who die in the **country**."
21:24 and the birds of the air will feed on those who die in the **country**."
2Ki 4:39 One of them went out into the **fields** to gather herbs and found a
4:39 them went out into the fields to gather herbs and found a **wild** vine.
4:39 some of its gourds **[RPH]** and filled the fold of his cloak.
7:12 so they have left the camp to hide in the **countryside**, thinking,
8: 3 the Philistines and went to the king to beg for her house and **land**.
8: 5 brought back to life came to beg the king for her house and **land**.
8: 6 including all the income from her **land** from the day she left the

2Ki 9:25 throw him on the **field** [+2754] *that belonged to* Naboth the
9:37 Jezebel's body will be like refuse on the **ground** in the plot at
14: 9 a **wild** beast in Lebanon came along and trampled the thistle
18:17 aqueduct of the Upper Pool, on the road to the Washerman's **Field**.
19:26 They are like plants in the **field**, like tender green shoots, like grass
1Ch 1:46 son of Bedad, who defeated Midian in the **country** *of* Moab,
6:56 [6:41] the **fields** and villages around the city were given to Caleb
8: 8 Sons were born to Shaharaim in **Moab** [+4566] after he had
11:13 At a place where there was a **field** [+2754] full of barley,
16:32 all that is in it; let the **fields** be jubilant, and everything in them!
19: 9 the kings who had come were by themselves in the **open country**.
27:25 Uzziah was in charge of the storehouses in the **outlying districts**,
27:26 Ezri son of Kelub was in charge of the **field** workers who farmed
2Ch 25:18 a **wild** beast in Lebanon came along and trampled the thistle
26:23 was buried near them in a **field** *for* burial that belonged to the
31: 5 new wine, oil and honey and all that the **fields** produced.
31:19 who lived on the farm **lands** around their towns or in any other
Ne 5: 3 "We are mortgaging our **fields**, our vineyards and our homes to get
5: 4 "We have had to borrow money to pay the king's tax on our **fields**
5: 5 because our **fields** and our vineyards belong to others."
5:11 Give back to them immediately their **fields**, vineyards, olive groves
5:16 were assembled there for the work; we did not acquire *any* **land**.
11:25 As for the villages with their **fields**, some of the people of Judah
11:30 in Lachish and its **fields**, and in Azekah and its settlements.
12:29 from Beth Gilgal, and from the **area** *of* Geba and Azmaveth,
12:44 From the **fields** *around* the towns they were to bring into the
13:10 responsible for the service had gone back to their own **fields**.
Job 5:23 For you will have a covenant with the stones of the **field**,
5:23 stones of the field, and the **wild** animals will be at peace with you.
24: 6 They gather fodder in the **fields** and glean in the vineyards of the
39:15 a foot may crush them, that some **wild** animal may trample them.
40:20 hills bring him their produce, and all the **wild** animals play nearby.
Ps 78:12 sight of their fathers in the land of Egypt, in the **region** *of* Zoan.
78:43 his miraculous signs in Egypt, his wonders in the **region** *of* Zoan.
103:15 his days are like grass, he flourishes like a flower of the **field**;
107:37 They sowed **fields** and planted vineyards that yielded a fruitful
132: 6 We heard it in Ephrathah, we came upon it in the **fields** *of* Jaar:
Pr 23:10 ancient boundary stone or encroach on the **fields** *of* the fatherless,
24:27 Finish your outdoor work and get your **fields** ready; after that,
24:30 I went past the **field** *of* the sluggard, past the vineyard of the man
27:26 provide you with clothing, and the goats with the price of a **field**.
31:16 She considers a **field** and buys it; out of her earnings she plants a
Ecc 5: 9 [5:8] land is taken by all; the king himself profits from the **fields**.
SS 2: 7 I charge you by the gazelles and by the does of the **field**:
3: 5 I charge you by the gazelles and by the does of the **field**:
7:11 [7:12] Come, my lover, let us go to the **countryside**, let us spend
Isa 5: 8 join **field** to field till no space is left and you live alone in the land.
5: 8 join field to **field** till no space is left and you live alone in the land.
7: 3 aqueduct of the Upper Pool, on the road to the Washerman's **Field**.
32:12 Beat your breasts for the pleasant **fields**, for the fruitful vines
36: 2 aqueduct of the Upper Pool, on the road to the Washerman's **Field**,
37:27 They are like plants in the **field**, like tender green shoots, like grass
40: 6 are like grass, and all their glory is like the flowers of the **field**.
43:20 The **wild** animals honor me, the jackals and the owls, because I
55:12 song before you, and all the trees of the **field** will clap their hands.
Jer 6:12 be turned over to others, together with their **fields** and their wives,
6:25 Do not go out to the **fields** or walk on the roads, for the enemy has
7:20 and beast, on the trees of the **field** and on the fruit of the ground,
8:10 I will give their wives to other men and their **fields** to new owners.
9:22 [9:21] dead bodies of men will lie like refuse on the open **field**,
12: 4 will the land lie parched and the grass in every **field** be withered?
12: 9 Go and gather all the **wild** beasts; bring them to devour.
13:27 I have seen your detestable acts on the hills and in the **fields**.
14: 5 Even the doe in the **field** deserts her newborn fawn because there is
14:18 If I go into the **country**, I see those slain by the sword; if I go into
17: 3 My mountain in the **land** and your wealth and all your treasures I
26:18 " 'Zion will be plowed like a **field**, Jerusalem will become a heap
27: 6 king of Babylon; I will make even the **wild** animals subject to him.
28:14 serve him. I will even give him control over the **wild** animals.' "
32: 7 uncle is going to come to you and say, 'Buy my **field** at Anathoth,
32: 8 and said, 'Buy my **field** at Anathoth in the territory of Benjamin.
32: 9 so I bought the **field** at Anathoth from my cousin Hanamel
32:15 Houses, **fields** and vineyards will again be bought in this land.'
32:25 'Buy the **field** with silver and have the transaction witnessed.' "
32:43 Once more **fields** will be bought in this land of which you say,
32:44 **Fields** will be bought for silver, and deeds will be signed,
35: 9 or built houses to live in or had vineyards, **fields** or crops.
40: 7 their men who were still in the **open country** heard that the king of
40:13 all the army officers still in the **open country** came to Gedaliah at
41: 8 We have wheat and barley, oil and honey, hidden in a **field**."
Eze 7:15 those in the **country** will die by the sword, and those in the city
16: 5 Rather, you were thrown out into the open **field**, for on the day you
16: 7 I made you grow like a plant of the **field**. You grew up
17: 5 " 'He took some of the seed of your land and put it in fertile **soil**.
17: 8 It had been planted in good **soil** by abundant water so that it would
17:24 All the trees of the **field** will know that I the LORD bring down
20:46 [21:2] and prophesy against the forest of the **southland** [+5582].
26: 6 and her settlements on the **mainland** will be ravaged by the sword.
26: 8 He will ravage your settlements on the **mainland** with the sword;
29: 5 You will fall on the open **field** and not be gathered or picked up.
31: 4 around its base and sent their channels to all the trees of the **field**.
31: 5 So it towered higher than all the trees of the **field**; its boughs
31: 6 its boughs, all the beasts of the **field** gave birth under its branches;
31:13 fallen tree, and all the beasts of the **field** were among its branches.
31:15 Lebanon with gloom, and all the trees of the **field** withered away.
32: 4 I will throw you on the land and hurl you on the open **field**.
33:27 those out in the **country** I will give to the wild animals to be
34: 5 when they were scattered they became food for all the **wild**
34: 8 has been plundered and has become food for all the **wild** animals,
34:27 The trees of the **field** will yield their fruit and the ground will yield
36:30 I will increase the fruit of the trees and the crops of the **field**,
38:20 The fish of the sea, the birds of the air, the beasts of the **field**,
39: 4 you as food to all kinds of carrion birds and to the **wild** animals.
39: 5 You will fall in the **open** field, for I have spoken,
39:10 They will not need to gather wood from the **fields** or cut it from the
39:17 Call out to every kind of bird and all the **wild** animals: 'Assemble
Hos 2:12 [2:14] make them a thicket, and **wild** animals will devour them.
2:18 [2:20] I will make a covenant for them with the beasts of the **field**
4: 3 the beasts of the **field** and the birds of the air and the fish of the sea
12:12 [12:13] Jacob fled to the **country** *of* Aram; Israel served to get a
13: 8 Like a lion I will devour them; a **wild** animal will tear them apart.
Joel 1:10 The **fields** are ruined, the ground is dried up; the grain is destroyed,
1:11 and the barley, because the harvest of the **field** is destroyed.
1:12 and the apple tree—all the trees of the **field**—are dried up.
1:19 open pastures and flames have burned up all the trees of the **field**.
1:20 Even the **wild** animals pant for you; the streams of water have
Ob 1:19 They will occupy the **fields** *of* Ephraim and Samaria,
1:19 They will occupy the fields of Ephraim and **[RPH]** Samaria,
Mic 1: 6 will make Samaria a heap of rubble, a **place** for planting vineyards.
2: 2 They covet **fields** and seize them, and houses, and take them.
2: 4 He takes it from me! He assigns our **fields** to traitors.' "
3:12 Therefore because of you, Zion will be plowed like a **field**,
4:10 for now you must leave the city to camp in the **open field**.
Zec 10: 1 gives showers of rain to men, and plants of the **field** to everyone.
Mal 3:11 the vines in your **fields** will not cast their fruit," says the LORD

8442 שָׂדַי **śāday**, n.m. [13] [√ 8441]

field [9], fields [2], slopes [1], wild [1]

Dt 32:13 on the heights of the land and fed him with the fruit of the **fields**.
Ps 8: 7 [8:8] all flocks and herds, and the beasts of the **field**,
50:11 every bird in the mountains, and the creatures of the **field** are mine.
80:13 [80:14] forest ravage it and the creatures of the **field** feed on it.
96:12 let the **fields** be jubilant, and everything in them. Then all the trees
104:11 They give water to all the beasts of the **field**; the wild donkeys
Isa 56: 9 Come, all you beasts of the **field**, come and devour, all you beasts
Jer 4:17 They surround her like men guarding a **field**, because she has
18:14 Does the snow of Lebanon ever vanish from its rocky **slopes**?
La 4: 9 with hunger, they waste away for lack of food from the **field**.
Hos 10: 4 lawsuits spring up like poisonous weeds in a plowed **field**.
12:11 [12:12] Their altars will be like piles of stones on a plowed **field**.
Joel 2:22 Be not afraid, O **wild** animals, for the open pastures are becoming

8443 שִׂדִּים **śiddîm**, n.pr.loc. [3] [√ 8440]

Siddim [3]

Ge 14: 3 All these latter kings joined forces in the Valley of **Siddim** (the
14: 8 marched out and drew up their battle lines in the Valley of **Siddim**
14:10 Now the Valley of **Siddim** was full of tar pits, and when the kings

8444 שְׂדֵרָה **śᵉdērâ**, n.f. [4] [cf. 6043, 8440]

ranks [3], planks [1]

1Ki 6: 9 and completed it, roofing it with beams and cedar **planks**.
2Ki 11: 8 Anyone who approaches your **ranks** must be put to death.
11:15 "Bring her out between the **ranks** and put to the sword anyone
2Ch 23:14 "Bring her out between the **ranks** and put to the sword anyone

8445 שֶׂה **śeh**, n.m. & f. [47]

sheep [26], lamb [11], another[s] [2], flock [2], animals [1], goat [+6436] [1], lamb [+928+2021+3897] [1], lamb [+928+2021+4166] [1], one[s] [1], sheep [+4166] [1]

Ge 22: 7 Isaac said, "but where is the **lamb** for the burnt offering?"
22: 8 "God himself will provide the **lamb** for the burnt offering,
30:32 and remove from them every speckled or spotted **sheep**,
30:32 every dark-colored **lamb** [+928+2021+4166] and every spotted or
Ex 12: 3 tenth day of this month each man is to take a **lamb** for his family,
12: 3 each man is to take a lamb for his family, **one**[s] for each household.

Ex 12: 4 If any household is too small for a *whole* **lamb**, they must share
12: 4 You are to determine the amount of **lamb** needed in accordance
12: 5 The **animals** you choose must be year-old males without defect,
13: 13 Redeem with a **lamb** every firstborn donkey, but if you do not
22: 1 [21:37] a man steals an ox or a **sheep** and slaughters it or sells it,
22: 1 [21:37] five head of cattle for the ox and four sheep for the **sheep**.
22: 4 [22:3] whether ox or donkey or **sheep**—he must pay back double.
22: 9 [22:8] illegal possession of an ox, a donkey, a **sheep**, a garment,
22: 10 [22:9] a **sheep** or any other animal to his neighbor for safekeeping
34: 19 the firstborn males of your livestock, whether from herd or **flock**.
34: 20 Redeem the firstborn donkey with a **lamb**, but if you do not
Lev 5: 7 " 'If he cannot afford a **lamb**, he is to bring two doves or two
12: 8 If she cannot afford a **lamb**, she is to bring two doves or two young
22: 23 as a freewill offering an ox or a **sheep** that is deformed or stunted,
22: 28 Do not slaughter a cow or a **sheep** and its young on the same day.
27: 26 to the LORD; whether an ox or a **sheep**, it is the LORD's.
Nu 15: 11 Each bull or ram, each **lamb** [+928+2021+3897] or young goat, is
Dt 14: 4 are the animals you may eat: the ox, the **sheep** [+4166], the goat,
14: 4 are the animals you may eat: the ox, the sheep, the **goat** [+6436],
17: 1 your God an ox or a **sheep** that has any defect or flaw in it,
18: 3 due the priests from the people who sacrifice a bull or a **sheep**:
22: 1 If you see your brother's ox or **sheep** straying, do not ignore it
Jos 6: 21 men and women, young and old, cattle, **sheep** and donkeys.
Jdg 6: 4 spare a living thing for Israel, neither **sheep** nor cattle nor donkeys.
1Sa 14: 34 and tell them, 'Each of you bring me your cattle and **sheep**,
15: 3 children and infants, cattle and **sheep**, camels and donkeys.' "
17: 34 When a lion or a bear came and carried off a **sheep** from the flock,
22: 19 its children and infants, and its cattle, donkeys and **sheep**.
Ps 119: 176 I have strayed like a lost **sheep**. Seek your servant, for I have not
Isa 7: 25 become places where cattle are turned loose and where **sheep** run.
43: 23 You have not brought me **sheep** for burnt offerings, nor honored
53: 7 he was led like a **lamb** to the slaughter, and as a sheep before her
66: 3 and whoever offers a **lamb**, like one who breaks a dog's neck;
Jer 50: 17 "Israel is a scattered **flock** that lions have chased away. The first to
Eze 34: 17 I will judge between *one* **sheep** and another, and between rams
34: 17 I will judge between one sheep and **another**[s], and between rams
34: 20 I myself will judge between the fat **sheep** and the lean sheep.
34: 20 I myself will judge between the fat sheep and the lean **sheep**.
34: 22 longer be plundered. I will judge between *one* **sheep** and another.
34: 22 longer be plundered. I will judge between one sheep and **another**[s].
45: 15 Also one **sheep** is to be taken from every flock of two hundred

8446 שָׂהֵד *śāhēd*, n.[m.]. [1] [→ Ar 10679]
advocate [1]

Job 16: 19 Even now my witness is in heaven; my **advocate** is on high.

8447 שָׂהֲדוּתָא *śahᵃdûtā'*, n.f. Not used in NIV/BHS [→ Ar 10679]

8448 שַׂהֲרֹנִים *śahᵃrōnîm*, n.m. [3]
ornaments [2], crescent necklaces [1]

Jdg 8: 21 and killed them, and took the **ornaments** off their camels' necks.
8: 26 not counting the **ornaments**, the pendants and the purple garments
Isa 3: 18 their finery: the bangles and headbands and **crescent necklaces**,

8449 שׂוֹבֶךְ *śôbek*, n.[m.]. [1] [√ 8422; cf. 6018]
thick branches [1]

2Sa 18: 9 and as the mule went under the **thick branches** *of* a large oak,

8450 ¹שׂוּג *śûg¹*, v. Not used in NIV/BHS [cf. 6047]

8451 ²שׂוּג *śûg²*, v. [1] [cf. 6048?]
make grow [1]

Isa 17: 11 [D] though on the day you set them out, *you* **make** them **grow**,

8452 שׂוּחַ *śûaḥ*, v. [1]
meditate [1]

Ge 24: 63 [A] He went out to the field one evening to **meditate**, and as he

8453 שַׂוְחָט *śawḥāṭ*, n.[?] Not used in NIV/BHS [√ 8759]

8454 שׂוּט *śûṭ*, v. [1] [→ 8473?; cf. 6091, 8474]
turn aside [1]

Ps 40: 4 [40:5] [A] to the proud, to *those who* **turn aside** *to* false gods.

8455 שׂוּךְ *śûk*, v. [2] [→ 8456, 8457, 8458?, 8459; cf. 5819, 6115, 6058, 8504]
block [1], put a hedge [1]

Job 1: 10 [A] "*Have* you not **put a hedge** around him and his household
Hos 2: 6 [2:8] [A] Therefore I *will* **block** her path with thornbushes; I

8456 שׂוֹךְ *śôk*, n.[m.]. [1] [√ 8455]
branches [1]

Jdg 9: 49 So all the men cut **branches** and followed Abimelech. They piled

8457 שׂוֹכָה *śôkâ*, n.f. [1] [√ 8455]
branches [+6770] [1]

Jdg 9: 48 He took an ax and cut off *some* **branches** [+6770], which he lifted

8458 שׂוֹכֹה *śôkōh*, n.pr.loc. [5] [√ 8455?]
Socoh [5]

Jos 15: 35 Jarmuth, Adullam, **Socoh**, Azekah,
15: 48 In the hill country: Shamir, Jattir, **Socoh**,
1Sa 17: 1 gathered their forces for war and assembled at **Socoh** in Judah.
17: 1 pitched camp at Ephes Dammim, between **Socoh** and Azekah.
1Ki 4: 10 in Arubboth (**Socoh** and all the land of Hepher were his);

8459 שׂוֹכוֹ *śôkô*, n.pr.loc. [3] [√ 8455]
Soco [3]

1Ch 4: 18 Heber the father of **Soco**, and Jekuthiel the father of Zanoah.)
2Ch 11: 7 Beth Zur, **Soco**, Adullam,
28: 18 Aijalon and Gederoth, as well as **Soco**, Timnah and Gimzo,

8460 שׂוּכָתִי *śûkātî*, a.g. [1]
Sucathites [1]

1Ch 2: 55 who lived at Jabez: the Tirathites, Shimeathites and **Sucathites**.

8461 שׂוּמָה *śûmâ*, n.f. [1] [√ 8492]
intention [1]

2Sa 13: 32 This has been Absalom's expressed **intention** ever since the day

8462 שׂוּר *śûr*, v. [1 / 0] [√ 8463?]

1Ch 20: 3 [a] consigning [BHS ***cutting***; NIV 8492] them to labor with saws

8463 שׂוֹרָה *śôrâ*, n.[f.]. [1] [√ 8462?; cf. 8555?]
place [1]

Isa 28: 25 Does he not plant wheat *in* its **place**, barley in its plot, and spelt in

8464 שׂוּשׂ *śûś*, v. [27] [→ 5375, 5376, 8607]
rejoice [11], delight greatly [+8464] [2], delight [2], glad [2], rejoicing [2], delighted [1], gladly [1], happy [1], please [1], pleased [1], rejoice greatly [+5375] [1], take delight [1], take great delight [+928+8525] [1]

Dt 28: 63 [A] Just as *it* **pleased** the LORD to make you prosper and
28: 63 [A] in number, so *it will* **please** him to ruin and destroy you.
30: 9 [A] The LORD *will* again **delight** in you and make you
30: 9 [A] make you prosperous, just as *he* **delighted** in your fathers,
Job 3: 22 [A] filled with gladness and **rejoice** when they reach the grave?
39: 21 [A] He paws fiercely, **rejoicing** in his strength, and charges into
Ps 19: 5 [19:6] [A] like a champion **rejoicing** to run his course.
35: 9 [A] soul will rejoice in the LORD and **delight** in his salvation.
40: 16 [40:17] [A] *may* all who seek you **rejoice** and be glad in you;
68: 3 [68:4] [A] rejoice before God; *may they be* **happy** and joyful.
70: 4 [70:5] [A] *may* all who seek you **rejoice** and be glad in you;
119: 14 [A] *I* **rejoice** in following your statutes as one rejoices in great
119: 162 [A] **I rejoice** in your promise like one who finds great spoil.
Isa 35: 1 [A] The desert and the parched land *will be* **glad**; the wilderness
61: 10 [A] *I* **delight** [+8464] **greatly** in the LORD; my soul rejoices in
61: 10 [A] *I* **delight greatly** [+8464] in the LORD; my soul rejoices in
62: 5 [A] rejoices over his bride, so *will* your God **rejoice** over you.
64: 5 [64:4] [A] You come to the help of *those who* **gladly** do right,
65: 18 [A] *be* **glad** and rejoice forever in what I will create, for I will
65: 19 [A] I will rejoice over Jerusalem and **take delight** in my people;
66: 10 [A] **rejoice** [+5375] **greatly** with her, all you who mourn over
66: 14 [A] your heart *will* **rejoice** and you will flourish like grass;
Jer 32: 41 [A] *I will* **rejoice** in doing them good and will assuredly plant
La 1: 21 [A] heard of my distress; *they* **rejoice** *at* what you have done.
4: 21 [A] **Rejoice** and be glad, O Daughter of Edom, you who live in
Eze 21: 10 [21:15] [A] " '*Shall we* **rejoice** *in* the scepter of my son
Zep 3: 17 [A] *He will* **take great delight** [+928+8525] in you, he will quiet

8465 שֵׂחַ śēaḥ, n.[m.]. [1] [√ 8488]
thoughts [1]
Am 4:13 the mountains, creates the wind, and reveals his **thoughts** to man,

8466 שָׂחָה śāḥâ, v. [3] [→ 8467]
flood [1], swim [1], swimmer [1]
Ps 6: 6 [6:7] [G] all night long *I* **flood** my bed with weeping and drench
Isa 25:11 [A] hands in it, as a **swimmer** spreads out his hands to swim.
25:11 [A] hands in it, as a swimmer spreads out his hands to **swim**.

8467 שָׂחוּ śāḥû, n.[m.]. [1] [√ 8466]
deep enough to swim in [1]
Eze 47: 5 because the water had risen and was **deep enough to swim in**—

8468 שְׂחוֹק śᵉḥôq, n.[m.]. [15] [√ 8471]
laughter [7], laughingstock [3], object of ridicule [3], pleasure [1], ridiculed [1]
Job 8:21 He will yet fill your mouth with **laughter** and your lips with shouts
12: 4 "I have become a **laughingstock** to my friends, though I called
12: 4 a mere **laughingstock**, though righteous and blameless!
Ps 126: 2 Our mouths were filled with **laughter**, our tongues with songs of
Pr 10:23 A fool finds **pleasure** in evil conduct, but a man of understanding
14:13 Even in **laughter** the heart may ache, and joy may end in grief.
Ecc 2: 2 "**Laughter**," I said, "is foolish. And what does pleasure
7: 3 Sorrow is better than **laughter**, because a sad face is good for the
7: 6 the crackling of thorns under the pot, so is the **laughter** *of* fools.
10:19 A feast is made for **laughter**, and wine makes life merry,
Jer 20: 7 and prevailed. I am **ridiculed** all day long; everyone mocks me.
48:26 Let Moab wallow in her vomit; let her be an **object of ridicule**.
48:27 Was not Israel the **object of** your **ridicule**? Was she caught among
48:39 Moab has become an **object of ridicule**, an object of horror to all
La 3:14 I became the **laughingstock** of all my people; they mock me in

8469 שָׂחַט śāḥaṭ, v. [1]
squeezed [1]
Ge 40:11 [A] **squeezed** them into Pharaoh's cup and put the cup in his

8470 שָׂחִיף śāḥîp, a. [1]
covered with [+6017+6017] [1]
Eze 41:16 including the threshold was **covered** [+6017+6017] **with** wood.

8471 שָׂחַק śāḥaq, v. [36] [→ 3773, 5377, 8468; cf. 7464]
laugh [7], laughs [6], celebrating [3], rejoicing [3], celebrate [1], danced [1], entertain [1], fight hand to hand [1], frolic [1], joking [1], joyful [1], laughed [1], make a pet [1], mock [1], perform [1], play [1], playing [1], revelers [1], scoffs [1], scorned [1], smiled [1]
Jdg 16:25 [D] they shouted, "Bring out Samson *to* **entertain** us."
16:27 [A] three thousand men and women watching Samson **perform**.
1Sa 18: 7 [D] As they **danced**, they sang: "Saul has slain his thousands,
2Sa 2:14 [D] the young men get up and **fight hand to hand** in front of us."
6: 5 [D] the whole house of Israel *were* **celebrating** with all their
6:21 [D] LORD's people Israel—*I will* **celebrate** before the LORD.
1Ch 13: 8 [D] all the Israelites *were* **celebrating** with all their might before
15:29 [D] when she saw King David dancing and **celebrating**, she
2Ch 30:10 [G] as far as Zebulun, but the people **scorned** and ridiculed them.
Job 5:22 [A] *You will* **laugh** at destruction and famine, and need not fear
29:24 [A] *When I* **smiled** at them, they scarcely believed it; the light of
30: 1 [A] "But now *they* **mock** me, men younger than I, whose fathers
39: 7 [A] *He* **laughs** at the commotion in the town; he does not hear a
39:18 [A] she spreads her feathers to run, *she* **laughs** at horse and rider.
39:22 [A] *He* **laughs** at fear, afraid of nothing; he does not shy away
40:20 [D] him their produce, and all the wild animals **play** nearby.
41: 5 [40:29] [D] *Can you* **make a pet** of him like a bird or put him
41:29 [41:21] [A] piece of straw; *he* **laughs** at the rattling of the lance.
Ps 2: 4 [A] The One enthroned in heaven **laughs**; the Lord scoffs at
37:13 [A] the Lord **laughs** at the wicked, for he knows their day is
52: 6 [52:8] [A] will see and fear; *they will* **laugh** at him, saying,
59: 8 [59:9] [A] you, O LORD, **laugh** at them; you scoff at all those
104:26 [D] and fro, and the leviathan, which you formed to **frolic** there.
Pr 1:26 [A] I in turn *will* **laugh** at your disaster; I will mock when
8:30 [D] with delight day after day, **rejoicing** always in his presence,
8:31 [D] **rejoicing** in his whole world and delighting in mankind.
26:19 [D] who deceives his neighbor and says, "I *was* only **joking**!"
29: 9 [A] with a fool, the fool rages and **scoffs**, and there is no peace.
31:25 [A] with strength and dignity; *she can* **laugh** at the days to come.
Ecc 3: 4 [A] a time to weep and a time to **laugh**, a time to mourn and a
Jer 15:17 [D] I never sat in the company of **revelers**, never made merry
30:19 [D] will come songs of thanksgiving and the sound of **rejoicing**.
31: 4 [D] up your tambourines and go out to dance with the **joyful**.
La 1: 7 [A] Her enemies looked at her and **laughed** at her destruction.
Hab 1:10 [A] They **laugh** at all fortified cities; they build earthen ramps
Zec 8: 5 [D] city streets will be filled with boys and girls **playing** there."

8472 שֻׂחֹת śuḥōt, n.f. Not used in NIV/BHS [cf. 6054]

8473 שֵׂט śēṭ, n.[m.]. [1] [√ 8454?]
rebels [1]
Hos 5: 2 The **rebels** are deep in slaughter. I will discipline all of them.

8474 שָׂטָה śāṭâ, v. [6] [cf. 8454]
goes astray [2], gone astray [2], turn [2]
Nu 5:12 [A] to them: 'If a man's wife **goes astray** and is unfaithful to him
5:19 [A] other man has slept with you and *you have* not **gone astray**
5:20 [A] But if you *have* **gone astray** while married to your husband
5:29 [A] is the law of jealousy when a woman **goes astray** and defiles
Pr 4:15 [A] do not travel on it; **turn** from it and go on your way.
7:25 [A] *Do* not *let* your heart **turn** to her ways or stray into her paths.

8475 שָׂטַם śāṭam, v. [6] [√ 5378; cf. 8476]
assails [1], attack [1], held a grudge against [1], holds a grudge against [1], hostility [1], revile [1]
Ge 27:41 [A] Esau **held a grudge against** Jacob because of the blessing
49:23 [A] archers attacked him; they shot at him *with* **hostility**.
50:15 [A] "What if Joseph **holds a grudge against** us and pays us back
Job 16: 9 [A] God **assails** me and tears me in his anger and gnashes his
30:21 [A] me ruthlessly; with the might of your hand *you* **attack** me.
Ps 55: 3 [55:4] [A] down suffering upon me and **revile** me in their anger.

8476 שָׂטַן śāṭan, v.den. [6] [→ 8477, 8478, 8479; cf. 8475]
accusers [3], accuse [2], slander [1]
Ps 38:20 [38:21] [A] Those who repay my good with evil **slander** me
71:13 [A] May my **accusers** perish in shame; may those who want to
109: 4 [A] In return for my friendship *they* **accuse** me, but I am a man
109:20 [A] May this be the LORD's payment to my **accusers**, to those
109:29 [A] My **accusers** will be clothed with disgrace and wrapped in
Zec 3: 1 [A] and Satan standing at his right side to **accuse** him.

8477 שָׂטָן śāṭān, n.m.[pr.]. [27] [√ 8476]
Satan [18], adversary [4], oppose [2], accuser [1], adversaries [1], turn against [+2118+4200+4200] [1]
Nu 22:22 and the angel of the LORD stood in the road to **oppose** him.
22:32 I have come here to **oppose** you because your path is a reckless
1Sa 29: 4 or *he will* **turn against** [+2118+4200+4200] us during the fighting.
2Sa 19:22 [19:23] of Zeruiah? This day you have become my **adversaries**!
1Ki 5: 4 [5:18] rest on every side, and there is no **adversary** or disaster.
11:14 Then the LORD raised up against Solomon an **adversary**,
11:23 God raised up against Solomon another **adversary**, Rezon son of
11:25 Rezon was Israel's **adversary** as long as Solomon lived, adding to
1Ch 21: 1 **Satan** rose up against Israel and incited David to take a census of
Job 1: 6 themselves before the LORD, and **Satan** also came with them.
1: 7 The LORD said to **Satan**, "Where have you come from?"
1: 7 **Satan** answered the LORD, "From roaming through the earth
1: 8 the LORD said to **Satan**, "Have you considered my servant Job?
1: 9 "Does Job fear God for nothing?" **Satan** replied.
1:12 The LORD said to **Satan**, "Very well, then, everything he has is
1:12 a finger." Then **Satan** went out from the presence of the LORD.
2: 1 and **Satan** also came with them to present himself before him.
2: 2 And the LORD said to **Satan**, "Where have you come from?"
2: 2 **Satan** answered the LORD, "From roaming through the earth
2: 3 the LORD said to **Satan**, "Have you considered my servant Job?
2: 4 "Skin for skin!" **Satan** replied. "A man will give all he has for his
2: 6 The LORD said to **Satan**, "Very well, then, he is in your hands;
2: 7 So **Satan** went out from the presence of the LORD and afflicted
Ps 109: 6 an evil man to oppose him; let an **accuser** stand at his right hand.
Zec 3: 1 of the LORD, and **Satan** standing at his right side to accuse him.
3: 2 The LORD said to **Satan**, "The LORD rebuke you, Satan!
3: 2 The LORD said to Satan, "The LORD rebuke you, **Satan**!

8478 ¹שִׂטְנָה śiṭnâ¹, n.f. [1] [→ 8479; cf. 8476]
accusation [1]
Ezr 4: 6 they lodged an **accusation** against the people of Judah

8479 ²שִׂטְנָה śiṭnâ², n.pr.loc. [1] [√ 8478]
Sitnah [1]
Ge 26:21 but they quarreled over that one also; so he named it **Sitnah**.

8480 שִׂיא śî', n.m. [1] [→ 8481; cf. 5951?, 8420?]
pride [1]

Job 20: 6 Though his **pride** reaches to the heavens and his head touches the

8481 שִׂיאֹן śî'ôn, n.pr.loc. [1] [√ 8480; cf. 5951?, 8420]
Siyon [1]

Dt 4:48 from Aroer on the rim of the Arnon Gorge to Mount **Siyon** (that is,

8482 שִׂיב śîb, v. [2] [→ 8483, 8484; Ar 10681]
gray [1], gray-haired [1]

1Sa 12: 2 [A] As for me, I am old and **gray**, and my sons are here with you.
Job 15:10 [A] The **gray-haired** and the aged are on our side, men even

8483 שֵׂיב śêb, n.[m.]. [1] [√ 8482]
age [1]

1Ki 14: 4 Now Ahijah could not see; his sight was gone because of his **age**.

8484 שֵׂיבָה śêbâ, n.f. [19] [√ 8482]
old age [6], gray head [5], gray hair [2], aged [1], gray hairs [1], gray [1], gray-haired [1], hair gray [1], white hair [1]

Ge 15:15 will go to your fathers in peace and be buried at a good **old age**.
25: 8 Then Abraham breathed his last and died at a good **old age**,
42:38 you will bring my **gray head** down to the grave in sorrow."
44:29 you will bring my **gray head** down to the grave in misery.'
44:31 Your servants will bring the **gray head** *of* our father down to the
Lev 19:32 " 'Rise in the presence of the **aged**, show respect for the elderly
Dt 32:25 and young women will perish, infants and **gray-haired** men.
Jdg 8:32 Gideon son of Joash died at a good **old age** and was buried in the
Ru 4:15 He will renew your life and sustain you in your **old age**. For your
1Ki 2: 6 but do not let his **gray head** go down to the grave in peace.
2: 9 to do to him. Bring his **gray head** down to the grave in blood."
1Ch 29:28 He died at a good **old age**, having enjoyed long life, wealth
Job 41:32 [41:24] one would think the deep had **white hair**.
Ps 71:18 Even when I am old and **gray**, do not forsake me, O God,
92:14 [92:15] They will still bear fruit in **old age**, they will stay fresh
Pr 16:31 **Gray hair** is a crown of splendor; it is attained by a righteous life.
20:29 of young men is their strength, **gray hair** the splendor of the old.
Isa 46: 4 Even to your old age and **gray hairs** I am he, I am he who will
Hos 7: 9 realize it. His **hair** is sprinkled with **gray**, but he does not notice.

8485 שִׂיג śîg, n.[m.]. [1] [cf. 6047, 6092]
busy [1]

1Ki 18:27 he is a god! Perhaps he is deep in thought, or **busy**, or traveling.

8486 שִׂיד¹ śîd¹, v.den. [2] [√ 8487]
coat [2]

Dt 27: 2 [A] set up some large stones and **coat** them with plaster.
27: 4 [A] as I command you today, and **coat** them with plaster.

8487 שִׂיד² śîd², n.[m.]. [4] [→ 8486; cf. 6093, 6167]
lime [2], plaster [2]

Dt 27: 2 is giving you, set up some large stones and coat them with **plaster**.
27: 4 Mount Ebal, as I command you today, and coat them with **plaster**.
Isa 33:12 The peoples will be burned as if to **lime**; like cut thornbushes they
Am 2: 1 Because he burned, as if to **lime**, the bones of Edom's king,

8488 שִׂיחַ¹ śîaḥ¹, v.den. [20] [→ 8465, 8490, 8491]
meditate [7], consider [3], speak [3], mused [2], tell [2], complain [1], in distress [1], mock [1]

Jdg 5:10 [A] saddle blankets, and you who walk along the road, **consider**
1Ch 16: 9 [A] Sing to him, sing praise to him; **tell** of all his wonderful acts.
Job 7:11 [A] of my spirit, *I will* **complain** in the bitterness of my soul.
12: 8 [A] or **speak** to the earth, and it will teach you, or let the fish of
Ps 55:17 [55:18] [A] Evening, morning and noon I cry out **in distress**,
69:12 [69:13] [A] Those who sit at the gate **mock** me, and I am the
77: 3 [77:4] [A] and I groaned; *I* **mused**, and my spirit grew faint.
77: 6 [77:7] [A] in the night. My heart **mused** and my spirit inquired:
77:12 [77:13] [A] all your works and **consider** all your mighty deeds.
105: 2 [A] Sing to him, sing praise to him; **tell** of all his wonderful acts.
119:15 [A] *I* **meditate** on your precepts and consider your ways.
119:23 [A] and slander me, your servant *will* **meditate** on your decrees.
119:27 [A] of your precepts; then *I will* **meditate** on your wonders.
119:48 [A] which I love, and *I* **meditate** on your decrees.
119:78 [A] me without cause; but I *will* **meditate** on your precepts.
119:148 [A] watches of the night, that I *may* **meditate** on your promises.
143: 5 [D] on all your works and **consider** what your hands have done.
145: 5 [A] your majesty, and *I will* **meditate** *on* your wonderful works.
Pr 6:22 [A] watch over you; when you awake, they *will* **speak** *to* you.
Isa 53: 8 [D] he was taken away. And who *can* **speak** *of* his descendants?

8489 שִׂיחַ² śîaḥ², n.[m.]. [4]
bushes [2], brush [1], shrub [+3972] [1]

Ge 2: 5 and no **shrub** [+3972] *of* the field had yet appeared on the earth
21:15 in the skin was gone, she put the boy under one of the **bushes**.
Job 30: 4 In the **brush** they gathered salt herbs, and their food was the root
30: 7 They brayed among the **bushes** and huddled in the undergrowth.

8490 שִׂיחַ³ śîaḥ³, n.m. [14] [√ 8488]
complaint [7], anguish [1], complaints [1], deep in thought [1], lament [1], meditation [1], sort of things he says [1], thoughts [1]

1Sa 1:16 I have been praying here out of my great **anguish** and grief."
1Ki 18:27 he is a god! Perhaps he is **deep in thought**, or busy, or traveling.
2Ki 9:11 "You know the man and the **sort of things he says**," Jehu replied.
Job 7:13 my bed will comfort me and my couch will ease my **complaint**,
9:27 If I say, 'I will forget my **complaint**, I will change my expression,
10: 1 therefore I will give free rein to my **complaint** and speak out in the
21: 4 "Is my **complaint** directed to man? Why should I not be impatient?
23: 2 "Even today my **complaint** is bitter; his hand is heavy in spite of
Ps 55: 2 [55:3] answer me. My **thoughts** trouble me and I am distraught
64: 1 [64:2] Hear me, O God, as I voice my **complaint**; protect my life
102: T [102:1] he is faint and pours out his **lament** before the LORD.
104:34 May my **meditation** be pleasing to him, as I rejoice in the LORD.
142: 2 [142:3] I pour out my **complaint** before him; before him I tell my
Pr 23:29 has woe? Who has sorrow? Who has strife? Who has **complaints**?

8491 שִׂיחָה śîḥâ, n.f. [3] [√ 8488]
meditate [2], devotion [1]

Job 15: 4 But you even undermine piety and hinder **devotion** to God.
Ps 119:97 Oh, how I love your law! I **meditate** *on* it all day long.
119:99 more insight than all my teachers, for I **meditate** *on* your statutes.

8492 שִׂים śîm, v. [583] [→ 3774, 8461, 9582; cf. 3775; Ar 10682]
put [106], set [50], make [48], made [35], *untranslated* [16], placed [16], set up [13], give [11], laid [11], appointed [8], lay [8], makes [7], place [7], turn [7], established [5], gave [5], give careful thought [+4222] [5], puts [5], bring [4], put in place [4], put up [4], putting [4], took [4], turned [4], appoint [3], brought [3], fasten [3], performed [3], provide [3], take [3], assign [2], attached [2], be sure to appoint [+8492] [2], charges [2], consigning to labor [2], determined [+7156+8492] [2], fastened [2], fix [2], given [2], giving [2], leaving [2], mark out [2], named [+9005] [2], pay [2], planted [2], posted [2], prepare [2], prepares [2], reduce [2], reduced [2], regard [+4200+5584] [2], seized [+3338+4200] [2], served [2], sets [2], turn into [2], accuse [+928+1821] [1], added [1], applied [1], attach [1], avenged [1], become [1], care [+448+4213] [1], care about [+448+4213] [1], cares [+4213+6584] [1], caused to turn [1], charge [1], clap [1], concerned about [+448+4213] [1], consider [+4213] [1], consider [+4213+6584] [1], consider [1], considered [+4213+6584] [1], considered [+448+4213] [1], controls [1], covered [+4200] [1], depends on [1], designate [1], destroy [+9039] [1], determine [+7156] [1], determined [+4200+7156] [1], determined [+7156] [1], determined [+906+7156] [1], determined [+928+4200+4200+7156] [1], did[s] [1], displayed [1], does [1], don't say a word [+3338+6584+7023] [1], drew up [1], end [+4200+7874] [1], erected [1], establish [1], establishes [1], exacted [1], examine [1], fastens [1], float [1], formed [1], gave a high rank in [+6584] [1], grants [1], had brought [1], had take up positions [1], had [1], harbor [1], headed for [+906+7156] [1], hung [1], ignored [+448+4202+4213] [1], imposed [1], increased [1], inflict [1], intention [+448+4213] [1], keep [1], keeps [1], lay up [1], left [1], lifted [1], light [1], list [1], loaded [1], look after [+6524+6584] [1], look after [+906+6524+6584] [1], looked [+7156] [1], make serve [+4200] [1], make sure hears [+265+928] [1], making [1], marked off [1], named [+906+9005] [1], offers [1], piled [1], pitched [1], plant [1], pondered [1], ponders [1], poured [1], prepared [1], presented [1], preserve [1], preserved [+928+2021+2645] [1], press charges [1], pressed [1], provided [1], put in charge [1], put on [+928+5516] [1], repay [1], replace [+9393] [1], replaced [1], require [1], resolved [+4213+6584] [1], see [+6524+6584] [1], seize [+928+3338] [1], separated [1], serve [1], set in place [1], sets up [1], setting [1], shave [+7947] [1], shedding [1], showed [1], shrouded [1], sing [+928+7023] [1], slandered [+1821+6613] [1], slanders [+1821+4200+6613] [1], spread [1], stared with a fixed gaze [+906+2256+6641+7156] [1], stationed [1], stirs up [1], strap [1], take up positions [1], think [+4013+4200] [1], throw [1], thrown [1], told [+928+7023] [1], trample down [+5330] [1], treat [1], turned [+7156] [1], turned into [1], unnoticed [+1172+4946] [1], use [1], used [1],

[A] Qal [B] Qal passive [C] Niphal [D] Piel (poel, polel, pilel, pilal, pealal, pilpel) [E] Pual (poal, polal, poalal, pulal, pualal)

was placed [1], was set [1], watch over [+6584] [1], waylaid [+928+2006+2021+4200] [1], worry [+906+4213] [1]

Ge 2: 8 [A] in the east, in Eden; and there *he* **put** the man he had formed.
4: 15 [A] the LORD **put** a mark on Cain so that no one who found
6: 16 [A] **Put** a door in the side of the ark and make lower, middle
9: 23 [A] and Japheth took a garment and **laid** it across their shoulders;
13: 16 [A] *I will* **make** your offspring like the dust of the earth, so that
21: 13 [A] *I will* **make** the son of the maidservant into a nation also,
21: 14 [A] *He* **set** them on her shoulders and then sent her off with the
21: 18 [A] him by the hand, for *I will* **make** him into a great nation."
22: 6 [A] wood for the burnt offering and **placed** it on his son Isaac,
22: 9 [A] He bound his son Isaac and **laid** him on the altar, on top of
24: 2 [A] in charge of all that he had, "**Put** your hand under my thigh.
24: 9 [A] So the servant **put** his hand under the thigh of his master
24: 33 [H] food **was set** before him, but he said, "I will not eat until I
24: 47 [A] "Then *I* **put** the ring in her nose and the bracelets on her
27: 37 [A] "*I have* **made** him lord over you and have made all his
28: 11 [A] stones there, *he* **put** it under his head and lay down to sleep.
28: 18 [A] Early the next morning Jacob took the stone *he had* **placed**
28: 18 [A] his head and **set** it **up** *as* a pillar and poured oil on top of it.
28: 22 [A] this stone that *I have* **set up** as a pillar will be God's house,
30: 36 [A] Then *he* **put** a three-day journey between himself and Jacob,
30: 41 [A] Jacob *would* **place** the branches in the troughs in front of the
30: 42 [A] but if the animals were weak, *he would* not **place** them there.
31: 21 [A] he **headed** [+906+7156] **for** the hill country of Gilead.
31: 34 [A] **put** them inside her camel's saddle and was sitting on them.
31: 37 [A] **Put** it here in front of your relatives and mine, and let them
32: 12 [32:13] [A] *will* **make** your descendants like the sand of the sea,
32: 16 [32:17] [A] of me, and **keep** some space between the herds."
33: 2 [A] *He* **put** the maidservants and their children in front, Leah and
37: 34 [A] **put** [+928+5516] **on** sackcloth and mourned for his son
40: 15 [A] even here I have done nothing *to deserve being* **put** in a
41: 42 [A] in robes of fine linen and **put** a gold chain around his neck.
43: 22 [A] buy food. We don't know who **put** our silver in our sacks."
43: 31 [A] he came out and, controlling himself, said, "**Serve** the food."
43: 32 [A] *They* **served** him by himself, the brothers by themselves, and
44: 1 [A] can carry, and **put** each man's silver in the mouth of his sack.
44: 2 [A] **put** my cup, the silver one, in the mouth of the youngest one's
44: 21 [A] him down to me so *I can* **see** [+6524+6584] him for myself.'
45: 7 [A] God sent me ahead of you to **preserve** for you a remnant on
45: 8 [A] *He* **made** me father to Pharaoh, lord of his entire household
45: 9 [A] God *has* **made** me lord of all Egypt. Come down to me;
46: 3 [A] down to Egypt, for *I will* **make** you into a great nation there.
47: 6 [A] special ability, **put** them in charge of my own livestock."
47: 26 [A] So Joseph **established** it as a law concerning land in Egypt—
47: 29 [A] **put** your hand under my thigh and promise that you will
48: 18 [A] this one is the firstborn; **put** your right hand on his head."
48: 20 [A] '*May* God **make** you like Ephraim and Manasseh.' " So he
48: 20 [A] and Manasseh.' " So *he* **put** Ephraim ahead of Manasseh.
50: 26 [B] after they embalmed him, *he* **was placed** in a coffin in Egypt.
Ex 1: 11 [A] So *they* **put** slave masters over them to oppress them with
2: 3 [A] *she* **placed** the child in it and put it among the reeds along
2: 3 [A] in it and **put** it among the reeds along the bank of the Nile.
2: 14 [A] The man said, "Who **made** you ruler and judge over us? Are
3: 22 [A] for clothing, which *you will* **put** on your sons and daughters.
4: 11 [A] The LORD said to him, "Who **gave** man his mouth? Who
4: 11 [A] Who **makes** him deaf or mute? Who gives him sight
4: 15 [A] You shall speak to him and **put** words in his mouth; I will
4: 21 [A] Pharaoh all the wonders *I have* **given** you the power to do.
5: 8 [A] **require** them to make the same number of bricks as before;
5: 14 [A] The Israelite foremen **appointed** *by* Pharaoh's slave drivers
8: 12 [8:8] [A] LORD about the frogs *he had* **brought** on Pharaoh.
8: 23 [8:19] [A] *I will* **make** a distinction between my people
9: 5 [A] The LORD **set** a time and said, "Tomorrow the LORD will
9: 21 [A] those who **ignored** [+448+4202+4213] the word of the LORD
10: 2 [A] the Egyptians and how *I* **performed** my signs among them,
14: 21 [A] sea back with a strong east wind and **turned** it into dry land.
15: 25 [A] There the LORD **made** a decree and a law for them,
15: 26 [A] *I will* not **bring** on you any of the diseases I brought on the
15: 26 [A] I will not bring on you any of the diseases *I* **brought** on the
17: 12 [A] they took a stone and **put** it under him and he sat on it.
17: 14 [A] and **make sure** *that* Joshua **hears** [+265+928] it,
18: 21 [A] **appoint** them as officials over thousands, hundreds, fifties
19: 7 [A] **set** before them all the words the LORD had commanded
21: 1 [A] "These are the laws *you are to* **set** before them:
21: 13 [A] God lets it happen, he is to flee to a place *I will* **designate**.
22: 25 [22:24] [A] not be like a moneylender; **charge** him no interest.
24: 6 [A] Moses took half of the blood and **put** it in bowls,
26: 35 [A] **Place** the table outside the curtain on the north side of the
28: 12 [A] **fasten** them on the shoulder pieces of the ephod as memorial
28: 26 [A] **attach** them to the other two corners of the breastpiece on the
28: 37 [A] **Fasten** a blue cord to it to attach it to the turban; it is to be on
29: 6 [A] **Put** the turban on his head and attach the sacred diadem to
29: 24 [A] **Put** all these in the hands of Aaron and his sons and wave
32: 27 [A] the God of Israel, says: 'Each man **strap** a sword to his side.
33: 22 [A] *I will* **put** you in a cleft in the rock and cover you with my
39: 7 [A] *they* **fastened** them on the shoulder pieces of the ephod as
39: 19 [A] **attached** them to the other two corners of the breastpiece on
40: 3 [A] **Place** the ark of the Testimony in it and shield the ark with
40: 5 [A] and **put** the curtain at the entrance to the tabernacle.
40: 8 [A] **Set up** the courtyard around it and put the curtain at the
40: 18 [A] **erected** the frames, inserted the crossbars and set up the
40: 19 [A] tent over the tabernacle and **put** the covering over the tent,
40: 20 [A] **attached** the poles to the ark and put the atonement cover
40: 21 [A] **hung** the shielding curtain and shielded the ark of the
40: 24 [A] *He* **placed** the lampstand in the Tent of Meeting opposite the
40: 26 [A] Moses **placed** the gold altar in the Tent of Meeting in front
40: 28 [A] Then *he* **put up** the curtain at the entrance to the tabernacle.
40: 29 [A] *He* **set** the altar of burnt offering near the entrance to the
40: 30 [A] *He* **placed** the basin between the Tent of Meeting and the
Lev 2: 15 [A] Put oil and **[RPH]** incense on it; it is a grain offering.
5: 11 [A] *He must* not **put** oil or incense on it, because it is a sin
6: 10 [6:3] [A] consumed on the altar and **place** them beside the altar.
8: 8 [A] *He* **placed** the breastpiece on him and put the Urim
8: 9 [A] *he* **placed** the turban on Aaron's head and set the gold plate,
8: 9 [A] he placed the turban on Aaron's head and **set** the gold plate,
8: 26 [A] *he* **put** these on the fat portions and on the right thigh.
9: 20 [A] these *they* **laid** on the breasts, and then Aaron burned the fat
10: 1 [A] Abihu took their censers, put fire in them and **added** incense;
20: 5 [A] I *will* **set** my face against that man and his family and will
24: 6 [A] **Set** them in two rows, six in each row, on the table of pure
Nu 4: 6 [A] a cloth of solid blue over that and **put** the poles **in place**.
4: 8 [A] cover that with hides of sea cows and **put** its poles **in place**.
4: 11 [A] cover that with hides of sea cows and **put** its poles **in place**.
4: 14 [A] a covering of hides of sea cows and **put** its poles **in place**.
4: 19 [A] and **assign** to each man his work and what he is to carry.
6: 26 [A] the LORD turn his face toward you and **give** you peace." '
6: 27 [A] "So *they will* **put** my name on the Israelites, and I will bless
11: 11 [A] What have I done to displease you that *you* **put** the burden of
11: 17 [A] take of the Spirit that is on you and **put** the Spirit on them.
16: 7 [A] tomorrow put **[RPH]** fire and incense in them before the
16: 18 [A] put **[RPH]** fire and incense in it, and stood with Moses
16: 46 [17:11] [A] "Take your censer and put **[RPH]** incense in it,
21: 8 [A] said to Moses, "Make a snake and **put** it **up** on a pole;
21: 9 [A] So Moses made a bronze snake and **put** it **up** on a pole.
22: 38 [A] I must speak only what God **puts** in my mouth."
23: 5 [A] The LORD **put** a message in Balaam's mouth and said,
23: 12 [A] "Must I not speak what the LORD **puts** in my mouth?"
23: 16 [A] met with Balaam and **put** a message in his mouth and said,
24: 21 [B] "Your dwelling place is secure, your nest *is* **set** in a rock;
24: 23 [A] he uttered his oracle: "Ah, who can live when God **does** this?
Dt 1: 13 [A] men from each of your tribes, and *I will* **set** them over you."
4: 44 [A] This is the law Moses **set** before the Israelites.
7: 15 [A] *He will* not **inflict** on you the horrible diseases you knew in
10: 2 [A] which you broke. Then *you are to* **put** them in the chest."
10: 5 [A] down the mountain and **put** the tablets in the ark I had made,
10: 22 [A] now the LORD your God *has* **made** you as numerous as the
11: 18 [A] **Fix** these words of mine in your hearts and minds; tie them
12: 5 [A] among all your tribes to **put** his Name there for his dwelling.
12: 21 [A] If the place where the LORD your God chooses to **put** his
14: 1 [A] or **shave** [+7947] the front of your heads for the dead,
14: 24 [A] (because the place where the LORD will choose to **put** his
17: 14 [A] "*Let us* **set** a king over us like all the nations around us,"
17: 15 [A] **be sure to appoint** [+8492] over you the king the LORD
17: 15 [A] **be sure to appoint** [+8492] over you the king the LORD
17: 15 [A] **[RPH]** Do not place a foreigner over you, one who is not a
22: 8 [A] so that *you may* not **bring** the guilt of bloodshed on your
22: 14 [A] **slanders** [+1821+4200+6613] her and gives her a bad name,
22: 17 [A] Now he *has* **slandered** [+1821+6613] her and said, 'I did not
26: 2 [A] the LORD your God is giving you and **put** them in a basket.
27: 15 [A] the work of the craftsman's hands—and **sets** it **up** in secret."
31: 19 [A] teach it to the Israelites and *have* them **sing** [+928+7023] it,
31: 26 [A] **place** it beside the ark of the covenant of the LORD your
32: 46 [A] "**Take** to heart all the words I have solemnly declared to you
33: 10 [A] *He* **offers** incense before you and whole burnt offerings on
Jos 6: 18 [A] Otherwise *you will* **make** the camp of Israel liable to
7: 11 [A] have lied, *they have* **put** them with their own possessions.
7: 19 [A] "My son, **give** glory to the LORD, the God of Israel,
8: 2 [A] and livestock for yourselves. **Set** an ambush behind the city."
8: 12 [A] and **set** them in ambush between Bethel and Ai,
8: 13 [A] *They* **had** the soldiers **take up** *their* **positions**—all those in the
8: 28 [A] So Joshua burned Ai and **made** it a permanent heap of ruins,
10: 24 [A] "Come here and **put** your feet on the necks of these kings."
10: 24 [A] So they came forward and **placed** their feet on their necks.
10: 27 [A] At the mouth of the cave *they* **placed** large rocks, which are
24: 7 [A] and *he* **put** darkness between you and the Egyptians;
24: 25 [A] and there at Shechem *he* **drew up** for them decrees and laws.

Jdg 1:28 [A] *they* **pressed** the Canaanites into forced labor but never
4:21 [A] picked up a tent peg and **[NIE]** a hammer and went quietly
6:19 [A] **Putting** the meat in a basket and its broth in a pot, he brought
6:19 [A] Putting the meat in a basket and its broth **[RPH]** in a pot,
7:22 [A] the LORD **caused** the men throughout the camp **to turn** on
8:31 [A] bore him a son, whom *he* **named** [+906+9005] Abimelech.
8:33 [A] to the Baals. *They* **set up** Baal-Berith as their god
9:24 [A] *might be* **avenged** on their brother Abimelech and on the
9:25 [A] In opposition to him these citizens of Shechem **set** men on
9:48 [A] off some branches, which he lifted **[RPH]** to his shoulders.
9:49 [A] *They* **piled** them against the stronghold and set it on fire over
11:11 [A] and the people **made** him head and commander over them.
12:3 [A] *I* **took** my life in my hands and crossed over to fight the
15:4 [A] to tail in pairs. *He* then **fastened** a torch to every pair of tails,
16:3 [A] *He* **lifted** them to his shoulders and carried them to the top of
18:19 [A] "Be quiet! **Don't say a word** [+3338+6584+7023]. Come with
18:21 [A] **Putting** their little children, their livestock and their
18:31 [A] *They continued to* **use** the idols Micah had made,
19:30 [A] **Think** [+4013+4200] about it! Consider it! Tell us what to
20:29 [A] Then Israel **set** an ambush around Gibeah.
20:36 [A] because they relied on the ambush *they had* **set** near Gibeah.
Ru 3:3 [A] Wash and perfume yourself, and **put** on your best clothes.
1Sa 2:20 [A] "*May* the LORD **give** you children by this woman to take
6:8 [A] in a chest beside it **put** the gold objects you are sending back
6:11 [A] *They* **placed** the ark of the LORD on the cart and along with it
6:15 [A] the gold objects, and **placed** them on the large rock.
7:12 [A] Samuel took a stone and **set** it **up** between Mizpah and Shen.
8:1 [A] Samuel grew old, *he* **appointed** his sons as judges for Israel.
8:5 [A] now **appoint** a king to lead us, such as all the other nations
8:11 [A] and **make** them **serve** [+4200] with his chariots and horses,
8:12 [A] Some he *will* **assign** to be commanders of thousands
9:20 [A] lost three days ago, *do* not **worry** [+906+4213] about them;
9:23 [A] the piece of meat I gave you, the one I told you *to* **lay** aside."
9:24 [A] took up the leg with what was on it and **set** it in front of Saul.
9:24 [A] Samuel said, "Here is what has been kept **[RPH]** for you.
10:19 [A] and distresses. And you have said, 'No, **set** a king over us.'
11:2 [A] eye of every one of you and so **bring** disgrace on all Israel."
11:11 [A] The next day Saul **separated** his men *into* three divisions;
15:2 [A] they did to Israel when *they* **waylaid** [+928+2006+2021+4200]
17:40 [A] **put** them in the pouch of his shepherd's bag and, with his
17:54 [A] and *he* **put** the Philistine's weapons in his own tent.
18:5 [A] so successfully that Saul **gave** [+6584] him **a high rank in**
18:13 [A] from him and **gave** him command over a thousand men,
19:5 [A] *He* **took** his life in his hands when he killed the Philistine.
19:13 [A] Michal took an idol and **laid** it on the bed, covering it with a
19:13 [A] it with a garment and **putting** some goats' hair at the head.
21:6 [21:7] [A] **replaced** *by* hot bread on the day it was taken away.
21:12 [21:13] [A] David **took** these words to heart and was very much
22:7 [A] *Will he* **make** all of you commanders of thousands
22:15 [A] *Let* not the king **accuse** [+928+1821] your servant or any of
25:18 [A] hundred cakes of pressed figs, and **loaded** them on donkeys.
25:25 [A] *May* my lord **pay** no attention to that wicked man Nabal. He
28:2 [A] "Very well, *I will* **make** you my bodyguard for life."
28:21 [A] *I* **took** my life in my hands and did what you told me to do.
28:22 [A] your servant and *let me* **give** you some food so you may eat
30:25 [A] David **made** this a statute and ordinance for Israel from that
31:10 [A] *They* **put** his armor *in* the temple of the Ashtoreths
2Sa 7:10 [A] *I will* **provide** a place for my people Israel and will plant
7:23 [A] to **make** a name for himself, and to perform great
8:6 [A] He **put** garrisons in the Aramean kingdom of Damascus,
8:14 [A] *He* **put** garrisons throughout Edom, and all the Edomites
8:14 [A] **[RPH]** and all the Edomites became subject to David.
12:20 [A] and at his request *they* **served** him food, and he ate.
12:31 [A] **consigning** them **to labor** with saws and with iron picks
13:19 [A] *She* **put** her hand on her head and went away, weeping aloud
13:33 [A] lord the king *should* not *be* **concerned** [+448+4213] **about**
14:3 [A] these words to him." And Joab **put** the words in her mouth.
14:7 [A] **leaving** my husband neither name nor descendant on the face
14:19 [A] and who **put** all these words into the mouth of your servant.
15:4 [A] would add, "If only I *were* **appointed** judge in the land!
17:25 [A] Absalom *had* **appointed** Amasa over the army in place of
18:1 [A] **appointed** over them commanders of thousands
18:3 [A] if we are forced to flee, *they* won't **care about** [+448+4213]
18:3 [A] Even if half of us die, *they* won't **care** [+448+4213]; but you
19:19 [19:20] [A] left Jerusalem. *May* the king **put** it out of his mind.
23:5 [A] *Has he* not **made** with me an everlasting covenant, arranged
23:23 [A] the Three. And David **put** him in charge of his bodyguard.
1Ki 2:5 [A] killed them, **shedding** their blood in peacetime as if in battle,
2:15 [A] All Israel **looked** [+7156] to me as their king. But things
2:19 [A] *He* **had** a throne **brought** for the king's mother, and she sat
5:9 [5:23] [A] I *will* **float** them *in* rafts by sea to the place you
8:21 [A] *I have* **provided** a place there for the ark, in which is the
9:3 [A] which you have built, by **putting** my Name there forever.
10:9 [A] *he has* **made** you king, to maintain justice
11:36 [A] me in Jerusalem, the city where I chose to **put** my Name.
12:29 [A] One *he* **set up** in Bethel, and the other in Dan.
14:21 [A] out of all the tribes of Israel in which to **put** his Name.
18:23 [A] cut it into pieces and **put** it on the wood but not set fire to it.
18:23 [A] cut it into pieces and put it on the wood but not **set** fire *to* it.
18:23 [A] the other bull and put it on the wood but not **set** fire *to* it.
18:25 [A] Call on the name of your god, but *do* not **light** the fire."
18:33 [A] the wood, cut the bull into pieces and **laid** it on the wood.
18:42 [A] bent down to the ground and **put** his face between his knees.
19:2 [A] if by this time tomorrow *I do* not **make** your life like that of
20:6 [A] *They will* **seize** [+928+3338] everything you value and carry
20:12 [A] in their tents, and he ordered his men: "**Prepare** to attack."
20:12 [A] "Prepare to attack." So *they* **prepared** to attack the city.
20:24 [A] and **replace** [+9393] them *with* other officers.
20:31 [A] Let us go to the king of Israel **[NIE]** with sackcloth around
20:34 [A] "*You may* **set up** your own market areas in Damascus,
20:34 [A] market areas in Damascus, as my father **did**[s] in Samaria."
21:27 [A] these words, he tore his clothes, **put** on sackcloth and fasted.
22:27 [A] **Put** this fellow *in* prison and give him nothing but bread
2Ki 2:20 [A] "Bring me a new bowl," he said, "and **put** salt in it." So they
4:10 [A] a small room on the roof and **put** in it a bed and a table,
4:29 [A] greets you, do not answer. **Lay** my staff on the boy's face."
4:31 [A] Gehazi went on ahead and **laid** the staff on the boy's face,
4:34 [A] **[NIE]** mouth to mouth, eyes to eyes, hands to hands.
6:22 [A] **Set** food and water before them so that they may eat
8:11 [A] He **stared** *at* him **with a fixed gaze** [+906+2256+6641+7156]
9:13 [A] their cloaks and **spread** them under him on the bare steps.
10:3 [A] of your master's sons and **set** him on his father's throne.
10:7 [A] *They* **put** their heads in baskets and sent them to Jehu in
10:8 [A] "**Put** them *in* two piles at the entrance of the city gate until
10:24 [A] Now Jehu *had* **posted** eighty men outside with this warning:
10:27 [A] of Baal, and *people have* **used** it for a latrine to this day.
11:16 [A] So *they* **seized** [+3338+4200] her as she reached the place
11:18 [A] Jehoiada the priest **posted** guards at the temple of the
12:17 [12:18] [A] Then he **turned** [+7156] to attack Jerusalem.
13:7 [A] the rest and **made** them like the dust at threshing time.
13:16 [A] he had taken it, Elisha **put** his hands on the king's hands.
17:34 [A] the descendants of Jacob, whom *he* **named** [+9005] Israel.
18:14 [A] The king of Assyria **exacted** from Hezekiah king of Judah
19:28 [A] *I will* **put** my hook in your nose and my bit in your mouth,
20:7 [A] They did so and **applied** it to the boil, and he recovered.
21:4 [A] the LORD had said, "In Jerusalem *I will* **put** my Name."
21:7 [A] carved Asherah pole he had made and **put** it in the temple,
21:7 [A] out of all the tribes of Israel, *I will* **put** my Name forever.
1Ch 10:10 [A] *They* **put** his armor in the temple of their gods and hung up
11:25 [A] the Three. And David **put** him in charge of his bodyguard.
17:9 [A] *I will* **provide** a place for my people Israel and will plant
17:21 [A] to **make** a name for yourself, and to perform great
18:6 [A] He **put** garrisons in the Aramean kingdom of Damascus,
18:13 [A] *He* **put** garrisons in Edom, and all the Edomites became
20:3 [A] **consigning** [BHS 8462] them **to labor** with saws and with
26:10 [A] was not the firstborn, his father *had* **appointed** him the first),
2Ch 1:5 [a] the assembly inquired of him there. [BHS ***he put***; NIV 9004]
6:11 [A] There *I have* **placed** the ark, in which is the covenant of the
6:20 [A] this place of which you said you *would* **put** your Name
12:13 [A] out of all the tribes of Israel in which to **put** his Name.
18:26 [A] **Put** this fellow *in* prison and give him nothing but bread
23:15 [A] So *they* **seized** [+3338+4200] her as she reached the entrance
23:18 [A] Jehoiada **placed** the oversight of the temple of the LORD in
33:7 [A] the carved image he had made and **put** it in God's temple,
33:7 [A] out of all the tribes of Israel, *I will* **put** my Name forever.
33:14 [A] *He* **stationed** military commanders in all the fortified cities
Ezr 8:17 [A] *I* **told** [+928+7023] them what to say to Iddo and his
10:44 [A] and some of them **had** children by these wives.
Ne 8:8 [A] making it clear and **giving** the meaning so that the people
9:7 [A] of Ur of the Chaldeans and **named** [+9005] him Abraham.
Est 2:17 [A] So *he* **set** a royal crown on her head and made her queen
3:1 [A] **giving** him a seat of honor higher than that of all the other
8:2 [A] And Esther **appointed** him over Haman's estate.
10:1 [A] King Xerxes **imposed** tribute throughout the empire, to its
Job 1:8 [A] "*Have you* **considered** [+4213+6584] my servant Job?
1:17 [A] "The Chaldeans **formed** three raiding parties and swept
2:3 [A] "*Have you* **considered** [+448+4213] my servant Job?
4:18 [A] no trust in his servants, if *he* **charges** his angels *with* error,
4:20 [G] broken to pieces; **unnoticed** [+1172+4946], they perish forever.
5:8 [A] I would appeal to God; *I would* **lay** my cause before him.
5:11 [A] The lowly he **sets** on high, and those who mourn are lifted to
7:12 [A] or the monster of the deep, that *you* **put** me under guard?
7:20 [A] O watcher of men? Why *have you* **made** me your target?
13:14 [A] do I put myself in jeopardy and **take** my life in my hands?
13:27 [A] *You* **fasten** my feet in shackles; you keep close watch on all
17:3 [A] "**Give** me, O God, the pledge you demand. Who else will put
17:12 [A] These men **turn** night into day; in the face of darkness they
18:2 [A] "When *will you* **end** [+4200+7874] these speeches?

Job 19: 8 [A] so I cannot pass; *he has* **shrouded** my paths *in* darkness.
20: 4 [A] been from of old, ever since man *was* **placed** on the earth,
21: 5 [A] at me and be astonished; **clap** your hand over your mouth.
22:22 [A] from his mouth and **lay up** his words in your heart.
23: 6 [A] great power? No, he *would* not **press charges** against me.
24:12 [A] cry out for help. But God **charges** no one *with* wrongdoing.
24:15 [A] 'No eye will see me,' and *he* **keeps** his face concealed.
24:25 [A] who can prove me false and **reduce** my words to nothing?"
28: 3 [A] *Man* **puts** an end to the darkness; he searches the farthest
29: 9 [A] and **covered** [+4200] their mouths *with* their hands;
31:24 [A] "If *I have* **put** my trust *in* gold or said to pure gold, 'You are
33:11 [A] *He* **fastens** my feet in shackles; he keeps close watch on all
34:13 [A] over the earth? Who **put** him **in charge** *of* the whole world?
34:14 [A] If it *were* his **intention** [+448+4213] and he withdrew his
34:23 [A] God *has* no *need to* **examine** men further, that they should
36:13 [A] "The godless in heart **harbor** resentment; even when he
37:15 [A] Do you know how God **controls** the clouds and makes his
38: 5 [A] Who **marked off** its dimensions? Surely you know! Who
38: 9 [A] when I **made** the clouds its garment and wrapped it in thick
38:10 [A] when I fixed limits for it and **set** its doors and bars **in place**,
38:33 [A] *Can you* **set up** ⌊God's⌋ dominion over the earth?
39: 6 [A] *I* **gave** him the wasteland as his home, the salt flats as his
40: 4 [A] how can I reply to you? *I* **put** my hand over my mouth.
41: 2 [40:26] [A] *Can you* **put** a cord through his nose or pierce his
41: 8 [40:32] [A] If *you* **lay** a hand on him, you will remember the
41:31 [41:23] [A] and **stirs up** the sea like a pot of ointment.
Ps 18:43 [18:44] [A] *you have* **made** me the head of nations; people I did
19: 4 [19:5] [A] In the heavens *he has* **pitched** a tent for the sun,
39: 8 [39:9] [A] *do* not **make** me the scorn of fools.
40: 4 [40:5] [A] Blessed is the man who **makes** the LORD his trust,
44:13 [44:14] [A] *You have* **made** us a reproach to our neighbors,
44:14 [44:15] [A] *You have* **made** us a byword among the nations;
46: 8 [46:9] [A] the desolations *he has* **brought** on the earth.
50:23 [A] *he* **prepares** the way so that I may show him the salvation of
52: 7 [52:9] [A] "Here now is the man *who did* not **make** God his
54: 3 [54:5] [A] men without **regard** [+4200+5584] *for* God.
56: 8 [56:9] [A] Record my lament; **list** my tears on your scroll—are
66: 2 [A] Sing the glory of his name; **make** his praise glorious!
66: 9 [A] he *has* **preserved** [+928+2021+2645] our lives and kept our
66:11 [A] You brought us into prison and **laid** burdens on our backs.
74: 4 [A] where you met with us; *they* **set up** their standards as signs.
78: 5 [A] decreed statutes for Jacob and **established** the law in Israel,
78: 7 [A] *they would* **put** their trust in God and would not forget his
78:43 [A] the day *he* **displayed** his miraculous signs in Egypt, his
79: 1 [A] your holy temple, *they have* **reduced** Jerusalem to rubble.
80: 6 [80:7] [A] *You have* **made** us a source of contention to our
81: 5 [81:6] [A] *He* **established** it as a statute for Joseph when he
85:13 [85:14] [A] goes before him and **prepares** the way for his steps.
86:14 [A] seeks my life—men without **regard** [+4200+5584] *for* you.
89:25 [89:26] [A] *I will* **set** his hand over the sea, his right hand over
89:29 [89:30] [A] *I will* **establish** his line forever, his throne as long
89:40 [89:41] [A] all his walls and **reduced** his strongholds *to* ruins.
91: 9 [A] If you **make** the Most High your dwelling—
104: 3 [A] He **makes** the clouds his chariot and rides on the wings of
104: 9 [A] *You* **set** a boundary they cannot cross; never again will they
105:21 [A] *He* **made** him master of his household, ruler over all he
105:27 [A] *They* **performed** his miraculous signs among them, his
107:33 [A] *He* **turned** rivers into a desert, flowing springs into thirsty
107:35 [A] *He* **turned** the desert into pools of water and the parched
107:41 [A] out of their affliction and **increased** their families like flocks.
109: 5 [A] *They* **repay** me evil for good, and hatred for my friendship.
147:14 [A] He **grants** peace *to* your borders and satisfies you with the
Pr 8:29 [A] when he **gave** the sea its boundary so the waters would not
23: 2 [A] and **put** a knife to your throat if you are given to gluttony.
30:26 [A] of little power, yet *they* **make** their home in the crags;
SS 1: 6 [A] were angry with me and **made** me take care of the vineyards;
6:12 [A] my desire **set** me *among* the royal chariots of my people.
8: 6 [A] **Place** me like a seal over your heart, like a seal on your arm;
Isa 3: 7 [A] in my house; *do* not **make** me the leader of the people."
5:20 [A] good evil, *who* **put** darkness for light and light for darkness,
5:20 [A] for darkness, *who* **put** bitter for sweet and sweet for bitter.
10: 6 [A] and to **trample** them **down** [+5330] like mud in the streets.
13: 9 [A] to **make** the land desolate and destroy the sinners within it.
14:17 [A] *the man who* **made** the world a desert, who overthrew its
14:23 [A] "*I will* **turn** her into a place for owls and into swampland;
21: 4 [A] fear makes me tremble; the twilight I longed for *has* **become**
23:13 [A] they stripped its fortresses bare and **turned** it into a ruin.
25: 2 [A] *You have* **made** the city a heap of rubble, the fortified town
27: 9 [A] When he **makes** all the altar stones to be like chalk stones
28:15 [A] for *we have* **made** a lie our refuge and falsehood our hiding
28:17 [A] *I will* **make** justice the measuring line and righteousness the
28:25 [A] *Does he* not **plant** wheat in its place, barley in its plot,
37:29 [A] *I will* **put** my hook in your nose and my bit in your mouth,
41:15 [A] *I will* **make** you into a threshing sledge, new and sharp,
41:15 [A] the mountains and crush them, and **reduce** the hills to chaff.
41:18 [A] *I will* **turn** the desert into pools of water, and the parched
41:19 [A] *I will* **set** pines in the wasteland, the fir and the cypress
41:20 [A] people may see and know, *may* **consider** and understand,
41:22 [A] so that we *may* **consider** [+4213] them and know their final
42: 4 [A] or be discouraged till *he* **establishes** justice on earth.
42:12 [A] *Let them* **give** glory to the LORD and proclaim his praise
42:15 [A] *I will* **turn** rivers into islands and dry up the pools.
42:16 [A] *I will* **turn** the darkness into light before them and make the
42:25 [A] it consumed them, but *they did* not **take** it to heart.
43:19 [A] *I am* **making** a way in the desert and streams in the
44: 7 [A] lay out before me what has happened since I **established** my
47: 6 [A] I gave them into your hand, and *you* **showed** them no mercy.
47: 7 [A] *you did* not **consider** [+4213+6584] these things or reflect
49: 2 [A] *He* **made** my mouth like a sharpened sword, in the shadow
49: 2 [A] *he* **made** me into a polished arrow and concealed me in his
49:11 [A] *I will* **turn** all my mountains into roads, and my highways
50: 2 [A] By a mere rebuke I dry up the sea, *I* **turn** rivers **into** a desert;
50: 3 [A] the sky with darkness and **make** sackcloth its covering."
50: 7 [A] Therefore *have I* **set** my face like flint, and I know I will not
51: 3 [A] *he will* **make** her deserts like Eden, her wastelands like the
51:10 [A] who **made** a road in the depths of the sea so that the
51:16 [A] *I have* **put** my words in your mouth and covered you with
51:23 [A] *I will* **put** it into the hands of your tormentors, who said to
51:23 [A] *you* **made** your back like the ground, like a street to be
53:10 [A] and though the LORD **makes** his life a guilt offering,
54:12 [A] *I will* **make** your battlements *of* rubies, your gates of
57: 1 [A] The righteous perish, and no one **ponders** it in his heart;
57: 7 [A] *You have* **made** your bed on a high and lofty hill; there you
57: 8 [A] and your doorposts *you have* **put** your pagan symbols.
57:11 [A] have neither remembered me nor **pondered** this in your
59:21 [A] my words that *I have* **put** in your mouth will not depart from
60:15 [A] *I will* **make** you the everlasting pride and the joy of all
60:17 [A] *I will* **make** peace your governor and righteousness your
61: 3 [A] **provide** for those who grieve in Zion—to bestow on them a
62: 7 [A] establishes Jerusalem and **makes** her the praise of the earth.
63:11 [A] his flock? Where is he *who* **set** his Holy Spirit among them,
66:19 [A] "*I will* **set** a sign among them, and I will send some of those
Jer 2: 7 [A] and defiled my land and **made** my inheritance detestable.
4: 7 [A] has set out. He has left his place to **lay** waste your land.
5:22 [A] *I* **made** the sand a boundary for the sea, an everlasting barrier
6: 8 [A] and **make** your land desolate so no one can live in it."
7:30 [A] *They have* **set up** their detestable idols in the house that
9: 8 [9:7] [A] to his neighbor, but in his heart *he* **sets** a trap for him.
10:22 [A] *It will* **make** the towns of Judah desolate, a haunt of jackals.
11:13 [A] the altars *you have* **set up** to burn incense to that shameful
12:11 [A] It *will be* **made** a wasteland, parched and desolate before me;
12:11 [A] laid waste because there is no one *who* **cares** [+4213+6584].
13: 1 [A] "Go and buy a linen belt and **put** it around your waist, but do
13: 2 [A] a belt, as the LORD directed, and **put** it around my waist.
13:16 [A] *he will* **turn** it to thick darkness and change it to deep gloom.
17: 5 [A] *who* **depends on** flesh *for* his strength and whose heart turns
18:16 [A] Their land *will be* **laid** waste, an object of lasting scorn; all
19: 8 [A] *I will* devastate this city and **make** it an object of scorn;
21:10 [A] *I have* **determined** [+928+4200+4200+7156] to do this city
24: 6 [A] My eyes *will* **watch** [+6584] **over** them for their good, and I
25: 9 [A] **make** them an object of horror and scorn, and an everlasting
25:12 [A] declares the LORD, "and *will* **make** it desolate forever.
29:22 [A] 'The LORD **treat** you like Zedekiah and Ahab,
31:21 [A] "Set up road signs; **put up** guideposts. Take note of the
32:20 [A] *You* **performed** miraculous signs and wonders in Egypt
32:34 [A] *They* **set up** their abominable idols in the house that bears
33:25 [A] 'If *I have* not **established** my covenant *with* day and night
38:12 [A] "**Put** these old rags and worn-out clothes under your arms to
39:12 [A] "Take him and **look after** [+6524+6584] him; don't harm
40: 4 [A] if you like, and I *will* **look after** [+906+6524+6584] you; but if
40:10 [A] summer fruit and oil, and **put** them in your storage jars,
42:15 [A] 'If you *are* **determined** [+7156+8492] to go to Egypt and you
42:15 [A] 'If you *are* **determined** [+7156+8492] to go to Egypt and you
42:17 [A] Indeed, all who *are* **determined** [+906+7156] to go to Egypt
43:10 [A] and *I will* **set** his throne over these stones I have buried here;
44:11 [A] I *am* **determined** [+4200+7156] to bring disaster on you and to
44:12 [A] who *were* **determined** [+7156] to go to Egypt to settle there.
49:38 [A] *I will* **set** my throne in Elam and destroy her king
51:29 [A] to **lay** waste the land of Babylon so that no one will live
La 3:11 [A] me from the path and mangled me and **left** me without help.
3:45 [A] *You have* **made** us scum and refuse among the nations.
Eze 4: 2 [A] to it, set up camps against it and **put** battering rams around it.
4: 4 [A] left side and **put** the sin of the house of Israel upon yourself.
5: 5 [A] is Jerusalem, which *I have* **set** in the center of the nations,
6: 2 [A] "Son of man, **set** your face against the mountains of Israel;
7:20 [A] **[NIE]** and used it to make their detestable idols and vile
11: 7 [A] The bodies *you have* **thrown** there are the meat and this city
13:17 [A] **set** your face against the daughters of your people who

Eze 14: 4 [A] **puts** a wicked stumbling block before his face and then goes
14: 7 [A] and **puts** a wicked stumbling block before his face and
14: 8 [G] against that man and **make** him an example and a byword.
15: 7 [A] when I **set** my face against them, you will know that I am the
16: 14 [A] because the splendor *I had* **given** you made your beauty
17: 4 [A] a land of merchants, where *he* **planted** it in a city of traders.
17: 5 [A] in fertile soil. *He* **planted** it like a willow by abundant water,
19: 5 [A] she took another of her cubs and **made** him a strong lion.
20: 28 [A] **presented** their fragrant incense and poured out their drink
20: 46 [21:2] [A] "Son of man, **set** your face toward the south; preach
21: 2 [21:7] [A] **set** your face against Jerusalem and preach against
21: 16 [21:21] [A] O sword, slash to the right, then **[NIE]** to the left,
21: 19 [21:24] [A] **mark out** two roads *for* the sword of the king of
21: 20 [21:25] [A] **Mark out** one road for the sword to come against
21: 22 [21:27] [A] where he is to **set up** battering rams, to give the
21: 22 [21:27] [A] to **set** battering rams against the gates, to build a
21: 27 [21:32] [G] A ruin! A ruin! *I will* **make** it a ruin! It will not be
23: 24 [A] *they will* **take up positions** against you on every side with
23: 41 [A] with a table spread before it on which *you had* **placed** the
24: 7 [A] *She* **poured** it on the bare rock; she did not pour it on the
24: 17 [A] your turban fastened and your sandals **[NIE]** on your feet;
25: 2 [A] **set** your face against the Ammonites and prophesy against
26: 12 [A] and demolish your fine houses and **throw** your stones,
28: 21 [A] "Son of man, **set** your face against Sidon; prophesy against
29: 2 [A] **set** your face against Pharaoh king of Egypt and prophesy
30: 21 [A] It has not been bound up for healing or **put** *in* a splint so as
35: 2 [A] "Son of man, **set** your face against Mount Seir; prophesy
35: 4 [A] *I will* **turn** your towns **into** ruins and you will be desolate.
38: 2 [A] "Son of man, **set** your face against Gog, of the land of
39: 21 [A] see the punishment I inflict and the hand *I* **lay** upon them.
40: 4 [A] and **pay** attention to everything I am going to show you,
44: 5 [A] **give** attention *to* everything I tell you concerning all the
44: 5 [A] **Give** attention to the entrance of the temple and all the exits
44: 8 [A] to my holy things, *you* **put** others in charge of my sanctuary.
Da 1: 7 [A] The chief official **gave** them new names: to Daniel, the name
1: 7 [A] **[RPH]** to Daniel, the name Belteshazzar; to Hananiah,
1: 8 [A] Daniel **resolved** [+4213+6584] not to defile himself with the
11: 17 [A] *He will* **determine** [+7156] to come with the might of his
11: 18 [g] [*he will* **turn** [Q; see K 8740] his attention to the coastlands]
Hos 1: 11 [2:2] [A] *they will* **appoint** one leader and will come up out of
2: 3 [2:5] [A] *I will* **make** her like a desert, turn her into a parched
2: 12 [2:14] [A] *I will* **make** them a thicket, and wild animals will
11: 8 [A] How *can I* **make** you like Zeboiim? My heart is changed
Joel 1: 7 [A] *It has* **laid** waste my vines and ruined my fig trees. It has
Am 7: 8 [A] "Look, I *am* **setting** a plumb line among my people Israel;
8: 10 [A] *I will* **make** that time like mourning for an only son
9: 4 [A] *I will* **fix** my eyes upon them for evil and not for good."
Ob 1: 4 [B] you soar like the eagle and **make** your nest among the stars,
1: 7 [A] those who eat your bread *will* **set** a trap for you, but you will
Mic 1: 6 [A] "Therefore *I will* **make** Samaria a heap of rubble, a place for
1: 7 [A] be burned with fire; *I will* **destroy** [+9039] all her images.
2: 12 [A] *I will* **bring** them together like sheep in a pen, like a flock in
4: 7 [A] *I will* **make** the lame a remnant, those driven away a strong
4: 13 [A] O Daughter of Zion, for *I will* **give** you horns of iron;
4: 13 [A] *I will* **give** you hoofs of bronze and you will break to pieces
5: 1 [4:14] [A] O city of troops, for a siege *is* **laid** against us.
7: 16 [A] *They will* **lay** their hands on their mouths and their ears will
Na 1: 14 [A] of your gods. *I will* **prepare** your grave, for you are vile."
3: 6 [A] I will treat you with contempt and **make** you a spectacle.
Hab 1: 12 [A] O LORD, *you have* **appointed** them to execute judgment;
2: 9 [A] "Woe to him who builds his realm by unjust gain to **set** his
3: 19 [A] *he* **makes** my feet like the feet of a deer, he enables me to go
Zep 2: 13 [A] **leaving** Nineveh utterly desolate and dry as the desert.
3: 19 [A] *I will* **give** them praise and honor in every land where they
Hag 1: 5 [A] the LORD Almighty says: "**Give careful thought** [+4222]
1: 7 [A] the LORD Almighty says: "**Give careful thought** [+4222]
2: 15 [A] " 'Now **give careful thought** [+4222] to this from this day
2: 15 [A] consider how things were before one stone *was* **laid** on
2: 18 [A] day of the ninth month, **give careful thought** [+4222]
2: 18 [A] LORD's temple was laid. **Give careful thought** [+4222]:
2: 23 [A] the LORD, 'and *I will* **make** you like my signet ring,
Zec 3: 5 [A] I said, "**Put** a clean turban on his head." So they put a clean
3: 5 [A] So *they* **put** a clean turban on his head and clothed him,
6: 11 [A] and make a crown, and **set** it on the head of the high priest,
7: 12 [A] *They* **made** their hearts as hard as flint and would not listen
7: 14 [A] or go. This is how *they* **made** the pleasant land desolate.' "
9: 13 [A] your sons, O Greece, and **make** you like a warrior's sword.
10: 3 [A] house of Judah, and **make** them like a proud horse in battle.
12: 2 [A] "I *am going to* **make** Jerusalem a cup that sends all the
12: 3 [A] *I will* **make** Jerusalem an immovable rock for all the nations.
12: 6 [A] "On that day *I will* **make** the leaders of Judah like a firepot
Mal 1: 3 [A] *I have* **turned** his mountains **into** a wasteland and left his
2: 2 [A] and if *you do* not **set** your heart to honor my name,"
2: 2 [A] because you *have* not **set** your heart to honor me.

8493 שֵׂךְ *śēk*, n.[m.]. [1] [√ 8504]
barbs [1]

Nu 33: 55 those you allow to remain will become **barbs** in your eyes

8494 שֹׂךְ *śōk*, n.[m.]. [1] [cf. 6108]
dwelling [1]

La 2: 6 He has laid waste his **dwelling** like a garden; he has destroyed his

8495 שָׂכָה *śākâ*, n.[m.]. Not used in NIV/BHS [→ 5381, 8499; cf. 8498?]

8496 שֻׂכָּה *śukkâ*, n.f. [1] [√ 8504]
harpoons [1]

Job 41: 7 [40:31] Can you fill his hide with **harpoons** or his head with

8497 שֶׂכוּ *śekû*, n.pr.loc. [1]
Secu [1]

1Sa 19: 22 he himself left for Ramah and went to the great cistern at **Secu**.

8498 שֶׂכְוִי *śekwî*, n.[m.]. [1] [cf. 8495?]
mind [1]

Job 38: 36 the heart with wisdom or gave understanding to the **mind**?

8499 שָׂכְיָה *śākᵉyâ*, n.pr.m. [1] [√ 8495 + 3378]
Sakia [1]

1Ch 8: 10 Jeuz, **Sakia** and Mirmah. These were his sons, heads of families.

8500 שְׂכִיָּה *śᵉkiyyâ*, n.f. [1]
vessel [1]

Isa 2: 16 for every trading ship and every stately **vessel**.

8501 שַׂכִּין *śakkîn*, n.[m.]. [1] [√ 8504]
knife [1]

Pr 23: 2 and put a **knife** to your throat if you are given to gluttony.

8502 שָׂכִיר *śākîr*, a. [18] [√ 8509]
hired man [5], hired worker [4], hired [3], servant bound by contract [2], hired hand [1], laborers [1], man hired [1], mercenaries [1]

Ex 12: 45 but a temporary resident and a **hired worker** may not eat of it.
22: 15 [22:14] If the animal was **hired**, the money paid for the hire
Lev 19: 13 rob him. " 'Do not hold back the wages of a **hired man** overnight.
22: 10 nor may the guest of a priest or his **hired worker** eat it.
25: 6 and the **hired worker** and temporary resident who live among you,
25: 40 He is to be treated as a **hired worker** or a temporary resident
25: 50 be based on the rate paid to a **hired man** for that number of years.
25: 53 He is to be treated as a **man hired** *from* year to year; you must see
Dt 15: 18 six years has been worth twice as much as that of a **hired hand**.
24: 14 Do not take advantage of a **hired** *man* who is poor and needy,
Job 7: 1 hard service on earth? Are not his days like those of a **hired man**?
7: 2 evening shadows, or a **hired man** waiting eagerly for his wages,
14: 6 and let him alone, till he has put in his time like a **hired man**.
Isa 7: 20 In that day the Lord will use a razor **hired** from beyond the River—
16: 14 as a **servant bound by contract** would count them, Moab's
21: 16 "Within one year, as a **servant bound by contract** would count it,
Jer 46: 21 The **mercenaries** in her ranks are like fattened calves. They too
Mal 3: 5 and perjurers, against those who defraud **laborers** of their wages,

8503 ¹שָׂכַךְ *śākak*[1], v. [1] [cf. 6058, 6114]
cover [1]

Ex 33: 22 [A] the rock and **cover** you *with* my hand until I have passed by.

8504 ²שָׂכַךְ *śākak*[2], v. Not used in NIV/BHS [→ 5372, 8493, 8496, 8501; cf. 5819, 6056, 6115, 8455]

8505 ¹שָׂכַל *śākal*[1], v. [60 / 61] [→ 5380, 8507; cf. 8506; Ar 10683]
wise [13], understand [6], successful [4], prosper [3], prudent [3], understanding [3], instruct [2], act wisely [1], careful [1], fail [+4202] [1], gaining wisdom [1], gave thought [1], gave understanding [1], give attention [1], give insight [1], gives heed [1], giving attention [1], guides [1], had great success [1], had regard for [1], has regard for [1], have insight [1], insight [1], instructed [1], met with success [1], ponder [1], showed understanding [+8507] [1], showing aptitude [1],

skilled [1], succeeds [1], successfully [1], takes note [1], understands [1], wisely [1]

Ge 3: 6 [G] also desirable for **gaining wisdom**, she took some and ate it.
Dt 29: 9 [29:8] [G] so that *you may* **prosper** *in* everything you do.
32:29 [G] If only they were wise and *would* **understand** this
Jos 1: 7 [G] or to the left, that *you may be* **successful** wherever you go.
1: 8 [G] written in it. Then you will be prosperous and **successful**.
1Sa 18: 5 [G] *so* **successfully** that Saul gave him a high rank in the army.
18:14 [G] In everything he did he **had great success**,
18:15 [G] When Saul saw how **successful** he *was*, he was afraid of him.
18:30 [A] David **met with** more **success** than the rest of Saul's officers,
1Ki 2: 3 [G] so that *you may* **prosper** in all you do and wherever you go,
2Ki 18: 7 [G] was with him; *he was* **successful** in whatever he undertook.
1Ch 28:19 [G] *he* **gave** me **understanding** *in* all the details of the plan."
2Ch 30:22 [G] who **showed** good **understanding** [+8507] of the service of
Ne 8:13 [G] gathered around Ezra the scribe to **give attention** to the
9:20 [G] You gave your good Spirit to **instruct** them. You did not
Job 22: 2 [G] man be of benefit to God? Can even a **wise** *man* benefit him?
34:27 [G] from following him and **had** no **regard for** any of his ways.
34:35 [G] 'Job speaks without knowledge; his words lack **insight**.'
Ps 2:10 [G] Therefore, *you* kings, *be* **wise**; be warned, you rulers of the
14: 2 [G] on the sons of men to see if there are *any who* **understand**,
32: 8 [G] *I will* **instruct** you and teach you in the way you should go;
36: 3 [36:4] [G] he has ceased to *be* **wise** and to do good.
41: 1 [41:2] [G] Blessed is *he who* **has regard for** the weak;
53: 2 [53:3] [G] sons of men to see if there are *any who* **understand**,
64: 9 [64:10] [G] the works of God and **ponder** what he has done.
94: 8 [G] among the people; you fools, when *will you become* **wise**?
101: 2 [G] *I will be* **careful** to lead a blameless life—when will you
106: 7 [G] were in Egypt, *they* **gave** no **thought** *to* your miracles;
119:99 [G] *I* **have** more **insight** than all my teachers, for I meditate on
Pr 1: 3 [G] for acquiring a disciplined and **prudent** *life*, doing what is
10: 5 [G] He who gathers crops in summer *is* a **wise** son, but he who
10:19 [G] sin is not absent, but he who holds his tongue *is* **wise**.
14:35 [G] A king delights in a **wise** servant, but a shameful servant
15:24 [G] The path of life leads upward for the **wise** to keep him from
16:20 [G] *Whoever* **gives heed** to instruction prospers, and blessed is
16:23 [G] A wise man's heart **guides** his mouth, and his lips promote
17: 2 [G] A **wise** servant will rule over a disgraceful son, and will
17: 8 [G] to the one who gives it; wherever he turns, *he* **succeeds**.
19:14 [G] from parents, but a **prudent** wife is from the LORD.
21:11 [G] when a wise man *is* **instructed**, he gets knowledge.
21:12 [G] The Righteous One **takes note** of the house of the wicked
21:16 [G] A man who strays from the path of **understanding** comes to
Isa 41:20 [G] people may see and know, may consider and **understand**,
44:18 [G] and their minds closed so they cannot **understand**.
52:13 [G] See, my servant *will* **act wisely**; he will be raised and lifted
Jer 3:15 [G] who will lead you with knowledge and **understanding**.
9:24 [9:23] [G] that *he* **understands** and knows me, that I am the
10:21 [G] so *they do* not **prosper** and all their flock is scattered.
20:11 [G] not prevail. *They will* **fail** [+4202] and be thoroughly
23: 5 [G] a King who will reign **wisely** and do what is just and right in
50: 9 [G] Their arrows will be like **skilled** [BHS 8897] warriors who
Da 1: 4 [G] handsome, **showing aptitude** for every kind of learning, well
1:17 [G] and **understanding** of all kinds of literature and learning.
9:13 [G] by turning from our sins and **giving attention** to your truth.
9:22 [G] I have now come to **give** you **insight** and understanding.
9:25 [G] "Know and **understand** this: From the issuing of the decree
11:33 [G] "Those *who are* **wise** will instruct many, though for a time
11:35 [G] Some of the **wise** will stumble, so that they may be refined,
12: 3 [G] Those *who are* **wise** will shine like the brightness of the
12:10 [G] will understand, but those *who are* **wise** will understand.
Am 5:13 [G] Therefore the **prudent** *man* keeps quiet in such times,

8506 ²שָׂכַל śākal², v. [1] [cf. 8505]

crossing [1]

Ge 48:14 [D] though he was the younger, and **crossing** his arms,

8507 שֶׂכֶל śekel, n.m. [16] [√ 8505; Ar 10684]

understanding [4], wisdom [3], *untranslated* [1], capable [1], discretion [1], intelligence [1], intelligent [+3202] [1], meaning [1], name [1], showed understanding [+8505] [1], wise [1]

1Sa 25: 3 She was an **intelligent** [+3202] and beautiful woman, but her
1Ch 22:12 May the LORD give you **discretion** and understanding when he
26:14 a **wise** counselor, and the lot for the North Gate fell to him.
2Ch 2:12 [2:11] a wise son, endowed with **intelligence** and discernment,
30:22 who **showed** good **understanding** [+8505] of the service of the
Ezr 8:18 they brought us Sherebiah, a **capable** man, from the descendants of
Ne 8: 8 making it clear and giving the **meaning** so that the people could
Job 17: 4 You have closed their minds to **understanding**; therefore you will
Ps 111:10 of wisdom; all who follow his precepts have good **understanding**.
Pr 3: 4 you will win favor and a good **name** in the sight of God and man.
12: 8 A man is praised according to his **wisdom**, but men with warped
13:15 Good **understanding** wins favor, but the way of the unfaithful is
16:22 **Understanding** is a fountain of life to those who have it, but folly
19:11 A man's **wisdom** gives him patience; it is to his glory to overlook
23: 9 not speak to a fool, for he will scorn the **wisdom** *of* your words.
Da 8:25 **[NIE]** He will cause deceit to prosper, and he will consider

8508 שִׂכְלוּת śiklût, n.f. [1] [cf. 6121]

folly [1]

Ecc 1:17 also of madness and **folly**, but I learned that this, too, is a chasing

8509 שָׂכַר śākar, v. [20] [→ 3779, 5382, 8502, 8510, 8511, 8512; cf. 6128]

hired [9], hire [3], earn wages [+8509] [2], hired [+8509] [2], *untranslated* [1], been hired [1], hire themselves out [1], hires [1]

Ge 30:16 [A] "*I have* **hired** [+8509] you with my son's mandrakes."
30:16 [A] "*I have* **hired** [+8509] you with my son's mandrakes."
Dt 23: 4 [23:5] [A] *they* **hired** Balaam son of Beor from Pethor in Aram
Jdg 9: 4 [A] Abimelech used it *to* **hire** reckless adventurers, who became
18: 4 [A] for him, and said, "*He has* **hired** me and I am his priest."
1Sa 2: 5 [C] Those who were full **hire themselves out** for food, but those
2Sa 10: 6 [A] **hired** twenty thousand Aramean foot soldiers from Beth Rehob
2Ki 7: 6 [A] the king of Israel *has* **hired** the Hittite and Egyptian kings to
1Ch 19: 6 [A] the Ammonites sent a thousand talents of silver to **hire**
19: 7 [A] *They* **hired** thirty-two thousand chariots and charioteers, as
2Ch 24:12 [A] *They* **hired** masons and carpenters to restore the LORD's
25: 6 [A] *He* also **hired** a hundred thousand fighting men from Israel
Ne 6:12 [A] against me because Tobiah and Sanballat *had* **hired** him.
6:13 [B] He *had* **been hired** to intimidate me so that I would commit
13: 2 [A] but *had* **hired** Balaam to call a curse down on them.
Pr 26:10 [A] Like an archer who wounds at random is *he who* **hires** a fool
26:10 [A] at random is he who hires a fool or **[RPH]** any passer-by.
Isa 46: 6 [A] *they* **hire** a goldsmith to make it into a god, and they bow
Hag 1: 6 [F] You **earn wages** [+8509], only to put them in a purse with
1: 6 [F] You **earn wages** [+8509], only to put them in a purse with

8510 ¹שָׂכָר śākār¹, n.m. [28] [→ 8511; cf. 8509; *also used with compound proper names*]

wages [10], reward [6], pay [2], rewarded [2], *untranslated* [1], fare [1], money paid for hire [1], paid [+906+9202] [1], pay [+906+5989] [1], return [1], rewarded [+5989] [1], worth [1]

Ge 15: 1 not be afraid, Abram. I am your shield, your very great **reward**."
30:18 "God *has* **rewarded** [+5989] me for giving my maidservant to my
30:28 He added, "Name your **wages**, and I will pay them."
30:32 and every spotted or speckled goat. They will be my **wages**.
30:33 in the future, whenever you check on the **wages** you *have paid* me.
31: 8 If he said, 'The speckled ones will be your **wages**,' then all the
31: 8 if he said, 'The streaked ones will be your **wages**,' then all the
Ex 2: 9 this baby and nurse him for me, and I *will* **pay** [+906+5989] you."
22:15 [22:14] was hired, the **money paid for** *the* **hire** covers the loss.
Nu 18:31 for it is your **wages** for your work at the Tent of Meeting.
Dt 15:18 six years has been **worth** twice as much as that *of* a hired hand.
24:15 Pay him his **wages** each day before sunset, because he is poor
1Ki 5: 6 [5:20] and I will pay you *for* your men whatever **wages** you set.
2Ch 15: 7 be strong and do not give up, for your work will be **rewarded**."
Ps 127: 3 Sons are a heritage from the LORD, children a **reward** from him.
Ecc 4: 9 better than one, because they have a good **return** for their work:
9: 5 they have no further **reward**, and even the memory of them is
Isa 40:10 See, his **reward** is with him, and his recompense accompanies
62:11 See, his **reward** is with him, and his recompense accompanies
Jer 31:16 from tears, for your work will be **rewarded**," declares the LORD.
Eze 29:18 his army got no **reward** from the campaign he led against Tyre.
29:19 its wealth. He will loot and plunder the land as **pay** for his army.
Jnh 1: 3 After paying the **fare**, he went aboard and sailed for Tarshish to
Zec 8:10 Before that time there were no **wages** *for* man or beast. No one
8:10 Before that time there were no wages for man or **[RPH]** beast.
11:12 I told them, "If you think it best, give me my **pay**; but if not,
11:12 keep it." So *they* **paid** [+906+9202] me thirty pieces of silver.
Mal 3: 5 and perjurers, against those who defraud laborers of their **wages**,

8511 ²שָׂכָר śākār², n.pr.m. [2] [√ 8510; cf. 8509]

Sacar [2]

1Ch 11:35 Ahiam son of **Sacar** the Hararite, Eliphal son of Ur,
26: 4 the second, Joah the third, **Sacar** the fourth, Nethanel the fifth,

8512 שֶׂכֶר śeker, n.[m.] [2] [√ 8509]

reward [1], wage [1]

Pr 11:18 but he who sows righteousness reaps a sure **reward**.
Isa 19:10 will be dejected, and all the **wage** earners will be sick at heart.

8513 שְׂלָו śelāw, n.f. [4]

quail [4]

Ex 16:13 That evening **quail** came and covered the camp, and in the
Nu 11:31 a wind went out from the LORD and drove **quail** in from the sea.
11:32 and all the next day the people went out and gathered **quail**.
Ps 105:40 he brought them **quail** and satisfied them with the bread of heaven.

8514 שַׂלְמָא śalmā', n.pr.m. [4 / 2] [→ 8516, 8517]

Salma [2]

1Ch 2:11 Nahshon was the father of Salmon, [BHS *Salma*; NIV 8517]
2:11 Salmon [BHS *Salma*; NIV 8517] the father of Boaz,
2:51 **Salma** the father of Bethlehem, and Hareph the father of Beth
2:54 The descendants of **Salma**: Bethlehem, the Netophathites,

8515 שַׂלְמָה śalmâ[1], n.f. [16] [cf. 8529]

clothes [5], cloak [4], garment [2], robes [2], clothing [1], garments [1], robe [1]

Ex 22:9 [22:8] illegal possession of an ox, a donkey, a sheep, a **garment**,
22:26 [22:25] If you take your neighbor's **cloak** as a pledge, return it to
Dt 24:13 Return his **cloak** to him by sunset so that he may sleep in it.
29:5 [29:4] your **clothes** did not wear out, nor did the sandals on your
Jos 9:5 put worn and patched sandals on their feet and wore old **clothes**.
9:13 our **clothes** and sandals are worn out by the very long journey."
22:8 gold, bronze and iron, and a great quantity of **clothing**—
1Ki 10:25 articles of silver and gold, **robes**, weapons and spices, and horses
11:29 the prophet of Shiloh met him on the way, wearing a new **cloak**.
11:30 Ahijah took hold of the new **cloak** he was wearing and tore it into
2Ch 9:24 articles of silver and gold, and **robes**, weapons and spices,
Ne 9:21 their **clothes** did not wear out nor did their feet become swollen.
Job 9:31 me into a slime pit so that even my **clothes** would detest me.
Ps 104:2 He wraps himself in light as with a **garment**; he stretches out the
SS 4:11 The fragrance of your **garments** is like that of Lebanon.
Mic 2:8 You strip off the rich **robe** from those who pass by without a care,

8516 שַׂלְמָה śalmâ[2], n.pr.m. [1 / 0] [√ 8514]

Ru 4:20 Nahshon the father of Salmon, [BHS *Salma*; NIV 8517]

8517 שַׂלְמוֹן śalmôn, n.pr.m. [1 / 4] [√ 8514]

Salmon [4]

Ru 4:20 the father of Nahshon, Nahshon the father of **Salmon**, [BHS 8516]
4:21 **Salmon** the father of Boaz, Boaz the father of Obed,
1Ch 2:11 Nahshon was the father of **Salmon**, [BHS 8514] Salmon the father
2:11 was the father of Salmon, **Salmon** [BHS 8514] the father of Boaz,

8518 שַׂלְמַי śalmay, n.pr.m. Not used in NIV/BHS [cf. 8978]

8519 שָׂלַק śālaq, v. Not used in NIV/BHS [cf. 5956]

8520 שְׂמֹאל śemō'l, n.[m.]. [54] [→ 8521, 8522; cf. 8619]

left [45], north [6], north [+4946] [2], which way [+196+3545+6584+6584] [1]

Ge 13:9 If you go to the **left**, I'll go to the right; if you go to the right,
14:15 pursuing them as far as Hobah, **north** [+4946] of Damascus.
24:49 so I may know **which way** [+196+3545+6584+6584] to turn."
48:13 Ephraim on his right toward Israel's **left** hand and Manasseh on his
48:13 left hand and Manasseh on his **left** toward Israel's right hand,
48:14 and crossing his arms, he put his **left** hand on Manasseh's head,
Ex 14:22 on dry ground, with a wall of water on their right and on their **left**.
14:29 on dry ground, with a wall of water on their right and on their **left**.
Nu 20:17 or to the **left** until we have passed through your territory."
22:26 where there was no room to turn, either to the right or to the **left**.
Dt 2:27 on the main road; we will not turn aside to the right or to the **left**.
5:32 has commanded you; do not turn aside to the right or to the **left**.
17:11 Do not turn aside from what they tell you, to the right or to the **left**.
17:20 than his brothers and turn from the law to the right or to the **left**.
28:14 to the right or to the **left**, following other gods and serving them.
Jos 1:7 do not turn from it to the right or to the **left**, that you may be
19:27 and went north to Beth Emek and Neiel, passing Cabul on the **left**.
23:6 the Law of Moses, without turning aside to the right or to the **left**.
Jdg 3:21 Ehud reached with his **left** hand, drew the sword from his right
7:20 Grasping the torches in their **left** hands and holding in their right
16:29 his right hand on the one and his **left** hand on the other,
1Sa 6:12 and lowing all the way; they did not turn to the right or to the **left**.
2Sa 2:19 turning neither to the right nor to the **left** as he pursued him.
2:21 Then Abner said to him, "Turn aside to the right or to the **left**;
16:6 all the troops and the special guard were on David's right and **left**.
1Ki 7:39 on the south side of the temple and five on the **north** [+4946].
7:49 the lampstands of pure gold (five on the right and five on the **left**,
22:19 the host of heaven standing around him on his right and on his **left**.
2Ki 22:2 of his father David, not turning aside to the right or to the **left**.
23:8 of Joshua, the city governor, which is on the **left** of the city gate.
1Ch 6:44 [6:29] from their associates, the Merarites, at his **left** hand:
2Ch 3:17 in the front of the temple, one to the south and one to the **north**.
4:6 and placed five on the south side and five on the **north**.
4:7 them in the temple, five on the south side and five on the **north**.
4:8 them in the temple, five on the south side and five on the **north**.
18:18 with all the host of heaven standing on his right and on his **left**.
34:2 of his father David, not turning aside to the right or to the **left**.
Ne 8:4 and on his **left** were Pedaiah, Mishael, Malkijah, Hashum,
Job 23:9 When he is at work in the **north**, I do not see him; when he turns to
Pr 3:16 Long life is in her right hand; in her **left** hand are riches and honor.
4:27 Do not swerve to the right or the **left**; keep your foot from evil.
Ecc 10:2 of the wise inclines to the right, but the heart of the fool to the **left**.
SS 2:6 His **left** arm is under my head, and his right arm embraces me.
8:3 His **left** arm is under my head and his right arm embraces me.
Isa 9:20 [9:19] be hungry; on the **left** they will eat, but not be satisfied.
54:3 For you will spread out to the right and to the **left**; your
Eze 1:10 side each had the face of a lion, and on the **left** the face of an ox;
16:46 was Samaria, who lived to the **north** *of* you with her daughters;
39:3 I will strike your bow from your **left** hand and make your arrows
Da 12:7 of the river, lifted his right hand and his **left** hand toward heaven,
Jnh 4:11 thousand people who cannot tell their right hand from their **left**,
Zec 4:3 trees by it, one on the right of the bowl and the other on its **left**."
4:11 these two olive trees on the right and the **left** *of* the lampstand?"
12:6 They will consume right and **left** all the surrounding peoples,

8521 שִׂמְאֵל śim'ēl, v.den. [5] [√ 8520]

to the left [3], go to the left [1], left-handed [1]

Ge 13:9 [G] I'll go to the right; if you go to the right, *I'll* **go to the left**."
2Sa 14:19 [G] the right or **to the left** from anything my lord the king says.
1Ch 12:2 [G] shoot arrows or to sling stones right-handed or **left-handed**;
Isa 30:21 [G] Whether you turn to the right or **to the left**, your ears will
Eze 21:16 [21:21] [G] O sword, slash to the right, then **to the left**,

8522 שְׂמָאלִי śemā'lî, a. [9] [√ 8520]

north [4], left [3], *untranslated* [2]

Lev 14:15 take some of the log of oil, pour it in the palm of his own **left** hand,
14:16 **[RPH]** and with his finger sprinkle some of it before the LORD
14:26 The priest is to pour some of the oil into the palm of his own **left**
14:27 of the oil from his palm **[RPH]** seven times before the LORD.
1Ki 7:21 pillar to the south he named Jakin and the one to the **north** Boaz.
2Ki 11:11 and the temple, from the south side to the **north** side of the temple.
2Ch 3:17 one to the south he named Jakin and the *one to the* **north** Boaz.
23:10 and the temple, from the south side to the **north** side of the temple.
Eze 4:4 "Then lie on your **left** side and put the sin of the house of Israel

8523 שָׂמַח śāmaḥ, v. [154] [→ 8524, 8525]

rejoice [42], glad [30], rejoiced [11], gloat [5], rejoices [5], brings joy [4], bring joy [3], delight [3], happy [3], joy [3], make glad [3], rejoicing [3], enjoy [2], gladly [2], joyful [2], let gloat [2], made very glad [+8523] [2], pleased [2], be[s] [1], bring happiness [1], cheers up [1], cheers [1], delights [1], elated [1], exult [1], filled with joy [1], give joy [1], given cause to rejoice [1], given joy [+8525] [1], giving joy [1], gladdens [1], gladness [1], glee [1], happy [+8525] [1], held a celebration [1], joyous [1], made rejoice [1], make merry [1], makes glad [1], makes merry [1], received gladly [+6584] [1], rejoiced [+8525] [1], share joy [+8525] [1], shines brightly [1], take pleasure [1]

Ex 4:14 [A] to meet you, and his heart *will be* **glad** when he sees you.
Lev 23:40 [A] and **rejoice** before the LORD your God for seven days.
Dt 12:7 [A] and *shall* **rejoice** in everything you have put your hand to,
12:12 [A] there **rejoice** before the LORD your God, you, your sons
12:18 [A] *you are to* **rejoice** before the LORD your God in
14:26 [A] there in the presence of the LORD your God and **rejoice**.
16:11 [A] **rejoice** before the LORD your God at the place he will
16:14 [A] *Be* **joyful** at your Feast—you, your sons and daughters, your
24:5 [D] at home and **bring happiness** *to* the wife he has married.
26:11 [A] the aliens among you *shall* **rejoice** in all the good things the
27:7 [A] and **rejoicing** in the presence of the LORD your God.
33:18 [A] "**Rejoice**, Zebulun, in your going out, and you, Issachar,
Jdg 9:13 [D] 'Should I give up my wine, which **cheers** both gods and men,
9:19 [A] *may* Abimelech *be your* **joy**, and may you be his, too!
9:19 [A] may Abimelech be your joy, and *may* you **be**[s] his, too!
19:3 [A] and when her father saw him, *he* **gladly** welcomed him.
1Sa 2:1 [A] boasts over my enemies, for *I* **delight** in your deliverance.
6:13 [A] they looked up and saw the ark, *they* **rejoiced** at the sight.
11:9 [A] and reported this to the men of Jabesh, *they were* **elated**.
11:15 [A] and Saul and all the Israelites **held a** great **celebration**.
19:5 [A] a great victory for all Israel, and you saw it and *were* **glad**.
2Sa 1:20 [A] of Ashkelon, lest the daughters of the Philistines *be* **glad**,
1Ki 5:7 [5:21] [A] *he was* greatly **pleased** and said, "Praise be to the

2Ki 11:20 [A] all the people of the land **rejoiced**. And the city was quiet,
1Ch 16:10 [A] *let* the hearts of those who seek the LORD **rejoice**.
16:31 [A] *Let* the heavens **rejoice**, let the earth be glad; let them say
29: 9 [A] The people **rejoiced** at the willing response of their leaders,
29: 9 [A] to the LORD. David the king also **rejoiced** [+8525] greatly.
2Ch 6:41 [A] with salvation, *may* your saints **rejoice** in your goodness.
15:15 [A] All Judah **rejoiced** about the oath because they had sworn it
20:27 [D] for the LORD *had* **given** them **cause to rejoice** over their
23:21 [A] all the people of the land **rejoiced**. And the city was quiet,
24:10 [A] and all the people brought their contributions **gladly**,
29:36 [A] all the people **rejoiced** at what God had brought about for his
30:25 [A] The entire assembly of Judah **rejoiced**, along with the priests
Ezr 6:22 [D] because the LORD *had* **filled** them **with joy** by changing
Ne 12:43 [A] **rejoicing** because God had given them great joy.
12:43 [D] rejoicing because God *had* **given** them great **joy** [+8525].
12:43 [A] given them great joy. The women and children also **rejoiced**.
Est 8:15 [A] of fine linen. And the city of Susa held a **joyous** celebration.
Job 21:12 [A] and harp; *they* **make merry** to the sound of the flute.
22:19 [A] "The righteous see their ruin and **rejoice**; the innocent mock
31:25 [A] if *I have* **rejoiced** *over* my great wealth, the fortune my
31:29 [A] "If *I have* **rejoiced** at my enemy's misfortune or gloated
Ps 5:11 [5:12] [A] *let* all who take refuge in you *be* **glad**; let them ever
9: 2 [9:3] [A] *I will be* **glad** and rejoice in you; I will sing praise to
14: 7 [A] fortunes of his people, let Jacob rejoice and Israel *be* **glad**!
16: 9 [A] Therefore my heart *is* **glad** and my tongue rejoices; my body
19: 8 [19:9] [D] of the LORD are right, **giving joy** *to* the heart.
21: 1 [21:2] [A] O LORD, the king **rejoices** in your strength. How
30: 1 [30:2] [D] the depths and *did* not **let** my enemies **gloat** over me.
31: 7 [31:8] [A] I will be glad and **rejoice** in your love, for you saw
32:11 [A] **Rejoice** in the LORD and be glad, you righteous; sing,
33:21 [A] In him our hearts **rejoice**, for we trust in his holy name.
34: 2 [34:3] [A] in the LORD; let the afflicted hear and **rejoice**.
35:15 [A] when I stumbled, they gathered *in* **glee**; attackers gathered
35:19 [A] *Let* not *those* **gloat** over me who are my enemies without
35:24 [A] O LORD my God; *do* not *let them* **gloat** over me.
35:27 [A] who delight in my vindication shout for joy and **gladness**;
38:16 [38:17] [A] "*Do* not *let them* **gloat** or exalt themselves over me
40:16 [40:17] [A] may all who seek you rejoice and *be* **glad** in you;
45: 8 [45:9] [D] with ivory the music of the strings **makes** you **glad**.
46: 4 [46:5] [D] There is a river whose streams **make glad** the city of
48:11 [48:12] [A] Mount Zion **rejoices**, the villages of Judah are glad
53: 6 [53:7] [A] of his people, let Jacob rejoice and Israel *be* **glad**!
58:10 [58:11] [A] The righteous *will be* **glad** when they are avenged,
63:11 [63:12] [A] the king *will* **rejoice** in God; all who swear by
64:10 [64:11] [A] *Let* the righteous **rejoice** in the LORD and take
66: 6 [A] through the waters on foot—*come, let us* **rejoice** in him.
67: 4 [67:5] [A] *May* the nations *be* **glad** and sing for joy, for you
68: 3 [68:4] [A] *may* the righteous *be* **glad** and rejoice before God;
69:32 [69:33] [A] The poor will see and *be* **glad**—you who seek God,
70: 4 [70:5] [A] may all who seek you rejoice and *be* **glad** in you;
85: 6 [85:7] [A] revive us again, that your people *may* **rejoice** in you?
86: 4 [D] **Bring joy** *to* your servant, for to you, O Lord, I lift up my
89:42 [89:43] [G] of his foes; *you have* **made** all his enemies **rejoice**.
90:14 [A] that we may sing for joy and *be* **glad** all our days.
90:15 [D] **Make** us **glad** for as many days as you have afflicted us,
92: 4 [92:5] [D] For *you* **make** me **glad** by your deeds, O LORD;
96:11 [A] *Let* the heavens **rejoice**, let the earth be glad; let the sea
97: 1 [A] The LORD reigns, *let* the earth *be* **glad**; let the distant
97: 8 [A] Zion hears and **rejoices** and the villages of Judah are glad
97:12 [A] **Rejoice** in the LORD, *you* who are righteous, and praise his
104:15 [D] wine *that* **gladdens** the heart of man, oil to make his face
104:31 [A] endure forever; *may* the LORD **rejoice** in his works—
104:34 [A] meditation be pleasing to him, *as* I **rejoice** in the LORD.
105: 3 [A] *let* the hearts of those who seek the LORD **rejoice**.
105:38 [A] Egypt *was* **glad** when they left, because dread of Israel had
106: 5 [A] that I *may* **share** in the **joy of** [+8525] your nation and join
107:30 [A] *They were* **glad** when it grew calm, and he guided them to
107:42 [A] The upright see and **rejoice**, but all the wicked shut their
109:28 [A] they will be put to shame, but your servant *will* **rejoice**.
118:24 [A] the day the LORD has made; let us rejoice and *be* **glad** in it.
119:74 [A] *May* those who fear you **rejoice** when they see me, for I
122: 1 [A] *I* **rejoiced** with those who said to me, "Let us go to the house
149: 2 [A] *Let* Israel **rejoice** in their Maker; let the people of Zion be
Pr 5:18 [A] be blessed, and *may you* **rejoice** in the wife of your youth.
10: 1 [D] A wise son **brings joy** *to* his father, but a foolish son grief to
12:25 [D] heart weighs a man down, but a kind word **cheers** him **up**.
13: 9 [A] The light of the righteous **shines brightly**, but the lamp of
15:20 [D] A wise son **brings joy** *to* his father, but a foolish man
15:30 [D] A cheerful look **brings joy** *to* the heart, and good news gives
17:21 [A] for a son brings grief; *there is* no **joy** *for* the father of a fool.
23:15 [A] My son, if your heart is wise, then my heart *will be* **glad**;
23:24 [A] man has great joy; he who has a wise son **delights** in him.
23:25 [A] *May* your father and mother *be* **glad**; may she who gave you
24:17 [A] *Do* not **gloat** when your enemy falls; when he stumbles,
27: 9 [D] Perfume and incense **bring joy** *to* the heart,
27:11 [D] Be wise, my son, and **bring joy** *to* my heart; then I can
29: 2 [A] When the righteous thrive, the people **rejoice**; when the
29: 3 [D] A man who loves wisdom **brings joy** *to* his father, but a
29: 6 [A] by his own sin, but a righteous one can sing and *be* **glad**.
Ecc 3:12 [A] I know that there is nothing better for men than to *be* **happy**
3:22 [A] So I saw that there is nothing better for a man than *to* **enjoy**
4:16 [A] those who came later *were* not **pleased** with the successor.
5:19 [5:18] [A] to accept his lot and *be* **happy** in his work—
8:15 [A] for a man under the sun than to eat and drink and *be* **glad**.
10:19 [D] A feast is made for laughter, and wine **makes** life **merry**,
11: 8 [A] However many years a man may live, *let him* **enjoy** them all.
11: 9 [A] *Be* **happy**, young man, while you are young, and let your
SS 1: 4 [A] We rejoice and **delight** in you; we will praise your love more
Isa 9: 3 [9:2] [A] *they* **rejoice** before you as people rejoice at the
9:17 [9:16] [A] Therefore the Lord *will* **take** no **pleasure** in the
14: 8 [A] pine trees and the cedars of Lebanon **exult** over you and say,
14:29 [A] *Do* not **rejoice**, all you Philistines, that the rod that struck
25: 9 [A] we trusted in him; let us rejoice and *be* **glad** in his salvation."
39: 2 [A] Hezekiah **received** the envoys **gladly** [+6584] and showed
56: 7 [D] my holy mountain and **give** them **joy** in my house of prayer.
65:13 [A] my servants *will* **rejoice**, but you will be put to shame.
66:10 [A] "**Rejoice** with Jerusalem and be glad for her, all you who
Jer 20:15 [D] *who* **made** him **very glad** [+8523], saying, "A child is born
20:15 [D] *who* **made** him **very glad** [+8523], saying, "A child is born
31:13 [A] maidens *will* dance and *be* **glad**, young men and old as well.
31:13 [D] I will give them comfort and **joy** instead of sorrow.
41:13 [A] and the army officers who were with him, *they were* **glad**.
50:11 [A] "Because *you* **rejoice** and are glad, you who pillage my
La 2:17 [D] *he has* **let** the enemy **gloat** over you, he has exalted the horn
4:21 [A] Rejoice and *be* **glad**, O Daughter of Edom, you who live in
Eze 7:12 [A] *Let* not the buyer **rejoice** nor the seller grieve, for wrath is
25: 6 [A] **rejoicing** with all the malice of your heart against the land of
35:14 [A] While the whole earth **rejoices**, I will make you desolate.
Hos 7: 3 [D] "*They* **delight** the king with their wickedness, the princes
9: 1 [A] *Do* not **rejoice**, O Israel; do not be jubilant like the other
Joel 2:21 [A] Be not afraid, O land; be glad and **rejoice**.
2:23 [A] Be glad, O people of Zion, **rejoice** in the LORD your God,
Ob 1:12 [A] nor **rejoice** over the people of Judah in the day of their
Jnh 4: 6 [A] and Jonah *was* very **happy** [+8525] about the vine.
Mic 7: 8 [A] *Do* not **gloat** over me, my enemy! Though I have fallen,
Hab 1:15 [A] them up in his dragnet; and so *he* **rejoices** and is glad.
Zep 3:14 [A] *Be* **glad** and rejoice with all your heart, O Daughter of
Zec 2:10 [2:14] [A] "Shout and *be* **glad**, O Daughter of Zion. For I am
4:10 [A] *Men will* **rejoice** when they see the plumb line in the hand of
10: 7 [A] like mighty men, and their hearts *will be* **glad** as with wine.
10: 7 [A] Their children will see it and *be* **joyful**; their hearts will

8524 שָׂמֵחַ *śāmēaḥ*, a.vbl. [21] [√ 8523]

happy [5], joyful [2], rejoicing [2], cheerful [1], cheering [1], delight in [1], delight [1], filled with gladness [+448+1637] [1], filled with joy [1], gloat [1], gloats [1], joy [1], merrymakers [+4213] [1], rejoice [1], rejoicing [+8525] [1]

Dt 16:15 and in all the work of your hands, and your **joy** will be complete.
1Ki 1:40 went up after him, playing flutes and **rejoicing** [+8525] greatly,
1:45 From there they have gone up **cheering**, and the city resounds with
4:20 sand on the seashore; they ate, they drank and they were **happy**.
8:66 **joyful** and glad in heart for all the good things the LORD had
2Ki 11:14 all the people of the land were **rejoicing** and blowing trumpets.
2Ch 7:10 **joyful** and glad in heart for the good things the LORD had done
23:13 all the people of the land were **rejoicing** and blowing trumpets,
Est 5: 9 Haman went out that day **happy** and in high spirits. But when he
5:14 go with the king to the dinner and be **happy**." This suggestion
Job 3:22 who are **filled with gladness** [+448+1637] and rejoice when they
Ps 35:26 May all *who* **gloat** *over* my distress be put to shame
113: 9 He settles the barren woman in her home as a **happy** mother of
126: 3 LORD has done great things for us, and we are **filled with joy**.
Pr 2:14 who **delight in** doing wrong and rejoice in the perverseness of evil,
15:13 A **happy** heart makes the face cheerful, but heartache crushes the
17: 5 their Maker; *whoever* **gloats** over disaster will not go unpunished.
17:22 A **cheerful** heart is good medicine, but a crushed spirit dries up the
Ecc 2:10 My heart *took* **delight** in all my work, and this was the reward for
Isa 24: 7 and the vine withers; all the **merrymakers** [+4213] groan.
Am 6:13 *you who* **rejoice** in the conquest of Lo Debar and say, "Did we not

8525 שִׂמְחָה *śimḥâ*, n.f. [94] [√ 8523]

joy [46], gladness [10], rejoicing [6], pleasure [5], rejoice [3], joyful [2], joyfully [+928] [2], joyfully [2], rejoiced [2], celebrate [1], delight [1], delights [1], enjoyment [1], given joy [+8523] [1], glad occasions [1], glee [1], happiness [1], happy [+8523] [1], joyful songs [1], pleased [1], rejoiced [+8523] [1], rejoicing [+8524] [1], revelry [1], share joy [+8523] [1], take great delight [+928+8464] [1]

Ge 31:27 so I could send you away with **joy** and singing to the music of
Nu 10:10 Also at your times of **rejoicing**—your appointed feasts and New
Dt 28:47 Because you did not serve the LORD your God **joyfully** [+928]
Jdg 16:23 to offer a great sacrifice to Dagon their god and to **celebrate**,
1Sa 18:6 and dancing, with **joyful songs** and with tambourines and lutes.
2Sa 6:12 from the house of Obed-Edom to the City of David with **rejoicing**.
1Ki 1:40 went up after him, playing flutes and **rejoicing** [+8524] greatly,
1Ch 12:40 [12:41] oil, cattle and sheep, for there was **joy** in Israel.
15:16 the Levites to appoint their brothers as singers to sing **joyful** songs,
15:25 of the LORD from the house of Obed-Edom, with **rejoicing**.
29:9 to the LORD. David the king also **rejoiced** [+8523] greatly.
29:17 now I have seen with **joy** how willingly your people who are here
29:22 and drank with great **joy** in the presence of the LORD that day.
2Ch 20:27 men of Judah and Jerusalem returned **joyfully** [+928] to Jerusalem,
23:18 Law of Moses, with **rejoicing** and singing, as David had ordered.
29:30 So they sang praises with **gladness** and bowed their heads
30:21 the Feast of Unleavened Bread for seven days with great **rejoicing**,
30:23 more days; so for another seven days they celebrated **joyfully**.
30:26 There was great **joy** in Jerusalem, for since the days of Solomon
Ezr 3:12 of this temple being laid, while many others shouted for **joy**.
3:13 No one could distinguish the sound of the shouts of **joy** from the
6:22 For seven days they celebrated with **joy** the Feast of Unleavened
Ne 8:12 and drink, to send portions of food and to celebrate with great **joy**,
8:17 had not celebrated it like this. And their **joy** was very great.
12:27 were brought to Jerusalem to celebrate **joyfully** the dedication with
12:43 rejoicing because God *had* **given** them great **joy** [+8523].
12:43 The sound of **rejoicing** *in* Jerusalem could be heard far away.
12:44 for Judah was **pleased** with the ministering priests and Levites.
Est 8:16 For the Jews it was a time of happiness and **joy**, gladness
8:17 there was **joy** and gladness among the Jews, with feasting
9:17 on the fourteenth they rested and made it a day of feasting and **joy**.
9:18 on the fifteenth they rested and made it a day of feasting and **joy**.
9:19 observe the fourteenth of the month of Adar as a day of **joy**
9:22 as the month when their sorrow was turned into **joy** and their
9:22 **joy** and giving presents of food to one another and gifts to the
Job 20:5 of the wicked is brief, the **joy** *of* the godless lasts but a moment.
Ps 4:7 [4:8] You have filled my heart with greater **joy** than when their
16:11 you will fill me with **joy** in your presence, with eternal pleasures at
21:6 [21:7] and made him glad with the **joy** of your presence.
30:11 [30:12] you removed my sackcloth and clothed me with **joy**,
43:4 Then will I go to the altar of God, to God, my **joy** and my delight.
45:15 [45:16] They are led in with **joy** and gladness; they enter the
51:8 [51:10] Let me hear joy and **gladness**; let the bones you have
68:3 [68:4] and rejoice before God; may they be happy and **joyful**.
97:11 Light is shed upon the righteous and **joy** on the upright in heart.
100:2 Worship the LORD with **gladness**; come before him with joyful
106:5 that I *may* **share** in the **joy** [+8523] *of* your nation and join your
137:3 captors asked us for songs, our tormentors demanded songs of **joy**;
137:6 not remember you, if I do not consider Jerusalem my highest **joy**.
Pr 10:28 The prospect of the righteous is **joy**, but the hopes of the wicked
12:20 hearts of those who plot evil, but **joy** for those who promote peace.
14:10 heart knows its own bitterness, and no one else can share its **joy**.
14:13 Even in laughter the heart may ache, and **joy** may end in grief.
15:21 Folly **delights** a man who lacks judgment, but a man of
15:23 A man finds **joy** in giving an apt reply—and how good is a timely
21:15 justice is done, it brings **joy** to the righteous but terror to evildoers.
21:17 He who loves **pleasure** will become poor; whoever loves wine
Ecc 2:1 I will test you with **pleasure** to find out what is good."
2:2 I said, "is foolish. And what does **pleasure** accomplish?"
2:10 myself nothing my eyes desired; I refused my heart no **pleasure**.
2:26 who pleases him, God gives wisdom, knowledge and **happiness**,
5:20 [5:19] because God keeps him occupied with **gladness** *of* heart.
7:4 of mourning, but the heart of fools is in the house of **pleasure**.
8:15 So I commend the **enjoyment** of life, because nothing is better for
9:7 Go, eat your food with **gladness**, and drink your wine with a joyful
SS 3:11 crowned him on the day of his wedding, the day his heart **rejoiced**.
Isa 9:3 [9:2] You have enlarged the nation and increased their **joy**;
9:3 [9:2] they rejoice before you as people **rejoice** at the harvest,
16:10 **Joy** and gladness are taken away from the orchards; no one sings
22:13 see, there is joy and **revelry**, slaughtering of cattle and killing of
24:11 all **joy** turns to gloom, all gaiety is banished from the earth.
29:19 Once more the humble will **rejoice** in the LORD; the needy will
30:29 your hearts will **rejoice** as when people go up with flutes to the
35:10 enter Zion with singing; everlasting **joy** will crown their heads.
35:10 Gladness and **joy** will overtake them, and sorrow and sighing will
51:3 Joy and **gladness** will be found in her, thanksgiving and the sound
51:11 enter Zion with singing; everlasting **joy** will crown their heads.
51:11 Gladness and **joy** will overtake them, and sorrow and sighing will
55:12 You will go out in **joy** and be led forth in peace; the mountains
61:7 a double portion in their land, and everlasting **joy** will be theirs.
66:5 have said, 'Let the LORD be glorified, that we may see your **joy**!'
Jer 7:34 **gladness** and to the voices of bride and bridegroom in the towns of
15:16 they were my joy and my heart's **delight**, for I bear your name,
16:9 **gladness** and to the voices of bride and bridegroom in this place.
25:10 I will banish from them the sounds of joy and **gladness**, the voices
31:7 "Sing with **joy** for Jacob; shout for the foremost of the nations.
33:11 the sounds of joy and **gladness**, the voices of bride
48:33 **Joy** and gladness are gone from the orchards and fields of Moab.
Eze 35:15 Because you **rejoiced** when the inheritance of the house of Israel
36:5 for with **glee** and with malice *in* their hearts they made my land
Joel 1:16 our very eyes—**joy** and gladness from the house of our God?
Jnh 4:6 his discomfort, and Jonah *was* very **happy** [+8523] about the vine.
Zep 3:17 *He will* **take great delight** [+928+8464] in you, he will quiet you
Zec 8:19 become joyful and **glad occasions** and happy festivals for Judah.

8526 שְׂמִיכָה *śᵉmîkâ*, n.f. [1] [√ 8527]

covering [1]

Jdg 4:18 be afraid." So he entered her tent, and she put a **covering** over him.

8527 שָׂמַךְ *śāmak*, v. Not used in NIV/BHS [→ 8526; cf. 6164]

8528 שַׂמְלָה *śamlâ*, n.pr.m. [4] [→ 8529, 8530]

Samlah [4]

Ge 36:36 When Hadad died, **Samlah** from Masrekah succeeded him as king.
36:37 When **Samlah** died, Shaul from Rehoboth on the river succeeded
1Ch 1:47 When Hadad died, **Samlah** from Masrekah succeeded him as king.
1:48 When **Samlah** died, Shaul from Rehoboth on the river succeeded

8529 שִׂמְלָה *śimlâ*, n.f. [29] [√ 8528; cf. 8515]

clothes [12], clothing [7], cloak [4], garment [3], cloth [2], best clothes [1]

Ge 9:23 Shem and Japheth took a **garment** and laid it across their
35:2 you have with you, and purify yourselves and change your **clothes**.
37:34 Jacob tore his **clothes**, put on sackcloth and mourned for his son
41:14 When he had shaved and changed his **clothes**, he came before
44:13 At this, they tore their **clothes**. Then they all loaded their donkeys
45:22 To each of them he gave new **clothing**, but to Benjamin he gave
45:22 he gave three hundred shekels of silver and five sets of **clothes**.
Ex 3:22 living in her house for articles of silver and gold and for **clothing**,
12:34 it on their shoulders in kneading troughs wrapped in **clothing**.
12:35 asked the Egyptians for articles of silver and gold and for **clothing**.
19:10 them today and tomorrow. Have them wash their **clothes**
19:14 to the people, he consecrated them, and they washed their **clothes**.
22:27 [22:26] because his **cloak** is the only covering he has for his body.
Dt 8:4 Your **clothes** did not wear out and your feet did not swell during
10:18 and the widow, and loves the alien, giving him food and **clothing**.
21:13 and put aside the **clothes** she was wearing when captured.
22:3 if you find your brother's donkey or his **cloak** or anything he loses.
22:5 must not wear men's clothing, nor a man wear women's **clothing**,
22:17 her parents shall display the **cloth** before the elders of the town,
Jos 7:6 Joshua tore his **clothes** and fell facedown to the ground before the
Jdg 8:25 So they spread out a **garment**, and each man threw a ring from his
Ru 3:3 Wash and perfume yourself, and put on your **best clothes**.
1Sa 21:9 [21:10] of Elah, is here; it is wrapped in a **cloth** behind the ephod.
2Sa 12:20 After he had washed, put on lotions and changed his **clothes**,
Pr 30:4 Who has wrapped up the waters in his **cloak**? Who has established
Isa 3:6 his father's home, and say, "You have a **cloak**, you be our leader;
3:7 I have no food or **clothing** in my house; do not make me the leader
4:1 and say, "We will eat our own food and provide our own **clothes**;
9:5 [9:4] every **garment** rolled in blood will be destined for burning,

8530 שַׂמְלַי *śamlay*, n.pr.m. Not used in NIV/BHS [√ 8528]

8531 שָׂמַם *śāmam*, v. [1] [cf. 6167]

painted [+928+2021+7037] [1]

2Ki 9:30 [A] Jezebel heard about it, *she* **painted** [+928+2021+7037] her eyes

8532 שְׂמָמִית *śᵉmāmît*, n.f. [1]

lizard [1]

Pr 30:28 a **lizard** can be caught with the hand, yet it is found in kings'

8533 שָׂנֵא *śānēʾ*, v. [146] [→ 2190, 6171, 6176, 8534, 8535; Ar 10686]

hate [59], hated [16], hates [14], foes [11], enemies [9], adversaries [3], dislikes [3], enemy [3], malice aforethought [+4200+4946+8997 +9453] [3], foe [2], thoroughly hated [+8533] [2], unloved [2], abhor [1], am not loved [1], are shunned [1], both[s] [+170+2021+2021+2256] [1], detest [1], enemies [+5883] [1], enemy's [1], hate [+8534] [1], have hatred [+8534] [1], hostile [1], is hated [1], malice aforethought

[+4946+8997+9453] [1], malicious [1], not love [1], not loved [1], not[s] [1], refuses [1], shunned [1], them[s] [+2157] [1]

Ge 24:60 [A] may your offspring possess the gates of their **enemies**."
26:27 [A] to me, since you *were* **hostile** *to* me and sent me away?"
29:31 [B] When the LORD saw that Leah *was* **not loved**, he opened
29:33 [B] "Because the LORD heard that I **am not loved**, he gave me
37: 4 [A] *they* **hated** him and could not speak a kind word to him.
37: 5 [A] when he told it to his brothers, *they* **hated** him all the more.
37: 8 [A] *they* **hated** him all the more because of his dream and what
Ex 1:10 [A] will join our **enemies**, fight against us and leave the
18:21 [A] who fear God, trustworthy men *who* **hate** dishonest gain—
20: 5 [A] to the third and fourth generation of *those who* **hate** me,
23: 5 [A] If you see the donkey of *someone who* **hates** you fallen
Lev 19:17 [A] " '*Do* not **hate** your brother in your heart. Rebuke your
26:17 [A] *those who* **hate** you will rule over you, and you will flee
Nu 10:35 [D] your enemies be scattered; may your **foes** flee before you."
Dt 4:42 [A] without **malice** [+4200+4946+8997+9453] **aforethought**.
5: 9 [A] to the third and fourth generation of *those who* **hate** me,
7:10 [A] *those who* **hate** him he will repay to their face by
7:10 [A] he will not be slow to repay to their face *those who* **hate**
7:15 [A] knew in Egypt, but he will inflict them on all *who* **hate** you.
12:31 [A] they do all kinds of detestable things the LORD **hates**.
16:22 [A] erect a sacred stone, for these the LORD your God **hates**.
19: 4 [A] without **malice** [+4200+4946+8997+9453] **aforethought**.
19: 6 [A] without **malice** [+4946+8997+9453] **aforethought**.
19:11 [A] if a man **hates** his neighbor and lies in wait for him, assaults
21:15 [B] and he loves one but **not**[s] the other, and both bear him sons
21:15 [B] and **both**[s] [+170+2021+2021+2256] bear him sons but the
21:16 [B] to his actual firstborn, the son of the wife *he does* **not love**.
21:17 [B] He must acknowledge the son of his **unloved** wife as the
22:13 [A] If a man takes a wife and, after lying with her, **dislikes** her
22:16 [A] my daughter in marriage to this man, but *he* **dislikes** her.
24: 3 [A] her second husband **dislikes** her and writes her a certificate
30: 7 [A] your God will put all these curses on your enemies who **hate**
32:41 [D] vengeance on my adversaries and repay *those who* **hate** me.
33:11 [D] rise up against him; strike his **foes** till they rise no more."
Jos 20: 5 [A] without **malice** [+4200+4946+8997+9453] **aforethought**.
Jdg 11: 7 [A] "Didn't you **hate** me and drive me from my father's house?
14:16 [A] wife threw herself on him, sobbing, "*You* **hate** me!
15: 2 [A] "I was so sure *you* **thoroughly hated** [+8533] her," he said,
15: 2 [A] "I was so sure *you* **thoroughly hated** [+8533] her," he said,
2Sa 5: 8 [A] those 'lame and blind' *who are* David's **enemies** [+5883]."
13:15 [A] Amnon **hated** her *with* intense hatred. In fact, he hated her
13:15 [A] In fact, *he* **hated** her more than he had loved her. Amnon
13:22 [A] he **hated** Amnon because he had disgraced his sister Tamar.
19: 6 [19:7] [A] You love *those who* **hate** you and hate those who
19: 6 [19:7] [A] those who hate you and **hate** those who love you.
22:18 [A] powerful enemy, from my **foes**, who were too strong for me.
22:41 [D] enemies turn their backs in flight, and I destroyed my **foes**.
1Ki 22: 8 [A] I **hate** him because he never prophesies anything good about
2Ch 1:11 [A] riches or honor, nor for the death of your **enemies**,
18: 7 [A] I **hate** him because he never prophesies anything good about
19: 2 [A] you help the wicked and love *those who* **hate** the LORD?
Est 9: 1 [A] and the Jews got the upper hand over *those who* **hated** them.
9: 5 [A] and they did what they pleased to *those who* **hated** them.
9:16 [A] They killed seventy-five thousand of **them**[s] [+2157] but did
Job 8:22 [A] Your **enemies** will be clothed in shame, and the tents of the
31:29 [D] "If I have rejoiced at my **enemy's** misfortune or gloated over
34:17 [A] *Can he who* **hates** justice govern? Will you condemn the
Ps 5: 5 [5:6] [A] stand in your presence; *you* **hate** all who do wrong.
9:13 [9:14] [A] O LORD, see how my **enemies** persecute me!
11: 5 [A] but the wicked and those who love violence his soul **hates**.
18:17 [18:18] [A] from my **foes**, who were too strong for me.
18:40 [18:41] [D] turn their backs in flight, and I destroyed my **foes**.
21: 8 [21:9] [A] your enemies; your right hand will seize your **foes**.
25:19 [A] have increased and how fiercely *they* **hate** [+8534] me!
26: 5 [A] *I* **abhor** the assembly of evildoers and refuse to sit with the
31: 6 [31:7] [A] *I* **hate** those who cling to worthless idols; I trust in
34:21 [34:22] [A] the **foes** *of* the righteous will be condemned.
35:19 [A] let not *those who* **hate** me without reason maliciously wink
36: 2 [36:3] [A] he flatters himself too much to detect or **hate** his sin.
38:19 [38:20] [A] *those who* **hate** me without reason are numerous.
41: 7 [41:8] [A] All my **enemies** whisper together against me;
44: 7 [44:8] [D] over our enemies, you put our **adversaries** to shame.
44:10 [44:11] [D] the enemy, and our **adversaries** have plundered us.
45: 7 [45:8] [A] You love righteousness and **hate** wickedness;
50:17 [A] You **hate** my instruction and cast my words behind you.
55:12 [55:13] [D] if a **foe** were raising himself against me, I could
68: 1 [68:2] [D] enemies be scattered; may his **foes** flee before him.
69: 4 [69:5] [A] *Those who* **hate** me without reason outnumber the
69:14 [69:15] [A] deliver me from *those who* **hate** me, from the deep
81:15 [81:16] [D] *Those who* **hate** the LORD would cringe before
83: 2 [83:3] [D] enemies are astir, how your **foes** rear their heads.
86:17 [A] that my **enemies** may see it and be put to shame, for you,
89:23 [89:24] [D] foes before him and strike down his **adversaries**.
97:10 [A] Let those who love the LORD **hate** evil, for he guards the
101: 3 [A] The deeds of faithless men *I* **hate**; they will not cling to me.
105:25 [A] whose hearts he turned to **hate** his people, to conspire against
106:10 [A] He saved them from the hand of the **foe**; from the hand of the
106:41 [A] them over to the nations, and their **foes** ruled over them.
118: 7 [A] he is my helper. I will look in triumph on my **enemies**.
119:104 [A] from your precepts; therefore *I* **hate** every wrong path.
119:113 [A] *I* **hate** double-minded men, but I love your law.
119:128 [A] I consider all your precepts right, *I* **hate** every wrong path.
119:163 [A] *I* **hate** and abhor falsehood but I love your law.
120: 6 [A] Too long have I lived among *those who* **hate** peace.
129: 5 [A] May all *who* **hate** Zion be turned back in shame.
139:21 [A] *Do I* not **hate** those who hate you, O LORD, and abhor
139:21 [D] Do I not hate *those who* **hate** you, O LORD, and abhor
139:22 [A] *I* **have** nothing but **hatred** [+8534] *for* them; I count them
Pr 1:22 [A] will mockers delight in mockery and fools **hate** knowledge?
1:29 [A] Since *they* **hated** knowledge and did not choose to fear the
5:12 [A] You will say, "How *I* **hated** discipline! How my heart
6:16 [A] There are six things the LORD **hates**, seven that are
8:13 [A] To fear the LORD is *to* **hate** evil; I hate pride
8:13 [A] *I* **hate** pride and arrogance, evil behavior and perverse
8:36 [D] fails to find me harms himself; all *who* **hate** me love death."
9: 8 [A] Do not rebuke a mocker or *he will* **hate** you; rebuke a wise
11:15 [A] but *whoever* **refuses** to strike hands in pledge is safe.
12: 1 [A] loves knowledge, but *he who* **hates** correction is stupid.
13: 5 [A] The righteous **hate** what is false, but the wicked bring shame
13:24 [A] He who spares the rod **hates** his son, but he who loves him is
14:17 [C] man does foolish things, and a crafty man **is hated**.
14:20 [C] The poor **are shunned** even by their neighbors, but the rich
15:10 [A] him who leaves the path; *he who* **hates** correction will die.
15:27 [A] trouble to his family, but *he who* **hates** bribes will live.
19: 7 [A] A poor man *is* **shunned** *by* all his relatives—how much more
25:17 [A] neighbor's house—too much of you, and *he will* **hate** you.
25:21 [A] If your **enemy** is hungry, give him food to eat; if he is thirsty,
26:24 [A] A **malicious** *man* disguises himself with his lips, but in his
26:28 [A] A lying tongue **hates** those it hurts, and a flattering mouth
27: 6 [A] from a friend can be trusted, but an **enemy** multiplies kisses.
28:16 [A] but *he who* **hates** ill-gotten gain will enjoy a long life.
29:10 [A] Bloodthirsty men **hate** a man of integrity and seek to kill the
29:24 [A] The accomplice of a thief is his own **enemy**; he is put under
30:23 [B] an **unloved** *woman* who is married, and a maidservant who
Ecc 2:17 [A] So *I* **hated** life, because the work that is done under the sun
2:18 [A] I **hated** all the things I had toiled for under the sun, because I
3: 8 [A] a time to love and a time to **hate**, a time for war and a time
Isa 1:14 [A] Moon festivals and your appointed feasts my soul **hates**.
60:15 [B] "Although you have been forsaken and **hated**, with no one
61: 8 [A] "For I, the LORD, love justice; I **hate** robbery and iniquity.
66: 5 [A] "Your brothers *who* **hate** you, and exclude you because of
Jer 12: 8 [A] like a lion in the forest. She roars at me; therefore *I* **hate** her.
44: 4 [A] who said, 'Do not do this detestable thing that *I* **hate**!'
Eze 16:27 [A] I gave you over to the greed of your **enemies**, the daughters
16:37 [A] found pleasure, those you loved as well as those *you* **hated**.
23:28 [A] I am about to hand you over to those *you* **hate**, to those you
35: 6 [A] Since *you did* not **hate** bloodshed, bloodshed will pursue
Hos 9:15 [A] of all their wickedness in Gilgal, *I* **hated** them there.
Am 5:10 [A] *you* **hate** the one who reproves in court and despise him who
5:15 [A] **Hate** evil, love good; maintain justice in the courts.
5:21 [A] "*I* **hate**, I despise your religious feasts; I cannot stand your
6: 8 [A] "I abhor the pride of Jacob and **detest** his fortresses; I will
Mic 3: 2 [A] *you who* **hate** good and love evil; who tear the skin from my
Zec 8:17 [A] love to swear falsely. *I* **hate** all this," declares the LORD.
Mal 1: 3 [A] Esau *I have* **hated**, and I have turned his mountains into a
2:16 [A] "*I* **hate** divorce," says the LORD God of Israel, "and I hate

8534 שִׂנְאָה *śin'â*, n.f. [17] [√ 8533]

hatred [8], hate [2], *untranslated* [1], hate [+8533] [1], hated [1], hates [1], have hatred [+8533] [1], malice aforethought [1], malice [1]

Nu 35:20 If anyone with **malice aforethought** shoves another or throws
Dt 1:27 You grumbled in your tents and said, "The LORD **hates** us;
9:28 because he **hated** them, he brought them out to put them to death
2Sa 13:15 Amnon hated her with intense **hatred**. In fact, he hated her more
13:15 In fact, he hated her more **[RPH]** than he had loved her. Amnon
Ps 25:19 enemies have increased and how fiercely *they* **hate** [+8533] me!
109: 3 With words of **hatred** they surround me; they attack me without
109: 5 They repay me evil for good, and **hatred** for my friendship.
139:22 *I* **have** nothing but **hatred for** [+8533] them; I count them my
Pr 10:12 **Hatred** stirs up dissension, but love covers over all wrongs.
10:18 He who conceals his **hatred** has lying lips, and whoever spreads
15:17 of vegetables where there is love than a fattened calf with **hatred**.
26:26 His **malice** may be concealed by deception, but his wickedness
Ecc 9: 1 God's hands, but no man knows whether love or **hate** awaits him.

Ecc 9: 6 Their love, their **hate** and their jealousy have long since vanished;
Eze 23:29 They will deal with you in **hatred** and take away everything you
35:11 with the anger and jealousy you showed in your **hatred** of them

8535 שָׂנִיא **śānî'**, a. [1] [√ 8533]

not love [1]

Dt 21:15 him sons but the firstborn is the son of the wife *he does* **not love**,

8536 שְׂנִיר **śᵉnîr**, n.pr.loc. [4]

Senir [4]

Dt 3: 9 is called Sirion by the Sidonians; the Amorites call it **Senir**.)
1Ch 5:23 from Bashan to Baal Hermon, that is, to **Senir** (Mount Hermon).
SS 4: 8 from the top of **Senir**, the summit of Hermon, from the lions' dens
Eze 27: 5 They made all your timbers of pine trees from **Senir**; they took a

8537 [1]שָׂעִיר **śā'îr[1]**, a. [3] [→ 8538, 8539, 8544; cf. 8547]

hairy [2], shaggy [1]

Ge 27:11 "But my brother Esau is a **hairy** man, and I'm a man with smooth
27:23 for his hands were **hairy** like those of his brother Esau;
Da 8:21 The **shaggy** goat is the king of Greece, and the large horn between

8538 [2]שָׂעִיר **śā'îr[2]**, n.m. [54] [√ 8537; cf. 8547]

male goat [+6436] [24], goat [10], male goat [7], goat's [3], goats [3], goat [+6436] [2], male goats [+6436] [2], wild goats [2], it[s] [+2021] [1]

Ge 37:31 slaughtered a **goat** [+6436] and dipped the robe in the blood.
Lev 4:23 he must bring as his offering a male **goat** [+6436] without defect.
4:24 He is to lay his hand on the **goat's** head and slaughter it at the
9: 3 'Take a **male goat** [+6436] for a sin offering, a calf and a lamb—
9:15 He took the **goat** for the people's sin offering and slaughtered it
10:16 When Moses inquired about the **goat** *of* the sin offering and found
16: 5 From the Israelite community he is to take two **male goats** [+6436]
16: 7 he is to take the two **goats** and present them before the LORD at
16: 8 He is to cast lots for the two **goats**—one lot for the LORD
16: 9 Aaron shall bring the **goat** whose lot falls to the LORD
16:10 the **goat** chosen by lot as the scapegoat shall be presented alive
16:15 "He shall then slaughter the **goat** *for* the sin offering for the people
16:18 and some of the **goat's** blood and put it on all the horns of the altar.
16:20 Tent of Meeting and the altar, he shall bring forward the live **goat**.
16:21 He is to lay both hands on the head of the live **goat** and confess
16:21 of the Israelites—all their sins—and put them on the **goat's** head.
16:22 The **goat** will carry on itself all their sins to a solitary place;
16:22 a solitary place; and the man shall release **it**[s] [+2021] in the desert.
16:26 "The man who releases the **goat** as a scapegoat must wash his
16:27 The bull and the **goat** *for* the sin offerings, whose blood was
23:19 sacrifice one **male goat** [+6436] for a sin offering and two lambs,
Nu 7:16 one **male goat** [+6436] for a sin offering;
7:22 one **male goat** [+6436] for a sin offering;
7:28 one **male goat** [+6436] for a sin offering;
7:34 one **male goat** [+6436] for a sin offering;
7:40 one **male goat** [+6436] for a sin offering;
7:46 one **male goat** [+6436] for a sin offering;
7:52 one **male goat** [+6436] for a sin offering;
7:58 one **male goat** [+6436] for a sin offering;
7:64 one **male goat** [+6436] for a sin offering;
7:70 one **male goat** [+6436] for a sin offering;
7:76 one **male goat** [+6436] for a sin offering;
7:82 one **male goat** [+6436] for a sin offering;
7:87 Twelve **male goats** [+6436] were used for the sin offering.
15:24 and drink offering, and a **male goat** [+6436] for a sin offering.
28:15 one **male goat** [+6436] is to be presented to the LORD as a sin
28:22 Include one **male goat** as a sin offering to make atonement for you.
28:30 Include one **male goat** [+6436] to make atonement for you.
29: 5 Include one **male goat** [+6436] as a sin offering to make
29:11 Include one **male goat** [+6436] as a sin offering, in addition to the
29:16 Include one **male goat** [+6436] as a sin offering, in addition to the
29:19 Include one **male goat** [+6436] as a sin offering, in addition to the
29:22 Include one **male goat** as a sin offering, in addition to the regular
29:25 Include one **male goat** [+6436] as a sin offering, in addition to the
29:28 Include one **male goat** as a sin offering, in addition to the regular
29:31 Include one **male goat** as a sin offering, in addition to the regular
29:34 Include one **male goat** as a sin offering, in addition to the regular
29:38 Include one **male goat** as a sin offering, in addition to the regular
2Ch 29:23 The **goats** *for* the sin offering were brought before the king
Isa 13:21 there the owls will dwell, and there the **wild goats** will leap about.
34:14 will meet with hyenas, and **wild goats** will bleat to each other;
Eze 43:22 "On the second day you are to offer a **male goat** [+6436] without
43:25 "For seven days you are to provide a **male goat** daily for a sin
45:23 offering to the LORD, and a **male goat** [+6436] for a sin offering.

8539 [3]שָׂעִיר **śā'îr[3]**, n.m. [2] [√ 8537; cf. 8547]

goat idols [2]

Lev 17: 7 They must no longer offer any of their sacrifices to the **goat idols**
2Ch 11:15 for the high places and for the **goat** and calf **idols** he had made.

8540 [4]שָׂעִיר **śā'îr[4]**, n.[m.]. [1]

showers [1]

Dt 32: 2 and my words descend like dew, like **showers** on new grass,

8541 [1]שֵׂעִיר **śē'îr[1]**, n.pr.loc. [35] [→ 8542, 8543, 8545; cf. 8547]

Seir [35]

Ge 14: 6 the Horites in the hill country of **Seir**, as far as El Paran near the
32: 3 [32:4] ahead of him to his brother Esau in the land of **Seir**,
33:14 before me and that of the children, until I come to my lord in **Seir**."
33:16 So that day Esau started on his way back to **Seir**.
36: 8 So Esau (that is, Edom) settled in the hill country of **Seir**.
36: 9 of Esau the father of the Edomites in the hill country of **Seir**.
36:30 the Horite chiefs, according to their divisions, in the land of **Seir**.
Nu 24:18 **Seir**, his enemy, will be conquered, but Israel will grow strong.
Dt 1: 2 days to go from Horeb to Kadesh Barnea by the Mount **Seir** road.)
1:44 of bees and beat you down from **Seir** all the way to Hormah.
2: 1 For a long time we made our way around the hill country of **Seir**.
2: 4 territory of your brothers the descendants of Esau, who live in **Seir**.
2: 5 your foot on. I have given Esau the hill country of **Seir** as his own.
2: 8 on past our brothers the descendants of Esau, who live in **Seir**.
2:12 Horites used to live in **Seir**, but the descendants of Esau drove
2:22 who lived in **Seir**, when he destroyed the Horites from before
2:29 who live in **Seir**, and the Moabites, who live in Ar, did for us—
33: 2 "The LORD came from Sinai and dawned over them from **Seir**;
Jos 11:17 from Mount Halak, which rises toward **Seir**, to Baal Gad in the
12: 7 which rises toward **Seir** (their lands Joshua gave as an inheritance
24: 4 I assigned the hill country of **Seir** to Esau, but Jacob and his sons
Jdg 5: 4 "O LORD, when you went out from **Seir**, when you marched
1Ch 4:42 and Uzziel, the sons of Ishi, invaded the hill country of **Seir**.
2Ch 20:10 "But now here are men from Ammon, Moab and Mount **Seir**,
20:22 of Ammon and Moab and Mount **Seir** who were invading Judah,
20:23 and Moab rose up against the men from Mount **Seir** to destroy
20:23 After they finished slaughtering the men from **Seir**, they helped to
25:11 to the Valley of Salt, where he killed ten thousand men of **Seir**.
25:14 the Edomites, he brought back the gods of the people of **Seir**.
Isa 21:11 Someone calls to me from **Seir**, "Watchman, what is left of the
Eze 25: 8 'Because Moab and **Seir** said, "Look, the house of Judah has
35: 2 "Son of man, set your face against Mount **Seir**; prophesy against it
35: 3 I am against you, Mount **Seir**, and I will stretch out my hand
35: 7 I will make Mount **Seir** a desolate waste and cut off from it all who
35:15 You will be desolate, O Mount **Seir**, you and all of Edom.

8542 [2]שֵׂעִיר **śē'îr[2]**, n.pr.loc. [1] [√ 8541; cf. 8547]

Seir [1]

Jos 15:10 it curved westward from Baalah to Mount **Seir**, ran along the

8543 [3]שֵׂעִיר **śē'îr[3]**, n.pr.m. [3] [√ 8541; cf. 8547]

Seir [3]

Ge 36:20 These were the sons of **Seir** the Horite, who were living in the
36:21 and Dishan. These sons of **Seir** in Edom were Horite chiefs.
1Ch 1:38 The sons of **Seir**: Lotan, Shobal, Zibeon, Anah, Dishon, Ezer

8544 [1]שְׂעִירָה **śᵉ'îrâ[1]**, n.f. [2] [√ 8537]

goat [+6436] [2]

Lev 4:28 for the sin he committed a female **goat** [+6436] without defect.
5: 6 a female lamb or **goat** [+6436] from the flock as a sin offering;

8545 [2]שְׂעִירָה **śᵉ'îrâ[2]**, n.pr.loc. [1] [√ 8541]

Seirah [1]

Jdg 3:26 Ehud got away. He passed by the idols and escaped to **Seirah**.

8546 שְׂעִפִּים **śᵉ'ippîm**, n.[m.]pl. [2] [√ 8595]

disquieting [1], troubled thoughts [1]

Job 4:13 Amid **disquieting** dreams in the night, when deep sleep falls on
20: 2 "My **troubled thoughts** prompt me to answer because I am greatly

8547 [1]שָׂעַר **śā'ar[1]**, v.den. [3] [→ 8537, 8538, 8539, 8541, 8542, 8543, 8544, 8545, 8550, 8552, 8553, 8555]

shudder [3]

Jer 2:12 [A] appalled at this, O heavens, and **shudder** *with* great horror,"

Eze 27:35 [A] their kings **shudder** *with* horror and their faces are distorted
32:10 [A] their kings *will* **shudder** *with* horror because of you when I

8548 [2]שָׂעַר ***śā'ar***[2], v. [4] [→ 8551, 8554; cf. 6192]

storm out [1], sweeps out [1], swept away [1], tempest rages [+4394] [1]

Job 27:21 [D] him off, and he is gone; *it* **sweeps** him **out** of his place.
Ps 50: 3 [C] before him, and around him a **tempest rages** [+4394].
58: 9 [58:10] [A] be green or dry—the wicked *will be* **swept away**.
Da 11:40 [F] the king of the North *will* **storm out** against him with

8549 [3]שָׂעַר ***śā'ar***[3], v. [1]

fear [1]

Dt 32:17 [A] gods that recently appeared, gods your fathers *did* not **fear**.

8550 [1]שַׂעַר ***śa'ar***[1], n.[m.]. [3] [√ 8547]

horror [3]

Job 18:20 are appalled at his fate; men of the east are seized with **horror**.
Eze 27:35 their kings shudder with **horror** and their faces are distorted with
32:10 their kings will shudder with **horror** because of you when I

8551 [2]שַׂעַר ***śa'ar***[2], n.[m.]. [1] [√ 8548]

wind [1]

Isa 28: 2 Like a hailstorm and a destructive **wind**, like a driving rain

8552 שֵׂעָר ***śē'ār***, n.m. [28] [√ 8547; Ar 10687]

hair [23], hairy [2], garment of hair [1], hair [+7279] [1], it[s] [+8031] [1]

Ge 25:25 to come out was red, and his whole body was like a **hairy** garment;
Lev 13: 3 if the **hair** in the sore has turned white and the sore appears to be
13: 4 to be more than skin deep and the **hair** *in* it has not turned white,
13:10 if there is a white swelling in the skin that has turned the **hair**
13:20 to be more than skin deep and the **hair** *in* it has turned white,
13:21 there is no white **hair** in it and it is not more than skin deep
13:25 priest is to examine the spot, and if the **hair** in it has turned white,
13:26 But if the priest examines it and there is no white **hair** in the spot
13:30 to be more than skin deep and the **hair** in it is yellow and thin,
13:31 not seem to be more than skin deep and there is no black **hair** in it,
13:32 and if the itch has not spread and there is no yellow **hair** in it
13:36 spread in the skin, the priest does not need to look for yellow **hair**;
13:37 in his judgment it is unchanged and black **hair** has grown in it,
14: 8 must wash his clothes, shave off all his **hair** and bathe with water;
14: 9 On the seventh day he must shave off all his **hair**; he must shave
14: 9 shave his head, his beard, his eyebrows and the rest of his **hair**.
Nu 6: 5 is over; he must let the **hair** [+7279] *of* his head grow long.
6:18 He is to take the **hair** and put it in the fire that is under the sacrifice
Jdg 16:22 the **hair** *on* his head began to grow again after it had been shaved.
2Sa 14:26 he would weigh **it**[s] [+8031], and its weight was two hundred
2Ki 1: 8 "He was a man with a **garment of hair** and with a leather belt
Ezr 9: 3 pulled **hair** from my head and beard and sat down appalled.
Ps 68:21 [68:22] the **hairy** crowns of those who go on in their sins.
SS 4: 1 Your **hair** is like a flock of goats descending from Mount Gilead.
6: 5 Your **hair** is like a flock of goats descending from Gilead.
Isa 7:20 to shave your head and the **hair** *of* your legs, and to take off your
Eze 16: 7 Your breasts were formed and your **hair** grew, you who were
Zec 13: 4 He will not put on a prophet's garment of **hair** in order to deceive.

8553 שַׂעֲרָה ***śa'ărâ***, n.f. [7] [√ 8547]

hair [3], hair of head [2], hairs [2]

Jdg 20:16 each of whom could sling a stone at a **hair** and not miss.
1Sa 14:45 as the LORD lives, not a **hair** of his head will fall to the ground,
2Sa 14:11 he said, "not one **hair of** your son's **head** will fall to the ground."
1Ki 1:52 to be a worthy man, not a **hair of** his **head** will fall to the ground;
Job 4:15 spirit glided past my face, and the **hair** *on* my body stood on end.
Ps 40:12 [40:13] They are more than the **hairs** *of* my head, and my heart
69: 4 [69:5] Those who hate me without reason outnumber the **hairs** *of*

8554 שְׂעָרָה ***śe'ārâ***, n.f. [2] [√ 8548]

storm [2]

Job 9:17 He would crush me with a **storm** and multiply my wounds for no
Na 1: 3 His way is in the whirlwind and the **storm**, and clouds are the dust

8555 שְׂעֹרָה ***śe'ōrâ***, n.f. [34] [√ 8547; cf. 8463?]

barley [33], *untranslated* [1]

Ex 9:31 (The flax and **barley** were destroyed, since the barley had headed
9:31 since the **barley** had headed and the flax was in bloom.
Lev 27:16 required for it—fifty shekels of silver to a homer of **barley** seed.
Nu 5:15 He must also take an offering of a tenth of an ephah of **barley** flour
Dt 8: 8 a land with wheat and **barley**, vines and fig trees, pomegranates,
Jdg 7:13 "A round loaf of **barley** bread came tumbling into the Midianite
Ru 1:22 arriving in Bethlehem as the **barley** harvest was beginning.
2:17 she threshed the **barley** she had gathered, and it amounted to about
2:23 stayed close to the servant girls of Boaz to glean until the **barley**
3: 2 Tonight he will be winnowing **barley** on the threshing floor.
3:15 he poured into it six measures of **barley** and put it on her.
3:17 and added, "He gave me these six measures of **barley**, saying,
2Sa 14:30 "Look, Joab's field is next to mine, and he has **barley** there.
17:28 They also brought wheat and **barley**, flour and roasted grain,
21: 9 first days of the harvest, just as the **barley** harvest was beginning.
1Ki 4:28 [5:8] They also brought to the proper place their quotas of **barley**
2Ki 4:42 bringing the man of God twenty loaves of **barley** bread baked from
7: 1 and two seahs of **barley** for a shekel at the gate of Samaria."
7:16 and two seahs of **barley** sold for a shekel, as the LORD had said.
7:18 and two seahs of **barley** for a shekel at the gate of Samaria."
1Ch 11:13 At a place where there was a field full of **barley**, the troops fled
2Ch 2:10 [2:9] twenty thousand cors of **barley**, twenty thousand baths of
2:15 [2:14] and **barley** and the olive oil and wine he promised,
27: 5 ten thousand cors of wheat and ten thousand cors of **barley**.
Job 31:40 let briers come up instead of wheat and weeds instead of **barley**."
Isa 28:25 not plant wheat in its place, **barley** in its plot, and spelt in its field?
Jer 41: 8 We have wheat and **barley**, oil and honey, hidden in a field."
Eze 4: 9 "Take wheat and **barley**, beans and lentils, millet and spelt;
4:12 Eat the food as you would a **barley** cake; bake it in the sight of the
13:19 have profaned me among my people for a few handfuls of **barley**
45:13 of wheat and a sixth of an ephah from each homer of **barley**.
Hos 3: 2 shekels of silver and about a homer **[RPH]** and a lethek of barley.
3: 2 fifteen shekels of silver and about a homer and a lethek of **barley**.
Joel 1:11 grieve for the wheat and the **barley**, because the harvest of the

8556 שְׂעֹרִים ***śe'ōrîm***, n.pr.m. [1]

Seorim [1]

1Ch 24: 8 the third to Harim, the fourth to **Seorim**,

8557 שָׂפָה ***śāpâ***, n.f. & m. [176] [→ 8559]

lips [97], rim [14], edge [10], bank [7], language [6], *untranslated* [5], seashore [+3542] [5], speech [5], chattering [2], empty words [+1821] [2], mouth [2], talk [2], tongue [2], band [1], banks [1], border [1], coast [+3542] [1], hurl insults [+928+7080] [1], mere talk [+1821] [1], object of malicious talk [+4383+6584+6590] [1], riverbank [+3284] [1], shore [+3542] [1], shore [1], speaks rashly [+7316] [1], talker [+408] [1], talks too much [+7331] [1], thoughtlessly [+928+1051+4200] [1], what said [1], whisper [1], words [1]

Ge 11: 1 Now the whole world had one **language** and a common speech.
11: 6 "If as one people speaking the same **language** they have begun to
11: 7 let us go down and confuse their **language** so they will not
11: 7 their language so they will not understand **[RPH]** each other."
11: 9 because there the LORD confused the **language** *of* the whole
22:17 as the stars in the sky and as the sand on the **seashore** [+3542].
41: 3 out of the Nile and stood beside those on the **riverbank** [+3284].
41:17 to Joseph, "In my dream I was standing on the **bank** *of* the Nile,
Ex 2: 3 child in it and put it among the reeds along the **bank** *of* the Nile.
6:12 why would Pharaoh listen to me, since I speak with faltering **lips**?"
6:30 But Moses said to the LORD, "Since I speak with faltering **lips**,
7:15 Wait on the **bank** *of* the Nile to meet him, and take in your hand
14:30 and Israel saw the Egyptians lying dead on the **shore** [+3542].
26: 4 Make loops of blue material along the **edge** *of* the end curtain in
26: 4 and do the same with **[RPH]** the end curtain in the other set.
26:10 Make fifty loops along the **edge** *of* the end curtain in one set
26:10 and also along the **edge** *of* the end curtain in the other set.
28:26 two corners of the breastpiece on the inside **edge** next to the ephod.
28:32 There shall be a woven **edge** like a collar around this opening,
36:11 they made loops of blue material along the **edge** *of* the end curtain
36:11 the same was done with **[RPH]** the end curtain in the other set.
36:17 they made fifty loops along the **edge** *of* the end curtain in one set
36:17 and also along the **edge** *of* the end curtain in the other set.
39:19 two corners of the breastpiece on the inside **edge** next to the ephod.
39:23 a collar, and a **band** around this opening, so that it would not tear.
Lev 5: 4 " 'Or if a person **thoughtlessly** [+928+1051+4200] takes an oath to
Nu 30: 6 [30:7] or after her **lips** utter a rash promise by which she
30: 8 [30:9] or the rash promise **[RPH]** by which she obligates herself,
30:12 [30:13] of the vows or pledges that came from her **lips** will stand.
Dt 2:36 From Aroer on the **rim** *of* the Arnon Gorge, and from the town in
4:48 This land extended from Aroer on the **rim** *of* the Arnon Gorge to
23:23 [23:24] Whatever your **lips** utter you must be sure to do,
Jos 11: 4 a huge army, as numerous as the sand on the **seashore** [+3542].
12: 2 He ruled from Aroer on the **rim** *of* the Arnon Gorge—from the
13: 9 It extended from Aroer on the **rim** *of* the Arnon Gorge, and from
13:16 The territory from Aroer on the **rim** *of* the Arnon Gorge, and from
Jdg 7:12 could no more be counted than the sand on the **seashore** [+3542].
7:22 Zererah as far as the **border** *of* Abel Meholah near Tabbath.
1Sa 1:13 in her heart, and her **lips** were moving but her voice was not heard.
13: 5 and soldiers as numerous as the sand on the **seashore** [+3542].

1Ki 4:29 [5:9] as measureless as the sand on the **seashore** [+3542].
7:23 measuring ten cubits from **rim** to rim and five cubits high.
7:23 measuring ten cubits from rim to **rim** and five cubits high.
7:24 Below the **rim**, gourds encircled it—ten to a cubit. The gourds
7:26 and its **rim** was like the rim of a cup, like a lily blossom.
7:26 and its rim was like the **rim** *of* a cup, like a lily blossom.
9:26 which is near Elath in Edom, on the **shore** *of* the Red Sea.
2Ki 2:13 from Elijah and went back and stood on the **bank** *of* the Jordan.
18:20 and military strength—but you speak only **empty words** [+1821].
19:28 I will put my hook in your nose and my bit in your **mouth**,
2Ch 4: 2 measuring ten cubits from **rim** to rim and five cubits high.
4: 2 measuring ten cubits from rim to **rim** and five cubits high.
4: 5 and its **rim** was like the rim of a cup, like a lily blossom.
4: 5 and its rim was like the **rim** *of* a cup, like a lily blossom.
8:17 went to Ezion Geber and Elath on the **coast** [+3542] of Edom.
Job 2:10 and not trouble?" In all this, Job did not sin in **what** he **said**.
8:21 yet fill your mouth with laughter and your **lips** with shouts of joy.
11: 2 words to go unanswered? Is this **talker** [+408] to be vindicated?
11: 5 that God would speak, that he would open his **lips** against you
12:20 He silences the **lips** of trusted advisers and takes away the
13: 6 Hear now my argument; listen to the plea of my **lips**.
15: 6 mouth condemns you, not mine; your own **lips** testify against you.
16: 5 encourage you; comfort from my **lips** would bring you relief.
23:12 I have not departed from the commands of his **lips**; I have
27: 4 my **lips** will not speak wickedness, and my tongue will utter no
32:20 I must speak and find relief; I must open my **lips** and reply.
33: 3 come from an upright heart; my **lips** sincerely speak what I know.
Ps 12: 2 [12:3] to his neighbor; their flattering **lips** speak with deception.
12: 3 [12:4] May the LORD cut off all flattering **lips** and every
12: 4 [12:5] with our tongues; we own our **lips**—who is our master?"
16: 4 pour out their libations of blood or take up their names on my **lips**.
17: 1 Give ear to my prayer—it does not rise from deceitful **lips**.
17: 4 by the word of your **lips** I have kept myself from the ways of the
21: 2 [21:3] of his heart and have not withheld the request of his **lips**.
22: 7 [22:8] All who see me mock me; *they* **hurl insults** [+928+7080],
31:18 [31:19] Let their lying **lips** be silenced, for with pride
34:13 [34:14] your tongue from evil and your **lips** from speaking lies.
40: 9 [40:10] I do not seal my **lips**, as you know, O LORD.
45: 2 [45:3] of men and your **lips** have been anointed with grace,
51:15 [51:17] O Lord, open my **lips**, and my mouth will declare your
59: 7 [59:8] they spew out swords from their **lips**, and they say, "Who
59:12 [59:13] For the sins of their mouths, for the words of their **lips**, let
63: 3 [63:4] your love is better than life, my **lips** will glorify you.
63: 5 [63:6] of foods; with singing **lips** my mouth will praise you.
66:14 vows my **lips** promised and my mouth spoke when I was in
71:23 My **lips** will shout for joy when I sing praise to you—I, whom you
81: 5 [81:6] where we heard a **language** we did not understand.
89:34 [89:35] violate my covenant or alter what my **lips** have uttered.
106:33 against the Spirit of God, and rash words came from Moses' **lips**.
119:13 With my **lips** I recount all the laws that come from your mouth.
119:171 May my **lips** overflow with praise, for you teach me your decrees.
120: 2 Save me, O LORD, from lying **lips** and from deceitful tongues.
140: 3 [140:4] sharp as a serpent's; the poison of vipers is on their **lips**.
140: 9 [140:10] me be covered with the trouble their **lips** have caused.
141: 3 over my mouth, O LORD; keep watch over the door of my **lips**.
Pr 4:24 perversity from your mouth; keep corrupt talk far from your **lips**.
5: 2 may maintain discretion and your **lips** may preserve knowledge.
5: 3 For the **lips** *of* an adulteress drip honey, and her speech is smoother
7:21 words she led him astray; she seduced him with her smooth **talk**.
8: 6 I have worthy things to say; I open my **lips** to speak what is right.
8: 7 My mouth speaks what is true, for my **lips** detest wickedness.
10: 8 in heart accept commands, but a **chattering** fool comes to ruin.
10:10 maliciously causes grief, and a **chattering** fool comes to ruin.
10:13 Wisdom is found on the **lips** *of* the discerning, but a rod is for the
10:18 He who conceals his hatred has lying **lips**, and whoever spreads
10:19 are many, sin is not absent, but he who holds his **tongue** is wise.
10:21 The **lips** *of* the righteous nourish many, but fools die for lack of
10:32 The **lips** *of* the righteous know what is fitting, but the mouth of the
12:13 An evil man is trapped by his sinful **talk**, but a righteous man
12:19 Truthful **lips** endure forever, but a lying tongue lasts only a
12:22 The LORD detests lying **lips**, but he delights in men who are
13: 3 his life, but he *who* **speaks** [+7316] **rashly** will come to ruin.
14: 3 talk brings a rod to his back, but the **lips** *of* the wise protect them.
14: 7 from a foolish man, for you will not find knowledge on his **lips**.
14:23 work brings a profit, but **mere talk** [+1821] leads only to poverty.
15: 7 The **lips** *of* the wise spread knowledge; not so the hearts of fools.
16:10 The **lips** *of* a king speak as an oracle, and his mouth should not
16:13 Kings take pleasure in honest **lips**; they value a man who speaks
16:21 are called discerning, and pleasant **words** promote instruction.
16:23 man's heart guides his mouth, and his **lips** promote instruction.
16:27 A scoundrel plots evil, and his **speech** is like a scorching fire.
16:30 his eye is plotting perversity; he who purses his **lips** is bent on evil.
17: 4 A wicked man listens to evil **lips**; a liar pays attention to a
17: 7 Arrogant **lips** are unsuited to a fool—how much worse lying lips to
17: 7 lips are unsuited to a fool—how much worse lying **lips** to a ruler!
17:28 wise if he keeps silent, and discerning if he holds his **tongue**.
18: 6 A fool's **lips** bring him strife, and his mouth invites a beating.
18: 7 A fool's mouth is his undoing, and his **lips** are a snare to his soul.
18:20 stomach is filled; with the harvest from his **lips** he is satisfied.
19: 1 Better a poor man whose walk is blameless than a fool whose **lips**
20:15 in abundance, but **lips** *that speak* knowledge are a rare jewel.
20:19 a confidence; so avoid a *man who* **talks** [+7331] **too much**.
22:11 and whose **speech** is gracious will have the king for his friend.
22:18 keep them in your heart and have all of them ready on your **lips**.
23:16 my inmost being will rejoice when your **lips** speak what is right.
24: 2 their hearts plot violence, and their **lips** talk about making trouble.
24:26 An honest answer is like a kiss on the **lips**.
24:28 against your neighbor without cause, or use your **lips** to deceive.
26:23 Like a coating of glaze over earthenware are fervent **lips** with an
26:24 A malicious man disguises himself with his **lips**, but in his heart he
27: 2 and not your own mouth; someone else, and not your own **lips**.
Ecc 10:12 man's mouth are gracious, but a fool is consumed by his own **lips**.
SS 4: 3 Your **lips** are like a scarlet ribbon; your mouth is lovely.
4:11 Your **lips** drop sweetness as the honeycomb, my bride; milk
5:13 spice yielding perfume. His **lips** are like lilies dripping with myrrh.
7: 9 [7:10] go straight to my lover, flowing gently over **lips** and teeth.
Isa 6: 5 For I am a man of unclean **lips**, and I live among a people of
6: 5 a man of unclean lips, and I live among a people of unclean **lips**,
6: 7 it he touched my mouth and said, "See, this has touched your **lips**;
11: 4 of his mouth; with the breath of his **lips** he will slay the wicked.
19:18 In that day five cities in Egypt will speak the **language** *of* Canaan
28:11 with foreign **lips** and strange tongues God will speak to this
29:13 come near to me with their mouth and honor me with their **lips**,
30:27 his **lips** are full of wrath, and his tongue is a consuming fire.
33:19 those people of an obscure **speech**, with their strange,
36: 5 and military strength—but you speak only **empty words** [+1821].
37:29 I will put my hook in your nose and my bit in your **mouth**,
57:19 creating praise on the **lips** of the mourners in Israel. Peace,
59: 3 Your **lips** have spoken lies, and your tongue mutters wicked things.
Jer 17:16 desired the day of despair. What passes my **lips** is open before you.
La 3:62 *what* my enemies **whisper** and mutter against me all day long.
Eze 3: 5 You are not being sent to a people of obscure **speech** and difficult
3: 6 not to many peoples of obscure **speech** and difficult language,
36: 3 and *the* **object of** people's **malicious talk** [+4383+6584+6590] and
43:13 and a cubit wide, with a rim of one span around the **edge**.
47: 6 do you see this?" Then he led me back to the **bank** *of* the river.
47: 7 I saw a great number of trees on each side of **[RPH]** the river.
47:12 Fruit trees of all kinds will grow on both **banks** *of* the river.
Da 10:16 one who looked like a man touched my **lips**, and I opened my
12: 5 one on this **bank** *of* the river and one on the opposite bank.
12: 5 one on this bank of the river and one on the opposite **bank**.
Hos 14: 2 [14:3] us graciously, that we may offer the fruit of our **lips**.
Hab 3:16 I heard and my heart pounded, my **lips** quivered at the sound;
Zep 3: 9 "Then will I purify the **lips** *of* the peoples, that all of them may call
Mal 2: 6 was in his mouth and nothing false was found on his **lips**.
2: 7 "For the **lips** *of* a priest ought to preserve knowledge, and from his

8558 שָׂפַח *śāpaḥ*, v.den. [1] [cf. 6202?, 6203?]

bring sores on [1]

Isa 3:17 [D] Therefore the Lord *will* **bring sores on** the heads of the

8559 שָׂפָם *śāpām*, n.[m.]. [5] [√ 8557]

lower part of face [3], faces [1], mustache [1]

Lev 13:45 cover the **lower part of** his **face** and cry out, 'Unclean!
2Sa 19:24 [19:25] had not taken care of his feet or trimmed his **mustache**
Eze 24:17 do not cover the **lower part of** your **face** or eat the customary food
24:22 You will not cover the **lower part of** your **face** or eat the
Mic 3: 7 They will all cover their **faces** because there is no answer from

8560 שִׂפְמוֹת *śipmôt*, n.pr.loc. [1] [cf. 9174]

Siphmoth [1]

1Sa 30:28 to those in Aroer, **Siphmoth**, Eshtemoa

8561 שָׂפַן *śāpan*, v. [1] [cf. 6211]

treasures hidden [+3243] [1]

Dt 33:19 [B] of the seas, on the **treasures hidden in** [+3243] the sand."

8562 שָׂפַק[1] *śāpaq*[1], v. [2] [→ 8564; cf. 6215]

claps in derision [1], clasp hands [1]

Job 27:23 [A] *It* **claps** its hands **in derision** and hisses him out of his place.
Isa 2: 6 [G] divination like the Philistines and **clasp hands** with pagans.

8563 ²שָׂפַק **śāpaq²**, v. [1] [→ 8565; cf. 6217]
enough [1]
1Ki 20:10 [A] if **enough** dust *remains* in Samaria to give each of my men a

8564 שֶׂפֶק **śepeq**, n.[m.]. Not used in NIV/BHS [√ 8562]

8565 שֵׂפֶק **śēpeq**, n.[m.]. [1] [√ 8563]
plenty [1]
Job 20:22 In the midst of his **plenty**, distress will overtake him; the full force

8566 שַׂק **śaq**, n.m. [48]
sackcloth [42], sack [3], sacks [2], sackcloth [+4680] [1]
Ge 37:34 his clothes, put on **sackcloth** and mourned for his son many days.
42:25 to put each man's silver back in his **sack**, and to give them
42:27 the night one of them opened his **sack** to get feed for his donkey,
42:35 As they were emptying their **sacks**, there in each man's sack was
42:35 their sacks, there in each man's **sack** was his pouch of silver!
Lev 11:32 be unclean, whether it is made of wood, cloth, hide or **sackcloth**.
Jos 9:4 as a delegation whose donkeys were loaded with worn-out **sacks**
2Sa 3:31 "Tear your clothes and put on **sackcloth** and walk in mourning in
21:10 Rizpah daughter of Aiah took **sackcloth** and spread it out for
1Ki 20:31 Let us go to the king of Israel with **sackcloth** around our waists
20:32 Wearing **sackcloth** around their waists and ropes around their
21:27 heard these words, he tore his clothes, put on **sackcloth** and fasted.
21:27 and fasted. He lay in **sackcloth** and went around meekly.
2Ki 6:30 and there, underneath, he had **sackcloth** on his body.
19:1 he tore his clothes and put on **sackcloth** and went into the temple
19:2 Shebna the secretary and the leading priests, all wearing **sackcloth**,
1Ch 21:16 Then David and the elders, clothed in **sackcloth**, fell facedown.
Ne 9:1 fasting and wearing **sackcloth** and having dust on their heads.
Est 4:1 he tore his clothes, put on **sackcloth** and ashes, and went out into
4:2 because no one clothed in **sackcloth** was allowed to enter it.
4:3 weeping and wailing. Many lay in **sackcloth** and ashes.
4:4 She sent clothes for him to put on instead of his **sackcloth**,
Job 16:15 "I have sewed **sackcloth** over my skin and buried my brow in the
Ps 30:11 [30:12] you removed my **sackcloth** and clothed me with joy,
35:13 they were ill, I put on **sackcloth** and humbled myself with fasting.
69:11 [69:12] when I put on **sackcloth**, people make sport of me.
Isa 3:24 baldness; instead of fine clothing, **sackcloth** [+4680];
15:3 In the streets they wear **sackcloth**; on the roofs and in the public
20:2 "Take off the **sackcloth** from your body and the sandals from your
22:12 day to weep and to wail, to tear out your hair and put on **sackcloth**.
37:1 he tore his clothes and put on **sackcloth** and went into the temple
37:2 the secretary, and the leading priests, all wearing **sackcloth**,
50:3 I clothe the sky with darkness and make **sackcloth** its covering."
58:5 one's head like a reed and for lying on **sackcloth** and ashes?
Jer 4:8 So put on **sackcloth**, lament and wail, for the fierce anger of the
6:26 O my people, put on **sackcloth** and roll in ashes; mourn with bitter
48:37 every hand is slashed and every waist is covered with **sackcloth**.
49:3 Put on **sackcloth** and mourn; rush here and there inside the walls,
La 2:10 they have sprinkled dust on their heads and put on **sackcloth**.
Eze 7:18 They will put on **sackcloth** and be clothed with terror. Their faces
27:31 will shave their heads because of you and will put on **sackcloth**.
Da 9:3 him in prayer and petition, in fasting, and in **sackcloth** and ashes.
Joel 1:8 Mourn like a virgin in **sackcloth** grieving for the husband of her
1:13 Come, spend the night in **sackcloth**, you who minister before my
Am 8:10 I will make all of you wear **sackcloth** and shave your heads.
Jnh 3:5 and all of them, from the greatest to the least, put on **sackcloth**.
3:6 covered himself with **sackcloth** and sat down in the dust.
3:8 let man and beast be covered with **sackcloth**. Let everyone call

8567 שָׂקַד **śāqad**, v. [1]
been bound [1]
La 1:14 [C] "My sins *have* **been bound** *into* a yoke; by his hands they

8568 שָׂקַר **śāqar**, v. [1]
flirting [1]
Isa 3:16 [D] **flirting** *with* their eyes, tripping along with mincing steps,

8569 שַׂר **śar**, n.m. [421] [→ 5552, 5947, 8576, 8593; cf. 6254, 8606]
officials [78], commanders [74], princes [41], commander [36], officers [31], leaders [29], nobles [18], chief [17], *untranslated* [15], ruler [14], prince [10], leader [8], captain [7], rulers [7], captain [+2822] [5], leading [3], officials in charge [3], warden [3], chief officer [+2021+7372] [2], command [2], governor [2], in charge [2], captains [+2822] [1], chief men [1], chief officials [1], commander-in-chief [+2256+8031] [1], commanders [+7372] [1], dignitaries [1], foremen [+5893] [1], head [1], heads [1], masters [1], mighty [1], officer [1], they^s [+2021+2256+2657+3405] [1], they^s [+2021] [1]
Ge 12:15 And when Pharaoh's **officials** saw her, they praised her to Pharaoh,
21:22 and Phicol the **commander** *of* his forces said to Abraham,
21:32 Phicol the **commander** *of* his forces returned to the land of the
26:26 his personal adviser and Phicol the **commander** *of* his forces.
37:36 to Potiphar, one of Pharaoh's officials, the **captain** *of* the guard.
39:1 who was one of Pharaoh's officials, the **captain** *of* the guard,
39:21 and granted him favor in the eyes of the prison **warden**.
39:22 So the **warden** put Joseph in charge of all those held in the prison,
39:23 The **warden** paid no attention to anything under Joseph's care,
40:2 with his two officials, the **chief** cupbearer and the chief baker,
40:2 with his two officials, the chief cupbearer and the **chief** baker,
40:3 and put them in custody in the house of the **captain** *of* the guard,
40:4 The **captain** *of* the guard assigned them to Joseph, and he attended
40:9 So the **chief** cupbearer told Joseph his dream. He said to him,
40:16 When the **chief** baker saw that Joseph had given a favorable
40:20 He lifted up the heads of the **chief** cupbearer and the chief baker in
40:20 chief cupbearer and the **chief** baker in the presence of his officials:
40:21 He restored the **chief** cupbearer to his position, so that he once
40:22 he hanged the **chief** baker, just as Joseph had said to them in his
40:23 The **chief** cupbearer, however, did not remember Joseph; he forgot
41:9 the **chief** cupbearer said to Pharaoh, "Today I am reminded of my
41:10 and the **chief** baker in the house of the captain of the guard.
41:10 and the chief baker in the house of the **captain** *of* the guard.
41:12 Hebrew was there with us, a servant of the **captain** *of* the guard.
47:6 with special ability, put them **in charge** of my own livestock."
Ex 1:11 So they put slave **masters** over them to oppress them with forced
2:14 The man said, "Who made you **ruler** and judge over us? Are you
18:21 and appoint them as **officials** over thousands, hundreds, fifties
18:21 as officials over thousands, **[RPH]** hundreds, fifties and tens.
18:21 as officials over thousands, hundreds, **[RPH]** fifties and tens.
18:21 as officials over thousands, hundreds, fifties and **[RPH]** tens.
18:25 of the people, **officials** *over* thousands, hundreds, fifties and tens.
18:25 officials over thousands, **[RPH]** hundreds, fifties and tens.
18:25 officials over thousands, hundreds, **[RPH]** fifties and tens.
18:25 officials over thousands, hundreds, fifties and **[RPH]** tens.
Nu 21:18 about the well that the **princes** dug, that the nobles of the people
22:8 the LORD gives me." So the Moabite **princes** stayed with him.
22:13 The next morning Balaam got up and said to Balak's **princes**,
22:14 So the Moabite **princes** returned to Balak and said,
22:15 Balak sent other **princes**, more numerous and more distinguished
22:21 saddled his donkey and went with the **princes** *of* Moab.
22:35 only what I tell you." So Balaam went with the **princes** *of* Balak.
22:40 and gave some to Balaam and the **princes** who were with him.
23:6 him standing beside his offering, with all the **princes** *of* Moab.
23:17 found him standing beside his offering, with the **princes** *of* Moab.
31:14 the **commanders** *of* thousands and commanders of hundreds—
31:14 the commanders of thousands and **commanders** *of* hundreds—
31:48 the **commanders** *of* thousands and commanders of hundreds—
31:48 the commanders of thousands and **commanders** *of* hundreds—
31:52 All the gold from the **commanders** *of* thousands and commanders
31:52 of thousands and **commanders** *of* hundreds that Moses
31:54 Eleazar the priest accepted the gold from the **commanders** *of*
Dt 1:15 as **commanders** *of* thousands, *of* hundreds, *of* fifties and *of* tens
1:15 of **[RPH]** hundreds, of fifties and of tens and as tribal officials.
1:15 of hundreds, **[RPH]** of fifties and of tens and as tribal officials.
1:15 of hundreds, of fifties and of **[RPH]** tens and as tribal officials.
20:9 to the army, they shall appoint **commanders** [+7372] over it.
Jos 5:14 "but as **commander** *of* the army of the LORD I have now come."
5:15 The **commander** *of* the LORD's army replied, "Take off your
Jdg 4:2 The **commander** *of* his army was Sisera, who lived in Harosheth
4:7 the **commander** *of* Jabin's army, with his chariots and his troops
5:15 The **princes** of Issachar were with Deborah; yes, Issachar was with
7:25 They also captured two of the Midianite **leaders**, Oreb and Zeeb.
8:3 God gave Oreb and Zeeb, the Midianite **leaders**, into your hands.
8:6 the **officials** *of* Succoth said, "Do you already have the hands of
8:14 down for him the names of the seventy-seven **officials** *of* Succoth,
9:30 When Zebul the **governor** *of* the city heard what Gaal son of Ebed
10:18 The **leaders** *of* the people of Gilead said to each other, "Whoever
1Sa 8:12 Some he will assign to be **commanders** *of* thousands
8:12 assign to be commanders of thousands and **commanders** *of* fifties,
12:9 the **commander** *of* the army of Hazor, and into the hands of the
14:50 The name of the **commander** *of* Saul's army was Abner son of
17:18 Take along these ten cheeses to the **commander** *of* their unit.
17:55 he said to Abner, **commander** *of* the army, "Abner, whose son is
18:13 away from him and gave him **command** *over* a thousand men,
18:30 The Philistine **commanders** continued to go out to battle,
22:2 or discontented gathered around him, and he became their **leader**.
22:7 Will he make all of you **commanders** *of* thousands
22:7 of you commanders of thousands and **commanders** *of* hundreds?
26:5 and Abner son of Ner, the **commander** *of* the army, had lain down.
29:3 The **commanders** *of* the Philistines asked, "What about these

1Sa 29: 3 Achish replied, **[RPH]** "Is this not David, who was an officer of
29: 4 But the Philistine **commanders** were angry with him and said,
29: 4 were angry with him and said, **[RPH]** "Send the man back,
29: 9 nevertheless, the Philistine **commanders** have said, 'He must not
2Sa 2: 8 Meanwhile, Abner son of Ner, the **commander** *of* Saul's army,
3: 38 "Do you not realize that a **prince** and a great man has fallen in
4: 2 Now Saul's son had two men who were **leaders** *of* raiding bands.
10: 3 the Ammonite **nobles** said to Hanun their lord, "Do you think
10: 16 with Shobach the **commander** *of* Hadadezer's army leading them.
10: 18 He also struck down Shobach the **commander** *of* their army,
18: 1 appointed over them **commanders** *of* thousands and commanders
18: 1 them commanders of thousands and **commanders** *of* hundreds.
18: 5 giving orders concerning Absalom to each of the **commanders**.
19: 6 [19:7] You have made it clear today that the **commanders**
19: 13 [19:14] if from now on you are not the **commander** *of* my army
23: 19 He became their **commander**, even though he was not included
24: 2 So the king said to Joab and the army **commanders** with him,
24: 4 king's word, however, overruled Joab and the army **commanders**;
24: 4 so **they**[s] [+2021+2256+2657+3405] left the presence of the king to
1Ki 1: 19 Abiathar the priest and Joab the **commander** *of* the army,
1: 25 king's sons, the **commanders** *of* the army and Abiathar the priest.
2: 5 what he did to the two **commanders** *of* Israel's armies, Abner son
2: 32 Abner son of Ner, **commander** *of* Israel's army, and Amasa son of
2: 32 and Amasa son of Jether, **commander** *of* Judah's army—
4: 2 And these were his **chief officials**: Azariah son of Zadok—
5: 16 [5:30] as well as thirty-three hundred **foremen** [+5893] who
9: 22 fighting men, his government officials, his **officers**, his captains,
9: 22 his captains, and the **commanders** *of* his chariots and charioteers.
9: 23 They were also the **chief** officials in charge of Solomon's
11: 15 Joab the **commander** *of* the army, who had gone up to bury the
11: 21 and that Joab the **commander** *of* the army was also dead.
11: 24 became the **leader** *of* a band of rebels when David destroyed the
14: 27 assigned these to the **commanders** *of* the guard on duty at the
15: 20 and sent the **commanders** *of* his forces against the towns of Israel.
16: 9 one of his officials, who had **command** *of* half his chariots,
16: 16 they proclaimed Omri, the **commander** *of* the army,
20: 14 'The young officers of the provincial **commanders** will do it.' "
20: 15 summoned the young officers of the provincial **commanders**,
20: 17 The young officers of the provincial **commanders** went out first.
20: 19 The young officers of the provincial **commanders** marched out of
22: 26 "Take Micaiah and send him back to Amon the **ruler** *of* the city
22: 31 the king of Aram had ordered his thirty-two chariot **commanders**,
22: 32 When the chariot **commanders** saw Jehoshaphat, they thought,
22: 33 the chariot **commanders** saw that he was not the king of Israel
2Ki 1: 9 he sent to Elijah a **captain** [+2822] with his company of fifty men.
1: 10 Elijah answered the **captain** [+2822], "If I am a man of God,
1: 11 At this the king sent to Elijah another **captain** [+2822] with his
1: 13 So the king sent a third **captain** [+2822] with his fifty men.
1: 13 This third **captain** [+2822] went up and fell on his knees before
1: 14 and consumed the first two **captains** [+2822] and all their men.
4: 13 behalf to the king or the **commander** *of* the army?' " She replied,
5: 1 Now Naaman was **commander** *of* the army of the king of Aram.
8: 21 The Edomites surrounded him and his chariot **commanders**,
9: 5 When he arrived, he found the army **officers** sitting together.
9: 5 "I have a message for you, **commander**," he said. "For which of
9: 5 which of us?" asked Jehu. "For you, **commander**," he replied.
10: 1 to the **officials** *of* Jezreel, to the elders and to the guardians of
11: 4 In the seventh year Jehoiada sent for the **commanders** *of* units of a
11: 9 The **commanders** *of* units of a hundred did just as Jehoiada the
11: 10 he gave the **commanders** the spears and shields that had belonged
11: 14 The **officers** and the trumpeters were beside the king, and all the
11: 15 Jehoiada the priest ordered the **commanders** *of* units of a hundred,
11: 19 He took with him the **commanders** *of* hundreds, the Carites,
23: 8 of Joshua, the city **governor**, which is on the left of the city gate.
24: 12 his attendants, his **nobles** and his officials all surrendered to him.
24: 14 all the **officers** and fighting men, and all the craftsmen
25: 19 He also took the secretary who was **chief officer** [+2021+7372] in
25: 23 When all the army **officers** and their men heard that the king of
25: 26 together with the army **officers**, fled to Egypt for fear of the
1Ch 11: 6 on the Jebusites will become **commander-in-chief** [+2256+8031]."
11: 21 doubly honored above the Three and became their **commander**,
12: 21 [12:22] brave warriors, and they were **commanders** in his army.
12: 28 [12:29] a brave young warrior, with 22 **officers** from his family;
12: 34 [12:35] 1,000 **officers**, together with 37,000 men carrying shields
13: 1 the **commanders** *of* thousands and commanders of hundreds.
15: 5 the descendants of Kohath, Uriel the **leader** and 120 relatives;
15: 6 the descendants of Merari, Asaiah the **leader** and 220 relatives;
15: 7 the descendants of Gershon, Joel the **leader** and 130 relatives;
15: 8 descendants of Elizaphan, Shemaiah the **leader** and 200 relatives;
15: 9 from the descendants of Hebron, Eliel the **leader** and 80 relatives;
15: 10 descendants of Uzziel, Amminadab the **leader** and 112 relatives.
15: 16 David told the **leaders** *of* the Levites to appoint their brothers as
15: 22 Kenaniah the **head** Levite was in charge of the singing; that was
15: 25 the **commanders** *of* units of a thousand went to bring up the ark of
15: 27 and Kenaniah, who was **in charge** *of* the singing of the choirs.
19: 3 the Ammonite **nobles** said to Hanun, "Do you think David is
19: 16 with Shophach the **commander** *of* Hadadezer's army leading
19: 18 He also killed Shophach the **commander** *of* their army.
21: 2 So David said to Joab and the **commanders** *of* the troops,
22: 17 David ordered all the **leaders** *of* Israel to help his son Solomon.
23: 2 He also gathered together all the **leaders** *of* Israel, as well as the
24: 5 for there were **officials** *of* the sanctuary and officials of God
24: 5 and **officials** *of* God among the descendants of both Eleazar
24: 6 their names in the presence of the king and of the **officials**:
25: 1 David, together with the **commanders** *of* the army, set apart some
26: 26 by the heads of families who were the **commanders** *of* thousands
26: 26 commanders of hundreds, and by the other army **commanders**.
27: 1 **commanders** *of* thousands and commanders of hundreds,
27: 3 of Perez and chief of all the army **officers** for the first month.
27: 5 The third army **commander**, for the third month, was Benaiah son
27: 8 for the fifth month, was the **commander** Shamhuth the Izrahite.
27: 22 son of Jeroham. These were the **officers** *over* the tribes of Israel.
27: 31 All these were the **officials in charge** *of* King David's property.
27: 34 and by Abiathar. Joab was the **commander** of the royal army.
28: 1 David summoned all the **officials** *of* Israel to assemble at
28: 1 the **officers** *over* the tribes, the commanders of the divisions in the
28: 1 the **commanders** *of* the divisions in the service of the king,
28: 1 the **commanders** *of* thousands and commanders of hundreds,
28: 1 the commanders of thousands and **commanders** *of* hundreds,
28: 1 the **officials in charge** *of* all the property and livestock belonging
28: 21 The **officials** and all the people will obey your every command."
29: 6 Then the **leaders** *of* families, the officers of the tribes of Israel,
29: 6 Then the leaders of families, the **officers** *of* the tribes of Israel,
29: 6 the **commanders** *of* thousands and commanders of hundreds,
29: 6 and the **officials in charge** *of* the king's work gave willingly.
29: 24 All the **officers** and mighty men, as well as all of King David's
2Ch 1: 2 to the **commanders** *of* thousands and commanders of hundreds,
8: 9 they were his fighting men, **commanders** *of* his captains,
8: 9 of his captains, and **commanders** *of* his chariots and charioteers.
8: 10 They were also King Solomon's **chief** officials—two hundred
12: 5 to the **leaders** *of* Judah who had assembled in Jerusalem for fear of
12: 6 The **leaders** *of* Israel and the king humbled themselves and said,
12: 10 assigned these to the **commanders** *of* the guard on duty at the
16: 4 and sent the **commanders** *of* his forces against the towns of Israel.
17: 7 In the third year of his reign he sent his **officials** Ben-Hail,
17: 14 From Judah, **commanders** *of* units of 1,000:
17: 14 units of 1,000: Adnah the **commander**, with 300,000 fighting men;
17: 15 next, Jehohanan the **commander**, with 280,000;
18: 25 "Take Micaiah and send him back to Amon the **ruler** *of* the city
18: 30 Now the king of Aram had ordered his chariot **commanders**,
18: 31 When the chariot **commanders** saw Jehoshaphat, they thought,
18: 32 for when the chariot **commanders** saw that he was not the king of
21: 4 his brothers to the sword along with some of the **princes** *of* Israel.
21: 9 So Jehoram went there with his **officers** and all his chariots.
21: 9 The Edomites surrounded him and his chariot **commanders**,
22: 8 he found the **princes** *of* Judah and the sons of Ahaziah's relatives,
23: 1 He made a covenant with the **commanders** *of* units of a hundred:
23: 9 Then he gave the **commanders** *of* units of a hundred the spears
23: 13 The **officers** and the trumpeters were beside the king, and all the
23: 14 Jehoiada the priest sent out the **commanders** *of* units of a hundred,
23: 20 He took with him the **commanders** *of* hundreds, the nobles,
24: 10 All the **officials** and all the people brought their contributions
24: 17 the **officials** *of* Judah came and paid homage to the king, and he
24: 23 and Jerusalem and killed all the **leaders** *of* the people.
25: 5 assigned them according to their families to **commanders** *of*
25: 5 and **commanders** *of* hundreds for all Judah and Benjamin.
26: 11 officer under the direction of Hananiah, one of the royal **officials**.
28: 14 and plunder in the presence of the **officials** and all the assembly.
28: 21 from the royal palace and from the **princes** and presented them to
29: 20 Early the next morning King Hezekiah gathered the city **officials**
29: 30 his **officials** ordered the Levites to praise the LORD with the
30: 2 The king and his **officials** and the whole assembly in Jerusalem
30: 6 and Judah with letters from the king and from his **officials**,
30: 12 of mind to carry out what the king and his **officials** had ordered,
30: 24 the **officials** provided them with a thousand bulls and ten thousand
31: 8 When Hezekiah and his **officials** came and saw the heaps,
32: 3 he consulted with his **officials** and military staff about blocking off
32: 6 He appointed military **officers** over the people and assembled them
32: 21 and the leaders and **officers** in the camp of the Assyrian king.
32: 31 when envoys were sent by the **rulers** *of* Babylon to ask him about
33: 11 So the LORD brought against them the army **commanders** of the
33: 14 He stationed military **commanders** in all the fortified cities in
34: 8 he sent Shaphan son of Azaliah and Maaseiah the **ruler** *of* the city,
35: 8 His **officials** also contributed voluntarily to the people and the
35: 9 and Hashabiah, Jeiel and Jozabad, the **leaders** *of* the Levites,
36: 14 all the **leaders** *of* the priests and the people became more and more
36: 18 the LORD's temple and the treasures of the king and his **officials**.
Ezr 7: 28 the king and his advisers and all the king's powerful **officials**.

Ezr 8:20 that David and the **officials** had established to assist the Levites.
8:24 I set apart twelve of the **leading** priests, together with Sherebiah,
8:25 his **officials** and all Israel present there had donated for the house
8:29 of the house of the LORD in Jerusalem before the **leading** priests
8:29 the leading priests and the Levites and the family **heads** of Israel."
9: 1 the **leaders** came to me and said, "The people of Israel,
9: 2 the **leaders** and officials have led the way in this unfaithfulness."
10: 5 So Ezra rose up and put the **leading** priests and Levites and all
10: 8 in accordance with the decision of the **officials** and elders,
10:14 Let our **officials** act for the whole assembly. Then let everyone in
Ne 2: 9 The king had also sent army **officers** and cavalry with me.
3: 9 Rephaiah son of Hur, **ruler** *of* a half-district of Jerusalem,
3:12 Shallum son of Hallohesh, **ruler** *of* a half-district of Jerusalem,
3:14 by Malkijah son of Recab, **ruler** *of* the district of Beth Hakkerem.
3:15 by Shallun son of Col-Hozeh, **ruler** *of* the district of Mizpah.
3:16 Nehemiah son of Azbuk, **ruler** *of* a half-district of Beth Zur,
3:17 Beside him, Hashabiah, **ruler** *of* half the district of Keilah,
3:18 Binnui son of Henadad, **ruler** *of* the other half-district of Keilah.
3:19 Next to him, Ezer son of Jeshua, **ruler** *of* Mizpah, repaired another
4:16 [4:10] The **officers** posted themselves behind all the people of
7: 2 along with Hananiah the **commander** *of* the citadel, because he
9:32 upon our kings and **leaders**, upon our priests and prophets,
9:34 our **leaders**, our priests and our fathers did not follow your law;
9:38 [10:1] our **leaders**, our Levites and our priests are affixing their
11: 1 Now the **leaders** *of* the people settled in Jerusalem, and the rest of
12:31 I had the **leaders** *of* Judah go up on top of the wall. I also assigned
12:32 Hoshaiah and half the **leaders** *of* Judah followed them,
Est 1: 3 in the third year of his reign he gave a banquet for all his **nobles**
1: 3 the princes, and the **nobles** *of* the provinces were present.
1:11 in order to display her beauty to the people and **nobles**,
1:14 the seven **nobles** *of* Persia and Media who had special access to the
1:16 Then Memucan replied in the presence of the king and the **nobles**,
1:16 not only against the king but also against all the **nobles** and the
1:18 conduct will respond to all the king's **nobles** in the same way.
1:21 The king and his **nobles** were pleased with this advice, so the king
2:18 a great banquet, Esther's banquet, for all his **nobles** and officials.
3: 1 giving him a seat of honor higher than that of all the other **nobles**.
3:12 of the various provinces and the **nobles** *of* the various peoples.
5:11 and how he had elevated him above the other **nobles** and officials.
6: 9 and horse be entrusted to one of the king's most noble **princes**.
8: 9 and **nobles** *of* the 127 provinces stretching from India to Cush.
9: 3 And all the **nobles** *of* the provinces, the satraps, the governors
Job 3:15 with **rulers** who had gold, who filled their houses with silver.
29: 9 the **chief men** refrained from speaking and covered their mouths
34:19 who shows no partiality to **princes** and does not favor the rich over
39:25 of battle from afar, the shout of **commanders** and the battle cry.
Ps 45:16 [45:17] you will make them **princes** throughout the land.
68:27 [68:28] leading them, there the great throng of Judah's **princes**,
68:27 [68:28] and there the **princes** *of* Zebulun and of Naphtali.
68:27 [68:28] and there the princes of Zebulun and **[RPH]** of Naphtali.
82: 7 you will die like mere men; you will fall like every other **ruler**."
105:22 to instruct his **princes** as he pleased and teach his elders wisdom.
119:23 Though **rulers** sit together and slander me, your servant will
119:161 **Rulers** persecute me without cause, but my heart trembles at your
148:11 of the earth and all nations, you **princes** and all rulers on earth,
Pr 8:16 by me **princes** govern, and all nobles who rule on earth.
19:10 live in luxury—how much worse for a slave to rule over **princes**!
28: 2 it has many **rulers**, but a man of understanding and knowledge
Ecc 10: 7 seen slaves on horseback, while **princes** go on foot like slaves.
10:16 whose king was a servant and whose **princes** feast in the morning.
10:17 king is of noble birth and whose **princes** eat at a proper time—
Isa 1:23 Your **rulers** are rebels, companions of thieves; they all love bribes
3: 3 the **captain** *of* fifty and man of rank, the counselor, skilled
3: 4 I will make boys their **officials**; mere children will govern them.
3:14 enters into judgment against the elders and **leaders** *of* his people:
9: 6 [9:5] Mighty God, Everlasting Father, **Prince** *of* Peace.
10: 8 'Are not my **commanders** all kings?' he says.
19:11 The **officials** *of* Zoan are nothing but fools; the wise counselors of
19:13 The **officials** *of* Zoan have become fools, the leaders of Memphis
19:13 of Zoan have become fools, the **leaders** *of* Memphis are deceived;
21: 5 the rugs, they eat, they drink! Get up, you **officers**, oil the shields!
23: 8 the bestower of crowns, whose merchants are **princes**,
30: 4 Though *they* have **officials** in Zoan and their envoys have arrived
31: 9 at sight of the battle standard their **commanders** will panic,"
32: 1 a king will reign in righteousness and **rulers** will rule with justice.
34:12 there to be called a kingdom, all her **princes** will vanish away.
43:28 So I will disgrace the **dignitaries** *of* your temple, and I will
49: 7 "Kings will see you and rise up, **princes** will see and bow down,
Jer 1:18 kings of Judah, its **officials**, its priests and the people of the land.
2:26 they, their kings and their **officials**, their priests and their prophets.
4: 9 declares the LORD, "the king and the **officials** will lose heart,
8: 1 declares the LORD, the bones of the kings and **officials** *of* Judah,
17:25 throne will come through the gates of this city with their **officials**.
17:25 They and their **officials** will come riding in chariots and on horses,
24: 1 After Jehoiachin son of Jehoiakim king of Judah and the **officials**,
24: 8 his **officials** and the survivors from Jerusalem, whether they
25:18 its kings and **officials**, to make them a ruin and an object of horror
25:19 king of Egypt, his attendants, his **officials** and all his people,
26:10 When the **officials** *of* Judah heard about these things, they went up
26:11 the priests and the prophets said to the **officials** and all the people,
26:12 Jeremiah said to all the **officials** and all the people: "The LORD
26:16 the **officials** and all the people said to the priests and the prophets,
26:21 King Jehoiakim and all his officers and **officials** heard his words,
29: 2 the court officials and the **leaders** *of* Judah and Jerusalem,
32:32 they, their kings and **officials**, their priests and prophets, the men
34:10 So all the **officials** and people who entered into this covenant
34:19 The **leaders** *of* Judah and Jerusalem, the court officials, the priests
34:19 The leaders of Judah and **[RPH]** Jerusalem, the court officials,
34:21 and his **officials** over to their enemies who seek their lives,
35: 4 It was next to the room of the **officials**, which was over that of
36:12 room in the royal palace, where all the **officials** were sitting:
36:12 of Shaphan, Zedekiah son of Hananiah, and all the other **officials**.
36:14 all the **officials** sent Jehudi son of Nethaniah, the son of Shelemiah,
36:19 Then the **officials** said to Baruch, "You and Jeremiah, go and hide.
36:21 and read it to the king and all the **officials** standing beside him.
37:14 instead, he arrested Jeremiah and brought him to the **officials**.
37:15 **They**[s] [+2021] were angry with Jeremiah and had him beaten
38: 4 the **officials** said to the king, "This man should be put to death.
38:17 'If you surrender to the **officers** *of* the king of Babylon, your life
38:18 But if you will not surrender to the **officers** *of* the king of Babylon,
38:22 of Judah will be brought out to the **officials** *of* the king of Babylon.
38:25 If the **officials** hear that I talked with you, and they come to you
38:27 All the **officials** did come to Jeremiah and question him, and he
39: 3 all the **officials** *of* the king of Babylon came and took seats in the
39: 3 a high official and all the other **officials** *of* the king of Babylon.
40: 7 When all the army **officers** and their men who were still in the
40:13 all the army **officers** still in the open country came to Gedaliah at
41:11 all the army **officers** who were with him heard about all the crimes
41:13 Johanan son of Kareah and the army **officers** who were with him,
41:16 all the army **officers** who were with him led away all the survivors
42: 1 Then all the army **officers**, including Johanan son of Kareah
42: 8 son of Kareah and all the army **officers** who were with him
43: 4 So Johanan son of Kareah and all the army **officers** and all the
43: 5 all the army **officers** led away all the remnant of Judah who had
44:17 our kings and our **officials** did in the towns of Judah and in the
44:21 your kings and your **officials** and the people of the land?
48: 7 Chemosh will go into exile, together with his priests and **officials**.
49: 3 Molech will go into exile, together with his priests and **officials**.
49:38 I will set my throne in Elam and destroy her king and **officials**,"
50:35 those who live in Babylon and against her **officials** and wise men!
51:57 I will make her **officials** and wise men drunk, her governors,
51:59 This is the message Jeremiah gave to the staff **officer** Seraiah son
52:10 Zedekiah before his eyes; he also killed all the **officials** *of* Judah.
52:25 He also took the secretary who was **chief officer** [+2021+7372] in
La 1: 6 Her **princes** are like deer that find no pasture; in weakness they
2: 2 her kingdom and its **princes** down to the ground in dishonor.
2: 9 Her king and her **princes** are exiled among the nations, the law is
5:12 **Princes** have been hung up by their hands; elders are shown no
Eze 11: 1 son of Azzur and Pelatiah son of Benaiah, **leaders** *of* the people.
17:12 Babylon went to Jerusalem and carried off her king and her **nobles**,
22:27 Her **officials** within her are like wolves tearing their prey;
Da 1: 7 The **chief** official gave them new names: to Daniel, the name
1: 8 he asked the **chief** official for permission not to defile himself this
1: 9 Now God had caused the **[RPH]** official to show favor
1:10 the **[RPH]** official told Daniel, "I am afraid of my lord the king,
1:11 said to the guard whom the **chief** official had appointed over
1:18 them in, the **chief** official presented them to Nebuchadnezzar.
8:11 It set itself up to be as great as the **Prince** *of* the host; it took away
8:25 will destroy many and take his stand against the **Prince** *of* princes.
8:25 will destroy many and take his stand against the Prince of **princes**.
9: 6 our **princes** and our fathers, and to all the people of the land.
9: 8 our **princes** and our fathers are covered with shame because we
10:13 the **prince** *of* the Persian kingdom resisted me twenty-one days.
10:13 Then Michael, one of the chief **princes**, came to help me,
10:20 Soon I will return to fight against the **prince** *of* Persia, and when I
10:20 prince of Persia, and when I go, the **prince** *of* Greece will come;
10:21 (No one supports me against them except Michael, your **prince**.
11: 5 but one of his **commanders** will become even stronger than he
12: 1 the great **prince** who protects your people, will arise.
Hos 3: 4 For the Israelites will live many days without king or **prince**,
5:10 Judah's **leaders** are like those who move boundary stones.
7: 3 delight the king with their wickedness, the **princes** with their lies.
7: 5 On the day of the festival of our king the **princes** become inflamed
7:16 Their **leaders** will fall by the sword because of their insolent
8:10 They will begin to waste away under the oppression of the **mighty**
9:15 I will no longer love them; all their **leaders** are rebellious.
13:10 in all your towns, of whom you said, 'Give me a king and **princes**'?
Am 1:15 will go into exile, he and his **officials** together," says the LORD.

Am 2: 3 I will destroy her ruler and kill all her **officials** with him,"
Mic 7: 3 the **ruler** demands gifts, the judge accepts bribes, the powerful
Zep 1: 8 On the day of the LORD's sacrifice I will punish the **princes**
3: 3 Her **officials** are roaring lions, her rulers are evening wolves,

8570 שַׂרְאֶצֶר śar'eṣer, שַׂר־אֶצֶר śar-'eṣer, n.pr.m. [3] [→ 5947]

Sharezer [3]

2Ki 19:37 sons Adrammelech and **Sharezer** cut him down with the sword,
Isa 37:38 sons Adrammelech and **Sharezer** cut him down with the sword,
Zec 7: 2 The people of Bethel had sent **Sharezer** and Regem-Melech,

8571 שָׂרַג śārag, v. [2] [→ 8585]

close-knit [1], woven together [1]

Job 40:17 [E] sways like a cedar; the sinews of his thighs *are* **close-knit**.
La 1:14 [F] bound into a yoke; by his hands *they were* **woven together**.

8572 שָׂרַד śārad, v. [1] (→ 8586]

left [1]

Jos 10:20 [A] but the few *who were* **left** reached their fortified cities.

8573 שְׂרָד śerād, n.[m.]. [4] [√ 8574?]

woven [4]

Ex 31:10 also the **woven** garments, both the sacred garments for Aaron the
35:19 the **woven** garments worn for ministering in the sanctuary—
39: 1 scarlet yarn they made **woven** garments for ministering in the
39:41 and the **woven** garments worn for ministering in the sanctuary,

8574 שֶׂרֶד śered, n.[m.]. [1] [√ 8573?]

marker [1]

Isa 44:13 measures with a line and makes an outline with a **marker**;

8575 שָׂרָה śārâ[1], v. [3] [→ 449, 3776, 3778, 8588, 8589]

struggled [3]

Ge 32:28 [32:29] [A] because *you have* **struggled** with God and with
Hos 12: 3 [12:4] [A] his brother's heel; as a man *he* **struggled** with God.
12: 4 [12:5] [A] *He* **struggled** with the angel and overcame him;

8576 ²שָׂרָה śārâ[2], n.f. [5] [→ 8569, 8577; cf. 8606]

ladies [1], of royal birth [1], queen [1], queens [1], women of nobility [1]

Jdg 5:29 The wisest of her **ladies** answer her; indeed, she keeps saying to
1Ki 11: 3 He had seven hundred wives **of royal birth** and three hundred
Est 1:18 Median **women of** the **nobility** who have heard about the queen's
Isa 49:23 will be your foster fathers, and their **queens** your nursing mothers.
La 1: 1 She who was **queen** among the provinces has now become a slave.

8577 ³שָׂרָה śārâ[3], n.pr.f. [38] [√ 8576; cf. 8584]

Sarah [35], *untranslated* [1], Sarah's [1], she[s] [1]

Ge 17:15 you are no longer to call her Sarai; her name will be **Sarah**.
17:17 a hundred years old? Will **Sarah** bear a child at the age of ninety?"
17:19 Then God said, "Yes, but your wife **Sarah** will bear you a son,
17:21 with Isaac, whom **Sarah** will bear to you by this time next year."
18: 6 So Abraham hurried into the tent to **Sarah**. "Quick," he said,
18: 9 "Where is your wife **Sarah**?" they asked him. "There, in the tent,"
18:10 about this time next year, and **Sarah** your wife will have a son."
18:10 Now **Sarah** was listening at the entrance to the tent, which was
18:11 Abraham and **Sarah** were already old and well advanced in years,
18:11 advanced in years, and **Sarah** was past the age of childbearing.
18:12 So **Sarah** laughed to herself as she thought, "After I am worn out
18:13 "Why did **Sarah** laugh and say, 'Will I really have a child,
18:14 to you at the appointed time next year and **Sarah** will have a son."
18:15 **Sarah** was afraid, so she lied and said, "I did not laugh." But he
20: 2 and there Abraham said of his wife **Sarah**, "She is my sister."
20: 2 Then Abimelech king of Gerar sent for **Sarah** and took her.
20:14 and gave them to Abraham, and he returned **Sarah** his wife to him.
20:16 To **Sarah** he said, "I am giving your brother a thousand shekels of
20:18 in Abimelech's household because of Abraham's wife **Sarah**.
21: 1 Now the LORD was gracious to **Sarah** as he had said,
21: 1 he had said, and the LORD did for **Sarah** what he had promised.
21: 2 **Sarah** became pregnant and bore a son to Abraham in his old age,
21: 3 Abraham gave the name Isaac to the son **Sarah** bore him.
21: 6 **Sarah** said, "God has brought me laughter, and everyone who
21: 7 "Who would have said to Abraham that **Sarah** would nurse
21: 9 **Sarah** saw that the son whom Hagar the Egyptian had borne to
21:12 Listen to whatever **Sarah** tells you, because it is through Isaac that
23: 1 **Sarah** lived to be a hundred and twenty-seven years old.
23: 1 Sarah lived to be a hundred and twenty-seven years old. **[RPH]**
23: 2 **She**[s] died at Kiriath Arba (that is, Hebron) in the land of Canaan,
23: 2 and Abraham went to mourn for **Sarah** and to weep over her.
23:19 Afterward Abraham buried his wife **Sarah** in the cave in the field
24:36 My master's wife **Sarah** has borne him a son in her old age,
24:67 Isaac brought her into the tent of his mother **Sarah**, and he married
25:10 from the Hittites. There Abraham was buried with his wife **Sarah**.
25:12 whom **Sarah's** maidservant, Hagar the Egyptian, bore to Abraham.
49:31 There Abraham and his wife **Sarah** were buried, there Isaac
Isa 51: 2 look to Abraham, your father, and to **Sarah**, who gave you birth.

8578 שְׂרוּג śerûg, n.pr.m. [5]

Serug [5]

Ge 11:20 When Reu had lived 32 years, he became the father of **Serug**.
11:21 And after he became the father of **Serug**, Reu lived 207 years
11:22 When **Serug** had lived 30 years, he became the father of Nahor.
11:23 of Nahor, **Serug** lived 200 years and had other sons and daughters.
1Ch 1:26 **Serug**, Nahor, Terah

8579 שְׂרוֹךְ śerôk, n.[m.]. [2] [√ 8592]

thong [2]

Ge 14:23 not even a thread or the **thong** *of* a sandal, so that you will never
Isa 5:27 not a belt is loosened at the waist, not a sandal **thong** is broken.

8580 שֶׂרַח seraḥ, n.pr.f. [3] [cf. 6243]

Serah [3]

Ge 46:17 of Asher: Imnah, Ishvah, Ishvi and Beriah. Their sister was **Serah**.
Nu 26:46 (Asher had a daughter named **Serah**.)
1Ch 7:30 of Asher: Imnah, Ishvah, Ishvi and Beriah. Their sister was **Serah**.

8581 שָׂרַט śāraṭ, v. [3] [→ 8582, 8583]

injure themselves [+8581] [2], cut [+928+8583] [1]

Lev 21: 5 [A] off the edges of their beards or **cut** [+928+8583] their bodies.
Zec 12: 3 [C] All who try to move it *will* **injure** [+8581] **themselves**.
12: 3 [A] All who try to move it *will* **injure themselves** [+8581].

8582 שֶׂרֶט śereṭ, n.[m.]. [1] [√ 8581]

cut [+928+5989] [1]

Lev 19:28 " '*Do* not **cut** [+928+5989] your bodies for the dead or put tattoo

8583 שָׂרֶטֶת śāreṭet, n.f. [1] [√ 8581]

cut [+928+8581] [1]

Lev 21: 5 off the edges of their beards or **cut** [+928+8581] their bodies.

8584 שָׂרַי śāray, n.pr.f. [17] [cf. 8577]

Sarai [15], *untranslated* [1], she[s] [1]

Ge 11:29 The name of Abram's wife was **Sarai**, and the name of Nahor's
11:30 Now **Sarai** was barren; she had no children.
11:31 and his daughter-in-law **Sarai**, the wife of his son Abram,
12: 5 He took his wife **Sarai**, his nephew Lot, all the possessions they
12:11 As he was about to enter Egypt, he said to his wife **Sarai**,
12:17 on Pharaoh and his household because of Abram's wife **Sarai**.
16: 1 Now **Sarai**, Abram's wife, had borne him no children. But she had
16: 2 so **she**[s] said to Abram, "The LORD has kept me from having
16: 2 can build a family through her." Abram agreed to what **Sarai** said.
16: 3 **Sarai** his wife took her Egyptian maidservant Hagar and gave her
16: 5 **Sarai** said to Abram, "You are responsible for the wrong I am
16: 6 Abram said. **[RPH]** "Do with her whatever you think best."
16: 6 think best." Then **Sarai** mistreated Hagar; so she fled from her.
16: 8 And he said, "Hagar, servant of **Sarai**, where have you come from,
16: 8 "I'm running away from my mistress **Sarai**," she answered.
17:15 God also said to Abraham, "*As for* **Sarai** your wife, you are no
17:15 "As for Sarai your wife, you are no longer to call her **Sarai**;

8585 שָׂרִיג śārîg, n.m. [3] [√ 8571]

branches [3]

Ge 40:10 and on the vine were three **branches**. As soon as it budded,
40:12 it means," Joseph said to him. "The three **branches** are three days.
Joel 1: 7 off their bark and thrown it away, leaving their **branches** white.

8586 ¹שָׂרִיד śārîd[1], n.m. [28] [√ 8572]

survivors [17], survive [4], left [2], survivor [2], few [1], men who were left [1], survived [1]

Nu 21:35 with his sons and his whole army, leaving them no **survivors**.
24:19 ruler will come out of Jacob and destroy the **survivors** of the city."
Dt 2:34 destroyed them—men, women and children. We left no **survivors**.
3: 3 and all his army. We struck them down, leaving no **survivors**.
Jos 8:22 Israel cut them down, leaving them neither **survivors** nor fugitives.
10:20 to a man—but the **few** who were left reached their fortified cities.

[A] Qal [B] Qal passive [C] Niphal [D] Piel (poel, polel, pilel, pilal, pealal, pilpel) [E] Pual (poal, polal, poalal, pulal, pualal)

Jos 10:28 and totally destroyed everyone in it. He left no **survivors**.
10:30 everyone in it Joshua put to the sword. He left no **survivors** there.
10:33 Joshua defeated him and his army—until no **survivors** were left.
10:37 They left no **survivors**. Just as at Eglon, they totally destroyed it
10:39 They left no **survivors**. They did to Debir and its king as they had
10:40 together with all their kings. He left no **survivors**.
11: 8 to the Valley of Mizpah on the east, until no **survivors** were left.
Jdg 5:13 "Then the **men who were left** came down to the nobles; the people
2Ki 10:11 his close friends and his priests, leaving him no **survivor**.
Job 18:19 descendants among his people, no **survivor** where once he lived.
20:21 Nothing is **left** for him to devour; his prosperity will not endure.
20:26 fire unfanned will consume him and devour *what* is **left** in his tent.
27:15 The plague will bury *those who* **survive** him, and their widows
Isa 1: 9 Unless the LORD Almighty had left us some **survivors**,
Jer 31: 2 "The people *who* **survive** the sword will find favor in the desert;
42:17 not one of them will **survive** or escape the disaster I will bring on
44:14 live in Egypt will escape or **survive** to return to the land of Judah,
47: 4 and to cut off all **survivors** who could help Tyre and Sidon.
La 2:22 In the day of the LORD's anger no one escaped or **survived**;
Joel 2:32 [3:5] has said, among the **survivors** whom the LORD calls.
Ob 1:14 nor hand over their **survivors** in the day of their trouble.
1:18 consume it. There will be no **survivors** from the house of Esau."

8587 ²שָׂרִיד śārîd², n.pr.loc. [2]

Sarid [2]

Jos 19:10 by clan: The boundary of their inheritance went as far as **Sarid**.
19:12 It turned east from **Sarid** toward the sunrise to the territory of

8588 שְׂרָיָה śᵉrāyâ, n.pr.m. [19] [√ 8575 + 3378]

Seraiah [17], *untranslated* [1], Seraiah's [1]

2Sa 8:17 Ahimelech son of Abiathar were priests; **Seraiah** was secretary;
2Ki 25:18 The commander of the guard took as prisoners **Seraiah** the chief
25:23 son of Kareah, **Seraiah** son of Tanhumeth the Netophathite,
1Ch 4:13 The sons of Kenaz: Othniel and **Seraiah**. The sons of Othniel:
4:14 **Seraiah** was the father of Joab, the father of Ge Harashim.
4:35 Jehu son of Joshibiah, the son of **Seraiah**, the son of Asiel,
6:14 [5:40] Azariah the father of **Seraiah**, and Seraiah the father of
6:14 [5:40] the father of Seraiah, and **Seraiah** the father of Jehozadak.
Ezr 2: 2 **Seraiah**, Reelaiah, Mordecai, Bilshan, Mispar, Bigvai, Rehum
7: 1 Ezra son of **Seraiah**, the son of Azariah, the son of Hilkiah,
Ne 10: 2 [10:3] **Seraiah**, Azariah, Jeremiah,
11:11 **Seraiah** son of Hilkiah, the son of Meshullam, the son of Zadok,
12: 1 son of Shealtiel and with Jeshua: **Seraiah**, Jeremiah, Ezra,
12:12 of **Seraiah's** family, Meraiah; of Jeremiah's, Hananiah;
Jer 40: 8 and Jonathan the sons of Kareah, **Seraiah** son of Tanhumeth,
51:59 This is the message Jeremiah gave to the staff officer **Seraiah** son
51:59 Zedekiah king of Judah in the fourth year of his reign. **[RPH]**
51:61 He said to **Seraiah**, "When you get to Babylon, see that you read
52:24 The commander of the guard took as prisoners **Seraiah** the chief

8589 שְׂרָיָהוּ śᵉrāyāhû, n.pr.m. [1] [√ 8575 + 3378]

Seraiah [1]

Jer 36:26 **Seraiah** son of Azriel and Shelemiah son of Abdeel to arrest

8590 שִׂרְיוֹן śiryôn, n.pr.loc. [2] [cf. 6246]

Sirion [2]

Dt 3: 9 (Hermon is called **Sirion** by the Sidonians; the Amorites call it
Ps 29: 6 He makes Lebanon skip like a calf, **Sirion** like a young wild ox.

8591 שָׂרִיק śārîq, a. [1] [√ 8600]

combed [1]

Isa 19: 9 Those who work with **combed** flax will despair, the weavers of

8592 שָׂרַךְ śārak, v. [1] [→ 8579]

running here and there [+2006] [1]

Jer 2:23 [D] You are a swift she-camel **running** [+2006] **here and there**,

8593 שַׂר־סְכִים śar-sᵉkîm, n.pr.m. Not used in NIV/BHS [√ 8569; cf. 5552]

8594 שָׂרַע śāraʿ, v. [3]

deformed [2], stretch out [1]

Lev 21:18 [B] no man who is blind or lame, disfigured or **deformed**;
22:23 [B] offering an ox or a sheep *that is* **deformed** or stunted,
Isa 28:20 [F] The bed is too short *to* **stretch out** *on*, the blanket too narrow

8595 שַׂרְעַפִּים śarʿappîm, n.[m.]pl. [2] [→ 8546]

anxiety [1], anxious thoughts [1]

Ps 94:19 When **anxiety** was great within me, your consolation brought joy
139:23 and know my heart; test me and know my **anxious thoughts**.

8596 שָׂרַף śārap, v. [117] [→ 5386, 5387, 8597, 8598, 8599; cf. 6251]

burned [27], burn [13], burn down [+836+928+2021] [7], burned [+836+906+928+2021] [5], be burned up [+836+928+2021] [4], burned down [+836+906+928+2021] [4], burns [4], set fire to [3], *untranslated* [2], are burned up [+836+928+2021+8596] [2], be burned [2], been burned up [2], burn down [+836+906+928+2021] [2], burn up [+836+906+928+2021] [2], burn up [2], burned [+836+928+2021] [2], set on fire [+836+906+928+2021] [2], set on fire [+836+928+2021] [2], bake thoroughly [+4200+8599] [1], be burned [+836+928+2021] [1], be burned down [+836+928+2021] [1], be destroyed [1], being burned [1], burn [+836+906+906+906+928+2021] [1], burn [+836+906+906+928+2021] [1], burn [+836+906+928+2021] [1], burn [+836+928+2021] [1], burn as sacrifices [1], burn down [1], burn to death [+836+906+906+928+2021] [1], burn up [+836+928+2021] [1], burned [+836+906+906+928+2021] [1], burned as sacrifices [1], burned to death [+836+906+906+928+2021] [1], burned to death [1], burned up [+836+906+906+906+906+928+2021] [1], burned up [+836+906+906+906+928+2021] [1], burned up [+836+906+906+928+2021] [1], burned up [+836+906+928+2021] [1], burned up [1], destroy [1], destroyed by fire [1], destroyed [1], is burned [1], made [1], make a fire [1], set fire to [+836+906+906+928+2021] [1], used for fuel [+836+1198] [1]

Ge 11: 3 [A] make bricks and **bake** [+4200+8599] them **thoroughly**."
38:24 [C] Judah said, "Bring her out and *have her* **burned to death**!"
Ex 12:10 [A] is left till morning, *you must* **burn** [+836+928+2021] it.
29:14 [A] But **burn** [+836+906+906+906+928+2021] the bull's flesh
29:34 [A] is left over till morning, **burn** [+836+906+906+928+2021] it **up**.
32:20 [A] And he took the calf they had made and **burned** it in the fire;
Lev 4:12 [A] ashes are thrown, and **burn** it in a wood fire on the ash heap.
4:12 [C] and burn it in a wood fire on the ash heap. **[RPH]**
4:21 [A] bull outside the camp and **burn** it as he burned the first bull.
4:21 [A] bull outside the camp and burn it as *he* **burned** the first bull.
6:30 [6:23] [C] not be eaten; *it must* **be burned** [+836+928+2021].
7:17 [C] till the third day *must* **be burned** [+836+928+2021] **up**.
7:19 [C] must not be eaten; *it must* **be burned** [+836+928+2021] **up**.
8:17 [A] its offal *he* **burned** [+836+906+906+906+906+928+2021] **up**
8:32 [A] **burn** [+836+928+2021] **up** the rest of the meat and the
9:11 [A] the hide *he* **burned** [+836+906+906+928+2021] **up** outside
10: 6 [A] may mourn for those the LORD *has* **destroyed by fire**.
10:16 [E] of the sin offering and found that *it had* **been burned up**,
13:52 [A] *He must* **burn up** the clothing, or the woven or knitted material
13:52 [C] the article *must* **be burned** [+836+928+2021] **up**.
13:55 [A] **Burn** it with fire, whether the mildew has affected one side
13:57 [A] and whatever has the mildew *must be* **burned** with fire.
16:27 [A] offal *are to be* **burned** [+836+906+906+928+2021] **up**.
16:28 [A] The *man who* **burns** them must wash his clothes and bathe
19: 6 [C] until the third day *must* **be burned** [+836+928+2021] **up**.
20:14 [A] Both he and they *must be* **burned** in the fire, so that no
21: 9 [C] she disgraces her father; *she must* **be burned** in the fire.
Nu 16:39 [17:4] [B] censers brought by those *who had* **been burned up**,
19: 5 [A] While he watches, the heifer *is to be* **burned**—its hide, flesh,
19: 5 [A] is to be burned—its hide, flesh, blood and offal. **[RPH]**
19: 8 [A] The *man who* **burns** it must also wash his clothes and bathe
31:10 [A] *They* **burned** [+836+906+906+928+2021] all the towns where
Dt 7: 5 [A] cut down their Asherah poles and **burn** their idols in the fire.
7:25 [A] The images of their gods *you are to* **burn** in the fire. Do not
9:21 [A] of yours, the calf you had made, and **burned** it in the fire.
12: 3 [A] their sacred stones and **burn** their Asherah poles in the fire;
12:31 [A] even **burn** their sons and daughters in the fire **as sacrifices**
13:16 [13:17] [A] completely **burn** [+836+906+906+928+2021] the town
Jos 6:24 [A] *they* **burned** [+836+928+2021] the whole city and everything
7:15 [C] the devoted things *shall* **be destroyed** by fire, along with
7:25 [A] stoned the rest, *they* **burned** [+836+906+928+2021] them.
8:28 [A] So Joshua **burned** Ai and made it a permanent heap of ruins,
11: 6 [A] their horses and **burn** [+836+906+928+2021] their chariots."
11: 9 [A] their horses and **burned** [+836+906+928+2021] their chariots.
11:11 [A] and *he* **burned** [+836+906+928+2021] **up** Hazor itself.
11:13 [A] Yet Israel *did* not **burn** any of the cities built on their
11:13 [A] built on their mounds—except Hazor, which Joshua **burned**.
Jdg 9:52 [A] the entrance to the tower to **set** it **on fire** [+836+928+2021],
12: 1 [A] *We're going to* **burn** [+836+928+2021] **down** your house
14:15 [A] or *we will* **burn** [+836+906+906+928+2021] you and your father's household **to death**.
15: 6 [A] So the Philistines went up and **burned** [+836+906+906 +928+2021] her and her father **to death**.
18:27 [A] the sword and **burned** [+836+906+928+2021] **down** their city.

1Sa 30: 1 [A] attacked Ziklag and **burned** [+836+906+928+2021] it,
30: 3 [B] they found *it* **destroyed** by fire and their wives and sons and
30: 14 [A] And *we* **burned** [+836+906+928+2021] Ziklag."
31: 12 [A] of Beth Shan and went to Jabesh, where *they* **burned** them.
2Sa 23: 7 [C] *they* **are burned** [+836+928+2021+8596] **up** where they lie."
23: 7 [A] *they* **are burned up** [+836+928+2021+8596] where they lie."
1Ki 9: 16 [A] and captured Gezer. *He had* **set** it **on fire** [+836+928+2021].
13: 2 [A] offerings here, and human bones *will be* **burned** on you.' "
15: 13 [A] Asa cut the pole down and **burned** it in the Kidron Valley.
16: 18 [A] and **set** the palace **on fire** [+836+906+928+2021] around him.
2Ki 10: 26 [A] the sacred stone out of the temple of Baal and **burned** it.
17: 31 [A] the Sepharvites **burned** their children in the fire **as sacrifices**
23: 4 [A] *He* **burned** them outside Jerusalem in the fields of the
23: 6 [A] to the Kidron Valley outside Jerusalem and **burned** it there.
23: 11 [A] Josiah then **burned** [+836+906+928+2021] the chariots
23: 15 [A] *He* **burned** the high place and ground it to powder,
23: 15 [A] and ground it to powder, and **burned** the Asherah pole also.
23: 16 [A] removed from them and **burned** on the altar to defile it,
23: 20 [A] high places on the altars and **burned** human bones on them.
25: 9 [A] *He* **set fire to** the temple of the LORD, the royal palace and
25: 9 [A] important building *he* **burned** [+836+906+928+2021] **down**.
1Ch 14: 12 [C] gods there, and David gave orders *to* **burn** *them* in the fire.
2Ch 15: 16 [A] pole down, broke it up and **burned** it in the Kidron Valley.
16: 14 [A] blended perfumes, and *they* **made** a huge fire in his honor.
34: 5 [A] *He* **burned** the bones of the priests on their altars, and so he
36: 19 [A] *They* **set fire to** God's temple and broke down the wall of
36: 19 [A] *they* **burned** [+836+928+2021] all the palaces and destroyed
Ne 4: 2 [3:34] [B] from those heaps of rubble—**burned** as they are?"
Ps 46: 9 [46:10] [A] shatters the spear, *he* **burns** the shields with fire.
74: 8 [A] *They* **burned** every place where God was worshiped in the
80: 16 [80:17] [B] Your vine is cut down, *it* **is burned** with fire;
Pr 6: 27 [C] scoop fire into his lap without his clothes **being burned**?
Isa 1: 7 [B] Your country is desolate, your cities **burned** *with* fire;
44: 16 [A] Half of the wood *he* **burns** in the fire; over it he prepares his
44: 19 [A] to say, "Half of it *I* **used for fuel** [+836+1198];
47: 14 [A] Surely they are like stubble; the fire *will* **burn** them **up**.
Jer 7: 31 [A] Topheth in the Valley of Ben Hinnom to **burn** their sons and
19: 5 [A] They have built the high places of Baal to **burn** their sons in
21: 10 [A] of the king of Babylon, and *he will* **destroy** it with fire.'
32: 29 [A] *they will* **burn** it **down**, along with the houses where the
34: 2 [A] of Babylon, and *he will* **burn** [+836+928+2021] it **down**.
34: 5 [A] so *they will* **make a fire** in your honor and lament, "Alas,
34: 22 [A] fight against it, take it and **burn** [+836+928+2021] it **down**.
36: 25 [A] Delaiah and Gemariah urged the king not *to* **burn** the scroll,
36: 27 [A] After the king **burned** the scroll containing the words that
36: 28 [A] the first scroll, which Jehoiakim king of Judah **burned up**.
36: 29 [A] You **burned** that scroll and said, "Why did you write on it
36: 32 [A] scroll that Jehoiakim king of Judah *had* **burned** in the fire.
37: 8 [A] they will capture it and **burn** [+836+928+2021] it **down**.'
37: 10 [A] come out and **burn** [+836+906+928+2021] this city **down**."
38: 17 [C] and this city *will* not **be burned** [+836+928+2021] **down**;
38: 18 [A] and *they will* **burn** [+836+928+2021] it **down**;
38: 23 [A] and this city *will be* **burned** [+836+906+928+2021] **down**."
39: 8 [A] The Babylonians **set fire** [+836+906+906+928+2021] **to** the
43: 12 [A] *he will* **burn** their temples and take their gods captive.
43: 13 [A] and *will* **burn** [+836+906+928+2021] **down** the temples of the
51: 32 [A] the marshes **set on fire** [+836+906+928+2021], and the
52: 13 [A] *He* **set fire to** the temple of the LORD, the royal palace and
52: 13 [A] important building *he* **burned** [+836+906+928+2021] **down**.
Eze 5: 4 [A] into the fire and **burn** [+836+906+928+2021] them **up**.
16: 41 [A] *They will* **burn** [+836+928+2021] **down** your houses
23: 47 [A] and **burn** [+836+928+2021] **down** their houses.
43: 21 [A] **burn** it in the designated part of the temple area outside the
Am 2: 1 [A] Because he **burned**, as if to lime, the bones of Edom's king,
Mic 1: 7 [C] all her temple gifts *will* **be burned** with fire; I will destroy all

8597 ¹שָׂרָף **śārāp[1]**, n.m. [7] [→ 8598; cf. 8596]

seraphs [2], venomous [2], snake [1], snakes [1], venomous serpent [1]

Nu 21: 6 the LORD sent **venomous** snakes among them; they bit the
21: 8 The LORD said to Moses, "Make a **snake** and put it up on a pole;
Dt 8: 15 and waterless land, with its **venomous** snakes and scorpions.
Isa 6: 2 Above him were **seraphs**, each with six wings: With two wings
6: 6 Then one of the **seraphs** flew to me with a live coal in his hand,
14: 29 spring up a viper, its fruit will be a darting, **venomous serpent**.
30: 6 and distress, of lions and lionesses, of adders and darting **snakes**,

8598 ²שָׂרָף **śārāp[2]**, n.pr.m. [1] [√ 8597; cf. 8596]

Saraph [1]

1Ch 4: 22 and Joash and **Saraph**, who ruled in Moab and Jashubi Lehem.

8599 שְׂרֵפָה **śᵉrēpâ**, n.f. [13] [√ 8596]

fire [3], burned [2], burning [2], *untranslated* [1], bake thoroughly [+4200+8596] [1], burned-out [1], burning waste [1], smoldering remains [1], those[s] [+2021] [1]

Ge 11: 3 let's make bricks and **bake** them **thoroughly** [+4200+8596]."
Lev 10: 6 may mourn for **those**[s] [+2021] the LORD has destroyed by fire.
Nu 16: 37 [17:2] to take the censers out of the **smoldering remains**
19: 6 and scarlet wool and throw them onto the **burning** heifer.
19: 17 put some ashes from the **burned** purification offering into a jar
Dt 29: 23 [29:22] The whole land will be a **burning waste** *of* salt
2Ch 16: 14 various blended perfumes, and they made a huge **fire** in his honor.
21: 19 His people made no **fire** in his honor, as they had for his fathers.
21: 19 made no fire in his honor, as they had **[RPH]** for his fathers.
Isa 9: 5 [9:4] every garment rolled in blood will be destined for **burning**,
64: 11 [64:10] where our fathers praised you, has been **burned** *with* fire,
Jer 51: 25 roll you off the cliffs, and make you a **burned-out** mountain.
Am 4: 11 You were like a burning stick snatched from the **fire**, yet you have

8600 שָׂרַק **śāraq**, a. Not used in NIV/BHS [→ 8591]

8601 ¹שָׂרֹק **śārōq[1]**, a. [1] [→ 5388, 8602, 8603, 8604, 8605]

brown [1]

Zec 1: 8 trees in a ravine. Behind him were red, **brown** and white horses.

8602 ²שָׂרֹק **śārōq[2]**, n.[m.]. [1] [√ 8601]

choicest vines [1]

Isa 16: 8 The rulers of the nations have trampled down the **choicest vines**,

8603 ¹שֹׂרֵק **śōrēq[1]**, n.[m.]. [2] [√ 8601]

choice vine [1], choicest vines [1]

Isa 5: 2 and cleared it of stones and planted it with the **choicest vines**.
Jer 2: 21 I had planted you like a **choice vine** of sound and reliable stock.

8604 ²שֹׂרֵק **śōrēq[2]**, n.pr.loc. [1] [√ 8601]

Sorek [1]

Jdg 16: 4 he fell in love with a woman in the Valley of **Sorek** whose name

8605 שְׂרֵקָה **śᵉrēqâ**, n.f. [1] [√ 8601]

choicest branch [1]

Ge 49: 11 He will tether his donkey to a vine, his colt to the **choicest branch**;

8606 שָׂרַר **śārar**, v.den. [7] [→ 5385, 8569; cf. 6233, 6254]

lord it [+8606] [2], choose princes [1], govern [1], governed [1], rule [1], ruler [1]

Nu 16: 13 [F] And now *you* also *want to* **lord** [+8606] **it** over us?
16: 13 [F] And now *you* also *want to* **lord it** [+8606] over us?
Jdg 9: 22 [A] After Abimelech *had* **governed** Israel three years,
Est 1: 22 [A] that every man should be **ruler** over his own household.
Pr 8: 16 [A] by me princes **govern**, and all nobles who rule on earth.
Isa 32: 1 [A] will reign in righteousness and rulers *will* **rule** with justice.
Hos 8: 4 [G] my consent; *they* **choose princes** without my approval.

8607 שָׂשׂוֹן **śāśôn**, n.m. [22] [√ 8464]

joy [14], gladness [6], joyful [1], rejoicing [1]

Est 8: 16 the Jews it was a time of happiness and joy, **gladness** and honor.
8: 17 there was joy and **gladness** among the Jews, with feasting
Ps 45: 7 [45:8] your companions by anointing you with the oil of **joy**.
51: 8 [51:10] Let me hear **joy** and gladness; let the bones you have
51: 12 [51:14] Restore to me the **joy** *of* your salvation and grant me a
105: 43 He brought out his people with **rejoicing**, his chosen ones with
119: 111 Your statutes are my heritage forever; they are the **joy** *of* my heart.
Isa 12: 3 With **joy** you will draw water from the wells of salvation.
22: 13 see, there is **joy** and revelry, slaughtering of cattle and killing of
35: 10 **Gladness** and joy will overtake them, and sorrow and sighing will
51: 3 **Joy** and gladness will be found in her, thanksgiving and the sound
51: 11 **Gladness** and joy will overtake them, and sorrow and sighing will
61: 3 the oil of **gladness** instead of mourning, and a garment of praise
Jer 7: 34 I will bring an end to the sounds of **joy** and gladness and to the
15: 16 they were my **joy** and my heart's delight, for I bear your name,
16: 9 in your days I will bring an end to the sounds of **joy** and gladness
25: 10 I will banish from them the sounds of **joy** and gladness, the voices
31: 13 I will turn their mourning into **gladness**; I will give them comfort
33: 9 **joy**, praise and honor before all nations on earth that hear of all the
33: 11 the sounds of **joy** and gladness, the voices of bride
Joel 1: 12 are dried up. Surely the **joy** of mankind is withered away.
Zec 8: 19 seventh and tenth months will become **joyful** and glad occasions

8608 שָׂתַם ***śātam***, v. [1] [cf. 6258]

shuts out [1]

La 3: 8 [A] Even when I call out or cry for help, *he* **shuts out** my prayer.

8609 שָׂתַר ***śātar***, v. [1] [→ Ar 10520]

outbreak [1]

1Sa 5: 9 [C] of the city, both young and old, with an **outbreak** of tumors.

שׁ, *š*

8610 שׁ ***š***, letter. Not used in NIV/BHS [→ Ar 10688]

8611 -שֶׁ ***ša-***, pt.rel.pref. [140] [→ 1417, 4792, 5499, 8724, 8975] See Select Index

untranslated [52], that [16], who [15], which [7], until [+6330] [6], the one[s] [4], whose [4], because [3], whom [3], he[s] [2], till [+6330] [2], allies[s] [+6640] [1], as [+3869] [1], as [+3972+6645] [1], body[s] [1], despite [+928+4200] [1], fault [+928+4200] [1], for [+928+1685] [1], future [+2118+4537] [1], how [1], it[s] [1], mine [+3276+4200] [1], my own [+3276+4200] [1], of [+4200+4946] [1], responsible for [+928+4200] [1], since [1], so that [1], Solomon's [+4200+8976] [1], successor [+132+339+995] [1], than [1], the produce[s] [1], therefore [+1826+6584] [1], when [+6330] [1], where [1], while [+6330] [1], why [+4200+4537] [1], wisdom[s] [1]

8612 שָׁאַב ***šāʾab***, v. [19] [→ 5393]

draw water [5], draw [4], drew [4], carriers [3], carry [1], drew water [1], filled [1]

Ge 24: 11 [A] toward evening, the time the *women* go out *to* **draw water**.
24: 13 [A] the daughters of the townspeople are coming out to **draw**
24: 19 [A] him a drink, she said, "*I'll* **draw water** for your camels too,
24: 20 [A] ran back to the well to **draw** *more* **water**, and drew enough
24: 20 [A] well to draw more water, and **drew** enough for all his camels.
24: 43 [A] if a maiden comes out to **draw water** and I say to her,
24: 44 [A] to me, "Drink, and *I'll* **draw water** for your camels too,"
24: 45 [A] She went down to the spring and **drew water**, and I said to
Dt 29: 11 [29:10] [A] camps who chop your wood and **carry** your water.
Jos 9: 21 [A] and water **carriers** for the entire community."
9: 23 [A] as woodcutters and water **carriers** for the house of my God."
9: 27 [A] and water **carriers** for the community
Ru 2: 9 [A] go and get a drink from the water jars the men *have* **filled**."
1Sa 7: 6 [A] *they* **drew** water and poured it out before the LORD.
9: 11 [A] they met some girls coming out to **draw** water, and they
2Sa 23: 16 [A] **drew** water from the well near the gate of Bethlehem and
1Ch 11: 18 [A] **drew** water from the well near the gate of Bethlehem and
Isa 12: 3 [A] With joy *you will* **draw** water from the wells of salvation.
Na 3: 14 [A] **Draw** water for the siege, strengthen your defenses!

8613 שָׁאַג ***šāʾag***, v. [20] [→ 8614]

roar [7], roaring [4], roared [3], roar mightily [+8613] [2], roars [2], comes roar [1], groan [1]

Jdg 14: 5 [A] of Timnah, suddenly a young lion came **roaring** toward him.
Job 37: 4 [A] After that **comes** the sound of *his* **roar**; he thunders with his
Ps 22: 13 [22:14] [A] **Roaring** lions tearing their prey open their mouths
38: 8 [38:9] [A] and utterly crushed; *I* **groan** in anguish of heart.
74: 4 [A] Your foes **roared** in the place where you met with us;
104: 21 [A] The lions **roar** for their prey and seek their food from God.
Isa 5: 29 [A] Their roar is like that of the lion, *they* **roar** like young lions;
Jer 2: 15 [A] Lions *have* **roared**; they have growled at him. They have
25: 30 [A] " 'The LORD *will* **roar** from on high; he will thunder from
25: 30 [A] holy dwelling and **roar** [+8613] **mightily** against his land.
25: 30 [A] holy dwelling and **roar mightily** [+8613] against his land.
51: 38 [A] Her *people* all **roar** like young lions, they growl like lion
Eze 22: 25 [A] There is a conspiracy of her princes within her like a **roaring**
Hos 11: 10 [A] They will follow the LORD; *he will* **roar** like a lion.
11: 10 [A] When he **roars**, his children will come trembling from the
Joel 3: 16 [4:16] [A] The LORD *will* **roar** from Zion and thunder from
Am 1: 2 [A] "The LORD **roars** from Zion and thunders from Jerusalem;
3: 4 [A] *Does* a lion **roar** in the thicket when he has no prey? Does he
3: 8 [A] The lion *has* **roared**—who will not fear? The Sovereign
Zep 3: 3 [A] Her officials are **roaring** lions, her rulers are evening wolves,

8614 שְׁאָגָה ***šᵉʾāgâ***, n.f. [7] [√ 8613]

roar [3], groaning [2], groans [1], roaring [+7754] [1]

Job 3: 24 comes to me instead of food; my **groans** pour out like water.
4: 10 The lions may **roar** and growl, yet the teeth of the great lions are
Ps 22: 1 [22:2] far from saving me, so far from the words of my **groaning**?
32: 3 my bones wasted away through my **groaning** all day long.
Isa 5: 29 Their **roar** is like that of the lion, they roar like young lions;
Eze 19: 7 and all who were in it were terrified by his **roaring** [+7754].
Zec 11: 3 Listen to the **roar** *of* the lions; the lush thicket of the Jordan is

8615 שָׁאָה[1] ***šāʾâ[1]***, v. [4] [→ 8619, 8622, 8625, 8643, 8858?, 8885?]

turned into [2], lie ruined [1], ruined [1]

2Ki 19: 25 [G] that you *have* **turned** fortified cities **into** piles of stone.
Isa 6: 11 [A] "Until the cities **lie ruined** and without inhabitant,
6: 11 [C] houses are left deserted and the fields **ruined** and ravaged,
37: 26 [G] that you *have* **turned** fortified cities **into** piles of stone.

8616 שָׁאָה[2] ***šāʾâ[2]***, v. [2] [→ 8623, 9583, 9589, 9594]

roar [2]

Isa 17: 12 [C] of the peoples—*they* **roar** like the roaring of great waters!
17: 13 [C] Although the peoples **roar** like the roar of surging waters,

8617 שָׁאָה[3] ***šāʾâ[3]***, v. [1] [cf. 9120]

watched closely [1]

Ge 24: 21 [F] the man **watched** her **closely** to learn whether or not the

8618 שֹׁאָה ***šaʾwâ***, n.f. [0]

Pr 1: 27 [when calamity overtakes you like a **storm**, [K; see Q 8739]]

8619 שְׁאוֹל ***šᵉʾôl***, n.f. & m. [65 / 66] [√ 8615; cf. 8520, 8628]

grave [55], death [6], depths of the grave [2], depths [2], realm of death [1]

Ge 37: 35 he said, "in mourning will I go down to the **grave** to my son."
42: 38 you will bring my gray head down to the **grave** in sorrow."
44: 29 you will bring my gray head down to the **grave** in misery.'
44: 31 will bring the gray head of our father down to the **grave** in sorrow.
Nu 16: 30 that belongs to them, and they go down alive into the **grave**,
16: 33 They went down alive into the **grave**, with everything they owned;
Dt 32: 22 kindled by my wrath, one that burns to the **realm of death** below.
1Sa 2: 6 and makes alive; he brings down to the **grave** and raises up.
2Sa 22: 6 The cords of the **grave** coiled around me; the snares of death
1Ki 2: 6 but do not let his gray head go down to the **grave** in peace.
2: 9 to do to him. Bring his gray head down to the **grave** in blood."
Job 7: 9 and is gone, so he who goes down to the **grave** does not return.
11: 8 They are deeper than the **depths of the grave**—what can you
14: 13 "If only you would hide me in the **grave** and conceal me till your
17: 13 If the only home I hope for is the **grave**, if I spread out my bed in
17: 16 Will it go down to the gates of **death**? Will we descend together
21: 13 spend their years in prosperity and go down to the **grave** in peace.
24: 19 melted snow, so the **grave** snatches away those who have sinned.
26: 6 **Death** is naked before God; Destruction lies uncovered.
Ps 6: 5 [6:6] you when he is dead. Who praises you from the **grave**?
9: 17 [9:18] The wicked return to the **grave**, all the nations that forget
16: 10 because you will not abandon me to the **grave**, nor will you let
18: 5 [18:6] The cords of the **grave** coiled around me; the snares of
30: 3 [30:4] O LORD, you brought me up from the **grave**; you spared
31: 17 [31:18] let the wicked be put to shame and lie silent in the **grave**.
49: 14 [49:15] Like sheep they are destined for the **grave**, and death will
49: 14 [49:15] their forms will decay in the **grave**, far from their princely
49: 15 [49:16] God will redeem my life from the **grave**; he will surely
55: 15 [55:16] let them go down alive to the **grave**, for evil finds lodging
86: 13 toward me; you have delivered me from the depths of the **grave**.
88: 3 [88:4] my soul is full of trouble and my life draws near the **grave**.
89: 48 [89:49] see death, or save himself from the power of the **grave**?
116: 3 of death entangled me, the anguish of the **grave** came upon me;
139: 8 you are there; if I make my bed in the **depths**, you are there.
141: 7 so our bones have been scattered at the mouth of the **grave**."
Pr 1: 12 let's swallow them alive, like the **grave**, and whole, like those who
5: 5 Her feet go down to death; her steps lead straight to the **grave**.
7: 27 Her house is a highway to the **grave**, leading down to the chambers
9: 18 the dead are there, that her guests are in the depths of the **grave**.
15: 11 **Death** and Destruction lie open before the LORD—how much
15: 24 upward for the wise to keep him from going down to the **grave**.
23: 14 Punish him with the rod and save his soul from **death**.
27: 20 **Death** and Destruction are never satisfied, and neither are the eyes
30: 16 the **grave**, the barren womb, land, which is never satisfied with
Ecc 9: 10 do it with all your might, for in the **grave**, where you are going,
SS 8: 6 for love is as strong as death, its jealousy unyielding as the **grave**.
Isa 5: 14 Therefore the **grave** enlarges its appetite and opens its mouth
7: 11 whether in the deepest **depths** [BHS 8628] or in the highest
14: 9 The **grave** below is all astir to meet you at your coming; it rouses
14: 11 All your pomp has been brought down to the **grave**, along with the
14: 15 But you are brought down to the **grave**, to the depths of the pit.

Isa 28:15 a covenant with death, with the **grave** we have made an agreement.
28:18 will be annulled; your agreement with the **grave** will not stand.
38:10 "In the prime of my life must I go through the gates of **death**
38:18 For the **grave** cannot praise you, death cannot sing your praise;
57: 9 sent your ambassadors far away; you descended to the **grave** *itself*!
Eze 31:15 On the day it was brought down to the **grave** I covered the deep
31:16 I brought it down to the **grave** with those who go down to the pit.
31:17 allies among the nations, had also gone down to the **grave** with it,
32:21 From within the **grave** the mighty leaders will say of Egypt
32:27 who went down to the **grave** with their weapons of war, whose
Hos 13:14 "I will ransom them from the power of the **grave**; I will redeem
13:14 O death, are your plagues? Where, O **grave**, is your destruction?
Am 9: 2 Though they dig down to the **depths of the grave**, from there my
Jnh 2: 2 [2:3] From the depths of the **grave** I called for help, and you
Hab 2: 5 Because he is as greedy as the **grave** and like death is never

8620 שָׁאוּל ***šā'ûl***, n.pr.m. [406] [→ 8621; cf. 8626]

Saul [327], Saul's [34], he[s] [12], *untranslated* [9], Shaul [9], him[s] [6], Saul's [+4200] [4], his[s] [3], his[s] [+4200] [1], they[s] [+6269] [1]

Ge 36:37 **Shaul** from Rehoboth on the river succeeded him as king.
36:38 When **Shaul** died, Baal-Hanan son of Acbor succeeded him as
46:10 Ohad, Jakin, Zohar and **Shaul** the son of a Canaanite woman.
Ex 6:15 Ohad, Jakin, Zohar and **Shaul** the son of a Canaanite woman.
Nu 26:13 through Zerah, the Zerahite clan; through **Shaul**, the Shaulite clan.
1Sa 9: 2 He had a son named **Saul**, an impressive young man without equal
9: 3 Now the donkeys belonging to **Saul's** father Kish were lost,
9: 3 and Kish said to his son **Saul**, "Take one of the servants with you
9: 5 **Saul** said to the servant who was with him, "Come, let's go back,
9: 7 **Saul** said to his servant, "If we go, what can we give the man?
9: 8 The servant answered **him**[s] again. "Look," he said, "I have a
9:10 "Good," **Saul** said to his servant. "Come, let's go." So they set out
9:15 Now the day before **Saul** came, the LORD had revealed this to
9:17 When Samuel caught sight of **Saul**, the LORD said to him,
9:18 **Saul** approached Samuel in the gateway and asked, "Would you
9:19 **[RPH]** "Go up ahead of me to the high place, for today you are to
9:21 **Saul** answered, "But am I not a Benjamite, from the smallest tribe
9:22 Samuel brought **Saul** and his servant into the hall and seated them
9:24 cook took up the leg with what was on it and set it in front of **Saul**.
9:24 'I have invited guests.' " And **Saul** dined with Samuel that day.
9:25 to the town, Samuel talked with **Saul** on the roof of his house.
9:26 They rose about daybreak and Samuel called to **Saul** on the roof,
9:26 When **Saul** got ready, he and Samuel went outside together.
9:27 Samuel said to **Saul**, "Tell the servant to go on ahead of us"—
10:11 happened to the son of Kish? Is **Saul** also among the prophets?"
10:12 So it became a saying: "Is **Saul** also among the prophets?"
10:14 Now **Saul's** uncle asked him and his servant, "Where have you
10:15 **Saul's** uncle said, "Tell me what Samuel said to you."
10:16 **Saul** replied, "He assured us that the donkeys had been found."
10:21 and Matri's clan was chosen. Finally **Saul** son of Kish was chosen.
10:26 **Saul** also went to his home in Gibeah, accompanied by valiant men
11: 4 When the messengers came to Gibeah of **Saul** and reported these
11: 5 Just then **Saul** was returning from the fields, behind his oxen,
11: 5 behind his oxen, and **he**[s] asked, "What is wrong with the people?
11: 6 When **Saul** heard their words, the Spirit of God came upon him in
11: 7 what will be done to the oxen of anyone who does not follow **Saul**
11:11 The next day **Saul** separated his men into three divisions; during
11:12 said to Samuel, "Who was it that asked, 'Shall **Saul** reign over us?'
11:13 **Saul** said, "No one shall be put to death today, for this day the
11:15 and confirmed **Saul** as king in the presence of the LORD.
11:15 the LORD, and **Saul** and all the Israelites held a great celebration.
13: 1 **Saul** was ⌊thirty⌋ years old when he became king, and he reigned
13: 2 **Saul** chose three thousand men from Israel; two thousand were
13: 2 two thousand were with **him**[s] at Micmash and in the hill country of
13: 3 Then **Saul** had the trumpet blown throughout the land and said,
13: 4 "**Saul** has attacked the Philistine outpost, and now Israel has
13: 4 And the people were summoned to join **Saul** at Gilgal.
13: 7 **Saul** remained at Gilgal, and all the troops with him were quaking
13: 9 So **he**[s] said, "Bring me the burnt offering and the fellowship
13:10 the offering, Samuel arrived, and **Saul** went out to greet him.
13:11 **Saul** replied, "When I saw that the men were scattering, and that
13:13 **[RPH]** "You have not kept the command the LORD your God
13:15 in Benjamin, and **Saul** counted the men who were with him.
13:16 **Saul** and his son Jonathan and the men with them were staying in
13:22 So on the day of the battle not a soldier with **Saul** and Jonathan
13:22 or spear in his hand; only **Saul** and his son Jonathan had them.
14: 1 One day Jonathan son of **Saul** said to the young man bearing his
14: 2 **Saul** was staying on the outskirts of Gibeah under a pomegranate
14:16 **Saul's** [+4200] lookouts at Gibeah in Benjamin saw the army
14:17 Then **Saul** said to the men who were with him, "Muster the forces
14:18 **Saul** said to Ahijah, "Bring the ark of God." (At that time it was
14:19 While **Saul** was talking to the priest, the tumult in the Philistine
14:19 and more. So **Saul** said to the priest, "Withdraw your hand."
14:20 Then **Saul** and all his men assembled and went to the battle.
14:21 them to their camp went over to the Israelites who were with **Saul**
14:24 because **Saul** had bound the people under an oath, saying,
14:33 someone said to **Saul**, "Look, the men are sinning against the
14:34 **he**[s] said, "Go out among the men and tell them, 'Each of you bring
14:35 **Saul** built an altar to the LORD; it was the first time he had done
14:36 **Saul** said, "Let us go down after the Philistines by night
14:37 So **Saul** asked God, "Shall I go down after the Philistines?
14:38 **Saul** therefore said, "Come here, all you who are leaders of the
14:40 over here." "Do what seems best to you," the men replied. **[RPH]**
14:41 **Saul** prayed to the LORD, the God of Israel, "Give me the right
14:41 Jonathan and **Saul** were taken by lot, and the men were cleared.
14:42 **Saul** said, "Cast the lot between me and Jonathan my son."
14:43 Then **Saul** said to Jonathan, "Tell me what you have done."
14:44 **Saul** said, "May God deal with me, be it ever so severely,
14:45 the men said to **Saul**, "Should Jonathan die—he who has brought
14:46 **Saul** stopped pursuing the Philistines, and they withdrew to their
14:47 After **Saul** had assumed rule over Israel, he fought against their
14:49 **Saul's** sons were Jonathan, Ishvi and Malki-Shua. The name of his
14:50 The name of the commander of **Saul's** army was Abner son of Ner,
14:50 of Saul's army was Abner son of Ner, and Ner was **Saul's** uncle.
14:51 **Saul's** father Kish and Abner's father Ner were sons of Abiel.
14:52 All the days of **Saul** there was bitter war with the Philistines,
14:52 whenever **Saul** saw a mighty or brave man, he took him into his
15: 1 Samuel said to **Saul**, "I am the one the LORD sent to anoint you
15: 4 So **Saul** summoned the men and mustered them at Telaim—
15: 5 **Saul** went to the city of Amalek and set an ambush in the ravine.
15: 6 Then **he**[s] said to the Kenites, "Go away, leave the Amalekites
15: 7 **Saul** attacked the Amalekites all the way from Havilah to Shur,
15: 9 But **Saul** and the army spared Agag and the best of the sheep
15:11 "I am grieved that I have made **Saul** king, because he has turned
15:12 Early in the morning Samuel got up and went to meet **Saul**,
15:12 and went to meet Saul, but he was told, "**Saul** has gone to Carmel.
15:13 When Samuel reached **him**[s], Saul said, "The LORD bless you!
15:13 When Samuel reached him, **Saul** said, "The LORD bless you!
15:15 **Saul** answered, "The soldiers brought them from the Amalekites;
15:16 "Stop!" Samuel said to **Saul**. "Let me tell you what the LORD
15:20 "But I did obey the LORD," **Saul** said. "I went on the mission the
15:24 **Saul** said to Samuel, "I have sinned. I violated the LORD's
15:26 Samuel said to **him**[s], "I will not go back with you. You have
15:31 So Samuel went back with **Saul**, and Saul worshiped the LORD.
15:31 So Samuel went back with Saul, and **Saul** worshiped the LORD.
15:34 left for Ramah, but **Saul** went up to his home in Gibeah of Saul.
15:34 left for Ramah, but Saul went up to his home in Gibeah of **Saul**.
15:35 Until the day Samuel died, he did not go to see **Saul** again,
15:35 he did not go to see Saul again, though Samuel mourned for **him**[s].
15:35 the LORD was grieved that he had made **Saul** king over Israel.
16: 1 The LORD said to Samuel, "How long will you mourn for **Saul**,
16: 2 Samuel said, "How can I go? **Saul** will hear about it and kill me."
16:14 Now the Spirit of the LORD had departed from **Saul**, and an evil
16:15 **Saul's** attendants said to him, "See, an evil spirit from God is
16:17 So **Saul** said to his attendants, "Find someone who plays well
16:19 **Saul** sent messengers to Jesse and said, "Send me your son David,
16:20 and a young goat and sent them with his son David to **Saul**.
16:21 David came to **Saul** and entered his service. Saul liked him very
16:22 **Saul** sent word to Jesse, saying, "Allow David to remain in my
16:23 Whenever the spirit from God came upon **Saul**, David would take
16:23 relief would come to **Saul**; he would feel better, and the evil spirit
17: 2 **Saul** and the Israelites assembled and camped in the Valley of Elah
17: 8 Am I not a Philistine, and are you not the servants of **Saul**?
17:11 **Saul** and all the Israelites were dismayed and terrified.
17:12 and in **Saul's** time he was old and well advanced in years.
17:13 Jesse's three oldest sons had followed **Saul** to the war: The
17:14 David was the youngest. The three oldest followed **Saul**,
17:15 and forth from **Saul** to tend his father's sheep at Bethlehem.
17:19 They are with **Saul** and all the men of Israel in the Valley of Elah,
17:31 What David said was overheard and reported to **Saul**, and Saul
17:32 David said to **Saul**, "Let no one lose heart on account of this
17:33 **Saul** replied, "You are not able to go out against this Philistine
17:34 David said to **Saul**, "Your servant has been keeping his father's
17:37 **Saul** said to David, "Go, and the LORD be with you."
17:38 **Saul** dressed David in his own tunic. He put a coat of armor on
17:39 "I cannot go in these," he said to **Saul**, "because I am not used to
17:55 As **Saul** watched David going out to meet the Philistine, he said to
17:57 Abner took him and brought him before **Saul**, with David still
17:58 **Saul** asked him. David said, "I am the son of your servant Jesse of
18: 1 After David had finished talking with **Saul**, Jonathan became one
18: 2 From that day **Saul** kept David with him and did not let him return
18: 5 Whatever **Saul** sent him to do, David did it so successfully that
18: 5 so successfully that **Saul** gave him a high rank in the army.
18: 5 the army. This pleased all the people, and **Saul's** officers as well.
18: 6 the women came out from all the towns of Israel to meet King **Saul**
18: 7 "**Saul** has slain his thousands, and David his tens of thousands."
18: 8 **Saul** was very angry; this refrain galled him. "They have credited
18: 9 And from that time on **Saul** kept a jealous eye on David.

1Sa 18:10 The next day an evil spirit from God came forcefully upon **Saul**.
18:10 playing the harp, as he usually did. **Saul** had a spear in his hand
18:11 and **he**[s] hurled it, saying to himself, "I'll pin David to the wall."
18:12 **Saul** was afraid of David, because the LORD was with David
18:12 of David, because the LORD was with David but had left **Saul**.
18:13 So **he**[s] sent David away from him and gave him command over a
18:15 When **Saul** saw how successful he was, he was afraid of him.
18:17 **Saul** said to David, "Here is my older daughter Merab. I will give
18:17 For **Saul** said to himself, "I will not raise a hand against him.
18:18 But David said to **Saul**, "Who am I, and what is my family
18:19 the time came for Merab, **Saul's** daughter, to be given to David,
18:20 Now **Saul's** daughter Michal was in love with David, and when
18:20 love with David, and when they told **Saul** about it, he was pleased.
18:21 "I will give her to him," **he**[s] thought, "so that she may be a snare to
18:21 So **Saul** said to David, "Now you have a second opportunity to
18:22 Then **Saul** ordered his attendants: "Speak to David privately
18:23 **They**[s] [+6269] repeated these words to David. But David said,
18:24 When **Saul's** servants told him what David had said,
18:25 **Saul** replied, "Say to David, 'The king wants no other price for the
18:25 to take revenge on his enemies.' " **Saul's** plan was to have David
18:27 Then **Saul** gave him his daughter Michal in marriage.
18:28 When **Saul** realized that the LORD was with David and that his
18:28 was with David and that **his**[s] daughter Michal loved David,
18:29 **Saul** became still more afraid of him, and he remained his enemy
18:29 afraid of him, and **he**[s] remained his enemy the rest of his days.
18:30 David met with more success than the rest of **Saul's** officers,
19: 1 **Saul** told his son Jonathan and all the attendants to kill David.
19: 1 to kill David. But Jonathan **[NIE]** was very fond of David
19: 2 warned him, "My father **Saul** is looking for a chance to kill you.
19: 4 Jonathan spoke well of David to **Saul** his father and said to him,
19: 6 **Saul** listened to Jonathan and took this oath: "As surely as the
19: 6 Saul listened to Jonathan and **[RPH]** took this oath: "As surely as
19: 7 He brought him to **Saul**, and David was with Saul as before.
19: 9 an evil spirit from the LORD came upon **Saul** as he was sitting in
19:10 **Saul** tried to pin him to the wall with his spear, but David eluded
19:10 but David eluded him as **Saul** drove the spear into the wall.
19:11 **Saul** sent men to David's house to watch it and to kill him in the
19:14 When **Saul** sent the men to capture David, Michal said, "He is ill."
19:15 **Saul** sent the men back to see David and told them, "Bring him up
19:17 **Saul** said to Michal, "Why did you deceive me like this and send
19:17 he escaped?" Michal told **him**[s], "He said to me, 'Let me get away.
19:18 to Samuel at Ramah and told him all that **Saul** had done to him.
19:19 Word came to **Saul**: "David is in Naioth at Ramah";
19:20 so **he**[s] sent men to capture him. But when they saw a group of
19:20 the Spirit of God came upon **Saul's** men and they also prophesied.
19:21 **Saul** was told about it, and he sent more men, and they prophesied
19:21 **Saul** sent men a third time, and they also prophesied.
19:24 This is why people say, "Is **Saul** also among the prophets?"
20:25 opposite Jonathan, and Abner sat next to **Saul**, but David's place
20:26 **Saul** said nothing that day, for he thought, "Something must have
20:27 **Saul** said to his son Jonathan, "Why hasn't the son of Jesse come
20:28 **[RPH]** "David earnestly asked me for permission to go to
20:30 **Saul's** anger flared up at Jonathan and he said to him, "You son of
20:32 to death? What has he done?" Jonathan asked his father. **[RPH]**
20:33 **Saul** hurled his spear at him to kill him. Then Jonathan knew that
21: 7 [21:8] Now one of **Saul's** servants was there that day,
21: 7 [21:8] he was Doeg the Edomite, **Saul's** [+4200] head shepherd.
21:10 [21:11] That day David fled from **Saul** and went to Achish king
21:11 [21:12] " '**Saul** has slain his thousands, and David his tens of
22: 6 Now **Saul** heard that David and his men had been discovered.
22: 6 **Saul**, spear in hand, was seated under the tamarisk tree on the hill
22: 7 **Saul** said to them, "Listen, men of Benjamin! Will the son of Jesse
22: 9 Doeg the Edomite, who was standing with **Saul's** officials, said,
22:12 **Saul** said, "Listen now, son of Ahitub." "Yes, my lord,"
22:13 **Saul** said to him, "Why have you conspired against me, you
22:21 He told David that **Saul** had killed the priests of the LORD.
22:22 Doeg the Edomite was there, I knew he would be sure to tell **Saul**.
23: 7 **Saul** was told that David had gone to Keilah, and he said,
23: 7 had gone to Keilah, and **he**[s] said, "God has handed him over to me,
23: 8 **Saul** called up all his forces for battle, to go down to Keilah to
23: 9 When David learned that **Saul** was plotting against him, he said to
23:10 your servant has heard definitely that **Saul** plans to come to Keilah
23:11 Will **Saul** come down, as your servant has heard? O LORD,
23:12 "Will the citizens of Keilah surrender me and my men to **Saul**?"
23:13 When **Saul** was told that David had escaped from Keilah,
23:14 Day after day **Saul** searched for him, but God did not give David
23:15 Desert of Ziph, he learned that **Saul** had come out to take his life.
23:16 **Saul's** son Jonathan went to David at Horesh and helped him find
23:17 be afraid," he said. "My father **Saul** will not lay a hand on you.
23:17 and I will be second to you. Even my father **Saul** knows this."
23:19 The Ziphites went up to **Saul** at Gibeah and said, "Is not David
23:21 **Saul** replied, "The LORD bless you for your concern for me.
23:24 So they set out and went to Ziph ahead of **Saul**. Now David
23:25 **Saul** and his men began the search, and when David was told about
23:25 When **Saul** heard this, he went into the Desert of Maon in pursuit
23:26 **Saul** was going along one side of the mountain, and David
23:26 his men were on the other side, hurrying to get away from **Saul**.
23:26 As **Saul** and his forces were closing in on David and his men to
23:27 a messenger came to **Saul**, saying, "Come quickly! The Philistines
23:28 **Saul** broke off his pursuit of David and went to meet the
24: 1 [24:2] After **Saul** returned from pursuing the Philistines, he was
24: 2 [24:3] So **Saul** took three thousand chosen men from all Israel
24: 3 [24:4] a cave was there, and **Saul** went in to relieve himself.
24: 4 [24:5] up unnoticed and cut off a corner of **Saul's** [+4200] robe.
24: 5 [24:6] for having cut off a corner of **his**[s] [+4200] robe.
24: 7 [24:8] rebuked his men and did not allow them to attack **Saul**.
24: 7 [24:8] to attack Saul. And **Saul** left the cave and went his way.
24: 8 [24:9] David went out of the cave and called out to **Saul**, "My
24: 8 [24:9] When **Saul** looked behind him, David bowed down
24: 9 [24:10] He said to **Saul**, "Why do you listen when men say,
24:16 [24:17] **[RPH]** Saul asked, "Is that your voice, David my son?"
24:16 [24:17] **Saul** asked, "Is that your voice, David my son?"
24:16 [24:17] "Is that your voice, David my son?" And **he**[s] wept aloud.
24:22 [24:23] So David gave his oath to **Saul**. Then Saul returned home,
24:22 [24:23] **Saul** returned home, but David and his men went up to
25:44 **Saul** had given his daughter Michal, David's wife, to Paltiel son of
26: 1 The Ziphites went to **Saul** at Gibeah and said, "Is not David hiding
26: 2 So **Saul** went down to the Desert of Ziph, with his three thousand
26: 3 **Saul** made his camp beside the road on the hill of Hakilah facing
26: 3 in the desert. When he saw that **Saul** had followed him there,
26: 4 he sent out scouts and learned that **Saul** had definitely arrived.
26: 5 Then David set out and went to the place where **Saul** had camped.
26: 5 He saw where **Saul** and Abner son of Ner, the commander of the
26: 5 **Saul** was lying inside the camp, with the army encamped around
26: 6 "Who will go down into the camp with me to **Saul**?"
26: 7 and Abishai went to the army by night, and there was **Saul**,
26:12 So David took the spear and water jug near **Saul's** head, and they
26:17 **Saul** recognized David's voice and said, "Is that your voice,
26:21 Then **Saul** said, "I have sinned. Come back, David my son.
26:25 Then **Saul** said to David, "May you be blessed, my son David;
26:25 So David went on his way, and **Saul** returned home.
27: 1 "One of these days I will be destroyed by the hand of **Saul**.
27: 1 Then **Saul** will give up searching for me anywhere in Israel,
27: 4 When **Saul** was told that David had fled to Gath, he no longer
28: 3 **Saul** had expelled the mediums and spiritists from the land.
28: 4 while **Saul** gathered all the Israelites and set up camp at Gilboa.
28: 5 When **Saul** saw the Philistine army, he was afraid; terror filled his
28: 6 **He**[s] inquired of the LORD, but the LORD did not answer him
28: 7 **Saul** then said to his attendants, "Find me a woman who is a
28: 8 So **Saul** disguised himself, putting on other clothes, and at night he
28: 9 But the woman said to him, "Surely you know what **Saul** has done.
28:10 **Saul** swore to her by the LORD, "As surely as the LORD lives,
28:12 she cried out at the top of her voice and said to **Saul**, "Why have
28:12 and said to Saul, "Why have you deceived me? You are **Saul**!"
28:13 woman said, **[RPH]** "I see a spirit coming up out of the ground."
28:14 **Saul** knew it was Samuel, and he bowed down and prostrated
28:15 Samuel said to **Saul**, "Why have you disturbed me by bringing me
28:15 "I am in great distress," **Saul** said. "The Philistines are fighting
28:20 Immediately **Saul** fell full length on the ground, filled with fear
28:21 When the woman came to **Saul** and saw that he was greatly
28:25 she set it before **Saul** and his men, and they ate. That same night
29: 3 "Is this not David, who was an officer of **Saul** king of Israel?
29: 5 " '**Saul** has slain his thousands, and David his tens of thousands'?"
31: 2 The Philistines pressed hard after **Saul** and his sons, and they
31: 2 and they killed **his**[s] sons Jonathan, Abinadab and Malki-Shua.
31: 3 The fighting grew fierce around **Saul**, and when the archers
31: 4 **Saul** said to his armor-bearer, "Draw your sword and run me
31: 4 and would not do it; so **Saul** took his own sword and fell on it.
31: 5 When the armor-bearer saw that **Saul** was dead, he too fell on his
31: 6 So **Saul** and his three sons and his armor-bearer and all his men
31: 7 that the Israelite army had fled and that **Saul** and his sons had died,
31: 8 they found **Saul** and his three sons fallen on Mount Gilboa.
31:11 of Jabesh Gilead heard of what the Philistines had done to **Saul**,
31:12 They took down the bodies of **Saul** and his sons from the wall of
2Sa 1: 1 After the death of **Saul**, David returned from defeating the
1: 2 On the third day a man arrived from **Saul's** camp, with his clothes
1: 4 of them fell and died. And **Saul** and his son Jonathan are dead."
1: 5 "How do you know that **Saul** and his son Jonathan are dead?"
1: 6 the young man said, "and there was **Saul**, leaning on his spear,
1:12 They mourned and wept and fasted till evening for **Saul** and his
1:17 David took up this lament concerning **Saul** and his son Jonathan,
1:21 For there the shield of the mighty was defiled, the shield of **Saul**—
1:22 did not turn back, the sword of **Saul** did not return unsatisfied.
1:23 "**Saul** and Jonathan—in life they were loved and gracious,
1:24 "O daughters of Israel, weep for **Saul**, who clothed you in scarlet
2: 4 was told that it was the men of Jabesh Gilead who had buried **Saul**,
2: 5 "The LORD bless you for showing this kindness to **Saul** your
2: 7 Now then, be strong and brave, for **Saul** your master is dead,

2Sa 2: 8 Abner son of Ner, the commander of **Saul's** [+4200] army,
2: 8 had taken Ish-Bosheth son of **Saul** and brought him over to
2: 10 Ish-Bosheth son of **Saul** was forty years old when he became king
2: 12 together with the men of Ish-Bosheth son of **Saul**, left Mahanaim
2: 15 twelve men for Benjamin and Ish-Bosheth son of **Saul**, and twelve
3: 1 The war between the house of **Saul** and the house of David lasted a
3: 1 and stronger, while the house of **Saul** grew weaker and weaker.
3: 6 During the war between the house of **Saul** and the house of David,
3: 6 had been strengthening his own position in the house of **Saul**.
3: 7 Now **Saul** had had a concubine named Rizpah daughter of Aiah.
3: 8 This very day I am loyal to the house of your father **Saul** and to his
3: 10 transfer the kingdom from the house of **Saul** and establish David's
3: 13 you bring Michal daughter of **Saul** when you come to see me."
3: 14 David sent messengers to Ish-Bosheth son of **Saul**, demanding,
4: 1 When Ish-Bosheth son of **Saul** heard that Abner had died in
4: 2 Now **Saul's** son had two men who were leaders of raiding bands.
4: 4 (Jonathan son of **Saul** had a son who was lame in both feet.
4: 4 He was five years old when the news about **Saul** and Jonathan
4: 8 "Here is the head of Ish-Bosheth son of **Saul**, your enemy,
4: 8 This day the LORD has avenged my lord the king against **Saul**
4: 10 when a man told me, '**Saul** is dead,' and thought he was bringing
5: 2 In the past, while **Saul** was king over us, you were the one who led
6: 16 City of David, Michal daughter of **Saul** watched from a window.
6: 20 Michal daughter of **Saul** came out to meet him and said,
6: 23 Michal daughter of **Saul** had no children to the day of her death.
7: 15 as I took it away from **Saul**, whom I removed from before you.
9: 1 "Is there anyone still left of the house of **Saul** to whom I can show
9: 2 Now there was a servant of **Saul's** household named Ziba.
9: 3 "Is there no one still left of the house of **Saul** to whom I can show
9: 6 the son of **Saul**, came to David, he bowed down to pay him honor.
9: 7 restore to you all the land that belonged to your grandfather **Saul**,
9: 9 Then the king summoned Ziba, **Saul's** servant, and said to him,
9: 9 given your master's grandson everything that belonged to **Saul**
12: 7 you king over Israel, and I delivered you from the hand of **Saul**.
16: 5 a man from the same clan as **Saul's** family came out from there.
16: 8 has repaid you for all the blood you shed in the household of **Saul**,
19: 17 [19:18] along with Ziba, the steward of **Saul's** household, and his
19: 24 [19:25] Mephibosheth, **Saul's** grandson, also went down to meet
21: 1 "It is on account of **Saul** and his blood-stained house;
21: 2 **Saul** in his zeal for Israel and Judah had tried to annihilate them.)
21: 4 have no right to demand silver or gold from **Saul** or his family,
21: 6 us to be killed and exposed before the LORD at Gibeah of **Saul**—
21: 7 The king spared Mephibosheth son of Jonathan, the son of **Saul**,
21: 7 oath before the LORD between David and Jonathan son of **Saul**.
21: 8 two sons of Aiah's daughter Rizpah, whom she had borne to **Saul**,
21: 8 to Saul, together with the five sons of **Saul's** daughter Merab,
21: 11 told what Aiah's daughter Rizpah, **Saul's** concubine, had done,
21: 12 he went and took the bones of **Saul** and his son Jonathan from the
21: 12 where the Philistines had hung them after they struck **Saul** down
21: 13 David brought the bones of **Saul** and his son Jonathan from there,
21: 14 They buried the bones of **Saul** and his son Jonathan in the tomb of
22: 1 him from the hand of all his enemies and from the hand of **Saul**.
1Ch 1: 48 **Shaul** from Rehoboth on the river succeeded him as king.
1: 49 When **Shaul** died, Baal-Hanan son of Acbor succeeded him as
4: 24 descendants of Simeon: Nemuel, Jamin, Jarib, Zerah and **Shaul**;
5: 10 During **Saul's** reign they waged war against the Hagrites,
6: 24 [6:9] his son, Uriel his son, Uzziah his son and **Shaul** his son.
8: 33 Ner was the father of Kish, Kish the father of **Saul**, and Saul the
8: 33 **Saul** the father of Jonathan, Malki-Shua, Abinadab and Esh-Baal.
9: 39 Ner was the father of Kish, Kish the father of **Saul**, and Saul the
9: 39 **Saul** the father of Jonathan, Malki-Shua, Abinadab and Esh-Baal.
10: 2 The Philistines pressed hard after **Saul** and his sons, and they
10: 2 and they killed **his**[s] sons Jonathan, Abinadab and Malki-Shua.
10: 3 The fighting grew fierce around **Saul**, and when the archers
10: 4 **Saul** said to his armor-bearer, "Draw your sword and run me
10: 4 and would not do it; so **Saul** took his own sword and fell on it.
10: 5 When the armor-bearer saw that **Saul** was dead, he too fell on his
10: 6 So **Saul** and his three sons died, and all his house died together.
10: 7 saw that the army had fled and that **Saul** and his sons had died,
10: 8 the dead, they found **Saul** and his sons fallen on Mount Gilboa.
10: 11 Jabesh Gilead heard of everything the Philistines had done to **Saul**,
10: 12 all their valiant men went and took the bodies of **Saul** and his sons
10: 13 **Saul** died because he was unfaithful to the LORD; he did not
11: 2 In the past, even while **Saul** was king, you were the one who led
12: 1 while he was banished from the presence of **Saul** son of Kish (they
12: 2 they were kinsmen of **Saul** from the tribe of Benjamin):
12: 19 [12:20] when he went with the Philistines to fight against **Saul**.
12: 19 [12:20] will cost us our heads if he deserts to his master **Saul**.")
12: 23 [12:24] to David at Hebron to turn **Saul's** kingdom over to him,
12: 29 [12:30] men of Benjamin, **Saul's** kinsmen—3,000, most of whom
12: 29 [12:30] most of whom had remained loyal to **Saul's** house until
13: 3 back to us, for we did not inquire of it during the reign of **Saul**."
15: 29 City of David, Michal daughter of **Saul** watched from a window.
26: 28 everything dedicated by Samuel the seer and by **Saul** son of Kish,
Ps 18: T [18:1] the hand of all his enemies and from the hand of **Saul**.
52: T [52:2] When Doeg the Edomite had gone to **Saul** and told him:
54: T [54:2] When the Ziphites had gone to **Saul** and said, "Is not David
57: T [57:1] A *miktam*. When he had fled from **Saul** into the cave.
59: T [59:1] When **Saul** had sent men to watch David's house in order
Isa 10: 29 camp overnight at Geba." Ramah trembles; Gibeah of **Saul** flees.

8621 שָׁאוּלִי ***šā'ûlî***, a.g. [1] [√ 8620]

Shaulite [1]

Nu 26: 13 through Zerah, the Zerahite clan; through Shaul, the **Shaulite** clan.

8622 שָׁאוֹן ***šā'ôn***[1], n.m. [1] [√ 8615]

slimy pit [+1014] [1]

Ps 40: 2 [40:3] He lifted me out of the **slimy pit** [+1014], out of the mud

8623 שָׁאוֹן ***šā'ôn***[2], n.m. [17] [√ 8616]

uproar [5], roaring [3], roar [2], brawlers [1], great tumult [1], loud noise [1], noise [1], noisy boasters [+1201] [1], roar of battle [1], tumult [1]

Ps 65: 7 [65:8] who stilled the **roaring** *of* the seas, the roaring of their
65: 7 [65:8] the **roaring** *of* their waves, and the turmoil of the nations.
74: 23 the **uproar** *of* your enemies, which rises continually.
Isa 5: 14 their nobles and masses with all their **brawlers** and revelers.
13: 4 Listen, an **uproar** *among* the kingdoms, like nations massing
17: 12 Oh, the **uproar** *of* the peoples—they roar like the roaring of great
17: 12 uproar of the peoples—they roar like the **roaring** *of* great waters!
17: 13 Although the peoples roar like the **roar** *of* surging waters,
24: 8 the **noise** *of* the revelers has stopped, the joyful harp is silent.
25: 5 You silence the **uproar** *of* foreigners; as heat is reduced by the
66: 6 Hear that **uproar** from the city, hear that noise from the temple!
Jer 25: 31 The **tumult** will resound to the ends of the earth, for the LORD
46: 17 they will exclaim, 'Pharaoh king of Egypt is only a **loud noise**;
48: 45 the foreheads of Moab, the skulls of the **noisy** [+1201] **boasters**.
51: 55 will rage like great waters; the **roar** *of* their voices will resound.
Hos 10: 14 the **roar of battle** will rise against your people, so that all your
Am 2: 2 Moab will go down in **great tumult** amid war cries and the blast of

8624 שְׁאָט ***še'āṭ***, n.[m.]. [3]

malice [3]

Eze 25: 6 rejoicing with all the **malice** of your heart against the land of
25: 15 acted in vengeance and took revenge with **malice** in their hearts,
36: 5 with **malice** in their hearts they made my land their own possession

8625 שְׁאִיָּה ***še'iyyâ***, n.f. [1] [√ 8615]

battered to pieces [+4198] [1]

Isa 24: 12 The city is left in ruins, its gate *is* **battered to pieces** [+4198].

8626 שָׁאַל ***šā'al***, v. [171] [→ 900, 901, 3781, 5399, 8620, 8621, 8924, 8927, 8929; Ar 10689; *also used with compound proper names*]

ask [39], asked [36], inquired of [+928] [15], question [6], *untranslated* [4], asks [4], greet [+4200+4200+8934] [4], greeted [+4200+4200+8934] [4], request [4], consult [3], questioned [3], asking [2], earnestly asked for permission [+4946+6643+8626] [2], earnestly asked permission [+4946+8626] [2], get answer [+8626] [2], have request to make [+8629] [2], questioned closely [+8626] [2], ask [+907+4946] [1], asked how they were [+4200+4200+8934] [1], be given over [1], beg [1], beggars [1], borrows [1], consulted [1], consulting [+7023] [1], demand [1], demanding [1], demands [1], desired [1], find out [1], gave what asked for [1], gave [1], give [1], have request [+8629] [1], inquire of [+906+7023] [1], inquire of [+928] [1], inquire [1], inquires of [+928+1821] [1], inquiring of [+928] [1], investigate [1], invoking [1], looks [1], make[s] [1], medium [+200] [1], obtain decisions [1], pray [1], prayed [1], require [1], said [1], tell [1], took [1], wanted [+906+5883] [1], was borrowed [1], wish [1]

Ge 24: 47 [A] "*I* **asked** her, 'Whose daughter are you?' "She said,
24: 57 [A] Then they said, "Let's call the girl and **ask** her *about* it."
26: 7 [A] When the men of that place **asked** him about his wife, he
32: 17 [32:18] [A] "When my brother Esau meets you and **asks**, 'To
32: 29 [32:30] [A] Jacob **said**, "Please tell me your name." But he
32: 29 [32:30] [A] he replied, "Why *do you* **ask** my name?" Then he
37: 15 [A] found him wandering around in the fields and **asked** him,
38: 21 [A] *He* **asked** the men who lived there, "Where is the shrine
40: 7 [A] So *he* **asked** Pharaoh's officials who were in custody with
43: 7 [A] "The man **questioned** [+8626] us **closely** about ourselves
43: 7 [A] "The man **questioned** us **closely** [+8626] about ourselves
43: 27 [A] *He* **asked** [+4200+4200+8934] them **how they were**, and then
44: 19 [A] My lord **asked** his servants, 'Do you have a father or a
Ex 3: 22 [A] *is to* **ask** her neighbor and any woman living in her house *for*

Ex 11: 2 [A] women alike *are to* **ask** their neighbors *for* articles of silver
12:35 [A] **asked** the Egyptians *for* articles of silver and gold and for
12:36 [G] toward the people, and *they* **gave** them **what** they **asked for**;
13:14 [A] "In days to come, when your son **asks** you, 'What does this
18: 7 [A] *They* **greeted** [+4200+4200+8934] each other and then went
22:14 [22:13] [A] "If a man **borrows** an animal from his neighbor
Nu 27:21 [A] *who will* **obtain decisions** for him by inquiring of the Urim
Dt 4:32 [A] **Ask** now about the former days, long before your time, from
6:20 [A] In the future, when your son **asks** you, "What is the meaning
10:12 [A] what *does* the LORD your God **ask** of you but to fear the
13:14 [13:15] [A] must inquire, probe and **investigate** it thoroughly.
14:26 [A] sheep, wine or other fermented drink, or anything you **wish**.
18:11 [A] or *who is a* **medium** [+200] or spiritist or who consults the
18:16 [A] For this is what *you* **asked** of the LORD your God at Horeb
32: 7 [A] **Ask** your father and he will tell you, your elders, and they
Jos 4: 6 [A] In the future, when your children **ask** you, 'What do these
4:21 [A] "In the future when your descendants **ask** their fathers,
9:14 [A] but *did* not **inquire** [+906+7023] **of** the LORD.
15:18 [A] she urged him to **ask** [+907+4946] her father for a field.
19:50 [A] They gave him the town *he* **asked** *for*—Timnath Serah in the
Jdg 1: 1 [A] After the death of Joshua, the Israelites **asked** the LORD,
1:14 [A] came to Othniel, she urged him to **ask** her father *for* a field.
4:20 [A] "If someone comes by and **asks** you, 'Is anyone here?' say
5:25 [A] *He* **asked** *for* water, and she gave him milk; in a bowl fit for
8:14 [A] He caught a young man of Succoth and **questioned** him,
8:24 [A] he said, "*I do* **have** *one* **request** [+8629], that each of you
8:26 [A] The weight of the gold rings *he* **asked** *for* came to seventeen
13: 6 [A] *I* didn't **ask** him where he came from, and he didn't tell me
13:18 [A] He replied, "Why *do you* **ask** my name? It is beyond
18: 5 [A] "Please **inquire** [+928] **of** God to learn whether our journey
18:15 [A] at Micah's place and **greeted** [+4200+4200+8934] him.
20:18 [A] The Israelites went up to Bethel and **inquired** [+928] **of** God.
20:23 [A] until evening, and *they* **inquired** [+928] **of** the LORD.
20:27 [A] the Israelites **inquired** [+928] **of** the LORD. (In those days
1Sa 1:17 [A] may the God of Israel grant you what *you have* **asked** of
1:20 [A] him Samuel, saying, "Because *I* **asked** the LORD *for* him."
1:27 [A] and the LORD has granted me what *I* **asked** of him.
1:28 [G] So now I **give** him to the LORD. For his whole life he will
1:28 [B] For his whole life he *will* **be given over** to the LORD."
2:20 [G] the place of the one she prayed for and **gave** to the LORD."
8:10 [A] the LORD to the people who *were* **asking** him *for* a king.
10: 4 [A] *They will* **greet** [+4200+4200+8934] you and offer you two
10:22 [A] So *they* **inquired** [+928] further **of** the LORD, "Has the
12:13 [A] here is the king you have chosen, the one *you* **asked** *for*;
12:17 [A] did in the eyes of the LORD when you **asked** for a king."
12:19 [A] for we have added to all our other sins the evil of **asking** for
14:37 [A] So Saul **asked** God, "Shall I go down after the Philistines?
17:22 [A] the battle lines and **greeted** [+4200+4200+8934] his brothers.
17:56 [A] The king said, "**Find out** whose son this young man is."
19:22 [A] *he* **asked**, "Where are Samuel and David?" "Over in Naioth
20: 6 [C] 'David **earnestly asked** [+4946+8626] my **permission** to
20: 6 [C] 'David **earnestly asked** my **permission** [+4946+8626] to
20:28 [C] **earnestly asked** [+4946+6643+8626] me **for permission** to go
20:28 [C] **earnestly asked** me **for permission** [+4946+6643+8626] to go
22:10 [A] Ahimelech **inquired** [+928] **of** the LORD for him; he also
22:13 [A] him bread and a sword and **inquiring** [+928] **of** God for him,
22:15 [A] Was that day the first time I **inquired** [+928] **of** God for
23: 2 [A] he **inquired** [+928] **of** the LORD, saying, "Shall I go
23: 4 [A] Once again David **inquired** [+928] **of** the LORD,
25: 5 [A] at Carmel and **greet** [+4200+4200+8934] him in my name.
25: 8 [A] **Ask** your own servants and they will tell you. Therefore be
28: 6 [A] He **inquired** [+928] **of** the LORD, but the LORD did not
28:16 [A] Samuel said, "Why *do you* **consult** me, now that the LORD
30: 8 [A] David **inquired** [+928] **of** the LORD, "Shall I pursue this
30:21 [A] and his men approached, *he* **greeted** [+4200+4200+8934] them.
2Sa 2: 1 [A] In the course of time, David **inquired** [+928] **of** the LORD.
3:13 [A] an agreement with you. But I **demand** one thing of you:
5:19 [A] so David **inquired** [+928] **of** the LORD, "Shall I go
5:23 [A] so David **inquired** [+928] **of** the LORD, and he answered,
8:10 [A] his son Joram to King David to **greet** [+4200+4200+8934] him
11: 7 [A] David **asked** him how Joab was, how the soldiers were
12:20 [A] and *at his* **request** they served him food, and he ate.
14:18 [A] "Do not keep from me the answer to what I *am going to* **ask**
16:23 [A] gave was like that of one *who* **inquires** [+928+1821] **of** God.
20:18 [D] to say, '**Get** *your* **answer** [+8626] at Abel,' and that settled it.
20:18 [A] to say, '**Get** *your* **answer** [+8626] at Abel,' and that settled it.
1Ki 2:16 [A] Now I **have** one **request** [+8629] **to make** of you. Do not
2:20 [A] "I **have** one small **request** [+8629] **to make** of you,"
2:20 [A] The king replied, "**Make**[s] it, my mother; I will not refuse
2:22 [A] "Why *do* you **request** Abishag the Shunammite for
2:22 [A] *You might as well* **request** the kingdom for him—after all,
3: 5 [A] and God said, "**Ask** *for* whatever you want me to give you."
3:10 [A] The Lord was pleased that Solomon *had* **asked** *for* this.
3:11 [A] "Since *you have* **asked** *for* this and not for long life
3:11 [A] for this and not **[RPH]** for long life or wealth for yourself,
3:11 [A] for this and not for long life or **[RPH]** wealth for yourself,
3:11 [A] nor *have* **asked** *for* the death of your enemies but for
3:11 [A] but **[RPH]** for discernment in administering justice,
3:13 [A] Moreover, I will give you what *you have* not **asked** *for*—
10:13 [A] gave the queen of Sheba all she desired and **asked** *for*,
19: 4 [A] a broom tree, sat down under it and **prayed** that he might die.
2Ki 2: 9 [A] When they had crossed, Elijah said to Elisha, "**Tell** me,
2:10 [A] "*You have* **asked** a difficult thing," Elijah said, "yet if you
4: 3 [A] "Go around and **ask** all your neighbors for empty jars.
4:28 [A] "*Did I* **ask** you for a son, my lord?" she said. "Didn't I tell
6: 5 [B] the water. "Oh, my lord," he cried out, "it **was borrowed**!"
8: 6 [A] The king **asked** the woman *about* it, and she told him.
1Ch 4:10 [A] that I will be free from pain." And God granted *his* **request**.
10:13 [A] of the LORD and even **consulted** a medium for guidance,
14:10 [A] so David **inquired** [+928] **of** God: "Shall I go and attack the
14:14 [A] so David **inquired** [+928] **of** God again, and God answered
18:10 [A] Hadoram to King David to **greet** [+4200+4200+8934] him and
2Ch 1: 7 [A] said to him, "**Ask** *for* whatever you want me to give you."
1:11 [A] *you have* not **asked** *for* wealth, riches or honor, nor for the
1:11 [A] and since *you have* not **asked** *for* a long life but for wisdom
1:11 [A] you have not asked for a long life but **[RPH]** for wisdom
9:12 [A] gave the queen of Sheba all she desired and **asked** *for*;
11:23 [A] them abundant provisions and **took** many wives for them.
Ezr 8:22 [A] I was ashamed to **ask** the king *for* soldiers and horsemen to
Ne 1: 2 [A] *I* **questioned** them about the Jewish remnant that survived
13: 6 [C] returned to the king. Some time later *I* **asked** his permission
Job 8: 8 [A] "**Ask** the former generations and find out what their fathers
12: 7 [A] "But **ask** the animals, and they will teach you, or the birds of
21:29 [A] *Have you* never **questioned** those who travel? Have you
31:30 [A] my mouth to sin by **invoking** a curse *against* his life—
38: 3 [A] like a man; *I will* **question** you, and you shall answer me.
40: 7 [A] like a man; *I will* **question** you, and you shall answer me.
42: 4 [A] I will speak; *I will* **question** you, and you shall answer me.'
Ps 2: 8 [A] **Ask** of me, and I will make the nations your inheritance,
21: 4 [21:5] [A] *He* **asked** you *for* life, and you gave it to him—
27: 4 [A] One thing *I* **ask** of the LORD, this is what I seek: that I may
35:11 [A] *they* **question** me on things I know nothing about.
40: 6 [40:7] [A] and sin offerings *you did* not **require**.
78:18 [A] They willfully put God to the test by **demanding** the food
105:40 [A] *They* **asked**, and he brought them quail and satisfied them
109:10 [D] May his children be wandering **beggars**; may they be driven
122: 6 [A] **Pray** *for* the peace of Jerusalem: "May those who love you
137: 3 [A] for there our captors **asked** us *for* songs, our tormentors
Pr 20: 4 [A] plow in season; so at harvest time *he* **looks** but finds nothing.
30: 7 [A] "Two things *I* **ask** of you, O LORD; do not refuse me
Ecc 2:10 [A] I denied myself nothing my eyes **desired**; I refused my heart
7:10 [A] better than these?" For it is not wise *to* **ask** such questions.
Isa 7:11 [A] "**Ask** the LORD your God for a sign, whether in the deepest
7:12 [A] Ahaz said, "*I will* not **ask**; I will not put the LORD to the
30: 2 [A] who go down to Egypt without **consulting** [+7023] me; who
41:28 [A] to give counsel, no one to give answer when *I* **ask** them.
45:11 [A] things to come, *do you* **question** me about my children,
58: 2 [A] *They* **ask** me *for* just decisions and seem eager for God to
65: 1 [A] "I revealed myself to *those who did* not **ask** for me; I was
Jer 6:16 [A] **ask** for the ancient paths, ask where the good way is,
15: 5 [A] Who will mourn for you? Who will stop to **ask** how you are?
18:13 [A] "**Inquire** among the nations: Who has ever heard anything
23:33 [A] "When these people, or a prophet or a priest, **ask** you, 'What
30: 6 [A] **Ask** and see: Can a man bear children? Then why do I see
36:17 [A] *they* **asked** Baruch, "Tell us, how did you come to write all
37:17 [A] had him brought to the palace, where he **asked** him privately,
38:14 [A] "I *am going to* **ask** you something," the king said to
38:27 [A] All the officials did come to Jeremiah and **question** him,
48:19 [A] **Ask** the man fleeing and the woman escaping, ask them,
50: 5 [A] *They will* **ask** the way to Zion and turn their faces toward it.
La 4: 4 [A] the children **beg** *for* bread, but no one gives it to them.
Eze 21:21 [21:26] [A] *he will* **consult** his idols, he will examine the liver.
Hos 4:12 [A] *They* **consult** a wooden idol and are answered by a stick of
Jnh 4: 8 [A] He **wanted** [+906+5883] to die, and said, "It would be better
Mic 7: 3 [A] the ruler **demands** gifts, the judge accepts bribes,
Hag 2:11 [A] LORD Almighty says: '**Ask** the priests what the law says:
Zec 10: 1 [A] **Ask** the LORD *for* rain in the springtime; it is the LORD

8627 שְׁאָל šᵉʾāl, n.pr.m. [1] [√ 8626]

Sheal [1]

Ezr 10:29 Meshullam, Malluch, Adaiah, Jashub, **Sheal** and Jeremoth.

8628 שְׁאָלָה šᵉʾālâ, var. [1 / 0] [√ 8619 + 2025]

Isa 7:11 whether in the deepest depths [BHS ***request*** ?; NIV 8619]

8629 שְׁאֵלָה še'ēlâ, n.f. [13] [→ 8924; cf. 8626; Ar 10690]
petition [6], have request to make [+8626] [2], have request [+8626] [1], prayed for [1], request [1], what asked for [1], what[s] [1]

Jdg 8:24 he said, "*I do* **have** *one* **request** [+8626], that each of you give me
1Sa 1:27 this child, and the LORD has granted me **what**[s] I asked of him.
2:20 children by this woman to take the place of the *one* she **prayed for**
1Ki 2:16 Now I **have** one **request to make** [+8626] of you. Do not refuse
2:20 "I **have** one small **request to make** [+8626] of you," she said.
Est 5:6 the king again asked Esther, "Now what is your **petition**?
5:7 Esther replied, "My **petition** and my request is this:
5:8 if it pleases the king to grant my **petition** and fulfill my request,
7:2 the king again asked, "Queen Esther, what is your **petition**?
7:3 if it pleases your majesty, grant me my life—this is my **petition**.
9:12 Now what is your **petition**? It will be given you. What is your
Job 6:8 "Oh, that I might have my **request**, that God would grant what I
Ps 106:15 So he gave them **what** they **asked for**, but sent a wasting disease

8630 שְׁאַלְתִּיאֵל še'altî'ēl, n.pr.m. [6] [√ 8626 + 446; cf. 9003]
Shealtiel [6]

1Ch 3:17 The descendants of Jehoiachin the captive: **Shealtiel** his son,
Ezr 3:2 of Jozadak and his fellow priests and Zerubbabel son of **Shealtiel**
3:8 Zerubbabel son of **Shealtiel**, Jeshua son of Jozadak and the rest of
Ne 12:1 and Levites who returned with Zerubbabel son of **Shealtiel**
Hag 1:1 came through the prophet Haggai to Zerubbabel son of **Shealtiel**,
2:23 'I will take you, my servant Zerubbabel son of **Shealtiel**,'

8631 שָׁאַן šā'an, v. [5] [→ 8633, 8916]
security [2], at ease [1], at rest [1], enjoy ease [1]

Job 3:18 [D] Captives also **enjoy** *their* **ease**; they no longer hear the slave
Pr 1:33 [D] but whoever listens to me will live in safety and *be* **at ease**,
Jer 30:10 [D] Jacob will again have peace and **security**, and no one will
46:27 [D] Jacob will again have peace and **security**, and no one will
48:11 [D] "Moab *has been* **at rest** from youth, like wine left on its

8632 שְׁאָן še'ān, n.pr.loc. Not used in NIV/BHS [→ 1126, 9093]

8633 שַׁאֲנָן ša'anān, a. [10] [√ 8631]
complacent [3], insolence [2], at ease [1], feel secure [1], peaceful [1], proud [1], undisturbed [1]

2Ki 19:28 you rage against me and your **insolence** has reached my ears,
Job 12:5 *Men* **at ease** have contempt for misfortune as the fate of those
Ps 123:4 We have endured much ridicule from the **proud**, much contempt
Isa 32:9 You women *who* are *so* **complacent**, rise up and listen to me;
32:11 Tremble, you **complacent** *women*; shudder, you daughters who
32:18 dwelling places, in secure homes, in **undisturbed** places of rest.
33:20 your eyes will see Jerusalem, a **peaceful** abode, a tent that will not
37:29 rage against me and because your **insolence** has reached my ears,
Am 6:1 Woe to *you who* are **complacent** in Zion, and to you who feel
Zec 1:15 I am very angry with the nations that **feel secure**. I was only a little

8634 ¹שָׁאַף šā'ap[1], v. [11] [cf. 8635]
pant [3], hotly pursue [2], hurries back [1], long for [1], longing for [1], pant [+8120] [1], pursue [1], sniffing [1]

Job 5:5 [A] from among thorns, and the thirsty **pant** *after* his wealth.
7:2 [A] Like a slave **longing for** the evening shadows, or a hired man
36:20 [A] *Do* not **long for** the night, to drag people away from their
Ps 56:1 [56:2] [A] Be merciful to me, O God, for men **hotly pursue** me;
56:2 [56:3] [A] My slanderers **pursue** me all day long; many are
57:3 [57:4] [A] and saves me, rebuking *those who* **hotly pursue** me;
119:131 [A] I open my mouth and **pant**, longing for your commands.
Ecc 1:5 [A] sun rises and the sun sets, and **hurries back** to where it rises.
Isa 42:14 [A] like a woman in childbirth, I cry out, I gasp and **pant**.
Jer 2:24 [A] accustomed to the desert, **sniffing** the wind in her craving—
14:6 [A] stand on the barren heights and **pant** [+8120] like jackals;

8635 ²שָׁאַף šā'ap[2], v. [3] [cf. 8634, 8789, 8790]
trample [2], hounded [1]

Eze 36:3 [A] Because they ravaged and **hounded** you from every side
Am 2:7 [A] They **trample** on the heads of the poor as upon the dust of
8:4 [A] *you who* **trample** the needy and do away with the poor of

8636 שָׁאַר šā'ar, v. [133] [→ 8637, 8639, 8641, 8642; Ar 10692]
left [52], remained [10], remain [9], *untranslated* [8], leave [7], left behind [6], leaving [5], rest [5], survived [5], survive [3], survivors [3], have left [2], leave alive [2], spare [2], been kept [1], can hardly breathe [+928+4202+5972] [1], left alone [1], left survivor [1], little left [+3856+7129] [1], remains [1], remnant spare [1], remnant [1], reserve [1], sparing [1], still [+6388] [1], still [1], survives [1], those[s] [+2021] [1]

Ge 7:23 [C] the earth. Only Noah *was* **left**, and those with him in the ark.
14:10 [C] some of the men fell into them and the **rest** fled to the hills.
32:8 [32:9] [C] attacks one group, the group that *is* **left** may escape."
42:38 [C] there with you; his brother is dead and he *is* the only one **left**.
47:18 [C] *there is* nothing **left** for our lord except our bodies and our
Ex 8:9 [8:5] [C] of the frogs, except for *those that* **remain** in the Nile."
8:11 [8:7] [C] and your people; *they will* **remain** only in the Nile."
8:31 [8:27] [C] and his officials and his people; not a fly **remained**.
10:5 [C] They will devour what **little** you have **left** [+3856+7129]
10:12 [G] everything growing in the fields, everything **left** *by* the hail."
10:19 [C] into the Red Sea. Not a locust *was* **left** anywhere in Egypt.
10:26 [C] livestock too must go with us; not a hoof *is to be* **left behind**.
14:28 [C] the Israelites into the sea. Not one of them **survived**.
Lev 5:9 [C] the **rest** of the blood must be drained out at the base of the
25:52 [C] If only a few years **remain** until the Year of Jubilee, he is to
26:36 [C] " 'As for those of you *who are* **left**, I will make their hearts
26:39 [C] Those of you *who are* **left** will waste away in the lands of
Nu 9:12 [G] *They must* not **leave** any of it till morning or break any of its
11:26 [C] names were Eldad and Medad, *had* **remained** in the camp.
21:35 [G] with his sons and his whole army, **leaving** them no survivors.
Dt 2:34 [G] men, women and children. *We* **left** no survivors.
3:3 [G] all his army. We struck them down, **leaving** no survivors.
3:11 [C] (Only Og king of Bashan *was* **left** of the remnant of the
4:27 [C] only a few of *you will* **survive** among the nations to which
7:20 [C] until even the **survivors** who hide from you have perished.
19:20 [C] The **rest** *of the people* will hear of this and be afraid,
28:51 [G] *They will* **leave** you no grain, new wine or oil, nor any
28:55 [G] It will be all he has **left** because of the suffering your enemy
28:62 [C] who were as numerous as the stars in the sky *will be* **left** but
Jos 8:17 [C] Not a man **remained** in Ai or Bethel who did not go after
8:22 [G] cut them down, **leaving** them neither survivors nor fugitives.
10:28 [G] and totally destroyed everyone in it. *He* **left** no survivors.
10:30 [G] in it Joshua put to the sword. *He* **left** no survivors there.
10:33 [G] defeated him and his army—until no survivors *were* **left**.
10:37 [G] *They* **left** no survivors. Just as at Eglon, they totally
10:39 [G] *They* **left** no survivors. They did to Debir and its king as they
10:40 [G] together with all their kings. *He* **left** no survivors.
11:8 [G] Valley of Mizpah on the east, until no survivors *were* **left**.
11:14 [G] destroyed them, not **sparing** anyone that breathed.
11:22 [C] only in Gaza, Gath and Ashdod *did any* **survive**.
13:1 [C] and *there are* **still** very large areas of land to be taken over.
13:2 [C] "This is the land that **remains**: all the regions of the
13:12 [C] and *had* **survived** as one of the last of the Rephaites.
23:4 [C] for your tribes all the land of the nations that **remain**—
23:7 [C] Do not associate with these nations that **remain** among you;
23:12 [C] yourselves with the survivors of these nations that **remain**
Jdg 4:16 [C] All the troops of Sisera fell by the sword; not a man *was* **left**.
6:4 [G] the way to Gaza and *did* not **spare** a living thing for Israel,
7:3 [C] twenty-two thousand men left, while ten thousand **remained**.
Ru 1:3 [C] Naomi's husband, died, and she *was* **left** with her two sons.
1:5 [C] and Naomi *was* **left** without her two sons and her husband.
1Sa 5:4 [C] and were lying on the threshold; only his body **remained**.
9:24 [C] Samuel said, "Here is what *has* **been kept** for you. Eat,
11:11 [C] Those *who* **survived** were scattered, so that no two of them
11:11 [C] were scattered, so that no two of them *were* **left** together.
14:36 [G] them till dawn, and *let us* not **leave** one of them **alive**."
16:11 [A] "*There is* **still** [+6388] the youngest," Jesse answered,
25:22 [G] if by morning *I* **leave alive** one male of all who belong to
2Sa 14:7 [C] They would put out the only burning coal I *have* **left**,
1Ki 15:29 [G] *He did* not **leave** Jeroboam anyone that breathed,
16:11 [G] *He did* not **spare** a single male, whether relative or friend.
19:18 [G] Yet *I* **reserve** seven thousand in Israel—all whose knees
22:46 [22:47] [C] **remained** there even after the reign of his father
2Ki 3:25 [G] Only Kir Hareseth *was* **left** with its stones in place, but men
7:13 [C] "Have some men take five of the horses **[RPH]** that are left
7:13 [C] "Have some men take five of the horses that *are* **left** in the
7:13 [C] Their plight will be like that of all the Israelites **left** here—
10:11 [C] So Jehu killed everyone in Jezreel who **remained** of the
10:11 [G] his close friends and his priests, **leaving** him no survivor.
10:14 [G] the well of Beth Eked—forty-two men. *He* **left** no **survivor**.
10:17 [C] he killed all who *were* **left** there of Ahab's family;
10:21 [C] all the ministers of Baal came; not one **[RPH]** stayed away.
13:7 [G] Nothing *had been* **left** *of* the army of Jehoahaz except fifty
17:18 [C] them from his presence. Only the tribe of Judah *was* **left**,
19:30 [C] Once more a remnant of the house of Judah **[RPH]** will take
24:14 [C] ten thousand. Only the poorest people of the land *were* **left**.
25:11 [C] guard carried into exile the people who **remained** in the city,
25:12 [G] the commander **left behind** some of the poorest people of the
25:22 [C] to be over the people **[RPH]** he had left behind in Judah.
25:22 [G] to be over the people *he had* **left behind** in Judah.
1Ch 13:2 [C] wide to the **rest** of our brothers throughout the territories of

2Ch 21:17 [C] Not a son *was* **left** to him except Ahaziah, the youngest.
30: 6 [C] Isaac and Israel, that he may return to you who *are* **left**,
34:21 [C] inquire of the LORD for me and for the **remnant** in Israel
Ezr 1: 4 [C] the people of any place where **survivors** may now be living
9: 8 [G] the LORD our God has been gracious in **leaving** us a
9:15 [C] you are righteous! *We are* **left** this day as a remnant.
Ne 1: 2 [C] I questioned them about the Jewish remnant that **survived** the
1: 3 [C] They said to me, "**Those**ˢ [+2021] who survived the exile
1: 3 [C] "Those who **survived** the exile and are back in the province
Job 21:34 [C] Nothing *is* **left** of your answers but falsehood!"
Isa 4: 3 [C] Those *who are* **left** in Zion, who remain in Jerusalem, will be
11:11 [C] to reclaim the remnant that *is* **left** *of* his people from Assyria,
11:16 [C] for the remnant of his people that *is* **left** from Assyria,
17: 6 [C] Yet some gleanings *will* **remain**, as when an olive tree is
24: 6 [C] earth's inhabitants are burned up, and very few *are* **left**.
24:12 [C] The city *is* **left** in ruins, its gate is battered to pieces.
37:31 [C] Once more a remnant of the house of Judah **[NIE]** will take
49:21 [C] I *was* **left** all alone, but these—where have they come
Jer 8: 3 [C] **[RPH]** all the survivors of this evil nation will prefer death
8: 3 [C] all the survivors **[RPH]** of this evil nation will prefer death
21: 7 [C] the people in this city who **survive** the plague, sword and
24: 8 [C] whether they **remain** in this land or live in Egypt.
34: 7 [C] These *were* the only fortified cities **left** in Judah.
37:10 [C] attacking you and only wounded men *were* **left** in their tents,
38: 4 [C] He is discouraging the soldiers who *are* **left** in this city,
38:22 [C] All the women **left** in the palace of the king of Judah will be
39: 9 [C] into exile to Babylon the people who **remained** in the city,
39: 9 [C] had gone over to him, and the rest of the people. **[RPH]**
39:10 [G] Nebuzaradan the commander of the guard **left behind** in the
40: 6 [C] stayed with him among the people who *were* **left behind** in
41:10 [C] the king's daughters along with all the others who *were* **left**
42: 2 [C] though we were once many, now only a few *are* **left**.
49: 9 [G] pickers came to you, *would they* not **leave** a few grapes?
50:20 [G] none will be found, for I will forgive *the* **remnant** *I* **spare**.
52:15 [C] of the poorest people and those *who* **remained** in the city,
52:16 [G] Nebuzaradan **left behind** the rest of the poorest people of the
Eze 6:12 [C] and he *that* **survives** and is spared will die of famine.
9: 8 [C] While they were killing and I *was* **left alone**, I fell facedown,
17:21 [C] the sword, and the **survivors** will be scattered to the winds.
36:36 [C] the nations around you that **remain** will know that I the
Da 10: 8 [C] So I *was* **left** alone, gazing at this great vision; I had no
10: 8 [C] I had no strength **left**, my face turned deathly pale and I was
10:17 [C] is gone and I **can hardly breathe** [+928+4202+5972]."
Joel 2:14 [G] He may turn and have pity and **leave** behind a blessing—
Am 5: 3 [G] out a thousand strong for Israel *will* **have** only a hundred **left**;
5: 3 [G] that marches out a hundred strong *will* **have** only ten **left**."
Ob 1: 5 [G] pickers came to you, *would they* not **leave** a few grapes?
Zep 3:12 [G] *I will* **leave** within you the meek and humble, who trust in
Hag 2: 3 [C] 'Who of you *is* **left** who saw this house in its former glory?
Zec 9: 7 [C] Those *who are* **left** will belong to our God and become
11: 9 [C] Let those *who are* **left** eat one another's flesh."
12:14 [C] and all the **rest** *of* the clans and their wives.

8637 שְׁאָר šᵉʾār, n.m. [26 / 25] [√ 8636; Ar 10692]

rest [10], remnant [9], survivors [3], other [1], remainder [1], remaining [1]

1Ch 11: 8 to the surrounding wall, while Joab restored the **rest** *of* the city.
16:41 With them were Heman and Jeduthun and the **rest** *of* those chosen
2Ch 9:29 As for the **other** events of Solomon's reign, from beginning to end,
24:14 they brought the **rest** *of* the money to the king and Jehoiada,
Ezr 3: 8 and the **rest** *of* their brothers (the priests and the Levites
4: 3 and the **rest** *of* the heads of the families of Israel answered,
4: 7 Tabeel and the **rest** *of* his associates wrote a letter to Artaxerxes.
Ne 10:28 [10:29] "The **rest** *of* the people—priests, Levites, gatekeepers,
11: 1 the **rest** *of* the people cast lots to bring one out of every ten to live
11:20 The **rest** *of* the Israelites, with the priests and Levites, were in all
Est 9:12 What have they done in the **rest** *of* the king's provinces?
9:16 the **remainder** *of* the Jews who were in the king's provinces also
Isa 10:19 the **remaining** trees of his forests will be so few that a child could
10:20 In that day the **remnant** *of* Israel, the survivors of the house of
10:21 A **remnant** will return, a remnant of Jacob will return to the
10:21 will return, a **remnant** *of* Jacob will return to the Mighty God.
10:22 O Israel, be like the sand by the sea, only a **remnant** will return.
11:11 time to reclaim the **remnant** that is left of his people from Assyria,
11:16 There will be a highway for the **remnant** *of* his people that is left
14:22 "I will cut off from Babylon her name and **survivors**, her offspring
16:14 will be despised, and her **survivors** will be very few and feeble."
17: 3 the **remnant** *of* Aram will be like the glory of the Israelites,"
21:17 The **survivors** *of* the bowmen, the warriors of Kedar, will be few."
28: 5 a glorious crown, a beautiful wreath for the **remnant** *of* his people.
Zep 1: 4 I will cut off from this place *every* **remnant** *of* Baal, the names of
Mal 2:15 *In* flesh [BHS *as life remained*; NIV 8638] and spirit they are his.

8638 שְׁאֵר šᵉʾēr, n.m. [16 / 18] [√ 8640]

flesh [5], close relative [3], meat [2], blood relative [+1414] [1], body [1], close relative [+1414] [1], close relative [+7940] [1], close relatives [1], food [1], himself [+2257] [1], relative [1]

Ex 21:10 he must not deprive the first one of her **food**, clothing and marital
Lev 18: 6 " 'No one is to approach any **close relative** [+1414] to have sexual
18:12 with your father's sister; she is your father's **close relative**.
18:13 your mother's sister, because she is your mother's **close relative**.
18:17 her daughter's daughter; they are her **close relatives**. [BHS 8640]
20:19 or your father, for that would dishonor a **close relative**;
21: 2 except for a **close relative** [+7940], such as his mother or father,
25:49 or any **blood relative** [+1414] in his clan may redeem him.
Nu 27:11 give his inheritance to the nearest **relative** in his clan, that he may
Ps 73:26 My **flesh** and my heart may fail, but God is the strength of my
78:20 But can he also give us food? Can he supply **meat** for his people?"
78:27 He rained **meat** down on them like dust, flying birds like sand on
Pr 5:11 of your life you will groan, when your flesh and **body** are spent.
11:17 but a cruel man brings trouble on **himself** [+2257].
Jer 51:35 May the violence done to our **flesh** be upon Babylon,"
Mic 3: 2 who tear the skin from my people and the **flesh** from their bones;
3: 3 who eat my people's **flesh**, strip off their skin and break their
Mal 2:15 *In* **flesh** [BHS 8637] and spirit they are his. And why one?

8639 שְׁאָר יָשׁוּב šᵉʾār yāšûb, n.pr.m. [1] [√ 8636 + 3782]

Shear-Jashub [1]

Isa 7: 3 LORD said to Isaiah, "Go out, you and your son **Shear-Jashub**,

8640 שַׁאֲרָה šaʾărâ, var. [1 / 0] [√ 8638 + 2023]

Lev 18:17 daughter; they are her **close** relatives. [BHS ?; NIV 8638]

8641 שֶׁאֱרָה šeʾĕrâ, n.pr.f. [1] [√ 8636; cf. 267]

Sheerah [1]

1Ch 7:24 His daughter was **Sheerah**, who built Lower and Upper Beth

8642 שְׁאֵרִית šᵉʾērît, n.f. [66] [√ 8636]

remnant [44], rest [7], survivors [7], remain [2], remaining [2], descendant [1], last [1], left [1], other [1]

Ge 45: 7 God sent me ahead of you to preserve for you a **remnant** on earth
2Sa 14: 7 leaving my husband neither name nor **descendant** on the face of
2Ki 19: 4 God has heard. Therefore pray for the **remnant** that still survives."
19:31 For out of Jerusalem will come a **remnant**, and out of Mount Zion
21:14 I will forsake the **remnant** *of* my inheritance and hand them over
1Ch 4:43 They killed the **remaining** Amalekites who had escaped, and they
12:38 [12:39] All the **rest** *of* the Israelites were also of one mind to
2Ch 34: 9 Ephraim and the entire **remnant** *of* Israel and from all the people
36:20 He carried into exile to Babylon the **remnant**, who escaped from
Ezr 9:14 enough with us to destroy us, leaving us no **remnant** or survivor?
Ne 7:72 [7:71] The total given by the **rest** *of* the people was 20,000
Ps 76:10 [76:11] and the **survivors** *of* your wrath are restrained.
Isa 14:30 But your root I will destroy by famine; it will slay your **survivors**.
15: 9 the fugitives of Moab and upon *those who* **remain** *in* the land.
37: 4 God has heard. Therefore pray for the **remnant** that still survives."
37:32 For out of Jerusalem will come a **remnant**, and out of Mount Zion
44:17 From the **rest** he makes a god, his idol; he bows down to it
46: 3 O house of Jacob, all you *who* **remain** *of* the house of Israel,
Jer 6: 9 "Let them glean the **remnant** *of* Israel as thoroughly as a vine;
8: 3 all the **survivors** of this evil nation will prefer death to life,
11:23 Not even a **remnant** will be left to them, because I will bring
15: 9 I will put the **survivors** to the sword before their enemies,"
23: 3 "I myself will gather the **remnant** *of* my flock out of all the
24: 8 his officials and the **survivors** *from* Jerusalem, whether they
25:20 (those of Ashkelon, Gaza, Ekron, and the *people* **left** *at* Ashdod);
31: 7 and say, 'O LORD, save your people, the **remnant** *of* Israel.'
39: 3 a high official and all the **other** officials of the king of Babylon.
40:11 heard that the king of Babylon had left a **remnant** in Judah
40:15 around you to be scattered and the **remnant** *of* Judah to perish?"
41:10 Ishmael made captives of all the **rest** *of* the people who were in
41:16 all the army officers who were with him led away all the **survivors**
42: 2 and pray to the LORD your God for this entire **remnant**.
42:15 hear the word of the LORD, O **remnant** *of* Judah. This is what
42:19 "O **remnant** *of* Judah, the LORD has told you, 'Do not go to
43: 5 all the army officers led away all the **remnant** *of* Judah who had
44: 7 and infants, and so leave yourselves without a **remnant**?
44:12 I will take away the **remnant** *of* Judah who were determined to go
44:14 None of the **remnant** *of* Judah who have gone to live in Egypt will
44:28 the whole **remnant** *of* Judah who came to live in Egypt will know
47: 4 to destroy the Philistines, the **remnant** *from* the coasts of Caphtor.
47: 5 O **remnant** *on* the plain, how long will you cut yourselves?
50:26 heaps of grain. Completely destroy her and leave her no **remnant**.
Eze 5:10 punishment on you and will scatter all your **survivors** to the winds.

Eze 9: 8 Are you going to destroy the entire **remnant** *of* Israel in this
11: 13 Will you completely destroy the **remnant** *of* Israel?"
25: 16 cut off the Kerethites and destroy those **remaining** *along* the coast.
36: 3 so that you became the possession of the **rest** *of* the nations
36: 4 and ridiculed by the **rest** *of* the nations around you—
36: 5 In my burning zeal I have spoken against the **rest** *of* the nations,
Am 1: 8 till the **last** *of* the Philistines is dead," says the Sovereign LORD.
5: 15 LORD God Almighty will have mercy on the **remnant** *of* Joseph.
9: 12 so that they may possess the **remnant** *of* Edom and all the nations
Mic 2: 12 O Jacob; I will surely bring together the **remnant** *of* Israel.
4: 7 I will make the lame a **remnant**, those driven away a strong
5: 7 [5:6] The **remnant** *of* Jacob will be in the midst of many peoples
5: 8 [5:7] The **remnant** *of* Jacob will be among the nations,
7: 18 and forgives the transgression of the **remnant** *of* his inheritance?
Zep 2: 7 It will belong to the **remnant** *of* the house of Judah; there they will
2: 9 The **remnant** *of* my people will plunder them; the survivors of my
3: 13 The **remnant** *of* Israel will do no wrong; they will speak no lies,
Hag 1: 12 the whole **remnant** *of* the people obeyed the voice of the LORD
1: 14 the high priest, and the spirit of the whole **remnant** *of* the people.
2: 2 of Jehozadak, the high priest, and to the **remnant** *of* the people.
Zec 8: 6 "It may seem marvelous to the **remnant** *of* this people at that time,
8: 11 now I will not deal with the **remnant** *of* this people as I did in the
8: 12 I will give all these things as an inheritance to the **remnant** *of* this

8643 שְׂאֵת *śē't*, n.f. [1] [√ 8615]

ruin [1]

La 3: 47 We have suffered terror and pitfalls, **ruin** and destruction."

8644 שְׁבָא *šᵉbā'*, n.pr.loc. & m. [23] [→ 8645]

Sheba [22], Sabeans [1]

Ge 10: 7 Raamah and Sabteca. The sons of Raamah: **Sheba** and Dedan.
10: 28 Obal, Abimael, **Sheba**,
25: 3 Jokshan was the father of **Sheba** and Dedan; the descendants of
1Ki 10: 1 When the queen of **Sheba** heard about the fame of Solomon
10: 4 When the queen of **Sheba** saw all the wisdom of Solomon
10: 10 so many spices brought in as those the queen of **Sheba** gave to
10: 13 King Solomon gave the queen of **Sheba** all she desired and asked
1Ch 1: 9 Raamah and Sabteca. The sons of Raamah: **Sheba** and Dedan.
1: 22 Obal, Abimael, **Sheba**,
1: 32 Ishbak and Shuah. The sons of Jokshan: **Sheba** and Dedan.
2Ch 9: 1 When the queen of **Sheba** heard of Solomon's fame, she came to
9: 3 When the queen of **Sheba** saw the wisdom of Solomon, as well as
9: 9 There had never been such spices as those the queen of **Sheba**
9: 12 King Solomon gave the queen of **Sheba** all she desired and asked
Job 1: 15 the **Sabeans** attacked and carried them off. They put the servants
6: 19 look for water, the traveling merchants of **Sheba** look in hope.
Ps 72: 10 tribute to him; the kings of **Sheba** and Seba will present him gifts.
72: 15 Long may he live! May gold from **Sheba** be given him. May
Isa 60: 6 all from **Sheba** will come, bearing gold and incense
Jer 6: 20 What do I care about incense from **Sheba** or sweet calamus from a
Eze 27: 22 " 'The merchants of **Sheba** and Raamah traded with you; for your
27: 23 Canneh and Eden and merchants of **Sheba**, Asshur and Kilmad
38: 13 **Sheba** and Dedan and the merchants of Tarshish and all her

8645 שְׁבָאִים *šᵉbā'îm*, a.g. [1] [√ 8644]

Sabeans [1]

Joel 3: 8 [4:8] and they will sell them to the **Sabeans**, a nation far away."

8646 שְׁבָבִים *šᵉbābîm*, n.[m.]pl. [1] [√ 8663]

broken in pieces [1]

Hos 8: 6 it is not God. It will be **broken in pieces**, that calf of Samaria.

8647 שָׁבָה *šābâ*, v. [47] [→ 8649, 8654, 8659, 8660, 8664, 8665, 8669, 8860]

captors [4], carried off [4], taken captive [4], takes captive [+8647] [4], captured [3], took captive [3], are held captive [2], captives [2], conquerors [2], take captive [2], be taken captive [1], been captured [1], been carried captive [1], been taken captive [1], captured [+8660] [1], carried away [1], held captive [1], is taken away [1], led in train [1], made captives of [1], make captives [1], seized [1], take captives [+8660] [1], taken as prisoners [+4946+8664] [1], taken [1], takes captive [1], took as prisoners [+8664] [1]

Ge 14: 14 [C] When Abram heard that his relative *had* **been taken captive**,
31: 26 [B] and you've carried off my daughters like **captives** *in* war.
34: 29 [A] *They* **carried off** all their wealth and all their women and
Ex 22: 10 [22:9] [C] is injured or **is taken away** while no one is looking,
Nu 21: 1 [A] attacked the Israelites and **captured** [+8660] some of them.
24: 22 [A] Kenites will be destroyed when Asshur **takes** you **captive**."
31: 9 [A] The Israelites **captured** the Midianite women and children
Dt 21: 10 [A] them into your hands and *you* **take captives** [+8660],
Jdg 5: 12 [A] O Barak! **Take captive** your captives, O son of Abinoam.'
1Sa 30: 2 [A] and *had* **taken captive** the women and all who were in it,
30: 3 [C] by fire and their wives and sons and daughters **taken captive**.
30: 5 [C] David's two wives *had* **been captured**—Ahinoam of Jezreel
1Ki 8: 46 [A] *who* **takes** them **captive** [+8647] to his own land, far away
8: 46 [A] *who* **takes** them **captive** [+8647] to his own land, far away
8: 47 [C] a change of heart in the land where *they* **are held captive**,
8: 47 [A] and plead with you in the land of their **conquerors** and say,
8: 48 [A] and soul in the land of their enemies who **took** them **captive**,
8: 50 [A] and cause their **conquerors** to show them mercy;
2Ki 5: 2 [A] had gone out and *had* **taken captive** a young girl from Israel,
6: 22 [A] "Would you kill men *you have* **captured** with your own
1Ch 5: 21 [A] *They* **seized** the livestock of the Hagrites—fifty thousand
2Ch 6: 36 [A] *who* **takes** them **captive** [+8647] to a land far away or near;
6: 36 [A] *who* **takes** them **captive** [+8647] to a land far away or near;
6: 37 [C] a change of heart in the land where *they* **are held captive**,
6: 38 [A] and soul in the land of their captivity where they *were* **taken**,
14: 15 [14:14] [A] **carried off** droves of sheep and goats and camels.
21: 17 [A] and **carried off** all the goods found in the king's palace,
25: 12 [A] The army of Judah also **captured** ten thousand men alive,
28: 5 [A] and **took** [+8664] many of his people **as prisoners**
28: 8 [A] The Israelites **took captive** from their kinsmen two hundred
28: 11 [A] countrymen *you have* **taken as prisoners** [+4946+8664], for
28: 17 [A] again come and attacked Judah and **carried away** prisoners,
30: 9 [A] and your children will be shown compassion by their **captors**
Ps 68: 18 [68:19] [A] ascended on high, *you* **led** captives **in** *your* **train**;
106: 46 [A] He caused them to be pitied by all *who* **held** them **captive**.
137: 3 [A] for there our **captors** asked us for songs, our tormentors
Isa 14: 2 [A] *They will* **make captives** of their captors and rule over their
14: 2 [A] They will make captives of their **captors** and rule over their
61: 1 [B] to proclaim freedom for the **captives** and release from
Jer 13: 17 [C] because the LORD's flock *will* **be taken captive**.
41: 10 [A] **made captives of** all the rest of the people who were in Mizpah
41: 10 [A] Ishmael son of Nethaniah **took** them **captive** and set out to
41: 14 [A] All the people Ishmael *had* **taken captive** at Mizpah turned
43: 12 [A] he will burn their temples and **take** their gods **captive**.
50: 33 [A] All their **captors** hold them fast, refusing to let them go.
Eze 6: 9 [C] Then in the nations where *they have* **been carried captive**,
Ob 1: 11 [A] On the day you stood aloof while strangers **carried off** his

8648 שְׁבוֹ *šᵉbô*, n.[f.]. [2]

agate [2]

Ex 28: 19 in the third row a jacinth, an **agate** and an amethyst;
39: 12 in the third row a jacinth, an **agate** and an amethyst;

8649 שְׁבוּאֵל *šᵉbû'ēl*, n.pr.m. [3 / 0] [√ 8647? + 446; cf. 8742]

1Ch 23: 16 The descendants of Gershom: Shubael [BHS *Shebuel*; NIV 8742]
25: 4 Bukkiah, Mattaniah, Uzziel, Shubael [BHS *Shebuel*; NIV 8742]
26: 24 Shubael, [BHS *Shebuel*; NIV 8742] a descendant of Gershom

8650 שְׁבוּל *šᵉbûl*, n.[m.]. Not used in NIV/BHS [cf. 8666]

8651 שָׁבוּעַ *šābûa'*, n.m. [20] [√ 8678]

weeks [7], sevens [4], seven [3], weeks [+3427] [2], *untranslated* [1], bridal week [1], Feast of Weeks [1], week [1]

Ge 29: 27 Finish this daughter's **bridal week**; then we will give you the
29: 28 He finished the **week** *with* Leah, and then Laban gave him his
Ex 34: 22 "Celebrate the Feast of **Weeks** with the firstfruits of the wheat
Lev 12: 5 *for two* **weeks** the woman will be unclean, as during her period.
Nu 28: 26 to the LORD an offering of new grain during the **Feast of Weeks**,
Dt 16: 9 Count off seven **weeks** from the time you begin to put the sickle to
16: 9 the time you begin to put the sickle to the standing grain. **[RPH]**
16: 10 celebrate the Feast of **Weeks** to the LORD your God by giving a
16: 16 the Feast of **Weeks** and the Feast of Tabernacles.
2Ch 8: 13 the Feast of **Weeks** and the Feast of Tabernacles.
Jer 5: 24 rains in season, who assures us of the regular **weeks** *of* harvest.'
Eze 45: 21 a feast lasting **seven** days, during which you shall eat bread made
Da 9: 24 "Seventy **'sevens'** are decreed for your people and your holy city to
9: 25 the ruler, comes, there will be seven **'sevens**,' and sixty-two
9: 25 comes, there will be seven 'sevens,' and sixty-two **'sevens.'**
9: 26 After the sixty-two **'sevens,'** the Anointed One will be cut off
9: 27 He will confirm a covenant with many *for* one **'seven.'** In the
9: 27 In the middle of the **'seven'** he will put an end to sacrifice
10: 2 At that time I, Daniel, mourned *for* three **weeks** [+3427].
10: 3 I used no lotions at all until the three **weeks** [+3427] were over.

8652 שְׁבוּעָה *šᵉbû'â*, n.f. [30 / 29] [√ 8678]

oath [17], swear [2], curse [1], denounce [1], oath swore [1], put oath [+906+8678] [1], sworn allegiance [+8678] [1], sworn judgments [1], sworn [1], takes an oath [+8678] [1], them[s] [1], under oath [+1251] [1]

Ge 24: 8 back with you, then you will be released from this **oath** *of* mine.

Ge 26: 3 and will confirm the **oath** I swore to your father Abraham.
Ex 22: 11 [22:10] **oath** *before* the LORD that the neighbor did not lay
Lev 5: 4 or evil—in any matter one might carelessly **swear** about—
Nu 5: 21 *is to* **put** the woman under this curse *of* the **oath** [+906+8678]—
5: 21 and **denounce** you when he causes your thigh to waste away
30: 2 [30:3] or **takes an oath** [+8678] to obligate himself by a pledge,
30: 10 [30:11] makes a vow or obligates herself by a pledge under **oath**
30: 13 [30:14] any vow she makes or any **sworn** pledge to deny herself.
Dt 7: 8 kept the **oath** he swore to your forefathers that he brought you out
Jos 2: 17 to her, "This **oath** you made us swear will not be binding on us
2: 20 are doing, we will be released from the **oath** you made us swear."
9: 20 so that wrath will not fall on us for breaking the **oath** we swore to
Jdg 21: 5 For they had taken a solemn **oath** that anyone who failed to
1Sa 14: 26 yet no one put his hand to his mouth, because they feared the **oath**.
2Sa 21: 7 because of the **oath** *before* the LORD between David
1Ki 2: 43 Why then did you not keep your **oath** *to* the LORD and obey the
1Ch 16: 16 the covenant he made with Abraham, the **oath** he **swore** to Isaac.
2Ch 15: 15 All Judah rejoiced about the **oath** because they had sworn it
Ne 6: 18 For many in Judah were **under oath** [+1251] to him, since he was
10: 29 [10:30] an **oath** to follow the Law of God given through Moses
Ps 105: 9 the covenant he made with Abraham, the **oath** he swore to Isaac.
Ecc 8: 2 the king's command, I say, because you took an **oath** *before* God.
9: 2 those who take oaths, so with those who are afraid to take **them**[s].
Isa 65: 15 You will leave your name to my chosen ones as a **curse**;
Jer 11: 5 I will fulfill the **oath** I swore to your forefathers, to give them a
Eze 21: 23 [21:28] to those *who have* **sworn allegiance** [+8678] to him,
Da 9: 11 the curses and **sworn judgments** written in the Law of Moses,
Hab 3: 9 you called for many [BHS *oaths*; NIV 8679] arrows.
Zec 8: 17 plot evil against your neighbor, and do not love to **swear** falsely.

8653 שָׁבוּר *šābûr*, a. *or* v.ptcp. [1] [√ 8689]

injured [1]

Lev 22: 22 the **injured** or the maimed, or anything with warts or festering

8654 שְׁבוּת *šᵉbût*, n.f. [24] [√ 8647]

fortunes [14], captivity [7], *untranslated* [1], exiled [1], made prosperous again [+906+8740] [1]

Dt 30: 3 the LORD your God will restore your **fortunes** and have
Job 42: 10 the LORD **made** him **prosperous again** [+906+8740] and gave
Ps 14: 7 When the LORD restores the **fortunes** *of* his people, let Jacob
53: 6 [53:7] When God restores the **fortunes** *of* his people, let Jacob
85: 1 [85:2] [you restored the **fortunes** [K; see Q 8669] *of* Jacob.]
126: 4 [Restore our **fortunes**, [K; see Q 8669] O LORD, like streams in the Negev.]
Jer 29: 14 the LORD, "and will bring you back from **captivity**. [K 8669]
30: 3 'when I will bring my people Israel and Judah back from **captivity**
30: 18 " 'I will restore the **fortunes** *of* Jacob's tents and have compassion
31: 23 "When I bring them back from **captivity**, the people in the land of
32: 44 and of the Negev, because I will restore their **fortunes**,
33: 7 I will bring Judah and Israel back from **captivity** and will rebuild
33: 7 from captivity **[RPH]** and will rebuild them as they were before.
33: 11 For I will restore the **fortunes** *of* the land as they were before,'
33: 26 For I will restore their **fortunes** and have compassion on them.' "
48: 47 "Yet I will restore the **fortunes** *of* Moab in days to come,"
49: 6 "Yet afterward, I will restore the **fortunes** *of* the Ammonites,"
49: 39 "Yet I will restore the **fortunes** [K 8669] *of* Elam in days to
La 2: 14 they did not expose your sin to ward off your **captivity**. [K 8669]
Eze 16: 53 [I will restore the fortunes of [RPH; K 8669] Sodom and her]
16: 53 [and her daughters and of [RPH; K 8669] Samaria and her]
16: 53 [her daughters, and [RPH; K 8669] your fortunes along with them,]
29: 14 I will bring them back from **captivity** and return them to Upper
39: 25 I will now bring Jacob back from **captivity** [K 8669] and will
Hos 6: 11 "Whenever I would restore the **fortunes** *of* my people,
Joel 3: 1 [4:1] when I restore the **fortunes** *of* Judah and Jerusalem,
Am 9: 14 I will bring back my **exiled** people Israel; they will rebuild the
Zep 2: 7 God will care for them; he will restore their **fortunes**. [Q 8669]
3: 20 of the earth when I restore your **fortunes** before your very eyes,"

8655 ¹שָׁבַח *šābaḥ*[1], v. [8 / 9] [→ 3786; Ar 10693]

commend [2], extol [2], glory [2], declared [1], glorify [1], receive praise [1]

1Ch 16: 35 [F] thanks to your holy name, that we *may* **glory** in your praise."
Ps 63: 3 [63:4] [D] your love is better than life, my lips *will* **glorify** you.
106: 47 [F] may give thanks to your holy name and **glory** in your praise.
117: 1 [D] the LORD, all you nations; **extol** him, all *you* peoples.
145: 4 [D] One generation *will* **commend** your works to another; they
147: 12 [D] **Extol** the LORD, O Jerusalem; praise your God, O Zion,
Ecc 4: 2 [D] I **declared** that the dead, who had already died, are happier
8: 10 [f] **receive praise** [BHS 8894] in the city where they did this.
8: 15 [D] So I **commend** the enjoyment of life, because nothing is

8656 ²שָׁבַח *šābaḥ*[2], v. [3]

keeps [1], still [1], stilled [1]

Ps 65: 7 [65:8] [G] *who* **stilled** the roaring of the seas, the roaring of
89: 9 [89:10] [D] when its waves mount up, you **still** them.
Pr 29: 11 [D] to his anger, but a wise man **keeps** himself under control.

8657 שֵׁבֶט *šēbeṭ*, n.m. [190] [→ 9222; Ar 10694]

tribes [74], tribe [44], rod [23], half-tribe [+2942] [18], scepter [15], tribal [3], *untranslated* [2], club [2], staff [2], chief men [1], javelins [1], peoples [1], punish [1], rulers [1], shepherd's rod [1], stick [1]

Ge 49: 10 The **scepter** will not depart from Judah, nor the ruler's staff from
49: 16 "Dan will provide justice for his people as one of the **tribes** *of*
49: 28 All these are the twelve **tribes** *of* Israel, and this is what their
Ex 21: 20 "If a man beats his male or female slave with a **rod** and the slave
24: 4 set up twelve stone pillars representing the twelve **tribes** *of* Israel.
28: 21 engraved like a seal with the name of one of the twelve **tribes**.
39: 14 engraved like a seal with the name of one of the twelve **tribes**.
Lev 27: 32 every tenth animal that passes under the **shepherd's rod**—
Nu 4: 18 "See that the Kohathite **tribal** clans are not cut off from the
18: 2 Bring your fellow Levites from your ancestral **tribe** to join you
24: 2 When Balaam looked out and saw Israel encamped tribe by **tribe**,
24: 17 A star will come out of Jacob; a **scepter** will rise out of Israel.
32: 33 the **half-tribe of** [+2942] Manasseh son of Joseph the kingdom of
36: 3 Now suppose they marry men from other Israelite **tribes**; then their
Dt 1: 13 understanding and respected men from each of your **tribes**,
1: 15 So I took the leading men of your **tribes**, wise and respected men,
1: 15 of hundreds, of fifties and of tens and as **tribal** officials.
1: 23 good to me; so I selected twelve of you, one man from each **tribe**.
3: 13 the kingdom of Og, I gave to the half **tribe** *of* Manasseh.
5: 23 all the leading men of your **tribes** and your elders came to me.
10: 8 At that time the LORD set apart the **tribe** *of* Levi to carry the ark
12: 5 from among all your **tribes** to put his Name there for his dwelling.
12: 14 only at the place the LORD will choose in one of your **tribes**,
16: 18 officials for each of your **tribes** in every town the LORD your
18: 1 The priests, who are Levites—indeed the whole **tribe** *of* Levi—
18: 5 chosen them and their descendants out of all your **tribes** to stand
29: 8 [29:7] the Gadites and the **half-tribe of** [+2942] Manasseh.
29: 10 [29:9] your leaders and **chief men**, your elders and officials, and
29: 18 [29:17] or **tribe** among you today whose heart turns away from
29: 21 [29:20] The LORD will single him out from all the **tribes** *of*
31: 28 Assemble before me all the elders of your **tribes** and all your
33: 5 the leaders of the people assembled, along with the **tribes** *of* Israel.
Jos 1: 12 the Gadites and the **half-tribe of** [+2942] Manasseh, Joshua said,
3: 12 Now then, choose twelve men from the **tribes** *of* Israel, one from
3: 12 choose twelve men from the tribes of Israel, one from each **tribe**.
4: 2 "Choose twelve men from among the people, one from each **tribe**,
4: 4 men he had appointed from the Israelites, one from each **tribe**,
4: 5 his shoulder, according to the number of the **tribes** *of* the Israelites,
4: 8 according to the number of the **tribes** *of* the Israelites, as the
4: 12 Gad and the **half-tribe of** [+2942] Manasseh crossed over,
7: 14 " 'In the morning, present yourselves tribe by **tribe**. The tribe that
7: 14 The **tribe** that the LORD takes shall come forward clan by clan;
7: 16 Early the next morning Joshua had Israel come forward by **tribes**,
7: 16 had Israel come forward by tribes, and **[RPH]** Judah was taken.
11: 23 he gave it as an inheritance to Israel according to their **tribal**
12: 6 and the **half-tribe of** [+2942] Manasseh to be their possession.
12: 7 to the **tribes** *of* Israel according to their tribal divisions—
13: 7 divide it as an inheritance among the nine **tribes** and half of the
13: 7 among the nine tribes and half of the **tribe** *of* Manasseh."
13: 14 to the **tribe** *of* Levi he gave no inheritance, since the offerings
13: 29 This is what Moses had given to the **half-tribe of** [+2942]
13: 33 to the **tribe** *of* Levi, Moses had given no inheritance; the LORD,
18: 2 there were still seven Israelite **tribes** who had not yet received their
18: 4 Appoint three men from each **tribe**. I will send them out to make a
18: 7 the **half-tribe of** [+2942] Manasseh have already received their
21: 16 with their pasturelands—nine towns from these two **tribes**.
22: 7 (To the **half-tribe of** [+2942] Manasseh Moses had given land in
22: 9 the **half-tribe of** [+2942] Manasseh left the Israelites at Shiloh in
22: 10 the **half-tribe of** [+2942] Manasseh built an imposing altar there
22: 11 of Canaan at Geliloth **[RPH]** near the Jordan on the Israelite side,
22: 13 to Reuben, Gad and the **half-tribe of** [+2942] Manasseh.
22: 15 to Reuben, Gad and the **half-tribe of** [+2942] Manasseh—
22: 21 the **half-tribe of** [+2942] Manasseh replied to the heads of the
23: 4 Remember how I have allotted as an inheritance for your **tribes** all
24: 1 Then Joshua assembled all the **tribes** *of* Israel at Shechem.
Jdg 5: 14 came down, from Zebulun those who bear a commander's **staff**.
18: 1 in those days the **tribe** *of* the Danites was seeking a place of their
18: 1 had not yet come into an inheritance among the **tribes** *of* Israel.
18: 19 Isn't it better that you serve a **tribe** and clan in Israel as priest
18: 30 his sons were priests for the **tribe** *of* Dan until the time of the
20: 2 The leaders of all the people of the **tribes** *of* Israel took their places
20: 10 We'll take ten men out of every hundred from all the **tribes** *of*

Jdg 20:12 The **tribes** *of* Israel sent men throughout the tribe of Benjamin,
20:12 The tribes of Israel sent men throughout the **tribe** *of* Benjamin,
21: 3 to Israel? Why should one **tribe** be missing from Israel today?"
21: 5 "Who from all the **tribes** *of* Israel has failed to assemble before the
21: 6 the Benjamites. "Today one **tribe** is cut off from Israel," they said.
21: 8 "Which one of the **tribes** *of* Israel failed to assemble before the
21:15 because the LORD had made a gap in the **tribes** *of* Israel.
21:17 they said, "so that a **tribe** of Israel will not be wiped out.
21:24 Israelites left that place and went home to their **tribes** and clans,
1Sa 2:28 I chose your father out of all the **tribes** *of* Israel to be my priest,
9:21 "But am I not a Benjamite, from the smallest **tribe** *of* Israel,
9:21 is not my clan the least of all the clans of the **tribe** *of* Benjamin?
10:19 So now present yourselves before the LORD by your **tribes**
10:20 When Samuel brought all the **tribes** *of* Israel near, the tribe of
10:20 all the tribes of Israel near, the **tribe** *of* Benjamin was chosen.
10:21 Then he brought forward the **tribe** *of* Benjamin, clan by clan,
15:17 own eyes, did you not become the head of the **tribes** *of* Israel?
2Sa 5: 1 All the **tribes** *of* Israel came to David at Hebron and said,
7: 7 did I ever say to any of their **rulers** whom I commanded to
7:14 When he does wrong, I will punish him with the **rod** *of* men,
15: 2 would answer, "Your servant is from one of the **tribes** *of* Israel."
15:10 Absalom sent secret messengers throughout the **tribes** *of* Israel to
18:14 So he took three **javelins** in his hand and plunged them into
19: 9 [19:10] Throughout the **tribes** *of* Israel, the people were all
20:14 Sheba passed through all the **tribes** *of* Israel to Abel Beth Maacah
23:21 had a spear in his hand, Benaiah went against him with a **club**.
24: 2 "Go throughout the **tribes** *of* Israel from Dan to Beersheba
1Ki 8:16 I have not chosen a city in any **tribe** *of* Israel to have a temple built
11:13 but will give him one **tribe** for the sake of David my servant
11:31 to tear the kingdom out of Solomon's hand and give you ten **tribes**.
11:32 which I have chosen out of all the **tribes** *of* Israel, he will have one
11:32 I have chosen out of all the tribes of Israel, he will have one **tribe**.
11:35 take the kingdom from his son's hands and give you ten **tribes**.
11:36 I will give one **tribe** to his son so that David my servant may
12:20 Only the **tribe** *of* Judah remained loyal to the house of David.
12:21 he mustered the whole house of Judah and the **tribe** *of* Benjamin—
14:21 the city the LORD had chosen out of all the **tribes** *of* Israel in
18:31 twelve stones, one for each of the **tribes** descended from Jacob,
2Ki 17:18 removed them from his presence. Only the **tribe** *of* Judah was left,
21: 7 in Jerusalem, which I have chosen out of all the **tribes** *of* Israel,
1Ch 5:18 the **half-tribe of** [+2942] Manasseh had 44,760 men ready for
5:23 The people of the **half-tribe of** [+2942] Manasseh were numerous;
5:26 the Gadites and the **half-tribe of** [+2942] Manasseh into exile.
11:23 a weaver's rod in his hand, Benaiah went against him with a **club**.
12:37 [12:38] of Reuben, Gad and the **half-tribe of** [+2942] Manasseh,
23:14 of Moses the man of God were counted as part of the **tribe** *of* Levi.
26:32 the **half-tribe of** [+2942] Manasseh for every matter pertaining to
27:16 The officers over the **tribes** *of* Israel: over the Reubenites:
27:20 Hoshea son of Azaziah; over half the **tribe** *of* Manasseh: Joel son
27:22 son of Jeroham. These were the officers over the **tribes** *of* Israel.
28: 1 the officers over the **tribes**, the commanders of the divisions in the
29: 6 Then the leaders of families, the officers of the **tribes** *of* Israel,
2Ch 6: 5 I have not chosen a city in any **tribe** *of* Israel to have a temple built
11:16 Those from every **tribe** *of* Israel who set their hearts on seeking
12:13 the city the LORD had chosen out of all the **tribes** *of* Israel in
33: 7 in Jerusalem, which I have chosen out of all the **tribes** *of* Israel,
Job 9:34 someone to remove God's **rod** from me, so that his terror would
21: 9 are safe and free from fear; the **rod** *of* God is not upon them.
37:13 He brings the clouds to **punish** men, or to water his earth and show
Ps 2: 9 You will rule them with an iron **scepter**; you will dash them to
23: 4 for you are with me; your **rod** and your staff, they comfort me.
45: 6 [45:7] a **scepter** *of* justice will be the scepter of your kingdom.
45: 6 [45:7] a scepter of justice will be the **scepter** *of* your kingdom.
74: 2 of old, the **tribe** *of* your inheritance, whom you redeemed—
78:55 as an inheritance; he settled the **tribes** *of* Israel in their homes.
78:67 the tents of Joseph, he did not choose the **tribe** *of* Ephraim;
78:68 but he chose the **tribe** *of* Judah, Mount Zion, which he loved.
89:32 [89:33] I will punish their sin with the **rod**, their iniquity with
105:37 with silver and gold, and from among their **tribes** no one faltered.
122: 4 That is where the **tribes** go up, the tribes of the LORD, to praise
122: 4 That is where the tribes go up, the **tribes** *of* the LORD, to praise
125: 3 The **scepter** *of* the wicked will not remain over the land allotted to
Pr 10:13 but a **rod** is for the back of him who lacks judgment.
13:24 He who spares the **rod** hates his son, but he who loves him is
22: 8 wickedness reaps trouble, and the **rod** *of* his fury will be destroyed.
22:15 heart of a child, but the **rod** *of* discipline will drive it far from him.
23:13 from a child; if you punish him with the **rod**, he will not die.
23:14 Punish him with the **rod** and save his soul from death.
26: 3 the horse, a halter for the donkey, and a **rod** for the backs of fools!
29:15 The **rod** of correction imparts wisdom, but a child left to himself
Isa 9: 4 [9:3] the bar across their shoulders, the **rod** *of* their oppressor.
10: 5 "Woe to the Assyrian, the **rod** *of* my anger, in whose hand is the
10:15 As if a **rod** were to wield him who lifts it up, or a club brandish
10:24 who beat you with a **rod** and lift up a club against you, as Egypt
11: 4 He will strike the earth with the **rod** *of* his mouth; with the breath
14: 5 LORD has broken the rod of the wicked, the **scepter** *of* the rulers,
14:29 all you Philistines, that the **rod** that struck you is broken;
19:13 the cornerstones of her **peoples** have led Egypt astray.
28:27 caraway is beaten out with a rod, and cummin with a **stick**.
30:31 will shatter Assyria; with his **scepter** he will strike them down.
49: 6 small a thing for you to be my servant to restore the **tribes** *of* Jacob
63:17 for the sake of your servants, the **tribes** that are your inheritance.
Jer 10:16 Maker of all things, including Israel, the **tribe** *of* his inheritance—
51:19 is the Maker of all things, including the **tribe** *of* his inheritance—
La 3: 1 I am the man who has seen affliction by the **rod** *of* his wrath.
Eze 19:11 Its branches were strong, fit for a ruler's **scepter**. It towered high
19:14 No strong branch is left on it fit for a ruler's **scepter**.' This is a
20:37 I will take note of you as you pass under my **rod**, and I will bring
21:10 [21:15] " 'Shall we rejoice in the **scepter** *of* my son ⌞Judah⌟?
21:13 [21:18] what if the **scepter** ⌞of Judah⌟, which the sword despises,
37:19 of the Israelite **tribes** associated with him, and join it to Judah's
45: 8 the house of Israel to possess the land according to their **tribes**.
47:13 the land for an inheritance among the twelve **tribes** *of* Israel,
47:21 this land among yourselves according to the **tribes** *of* Israel.
47:22 they are to be allotted an inheritance among the **tribes** *of* Israel.
47:23 In whatever **tribe** the alien settles, there you are to give him his
48: 1 "These are the **tribes**, listed by name: At the northern frontier,
48:19 from the city who farm it will come from all the **tribes** *of* Israel.
48:23 "As for the rest of the **tribes**: Benjamin will have one portion;
48:29 "This is the land you are to allot as an inheritance to the **tribes** *of*
48:31 the gates of the city will be named after the **tribes** *of* Israel.
Hos 5: 9 of reckoning. Among the **tribes** *of* Israel I proclaim what is certain.
Am 1: 5 Valley of Aven and the one who holds the **scepter** in Beth Eden.
1: 8 king of Ashdod and the one who holds the **scepter** in Ashkelon.
Mic 5: 1 [4:14] They will strike Israel's ruler on the cheek with a **rod**.
7:14 Shepherd your people with your **staff**, the flock of your
Zec 9: 1 for the eyes of men and all the **tribes** *of* Israel are on the LORD—
10:11 pride will be brought down and Egypt's **scepter** will pass away.

8658 שְׁבָט šᵉbāṭ, n.pr.m. [1]

Shebat [1]

Zec 1: 7 eleventh month, the month of **Shebat**, in the second year of Darius,

8659 שָׁבִי šābî, a. *or* n.m. Not used in NIV/BHS [√ 8647]

8660 שְׁבִי šᵉbî, n.m. [48] [√ 8647]

captivity [17], exile [13], captives [8], captured [4], prisoners [2], captured [+8647] [1], carry off [+928+995+2021] [1], prisoner [1], take captives [+8647] [1]

Ex 12:29 who sat on the throne, to the firstborn of the **prisoner**, who was in
Nu 21: 1 he attacked the Israelites and **captured** [+8647] some of them.
31:12 brought the **captives**, spoils and plunder to Moses and Eleazar the
31:19 and seventh days you must purify yourselves and your **captives**.
31:26 are to count all the people and animals that were **captured**.
Dt 21:10 God delivers them into your hands and *you* **take captives** [+8647],
21:13 and put aside the clothes she was wearing when **captured**.
28:41 but you will not keep them, because they will go into **captivity**.
Jdg 5:12 O Barak! Take captive your **captives**, O son of Abinoam.'
2Ch 6:37 and plead with you in the land of their **captivity** and say,
6:38 and soul in the land of their **captivity** where they were taken,
28:17 had again come and attacked Judah and carried away **prisoners**,
29: 9 and why our sons and daughters and our wives are in **captivity**.
Ezr 2: 1 of the province who came up from the **captivity** *of* the exiles,
3: 8 and all who had returned from the **captivity** to Jerusalem)
8:35 the exiles who had returned from **captivity** sacrificed burnt
9: 7 and our priests have been subjected to the sword and **captivity**,
Ne 1: 2 I questioned them about the Jewish remnant that survived the **exile**,
1: 3 "Those who survived the **exile** and are back in the province are in
7: 6 **captivity** *of* the exiles whom Nebuchadnezzar king of Babylon had
8:17 The whole company that had returned from **exile** built booths
Ps 68:18 [68:19] you ascended on high, you led **captives** in your train;
78:61 He sent ⌞the ark of⌟ his might into **captivity**, his splendor into the
Isa 20: 4 and barefoot the Egyptian **captives** and Cushite exiles,
46: 2 unable to rescue the burden, they themselves go off into **captivity**.
49:24 be taken from warriors, or **captives** rescued from the fierce?
49:25 "Yes, **captives** will be taken from warriors, and plunder retrieved
Jer 15: 2 those for starvation, to starvation; those for **captivity**, to captivity.'
15: 2 those for starvation, to starvation; those for captivity, to **captivity**.'
20: 6 and all who live in your house will go into **exile** to Babylon.
22:22 drive all your shepherds away, and your allies will go into **exile**.
30:10 out of a distant place, your descendants from the land of their **exile**.
30:16 devour you will be devoured; all your enemies will go into **exile**.
43:11 those destined for death, **captivity** to those destined for captivity,
43:11 those destined for death, captivity to those destined for **captivity**,
46:27 out of a distant place, your descendants from the land of their **exile**.
48:46 your sons are taken into **exile** and your daughters into captivity.

La 1: 5 Her children have gone into **exile**, captive before the foe.
1: 18 my suffering. My young men and maidens have gone into **exile**.
Eze 12: 11 so it will be done to them. They will go into exile as **captives**.
30: 17 fall by the sword, and the cities themselves will go into **captivity**.
30: 18 will be covered with clouds, and her villages will go into **captivity**.
Da 11: 8 and gold and **carry** them **off to** [+928+995+2021] Egypt.
11: 33 they will fall by the sword or be burned or **captured** or plundered.
Am 4: 10 your young men with the sword, along with your **captured** horses.
9: 4 Though they are driven into **exile** by their enemies, there I will
Na 3: 10 Yet she was taken captive and went into **exile**. Her infants were
Hab 1: 9 hordes advance like a desert wind and gather **prisoners** like sand.

8661 שֹׁבִי šōbî, n.pr.m. [1]

Shobi [1]

2Sa 17: 27 **Shobi** son of Nahash from Rabbah of the Ammonites,

8662 שֹׁבַי šōbay, n.pr.m. [2]

Shobai [2]

Ezr 2: 42 of Shallum, Ater, Talmon, Akkub, Hatita and **Shobai** 139
Ne 7: 45 of Shallum, Ater, Talmon, Akkub, Hatita and **Shobai** 138

8663 שָׁבִיב šābîb, n.m. [1] [→ 8646; Ar 10695]

flame [1]

Job 18: 5 of the wicked is snuffed out; the **flame** *of* his fire stops burning.

8664 שִׁבְיָה šibyâ, n.f. [9] [√ 8647]

prisoners [3], captives [2], captivity [2], taken as prisoners [+4946+8647] [1], took as prisoners [+8647] [1]

Dt 21: 11 if you notice among the **captives** a beautiful woman and are
32: 42 the blood of the slain and the **captives**, the heads of the enemy
2Ch 28: 5 defeated him and **took** many of his people **as prisoners** [+8647]
28: 11 countrymen *you have* **taken as prisoners** [+4946+8647], for the
28: 13 "You must not bring those **prisoners** here," they said, "or we will
28: 14 So the soldiers gave up the **prisoners** and plunder in the presence
28: 15 The men designated by name took the **prisoners**, and from the
Ne 4: 4 [3:36] Give them over as plunder in a land of **captivity**.
Jer 48: 46 your sons are taken into exile and your daughters into **captivity**.

8665 שְׁבִיָּה šᵉbiyyâ, n.f. [1] [√ 8647]

captive [1]

Isa 52: 2 from the chains on your neck, O **captive** Daughter of Zion.

8666 שְׁבִיל šᵉbîl, n.[m.]. [2] [√ 8670; cf. 8650]

paths [1], way [1]

Ps 77: 19 [77:20] led through the sea, your **way** through the mighty waters,
Jer 18: 15 which made them stumble in their ways and in the ancient **paths**.

8667 שָׁבִיס šābîs, n.[m.]. [1]

headbands [1]

Isa 3: 18 their finery: the bangles and **headbands** and crescent necklaces,

8668 שְׁבִיעִי šᵉbîʿî, a.num.ord. [98 / 97] [√ 8679]

seventh [97]

Ge 2: 2 By the **seventh** day God had finished the work he had been doing;
2: 2 had been doing; so on the **seventh** day he rested from all his work.
2: 3 God blessed the **seventh** day and made it holy, because on it he
8: 4 on the seventeenth day of the **seventh** month the ark came to rest
Ex 12: 15 from the first day through the **seventh** must be cut off from Israel.
12: 16 day hold a sacred assembly, and another one on the **seventh** day.
13: 6 and on the **seventh** day hold a festival to the LORD.
16: 26 but on the **seventh** day, the Sabbath, there will not be any."
16: 27 some of the people went out on the **seventh** day to gather it,
16: 29 Everyone is to stay where he is on the **seventh** day; no one is to go
16: 30 So the people rested on the **seventh** day.
20: 10 but the **seventh** day is a Sabbath to the LORD your God.
20: 11 the sea, and all that is in them, but he rested on the **seventh** day.
21: 2 But in the **seventh** year, he shall go free, without paying anything.
23: 11 but during the **seventh** year let the land lie unplowed and unused.
23: 12 on the **seventh** day do not work, so that your ox and your donkey
24: 16 on the **seventh** day the LORD called to Moses from within the
31: 15 work is to be done, but the **seventh** day is a Sabbath of rest,
31: 17 and on the **seventh** day he abstained from work and rested.' "
34: 21 "Six days you shall labor, but on the **seventh** day you shall rest;
35: 2 work is to be done, but the **seventh** day shall be your holy day,
Lev 13: 5 On the **seventh** day the priest is to examine him, and if he sees that
13: 6 On the **seventh** day the priest is to examine him again, and if the
13: 27 On the **seventh** day the priest is to examine him, and if it is
13: 32 On the **seventh** day the priest is to examine the sore, and if the itch
13: 34 On the **seventh** day the priest is to examine the itch, and if it has
13: 51 On the **seventh** day he is to examine it, and if the mildew has
14: 9 On the **seventh** day he must shave off all his hair; he must shave
14: 39 On the **seventh** day the priest shall return to inspect the house.
16: 29 On the tenth day of the **seventh** month you must deny yourselves
23: 3 but the **seventh** day is a Sabbath of rest, a day of sacred assembly.
23: 8 on the **seventh** day hold a sacred assembly and do no regular
23: 16 Count off fifty days up to the day after the **seventh** Sabbath,
23: 24 'On the first day of the **seventh** month you are to have a day of
23: 27 "The tenth day of this **seventh** month is the Day of Atonement.
23: 34 'On the fifteenth day of the **seventh** month the LORD's Feast of
23: 39 " 'So beginning with the fifteenth day of the **seventh** month,
23: 41 for the generations to come; celebrate it in the **seventh** month.
25: 4 But in the **seventh** year the land is to have a sabbath of rest,
25: 9 sounded everywhere on the tenth day of the **seventh** month;
25: 20 "What will we eat in the **seventh** year if we do not plant or harvest
Nu 6: 9 must shave his head on the day of his cleansing—the **seventh** day.
7: 48 On the **seventh** day Elishama son of Ammihud, the leader of the
19: 12 himself with the water on the third day and on the **seventh** day;
19: 12 But if he does not purify himself on the third and **seventh** days,
19: 19 is to sprinkle the unclean person on the third and **seventh** days,
19: 19 and seventh days, and on the **seventh** day he is to purify him.
28: 25 On the **seventh** day hold a sacred assembly and do no regular
29: 1 " 'On the first day of the **seventh** month hold a sacred assembly
29: 7 " 'On the tenth day of this **seventh** month hold a sacred assembly.
29: 12 " 'On the fifteenth day of the **seventh** month, hold a sacred
29: 32 " 'On the **seventh** day prepare seven bulls, two rams and fourteen
31: 19 On the third and **seventh** days you must purify yourselves
31: 24 On the **seventh** day wash your clothes and you will be clean.
Dt 5: 14 but the **seventh** day is a Sabbath to the LORD your God.
15: 12 serves you six years, in the **seventh** year you must let him go free.
16: 8 and on the **seventh** day hold an assembly to the LORD your God
Jos 6: 4 On the **seventh** day, march around the city seven times,
6: 15 On the **seventh** day, they got up at daybreak and marched around
6: 16 The **seventh** time around, when the priests sounded the trumpet
19: 40 The **seventh** lot came out for the tribe of Dan, clan by clan.
Jdg 14: 15 On the fourth [BHS ***seventh***; NIV 8055] day, they said
14: 17 So on the **seventh** day he finally told her, because she continued to
14: 18 Before sunset on the **seventh** day the men of the town said to him,
2Sa 12: 18 On the **seventh** day the child died. David's servants were afraid to
1Ki 8: 2 time of the festival in the month of Ethanim, the **seventh** month.
18: 44 The **seventh** time the servant reported, "A cloud as small as a
20: 29 opposite each other, and on the **seventh** day the battle was joined.
2Ki 11: 4 In the **seventh** year Jehoiada sent for the commanders of units of a
18: 9 which was the **seventh** year of Hoshea son of Elah king of Israel,
25: 25 In the **seventh** month, however, Ishmael son of Nethaniah,
1Ch 2: 15 the sixth Ozem and the **seventh** David.
12: 11 [12:12] Attai the sixth, Eliel the **seventh**,
24: 10 the **seventh** to Hakkoz, the eighth to Abijah,
25: 14 the **seventh** to Jesarelah, his sons and relatives, 12
26: 3 Elam the fifth, Jehohanan the sixth and Eliehoenai the **seventh**.
26: 5 Ammiel the sixth, Issachar the **seventh** and Peullethai the eighth.
27: 10 The **seventh**, for the seventh month, was Helez the Pelonite,
27: 10 The seventh, for the **seventh** month, was Helez the Pelonite,
2Ch 5: 3 to the king at the time of the festival in the **seventh** month.
7: 10 On the twenty-third day of the **seventh** month he sent the people to
23: 1 In the **seventh** year Jehoiada showed his strength. He made a
31: 7 doing this in the third month and finished in the **seventh** month.
Ezr 3: 1 When the **seventh** month came and the Israelites had settled in
3: 6 On the first day of the **seventh** month they began to offer burnt
7: 8 Ezra arrived in Jerusalem in the fifth month of the **seventh** year of
Ne 7: 73 [7:72] When the **seventh** month came and the Israelites had
8: 2 So on the first day of the **seventh** month Ezra the priest brought the
8: 14 were to live in booths during the feast of the **seventh** month
10: 31 [10:32] Every **seventh** year we will forgo working the land
Est 1: 10 On the **seventh** day, when King Xerxes was in high spirits from
Jer 28: 17 In the **seventh** month of that same year, Hananiah the prophet died.
41: 1 In the **seventh** month Ishmael son of Nethaniah, the son of
Eze 20: 1 In the **seventh** year, in the fifth month on the tenth day, some of
45: 25 the Feast, which begins in the **seventh** month on the fifteenth day,
Hag 2: 1 On the twenty-first day of the **seventh** month, the word of the
Zec 7: 5 in the fifth and **seventh** months for the past seventy years,
8: 19 **seventh** and tenth months will become joyful and glad occasions

8669 שְׁבִית šᵉbît, n.f. [8] [√ 8647]

fortunes [4], *untranslated* [3], captives [1]

Nu 21: 29 and his daughters as **captives** to Sihon king of the Amorites.
Job 42: 10 [the LORD **made** him **prosperous again** [+906+8740] and gave]
Ps 85: 1 [85:2] O LORD; you restored the **fortunes** [K 8654] *of* Jacob.
126: 4 Restore our **fortunes**, [K 8654] O LORD, like streams in the
Jer 29: 14 ["and will bring you back from **captivity**. [K; see Q 8654]]
49: 39 ["Yet I will restore the **fortunes** [K; see Q 8654] *of* Elam]
La 2: 14 [not expose your sin to ward off your **captivity**. [K; see Q 8654]]

Eze 16:53 I will restore the **fortunes** *of* Sodom and her daughters and of
16:53 I will restore the fortunes of [RPH; Q 8654] Sodom and her
16:53 and her daughters and of [RPH; Q 8654] Samaria and her daughters,
16:53 her daughters, and [RPH; Q 8654] your fortunes along with them,
16:53 of Samaria and her daughters, and your **fortunes** along with them,
39:25 [I will now bring Jacob back from **captivity** [K; see Q 8654]]
Zep 2:7 [care for them; he will restore their **fortunes**. [Q; see K 8654]]

8670 שֹׁבֶל *šōbel*, n.[m.]. [1] [→ 839, 840, 8666, 8672, 8673]

skirts [1]

Isa 47:2 Lift up your **skirts**, bare your legs, and wade through the streams.

8671 שַׁבְּלוּל *šabbᵉlûl*, n.m. [1] [√ 1176?]

slug [1]

Ps 58:8 [58:9] Like a **slug** melting away as it moves along, like a stillborn

8672 שִׁבֹּלֶת¹ *šibbōlet¹*, n.f. [16] [√ 8670; cf. 6027]

heads of grain [8], heads [3], grain [2], branches [1], leftover grain [1], Shibboleth [1]

Ge 41:5 Seven **heads of grain**, healthy and good, were growing on a single
41:6 After them, seven other **heads of grain** sprouted—thin
41:7 The thin **heads of grain** swallowed up the seven healthy, full
41:7 thin heads of grain swallowed up the seven healthy, full **heads**.
41:22 "In my dreams I also saw seven **heads of grain**, full and good,
41:23 After them, seven other **heads** sprouted—withered and thin
41:24 The thin **heads of grain** swallowed up the seven good heads.
41:24 The thin heads of grain swallowed up the seven good **heads**.
41:26 seven years, and the seven good **heads of grain** are seven years;
41:27 so are the seven worthless **heads of grain** scorched by the east
Jdg 12:6 they said, "All right, say '**Shibboleth**.' " If he said, "Sibboleth,"
Ru 2:2 pick up the **leftover grain** behind anyone in whose eyes I find
Job 24:24 and gathered up like all others; they are cut off like heads of **grain**.
Isa 17:5 gathers the standing grain and harvests the **grain** with his arm—
17:5 as when a man gleans **heads of grain** in the Valley of Rephaim.
Zec 4:12 "What are these two olive **branches** beside the two gold pipes that

8673 שִׁבֹּלֶת² *šibbōlet²*, n.f. [3] [√ 8670; cf. 6027]

floods [1], floodwaters [+4784] [1], flowing [1]

Ps 69:2 [69:3] I have come into the deep waters; the **floods** engulf me.
69:15 [69:16] Do not let the **floodwaters** [+4784] engulf me or the
Isa 27:12 In that day the LORD will thresh from the **flowing** Euphrates to

8674 שֶׁבְנָא *šebnā'*, n.pr.m. [7] [√ 8676?; cf. 8675]

Shebna [7]

2Ki 18:37 **Shebna** the secretary and Joah son of Asaph the recorder went to
19:2 **Shebna** the secretary and the leading priests, all wearing sackcloth,
Isa 22:15 "Go, say to this steward, to **Shebna**, who is in charge of the palace:
36:3 son of Hilkiah the palace administrator, **Shebna** the secretary,
36:11 Then Eliakim, **Shebna** and Joah said to the field commander,
36:22 son of Hilkiah the palace administrator, **Shebna** the secretary,
37:2 **Shebna** the secretary, and the leading priests, all wearing

8675 שֶׁבְנָה *šebnâ*, n.pr.m. [2] [cf. 8674]

Shebna [2]

2Ki 18:18 son of Hilkiah the palace administrator, **Shebna** the secretary,
18:26 son of Hilkiah, and **Shebna** and Joah said to the field commander,

8676 שְׁבַנְיָה *šᵉbanyâ*, n.pr.m. [6 / 5] [→ 8674?, 8677]

Shebaniah [5]

Ne 9:4 Jeshua, Bani, Kadmiel, **Shebaniah**, Bunni, Sherebiah, Bani
9:5 Hashabneiah, Sherebiah, Hodiah, **Shebaniah** and Pethahiah—
10:4 [10:5] Hattush, **Shebaniah**, Malluch,
10:10 [10:11] **Shebaniah**, Hodiah, Kelita, Pelaiah, Hanan,
10:12 [10:13] Zaccur, Sherebiah, **Shebaniah**,
12:14 of Shecaniah's, [BHS ***Shebaniah's***; NIV 8908] Joseph;

8677 שְׁבַנְיָהוּ *šᵉbanyāhû*, n.pr.m. [1] [√ 8676]

Shebaniah [1]

1Ch 15:24 **Shebaniah**, Joshaphat, Nethanel, Amasai, Zechariah, Benaiah

8678 שָׁבַע *šāba'*, v. [186] [→ 937, 8651, 8652, 8668, 8679, 8684, 8685, 8686]

swore [35], swear [29], promised on oath [21], sworn [21], took an oath [7], swore an oath [6], charge [5], made swear [4], take oaths [4], made swear an oath [3], made take an oath [3], make swear [3], oath [3], put under oath [3], taken an oath [3], bound under a strict oath [+906+8678] [2], made swear an oath [+906+8678] [2], solemnly swore [2], swears [2], swore oath [2], takes an oath [2], bound with the oath [1], confirmed by oath [1], declared on oath [1], gave oath [1], gave solemn oath [1], given oath [1], perjurers [+2021+4200+9214] [1], perjury [+2021+4200+9214] [1], pledged on oath [1], pronounced solemn oath [1], put oath [+906+8652] [1], ratified by oath [1], solemnly promised [1], swear allegiance [1], swearing [1], swears falsely [1], sworn allegiance [+8652] [1], sworn an oath [1], taken oath [1], takes an oath [+8652] [1], took oath [1], took the oath [1], use name as a curse [+928] [1], want to swear [1]

Ge 21:23 [C] Now **swear** to me here before God *that* you will not deal
21:24 [C] Abraham said, "I **swear** it."
21:31 [C] called Beersheba, because the two men **swore an oath** there.
22:16 [C] said, "*I* **swear** by myself, declares the LORD, that
24:3 [G] *I* **want** you **to swear** by the LORD, the God of heaven
24:7 [C] native land and who spoke to me and **promised** me **on oath**,
24:9 [C] and **swore an oath** to him concerning this matter.
24:37 [G] my master **made** me **swear an oath**, and said, 'You must not
25:33 [C] Jacob said, "**Swear** to me first." So he swore an oath to him,
25:33 [C] So *he* **swore an oath** to him, selling his birthright to Jacob.
26:3 [C] and will confirm the oath *I* **swore** to your father Abraham.
26:31 [C] Early the next morning *the men* **swore an oath** to each
31:53 [C] So Jacob **took an oath** in the name of the Fear of his father
47:31 [C] "**Swear** to me," he said. Then Joseph swore to him,
47:31 [C] Joseph **swore** to him, and Israel worshiped as he leaned on
50:5 [G] 'My father **made** me **swear an oath** and said, "I am about to
50:6 [G] "Go up and bury your father, as *he* **made** you **swear** *to do*."
50:24 [C] land to the land *he* **promised on oath** to Abraham, Isaac and
50:25 [G] And Joseph **made** the sons of Israel **swear an oath** and said,
Ex 13:5 [C] the land *he* **swore** to your forefathers to give you, a land
13:11 [C] to you, as *he* **promised on oath** to you and your forefathers,
13:19 [G] *had* **made** the sons of Israel **swear** [+906+8678] **an oath**.
13:19 [G] *had* **made** the sons of Israel **swear an oath** [+906+8678].
32:13 [C] and Israel, to whom *you* **swore** by your own self:
33:1 [C] and go up to the land *I* **promised on oath** to Abraham, Isaac
Lev 5:4 [C] " 'Or if a person thoughtlessly **takes an oath** to do anything,
6:3 [5:22] [C] lost property and lies about it, or if *he* **swears** falsely,
6:5 [5:24] [C] or whatever it was *he* **swore** falsely about. He must
19:12 [C] " '*Do* not **swear** falsely by my name and so profane the name
Nu 5:19 [G] the priest *shall* **put** the woman **under oath** and say to her,
5:21 [G] *is to* **put** the woman under this curse *of* the **oath** [+906+8652]
11:12 [C] to the land *you* **promised on oath** to their forefathers?
14:16 [C] bring these people into the land *he* **promised** them **on oath**;
14:23 [C] not one of them will ever see the land *I* **promised on oath** to
30:2 [30:3] [C] or **takes an oath** [+8652] to obligate himself by a
32:10 [C] anger was aroused that day and *he* **swore** *this* **oath**:
32:11 [C] of Egypt will see the land *I* **promised on oath** to Abraham,
Dt 1:8 [C] take possession of the land that the LORD **swore** he would
1:34 [C] heard what you said, he was angry and **solemnly swore**:
1:35 [C] shall see the good land *I* **swore** to give your forefathers,
2:14 [C] perished from the camp, as the LORD *had* **sworn** to them.
4:21 [C] *he* **solemnly swore** that I would not cross the Jordan
4:31 [C] with your forefathers, which *he* **confirmed** to them **by oath**.
6:10 [C] your God brings you into the land *he* **swore** to your fathers,
6:13 [C] your God, serve him only and **take** *your* **oaths** in his name.
6:18 [C] take over the good land that the LORD **promised on oath**
6:23 [C] give us the land that *he* **promised on oath** to our forefathers.
7:8 [C] kept the oath *he* **swore** to your forefathers that he brought
7:12 [C] covenant of love with you, as *he* **swore** to your forefathers.
7:13 [C] the lambs of your flocks in the land that *he* **swore** to your
8:1 [C] possess the land that the LORD **promised on oath** to your
8:18 [C] which *he* **swore** to your forefathers, as it is today.
9:5 [C] to accomplish what he **swore** to your fathers, to Abraham,
10:11 [C] possess the land that *I* **swore** to their fathers to give them."
10:20 [C] serve him. Hold fast to him and **take** *your* **oaths** in his name.
11:9 [C] so that you may live long in the land that the LORD **swore**
11:21 [C] in the land that the LORD **swore** to give your forefathers,
13:17 [13:18] [C] as *he* **promised on oath** to your forefathers,
19:8 [C] your territory, as *he* **promised on oath** to your forefathers,
26:3 [C] to the land the LORD **swore** to our forefathers to give us."
26:15 [C] the land you have given us as *you* **promised on oath** to our
28:9 [C] you as his holy people, as *he* **promised** you **on oath**,
28:11 [C] in the land he **swore** to your forefathers to give you.
29:13 [29:12] [C] as he promised you and as *he* **swore** to your fathers,
30:20 [C] he will give you many years in the land he **swore** to give to
31:7 [C] land that the LORD **swore** to their forefathers to give them,
31:20 [C] and honey, the land *I* **promised on oath** to their forefathers,
31:21 [C] before I bring them into the land *I* **promised** them **on oath**."
31:23 [C] bring the Israelites into the land *I* **promised** them **on oath**,
34:4 [C] "This is the land *I* **promised on oath** to Abraham, Isaac
Jos 1:6 [C] because you will lead these people to inherit the land *I* **swore**
2:12 [C] please **swear** to me by the LORD that you will show
2:17 [G] "This oath *you* **made** us **swear** will not be binding on us
2:20 [G] we will be released from the oath *you* **made** us **swear**."

Jos 5: 6 [C] For the LORD *had* **sworn** to them that they would not see
5: 6 [C] land that he *had* **solemnly promised** their fathers to give us,
6: 22 [C] all who belong to her, in accordance with *your* **oath** to her."
6: 26 [G] At that time Joshua **pronounced** *this* **solemn oath**: "Cursed
9: 15 [C] them live, and the leaders of the assembly **ratified** it **by oath**.
9: 18 [C] because the leaders of the assembly *had* **sworn an oath** to
9: 19 [C] "We *have* **given** them *our* **oath** by the LORD, the God of
9: 20 [C] will not fall on us for breaking the oath *we* **swore** to them."
14: 9 [C] So on that day Moses **swore** to me, 'The land on which your
21: 43 [C] So the LORD gave Israel all the land *he had* **sworn** to give
21: 44 [C] rest on every side, just as *he had* **sworn** to their forefathers.
23: 7 [G] do not invoke the names of their gods or **swear** by them.
Jdg 2: 1 [C] led you into the land that *I* **swore** to give to your forefathers.
2: 15 [C] against them to defeat them, just as he *had* **sworn** to them.
15: 12 [C] "**Swear** to me that you won't kill me yourselves."
21: 1 [C] The men of Israel *had* **taken an oath** at Mizpah: "Not one of
21: 7 [C] since we *have* **taken an oath** by the LORD not to give
21: 18 [C] daughters as wives, since *we* Israelites *have* **taken** *this* **oath**:
1Sa 3: 14 [C] Therefore, *I* **swore** to the house of Eli, 'The guilt of Eli's
14: 27 [G] heard that his father *had* **bound** the people **with the oath**,
14: 28 [G] father **bound** the army **under a strict oath** [+906+8678],
14: 28 [G] father **bound** the army **under a strict oath** [+906+8678],
19: 6 [C] Saul listened to Jonathan and **took** *this* **oath**: "As surely as
20: 3 [C] David **took an oath** and said, "Your father knows very well
20: 17 [G] Jonathan had David reaffirm his **oath** out of love for him,
20: 42 [C] for we *have* **sworn** friendship with each other in the name of
24: 21 [24:22] [C] Now **swear** to me by the LORD that you will not
24: 22 [24:23] [C] So David **gave** *his* **oath** to Saul. Then Saul returned
28: 10 [C] Saul **swore** to her by the LORD, "As surely as the LORD
30: 15 [C] "**Swear** to me before God that you will not kill me or hand
2Sa 3: 9 [C] not do for David what the LORD **promised** him **on oath**
3: 35 [C] but David **took an oath**, saying, "May God deal with me,
19: 7 [19:8] [C] *I* **swear** by the LORD that if you don't go out, not a
19: 23 [19:24] [C] shall not die." And the king **promised** him **on oath**.
21: 2 [C] the Israelites *had* **sworn** to ⌊spare⌋ them, but Saul in his zeal
21: 17 [C] David's men **swore** to him, saying, "Never again will you go
1Ki 1: 13 [C] 'My lord the king, *did* you not **swear** to me your servant:
1: 17 [C] *you* yourself **swore** to me your servant by the LORD your
1: 29 [C] The king then **took an oath**: "As surely as the LORD lives,
1: 30 [C] I will surely carry out today what *I* **swore** to you by the
1: 51 [C] '*Let* King Solomon **swear** to me today that he will not put
2: 8 [C] to meet me at the Jordan, *I* **swore** to him by the LORD:
2: 23 [C] King Solomon **swore** by the LORD: "May God deal with
2: 42 [G] "*Did I* not **make** you **swear** by the LORD and warn you,
18: 10 [G] were not there, *he* **made** them **swear** they could not find you.
22: 16 [G] "How many times *must* I **make** you **swear** to tell me nothing
2Ki 11: 4 [G] and **put** them **under oath** at the temple of the LORD.
25: 24 [C] Gedaliah **took an oath** to reassure them and their men. "Do
2Ch 15: 14 [C] *They* **took an oath** to the LORD with loud acclamation,
15: 15 [C] about the oath because *they had* **sworn** it wholeheartedly.
18: 15 [G] "How many times *must* I **make** you **swear** to tell me nothing
36: 13 [G] who *had* **made** him **take an oath** in God's name.
Ezr 10: 5 [G] **put** the leading priests and Levites and all Israel **under oath**
10: 5 [C] oath to do what had been suggested. And *they* **took the oath**.
Ne 5: 12 [G] **made** the nobles and officials **take an oath** to do what they
13: 25 [G] *I* **made** them **take an oath** in God's name and said:
Ps 15: 4 [C] who fear the LORD, who keeps *his* **oath** even when it hurts,
24: 4 [C] does not lift up his soul to an idol or **swear** by what is false.
63: 11 [63:12] [C] all who **swear** by God's name will praise him,
89: 3 [89:4] [C] my chosen one, *I have* **sworn** to David my servant,
89: 35 [89:36] [C] Once for all, *I have* **sworn** by my holiness—and I
89: 49 [89:50] [C] *which* in your faithfulness *you* **swore** to David?
95: 11 [C] So *I* **declared on oath** in my anger, "They shall never enter
102: 8 [102:9] [C] rail against me **use** my **name as a curse** [+928].
110: 4 [C] The LORD *has* **sworn** and will not change his mind:
119:106 [C] *I have* **taken an oath** and confirmed it, that I will follow
132: 2 [C] He **swore an oath** to the LORD and made a vow to the
132: 11 [C] The LORD **swore an oath** to David, a sure oath that he will
Ecc 9: 2 [C] as it is with those *who* **take oaths**, so with those who are
SS 2: 7 [G] *I* **charge** you by the gazelles and by the does of the field:
3: 5 [G] *I* **charge** you by the gazelles and by the does of the field:
5: 8 [G] O daughters of Jerusalem, *I* **charge** you—if you find my
5: 9 [G] is your beloved better than others, that *you* **charge** us so?
8: 4 [G] Daughters of Jerusalem, *I* **charge** you: Do not arouse or
Isa 14: 24 [C] The LORD Almighty *has* **sworn**, "Surely, as I have
19: 18 [C] of Canaan and **swear allegiance** to the LORD Almighty.
45: 23 [C] By myself *I have* **sworn**, my mouth has uttered in all
45: 23 [C] me every knee will bow; by me every tongue *will* **swear**.
48: 1 [C] you who **take oaths** in the name of the LORD and invoke
54: 9 [C] when *I* **swore** that the waters of Noah would never again
54: 9 [C] So now *I have* **sworn** not to be angry with you, never to
62: 8 [C] The LORD *has* **sworn** by his right hand and by his mighty
65: 16 [C] he *who* **takes an oath** in the land will swear by the God of
65: 16 [C] he who takes an oath in the land *will* **swear** by the God of
Jer 4: 2 [C] if in a truthful, just and righteous way *you* **swear**, 'As surely
5: 2 [C] surely as the LORD lives,' still *they are* **swearing** falsely."
5: 7 [C] have forsaken me and **sworn** by gods that are not gods.
7: 9 [C] adultery and **perjury** [+2021+4200+9214], burn incense to
11: 5 [C] I will fulfill the oath *I* **swore** to your forefathers, to give them
12: 16 [C] learn well the ways of my people and **swear** by my name,
12: 16 [C] even as they once taught my people to **swear** by Baal—
22: 5 [C] *I* **swear** by myself that this palace will become a ruin.' "
32: 22 [C] You gave them this land *you had* **sworn** to give their
38: 16 [C] King Zedekiah **swore** *this* **oath** secretly to Jeremiah: "As
40: 9 [C] of Shaphan, **took an oath** to reassure them and their men.
44: 26 [C] 'I **swear** by my great name,' says the LORD, 'that no one
49: 13 [C] *I* **swear** by myself," declares the LORD, "that Bozrah will
51: 14 [C] The LORD Almighty *has* **sworn** by himself: I will surely
Eze 16: 8 [C] *I* **gave** you *my* **solemn oath** and entered into a covenant with
21: 23 [21:28] [B] those *who have* **sworn** [+8652] **allegiance** to him,
Da 12: 7 [C] I heard him **swear** by him who lives forever, saying, "It will
Hos 4: 15 [C] And *do* not **swear**, 'As surely as the LORD lives!'
Am 4: 2 [C] The Sovereign LORD *has* **sworn** by his holiness: "The time
6: 8 [C] The Sovereign LORD *has* **sworn** by himself—the LORD
8: 7 [C] The LORD *has* **sworn** by the Pride of Jacob: "I will never
8: 14 [C] They *who* **swear** by the shame of Samaria, or say, 'As surely
Mic 7: 20 [C] as *you* **pledged on oath** to our fathers in days long ago.
Zep 1: 5 [C] those who bow down and **swear** by the LORD and who also
1: 5 [C] and swear by the LORD and who also **swear** by Molech,
Zec 5: 3 [C] on the other, everyone who **swears falsely** will be banished.
5: 4 [C] and the house of him *who* **swears** falsely by my name.
Mal 3: 5 [C] sorcerers, adulterers and **perjurers** [+2021+4200+9214],

8679 שֶׁבַע¹ ***šeba'***[1], n.m. & f. [489 / 492] [→ 937, 1445?, 8668, 8685; cf. 8678; Ar 10696]

seven [286], seventy [57], seventh [9], *untranslated* [6], seventy-seven [+2256+8679] [6], twenty-seventh [+2256+6929] [6], 70 [5], seventeen [+6926] [5], 1,775 [+547+2256+2256+2256+2822+4395 +8679] [4], 7,337 [+547+2256+4395+8679+8993+8993] [4], seven [+8679] [4], seventeenth [+6925] [4], 127 [+2256+2256+4395+6929] [3], 777 [+2256+2256+4395+8679+8679] [3], seventy-five [+2256+2822] [3], thirty-seventh [+2256+8993] [3], 1,247 [+547+752+2256+4395] [2], 137 [+2256+2256+4395+8993] [2], 372 [+2256+4395+8993+9109] [2], 57,400 [+547+752+2256+2256+2822 +4395] [2], 6,720 [+547+2256+4395+6929+9252] [2], 62,700 [+547+2256+2256+4395+9109+9252] [2], 736 [+2256+4395+8993 +9252] [2], 74 [+752+2256] [2], 74,600 [+547+752+2256+2256 +4395+9252] [2], 760 [+2256+4395+9252] [2], 775 [+2256+2822 +4395+8679] [2], 973 [+2256+4395+8993+9596] [2], seventeen hundred [+547+2256+4395] [2], seventeenth [+6926] [2], thirty-seven [+2256+8993] [2], twenty-seven [+2256+6929] [2], 1,017 [+547+2256 +6925] [1], 1,017 [+547+6925] [1], 1,760 [+547+2256+2256+4395 +9252] [1], 14,700 [+547+752+2256+4395+6925] [1], 157,600 [+547+547+2256+2256+2256+2822+4395+4395+9252] [1], 16,750 [+547+2256+2822+4395+6925+9252] [1], 17,200 [+547+2256+4395 +6925] [1], 172 [+2256+4395+9109] [1], 187 [+2256+2256+4395 +9046] [1], 2,067 [+547+2256+9252] [1], 2,172 [+547+2256+2256 +4395+9109] [1], 2,172 [+547+2256+4395+9109] [1], 2,750 [+547+2256+2822+4395] [1], 207 [+2256+4395] [1], 22,273 [+547+2256+2256+2256+4395+6929+8993+9109] [1], 273 [+2256+2256+4395+8993] [1], 3,700 [+547+2256+4395+8993] [1], 307,500 [+547+547+2256+2256+2822+4395+4395+8993] [1], 337,500 [+547+547+547+2256+2256+2256+2822+4395+4395 +8993+8993] [1], 337,500 [+547+547+547+2256+2256+2822+4395 +4395+8993+8993] [1], 37,000 [+547+2256+8993] [1], 43,730 [+547+752+2256+2256+2256+4395+8993+8993] [1], 44,760 [+547+752+752+2256+2256+2256+4395+9252] [1], 52,700 [+547+2256+2256+2822+4395+9109] [1], 601,730 [+547+547+2256 +2256+4395+4395+8993+9252] [1], 667 [+2256+4395+9252+9252] [1], 67 [+2256+9252] [1], 675 [+2256+2822+4395+9252] [1], 675,000 [+547+547+547+2256+2256+2822+4395+9252] [1], 7,000 [+547] [1], 7,100 [+547+2256+4395] [1], 7,500 [+547+2256+2822+4395] [1], 70,000 [+547] [1], 72 [+2256+9109] [1], 72,000 [+547+2256 +9109] [1], 721 [+285+2256+2256+4395+6929] [1], 725 [+2256+2822+4395+6929] [1], 730 [+2256+4395+8993] [1], 743 [+752+2256+2256+4395+8993] [1], 743 [+752+2256+4395+8993] [1], 745 [+752+2256+2822+4395] [1], 76,500 [+547+2256+2256 +2822+4395+9252] [1], 782 [+2256+2256+4395+9046+9109] [1], 807 [+2256+4395+9046] [1], 87,000 [+547+2256+9046] [1], forty-seven [+752+2256] [1], many [1], seven-day [+3427] [1], seven-day periods [+2021+3427] [1], sevenfold [1], seventeen [+2256+6927] [1], twenty-seven hundred [+547+2256+4395] [1]

Ge 4: 15 if anyone kills Cain, he will suffer vengeance **seven** *times over*."
4: 24 If Cain is avenged **seven** *times*, then Lamech seventy-seven
4: 24 seven times, then Lamech **seventy-seven** [+2256+8679] *times*."
4: 24 seven times, then Lamech **seventy-seven times** [+2256+8679]."
5: 7 Seth lived **807** [+2256+4395+9046] years and had other sons and

Ge 5:12 When Kenan had lived **70** years, he became the father of
5:25 When Methuselah had lived **187** [+2256+2256+4395+9046] years,
5:26 Methuselah lived **782** [+2256+2256+4395+9046+9109] years and
5:31 Lamech lived **777** [+2256+2256+4395+8679+8679] years, and
5:31 Lamech lived **777** [+2256+2256+4395+8679+8679] years, and
5:31 Lamech lived **777** [+2256+2256+4395+8679+8679] years, and
7:2 Take with you **seven** [+8679] of every kind of clean animal,
7:2 Take with you **seven** [+8679] of every kind of clean animal,
7:3 and also **seven** [+8679] of every kind of bird, male and female,
7:3 and also **seven** [+8679] of every kind of bird, male and female,
7:4 **Seven** days from now I will send rain on the earth for forty days
7:10 And after the **seven** days the floodwaters came on the earth.
7:11 Noah's life, on the **seventeenth** [+6925] day of the second month—
8:4 on the **seventeenth** [+6925] day of the seventh month the ark came
8:10 He waited **seven** more days and again sent out the dove from the
8:12 He waited **seven** more days and sent the dove out again, but this
8:14 By the **twenty-seventh** [+2256+6929] day of the second month the
11:21 Reu lived **207** [+2256+4395] years and had other sons
11:26 After Terah had lived **70** years, he became the father of Abram,
12:4 Abram was **seventy-five** [+2256+2822] years old when he set out
21:28 Abraham set apart **seven** ewe lambs from the flock,
21:29 "What is the meaning of these **seven** ewe lambs you have set apart
21:30 "Accept these **seven** lambs from my hand as a witness that I dug
23:1 Sarah lived to be a hundred and **twenty-seven** [+2256+6929] years
25:7 Abraham lived a hundred and **seventy-five** [+2256+2822] years.
25:17 Ishmael lived a hundred and **thirty-seven** [+2256+8993] years.
29:18 "I'll work for you **seven** years in return for your younger daughter
29:20 So Jacob served **seven** years to get Rachel, but they seemed like
29:27 the younger one also, in return for another **seven** years of work."
29:30 more than Leah. And he worked for Laban another **seven** years.
31:23 he pursued Jacob for **seven** days and caught up with him in the hill
33:3 bowed down to the ground **seven** times as he approached his
37:2 Joseph, a young man *of* **seventeen** [+6926], was tending the flocks
41:2 when out of the river there came up **seven** cows, sleek and fat,
41:3 After them, **seven** other cows, ugly and gaunt, came up out of the
41:4 And the cows that were ugly and gaunt ate up the **seven** sleek,
41:5 **Seven** heads of grain, healthy and good, were growing on a single
41:6 After them, **seven** other heads of grain sprouted—thin
41:7 The thin heads of grain swallowed up the **seven** healthy, full heads.
41:18 when out of the river there came up **seven** cows, fat and sleek,
41:19 After them, **seven** other cows came up—scrawny and very ugly
41:20 The lean, ugly cows ate up the **seven** fat cows that came up first.
41:22 "In my dreams I also saw **seven** heads of grain, full and good,
41:23 After them, **seven** other heads sprouted—withered and thin
41:24 The thin heads of grain swallowed up the **seven** good heads.
41:26 The **seven** good cows are seven years, and the seven good heads of
41:26 The seven good cows are **seven** years, and the seven good heads of
41:26 are seven years, and the **seven** good heads of grain are seven years;
41:26 are seven years, and the seven good heads of grain are **seven** years;
41:27 The **seven** lean, ugly cows that came up afterward are seven years,
41:27 ugly cows that came up afterward are **seven** years, and so are the
41:27 so are the **seven** worthless heads of grain scorched by the east
41:27 grain scorched by the east wind: They are **seven** years of famine.
41:29 **Seven** years of great abundance are coming throughout the land of
41:30 **seven** years of famine will follow them. Then all the abundance in
41:34 a fifth of the harvest of Egypt during the **seven** years of abundance.
41:36 to be used during the **seven** years of famine that will come upon
41:47 During the **seven** years of abundance the land produced plentifully.
41:48 Joseph collected all the food produced in those **seven** years of
41:53 The **seven** years of abundance in Egypt came to an end,
41:54 and the **seven** years of famine began, just as Joseph had said.
46:25 whom Laban had given to his daughter Rachel—**seven** in all.
46:27 of Jacob's family, which went to Egypt, were **seventy** in all.
47:28 Jacob lived in Egypt **seventeen** [+6926] years, and the years of his
47:28 the years of his life were a hundred and **forty-seven** [+752+2256].
50:3 for embalming. And the Egyptians mourned for him **seventy** days.
50:10 there Joseph observed a **seven-day** [+3427] period of mourning for
Ex 1:5 The descendants of Jacob numbered **seventy** in all; Joseph was
2:16 Now a priest of Midian had **seven** daughters, and they came to
6:16 Levi lived **137** [+2256+2256+4395+8993] years.
6:20 Amram lived **137** [+2256+2256+4395+8993] years.
7:25 **Seven** days passed after the LORD struck the Nile.
12:15 For **seven** days you are to eat bread made without yeast. On the
12:19 For **seven** days no yeast is to be found in your houses. And
13:6 For **seven** days eat bread made without yeast and on the seventh
13:7 Eat unleavened bread during those **seven** days; nothing with yeast
15:27 to Elim, where there were twelve springs and **seventy** palm trees,
22:30 [22:29] Let them stay with their mothers for **seven** days, but give
23:15 for **seven** days eat bread made without yeast, as I commanded you.
24:1 and Aaron, Nadab and Abihu, and **seventy** of the elders of Israel.
24:9 Nadab and Abihu, and the **seventy** elders of Israel went up
25:37 "Then make its **seven** lamps and set them up on it so that they light
29:30 Meeting to minister in the Holy Place is to wear them **seven** days.
29:35 I have commanded you, taking **seven** days to ordain them.
29:37 For **seven** days make atonement for the altar and consecrate it.
34:18 For **seven** days eat bread made without yeast, as I commanded you.
37:23 They made its **seven** lamps, as well as its wick trimmers and trays,
38:24 the sanctuary was 29 talents and **730** [+2256+4395+8993] shekels,
38:25 and **1,775** [+547+2256+2256+2822+4395+8679] shekels,
38:25 and **1,775** [+547+2256+2256+2256+2822+4395+8679] shekels,
38:28 They used the **1,775** [+547+2256+2256+2256+2822+4395+8679]
38:28 They used the **1,775** [+547+2256+2256+2256+2822+4395+8679]
38:29 The bronze from the wave offering was **70** talents and 2,400
Lev 4:6 the blood and sprinkle some of it **seven** times before the LORD,
4:17 sprinkle it before the LORD **seven** times in front of the curtain.
8:11 He sprinkled some of the oil on the altar **seven** times, anointing the
8:33 Do not leave the entrance to the Tent of Meeting for **seven** days,
8:33 ordination are completed, for your ordination will last **seven** days.
8:35 and night for **seven** days and do what the LORD requires,
12:2 gives birth to a son will be ceremonially unclean for **seven** days,
13:4 the priest is to put the infected person in isolation for **seven** days.
13:5 in the skin, he is to keep him in isolation another **seven** days.
13:21 has faded, then the priest is to put him in isolation for **seven** days.
13:26 has faded, then the priest is to put him in isolation for **seven** days.
13:31 the priest is to put the infected person in isolation for **seven** days.
13:33 and the priest is to keep him in isolation another **seven** days.
13:50 examine the mildew and isolate the affected article for **seven** days.
13:54 article be washed. Then he is to isolate it for another **seven** days.
14:7 **Seven** times he shall sprinkle the one to be cleansed of the
14:8 into the camp, but he must stay outside his tent for **seven** days.
14:16 with his finger sprinkle some of it before the LORD **seven** times.
14:27 some of the oil from his palm **seven** times before the LORD.
14:38 go out the doorway of the house and close it up for **seven** days.
14:51 dead bird and the fresh water, and sprinkle the house **seven** times.
15:13 he is to count off **seven** days for his ceremonial cleansing;
15:19 of blood, the impurity of her monthly period will last **seven** days,
15:24 her monthly flow touches him, he will be unclean for **seven** days;
15:28 she is cleansed from her discharge, she must count off **seven** days,
16:14 he shall sprinkle some of it with his finger **seven** times before the
16:19 He shall sprinkle some of the blood on it with his finger **seven**
22:27 or a goat is born, it is to remain with its mother for **seven** days.
23:6 for **seven** days you must eat bread made without yeast.
23:8 For **seven** days present an offering made to the LORD by fire.
23:15 brought the sheaf of the wave offering, count off **seven** full weeks.
23:18 Present with this bread **seven** male lambs, each a year old
23:34 LORD's Feast of Tabernacles begins, and it lasts for **seven** days.
23:36 For **seven** days present offerings made to the LORD by fire,
23:39 of the land, celebrate the festival to the LORD for **seven** days;
23:40 and rejoice before the LORD your God for **seven** days.
23:41 Celebrate this as a festival to the LORD for **seven** days each year.
23:42 Live in booths for **seven** days: All native-born Israelites are to live
25:8 " 'Count off **seven** sabbaths of years—seven times seven years—
25:8 " 'Count off seven sabbaths of years—**seven** times seven years—
25:8 " 'Count off seven sabbaths of years—seven times **seven** years—
25:8 so that the **seven** sabbaths of years amount to a period of forty-nine
26:18 not listen to me, I will punish you for your sins **seven** *times* over.
26:21 I will multiply your afflictions **seven** *times over*, as your sins
26:24 toward you and will afflict you for your sins **seven** *times over*.
26:28 and I myself will punish you for your sins **seven** *times over*.
Nu 1:27 the tribe of Judah was **74,600** [+547+752+2256+2256+4395+9252].
1:31 tribe of Zebulun was **57,400** [+547+752+2256+2256+2822+4395].
1:39 the tribe of Dan was **62,700** [+547+2256+2256+4395+9109+9252].
2:4 His division numbers **74,600** [+547+752+2256+2256+4395+9252].
2:8 His division numbers **57,400** [+547+752+2256+2256+2822+4395].
2:26 division numbers **62,700** [+547+2256+2256+4395+9109+9252].
2:31 **157,600** [+547+547+2256+2256+2256+2822+4395+4395+9252].
3:22 who were counted was **7,500** [+547+2256+2822+4395].
3:43 was **22,273** [+547+2256+2256+2256+4395+6929+8993+9109].
3:46 To redeem the **273** [+2256+2256+4395+8993] firstborn Israelites
4:36 counted by clans, were **2,750** [+547+2256+2822+4395].
7:13 and one silver sprinkling bowl weighing **seventy** shekels,
7:19 and one silver sprinkling bowl weighing **seventy** shekels,
7:25 and one silver sprinkling bowl weighing **seventy** shekels,
7:31 and one silver sprinkling bowl weighing **seventy** shekels,
7:37 and one silver sprinkling bowl weighing **seventy** shekels,
7:43 and one silver sprinkling bowl weighing **seventy** shekels,
7:49 and one silver sprinkling bowl weighing **seventy** shekels,
7:55 and one silver sprinkling bowl weighing **seventy** shekels,
7:61 and one silver sprinkling bowl weighing **seventy** shekels,
7:67 and one silver sprinkling bowl weighing **seventy** shekels,
7:73 and one silver sprinkling bowl weighing **seventy** shekels,
7:79 and one silver sprinkling bowl weighing **seventy** shekels,
7:85 and thirty shekels, and each sprinkling bowl **seventy** shekels.
8:2 to Aaron and say to him, 'When you set up the **seven** lamps,
11:16 "Bring me **seventy** of Israel's elders who are known to you as
11:24 He brought together **seventy** of their elders and had them stand
11:25 the Spirit that was on him and put the Spirit on the **seventy** elders.
12:14 in her face, would she not have been in disgrace for **seven** days?

Nu 12:14 Confine her outside the camp for **seven** days; after that she can be
12:15 So Miriam was confined outside the camp for **seven** days,
13:22 (Hebron had been built **seven** years before Zoan in Egypt.)
16:49 [17:14] But **14,700** [+547+752+2256+4395+6925] people died
19: 4 and sprinkle it **seven** times toward the front of the Tent of Meeting.
19:11 touches the dead body of anyone will be unclean for **seven** days.
19:14 the tent and anyone who is in it will be unclean for **seven** days,
19:16 touches a human bone or a grave, will be unclean for **seven** days.
23: 1 Balaam said, "Build me **seven** altars here, and prepare seven bulls
23: 1 seven altars here, and prepare **seven** bulls and seven rams for me."
23: 1 seven altars here, and prepare seven bulls and **seven** rams for me."
23: 4 God met with him, and Balaam said, "I have prepared **seven** altars,
23:14 there he built **seven** altars and offered a bull and a ram on each
23:29 Balaam said, "Build me **seven** altars here, and prepare seven bulls
23:29 seven altars here, and prepare **seven** bulls and seven rams for me."
23:29 seven altars here, and prepare seven bulls and **seven** rams for me."
26: 7 were **43,730** [+547+752+2256+2256+2256+4395+8993+8993].
26:22 numbered were **76,500** [+547+2256+2256+2822+4395+9252].
26:34 numbered were **52,700** [+547+2256+2256+2822+4395+9109].
26:51 was **601,730** [+547+547+2256+2256+4395+4395+8993+9252].
28:11 one ram and **seven** male lambs a year old, all without defect.
28:17 is to be a festival; for **seven** days eat bread made without yeast.
28:19 one ram and **seven** male lambs a year old, all without defect.
28:21 and with each of the **seven** lambs, one-tenth.
28:24 fire every day for **seven** days as an aroma pleasing to the LORD;
28:27 **seven** male lambs a year old as an aroma pleasing to the LORD.
28:29 and with each of the **seven** lambs, one-tenth.
29: 2 one ram and **seven** male lambs a year old, all without defect.
29: 4 and with each of the **seven** lambs, one-tenth.
29: 8 one ram and **seven** male lambs a year old, all without defect.
29:10 and with each of the **seven** lambs, one-tenth.
29:12 no regular work. Celebrate a festival to the LORD for **seven** days.
29:32 " 'On the seventh day prepare **seven** bulls, two rams and fourteen
29:36 one ram and **seven** male lambs a year old, all without defect.
31:19 anyone who was killed must stay outside the camp **seven** days.
31:32 **675,000** [+547+547+547+2256+2256+2822+4395+9252] sheep,
31:33 **72,000** [+547+2256+9109] cattle,
31:36 share of those who fought in the battle was: **337,500** [+547+547
+547+2256+2256+2256+2822+4395+4395+8993+8993] sheep,
31:37 the tribute for the LORD was **675** [+2256+2822+4395+9252];
31:38 of which the tribute for the LORD was **72** [+2256+9109];
31:43 the community's half—was **337,500** [+547+547+547+2256+2256
+2822+4395+4395+8993+8993] sheep,
31:52 weighed **16,750** [+547+2256+2822+4395+6925+9252] shekels.
33: 9 to Elim, where there were twelve springs and **seventy** palm trees,
Dt 7: 1 and Jebusites, **seven** nations larger and stronger than you—
10:22 Your forefathers who went down into Egypt were **seventy** in all,
15: 1 At the end of every **seven** years you must cancel debts.
15: 9 "The **seventh** year, the year for canceling debts, is near," so that
16: 3 but for **seven** days eat unleavened bread, the bread of affliction,
16: 4 Let no yeast be found in your possession in all your land for **seven**
16: 9 Count off **seven** weeks from the time you begin to put the sickle to
16: 9 the time you begin to put the sickle to the standing grain. **[RPH]**
16:13 Celebrate the Feast of Tabernacles for **seven** days after you have
16:15 For **seven** days celebrate the Feast to the LORD your God at the
28: 7 will come at you from one direction but flee from you in **seven**.
28:25 will come at them from one direction but flee from them in **seven**,
31:10 "At the end of every **seven** years, in the year for canceling debts,
Jos 6: 4 Have **seven** priests carry trumpets of rams' horns in front of the
6: 4 Have seven priests carry **[RPH]** trumpets of rams' horns in front
6: 4 On the seventh day, march around the city **seven** times,
6: 6 of the LORD and have **seven** priests carry trumpets in front of it."
6: 6 and have seven priests carry **[RPH]** trumpets in front of it."
6: 8 the **seven** priests carrying the seven trumpets before the LORD
6: 8 the seven priests carrying the **seven** trumpets before the LORD
6:13 The **seven** priests carrying the seven trumpets went forward,
6:13 The seven priests carrying the **seven** trumpets went forward,
6:15 and marched around the city **seven** times in the same manner,
6:15 except that on that day they circled the city **seven** times.
18: 2 there were still **seven** Israelite tribes who had not yet received their
18: 5 You are to divide the land into **seven** parts. Judah is to remain in its
18: 6 After you have written descriptions of the **seven** parts of the land,
18: 9 wrote its description on a scroll, town by town, in **seven** parts,
Jdg 1: 7 "**Seventy** kings with their thumbs and big toes cut off have picked
6: 1 and for **seven** years he gave them into the hands of the Midianites.
6:25 the second bull from your father's herd, the one **seven** years old.
8:14 the names of the **seventy-seven** [+2256+8679] officials of Succoth,
8:14 the names of the **seventy-seven** [+2256+8679] officials of Succoth,
8:26 came to **seventeen** [+547+2256+4395] **hundred** shekels,
8:30 He had **seventy** sons of his own, for he had many wives.
9: 2 to have all **seventy** of Jerub-Baal's sons rule over you, or just one
9: 4 They gave him **seventy** shekels of silver from the temple of
9: 5 home in Ophrah and on one stone murdered his **seventy** brothers,
9:18 murdered his **seventy** sons on a single stone, and made Abimelech,
9:24 God did this in order that the crime against Jerub-Baal's **seventy**
9:56 had done to his father by murdering his **seventy** brothers.
12: 9 as wives from outside his clan. Ibzan led Israel **seven** years.
12:14 had forty sons and thirty grandsons, who rode on **seventy** donkeys.
14:12 "If you can give me the answer within the **seven** days of the feast,
14:17 She cried the whole **seven** days of the feast. So on the seventh day
16: 7 "If anyone ties me with **seven** fresh thongs that have not been
16: 8 the rulers of the Philistines brought her **seven** fresh thongs that had
16:13 "If you weave the **seven** braids of my head into the fabric ⌞on the
16:13 was sleeping, Delilah took the **seven** [BHS-] braids of his head,
16:19 she called a man to shave off the **seven** braids of his hair, and
20:15 in addition to **seven** hundred chosen men from those living in
20:16 Among all these soldiers there were **seven** hundred chosen men
Ru 4:15 who loves you and who is better to you than **seven** sons, has given
1Sa 2: 5 She who was barren has borne **seven** children, but she who has had
6: 1 When the ark of the LORD had been in Philistine territory **seven**
6:19 putting **seventy** of them to death because they had looked into the
10: 8 you must wait **seven** days until I come to you and tell you what
11: 3 "Give us **seven** days so we can send messengers throughout Israel;
13: 8 He waited **seven** days, the time set by Samuel; but Samuel did not
16:10 Jesse had **seven** *of* his sons pass before Samuel, but Samuel said to
31:13 them under a tamarisk tree at Jabesh, and they fasted **seven** days.
2Sa 2:11 was king in Hebron over the house of Judah was **seven** years
5: 5 In Hebron he reigned over Judah **seven** years and six months,
8: 4 **seven** thousand charioteers and twenty thousand foot soldiers.
10:18 David killed **seven** hundred of their charioteers and forty thousand
21: 6 let **seven** of his male descendants be given to us to be killed
21: 9 *All* **seven** *of* them fell together; they were put to death during the
23:39 and Uriah the Hittite. There were **thirty-seven** [+2256+8993] in all.
24:13 "Shall there come upon you <u>three</u> [BHS *seven*; NIV 8993] years
24:15 and **seventy** thousand of the people from Dan to Beersheba died.
1Ki 2:11 over Israel—**seven** years in Hebron and thirty-three in Jerusalem.
5:15 [5:29] Solomon had **seventy** thousand carriers and eighty
6: 6 cubits wide, the middle floor six cubits and the third floor **seven**.
6:38 to its specifications. He had spent **seven** years building it.
7:17 festooned the capitals on top of the pillars, **seven** for each capital.
7:17 the capitals on top of the pillars, seven for each capital. **[RPH]**
8:65 They celebrated it before the LORD our God for **seven** days
8:65 it before the LORD our God for seven days and **seven** days more,
11: 3 He had **seven** hundred wives of royal birth and three hundred
14:21 and he reigned **seventeen** [+6926] years in Jerusalem,
16:10 and killed him in the **twenty-seventh** [+2256+6929] year of Asa
16:15 In the **twenty-seventh** [+2256+6929] year of Asa king of Judah,
16:15 year of Asa king of Judah, Zimri reigned in Tirzah **seven** days.
18:43 is nothing there," he said. **Seven** times Elijah said, "Go back."
19:18 Yet I reserve **seven** thousand in Israel—all whose knees have not
20:15 Then he assembled the rest of the Israelites, **7,000** [+547] in all.
20:29 For **seven** days they camped opposite each other, and on the
20:30 where the wall collapsed on **twenty-seven** [+2256+6929] thousand
22:51 [22:52] **seventeenth** [+6926] year of Jehoshaphat king of Judah,
2Ki 3: 9 After a roundabout march of **seven** days, the army had no more
3:26 he took with him **seven** hundred swordsmen to break through to
4:35 him once more. The boy sneezed **seven** times and opened his eyes.
5:10 "Go, wash yourself **seven** times in the Jordan, and your flesh will
5:14 So he went down and dipped himself in the Jordan **seven** times,
8: 1 has decreed a famine in the land that will last **seven** years."
8: 2 went away and stayed in the land of the Philistines **seven** years.
8: 3 At the end of the **seven** years she came back from the land of the
10: 1 Now there were in Samaria **seventy** sons of the house of Ahab.
10: 6 Now the royal princes, **seventy** of them, were with the leading men
10: 7 these men took the princes and slaughtered all **seventy** of them.
11:21 [12:1] Joash was **seven** years old when he began to reign.
12: 1 [12:2] In the **seventh** year of Jehu, Joash became king, and he
13: 1 king of Israel in Samaria, and he reigned **seventeen** [+6926] years.
13:10 In the **thirty-seventh** [+2256+8993] year of Joash king of Judah,
15: 1 In the **twenty-seventh** [+2256+6929] year of Jeroboam king of
16: 1 In the **seventeenth** [+6926] year of Pekah son of Remaliah,
24:16 to Babylon the entire force of **seven** thousand fighting men,
25: 8 On the **seventh** day of the fifth month, in the nineteenth year of
25:27 In the **thirty-seventh** [+2256+8993] year of the exile of Jehoiachin
25:27 on the **twenty-seventh** [+2256+6929] day of the twelfth month.
1Ch 3: 4 to David in Hebron, where he reigned **seven** years and six months.
3:24 Pelaiah, Akkub, Johanan, Delaiah and Anani—**seven** in all.
5:13 Meshullam, Sheba, Jorai, Jacan, Zia and Eber—**seven** in all.
5:18 had **44,760** [+547+752+752+2256+2256+2256+4395+9252] men
7: 5 listed in their genealogy, were **87,000** [+547+2256+9046] in all.
7:11 There were **17,200** [+547+2256+4395+6925] fighting men ready
9:13 of families, numbered **1,760** [+547+2256+2256+4395+9252].
9:25 and share their duties for **seven-day** [+2021+3427] **periods**.
10:12 bones under the great tree in Jabesh, and they fasted **seven** days.
12:25 [12:26] warriors ready for battle—**7,100** [+547+2256+4395];
12:27 [12:28] of Aaron, with **3,700** [+547+2256+4395+8993] men,
12:34 [12:35] officers, together with **37,000** [+547+2256+8993] men
15:26 of the LORD, **seven** bulls and seven rams were sacrificed.

1Ch 15:26 of the LORD, seven bulls and **seven** rams were sacrificed.
18: 4 **seven** thousand charioteers and twenty thousand foot soldiers.
19:18 David killed **seven** thousand of their charioteers and forty thousand
21: 5 a sword, including four hundred and **seventy** thousand in Judah.
21:14 a plague on Israel, and **seventy** thousand men of Israel fell dead.
24:15 the **seventeenth** [+6925] to Hezir, the eighteenth to Happizzez,
25:24 the **seventeenth** [+6925] to Joshbekashah, his sons and relatives,
26:30 his relatives—**seventeen** [+547+2256+4395] **hundred** able men—
26:32 Jeriah had **twenty-seven hundred** [+547+2256+4395] relatives,
29: 4 **seven** thousand talents of refined silver, for the overlaying of the
29:27 Israel forty years—**seven** in Hebron and thirty-three in Jerusalem.
2Ch 2: 2 [2:1] He conscripted **seventy** thousand men as carriers and eighty
2:18 [2:17] He assigned **70,000** [+547] of them to be carriers
7: 8 So Solomon observed the festival at that time for **seven** days,
7: 9 for they had celebrated the dedication of the altar for **seven** days
7: 9 of the altar for seven days and the festival for **seven** days more.
12:13 and he reigned **seventeen** [+6926] years in Jerusalem,
13: 9 and **seven** rams may become a priest of what are not gods.
15:11 At that time they sacrificed to the LORD **seven** hundred head of
15:11 **seven** thousand sheep and goats from the plunder they had brought
17:11 **seven** thousand seven hundred rams and seven thousand seven
17:11 seven thousand **seven** hundred rams and seven thousand seven
17:11 seven hundred rams and **seven** thousand seven hundred goats.
17:11 seven hundred rams and seven thousand **seven** hundred goats.
24: 1 Joash was **seven** years old when he became king, and he reigned in
26:13 of **307,500** [+547+547+2256+2256+2822+4395+4395+8993] men
29:21 They brought **seven** bulls, seven rams, seven male lambs and seven
29:21 **seven** rams, seven male lambs and seven male goats as a sin
29:21 **seven** male lambs and seven male goats as a sin offering for the
29:21 male lambs and **seven** male goats as a sin offering for the kingdom,
29:32 The number of burnt offerings the assembly brought was **seventy**
30:21 the Feast of Unleavened Bread for **seven** days with great rejoicing,
30:22 For the **seven** days they ate their assigned portion and offered
30:23 then agreed to celebrate the festival **seven** more days;
30:23 more days; so for another **seven** days they celebrated joyfully.
30:24 and **seven** thousand sheep and goats for the assembly,
35:17 and observed the Feast of Unleavened Bread for **seven** days.
36:21 until the **seventy** years were completed in fulfillment of the word
Ezr 2: 3 the descendants of Parosh **2,172** [+547+2256+4395+9109]
2: 4 of Shephatiah **372** [+2256+4395+8993+9109]
2: 5 of Arah **775** [+2256+2822+4395+8679]
2: 5 of Arah **775** [+2256+2822+4395+8679]
2: 9 of Zaccai **760** [+2256+4395+9252]
2:25 Kephirah and Beeroth **743** [+752+2256+2256+4395+8993]
2:33 of Lod, Hadid and Ono **725** [+2256+2822+4395+6929]
2:36 (through the family of Jeshua) **973** [+2256+4395+8993+9596]
2:38 of Pashhur **1,247** [+547+752+2256+4395]
2:39 of Harim **1,017** [+547+2256+6925]
2:40 and Kadmiel (through the line of Hodaviah) **74** [+752+2256]
2:65 their **7,337** [+547+2256+4395+8679+8993+8993] menservants and
2:65 their **7,337** [+547+2256+4395+8679+8993+8993] menservants and
2:66 They had **736** [+2256+4395+8993+9252] horses, 245 mules,
2:67 435 camels and **6,720** [+547+2256+4395+6929+9252] donkeys.
6:22 For **seven** days they celebrated with joy the Feast of Unleavened
7: 7 also came up to Jerusalem in the **seventh** year of King Artaxerxes.
8: 7 of Elam, Jeshaiah son of Athaliah, and with him **70** men;
8:14 descendants of Bigvai, Uthai and Zaccur, and with them **70** men.
8:35 ninety-six rams, **seventy-seven** [+2256+8679] male lambs and, as a
8:35 ninety-six rams, **seventy-seven** [+2256+8679] male lambs and, as a
Ne 7: 8 the descendants of Parosh **2,172** [+547+2256+2256+4395+9109]
7: 9 of Shephatiah **372** [+2256+4395+8993+9109]
7:14 of Zaccai **760** [+2256+4395+9252]
7:18 of Adonikam **667** [+2256+4395+9252+9252]
7:19 of Bigvai **2,067** [+547+2256+9252]
7:29 Kephirah and Beeroth **743** [+752+2256+4395+8993]
7:37 of Lod, Hadid and Ono **721** [+285+2256+2256+4395+6929]
7:39 (through the family of Jeshua) **973** [+2256+4395+8993+9596]
7:41 of Pashhur **1,247** [+547+752+2256+4395]
7:42 of Harim **1,017** [+547+6925]
7:43 (through Kadmiel through the line of Hodaviah) **74** [+752+2256]
7:67 their **7,337** [+547+2256+4395+8679+8993+8993] menservants and
7:67 their **7,337** [+547+2256+4395+8679+8993+8993] menservants and
7:68 [7:67] There were **736** [+2256+4395+8993+9252] [BHS-] horses,
7:69 [7:68] camels and **6,720** [+547+2256+4395+6929+9252] donkeys.
7:72 [7:71] minas of silver and **67** [+2256+9252] garments for priests.
8:18 They celebrated the feast for **seven** days, and on the eighth day,
11:19 who kept watch at the gates—**172** [+2256+4395+9109] men.
Est 1: 1 Xerxes who ruled over **127** [+2256+2256+4395+6929] provinces
1: 5 these days were over, the king gave a banquet, lasting **seven** days,
1:10 from wine, he commanded the **seven** eunuchs who served him—
1:14 the **seven** nobles of Persia and Media who had special access to the
2: 9 He assigned to her **seven** maids selected from the king's palace
2:16 tenth month, the month of Tebeth, in the **seventh** year of his reign.
8: 9 and nobles of the **127** [+2256+2256+4395+6929] provinces
9:16 They killed **seventy-five** [+2256+2822] thousand of them but did
9:30 to all the Jews in the **127** [+2256+2256+4395+6929] provinces of
Job 1: 2 He had **seven** sons and three daughters,
1: 3 and he owned **seven** thousand sheep, three thousand camels,
2:13 they sat on the ground with him for **seven** days and seven nights.
2:13 they sat on the ground with him for seven days and **seven** nights.
5:19 six calamities he will rescue you; in **seven** no harm will befall you.
42: 8 So now take **seven** bulls and seven rams and go to my servant Job
42: 8 So now take seven bulls and **seven** rams and go to my servant Job
Ps 12: 6 [12:7] silver refined in a furnace of clay, purified **seven** *times*.
79:12 Pay back into the laps of our neighbors **seven** *times* the reproach
90:10 The length of our days is **seventy** years—or eighty, if we have the
119:164 **Seven** *times* a day I praise you for your righteous laws.
Pr 6:16 are six things the LORD hates, **seven** that are detestable to him:
6:31 Yet if he is caught, he must pay **sevenfold**, though it costs him all
9: 1 Wisdom has built her house; she has hewn out its **seven** pillars.
24:16 for though a righteous man falls **seven** *times*, he rises again,
26:16 The sluggard is wiser in his own eyes than **seven** men who answer
26:25 do not believe him, for **seven** abominations fill his heart.
Ecc 11: 2 Give portions to **seven**, yes to eight, for you do not know what
Isa 4: 1 In that day **seven** women will take hold of one man and say,
11:15 He will break it up into **seven** streams so that men can cross over
23:15 At that time Tyre will be forgotten for **seventy** years, the span of a
23:15 at the end of these **seventy** years, it will happen to Tyre as in the
23:17 At the end of **seventy** years, the LORD will deal with Tyre.
30:26 the sunlight will be **seven** *times brighter*, like the light of seven
30:26 will be seven times brighter, like the light of **seven** full days,
Jer 15: 9 The mother of **seven** will grow faint and breathe her last. Her sun
25:11 and these nations will serve the king of Babylon **seventy** years.
25:12 "But when the **seventy** years are fulfilled, I will punish the king of
29:10 "When **seventy** years are completed for Babylon, I will come to
32: 9 and weighed out for him **seventeen** [+2256+6927] shekels of silver.
34:14 'Every **seventh** year each of you must free any fellow Hebrew who
52:25 the officer in charge of the fighting men, and **seven** royal advisers.
52:28 carried into exile: in the **seventh** year, 3,023 Jews;
52:30 **745** [+752+2256+2822+4395] Jews taken into exile by
52:31 In the **thirty-seventh** [+2256+8993] year of the exile of Jehoiachin
Eze 3:15 where they were living, I sat among them for **seven** days—
3:16 At the end of **seven** days the word of the LORD came to me:
8:11 In front of them stood **seventy** elders of the house of Israel,
29:17 In the **twenty-seventh** [+2256+6929] year, in the first month on the
30:20 In the eleventh year, in the first month on the **seventh** day,
39: 9 war clubs and spears. For **seven** years they will use them for fuel.
39:12 " 'For **seven** months the house of Israel will be burying them in
39:14 At the end of the **seven** months they will begin their search.
40:22 facing east. **Seven** steps led up to it, with its portico opposite them.
40:26 **Seven** steps led up to it, with its portico opposite them; it had palm
41: 3 and the projecting walls on each side of it were **seven** cubits wide.
41:12 the temple courtyard on the west side was **seventy** cubits wide.
43:25 "For **seven** days you are to provide a male goat daily for a sin
43:26 For **seven** days they are to make atonement for the altar
44:26 After he is cleansed, he must wait **seven** days.
45:20 You are to do the same on the **seventh** day of the month for
45:23 Every day during the **seven** days of the Feast he is to provide seven
45:23 Every day during the seven days of the Feast he is to provide **seven**
45:23 and **seven** rams without defect as a burnt offering to the LORD,
45:23 offering to the LORD, **[RPH]** and a male goat for a sin offering.
45:25 " 'During the **seven** days of the Feast, which begins in the seventh
Da 9: 2 that the desolation of Jerusalem would last **seventy** years.
9:24 "**Seventy** 'sevens' are decreed for your people and your holy city to
9:25 the ruler, comes, there will be **seven** 'sevens,' and sixty-two
Mic 5: 5 [5:4] we will raise against him **seven** shepherds, even eight
Hab 3: 9 You uncovered your bow, you called for **many** [BHS 8652] arrows.
Zec 1:12 of Judah, which you have been angry with these **seventy** years?"
3: 9 There are **seven** eyes on that one stone, and I will engrave an
4: 2 a solid gold lampstand with a bowl at the top and **seven** lights on it,
4: 2 and seven lights on it, **[RPH]** with seven channels to the lights.
4: 2 at the top and seven lights on it, with **seven** channels to the lights.
4:10 "(These **seven** are the eyes of the LORD, which range throughout
7: 5 mourned in the fifth and seventh months for the past **seventy** years,

8680 ²שֶׁבַע *šeba* ², n.pr.m. [9] [√ 8682]

Sheba [9]

2Sa 20: 1 Now a troublemaker named **Sheba** son of Bicri, a Benjamite,
20: 2 So all the men of Israel deserted David to follow **Sheba** son of
20: 6 "Now **Sheba** son of Bicri will do us more harm than Absalom did.
20: 7 They marched out from Jerusalem to pursue **Sheba** son of Bicri.
20:10 Then Joab and his brother Abishai pursued **Sheba** son of Bicri.
20:13 all the men went on with Joab to pursue **Sheba** son of Bicri.
20:21 A man named **Sheba** son of Bicri, from the hill country of
20:22 they cut off the head of **Sheba** son of Bicri and threw it to Joab.
1Ch 5:13 Michael, Meshullam, **Sheba**, Jorai, Jacan, Zia and Eber—seven in

8681 ³שְׁבַע **šeba'³**, n.pr.loc. [1] [√ 8682]

Sheba [1]

Jos 19: 2 It included: Beersheba (or **Sheba**), Moladah,

8682 ⁴שְׁבַע **šeba'⁴**, n.m. Not used in NIV/BHS [→ 510, 1444, 3394, 3395, 8680, 8681, 8683]

8683 שִׁבְעָה **šib'â**, n.pr.loc. [1] [√ 8682]

Shibah [1]

Ge 26: 33 He called it **Shibah**, and to this day the name of the town has been

8684 שְׁבָעִים **šib'îm**, n.pl. Not used in NIV/BHS [√ 8678]

8685 שִׁבְעָנָה **šib'ānâ**, n.m. [1] [√ 8679; cf. 8678]

seven [1]

Job 42: 13 And he also had **seven** sons and three daughters.

8686 שִׁבְעָתַיִם **šib'ātayim**, n.f.du. Not used in NIV/BHS [√ 8678]

8687 שָׁבַץ **šābaṣ**, v. [2] [→ 5401, 8688, 9587]

filigree settings [1], weave [1]

Ex 28: 20 [E] an onyx and a jasper. Mount them in gold **filigree settings**.
28: 39 [D] "**Weave** the tunic of fine linen and make the turban of fine

8688 שָׁבָץ **šābāṣ**, n.m. [1] [√ 8687]

throes of death [1]

2Sa 1: 9 and kill me! I am in the **throes of death**, but I'm still alive.'

8689 ¹שָׁבַר **šābar¹**, v. [146] [→ 5402, 5403, 8653, 8691, 8693, 8695, 8696; Ar 10752]

break [19], broken [16], smashed [10], be broken [9], broke [9], be destroyed [5], break down [4], cut off [4], shattered [4], smash [4], brokenhearted [+4213] [3], injured [3], is broken [3], are broken [2], are crushed [2], break to pieces [+8689] [2], breaking to pieces [2], breaks [2], broke up [2], crush [2], destroy [2], destroyed [2], is injured [2], mauled [2], was broken off [2], were wrecked [2], abolish [1], are broken off [1], are shattered [1], be broken off [1], be broken up [1], be injured [1], be smashed [1], been broken [1], been grieved [1], break to pieces [1], break up [1], breaks down [1], breaks in pieces [1], bring to the moment of birth [1], broke off [1], broken off [1], crushed [1], demolish [1], desolate [1], fixed [1], is shattered [1], quench [1], shattering [1], stripped [1], suffered [1], was broken [1], were crushed [1]

Ge 19: 9 [A] pressure on Lot and moved forward to **break down** the door.
Ex 9: 25 [D] everything growing in the fields and **stripped** every tree.
12: 46 [A] the meat outside the house. *Do* not **break** any of the bones.
22: 10 [22:9] [C] it dies or **is injured** or is taken away while no one is
22: 14 [22:13] [C] *it* **is injured** or dies while the owner is not present,
23: 24 [D] and **break** [+8689] their sacred stones **to pieces**.
23: 24 [D] and **break** their sacred stones **to pieces** [+8689].
32: 19 [D] **breaking** them **to pieces** at the foot of the mountain.
34: 1 [D] the words that were on the first tablets, which *you* **broke**.
34: 13 [D] **smash** their sacred stones and cut down their Asherah poles.
Lev 6: 28 [6:21] [C] The clay pot the meat is cooked in *must* **be broken**;
11: 33 [A] everything in it will be unclean, and *you must* **break** the pot.
15: 12 [C] " 'A clay pot that the man touches *must* **be broken**, and any
26: 13 [A] *I* **broke** the bars of your yoke and enabled you to walk with
26: 19 [A] *I will* **break down** your stubborn pride and make the sky
26: 26 [A] When I **cut off** your supply of bread, ten women will be able
Nu 9: 12 [A] not leave any of it till morning or **break** any of its bones.
Dt 7: 5 [D] Break down their altars, **smash** their sacred stones, cut down
9: 17 [D] out of my hands, **breaking** them **to pieces** before your eyes.
10: 2 [D] the words that were on the first tablets, which *you* **broke**.
12: 3 [D] **smash** their sacred stones and burn their Asherah poles in the
Jdg 7: 20 [A] three companies blew the trumpets and **smashed** the jars.
1Sa 4: 18 [C] His neck **was broken** and he died, for he was an old man
1Ki 13: 26 [A] him over to the lion, *which has* **mauled** him and killed him,
13: 28 [A] The lion had neither eaten the body nor **mauled** the donkey.
19: 11 [D] mountains apart and **shattered** the rocks before the LORD,
22: 48 [22:49] [C] never set sail—they **were wrecked** at Ezion Geber.
2Ki 11: 18 [D] *They* **smashed** the altars and idols to pieces and killed
18: 4 [D] **smashed** the sacred stones and cut down the Asherah poles.
23: 14 [D] Josiah **smashed** the sacred stones and cut down the Asherah
25: 13 [D] The Babylonians **broke up** the bronze pillars, the movable
2Ch 14: 3 [14:2] [D] **smashed** the sacred stones and cut down the Asherah
14: 13 [14:12] [C] *they* **were crushed** before the LORD and his
20: 37 [C] The ships **were wrecked** and were not able to set sail to
23: 17 [D] *They* **smashed** the altars and idols and killed Mattan the
31: 1 [D] **smashed** the sacred stones and cut down the Asherah poles.
34: 4 [D] and **smashed** the Asherah poles, the idols and the images.
Job 24: 20 [C] men are no longer remembered but **are broken** like a tree.
29: 17 [D] *I* **broke** the fangs of the wicked and snatched the victims
31: 22 [C] arm fall from the shoulder, *let* it **be broken off** at the joint.
38: 10 [A] when *I* **fixed** limits for it and set its doors and bars in place,
38: 15 [C] are denied their light, and their upraised arm **is broken**.
Ps 3: 7 [3:8] [D] my enemies on the jaw; **break** the teeth of the wicked.
10: 15 [A] **Break** the arm of the wicked and evil man; call him to
29: 5 [A] The voice of the LORD **breaks** the cedars; the LORD
29: 5 [D] the LORD **breaks in pieces** the cedars of Lebanon.
34: 18 [34:19] [C] The LORD is close to the **brokenhearted** [+4213]
34: 20 [34:21] [C] all his bones, not one of them *will* **be broken**.
37: 15 [C] will pierce their own hearts, and their bows *will* **be broken**.
37: 17 [C] for the power of the wicked *will* **be broken**, but the LORD
46: 9 [46:10] [D] *he* **breaks** the bow and shatters the spear, he burns
48: 7 [48:8] [D] *You* **destroyed** them like ships of Tarshish shattered
51: 17 [51:19] [C] The sacrifices of God are a **broken** spirit; a broken
51: 17 [51:19] [C] **broken** and contrite heart, O God, you will not
69: 20 [69:21] [A] Scorn *has* **broken** my heart and has left me
74: 13 [D] *you* **broke** the heads of the monster in the waters.
76: 3 [76:4] [D] There *he* **broke** the flashing arrows, the shields
104: 11 [A] the beasts of the field; the wild donkeys **quench** their thirst.
105: 16 [A] famine on the land and **destroyed** all their supplies of food;
105: 33 [D] and fig trees and **shattered** the trees of their country.
107: 16 [D] for *he* **breaks down** gates of bronze and cuts through bars of
124: 7 [C] the snare *has* **been broken**, and we have escaped.
147: 3 [B] He heals the **brokenhearted** [+4213] and binds up their
Pr 6: 15 [C] an instant; *he will* suddenly **be destroyed**—without remedy.
25: 15 [A] can be persuaded, and a gentle tongue *can* **break** a bone.
29: 1 [C] after many rebukes *will* suddenly **be destroyed**—
Ecc 12: 6 [C] before the pitcher **is shattered** at the spring, or the wheel
Isa 8: 15 [C] they will fall and **be broken**, they will be snared
14: 5 [A] The LORD *has* **broken** the rod of the wicked, the scepter of
14: 25 [A] I *will* **crush** the Assyrian in my land; on my mountains I will
14: 29 [C] all you Philistines, that the rod that struck you *is* **broken**;
21: 9 [D] All the images of its gods *lie* **shattered** on the ground!' "
24: 10 [C] The ruined city *lies* **desolate**; the entrance to every house is
27: 11 [C] *they* **are broken off** and women come and make fires with
28: 13 [C] and fall backward, **be injured** and snared and captured.
38: 13 [D] patiently till dawn, but like a lion *he* **broke** all my bones;
42: 3 [A] A bruised reed *he will* not **break**, and a smoldering wick he
45: 2 [D] *I will* **break down** gates of bronze and cut through bars of
61: 1 [C] He has sent me to bind up the **brokenhearted** [+4213], to
66: 9 [G] *Do* I **bring to the moment of birth** and not give delivery?"
Jer 2: 13 [C] their own cisterns, **broken** cisterns that cannot hold water.
2: 20 [A] "Long ago *you* **broke off** your yoke and tore off your bonds;
5: 5 [A] with one accord they too *had* **broken off** the yoke and torn
8: 21 [H] Since my people are crushed, *I am* **crushed**; I mourn,
14: 17 [C] *has* **suffered** a grievous wound, a crushing blow.
17: 18 [A] the day of disaster; **destroy** them *with* double destruction.
19: 10 [A] "Then **break** the jar while those who go with you are
19: 11 [A] *I will* **smash** this nation and this city just as this potter's jar is
19: 11 [A] this city just as this potter's jar *is* **smashed** and cannot be
22: 20 [C] cry out from Abarim, for all your allies **are crushed**.
23: 9 [C] My heart *is* **broken** within me; all my bones tremble. I am
28: 2 [A] of Israel, says: '*I will* **break** the yoke of the king of Babylon.
28: 4 [A] 'for *I will* **break** the yoke of the king of Babylon.' "
28: 10 [A] the yoke off the neck of the prophet Jeremiah and **broke** it,
28: 11 [A] 'In the same way *will I* **break** the yoke of Nebuchadnezzar
28: 12 [A] Shortly after the prophet Hananiah *had* **broken** the yoke off
28: 13 [A] *You have* **broken** a wooden yoke, but in its place you will
30: 8 [A] '*I will* **break** the yoke off their necks and will tear off their
43: 13 [D] There in the temple of the sun in Egypt *he will* **demolish** the
48: 4 [C] Moab *will* **be broken**; her little ones will cry out.
48: 17 [C] say, 'How **broken** *is* the mighty scepter, how broken the
48: 25 [C] horn is cut off; her arm **is broken**," declares the LORD.
48: 38 [A] for *I have* **broken** Moab like a jar that no one wants,"
49: 35 [A] "See, I *will* **break** the bow of Elam, the mainstay of their
50: 23 [C] How broken and **shattered** *is* the hammer of the whole earth!
51: 8 [C] Babylon will suddenly fall and **be broken**. Wail over her!
51: 30 [C] dwellings are set on fire; the bars of her gates **are broken**.
52: 17 [D] **broke up** the bronze pillars, the movable stands and
La 1: 15 [A] he has summoned an army against me to **crush** my young
2: 9 [D] into the ground; their bars *he has* **broken** and destroyed.
3: 4 [D] my skin and my flesh grow old and *has* **broken** my bones.
Eze 4: 16 [A] "Son of man, I *will* **cut off** the supply of food in Jerusalem.
5: 16 [A] and more famine upon you and **cut off** your supply of food.
6: 4 [C] will be demolished and your incense altars *will* **be smashed**;
6: 6 [C] be laid waste and devastated, your idols **smashed** and ruined,
6: 9 [C] *I have* **been grieved** *by* their adulterous hearts, which have
14: 13 [A] and I stretch out my hand against it *to* **cut off** its food supply
26: 2 [C] The gate to the nations **is broken**, and its doors have swung

Eze 27:26 [A] the east wind *will* **break** you **to pieces** in the heart of the sea.
27:34 [C] Now *you* **are shattered** by the sea in the depths of the
29: 7 [C] leaned on you, *you* **broke** and their backs were wrenched.
30: 8 [C] when I set fire to Egypt and all her helpers **are crushed**.
30:18 [A] Dark will be the day at Tahpanhes when I **break** the yoke of
30:21 [A] of man, *I have* **broken** the arm of Pharaoh king of Egypt.
30:22 [A] *I will* **break** both his arms, the good arm as well as the
30:22 [C] break both his arms, the good arm as well as the **broken** *one*,
30:24 [A] my sword in his hand, but *I will* **break** the arms of Pharaoh,
31:12 [C] its branches *lay* **broken** in all the ravines of the land.
32:28 [C] *will* **be broken** and will lie among the uncircumcised,
34: 4 [C] the weak or healed the sick or bound up the **injured**.
34:16 [C] I will bind up the **injured** and strengthen the weak, but the
34:27 [A] when I **break** the bars of their yoke and rescue them from the
Da 8: 7 [D] ram furiously, striking the ram and **shattering** his two horns.
8: 8 [C] but at the height of his power his large horn **was broken off**,
8:22 [C] The four horns that replaced the *one that* **was broken off**
8:25 [C] Yet *he will* **be destroyed**, but not by human power.
11: 4 [C] his empire *will* **be broken up** and parceled out toward the
11:20 [C] In a few years, however, *he will* **be destroyed**, yet not in
11:22 [C] both *it* and a prince of the covenant *will* **be destroyed**.
11:26 [A] Those who eat from the king's provisions *will try to* **destroy**
Hos 1: 5 [A] In that day *I will* **break** Israel's bow in the Valley of
2:18 [2:20] [A] Bow and sword and battle *I will* **abolish** from the
Am 1: 5 [A] *I will* **break down** the gate of Damascus; I will destroy the
Jnh 1: 4 [C] a violent storm arose that the ship threatened to **break up**.
Na 1:13 [A] Now *I will* **break** their yoke from your neck and tear your
Zec 11:16 [C] or seek the young, or heal the **injured**, or feed the healthy,

8690 [2]שָׁבַר *šābar*[2], v.den. [21] [√ 8692]

buy [11], sell [3], buy grain [2], sold grain [2], buying [1], pay for [1], selling [1]

Ge 41:56 [A] opened the storehouses and **sold grain** to the Egyptians,
41:57 [A] all the countries came to Egypt to **buy grain** from Joseph,
42: 2 [A] Go down there and **buy** some for us, so that we may live
42: 3 [A] ten of Joseph's brothers went down to **buy** grain from Egypt.
42: 5 [A] So Israel's sons were among those who went to **buy grain**,
42: 6 [G] of the land, the *one who* **sold grain** to all its people.
42: 7 [A] "From the land of Canaan," they replied, "to **buy** food."
42:10 [A] they answered. "Your servants have come to **buy** food.
43: 2 [A] father said to them, "Go back and **buy** us a little more food."
43: 4 [A] along with us, we will go down and **buy** food for you.
43:20 [A] they said, "we came down here the first time to **buy** food.
43:22 [A] We have also brought additional silver with us to **buy** food.
44:25 [A] "Then our father said, 'Go back and **buy** a little more food.'
47:14 [A] and Canaan in payment for the grain they *were* **buying**,
Dt 2: 6 [A] *You are to* **pay** them in silver **for** the food you eat and the
2:28 [G] **Sell** us food to eat and water to drink for their price in silver.
Pr 11:26 [G] hoards grain, but blessing crowns *him who is willing to* **sell**.
Isa 55: 1 [A] the waters; and you who have no money, come, **buy** and eat!
55: 1 [A] Come, **buy** wine and milk without money and without cost.
Am 8: 5 [G] "When will the New Moon be over that *we may* **sell** grain,
8: 6 [G] a pair of sandals, **selling** even the sweepings with the wheat.

8691 [1]שֶׁבֶר *šeber*[1], n.m. [44] [→ 8696; cf. 8689]

destruction [14], wound [7], destroyed [3], *untranslated* [2], disaster [2], fracture [2], break in pieces [1], broken [1], brokenness [1], bruises [1], collapses [+995] [1], crash [1], crippled [1], crushed [1], crushes [1], downfall [1], fractures [1], injury [1], ruin [1], thrashing [1]

Lev 21:19 no man with a **crippled** foot or hand,
21:19 no man with a crippled foot or **[RPH]** hand,
24:20 **fracture** for fracture, eye for eye, tooth for tooth. As he has injured
24:20 fracture for **fracture**, eye for eye, tooth for tooth. As he has injured
Job 41:25 [41:17] the mighty are terrified; they retreat before his **thrashing**.
Ps 60: 2 [60:4] and torn it open; mend its **fractures**, for it is quaking.
Pr 15: 4 healing is a tree of life, but a deceitful tongue **crushes** the spirit.
16:18 Pride goes before **destruction**, a haughty spirit before a fall.
17:19 a quarrel loves sin; he who builds a high gate invites **destruction**.
18:12 Before his **downfall** a man's heart is proud, but humility comes
Isa 1:28 rebels and sinners will both be **broken**, and those who forsake the
15: 5 as they go; on the road to Horonaim they lament their **destruction**.
30:13 cracked and bulging, that **collapses** [+995] suddenly, in an instant.
30:14 It will **break in pieces** like pottery, shattered so mercilessly that
30:14 It will break in pieces like **[RPH]** pottery, shattered so mercilessly
30:26 when the LORD binds up the **bruises** *of* his people and heals the
51:19 ruin and **destruction**, famine and sword—who can console you?
59: 7 thoughts are evil thoughts; ruin and **destruction** mark their ways.
60:18 nor ruin or **destruction** within your borders, but you will call your
65:14 will cry out from anguish of heart and wail in **brokenness** *of* spirit.
Jer 4: 6 I am bringing disaster from the north, even terrible **destruction**."
4:20 **Disaster** follows disaster; the whole land lies in ruins. In an instant
4:20 Disaster follows **disaster**; the whole land lies in ruins. In an instant
6: 1 For disaster looms out of the north, even terrible **destruction**.
6:14 They dress the **wound** *of* my people as though it were not serious.
8:11 They dress the **wound** *of* my people as though it were not serious.
8:21 Since my people are **crushed**, I am crushed; I mourn, and horror
10:19 Woe to me because of my **injury**! My wound is incurable!
14:17 my people—has suffered a grievous **wound**, a crushing blow.
30:12 " 'Your **wound** is incurable, your injury beyond healing.
30:15 Why do you cry out over your **wound**, your pain that has no cure?
48: 3 to the cries from Horonaim, cries of great havoc and **destruction**.
48: 5 down to Horonaim anguished cries over the **destruction** are heard.
50:22 The noise of battle is in the land, the noise of great **destruction**!
51:54 the sound of great **destruction** from the land of the Babylonians.
La 2:11 is poured out on the ground because my people are **destroyed**,
2:13 of Zion? Your **wound** is as deep as the sea. Who can heal you?
3:47 We have suffered terror and pitfalls, ruin and **destruction**."
3:48 of tears flow from my eyes because my people are **destroyed**.
4:10 who became their food when my people were **destroyed**.
Eze 32: 9 peoples when I bring about your **destruction** among the nations,
Am 6: 6 the finest lotions, but you do not grieve over the **ruin** *of* Joseph.
Na 3:19 Nothing can heal your **wound**; your injury is fatal. Everyone who
Zep 1:10 wailing from the New Quarter, and a loud **crash** from the hills.

8692 [2]שֶׁבֶר *šeber*[2], n.[m.]. [9] [→ 8690]

grain [9]

Ge 42: 1 When Jacob learned that there was **grain** in Egypt, he said to his
42: 2 He continued, "I have heard that there is **grain** in Egypt. Go down
42:19 rest of you go and take **grain** back for your starving households.
42:26 they loaded their **grain** on their donkeys and left.
43: 2 So when they had eaten all the **grain** they had brought from Egypt,
44: 2 of the youngest one's sack, along with the silver for his **grain**."
47:14 in Egypt and Canaan in payment for the **grain** they were buying,
Ne 10:31 [10:32] bring merchandise or **grain** to sell on the Sabbath,
Am 8: 5 "When will the New Moon be over that we may sell **grain**,

8693 [3]שֶׁבֶר *šeber*[3], n.pr.m. [1] [√ 8691 *or* 8692]

Sheber [1]

1Ch 2:48 Caleb's concubine Maacah was the mother of **Sheber**

8694 שֵׁבֶר *šēber*, n.m. [1]

interpretation [1]

Jdg 7:15 When Gideon heard the dream and its **interpretation**, he

8695 שִׁבָּרוֹן *šibbārôn*, n.[m.]. [2] [√ 8689]

broken [1], destruction [1]

Jer 17:18 on them the day of disaster; destroy them with double **destruction**.
Eze 21: 6 [21:11] Groan before them with **broken** heart and bitter grief.

8696 שְׁבָרִים *šᵉbārîm*, n.m.[pl.]. [1] [√ 8691]

stone quarries [1]

Jos 7: 5 chased the Israelites from the city gate as far as the **stone quarries**

8697 [1]שָׁבַת *šābat*[1], v. [72] [→ 5404, 8698, 8700, 8701, 8702, 8703]

put an end [14], rested [4], stopped [4], come to an end [3], remove [3], rest [3], stop [3], bring an end [2], cease [2], ended [2], gone [2], put a stop [2], abandoned [1], abstained from work [1], blot out [1], bring to an end [1], cause to stop [1], cut off [1], did away with [1], disappear [1], discard [1], do away with [1], do not work [1], have rest [1], have[s] [1], leave [1], left without [1], makes cease [1], must observe a sabbath [+8701] [1], need not [1], no [1], observe sabbath [+8701] [1], removed [1], revert [1], rid [1], ruined [1], settles [1], silence [1], stilled [1], stopping [1]

Ge 2: 2 [A] so on the seventh day *he* **rested** from all his work.
2: 3 [A] because on it *he* **rested** from all the work of creating that he
8:22 [A] summer and winter, day and night *will* never **cease**."
Ex 5: 5 [G] now numerous, and *you are* **stopping** them from working."
12:15 [G] On the first day **remove** the yeast from your houses,
16:30 [A] So the people **rested** on the seventh day.
23:12 [A] on the seventh day **do not work**, so that your ox and your
31:17 [A] on the seventh day *he* **abstained from work** and rested.' "
34:21 [A] days you shall labor, but on the seventh day *you shall* **rest**;
34:21 [A] even during the plowing season and harvest *you must* **rest**.
Lev 2:13 [G] *Do* not **leave** the salt of the covenant of your God out of your
23:32 [A] evening *you are to* **observe** your **sabbath** [+8701]."
25: 2 [A] the land itself **must observe a sabbath** [+8701] to the
26: 6 [G] *I will* **remove** savage beasts from the land, and the sword
26:34 [A] your enemies; then the land *will* **rest** and enjoy its sabbaths.
26:35 [A] the land *will* **have** *the* **rest** *it* did not have during the
26:35 [A] the land will have the rest *it did* not **have**[s] during the

Dt 32:26 [G] scatter them and **blot out** their memory from mankind,
Jos 5:12 [A] The manna **stopped** the day after they ate this food from the
22:25 [G] So your descendants *might* **cause** ours **to stop** fearing the
Ru 4:14 [G] who this day *has* not **left** you **without** a kinsman-redeemer.
2Ki 23: 5 [G] *He* **did away with** the pagan priests appointed by the kings
23:11 [G] *He* **removed** from the entrance to the temple of the LORD
2Ch 16: 5 [G] he stopped building Ramah and **abandoned** his work.
36:21 [A] all the time of its desolation *it* **rested**, until the seventy years
Ne 4:11 [4:5] [G] and will kill them and **put an end** *to* the work."
6: 3 [A] Why *should* the work **stop** while I leave it and go down to
Job 32: 1 [A] So these three men **stopped** answering Job, because he was
Ps 8: 2 [8:3] [G] of your enemies, to **silence** the foe and the avenger.
46: 9 [46:10] [G] *He* **makes** wars **cease** to the ends of the earth;
89:44 [89:45] [G] *You have* **put an end** to his splendor and cast his
119:119 [G] All the wicked of the earth *you* **discard** like dross; therefore
Pr 18:18 [G] Casting the lot **settles** disputes and keeps strong opponents
22:10 [A] and out goes strife; quarrels and insults *are* **ended**.
Isa 13:11 [G] *I will* **put an end** *to* the arrogance of the haughty and will
14: 4 [A] How the oppressor *has* **come to an end**! How his fury has
14: 4 [A] the oppressor has come to an end! How his fury *has* **ended**!
16:10 [G] wine at the presses, for *I have* **put an end** *to* the shouting.
17: 3 [C] The fortified city *will* **disappear** from Ephraim, and royal
21: 2 [G] lay siege! *I will* **bring to an end** all the groaning she caused.
24: 8 [A] The gaiety of the tambourines *is* **stilled**, the noise of the
24: 8 [A] the noise of the revelers *has* **stopped**, the joyful harp is
30:11 [G] and **stop** confronting us with the Holy One of Israel!"
33: 8 [A] The highways are deserted, **no** travelers *are* on the roads.
Jer 7:34 [G] *I will* **bring an end** *to* the sounds of joy and gladness and to
16: 9 [G] in your days I *will* **bring an end** *to* the sounds of joy
31:36 [A] "*will* the descendants of Israel ever **cease** to be a nation
36:29 [G] destroy this land and **cut off** both men and animals from it?"
48:33 [G] *I have* **stopped** the flow of wine from the presses; no one
48:35 [G] In Moab *I will* **put an end** *to* those who make offerings on
La 5:14 [A] The elders *are* **gone** from the city gate; the young men have
5:15 [A] Joy *is* **gone** *from* our hearts; our dancing has turned to
Eze 6: 6 [C] be laid waste and devastated, your idols smashed and **ruined**,
7:24 [G] *I will* **put an end** *to* the pride of the mighty, and their
12:23 [G] *I am going to* **put an end** *to* this proverb, and they will no
16:41 [G] *I will* **put a stop** to your prostitution, and you will no longer
23:27 [G] So *I will* **put a stop** *to* the lewdness and prostitution you
23:48 [G] "So *I will* **put an end** *to* lewdness in the land, that all women
26:13 [G] *I will* **put an end** *to* your noisy songs, and the music of your
30:10 [G] " '*I will* **put an end** *to* the hordes of Egypt by the hand of
30:13 [G] destroy the idols and **put an end** *to* the images in Memphis.
30:18 [C] yoke of Egypt; there her proud strength *will* **come to an end**.
33:28 [C] a desolate waste, and her proud strength *will* **come to an end**,
34:10 [G] *I will* **remove** them from tending the flock so that the
34:25 [G] **rid** the land of wild beasts so that they may live in the desert
46:17 [A] it until the year of freedom; then *it will* **revert** to the prince.
Da 9:27 [G] In the middle of the 'seven' *he will* **put an end** *to* sacrifice
11:18 [G] a commander *will* **put an end** *to* his insolence and will turn
Hos 1: 4 [G] at Jezreel, and *I will* **put an end** *to* the kingdom of Israel.
2:11 [2:13] [G] *I will* **stop** all her celebrations: her yearly festivals,
7: 4 [A] burning like an oven whose fire the baker **need not** stir from
Am 8: 4 [G] trample the needy and **do away with** the poor of the land,

8698 ²שָׁבַת *šābat²*, v.den. Not used in NIV/BHS [√ 8697]

8699 ¹שֶׁבֶת *šebet¹*, n.f. [6] [√ 3782]

seat [+5226] [2], home [1], lie [1], reign [1], site [1]

Nu 21:15 the slopes of the ravines that lead to the **site** *of* Ar and lie along the
2Sa 23: 7 or the shaft of a spear; they are burned up where they **lie**."
1Ki 10:19 On both sides of the **seat** [+5226] were armrests, with a lion
2Ch 9:18 On both sides of the **seat** [+5226] were armrests, with a lion
Am 6: 3 You put off the evil day and bring near a **reign** *of* terror.
Ob 1: 3 live in the clefts of the rocks and make your **home** on the heights,

8700 ²שֶׁבֶת *šebet²*, n.f. [2] [√ 8697]

Do-Nothing [1], loss of time [1]

Ex 21:19 he must pay the injured man for the **loss of** his **time** and see that he
Isa 30: 7 help is utterly useless. Therefore I call her Rahab the **Do-Nothing**.

8701 שַׁבָּת *šabbāt*, n.f. & m. [111] [→ 8702, 8703; cf. 8697]

sabbath [66], sabbaths [30], *untranslated* [2], every Sabbath [+8701] [2], every Sabbath [+928+8701] [2], Sabbath after Sabbath [+928+928+2021+2021+3427+3427+8701] [2], another[s] [1], it[s] [+2021] [1], must observe a sabbath [+8697] [1], observe sabbath [+8697] [1], Sabbath days [1], sabbath rests [1], weeks [1]

Ex 16:23 'Tomorrow is to be a day of rest, a holy **Sabbath** to the LORD.
16:25 it today," Moses said, "because today is a **Sabbath** to the LORD.
16:26 but on the seventh day, the **Sabbath**, there will not be any."
16:29 Bear in mind that the LORD has given you the **Sabbath**;
20: 8 "Remember the **Sabbath** day by keeping it holy.
20:10 but the seventh day is a **Sabbath** to the LORD your God.
20:11 Therefore the LORD blessed the **Sabbath** day and made it holy.
31:13 "Say to the Israelites, 'You must observe my **Sabbaths**. This will
31:14 " 'Observe the **Sabbath**, because it is holy to you. Anyone who
31:15 work is to be done, but the seventh day is a **Sabbath** *of* rest,
31:15 Whoever does any work on the **Sabbath** day must be put to death.
31:16 The Israelites are to observe the **Sabbath**, celebrating it for the
31:16 celebrating **it**[s] [+2021] for the generations to come as a lasting
35: 2 day shall be your holy day, a **Sabbath** *of* rest to the LORD.
35: 3 Do not light a fire in any of your dwellings on the **Sabbath** day."
Lev 16:31 It is a **sabbath** *of* rest, and you must deny yourselves; it is a lasting
19: 3 respect his mother and father, and you must observe my **Sabbaths**.
19:30 " 'Observe my **Sabbaths** and have reverence for my sanctuary.
23: 3 but the seventh day is a **Sabbath** *of* rest, a day of sacred assembly.
23: 3 to do any work; wherever you live, it is a **Sabbath** to the LORD.
23:11 your behalf; the priest is to wave it on the day after the **Sabbath**.
23:15 " 'From the day after the **Sabbath**, the day you brought the sheaf of
23:15 brought the sheaf of the wave offering, count off seven full **weeks**.
23:16 Count off fifty days up to the day after the seventh **Sabbath**,
23:32 It is a **sabbath** *of* rest for you, and you must deny yourselves.
23:32 the following evening *you are to* **observe** your **sabbath** [+8697]."
23:38 These offerings are in addition to those for the LORD's **Sabbaths**
24: 8 This bread is to be set out before the LORD regularly, **Sabbath**
[+928+928+2021+2021+3427+3427+8701] **after Sabbath**,
24: 8 This bread is to be set out before the LORD regularly, **Sabbath**
after Sabbath [+928+928+2021+2021+3427+3427+8701],
25: 2 the land itself **must observe a sabbath** [+8697] to the LORD.
25: 4 But in the seventh year the land is to have a **sabbath** *of* rest,
25: 4 year the land is to have a sabbath of rest, a **sabbath** to the LORD.
25: 6 Whatever the land yields during the **sabbath** year will be food for
25: 8 " 'Count off seven **sabbaths** *of* years—seven times seven years—
25: 8 so that the seven **sabbaths** *of* years amount to a period of
26: 2 " 'Observe my **Sabbaths** and have reverence for my sanctuary.
26:34 the land will enjoy its **sabbath** years all the time that it lies
26:34 of your enemies; then the land will rest and enjoy its **sabbaths**.
26:35 the land will have the rest it did not have during the **sabbaths** you
26:43 and will enjoy its **sabbaths** while it lies desolate without them.
Nu 15:32 the desert, a man was found gathering wood on the **Sabbath** day.
28: 9 " 'On the **Sabbath** day, make an offering of two lambs a year old
28:10 This is the burnt offering for **every Sabbath** [+928+8701],
28:10 This is the burnt offering for **every Sabbath** [+928+8701],
Dt 5:12 "Observe the **Sabbath** day by keeping it holy, as the LORD your
5:14 but the seventh day is a **Sabbath** to the LORD your God.
5:15 your God has commanded you to observe the **Sabbath** day.
2Ki 4:23 he asked. "It's not the New Moon or the **Sabbath**." "It's all right,"
11: 5 are in the three companies that are going on duty on the **Sabbath**—
11: 7 who are in the other two companies that normally go off **Sabbath**
11: 9 those who were going on duty on the **Sabbath** and those who were
11: 9 were going off duty—**[RPH]** and came to Jehoiada the priest.
16:18 He took away the **Sabbath** canopy that had been built at the
1Ch 9:32 *for* **every Sabbath** [+8701] the bread set out on the table.
9:32 *for* **every Sabbath** [+8701] the bread set out on the table.
23:31 burnt offerings were presented to the LORD on **Sabbaths**
2Ch 2: 4 [2:3] and evening and on **Sabbaths** and New Moons
8:13 requirement for offerings commanded by Moses for **Sabbaths**,
23: 4 Levites who are going on duty on the **Sabbath** are to keep watch at
23: 8 those who were going on duty on the **Sabbath** and those who were
23: 8 **[RPH]** for Jehoiada the priest had not released any of the
31: 3 burnt offerings and for the burnt offerings on the **Sabbaths**,
36:21 The land enjoyed its **sabbath rests**; all the time of its desolation it
Ne 9:14 You made known to them your holy **Sabbath** and gave them
10:31 [10:32] bring merchandise or grain to sell on the **Sabbath**,
10:31 [10:32] we will not buy from them on the **Sabbath** or on any holy
10:33 [10:34] for the offerings on the **Sabbaths**, New Moon festivals
13:15 days I saw men in Judah treading winepresses on the **Sabbath**
13:15 And they were bringing all this into Jerusalem on the **Sabbath**.
13:16 selling them in Jerusalem on the **Sabbath** to the people of Judah.
13:17 is this wicked thing you are doing—desecrating the **Sabbath** day?
13:18 stirring up more wrath against Israel by desecrating the **Sabbath**."
13:19 shadows fell on the gates of Jerusalem before the **Sabbath**,
13:19 the doors to be shut and not opened until the **Sabbath** was over.
13:19 the gates so that no load could be brought in on the **Sabbath** day.
13:21 on you." From that time on they no longer came on the **Sabbath**.
13:22 and guard the gates in order to keep the **Sabbath** day holy.
Ps 92: T [92:1] A psalm. A song. For the **Sabbath** day.
Isa 1:13 New Moons, **Sabbaths** and convocations—I cannot bear your evil
56: 2 who holds it fast, who keeps the **Sabbath** without desecrating it,
56: 4 "To the eunuchs who keep my **Sabbaths**, who choose what pleases
56: 6 all who keep the **Sabbath** without desecrating it and who hold fast
58:13 "If you keep your feet from breaking the **Sabbath** and from doing
58:13 if you call the **Sabbath** a delight and the LORD's holy day
66:23 From one New Moon to another and from *one* **Sabbath** to another,

Isa 66:23 one New Moon to another and from one Sabbath to **another**,
Jer 17:21 Be careful not to carry a load on the **Sabbath** day or bring it
17:22 bring a load out of your houses or do any work on the **Sabbath**,
17:22 or do any work on the Sabbath, but keep the **Sabbath** day holy,
17:24 and bring no load through the gates of this city on the **Sabbath**,
17:24 but keep the **Sabbath** day holy by not doing any work on it,
17:27 if you do not obey me to keep the **Sabbath** day holy by not
17:27 as you come through the gates of Jerusalem on the **Sabbath** day,
La 2:6 has made Zion forget her appointed feasts and her **Sabbaths**;
Eze 20:12 Also I gave them my **Sabbaths** as a sign between us, so they
20:13 them will live by them—and they utterly desecrated my **Sabbaths**.
20:16 and did not follow my decrees and desecrated my **Sabbaths**.
20:20 Keep my **Sabbaths** holy, that they may be a sign between us.
20:21 obeys them will live by them—and they desecrated my **Sabbaths**.
20:24 but had rejected my decrees and desecrated my **Sabbaths**,
22:8 You have despised my holy things and desecrated my **Sabbaths**.
22:26 they shut their eyes to the keeping of my **Sabbaths**, so that I am
23:38 same time they defiled my sanctuary and desecrated my **Sabbaths**.
44:24 all my appointed feasts, and they are to keep my **Sabbaths** holy.
45:17 drink offerings at the festivals, the New Moons and the **Sabbaths**—
46:1 on the **Sabbath** day and on the day of the New Moon it is to be
46:3 On the **Sabbaths** and New Moons the people of the land are to
46:4 The burnt offering the prince brings to the LORD on the **Sabbath**
46:12 or his fellowship offerings as he does on the **Sabbath** day.
Hos 2:11 [2:13] her yearly festivals, her New Moons, her **Sabbath days**—
Am 8:5 and the **Sabbath** be ended that we may market wheat?"—

8702 שַׁבָּתוֹן *šabbātôn*, n.m. [11] [√ 8701]

rest [7], day of rest [4]

Ex 16:23 'Tomorrow is to be a **day of rest**, a holy Sabbath to the LORD.
31:15 work is to be done, but the seventh day is a Sabbath of **rest**,
35:2 day shall be your holy day, a Sabbath of **rest** to the LORD.
Lev 16:31 It is a sabbath of **rest**, and you must deny yourselves; it is a lasting
23:3 but the seventh day is a Sabbath of **rest**, a day of sacred assembly.
23:24 the first day of the seventh month you are to have a **day of rest**,
23:32 It is a sabbath of **rest** for you, and you must deny yourselves.
23:39 the first day is a **day of rest**, and the eighth day also is a day of
23:39 first day is a day of rest, and the eighth day also is a **day of rest**.
25:4 But in the seventh year the land is to have a sabbath of **rest**,
25:5 grapes of your untended vines. The land is to have a year of **rest**.

8703 שַׁבְּתַי *šabbᵉtay*, n.pr.m. [3] [√ 8701]

Shabbethai [3]

Ezr 10:15 supported by Meshullam and **Shabbethai** the Levite, opposed this.
Ne 8:7 Jamin, Akkub, **Shabbethai**, Hodiah, Maaseiah, Kelita, Azariah,
11:16 **Shabbethai** and Jozabad, two of the heads of the Levites,

8704 שָׁגַג *šāgag*, v. [4] [→ 54; cf. 5413, 8706]

deceived [1], erred [1], went astray [1], wrong committed unintentionally [+8705] [1]

Lev 5:18 [A] for the **wrong** *he has* **committed unintentionally** [+8705],
Nu 15:28 [A] LORD for the one who **erred** by sinning unintentionally,
Job 12:16 [A] and victory; both **deceived** and deceiver are his.
Ps 119:67 [A] Before I was afflicted I **went astray**, but now I obey your

8705 שְׁגָגָה *šᵉgāgâ*, n.f. [19] [cf. 8706]

unintentionally [+928] [6], accidentally [+928] [4], mistake [2], error [1], not intentional [1], sins unintentionally [+928+6913] [1], unintentional wrong [1], unintentionally [+4200] [1], wrong committed unintentionally [+8704] [1], wrong [1]

Lev 4:2 'When anyone sins **unintentionally** [+928] and does what is
4:22 " 'When a leader sins **unintentionally** [+928] and does what is
4:27 " 'If a member of the community sins **unintentionally** [+928]
5:15 sins **unintentionally** [+928] in regard to any of the LORD's holy
5:18 for the **wrong** *he has* **committed unintentionally** [+8704],
22:14 " 'If anyone eats a sacred offering by **mistake**, he must make
Nu 15:24 if this is done **unintentionally** [+4200] without the community
15:25 for it was **not intentional** and they have brought to the LORD for
15:25 they have brought to the LORD for their **wrong** an offering made
15:26 because all the people were involved in the **unintentional wrong**.
15:27 " 'But if just one person sins **unintentionally** [+928], he must
15:28 LORD for the one who erred by sinning **unintentionally** [+928],
15:29 law applies to everyone *who* **sins unintentionally** [+928+6913],
35:11 to which a person who has killed someone **accidentally** [+928]
35:15 so that anyone who has killed another **accidentally** [+928] can flee
Jos 20:3 so that anyone who kills a person **accidentally** [+928]
20:9 someone **accidentally** [+928] could flee to these designated cities
Ecc 5:6 [5:5] to the ˻temple˼ messenger, "My vow was a **mistake**."
10:5 I have seen under the sun, the sort of **error** that arises from a ruler:

8706 שָׁגָה *šāgâ*, v. [21] [→ 5405; cf. 5413, 8704, 8705, 8707?, 8709]

stagger [3], stray [3], captivated [2], led astray [2], sins unintentionally [2], deceiver [1], erred [1], gone astray [1], leads astray [1], leads [1], let stray [1], unintentionally [1], wandered [1], wrong [1]

Lev 4:13 [A] " 'If the whole Israelite community **sins unintentionally**
Nu 15:22 [A] " 'Now if *you* **unintentionally** fail to keep any of these
Dt 27:18 [G] "Cursed is the man *who* **leads** the blind **astray** on the road."
1Sa 26:21 [A] Surely I have acted like a fool and *have* **erred** greatly."
Job 6:24 [A] and I will be quiet; show me where *I have been* **wrong**.
12:16 [G] and victory; both deceived and **deceiver** are his.
19:4 [A] If it is true that *I have* **gone astray**, my error remains my
Ps 119:10 [G] with all my heart; *do* not **let** me **stray** from your commands.
119:21 [A] who are cursed and who **stray** from your commands.
119:118 [A] You reject all *who* **stray** from your decrees, for their
Pr 5:19 [A] satisfy you always, *may you* ever *be* **captivated** by her love.
5:20 [A] Why *be* **captivated**, my son, by an adulteress? Why embrace
5:23 [A] die for lack of discipline, **led astray** by his own great folly.
19:27 [A] my son, and you *will* **stray** from the words of knowledge.
20:1 [A] beer a brawler; whoever *is* **led astray** by them is not wise.
28:10 [G] *He who* **leads** the upright along an evil path will fall into his
Isa 28:7 [A] And these also **stagger** from wine and reel from beer: Priests
28:7 [A] Priests and prophets **stagger** from beer and are befuddled
28:7 [A] they reel from beer, *they* **stagger** when seeing visions,
Eze 34:6 [A] My sheep **wandered** over all the mountains and on every
45:20 [A] day of the month for anyone *who* **sins unintentionally**

8707 שָׁגֵה *šāgēh*, n.pr.m. [1] [√ 8706?]

Shagee [1]

1Ch 11:34 sons of Hashem the Gizonite, Jonathan son of **Shagee** the Hararite,

8708 שָׁגַח *šāgaḥ*, v. [3]

gazing [1], stare [1], watches [1]

Ps 33:14 [G] from his dwelling place *he* **watches** all who live on earth—
SS 2:9 [G] **gazing** through the windows, peering through the lattice.
Isa 14:16 [G] Those who see you **stare** at you, they ponder your fate: "Is

8709 שְׁגִיאָה *šᵉgîʾâ*, n.f. [1] [cf. 8706]

errors [1]

Ps 19:12 [19:13] Who can discern his **errors**? Forgive my hidden faults.

8710 שִׁגָּיוֹן *šiggāyôn*, tt. *or* n.m. [2]

shiggaion [1], shigionoth [1]

Ps 7:T [7:1] A ***shiggaion*** of David, which he sang to the LORD
Hab 3:1 A prayer of Habakkuk the prophet. On ***shigionoth***.

8711 שָׁגַל *šāgal*, v. [4] [√ 8712]

been ravished [1], raped [1], ravish [1], ravished [1]

Dt 28:30 [A] a woman, but another *will* take her and **ravish** [Q 8886] her.
Isa 13:16 [C] houses will be looted and their wives **ravished**. [Q 8886]
Jer 3:2 [E] any place where *you have* not **been ravished**? [Q 8886]
Zec 14:2 [C] the houses ransacked, and the women **raped**. [Q 8886]

8712 שֵׁגַל *šēgal*, n.f. [2] [→ 8711; Ar 10699]

queen [1], royal bride [1]

Ne 2:6 Then the king, with the **queen** sitting beside him, asked me,
Ps 45:9 [45:10] at your right hand is the **royal bride** in gold of Ophir.

8713 שָׁגַע *šāgaʿ*, v. [7] [→ 8714]

carry on [1], drive mad [1], insane [1], madman [+408] [1], madman [1], madmen [1], maniac [1]

Dt 28:34 [E] The sights you see will **drive** you **mad**.
1Sa 21:14 [21:15] [F] said to his servants, "Look at the man! *He is* **insane**!
21:15 [21:16] [E] so short of **madmen** that you have to bring this
21:15 [21:16] [F] this fellow here to **carry on** like this in front of me?
2Ki 9:11 [E] Why did this **madman** come to you?" "You know the man
Jer 29:26 [E] you should put any **madman** [+408] who acts like a prophet
Hos 9:7 [E] the prophet is considered a fool, the inspired man a **maniac**.

8714 שִׁגָּעוֹן *šiggāʿôn*, n.m. [3] [√ 8713]

madness [2], madman [1]

Dt 28:28 The LORD will afflict you with **madness**, blindness
2Ki 9:20 is like that of Jehu son of Nimshi—he drives like a **madman**."
Zec 12:4 I will strike every horse with panic and its rider with **madness**,"

8715 שֶׁגֶר *šeger*, n.f. [5]

calves [4], firstborn [+7081] [1]

Ex 13:12 All the **firstborn** males **of** [+7081] your livestock belong to the
Dt 7:13 the **calves** *of* your herds and the lambs of your flocks in the land
28:4 the **calves** *of* your herds and the lambs of your flocks.
28:18 and the **calves** *of* your herds and the lambs of your flocks.
28:51 nor any **calves** *of* your herds or lambs of your flocks until you are

8716 שַׁד *šad*, n.m. [21] [→ 8718, 8721]

breasts [17], breast [4]

Ge 49:25 of the deep that lies below, blessings of the **breast** and womb.
Job 3:12 were there knees to receive me and **breasts** that I might be nursed?
Ps 22:9 [22:10] you made me trust in you even at my mother's **breast**.
SS 1:13 My lover is to me a sachet of myrrh resting between my **breasts**.
4:5 Your two **breasts** are like two fawns, like twin fawns of a gazelle
7:3 [7:4] Your **breasts** are like two fawns, twins of a gazelle.
7:7 [7:8] like that of the palm, and your **breasts** like clusters of fruit.
7:8 [7:9] May your **breasts** be like the clusters of the vine,
8:1 were to me like a brother, who was nursed at my mother's **breasts**!
8:8 We have a young sister, and her **breasts** are not yet grown.
8:10 I am a wall, and my **breasts** are like towers. Thus I have become in
Isa 28:9 weaned from their milk, to those just taken from the **breast**?
32:12 Beat your **breasts** for the pleasant fields, for the fruitful vines
La 4:3 Even jackals offer their **breasts** to nurse their young, but my
Eze 16:7 Your **breasts** were formed and your hair grew, you who were
23:3 In that land their **breasts** were fondled and their virgin bosoms
23:21 Egypt your bosom was caressed and your young **breasts** fondled.
23:34 and drain it dry; you will dash it to pieces and tear your **breasts**.
Hos 2:2 [2:4] her face and the unfaithfulness from between her **breasts**.
9:14 Give them wombs that miscarry and **breasts** that are dry.
Joel 2:16 together the elders, gather the children, those nursing at the **breast**.

8717 שֵׁד *šēd*, n.[m.]. [2]

demons [2]

Dt 32:17 They sacrificed to **demons**, which are not God—gods they had not
Ps 106:37 They sacrificed their sons and their daughters to **demons**.

8718 שֹׁד¹ *šōd¹*, n.m. [3] [√ 8716]

breasts [2], breast [1]

Job 24:9 The fatherless child is snatched from the **breast**; the infant of the
Isa 60:16 You will drink the milk of nations and be nursed at royal **breasts**.
66:11 For you will nurse and be satisfied at her comforting **breasts**;

8719 שֹׁד² *šōd²*, n.m. [24] [√ 8720]

destruction [13], ruin [4], violence [3], oppression [2], havoc [1], loot [1]

Job 5:21 the lash of the tongue, and need not fear when **destruction** comes.
5:22 You will laugh at **destruction** and famine, and need not fear the
Ps 12:5 [12:6] "Because of the **oppression** *of* the weak and the groaning
Pr 11:3 [the unfaithful *are* **destroyed** [K; see Q 8720] *by* their duplicity.]
21:7 The **violence** *of* the wicked will drag them away, for they refuse to
24:2 for their hearts plot **violence**, and their lips talk about making
Isa 13:6 LORD is near; it will come like **destruction** from the Almighty.
16:4 The oppressor will come to an end, and **destruction** will cease;
22:4 Do not try to console me over the **destruction** *of* my people."
51:19 **ruin** and destruction, famine and sword—who can console you?
59:7 thoughts are evil thoughts; **ruin** and destruction mark their ways.
60:18 nor **ruin** or destruction within your borders, but you will call your
Jer 6:7 Violence and **destruction** resound in her; her sickness and wounds
20:8 Whenever I speak, I cry out proclaiming violence and **destruction**.
48:3 to the cries from Horonaim, cries of great **havoc** and destruction.
Eze 45:9 up your violence and **oppression** and do what is just and right.
Hos 7:13 **Destruction** to them, because they have rebelled against me!
9:6 Even if they escape from **destruction**, Egypt will gather them,
12:1 [12:2] the east wind all day and multiplies lies and **violence**.
Joel 1:15 LORD is near; it will come like **destruction** from the Almighty.
Am 3:10 the LORD, "who hoard plunder and **loot** in their fortresses."
5:9 he flashes **destruction** on the stronghold and brings the fortified
5:9 destruction on the stronghold and brings the fortified city to **ruin**),
Hab 1:3 **Destruction** and violence are before me; there is strife,
2:17 overwhelm you, and your **destruction** *of* animals will terrify you.

8720 שָׁדַד *šādad*, v. [59] [→ 8719, 8722]

destroyer [7], destroyed [6], destroy [5], ruined [4], destroyers [3], is destroyed [3], are destroyed [2], be destroyed [2], destroying [2], destroys [2], devastated [2], marauders [2], utterly ruined [+8720] [2], are ruined [1], assail [1], be devastated [1], be ruined [1], been destroyed [1], dead [1], doomed to destruction [1], in ruins [1], lies in ruins [1], looter [1], perish [1], raid [1], ravage [1], robbers [1], robs [1], shatter [1], takes loot [1]

Jdg 5:27 [B] her feet he sank, he fell; where he sank, there he fell—**dead**.
Job 12:6 [A] The tents of **marauders** are undisturbed, and those who
15:21 [A] fill his ears; when all seems well, **marauders** attack him.
Ps 17:9 [A] from the wicked who **assail** me, from my mortal enemies
91:6 [A] in the darkness, nor the plague *that* **destroys** at midday.
137:8 [B] O Daughter of Babylon, **doomed to destruction**, happy is he
Pr 11:3 [A] but the unfaithful *are* **destroyed** [K 8719] *by* their duplicity.
19:26 [D] *He who* **robs** his father and drives out his mother is a son
24:15 [D] a righteous man's house, *do* not **raid** his dwelling place;
Isa 15:1 [E] Ar in Moab is ruined, **destroyed** in a night! Kir in Moab is
15:1 [E] in a night! Kir in Moab is ruined, **destroyed** in a night!
16:4 [A] fugitives stay with you; be their shelter from the **destroyer**."
21:2 [A] The traitor betrays, the **looter** takes loot. Elam, attack!
21:2 [A] The traitor betrays, the looter **takes loot**. Elam, attack!
23:1 [E] For Tyre *is* **destroyed** and left without house or harbor.
23:14 [E] Wail, you ships of Tarshish; your fortress *is* **destroyed**!
33:1 [A] Woe to you, O **destroyer**, you who have not been destroyed!
33:1 [B] Woe to you, O destroyer, you *who have* not **been destroyed**!
33:1 [A] When you stop **destroying**, you will be destroyed; when you
33:1 [H] When you stop destroying, *you will* **be destroyed**; when you
Jer 4:13 [E] horses are swifter than eagles. Woe to us! *We* **are ruined**!
4:20 [E] Disaster follows disaster; the whole land **lies in ruins**. In an
4:20 [E] In an instant my tents **are destroyed**, my shelter in a
4:30 [B] What are you doing, O **devastated** *one*? Why dress yourself
5:6 [A] will attack them, a wolf from the desert *will* **ravage** them,
6:26 [A] an only son, for suddenly the **destroyer** will come upon us.
9:19 [9:18] [E] 'How **ruined** *we are*! How great is our shame! We
10:20 [E] My tent **is destroyed**; all its ropes are snapped. My sons are
12:12 [A] Over all the barren heights in the desert **destroyers** will
15:8 [A] At midday I will bring a **destroyer** against the mothers of
25:36 [A] of the flock, for the LORD *is* **destroying** their pasture.
47:4 [A] For the day has come to **destroy** all the Philistines and to cut
47:4 [A] The LORD *is about to* **destroy** the Philistines, the remnant
48:1 [E] the God of Israel, says: "Woe to Nebo, for *it will* **be ruined**.
48:8 [A] The **destroyer** will come against every town, and not a town
48:15 [E] Moab *will* **be destroyed** and her towns invaded; her finest
48:18 [A] for *he who* **destroys** Moab will come up against you and ruin
48:20 [E] and cry out! Announce by the Arnon that Moab **is destroyed**.
48:32 [A] The **destroyer** has fallen on your ripened fruit and grapes.
49:3 [E] "Wail, O Heshbon, for Ai **is destroyed**! Cry out,
49:10 [E] His children, relatives and neighbors *will* **perish**, and he will
49:28 [A] "Arise, and attack Kedar and **destroy** the people of the East.
51:48 [A] for out of the north **destroyers** will attack her,"
51:53 [A] I will send **destroyers** against her," declares the LORD.
51:55 [A] The LORD *will* **destroy** Babylon; he will silence her noisy
51:56 [A] A **destroyer** will come against Babylon; her warriors will be
Eze 32:12 [A] *They will* **shatter** the pride of Egypt, and all her hordes will
Hos 10:2 [D] will demolish their altars and **destroy** their sacred stones.
10:14 [H] your people, so that all your fortresses *will* **be devastated**—
10:14 [A] as Shalman **devastated** Beth Arbel on the day of battle,
Joel 1:10 [E] The fields *are* **ruined**, the ground is dried up; the grain is
1:10 [E] the grain *is* **destroyed**, the new wine is dried up, the oil fails.
Ob 1:5 [A] "If thieves came to you, if **robbers** *in* the night—Oh, what a
Mic 2:4 [C] '*We are* **utterly ruined** [+8720]; my people's possession is
2:4 [A] '*We are* **utterly ruined** [+8720]; my people's possession is
Na 3:7 [E] see you will flee from you and say, 'Nineveh *is* **in ruins**—
Zec 11:2 [E] for the cedar has fallen; the stately trees *are* **ruined**!
11:3 [E] the wail of the shepherds; their rich pastures **are destroyed**!
11:3 [E] the roar of the lions; the lush thicket of the Jordan *is* **ruined**!

8721 שִׁדָּה *šiddâ*, n.f. [2] [√ 8716]

harem [+2256+8721] [2]

Ecc 2:8 and women singers, and a **harem** [+2256+8721] as well—
2:8 and women singers, and a **harem** [+2256+8721] as well—

8722 שָׁדוּד *šādûd*, n.pr.loc. Not used in NIV/BHS [√ 8720; cf. 8587]

8723 שַׁדּוּן *šaddûn*, n.[m.]. Not used in NIV/BHS [√ 1906; cf. 8726]

8724 שַׁדַּי *šadday*, n.[pr.m.]. [48] [→ 7453, 8725?; cf. 8716 *or* 8717 *or* 8720 *or* 8611 + 1896; *also used with compound proper names*]

Almighty [48]

Ge 17:1 the LORD appeared to him and said, "I am God **Almighty**;
28:3 May God **Almighty** bless you and make you fruitful and increase
35:11 God said to him, "I am God **Almighty**; be fruitful and increase in

Ge 43:14 may God **Almighty** grant you mercy before the man so that he will
48: 3 "God **Almighty** appeared to me at Luz in the land of Canaan,
49:25 of your father's God, who helps you, because of the **Almighty**,
Ex 6: 3 I appeared to Abraham, to Isaac and to Jacob as God **Almighty**,
Nu 24: 4 who sees a vision from the **Almighty**, who falls prostrate,
24:16 who sees a vision from the **Almighty**, who falls prostrate,
Ru 1:20 me Mara, because the **Almighty** has made my life very bitter.
1:21 has afflicted me; the **Almighty** has brought misfortune upon me."
Job 5:17 God corrects; so do not despise the discipline of the **Almighty**.
6: 4 The arrows of the **Almighty** are in me, my spirit drinks in their
6:14 of his friends, even though he forsakes the fear of the **Almighty**.
8: 3 God pervert justice? Does the **Almighty** pervert what is right?
8: 5 But if you will look to God and plead with the **Almighty**,
11: 7 the mysteries of God? Can you probe the limits of the **Almighty**?
13: 3 I desire to speak to the **Almighty** and to argue my case with God.
15:25 he shakes his fist at God and vaunts himself against the **Almighty**,
21:15 Who is the **Almighty**, that we should serve him? What would we
21:20 see his destruction; let him drink of the wrath of the **Almighty**.
22: 3 What pleasure would it give the **Almighty** if you were righteous?
22:17 said to God, 'Leave us alone! What can the **Almighty** do to us?'
22:23 If you return to the **Almighty**, you will be restored: If you remove
22:25 then the **Almighty** will be your gold, the choicest silver for you.
22:26 Surely then you will find delight in the **Almighty** and will lift up
23:16 God has made my heart faint; the **Almighty** has terrified me.
24: 1 "Why does the **Almighty** not set times for judgment? Why must
27: 2 "As surely as God lives, who has denied me justice, the **Almighty**,
27:10 Will he find delight in the **Almighty**? Will he call upon God at all
27:11 the power of God; the ways of the **Almighty** I will not conceal.
27:13 the heritage a ruthless man receives from the **Almighty**:
29: 5 when the **Almighty** was still with me and my children were around
31: 2 lot from God above, his heritage from the **Almighty** on high?
31:35 I sign now my defense—let the **Almighty** answer me; let my
32: 8 it is the spirit in a man, the breath of the **Almighty**, that gives him
33: 4 of God has made me; the breath of the **Almighty** gives me life.
34:10 Far be it from God to do evil, from the **Almighty** to do wrong.
34:12 that God would do wrong, that the **Almighty** would pervert justice.
35:13 not listen to their empty plea; the **Almighty** pays no attention to it.
37:23 The **Almighty** is beyond our reach and exalted in power; in his
40: 2 "Will the one who contends with the **Almighty** correct him?
Ps 68:14 [68:15] When the **Almighty** scattered the kings in the land, it was
91: 1 shelter of the Most High will rest in the shadow of the **Almighty**.
Isa 13: 6 LORD is near; it will come like destruction from the **Almighty**.
Eze 1:24 like the voice of the **Almighty**, like the tumult of an army.
10: 5 as the outer court, like the voice of God **Almighty** when he speaks.
Joel 1:15 LORD is near; it will come like destruction from the **Almighty**.

8725 שְׁדֵיאוּר šᵉdê'ûr, n.pr.m. [5] [√ 8724? + 329]

Shedeur [5]

Nu 1: 5 men who are to assist you: from Reuben, Elizur son of **Shedeur**;
2:10 The leader of the people of Reuben is Elizur son of **Shedeur**.
7:30 On the fourth day Elizur son of **Shedeur**, the leader of the people
7:35 This was the offering of Elizur son of **Shedeur**.
10:18 under their standard. Elizur son of **Shedeur** was in command.

8726 שַׁדִּין šaddîn, n.m. Not used in NIV/BHS [√ 1906; cf. 8723]

8727 שְׁדֵמָה šᵉdēmâ, n.f. [6 / 5]

fields [4], terraces [1]

Dt 32:32 comes from the vine of Sodom and from the **fields** *of* Gomorrah.
2Ki 23: 4 He burned them outside Jerusalem in the **fields** *of* the Kidron
Isa 16: 8 The **fields** *of* Heshbon wither, the vines of Sibmah also. The rulers
37:27 on the roof, scorched [BHS ***and terraces***; NIV 8729] before it
Jer 31:40 all the **terraces** [K 9236] out to the Kidron Valley on the east as
Hab 3:17 though the olive crop fails and the **fields** produce no food,

8728 שָׁדַף šādap, v. [3] [→ 8729, 8730; cf. 8812]

scorched [3]

Ge 41: 6 [B] heads of grain sprouted—thin and **scorched** *by* the east wind.
41:23 [B] withered and thin and **scorched** *by* the east wind.
41:27 [B] so are the seven worthless heads of grain **scorched** *by* the

8729 שְׁדֵפָה šᵉdēpâ, n.f. [1 / 2] [√ 8728]

scorched [2]

2Ki 19:26 like grass sprouting on the roof, **scorched** before it grows up.
Isa 37:27 sprouting on the roof, **scorched** [BHS 8727] before it grows up.

8730 שִׁדָּפוֹן šiddāpôn, n.m. [5] [√ 8728]

blight [5]

Dt 28:22 with scorching heat and drought, with **blight** and mildew,
1Ki 8:37 comes to the land, or **blight** or mildew, locusts or grasshoppers,
2Ch 6:28 comes to the land, or **blight** or mildew, locusts or grasshoppers,
Am 4: 9 your gardens and vineyards, I struck them with **blight** and mildew.
Hag 2:17 I struck all the work of your hands with **blight**, mildew and hail,

8731 שַׁדְרַךְ šadrak, n.pr.m. [1] [→ Ar 10701]

Shadrach [1]

Da 1: 7 to Hananiah, **Shadrach**; to Mishael, Meshach; and to Azariah,

8732 שֹׁהַם šōham[1], n.m. [11] [→ 8733]

onyx [9], onyx [+74] [2]

Ge 2:12 of that land is good; aromatic resin and **onyx** [+74] are also there.)
Ex 25: 7 and **onyx** stones and other gems to be mounted on the ephod
28: 9 "Take two **onyx** stones and engrave on them the names of the sons
28:20 in the fourth row a chrysolite, an **onyx** and a jasper. Mount them in
35: 9 and **onyx** stones and other gems to be mounted on the ephod
35:27 The leaders brought **onyx** stones and other gems to be mounted on
39: 6 They mounted the **onyx** stones in gold filigree settings
39:13 in the fourth row a chrysolite, an **onyx** and a jasper. They were
1Ch 29: 2 for the wood, as well as **onyx** [+74] for the settings, turquoise,
Job 28:16 be bought with the gold of Ophir, with precious **onyx** or sapphires.
Eze 28:13 chrysolite, **onyx** and jasper, sapphire, turquoise and beryl.

8733 שֹׁהַם šōham[2], n.pr.m. [1] [√ 8732]

Shoham [1]

1Ch 24:27 The sons of Merari: from Jaaziah: Beno, **Shoham**, Zaccur and Ibri.

8734 שַׁו šāw, n.[m.]. Not used in NIV/BHS [√ 8736]

8735 שׁוֹא šû', v. Not used in NIV/BHS [→ 5409, 8738, 8739; cf. 5957, 5958; 8615]

8736 שָׁוְא šāw', n.[m.]. [53] [→ 7417?, 8734]

false [15], in vain [+2021+4200] [4], worthless [4], in vain [3], lies [3], deceitful [2], falsehood [2], futility [2], misuse [+906+2021+4200+5951] [2], misuses [+906+2021+4200+5951] [2], deceit [1], destruction [1], empty plea [1], falsely [1], futile [1], idol [1], idols [1], lies [+1819] [1], meaningless [1], misuse [+2021+4200+5951] [1], nothing [1], worthless idols [+2039] [1], worthless idols [1], worthless things [1]

Ex 20: 7 "*You shall* not **misuse** [+906+2021+4200+5951] the name of the
20: 7 anyone guiltless who **misuses** [+906+2021+4200+5951] his name.
23: 1 "Do not spread **false** reports. Do not help a wicked man by being a
Dt 5:11 "*You shall* not **misuse** [+906+2021+4200+5951] the name of the
5:11 anyone guiltless *who* **misuses** [+906+2021+4200+5951] his name.
5:20 "You shall not give **false** testimony against your neighbor.
Job 7: 3 so I have been allotted months of **futility**, and nights of misery
11:11 Surely he recognizes **deceitful** men; and when he sees evil,
15:31 Let him not deceive himself by trusting what is **worthless**,
15:31 by trusting what is worthless, for he will get **nothing** in return.
31: 5 "If I have walked in **falsehood** or my foot has hurried after deceit—
35:13 Indeed, God does not listen to their **empty plea**; the Almighty pays
Ps 12: 2 [12:3] Everyone **lies** [+1819] to his neighbor; their flattering lips
24: 4 who does not lift up his soul to an **idol** or swear by what is false.
26: 4 I do not sit with **deceitful** men, nor do I consort with hypocrites;
31: 6 [31:7] I hate those who cling to **worthless idols** [+2039]; I trust in
41: 6 [41:7] see me, he speaks **falsely**, while his heart gathers slander;
60:11 [60:13] aid against the enemy, for the help of man is **worthless**.
89:47 [89:48] is my life. For what **futility** you have created all men!
108:12 [108:13] aid against the enemy, for the help of man is **worthless**.
119:37 Turn my eyes away from **worthless things**; preserve my life
127: 1 Unless the LORD builds the house, its builders labor **in vain**.
127: 1 LORD watches over the city, the watchmen stand guard **in vain**.
127: 2 **In vain** you rise early and stay up late, toiling for food to eat—
139:20 your adversaries **misuse** [+2021+4200+5951] your name.
144: 8 whose mouths are full of **lies**, whose right hands are deceitful.
144:11 me from the hands of foreigners whose mouths are full of **lies**,
Pr 30: 8 Keep **falsehood** and lies far from me; give me neither poverty nor
Isa 1:13 Stop bringing **meaningless** offerings! Your incense is detestable to
5:18 Woe to those who draw sin along with cords of **deceit**,
30:28 He shakes the nations in the sieve of **destruction**; he places in the
59: 4 They rely on empty arguments and speak **lies**; they conceive
Jer 2:30 "**In vain** [+2021+4200] I punished your people; they did not
4:30 You adorn yourself **in vain** [+2021+4200]. Your lovers despise
6:29 the lead with fire, but the refining goes on **in vain** [+2021+4200];
18:15 they burn incense to **worthless idols**, which made them stumble in
46:11 you multiply remedies **in vain** [+2021+4200]; there is no healing
La 2:14 The visions of your prophets were **false** and worthless; they did not
2:14 The oracles they gave you were **false** and misleading.
Eze 12:24 For there will be no more **false** visions or flattering divinations
13: 6 Their visions are **false** and their divinations a lie. They say,

Eze 13: 7 Have you not seen **false** visions and uttered lying divinations when
13: 8 Because of your **false** words and lying visions, I am against you,
13: 9 My hand will be against the prophets who see **false** visions
13: 23 therefore you will no longer see **false** visions or practice
21: 23 [21:28] It will seem like a **false** omen to those who have sworn
21: 29 [21:34] Despite **false** visions concerning you and lying
22: 28 Her prophets whitewash these deeds for them by **false** visions
Hos 10: 4 They make many promises, take **false** oaths and make agreements;
12: 11 [12:12] Is Gilead wicked? Its people are **worthless**! Do they
Jnh 2: 8 [2:9] "Those who cling to worthless **idols** forfeit the grace that
Zec 10: 2 that lie; they tell dreams that are **false**, they give comfort in vain.
Mal 3: 14 "You have said, 'It is **futile** to serve God. What did we gain by

8737 שָׁוְא **š[e]wā'**, n.pr.m. [2] [√ 8750; cf. 8857]

Sheva [2]

2Sa 20: 25 **Sheva** [K 8857] was secretary; Zadok and Abiathar were priests;
1Ch 2: 49 of Madmannah and to **Sheva** the father of Macbenah and Gibea.

8738 שׁוֹא **šô'**, n.[m.]. [1] [√ 8735]

ravages [1]

Ps 35: 17 Rescue my life from their **ravages**, my precious life from these

8739 שׁוֹאָה **šô'â**, n.f. [12] [√ 8735]

ruin [3], desolate [2], storm [2], catastrophe [1], destroyed [1], disaster [1], ruins [1], trouble [1]

Job 30: 3 they roamed the parched land in **desolate** wastelands at night.
30: 14 as through a gaping breach; amid the **ruins** they come rolling in.
38: 27 to satisfy a **desolate** wasteland and make it sprout with grass?
Ps 35: 8 may **ruin** overtake them by surprise—may the net they hid
35: 8 net they hid entangle them, may they fall into the pit, to their **ruin**.
63: 9 [63:10] They who seek my life will be **destroyed**; they will go
Pr 1: 27 when calamity overtakes you like a **storm**, [K 8618] when disaster
3: 25 no fear of sudden disaster or of the **ruin** that overtakes the wicked,
Isa 10: 3 you do on the day of reckoning, when **disaster** comes from afar?
47: 11 a **catastrophe** you cannot foresee will suddenly come upon you.
Eze 38: 9 and the many nations with you will go up, advancing like a **storm**;
Zep 1: 15 a day of distress and anguish, a day of **trouble** and ruin, a day of

8740 שׁוּב **šûb[1]**, v. [1054 / 1053] [→ 3793, 3795, 5411, 5412, 8743, 8744, 8745, 8746, 9588; Ar 10754; *also used with compound proper names*]

return [157], returned [99], turn [50], bring back [39], go back [37], again [34], restore [34], turn back [34], come back [23], brought back [21], went back [21], back [20], *untranslated* [16], turned [16], turn away [15], restored [14], turned away [13], put back [10], repent [10], turned back [10], give back [9], send back [9], repay [8], came back [7], take back [7], turns away [7], turns [7], recovered [6], returns [6], answer [5], bring [5], change [5], go [5], reported [+906+1821] [5], took back [5], answer [+906+1821] [4], be sure to take back [+8740] [4], ever return [+8740] [4], go [+2143+2256+4200] [4], pay back [4], refuse [4], relent [4], rewarded [4], take [4], turn away [+8740] [4], withdrew [4], answer [+1821] [3], bringing back [3], make return [3], regain [3], restores [3], returning [3], started back [3], stop [3], stopped [3], turned around [3], again and again [2], answered [+906+1821] [2], bring down [2], brought [2], by all means send [+8740] [2], come [2], coming back [2], give [2], keep [2], left [2], once more [2], oppose [2], pay [2], pays back [+906+4200+8740] [2], rebuilt [+906+1215+2256] [2], receded steadily [+2143+2256+8740] [2], reject [+7156] [2], repaid [2], repented [2], reply [2], repulse [+906+7156] [2], restrain [2], retreat [2], return [+906+8740] [2], revert [2], revoked [2], rewards [2], sent back [2], sent [2], surely return [+8740] [2], take back [+906+8740] [2], take vengeance [+5934] [2], takes back [+8740] [2], turn around [2], turning [2], withdraw [2], withholds [2], again [+9108] [1], again be used [1], again give allegiance [+4213] [1], another [1], answer [+1821+4200] [1], answer give [1], answered [+1821] [1], answered [1], answers [+1821] [1], arrived [1], back again [1], be brought back [1], been returned [1], break [1], bring in [1], broke off [+4946] [1], brought down [1], call to mind [+448+4213] [1], came again [1], carry the battle [+1741+2256] [1], caused to roam [1], changed mind [1], changed minds [1], changed [1], continually [1], cover up [+906+2256+4059] [1], depart [1], departs [1], did[s] [1], do[s] so [+2006+4946] [1], dole out [1], draw back [1], drew back [1], drives [1], escaping [1], flow back [1], flowed back [1], forced to restore [1], gave [1], get back [1], give up [+4946+4946] [1], gives back [1], go back [+345] [1], go on [1], going back [1], hold back [1], keep themselves alive [+5883] [1], keep themselves alive [+906+4392+5883] [1], keeps saying [+609] [1], lose [1], made go back [1], made pay for [+906+928+8031] [1], made prosperous again [+906+8669] [1], made retreat [+294] [1], make full restitution [+906+928+8031] [1], make go [1], make right [1], marauding [+2256+6296] [1], mislead [1], no longer [1], not angry [+678] [1], overruling [1], overthrows [+294] [1], paid [+868] [1], paid back [1], paid [1], pass again [1], passed [1], pay [+4084+4200] [1], pays back [1], penitent [1], prompt to answer [1], pull back [1], pursues [+928] [1], raised [1], ran [1], reappears [+2256+7255] [1], rebuild [+1215+2256] [1], recaptured [+906+2256+4374] [1], recoil [1], recoils [1], reconsider [+6388] [1], recover [1], reentered [+995+2256] [1], refreshes [1], refund [1], renew [1], renounce [+4946+6584+7156] [1], reopened [+906+2256+2916] [1], repay [+906+6584+8031] [1], repay [+906+928+8031] [1], repaying [1], repents [1], reply [+906+4863] [1], reported [+906+906+1821] [1], rescue [1], respond [1], responded [1], rest [1], restitution [+871] [1], restitution made [1], restore again [1], restorer [1], restrained [1], retire [1], retreats [1], return [+2143] [1], returned unanswered [+2668] [1], reverse [1], reversed [1], revived [+448+8120] [1], reviving [1], revoke [1], roll back [1], say [1], send [1], sending back [1], shy away [1], something else [1], stops to think [+448+4213] [1], strayed [1], subsides [1], supply [1], take away [1], taken back [1], try again [1], turn again [1], turned again [1], turned to go [1], turning away [1], vent [1], ward off [1], were brought back [1], withdrawn [+294] [1], withheld [1], withhold [1]

Ge 3: 19 [A] brow you will eat your food until you **return** to the ground,
3: 19 [A] were taken; for dust you are and to dust *you will* **return**."
8: 3 [A] water **receded** [+2143+2256+8740] **steadily** from the earth.
8: 3 [A] water **receded steadily** [+2143+2256+8740] from the earth.
8: 7 [A] it kept flying **back** and forth until the water had dried up
8: 9 [A] all the surface of the earth; so *it* **returned** to Noah in the ark.
8: 12 [A] the dove out again, but this time *it did* not **return** to him.
14: 7 [A] *they* **turned back** and went to En Mishpat (that is, Kadesh),
14: 16 [G] *He* **recovered** all the goods and brought back his relative Lot
14: 16 [G] **brought back** his relative Lot and his possessions, together
14: 17 [A] After Abram **returned** from defeating Kedorlaomer and the
15: 16 [A] In the fourth generation your descendants *will* **come back**
16: 9 [A] told her, "**Go back** to your mistress and submit to her."
18: 10 [A] "*I will* **surely return** [+8740] to you about this time next
18: 10 [A] "*I will* **surely return** [+8740] to you about this time next
18: 14 [A] *I will* **return** to you at the appointed time next year
18: 33 [A] with Abraham, he left, and Abraham **returned** home.
20: 7 [G] Now **return** the man's wife, for he is a prophet, and he will
20: 7 [G] if you *do* not **return** her, you may be sure that you and all
20: 14 [G] them to Abraham, and *he* **returned** Sarah his wife to him.
21: 32 [A] Phicol the commander of his forces **returned** to the land of
22: 5 [A] We will worship and then *we will* **come back** to you."
22: 19 [A] Abraham **returned** to his servants, and they set off together
24: 5 [G] *Shall I then* **take** your son **back** [+906+8740] to the country
24: 5 [G] *Shall I then* **take** your son **back** [+906+8740] to the country
24: 6 [G] "Make sure that *you do* not **take** my son **back** there,"
24: 8 [G] this oath of mine. Only *do* not **take** my son **back** there."
26: 18 [A] Isaac **reopened** [+906+2256+2916] the wells that had been
27: 44 [A] Stay with him for a while until your brother's fury **subsides**.
27: 45 [A] When your brother *is* **no longer** angry with you and forgets
28: 15 [G] you wherever you go, and *I will* **bring** you **back** to this land.
28: 21 [A] so that *I* **return** safely to my father's house,
29: 3 [G] *they would* **return** the stone to its place over the mouth of
30: 31 [A] *I will* **go on** tending your flocks and watching over them:
31: 3 [A] "**Go back** to the land of your fathers and to your relatives,
31: 13 [A] leave this land at once and **go back** to your native land.' "
31: 55 [32:1] [A] and blessed them. Then he left and **returned** home.
32: 6 [32:7] [A] When the messengers **returned** to Jacob, they said,
32: 9 [32:10] [A] to me, '**Go back** to your country and your relatives,
33: 16 [A] So that day Esau **started** on his way **back** to Seir.
37: 14 [G] and with the flocks, and **bring** word **back** *to* me."
37: 22 [G] this to rescue him from them and **take** him **back** to his father.
37: 29 [A] When Reuben **returned** to the cistern and saw that Joseph
37: 30 [A] *He* **went back** to his brothers and said, "The boy isn't there!
38: 22 [A] So *he* **went back** to Judah and said, "I didn't find her.
38: 29 [G] when *he* **drew back** his hand, his brother came out, and she
40: 13 [G] will lift up your head and **restore** you to your position,
40: 21 [G] *He* **restored** the chief cupbearer to his position, so that he
41: 13 [G] out exactly as he interpreted them to us: I *was* **restored**
42: 24 [A] to weep, but then **turned back** and spoke to them again.
42: 25 [G] to **put** each man's silver **back** in his sack, and to give them
42: 28 [H] "My silver *has* **been returned**," he said to his brothers.
42: 37 [G] to you. Entrust him to my care, and I *will* **bring** him **back**."
43: 2 [A] father said to them, "**Go back** and buy us a little more food."
43: 10 [A] had not delayed, *we could have* gone and **returned** twice."
43: 12 [G] for *you must* **return** the silver that was put back into the
43: 12 [H] for you must return the silver that *was* **put back** into the
43: 13 [A] Take your brother also and **go back** to the man at once.
43: 18 [A] because of the silver that *was* **put back** into our sacks the
43: 21 [G] the mouth of his sack. So *we have* **brought** it **back** with us.
44: 8 [G] *We* even **brought back** to you from the land of Canaan the

Ge 44:13 [A] Then they all loaded their donkeys and **returned** to the city.
44:25 [A] "Then our father said, '**Go back** and buy a little more food.'
48:21 [G] be with you and **take** you **back** to the land of your fathers.
50: 5 [A] Now let me go up and bury my father; then *I will* **return**.' "
50:14 [A] After burying his father, Joseph **returned** to Egypt, together
50:15 [G] and **pays** [+906+4200+8740] us **back** *for* all the wrongs we did
50:15 [G] **pays** us **back for** [+906+4200+8740] all the wrongs we did
Ex 4: 7 [G] "Now **put** it **back** into your cloak," he said. So Moses put his
4: 7 [G] So Moses **put** his hand **back** into his cloak, and when he
4: 7 [A] when he took it out, *it was* **restored**, like the rest of his flesh.
4:18 [A] Moses went **back** to Jethro his father-in-law and said to him,
4:18 [A] "Let me go **back** to my own people in Egypt to see if any of
4:19 [A] LORD had said to Moses in Midian, "Go **back** *to* Egypt,
4:20 [A] and sons, put them on a donkey and **started back** to Egypt.
4:21 [A] LORD said to Moses, "When you **return** [+2143] to Egypt,
5:22 [A] Moses **returned** to the LORD and said, "O Lord, why have
10: 8 [H] Then Moses and Aaron **were brought back** to Pharaoh. "Go,
13:17 [A] they might change their minds and **return** to Egypt."
14: 2 [A] "Tell the Israelites *to* **turn back** and encamp near Pi
14:26 [A] so that the waters *may* **flow back** over the Egyptians
14:27 [A] over the sea, and at daybreak the sea **went back** to its place.
14:28 [A] The water **flowed back** and covered the chariots
15:19 [G] the LORD **brought** the waters of the sea **back** over them,
19: 8 [G] So Moses **brought** their answer **back** to the LORD.
21:34 [G] of the pit must pay for the loss; *he must* **pay** [+4084+4200]
22:26 [22:25] [G] cloak as a pledge, **return** it to him by sunset,
23: 4 [G] wandering off, **be sure to take** it **back** [+8740] to him.
23: 4 [G] wandering off, **be sure to take** it **back** [+8740] to him.
24:14 [A] to the elders, "Wait here for us until *we* **come back** to you.
32:12 [A] **Turn** from your fierce anger; relent and do not bring disaster
32:27 [A] **Go back** and forth through the camp from one end to the
32:31 [A] So Moses **went back** to the LORD and said, "Oh, what a
33:11 [A] Moses *would* **return** to the camp, but his young aide Joshua
34:31 [A] and all the leaders of the community **came back** to him,
34:35 [G] Moses *would* **put** the veil **back** over his face until he went in
Lev 6: 4 [5:23] [G] *he must* **return** what he has stolen or taken by
13:16 [A] Should the raw flesh **change** and turn white, he must go to
14:39 [A] On the seventh day the priest *shall* **return** to inspect the
14:43 [A] "If the mildew **reappears** [+2256+7255] in the house after the
22:13 [A] and *she* **returns** to live in her father's house as in her youth,
25:10 [A] each one of *you is to* **return** to his family property and each
25:10 [A] to his family property and each to his own clan. **[RPH]**
25:13 [A] " 'In this Year of Jubilee everyone *is to* **return** to his own
25:27 [G] sold it and **refund** the balance to the man to whom he sold it;
25:27 [A] to whom he sold it; *he can* then **go back** to his own property.
25:28 [G] if he does not acquire the means *to* **repay** him, what he sold
25:28 [A] in the Jubilee, and *he can* then **go back** to his property.
25:41 [A] *he will* **go back** to his own clan and to the property of his
25:41 [A] his own clan and to the property of his forefathers. **[RPH]**
25:51 [G] *he must* **pay** *for* his redemption a larger share of the price
25:52 [G] is to compute that and **pay** *for* his redemption accordingly.
26:26 [G] in one oven, and *they will* **dole out** the bread by weight.
27:24 [A] In the Year of Jubilee the field *will* **revert** to the person from
Nu 5: 7 [G] *He must* **make full restitution** [+906+928+8031] *for* his wrong
5: 8 [G] relative to whom **restitution** *can be* **made** *for* the wrong,
5: 8 [H] the **restitution** [+871] belongs to the LORD and must be
8:25 [A] *they must* **retire** from their regular service and work no
10:36 [A] "**Return**, O LORD, *to* the countless thousands of Israel."
11: 4 [A] **again** the Israelites started wailing and said, "If only we had
13:25 [A] At the end of forty days *they* **returned** from exploring the
13:26 [G] There *they* **reported to** [+906+906+1821] them and to the
14: 3 [A] Wouldn't it be better for us *to* **go back** to Egypt?"
14: 4 [A] "We should choose a leader and **go back** to Egypt."
14:36 [A] *who* **returned** and made the whole community grumble
14:43 [A] Because *you have* **turned away** from the LORD, he will
16:50 [17:15] [A] Aaron **returned** to Moses at the entrance to the
17:10 [17:25] [G] "**Put back** Aaron's staff in front of the Testimony,
18: 9 [A] From all the gifts *they* **bring** me as most holy offerings,
22: 8 [G] "and *I will* **bring** you **back** the answer the LORD gives
22:34 [A] to oppose me. Now if you are displeased, *I will* **go back**."
23: 5 [A] and said, "**Go back** to Balak and give him this message."
23: 6 [A] So *he* **went back** to him and found him standing beside his
23:16 [A] and said, "**Go back** to Balak and give him this message."
23:20 [G] a command to bless; he has blessed, and *I* cannot **change** it.
24:25 [A] Balaam got up and **returned** home and Balak went his own
25: 4 [A] so that the LORD's fierce anger *may* **turn away** from
25:11 [G] the priest, *has* **turned** my anger **away** from the Israelites;
32:15 [A] If *you* **turn away** from following him, he will again leave all
32:18 [A] *We will* not **return** to our homes until every Israelite has
32:22 [A] *you may* **return** and be free from your obligation to the
33: 7 [A] They left Etham, **turned back** to Pi Hahiroth, to the east of
35:25 [G] and **send** him **back** to the city of refuge to which he fled.
35:28 [A] only after the death of the high priest *may* he **return** to his
35:32 [A] so *allow* him *to* **go back** and live on his own land before the
Dt 1:22 [G] **bring back** a report about the route we are to take and the
1:25 [G] they brought it down to us and **reported** [+906+1821],
1:45 [A] *You* **came back** and wept before the LORD, but he paid no
3:20 [A] each of you *may* **go back** to the possession I have given
4:30 [A] then in later days *you will* **return** to the LORD your God
4:39 [G] **take** to heart this day that the LORD is God in heaven
5:30 [A] "Go, tell them *to* **return** to their tents.
13:17 [13:18] [A] so that the LORD *will* **turn** from his fierce anger;
17:16 [G] or **make** the people **return** to Egypt to get more of them,
17:16 [A] has told you, "*You are* not to **go back** that way again."
20: 5 [A] *Let him* **go** [+2143+2256+4200] home, or he may die in
20: 6 [A] *Let him* **go** [+2143+2256+4200] home, or he may die in
20: 7 [A] *Let him* **go** [+2143+2256+4200] home, or he may die in
20: 8 [A] *Let him* **go** [+2143+2256+4200] home so that his brothers
22: 1 [G] do not ignore it but **be sure to take** it **back** [+8740] to him.
22: 1 [G] do not ignore it but **be sure to take** it **back** [+8740] to him.
22: 2 [G] it until he comes looking for it. Then **give** it **back** to him.
23:13 [23:14] [A] and **cover up** [+906+2256+4059] your excrement.
23:14 [23:15] [A] you anything indecent and **turn** away from you.
24: 4 [A] is not allowed to marry her **again** after she has been defiled.
24:13 [G] **Return** [+906+8740] his cloak to him by sunset so that he
24:13 [G] **Return** [+906+8740] his cloak to him by sunset so that he
24:19 [A] your field and you overlook a sheaf, *do* not **go back** to get it.
28:31 [A] will be forcibly taken from you and *will* not *be* **returned**.
28:60 [G] *He will* **bring** upon you all the diseases of Egypt that you
28:68 [G] The LORD *will* **send** you **back** in ships *to* Egypt on a
30: 1 [G] *you* **take** them to heart wherever the LORD your God
30: 2 [A] when you and your children **return** to the LORD your God
30: 3 [A] the LORD your God *will* **restore** your fortunes and have
30: 3 [A] gather you **again** from all the nations where he scattered you.
30: 8 [A] You will **again** obey the LORD and follow all his
30: 9 [A] The LORD will **again** delight in you and make you
30:10 [A] **turn** to the LORD your God with all your heart and with all
32:41 [G] hand grasps it in judgment, *I will* **take vengeance** [+5934]
32:43 [G] the blood of his servants; *he will* **take vengeance** [+5934]
Jos 1:15 [A] After that, *you may* **go back** and occupy your own land,
2:16 [A] Hide yourselves there three days until they **return**, and
2:22 [A] all along the road and **returned** without finding them.
2:23 [A] the two men **started back**. They went down out of the hills,
4:18 [A] ground than the waters of the Jordan **returned** to their place
5: 2 [A] flint knives and circumcise the Israelites **again** [+9108]."
6:14 [A] marched around the city once and **returned** *to* the camp.
7: 3 [A] When *they* **returned** to Joshua, they said, "Not all the people
7:26 [A] to this day. Then the LORD **turned** from his fierce anger.
8:21 [A] the city, *they* **turned around** and attacked the men of Ai.
8:24 [A] all the Israelites **returned** *to* Ai and killed those who were in
8:26 [G] For Joshua *did* not **draw back** the hand that held out his
10:15 [A] Then Joshua **returned** with all Israel to the camp at Gilgal.
10:21 [A] then **returned** safely to Joshua in the camp at Makkedah,
10:38 [A] Joshua and all Israel with him **turned around** and attacked
10:43 [A] Then Joshua **returned** with all Israel to the camp at Gilgal.
11:10 [A] At that time Joshua **turned back** and captured Hazor and put
14: 7 [G] *I* **brought** him **back** a report according to my convictions,
18: 8 [A] **return** to me, and I will cast lots for you here at Shiloh in the
19:12 [A] *It* **turned** east from Sarid toward the sunrise to the territory
19:27 [A] *It* then **turned** east *toward* Beth Dagon, touched Zebulun
19:29 [A] The boundary then **turned back** *toward* Ramah and went to
19:29 [A] **turned** *toward* Hosah and came out at the sea in the region
19:34 [A] The boundary **ran** west *through* Aznoth Tabor and came out
20: 6 [A] he *may* go **back** to his own home in the town from which he
22: 8 [A] saying, "**Return** to your homes with your great wealth—with
22: 9 [A] left the Israelites at Shiloh in Canaan to **return** to Gilead,
22:16 [A] How could you **turn away** from the LORD and build
22:18 [A] *are* you now **turning away** from the LORD? " 'If you rebel
22:23 [A] If we have built our own altar to **turn away** from the LORD
22:29 [A] **turn away** from him today by building an altar for burnt
22:32 [A] the leaders **returned** to Canaan from their meeting with the
22:32 [G] in Gilead and **reported to** [+906+1821] the Israelites.
23:12 [A] "But if *you* **turn** [+8740] **away** and ally yourselves with the
23:12 [A] "But if *you* **turn away** [+8740] and ally yourselves with the
24:20 [A] *he will* **turn** and bring disaster on you and make an end of
Jdg 2:19 [A] *the people* **returned** *to* ways even more corrupt than those
3:19 [A] At the idols near Gilgal *he* himself **turned back** and said,
5:29 [G] answer her; indeed, she **keeps saying** [+609] to herself,
6:18 [A] And the LORD said, "I will wait until you **return**."
7: 3 [A] 'Anyone who trembles with fear *may* **turn back** and leave
7: 3 [A] and leave Mount Gilead.' " So twenty-two thousand men **left**,
7:15 [A] *He* **returned** to the camp of Israel and called out, "Get up!
8: 9 [A] "When I **return** in triumph, I will tear down this tower."
8:13 [A] of Joash then **returned** from the battle by the Pass of Heres.
8:33 [A] No sooner had Gideon died than the Israelites **again**
9:56 [G] Thus God **repaid** the wickedness that Abimelech had done to
9:57 [G] **made** the men of Shechem **pay** [+906+928+8031] **for** all
11: 8 [A] said to him, "Nevertheless, *we are* **turning** to you now;

Jdg 11: 9 [G] "Suppose you **take** me **back** to fight the Ammonites
11:13 [G] all the way to the Jordan. Now **give** it **back** peaceably."
11:31 [A] **return** in triumph from the Ammonites will be the
11:35 [A] I have made a vow to the LORD that I cannot **break**."
11:39 [A] *she* **returned** to her father and he did to her as he had vowed.
14: 8 [A] Some time later, when *he* **went back** to marry her, he turned
15:19 [A] When Samson drank, his strength **returned** and he revived.
17: 3 [G] When *he* **returned** the eleven hundred shekels of silver to
17: 3 [G] a carved image and a cast idol. *I will* **give** it **back** to you."
17: 4 [G] So *he* **returned** the silver to his mother, and she took two
18:26 [A] were too strong for him, turned around and **went back** home.
19: 3 [G] her husband went to her to persuade her to **return**. He had
20:48 [A] The men of Israel **went back** to Benjamin and put all the
21:14 [A] So the Benjamites **returned** at that time and were given the
21:23 [A] Then *they* **returned** to their inheritance and rebuilt the towns
Ru 1: 6 [A] her daughters-in-law prepared *to* **return** home from there.
1: 7 [A] set out on the road that *would* **take** them **back** to the land of
1: 8 [A] "Go **back**, each of you, to your mother's home.
1:10 [A] and said to her, "*We will* **go back** with you to your people."
1:11 [A] Naomi said, "**Return** home, my daughters. Why would you
1:12 [A] **Return** home, my daughters; I am too old to have another
1:15 [A] "your sister-in-law *is* **going back** to her people and her gods.
1:15 [A] is going back to her people and her gods. **Go back** with her."
1:16 [A] "Don't urge me to leave you or to **turn back** from you.
1:21 [G] away full, but the LORD *has* **brought** me **back** empty.
1:22 [A] So Naomi **returned** from Moab accompanied by Ruth the
1:22 [A] **[RPH]** arriving in Bethlehem as the barley harvest was
2: 6 [A] "She is the Moabitess who **came back** from Moab with
4: 3 [A] "Naomi, who *has* **come back** from Moab,
4:15 [G] He will **renew** your life and sustain you in your old age.
1Sa 1:19 [A] the LORD and then went **back** to their home at Ramah.
3: 5 [A] Eli said, "I did not call; **go back** and lie down." So he went
3: 6 [A] "My son," Eli said, "I did not call; **go back** and lie down."
5: 3 [G] They took Dagon and **put** him **back** in his place.
5:11 [A] *let* it **go back** to its own place, or it will kill us and our
6: 3 [G] but **by all means send** [+8740] a guilt offering to him.
6: 3 [G] but **by all means send** [+8740] a guilt offering to him.
6: 4 [G] "What guilt offering *should we* **send** to him?"
6: 7 [G] cows to the cart, but **take** their calves **away** and pen them up.
6: 8 [G] gold objects *you are* **sending back** to him as a guilt offering.
6:16 [A] saw all this and then **returned** that same day *to* Ekron.
6:17 [G] These are the gold tumors the Philistines **sent** as a guilt
6:21 [G] "The Philistines *have* **returned** the ark of the LORD.
7: 3 [A] "If you *are* **returning** to the LORD with all your hearts,
7:14 [A] the Philistines had captured from Israel *were* **restored** to her,
9: 5 [A] said to the servant who was with him, "Come, *let's* **go back**,
12: 3 [G] my eyes? If I have done any of these, *I will* **make** it **right**."
14:27 [G] *He* **raised** his hand to his mouth, and his eyes brightened.
15:11 [A] because *he has* **turned** away from me and has not carried out
15:25 [A] Now I beg you, forgive my sin and **come back** with me,
15:26 [A] Samuel said to him, "*I will* not **go back** with you. You have
15:30 [A] **come back** with me, so that I may worship the LORD your
15:31 [A] So Samuel **went back** with Saul, and Saul worshiped the
17:15 [A] David went **back** and forth from Saul to tend his father's
17:30 [G] same matter, and the men **answered** [+1821] him as before.
17:53 [A] When the Israelites **returned** from chasing the Philistines,
17:57 [A] As soon as David **returned** from killing the Philistine, Abner
18: 2 [A] with him and did not let him **return** *to* his father's house.
18: 6 [A] When the men were returning home after David **[NIE]** had
23:23 [A] he uses and **come back** to me with definite information.
23:28 [A] Saul **broke** [+4946] **off** his pursuit of David and went to
24: 1 [24:2] [A] After Saul **returned** from pursuing the Philistines, he
25:12 [A] David's men turned around and **went back**. When they
25:21 [G] of his was missing. *He has* **paid** me **back** evil for good.
25:39 [G] *has* **brought** Nabal's wrongdoing **down** on his own head."
26:21 [A] Then Saul said, "I have sinned. **Come back**, David my son.
26:23 [G] The LORD **rewards** every man *for* his righteousness and
26:25 [A] So David went on his way, and Saul **returned** home.
27: 9 [A] and camels, and clothes. Then *he* **returned** to Achish.
29: 4 [G] were angry with him and said, "**Send** the man **back**,
29: 4 [A] man back, that *he may* **return** to the place you assigned him.
29: 7 [A] **Turn back** and go in peace; do nothing to displease the
29:11 [A] his men got up early in the morning to go **back** to the land of
30:12 [A] He ate and *was* **revived** [+448+8120], for he had not eaten
30:19 [G] else they had taken. David **brought** everything **back**.
2Sa 1: 1 [A] David **returned** from defeating the Amalekites and stayed in
1:22 [A] not turn back, the sword of Saul *did* not **return** unsatisfied.
2:26 [A] How long before you order your men to **stop** pursuing their
2:30 [A] Joab **returned** from pursuing Abner and assembled all his
3:11 [G] Ish-Bosheth did not dare to **say** another word *to* Abner,
3:16 [A] Then Abner said to him, "Go **back** home!" So he went back.
3:16 [A] Then Abner said to him, "Go back home!" So *he* **went back**.
3:26 [G] and *they* **brought** him **back** from the well of Sirah.
3:27 [A] Now when Abner **returned** *to* Hebron, Joab took him aside
6:20 [A] When David **returned** home to bless his household, Michal
8: 3 [G] when he went to **restore** his control along the Euphrates
8:13 [A] David became famous after he **returned** from striking down
9: 7 [G] *I will* **restore** to you all the land that belonged to your
10: 5 [A] at Jericho till your beards have grown, and then **come back**."
10:14 [A] So Joab **returned** from fighting the Ammonites and came to
11: 4 [A] herself from her uncleanness.) Then *she* **went back** home.
11:15 [A] **withdraw** from him so he will be struck down and die."
12:23 [G] Can I **bring** him **back** again? I will go to him, but he will not
12:23 [A] back again? I will go to him, but he *will* not **return** to me."
12:31 [A] Then David and his entire army **returned** *to* Jerusalem.
14:13 [G] for the king *has* not **brought back** his banished son?
14:21 [G] I will do it. Go, **bring back** the young man Absalom."
15: 8 [G] 'If the LORD **takes** me **back** [+8740] *to* Jerusalem, I will
15: 8 [A] 'If the LORD **takes** me **back to** [+8740] Jerusalem, I will
15:19 [A] **Go back** and stay with King Absalom. You are a foreigner,
15:20 [A] **Go back**, and take your countrymen. May kindness
15:20 [G] Go back, and **take** your countrymen. May kindness
15:25 [G] king said to Zadok, "**Take** the ark of God **back** *into* the city.
15:25 [G] *he will* **bring** me **back** and let me see it and his dwelling
15:27 [A] **Go back** *to* the city in peace, with your son Ahimaaz
15:29 [G] and Abiathar **took** the ark of God **back** *to* Jerusalem
15:34 [A] if *you* **return** *to* the city and say to Absalom, 'I will be your
16: 3 [G] 'Today the house of Israel *will* **give** me **back** my
16: 8 [G] The LORD *has* **repaid** you *for* all the blood you shed in the
16:12 [G] **repay** me *with* good for the cursing I am receiving today."
17: 3 [G] **bring** all the people **back** to you. The death of the man you
17: 3 [A] The death of the man you seek will mean the **return** *of* all;
17:20 [A] but found no one, so *they* **returned** *to* Jerusalem.
18:16 [A] and the troops **stopped** pursuing Israel, for Joab halted them.
19:10 [19:11] [G] do you say nothing about **bringing** the king **back**?"
19:11 [19:12] [G] 'Why should you be the last to **bring** the king **back**
19:12 [19:13] [G] why should you be the last to **bring back** the king?'
19:14 [19:15] [A] word to the king, "**Return**, you and all your men."
19:15 [19:16] [A] the king **returned** and went as far as the Jordan.
19:37 [19:38] [A] *Let* your servant **return**, that I may die in my own
19:39 [19:40] [A] his blessing, and Barzillai **returned** to his home.
19:43 [19:44] [G] Were we not the first to speak of **bringing back** our
20:22 [A] to his home. And Joab **went back** to the king in Jerusalem.
22:21 [G] according to the cleanness of my hands *he has* **rewarded**
22:25 [G] The LORD *has* **rewarded** me according to my
22:38 [A] crushed them; *I did* not **turn back** till they were destroyed.
23:10 [A] The troops **returned** to Eleazar, but only to strip the dead.
24:13 [G] decide how *I should* **answer** [+1821] the one who sent me."
1Ki 2:16 [G] of you. *Do* not **refuse** me." "You may make it," she said.
2:17 [G] "Please ask King Solomon—*he will* not **refuse** you—
2:20 [G] small request to make of you," she said. "*Do* not **refuse** me."
2:20 [G] king replied, "Make it, my mother; *I will* not **refuse** you."
2:30 [G] Benaiah **reported to** [+906+1821] the king, "This is how
2:32 [G] The LORD *will* **repay** [+906+6584+8031] him *for* the blood he
2:33 [A] *May* the guilt of their blood **rest** on the head of Joab and his
2:41 [A] Shimei had gone from Jerusalem to Gath and *had* **returned**,
2:44 [G] Now the LORD *will* **repay** [+906+928+8031] you *for* your
8:33 [A] when *they* **turn back** to you and confess your name, praying
8:34 [G] and **bring** them **back** to the land you gave to their fathers.
8:35 [A] confess your name and **turn** from their sin because you have
8:47 [G] if *they have a* **change** *of* heart in the land where they are
8:47 [A] and **repent** and plead with you in the land of their conquerors
8:48 [A] if *they* **turn back** to you with all their heart and soul in the
9: 6 [A] "But if you or your sons **turn** [+8740] **away** from me and do
9: 6 [A] "But if you or your sons **turn away** [+8740] from me and do
12: 2 [a] from King Solomon), he **returned** [BHS 3782] from Egypt.
12: 5 [A] "Go away for three days and then **come back** to me."
12: 6 [G] "How would you advise me to **answer** [+906+1821] these
12: 9 [G] How *should we* **answer** [+906+1821] these people who say
12:12 [A] as the king had said, "**Come back** to me in three days."
12:16 [G] to listen to them, they **answered** [+906+1821] the king:
12:20 [A] When all the Israelites heard that Jeroboam *had* **returned**,
12:21 [G] and to **regain** the kingdom for Rehoboam son of Solomon.
12:24 [A] **Go** home, every one of you, for this is my doing.' " So they
12:24 [A] they obeyed the word of the LORD and went home **again**,
12:26 [A] "The kingdom *will* now *likely* **revert** to the house of David.
12:27 [A] they *will* **again give** their **allegiance** [+4213] to their lord,
12:27 [A] of Judah. They will kill me and **return** to King Rehoboam."
13: 4 [G] the man shriveled up, so that he could not **pull** it **back**.
13: 6 [A] your God and pray for me that my hand *may be* **restored**."
13: 6 [A] the king's hand *was* **restored** and became as it was before.
13: 9 [A] eat bread or drink water or **return** by the way you came.' "
13:10 [A] and *did* not **return** by the way he had come to Bethel.
13:16 [A] "I cannot **turn back** and go with you, nor can I eat bread
13:17 [A] or drink water there or **return** by the way you came.' "
13:18 [G] '**Bring** him **back** with you to your house so that he may eat
13:19 [A] So the man of God **returned** with him and ate and drank in
13:20 [G] came to the old prophet who *had* **brought** him **back**.

1Ki 13:22 [A] *You* **came back** and ate bread and drank water in the place
13:23 [G] the prophet who *had* **brought** him **back** saddled his donkey
13:26 [G] When the prophet who *had* **brought** him **back** from his
13:29 [G] **brought** it **back** to his own city to mourn for him and bury
13:33 [A] Even after this, Jeroboam *did* not **change** his evil ways,
13:33 [A] **once more** appointed priests for the high places from all
14:28 [G] and afterward *they* **returned** them to the guardroom.
17:21 [A] "O LORD my God, *let* this boy's life **return** to him!"
17:22 [A] Elijah's cry, and the boy's life **returned** to him, and he lived.
18:43 [A] nothing there," he said. Seven times Elijah said, "**Go back**."
19: 6 [A] a jar of water. He ate and drank and then lay down **again**.
19: 7 [A] The angel of the LORD **came back** a second time
19:15 [A] The LORD said to him, "Go **back** the way you came,
19:20 [A] "and then I will come with you." "Go **back**," Elijah replied.
19:21 [A] So Elisha left him and **went back**. He took his yoke of oxen
20: 5 [A] The messengers **came again** and said, "This is what
20: 9 [G] meet.' " They left and **took** the answer **back** *to* Ben-Hadad.
20:34 [G] "*I will* **return** the cities my father took from your father,"
22:17 [A] people have no master. *Let* each one **go** home in peace.' "
22:26 [G] and **send** him **back** to Amon the ruler of the city
22:28 [A] Micaiah declared, "If *you* **ever return** [+8740] safely,
22:28 [A] Micaiah declared, "If *you* **ever return** [+8740] safely,
22:33 [A] that he was not the king of Israel and **stopped** pursuing him.
2Ki 1: 5 [A] When the messengers **returned** to the king, he asked them,
1: 5 [A] to the king, he asked them, "Why *have you* **come back**?"
1: 6 [A] he said to us, 'Go **back** to the king who sent you and tell him,
1:11 [A] At this the king **[NIE]** sent to Elijah another captain with his
1:13 [A] So the king **[NIE]** sent a third captain with his fifty men.
2:13 [A] and **went back** and stood on the bank of the Jordan.
2:18 [A] When *they* **returned** to Elisha, who was staying in Jericho,
2:25 [A] on to Mount Carmel and from there **returned** *to* Samaria.
3: 4 [G] *he had to* **supply** the king of Israel *with* a hundred thousand
3:27 [A] was great; they withdrew and **returned** to their own land.
4:22 [A] a donkey so I can go to the man of God quickly and **return**."
4:31 [A] So Gehazi **went back** to meet Elisha and told him, "The boy
4:35 [A] Elisha **turned away** and walked back and forth in the room
4:38 [A] Elisha **returned** to Gilgal and there was a famine in that
5:10 [A] and your flesh *will be* **restored** and you will be cleansed."
5:14 [A] his flesh *was* **restored** and became clean like that of a young
5:15 [A] and all his attendants **went back** to the man of God.
7: 8 [A] *They* **returned** and entered another tent and took some
7:15 [A] So the messengers **returned** and reported to the king.
8: 3 [A] At the end of the seven years she **came back** from the land of
8: 6 [G] "**Give back** everything that belonged to her, including all the
8:29 [A] so King Joram **returned** to Jezreel to recover from the
9:15 [A] King Joram *had* **returned** to Jezreel to recover from the
9:18 [A] messenger has reached them, but *he* isn't **coming back**."
9:20 [A] "He has reached them, but *he* isn't **coming back** either.
9:36 [A] *They* **went back** and told Jehu, who said, "This is the word
13:25 [A] Jehoash son of Jehoahaz **recaptured** [+906+2256+4374] from
13:25 [G] defeated him, and so *he* **recovered** the Israelite towns.
14:14 [A] royal palace. He also took hostages and **returned** to Samaria.
14:22 [G] **restored** it to Judah after Amaziah rested with his fathers.
14:25 [G] He was the *one who* **restored** the boundaries of Israel from
14:28 [G] including how *he* **recovered** for Israel both Damascus and
15:20 [A] So the king of Assyria **withdrew** and stayed in the land no
16: 6 [G] Rezin king of Aram **recovered** Elath for Aram by driving out
17: 3 [G] had been Shalmaneser's vassal and *had* **paid** him tribute.
17:13 [A] all his prophets and seers: "**Turn** from your evil ways.
18:14 [A] **Withdraw** from me, and I will pay whatever you demand of
18:24 [G] How *can you* **repulse** [+906+7156] one officer of the least
19: 7 [A] *he will* **return** to his own country, and there I will have him
19: 8 [A] *he* **withdrew** and found the king fighting against Libnah.
19: 9 [A] So *he* **again** sent messengers to Hezekiah with this word:
19:28 [G] and *I will* **make** you **return** by the way you came.'
19:33 [A] By the way that he came *he will* **return**; he will not enter this
19:36 [A] and withdrew. *He* **returned** to Nineveh and stayed there.
20: 5 [A] "**Go back** and tell Hezekiah, the leader of my people, 'This is
20: 9 [A] shadow go forward ten steps, or *shall it* **go back** ten steps?"
20:10 [A] said Hezekiah. "Rather, *have* it **go back** [+345] ten steps."
20:11 [G] the LORD **made** the shadow **go back** the ten steps it had
21: 3 [A] *He* **rebuilt** [+906+1215+2256] the high places his father
22: 9 [G] secretary went to the king and **reported to** [+906+1821] him:
22:20 [G] on this place.' " So *they* **took** her answer **back** *to* the king.
23:20 [A] human bones on them. Then *he* **went back** *to* Jerusalem.
23:25 [A] there a king like him who **turned** to the LORD as he did—
23:26 [A] the LORD *did* not **turn away** from the heat of his fierce
24: 1 [A] then *he* **changed** *his* **mind** and rebelled against
1Ch 19: 5 [A] at Jericho till your beards have grown, and then **come back**."
20: 3 [A] Then David and his entire army **returned** *to* Jerusalem.
21:12 [G] decide how *I should* **answer** [+906+1821] the one who sent
21:20 [A] Araunah was threshing wheat, he **turned** and saw the angel;
21:27 [G] spoke to the angel, and *he* **put** his sword **back** into its sheath.
2Ch 6:23 [G] **repaying** the guilty by bringing down on his own head what
6:24 [A] and when *they* **turn back** and confess your name,
6:25 [G] **bring** them **back** to the land you gave to them and their
6:26 [A] confess your name and **turn** from their sin because you have
6:37 [G] if *they have a* **change** *of* heart in the land where they are
6:37 [A] and **repent** and plead with you in the land of their captivity
6:38 [A] if *they* **turn back** to you with all their heart and soul in the
6:42 [G] O LORD God, *do* not **reject** [+7156] your anointed one.
7:14 [A] and pray and seek my face and **turn** from their wicked ways,
7:19 [A] "But if you **turn away** and forsake the decrees
10: 2 [A] he had fled from King Solomon), he **returned** from Egypt.
10: 5 [A] Rehoboam answered, "**Come back** to me in three days."
10: 6 [G] "How would you advise me to **answer** [+1821+4200] these
10: 9 [G] How *should we* **answer** [+906+1821] these people who say
10:12 [A] as the king had said, "**Come back** to me in three days."
10:16 [G] the king refused to listen to them, they **answered** the king:
11: 1 [G] war against Israel and to **regain** the kingdom for Rehoboam.
11: 4 [A] **Go** home, every one of you, for this is my doing.' " So they
11: 4 [A] and **turned back** from marching against Jeroboam.
12:11 [G] and afterward *they* **returned** them to the guardroom.
12:12 [A] the LORD's anger **turned** from him, and he was not totally
14:15 [14:14] [A] and camels. Then *they* **returned** *to* Jerusalem.
15: 4 [A] in their distress *they* **turned** to the LORD, the God of
18:16 [A] people have no master. *Let* each one **go** home in peace.' "
18:25 [G] and **send** him **back** to Amon the ruler of the city
18:26 [A] him nothing but bread and water until I **return** safely.' "
18:27 [A] Micaiah declared, "If *you* **ever return** [+8740] safely,
18:27 [A] Micaiah declared, "If *you* **ever return** [+8740] safely,
18:32 [A] he was not the king of Israel, *they* **stopped** pursuing him.
19: 1 [A] When Jehoshaphat king of Judah **returned** safely to his
19: 4 [A] he went out **again** among the people from Beersheba to the
19: 4 [G] country of Ephraim and **turned** them **back** to the LORD,
19: 8 [a] And *they* lived [BHS *returned to*; NIV 3782] **in** Jerusalem.
20:27 [A] men of Judah and Jerusalem **returned** joyfully to Jerusalem,
20:27 [A] and Jerusalem returned joyfully **[RPH]** to Jerusalem,
22: 6 [A] so *he* **returned** to Jezreel to recover from the wounds they
24:11 [G] and empty the chest and carry it **back** to its place.
24:19 [G] sent prophets to the people to **bring** them **back** to him,
25:10 [A] were furious with Judah and **left** for home in a great rage.
25:13 [G] Meanwhile the troops that Amaziah *had* **sent back** and had
25:24 [A] palace treasures and the hostages, and **returned** *to* Samaria.
26: 2 [G] **restored** it to Judah after Amaziah rested with his fathers.
27: 5 [G] The Ammonites **brought** him the same amount also in the
28:11 [G] **Send back** your fellow countrymen you have taken as
28:15 [A] at Jericho, the City of Palms, and **returned** *to* Samaria.
29:10 [A] of Israel, so that his fierce anger *will* **turn away** from us.
30: 6 [A] "People of Israel, **return** to the LORD, the God of
30: 6 [A] Isaac and Israel, that *he may* **return** to you who are left,
30: 8 [A] your God, so that his fierce anger *will* **turn away** from you.
30: 9 [A] If you **return** to the LORD, then your brothers and your
30: 9 [A] compassion by their captors and *will* **come back** to this land,
30: 9 [A] He will not turn his face from you if *you* **return** to him."
31: 1 [A] the Israelites **returned** to their own towns and to their own
32:21 [A] So *he* **withdrew** to his own land in disgrace. And when he
32:25 [G] and he *did* not **respond** to the kindness shown him;
33: 3 [A] *He* **rebuilt** [+906+1215+2256] the high places his father
33:13 [G] so *he* **brought** him **back** *to* Jerusalem and to his kingdom.
34: 7 [A] altars throughout Israel. Then *he* **went back** to Jerusalem.
34: 9 [a] [Benjamin and the **inhabitants** [Q; see K 3782] *of* Jerusalem.]
34:16 [G] took the book to the king and **reported to** [+906+1821] him:
34:28 [G] on those who live here.' " So *they* **took** her answer **back** *to*
36:13 [A] and hardened his heart and *would* not **turn** to the LORD,
Ezr 2: 1 [A] had taken captive to Babylon (*they* **returned** to Jerusalem
6:21 [A] So the Israelites who *had* **returned** from the exile ate it,
9:14 [A] *Shall we* **again** break your commands and intermarry with
10:14 [G] anger of our God in this matter *is* **turned away** from us."
Ne 1: 9 [A] if *you* **return** to me and obey my commands, then even if
2: 6 [A] long will your journey take, and when *will you* **get back**?"
2:15 [A] *I* **turned back** and reentered through the Valley Gate.
2:15 [A] and **reentered** [+995+2256] through the Valley Gate.
2:20 [G] *I* **answered** [+906+1821] them by saying, "The God of
4: 4 [3:36] [G] **Turn** their insults **back** on their own heads.
4:12 [4:6] [A] times over, "Wherever *you* **turn**, they will attack us."
4:15 [4:9] [A] we all **returned** to the wall, each to his own work.
5:11 [G] **Give back** to them immediately their fields, vineyards, olive
5:12 [G] "*We will* **give** it **back**," they said. "And we will not demand
6: 4 [G] same message, and each time *I* **gave** them the same answer.
7: 6 [A] of Babylon had taken captive (*they* **returned** to Jerusalem
8:17 [A] The whole company that *had* **returned** from exile built
9:17 [A] in their rebellion appointed a leader in order to **return** to
9:26 [G] who had admonished them in order to **turn** them **back** to
9:28 [A] they were at rest, *they* **again** did what was evil in your sight.
9:28 [A] when they cried out to you **again**, you heard from heaven,
9:29 [G] "You warned them to **return** to your law, but they became
9:35 [A] they did not serve you or **turn** from their evil ways.

Ne 13: 9 [G] *I* **put back** *into* them the equipment of the house of God,
Est 2: 14 [A] in the morning **return** to another part of the harem to the
4: 13 [G] he **sent back** this answer: "Do not think that because you are
4: 15 [G] Then Esther **sent** this reply to Mordecai:
6: 12 [A] Afterward Mordecai **returned** to the king's gate. But Haman
7: 8 [A] Just as the king **returned** from the palace garden to the
8: 5 [G] let an order be written **overruling** the dispatches that Haman
8: 8 [G] in the king's name and sealed with his ring *can be* **revoked**."
9: 25 [A] against the Jews *should* **come back** onto his own head,
Job 1: 21 [A] I came from my mother's womb, and naked *I will* **depart**.
6: 29 [A] **Relent**, do not be unjust; reconsider, for my integrity is at
6: 29 [A] be unjust; **reconsider** [+6388], for my integrity is at stake.
7: 7 [A] life is but a breath; my eyes will never see happiness **again**.
7: 10 [A] *He will* never **come** to his house again; his place will know
9: 12 [G] If he snatches away, who *can* **stop** him? Who can say to him,
9: 13 [G] God *does* not **restrain** his anger; even the cohorts of Rahab
9: 18 [G] He would not let me **regain** my breath but would overwhelm
10: 9 [G] molded me like clay. *Will you* now **turn** me to dust **again**?
10: 16 [A] a lion and **again** display your awesome power against me.
10: 21 [A] before I go to the place of no **return**, to the land of gloom
11: 10 [G] you in prison and convenes a court, who *can* **oppose** him?
13: 22 [G] and I will answer, or let me speak, and *you* **reply**.
14: 13 [A] me in the grave and conceal me till your anger *has* **passed**!
15: 13 [G] so that *you* **vent** your rage against God and pour out such
15: 22 [A] He despairs of **escaping** the darkness; he is marked for the
16: 22 [A] a few years will pass before I go on the journey of no **return**.
17: 10 [A] "But come on, all of you, **try again**! I will not find a wise
20: 2 [G] "My troubled thoughts **prompt** me **to answer** because I am
20: 10 [G] to the poor; his own hands *must* **give back** his wealth.
20: 18 [G] What he toiled for *he must* **give back** uneaten; he will not
22: 23 [A] If *you* **return** to the Almighty, you will be restored: If you
23: 13 [G] "But he stands alone, and who *can* **oppose** him? He does
30: 23 [G] I know *you will* **bring** me **down** *to* death, to the place
31: 14 [G] confronts me? What *will I* **answer** when called to account?
32: 14 [G] against me, and *I will* not **answer** him with your arguments.
33: 5 [G] **Answer** me then, if you can; prepare yourself and confront
33: 25 [A] like a child's; *it is* **restored** as in the days of his youth.
33: 26 [G] shouts for joy; he *is* **restored** by God *to* his righteous state.
33: 30 [G] to **turn back** his soul from the pit, that the light of life may
33: 32 [G] If you have anything to say, **answer** me; speak up, for I want
34: 15 [A] would perish together and man *would* **return** to the dust.
35: 4 [G] "I *would like to* **reply** [+906+4863] *to* you and to your
36: 10 [A] to correction and commands them *to* **repent** of their evil.
39: 4 [A] and grow strong in the wilds; they leave and *do* not **return**.
39: 12 [G] Can you trust him *to* **bring in** your grain and gather it to your
39: 22 [A] afraid of nothing; *he does* not **shy away** from the sword.
40: 4 [G] "I am unworthy—how *can I* **reply** *to* you? I put my hand
42: 10 [A] the LORD **made** him **prosperous** [+906+8669] **again** and gave
Ps 6: 4 [6:5] [A] **Turn**, O LORD, and deliver me; save me because of
6: 10 [6:11] [A] *they will* **turn back** in sudden disgrace.
7: 7 [7:8] [a] Rule [BHS *Return*; NIV 3782] over them from on high;
7: 12 [7:13] [A] If *he does* not **relent**, he will sharpen his sword;
7: 16 [7:17] [A] The trouble he causes **recoils** on himself; his violence
9: 3 [9:4] [A] My enemies **turn** back; they stumble and perish before
9: 17 [9:18] [A] The wicked **return** to the grave, all the nations that
14: 7 [A] When the LORD **restores** the fortunes of his people,
18: 20 [18:21] [G] to the cleanness of my hands *he has* **rewarded** me.
18: 24 [18:25] [G] The LORD *has* **rewarded** me according to my
18: 37 [18:38] [A] *I did* not **turn back** till they were destroyed.
19: 7 [19:8] [G] The law of the LORD is perfect, **reviving** the soul.
22: 27 [22:28] [A] of the earth will remember and **turn** to the LORD,
23: 3 [D] *he* **restores** my soul. He guides me in paths of righteousness
28: 4 [G] have done and **bring back** upon them what they deserve.
35: 13 [A] When my prayers **returned** [+2668] to me **unanswered**,
35: 17 [G] **Rescue** my life from their ravages, my precious life from
44: 10 [44:11] [G] *You* **made** us **retreat** [+294] before the enemy,
51: 12 [51:14] [G] **Restore** to me the joy of your salvation and grant
51: 13 [51:15] [A] your ways, and sinners *will* **turn back** to you.
53: 6 [53:7] [A] When God **restores** the fortunes of his people,
54: 5 [54:7] [G] *Let* evil **recoil** on those who slander me; in your
56: 9 [56:10] [A] my enemies *will* **turn** back when I call for help.
59: 6 [59:7] [A] *They* **return** at evening, snarling like dogs,
59: 14 [59:15] [A] *They* **return** at evening, snarling like dogs,
60: T [60:2] [A] *when* Joab **returned** and struck down twelve
60: 1 [60:3] [D] upon us; you have been angry—now **restore** us!
68: 22 [68:23] [G] The Lord says, "*I will* **bring** them from Bashan;
68: 22 [68:23] [G] *I will* **bring** them from the depths of the sea,
69: 4 [69:5] [G] *I am* **forced to restore** what I did not steal.
70: 3 [70:4] [A] *May* those who say to me, "Aha! Aha!" **turn back**
71: 20 [A] see troubles, many and bitter, you will restore my life **again**;
71: 20 [A] from the depths of the earth *you will* **again** bring me up.
72: 10 [G] of Tarshish and of distant shores *will* **bring** tribute to him;
73: 10 [A] Therefore their people **turn** to them and drink up waters in
74: 11 [G] Why *do you* **hold back** your hand, your right hand? Take it
74: 21 [A] *Do* not *let* the oppressed **retreat** in disgrace; may the poor
78: 34 [A] they would seek him; *they* eagerly **turned** *to* him **again**.
78: 38 [G] Time after time he **restrained** his anger and did not stir up
78: 39 [A] they were but flesh, a passing breeze *that does* not **return**.
78: 41 [A] **Again and again** they put God to the test; they vexed the
79: 12 [G] **Pay back** into the laps of our neighbors seven times the
80: 3 [80:4] [G] **Restore** us, O God; make your face shine upon us,
80: 7 [80:8] [G] **Restore** us, O God Almighty; make your face shine
80: 14 [80:15] [A] **Return** to us, O God Almighty! Look down from
80: 19 [80:20] [G] **Restore** us, O LORD God Almighty; make your
81: 14 [81:15] [G] their enemies and **turn** my hand against their foes!
85: 1 [85:2] [A] O LORD; *you* **restored** the fortunes of Jacob.
85: 3 [85:4] [G] all your wrath and **turned** from your fierce anger.
85: 4 [85:5] [A] **Restore** us **again**, O God our Savior, and put away
85: 6 [85:7] [A] Will you not revive us **again**, that your people may
85: 8 [85:9] [A] his saints—but *let them* not **return** to folly.
89: 43 [89:44] [G] *You have* **turned back** the edge of his sword
90: 3 [G] *You* **turn** men **back** to dust, saying, "Return to dust, O sons
90: 3 [A] men back to dust, saying, "**Return** to dust, O sons of men."
90: 13 [A] **Relent**, O LORD! How long will it be? Have compassion
94: 2 [G] Judge of the earth; **pay back** to the proud what they deserve.
94: 15 [A] Judgment *will* **again** be founded on righteousness, and all the
94: 23 [G] *He will* **repay** them *for* their sins and destroy them for their
104: 9 [A] they cannot cross; never **again** will they cover the earth.
104: 29 [A] you take away their breath, they die and **return** to the dust.
106: 23 [G] stood in the breach before him to **keep** his wrath from
116: 7 [A] *Be* at rest **once more**, O my soul, for the LORD has been
116: 12 [G] How *can I* **repay** the LORD *for* all his goodness to me?
119: 59 [G] my ways and *have* **turned** my steps to your statutes.
119: 79 [A] *May* those who fear you **turn** to me, those who understand
126: 1 [A] When the LORD **brought back** the captives *to* Zion,
126: 4 [A] **Restore** our fortunes, O LORD, like streams in the Negev.
132: 10 [G] David your servant, *do* not **reject** [+7156] your anointed one.
132: 11 [A] swore an oath to David, a sure oath that *he will* not **revoke**:
146: 4 [A] When their spirit departs, *they* **return** to the ground; on that
Pr 1: 23 [A] If *you had* **responded** to my rebuke, I would have poured
2: 19 [A] None who go to her **return** or attain the paths of life.
3: 28 [A] Do not say to your neighbor, "Come **back** later; I'll give it
12: 14 [G] good things as surely as the work of his hands **rewards** him.
15: 1 [G] A gentle answer **turns away** wrath, but a harsh word stirs up
17: 13 [G] If a *man* **pays back** evil for good, evil will never leave his
18: 13 [G] *He who* **answers** [+1821] before listening—that is his folly
19: 24 [G] hand in the dish; *he will* not even **bring** it **back** to his mouth!
20: 26 [G] out the wicked; *he* **drives** the threshing wheel over them.
22: 21 [G] so that *you can* **give** sound answers to him who sent you?
24: 12 [G] *Will he* not **repay** each person according to what he has
24: 18 [G] will see and disapprove and **turn** his wrath **away** from him.
24: 26 [G] An honest **answer** [+1821] is like a kiss on the lips.
24: 29 [G] he has done to me; *I'll* **pay** that man **back** *for* what he did."
25: 10 [A] may shame you and *you will* never **lose** your bad reputation.
25: 13 [G] to those who send him; *he* **refreshes** the spirit of his masters.
26: 11 [A] As a dog **returns** to its vomit, so a fool repeats his folly.
26: 15 [G] hand in the dish; he is too lazy to **bring** it **back** to his mouth.
26: 16 [G] in his own eyes than seven *men who* **answer** discreetly.
26: 27 [A] fall into it; if a man rolls a stone, *it will* **roll back** on him.
27: 11 [G] *I can* **answer** [+1821] anyone who treats me with contempt.
29: 8 [G] Mockers stir up a city, but wise men **turn away** anger.
30: 30 [A] a lion, mighty among beasts, *who* **retreats** before nothing;
Ecc 1: 6 [A] round and round it goes, *ever* **returning** on its course.
1: 7 [A] To the place the streams come from, there they return **again**.
3: 20 [A] to the same place; all come from dust, and to dust all **return**.
4: 1 [A] **Again** I looked and saw all the oppression that was taking
4: 7 [A] **Again** I saw something meaningless under the sun:
5: 15 [5:14] [A] his mother's womb, and as he comes, so *he* **departs**.
9: 11 [A] I have seen **something else** under the sun: The race is not to
12: 2 [A] and the stars grow dark, and the clouds **return** after the rain;
12: 7 [A] the dust **returns** to the ground it came from, and the spirit
12: 7 [A] it came from, and the spirit **returns** to God who gave it.
SS 6: 13 [7:1] [A] **Come back**, come back, O Shulammite; come back,
6: 13 [7:1] [A] Come back, **come back**, O Shulammite; come back,
6: 13 [7:1] [A] **come back**, come back, that we may gaze on you!
6: 13 [7:1] [A] come back, **come back**, that we may gaze on you!
Isa 1: 25 [G] *I will* **turn** my hand against you; I will thoroughly purge
1: 26 [G] *I will* **restore** your judges as in days of old, your counselors
1: 27 [A] redeemed with justice, her **penitent** *ones* with righteousness.
5: 25 [A] Yet for all this, his anger *is* not **turned away**, his hand is still
6: 10 [A] understand with their hearts, and **turn** and be healed."
6: 13 [A] a tenth remains in the land, *it will* **again** be laid waste.
9: 12 [9:11] [A] Yet for all this, his anger *is* not **turned away**, his
9: 13 [9:12] [A] the people *have* not **returned** to him who struck
9: 17 [9:16] [A] Yet for all this, his anger *is* not **turned away**, his
9: 21 [9:20] [A] Yet for all this, his anger *is* not **turned away**, his
10: 4 [A] Yet for all this, his anger *is* not **turned away**, his hand is still
10: 21 [A] A remnant *will* **return**, a remnant of Jacob will return to the

Isa 10:22 [A] be like the sand by the sea, only a remnant *will* **return**.
12: 1 [A] your anger *has* **turned away** and you have comforted me.
14:27 [G] His hand is stretched out, and who *can* **turn** it **back**?
19:22 [A] *They will* **turn** to the LORD, and he will respond to their
21:12 [A] If you would ask, then ask; and come **back** yet **again**."
23:17 [A] *She will* **return** to her hire as a prostitute and will ply her
28: 6 [G] a source of strength to *those who* **turn back** the battle at the
29:17 [A] *will* not Lebanon *be* **turned** into a fertile field and the fertile
31: 6 [A] **Return** to him you have so greatly revolted against,
35:10 [A] the ransomed of the LORD *will* **return**. They will enter
36: 9 [G] *can you* **repulse** [+906+7156] one officer of the least of my
37: 7 [A] he hears a certain report, *he will* **return** to his own country,
37: 8 [A] *he* **withdrew** and found the king fighting against Libnah.
37:29 [G] and *I will* **make** you **return** by the way you came.
37:34 [A] By the way that he came *he will* **return**; he will not enter this
37:37 [A] and withdrew. *He* **returned** to Nineveh and stayed there.
38: 8 [G] I *will* **make** the shadow cast by the sun **go** back the ten steps
38: 8 [A] So the sunlight **went back** the ten steps it had gone down.
41:28 [G] to give counsel, no *one to* **give** answer when I ask them.
42:22 [G] have been made loot, with no one to say, "**Send** them **back**."
43:13 [G] can deliver out of my hand. When I act, who *can* **reverse** it?"
44:19 [G] No one **stops to think** [+448+4213], no one has the
44:22 [A] the morning mist. **Return** to me, for I have redeemed you."
44:25 [G] *who* **overthrows** [+294] the learning of the wise and turns it
45:23 [A] has uttered in all integrity a word *that will* not *be* **revoked**:
46: 8 [G] "Remember this, fix it in mind, **take** it to heart, *you* rebels.
47:10 [A] and knowledge **mislead** you when you say to yourself,
49: 5 [D] me in the womb to be his servant to **bring** Jacob **back** to him
49: 6 [G] tribes of Jacob and **bring back** those of Israel I have kept.
51:11 [A] The ransomed of the LORD *will* **return**. They will enter
52: 8 [A] When the LORD **returns** *to* Zion, they will see it with their
55: 7 [A] *Let him* **turn** to the LORD, and he will have mercy on him,
55:10 [A] *do* not **return** to it without watering the earth and making it
55:11 [A] *It will* not **return** to me empty, but will accomplish what I
58:12 [D] of Broken Walls, **Restorer** *of* Streets with Dwellings.
58:13 [G] "If *you* **keep** your feet from breaking the Sabbath and from
59:20 [A] to *those* in Jacob *who* **repent** *of* their sins,"
63:17 [A] **Return** for the sake of your servants, the tribes that are your
66:15 [G] *he will* **bring down** his anger with fury, and his rebuke with
Jer 2:24 [G] the wind in her craving—in her heat who *can* **restrain** her?
2:35 [A] you say, 'I am innocent; he *is* **not angry** [+678] with me.'
3: 1 [A] and marries another man, *should he* **return** to her again?
3: 1 [A] with many lovers—*would* you now **return** to me?"
3: 7 [A] I thought that after she had done all this *she would* **return** to
3: 7 [A] she had done all this she would return to me but *she* **did**[s] not,
3:10 [A] her unfaithful sister Judah *did* not **return** to me with all her
3:12 [A] " '**Return**, faithless Israel,' declares the LORD, 'I will frown
3:14 [A] "**Return**, faithless people," declares the LORD, "for I am
3:19 [A] call me 'Father' and not **turn away** from following me.
3:22 [A] "**Return**, faithless people; I will cure you of backsliding."
4: 1 [A] "If *you will* **return**, O Israel, return to me,"
4: 1 [A] "If you will return, O Israel, **return** to me,"
4: 8 [A] for the fierce anger of the LORD *has* not **turned away** from
4:28 [A] and will not relent, I have decided and *will* not **turn back**."
5: 3 [A] made their faces harder than stone and refused to **repent**.
6: 9 [G] **pass** your hand over the branches **again**, like one gathering
8: 4 [A] not get up? When *a man* **turns away**, does he not return?
8: 4 [A] not get up? When a man turns away, *does he* not **return**?
8: 5 [D] Why then *have* these people **turned away**? Why does
8: 5 [A] turn away? They cling to deceit; they refuse to **return**.
8: 6 [A] Each **pursues** [+928] his own course like a horse charging
11:10 [A] *They have* **returned** to the sins of their forefathers, who
12:15 [A] *I will* **again** have compassion and will bring each of them
12:15 [G] *will* **bring** each of them **back** to his own inheritance and his
14: 3 [A] *They* **return** with their jars unfilled; dismayed
15: 7 [A] on my people, for *they have* not **changed** their ways.
15:19 [A] "If *you* **repent**, I will restore you that you may serve me; if
15:19 [G] "If you repent, *I will* **restore** you that you may serve me; if
15:19 [A] *Let* this people **turn** to you, but you must not turn to them.
15:19 [A] Let this people turn to you, but you *must* not **turn** to them.
16:15 [G] For *I will* **restore** them to the land I gave their forefathers.
18: 4 [A] so the potter **[NIE]** formed it into another pot, shaping it as
18: 8 [A] if that nation I warned **repents** of its evil, then I will relent
18:11 [A] So **turn** from your evil ways, each one of you, and reform
18:20 [G] spoke in their behalf to **turn** your wrath **away** from them.
22:10 [A] because *he will* never **return** nor see his native land again.
22:11 [A] but has gone from this place: "*He will* never **return**.
22:27 [A] *You will* never **come back** to the land you long to return to."
22:27 [A] You will never come back to the land you long to **return** to."
23: 3 [G] I have driven them and *will* **bring** them **back** to their pasture,
23:14 [A] hands of evildoers, so that no one **turns** from his wickedness.
23:20 [A] The anger of the LORD *will* not **turn back** until he fully
23:22 [G] *would have* **turned** them from their evil ways and from their
24: 6 [G] them for their good, and *I will* **bring** them **back** to this land.
24: 7 [A] be their God, for *they will* **return** to me with all their heart.
25: 5 [A] They said, "**Turn** now, each of you, from your evil ways
26: 3 [A] Perhaps they will listen and each *will* **turn** from his evil way.
27:16 [H] the LORD's house *will* **be brought back** from Babylon.'
27:22 [G] I will bring them back and **restore** them to this place.' "
28: 3 [G] Within two years I *will* **bring back** to this place all the
28: 4 [G] I *will* also **bring back** to this place Jehoiachin son of
28: 6 [G] **bringing** the articles of the LORD's house … **back**
29:10 [G] fulfill my gracious promise to **bring** you **back** to this place.
29:14 [A] the LORD, "and *will* **bring** you **back** *from* captivity.
29:14 [G] "and *will* **bring** you **back** to the place from which I carried
30: 3 [A] 'when *I will* **bring** my people Israel and Judah **back** *from*
30: 3 [G] **restore** them to the land I gave their forefathers to possess,'
30:10 [A] Jacob *will* **again** have peace and security, and no one will
30:18 [A] " 'I *will* **restore** the fortunes of Jacob's tents and have
30:24 [A] The fierce anger of the LORD *will* not **turn back** until he
31: 8 [A] and women in labor; a great throng *will* **return**.
31:16 [A] the LORD. "*They will* **return** from the land of the enemy.
31:17 [A] the LORD. "Your children *will* **return** to their own land.
31:18 [G] **Restore** me, and I will return, because you are the LORD
31:18 [A] Restore me, and *I will* **return**, because you are the LORD
31:19 [A] After I **strayed**, I repented; after I came to understand, I beat
31:21 [A] that you take. **Return**, O Virgin Israel, return to your towns.
31:21 [A] that you take. Return, O Virgin Israel, **return** to your towns.
31:23 [A] "When I **bring** them **back** *from* captivity, the people in the
32:37 [G] *I will* **bring** them **back** to this place and let them live in
32:40 [A] *I will* never **stop** doing good to them, and I will inspire them
32:44 [G] and of the Negev, because *I will* **restore** their fortunes,
33: 7 [G] *I will* **bring** Judah and Israel **back** *from* captivity and will
33:11 [G] For *I will* **restore** the fortunes of the land as they were
33:26 [G] For *I will* **restore** their fortunes and have compassion on
34:11 [A] afterward *they* **changed** *their* **minds** and took back the
34:11 [G] **took back** the slaves they had freed and enslaved them again.
34:15 [A] Recently you **repented** and did what is right in my sight:
34:16 [A] But now *you have* **turned around** and profaned my name;
34:16 [G] each of *you has* **taken back** the male and female slaves you
34:22 [G] declares the LORD, and *I will* **bring** them **back** to this city.
35:15 [A] "Each of *you must* **turn** from your wicked ways and reform
36: 3 [A] inflict on them, each of *them will* **turn** from his wicked way;
36: 7 [A] each *will* **turn** from his wicked ways, for the anger and wrath
36:28 [A] **[NIE]** "Take another scroll and write on it all the words that
37: 7 [A] out to support you, *will* **go back** to its own land, to Egypt.
37: 8 [A] the Babylonians *will* **return** and attack this city; they will
37:20 [G] *Do* not **send** me **back** *to* the house of Jonathan the secretary,
38:26 [G] 'I was pleading with the king not *to* **send** me **back** *to*
40: 5 [A] However, before Jeremiah **turned to go**, Nebuzaradan
40: 5 [A] "**Go back** to Gedaliah son of Ahikam, the son of Shaphan,
40:12 [A] they all **came back** to the land of Judah, to Gedaliah at
41:14 [A] **[RPH]** and went over to Johanan son of Kareah.
41:16 [G] *he had* **recovered** from Ishmael son of Nethaniah after he
41:16 [G] children and court officials *he had* **brought** from Gibeon.
42:10 [a] 'If *you* stay [BHS *return*; NIV 3782] in this land,
42:12 [G] will have compassion on you and **restore** you to your land.'
43: 5 [A] *had* **come back** to live in the land of Judah from all the
44: 5 [A] they *did* not **turn** from their wickedness or stop burning
44:14 [A] Egypt will escape or survive to **return** *to* the land of Judah,
44:14 [A] to the land of Judah, to which they long to **return** and live;
44:14 [A] to return and live; none *will* **return** except a few fugitives."
44:28 [A] and **return** *to* the land of Judah from Egypt will be very few.
46:16 [A] *let us* **go back** to our own people and our native lands,
46:27 [A] Jacob *will* **again** have peace and security, and no one will
48:47 [A] "Yet *I will* **restore** the fortunes of Moab in days to come,"
49: 6 [G] *I will* **restore** the fortunes of the Ammonites,"
49:39 [G] "Yet *I will* **restore** the fortunes of Elam in days to come,"
50: 6 [D] led them astray and **caused** them **to roam** on the mountains.
50: 9 [A] Their arrows will be like skilled warriors *who do* not **return**
50:19 [D] *I will* **bring** Israel **back** to his own pasture and he will graze
La 1: 8 [A] have seen her nakedness; she herself groans and **turns** away.
1:11 [G] their treasures for food to **keep themselves alive** [+5883].
1:13 [G] He spread a net for my feet and **turned** me back. He made
1:16 [G] No one is near to comfort me, no *one to* **restore** my spirit.
1:19 [G] for food *to* **keep themselves alive** [+906+4392+5883].
2: 3 [G] *He has* **withdrawn** [+294] his right hand at the approach of
2: 8 [G] and *did* not **withhold** his hand from destroying.
2:14 [G] they did not expose your sin to **ward off** your captivity.
3: 3 [A] indeed, he has turned his hand against me **again and again**,
3:21 [G] Yet this I **call to mind** [+448+4213] and therefore I have
3:40 [A] our ways and test them, and *let us* **return** to the LORD.
3:64 [G] **Pay** them **back** what they deserve, O LORD, for what their
5:21 [G] **Restore** us to yourself, O LORD, that we may return;
5:21 [A] Restore us to yourself, O LORD, that *we may* **return**;
Eze 1:14 [A] The creatures sped **back** and forth like flashes of lightning.
3:19 [A] *he does* not **turn** from his wickedness or from his evil ways,
3:20 [A] when a righteous man **turns** from his righteousness and does

Eze 7:13 [A] The seller *will* not **recover** the land he has sold as long as
7:13 [A] the vision concerning the whole crowd *will* not *be* **reversed**.
8: 6 [A] **[NIE]** you will see things that are even more detestable."
8:13 [A] **[NIE]** "You will see them doing things that are even more
8:15 [A] **[NIE]** You will see things that are even more detestable
8:17 [A] the land with violence and **continually** provoke me to anger?
9:11 [G] the man in linen with the writing kit at his side **brought back**
13:22 [A] because you encouraged the wicked not *to* **turn** from their
14: 6 [A] **Repent**! Turn from your idols and renounce all your
14: 6 [G] **Turn** from your idols and renounce all your detestable
14: 6 [G] **renounce** [+4946+6584+7156] all your detestable practices!
16:53 [A] *I will* **restore** the fortunes of Sodom and her daughters and
16:55 [A] with her daughters, *will* **return** to what they were before;
16:55 [A] **[RPH]** and you and your daughters will return to what you
16:55 [A] and your daughters *will* **return** to what you were before.
18: 7 [G] but **returns** what he took in pledge for a loan.
18: 8 [G] *He* **withholds** his hand from doing wrong and judges fairly
18:12 [G] *He does* not **return** what he took in pledge.
18:17 [G] *He* **withholds** his hand from sin and takes no usury
18:21 [A] "But if a wicked man **turns away** from all the sins he has
18:23 [A] am I not pleased when they **turn** from their ways and live?
18:24 [A] "But if a righteous man **turns** from his righteousness
18:26 [A] If a righteous man **turns** from his righteousness and commits
18:27 [A] if a wicked man **turns away** from the wickedness he has
18:28 [A] the offenses he has committed and **turns away** from them,
18:30 [A] to his ways, declares the Sovereign LORD. **Repent**!
18:30 [G] **Turn away** from all your offenses; then sin will not be your
18:32 [G] of anyone, declares the Sovereign LORD. **Repent** and live!
20:22 [G] *I* **withheld** my hand, and for the sake of my name I did what
21: 5 [21:10] [A] sword from its scabbard; *it will* not **return** again.'
21:30 [21:35] [G] **Return** the sword to its scabbard. In the place
26:20 [a] *you will* not **return** [BHS 3782] or take your place in the
27:15 [G] coastlands were your customers; *they* **paid** you **with** [+868]
29:14 [A] *I will* **bring** them **back** *from* captivity and return them to
29:14 [G] them back from captivity and **return** them to Upper Egypt,
33: 9 [A] But if you do warn the wicked man to **turn** from his ways
33: 9 [A] to turn from his ways and *he does* not **do**[s] [+2006+4946] **so**,
33:11 [A] but rather that they **turn** from their ways and live.
33:11 [A] but rather that they turn from their ways and live. **Turn**!
33:11 [A] from their ways and live. Turn! **Turn** from your evil ways!
33:12 [A] wicked man will not cause him to fall when he **turns** from it.
33:14 [A] but *he* then **turns away** from his sin and does what is just
33:15 [G] if he **gives back** what he took in pledge for a loan,
33:18 [A] If a righteous man **turns** from his righteousness and does
33:19 [A] if a wicked man **turns away** from his wickedness and does
34: 4 [G] *You have* not **brought back** the strays or searched for the
34:16 [G] I will search for the lost and **bring back** the strays. I will
35: 7 [A] a desolate waste and cut off from it all who come and **go**.
35: 9 [a] [your towns *will* not *be* **inhabited**. [Q; see K 3782]
38: 4 [D] *I will* **turn** you **around**, put hooks in your jaws and bring
38: 8 [E] In future years you will invade a land *that has* **recovered**
38:12 [G] and loot and **turn** my hand against the resettled ruins
39: 2 [D] *I will* **turn** you **around** and drag you along. I will bring you
39:25 [G] *I will* now **bring** Jacob **back** *from* captivity and will have
39:27 [D] When I *have* **brought** them **back** from the nations and have
44: 1 [G] the man **brought** me **back** to the outer gate of the sanctuary,
46: 9 [A] No *one is to* **return** through the gate by which he entered,
47: 1 [G] The man **brought** me **back** to the entrance of the temple,
47: 6 [G] you see this?" Then he led me **back** *to* the bank of the river.
47: 7 [A] When I **arrived** there, I saw a great number of trees on each
Da 9:13 [A] the favor of the LORD our God by **turning** from our sins
9:16 [A] **turn away** your anger and your wrath from Jerusalem,
9:25 [G] From the issuing of the decree to **restore** and rebuild
9:25 [A] **[RPH]** It will be rebuilt with streets and a trench, but in
10:20 [A] Soon *I will* **return** to fight against the prince of Persia,
11: 9 [A] of the king of the South but *will* **retreat** to his own country.
11:10 [A] and **carry the battle** [+1741+2256] as far as his fortress.
11:13 [A] For the king of the North will muster **another** army,
11:18 [G] Then *he will* **turn** [Q 8492] his attention to the coastlands
11:18 [G] to his insolence and *will* **turn** his insolence **back** upon him.
11:19 [G] *he will* **turn back** toward the fortresses of his own country
11:28 [A] The king of the North *will* **return** *to* his own country with
11:28 [A] take action against it and then **return** to his own country.
11:29 [A] "At the appointed time he will invade the South **again**,
11:30 [A] *he will* **turn back** and vent his fury against the holy
11:30 [A] *He will* **return** and show favor to those who forsake the holy
Hos 2: 7 [2:9] [A] 'I will go **back** to my husband as at first, for then I was
2: 9 [2:11] [A] "Therefore **[NIE]** I will take away my grain when it
3: 5 [A] Afterward the Israelites *will* **return** and seek the LORD
4: 9 [G] both of them for their ways and **repay** them *for* their deeds.
5: 4 [A] "Their deeds do not permit them to **return** to their God. A
5:15 [A] Then I will go **back** to my place until they admit their guilt.
6: 1 [A] "Come, *let us* **return** to the LORD. He has torn us to pieces
6:11 [A] "Whenever I *would* **restore** the fortunes of my people,
7:10 [A] but despite all this *he does* not **return** to the LORD his God
7:16 [A] *They do* not **turn** *to* the Most High; they are like a faulty
8:13 [A] and punish their sins: They *will* **return** *to* Egypt.
9: 3 [A] Ephraim *will* **return** *to* Egypt and eat unclean food in
11: 5 [A] "*Will they* not **return** to Egypt and will not Assyria rule
11: 5 [A] not Assyria rule over them because they refuse to **repent**?
11: 9 [A] out my fierce anger, nor *will I* **turn** and devastate Ephraim.
12: 2 [12:3] [G] to his ways and **repay** him according to his deeds.
12: 6 [12:7] [A] you *must* **return** to your God; maintain love
12:14 [12:15] [G] his bloodshed and *will* **repay** him *for* his contempt.
14: 1 [14:2] [A] **Return**, O Israel, to the LORD your God. Your sins
14: 2 [14:3] [A] Take words with you and **return** to the LORD.
14: 4 [14:5] [A] for my anger *has* **turned away** from them.
14: 7 [14:8] [A] Men will dwell **again** in his shade. He will flourish
Joel 2:12 [A] "**return** to me with all your heart, with fasting and weeping
2:13 [A] **Return** to the LORD your God, for he is gracious
2:14 [A] *He may* **turn** and have pity and leave behind a blessing—
3: 1 [4:1] [G] when *I* **restore** the fortunes of Judah and Jerusalem,
3: 4 [4:4] [G] *I will* swiftly and speedily **return** on your own heads
3: 7 [4:7] [G] *I will* **return** on your own heads what you have done.
Am 1: 3 [G] of Damascus, even for four, *I will* not **turn back** ⌊my wrath⌋.
1: 6 [G] sins of Gaza, even for four, *I will* not **turn back** ⌊my wrath⌋.
1: 8 [G] *I will* **turn** my hand against Ekron, till the last of the
1: 9 [G] sins of Tyre, even for four, *I will* not **turn back** ⌊my wrath⌋.
1:11 [G] sins of Edom, even for four, *I will* not **turn back** ⌊my wrath⌋.
1:13 [G] of Ammon, even for four, *I will* not **turn back** ⌊my wrath⌋.
2: 1 [G] sins of Moab, even for four, *I will* not **turn back** ⌊my wrath⌋.
2: 4 [G] sins of Judah, even for four, *I will* not **turn back** ⌊my wrath⌋.
2: 6 [G] sins of Israel, even for four, *I will* not **turn back** ⌊my wrath⌋.
4: 6 [A] yet *you have* not **returned** to me," declares the LORD.
4: 8 [A] yet *you have* not **returned** to me," declares the LORD.
4: 9 [A] your fig and olive trees, yet *you have* not **returned** to me,"
4:10 [A] yet *you have* not **returned** to me," declares the LORD.
4:11 [A] yet *you have* not **returned** to me," declares the LORD.
9:14 [A] *I will* **bring back** my exiled people Israel; they will rebuild
Ob 1:15 [A] be done to you; your deeds *will* **return** upon your own head.
Jnh 1:13 [G] Instead, the men did their best to row **back** to land. But they
3: 8 [A] *Let* them **give** [+4946+4946] **up** their evil ways and their
3: 9 [A] God *may* yet **relent** and with compassion turn from his
3: 9 [A] yet relent and with compassion **turn** from his fierce anger
3:10 [A] what they did and how *they* **turned** from their evil ways,
Mic 1: 7 [A] as the wages of prostitutes *they will* **again be used**."
2: 8 [B] who pass by without a care, like *men* **returning** *from* battle.
5: 3 [5:2] [A] the rest of his brothers **return** to join the Israelites.
7:19 [A] *You will* **again** have compassion on us; you will tread our
Na 2: 2 [2:3] [A] The LORD *will* **restore** the splendor of Jacob like
Hab 2: 1 [G] say to me, and what **answer** *I am to* **give** to this complaint.
Zep 2: 7 [A] their God will care for them; *he will* **restore** their fortunes.
3:20 [A] praise among all the peoples of the earth when I **restore** your
Zec 1: 3 [A] '**Return** to me,' declares the LORD Almighty, 'and I will
1: 3 [A] 'and *I will* **return** to you,' says the LORD Almighty.
1: 4 [A] '**Turn** from your evil ways and your evil practices.' But they
1: 6 [A] "Then *they* **repented** and said, 'The LORD Almighty has
1:16 [A] '*I will* **return** to Jerusalem with mercy, and there my house
4: 1 [A] the angel who talked with me **returned** and wakened me,
5: 1 [A] I looked **again**—and there before me was a flying scroll!
6: 1 [A] I looked up **again**—and there before me were four chariots
7:14 [A] so desolate behind them that no *one could* **come** or go.
8: 3 [A] LORD says: "*I will* **return** to Zion and dwell in Jerusalem.
8:15 [A] "so now I have determined to do good **again** *to* Jerusalem
9: 8 [A] defend my house against **marauding** [+2256+6296] forces.
9:12 [A] **Return** to your fortress, O prisoners of hope; even now I
9:12 [G] even now I announce that *I will* **restore** twice as much to
10: 9 [A] They and their children will survive, and *they will* **return**.
10:10 [G] *I will* **bring** them **back** from Egypt and gather them from
13: 7 [G] be scattered, and *I will* **turn** my hand against the little ones.
Mal 1: 4 [A] have been crushed, *we will* **rebuild** [+1215+2256] the ruins."
2: 6 [G] me in peace and uprightness, and **turned** many from sin.
3: 7 [A] **Return** to me, and I will return to you," says the LORD
3: 7 [A] Return to me, and *I will* **return** to you," says the LORD
3: 7 [A] LORD Almighty. "But you ask, 'How *are we to* **return**?'
3:18 [A] And you will **again** see the distinction between the righteous
4: 6 [3:24] [G] *He will* **turn** the hearts of the fathers to their

8741 ²שׁוּב **šûb²**, n.f. Not used in NIV/BHS

8742 שׁוּבָאֵל **šûbā'ēl**, n.pr.m. [3 / 6] [cf. 8649]

Shubael [6]

1Ch 23:16 The descendants of Gershom: **Shubael** [BHS 8649] was the first.
24:20 the sons of Amram: **Shubael**; from the sons of Shubael: Jehdeiah.
24:20 the sons of Amram: Shubael; from the sons of **Shubael**: Jehdeiah.
25: 4 Bukkiah, Mattaniah, Uzziel, **Shubael** [BHS 8649] and Jerimoth;
25:20 the thirteenth to **Shubael**, his sons and relatives, 12

1Ch 26:24 **Shubael,** [BHS 8649] a descendant of Gershom son of Moses,

8743 ¹שׁוֹבָב **šôbāb¹**, a. [3] [√ 8740]
faithless [2], kept on [+2143] [1]

Isa 57:17 hid my face in anger, yet *he* **kept on** [+2143] in his willful ways.
Jer 3:14 "Return, **faithless** people," declares the LORD, "for I am your
3:22 "Return, **faithless** people; I will cure you of backsliding."

8744 ²שׁוֹבָב **šôbāb²**, n.pr.m. [4] [√ 8740]
Shobab [4]

2Sa 5:14 children born to him there: Shammua, **Shobab**, Nathan, Solomon,
1Ch 2:18 (and by Jerioth). These were her sons: Jesher, **Shobab** and Ardon.
3:5 born to him there: Shammua, **Shobab**, Nathan and Solomon.
14:4 children born to him there: Shammua, **Shobab**, Nathan, Solomon,

8745 שׁוֹבֵב **šôbēb**, a. [3] [√ 8740]
unfaithful [2], traitors [1]

Jer 31:22 How long will you wander, O **unfaithful** daughter? The LORD
49:4 O **unfaithful** daughter, you trust in your riches and say, 'Who will
Mic 2:4 He takes it from me! He assigns our fields to **traitors**.' "

8746 שׁוּבָה **šûbâ**, n.f. [1] [√ 8740]
repentance [1]

Isa 30:15 "In **repentance** and rest is your salvation, in quietness and trust is

8747 שׁוֹבַךְ **šôbak**, n.pr.m. [2] [cf. 8791]
Shobach [2]

2Sa 10:16 with **Shobach** the commander of Hadadezer's army leading them.
10:18 He also struck down **Shobach** the commander of their army,

8748 שׁוֹבָל **šôbāl**, n.pr.m. [9]
Shobal [9]

Ge 36:20 who were living in the region: Lotan, **Shobal**, Zibeon, Anah,
36:23 The sons of **Shobal**: Alvan, Manahath, Ebal, Shepho and Onam.
36:29 These were the Horite chiefs: Lotan, **Shobal**, Zibeon, Anah,
1Ch 1:38 of Seir: Lotan, **Shobal**, Zibeon, Anah, Dishon, Ezer and Dishan.
1:40 The sons of **Shobal**: Alvan, Manahath, Ebal, Shepho and Onam.
2:50 Hur the firstborn of Ephrathah: **Shobal** the father of Kiriath Jearim,
2:52 The descendants of **Shobal** the father of Kiriath Jearim were:
4:1 The descendants of Judah: Perez, Hezron, Carmi, Hur and **Shobal**.
4:2 Reaiah son of **Shobal** was the father of Jahath, and Jahath the

8749 שׁוֹבֵק **šôbēq**, n.pr.m. [1] [√ 3791]
Shobek [1]

Ne 10:24 [10:25] Hallohesh, Pilha, **Shobek**,

8750 ¹שָׁוָה **šāwâ¹**, v. [14] [→ 3796, 3798, 3799, 8737, 8752, 8753, 8754, 8856, 9590; Ar 10702]
compare [2], be like [1], count equal [1], equal [1], get what deserved [1], gives satisfaction [1], in best interest [1], is like [1], justify [1], leveled [1], liken [1], stilled [1], waited patiently [1]

Est 3:8 [A] it is not **in** the king's **best interest** to tolerate them.
5:13 [A] all this **gives** me no **satisfaction** as long as I see that Jew
7:4 [A] because no such distress *would* **justify** disturbing the king."
Job 33:27 [A] perverted what was right, but I *did* not **get what I deserved**.
Ps 131:2 [D] *I have* **stilled** and quieted my soul; like a weaned child with
Pr 3:15 [A] than rubies; nothing you desire *can* **compare** with her.
8:11 [A] than rubies, and nothing you desire *can* **compare** with her.
26:4 [A] a fool according to his folly, or *you will* **be like** him yourself.
27:15 [C] A quarrelsome wife **is like** a constant dripping on a rainy
Isa 28:25 [D] When *he has* **leveled** the surface, does he not sow caraway
38:13 [D] *I* **waited patiently** till dawn, but like a lion he broke all my
40:25 [A] you compare me? Or who *is my* **equal**?" says the Holy One.
46:5 [G] "To whom will you compare me or **count** me **equal**? To
La 2:13 [G] To what *can I* **liken** you, that I may comfort you, O Virgin

8751 ²שָׁוָה **šāwâ²**, v. [7]
bestowed [2], makes [2], brought forth [1], set heart [1], set [1]

2Sa 22:34 [D] *He* **makes** my feet like the feet of a deer; he enables me to
Ps 16:8 [D] *I have* **set** the LORD always before me. Because he is at
18:33 [18:34] [D] *He* **makes** my feet like the feet of a deer; he enables
21:5 [21:6] [D] *you have* **bestowed** on him splendor and majesty.
89:19 [89:20] [D] "*I have* **bestowed** strength on a warrior; I have
119:30 [D] chosen the way of truth; *I have* **set** *my* **heart** *on* your laws.
Hos 10:1 [D] was a spreading vine; *he* **brought forth** fruit for himself.

8752 שָׁוֵה **šāweh**, n.m.[loc.?]. Not used in NIV/BHS [→ 8753; cf. 8750]

8753 שָׁוֵה **šāwēh**, n.pr.loc. [1] [√ 8752; cf. 8750]
Shaveh [1]

Ge 14:17 the king of Sodom came out to meet him in the Valley of **Shaveh**

8754 שָׁוֵה קִרְיָתַיִם **šāwēh qiryātayim**, n.pr.loc. [1] [√ 8750 + 7984]
Shaveh Kiriathaim [1]

Ge 14:5 the Zuzites in Ham, the Emites in **Shaveh Kiriathaim**

8755 ¹שׁוּחַ **šûaḥ¹**, v. [1] [→ 8757, 8758?, 8846; cf. 8817, 8820]
leads down [1]

Pr 2:18 [A] For her house **leads down** to death and her paths to the

8756 ²שׁוּחַ **šûaḥ²**, n.pr.m. [2] [→ 8760]
Shuah [2]

Ge 25:2 She bore him Zimran, Jokshan, Medan, Midian, Ishbak and **Shuah**.
1Ch 1:32 Zimran, Jokshan, Medan, Midian, Ishbak and **Shuah**. The sons of

8757 ¹שׁוּחָה **šûḥâ¹**, n.f. [5] [→ 8758?; cf. 8755, 8864]
pit [4], rifts [1]

Pr 22:14 The mouth of an adulteress is a deep **pit**; he who is under the
23:27 for a prostitute is a deep **pit** and a wayward wife is a narrow well.
Jer 2:6 through a land of deserts and **rifts**, a land of drought and darkness,
18:20 Should good be repaid with evil? Yet they have dug a **pit** for me.
18:22 for they have dug a **pit** [K 8864] to capture me and have hidden

8758 ²שׁוּחָה **šûḥâ²**, n.pr.[m.?]. [1] [√ 8757?; cf. 8755?]
Shuhah's [1]

1Ch 4:11 Kelub, **Shuhah's** brother, was the father of Mehir, who was the

8759 שׁוּחָט **šawḥāṭ**, n.[?] Not used in NIV/BHS [→ 8453]

8760 שׁוּחִי **šûḥî**, a.g. [5] [√ 8756]
Shuhite [5]

Job 2:11 the Temanite, Bildad the **Shuhite** and Zophar the Naamathite,
8:1 Then Bildad the **Shuhite** replied:
18:1 Then Bildad the **Shuhite** replied:
25:1 Then Bildad the **Shuhite** replied:
42:9 Bildad the **Shuhite** and Zophar the Naamathite did what the

8761 שׁוּחָם **šûḥām**, n.pr.m. [1] [→ 8762]
Shuham [1]

Nu 26:42 through **Shuham**, the Shuhamite clan. These were the clans of

8762 שׁוּחָמִי **šûḥāmî**, a.g. [2] [√ 8761]
Shuhamite [2]

Nu 26:42 through Shuham, the **Shuhamite** clan. These were the clans of
26:43 All of them were **Shuhamite** clans; and those numbered were

8763 ¹שׁוּט **šûṭ¹**, v.den. [13] [→ 5414, 5415, 8765, 8849, 8868]
oarsmen [2], range [2], roaming [2], go here and there [1], go up and down [1], go [1], gone [1], rush here and there [1], wander [1], went around [1]

Nu 11:8 [A] The people **went around** gathering it, and then ground it in a
2Sa 24:2 [A] "**Go** throughout the tribes of Israel from Dan to Beersheba
24:8 [A] After *they had* **gone** through the entire land, they came back
2Ch 16:9 [D] For the eyes of the LORD **range** throughout the earth to
Job 1:7 [A] "From **roaming** through the earth and going back and forth
2:2 [A] "From **roaming** through the earth and going back and forth
Jer 5:1 [D] "**Go up and down** the streets of Jerusalem, look around and
49:3 [F] **rush here and there** inside the walls, for Molech will go into
Eze 27:8 [A] Men of Sidon and Arvad were your **oarsmen**; your skilled
27:26 [A] Your **oarsmen** take you out to the high seas. But the east
Da 12:4 [D] Many *will* **go here and there** to increase knowledge."
Am 8:12 [D] will stagger from sea to sea and **wander** from north to east,
Zec 4:10 [D] the eyes of the LORD, *which* **range** throughout the earth.)"

8764 ²שׁוּט **šûṭ²**, v. [3]
despise [1], malicious [1], maligned [1]

Eze 16:57 [A] of the Philistines—all those around you who **despise** you.
28:24 [A] " 'No longer will the people of Israel have **malicious**
28:26 [A] punishment on all their neighbors who **maligned** them.

8765 שׁוֹט¹ ***šôṭ¹***, n.m. [11] [→ 8849; cf. 8763, 8867]

whips [5], scourge [3], whip [2], lash [1]

1Ki 12:11 My father scourged you with **whips**; I will scourge you with
12:14 My father scourged you with **whips**; I will scourge you with
2Ch 10:11 My father scourged you with **whips**; I will scourge you with
10:14 My father scourged you with **whips**; I will scourge you with
Job 5:21 You will be protected from the **lash** *of* the tongue, and need not
9:23 When a **scourge** brings sudden death, he mocks the despair of the
Pr 26:3 A **whip** for the horse, a halter for the donkey, and a rod for the
Isa 10:26 The LORD Almighty will lash them with a **whip**, as when he
28:15 When an overwhelming **scourge** sweeps by, it cannot touch us,
28:18 When the overwhelming **scourge** sweeps by, you will be beaten
Na 3:2 The crack of **whips**, the clatter of wheels, galloping horses

8766 שׁוֹט² ***šôṭ²***, n.m. Not used in NIV/BHS

8767 שׁוּל ***šûl***, n.m. [11] [cf. 8870]

hem [5], skirts [4], *untranslated* [1], train of robe [1]

Ex 28:33 of blue, purple and scarlet yarn around the **hem** *of* the robe,
28:33 around the hem of the robe, **[RPH]** with gold bells between them.
28:34 and the pomegranates are to alternate around the **hem** *of* the robe.
39:24 scarlet yarn and finely twisted linen around the **hem** *of* the robe.
39:25 and attached them around the **hem** between the pomegranates.
39:26 pomegranates alternated around the **hem** *of* the robe to be worn for
Isa 6:1 high and exalted, and the **train of** his **robe** filled the temple.
Jer 13:22 because of your many sins that your **skirts** have been torn off
13:26 I will pull up your **skirts** over your face that your shame may be
La 1:9 Her filthiness clung to her **skirts**; she did not consider her future.
Na 3:5 the LORD Almighty. "I will lift your **skirts** over your face.

8768 שׁוֹלָל ***šôlāl***, a. [3] [√ 8964; cf. 8871]

stripped [2], barefoot [1]

Job 12:17 He leads counselors away **stripped** and makes fools of judges.
12:19 He leads priests away **stripped** and overthrows men long
Mic 1:8 of this I will weep and wail; I will go about **barefoot** and naked.

8769 שׁוּלַמִּית ***šûlammît***, a.g.[f.]. [2]

Shulammite [2]

SS 6:13 [7:1] Come back, come back, O **Shulammite**; come back,
6:13 [7:1] Why would you gaze on the **Shulammite** as on the dance of

8770 שׁוּמִים ***šûmîm***, n.[m.]. [1]

garlic [1]

Nu 11:5 at no cost—also the cucumbers, melons, leeks, onions and **garlic**.

8771 שׁוּנִי¹ ***šûnî¹***, n.pr.m. [2] [→ 8772]

Shuni [2]

Ge 46:16 sons of Gad: Zephon, Haggi, **Shuni**, Ezbon, Eri, Arodi and Areli.
Nu 26:15 through Haggi, the Haggite clan; through **Shuni**, the Shunite clan;

8772 שׁוּנִי² ***šûnî²***, a.g. [1] [√ 8771]

Shunite [1]

Nu 26:15 through Haggi, the Haggite clan; through Shuni, the **Shunite** clan;

8773 שׁוּנֵם ***šûnēm***, n.pr.loc. [3] [→ 8774]

Shunem [3]

Jos 19:18 Their territory included: Jezreel, Kesulloth, **Shunem**,
1Sa 28:4 The Philistines assembled and came and set up camp at **Shunem**,
2Ki 4:8 One day Elisha went to **Shunem**. And a well-to-do woman was

8774 שׁוּנַמִּי ***šûnammî***, a.g. [8] [√ 8773]

Shunammite [8]

1Ki 1:3 Israel for a beautiful girl and found Abishag, a **Shunammite**,
1:15 in his room, where Abishag the **Shunammite** was attending him.
2:17 not refuse you—to give me Abishag the **Shunammite** as my wife."
2:21 "Let Abishag the **Shunammite** be given in marriage to your
2:22 "Why do you request Abishag the **Shunammite** for Adonijah?
2Ki 4:12 He said to his servant Gehazi, "Call the **Shunammite**." So he
4:25 God said to his servant Gehazi, "Look! There's the **Shunammite**!
4:36 Elisha summoned Gehazi and said, "Call the **Shunammite**."

8775 שָׁוַע ***šāwa'***, v. [21 / 22] [→ 8776, 8779, 8780, 8784; cf. 8782; *also used with compound proper names*]

cry for help [7], cried for help [4], call for help [3], called for help [3], cry out [3], cry out for help [1], plead for relief [1]

2Sa 22:42 [d] *They* **cried** [BHS 9120] **for help**, but there was no one to
Job 19:7 [D] I get no response; though *I* **call for help**, there is no justice.
24:12 [D] from the city, and the souls of the wounded **cry out for help**.
29:12 [D] because I rescued the poor *who* **cried for help**,
30:20 [D] "*I* **cry out** to you, O God, but you do not answer; I stand up,
30:28 [D] not by the sun; I stand up in the assembly and **cry for help**.
35:9 [D] *they* **plead for relief** from the arm of the powerful.
36:13 [D] even when he fetters them, *they do* not **cry for help**.
38:41 [D] Who provides food for the raven when its young **cry out** to
Ps 18:6 [18:7] [D] I called to the LORD; *I* **cried** to my God **for help**.
18:41 [18:42] [D] *They* **cried for help**, but there was no one to save
22:24 [22:25] [D] face from him but has listened to his **cry for help**.
28:2 [D] Hear my cry for mercy as I **call** to you **for help**, as I lift up
30:2 [30:3] [D] my God, *I* **called** to you **for help** and you healed me.
31:22 [31:23] [D] my cry for mercy when I **called** to you **for help**.
72:12 [D] For he will deliver the needy *who* **cry out**, the afflicted who
88:13 [88:14] [D] I **cry** to you **for help**, O LORD; in the morning my
119:147 [D] I rise before dawn and **cry for help**; I have put my hope in
Isa 58:9 [D] LORD will answer; *you will* **cry for help**, and he will say:
La 3:8 [D] Even when I call out or **cry for help**, he shuts out my prayer.
Jnh 2:2 [2:3] [D] From the depths of the grave *I* **called for help**,
Hab 1:2 [D] How long, O LORD, *must I* **call for help**, but you do not

8776 שֶׁוַע ***šewa'***, n.[m.]. [1] [√ 8775]

cry for help [+7754] [1]

Ps 5:2 [5:3] Listen to my **cry for help** [+7754], my King and my God,

8777 שׁוֹעַ¹ ***šôa'¹***, a. [2] [→ 55, 8781, 8782]

highly respected [1], rich [1]

Job 34:19 no partiality to princes and does not favor the **rich** over the poor,
Isa 32:5 the fool be called noble nor the scoundrel be **highly respected**.

8778 שׁוֹעַ² ***šôa'²***, n.pr.g. [1] [cf. 7760]

Shoa [1]

Eze 23:23 and all the Chaldeans, the men of Pekod and **Shoa** and Koa,

8779 שׁוֹעַ³ ***šôa'³***, n.[m.]. [1] [√ 8775]

crying out [1]

Isa 22:5 a day of battering down walls and of **crying out** to the mountains.

8780 שׁוּעַ¹ ***šûa'¹***, n.[m.]. [1] [√ 8775]

cries for help [1]

Job 30:24 no one lays a hand on a broken man when *he* **cries for help**

8781 שׁוּעַ² ***šûa'²***, n.pr.m. [3] [√ 8782; cf. 8777]

Shua [3]

Ge 38:2 There Judah met the daughter of a Canaanite man named **Shua**.
38:12 After a long time Judah's wife, the daughter of **Shua**, died.
1Ch 2:3 were born to him by a Canaanite woman, the daughter of **Shua**.

8782 שׁוּעַ³ ***šûa'³***, n.m. [1] [→ 8781; cf. 8775, 8777]

wealth [1]

Job 36:19 Would your **wealth** or even all your mighty efforts sustain you

8783 שׁוּעָא ***šû'ā'***, n.pr.f. [1]

Shua [1]

1Ch 7:32 the father of Japhlet, Shomer and Hotham and of their sister **Shua**.

8784 שַׁוְעָה ***šaw'â***, n.f. [11] [√ 8775]

cry [7], cry for help [3], outcry [1]

Ex 2:23 and their **cry for help** because of their slavery went up to God.
1Sa 5:12 afflicted with tumors, and the **outcry** *of* the city went up to heaven.
2Sa 22:7 From his temple he heard my voice; my **cry** came to his ears.
Ps 18:6 [18:7] he heard my voice; my **cry** came before him, into his ears.
34:15 [34:16] are on the righteous and his ears are attentive to their **cry**;
39:12 [39:13] "Hear my prayer, O LORD, listen to my **cry for help**;
40:1 [40:2] for the LORD; he turned to me and heard my **cry**.
102:1 [102:2] my prayer, O LORD; let my **cry for help** come to you.
145:19 desires of those who fear him; he hears their **cry** and saves them.
Jer 8:19 Listen to the **cry** *of* my people from a land far away: "Is the
La 3:56 You heard my plea: "Do not close your ears to my **cry** for relief."

8785 שׁוּעָל¹ ***šû'āl¹***, n.m. [7] [→ 2967, 8786, 8787]

foxes [3], jackals [3], fox [1]

Jdg 15:4 So he went out and caught three hundred **foxes** and tied them tail to
Ne 4:3 [3:35] if even a **fox** climbed up on it, he would break down their
Ps 63:10 [63:11] be given over to the sword and become food for **jackals**.
SS 2:15 Catch for us the **foxes**, the little foxes that ruin the vineyards,

SS 2:15 Catch for us the foxes, the little **foxes** that ruin the vineyards,
La 5:18 for Mount Zion, which lies desolate, with **jackals** prowling over it.
Eze 13: 4 Your prophets, O Israel, are like **jackals** among ruins.

8786 ²שׁוּעָל ***šû'āl²***, n.pr.m. [1] [√ 8785]

Shual [1]

1Ch 7:36 The sons of Zophah: Suah, Harnepher, **Shual**, Beri, Imrah,

8787 ³שׁוּעָל ***šû'āl³***, n.pr.loc. [1] [√ 8785]

Shual [1]

1Sa 13:17 One turned toward Ophrah in the vicinity of **Shual**,

8788 שׁוֹעֵר ***šō'ēr***, n.m. [37] [√ 9133; Ar 10777]

gatekeepers [29], doorkeepers [4], gatekeeper [2], keep watch [1], keeper of gate [1]

2Sa 18:26 he called down to the **gatekeeper**, "Look, another man running
2Ki 7:10 So they went and called out to the city **gatekeepers** and told them,
7:11 The **gatekeepers** shouted the news, and it was reported within the
1Ch 9:17 The **gatekeepers**: Shallum, Akkub, Talmon, Ahiman and their
9:18 These were the **gatekeepers** belonging to the camp of the Levites.
9:21 Zechariah son of Meshelemiah was the **gatekeeper** *at* the entrance
9:22 those chosen to be **gatekeepers** at the thresholds numbered 212.
9:24 The **gatekeepers** were on the four sides: east, west, north and
9:26 the four principal **gatekeepers**, who were Levites, were entrusted
15:18 Eliphelehu, Mikneiah, Obed-Edom and Jeiel, the **gatekeepers**.
15:23 Berekiah and Elkanah were to be **doorkeepers** for the ark.
15:24 Obed-Edom and Jehiah were also to be **doorkeepers** for the ark.
16:38 Obed-Edom son of Jeduthun, and also Hosah, were **gatekeepers**.
23: 5 Four thousand are to be **gatekeepers** and four thousand are to
26: 1 The divisions of the **gatekeepers**: From the Korahites:
26:12 These divisions of the **gatekeepers**, through their chief men,
26:19 These were the divisions of the **gatekeepers** who were descendants
2Ch 8:14 He also appointed the **gatekeepers** by divisions for the various
23: 4 Levites who are going on duty on the Sabbath are to **keep watch** *at*
23:19 He also stationed **doorkeepers** at the gates of the LORD's temple
31:14 Kore son of Imnah the Levite, **keeper of** the East **Gate**, was in
34:13 Some of the Levites were secretaries, scribes and **doorkeepers**.
35:15 The **gatekeepers** at each gate did not need to leave their posts,
Ezr 2:42 The **gatekeepers** of the temple: the descendants of Shallum,
2:70 the **gatekeepers** and the temple servants settled in their own towns,
7: 7 Levites, singers, **gatekeepers** and temple servants,
10:24 Eliashib. From the **gatekeepers**: Shallum, Telem and Uri.
Ne 7: 1 the **gatekeepers** and the singers and the Levites were appointed.
7:45 The **gatekeepers**: the descendants of Shallum, Ater, Talmon,
7:73 [7:72] the **gatekeepers**, the singers and the temple servants,
10:28 [10:29] priests, Levites, **gatekeepers**, singers, temple servants
10:39 [10:40] ministering priests, the **gatekeepers** and the singers stay.
11:19 The **gatekeepers**: Akkub, Talmon and their associates, who kept
12:25 Akkub were **gatekeepers** who guarded the storerooms at the gates.
12:45 the service of purification, as did also the singers and **gatekeepers**,
12:47 contributed the daily portions for the singers and **gatekeepers**.
13: 5 and oil prescribed for the Levites, singers and **gatekeepers**,

8789 ¹שׁוּף ***šûp¹***, v. [3] [cf. 8790, 8635]

crush [2], hide [1]

Ge 3:15 [A] he *will* **crush** your head, and you will strike his heel."
Job 9:17 [A] He *would* **crush** me with a storm and multiply my wounds
Ps 139:11 [A] "Surely the darkness *will* **hide** me and the light become night

8790 ²שׁוּף ***šûp²***, v. [1] [cf. 8789, 8635]

strike [1]

Ge 3:15 [A] he will crush your head, and you *will* **strike** his heel."

8791 שׁוֹפָךְ ***šôpak***, n.pr.m. [2] [cf. 8747]

Shophach [2]

1Ch 19:16 with **Shophach** the commander of Hadadezer's army leading them.
19:18 He also killed **Shophach** the commander of their army.

8792 שׁוּפָם ***šûpām***, n.pr.m. [0 / 1] [→ 8793; cf. 9145]

Shupham [1]

Nu 26:39 through **Shupham**, [BHS 9145] the Shuphamite clan;

8793 שׁוּפָמִי ***šûpāmî***, a.g. [1] [√ 8792]

Shuphamite [1]

Nu 26:39 through Shupham, the **Shuphamite** clan; through Hupham,

8794 שׁוֹפָן ***šôpān***, n.pr.loc. Not used in NIV/BHS [→ 6503]

8795 שׁוֹפָר ***šôpār***, n.m. [72] [→ 882; cf. 9182]

trumpet [44], trumpets [18], trumpets [+3413] [3], ram's horn [2], *untranslated* [1], blast [+7754] [1], horns [1], rams horns [1], trumpet [+9558] [1]

Ex 19:16 a thick cloud over the mountain, and a very loud **trumpet** blast.
19:19 the sound of the **trumpet** grew louder and louder. Then Moses
20:18 lightning and heard the **trumpet** and saw the mountain in smoke,
Lev 25: 9 have the **trumpet** [+9558] sounded everywhere on the tenth day of
25: 9 on the Day of Atonement sound the **trumpet** throughout your land.
Jos 6: 4 Have seven priests carry **trumpets** *of* rams' horns in front of the
6: 4 around the city seven times, with the priests blowing the **trumpets**.
6: 5 When you hear them sound a long **blast** [+7754] on the trumpets,
6: 6 and have seven priests carry **trumpets** [+3413] in front of it."
6: 8 the seven priests carrying the seven **trumpets** [+3413] before the
6: 8 blowing their **trumpets**, and the ark of the LORD's covenant
6: 9 armed guard marched ahead of the priests who blew the **trumpets**,
6: 9 guard followed the ark. All this time the **trumpets** were sounding.
6:13 The seven priests carrying the seven **trumpets** [+3413] went
6:13 marching before the ark of the LORD and blowing the **trumpets**.
6:13 the ark of the LORD, while the **trumpets** kept sounding.
6:16 seventh time around, when the priests sounded the **trumpet** blast,
6:20 When the **trumpets** sounded, the people shouted, and at the sound
6:20 the people shouted, and at the sound of the **trumpet**,
Jdg 3:27 he arrived there, he blew a **trumpet** in the hill country of Ephraim,
6:34 and he blew a **trumpet**, summoning the Abiezrites to follow him.
7: 8 who took over the provisions and **trumpets** *of* the others.
7:16 he placed **trumpets** and empty jars in the hands of all of them,
7:18 When I and all who are with me blow our **trumpets**, then from all
7:18 then from all around the camp blow **[RPH]** yours and shout,
7:19 They blew their **trumpets** and broke the jars that were in their
7:20 The three companies blew the **trumpets** and smashed the jars.
7:20 and holding in their right hands the **trumpets** they were to blow,
7:22 When the three hundred **trumpets** sounded, the LORD caused the
1Sa 13: 3 Then Saul had the **trumpet** blown throughout the land and said,
2Sa 2:28 So Joab blew the **trumpet**, and all the men came to a halt;
6:15 up the ark of the LORD with shouts and the sound of **trumpets**.
15:10 "As soon as you hear the sound of the **trumpets**, then say,
18:16 Joab sounded the **trumpet**, and the troops stopped pursuing Israel,
20: 1 He sounded the **trumpet** and shouted, "We have no share in
20:22 So he sounded the **trumpet**, and his men dispersed from the city,
1Ki 1:34 Blow the **trumpet** and shout, 'Long live King Solomon!'
1:39 Then they sounded the **trumpet** and all the people shouted,
1:41 On hearing the sound of the **trumpet**, Joab asked, "What's the
2Ki 9:13 Then they blew the **trumpet** and shouted, "Jehu is king!"
1Ch 15:28 with the sounding of **rams' horns** and trumpets, and of cymbals,
2Ch 15:14 with loud acclamation, with shouting and with trumpets and **horns**.
Ne 4:18 [4:12] But the man who sounded the **trumpet** stayed with me.
4:20 [4:14] Wherever you hear the sound of the **trumpet**, join us there.
Job 39:24 eats up the ground; he cannot stand still when the **trumpet** sounds.
39:25 At the blast of the **trumpet** he snorts, 'Aha!' He catches the scent
Ps 47: 5 [47:6] shouts of joy, the LORD amid the sounding of **trumpets**.
81: 3 [81:4] Sound the **ram's horn** at the New Moon, and when the
98: 6 with trumpets and the blast of the **ram's horn**—shout for joy
150: 3 Praise him with the sounding of the **trumpet**, praise him with the
Isa 18: 3 you will see it, and when a **trumpet** sounds, you will hear it.
27:13 in that day a great **trumpet** will sound. Those who were perishing
58: 1 "Shout it aloud, do not hold back. Raise your voice like a **trumpet**.
Jer 4: 5 in Jerusalem and say: 'Sound the **trumpet** throughout the land!'
4:19 For I have heard the sound of the **trumpet**; I have heard the battle
4:21 must I see the battle standard and hear the sound of the **trumpet**?
6: 1 of Benjamin! Flee from Jerusalem! Sound the **trumpet** in Tekoa!
6:17 watchmen over you and said, 'Listen to the sound of the **trumpet**!'
42:14 we will not see war or hear the **trumpet** or be hungry for bread,'
51:27 up a banner in the land! Blow the **trumpet** among the nations!
Eze 33: 3 coming against the land and blows the **trumpet** to warn the people,
33: 4 then if anyone hears the **trumpet** but does not take warning
33: 5 Since he heard the sound of the **trumpet** but did not take warning,
33: 6 does not blow the **trumpet** to warn the people and the sword
Hos 5: 8 "Sound the **trumpet** in Gibeah, the horn in Ramah. Raise the battle
8: 1 "Put the **trumpet** to your lips! An eagle is over the house of the
Joel 2: 1 Blow the **trumpet** in Zion; sound the alarm on my holy hill.
2:15 Blow the **trumpet** in Zion, declare a holy fast, call a sacred
Am 2: 2 down in great tumult amid war cries and the blast of the **trumpet**.
3: 6 When a **trumpet** sounds in a city, do not the people tremble?
Zep 1:16 a day of **trumpet** and battle cry against the fortified cities
Zec 9:14 The Sovereign LORD will sound the **trumpet**; he will march in

8796 ¹שׁוּק ***šûq¹***, v. [3] [→ 8797, 8798, 8799; cf. 9212?]

overflow [2], water [1]

Ps 65: 9 [65:10] [D] You care for the land and **water** it; you enrich it
Joel 2:24 [G] with grain; the vats *will* **overflow** *with* new wine and oil.
3:13 [4:13] [G] for the winepress is full and the vats **overflow**—

8797 שׁוֹק *šôq*, n.[f.]. [19] [√ 8796; Ar 10741]

thigh [12], legs [5], attacked viciously [+906+3751+5782+6584] [1], leg [1]

Ex 29:22 of the liver, both kidneys with the fat on them, and the right **thigh**.
29:27 the breast that was waved and the **thigh** that was presented.
Lev 7:32 You are to give the right **thigh** of your fellowship offerings to the
7:33 the fat of the fellowship offering shall have the right **thigh** as his
7:34 I have taken the breast that is waved and the **thigh** that is presented
8:25 covering of the liver, both kidneys and their fat and the right **thigh**.
8:26 and a wafer; he put these on the fat portions and on the right **thigh**.
9:21 and the right **thigh** before the LORD as a wave offering,
10:14 eat the breast that was waved and the **thigh** that was presented.
10:15 The **thigh** that was presented and the breast that was waved must
Nu 6:20 with the breast that was waved and the **thigh** that was presented.
18:18 just as the breast of the wave offering and the right **thigh** are yours.
Dt 28:35 afflict your knees and **legs** with painful boils that cannot be cured,
Jdg 15:8 *He* **attacked** them **viciously** [+906+3751+5782+6584] and
1Sa 9:24 So the cook took up the **leg** with what was on it and set it in front
Ps 147:10 not in the strength of the horse, nor his delight in the **legs** *of* a man;
Pr 26:7 Like a lame man's **legs** that hang limp is a proverb in the mouth of
SS 5:15 His **legs** are pillars of marble set on bases of pure gold.
Isa 47:2 Lift up your skirts, bare your **legs**, and wade through the streams.

8798 [2]שׁוּק *šûq*[2], n.m. [4] [√ 8796]

street [2], streets [2]

Pr 7:8 He was going down the **street** near her corner, walking along in
Ecc 12:4 when the doors to the **street** are closed and the sound of grinding
12:5 man goes to his eternal home and mourners go about the **streets**.
SS 3:2 get up now and go about the city, through its **streets** and squares;

8799 שֹׁקֵק *šôqēq*, a. *or* v.ptcp. [2] [√ 8796]

thirsty [+5883] [1], unquenched [1]

Ps 107:9 for he satisfies the **thirsty** [+5883] and fills the hungry with good
Isa 29:8 he is drinking, but he awakens faint, with his thirst **unquenched**.

8800 [1]שׁוּר *šûr*[1], v. [15 / 14] [→ 8803, 8804?, 8805, 9224]

see [5], behold [1], care for [1], gaze [1], lie in wait [1], look [1], lurk [1], pays attention [1], perceive [1], view [1]

Nu 23:9 [A] the rocky peaks I see them, from the heights *I* **view** them.
24:17 [A] "I see him, but not now; *I* **behold** him, but not near. A star
Job 7:8 [A] The eye that now sees me *will* **see** me no longer; you will
17:15 [A] where then is my hope? Who *can* **see** any hope for me?
20:9 [A] will not see him again; his place *will* **look** *on* him no more.
24:15 [A] he thinks, 'No eye *will* **see** me,' and he keeps his face
33:14 [A] one way, now another—though *man may* not **perceive** it.
34:29 [A] If he hides his face, who *can* **see** him? Yet he is over man
35:5 [A] at the heavens and see; **gaze** *at* the clouds so high above you.
35:13 [A] to their empty plea; the Almighty **pays** no **attention** *to* it.
35:14 [A] then, will he listen when you say that *you do* not **see** him,
Ps 92:11 [92:12] [a] defeat of my adversaries; [BHS *watchers*; NIV 8806]
Jer 5:26 [A] "Among my people are wicked men *who* **lie in wait** like men
Hos 13:7 [A] upon them like a lion, like a leopard *I will* **lurk** by the path.
14:8 [14:9] [A] I will answer him and **care for** him. I am like a green

8801 [2]שׁוּר *šûr*[2], v. [4]

carriers [1], comes [1], descend [1], went [1]

Job 33:27 [A] *he* **comes** to men and says, 'I sinned, and perverted what was
SS 4:8 [A] **Descend** from the crest of Amana, from the top of Senir,
Isa 57:9 [A] *You* **went** to Molech with olive oil and increased your
Eze 27:25 [A] " 'The ships of Tarshish *serve as* **carriers** *for* your wares.

8802 שׁוֹר *šôr*, n.m. [79] [→ 56, 9593; Ar 10756]

ox [38], bull [16], cattle [13], animal [2], bulls [2], calf [2], herd [2], oxen [2], cow [1], one[s] [1]

Ge 32:5 [32:6] I have **cattle** and donkeys, sheep and goats, menservants
49:6 have killed men in their anger and hamstrung **oxen** as they pleased.
Ex 20:17 or his manservant or maidservant, his **ox** or donkey,
21:28 "If a **bull** gores a man or a woman to death, the bull must be stoned
21:28 gores a man or a woman to death, the **bull** must be stoned to death,
21:28 not be eaten. But the owner of the **bull** will not be held responsible.
21:29 the **bull** has had the habit of goring and the owner has been warned
21:29 the **bull** must be stoned and the owner also must be put to death.
21:32 If the **bull** gores a male or female slave, the owner must pay thirty
21:32 of silver to the master of the slave, and the **bull** must be stoned.
21:33 or digs one and fails to cover it and an **ox** or a donkey falls into it,
21:35 "If a man's **bull** injures the bull of another and it dies, they are to
21:35 "If a man's bull injures the **bull** *of* another and it dies, they are to
21:35 they are to sell the live **one**[s] and divide both the money and the
21:36 However, if it was known that the **bull** had the habit of goring,
21:36 the owner must pay, **animal** for animal, and the dead animal will
21:36 the owner must pay, animal for **animal**, and the dead animal will
22:1 [21:37] "If a man steals an **ox** or a sheep and slaughters it or sells
22:1 [21:37] he must pay back five head of cattle for the **ox** and four
22:4 [22:3] whether **ox** or donkey or sheep—he must pay back double.
22:9 [22:8] In all cases of illegal possession of an **ox**, a donkey, a
22:10 [22:9] an **ox**, a sheep or any other animal to his neighbor for
22:30 [22:29] Do the same with your **cattle** and your sheep. Let them
23:4 "If you come across your enemy's **ox** or donkey wandering off,
23:12 so that your **ox** and your donkey may rest and the slave born in
34:19 the firstborn males of your livestock, whether from **herd** or flock.
Lev 4:10 just as the fat is removed from the **ox** sacrificed as a fellowship
7:23 to the Israelites: 'Do not eat any of the fat of **cattle**, sheep or goats.
9:4 an **ox** and a ram for a fellowship offering to sacrifice before the
9:18 He slaughtered the **ox** and the ram as the fellowship offering for
9:19 the fat portions of the **ox** and the ram—the fat tail, the layer of fat,
17:3 Any Israelite who sacrifices an **ox**, a lamb or a goat in the camp
22:23 present as a freewill offering an **ox** or a sheep that is deformed
22:27 "When a **calf**, a lamb or a goat is born, it is to remain with its
22:28 Do not slaughter a **cow** or a sheep and its young on the same day.
27:26 to the LORD; whether an **ox** or a sheep, it is the LORD's.
Nu 7:3 twelve oxen—an **ox** from each leader and a cart from every two.
15:11 Each **bull** or ram, each lamb or young goat, is to be prepared in
18:17 "But you must not redeem the firstborn of an **ox**, a sheep or a goat;
22:4 up everything around us, as an **ox** licks up the grass of the field."
Dt 5:14 or maidservant, nor your **ox**, your donkey or any of your animals,
5:21 or land, his manservant or maidservant, his **ox** or donkey,
14:4 These are the animals you may eat: the **ox**, the sheep, the goat,
15:19 Do not put the firstborn of your **oxen** to work, and do not shear the
17:1 Do not sacrifice to the LORD your God an **ox** or a sheep that has
18:3 is the share due the priests from the people who sacrifice a **bull**
22:1 If you see your brother's **ox** or sheep straying, do not ignore it
22:4 If you see your brother's donkey or his **ox** fallen on the road,
22:10 Do not plow with an **ox** and a donkey yoked together.
25:4 Do not muzzle an **ox** while it is treading out the grain.
28:31 Your **ox** will be slaughtered before your eyes, but you will eat none
33:17 In majesty he is like a firstborn **bull**; his horns are the horns of a
Jos 6:21 men and women, young and old, **cattle**, sheep and donkeys.
7:24 his **cattle**, donkeys and sheep, his tent and all that he had,
Jdg 6:4 spare a living thing for Israel, neither sheep nor **cattle** nor donkeys.
6:25 "Take the second bull from your father's **herd**, the one seven years
1Sa 12:3 presence of the LORD and his anointed. Whose **ox** have I taken?
14:34 and tell them, 'Each of you bring me your **cattle** and sheep,
14:34 meat with blood still in it.' " So everyone brought his **ox** that night
15:3 children and infants, **cattle** and sheep, camels and donkeys.' "
22:19 its children and infants, and its **cattle**, donkeys and sheep.
2Sa 6:13 had taken six steps, he sacrificed a **bull** and a fattened calf.
1Ki 1:19 He has sacrificed great numbers of **cattle**, fattened calves,
1:25 Today he has gone down and sacrificed great numbers of **cattle**,
Ne 5:18 Each day one **ox**, six choice sheep and some poultry were prepared
Job 6:5 donkey bray when it has grass, or an **ox** bellow when it has fodder?
21:10 Their **bulls** never fail to breed; their cows calve and do not
24:3 away the orphan's donkey and take the widow's **ox** in pledge.
Ps 69:31 [69:32] This will please the LORD more than an **ox**, more than a
106:20 They exchanged their Glory for an image of a **bull**, which eats
Pr 7:22 All at once he followed her like an **ox** going to the slaughter,
14:4 but from the strength of an **ox** comes an abundant harvest.
15:17 Better a meal of vegetables where there is love than a fattened **calf**
Isa 1:3 The **ox** knows his master, the donkey his owner's manger,
7:25 they will become places where **cattle** are turned loose and where
32:20 by every stream, and letting your **cattle** and donkeys range free.
66:3 But whoever sacrifices a **bull** is like one who kills a man,
Eze 1:10 side each had the face of a lion, and on the left the face of an **ox**;
Hos 12:11 [12:12] people are worthless! Do they sacrifice **bulls** in Gilgal?

8803 [3]שׁוּר *šûr*[3], n.[m.]. [3] [→ 8804; cf. 8800; Ar 10703]

wall [3]

Ge 49:22 a fruitful vine near a spring, whose branches climb over a **wall**.
2Sa 22:30 help I can advance against a troop; with my God I can scale a **wall**.
Ps 18:29 [18:30] advance against a troop; with my God I can scale a **wall**.

8804 [4]שׁוּר *šûr*[4], n.pr.loc. [6] [√ 8803?; cf. 8800?]

Shur [6]

Ge 16:7 in the desert; it was the spring that is beside the road to **Shur**.
20:1 into the region of the Negev and lived between Kadesh and **Shur**.
25:18 His descendants settled in the area from Havilah to **Shur**,
Ex 15:22 led Israel from the Red Sea and they went into the Desert of **Shur**.
1Sa 15:7 Saul attacked the Amalekites all the way from Havilah to **Shur**,
27:8 ancient times these peoples had lived in the land extending to **Shur**

8805 שׁוּרָה šûrâ, n.f. [1] [→ 9224; cf. 8800]

terraces [1]

Job 24: 11 They crush olives among the **terraces**; they tread the winepresses,

8806 שׁוֹרֵר šôrēr, n.m. [5 / 6]

slander [2], adversaries [1], enemies [1], oppressors [1], slanderers [1]

Ps 5: 8 [5:9] O LORD, in your righteousness because of my **enemies**—
27: 11 O LORD; lead me in a straight path because of my **oppressors**.
54: 5 [54:7] Let evil recoil on *those who* **slander** me; in your
56: 2 [56:3] My **slanderers** pursue me all day long; many are attacking
59: 10 [59:11] and will let me gloat over *those who* **slander** me.
92: 11 [92:12] eyes have seen the defeat of my **adversaries**; [BHS 8800]

8807 שַׁוְשָׁא šawšā', n.pr.m. [1]

Shavsha [1]

1Ch 18: 16 Ahimelech son of Abiathar were priests; **Shavsha** was secretary;

8808 שׁוּשַׁן šûšan¹, n.m. [17]

lilies [11], lily [6]

1Ki 7: 19 on top of the pillars in the portico were in the shape of **lilies**,
7: 22 The capitals on top were in the shape of **lilies**. And so the work on
7: 26 and its rim was like the rim of a cup, like a **lily** blossom.
2Ch 4: 5 and its rim was like the rim of a cup, like a **lily** blossom.
Ps 45: T [45:1] To ⌊the tune of⌋ "Lilies." Of the Sons of Korah.
60: T [60:1] To ⌊the tune of⌋ "The **Lily** *of* the Covenant." A *miktam*
69: T [69:1] the director of music. To ⌊the tune of⌋ "**Lilies**." Of David.
80: T [80:1] To ⌊the tune of⌋ "The **Lilies** *of* the Covenant." Of Asaph.
SS 2: 1 I am a rose of Sharon, a **lily** *of* the valleys.
2: 2 Like a **lily** among thorns is my darling among the maidens.
2: 16 My lover is mine and I am his; he browses among the **lilies**.
4: 5 like twin fawns of a gazelle that browse among the **lilies**.
5: 13 spice yielding perfume. His lips are like **lilies** dripping with myrrh.
6: 2 to the beds of spices, to browse in the gardens and to gather **lilies**.
6: 3 I am my lover's and my lover is mine; he browses among the **lilies**.
7: 2 [7:3] Your waist is a mound of wheat encircled by **lilies**.
Hos 14: 5 [14:6] I will be like the dew to Israel; he will blossom like a **lily**.

8809 שׁוּשַׁן šûšan², n.pr.loc. [21] [→ Ar 10704]

Susa [21]

Ne 1: 1 of Kislev in the twentieth year, while I was in the citadel of **Susa**,
Est 1: 2 King Xerxes reigned from his royal throne in the citadel of **Susa**,
1: 5 from the least to the greatest, who were in the citadel of **Susa**.
2: 3 bring all these beautiful girls into the harem at the citadel of **Susa**.
2: 5 Now there was in the citadel of **Susa** a Jew of the tribe of
2: 8 many girls were brought to the citadel of **Susa** and put under the
3: 15 couriers went out, and the edict was issued in the citadel of **Susa**.
3: 15 and Haman sat down to drink, but the city of **Susa** was bewildered.
4: 8 which had been published in **Susa**, to show to Esther and explain it
4: 16 "Go, gather together all the Jews who are in **Susa**, and fast for me.
8: 14 And the edict was also issued in the citadel of **Susa**.
8: 15 robe of fine linen. And the city of **Susa** held a joyous celebration.
9: 6 In the citadel of **Susa**, the Jews killed and destroyed five hundred
9: 11 The number of those slain in the citadel of **Susa** was reported to
9: 12 five hundred men and the ten sons of Haman in the citadel of **Susa**.
9: 13 "give the Jews in **Susa** permission to carry out this day's edict
9: 14 An edict was issued in **Susa**, and they hanged the ten sons of
9: 15 The Jews in **Susa** came together on the fourteenth day of the
9: 15 they put to death in **Susa** three hundred men, but they did not lay
9: 18 The Jews in **Susa**, however, had assembled on the thirteenth
Da 8: 2 In my vision I saw myself in the citadel of **Susa** in the province of

8810 שׁוּשַׁק šûšaq, n.pr.m. [0] [cf. 8882]

1Ki 14: 25 [**Shishak** [K; see Q 8882] king of Egypt attacked Jerusalem.]

8811 שׁוּתֶלַח šûtelaḥ, n.pr.m. [4] [→ 9279]

Shuthelah [4]

Nu 26: 35 through **Shuthelah**, the Shuthelahite clan; through Beker,
26: 36 These were the descendants of **Shuthelah**: through Eran,
1Ch 7: 20 **Shuthelah**, Bered his son, Tahath his son, Eleadah his son,
7: 21 Zabad his son and **Shuthelah** his son. Ezer and Elead were killed

8812 שָׁזַף šāzap, v. [3] [cf. 8728]

darkened [1], saw [1], seen [1]

Job 20: 9 [A] The eye *that* **saw** him will not see him again; his place will
28: 7 [A] of prey knows that hidden path, no falcon's eye *has* **seen** it.
SS 1: 6 [A] at me because I am dark, because I *am* **darkened** *by* the sun.

8813 שָׁזַר šāzar, v. [21]

finely twisted [21]

Ex 26: 1 [H] "Make the tabernacle with ten curtains of **finely twisted**
26: 31 [H] of blue, purple and scarlet yarn and **finely twisted** linen,
26: 36 [H] of blue, purple and scarlet yarn and **finely twisted** linen—
27: 9 [H] cubits long and is to have curtains of **finely twisted** linen,
27: 16 [H] of blue, purple and scarlet yarn and **finely twisted** linen—
27: 18 [H] with curtains of **finely twisted** linen five cubits high,
28: 6 [H] of blue, purple and scarlet yarn, and of **finely twisted** linen—
28: 8 [H] purple and scarlet yarn, and with **finely twisted** linen.
28: 15 [H] of blue, purple and scarlet yarn, and of **finely twisted** linen.
36: 8 [H] made the tabernacle with ten curtains of **finely twisted** linen
36: 35 [H] of blue, purple and scarlet yarn and **finely twisted** linen,
36: 37 [H] of blue, purple and scarlet yarn and **finely twisted** linen—
38: 9 [H] hundred cubits long and had curtains of **finely twisted** linen,
38: 16 [H] All the curtains around the courtyard were of **finely twisted**
38: 18 [H] of blue, purple and scarlet yarn and **finely twisted** linen—
39: 2 [H] of blue, purple and scarlet yarn, and of **finely twisted** linen.
39: 5 [H] purple and scarlet yarn, and with **finely twisted** linen,
39: 8 [H] of blue, purple and scarlet yarn, and of **finely twisted** linen.
39: 24 [H] and **finely twisted** linen around the hem of the robe.
39: 28 [H] and the undergarments of **finely twisted** linen.
39: 29 [H] The sash was of **finely twisted** linen and blue, purple

8814 שַׁח šaḥ, a. [1] [√ 8820]

downcast [+6524] [1]

Job 22: 29 you say, 'Lift them up!' then he will save the **downcast** [+6524].

8815 שָׁחַד šāḥad, v. [2] [→ 8816; cf. 8610]

bribing [1], pay a ransom [1]

Job 6: 22 [A] on my behalf, **pay a ransom** for me from your wealth,
Eze 16: 33 [A] **bribing** them to come to you from everywhere for your illicit

8816 שֹׁחַד šōḥad, n.m. [23] [√ 8815]

bribe [12], bribes [6], gift [2], bribery [+5228] [1], reward [1], those who love bribes [1]

Ex 23: 8 "Do not accept a **bribe**, for a bribe blinds those who see and twists
23: 8 for a **bribe** blinds those who see and twists the words of the
Dt 10: 17 and awesome, who shows no partiality and accepts no **bribes**.
16: 19 Do not accept a **bribe**, for a bribe blinds the eyes of the wise
16: 19 for a **bribe** blinds the eyes of the wise and twists the words of the
27: 25 "Cursed is the man who accepts a **bribe** to kill an innocent
1Sa 8: 3 after dishonest gain and accepted **bribes** and perverted justice.
1Ki 15: 19 and your father. See, I am sending you a **gift** *of* silver and gold.
2Ki 16: 8 of the royal palace and sent it as a **gift** to the king of Assyria.
2Ch 19: 7 our God there is no injustice or partiality or **bribery** [+5228]."
Job 15: 34 and fire will consume the tents of **those who love bribes**.
Ps 15: 5 without usury and does not accept a **bribe** against the innocent.
26: 10 hands are wicked schemes, whose right hands are full of **bribes**.
Pr 6: 35 any compensation; he will refuse the **bribe**, however great it is.
17: 8 A **bribe** is a charm to the one who gives it; wherever he turns,
17: 23 A wicked man accepts a **bribe** in secret to pervert the course of
21: 14 and a **bribe** concealed in the cloak pacifies great wrath.
Isa 1: 23 companions of thieves; they all love **bribes** and chase after gifts.
5: 23 who acquit the guilty for a **bribe**, but deny justice to the innocent.
33: 15 gain from extortion and keeps his hand from accepting **bribes**,
45: 13 my city and set my exiles free, but not for a price or **reward**,
Eze 22: 12 In you men accept **bribes** to shed blood; you take usury
Mic 3: 11 Her leaders judge for a **bribe**, her priests teach for a price,

8817 שָׁחָה šāḥâ, v. [2] [cf. 2556, 8755, 8820]

fall prostrate [1], weighs down [1]

Pr 12: 25 [G] An anxious heart **weighs** a man **down**, but a kind word
Isa 51: 23 [A] who said to you, '**Fall prostrate** that we may walk over you.'

8818 שְׁחוֹר šᵉḥôr, n.[m.]. [1] [√ 8837]

soot [1]

La 4: 8 now they are blacker than **soot**; they are not recognized in the

8819 שְׁחוּת šᵉḥût, n.f. [1] [→ 8827]

trap [1]

Pr 28: 10 who leads the upright along an evil path will fall into his own **trap**,

8820 שָׁחַח šāḥaḥ, v. [18] [→ 8814; cf. 8755, 8817]

brought low [3], be brought low [2], bow down [1], bowed head [1], bowing [1], bring down [1], collapse [1], collapsed [1], cowered [1], crouch [1], downcast [1], faint [1], humbled [1], humbles [1], mumble [1]

Job 9:13 [A] his anger; even the cohorts of Rahab **cowered** at his feet.
38:40 [A] when *they* **crouch** in their dens or lie in wait in a thicket?
Ps 10:10 [A] His victims are crushed, *they* **collapse**; they fall under his
35:14 [A] *I* **bowed** *my* **head** in grief as though weeping for my mother.
38:6 [38:7] [A] I am bowed down and **brought** very **low**; all day
107:39 [A] and *they were* **humbled** by oppression, calamity and sorrow;
Pr 14:19 [A] Evil men *will* **bow down** in the presence of the good,
Ecc 12:4 [C] rise up at the sound of birds, but all their songs *grow* **faint**;
Isa 2:9 [C] So man *will* **be brought low** and mankind humbled—do not
2:11 [A] man will be humbled and the pride of men **brought low**;
2:17 [A] The arrogance of man *will be* **brought low** and the pride of
5:15 [C] So man *will* **be brought low** and mankind humbled, the eyes
25:12 [G] *He will* **bring down** your high fortified walls and lay them
26:5 [G] *He* **humbles** those who dwell on high, he lays the lofty city
29:4 [C] from the ground; your speech *will* **mumble** out of the dust.
60:14 [A] The sons of your oppressors will come **bowing** before you;
La 3:20 [A] I well remember them, and my soul *is* **downcast** within me.
Hab 3:6 [A] ancient mountains crumbled and the age-old hills **collapsed**.

8821 1שָׁחַט šāḥaṭ[1], v. [80] [→ 8823, 8824]

slaughtered [35], slaughter [23], killed [5], sacrifices [2], *untranslated* [1], be slaughtered [1], butchered [1], dead [1], deadly [1], kill [1], killing [1], offer [1], sacrifice [1], sacrificed [1], sacrifices slaughtered [1], slaughtering [1], slay [1], was killed [1], were slaughtered [1]

Ge 22:10 [A] he reached out his hand and took the knife to **slay** his son.
37:31 [A] **slaughtered** a goat and dipped the robe in the blood.
Ex 12:6 [A] of the community of Israel *must* **slaughter** them at twilight.
12:21 [A] animals for your families and **slaughter** the Passover lamb.
29:11 [A] **Slaughter** it in the LORD's presence at the entrance to the
29:16 [A] **Slaughter** it and take the blood and sprinkle it against the
29:20 [A] **Slaughter** it, take some of its blood and put it on the lobes of
34:25 [A] "*Do* not **offer** the blood of a sacrifice to me along with
Lev 1:5 [A] *He is to* **slaughter** the young bull before the LORD, and
1:11 [A] *He is to* **slaughter** it at the north side of the altar before the
3:2 [A] and **slaughter** it at the entrance to the Tent of Meeting.
3:8 [A] his offering and **slaughter** it in front of the Tent of Meeting.
3:13 [A] on its head and **slaughter** it in front of the Tent of Meeting.
4:4 [A] lay his hand on its head and **slaughter** it before the LORD.
4:15 [A] and the bull *shall be* **slaughtered** before the LORD.
4:24 [A] **slaughter** it at the place where the burnt offering is
4:24 [A] where the burnt offering *is* **slaughtered** before the LORD.
4:29 [A] and **slaughter** it at the place of the burnt offering.
4:33 [A] **slaughter** it for a sin offering at the place where the burnt
4:33 [A] offering at the place where the burnt offering *is* **slaughtered**.
6:25 [6:18] [C] The sin offering *is to* **be slaughtered** before the
6:25 [6:18] [C] in the place the burnt offering *is* **slaughtered**;
7:2 [A] The guilt offering *is to be* **slaughtered** in the place where the
7:2 [A] in the place where the burnt offering *is* **slaughtered**,
8:15 [A] Moses **slaughtered** the bull and took some of the blood,
8:19 [A] Moses **slaughtered** the ram and sprinkled the blood against
8:23 [A] Moses **slaughtered** the ram and took some of its blood
9:8 [A] and **slaughtered** the calf as a sin offering for himself.
9:12 [A] *he* **slaughtered** the burnt offering. His sons handed him the
9:15 [A] took the goat for the people's sin offering and **slaughtered** it
9:18 [A] *He* **slaughtered** the ox and the ram as the fellowship offering
14:5 [A] the priest shall order that one of the birds *be* **killed** over fresh
14:6 [B] into the blood of the bird that **was killed** over the fresh water.
14:13 [A] *He is to* **slaughter** the lamb in the holy place where the sin
14:13 [A] the sin offering and the burnt offering *are* **slaughtered**.
14:19 [A] After that, the priest *shall* **slaughter** the burnt offering
14:25 [A] *He shall* **slaughter** the lamb for the guilt offering and take
14:50 [A] *He shall* **kill** one of the birds over fresh water in a clay pot.
14:51 [B] dip them into the blood of the **dead** bird and the fresh water,
16:11 [A] and *he is to* **slaughter** the bull for his own sin offering.
16:15 [A] "*He shall* then **slaughter** the goat for the sin offering for the
17:3 [A] Any Israelite who **sacrifices** an ox, a lamb or a goat in the
17:3 [A] an ox, a lamb or a goat in the camp or **[RPH]** outside of it
22:28 [A] *Do* not **slaughter** a cow or a sheep and its young on the same
Nu 11:22 [C] have enough if flocks and herds **were slaughtered** for them?
14:16 [A] them on oath; so *he* **slaughtered** them in the desert.'
19:3 [A] be taken outside the camp and **slaughtered** in his presence.
Jdg 12:6 [A] they seized him and **killed** him at the fords of the Jordan.
1Sa 1:25 [A] When *they had* **slaughtered** the bull, they brought the boy to
14:32 [A] and calves, they **butchered** them on the ground and ate them,
14:34 [A] your cattle and sheep, and **slaughter** them here and eat them.
14:34 [A] everyone brought his ox that night and **slaughtered** it there.
1Ki 18:40 [A] brought down to the Kishon Valley and **slaughtered** there.
2Ki 10:7 [A] men took the princes and **slaughtered** all seventy of them.
10:14 [A] them alive and **slaughtered** them by the well of Beth Eked—
25:7 [A] *They* **killed** the sons of Zedekiah before his eyes. Then they
2Ch 29:22 [A] So *they* **slaughtered** the bulls, and the priests took the blood
29:22 [A] next *they* **slaughtered** the rams and sprinkled their blood on
29:22 [A] *they* **slaughtered** the lambs and sprinkled their blood on the
29:24 [A] The priests then **slaughtered** the goats and presented their
30:15 [A] *They* **slaughtered** the Passover lamb on the fourteenth day
35:1 [A] the Passover lamb *was* **slaughtered** on the fourteenth day of
35:6 [A] **Slaughter** the Passover lambs, consecrate yourselves
35:11 [A] The Passover lambs *were* **slaughtered**, and the priests
Ezr 6:20 [A] The Levites **slaughtered** the Passover lamb for all the exiles,
Isa 22:13 [A] is joy and revelry, slaughtering of cattle and **killing** *of* sheep,
57:5 [A] you **sacrifice** your children in the ravines and under the
66:3 [A] But *whoever* **sacrifices** a bull is like one who kills a man,
Jer 9:8 [9:7] [A] Their tongue is a **deadly** arrow; it speaks with deceit.
39:6 [A] There at Riblah the king of Babylon **slaughtered** the sons of
39:6 [A] before his eyes and also **killed** all the nobles of Judah.
41:7 [A] and the men who were with him **slaughtered** them
52:10 [A] There at Riblah the king of Babylon **slaughtered** the sons of
52:10 [A] before his eyes; *he* also **killed** all the officials of Judah.
Eze 16:21 [A] *You* **slaughtered** my children and sacrificed them to the
23:39 [A] On the very day they **sacrificed** their children to their idols,
40:39 [A] sin offerings and guilt offerings *were* **slaughtered**.
40:41 [A] tables in all—on which *the* **sacrifices** *were* **slaughtered**.
40:42 [A] On them were placed the utensils *for* **slaughtering** the burnt
44:11 [A] they *may* **slaughter** the burnt offerings and sacrifices for the

8822 2שָׁחַט šāḥaṭ[2], v. [5]

hammered [5]

1Ki 10:16 [B] made two hundred large shields of **hammered** gold;
10:17 [B] He also made three hundred small shields of **hammered**
2Ch 9:15 [B] made two hundred large shields of **hammered** gold;
9:15 [B] six hundred bekas of **hammered** gold went into each shield.
9:16 [B] He also made three hundred small shields of **hammered**

8823 שַׁחֲטָה šaḥ^{a}ṭâ, n.f. [1] [√ 8821]

slaughter [1]

Hos 5:2 The rebels are deep in **slaughter**. I will discipline all of them.

8824 שְׁחִיטָה š^{e}ḥîṭâ, n.f. [1] [√ 8821]

kill [1]

2Ch 30:17 the Levites had to **kill** the Passover lambs for all those who were

8825 שְׁחִין š^{e}ḥîn, n.m. [13]

boil [6], boils [5], *untranslated* [1], sores [1]

Ex 9:9 festering **boils** will break out on men and animals throughout the
9:10 it into the air, and festering **boils** broke out on men and animals.
9:11 because of the **boils** that were on them and on all the Egyptians.
9:11 because of the boils that were **[RPH]** on them and on all the
Lev 13:18 "When someone has a **boil** on his skin and it heals,
13:19 in the place where the **boil** was, a white swelling or reddish-white
13:20 It is an infectious skin disease that has broken out where the **boil**
13:23 is unchanged and has not spread, it is only a scar from the **boil**,
Dt 28:27 The LORD will afflict you with the **boils** *of* Egypt and with
28:35 afflict your knees and legs with painful **boils** that cannot be cured,
2Ki 20:7 of figs." They did so and applied it to the **boil**, and he recovered.
Job 2:7 afflicted Job with painful **sores** from the soles of his feet to the top
Isa 38:21 Isaiah had said, "Prepare a poultice of figs and apply it to the **boil**,

8826 שָׁחִיס šāḥîs, n.[m.]. [1] [cf. 6084]

what springs from [1]

Isa 37:30 what grows by itself, and the second year **what springs from** *that*.

8827 שְׁחִית š^{e}ḥît, n.f. [2] [√ 8819]

grave [1], traps [1]

Ps 107:20 forth his word and healed them; he rescued them from the **grave**.
La 4:20 LORD's anointed, our very life breath, was caught in their **traps**.

8828 שַׁחַל šaḥal, n.m. [7] [√ 8829]

lion [6], *untranslated* [1]

Job 4:10 and growl, **[RPH]** yet the teeth of the great lions are broken.
10:16 you stalk me like a **lion** and again display your awesome power
28:8 Proud beasts do not set foot on it, and no **lion** prowls there.
Ps 91:13 You will tread upon the **lion** and the cobra; you will trample the
Pr 26:13 The sluggard says, "There is a **lion** in the road, a fierce lion
Hos 5:14 For I will be like a **lion** to Ephraim, like a great lion to Judah.
13:7 So I will come upon them like a **lion**, like a leopard I will lurk by

8829 שְׁחֵלֶת š^{e}ḥēlet, n.f. [1] [→ 8828]

onycha [1]

Ex 30:34 gum resin, **onycha** and galbanum—and pure frankincense,

8830 שַׁחַף šaḥap, n.[m.]. [2]

gull [2]

Lev 11:16 the horned owl, the screech owl, the **gull**, any kind of hawk,
Dt 14:15 the horned owl, the screech owl, the **gull**, any kind of hawk,

8831 שַׁחֶפֶת šaḥepet, n.f. [2]

wasting disease [1], wasting diseases [1]

Lev 26:16 **wasting diseases** and fever that will destroy your sight and drain
Dt 28:22 The LORD will strike you with **wasting disease**, with fever

8832 שַׁחַץ šaḥaṣ, n.[m.]. [2] [→ 8833, 8834]

proud [+1201] [1], proud beasts [+1201] [1]

Job 28:8 **Proud** [+1201] **beasts** do not set foot on it, and no lion prowls
41:34 [41:26] are haughty; he is king over all that are **proud** [+1201]."

8833 שַׁחֲצוּמָה šaḥᵃṣûmâ, n.pr.loc. [1] [√ 8832]

Shahazumah [1]

Jos 19:22 **Shahazumah** [Q 8834] and Beth Shemesh, and ended at the

8834 שַׁחֲצִימָה šaḥᵃṣîmâ, n.pr.loc. [0] [√ 8832]

Jos 19:22 [The boundary touched Tabor, **Shahazumah** [Q; see K 8833]]

8835 שָׁחַק šāḥaq, v. [4] [→ 8836]

beat fine [2], grind [1], wears away [1]

Ex 30:36 [A] **Grind** some of it to powder and place it in front of the
2Sa 22:43 [A] *I* **beat** them as **fine** as the dust of the earth; I pounded and
Job 14:19 [A] as water **wears away** stones and torrents wash away the soil,
Ps 18:42 [18:43] [A] *I* **beat** them as **fine** as dust borne on the wind;

8836 שַׁחַק šaḥaq, n.m. [21] [√ 8835]

clouds [8], skies [8], clouds of the sky [+6265] [2], dust [1], skies above [1], sky [1]

Dt 33:26 rides on the heavens to help you and on the **clouds** in his majesty.
2Sa 22:12 his canopy around him—the dark rain **clouds** [+6265] **of the sky**.
Job 35:5 up at the heavens and see; gaze at the **clouds** so high above you.
36:28 the **clouds** pour down their moisture and abundant showers fall on
37:18 can you join him in spreading out the **skies**, hard as a mirror of cast
37:21 bright as it is in the **skies** after the wind has swept them clean.
38:37 Who has the wisdom to count the **clouds**? Who can tip over the
Ps 18:11 [18:12] around him—the dark rain **clouds** [+6265] **of the sky**.
36:5 [36:6] reaches to the heavens, your faithfulness to the **skies**.
57:10 [57:11] to the heavens; your faithfulness reaches to the **skies**.
68:34 [68:35] whose majesty is over Israel, whose power is in the **skies**.
77:17 [77:18] poured down water, the **skies** resounded with thunder;
78:23 Yet he gave a command to the **skies** above and opened the doors of
89:6 [89:7] For who in the **skies above** can compare with the LORD?
89:37 [89:38] forever like the moon, the faithful witness in the **sky**."
108:4 [108:5] than the heavens; your faithfulness reaches to the **skies**.
Pr 3:20 the deeps were divided, and the **clouds** let drop the dew.
8:28 when he established the **clouds** above and fixed securely the
Isa 40:15 are like a drop in a bucket; they are regarded as **dust** *on* the scales;
45:8 rain down righteousness; let the **clouds** shower it down.
Jer 51:9 for her judgment reaches to the skies, it rises as high as the **clouds**.'

8837 [1]שָׁחַר šāḥar[1], v. [1] [→ 328, 5423, 8818, 8839, 8040, 8841, 8842, 8844]

grows black [1]

Job 30:30 [A] My skin **grows black** and peels; my body burns with fever.

8838 [2]שָׁחַר šāḥar[2], v.den. [13] [→ 8843; cf. 8840?]

earnestly seek [2], careful [1], conjure away [1], eagerly [1], foraging [1], longs for [1], look for [1], look [1], looked for [1], search for [1], seek [1], seeks [1]

Job 7:21 [D] in the dust; *you will* **search for** me, but I will be no more."
8:5 [D] But if you *will* **look** to God and plead with the Almighty,
24:5 [D] in the desert, the poor go about their labor of **foraging** food;
Ps 63:1 [63:2] [D] O God, you are my God, **earnestly** *I* **seek** you;
78:34 [D] they would seek him; they **eagerly** turned to him again.
Pr 1:28 [D] I will not answer; *they will* **look for** me but will not find me.
7:15 [D] came out to meet you; I **looked for** you and have found you!
8:17 [D] I love those who love me, and *those who* **seek** me find me.
11:27 [A] *He who* **seeks** good finds goodwill, but evil comes to him
13:24 [D] his son, but he who loves him *is* **careful** to discipline him.
Isa 26:9 [D] for you in the night; in the morning my spirit **longs for** you.
47:11 [D] upon you, and you will not know how *to* **conjure** it **away**.
Hos 5:15 [D] seek my face; in their misery *they will* **earnestly seek** me."

8839 שָׁחֹר šāḥōr, a. [6] [√ 8837]

black [5], dark [1]

Lev 13:31 not seem to be more than skin deep and there is no **black** hair in it,
13:37 in his judgment it is unchanged and **black** hair has grown in it,
SS 1:5 **Dark** am I, yet lovely, O daughters of Jerusalem, dark like the
5:11 His head is purest gold; his hair is wavy and **black** as a raven.
Zec 6:2 The first chariot had red horses, the second **black**,
6:6 The one with the **black** horses is going toward the north country,

8840 שַׁחַר šaḥar, n.m. [23] [√ 8037, 8844; cf. 8838?]

dawn [14], daybreak [+2021+6590] [2], daybreak [2], day dawns [1], first light of dawn [+6590] [1], light of dawn [1], morning [1], sun rises [1]

Ge 19:15 With the coming of **dawn**, the angels urged Lot, saying, "Hurry!
32:24 [32:25] left alone, and a man wrestled with him till **daybreak**.
32:26 [32:27] the man said, "Let me go, for it is **daybreak**." But Jacob
Jos 6:15 On the seventh day, they got up at **daybreak** [+2021+6590] and
Jdg 19:25 and abused her throughout the night, and at **dawn** they let her go.
1Sa 9:26 They rose about **daybreak** [+2021+6590] and Samuel called to
Ne 4:21 [4:15] from the **first light of dawn** [+6590] till the stars came out.
Job 3:9 may it wait for daylight in vain and not see the first rays of **dawn**,
38:12 given orders to the morning, or shown the **dawn** its place,
41:18 [41:10] out flashes of light; his eyes are like the rays of **dawn**.
Ps 22:T [22:1] To ⌊the tune of⌋ "The Doe of the **Morning**." A psalm of
57:8 [57:9] my soul! Awake, harp and lyre! I will awaken the **dawn**.
108:2 [108:3] Awake, harp and lyre! I will awaken the **dawn**.
139:9 If I rise on the wings of the **dawn**, if I settle on the far side of the
SS 6:10 Who is this that appears like the **dawn**, fair as the moon, bright as
Isa 8:20 do not speak according to this word, they have no **light of dawn**.
14:12 you have fallen from heaven, O morning star, son of the **dawn**!
58:8 your light will break forth like the **dawn**, and your healing will
Hos 6:3 As surely as the **sun rises**, he will appear; he will come to us like
10:15 When that **day dawns**, the king of Israel will be completely
Joel 2:2 Like **dawn** spreading across the mountains a large and mighty
Am 4:13 and reveals his thoughts to man, he who turns **dawn** to darkness,
Jnh 4:7 at **dawn** the next day God provided a worm, which chewed the

8841 שַׁחֲרוּת šaḥᵃrût, n.f. [1] [√ 8837]

vigor [1]

Ecc 11:10 off the troubles of your body, for youth and **vigor** are meaningless.

8842 שְׁחַרְחֹר šᵉḥarḥōr, a. [1] [√ 8837]

dark [1]

SS 1:6 Do not stare at me because I am **dark**, because I am darkened by

8843 שְׁחַרְיָה šᵉḥaryâ, n.pr.m. [1] [√ 8838]

Shehariah [1]

1Ch 8:26 Shamsherai, **Shehariah**, Athaliah,

8844 שַׁחֲרַיִם šaḥᵃrayim, n.pr.m. [1] [√ 8840; cf. 8837]

Shaharaim [1]

1Ch 8:8 Sons were born to **Shaharaim** in Moab after he had divorced his

8845 שָׁחַת šāḥat, v. [146] [→ 5422, 5424, 5425, 5426; Ar 10705]

destroy [60], destroyed [11], corrupt [10], destroying [5], cut down [3], destroys [3], ruin [3], ruined [3], act corruptly [2], corrupted [2], depraved [2], destruction [2], devastate [2], raiding parties [2], ravage [2], sure to become utterly corrupt [+8845] [2], *untranslated* [1], acted corruptly [1], afflicting [1], allowed to fall into ruin [1], battering [1], blemished [1], cause devastation [1], cause of destruction [1], clip off [1], corrupt practices [1], corruption [1], devastated [1], devouring [1], doing[s] so [1], downfall [1], endanger [1], given to corruption [1], killed [1], laid waste [1], overthrow [1], polluted [1], ravaging [1], ravening [1], spilled [1], steal [1], stifling [1], struck down [1], tear down [1], violated [1], was marred [1], was ruined [1], wasted [1]

Ge 6:11 [C] Now the earth *was* **corrupt** in God's sight and was full of
6:12 [C] God saw *how* **corrupt** the earth *had become*, for all the
6:12 [G] for all the people on earth *had* **corrupted** their ways.
6:13 [G] I *am* surely *going to* **destroy** both them and the earth.
6:17 [D] I am going to bring floodwaters on the earth to **destroy** all
9:11 [D] never again will there be a flood to **destroy** the earth."
9:15 [D] Never again will the waters become a flood to **destroy** all
13:10 [D] (This was before the LORD **destroyed** Sodom and
18:28 [G] *Will you* **destroy** the whole city because of five people?"
18:28 [G] "If I find forty-five there," he said, "*I will* not **destroy** it."
18:31 [G] He said, "For the sake of twenty, *I will* not **destroy** it."
18:32 [G] He answered, "For the sake of ten, *I will* not **destroy** it."

Ge 19:13 [G] because we *are going to* **destroy** this place. The outcry to
19:13 [D] its people is so great that he has sent us to **destroy** it."
19:14 [G] this place, because the LORD *is about to* **destroy** the city!"
19:29 [D] So when God **destroyed** the cities of the plain, he
38: 9 [D] *he* **spilled** his semen on the ground to keep from producing
Ex 8:24 [8:20] [C] throughout Egypt the land **was ruined** by the flies.
21:26 [D] hits a manservant or maidservant in the eye and **destroys** it,
32: 7 [D] whom you brought up out of Egypt, *have become* **corrupt**.
Lev 19:27 [G] at the sides of your head or **clip off** the edges of your beard.
Nu 32:15 [D] the desert, and *you will be the* **cause of** their **destruction**."
Dt 4:16 [G] so that *you do* not *become* **corrupt** and make for yourselves
4:25 [G] if *you* then *become* **corrupt** and make any kind of idol,
4:31 [G] he will not abandon or **destroy** you or forget the covenant
9:12 [D] whom you brought out of Egypt *have become* **corrupt**.
9:26 [G] and said, "O Sovereign LORD, *do* not **destroy** your people,
10:10 [G] to me at this time also. It was not his will *to* **destroy** you.
20:19 [G] *do* not **destroy** its trees by putting an ax to them,
20:20 [G] **[RPH]** and use them to build siege works until the city at
31:29 [G] my death *you are* **sure to become utterly corrupt** [+8845]
31:29 [G] my death *you are* **sure to become utterly corrupt** [+8845]
32: 5 [D] *They have* **acted corruptly** toward him; to their shame they
Jos 22:33 [D] against them to **devastate** the country where the Reubenites
Jdg 2:19 [G] the people returned to ways even more **corrupt** than those of
6: 4 [G] camped on the land and **ruined** the crops all the way to Gaza
6: 5 [D] the men and their camels; they invaded the land to **ravage** it.
20:21 [G] **cut down** twenty-two thousand Israelites on the battlefield
20:25 [G] *they* **cut down** another eighteen thousand Israelites, all of
20:35 [G] on that day the Israelites **struck down** 25,100 Benjamites,
20:42 [G] the men of Israel who came out of the towns **cut** them **down**
Ru 4: 6 [G] I cannot redeem it because *I might* **endanger** my own estate.
1Sa 6: 5 [G] of the tumors and of the rats that *are* **destroying** the country,
13:17 [G] **Raiding parties** went out from the Philistine camp in three
14:15 [G] and field, and those in the outposts and **raiding parties**—
23:10 [D] to come to Keilah and **destroy** the town on account of me.
26: 9 [G] David said to Abishai, "Don't **destroy** him! Who can lay a
26:15 [G] lord the king? Someone came to **destroy** your lord the king.
2Sa 1:14 [D] "Why were you not afraid to lift your hand to **destroy** the
11: 1 [G] *They* **destroyed** the Ammonites and besieged Rabbah.
14:11 [D] prevent the avenger of blood from adding to the **destruction**,
20:15 [G] While *they were* **battering** the wall to bring it down,
20:20 [G] Joab replied, "Far be it from me to swallow up or **destroy**!
24:16 [D] When the angel stretched out his hand to **destroy** Jerusalem,
24:16 [G] and said to the angel who *was* **afflicting** the people,
2Ki 8:19 [G] servant David, the LORD was not willing to **destroy** Judah.
13:23 [G] To this day he has been unwilling *to* **destroy** them or banish
18:25 [G] and **destroy** this place without word from the LORD?
18:25 [G] told me to march against this country and **destroy** it.' "
19:12 [D] Did the gods of the nations that *were* **destroyed** *by* my
1Ch 20: 1 [G] *He* **laid waste** the land of the Ammonites and went to
21:12 [G] with the angel of the LORD **ravaging** every part of Israel.'
21:15 [G] God sent an angel to **destroy** Jerusalem. But as the angel was
21:15 [G] as the angel *was* **doing** so, the LORD saw it and was
21:15 [G] and said to the angel who *was* **destroying** the people,
2Ch 12: 7 [G] *I will* not **destroy** them but will soon give them deliverance.
12:12 [G] anger turned from him, and he *was* not totally **destroyed**.
20:23 [G] the men from Seir, they helped to **destroy** one another.
21: 7 [G] the LORD was not willing to **destroy** the house of David.
24:23 [G] and Jerusalem and **killed** all the leaders of the people.
25:16 [G] but said, "I know that God has determined to **destroy** you,
26:16 [G] after Uzziah became powerful, his pride led to his **downfall**.
27: 2 [G] The people, however, continued *their* **corrupt practices**.
34:11 [G] that the kings of Judah *had* **allowed to fall into ruin**.
35:21 [G] stop opposing God, who is with me, or *he will* **destroy** you."
36:19 [G] all the palaces and **destroyed** everything of value there.
Ps 14: 1 [G] *They are* **corrupt**, their deeds are vile; there is no one who
53: 1 [53:2] [G] *They are* **corrupt**, and their ways are vile; there is
57: T [57:1] [G] ⌞To the tune of⌟ "*Do* Not **Destroy**." Of David.
58: T [58:1] [G] ⌞To the tune of⌟ "*Do* Not **Destroy**." Of David.
59: T [59:1] [G] ⌞To the tune of⌟ "*Do* Not **Destroy**." Of David.
75: T [75:1] [G] ⌞To the tune of⌟ "*Do* Not **Destroy**." A psalm of
78:38 [G] he forgave their iniquities and *did* not **destroy** them.
78:45 [G] of flies that devoured them, and frogs that **devastated** them.
106:23 [G] breach before him to keep his wrath from **destroying** them.
Pr 6:32 [G] adultery lacks judgment; whoever does so **destroys** himself.
11: 9 [G] With his mouth the godless **destroys** his neighbor,
23: 8 [D] you have eaten and *will have* **wasted** your compliments.
25:26 [H] or a **polluted** well is a righteous man who gives way to the
Isa 1: 4 [G] a brood of evildoers, children **given to corruption**!
11: 9 [G] They will neither harm nor **destroy** on all my holy mountain,
14:20 [D] for *you have* **destroyed** your land and killed your people.
36:10 [G] I come to attack and **destroy** this land without the LORD?
36:10 [G] told me to march against this country and **destroy** it.' "
37:12 [G] Did the gods of the nations that *were* **destroyed** *by* my
51:13 [G] of the wrath of the oppressor, who is bent on **destruction**?
65: 8 [G] found in a cluster of grapes and men say, 'Don't **destroy** it,
65: 8 [G] I do in behalf of my servants; *I will* not **destroy** them all.
65:25 [G] They will neither harm nor **destroy** on all my holy
Jer 2:30 [G] Your sword has devoured your prophets like a **ravening** lion.
5:10 [D] "Go through her vineyards and **ravage** them, but do not
6: 5 [G] So arise, let us attack at night and **destroy** her fortresses!"
6:28 [G] to slander. They are bronze and iron; they all **act corruptly**.
11:19 [G] against me, saying, "*Let us* **destroy** the tree and its fruit;
12:10 [D] Many shepherds *will* **ruin** my vineyard and trample down
13: 7 [C] had hidden it, but now it *was* **ruined** and completely useless.
13: 9 [G] 'In the same way *I will* **ruin** the pride of Judah and the great
13:14 [G] or compassion *to* keep me from **destroying** them.' "
15: 3 [G] of the air and the beasts of the earth to devour and **destroy**.
15: 6 [G] So I will lay hands on you and **destroy** you; I can no longer
18: 4 [C] the pot he was shaping from the clay **was marred** in his
36:29 [G] **destroy** this land and cut off both men and animals from it?"
48:18 [D] Moab will come up against you and **ruin** your fortified cities.
49: 9 [G] the night, *would they* not **steal** only as much as they wanted?
51:11 [G] of the Medes, because his purpose is to **destroy** Babylon.
51:20 [G] with you I shatter nations, with you *I* **destroy** kingdoms,
51:25 [G] "I am against you, O **destroying** mountain, you who destroy
51:25 [G] you who **destroy** the whole earth," declares the LORD.
La 2: 5 [D] swallowed up all her palaces and **destroyed** her strongholds.
2: 6 [D] like a garden; *he has* **destroyed** his place of meeting.
2: 8 [G] The LORD determined to **tear down** the wall around the
Eze 5:16 [D] and destructive arrows of famine, I will shoot to **destroy** you.
9: 8 [G] *Are* you *going to* **destroy** the entire remnant of Israel in this
16:47 [G] in all your ways *you* soon *became* more **depraved** than they.
20:17 [D] Yet I looked on them with pity and *did* not **destroy** them
20:44 [C] not according to your evil ways and your **corrupt** practices,
22:30 [D] gap on behalf of the land so I *would* not *have to* **destroy** it,
23:11 [G] and prostitution *she was* more **depraved** than her sister.
26: 4 [D] *They will* **destroy** the walls of Tyre and pull down her
28:17 [D] and *you* **corrupted** your wisdom because of your splendor.
30:11 [D] ruthless of nations—will be brought in to **destroy** the land.
43: 3 [D] like the vision I had seen when he came to **destroy** the city
Da 8:24 [G] *He will* **cause** astounding **devastation** and will succeed in
8:24 [G] *He will* **destroy** the mighty men and the holy people.
8:25 [G] *he will* **destroy** many and take his stand against the Prince of
9:26 [G] The people of the ruler who will come *will* **destroy** the city
11:17 [G] a daughter in marriage in order to **overthrow** the kingdom,
Hos 9: 9 [D] They have sunk deep into **corruption**, as in the days of
11: 9 [D] out my fierce anger, nor will I turn and **devastate** Ephraim.
13: 9 [D] "You *are* **destroyed**, O Israel, because you are against me,
Am 1:11 [D] **stifling** all compassion, because his anger raged continually
Na 2: 2 [2:3] [D] have laid them waste and *have* **ruined** their vines.
Zep 3: 7 [G] But they were still eager *to* **act corruptly** in all they did.
Mal 1:14 [H] give it, but then sacrifices a **blemished** *animal* to the Lord.
2: 8 [D] *you have* **violated** the covenant with Levi," says the LORD
3:11 [G] I will prevent pests from **devouring** your crops, and the vines

8846 שַׁחַת *šaḥat*, n.f. [23] [√ 8755]

pit [17], corruption [2], decay [2], dungeon [1], slime pit [1]

Job 9:31 you would plunge me into a **slime pit** so that even my clothes
17:14 if I say to **corruption**, 'You are my father,' and to the worm,
33:18 to preserve his soul from the **pit**, his life from perishing by the
33:22 His soul draws near to the **pit**, and his life to the messengers of
33:24 be gracious to him and say, 'Spare him from going down to the **pit**;
33:28 He redeemed my soul from going down to the **pit**, and I will live to
33:30 to turn back his soul from the **pit**, that the light of life may shine on
Ps 7:15 [7:16] digs a hole and scoops it out falls into the **pit** he has made.
9:15 [9:16] The nations have fallen into the **pit** they have dug;
16:10 me to the grave, nor will you let your Holy One see **decay**.
30: 9 [30:10] is there in my destruction, in my going down into the **pit**?
35: 7 their net for me without cause and without cause dug a **pit** for me,
49: 9 [49:10] that he should live on forever and not see **decay**.
55:23 [55:24] will bring down the wicked into the pit of **corruption**;
94:13 him relief from days of trouble, till a **pit** is dug for the wicked.
103: 4 who redeems your life from the **pit** and crowns you with love
Pr 26:27 If a man digs a **pit**, he will fall into it; if a man rolls a stone,
Isa 38:17 In your love you kept me from the **pit** *of* destruction; you have put
51:14 they will not die in their **dungeon**, nor will they lack bread.
Eze 19: 4 The nations heard about him, and he was trapped in their **pit**.
19: 8 They spread their net for him, and he was trapped in their **pit**.
28: 8 They will bring you down to the **pit**, and you will die a violent
Jnh 2: 6 [2:7] you brought my life up from the **pit**, O LORD my God.

8847 שִׁטָּה *šiṭṭâ*, n.f. [29] [→ 8850]

acacia [25], acacia wood [3], acacias [1]

Ex 25: 5 ram skins dyed red and hides of sea cows; **acacia** wood;
25:10 "Have them make a chest of **acacia** wood—two and a half cubits
25:13 Then make poles of **acacia** wood and overlay them with gold.

[F] Hitpael (hitpoel, hitpoal, hitpolel, hitpolal, hitpalel, hitpalal, hitpalpel, hitpalpal, hotpael, hotpaal) [G] Hiphil (hiphtil) [H] Hophal [I] Hishtaphel

Ex 25: 23 "Make a table of **acacia** wood—two cubits long, a cubit wide
25: 28 Make the poles of **acacia** wood, overlay them with gold and carry
26: 15 "Make upright frames of **acacia** wood for the tabernacle.
26: 26 "Also make crossbars of **acacia** wood: five for the frames on one
26: 32 Hang it with gold hooks on four posts of **acacia wood** overlaid
26: 37 for this curtain and five posts of **acacia wood** overlaid with gold.
27: 1 "Build an altar of **acacia** wood, three cubits high; it is to be square,
27: 6 Make poles of **acacia** wood for the altar and overlay them with
30: 1 "Make an altar of **acacia** wood for burning incense.
30: 5 Make the poles of **acacia** wood and overlay them with gold.
35: 7 ram skins dyed red and hides of sea cows; **acacia** wood;
35: 24 everyone who had **acacia** wood for any part of the work brought it.
36: 20 They made upright frames of **acacia** wood for the tabernacle.
36: 31 They also made crossbars of **acacia** wood: five for the frames on
36: 36 They made four posts of **acacia wood** for it and overlaid them with
37: 1 Bezalel made the ark of **acacia** wood—two and a half cubits long,
37: 4 Then he made poles of **acacia** wood and overlaid them with gold.
37: 10 They made the table of **acacia** wood—two cubits long, a cubit
37: 15 The poles for carrying the table were made of **acacia** wood
37: 25 They made the altar of incense out of **acacia** wood. It was square,
37: 28 They made the poles of **acacia** wood and overlaid them with gold.
38: 1 They built the altar of burnt offering of **acacia** wood, three cubits
38: 6 They made the poles of **acacia** wood and overlaid them with
Dt 10: 3 So I made the ark out of **acacia** wood and chiseled out two stone
Isa 41: 19 I will put in the desert the cedar and the **acacia**, the myrtle
Joel 3: 18 [4:18] of the LORD's house and will water the valley of **acacias**.

8848 שָׁטַח šāṭaḥ, v. [6] [→ 5427]

spread out [+4200+8848] [2], enlarges [1], exposed [1], scattered [1], spread out [1]

Nu 11: 32 [A] *they* **spread** [+4200+8848] them **out** all around the camp.
11: 32 [A] *they* **spread** them **out** [+4200+8848] all around the camp.
2Sa 17: 19 [A] out over the opening of the well and **scattered** grain over it.
Job 12: 23 [A] and destroys them; *he* **enlarges** nations, and disperses them.
Ps 88: 9 [88:10] [D] every day; *I* **spread out** my hands to you.
Jer 8: 2 [A] They *will be* **exposed** to the sun and the moon and all the

8849 שׁוֹטֵט šōṭēṭ, n.[m.] [1] [√ 8765; cf. 8763]

whips [1]

Jos 23: 13 and traps for you, **whips** on your backs and thorns in your eyes,

8850 שִׁטִּים šiṭṭîm, n.pr.loc. [4] [√ 8847]

Shittim [4]

Nu 25: 1 While Israel was staying in **Shittim**, the men began to indulge in
Jos 2: 1 Then Joshua son of Nun secretly sent two spies from **Shittim**.
3: 1 and all the Israelites set out from **Shittim** and went to the Jordan,
Mic 6: 5 Remember ⌞your journey⌟ from **Shittim** to Gilgal, that you may

8851 שָׁטַף šāṭap, v. [31] [→ 8852; cf. 9192]

overwhelming [3], torrents [3], engulf [2], flood [2], overflow [2], wash away [2], washed [2], be rinsed [1], be swept away [1], charging [1], engulfed [1], flooding downpour [+3888] [1], flooding [1], flowed abundantly [1], flowed [1], overflowing [1], rinsed [1], rinsing [1], rushing [1], sweep over [1], swept away [1], swirling over [1]

Lev 6: 28 [6:21] [E] the pot is to be scoured and **rinsed** with water.
15: 11 [A] " 'Anyone the man with a discharge touches without **rinsing**
15: 12 [C] be broken, and any wooden article *is to* **be rinsed** with water.
1Ki 22: 38 [A] *They* **washed** the chariot at a pool in Samaria (where the
2Ch 32: 4 [A] all the springs and the stream that **flowed** through the land.
Job 14: 19 [A] as water wears away stones and torrents **wash away** the soil,
Ps 69: 2 [69:3] [A] come into the deep waters; the floods **engulf** me.
69: 15 [69:16] [A] *Do* not *let* the floodwaters **engulf** me or the depths
78: 20 [A] the rock, water gushed out, and streams **flowed abundantly**.
124: 4 [A] the flood *would have* **engulfed** us, the torrent would have
SS 8: 7 [A] waters cannot quench love; rivers cannot **wash it away**.
Isa 8: 8 [A] **swirling over** it, passing through it and reaching up to the
10: 22 [A] Destruction has been decreed, **overwhelming** and righteous.
28: 2 [A] like a driving rain and a **flooding** [+3888] **downpour**,
28: 15 [A] When an **overwhelming** scourge sweeps by, it cannot touch
28: 17 [A] the lie, and water *will* **overflow** your hiding place.
28: 18 [A] When the **overwhelming** scourge sweeps by, you will be
30: 28 [A] His breath *is* like a **rushing** torrent, rising up to the neck.
43: 2 [A] you pass through the rivers, *they will* not **sweep over** you.
66: 12 [A] like a river, and the wealth of nations like a **flooding** stream;
Jer 8: 6 [A] Each pursues his own course like a horse **charging** into
47: 2 [A] rising in the north; they will become an **overflowing** torrent.
47: 2 [A] *They will* **overflow** the land and everything in it, the towns
Eze 13: 11 [A] Rain will come *in* **torrents**, and I will send hailstones
13: 13 [A] and **torrents** *of* rain will fall with destructive fury.
16: 9 [A] " 'I bathed you with water and **washed** the blood from you
38: 22 [A] I will pour down **torrents** *of* rain, hailstones and burning
Da 11: 10 [A] which will sweep on like an irresistible **flood** and carry the
11: 22 [C] Then an overwhelming army *will* **be swept away** before him;
11: 26 [A] his army *will be* **swept away**, and many will fall in battle.
11: 40 [A] invade many countries and sweep through them like *a* **flood**.

8852 שֶׁטֶף šeṭep, n.m. [6] [√ 8851; cf. 9192]

flood [2], overwhelming [2], rise [1], torrents of rain [1]

Job 38: 25 Who cuts a channel for the **torrents of rain**, and a path for the
Ps 32: 6 surely when the mighty waters **rise**, they will not reach him.
Pr 27: 4 Anger is cruel and fury **overwhelming**, but who can stand before
Da 9: 26 destroy the city and the sanctuary. The end will come like a **flood**:
11: 22 Then an **overwhelming** army will be swept away before him;
Na 1: 8 but with an overwhelming **flood** he will make an end of ⌞Nineveh⌟;

8853 שֹׁטֵר šāṭar, n.m. [25] [→ 5428, 8854, 8855]

officials [10], officers [6], foremen [5], officer [1], overseer [1], scribes [1], serve as officials [1]

Ex 5: 6 [A] to the slave drivers and **foremen** in charge of the people:
5: 10 [A] the slave drivers and the **foremen** went out and said to the
5: 14 [A] The Israelite **foremen** appointed by Pharaoh's slave drivers
5: 15 [A] Then the Israelite **foremen** went and appealed to Pharaoh:
5: 19 [A] The Israelite **foremen** realized they were in trouble when
Nu 11: 16 [A] are known to you as leaders and **officials** *among* the people.
Dt 1: 15 [A] of hundreds, of fifties and of tens and as tribal **officials**.
16: 18 [A] **officials** for each of your tribes in every town the LORD
20: 5 [A] The **officers** shall say to the army: "Has anyone built a new
20: 8 [A] the **officers** shall add, "Is any man afraid or fainthearted?
20: 9 [A] When the **officers** have finished speaking to the army, they
29: 10 [29:9] [A] your leaders and chief men, your elders and **officials**,
31: 28 [A] before me all the elders of your tribes and all your **officials**,
Jos 1: 10 [A] So Joshua ordered the **officers** *of* the people:
3: 2 [A] After three days the **officers** went throughout the camp,
8: 33 [A] and citizens alike, with their elders, **officials** and judges,
23: 2 [A] their elders, leaders, judges and **officials**—and said to them:
24: 1 [A] summoned the elders, leaders, judges and **officials** *of* Israel,
1Ch 23: 4 [A] the LORD and six thousand *are to be* **officials** and judges.
26: 29 [A] away from the temple, as **officials** and judges over Israel.
27: 1 [A] and commanders of hundreds, and their **officers**,
2Ch 19: 11 [A] the king, and the Levites *will* **serve as officials** before you.
26: 11 [A] and Maaseiah the **officer** under the direction of Hananiah,
34: 13 [A] of the Levites were secretaries, **scribes** and doorkeepers.
Pr 6: 7 [A] It has no commander, no **overseer** or ruler,

8854 שֹׁטֵר šōṭēr, n.m. Not used in NIV/BHS [√ 8853]

8855 שִׁטְרַי šiṭray, n.pr.m. [1] [√ 8853; cf. 9231]

Shitrai [1]

1Ch 27: 29 **Shitrai** [Q 9231] the Sharonite was in charge of the herds grazing

8856 שַׁי šay, n.m. [3] [√ 8750; cf. 2593?]

gifts [3]

Ps 68: 29 [68:30] of your temple at Jerusalem kings will bring you **gifts**.
76: 11 [76:12] let all the neighboring lands bring **gifts** to the One to be
Isa 18: 7 At that time **gifts** will be brought to the LORD Almighty from a

8857 שְׁיָא š^eyā', n.pr.m. [0] [cf. 8737]

2Sa 20: 25 [**Sheva** [K; see Q 8737] was secretary; Zadok and Abiathar were]

8858 שִׁיאֹן šî'ōn, n.pr.loc. [1] [√ 8615?]

Shion [1]

Jos 19: 19 Hapharaim, **Shion**, Anaharath,

8859 שִׁיבָה¹ šîbâ¹, n.f. [1] [√ 3782?]

stay [1]

2Sa 19: 32 [19:33] He had provided for the king during his **stay** in

8860 שִׁיבָה² šîbâ², n.f. [1] [√ 8647; cf. 8669]

captives [1]

Ps 126: 1 When the LORD brought back the **captives** to Zion, we were like

8861 שָׁיָה šāyâ, v. [1] [cf. 5960]

deserted [1]

Dt 32: 18 [A] *You* **deserted** the Rock, who fathered you; you forgot the

8862 שִׁיזָא šîzā', n.pr.m. [1]

Shiza [1]

1Ch 11: 42 Adina son of **Shiza** the Reubenite, who was chief of the

8863 שִׂיחַ šîaḥ, v. [5]

downcast [4], down [1]

Ps 42: 5 [42:6] [F] Why *are you* **downcast**, O my soul? Why
42: 6 [42:7] [F] My soul *is* **downcast** within me; therefore I will
42: 11 [42:12] [F] Why *are you* **downcast**, O my soul? Why
43: 5 [F] Why *are you* **downcast**, O my soul? Why so disturbed within
44: 25 [44:26] [A] We *are brought* **down** to the dust; our bodies cling

8864 שִׁיחָה šîḥâ, n.f. [2] [cf. 8757]

pit [1], pitfalls [1]

Ps 57: 6 [57:7] They dug a **pit** in my path—but they have fallen into it
119: 85 The arrogant dig **pitfalls** for me, contrary to your law.
Jer 18: 22 [for they have dug a **pit** [K; see Q 8757] to capture me and have]

8865 שִׁיחוֹר šîḥôr, n.pr.loc. [4] [→ 8866]

Shihor [4]

Jos 13: 3 from the **Shihor** River on the east of Egypt to the territory of
1Ch 13: 5 all the Israelites, from the **Shihor** River *in* Egypt to Lebo Hamath,
Isa 23: 3 On the great waters came the grain of the **Shihor**; the harvest of
Jer 2: 18 Now why go to Egypt to drink water from the **Shihor**? And why

8866 שִׁיחוֹר לִבְנָת šîḥôr libnāt, n.pr.loc. [1] [√ 4251 + 8865]

Shihor Libnath [1]

Jos 19: 26 On the west the boundary touched Carmel and **Shihor Libnath**.

8867 שִׁיט šîṭ, n.[m.]. Not used in NIV/BHS [cf. 8765]

8868 שַׁיִט šayiṭ, n.[m.]. [1] [√ 8763]

oars [1]

Isa 33: 21 No galley with **oars** will ride them, no mighty ship will sail them.

8869 שִׁילֹה šîlōh, n.pr.loc.?. [0] [√ 8870]

Ge 49: 10 [until he comes to **whom** [K; see Q 8611] it belongs]

8870 שִׁילוֹ šîlô, n.pr.loc. [3] [→ 8869, 8872; cf. 8767]

Shiloh [3]

Jdg 21: 21 When the girls of **Shiloh** come out to join in the dancing, then rush
21: 21 the vineyards and each of you seize a wife from the girls of **Shiloh**
Jer 7: 12 " 'Go now to the place in **Shiloh** where I first made a dwelling for

8871 שֶׁלָל šēlāl, a. Not used in NIV/BHS [cf. 8768]

8872 שִׁילֹנִי šîlōnî, a.g. [7 / 6] [√ 8870; cf. 8926]

Shilonite [4], of Shiloh [1], Shilonites [1]

1Ki 11: 29 Ahijah the prophet **of Shiloh** met him on the way, wearing a new
12: 15 spoken to Jeroboam son of Nebat through Ahijah the **Shilonite**.
15: 29 of the LORD given through his servant Ahijah the **Shilonite**—
1Ch 9: 5 Of the **Shilonites**: Asaiah the firstborn and his sons.
2Ch 9: 29 in the prophecy of Ahijah the **Shilonite** and in the visions of Iddo
10: 15 spoken to Jeroboam son of Nebat through Ahijah the **Shilonite**.
Ne 11: 5 Zechariah, a descendant of Shelah. [BHS *the Shilonite*; NIV 8989]

8873 שִׁימוֹן šîmôn, n.pr.m. [1]

Shimon [1]

1Ch 4: 20 The sons of **Shimon**: Amnon, Rinnah, Ben-Hanan and Tilon.

8874 שִׁין šîn, v. [6] [→ 8875; cf. 9282]

every last male [+928+7815] [3], male [+928+7815] [3]

1Sa 25: 22 [G] if by morning I leave alive *one* **male** [+928+7815] of all who
25: 34 [G] not *one* **male** [+928+7815] belonging to Nabal would have
1Ki 14: 10 [G] I will cut off from Jeroboam **every last male** [+928+7815] in
16: 11 [G] He did not spare a *single* **male** [+928+7815], whether
21: 21 [G] cut off from Ahab **every last male** [+928+7815] in Israel—
2Ki 9: 8 [G] I will cut off from Ahab **every last male** [+928+7815] in

8875 שַׁיִן šayin, n.[m.]. [2] [√ 8874]

urine [2]

2Ki 18: 27 eat their own filth and drink their own **urine**?" [Q 4784+8079]
Isa 36: 12 eat their own filth and drink their own **urine**?" [Q 4784+8079]

8876 שִׁיר¹ šîr[1], v. [87 / 86] [→ 8877, 8878; cf. 3938]

sing [33], singers [27], musicians [6], sang [5], women[s] [5], choirs [2], be sung [1], echo [1], musician [1], praised in song [1], sang song [1], singers [+1201] [1], singing [1], sings [1]

Ex 15: 1 [A] Then Moses and the Israelites **sang** this song to the LORD:
15: 1 [A] "*I will* **sing** to the LORD, for he is highly exalted. The
15: 21 [A] "**Sing** to the LORD, for he is highly exalted. The horse
Nu 21: 17 [A] Then Israel **sang** this song: "Spring up, O well! Sing about it,
Jdg 5: 1 [A] that day Deborah and Barak son of Abinoam **sang** *this* **song**:
5: 3 [A] I *will* **sing** to the LORD, I will sing; I will make music to
1Sa 18: 6 [A] from all the towns of Israel to meet King Saul with **singing**
2Sa 19: 35 [19:36] [A] I still hear the voices of men and **women**[s] singers?
19: 35 [19:36] [A] I still hear the voices of *men* and women **singers**?
1Ki 10: 12 [A] royal palace, and to make harps and lyres for the **musicians**.
1Ch 6: 33 [6:18] [D] the **musician**, the son of Joel, the son of Samuel,
9: 33 [D] Those who *were* **musicians**, heads of Levite families,
15: 16 [D] to appoint their brothers as **singers** to sing joyful songs,
15: 19 [D] The **musicians** Heman, Asaph and Ethan were to sound the
15: 27 [D] as were the **singers**, and Kenaniah, who was in charge of the
15: 27 [D] who was in charge of the singing of the **choirs**.
16: 9 [A] **Sing** to him, sing praise to him; tell of all his wonderful acts.
16: 23 [A] **Sing** to the LORD, all the earth; proclaim his salvation day
2Ch 5: 12 [D] All the Levites who *were* **musicians**—Asaph, Heman,
5: 13 [D] The trumpeters and **singers** joined in unison, as with one
9: 11 [A] royal palace, and to make harps and lyres for the **musicians**.
20: 21 [D] Jehoshaphat appointed *men to* **sing** to the LORD and to
23: 13 [D] **singers** with musical instruments were leading the praises.
29: 28 [D] in worship, while the singers **sang** and the trumpeters played.
35: 15 [D] The **musicians**, the descendants of Asaph, were in the places
35: 25 [A] and **women**[s] singers commemorate Josiah in the laments.
35: 25 [A] to this day all the *men* and women **singers** commemorate
Ezr 2: 41 [D] The **singers**: the descendants of Asaph 128
2: 65 [D] and they also had 200 men and **women**[s] singers.
2: 65 [D] and they also had 200 *men* and women **singers**.
2: 70 [D] The priests, the Levites, the **singers**, the gatekeepers
7: 7 [D] Levites, **singers**, gatekeepers and temple servants,
10: 24 [D] From the **singers**: Eliashib. From the gatekeepers: Shallum,
Ne 7: 1 [D] the gatekeepers and the **singers** and the Levites were
7: 44 [D] The **singers**: the descendants of Asaph 148
7: 67 [D] and they also had 245 men and **women**[s] singers.
7: 67 [D] and they also had 245 *men* and women **singers**.
7: 73 [7:72] [D] the gatekeepers, the **singers** and the temple servants,
10: 28 [10:29] [D] priests, Levites, gatekeepers, **singers**, temple
10: 39 [10:40] [D] the gatekeepers and the **singers** stay.
11: 22 [D] who *were* the **singers** responsible for the service of the house
11: 23 [D] The **singers** were under the king's orders, which regulated
12: 28 [D] The **singers** [+1201] also were brought together from the
12: 29 [D] for the **singers** had built villages for themselves around
12: 42 [D] and Ezer. The **choirs** sang under the direction of Jezrahiah.
12: 45 [D] of purification, as did also the **singers** and gatekeepers,
12: 46 [D] there had been directors for the **singers** and for the songs of
12: 47 [D] all Israel contributed the daily portions for the **singers** and
13: 5 [D] and oil prescribed for the Levites, **singers** and gatekeepers,
13: 10 [D] **singers** responsible for the service had gone back to their
Job 36: 24 [D] to extol his work, which men *have* **praised in song**.
Ps 7: T [7:1] [A] which *he* **sang** to the LORD concerning Cush,
13: 6 [A] *I will* **sing** to the LORD, for he has been good to me.
21: 13 [21:14] [A] in your strength; *we will* **sing** and praise your might.
27: 6 [A] shouts of joy; *I will* **sing** and make music to the LORD.
33: 3 [A] **Sing** to him a new song; play skillfully, and shout for joy.
57: 7 [57:8] [A] my heart is steadfast; *I will* **sing** and make music.
59: 16 [59:17] [A] I *will* **sing** *of* your strength, in the morning I will
65: 13 [65:14] [A] are mantled with grain; they shout for joy and **sing**.
68: 4 [68:5] [A] **Sing** to God, sing praise to his name, extol him who
68: 25 [68:26] [A] In front are the **singers**, after them the musicians;
68: 32 [68:33] [A] **Sing** to God, O kingdoms of the earth, sing praise to
87: 7 [A] As they make music *they will* **sing**, "All my fountains are in
89: 1 [89:2] [A] *I will* **sing** *of* the LORD's great love forever;
96: 1 [A] **Sing** to the LORD a new song; sing to the LORD,
96: 1 [A] to the LORD a new song; **sing** to the LORD, all the earth.
96: 2 [A] **Sing** to the LORD, praise his name; proclaim his salvation
98: 1 [A] **Sing** to the LORD a new song, for he has done marvelous
101: 1 [A] *I will* **sing** *of* your love and justice; to you, O LORD, I will
104: 33 [A] *I will* **sing** to the LORD all my life; I will sing praise to my
105: 2 [A] **Sing** to him, sing praise to him; tell of all his wonderful acts.
106: 12 [A] Then they believed his promises and **sang** his praise.
108: 1 [108:2] [A] *I will* **sing** and make music with all my soul.
137: 3 [A] songs of joy; they said, "**Sing** us one of the songs of Zion!"
137: 4 [A] How *can we* **sing** the songs of the LORD while in a foreign
138: 5 [A] *May they* **sing** of the ways of the LORD, for the glory of
144: 9 [A] *I will* **sing** a new song to you, O God; on the ten-stringed
149: 1 [A] **Sing** to the LORD a new song, his praise in the assembly of
Pr 25: 20 [A] poured on soda, is *one who* **sings** songs to a heavy heart.
Ecc 2: 8 [A] I acquired men and **women**[s] singers, and a harem as well—
2: 8 [A] I acquired *men* and women **singers**, and a harem as well—
Isa 5: 1 [A] *I will* **sing** for the one I love a song about his vineyard:
26: 1 [H] In that day this song *will* **be sung** in the land of Judah:
42: 10 [A] **Sing** to the LORD a new song, his praise from the ends of
Jer 20: 13 [A] **Sing** to the LORD! Give praise to the LORD! He rescues

Eze 40: 44 [a] the inner court, were two [BHS *the singers'*; NIV 9109] rooms,
Zep 2: 14 [D] Their calls *will* **echo** through the windows, rubble will be in

8877 ²שִׁיר ***šîr²***, n.m. [77 / 78] [√ 8876]

song [47], songs [11], musical [6], music [5], singing [4], instruments [+3998] [1], sing [1], singers [1], songs [+1426] [1], songs [+1821] [1]

Ge 31: 27 away with joy and **singing** to the music of tambourines and harps?
Jdg 5: 12 Deborah! Wake up, wake up, break out in **song**! Arise, O Barak!
2Sa 6: 5 with **songs** [BHS 1360] and with harps, lyres, tambourines,
1Ki 4: 32 [5:12] and his **songs** numbered a thousand and five.
1Ch 6: 31 [6:16] These are the men David put in charge of the **music** *in* the
6: 32 [6:17] They ministered with **music** before the tabernacle, the Tent
13: 8 with **songs** and with harps, lyres, tambourines, cymbals
15: 16 singers to sing joyful songs, accompanied by **musical** instruments:
16: 42 and for the playing of the other instruments for sacred **song**.
25: 6 of their fathers for the **music** of the temple of the LORD,
25: 7 all of them trained and skilled in **music** for the LORD—
2Ch 5: 13 by trumpets, cymbals and other **instruments** [+3998],
7: 6 as did the Levites with the LORD's **musical** instruments,
23: 13 and singers with **musical** instruments were leading the praises.
23: 18 Law of Moses, with rejoicing and **singing**, as David had ordered.
29: 27 As the offering began, **singing** *to* the LORD began also,
29: 28 in worship, while the **singers** sang and the trumpeters played.
34: 12 all who were skilled in playing **musical** instruments—
Ne 12: 27 with songs of thanksgiving and with the **music** *of* cymbals,
12: 36 with **musical** instruments ⸤*prescribed by*⸥ David the man of God.
12: 46 for the singers and for the **songs** *of* praise and thanksgiving to God.
Ps 28: 7 My heart leaps for joy and I will give thanks to him in **song**.
30: T [30:1] A psalm. A **song**. *For* the dedication of the temple.
33: 3 Sing to him a new **song**; play skillfully, and shout for joy.
40: 3 [40:4] He put a new **song** in my mouth, a hymn of praise to our
42: 8 [42:9] the LORD directs his love, at night his **song** is with me—
45: T [45:1] Of the Sons of Korah. A *maskil*. A wedding **song**.
46: T [46:1] Of the Sons of Korah. According to *alamoth*. A **song**.
48: T [48:1] A **song**. A psalm of the Sons of Korah.
65: T [65:1] For the director of music. A psalm of David. A **song**.
66: T [66:1] For the director of music. A **song**. A psalm.
67: T [67:1] of music. With stringed instruments. A psalm. A **song**.
68: T [68:1] For the director of music. Of David. A psalm. A **song**.
69: 30 [69:31] I will praise God's name in **song** and glorify him with
75: T [75:1] the tune of⸥ "Do Not Destroy." A psalm of Asaph. A **song**.
76: T [76:1] With stringed instruments. A psalm of Asaph. A **song**.
83: T [83:1] A **song**. A psalm of Asaph.
87: T [87:1] Of the Sons of Korah. A psalm. A **song**.
88: T [88:1] A **song**. A psalm of the Sons of Korah. For the director of
92: T [92:1] A psalm. A **song**. For the Sabbath day.
96: 1 Sing to the LORD a new **song**; sing to the LORD, all the earth.
98: 1 Sing to the LORD a new **song**, for he has done marvelous things;
108: T [108:1] A **song**. A psalm of David.
120: T [120:1] A **song** *of* ascents.
121: T [121:1] A **song** *of* ascents.
122: T [122:1] A **song** *of* ascents. Of David.
123: T [123:1] A **song** *of* ascents.
124: T [124:1] A **song** *of* ascents. Of David.
125: T [125:1] A **song** *of* ascents.
126: T [126:1] A **song** *of* ascents.
127: T [127:1] A **song** *of* ascents. Of Solomon.
128: T [128:1] A **song** *of* ascents.
129: T [129:1] A **song** *of* ascents.
130: T [130:1] A **song** *of* ascents.
131: T [131:1] A **song** *of* ascents. Of David.
132: T [132:1] A **song** *of* ascents.
133: T [133:1] A **song** *of* ascents. Of David.
134: T [134:1] A **song** *of* ascents.
137: 3 for there our captors asked us for **songs** [+1821], our tormentors
137: 3 songs of joy; they said, "Sing us one of the **songs** *of* Zion!"
137: 4 How can we sing the **songs** *of* the LORD while in a foreign land?
144: 9 I will sing a new **song** to you, O God; on the ten-stringed lyre I
149: 1 Sing to the LORD a new **song**, his praise in the assembly of the
Pr 25: 20 vinegar poured on soda, is one who sings **songs** to a heavy heart.
Ecc 7: 5 It is better to heed a wise man's rebuke than to listen to the **song** *of*
12: 4 rise up at the sound of birds, but all their **songs** [+1426] grow faint;
SS 1: 1 Solomon's **Song** *of* Songs.
1: 1 Solomon's Song of **Songs**.
Isa 23: 16 play the harp well, sing many a **song**, so that you will be
24: 9 No longer do they drink wine with a **song**; the beer is bitter to its
26: 1 In that day this **song** will be sung in the land of Judah: We have a
30: 29 And you will **sing** as on the night you celebrate a holy festival;
42: 10 Sing to the LORD a new **song**, his praise from the ends of the
Eze 26: 13 I will put an end to your noisy **songs**, and the music of your harps
33: 32 to them you are nothing more than one who sings love **songs** with
Am 5: 23 Away with the noise of your **songs**! I will not listen to the music of
6: 5 on your harps like David and improvise on **musical** instruments.
8: 10 religious feasts into mourning and all your **singing** into weeping.

8878 שִׁירָה ***šîrâ***, n.f. [13] [√ 8876]

song [11], it^s [+2021+2021+2296] [1], songs [1]

Ex 15: 1 Then Moses and the Israelites sang this **song** to the LORD:
Nu 21: 17 Then Israel sang this **song**: "Spring up, O well! Sing about it,
Dt 31: 19 "Now write down for yourselves this **song** and teach it to the
31: 19 so that **it**^s [+2021+2021+2296] may be a witness for me against
31: 21 difficulties come upon them, this **song** will testify against them,
31: 22 So Moses wrote down this **song** that day and taught it to the
31: 30 Moses recited the words of this **song** from beginning to end in the
32: 44 and spoke all the words of this **song** in the hearing of the people.
2Sa 22: 1 David sang to the LORD the words of this **song** when the LORD
Ps 18: T [18:1] He sang to the LORD the words of this **song** when the
Isa 5: 1 I will sing for the one I love a **song** about his vineyard: My loved
23: 15 it will happen to Tyre as in the **song** *of* the prostitute:
Am 8: 3 Sovereign LORD, "the **songs** *in* the temple will turn to wailing.

8879 שְׁיָרָה ***šᵉyārâ***, n.[f.]. Not used in NIV/BHS

8880 שַׁיִשׁ ***šayiš***, n.[m.]. [1] [√ 9253]

marble [+74] [1]

1Ch 29: 2 of various colors, and all kinds of fine stone and **marble** [+74]—

8881 שִׁישָׁא ***šîšā'***, n.pr.m. [1]

Shisha [1]

1Ki 4: 3 Elihoreph and Ahijah, sons of **Shisha**—secretaries;

8882 שִׁישַׁק ***šîšaq***, n.pr.m. [7] [cf. 8810]

Shishak [7]

1Ki 11: 40 to kill Jeroboam, but Jeroboam fled to Egypt, to **Shishak** the king,
14: 25 **Shishak** [K 8810] king of Egypt attacked Jerusalem.
2Ch 12: 2 **Shishak** king of Egypt attacked Jerusalem in the fifth year of King
12: 5 of Judah who had assembled in Jerusalem for fear of **Shishak**,
12: 5 have abandoned me; therefore, I now abandon you to **Shishak**.' "
12: 7 My wrath will not be poured out on Jerusalem through **Shishak**.
12: 9 When **Shishak** king of Egypt attacked Jerusalem, he carried off the

8883 ¹שִׁית ***šît¹***, v. [83] [→ 8884, 9269; cf. 9286]

make [9], put [9], set [7], made [6], laid [3], bring [2], give [2], granted [2], is demanded [2], lay [2], place [2], posted [+8883] [2], take [2], turn [2], alert [1], applied [1], apply [1], appointed [1], assign [1], change [1], close [1], consider well [+4200+4213] [1], demands [1], drawn up [1], endowed [1], establish [1], gave a place [1], halt [1], harbors [1], have [1], help [+3338+6640] [1], hold [1], make turn [1], makes [1], pay [1], perform [1], placed [1], placing [1], protect [+928+3829] [1], set out [1], strike [1], take note [+4213] [1], treat [1], turned [1], wrestle [1]

Ge 3: 15 [A] *I will* **put** enmity between you and the woman, and between
4: 25 [A] saying, "God *has* **granted** me another child in place of Abel,
30: 40 [A] Thus *he* **made** separate flocks for himself and did not put
30: 40 [A] for himself and *did* not **put** them with Laban's animals.
41: 33 [A] and wise man and **put** him in charge of the land of Egypt.
46: 4 [A] back again. And Joseph's own hand *will* **close** your eyes."
48: 14 [A] reached out his right hand and **put** it on Ephraim's head,
48: 17 [A] When Joseph saw his father **placing** his right hand on
Ex 7: 23 [A] and went into his palace, and *did* not **take** even this *to* heart.
10: 1 [A] so that I *may* **perform** these miraculous signs of mine
21: 22 [A] must be fined whatever the woman's husband **demands**
21: 30 [H] However, if payment **is demanded** of him, he may redeem
21: 30 [H] he may redeem his life by paying whatever **is demanded**.
23: 1 [A] *Do* not **help** [+3338+6640] a wicked man by being a
23: 31 [A] "*I will* **establish** your borders from the Red Sea to the Sea of
33: 4 [A] they began to mourn and no one **put** on any ornaments.
Nu 12: 11 [A] *do* not **hold** against us the sin we have so foolishly
24: 1 [A] as at other times, but **turned** his face toward the desert.
Ru 3: 15 [A] he poured into it six measures of barley and **put** it on her.
4: 16 [A] Naomi took the child, **laid** him in her lap and cared for him.
1Sa 2: 8 [A] the earth are the LORD's; upon them *he has* **set** the world.
4: 20 [A] birth to a son." But she did not respond or **pay** any attention.
2Sa 13: 20 [A] my sister; he is your brother. Don't **take** this thing *to* heart."
19: 28 [19:29] [A] *you* **gave** your servant **a place** among those who sat
22: 12 [A] *He* **made** darkness his canopy around him—the dark rain
1Ki 11: 34 [A] *I have* **made** him ruler all the days of his life for the sake of
Job 7: 17 [A] so much of him, that *you* **give** him so much attention,
9: 33 [A] to arbitrate between us, *to* **lay** his hand upon us both,
10: 20 [A] **Turn** away from me so I can have a moment's joy
14: 13 [A] If only *you would* **set** me a time and then remember me!
22: 24 [A] **assign** your nuggets to the dust, your gold of Ophir to the
30: 1 [A] whose fathers I would have disdained to **put** with my sheep

Job 38: 11 [A] and no farther; here is where your proud waves **halt**'?
38: 36 [A] Who **endowed** the heart *with* wisdom or gave understanding
Ps 3: 6 [3:7] [A] I will not fear the tens of thousands **drawn up** against
8: 6 [8:7] [A] of your hands; *you* **put** everything under his feet:
9: 20 [9:21] [A] **Strike** them *with* terror, O LORD; let the nations
12: 5 [12:6] [A] the LORD. "*I will* **protect** them **from** [+928+3829]
13: 2 [13:3] [A] How long *must I* **wrestle** *with* my thoughts and
17: 11 [A] they now surround me, with eyes **alert**, to throw me to the
18: 11 [18:12] [A] *He* **made** darkness his covering, his canopy around
21: 3 [21:4] [A] and **placed** a crown of pure gold on his head.
21: 6 [21:7] [A] Surely *you have* **granted** him eternal blessings
21: 9 [21:10] [A] At the time of your appearing *you will* **make** them
21: 12 [21:13] [A] for *you will* **make** them **turn** their backs when you
45: 16 [45:17] [A] *you will* **make** them princes throughout the land.
48: 13 [48:14] [A] **consider** [+4200+4213] **well** her ramparts, view her
62: 10 [62:11] [A] your riches increase, *do* not **set** your heart on them.
73: 18 [A] Surely *you* **place** them on slippery ground; you cast them
73: 28 [A] *I have* **made** the Sovereign LORD my refuge; I will tell of
83: 11 [83:12] [A] **Make** their nobles like Oreb and Zeeb, all their
83: 13 [83:14] [A] **Make** them like tumbleweed, O my God, like chaff
84: 3 [84:4] [A] a nest for herself, where *she may* **have** her young—
84: 6 [84:7] [A] the Valley of Baca, *they* **make** it a place of springs;
88: 6 [88:7] [A] *You have* **put** me in the lowest pit, in the darkest
88: 8 [88:9] [A] closest friends and *have* **made** me repulsive to them.
90: 8 [A] *You have* **set** our iniquities before you, our secret sins in the
101: 3 [A] *I will* **set** before my eyes no vile thing. The deeds of faithless
104: 20 [A] *You* **bring** darkness, it becomes night, and all the beasts of
110: 1 [A] "Sit at my right hand until *I* **make** your enemies a footstool
132: 11 [A] "One of your own descendants *I will* **place** on your throne—
139: 5 [A] behind and before; *you have* **laid** your hand upon me.
140: 5 [140:6] [A] of their net and *have* **set** traps for me along my path.
141: 3 [A] **Set** a guard over my mouth, O LORD; keep watch over the
Pr 22: 17 [A] to the sayings of the wise; **apply** your heart to what I teach,
24: 32 [A] I **applied** my heart *to* what I observed and learned a lesson
26: 24 [A] himself with his lips, but in his heart *he* **harbors** deceit.
27: 23 [A] condition of your flocks, **give** careful attention to your herds;
Isa 5: 6 [A] *I will* **make** it a wasteland, neither pruned nor cultivated,
15: 9 [A] are full of blood, but *I will* **bring** still more upon Dimon—
16: 3 [A] a decision. **Make** your shadow like night—at high noon.
22: 7 [A] and horsemen *are* **posted** [+8883] at the city gates;
22: 7 [A] and horsemen *are* **posted** [+8883] at the city gates;
26: 1 [A] a strong city; God **makes** salvation its walls and ramparts.
Jer 2: 15 [A] *They have* **laid** waste his land; his towns are burned and
3: 19 [A] " 'How gladly *would I* **treat** you like sons and give you a
13: 16 [A] he will turn it to thick darkness and **change** it to deep gloom.
22: 6 [A] *I will* surely **make** you like a desert, like towns not inhabited.
31: 21 [A] **Take note** [+4213] of the highway, the road that you take.
50: 3 [A] nation from the north will attack her and **lay** waste her land.
51: 39 [A] *I will* **set out** a feast for them and make them drunk,
Hos 2: 3 [2:5] [A] **turn** her into a parched land, and slay her with thirst.
6: 11 [A] "Also for you, Judah, a harvest *is* **appointed**. "Whenever I

8884 ²שִׁית ***šît²***, n.m. [2] [√ 8883]

clothe [+4200+6493] [1], dressed [1]

Ps 73: 6 *they* **clothe** themselves **with** [+4200+6493] violence.
Pr 7: 10 to meet him, **dressed** *like* a prostitute and with crafty intent.

8885 שַׁיִת ***šayit***, n.[m.]. [7] [√ 8615?]

thorns [7]

Isa 5: 6 pruned nor cultivated, and briers and **thorns** will grow there.
7: 23 a thousand silver shekels, there will be only briers and **thorns**.
7: 24 and arrow, for the land will be covered with briers and **thorns**.
7: 25 you will no longer go there for fear of the briers and **thorns**;
9: 18 [9:17] it consumes briers and **thorns**, it sets the forest thickets
10: 17 in a single day it will burn and consume his **thorns** and his briers.
27: 4 am not angry. If only there were briers and **thorns** confronting me!

8886 שָׁכַב ***šākab***, v. [207] [→ 5435, 8887, 8888]

rested [36], lie down [20], lie [18], lay down [13], lying [10], lay [8], rest [8], lies [7], sleep [5], sleeps with [+6640] [5], slept with [+907] [5], lie with [+6640] [4], lying down [4], laid [3], lies down [3], lies with [+907] [3], sleeps with [+907] [3], slept with [+6640] [3], be laid [2], come to bed with [+6640] [2], has sexual relations with [+6640] [2], lay with [+6640] [2], lay with [+907] [2], lies with [+907+8886] [2], put [2], sleep with [+6640] [2], slept [2], bed with [+6640] [1], done[s] this [+6640] [1], go to bed with [+725] [1], go to sleep [1], go [1], gone to bed [1], he[s] [+408+2021+2021+6640] [1], laid low [1], laid to rest [1], lain down [1], lay down to sleep [1], lie around [1], lie in state [+928+3883] [1], lie with [+907] [1], lies with [+6640] [1], lying with [+907] [1], made lie down [1], raped [+906+2256+6700] [1], rapes [+2256+2616+6640] [1], rapes [+2256+6640+9530] [1], resting [1], sleeping with [+6640] [1], sleeping with [+907+2446+8887] [1], sleeping [1], sleeps with [+907+2446+8887] [1], sleeps [1], stayed [1], take rest [1], taking rest [+906+5435] [1], tip over [1], violated [+906+2256+6700] [1]

Ge 19: 4 [A] Before *they had* **gone to bed**, all the men from every part of
19: 32 [A] get our father to drink wine and then **lie** [+6640] **with** him
19: 33 [A] and the older daughter went in and **lay** [+907] **with** him.
19: 33 [A] He was not aware of it when she **lay down** or when she got
19: 34 [A] said to the younger, "Last night *I* **lay** [+907] **with** my father.
19: 34 [A] you go in and **lie** [+6640] **with** him so we can preserve our
19: 35 [A] and the younger daughter went and **lay** [+6640] **with** him.
19: 35 [A] Again he was not aware of it when she **lay down** or when she
26: 10 [A] One of the men might well have **slept** [+907] **with** your wife,
28: 11 [A] stones there, he put it under his head and **lay down to sleep**.
28: 13 [A] and your descendants the land on which you *are* **lying**.
30: 15 [A] "*he can* **sleep** [+6640] **with** you tonight in return for your
30: 16 [A] son's mandrakes." So *he* **slept** [+6640] **with** her that night.
34: 2 [A] saw her, he took her and **violated** [+906+2256+6700] her.
34: 7 [A] thing in Israel by **lying** [+907] **with** Jacob's daughter—
35: 22 [A] went in and **slept** [+907] **with** his father's concubine Bilhah,
39: 7 [A] notice of Joseph and said, "**Come to bed** [+6640] **with** me!"
39: 10 [A] he refused to **go to bed** [+725] **with** her or even be with her.
39: 12 [A] him by his cloak and said, "**Come to bed** [+6640] **with** me!"
39: 14 [A] He came in here to **sleep** [+6640] **with** me, but I screamed.
47: 30 [A] when *I* **rest** with my fathers, carry me out of Egypt and bury
Ex 22: 16 [22:15] [A] pledged to be married and **sleeps** [+6640] **with** her,
22: 19 [22:18] [A] "Anyone *who* **has sexual** [+6640] **relations with** an
22: 27 [22:26] [A] What else *will he* **sleep** in? When he cries out to
Lev 14: 47 [A] Anyone *who* **sleeps** or eats in the house must wash his
15: 4 [A] " 'Any bed the man with a discharge **lies** on will be unclean,
15: 18 [A] When a man **lies** [+907] **with** a woman and there is an
15: 20 [A] " 'Anything *she* **lies** on during her period will be unclean,
15: 24 [A] " 'If a man **lies** [+907+8886] **with** her and her monthly flow
15: 24 [A] " 'If a man **lies with** [+907+8886] her and her monthly flow
15: 24 [A] unclean for seven days; any bed *he* **lies** on will be unclean.
15: 26 [A] Any bed *she* **lies** on while her discharge continues will be
15: 33 [A] for a man who **lies** [+6640] **with** a woman who is
18: 22 [A] " '*Do* not **lie** [+907] **with** a man as one lies with a woman;
19: 20 [A] " 'If a man **sleeps** [+907+2446+8887] **with** a woman who is a
20: 11 [A] " 'If a man **sleeps** [+907] **with** his father's wife, he has
20: 12 [A] " 'If a man **sleeps** [+907] **with** his daughter-in-law, both of
20: 13 [A] " 'If a man **lies** [+907] **with** a man as one lies with a woman,
20: 18 [A] " 'If a man **lies** [+907] **with** a woman during her monthly
20: 20 [A] " 'If a man **sleeps** [+907] **with** his aunt, he has dishonored his
26: 6 [A] and *you will* **lie down** and no one will make you afraid.
Nu 5: 13 [A] *by* **sleeping** [+907+2446+8887] **with** another man, and this is
5: 19 [A] "If no other man *has* **slept** [+907] **with** you and you have not
23: 24 [A] they rouse themselves like a lion *that does* not **rest** till he
24: 9 [A] Like a lion they crouch and **lie down**, like a lioness—
Dt 6: 7 [A] along the road, when you **lie down** and when you get up.
11: 19 [A] along the road, when you **lie down** and when you get up.
22: 22 [A] If a man is found **sleeping** [+6640] **with** another man's wife,
22: 22 [A] both the man who **slept** [+6640] **with** her and the woman
22: 23 [A] virgin pledged to be married and *he* **sleeps** [+6640] **with** her,
22: 25 [A] girl pledged to be married and **rapes** [+2256+2616+6640] her,
22: 25 [A] only the man who *has* **done**[s] [+6640] **this** shall die.
22: 28 [A] and **rapes** [+2256+6640+9530] her and they are discovered,
22: 29 [A] **he**[s] [+408+2021+2021+6640] shall pay the girl's father fifty
24: 12 [A] *do* not **go to sleep** with his pledge in your possession.
24: 13 [A] Return his cloak to him by sunset so that *he may* **sleep** in it.
27: 20 [A] "Cursed is the man *who* **sleeps** [+6640] **with** his father's
27: 21 [A] "Cursed is the man *who* **has sexual** [+6640] **relations with**
27: 22 [A] "Cursed is the man *who* **sleeps** [+6640] **with** his sister,
27: 23 [A] "Cursed is the man *who* **sleeps** [+6640] **with** his
28: 30 [a] [but another *will* take her and **ravish** [Q; see K 8711] her.]
31: 16 [A] "You *are going to* **rest** with your fathers, and these people
Jos 2: 1 [A] the house of a prostitute named Rahab and **stayed** there.
2: 8 [A] Before the spies **lay down** for the night, she went up on the
Jdg 5: 27 [A] At her feet he sank, he fell; there *he* **lay**. At her feet he sank,
16: 3 [A] Samson **lay** there only until the middle of the night. Then he
Ru 3: 4 [A] When he **lies down**, note the place where he is lying.
3: 4 [A] When he lies down, note the place where *he is* **lying**.
3: 4 [A] go and uncover his feet and **lie down**. He will tell you what
3: 7 [A] he went over to **lie down** at the far end of the grain pile.
3: 7 [A] Ruth approached quietly, uncovered his feet and **lay down**.
3: 8 [A] and he turned and discovered a woman **lying** *at* his feet.
3: 13 [A] as the LORD lives I will do it. **Lie** here until morning."
3: 14 [A] So *she* **lay** at his feet until morning, but got up before anyone
1Sa 2: 22 [A] how *they* **slept** [+907] **with** the women who served at the
3: 2 [A] that he could barely see, *was* **lying down** in his usual place.
3: 3 [A] and Samuel *was* **lying down** in the temple of the LORD,
3: 5 [A] Eli said, "I did not call; go back and **lie down**." So he went
3: 5 [A] not call; go back and lie down." So he went and **lay down**.
3: 6 [A] "My son," Eli said, "I did not call; go back and **lie down**."

1Sa 3: 9 [A] "Go and **lie down**, and if he calls you, say, 'Speak, LORD,
3: 9 [A] is listening.' " So Samuel went and **lay down** in his place.
3: 15 [A] Samuel **lay down** until morning and then opened the doors of
26: 5 [A] son of Ner, the commander of the army, *had* **lain down**.
26: 5 [A] Saul *was* **lying** inside the camp, with the army encamped
26: 7 [A] **lying** asleep inside the camp with his spear stuck in the
26: 7 [A] near his head. Abner and the soldiers *were* **lying** around him.
2Sa 4: 5 [A] the day while he *was* **taking** his noonday **rest** [+906+5435].
4: 7 [A] They had gone into the house while he *was* **lying** on the bed
7: 12 [A] When your days are over and *you* **rest** with your fathers, I
8: 2 [G] *He* **made** them **lie down** on the ground and measured them
11: 4 [A] to get her. She came to him, and *he* **slept** [+6640] **with** her.
11: 9 [A] Uriah **slept** *at* the entrance to the palace with all his master's
11: 11 [A] to my house to eat and drink and **lie** [+6640] **with** my wife?
11: 13 [A] in the evening Uriah went out to **sleep** on his mat among his
12: 3 [A] his food, drank from his cup and even **slept** in his arms.
12: 11 [A] and *he will* **lie** [+6640] **with** your wives in broad daylight.
12: 16 [A] went into his house and spent the nights **lying** on the ground.
12: 24 [A] wife Bathsheba, and he went to her and **lay** [+6640] **with** her.
13: 5 [A] "**Go** to bed and pretend to be ill," Jonadab said. "When your
13: 6 [A] So Amnon **lay down** and pretended to be ill. When the king
13: 8 [A] to the house of her brother Amnon, who *was* **lying down**.
13: 11 [A] he grabbed her and said, "Come *to* **bed** [+6640] **with** me,
13: 14 [A] he was stronger than she, *he* **raped** [+906+2256+6700] her.
13: 31 [A] king stood up, tore his clothes and **lay down** on the ground;
1Ki 1: 2 [A] *She can* **lie** beside him so that our lord the king may keep
1: 21 [A] as soon as my lord the king *is* **laid to rest** with his fathers,
2: 10 [A] David **rested** with his fathers and was buried in the City of
3: 19 [A] the night this woman's son died because *she* **lay** on him.
3: 20 [G] *She* **put** him by her breast and put her dead son by my breast.
3: 20 [G] She put him by her breast and **put** her dead son by my breast.
11: 21 [A] Hadad heard that David **rested** with his fathers and that Joab
11: 43 [A] he **rested** with his fathers and was buried in the city of David
14: 20 [A] for twenty-two years and then **rested** with his fathers.
14: 31 [A] Rehoboam **rested** with his fathers and was buried with them
15: 8 [A] Abijah **rested** with his fathers and was buried in the City of
15: 24 [A] Asa **rested** with his fathers and was buried with them in the
16: 6 [A] Baasha **rested** with his fathers and was buried in Tirzah.
16: 28 [A] Omri **rested** with his fathers and was buried in Samaria.
17: 19 [G] upper room where he was staying, and **laid** him on his bed.
19: 5 [A] *he* **lay down** under the tree and fell asleep. All at once an
19: 6 [A] a jar of water. He ate and drank and then **lay down** again.
21: 4 [A] of my fathers." *He* **lay** on his bed sulking and refused to eat.
21: 27 [A] and fasted. *He* **lay** in sackcloth and went around meekly.
22: 40 [A] Ahab **rested** with his fathers. And Ahaziah his son succeeded
22: 50 [22:51] [A] Jehoshaphat **rested** with his fathers and was buried
2Ki 4: 11 [A] Elisha came, he went up to his room and **lay down** there.
4: 21 [G] She went up and **laid** him on the bed of the man of God,
4: 32 [H] the house, there was the boy **lying** dead on his couch.
4: 34 [A] he got on the bed and **lay** upon the boy, mouth to mouth,
8: 24 [A] Jehoram **rested** with his fathers and was buried with them in
9: 16 [A] because Joram *was* **resting** there and Ahaziah king of Judah
10: 35 [A] Jehu **rested** with his fathers and was buried in Samaria.
13: 9 [A] Jehoahaz **rested** with his fathers and was buried in Samaria.
13: 13 [A] Jehoash **rested** with his fathers, and Jeroboam succeeded him
14: 16 [A] Jehoash **rested** with his fathers and was buried in Samaria
14: 22 [A] restored it to Judah after Amaziah **rested** with his fathers.
14: 29 [A] Jeroboam **rested** with his fathers, the kings of Israel.
15: 7 [A] Azariah **rested** with his fathers and was buried near them in
15: 22 [A] Menahem **rested** with his fathers. And Pekahiah his son
15: 38 [A] Jotham **rested** with his fathers and was buried with them in
16: 20 [A] Ahaz **rested** with his fathers and was buried with them in the
20: 21 [A] Hezekiah **rested** with his fathers. And Manasseh his son
21: 18 [A] Manasseh **rested** with his fathers and was buried in his
24: 6 [A] Jehoiakim **rested** with his fathers. And Jehoiachin his son
2Ch 9: 31 [A] he **rested** with his fathers and was buried in the city of David
12: 16 [A] Rehoboam **rested** with his fathers and was buried in the City
14: 1 [13:23] [A] Abijah **rested** with his fathers and was buried in the
16: 13 [A] year of his reign Asa died and **rested** with his fathers.
16: 14 [G] *They* **laid** him on a bier covered with spices and various
21: 1 [A] Jehoshaphat **rested** with his fathers and was buried with
26: 2 [A] restored it to Judah after Amaziah **rested** with his fathers.
26: 23 [A] Uzziah **rested** with his fathers and was buried near them in a
27: 9 [A] Jotham **rested** with his fathers and was buried in the City of
28: 27 [A] Ahaz **rested** with his fathers and was buried in the city of
32: 33 [A] Hezekiah **rested** with his fathers and was buried on the hill
33: 20 [A] Manasseh **rested** with his fathers and was buried in his
Job 3: 13 [A] For now *I would be* **lying down** in peace; I would be asleep
7: 4 [A] When *I* **lie down** I think, 'How long before I get up?' The
7: 21 [A] For *I will* soon **lie down** in the dust; you will search for me,
11: 18 [A] you will look about you and **take** *your* **rest** in safety.
14: 12 [A] so man **lies down** and does not rise; till the heavens are no
20: 11 [A] The youthful vigor that fills his bones *will* **lie** with him in the
21: 26 [A] Side by side *they* **lie** in the dust, and worms cover them both.
27: 19 [A] *He* **lies down** wealthy, but will do so no more; when he
30: 17 [A] Night pierces my bones; my gnawing pains never **rest**.
38: 37 [G] the clouds? Who *can* **tip over** the water jars of the heavens
40: 21 [A] Under the lotus plants *he* **lies**, hidden among the reeds in the
Ps 3: 5 [3:6] [A] I **lie down** and sleep; I wake again,
4: 8 [4:9] [A] *I will* **lie down** and sleep in peace, for you alone,
41: 8 [41:9] [A] he will never get up from the place where *he* **lies**."
57: 4 [57:5] [A] I am in the midst of lions; *I* **lie** among ravenous
68: 13 [68:14] [A] Even while *you* **sleep** among the campfires,
Pr 3: 24 [A] when *you* **lie down**, you will not be afraid; when you lie
3: 24 [A] not be afraid; when *you* **lie down**, your sleep will be sweet.
6: 9 [A] How long *will you* **lie** there, you sluggard? When will you
6: 10 [A] a little slumber, a little folding of the hands to **rest**—
6: 22 [A] when you **sleep**, they will watch over you; when you awake,
23: 34 [A] You will be like *one* **sleeping** on the high seas, lying on top
23: 34 [A] one sleeping on the high seas, **lying** on top of the rigging.
24: 33 [A] a little slumber, a little folding of the hands to **rest**—
Ecc 2: 23 [A] work is pain and grief; even at night his mind *does* not **rest**.
4: 11 [A] Also, if two **lie down** *together*, they will keep warm. But
Isa 13: 16 [c] [looted and their wives **ravished**. [Q; see K 8711]]
14: 8 [A] exult over you and say, "Now that *you have been* **laid low**,
14: 18 [A] All the kings of the nations **lie** [+928+3883] **in state**, each in
43: 17 [A] *they* **lay** there, never to rise again, extinguished, snuffed out
50: 11 [A] shall receive from my hand: *You will* **lie down** in torment.
51: 20 [A] *they* **lie** at the head of every street, like antelope caught in a
56: 10 [A] cannot bark; *they* **lie around** and dream, they love to sleep.
Jer 3: 2 [e] [any place where *you have* not **been ravished**? [Q; see K 8711]]
3: 25 [A] *Let us* **lie down** in our shame, and let our disgrace cover us.
La 2: 21 [A] "Young and old **lie** *together* in the dust of the streets;
Eze 4: 4 [A] "Then **lie** on your left side and put the sin of the house of
4: 4 [A] You are to bear their sin for the number of days *you* **lie** on
4: 6 [A] finished this, **lie down** again, this time on your right side,
4: 9 [A] You are to eat it during the 390 days you **lie** on your side.
23: 8 [A] when during her youth *men* **slept** [+907] **with** her, caressed
31: 18 [A] *you will* **lie** among the uncircumcised, with those killed by
32: 19 [H] than others? Go down and **be laid** among the uncircumcised.'
32: 21 [A] *they* **lie** *with* the uncircumcised, *with* those killed by the
32: 27 [A] *Do they* not **lie** with the other uncircumcised warriors who
32: 28 [A] will be broken and *will* **lie** among the uncircumcised,
32: 29 [A] They **lie** with the uncircumcised, with those who go down to
32: 30 [A] *They* **lie** uncircumcised with those killed by the sword
32: 32 [H] and all his hordes *will* **be laid** among the uncircumcised,
Hos 2: 18 [2:20] [G] from the land, so that all *may* **lie down** in safety.
Am 6: 4 [A] *You* **lie** on beds inlaid with ivory and lounge on your
Jnh 1: 5 [A] below deck, where *he* **lay down** and fell into a deep sleep.
Mic 7: 5 [A] Even with *her who* **lies** *in* your embrace be careful of your
Zec 14: 2 [c] [houses ransacked, and the women **raped**. [Q; see K 8711]]

8887 שִׁכְבָה šikbâ, n.f. [9] [√ 8886]

emission [4], *untranslated* [2], layer [1], sleeping with [+907+2446+8886] [1], sleeps with [+907+2446+8886] [1]

Ex 16: 13 and in the morning there was a **layer** *of* dew around the camp.
16: 14 When **[RPH]** the dew was gone, thin flakes like frost on the
Lev 15: 16 " 'When a man has an **emission** *of* semen, he must bathe his whole
15: 17 or leather that has **[RPH]** semen on it must be washed with water,
15: 18 When a man lies with a woman and there is an **emission** *of* semen,
15: 32 a discharge, for anyone made unclean by an **emission** *of* semen,
19: 20 " 'If a man **sleeps with** [+907+2446+8886] a woman who is a slave
22: 4 defiled by a corpse or by anyone who has an **emission** *of* semen,
Nu 5: 13 *by* **sleeping with** [+907+2446+8886] another man, and this is

8888 שְׁכֹבֶת šᵉkōbet, n.f. [4] [√ 8886]

has sexual relations [+5989] [1], have sexual relations [+2446+4200+5989] [1], have sexual relations [+5989] [1], sleeping with [+906+928+5989] [1]

Lev 18: 20 " '*Do* not **have sexual relations** [+2446+4200+5989] with your
18: 23 " '*Do* not **have sexual relations** [+5989] with an animal and defile
20: 15 " 'If a man **has sexual relations** [+5989] with an animal, he must
Nu 5: 20 you have defiled yourself *by* **sleeping with** [+906+928+5989] a

8889 שָׂכָה šākâ, v. [1]

well-fed [1]

Jer 5: 8 [G] They are **well-fed**, lusty stallions, each neighing for another

8890 שְׁכוֹל šᵉkōl, n.[m.]. [3] [√ 8897]

loss of children [2], forlorn [1]

Ps 35: 12 They repay me evil for good and leave my soul **forlorn**.
Isa 47: 8 besides me. I will never be a widow or suffer the **loss of children**.'
47: 9 in a moment, on a single day: **loss of children** and widowhood.

8891 שָׁכוּל šakkûl, a. [6] [√ 8897]

alone [2], robbed of cubs [2], childless [1], robbed [1]

2Sa 17: 8 they are fighters, and as fierce as a wild bear **robbed of** her **cubs**.
Pr 17:12 Better to meet a bear **robbed** of her cubs than a fool in his folly.
SS 4: 2 up from the washing. Each has its twin; not one of them is **alone**.
6: 6 up from the washing. Each has its twin, not one of them is **alone**.
Jer 18:21 Let their wives be made **childless** and widows; let their men be put
Hos 13: 8 Like a bear **robbed of** *her* **cubs**, I will attack them and rip them

8892 שְׁכוּלָה šᵉkûlâ, a. [1] [√ 8897]

bereaved [1]

Isa 49:21 me these? I was **bereaved** and barren; I was exiled and rejected.

8893 שִׁכּוֹר šikkôr, a. [13] [√ 8910]

drunkards [4], drunk [2], drunkard [2], getting drunk [+9272] [2], drunkard's [1], drunken men [1], drunken [1]

1Sa 1:13 but her voice was not heard. Eli thought she was **drunk**
25:36 He was in high spirits and very **drunk**. So she told him nothing
1Ki 16: 9 Elah was in Tirzah at the time, **getting drunk** [+9272] in the home
20:16 32 kings allied with him were in their tents **getting drunk** [+9272].
Job 12:25 in darkness with no light; he makes them stagger like **drunkards**.
Ps 107:27 They reeled and staggered like **drunken men**; they were at their
Pr 26: 9 Like a thornbush in a **drunkard's** hand is a proverb in the mouth
Isa 19:14 in all that she does, as a **drunkard** staggers around in his vomit.
24:20 The earth reels like a **drunkard**, it sways like a hut in the wind;
28: 1 Woe to that wreath, the pride of Ephraim's **drunkards**, to the
28: 3 That wreath, the pride of Ephraim's **drunkards**, will be trampled
Jer 23: 9 I am like a **drunken** man, like a man overcome by wine,
Joel 1: 5 Wake up, you **drunkards**, and weep! Wail, all you drinkers of

8894 שָׁכַח šākaḥ, v. [102 / 101] [→ 8895; Ar 10708]

forget [42], forgotten [22], forgot [11], be forgotten [9], ignore [4], ever forget [+906+8894] [2], forgets [2], ignored [2], am forgotten [+4213+4946] [1], is forgotten [1], made forget [1], make forget [1], neglect [1], overlook [1], unmindful [1]

Ge 27:45 [A] is no longer angry with you and **forgets** what you did to him,
40:23 [A] however, did not remember Joseph; *he* **forgot** him.
41:30 [C] all the abundance in Egypt *will* **be forgotten**, and the famine
Dt 4: 9 [A] so that *you do* not **forget** the things your eyes have seen
4:23 [A] Be careful not *to* **forget** the covenant of the LORD your
4:31 [A] or destroy you or **forget** the covenant with your forefathers,
6:12 [A] be careful that *you do* not **forget** the LORD, who brought
8:11 [A] Be careful that *you do* not **forget** the LORD your God,
8:14 [A] become proud and *you will* **forget** the LORD your God,
8:19 [A] If *you* **ever forget** [+906+8894] the LORD your God
8:19 [A] If *you* **ever forget** [+906+8894] the LORD your God
9: 7 [A] never **forget** how you provoked the LORD your God to
24:19 [A] you are harvesting in your field and *you* **overlook** a sheaf,
25:19 [A] the memory of Amalek from under heaven. *Do* not **forget**!
26:13 [A] from your commands nor *have I* **forgotten** any of them.
31:21 [C] because *it will* not **be forgotten** by their descendants.
32:18 [A] who fathered you; *you* **forgot** the God who gave you birth.
Jdg 3: 7 [A] *they* **forgot** the LORD their God and served the Baals
1Sa 1:11 [A] remember me, and not **forget** your servant but give her a son,
12: 9 [A] "But *they* **forgot** the LORD their God; so he sold them into
2Ki 17:38 [A] *Do* not **forget** the covenant I have made with you, and do not
Job 8:13 [A] Such is the destiny of all *who* **forget** God; so perishes the
9:27 [A] If I say, '*I will* **forget** my complaint, I will change my
11:16 [A] You *will* surely **forget** your trouble, recalling it only as
19:14 [A] kinsmen have gone away; my friends *have* **forgotten** me.
24:20 [A] The womb **forgets** them, the worm feasts on them; evil men
28: 4 [C] dwell he cuts a shaft, in places **forgotten** by the foot of man;
39:15 [A] **unmindful** that a foot may crush them, that some wild
Ps 9:12 [9:13] [A] *he does* not **ignore** the cry of the afflicted.
9:18 [9:19] [C] the needy *will* not always **be forgotten**, nor the hope
10:11 [A] He says to himself, "God *has* **forgotten**; he covers his face
10:12 [A] Lift up your hand, O God. *Do* not **forget** the helpless.
13: 1 [13:2] [A] How long, O LORD? *Will you* **forget** me forever?
31:12 [31:13] [C] *I* **am forgotten** [+4213+4946] by them as though I
42: 9 [42:10] [A] I say to God my Rock, "Why *have you* **forgotten**
44:17 [44:18] [A] though *we had* not **forgotten** you or been false to
44:20 [44:21] [A] If *we had* **forgotten** the name of our God or spread
44:24 [44:25] [A] your face and **forget** our misery and oppression?
45:10 [45:11] [A] **Forget** your people and your father's house.
50:22 [A] "Consider this, you *who* **forget** God, or I will tear you to
59:11 [59:12] [A] O Lord our shield, or my people *will* **forget**.
74:19 [A] *do* not **forget** the lives of your afflicted people forever.
74:23 [A] *Do* not **ignore** the clamor of your adversaries, the uproar of
77: 9 [77:10] [A] *Has* God **forgotten** to be merciful? Has he in anger
78: 7 [A] *would* not **forget** his deeds but would keep his commands.
78:11 [A] *They* **forgot** what he had done, the wonders he had shown
102: 4 [102:5] [A] and withered like grass; *I* **forget** to eat my food.
103: 2 [A] the LORD, O my soul, and **forget** not all his benefits—
106:13 [A] *they* soon **forgot** what he had done and did not wait for his
106:21 [A] *They* **forgot** the God who saved them, who had done great
119:16 [A] I delight in your decrees; *I will* not **neglect** your word.
119:61 [A] the wicked bind me with ropes, *I will* not **forget** your law.
119:83 [A] like a wineskin in the smoke, *I do* not **forget** your decrees.
119:93 [A] *I will* never **forget** your precepts, for by them you have
119:109 [A] take my life in my hands, *I will* not **forget** your law.
119:139 [A] My zeal wears me out, for my enemies **ignore** your words.
119:141 [A] I am lowly and despised, *I do* not **forget** your precepts.
119:153 [A] and deliver me, for *I have* not **forgotten** your law.
119:176 [A] Seek your servant, for *I have* not **forgotten** your commands.
137: 5 [A] If *I* **forget** you, O Jerusalem, may my right hand forget ⌊its
137: 5 [A] forget you, O Jerusalem, *may* my right hand **forget** ⌊its skill⌋.
Pr 2:17 [A] of her youth and **ignored** the covenant she made before God.
3: 1 [A] My son, *do* not **forget** my teaching, but keep my commands
4: 5 [A] do not **forget** my words or swerve from them.
31: 5 [A] lest they drink and **forget** what the law decrees, and deprive
31: 7 [A] let them drink and **forget** their poverty and remember their
Ecc 2:16 [C] be long remembered; in days to come both *will* **be forgotten**.
8:10 [f] and **receive** praise [BHS *are forgotten*; NIV 8655] in the city
9: 5 [C] further reward, and even the memory of them **is forgotten**.
Isa 17:10 [A] *You have* **forgotten** God your Savior; you have not
23:15 [C] At that time Tyre *will* **be forgotten** for seventy years,
23:16 [C] up a harp, walk through the city, O prostitute **forgotten**;
49:14 [A] "The LORD has forsaken me, the Lord *has* **forgotten** me."
49:15 [A] "*Can* a mother **forget** the baby at her breast and have no
49:15 [A] she has borne? Though she *may* **forget**, I will not forget you!
49:15 [A] she has borne? Though she may forget, I *will* not **forget** you!
51:13 [A] that *you* **forget** the LORD your Maker, who stretched out
54: 4 [A] *You will* **forget** the shame of your youth and remember no
65:16 [C] For the past troubles *will* **be forgotten** and hidden from my
Jer 2:32 [A] *Does* a maiden **forget** her jewelry, a bride her wedding
2:32 [A] Yet my people *have* **forgotten** me, days without number.
3:21 [A] their ways and *have* **forgotten** the LORD their God.
13:25 [A] "because *you have* **forgotten** me and trusted in false gods.
18:15 [A] Yet my people *have* **forgotten** me; they burn incense to
20:11 [C] thoroughly disgraced; their dishonor *will* never **be forgotten**.
23:27 [G] they tell one another *will* **make** my people **forget** my name,
23:27 [A] just as their fathers **forgot** my name through Baal worship.
23:40 [C] everlasting shame that *will* not **be forgotten**."
30:14 [A] All your allies *have* **forgotten** you; they care nothing for
44: 9 [A] *Have you* **forgotten** the wickedness committed by your fathers
50: 5 [C] in an everlasting covenant *that will* not **be forgotten**.
50: 6 [A] over mountain and hill and **forgot** their own resting place.
La 2: 6 [D] The LORD *has* **made** Zion **forget** her appointed feasts
5:20 [A] Why *do you* always **forget** us? Why do you forsake us so
Eze 22:12 [A] *you have* **forgotten** me, declares the Sovereign LORD.
23:35 [A] Since *you have* **forgotten** me and thrust me behind your
Hos 2:13 [2:15] [A] her lovers, but me *she* **forgot**," declares the LORD.
4: 6 [A] because *you have* **ignored** the law of your God, I also will
4: 6 [A] ignored the law of your God, I also *will* **ignore** your children.
8:14 [A] Israel *has* **forgotten** his Maker and built palaces; Judah has
13: 6 [A] they were satisfied, they became proud; then *they* **forgot** me.
Am 8: 7 [A] Pride of Jacob: "*I will* never **forget** anything they have done.

8895 שָׁכֵחַ šākēaḥ, a. [2] [√ 8894]

forget [2]

Ps 9:17 [9:18] wicked return to the grave, all the nations *that* **forget** God.
Isa 65:11 as for you who forsake the LORD and **forget** my holy mountain,

8896 שָׁכַךְ šākak, v. [5]

subsided [2], *untranslated* [1], receded [1], rid [1]

Ge 8: 1 [A] and he sent a wind over the earth, and the waters **receded**.
Nu 17: 5 [17:20] [G] *I will* **rid** myself *of* this constant grumbling against
Est 2: 1 [A] Later when the anger of King Xerxes *had* **subsided**,
7:10 [A] had prepared for Mordecai. Then the king's fury **subsided**.
Jer 5:26 [A] men who lie in wait like **[RPH]** men who snare birds

8897 שָׁכַל šākal, v. [24 / 23] [→ 864, 5437, 8890, 8891, 8892, 8898]

miscarry [3], bereaved [2], deprive of children [2], leave childless [2], make childless [2], bereave [1], bereaves [1], bring bereavement [1], cast fruit [1], childless [1], deprived of children [1], lose [1], made childless [1], make unproductive [1], miscarried [1], rob of children [1], unproductive [1]

Ge 27:45 [A] back from there. Why *should I* **lose** both of you in one day?"
31:38 [D] Your sheep and goats *have* not **miscarried**, nor have I eaten
42:36 [D] Jacob said to them, "*You have* **deprived** me **of** my **children**.
43:14 [A] back with you. As for me, if *I am* **bereaved**, I am bereaved."

Ge 43:14 [A] back with you. As for me, if I am bereaved, *I am* **bereaved**."
Ex 23:26 [D] none will **miscarry** or be barren in your land. I will give you
Lev 26:22 [D] and *they will* **rob** you **of** your **children**, destroy your cattle
Dt 32:25 [D] In the street the sword *will* **make** them **childless**; in their
1Sa 15:33 [D] Samuel said, "As your sword *has* **made** women **childless**,
15:33 [A] so *will* your mother *be* **childless** among women."
2Ki 2:19 [D] can see, but the water is bad and the land *is* **unproductive**."
2:21 [D] again will it cause death or **make** the land **unproductive**.' "
Job 21:10 [D] never fail to breed; their cows calve and *do* not **miscarry**.
Jer 15:7 [D] *I will* **bring bereavement** and destruction on my people,
50:9 [g] arrows will be like skilled [BHS ***bereaving***; NIV 8505] warriors
La 1:20 [D] the sword **bereaves**; inside, there is only death.
Eze 5:17 [D] wild beasts against you, and *they will* **leave** you **childless**.
14:15 [D] *they* **leave** it **childless** and it becomes desolate so that no one
36:12 [D] you will never again **deprive** them **of** their **children**.
36:13 [D] "You devour men and **deprive** your nation of *its* **children**,"
36:14 [D] longer devour men or **make** your nation **childless**, [K 4173]
Hos 9:12 [D] Even if they rear children, *I will* **bereave** them of every one.
9:14 [G] Give them wombs *that* **miscarry** and breasts that are dry.
Mal 3:11 [D] the vines in your fields *will* not **cast** *their* **fruit**,"

8898 שִׁכֻּלִים *šikkulîm*, n.[m.]pl.abst. [1] [√ 8897]

bereavement [1]

Isa 49:20 The children born during your **bereavement** will yet say in your

8899 שָׁכַם *šākam*, v.den. [65] [√ 8900]

early [18], again and again [11], got up early [5], get up early [4], got up [4], early got up [3], early in the morning [3], rose early [3], rose [3], *untranslated* [2], early the next morning [2], again and again [+2256+8938] [1], eager [1], early arose [1], early morning get up [1], go early [1], morning [1], rise early [1]

Ge 19:2 [G] the night and then go on your way **early in the morning**."
19:27 [G] **Early** the next morning Abraham **got up** and returned to the
20:8 [G] **Early** the next morning Abimelech summoned all his
21:14 [G] **Early** the next morning Abraham took some food and a skin
22:3 [G] **Early** the next morning Abraham **got up** and saddled his
26:31 [G] **Early** the next morning the men swore an oath to each other.
28:18 [G] **Early** the next morning Jacob took the stone he had placed
31:55 [32:1] [G] **Early** the next morning Laban kissed his
Ex 8:20 [8:16] [G] "**Get up early** in the morning and confront Pharaoh
9:13 [G] "**Get up early** in the morning, confront Pharaoh and say to
24:4 [G] *He* **got up early** the next morning and built an altar at the
32:6 [G] So the next day the people **rose early** and sacrificed burnt
34:4 [G] the first ones and went up Mount Sinai **early** in the morning,
Nu 14:40 [G] **Early** the next morning they went up toward the high hill
Jos 3:1 [G] **Early** in the morning Joshua and all the Israelites set out
6:12 [G] Joshua **got up early** the next morning and the priests took up
6:15 [G] *they* **got up** at daybreak and marched around the city seven
7:16 [G] **Early** the next morning Joshua had Israel come forward by
8:10 [G] **Early** the next morning Joshua mustered his men, and he
8:14 [G] all the men of the city hurried out **early in the morning** to
Jdg 6:28 [G] In the morning when the men of the town **got up**, there was
6:38 [G] Gideon **rose early** the next day; he squeezed the fleece
7:1 [G] **Early in the morning**, Jerub-Baal (that is, Gideon) and all
9:33 [G] In the morning at sunrise, **[NIE]** advance against the city.
19:5 [G] On the fourth day *they* **got up early** and he prepared to
19:8 [G] when *he* **rose** to go, the girl's father said, "Refresh yourself.
19:9 [G] **Early** tomorrow **morning** *you can* **get up** and be on your
21:4 [G] **Early** the next day the people built an altar and presented
1Sa 1:19 [G] **Early** the next morning *they* **arose** and worshiped before the
5:3 [G] When the people of Ashdod **rose early** the next day, there
5:4 [G] the following morning *when they* **rose**, there was Dagon,
9:26 [G] *They* **rose** about daybreak and Samuel called to Saul on the
15:12 [G] **Early** in the morning Samuel **got up** and went to meet Saul,
17:16 [G] For forty days the Philistine came forward *every* **morning**
17:20 [G] **Early** in the morning David left the flock with a shepherd,
29:10 [G] Now **get up early**, along with your master's servants who
29:10 [G] and leave **[RPH]** in the morning as soon as it is light."
29:11 [G] his men **got up early** in the morning to go back to the land of
2Sa 15:2 [G] He *would* **get up early** and stand by the side of the road
2Ki 3:22 [G] When *they* **got up early** in the morning, the sun was shining
6:15 [G] the man of God got up and went out **early the next morning**,
19:35 [G] When *the people* **got up** the next morning—there were all
2Ch 20:20 [G] **Early** in the morning they left for the Desert of Tekoa. As
29:20 [G] **Early the next morning** King Hezekiah gathered the city
36:15 [G] through his messengers **again** [+2256+8938] **and again**,
Job 1:5 [G] **Early** in the morning he would sacrifice a burnt offering for
Ps 127:2 [G] In vain you rise **early** and stay up late, toiling for food to
Pr 27:14 [G] If a man loudly blesses his neighbor **early** in the morning,
SS 7:12 [7:13] [G] *Let us* **go early** to the vineyards to see if the vines
Isa 5:11 [G] Woe to *those who* **rise early** in the morning to run after their
37:36 [G] When *the people* **got up** the next morning—there were all
Jer 7:13 [G] declares the LORD, I spoke to you **again and again**, but
7:25 [G] **again and again** I sent you my servants the prophets.
11:7 [G] I warned them **again and again**, saying, "Obey me."
25:3 [G] has come to me and I have spoken to you **again and again**,
25:4 [G] has sent all his servants the prophets to you **again and again**,
26:5 [G] whom I have sent to you **again and again** (though you have
29:19 [G] "words that I sent to them **again and again** by my servants
32:33 [G] though I taught them **again and again**, they would not listen
35:14 [G] I have spoken to you **again and again**, yet you have not
35:15 [G] **Again and again** I sent all my servants the prophets to you.
44:4 [G] **Again and again** I sent my servants the prophets, who said,
Hos 6:4 [G] is like the morning mist, like the **early** dew that disappears.
13:3 [G] like the **early** dew that disappears, like chaff swirling from a
Zep 3:7 [G] But *they were still* **eager** to act corruptly in all they did.

8900 שְׁכֶם¹ *šᵉkem*[1], n.m. [22] [→ 8899, 8901, 8902, 8903, 8904]

shoulders [9], shoulder [7], head [+2025+2256+4946+5087] [2], backs [1], ridge of land [1], shoulder to shoulder [+285] [1], turned [+7155] [1]

Ge 9:23 and Japheth took a garment and laid it across their **shoulders**;
21:14 He set them on her **shoulders** and then sent her off with the boy.
24:15 finished praying, Rebekah came out with her jar on her **shoulder**.
24:45 in my heart, Rebekah came out, with her jar on her **shoulder**.
48:22 I give the **ridge of land** I took from the Amorites with my sword
49:15 he will bend his **shoulder** to the burden and submit to forced labor.
Ex 12:34 carried it on their **shoulders** in kneading troughs wrapped in
Jos 4:5 Each of you is to take up a stone on his **shoulder**, according to the
Jdg 9:48 and cut off some branches, which he lifted to his **shoulders**.
1Sa 9:2 a **head** [+2025+2256+4946+5087] taller than any of the others.
10:9 As Saul **turned** [+7155] to leave Samuel, God changed Saul's
10:23 a **head** [+2025+2256+4946+5087] taller than any of the others.
Job 31:22 let my arm fall from the **shoulder**, let it be broken off at the joint.
31:36 Surely I would wear it on my **shoulder**, I would put it on like a
Ps 21:12 [21:13] for you will make them turn their **backs** when you aim at
81:6 [81:7] He says, "I removed the burden from their **shoulders**;
Isa 9:4 [9:3] the bar across their **shoulders**, the rod of their oppressor.
9:6 [9:5] a son is given, and the government will be on his **shoulders**.
10:27 In that day their burden will be lifted from your **shoulders**,
14:25 from my people, and his burden removed from their **shoulders**."
22:22 I will place on his **shoulder** the key to the house of David;
Zep 3:9 name of the LORD and serve him **shoulder** [+285] **to shoulder**.

8901 שְׁכֶם² *šᵉkem*[2], n.pr.loc. [48] [√ 8900]

Shechem [43], there[s] [2], its[s] [1], they[s] [+1251+3972+4463] [1], who[s] [+1251] [1]

Ge 12:6 the land as far as the site of the great tree of Moreh at **Shechem**.
33:18 he arrived safely at the city of **Shechem** in Canaan and camped
35:4 in their ears, and Jacob buried them under the oak at **Shechem**.
37:12 his brothers had gone to graze their father's flocks near **Shechem**,
37:13 "As you know, your brothers are grazing the flocks near **Shechem**.
37:14 off from the Valley of Hebron. When Joseph arrived at **Shechem**,
Jos 17:7 Manasseh extended from Asher to Micmethath east of **Shechem**.
20:7 **Shechem** in the hill country of Ephraim, and Kiriath Arba (that is,
21:21 In the hill country of Ephraim they were given **Shechem** (a city of
24:1 Then Joshua assembled all the tribes of Israel at **Shechem**.
24:25 and there at **Shechem** he drew up for them decrees and laws.
24:32 were buried at **Shechem** in the tract of land that Jacob bought for a
Jdg 8:31 His concubine, who lived in **Shechem**, also bore him a son,
9:1 son of Jerub-Baal went to his mother's brothers in **Shechem**
9:2 "Ask all the citizens of **Shechem**, 'Which is better for you:
9:3 When the brothers repeated all this to the citizens of **Shechem**,
9:6 all the citizens of **Shechem** and Beth Millo gathered beside the
9:6 Beth Millo gathered beside the great tree at the pillar in **Shechem**
9:7 and shouted to them, "Listen to me, citizens of **Shechem**,
9:18 king over the citizens of **Shechem** because he is your brother)—
9:20 and consume you, citizens of **Shechem** and Beth Millo,
9:20 citizens of **Shechem** and Beth Millo, and consume Abimelech!"
9:23 sent an evil spirit between Abimelech and the citizens of **Shechem**,
9:23 the citizens of Shechem, **who**[s] [+1251] acted treacherously against
9:24 on their brother Abimelech and on the citizens of **Shechem**,
9:25 In opposition to him these citizens of **Shechem** set men on the
9:26 Now Gaal son of Ebed moved with his brothers into **Shechem**,
9:26 into Shechem, and **its**[s] citizens put their confidence in him.
9:31 "Gaal son of Ebed and his brothers have come to **Shechem**
9:34 and took up concealed positions near **Shechem** in four companies.
9:39 So Gaal led out the citizens of **Shechem** and fought Abimelech.
9:41 and Zebul drove Gaal and his brothers out of **Shechem**.
9:46 the citizens in the tower of **Shechem** went into the stronghold of
9:47 Abimelech heard that **they**[s] [+1251+3972+4463] had assembled
9:49 So all the people in the tower of **Shechem**, about a thousand men
9:57 God also made the men of **Shechem** pay for all their wickedness.

Jdg 21:19 of Bethel, and east of the road that goes from Bethel to **Shechem**,
1Ki 12: 1 Rehoboam went to **Shechem**, for all the Israelites had gone there
12: 1 for all the Israelites had gone **there**ˢ to make him king.
12:25 Then Jeroboam fortified **Shechem** in the hill country of Ephraim
1Ch 6:67 [6:52] In the hill country of Ephraim they were given **Shechem** (a
7:28 and **Shechem** and its villages all the way to Ayyah and its villages.
2Ch 10: 1 Rehoboam went to **Shechem**, for all the Israelites had gone there
10: 1 for all the Israelites had gone **there**ˢ to make him king.
Ps 60: 6 [60:8] "In triumph I will parcel out **Shechem** and measure off the
108: 7 [108:8] "In triumph I will parcel out **Shechem** and measure off
Jer 41: 5 torn their clothes and cut themselves came from **Shechem**,
Hos 6: 9 they murder on the road to **Shechem**, committing shameful crimes.

8902 ³שְׁכֶם ***šᵉkem³***, n.pr.m. [15] [√ 8900]

Shechem [12], Shechem's [3]

Ge 33:19 he bought from the sons of Hamor, the father of **Shechem**,
34: 2 When **Shechem** son of Hamor the Hivite, the ruler of that area,
34: 4 **Shechem** said to his father Hamor, "Get me this girl as my wife."
34: 6 Then **Shechem's** father Hamor went out to talk with Jacob.
34: 8 said to them, "My son **Shechem** has his heart set on your daughter.
34:11 **Shechem** said to Dinah's father and brothers, "Let me find favor in
34:13 Jacob's sons replied deceitfully as they spoke to **Shechem**
34:18 Their proposal seemed good to Hamor and his son **Shechem**.
34:20 his son **Shechem** went to the gate of their city to speak to their
34:24 went out of the city gate agreed with Hamor and his son **Shechem**,
34:26 They put Hamor and his son **Shechem** to the sword and took
34:26 to the sword and took Dinah from **Shechem's** house and left.
Jos 24:32 pieces of silver from the sons of Hamor, the father of **Shechem**.
Jdg 9:28 Gaal son of Ebed said, "Who is Abimelech, and who is **Shechem**,
9:28 Zebul his deputy? Serve the men of Hamor, **Shechem's** father!

8903 שֶׁכֶם ***šekem***, n.pr.m. [3] [→ 8904; cf. 8900]

Shechem [3]

Nu 26:31 the Asrielite clan; through **Shechem**, the Shechemite clan;
Jos 17: 2 clans of Abiezer, Helek, Asriel, **Shechem**, Hepher and Shemida.
1Ch 7:19 The sons of Shemida were: Ahian, **Shechem**, Likhi and Aniam.

8904 שִׁכְמִי ***šikmî***, a.g. [1] [√ 8903]

Shechemite [1]

Nu 26:31 the Asrielite clan; through Shechem, the **Shechemite** clan;

8905 שָׁכַן ***šākan***, v. [130] [→ 5438, 8906, 8907, 8908, 8909; Ar 10709]

live [26], dwell [21], dwelling [8], live in [6], settled [5], dwell in [4], dwells [4], nest [3], stayed [3], dwelt in [2], dwelt [2], have a home [+9393] [2], let live [2], lived in [2], lives [2], living [2], remain [2], rest [2], set up [2], settle [2], abode [1], allow to dwell [1], among [+907] [1], at rest [1], came to rest [1], camp [1], come to dwell [1], dwells in [1], encamped [1], find shelter [1], inhabit [1], inhabited [1], let settle [1], lie down to rest [1], lie [1], lived [1], lives in [1], made a dwelling [1], make home [1], make sleep [1], nomads [+185+928] [1], placed [1], resides [1], rests [1], settled in [1], stands [1], stay [1], stayed [+799] [1]

Ge 3:24 [G] *he* **placed** on the east side of the Garden of Eden cherubim and
9:27 [A] *may* Japheth **live** in the tents of Shem, and may Canaan be
14:13 [A] Now Abram *was* **living** near the great trees of Mamre the
16:12 [A] and *he will* **live** in hostility toward all his brothers."
25:18 [A] His descendants **settled in** the area from Havilah to Shur,
26: 2 [A] go down to Egypt; **live** in the land where I tell you to live.
35:22 [A] While Israel *was* **living** in that region, Reuben went in
49:13 [A] "Zebulun *will* **live** by the seashore and become a haven for
Ex 24:16 [A] the glory of the LORD **settled** on Mount Sinai. For six days
25: 8 [A] them make a sanctuary for me, and *I will* **dwell** among them.
29:45 [A] Then *I will* **dwell** among the Israelites and be their God.
29:46 [A] them out of Egypt so that I *might* **dwell** among them.
40:35 [A] the Tent of Meeting because the cloud *had* **settled** upon it,
Lev 16:16 [A] which *is* **among** [+907] them in the midst of their
Nu 5: 3 [A] they will not defile their camp, where I **dwell** among them."
9:17 [A] set out; wherever the cloud **settled**, the Israelites encamped.
9:18 [A] As long as the cloud **stayed** over the tabernacle,
9:22 [A] Whether the cloud **stayed** [+799] over the tabernacle for two
10:12 [A] traveled from place to place until the cloud **came to rest** in
14:30 [D] the land I swore with uplifted hand to **make** your **home**,
23: 9 [A] I see a people *who* **live** apart and do not consider themselves
24: 2 [A] Balaam looked out and saw Israel **encamped** tribe by tribe,
35:34 [A] Do not defile the land where you live and where I **dwell**, for
35:34 [A] I dwell, for I, the LORD, **dwell** among the Israelites.' "
Dt 12: 5 [A] among all your tribes to put his Name there for his **dwelling**.
12:11 [D] LORD your God will choose as a **dwelling** *for* his Name—
14:23 [D] God at the place he will choose as a **dwelling** *for* his Name,
16: 2 [D] or herd at the place the LORD will choose as a **dwelling** *for*
16: 6 [D] except in the place he will choose as a **dwelling** *for* his
16:11 [D] God at the place he will choose as a **dwelling** *for* his Name—
26: 2 [D] LORD your God will choose as a **dwelling** *for* his Name
33:12 [A] "*Let* the beloved of the LORD **rest** secure in him, for he
33:12 [A] and the one the LORD loves **rests** between his shoulders."
33:16 [A] and the favor of *him who* **dwelt in** the burning bush.
33:20 [A] Gad **lives** there like a lion, tearing at arm or head.
33:28 [A] So Israel *will* **live** in safety alone; Jacob's spring is secure in
Jos 18: 1 [G] gathered at Shiloh and **set up** the Tent of Meeting there.
22:19 [A] where the LORD's tabernacle **stands**, and share the land
Jdg 5:17 [A] Gilead **stayed** beyond the Jordan. And Dan, why did he
5:17 [A] Asher remained on the coast and **stayed** in his coves.
8:11 [B] Gideon went up by the route of the **nomads** [+185+928] east
2Sa 7:10 [A] so that *they can* **have a home** [+9393] *of* their own
1Ki 6:13 [A] *I will* **live** among the Israelites and will not abandon my
8:12 [A] "The LORD has said that he *would* **dwell** in a dark cloud;
1Ch 17: 9 [A] so that *they can* **have a home** [+9393] *of their own*
23:25 [A] to his people and *has* **come to dwell** in Jerusalem forever,
2Ch 6: 1 [A] "The LORD has said that he *would* **dwell** in a dark cloud;
Ne 1: 9 [D] bring them to the place I have chosen as a **dwelling** *for* my
Job 3: 5 [A] *may* a cloud **settle** over it; may blackness overwhelm its
4:19 [A] how much more *those who* **live in** houses of clay,
11:14 [G] that is in your hand and **allow** no evil **to dwell** in your tent,
15:28 [A] *he will* **inhabit** ruined towns and houses where no one lives,
18:15 [A] Fire **resides** in his tent; burning sulfur is scattered over his
26: 5 [A] those beneath the waters and *all that* **live in** them.
29:25 [A] and sat as their chief; *I* **dwelt** as a king among his troops;
30: 6 [A] They were forced to **live** in the dry stream beds,
37: 8 [A] The animals take cover; *they* **remain** in their dens.
38:19 [A] "What is the way to the **abode** *of* light? And where does
39:28 [A] *He* **dwells** on a cliff and stays there at night; a rocky crag is
Ps 7: 5 [7:6] [G] my life to the ground and **make** me **sleep** in the dust.
15: 1 [A] dwell in your sanctuary? Who *may* **live** on your holy hill?
16: 9 [A] and my tongue rejoices; my body also *will* **rest** secure,
37: 3 [A] and do good; **dwell in** the land and enjoy safe pasture.
37:27 [A] and do good; then *you will* **dwell in** the land forever.
37:29 [A] the righteous will inherit the land and **dwell** in it forever.
55: 6 [55:7] [A] wings of a dove! I would fly away and *be* **at rest**—
65: 4 [65:5] [A] you choose and bring near *to* **live in** your courts!
68: 6 [68:7] [A] but the rebellious **live in** a sun-scorched land.
68:16 [68:17] [A] where the LORD himself *will* **dwell** forever?
68:18 [68:19] [A] that you, O LORD God, *might* **dwell** there.
69:36 [69:37] [A] and those who love his name *will* **dwell** there.
74: 2 [A] whom you redeemed—Mount Zion, where *you* **dwelt**.
78:55 [G] an inheritance; *he* **settled** the tribes of Israel in their homes.
78:60 [D] the tabernacle of Shiloh, the tent *he had* **set up** among men.
85: 9 [85:10] [A] who fear him, that his glory *may* **dwell** in our land.
88: 5 [88:6] [A] with the dead, like the slain *who* **lie** *in* the grave,
94:17 [A] me help, I *would* soon *have* **dwelt in** the silence of death.
102:28 [102:29] [A] The children of your servants *will* **live** in your
104:12 [A] The birds of the air **nest** by the waters; they sing among the
120: 5 [A] that I dwell in Meshech, that *I* **live** among the tents of Kedar!
120: 6 [A] Too long *have* I **lived** among those who hate peace.
135:21 [A] to the LORD from Zion, to *him who* **dwells in** Jerusalem.
139: 9 [A] on the wings of the dawn, if *I* **settle** on the far side of the sea,
Pr 1:33 [A] but whoever listens to me *will* **live** in safety and be at ease,
2:21 [A] For the upright *will* **live in** the land, and the blameless will
7:11 [A] (She is loud and defiant, her feet never **stay** at home;
8:12 [A] "I, wisdom, **dwell** *together with* prudence; I possess
10:30 [A] be uprooted, but the wicked *will* not **remain** *in* the land.
Isa 8:18 [A] from the LORD Almighty, who **dwells** on Mount Zion.
13:20 [A] will never be inhabited or **lived in** through all generations;
13:21 [A] there the owls *will* **dwell**, and there the wild goats will leap
18: 3 [A] All you people of the world, you *who* **live** *on* the earth,
26:19 [A] *You who* **dwell in** the dust, wake up and shout for joy.
32:16 [A] Justice *will* **dwell** in the desert and righteousness live in the
33: 5 [A] The LORD is exalted, for *he* **dwells** on high; he will fill
33:16 [A] this is the *man who will* **dwell** on the heights, whose refuge
34:11 [A] will possess it; the great owl and the raven *will* **nest** there.
34:17 [A] it forever and **dwell** there from generation to generation.
57:15 [A] lofty One says—*he who* **lives** forever, whose name is holy:
57:15 [A] "*I* **live in** a high and holy place, but also with him who is
65: 9 [A] people will inherit them, and there *will* my servants **live**.
Jer 7: 3 [D] and your actions, and *I will* **let** you **live** in this place.
7: 7 [D] *I will* **let** you **live** in this place, in the land I gave your
7:12 [D] place in Shiloh where *I* first **made a dwelling** *for* my Name,
17: 6 [A] *He will* **dwell in** the parched places of the desert, in a salt
23: 6 [A] In his days Judah will be saved and Israel *will* **live** in safety.
25:24 [A] and all the kings of the foreign people who **live** in the desert;
33:16 [A] days Judah will be saved and Jerusalem *will* **live** in safety.
46:26 [A] Later, however, Egypt *will be* **inhabited** as in times past,"
48:28 [A] Abandon your towns and **dwell** among the rocks, you who
49:16 [A] you *who* **live** in the clefts of the rocks, who occupy the
49:31 [A] nation that has neither gates nor bars; its *people* **live** alone.

Jer 50:39 [A] again be inhabited or **lived in** from generation to generation.
51:13 [A] *You who* **live** by many waters and are rich in treasures,
Eze 17:23 [A] Birds of every kind *will* **nest** in it; they will find shelter in the
17:23 [A] nest in it; *they will* **find shelter** in the shade of its branches.
31:13 [A] All the birds of the air **settled** on the fallen tree, and all the
32: 4 [G] *I will* **let** all the birds of the air **settle** on you and all the
43: 7 [A] This is where *I will* **live** among the Israelites forever.
43: 9 [A] idols of their kings, and *I will* **live** among them forever.
Joel 3:17 [4:17] [A] the LORD your God, **dwell** in Zion, my holy hill.
3:21 [4:21] [A] I will pardon." The LORD **dwells** in Zion!
Ob 1: 3 [A] you *who* **live** in the clefts of the rocks and make your home
Mic 4:10 [A] for now you must leave the city *to* **camp** in the open field.
7:14 [A] *which* **lives** by itself **in** a forest, in fertile pasturelands.
Na 3:18 [A] your shepherds slumber; your nobles **lie down to rest**.
Zec 2:10 [2:14] [A] For I am coming, and *I will* **live** among you,"
2:11 [2:15] [A] *I will* **live** among you and you will know that the
8: 3 [A] LORD says: "I will return to Zion and **dwell** in Jerusalem.
8: 8 [A] I will bring them back *to* **live** in Jerusalem; they will be my

8906 שֶׁכֶן šeken, n.m. Not used in NIV/BHS [√ 8905]

8907 שָׁכֵן šākēn, a. [20] [√ 8905]

neighbors [11], neighbor [3], neighboring [2], living [1], neighboring peoples [1], one living in [1], people who live in [1]

Ex 3:22 Every woman is to ask her **neighbor** and any woman living in her
12: 4 for a whole lamb, they must share one with their nearest **neighbor**,
Dt 1: 7 go to all the **neighboring peoples** in the Arabah, in the mountains,
Ru 4:17 The *women* **living** there said, "Naomi has a son." And they named
2Ki 4: 3 Elisha said, "Go around and ask all your **neighbors** for empty jars.
Ps 31:11 [31:12] all my enemies, I am the utter contempt of my **neighbors**;
44:13 [44:14] You have made us a reproach to our **neighbors**, the scorn
79: 4 We are objects of reproach to our **neighbors**, of scorn and derision
79:12 Pay back into the laps of our **neighbors** seven times the reproach
80: 6 [80:7] You have made us a source of contention to our **neighbors**,
89:41 [89:42] plundered him; he has become the scorn of his **neighbors**.
Pr 27:10 strikes you—better a **neighbor** nearby than a brother far away.
Isa 33:24 No **one living in** Zion will say, "I am ill"; and the sins of those
Jer 6:21 alike will stumble over them; **neighbors** and friends will perish."
12:14 "As for all my wicked **neighbors** who seize the inheritance I gave
49:10 His children, relatives and **neighbors** will perish, and he will be no
49:18 along with their **neighboring** towns," says the LORD, "so no one
50:40 and Gomorrah along with their **neighboring** towns,"
Eze 16:26 engaged in prostitution with the Egyptians, your lustful **neighbors**,
Hos 10: 5 The **people who live in** Samaria fear for the calf-idol of Beth

8908 שְׁכַנְיָה š^ekanyâ, n.pr.m. [8 / 9] [√ 8905 + 3378]

Shecaniah [8], Shecaniah's [1]

1Ch 3:21 and the sons of Rephaiah, of Arnan, of Obadiah and of **Shecaniah**.
3:22 The descendants of **Shecaniah**: Shemaiah and his sons: Hattush,
Ezr 8: 3 of the descendants of **Shecaniah**; of the descendants of Parosh,
8: 5 of Zattu, **Shecaniah** son of Jahaziel, and with him 300 men;
10: 2 Then **Shecaniah** son of Jehiel, one of the descendants of Elam,
Ne 3:29 Next to him, Shemaiah son of **Shecaniah**, the guard at the East
6:18 oath to him, since he was son-in-law to **Shecaniah** son of Arah,
12: 3 **Shecaniah**, Rehum, Meremoth,
12:14 of Malluch's, Jonathan; of **Shecaniah's**, [BHS 8676] Joseph;

8909 שְׁכַנְיָהוּ š^ekanyāhû, n.pr.m. [2] [√ 8905 + 3378]

Shecaniah [2]

1Ch 24:11 the ninth to Jeshua, the tenth to **Shecaniah**,
2Ch 31:15 and **Shecaniah** assisted him faithfully in the towns of the priests,

8910 שָׁכַר šākar, v. [18] [→ 8893, 8911, 8912, 8913]

drunk [6], make drunk [4], made drunk [3], drank freely [1], drink fill [1], get drunk [1], have fill [1], keep on getting drunk [1]

Ge 9:21 [A] its wine, *he became* **drunk** and lay uncovered inside his tent.
43:34 [A] as anyone else's. So they feasted and **drank freely** with him.
Dt 32:42 [G] *I will* **make** my arrows **drunk** with blood, while my sword
1Sa 1:14 [F] and said to her, "How long *will you* **keep on getting drunk**?
2Sa 11:13 [D] he ate and drank with him, and David **made him drunk**.
SS 5: 1 [A] my milk. Eat, O friends, and drink; **drink** *your* **fill**, O lovers.
Isa 29: 9 [A] *be* **drunk**, but not from wine, stagger, but not from beer.
49:26 [A] *they will be* **drunk** *on* their own blood, as with wine.
63: 6 [D] in my wrath *I* **made** them **drunk** and poured their blood on
Jer 25:27 [A] Drink, **get drunk** and vomit, and fall to rise no more
48:26 [G] "**Make** her **drunk**, for she has defied the LORD. Let Moab
51: 7 [D] cup in the LORD's hand; *she* **made** the whole earth **drunk**.
51:39 [G] I will set out a feast for them and **make** them **drunk**,
51:57 [G] *I will* **make** her officials and wise men **drunk**, her
La 4:21 [A] cup will be passed; *you will be* **drunk** and stripped naked.
Na 3:11 [A] You too *will become* **drunk**; you will go into hiding
Hab 2:15 [D] pouring it from the wineskin till *they are* **drunk**, so that he
Hag 1: 6 [A] You drink, but never **have** *your* **fill**. You put on clothes,

8911 שֵׁכָר šēkār, n.[m.]. [23] [√ 8910]

beer [11], fermented drink [9], drinks [2], drunkards [+9272] [1]

Lev 10: 9 or other **fermented drink** whenever you go into the Tent of
Nu 6: 3 he must abstain from wine and other **fermented drink** and must
6: 3 not drink vinegar made from wine or from other **fermented drink**.
28: 7 is to be a quarter of a hin of **fermented drink** with each lamb.
Dt 14:26 cattle, sheep, wine or other **fermented drink**, or anything you
29: 6 [29:5] ate no bread and drank no wine or other **fermented drink**.
Jdg 13: 4 Now see to it that you drink no wine or other **fermented drink**
13: 7 drink no wine or other **fermented drink** and do not eat anything
13:14 drink any wine or other **fermented drink** nor eat anything unclean.
1Sa 1:15 I have not been drinking wine or **beer**; I was pouring out my soul
Ps 69:12 [69:13] mock me, and I am the song of the **drunkards** [+9272].
Pr 20: 1 Wine is a mocker and **beer** a brawler; whoever is led astray by
31: 4 not for kings to drink wine, not for rulers to crave **beer**,
31: 6 Give **beer** to those who are perishing, wine to those who are in
Isa 5:11 to those who rise early in the morning to run after their **drinks**,
5:22 who are heroes at drinking wine and champions at mixing **drinks**,
24: 9 do they drink wine with a song; the **beer** is bitter to its drinkers.
28: 7 And these also stagger from wine and reel from **beer**: Priests
28: 7 Priests and prophets stagger from **beer** and are befuddled with
28: 7 they reel from **beer**, they stagger when seeing visions,
29: 9 be drunk, but not from wine, stagger, but not from **beer**.
56:12 each one cries, "let me get wine! Let us drink our fill of **beer**!
Mic 2:11 and says, 'I will prophesy for you plenty of wine and **beer**,'

8912 שָׁכֻר šākur, a. *or* v.ptcp. [1] [√ 8910]

made drunk [1]

Isa 51:21 hear this, you afflicted one, **made drunk**, but not with wine.

8913 שִׁכָּרוֹן šikkārôn[1], n.[m.]. [3] [√ 8910]

drunkenness [2], drunk [1]

Jer 13:13 I am going to fill with **drunkenness** all who live in this land,
Eze 23:33 You will be filled with **drunkenness** and sorrow, the cup of ruin
39:19 will eat fat till you are glutted and drink blood till you are **drunk**.

8914 שִׁכָּרוֹן[2] šikkārôn[2], n.pr.loc. [1]

Shikkeron [1]

Jos 15:11 turned toward **Shikkeron**, passed along to Mount Baalah

8915 שַׁל šal, n.[m.]. [1]

irreverent act [1]

2Sa 6: 7 anger burned against Uzzah because of his **irreverent act**;

8916 שַׁלְאֲנָן šal^anan, a. [1] [√ 8631]

secure [1]

Job 21:23 One man dies in full vigor, completely **secure** and at ease,

8917 שָׁלַב šālab, v. [2] [√ 8918]

set parallel [2]

Ex 26:17 [E] with two projections **set parallel** to each other. Make all the
36:22 [E] with two projections **set parallel** to each other. They made all

8918 שָׁלָב šālāb, n.[m.]pl. [3] [→ 8917]

uprights [3]

1Ki 7:28 the stands were made: They had side panels attached to **uprights**.
7:29 On the panels between the **uprights** were lions, bulls
7:29 were lions, bulls and cherubim—and on the **uprights** as well.

8919 שָׁלַג šālag, v.den. [1] [√ 8920]

snow fallen [1]

Ps 68:14 [68:15] [G] in the land, *it was like* **snow fallen** on Zalmon.

8920 שֶׁלֶג[1] šeleg[1], n.m. [19] [→ 8919, 8921; Ar 10758]

snow [16], snowy [2], snows [1]

Ex 4: 6 into his cloak, and when he took it out, it was leprous, like **snow**.
Nu 12:10 from above the Tent, there stood Miriam—leprous, like **snow**.
2Sa 23:20 He also went down into a pit on a **snowy** day and killed a lion.
2Ki 5:27 went from Elisha's presence and he was leprous, as white as **snow**.
1Ch 11:22 He also went down into a pit on a **snowy** day and killed a lion.
Job 6:16 when darkened by thawing ice and swollen with melting **snow**,
24:19 As heat and drought snatch away the melted **snow**, so the grave
37: 6 He says to the **snow**, 'Fall on the earth,' and to the rain shower,
38:22 "Have you entered the storehouses of the **snow** or seen the

Ps 51: 7 [51:9] I will be clean; wash me, and I will be whiter than **snow**.
147: 16 He spreads the **snow** like wool and scatters the frost like ashes.
148: 8 lightning and hail, **snow** and clouds, stormy winds that do his
Pr 25: 13 Like the coolness of **snow** at harvest time is a trustworthy
26: 1 Like **snow** in summer or rain in harvest, honor is not fitting for a
31: 21 When it **snows**, she has no fear for her household; for all of them
Isa 1: 18 "Though your sins are like scarlet, they shall be as white as **snow**;
55: 10 As the rain and the **snow** come down from heaven, and do not
Jer 18: 14 Does the **snow** *of* Lebanon ever vanish from its rocky slopes?
La 4: 7 Their princes were brighter than **snow** and whiter than milk,

8921 [2]שֶׁלֶג ***šeleg***[2], n.m. [1] [√ 8920]

soap [1]

Job 9: 30 Even if I washed myself with **soap** and my hands with washing

8922 [1]שָׁלָה ***šālā***[1], v. [7] [→ 8929, 8930, 8932, 8937, 8952, 8953; cf. 8923]

at ease [1], have peace [1], live at ease [1], negligent [1], raise hopes [1], secure [1], undisturbed [1]

2Ki 4: 28 [G] she said. "Didn't I tell you, 'Don't **raise** my **hopes**'?"
2Ch 29: 11 [C] My sons, *do* not *be* **negligent** now, for the LORD has
Job 3: 26 [A] *I* **have** no **peace**, no quietness; I have no rest, but only
12: 6 [A] The tents of marauders *are* **undisturbed**, and those who
Ps 122: 6 [A] the peace of Jerusalem: "*May* those who love you *be* **secure**.
Jer 12: 1 [A] of the wicked prosper? Why *do* all the faithless **live at ease**?
La 1: 5 [A] Her foes have become her masters; her enemies *are* **at ease**.

8923 [2]שָׁלָה ***šālâ***[2], v. [1] [cf. 8922]

takes away [1]

Job 27: 8 [A] godless when he is cut off, when God **takes away** his life?

8924 [1]שְׁלָה ***šēlâ***[1], n.f. [1] [√ 8629; cf. 8626]

what[s] [1]

1Sa 1: 17 may the God of Israel grant you **what**[s] you have asked of him."

8925 [2]שֵׁלָה ***šēlâ***[2], n.pr.m. [8] [→ 8924, 8989]

Shelah [8]

Ge 38: 5 She gave birth to still another son and named him **Shelah**.
38: 11 "Live as a widow in your father's house until my son **Shelah**
38: 14 For she saw that, though **Shelah** had now grown up, she had not
38: 26 righteous than I, since I wouldn't give her to my son **Shelah**."
46: 12 **Shelah**, Perez and Zerah (but Er and Onan had died in the land of
Nu 26: 20 through **Shelah**, the Shelanite clan; through Perez, the Perezite
1Ch 2: 3 The sons of Judah: Er, Onan and **Shelah**. These three were born to
4: 21 The sons of **Shelah** son of Judah: Er the father of Lecah, Laadah

8926 שִׁלֹה ***šilōh***, n.pr.loc. [22] [cf. 8872, 8931, 9304]

Shiloh [22]

Jos 18: 1 The whole assembly of the Israelites gathered at **Shiloh** and set up
18: 8 I will cast lots for you here at **Shiloh** in the presence of the
18: 9 in seven parts, and returned to Joshua in the camp at **Shiloh**.
18: 10 then cast lots for them in **Shiloh** in the presence of the LORD,
19: 51 the heads of the tribal clans of Israel assigned by lot at **Shiloh** in
21: 2 at **Shiloh** in Canaan and said to them, "The LORD commanded
22: 9 the half-tribe of Manasseh left the Israelites at **Shiloh** in Canaan to
22: 12 the whole assembly of Israel gathered at **Shiloh** to go to war
Jdg 18: 31 idols Micah had made, all the time the house of God was in **Shiloh**.
21: 12 with a man, and they took them to the camp at **Shiloh** in Canaan.
1Sa 1: 3 town to worship and sacrifice to the LORD Almighty at **Shiloh**,
1: 9 Once when they had finished eating and drinking in **Shiloh**,
2: 14 This is how they treated all the Israelites who came to **Shiloh**.
3: 21 The LORD continued to appear at **Shiloh**, and there he revealed
4: 3 Let us bring the ark of the LORD's covenant from **Shiloh**,
4: 4 So the people sent men to **Shiloh**, and they brought back the ark of
4: 12 same day a Benjamite ran from the battle line and went to **Shiloh**,
1Ki 2: 27 fulfilling the word the LORD had spoken at **Shiloh** about the
14: 2 go to **Shiloh**. Ahijah the prophet is there—the one who told me I
14: 4 wife did what he said and went to Ahijah's house in **Shiloh**.
Jer 26: 6 I will make this house like **Shiloh** and this city an object of
41: 5 **Shiloh** and Samaria, bringing grain offerings and incense with

8927 שַׁלְהֶבֶת ***šalhebet***, n.f. [2] [√ 4258]

flame [2]

Job 15: 30 a **flame** will wither his shoots, and the breath of God's mouth will
Eze 20: 47 [21:3] The blazing **flame** will not be quenched, and every face

8928 שַׁלְהֶבֶתְיָה ***šalhebetyâ***, n.f. [+n.pr.?]. [1]

mighty flame [1]

SS 8: 6 as the grave. It burns like blazing fire, like a **mighty flame**.

8929 שָׁלֵו ***šālēw***, a. [8] [√ 8922; Ar 10710]

at ease [2], carefree [2], prosperous [1], quiet [1], respite [1], well [1]

1Ch 4: 40 good pasture, and the land was spacious, peaceful and **quiet**.
Job 16: 12 *All* was **well** with me, but he shattered me; he seized me by the
20: 20 "Surely he will have no **respite** from his craving; he cannot save
21: 23 One man dies in full vigor, completely secure and **at ease**,
Ps 73: 12 the wicked are like—always **carefree**, they increase in wealth.
Jer 49: 31 "Arise and attack a nation **at ease**, which lives in confidence,"
Eze 23: 42 "The noise of a **carefree** crowd was around her; Sabeans were
Zec 7: 7 and its surrounding towns were at rest and **prosperous**,

8930 שָׁלוּ ***šālû***, n.[m.]. [1] [√ 8922; Ar 10711, 10712]

felt secure [1]

Ps 30: 6 [30:7] When I **felt secure**, I said, "I will never be shaken."

8931 שִׁלוֹ ***šilō***, n.pr.loc. [7] [cf. 8926]

Shiloh [6], there[s] [+928] [1]

Jdg 21: 19 But look, there is the annual festival of the LORD in **Shiloh**,
1Sa 1: 24 of wine, and brought him to the house of the LORD at **Shiloh**.
3: 21 and **there**[s] [+928] he revealed himself to Samuel through his word.
14: 3 son of Phinehas, the son of Eli, the LORD's priest in **Shiloh**.
Ps 78: 60 He abandoned the tabernacle of **Shiloh**, the tent he had set up
Jer 7: 14 what I did to **Shiloh** I will now do to the house that bears my
26: 9 prophesy in the LORD's name that this house will be like **Shiloh**

8932 שַׁלְוָה ***šalwâ***, n.f. [8] [√ 8922; Ar 10713]

feel secure [3], complacency [1], felt secure [1], peace and quiet [1], security [1], unconcerned [+9200] [1]

Ps 122: 7 be peace within your walls and **security** within your citadels."
Pr 1: 32 will kill them, and the **complacency** *of* fools will destroy them;
17: 1 Better a dry crust with **peace and quiet** than a house full of
Jer 22: 21 I warned you when you **felt secure**, but you said, 'I will not listen!'
Eze 16: 49 her daughters were arrogant, overfed and **unconcerned** [+9200];
Da 8: 25 When they **feel secure**, he will destroy many and take his stand
11: 21 He will invade the kingdom when its people **feel secure**, and he
11: 24 When the richest provinces **feel secure**, he will invade them

8933 שִׁלּוּחִים ***šillûḥîm***, n.[m.]pl. [3] [√ 8938]

parting gifts [1], sent away [1], wedding gift [1]

Ex 18: 2 After Moses had **sent away** his wife Zipporah, his father-in-law
1Ki 9: 16 and then gave it as a **wedding gift** to his daughter,
Mic 1: 14 Therefore you will give **parting gifts** to Moresheth Gath. The town

8934 שָׁלוֹם ***šālôm***, n.m. [237 / 236] [→ 58, 94, 8976, 8979, 8984, 8985; cf. 8966; Ar 10720]

peace [113], all right [9], safe [9], safely [+928] [9], come in peace [5], prosperity [5], greet [+4200+4200+8626] [4], greeted [+4200+4200+8626] [4], well [4], *untranslated* [3], how are [3], success [3], cordially [2], good health [2], in peace [2], peaceful [2], peacefully [2], perfect peace [+8934] [2], prosper [2], treaty of friendship [+2256+3208] [2], triumph [2], all is well [1], asked how they were [+4200+4200+8626] [1], benefit [1], blessing [1], close friend [+408] [1], completely [1], contentment [1], desires [1], friendly relations [1], friends [+408] [1], friends [+632] [1], friends [1], good [1], goodwill [1], greet [1], grow well [1], harmony [+6783] [1], how is [1], how was [+4200] [1], how was going [+4200] [1], how was [1], how were [+4200] [1], kind [1], order [1], peace and prosperity [1], peaceably [+928] [1], peaceably [1], peaceful relations [1], peacefully [+928] [1], peacetime [1], prospers [1], safely [+2021+4200] [1], safely [+4200] [1], satisfied [+928] [1], secure [1], sound [1], soundness [1], trusted friends [+408] [1], unharmed [+928] [1], unharmed [1], unscathed [+928] [1], unscathed [1], welcome [1], welfare [1], well-being [1], wish well [+4200] [1], yes[s] [1]

Ge 15: 15 will go to your fathers in **peace** and be buried at a good old age.
26: 29 but always treated you well and sent you away in **peace**.
26: 31 Then Isaac sent them on their way, and they left him in **peace**.
28: 21 so that I return **safely** [+928] to my father's house,
29: 6 Then Jacob asked them, "Is he **well**?" "Yes, he is," they said,
29: 6 "**Yes**[s], he is," they said, "and here comes his daughter Rachel with
37: 4 of them, they hated him and could not speak a **kind** word to him.
37: 14 "Go and see if all is **well** *with* your brothers and with the flocks,
37: 14 see if all is well with your brothers and **[RPH]** with the flocks,
41: 16 to Pharaoh, "but God will give Pharaoh the answer he **desires**."
43: 23 "It's **all right**," he said. "Don't be afraid. Your God, the God of

Ge 43:27 *He* **asked** them **how they were** [+4200+4200+8626], and then he
43:27 then he said, "**How is** your aged father you told me about?
43:28 They replied, "Your servant our father is still alive and **well**."
44:17 my slave. The rest of you, go back to your father in **peace**."
Ex 4:18 are still alive." Jethro said, "Go, and I **wish** you **well** [+4200]."
18:7 *They* **greeted** [+4200+4200+8626] each other and then went into
18:23 the strain, and all these people will go home **satisfied** [+928]."
Lev 26:6 " 'I will grant **peace** in the land, and you will lie down and no one
Nu 6:26 the LORD turn his face toward you and give you **peace**." '
25:12 Therefore tell him I am making my covenant of **peace** with him.
Dt 2:26 I sent messengers to Sihon king of Heshbon offering **peace**
20:10 you march up to attack a city, make its people an offer of **peace**.
20:11 If **[RPH]** they accept and open their gates, all the people in it
23:6 [23:7] Do not seek a **treaty of friendship** [+2256+3208] *with* them
29:19 [29:18] a blessing on himself and therefore thinks, "I will be **safe**,
Jos 9:15 Then Joshua made a treaty of **peace** with them to let them live,
10:21 then returned **safely** [+928] to Joshua in the camp at Makkedah,
Jdg 4:17 because there were **friendly relations** between Jabin king of Hazor
6:23 the LORD said to him, "**Peace**! Do not be afraid. You are not
6:24 an altar to the LORD there and called it The LORD is **Peace**.
8:9 of Peniel, "When I return in **triumph**, I will tear down this tower."
11:13 all the way to the Jordan. Now give it back **peaceably** [+928]."
11:31 I return in **triumph** from the Ammonites will be the LORD's,
18:6 The priest answered them, "Go in **peace**. Your journey has the
18:15 at Micah's place and **greeted** [+4200+4200+8626] him.
19:20 "You are **welcome** at my house," the old man said. "Let me supply
21:13 the whole assembly sent an offer of **peace** to the Benjamites at the
1Sa 1:17 Eli answered, "Go in **peace**, and may the God of Israel grant you
7:14 And there was **peace** between Israel and the Amorites.
10:4 *They will* **greet** [+4200+4200+8626] you and offer you two loaves
16:4 when they met him. They asked, "Do you come **in peace**?"
16:5 Samuel replied, "Yes, **in peace**; I have come to sacrifice to the
17:18 See **how** your brothers **are** and bring back some assurance from
17:22 to the battle lines and **greeted** [+4200+4200+8626] his brothers.
20:7 If he says, 'Very well,' then your servant is **safe**. But if he loses his
20:13 if I do not let you know and send you away **safely** [+4200].
20:21 then come, because, as surely as the LORD lives, you are **safe**;
20:42 Jonathan said to David, "Go in **peace**, for we have sworn
25:5 at Carmel and **greet** [+4200+4200+8626] him in my name.
25:6 'Long life to you! **Good health** to you and your household!
25:6 and your household! **[RPH]** And good health to all that is yours!
25:6 and your household! And **good health** to all that is yours!
25:35 her hand what she had brought him and said, "Go home in **peace**.
29:7 Turn back and go in **peace**; do nothing to displease the Philistine
30:21 and his men approached, *he* **greeted** [+4200+4200+8626] them.
2Sa 3:21 heart desires." So David sent Abner away, and he went in **peace**.
3:22 because David had sent him away, and he had gone in **peace**.
3:23 and that the king had sent him away and that he had gone in **peace**.
8:10 his son Joram to King David to **greet** [+4200+4200+8626] him and
11:7 David asked him **how** [+4200] Joab **was**, how the soldiers were
11:7 David asked him how Joab was, **how** [+4200] the soldiers **were**
11:7 how the soldiers were and **how** [+4200] the war **was going**.
15:9 The king said to him, "Go in **peace**." So he went to Hebron.
15:27 Go back to the city in **peace**, with your son Ahimaaz and Jonathan
17:3 seek will mean the return of all; all the people will be **unharmed**."
18:28 Ahimaaz called out to the king, "**All is well**!" He bowed down
18:29 The king asked, "Is the young man Absalom **safe**?" Ahimaaz
18:32 The king asked the Cushite, "Is the young man Absalom **safe**?"
19:24 [19:25] day the king left until the day he returned **safely** [+928].
19:30 [19:31] that my lord the king has arrived home **safely** [+928]."
20:9 Joab said to Amasa, "**How are** you, my brother?" Then Joab took
1Ki 2:5 He killed them, shedding their blood in **peacetime** as if in battle,
2:6 but do not let his gray head go down to the grave in **peace**.
2:13 Bathsheba asked him, "Do you come **peacefully**?" He answered,
2:13 "Do you come peacefully?" He answered, "Yes, **peacefully**."
2:33 and his throne, may there be the LORD's **peace** forever."
4:24 [5:4] the River, from Tiphsah to Gaza, and had **peace** on all sides.
5:12 [5:26] There were **peaceful relations** between Hiram
20:18 He said, "If they have come out for **peace**, take them alive;
22:17 'These people have no master. Let each one go home in **peace**.' "
22:27 him nothing but bread and water until I return **safely** [+928].' "
22:28 Micaiah declared, "If you ever return **safely** [+928], the LORD
2Ki 4:23 "It's not the New Moon or the Sabbath." "It's **all right**," she said.
4:26 Run to meet her and ask her, 'Are you **all right**? Is your husband
4:26 and ask her, 'Are you all right? Is your husband **all right**?
4:26 Is your child **all right**?' " "Everything is all right," she said.
4:26 Is your child all right?' " "Everything is **all right**," she said.
5:19 "Go in **peace**," Elisha said. After Naaman had traveled some
5:21 from the chariot to meet him. "Is everything **all right**?" he asked.
5:22 "Everything is **all right**," Gehazi answered. "My master sent me to
9:11 fellow officers, one of them asked him, "Is everything **all right**?
9:17 "Send him to meet them and ask, 'Do you **come in peace**?' "
9:18 'Do you **come in peace**?' " "What do you have to do with peace?"
9:18 'Do you come in peace?' " "What do you have to do with **peace**?"
9:19 'Do you **come in peace**?' " Jehu replied, "What do you have to do
9:19 in peace?' " Jehu replied, "What do you have to do with **peace**?
9:22 When Joram saw Jehu he asked, "Have you **come in peace**, Jehu?"
9:22 "How can there be **peace**," Jehu replied, "as long as all the idolatry
9:31 Jehu entered the gate, she asked, "Have you **come in peace**, Zimri,
10:13 we have come down to **greet** the families of the king and of the
20:19 he thought, "Will there not be **peace** and security in my lifetime?"
22:20 I will gather you to your fathers, and you will be buried in **peace**.
1Ch 12:17 [12:18] to them, "If you have come to me in **peace**, to help me,
12:18 [12:19] **Success**, success to you, and success to those who help
12:18 [12:19] Success, **success** to you, and success to those who help
12:18 [12:19] success to you, and **success** to those who help you,
18:10 Hadoram to King David to **greet** [+4200+4200+8626] him and
22:9 and I will grant Israel **peace** and quiet during his reign.
2Ch 15:5 In those days it was not **safe** to travel about, for all the inhabitants
18:16 'These people have no master. Let each one go home in **peace**.' "
18:26 him nothing but bread and water until I return **safely** [+928].' "
18:27 Micaiah declared, "If you ever return **safely** [+928], the LORD
19:1 When Jehoshaphat king of Judah returned **safely** [+928] to his
34:28 I will gather you to your fathers, and you will be buried in **peace**.
Ezr 9:12 Do not seek a **treaty of friendship** [+2256+3208] *with* them at any
Est 2:11 forth near the courtyard of the harem to find out **how** Esther **was**
9:30 of the kingdom of Xerxes—words of **goodwill** and assurance—
10:3 the good of his people and spoke up for the **welfare** of all the Jews.
Job 5:24 You will know that your tent is **secure**; you will take stock of your
15:21 sounds fill his ears; when all seems **well**, marauders attack him.
21:9 Their homes are **safe** and free from fear; the rod of God is not upon
25:2 awe belong to God; he establishes **order** in the heights of heaven.
Ps 4:8 [4:9] I will lie down and sleep in **peace**, for you alone, O LORD,
28:3 who speak **cordially** with their neighbors but harbor malice in their
29:11 strength to his people; the LORD blesses his people with **peace**.
34:14 [34:15] Turn from evil and do good; seek **peace** and pursue it.
35:20 They do not speak **peaceably**, but devise false accusations against
35:27 LORD be exalted, who delights in the **well-being** *of* his servant."
37:11 But the meek will inherit the land and enjoy great **peace**.
37:37 observe the upright; there is a future for the man of **peace**.
38:3 [38:4] my body; my bones have no **soundness** because of my sin.
41:9 [41:10] Even my **close friend** [+408], whom I trusted, he who
55:18 [55:19] He ransoms me **unharmed** [+928] from the battle waged
55:20 [55:21] My companion attacks his **friends**; he violates his
69:22 [69:23] may it become retribution [BHS *fellowship*; NIV 8936] and
72:3 The mountains will bring **prosperity** to the people, the hills the
72:7 will flourish; **prosperity** will abound till the moon is no more.
73:3 For I envied the arrogant when I saw the **prosperity** *of* the wicked.
85:8 [85:9] he promises **peace** to his people, his saints—but let them
85:10 [85:11] meet together; righteousness and **peace** kiss each other.
119:165 Great **peace** have they who love your law, and nothing can make
120:6 Too long have I lived among those who hate **peace**.
120:7 I am a man of **peace**; but when I speak, they are for war.
122:6 Pray for the **peace** *of* Jerusalem: "May those who love you be
122:7 May there be **peace** within your walls and security within your
122:8 sake of my brothers and friends, I will say, "**Peace** be within you."
125:5 the LORD will banish with the evildoers. **Peace** be upon Israel.
128:6 may you live to see your children's children. **Peace** be upon Israel.
147:14 He grants **peace** to your borders and satisfies you with the finest of
Pr 3:2 they will prolong your life many years and bring you **prosperity**.
3:17 Her ways are pleasant ways, and all her paths are **peace**.
12:20 hearts of those who plot evil, but joy for those who promote **peace**.
Ecc 3:8 time to love and a time to hate, a time for war and a time for **peace**.
SS 8:10 Thus I have become in his eyes like one bringing **contentment**.
Isa 9:6 [9:5] Mighty God, Everlasting Father, Prince of **Peace**.
9:7 [9:6] increase of his government and **peace** there will be no end.
26:3 You will keep in **perfect peace** [+8934] him whose mind is
26:3 You will keep in **perfect peace** [+8934] him whose mind is
26:12 LORD, you establish **peace** for us; all that we have accomplished
27:5 let them make **peace** with me, yes, let them make peace with me."
27:5 let them make peace with me, yes, let them make **peace** with me."
32:17 The fruit of righteousness will be **peace**; the effect of righteousness
32:18 My people will live in **peaceful** dwelling places, in secure homes,
33:7 men cry aloud in the streets; the envoys of **peace** weep bitterly.
38:17 Surely it was for my **benefit** that I suffered such anguish. In your
39:8 For he thought, "There will be **peace** and security in my lifetime."
41:3 He pursues them and moves on **unscathed**, by a path his feet have
45:7 and create darkness, I bring **prosperity** and create disaster;
48:18 your **peace** would have been like a river, your righteousness like
48:22 "There is no **peace**," says the LORD, "for the wicked."
52:7 who proclaim **peace**, who bring good tidings, who proclaim
53:5 the punishment that brought us **peace** was upon him, and by his
54:10 for you will not be shaken nor my covenant of **peace** be removed,"
54:13 be taught by the LORD, and great will be your children's **peace**.
55:12 You will go out in joy and be led forth in **peace**; the mountains
57:2 Those who walk uprightly enter into **peace**; they find rest as they
57:19 **Peace**, peace, to those far and near," says the LORD. "And I will
57:19 Peace, **peace**, to those far and near," says the LORD. "And I will

Isa 57:21 "There is no **peace**," says my God, "for the wicked."
59: 8 The way of **peace** they do not know; there is no justice in their
59: 8 into crooked roads; no one who walks in them will know **peace**.
60:17 I will make **peace** your governor and righteousness your ruler.
66:12 "I will extend **peace** to her like a river, and the wealth of nations
Jer 4:10 this people and Jerusalem by saying, 'You will have **peace**,'
6:14 were not serious. '**Peace**, peace,' they say, when there is no peace.
6:14 were not serious. 'Peace, **peace**,' they say, when there is no peace.
6:14 were not serious. 'Peace, peace,' they say, when there is no **peace**.
8:11 were not serious. "**Peace**, peace," they say, when there is no peace.
8:11 were not serious. "Peace, **peace**," they say, when there is no peace.
8:11 were not serious. "Peace, peace," they say, when there is no **peace**.
8:15 We hoped for **peace** but no good has come, for a time of healing
9: 8 [9:7] With his mouth each speaks **cordially** to his neighbor, but in
12: 5 If you stumble in **safe** country, how will you manage in the
12:12 devour from one end of the land to the other; no one will be **safe**.
13:19 All Judah will be carried into exile, carried **completely** away.
14:13 suffer famine. Indeed, I will give you lasting **peace** in this place.' "
14:19 We hoped for **peace** but no good has come, for a time of healing
15: 5 Who will mourn for you? Who will stop to ask **how** you **are**?
16: 5 because I have withdrawn my **blessing**, my love and my pity from
20:10 All my **friends** [+632] are waiting for me to slip, saying,
23:17 to those who despise me, 'The LORD says: You will have **peace**.'
25:37 The **peaceful** meadows will be laid waste because of the fierce
28: 9 the prophet who prophesies **peace** will be recognized as one truly
29: 7 seek the **peace and prosperity** *of* the city to which I have carried
29: 7 to the LORD for it, because if it **prospers**, you too will prosper."
29: 7 to the LORD for it, because if it prospers, you too will **prosper**."
29:11 declares the LORD, "plans to **prosper** you and not to harm you,
30: 5 the LORD says: " 'Cries of fear are heard—terror, not **peace**.
33: 6 my people and will let them enjoy abundant **peace** and security.
33: 9 will tremble at the abundant prosperity and **peace** I provide for it.'
34: 5 you will die **peacefully** [+928]. As people made a funeral fire in
38: 4 This man is not seeking the **good** of these people but their ruin."
38:22 and overcame you—those **trusted friends** [+408] *of* yours.
43:12 Egypt around himself and depart from there **unscathed** [+928].
La 3:17 I have been deprived of **peace**; I have forgotten what prosperity is.
Eze 7:25 When terror comes, they will seek **peace**, but there will be none.
13:10 saying, "**Peace**," when there is no peace, and because, when a
13:10 saying, "Peace," when there is no **peace**, and because, when a
13:16 and saw visions of **peace** for her when there was no peace,
13:16 and saw visions of peace for her when there was no **peace**,
34:25 " 'I will make a covenant of **peace** with them and rid the land of
37:26 I will make a covenant of **peace** with them; it will be an everlasting
Da 10:19 "Do not be afraid, O man highly esteemed," he said. "**Peace**!
Ob 1: 7 the border; your **friends** [+408] will deceive and overpower you;
Mic 3: 5 lead my people astray, if one feeds them, they proclaim '**peace**';
5: 5 [5:4] he will be their **peace**. When the Assyrian invades our land
Na 1:15 [2:1] feet of one who brings good news, who proclaims **peace**!
Hag 2: 9 'And in this place I will grant **peace**,' declares the LORD
Zec 6:13 his throne. And there will be **harmony** [+6783] between the two.'
8:10 No one could go about his business **safely** [+2021+4200]
8:12 "The seed will **grow well**, the vine will yield its fruit, the ground
8:16 to each other, and render true and **sound** judgment in your courts;
8:19 and happy festivals for Judah. Therefore love truth and **peace**."
9:10 battle bow will be broken. He will proclaim **peace** to the nations.
Mal 2: 5 with him, a covenant of life and **peace**, and I gave them to him;
2: 6 He walked with me in **peace** and uprightness, and turned many

8935 שַׁלּוּם šallûm, n.pr.m. [27 / 26] [√ 8966]

Shallum [25], Shallum's [1]

2Ki 15:10 **Shallum** son of Jabesh conspired against Zechariah. He attacked
15:13 **Shallum** son of Jabesh became king in the thirty-ninth year of
15:14 He attacked **Shallum** son of Jabesh in Samaria, assassinated him
15:15 The other events of **Shallum's** reign, and the conspiracy he led,
22:14 who was the wife of **Shallum** son of Tikvah, the son of Harhas,
1Ch 2:40 Eleasah the father of Sismai, Sismai the father of **Shallum**,
2:41 **Shallum** the father of Jekamiah, and Jekamiah the father of
3:15 Jehoiakim the second son, Zedekiah the third, **Shallum** the fourth.
4:25 **Shallum** was Shaul's son, Mibsam his son and Mishma his son.
6:12 [5:38] Ahitub the father of Zadok, Zadok the father of **Shallum**,
6:13 [5:39] **Shallum** the father of Hilkiah, Hilkiah the father of
7:13 Jahziel, Guni, Jezer and Shillem—[BHS ***Shallum***; NIV 8973]
9:17 **Shallum**, Akkub, Talmon, Ahiman and their brothers,
9:17 Akkub, Talmon, Ahiman and their brothers, **Shallum** their chief
9:19 **Shallum** son of Kore, the son of Ebiasaph, the son of Korah,
9:31 named Mattithiah, the firstborn son of **Shallum** the Korahite,
2Ch 28:12 Jehizkiah son of **Shallum**, and Amasa son of Hadlai—
34:22 who was the wife of **Shallum** son of Tokhath, the son of Hasrah,
Ezr 2:42 the descendants of **Shallum**, Ater, Talmon, Akkub, Hatita
7: 2 the son of **Shallum**, the son of Zadok, the son of Ahitub,
10:24 Eliashib. From the gatekeepers: **Shallum**, Telem and Uri.
10:42 **Shallum**, Amariah and Joseph.
Ne 3:12 **Shallum** son of Hallohesh, ruler of a half-district of Jerusalem,
7:45 the descendants of **Shallum**, Ater, Talmon, Akkub, Hatita
Jer 22:11 For this is what the LORD says about **Shallum** son of Josiah,
32: 7 Hanamel son of **Shallum** your uncle is going to come to you
35: 4 which was over that of Maaseiah son of **Shallum** the doorkeeper.

8936 שִׁלּוּם šillûm, n.[m.], [3 / 4] [√ 8966]

retribution [2], bribes [1], reckoning [1]

Ps 69:22 [69:23] a snare; may it become **retribution** [BHS 8934] and a trap.
Isa 34: 8 a day of vengeance, a year of **retribution**, to uphold Zion's cause.
Hos 9: 7 days of punishment are coming, the days of **reckoning** are at hand.
Mic 7: 3 the ruler demands gifts, the judge accepts **bribes**, the powerful

8937 שַׁלּוּן šallûn, n.pr.m. [1] [√ 8922]

Shallun [1]

Ne 3:15 The Fountain Gate was repaired by **Shallun** son of Col-Hozeh,

8938 שָׁלַח šālaḥ, v. [847] [→ 5447, 5448, 5449, 8933, 8939, 8940, 8941, 8942, 8943, 8944; Ar 10714]

sent [310], send [113], let go [55], sent away [22], sending [20], *untranslated* [17], sent out [17], lay [11], sent word [11], reached out [10], sends [10], send away [9], stretched out [7], sent for [+2256+4200+7924] [6], send on way [5], sent on way [5], set free [5], lift [4], release [4], send word [4], sent off [4], set [4], stretch out [4], divorce [3], reach out [3], sent back [3], sent for [3], shoot [3], stirs up [3], assassinate [+928+3338] [2], be sure to let go [+906+8938] [2], been sent [2], called together [+665+906+2256] [2], dismissed [2], divorced [2], do let go [+8938] [2], drive out [2], extend [2], free [+906+906+2930] [2], free [2], gave orders [2], gave over [2], pursue [+339+906] [2], raise [2], reached down [2], reached [2], replied [+606] [2], send back [2], send forth [2], send out [2], send urgent [+448+8938] [2], sent message [2], shot [2], thrust [2], unleashed [2], was sent [2], abandoned [1], again and again [+2256+8899] [1], appealed [1], assaults [+928] [1], assigned [1], attack [+928+3338] [1], attacked [+928+3338] [1], attacks [+928+3338] [1], banished [1], be sent [1], being sent [1], brought [1], burned [+836+928+2021] [1], called together [+448+665+2256] [1], called together [+448+665+906+2256] [1], calling together [+906+906+995+2256] [1], cast [1], checked on [+448] [1], come back [1], delivered [1], demanded [1], directed [1], dispatched [1], divorces [1], does[s] [1], ended [1], exile [1], extends [1], force [1], freed [+2930] [1], give away in marriage [1], gave [1], get out of here [+906+2021+2025+2575+4946+6584] [1], give an order [1], had brought [+2256+4374] [1], had removed [+906+2256+4374] [1], holds [1], invite [+2256+4200+7924] [1], killing [+928+3338] [1], laid [1], lay snares [1], lays [1], leave [1], left to himself [1], let down [1], let get away [+928+2006] [1], let get away [1], let grow [1], let loose [1], lets loose [1], lets stray [1], letting go [1], letting range free [+8079] [1], lowered [1], made flourish [1], makes pour [1], mission [+889 +1821] [1], ordered [1], pointing [1], provided [1], pushed [1], put out [1], put [1], putting [1], reach down [1], reached out [+906+3338] [1], reaches out [+3338] [1], reaching [+906+3338] [1], reject [+906 +4946+6584+7156] [1], released [1], releases [1], remove [1], return [1], rushing [1], see on way [1], seize [1], send a message [1], send for [+2256+4374] [1], send for [+906+2256+4374] [1], send for [1], sending away [1], sends out [1], sent a message [1], sent for [+906+2256+4200+4200+4374] [1], sent for [+906+2256+7924] [1], sent for [+906+906+2256+7924] [1], sent for [+906+906+4200+7924] [1], sent for help [1], sent forth [1], sent messengers [1], sent on way [+906+906+906] [1], sent word [+2256+5583] [1], sent word [+2256 +7924] [1], set fire to [+836+928+2021] [1], set free [+906+2930 +4946+6640] [1], set free [+906+3338+4946] [1], shooting [1], spared [1], specify [1], spreading [1], summon [+448+906+2256 +4374] [1], summon [1], summoned [+2256+4200+4200+7924] [1], summoned [+2256+4200+7924] [1], summoned [+4200+4200+4200 +7924] [1], summoned [1], swing [1], throw off [1], told [+448+606 +4200] [1], took back [+906+995+2256] [1], turned [1], unleash [1], use to do [1], use [1], vent [1], was sent away [1], were sent on way [1], were sent [1]

Ge 3:22 [A] *He must* not be allowed *to* **reach out** his hand and take also
3:23 [D] So the LORD God **banished** him from the Garden of Eden
8: 7 [D] **sent out** a raven, and it kept flying back and forth until the
8: 8 [D] *he* **sent out** a dove to see if the water had receded from the
8: 9 [A] *He* **reached out** his hand and took the dove and brought it
8:10 [D] seven more days and again **sent out** the dove from the ark.
8:12 [D] He waited seven more days and **sent** the dove **out** again,
12:20 [D] *they* **sent** [+906+906+906] him **on** his **way**, with his wife and

Ge 18:16 [D] Abraham walked along with them to **see** them **on** their **way**.
19:10 [A] the men inside **reached** [+906+3338] **out** and pulled Lot
19:13 [D] its people is so great that he *has* **sent** us to destroy it."
19:29 [D] *he* **brought** Lot out of the catastrophe that overthrew the
20: 2 [A] Then Abimelech king of Gerar **sent for** Sarah and took her.
21:14 [D] set them on her shoulders and then **sent** her **off** with the boy.
22:10 [A] he **reached out** his hand and took the knife to slay his son.
22:12 [A] "*Do* not **lay** a hand on the boy," he said. "Do not do anything
24: 7 [A] he *will* **send** his angel before you so that you can get a wife
24:40 [A] *will* **send** his angel with you and make your journey a
24:54 [D] next morning, he said, "**Send** me **on** my **way** to my master."
24:56 [D] my journey. **Send** me **on** my **way** so I may go to my master."
24:59 [D] *they* **sent** their sister Rebekah **on** her **way**, along with her nurse
25: 6 [D] **sent** them **away** from his son Isaac to the land of the east.
26:27 [D] to me, since you were hostile to me and **sent** me away?"
26:29 [D] but always treated you well and **sent** you **away** in peace.
26:31 [D] Isaac **sent** them **on** their **way**, and they left him in peace.
27:42 [A] *she* **sent** [+2256+4200+7924] **for** her younger son Jacob and
27:45 [A] did to him, *I'll* **send word** *for* you to come back from there.
28: 5 [A] Isaac **sent** Jacob **on** *his* **way**, and he went to Paddan Aram,
28: 6 [D] and *had* **sent** him to Paddan Aram to take a wife from there,
30:25 [D] "**Send** me **on** my **way** so I can go back to my own homeland.
31: 4 [A] So Jacob **sent** [+2256+7924] **word** to Rachel and Leah to
31:27 [D] so *I could* **send** you **away** with joy and singing to the music
31:42 [D] *you would* surely *have* **sent** me **away** empty-handed.
32: 3 [32:4] [A] Jacob **sent** messengers ahead of him to his brother
32: 5 [32:6] [A] Now *I am* **sending** this message to my lord, that I
32:18 [32:19] [B] They are a gift **sent** to my lord Esau, and he is
32:26 [32:27] [D] the man said, "**Let** me **go**, for it is daybreak."
32:26 [32:27] [D] "*I will* not **let** you **go** unless you bless me."
37:13 [A] Come, *I am going to* **send** you to them." "Very well," he
37:14 [A] to me." Then *he* **sent** him **off** from the Valley of Hebron.
37:22 [A] this cistern here in the desert, but don't **lay** a hand on him."
37:32 [D] *They* **took** the ornamented robe **back** [+906+995+2256] to
38:17 [D] "I'll **send** you a young goat from my flock," he said. "Will
38:17 [A] "Will you give me something as a pledge until you **send** it?"
38:20 [A] Meanwhile Judah **sent** the young goat by his friend the
38:23 [A] After all, *I did* **send** her this young goat, but you didn't find
38:25 [A] being brought out, she **sent a message** to her father-in-law.
41: 8 [A] so *he* **sent** [+906+906+2256+7924] **for** all the magicians and
41:14 [A] So Pharaoh **sent** [+906+2256+7924] **for** Joseph, and he was
42: 4 [A] Jacob *did* not **send** Benjamin, Joseph's brother,
42:16 [A] **Send** one of your number to get your brother; the rest of you
43: 4 [D] If you will **send** our brother along with us, we will go down
43: 5 [D] if you will not **send** him, we will not go down,
43: 8 [A] "**Send** the boy along with me and we will go at once, so that
43:14 [D] that *he will let* your other brother and Benjamin **come back**
44: 3 [E] the men **were sent on** *their* **way** with their donkeys.
45: 5 [A] because it was to save lives *that* God **sent** me ahead of you.
45: 7 [A] God **sent** me ahead of you to preserve for you a remnant on
45: 8 [A] "So then, it was not you *who* **sent** me here, but God. He
45:23 [A] this is what *he* **sent** to his father: ten donkeys loaded with the
45:24 [D] *he* **sent** his brothers **away**, and as they were leaving he said
45:27 [A] when he saw the carts Joseph *had* **sent** to carry him back,
46: 5 [A] their wives in the carts that Pharaoh *had* **sent** to transport
46:28 [A] Now Jacob **sent** Judah ahead of him to Joseph to get
48:14 [A] **reached out** his right hand and put it on Ephraim's head,
49:21 [B] "Naphtali is a doe **set free** that bears beautiful fawns.
Ex 2: 5 [A] the basket among the reeds and **sent** her slave girl to get it.
3:10 [A] *I am* **sending** you to Pharaoh to bring my people the
3:12 [A] this will be the sign to you that it is I *who have* **sent** you:
3:13 [A] say to them, 'The God of your fathers *has* **sent** me to you,'
3:14 [A] you are to say to the Israelites: 'I AM *has* **sent** me to you.' "
3:15 [A] the God of Isaac and the God of Jacob—*has* **sent** me to you.'
3:20 [A] So *I will* **stretch out** my hand and strike the Egyptians with
3:20 [D] I will perform among them. After that, *he will* **let** you **go**.
4: 4 [A] said to him, "**Reach out** your hand and take it by the tail."
4: 4 [A] So Moses **reached out** and took hold of the snake and it
4:13 [A] But Moses said, "O Lord, please **send** someone else to do it."
4:13 [A] "O Lord, please send someone else **[RPH]** to do it."
4:21 [D] I will harden his heart so that *he will* not **let** the people **go**.
4:23 [D] I told you, "**Let** my son **go**, so he may worship me." But you
4:23 [D] you refused to **let** him **go**; so I will kill your firstborn son.' "
4:28 [A] Moses told Aaron everything the LORD *had* **sent** him to
5: 1 [D] '**Let** my people **go**, so that they may hold a festival to me in
5: 2 [D] is the LORD, that I should obey him and **let** Israel **go**?
5: 2 [D] I do not know the LORD and *I will* not **let** Israel **go**."
5:22 [A] brought trouble upon this people? Is this why *you* **sent** me?
6: 1 [D] Because of my mighty hand *he will* **let** them **go**; because of
6:11 [D] tell Pharaoh king of Egypt *to* **let** the Israelites **go** out of his
7: 2 [D] your brother Aaron is to tell Pharaoh *to* **let** the Israelites **go**
7:14 [D] heart is unyielding; he refuses to **let** the people **go**.
7:16 [A] the God of the Hebrews, *has* **sent** me to say to you:
7:16 [D] **Let** my people **go**, so that they may worship me in the desert.
8: 1 [7:26] [D] **Let** my people **go**, so that they may worship me.
8: 2 [7:27] [D] If you refuse to **let** them **go**, I will plague your whole
8: 8 [8:4] [D] *I will* **let** your people **go** to offer sacrifices to the
8:20 [8:16] [D] **Let** my people **go**, so that they may worship me.
8:21 [8:17] [D] If you *do* not **let** my people **go**, I will send swarms of
8:21 [8:17] [G] I *will* **send** swarms of flies on you and your officials,
8:28 [8:24] [D] "I *will* **let** you **go** to offer sacrifices to the LORD
8:29 [8:25] [D] **letting** the people **go** to offer sacrifices to the
8:32 [8:28] [D] hardened his heart and *would* not **let** the people **go**.
9: 1 [D] says: "**Let** my people **go**, so that they may worship me."
9: 2 [D] If you refuse to **let** them **go** and continue to hold them back,
9: 7 [A] Pharaoh **sent** men to investigate and found that not even one
9: 7 [D] his heart was unyielding and *he would* not **let** the people **go**.
9:13 [D] says: **Let** my people **go**, so that they may worship me,
9:14 [A] or this time I *will* **send** the full force of my plagues against
9:15 [A] For by now *I could have* **stretched out** my hand and struck
9:17 [D] still set yourself against my people and *will* not **let** them **go**.
9:19 [A] **Give an order** now to bring your livestock and everything
9:27 [A] Pharaoh **summoned** [+2256+4200+4200+7924] Moses and
9:28 [D] *I will* **let** you **go**; you don't have to stay any longer."
9:35 [D] heart was hard and *he would* not **let** the Israelites **go**,
10: 3 [D] before me? **Let** my people **go**, so that they may worship me.
10: 4 [D] If you refuse to **let** them **go**, I will bring locusts into your
10: 7 [D] **Let** the people **go**, so that they may worship the LORD their
10:10 [D] if *I* **let** you **go**, along with your women and children!
10:20 [D] Pharaoh's heart, and *he would* not **let** the Israelites **go**.
10:27 [D] Pharaoh's heart, and he was not willing to **let** them **go**.
11: 1 [D] After that, *he will* **let** you **go** from here, and when he does,
11: 1 [D] After that, he will let you go from here, and when he **does**[*],
11:10 [D] and *he would* not **let** the Israelites **go** out of his country.
12:33 [D] Egyptians urged the people to hurry and **leave** the country.
13:15 [D] When Pharaoh stubbornly refused to **let** us **go**, the LORD
13:17 [D] When Pharaoh **let** the people **go**, God did not lead them on
14: 5 [D] *We have* **let** the Israelites **go** and have lost their services!"
15: 7 [D] *You* **unleashed** your burning anger; it consumed them like
18:27 [D] Moses **sent** his father-in-law **on** *his* **way**, and Jethro returned
21:26 [D] *he must* **let** the servant **go** free to compensate for the eye.
21:27 [D] *he must* **let** the servant **go** free to compensate for the tooth.
22: 5 [22:4] [D] or vineyard and **lets** them **stray** and they graze in
22: 8 [22:7] [A] *he has* **laid** his hands on the other man's property.
22:11 [22:10] [A] *did* not **lay** hands on the other person's property.
23:20 [A] I *am* **sending** an angel ahead of you to guard you along the
23:27 [D] "*I will* **send** my terror ahead of you and throw into confusion
23:28 [A] *I will* **send** the hornet ahead of you to drive the Hivites,
24: 5 [A] *he* **sent** young Israelite men, and they offered burnt offerings
24:11 [A] God *did* not **raise** his hand against these leaders of the
33: 2 [A] *I will* **send** an angel before you and drive out the Canaanites,
33:12 [A] but you have not let me know whom *you will* **send** with me.
Lev 14: 7 [D] Then *he is to* **release** the live bird in the open fields.
14:53 [D] *he is to* **release** the live bird in the open fields outside the
16:10 [D] atonement by **sending** it into the desert as a scapegoat.
16:21 [D] *He shall* **send** the goat **away** into the desert in the care of a
16:22 [D] to a solitary place; and the man *shall* **release** it in the desert.
16:26 [D] "The *man who* **releases** the goat as a scapegoat must wash
18:24 [D] because this is how the nations that I *am going to* **drive out**
20:23 [D] customs of the nations I *am going to* **drive out** before you.
26:22 [G] *I will* **send** wild animals against you, and they will rob you
26:25 [D] withdraw into your cities, *I will* **send** a plague among you,
Nu 5: 2 [D] "Command the Israelites *to* **send away** from the camp
5: 3 [D] **Send away** male and female alike; send them outside the
5: 3 [D] **send** them outside the camp so they will not defile their
5: 4 [D] The Israelites did this; *they* **sent** them outside the camp.
13: 2 [A] "**Send** some men to explore the land of Canaan, which I am
13: 2 [A] From each ancestral tribe **send** one of its leaders."
13: 3 [A] So at the LORD's command Moses **sent** them **out** from the
13:16 [A] These are the names of the men Moses **sent** to explore the
13:17 [A] When Moses **sent** them to explore Canaan, he said, "Go up
13:27 [A] "We went into the land *to* which *you* **sent** us, and it does
14:36 [A] So the men Moses *had* **sent** to explore the land, who
16:12 [A] Then Moses **summoned** [+4200+4200+4200+7924] Dathan
16:28 [A] "This is how you will know that the LORD *has* **sent** me to
16:29 [A] usually happens to men, then the LORD *has* not **sent** me.
20:14 [A] Moses **sent** messengers from Kadesh to the king of Edom,
20:16 [A] he heard our cry and **sent** an angel and brought us out of
21: 6 [D] the LORD **sent** venomous snakes among them; they bit the
21:21 [A] Israel **sent** messengers to say to Sihon king of the Amorites:
21:32 [A] After Moses *had* **sent** spies *to* Jazer, the Israelites captured
22: 5 [A] **sent** messengers to summon Balaam son of Beor, who was at
22:10 [A] "Balak son of Zippor, king of Moab, **sent** me *this* **message**:
22:15 [A] Balak **sent** other princes, more numerous and more
22:37 [A] "*Did I* not **send** [+448+8938] you an **urgent** summons?
22:37 [A] "*Did I* not **send** you an **urgent** [+448+8938] summons?
22:40 [D] **gave** some to Balaam and the princes who were with him.
24:12 [A] answered Balak, "Did I not tell the messengers *you* **sent** me,

Nu 31: 4 [A] **Send** into battle a thousand men from each of the tribes of
31: 6 [A] **sent** them into battle, a thousand from each tribe, along with
32: 8 [A] This is what your fathers did when I **sent** them from Kadesh
Dt 1:22 [A] "*Let us* **send** men ahead to spy out the land for us and bring
2:26 [A] From the desert of Kedemoth *I* **sent** messengers to Sihon
7:20 [D] the LORD your God *will* **send** the hornet among them until
9:23 [A] And when the LORD **sent** you out from Kadesh Barnea,
15:12 [D] you six years, in the seventh year *you must* **let** him **go** free.
15:13 [D] when *you* **release** him, do not send him away empty-handed.
15:13 [D] when you release him, *do* not **send** him away empty-handed.
15:18 [D] a hardship *to* **set** your servant **free** [+906+2930+4946+6640],
19:12 [A] the elders of his town *shall* **send for** him, bring him back
21:14 [D] you are not pleased with her, **let** her **go** wherever she wishes.
22: 7 [D] the young, but **be sure to let** the mother **go** [+906+8938],
22: 7 [D] the young, but **be sure to let** the mother **go** [+906+8938],
22:19 [D] to be his wife; he must not **divorce** her as long as he lives.
22:29 [D] violated her. He can never **divorce** her as long as he lives.
24: 1 [D] of divorce, gives it to her and **sends** her from his house,
24: 3 [D] gives it to her and **sends** her from his house, or if he dies,
24: 4 [D] her first husband, who **divorced** her, is not allowed to marry
25:11 [A] *she* **reaches** [+3338] **out** and seizes him by his private parts,
28:20 [D] The LORD *will* **send** on you curses, confusion and rebuke
28:48 [D] you will serve the enemies the LORD **sends** against you.
32:24 [D] *I will* **send** wasting famine against them, consuming
34:11 [A] and wonders the LORD **sent** him to do in Egypt—
Jos 1:16 [A] us we will do, and wherever *you* **send** us we will go.
2: 1 [A] Then Joshua son of Nun secretly **sent** two spies from Shittim.
2: 3 [A] So the king of Jericho **sent** *this* **message** to Rahab: "Bring
2:21 [D] it be as you say." So *she* **sent** them **away** and they departed.
6:17 [A] her house shall be spared, because she hid the spies *we* **sent**.
6:25 [A] because she hid the men Joshua *had* **sent** as spies to
7: 2 [A] Now Joshua **sent** men from Jericho to Ai, which is near Beth
7:22 [A] So Joshua **sent** messengers, and they ran to the tent,
8: 3 [A] thousand of his best fighting men and **sent** them **out** at night
8: 9 [A] Joshua **sent** them **off**, and they went to the place of ambush
10: 3 [A] So Adoni-Zedek king of Jerusalem **appealed** to Hoham king
10: 6 [A] then **sent** word to Joshua in the camp at Gilgal:
11: 1 [A] *he* **sent word** to Jobab king of Madon, to the kings of
14: 7 [A] the LORD **sent** me from Kadesh Barnea to explore the land.
14:11 [A] I am still as strong today as the day Moses **sent** me **out**;
18: 4 [A] *I will* **send** them **out** to make a survey of the land and to
22: 6 [D] Joshua blessed them and **sent** them **away**, and they went to
22: 7 [D] When Joshua **sent** them home, he blessed them,
22:13 [A] So the Israelites **sent** Phinehas son of Eleazar, the priest,
24: 5 [A] " 'Then *I* **sent** Moses and Aaron, and I afflicted the Egyptians
24: 9 [A] *he* **sent** [+2256+4200+7924] **for** Balaam son of Beor to put a
24:12 [A] *I* **sent** the hornet ahead of you, which drove them out before
24:28 [D] Joshua **sent** the people **away**, each to his own inheritance.
Jdg 1: 8 [D] and took it. They put the city to the sword and **set** it on fire.
1:25 [D] city to the sword but **spared** the man and his whole family.
2: 6 [D] After Joshua *had* **dismissed** the Israelites, they went to take
3:15 [A] The Israelites **sent** him with tribute to Eglon king of Moab.
3:18 [D] the tribute, *he* **sent on** their **way** the men who had carried it.
3:21 [A] Ehud **reached** *with* his left hand, drew the sword from his
4: 6 [A] *She* **sent** [+2256+4200+7924] **for** Barak son of Abinoam from
5:15 [E] Issachar was with Barak, **rushing** after him into the valley.
5:26 [A] Her hand **reached** for the tent peg, her right hand for the
6: 8 [A] he **sent** them a prophet, who said, "This is what the LORD,
6:14 [A] save Israel out of Midian's hand. *Am I* not **sending** you?"
6:21 [A] the angel of the LORD **[NIE]** touched the meat and the
6:35 [A] *He* **sent** messengers throughout Manasseh, calling them to
6:35 [A] to arms, and also **[RPH]** into Asher, Zebulun and Naphtali,
7: 8 [D] So Gideon **sent** the rest of the Israelites to their tents but kept
7:24 [A] Gideon **sent** messengers throughout the hill country of
9:23 [A] God **sent** an evil spirit between Abimelech and the citizens
9:31 [A] Under cover *he* **sent** messengers to Abimelech, saying, "Gaal
11:12 [A] Jephthah **sent** messengers to the Ammonite king with the
11:14 [A] Jephthah **sent** back messengers to the Ammonite king,
11:17 [A] Israel **sent** messengers to the king of Edom, saying, 'Give us
11:17 [A] *They* **sent** also to the king of Moab, and he refused. So Israel
11:19 [A] "Then Israel **sent** messengers to Sihon king of the Amorites,
11:28 [A] however, paid no attention to the message Jephthah **sent** him.
11:38 [A] *he* **let** her **go** for two months. She and the girls went into the
12: 9 [D] *He* **gave** his daughters **away in marriage** to those outside his
13: 8 [A] let the man of God *you* **sent** to us come again to teach us
15: 5 [D] and **let** the foxes **loose** in the standing grain of the Philistines.
15:15 [A] **[RPH]** he grabbed it and struck down a thousand men.
16:18 [A] *she* **sent** word to the rulers of the Philistines, "Come back
18: 2 [A] So the Danites **sent** five warriors from Zorah and Eshtaol to
19:25 [D] abused her throughout the night, and at dawn *they* **let** her **go**.
19:29 [D] into twelve parts and **sent** them into all the areas of Israel.
20: 6 [D] and **sent** one piece to each region of Israel's inheritance,
20:12 [A] The tribes of Israel **sent** men throughout the tribe of
20:48 [D] they found. All the towns they came across *they* **set** on fire.
21:10 [A] So the assembly **sent** twelve thousand fighting men with
21:13 [A] the whole assembly **sent** an offer of peace to the Benjamites
1Sa 4: 4 [A] So the people **sent** men to Shiloh, and they brought back the
5: 8 [A] So *they* **called together** [+448+665+906+2256] all the rulers
5:10 [D] So *they* **sent** the ark of God to Ekron. As the ark of God was
5:11 [A] So *they* **called together** [+665+906+2256] all the rulers of the
5:11 [D] and said, "**Send** the ark of the god of Israel **away**;
6: 2 [D] Tell us how *we should* **send** it **back** to its place."
6: 3 [D] They answered, "If *you* **return** the ark of the god of Israel,
6: 3 [D] the ark of the god of Israel, *do* not **send** it **away** empty,
6: 6 [D] *did they* not **send** the Israelites **out** so they could go on their
6: 8 [D] sending back to him as a guilt offering. **Send** it on its way,
6:21 [A] Then *they* **sent** messengers to the people of Kiriath Jearim,
9:16 [A] "About this time tomorrow *I will* **send** you a man from the
9:19 [D] in the morning *I will* **let** you **go** and will tell you all that is in
9:26 [D] on the roof, "Get ready, and *I will* **send** you **on** *your* **way**."
10:25 [D] Then Samuel **dismissed** the people, each to his own home.
11: 3 [A] us seven days so *we can* **send** messengers throughout Israel;
11: 7 [D] **sent** the pieces by messengers throughout Israel,
12: 8 [A] the LORD for help, and the LORD **sent** Moses and Aaron,
12:11 [A] the LORD **sent** Jerub-Baal, Barak, Jephthah and Samuel,
13: 2 [D] The rest of the men *he* **sent back** to their homes.
14:27 [A] so *he* **reached out** the end of the staff that was in his hand
15: 1 [A] Samuel said to Saul, "I am the one the LORD **sent** to anoint
15:18 [A] he **sent** you on a mission, saying, 'Go and completely destroy
15:20 [A] Saul said. "I went on the mission the LORD **assigned** me.
16: 1 [A] be on your way; *I am* **sending** you to Jesse of Bethlehem.
16:11 [A] Samuel said, "**Send** [+2256+4374] **for** him; we will not sit
16:12 [A] So *he* **sent** and had him brought in. He was ruddy, with a fine
16:19 [A] Saul **sent** messengers to Jesse and said, "Send me your son
16:19 [A] sent messengers to Jesse and said, "**Send** me your son David,
16:20 [A] and a young goat and **sent** them with his son David to Saul.
16:22 [A] Saul **sent word** to Jesse, saying, "Allow David to remain in
17:49 [A] **Reaching** [+906+3338] into his bag and taking out a stone,
18: 5 [A] Whatever Saul **sent** him to do, David did it so successfully
19:11 [A] Saul **sent** men to David's house to watch it and to kill him in
19:14 [A] When Saul **sent** the men to capture David, Michal said,
19:15 [A] Then Saul **sent** the men **back** to see David and told them,
19:17 [D] me like this and **send** my enemy **away** so that he escaped?"
19:17 [D] Michal told him, "He said to me, '**Let** me **get away**.
19:20 [A] so he **sent** men to capture him. But when they saw a group of
19:21 [A] Saul was told about it, and *he* **sent** more men, and they
19:21 [A] Saul **sent** men a third time, and they also prophesied.
20: 5 [D] **let** me **go** and hide in the field until the evening of the day
20:12 [A] toward you, *will I* not **send** you **word** and let you know?
20:13 [D] if I do not let you know and **send** you away safely.
20:20 [D] arrows to the side of it, as though I *were* **shooting** at a target.
20:21 [A] *I will* **send** a boy and say, 'Go, find the arrows.' If I say to
20:22 [D] then you must go, because the LORD *has* **sent** you **away**.
20:29 [D] He said, '**Let** me **go**, because our family is observing a
20:31 [A] Now **send** and bring him to me, for he must die!"
21: 2 [21:3] [A] is to know anything about your **mission** [+889+1821]
22:11 [A] king **sent** [+906+906+4200+7924] **for** the priest Ahimelech
22:17 [A] the king's officials were not willing to **raise** a hand to strike
24: 6 [24:7] [A] the LORD's anointed, or **lift** my hand against him;
24:10 [24:11] [A] I said, '*I will* not **lift** my hand against my master,
24:19 [24:20] [D] *does he* **let** him **get away** [+928+2006] unharmed?
25: 5 [A] So he **sent** ten young men and said to them, "Go up to Nabal
25:14 [A] "David **sent** messengers from the desert to give our master
25:25 [A] for me, your servant, I did not see the men my master **sent**.
25:32 [A] the God of Israel, who *has* **sent** you today to meet me.
25:39 [A] David **sent word** to Abigail, asking her to become his wife.
25:40 [A] "David *has* **sent** us to you to take you to become his wife."
26: 4 [A] he **sent out** scouts and learned that Saul had definitely
26: 9 [A] Who *can* **lay** a hand on the LORD's anointed and be
26:11 [A] the LORD forbid that I *should* **lay** a hand on the LORD's
26:23 [A] but I would not **lay** a hand on the LORD's anointed.
30:26 [A] *he* **sent** some of the plunder to the elders of Judah, who were
31: 9 [A] *they* **sent** messengers throughout the land of the Philistines
2Sa 1:14 [A] "Why were you not afraid to **lift** your hand to destroy the
2: 5 [A] he **sent** messengers to the men of Jabesh Gilead to say to
3:12 [A] Then Abner **sent** messengers on his behalf to say to David,
3:14 [A] David **sent** messengers to Ish-Bosheth son of Saul,
3:15 [A] So Ish-Bosheth **gave orders** and had her taken away from
3:21 [D] So David **sent** Abner **away**, and he went in peace.
3:22 [D] because David *had* **sent** him **away**, and he had gone in
3:23 [D] that the king *had* **sent** him **away** and that he had gone in
3:24 [D] came to you. Why *did you* **let** him **go**? Now he is gone!
3:26 [A] Joab then left David and **sent** messengers after Abner,
5:11 [A] Now Hiram king of Tyre **sent** messengers to David,
6: 6 [A] Uzzah **reached out** and took hold of the ark of God, because
8:10 [A] he **sent** his son Joram to King David to greet him
9: 5 [A] So King David **had** him **brought** [+2256+4374] from Lo
10: 2 [A] So David **sent** a delegation to express his sympathy to Hanun

2Sa 10: 3 [A] "Do you think David is honoring your father by **sending** men
10: 3 [A] Hasn't David **sent** them to you to explore the city and spy it
10: 4 [D] garments in the middle at the buttocks, and **sent** them **away**.
10: 5 [A] was told about this, *he* **sent** messengers to meet the men,
10: 6 [A] **[RPH]** they hired twenty thousand Aramean foot soldiers
10: 7 [A] David **sent** Joab **out** with the entire army of fighting men.
10: 16 [A] Hadadezer **[RPH]** had Arameans brought from beyond the
11: 1 [A] David **sent** Joab **out** with the king's men and the whole
11: 3 [A] and David **sent** someone to find out about her. The man said,
11: 4 [A] Then David **sent** messengers to get her. She came to him,
11: 5 [A] woman conceived and **sent** [+2256+5583] **word** to David,
11: 6 [A] So David **sent** *this* **word** to Joab: "Send me Uriah the
11: 6 [A] "**Send** me Uriah the Hittite." And Joab sent him to David.
11: 6 [A] "Send me Uriah the Hittite." And Joab **sent** him to David.
11: 12 [D] here one more day, and tomorrow *I will* **send** you **back**."
11: 14 [A] morning David wrote a letter to Joab and **sent** it with Uriah.
11: 18 [A] Joab **sent** David a full account of the battle.
11: 22 [A] when he arrived he told David everything Joab *had* **sent** him
11: 27 [A] David **[NIE]** had her brought to his house, and she became
12: 1 [A] The LORD **sent** Nathan to David. When he came to him,
12: 25 [A] *he* **sent word** through Nathan the prophet to name him
12: 27 [A] Joab then **sent** messengers to David, saying, "I have fought
13: 7 [A] David **sent** word to Tamar at the palace: "Go to the house of
13: 16 [D] "**Sending** me **away** would be a greater wrong than what you
13: 17 [A] "**Get** this woman **out** [+906+2021+2025+2575+4946+6584] **of here** and bolt the door after her."
13: 27 [A] so *he* **sent** with him Amnon and the rest of the king's sons.
14: 2 [A] So Joab **sent** someone to Tekoa and had a wise woman
14: 29 [A] Then Absalom **sent** for Joab in order to send him to the king,
14: 29 [A] Then Absalom sent for Joab in order to **send** him to the king,
14: 29 [A] to him. So *he* **sent** a second time, but he refused to come.
14: 32 [A] "Look, *I* **sent word** to you and said, 'Come here so I can send
14: 32 [A] and said, 'Come here so *I can* **send** you to the king to ask,
15: 5 [A] Absalom *would* **reach out** his hand, take hold of him
15: 10 [A] Absalom **sent** secret messengers throughout the tribes of
15: 12 [A] he also **sent** *for* Ahithophel the Gilonite, David's counselor,
15: 36 [A] there with them. **Send** them to me with anything you hear."
17: 16 [A] Now **send a message** immediately and tell David, 'Do not
18: 2 [D] David **sent** the troops **out**—a third under the command of
18: 12 [A] my hands, *I would* not **lift** my hand against the king's son.
18: 29 [A] "I saw great confusion just as Joab was about to **send** the
19: 11 [19:12] [A] King David **sent** this message to Zadok
19: 14 [19:15] [A] *They* **sent word** to the king, "Return, you and all
19: 31 [19:32] [D] the king and to **send** him **on** his **way** *from* there.
22: 15 [A] *He* **shot** arrows and scattered ⌞the enemies⌟, bolts of
22: 17 [A] "*He* **reached down** from on high and took hold of me;
24: 13 [A] and decide how I should answer the *one who* **sent** me."
24: 16 [A] When the angel **stretched out** his hand to destroy Jerusalem,
1Ki 1: 44 [A] The king *has* **sent** with him Zadok the priest, Nathan the
1: 53 [A] King Solomon **sent** men, and they brought him down from
2: 25 [A] So King Solomon **gave orders** to Benaiah son of Jehoiada,
2: 29 [A] Solomon **ordered** Benaiah son of Jehoiada, "Go, strike him
2: 36 [A] the king **sent** [+2256+4200+7924] **for** Shimei and said to him,
2: 42 [A] the king **summoned** [+2256+4200+7924] Shimei and said to
5: 1 [5:15] [A] *he* **sent** his envoys to Solomon, because he had
5: 2 [5:16] [A] Solomon **sent back** this message to Hiram:
5: 8 [5:22] [A] So Hiram **sent** word to Solomon: "I have received
5: 8 [5:22] [A] "I have received the message *you* **sent** me and will
5: 9 [5:23] [A] float them in rafts by sea to the place *you* **specify**.
5: 14 [5:28] [A] *He* **sent** them **off** to Lebanon in shifts of ten thousand
7: 13 [A] King Solomon **sent** to Tyre and brought Huram,
8: 44 [A] go to war against their enemies, wherever *you* **send** them,
8: 66 [D] On the following day *he* **sent** the people **away**. They blessed
9: 7 [D] and *will* **reject** [+906+4946+6584+7156] this temple I have
9: 14 [A] Now Hiram *had* **sent** to the king 120 talents of gold.
9: 27 [A] Hiram **sent** his men—sailors who knew the sea—to serve in
11: 21 [D] Hadad said to Pharaoh, "**Let** me **go**, that I may return to my
11: 22 [D] Hadad replied, "but **do let** me **go** [+8938]!"
11: 22 [D] Hadad replied, "but **do let** me **go** [+8938]!"
12: 3 [A] So *they* **sent** [+2256+4200+7924] **for** Jeroboam, and he and the
12: 18 [A] King Rehoboam **sent out** Adoniram, who was in charge of
12: 20 [A] *they* **sent** and called him to the assembly and made him king
13: 4 [A] *he* **stretched out** his hand from the altar and said,
13: 4 [A] But the hand *he* **stretched out** toward the man shriveled up,
14: 6 [B] Why this pretense? I *have* **been sent** to you *with* bad news.
15: 18 [A] his officials and **sent** them to Ben-Hadad son of Tabrimmon,
15: 19 [A] your father. See, *I am* **sending** you a gift of silver and gold.
15: 20 [A] **sent** the commanders of his forces against the towns of
18: 10 [A] or kingdom where my master *has* not **sent** someone to look
18: 19 [A] Now **summon** the people from all over Israel to meet me on
18: 20 [A] So Ahab **sent word** throughout all Israel and assembled the
19: 2 [A] So Jezebel **sent** a messenger to Elijah to say, "May the gods
20: 2 [A] *He* **sent** messengers into the city to Ahab king of Israel,
20: 5 [A] '*I* **sent** to demand your silver and gold, your wives and your
20: 6 [A] about this time tomorrow *I am going to* **send** my officials to
20: 7 [A] When *he* **sent** for my wives and my children, my silver
20: 9 [A] 'Your servant will do all *you* **demanded** the first time,
20: 10 [A] Ben-Hadad **sent** another message to Ahab: "May the gods
20: 17 [A] Now Ben-Hadad *had* **dispatched** scouts, who reported,
20: 34 [D] ⌞Ahab said⌟ "On the basis of a treaty I *will* **set** you **free**."
20: 34 [D] set you free." So he made a treaty with him, and **let** him **go**.
20: 42 [D] '*You have* **set free** [+906+3338+4946] a man I had
21: 8 [A] **sent** them to the elders and nobles who lived in Naboth's city
21: 11 [A] nobles who lived in Naboth's city did as Jezebel **directed** in
21: 11 [A] directed in the letters she had written **[RPH]** to them.
21: 14 [A] Then *they* **sent** word to Jezebel: "Naboth has been stoned
2Ki 1: 2 [A] So *he* **sent** messengers, saying to them, "Go and consult
1: 6 [A] he said to us, 'Go back to the king who **sent** you and tell him,
1: 6 [A] because there is no God in Israel that you *are* **sending** men
1: 9 [A] *he* **sent** to Elijah a captain with his company of fifty men.
1: 11 [A] At this the king **sent** to Elijah another captain with his fifty
1: 13 [A] So the king **sent** a third captain with his fifty men. This third
1: 16 [A] that *you have* **sent** messengers to consult Baal-Zebub,
2: 2 [A] to Elisha, "Stay here; the LORD *has* **sent** me to Bethel."
2: 4 [A] "Stay here, Elisha; the LORD *has* **sent** me *to* Jericho."
2: 6 [A] to him, "Stay here; the LORD *has* **sent** me to the Jordan."
2: 16 [A] or in some valley." "No," Elisha replied, "*do* not **send** them."
2: 17 [A] So he said, "**Send** them." And they sent fifty men, who
2: 17 [A] *they* **sent** fifty men, who searched for three days but did not
3: 7 [A] *He* also **sent** this message to Jehoshaphat king of Judah:
4: 22 [A] "Please **send** me one of the servants and a donkey so I can go
5: 5 [A] "*I will* **send** a letter to the king of Israel." So Naaman left,
5: 6 [A] "With this letter *I am* **sending** my servant Naaman to you
5: 7 [A] Why *does* this fellow **send** someone to me to be cured of his
5: 8 [A] king of Israel had torn his robes, *he* **sent** him this message:
5: 10 [A] Elisha **sent** a messenger to say to him, "Go, wash yourself
5: 22 [A] "My master **sent** me to say, 'Two young men from the
5: 24 [D] them away in the house. *He* **sent** the men **away** and they left.
6: 7 [A] he said. Then the man **reached out** his hand and took it.
6: 9 [A] The man of God **sent** word to the king of Israel: "Beware of
6: 10 [A] So the king of Israel **checked** [+448] **on** the place indicated
6: 13 [A] the king ordered, "so *I can* **send** men and capture him."
6: 14 [A] Then *he* **sent** horses and chariots and a strong force there.
6: 23 [D] they had finished eating and drinking, *he* **sent** them **away**,
6: 32 [A] The king **sent** a messenger ahead, but before he arrived,
6: 32 [A] "Don't you see how this murderer *is* **sending** someone to cut
7: 13 [A] are doomed. So *let us* **send** them to find out what happened."
7: 14 [A] their horses, and the king **sent** them after the Aramean army.
8: 9 [A] "Your son Ben-Hadad king of Aram *has* **sent** me to ask,
8: 12 [D] he answered. "*You will* **set fire to** [+836+928+2021] their
9: 17 [A] "**Send** him to meet them and ask, 'Do you come in peace?' "
9: 19 [A] So the king **sent out** a second horseman. When he came to
10: 1 [A] So Jehu wrote letters and **sent** them *to* Samaria:
10: 5 [A] the elders and the guardians **sent** this message to Jehu:
10: 7 [A] put their heads in baskets and **sent** them to Jehu in Jezreel.
10: 21 [A] he **sent word** throughout Israel, and all the ministers of Baal
11: 4 [A] Jehoiada **sent** [+906+2256+4200+4200+4374] **for** the
12: 18 [12:19] [A] *he* **sent** them to Hazael king of Aram, who
14: 8 [A] Then Amaziah **sent** messengers to Jehoash son of Jehoahaz,
14: 9 [A] Jehoash king of Israel **replied** [+606] to Amaziah king of
14: 9 [A] "A thistle in Lebanon **sent** a message to a cedar in Lebanon,
14: 19 [A] but *they* **sent** men after him to Lachish and killed him there.
15: 37 [G] days the LORD began to **send** Rezin king of Aram and
16: 7 [A] Ahaz **sent** messengers to say to Tiglath-Pileser king of
16: 8 [A] of the royal palace and **sent** it as a gift to the king of Assyria.
16: 10 [A] **sent** to Uriah the priest a sketch of the altar, with detailed
16: 11 [A] with all the plans that King Ahaz *had* **sent** from Damascus
17: 4 [A] for *he had* **sent** envoys to So king of Egypt, and he no longer
17: 13 [A] that *I* **delivered** to you through my servants the prophets."
17: 25 [D] so he **sent** lions among them and they killed some of the
17: 26 [D] *He has* **sent** lions among them, which are killing them off,
18: 14 [A] So Hezekiah king of Judah **sent** this message to the king of
18: 17 [A] of Assyria **sent** his supreme commander, his chief officer and
18: 27 [A] and you that my master **sent** me to say these things,
19: 2 [A] *He* **sent** Eliakim the palace administrator, Shebna the secretary
19: 4 [A] the king of Assyria, *has* **sent** to ridicule the living God,
19: 9 [A] So he again **sent** messengers to Hezekiah with this word:
19: 16 [A] listen to the words Sennacherib *has* **sent** to insult the living
19: 20 [A] Isaiah son of Amoz **sent** a message to Hezekiah: "This is
20: 12 [A] son of Baladan king of Babylon **sent** Hezekiah letters
22: 3 [A] **sent** the secretary, Shaphan son of Azaliah, the son of
22: 15 [A] the God of Israel, says: Tell the man who **sent** you to me,
22: 18 [A] the king of Judah, who **sent** you to inquire of the LORD,
23: 1 [A] Then the king **called together** [+448+665+2256] all the elders
23: 16 [A] *he* **had** the bones **removed** [+906+2256+4374] from them and
24: 2 [D] The LORD **sent** Babylonian, Aramean, Moabite and
24: 2 [D] *He* **sent** them to destroy Judah, in accordance with the word
1Ch 8: 8 [D] in Moab after he *had* **divorced** his wives Hushim and

1Ch 10: 9 [D] **sent messengers** throughout the land of the Philistines to
12:19 [12:20] [D] after consultation, their rulers **sent** him **away**.
13: 2 [A] *let us* **send word** far and wide to the rest of our brothers
13: 9 [A] Uzzah **reached out** his hand to steady the ark,
13:10 [A] he struck him down because *he had* **put** his hand on the ark.
14: 1 [A] Now Hiram king of Tyre **sent** messengers to David,
18:10 [A] *he* **sent** his son Hadoram to King David to greet him
19: 2 [A] So David **sent** a delegation to express his sympathy to Hanun
19: 3 [A] "Do you think David is honoring your father by **sending** men
19: 4 [D] garments in the middle at the buttocks, and **sent** them **away**.
19: 5 [A] told David about the men, *he* **sent** messengers to meet them,
19: 6 [A] the Ammonites **sent** a thousand talents of silver to hire
19: 8 [A] David **sent** Joab **out** with the entire army of fighting men.
19:16 [A] *they* **sent** messengers and had Arameans brought from
21:12 [A] decide how I should answer the *one who* **sent** me."
21:15 [A] God **sent** an angel to destroy Jerusalem. But as the angel was
2Ch 2: 3 [2:2] [A] Solomon **sent** this message to Hiram king of Tyre:
2: 3 [2:2] [A] when *you* **sent** him cedar to build a palace to live in.
2: 7 [2:6] [A] "**Send** me, therefore, a man skilled to work in gold
2: 8 [2:7] [A] "**Send** me also cedar, pine and algum logs from
2:11 [2:10] [A] Hiram king of Tyre replied by letter **[NIE]** to
2:13 [2:12] [A] "*I am* **sending** you Huram-Abi, a man of great skill,
2:15 [2:14] [A] "Now *let* my lord **send** his servants the wheat
6:34 [A] go to war against their enemies, wherever *you* **send** them,
7:10 [D] On the twenty-third day of the seventh month *he* **sent** the
7:13 [D] to devour the land or **send** a plague among my people,
8:18 [A] And Hiram **sent** him ships commanded by his own officers,
10: 3 [A] So *they* **sent** [+2256+4200+7924] **for** Jeroboam, and he and all
10:18 [A] King Rehoboam **sent out** Adoniram, who was in charge of
16: 2 [A] of his own palace and **sent** it to Ben-Hadad king of Aram,
16: 3 [A] and your father. See, *I am* **sending** you silver and gold.
16: 4 [A] **sent** the commanders of his forces against the towns of
17: 7 [A] In the third year of his reign *he* **sent** his officials Ben-Hail,
24:19 [A] Although the LORD **sent** prophets to the people to bring
24:23 [D] *They* **sent** all the plunder to their king in Damascus.
25:15 [A] *he* **sent** a prophet to him, who said, "Why do you consult this
25:17 [A] *he* **sent** this challenge to Jehoash son of Jehoahaz, the son of
25:18 [A] Jehoash king of Israel **replied** [+606] to Amaziah king of
25:18 [A] "A thistle in Lebanon **sent** a message to a cedar in Lebanon,
25:27 [A] but *they* **sent** men after him to Lachish and killed him there.
28:16 [A] At that time King Ahaz **sent** to the king of Assyria for help.
30: 1 [A] Hezekiah **sent word** to all Israel and Judah and also wrote
32: 9 [A] he **sent** his officers to Jerusalem with this message for
32:21 [A] the LORD **sent** an angel, who annihilated all the fighting
32:31 [D] when envoys *were* **sent** by the rulers of Babylon to ask him
34: 8 [A] *he* **sent** Shaphan son of Azaliah and Maaseiah the ruler of the
34:23 [A] the God of Israel, says: Tell the man who **sent** you to me,
34:26 [A] the king of Judah, who **sent** you to inquire of the LORD,
34:29 [A] Then the king **called together** [+665+906+2256] all the elders
35:21 [A] Neco **sent** messengers to him, saying, "What quarrel is there
36:10 [A] King Nebuchadnezzar **sent** *for* him and brought him to
36:15 [A] **sent word** to them through his messengers again and again,
36:15 [A] through his messengers **again and again** [+2256+8899],
Ezr 8:16 [A] *I* **summoned** Eliezer, Ariel, Shemaiah, Elnathan, Jarib,
Ne 2: 5 [A] *let him* **send** me to the city in Judah where my fathers are
2: 6 [A] you get back?" It pleased the king *to* **send** me; so I set a time.
2: 9 [A] The king *had* also **sent** army officers and cavalry with me.
6: 2 [A] Sanballat and Geshem **sent** me this message: "Come, let us
6: 3 [A] so *I* **sent** messengers to them with this reply: "I am carrying
6: 4 [A] Four times *they* **sent** me the same message, and each time I
6: 5 [A] Sanballat **sent** his aide to me with the same message,
6: 8 [A] *I* **sent** him this reply: "Nothing like what you are saying is
6:12 [A] I realized that God *had* not **sent** him, but that he had
6:19 [A] him what I said. And Tobiah **sent** letters to intimidate me.
8:10 [A] and **send** some to those who have nothing prepared.
8:12 [A] to **send** portions of food and to celebrate with great joy,
13:21 [A] by the wall? If you do this again, *I will* **lay** hands on you."
Est 1:22 [A] *He* **sent** dispatches to all parts of the kingdom, to each
2:21 [A] and conspired to **assassinate** [+928+3338] King Xerxes.
3: 6 [A] he scorned the idea of **killing** [+928+3338] only Mordecai.
3:13 [C] Dispatches **were sent** by couriers to all the king's provinces
4: 4 [A] *She* **sent** clothes *for* him to put on instead of his sackcloth,
5:10 [A] **Calling** [+906+906+995+2256] **together** his friends and
6: 2 [A] who had conspired to **assassinate** [+928+3338] King Xerxes.
8: 7 [A] the Jew, "Because Haman **attacked** [+928+3338] the Jews,
8:10 [A] the king's signet ring, and **sent** them by mounted couriers,
9: 2 [A] to **attack** [+928+3338] those seeking their destruction.
9:10 [A] of the Jews. But *they did* not **lay** their hands on the plunder.
9:15 [A] but *they did* not **lay** their hands on the plunder.
9:16 [A] thousand of them but *did* not **lay** their hands on the plunder.
9:20 [A] *he* **sent** letters to all the Jews throughout the provinces of
9:30 [A] Mordecai **sent** letters to all the Jews in the 127 provinces of
Job 1: 4 [A] and *they would* **invite** [+2256+4200+7924] their three sisters to
1: 5 [A] had run its course, Job *would* **send** and have them purified.
1:11 [A] **stretch out** your hand and strike everything he has, and he
1:12 [A] is in your hands, but on the man himself *do* not **lay** a finger."
2: 5 [A] **stretch out** your hand and strike his flesh and bones, and he
5:10 [A] rain on the earth; *he* **sends** water upon the countryside.
8: 4 [D] against him, *he* **gave** them **over** to the penalty of their sin.
12:15 [D] is drought; if *he* **lets** them **loose**, they devastate the land.
14:20 [D] he is gone; you change his countenance and **send** him **away**.
18: 8 [E] His feet **thrust** *him* into a net and he wanders into its mesh.
20:23 [D] God *will* **vent** his burning anger against him and rain down
21:11 [D] *They* **send forth** their children as a flock; their little ones
22: 9 [D] *you* **sent** widows **away** empty-handed and broke the strength
28: 9 [A] Man's hand **assaults** [+928] the flinty rock and lays bare the
30:11 [D] and afflicted me, *they* **throw off** restraint in my presence.
30:12 [D] *they* **lay snares** *for* my feet, they build their siege ramps
30:24 [A] "Surely no *one* **lays** a hand on a broken man when he cries
38:35 [D] *Do you* **send** the lightning bolts on their way? Do they report
39: 3 [D] and bring forth their young; their labor pains *are* **ended**.
39: 5 [D] "Who **let** the wild donkey **go** free? Who untied his ropes?
Ps 18:14 [18:15] [A] *He* **shot** his arrows and scattered ⌊the enemies⌋,
18:16 [18:17] [A] *He* **reached down** from on high and took hold of
20: 2 [20:3] [A] *May he* **send** you help from the sanctuary and grant
43: 3 [A] **Send forth** your light and your truth, let them guide me;
44: 2 [44:3] [D] crushed the peoples and **made** our fathers **flourish**.
50:19 [A] *You* **use** your mouth for evil and harness your tongue to
55:20 [55:21] [A] My companion **attacks** [+928+3338] his friends;
57: 3 [57:4] [A] *He* **sends** from heaven and saves me, rebuking those
57: 3 [57:4] [A] *Selah* God **sends** his love and his faithfulness.
59: T [59:1] [A] When Saul *had* **sent** men to watch David's house in
74: 7 [A] *They* **burned** [+836+928+2021] your sanctuary to the ground;
78:25 [A] the bread of angels; *he* **sent** them all the food they could eat.
78:45 [D] *He* **sent** swarms of flies that devoured them, and frogs that
78:49 [D] *He* **unleashed** against them his hot anger, his wrath,
80:11 [80:12] [D] *It* **sent out** its boughs to the Sea, its shoots as far as
81:12 [81:13] [D] So *I* **gave** them **over** to their stubborn hearts to
104:10 [D] He **makes** springs **pour** water into the ravines; it flows
104:30 [D] *When you* **send** your Spirit, they are created, and you renew
105:17 [A] and *he* **sent** a man before them—Joseph, sold as a slave.
105:20 [A] The king **sent** and released him, the ruler of peoples set him
105:26 [A] *He* **sent** Moses his servant, and Aaron, whom he had chosen.
105:28 [A] *He* **sent** darkness and made the land dark—for had they not
106:15 [D] what they asked for, but **sent** a wasting disease upon them.
107:20 [A] *He* **sent forth** his word and healed them; he rescued them
110: 2 [A] The LORD *will* **extend** your mighty scepter from Zion;
111: 9 [A] *He* **provided** redemption for his people; he ordained his
125: 3 [A] then the righteous *might* **use** their hands **to do** evil.
135: 9 [A] *He* **sent** his signs and wonders into your midst, O Egypt,
138: 7 [A] *you* **stretch out** your hand against the anger of my foes, with
144: 6 [A] and scatter ⌊the enemies⌋; **shoot** your arrows and rout them.
144: 7 [A] **Reach down** your hand from on high; deliver me and rescue
147:15 [A] He **sends** his command *to* the earth; his word runs swiftly.
147:18 [A] *He* **sends** his word and melts them; he stirs up his breezes,
Pr 6:14 [D] evil with deceit in his heart—*he* always **stirs up** dissension.
6:19 [D] out lies and *a man who* **stirs up** dissension among brothers.
9: 3 [A] *She has* **sent out** her maids, and she calls from the highest
10:26 [A] smoke to the eyes, so is a sluggard to *those who* **send** him.
16:28 [D] A perverse man **stirs up** dissension, and a gossip separates
17:11 [E] on rebellion; a merciless official *will* **be sent** against him.
22:21 [A] so that you can give sound answers to *him who* **sent** you?
25:13 [A] time is a trustworthy messenger to *those who* **send** him;
26: 6 [A] or drinking violence is the **sending** *of* a message by the hand
29:15 [E] but a child **left to himself** disgraces his mother.
31:19 [D] In her hand *she* **holds** the distaff and grasps the spindle with
31:20 [D] her arms to the poor and **extends** her hands to the needy.
Ecc 11: 1 [D] **Cast** your bread upon the waters, for after many days you
SS 5: 4 [A] My lover **thrust** his hand through the latch-opening; my
Isa 6: 8 [A] I heard the voice of the Lord saying, "Whom *shall I* **send**?
6: 8 [A] And who will go for us?" And I said, "Here am I. **Send** me!"
9: 8 [9:7] [A] The Lord *has* **sent** a message against Jacob; it will fall
10: 6 [D] *I* **send** him against a godless nation, I dispatch him against a
10:16 [D] *will* **send** a wasting disease upon his sturdy warriors;
16: 1 [A] **Send** lambs as tribute *to* the ruler of the land, from Sela,
16: 2 [E] Like fluttering birds **pushed** *from* the nest, so are the women
18: 2 [A] which **sends** envoys by sea in papyrus boats over the water.
19:20 [A] *he will* **send** them a savior and defender, and he will rescue
20: 1 [A] **sent** *by* Sargon king of Assyria, came to Ashdod
27: 8 [D] By warfare and **exile** you contend with her—with his fierce
27:10 [E] an **abandoned** settlement, forsaken like the desert;
32:20 [D] and **letting** your cattle and donkeys **range** [+8079] **free**.
36: 2 [A] the king of Assyria **sent** his field commander with a large
36:12 [A] and you that my master **sent** me to say these things,
37: 2 [A] *He* **sent** Eliakim the palace administrator, Shebna the secretary,
37: 4 [A] the king of Assyria, *has* **sent** to ridicule the living God,
37: 9 [A] he heard it, *he* **sent** messengers to Hezekiah with this word:
37:17 [A] listen to all the words Sennacherib *has* **sent** to insult the

Isa 37:21 [A] Isaiah son of Amoz **sent** a message to Hezekiah: "This is
39: 1 [A] son of Baladan king of Babylon **sent** Hezekiah letters
42:19 [A] is blind but my servant, and deaf like the messenger *I* **send**?
43:14 [D] "For your sake *I will* **send** to Babylon and bring down as
45:13 [D] He will rebuild my city and **set** my exiles **free**, but not for a
48:16 [A] And now the Sovereign LORD *has* **sent** me, with his Spirit.
50: 1 [D] mother's certificate of divorce with which *I* **sent** her **away**?
50: 1 [E] because of your transgressions your mother **was sent away**.
55:11 [A] what I desire and achieve the purpose for which *I* **sent** it.
57: 9 [D] *You* **sent** your ambassadors far away; you descended to the
58: 6 [D] of the yoke, *to* **set** the oppressed free and break every yoke?
58: 9 [A] of oppression, *with the* **pointing** finger and malicious talk,
61: 1 [A] *He has* **sent** me to bind up the brokenhearted, to proclaim
66:19 [D] and *I will* **send** some of those who survive to the nations—
Jer 1: 7 [A] You must go to everyone *I* **send** you to and say whatever I
1: 9 [A] the LORD **reached out** his hand and touched my mouth
2:10 [A] of Kittim and look, **send** *to* Kedar and observe closely;
3: 1 [D] "If a man **divorces** his wife and she leaves him and marries
3: 8 [D] of divorce and **sent** her **away** because of all her adulteries.
7:25 [A] again and again **[RPH]** I sent you my servants the prophets.
7:25 [A] again and again *I* **sent** you my servants the prophets.
8:17 [D] "See, I *will* **send** venomous snakes among you, vipers that
9:16 [9:15] [D] *I will* **pursue** [+339+906] them *with* the sword until
9:17 [9:16] [A] women to come; **send** for the most skillful of them.
14: 3 [A] The nobles **send** their servants for water; they go to the
14:14 [A] *I have* not **sent** them or appointed them or spoken to them.
14:15 [A] I *did* not **send** them, yet they are saying, 'No sword or famine
15: 1 [D] **Send** them **away** from my presence! Let them go!
16:16 [A] "But now I *will* **send** for many fishermen," declares the
16:16 [A] After that *I will* **send** for many hunters, and they will hunt
17: 8 [D] He will be like a tree planted by the water *that* **sends out** its
19:14 [A] from Topheth, where the LORD *had* **sent** him to prophesy,
21: 1 [A] King Zedekiah **sent** to him Pashhur son of Malkijah and
23:21 [A] *I did* not **send** these prophets, yet they have run with their
23:32 [A] with their reckless lies, yet I *did* not **send** or appoint them.
23:38 [A] even though *I* **told** [+448+606+4200] you that you must not
24: 5 [D] whom *I* **sent away** from this place *to* the land of the
24:10 [D] *I will* **send** the sword, famine and plague against them until
25: 4 [A] though the LORD *has* **sent** all his servants the prophets to
25: 4 [A] **[RPH]** you have not listened or paid any attention.
25: 9 [A] I *will* **summon** [+448+906+2256+4374] all the peoples of the
25:15 [A] and make all the nations to whom I **send** you drink it.
25:16 [A] and go mad because of the sword I *will* **send** among them."
25:17 [A] and made all the nations to whom he **sent** me drink it:
25:27 [A] to rise no more because of the sword I *will* **send** among you.'
26: 5 [A] whom I *have* **sent** to you again and again (though you have
26: 5 [A] you again and again **[RPH]** (though you have not listened),
26:12 [A] "The LORD **sent** me to prophesy against this house and this
26:15 [A] for in truth the LORD *has* **sent** me to you to speak all these
26:22 [A] however, **sent** Elnathan son of Acbor to Egypt,
27: 3 [D] Then **send word** to the kings of Edom, Moab, Ammon, Tyre
27:15 [A] '*I have* not **sent** them,' declares the LORD. 'They are
28: 9 [A] truly **sent** *by* the LORD only if his prediction comes true."
28:15 [A] The LORD *has* not **sent** you, yet you have persuaded this
28:16 [D] 'I *am about to* **remove** you from the face of the earth.
29: 1 [A] This is the text of the letter that the prophet Jeremiah **sent**
29: 3 [A] whom Zedekiah king of Judah **sent** to King Nebuchadnezzar
29: 9 [A] in my name. *I have* not **sent** them," declares the LORD.
29:17 [D] "I *will* **send** the sword, famine and plague against them and I
29:19 [A] "words that *I* **sent** to them again and again by my servants
29:19 [A] **[RPH]** And you exiles have not listened either,"
29:20 [D] all you exiles whom *I have* **sent away** from Jerusalem to
29:25 [A] You **sent** letters in your own name to all the people in
29:28 [A] *He has* **sent** this message to us in Babylon: It will be a long
29:31 [A] "**Send** this message to all the exiles: 'This is what the
29:31 [A] even though I *did* not **send** him, and has led you to believe a
34: 9 [D] to **free** [+906+906+2930] his Hebrew slaves, both male and
34:10 [D] agreed that they *would* **free** [+906+906+2930] their male
34:10 [D] hold them in bondage. They agreed, and **set** them **free**.
34:11 [D] took back the slaves *they had* **freed** [+2930] and enslaved
34:14 [D] 'Every seventh year each of *you must* **free** any fellow
34:14 [D] After he has served you six years, *you must* **let** him **go** free.'
34:16 [D] and female slaves *you had* **set** free to go where they wished.
35:15 [A] and again **[RPH]** I sent all my servants the prophets to you.
35:15 [A] Again and again *I* **sent** all my servants the prophets to you.
36:14 [A] all the officials **sent** Jehudi son of Nethaniah, the son of
36:21 [A] The king **sent** Jehudi to get the scroll, and Jehudi brought it
37: 3 [A] **sent** Jehucal son of Shelemiah with the priest Zephaniah son
37: 7 [A] of Judah, who **sent** you to inquire of me, 'Pharaoh's army,
37:17 [A] King Zedekiah **sent for** him and had him brought to the
38: 6 [D] *They* **lowered** Jeremiah by ropes into the cistern; it had no
38:11 [D] and **let** them **down** with ropes to Jeremiah in the cistern.
38:14 [A] King Zedekiah **sent for** Jeremiah the prophet and had him
39:13 [A] and all the other officers of the king of Babylon **[RPH]**
39:14 [A] **sent** and had Jeremiah taken out of the courtyard of the
40: 1 [D] of the imperial guard *had* **released** him at Ramah.
40: 5 [D] gave him provisions and a present and **let** him **go**.
40:14 [A] "Don't you know that Baalis king of the Ammonites *has* **sent**
42: 5 [A] with everything the LORD your God **sends** you to tell us.
42: 6 [A] to whom we *are* **sending** you, so that it will go well with us,
42: 9 [A] of Israel, to whom *you* **sent** me to present your petition, says:
42:20 [A] that you made a fatal mistake when you **sent** me to the
42:21 [A] obeyed the LORD your God in all *he* **sent** me to tell you.
43: 1 [A] everything the LORD *had* **sent** him to tell them—
43: 2 [A] The LORD our God *has* not **sent** you to say, 'You must not
43:10 [A] I *will* **send** [+906+2256+4374] **for** my servant Nebuchadnezzar
44: 4 [A] Again and again *I* **sent** my servants the prophets, who said,
44: 4 [A] Again and again I sent **[RPH]** my servants the prophets,
48:12 [D] the LORD, "when *I will* **send** men who pour from jars,
49:14 [B] An envoy **was sent** to the nations to say,
49:37 [D] "*I will* **pursue** [+339+906] them *with* the sword until I have
50:33 [D] All their captors hold them fast, refusing *to* **let** them **go**.
51: 2 [D] *I will* **send** foreigners to Babylon to winnow her and to
La 1:13 [A] "From on high *he* **sent** fire, sent it down into my bones.
Eze 2: 3 [A] "Son of man, I *am* **sending** you to the Israelites, to a
2: 4 [A] The people to whom I *am* **sending** you are obstinate and
2: 9 [B] I looked, and I saw a hand **stretched out** to me. In it was a
3: 5 [B] You *are* not **being sent** to a people of obscure speech
3: 6 [A] Surely if *I had* **sent** you to them, they would have listened to
5:16 [D] When I **shoot** at you with my deadly and destructive arrows
5:16 [D] and destructive arrows of famine, *I will* **shoot** to destroy you.
5:17 [D] *I will* **send** famine and wild beasts against you, and they will
7: 3 [D] is now upon you and *I will* **unleash** my anger against you.
8: 3 [A] *He* **stretched out** what looked like a hand and took me by
8:17 [A] me to anger? Look at them **putting** the branch to their nose!
10: 7 [A] one of the cherubim **reached out** his hand to the fire that was
13: 6 [A] LORD declares," when the LORD *has* not **sent** them;
13:20 [D] *I will* **set free** the people that you ensnare like birds.
14:13 [G] and **send** famine upon it and kill its men and their animals,
14:19 [D] "Or if *I* **send** a plague into that land and pour out my wrath
14:21 [A] How much worse will it be *when I* **send** against Jerusalem
17: 6 [D] a vine and produced branches and **put out** leafy boughs.
17: 7 [A] was planted and **stretched out** its branches to him for water.
17:15 [A] the king rebelled against him by **sending** his envoys *to* Egypt
23:16 [A] lusted after them and **sent** messengers to them in Chaldea.
23:40 [A] "*They* even **sent** messengers for men who came from far
23:40 [B] **[RPH]** and when they arrived you bathed yourself for them,
28:23 [D] *I will* **send** a plague upon her and make blood flow in her
31: 4 [D] its base and **sent** their channels to all the trees of the field.
31: 5 [D] branches grew long, **spreading** because of abundant waters.
39: 6 [D] *I will* **send** fire on Magog and on those who live in safety in
44:20 [D] must not shave their heads or **let** their hair **grow** long,
Da 10:11 [E] to you, and stand up, for *I have* now **been sent** to you."
11:42 [A] *He will* **extend** his power over many countries; Egypt will
Hos 5:13 [A] turned to Assyria, and **sent** to the great king **for help**.
8:14 [D] *I will* **send** fire upon their cities that will consume their
Joel 2:19 [A] "I *am* **sending** you grain, new wine and oil, enough to satisfy
2:25 [D] and the locust swarm—my great army that *I* **sent** among you.
3:13 [4:13] [A] **Swing** the sickle, for the harvest is ripe. Come,
Am 1: 4 [D] *I will* **send** fire upon the house of Hazael that will consume
1: 7 [D] *I will* **send** fire upon the walls of Gaza that will consume her
1:10 [D] *I will* **send** fire upon the walls of Tyre that will consume her
1:12 [D] *I will* **send** fire upon Teman that will consume the fortresses
2: 2 [D] *I will* **send** fire upon Moab that will consume the fortresses
2: 5 [D] *I will* **send** fire upon Judah that will consume the fortresses
4:10 [D] "*I* **sent** plagues among you as I did to Egypt. I killed your
7:10 [A] Amaziah the priest of Bethel **sent** a message to Jeroboam
8:11 [G] "when *I will* **send** a famine through the land—
Ob 1: 1 [E] An envoy **was sent** to the nations to say, "Rise, and let us go
1: 7 [D] All your allies *will* **force** you to the border; your friends will
1:13 [A] nor **seize** their wealth in the day of their disaster.
Mic 6: 4 [A] of slavery. *I* **sent** Moses to lead you, also Aaron and Miriam.
Hag 1:12 [A] because the LORD their God *had* **sent** him.
Zec 1:10 [A] "They are the ones the LORD *has* **sent** to go throughout the
2: 8 [2:12] [A] *has* **sent** me against the nations that have plundered
2: 9 [2:13] [A] you will know that the LORD Almighty *has* **sent**
2:11 [2:15] [A] you will know that the LORD Almighty *has* **sent**
4: 9 [A] you will know that the LORD Almighty *has* **sent** me to
6:15 [A] you will know that the LORD Almighty *has* **sent** me to
7: 2 [A] The people of Bethel *had* **sent** Sharezer and Regem-Melech,
7:12 [A] or to the words that the LORD Almighty *had* **sent** by his
8:10 [D] his enemy, for *I had* **turned** every man against his neighbor.
9:11 [D] with you, *I will* **free** your prisoners from the waterless pit.
Mal 2: 2 [D] says the LORD Almighty, "*I will* **send** a curse upon you,
2: 4 [D] you will know that *I have* **sent** you this admonition so that
2:16 [D] "I hate **divorce**," says the LORD God of Israel, "and I hate
3: 1 [A] "See, I *will* **send** my messenger, who will prepare the way
4: 5 [3:23] [A] I *will* **send** you the prophet Elijah before that great

8939 [1]שֶׁלַח **šelaḥ[1]**, n.[m.]. [7] [√ 8938]

weapon [3], sword [2], defenses [1], weapons [1]

2Ch 23:10 all the men, each with his **weapon** in his hand, around the king—
32: 5 of David. He also made large numbers of **weapons** and shields.
Ne 4:17 [4:11] their work with one hand and held a **weapon** in the other,
4:23 [4:17] each had his **weapon**, even when he went for water.
Job 33:18 preserve his soul from the pit, his life from perishing by the **sword**.
36:12 they will perish by the **sword** and die without knowledge.
Joel 2: 8 They plunge through **defenses** without breaking ranks.

8940 [2]שֶׁלַח **šelaḥ[2]**, n.pr.loc. [1] [√ 8938]

Siloam [1]

Ne 3:15 He also repaired the wall of the Pool of **Siloam**, by the King's

8941 [3]שֶׁלַח **šelaḥ[3]**, n.pr.m. [9] [→ 8939?; cf. 8938]

Shelah [9]

Ge 10:24 Arphaxad was the father of **Shelah**, and Shelah the father of Eber.
10:24 Arphaxad was the father of Shelah, and **Shelah** the father of Eber.
11:12 Arphaxad had lived 35 years, he became the father of **Shelah**.
11:13 after he became the father of **Shelah**, Arphaxad lived 403 years
11:14 When **Shelah** had lived 30 years, he became the father of Eber.
11:15 **Shelah** lived 403 years and had other sons and daughters.
1Ch 1:18 Arphaxad was the father of **Shelah**, and Shelah the father of Eber.
1:18 Arphaxad was the father of Shelah, and **Shelah** the father of Eber.
1:24 Shem, Arphaxad, **Shelah**,

8942 שִׁלֹחַ **šilōaḥ**, n.pr.loc. [1] [√ 8938]

Shiloah [1]

Isa 8: 6 this people has rejected the gently flowing waters of **Shiloah**

8943 שְׁלֻחוֹת **šᵉluḥôt**, n.f. [1] [√ 8938]

shoots [1]

Isa 16: 8 the desert. Their **shoots** spread out and went as far as the sea.

8944 שִׁלְחִי **šilḥî**, n.pr.m. [2] [√ 8938]

Shilhi [2]

1Ki 22:42 His mother's name was Azubah daughter of **Shilhi**.
2Ch 20:31 His mother's name was Azubah daughter of **Shilhi**.

8945 שְׁלָחִים **šᵉlāḥîm**, n.[m.]. [1] [√ 8938]

plants [1]

SS 4:13 Your **plants** are an orchard of pomegranates with choice fruits,

8946 שִׁלְחִים **šilḥîm**, n.pr.loc. [1]

Shilhim [1]

Jos 15:32 Lebaoth, **Shilhim**, Ain and Rimmon—a total of twenty-nine towns

8947 שֻׁלְחָן **šulḥān**, n.m. [71]

table [52], tables [12], *untranslated* [4], each table [+2256+8947] [2], it[s] [+2021] [1]

Ex 25:23 "Make a **table** *of* acacia wood—two cubits long, a cubit wide
25:27 to be close to the rim to hold the poles used in carrying the **table**.
25:28 overlay them with gold and carry the **table** with them.
25:30 Put the bread of the Presence on this **table** to be before me at all
26:35 Place the **table** outside the curtain on the north side of the
26:35 and put the lampstand opposite **it**[s] [+2021] on the south side.
26:35 and put the lampstand opposite it on the south side. **[RPH]**
30:27 the **table** and all its articles, the lampstand and its accessories,
31: 8 the **table** and its articles, the pure gold lampstand and all its
35:13 the **table** with its poles and all its articles and the bread of the
37:10 They made the **table** of acacia wood—two cubits long, a cubit
37:14 put close to the rim to hold the poles used in carrying the **table**.
37:15 The poles for carrying the **table** were made of acacia wood
37:16 And they made from pure gold the articles for the **table**—its plates
39:36 the **table** with all its articles and the bread of the Presence;
40: 4 Bring in the **table** and set out what belongs on it. Then bring in the
40:22 Moses placed the **table** in the Tent of Meeting on the north side of
40:24 He placed the lampstand in the Tent of Meeting opposite the **table**
Lev 24: 6 six in each row, on the **table** of pure gold before the LORD.
Nu 3:31 for the care of the ark, the **table**, the lampstand, the altars,
4: 7 "Over the **table** *of* the Presence they are to spread a blue cloth
Jdg 1: 7 and big toes cut off have picked up scraps under my **table**.
1Sa 20:29 see my brothers.' That is why he has not come to the king's **table**."
20:34 Jonathan got up from the **table** in fierce anger; on that second day
2Sa 9: 7 to your grandfather Saul, and you will always eat at my **table**."
9:10 grandson of your master, will always eat at my **table**."
9:11 So Mephibosheth ate at David's **table** like one of the king's sons.
9:13 because he always ate at the king's **table**, and he was crippled in
19:28 [19:29] your servant a place among those who sat at your **table**.
1Ki 2: 7 of Gilead and let them be among those who eat at your **table**.
4:27 [5:7] for King Solomon and all who came to the king's **table**.
7:48 the golden **table** on which was the bread of the Presence;
10: 5 the food on his **table**, the seating of his officials, the attending
13:20 While they were sitting at the **table**, the word of the LORD came
18:19 the four hundred prophets of Asherah, who eat at Jezebel's **table**."
2Ki 4:10 Let's make a small room on the roof and put in it a bed and a **table**,
1Ch 28:16 the weight of gold for **each table** [+2256+8947] for consecrated
28:16 the weight of gold for **each table** [+2256+8947] for consecrated
28:16 the weight of gold for each table for **[RPH]** consecrated bread;
28:16 for consecrated bread; the weight of silver for the silver **tables**;
2Ch 4: 8 He made ten **tables** and placed them in the temple, five on the
4:19 golden altar; the **tables** on which was the bread of the Presence;
9: 4 the food on his **table**, the seating of his officials, the attending
13:11 They set out the bread on the ceremonially clean **table** and light
29:18 the **table** *for* setting out the consecrated bread, with all its articles.
Ne 5:17 a hundred and fifty Jews and officials ate at my **table**,
Job 36:16 to the comfort of your **table** laden with choice food.
Ps 23: 5 You prepare a **table** before me in the presence of my enemies.
69:22 [69:23] May the **table** set before them become a snare; may it
78:19 spoke against God, saying, "Can God spread a **table** in the desert?
128: 3 your house; your sons will be like olive shoots around your **table**.
Pr 9: 2 prepared her meat and mixed her wine; she has also set her **table**.
Isa 21: 5 They set the **tables**, they spread the rugs, they eat, they drink!
28: 8 All the **tables** are covered with vomit and there is not a spot
65:11 who spread a **table** for Fortune and fill bowls of mixed wine for
Eze 23:41 with a **table** spread before it on which you had placed the incense
39:20 At my **table** you will eat your fill of horses and riders, mighty men
40:39 In the portico of the gateway were two **tables** on each side,
40:39 **[RPH]** on which the burnt offerings, sin offerings and guilt
40:40 near the steps at the entrance to the north gateway were two **tables**,
40:40 were two tables, and on the other side of the steps were two **tables**.
40:41 So there were four **tables** on one side of the gateway and four on
40:41 tables on one side of the gateway and four **[RPH]** on the other—
40:41 one side of the gateway and four on the other—eight **tables** in all—
40:42 There were also four **tables** of dressed stone for the burnt
40:43 the wall all around. The **tables** were for the flesh of the offerings.
41:22 The man said to me, "This is the **table** that is before the LORD."
44:16 they alone are to come near my **table** to minister before me
Da 11:27 will sit at the same **table** and lie to each other, but to no avail,
Mal 1: 7 defiled you?' "By saying that the LORD's **table** is contemptible.
1:12 "But you profane it by saying of the Lord's **table**, 'It is defiled,'

8948 שָׁלַט **šālaṭ**, v. [8] [→ 8950, 8951, 8954; Ar 10715]

enable [1], enables [1], got the upper hand [1], have control [1], let rule [1], lorded it over [1], lords it over [1], overpower [1]

Ne 5:15 [A] and wine. Their assistants also **lorded it over** the people.
Est 9: 1 [A] On this day the enemies of the Jews had hoped to **overpower**
9: 1 [A] the Jews **got the upper hand** over those who hated them.
Ps 119:133 [G] footsteps according to your word; **let** no sin **rule** over me.
Ecc 2:19 [A] Yet *he will* **have control** over all the work into which I have
5:19 [5:18] [G] **enables** him to enjoy them, to accept his lot and be
6: 2 [G] God *does* not **enable** him to enjoy them, and a stranger
8: 9 [A] There is a time when a man **lords it over** others to his own

8949 שֶׁלֶט **šeleṭ**, n.m. [7]

shields [6], small shields [1]

2Sa 8: 7 David took the gold **shields** that belonged to the officers of
2Ki 11:10 the spears and **shields** that had belonged to King David
1Ch 18: 7 David took the gold **shields** carried by the officers of Hadadezer
2Ch 23: 9 and the large and **small shields** that had belonged to King David
SS 4: 4 on it hang a thousand shields, all of them **shields** *of* warriors.
Jer 51:11 "Sharpen the arrows, take up the **shields**! The LORD has stirred
Eze 27:11 They hung their **shields** around your walls; they brought your

8950 שִׁלְטוֹן **šilṭôn**, n.[m.]. [2] [√ 8948; Ar 10717]

power [1], supreme [1]

Ecc 8: 4 Since a king's word is **supreme**, who can say to him, "What are
8: 8 wind to contain it; so no one has **power** over the day of his death.

8951 שַׁלֶּטֶת **šalleṭet**, a. [1] [√ 8948]

brazen [1]

Eze 16:30 when you do all these things, acting like a **brazen** prostitute!

8952 שְׁלִי **šᵉlî**, n.[m.]. [1] [√ 8922]

privately [+928+2021] [1]

2Sa 3:27 the gateway, as though to speak with him **privately** [+928+2021].

8953 שִׁלְיָה šilyâ, n.f. [1] [√ 8922]

afterbirth [1]

Dt 28:57 the **afterbirth** from her womb and the children she bears.

8954 שַׁלִּיט šallîṭ, a. [4] [√ 8948; Ar 10718]

governor [1], power [1], ruler [1], rulers [1]

Ge 42: 6 Now Joseph was the **governor** of the land, the one who sold grain
Ecc 7:19 Wisdom makes one wise man more powerful than ten **rulers** in a
8: 8 No man has **power** over the wind to contain it; so no one has
10: 5 I have seen under the sun, the sort of error that arises from a **ruler**:

8955 שָׁלִישׁ¹ šālîš¹, n.[m.]. [2] [√ 8993]

basket [1], bowlful [1]

Ps 80: 5 [80:6] of tears; you have made them drink tears *by* the **bowlful**.
Isa 40:12 Who has held the dust of the earth in a **basket**, or weighed the

8956 שָׁלִישׁ² šālîš², n.[m.]. [1] [√ 8993]

lutes [1]

1Sa 18: 6 and dancing, with joyful songs and with tambourines and **lutes**.

8957 שָׁלִישׁ³ šālîš³, n.m. [14] [√ 8993; Ar 10761]

officers [5], officer [3], captains [2], chariot officers [2], chariot officer [1], chief officers [1]

Ex 14: 7 with all the other chariots of Egypt, with **officers** over all of them.
15: 4 The best of Pharaoh's **officers** are drowned in the Red Sea.
1Ki 9:22 fighting men, his government officials, his officers, his **captains**,
2Ki 7: 2 The **officer** on whose arm the king was leaning said to the man of
7:17 Now the king had put the **officer** on whose arm he leaned in charge
7:19 The **officer** had said to the man of God, "Look, even if the LORD
9:25 his **chariot officer**, "Pick him up and throw him on the field that
10:25 making the burnt offering, he ordered the guards and **officers**:
10:25 The guards and **officers** threw the bodies out and then entered the
15:25 One of his **chief officers**, Pekah son of Remaliah,
1Ch 11:11 Jashobeam, a Hacmonite, was chief of the **officers**; [K 8993]
12:18 [12:19] [chief of the **Thirty**, [Q; see K 8993] and he said:]
2Ch 8: 9 they were his fighting men, commanders of his **captains**,
Eze 23:15 all of them looked like Babylonian **chariot officers**, natives of
23:23 and commanders, **chariot officers** and men of high rank,

8958 שְׁלִישִׁי šᵉlîšî, a.num.ord. [105] [√ 8993; Ar 10759, 10761]

third [93], three [7], day after tomorrow [1], day after [1], one-third [1], that[s] [1], upper [1]

Ge 1:13 And there was evening, and there was morning—the **third** day.
2:14 The name of the **third** river is the Tigris; it runs along the east side
6:16 in the side of the ark and make lower, middle and **upper** *decks*.
22: 4 On the **third** day Abraham looked up and saw the place in the
31:22 On the **third** day Laban was told that Jacob had fled.
32:19 [32:20] the **third** and all the others who followed the herds:
34:25 **Three** days later, while all of them were still in pain, two of
40:20 Now the **third** day was Pharaoh's birthday, and he gave a feast for
42:18 On the **third** day, Joseph said to them, "Do this and you will live,
Ex 19: 1 In the **third** month after the Israelites left Egypt—on the very
19:11 be ready by the **third** day, because on that day the LORD will
19:11 because on **that**[s] day the LORD will come down on Mount Sinai
19:16 On the morning of the **third** day there was thunder and lightning,
28:19 in the **third** row a jacinth, an agate and an amethyst;
39:12 in the **third** row a jacinth, an agate and an amethyst;
Lev 7:17 Any meat of the sacrifice left over till the **third** day must be
7:18 If any meat of the fellowship offering is eaten on the **third** day,
19: 6 next day; anything left over until the **third** day must be burned up.
19: 7 If any of it is eaten on the **third** day, it is impure and will not be
Nu 2:24 to their divisions, number 108,100. They will set out **third**.
7:24 On the **third** day, Eliab son of Helon, the leader of the people of
15: 6 of an ephah of fine flour mixed with a **third** *of* a hin of oil,
15: 7 a **third** *of* a hin of wine as a drink offering. Offer it as an aroma
19:12 He must purify himself with the water on the **third** day and on the
19:12 But if he does not purify himself on the **third** and seventh days,
19:19 man who is clean is to sprinkle the unclean person on the **third**
28:14 with the ram, a **third** *of* a hin; and with each lamb, a quarter of a
29:20 " 'On the **third** day prepare eleven bulls, two rams and fourteen
31:19 On the **third** and seventh days you must purify yourselves
Dt 23: 8 [23:9] The **third** generation of children born to them may enter
26:12 finished setting aside a tenth of all your produce in the **third** year,
Jos 9:17 So the Israelites set out and on the **third** day came to their cities:
19:10 The **third** lot came up for Zebulun, clan by clan: The boundary of
Jdg 20:30 They went up against the Benjamites on the **third** day and took up
1Sa 3: 8 The LORD called Samuel a **third** *time*, and Samuel got up
17:13 was Eliab; the second, Abinadab; and the **third**, Shammah.
19:21 Saul sent men a **third** *time*, and they also prophesied.
20: 5 and hide in the field until the evening of the **day after tomorrow**.
20:12 I will surely sound out my father by this time the **day after**
30: 1 David and his men reached Ziklag on the **third** day.
2Sa 1: 2 On the **third** day a man arrived from Saul's camp, with his clothes
3: 3 the **third**, Absalom the son of Maacah daughter of Talmai king of
18: 2 a **third** under the command of Joab, a third under Joab's brother
18: 2 a **third** under Joab's brother Abishai son of Zeruiah, and a third
18: 2 brother Abishai son of Zeruiah, and a **third** under Ittai the Gittite.
1Ki 3:18 The **third** day after my child was born, this woman also had a
6: 6 cubits wide, the middle floor six cubits and the **third** floor seven.
6: 8 a stairway led up to the middle level and from there to the **third**.
12:12 **Three** days later Jeroboam and all the people returned to
12:12 as the king had said, "Come back to me in **three** days."
18: 1 After a long time, in the **third** year, the word of the LORD came
22: 2 in the **third** year Jehoshaphat king of Judah went down to see the
2Ki 1:13 So the king sent a **third** captain with his fifty men. This third
1:13 This **third** captain went up and fell on his knees before Elijah.
11: 5 on duty on the Sabbath—a **third** of you guarding the royal palace,
11: 6 a **third** at the Sur Gate, and a third at the gate behind the guard,
11: 6 a third at the Sur Gate, and a **third** at the gate behind the guard,
19:29 in the **third** year sow and reap, plant vineyards and eat their fruit.
20: 5 On the **third** day from now you will go up to the temple of the
20: 8 that I will go up to the temple of the LORD on the **third** day from
1Ch 2:13 his firstborn; the second son was Abinadab, the **third** Shimea,
3: 2 the **third**, Absalom the son of Maacah daughter of Talmai king of
3:15 Jehoiakim the second son, Zedekiah the **third**, Shallum the fourth.
8: 1 of Bela his firstborn, Ashbel the second son, Aharah the **third**,
8:39 Ulam his firstborn, Jeush the second son and Eliphelet the **third**.
12: 9 [12:10] Obadiah the second in command, Eliab the **third**,
23:19 Amariah the second, Jahaziel the **third** and Jekameam the fourth.
24: 8 the **third** to Harim, the fourth to Seorim,
24:23 Amariah the second, Jahaziel the **third** and Jekameam the fourth.
25:10 the **third** to Zaccur, his sons and relatives, 12
26: 2 Jediael the second, Zebadiah the **third**, Jathniel the fourth,
26: 4 the second, Joah the **third**, Sacar the fourth, Nethanel the fifth,
26:11 Hilkiah the second, Tabaliah the **third** and Zechariah the fourth.
27: 5 The **third** army commander, for the third month, was Benaiah son
27: 5 The third army commander, for the **third** month, was Benaiah son
2Ch 10:12 **Three** days later Jeroboam and all the people returned to
10:12 as the king had said, "Come back to me in **three** days."
15:10 They assembled at Jerusalem in the **third** month of the fifteenth
23: 4 A **third** of you priests and Levites who are going on duty on the
23: 5 a **third** of you at the royal palace and a third at the Foundation
23: 5 third of you at the royal palace and a **third** at the Foundation Gate,
27: 5 brought him the same amount also in the second and **third** years.
31: 7 They began doing this in the **third** month and finished in the
Ne 10:32 [10:33] **third** *of* a shekel each year for the service of the house of
Est 5: 1 On the **third** day Esther put on her royal robes and stood in the
8: 9 on the twenty-third day of the **third** month, the month of Sivan.
Job 42:14 named Jemimah, the second Keziah and the **third** Keren-Happuch.
Isa 19:24 In that day Israel will be the **third**, along with Egypt and Assyria,
37:30 in the **third** year sow and reap, plant vineyards and eat their fruit.
Jer 38:14 had him brought to the **third** entrance to the temple of the LORD.
Eze 5: 2 come to an end, burn a **third** of the hair with fire inside the city.
5: 2 Take a **third** and strike it with the sword all around the city.
5: 2 scatter a **third** to the wind. For I will pursue them with drawn
5:12 A **third** *of* your *people* will die of the plague or perish by famine
5:12 inside you; a **third** will fall by the sword outside your walls;
5:12 a **third** I will scatter to the winds and pursue with drawn sword.
10:14 a cherub, the second the face of a man, the **third** the face of a lion,
21:14 [21:19] Let the sword strike twice, even **three** *times*. It is a sword
31: 1 In the eleventh year, in the **third** month on the first day, the word
42: 3 of the outer court, gallery faced gallery at the **three** *levels*.
46:14 consisting of a sixth of an ephah with a **third** *of* a hin of oil to
Hos 6: 2 on the **third** day he will restore us, that we may live in his
Zec 6: 3 the **third** white, and the fourth dappled—all of them powerful.
13: 8 will be struck down and perish; yet **one-third** will be left in it.
13: 9 This **third** I will bring into the fire; I will refine them like silver

8959 שָׁלַךְ šālak, v. [125] [→ 8960?, 8961]

threw [26], throw [14], cast [8], thrust [7], thrown [6], put [5], throw away [3], throw down [3], thrown down [3], get rid of [2], hurled down [2], hurled [2], threw down [2], thrown away [2], thrown out [2], throws [2], toss [2], are cast [1], banish [1], be thrown out [1], be thrown [1], cast away [1], cast out [1], did[s] [1], divide [1], dropped [1], dropping [1], flung [1], hurl [1], hurls down [1], hurls [1], in ruins [1], knocked [1], pelt [1], pushed back [1], pushed down [1], reject [+906+4946+6584+7156] [1], rid [+906+4946+6584] [1], risked [+906+4946+5584] [1], scatter [1], scattered [1], set down [1], shedding [1], snatched [1], sprinkle [1], threw away [1], threw out [1], throw off [1], thrown aside [1], was brought low [1], were thrown out [1]

Ge 21:15 [G] the skin was gone, *she* **put** the boy under one of the bushes.
37:20 [G] let's kill him and **throw** him into one of these cisterns

Ge 37:22 [G] **Throw** him into this cistern here in the desert, but don't lay a
37:24 [G] they took him and **threw** him into the cistern.
Ex 1:22 [G] "Every boy that is born *you must* **throw** into the Nile, but let
4:3 [G] The LORD said, "**Throw** it on the ground." Moses threw it
4:3 [G] Moses **threw** it on the ground and it became a snake, and he
7:9 [G] 'Take your staff and **throw** it **down** before Pharaoh,'
7:10 [G] Aaron **threw** his staff **down** in front of Pharaoh and his
7:12 [G] Each one **threw down** his staff and it became a snake.
15:25 [G] *He* **threw** it into the water, and the water became sweet.
22:31 [22:30] [G] an animal torn by wild beasts; **throw** it to the dogs.
32:19 [G] his anger burned and *he* **threw** the tablets out of his hands,
32:24 [G] the gold, and *I* **threw** it into the fire, and out came this calf!"
Lev 1:16 [G] with its contents and **throw** it to the east side of the altar,
14:40 [G] torn out and **thrown** into an unclean place outside the town.
Nu 19:6 [G] and scarlet wool and **throw** them onto the burning heifer.
35:20 [G] or **throws** something at him intentionally so that he dies
35:22 [G] shoves another or **throws** something at him unintentionally
Dt 9:17 [G] So I took the two tablets and **threw** them out of my hands,
9:21 [G] **threw** the dust into a stream that flowed down the mountain.
29:28 [29:27] [G] from their land and **thrust** them into another land,
Jos 8:29 [G] the tree and **throw** it **down** at the entrance of the city gate.
10:11 [G] the LORD **hurled** large hailstones **down** on them from the
10:27 [G] and **threw** them into the cave where they had been hiding.
18:8 [G] *I will* **cast** lots for you here at Shiloh in the presence of the
18:10 [G] **cast** lots for them in Shiloh in the presence of the LORD,
Jdg 8:25 [G] and each man **threw** a ring from his plunder onto it.
9:17 [G] my father fought for you, **risked** [+906+4946+5584] his life to
9:53 [G] a woman **dropped** an upper millstone on his head
15:17 [G] When he finished speaking, *he* **threw away** the jawbone; and
2Sa 11:21 [G] Didn't a woman **throw** an upper millstone on him from the
18:17 [G] **threw** him into a big pit in the forest and piled up a large
20:12 [G] him from the road into a field and **threw** a garment over him.
20:21 [H] to Joab, "His head *will* **be thrown** to you from the wall."
20:22 [G] cut off the head of Sheba son of Bicri and **threw** it to Joab.
1Ki 13:24 [H] and killed him, and his body was **thrown down** on the road,
13:25 [H] Some people who passed by saw the body **thrown down**
13:28 [H] he went out and found the body **thrown down** on the road,
14:9 [G] have provoked me to anger and **thrust** me behind your back.
19:19 [G] Elijah went up to him and **threw** his cloak around him.
2Ki 2:16 [G] and **set** him **down** on some mountain or in some valley."
2:21 [G] he went out to the spring and **threw** the salt into it, saying,
3:25 [G] each man **threw** a stone *on* every good field until it was
4:41 [G] *He* **put** it into the pot and said, "Serve it to the people to eat."
6:6 [G] Elisha cut a stick and **threw** it there, and made the iron float.
7:15 [G] equipment the Arameans *had* **thrown away** in their
9:25 [G] **throw** him on the field that belonged to Naboth the
9:26 [G] Now then, pick him up and **throw** him on that plot,
10:25 [G] The guards and officers **threw** the bodies **out** and
13:21 [G] of raiders; so *they* **threw** the man's body into Elisha's tomb.
13:23 [G] unwilling to destroy them or **banish** them from his presence.
17:20 [G] hands of plunderers, until *he* **thrust** them from his presence.
23:6 [G] **scattered** the dust over the graves of the common people.
23:12 [G] them to pieces and **threw** the rubble into the Kidron Valley.
24:20 [G] and Judah, and in the end he **thrust** them from his presence.
2Ch 7:20 [G] and *will* **reject** [+906+4946+6584+7156] this temple I have
24:10 [G] **dropping** them into the chest until it was full.
25:12 [G] took them to the top of a cliff and **threw** them down so that
30:14 [G] the incense altars and **threw** them into the Kidron Valley.
33:15 [G] and in Jerusalem; and *he* **threw** them out of the city.
Ne 9:11 [G] *you* **hurled** their pursuers into the depths, like a stone into
9:26 [G] rebelled against you; *they* **put** your law behind their backs.
13:8 [G] and **threw** all Tobiah's household goods out of the room.
Job 15:33 [G] of its unripe grapes, like an olive tree **shedding** its blossoms.
18:7 [G] of his step is weakened; his own schemes **throw** him **down**.
27:22 [G] *It* **hurls** *itself* against him without mercy as he flees
29:17 [G] of the wicked and **snatched** the victims from their teeth.
Ps 2:3 [G] us break their chains," they say, "and **throw off** their fetters."
22:10 [22:11] [H] From birth *I was* **cast** upon you; from my mother's
50:17 [G] You hate my instruction and **cast** my words behind you.
51:11 [51:13] [G] *Do* not **cast** me from your presence or take your
55:22 [55:23] [G] **Cast** your cares on the LORD and he will sustain
60:8 [60:10] [G] Moab is my washbasin, upon Edom *I* **toss** my
71:9 [G] *Do* not **cast** me **away** when I am old; do not forsake me
102:10 [102:11] [G] for you have taken me up and **thrown** me **aside**.
108:9 [108:10] [G] Moab is my washbasin, upon Edom *I* **toss** my
147:17 [G] *He* **hurls down** his hail like pebbles. Who can withstand his
Ecc 3:5 [G] a time to **scatter** stones and a time to gather them, a time to
3:6 [G] a time to give up, a time to keep and a time to **throw away**,
Isa 2:20 [G] In that day men *will* **throw away** to the rodents and bats their
14:19 [H] you **are cast** out of your tomb like a rejected branch; you are
19:8 [G] will groan and lament, all *who* **cast** hooks into the Nile;
34:3 [H] Their slain *will* **be thrown out**, their dead bodies will send
38:17 [G] of destruction; *you have* **put** all my sins behind your back.
Jer 7:15 [G] *I will* **thrust** you from my presence, just as I did all your
7:15 [G] just as *I* **did**[s] all your brothers, the people of Ephraim.'
7:29 [G] Cut off your hair and **throw** it **away**; take up a lament on the
9:19 [9:18] [G] leave our land because our houses *are* **in ruins**.' "
14:16 [H] the people they are prophesying to will be **thrown out** into
22:19 [G] dragged away and **thrown** outside the gates of Jerusalem."
22:28 [H] his children be hurled out, **cast** into a land they do not know?
26:23 [G] his body **thrown** into the burial place of the common
36:23 [G] off with a scribe's knife and **threw** them into the firepot,
36:30 [H] his body will be **thrown out** and exposed to the heat by day
38:6 [G] they took Jeremiah and **put** him into the cistern of Malkijah,
38:9 [G] *They have* **thrown** him into a cistern, where he will starve to
41:9 [G] Now the cistern where he **threw** all the bodies of the men he
51:63 [G] this scroll, tie a stone to it and **throw** it into the Euphrates.
52:3 [G] and Judah, and in the end he **thrust** them from his presence.
La 2:1 [G] *He has* **hurled down** the splendor of Israel from heaven to
Eze 5:4 [G] few of these and **throw** them into the fire and burn them up.
7:19 [G] *They will* **throw** their silver into the streets, and their gold
16:5 [H] Rather, *you* **were thrown out** into the open field, for on the
18:31 [G] **Rid** [+906+4946+6584] yourselves *of* all the offenses you
19:12 [H] it was uprooted in fury and **thrown** to the ground. The east
20:7 [G] of you, **get rid of** the vile images you have set your eyes on,
20:8 [G] they *did* not **get rid of** the vile images they had set their eyes
23:35 [G] you have forgotten me and **thrust** me behind your back,
28:17 [G] So *I* **threw** you to the earth; I made a spectacle of you before
43:24 [G] the priests *are to* **sprinkle** salt on them and sacrifice them as
Da 8:7 [G] the goat **knocked** him to the ground and trampled on him,
8:11 [H] from him, and the place of his sanctuary **was brought low**.
8:12 [G] in everything it did, and truth *was* **thrown** to the ground.
Joel 1:7 [G] It has stripped off their bark and **thrown** it **away**,
Am 4:3 [G] *you will be* **cast out** toward Harmon," declares the LORD.
8:3 [G] Many, many bodies—**flung** everywhere! Silence!"
Jnh 2:3 [2:4] [G] *You* **hurled** me into the deep, into the very heart of
Mic 2:5 [G] *one* in the assembly of the LORD *to* **divide** the land by lot.
7:19 [G] and **hurl** all our iniquities into the depths of the sea.
Na 3:6 [G] *I will* **pelt** you *with* filth, I will treat you with contempt
Zec 5:8 [G] *he* **pushed** her **back** into the basket and pushed the lead
5:8 [G] the basket and **pushed** the lead cover **down** over its mouth.
11:13 [G] the LORD said to me, "**Throw** it to the potter"—
11:13 [G] and **threw** them *into* the house of the LORD to the potter.

8960 שָׁלָךְ ***šālāk***, n.[m.]. [2] [√ 8959?]

cormorant [2]

Lev 11:17 the little owl, the **cormorant**, the great owl,
Dt 14:17 the desert owl, the osprey, the **cormorant**,

8961 שַׁלֶּכֶת¹ ***šalleket***[1], n.f. [1] [√ 8959]

cut down [1]

Isa 6:13 But as the terebinth and oak leave stumps when they are **cut down**,

8962 שַׁלֶּכֶת² ***šalleket***[2], n.pr.loc. [1]

Shalleketh [1]

1Ch 26:16 and the **Shalleketh** Gate on the upper road fell to Shuppim

8963 שָׁלַל¹ ***šālal***[1], v. [2]

pull out [+8963] [2]

Ru 2:16 [A] **pull** [+8963] **out** some stalks for her from the bundles
2:16 [A] **pull out** [+8963] some stalks for her from the bundles

8964 שָׁלַל² ***šālal***[2], v. [14] [→ 8768, 8965]

plunder [4], plundered [4], plunder [+8965] [2], seize [2], becomes prey [1], loot [+8965] [1]

Ps 76:5 [76:6] [F] Valiant men *lie* **plundered**, they sleep their last sleep;
Isa 10:6 [A] a people who anger me, to **seize** loot and snatch plunder,
59:15 [F] to be found, and whoever shuns evil **becomes** *a* **prey**.
Jer 50:10 [A] all *who* **plunder** her will have their fill,"
Eze 26:12 [A] *They will* **plunder** your wealth and loot your merchandise;
29:19 [A] *He will* **loot** [+8965] and plunder the land as pay for his
38:12 [A] I *will* **plunder** [+8965] and loot and turn my hand against the
38:13 [A] will say to you, "Have you come to **plunder** [+8965]?
38:13 [A] take away livestock and goods and to **seize** much plunder?" '
39:10 [A] *they will* **plunder** those who plundered them and loot those
39:10 [A] they will plunder *those who* **plundered** them and loot those
Hab 2:8 [A] Because you *have* **plundered** many nations, the peoples who
2:8 [A] many nations, the peoples who are left *will* **plunder** you.
Zec 2:8 [2:12] [A] has sent me against the nations that *have* **plundered**

8965 שָׁלָל ***šālāl***, n.m. [73] [→ 4561; cf. 8964]

plunder [49], escape with [+4200] [4], spoils [4], loot [3], plunder [+8964] [2], *untranslated* [1], booty [1], goods [1], loot [+8964] [1],

[F] Hitpael (hitpoel, hitpoal, hitpolel, hitpolal, hitpalel, hitpalal, hitpalpel, hitpalpal, hotpael, hotpaal) [G] Hiphil (hiphtil) [H] Hophal [I] Hishtaphel

plundered [1], prey [1], property [1], share of plunder [1], spoil [1], value [1], which[s] [+2021] [1]

Ge 49:27 he devours the prey, in the evening he divides the **plunder**."
Ex 15: 9 I will divide the **spoils**; I will gorge myself on them.
Nu 31:11 They took all the **plunder** and spoils, including the people
31:12 spoils and **plunder** to Moses and Eleazar the priest and the
Dt 2:35 the **plunder** *from* the towns we had captured we carried off for
3: 7 and the **plunder** *from* their cities we carried off for ourselves.
13:16 [13:17] Gather all the **plunder** *of* the town into the middle of the
13:16 [13:17] all its **plunder** as a whole burnt offering to the LORD
20:14 else in the city, you may take these as **plunder** for yourselves.
20:14 you may use the **plunder** the LORD your God gives you *from*
Jos 7:21 When I saw in the **plunder** a beautiful robe from Babylonia,
8: 2 except that you may carry off their **plunder** and livestock for
8:27 did carry off for themselves the livestock and **plunder** *of* this city,
11:14 carried off for themselves all the **plunder** and livestock *of*
22: 8 and divide with your brothers the **plunder** *from* your enemies."
Jdg 5:30 'Are they not finding and dividing the **spoils**: a girl or two for each
5:30 or two for each man, colorful garments as **plunder** for Sisera,
5:30 as plunder for Sisera, **[RPH]** colorful garments embroidered,
5:30 highly embroidered garments for my neck—all this as **plunder**?'
8:24 each of you give me an earring from your **share of the plunder**."
8:25 out a garment, and each man threw a ring from his **plunder** onto it.
1Sa 14:30 eaten today some of the **plunder** they took *from* their enemies.
14:32 They pounced on the **plunder** and, taking sheep, cattle and calves,
15:19 Why did you pounce on the **plunder** and do evil in the eyes of the
15:21 The soldiers took sheep and cattle from the **plunder**, the best of
30:16 because of the great amount of **plunder** they had taken from the
30:19 or old, boy or girl, **plunder** or anything else they had taken.
30:20 ahead of the other livestock, saying, "This is David's **plunder**."
30:22 with us, we will not share with them the **plunder** we recovered.
30:26 he sent some of the **plunder** to the elders of Judah, who were his
30:26 "Here is a present for you from the **plunder** *of* the LORD's
2Sa 3:22 from a raid and brought with them a great deal of **plunder**.
8:12 He also dedicated the **plunder** taken from Hadadezer son of
12:30 David's head. He took a great quantity of **plunder** from the city
2Ki 3:23 and slaughtered each other. Now to the **plunder**, Moab!"
1Ch 20: 2 David's head. He took a great quantity of **plunder** from the city
26:27 Some of the **plunder** taken in battle they dedicated for the repair of
2Ch 14:13 [14:12] The men of Judah carried off a large amount of **plunder**.
15:11 thousand sheep and goats from the **plunder** they had brought back.
20:25 So Jehoshaphat and his men went to carry off their **plunder**,
20:25 There was so much **plunder** that it took three days to collect it.
24:23 of the people. They sent all the **plunder** to their king in Damascus.
28: 8 They also took a great deal of **plunder**, which they carried back to
28: 8 They also took a great deal of plunder, **which**[s] [+2021] they
28:15 and from the **plunder** they clothed all who were naked.
Est 3:13 the twelfth month, the month of Adar, and to plunder their **goods**.
8:11 and children; and to plunder the **property** *of* their enemies.
Ps 68:12 [68:13] flee in haste; in the camps men divide the **plunder**.
119:162 I rejoice in your promise like one who finds great **spoil**.
Pr 1:13 get all sorts of valuable things and fill our houses with **plunder**;
16:19 and among the oppressed than to share **plunder** with the proud.
31:11 Her husband has full confidence in her and lacks nothing of **value**.
Isa 8: 4 the **plunder** *of* Samaria will be carried off by the king of Assyria."
9: 3 [9:2] at the harvest, as men rejoice when dividing the **plunder**.
10: 2 my people, making widows their **prey** and robbing the fatherless.
10: 6 against a people who anger me, to seize **loot** and snatch plunder,
33: 4 Your **plunder**, O nations, is harvested as by young locusts;
33:23 an abundance of **spoils** will be divided and even the lame will
53:12 he will divide the **spoils** with the strong, because he poured out his
Jer 21: 9 are besieging you will live; he will **escape** [+4200] **with** his life.
38: 2 will live. He will **escape** [+4200] **with** his life; he will live.'
39:18 will not fall by the sword but will **escape** [+4200] **with** your life,
45: 5 wherever you go I will let you **escape** [+4200] **with** your life.' "
49:32 camels will become plunder, and their large herds will be **booty**.
50:10 So Babylonia will be **plundered**; all who plunder her will have
Eze 7:21 over as plunder to foreigners and as **loot** to the wicked of the earth,
29:19 *He will* **loot** [+8964] and plunder the land as pay for his army.
38:12 I *will* **plunder** [+8964] and loot and turn my hand against the
38:13 her villages will say to you, "Have you come to **plunder** [+8964]?
38:13 to take away livestock and goods and to seize much **plunder**?" '
Da 11:24 He will distribute plunder, **loot** and wealth among his followers.
Zec 2: 9 [2:13] hand against them so that their slaves will **plunder** them.
14: 1 A day of the LORD is coming when your **plunder** will be divided

8966 שָׁלֵם¹ ***šālēm¹***, v. [118] [→ 5450, 5451, 5454, 5455, 8934, 8935, 8936, 8967, 8968, 8969, 8970, 8971, 8972, 8973, 8974, 8976, 8977, 8979, 8980, 8984, 8985, 8986, 8988; *also used with compo]*

repay [18], fulfill [12], pay [9], make restitution [6], pay back [6], reward [6], at peace [4], must make restitution [+8966] [4], finished [3], made peace [3], repays [3], made a treaty of peace [2], made an end [2], must certainly make restitution [+8966] [2], must pay [+8966] [2], repay in full [+8966] [2], repaying [2], restore [2], accomplish [1], be fulfilled [1], be repaid [1], bring punishment [1], carries out [1], committed [1], completed [1], end [1], fulfilled obligations [1], fulfilled [1], fulfilling [1], fulfills [1], is rewarded [1], keep [1], make good [1], make pay [1], make peace [1], makes live at peace [1], offer [1], paid back [1], pay back in full [1], pay for the loss [1], pays back [1], peaceful [1], present [1], receive due [1], repaid [1], restitution [1], returns [1], unscathed [1]

Ge 44: 4 [D] say to them, 'Why *have you* **repaid** good with evil?
Ex 21:34 [D] the owner of the pit *must* **pay for the loss**; he must pay its
21:36 [D] the owner **must pay** [+8966], animal for animal,
21:36 [D] the owner **must pay** [+8966], animal for animal,
22: 1 [21:37] [D] *he must* **pay back** five head of cattle for the ox
22: 3 [22:2] [D] "A thief **must certainly make restitution** [+8966],
22: 3 [22:2] [D] "A thief **must certainly make restitution** [+8966],
22: 4 [22:3] [D] or donkey or sheep—*he must* **pay back** double.
22: 5 [22:4] [D] *he must* **make restitution** *from* the best of his own
22: 6 [22:5] [D] who started the fire **must make restitution** [+8966].
22: 6 [22:5] [D] who started the fire **must make restitution** [+8966].
22: 7 [22:6] [D] the thief, if he is caught, *must* **pay back** double.
22: 9 [22:8] [D] declare guilty *must* **pay back** double to his neighbor.
22:11 [22:10] [D] is to accept this, and no **restitution** *is required*.
22:12 [22:11] [D] *he must* **make restitution** to the owner.
22:13 [22:12] [D] *he will* not *be required to* **pay** *for* the torn animal.
22:14 [22:13] [D] is not present, *he* **must make restitution** [+8966].
22:14 [22:13] [D] is not present, *he* **must make restitution** [+8966].
22:15 [22:14] [D] with the animal, the borrower *will* not *have to* **pay**.
Lev 5:16 [D] *He must* **make restitution** *for* what he has failed to do in
6: 5 [5:24] [D] *He must* **make restitution** in full, add a fifth of the
24:18 [D] takes the life of someone's animal *must* **make restitution**—
24:21 [D] Whoever kills an animal *must* **make restitution**, but
Dt 7:10 [D] those who hate him *he will* **repay** to their face by
7:10 [D] he will not be slow *to* **repay** to their face those who hate
20:12 [G] If *they* refuse *to* **make peace** and they engage you in battle,
23:21 [23:22] [D] to the LORD your God, do not be slow to **pay** it,
32:35 [D] It is mine to avenge; *I will* **repay**. In due time their foot will
32:41 [D] vengeance on my adversaries and **repay** those who hate me.
Jos 10: 1 [G] that the people of Gibeon *had* **made a treaty of peace** with
10: 4 [G] "because *it has* **made peace** with Joshua and the Israelites."
11:19 [G] not one city **made a treaty of peace** with the Israelites,
Jdg 1: 7 [D] Now God *has* **paid** me **back** *for* what I did to them." They
Ru 2:12 [D] *May* the LORD **repay** you *for* what you have done. May
1Sa 24:19 [24:20] [D] *May* the LORD **reward** you well for the way you
2Sa 3:39 [D] *May* the LORD **repay** the evildoer according to his evil
10:19 [G] *they* **made peace** with the Israelites and became subject to
12: 6 [D] *He must* **pay** *for* that lamb four times over, because he did
15: 7 [D] me go to Hebron and **fulfill** a vow I made to the LORD.
20:19 [B] We are the **peaceful** and faithful in Israel. You are trying to
1Ki 7:51 [A] had done for the temple of the LORD *was* **finished**,
9:25 [D] along with them, and so **fulfilled** the temple **obligations**.
22:44 [22:45] [G] Jehoshaphat *was* also **at peace** with the king of
2Ki 4: 7 [D] of God, and he said, "Go, sell the oil and **pay** your debts.
9:26 [D] and *I will* surely **make** you **pay** *for* it on this plot of ground,
1Ch 19:19 [G] *they* **made peace** with David and became subject to him.
2Ch 5: 1 [A] had done for the temple of the LORD *was* **finished**,
8:16 [A] its completion. So the temple of the LORD *was* **finished**.
Ne 6:15 [A] So the wall *was* **completed** on the twenty-fifth of Elul,
Job 5:23 [H] of the field, and the wild animals *will be* **at peace** with you.
8: 6 [D] on your behalf and **restore** you *to* your rightful place.
9: 4 [A] is vast. Who has resisted him and *come out* **unscathed**?
21:19 [D] *Let him* **repay** the man himself, so that he will know it!
21:31 [D] conduct to his face? Who **repays** him for what he has done?
22:21 [A] "Submit to God and *be* **at peace** with him; in this way
22:27 [D] to him, and he will hear you, and *you will* **fulfill** your vows.
23:14 [G] *He* **carries out** his decree against me, and many such plans
34:11 [D] *He* **repays** a man *for* what he has done; he brings upon him
34:33 [D] *Should* God then **reward** you on your terms, when you
41:11 [41:3] [D] Who has a claim against me that *I must* **pay**?
Ps 7: 4 [7:5] [A] if I have done evil to *him who is* **at peace** *with* me
22:25 [22:26] [D] before those who fear you *will I* **fulfill** my vows.
31:23 [31:24] [D] the faithful, but the proud *he* **pays back** in full.
35:12 [D] *They* **repay** me evil for good and leave my soul forlorn.
37:21 [D] The wicked borrow and *do* not **repay**, but the righteous give
38:20 [38:21] [D] *Those who* **repay** my good with evil slander me
41:10 [41:11] [D] mercy on me; raise me up, that *I may* **repay** them.
50:14 [D] thank offerings to God, **fulfill** your vows to the Most High,
56:12 [56:13] [D] O God; *I will* **present** my thank offerings to you.
61: 8 [61:9] [D] to your name and **fulfill** my vows day after day.
62:12 [62:13] [D] Surely you *will* **reward** each person according to
65: 1 [65:2] [E] O God, in Zion; to you our vows *will* **be fulfilled**.
66:13 [D] temple with burnt offerings and **fulfill** my vows to you—

Ps 76: 11 [76:12] [D] Make vows to the LORD your God and **fulfill**
116: 14 [D] *I will* **fulfill** my vows to the LORD in the presence of all his
116: 18 [D] *I will* **fulfill** my vows to the LORD in the presence of all his
137: 8 [D] happy is *he* who **repays** you *for* what you have done to us—
Pr 6: 31 [D] Yet if he is caught, *he must* **pay** sevenfold, though it costs
7: 14 [D] fellowship offerings at home; today *I* **fulfilled** my vows.
11: 31 [E] If the righteous **receive** *their* **due** on earth, how much more
13: 13 [E] will pay for it, but he who respects a command **is rewarded**.
13: 21 [D] the sinner, but prosperity *is the* **reward** *of* the righteous.
16: 7 [G] *he* **makes** even his enemies **live at peace** with him.
19: 17 [D] the LORD, and *he will* **reward** him *for* what he has done.
20: 22 [D] Do not say, "*I'll* **pay** you **back** *for* this wrong!" Wait for the
22: 27 [D] if you lack the means to **pay**, your very bed will be snatched
25: 22 [D] burning coals on his head, and the LORD *will* **reward** you.
Ecc 5: 4 [5:3] [D] you make a vow to God, do not delay in **fulfilling** it.
5: 4 [5:3] [D] He has no pleasure in fools; **fulfill** your vow.
5: 5 [5:4] [D] better not to vow than to make a vow and not **fulfill** it.
Isa 19: 21 [D] they will make vows to the LORD and **keep** them.
38: 12 [G] off from the loom; day and night *you* **made an end** *of* me.
38: 13 [G] broke all my bones; day and night *you* **made an end** *of* me.
42: 19 [E] Who is blind like the *one* **committed** to me, blind like the
44: 26 [G] of his servants and **fulfills** the predictions of his messengers,
44: 28 [G] 'He is my shepherd and *will* **accomplish** all that I please;
57: 18 [D] I will heal him; I will guide him and **restore** comfort to him,
59: 18 [D] so *will he* **repay** wrath to his enemies and retribution to his
59: 18 [D] retribution to his foes; *he will* **repay** the islands their due.
60: 20 [A] be your everlasting light, and your days of sorrow *will* **end**.
65: 6 [D] I will not keep silent but *will* **pay back in full**; I will pay it
65: 6 [D] but will pay back in full; *I will* **pay** it **back** into their laps—
66: 6 [D] It is the sound of the LORD **repaying** his enemies all they
Jer 16: 18 [D] *I will* **repay** them double *for* their wickedness and their sin,
18: 20 [E] *Should* good **be repaid** with evil? Yet they have dug a pit for
25: 14 [D] *I will* **repay** them according to their deeds and the work of
32: 18 [D] **bring** *the* **punishment** *for* the fathers' sins into the laps of
50: 29 [D] **Repay** her for her deeds; do to her as she has done.
51: 6 [D] the LORD's vengeance; he *will* **pay** her what she deserves.
51: 24 [D] eyes *I will* **repay** Babylon and all who live in Babylonia *for*
51: 56 [D] is a God of retribution; *he will* **repay** [+8966] **in full**.
51: 56 [D] is a God of retribution; *he will* **repay in full** [+8966].
Eze 33: 15 [D] **returns** what he has stolen, follows the decrees that give life,
Hos 14: 2 [14:3] [D] us graciously, that *we may* **offer** the fruit of our lips.
Joel 2: 25 [D] "*I will* **repay** you *for* the years the locusts have eaten—
3: 4 [4:4] [D] *Are* you **repaying** me *for* something I have done? If
Jnh 2: 9 [2:10] [D] to you. What I have vowed *I will* **make good**.
Na 1: 15 [2:1] [D] your festivals, O Judah, and **fulfill** your vows.

8967 שְׁלָם ***šᵉlām***, n.m. Not used in NIV/BHS [→ 1420; cf. 8966; Ar 10720]

8968 שֶׁלֶם ***šelem***, n.[m.]. [87] [√ 8966]

fellowship [34], fellowship offerings [32], fellowship offering [20], it[s] [+2285] [1]

Ex 20: 24 and sacrifice on it your burnt offerings and **fellowship offerings**,
24: 5 and sacrificed young bulls as **fellowship** offerings to the LORD.
29: 28 are to make to the LORD from their **fellowship** offerings.
32: 6 and sacrificed burnt offerings and presented **fellowship offerings**.
Lev 3: 1 " 'If someone's offering is a **fellowship** offering, and he offers an
3: 3 From the **fellowship** offering he is to bring a sacrifice made to the
3: 6 " 'If he offers an animal from the flock as a **fellowship** offering to
3: 9 From the **fellowship** offering he is to bring a sacrifice made to the
4: 10 the fat is removed from the ox sacrificed as a **fellowship offering**.
4: 26 the fat on the altar as he burned the fat of the **fellowship** offering.
4: 31 all the fat, just as the fat is removed from the **fellowship** offering,
4: 35 just as the fat is removed from the lamb of the **fellowship** offering,
6: 12 [6:5] on the fire and burn the fat of the **fellowship offerings** on it.
7: 11 " 'These are the regulations for the **fellowship** offering a person
7: 13 Along with his **fellowship** offering of thanksgiving he is to present
7: 14 to the priest who sprinkles the blood of the **fellowship offerings**.
7: 15 The meat of his **fellowship** offering of thanksgiving must be eaten
7: 18 If any meat of the **fellowship** offering is eaten on the third day,
7: 20 if anyone who is unclean eats any meat of the **fellowship** offering
7: 21 eats any of the meat of the **fellowship** offering belonging to the
7: 29 'Anyone who brings a **fellowship** offering to the LORD is to
7: 29 is to bring part of **it**[s] [+2285] as his sacrifice to the LORD.
7: 32 You are to give the right thigh of your **fellowship** offerings to the
7: 33 the fat of the **fellowship offering** shall have the right thigh as his
7: 34 From the **fellowship** offerings of the Israelites, I have taken the
7: 37 guilt offering, the ordination offering and the **fellowship** offering,
9: 4 and a ram for a **fellowship offering** to sacrifice before the LORD,
9: 18 the ox and the ram as the **fellowship** offering for the people.
9: 22 the burnt offering and the **fellowship offering**, he stepped down.
10: 14 your children as your share of the Israelites' **fellowship** offerings.
17: 5 to the Tent of Meeting and sacrifice them as **fellowship** offerings.
19: 5 " 'When you sacrifice a **fellowship** offering to the LORD,
22: 21 or flock a **fellowship** offering to the LORD to fulfill a special
23: 19 and two lambs, each a year old, for a **fellowship** offering.
Nu 6: 14 for a sin offering, a ram without defect for a **fellowship offering**,
6: 17 and is to sacrifice the ram as a **fellowship** offering to the LORD,
6: 18 it in the fire that is under the sacrifice of the **fellowship offering**.
7: 17 male lambs a year old, to be sacrificed as a **fellowship offering**.
7: 23 male lambs a year old, to be sacrificed as a **fellowship offering**.
7: 29 male lambs a year old, to be sacrificed as a **fellowship offering**.
7: 35 male lambs a year old, to be sacrificed as a **fellowship offering**.
7: 41 male lambs a year old, to be sacrificed as a **fellowship offering**.
7: 47 male lambs a year old, to be sacrificed as a **fellowship offering**.
7: 53 male lambs a year old, to be sacrificed as a **fellowship offering**.
7: 59 male lambs a year old, to be sacrificed as a **fellowship offering**.
7: 65 male lambs a year old, to be sacrificed as a **fellowship offering**.
7: 71 male lambs a year old, to be sacrificed as a **fellowship offering**.
7: 77 male lambs a year old, to be sacrificed as a **fellowship offering**.
7: 83 male lambs a year old, to be sacrificed as a **fellowship offering**.
7: 88 the sacrifice of the **fellowship offering** came to twenty-four oxen,
10: 10 the trumpets over your burnt offerings and **fellowship** offerings,
15: 8 for a special vow or a **fellowship offering** to the LORD,
29: 39 grain offerings, drink offerings and **fellowship offerings**.' "
Dt 27: 7 Sacrifice **fellowship offerings** there, eating them and rejoicing in
Jos 8: 31 to the LORD burnt offerings and sacrificed **fellowship offerings**.
22: 23 and grain offerings, or to sacrifice **fellowship** offerings on it,
22: 27 with our burnt offerings, sacrifices and **fellowship offerings**.
Jdg 20: 26 presented burnt offerings and **fellowship offerings** to the LORD.
21: 4 an altar and presented burnt offerings and **fellowship offerings**.
1Sa 10: 8 down to you to sacrifice burnt offerings and **fellowship** offerings,
11: 15 There they sacrificed **fellowship** offerings before the LORD,
13: 9 "Bring me the burnt offering and the **fellowship offerings**."
2Sa 6: 17 burnt offerings and **fellowship offerings** before the LORD.
6: 18 finished sacrificing the burnt offerings and **fellowship offerings**,
24: 25 and sacrificed burnt offerings and **fellowship offerings**.
1Ki 3: 15 and sacrificed burnt offerings and **fellowship offerings**.
8: 63 Solomon offered a sacrifice of **fellowship** offerings to the LORD:
8: 64 grain offerings and the fat of the **fellowship offerings**,
8: 64 the grain offerings and the fat of the **fellowship offerings**.
9: 25 and **fellowship offerings** on the altar he had built for the LORD,
2Ki 16: 13 and sprinkled the blood of his **fellowship offerings** on the altar.
1Ch 16: 1 presented burnt offerings and **fellowship offerings** before God.
16: 2 finished sacrificing the burnt offerings and **fellowship offerings**,
21: 26 and sacrificed burnt offerings and **fellowship offerings**.
2Ch 7: 7 he offered burnt offerings and the fat of the **fellowship offerings**,
29: 35 together with the fat of the **fellowship offerings** and the drink
30: 22 and offered **fellowship** offerings and praised the LORD,
31: 2 to offer burnt offerings and **fellowship offerings**, to minister,
33: 16 and sacrificed **fellowship** offerings and thank offerings on it,
Pr 7: 14 "I have **fellowship** offerings at home; today I fulfilled my vows.
Eze 43: 27 present your burnt offerings and **fellowship offerings** on the altar.
45: 15 and **fellowship offerings** to make atonement for the people,
45: 17 **fellowship offerings** to make atonement for the house of Israel.
46: 2 are to sacrifice his burnt offering and his **fellowship offerings**.
46: 12 whether a burnt offering or **fellowship offerings**—the gate facing
46: 12 or his **fellowship offerings** as he does on the Sabbath day.
Am 5: 22 Though you bring choice **fellowship offerings**, I will have no

8969 ²שָׁלֵם ***šālēm²***, a. [27] [√ 8966; Ar 10719]

fully committed [4], accurate [2], fully devoted [2], whole [2], wholehearted devotion [+4213] [2], wholehearted devotion [+4222] [2], wholeheartedly [+928+4222] [2], *untranslated* [1], allies [1], dressed [1], fieldstones [+74] [1], friendly [1], full measure [1], fully determined [+928+4222] [1], richly [1], safely [1], uncut [1], wholeheartedly [+928+4213] [1]

Ge 15: 16 for the sin of the Amorites has not yet reached its **full measure**."
33: 18 he arrived **safely** at the city of Shechem in Canaan and camped
34: 21 "These men are **friendly** toward us," they said. "Let them live in
Dt 25: 15 You must have **accurate** and honest weights and measures,
25: 15 **[RPH]** so that you may live long in the land the LORD your
27: 6 Build the altar of the LORD your God with **fieldstones** [+74]
Jos 8: 31 an altar of **uncut** stones, on which no iron tool had been used.
Ru 2: 12 May you be **richly** rewarded by the LORD, the God of Israel,
1Ki 6: 7 only blocks **dressed** *at* the quarry were used, and no hammer,
8: 61 But your hearts must be **fully committed** to the LORD our God,
11: 4 and his heart was not **fully devoted** to the LORD his God,
15: 3 his heart was not **fully devoted** to the LORD his God, as the heart
15: 14 Asa's heart was **fully committed** to the LORD all his life.
2Ki 20: 3 before you faithfully and with **wholehearted devotion** [+4222]
1Ch 12: 38 [12:39] They came to Hebron **fully determined** [+928+4222] to

1Ch 28: 9 serve him with **wholehearted devotion** [+4213] and with a willing
29: 9 had given freely and **wholeheartedly** [+928+4213] to the LORD.
29: 19 give my son Solomon the **wholehearted devotion** [+4222] to keep
2Ch 15: 17 Asa's heart was **fully committed** ⌞to the LORD⌟ all his life.
16: 9 earth to strengthen those whose hearts are **fully committed** to him.
19: 9 "You must serve faithfully and **wholeheartedly** [+928+4222] in
25: 2 in the eyes of the LORD, but not **wholeheartedly** [+928+4222].
Pr 11: 1 abhors dishonest scales, but **accurate** weights are his delight.
Isa 38: 3 before you faithfully and with **wholehearted devotion** [+4213]
Am 1: 6 Because she took captive **whole** communities and sold them to
1: 9 Because she sold **whole** communities of captives to Edom,
Na 1: 12 "Although *they have* **allies** and are numerous, they will be cut off

8970 [3]שָׁלֵם *šālēm*[3], n.pr.loc. [2] [√ 8966]

Salem [2]

Ge 14: 18 Then Melchizedek king of **Salem** brought out bread and wine.
Ps 76: 2 [76:3] His tent is in **Salem**, his dwelling place in Zion.

8971 [4]שָׁלֵם *šālēm*[4], v.den. Not used in NIV/BHS [√ 8966]

8972 [1]שִׁלֵּם *šillēm*[1], n.pr.loc. Not used in NIV/BHS [√ 8966]

8973 [2]שִׁלֵּם *šillēm*[2], n.pr.m. [2 / 3] [→ 8980; cf. 8966]

Shillem [3]

Ge 46: 24 The sons of Naphtali: Jahziel, Guni, Jezer and **Shillem**.
Nu 26: 49 the Jezerite clan; through **Shillem**, the Shillemite clan.
1Ch 7: 13 Jahziel, Guni, Jezer and **Shillem**—[BHS 8935] the descendants of

8974 שִׁלֻּמָה *sillumâ*, n.f. [1] [√ 8966]

punishment [1]

Ps 91: 8 observe with your eyes and see the **punishment** *of* the wicked.

8975 שַׁלָּמָה *šallāmâ*, rel.+pp.+p.indef. Not used in NIV/BHS [√ 8611 + 4200 + 4537]

8976 שְׁלֹמֹה *šᵉlōmōh*, n.pr.m. [293] [√ 8934; cf. 8966]

Solomon [235], Solomon's [26], he[s] [12], Solomon's [+4200] [7], him[s] [6], *untranslated* [2], his[s] [+4200] [2], his[s] [2], Solomon's [+4200+8611] [1]

2Sa 5: 14 children born to him there: Shammua, Shobab, Nathan, **Solomon**,
12: 24 with her. She gave birth to a son, and they named him **Solomon**.
1Ki 1: 10 or Benaiah or the special guard or his brother **Solomon**.
1: 11 Nathan asked Bathsheba, **Solomon's** mother, "Have you not heard
1: 12 how you can save your own life and the life of your son **Solomon**.
1: 13 "Surely **Solomon** your son shall be king after me, and he will sit
1: 17 '**Solomon** your son shall be king after me, and he will sit on my
1: 19 of the army, but he has not invited **Solomon** your servant.
1: 21 his fathers, I and my son **Solomon** will be treated as criminals."
1: 26 son of Jehoiada, and your servant **Solomon** he did not invite.
1: 30 **Solomon** your son shall be king after me, and he will sit on my
1: 33 set **Solomon** my son on my own mule and take him down to
1: 34 Blow the trumpet and shout, 'Long live King **Solomon**!'
1: 37 so may he be with **Solomon** to make his throne even greater than
1: 38 put **Solomon** on King David's mule and escorted him to Gihon.
1: 39 took the horn of oil from the sacred tent and anointed **Solomon**.
1: 39 and all the people shouted, "Long live King **Solomon**!"
1: 43 "Our lord King David has made **Solomon** king.
1: 46 Moreover, **Solomon** has taken his seat on the royal throne.
1: 47 'May your God make **Solomon's** name more famous than yours
1: 50 in fear of **Solomon**, went and took hold of the horns of the altar.
1: 51 Then **Solomon** was told, "Adonijah is afraid of King Solomon
1: 51 "Adonijah is afraid of King **Solomon** and is clinging to the horns
1: 51 'Let King **Solomon** swear to me today that he will not put his
1: 52 **Solomon** replied, "If he shows himself to be a worthy man,
1: 53 King **Solomon** sent men, and they brought him down from the
1: 53 Adonijah came and bowed down to King **Solomon**, and Solomon
1: 53 down to King Solomon, and **Solomon** said, "Go to your home."
2: 1 drew near for David to die, he gave a charge to **Solomon** his son.
2: 12 So **Solomon** sat on the throne of his father David, and his rule was
2: 13 the son of Haggith, went to Bathsheba, **Solomon's** mother.
2: 17 So he continued, "Please ask King **Solomon**—he will not refuse
2: 19 When Bathsheba went to King **Solomon** to speak to him for
2: 22 King **Solomon** answered his mother, "Why do you request
2: 23 King **Solomon** swore by the LORD: "May God deal with me,
2: 25 So King **Solomon** gave orders to Benaiah son of Jehoiada,
2: 27 So **Solomon** removed Abiathar from the priesthood of the LORD,
2: 29 King **Solomon** was told that Joab had fled to the tent of the
2: 29 **Solomon** ordered Benaiah son of Jehoiada, "Go, strike him down!"
2: 41 When **Solomon** was told that Shimei had gone from Jerusalem to
2: 45 King **Solomon** will be blessed, and David's throne will remain
2: 46 The kingdom was now firmly established in **Solomon's** hands.
3: 1 **Solomon** made an alliance with Pharaoh king of Egypt
3: 3 **Solomon** showed his love for the LORD by walking according to
3: 4 and **Solomon** offered a thousand burnt offerings on that altar.
3: 5 At Gibeon the LORD appeared to **Solomon** during the night in a
3: 6 **Solomon** answered, "You have shown great kindness to your
3: 10 The Lord was pleased that **Solomon** had asked for this.
3: 15 Then **Solomon** awoke—and he realized it had been a dream.
4: 1 So King **Solomon** ruled over all Israel.
4: 7 **Solomon** also had twelve district governors over all Israel,
4: 11 in Naphoth Dor (he was married to Taphath daughter of **Solomon**);
4: 15 in Naphtali (he had married Basemath daughter of **Solomon**);
4: 21 [5:1] **Solomon** ruled over all the kingdoms from the River to the
4: 21 [5:1] brought tribute and were **Solomon's** subjects all his life.
4: 22 [5:2] **Solomon's** daily provisions were thirty cors of fine flour
4: 25 [5:5] During **Solomon's** lifetime Judah and Israel, from Dan to
4: 26 [5:6] **Solomon** had four thousand stalls for chariot horses,
4: 27 [5:7] supplied provisions for King **Solomon** and all who came to
4: 27 [5:7] King Solomon and all who came to the king's **[RPH]** table.
4: 29 [5:9] God gave **Solomon** wisdom and very great insight, and a
4: 30 [5:10] **Solomon's** wisdom was greater than the wisdom of all the
4: 34 [5:14] Men of all nations came to listen to **Solomon's** wisdom,
5: 1 [5:15] he sent his envoys to **Solomon**, because he had always
5: 2 [5:16] **Solomon** sent back this message to Hiram:
5: 7 [5:21] When Hiram heard **Solomon's** message, he was greatly
5: 8 [5:22] So Hiram sent word to **Solomon**: "I have received the
5: 10 [5:24] In this way Hiram kept **Solomon** supplied with all the
5: 11 [5:25] **Solomon** gave Hiram twenty thousand cors of wheat as
5: 11 [5:25] **Solomon** continued to do this for Hiram year after year.
5: 12 [5:26] The LORD gave **Solomon** wisdom, just as he had
5: 12 [5:26] were peaceful relations between Hiram and **Solomon**,
5: 13 [5:27] King **Solomon** conscripted laborers from all Israel—thirty
5: 15 [5:29] **Solomon** had seventy thousand carriers and eighty
5: 16 [5:30] as well as thirty-three hundred foremen **[RPH]** who
5: 18 [5:32] The craftsmen of **Solomon** and Hiram and the men of
6: 1 in the fourth year of **Solomon's** reign over Israel, in the month of
6: 2 The temple that King **Solomon** built for the LORD was sixty
6: 11 The word of the LORD came to **Solomon**:
6: 14 So **Solomon** built the temple and completed it.
6: 21 **Solomon** covered the inside of the temple with pure gold,
7: 1 It took **Solomon** thirteen years, however, to complete the
7: 8 **Solomon** also made a palace like this hall for Pharaoh's daughter,
7: 13 King **Solomon** sent to Tyre and brought Huram,
7: 14 He came to King **Solomon** and did all the work assigned to him.
7: 40 he had undertaken for King **Solomon** in the temple of the LORD:
7: 45 All these objects that Huram made for King **Solomon** for the
7: 47 **Solomon** left all these things unweighed, because there were
7: 48 **Solomon** also made all the furnishings that were in the LORD's
7: 51 When all the work King **Solomon** had done for the temple of the
7: 51 **he**[s] brought in the things his father David had dedicated—
8: 1 King **Solomon** summoned into his presence at Jerusalem the elders
8: 1 King Solomon summoned into **his**[s] presence at Jerusalem the
8: 2 All the men of Israel came together to King **Solomon** at the time of
8: 5 King **Solomon** and the entire assembly of Israel that had gathered
8: 12 **Solomon** said, "The LORD has said that he would dwell in a dark
8: 22 **Solomon** stood before the altar of the LORD in front of the whole
8: 54 When **Solomon** had finished all these prayers and supplications to
8: 63 **Solomon** offered a sacrifice of fellowship offerings to the LORD:
8: 65 So **Solomon** observed the festival at that time, and all Israel with
9: 1 When **Solomon** had finished building the temple of the LORD
9: 1 and the royal palace, and had achieved all **he**[s] had desired to do,
9: 2 the LORD appeared to **him**[s] a second time, as he had appeared to
9: 10 of twenty years, during which **Solomon** built these two buildings—
9: 11 King **Solomon** gave twenty towns in Galilee to Hiram king of
9: 11 because Hiram had supplied **him**[s] with all the cedar and pine
9: 12 when Hiram went from Tyre to see the towns that **Solomon** had
9: 15 Here is the account of the forced labor King **Solomon** conscripted
9: 16 then gave it as a wedding gift to his daughter, **Solomon's** wife.
9: 17 And **Solomon** rebuilt Gezer.) He built up Lower Beth Horon,
9: 19 as well as all **his**[s] [+4200] store cities and the towns for his
9: 19 whatever **he**[s] desired to build in Jerusalem, in Lebanon
9: 21 these **Solomon** conscripted for his slave labor force, as it is to this
9: 22 But **Solomon** did not make slaves of any of the Israelites;
9: 23 They were also the chief officials in charge of **Solomon's** [+4200]
9: 25 Three times a year **Solomon** sacrificed burnt offerings
9: 26 King **Solomon** also built ships at Ezion Geber, which is near Elath
9: 27 who knew the sea—to serve in the fleet with **Solomon's** men.
9: 28 back 420 talents of gold, which they delivered to King **Solomon**.
10: 1 When the queen of Sheba heard about the fame of **Solomon**
10: 2 she came to **Solomon** and talked with him about all that she had on
10: 3 **Solomon** answered all her questions; nothing was too hard for the
10: 4 When the queen of Sheba saw all the wisdom of **Solomon**
10: 10 brought in as those the queen of Sheba gave to King **Solomon**.
10: 13 King **Solomon** gave the queen of Sheba all she desired and asked

1Ki 10:13 asked for, besides what he had given her out of **his**[s] royal bounty.
10:14 The weight of the gold that **Solomon** received yearly was 666
10:16 King **Solomon** made two hundred large shields of hammered gold;
10:21 All King **Solomon's** goblets were gold, and all the household
10:21 because silver was considered of little value in **Solomon's** days.
10:23 King **Solomon** was greater in riches and wisdom than all the other
10:24 The whole world sought audience with **Solomon** to hear the
10:26 **Solomon** accumulated chariots and horses; he had fourteen
10:28 **Solomon's** [+4200] horses were imported from Egypt and from
11: 1 King **Solomon**, however, loved many foreign women besides
11: 2 after their gods." Nevertheless, **Solomon** held fast to them in love.
11: 4 As **Solomon** grew old, his wives turned his heart after other gods,
11: 5 **He**[s] followed Ashtoreth the goddess of the Sidonians, and Molech
11: 6 So **Solomon** did evil in the eyes of the LORD; he did not follow
11: 7 **Solomon** built a high place for Chemosh the detestable god of
11: 9 The LORD became angry with **Solomon** because his heart had
11:11 So the LORD said to **Solomon**, "Since this is your attitude
11:14 Then the LORD raised up against **Solomon** an adversary,
11:25 Rezon was Israel's adversary as long as **Solomon** lived, adding to
11:26 He was one of **Solomon's** [+4200] officials, an Ephraimite from
11:27 **Solomon** had built the supporting terraces and had filled in the gap
11:28 and when **Solomon** saw how well the young man did his work,
11:31 I am going to tear the kingdom out of **Solomon's** hand and give
11:40 **Solomon** tried to kill Jeroboam, but Jeroboam fled to Egypt,
11:40 to Shishak the king, and stayed there until **Solomon's** death.
11:41 As for the other events of **Solomon's** reign—all he did
11:41 are they not written in the book of the annals of **Solomon**?
11:42 **Solomon** reigned in Jerusalem over all Israel forty years.
11:43 **he**[s] rested with his fathers and was buried in the city of David his
12: 2 where he had fled from King **Solomon**), he returned from Egypt.
12: 6 the elders who had served his father **Solomon** during his lifetime.
12:21 and to regain the kingdom for Rehoboam son of **Solomon**.
12:23 "Say to Rehoboam son of **Solomon** king of Judah, to the whole
14:21 Rehoboam son of **Solomon** was king in Judah. He was forty-one
14:26 took everything, including all the gold shields **Solomon** had made.
2Ki 21: 7 of which the LORD had said to David and to his son **Solomon**,
23:13 the ones **Solomon** king of Israel had built for Ashtoreth the vile
24:13 took away all the gold articles that **Solomon** king of Israel had
25:16 which **Solomon** had made for the temple of the LORD,
1Ch 3: 5 born to him there: Shammua, Shobab, Nathan and **Solomon**.
3:10 **Solomon's** son was Rehoboam, Abijah his son, Asa his son,
6:10 [5:36] served as priest in the temple **Solomon** built in Jerusalem),
6:32 [6:17] until **Solomon** built the temple of the LORD in Jerusalem.
14: 4 children born to him there: Shammua, Shobab, Nathan, **Solomon**,
18: 8 which **Solomon** used to make the bronze Sea, the pillars
22: 5 David said, "My son **Solomon** is young and inexperienced,
22: 6 he called for his son **Solomon** and charged him to build a house for
22: 7 David said to **Solomon**: "My son, I had it in my heart to build a
22: 9 His name will be **Solomon**, and I will grant Israel peace and quiet
22:17 David ordered all the leaders of Israel to help his son **Solomon**.
23: 1 and full of years, he made his son **Solomon** king over Israel.
28: 5 he has chosen my son **Solomon** to sit on the throne of the kingdom
28: 6 '**Solomon** your son is the one who will build my house and my
28: 9 "And you, my son **Solomon**, acknowledge the God of your father,
28:11 David gave his son **Solomon** the plans for the portico of the
28:20 David also said to **Solomon** his son, "Be strong and courageous,
29: 1 "My son **Solomon**, the one whom God has chosen, is young
29:19 give my son **Solomon** the wholehearted devotion to keep your
29:22 they acknowledged **Solomon** son of David as king a second time,
29:23 So **Solomon** sat on the throne of the LORD as king in place of his
29:24 of King David's sons, pledged their submission to King **Solomon**.
29:25 The LORD highly exalted **Solomon** in the sight of all Israel
29:28 wealth and honor. His son **Solomon** succeeded him as king.
2Ch 1: 1 **Solomon** son of David established himself firmly over his
1: 2 **Solomon** spoke to all Israel—to the commanders of thousands
1: 3 **Solomon** and the whole assembly went to the high place at
1: 5 the LORD; so **Solomon** and the assembly inquired of him there.
1: 6 **Solomon** went up to the bronze altar before the LORD in the Tent
1: 7 That night God appeared to **Solomon** and said to him, "Ask for
1: 8 **Solomon** answered God, "You have shown great kindness to
1:11 God said to **Solomon**, "Since this is your heart's desire and you
1:13 Then **Solomon** went to Jerusalem from the high place at Gibeon,
1:14 **Solomon** accumulated chariots and horses; he had fourteen
1:16 **Solomon's** [+4200] horses were imported from Egypt and from
2: 1 [1:18] **Solomon** gave orders to build a temple for the Name of the
2: 2 [2:1] **He**[s] conscripted seventy thousand men as carriers and eighty
2: 3 [2:2] **Solomon** sent this message to Hiram king of Tyre:
2:11 [2:10] Hiram king of Tyre replied by letter to **Solomon**:
2:17 [2:16] **Solomon** took a census of all the aliens who were in Israel,
3: 1 **Solomon** began to build the temple of the LORD in Jerusalem on
3: 3 The foundation **Solomon** laid for building the temple of God was
4:11 So Huram finished the work he had undertaken for King **Solomon**
4:16 All the objects that Huram-Abi made for King **Solomon** for the
4:18 All these things that **Solomon** made amounted to so much that the
4:19 **Solomon** also made all the furnishings that were in God's temple:
5: 1 When all the work **Solomon** had done for the temple of the
5: 1 **he**[s] brought in the things his father David had dedicated—
5: 2 Then **Solomon** summoned to Jerusalem the elders of Israel,
5: 6 King **Solomon** and the entire assembly of Israel that had gathered
6: 1 **Solomon** said, "The LORD has said that he would dwell in a dark
6:13 Now **he**[s] had made a bronze platform, five cubits long, five cubits
7: 1 When **Solomon** finished praying, fire came down from heaven
7: 5 King **Solomon** offered a sacrifice of twenty-two thousand head of
7: 7 **Solomon** consecrated the middle part of the courtyard in front of
7: 7 because the bronze altar **he**[s] had made could not hold the burnt
7: 8 So **Solomon** observed the festival at that time for seven days,
7:10 had done for David and **Solomon** and for his people Israel.
7:11 When **Solomon** had finished the temple of the LORD and the
7:11 had succeeded in carrying out all **he**[s] had in mind to do in the
7:12 the LORD appeared to **him**[s] at night and said: "I have heard your
8: 1 during which **Solomon** built the temple of the LORD and his own
8: 2 **Solomon** rebuilt the villages that Hiram had given him, and settled
8: 2 Solomon rebuilt the villages that Hiram had given **him**[s],
8: 3 **Solomon** then went to Hamath Zobah and captured it.
8: 6 as well as Baalath and all **his**[s] [+4200] store cities, and all the
8: 6 whatever **he**[s] desired to build in Jerusalem, in Lebanon
8: 8 these **Solomon** conscripted for his slave labor force, as it is to this
8: 9 But **Solomon** did not make slaves of the Israelites for his work;
8:10 They were also King **Solomon's** [+4200] chief officials—
8:11 **Solomon** brought Pharaoh's daughter up from the City of David to
8:12 of the portico, **Solomon** sacrificed burnt offerings to the LORD,
8:16 All **Solomon's** work was carried out, from the day the foundation
8:17 **Solomon** went to Ezion Geber and Elath on the coast of Edom.
8:18 These, with **Solomon's** men, sailed to Ophir and brought back four
8:18 and fifty talents of gold, which they delivered to King **Solomon**.
9: 1 When the queen of Sheba heard of **Solomon's** fame, she came to
9: 1 she came to Jerusalem to test **him**[s] with hard questions.
9: 1 she came to **Solomon** and talked with him about all she had on her
9: 2 **Solomon** answered all her questions; nothing was too hard for him
9: 2 all her questions; nothing was too hard for **him**[s] to explain to her.
9: 3 When the queen of Sheba saw the wisdom of **Solomon**, as well as
9: 9 such spices as those the queen of Sheba gave to King **Solomon**.
9:10 men of Hiram and the men of **Solomon** brought gold from Ophir;
9:12 King **Solomon** gave the queen of Sheba all she desired and asked
9:13 The weight of the gold that **Solomon** received yearly was 666
9:14 and the governors of the land brought gold and silver to **Solomon**.
9:15 King **Solomon** made two hundred large shields of hammered gold;
9:20 All King **Solomon's** goblets were gold, and all the household
9:20 because silver was considered of little value in **Solomon's** day.
9:22 King **Solomon** was greater in riches and wisdom than all the other
9:23 All the kings of the earth sought audience with **Solomon** to hear
9:25 **Solomon** had four thousand stalls for horses and chariots,
9:28 **Solomon's** [+4200] horses were imported from Egypt and from all
9:29 As for the other events of **Solomon's** reign, from beginning to end,
9:30 **Solomon** reigned in Jerusalem over all Israel forty years.
9:31 **he**[s] rested with his fathers and was buried in the city of David his
10: 2 where he had fled from King **Solomon**), he returned from Egypt.
10: 6 the elders who had served his father **Solomon** during his lifetime.
11: 3 "Say to Rehoboam son of **Solomon** king of Judah and to all the
11:17 of Judah and supported Rehoboam son of **Solomon** three years,
11:17 walking in the ways of David and **Solomon** during this time.
12: 9 He took everything, including the gold shields **Solomon** had made.
13: 6 an official of **Solomon** son of David, rebelled against his master.
13: 7 and opposed Rehoboam son of **Solomon** when he was young
30:26 for since the days of **Solomon** son of David king of Israel there had
33: 7 of which God had said to David and to his son **Solomon**, "In this
35: 3 "Put the sacred ark in the temple that **Solomon** son of David king
35: 4 directions written by David king of Israel and by his son **Solomon**.
Ezr 2:55 The descendants of the servants of **Solomon**: the descendants of
2:58 and the descendants of the servants of **Solomon** 392
Ne 7:57 The descendants of the servants of **Solomon**: the descendants of
7:60 and the descendants of the servants of **Solomon** 392
11: 3 descendants of **Solomon's** servants lived in the towns of Judah,
12:45 according to the commands of David and his son **Solomon**.
13:26 because of marriages like these that **Solomon** king of Israel
Ps 72: T [72:1] Of **Solomon**.
127: T [127:1] A song of ascents. Of **Solomon**.
Pr 1: 1 The proverbs of **Solomon** son of David, king of Israel:
10: 1 The proverbs of **Solomon**: A wise son brings joy to his father,
25: 1 These are more proverbs of **Solomon**, copied by the men of
SS 1: 1 **Solomon's** [+4200] Song of Songs.
1: 5 dark like the tents of Kedar, like the tent curtains of **Solomon**.
3: 7 It is **Solomon's** [+4200+8611] carriage, escorted by sixty warriors,
3: 9 King **Solomon** made for himself the carriage; he made it of wood
3:11 daughters of Zion, and look at King **Solomon** wearing the crown,
8:11 **Solomon** had a vineyard in Baal Hamon; he let out his vineyard to
8:12 the thousand shekels are for you, O **Solomon**, and two hundred are
Jer 52:20 which King **Solomon** had made for the temple of the LORD,

8977 שְׁלֹמוֹת *šᵉlōmôt*, n.pr.m. [4 / 3] [√ 8966]

Shelomoth [3]

1Ch 23: 9 of Shimei: **Shelomoth**, [Q 8984] Haziel and Haran—three in all.
24: 22 the Izharites: **Shelomoth**; from the sons of Shelomoth: Jahath.
24: 22 the Izharites: Shelomoth; from the sons of **Shelomoth**: Jahath.
26: 25 [his son, Zicri his son and **Shelomith** [K; see Q 8984] his son.]
26: 26 Shelomith [BHS *Shelomoth*; NIV 8984] and his relatives

8978 שַׁלְמַי *šalmay*, n.pr.m. [2] [cf. 8518, 9036]

Shalmai [2]

Ezr 2: 46 Hagab, **Shalmai**, [K 9036] Hanan,
Ne 7: 48 Lebana, Hagaba, **Shalmai**,

8979 שְׁלֹמִי *šᵉlōmî*, n.pr.m. [1] [→ 8984, 8985; cf. 8934]

Shelomi [1]

Nu 34: 27 Ahihud son of **Shelomi**, the leader from the tribe of Asher;

8980 שִׁלֵּמִי *šillēmî*, a.g. [1] [√ 8973]

Shillemite [1]

Nu 26: 49 the Jezerite clan; through Shillem, the **Shillemite** clan.

8981 שְׁלֻמִיאֵל *šᵉlumîʾēl*, n.pr.m. [5] [√ 8966 + 446]

Shelumiel [5]

Nu 1: 6 from Simeon, **Shelumiel** son of Zurishaddai;
2: 12 The leader of the people of Simeon is **Shelumiel** son of
7: 36 On the fifth day **Shelumiel** son of Zurishaddai, the leader of the
7: 41 This was the offering of **Shelumiel** son of Zurishaddai.
10: 19 **Shelumiel** son of Zurishaddai was over the division of the tribe of

8982 שֶׁלֶמְיָה *šelemyâ*, n.pr.m. [5] [√ 8966 + 3378]

Shelemiah [5]

Ezr 10: 39 **Shelemiah**, Nathan, Adaiah,
Ne 3: 30 Next to him, Hananiah son of **Shelemiah**, and Hanun, the sixth son
13: 13 I put **Shelemiah** the priest, Zadok the scribe, and a Levite named
Jer 37: 3 sent Jehucal son of **Shelemiah** with the priest Zephaniah son of
37: 13 whose name was Irijah son of **Shelemiah**, the son of Hananiah,

8983 שֶׁלֶמְיָהוּ *šelemyāhû*, n.pr.m. [5] [√ 8966 + 3378]

Shelemiah [5]

1Ch 26: 14 The lot for the East Gate fell to **Shelemiah**. Then lots were cast for
Ezr 10: 41 Azarel, **Shelemiah**, Shemariah,
Jer 36: 14 the son of **Shelemiah**, the son of Cushi, to say to Baruch,
36: 26 of Azriel and **Shelemiah** son of Abdeel to arrest Baruch the scribe
38: 1 son of Mattan, Gedaliah son of Pashhur, Jehucal son of **Shelemiah**,

8984 שְׁלֹמִית *šᵉlōmît¹*, n.pr.m. [5 / 6] [√ 8979; cf. 8966]

Shelomith [6]

1Ch 23: 9 [The sons of Shimei: **Shelomoth**, [Q; see K 8977]]
23: 18 The sons of Izhar: **Shelomith** was the first.
26: 25 Joram his son, Zicri his son and **Shelomith** [K 8977] his son.
26: 26 **Shelomith** [BHS 8977] and his relatives were in charge of all the
26: 28 and all the other dedicated things were in the care of **Shelomith**
2Ch 11: 20 of Absalom, who bore him Abijah, Attai, Ziza and **Shelomith**.
Ezr 8: 10 of Bani, **Shelomith** son of Josiphiah, and with him 160 men;

8985 שְׁלֹמִית *šᵉlōmît²*, n.pr.f. [2] [√ 8979; cf. 8966]

Shelomith [2]

Lev 24: 11 (His mother's name was **Shelomith**, the daughter of Dibri the
1Ch 3: 19 Meshullam and Hananiah. **Shelomith** was their sister.

8986 שַׁלְמַן *šalman*, n.pr.m. [1] [√ 8966]

Shalman [1]

Hos 10: 14 as **Shalman** devastated Beth Arbel on the day of battle,

8987 שַׁלְמַנְאֶסֶר *šalmanʾeser*, n.pr.m. [2]

Shalmaneser [2]

2Ki 17: 3 **Shalmaneser** king of Assyria came up to attack Hoshea, who had
18: 9 **Shalmaneser** king of Assyria marched against Samaria and laid

8988 שַׁלְמֹנִים *šalmōnîm*, n.[m.pl.]. [1] [√ 8966]

gifts [1]

Isa 1: 23 companions of thieves; they all love bribes and chase after **gifts**.

8989 שֵׁלָנִי *šēlānî*, a.g. [1 / 2] [√ 8925]

of Shelah [1], Shelanite [1]

Nu 26: 20 through Shelah, the **Shelanite** clan; through Perez, the Perezite
Ne 11: 5 the son of Zechariah, a descendant **of Shelah**. [BHS 8872]

8990 שָׁלַף *šālap*, v. [25]

swordsmen [+408+2995] [5], draw [4], drawn [4], armed [3], handle [2], *untranslated* [1], drew [1], grow [1], pull out [1], pulls [1], removed [1], took off [1]

Nu 22: 23 [B] LORD standing in the road with a **drawn** sword in his hand,
22: 31 [B] of the LORD standing in the road with his sword **drawn**.
Jos 5: 13 [B] saw a man standing in front of him with a **drawn** sword in
Jdg 3: 22 [A] Ehud *did* not **pull** the sword **out**, and the fat closed in over it.
8: 10 [A] and twenty thousand **swordsmen** [+408+2995] had fallen.
8: 20 [A] Jether *did* not **draw** his sword, because he was only a boy
9: 54 [A] "**Draw** your sword and kill me, so that they can't say,
20: 2 [A] of God, four hundred thousand soldiers **armed** *with* swords.
20: 15 [A] twenty-six thousand **swordsmen** [+408+2995] from their towns
20: 17 [A] mustered four hundred thousand **swordsmen** [+408+2995], all
20: 25 [A] eighteen thousand Israelites, all of them **armed** *with* swords.
20: 35 [A] struck down 25,100 Benjamites, all **armed** *with* swords.
20: 46 [A] twenty-five thousand Benjamite **swordsmen** [+408+2995] fell,
Ru 4: 7 [A] one party **took off** his sandal and gave it to the other.
4: 8 [A] said to Boaz, "Buy it yourself." And *he* **removed** his sandal.
1Sa 17: 51 [A] hold of the Philistine's sword and **drew** it from the scabbard.
31: 4 [A] to his armor-bearer, "**Draw** your sword and run me through,
2Sa 24: 9 [A] thousand able-bodied men *who could* **handle** a sword,
2Ki 3: 26 [A] he took with him seven hundred **swordsmen** [+408+2995] to
1Ch 10: 4 [A] to his armor-bearer, "**Draw** your sword and run me through,
21: 5 [A] one hundred thousand men *who could* **handle** a sword,
21: 5 [A] four hundred and seventy thousand in Judah. **[RPH]**
21: 16 [B] with a **drawn** sword in his hand extended over Jerusalem.
Job 20: 25 [A] *He* **pulls** it out of his back, the gleaming point out of his
Ps 129: 6 [A] be like grass on the roof, which withers before *it can* **grow**;

8991 שֶׁלֶף *šelep*, n.pr.m. [2]

Sheleph [2]

Ge 10: 26 Joktan was the father of Almodad, **Sheleph**, Hazarmaveth, Jerah,
1Ch 1: 20 Joktan was the father of Almodad, **Sheleph**, Hazarmaveth, Jerah,

8992 שָׁלַשׁ *šālaš*, v.den. [9 / 10] [√ 8993]

untranslated [2], did the third time [1], divide into three [1], do a third time [1], the day after tomorrow [1], third [1], three years old [1], three [1], three-year-old [1]

Ge 15: 9 [E] "Bring me a heifer, **[RPH]** a goat and a ram, each three
15: 9 [E] "Bring me a heifer, a goat **[RPH]** and a ram, each three
15: 9 [E] a goat and a ram, each **three years old**, along with a dove
Dt 19: 3 [D] **divide into three** parts the land the LORD your God is
1Sa 1: 24 [E] young as he was, along with a **three-year-old** [BHS 8993] bull,
20: 19 [D] **The day after tomorrow**, toward evening, go to the place
1Ki 18: 34 [D] "**Do** *it* **a third time**," he ordered, and they did it the third
18: 34 [D] it a third time," he ordered, and *they* **did** *it* **the third time**.
Ecc 4: 12 [E] A cord of **three** *strands* is not quickly broken.
Eze 42: 6 [E] The rooms *on the* **third** *floor* had no pillars, as the courts

8993 שָׁלֹשׁ *šālōš*, n.m. & f. [601 / 605] [→ 5456, 8955, 8956, 8957, 8958, 8992, 8994, 8996, 8997, 8998, 8999, 9000, 9001; Ar 10760]

three [282], thirty [83], third [12], thirty-three [+2256+8993] [12], thirteen [+6926] [10], thirteenth [+6925] [8], three-tenths [+6928] [8], twenty-third [+2256+6929] [7], *untranslated* [6], thirty-two [+2256+9109] [6], twenty-three [+2256+6929] [6], 30 [5], 7,337 [+547+2256+4395+8679+8679+8993] [4], three-day [+3427] [4], 32 [+2256+9109] [3], 36,000 [+547+2256+9252] [3], 430 [+752+2256 +4395] [3], 53,400 [+547+752+2256+2256+2822+4395] [3], 603,550 [+547+547+2256+2256+2256+2822+2822+4395+4395+9252] [3], thirteenth [+6926] [3], thirty-five [+2256+2822] [3], thirty-ninth [+2256+9596] [3], thirty-one [+285+2256] [3], thirty-seventh [+2256+8679] [3], 1,335 [+547+2256+2822+4395+8993] [2], 123 [+2256+4395+6929] [2], 130 [+2256+4395] [2], 133 [+2256+2256 +4395+8993] [2], 137 [+2256+2256+4395+8679] [2], 223 [+2256+4395+6929] [2], 3,023 [+547+2256+2256+6929+8993] [2], 3,630 [+547+2256+2256+4395+8993+9252] [2], 3,930 [+547+2256 +4395+8993+9596] [2], 30,500 [+547+2256+2822+4395] [2], 300 [+4395] [2], 32,200 [+547+2256+2256+4395+9109] [2], 320 [+2256+4395+6929] [2], 323 [+2256+4395+6929+8993] [2], 337,500 [+547+547+547+2256+2256+2256+2822+4395+4395+8679+8993] [2], 337,500 [+547+547+547+2256+2256+2822+4395+4395+8679 +8993] [2], 345 [+752+2256+2822+4395] [2], 35,400 [+547+752 +2256+2256+2822+4395] [2], 372 [+2256+4395+8679+9109] [2],

[A] Qal [B] Qal passive [C] Niphal [D] Piel (poel, polel, pilel, pilal, pealal, pilpel) [E] Pual (poal, polal, poalal, pulal, pualal)

390 [+2256+4395+9596] [2], 392 [+2256+4395+9109+9596] [2], 403 [+752+2256+4395] [2], 43,730 [+547+752+2256+2256+2256+4395 +8679+8993] [2], 435 [+752+2256+2822+4395] [2], 59,300 [+547+2256+2256+2822+4395+9596] [2], 736 [+2256+4395+8679 +9252] [2], 973 [+2256+4395+8679+9596] [2], them[s] [+2021] [2], thirteen [+6925] [2], thirty-eight [+2256+9046] [2], thirty-eighth [+2256+9046] [2], thirty-second [+2256+9109] [2], thirty-seven [+2256+8679] [2], thirty-three hundred [+547+2256+4395+8993] [2], 1,365 [+547+2256+2256+2256+2822+4395+9252] [1], 13 [+6925] [1], 138 [+2256+4395+9046] [1], 139 [+2256+4395+9596] [1], 153,600 [+547+547+2256+2256+2822+4395+4395+9252] [1], 2,300 [+547+2256+4395] [1], 2,322 [+547+2256+4395+6929+9109] [1], 2,630 [+547+2256+2256+4395+9252] [1], 22,034 [+547+752 +2256+2256+2256+6929+9109] [1], 22,273 [+547+2256+2256+2256 +4395+6929+8679+9109] [1], 23,000 [+547+2256+6929] [1], 232 [+2256+4395+9109] [1], 273 [+2256+2256+4395+8679] [1], 3,000 [+547] [1], 3,200 [+547+2256+4395] [1], 3,600 [+547+2256+4395 +9252] [1], 3,700 [+547+2256+4395+8679] [1], 300,000 [+547+4395] [1], 307,500 [+547+547+2256+2256+2822+4395+4395+8679] [1], 318 [+2256+4395+6925+9046] [1], 32,000 [+547+2256+9109] [1], 32,500 [+547+2256+2256+2822+4395+9109] [1], 324 [+752+2256 +4395+6929] [1], 328 [+2256+4395+6929+9046] [1], 34 [+752+2256] [1], 35 [+2256+2822] [1], 350 [+2256+2822+4395] [1], 365 [+2256+2256+2822+4395+9252] [1], 37,000 [+547+2256+8679] [1], 42,360 [+547+752+2256+4395+8052+9252] [1], 42,360 [+547+752+4395+8052+9252] [1], 45 feet [+564] [1], 450 feet [+564+4395] [1], 530 [+2256+2822+4395] [1], 601,730 [+547+547 +2256+2256+4395+4395+8679+9252] [1], 623 [+2256+4395+6929 +9252] [1], 64,300 [+547+752+2256+2256+4395+9252] [1], 730 [+2256+4395+8679] [1], 743 [+752+2256+2256+4395+8679] [1], 743 [+752+2256+4395+8679] [1], 830 [+2256+4395+9046] [1], 832 [+2256+4395+9046+9109] [1], 930 [+2256+4395+9596] [1], eighty-three [+2256+9046] [1], four and a half feet [+564] [1], people[s] [+9109] [1], thirtieth [1], thirty-fifth [+2256+2822] [1], thirty-first [+285+2256] [1], thirty-six [+2256+9252] [1], thirty-six hundred [+547+2256+4395+9252] [1], thirty-sixth [+2256+9252] [1], this time[s] [+9102] [1], three-pronged [+9094] [1]

Ge 5: 3 When Adam had lived **130** [+2256+4395] years, he had a son in
5: 5 Adam lived **930** [+2256+4395+9596] years, and then he died.
5: 16 Mahalalel lived **830** [+2256+4395+9046] years and had other sons
5: 22 Enoch walked with God **300** [+4395] years and had other sons
5: 23 Enoch lived **365** [+2256+2256+2822+4395+9252] years.
6: 10 Noah had **three** sons: Shem, Ham and Japheth.
6: 15 The ark is to be **450 feet** [+564+4395] long, 75 feet wide and 45
6: 15 ark is to be 450 feet long, 75 feet wide and **45 feet** [+564] high.
7: 13 and Japheth, together with his wife and the wives of his **three** sons,
9: 19 These were the **three** sons of Noah, and from them came the
9: 28 After the flood Noah lived **350** [+2256+2822+4395] years.
11: 12 When Arphaxad had lived **35** [+2256+2822] years, he became the
11: 13 Arphaxad lived **403** [+752+2256+4395] years and had other sons
11: 14 When Shelah had lived **30** years, he became the father of Eber.
11: 15 Shelah lived **403** [+752+2256+4395] years and had other sons
11: 16 When Eber had lived **34** [+752+2256] years, he became the father
11: 17 Eber lived **430** [+752+2256+4395] years and had other sons
11: 18 When Peleg had lived **30** years, he became the father of Reu.
11: 20 When Reu had lived **32** [+2256+9109] years, he became the father
11: 22 When Serug had lived **30** years, he became the father of Nahor.
14: 4 to Kedorlaomer, but in the **thirteenth** [+6926] year they rebelled.
14: 14 he called out the **318** [+2256+4395+6925+9046] trained men born
17: 25 and his son Ishmael was **thirteen** [+6926];
18: 2 Abraham looked up and saw **three** men standing nearby. When he
18: 6 "get **three** seahs of fine flour and knead it and bake some bread."
18: 30 What if only **thirty** can be found there?" He answered, "I will not
18: 30 found there?" He answered, "I will not do it if I find **thirty** there."
25: 17 Ishmael lived a hundred and **thirty-seven** [+2256+8679] years.
29: 2 with **three** flocks of sheep lying near it because the flocks were
29: 34 will become attached to me, because I have borne him **three** sons."
30: 36 Then he put a **three-day** [+3427] journey between himself
32: 15 [32:16] **thirty** female camels with their young, forty cows and ten
38: 24 About **three** months later Judah was told, "Your daughter-in-law
40: 10 and on the vine were **three** branches. As soon as it budded,
40: 12 it means," Joseph said to him. "The **three** branches are three days.
40: 12 it means," Joseph said to him. "The three branches are **three** days.
40: 13 Within **three** days Pharaoh will lift up your head and restore you to
40: 16 "I too had a dream: On my head were **three** baskets of bread.
40: 18 is what it means," Joseph said. "The **three** baskets are three days.
40: 18 is what it means," Joseph said. "The three baskets are **three** days.
40: 19 Within **three** days Pharaoh will lift off your head and hang you on
41: 46 Joseph was **thirty** years old when he entered the service of
42: 17 And he put them all in custody for **three** days.
45: 22 to Benjamin he gave **three** hundred shekels of silver and five sets
46: 15 sons and daughters of his were **thirty-three** [+2256+8993] in all.
46: 15 sons and daughters of his were **thirty-three** [+2256+8993] in all.
47: 9 to Pharaoh, "The years of my pilgrimage are a hundred and **thirty**.

Ex 2: 2 she saw that he was a fine child, she hid him for **three** months.
3: 18 Let us take a **three-day** [+3427] journey into the desert to offer
5: 3 Now let us take a **three-day** [+3427] journey into the desert to
6: 16 Levi lived **137** [+2256+2256+4395+8679] years.
6: 18 Kohath lived **133** [+2256+2256+4395+8993] years.
6: 18 Kohath lived **133** [+2256+2256+4395+8993] years.
6: 20 Amram lived **137** [+2256+2256+4395+8679] years.
7: 7 Moses was eighty years old and Aaron **eighty-three** [+2256+9046]
8: 27 [8:23] We must take a **three-day** [+3427] journey into the desert
10: 22 the sky, and total darkness covered all Egypt for **three** days.
10: 23 No one could see anyone else or leave his place for **three** days.
12: 40 Israelite people lived in Egypt was **430** [+752+2256+4395] years.
12: 41 At the end of the **430** [+752+2256+4395] years, to the very day,
15: 22 For **three** days they traveled in the desert without finding water.
19: 15 Then he said to the people, "Prepare yourselves for the **third** day.
21: 11 If he does not provide her with these **three** *things*, she is to go
21: 32 the owner must pay **thirty** shekels of silver to the master of the
23: 14 "**Three** times a year you are to celebrate a festival to me.
23: 17 "**Three** times a year all the men are to appear before the Sovereign
25: 32 sides of the lampstand—**three** on one side and three on the other.
25: 32 sides of the lampstand—three on one side and **three** on the other.
25: 33 **Three** cups shaped like almond flowers with buds and blossoms
25: 33 and blossoms are to be on one branch, **three** on the next branch,
26: 8 are to be the same size—**thirty** cubits long and four cubits wide.
27: 1 "Build an altar of acacia wood, **three** cubits high; it is to be square,
27: 14 to be on one side of the entrance, with **three** posts and three bases,
27: 14 to be on one side of the entrance, with three posts and **three** bases,
27: 15 long are to be on the other side, with **three** posts and three bases.
27: 15 long are to be on the other side, with three posts and **three** bases.
32: 28 and that day about **three** thousand of the people died.
34: 23 **Three** times a year all your men are to appear before the Sovereign
34: 24 no one will covet your land when you go up **three** times each year
36: 15 were the same size—**thirty** cubits long and four cubits wide.
37: 18 sides of the lampstand—**three** on one side and three on the other.
37: 18 sides of the lampstand—three on one side and **three** on the other.
37: 19 **Three** cups shaped like almond flowers with buds and blossoms
37: 19 **three** on the next branch and the same for all six branches
38: 1 built the altar of burnt offering of acacia wood, **three** cubits high;
38: 14 were on one side of the entrance, with **three** posts and three bases,
38: 14 were on one side of the entrance, with three posts and **three** bases,
38: 15 of the entrance to the courtyard, with **three** posts and three bases.
38: 15 of the entrance to the courtyard, with three posts and **three** bases.
38: 24 the sanctuary was 29 talents and **730** [+2256+4395+8679] shekels,
38: 26 twenty years old or more, a total of **603,550** [+547+547+2256 +2256+2256+2822+2822+4395+4395+9252] men.

Lev 12: 4 Then the woman must wait **thirty-three** [+2256+8993] days to be
12: 4 Then the woman must wait **thirty-three** [+2256+8993] days to be
14: 10 along with **three-tenths** [+6928] of an ephah of fine flour mixed
19: 23 For **three** years you are to consider it forbidden; it must not be
25: 21 in the sixth year that the land will yield enough for **three** years.
27: 4 and if it is a female, set her value at **thirty** shekels.
27: 6 five shekels of silver and that of a female at **three** shekels of silver.

Nu 1: 23 tribe of Simeon was **59,300** [+547+2256+2256+2822+4395+9596].
1: 35 tribe of Manasseh was **32,200** [+547+2256+2256+4395+9109].
1: 37 of Benjamin was **35,400** [+547+752+2256+2256+2822+4395].
1: 43 tribe of Naphtali was **53,400** [+547+752+2256+2256+2822+4395].
1: 46 The total number was **603,550** [+547+547+2256+2256+2256 +2822+2822+4395+4395+9252].
2: 13 division numbers **59,300** [+547+2256+2256+2822+4395+9596].
2: 21 His division numbers **32,200** [+547+2256+2256+4395+9109].
2: 23 His division numbers **35,400** [+547+752+2256+2256+2822+4395].
2: 30 His division numbers **53,400** [+547+752+2256+2256+2822+4395].
2: 32 their divisions, number **603,550** [+547+547+2256+2256+2256 +2822+2822+4395+4395+9252].
3: 43 was **22,273** [+547+2256+2256+2256+4395+6929+8679+9109].
3: 46 To redeem the **273** [+2256+2256+4395+8679] firstborn Israelites
3: 50 **1,365** [+547+2256+2256+2256+2822+4395+9252] shekels,
4: 3 Count all the men from **thirty** to fifty years of age who come to
4: 23 Count all the men from **thirty** to fifty years of age who come to
4: 30 Count all the men from **thirty** to fifty years of age who come to
4: 35 All the men from **thirty** to fifty years of age who came to serve in
4: 39 All the men from **thirty** to fifty years of age who came to serve in
4: 40 clans and families, were **2,630** [+547+2256+2256+4395+9252].
4: 43 All the men from **thirty** to fifty years of age who came to serve in
4: 44 counted by their clans, were **3,200** [+547+2256+4395].
4: 47 All the men from **thirty** to fifty years of age who came to do the
7: 13 was one silver plate weighing a hundred and **thirty** shekels,
7: 19 was one silver plate weighing a hundred and **thirty** shekels,
7: 25 was one silver plate weighing a hundred and **thirty** shekels,
7: 31 was one silver plate weighing a hundred and **thirty** shekels,
7: 37 was one silver plate weighing a hundred and **thirty** shekels,
7: 43 was one silver plate weighing a hundred and **thirty** shekels,
7: 49 was one silver plate weighing a hundred and **thirty** shekels,

Nu 7:55 was one silver plate weighing a hundred and **thirty** shekels,
7:61 was one silver plate weighing a hundred and **thirty** shekels,
7:67 was one silver plate weighing a hundred and **thirty** shekels,
7:73 was one silver plate weighing a hundred and **thirty** shekels,
7:79 was one silver plate weighing a hundred and **thirty** shekels,
7:85 Each silver plate weighed a hundred and **thirty** shekels, and each
10:33 out from the mountain of the LORD and traveled for **three** days.
10:33 before them during those **three** days to find them a place to rest.
12: 4 and Miriam, "Come out to the Tent of Meeting, *all* **three** *of* you."
12: 4 Tent of Meeting, all three of you." So the **three** *of* them came out.
15: 9 bring with the bull a grain offering of **three-tenths** [+6928] of an
20:29 had died, the entire house of Israel mourned for him **thirty** days.
22:28 "What have I done to you to make you beat me these **three** times?"
22:32 asked him, "Why have you beaten your donkey these **three** times?
22:33 The donkey saw me and turned away from me these **three** times.
24:10 to curse my enemies, but you have blessed them these **three** times.
26: 7 were **43,730** [+547+752+2256+2256+2256+4395+8679+8993].
26: 7 were **43,730** [+547+752+2256+2256+2256+4395+8679+8993].
26:25 those numbered were **64,300** [+547+752+2256+2256+4395+9252].
26:37 numbered were **32,500** [+547+2256+2256+2822+4395+9109].
26:47 those numbered were **53,400** [+547+752+2256+2256+2822+4395].
26:51 was **601,730** [+547+547+2256+2256+4395+4395+8679+9252].
26:62 Levites a month old or more numbered **23,000** [+547+2256+6929].
28:12 of **three-tenths** [+6928] of an ephah of fine flour mixed with oil;
28:20 With each bull prepare a grain offering of **three-tenths** [+6928] of
28:28 of **three-tenths** [+6928] of an ephah of fine flour mixed with oil;
29: 3 With the bull prepare a grain offering of **three-tenths** [+6928] of
29: 9 With the bull prepare a grain offering of **three-tenths** [+6928] of
29:13 a burnt offering of **thirteen** [+6925] young bulls, two rams
29:14 With each of the **thirteen** [+6925] bulls prepare a grain offering of
29:14 of **three-tenths** [+6928] of an ephah of fine flour mixed with oil;
31:35 **32,000** [+547+2256+9109] women who had never slept with a man.
31:36 share of those who fought in the battle was: **337,500** [+547+547 +547+2256+2256+2256+2822+4395+4395+8679+8993] sheep,
31:36 share of those who fought in the battle was: **337,500** [+547+547 +547+2256+2256+2256+2822+4395+4395+8679+8993] sheep,
31:38 **36,000** [+547+2256+9252] cattle, of which the tribute for the LORD
31:39 **30,500** [+547+2256+2822+4395] donkeys, of which the tribute for
31:40 of which the tribute for the LORD was **32** [+2256+9109].
31:43 the community's half—was **337,500** [+547+547+547+2256+2256 +2822+4395+4395+8679+8993] sheep,
31:43 the community's half—was **337,500** [+547+547+547+2256+2256 +2822+4395+4395+8679+8993] sheep,
31:44 **36,000** [+547+2256+9252] cattle,
31:45 **30,500** [+547+2256+2822+4395] donkeys
33: 8 and when they had traveled for **three** days in the Desert of Etham,
33:39 Aaron was a hundred and **twenty-three** [+2256+6929] years old
35:14 Give **three** on this side of the Jordan and three in Canaan as cities
35:14 on this side of the Jordan and **three** in Canaan as cities of refuge.
Dt 2:14 **Thirty-eight** [+2256+9046] years passed from the time we left
4:41 Then Moses set aside **three** cities east of the Jordan,
14:28 At the end of every **three** years, bring all the tithes of that year's
16:16 **Three** times a year all your men must appear before the LORD
17: 6 testimony of two or **three** witnesses a man shall be put to death,
19: 2 set aside for yourselves **three** cities centrally located in the land the
19: 7 This is why I command you to set aside for yourselves **three** cities.
19: 9 always in his ways—then you are to set aside **three** more cities.
19: 9 in his ways—then you are to set aside three more cities. **[RPH]**
19:15 must be established by the testimony of two or **three** witnesses.
34: 8 The Israelites grieved for Moses in the plains of Moab **thirty** days,
Jos 1:11 **Three** days from now you will cross the Jordan here to go in
2:16 Hide yourselves there **three** days until they return, and then go on
2:22 they left, they went into the hills and stayed there **three** days,
3: 2 After **three** days the officers went throughout the camp,
7: 3 Send two or **three** thousand men to take it and do not weary all the
7: 4 So about **three** thousand men went up; but they were routed by the
7: 5 who killed about **thirty-six** [+2256+9252] of them. They chased
8: 3 He chose **thirty** thousand of his best fighting men and sent them
9:16 **Three** days after they made the treaty with the Gibeonites,
12:24 the king of Tirzah one **thirty-one** [+285+2256] kings in all.
15:14 From Hebron Caleb drove out the **three** Anakites—Sheshai,
17:11 together with their surrounding settlements (the **third** in the list is
18: 4 Appoint **three** men from each tribe. I will send them out to make a
19: 6 and Sharuhen—**thirteen** [+6926] towns and their villages;
21: 4 were allotted **thirteen** [+6926] towns from the tribes of Judah,
21: 6 The descendants of Gershon were allotted **thirteen** [+6926] towns
21:19 for the priests, the descendants of Aaron, were **thirteen** [+6926],
21:32 and Kartan, together with their pasturelands—**three** towns.
21:33 All the towns of the Gershonite clans were **thirteen** [+6926],
Jdg 1:20 was given to Caleb, who drove from it the **three** sons of Anak.
7: 6 **Three** hundred men lapped with their hands to their mouths.
7: 7 "With the **three** hundred men that lapped I will save you and give
7: 8 the rest of the Israelites to their tents but kept the **three** hundred,
7:16 Dividing the **three** hundred men into three companies, he placed
7:16 Dividing the three hundred men into **three** companies, he placed
7:20 The **three** companies blew the trumpets and smashed the jars.
7:22 When the **three** hundred trumpets sounded, the LORD caused the
8: 4 Gideon and his **three** hundred men, exhausted yet keeping up the
9:22 After Abimelech had governed Israel **three** years,
9:43 divided them into **three** companies and set an ambush in the fields.
10: 2 He led Israel **twenty-three** [+2256+6929] years; then he died, and
10: 4 He had **thirty** sons, who rode thirty donkeys. They controlled
10: 4 He had thirty sons, who rode **thirty** donkeys. They controlled
10: 4 They controlled **thirty** towns in Gilead, which to this day are
11:26 For **three** hundred years Israel occupied Heshbon, Aroer, the
12: 9 He had **thirty** sons and thirty daughters. He gave his daughters
12: 9 He had thirty sons and **thirty** daughters. He gave his daughters
12: 9 for his sons he brought in **thirty** young women as wives from
12:14 He had forty sons and **thirty** grandsons, who rode on seventy
14:11 When he appeared, he was given **thirty** companions.
14:12 I will give you **thirty** linen garments and thirty sets of clothes.
14:12 I will give you thirty linen garments and **thirty** sets of clothes.
14:13 you must give me **thirty** linen garments and thirty sets of clothes."
14:13 you must give me thirty linen garments and **thirty** sets of clothes."
14:14 something sweet." For **three** days they could not give the answer.
14:19 He went down to Ashkelon, struck down **thirty** of their men,
15: 4 So he went out and caught **three** hundred foxes and tied them tail
15:11 **three** thousand men from Judah went down to the cave in the rock
16:15 This is the **third** time you have made a fool of me and haven't told
16:27 on the roof were about **three** thousand men and women watching
19: 4 so he remained with him **three** days, eating and drinking,
20:31 so that about **thirty** men fell in the open field and on the roads—
20:39 had begun to inflict casualties on the men of Israel (about **thirty**),
1Sa 1:24 along with a <u>three-year-old</u> [BHS *three bulls*; NIV 8992] bull,
2:13 priest would come with a **three-pronged** [+9094] fork in his hand.
2:21 she conceived and gave birth to **three** sons and two daughters.
4:10 slaughter was very great; Israel lost **thirty** thousand foot soldiers.
9:20 As for the donkeys you lost **three** days ago, do not worry about
9:22 at the head of those who were invited—about **thirty** in number.
10: 3 **Three** men going up to God at Bethel will meet you there.
10: 3 One will be carrying **three** young goats, another three loaves of
10: 3 another **three** loaves of bread, and another a skin of wine.
11: 8 the men of Israel numbered **three** hundred thousand and the men
11: 8 three hundred thousand and the men of Judah **thirty** thousand.
11:11 The next day Saul separated his men into **three** divisions;
13: 1 Saul was ⌞**thirty**⌟ [BHS-] years old when he became king,
13: 2 Saul chose **three** thousand men from Israel; two thousand were
13: 5 fight Israel, with **three** thousand chariots, six thousand charioteers,
13:17 Raiding parties went out from the Philistine camp in **three**
13:21 a **third** *of* a shekel for sharpening forks and axes and for repointing
17:13 Jesse's **three** oldest sons had followed Saul to the war: The
17:13 **[RPH]** The firstborn was Eliab; the second, Abinadab;
17:14 David was the youngest. The **three** oldest followed Saul,
20:20 I will shoot **three** arrows to the side of it, as though I were
20:41 side ⌞of the stone⌟ and bowed down before Jonathan **three** times,
24: 2 [24:3] So Saul took **three** thousand chosen men from all Israel
25: 2 He had a thousand goats and **three** thousand sheep, which he was
26: 2 with his **three** thousand chosen men of Israel, to search there for
30:12 eaten any food or drunk any water for **three** days and three nights.
30:12 eaten any food or drunk any water for three days and **three** nights.
30:13 My master abandoned me when I became ill **three** days *ago*.
31: 6 So Saul and his **three** sons and his armor-bearer and all his men
31: 8 they found Saul and his **three** sons fallen on Mount Gilboa.
2Sa 2:18 The **three** sons of Zeruiah were there: Joab, Abishai and Asahel.
2:31 David's men had killed **three** hundred and sixty Benjamites who
5: 4 David was **thirty** years old when he became king, and he reigned
5: 5 reigned over all Israel and Judah **thirty-three** [+2256+8993] years.
5: 5 reigned over all Israel and Judah **thirty-three** [+2256+8993] years.
6: 1 brought together out of Israel chosen men, **thirty** thousand in all.
6:11 remained in the house of Obed-Edom the Gittite for **three** months,
13:38 Absalom fled and went to Geshur, he stayed there **three** years.
14:27 **Three** sons and a daughter were born to Absalom. The daughter's
18:14 So he took **three** javelins in his hand and plunged them into
20: 4 "Summon the men of Judah to come to me within **three** days,
21: 1 the reign of David, there was a famine for **three** successive years;
21:16 whose bronze spearhead weighed **three** hundred shekels and who
23: 9 As one of the **three** mighty men, he was with David when they
23:13 **three** of the thirty chief men came down to David at the cave of
23:13 three of the **thirty** chief men came down to David at the cave of
23:16 So the **three** mighty men broke through the Philistine lines,
23:17 not drink it. Such were the exploits of the **three** mighty men.
23:18 [of Joab son of Zeruiah was chief of the **Three**. [Q; see K 8998]]
23:18 He raised his spear against **three** hundred men, whom he killed,
23:18 whom he killed, and so he became as famous as the **Three**.
23:19 Was he not held in greater honor than the **Three**? He became their
23:19 even though he was not included among **them**' [+2021].
23:22 son of Jehoiada; he too was as famous as the **three** mighty men.
23:23 He was held in greater honor than any of the **Thirty**, but he was

2Sa 23:23 than any of the Thirty, but he was not included among the **Three**.
23:24 Among the **Thirty** were: Asahel the brother of Joab, Elhanan son
23:39 and Uriah the Hittite. There were **thirty-seven** [+2256+8679] in all.
24:12 'This is what the LORD says: I am giving you **three** *options*.
24:13 "Shall there come upon you **three** [BHS 8679] years of famine in
24:13 Or **three** months of fleeing from your enemies while they pursue
24:13 Or **three** days of plague in your land? Now then, think it over
1Ki 2:11 years in Hebron and **thirty-three** [+2256+8993] in Jerusalem.
2:11 years in Hebron and **thirty-three** [+2256+8993] in Jerusalem.
2:39 **three** years later, two of Shimei's slaves ran off to Achish son of
4:22 [5:2] Solomon's daily provisions were **thirty** cors of fine flour
4:32 [5:12] He spoke **three** thousand proverbs and his songs numbered
5:13 [5:27] conscripted laborers from all Israel—**thirty** thousand men.
5:16 [5:30] as **thirty-three** [+547+2256+4395+8993] **hundred** foremen
5:16 [5:30] as **thirty-three hundred** [+547+2256+4395+8993] foremen
6:2 for the LORD was sixty cubits long, twenty wide and **thirty** high.
6:36 And he built the inner courtyard of **three** courses of dressed stone
7:1 It took Solomon **thirteen** [+6926] years, however, to complete the
7:2 fifty wide and **thirty** high, with four rows of cedar columns
7:4 Its windows were placed high in sets of **three**, facing each other.
7:4 were placed high in sets of three, facing each other. **[RPH]**
7:5 they were in the front part in sets of **three**, facing each other.
7:6 He made a colonnade fifty cubits long and **thirty** wide. In front of
7:12 The great courtyard was surrounded by a wall of **three** courses of
7:23 five cubits high. It took a line of **thirty** cubits to measure around it.
7:25 **three** facing north, three facing west, three facing south and three
7:25 **three** facing west, three facing south and three facing east.
7:25 three facing west, **three** facing south and three facing east.
7:25 three facing west, three facing south and **three** facing east.
7:27 of bronze; each was four cubits long, four wide and **three** high.
9:25 **Three** times a year Solomon sacrificed burnt offerings
10:17 He also made **three** hundred small shields of hammered gold,
10:17 shields of hammered gold, with **three** minas of gold in each shield.
10:22 Once every **three** years it returned, carrying gold, silver and ivory,
11:3 seven hundred wives of royal birth and **three** hundred concubines,
12:5 "Go away for **three** days and then come back to me."
15:2 he reigned in Jerusalem **three** years. His mother's name was
15:28 Baasha killed Nadab in the **third** year of Asa king of Judah
15:33 In the **third** year of Asa king of Judah, Baasha son of Ahijah
16:23 In the **thirty-first** [+285+2256] year of Asa king of Judah, Omri
16:29 In the **thirty-eighth** [+2256+9046] year of Asa king of Judah,
17:21 he stretched himself out on the boy **three** times and cried to the
20:1 Accompanied by **thirty-two** [+2256+9109] kings with their horses
20:15 of the provincial commanders, **232** [+2256+4395+9109] men.
20:16 the **32** [+2256+9109] kings allied with him were in their tents
22:1 For **three** years there was no war between Aram and Israel.
22:31 had ordered his **thirty-two** [+2256+9109] chariot commanders,
22:42 Jehoshaphat was **thirty-five** [+2256+2822] years old when he
2Ki 2:17 sent fifty men, who searched for **three** days but did not find him.
3:10 "Has the LORD called us **three** kings together only to hand us
3:13 "because it was the LORD who called us **three** kings together to
8:17 He was **thirty-two** [+2256+9109] years old when he became king,
9:32 is on my side? Who?" Two or **three** eunuchs looked down at him.
12:6 [12:7] But by the **twenty-third** [+2256+6929] year of King Joash
13:1 In the **twenty-third** [+2256+6929] year of Joash son of Ahaziah
13:10 In the **thirty-seventh** [+2256+8679] year of Joash king of Judah,
13:18 "Strike the ground." He struck it **three** times and stopped.
13:19 destroyed it. But now you will defeat it only **three** times."
13:25 **Three** times Jehoash defeated him, and so he recovered the
15:8 In the **thirty-eighth** [+2256+9046] year of Azariah king of Judah,
15:13 became king in the **thirty-ninth** [+2256+9596] year of Uzziah
15:17 In the **thirty-ninth** [+2256+9596] year of Azariah king of Judah,
17:5 marched against Samaria and laid siege to it for **three** years.
18:1 In the **third** year of Hoshea son of Elah king of Israel,
18:10 At the end of **three** years the Assyrians took it. So Samaria was
18:14 The king of Assyria exacted from Hezekiah king of Judah **three**
18:14 of Judah three hundred talents of silver and **thirty** talents of gold.
22:1 and he reigned in Jerusalem **thirty-one** [+285+2256] years.
23:31 Jehoahaz was **twenty-three** [+2256+6929] years old when he
23:31 when he became king, and he reigned in Jerusalem **three** months.
24:1 invaded the land, and Jehoiakim became his vassal for **three** years.
24:8 when he became king, and he reigned in Jerusalem **three** months.
25:17 bronze capital on top of one pillar was **four and a half feet** [+564]
25:18 Zephaniah the priest next in rank and the **three** doorkeepers.
25:27 In the **thirty-seventh** [+2256+8679] year of the exile of Jehoiachin
1Ch 2:3 These **three** were born to him by a Canaanite woman, the daughter
2:16 and Abigail. Zeruiah's **three** sons were Abishai, Joab and Asahel.
2:22 who controlled **twenty-three** [+2256+6929] towns in Gilead.
3:4 David reigned in Jerusalem **thirty-three** [+2256+8993] years,
3:4 David reigned in Jerusalem **thirty-three** [+2256+8993] years,
3:23 The sons of Neariah: Elioenai, Hizkiah and Azrikam—**three** in all.
6:60 [6:45] among the Kohathite clans, were **thirteen** [+6926] in all.
6:62 [6:47] were allotted **thirteen** [+6926] towns from the tribes of
7:4 they had **36,000** [+547+2256+9252] men ready for battle, for they
7:6 **Three** sons of Benjamin: Bela, Beker and Jediael.
7:7 **22,034** [+547+752+2256+2256+2256+6929+9109] fighting men.
10:6 So Saul and his **three** sons died, and all his house died together.
11:11 [was chief of the **officers**; [K; see Q 8957] he raised his spear]
11:11 he raised his spear against **three** hundred men, whom he killed in
11:12 Eleazar son of Dodai the Ahohite, one of the **three** mighty men.
11:15 **Three** of the thirty chiefs came down to David to the rock at the
11:15 Three of the **thirty** chiefs came down to David to the rock at the
11:18 So the **Three** broke through the Philistine lines, drew water from
11:19 not drink it. Such were the exploits of the **three** mighty men.
11:20 Abishai the brother of Joab was chief of the **Three**. He raised his
11:20 He raised his spear against **three** hundred men, whom he killed,
11:20 whom he killed, and so he became as famous as the **Three**.
11:21 He was doubly honored above the **Three** and became their
11:21 even though he was not included among **them**[s] [+2021].
11:24 son of Jehoiada; he too was as famous as the **three** mighty men.
11:25 He was held in greater honor than any of the **Thirty**, but he was
11:25 than any of the Thirty, but he was not included among the **Three**.
11:42 who was chief of the Reubenites, and the **thirty** with him,
12:4 and Ishmaiah the Gibeonite, a mighty man among the **Thirty**,
12:4 a mighty man among the Thirty, who was a leader of the **Thirty**;
12:18 [12:19] upon Amasai, chief of the **Thirty**, [Q 8957] and he said:
12:27 [12:28] of Aaron, with **3,700** [+547+2256+4395+8679] men,
12:29 [12:30] **3,000** [+547], most of whom had remained loyal to Saul's
12:34 [12:35] officers, together with **37,000** [+547+2256+8679] men
12:39 [12:40] The men spent **three** days there with David, eating
13:14 with the family of Obed-Edom in his house for **three** months,
15:7 of Gershon, Joel the leader and **130** [+2256+4395] relatives;
19:7 They hired **thirty-two** [+2256+9109] thousand chariots and
21:10 'This is what the LORD says: I am giving you **three** *options*.
21:12 **three** years of famine, three months of being swept away before
21:12 of famine, **three** months of being swept away before your enemies,
21:12 swords overtaking you, or **three** days of the sword of the LORD—
23:3 The Levites **thirty** years old or more were counted, and the total
23:3 the total number of men was **thirty-eight** [+2256+9046] thousand.
23:8 The sons of Ladan: Jehiel the first, Zetham and Joel—**three** in all.
23:9 The sons of Shimei: Shelomoth, Haziel and Haran—**three** in all.
23:23 The sons of Mushi: Mahli, Eder and Jerimoth—**three** in all.
24:13 the **thirteenth** [+6925] to Huppah, the fourteenth to Jeshebeab,
24:18 the **twenty-third** [+2256+6929] to Delaiah and the twenty-fourth
25:5 to exalt him. God gave Heman fourteen sons and **three** daughters.
25:20 the **thirteenth** [+6925] to Shubael, his sons and relatives,
25:30 the **twenty-third** [+2256+6929] to Mahazioth, his sons and
26:11 the fourth. The sons and relatives of Hosah were **13** [+6925] in all.
27:6 This was the Benaiah who was a mighty man among the **Thirty**
27:6 who was a mighty man among the Thirty and was over the **Thirty**.
29:4 **three** thousand talents of gold (gold of Ophir) and seven thousand
29:27 seven in Hebron and **thirty-three** [+2256+8993] in Jerusalem.
29:27 seven in Hebron and **thirty-three** [+2256+8993] in Jerusalem.
2Ch 2:2 [2:1] and **thirty-six** [+547+2256+4395+9252] **hundred** as foremen
2:17 [2:16] his father David had taken; and they were found to be
153,600 [+547+547+2256+2256+2256+2822+4395+4395+9252].
2:18 [2:17] with **3,600** [+547+2256+4395+9252] foremen over them to
3:15 were **thirty-five** [+2256+2822] cubits long, each with a capital on
4:2 five cubits high. It took a line of **thirty** cubits to measure around it.
4:4 **three** facing north, three facing west, three facing south and three
4:4 **three** facing west, three facing south and three facing east.
4:4 three facing west, **three** facing south and three facing east.
4:4 three facing west, three facing south and **three** facing east.
4:5 the rim of a cup, like a lily blossom. It held **three** thousand baths.
6:13 five cubits long, five cubits wide and **three** cubits high,
7:10 On the **twenty-third** [+2256+6929] day of the seventh month he
8:13 by Moses for Sabbaths, New Moons and the **three** annual feasts—
9:16 He also made **three** hundred small shields of hammered gold,
9:16 hammered gold, with **three** hundred bekas of gold in each shield.
9:21 Once every **three** years it returned, carrying gold, silver and ivory,
10:5 Rehoboam answered, "Come back to me in **three** days."
11:17 of Judah and supported Rehoboam son of Solomon **three** years,
11:17 in the ways of David and Solomon during **this time**[s] [+9102].
13:2 he reigned in Jerusalem **three** years. His mother's name was
14:8 [14:7] Asa had an army of **three** hundred thousand men from
14:9 [14:8] against them with a vast army and **three** hundred chariots,
15:19 until the **thirty-fifth** [+2256+2822] year of Asa's reign.
16:1 In the **thirty-sixth** [+2256+9252] year of Asa's reign Baasha king
16:12 In the **thirty-ninth** [+2256+9596] year of his reign Asa was
17:7 In the **third** year of his reign he sent his officials Ben-Hail,
17:14 Adnah the commander, with **300,000** [+547+4395] fighting men;
20:25 There was so much plunder that it took **three** days to collect it.
20:31 He was **thirty-five** [+2256+2822] years old when he became king
21:5 Jehoram was **thirty-two** [+2256+9109] years old when he became
21:20 Jehoram was **thirty-two** [+2256+9109] years old when he became
24:15 and full of years, and he died at the age of a hundred and **thirty**.
25:5 found that there were **three** hundred thousand men ready for
25:13 They killed **three** thousand people and carried off great quantities

2Ch 26:13 army of **307,500** [+547+547+2256+2256+2822+4395+4395+8679]
29:33 amounted to six hundred bulls and **three** thousand sheep and goats.
31:16 they distributed to the males **three** years old or more whose names
34: 1 and he reigned in Jerusalem **thirty-one** [+285+2256] years.
35: 7 all the lay people who were there a total of **thirty** thousand sheep
35: 7 goats for the Passover offerings, and also **three** thousand cattle—
35: 8 twenty-six hundred Passover offerings and **three** hundred cattle.
36: 2 Jehoahaz was **twenty-three** [+2256+6929] years old when he
36: 2 when he became king, and he reigned in Jerusalem **three** months.
36: 9 and he reigned in Jerusalem **three** months and ten days.
Ezr 1: 9 the inventory: gold dishes **30** silver dishes 1,000 silver pans 29
1:10 gold bowls **30** matching silver bowls 410 other articles 1,000
2: 4 of Shephatiah **372** [+2256+4395+8679+9109]
2:11 of Bebai **623** [+2256+4395+6929+9252]
2:17 of Bezai **323** [+2256+4395+6929+8993]
2:17 of Bezai **323** [+2256+4395+6929+8993]
2:19 of Hashum **223** [+2256+4395+6929]
2:21 the men of Bethlehem **123** [+2256+4395+6929]
2:25 Kephirah and Beeroth **743** [+752+2256+2256+4395+8679]
2:28 of Bethel and Ai **223** [+2256+4395+6929]
2:32 of Harim **320** [+2256+4395+6929]
2:34 of Jericho **345** [+752+2256+2822+4395]
2:35 of Senaah **3,630** [+547+2256+2256+4395+8993+9252]
2:35 of Senaah **3,630** [+547+2256+2256+4395+8993+9252]
2:36 (through the family of Jeshua) **973** [+2256+4395+8679+9596]
2:42 Ater, Talmon, Akkub, Hatita and Shobai **139** [+2256+4395+9596]
2:58 the servants of Solomon **392** [+2256+4395+9109+9596]
2:64 whole company numbered **42,360** [+547+752+4395+8052+9252],
2:65 their **7,337** [+547+2256+4395+8679+8679+8993] menservants and
2:65 their **7,337** [+547+2256+4395+8679+8679+8993] menservants and
2:66 They had **736** [+2256+4395+8679+9252] horses, 245 mules,
2:67 **435** [+752+2256+2822+4395] camels and 6,720 donkeys.
8: 5 Shecaniah son of Jahaziel, and with him **300** [+4395] men;
8:15 canal that flows toward Ahava, and we camped there **three** days.
8:32 So we arrived in Jerusalem, where we rested **three** days.
10: 8 Anyone who failed to appear within **three** days would forfeit all
10: 9 Within the **three** days, all the men of Judah and Benjamin had
Ne 2:11 I went to Jerusalem, and after staying there **three** days
5:14 in the land of Judah, until his **thirty-second** [+2256+9109] year—
7: 9 of Shephatiah **372** [+2256+4395+8679+9109]
7:17 of Azgad **2,322** [+547+2256+4395+6929+9109]
7:22 of Hashum **328** [+2256+4395+6929+9046]
7:23 of Bezai **324** [+752+2256+4395+6929]
7:29 Kephirah and Beeroth **743** [+752+2256+4395+8679]
7:32 of Bethel and Ai **123** [+2256+4395+6929]
7:35 of Harim **320** [+2256+4395+6929]
7:36 of Jericho **345** [+752+2256+2822+4395]
7:38 of Senaah **3,930** [+547+2256+4395+8993+9596]
7:38 of Senaah **3,930** [+547+2256+4395+8993+9596]
7:39 (through the family of Jeshua) **973** [+2256+4395+8679+9596]
7:45 Ater, Talmon, Akkub, Hatita and Shobai **138** [+2256+4395+9046]
7:60 the servants of Solomon **392** [+2256+4395+9109+9596]
7:66 company numbered **42,360** [+547+752+2256+4395+8052+9252],
7:67 their **7,337** [+547+2256+4395+8679+8679+8993] menservants and
7:67 their **7,337** [+547+2256+4395+8679+8679+8993] menservants and
7:68 [7:67] There were **736** [+2256+4395+8679+9252] [BHS-] horses,
7:69 [7:68] **435** [+752+2256+2822+4395] camels and 6,720 donkeys.
7:70 [7:69] and **530** [+2256+2822+4395] garments for priests.
13: 6 for in the **thirty-second** [+2256+9109] year of Artaxerxes king of
Est 1: 3 in the **third** year of his reign he gave a banquet for all his nobles
3:12 on the **thirteenth** [+6925] day of the first month the royal
3:13 on a single day, the **thirteenth** [+6925] day of the twelfth month,
4:11 But **thirty** days have passed since I was called to go to the king."
4:16 Do not eat or drink for **three** days, night or day. I and my maids
8: 9 on the **twenty-third** [+2256+6929] day of the third month, the
8:12 King Xerxes was the **thirteenth** [+6925] day of the twelfth month,
9: 1 On the **thirteenth** [+6925] day of the twelfth month, the month of
9:15 they put to death in Susa **three** hundred men, but they did not lay
9:17 This happened on the **thirteenth** [+6925] day of the month of
9:18 had assembled on the **thirteenth** [+6925] and fourteenth, and
Job 1: 2 He had seven sons and **three** daughters,
1: 3 **three** thousand camels, five hundred yoke of oxen and five
1: 4 and they would invite their **three** sisters to eat and drink with them.
1:17 "The Chaldeans formed **three** raiding parties and swept down on
2:11 When Job's **three** friends, Eliphaz the Temanite, Bildad the
32: 1 So these **three** men stopped answering Job, because he was
32: 3 He was also angry with the **three** friends, because they had found
32: 5 But when he saw that the **three** men had nothing more to say,
33:29 "God does all these things to a man—twice, even **three** *times*—
42:13 And he also had seven sons and **three** daughters.
Pr 22:20 Have I not written **thirty** [BHS 8997] sayings for you, sayings of
30:15 "There are **three** things that are never satisfied, four that never say,
30:18 "There are **three** things that are too amazing for me, four that I do
30:21 "Under **three** *things* the earth trembles, under four it cannot bear
30:29 "There are **three** things that are stately in their stride, four that
Isa 16:14 "Within **three** years, as a servant bound by contract would count
17: 6 leaving two or **three** olives on the topmost branches, four
20: 3 my servant Isaiah has gone stripped and barefoot for **three** years,
Jer 1: 2 The word of the LORD came to him in the **thirteenth** [+6926]
25: 3 *For* **twenty-three** [+2256+6929] years—from the thirteenth year of
25: 3 from the **thirteenth** [+6926] year of Josiah son of Amon king of
36:23 Whenever Jehudi had read **three** or four columns of the scroll,
38:10 "Take **thirty** men from here with you and lift Jeremiah the prophet
52:24 Zephaniah the priest next in rank and the **three** doorkeepers.
52:28 in the seventh year, **3,023** [+547+2256+2256+6929+8993] Jews;
52:28 in the seventh year, **3,023** [+547+2256+2256+6929+8993] Jews;
52:29 year, **832** [+2256+4395+9046+9109] people from Jerusalem;
52:30 in his **twenty-third** [+2256+6929] year, 745 Jews taken into exile
52:31 In the **thirty-seventh** [+2256+8679] year of the exile of Jehoiachin
Eze 1: 1 In the **thirtieth** year, in the fourth month on the fifth day, while I
4: 5 So for **390** [+2256+4395+9596] days you will bear the sin of the
4: 9 eat it during the **390** [+2256+4395+9596] days you lie on your side.
14:14 even if these **three** men—Noah, Daniel and Job—were in it,
14:16 declares the Sovereign LORD, even if these **three** men were in it,
14:18 declares the Sovereign LORD, even if these **three** men were in it,
40:10 Inside the east gate were **three** alcoves on each side; the three had
40:10 **[RPH]** the three had the same measurements, and the faces of the
40:10 the **three** had the same measurements, and the faces of the
40:11 it was ten cubits and its length was **thirteen** [+6926] cubits.
40:17 all around the court; there were **thirty** rooms along the pavement.
40:21 Its alcoves—**three** on each side—its projecting walls and its
40:21 **[RPH]** its projecting walls and its portico had the same
40:48 and its projecting walls were **three** cubits wide on either side.
40:48 its projecting walls were three cubits wide on either side. **[RPH]**
41: 6 The side rooms were on **three** levels, one above another, thirty on
41: 6 were on three levels, one above another, **thirty** on each level.
41:16 and the narrow windows and galleries around the **three** *of* them—
41:22 There was a wooden altar **three** cubits high and two cubits square;
46:22 were enclosed courts, forty cubits long and **thirty** cubits wide;
48:31 The **three** gates on the north side will be the gate of Reuben,
48:32 "On the east side, which is 4,500 cubits long, will be **three** gates:
48:33 the south side, which measures 4,500 cubits, will be **three** gates:
48:34 "On the west side, which is 4,500 cubits long, will be **three** gates:
Da 1: 1 In the **third** year of the reign of Jehoiakim king of Judah,
1: 5 They were to be trained for **three** years, and after that they were to
8: 1 In the **third** year of King Belshazzar's reign, I, Daniel, had a
8:14 "It will take **2,300** [+547+2256+4395] evenings and mornings;
10: 1 In the **third** year of Cyrus king of Persia, a revelation was given to
10: 2 At that time I, Daniel, mourned for **three** weeks.
10: 3 and I used no lotions at all until the **three** weeks were over.
11: 2 **Three** more kings will appear in Persia, and then a fourth,
12:12 reaches the end of the **1,335** [+547+2256+2822+4395+8993] days.
12:12 reaches the end of the **1,335** [+547+2256+2822+4395+8993] days.
Am 1: 3 "For **three** sins of Damascus, even for four, I will not turn back
1: 6 "For **three** sins of Gaza, even for four, I will not turn back ⌊my
1: 9 "For **three** sins of Tyre, even for four, I will not turn back ⌊my
1:11 "For **three** sins of Edom, even for four, I will not turn back ⌊my
1:13 "For **three** sins of Ammon, even for four, I will not turn back ⌊my
2: 1 "For **three** sins of Moab, even for four, I will not turn back ⌊my
2: 4 "For **three** sins of Judah, even for four, I will not turn back ⌊my
2: 6 "For **three** sins of Israel, even for four, I will not turn back ⌊my
4: 4 Bring your sacrifices every morning, your tithes every **three** years.
4: 7 "I also withheld rain from you when the harvest was still **three**
4: 8 **People**° [+9109] staggered from town to town for water but did not
Jnh 1:17 [2:1] and Jonah was inside the fish **three** days and three nights.
1:17 [2:1] and Jonah was inside the fish three days and **three** nights.
3: 3 Nineveh was a very important city—a visit required **three** days.
Zec 11: 8 In one month I got rid of the **three** shepherds. The flock detested
11:12 but if not, keep it." So they paid me **thirty** *pieces of* silver.
11:13 So I took the **thirty** *pieces of* silver and threw them into the house

8994 שֶׁלֶשׁ *šeleš*, n.pr.m. [1] [√ 8993]

Shelesh [1]

1Ch 7:35 The sons of his brother Helem: Zophah, Imna, **Shelesh** and Amal.

8995 שָׁלִשָׁה *šālišâ*, n.pr.loc. [1] [→ 1264]

Shalisha [1]

1Sa 9: 4 the hill country of Ephraim and through the area around **Shalisha**,

8996 שִׁלְשָׁה *šilšâ*, n.pr.m. [1] [√ 8993]

Shilshah [1]

1Ch 7:37 Bezer, Hod, Shamma, **Shilshah**, Ithran and Beera.

8997 שִׁלְשׁוֹם **šilšōm**, adv. [25 / 24] [√ 8993]

before [+9453] [6], malice aforethought [+4200+4946+8533+9453] [3], before [+919] [2], had the habit [+4946+9453] [2], *untranslated* [1], as usual [+3869+9453] [1], before [+4946+9453] [1], for some time [+1685+1685+9453] [1], formerly [+919+4946] [1], had been [+9453] [1], in the past [+919+1685+1685] [1], in the past [+9453] [1], malice aforethought [+4946+8533+9453] [1], past [+9453] [1], previously [+919+3869] [1]

Ge 31: 2 Laban's attitude toward him was not what *it* **had been** [+9453].
31: 5 your father's attitude toward me is not what it was **before** [+9453],
Ex 4: 10 neither in the **past** [+9453] nor since you have spoken to your
5: 7 for making bricks; let them go and gather their own straw. **[RPH]**
5: 8 them to make the same number of bricks as **before** [+9453];
5: 14 meet your quota of bricks yesterday or today, as **before** [+9453]?"
21: 29 the bull has **had the habit** [+4946+9453] of goring and the owner
21: 36 if it was known that the bull **had the habit** [+4946+9453] of
Dt 4: 42 neighbor without **malice aforethought** [+4200+4946+8533+9453].
19: 4 without **malice aforethought** [+4200+4946+8533+9453].
19: 6 to his neighbor without **malice aforethought** [+4946+8533+9453].
Jos 3: 4 since you have never been this way **before** [+4946+9453].
4: 18 returned to their place and ran at flood stage as **before** [+9453].
20: 5 and without **malice aforethought** [+4200+4946+8533+9453].
Ru 2: 11 and came to live with a people you did not know **before** [+9453].
1Sa 4: 7 "We're in trouble! Nothing like this has happened **before** [+919].
10: 11 When all those who had **formerly** [+919+4946] known him saw
14: 21 Those Hebrews who had **previously** [+919+3869] been with the
19: 7 brought him to Saul, and David was with Saul as **before** [+919].
21: 5 [21:6] kept from us, **as usual** [+3869+9453] whenever I set out.
2Sa 3: 17 and said, "**For some time** [+1685+1685+9453] you have wanted to
5: 2 **In the past** [+919+1685+1685], while Saul was king over us, you
2Ki 13: 5 the Israelites lived in their own homes as they had **before** [+9453].
1Ch 11: 2 **In the past** [+9453], even while Saul was king, you were the one
Pr 22: 20 Have I not written thirty [BHS *former*; NIV 8993] sayings for you,

8998 שָׁלִשִׁי **šālišî**, a.num.ord. (used as noun). [2] [√ 8993]

Three [2]

2Sa 23: 8 Josheb-Basshebeth, a Tahkemonite, was chief of the **Three**;
23: 18 brother of Joab son of Zeruiah was chief of the **Three**. [Q 8993]

8999 שְׁלִשִׁיָּה **šᵉlišiyyâ**, n.pr.loc. Not used in NIV/BHS → 6326; cf. 8993

9000 שִׁלֵּשִׁים **sillēšîm**, a. [5] [√ 8993]

third generation [5]

Ge 50: 23 and saw the **third generation** of Ephraim's children.
Ex 20: 5 for the sin of the fathers to the **third** and fourth **generation**
34: 7 for the sin of the fathers to the **third** and fourth **generation**."
Nu 14: 18 for the sin of the fathers to the **third** and fourth **generation**.'
Dt 5: 9 for the sin of the fathers to the **third** and fourth **generation**

9001 שְׁלֹשִׁים **šᵉlōšîm**, n.indecl. Not used in NIV/BHS [√ 8993]

9002 שִׁלְתָּה **šiltâ**, n.pr.loc. Not used in NIV/BHS [√ 9434; cf. 3849]

9003 שַׁלְתִּיאֵל **šaltî'ēl**, n.pr.m. [3] [cf. 8630]

Shealtiel [3]

Hag 1: 12 Then Zerubbabel son of **Shealtiel**, Joshua son of Jehozadak,
1: 14 So the LORD stirred up the spirit of Zerubbabel son of **Shealtiel**,
2: 2 "Speak to Zerubbabel son of **Shealtiel**, governor of Judah,

9004 שָׁם **šām**, adv. [834 / 835] [→ Ar 10764] See Select Index

there [400], *untranslated* [140], where [101], there [+2025] [58], which[s] [18], it[s] [17], where [+2025] [16], here [9], in which[s] [5], in it[s] [4], the Jordan[s] [+2025] [4], back [+4946] [3], in it[s] [+2025] [3], out [+4946] [3], them[s] [3], away [+4946] [2], behind [2], in Zion[s] [2], in [2], it[s] [+2025] [2], that place[s] [2], where [+4946] [2], wherever [+2025] [2], whom[s] [2], among which[s] [1], at Pas[s] Dammim [1], back [1], back[s] [+2025] [1], because of [+4946] [1], beside [1], Gath[s] [1], Hebron[s] [1], in such places[s] [1], in that place[s] [1], in them[s] [1], inside[s] [+2025] [1], into it[s] [1], invade [+995+2025] [1], leave [+4946] [1], nearby [1], place [1], proper place [+889+2118+5226] [1], right there [1], Samaria[s] [1], see [1], that land[s] [1], the chest[s] [1], the city[s] [1], the land[s] [+2025] [1], the north[s] [1], there [+4946] [1], to [+2025] [1], what[s] [1], when [1], wherever [+889+2025] [1], wherever [+889+3972] [1], wherever [1]

9005 שֵׁם **šēm¹**, n.m. [864] [→ 9006?, 9017, 9026, 9027; Ar 10721]

name [563], names [62], named [44], *untranslated* [28], named [+7924] [28], named [+906+7924] [23], called [+7924] [21], called [10], fame [10], name's [7], called [+906+7924] [6], renown [6], famous [5], call [+7924] [4], honor [3], name [+7924] [3], call [+906+7924] [2], chosen [+928+7924] [2], famous [+7924] [2], named [+4200+7924] [2], named [+8492] [2], after [+3869] [1], after [+928] [1], be called [+7924] [1], be called [+906+7924] [1], be known as [+7924] [1], be named [+7924] [1], became famous [+6913] [1], been named [+7924] [1], byword [1], calling [+906+7924] [1], famous [+408] [1], giving credit to [+928] [1], himself [+2257] [1], infamous [+2021+3238] [1], is called [+7924] [1], it[s] [+2257] [1], memorable [1], name [+906+7924] [1], named [+6584+7924] [1], named [+906+8492] [1], named [+906+906+7924] [1], named [+906+928+7924] [1], nameless [+1172] [1], perpetuate memory [+2349] [1], record [+906+906+4180+4200] [1], renowned [+4200] [1], that[s] [1], to each man [+928] [1], was called [+7924] [1], well-known [+408] [1], word [1]

Ge 2: 11 The **name** *of* the first is the Pishon; it winds through the entire land
2: 13 The **name** *of* the second river is the Gihon; it winds through the
2: 14 The **name** *of* the third river is the Tigris; it runs along the east side
2: 19 whatever the man called each living creature, that was its **name**.
2: 20 So the man gave **names** to all the livestock, the birds of the air
3: 20 Adam **named** [+7924] his wife Eve, because she would become
4: 17 then building a city, and *he* **named** [+7924] it after his son Enoch.
4: 17 then building a city, and he named it after **[RPH]** his son Enoch.
4: 19 married two women, one **named** Adah and the other Zillah.
4: 19 two women, one named Adah and the other **[RPH]** Zillah.
4: 21 His brother's **name** was Jubal; he was the father of all who play
4: 25 and she gave birth to a son and **named** [+906+7924] him Seth,
4: 26 Seth also had a son, and *he* **named** [+906+7924] him Enosh.
4: 26 At that time men began to call on the **name** *of* the LORD.
5: 2 And when they were created, *he* **called** [+906+7924] them "man."
5: 3 in his own image; and *he* **named** [+906+7924] him Seth.
5: 29 *He* **named** [+906+7924] him Noah and said, "He will comfort us
6: 4 children by them. They were the heroes of old, men of **renown**.
10: 25 One was **named** Peleg, because in his time the earth was divided;
10: 25 in his time the earth was divided; his brother was **named** Joktan.
11: 4 so that we may make a **name** for ourselves and not be scattered
11: 9 That is why it *was* **called** [+7924] Babel—because there the
11: 29 The **name** *of* Abram's wife was Sarai, and the name of Nahor's
11: 29 wife was Sarai, and the **name** *of* Nahor's wife was Milcah;
12: 2 bless you; I will make your **name** great, and you will be a blessing.
12: 8 built an altar to the LORD and called on the **name** *of* the LORD.
13: 4 first built an altar. There Abram called on the **name** *of* the LORD.
16: 1 no children. But she had an Egyptian maidservant **named** Hagar;
16: 11 *You shall* **name** [+7924] him Ishmael, for the LORD has heard
16: 13 She gave this **name** to the LORD who spoke to her: "You are the
16: 15 and Abram gave the **name** Ishmael *to* the son she had borne.
17: 5 No longer *will* you **be called** [+906+7924] Abram; your name will
17: 5 your **name** will be Abraham, for I have made you a father of many
17: 15 Sarai your wife, *you are* no longer *to* **call** [+906+7924] her Sarai;
17: 15 you are no longer to call her Sarai; her **name** will be Sarah.
17: 19 will bear you a son, and *you will* **call** [+906+7924] him Isaac.
19: 22 you reach it." (That is why the town *was* **called** [+7924] Zoar.)
19: 37 The older daughter had a son, and *she* **named** [+7924] him Moab;
19: 38 daughter also had a son, and *she* **named** [+7924] him Ben-Ammi;
21: 3 Abraham gave the **name** Isaac to the son Sarah bore him.
21: 33 and there he called upon the **name** *of* the LORD, the Eternal God.
22: 14 So Abraham **called** [+7924] that place The LORD Will Provide.
22: 24 His concubine, whose **name** was Reumah, also had sons: Tebah,
24: 29 Now Rebekah had a brother **named** Laban, and he hurried out to
25: 1 Abraham took another wife, whose **name** was Keturah.
25: 13 These are the **names** *of* the sons of Ishmael, listed in the order of
25: 13 of the sons of Ishmael, **[RPH]** listed in the order of their birth:
25: 16 these are the **names** of the twelve tribal rulers according to their
25: 25 body was like a hairy garment; so *they* **named** [+7924] him Esau.
25: 26 his hand grasping Esau's heel; so he *was* **named** [+7924] Jacob.
25: 30 I'm famished!" (That is why he *was* also **called** [+7924] Edom.)
26: 18 and he gave them the same **names** his father had given them.
26: 18 he gave them the same names **[RPH]** his father had given them.
26: 20 So *he* **named** [+7924] the well Esek, because they disputed with
26: 21 they quarreled over that one also; so *he* **named** [+7924] it Sitnah.
26: 22 *He* **named** [+7924] it Rehoboth, saying, "Now the LORD has
26: 25 Isaac built an altar there and called on the **name** *of* the LORD.
26: 33 and to this day the **name** *of* the town has been Beersheba.
27: 36 Esau said, "*Isn't* he rightly **named** [+7924] Jacob? He has
28: 19 *He* **called** [+906+7924] that place Bethel, though the city used to
28: 19 He called that place Bethel, though the city used to *be* **called** Luz.
29: 16 the **name** *of* the older was Leah, and the name of the younger was
29: 16 of the older was Leah, and the **name** *of* the younger was Rachel.

Ge 29:32 *She* **named** [+7924] him Reuben, for she said, "It is
29:33 he gave me this one too." So *she* **named** [+7924] him Simeon.
29:34 I have borne him three sons." So he *was* **named** [+7924] Levi.
29:35 So *she* **named** [+7924] him Judah. Then she stopped having
30: 6 and given me a son." Because of this *she* **named** [+7924] him Dan.
30: 8 my sister, and I have won." So *she* **named** [+7924] him Naphtali.
30:11 "What good fortune!" So *she* **named** [+906+7924] him Gad.
30:13 will call me happy." So *she* **named** [+906+7924] him Asher.
30:18 maidservant to my husband." So *she* **named** [+7924] him Issachar.
30:20 borne him six sons." So *she* **named** [+906+7924] him Zebulun.
30:21 she gave birth to a daughter and **named** [+906+7924] her Dinah.
30:24 *She* **named** [+906+7924] him Joseph, and said, "May the LORD
31:48 and me today." That is why it *was* **called** [+7924] Galeed.
32: 2 [32:3] of God!" So *he* **named** [+7924] that place Mahanaim.
32:27 [32:28] The man asked him, "What is your **name**?" "Jacob,"
32:28 [32:29] man said, "Your **name** will no longer be Jacob, but Israel,
32:29 [32:30] Jacob said, "Please tell me your **name**." But he replied,
32:29 [32:30] he replied, "Why do you ask my **name**?" Then he blessed
32:30 [32:31] So Jacob **called** [+7924] the place Peniel, saying, "It is
33:17 for his livestock. That is why the place *is* **called** [+7924] Succoth.
35: 8 the oak below Bethel. So it *was* **named** [+7924] Allon Bacuth.
35:10 God said to him, "Your **name** is Jacob, but you will no longer be
35:10 name is Jacob, but you *will* no longer **be called** [+7924] Jacob;
35:10 but you will no longer be called Jacob; your **name** will be Israel."
35:10 your name will be Israel." So *he* **named** [+906+7924] him Israel.
35:15 Jacob **called** [+906+7924] the place where God had talked with
35:18 for she was dying—*she* **named** [+7924] her son Ben-Oni.
36:10 These are the **names** *of* Esau's sons: Eliphaz, the son of Esau's
36:32 son of Beor became king of Edom. His city was **named** Dinhabah.
36:35 of Moab, succeeded him as king. His city was **named** Avith.
36:39 His city was **named** Pau, and his wife's name was Mehetabel
36:39 and his wife's **name** was Mehetabel daughter of Matred,
36:40 These were **[RPH]** the chiefs descended from Esau, by name,
36:40 from Esau, by **name**, according to their clans and regions:
38: 1 and went down to stay with a man of Adullam **named** Hirah.
38: 2 There Judah met the daughter of a Canaanite man **named** Shua.
38: 3 and gave birth to a son, who *was* **named** [+906+7924] Er.
38: 4 and gave birth to a son and **named** [+906+7924] him Onan.
38: 5 birth to still another son and **named** [+906+7924] him Shelah.
38: 6 Judah got a wife for Er, his firstborn, and her **name** was Tamar.
38:29 is how you have broken out!" And he *was* **named** [+7924] Perez.
38:30 thread on his wrist, came out and he was given the **name** Zerah.
41:45 Pharaoh gave Joseph the **name** Zaphenath-Paneah and gave him
41:51 Joseph **named** [+906+7924] his firstborn Manasseh and said,
41:52 The second son *he* **named** [+906+7924] Ephraim and said,
46: 8 These are the **names** *of* the sons of Israel (Jacob and his
48: 6 inherit they will be reckoned under the **names** *of* their brothers.
48:16 May they be called by my **name** and the names of my fathers
48:16 by my name and the **names** *of* my fathers Abraham and Isaac,
50:11 That is why that place near the Jordan *is* **called** [+7924] Abel
Ex 1: 1 These are the **names** *of* the sons of Israel who went to Egypt with
1:15 to the Hebrew midwives, whose **names** were Shiphrah and Puah,
1:15 Hebrew midwives, whose names were Shiphrah and **[RPH]** Puah,
2:10 *She* **named** [+7924] him Moses, saying, "I drew him out of the
2:22 to a son, and Moses **named** [+906+7924] him Gershom, saying,
3:13 fathers has sent me to you,' and they ask me, 'What is his **name**?'
3:15 This is my **name** forever, the name by which I am to be
5:23 Ever since I went to Pharaoh to speak in your **name**, he has
6: 3 *by* my **name** the LORD I did not make myself known to them.
6:16 These were the **names** *of* the sons of Levi according to their
9:16 my power and that my **name** might be proclaimed in all the earth.
15: 3 The LORD is a warrior; the LORD is his **name**.
15:23 it was bitter. (That is why the place *is* **called** [+7924] Marah.)
16:31 The people of Israel **called** [+906+7924] the bread manna.
17: 7 *he* **called** [+7924] the place Massah and Meribah
17:15 built an altar and **called** [+7924] it The LORD is my Banner.
18: 3 One son was **named** Gershom, for Moses said, "I have become an
18: 4 the other was **named** Eliezer, for he said, "My father's God was
20: 7 "You shall not misuse the **name** *of* the LORD your God,
20: 7 the LORD will not hold anyone guiltless who misuses his **name**.
20:24 Wherever I cause my **name** to be honored, I will come to you
23:13 Do not invoke the **names** *of* other gods; do not let them be heard
23:21 he will not forgive your rebellion, since my **Name** is in him.
28: 9 onyx stones and engrave on them the **names** *of* the sons of Israel
28:10 six **names** on one stone and the remaining six on the other.
28:10 six names on one stone and the remaining six **[RPH]** on the other.
28:11 Engrave the **names** *of* the sons of Israel on the two stones the way
28:12 Aaron is to bear the **names** on his shoulders as a memorial before
28:21 to be twelve stones, one for each of the **names** *of* the sons of Israel,
28:21 **[RPH]** each engraved like a seal with the name of one of the
28:21 each engraved like a seal with the **name** *of* one of the twelve
28:29 he will bear the **names** *of* the sons of Israel over his heart on the
31: 2 "See, *I have* **chosen** [+928+7924] Bezalel son of Uri, the son of
33:12 'I know you by **name** and you have found favor with me.'
33:17 because I am pleased with you and I know you by **name**."
33:19 and I will proclaim my **name**, the LORD, in your presence.
34: 5 in the cloud and stood there with him and proclaimed his **name**,
34:14 for the LORD, whose **name** is Jealous, is a jealous God.
35:30 "See, the LORD *has* **chosen** [+928+7924] Bezalel son of Uri,
39: 6 and engraved them like a seal with the **names** *of* the sons of Israel.
39:14 were twelve stones, one for each of the **names** *of* the sons of Israel,
39:14 **[RPH]** each engraved like a seal with the name of one of the
39:14 each engraved like a seal with the **name** of one of the twelve
Lev 18:21 to Molech, for you must not profane the **name** *of* your God.
19:12 " 'Do not swear falsely by my **name** and so profane the name of
19:12 swear falsely by my name and so profane the **name** *of* your God.
20: 3 he has defiled my sanctuary and profaned my holy **name**.
21: 6 be holy to their God and must not profane the **name** *of* their God.
22: 2 Israelites consecrate to me, so they will not profane my holy **name**.
22:32 Do not profane my holy **name**. I must be acknowledged as holy by
24:11 The son of the Israelite woman blasphemed the **Name** with a curse;
24:11 (His mother's **name** was Shelomith, the daughter of Dibri the
24:16 anyone who blasphemes the **name** *of* the LORD must be put to
24:16 Whether an alien or native-born, when he blasphemes the **Name**,
Nu 1: 2 by their clans and families, listing every man by **name**, one by one.
1: 5 These are the **names** *of* the men who are to assist you:
1:17 Moses and Aaron took these men whose **names** had been given,
1:18 and the men twenty years old or more were listed by **name**,
1:20 or more who were able to serve in the army were listed by **name**,
1:22 were able to serve in the army were counted and listed by **name**,
1:24 or more who were able to serve in the army were listed by **name**,
1:26 or more who were able to serve in the army were listed by **name**,
1:28 or more who were able to serve in the army were listed by **name**,
1:30 or more who were able to serve in the army were listed by **name**,
1:32 or more who were able to serve in the army were listed by **name**,
1:34 or more who were able to serve in the army were listed by **name**,
1:36 or more who were able to serve in the army were listed by **name**,
1:38 or more who were able to serve in the army were listed by **name**,
1:40 or more who were able to serve in the army were listed by **name**,
1:42 or more who were able to serve in the army were listed by **name**,
3: 2 The **names** *of* the sons of Aaron were Nadab the firstborn
3: 3 Those were the **names** *of* Aaron's sons, the anointed priests,
3:17 These were the **names** *of* the sons of Levi: Gershon, Kohath
3:18 These were the **names** *of* the Gershonite clans: Libni and Shimei.
3:40 males who are a month old or more and make a list of their **names**.
3:43 number of firstborn males a month old or more, listed by **name**,
4:32 Assign **to each man** [+928] the specific things he is to carry.
6:27 "So they will put my **name** on the Israelites, and I will bless them."
11: 3 So that place *was* **called** [+7924] Taberah, because fire from the
11:26 However, two men, whose **names** were Eldad and Medad,
11:26 However, two men, whose names were Eldad and **[RPH]** Medad,
11:34 Therefore the place *was* **named** [+906+7924] Kibroth Hattaavah,
13: 4 These are their **names**: from the tribe of Reuben, Shammua son of
13:16 These are the **names** *of* the men Moses sent to explore the land.
16: 2 With them were 250 Israelite men, **well-known** [+408] community
17: 2 [17:17] ancestral tribes. Write the **name** *of* each man on his staff.
17: 3 [17:18] On the staff of Levi write Aaron's **name**, for there must
21: 3 and their towns; so the place *was* **named** [+7924] Hormah.
25:14 The **name** *of* the Israelite who was killed with the Midianite
25:15 the **name** *of* the Midianite woman who was put to death was Cozbi
26:33 whose **names** were Mahlah, Noah, Hoglah, Milcah and Tirzah.)
26:46 (Asher had a daughter **named** Serah.)
26:53 allotted to them as an inheritance based on the number of **names**.
26:55 What each group inherits will be according to the **names** *for* its
26:59 the **name** *of* Amram's wife was Jochebed, a descendant of Levi,
27: 1 The **names** *of* the daughters were Mahlah, Noah, Hoglah,
27: 4 Why should our father's **name** disappear from his clan because he
32:38 as well as Nebo and Baal Meon (these **names** were changed)
32:38 and Sibmah. They gave **names** to the cities they rebuilt.
32:38 and Sibmah. They gave names to **[RPH]** the cities they rebuilt.
32:42 surrounding settlements and called it Nobah after **himself** [+2257].
34:17 "These are the **names** *of* the men who are to assign the land for
34:19 These are their **names**: Caleb son of Jephunneh, from the tribe of
Dt 3:14 it *was* **named** [+906+906+7924] after him, so that to this day
5:11 "You shall not misuse the **name** *of* the LORD your God,
5:11 the LORD will not hold anyone guiltless who misuses his **name**.
6:13 your God, serve him only and take your oaths in his **name**.
7:24 your hand, and you will wipe out their **names** from under heaven.
9:14 I may destroy them and blot out their **name** from under heaven.
10: 8 the LORD to minister and to pronounce blessings in his **name**,
10:20 and serve him. Hold fast to him and take your oaths in his **name**.
12: 3 the idols of their gods and wipe out their **names** from those places.
12: 5 from among all your tribes to put his **Name** there for his dwelling.
12:11 the LORD your God will choose as a dwelling for his **Name**—
12:21 If the place where the LORD your God chooses to put his **Name**
14:23 your God at the place he will choose as a dwelling for his **Name**,
14:24 (because the place where the LORD will choose to put his **Name**
16: 2 at the place the LORD will choose as a dwelling for his **Name**.

Dt 16: 6 except in the place he will choose as a dwelling for his **Name**.
16: 11 your God at the place he will choose as a dwelling for his **Name**—
18: 5 all your tribes to stand and minister in the LORD's **name** always.
18: 7 he may minister in the **name** *of* the LORD his God like all his
18: 19 does not listen to my words that the prophet speaks in my **name**,
18: 20 a prophet who presumes to speak in my **name** anything I have not
18: 20 or a prophet who speaks in the **name** *of* other gods, must be put to
18: 22 If what a prophet proclaims in the **name** *of* the LORD does not
21: 5 to pronounce blessings in the **name** *of* the LORD and to decide
22: 14 slanders her and gives her a bad **name**, saying, "I married this
22: 19 because this man has given an Israelite virgin a bad **name**.
25: 6 The first son she bears shall carry on the **name** *of* the dead brother
25: 6 dead brother so that his **name** will not be blotted out from Israel.
25: 7 "My husband's brother refuses to carry on his brother's **name** in
25: 10 That man's line *shall* **be known** in Israel **as** [+7924] The Family of
26: 2 the LORD your God will choose as a dwelling for his **Name**
26: 19 **fame** and honor high above all the nations he has made and that
28: 10 all the peoples on earth will see that you are called by the **name** *of*
28: 58 in this book, and do not revere this glorious and awesome **name**—
29: 20 [29:19] the LORD will blot out his **name** from under heaven.
32: 3 I will proclaim the **name** *of* the LORD. Oh, praise the greatness
Jos 2: 1 So they went and entered the house of a prostitute **named** Rahab
5: 9 So the place *has been* **called** [+7924] Gilgal to this day.
7: 9 and they will surround us and wipe out our **name** from the earth.
7: 9 from the earth. What then will you do for your own great **name**?"
7: 26 Therefore that place *has been* **called** [+7924] the Valley of Achor
9: 9 very distant country because of the **fame** *of* the LORD your God.
14: 15 (Hebron used to be **called** Kiriath Arba after Arba, who was the
15: 15 against the people living in Debir (formerly **called** Kiriath Sepher).
17: 3 whose **names** were Mahlah, Noah, Hoglah, Milcah and Tirzah.
19: 47 settled in Leshem and named it Dan **after** [+3869] their forefather.)
21: 9 of Judah and Simeon they allotted the following towns by **name**
23: 7 do not invoke the **names** *of* their gods or swear by them.
Jdg 1: 10 the Canaanites living in Hebron (formerly **called** Kiriath Arba)
1: 11 against the people living in Debir (formerly **called** Kiriath Sepher).
1: 17 destroyed the city. Therefore it *was* **called** [+906+7924] Hormah.
1: 23 When they sent men to spy out Bethel (formerly **called** Luz),
1: 26 where he built a city and **called** [+7924] it Luz, which is its name
1: 26 he built a city and called it Luz, which is its **name** to this day.
2: 5 *they* **called** [+7924] that place Bokim. There they offered
8: 31 also bore him a son, whom *he* **named** [+906+8492] Abimelech.
13: 2 A certain man of Zorah, **named** Manoah, from the clan of the
13: 6 ask him where he came from, and he didn't tell me his **name**.
13: 17 Manoah inquired of the angel of the LORD, "What is your **name**,
13: 18 He replied, "Why do you ask my **name**? It is beyond
13: 24 woman gave birth to a boy and **named** [+906+7924] him Samson.
15: 19 So the spring *was* **called** [+7924] En Hakkore, and it is still there
16: 4 he fell in love with a woman in the Valley of Sorek whose **name**
17: 1 Now a man **named** Micah from the hill country of Ephraim
18: 29 *They* **named** [+7924] it Dan after their forefather Dan, who was
18: 29 They named it Dan **after** [+928] their forefather Dan, who was
18: 29 who was born to Israel—though the city used to be **called** Laish.
Ru 1: 2 The man's **name** was Elimelech, his wife's name Naomi,
1: 2 The man's name was Elimelech, his wife's **name** Naomi,
1: 2 and the **names** *of* his two sons were Mahlon and Kilion.
1: 4 married Moabite women, one **named** Orpah and the other Ruth.
1: 4 Moabite women, one named Orpah and **[RPH]** the other Ruth.
2: 1 the clan of Elimelech, a man of standing, whose **name** was Boaz.
2: 19 "The **name** *of* the man I worked with today is Boaz," she said.
4: 5 in order to maintain the **name** *of* the dead with his property."
4: 10 in order to maintain the **name** *of* the dead with his property,
4: 10 so that his **name** will not disappear from among his family
4: 11 have standing in Ephrathah and *be* **famous** [+7924] in Bethlehem.
4: 14 without a kinsman-redeemer. *May* he *become* **famous** [+7924]
4: 17 "Naomi has a son." And *they* **named** [+4200+7924] him Obed.
4: 17 him Obed. **[RPH]** He was the father of Jesse, the father of David.
1Sa 1: 1 whose **name** was Elkanah son of Jeroham, the son of Elihu,
1: 2 He had two wives; one was **called** Hannah and the other Peninnah.
1: 2 two wives; one was called Hannah and the other **[RPH]** Peninnah.
1: 20 *She* **named** [+906+7924] him Samuel, saying, "Because I asked
7: 12 between Mizpah and Shen. *He* **named** [+906+7924] it Ebenezer,
8: 2 The **name** *of* his firstborn was Joel and the name of his second was
8: 2 of his firstborn was Joel and the **name** *of* his second was Abijah,
9: 1 of standing, whose **name** was Kish son of Abiel, the son of Zeror,
9: 2 He had a son **named** Saul, an impressive young man without equal
12: 22 For the sake of his great **name** the LORD will not reject his
14: 4 outpost was a cliff; one was **called** Bozez, and the other Seneh.
14: 4 was a cliff; one was called Bozez, and **[RPH]** the other Seneh.
14: 49 **[RPH]** The name of his older daughter was Merab, and that of the
14: 49 The **name** *of* his older daughter was Merab, and that of the
14: 49 older daughter was Merab, and **that** *of* the younger was Michal.
14: 50 His wife's **name** was Ahinoam daughter of Ahimaaz. The name of
14: 50 The **name** *of* the commander of Saul's army was Abner son of
17: 4 A champion **named** Goliath, who was from Gath, came out of the
17: 12 Now David was the son of an Ephrathite **named** Jesse, who was
17: 13 **[RPH]** The firstborn was Eliab; the second, Abinadab;
17: 23 Goliath, the Philistine **[RPH]** champion from Gath, stepped out
17: 45 but I come against you in the **name** *of* the LORD Almighty,
18: 30 than the rest of Saul's officers, and his **name** became well known.
20: 42 for we have sworn friendship with each other in the **name** *of* the
21: 7 [21:8] **[NIE]** he was Doeg the Edomite, Saul's head shepherd.
22: 20 **[NIE]** a son of Ahimelech son of Ahitub, escaped and fled to join
24: 21 [24:22] or wipe out my **name** from my father's family."
25: 3 His **name** was Nabal and his wife's name was Abigail. She was an
25: 3 His name was Nabal and his wife's **name** was Abigail. She was an
25: 5 to them, "Go up to Nabal at Carmel and greet him in my **name**.
25: 9 men arrived, they gave Nabal this message in David's **name**.
25: 25 He is just like his **name**—his name is Fool, and folly goes with
25: 25 is just like his name—his **name** is Fool, and folly goes with him.
2Sa 3: 7 Now Saul had had a concubine **named** Rizpah daughter of Aiah.
4: 2 One was **named** Baanah and the other Recab; they were sons of
4: 2 One was named Baanah and **[RPH]** the other Recab; they were
4: 4 he fell and became crippled. His **name** was Mephibosheth.)
5: 14 These are the **names** *of* the children born to him there: Shammua,
5: 20 before me." So that place *was* **called** [+7924] Baal Perazim.
6: 2 which is called by the **Name**, the name of the LORD Almighty,
6: 2 which is called by the Name, the **name** *of* the LORD Almighty,
6: 18 he blessed the people in the **name** *of* the LORD Almighty.
7: 9 Now I will make your **name** great, like the names of the greatest
7: 9 your name great, like the **names** *of* the greatest men of the earth.
7: 13 He is the one who will build a house for my **Name**, and I will
7: 23 to make a **name** for himself, and to perform great and awesome
7: 26 so that your **name** will be great forever. Then men will say,
8: 13 David **became famous** [+6913] after he returned from striking
9: 2 Now there was a servant of Saul's household **named** Ziba.
9: 12 Mephibosheth had a young son **named** Mica, and all the members
12: 24 gave birth to a son, and *they* **named** [+906+7924] him Solomon.
12: 25 he sent word through Nathan the prophet *to* **name** [+906+7924]
12: 28 I will take the city, and it *will* **be named** [+7924] after me."
13: 1 with Tamar, the beautiful sister of Absalom son of David. **[NIE]**
13: 3 Now Amnon had a friend **named** Jonadab son of Shimeah,
14: 7 leaving my husband neither **name** nor descendant on the face of
14: 27 The daughter's **name** was Tamar, and she became a beautiful
16: 5 His **name** was Shimei son of Gera, and he cursed as he came out.
17: 25 Amasa was the son of a man **named** Jether, an Israelite who had
18: 18 he thought, "I have no son to carry on the memory of my **name**."
18: 18 to carry on the memory of my name." *He* **named** [+4200+7924]
20: 1 Now a troublemaker **named** Sheba son of Bicri, a Benjamite,
20: 21 A man **named** Sheba son of Bicri, from the hill country of
22: 50 O LORD, among the nations; I will sing praises to your **name**.
23: 8 These are the **names** *of* David's mighty men: Josheb-Basshebeth,
23: 18 whom he killed, and so he became as **famous** as the Three.
23: 22 son of Jehoiada; he too was as **famous** as the three mighty men.
1Ki 1: 47 'May your God make Solomon's **name** more famous than yours
1: 47 famous than yours **[RPH]** and his throne greater than yours!'
3: 2 because a temple had not yet been built for the **Name** *of* the
4: 8 These are their **names**: Ben-Hur—in the hill country of Ephraim;
4: 31 [5:11] And his **fame** spread to all the surrounding nations.
5: 3 [5:17] he could not build a temple for the **Name** *of* the LORD
5: 5 [5:19] to build a temple for the **Name** *of* the LORD my God,
5: 5 [5:19] throne in your place will build the temple for my **Name**.'
7: 21 The pillar to the south *he* **named** [+906+7924] Jakin and the one to
7: 21 to the south he named Jakin and the one to the north **[RPH]** Boaz.
8: 16 any tribe of Israel to have a temple built for my **Name** to be there,
8: 17 had it in his heart to build a temple for the **Name** *of* the LORD,
8: 18 'Because it was in your heart to build a temple for my **Name**,
8: 19 and blood—he is the one who will build the temple for my **Name**.'
8: 20 I have built the temple for the **Name** *of* the LORD, the God of
8: 29 and day, this place of which you said, 'My **Name** shall be there,'
8: 33 and when they turn back to you and confess your **name**, praying
8: 35 confess your **name** and turn from their sin because you have
8: 41 but has come from a distant land because of your **name**—
8: 42 for men will hear of your great **name** and your mighty hand
8: 43 so that all the peoples of the earth may know your **name** and fear
8: 43 and may know that this house I have built bears your **Name**.
8: 44 city you have chosen and the temple I have built for your **Name**,
8: 48 city you have chosen and the temple I have built for your **Name**;
9: 3 which you have built, by putting my **Name** there forever.
9: 7 and will reject this temple I have consecrated for my **Name**.
10: 1 the fame of Solomon and his relation to the **name** *of* the LORD,
11: 26 from Zeredah, and his mother was a widow **named** Zeruah.
11: 36 before me in Jerusalem, the city where I chose to put my **Name**.
13: 2 'A son **named** Josiah will be born to the house of David.
14: 21 had chosen out of all the tribes of Israel in which to put his **Name**.
14: 21 His mother's **name** was Naamah; she was an Ammonite.
14: 31 His mother's **name** was Naamah; she was an Ammonite.
15: 2 His mother's **name** was Maacah daughter of Abishalom.
15: 10 His grandmother's **name** was Maacah daughter of Abishalom.

1Ki 16:24 a city on the hill, **calling** [+906+7924] it Samaria, after Shemer,
16:24 it Samaria, after Shemer, the **name** *of* the former owner of the hill.
18:24 you call on the **name** *of* your god, and I will call on the name of
18:24 the name of your god, and I will call on the **name** *of* the LORD.
18:25 of you. Call on the **name** *of* your god, but do not light the fire."
18:26 Then they called on the **name** *of* Baal from morning till noon.
18:31 of the LORD had come, saying, "Your **name** shall be Israel."
18:32 With the stones he built an altar in the **name** *of* the LORD,
21: 8 So she wrote letters in Ahab's **name**, placed his seal on them,
22:16 swear to tell me nothing but the truth in the **name** *of* the LORD?"
22:42 His mother's **name** was Azubah daughter of Shilhi.
2Ki 2:24 and called down a curse on them in the **name** *of* the LORD.
5:11 out to me and stand and call on the **name** *of* the LORD his God,
8:26 His mother's **name** was Athaliah, a granddaughter of Omri king of
12: 1 [12:2] His mother's **name** was Zibiah; she was from Beersheba.
14: 2 His mother's **name** was Jehoaddin; she was from Jerusalem.
14: 7 Sela in battle, calling it Joktheel, the **name** it has to this day.
14:27 since the LORD had not said he would blot out the **name** *of* Israel
15: 2 His mother's **name** was Jecoliah; she was from Jerusalem.
15:33 sixteen years. His mother's **name** was Jerusha daughter of Zadok.
17:34 gave the descendants of Jacob, whom *he* **named** [+8492] Israel.
18: 2 His mother's **name** was Abijah daughter of Zechariah.
21: 1 in Jerusalem fifty-five years. His mother's **name** was Hephzibah.
21: 4 of which the LORD had said, "In Jerusalem I will put my **Name**."
21: 7 chosen out of all the tribes of Israel, I will put my **Name** forever.
21:19 His mother's **name** was Meshullemeth daughter of Haruz;
22: 1 His mother's **name** was Jedidah daughter of Adaiah; she was from
23:27 and this temple, about which I said, 'There shall my **Name** be.' "
23:31 His mother's **name** was Hamutal daughter of Jeremiah; she was
23:34 of his father Josiah and changed Eliakim's **name** to Jehoiakim.
23:36 His mother's **name** was Zebidah daughter of Pedaiah; she was
24: 8 His mother's **name** was Nehushta daughter of Elnathan; she was
24:17 king in his place and changed his **name** to Zedekiah.
24:18 His mother's **name** was Hamutal daughter of Jeremiah; she was
1Ch 1:19 One was **named** Peleg, because in his time the earth was divided;
1:19 in his time the earth was divided; his brother was **named** Joktan.
1:43 king reigned: Bela son of Beor, whose city was **named** Dinhabah.
1:46 of Moab, succeeded him as king. His city was **named** Avith.
1:50 His city was **named** Pau, and his wife's name was Mehetabel
1:50 and his wife's **name** was Mehetabel daughter of Matred,
2:26 Jerahmeel had another wife, whose **name** was Atarah; she was the
2:29 Abishur's wife was **named** Abihail, who bore him Ahban
2:34 only daughters. He had an Egyptian servant **named** Jarha.
4: 3 Jezreel, Ishma and Idbash. Their sister was **named** Hazzelelponi.
4: 9 His mother *had* **named** [+7924] him Jabez, saying, "I gave birth to
4:38 The men listed above by **name** were leaders of their clans.
4:41 The men whose **names** were listed came in the days of Hezekiah
5:24 They were brave warriors, **famous** men, and heads of their
6:17 [6:2] These are the **names** *of* the sons of Gershon: Libni
6:65 [6:50] they allotted the *previously* **named** [+906+928+7924] towns.
7:15 among the Huppites and Shuppites. His sister's **name** was Maacah.
7:15 Another descendant was **named** Zelophehad, who had only
7:16 wife Maacah gave birth to a son and **named** [+7924] him Peresh.
7:16 His brother was **named** Sheresh, and his sons were Ulam
7:23 and gave birth to a son. *He* **named** [+906+7924] him Beriah,
8:29 father of Gibeon lived in Gibeon. His wife's **name** was Maacah,
8:38 Azel had six sons, and these were their **names**: Azrikam, Bokeru,
9:35 father of Gibeon lived in Gibeon. His wife's **name** was Maacah,
9:44 Azel had six sons, and these were their **names**: Azrikam, Bokeru,
11:20 whom he killed, and so he became as **famous** as the Three.
11:24 son of Jehoiada; he too was as **famous** as the three mighty men.
12:30 [12:31] brave warriors, **famous** [+408] in their own clans—
12:31 [12:32] designated by **name** to come and make David king—
13: 6 between the cherubim—the ark that is called by the **Name**.
14: 4 These are the **names** *of* the children born to him there: Shammua,
14:11 by my hand." So that place *was* **called** [+7924] Baal Perazim.
14:17 So David's **fame** spread throughout every land, and the LORD
16: 2 he blessed the people in the **name** *of* the LORD.
16: 8 Give thanks to the LORD, call on his **name**; make known among
16:10 Glory in his holy **name**; let the hearts of those who seek the
16:29 ascribe to the LORD the glory due his **name**. Bring an offering
16:35 us from the nations, that we may give thanks to your holy **name**,
16:41 and designated by **name** to give thanks to the LORD,
17: 8 Now I will make your **name** like the names of the greatest men of
17: 8 Now I will make your name like the **names** *of* the greatest men of
17:21 to make a **name** for yourself, and to perform great and awesome
17:24 that it will be established and that your **name** will be great forever.
21:19 to the word that Gad had spoken in the **name** *of* the LORD.
22: 5 and **fame** and splendor in the sight of all the nations.
22: 7 I had it in my heart to build a house for the **Name** *of* the LORD
22: 8 You are not to build a house for my **Name**, because you have shed
22: 9 His **name** will be Solomon, and I will grant Israel peace and quiet
22:10 He is the one who will build a house for my **Name**. He will be my
22:19 into the temple that will be built for the **Name** *of* the LORD."
23:13 before him and to pronounce blessings in his **name** forever.
23:24 the heads of families as they were registered under their **names**
28: 3 But God said to me, 'You are not to build a house for my **Name**,
29:13 our God, we give you thanks, and praise your glorious **name**.
29:16 we have provided for building you a temple for your Holy **Name**,
2Ch 2: 1 [1:18] Solomon gave orders to build a temple for the **Name** *of* the
2: 4 [2:3] Now I am about to build a temple for the **Name** *of* the
3:17 The one to the south *he* **named** [+7924] Jakin and the one to the
3:17 to the south he named Jakin and the one to the north Boaz. **[NIE]**
6: 5 any tribe of Israel to have a temple built for my **Name** to be there,
6: 6 But now I have chosen Jerusalem for my **Name** to be there,
6: 7 had it in his heart to build a temple for the **Name** *of* the LORD,
6: 8 'Because it was in your heart to build a temple for my **Name**,
6: 9 and blood—he is the one who will build the temple for my **Name**.'
6:10 I have built the temple for the **Name** *of* the LORD, the God of
6:20 this place of which you said you would put your **Name** there.
6:24 against you and when they turn back and confess your **name**,
6:26 confess your **name** and turn from their sin because you have
6:32 because of your great **name** and your mighty hand and your
6:33 so that all the peoples of the earth may know your **name** and fear
6:33 and may know that this house I have built bears your **Name**.
6:34 city you have chosen and the temple I have built for your **Name**,
6:38 have chosen and toward the temple I have built for your **Name**;
7:14 if my people, who are called by my **name**, will humble themselves
7:16 consecrated this temple so that my **Name** may be there forever.
7:20 and will reject this temple I have consecrated for my **Name**.
12:13 had chosen out of all the tribes of Israel in which to put his **Name**.
12:13 His mother's **name** was Naamah; she was an Ammonite.
13: 2 His mother's **name** was Maacah, a daughter of Uriel of Gibeah.
14:11 [14:10] and in your **name** we have come against this vast army.
18:15 swear to tell me nothing but the truth in the **name** *of* the LORD?"
20: 8 have lived in it and have built in it a sanctuary for your **Name**,
20: 9 stand in your presence before this temple that bears your **Name**
20:26 This is why it *is* **called** [+906+7924] the Valley of Beracah to this
20:31 His mother's **name** was Azubah daughter of Shilhi.
22: 2 His mother's **name** was Athaliah, a granddaughter of Omri.
24: 1 His mother's **name** was Zibiah; she was from Beersheba.
25: 1 His mother's **name** was Jehoaddin; she was from Jerusalem.
26: 3 His mother's **name** was Jecoliah; she was from Jerusalem.
26: 8 his **fame** spread as far as the border of Egypt, because he had
26:15 His **fame** spread far and wide, for he was greatly helped until he
27: 1 sixteen years. His mother's **name** was Jerusha daughter of Zadok.
28: 9 a prophet of the LORD **named** Oded was there, and he went out
28:15 The men designated by **name** took the prisoners, and from the
29: 1 His mother's **name** was Abijah daughter of Zechariah.
31:19 men were designated by **name** to distribute portions to every male
33: 4 LORD had said, "My **Name** will remain in Jerusalem forever."
33: 7 chosen out of all the tribes of Israel, I will put my **Name** forever.
33:18 and the words the seers spoke to him in the **name** *of* the LORD,
36: 4 and Jerusalem and changed Eliakim's **name** to Jehoiakim.
Ezr 2:61 a daughter of Barzillai the Gileadite and was called by that **name**).
8:13 the last ones, whose **names** were Eliphelet, Jeuel and Shemaiah,
8:20 had established to assist the Levites. All were registered by **name**.
10:16 from each family division, and all of them designated by **name**.
Ne 1: 9 bring them to the place I have chosen as a dwelling for my **Name**.'
1:11 to the prayer of your servants who delight in revering your **name**.
6:13 and then they would give me a bad **name** to discredit me.
7:63 a daughter of Barzillai the Gileadite and was called by that **name**).
9: 5 "Blessed be your glorious **name**, and may it be exalted above all
9: 7 him out of Ur of the Chaldeans and **named** [+8492] him Abraham.
9:10 You made a **name** for yourself, which remains to this day.
Est 2: 5 **named** Mordecai son of Jair, the son of Shimei, the son of Kish,
2:14 king unless he was pleased with her and summoned her by **name**.
2:22 who in turn reported it to the king, **giving credit** [+928] **to**
3:12 These were written in the **name** *of* King Xerxes himself and sealed
8: 8 Now write another decree in the king's **name** in behalf of the Jews
8: 8 for no document written in the king's **name** and sealed with his
8:10 Mordecai wrote in the **name** *of* King Xerxes, sealed the dispatches
9:26 (Therefore these days were called Purim, from the **word** *pur*.)
Job 1: 1 In the land of Uz there lived a man whose **name** was Job.
1:21 LORD has taken away; may the **name** *of* the LORD be praised."
18:17 of him perishes from the earth; he has no **name** in the land.
30: 8 A base and **nameless** [+1172] brood, they were driven out of the
42:14 The first daughter *he* **named** [+7924] Jemimah, the second Keziah
42:14 **[RPH]** the second Keziah and the third Keren-Happuch.
42:14 the second Keziah and **[RPH]** the third Keren-Happuch.
Ps 5:11 [5:12] that those who love your **name** may rejoice in you.
7:17 [7:18] and will sing praise to the **name** *of* the LORD Most High.
8: 1 [8:2] our Lord, how majestic is your **name** in all the earth!
8: 9 [8:10] our Lord, how majestic is your **name** in all the earth!
9: 2 [9:3] in you; I will sing praise to your **name**, O Most High.
9: 5 [9:6] you have blotted out their **name** for ever and ever.
9:10 [9:11] Those who know your **name** will trust in you, for you,
16: 4 pour out their libations of blood or take up their **names** on my lips.

Ps 18:49 [18:50] the nations, O LORD; I will sing praises to your **name**.
20: 1 [20:2] in distress; may the **name** *of* the God of Jacob protect you.
20: 5 [20:6] and will lift up our banners in the **name** *of* our God.
20: 7 [20:8] in horses, but we trust in the **name** *of* the LORD our God.
22:22 [22:23] I will declare your **name** to my brothers; in the
23: 3 He guides me in paths of righteousness for his **name's** sake.
25:11 For the sake of your **name**, O LORD, forgive my iniquity,
29: 2 Ascribe to the LORD the glory due his **name**; worship the
31: 3 [31:4] my fortress, for the sake of your **name** lead and guide me.
33:21 In him our hearts rejoice, for we trust in his holy **name**.
34: 3 [34:4] the LORD with me; let us exalt his **name** together.
41: 5 [41:6] of me in malice, "When will he die and his **name** perish?"
44: 5 [44:6] back our enemies; through your **name** we trample our foes.
44: 8 [44:9] boast all day long, and we will praise your **name** forever.
44:20 [44:21] If we had forgotten the **name** *of* our God or spread out
45:17 [45:18] *I will* **perpetuate** your **memory** [+2349] through all
48:10 [48:11] Like your **name**, O God, your praise reaches to the ends
49:11 [49:12] though *they had* **named** [+6584+7924] lands after
52: 9 [52:11] in your **name** I will hope, for your name is good.
54: 1 [54:3] Save me, O God, by your **name**; vindicate me by your
54: 6 [54:8] to you; I will praise your **name**, O LORD, for it is good.
61: 5 [61:6] have given me the heritage of those who fear your **name**.
61: 8 [61:9] will I ever sing praise to your **name** and fulfill my vows
63: 4 [63:5] as long as I live, and in your **name** I will lift up my hands.
66: 2 Sing the glory of his **name**; make his praise glorious!
66: 4 to you; they sing praise to you, they sing praise to your **name**."
68: 4 [68:5] Sing to God, sing praise to his **name**, extol him who rides
68: 4 [68:5] his **name** is the LORD—and rejoice before him.
69:30 [69:31] I will praise God's **name** in song and glorify him with
69:36 [69:37] inherit it, and those who love his **name** will dwell there.
72:17 May his **name** endure forever; may it continue as long as the sun.
72:17 name endure forever; may **it**[s] [+2257] continue as long as the sun.
72:19 Praise be to his glorious **name** forever; may the whole earth be
74: 7 to the ground; they defiled the dwelling place of your **Name**.
74:10 enemy mock you, O God? Will the foe revile your **name** forever?
74:18 O LORD, how foolish people have reviled your **name**.
74:21 retreat in disgrace; may the poor and needy praise your **name**.
75: 1 [75:2] to you, O God, we give thanks, for your **Name** is near;
76: 1 [76:2] In Judah God is known; his **name** is great in Israel.
79: 6 acknowledge you, on the kingdoms that do not call on your **name**;
79: 9 Help us, O God our Savior, for the glory of your **name**; deliver us
79: 9 your name; deliver us and forgive our sins for your **name's** sake.
80:18 [80:19] away from you; revive us, and we will call on your **name**.
83: 4 [83:5] a nation, that the **name** *of* Israel be remembered no more."
83:16 [83:17] their faces with shame so that men will seek your **name**,
83:18 [83:19] Let them know that you, whose **name** is the LORD—
86: 9 worship before you, O Lord; they will bring glory to your **name**.
86:11 your truth; give me an undivided heart, that I may fear your **name**.
86:12 Lord my God, with all my heart; I will glorify your **name** forever.
89:12 [89:13] the south; Tabor and Hermon sing for joy at your **name**.
89:16 [89:17] They rejoice in your **name** all day long; they exult in your
89:24 [89:25] with him, and through my **name** his horn will be exalted.
91:14 will rescue him; I will protect him, for he acknowledges my **name**.
92: 1 [92:2] good to praise the LORD and make music to your **name**,
96: 2 Sing to the LORD, praise his **name**; proclaim his salvation day
96: 8 Ascribe to the LORD the glory due his **name**; bring an offering
99: 3 Let them praise your great and awesome **name**—he is holy.
99: 6 his priests, Samuel was among those who called on his **name**;
100: 4 and his courts with praise; give thanks to him and praise his **name**.
102:15 [102:16] The nations will fear the **name** *of* the LORD, all the
102:21 [102:22] So the **name** *of* the LORD will be declared in Zion
103: 1 the LORD, O my soul; all my inmost being, praise his holy **name**.
105: 1 Give thanks to the LORD, call on his **name**; make known among
105: 3 Glory in his holy **name**; let the hearts of those who seek the
106: 8 Yet he saved them for his **name's** sake, to make his mighty power
106:47 that we may give thanks to your holy **name** and glory in your
109:13 be cut off, their **names** blotted out from the next generation.
109:21 O Sovereign LORD, deal well with me for your **name's** sake;
111: 9 he ordained his covenant forever—holy and awesome is his **name**.
113: 1 O servants of the LORD, praise the **name** *of* the LORD.
113: 2 Let the **name** *of* the LORD be praised, both now
113: 3 to the place where it sets, the **name** *of* the LORD is to be praised.
115: 1 Not to us, O LORD, not to us but to your **name** be the glory,
116: 4 Then I called on the **name** *of* the LORD: "O LORD, save me!"
116:13 lift up the cup of salvation and call on the **name** *of* the LORD.
116:17 a thank offering to you and call on the **name** *of* the LORD.
118:10 surrounded me, but in the **name** *of* the LORD I cut them off.
118:11 me on every side, but in the **name** *of* the LORD I cut them off.
118:12 as burning thorns; in the **name** *of* the LORD I cut them off.
118:26 Blessed is he who comes in the **name** *of* the LORD.
119:55 In the night I remember your **name**, O LORD, and I will keep
119:132 have mercy on me, as you always do to those who love your **name**.
122: 4 to praise the **name** *of* the LORD according to the statute given to
124: 8 Our help is in the **name** *of* the LORD, the Maker of heaven
129: 8 LORD be upon you; we bless you in the **name** *of* the LORD."
135: 1 Praise the **name** *of* the LORD; praise him, you servants of the
135: 3 the LORD is good; sing praise to his **name**, for that is pleasant.
135:13 Your **name**, O LORD, endures forever, your renown, O LORD,
138: 2 and will praise your **name** for your love and your faithfulness,
138: 2 for you have exalted above all things your **name** and your word.
140:13 [140:14] Surely the righteous will praise your **name**
142: 7 [142:8] Set me free from my prison, that I may praise your **name**.
143:11 For your **name's** sake, O LORD, preserve my life; in your
145: 1 my God the King; I will praise your **name** for ever and ever.
145: 2 Every day I will praise you and extol your **name** for ever and ever.
145:21 Let every creature praise his holy **name** for ever and ever.
147: 4 determines the number of the stars and calls them each *by* **name**.
148: 5 Let them praise the **name** *of* the LORD, for he commanded
148:13 Let them praise the **name** *of* the LORD, for his name alone is
148:13 them praise the name of the LORD, for his **name** alone is exalted;
149: 3 Let them praise his **name** with dancing and make music to him
Pr 10: 7 righteous will be a blessing, but the **name** *of* the wicked will rot.
18:10 The **name** *of* the LORD is a strong tower; the righteous run to it
21:24 The proud and arrogant man—"Mocker" is his **name**; he behaves
22: 1 A good **name** is more desirable than great riches; to be esteemed is
30: 4 What is his **name**, and the name of his son? Tell me if you know!
30: 4 What is his name, and the **name** *of* his son? Tell me if you know!
30: 9 may become poor and steal, and so dishonor the **name** *of* my God.
Ecc 6: 4 it departs in darkness, and in darkness its **name** is shrouded.
6:10 Whatever exists *has* already **been named** [+7924], and what man
7: 1 A good **name** is better than fine perfume, and the day of death
SS 1: 3 fragrance of your perfumes; your **name** is like perfume poured out.
Isa 4: 1 and provide our own clothes; only let us be called by your **name**.
7:14 and will give birth to a son, and *will* **call** [+7924] him Immanuel.
8: 3 the LORD said to me, "**Name** [+7924] him
9: 6 [9:5] he *will be* **called** [+7924] Wonderful Counselor,
12: 4 "Give thanks to the LORD, call on his **name**; make known
12: 4 nations what he has done, and proclaim that his **name** is exalted.
14:22 "I will cut off from Babylon her **name** and survivors, her offspring
18: 7 to Mount Zion, the place of the **Name** *of* the LORD Almighty.
24:15 exalt the **name** *of* the LORD, the God of Israel, in the islands of
25: 1 I will exalt you and praise your **name**, for in perfect faithfulness
26: 8 wait for you; your **name** and renown are the desire of our hearts.
26:13 besides you have ruled over us, but your **name** alone do we honor.
29:23 the work of my hands, they will keep my **name** holy;
30:27 See, the **Name** *of* the LORD comes from afar, with burning anger
40:26 brings out the starry host one by one, and calls them each by **name**.
41:25 and he comes—one from the rising sun who calls on my **name**.
42: 8 "I am the LORD; that is my **name**! I will not give my glory to
43: 1 have redeemed you; I have summoned you by **name**; you are mine.
43: 7 everyone who is called by my **name**, whom I created for my glory,
44: 5 to the LORD'; another will call himself by the **name** *of* Jacob;
44: 5 write on his hand, 'The LORD's,' and will take the **name** Israel.
45: 3 I am the LORD, the God of Israel, who summons you by **name**.
45: 4 I summon you by **name** and bestow on you a title of honor,
47: 4 Our Redeemer—the LORD Almighty is his **name**—is the Holy
48: 1 you who are called by the **name** *of* Israel and come from the line
48: 1 you who take oaths in the **name** *of* the LORD and invoke the God
48: 2 and rely on the God of Israel—the LORD Almighty is his **name**:
48: 9 For my own **name's** sake I delay my wrath; for the sake of my
48:19 their **name** would never be cut off nor destroyed from before me."
49: 1 called me; from my birth he has made mention of my **name**.
50:10 has no light, trust in the **name** *of* the LORD and rely on his God.
51:15 so that its waves roar—the LORD Almighty is his **name**.
52: 5 the LORD. "And all day long my **name** is constantly blasphemed.
52: 6 Therefore my people will know my **name**; therefore in that day
54: 5 your Maker is your husband—the LORD Almighty is his **name**—
55:13 This will be for the LORD's **renown**, for an everlasting sign,
56: 5 its walls a memorial and a **name** better than sons and daughters;
56: 5 I will give them an everlasting **name** that will not be cut off.
56: 6 to love the **name** *of* the LORD, and to worship him, all who keep
57:15 and lofty One says—he who lives forever, whose **name** is holy:
59:19 From the west, men will fear the **name** *of* the LORD, and from
60: 9 with their silver and gold, to the **honor** *of* the LORD your God,
62: 2 you will be called by a new **name** that the mouth of the LORD
63:12 the waters before them, to gain for himself everlasting **renown**,
63:14 how you guided your people to make for yourself a glorious **name**.
63:16 are our Father, our Redeemer from of old is your **name**.
63:19 have not ruled over them, they have not been called by your **name**.
64: 2 [64:1] come down to make your **name** known to your enemies
64: 7 [64:6] No one calls on your **name** or strives to lay hold of you;
65: 1 To a nation that did not call on my **name**, I said, 'Here am I,
65:15 You will leave your **name** to my chosen ones as a curse;
65:15 put you to death, but to his servants he will give another **name**.
66: 5 exclude you because of my **name**, have said, 'Let the LORD be
66:22 declares the LORD, "so will your **name** and descendants endure.
Jer 3:17 all nations will gather in Jerusalem to honor the **name** *of* the
7:10 me in this house, which bears my **Name**, and say, "We are safe"—

Jer 7: 11 Has this house, which bears my **Name**, become a den of robbers to
7: 12 to the place in Shiloh where I first made a dwelling for my **Name**,
7: 14 I did to Shiloh I will now do to the house that bears my **Name**,
7: 30 have set up their detestable idols in the house that bears my **Name**
10: 6 O LORD; you are great, and your **name** is mighty in power.
10: 16 the tribe of his inheritance—the LORD Almighty is his **name**.
10: 25 acknowledge you, on the peoples who do not call on your **name**.
11: 16 The LORD **called** [+7924] you a thriving olive tree with fruit
11: 19 the land of the living, that his **name** be remembered no more."
11: 21 'Do not prophesy in the **name** *of* the LORD or you will die by our
12: 16 if they learn well the ways of my people and swear by my **name**,
13: 11 'to be my people for my **renown** and praise and honor.
14: 7 against us, O LORD, do something for the sake of your **name**.
14: 9 You are among us, O LORD, and we bear your **name**; do not
14: 14 said to me, "The prophets are prophesying lies in my **name**.
14: 15 LORD says about the prophets who are prophesying in my **name**:
14: 21 For the sake of your **name** do not despise us; do not dishonor your
15: 16 they were my joy and my heart's delight, for I bear your **name**,
16: 21 and might. Then they will know that my **name** is the LORD.
20: 3 "The LORD's **name** [+7924] *for* you is not Pashhur,
20: 9 if I say, "I will not mention him or speak any more in his **name**,"
23: 6 will live in safety. This is the **name** by which he will be called:
23: 25 have heard what the prophets say who prophesy lies in my **name**.
23: 27 dreams they tell one another will make my people forget my **name**,
23: 27 just as their fathers forgot my **name** through Baal worship.
25: 29 I am beginning to bring disaster on the city that bears my **Name**,
26: 9 Why do you prophesy in the LORD's **name** that this house will
26: 16 He has spoken to us in the **name** *of* the LORD our God."
26: 20 was another man who prophesied in the **name** *of* the LORD;
27: 15 'They are prophesying lies in my **name**. Therefore, I will banish
29: 9 They are prophesying lies to you in my **name**. I have not sent
29: 21 son of Maaseiah, who are prophesying lies to you in my **name**:
29: 23 with their neighbors' wives and in my **name** have spoken lies,
29: 25 You sent letters in your own **name** to all the people in Jerusalem,
31: 35 so that its waves roar—the LORD Almighty is his **name**:
32: 18 and powerful God, whose **name** is the LORD Almighty,
32: 20 among all mankind, and have gained the **renown** that is still yours.
32: 34 set up their abominable idols in the house that bears my **Name**
33: 2 who formed it and established it—the LORD is his **name**:
33: 9 this city will bring me **renown**, joy, praise and honor before all
34: 15 even made a covenant before me in the house that bears my **Name**.
34: 16 But now you have turned around and profaned my **name**;
37: 13 whose **name** was Irijah son of Shelemiah, the son of Hananiah,
44: 16 to the message you have spoken to us in the **name** *of* the LORD!
44: 26 'I swear by my great **name**,' says the LORD, 'that no one from
44: 26 Judah living anywhere in Egypt will ever again invoke my **name**
46: 18 as I live," declares the King, whose **name** is the LORD Almighty,
48: 15 declares the King, whose **name** is the LORD Almighty.
48: 17 Mourn for her, all who live around her, all who know her **fame**;
50: 34 Yet their Redeemer is strong; the LORD Almighty is his **name**.
51: 19 the tribe of his inheritance—the LORD Almighty is his **name**.
51: 57 declares the King, whose **name** is the LORD Almighty.
52: 1 His mother's **name** was Hamutal daughter of Jeremiah; she was
La 3: 55 I called on your **name**, O LORD, from the depths of the pit.
Eze 16: 14 your **fame** spread among the nations on account of your beauty,
16: 15 trusted in your beauty and used your **fame** to become a prostitute.
20: 9 for the sake of my **name** I did what would keep it from being
20: 14 for the sake of my **name** I did what would keep it from being
20: 22 for the sake of my **name** I did what would keep it from being
20: 29 What is this high place you go to?' " (It **is called** [+7924] Bamah to
20: 39 and no longer profane my holy **name** with your gifts and idols.
20: 44 when I deal with you for my **name's** sake and not according to
22: 5 will mock you, O **infamous** [+2021+3238] city, full of turmoil.
23: 4 The older was **named** Oholah, and her sister was Oholibah.
23: 4 **[NIE]** Oholah is Samaria, and Oholibah is Jerusalem.
23: 10 She became a **byword** among women, and punishment was
24: 2 "Son of man, **record** [+906+906+4180+4200] this date, this very
34: 29 I will provide for them a land **renowned** [+4200] for its crops,
36: 20 they went among the nations they profaned my holy **name**,
36: 21 I had concern for my holy **name**, which the house of Israel
36: 22 I am going to do these things, but for the sake of my holy **name**,
36: 23 I will show the holiness of my great **name**, which has been
39: 7 " 'I will make known my holy **name** among my people Israel.
39: 7 I will no longer let my holy **name** be profaned, and the nations will
39: 13 and the day I am glorified will be a **memorable** day for them,
39: 16 (Also a town **called** Hamonah will be there.) And so they will
39: 25 on all the people of Israel, and I will be zealous for my holy **name**.
43: 7 The house of Israel will never again defile my holy **name**—
43: 8 and them, they defiled my holy **name** by their detestable practices.
48: 1 "These are the tribes, listed by **name**: At the northern frontier,
48: 31 the gates of the city will be **named** after the tribes of Israel.
48: 35 "And the **name** *of* the city from that time on will be: THE LORD
Da 1: 7 The chief official gave them new **names**: to Daniel, the name
9: 6 who spoke in your **name** to our kings, our princes and our fathers,
9: 15 and who made for yourself a **name** that endures to this day,
9: 18 your eyes and see the desolation of the city that bears your **Name**.
9: 19 do not delay, because your city and your people bear your **Name**."
10: 1 a revelation was given to Daniel (who **was called** [+7924]
Hos 1: 4 Then the LORD said to Hosea, "**Call** [+7924] him Jezreel,
1: 6 Then the LORD said to Hosea, "**Call** [+7924] her Lo-Ruhamah,
1: 9 the LORD said, "**Call** [+7924] him Lo-Ammi, for you are not my
2: 17 [2:19] I will remove the **names** *of* the Baals from her lips; no
2: 17 [2:19] Baals from her lips; no longer will their **names** be invoked.
Joel 2: 26 are full, and you will praise the **name** *of* the LORD your God,
2: 32 [3:5] everyone who calls on the **name** *of* the LORD will be
Am 2: 7 Father and son use the same girl and so profane my holy **name**.
4: 13 high places of the earth—the LORD God Almighty is his **name**.
5: 8 them out over the face of the land—the LORD is his **name**—
5: 27 says the LORD, whose **name** is God Almighty.
6: 10 will say, "Hush! We must not mention the **name** *of* the LORD."
9: 6 pours them out over the face of the land—the LORD is his **name**.
9: 12 the remnant of Edom and all the nations that bear my **name**,"
Mic 4: 5 All the nations may walk in the **name** *of* their gods; we will walk
4: 5 we will walk in the **name** *of* the LORD our God for ever
5: 4 [5:3] in the majesty of the **name** *of* the LORD his God.
6: 9 to fear your **name** is wisdom—"Heed the rod and the One who
Na 1: 14 ⌊Nineveh⌋: "You will have no descendants to bear your **name**.
Zep 1: 4 of Baal, the **names** *of* the pagan and the idolatrous priests—
3: 9 that all of them may call on the **name** *of* the LORD and serve him
3: 12 you the meek and humble, who trust in the **name** *of* the LORD.
3: 19 and **honor** in every land where they were put to shame.
3: 20 I will give you **honor** and praise among all the peoples of the earth
Zec 5: 4 of the thief and the house of him who swears falsely by my **name**.
6: 12 'Here is the man whose **name** is the Branch, and he will branch out
10: 12 strengthen them in the LORD and in his **name** they will walk,"
13: 2 "On that day, I will banish the **names** of the idols from the land,
13: 3 'You must die, because you have told lies in the LORD's **name**.'
13: 9 They will call on my **name** and I will answer them; I will say,
14: 9 that day there will be one LORD, and his **name** the only name.
Mal 1: 6 "It is you, O priests, who show contempt for my **name**. "But you
1: 6 "But you ask, 'How have we shown contempt for your **name**?'
1: 11 My **name** will be great among the nations, from the rising to the
1: 11 place incense and pure offerings will be brought to my **name**,
1: 11 because my **name** will be great among the nations,"
1: 14 "and my **name** is to be feared among the nations.
2: 2 do not listen, and if you do not set your heart to honor my **name**,"
2: 5 for reverence and he revered me and stood in awe of my **name**.
3: 16 concerning those who feared the LORD and honored his **name**.
4: 2 [3:20] for you who revere my **name**, the sun of righteousness will

9006 ²שֵׁם *šēm²*, n.pr.m. [17] [√ 9005?]

Shem [17]

Ge 5: 32 500 years old, he became the father of **Shem**, Ham and Japheth.
6: 10 Noah had three sons: **Shem**, Ham and Japheth.
7: 13 On that very day Noah and his sons, **Shem**, Ham and Japheth,
9: 18 The sons of Noah who came out of the ark were **Shem**, Ham
9: 23 **Shem** and Japheth took a garment and laid it across their
9: 26 He also said, "Blessed be the LORD, the God of **Shem**! May
9: 27 may Japheth live in the tents of **Shem**, and may Canaan be his
10: 1 This is the account of **Shem**, Ham and Japheth, Noah's sons,
10: 21 Sons were also born to **Shem**, whose older brother was Japheth;
10: 22 The sons of **Shem**: Elam, Asshur, Arphaxad, Lud and Aram.
10: 31 These are the sons of **Shem** by their clans and languages, in their
11: 10 This is the account of **Shem**. Two years after the flood,
11: 10 Two years after the flood, when **Shem** was 100 years old,
11: 11 **Shem** lived 500 years and had other sons and daughters.
1Ch 1: 4 The sons of Noah: **Shem**, Ham and Japheth.
1: 17 The sons of **Shem**: Elam, Asshur, Arphaxad, Lud and Aram.
1: 24 **Shem**, Arphaxad, Shelah,

9007 שַׁמָּא *šammā'*, n.pr.m. [2] [cf. 9015]

Shamma [1], Shammah [1]

2Sa 23: 11 Next to him was **Shammah** son of Agee the Hararite.
1Ch 7: 37 Bezer, Hod, **Shamma**, Shilshah, Ithran and Beera.

9008 שֶׁמְאֵבֶר *šem'ēber*, n.pr.m. [1]

Shemeber [1]

Ge 14: 2 of Gomorrah, Shinab king of Admah, **Shemeber** king of Zeboiim,

9009 שִׁמְאָה *šim'â*, n.pr.m. [1] [cf. 9010]

Shimeah [1]

1Ch 8: 32 Mikloth, who was the father of **Shimeah**. They too lived near their

9010 שִׁמְאָם ***šim'ām***, n.pr.m. [1] [cf. 9009]

Shimeam [1]

1Ch 9:38 Mikloth was the father of **Shimeam**. They too lived near their

9011 שַׁמְגַּר ***šamgar***, n.pr.m. [2]

Shamgar [2]

Jdg 3:31 After Ehud came **Shamgar** son of Anath, who struck down six
5:6 "In the days of **Shamgar** son of Anath, in the days of Jael,

9012 שָׁמַד ***šāmad***, v. [90] [→ Ar 10722]

destroy [31], destroyed [24], be destroyed [6], are destroyed [5], destruction [3], certainly be destroyed [+9012] [2], demolish [2], totally destroy [+906+9012] [2], wipe out [2], annihilate [1], annihilation [1], be overthrown [1], been decimated [1], been destroyed [1], brought to ruin [1], completely destroyed [1], crushed [1], cut off [1], exterminating [1], get rid of [1], perished [1], shatter [1]

Ge 34:30 [C] and attack me, I and my household *will* **be destroyed**."
Lev 26:30 [G] *I will* **destroy** your high places, cut down your incense altars
Nu 33:52 [G] and their cast idols, and **demolish** all their high places.
Dt 1:27 [G] to deliver us into the hands of the Amorites to **destroy** us.
2:12 [G] *They* **destroyed** the Horites from before them and settled in
2:21 [G] The LORD **destroyed** them from before the Ammonites,
2:22 [G] in Seir, when *he* **destroyed** the Horites from before them.
2:23 [G] the Caphtorites coming out from Caphtor **destroyed** them
4:3 [G] The LORD your God **destroyed** from among you everyone
4:26 [C] not live there long but *will* **certainly be destroyed** [+9012].
4:26 [C] not live there long but *will* **certainly be destroyed** [+9012].
6:15 [G] and *he will* **destroy** you from the face of the land.
7:4 [G] anger will burn against you and *will* quickly **destroy** you.
7:23 [C] throwing them into great confusion until they **are destroyed**.
7:24 [G] will be able to stand up against you; you *will* **destroy** them.
9:3 [G] He *will* **destroy** them; he will subdue them before you.
9:8 [G] LORD's wrath so that he was angry enough to **destroy** you.
9:14 [G] so that *I may* **destroy** them and blot out their name from
9:19 [G] for he was angry enough with you to **destroy** you.
9:20 [G] the LORD was angry enough with Aaron to **destroy** him,
9:25 [G] because the LORD had said *he would* **destroy** you.
12:30 [C] after they *have* **been destroyed** before you, be careful not to
28:20 [C] until you **are destroyed** and come to sudden ruin because of
28:24 [C] it will come down from the skies until you **are destroyed**.
28:45 [C] will pursue you and overtake you until you *are* **destroyed**,
28:48 [G] He will put an iron yoke on your neck until he *has* **destroyed**
28:51 [C] and the crops of your land until you **are destroyed**.
28:61 [C] recorded in this Book of the Law, until you **are destroyed**.
28:63 [G] in number, so it will please him to ruin and **destroy** you.
31:3 [G] He *will* **destroy** these nations before you, and you will take
31:4 [G] of the Amorites, whom *he* **destroyed** along with their land.
33:27 [G] will drive out your enemy before you, saying, '**Destroy** him!'
Jos 7:12 [G] I will not be with you anymore unless *you* **destroy** whatever
9:24 [G] and to **wipe out** all its inhabitants from before you.
11:14 [G] they put to the sword until they **completely destroyed** them,
11:20 [G] destroy them totally, **exterminating** them without mercy,
23:15 [G] until he *has* **destroyed** you from this good land he has given
24:8 [G] *I* **destroyed** them from before you, and you took possession
Jdg 21:16 [C] the assembly said, "With the women of Benjamin **destroyed**,
1Sa 24:21 [24:22] [G] or **wipe out** my name from my father's family."
2Sa 14:7 [G] whom he killed; then *we will* **get rid of** the heir as well.'
14:11 [G] to the destruction, so that my son *will* not *be* **destroyed**."
14:16 [G] the hand of the man *who is trying to* **cut off** both me and
21:5 [C] and plotted against us so that *we have* **been decimated**
22:38 [G] "I pursued my enemies and **crushed** them; I did not turn
1Ki 13:34 [G] its downfall and to its **destruction** from the face of the earth.
15:29 [G] Jeroboam anyone that breathed, but **destroyed** them all,
16:12 [G] So Zimri **destroyed** the whole family of Baasha,
2Ki 10:17 [G] *he* **destroyed** them, according to the word of the LORD
10:28 [G] So Jehu **destroyed** Baal worship in Israel.
21:9 [G] the nations the LORD *had* **destroyed** before the Israelites.
1Ch 5:25 [G] peoples of the land, whom God *had* **destroyed** before them.
2Ch 20:10 [G] so they turned away from them and *did* not **destroy** them.
20:23 [G] the men from Mount Seir to destroy and **annihilate** them.
33:9 [G] the nations the LORD *had* **destroyed** before the Israelites.
Est 3:6 [G] Instead Haman looked for a way to **destroy** all Mordecai's
3:13 [G] couriers to all the king's provinces with the order to **destroy**,
4:8 [G] him a copy of the text of the edict for their **annihilation**,
7:4 [G] For I and my people have been sold for **destruction**
8:11 [G] to **destroy**, kill and annihilate any armed force of any
Ps 37:38 [C] all sinners *will* **be destroyed**; the future of the wicked will be
83:10 [83:11] [C] *who* **perished** at Endor and became like refuse on
92:7 [92:8] [C] all evildoers flourish, they *will* be forever **destroyed**.
106:23 [G] So he said *he would* **destroy** them—had not Moses,
106:34 [G] *They did* not **destroy** the peoples as the LORD had
145:20 [G] over all who love him, but all the wicked *he will* **destroy**.
Pr 14:11 [C] The house of the wicked *will* **be destroyed**, but the tent of
Isa 10:7 [G] his purpose is to **destroy**, to put an end to many nations.
13:9 [G] to make the land desolate and **destroy** the sinners within it.
14:23 [G] I will sweep her with the broom of **destruction**,"
23:11 [G] order concerning Phoenicia that her fortresses *be* **destroyed**.
26:14 [G] You punished them and **brought** them **to ruin**; you wiped
48:19 [C] their name would never be cut off nor **destroyed** from before
Jer 48:8 [C] The valley will be ruined and the plateau **destroyed**,
48:42 [C] Moab *will* **be destroyed** as a nation because she defied the
La 3:66 [G] and **destroy** them from under the heavens of the LORD.
Eze 14:9 [G] against him and **destroy** him from among my people Israel.
25:7 [G] *I will* **destroy** you, and you will know that I am the
32:12 [C] the pride of Egypt, and all her hordes *will* **be overthrown**.
34:16 [G] the weak, but the sleek and the strong *I will* **destroy**.
Da 11:44 [G] he will set out in a great rage to **destroy** and annihilate many.
Hos 10:8 [C] The high places of wickedness *will* **be destroyed**—it is the
Am 2:9 [G] "I **destroyed** the Amorite before them, though he was tall as
2:9 [G] as the oaks. *I* **destroyed** his fruit above and his roots below.
9:8 [G] *I will* **destroy** it from the face of the earth—yet I will not
9:8 [G] yet *I will* not **totally destroy** [+906+9012] the house of
9:8 [G] yet *I will* not **totally destroy** [+906+9012] the house of
Mic 5:14 [5:13] [G] you your Asherah poles and **demolish** your cities.
Hag 2:22 [G] royal thrones and **shatter** the power of the foreign kingdoms.
Zec 12:9 [G] On that day I will set out to **destroy** all the nations that attack

9013 שֶׁמֶד ***šemed***, n.pr.m. [1]

Shemed [1]

1Ch 8:12 **Shemed** (who built Ono and Lod with its surrounding villages),

9014 ¹שַׁמָּה ***šammâ¹***, n.f. [40] [√ 9037]

desolate [7], waste [7], horror [6], object of horror [5], ruin [4], laid waste [3], desolation [1], desolations [1], destroyed [1], devastate [1], horrible [1], in ruins [1], thing of horror [1], wasteland [1]

Dt 28:37 You will become a **thing of horror** and an object of scorn
2Ki 22:19 that they would become accursed and **laid waste**, and because you
2Ch 29:8 he has made them an object of dread and **horror** and scorn,
30:7 their fathers, so that he made them an **object of horror**, as you see.
36:21 all the time of its **desolation** it rested, until the seventy years were
Ps 46:8 [46:9] of the LORD, the **desolations** he has brought on the earth.
73:19 How suddenly are they **destroyed**, completely swept away by
Isa 5:9 "Surely the great houses will become **desolate**, the fine mansions
13:9 to make the land **desolate** and destroy the sinners within it.
24:12 The city is left **in ruins**, its gate is battered to pieces.
Jer 2:15 They have laid **waste** his land; his towns are burned and deserted.
4:7 of nations has set out. He has left his place to lay **waste** your land.
5:30 "A **horrible** and shocking thing has happened in the land:
8:21 people are crushed, I am crushed; I mourn, and **horror** grips me.
18:16 Their land will be laid **waste**, an object of lasting scorn; all who
19:8 I will **devastate** this city and make it an object of scorn; all who
25:9 destroy them and make them an **object of horror** and scorn,
25:11 This whole country will become a desolate **wasteland**, and these
25:18 make them a ruin and an **object of horror** and scorn and cursing,
25:38 their land will become **desolate** because of the sword of the
29:18 all the kingdoms of the earth and an object of cursing and **horror**,
42:18 You will be an object of cursing and **horror**, of condemnation
44:12 They will become an object of cursing and **horror**, of
44:22 an object of cursing and a desolate **waste** without inhabitants,
46:19 for Memphis will be **laid waste** and lie in ruins without inhabitant.
48:9 her towns will become **desolate**, with no one to live in them.
49:13 "that Bozrah will become a **ruin** and an object of horror, of
49:17 "Edom will become an **object of horror**; all who pass by will be
50:3 A nation from the north will attack her and lay **waste** her land.
50:23 of the whole earth! How **desolate** is Babylon among the nations!
51:29 to lay **waste** the land of Babylon so that no one will live there.
51:37 a haunt of jackals, an **object of horror** and scorn, a place where no
51:41 earth seized! What a **horror** Babylon will be among the nations!
51:43 Her towns will be **desolate**, a dry and desert land, a land where no
Eze 23:33 filled with drunkenness and sorrow, the cup of **ruin** and desolation,
Hos 5:9 Ephraim will be **laid waste** on the day of reckoning.
Joel 1:7 It has laid **waste** my vines and ruined my fig trees. It has stripped
Mic 6:16 Therefore I will give you over to **ruin** and your people to derision;
Zep 2:15 What a **ruin** she has become, a lair for wild beasts! All who pass
Zec 7:14 or go. This is how they made the pleasant land **desolate**.' "

9015 ²שַׁמָּה ***šammâ²***, n.pr.m. [7] [→ 9016, 9021, 9025?; cf. 9007, 9048? *or* 9087?]

Shammah [7]

Ge 36:13 The sons of Reuel: Nahath, Zerah, **Shammah** and Mizzah.
36:17 Esau's son Reuel: Chiefs Nahath, Zerah, **Shammah** and Mizzah.
1Sa 16:9 Jesse then had **Shammah** pass by, but Samuel said, "Nor has the

1Sa 17: 13 was Eliab; the second, Abinadab; and the third, **Shammah**.
2Sa 23: 25 **Shammah** the Harodite, Elika the Harodite,
23: 33 son of **Shammah** the Hararite, Ahiam son of Sharar the Hararite,
1Ch 1: 37 The sons of Reuel: Nahath, Zerah, **Shammah** and Mizzah.

9016 שַׁמְהוּת *šamhût*, n.pr.m. [1] [√ 9021; cf. 9015]

Shamhuth [1]

1Ch 27: 8 for the fifth month, was the commander **Shamhuth** the Izrahite.

9017 שְׁמוּאֵל *šᵉmû'ēl*, n.pr.m. [140 / 141] [√ 9005 + 446]

Samuel [127], he^s [5], Samuel's [4], *untranslated* [2], him^s [2], Shemuel [1]

Nu 34: 20 **Shemuel** son of Ammihud, from the tribe of Simeon;
1Sa 1: 20 She named him **Samuel**, saying, "Because I asked the LORD for
2: 18 **Samuel** was ministering before the LORD—a boy wearing a
2: 21 the boy **Samuel** grew up in the presence of the LORD.
2: 26 the boy **Samuel** continued to grow in stature and in favor with the
3: 1 The boy **Samuel** ministered before the LORD under Eli.
3: 3 and **Samuel** was lying down in the temple of the LORD,
3: 4 Then the LORD called **Samuel**. Samuel answered, "Here I am."
3: 6 Again the LORD called, "**Samuel**!" And Samuel got up and went
3: 6 And **Samuel** got up and went to Eli and said, "Here I am;
3: 7 Now **Samuel** did not yet know the LORD: The word of the
3: 8 The LORD called **Samuel** a third time, and Samuel got up
3: 9 So Eli told **Samuel**, "Go and lie down, and if he calls you,
3: 9 for your servant is listening.' " So **Samuel** went and lay down in
3: 10 and stood there, calling as at the other times, "**Samuel**!
3: 10 and stood there, calling as at the other times, "Samuel! **Samuel**!"
3: 10 Samuel!" Then **Samuel** said, "Speak, for your servant is listening."
3: 11 the LORD said to **Samuel**: "See, I am about to do something in
3: 15 **Samuel** lay down until morning and then opened the doors of the
3: 15 of the house of the LORD. **He**^s was afraid to tell Eli the vision,
3: 16 but Eli called **him**^s and said, "Samuel, my son." Samuel answered,
3: 16 but Eli called him and said, "**Samuel**, my son." Samuel answered,
3: 18 So **Samuel** told him everything, hiding nothing from him.
3: 19 The LORD was with **Samuel** as he grew up, and he let none of
3: 20 all Israel from Dan to Beersheba recognized that **Samuel** was
3: 21 and there he revealed himself to **Samuel** through his word.
4: 1 **Samuel's** word came to all Israel. Now the Israelites went out to
7: 3 **Samuel** said to the whole house of Israel, "If you are returning to
7: 5 **Samuel** said, "Assemble all Israel at Mizpah and I will intercede
7: 6 against the LORD." And **Samuel** was leader of Israel at Mizpah.
7: 8 They said to **Samuel**, "Do not stop crying out to the LORD our
7: 9 **Samuel** took a suckling lamb and offered it up as a whole burnt
7: 9 **He**^s cried out to the LORD on Israel's behalf, and the LORD
7: 10 While **Samuel** was sacrificing the burnt offering, the Philistines
7: 12 Then **Samuel** took a stone and set it up between Mizpah and Shen.
7: 13 Throughout **Samuel's** lifetime, the hand of the LORD was
7: 15 **Samuel** continued as judge over Israel all the days of his life.
8: 1 When **Samuel** grew old, he appointed his sons as judges for Israel.
8: 4 elders of Israel gathered together and came to **Samuel** at Ramah.
8: 6 they said, "Give us a king to lead us," this displeased **Samuel**;
8: 6 to lead us," this displeased Samuel; so **he**^s prayed to the LORD.
8: 7 the LORD told **him**^s: "Listen to all that the people are saying to
8: 10 **Samuel** told all the words of the LORD to the people who were
8: 19 But the people refused to listen to **Samuel**. "No!" they said.
8: 21 When **Samuel** heard all that the people said, he repeated it before
8: 22 LORD answered, **[RPH]** "Listen to them and give them a king."
8: 22 **Samuel** said to the men of Israel, "Everyone go back to his town."
9: 14 up to the town, and as they were entering it, there was **Samuel**,
9: 15 day before Saul came, the LORD had revealed this to **Samuel**:
9: 17 When **Samuel** caught sight of Saul, the LORD said to him,
9: 18 Saul approached **Samuel** in the gateway and asked, "Would you
9: 19 "I am the seer," **Samuel** replied. "Go up ahead of me to the high
9: 22 **Samuel** brought Saul and his servant into the hall and seated them
9: 23 **Samuel** said to the cook, "Bring the piece of meat I gave you,
9: 24 'I have invited guests.' " And Saul dined with **Samuel** that day.
9: 26 They rose about daybreak and **Samuel** called to Saul on the roof,
9: 26 When Saul got ready, he and **Samuel** went outside together.
9: 27 **Samuel** said to Saul, "Tell the servant to go on ahead of us"—
10: 1 Then **Samuel** took a flask of oil and poured it on Saul's head
10: 9 As Saul turned to leave **Samuel**, God changed Saul's heart,
10: 14 "But when we saw they were not to be found, we went to **Samuel**."
10: 15 Saul's uncle said, "Tell me what **Samuel** said to you."
10: 16 he did not tell his uncle what **Samuel** had said about the kingship.
10: 17 **Samuel** summoned the people of Israel to the LORD at Mizpah
10: 20 When **Samuel** brought all the tribes of Israel near, the tribe of
10: 24 **Samuel** said to all the people, "Do you see the man the LORD
10: 25 **Samuel** explained to the people the regulations of the kingship.
10: 25 Then **Samuel** dismissed the people, each to his own home.
11: 7 to the oxen of anyone who does not follow Saul and **Samuel**."
11: 12 The people then said to **Samuel**, "Who was it that asked,
11: 14 Then **Samuel** said to the people, "Come, let us go to Gilgal
12: 1 **Samuel** said to all Israel, "I have listened to everything you said to
12: 6 **Samuel** said to the people, "It is the LORD who appointed Moses
12: 11 Then the LORD sent Jerub-Baal, Barak, Jephthah and **Samuel**,
12: 18 **Samuel** called upon the LORD, and that same day the LORD
12: 18 So all the people stood in awe of the LORD and of **Samuel**.
12: 19 The people all said to **Samuel**, "Pray to the LORD your God for
12: 20 "Do not be afraid," **Samuel** replied. "You have done all this evil;
13: 8 He waited seven days, the time set by **Samuel**; but Samuel did not
13: 8 **Samuel** did not come to Gilgal, and Saul's men began to scatter.
13: 10 the offering, **Samuel** arrived, and Saul went out to greet him.
13: 11 asked **Samuel**. Saul replied, "When I saw that the men were
13: 13 "You acted foolishly," **Samuel** said. "You have not kept the
13: 15 Then **Samuel** left Gilgal and went up to Gibeah in Benjamin,
15: 1 **Samuel** said to Saul, "I am the one the LORD sent to anoint you
15: 10 Then the word of the LORD came to **Samuel**:
15: 11 **Samuel** was troubled, and he cried out to the LORD all that night.
15: 12 Early in the morning **Samuel** got up and went to meet Saul,
15: 12 morning Samuel got up and went to meet Saul, but **he**^s was told,
15: 13 When **Samuel** reached him, Saul said, "The LORD bless you!
15: 14 But **Samuel** said, "What then is this bleating of sheep in my ears?
15: 16 "Stop!" **Samuel** said to Saul. "Let me tell you what the LORD
15: 17 **Samuel** said, "Although you were once small in your own eyes,
15: 20 Saul said. **[RPH]** "I went on the mission the LORD assigned me.
15: 22 But **Samuel** replied: "Does the LORD delight in burnt offerings
15: 24 Saul said to **Samuel**, "I have sinned. I violated the LORD's
15: 26 **Samuel** said to him, "I will not go back with you. You have
15: 27 As **Samuel** turned to leave, Saul caught hold of the hem of his
15: 28 **Samuel** said to him, "The LORD has torn the kingdom of Israel
15: 31 So **Samuel** went back with Saul, and Saul worshiped the LORD.
15: 32 Then **Samuel** said, "Bring me Agag king of the Amalekites."
15: 33 But **Samuel** said, "As your sword has made women childless,
15: 33 And **Samuel** put Agag to death before the LORD at Gilgal.
15: 34 **Samuel** left for Ramah, but Saul went up to his home in Gibeah of
15: 35 Until the day **Samuel** died, he did not go to see Saul again,
15: 35 he did not go to see Saul again, though **Samuel** mourned for him.
16: 1 The LORD said to **Samuel**, "How long will you mourn for Saul,
16: 2 **Samuel** said, "How can I go? Saul will hear about it and kill me."
16: 4 **Samuel** did what the LORD said. When he arrived at Bethlehem,
16: 7 But the LORD said to **Samuel**, "Do not consider his appearance
16: 8 Then Jesse called Abinadab and had him pass in front of **Samuel**.
16: 10 Jesse had seven of his sons pass before **Samuel**, but Samuel said to
16: 10 but **Samuel** said to him, "The LORD has not chosen these."
16: 11 So **he**^s asked Jesse, "Are these all the sons you have?" "There is
16: 11 **Samuel** said, "Send for him; we will not sit down until he arrives."
16: 13 So **Samuel** took the horn of oil and anointed him in the presence of
16: 13 LORD came upon David in power. **Samuel** then went to Ramah.
19: 18 he went to **Samuel** at Ramah and told him all that Saul had done to
19: 18 done to him. Then he and **Samuel** went to Naioth and stayed there.
19: 20 with **Samuel** standing there as their leader, the Spirit of God came
19: 22 he asked, "Where are **Samuel** and David?" "Over in Naioth at
19: 24 stripped off his robes and also prophesied in **Samuel's** presence.
25: 1 Now **Samuel** died, and all Israel assembled and mourned for him;
28: 3 Now **Samuel** was dead, and all Israel had mourned for him
28: 11 "Whom shall I bring up for you?" "Bring up **Samuel**," he said.
28: 12 When the woman saw **Samuel**, she cried out at the top of her voice
28: 14 Saul knew it was **Samuel**, and he bowed down and prostrated
28: 15 **Samuel** said to Saul, "Why have you disturbed me by bringing me
28: 16 **Samuel** said, "Why do you consult me, now that the LORD has
28: 20 length on the ground, filled with fear because of **Samuel's** words.
1Ch 6: 27 [6:12] his son, Elkanah his son and **Samuel** [BHS-] his son.
6: 28 [6:13] The sons of **Samuel**: Joel the firstborn and Abijah the
6: 33 [6:18] Heman, the musician, the son of Joel, the son of **Samuel**,
7: 2 Uzzi, Rephaiah, Jeriel, Jahmai, Ibsam and **Samuel**—heads of their
9: 22 assigned to their positions of trust by David and **Samuel** the seer.
11: 3 king over Israel, as the LORD had promised through **Samuel**.
26: 28 everything dedicated by **Samuel** the seer and by Saul son of Kish,
29: 29 to end, they are written in the records of **Samuel** the seer,
2Ch 35: 18 observed like this in Israel since the days of the prophet **Samuel**;
Ps 99: 6 his priests, **Samuel** was among those who called on his name;
Jer 15: 1 "Even if Moses and **Samuel** were to stand before me, my heart

9018 שַׁמּוּעַ *šammûa'*, n.pr.m. [5] [√ 9048 + 3378?]

Shammua [5]

Nu 13: 4 their names: from the tribe of Reuben, **Shammua** son of Zaccur;
2Sa 5: 14 children born to him there: **Shammua**, Shobab, Nathan, Solomon,
1Ch 14: 4 children born to him there: **Shammua**, Shobab, Nathan, Solomon,
Ne 11: 17 and Abda son of **Shammua**, the son of Galal, the son of Jeduthun.
12: 18 of Bilgah's, **Shammua**; of Shemaiah's, Jehonathan;

9019 שְׁמוּעָה *šᵉmûʿâ*, n.f. [27] [√ 9048]

news [8], report [7], message [5], rumor [3], another[s] [+2021] [1], mention [+928+7023] [1], reports [1], rumors [1]

1Sa 2: 24 it is not a good **report** that I hear spreading among the LORD's
4: 19 When she heard the **news** that the ark of God had been captured
2Sa 4: 4 He was five years old when the **news** *about* Saul and Jonathan
13: 30 While they were on their way, the **report** came to David:
1Ki 2: 28 When the **news** reached Joab, who had conspired with Adonijah
10: 7 in wisdom and wealth you have far exceeded the **report** I heard.
2Ki 19: 7 to put such a spirit in him that when he hears a certain **report**,
2Ch 9: 6 wisdom was told me; you have far exceeded the **report** I heard.
Ps 112: 7 He will have no fear of bad **news**; his heart is steadfast, trusting in
Pr 15: 30 brings joy to the heart, and good **news** gives health to the bones.
25: 25 Like cold water to a weary soul is good **news** from a distant land.
Isa 28: 9 is it he is trying to teach? To whom is he explaining his **message**?
28: 19 The understanding of this **message** will bring sheer terror.
37: 7 going to put a spirit in him so that when he hears a certain **report**,
53: 1 Who has believed our **message** and to whom has the arm of the
Jer 10: 22 The **report** is coming—a great commotion from the land of the
49: 14 I have heard a **message** from the LORD: An envoy was sent to
49: 23 "Hamath and Arpad are dismayed, for they have heard bad **news**.
51: 46 Do not lose heart or be afraid when **rumors** are heard in the land;
51: 46 *one* **rumor** comes this year, another the next, rumors of violence in
51: 46 one rumor comes this year, **another**[s] [+2021] the next, rumors of
Eze 7: 26 Calamity upon calamity will come, and **rumor** upon rumor.
7: 26 Calamity upon calamity will come, and rumor upon **rumor**.
16: 56 You would not even **mention** [+928+7023] your sister Sodom in
21: 7 [21:12] you shall say, 'Because of the **news** that is coming. Every
Da 11: 44 **reports** from the east and the north will alarm him, and he will set
Ob 1: 1 says about Edom—We have heard a **message** from the LORD:

9020 שָׁמוּר *šāmûr*, n.pr.m. [0] [cf 9033]

1Ch 24: 24 [Micah; from the sons of Micah: **Shamir**. [K; see Q 9033]]

9021 שַׁמּוֹת *šammôt*, n.pr.m. [1] [→ 9016; cf. 9015]

Shammoth [1]

1Ch 11: 27 **Shammoth** the Harorite, Helez the Pelonite,

9022 שָׁמַח *šāmaḥ*, v. Not used in NIV/BHS

9023 שָׁמַט *šāmaṭ*, v. [9] [→ 9024]

stumbled [2], be thrown down [1], cancel debt [1], cancel [1], lie unplowed [1], lose [1], threw down [1], throw down [1]

Ex 23: 11 [A] during the seventh year *let* the land **lie unplowed**
Dt 15: 2 [A] Every creditor *shall* **cancel** the loan he has made to his
15: 3 [G] but you *must* **cancel** *any* **debt** your brother owes you.
2Sa 6: 6 [A] and took hold of the ark of God, because the oxen **stumbled**.
2Ki 9: 33 [A] "**Throw** her **down**!" Jehu said. So they threw her down,
9: 33 [A] So *they* **threw** her **down**, and some of her blood spattered
1Ch 13: 9 [A] out his hand to steady the ark, because the oxen **stumbled**.
Ps 141: 6 [C] their rulers *will* **be thrown down** from the cliffs,
Jer 17: 4 [A] Through your own fault *you will* **lose** the inheritance I gave

9024 שְׁמִטָּה *šᵉmiṭṭâ*, n.f. [5] [√ 9023]

canceling debts [2], cancel debts [+6913] [1], it[s] [+2021] [1], time for canceling debts [1]

Dt 15: 1 At the end of every seven years *you must* **cancel** [+6913] **debts**.
15: 2 This is how **it**[s] [+2021] is to be done: Every creditor shall cancel
15: 2 because the LORD's **time for canceling debts** has been
15: 9 "The seventh year, the year for **canceling debts**, is near,"
31: 10 in the year for **canceling debts**, during the Feast of Tabernacles,

9025 שַׁמַּי *šammay*, n.pr.m. [6] [√ 9048? *or* 9015?]

Shammai [5], Shammai's [1]

1Ch 2: 28 The sons of Onam: **Shammai** and Jada. The sons of Shammai:
2: 28 Shammai and Jada. The sons of **Shammai**: Nadab and Abishur.
2: 32 The sons of Jada, **Shammai's** brother: Jether and Jonathan.
2: 44 Raham the father of Jorkeam. Rekem was the father of **Shammai**.
2: 45 The son of **Shammai** was Maon, and Maon was the father of Beth
4: 17 birth to Miriam, **Shammai** and Ishbah the father of Eshtemoa.

9026 שְׁמִידָע *šᵉmîdāʿ*, n.pr.m. [3] [→ 9027; cf. 9005 + 3359]

Shemida [3]

Nu 26: 32 through **Shemida**, the Shemidaite clan; through Hepher,
Jos 17: 2 clans of Abiezer, Helek, Asriel, Shechem, Hepher and **Shemida**.
1Ch 7: 19 The sons of **Shemida** were: Ahian, Shechem, Likhi and Aniam.

9027 שְׁמִידָעִי *šᵉmîdāʿî*, a.g. [1] [√ 9026; cf. 9005]

Shemidaite [1]

Nu 26: 32 through Shemida, the **Shemidaite** clan; through Hepher,

9028 שָׁמַיִם *šāmayim*, n.m. [421] [→ Ar 10723]

heaven [154], heavens [141], sky [46], air [40], highest heavens [+9028] [12], starry [9], skies [6], *untranslated* [2], heavenly [2], highest heaven [+9028] [2], skies above [+9028] [2], astrologers [+2042] [1], heaven's [1], horizon [1], in midair [+824+1068+1068 +2021+2021+2256] [1], other[s] [+7895] [1]

Ge 1: 1 In the beginning God created the **heavens** and the earth.
1: 8 God called the expanse "**sky**." And there was evening, and there
1: 9 God said, "Let the water under the **sky** be gathered to one place,
1: 14 "Let there be lights in the expanse of the **sky** to separate the day
1: 15 let them be lights in the expanse of the **sky** to give light on the
1: 17 God set them in the expanse of the **sky** to give light on the earth,
1: 20 and let birds fly above the earth across the expanse of the **sky**."
1: 26 and let them rule over the fish of the sea and the birds of the **air**,
1: 28 Rule over the fish of the sea and the birds of the **air** and over every
1: 30 And to all the beasts of the earth and all the birds of the **air**
2: 1 Thus the **heavens** and the earth were completed in all their vast
2: 4 This is the account of the **heavens** and the earth when they were
2: 4 When the LORD God made the earth and the **heavens**—
2: 19 of the ground all the beasts of the field and all the birds of the **air**.
2: 20 all the livestock, the birds of the **air** and all the beasts of the field.
6: 7 and creatures that move along the ground, and birds of the **air**—
6: 17 bring floodwaters on the earth to destroy all life under the **heavens**,
7: 3 and also seven of every kind of bird, **[NIE]** male and female,
7: 11 deep burst forth, and the floodgates of the **heavens** were opened.
7: 19 and all the high mountains under the entire **heavens** were covered.
7: 23 the ground and the birds of the **air** were wiped from the earth.
8: 2 of the deep and the floodgates of the **heavens** had been closed,
8: 2 had been closed, and the rain had stopped falling from the **sky**.
9: 2 will fall upon all the beasts of the earth and all the birds of the **air**,
11: 4 us build ourselves a city, with a tower that reaches to the **heavens**,
14: 19 be Abram by God Most High, Creator of **heaven** and earth.
14: 22 God Most High, Creator of **heaven** and earth, and have taken an
15: 5 and said, "Look up at the **heavens** and count the stars—
19: 24 on Sodom and Gomorrah—from the LORD out of the **heavens**.
21: 17 and the angel of God called to Hagar from **heaven** and said to her,
22: 11 But the angel of the LORD called out to him from **heaven**,
22: 15 The angel of the LORD called to Abraham from **heaven** a
22: 17 and make your descendants as numerous as the stars in the **sky**
24: 3 to swear by the LORD, the God of **heaven** and the God of earth,
24: 7 "The LORD, the God of **heaven**, who brought me out of my
26: 4 I will make your descendants as numerous as the stars in the **sky**
27: 28 May God give you of **heaven's** dew and of earth's richness—
27: 39 from the earth's richness, away from the dew of **heaven** above.
28: 12 with its top reaching to **heaven**, and the angels of God were
28: 17 is none other than the house of God; this is the gate of **heaven**."
49: 25 who blesses you with blessings of the **heavens** above,
Ex 9: 8 and have Moses toss it into the **air** in the presence of Pharaoh.
9: 10 Moses tossed it into the **air**, and festering boils broke out on men
9: 22 "Stretch out your hand toward the **sky** so that hail will fall all over
9: 23 When Moses stretched out his staff toward the **sky**, the LORD
10: 21 "Stretch out your hand toward the **sky** so that darkness will spread
10: 22 So Moses stretched out his hand toward the **sky**, and total darkness
16: 4 said to Moses, "I will rain down bread from **heaven** for you.
17: 14 completely blot out the memory of Amalek from under **heaven**."
20: 4 make for yourself an idol in the form of anything in **heaven** above
20: 11 For in six days the LORD made the **heavens** and the earth,
20: 22 have seen for yourselves that I have spoken to you from **heaven**:
24: 10 like a pavement made of sapphire, clear as the **sky** itself.
31: 17 for in six days the LORD made the **heavens** and the earth,
32: 13 'I will make your descendants as numerous as the stars in the **sky**
Lev 26: 19 down your stubborn pride and make the **sky** *above* you like iron
Dt 1: 10 your numbers so that today you are as many as the stars in the **sky**.
1: 28 and taller than we are; the cities are large, with walls up to the **sky**.
2: 25 to put the terror and fear of you on all the nations under **heaven**.
3: 24 For what god is there in **heaven** or on earth who can do the deeds
4: 11 foot of the mountain while it blazed with fire to the very **heavens**,
4: 17 or like any animal on earth or any bird that flies in the **air**,
4: 19 And when you look up to the **sky** and see the sun, the moon
4: 19 and see the sun, the moon and the stars—all the **heavenly** array—
4: 19 LORD your God has apportioned to all the nations under **heaven**.
4: 26 I call **heaven** and earth as witnesses against you this day that you
4: 32 man on the earth; ask from one end of the **heavens** to the other.
4: 32 the earth; ask from one end of the heavens to the **other**[s] [+7895].
4: 36 From **heaven** he made you hear his voice to discipline you.
4: 39 and take to heart this day that the LORD is God in **heaven** above
5: 8 make for yourself an idol in the form of anything in **heaven** above
7: 24 your hand, and you will wipe out their names from under **heaven**.

Dt 9: 1 stronger than you, with large cities that have walls up to the **sky**.
9: 14 I may destroy them and blot out their name from under **heaven**.
10: 14 To the LORD your God belong the **heavens**, even the highest
10: 14 even the **highest heavens** [+9028], the earth and everything in it.
10: 14 even the **highest heavens** [+9028], the earth and everything in it.
10: 22 your God has made you as numerous as the stars in the **sky**.
11: 11 of is a land of mountains and valleys that drinks rain from **heaven**.
11: 17 he will shut the **heavens** so that it will not rain and the ground will
11: 21 as many as the days that the **heavens** are above the earth.
17: 3 down to them or to the sun or the moon or the stars of the **sky**,
25: 19 you shall blot out the memory of Amalek from under **heaven**.
26: 15 Look down from **heaven**, your holy dwelling place, and bless your
28: 12 The LORD will open the **heavens**, the storehouse of his bounty,
28: 23 The **sky** over your head will be bronze, the ground beneath you
28: 24 it will come down from the **skies** until you are destroyed.
28: 26 Your carcasses will be food for all the birds of the **air** and the
28: 62 You who were as numerous as the stars in the **sky** will be left
29: 20 [29:19] the LORD will blot out his name from under **heaven**.
30: 4 have been banished to the most distant land under the **heavens**,
30: 12 It is not up in **heaven**, so that you have to ask, "Who will ascend
30: 12 "Who will ascend into **heaven** to get it and proclaim it to us
30: 19 This day I call **heaven** and earth as witnesses against you that I
31: 28 in their hearing and call **heaven** and earth to testify against them.
32: 1 Listen, O **heavens**, and I will speak; hear, O earth, the words of my
32: 40 I lift my hand to **heaven** and declare: As surely as I live forever,
33: 13 LORD bless his land with the precious dew from **heaven** above
33: 26 who rides on the **heavens** to help you and on the clouds in his
33: 28 in a land of grain and new wine, where the **heavens** drop dew.
Jos 2: 11 for the LORD your God is God in **heaven** above and on the earth
8: 20 looked back and saw the smoke of the city rising against the **sky**,
10: 11 the LORD hurled large hailstones down on them from the **sky**,
10: 13 The sun stopped in the middle of the **sky** and delayed going down
Jdg 5: 4 the earth shook, the **heavens** poured, the clouds poured down
5: 20 From the **heavens** the stars fought, from their courses they fought
13: 20 As the flame blazed up from the altar toward **heaven**, the angel of
20: 40 and saw the smoke of the whole city going up into the **sky**.
1Sa 2: 10 He will thunder against them from **heaven**; the LORD will judge
5: 12 afflicted with tumors, and the outcry of the city went up to **heaven**.
17: 44 "and I'll give your flesh to the birds of the **air** and the beasts of the
17: 46 will give the carcasses of the Philistine army to the birds of the **air**
2Sa 18: 9 was left hanging **in midair** [+824+1068+1068+2021+2021+2256],
21: 10 harvest till the rain poured down from the **heavens** on the bodies,
21: 10 she did not let the birds of the **air** touch them by day or the wild
22: 8 earth trembled and quaked, the foundations of the **heavens** shook;
22: 10 He parted the **heavens** and came down; dark clouds were under his
22: 14 The LORD thundered from **heaven**; the voice of the Most High
1Ki 8: 22 the whole assembly of Israel, spread out his hands toward **heaven**
8: 23 there is no God like you in **heaven** above or on earth below—
8: 27 The **heavens**, even the highest heaven, cannot contain you.
8: 27 The heavens, even the **highest heaven** [+9028], cannot contain
8: 27 The heavens, even the **highest heaven** [+9028], cannot contain
8: 30 Hear from **heaven**, your dwelling place, and when you hear,
8: 32 then hear from **heaven** and act. Judge between your servants,
8: 34 then hear from **heaven** and forgive the sin of your people Israel
8: 35 "When the **heavens** are shut up and there is no rain because your
8: 36 then hear from **heaven** and forgive the sin of your servants,
8: 39 then hear from **heaven**, your dwelling place. Forgive and act;
8: 43 hear from **heaven**, your dwelling place, and do whatever the
8: 45 hear from **heaven** their prayer and their plea, and uphold their
8: 49 from **heaven**, your dwelling place, hear their prayer and their plea,
8: 54 he had been kneeling with his hands spread out toward **heaven**.
14: 11 and the birds of the **air** will feed on those who die in the country.
16: 4 and the birds of the **air** will feed on those who die in the country."
18: 45 Meanwhile, the **sky** grew black with clouds, the wind rose,
21: 24 and the birds of the **air** will feed on those who die in the country."
22: 19 I saw the LORD sitting on his throne with all the host of **heaven**
2Ki 1: 10 may fire come down from **heaven** and consume you and your fifty
1: 10 Then fire fell from **heaven** and consumed the captain and his men.
1: 12 "may fire come down from **heaven** and consume you and your
1: 12 Then the fire of God fell from **heaven** and consumed him
1: 14 fire has fallen from **heaven** and consumed the first two captains
2: 1 When the LORD was about to take Elijah up to **heaven** in a
2: 11 the two of them, and Elijah went up to **heaven** in a whirlwind.
7: 2 even if the LORD should open the floodgates of the **heavens**,
7: 19 even if the LORD should open the floodgates of the **heavens**,
14: 27 not said he would blot out the name of Israel from under **heaven**,
17: 16 They bowed down to all the **starry** hosts, and they worshiped Baal.
19: 15 all the kingdoms of the earth. You have made **heaven** and earth.
21: 3 He bowed down to all the **starry** hosts and worshiped them.
21: 5 of the temple of the LORD, he built altars to all the **starry** hosts.
23: 4 all the articles made for Baal and Asherah and all the **starry** hosts.
23: 5 and moon, to the constellations and to all the **starry** hosts.
1Ch 16: 26 gods of the nations are idols, but the LORD made the **heavens**.
16: 31 Let the **heavens** rejoice, let the earth be glad; let them say among
21: 16 and saw the angel of the LORD standing between **heaven**
21: 26 the LORD answered him with fire from **heaven** on the altar of
27: 23 had promised to make Israel as numerous as the stars in the **sky**.
29: 11 and the splendor, for everything in **heaven** and earth is yours.
2Ch 2: 6 [2:5] since the **heavens**, even the highest heavens, cannot contain
2: 6 [2:5] since the heavens, even the **highest heavens** [+9028],
2: 6 [2:5] since the heavens, even the **highest heavens** [+9028],
2: 12 [2:11] the God of Israel, who made **heaven** and earth!
6: 13 whole assembly of Israel and spread out his hands toward **heaven**.
6: 14 God of Israel, there is no God like you in **heaven** or on earth—
6: 18 The **heavens**, even the highest heavens, cannot contain you.
6: 18 The heavens, even the **highest heavens** [+9028], cannot contain
6: 18 The heavens, even the **highest heavens** [+9028], cannot contain
6: 21 Hear from **heaven**, your dwelling place; and when you hear,
6: 23 then hear from **heaven** and act. Judge between your servants,
6: 25 then hear from **heaven** and forgive the sin of your people Israel
6: 26 "When the **heavens** are shut up and there is no rain because your
6: 27 then hear from **heaven** and forgive the sin of your servants,
6: 30 hear from **heaven**, your dwelling place. Forgive, and deal with
6: 33 hear from **heaven**, your dwelling place, and do whatever the
6: 35 hear from **heaven** their prayer and their plea, and uphold their
6: 39 from **heaven**, your dwelling place, hear their prayer and their
7: 1 fire came down from **heaven** and consumed the burnt offering
7: 13 "When I shut up the **heavens** so that there is no rain, or command
7: 14 will I hear from **heaven** and will forgive their sin and will heal
18: 18 I saw the LORD sitting on his throne with all the host of **heaven**
20: 6 God of our fathers, are you not the God who is in **heaven**?
28: 9 But you have slaughtered them in a rage that reaches to **heaven**.
30: 27 God heard them, for their prayer reached **heaven**, his holy
32: 20 the prophet Isaiah son of Amoz cried out in prayer to **heaven** about
33: 3 He bowed down to all the **starry** hosts and worshiped them.
33: 5 of the temple of the LORD, he built altars to all the **starry** hosts.
36: 23 " 'The LORD, the God of **heaven**, has given me all the kingdoms
Ezr 1: 2 " 'The LORD, the God of **heaven**, has given me all the kingdoms
9: 6 are higher than our heads and our guilt has reached to the **heavens**.
Ne 1: 4 days I mourned and fasted and prayed before the God of **heaven**.
1: 5 "O LORD, God of **heaven**, the great and awesome God,
1: 9 then even if your exiled people are at the farthest **horizon**,
2: 4 "What is it you want?" Then I prayed to the God of **heaven**,
2: 20 them by saying, "The God of **heaven** will give us success.
9: 6 You made the **heavens**, even the highest heavens, and all their
9: 6 You made the heavens, even the **highest heavens** [+9028],
9: 6 You made the heavens, even the **highest heavens** [+9028],
9: 6 give life to everything, and the multitudes of **heaven** worship you.
9: 13 came down on Mount Sinai; you spoke to them from **heaven**.
9: 15 In their hunger you gave them bread from **heaven** and in their
9: 23 You made their sons as numerous as the stars in the **sky**, and you
9: 27 From **heaven** you heard them, and in your great compassion you
9: 28 And when they cried out to you again, you heard from **heaven**,
Job 1: 16 "The fire of God fell from the **sky** and burned up the sheep
2: 12 and they tore their robes and sprinkled dust on their heads. **[NIE]**
9: 8 He alone stretches out the **heavens** and treads on the waves of the
11: 8 They are higher than the **heavens**—what can you do? They are
12: 7 they will teach you, or the birds of the **air**, and they will tell you;
14: 12 till the **heavens** are no more, men will not awake or be roused from
15: 15 trust in his holy ones, if even the **heavens** are not pure in his eyes,
16: 19 Even now my witness is in **heaven**; my advocate is on high.
20: 6 Though his pride reaches to the **heavens** and his head touches the
20: 27 The **heavens** will expose his guilt; the earth will rise up against
22: 12 "Is not God in the heights of **heaven**? And see how lofty are the
22: 14 so he does not see us as he goes about in the vaulted **heavens**.'
26: 11 The pillars of the **heavens** quake, aghast at his rebuke.
26: 13 By his breath the **skies** became fair; his hand pierced the gliding
28: 21 of every living thing, concealed even from the birds of the **air**.
28: 24 views the ends of the earth and sees everything under the **heavens**.
35: 5 Look up at the **heavens** and see; gaze at the clouds so high above
35: 11 beasts of the earth and makes us wiser than the birds of the **air**?'
37: 3 He unleashes his lightning beneath the whole **heaven** and sends it
38: 29 comes the ice? Who gives birth to the frost from the **heavens**
38: 33 Do you know the laws of the **heavens**? Can you set up ⌊God's⌋
38: 37 count the clouds? Who can tip over the water jars of the **heavens**
41: 11 [41:3] that I must pay? Everything under **heaven** belongs to me.
Ps 2: 4 The One enthroned in **heaven** laughs; the Lord scoffs at them.
8: 1 [8:2] in all the earth! You have set your glory above the **heavens**.
8: 3 [8:4] When I consider your **heavens**, the work of your fingers,
8: 8 [8:9] the birds of the **air**, and the fish of the sea, all that swim the
11: 4 is in his holy temple; the LORD is on his **heavenly** throne.
14: 2 The LORD looks down from **heaven** on the sons of men to see if
18: 9 [18:10] He parted the **heavens** and came down; dark clouds were
18: 13 [18:14] The LORD thundered from **heaven**; the voice of the
19: 1 [19:2] The **heavens** declare the glory of God; the skies proclaim
19: 6 [19:7] It rises at one end of the **heavens** and makes its circuit to
20: 6 [20:7] he answers him from his holy **heaven** with the saving
33: 6 By the word of the LORD were the **heavens** made, their starry

Ps 33:13 From **heaven** the LORD looks down and sees all mankind;
36:5 [36:6] Your love, O LORD, reaches to the **heavens**,
50:4 He summons the **heavens** above, and the earth, that he may judge
50:6 the **heavens** proclaim his righteousness, for God himself is judge.
53:2 [53:3] God looks down from **heaven** on the sons of men to see if
57:3 [57:4] He sends from **heaven** and saves me, rebuking those who
57:5 [57:6] Be exalted, O God, above the **heavens**; let your glory be
57:10 [57:11] For great is your love, reaching to the **heavens**; your
57:11 [57:12] Be exalted, O God, above the **heavens**; let your glory be
68:8 [68:9] earth shook, the **heavens** poured down rain, before God,
68:33 [68:34] to him who rides the ancient **skies** [+9028] **above**, who
68:33 [68:34] to him who rides the ancient **skies above** [+9028], who
69:34 [69:35] Let **heaven** and earth praise him, the seas and all that
73:9 Their mouths lay claim to **heaven**, and their tongues take
73:25 Whom have I in **heaven** but you? And earth has nothing I desire
76:8 [76:9] From **heaven** you pronounced judgment, and the land
78:23 command to the skies above and opened the doors of the **heavens**;
78:24 manna for the people to eat, he gave them the grain of **heaven**.
78:26 He let loose the east wind from the **heavens** and led forth the south
79:2 the dead bodies of your servants as food to the birds of the **air**,
80:14 [80:15] to us, O God Almighty! Look down from **heaven** and see!
85:11 [85:12] the earth, and righteousness looks down from **heaven**.
89:2 [89:3] that you established your faithfulness in **heaven** itself.
89:5 [89:6] The **heavens** praise your wonders, O LORD,
89:11 [89:12] The **heavens** are yours, and yours also the earth;
89:29 [89:30] his line forever, his throne as long as the **heavens** endure.
96:5 gods of the nations are idols, but the LORD made the **heavens**.
96:11 Let the **heavens** rejoice, let the earth be glad; let the sea resound,
97:6 The **heavens** proclaim his righteousness, and all the peoples see his
102:19 [102:20] his sanctuary on high, from **heaven** he viewed the earth,
102:25 [102:26] of the earth, and the **heavens** are the work of your hands.
103:11 For as high as the **heavens** are above the earth, so great is his love
103:19 The LORD has established his throne in **heaven**, and his kingdom
104:2 in light as with a garment; he stretches out the **heavens** like a tent
104:12 The birds of the **air** nest by the waters; they sing among the
105:40 he brought them quail and satisfied them with the bread of **heaven**.
107:26 They mounted up to the **heavens** and went down to the depths;
108:4 [108:5] For great is your love, higher than the **heavens**; your
108:5 [108:6] Be exalted, O God, above the **heavens**, and let your glory
113:4 is exalted over all the nations, his glory above the **heavens**.
113:6 who stoops down to look on the **heavens** and the earth?
115:3 Our God is in **heaven**; he does whatever pleases him.
115:15 you be blessed by the LORD, the Maker of **heaven** and earth.
115:16 The **highest heavens** [+9028] belong to the LORD, but the earth
115:16 The **highest heavens** [+9028] belong to the LORD, but the earth
119:89 Your word, O LORD, is eternal; it stands firm in the **heavens**.
121:2 My help comes from the LORD, the Maker of **heaven** and earth.
123:1 I lift up my eyes to you, to you whose throne is in **heaven**.
124:8 help is in the name of the LORD, the Maker of **heaven** and earth.
134:3 May the LORD, the Maker of **heaven** and earth, bless you from
135:6 in the **heavens** and on the earth, in the seas and all their depths.
136:5 who by his understanding made the **heavens**, *His love*
136:26 Give thanks to the God of **heaven**. *His love endures*
139:8 If I go up to the **heavens**, you are there; if I make my bed in the
144:5 Part your **heavens**, O LORD, and come down; touch the
146:6 the Maker of **heaven** and earth, the sea, and everything in them—
147:8 He covers the **sky** with clouds; he supplies the earth with rain
148:1 Praise the LORD from the **heavens**, praise him in the heights
148:4 you **highest heavens** [+9028] and you waters above the skies.
148:4 you **highest heavens** [+9028] and you waters above the skies.
148:4 Praise him, you highest heavens and you waters above the **skies**.
148:13 alone is exalted; his splendor is above the earth and the **heavens**.
Pr 3:19 earth's foundations, by understanding he set the **heavens** in place;
8:27 I was there when he set the **heavens** in place, when he marked out
23:5 they will surely sprout wings and fly off to the **sky** like an eagle.
25:3 As the **heavens** are high and the earth is deep, so the hearts of
30:4 Who has gone up to **heaven** and come down? Who has gathered up
30:19 the way of an eagle in the **sky**, the way of a snake on a rock,
Ecc 1:13 to study and to explore by wisdom all that is done under **heaven**.
2:3 I wanted to see what was worthwhile for men to do under **heaven**
3:1 time for everything, and a season for every activity under **heaven**:
5:2 [5:1] God is in **heaven** and you are on earth, so let your words be
10:20 in your bedroom, because a bird of the **air** may carry your words,
Isa 1:2 Hear, O **heavens**! Listen, O earth! For the LORD has spoken:
13:5 They come from faraway lands, from the ends of the **heavens**—
13:10 The stars of **heaven** and their constellations will not show their
13:13 Therefore I will make the **heavens** tremble; and the earth will
14:12 How you have fallen from **heaven**, O morning star, son of the
14:13 You said in your heart, "I will ascend to **heaven**; I will raise my
34:4 All the stars of the **heavens** will be dissolved and the sky rolled up
34:4 of the heavens will be dissolved and the **sky** rolled up like a scroll;
34:5 My sword has drunk its fill in the **heavens**; see, it descends in
37:16 all the kingdoms of the earth. You have made **heaven** and earth.
40:12 his hand, or with the breadth of his hand marked off the **heavens**?
40:22 He stretches out the **heavens** like a canopy, and spreads them out
42:5 he who created the **heavens** and stretched them out, who spread
44:23 Sing for joy, O **heavens**, for the LORD has done this;
44:24 who has made all things, who alone stretched out the **heavens**,
45:8 "You **heavens** above, rain down righteousness; let the clouds
45:12 My own hands stretched out the **heavens**; I marshaled their starry
45:18 he who created the **heavens**, he is God; he who fashioned
47:13 Let your **astrologers** [+2042] come forward, those stargazers who
48:13 of the earth, and my right hand spread out the **heavens**;
49:13 Shout for joy, O **heavens**; rejoice, O earth; burst into song,
50:3 I clothe the **sky** with darkness and make sackcloth its covering."
51:6 Lift up your eyes to the **heavens**, look at the earth beneath;
51:6 the **heavens** will vanish like smoke, the earth will wear out like a
51:13 who stretched out the **heavens** and laid the foundations of the
51:16 I who set the **heavens** in place, who laid the foundations of the
55:9 "As the **heavens** are higher than the earth, so are my ways higher
55:10 As the rain and the snow come down from **heaven**, and do not
63:15 Look down from **heaven** and see from your lofty throne, holy
64:1 [63:19] Oh, that you would rend the **heavens** and come down,
65:17 "Behold, I will create new **heavens** and a new earth. The former
66:1 LORD says: "**Heaven** is my throne, and the earth is my footstool.
66:22 "As the new **heavens** and the new earth that I make will endure
Jer 2:12 Be appalled at this, O **heavens**, and shudder with great horror,"
4:23 and empty; and at the **heavens**, and their light was gone.
4:25 and there were no people; every bird in the **sky** had flown away.
4:28 Therefore the earth will mourn and the **heavens** above grow dark,
7:18 the dough and make cakes of bread for the Queen of **Heaven**.
7:33 carcasses of this people will become food for the birds of the **air**
8:2 exposed to the sun and the moon and all the stars of the **heavens**,
8:7 Even the stork in the **sky** knows her appointed seasons,
9:10 [9:9] The birds of the **air** have fled and the animals are gone.
10:2 not learn the ways of the nations or be terrified by signs in the **sky**,
10:12 by his wisdom and stretched out the **heavens** by his understanding.
10:13 When he thunders, the waters in the **heavens** roar; he makes clouds
14:22 Do the **skies** themselves send down showers? No, it is you,
15:3 sword to kill and the dogs to drag away and the birds of the **air**
16:4 and their dead bodies will become food for the birds of the **air**
19:7 and I will give their carcasses as food to the birds of the **air**
19:13 where they burned incense on the roofs to all the **starry** hosts
23:24 "Do not I fill **heaven** and earth?" declares the LORD.
31:37 "Only if the **heavens** above can be measured and the foundations
32:17 you have made the **heavens** and the earth by your great power
33:22 Levites who minister before me as countless as the stars of the **sky**
33:25 with day and night and the fixed laws of **heaven** and earth,
34:20 Their dead bodies will become food for the birds of the **air**
44:17 We will burn incense to the Queen of **Heaven** and will pour out
44:18 But ever since we stopped burning incense to the Queen of **Heaven**
44:19 "When we burned incense to the Queen of **Heaven** and poured out
44:25 burn incense and pour out drink offerings to the Queen of **Heaven**.'
49:36 against Elam the four winds from the four quarters of the **heavens**;
51:9 and each go to his own land, for her judgment reaches to the **skies**,
51:15 by his wisdom and stretched out the **heavens** by his understanding.
51:16 When he thunders, the waters in the **heavens** roar; he makes clouds
51:48 **heaven** and earth and all that is in them will shout for joy over
51:53 Even if Babylon reaches the **sky** and fortifies her lofty stronghold,
La 2:1 He has hurled down the splendor of Israel from **heaven** to earth;
3:41 Let us lift up our hearts and our hands to God in **heaven**, and say:
3:50 until the LORD looks down from **heaven** and sees.
3:66 and destroy them from under the **heavens** *of* the LORD.
4:19 Our pursuers were swifter than eagles in the **sky**; they chased us
Eze 1:1 Kebar River, the **heavens** were opened and I saw visions of God.
8:3 The Spirit lifted me up between earth and **heaven** and in visions of
29:5 give you as food to the beasts of the earth and the birds of the **air**.
31:6 All the birds of the **air** nested in its boughs, all the beasts of the
31:13 All the birds of the **air** settled on the fallen tree, and all the beasts
32:4 I will let all the birds of the **air** settle on you and all the beasts of
32:7 I snuff you out, I will cover the **heavens** and darken their stars;
32:8 All the shining lights in the **heavens** I will darken over you;
38:20 The fish of the sea, the birds of the **air**, the beasts of the field,
Da 8:8 four prominent horns grew up toward the four winds of **heaven**.
8:10 It grew until it reached the host of the **heavens**, and it threw some
9:12 Under the whole **heaven** nothing has ever been done like what has
11:4 be broken up and parceled out toward the four winds of **heaven**.
12:7 of the river, lifted his right hand and his left hand toward **heaven**,
Hos 2:18 [2:20] the birds of the **air** and the creatures that move along the
2:21 [2:23] "I will respond to the **skies**, and they will respond to the
4:3 the beasts of the field and the birds of the **air** and the fish of the sea
7:12 my net over them; I will pull them down like birds of the **air**.
Joel 2:10 the **sky** trembles, the sun and moon are darkened, and the stars no
2:30 [3:3] I will show wonders in the **heavens** and on the earth, blood
3:16 [4:16] thunder from Jerusalem; the earth and the **sky** will tremble.
Am 9:2 Though they climb up to the **heavens**, from there I will bring them
9:6 he who builds his lofty palace in the **heavens** and sets its
Jnh 1:9 the LORD, the God of **heaven**, who made the sea and the land."

Na 3: 16 of your merchants till they are more than the stars of the **sky**,
Hab 3: 3 His glory covered the **heavens** and his praise filled the
Zep 1: 3 I will sweep away the birds of the **air** and the fish of the sea.
1: 5 those who bow down on the roofs to worship the **starry** host,
Hag 1: 10 because of you the **heavens** have withheld their dew and the earth
2: 6 'In a little while I will once more shake the **heavens** and the earth,
2: 21 "Tell Zerubbabel governor of Judah that I will shake the **heavens**
Zec 2: 6 [2:10] "for I have scattered you to the four winds of **heaven**,"
5: 9 of a stork, and they lifted up the basket between **heaven** and earth.
6: 5 The angel answered me, "These are the four spirits of **heaven**,
8: 12 ground will produce its crops, and the **heavens** will drop their dew.
12: 1 The LORD, who stretches out the **heavens**, who lays the
Mal 3: 10 "and see if I will not throw open the floodgates of **heaven**

9029 שְׁמִינִי *šᵉmînî*, a.num.ord. [28] [√ 9046]

eighth [27], following[s] [1]

Ex 22: 30 [22:29] for seven days, but give them to me on the **eighth** day.
Lev 9: 1 On the **eighth** day Moses summoned Aaron and his sons and the
12: 3 On the **eighth** day the boy is to be circumcised.
14: 10 "On the **eighth** day he must bring two male lambs and one ewe
14: 23 "On the **eighth** day he must bring them for his cleansing to the
15: 14 On the **eighth** day he must take two doves or two young pigeons
15: 29 On the **eighth** day she must take two doves or two young pigeons
22: 27 From the **eighth** day on, it will be acceptable as an offering made
23: 36 on the **eighth** day hold a sacred assembly and present an offering
23: 39 first day is a day of rest, and the **eighth** day also is a day of rest.
25: 22 While you plant during the **eighth** year, you will eat from the old
Nu 6: 10 on the **eighth** day he must bring two doves or two young pigeons
7: 54 On the **eighth** day Gamaliel son of Pedahzur, the leader of the
29: 35 " 'On the **eighth** day hold an assembly and do no regular work.
1Ki 6: 38 In the eleventh year in the month of Bul, the **eighth** month,
8: 66 On the **following**[s] day he sent the people away. They blessed the
12: 32 He instituted a festival on the fifteenth day of the **eighth** month,
12: 33 On the fifteenth day of the **eighth** month, a month of his own
1Ch 12: 12 [12:13] Johanan the **eighth**, Elzabad the ninth,
24: 10 the seventh to Hakkoz, the **eighth** to Abijah,
25: 15 the **eighth** to Jeshaiah, his sons and relatives, 12
26: 5 Ammiel the sixth, Issachar the seventh and Peullethai the **eighth**.
27: 11 The **eighth**, for the eighth month, was Sibbecai the Hushathite,
27: 11 The eighth, for the **eighth** month, was Sibbecai the Hushathite,
2Ch 7: 9 On the **eighth** day they held an assembly, for they had celebrated
Ne 8: 18 on the **eighth** day, in accordance with the regulation, there was an
Eze 43: 27 At the end of these days, from the **eighth** day on, the priests are to
Zec 1: 1 In the **eighth** month of the second year of Darius, the word of the

9030 שְׁמִינִית *šᵉmînît*, tt. [3] [√ 9046]

sheminith [3]

1Ch 15: 21 were to play the harps, directing according to ***sheminith***.
Ps 6: T [6:1] According to ***sheminith***. A psalm of David.
12: T [12:1] of music. According to ***sheminith***. A psalm of David.

9031 שָׁמִיר¹ *šāmîr*[1], n.m. [8] [√ 9068; cf. 9033?]

briers [8]

Isa 5: 6 pruned nor cultivated, and **briers** and thorns will grow there.
7: 23 a thousand silver shekels, there will be only **briers** and thorns.
7: 24 and arrow, for the land will be covered with **briers** and thorns.
7: 25 you will no longer go there for fear of the **briers** and thorns;
9: 18 [9:17] it consumes **briers** and thorns, it sets the forest thickets
10: 17 in a single day it will burn and consume his thorns and his **briers**.
27: 4 am not angry. If only there were **briers** and thorns confronting me!
32: 13 the land of my people, a land overgrown with thorns and **briers**—

9032 שָׁמִיר² *šāmîr*[2], n.m. [3] [cf. 9033?]

as hard as flint [1], flint [1], hardest stone [1]

Jer 17: 1 inscribed with a **flint** point, on the tablets of their hearts and on the
Eze 3: 9 I will make your forehead like the **hardest stone**, harder than flint.
Zec 7: 12 They made their hearts **as hard as flint** and would not listen to the

9033 שָׁמִיר³ *šāmîr*[3], n.pr.m. [1] [cf. 9020, 9031?, 9032?]

Shamir [1]

1Ch 24: 24 son of Uzziel: Micah; from the sons of Micah: **Shamir**. [K 9020]

9034 שָׁמִיר⁴ *šāmîr*[4], n.pr.loc. [3]

Shamir [3]

Jos 15: 48 In the hill country: **Shamir**, Jattir, Socoh,
Jdg 10: 1 to save Israel. He lived in **Shamir**, in the hill country of Ephraim.
10: 2 Israel twenty-three years; then he died, and was buried in **Shamir**.

9035 שְׁמִירָמוֹת *šᵉmîrāmôt*, n.pr.m. [4] [cf. 9082]

Shemiramoth [4]

1Ch 15: 18 Jaaziel, **Shemiramoth**, Jehiel, Unni, Eliab, Benaiah, Maaseiah,
15: 20 Aziel, **Shemiramoth**, Jehiel, Unni, Eliab, Maaseiah and Benaiah
16: 5 then Jeiel, **Shemiramoth**, Jehiel, Mattithiah, Eliab, Benaiah,
2Ch 17: 8 Shemaiah, Nethaniah, Zebadiah, Asahel, **Shemiramoth**,

9036 שַׁמְלַי *šamlay*, n.pr.m. [0] [cf. 8978]

Ezr 2: 46 [Hagab, **Shalmai**, [K; see Q 8978] Hanan,]

9037 שָׁמֵם¹ *šāmēm*[1], v. [93] [→ 5457, 9014, 9038, 9039, 9040, 9041; cf. 3815; Ar 10724]

appalled [19], desolate [15], causes desolation [4], deserted [4], devastated [4], lay waste [4], lies desolate [4], completely destroy [2], demolished [2], destitute [2], destroyed [2], horrified [2], ruin [2], was laid waste [2], are appalled [1], are demolished [1], astonished [1], be demolished [1], be destroyed [1], be laid waste [1], brought devastation [1], cause to be appalled [1], desolation [1], desolations [1], destroy yourself [1], dismayed [1], fill with horror [1], him[s] [1], in ruins [1], laid waste [1], made desolate [1], overwhelmed [1], ravaged [1], ruined [1], strip [1], stripped [1], was left so desolate [1], were terrified [1], without help [1]

Ge 47: 19 [A] and not die, and that the land *may* not *become* **desolate**."
Lev 26: 22 [C] make you so few in number that your roads *will be* **deserted**.
26: 31 [G] turn your cities into ruins and **lay waste** your sanctuaries,
26: 32 [G] I *will* **lay waste** the land, so that your enemies who live there
26: 32 [A] so that your enemies who live there *will be* **appalled**.
26: 34 [H] will enjoy its sabbath years all the time that *it* **lies desolate**
26: 35 [H] All the time *that it* **lies desolate**, the land will have the rest it
26: 43 [H] will enjoy its sabbaths while *it* **lies desolate** without them.
Nu 21: 30 [G] *We have* **demolished** them as far as Nophah, which extends
1Sa 5: 6 [G] *he* **brought devastation** *upon* them and afflicted them with
2Sa 13: 20 [A] lived in her brother Absalom's house, a **desolate** *woman*.
1Ki 9: 8 [A] all who pass by *will be* **appalled** and will scoff and say,
2Ch 7: 21 [A] so imposing, all who pass by *will be* **appalled** and say,
Ezr 9: 3 [D] pulled hair from my head and beard and sat down **appalled**.
9: 4 [D] And I sat there **appalled** until the evening sacrifice.
Job 16: 7 [G] worn me out; *you have* **devastated** my entire household.
17: 8 [A] Upright men *are* **appalled** at this; the innocent are aroused
18: 20 [C] Men of the west **are appalled** at his fate; men of the east are
21: 5 [G] Look at me and *be* **astonished**; clap your hand over your
Ps 40: 15 [40:16] [A] *May* those who say to me, "Aha! Aha!" *be* **appalled**
69: 25 [69:26] [C] May their place be **deserted**; let there be no one to
79: 7 [G] for they have devoured Jacob and **destroyed** his homeland.
143: 4 [F] grows faint within me; my heart within me *is* **dismayed**.
Ecc 7: 16 [F] neither be overwise—why **destroy yourself**?
Isa 33: 8 [C] The highways *are* **deserted**, no travelers are on the roads.
49: 8 [A] to restore the land and to reassign its **desolate** inheritances,
49: 19 [A] were ruined and **made desolate** and your land laid waste,
52: 14 [A] Just as there were many *who were* **appalled** at him—
54: 1 [A] because more are the children of the **desolate** *woman* than of
54: 3 [C] will dispossess nations and settle in their **desolate** cities.
59: 16 [F] no one, *he was* **appalled** that there was no one to intervene;
61: 4 [A] the ancient ruins and restore the *places* long **devastated**;
61: 4 [A] the ruined cities *that have been* **devastated** *for* generations.
63: 5 [F] was no one to help, *I was* **appalled** that no one gave support;
Jer 2: 12 [A] *Be* **appalled** at this, O heavens, and shudder with great
4: 9 [C] and the officials will lose heart, the priests *will be* **horrified**,
10: 25 [G] have devoured him completely and **destroyed** his homeland.
12: 11 [C] the whole land *will* **be laid waste** because there is no one
18: 16 [A] all who pass by *will be* **appalled** and will shake their heads.
19: 8 [A] all who pass by *will be* **appalled** and will scoff because of all
33: 10 [C] of Judah and the streets of Jerusalem that *are* **deserted**,
49: 17 [A] all who pass by *will be* **appalled** and will scoff because of all
49: 20 [G] *he will* **completely destroy** their pasture because of them.
50: 13 [A] All who pass Babylon *will be* **horrified** and scoff because of
50: 45 [G] *he will* **completely destroy** their pasture because of them.
La 1: 4 [A] All her gateways are **desolate**, her priests groan, her maidens
1: 13 [A] turned me back. He made me **desolate**, faint all the day long.
1: 16 [A] My children are **destitute** because the enemy has prevailed."
3: 11 [A] me from the path and mangled me and left me **without help**.
4: 5 [C] Those who once ate delicacies *are* **destitute** in the streets.
5: 18 [A] for Mount Zion, which **lies desolate**, with jackals prowling
Eze 3: 15 [G] I sat among them for seven days—**overwhelmed**.
4: 17 [C] *They will be* **appalled** at the sight of each other and will
6: 4 [C] Your altars *will* **be demolished** and your incense altars will
6: 6 [A] the towns will be laid waste and the high places **demolished**,
12: 19 [A] for their land *will be* **stripped** of everything in it because of
19: 7 [A] The land and all who were in it **were terrified** by his roaring.
20: 26 [G] that *I might* **fill** them **with horror** so they would know that I
25: 3 [C] and over the land of Israel when *it* **was laid waste**

Eze 26:16 [A] sit on the ground, trembling every moment, **appalled** at you.
27:35 [A] All who live in the coastlands *are* **appalled** at you; their
28:19 [A] All the nations who knew you *are* **appalled** at you; you have
29:12 [C] I will make the land of Egypt desolate among **devastated**
30:7 [C] " '*They will be* **desolate** among desolate lands, and their
30:7 [C] " 'They will be desolate among **desolate** lands, and their
30:12 [G] by the hand of foreigners *I will* **lay waste** the land
30:14 [G] *I will* **lay waste** Upper Egypt, set fire to Zoan and inflict
32:10 [G] *I will* **cause** many peoples **to be appalled** at you, and their
32:15 [C] I make Egypt desolate and **strip** the land of everything in it,
33:28 [A] the mountains of Israel *will become* **desolate** so that no one
35:12 [A] "*They have been* **laid waste** and have been given over to us
35:15 [A] when the inheritance of the house of Israel *became* **desolate**,
36:3 [A] Because *they* **ravaged** and hounded you from every side
36:4 [A] to the **desolate** ruins and the deserted towns that have been
36:34 [C] The **desolate** land will be cultivated instead of lying desolate
36:35 [C] "This land that **was laid waste** has become like the garden of
36:35 [C] **desolate** and destroyed, are now fortified and inhabited."
36:36 [C] what was destroyed and have replanted what *was* **desolate**.
Da 8:13 [D] the rebellion *that* **causes desolation**, and the surrender of the
8:27 [F] *I was* **appalled** by the vision; it was beyond understanding.
9:18 [A] and see the **desolation** *of* the city that bears your Name.
9:26 [A] continue until the end, and **desolations** have been decreed.
9:27 [D] he will set up an abomination *that* **causes desolation**,
9:27 [D] until the end that is decreed is poured out on **him**[s]."
11:31 [D] they will set up the abomination *that* **causes desolation**.
12:11 [D] and the abomination *that* **causes desolation** is set up,
Hos 2:12 [2:14] [G] *I will* **ruin** her vines and her fig trees, which she said
Joel 1:17 [C] The storehouses *are* **in ruins**, the granaries have been broken
Am 7:9 [C] "The high places of Isaac *will* **be destroyed**
9:14 [C] they will rebuild the **ruined** cities and live in them.
Mic 6:13 [G] have begun to destroy you, *to* **ruin** you because of your sins.
Zep 3:6 [C] "I have cut off nations; their strongholds **are demolished**.
Zec 7:14 [C] The land **was left so desolate** behind them that no one could

9038 [2]שָׁמֵם ***šāmēm²***, a. [2] [√ 9037]
desolate [2]

Jer 12:11 It will be made a wasteland, parched and **desolate** before me;
Da 9:17 For your sake, O Lord, look with favor on your **desolate** sanctuary.

9039 שְׁמָמָה ***š^emāmâ***, n.f. [56] [√ 9037]
desolate [30], waste [5], desolation [3], ruins [3], wasteland [3], desolate place [2], laid waste [2], barren [1], demolished [1], desolate waste [1], despair [1], destroy [+8492] [1], ravaged [1], ruined [1], utterly desolate [1]

Ex 23:29 because the land would become **desolate** and the wild animals too
Lev 26:33 Your land will be **laid waste**, and your cities will lie in ruins.
Jos 8:28 made it a permanent heap of ruins, a **desolate place** to this day.
Isa 1:7 Your country is **desolate**, your cities burned with fire; your fields
1:7 right before you, **laid waste** as when overthrown by strangers.
6:11 until the houses are left deserted and the fields ruined and **ravaged**,
17:9 to thickets and undergrowth. And all will be **desolation**.
62:4 No longer will they call you Deserted, or name your land **Desolate**.
64:10 [64:9] a desert; even Zion is a desert, Jerusalem a **desolation**.
Jer 4:27 "The whole land will be **ruined**, though I will not destroy it
6:8 from you and make your land **desolate** so no one can live in it."
9:11 [9:10] I will lay **waste** the towns of Judah so no one can live
10:22 It will make the towns of Judah **desolate**, a haunt of jackals.
12:10 they will turn my pleasant field into a **desolate** wasteland.
12:11 It will be made a **wasteland**, parched and desolate before me;
25:12 declares the LORD, "and will make it **desolate** forever.
32:43 'It is a **desolate waste**, without men or animals, for it has been
34:22 And I will lay **waste** the towns of Judah so no one can live there."
44:6 of Jerusalem and made them the desolate **ruins** they are today.
49:2 it will become a mound of **ruins**, and its surrounding villages will
49:33 "Hazor will become a haunt of jackals, a **desolate place** forever.
50:13 anger she will not be inhabited but will be completely **desolate**.
51:26 for you will be **desolate** forever," declares the LORD.
51:62 neither man nor animal will live in it; it will be **desolate** forever.'
Eze 6:14 and make the land a **desolate** waste from the desert to Diblah—
7:27 The king will mourn, the prince will be clothed with **despair**,
12:20 inhabited towns will be laid waste and the land will be **desolate**.
14:15 they leave it childless and it becomes **desolate** so that no one can
14:16 They alone would be saved, but the land would be **desolate**.
15:8 I will make the land **desolate** because they have been unfaithful,
23:33 filled with drunkenness and sorrow, the cup of ruin and **desolation**,
29:9 Egypt will become a **desolate** wasteland. Then they will know that
29:10 land of Egypt a ruin and a **desolate** waste from Migdol to Aswan,
29:12 I will make the land of Egypt **desolate** among devastated lands,
29:12 and her cities will lie **desolate** forty years among ruined cities.
32:15 When I make Egypt **desolate** and strip the land of everything in it,
33:28 I will make the land a **desolate** waste, and her proud strength will
33:29 when I have made the land a **desolate** waste because of all the
35:3 stretch out my hand against you and make you a **desolate** waste.
35:4 I will turn your towns into ruins and you will be **desolate**.
35:7 I will make Mount Seir a desolate **waste** and cut off from it all who
35:9 I will make you **desolate** forever; your towns will not be inhabited.
35:14 While the whole earth rejoices, I will make you **desolate**.
35:15 You will be **desolate**, O Mount Seir, you and all of Edom.
36:34 The desolate land will be cultivated instead of lying **desolate** in the
Joel 2:3 the land is like the garden of Eden, behind them, a desert **waste**—
2:20 army far from you, pushing it into a parched and **barren** land,
3:19 [4:19] Egypt will be **desolate**, Edom a desert waste, because of
3:19 [4:19] Egypt will be desolate, Edom a desert **waste**, because of
Mic 1:7 will be burned with fire; *I will* **destroy** [+8492] all her images.
7:13 The earth will become **desolate** because of its inhabitants,
Zep 1:13 Their wealth will be plundered, their houses **demolished**. They
2:4 Gaza will be abandoned and Ashkelon left in **ruins**. At midday
2:9 a place of weeds and salt pits, a **wasteland** forever.
2:13 leaving Nineveh **utterly desolate** and dry as the desert.
Mal 1:3 I have turned his mountains into a **wasteland** and left his

9040 שִׁמְמָה ***šim^emâ***, n.f. [1] [√ 9037]
desolate [1]

Eze 35:7 I will make Mount Seir a **desolate** waste and cut off from it all

9041 שִׁמָּמוֹן ***šimmāmôn***, n.[m.]. [2] [√ 9037]
despair [2]

Eze 4:16 eat rationed food in anxiety and drink rationed water in **despair**,
12:19 They will eat their food in anxiety and drink their water in **despair**,

9042 [1]שָׁמֵן ***šāmēn¹***, v. [5] [√ 9043]
fat [1], filled with food [1], grew fat [1], make calloused [1], well-nourished [1]

Dt 32:15 [A] Jeshurun **grew fat** and kicked; filled with food, he became
32:15 [A] and kicked; **filled with food**, he became heavy and sleek.
Ne 9:25 [G] They ate to the full and *were* **well-nourished**; they reveled in
Isa 6:10 [G] **Make** the heart of this people **calloused**; make their ears dull
Jer 5:28 [A] *have grown* **fat** and sleek. Their evil deeds have no limit;

9043 שֶׁמֶן ***šemen***, n.m. [193] [→ 875?, 5458, 5459, 5460, 9042, 9044, 9045]
oil [155], olive oil [13], olive [4], perfume [3], fertile [2], *untranslated* [1], best [1], cosmetic lotions [1], fat [1], fertile [+1201] [1], fine perfume [1], gaunt [+4946] [1], it[s] [+2021] [1], lotions [1], oils [1], ointments [1], olive [+6770] [1], perfume [+8379] [1], perfumes [1], rich food [1], wild olive [1]

Ge 28:18 under his head and set it up as a pillar and poured **oil** on top of it.
35:14 and he poured out a drink offering on it; he also poured **oil** on it.
Ex 25:6 **olive oil** for the light; spices for the anointing oil and for the
25:6 the light; spices for the anointing **oil** and for the fragrant incense;
27:20 "Command the Israelites to bring you clear **oil** *of* pressed olives for
29:2 without yeast, make bread, and cakes mixed with **oil**, and wafers
29:2 make bread, and cakes mixed with oil, and wafers spread with **oil**.
29:7 Take the anointing **oil** and anoint him by pouring it on his head.
29:21 some of the anointing **oil** and sprinkle it on Aaron and his garments
29:23 the LORD, take a loaf, and a cake made with **oil**, and a wafer.
29:40 fine flour mixed with a quarter of a hin of **oil** *from* pressed olives,
30:24 all according to the sanctuary shekel—and a hin of olive **oil**.
30:25 Make these into a sacred anointing **oil**, a fragrant blend, the work
30:25 the work of a perfumer. It will be the sacred anointing **oil**.
30:31 'This is to be my sacred anointing **oil** for the generations to come.
31:11 and the anointing **oil** and fragrant incense for the Holy Place.
35:8 **olive oil** for the light; spices for the anointing oil and for the
35:8 the light; spices for the anointing **oil** and for the fragrant incense;
35:14 that is for light with its accessories, lamps and **oil** *for* the light;
35:15 of incense with its poles, the anointing **oil** and the fragrant incense;
35:28 brought spices and **olive oil** for the light and for the anointing oil
35:28 brought spices and olive oil for the light and for the anointing **oil**
37:29 They also made the sacred anointing **oil** and the pure,
39:37 its row of lamps and all its accessories, and the **oil** *for* the light;
39:38 the gold altar, the anointing **oil**, the fragrant incense, and the
40:9 "Take the anointing **oil** and anoint the tabernacle and everything in
Lev 2:1 is to be of fine flour. He is to pour **oil** on it, put incense on it
2:2 The priest shall take a handful of the fine flour and **oil**, together
2:4 cakes made without yeast and mixed with **oil**, or wafers made
2:4 mixed with oil, or wafers made without yeast and spread with **oil**.
2:5 it is to be made of fine flour mixed with **oil**, and without yeast.
2:6 Crumble it and pour **oil** on it; it is a grain offering.
2:7 offering is cooked in a pan, it is to be made of fine flour and **oil**.
2:15 Put **oil** and incense on it; it is a grain offering.
2:16 shall burn the memorial portion of the crushed grain and the **oil**,

[F] Hitpael (hitpoel, hitpoal, hitpolel, hitpolal, hitpalel, hitpalal, hitpalpel, hitpalpal, hotpael, hotpaal) [G] Hiphil (hiphtil) [H] Hophal [I] Hishtaphel

Lev 5: 11 He must not put **oil** or incense on it, because it is a sin offering.
6: 15 [6:8] The priest is to take a handful of fine flour and **oil**, together
6: 21 [6:14] Prepare it with **oil** on a griddle; bring it well-mixed
7: 10 every grain offering, whether mixed with **oil** or dry,
7: 12 is to offer cakes of bread made without yeast and mixed with **oil**,
7: 12 and mixed with oil, wafers made without yeast and spread with **oil**,
7: 12 with oil, and cakes of fine flour well-kneaded and mixed with **oil**.
8: 2 "Bring Aaron and his sons, their garments, the anointing **oil**,
8: 10 Then Moses took the anointing **oil** and anointed the tabernacle
8: 12 He poured some of the anointing **oil** on Aaron's head and anointed
8: 26 he took a cake of bread, and one made with **oil**, and a wafer;
8: 30 Moses took some of the anointing **oil** and some of the blood from
9: 4 before the LORD, together with a grain offering mixed with **oil**.
10: 7 or you will die, because the LORD's anointing **oil** is on you."
14: 10 along with three-tenths of an ephah of fine flour mixed with **oil** for
14: 10 of fine flour mixed with oil for a grain offering, and one log of **oil**.
14: 12 male lambs and offer it as a guilt offering, along with the log of **oil**;
14: 15 The priest shall then take some of the log of **oil**, pour it in the palm
14: 16 dip his right forefinger into the **oil** in his palm, and with his finger
14: 16 with his finger sprinkle some of **it**[s] [+2021] before the LORD
14: 17 The priest is to put some of the **oil** remaining in his palm on the
14: 18 The rest of the **oil** in his palm the priest shall put on the head of the
14: 21 together with a tenth of an ephah of fine flour mixed with **oil** for a
14: 21 ephah of fine flour mixed with oil for a grain offering, a log of **oil**,
14: 24 to take the lamb for the guilt offering, together with the log of **oil**,
14: 26 The priest is to pour some of the **oil** into the palm of his own left
14: 27 with his right forefinger sprinkle some of the **oil** from his palm
14: 28 Some of the **oil** in his palm he is to put on the same places he put
14: 29 The rest of the **oil** in his palm the priest shall put on the head of the
21: 10 the one among his brothers who has had the anointing **oil** poured
21: 12 because he has been dedicated by the anointing **oil** *of* his God.
23: 13 offering of two-tenths of an ephah of fine flour mixed with **oil**—
24: 2 "Command the Israelites to bring you clear **oil** *of* pressed olives for
Nu 4: 9 and trays, and all its jars for the **oil** used to supply it.
4: 16 the priest, is to have charge of the **oil** *for* the light, the fragrant
4: 16 fragrant incense, the regular grain offering and the anointing **oil**.
5: 15 He must not pour **oil** on it or put incense on it, because it is a grain
6: 15 cakes made of fine flour mixed with **oil**, and wafers spread with
6: 15 made of fine flour mixed with oil, and wafers spread with **oil**.
7: 13 each filled with fine flour mixed with **oil** as a grain offering;
7: 19 each filled with fine flour mixed with **oil** as a grain offering;
7: 25 each filled with fine flour mixed with **oil** as a grain offering;
7: 31 each filled with fine flour mixed with **oil** as a grain offering;
7: 37 each filled with fine flour mixed with **oil** as a grain offering;
7: 43 each filled with fine flour mixed with **oil** as a grain offering;
7: 49 each filled with fine flour mixed with **oil** as a grain offering;
7: 55 each filled with fine flour mixed with **oil** as a grain offering;
7: 61 each filled with fine flour mixed with **oil** as a grain offering;
7: 67 each filled with fine flour mixed with **oil** as a grain offering;
7: 73 each filled with fine flour mixed with **oil** as a grain offering;
7: 79 each filled with fine flour mixed with **oil** as a grain offering;
8: 8 a young bull with its grain offering of fine flour mixed with **oil**;
11: 8 it into cakes. And it tasted like something made with **olive oil**.
15: 4 tenth of an ephah of fine flour mixed with a quarter of a hin of **oil**.
15: 6 of an ephah of fine flour mixed with a third of a hin of **oil**,
15: 9 three-tenths of an ephah of fine flour mixed with half a hin of **oil**.
28: 5 fine flour mixed with a quarter of a hin of **oil** *from* pressed olives.
28: 9 offering of two-tenths of an ephah of fine flour mixed with **oil**.
28: 12 offering of three-tenths of an ephah of fine flour mixed with **oil**;
28: 12 offering of two-tenths of an ephah of fine flour mixed with **oil**;
28: 13 a grain offering of a tenth of an ephah of fine flour mixed with **oil**.
28: 20 offering of three-tenths of an ephah of fine flour mixed with **oil**;
28: 28 offering of three-tenths of an ephah of fine flour mixed with **oil**;
29: 3 offering of three-tenths of an ephah of fine flour mixed with **oil**;
29: 9 offering of three-tenths of an ephah of fine flour mixed with **oil**;
29: 14 offering of three-tenths of an ephah of fine flour mixed with **oil**;
35: 25 the death of the high priest, who was anointed with the holy **oil**.
Dt 8: 8 and barley, vines and fig trees, pomegranates, olive **oil** and honey;
28: 40 olive trees throughout your country but you will not use the **oil**,
32: 13 him with honey from the rock, and with **oil** from the flinty crag,
33: 24 let him be favored by his brothers, and let him bathe his feet in **oil**.
1Sa 10: 1 Then Samuel took a flask of **oil** and poured it on Saul's head
16: 1 Fill your horn with **oil** and be on your way; I am sending you to
16: 13 So Samuel took the horn of **oil** and anointed him in the presence of
2Sa 1: 21 mighty was defiled, the shield of Saul—no longer rubbed with **oil**.
14: 2 Dress in mourning clothes, and don't use any **cosmetic lotions**.
1Ki 1: 39 Zadok the priest took the horn of **oil** from the sacred tent
5: 11 [5:25] in addition to twenty thousand baths of pressed olive **oil**.
6: 23 In the inner sanctuary he made a pair of cherubim of **olive** wood,
6: 31 For the entrance of the inner sanctuary he made doors of **olive**
6: 32 And on the two **olive** wood doors he carved cherubim, palm trees
6: 33 In the same way he made four-sided jambs of **olive** wood for the
17: 12 any bread—only a handful of flour in a jar and a little **oil** in a jug.
17: 14 the jug of **oil** will not run dry until the day the LORD gives rain
17: 16 the jar of flour was not used up and the jug of **oil** did not run dry,
2Ki 4: 2 servant has nothing there at all," she said, "except a little **oil**."
4: 6 he replied, "There is not a jar left." Then the **oil** stopped flowing.
4: 7 the man of God, and he said, "Go, sell the **oil** and pay your debts.
9: 1 your belt, take this flask of **oil** with you and go to Ramoth Gilead.
9: 3 Then take the flask and pour the **oil** on his head and declare,
9: 6 Then the prophet poured the **oil** on Jehu's head and declared,
20: 13 the silver, the gold, the spices and the fine **oil**—his armory
1Ch 9: 29 as well as the flour and wine, and the **oil**, incense and spices.
12: 40 [12:41] fig cakes, raisin cakes, wine, **oil**, cattle and sheep,
27: 28 western foothills. Joash was in charge of the supplies of **olive oil**.
2Ch 2: 10 [2:9] baths of wine and twenty thousand baths of **olive oil**."
2: 15 [2:14] and barley and the **olive oil** and wine he promised,
11: 11 put commanders in them, with supplies of food, **olive oil** and wine.
Ezr 3: 7 and gave food and drink and **oil** to the people of Sidon and Tyre,
Ne 8: 15 and bring back branches from olive and **wild olive** trees,
Est 2: 12 six months with **oil** *of* myrrh and six with perfumes and cosmetics.
Job 29: 6 with cream and the rock poured out for me streams of **olive oil**.
Ps 23: 5 of my enemies. You anoint my head with **oil**; my cup overflows.
45: 7 [45:8] your companions by anointing you with the **oil** *of* joy.
55: 21 [55:22] his words are more soothing than **oil**, yet they are drawn
89: 20 [89:21] my servant; with my sacred **oil** I have anointed him.
92: 10 [92:11] like that of a wild ox; fine **oils** have been poured upon me.
104: 15 **oil** to make his face shine, and bread that sustains his heart.
109: 18 it entered into his body like water, into his bones like **oil**.
109: 24 knees give way from fasting; my body is thin and **gaunt** [+4946].
133: 2 It is like precious **oil** poured on the head, running down on the
141: 5 it is a kindness; let him rebuke me—it is **oil** *on* my head.
Pr 5: 3 of an adulteress drip honey, and her speech is smoother than **oil**;
21: 17 will become poor; whoever loves wine and **oil** will never be rich.
21: 20 In the house of the wise are stores of choice food and **oil**, but a
27: 9 **Perfume** and incense bring joy to the heart, and the pleasantness of
27: 16 her is like restraining the wind or grasping **oil** with the hand.
Ecc 7: 1 A good name is better than **fine perfume**, and the day of death
9: 8 Always be clothed in white, and always anoint your head with **oil**.
10: 1 As dead flies give **perfume** [+8379] a bad smell, so a little folly
SS 1: 3 Pleasing is the fragrance of your **perfumes**; your name is like
1: 3 fragrance of your perfumes; your name is like **perfume** poured out.
4: 10 love than wine, and the fragrance of your **perfume** than any spice!
Isa 1: 6 and open sores, not cleansed or bandaged or soothed with **oil**.
5: 1 My loved one had a vineyard on a **fertile** [+1201] hillside.
10: 27 your neck; the yoke will be broken because you have grown so **fat**.
25: 6 LORD Almighty will prepare a feast of **rich food** for all peoples,
25: 6 a banquet of aged wine—the **best** *of* meats and the finest of wines.
28: 1 his glorious beauty, set on the head of a **fertile** valley—
28: 4 his glorious beauty, set on the head of a **fertile** valley,
39: 2 the silver, the gold, the spices, the fine **oil**, his entire armory
41: 19 desert the cedar and the acacia, the myrtle and the **olive** [+6770].
57: 9 You went to Molech with **olive oil** and increased your perfumes.
61: 3 the **oil** *of* gladness instead of mourning, and a garment of praise
Jer 40: 10 you are to harvest the wine, summer fruit and **oil**, and put them in
41: 8 We have wheat and barley, **oil** and honey, hidden in a field."
Eze 16: 9 and washed the blood from you and put **ointments** on you.
16: 13 embroidered cloth. Your food was fine flour, honey and **olive oil**.
16: 18 to put on them, and you offered my **oil** and incense before them.
16: 19 for you—the fine flour, **olive oil** and honey I gave you to eat—
23: 41 on which you had placed the incense and **oil** *that belonged to* me.
27: 17 from Minnith and confections, honey, **oil** and balm for your wares.
32: 14 Then I will let her waters settle and make her streams flow like **oil**,
45: 14 The prescribed portion of **oil**, measured by the bath, is a tenth of a
45: 14 **[RPH]** is a tenth of a bath from each cor (which consists of ten
45: 24 and an ephah for each ram, along with a hin of **oil** for each ephah.
45: 25 provision for sin offerings, burnt offerings, grain offerings and **oil**.
46: 5 to be as much as he pleases, along with a hin of **oil** for each ephah.
46: 7 much as he wants to give, along with a hin of **oil** with each ephah.
46: 11 as much as one pleases, along with a hin of **oil** for each ephah.
46: 14 consisting of a sixth of an ephah with a third of a hin of **oil** to
46: 15 the **oil** shall be provided morning by morning for a regular burnt
Hos 2: 5 [2:7] and my water, my wool and my linen, my **oil** and my drink.'
12: 1 [12:2] makes a treaty with Assyria and sends **olive oil** to Egypt.
Am 6: 6 You drink wine by the bowlful and use the finest **lotions**, but you
Mic 6: 7 be pleased with thousands of rams, with ten thousand rivers of **oil**?
6: 15 you will press olives but not use the **oil** on yourselves, you will
Hag 2: 12 that fold touches some bread or stew, some wine, **oil** or other food,

9044 שָׁמָן ***šāmān***, n.[m.]. [2] [√ 9043]
richness [2]

Ge 27: 28 May God give you of heaven's dew and of earth's **richness**—
27: 39 "Your dwelling will be away from the earth's **richness**,

9045 ²שָׁמֵן ***šāmēn²***, a. [10] [√ 9043]

fertile [3], rich [3], luxury [1], plentiful [1], sleek [1], vigorous [1]

Ge 49:20 "Asher's food will be **rich**; he will provide delicacies fit for a king.
Nu 13:20 How is the soil? Is it **fertile** or poor? Are there trees on it or not?
Jdg 3:29 struck down about ten thousand Moabites, all **vigorous** and strong;
1Ch 4:40 They found **rich**, good pasture, and the land was spacious,
Ne 9:25 They captured fortified cities and **fertile** land; they took possession
9:35 goodness to them in the spacious and **fertile** land you gave them,
Isa 30:23 and the food that comes from the land will be rich and **plentiful**.
Eze 34:14 there they will feed in a **rich** pasture on the mountains of Israel.
34:16 strengthen the weak, but the **sleek** and the strong I will destroy.
Hab 1:16 for by his net he lives in **luxury** and enjoys the choicest food.

9046 שְׁמֹנֶה ***šᵉmōneh***, n.m. & f. [147] [→ 9029, 9030, 9047]

eight [29], eighty [16], eighteenth [+6926] [9], eighteen [+6926] [6], 128 [+2256+4395+6929] [4], eighteen [+6925] [4], eighty-five [+2256+2822] [4], twenty-eight [+2256+6929] [4], eighth [3], 18 [+6925] [2], 18,000 [+547+6925] [2], 188 [+2256+4395+9046] [2], 2,818 [+547+2256+4395+6925+9046] [2], 288 [+2256+4395+9046] [2], 8,580 [+547+2256+2256+2822+4395+9046] [2], 80 [2], 800 [+4395] [2], 98 [+2256+9596] [2], eighteenth [+6925] [2], forty-eight [+752+2256] [2], thirty-eight [+2256+8993] [2], thirty-eighth [+2256+8993] [2], 108,100 [+547+547+2256+2256+4395+4395] [1], 138 [+2256+4395+8993] [1], 148 [+752+2256+4395] [1], 180 [+2256+4395] [1], 180,000 [+547+2256+4395] [1], 182 [+2256+2256+4395+9109] [1], 186,400 [+547+547+547+752+2256+2256+2256+4395+4395+9252] [1], 187 [+2256+2256+4395+8679] [1], 2,812 [+547+2256+4395+6925+9109] [1], 20,800 [+547+2256+4395+6929] [1], 218 [+2256+4395+6925] [1], 28 [+2256+6929] [1], 28,600 [+547+2256+2256+4395+6929+9252] [1], 280,000 [+547+2256+4395] [1], 284 [+752+2256+4395] [1], 318 [+2256+4395+6925+8993] [1], 328 [+2256+4395+6929+8993] [1], 468 [+752+2256+4395+9252] [1], 6,800 [+547+2256+4395+9252] [1], 628 [+2256+4395+6929+9252] [1], 648 [+752+2256+4395+9252] [1], 782 [+2256+2256+4395+8679+9109] [1], 8,600 [+547+2256+4395+9252] [1], 80,000 [+547] [1], 807 [+2256+4395+8679] [1], 815 [+2256+2822+4395+6926] [1], 822 [+2256+4395+6929+9109] [1], 830 [+2256+4395+8993] [1], 832 [+2256+4395+8993+9109] [1], 840 [+752+2256+4395] [1], 845 [+752+2256+2822+4395] [1], 87,000 [+547+2256+8679] [1], 895 [+2256+2256+2822+4395+9596] [1], 928 [+2256+4395+6929+9596] [1], eighteen thousand [+547+2256+8052] [1], eighteen [+6926] [1], eightieth [1], eighty-six [+2256+9252] [1], eighty-three [+2256+8993] [1], ninety-eight [+2256+9596] [1], sixty-eight [+2256+9252] [1], twenty-seven feet [+564+6926] [1]

Ge 5:4 Adam lived **800** [+4395] years and had other sons and daughters.
5:7 Seth lived **807** [+2256+4395+8679] years and had other sons and
5:10 Enosh lived **815** [+2256+2822+4395+6926] years and had other
5:13 Kenan lived **840** [+752+2256+4395] years and had other sons
5:16 Mahalalel lived **830** [+2256+4395+8993] years and had other sons
5:17 Mahalalel lived **895** [+2256+2256+2822+4395+9596] years, and
5:19 Jared lived **800** [+4395] years and had other sons and daughters.
5:25 When Methuselah had lived **187** [+2256+2256+4395+8679] years,
5:26 Methuselah lived **782** [+2256+2256+4395+8679+9109] years and
5:28 When Lamech had lived **182** [+2256+2256+4395+9109] years,
14:14 he called out the **318** [+2256+4395+6925+8993] trained men born
16:16 Abram was **eighty-six** [+2256+9252] years old when Hagar bore
17:12 For the generations to come every male among you who is **eight**
21:4 When his son Isaac was **eight** days old, Abraham circumcised him,
22:23 Milcah bore these **eight** sons to Abraham's brother Nahor.
35:28 Isaac lived a hundred and **eighty** years.
Ex 7:7 Moses was **eighty** years old and Aaron eighty-three when they
7:7 Aaron **eighty-three** [+2256+8993] when they spoke to Pharaoh.
26:2 the same size—**twenty-eight** [+2256+6929] cubits long and four
26:25 So there will be **eight** frames and sixteen silver bases—two under
36:9 the same size—**twenty-eight** [+2256+6929] cubits long and four
36:30 So there were **eight** frames and sixteen silver bases—two under
Nu 2:9 to the camp of Judah, according to their divisions, number **186,400** [+547+547+547+752+2256+2256+2256+4395+4395+9252].
2:24 divisions, number **108,100** [+547+547+2256+2256+4395+4395].
3:28 males a month old or more was **8,600** [+547+2256+4395+9252].
4:48 numbered **8,580** [+547+2256+2256+2822+4395+9046].
4:48 numbered **8,580** [+547+2256+2256+2822+4395+9046].
7:8 he gave four carts and **eight** oxen to the Merarites, as their work
29:29 " 'On the sixth day prepare **eight** bulls, two rams and fourteen male
35:7 In all you must give the Levites **forty-eight** [+752+2256] towns,
Dt 2:14 **Thirty-eight** [+2256+8993] years passed from the time we left
Jos 14:10 So here I am today, **eighty-five** [+2256+2822] years old!
21:41 in the territory held by the Israelites were **forty-eight** [+752+2256]
Jdg 3:8 to whom the Israelites were subject for **eight** years.
3:14 were subject to Eglon king of Moab for **eighteen** [+6926] years.
3:30 made subject to Israel, and the land had peace for **eighty** years.
10:8 For **eighteen** [+6926] years they oppressed all the Israelites on the
12:14 who rode on seventy donkeys. He led Israel **eight** years.
20:25 they cut down another **eighteen** [+6925] thousand Israelites,
20:44 **Eighteen** [+6925] thousand Benjamites fell, all of them valiant
1Sa 4:15 who was **ninety-eight** [+2256+9596] years old and whose eyes
17:12 Jesse had **eight** sons, and in Saul's time he was old and well
22:18 he killed **eighty-five** [+2256+2822] men who wore the linen ephod.
2Sa 8:13 down **eighteen** [+6925] thousand Edomites in the Valley of Salt.
19:32 [19:33] Now Barzillai was a very old man, **eighty** years of age.
19:35 [19:36] I am now **eighty** years old. Can I tell the difference
23:8 he raised his spear against **eight** hundred men, whom he killed in
24:9 In Israel there were **eight** hundred thousand able-bodied men who
1Ki 5:15 [5:29] and **eighty** thousand stonecutters in the hills,
6:1 and **eightieth** year after the Israelites had come out of Egypt,
7:10 stones of good quality, some measuring ten cubits and some **eight**.
7:15 each **eighteen** [+6926] cubits high and twelve cubits around,
12:21 tribe of Benjamin—a hundred and **eighty** thousand fighting men—
15:1 In the **eighteenth** [+6926] year of the reign of Jeroboam son of
16:29 In the **thirty-eighth** [+2256+8993] year of Asa king of Judah,
2Ki 3:1 in the **eighteenth** [+6926] year of Jehoshaphat king of Judah,
6:25 so long that a donkey's head sold for **eighty** shekels of silver,
8:17 old when he became king, and he reigned in Jerusalem **eight** years.
10:24 Now Jehu had posted **eighty** men outside with this warning:
10:36 over Israel in Samaria was **twenty-eight** [+2256+6929] years.
15:8 In the **thirty-eighth** [+2256+8993] year of Azariah king of Judah,
19:35 to death a hundred and **eighty-five** [+2256+2822] thousand men in
22:1 Josiah was **eight** years old when he became king, and he reigned in
22:3 In the **eighteenth** [+6926] year of his reign, King Josiah sent the
23:23 in the **eighteenth** [+6926] year of King Josiah, this Passover was
24:8 Jehoiachin was **eighteen** [+6926] years old when he became king,
24:12 In the **eighth** year of the reign of the king of Babylon, he took
25:17 Each pillar was **twenty-seven feet** [+564+6926] high. The bronze
1Ch 7:5 as listed in their genealogy, were **87,000** [+547+2256+8679] in all.
12:24 [12:25] spear—**6,800** [+547+2256+4395+9252] armed for battle;
12:30 [12:31] in their own clans—**20,800** [+547+2256+4395+6929];
12:31 [12:32] to come and make David king—**18,000** [+547+6925];
12:35 [12:36] for battle—**28,600** [+547+2256+2256+4395+6929+9252];
15:9 from the descendants of Hebron, Eliel the leader and **80** relatives;
16:38 left Obed-Edom and his **sixty-eight** [+2256+9252] associates to
18:12 Abishai son of Zeruiah struck down **eighteen** [+6925] thousand
23:3 the total number of men was **thirty-eight** [+2256+8993] thousand.
24:4 and **eight** heads of families from Ithamar's descendants.
24:15 the seventeenth to Hezir, the **eighteenth** [+6925] to Happizzez,
25:7 in music for the LORD—they numbered **288** [+2256+4395+9046].
25:7 in music for the LORD—they numbered **288** [+2256+4395+9046].
25:25 the **eighteenth** [+6925] to Hanani, his sons and relatives, 12
26:9 had sons and relatives, who were able men—**18** [+6925] in all.
29:7 of silver, **eighteen** [+547+2256+8052] **thousand** talents of bronze
2Ch 2:2 [2:1] **eighty** thousand as stonecutters in the hills and thirty-six
2:18 [2:17] be carriers and **80,000** [+547] to be stonecutters in the hills,
11:1 and Benjamin—a hundred and **eighty** thousand fighting men—
11:21 In all, he had **eighteen** [+6926] wives and sixty concubines,
11:21 concubines, **twenty-eight** [+2256+6929] sons and sixty daughters.
13:1 In the **eighteenth** [+6926] year of the reign of Jeroboam, Abijah
13:3 Jeroboam drew up a battle line against him with **eight** hundred
14:8 [14:7] and two hundred and **eighty** thousand from Benjamin,
17:15 next, Jehohanan the commander, with **280,000** [+547+2256+4395];
17:18 Jehozabad, with **180,000** [+547+2256+4395] men armed for battle.
21:5 old when he became king, and he reigned in Jerusalem **eight** years.
21:20 old when he became king, and he reigned in Jerusalem **eight** years.
26:17 Azariah the priest with **eighty** other courageous priests of the
29:17 by the **eighth** day of the month they reached the portico of the
29:17 For **eight** more days they consecrated the temple of the LORD
34:1 Josiah was **eight** years old when he became king, and he reigned in
34:3 In the **eighth** year of his reign, while he was still young, he began
34:8 In the **eighteenth** [+6926] year of Josiah's reign, to purify the land
35:19 This Passover was celebrated in the **eighteenth** [+6926] year of
36:9 Jehoiachin was **eighteen** [+6926] [BHS *eight* -6926] years old
Ezr 2:6 the line of Jeshua and Joab) **2,812** [+547+2256+4395+6925+9109]
2:16 of Ater (through Hezekiah) **98** [+2256+9596]
2:23 of Anathoth **128** [+2256+4395+6929]
2:41 The singers: the descendants of Asaph **128** [+2256+4395+6929]
8:8 of Shephatiah, Zebadiah son of Michael, and with him **80** men;
8:9 Obadiah son of Jehiel, and with him **218** [+2256+4395+6925] men;
8:11 Zechariah son of Bebai, and with him **28** [+2256+6929] men;
8:18 son of Israel, and Sherebiah's sons and brothers, **18 men** [+6925];
Ne 7:11 the line of Jeshua and Joab) **2,818** [+547+2256+4395+6925+9046]
7:11 the line of Jeshua and Joab) **2,818** [+547+2256+4395+6925+9046]
7:13 of Zattu **845** [+752+2256+2822+4395]
7:15 of Binnui **648** [+752+2256+4395+9252]
7:16 of Bebai **628** [+2256+4395+6929+9252]
7:21 of Ater (through Hezekiah) **98** [+2256+9596]
7:22 of Hashum **328** [+2256+4395+6929+8993]
7:26 the men of Bethlehem and Netophah **188** [+2256+4395+9046]
7:26 the men of Bethlehem and Netophah **188** [+2256+4395+9046]

Ne 7:27 of Anathoth **128** [+2256+4395+6929]
7:44 The singers: the descendants of Asaph **148** [+752+2256+4395]
7:45 Ater, Talmon, Akkub, Hatita and Shobai **138** [+2256+4395+8993]
11: 6 in Jerusalem totaled **468** [+752+2256+4395+9252] able men.
11: 8 followers, Gabbai and Sallai—**928** [+2256+4395+6929+9596] men.
11:12 **822** [+2256+4395+6929+9109] men; Adaiah son of Jeroham,
11:14 and his associates, who were able men—**128** [+2256+4395+6929].
11:18 The Levites in the holy city totaled **284** [+752+2256+4395].
Est 1: 4 For a full **180** [+2256+4395] days he displayed the vast wealth of
Ps 90:10 or **eighty**, if we have the strength; yet their span is but trouble
Ecc 11: 2 Give portions to seven, yes to **eight**, for you do not know what
SS 6: 8 Sixty queens there may be, and **eighty** concubines, and virgins
Isa 37:36 put to death a hundred and **eighty-five** [+2256+2822] thousand
Jer 32: 1 which was the **eighteenth** [+6926] year of Nebuchadnezzar.
41: 5 **eighty** men who had shaved off their beards, torn their clothes
41:15 **eight** *of* his men escaped from Johanan and fled to the Ammonites.
52:21 Each of the pillars was **eighteen** [+6926] cubits high and twelve
52:29 in Nebuchadnezzar's **eighteenth** [+6926] year, 832 people from
52:29 year, **832** [+2256+4395+8993+9109] people from Jerusalem;
Eze 40: 9 it was **eight** cubits deep and its jambs were two cubits thick.
40:31 palm trees decorated its jambs, and **eight** steps led up to it.
40:34 decorated the jambs on either side, and **eight** steps led up to it.
40:37 decorated the jambs on either side, and **eight** steps led up to it.
40:41 one side of the gateway and four on the other—**eight** tables in all—
48:35 "The distance all around will be **18,000** [+547+6925] cubits.
Mic 5: 5 [5:4] against him seven shepherds, even **eight** leaders of men.

9047 שְׁמֹנִים ***š^e^mōnîm***, n.pl.indecl. Not used in NIV/BHS [√ 9046]

9048 שָׁמַע ***šāma'***, v. [1159] [→ 904, 2245, 3816-21, 5461, 5462, 5463, 9015, 9016, 9021, 9019, 9025, 9049, 9050, 9051, 9053, 9054, 9056, 9057, 9058, 9059, 9060, 9063, 9064, 9065; cf. 1072]

heard [293], hear [238], listen [225], listened [40], obey [+928+7754] [36], hears [27], obey [19], obeyed [+928+7754] [17], proclaim [15], obeyed [13], agreed [9], be heard [9], hearing [8], listen carefully [+9048] [8], listening [8], understand [8], is heard [6], *untranslated* [4], fully obey [+928+7754+9048] [4], listens [4], paid attention [4], was heard [4], do [3], heed [3], let hear [3], pay attention [3], proclaimed [3], resound [3], sound [3], agree [2], are heard [2], careful to obey [+448+9048] [2], certainly hear [+9048] [2], declare [2], diligently obey [+928+7754+9048] [2], discerning [2], disobeyed [+928+4202+7754] [2], ever hearing [+9048] [2], faithfully obey [+448+9048] [2], foretold [2], give [2], heard [+928+7754] [2], heard definitely [+9048] [2], hears [+9048] [2], hears [+906+7754+9048] [2], mark my words [2], obedient [2], obey fully [+928+7754+9048] [2], obeying [2], proclaiming [2], raise [2], received a report [2], sang [2], summon [2], surely heard [+9048] [2], administering [1], agreed with [+4200+7754] [1], announce [1], announced [1], are heeded [1], argue [+7754] [1], be heeded [1], been brought to attention [+2256 +4200+5583] [1], been heard of [1], been heard [1], been proclaimed [1], been^s^ [1], boast [1], bring word [1], called up [1], cause to hear [1], caused to hear [1], complied [1], comply [1], cry out [+2411] [1], cry out [1], deaf [+4946] [1], did [1], disobedience [+928+4202 +7754] [1], disobey [+448+4202] [1], disobey [+928+1194+7754] [1], disobeyed [+4200+4202] [1], disobeyed [+928+4202] [1], expect to be heard [1], find out [1], fully obeyed [+2256+3869+6913] [1], gave in [+928+7754] [1], get back to [1], have^s^ [1], heard [+9051] [1], hears [+7754] [1], heeds [1], is proclaimed [1], is reported [1], issued an order [1], learn [1], let be heard [1], listen [+7754] [1], listen carefully [+265+928] [1], listen carefully [+928+4200+7754] [1], listen closely [+265+928] [1], listen in [1], listened to [1], listens [+265] [1], made hear [1], made known [1], made proclamation [1], make hear [1], make heard [1], obedience [1], obey [+4200+7754] [1], obeyed [+928+4200+7754] [1], obeying [+928+7754] [1], obeys [+928+7754] [1], obeys [1], obscure [+4946+6680] [1], overheard [1], paid any attention [+265+906+4200+5742] [1], pay close attention [+2256+7992] [1], playing [1], plots [1], proclaims [1], pronounced [1], put under oath [+460] [1], reached [+928] [1], reached [1], received message [1], received [1], refused [+448+4202] [1], resounds [1], sing songs [+928+4200+7754+8123] [1], sound be heard [1], sounding [1], stopped up [+3877+4946] [1], summoned [1], tell [1], told [+907+4946] [1], told [1], was overheard [1], were heard [1], witness [+1068] [1], word came [1]

Ge 3: 8 [A] his wife **heard** the sound of the LORD God as he was
3:10 [A] He answered, "*I* **heard** you in the garden, and I was afraid
3:17 [A] "Because *you* **listened** to your wife and ate from the tree
4:23 [A] Lamech said to his wives, "Adah and Zillah, **listen** *to* me;
11: 7 [A] their language so *they will* not **understand** each other."
14:14 [A] When Abram **heard** that his relative had been taken captive,
16: 2 [A] a family through her." Abram **agreed** to what Sarai said.
16:11 [A] him Ishmael, for the LORD *has* **heard** of your misery.
17:20 [A] as for Ishmael, *I have* **heard** you: I will surely bless him;
18:10 [A] Now Sarah *was* **listening** *at* the entrance to the tent, which
21: 6 [A] and everyone who **hears** *about* this will laugh with me."
21:12 [A] **Listen** to whatever Sarah tells you, because it is through
21:17 [A] God **heard** the boy crying, and the angel of God called to
21:17 [A] not be afraid; God *has* **heard** the boy crying as he lies there.
21:26 [A] You did not tell me, and I **heard** *about* it only today."
22:18 [A] will be blessed, because *you have* **obeyed** [+928+7754] me."
23: 6 [A] "Sir, **listen** *to* us. You are a mighty prince among us.
23: 8 [A] **listen** *to* me and intercede with Ephron son of Zohar on my
23:11 [A] "**Listen** *to* me; I give you the field, and I give you the cave
23:13 [A] he said to Ephron in their hearing, "**Listen** *to* me, if you will.
23:15 [A] "**Listen** *to* me, my lord; the land is worth four hundred
23:16 [A] Abraham **agreed** to Ephron's *terms* and weighed out for him
24:30 [A] *had* **heard** Rebekah tell what the man said to her, he went
24:52 [A] When Abraham's servant **heard** what they said, he bowed
26: 5 [A] because Abraham **obeyed** [+928+7754] me and kept my
27: 5 [A] Now Rebekah *was* **listening** as Isaac spoke to his son Esau.
27: 6 [A] "Look, *I* **overheard** your father say to your brother Esau,
27: 8 [A] Now, my son, **listen** [+928+4200+7754] **carefully** and do what
27:13 [A] curse fall on me. Just **do** what I say; go and get them for me."
27:34 [A] When Esau **heard** his father's words, he burst out with a
27:43 [A] Now then, my son, **do** what I say: Flee at once to my brother
28: 7 [A] that Jacob *had* **obeyed** his father and mother and had gone to
29:13 [A] As soon as Laban **heard** the news about Jacob, his sister's
29:33 [A] "Because the LORD **heard** that I am not loved, he gave me
30: 6 [A] *he has* **listened** to my plea and given me a son."
30:17 [A] God **listened** to Leah, and she became pregnant and bore
30:22 [A] he **listened** to her and opened her womb.
31: 1 [A] Jacob **heard** that Laban's sons were saying, "Jacob has taken
34: 5 [A] When Jacob **heard** that his daughter Dinah had been defiled,
34: 7 [A] in from the fields as soon as they **heard** what had happened.
34:17 [A] if *you will* not **agree** to be circumcised, we'll take our sister
34:24 [A] All the men who went out of the city gate **agreed** with
35:22 [A] with his father's concubine Bilhah, and Israel **heard** *of* it.
37: 6 [A] He said to them, "**Listen** *to* this dream I had:
37:17 [A] "*I* **heard** them say, 'Let's go to Dothan.' " So Joseph went
37:21 [A] When Reuben **heard** this, he tried to rescue him from their
37:27 [A] our brother, our own flesh and blood." His brothers **agreed**.
39:10 [A] *he* **refused** [+448+4202] to go to bed with her or even be
39:15 [A] When he **heard** me scream for help, he left his cloak beside
39:19 [A] When his master **heard** the story his wife told him, saying,
41:15 [A] I *have* **heard** it said of you *that* when you hear a dream you
41:15 [A] I have heard it said of you that *when you* **hear** a dream you
42: 2 [A] He continued, "*I have* **heard** that there is grain in Egypt.
42:21 [A] when he pleaded with us for his life, but *we would* not **listen**;
42:22 [A] I tell you not to sin against the boy? But *you* wouldn't **listen**!
42:23 [A] They did not realize that Joseph *could* **understand** them,
43:25 [A] at noon, because *they had* **heard** that they were to eat there.
45: 2 [A] he wept so loudly that the Egyptians **heard** him,
45: 2 [A] heard him, and Pharaoh's household **heard** *about* it.
45:16 [C] When the news **reached** Pharaoh's palace that Joseph's
49: 2 [A] "Assemble and **listen**, sons of Jacob; listen to your father
49: 2 [A] and listen, sons of Jacob; **listen** to your father Israel.
Ex 2:15 [A] When Pharaoh **heard** *of* this, he tried to kill Moses,
2:24 [A] God **heard** their groaning and he remembered his covenant
3: 7 [A] *I have* **heard** them crying out because of their slave drivers,
3:18 [A] "The elders of Israel *will* **listen** to you. Then you
4: 1 [A] "What if they do not believe me or **listen** to me and say,
4: 8 [A] not believe you or **pay attention** to the first miraculous sign,
4: 9 [A] But if they do not believe these two signs or **listen** to you,
4:31 [A] when *they* **heard** that the LORD was concerned about them
5: 2 [A] that *I should* **obey** [+928+7754] him and let Israel go?
6: 5 [A] Moreover, I *have* **heard** the groaning of the Israelites,
6: 9 [A] *they did* not **listen** to him because of their discouragement
6:12 [A] said to the LORD, "If the Israelites *will* not **listen** to me,
6:12 [A] why *would* Pharaoh **listen** *to* me, since I speak with faltering
6:30 [A] speak with faltering lips, why *would* Pharaoh **listen** to me?"
7: 4 [A] he *will* not **listen** to you. Then I will lay my hand on Egypt
7:13 [A] heart became hard and *he would* not **listen** to them,
7:16 [A] me in the desert. But until now *you have* not **listened.**
7:22 [A] *he would* not **listen** to Moses and Aaron, just as the LORD
8:15 [8:11] [A] his heart and *would* not **listen** to Moses and Aaron,
8:19 [8:15] [A] Pharaoh's heart was hard and *he would* not **listen**,
9:12 [A] Pharaoh's heart and *he would* not **listen** to Moses and Aaron,
11: 9 [A] had said to Moses, "Pharaoh *will* refuse *to* **listen** to you—
15:14 [A] The nations *will* **hear** and tremble; anguish will grip the
15:26 [A] "If *you* **listen** [+9048] **carefully** to the voice of the LORD
15:26 [A] "If *you* **listen carefully** [+9048] to the voice of the LORD
16: 7 [A] because he *has* **heard** your grumbling against him.
16: 8 [A] because he *has* **heard** your grumbling against him.
16: 9 [A] before the LORD, for *he has* **heard** your grumbling.' "

Ex 16:12 [A] "*I have* **heard** the grumbling of the Israelites. Tell them, 'At
16:20 [A] However, some of them **paid** no **attention** to Moses; they
18: 1 [A] **heard** *of* everything God had done for Moses and for his
18:19 [A] **Listen** now to me and I will give you some advice, and may
18:24 [A] Moses **listened** to his father-in-law and did everything he
19: 5 [A] Now if *you* **obey** [+928+7754+9048] me **fully** and keep my
19: 5 [A] Now if *you* **obey** me **fully** [+928+7754+9048] and keep my
19: 9 [A] so that the people *will* **hear** me speaking with you and will
20:19 [A] and said to Moses, "Speak to us yourself and *we will* **listen**.
22:23 [22:22] [A] out to me, *I will* **certainly hear** [+9048] their cry.
22:23 [22:22] [A] out to me, *I will* **certainly hear** [+9048] their cry.
22:27 [22:26] [A] cries out to me, *I will* **hear**, for I am compassionate.
23:13 [C] names of other gods; *do* not *let them* **be heard** on your lips.
23:21 [A] Pay attention to him and **listen** to what he says. Do not rebel
23:22 [A] If *you* **listen** [+9048] **carefully** to what he says and do all
23:22 [A] If *you* **listen carefully** [+9048] to what he says and do all
24: 7 [A] "We will do everything the LORD has said; *we will* **obey**."
28:35 [C] The sound of the bells *will* **be heard** when he enters the Holy
32:17 [A] When Joshua **heard** the noise of the people shouting, he said
32:18 [A] the sound of defeat; it is the sound of singing that I **hear**."
33: 4 [A] When the people **heard** these distressing words, they began
Lev 5: 1 [A] because he does not speak up when *he* **hears** [+7754] a
10:20 [A] When Moses **heard** this, he was satisfied.
24:14 [A] All those *who* **heard** him are to lay their hands on his head,
26:14 [A] " 'But if *you will* not **listen** to me and carry out all these
26:18 [A] " 'If after all this *you will* not **listen** to me, I will punish you
26:21 [A] " 'If you remain hostile toward me and refuse to **listen** to me,
26:27 [A] " 'If in spite of this *you still do* not **listen** to me but continue
Nu 7:89 [A] *he* **heard** the voice speaking to him from between the two
9: 8 [A] "Wait until *I* **find out** what the LORD commands
11: 1 [A] the LORD, and when he **heard** them his anger was aroused.
11:10 [A] Moses **heard** the people of every family wailing, each at the
12: 2 [A] he also spoken through us?" And the LORD **heard** this.
12: 6 [A] he said, "**Listen** *to* my words: "When a prophet of the
14:13 [A] said to the LORD, "Then the Egyptians *will* **hear** *about* it!
14:14 [A] *They have already* **heard** that you, O LORD, are with
14:15 [A] the nations who *have* **heard** this report about you will say,
14:22 [A] but *who* **disobeyed** [+928+4202+7754] me and tested me ten
14:27 [A] *I have* **heard** the complaints of these grumbling Israelites.
16: 4 [A] When Moses **heard** this, he fell facedown.
16: 8 [A] Moses also said to Korah, "Now **listen**, *you* Levites!
20:10 [A] of the rock and Moses said to them, "**Listen**, you rebels,
20:16 [A] *he* **heard** our cry and sent an angel and brought us out of
21: 1 [A] **heard** that Israel was coming along the road to Atharim,
21: 3 [A] The LORD **listened** to Israel's plea and gave the Canaanites
22:36 [A] When Balak **heard** that Balaam was coming, he went out to
23:18 [A] his oracle: "Arise, Balak, and **listen**; hear me, son of Zippor.
24: 4 [A] the oracle of *one who* **hears** the words of God, who sees a
24:16 [A] the oracle of *one who* **hears** the words of God, who has
27:20 [A] so the whole Israelite community *will* **obey** him.
30: 4 [30:5] [A] her father **hears** *about* her vow or pledge but says
30: 5 [30:6] [A] if her father forbids her when he **hears** *about* it,
30: 7 [30:8] [A] her husband **hears** *about* it but says nothing to her,
30: 7 [30:8] [A] hears about it **[RPH]** but says nothing to her,
30: 8 [30:9] [A] if her husband forbids her when he **hears** *about* it, he
30:11 [30:12] [A] her husband **hears** *about* it but says nothing to her
30:12 [30:13] [A] if her husband nullifies them when he **hears** *about*
30:14 [30:15] [A] saying nothing to her when he **hears** *about* them.
30:15 [30:16] [A] nullifies them some time after he **hears** *about* them,
33:40 [A] the Negev of Canaan, **heard** that the Israelites were coming.
Dt 1:16 [A] **Hear** the disputes between your brothers and judge fairly,
1:17 [A] show partiality in judging; **hear** both small and great alike.
1:17 [A] Bring me any case too hard for you, and *I will* **hear** it.
1:34 [A] When the LORD **heard** what you said, he was angry
1:43 [A] So I told you, but *you would* not **listen**. You rebelled against
1:45 [A] he **paid** no **attention** to your weeping and turned a deaf ear
2:25 [A] *They will* **hear** reports of you and will tremble and be in
3:26 [A] the LORD was angry with me and *would* not **listen** to me.
4: 1 [A] **Hear** now, O Israel, the decrees and laws I am about to teach
4: 6 [A] to the nations, who *will* **hear** *about* all these decrees and say,
4:10 [G] "Assemble the people before me *to* **hear** my words so that
4:12 [A] You **heard** the sound of words but saw no form; there was
4:28 [A] of wood and stone, which cannot see or **hear** or eat or smell.
4:30 [A] return to the LORD your God and **obey** [+928+7754] him.
4:32 [C] ever happened, or *has* anything like it *ever* **been heard of**?
4:33 [A] *Has* any other people **heard** the voice of God speaking out of
4:33 [A] voice of God speaking out of fire, as you **have**[s], and lived?
4:36 [G] From heaven *he* **made** you **hear** his voice to discipline you.
4:36 [A] his great fire, and *you* **heard** his words from out of the fire.
5: 1 [A] **Hear**, O Israel, the decrees and laws I declare in your hearing
5:23 [A] When you **heard** the voice out of the darkness,
5:24 [A] and his majesty, and *we have* **heard** his voice from the fire.
5:25 [A] we will die if we **hear** the voice of the LORD our God any
5:26 [A] For what mortal man *has* ever **heard** the voice of the living
5:27 [A] Go near and **listen** *to* all that the LORD our God says.
5:27 [A] the LORD our God tells you. *We will* **listen** and obey."
5:28 [A] The LORD **heard** you when you spoke to me
5:28 [A] said to me, "*I have* **heard** what this people said to you.
6: 3 [A] **Hear**, O Israel, and be careful to obey so that it may go well
6: 4 [A] **Hear**, O Israel: The LORD our God, the LORD is one.
7:12 [A] If *you* **pay attention** *to* these laws and are careful to follow
8:20 [A] so you will be destroyed for not **obeying** [+928+7754] the
9: 1 [A] **Hear**, O Israel. You are now about to cross the Jordan to go
9: 2 [A] You know about them and *have* **heard** it said:
9:19 [A] you to destroy you. But again the LORD **listened** to me.
9:23 [A] your God. You did not trust him or **obey** [+928+7754] him.
10:10 [A] first time, and the LORD **listened** to me at this time also.
11:13 [A] So if *you* **faithfully obey** [+448+9048] the commands I am
11:13 [A] So if *you* **faithfully obey** [+448+9048] the commands I am
11:27 [A] the blessing if *you* **obey** the commands of the LORD your
11:28 [A] the curse if *you* **disobey** [+448+4202] the commands of the
12:28 [A] Be careful *to* **obey** all these regulations I am giving you, so
13: 3 [13:4] [A] *you must* not **listen** to the words of that prophet or
13: 4 [13:5] [A] Keep his commands and **obey** [+928+7754] him;
13: 8 [13:9] [A] do not yield to him or **listen** to him. Show him no
13:11 [13:12] [A] all Israel *will* **hear** and be afraid, and no one among
13:12 [13:13] [A] If *you* **hear** it said about one of the towns the
13:18 [13:19] [A] because *you* **obey** [+928+7754] the LORD your
15: 5 [A] if only *you* **fully obey** [+928+7754+9048] the LORD your God
15: 5 [A] if only *you* **fully obey** [+928+7754+9048] the LORD your God
17: 4 [A] *this has* **been brought to** your **attention** [+2256+4200+5583],
17:12 [A] or **[NIE]** for the priest who stands ministering there to the
17:13 [A] All the people *will* **hear** and be afraid, and will not be
18:14 [A] The nations you will dispossess **listen** to those who practice
18:15 [A] me from among your own brothers. *You must* **listen** to him.
18:16 [A] "*Let us* not **hear** the voice of the LORD our God nor see
18:19 [A] If anyone *does* not **listen** to my words that the prophet speaks
19:20 [A] The rest of the people *will* **hear** of this and be afraid,
20: 3 [A] "**Hear**, O Israel, today you are going into battle against your
21:18 [A] rebellious son who *does* not **obey** [+928+7754] his father
21:18 [A] and *will* not **listen** to them when they discipline him,
21:20 [A] is stubborn and rebellious. He *will* not **obey** [+928+7754] us.
21:21 [A] evil from among you. All Israel *will* **hear** of it and be afraid.
23: 5 [23:6] [A] the LORD your God would not **listen** to Balaam
26: 7 [A] and the LORD **heard** our voice and saw our misery, toil
26:14 [A] *I have* **obeyed** [+928+7754] the LORD my God; I have
26:17 [A] and laws, and that you *will* **obey** [+928+7754] him.
27: 9 [A] are Levites, said to all Israel, "Be silent, O Israel, and **listen**!
27:10 [A] **Obey** [+928+7754] the LORD your God and follow his
28: 1 [A] If *you* **fully obey** [+928+7754+9048] the LORD your God and
28: 1 [A] If *you* **fully obey** [+928+7754+9048] the LORD your God and
28: 2 [A] accompany you if *you* **obey** [+928+7754] the LORD your
28:13 [A] If *you* **pay attention** to the commands of the LORD your
28:15 [A] if *you do* not **obey** [+928+7754] the LORD your God
28:45 [A] because *you did* not **obey** [+928+7754] the LORD your
28:49 [A] a nation whose language *you will* not **understand**,
28:62 [A] because *you did* not **obey** [+928+7754] the LORD your
29: 4 [29:3] [A] that understands or eyes that see or ears that **hear**.
29:19 [29:18] [A] When such a person **hears** the words of this oath, he
30: 2 [A] your God and **obey** [+928+7754] him with all your heart
30: 8 [A] You *will* again **obey** [+928+7754] the LORD and follow all
30:10 [A] if *you* **obey** [+928+7754] the LORD your God and keep his
30:12 [G] heaven to get it and **proclaim** it *to* us so we may obey it?"
30:13 [G] the sea to get it and **proclaim** it *to* us so we may obey it?"
30:17 [A] if your heart turns away and *you are* not **obedient**, and if you
30:20 [A] LORD your God, **listen** to his voice, and hold fast to him.
31:12 [A] so *they can* **listen** and learn to fear the LORD your God
31:13 [A] *must* **hear** it and learn to fear the LORD your God as long
32: 1 [A] and I will speak; **hear**, O earth, the words of my mouth.
33: 7 [A] "**Hear**, O LORD, the cry of Judah; bring him to his people.
34: 9 [A] So the Israelites **listened** to him and did what the LORD
Jos 1:17 [A] Just as *we* fully **obeyed** Moses, so we will obey you.
1:17 [A] Just as we fully obeyed Moses, so *we will* **obey** you.
1:18 [A] rebels against your word and *does* not **obey** your words,
2:10 [A] *We have* **heard** how the LORD dried up the water of the
2:11 [A] When *we* **heard** of it, our hearts melted and everyone's
3: 9 [A] "Come here and **listen** *to* the words of the LORD your God.
5: 1 [A] all the Canaanite kings along the coast **heard** how the
5: 6 [A] since *they had* not **obeyed** [+928+7754] the LORD.
6: 5 [A] When you **hear** them sound a long blast on the trumpets,
6:10 [G] the people, "Do not give a war cry, *do* not **raise** your voices,
6:20 [A] the people shouted, and at **[NIE]** the sound of the trumpet,
7: 9 [A] and the other people of the country *will* **hear** *about* this
9: 1 [A] Now when all the kings west of the Jordan **heard** *about*
9: 3 [A] when the people of Gibeon **heard** what Joshua had done to
9: 9 [A] For *we have* **heard** reports of him: all that he did in Egypt,
9:16 [A] the Israelites **heard** that they were neighbors, living near
10: 1 [A] Now Adoni-Zedek king of Jerusalem **heard** that Joshua had

Jos 10:14 [A] it before or since, a day when the LORD **listened** to a man.
11: 1 [A] When Jabin king of Hazor **heard** of this, he sent word to
14:12 [A] *You* yourself **heard** then that the Anakites were there
22: 2 [A] *you have* **obeyed** [+928+7754] me in everything I
22:11 [A] *when* the Israelites **heard** that they had built the altar on the
22:12 [A] **[RPH]** the whole assembly of Israel gathered at Shiloh to
22:30 [A] **heard** what Reuben, Gad and Manasseh had to say, they
24:10 [A] But I would not **listen** to Balaam, so he blessed you again
24:24 [A] will serve the LORD our God and **obey** [+928+7754] him."
24:27 [A] It *has* **heard** all the words the LORD has said to us.
Jdg 2: 2 [A] Yet *you have* **disobeyed** [+928+4202+7754] me. Why have
2:17 [A] Yet *they would* not **listen** to their judges but prostituted
2:17 [A] the way of **obedience** *to* the LORD's commands.
2:20 [A] I laid down for their forefathers and *has* not **listened** to me,
3: 4 [A] to see whether *they would* **obey** the LORD's commands,
5: 3 [A] "**Hear** this, *you* kings! Listen, you rulers! I will sing to the
5:16 [A] Why did you stay among the campfires to **hear** the whistling
6:10 [A] in whose land you live.' But *you have* not **listened** to me."
7:11 [A] **listen** *to* what they are saying. Afterward, you will be
7:15 [A] When Gideon **heard** the dream and its interpretation, he
9: 7 [A] and shouted to them, "**Listen** to me, citizens of Shechem,
9: 7 [A] to me, citizens of Shechem, so that God *may* **listen** to you.
9:30 [A] When Zebul the governor of the city **heard** what Gaal son of
9:46 [A] On **hearing** this, the citizens in the tower of Shechem went
11:10 [A] of Gilead replied, "The LORD is our **witness** [+1068];
11:17 [A] your country,' but the king of Edom *would* not **listen**.
11:28 [A] **paid** no **attention** to the message Jephthah sent him.
13: 9 [A] God **heard** [+928+7754] Manoah, and the angel of God
13:23 [G] our hands, nor shown us all these things or now **told** us this."
14:13 [A] of clothes." "Tell us your riddle," they said. "*Let's* **hear** it."
18:25 [G] The Danites answered, "Don't **argue** [+7754] with us,
19:25 [A] the men would not **listen** to him. So the man took his
20: 3 [A] (The Benjamites **heard** that the Israelites had gone up to
20:13 [A] But the Benjamites would not **listen** to their fellow Israelites.
Ru 1: 6 [A] When *she* **heard** in Moab that the LORD had come to the
2: 8 [A] So Boaz said to Ruth, "My daughter, **listen** *to* me. Don't go
1Sa 1:13 [C] and her lips were moving but her voice **was** not **heard.**
2:22 [A] **heard** *about* everything his sons were doing to all Israel and
2:23 [A] I **hear** from all the people *about* these wicked deeds of
2:24 [A] it is not a good report that I **hear** spreading among the
2:25 [A] His sons, however, *did* not **listen** to their father's rebuke,
3: 9 [A] for your servant *is* **listening**.' " So Samuel went and lay down
3:10 [A] Then Samuel said, "Speak, for your servant *is* **listening**."
3:11 [A] that will make the ears of everyone *who* **hears** *of* it tingle.
4: 6 [A] **Hearing** the uproar, the Philistines asked, "What's all this
4:14 [A] Eli **heard** the outcry and asked, "What is the meaning of this
4:19 [A] When *she* **heard** the news that the ark of God had been
7: 7 [A] When the Philistines **heard** that Israel had assembled at
7: 7 [A] when the Israelites **heard** *of* it, they were afraid because of
8: 7 [A] "**Listen** to all that the people are saying to you; it is not you
8: 9 [A] Now **listen** to them; but warn them solemnly and let them
8:19 [A] But the people refused to **listen** to Samuel. "No!" they said.
8:21 [A] When Samuel **heard** all that the people said, he repeated it
8:22 [A] LORD answered, "**Listen** to them and give them a king."
9:27 [G] here awhile, so that *I may* **give** you a message from God."
11: 6 [A] When Saul **heard** their words, the Spirit of God came upon
12: 1 [A] "*I have* **listened** to everything you said to me and have set a
12:14 [A] If you fear the LORD and serve and **obey** [+928+7754] him
12:15 [A] if *you do* not **obey** [+928+7754] the LORD, and if you
13: 3 [A] Philistine outpost at Geba, and the Philistines **heard** *about* it.
13: 3 [A] throughout the land and said, "*Let* the Hebrews **hear**!"
13: 4 [A] So all Israel **heard** the news: "Saul has attacked the
14:22 [A] of Ephraim **heard** that the Philistines were on the run,
14:27 [A] Jonathan *had* not **heard** that his father had bound the people
15: 1 [A] people Israel; so **listen** now to the message from the LORD.
15: 4 [D] So Saul **summoned** the men and mustered them at Telaim—
15:14 [A] sheep in my ears? What is this lowing of cattle that I **hear**?"
15:19 [A] Why *did you* not **obey** [+928+7754] the LORD? Why did
15:20 [A] "But *I did* **obey** [+928+7754] the LORD," Saul said. "I
15:22 [A] sacrifices as much as *in* **obeying** the voice of the LORD?
15:22 [A] *To* **obey** is better than sacrifice, and to heed is better than the
15:24 [A] afraid of the people and so *I* **gave** [+928+7754] **in** *to* them.
16: 2 [A] "How can I go? Saul *will* **hear** *about* it and kill me."
17:11 [A] On **hearing** the Philistine's words, Saul and all the Israelites
17:23 [A] his lines and shouted his usual defiance, and David **heard** it.
17:28 [A] David's oldest brother, **heard** him speaking with the men,
17:31 [C] What David said **was overheard** and reported to Saul,
19: 6 [A] Saul **listened** to Jonathan and took this oath: "As surely as
22: 1 [A] When his brothers and his father's household **heard** *about* it,
22: 6 [A] Now Saul **heard** that David and his men had been
22: 7 [A] Saul said to them, "**Listen**, men of Benjamin! Will the son of
22:12 [A] Saul said, "**Listen** now, son of Ahitub." "Yes, my lord,"
23: 8 [D] Saul **called up** all his forces for battle, to go down to Keilah
23:10 [A] your servant *has* **heard** [+9048] **definitely** that Saul plans to
23:10 [A] your servant *has* **heard definitely** [+9048] that Saul plans to
23:11 [A] Will Saul come down, as your servant *has* **heard**?
23:25 [A] When Saul **heard** this, he went into the Desert of Maon in
24: 9 [24:10] [A] He said to Saul, "Why *do you* **listen** when men say,
25: 4 [A] was in the desert, *he* **heard** that Nabal was shearing sheep.
25: 7 [A] " 'Now *I* **hear** that it is sheep-shearing time. When your
25:24 [A] your servant speak to you; **hear** what your servant has to say.
25:35 [A] *I have* **heard** your words and granted your request."
25:39 [A] When David **heard** that Nabal was dead, he said, "Praise be
26:19 [A] Now *let* my lord the king **listen** *to* his servant's words.
28:18 [A] Because *you did* not **obey** [+928+7754] the LORD or carry
28:21 [A] "Look, your maidservant *has* **obeyed** [+928+7754] you.
28:21 [A] I took my life in my hands and **did** what you told me to do.
28:22 [A] Now please **listen** to your servant and let me give you some
28:23 [A] joined the woman in urging him, and *he* **listened** to them.
30:24 [A] Who *will* **listen** to what you say? The share of the man who
31:11 [A] When the people of Jabesh Gilead **heard** of what the
2Sa 3:28 [A] Later, when David **heard** *about* this, he said, "I and my
4: 1 [A] When Ish-Bosheth son of Saul **heard** that Abner had died in
5:17 [A] When the Philistines **heard** that David had been anointed
5:17 [A] but David **heard** *about* it and went down to the stronghold.
5:24 [A] As soon as you **hear** the sound of marching in the tops of the
7:22 [A] is no God but you, as *we have* **heard** with our own ears.
8: 9 [A] When Tou king of Hamath **heard** that David had defeated
10: 7 [A] On **hearing** this, David sent Joab out with the entire army of
11:26 [A] When Uriah's wife **heard** that her husband was dead, she
12:18 [A] still living, we spoke to David but *he would* not **listen** to us.
13:14 [A] he refused to **listen** to her, and since he was stronger than
13:16 [A] you have already done to me." But he refused to **listen** to her.
13:21 [A] When King David **heard** all this, he was furious.
14:16 [A] Perhaps the king *will* **agree** to deliver his servant from the
14:17 [A] for my lord the king is like an angel of God in **discerning**
15: 3 [A] but there is no representative of the king *to* **hear** you."
15:10 [A] "As soon as you **hear** the sound of the trumpets, then say,
15:35 [A] with you? Tell them anything *you* **hear** in the king's palace.
15:36 [A] there with them. Send them to me with anything *you* **hear**."
16:21 [A] all Israel *will* **hear** that you have made yourself a stench in
17: 5 [A] also Hushai the Arkite, so *we can* **hear** what he has to say."
17: 9 [A] your troops first, whoever **hears** [+9048] *about* it will say,
17: 9 [A] your troops first, whoever **hears about** [+9048] it will say,
18: 5 [A] all the troops **heard** the king giving orders concerning
19: 2 [19:3] [A] because on that day the troops **heard** it said,
19:35 [19:36] [A] *Can I* still **hear** the voices of men and women
20:16 [A] a wise woman called from the city, "**Listen**! Listen!
20:16 [A] a wise woman called from the city, "Listen! **Listen**!
20:17 [A] She said, "**Listen** *to* what your servant has to say."
20:17 [A] to what your servant has to say." "I'm **listening**," he said.
22: 7 [A] From his temple *he* **heard** my voice; my cry came to his
22:45 [A] come cringing to me; as soon as they **hear** me, they obey me.
22:45 [C] come cringing to me; as soon as they hear me, *they* **obey** me.
1Ki 1:11 [A] "*Have you* not **heard** that Adonijah, the son of Haggith,
1:41 [A] all the guests who were with him **heard** it as they were
1:41 [A] *On* **hearing** the sound of the trumpet, Joab asked,
1:45 [A] and the city resounds with it. That's the noise *you* **hear**.
2:42 [A] that time you said to me, 'What you say is good. *I will* **obey**.'
3: 9 [A] So give your servant a **discerning** heart to govern your
3:11 [A] your enemies but for discernment in **administering** justice,
3:28 [A] When all Israel **heard** the verdict the king had given, they
4:34 [5:14] [A] Men of all nations came to **listen** *to* Solomon's
4:34 [5:14] [A] kings of the world, who *had* **heard** *of* his wisdom.
5: 1 [5:15] [A] When Hiram king of Tyre **heard** that Solomon had
5: 7 [5:21] [A] When Hiram **heard** Solomon's message, he was
5: 8 [5:22] [A] "*I have* **received** *the* **message** you sent me and will
6: 7 [C] or any other iron tool **was heard** at the temple site while it
8:28 [A] **Hear** the cry and the prayer that your servant is praying in
8:29 [A] so that you *will* **hear** the prayer your servant prays toward
8:30 [A] **Hear** the supplication of your servant and of your people
8:30 [A] **Hear** from heaven, your dwelling place, and when you hear,
8:30 [A] your dwelling place, and when *you* **hear**, forgive.
8:32 [A] then **hear** from heaven and act. Judge between your servants,
8:34 [A] **hear** from heaven and forgive the sin of your people Israel
8:36 [A] then **hear** from heaven and forgive the sin of your servants,
8:39 [A] then **hear** from heaven, your dwelling place. Forgive and act;
8:42 [A] for *men will* **hear** *of* your great name and your mighty hand
8:43 [A] **hear** from heaven, your dwelling place, and do whatever the
8:45 [A] **hear** from heaven their prayer and their plea, and uphold
8:49 [A] your dwelling place, **hear** their prayer and their plea,
8:52 [A] and *may* you **listen** to them whenever they cry out to you.
9: 3 [A] "*I have* **heard** the prayer and plea you have made before me;
10: 1 [A] When the queen of Sheba **heard** *about* the fame of Solomon
10: 6 [A] "The report *I* **heard** in my own country about your
10: 7 [A] and wealth you have far exceeded the report *I* **heard**.
10: 8 [A] who continually stand before you and **hear** your wisdom!
10:24 [A] The whole world sought audience with Solomon to **hear** the

1Ki 11:21 [A] Hadad **heard** that David rested with his fathers and that Joab
11:38 [A] If *you* **do** whatever I command you and walk in my ways
12: 2 [A] When Jeroboam son of Nebat **heard** this (he was still in
12:15 [A] So the king *did* not **listen** to the people, for this turn of
12:16 [A] When all Israel saw that the king refused *to* **listen** to them,
12:20 [A] When all the Israelites **heard** that Jeroboam had returned,
12:24 [A] for this is my doing.' " So *they* **obeyed** the word of the
13: 4 [A] When King Jeroboam **heard** what the man of God cried out
13:26 [A] who had brought him back from his journey **heard** *of* it,
14: 6 [A] So when Ahijah **heard** the sound of her footsteps at the door,
15:20 [A] Ben-Hadad **agreed** with King Asa and sent the commanders
15:21 [A] When Baasha **heard** this, he stopped building Ramah
15:22 [G] King Asa **issued an order** *to* all Judah—no one was
16:16 [A] When the Israelites in the camp **heard** that Zimri had plotted
17:22 [A] The LORD **heard** Elijah's cry, and the boy's life returned
19:13 [A] When Elijah **heard** it, he pulled his cloak over his face
20: 8 [A] all answered, "Don't **listen** to him or agree to his demands."
20:12 [A] Ben-Hadad **heard** this message while he and the kings were
20:25 [A] *He* **agreed** [+4200+7754] **with** them and acted accordingly.
20:31 [A] *we have* **heard** that the kings of the house of Israel are
20:36 [A] "Because *you have* not **obeyed** [+928+7754] the LORD,
21:15 [A] As soon as Jezebel **heard** that Naboth had been stoned to
21:16 [A] When Ahab **heard** that Naboth was dead, he got up and went
21:27 [A] When Ahab **heard** these words, he tore his clothes, put on
22:19 [A] Micaiah continued, "Therefore **hear** the word of the LORD:
22:28 [A] Then he added, "**Mark my words**, all you people!"
2Ki 3:21 [A] Now all the Moabites *had* **heard** that the kings had come to
5: 8 [A] When Elisha the man of God **heard** that the king of Israel
6:30 [A] When the king **heard** the woman's words, he tore his robes.
7: 1 [A] Elisha said, "**Hear** the word of the LORD. This is what the
7: 6 [G] for the Lord *had* **caused** the Arameans **to hear** the sound of
9:30 [A] When Jezebel **heard** *about* it, she painted her eyes, arranged
10: 6 [A] "If you are on my side and *will* **obey** [+4200+7754] me,
11:13 [A] When Athaliah **heard** the noise made by the guards
13: 4 [A] sought the LORD's favor, and the LORD **listened** to him,
14:11 [A] Amaziah, however, *would* not **listen**, so Jehoash king of
16: 9 [A] The king of Assyria **complied** *by* attacking Damascus
17:14 [A] *they would* not **listen** and were as stiff-necked as their
17:40 [A] They *would* not **listen**, however, but persisted in their former
18:12 [A] because *they had* not **obeyed** [+928+7754] the LORD their
18:12 [A] *They* neither **listened** to the commands nor carried them out.
18:26 [A] speak to your servants in Aramaic, since we **understand** it.
18:28 [A] "**Hear** the word of the great king, the king of Assyria!
18:31 [A] "*Do* not **listen** to Hezekiah. This is what the king of Assyria
18:32 [A] "*Do* not **listen** to Hezekiah, for he is misleading you when he
19: 1 [A] When King Hezekiah **heard** this, he tore his clothes and put
19: 4 [A] It may be that the LORD your God *will* **hear** all the words
19: 4 [A] rebuke him for the words the LORD your God *has* **heard**.
19: 6 [A] Do not be afraid of what *you have* **heard**—those words with
19: 7 [A] I am going to put such a spirit in him that when *he* **hears** a
19: 8 [A] When the field commander **heard** that the king of Assyria
19: 9 [A] Now Sennacherib **received a report** that Tirhakah,
19:11 [A] Surely you *have* **heard** what the kings of Assyria have done
19:16 [A] Give ear, O LORD, and **hear**; open your eyes, O LORD,
19:16 [A] **listen** *to* the words Sennacherib has sent to insult the living
19:20 [A] *I have* **heard** your prayer concerning Sennacherib king of
19:25 [A] " '*Have you* not **heard**? Long ago I ordained it. In days of
20: 5 [A] *I have* **heard** your prayer and seen your tears; I will heal
20:12 [A] and a gift, because *he had* **heard** *of* Hezekiah's illness.
20:13 [A] Hezekiah **received** the messengers and showed them all that
20:16 [A] Isaiah said to Hezekiah, "**Hear** the word of the LORD:
21: 9 [A] *the people did* not **listen**. Manasseh led them astray, so that
21:12 [A] Judah that the ears of everyone *who* **hears** *of* it will tingle.
22:11 [A] When the king **heard** the words of the Book of the Law, he
22:13 [A] because our fathers *have* not **obeyed** the words of this book;
22:18 [A] the God of Israel, says concerning the words *you* **heard**:
22:19 [A] you humbled yourself before the LORD when you **heard**
22:19 [A] in my presence, I *have* **heard** you, declares the LORD.
25:23 [A] their men **heard** that the king of Babylon had appointed
1Ch 10:11 [A] When all the inhabitants of Jabesh Gilead **heard** *of*
14: 8 [A] When the Philistines **heard** that David had been anointed
14: 8 [A] but David **heard** *about* it and went out to meet them.
14:15 [A] As soon as you **hear** the sound of marching in the tops of the
15:16 [G] as singers *to* **sing** [+928+4200+7754+8123] joyful **songs**,
15:19 [G] Asaph and Ethan were to **sound** the bronze cymbals;
15:28 [G] and of cymbals, and the **playing** of lyres and harps.
16: 5 [G] to play the lyres and harps, Asaph *was to* **sound** the cymbals,
16:42 [G] Jeduthun were responsible for *the* **sounding** *of* the trumpets
17:20 [A] is no God but you, as *we have* **heard** with our own ears.
18: 9 [A] When Tou king of Hamath **heard** that David had defeated
19: 8 [A] On **hearing** this, David sent Joab out with the entire army of
28: 2 [A] his feet and said: "**Listen** *to* me, my brothers and my people.
29:23 [A] of his father David. He prospered and all Israel **obeyed** him.
2Ch 5:13 [G] they raised their voices in praise to the LORD and **sang**:
6:19 [A] **Hear** the cry and the prayer that your servant is praying in
6:20 [A] *May* you **hear** the prayer your servant prays toward this
6:21 [A] **Hear** the supplications of your servant and of your people
6:21 [A] **Hear** from heaven, your dwelling place; and when you hear,
6:21 [A] your dwelling place; and when *you* **hear**, forgive.
6:23 [A] then **hear** from heaven and act. Judge between your servants,
6:25 [A] **hear** from heaven and forgive the sin of your people Israel
6:27 [A] then **hear** from heaven and forgive the sin of your servants,
6:30 [A] **hear** from heaven, your dwelling place. Forgive, and deal
6:33 [A] **hear** from heaven, your dwelling place, and do whatever the
6:35 [A] **hear** from heaven their prayer and their plea, and uphold
6:39 [A] your dwelling place, **hear** their prayer and their pleas,
7:12 [A] "*I have* **heard** your prayer and have chosen this place for
7:14 [A] *will* I **hear** from heaven and will forgive their sin and will
9: 1 [A] When the queen of Sheba **heard** *of* Solomon's fame, she
9: 5 [A] "The report *I* **heard** in my own country about your
9: 6 [A] was told me; you have far exceeded the report *I* **heard**.
9: 7 [A] who continually stand before you and **hear** your wisdom!
9:23 [A] with Solomon to **hear** the wisdom God had put in his heart.
10: 2 [A] When Jeroboam son of Nebat **heard** this (he was in Egypt,
10:15 [A] So the king *did* not **listen** to the people, for this turn of
10:16 [A] When all Israel saw that the king refused *to* **listen** to them,
11: 4 [A] for this is my doing.' " So *they* **obeyed** the words of the
13: 4 [A] of Ephraim, and said, "Jeroboam and all Israel, **listen** *to* me!
15: 2 [A] said to him, "**Listen** *to* me, Asa and all Judah and Benjamin.
15: 8 [A] When Asa **heard** these words and the prophecy of Azariah
16: 4 [A] Ben-Hadad **agreed** with King Asa and sent the commanders
16: 5 [A] When Baasha **heard** this, he stopped building Ramah
18:18 [A] Micaiah continued, "Therefore **hear** the word of the LORD:
18:27 [A] Then he added, "**Mark my words**, all you people!"
20: 9 [A] out to you in our distress, and *you will* **hear** us and save us.'
20:20 [A] and said, "**Listen** *to* me, Judah and people of Jerusalem!
20:29 [A] **heard** how the LORD had fought against the enemies of
23:12 [A] When Athaliah **heard** the noise of the people running
24:17 [A] and paid homage to the king, and he **listened** to them.
25:16 [A] you have done this and *have* not **listened** to my counsel."
25:20 [A] *would* not **listen**, for God so worked that he might hand them
28:11 [A] Now **listen** *to* me! Send back your fellow countrymen you
29: 5 [A] and said: "**Listen** *to* me, Levites! Consecrate yourselves now
30:20 [A] And the LORD **heard** Hezekiah and healed the people.
30:27 [A] God **heard** [+928+7754] them, for their prayer reached
33:13 [A] LORD was moved by his entreaty and **listened** *to* his plea;
34:19 [A] When the king **heard** the words of the Law, he tore his
34:26 [A] the God of Israel, says concerning the words *you* **heard**:
34:27 [A] you humbled yourself before God when you **heard** what he
34:27 [A] in my presence, I *have* **heard** you, declares the LORD.
35:22 [A] *He would* not **listen** to what Neco had said at God's
Ezr 3:13 [C] so much noise. And the sound **was heard** far away.
4: 1 [A] Benjamin **heard** that the exiles were building a temple for
9: 3 [A] When I **heard** this, I tore my tunic and cloak, pulled hair
Ne 1: 4 [A] When I **heard** these things, I sat down and wept. For some
1: 6 [A] your eyes open to **hear** the prayer your servant is praying
2:10 [A] and Tobiah the Ammonite official **heard** *about* this,
2:19 [A] the Ammonite official and Geshem the Arab **heard** *about* it,
4: 1 [3:33] [A] When Sanballat **heard** that we were rebuilding the
4: 4 [3:36] [A] **Hear** us, O our God, for we are despised. Turn their
4: 7 [4:1] [A] the men of Ashdod **heard** that the repairs to
4:15 [4:9] [A] When our enemies **heard** that we were aware of their
4:20 [4:14] [A] Wherever *you* **hear** the sound of the trumpet, join us
5: 6 [A] When *I* **heard** their outcry and these charges, I was very
6: 1 [C] When **word came** to Sanballat, Tobiah, Geshem the Arab
6: 6 [C] "*It* **is reported** among the nations—and Geshem says it is
6: 7 [C] Now this report *will* **get back to** the king; so come, let us
6:16 [A] When all our enemies **heard** *about* this, all the surrounding
8: 2 [A] up of men and women and all who were able to **understand**.
8: 9 [A] For all the people had been weeping as they **listened** *to* the
8:15 [G] that *they should* **proclaim** this word and spread it
9: 9 [A] our forefathers in Egypt; *you* **heard** their cry at the Red Sea.
9:16 [A] and stiff-necked, and *did* not **obey** your commands.
9:17 [A] They refused to **listen** and failed to remember the miracles
9:27 [A] From heaven you **heard** them, and in your great compassion
9:28 [A] when they cried out to you again, you **heard** from heaven,
9:29 [A] arrogant and **disobeyed** [+4200+4202] your commands.
9:29 [A] their backs on you, became stiff-necked and refused *to* **listen**.
12:42 [G] and Ezer. The choirs **sang** under the direction of Jezrahiah.
12:43 [C] *The* **sound** of rejoicing in Jerusalem *could* **be heard** far
13: 3 [A] When the people **heard** this law, they excluded from Israel
13:27 [A] *Must we* **hear** now that you too are doing all this terrible
Est 1:18 [A] Median women of the nobility who *have* **heard** *about* the
1:20 [C] when the king's edict **is proclaimed** throughout all his vast
2: 8 [C] When the king's order and edict *had* **been proclaimed**,
3: 4 [A] Day after day they spoke to him but *he* refused *to* **comply**.
Job 2:11 [A] **heard** *about* all the troubles that had come upon him,
3:18 [A] enjoy their ease; *they* no longer **hear** the slave driver's shout.

Job 4:16 [A] A form stood before my eyes, and *I* **heard** a hushed voice:
5:27 [A] and it is true. So **hear** it and apply it to yourself."
13: 1 [A] have seen all this, my ears *have* **heard** and understood it.
13: 6 [A] **Hear** now my argument; listen to the plea of my lips.
13:17 [A] **Listen** [+9048] **carefully** *to* my words; let your ears take in
13:17 [A] **Listen carefully to** [+9048] my words; let your ears take in
15: 8 [A] *Do you* **listen in** on God's council? Do you limit wisdom to
15:17 [A] "**Listen** to me and I will explain to you; let me tell you what
16: 2 [A] "*I have* **heard** many things like these; miserable comforters
20: 3 [A] *I* **hear** a rebuke that dishonors me, and my understanding
21: 2 [A] "**Listen** [+9048] **carefully** *to* my words; let this be the
21: 2 [A] "**Listen carefully to** [+9048] my words; let this be the
22:27 [A] You will pray to him, and *he will* **hear** you, and you will
26:14 [A] fringe of his works; how faint the whisper *we* **hear** of him!
27: 9 [A] *Does* God **listen** *to* his cry when distress comes upon him?
28:22 [A] Death say, 'Only a rumor of it *has* **reached** [+928] our ears.'
29:11 [A] Whoever **heard** me spoke well of me, and those who saw me
29:21 [A] "*Men* **listened** to me expectantly, waiting in silence for my
31:35 [A] ("Oh, that I had *someone to* **hear** me! I sign now my
32:10 [A] I say: **Listen** to me; I too will tell you what I know.
33: 1 [A] "But now, Job, **listen** *to* my words; pay attention to
33: 8 [A] "But you have said in my hearing—*I* **heard** the very words—
33:31 [A] "Pay attention, Job, and **listen** to me; be silent, and I will
33:33 [A] if not, then **listen** to me; be silent, and I will teach you
34: 2 [A] "**Hear** my words, you wise men; listen to me, you men of
34:10 [A] "So **listen** to me, you men of understanding. Far be it from
34:16 [A] "If you have understanding, **hear** this; listen to what I say.
34:28 [A] to come before him, so that *he* **heard** the cry of the needy.
34:34 [A] of understanding declare, wise men *who* **hear** me say to me,
35:13 [A] Indeed, God *does* not **listen** *to* their empty plea;
36:11 [A] If *they* **obey** and serve him, they will spend the rest of their
36:12 [A] if *they do* not **listen**, they will perish by the sword and die
37: 2 [A] **Listen**! Listen to the roar of his voice, to the rumbling that
37: 2 [A] **Listen** to the roar of his voice, to the rumbling that comes
37: 4 [C] When his voice **resounds**, he holds nothing back.
39: 7 [A] commotion in the town; *he does* not **hear** a driver's shout.
42: 4 [A] ⌞"You said,⌟ '**Listen** now, and I will speak; I will question
42: 5 [A] My ears *had* **heard** [+9051] *of* you but now my eyes have
Ps 4: 1 [4:2] [A] my distress; be merciful to me and **hear** my prayer.
4: 3 [4:4] [A] for himself; the LORD *will* **hear** when I call to him.
5: 3 [5:4] [A] In the morning, O LORD, *you* **hear** my voice;
6: 8 [6:9] [A] who do evil, for the LORD *has* **heard** my weeping.
6: 9 [6:10] [A] The LORD *has* **heard** my cry for mercy;
10:17 [A] *You* **hear**, O LORD, the desire of the afflicted;
17: 1 [A] **Hear**, O LORD, my righteous plea; listen to my cry.
17: 6 [A] for you will answer me; give ear to me and **hear** my prayer.
18: 6 [18:7] [A] From his temple *he* **heard** my voice; my cry came
18:44 [18:45] [C] As soon as they hear me, *they* **obey** me; foreigners
19: 3 [19:4] [C] no speech or language where their voice **is** not **heard**.
22:24 [22:25] [A] face from him but *has* **listened** to his cry for help.
26: 7 [G] **proclaiming** aloud your praise and telling of all your
27: 7 [A] **Hear** my voice when I call, O LORD; be merciful to me
28: 2 [A] **Hear** my cry for mercy as I call to you for help, as I lift up
28: 6 [A] Praise be to the LORD, for *he has* **heard** my cry for mercy.
30:10 [30:11] [A] **Hear**, O LORD, and be merciful to me;
31:13 [31:14] [A] For *I* **hear** the slander of many; there is terror on
31:22 [31:23] [A] Yet *you* **heard** my cry for mercy when I called to
34: 2 [34:3] [A] in the LORD; *let* the afflicted **hear** and rejoice.
34: 6 [34:7] [A] This poor man called, and the LORD **heard** him; he
34:11 [34:12] [A] Come, my children, **listen** to me; I will teach you
34:17 [34:18] [A] The righteous cry out, and the LORD **hears** them;
38:13 [38:14] [A] I am like a deaf man, *who* cannot **hear**, like a mute,
38:14 [38:15] [A] I have become like a man who *does* not **hear**,
39:12 [39:13] [A] "**Hear** my prayer, O LORD, listen to my cry for
40: 1 [40:2] [A] for the LORD; he turned to me and **heard** my cry.
44: 1 [44:2] [A] *We have* **heard** with our ears, O God; our fathers
45:10 [45:11] [A] **Listen**, O daughter, consider and give ear: Forget
48: 8 [48:9] [A] As *we have* **heard**, so have we seen in the city of the
49: 1 [49:2] [A] **Hear** this, all you peoples; listen, all who live in this
50: 7 [A] "**Hear**, O my people, and I will speak, O Israel, and I will
51: 8 [51:10] [G] **Let** me **hear** joy and gladness; let the bones you
54: 2 [54:4] [A] **Hear** my prayer, O God; listen to the words of my
55:17 [55:18] [A] noon I cry out in distress, and *he* **hears** my voice.
55:19 [55:20] [A] enthroned forever, *will* **hear** them and afflict them—
58: 5 [58:6] [A] that *will* not **heed** the tune of the charmer,
59: 7 [59:8] [A] from their lips, and they say, "Who *can* **hear** us?"
61: 1 [61:2] [A] **Hear** my cry, O God; listen to my prayer.
61: 5 [61:6] [A] For you *have* **heard** my vows, O God; you have
62:11 [62:12] [A] thing God has spoken, two things *have I* **heard**:
64: 1 [64:2] [A] **Hear** me, O God, as I voice my complaint;
65: 2 [65:3] [A] O you *who* **hear** prayer, to you all men will come.
66: 8 [G] our God, O peoples, **let** the sound of his praise **be heard**;
66:16 [A] Come and **listen**, all *you* who fear God; let me tell you what
66:18 [A] cherished sin in my heart, the Lord *would* not *have* **listened**;
66:19 [A] but God *has* surely **listened** and heard my voice in prayer.
69:33 [69:34] [A] The LORD **hears** the needy and does not despise
76: 8 [76:9] [G] From heaven *you* **pronounced** judgment,
78: 3 [A] what *we have* **heard** and known, what our fathers have told
78:21 [A] *When* the LORD **heard** them, he was very angry; his fire
78:59 [A] *When* God **heard** them, he was very angry; he rejected Israel
81: 5 [81:6] [A] where *we* **heard** a language we did not understand.
81: 8 [81:9] [A] "**Hear**, O my people, and I will warn you—if you
81: 8 [81:9] [A] warn you—if *you would but* **listen** to me, O Israel!
81:11 [81:12] [A] "But my people *would* not **listen** to me; Israel
81:13 [81:14] [A] "If my people *would but* **listen** to me, if Israel
84: 8 [84:9] [A] **Hear** my prayer, O LORD God Almighty; listen to
85: 8 [85:9] [A] *I will* **listen** *to* what God the LORD will say; he
92:11 [92:12] [A] my ears *have* **heard** the rout of my wicked foes.
94: 9 [A] *Does he* who implanted the ear not **hear**? Does he who
95: 7 [A] the flock under his care. Today, if *you* **hear** his voice,
97: 8 [A] Zion **hears** and rejoices and the villages of Judah are glad
102: 1 [102:2] [A] **Hear** my prayer, O LORD; let my cry for help
102:20 [102:21] [A] to **hear** the groans of the prisoners and release
103:20 [A] ones who do his bidding, *who* **obey** [+928+7754] his word.
106: 2 [G] the mighty acts of the LORD or fully **declare** his praise?
106:25 [A] in their tents and *did* not **obey** [+928+7754] the LORD.
106:44 [A] But he took note of their distress when he **heard** their cry;
115: 6 [A] they have ears, but cannot **hear**, noses, but they cannot smell;
116: 1 [A] I love the LORD, for *he* **heard** my voice; he heard my cry
119:149 [A] **Hear** my voice in accordance with your love; preserve my
130: 2 [A] O Lord, **hear** my voice. Let your ears be attentive to my cry
132: 6 [A] *We* **heard** it in Ephrathah, we came upon it in the fields of
138: 4 [A] O LORD, when *they* **hear** the words of your mouth.
141: 6 [A] and the wicked *will* **learn** that my words were well spoken.
143: 1 [A] O LORD, **hear** my prayer, listen to my cry for mercy;
143: 8 [G] *Let* the morning **bring** me **word** *of* your unfailing love, for I
145:19 [A] of those who fear him; *he* **hears** their cry and saves them.
Pr 1: 5 [A] *let* the wise **listen** and add to their learning, and let the
1: 8 [A] **Listen**, my son, *to* your father's instruction and do not
1:33 [A] but *whoever* **listens** to me will live in safety and be at ease,
4: 1 [A] **Listen**, my sons, *to* a father's instruction; pay attention
4:10 [A] **Listen**, my son, accept what I say, and the years of your life
5: 7 [A] Now then, my sons, **listen** to me; do not turn aside from what
5:13 [A] *I would* not **obey** [+928+7754] my teachers or listen to my
7:24 [A] Now then, my sons, **listen** to me; pay attention to what I say.
8: 6 [A] **Listen**, for I have worthy things to say; I open my lips to
8:32 [A] "Now then, my sons, **listen** to me; blessed are those who
8:33 [A] **Listen** *to* my instruction and be wise; do not ignore it.
8:34 [A] Blessed is the man *who* **listens** to me, watching daily at my
12:15 [A] of a fool seems right to him, but a wise man **listens** to advice.
13: 1 [A] father's instruction, but a mocker *does* not **listen** *to* rebuke.
13: 8 [A] riches may ransom his life, but a poor man **hears** no threat.
15:29 [A] far from the wicked but *he* **hears** the prayer of the righteous.
15:31 [A] *He who* **listens** [+265] *to* a life-giving rebuke will be at
15:32 [A] but *whoever* **heeds** correction gains understanding.
18:13 [A] He who answers before **listening**—that is his folly and his
19:20 [A] **Listen** *to* advice and accept instruction, and in the end you
19:27 [A] Stop **listening** *to* instruction, my son, and you will stray from
20:12 [A] Ears *that* **hear** and eyes that see—the LORD has made
21:28 [A] and whoever **listens** to him will be destroyed forever.
22:17 [A] Pay attention and **listen** *to* the sayings of the wise; apply
23:19 [A] **Listen**, my son, and be wise, and keep your heart on the right
23:22 [A] **Listen** to your father, who gave you life, and do not despise
25:10 [A] or *he who* **hears** it may shame you and you will never lose
25:12 [A] of fine gold is a wise man's rebuke to a **listening** ear.
28: 9 [A] If anyone turns a **deaf** [+4946] ear *to* the law, even his
29:24 [A] *he is* **put under oath** [+460] and dare not testify.
Ecc 1: 8 [A] never has enough of seeing, nor the ear its fill of **hearing**.
5: 1 [4:17] [A] Go near to **listen** rather than to offer the sacrifice of
7: 5 [A] It is better to **heed** a wise man's rebuke than to listen to the
7: 5 [A] It is better to heed a wise man's rebuke than *to* **listen** *to* the
7:21 [A] people say, or *you may* **hear** your servant cursing you—
9:16 [C] wisdom is despised, and his words **are** no longer **heeded**.
9:17 [C] The quiet words of the wise *are* more *to* **be heeded** than the
12:13 [C] Now all *has* **been heard**; here is the conclusion of the matter:
SS 2:12 [C] singing has come, the cooing of doves **is heard** in our land.
2:14 [G] show me your face, **let** me **hear** your voice;
8:13 [G] gardens with friends in attendance, **let** me **hear** your voice!
Isa 1: 2 [A] **Hear**, O heavens! Listen, O earth! For the LORD has
1:10 [A] **Hear** the word of the LORD, you rulers of Sodom; listen to
1:15 [A] from you; even if you offer many prayers, I *will* not **listen**.
1:19 [A] If you are willing and **obedient**, you will eat the best from
6: 8 [A] *I* **heard** the voice of the Lord saying, "Whom shall I send?
6: 9 [A] " '*Be* **ever hearing** [+9048], but never understanding; be
6: 9 [A] " '*Be* **ever hearing** [+9048], but never understanding; be
6:10 [A] **hear** with their ears, understand with their hearts, and turn
7:13 [A] Isaiah said, "**Hear** now, you house of David! Is it not enough
15: 4 [C] Elealeh cry out, their voices **are heard** all the way to Jahaz.

Isa 16: 6 [A] *We have* **heard** *of* Moab's pride—her overweening pride
18: 3 [A] you will see it, and when a trumpet sounds, *you will* **hear** it.
21: 3 [A] I am staggered by *what* I **hear**, I am bewildered by what I
21: 10 [A] I tell you what *I have* **heard** from the LORD Almighty,
24: 16 [A] From the ends of the earth *we* **hear** singing: "Glory to the
28: 12 [A] and, "This is the place of repose"—but they would not **listen**.
28: 14 [A] Therefore **hear** the word of the LORD, *you* scoffers who
28: 22 [A] *has* **told** [+907+4946] *me of* the destruction decreed against
28: 23 [A] Listen and **hear** my voice; pay attention and hear what I say.
28: 23 [A] Listen and hear my voice; pay attention and **hear** what I say.
29: 18 [A] In that day the deaf *will* **hear** the words of the scroll, and out
30: 9 [A] children unwilling *to* **listen** *to* the LORD's instruction.
30: 19 [A] you cry for help! As soon as he **hears**, he will answer you.
30: 21 [A] or to the left, your ears *will* **hear** a voice behind you, saying,
30: 30 [G] The LORD *will* **cause** men **to hear** his majestic voice
32: 3 [A] longer be closed, and the ears of *those who* **hear** will listen.
32: 9 [A] and **listen** [+7754] *to* me; *you* daughters who feel secure,
33: 13 [A] You who are far away, **hear** what I have done; you who are
33: 15 [A] who stops his ears against **plots** *of* murder and shuts his eyes
33: 19 [A] those people of an **obscure** [+4946+6680] speech, with their
34: 1 [A] Come near, you nations, and **listen**; pay attention,
34: 1 [A] *Let* the earth **hear**, and all that is in it, the world, and all that
36: 11 [A] speak to your servants in Aramaic, since we **understand** it.
36: 13 [A] "**Hear** the words of the great king, the king of Assyria!
36: 16 [A] "*Do* not **listen** to Hezekiah. This is what the king of Assyria
37: 1 [A] When King Hezekiah **heard** this, he tore his clothes and put
37: 4 [A] It may be that the LORD your God *will* **hear** the words of
37: 4 [A] rebuke him for the words the LORD your God *has* **heard**.
37: 6 [A] Do not be afraid of what *you have* **heard**—those words with
37: 7 [A] to put a spirit in him so that *when he* **hears** a certain report,
37: 8 [A] When the field commander **heard** that the king of Assyria
37: 9 [A] Now Sennacherib **received a report** that Tirhakah,
37: 9 [A] When *he* **heard** it, he sent messengers to Hezekiah with this
37: 11 [A] Surely you *have* **heard** what the kings of Assyria have done
37: 17 [A] Give ear, O LORD, and **hear**; open your eyes, O LORD,
37: 17 [A] **listen** *to* all the words Sennacherib has sent to insult the
37: 26 [A] "*Have you* not **heard**? Long ago I ordained it. In days of old
38: 5 [A] *I have* **heard** your prayer and seen your tears; I will add
39: 1 [A] and a gift, because *he had* **heard** *of* his illness and recovery.
39: 5 [A] said to Hezekiah, "**Hear** the word of the LORD Almighty:
40: 21 [A] Do you not know? *Have you* not **heard**? Has it not been told
40: 28 [A] Do you not know? *Have you* not **heard**? The LORD is the
41: 22 [G] their final outcome. Or **declare** *to* us the things to come,
41: 26 [G] No one told of this, no *one* **foretold** it, no one heard any
41: 26 [A] of this, no one foretold it, no *one* **heard** any words from you.
42: 2 [G] He will not shout or **cry out**, or raise his voice in the streets.
42: 9 [G] before they spring into being *I* **announce** them *to* you."
42: 18 [A] "**Hear**, *you* deaf; look, you blind, and see!
42: 20 [A] paid no attention; your ears are open, but *you* **hear** nothing."
42: 23 [A] or **pay close attention** [+2256+7992] in time to come?
42: 24 [A] they would not follow his ways; *they did* not **obey** his law.
43: 9 [G] them foretold this and **proclaimed** *to* us the former things?
43: 9 [A] they were right, so that *others may* **hear** and say, "It is true."
43: 12 [G] I have revealed and saved and **proclaimed**—I, and not some
44: 1 [A] "But now **listen**, O Jacob, my servant, Israel, whom I have
44: 8 [G] be afraid. *Did I* not **proclaim** this and foretell it long ago?
45: 21 [G] Who **foretold** this long ago, who declared it from the distant
46: 3 [A] "**Listen** to me, O house of Jacob, all you who remain of the
46: 12 [A] **Listen** to me, *you* stubborn-hearted, you who are far from
47: 8 [A] "Now then, **listen**, *you* wanton creature, lounging in your
48: 1 [A] "**Listen** *to* this, O house of Jacob, you who are called by the
48: 3 [G] my mouth announced them and *I* **made** them **known**;
48: 5 [G] before they happened *I* **announced** them *to* you so that you
48: 6 [A] *You have* **heard** these things; look at them all. Will you not
48: 6 [G] "From now on *I will* **tell** you *of* new things, *of* hidden things
48: 7 [A] and not long ago; *you have* not **heard** *of* them before today.
48: 8 [A] *You have* neither **heard** nor understood; from of old your
48: 12 [A] "**Listen** to me, O Jacob, Israel, whom I have called: I am he;
48: 14 [A] "Come together, all of you, and **listen**: Which of ⌞the idols⌟
48: 16 [A] "Come near me and **listen** *to* this: "From the first
48: 20 [G] Announce this with shouts of joy and **proclaim** it.
49: 1 [A] **Listen** to me, *you* islands; hear this, you distant nations:
50: 4 [A] by morning, wakens my ear to **listen** like one being taught.
50: 10 [A] you fears the LORD and **obeys** the word of his servant?
51: 1 [A] "**Listen** to me, you who pursue righteousness and who seek
51: 7 [A] "**Hear** me, you who know what is right, you people who
51: 21 [A] Therefore **hear** this, *you* afflicted one, made drunk, but not
52: 7 [G] *who* **proclaim** peace, who bring good tidings, who proclaim
52: 7 [G] *who* **proclaim** salvation, who say to Zion, "Your God
52: 15 [A] they will see, and what *they have* not **heard**, they will
55: 2 [A] **Listen**, listen to me, and eat what is good, and your soul will
55: 2 [A] Listen, **listen** to me, and eat what is good, and your soul will
55: 3 [A] Give ear and come to me; **hear** me, that your soul may live.
58: 4 [G] as you do today and **expect** your voice **to be heard** on high.
59: 1 [A] LORD is not too short to save, nor his ear too dull *to* **hear**.
59: 2 [A] sins have hidden his face from you, so that *he will* not **hear**.
60: 18 [C] No longer *will* violence **be heard** in your land, nor ruin
62: 11 [G] The LORD *has* **made proclamation** to the ends of the
64: 4 [64:3] [A] Since ancient times no *one has* **heard**, no ear has
65: 12 [A] but you did not answer, I spoke but *you did* not **listen**.
65: 19 [C] sound of weeping and of crying *will* **be heard** in it no more.
65: 24 [A] call I will answer; while they are still speaking I *will* **hear**.
66: 4 [A] I called, no one answered, when I spoke, no *one* **listened**.
66: 5 [A] **Hear** the word of the LORD, you who tremble at his word:
66: 8 [A] Who *has ever* **heard** *of* such a thing? Who has ever seen
66: 19 [A] and to the distant islands that *have* not **heard** *of* my fame
Jer 2: 4 [A] **Hear** the word of the LORD, O house of Jacob, all you
3: 13 [A] *have* not **obeyed** [+928+7754] me,' " declares the LORD.
3: 21 [C] A cry **is heard** on the barren heights, the weeping
3: 25 [A] day *we have* not **obeyed** [+928+7754] the LORD our God."
4: 5 [G] "Announce in Judah and **proclaim** in Jerusalem and say:
4: 15 [G] from Dan, **proclaiming** disaster from the hills of Ephraim.
4: 16 [G] "Tell this to the nations, **proclaim** it to Jerusalem:
4: 19 [A] For I *have* **heard** the sound of the trumpet; I have heard the
4: 21 [A] I see the battle standard and **hear** the sound of the trumpet?
4: 31 [A] *I* **hear** a cry as of a woman in labor, a groan as of one
5: 15 [A] you do not know, whose speech *you do* not **understand**.
5: 20 [G] this to the house of Jacob and **proclaim** it in Judah:
5: 21 [A] **Hear** this, *you* foolish and senseless people, who have eyes
5: 21 [A] have eyes but do not see, who have ears but *do* not **hear**:
6: 7 [C] Violence and destruction **resound** in her; her sickness
6: 10 [A] whom can I speak and give warning? *Who will* **listen** *to* me?
6: 18 [A] Therefore **hear**, O nations; observe, O witnesses, what will
6: 19 [A] **Hear**, O earth: I am bringing disaster on this people, the fruit
6: 24 [A] *We have* **heard** reports about them, and our hands hang
7: 2 [A] " '**Hear** the word of the LORD, all you people of Judah who
7: 13 [A] I spoke to you again and again, but *you did* not **listen**;
7: 16 [A] for them; do not plead with me, for I *will* not **listen** *to* you.
7: 23 [A] **Obey** [+928+7754] me, and I will be your God and you will
7: 24 [A] *they did* not **listen** or pay attention; instead, they followed
7: 26 [A] *they did* not **listen** to me or pay attention. They were
7: 27 [A] "When you tell them all this, *they will* not **listen** to you;
7: 28 [A] 'This is the nation that *has* not **obeyed** [+928+7754] the
8: 6 [A] *I have* **listened** attentively, but they do not say what is right.
8: 16 [C] The snorting of the enemy's horses **is heard** from Dan; at the
9: 10 [9:9] [A] and untraveled, and the lowing of cattle *is* not **heard**.
9: 13 [9:12] [A] *they have* not **obeyed** [+928+7754] me or followed
9: 19 [9:18] [C] The sound of wailing **is heard** from Zion:
9: 20 [9:19] [A] Now, O women, **hear** the word of the LORD; open
10: 1 [A] **Hear** what the LORD says to you, O house of Israel.
11: 2 [A] "**Listen** *to* the terms of this covenant and tell them to the
11: 3 [A] 'Cursed is the man who *does* not **obey** the terms of this
11: 4 [A] '**Obey** [+928+7754] me and do everything I command you,
11: 6 [A] '**Listen** *to* the terms of this covenant and follow them.
11: 7 [A] them again and again, saying, "**Obey** [+928+7754] me."
11: 8 [A] *they did* not **listen** or pay attention; instead, they followed
11: 10 [A] sins of their forefathers, who refused to **listen** *to* my words.
11: 11 [A] Although they cry out to me, *I will* not **listen** to them.
11: 14 [A] because I *will* not **listen** when they call to me in the time of
12: 17 [A] But if any nation *does* not **listen**, I will completely uproot
13: 10 [A] These wicked people, who refuse to **listen** *to* my words,
13: 11 [A] and praise and honor. But *they have* not **listened**.'
13: 15 [A] **Hear** and pay attention, do not be arrogant, for the LORD
13: 17 [A] if *you do* not **listen**, I will weep in secret because of your
14: 12 [A] Although they fast, I *will* not **listen** to their cry; though they
16: 12 [A] the stubbornness of his evil heart instead of **obeying** me.
17: 20 [A] Say to them, '**Hear** the word of the LORD, O kings of
17: 23 [A] Yet *they did* not **listen** or pay attention; they were
17: 23 [A] they were stiff-necked and *would* not **listen** or respond to
17: 24 [A] if *you are* **careful to obey** [+448+9048] me,
17: 24 [A] if *you are* **careful to obey** [+448+9048] me,
17: 27 [A] if *you do* not **obey** me to keep the Sabbath day holy by not
18: 2 [G] to the potter's house, and there *I will* **give** you my message."
18: 10 [A] it does evil in my sight and *does* not **obey** [+928+7754] me,
18: 13 [A] among the nations: Who *has ever* **heard** anything like this?
18: 19 [A] Listen to me, O LORD; **hear** what my accusers are saying!
18: 22 [C] *Let* a cry **be heard** from their houses when you suddenly
19: 3 [A] say, '**Hear** the word of the LORD, O kings of Judah
19: 3 [A] that will make the ears of everyone *who* **hears** *of* it tingle.
19: 15 [A] they were stiff-necked and *would* not **listen** *to* my words.' "
20: 1 [A] of the LORD, **heard** Jeremiah prophesying these things,
20: 10 [A] *I* **hear** many whispering, "Terror on every side! Report him!
20: 16 [A] *May he* **hear** wailing in the morning, a battle cry at noon.
21: 11 [A] to the royal house of Judah, '**Hear** the word of the LORD;
22: 2 [A] '**Hear** the word of the LORD, O king of Judah, you who sit
22: 5 [A] if *you do* not **obey** these commands, declares the LORD,
22: 21 [A] you when you felt secure, but you said, '*I will* not **listen**!'
22: 21 [A] from your youth; *you have* not **obeyed** [+928+7754] me.

[F] Hitpael (hitpoel, hitpoal, hitpolel, hitpolal, hitpalel, hitpalal, hitpalpel, hitpalpal, hotpael, hotpaal) [G] Hiphil (hiphtil) [H] Hophal [I] Hishtaphel

Jer 22:29 [A] O land, land, land, **hear** the word of the LORD!
23:16 [A] "*Do* not **listen** to what the prophets are prophesying to you;
23:18 [A] in the council of the LORD to see or *to* **hear** his word?
23:18 [A] or to hear his word? Who has listened and **heard** his word?
23:22 [G] *they would have* **proclaimed** my words *to* my people
23:25 [A] "*I have* **heard** what the prophets say who prophesy lies in
25: 3 [A] spoken to you again and again, but *you have* not **listened**.
25: 4 [A] and again, *you have* not **listened** or paid any attention.
25: 4 [A] not listened or **paid any attention** [+265+906+4200+5742].
25: 7 [A] "But *you did* not **listen** to me," declares the LORD, "and
25: 8 [A] says this: "Because *you have* not **listened** *to* my words,
26: 3 [A] Perhaps *they will* **listen** and each will turn from his evil way.
26: 4 [A] If *you do* not **listen** to me and follow my law, which I have
26: 5 [A] if you *do* not **listen** to the words of my servants the prophets,
26: 5 [A] sent to you again and again (though *you have* not **listened**),
26: 7 [A] all the people **heard** Jeremiah speak these words in the house
26:10 [A] When the officials of Judah **heard** *about* these things, they
26:11 [A] against this city. *You have* **heard** it with your own ears!"
26:12 [A] this house and this city all the things *you have* **heard**.
26:13 [A] your actions and **obey** [+928+7754] the LORD your God.
26:21 [A] and all his officers and officials **heard** his words,
26:21 [A] him to death. But Uriah **heard** of it and fled in fear to Egypt.
27: 9 [A] So *do* not **listen** to your prophets, your diviners, your
27:14 [A] *Do* not **listen** to the words of the prophets who say to you,
27:16 [A] *Do* not **listen** to the prophets who say, 'Very soon now the
27:17 [A] *Do* not **listen** to them. Serve the king of Babylon, and you
28: 7 [A] **listen** *to* what I have to say in your hearing and in the hearing
28:15 [A] Jeremiah said to Hananiah the prophet, "**Listen**, Hananiah!
29: 8 [A] *Do* not **listen** to the dreams you encourage them to have.
29:12 [A] upon me and come and pray to me, and *I will* **listen** to you.
29:19 [A] For *they have* not **listened** to my words,"
29:19 [A] *you* exiles *have* not **listened** either," declares the LORD.
29:20 [A] Therefore, **hear** the word of the LORD, all you exiles
30: 5 [A] LORD says: " 'Cries of fear *are* **heard**—terror, not peace.
31: 7 [G] **Make** your praises **heard**, and say, 'O LORD, save your
31:10 [A] "**Hear** the word of the LORD, O nations; proclaim it in
31:15 [C] "A voice **is heard** in Ramah, mourning and great weeping,
31:18 [A] "*I have* **surely heard** [+9048] Ephraim's moaning: 'You
31:18 [A] "*I have* **surely heard** [+9048] Ephraim's moaning: 'You
32:23 [A] but *they did* not **obey** [+928+7754] you or follow your law;
32:33 [A] and again, they *would* not **listen** or respond to discipline.
33: 9 [A] honor before all nations on earth that **hear** *of* all the good
33:10 [C] by neither men nor animals, *there will* **be heard** once more
34: 4 [A] " 'Yet **hear** the promise of the LORD, O Zedekiah king of
34:10 [A] people who entered into this covenant **agreed** that they
34:10 [A] hold them in bondage. *They* **agreed**, and set them free.
34:14 [A] however, *did* not **listen** to me or pay attention to me.
34:17 [A] You *have* not **obeyed** me; you have not proclaimed freedom
35: 8 [A] *We have* **obeyed** [+928+4200+7754] everything our forefather
35:10 [A] and *have* **fully obeyed** [+2256+3869+6913] everything our
35:13 [A] 'Will you not learn a lesson and **obey** my words?'
35:14 [A] drink wine, because *they* **obey** their forefather's command.
35:14 [A] spoken to you again and again, yet *you have* not **obeyed** me.
35:15 [A] But you have not paid attention or **listened** to me.
35:16 [A] forefather gave them, but these people *have* not **obeyed** me.'
35:17 [A] I spoke to them, but *they did* not **listen**; I called to them,
35:18 [A] '*You have* **obeyed** the command of your forefather Jonadab
36: 3 [A] Perhaps *when* the people of Judah **hear** *about* every disaster
36:11 [A] **heard** all the words of the LORD from the scroll,
36:13 [A] After Micaiah told them everything *he had* **heard** Baruch
36:16 [A] When they **heard** all these words, they looked at each other
36:24 [A] all his attendants who **heard** all these words showed no fear,
36:25 [A] the king not to burn the scroll, *he would* not **listen** to them.
36:31 [A] pronounced against them, because *they have* not **listened**.' "
37: 2 [A] **paid** *any* **attention** to the words the LORD had spoken
37: 5 [A] *when* the Babylonians who were besieging Jerusalem **heard**
37:14 [A] Irijah *would* not **listen** to him; instead, he arrested Jeremiah
37:20 [A] now, my lord the king, please **listen**. Let me bring my
38: 1 [A] Pashhur son of Malkijah **heard** what Jeremiah was telling all
38: 7 [A] **heard** that they had put Jeremiah into the cistern.
38:15 [A] Even if I did give you counsel, *you would* not **listen** to me."
38:20 [A] "**Obey** [+928+7754] the LORD by doing what I tell you.
38:25 [A] If the officials **hear** that I talked with you, and they come to
38:27 [C] to him, for no *one had* **heard** his conversation with the king.
40: 3 [A] against the LORD and *did* not **obey** [+928+7754] him.
40: 7 [A] their men who were still in the open country **heard** that the
40:11 [A] all the other countries **heard** that the king of Babylon had left
41:11 [A] all the army officers who were with him **heard** *about* all the
42: 4 [A] "*I have* **heard** you," replied Jeremiah the prophet. "I will
42: 6 [A] *we will* **obey** [+928+7754] the LORD our God,
42: 6 [A] for *we will* **obey** [+928+7754] the LORD our God."
42:13 [A] and so **disobey** [+928+1194+7754] the LORD your God,
42:14 [A] will not see war or **hear** the trumpet or be hungry for bread,'
42:15 [A] **hear** the word of the LORD, O remnant of Judah. This is
42:21 [A] *you still have* not **obeyed** [+928+7754] the LORD your
43: 4 [A] all the people **disobeyed** [+928+4202] the LORD's
43: 7 [A] So they entered Egypt *in* **disobedience** [+928+4202+7754] *to*
44: 5 [A] *they did* not **listen** or pay attention; they did not turn from
44:16 [A] "We *will* not **listen** to the message you have spoken to us in
44:23 [A] and *have* not **obeyed** [+928+7754] him or followed his law
44:24 [A] "**Hear** the word of the LORD, all *you people* of Judah in
44:26 [A] But **hear** the word of the LORD, all Jews living in Egypt:
46:12 [A] The nations *will* **hear** *of* your shame; your cries will fill the
46:14 [G] "Announce this in Egypt, and **proclaim** it in Migdol;
46:14 [G] it in Migdol; **proclaim** it also in Memphis and Tahpanhes:
48: 4 [G] Moab will be broken; her little ones *will* **cry out** [+2411].
48: 5 [A] to Horonaim anguished cries over the destruction *are* **heard**.
48:29 [A] "*We have* **heard** *of* Moab's pride—her overweening pride
49: 2 [G] "when *I will* **sound** the battle cry against Rabbah of the
49:14 [A] *I have* **heard** a message from the LORD: An envoy was
49:20 [A] Therefore, **hear** what the LORD has planned against Edom,
49:21 [C] the earth will tremble; their cry *will* **resound** to the Red Sea.
49:23 [A] and Arpad are dismayed, for *they have* **heard** bad news.
50: 2 [G] "Announce and **proclaim** among the nations, lift up a banner
50: 2 [G] proclaim among the nations, lift up a banner and **proclaim** it;
50:29 [G] "**Summon** archers against Babylon, all those who draw the
50:43 [A] The king of Babylon *has* **heard** reports about them, and his
50:45 [A] **hear** what the LORD has planned against Babylon,
50:46 [C] earth will tremble; its cry *will* **resound** among the nations.
51:27 [G] for battle against her; **summon** against her these kingdoms:
51:46 [C] lose heart or be afraid when rumors **are heard** in the land;
51:51 [A] for *we have* **been**[s] insulted and shame covers our faces,
La 1:18 [A] **Listen**, all you peoples; look upon my suffering. My young
1:21 [A] "*People have* **heard** my groaning, but there is no one to
1:21 [A] All my enemies *have* **heard** *of* my distress; they rejoice at
3:56 [A] *You* **heard** my plea: "Do not close your ears to my cry for
3:61 [A] O LORD, *you have* **heard** their insults, all their plots
Eze 1:24 [A] When the creatures moved, *I* **heard** the sound of their wings,
1:28 [A] I fell facedown, and *I* **heard** the voice of one speaking.
2: 2 [A] and raised me to my feet, and *I* **heard** him speaking to me.
2: 5 [A] whether they **listen** or fail to listen—for they are a rebellious
2: 7 [A] whether *they* **listen** or fail to listen, for they are rebellious.
2: 8 [A] you, son of man, **listen** *to* what I say to you. Do not rebel like
3: 6 [A] and difficult language, whose words *you* cannot **understand**.
3: 6 [A] if I had sent you to them, they *would have* **listened** to you.
3: 7 [A] the house of Israel is not willing to **listen** to you because they
3: 7 [A] to listen to you because they are not willing to **listen** to me,
3:10 [A] "Son of man, **listen** [+265+928] **carefully** and take to heart
3:11 [A] LORD says,' whether *they* **listen** or fail to listen."
3:12 [A] lifted me up, and *I* **heard** behind me a loud rumbling sound—
3:17 [A] so **hear** the word I speak and give them warning from me.
3:27 [A] Whoever *will* **listen** let him listen, and whoever will refuse
3:27 [A] Whoever will listen *let him* **listen**, and whoever will refuse
6: 3 [A] mountains of Israel, **hear** the word of the Sovereign LORD.
8:18 [A] Although they shout in my ears, *I will* not **listen** *to* them."
10: 5 [C] The sound of the wings of the cherubim *could* **be heard** as
12: 2 [A] eyes to see but do not see and ears to **hear** but do not hear,
12: 2 [A] eyes to see but do not see and ears to hear but *do* not **hear**,
13: 2 [A] out of their own imagination: '**Hear** the word of the LORD!
13:19 [A] By lying to my people, *who* **listen** *to* lies, you have killed
16:35 [A] " 'Therefore, you prostitute, **hear** the word of the LORD!
18:25 [A] Lord is not just.' **Hear**, O house of Israel: Is my way unjust?
19: 4 [A] The nations **heard** about him, and he was trapped in their pit.
19: 9 [C] so his roar **was heard** no longer on the mountains of Israel.
20: 8 [A] " 'But they rebelled against me and would not **listen** to me;
20:39 [A] afterward you *will* surely **listen** to me and no longer profane
20:47 [21:3] [A] to the southern forest: '**Hear** the word of the LORD.
25: 3 [A] Say to them, '**Hear** the word of the Sovereign LORD.
26:13 [C] and the music of your harps *will* **be heard** no more.
27:30 [G] *They will* **raise** their voice and cry bitterly over you; they
33: 4 [A] if *anyone* **hears** [+906+7754+9048] the trumpet but does not
33: 4 [A] if *anyone* **hears** [+906+7754+9048] the trumpet but does not
33: 5 [A] Since *he* **heard** the sound of the trumpet but did not take
33: 7 [A] so **hear** the word I speak and give them warning from me.
33:30 [A] and **hear** the message that has come from the LORD.'
33:31 [A] as they usually do, and sit before you *to* **listen** *to* your words,
33:32 [A] for *they* **hear** your words but do not put them into practice.
34: 7 [A] " 'Therefore, you shepherds, **hear** the word of the LORD:
34: 9 [A] therefore, O shepherds, **hear** the word of the LORD:
35:12 [A] you will know that I the LORD *have* **heard** all the
35:13 [A] and spoke against me without restraint, and I **heard** it.
36: 1 [A] 'O mountains of Israel, **hear** the word of the LORD.
36: 4 [A] mountains of Israel, **hear** the word of the Sovereign LORD:
36:15 [G] No longer *will I* **make** you **hear** the taunts of the nations,
37: 4 [A] and say to them, 'Dry bones, **hear** the word of the LORD!
40: 4 [A] look with your eyes and **hear** with your ears and pay
43: 6 [A] *I* **heard** someone speaking to me from inside the temple.
44: 5 [A] **listen** [+265+928] **closely** and give attention to everything I

Da 1:14 [A] So *he* **agreed** to this and tested them for ten days.
8:13 [A] *I* **heard** a holy one speaking, and another holy one said to
8:16 [A] And *I* **heard** a man's voice from the Ulai calling, "Gabriel,
9:6 [A] *We have* not **listened** to your servants the prophets,
9:10 [A] *we have* not **obeyed** [+928+7754] the LORD our God
9:11 [A] and turned away, refusing *to* **obey** [+928+7754] you.
9:14 [A] he does; yet *we have* not **obeyed** [+928+7754] him.
9:17 [A] our God, **hear** the prayers and petitions of your servant.
9:18 [A] Give ear, O God, and **hear**; open your eyes and see the
9:19 [A] O Lord, **listen**! O Lord, forgive! O Lord, hear and act! For
10:9 [A] *I* **heard** him speaking, and as I listened to him, I fell into a
10:9 [A] as I **listened** *to* him, I fell into a deep sleep, my face to the
10:12 [C] your words **were heard**, and I have come in response to
12:7 [A] *I* **heard** him swear by him who lives forever, saying, "It will
12:8 [A] I **heard**, but I did not understand. So I asked, "My lord,
Hos 4:1 [A] **Hear** the word of the LORD, you Israelites,
5:1 [A] "**Hear** this, *you* priests! Pay attention, you Israelites! Listen,
9:17 [A] My God will reject them because *they have* not **obeyed** him;
Joel 1:2 [A] **Hear** this, you elders; listen, all who live in the land. Has
Am 3:1 [A] **Hear** this word the LORD has spoken against you,
3:9 [G] **Proclaim** to the fortresses of Ashdod and to the fortresses of
3:13 [A] "**Hear** this and testify against the house of Jacob,"
4:1 [A] **Hear** this word, you cows of Bashan on Mount Samaria,
4:5 [G] **boast** *about* them, you Israelites, for this is what you love to
5:1 [A] **Hear** this word, O house of Israel, this lament I take up
5:23 [A] of your songs! *I will* not **listen** *to* the music of your harps.
7:16 [A] Now then, **hear** the word of the LORD. You say, " 'Do not
8:4 [A] **Hear** this, you who trample the needy and do away with the
8:11 [A] for water, but a famine of **hearing** the words of the LORD.
Ob 1:1 [A] about Edom—*We have* **heard** a message from the LORD:
Jnh 2:2 [2:3] [A] the grave I called for help, and *you* **listened to** my cry.
Mic 1:2 [A] **Hear**, O peoples, all of you, listen, O earth and all who are in
3:1 [A] I said, "**Listen**, you leaders of Jacob, you rulers of the house
3:9 [A] **Hear** this, you leaders of the house of Jacob, you rulers of
5:15 [5:14] [A] wrath upon the nations that *have* not **obeyed** me."
6:1 [A] **Listen** *to* what the LORD says: "Stand up, plead your case
6:1 [A] before the mountains; *let* the hills **hear** what you have to say.
6:2 [A] **Hear**, O mountains, the LORD's accusation; listen,
6:9 [A] is wisdom—"**Heed** the rod and the One who appointed it.
7:7 [A] I wait for God my Savior; my God *will* **hear** me.
Na 1:15 [2:1] [G] of one who brings good news, *who* **proclaims** peace!
2:13 [2:14] [C] voices of your messengers *will* no longer **be heard**."
3:19 [A] Everyone *who* **hears** the news about you claps his hands at
Hab 1:2 [A] O LORD, must I call for help, but *you do* not **listen**?
3:2 [A] LORD, *I have* **heard** *of* your fame; I stand in awe of your
3:16 [A] *I* **heard** and my heart pounded, my lips quivered at the
Zep 2:8 [A] "*I have* **heard** the insults of Moab and the taunts of the
3:2 [A] *She* **obeys** [+928+7754] no one, she accepts no correction.
Hag 1:12 [A] the whole remnant of the people **obeyed** the voice of the
Zec 1:4 [A] *they would* not **listen** or pay attention to me,
3:8 [A] " '**Listen**, O high priest Joshua and your associates seated
6:15 [A] *you* **diligently obey** [+928+7754+9048] the LORD your God."
6:15 [A] *you* **diligently obey** [+928+7754+9048] the LORD your God."
7:11 [A] turned their backs and **stopped up** [+3877+4946] their ears.
7:12 [A] *would* not **listen** *to* the law or *to* the words that the LORD
7:13 [A] " 'When I called, *they did* not **listen**; so when they called,
7:13 [A] so when they called, *I would* not **listen**,' says the LORD
8:9 [A] "*You* who now **hear** these words spoken by the prophets
8:23 [A] go with you, because *we have* **heard** that God is with you.' "
Mal 2:2 [A] If *you do* not **listen**, and if you do not set your heart to honor
3:16 [A] talked with each other, and the LORD listened and **heard**.

9049 [1]שֶׁמַע ***šema'***[1], n.[m.]. [1] [→ 9050; cf. 9048]

clash [1]

Ps 150:5 praise him with the **clash** *of* cymbals, praise him with resounding

9050 [2]שֶׁמַע ***šema'***[2], n.pr.m. [5] [√ 9049]

Shema [5]

1Ch 2:43 The sons of Hebron: Korah, Tappuah, Rekem and **Shema**.
2:44 **Shema** was the father of Raham, and Raham the father of Jorkeam.
5:8 Bela son of Azaz, the son of **Shema**, the son of Joel. They settled
8:13 Beriah and **Shema**, who were heads of families of those living in
Ne 8:4 stood Mattithiah, **Shema**, Anaiah, Uriah, Hilkiah and Maaseiah;

9051 שֵׁמַע ***šēma'***, n.[m.]. [17] [√ 9048]

fame [4], report [3], reports [3], hear [2], news [2], heard [+9048] [1], rumor [1], word [1]

Ge 29:13 As soon as Laban heard the **news** *about* Jacob, his sister's son,
Ex 23:1 "Do not spread false **reports**. Do not help a wicked man by being a
Nu 14:15 the nations who have heard this **report** *about* you will say,
Dt 2:25 They will hear **reports** *of* you and will tremble and be in anguish
1Ki 10:1 When the queen of Sheba heard about the **fame** *of* Solomon
2Ch 9:1 When the queen of Sheba heard of Solomon's **fame**, she came to
Job 28:22 and Death say, 'Only a **rumor** *of* it has reached our ears.'
42:5 My ears *had* **heard of** [+9048] you but now my eyes have seen
Ps 18:44 [18:45] As soon as they **hear** me, they obey me; foreigners cringe
Isa 23:5 When **word** comes to Egypt, they will be in anguish at the report
23:5 comes to Egypt, they will be in anguish at the **report** *from* Tyre.
66:19 to the distant islands that have not heard of my **fame** or seen my
Jer 37:5 who were besieging Jerusalem heard the **report** *about* them,
50:43 The king of Babylon has heard **reports** *about* them, and his hands
Hos 7:12 of the air. When I **hear** them flocking together, I will catch them.
Na 3:19 Everyone who hears the **news** *about* you claps his hands at your
Hab 3:2 LORD, I have heard of your **fame**; I stand in awe of your deeds,

9052 שָׁמָע ***šāmā'***, n.pr.m. [1] [√ 9048 + 3378?]

Shama [1]

1Ch 11:44 the Ashterathite, **Shama** and Jeiel the sons of Hotham the Aroerite,

9053 שֹׁמַע ***šōma'***, n.m. [4] [√ 9048]

reports [2], fame [1], reputation [1]

Jos 6:27 LORD was with Joshua, and his **fame** spread throughout the land.
9:9 For we have heard **reports** *of* him: all that he did in Egypt,
Est 9:4 his **reputation** spread throughout the provinces, and he became
Jer 6:24 We have heard **reports** *about* them, and our hands hang limp.

9054 שְׁמַע ***šᵉma'***, n.pr.loc. [1] [√ 9048]

Shema [1]

Jos 15:26 Amam, **Shema**, Moladah,

9055 שִׁמְעָא ***šim'ā'***, n.pr.m. [5] [√ 9048 + 3378?]

Shimea [4], Shammua [1]

1Ch 2:13 his firstborn; the second son was Abinadab, the third **Shimea**,
3:5 born to him there: **Shammua**, Shobab, Nathan and Solomon.
6:30 [6:15] **Shimea** his son, Haggiah his son and Asaiah his son.
6:39 [6:24] his right hand: Asaph son of Berekiah, the son of **Shimea**,
20:7 Jonathan son of **Shimea**, David's brother, killed him.

9056 שִׁמְעָה ***šim'â***, n.pr.m. [3] [→ 9065; cf. 9048 + 3378?]

Shimeah [3]

2Sa 13:3 Now Amnon had a friend named Jonadab son of **Shimeah**,
13:32 Jonadab son of **Shimeah**, David's brother, said, "My lord should
21:21 Jonathan son of **Shimeah**, [K 9059] David's brother, killed him.

9057 שְׁמָעָה ***šᵉmā'â***, n.pr.m. [1] [√ 9048]

Shemaah [1]

1Ch 12:3 Ahiezer their chief and Joash the sons of **Shemaah** the Gibeathite;

9058 שִׁמְעוֹן ***šim'ôn***, n.pr.m. [44] [→ 9063; cf. 9048]

Simeon [30], Simeon [+1201] [5], Simeonites [+1201] [4], Simeonites [3], *untranslated* [1], Shimeon [1]

Ge 29:33 not loved, he gave me this one too." So she named him **Simeon**.
34:25 **Simeon** and Levi, Dinah's brothers, took their swords and attacked
34:30 Jacob said to **Simeon** and Levi, "You have brought trouble on me
35:23 the firstborn of Jacob, **Simeon**, Levi, Judah, Issachar and Zebulun.
42:24 He had **Simeon** taken from them and bound before their eyes.
42:36 Joseph is no more and **Simeon** is no more, and now you want to
43:23 I received your silver." Then he brought **Simeon** out to them.
46:10 The sons of **Simeon**: Jemuel, Jamin, Ohad, Jakin, Zohar and Shaul
48:5 and Manasseh will be mine, just as Reuben and **Simeon** are mine.
49:5 "**Simeon** and Levi are brothers—their swords are weapons of
Ex 1:2 Reuben, **Simeon**, Levi and Judah;
6:15 The sons of **Simeon** were Jemuel, Jamin, Ohad, Jakin, Zohar
6:15 the son of a Canaanite woman. These were the clans of **Simeon**.
Nu 1:6 from **Simeon**, Shelumiel son of Zurishaddai;
1:22 From the descendants of **Simeon**: All the men twenty years old
1:23 The number from the tribe of **Simeon** was 59,300.
2:12 The tribe of **Simeon** will camp next to them. The leader of the
2:12 The leader of the people of **Simeon** is Shelumiel son of
7:36 the leader of the people of **Simeon**, brought his offering.
10:19 Zurishaddai was over the division of the tribe of **Simeon** [+1201],
13:5 from the tribe of **Simeon**, Shaphat son of Hori;
26:12 The descendants of **Simeon** by their clans were: through Nemuel,
34:20 Shemuel son of Ammihud, from the tribe of **Simeon** [+1201];
Dt 27:12 the people: **Simeon**, Levi, Judah, Issachar, Joseph and Benjamin.
Jos 19:1 The second lot came out for the tribe of **Simeon** [+1201], clan by
19:1 second lot came out for the tribe of Simeon, **[RPH]** clan by clan.
19:8 This was the inheritance of the tribe of the **Simeonites** [+1201],
19:9 The inheritance of the **Simeonites** [+1201] was taken from the
19:9 So the **Simeonites** [+1201] received their inheritance within the

Jos 21: 9 and **Simeon** [+1201] they allotted the following towns by name
Jdg 1: 3 Then the men of Judah said to the **Simeonites** their brothers,
1: 3 will go with you into yours." So the **Simeonites** went with them.
1: 17 Then the men of Judah went with the **Simeonites** their brothers
1Ch 2: 1 sons of Israel: Reuben, **Simeon**, Levi, Judah, Issachar, Zebulun,
4: 24 The descendants of **Simeon**: Nemuel, Jamin, Jarib, Zerah
4: 42 And five hundred of these **Simeonites** [+1201], led by Pelatiah,
6: 65 [6:50] From the tribes of Judah, **Simeon** [+1201] and Benjamin
12: 25 [12:26] men of **Simeon**, warriors ready for battle—7,100;
2Ch 15: 9 Manasseh and **Simeon** who had settled among them,
34: 6 the towns of Manasseh, Ephraim and **Simeon**, as far as Naphtali,
Ezr 10: 31 of Harim: Eliezer, Ishijah, Malkijah, Shemaiah, **Shimeon**,
Eze 48: 24 "**Simeon** will have one portion; it will border the territory of
48: 25 it will border the territory of **Simeon** from east to west.
48: 33 the gate of **Simeon**, the gate of Issachar and the gate of Zebulun.

9059 שִׁמְעִי *šim'î¹*, n.pr.m. [43 / 44] [→ 9060; cf. 9048 + 3378?]

Shimei [42], he[s] [1], Shimei's [+4200] [1]

Ex 6: 17 The sons of Gershon, by clans, were Libni and **Shimei**.
Nu 3: 18 These were the names of the Gershonite clans: Libni and **Shimei**.
2Sa 16: 5 His name was **Shimei** son of Gera, and he cursed as he came out.
16: 7 As he cursed, **Shimei** said, "Get out, get out, you man of blood,
16: 13 his men continued along the road while **Shimei** was going along
19: 16 [19:17] **Shimei** son of Gera, the Benjamite from Bahurim,
19: 18 [19:19] When **Shimei** son of Gera crossed the Jordan, he fell
19: 21 [19:22] Zeruiah said, "Shouldn't **Shimei** be put to death for this?
19: 23 [19:24] So the king said to **Shimei**, "You shall not die."
21: 21 [Jonathan son of **Shimeah**, [K; see Q 9056] David's brother, killed]
1Ki 1: 8 **Shimei** and Rei and David's special guard did not join Adonijah.
2: 8 "And remember, you have with you **Shimei** son of Gera,
2: 36 the king sent for **Shimei** and said to him, "Build yourself a house
2: 38 **Shimei** answered the king, "What you say is good. Your servant
2: 38 king has said." And **Shimei** stayed in Jerusalem for a long time.
2: 39 two of **Shimei's** [+4200] slaves ran off to Achish son of Maacah,
2: 39 king of Gath, and **Shimei** was told, "Your slaves are in Gath."
2: 40 **he**[s] saddled his donkey and went to Achish at Gath in search of his
2: 40 So **Shimei** went away and brought the slaves back from Gath.
2: 41 When Solomon was told that **Shimei** had gone from Jerusalem to
2: 42 the king summoned **Shimei** and said to him, "Did I not make you
2: 44 The king also said to **Shimei**, "You know in your heart all the
4: 18 **Shimei** son of Ela—in Benjamin;
1Ch 3: 19 The sons of Pedaiah: Zerubbabel and **Shimei**. The sons of
4: 26 of Mishma: Hammuel his son, Zaccur his son and **Shimei** his son.
4: 27 **Shimei** had sixteen sons and six daughters, but his brothers did not
5: 4 of Joel: Shemaiah his son, Gog his son, **Shimei** his son,
6: 17 [6:2] are the names of the sons of Gershon: Libni and **Shimei**.
6: 29 [6:14] Mahli, Libni his son, **Shimei** his son, Uzzah his son,
6: 42 [6:27] the son of Ethan, the son of Zimmah, the son of **Shimei**,
8: 21 Adaiah, Beraiah and Shimrath were the sons of **Shimei**.
23: 7 Belonging to the Gershonites: Ladan and **Shimei**.
23: 9 The sons of **Shimei**: Shelomoth, Haziel and Haran—three in all.
23: 10 the sons of **Shimei**: Jahath, Ziza, Jeush and Beriah. These were the
23: 10 Jeush and Beriah. These were the sons of **Shimei**—four in all.
25: 3 Gedaliah, Zeri, Jeshaiah, **Shimei**, [BHS-] Hashabiah
25: 17 the tenth to **Shimei**, his sons and relatives, 12
27: 27 **Shimei** the Ramathite was in charge of the vineyards. Zabdi the
2Ch 29: 14 from the descendants of Heman, Jehiel and **Shimei**; from the
31: 12 in charge of these things, and his brother **Shimei** was next in rank.
31: 13 Benaiah were supervisors under Conaniah and **Shimei** his brother,
Ezr 10: 23 Jozabad, **Shimei**, Kelaiah (that is, Kelita), Pethahiah, Judah
10: 33 Mattattah, Zabad, Eliphelet, Jeremai, Manasseh and **Shimei**.
10: 38 From the descendants of Binnui: **Shimei**,
Est 2: 5 named Mordecai son of Jair, the son of **Shimei**, the son of Kish,

9060 שִׁמְעִי² *šim'î²*, a.g. [2] [√ 9059]

Shimei [1], Shimeites [1]

Nu 3: 21 To Gershon belonged the clans of the Libnites and **Shimeites**;
Zec 12: 13 house of Levi and their wives, the clan of **Shimei** and their wives,

9061 שְׁמַעְיָה *šᵉma'yâ*, n.pr.m. [34] [√ 9048 + 3378]

Shemaiah [32], his[s] [1], Shemaiah's [1]

1Ki 12: 22 But this word of God came to **Shemaiah** the man of God:
1Ch 3: 22 **Shemaiah** and his sons: Hattush, Igal, Bariah, Neariah
3: 22 Shemaiah and **his**[s] sons: Hattush, Igal, Bariah, Neariah
4: 37 the son of Jedaiah, the son of Shimri, the son of **Shemaiah**.
5: 4 of Joel: **Shemaiah** his son, Gog his son, Shimei his son,
9: 14 **Shemaiah** son of Hasshub, the son of Azrikam, the son of
9: 16 Obadiah son of **Shemaiah**, the son of Galal, the son of Jeduthun;
15: 8 descendants of Elizaphan, **Shemaiah** the leader and 200 relatives;
15: 11 Asaiah, Joel, **Shemaiah**, Eliel and Amminadab the Levites.
24: 6 The scribe **Shemaiah** son of Nethanel, a Levite, recorded their
26: 4 **Shemaiah** the firstborn, Jehozabad the second, Joah the third,
26: 6 His son **Shemaiah** also had sons, who were leaders in their father's
26: 7 The sons of **Shemaiah**: Othni, Rephael, Obed and Elzabad;
2Ch 12: 5 the prophet **Shemaiah** came to Rehoboam and to the leaders of
12: 7 humbled themselves, this word of the LORD came to **Shemaiah**:
12: 15 are they not written in the records of **Shemaiah** the prophet
29: 14 from the descendants of Jeduthun, **Shemaiah** and Uzziel.
Ezr 8: 13 were Eliphelet, Jeuel and **Shemaiah**, and with them 60 men;
8: 16 Ariel, **Shemaiah**, Elnathan, Jarib, Elnathan, Nathan, Zechariah
10: 21 of Harim: Maaseiah, Elijah, **Shemaiah**, Jehiel and Uzziah.
10: 31 of Harim: Eliezer, Ishijah, Malkijah, **Shemaiah**, Shimeon,
Ne 3: 29 Next to him, **Shemaiah** son of Shecaniah, the guard at the East
6: 10 One day I went to the house of **Shemaiah** son of Delaiah,
10: 8 [10:9] Maaziah, Bilgai and **Shemaiah**. These were the priests.
11: 15 **Shemaiah** son of Hasshub, the son of Azrikam, the son of
12: 6 **Shemaiah**, Joiarib, Jedaiah,
12: 18 of Bilgah's, Shammua; of **Shemaiah's**, Jehonathan;
12: 34 Judah, Benjamin, **Shemaiah**, Jeremiah,
12: 35 the son of **Shemaiah**, the son of Mattaniah, the son of Micaiah,
12: 36 **Shemaiah**, Azarel, Milalai, Gilalai, Maai, Nethanel, Judah
12: 42 **Shemaiah**, Eleazar, Uzzi, Jehohanan, Malkijah, Elam and Ezer.
Jer 29: 31 'This is what the LORD says about **Shemaiah** the Nehelamite:
29: 31 Because **Shemaiah** has prophesied to you, even though I did not
29: 32 I will surely punish **Shemaiah** the Nehelamite and his descendants.

9062 שְׁמַעְיָהוּ *šᵉma'yāhû*, n.pr.m. [7] [√ 9048 + 3378]

Shemaiah [7]

2Ch 11: 2 But this word of the LORD came to **Shemaiah** the man of God:
17: 8 **Shemaiah**, Nethaniah, Zebadiah, Asahel, Shemiramoth,
31: 15 Jeshua, **Shemaiah**, Amariah and Shecaniah assisted him faithfully
35: 9 Also Conaniah along with **Shemaiah** and Nethanel, his brothers,
Jer 26: 20 (Now Uriah son of **Shemaiah** from Kiriath Jearim was another
29: 24 Tell **Shemaiah** the Nehelamite,
36: 12 the secretary, Delaiah son of **Shemaiah**, Elnathan son of Acbor,

9063 שִׁמְעֹנִי *šim'ōnî*, a.g. [4] [√ 9058]

Simeon [2], Simeonite [1], Simeonites [1]

Nu 25: 14 woman was Zimri son of Salu, the leader of a **Simeonite** family.
26: 14 These were the clans of **Simeon**; there were 22,200 men.
Jos 21: 4 thirteen towns from the tribes of Judah, **Simeon** and Benjamin.
1Ch 27: 16 over the Reubenites: Eliezer son of Zicri; over the **Simeonites**:

9064 שִׁמְעָת *šim'āt*, n.pr.f. [2] [√ 9048]

Shimeath [2]

2Ki 12: 21 [12:22] who murdered him were Jozabad son of **Shimeath**
2Ch 24: 26 son of **Shimeath** an Ammonite woman, and Jehozabad, son of

9065 שִׁמְעָתִי *šim'ātî*, a.g. [1] [√ 9056]

Shimeathites [1]

1Ch 2: 55 who lived at Jabez: the Tirathites, **Shimeathites** and Sucathites.

9066 שֶׁמֶץ *šemeṣ*, n.[m.] [2] [→ 9067?]

faint [1], whisper [1]

Job 4: 12 word was secretly brought to me, my ears caught a **whisper** of it.
26: 14 outer fringe of his works; how **faint** the whisper we hear of him!

9067 שִׁמְצָה *šimṣâ*, v. [1] [√ 9066?]

laughingstock [1]

Ex 32: 25 get out of control and so become a **laughingstock** to their enemies.

9068 שָׁמַר *šāmar*, v. [468] [→ 0874, 5464, 5465, 5466, 9031, 9069, 9070?, 9072, 9073, 9074, 9076, 9078, 9081, 9085, 9086; *also used with compound proper names*]

keep [83], careful [46], obey [21], observe [20], kept [19], carefully [16], guard [16], keeps [10], watch [9], watchmen [8], keeping [7], guards [6], watches over [6], doorkeepers [+6197] [5], in charge [5], keeper [5], maintain [5], obeyed [5], protect [5], take care of [5], watch over [5], celebrate [4], responsible [4], be sure [3], care [3], do [3], guarded [3], guarding [3], heeds [3], observed [3], on guard [3], protects [3], watched over [3], watchman [3], be careful [2], be sure to keep [+906+9068] [2], beware [2], careful [+9068] [2], carefully observe [+906+9068] [2], carried out [2], carrying out [2], cling [2], faithful [2], follow [2], followed [2], guard yourself [2], have charge of [+5466] [2], keep safe [2], kept myself [2], make sure [2], obeys [2], perform [2], protected [2], safekeeping [2], see [2], serve [2], waiting [2], watches [2], watching over [2], watching [2], assures [1], be protected [1], beware [+440] [1], bodyguard [+4200+8031] [1], cared for [1], careful to do [1], cherishes [1], consider [1], continue [1], continued [1], defending [1], did[s] [1], done [1], doorkeeper [+6197] [1], eyed [1], faithfully carried out [1], flamed unchecked [+5905] [1], give [1], guard [+906+5466] [1], guarded [+928+5464] [1], guarding [+5466] [1], guarding [+906+5466] [1], had charge of [1], have charge of [1], heed [1], hoarded [1], keep away [1], keep close watch on [1], keep penned up [1], keep track of [1], keepers [1], keeps close watch [1], kept a record [1], kept in mind [1], kept penned up [1], kept themselves [1], kept watch [1], living [1], looks after [1], loyal [+5466] [1], must [1], obey [+906+2256+6913] [1], obeying [1], observing [1], on duty at [1], on duty [1], paid attention [1], pay attention [1], performed [1], performing [1], preserve [1], preserved [1], put [1], regardless [+401+4200] [1], remains [1], responsible [+5466] [1], responsible for [1], secured [1], see to it [1], shepherd [1], spare [1], spies [1], take care [1], tended sheep [1], under siege [1], wait to kill [+5883] [1], was set aside [1], watch carefully [1]

Ge 2:15 [A] put him in the Garden of Eden to work it and **take care of** it.
3:24 [A] flashing back and forth to **guard** the way to the tree of life.
4:9 [A] "I don't know," he replied. "Am I my brother's **keeper**?"
17:9 [A] *you must* **keep** my covenant, you and your descendants after
17:10 [A] your descendants after you, the covenant *you are to* **keep**:
18:19 [A] his household after him *to* **keep** the way of the LORD by
24:6 [C] "**Make sure** *that* you do not take my son back there,"
26:5 [A] because Abraham obeyed me and **kept** my requirements,
28:15 [A] I am with you and *will* **watch over** you wherever you go,
28:20 [A] with me and *will* **watch over** me on this journey I am taking
30:31 [A] I will go on tending your flocks and **watching over** them:
31:24 [C] "**Be careful** not to say anything to Jacob, either good or bad."
31:29 [C] '**Be careful** not to say anything to Jacob, either good or bad.'
37:11 [A] were jealous of him, but his father **kept** the matter **in mind**.
41:35 [A] the authority of Pharaoh, *to be* **kept** in the cities *for* food.
Ex 10:28 [C] of my sight! **Make sure** you do not appear before me again!
12:17 [A] "**Celebrate** the Feast of Unleavened Bread, because it was
12:17 [A] **Celebrate** this day as a lasting ordinance for the generations
12:24 [A] "**Obey** these instructions as a lasting ordinance for you
12:25 [A] will give you as he promised, **observe** this ceremony.
13:10 [A] *You must* **keep** this ordinance at the appointed time year
15:26 [A] you pay attention to his commands and **keep** all his decrees,
16:28 [A] "How long will you refuse to **keep** my commands and my
19:5 [A] Now if you obey me fully and **keep** my covenant, then out of
19:12 [C] '*Be* **careful** *that* you do not go up the mountain or touch the
20:6 [A] of those who love me and **keep** my commandments.
21:29 [A] but *has* not **kept** it **penned up** and it kills a man or woman,
21:36 [A] yet the owner *did* not **keep** it **penned up**, the owner must
22:7 [22:6] [A] gives his neighbor silver or goods for **safekeeping**
22:10 [22:9] [A] or any other animal to his neighbor for **safekeeping**
23:13 [C] "*Be* **careful to do** everything I have said to you. Do not
23:15 [A] "**Celebrate** the Feast of Unleavened Bread; for seven days
23:20 [A] I am sending an angel ahead of you to **guard** you along the
23:21 [C] **Pay attention** to him and listen to what he says. Do not rebel
31:13 [A] "Say to the Israelites, '*You must* **observe** my Sabbaths. This
31:14 [A] " '**Observe** the Sabbath, because it is holy to you.
31:16 [A] The Israelites *are to* **observe** the Sabbath, celebrating it for
34:11 [A] **Obey** what I command you today. I will drive out before you
34:12 [C] *Be* **careful** not to make a treaty with those who live in the
34:18 [A] "**Celebrate** the Feast of Unleavened Bread. For seven days
Lev 8:35 [A] and night for seven days and **do** what the LORD requires,
18:4 [A] must obey my laws and *be* **careful** to follow my decrees.
18:5 [A] **Keep** my decrees and laws, for the man who obeys them will
18:26 [A] you *must* **keep** my decrees and my laws. The native-born
18:30 [A] **Keep** my requirements and do not follow any of the
19:3 [A] his mother and father, and *you must* **observe** my Sabbaths.
19:19 [A] " '**Keep** my decrees. " 'Do not mate different kinds of
19:30 [A] " '**Observe** my Sabbaths and have reverence for my
19:37 [A] " '**Keep** all my decrees and all my laws and follow them.
20:8 [A] **Keep** my decrees and follow them. I am the LORD,
20:22 [A] " '**Keep** all my decrees and laws and follow them, so that the
22:9 [A] " 'The priests *are to* **keep** my requirements so that they do
22:31 [A] "**Keep** my commands and follow them. I am the LORD.
25:18 [A] " 'Follow my decrees and *be* **careful** to obey my laws, and
26:2 [A] " '**Observe** my Sabbaths and have reverence for my
26:3 [A] follow my decrees and *are* **careful** to obey my commands,
Nu 1:53 [A] The Levites *are to be* **responsible for** the care of the
3:7 [A] *They are to* **perform** duties for him and for the whole
3:8 [A] *They are to* **take care of** all the furnishings of the Tent of
3:10 [A] Appoint Aaron and his sons *to* **serve** as priests; anyone else
3:28 [A] The Kohathites were responsible for the **care** *of* the
3:32 [A] *those who were* responsible for the **care** *of* the sanctuary.
3:38 [A] *They were* responsible for the **care** *of* the sanctuary on
6:24 [A] " ' "The LORD bless you and **keep** you;
8:26 [A] They may assist their brothers in **performing** their duties at
9:19 [A] the Israelites **obeyed** the LORD's order and did not set out.
9:23 [A] *They* **obeyed** the LORD's order, in accordance with his
18:3 [A] *They are to be* **responsible** [+5466] *to* you and are to
18:4 [A] and *be* **responsible** *for* the care of the Tent of Meeting—
18:5 [A] "*You are to be* **responsible** *for* the care of the sanctuary and
18:7 [A] your sons *may* **serve** as priests in connection with everything
23:12 [A] "**Must** *I* not speak what the LORD puts in my mouth?"
28:2 [A] '**See** that you present to me at the appointed time the food for
31:30 [A] *who are* **responsible** *for* the care of the LORD's
31:47 [A] *who were* **responsible** *for* the care of the LORD's
Dt 2:4 [C] live in Seir. They will be afraid of you, but *be* very **careful**.
4:2 [A] **keep** the commands of the LORD your God that I give you.
4:6 [A] Observe them **carefully**, for this will show your wisdom
4:9 [C] Only *be* **careful**, and watch yourselves closely so that you do
4:9 [A] **watch** yourselves closely so that you do not forget the things
4:15 [C] out of the fire. Therefore **watch** yourselves very **carefully**,
4:23 [C] *Be* **careful** not to forget the covenant of the LORD your
4:40 [A] **Keep** his decrees and commands, which I am giving you
5:1 [A] your hearing today. Learn them and **be sure** to follow them.
5:10 [A] of those who love me and **keep** my commandments.
5:12 [A] "**Observe** the Sabbath day by keeping it holy, as the LORD
5:29 [A] be inclined to fear me and **keep** all my commands always,
5:32 [A] So *be* **careful** to do what the LORD your God has
6:2 [A] your God as long as you live by **keeping** all his decrees
6:3 [A] *be* **careful** to obey so that it may go well with you and that
6:12 [C] *be* **careful** that you do not forget the LORD, who brought
6:17 [A] **Be sure to keep** [+906+9068] the commands of the LORD
6:17 [A] **Be sure to keep** [+906+9068] the commands of the LORD
6:25 [A] if *we are* **careful** to obey all this law before the LORD our
7:8 [A] **kept** the oath he swore to your forefathers that he brought
7:9 [A] **keeping** his covenant of love to a thousand generations of
7:9 [A] generations of those who love him and **keep** his commands.
7:11 [A] **take care** to follow the commands, decrees and laws I give
7:12 [A] pay attention to these laws and *are* **careful** to follow them,
7:12 [A] the LORD your God *will* **keep** his covenant of love with
8:1 [A] *Be* **careful** to follow every command I am giving you today,
8:2 [A] in your heart, whether or not *you would* **keep** his commands.
8:6 [A] **Observe** the commands of the LORD your God, walking in
8:11 [C] *Be* **careful** that you do not forget the LORD your God,
8:11 [A] failing *to* **observe** his commands, his laws and his decrees
10:13 [A] to **observe** the LORD's commands and decrees that I am
11:1 [A] Love the LORD your God and **keep** his requirements, his
11:8 [A] **Observe** therefore all the commands I am giving you today,
11:16 [C] *Be* **careful**, or you will be enticed to turn away and worship
11:22 [A] If *you* **carefully observe** [+906+9068] all these commands I
11:22 [A] If *you* **carefully observe** [+906+9068] all these commands I
11:32 [A] **be sure** that you obey all the decrees and laws I am setting
12:1 [A] laws *you must be* **careful** to follow in the land that the
12:13 [C] *Be* **careful** not to sacrifice your burnt offerings anywhere you
12:19 [C] *Be* **careful** not to neglect the Levites as long as you live in
12:28 [A] *Be* **careful** to obey all these regulations I am giving you, so
12:30 [C] *be* **careful** not to be ensnared by inquiring about their gods,
12:32 [13:1] [A] **See** that you do all I command you; do not add to it
13:4 [13:5] [A] **Keep** his commands and obey him; serve him
13:18 [13:19] [A] **keeping** all his commands that I am giving you
15:5 [A] *are* **careful** to follow all these commands I am giving you
15:9 [C] *Be* **careful** not to harbor this wicked thought: "The seventh
16:1 [A] **Observe** the month of Abib and celebrate the Passover of the
16:12 [A] you were slaves in Egypt, and follow **carefully** these decrees.
17:10 [A] *Be* **careful** to do everything they direct you to do.
17:19 [A] follow **carefully** all the words of this law and these decrees
19:9 [A] because *you* **carefully** follow all these laws I command you
23:9 [23:10] [C] your enemies, **keep** away from everything impure.
23:23 [23:24] [A] Whatever your lips utter *you must* **be sure** to do,
24:8 [C] In cases of leprous diseases *be* very **careful** [+9068] to do
24:8 [A] In cases of leprous diseases *be* very **careful** [+9068] to do
24:8 [A] You must follow **carefully** what I have commanded them.
26:16 [A] **carefully** observe them with all your heart and with all your
26:17 [A] that you *will* **keep** his decrees, commands and laws, and that
26:18 [A] as he promised, and that you *are to* **keep** all his commands.
27:1 [A] the people: "**Keep** all these commands that I give you today.
28:1 [A] and **carefully** follow all his commands I give you today,
28:9 [A] if *you* **keep** the commands of the LORD your God and walk
28:13 [A] your God that I give you this day and **carefully** follow them,
28:15 [A] do not **carefully** follow all his commands and decrees I am
28:45 [A] and **observe** the commands and decrees he gave you.
28:58 [A] If *you do* not **carefully** follow all the words of this law,
29:9 [29:8] [A] **Carefully** follow the terms of this covenant, so that
30:10 [A] if you obey the LORD your God and **keep** his commands
30:16 [A] in his ways, and to **keep** his commands, decrees and laws;
31:12 [A] your God and follow **carefully** all the words of this law.
32:46 [A] so that you may command your children to obey **carefully** all
33:9 [A] but *he* **watched over** your word and guarded your covenant.
Jos 1:7 [A] *Be* **careful** to obey all the law my servant Moses gave you;
1:8 [A] so that *you may be* **careful** to do everything written in it.
6:18 [A] **keep away** from the devoted things, so that you will not

Jos 10:18 [A] the mouth of the cave, and post some men there to **guard** it.
22: 2 [A] "You *have* **done** all that Moses the servant of the LORD
22: 3 [A] *have* **carried out** the mission the LORD your God gave
22: 5 [A] *be* very **careful** to keep the commandment and the law that
22: 5 [A] to **obey** his commands, to hold fast to him and to serve him
23: 6 [A] *be* **careful** to obey all that is written in the Book of the Law
23:11 [C] So *be* very **careful** to love the LORD your God.
24:17 [A] *He* **protected** us on our entire journey and among all the
Jdg 1:24 [A] the **spies** saw a man coming out of the city and they said to
2:22 [A] and see whether they *will* **keep** the way of the LORD
2:22 [A] way of the LORD and walk in it as their forefathers **did**[s]."
7:19 [A] of the middle watch, just after they had changed the **guard**.
13: 4 [C] Now **see to it** that you drink no wine or other fermented
13:13 [C] "Your wife *must* **do** all that I have told her.
13:14 [A] *She must* **do** everything I have commanded her."
1Sa 1:12 [A] she kept on praying to the LORD, Eli **observed** her mouth.
2: 9 [A] *He will* **guard** the feet of his saints, but the wicked will be
7: 1 [A] consecrated Eleazar his son to **guard** the ark of the LORD.
9:24 [B] Eat, because *it* **was set aside** for you for this occasion,
13:13 [A] "*You have* not **kept** the command the LORD your God
13:14 [A] because *you have* not **kept** the LORD's command."
17:20 [A] Early in the morning David left the flock with a **shepherd**,
17:22 [A] David left his things with the **keeper** *of* supplies, ran to the
19: 2 [C] *Be* **on** *your* **guard** tomorrow morning; go into hiding
19:11 [A] Saul sent men to David's house to **watch** it and to kill him in
21: 4 [21:5] [C] the men *have* **kept themselves** from women."
25:21 [A] "It's been useless—all *my* **watching over** this fellow's
26:15 [A] like you in Israel? Why didn't *you* **guard** your lord the king?
26:16 [A] because *you did* not **guard** your master, the LORD's
28: 2 [A] I will make you my **bodyguard** [+4200+8031] for life."
30:23 [A] *He has* **protected** us and handed over to us the forces that
2Sa 11:16 [A] So while Joab *had* the city **under siege**, he put Uriah at a
15:16 [A] but he left ten concubines to **take care of** the palace.
16:21 [A] father's concubines whom he left to **take care of** the palace.
18:12 [A] and Ittai, '**Protect** the young man Absalom for my sake.'
20: 3 [A] he took the ten concubines he had left to **take care of** the
20:10 [C] Amasa *was* not **on** *his* **guard** against the dagger in Joab's
22:22 [A] For *I have* **kept** the ways of the LORD; I have not done evil
22:24 [F] been blameless before him and *have* **kept myself** from sin.
22:44 [A] my people; *you have* **preserved** me as the head of nations.
23: 5 [B] an everlasting covenant, arranged and **secured** in every part?
1Ki 2: 3 [A] **observe** what the LORD your God requires: Walk in his
2: 3 [A] **keep** his decrees and commands, his laws and requirements,
2: 4 [A] 'If your descendants **watch** how they live, and if they walk
2:43 [A] *did you* not **keep** your oath to the LORD and obey the
3: 6 [A] *You have* **continued** this great kindness to him and have
3:14 [A] if you walk in my ways and **obey** my statutes and commands
6:12 [A] my regulations and **keep** all my commands and obey them,
8:23 [A] you *who* **keep** your covenant of love with your servants who
8:24 [A] *You have* **kept** your promise to your servant David my
8:25 [A] **keep** for your servant David my father the promises you
8:25 [A] if only your sons *are* **careful** in all they do to walk before me
8:58 [A] to walk in all his ways and to **keep** the commands, decrees
8:61 [A] to live by his decrees and **obey** his commands, as at this
9: 4 [A] and do all I command and **observe** my decrees and laws,
9: 6 [A] *do* not **observe** the commands and decrees I have given you
11:10 [A] other gods, Solomon *did* not **keep** the LORD's command.
11:11 [A] and *you have* not **kept** my covenant and my decrees,
11:34 [A] whom I chose and who **observed** my commands and statutes.
11:38 [A] do what is right in my eyes by **keeping** my statutes
13:21 [A] *have* not **kept** the command the LORD your God gave you.
14: 8 [A] who **kept** my commands and followed me with all his heart,
14:27 [A] assigned these to the commanders of the guard **on duty** at the
20:39 [A] came to me with a captive and said, '**Guard** this man.
2Ki 6: 9 [C] "**Beware** of passing that place, because the Arameans are
6:10 [C] warned the king, so that *he was* **on** *his* **guard** in such places.
9:14 [A] all Israel had been **defending** Ramoth Gilead against Hazael
10:31 [A] Yet Jehu *was* not **careful** to keep the law of the LORD,
11: 5 [A] a third of you **guarding** [+5466] the royal palace,
11: 6 [A] *who* take turns **guarding** [+906+5466] the temple—
11: 7 [A] duty *are* all *to* **guard** [+906+5466] the temple for the king.
12: 9 [12:10] [A] The priests *who* **guarded** the entrance put into the
17:13 [A] **Observe** my commands and decrees, in accordance with the
17:19 [A] even Judah *did* not **keep** the commands of the LORD their
17:37 [A] *You must* always *be* **careful** to keep the decrees
18: 6 [A] *he* **kept** the commands the LORD had given Moses.
21: 8 [A] if only *they will be* **careful** to do everything I commanded
22: 4 [A] which the **doorkeepers** [+6197] have collected from the
22:14 [A] son of Tikvah, the son of Harhas, **keeper** *of* the wardrobe.
23: 3 [A] **keep** his commands, regulations and decrees with all his
23: 4 [A] the **doorkeepers** [+6197] to remove from the temple of the
25:18 [A] the priest next in rank and the three **doorkeepers** [+6197].
1Ch 9:19 [A] were responsible for **guarding** the thresholds of the Tent just
9:19 [A] for **guarding** the entrance to the dwelling of the LORD.
10:13 [A] *he did* not **keep** the word of the LORD and even consulted
12:29 [12:30] [A] most of whom *had remained* **loyal** [+5466] *to*
22:12 [A] so that you *may* **keep** the law of the LORD your God.
22:13 [A] you will have success if *you are* **careful** to observe the
23:32 [A] so the Levites **carried out** their responsibilities for the Tent
28: 8 [A] *Be* **careful** to follow all the commands of the LORD your
29:18 [A] **keep** this desire in the hearts of your people forever,
29:19 [A] give my son Solomon the wholehearted devotion to **keep**
2Ch 5:11 [A] there had consecrated themselves, **regardless** [+401+4200]
6:14 [A] you *who* **keep** your covenant of love with your servants who
6:15 [A] You *have* **kept** your promise to your servant David my
6:16 [A] **keep** for your servant David my father the promises you
6:16 [A] if only your sons *are* **careful** in all they do to walk before me
7:17 [A] and do all I command, and **observe** my decrees and laws,
12:10 [A] assigned these to the commanders of the guard **on duty at**
13:11 [A] We *are* **observing** the requirements of the LORD our God.
19: 7 [A] Judge **carefully**, for with the LORD our God there is no
23: 6 [A] all the other men *are to* **guard** what the LORD has assigned
33: 8 [A] if only *they will be* **careful** to do everything I commanded
34: 9 [A] which the Levites *who were* the **doorkeepers** [+6197] had
34:21 [A] because our fathers *have* not **kept** the word of the LORD;
34:22 [A] son of Tokhath, the son of Hasrah, **keeper** *of* the wardrobe.
34:31 [A] to follow the LORD and **keep** his commands, regulations
Ezr 8:29 [A] Guard them **carefully** until you weigh them out in the
Ne 1: 5 [A] *who* **keeps** his covenant of love with those who love him
1: 5 [A] of love with those who love him and **obey** his commands,
1: 7 [A] *We have* not **obeyed** the commands, decrees and laws you
1: 9 [A] return to me and **obey** [+906+2256+6913] my commands,
2: 8 [A] may I have a letter to Asaph, **keeper** *of* the king's forest,
3:29 [A] son of Shecaniah, the **guard** *at* the East Gate, made repairs.
9:32 [A] mighty and awesome God, *who* **keeps** his covenant of love,
10:29 [10:30] [A] of God and to obey **carefully** all the commands,
11:19 [A] Talmon and their associates, who **kept watch** at the gates—
12:25 [A] Akkub were gatekeepers *who* **guarded** [+928+5464] the
12:45 [A] *They* **performed** the service of their God and the service of
13:22 [A] and **guard** the gates in order to keep the Sabbath day holy.
Est 2: 3 [A] of Hegai, the king's eunuch, *who is* **in charge** *of* the women;
2: 8 [A] and entrusted to Hegai, *who* **had charge of** the harem.
2:14 [A] the king's eunuch *who was* **in charge** *of* the concubines.
2:15 [A] the king's eunuch *who was* **in charge** *of* the harem,
2:21 [A] two of the king's officers *who* **guarded** the doorway,
6: 2 [A] two of the king's officers *who* **guarded** the doorway,
Job 2: 6 [A] then, he is in your hands; but *you must* **spare** his life."
10:12 [A] and in your providence **watched over** my spirit.
10:14 [A] *you would be* **watching** me and would not let my offense go
13:27 [A] *you* **keep close watch on** all my paths by putting marks on
14:16 [A] then you will count my steps but not **keep track of** my sin.
22:15 [A] *Will you* **keep** *to* the old path that evil men have trod?
23:11 [A] his steps; *I have* **kept** *to* his way without turning aside.
24:15 [A] The eye of the adulterer **watches** *for* dusk; he thinks, 'No eye
29: 2 [A] months gone by, for the days when God **watched over** me,
33:11 [A] my feet in shackles; *he* **keeps close watch** *on* all my paths.'
36:21 [C] **Beware** [+440] *of* turning to evil, which you seem to prefer
39: 1 [A] give birth? *Do you* **watch** when the doe bears her fawn?
Ps 12: 7 [12:8] [A] you *will* **keep** us **safe** and protect us from such
16: 1 [A] **Keep** me **safe**, O God, for in you I take refuge.
17: 4 [A] by the word of your lips I *have* **kept** *myself from* the ways
17: 8 [A] **Keep** me as the apple of your eye; hide me in the shadow of
18:21 [18:22] [A] For *I have* **kept** the ways of the LORD; I have not
18:23 [18:24] [F] before him and *have* **kept myself** from sin.
19:11 [19:12] [A] in **keeping** them there is great reward.
25:20 [A] **Guard** my life and rescue me; let me not be put to shame,
31: 6 [31:7] [A] I hate those *who* **cling** *to* worthless idols; I trust in
34:20 [34:21] [A] *he* **protects** all his bones, not one of them will be
37:28 [C] *They will* **be protected** forever, but the offspring of the
37:34 [A] Wait for the LORD and **keep** his way. He will exalt you to
37:37 [A] **Consider** the blameless, observe the upright; there is a future
39: 1 [39:2] [A] "*I will* **watch** my ways and keep my tongue from sin;
39: 1 [39:2] [A] *I will* **put** a muzzle on my mouth as long as the
41: 2 [41:3] [A] The LORD *will* **protect** him and preserve his life;
56: 6 [56:7] [A] They conspire, they lurk, *they* **watch** my steps, eager
59: T [59:1] [A] When Saul had sent men *to* **watch** David's house in
59: 9 [59:10] [A] O my Strength, *I* **watch** for you; you, O God,
71:10 [A] *those who* **wait** [+5883] **to kill** me conspire together.
78:10 [A] *they did* not **keep** God's covenant and refused to live by his
78:56 [A] against the Most High; *they did* not **keep** his statutes.
86: 2 [A] **Guard** my life, for I am devoted to you. You are my God;
89:28 [89:29] [A] *I will* **maintain** my love to him forever, and my
89:31 [89:32] [A] violate my decrees and fail *to* **keep** my commands,
91:11 [A] For he will command his angels concerning you to **guard**
97:10 [A] for *he* **guards** the lives of his faithful ones and delivers them
99: 7 [A] *they* **kept** his statutes and the decrees he gave them.
103:18 [A] with *those who* **keep** his covenant and remember to obey his
105:45 [A] that *they might* **keep** his precepts and observe his laws.

Ps 106: 3 [A] Blessed are *they who* **maintain** justice, who constantly do
107:43 [A] *let him* **heed** these things and consider the great love of the
116: 6 [A] The LORD **protects** the simplehearted; when I was in great
119: 4 [A] You have laid down precepts that *are to be* fully **obeyed**.
119: 5 [A] Oh, that my ways were steadfast *in* **obeying** your decrees!
119: 8 [A] *I will* **obey** your decrees; do not utterly forsake me.
119: 9 [A] man keep his way pure? *By* **living** according to your word.
119:17 [A] good to your servant, and I will live; *I will* **obey** your word.
119:34 [A] and I will keep your law and **obey** it with all my heart.
119:44 [A] *I will* always **obey** your law, for ever and ever.
119:55 [A] I remember your name, O LORD, and *I will* **keep** your law.
119:57 [A] my portion, O LORD; I have promised to **obey** your words.
119:60 [A] I will hasten and not delay to **obey** your commands.
119:63 [A] a friend to all who fear you, to *all who* **follow** your precepts.
119:67 [A] I was afflicted I went astray, but now *I* **obey** your word.
119:88 [A] to your love, and *I will* **obey** the statutes of your mouth.
119:101 [A] my feet from every evil path so that *I might* **obey** your word.
119:106 [A] and confirmed it, that I *will* **follow** your righteous laws.
119:134 [A] from the oppression of men, that *I may* **obey** your precepts.
119:136 [A] of tears flow from my eyes, for your law *is* not **obeyed**.
119:146 [A] I call out to you; save me and *I will* **keep** your statutes.
119:158 [A] the faithless with loathing, for *they do* not **obey** your word.
119:167 [A] I **obey** your statutes, for I love them greatly.
119:168 [A] *I* **obey** your precepts and your statutes, for all my ways are
121: 3 [A] your foot slip—*he who* **watches over** you will not slumber;
121: 4 [A] *he who* **watches over** Israel will neither slumber nor sleep.
121: 5 [A] The LORD **watches over** you—the LORD is your shade
121: 7 [A] The LORD *will* **keep** you from all harm—he will watch
121: 7 [A] will keep you from all harm—*he will* **watch over** your life;
121: 8 [A] the LORD *will* **watch over** your coming and going both
127: 1 [A] Unless the LORD **watches over** the city, the watchmen
127: 1 [A] watches over the city, the **watchmen** stand guard in vain.
130: 3 [A] If *you*, O LORD, **kept a record** *of* sins, O Lord, who could
130: 6 [A] My soul waits for the Lord more than **watchmen** wait for the
130: 6 [A] for the morning, more than **watchmen** wait for the morning.
132:12 [A] if your sons **keep** my covenant and the statutes I teach them,
140: 4 [140:5] [A] **Keep** me, O LORD, from the hands of the wicked;
141: 9 [A] **Keep** me from the snares they have laid for me, from the
145:20 [A] The LORD **watches over** all who love him, but all the
146: 6 [A] in them—the LORD, who **remains** faithful forever.
146: 9 [A] The LORD **watches over** the alien and sustains the
Pr 2: 8 [A] course of the just and **protects** the way of his faithful ones.
2:11 [A] Discretion *will* **protect** you, and understanding will guard
2:20 [A] the ways of good men and **keep** *to* the paths of the righteous.
3:26 [A] your confidence and *will* **keep** your foot from being snared.
4: 4 [A] with all your heart; **keep** my commands and you will live.
4: 6 [A] Do not forsake wisdom, and *she will* **protect** you; love her,
4:21 [A] not let them out of your sight, **keep** them within your heart;
5: 2 [A] that you *may* **maintain** discretion and your lips may preserve
6:22 [A] when you sleep, *they will* **watch** over you; when you awake,
6:24 [A] **keeping** you from the immoral woman, from the smooth
7: 1 [A] **keep** my words and store up my commands within you.
7: 2 [A] **Keep** my commands and you will live; guard my teachings
7: 5 [A] they *will* **keep** you from the adulteress, from the wayward
8:32 [A] my sons, listen to me; blessed are *those who* **keep** my ways.
8:34 [A] to me, watching daily at my doors, **waiting** *at* my doorway.
10:17 [A] *He who* **heeds** discipline shows the way to life, but whoever
13: 3 [A] He who guards his lips **guards** his life, but he who speaks
13:18 [A] and shame, but *whoever* **heeds** correction is honored.
14: 3 [A] a rod to his back, but the lips of the wise **protect** them.
15: 5 [A] but *whoever* **heeds** correction shows prudence.
16:17 [A] upright avoids evil; he who guards his way **guards** his life.
19: 8 [A] his own soul; *he who* **cherishes** understanding prospers.
19:16 [A] *He who* **obeys** instructions guards his life, but he who is
19:16 [A] He who obeys instructions **guards** his life, but he who is
21:23 [A] *He who* **guards** his mouth and his tongue keeps himself
21:23 [A] his mouth and his tongue **keeps** himself from calamity.
22: 5 [A] and snares, but *he who* **guards** his soul stays far from them.
22:18 [A] for it is pleasing when *you* **keep** them in your heart and have
27:18 [A] its fruit, and *he who* **looks after** his master will be honored.
28: 4 [A] praise the wicked, but *those who* **keep** the law resist them.
29:18 [A] people cast off restraint; but blessed is he *who* **keeps** the law.
Ecc 3: 6 [A] a time to give up, a time to **keep** and a time to throw away,
5: 1 [4:17] [A] **Guard** your steps when you go to the house of God.
5: 8 [5:7] [A] for one official *is* **eyed** *by* a higher one, and over them
5:13 [5:12] [B] the sun: wealth **hoarded** to the harm of its owner,
8: 2 [A] **Obey** the king's command, I say, because you took an oath
8: 5 [A] *Whoever* **obeys** his command will come to no harm,
11: 4 [A] *Whoever* **watches** the wind will not plant; whoever looks at
12: 3 [A] when the **keepers** *of* the house tremble, and the strong men
12:13 [A] Fear God and **keep** his commandments, for this is the whole
SS 3: 3 [A] The **watchmen** found me as they made their rounds in the
5: 7 [A] The **watchmen** found me as they made their rounds in the
5: 7 [A] they took away my cloak, those **watchmen** *of* the walls!

Isa 7: 4 [C] Say to him, '*Be* **careful**, keep calm and don't be afraid. Do
21:11 [A] calls to me from Seir, "**Watchman**, what is left of the night?
21:11 [A] is left of the night? **Watchman**, what is left of the night?"
21:12 [A] The **watchman** replies, "Morning is coming, but also the
26: 2 [A] the righteous nation may enter, the nation *that* **keeps** faith.
42:20 [A] You have seen many things, but *have* **paid** no **attention**;
56: 1 [A] "**Maintain** justice and do what is right, for my salvation is
56: 2 [A] holds it fast, *who* **keeps** the Sabbath without desecrating it,
56: 2 [A] desecrating it, and **keeps** his hand from doing any evil."
56: 4 [A] "To the eunuchs who **keep** my Sabbaths, who choose what
56: 6 [A] all *who* **keep** the Sabbath without desecrating it and who
62: 6 [A] I have posted **watchmen** on your walls, O Jerusalem;
Jer 3: 5 [A] *Will* your wrath **continue** forever?' This is how you talk, but
4:17 [A] They surround her like *men* **guarding** a field, because she
5:24 [A] in season, *who* **assures** us *of* the regular weeks of harvest.'
8: 7 [A] the swift and the thrush **observe** the time of their migration.
9: 4 [9:3] [C] "**Beware** of your friends; do not trust your brothers.
16:11 [A] worshiped them. They forsook me and *did* not **keep** my law.
17:21 [C] *Be* **careful** not to carry a load on the Sabbath day or bring it
20:10 [A] All my friends *are* **waiting** *for* me to slip, saying,
31:10 [A] gather them and *will* **watch over** his flock like a shepherd.'
35: 4 [A] that of Maaseiah son of Shallum the **doorkeeper** [+6197].
35:18 [A] *have* **followed** all his instructions and have done everything
51:12 [A] the guard, station the **watchmen**, prepare an ambush!
52:24 [A] the priest next in rank and the three **doorkeepers** [+6197].
Eze 11:20 [A] they will follow my decrees and *be* **careful** to keep my laws.
17:14 [A] unable to rise again, surviving only by **keeping** his treaty.
18: 9 [A] He follows my decrees and faithfully **keeps** my laws.
18:19 [A] is just and right and *has been* **careful** to keep all my decrees,
18:21 [A] and **keeps** all my decrees and does what is just and right,
20:18 [A] or **keep** their laws or defile yourselves with their idols.
20:19 [A] follow my decrees and *be* **careful** to keep my laws.
20:21 [A] follow my decrees, *they were* not **careful** to keep my laws—
36:27 [A] you to follow my decrees and *be* **careful** to keep my laws.
37:24 [A] will follow my laws and *be* **careful** to keep my decrees.
40:45 [A] is for the priests *who* **have charge** [+5466] **of** the temple,
40:46 [A] north is for the priests *who* **have charge** [+5466] **of** the altar.
43:11 [A] so that *they may be* **faithful** *to* its design and follow all its
44: 8 [A] Instead of **carrying out** *your* duty in regard to my holy
44: 8 [A] to my holy things, you put *others* **in charge** of my sanctuary.
44:14 [A] them **in charge** *of* the duties of the temple and all the work
44:15 [A] who **faithfully carried out** the duties of my sanctuary when
44:16 [A] near my table to minister before me and **perform** my service.
44:24 [A] *They are to* **keep** my laws and my decrees for all my
48:11 [A] who *were* **faithful** *in* serving me and did not go astray as the
Da 9: 4 [A] *who* **keeps** his covenant of love with all who love him
9: 4 [A] of love with all who love him and **obey** his commands,
Hos 4:10 [A] because they have deserted the LORD to **give** *themselves*
12: 6 [12:7] [A] **maintain** love and justice, and wait for your God
12:12 [12:13] [A] to get a wife, and to pay for her *he* **tended sheep**.
12:13 [12:14] [C] up from Egypt, by a prophet *he* **cared for** *him*.
Am 1:11 [A] raged continually and his fury **flamed unchecked** [+5905],
2: 4 [A] the law of the LORD and *have* not **kept** his decrees,
Jnh 2: 8 [2:9] [D] "*Those who* **cling** *to* worthless idols forfeit the grace
Mic 6:16 [F] *You have* **observed** the statutes of Omri and all the practices
7: 5 [A] Even with her who lies in your embrace *be* **careful** *of* your
Zec 3: 7 [A] 'If you will walk in my ways and **keep** my requirements, then
3: 7 [A] you will govern my house and **have charge of** my courts,
11:11 [A] so the afflicted of the flock who *were* **watching** me knew it
Mal 2: 7 [A] "For the lips of a priest *ought to* **preserve** knowledge,
2: 9 [A] because you *have* not **followed** my ways but have shown
2:15 [C] So **guard yourself** in your spirit, and do not break faith with
2:16 [C] So **guard yourself** in your spirit, and do not break faith.
3: 7 [A] have turned away from my decrees and *have* not **kept** them.
3:14 [A] What did we gain by **carrying out** his requirements

9069 ¹שֶׁמֶר **šemer¹**, n.m. [5] [→ 9070?; cf. 9068]
dregs [3], aged wine [1], wines [1]

Ps 75: 8 [75:9] all the wicked of the earth drink it down to its very **dregs**.
Isa 25: 6 a feast of rich food for all peoples, a banquet of **aged wine**—
25: 6 a banquet of aged wine—the best of meats and the finest of **wines**.
Jer 48:11 "Moab has been at rest from youth, like wine left on its **dregs**,
Zep 1:12 who are like wine left on its **dregs**, who think, 'The LORD will do

9070 ²שֶׁמֶר **šemer²**, n.pr.m. [4 / 3] [√ 9069?]
Shemer [3]

1Ki 16:24 He bought the hill of Samaria from **Shemer** for two talents of
16:24 and built a city on the hill, calling it Samaria, after **Shemer**,
1Ch 6:46 [6:31] the son of Amzi, the son of Bani, the son of **Shemer**,
7:34 The sons of Shomer: [BHS ***Shemer***; NIV 9071] Ahi, Rohgah,

9071 שֹׁמֵר ***šōmēr***, n.pr.m. [2 / 3] [√ 9083]

Shomer [3]

2Ki 12:21 [12:22] Jozabad son of Shimeath and Jehozabad son of **Shomer**.
1Ch 7:32 the father of Japhlet, **Shomer** and Hotham and of their sister Shua.
7:34 The sons of **Shomer**: [BHS 9070] Ahi, Rohgah, Hubbah and

9072 שָׁמְרָה ***šomrâ***, n.f. [1] [√ 9068]

guard [1]

Ps 141: 3 Set a **guard** over my mouth, O LORD; keep watch over the door

9073 שְׁמֻרָה ***šᵉmurâ***, n.f. [1] [√ 9068]

kept from closing [+296] [1]

Ps 77: 4 [77:5] *You* **kept** my eyes **from closing** [+296]; I was too troubled

9074 שִׁמְרוֹן ***šimrôn[1]***, n.pr.loc. [2] [√ 9068]

Shimron [2]

Jos 11: 1 to Jobab king of Madon, to the kings of **Shimron** and Acshaph,
19:15 Included were Kattath, Nahalal, **Shimron**, Idalah and Bethlehem.

9075 שִׁמְרוֹן ***šimrôn[2]***, n.pr.m. [3] [→ 9084]

Shimron [3]

Ge 46:13 The sons of Issachar: Tola, Puah, Jashub and **Shimron**.
Nu 26:24 the Jashubite clan; through **Shimron**, the Shimronite clan.
1Ch 7: 1 sons of Issachar: Tola, Puah, Jashub and **Shimron**—four in all.

9076 שֹׁמְרוֹן ***šōm^{e}rôn***, n.pr.m. [109] [→ 9085; cf. 9068; Ar 10726]

Samaria [105], the city[s] [2], there[s] [+928] [2]

1Ki 13:32 against all the shrines on the high places in the towns of **Samaria**
16:24 He bought the hill of **Samaria** from Shemer for two talents of
16:24 and built a city on the hill, calling it **Samaria**, after Shemer,
16:28 Omri rested with his fathers and was buried in **Samaria**. And Ahab
16:29 of Israel, and he reigned in **Samaria** over Israel twenty-two years.
16:32 up an altar for Baal in the temple of Baal that he built in **Samaria**.
18: 2 present himself to Ahab. Now the famine was severe in **Samaria**,
20: 1 and chariots, he went up and besieged **Samaria** and attacked it.
20:10 if enough dust remains in **Samaria** to give each of my men a
20:17 who reported, "Men are advancing from **Samaria**."
20:34 own market areas in Damascus, as my father did in **Samaria**."
20:43 and angry, the king of Israel went to his palace in **Samaria**.
21: 1 was in Jezreel, close to the palace of Ahab king of **Samaria**.
21:18 "Go down to meet Ahab king of Israel, who rules in **Samaria**.
22:10 at the threshing floor by the entrance of the gate of **Samaria**,
22:37 So the king died and was brought to **Samaria**, and they buried him
22:37 and was brought to Samaria, and they buried him **there**[s] [+928].
22:38 They washed the chariot at a pool in **Samaria** (where the
22:51 [22:52] Ahaziah son of Ahab became king of Israel in **Samaria** in
2Ki 1: 2 had fallen through the lattice of his upper room in **Samaria**
1: 3 "Go up and meet the messengers of the king of **Samaria** and ask
2:25 he went on to Mount Carmel and from there returned to **Samaria**.
3: 1 Joram son of Ahab became king of Israel in **Samaria** in the
3: 6 So at that time King Joram set out from **Samaria** and mobilized all
5: 3 "If only my master would see the prophet who is in **Samaria**!
6:19 you to the man you are looking for." And he led them to **Samaria**.
6:20 After they entered **the city**[s], Elisha said, "LORD, open the eyes
6:20 their eyes and they looked, and there they were, inside **Samaria**.
6:24 his entire army and marched up and laid siege to **Samaria**.
6:25 There was a great famine in **the city**[s]; the siege lasted so long that
7: 1 and two seahs of barley for a shekel at the gate of **Samaria**."
7:18 and two seahs of barley for a shekel at the gate of **Samaria**."
10: 1 Now there were in **Samaria** seventy sons of the house of Ahab.
10: 1 So Jehu wrote letters and sent them to **Samaria**: to the officials of
10:12 Jehu then set out and went toward **Samaria**. At Beth Eked of the
10:17 When Jehu came to **Samaria**, he killed all who were left there of
10:17 he killed all who were left **there**[s] [+928] of Ahab's family;
10:35 Jehu rested with his fathers and was buried in **Samaria**.
10:36 The time that Jehu reigned over Israel in **Samaria** was
13: 1 Jehoahaz son of Jehu became king of Israel in **Samaria**, and he
13: 6 in them. Also, the Asherah pole remained standing in **Samaria**.
13: 9 Jehoahaz rested with his fathers and was buried in **Samaria**.
13:10 Jehoash son of Jehoahaz became king of Israel in **Samaria**,
13:13 the throne. Jehoash was buried in **Samaria** with the kings of Israel.
14:14 the royal palace. He also took hostages and returned to **Samaria**.
14:16 his fathers and was buried in **Samaria** with the kings of Israel.
14:23 Jeroboam son of Jehoash king of Israel became king in **Samaria**,
15: 8 Zechariah son of Jeroboam became king of Israel in **Samaria**,
15:13 of Uzziah king of Judah, and he reigned in **Samaria** one month.
15:14 Then Menahem son of Gadi went from Tirzah up to **Samaria**.
15:14 He attacked Shallum son of Jabesh in **Samaria**, assassinated him
15:17 Gadi became king of Israel, and he reigned in **Samaria** ten years.
15:23 Pekahiah son of Menahem became king of Israel in **Samaria**,
15:25 and Arieh, in the citadel of the royal palace at **Samaria**.
15:27 Pekah son of Remaliah became king of Israel in **Samaria**,
17: 1 Hoshea son of Elah became king of Israel in **Samaria**, and he
17: 5 marched against **Samaria** and laid siege to it for three years.
17: 6 the king of Assyria captured **Samaria** and deported the Israelites to
17:24 and settled them in the towns of **Samaria** to replace the Israelites.
17:24 the Israelites. They took over **Samaria** and lived in its towns.
17:26 resettled in the towns of **Samaria** do not know what the god of that
17:28 So one of the priests who had been exiled from **Samaria** came to
18: 9 Shalmaneser king of Assyria marched against **Samaria** and laid
18:10 So **Samaria** was captured in Hezekiah's sixth year, which was the
18:34 Hena and Ivvah? Have they rescued **Samaria** from my hand?
21:13 out over Jerusalem the measuring line used against **Samaria**
23:18 his bones and those of the prophet who had come from **Samaria**.
23:19 in the towns of **Samaria** that had provoked the LORD to anger.
2Ch 18: 2 Some years later he went down to visit Ahab in **Samaria**.
18: 9 at the threshing floor by the entrance to the gate of **Samaria**,
22: 9 and his men captured him while he was hiding in **Samaria**.
25:13 part in the war raided Judean towns from **Samaria** to Beth Horon.
25:24 the palace treasures and the hostages, and returned to **Samaria**.
28: 8 took a great deal of plunder, which they carried back to **Samaria**.
28: 9 and he went out to meet the army when it returned to **Samaria**.
28:15 countrymen at Jericho, the City of Palms, and returned to **Samaria**.
Ne 4: 2 [3:34] in the presence of his associates and the army of **Samaria**,
Isa 7: 9 The head of Ephraim is **Samaria**, and the head of Samaria is only
7: 9 is Samaria, and the head of **Samaria** is only Remaliah's son.
8: 4 the plunder of **Samaria** will be carried off by the king of Assyria."
9: 9 [9:8] Ephraim and the inhabitants of **Samaria**—who say with
10: 9 Is not Hamath like Arpad, and **Samaria** like Damascus?
10:10 whose images excelled those of Jerusalem and **Samaria**—
10:11 and her images as I dealt with **Samaria** and her idols?' "
36:19 gods of Sepharvaim? Have they rescued **Samaria** from my hand?
Jer 23:13 "Among the prophets of **Samaria** I saw this repulsive thing:
31: 5 Again you will plant vineyards on the hills of **Samaria**;
41: 5 Shiloh and **Samaria**, bringing grain offerings and incense with
Eze 16:46 Your older sister was **Samaria**, who lived to the north of you with
16:51 **Samaria** did not commit half the sins you did. You have done
16:53 of Sodom and her daughters and of **Samaria** and her daughters,
16:55 Sodom with her daughters and **Samaria** with her daughters,
23: 4 and daughters. Oholah is **Samaria**, and Oholibah is Jerusalem.
23:33 the cup of ruin and desolation, the cup of your sister **Samaria**.
Hos 7: 1 sins of Ephraim are exposed and the crimes of **Samaria** revealed.
8: 5 Throw out your calf-idol, O **Samaria**! My anger burns against
8: 6 it is not God. It will be broken in pieces, that calf of **Samaria**.
10: 5 The people who live in **Samaria** fear for the calf-idol of Beth
10: 7 **Samaria** and its king will float away like a twig on the surface of
13:16 [14:1] The people of **Samaria** must bear their guilt, because they
Am 3: 9 "Assemble yourselves on the mountains of **Samaria**; see the great
3:12 those who sit in **Samaria** on the edge of their beds and in
4: 1 Hear this word, you cows of Bashan on Mount **Samaria**,
6: 1 to you who feel secure on Mount **Samaria**, you notable men of the
8:14 They who swear by the shame of **Samaria**, or say, 'As surely as
Ob 1:19 They will occupy the fields of Ephraim and **Samaria**,
Mic 1: 1 of Judah—the vision he saw concerning **Samaria** and Jerusalem.
1: 5 Is it not **Samaria**? What is Judah's high place? Is it not Jerusalem?
1: 6 "Therefore I will make **Samaria** a heap of rubble, a place for

9077 שִׁמְרוֹן מְרֹאוֹן ***šimrôn m^{e}r'ôn***, n.pr.loc. [1] [cf. 5264]

Shimron Meron [1]

Jos 12:20 the king of **Shimron Meron** one the king of Acshaph one

9078 שִׁמְרִי ***šimrî***, n.pr.m. [4] [√ 9068]

Shimri [4]

1Ch 4:37 the son of Allon, the son of Jedaiah, the son of **Shimri**, the son of
11:45 Jediael son of **Shimri**, his brother Joha the Tizite,
26:10 **Shimri** the first (although he was not the firstborn, his father had
2Ch 29:13 from the descendants of Elizaphan, **Shimri** and Jeiel; from the

9079 שְׁמַרְיָה ***š^{e}maryâ***, n.pr.m. [3] [√ 9068 + 3378]

Shemariah [3]

2Ch 11:19 She bore him sons: Jeush, **Shemariah** and Zaham.
Ezr 10:32 Benjamin, Malluch and **Shemariah**.
10:41 Azarel, Shelemiah, **Shemariah**,

9080 שְׁמַרְיָהוּ ***š^{e}maryāhû***, n.pr.m. [1] [√ 9068 + 3378]

Shemariah [1]

1Ch 12: 5 [12:6] **Shemariah** and Shephatiah the Haruphite;

9081 שִׁמֻּרִים šimmurîm, n.[m.pl.]. [2] [√ 9068]
vigil [2]
Ex 12:42 Because the LORD kept **vigil** that night to bring them out of
12:42 on this night all the Israelites are to keep **vigil** to honor the LORD

9082 שְׁמִרִימוֹת š^e^mirîmôt, n.pr.m. Not used in NIV/BHS [cf. 9035]

9083 שִׁמְרִית šimrît, n.pr.f. [1] [→ 9071]
Shimrith [1]
2Ch 24:26 and Jehozabad, son of **Shimrith** a Moabite woman.

9084 שִׁמְרֹנִי šimrōnî, a.g. [1] [√ 9075]
Shimronite [1]
Nu 26:24 the Jashubite clan; through Shimron, the **Shimronite** clan.

9085 שֹׁמְרֹנִי šōm^e^rōnî, a.g. [1] [√ 9076]
people of Samaria [1]
2Ki 17:29 set them up in the shrines the **people of Samaria** had made at the

9086 שִׁמְרָת šimrāt, n.pr.m. [1] [√ 9068]
Shimrath [1]
1Ch 8:21 Adaiah, Beraiah and **Shimrath** were the sons of Shimei.

9087 שֶׁמֶשׁ šemeš, n.f. & m. [135] [→ 1127, 1128, 6539, 6561, 9015, 9088, 9089, 9090; Ar 10728]
sun [102], sunset [+995+2021] [6], east [+2021+4667] [3], sunrise [+4667] [3], east [+2021+2025+4667] [2], east [+4667] [2], sunrise [+2021+2436] [2], sunset [+995+2021+6961] [2], west [+4427] [2], battlements [1], broad daylight [1], east [+928+2025+4667+6298] [1], east [+928+4667+6298] [1], eastern [+4667] [1], in broad daylight [+2021+2021+2296+4200+6524] [1], in broad daylight [+2021+5584] [1], on the west [+2021+4427] [1], sunlight [1], sunrise [+2436] [1], sunshine [1]
Ge 15:12 As the **sun** was setting, Abram fell into a deep sleep, and a thick
15:17 When the **sun** had set and darkness had fallen, a smoking firepot
19:23 By the time Lot reached Zoar, the **sun** had risen over the land.
28:11 a certain place, he stopped for the night because the **sun** had set.
32:31 [32:32] The **sun** rose above him as he passed Peniel, and he was
37: 9 this time the **sun** and moon and eleven stars were bowing down to
Ex 16:21 as much as he needed, and when the **sun** grew hot, it melted away.
17:12 so that his hands remained steady till **sunset** [+995+2021].
22: 3 [22:2] if it happens *after* **sunrise** [+2021+2436], he is guilty of
22:26 [22:25] cloak as a pledge, return it to him by **sunset** [+995+2021],
Lev 22: 7 When the **sun** goes down, he will be clean, and after that he may
Nu 21:11 in the desert that faces Moab toward the **sunrise** [+4667].
25: 4 kill them and expose them in **broad daylight** before the LORD,
Dt 4:19 And when you look up to the sky and see the **sun**, the moon
4:41 set aside three cities **east of** [+928+2025+4667+6298] the Jordan,
4:47 the two Amorite kings **east of** [+928+4667+6298] the Jordan.
11:30 west of the road, toward the setting **sun**, near the great trees of
16: 6 when the **sun** goes down, on the anniversary of your departure
17: 3 bowing down to them or to the **sun** or the moon or the stars of the
23:11 [23:12] and at **sunset** [+995+2021] he may return to the camp.
24:13 Return his cloak to him by **sunset** [+995+2021] so that he may
24:15 Pay him his wages each day before **sunset** [+995+2021], because
33:14 with the best the **sun** brings forth and the finest the moon can
Jos 1: 4 the Hittite country—to the Great Sea **on the west** [+2021+4427].
1:15 LORD gave you east of the Jordan toward the **sunrise** [+4667]."
8:29 At **sunset** [+995+2021], Joshua ordered them to take his body from
10:12 "O **sun**, stand still over Gibeon, O moon, over the Valley of
10:13 So the **sun** stood still, and the moon stopped, till the nation
10:13 The **sun** stopped in the middle of the sky and delayed going down
10:27 At **sunset** [+995+2021+6961] Joshua gave the order and they took
12: 1 whose territory they took over **east of** [+2021+2025+4667] the
13: 5 all Lebanon to the **east** [+2021+4667], from Baal Gad below
19:12 It turned east from Sarid *toward* the **sunrise** [+4667] to the
19:27 It then turned **east** [+2021+4667] toward Beth Dagon, touched
19:34 on the south, Asher on the west and the Jordan on the **east** [+4667].
23: 4 between the Jordan and the Great Sea in the **west** [+4427].
Jdg 5:31 may they who love you be like the **sun** when it rises in its
9:33 In the morning at **sunrise** [+2021+2436], advance against the city.
11:18 passed along the **eastern** [+4667] side of the country of Moab,
19:14 they went on, and the **sun** set as they neared Gibeah in Benjamin.
20:43 easily overran them in the vicinity of Gibeah on the **east** [+4667].
21:19 and **east** [+2021+2025+4667] of the road that goes from Bethel to
1Sa 11: 9 to the men of Jabesh Gilead, 'By the time the **sun** is hot tomorrow,
2Sa 2:24 But Joab and Abishai pursued Abner, and as the **sun** was setting,
3:35 so severely, if I taste bread or anything else before the **sun** sets!"
12:11 your wives **in broad daylight** [+2021+2021+2296+4200+6524].
12:12 I will do this thing **in broad daylight** [+2021+5584] before all
23: 4 he is like the light of morning at **sunrise on** [+2436] a cloudless
1Ki 22:36 As the **sun** was setting, a cry spread through the army: "Every man
2Ki 3:22 they got up early in the morning, the **sun** was shining on the water.
10:33 **east** [+2021+4667] of the Jordan in all the land of Gilead (the
23: 5 to the **sun** and moon, to the constellations and to all the starry
23:11 the horses that the kings of Judah had dedicated to the **sun**.
23:11 then burned the chariots dedicated to the **sun**.
2Ch 18:34 Then at **sunset** [+995+2021+6961] he died.
Ne 7: 3 "The gates of Jerusalem are not to be opened until the **sun** is hot.
Job 8:16 He is like a well-watered plant in the **sunshine**, spreading its
Ps 19: 4 [19:5] the world. In the heavens he has pitched a tent for the **sun**,
50: 1 summons the earth from the rising of the **sun** to the place where it
58: 8 [58:9] like a stillborn child, may they not see the **sun**.
72: 5 He will endure as long as the **sun**, as long as the moon, through all
72:17 May his name endure forever; may it continue as long as the **sun**.
74:16 and yours also the night; you established the **sun** and moon.
84:11 [84:12] For the LORD God is a **sun** and shield; the LORD
89:36 [89:37] and his throne endure before me like the **sun**;
104:19 moon marks off the seasons, and the **sun** knows when to go down.
104:22 The **sun** rises, and they steal away; they return and lie down in
113: 3 From the rising of the **sun** to the place where it sets, the name of
121: 6 the **sun** will not harm you by day, nor the moon by night.
136: 8 the **sun** to govern the day, *His love endures forever.*
148: 3 Praise him, **sun** and moon, praise him, all you shining stars.
Ecc 1: 3 does man gain from all his labor at which he toils under the **sun**?
1: 5 The **sun** rises and the sun sets, and hurries back to where it rises.
1: 5 The sun rises and the **sun** sets, and hurries back to where it rises.
1: 9 been done will be done again; there is nothing new under the **sun**.
1:14 I have seen all the things that are done under the **sun**; all of them
2:11 a chasing after the wind; nothing was gained under the **sun**.
2:17 because the work that is done under the **sun** was grievous to me.
2:18 I hated all the things I had toiled for under the **sun**, because I must
2:19 work into which I have poured my effort and skill under the **sun**.
2:20 heart began to despair over all my toilsome labor under the **sun**.
2:22 the toil and anxious striving with which he labors under the **sun**?
3:16 I saw something else under the **sun**: In the place of judgment—
4: 1 and saw all the oppression that was taking place under the **sun**:
4: 3 not yet been, who has not seen the evil that is done under the **sun**.
4: 7 Again I saw something meaningless under the **sun**:
4:15 that all who lived and walked under the **sun** followed the youth,
5:13 [5:12] I have seen a grievous evil under the **sun**: wealth hoarded
5:18 [5:17] to find satisfaction in his toilsome labor under the **sun**
6: 1 I have seen another evil under the **sun**, and it weighs heavily on
6: 5 Though it never saw the **sun** or knew anything, it has more rest
6:12 Who can tell him what will happen under the **sun** after he is gone?
7:11 an inheritance, is a good thing and benefits those who see the **sun**.
8: 9 this I saw, as I applied my mind to everything done under the **sun**.
8:15 because nothing is better for a man under the **sun** than to eat
8:15 his work all the days of the life God has given him under the **sun**.
8:17 has done. No one can comprehend what goes on under the **sun**.
9: 3 This is the evil in everything that happens under the **sun**: The same
9: 6 again will they have a part in anything that happens under the **sun**.
9: 9 of this meaningless life that God has given you under the **sun**—
9: 9 For this is your lot in life and in your toilsome labor under the **sun**.
9:11 I have seen something else under the **sun**: The race is not to the
9:13 I also saw under the **sun** this example of wisdom that greatly
10: 5 There is an evil I have seen under the **sun**, the sort of error that
11: 7 Light is sweet, and it pleases the eyes to see the **sun**.
12: 2 before the **sun** and the light and the moon and the stars grow dark,
SS 1: 6 stare at me because I am dark, because I am darkened by the **sun**.
Isa 13:10 The rising **sun** will be darkened and the moon will not give its
38: 8 I will make the shadow cast by the **sun** go back the ten steps it has
38: 8 Ahaz.' " So the **sunlight** went back the ten steps it had gone down.
41:25 and he comes—one from the rising **sun** who calls on my name.
45: 6 so that from the rising of the **sun** to the place of its setting men
49:10 nor thirst, nor will the desert heat or the **sun** beat upon them.
54:12 I will make your **battlements** of rubies, your gates of sparkling
59:19 and from the rising of the **sun**, they will revere his glory.
60:19 The **sun** will no more be your light by day, nor will the brightness
60:20 Your **sun** will never set again, and your moon will wane no more;
Jer 8: 2 They will be exposed to the **sun** and the moon and all the stars of
15: 9 Her **sun** will set while it is still day; she will be disgraced
31:35 he who appoints the **sun** to shine by day, who decrees the moon
43:13 There in the temple of the **sun** in Egypt he will demolish the sacred
Eze 8:16 toward the east, they were bowing down to the **sun** in the east.
32: 7 I will cover the **sun** with a cloud, and the moon will not give its
Joel 2:10 the sky trembles, the **sun** and moon are darkened, and the stars no
2:31 [3:4] The **sun** will be turned to darkness and the moon to blood
3:15 [4:15] The **sun** and moon will be darkened, and the stars no
Am 8: 9 "I will make the **sun** go down at noon and darken the earth in
Jnh 4: 8 When the **sun** rose, God provided a scorching east wind,

Jnh 4: 8 and the **sun** blazed on Jonah's head so that he grew faint.
Mic 3: 6 The **sun** will set for the prophets, and the day will go dark for
Na 3: 17 but when the **sun** appears they fly away, and no one knows where.
Hab 3: 11 **Sun** and moon stood still in the heavens at the glint of your flying
Zec 8: 7 my people from the countries of the east and the **west** [+4427].
Mal 1: 11 great among the nations, from the rising to the setting of the **sun**.
4: 2 [3:20] the **sun** *of* righteousness will rise with healing in its wings.

9088 שִׁמְשׁוֹן *šimšôn*, n.pr.m. [38] [√ 9087]

Samson [33], Samson's [3], he[s] [2]

Jdg 13: 24 The woman gave birth to a boy and named him **Samson**. He grew
14: 1 **Samson** went down to Timnah and saw there a young Philistine
14: 3 **Samson** said to his father, "Get her for me. She's the right one for
14: 5 **Samson** went down to Timnah together with his father and mother.
14: 7 Then he went down and talked with the woman, and **he**[s] liked her.
14: 10 **Samson** made a feast there, as was customary for bridegrooms.
14: 12 "Let me tell you a riddle," **Samson** said to them. "If you can give
14: 15 On the fourth day, they said to **Samson's** wife, "Coax your
14: 16 Then **Samson's** wife threw herself on him, sobbing, "You hate me!
14: 20 **Samson's** wife was given to the friend who had attended him at his
15: 1 **Samson** took a young goat and went to visit his wife.
15: 3 **Samson** said to them, "This time I have a right to get even with the
15: 4 So **he**[s] went out and caught three hundred foxes and tied them tail
15: 6 they were told, "**Samson**, the Timnite's son-in-law, because his
15: 7 **Samson** said to them, "Since you've acted like this, I won't stop
15: 10 "We have come to take **Samson** prisoner," they answered,
15: 11 went down to the cave in the rock of Etam and said to **Samson**,
15: 12 **Samson** said, "Swear to me that you won't kill me yourselves."
15: 16 **Samson** said, "With a donkey's jawbone I have made donkeys of
16: 1 One day **Samson** went to Gaza, where he saw a prostitute.
16: 2 The people of Gaza were told, "**Samson** is here!" So they
16: 3 **Samson** lay there only until the middle of the night. Then he got
16: 6 So Delilah said to **Samson**, "Tell me the secret of your great
16: 7 **Samson** answered her, "If anyone ties me with seven fresh thongs
16: 9 she called to him, "**Samson**, the Philistines are upon you!"
16: 10 Then Delilah said to **Samson**, "You have made a fool of me;
16: 12 with men hidden in the room, she called to him, "**Samson**,
16: 13 Delilah then said to **Samson**, "Until now, you have been making a
16: 14 Again she called to him, "**Samson**, the Philistines are upon you!"
16: 20 she called, "**Samson**, the Philistines are upon you!" He awoke
16: 23 saying, "Our god has delivered **Samson**, our enemy, into our
16: 25 in high spirits, they shouted, "Bring out **Samson** to entertain us."
16: 25 So they called **Samson** out of the prison, and he performed for
16: 26 **Samson** said to the servant who held his hand, "Put me where I
16: 27 about three thousand men and women watching **Samson** perform.
16: 28 Then **Samson** prayed to the LORD, "O Sovereign LORD,
16: 29 **Samson** reached toward the two central pillars on which the
16: 30 **Samson** said, "Let me die with the Philistines!" Then he pushed

9089 שִׁמְשַׁי *šimšay*, n.pr.m. [4] [√ 9087; Ar 10729]

Shimshai [4]

Ezr 4: 8 **Shimshai** the secretary wrote a letter against Jerusalem to
4: 9 Rehum the commanding officer and **Shimshai** the secretary,
4: 17 **Shimshai** the secretary and the rest of their associates living in
4: 23 read to Rehum and **Shimshai** the secretary and their associates,

9090 שִׁמְשִׁי *šimšî*, n.pr. *or* a.g. Not used in NIV/BHS [→ 1128; cf. 9087]

9091 שַׁמְשְׁרַי *šamš[e]ray*, n.pr.m. [1]

Shamsherai [1]

1Ch 8: 26 **Shamsherai**, Shehariah, Athaliah,

9092 שֻׁמָתִי *šumātî*, a.g. [1]

Shumathites [1]

1Ch 2: 53 Kiriath Jearim: the Ithrites, Puthites, **Shumathites** and Mishraites.

9093 שָׁן *šan*, n.pr.loc. Not used in NIV/BHS [√ 8632]

9094 שֵׁן¹ *šēn[1]*, n.f. & m. [55 / 56] [→ 9105; cf. 9111; Ar 10730]

teeth [26], ivory [10], tooth [9], *untranslated* [3], cliff [+6152] [1], cliff [1], crag [1], empty stomachs [+5931] [1], fangs [1], feeds [+928+5966] [1], put in jeopardy [+928+1414+5951] [1], three-pronged [+8993] [1]

Ge 49: 12 His eyes will be darker than wine, his **teeth** whiter than milk.
Ex 21: 24 eye for eye, **tooth** for tooth, hand for hand, foot for foot,
21: 24 eye for eye, tooth for **tooth**, hand for hand, foot for foot,
21: 27 And if he knocks out the **tooth** *of* a manservant or maidservant,
21: 27 if he knocks out the tooth of a manservant or **[RPH]** maidservant,
21: 27 he must let the servant go free to compensate for the **tooth**.
Lev 24: 20 fracture for fracture, eye for eye, **tooth** for tooth. As he has injured
24: 20 fracture for fracture, eye for eye, tooth for **tooth**. As he has injured
Nu 11: 33 while the meat was still between their **teeth** and before it could be
Dt 19: 21 life for life, eye for eye, **tooth** for tooth, hand for hand, foot for
19: 21 life for life, eye for eye, tooth for **tooth**, hand for hand, foot for
32: 24 I will send against them the **fangs** *of* wild beasts, the venom of
1Sa 2: 13 priest would come with a **three-pronged** [+8993] fork in his hand.
14: 4 to cross to reach the Philistine outpost was a **cliff** [+6152];
14: 4 was a cliff; **[RPH]** one was called Bozez, and the other Seneh.
14: 5 One **cliff** stood to the north toward Micmash, the other to the south
1Ki 10: 18 the king made a great throne inlaid with **ivory** and overlaid with
22: 39 including all he did, the palace he built and inlaid with **ivory**,
2Ch 9: 17 the king made a great throne inlaid with **ivory** and overlaid with
Job 4: 10 may roar and growl, yet the **teeth** *of* the great lions are broken.
13: 14 Why *do I* **put** myself **in jeopardy** [+928+1414+5951] and take my
16: 9 assails me and tears me in his anger and gnashes his **teeth** at me;
19: 20 and bones; I have escaped with only the skin of my **teeth**.
29: 17 the fangs of the wicked and snatched the victims from their **teeth**.
39: 28 on a cliff and stays there at night; a rocky **crag** is his stronghold.
41: 14 [41:6] doors of his mouth, ringed about with his fearsome **teeth**?
Ps 3: 7 [3:8] all my enemies on the jaw; break the **teeth** *of* the wicked.
35: 16 ungodly they maliciously mocked; they gnashed their **teeth** at me.
37: 12 wicked plot against the righteous and gnash their **teeth** at them;
45: 8 [45:9] from palaces adorned with **ivory** the music of the strings
57: 4 [57:5] men whose **teeth** are spears and arrows, whose tongues are
58: 6 [58:7] Break the **teeth** in their mouths, O God; tear out,
112: 10 will see and be vexed, he will gnash his **teeth** and waste away;
124: 6 Praise be to the LORD, who has not let us be torn by their **teeth**.
Pr 10: 26 As vinegar to the **teeth** and smoke to the eyes, so is a sluggard to
25: 19 Like a bad **tooth** or a lame foot is reliance on the unfaithful in
30: 14 those whose **teeth** are swords and whose jaws are set with knives
SS 4: 2 Your **teeth** are like a flock of sheep just shorn, coming up from the
5: 14 His body is like polished **ivory** decorated with sapphires.
6: 6 Your **teeth** are like a flock of sheep coming up from the washing.
7: 4 [7:5] Your neck is like an **ivory** tower. Your eyes are the pools of
7: 9 [7:10] my lover, flowing gently over lips and **teeth**. [BHS 3825]
Jer 31: 29 have eaten sour grapes, and the children's **teeth** are set on edge.'
31: 30 whoever eats sour grapes—his own **teeth** will be set on edge.
La 2: 16 they scoff and gnash their **teeth** and say, "We have swallowed her
3: 16 He has broken my **teeth** with gravel; he has trampled me in the
Eze 18: 2 fathers eat sour grapes, and the children's **teeth** are set on edge'?
27: 6 from the coasts of Cyprus they made your deck, inlaid with **ivory**.
27: 15 were your customers; they paid you with **ivory** tusks and ebony.
Joel 1: 6 without number; it has the **teeth** *of* a lion, the fangs of a lioness.
1: 6 it has the teeth of **[RPH]** a lion, the fangs of a lioness.
Am 3: 15 the houses adorned with **ivory** will be destroyed and the mansions
4: 6 "I gave you **empty stomachs** [+5931] in every city and lack of
6: 4 You lie on beds inlaid with **ivory** and lounge on your couches.
Mic 3: 5 if one **feeds** [+928+5966] them, they proclaim 'peace';
Zec 9: 7 from their mouths, the forbidden food from between their **teeth**.

9095 שֵׁן² *šēn[2]*, n.pr.loc. [1] [√ 9111]

Shen [1]

1Sa 7: 12 Then Samuel took a stone and set it up between Mizpah and **Shen**.

9096 שָׁנָא *šānā'*, v. [1] [√ 9091?]

dull [1]

La 4: 1 [A] How the gold has lost its luster, the fine gold *become* **dull**!

9097 שֵׁנָא *šēnā'*, n.f. [1] [√ 9104; cf. 3822]

sleep [1]

Ps 127: 2 toiling for food to eat—for he grants **sleep** to those he loves.

9098 שִׁנְאָב *šin'āb*, n.pr.m. [1]

Shinab [1]

Ge 14: 2 Birsha king of Gomorrah, **Shinab** king of Admah, Shemeber king

9099 שִׁנְאָן *šin'ān*, n.[m.] [1] [√ 9091?]

thousands [1]

Ps 68: 17 [68:18] of God are tens of thousands and thousands of **thousands**;

9100 שֶׁנְאַצַּר *šen'aṣṣar*, n.pr.m. [1]

Shenazzar [1]

1Ch 3: 18 **Shenazzar**, Jekamiah, Hoshama and Nedabiah.

9101 [1]שָׁנָה ***šānâ*[1]**, v. [24] [→ 5467, 9096?, 9099?, 9102, 9103, 9106?, 9108, 9109; cf. 9112; Ar 10731]

change [2], different [2], do again [2], pretended to be insane [+906+3248] [2], put aside [2], repeats [2], again [1], alter [1], changes [1], changing [1], deprive [1], did again [1], disguise yourself [1], more [1], moved [1], rebellious [1], strike twice [1], was given [1]

Ge 41:32 [C] The reason the dream **was given** to Pharaoh in two forms is
1Sa 21:13 [21:14] [D] So *he* **pretended** [+906+3248] **to be insane** in their
26: 8 [A] with one thrust of my spear; *I* won't **strike** him **twice**."
2Sa 20:10 [A] Without being stabbed **again**, Amasa died. Then Joab and his
1Ki 14: 2 [F] Jeroboam said to his wife, "Go, **disguise yourself**, so you
18:34 [A] "**Do** *it* **again**," he said, and they did it again. "Do it a third
18:34 [A] "Do it again," he said, and *they* **did** *it* **again**. "Do it a third
2Ki 25:29 [D] So Jehoiachin **put aside** his prison clothes and for the rest of
Ne 13:21 [A] by the wall? If *you* **do** *this* **again**, I will lay hands on you."
Est 1: 7 [A] each one **different** from the other, and the royal wine was
2: 9 [D] **moved** her and her maids into the best place in the harem.
3: 8 [A] whose customs *are* **different** from those of all other people
Job 14:20 [D] he is gone; *you* **change** his countenance and send him away.
29:22 [A] After I had spoken, *they* spoke no **more**; my words fell
Ps 34: T [34:1] [D] When he **pretended** [+906+3248] **to be insane**
89:34 [89:35] [D] my covenant or **alter** what my lips have uttered.
Pr 17: 9 [A] but *whoever* **repeats** the matter separates close friends.
24:21 [A] and the king, my son, and do not join with the **rebellious**,
26:11 [A] As a dog returns to its vomit, so a fool **repeats** his folly.
31: 5 [D] the law decrees, and **deprive** all the oppressed *of* their rights.
Ecc 8: 1 [E] brightens a man's face and **changes** its hard appearance.
Jer 2:36 [D] Why do you go about so much, **changing** your ways?
52:33 [D] So Jehoiachin **put aside** his prison clothes and for the rest of
Mal 3: 6 [A] "I the LORD *do* not **change**. So you, O descendants of

9102 [2]שָׁנָה ***šānâ*[2]**, n.f. [877] [√ 9101; Ar 10732]

years [409], year [303], *untranslated* [100], years [+3427] [8], each year [+928+9102] [6], year-old [+1201] [5], age [+1201] [4], spring [+9588] [3], ages [+1201] [2], annually [+928+2256+3972+9102] [2], due annually [+928+1896+4946+9102] [2], each year [+9102] [2], successive years [+339+9102] [2], them[s] [2], year-old [+1426] [2], yearly [+285+928] [2], age [+1426] [1], ages [1], annual [+285+928+2021] [1], annual [+928+2021+7193] [1], day [1], every spring [+995] [1], full years [+3427] [1], generations long past [+1887+1887+2256] [1], it[s] [1], its[s] [1], length of days [+3427] [1], lives [+3427] [1], many years [+2256+3427] [1], old [+2644+3427] [1], over a year [+196+2296+2296+3427] [1], some years later [+4200+7891] [1], spring [+2021+9588] [1], spring [+6961+9588] [1], this time[s] [+8993] [1], time [1], year [+1821] [1], year's [1], years [+2021+6961] [1]

Ge 1:14 and let them serve as signs to mark seasons and days and **years**,
5: 3 When Adam had lived 130 **years**, he had a son in his own likeness,
5: 4 was born, Adam lived 800 **years** and had other sons and daughters.
5: 5 Altogether, Adam lived 930 **years**, and then he died.
5: 5 Altogether, Adam lived 930 years, **[RPH]** and then he died.
5: 6 When Seth had lived 105 **years**, he became the father of Enosh.
5: 6 Seth had lived 105 years, **[RPH]** he became the father of Enosh.
5: 7 of Enosh, Seth lived 807 **years** and had other sons and daughters.
5: 7 Seth lived 807 years **[RPH]** and had other sons and daughters.
5: 8 Altogether, Seth lived 912 **years**, and then he died.
5: 8 Altogether, Seth lived 912 years, **[RPH]** and then he died.
5: 9 When Enosh had lived 90 **years**, he became the father of Kenan.
5:10 of Kenan, Enosh lived 815 **years** and had other sons and daughters.
5:10 Enosh lived 815 years **[RPH]** and had other sons and daughters.
5:11 Altogether, Enosh lived 905 **years**, and then he died.
5:11 Altogether, Enosh lived 905 years, **[RPH]** and then he died.
5:12 When Kenan had lived 70 **years**, he became the father of
5:13 Kenan lived 840 **years** and had other sons and daughters.
5:13 Kenan lived 840 years **[RPH]** and had other sons and daughters.
5:14 Altogether, Kenan lived 910 **years**, and then he died.
5:14 Altogether, Kenan lived 910 years, **[RPH]** and then he died.
5:15 When Mahalalel had lived 65 **years**, he became the father of Jared.
5:15 had lived 65 years, **[RPH]** he became the father of Jared.
5:16 Mahalalel lived 830 **years** and had other sons and daughters.
5:16 lived 830 years **[RPH]** and had other sons and daughters.
5:17 Altogether, Mahalalel lived 895 **years**, and then he died.
5:17 Altogether, Mahalalel lived 895 years, **[RPH]** and then he died.
5:18 When Jared had lived 162 **years**, he became the father of Enoch.
5:18 Jared had lived 162 years, **[RPH]** he became the father of Enoch.
5:19 of Enoch, Jared lived 800 **years** and had other sons and daughters.
5:20 Altogether, Jared lived 962 **years**, and then he died.
5:20 Altogether, Jared lived 962 years, **[RPH]** and then he died.
5:21 When Enoch had lived 65 **years**, he became the father of
5:22 Enoch walked with God 300 **years** and had other sons
5:23 Altogether, Enoch lived 365 **years**.
5:23 Altogether, Enoch lived 365 years. **[RPH]**
5:25 When Methuselah had lived 187 **years**, he became the father of
5:25 had lived 187 years, **[RPH]** he became the father of Lamech.
5:26 Methuselah lived 782 **years** and had other sons and daughters.
5:26 lived 782 years **[RPH]** and had other sons and daughters.
5:27 Altogether, Methuselah lived 969 **years**, and then he died.
5:27 Altogether, Methuselah lived 969 years, **[RPH]** and then he died.
5:28 When Lamech had lived 182 **years**, he had a son.
5:28 When Lamech had lived 182 years, **[RPH]** he had a son.
5:30 Lamech lived 595 **years** and had other sons and daughters.
5:30 Lamech lived 595 years **[RPH]** and had other sons and daughters.
5:31 Altogether, Lamech lived 777 **years**, and then he died.
5:31 Altogether, Lamech lived 777 years, **[RPH]** and then he died.
5:32 After Noah was 500 **years** old, he became the father of Shem,
6: 3 for he is mortal; his days will be a hundred and twenty **years**."
7: 6 Noah was six hundred **years** old when the floodwaters came on the
7:11 In the six hundredth **year** of Noah's life, on the seventeenth day of
7:11 In the six hundredth year **[RPH]** of Noah's life,
8:13 first day of the first month of Noah's six hundred and first **year**,
9:28 After the flood Noah lived 350 **years**.
9:28 After the flood Noah lived 350 years. **[RPH]**
9:29 Altogether, Noah lived 950 **years**, and then he died.
9:29 Altogether, Noah lived 950 years, **[RPH]** and then he died.
11:10 *Two* **years** after the flood, when Shem was 100 years old,
11:10 Two years after the flood, when Shem was 100 **years** old,
11:11 Shem lived 500 **years** and had other sons and daughters.
11:12 When Arphaxad had lived 35 **years**, he became the father of
11:13 Arphaxad lived 403 **years** and had other sons and daughters.
11:13 lived 403 years **[RPH]** and had other sons and daughters.
11:14 When Shelah had lived 30 **years**, he became the father of Eber.
11:15 Shelah lived 403 **years** and had other sons and daughters.
11:15 Shelah lived 403 years **[RPH]** and had other sons and daughters.
11:16 When Eber had lived 34 **years**, he became the father of Peleg.
11:17 of Peleg, Eber lived 430 **years** and had other sons and daughters.
11:17 Eber lived 430 years **[RPH]** and had other sons and daughters.
11:18 When Peleg had lived 30 **years**, he became the father of Reu.
11:19 of Reu, Peleg lived 209 **years** and had other sons and daughters.
11:19 Peleg lived 209 years **[RPH]** and had other sons and daughters.
11:20 When Reu had lived 32 **years**, he became the father of Serug.
11:21 of Serug, Reu lived 207 **years** and had other sons and daughters.
11:21 Reu lived 207 years **[RPH]** and had other sons and daughters.
11:22 When Serug had lived 30 **years**, he became the father of Nahor.
11:23 of Nahor, Serug lived 200 **years** and had other sons and daughters.
11:24 When Nahor had lived 29 **years**, he became the father of Terah.
11:25 of Terah, Nahor lived 119 **years** and had other sons and daughters.
11:25 Nahor lived 119 years **[RPH]** and had other sons and daughters.
11:26 After Terah had lived 70 **years**, he became the father of Abram,
11:32 Terah lived 205 **years**, and he died in Haran.
11:32 Terah lived 205 years, **[RPH]** and he died in Haran.
12: 4 Abram was seventy-five **years** old when he set out from Haran.
12: 4 Abram was seventy-five years old **[RPH]** when he set out from
14: 4 For twelve **years** they had been subject to Kedorlaomer, but in the
14: 4 subject to Kedorlaomer, but in the thirteenth **year** they rebelled.
14: 5 In the fourteenth **year**, Kedorlaomer and the kings allied with him
15:13 and they will be enslaved and mistreated four hundred **years**.
16: 3 So after Abram had been living in Canaan ten **years**, Sarai his wife
16:16 Abram was eighty-six **years** old when Hagar bore him Ishmael.
16:16 Abram was eighty-six years **[RPH]** old when Hagar bore him
17: 1 When Abram was ninety-nine **years** old, the LORD appeared to
17: 1 When Abram was ninety-nine years **[RPH]** old, the LORD
17:17 said to himself, "Will a son be born to a man a hundred **years** old?
17:17 years old? Will Sarah bear a child *at* the **age of** [+1426] ninety?"
17:21 with Isaac, whom Sarah will bear to you by this time next **year**."
17:24 Abraham was ninety-nine **years** old when he was circumcised,
17:25 and his son Ishmael was thirteen; **[RPH]**
21: 5 Abraham was a hundred **years** old when his son Isaac was born to
23: 1 Sarah lived to be a hundred and twenty-seven **years** *old*.
23: 1 Sarah lived to be a hundred and twenty-seven years old. **[RPH]**
23: 1 Sarah lived to be a hundred and twenty-seven years old. **[RPH]**
23: 1 Sarah lived to be a hundred and twenty-seven years old. **[RPH]**
25: 7 **[RPH]** Abraham lived a hundred and seventy-five years.
25: 7 Altogether, Abraham lived a hundred and seventy-five **years**.
25: 7 Abraham lived a hundred and seventy-five years. **[RPH]**
25: 7 Abraham lived a hundred and seventy-five years. **[RPH]**
25:17 **[RPH]** Ishmael lived a hundred and thirty-seven years.
25:17 Altogether, Ishmael lived a hundred and thirty-seven **years**.
25:17 **[RPH]** He breathed his last and died, and he was gathered to his
25:17 **[RPH]** He breathed his last and died, and he was gathered to his
25:20 Isaac was forty **years** old when he married Rebekah daughter of
25:26 Isaac was sixty **years** old when Rebekah gave birth to them.
26:12 planted crops in that land and the same **year** reaped a hundredfold,
26:34 When Esau was forty **years** old, he married Judith daughter of
29:18 "I'll work for you seven **years** in return for your younger daughter
29:20 So Jacob served seven **years** to get Rachel, but they seemed like
29:27 the younger one also, in return for another seven **years** *of* work."

Ge 29:30 more than Leah. And he worked for Laban another seven **years**.
31:38 "I have been with you for twenty **years** now. Your sheep and goats
31:41 It was like this for the twenty **years** I was in your household.
31:41 I worked for you fourteen **years** for your two daughters and six
31:41 years for your two daughters and six **years** for your flocks,
35:28 Isaac lived a hundred and eighty **years**.
35:28 Isaac lived a hundred and eighty years. **[RPH]**
37: 2 **[NIE]** was tending the flocks with his brothers, the sons of Bilhah
41: 1 When *two* **full years** [+3427] had passed, Pharaoh had a dream:
41:26 The seven good cows are seven **years**, and the seven good heads of
41:26 are seven years, and the seven good heads of grain are seven **years**;
41:27 ugly cows that came up afterward are seven **years**, and so are the
41:27 grain scorched by the east wind: They are seven **years** *of* famine.
41:29 Seven **years** *of* great abundance are coming throughout the land of
41:30 seven **years** *of* famine will follow them. Then all the abundance in
41:34 fifth of the harvest of Egypt during the seven **years** *of* abundance.
41:35 They should collect all the food of these good **years** that are
41:36 to be used during the seven **years** *of* famine that will come upon
41:46 Joseph was thirty **years** old when he entered the service of Pharaoh
41:47 During the seven **years** *of* abundance the land produced
41:48 Joseph collected all the food produced in those seven **years** of
41:50 Before the **years** *of* famine came, two sons were born to Joseph by
41:53 The seven **years** *of* abundance in Egypt came to an end,
41:54 and the seven **years** *of* famine began, just as Joseph had said.
45: 6 *For two* **years** now there has been famine in the land, and for the
45: 6 and *for* the next five **years** there will not be plowing and reaping.
45:11 for you there, because five **years** *of* famine are still to come.
47: 8 Pharaoh asked him, "How **old** [+2644+3427] are you?"
47: 9 "The **years** [+3427] *of* my pilgrimage are a hundred and thirty.
47: 9 **[RPH]** My years have been few and difficult, and they do not
47: 9 My **years** [+3427] have been few and difficult, and they do not
47: 9 they do not equal the **years** [+3427] of the pilgrimage of my
47:17 he brought them through that **year** with food in exchange for all
47:18 When that **year** was over, they came to him the following year
47:18 that year was over, they came to him the following **year** and said,
47:28 Jacob lived in Egypt seventeen **years**, and the years of his life were
47:28 and the **years** [+3427] *of* his life were a hundred and forty-seven.
47:28 and the years of his life were a hundred and forty-seven. **[RPH]**
47:28 and the years of his life were a hundred and forty-seven. **[RPH]**
50:22 with all his father's family. He lived a hundred and ten **years**
50:26 So Joseph died at the **age of** [+1201] a hundred and ten. And after
Ex 6:16 Gershon, Kohath and Merari. Levi **[RPH]** lived 137 years.
6:16 their records: Gershon, Kohath and Merari. Levi lived 137 **years**.
6:18 Izhar, Hebron and Uzziel. Kohath **[RPH]** lived 133 years.
6:18 were Amram, Izhar, Hebron and Uzziel. Kohath lived 133 **years**.
6:20 who bore him Aaron and Moses. Amram **[RPH]** lived 137 years.
6:20 who bore him Aaron and Moses. Amram lived 137 **years**.
7: 7 Moses was eighty **years** old and Aaron eighty-three when they
7: 7 and Aaron eighty-three **[RPH]** when they spoke to Pharaoh.
12: 2 month is to be for you the first month, the first month of your **year**.
12: 5 The animals you choose must be **year-old** [+1201] males without
12:40 length of time the Israelite people lived in Egypt was 430 **years**.
12:40 of time the Israelite people lived in Egypt was 430 years. **[RPH]**
12:41 At the end of the 430 **years**, to the very day, all the LORD's
12:41 At the end of the 430 years, **[RPH]** to the very day, all the
16:35 The Israelites ate manna forty **years**, until they came to a land that
21: 2 "If you buy a Hebrew servant, he is to serve you *for* six **years**.
23:10 "*For* six **years** you are to sow your fields and harvest the crops,
23:14 "Three times a **year** you are to celebrate a festival to me.
23:16 "Celebrate the Feast of Ingathering at the end of the **year**,
23:17 "Three times a **year** all the men are to appear before the Sovereign
23:29 I will not drive them out in a single **year**, because the land would
29:38 are to offer on the altar regularly each day: two lambs a **year** old.
30:10 Once a **year** Aaron shall make atonement on its horns. This annual
30:10 This **annual** [+285+928+2021] atonement must be made with the
30:14 All who cross over, those twenty **years** old or more, are to give an
34:22 wheat harvest, and the Feast of Ingathering at the turn of the **year**.
34:23 Three times a **year** all your men are to appear before the Sovereign
34:24 no one will covet your land when you go up three times each **year**
38:26 to those counted, twenty **years** old or more, a total of 603,550 men.
40:17 was set up on the first day of the first month in the second **year**.
Lev 9: 3 a calf and a lamb—both a **year** old and without defect—
12: 6 the Tent of Meeting a **year-old** [+1201] lamb for a burnt offering
14:10 day he must bring two male lambs and one ewe lamb a **year** old,
16:34 Atonement is to be made once a **year** for all the sins of the
19:23 *For* three **years** you are to consider it forbidden; it must not be
19:24 In the fourth **year** all its fruit will be holy, an offering of praise to
19:25 in the fifth **year** you may eat its fruit. In this way your harvest will
23:12 you must sacrifice as a burnt offering to the LORD a lamb a **year**
23:18 each a **year** old and without defect, one young bull and two rams.
23:19 one male goat for a sin offering and two lambs, each a **year** old,
23:41 Celebrate this as a festival to the LORD for seven days each **year**.
25: 3 *For* six **years** sow your fields, and for six years prune your
25: 3 and *for* six **years** prune your vineyards and gather their crops.
25: 4 But in the seventh **year** the land is to have a sabbath of rest,
25: 5 grapes of your untended vines. The land is to have a **year** *of* rest.
25: 8 " 'Count off seven sabbaths of **years**—seven times seven years—
25: 8 " 'Count off seven sabbaths of years—seven times seven **years**—
25: 8 so that the seven sabbaths of **years** amount to a period of
25: 8 the seven sabbaths of years amount to a period of forty-nine **years**.
25:10 Consecrate the fiftieth **year** and proclaim liberty throughout the
25:10 **[RPH]** and proclaim liberty throughout the land to all its
25:11 The fiftieth **year** shall be a jubilee for you; do not sow and do not
25:11 The fiftieth year **[RPH]** shall be a jubilee for you; do not sow
25:13 " 'In this **Year** *of* Jubilee everyone is to return to his own property.
25:15 countryman on the basis of the number of **years** since the Jubilee.
25:15 he is to sell to you on the basis of the number of **years** *left for*
25:16 When the **years** are many, you are to increase the price, and when
25:16 you are to increase the price, and when the **years** are few,
25:20 "What will we eat in the seventh **year** if we do not plant or harvest
25:21 I will send you such a blessing in the sixth **year** that the land will
25:21 in the sixth year that the land will yield enough for three **years**.
25:22 While you plant during the eighth **year**, you will eat from the old
25:22 will continue to eat from it until the harvest of the ninth **year**
25:27 he is to determine the value for the **years** *since* he sold it
25:28 will remain in the possession of the buyer until the **Year** *of* Jubilee.
25:29 he retains the right of redemption a full **year** after its sale.
25:30 If it is not redeemed before a full **year** has passed, the house in the
25:40 among you; he is to work for you until the **Year** *of* Jubilee.
25:50 his buyer are to count the time from the **year** he sold himself up to
25:50 the time from the year he sold himself up to the **Year** *of* Jubilee.
25:50 be based on the rate paid to a hired man for that number of **years**.
25:51 If many **years** remain, he must pay for his redemption a larger
25:52 If only a few **years** remain until the Year of Jubilee, he is to
25:52 If only a few years remain until the **Year** *of* Jubilee, he is to
25:52 to compute that and pay for his redemption accordingly. **[RPH]**
25:53 He is to be treated as a man hired from **year** to year; you must see
25:53 He is to be treated as a man hired from year to **year**; you must see
25:54 he and his children are to be released in the **Year** *of* Jubilee,
27: 3 set the value of a male between the **ages** [+1201] *of* twenty
27: 3 the ages of twenty and **[RPH]** sixty at fifty shekels of silver,
27: 5 If it is a person between the **ages** [+1201] *of* five and twenty,
27: 5 If it is a person between the ages of five and **[RPH]** twenty,
27: 6 If it is a person between one month and five **years**, set the value of
27: 7 If it is a person sixty **years** old or more, set the value of a male at
27:17 If he dedicates his field during the **Year** *of* Jubilee, the value that
27:18 to the number of **years** that remain until the next Year of Jubilee,
27:18 to the number of years that remain until the next **Year** *of* Jubilee,
27:23 the priest will determine its value up to the **Year** *of* Jubilee,
27:24 In the **Year** *of* Jubilee the field will revert to the person from
Nu 1: 1 month of the second **year** after the Israelites came out of Egypt.
1: 3 to number by their divisions all the men in Israel twenty **years** old
1:18 and the men twenty **years** old or more were listed by name,
1:20 All the men twenty **years** old or more who were able to serve in
1:22 All the men twenty **years** old or more who were able to serve in
1:24 All the men twenty **years** old or more who were able to serve in
1:26 All the men twenty **years** old or more who were able to serve in
1:28 All the men twenty **years** old or more who were able to serve in
1:30 All the men twenty **years** old or more who were able to serve in
1:32 All the men twenty **years** old or more who were able to serve in
1:34 All the men twenty **years** old or more who were able to serve in
1:36 All the men twenty **years** old or more who were able to serve in
1:38 All the men twenty **years** old or more who were able to serve in
1:40 All the men twenty **years** old or more who were able to serve in
1:42 All the men twenty **years** old or more who were able to serve in
1:45 All the Israelites twenty **years** old or more who were able to serve
4: 3 Count all the men from thirty to fifty **years** of age who come to
4: 3 Count all the men from thirty to fifty years of age **[RPH]** who
4:23 Count all the men from thirty to fifty **years** of age who come to
4:23 Count all the men from thirty to fifty years of age **[RPH]** who
4:30 Count all the men from thirty to fifty **years** of age who come to
4:30 Count all the men from thirty to fifty years of age **[RPH]** who
4:35 All the men from thirty to fifty **years** of age who came to serve in
4:35 All the men from thirty to fifty years of age **[RPH]** who came to
4:39 All the men from thirty to fifty **years** of age who came to serve in
4:39 All the men from thirty to fifty years of age **[RPH]** who came to
4:43 All the men from thirty to fifty **years** of age who came to serve in
4:43 All the men from thirty to fifty years of age **[RPH]** who came to
4:47 All the men from thirty to fifty **years** of age who came to do the
4:47 All the men from thirty to fifty years of age **[RPH]** who came to
6:12 and must bring a **year-old** [+1201] male lamb as a guilt offering.
6:14 a **year-old** [+1201] male lamb without defect for a burnt offering,
6:14 a **year-old** [+1426] ewe lamb without defect for a sin offering,
7:15 one young bull, one ram and one male lamb a **year** old, for a burnt
7:17 five rams, five male goats and five male lambs a **year** old,
7:21 one young bull, one ram and one male lamb a **year** old, for a burnt
7:23 five rams, five male goats and five male lambs a **year** old,
7:27 one young bull, one ram and one male lamb a **year** old, for a burnt

Nu 7:29 five rams, five male goats and five male lambs a **year** old,
7:33 one young bull, one ram and one male lamb a **year** old, for a burnt
7:35 five rams, five male goats and five male lambs a **year** old,
7:39 one young bull, one ram and one male lamb a **year** old, for a burnt
7:41 five rams, five male goats and five male lambs a **year** old,
7:45 one young bull, one ram and one male lamb a **year** old, for a burnt
7:47 five rams, five male goats and five male lambs a **year** old,
7:51 one young bull, one ram and one male lamb a **year** old, for a burnt
7:53 five rams, five male goats and five male lambs a **year** old,
7:57 one young bull, one ram and one male lamb a **year** old, for a burnt
7:59 five rams, five male goats and five male lambs a **year** old,
7:63 one young bull, one ram and one male lamb a **year** old, for a burnt
7:65 five rams, five male goats and five male lambs a **year** old,
7:69 one young bull, one ram and one male lamb a **year** old, for a burnt
7:71 five rams, five male goats and five male lambs a **year** old,
7:75 one young bull, one ram and one male lamb a **year** old, for a burnt
7:77 five rams, five male goats and five male lambs a **year** old,
7:81 one young bull, one ram and one male lamb a **year** old, for a burnt
7:83 five rams, five male goats and five male lambs a **year** old,
7:87 twelve rams and twelve male lambs a **year** old, together with their
7:88 sixty rams, sixty male goats and sixty male lambs a **year** old.
8:24 Men twenty-five **years** old or more shall come to take part in the
8:25 **[RPH]** they must retire from their regular service and work no
9:1 in the first month of the second **year** after they came out of Egypt.
10:11 On the twentieth day of the second month of the second **year**,
13:22 (Hebron had been built seven **years** before Zoan in Egypt.)
14:29 every one of you twenty **years** old or more who was counted in the
14:33 Your children will be shepherds here *for* forty **years**, suffering for
14:34 *For* forty **years**—one year for each of the forty days you explored
14:34 one **year** for each of the forty days you explored the land—
14:34 one year for each of the **[RPH]** forty days you explored the land—
15:27 he must bring a **year-old** [+1426] *female* goat for a sin offering.
26:2 all those twenty **years** old or more who are able to serve in the
26:4 "Take a census of the men twenty **years** old or more, as the
28:3 two lambs a **year** old without defect, as a regular burnt offering
28:9 make an offering of two lambs a **year** old without defect,
28:11 one ram and seven male lambs a **year** old, all without defect.
28:14 burnt offering to be made at each new moon during the **year**.
28:19 one ram and seven male lambs a **year** old, all without defect.
28:27 seven male lambs a **year** old as an aroma pleasing to the LORD.
29:2 one ram and seven male lambs a **year** old, all without defect.
29:8 one ram and seven male lambs a **year** old, all without defect.
29:13 two rams and fourteen male lambs a **year** old, all without defect.
29:17 two rams and fourteen male lambs a **year** old, all without defect.
29:20 two rams and fourteen male lambs a **year** old, all without defect.
29:23 two rams and fourteen male lambs a **year** old, all without defect.
29:26 two rams and fourteen male lambs a **year** old, all without defect.
29:29 two rams and fourteen male lambs a **year** old, all without defect.
29:32 two rams and fourteen male lambs a **year** old, all without defect.
29:36 one ram and seven male lambs a **year** old, all without defect.
32:11 not one of the men twenty **years** old or more who came up out of
32:13 against Israel and he made them wander in the desert forty **years**,
33:38 he died on the first day of the fifth month of the fortieth **year**
33:39 a hundred and twenty-three **years** old when he died on Mount Hor.
Dt 1:3 In the fortieth **year**, on the first day of the eleventh month,
2:7 These forty **years** the LORD your God has been with you,
2:14 Thirty-eight **years** passed from the time we left Kadesh Barnea
8:2 your God led you all the way in the desert these forty **years**,
8:4 not wear out and your feet did not swell *during* these forty **years**.
11:12 God are continually on it from the beginning of the **year** to its end.
11:12 are continually on it from the beginning of the year to **its**[s] end.
14:22 set aside a tenth of all that your fields produce **each year** [+9102].
14:22 set aside a tenth of all that your fields produce **each year** [+9102].
14:28 At the end of every three **years**, bring all the tithes of that year's
14:28 bring all the tithes of that **year's** produce and store it in your
15:1 At the end of every seven **years** you must cancel debts.
15:9 "The seventh **year**, the year for canceling debts, is near," so that
15:9 "The seventh year, the **year** *for* canceling debts, is near," so that
15:12 or a woman, sells himself to you and serves you six **years**,
15:12 serves you six years, in the seventh **year** you must let him go free.
15:18 because his service to you these six **years** has been worth twice as
15:20 **Each year** [+928+9102] you and your family are to eat them in the
15:20 **Each year** [+928+9102] you and your family are to eat them in the
16:16 Three times a **year** all your men must appear before the LORD
24:5 *For* one **year** he is to be free to stay at home and bring happiness
26:12 finished setting aside a tenth of all your produce in the third **year**,
26:12 the **year** *of* the tithe, you shall give it to the Levite, the alien,
29:5 [29:4] *During* the forty **years** that I led you through the desert,
31:2 "I am now a hundred and twenty **years** old and I am no longer able
31:10 "At the end of every seven **years**, in the year for canceling debts,
31:10 in the **year** *for* canceling debts, during the Feast of Tabernacles,
32:7 of old; consider the **generations long past** [+1887+1887+2256].
34:7 Moses was a hundred and twenty **years** old when he died,
Jos 5:6 The Israelites had moved about in the desert forty **years** until all
5:12 for the Israelites, but that **year** they ate of the produce of Canaan.
14:7 I was forty **years** old when Moses the servant of the LORD sent
14:10 he has kept me alive *for* forty-five **years** since the time he said this
14:10 about in the desert. So here I am today, eighty-five **years** old!
24:29 of the LORD, died at the **age of** [+1201] a hundred and ten.
Jdg 2:8 of the LORD, died at the **age of** [+1201] a hundred and ten.
3:8 to whom the Israelites were subject *for* eight **years**.
3:11 So the land had peace *for* forty **years**, until Othniel son of Kenaz
3:14 Israelites were subject to Eglon king of Moab *for* eighteen **years**.
3:30 made subject to Israel, and the land had peace *for* eighty **years**.
4:3 and had cruelly oppressed the Israelites *for* twenty **years**,
5:31 when it rises in its strength." Then the land had peace forty **years**.
6:1 and *for* seven **years** he gave them into the hands of the Midianites.
6:25 the second bull from your father's herd, the one seven **years** old.
8:28 During Gideon's lifetime, the land enjoyed peace forty **years**.
9:22 After Abimelech had governed Israel three **years**,
10:2 He led Israel twenty-three **years**; then he died, and was buried in
10:3 was followed by Jair of Gilead, who led Israel twenty-two **years**.
10:8 who that **year** shattered and crushed them. For eighteen years they
10:8 *For* eighteen **years** they oppressed all the Israelites on the east side
11:26 *For* three hundred **years** Israel occupied Heshbon, Aroer,
11:40 that each year the young women of **[NIE]** Israel go out for four
12:7 Jephthah led Israel six **years**. Then Jephthah the Gileadite died,
12:9 as wives from outside his clan. Ibzan led Israel seven **years**.
12:11 After him, Elon the Zebulunite led Israel ten **years**.
12:14 who rode on seventy donkeys. He led Israel eight **years**.
13:1 delivered them into the hands of the Philistines *for* forty **years**.
15:20 Samson led Israel *for* twenty **years** in the days of the Philistines.
16:31 in the tomb of Manoah his father. He had led Israel twenty **years**.
Ru 1:4 and the other Ruth. After they had lived there about ten **years**,
1Sa 1:7 This went on **year** after year. Whenever Hannah went up to the
1:7 This went on year after **year**. Whenever Hannah went up to the
4:15 who was ninety-eight **years** old and whose eyes were set so that he
4:18 for he was an old man and heavy. He had led Israel forty **years**.
7:2 It was a long time, twenty **years** in all, that the ark remained at
7:16 From **year** to year he went on a circuit from Bethel to Gilgal to
7:16 From year to **year** he went on a circuit from Bethel to Gilgal to
13:1 Saul was ⌞thirty⌟ **years** old when he became king, and he reigned
13:1 he became king, and he reigned over Israel ⌞forty-⌟two **years**.
29:3 already been with me for **over a year** [+196+2296+2296+3427],
2Sa 2:10 Ish-Bosheth son of Saul was forty **years** old when he became king
2:10 old when he became king over Israel, and he reigned two **years**.
2:11 was king in Hebron over the house of Judah was seven **years**
4:4 He was five **years** old when the news about Saul and Jonathan
5:4 David was thirty **years** old when he became king, and he reigned
5:4 thirty years old when he became king, and he reigned forty **years**.
5:5 In Hebron he reigned over Judah seven **years** and six months,
5:5 in Jerusalem he reigned over all Israel and Judah thirty-three **years**.
11:1 In the **spring** [+9588], at the time when kings go off to war,
13:23 *Two* **years** [+3427] later, when Absalom's sheepshearers were at
13:38 Absalom fled and went to Geshur, he stayed there three **years**.
14:28 Absalom lived *two* **years** [+3427] in Jerusalem without seeing the
15:7 At the end of four **years**, Absalom said to the king, "Let me go to
19:32 [19:33] Now Barzillai was a very old man, eighty **years** of age.
19:34 [19:35] answered the king, "How many more **years** will I live,
19:35 [19:36] I am now eighty **years** old. Can I tell the difference
21:1 there was a famine *for* three **successive years** [+339+9102];
21:1 there was a famine *for* three **successive years** [+339+9102];
21:1 successive years; **[RPH]** so David sought the face of the LORD.
24:13 "Shall there come upon you three **years** of famine in your land?
1Ki 2:11 He had reigned forty **years** over Israel—seven years in Hebron
2:11 over Israel—seven **years** in Hebron and thirty-three in Jerusalem.
2:11 seven years in Hebron and thirty-three **[RPH]** in Jerusalem.
2:39 three **years** later, two of Shimei's slaves ran off to Achish son of
4:7 Each one had to provide supplies for one month in the **year**.
5:11 [5:25] Solomon continued to do this for Hiram **year** after year.
5:11 [5:25] Solomon continued to do this for Hiram year after **year**.
6:1 **[RPH]** and eightieth year after the Israelites had come out of
6:1 and eightieth **year** after the Israelites had come out of Egypt,
6:1 in the fourth **year** of Solomon's reign over Israel, in the month of
6:37 foundation of the temple of the LORD was laid in the fourth **year**,
6:38 In the eleventh **year** in the month of Bul, the eighth month,
6:38 to its specifications. He had spent seven **years** building it.
7:1 It took Solomon thirteen **years**, however, to complete the
9:10 At the end of twenty **years**, during which Solomon built these two
9:25 Three times a **year** Solomon sacrificed burnt offerings
10:14 The weight of the gold that Solomon received **yearly** [+285+928]
10:22 Once every three **years** it returned, carrying gold, silver and ivory,
10:25 **Year** after year, everyone who came brought a gift—articles of
10:25 Year after **year**, everyone who came brought a gift—articles of
11:42 Solomon reigned in Jerusalem over all Israel forty **years**.
14:20 He reigned *for* twenty-two **years** and then rested with his fathers.
14:21 He was forty-one **years** old when he became king, and he reigned
14:21 he became king, and he reigned seventeen **years** in Jerusalem,

1Ki 14:25 In the fifth **year** of King Rehoboam, Shishak king of Egypt
15: 1 In the eighteenth **year** of the reign of Jeroboam son of Nebat,
15: 2 he reigned in Jerusalem three **years**. His mother's name was
15: 9 In the twentieth **year** of Jeroboam king of Israel, Asa became king
15:10 he reigned in Jerusalem forty-one **years**. His grandmother's name
15:25 Nadab son of Jeroboam became king of Israel in the second **year**
15:25 year of Asa king of Judah, and he reigned over Israel *two* **years**.
15:28 Baasha killed Nadab in the third **year** of Asa king of Judah
15:33 In the third **year** of Asa king of Judah, Baasha son of Ahijah
15:33 king of all Israel in Tirzah, and he reigned twenty-four **years**.
16: 8 In the twenty-sixth **year** of Asa king of Judah, Elah son of B aasha
16: 8 In the twenty-sixth year **[RPH]** of Asa king of Judah, Elah son of
16: 8 Baasha became king of Israel, and he reigned in Tirzah *two* **years**.
16:10 and killed him in the twenty-seventh **year** of Asa king of Judah.
16:15 In the twenty-seventh **year** of Asa king of Judah, Zimri reigned in
16:15 In the twenty-seventh year of **[RPH]** Asa king of Judah,
16:23 In the thirty-first **year** of Asa king of Judah, Omri became king of
16:23 In the thirty-first year **[RPH]** of Asa king of Judah, Omri became
16:23 king of Israel, and he reigned twelve **years**, six of them in Tirzah.
16:23 king of Israel, and he reigned twelve years, six of **them**[s] in Tirzah.
16:29 In the thirty-eighth **year** of Asa king of Judah, Ahab son of Omri
16:29 In the thirty-eighth year of **[RPH]** Asa king of Judah, Ahab son of
16:29 of Israel, and he reigned in Samaria over Israel twenty-two **years**.
17: 1 there will be neither dew nor rain *in* the next few **years** except at
18: 1 After a long time, in the third **year**, the word of the LORD came
20:22 because next **spring** [+2021+9588] the king of Aram will attack
20:26 The next **spring** [+9588] Ben-Hadad mustered the Arameans
22: 1 *For* three **years** there was no war between Aram and Israel.
22: 2 in the third **year** Jehoshaphat king of Judah went down to see the
22:41 Jehoshaphat son of Asa became king of Judah in the fourth **year** of
22:42 Jehoshaphat was thirty-five **years** old when he became king,
22:42 he became king, and he reigned in Jerusalem twenty-five **years**.
22:51 [22:52] in the seventeenth **year** of Jehoshaphat king of Judah,
22:51 [22:52] king of Judah, and he reigned over Israel *two* **years**.
2Ki 1:17 Joram succeeded him as king in the second **year** of Jehoram son of
3: 1 in Samaria in the eighteenth **year** of Jehoshaphat king of Judah,
3: 1 year of Jehoshaphat king of Judah, and he reigned twelve **years**.
8: 1 has decreed a famine in the land that will last seven **years**."
8: 2 went away and stayed in the land of the Philistines seven **years**.
8: 3 At the end of the seven **years** she came back from the land of the
8:16 In the fifth **year** of Joram son of Ahab king of Israel,
8:17 He was thirty-two **years** old when he became king, and he reigned
8:17 old when he became king, and he reigned in Jerusalem eight **years**.
8:25 In the twelfth **year** of Joram son of Ahab king of Israel,
8:25 In the twelfth year **[RPH]** of Joram son of Ahab king of Israel,
8:26 Ahaziah was twenty-two **years** old when he became king,
8:26 old when he became king, and he reigned in Jerusalem one **year**.
9:29 (In the eleventh **year** of Joram son of Ahab, Ahaziah had become
9:29 (In the eleventh year **[RPH]** of Joram son of Ahab, Ahaziah had
10:36 that Jehu reigned over Israel in Samaria was twenty-eight **years**.
11: 3 temple of the LORD *for* six **years** while Athaliah ruled the land.
11: 4 In the seventh **year** Jehoiada sent for the commanders of units of a
11:21 [12:1] Joash was seven **years** old when he began to reign.
12: 1 [12:2] In the seventh **year** of Jehu, Joash became king, and he
12: 1 [12:2] became king, and he reigned in Jerusalem forty **years**.
12: 6 [12:7] by the twenty-third **year** of King Joash the priests still had
12: 6 [12:7] by the twenty-third year **[RPH]** of King Joash the priests
13: 1 In the twenty-third **year** of Joash son of Ahaziah king of Judah,
13: 1 In the twenty-third year **[RPH]** of Joash son of Ahaziah king of
13: 1 became king of Israel in Samaria, and he reigned seventeen **years**.
13:10 In the thirty-seventh **year** of Joash king of Judah, Jehoash son of
13:10 In the thirty-seventh year **[RPH]** of Joash king of Judah,
13:10 became king of Israel in Samaria, and he reigned sixteen **years**.
13:20 Moabite raiders used to enter the country **every spring** [+995].
14: 1 In the second **year** of Jehoash son of Jehoahaz king of Israel,
14: 2 He was twenty-five **years** old when he became king, and he
14: 2 he became king, and he reigned in Jerusalem twenty-nine **years**.
14:17 Amaziah son of Joash king of Judah lived *for* fifteen **years** after
14:21 all the people of Judah took Azariah, who was sixteen **years** old,
14:23 In the fifteenth **year** of Amaziah son of Joash king of Judah,
14:23 In the fifteenth year **[RPH]** of Amaziah son of Joash king of
14:23 of Israel became king in Samaria, and he reigned forty-one **years**.
15: 1 In the twenty-seventh **year** of Jeroboam king of Israel, Azariah son
15: 1 In the twenty-seventh year **[RPH]** of Jeroboam king of Israel,
15: 2 He was sixteen **years** old when he became king, and he reigned in
15: 2 when he became king, and he reigned in Jerusalem fifty-two **years**.
15: 8 In the thirty-eighth **year** of Azariah king of Judah, Zechariah son
15: 8 In the thirty-eighth year **[RPH]** of Azariah king of Judah,
15:13 Shallum son of Jabesh became king in the thirty-ninth **year** of
15:13 king in the thirty-ninth year **[RPH]** of Uzziah king of Judah,
15:17 In the thirty-ninth **year** of Azariah king of Judah, Menahem son of
15:17 In the thirty-ninth year **[RPH]** of Azariah king of Judah,
15:17 Gadi became king of Israel, and he reigned in Samaria ten **years**.
15:23 In the fiftieth **year** of Azariah king of Judah, Pekahiah son of
15:23 In the fiftieth year **[RPH]** of Azariah king of Judah, Pekahiah son
15:23 became king of Israel in Samaria, and he reigned *two* **years**.
15:27 In the fifty-second **year** of Azariah king of Judah, Pekah son of
15:27 In the fifty-second year **[RPH]** of Azariah king of Judah,
15:27 became king of Israel in Samaria, and he reigned twenty **years**.
15:30 succeeded him as king in the twentieth **year** of Jotham son of
15:32 In the second **year** of Pekah son of Remaliah king of Israel,
15:33 He was twenty-five **years** old when he became king, and he
15:33 when he became king, and he reigned in Jerusalem sixteen **years**.
16: 1 In the seventeenth **year** of Pekah son of Remaliah, Ahaz son of
16: 1 In the seventeenth year **[RPH]** of Pekah son of Remaliah,
16: 2 Ahaz was twenty **years** old when he became king, and he reigned
16: 2 when he became king, and he reigned in Jerusalem sixteen **years**.
17: 1 In the twelfth **year** of Ahaz king of Judah, Hoshea son of Elah
17: 1 Elah became king of Israel in Samaria, and he reigned nine **years**.
17: 4 paid tribute to the king of Assyria, as he had done **year** by year.
17: 4 paid tribute to the king of Assyria, as he had done year by **year**.
17: 5 marched against Samaria and laid siege to it *for* three **years**.
17: 6 In the ninth **year** of Hoshea, the king of Assyria captured Samaria
18: 1 In the third **year** of Hoshea son of Elah king of Israel,
18: 2 He was twenty-five **years** old when he became king, and he
18: 2 he became king, and he reigned in Jerusalem twenty-nine **years**.
18: 9 In King Hezekiah's fourth **year**, which was the seventh year of
18: 9 which was the seventh **year** of Hoshea son of Elah king of Israel,
18:10 At the end of three **years** the Assyrians took it. So Samaria was
18:10 So Samaria was captured in Hezekiah's sixth **year**, which was the
18:10 sixth year, which was the ninth **year** of Hoshea king of Israel.
18:13 In the fourteenth **year** of King Hezekiah's reign, Sennacherib king
19:29 "This **year** you will eat what grows by itself, and the second year
19:29 what grows by itself, and the second **year** what springs from that.
19:29 in the third **year** sow and reap, plant vineyards and eat their fruit.
20: 6 I will add fifteen **years** to your life. And I will deliver you
21: 1 Manasseh was twelve **years** old when he became king, and he
21: 1 when he became king, and he reigned in Jerusalem fifty-five **years**.
21:19 Amon was twenty-two **years** old when he became king, and he
21:19 old when he became king, and he reigned in Jerusalem two **years**.
22: 1 Josiah was eight **years** old when he became king, and he reigned in
22: 1 he became king, and he reigned in Jerusalem thirty-one **years**.
22: 3 In the eighteenth **year** of his reign, King Josiah sent the secretary,
23:23 in the eighteenth **year** of King Josiah, this Passover was celebrated
23:31 Jehoahaz was twenty-three **years** old when he became king,
23:36 Jehoiakim was twenty-five **years** old when he became king,
23:36 when he became king, and he reigned in Jerusalem eleven **years**.
24: 1 invaded the land, and Jehoiakim became his vassal *for* three **years**.
24: 8 Jehoiachin was eighteen **years** old when he became king, and he
24:12 In the eighth **year** of the reign of the king of Babylon, he took
24:18 Zedekiah was twenty-one **years** old when he became king,
24:18 when he became king, and he reigned in Jerusalem eleven **years**.
25: 1 So in the ninth **year** of Zedekiah's reign, on the tenth day of the
25: 2 The city was kept under siege until the eleventh **year** of King
25: 8 in the nineteenth **year** of Nebuchadnezzar king of Babylon,
25: 8 in the nineteenth year **[RPH]** of Nebuchadnezzar king of
25:27 In the thirty-seventh **year** of the exile of Jehoiachin king of Judah,
25:27 king of Judah, in the **year** Evil-Merodach became king of Babylon,
1Ch 2:21 father of Gilead (he had married her when he was sixty **years** old),
3: 4 to David in Hebron, where he reigned seven **years** and six months.
3: 4 and six months. David reigned in Jerusalem thirty-three **years**,
20: 1 In the **spring** [+6961+9588], at the time when kings go off to war,
21:12 three **years** of famine, three months of being swept away before
23: 3 The Levites thirty **years** old or more were counted, and the total
23:24 the workers twenty **years** old or more who served in the temple of
23:27 the Levites were counted from those twenty **years** old or more.
26:31 In the fortieth **year** of David's reign a search was made in the
27: 1 divisions that were on duty month by month throughout the **year**.
27:23 David did not take the number of the men twenty **years** old
29:27 He ruled over Israel forty **years**—seven in Hebron and thirty-three
29:27 seven **[RPH]** in Hebron and thirty-three in Jerusalem.
2Ch 3: 2 the second day of the second month in the fourth **year** of his reign.
8: 1 At the end of twenty **years**, during which Solomon built the temple
8:13 New Moons and the three **annual** [+928+2021+7193] feasts—
9:13 The weight of the gold that Solomon received **yearly** [+285+928]
9:21 Once every three **years** it returned, carrying gold, silver and ivory,
9:24 **Year** [+1821] after year, everyone who came brought a gift—
9:24 Year after **year**, everyone who came brought a gift—articles of
9:30 Solomon reigned in Jerusalem over all Israel forty **years**.
11:17 of Judah and supported Rehoboam son of Solomon three **years**,
11:17 in the ways of David and Solomon during **this time**[s] [+8993].
12: 2 Shishak king of Egypt attacked Jerusalem in the fifth **year** of King
12:13 He was forty-one **years** old when he became king, and he reigned
12:13 he became king, and he reigned seventeen **years** in Jerusalem,
13: 1 In the eighteenth **year** of the reign of Jeroboam, Abijah became
13: 2 he reigned in Jerusalem three **years**. His mother's name was
14: 1 [13:23] and in his days the country was at peace *for* ten **years**.
14: 6 [14:5] No one was at war with him during those **years**,

2Ch 15:10 at Jerusalem in the third month of the fifteenth **year** of Asa's reign.
15:19 There was no more war until the thirty-fifth **year** of Asa's reign.
16: 1 In the thirty-sixth **year** of Asa's reign Baasha king of Israel went
16:12 In the thirty-ninth **year** of his reign Asa was afflicted with a
16:13 in the forty-first **year** *of* his reign Asa died and rested with his
17: 7 In the third **year** of his reign he sent his officials Ben-Hail,
18: 2 **Some years** [+4200+7891] **later** he went down to visit Ahab in
20:31 He was thirty-five **years** old when he became king of Judah,
20:31 king of Judah, and he reigned in Jerusalem twenty-five **years**.
21: 5 Jehoram was thirty-two **years** old when he became king, and he
21: 5 old when he became king, and he reigned in Jerusalem eight **years**.
21:20 old when he became king, and he reigned in Jerusalem eight **years**.
22: 2 Ahaziah was twenty-two **years** old when he became king,
22: 2 old when he became king, and he reigned in Jerusalem one **year**.
22:12 He remained hidden with them at the temple of God *for* six **years**
23: 1 In the seventh **year** Jehoiada showed his strength. He made a
24: 1 Joash was seven **years** old when he became king, and he reigned in
24: 1 old when he became king, and he reigned in Jerusalem forty **years**.
24: 5 the money **due annually** [+928+1896+4946+9102] from all Israel,
24: 5 the money **due annually** [+928+1896+4946+9102] from all Israel,
24:15 of years, and he died at the **age of** [+1201] a hundred and thirty.
24:23 At the turn of the **year**, the army of Aram marched against Joash;
25: 1 Amaziah was twenty-five **years** old when he became king,
25: 1 he became king, and he reigned in Jerusalem twenty-nine **years**.
25: 5 He then mustered those twenty **years** old or more and found that
25:25 Amaziah son of Joash king of Judah lived *for* fifteen **years** after
26: 1 all the people of Judah took Uzziah, who was sixteen **years** old,
26: 3 Uzziah was sixteen **years** old when he became king, and he
26: 3 when he became king, and he reigned in Jerusalem fifty-two **years**.
27: 1 Jotham was twenty-five **years** old when he became king, and he
27: 1 when he became king, and he reigned in Jerusalem sixteen **years**.
27: 5 That **year** the Ammonites paid him a hundred talents of silver,
27: 5 brought him the same amount also in the second and third **years**.
27: 8 He was twenty-five **years** old when he became king, and he
27: 8 when he became king, and he reigned in Jerusalem sixteen **years**.
28: 1 Ahaz was twenty **years** old when he became king, and he reigned
28: 1 when he became king, and he reigned in Jerusalem sixteen **years**.
29: 1 Hezekiah was twenty-five **years** old when he became king,
29: 1 he became king, and he reigned in Jerusalem twenty-nine **years**.
29: 3 In the first month of the first **year** of his reign, he opened the doors
31:16 they distributed to the males three **years** old or more whose names
31:17 and likewise to the Levites twenty **years** old or more,
33: 1 Manasseh was twelve **years** old when he became king, and he
33: 1 when he became king, and he reigned in Jerusalem fifty-five **years**.
33:21 Amon was twenty-two **years** old when he became king, and he
33:21 old when he became king, and he reigned in Jerusalem two **years**.
34: 1 Josiah was eight **years** old when he became king, and he reigned in
34: 1 he became king, and he reigned in Jerusalem thirty-one **years**.
34: 3 In the eighth **year** *of* his reign, while he was still young, he began
34: 3 In his twelfth **year** he began to purge Judah and Jerusalem of high
34: 8 In the eighteenth **year** *of* Josiah's reign, to purify the land
35:19 This Passover was celebrated in the eighteenth **year** of Josiah's
36: 2 Jehoahaz was twenty-three **years** old when he became king,
36: 5 Jehoiakim was twenty-five **years** old when he became king,
36: 5 when he became king, and he reigned in Jerusalem eleven **years**.
36: 9 Jehoiachin was eighteen **years** old when he became king, and he
36:10 In the **spring** [+9588], King Nebuchadnezzar sent for him
36:11 Zedekiah was twenty-one **years** old when he became king,
36:11 when he became king, and he reigned in Jerusalem eleven **years**.
36:21 until the seventy **years** were completed in fulfillment of the word
36:22 In the first **year** of Cyrus king of Persia, in order to fulfill the word
Ezr 1: 1 In the first **year** of Cyrus king of Persia, in order to fulfill the word
3: 8 In the second month of the second **year** after their arrival at the
3: 8 appointing Levites twenty **years** of age and older to supervise the
7: 7 also came up to Jerusalem in the seventh **year** of King Artaxerxes.
7: 8 Ezra arrived in Jerusalem in the fifth month of the seventh **year** of
Ne 1: 1 In the month of Kislev in the twentieth **year**, while I was in the
2: 1 In the month of Nisan in the twentieth **year** of King Artaxerxes,
5:14 Moreover, from the twentieth **year** of King Artaxerxes, when I was
5:14 their governor in the land of Judah, until his thirty-second **year**—
5:14 in the land of Judah, until his thirty-second year—twelve **years**—
9:21 *For* forty **years** you sustained them in the desert; they lacked
9:30 *For* many **years** you were patient with them. By your Spirit you
10:31 [10:32] Every seventh **year** we will forgo working the land
10:32 [10:33] shekel each **year** for the service of the house of our God:
10:34 [10:35] **each year** [+928+9102] a contribution of wood to burn on
10:34 [10:35] **each year** [+928+9102] a contribution of wood to burn on
10:35 [10:36] **each year** [+928+9102] the firstfruits of our crops
10:35 [10:36] **each year** [+928+9102] the firstfruits of our crops
13: 6 for in the thirty-second **year** of Artaxerxes king of Babylon I had
Est 1: 3 in the third **year** of his reign he gave a banquet for all his nobles
2:16 tenth month, the month of Tebeth, in the seventh **year** of his reign.
3: 7 In the twelfth **year** of King Xerxes, in the first month, the month of
9:21 to have them celebrate **annually** [+928+2256+3972+9102] the
9:21 to have them celebrate **annually** [+928+2256+3972+9102] the
9:27 join them should without fail observe these two days every **year**,
9:27 **[RPH]** in the way prescribed and at the time appointed.
Job 3: 6 may it not be included among the days of the **year** nor be entered
10: 5 your days like those of a mortal or your **years** like those of a man,
15:20 the ruthless through all the **years** stored up for him.
16:22 "Only a few **years** will pass before I go on the journey of no
32: 7 'Age should speak; advanced **years** should teach wisdom.'
36:11 the rest of their days in prosperity and their **years** in contentment.
36:26 our understanding! The number of his **years** is past finding out.
42:16 After this, Job lived a hundred and forty **years**; he saw his children
Ps 31:10 [31:11] life is consumed by anguish and my **years** by groaning;
61: 6 [61:7] the days of the king's life, his **years** for many generations.
65:11 [65:12] You crown the **year** with your bounty, and your carts
77: 5 [77:6] I thought about the former days, the **years** *of* long ago;
77:10 [77:11] will appeal: the **years** *of* the right hand of the Most High."
78:33 So he ended their days in futility and their **years** in terror.
90: 4 For a thousand **years** in your sight are like a day that has just gone
90: 9 pass away under your wrath; we finish our **years** with a moan.
90:10 The **length of** our **days** [+3427] is seventy years—or eighty,
90:10 The length of our days is seventy **years**—or eighty, if we have the
90:10 or eighty, **[RPH]** if we have the strength; yet their span is
90:15 you have afflicted us, *for* as many **years** as we have seen trouble.
95:10 *For* forty **years** I was angry with that generation; I said, "They are
102:24 [102:25] of my days; your **years** go on through all generations.
102:27 [102:28] But you remain the same, and your **years** will never end.
Pr 3: 2 for they will prolong your life **many years** [+2256+3427]
4:10 accept what I say, and the **years** *of* your life will be many.
5: 9 your best strength to others and your **years** to one who is cruel,
9:11 me your days will be many, and **years** will be added to your life.
10:27 adds length to life, but the **years** *of* the wicked are cut short.
Ecc 6: 3 A man may have a hundred children and live many **years**;
6: 3 yet no matter how long he **lives** [+3427], if he cannot enjoy his
6: 6 even if he lives a thousand **years** twice over but fails to enjoy his
11: 8 However many **years** a man may live, let him enjoy them all.
12: 1 days of trouble come and the **years** approach when you will say,
Isa 6: 1 In the **year** *that* King Uzziah died, I saw the Lord seated on a
7: 8 Within sixty-five **years** Ephraim will be too shattered to be a
14:28 This oracle came in the **year** King Ahaz died:
16:14 "Within three **years**, as a servant bound by contract would count
16:14 as a servant bound by contract would count **them**[s], Moab's
20: 1 In the **year** that the supreme commander, sent by Sargon king of
20: 3 my servant Isaiah has gone stripped and barefoot *for* three **years**,
21:16 "Within *one* **year**, as a servant bound by contract would count it,
21:16 "Within one year, as a servant bound by contract would count **it**[s],
23:15 At that time Tyre will be forgotten *for* seventy **years**, the span of a
23:15 at the end of these seventy **years**, it will happen to Tyre as in the
23:17 At the end of seventy **years**, the LORD will deal with Tyre.
29: 1 Add **year** to year and let your cycle of festivals go on.
29: 1 Add year to **year** and let your cycle of festivals go on.
32:10 In little more than a **year** you who feel secure will tremble;
34: 8 a day of vengeance, a **year** *of* retribution, to uphold Zion's cause.
36: 1 In the fourteenth **year** of King Hezekiah's reign, Sennacherib king
37:30 "This **year** you will eat what grows by itself, and the second year
37:30 what grows by itself, and the second **year** what springs from that.
37:30 in the third **year** sow and reap, plant vineyards and eat their fruit.
38: 5 and seen your tears; I will add fifteen **years** to your life.
38:10 through the gates of death and be robbed of the rest of my **years**?"
38:15 I will walk humbly all my **years** because of this anguish of my
61: 2 to proclaim the **year** *of* the LORD's favor and the day of
63: 4 was in my heart, and the **year** *of* my redemption has come.
65:20 he who dies at a hundred **[NIE]** will be thought a mere youth;
65:20 he who fails to reach a hundred **[NIE]** will be considered
Jer 1: 2 The word of the LORD came to him in the thirteenth **year** of the
1: 3 down to the fifth month of the eleventh **year** of Zedekiah son of
11:23 because I will bring disaster on the men of Anathoth in the **year** *of*
17: 8 It has no worries in a **year** *of* drought and never fails to bear fruit."
23:12 I will bring disaster on them in the **year** they are punished,"
25: 1 Judah in the fourth **year** of Jehoiakim son of Josiah king of Judah,
25: 1 which was the first **year** of Nebuchadnezzar king of Babylon.
25: 3 For twenty-three **years**—from the thirteenth year of Josiah son of
25: 3 from the thirteenth **year** of Josiah son of Amon king of Judah until
25:11 and these nations will serve the king of Babylon seventy **years**.
25:12 "But when the seventy **years** are fulfilled, I will punish the king of
28: 1 In the fifth month of that same **year**, the fourth year, early in the
28: 1 In the fifth month of that same year, the fourth **year**, early in the
28: 3 Within *two* **years** [+3427] I will bring back to this place all the
28:11 off the neck of all the nations within *two* **years** [+3427].' " At this,
28:16 This very **year** you are going to die, because you have preached
28:17 In the seventh month of that same **year**, Hananiah the prophet died.
29:10 "When seventy **years** are completed for Babylon, I will come to
32: 1 from the LORD in the tenth **year** of Zedekiah king of Judah,
32: 1 king of Judah, which was the eighteenth **year** of Nebuchadnezzar.
32: 1 which was the eighteenth year **[RPH]** of Nebuchadnezzar.

Jer 34: 14 'Every seventh **year** each of you must free any fellow Hebrew who
34: 14 After he has served you six **years**, you must let him go free.'
36: 1 In the fourth **year** of Jehoiakim son of Josiah king of Judah,
36: 9 In the ninth month of the fifth **year** of Jehoiakim son of Josiah king
39: 1 In the ninth **year** of Zedekiah king of Judah, in the tenth month,
39: 2 on the ninth day of the fourth month of Zedekiah's eleventh **year**,
45: 1 Neriah in the fourth **year** of Jehoiakim son of Josiah king of Judah,
46: 2 in the fourth **year** of Jehoiakim son of Josiah king of Judah:
48: 44 for I will bring upon Moab the **year** *of* her punishment,"
51: 46 one rumor comes this **year**, another the next, rumors of violence in
51: 46 one rumor comes this year, another **[RPH]** the next, rumors of
51: 59 with Zedekiah king of Judah in the fourth **year** of his reign.
52: 1 Zedekiah was twenty-one **years** old when he became king,
52: 1 when he became king, and he reigned in Jerusalem eleven **years**.
52: 4 So in the ninth **year** of Zedekiah's reign, on the tenth day of the
52: 5 The city was kept under siege until the eleventh **year** of King
52: 12 in the nineteenth **year** of Nebuchadnezzar king of Babylon,
52: 12 in the nineteenth year **[RPH]** of Nebuchadnezzar king of
52: 28 carried into exile: in the seventh **year**, 3,023 Jews;
52: 29 in Nebuchadnezzar's eighteenth **year**, 832 people from Jerusalem;
52: 30 in his twenty-third **year**, 745 Jews taken into exile by Nebuzaradan
52: 31 In the thirty-seventh **year** of the exile of Jehoiachin king of Judah,
52: 31 in the **year** Evil-Merodach became king of Babylon, he released
Eze 1: 1 In the thirtieth **year**, in the fourth month on the fifth day, while I
1: 2 the month—it was the fifth **year** of the exile of King Jehoiachin—
4: 5 I have assigned you the same number of days as the **years** *of* their
4: 6 house of Judah. I have assigned you 40 days, a day for each **year**.
4: 6 I have assigned you 40 days, a day for each year. **[RPH]**
8: 1 In the sixth **year**, in the sixth month on the fifth day, while I was
20: 1 In the seventh **year**, in the fifth month on the tenth day, some of
22: 4 brought your days to a close, and the end of your **years** has come.
24: 1 In the ninth **year**, in the tenth month on the tenth day, the word of
26: 1 In the eleventh **year**, on the first day of the month, the word of the
29: 1 In the tenth **year**, in the tenth month on the twelfth day, the word
29: 11 animal will pass through it; no one will live there *for* forty **years**.
29: 12 and her cities will lie desolate forty **years** among ruined cities.
29: 13 At the end of forty **years** I will gather the Egyptians from the
29: 17 In the twenty-seventh **year**, in the first month on the first day,
30: 20 In the eleventh **year**, in the first month on the seventh day,
31: 1 In the eleventh **year**, in the third month on the first day, the word
32: 1 In the twelfth **year**, in the twelfth month on the first day, the word
32: 17 In the twelfth **year**, on the fifteenth day of the month, the word of
33: 21 In the twelfth **year** of our exile, in the tenth month on the fifth day,
38: 8 In future **years** you will invade a land that has recovered from war,
38: 17 At that time they prophesied *for* **years** that I would bring you
39: 9 war clubs and spears. *For* seven **years** they will use them for fuel.
40: 1 In the twenty-fifth **year** of our exile, at the beginning of the year,
40: 1 our exile, at the beginning of the **year**, on the tenth of the month,
40: 1 tenth of the month, in the fourteenth **year** after the fall of the city—
46: 13 " 'Every day you are to provide a **year-old** [+1201] lamb without
46: 17 of his servants, the servant may keep it until the **year** *of* freedom;
Da 1: 1 In the third **year** of the reign of Jehoiakim king of Judah,
1: 5 They were to be trained *for* three **years**, and after that they were to
1: 21 And Daniel remained there until the first **year** of King Cyrus.
2: 1 In the second **year** of his reign, Nebuchadnezzar had dreams;
8: 1 In the third **year** of King Belshazzar's reign, I, Daniel, had a
9: 1 In the first **year** of Darius son of Xerxes (a Mede by descent),
9: 2 in the first **year** *of* his reign, I, Daniel, understood from the
9: 2 that the desolation of Jerusalem would last seventy **years**.
9: 2 that the desolation of Jerusalem would last seventy years. **[RPH]**
10: 1 In the third **year** of Cyrus king of Persia, a revelation was given to
11: 1 in the first **year** of Darius the Mede, I took my stand to support
11: 6 After *some* **years**, they will become allies. The daughter of the
11: 8 *For some* **years** he will leave the king of the North alone.
11: 13 after *several* **years** [+2021+6961], he will advance with a huge
Joel 2: 2 such as never was of old nor ever will be in **ages** to come.
2: 25 "I will repay you for the **years** the locusts have eaten—the great
Am 1: 1 what he saw concerning Israel *two* **years** before the earthquake,
2: 10 I led you forty **years** in the desert to give you the land of the
5: 25 you bring me sacrifices and offerings forty **years** in the desert,
Mic 6: 6 I come before him with burnt offerings, with calves a **year** old?
Hab 3: 2 Renew them in our **day**, in our time make them known; in wrath
3: 2 Renew them in our day, in our **time** make them known; in wrath
Hag 1: 1 In the second **year** of King Darius, on the first day of the sixth
1: 15 on the twenty-fourth day of the sixth month in the second **year** of
2: 10 twenty-fourth day of the ninth month, in the second **year** of Darius,
Zec 1: 1 In the eighth month of the second **year** of Darius, the word of the
1: 7 eleventh month, the month of Shebat, in the second **year** of Darius,
1: 12 of Judah, which you have been angry with these seventy **years**?"
7: 1 In the fourth **year** of King Darius, the word of the LORD came to
7: 3 and fast in the fifth month, as I have done for so many **years**?"
7: 5 in the fifth and seventh months for the past seventy **years**,
14: 16 attacked Jerusalem will go up **year** after year to worship the King,
14: 16 attacked Jerusalem will go up year after **year** to worship the King,
Mal 3: 4 acceptable to the LORD, as in days gone by, as in former **years**.

9103 ³שָׁנָה *šānâ³*, v. Not used in NIV/BHS [√ 9101]

9104 שֵׁנָה *šēnâ*, n.f. [23] [√ 3822; cf. 9097; Ar 10733]

sleep [18], sleep [+3822] [2], last sleep [1], sleep of death [1], slumber [1]

Ge 28: 16 When Jacob awoke from his **sleep**, he thought, "Surely the LORD
31: 40 in the daytime and the cold at night, and **sleep** fled from my eyes.
Jdg 16: 14 He awoke from his **sleep** and pulled up the pin and the loom,
16: 20 He awoke from his **sleep** and thought, "I'll go out as before
Est 6: 1 That night the king could not **sleep**; so he ordered the book of the
Job 14: 12 are no more, men will not awake or be roused from their **sleep**.
Ps 76: 5 [76:6] Valiant men lie plundered, they sleep their **last sleep**; not
90: 5 You sweep men away in the **sleep of death**; they are like the new
132: 4 I will allow no **sleep** to my eyes, no slumber to my eyelids,
Pr 3: 24 will not be afraid; when you lie down, your **sleep** will be sweet.
4: 16 do evil; they are robbed of **slumber** till they make someone fall.
6: 4 Allow no **sleep** to your eyes, no slumber to your eyelids.
6: 9 lie there, you sluggard? When will you get up from your **sleep**?
6: 10 A little **sleep**, a little slumber, a little folding of the hands to rest—
20: 13 Do not love **sleep** or you will grow poor; stay awake and you will
24: 33 A little **sleep**, a little slumber, a little folding of the hands to rest—
Ecc 5: 12 [5:11] The **sleep** *of* a laborer is sweet, whether he eats little
8: 16 man's labor on earth—his eyes not seeing **sleep** day or night—
Jer 31: 26 this I awoke and looked around. My **sleep** had been pleasant to me.
51: 39 then **sleep** [+3822] forever and not awake," declares the LORD.
51: 57 *they will* **sleep** [+3822] forever and not awake," declares the King,
Da 2: 1 had dreams; his mind was troubled and he could not **sleep**.
Zec 4: 1 me returned and wakened me, as a man is wakened from his **sleep**.

9105 שֶׁנְהַבִּים *šenhabbîm*, n.m.[pl.]. [2] [√ 9094 + 2036]

ivory [2]

1Ki 10: 22 it returned, carrying gold, silver and **ivory**, and apes and baboons.
2Ch 9: 21 it returned, carrying gold, silver and **ivory**, and apes and baboons.

9106 שָׁנִי *šānî¹*, n.[m.]. [42] [√ 9101?]

scarlet yarn [+9357] [31], scarlet [7], scarlet thread [2], scarlet [+9357] [1], scarlet wool [+9357] [1]

Ge 38: 28 so the midwife took a **scarlet thread** and tied it on his wrist
38: 30 who had the **scarlet thread** on his wrist, came out and he was
Ex 25: 4 blue, purple and **scarlet yarn** [+9357] and fine linen; goat hair;
26: 1 of finely twisted linen and blue, purple and **scarlet yarn** [+9357],
26: 31 of blue, purple and **scarlet yarn** [+9357] and finely twisted linen,
26: 36 purple and **scarlet yarn** [+9357] and finely twisted linen—
27: 16 purple and **scarlet yarn** [+9357] and finely twisted linen—
28: 5 and blue, purple and **scarlet yarn** [+9357], and fine linen.
28: 6 the ephod of gold, and of blue, purple and **scarlet yarn** [+9357],
28: 8 made with gold, and with blue, purple and **scarlet yarn** [+9357],
28: 15 of gold, and of blue, purple and **scarlet yarn** [+9357], and of finely
28: 33 purple and **scarlet yarn** [+9357] around the hem of the robe,
35: 6 blue, purple and **scarlet yarn** [+9357] and fine linen; goat hair;
35: 23 purple or **scarlet yarn** [+9357] or fine linen, or goat hair, ram
35: 25 she had spun—blue, purple or **scarlet yarn** [+9357] or fine linen.
35: 35 purple and **scarlet yarn** [+9357] and fine linen, and weavers—
36: 8 of finely twisted linen and blue, purple and **scarlet yarn** [+9357],
36: 35 of blue, purple and **scarlet yarn** [+9357] and finely twisted linen,
36: 37 purple and **scarlet yarn** [+9357] and finely twisted linen—
38: 18 purple and **scarlet yarn** [+9357] and finely twisted linen—
38: 23 in blue, purple and **scarlet yarn** [+9357] and fine linen.)
39: 1 **scarlet yarn** [+9357] they made woven garments for ministering in
39: 2 of blue, purple and **scarlet yarn** [+9357], and of finely twisted
39: 3 into the blue, purple and **scarlet yarn** [+9357] and fine linen—
39: 5 made with gold, and with blue, purple and **scarlet yarn** [+9357],
39: 8 of gold, and of blue, purple and **scarlet yarn** [+9357], and of finely
39: 24 purple and **scarlet yarn** [+9357] and finely twisted linen around
39: 29 of finely twisted linen and blue, purple and **scarlet yarn** [+9357]—
Lev 14: 4 **scarlet yarn** [+9357] and hyssop be brought for the one to be
14: 6 with the cedar wood, the **scarlet yarn** [+9357] and the hyssop,
14: 49 two birds and some cedar wood, **scarlet yarn** [+9357] and hyssop.
14: 51 cedar wood, the hyssop, the **scarlet yarn** [+9357] and the live bird,
14: 52 the cedar wood, the hyssop and the **scarlet yarn** [+9357].
Nu 4: 8 Over these they are to spread a **scarlet** [+9357] cloth, cover that
19: 6 hyssop and **scarlet wool** [+9357] and throw them onto the burning
Jos 2: 18 you have tied this **scarlet** cord in the window through which you
2: 21 and they departed. And she tied the **scarlet** cord in the window.
2Sa 1: 24 of Israel, weep for Saul, who clothed you in **scarlet** and finery,
Pr 31: 21 has no fear for her household; for all of them are clothed in **scarlet**.
SS 4: 3 Your lips are like a **scarlet** ribbon; your mouth is lovely.
Isa 1: 18 "Though your sins are like **scarlet**, they shall be as white as snow;
Jer 4: 30 Why dress yourself in **scarlet** and put on jewels of gold?

9107 שָׁנִי² ***šānî²***, a. Not used in NIV/BHS

9108 שֵׁנִי ***šēnî***, a.num.ord. [157] [√ 9109; cf. 9101; Ar 10765, 10766]

second [75], other [33], another [12], second time [10], *untranslated* [8], again [5], after [1], again [+8740] [1], all alone [+401] [1], another part [1], each [1], following [1], furthermore [+2021+2256] [1], middle [1], next [1], one [1], second in command [1], this time [1], this[s] [+2021] [1], whose[s] [+285+2021+2021] [1]

Ge 1: 8 And there was evening, and there was morning—the **second** day.
2: 13 The name of the **second** river is the Gihon; it winds through the
4: 19 married two women, one named Adah and the **other** Zillah.
6: 16 in the side of the ark and make lower, **middle** and upper decks.
7: 11 year of Noah's life, on the seventeenth day of the **second** month—
8: 14 By the twenty-seventh day of the **second** month the earth was
22: 15 of the LORD called to Abraham from heaven a **second time**
30: 7 servant Bilhah conceived again and bore Jacob a **second** son.
30: 12 Leah's servant Zilpah bore Jacob a **second** son.
32: 19 [32:20] He also instructed the **second**, the third and all the others
41: 5 He fell asleep again and had a **second** dream: Seven heads of grain,
41: 52 The **second** son he named Ephraim and said, "It is because God
47: 18 that year was over, they came to him the **following** year and said,
Ex 1: 15 Hebrew midwives, whose names were Shiphrah and **[NIE]** Puah,
2: 13 The **next** day he went out and saw two Hebrews fighting. He asked
16: 1 on the fifteenth day of the **second** month after they had come out
25: 12 its four feet, with two rings on one side and two rings on the **other**.
25: 32 sides of the lampstand—three on one side and three on the **other**.
26: 4 in one set, and do the same with the end curtain in the **other** set.
26: 5 on one curtain and fifty loops on the end curtain of the **other** set,
26: 10 and also along the edge of the end curtain in the **other** set.
26: 20 For the **other** side, the north side of the tabernacle, make twenty
26: 27 five for those on the **other** side, and five for the frames on the
27: 15 and curtains fifteen cubits long are to be on the **other** side,
28: 10 six names on one stone and the remaining six on the **other**.
28: 18 in the **second** row a turquoise, a sapphire and an emerald;
29: 19 "Take the **other** ram, and Aaron and his sons shall lay their hands
29: 39 Offer one in the morning and the **other** at twilight.
29: 41 Sacrifice the **other** lamb at twilight with the same grain offering
36: 11 and the same was done with the end curtain in the **other** set.
36: 12 on one curtain and fifty loops on the end curtain of the **other** set,
36: 17 and also along the edge of the end curtain in the **other** set.
36: 25 For the **other** side, the north side of the tabernacle, they made
36: 32 five for those on the **other** side, and five for the frames on the
37: 3 its four feet, with two rings on one side and two rings on the **other**.
37: 18 sides of the lampstand—three on one side and three on the **other**.
38: 15 curtains fifteen cubits long were on the **other** side of the entrance
39: 11 in the **second** row a turquoise, a sapphire and an emerald;
40: 17 was set up on the first day of the first month in the **second** year.
Lev 5: 10 then offer the **other** as a burnt offering in the prescribed way
8: 22 He then presented the **other** ram, the ram for the ordination,
13: 5 in the skin, he is to keep him in isolation **another** seven days.
13: 6 On the seventh day the priest is to examine him **again**, and if the
13: 7 to be pronounced clean, he must appear before the priest **again**.
13: 33 and the priest is to keep him in isolation **another** seven days.
13: 54 article be washed. Then he is to isolate it for **another** seven days.
13: 58 is rid of the mildew, must be washed **again**, and it will be clean."
Nu 1: 1 **second** month of the second year after the Israelites came out of
1: 1 month of the **second** year after the Israelites came out of Egypt.
1: 18 whole community together on the first day of the **second** month.
2: 16 to their divisions, number 151,450. They will set out **second**.
7: 18 On the **second** day Nethanel son of Zuar, the leader of Issachar,
8: 8 then you are to take a **second** young bull for a sin offering.
9: 1 in the first month of the **second** year after they came out of Egypt.
9: 11 They are to celebrate it on the fourteenth day of the **second** month
10: 6 At the sounding of a **second** blast, the camps on the south are to set
10: 11 On the twentieth day of the **second** month of the second year,
10: 11 On the twentieth day of the second month of the **second** year,
11: 26 men, **whose**[s] [+285+2021+2021] names were Eldad and Medad,
28: 4 Prepare one lamb in the morning and the **other** at twilight,
28: 8 Prepare the **second** lamb at twilight, along with the same kind of
29: 17 " 'On the **second** day prepare twelve young bulls, two rams
Jos 5: 2 "Make flint knives and circumcise the Israelites **again** [+8740]."
6: 14 So on the **second** day they marched around the city once
10: 32 Lachish over to Israel, and Joshua took it on the **second** day.
19: 1 The **second** lot came out for the tribe of Simeon, clan by clan.
Jdg 6: 25 "Take the **second** bull from your father's herd, the one seven years
6: 26 pole that you cut down, offer the **second** bull as a burnt offering."
6: 28 it cut down and the **second** bull sacrificed on the newly built altar!
20: 24 Then the Israelites drew near to Benjamin the **second** day.
20: 25 **This**[s] [+2021] time, when the Benjamites came out from Gibeah to
Ru 1: 4 married Moabite women, one named Orpah and the **other** Ruth.
1Sa 1: 2 He had two wives; one was called Hannah and the **other** Peninnah.
20: 27 the next day, the **second** day *of* the month, David's place was
20: 34 on that **second** day of the month he did not eat, because he was
2Sa 4: 2 One was named Baanah and the **other** Recab; they were sons of
14: 29 to come to him. So he sent a **second** time, but he refused to come.
16: 19 **Furthermore** [+2021+2256], whom should I serve? Should I not
1Ki 6: 1 in the month of Ziv, the **second** month, he began to build the
6: 24 first cherub was five cubits long, and the **other** wing five cubits—
6: 25 The **second** cherub also measured ten cubits, for the two cherubim
6: 26 The height of each cherub was ten cubits. **[RPH]**
6: 27 one wall, while the wing of the **other** touched the other wall,
6: 27 one wall, while the wing of the other touched the **other** wall,
6: 34 pine doors, each having two leaves that turned in sockets. **[RPH]**
7: 15 eighteen cubits high and twelve cubits around, by line. **[NIE]**
7: 16 the tops of the pillars; each capital was five cubits high. **[RPH]**
7: 17 the capitals on top of the pillars, seven for each capital. **[NIE]**
7: 18 the capitals on top of the pillars. He did the same for **each** capital.
7: 20 were the two hundred pomegranates in rows all around. **[NIE]**
9: 2 the LORD appeared to him a **second time**, as he had appeared to
19: 7 The angel of the LORD came back a **second time** and touched
2Ki 9: 19 So the king sent out a **second** horseman. When he came to them he
10: 6 Jehu wrote them a **second** letter, saying, "If you are on my side
19: 29 what grows by itself, and the **second** year what springs from that.
25: 17 bronze all around. The **other** pillar, with its network, was similar.
1Ch 2: 13 his firstborn; the **second** son was Abinadab, the third Shimea,
3: 1 of Jezreel; the **second**, Daniel the son of Abigail of Carmel;
3: 15 Jehoiakim the **second** son, Zedekiah the third, Shallum the fourth.
6: 28 [6:13] of Samuel: Joel the firstborn and Abijah the **second** son.
7: 15 **Another** descendant was named Zelophehad, who had only
8: 1 of Bela his firstborn, Ashbel the **second** son, Aharah the third,
8: 39 Ulam his firstborn, Jeush the **second** son and Eliphelet the third.
12: 9 [12:10] Obadiah the **second in command**, Eliab the third,
23: 11 Jahath was the first and Ziza the **second**, but Jeush and Beriah did
23: 19 Jeriah the first, Amariah the **second**, Jahaziel the third
23: 20 The sons of Uzziel: Micah the first and Isshiah the **second**.
24: 7 The first lot fell to Jehoiarib, the **second** to Jedaiah,
24: 23 Jeriah the first, Amariah the **second**, Jahaziel the third
25: 9 12 the **second** to Gedaliah, he and his relatives and sons, 12
26: 2 Jediael the **second**, Zebadiah the third, Jathniel the fourth,
26: 4 Jehozabad the **second**, Joah the third, Sacar the fourth, Nethanel
26: 11 Hilkiah the **second**, Tabaliah the third and Zechariah the fourth.
27: 4 In charge of the division for the **second** month was Dodai the
29: 22 they acknowledged Solomon son of David as king a **second time**,
2Ch 3: 2 He began building on the **second** day of the second month in the
3: 2 He began building on the second day of the **second** month in the
27: 5 The Ammonites brought him the same amount also in the **second**
30: 2 Jerusalem decided to celebrate the Passover in the **second** month.
30: 13 to celebrate the Feast of Unleavened Bread in the **second** month.
30: 15 the Passover lamb on the fourteenth day of the **second** month.
Ezr 3: 8 In the **second** month of the second year after their arrival at the
3: 8 In the second month of the **second** year after their arrival at the
Ne 3: 11 and Hasshub son of Pahath-Moab repaired **another** section
3: 19 Ezer son of Jeshua, ruler of Mizpah, repaired **another** section,
3: 20 Baruch son of Zabbai zealously repaired **another** section,
3: 21 son of Uriah, the son of Hakkoz, repaired **another** section,
3: 24 Next to him, Binnui son of Henadad repaired **another** section,
3: 27 Next to them, the men of Tekoa repaired **another** section,
3: 30 and Hanun, the sixth son of Zalaph, repaired **another** section.
8: 13 On the **second** day of the month, the heads of all the families,
12: 38 The **second** choir proceeded in the opposite direction. I followed
Est 2: 14 in the morning return to **another part** *of* the harem to the care of
2: 19 When the virgins were assembled a **second time**, Mordecai was
7: 2 as they were drinking wine on that **second** day, the king again
9: 29 wrote with full authority to confirm this **second** letter concerning
Job 42: 14 named Jemimah, the **second** Keziah and the third Keren-Happuch.
Ecc 4: 8 There was a man **all alone** [+401]; he had neither son nor brother.
4: 10 But pity the man who falls and has no **one** to help him up!
4: 15 under the sun followed the youth, **[NIE]** the king's successor.
Isa 11: 11 In that day the Lord will reach out his hand a **second time** to
37: 30 what grows by itself, and the **second** year what springs from that.
Jer 1: 13 The word of the LORD came to me **again**: "What do you see?"
13: 3 Then the word of the LORD came to me a **second time**:
33: 1 of the guard, the word of the LORD came to him a **second time**:
41: 4 The day **after** Gedaliah's assassination, before anyone knew about
52: 22 all around. The **other** pillar, with its pomegranates, was similar.
Eze 4: 6 you have finished this, lie down again, **this time** on your right side,
10: 14 a cherub, the **second** the face of a man, the third the face of a lion,
43: 22 "On the **second** day you are to offer a male goat without defect for
Da 8: 3 One of the horns was longer than the **other** but grew up later.
Jnh 3: 1 Then the word of the LORD came to Jonah a **second time**:
Hag 2: 20 The word of the LORD came to Haggai a **second time** on the
Zec 4: 12 **Again** I asked him, "What are these two olive branches beside the
6: 2 The first chariot had red horses, the **second** black,
11: 14 I broke my **second** staff called Union, breaking the brotherhood
Mal 2: 13 **Another** thing you do: You flood the LORD's altar with tears.

9109 שְׁנַיִם **šᵉnayim**, n.m. & f. [768 / 772] [→ 9108; cf. 9101; Ar 10775]

two [374], both [52], twelve [+6925] [52], *untranslated* [37], twelve [+6926] [30], 12 [+6925] [23], each [16], twelfth [+6925] [15], twenty-two [+2256+6929] [14], second [12], two-tenths [+6928] [11], pair [9], double [8], twelfth [+6926] [7], thirty-two [+2256+8993] [6], forty-two [+752+2256] [4], pairs [+9109] [4], 32 [+2256+8993] [3], fifty-two [+2256+2822] [3], together [3], 1,052 [+547+2256+2822] [2], 112 [+2256+4395+6925] [2], 20,000 [+8052] [2], 32,200 [+547+2256 +2256+4395+8993] [2], 372 [+2256+4395+8679+8993] [2], 392 [+2256+4395+8993+9596] [2], 42 [+752+2256] [2], 52 [+2256+2822] [2], 62,700 [+547+2256+2256+4395+8679+9252] [2], 652 [+2256 +2822+4395+9252] [2], other[s] [2], sides [2], sixty-two [+2256+9252] [2], thirty-second [+2256+8993] [2], twenty-second [+2256+6929] [2], twice [2], two at a time [+9109] [2], 1,222 [+547+2256+4395+6929] [1], 112 [+4395+6925] [1], 122 [+2256+2256+4395+6929] [1], 122 [+2256+4395+6929] [1], 162 [+2256+2256+4395+9252] [1], 172 [+2256+4395+8679] [1], 182 [+2256+2256+4395+9046] [1], 2,172 [+547+2256+2256+4395+8679] [1], 2,172 [+547+2256+4395+8679] [1], 2,322 [+547+2256+4395+6929+8993] [1], 2,812 [+547+2256 +4395+6925+9046] [1], 212 [+2256+4395+6925] [1], 22 [+2256 +6929] [1], 22,000 [+547+2256+6929] [1], 22,034 [+547+752+2256 +2256+2256+6929+8993] [1], 22,200 [+547+2256+2256+4395 +6929] [1], 22,273 [+547+2256+2256+2256+4395+6929+8679 +8993] [1], 22,600 [+547+2256+2256+4395+6929+9252] [1], 232 [+2256+4395+8993] [1], 242 [+752+2256+4395] [1], 32,000 [+547 +2256+8993] [1], 32,500 [+547+2256+2256+2822+4395+8993] [1], 52,700 [+547+2256+2256+2822+4395+8679] [1], 62 [+2256+9252] [1], 642 [+752+2256+2256+4395+9252] [1], 642 [+752+2256+4395 +9252] [1], 72 [+2256+8679] [1], 72,000 [+547+2256+8679] [1], 782 [+2256+2256+4395+8679+9046] [1], 822 [+2256+4395+6929+9046] [1], 832 [+2256+4395+8993+9046] [1], 912 [+2256+4395+6926 +9596] [1], 962 [+2256+2256+4395+9252+9596] [1], another [1], both sides [1], double-edged [+7023] [1], doubly [+928+2021] [1], each other [+5646] [1], each other[s] [+2157] [1], each[s] [1], Elijah[s] and Elisha [+2157] [1], few [1], fifty-second [+2256+2822] [1], forty [+2256] [1], hundred and twenty thousand [+6926+8052] [1], inner[s] and outer [1], people[s] [+8993] [1], some[s] [1], them[s] [+2021+3192] [1], them[s] [+74+2021] [1], time and again [+285+2256+4202+4202] [1], tore apart [+4200+7973+7974] [1], twenty-two [+752+2256] [1], two-and-a-half [+2256+2942] [1], two-thirds [+7023] [1]

Ge 1:16 God made **two** great lights—the greater light to govern the day
2:25 The man and his wife were **both** naked, and they felt no shame.
3:7 the eyes of **both** *of* them were opened, and they realized they were
4:19 Lamech married **two** women, one named Adah and the other
5:8 Seth lived **912** [+2256+4395+6926+9596] years, and then he died.
5:18 When Jared had lived **162** [+2256+2256+4395+9252] years, he
5:20 Jared lived **962** [+2256+2256+4395+9252+9596] years, and then
5:26 Methuselah lived **782** [+2256+2256+4395+8679+9046] years and
5:28 When Lamech had lived **182** [+2256+2256+4395+9046] years, he
6:19 You are to bring into the ark **two** of all living creatures, male
6:20 **Two** of every kind of bird, of every kind of animal and of every
7:2 and **two** of every kind of unclean animal, a male and its mate,
7:8 [7:9] **Pairs** [+9109] of clean and unclean animals, of birds and of
7:8 [7:9] **Pairs** [+9109] of clean and unclean animals, of birds and of
7:15 **Pairs** [+9109] of all creatures that have the breath of life in them
7:15 **Pairs** [+9109] of all creatures that have the breath of life in them
9:22 saw his father's nakedness and told his **two** brothers outside.
9:23 **[RPH]** then they walked in backward and covered their father's
10:25 **Two** sons were born to Eber: One was named Peleg, because in his
11:20 When Reu had lived **32** [+2256+8993] years, he became the father
14:4 For **twelve** [+6926] years they had been subject to Kedorlaomer,
17:20 He will be the father of **twelve** [+6925] rulers, and I will make him
19:1 The **two** angels arrived at Sodom in the evening, and Lot was
19:8 Look, I have **two** daughters who have never slept with a man.
19:15 Take your wife and your **two** daughters who are here, or you will
19:16 his hand and the hands of his wife and of his **two** daughters
19:30 Lot and his **two** daughters left Zoar and settled in the mountains,
19:30 afraid to stay in Zoar. He and his **two** daughters lived in a cave.
19:36 So **both** *of* Lot's daughters became pregnant by their father.
21:27 and gave them to Abimelech, and the **two** men made a treaty.
21:31 was called Beersheba, because the **two** men swore an oath there.
22:3 his donkey. He took with him **two** *of* his servants and his son Isaac.
22:6 carried the fire and the knife. As the **two** *of* them went on together,
22:8 the burnt offering, my son." And the **two** *of* them went on together.
24:22 ring weighing a beka and **two** gold bracelets weighing ten shekels.
25:16 these are the names of the **twelve** [+6925] tribal rulers according to
25:23 The LORD said to her, "**Two** nations are in your womb,
25:23 in your womb, and **two** peoples from within you will be separated;
27:9 Go out to the flock and bring me **two** choice young goats,
27:45 come back from there. Why should I lose **both** *of* you in one day?"
29:16 Now Laban had **two** daughters; the name of the older was Leah,
31:33 and into Leah's tent and into the tent of the **two** maidservants,
31:37 your relatives and mine, and let them judge between the **two** *of* us.
31:41 I worked for you fourteen years for your **two** daughters and six
32:7 [32:8] divided the people who were with him into **two** groups,
32:10 [32:11] I crossed this Jordan, but now I have become **two** groups.
32:22 [32:23] That night Jacob got up and took his **two** wives, his two
32:22 [32:23] his **two** maidservants and his eleven sons and crossed the
33:1 the children among Leah, Rachel and the **two** maidservants.
34:25 **two** *of* Jacob's sons, Simeon and Levi, Dinah's brothers, took their
35:22 and Israel heard of it. Jacob had **twelve** [+6925] sons:
40:2 Pharaoh was angry with his **two** officials, the chief cupbearer
40:5 each *of* the **two** men—the cupbearer and the baker of the king of
41:50 **two** sons were born to Joseph by Asenath daughter of Potiphera,
42:13 But they replied, "Your servants were **twelve** [+6925] brothers,
42:32 We were **twelve** [+6925] brothers, sons of one father. One is no
42:37 "You may put **both** *of* my sons to death if I do not bring him back
44:27 my father said to us, 'You know that my wife bore me **two** *sons*.
46:27 With the **two** sons who had been born to Joseph in Egypt,
48:1 So he took his **two** sons Manasseh and Ephraim along with him.
48:5 your **two** sons born to you in Egypt before I came to you here will
48:13 Joseph took **both** *of* them, Ephraim on his right toward Israel's left
49:28 All these are the **twelve** [+6925] tribes of Israel, and this is what
Ex 2:13 The next day he went out and saw **two** Hebrews fighting. He asked
4:9 But if they do not believe these **two** signs or listen to you,
12:7 put it on the **sides** and tops *of* the doorframes of the houses where
12:22 some of the blood on the top and on **both sides** *of* the doorframe.
12:23 he will see the blood on the top and **sides** *of* the doorframe
15:27 where there were **twelve** [+6926] springs and seventy palm trees,
16:22 they gathered twice as much—**two** omers for each person—
18:3 and her **two** sons. One son was named Gershom, for Moses said,
18:6 am coming to you with your wife and her **two** sons."
22:4 [22:3] whether ox or donkey or sheep—he must pay back **double**.
22:7 [22:6] the thief, if he is caught, must pay back **double**.
22:9 [22:8] **both** *parties* are to bring their cases before the judges.
22:9 [22:8] declare guilty must pay back **double** to his neighbor.
22:11 [22:10] the issue between **[NIE]** them will be settled by the
24:4 set up **twelve** [+6926] stone pillars representing the twelve tribes
24:4 set up twelve stone pillars representing the **twelve** [+6925] tribes
25:12 its four feet, with **two** rings on one side and two rings on the other.
25:12 its four feet, with two rings on one side and **two** rings on the other.
25:18 make **two** cherubim out of hammered gold at the ends of the cover.
25:18 make two cherubim out of hammered gold at **[RPH]** the ends of
25:19 make the cherubim of one piece with the cover, at the **two** ends.
25:22 above the cover between the **two** cherubim that are over the ark of
25:35 One bud shall be under the first **pair** *of* branches extending from
25:35 a second bud under the second **pair**, and a third bud under the third
25:35 bud under the second pair, and a third bud under the third **pair**—
26:17 with **two** projections set parallel to each other. Make all the frames
26:19 under them—**two** bases for each frame, one under each projection.
26:19 under them—two bases for each frame, one under **each** projection.
26:19 two bases for each frame, one under each projection. **[RPH]**
26:19 two bases for each frame, one under each projection. **[RPH]**
26:21 and forty silver bases—**two** under each frame.
26:21 and forty silver bases—two under each frame. **[RPH]**
26:23 and make **two** frames for the corners at the far end.
26:24 At these **two** corners they must be double from the bottom all the
26:24 way to the top, and fitted into a single ring; **both** shall be like that.
26:25 be eight frames and sixteen silver bases—**two** under each frame.
26:25 and sixteen silver bases—two under each frame. **[RPH]**
27:7 so they will be on **two** sides of the altar when it is carried.
28:7 It is to have **two** shoulder pieces attached to two of its corners,
28:7 It is to have two shoulder pieces attached to **two** *of* its corners,
28:9 "Take **two** onyx stones and engrave on them the names of the sons
28:11 Engrave the names of the sons of Israel on the **two** stones the way
28:12 fasten **them**[s] [+74+2021] on the shoulder pieces of the ephod as
28:12 Aaron is to bear the names on his **[RPH]** shoulders as a memorial
28:14 **two** braided chains of pure gold, like a rope, and attach the chains
28:21 There are to be **twelve** [+6926] stones, one for each of the names
28:21 like a seal with the name of one of the **twelve** [+6925] tribes.
28:23 Make **two** gold rings for it and fasten them to two corners of the
28:23 and fasten **them**[s] [+2021+3192] to two corners of the breastpiece.
28:23 gold rings for it and fasten them to **two** corners of the breastpiece.
28:24 Fasten the **two** gold chains to the rings at the corners of the
28:24 Fasten the two gold chains to **[RPH]** the rings at the corners of
28:25 the **other**[s] ends of the chains to the two settings, attaching them to
28:25 and the other ends of **[RPH]** the chains to the two settings,
28:25 the other ends of the chains to the **two** settings, attaching them to
28:26 Make **two** gold rings and attach them to the other two corners of
28:26 attach them to the other **two** corners of the breastpiece on the
28:27 Make **two** more gold rings and attach them to the bottom of the
28:27 attach them to the bottom of the **[RPH]** shoulder pieces on the
29:1 me as priests: Take a young bull and **two** rams without defect.
29:3 and present them in it—along with the bull and the **two** rams.
29:13 the covering of the liver, and **both** kidneys with the fat on them,

Ex 29:22 of the liver, **both** kidneys with the fat on them, and the right thigh.
29:38 are to offer on the altar regularly each day: **two** lambs a year old.
30: 4 Make **two** gold rings for the altar below the molding—two on
30: 4 **two** on opposite sides—to hold the poles used to carry it.
30: 4 two on opposite sides—**[RPH]** to hold the poles used to carry it.
31:18 he gave him the **two** tablets of the Testimony, the tablets of stone
32:15 went down the mountain with the **two** tablets of the Testimony in
32:15 in his hands. They were inscribed on **both** sides, front and back.
34: 1 said to Moses, "Chisel out **two** stone tablets like the first ones,
34: 4 So Moses chiseled out **two** stone tablets like the first ones
34: 4 commanded him; and he carried the **two** stone tablets in his hands.
34:29 When Moses came down from Mount Sinai with the **two** tablets of
36:22 with **two** projections set parallel to each other. They made all the
36:24 under them—**two** bases for each frame, one under each projection.
36:24 under them—two bases for each frame, one under **each** projection.
36:24 two bases for each frame, one under each projection. **[RPH]**
36:24 two bases for each frame, one under each projection. **[RPH]**
36:26 and forty silver bases—**two** under each frame.
36:26 and forty silver bases—two under each frame. **[RPH]**
36:28 **two** frames were made for the corners of the tabernacle at the far
36:29 At these **two** corners the frames were double from the bottom all
36:29 way to the top and fitted into a single ring; **both** were made alike.
36:30 were eight frames and sixteen silver bases—**two** under each frame.
36:30 and sixteen silver bases—two **[RPH]** under each frame.
37: 3 its four feet, with **two** rings on one side and two rings on the other.
37: 3 its four feet, with two rings on one side and **two** rings on the other.
37: 7 he made **two** cherubim out of hammered gold at the ends of the
37: 7 he made two cherubim out of hammered gold at **[NIE]** the ends of
37: 8 at the **two** ends he made them of one piece with the cover.
37:21 One bud was under the first **pair** *of* branches extending from the
37:21 a second bud under the second **pair**, and a third bud under the third
37:21 bud under the second pair, and a third bud under the third **pair**—
37:27 They made **two** gold rings below the molding—two on opposite
37:27 **two** on opposite sides—to hold the poles used to carry it.
37:27 two on opposite sides—**[RPH]** to hold the poles used to carry it.
39: 4 which were attached to **two** *of* its corners, so it could be fastened.
39:14 There were **twelve** [+6926] stones, one for each of the names of
39:14 like a seal with the name of one of the **twelve** [+6925] tribes.
39:16 They made **two** gold filigree settings and two gold rings,
39:16 They made two gold filigree settings and **two** gold rings,
39:16 fastened **[RPH]** the rings to two of the corners of the breastpiece.
39:16 and fastened the rings to **two** *of* the corners of the breastpiece.
39:17 They fastened the **two** gold chains to the rings at the corners of the
39:17 They fastened the two gold chains to **[RPH]** the rings at the
39:18 the **other**ˢ ends of the chains to the two settings, attaching them to
39:18 and the other ends of **[RPH]** the chains to the two settings,
39:18 the other ends of the chains to the **two** settings, attaching them to
39:19 They made **two** gold rings and attached them to the other two
39:19 attached them to the other **two** corners of the breastpiece on the
39:20 they made **two** more gold rings and attached them to the bottom of
39:20 attached them to the bottom of the **[RPH]** shoulder pieces on the
Lev 3: 4 **both** kidneys with the fat on them near the loins, and the covering
3:10 **both** kidneys with the fat on them near the loins, and the covering
3:15 **both** kidneys with the fat on them near the loins, and the covering
4: 9 **both** kidneys with the fat on them near the loins, and the covering
5: 7 he is to bring **two** doves or two young pigeons to the LORD as a
5: 7 or **two** young pigeons to the LORD as a penalty for his sin—
5:11 however, he cannot afford **two** doves or two young pigeons,
5:11 however, he cannot afford two doves or **two** young pigeons,
7: 4 **both** kidneys with the fat on them near the loins, and the covering
8: 2 the **two** rams and the basket containing bread made without yeast,
8:16 the covering of the liver, and **both** kidneys and their fat,
8:25 covering of the liver, **both** kidneys and their fat and the right thigh.
12: 8 she is to bring **two** doves or two young pigeons, one for a burnt
12: 8 she is to bring two doves or **two** young pigeons, one for a burnt
14: 4 the priest shall order that **two** live clean birds and some cedar
14:10 "On the eighth day he must bring **two** male lambs and one ewe
14:22 and **two** doves or two young pigeons, which he can afford,
14:22 and two doves or **two** young pigeons, which he can afford,
14:49 To purify the house he is to take **two** birds and some cedar wood,
15:14 On the eighth day he must take **two** doves or two young pigeons
15:14 On the eighth day he must take two doves or **two** young pigeons
15:29 On the eighth day she must take **two** doves or two young pigeons
15:29 On the eighth day she must take two doves or **two** young pigeons
16: 1 The LORD spoke to Moses after the death of the **two** sons of
16: 5 From the Israelite community he is to take **two** male goats for a sin
16: 7 he is to take the **two** goats and present them before the LORD at
16: 8 He is to cast lots for the **two** goats—one lot for the LORD
16:21 He is to lay **both** hands on the head of the live goat and confess
20:11 **Both** the man and the woman must be put to death; their blood will
20:12 sleeps with his daughter-in-law, **both** *of* them must be put to death.
20:13 one lies with a woman, **both** *of* them have done what is detestable.
20:18 also uncovered it. **Both** *of* them must be cut off from their people.
23:13 together with its grain offering of **two-tenths of** [+6928] an ephah
23:17 bring **two** loaves made of two-tenths of an ephah of fine flour,
23:17 bring two loaves made of **two-tenths of** [+6928] an ephah of fine
23:18 each a year old and without defect, one young bull and **two** rams.
23:19 Then sacrifice one male goat for a sin offering and **two** lambs,
23:20 The priest is to wave the **two** lambs before the LORD as a wave
24: 5 "Take fine flour and bake **twelve** [+6926] loaves of bread,
24: 5 of bread, using **two-tenths** [+6928] of an ephah for each loaf.
24: 6 Set them in **two** rows, six in each row, on the table of pure gold
Nu 1:35 the tribe of Manasseh was **32,200** [+547+2256+2256+4395+8993].
1:39 the tribe of Dan was **62,700** [+547+2256+2256+4395+8679+9252].
1:44 by Moses and Aaron and the **twelve** [+6925] leaders of Israel,
2:21 His division numbers **32,200** [+547+2256+2256+4395+8993].
2:26 division numbers **62,700** [+547+2256+2256+4395+8679+9252].
3:39 every male a month old or more, was **22,000** [+547+2256+6929].
3:43 was **22,273** [+547+2256+2256+4395+6929+8679+8993].
6:10 on the eighth day he must bring **two** doves or two young pigeons to
6:10 or **two** young pigeons to the priest at the entrance to the Tent of
7: 3 before the LORD six covered carts and **twelve** [+6925] oxen—
7: 3 twelve oxen—an ox from each leader and a cart from every **two**.
7: 7 He gave **two** carts and four oxen to the Gershonites, as their work
7:13 **each** filled with fine flour mixed with oil as a grain offering;
7:17 **two** oxen, five rams, five male goats and five male lambs a year
7:19 **each** filled with fine flour mixed with oil as a grain offering;
7:23 **two** oxen, five rams, five male goats and five male lambs a year
7:25 **each** filled with fine flour mixed with oil as a grain offering;
7:29 **two** oxen, five rams, five male goats and five male lambs a year
7:31 **each** filled with fine flour mixed with oil as a grain offering;
7:35 **two** oxen, five rams, five male goats and five male lambs a year
7:37 **each** filled with fine flour mixed with oil as a grain offering;
7:41 **two** oxen, five rams, five male goats and five male lambs a year
7:43 **each** filled with fine flour mixed with oil as a grain offering;
7:47 **two** oxen, five rams, five male goats and five male lambs a year
7:49 **each** filled with fine flour mixed with oil as a grain offering;
7:53 **two** oxen, five rams, five male goats and five male lambs a year
7:55 **each** filled with fine flour mixed with oil as a grain offering;
7:59 **two** oxen, five rams, five male goats and five male lambs a year
7:61 **each** filled with fine flour mixed with oil as a grain offering;
7:65 **two** oxen, five rams, five male goats and five male lambs a year
7:67 **each** filled with fine flour mixed with oil as a grain offering;
7:71 **two** oxen, five rams, five male goats and five male lambs a year
7:73 **each** filled with fine flour mixed with oil as a grain offering;
7:77 **two** oxen, five rams, five male goats and five male lambs a year
7:78 On the **twelfth** [+6925] day Ahira son of Enan, the leader of the
7:79 **each** filled with fine flour mixed with oil as a grain offering;
7:83 **two** oxen, five rams, five male goats and five male lambs a year
7:84 **twelve** [+6926] silver plates, twelve silver sprinkling bowls
7:84 **twelve** [+6925] silver sprinkling bowls and twelve gold dishes.
7:84 twelve silver sprinkling bowls and **twelve** [+6926] gold dishes.
7:86 The **twelve** [+6926] gold dishes filled with incense weighed ten
7:87 animals for the burnt offering came to **twelve** [+6925] young bulls,
7:87 **twelve** [+6925] rams and twelve male lambs a year old, together
7:87 twelve rams and **twelve** [+6925] male lambs a year old, together
7:87 **Twelve** [+6925] male goats were used for the sin offering.
7:89 he heard the voice speaking to him from between the **two** cherubim
10: 2 "Make **two** trumpets of hammered silver, and use them for calling
11:26 However, **two** men, whose names were Eldad and Medad,
12: 5 and Miriam. When **both** *of* them stepped forward,
13:23 **Two** of them carried it on a pole between them, along with some
15: 6 " 'With a ram prepare a grain offering of **two-tenths** [+6928] of an
17: 2 [17:17] to the Israelites and get **twelve** [+6925] staffs from them,
17: 6 [17:21] and their leaders gave him **twelve** [+6925] staffs,
22:22 was riding on his donkey, and his **two** servants were with him.
25: 8 He drove the spear through **both** *of* them—through the Israelite
26:14 Simeon; there were **22,200** [+547+2256+2256+4395+6929] men.
26:34 numbered were **52,700** [+547+2256+2256+2822+4395+8679].
26:37 numbered were **32,500** [+547+2256+2256+2822+4395+8993].
28: 3 **two** lambs a year old without defect, as a regular burnt offering
28: 9 make an offering of **two** lambs a year old without defect,
28: 9 a grain offering of **two-tenths** [+6928] of an ephah of fine flour
28:11 present to the LORD a burnt offering of **two** young bulls,
28:12 a grain offering of **two-tenths** [+6928] of an ephah of fine flour
28:19 a burnt offering of **two** young bulls, one ram and seven male lambs
28:20 of fine flour mixed with oil; with the ram, **two-tenths** [+6928];
28:27 Present a burnt offering of **two** young bulls, one ram and seven
28:28 of fine flour mixed with oil; with the ram, **two-tenths** [+6928];
29: 3 of fine flour mixed with oil; with the ram, **two-tenths** [+6928];
29: 9 of fine flour mixed with oil; with the ram, **two-tenths** [+6928];
29:13 **two** rams and fourteen male lambs a year old, all without defect.
29:14 of fine flour mixed with oil; with each of the **two** rams, two-tenths;
29:14 mixed with oil; with each of the two rams, **two-tenths** [+6928];
29:17 " 'On the second day prepare **twelve** [+6925] young bulls,
29:17 **two** rams and fourteen male lambs a year old, all without defect.
29:20 **two** rams and fourteen male lambs a year old, all without defect.
29:23 **two** rams and fourteen male lambs a year old, all without defect.

Nu 29: 26 **two** rams and fourteen male lambs a year old, all without defect.
29: 29 **two** rams and fourteen male lambs a year old, all without defect.
29: 32 **two** rams and fourteen male lambs a year old, all without defect.
31: 5 So **twelve** [+6925] thousand men armed for battle, a thousand from
31: 33 **72,000** [+547+2256+8679] cattle,
31: 35 **32,000** [+547+2256+8993] women who had never slept with a man.
31: 38 of which the tribute for the LORD was **72** [+2256+8679];
31: 40 of which the tribute for the LORD was **32** [+2256+8993].
33: 9 where there were **twelve** [+6926] springs and seventy palm trees,
34: 15 These **two** and a half tribes have received their inheritance on the
35: 6 In addition, give them **forty-two** [+752+2256] other towns.
Dt 1: 23 so I selected **twelve** [+6925] of you, one man from each tribe.
3: 8 So at that time we took from these **two** kings of the Amorites the
3: 21 eyes all that the LORD your God has done to these **two** kings.
4: 13 you to follow and then wrote them on **two** stone tablets.
4: 47 of Og king of Bashan, the **two** Amorite kings east of the Jordan.
5: 22 Then he wrote them on **two** stone tablets and gave them to me.
9: 10 The LORD gave me **two** stone tablets inscribed by the finger of
9: 11 and forty nights, the LORD gave me the **two** stone tablets,
9: 15 with fire. And the **two** tablets of the covenant were in my hands.
9: 15 And the two tablets of the covenant were in **[RPH]** my hands.
9: 17 So I took the **two** tablets and threw them out of my hands,
9: 17 So I took the two tablets and threw them out of **[RPH]** my hands,
10: 1 "Chisel out **two** stone tablets like the first ones and come up to me
10: 3 acacia wood and chiseled out **two** stone tablets like the first ones,
10: 3 and I went up on the mountain with the **two** tablets in my hands.
14: 6 You may eat any animal that has a split hoof divided in **two**
17: 6 On the testimony of **two** or three witnesses a man shall be put to
19: 15 A matter must be established by the testimony of **two** or three
19: 17 the **two** men involved in the dispute must stand in the presence of
21: 15 If a man has **two** wives, and he loves one but not the other,
21: 17 wife as the firstborn by giving him a **double** share of all he has.
22: 22 **both** the man who slept with her and the woman must die.
22: 24 you shall take **both** *of* them to the gate of that town and stone them
23: 18 [23:19] because the LORD your God detests them **both**.
32: 30 or **two** put ten thousand to flight, unless their Rock had sold them,
Jos 2: 1 Then Joshua son of Nun secretly sent **two** spies from Shittim.
2: 4 But the woman had taken the **two** men and hidden them. She said,
2: 10 to Sihon and Og, the **two** kings of the Amorites east of the Jordan,
2: 23 Then the **two** men started back. They went down out of the hills,
3: 12 Now then, choose **twelve** [+6925] men from the tribes of Israel,
4: 2 "Choose **twelve** [+6925] men from among the people, one from
4: 3 tell them to take up **twelve** [+6926] stones from the middle of the
4: 4 So Joshua called together the **twelve** [+6925] men he had
4: 8 They took **twelve** [+6926] stones from the middle of the Jordan,
4: 9 Joshua set up the **twelve** [+6926] stones that had been in the
4: 20 Joshua set up at Gilgal the **twelve** [+6926] stones they had taken
6: 22 Joshua said to the **two** men who had spied out the land, "Go into
8: 25 **Twelve** [+6925] thousand men and women fell that day—
9: 10 all that he did to the **two** kings of the Amorites east of the Jordan—
14: 3 Moses had granted the **two-and-a-half** [+2256+2942] tribes their
14: 4 for the sons of Joseph had become **two** tribes—Manasseh
15: 60 Kiriath Jearim) and Rabbah—**two** towns and their villages.
18: 24 Ophni and Geba—**twelve** [+6926] towns and their villages.
19: 15 There were **twelve** [+6926] towns and their villages.
19: 30 There were **twenty-two** [+2256+6929] towns and their villages.
21: 7 received **twelve** [+6926] towns from the tribes of Reuben,
21: 16 together with their pasturelands—nine towns from these **two** tribes.
21: 25 and Gath Rimmon, together with their pasturelands—**two** towns.
21: 27 and Be Eshtarah, together with their pasturelands—**two** towns;
21: 40 who were the rest of the Levites, were **twelve** [+6926].
24: 12 which drove them out before you—also the **two** Amorite kings.
Jdg 3: 16 Now Ehud had made a **double-edged** [+7023] sword about a foot
7: 3 So **twenty-two** [+2256+6929] thousand men left,
7: 25 They also captured **two** *of* the Midianite leaders, Oreb and Zeeb.
8: 12 Zebah and Zalmunna, the **two** kings of Midian, fled, but he
9: 44 **two** companies rushed upon those in the fields and struck them
10: 3 Jair of Gilead, who led Israel **twenty-two** [+2256+6929] years.
11: 37 "Give me **two** months to roam the hills and weep with my friends,
11: 38 he let her go for **two** months. She and the girls went into the hills
11: 39 After the **two** months, she returned to her father and he did to her
12: 6 **Forty-two** [+752+2256] thousand Ephraimites were killed at that
15: 4 tail to tail in pairs. He then fastened a torch to every **pair** *of* tails,
15: 13 So they bound him with **two** new ropes and led him up from the
16: 3 together with the **two** posts, and tore them loose, bar and all.
16: 28 let me with one blow get revenge on the Philistines for my **two**
16: 29 Samson reached toward the **two** central pillars on which the temple
19: 6 So the **two** *of* them sat down to eat and drink together.
19: 8 Wait till afternoon!" So the **two** *of* them ate together.
19: 29 into **twelve** [+6925] parts and sent them into all the areas of Israel.
20: 21 and cut down **twenty-two** [+2256+6929] thousand Israelites on the
21: 10 So the assembly sent **twelve** [+6925] thousand fighting men with
Ru 1: 1 from Bethlehem in Judah, together with his wife and **two** sons,
1: 2 and the names of his **two** sons were Mahlon and Kilion.
1: 3 Naomi's husband, died, and she was left with her **two** sons.
1: 5 **both** Mahlon and Kilion also died, and Naomi was left without her
1: 5 and Naomi was left without her **two** sons and her husband.
1: 7 With her **two** daughters-in-law she left the place where she had
1: 8 Naomi said to her **two** daughters-in-law, "Go back, each of you,
1: 19 So the **two** women went on until they came to Bethlehem.
4: 11 like Rachel and Leah, who **together** built up the house of Israel.
1Sa 1: 2 He had **two** wives; one was called Hannah and the other Peninnah.
1: 3 where Hophni and Phinehas, the **two** sons of Eli, were priests of
2: 21 she conceived and gave birth to three sons and **two** daughters.
2: 34 " 'And what happens to your **two** sons, Hophni and Phinehas,
2: 34 will be a sign to you—they will **both** die on the same day.
3: 11 I am about to do something in Israel that will make the **[NIE]** ears
4: 4 Eli's **two** sons, Hophni and Phinehas, were there with the ark of
4: 11 God was captured, and Eli's **two** sons, Hophni and Phinehas, died.
4: 17 Also your **two** sons, Hophni and Phinehas, are dead, and the ark of
5: 4 His head and **[NIE]** hands had been broken off and were lying on
6: 7 with **two** cows that have calved and have never been yoked.
6: 10 They took **two** such cows and hitched them to the cart and penned
9: 26 When Saul got ready, he and Samuel went outside **together**.
10: 2 you leave me today, you will meet **two** men near Rachel's tomb,
10: 4 They will greet you and offer you **two** loaves of bread, which you
11: 11 survived were scattered, so that no **two** of them were left together.
13: 1 became king, and he reigned over Israel ⌞**forty-** [+2256]⌟two years.
14: 11 So **both** *of* them showed themselves to the Philistine outpost.
14: 49 **[NIE]** The name of his older daughter was Merab, and that of the
18: 21 "Now you have a **second** *opportunity* to become my son-in-law."
20: 11 "let's go out into the field." So they went there **together**.
20: 42 for we have sworn friendship with **each** [+5646] **other** in the name
23: 18 The **two** *of* them made a covenant before the LORD.
25: 18 **two** skins of wine, five dressed sheep, five seahs of roasted grain,
25: 43 also married Ahinoam of Jezreel, and they **both** were his wives.
27: 3 Each man had his family with him, and David had his **two** wives:
28: 8 on other clothes, and at night he and **two** men went to the woman.
30: 5 David's **two** wives had been captured—Ahinoam of Jezreel
30: 12 part of a cake of pressed figs and **two** cakes of raisins. He ate
30: 18 everything the Amalekites had taken, including his **two** wives.
2Sa 1: 1 from defeating the Amalekites and stayed in Ziklag **two** days.
2: 2 So David went up there with his **two** wives, Ahinoam of Jezreel
2: 10 old when he became king over Israel, and he reigned **two** years.
2: 15 **twelve** [+6925] men for Benjamin and Ish-Bosheth son of Saul,
2: 15 and Ish-Bosheth son of Saul, and **twelve** [+6925] for David.
4: 2 Now Saul's son had **two** men who were leaders of raiding bands.
8: 2 Every **two** lengths of them were put to death, and the third length
8: 5 David struck down **twenty-two** [+2256+6929] thousand of them.
9: 13 he always ate at the king's table, and he was crippled in **both** feet.
10: 6 a thousand men, and also **twelve** [+6925] thousand men from Tob.
12: 1 he said, "There were **two** men in a certain town, one rich
13: 6 sister Tamar to come and make **some**[s] special bread in my sight,
14: 6 I your servant had **two** sons. They got into a fight with each other
14: 6 They got into a fight with **each other**[s] [+2157] in the field,
15: 27 son of Abiathar. You and Abiathar take your **two** sons with you.
15: 36 Their **two** sons, Ahimaaz son of Zadok and Jonathan son of
17: 1 "I would choose **twelve** [+6925] thousand men and set out tonight
17: 18 So the **two** *of* them left quickly and went to the house of a man in
18: 24 While David was sitting between the **inner**[s] **and outer** gates,
21: 8 and Mephibosheth, the **two** sons of Aiah's daughter Rizpah,
23: 20 performed great exploits. He struck down **two** *of* Moab's best men.
1Ki 2: 5 what he did to the **two** commanders of Israel's armies, Abner son
2: 32 without the knowledge of my father David he attacked **two** men
2: 39 **two** *of* Shimei's slaves ran off to Achish son of Maacah, king of
3: 16 Now **two** prostitutes came to the king and stood before him.
3: 18 We were alone; there was no one in the house but the **two** of us.
3: 25 "Cut the living child in **two** and give half to one and half to the
4: 7 Solomon also had **twelve** [+6925] district governors over all Israel,
4: 26 [5:6] for chariot horses, and **twelve** [+6925] thousand horses.
5: 12 [5:26] and Solomon, and the **two** *of* them made a treaty.
5: 14 [5:28] they spent one month in Lebanon and **two** months at home.
6: 23 In the inner sanctuary he made a **pair** *of* cherubim of olive wood,
6: 25 ten cubits, for the **two** cherubim were identical in size and shape.
6: 32 And on the **two** olive wood doors he carved cherubim, palm trees
6: 34 He also made **two** pine doors, each having two leaves that turned
6: 34 two pine doors, each having **two** leaves that turned in sockets.
6: 34 pine doors, each having two leaves that turned in sockets. **[RPH]**
7: 15 He cast **two** bronze pillars, each eighteen cubits high and twelve
7: 15 each eighteen cubits high and **twelve** [+6926] cubits around,
7: 16 He also made **two** capitals of cast bronze to set on the tops of the
7: 18 He made pomegranates in **two** rows encircling each network to
7: 20 On the capitals of **both** pillars, above the bowl-shaped part next to
7: 24 The gourds were cast in **two** rows in one piece with the Sea.
7: 25 The Sea stood on **twelve** [+6925] bulls, three facing north,
7: 41 the **two** pillars; the two bowl-shaped capitals on top of the pillars;
7: 41 the two pillars; the **two** bowl-shaped capitals on top of the pillars;
7: 41 the **two** *sets* of network decorating the two bowl-shaped capitals

1Ki 7:41 the two sets of network decorating the **two** bowl-shaped capitals on
7:42 the four hundred pomegranates for the **two** *sets* of network (two
7:42 the four hundred pomegranates for the two sets of network (**two**
7:42 decorating the **[RPH]** bowl-shaped capitals on top of the pillars);
7:44 the Sea and the **twelve** [+6925] bulls under it;
8:9 There was nothing in the ark except the **two** stone tablets that
8:63 **twenty-two** [+2256+6929] thousand cattle and a hundred and
9:10 of twenty years, during which Solomon built these **two** buildings—
10:19 of the seat were armrests, with a lion standing beside **each** of them.
10:20 **Twelve** [+6925] lions stood on the six steps, one at either end of
10:26 had fourteen hundred chariots and **twelve** [+6925] thousand horses,
11:29 a new cloak. The **two** *of* them were alone out in the country,
11:30 new cloak he was wearing and tore it into **twelve** [+6925] pieces.
12:28 After seeking advice, the king made **two** golden calves. He said to
14:20 He reigned for **twenty-two** [+2256+6929] years and then rested
15:25 Nadab son of Jeroboam became king of Israel in the **second** year
16:23 and he reigned **twelve** [+6926] years, six of them in Tirzah.
16:29 he reigned in Samaria over Israel **twenty-two** [+2256+6929] years.
17:12 I am gathering a **few** sticks to take home and make a meal for
18:21 and said, "How long will you waver between **two** opinions?
18:23 Get **two** bulls for us. Let them choose one for themselves,
18:31 Elijah took **twelve** [+6926] stones, one for each of the tribes
19:19 He was plowing with **twelve** [+6925] yoke of oxen, and he himself
19:19 yoke of oxen, and he himself was driving the **twelfth** [+6925] pair.
20:1 Accompanied by **thirty-two** [+2256+8993] kings with their horses
20:15 of the provincial commanders, **232** [+2256+4395+8993] men.
20:16 the **32** [+2256+8993] kings allied with him were in their tents
20:27 The Israelites camped opposite them like **two** small flocks of goats,
21:10 seat **two** scoundrels opposite him and have them testify that he has
21:13 **two** scoundrels came and sat opposite him and brought charges
22:31 had ordered his **thirty-two** [+2256+8993] chariot commanders,
2Ki 1:14 from heaven and consumed the first **two** captains and all their men.
1:17 Joram succeeded him as king in the **second** year of Jehoram son of
2:6 as you live, I will not leave you." So the **two** *of* them walked on.
2:7 facing the place where **Elijah**[s] [+2157] **and Elisha** had stopped at
2:8 and to the left, and the **two** *of* them crossed over on dry ground.
2:9 "Let me inherit a **double** portion of your spirit," Elisha replied.
2:11 and horses of fire appeared and separated the **two** *of* them,
2:12 hold of his own clothes and **tore** them **apart** [+4200+7973+7974].
2:24 **two** bears came out of the woods and mauled forty-two of the
2:24 of the woods and mauled **forty-two** [+752+2256] of the youths.
3:1 Jehoshaphat king of Judah, and he reigned **twelve** [+6926] years.
4:1 But now his creditor is coming to take my **two** boys as his slaves."
4:33 shut the door on the **two** *of* them and prayed to the LORD.
5:22 '**Two** young men from the company of the prophets have just come
5:22 Please give them a talent of silver and **two** sets of clothing.' "
5:23 then tied up the two talents of silver in **two** bags, with two sets of
5:23 up the two talents of silver in two bags, with **two** sets of clothing.
5:23 He gave them to **two** *of* his servants, and they carried them ahead
6:10 **Time and again** [+285+2256+4202+4202] Elisha warned the
7:14 So they selected **two** chariots with their horses, and the king sent
8:17 He was **thirty-two** [+2256+8993] years old when he became king,
8:25 In the **twelfth** [+6926] year of Joram son of Ahab king of Israel,
8:26 Ahaziah was **twenty-two** [+2256+6929] years old when he became
9:32 is on my side? Who?" **Two** or three eunuchs looked down at him.
10:4 But they were terrified and said, "If **two** kings could not resist him,
10:8 "Put them in **two** piles at the entrance of the city gate until
10:14 them by the well of Beth Eked—**forty-two** [+752+2256] men.
11:7 you who are in the other **two** companies that normally go off
14:1 In the **second** year of Jehoash son of Jehoahaz king of Israel,
15:2 and he reigned in Jerusalem **fifty-two** [+2256+2822] years.
15:27 In the **fifty-second** [+2256+2822] year of Azariah king of Judah,
15:32 In the **second** year of Pekah son of Remaliah king of Israel,
17:1 In the **twelfth** [+6926] year of Ahaz king of Judah, Hoshea son of
17:16 and made for themselves **two** idols cast in the shape of calves,
21:1 Manasseh was **twelve** [+6926] years old when he became king,
21:5 In **both** courts of the temple of the LORD, he built altars to all the
21:12 Judah that **[NIE]** the ears of everyone who hears of it will tingle.
21:19 Amon was **twenty-two** [+2256+6929] years old when he became
21:19 old when he became king, and he reigned in Jerusalem **two** years.
23:12 the altars Manasseh had built in the **two** courts of the temple of the
25:16 The bronze from the **two** pillars, the Sea and the movable stands,
25:27 prison on the twenty-seventh day of the **twelfth** [+6925] month.
1Ch 1:19 **Two** sons were born to Eber: One was named Peleg, because in his
4:5 Ashhur the father of Tekoa had **two** wives, Helah and Naarah.
6:63 [6:48] were allotted **twelve** [+6926] towns from the tribes of
7:2 numbered **22,600** [+547+2256+2256+4395+6929+9252].
7:7 **22,034** [+547+752+2256+2256+2256+6929+8993] fighting men.
9:22 gatekeepers at the thresholds numbered **212** [+2256+4395+6925].
11:21 He was **doubly** [+928+2021] honored above the Three and became
11:22 performed great exploits. He struck down **two** *of* Moab's best men.
12:28 [12:29] with **22** [+2256+6929] officers from his family;
15:10 Amminadab the leader and **112** [+2256+4395+6925] relatives.
18:5 David struck down **twenty-two** [+2256+6929] thousand of them.
19:7 They hired **thirty-two** [+2256+8993] thousand chariots and
24:12 the eleventh to Eliashib, the **twelfth** [+6925] to Jakim,
24:17 to Jakin, the **twenty-second** [+2256+6929] to Gamul,
25:9 fell to Joseph, his sons and relatives, **12** [+6925]
25:9 the second to Gedaliah, he and his relatives and sons, **12** [+6925]
25:10 the third to Zaccur, his sons and relatives, **12** [+6925]
25:11 the fourth to Izri, his sons and relatives, **12** [+6925]
25:12 the fifth to Nethaniah, his sons and relatives, **12** [+6925]
25:13 the sixth to Bukkiah, his sons and relatives, **12** [+6925]
25:14 the seventh to Jesarelah, his sons and relatives, **12** [+6925]
25:15 the eighth to Jeshaiah, his sons and relatives, **12** [+6925]
25:16 the ninth to Mattaniah, his sons and relatives, **12** [+6925]
25:17 the tenth to Shimei, his sons and relatives, **12** [+6925]
25:18 the eleventh to Azarel, his sons and relatives, **12** [+6925]
25:19 the **twelfth** [+6925] to Hashabiah, his sons and relatives, 12
25:19 the twelfth to Hashabiah, his sons and relatives, **12** [+6925]
25:20 the thirteenth to Shubael, his sons and relatives, **12** [+6925]
25:21 the fourteenth to Mattithiah, his sons and relatives, **12** [+6925]
25:22 the fifteenth to Jerimoth, his sons and relatives, **12** [+6925]
25:23 the sixteenth to Hananiah, his sons and relatives, **12** [+6925]
25:24 seventeenth to Joshbekashah, his sons and relatives, **12** [+6925]
25:25 the eighteenth to Hanani, his sons and relatives, **12** [+6925]
25:26 the nineteenth to Mallothi, his sons and relatives, **12** [+6925]
25:27 the twentieth to Eliathah, his sons and relatives, **12** [+6925]
25:28 the twenty-first to Hothir, his sons and relatives, **12** [+6925]
25:29 the **twenty-second** [+2256+6929] to Giddalti, his sons and
25:29 the twenty-second to Giddalti, his sons and relatives, **12** [+6925]
25:30 the twenty-third to Mahazioth, his sons and relatives, **12** [+6925]
25:31 twenty-fourth to Romamti-Ezer, his sons and relatives, **12** [+6925]
26:8 do the work—descendants of Obed-Edom, **62** [+2256+9252] in all.
26:17 a day on the south and **two** [+9109] **at a time** at the storehouse.
26:17 a day on the south and **two at a time** [+9109] at the storehouse.
26:18 to the west, there were four at the road and **two** at the court itself.
27:15 The **twelfth** [+6925], for the twelfth month, was Heldai the
27:15 The twelfth, for the **twelfth** [+6925] month, was Heldai the
2Ch 1:14 had fourteen hundred chariots and **twelve** [+6925] thousand horses,
3:10 In the Most Holy Place he made a **pair** of sculptured cherubim
3:15 In the front of the temple he made **two** pillars, which ⌞together⌟
4:3 The bulls were cast in **two** rows in one piece with the Sea.
4:4 The Sea stood on **twelve** [+6925] bulls, three facing north,
4:12 the **two** pillars; the two bowl-shaped capitals on top of the pillars;
4:12 the two pillars; the **two** bowl-shaped capitals on top of the pillars;
4:12 the **two** *sets* of network decorating the two bowl-shaped capitals
4:12 the two sets of network decorating the **two** bowl-shaped capitals on
4:13 the four hundred pomegranates for the **two** *sets of* network (two
4:13 the four hundred pomegranates for the two sets of network (**two**
4:13 decorating the **[RPH]** bowl-shaped capitals on top of the pillars);
4:15 the Sea and the **twelve** [+6925] bulls under it;
5:10 There was nothing in the ark except the **two** tablets that Moses had
7:5 offered a sacrifice of **twenty-two** [+2256+6929] thousand head of
9:18 of the seat were armrests, with a lion standing beside **each** of them.
9:19 **Twelve** [+6925] lions stood on the six steps, one at either end of
9:25 stalls for horses and chariots, and **twelve** [+6925] thousand horses,
13:21 and had **twenty-two** [+2256+6929] sons and sixteen daughters.
21:5 Jehoram was **thirty-two** [+2256+8993] years old when he became
21:19 at the end of the **second** year, his bowels came out because of the
21:20 Jehoram was **thirty-two** [+2256+8993] years old when he became
22:2 Ahaziah was **twenty-two** [+752+2256] years old when he became
24:3 Jehoiada chose **two** wives for him, and he had sons and daughters.
26:3 and he reigned in Jerusalem **fifty-two** [+2256+2822] years.
33:1 Manasseh was **twelve** [+6926] years old when he became king,
33:5 In **both** courts of the temple of the LORD, he built altars to all the
33:21 Amon was **twenty-two** [+2256+6929] years old when he became
33:21 old when he became king, and he reigned in Jerusalem **two** years.
34:3 In his **twelfth** [+6926] year he began to purge Judah and Jerusalem
Ezr 2:3 the descendants of Parosh **2,172** [+547+2256+4395+8679]
2:4 of Shephatiah **372** [+2256+4395+8679+8993]
2:6 the line of Jeshua and Joab) **2,812** [+547+2256+4395+6925+9046]
2:10 of Bani **642** [+752+2256+4395+9252]
2:12 of Azgad **1,222** [+547+2256+4395+6929]
2:18 of Jorah **112** [+2256+4395+6925]
2:24 of Azmaveth **42** [+752+2256]
2:27 of Micmash **122** [+2256+4395+6929]
2:29 of Nebo **52** [+2256+2822]
2:37 of Immer **1,052** [+547+2256+2822]
2:58 of the servants of Solomon **392** [+2256+4395+8993+9596]
2:60 of Delaiah, Tobiah and Nekoda **652** [+2256+2822+4395+9252]
8:24 I set apart **twelve** [+6925] of the leading priests, together with
8:27 and **two** fine articles of polished bronze, as precious as gold.
8:31 On the **twelfth** [+6925] day of the first month we set out from the
8:35 **twelve** [+6925] bulls for all Israel, ninety-six rams,
8:35 male lambs and, as a sin offering, **twelve** [+6925] male goats.
10:13 Besides, this matter cannot be taken care of in a day or **two**,
Ne 5:14 in the land of Judah, until his **thirty-second** [+2256+8993] year—

Ne 5:14 land of Judah, until his thirty-second year—**twelve** [+6926] years—
6:15 on the twenty-fifth of Elul, in **fifty-two** [+2256+2822] days.
7:8 the descendants of Parosh **2,172** [+547+2256+2256+4395+8679]
7:9 of Shephatiah **372** [+2256+4395+8679+8993]
7:10 of Arah **652** [+2256+2822+4395+9252]
7:17 of Azgad **2,322** [+547+2256+4395+6929+8993]
7:24 of Hariph **112** [+4395+6925]
7:28 of Beth Azmaveth **42** [+752+2256]
7:31 of Micmash **122** [+2256+2256+4395+6929]
7:33 of the other Nebo **52** [+2256+2822]
7:40 of Immer **1,052** [+547+2256+2822]
7:60 of the servants of Solomon **392** [+2256+4395+8993+9596]
7:62 Delaiah, Tobiah and Nekoda **642** [+752+2256+2256+4395+9252]
7:71 [7:70] the treasury for the work **20,000** [+8052] drachmas of gold
7:72 [7:71] rest of the people was **20,000** [+8052] drachmas of gold,
11:12 **822** [+2256+4395+6929+9046] men; Adaiah son of Jeroham, the
11:13 **242** [+752+2256+4395] men; Amashsai son of Azarel, the son of
11:19 who kept watch at the gates—**172** [+2256+4395+8679] men.
12:31 I also assigned **two** large choirs to give thanks. One was to proceed
12:40 The **two** choirs that gave thanks then took their places in the house
13:6 I was not in Jerusalem, for in the **thirty-second** [+2256+8993] year
13:20 Once or **twice** the merchants and sellers of all kinds of goods spent
Est 2:12 she had to complete **twelve** [+6925] months of beauty treatments
2:21 and Teresh, **two** of the king's officers who guarded the doorway,
2:23 and found to be true, the **two** officials were hanged on a gallows.
3:7 In the **twelfth** [+6926] year of King Xerxes, in the first month,
3:7 And the lot fell on the **twelfth** [+6925] month, the month of Adar.
3:13 on a single day, the thirteenth day of the **twelfth** [+6925] month,
6:2 and Teresh, **two** of the king's officers who guarded the doorway,
8:12 King Xerxes was the thirteenth day of the **twelfth** [+6925] month,
9:1 On the thirteenth day of the **twelfth** [+6925] month, the month of
9:27 all who join them should without fail observe these **two** days every
Job 9:33 someone to arbitrate between us, to lay his hand upon us **both**,
13:20 "Only grant me these **two** *things*, O God, and then I will not hide
33:14 For God does speak—now one way, now **another**—though man
40:5 spoke once, but I have no answer—**twice**, but I will say no more."
42:7 Eliphaz the Temanite, "I am angry with you and your **two** friends,
Ps 60:T [60:2] struck down **twelve** [+6925] thousand Edomites in the
62:11 [62:12] One thing God has spoken, **two** things have I heard:
Pr 17:15 and condemning the innocent—the LORD detests them **both**.
20:10 and differing measures—the LORD detests them **both**.
20:12 Ears that hear and eyes that see—the LORD has made them **both**.
24:22 for those **two** will send sudden destruction upon them, and who
27:3 and sand a burden, but provocation by a fool is heavier than **both**.
29:13 have this in common: The LORD gives sight to the eyes of **both**.
30:7 "**Two** *things* I ask of you, O LORD; do not refuse me before I
30:15 "The leech has **two** daughters. 'Give! Give!' they cry. "There are
Ecc 4:3 better than **both** is he who has not yet been, who has not seen the
4:9 **Two** are better than one, because they have a good return for their
4:11 Also, if **two** lie down together, they will keep warm. But how can
4:12 Though one may be overpowered, **two** can defend themselves.
11:6 whether this or that, or whether **both** will do equally well.
SS 4:5 Your **two** breasts are like two fawns, like twin fawns of a gazelle
4:5 Your two breasts are like **two** fawns, like twin fawns of a gazelle
7:3 [7:4] Your **[RPH]** breasts are like two fawns, twins of a gazelle.
7:3 [7:4] Your breasts are like **two** fawns, twins of a gazelle.
Isa 1:31 a spark; **both** will burn together, with no one to quench the fire."
6:2 With **two** wings they covered their faces, with two they covered
6:2 with **two** they covered their feet, and with two they were flying.
6:2 with two they covered their feet, and with **two** they were flying.
7:4 not lose heart because of these **two** smoldering stubs of firewood—
7:16 the right, the land of the **two** kings you dread will be laid waste.
7:21 In that day, a man will keep alive a young cow and **two** goats.
8:14 for **both** houses of Israel he will be a stone that causes men to
17:6 leaving **two** or three olives on the topmost branches, four or five on
47:9 **Both** *of* these will overtake you in a moment, on a single day:
51:19 These **double** calamities have come upon you—who can comfort
Jer 2:13 "My people have committed **two** sins: They have forsaken me,
3:14 I will choose you—one from a town and **two** from a clan—
24:1 the LORD showed me **two** baskets of figs placed in front of the
33:24 are saying, 'The LORD has rejected the **two** kingdoms he chose'?
34:18 I will treat like the calf they cut in **two** and then walked between its
46:12 warrior will stumble over another; **both** will fall down together."
52:20 The bronze from the **two** pillars, the Sea and the twelve bronze
52:20 the Sea and the **twelve** [+6925] bronze bulls under it,
52:21 eighteen cubits high and **twelve** [+6926] cubits in circumference;
52:29 year, **832** [+2256+4395+8993+9046] people from Jerusalem;
52:31 from prison on the twenty-fifth day of the **twelfth** [+6925] month.
Eze 1:11 each had **two** wings, one touching the wing of another creature on
1:11 of another creature on either side, and **two** wings covering its body.
1:23 one toward the other, and each had **two** wings covering its body.
1:23 the other, and each had two wings covering its body. **[RPH]**
15:4 the fire as fuel and the fire burns **both** ends and chars the middle,
21:19 [21:24] mark out **two** roads for the sword of the king of Babylon
21:19 [21:24] of Babylon to take, **both** starting from the same country.
21:21 [21:26] at the junction of the **two** roads, to seek an omen:
23:2 "Son of man, there were **two** women, daughters of the same
23:13 I saw that she too defiled herself; **both** *of* them went the same way.
29:1 In the tenth year, in the tenth month on the **twelfth** [+6925] day,
32:1 In the **twelfth** [+6926] year, in the twelfth month on the first day,
32:1 In the twelfth year, in the **twelfth** [+6925] month on the first day,
32:17 In the **twelfth** [+6926] year, on the fifteenth day of the month,
33:21 In the **twelfth** [+6926] year of our exile, in the tenth month on the
35:10 "These **two** nations and countries will be ours and we will take
35:10 "These two nations and **[RPH]** countries will be ours and we will
37:22 they will never again be **two** nations or be divided into two
37:22 will never again be two nations or be divided into **two** kingdoms.
40:9 it was eight cubits deep and its jambs were **two** cubits thick.
40:39 In the portico of the gateway were **two** tables on each side,
40:39 **[RPH]** on which the burnt offerings, sin offerings and guilt
40:40 near the steps at the entrance to the north gateway were **two** tables,
40:40 were two tables, and on the other side of the steps were **two** tables.
40:44 inner gate, within the inner court, were **two** [BHS 8876] rooms,
40:49 and **twelve** [+6926] [BHS 6954] cubits from front to back.
41:3 and measured the jambs of the entrance; each was **two** cubits wide.
41:18 Palm trees alternated with cherubim. Each cherub had **two** faces:
41:22 There was a wooden altar three cubits high and **two** cubits square;
41:22 **[RPH; BHS-]** its corners, its base and its sides were of wood.
41:23 the outer sanctuary and the Most Holy Place had **double** doors.
41:24 **Each**[s] door had two leaves—two hinged leaves for each door.
41:24 Each door had **two** leaves—two hinged leaves for each door.
41:24 Each door had two leaves—**two** hinged leaves for each door.
41:24 door had two leaves—two hinged leaves for each door. **[RPH]**
43:14 From the gutter on the ground up to the lower ledge it is **two** cubits
43:16 is square, **twelve** [+6926] cubits long and twelve cubits wide.
43:16 is square, twelve cubits long and **twelve** [+6926] cubits wide.
47:13 land for an inheritance among the **twelve** [+6925] tribes of Israel,
Da 2:1 In the **second** year of his reign, Nebuchadnezzar had dreams;
8:7 the ram furiously, striking the ram and shattering his **two** horns.
9:25 there will be seven 'sevens,' and **sixty-two** [+2256+9252] 'sevens.'
9:26 After the **sixty-two** [+2256+9252] 'sevens,' the Anointed One will
11:27 The **two** kings, with their hearts bent on evil, will sit at the same
12:5 Then I, Daniel, looked, and there before me stood **two** others,
Hos 10:10 be gathered against them to put them in bonds for their **double** sin.
Am 3:3 Do **two** walk together unless they have agreed to do so?
3:12 "As a shepherd saves from the lion's mouth only **two** leg bones
4:8 **People**[s] [+8993] staggered from town to town for water but did not
Jnh 4:11 has more than a **hundred and twenty thousand** [+6926+8052]
Hag 1:1 In the **second** year of King Darius, on the first day of the sixth
1:15 on the twenty-fourth day of the sixth month in the **second** year of
2:10 twenty-fourth day of the ninth month, in the **second** year of Darius,
Zec 1:1 In the eighth month of the **second** year of Darius, the word of the
1:7 eleventh month, the month of Shebat, in the **second** year of Darius,
4:3 Also there are **two** olive trees by it, one on the right of the bowl
4:11 "What are these **two** olive trees on the right and the left of the
4:12 "What are these **two** olive branches beside the two gold pipes that
4:12 "What are these two olive branches beside the **two** gold pipes that
4:14 "These are the **two** who are anointed to serve the Lord of all the
5:9 there before me were **two** women, with the wind in their wings!
6:1 there before me were four chariots coming out from between **two**
6:13 a priest on his throne. And there will be harmony between the **two**.'
11:7 Then I took **two** staffs and called one Favor and the other Union,
13:8 declares the LORD, "**two-thirds** [+7023] will be struck down

9110 שְׁנִינָה šᵉnînâ, n.f. [4] [√ 9111]

object of ridicule [3], ridicule [1]

Dt 28:37 and **ridicule** to all the nations where the LORD will drive you.
1Ki 9:7 become a byword and an **object of ridicule** among all peoples.
2Ch 7:20 will make it a byword and an **object of ridicule** among all peoples.
Jer 24:9 a reproach and a byword, an **object of ridicule** and cursing,

9111 [1]שָׁנַן šānan[1], v. [8] [→ 9094, 9095, 9105, 9110]

sharp [4], sharpen [2], embittered [1], make sharp [1]

Dt 32:41 [A] when *I* **sharpen** my flashing sword and my hand grasps it in
Ps 45:5 [45:6] [B] Let your **sharp** arrows pierce the hearts of the king's
64:3 [64:4] [A] *They* **sharpen** their tongues like swords and aim
73:21 [F] When my heart was grieved and my spirit **embittered**,
120:4 [B] He will punish you with a warrior's **sharp** arrows,
140:3 [140:4] [A] *They* **make** their tongues as **sharp** as a serpent's;
Pr 25:18 [B] or a **sharp** arrow is the man who gives false testimony
Isa 5:28 [B] Their arrows *are* **sharp**, all their bows are strung;

9112 [2]שָׁנַן šānan[2], v. [1] [cf. 9101]

impress [1]

Dt 6:7 [D] **Impress** them on your children. Talk about them when you

9113 שָׁנַס **šānas**, v. [1]

tucking cloak into belt [+5516] [1]

1Ki 18:46 [D] **tucking** [+5516] his **cloak into** *his* **belt**, he ran ahead of

9114 שִׁנְעָר **šinʿār**, n.pr.loc. [8]

Babylonia [3], Shinar [+824] [2], Shinar [2], Babylonia [+824] [1]

Ge 10:10 were Babylon, Erech, Akkad and Calneh, in **Shinar** [+824].
11: 2 they found a plain in **Shinar** [+824] and settled there.
14: 1 At this time Amraphel king of **Shinar**, Arioch king of Ellasar,
14: 9 of Goiim, Amraphel king of **Shinar** and Arioch king of Ellasar—
Jos 7:21 When I saw in the plunder a beautiful robe from **Babylonia**,
Isa 11:11 from Cush, from Elam, from **Babylonia**, from Hamath and from
Da 1: 2 These he carried off to the temple of his god in **Babylonia** [+824]
Zec 5:11 He replied, "To the country of **Babylonia** to build a house for it.

9115 שָׁסָה **šāsâ**, v. [11] [cf. 9116]

plundered [4], raiders [2], loot [1], looted [1], looting [1], pillage [1], plunderers [1]

Jdg 2:14 [A] LORD handed them over to **raiders** who plundered them.
2:16 [A] up judges, who saved them out of the hands of these **raiders**.
1Sa 14:48 [A] Israel from the hands of *those who had* **plundered** them.
23: 1 [A] fighting against Keilah and *are* **looting** the threshing floors,"
2Ki 17:20 [A] afflicted them and gave them into the hands of **plunderers**,
Ps 44:10 [44:11] [A] the enemy, and our adversaries *have* **plundered** us.
Isa 10:13 [D] the boundaries of nations, *I* **plundered** their treasures;
17:14 [A] This is the portion of *those who* **loot** us, the lot of those who
42:22 [B] this is a people plundered and **looted**, all of them trapped in
Jer 50:11 [A] you rejoice and are glad, you *who* **pillage** my inheritance,
Hos 13:15 [A] dry up. His storehouse *will be* **plundered** *of* all its treasures.

9116 שָׁסַס **šāsas**, v. [6] [→ 5468; cf. 9115]

plundered [3], be looted [1], plunder [1], ransacked [1]

Jdg 2:14 [A] LORD handed them over to raiders *who* **plundered** them.
1Sa 17:53 [A] from chasing the Philistines, *they* **plundered** their camp.
Ps 89:41 [89:42] [A] All who pass by *have* **plundered** him; he has
Isa 13:16 [C] their houses *will* **be looted** and their wives ravished.
Jer 30:16 [A] *Those who* **plunder** you will be plundered; all who make
Zec 14: 2 [C] be captured, the houses **ransacked**, and the women raped.

9117 שָׁסַע **šāsaʿ**, v. [9] [→ 9118]

completely divided [+9118] [3], completely divided [1], divided [+9118] [1], rebuked [1], tear open [1], tore apart [1], torn [1]

Lev 1:17 [D] *He shall* **tear** it **open** by the wings, not severing it
11: 3 [A] any animal that has a split hoof **completely divided** [+9118]
11: 7 [A] though it has a split hoof **completely divided** [+9118],
11:26 [A] animal that has a split hoof not **completely divided** [+9118]
Dt 14: 6 [A] eat any animal that has a split hoof **divided** [+9118] *in* two
14: 7 [B] or that have a split hoof **completely divided** you may not eat
Jdg 14: 6 [D] so that *he* **tore** the lion **apart** with his bare hands as he might
14: 6 [D] with his bare hands as *he might have* **torn** a young goat.
1Sa 24: 7 [24:8] [D] With these words David **rebuked** his men and did

9118 שֶׁסַע **šesaʿ**, n.[m.]. [4] [√ 9117]

completely divided [+9117] [3], divided [+9117] [1]

Lev 11: 3 eat any animal that has a split hoof **completely divided** [+9117]
11: 7 the pig, though it has a split hoof **completely divided** [+9117],
11:26 animal that has a split hoof not **completely divided** [+9117]
Dt 14: 6 You may eat any animal that has a split hoof **divided in** [+9117]

9119 שָׁסַף **šāsap**, v. [1]

put to death [1]

1Sa 15:33 [D] And Samuel **put** Agag **to death** before the LORD at Gilgal.

9120 שָׁעָה **šāʿâ**, v. [13 / 11] [cf. 8617, 9283]

look [6], have regard [1], look with favor [1], looked with favor [1], pay attention [1], turn away [1]

Ge 4: 4 [A] The LORD **looked with favor** on Abel and his offering,
4: 5 [A] on Cain and his offering *he did* not **look with favor**.
Ex 5: 9 [A] so that they keep working and **pay** no **attention** to lies."
2Sa 22:42 [a] *They* cried **for help**, [BHS *looked*; NIV 8775]
Job 7:19 [A] *Will you* never **look** away from me, or let me alone even for
14: 6 [A] So **look** away from him and let him alone, till he has put in
Ps 39:13 [39:14] [G] **Look** away from me, that I may rejoice again before
119:117 [A] be delivered; *I will* always **have regard** for your decrees.
Isa 17: 7 [A] In that day men *will* **look** to their Maker and turn their eyes
17: 8 [A] *They will* not **look** to the altars, the work of their hands,
22: 4 [A] Therefore I said, "**Turn away** from me; let me weep bitterly.
31: 1 [A] *do* not **look** to the Holy One of Israel, or seek help from the
32: 3 [a] those who see *will* no *longer be* closed, [BHS *look*; NIV 9129]

9121 שְׁעָטָה **šeʿāṭâ**, n.f. [1]

galloping [1]

Jer 47: 3 at the sound of the hoofs of **galloping** steeds, at the noise of enemy

9122 שַׁעַטְנֵז **šaʿaṭnēz**, n.m. [2]

woven material [1], woven [1]

Lev 19:19 of seed. " 'Do not wear clothing **woven** of two kinds of **material**.
Dt 22:11 Do not wear clothes of wool and linen **woven** together.

9123 שֹׁעַל **šōʿal**, n.[m.]. [3] [→ 5469, 9127?]

handful [1], handfuls [1], hollow of hand [1]

1Ki 20:10 dust remains in Samaria to give each of my men a **handful**."
Isa 40:12 Who has measured the waters in the **hollow of** his **hand**, or with
Eze 13:19 You have profaned me among my people for a *few* **handfuls** *of*

9124 שַׁעַלְבִים **šaʿalbîm**, n.pr.loc. [2] [→ 9125]

Shaalbim [2]

Jdg 1:35 Aijalon and **Shaalbim**, but when the power of the house of Joseph
1Ki 4: 9 in Makaz, **Shaalbim**, Beth Shemesh and Elon Bethhanan;

9125 שַׁעֲלַבִּין **šaʿalabbîn**, n.pr.loc. [1] [√ 9124]

Shaalabbin [1]

Jos 19:42 **Shaalabbin**, Aijalon, Ithlah,

9126 שַׁעַלְבֹנִי **šaʿalbōnî**, a.g. [2]

Shaalbonite [2]

2Sa 23:32 Eliahba the **Shaalbonite**, the sons of Jashen, Jonathan
1Ch 11:33 Azmaveth the Baharumite, Eliahba the **Shaalbonite**,

9127 שַׁעֲלִים **šaʿalîm**, n.pr.loc. [1] [√ 9123?]

Shaalim [1]

1Sa 9: 4 They went on into the district of **Shaalim**, but the donkeys were

9128 שָׁעַן **šāʿan**, v. [22] [→ 5472, 5473, 5474, 5475]

rely [5], lean [3], leaning [3], relied [3], leaned [2], rest [2], *untranslated* [1], depended [1], leans [1], lie [1]

Ge 18: 4 [C] and then you may all wash your feet and **rest** under this tree.
Nu 21:15 [C] that lead to the site of Ar and **lie** along the border of Moab."
Jdg 16:26 [C] that support the temple, so that *I may* **lean** against them."
2Sa 1: 6 [C] **leaning** on his spear, with the chariots and riders almost upon
2Ki 5:18 [C] and he *is* **leaning** on my arm and I bow there also—
7: 2 [C] The officer on whose arm the king *was* **leaning** said to the
7:17 [C] Now the king had put the officer on whose arm *he* **leaned** in
2Ch 13:18 [C] of Judah were victorious because *they* **relied** on the LORD,
14:11 [14:10] [C] Help us, O LORD our God, for *we* **rely** on you,
16: 7 [C] "Because you **relied** on the king of Aram and not on the
16: 7 [C] the army of **[RPH]** the king of Aram has escaped from your
16: 8 [C] Yet when you **relied** on the LORD, he delivered them into
Job 8:15 [C] *He* **leans** on his web, but it gives way; he clings to it, but it
24:23 [C] He may let them **rest** in a feeling of security, but his eyes are
Pr 3: 5 [C] with all your heart and **lean** not on your own understanding;
Isa 10:20 [C] will no longer **rely** on him who struck them down but will
10:20 [C] who struck them down but *will* truly **rely** on the LORD,
30:12 [C] this message, relied on oppression and **depended** on deceit,
31: 1 [C] *who* **rely** on horses, who trust in the multitude of their
50:10 [C] trust in the name of the LORD and **rely** on his God.
Eze 29: 7 [C] when they **leaned** on you, you broke and their backs were
Mic 3:11 [C] Yet *they* **lean** upon the LORD and say, "Is not the LORD

9129 ¹שָׁעַע **šāʿaʿ¹**, v. [3 / 4]

blind yourselves [1], close [1], closed [1], sightless [1]

Isa 6:10 [G] people calloused; make their ears dull and **close** their eyes.
29: 9 [F] Be stunned and amazed, **blind yourselves** and be sightless;
29: 9 [A] Be stunned and amazed, blind yourselves and *be* **sightless**;
32: 3 [a] eyes of those who see *will* no *longer be* **closed**, [BHS 9120]

9130 ²שָׁעַע **šāʿaʿ²**, v. [6] [→ 9141]

delight [3], brought joy [1], dandled [1], play [1]

Ps 94:19 [D] great within me, your consolation **brought joy** *to* my soul.
119:16 [F] *I* **delight** in your decrees; I will not neglect your word.
119:47 [F] for *I* **delight** in your commands because I love them.
119:70 [D] hearts are callous and unfeeling, but I **delight** *in* your law.
Isa 11: 8 [D] The infant *will* **play** near the hole of the cobra, and the young
66:12 [E] and be carried on her arm and **dandled** on her knees.

9131 שַׁ֫עַף ša'ap, n.pr.m. [2]

Shaaph [2]

1Ch 2:47 sons of Jahdai: Regem, Jotham, Geshan, Pelet, Ephah and **Shaaph**.
2:49 She also gave birth to **Shaaph** the father of Madmannah and to

9132 שָׁעַר šā'ar, v. [1] [→ 9134]

thinking [1]

Pr 23: 7 [A] for he is the kind of *man who is always* **thinking** about the

9133 שַׁ֫עַר ša'ar[1], n.m. [374 / 373] [→ 8788, 9135, 9139; Ar 10776]

gate [177], gates [75], gateway [29], towns [18], city gate [11], entrance [10], cities [6], court [5], city gates [4], courts [4], each gate [+2256+9133] [4], gateways [4], *untranslated* [3], town [3], cities [+824] [2], its[s] [+2021] [2], town gate [2], various gates [+2256+9133] [2], assembly at the gate [1], end[s] [1], entrance [+7339] [1], fellow townsmen [+6639] [1], gatepost [+4647] [1], gateposts [+4647] [1], gateways [+7339] [1], it[s] [+2021+4889] [1], opposite[s] [1], other[s] [1], they[s] [+2021] [1], town records [+5226] [1]

Ge 19: 1 in the evening, and Lot was sitting in the **gateway** *of* the city.
22:17 Your descendants will take possession of the **cities** *of* their
23:10 the hearing of all the Hittites who had come to the **gate** *of* his city.
23:18 presence of all the Hittites who had come to the **gate** *of* the city.
24:60 may your offspring possess the **gates** *of* their enemies."
28:17 is none other than the house of God; this is the **gate** *of* heaven."
34:20 his son Shechem went to the **gate** *of* their city to speak to their
34:24 All the men who went out of the city **gate** agreed with Hamor
34:24 son Shechem, and every male in the city **[RPH]** was circumcised.
Ex 20:10 or maidservant, nor your animals, nor the alien within your **gates**.
27:16 "For the **entrance** *to* the courtyard, provide a curtain twenty cubits
32:26 So he stood at the **entrance** *to* the camp and said, "Whoever is for
32:27 Go back and forth through the camp from *one* **end**[s] to the other,
32:27 Go back and forth through the camp from one end to the **other**[s],
35:17 and bases, and the curtain for the **entrance** *to* the courtyard;
38:15 cubits long were on the other side of the **entrance** *to* the courtyard,
38:18 The curtain for the **entrance** *to* the courtyard was of blue,
38:31 and those for its **entrance** and all the tent pegs for the tabernacle
39:40 and bases, and the curtain for the **entrance** *to* the courtyard;
40: 8 around it and put the curtain at the **entrance** *to* the courtyard.
40:33 and altar and put up the curtain at the **entrance** *to* the courtyard.
Nu 4:26 the curtain for the **entrance** [+7339], the ropes and all the
Dt 5:14 or any of your animals, nor the alien within your **gates**.
6: 9 Write them on the doorframes of your houses and on your **gates**.
11:20 Write them on the doorframes of your houses and on your **gates**,
12:12 and maidservants, and the Levites from your **towns**,
12:15 you may slaughter your animals in any of your **towns** and eat as
12:17 You must not eat in your own **towns** the tithe of your grain
12:18 and maidservants, and the Levites from your **towns**—
12:21 and in your own **towns** you may eat as much of them as you want.
14:21 You may give it to an alien living in any of your **towns**, and he
14:27 do not neglect the Levites living in your **towns**, for they have no
14:28 all the tithes of that year's produce and store it in your **towns**,
14:29 and the widows who live in your **towns** may come and eat
15: 7 If there is a poor man among your brothers in any of the **towns** of
15:22 You are to eat it in your own **towns**. Both the ceremonially unclean
16: 5 You must not sacrifice the Passover in any **town** the LORD your
16:11 the Levites in your **towns**, and the aliens, the fatherless
16:14 the aliens, the fatherless and the widows who live in your **towns**.
16:18 officials for each of your tribes in every **town** the LORD your
17: 2 or woman living among you in one of the **towns** the LORD gives
17: 5 the man or woman who has done this evil deed to your **city gate**
17: 8 If cases come before your **courts** that are too difficult for you to
18: 6 If a Levite moves from one of your **towns** anywhere in Israel
21:19 hold of him and bring him to the elders at the **gate** *of* his town.
22:15 bring proof that she was a virgin to the town elders at the **gate**.
22:24 you shall take both of them to the **gate** *of* that town and stone them
23:16 [23:17] you wherever he likes and in whatever **town** he chooses.
24:14 he is a brother Israelite or an alien living in one of your **towns**.
25: 7 brother's wife, she shall go to the elders at the **town gate** and say,
26:12 and the widow, so that they may eat in your **towns** and be satisfied.
28:52 They will lay siege to all the **cities** throughout your land until the
28:52 They will besiege all the **cities** throughout the land the LORD
28:55 your enemy will inflict on you during the siege of all your **cities**.
28:57 in the distress that your enemy will inflict on you in your **cities**.
31:12 women and children, and the aliens living in your **towns**—
Jos 2: 5 At dusk, when it was time to close the **city gate**, the men left.
2: 7 and as soon as the pursuers had gone out, the **gate** was shut.
7: 5 They chased the Israelites from the **city gate** as far as the stone
8:29 from the tree and threw it down at the entrance of the city **gate**.
20: 4 he is to stand in the entrance of the city **gate** and state his case
Jdg 5: 8 war came to the **city gates**, and not a shield or spear was seen
5:11 "Then the people of the LORD went down to the **city gates**.
9:35 and was standing at the entrance to the city **gate** just as Abimelech
9:40 fell wounded in the flight—all the way to the entrance to the **gate**.
9:44 him rushed forward to a position at the entrance to the city **gate**.
16: 2 the place and lay in wait for him all night at the city **gate**.
16: 3 Then he got up and took hold of the doors of the city **gate**,
18:16 hundred Danites, armed for battle, stood at the entrance to the **gate**.
18:17 and the six hundred armed men stood at the entrance to the **gate**.
Ru 3:11 All my **fellow townsmen** [+6639] know that you are a woman of
4: 1 Meanwhile Boaz went up to the **town gate** and sat there. When the
4:10 from among his family or from the **town** [+5226] **records**.
4:11 Then the elders and all those at the **gate** said, "We are witnesses.
1Sa 4:18 ark of God, Eli fell backward off his chair by the side of the **gate**.
9:18 Saul approached Samuel in the **gateway** and asked, "Would you
17:52 the Philistines to the entrance of Gath and to the **gates** *of* Ekron.
21:13 [21:14] making marks on the doors of the **gate** and letting saliva
2Sa 3:27 Abner returned to Hebron, Joab took him aside into the **gateway**,
10: 8 and drew up in battle formation at the entrance to their **city gate**,
11:23 the open, but we drove them back to the entrance to the **city gate**.
15: 2 up early and stand by the side of the road leading to the **city gate**.
18: 4 So the king stood beside the **gate** while all the men marched out in
18:24 While David was sitting between the inner and outer **gates**,
18:24 the watchman went up to the roof of the **gateway** by the wall.
18:33 [19:1] He went up to the room over the **gateway** and wept. As he
19: 8 [19:9] So the king got up and took his seat in the **gateway**.
19: 8 [19:9] the men were told, "The king is sitting in the **gateway**,"
23:15 get me a drink of water from the well near the **gate** of Bethlehem!"
23:16 drew water from the well near the **gate** of Bethlehem and carried it
1Ki 8:37 or when an enemy besieges them in any of their **cities** [+824],
22:10 at the threshing floor by the entrance of the **gate** *of* Samaria,
2Ki 7: 1 and two seahs of barley for a shekel at the **gate** *of* Samaria."
7: 3 there were four men with leprosy at the entrance of the **city gate**.
7:17 had put the officer on whose arm he leaned in charge of the **gate**,
7:17 and the people trampled him in the **gateway**, and he died,
7:18 and two seahs of barley for a shekel at the **gate** *of* Samaria."
7:20 to him, for the people trampled him in the **gateway**, and he died.
9:31 As Jehu entered the **gate**, she asked, "Have you come in peace,
10: 8 "Put them in two piles at the entrance of the **city gate** until
11: 6 a third at the Sur **Gate**, and a third at the gate behind the guard,
11: 6 a third at the Sur Gate, and a third at the **gate** behind the guard,
11:19 and went into the palace, entering by way of the **gate** *of* the guards.
14:13 broke down the wall of Jerusalem from the Ephraim **Gate** to the
14:13 the wall of Jerusalem from the Ephraim Gate to the Corner **Gate**—
15:35 Jotham rebuilt the Upper **Gate** *of* the temple of the LORD.
23: 8 He broke down the shrines at the **gates**—at the entrance to the
23: 8 at the entrance to the **Gate** *of* Joshua, the city governor, which is
23: 8 of Joshua, the city governor, which is on the left of the city **gate**.
25: 4 the whole army fled at night through the **gate** between the two
1Ch 9:18 being stationed at the King's **Gate** on the east, up to the present
9:23 their descendants were in charge of guarding the **gates** of the house
11:17 get me a drink of water from the well near the **gate** of Bethlehem!"
11:18 drew water from the well near the **gate** of Bethlehem and carried it
16:42 for sacred song. The sons of Jeduthun were stationed at the **gate**.
22: 3 a large amount of iron to make nails for the doors of the **gateways**
26:13 Lots were cast for **each gate** [+2256+9133], according to their
26:13 Lots were cast for **each gate** [+2256+9133], according to their
26:16 and the Shalleketh **Gate** on the upper road fell to Shuppim
2Ch 6:28 or when enemies besiege them in any of their **cities** [+824],
8:14 the gatekeepers by divisions for the **various gates** [+2256+9133],
8:14 the gatekeepers by divisions for the **various gates** [+2256+9133],
18: 9 at the threshing floor by the entrance to the **gate** *of* Samaria,
23: 5 third of you at the royal palace and a third at the Foundation **Gate**,
23:15 So they seized her as she reached the entrance of the Horse **Gate**
23:19 He also stationed doorkeepers at the **gates** *of* the LORD's temple
23:20 They went into the palace through the Upper **Gate** and seated the
24: 8 and placed outside, at the **gate** *of* the temple of the LORD.
25:23 broke down the wall of Jerusalem from the Ephraim **Gate** to the
25:23 the wall of Jerusalem from the Ephraim Gate to the Corner **Gate**—
26: 9 Uzziah built towers in Jerusalem at the Corner **Gate**, at the Valley
26: 9 at the Valley **Gate** and at the angle of the wall, and he fortified
27: 3 Jotham rebuilt the Upper **Gate** *of* the temple of the LORD
31: 2 and to sing praises at the **gates** *of* the LORD's dwelling.
32: 6 and assembled them before him in the square at the city **gate**
33:14 as far as the entrance of the Fish **Gate** and encircling the hill of
35:15 The gatekeepers at **each gate** [+2256+9133] did not need to leave
35:15 The gatekeepers at **each gate** [+2256+9133] did not need to leave
Ne 1: 3 is broken down, and its **gates** have been burned with fire."
2: 3 are buried lies in ruins, and its **gates** have been destroyed by fire?"
2: 8 so he will give me timber to make beams for the **gates** *of* the
2:13 By night I went out through the Valley **Gate** toward the Jackal
2:13 the Valley Gate toward the Jackal Well and the Dung **Gate**,
2:13 which had been broken down, and its **gates**, which had been
2:14 Then I moved on toward the Fountain **Gate** and the King's Pool,
2:15 Finally, I turned back and reentered through the Valley **Gate**.

Ne 2:17 Jerusalem lies in ruins, and its **gates** have been burned with fire.
3: 1 and his fellow priests went to work and rebuilt the Sheep **Gate**.
3: 3 The Fish **Gate** was rebuilt by the sons of Hassenaah. They laid its
3: 6 The Jeshanah **Gate** was repaired by Joiada son of Paseah
3:13 The Valley **Gate** was repaired by Hanun and the residents of
3:13 repaired five hundred yards of the wall as far as the Dung **Gate**.
3:14 The Dung **Gate** was repaired by Malkijah son of Recab, ruler of
3:15 The Fountain **Gate** was repaired by Shallun son of Col-Hozeh,
3:26 made repairs up to a point opposite the Water **Gate** toward the east
3:28 Above the Horse **Gate**, the priests made repairs, each in front of
3:29 son of Shecaniah, the guard at the East **Gate**, made repairs.
3:31 temple servants and the merchants, opposite the Inspection **Gate**,
3:32 and the Sheep **Gate** the goldsmiths and merchants made repairs.
6: 1 though up to that time I had not set the doors in the **gates**—
7: 3 "The **gates** *of* Jerusalem are not to be opened until the sun is hot.
8: 1 people assembled as one man in the square before the Water **Gate**.
8: 3 faced the square before the Water **Gate** in the presence of the men,
8:16 the courts of the house of God and in the square by the Water **Gate**
8:16 the square by the Water Gate and the one by the **Gate** *of* Ephraim.
11:19 Talmon and their associates, who kept watch at the **gates**—
12:25 Akkub were gatekeepers who guarded the storerooms at the **gates**.
12:30 they purified the people, the **gates** and the wall.
12:31 to proceed on top of the wall to the right, toward the Dung **Gate**.
12:37 At the Fountain **Gate** they continued directly up the steps of the
12:37 passed above the house of David to the Water **Gate** on the east.
12:39 over the **Gate** *of* Ephraim, the Jeshanah Gate, the Fish Gate,
12:39 the Jeshanah **Gate**, the Fish Gate, the Tower of Hananel
12:39 the Jeshanah Gate, the Fish **Gate**, the Tower of Hananel
12:39 and the Tower of the Hundred, as far as the Sheep **Gate**.
12:39 as far as the Sheep Gate. At the **Gate** *of* the Guard they stopped.
13:19 When evening shadows fell on the **gates** *of* Jerusalem before the
13:19 I stationed some of my own men at the **gates** so that no load could
13:22 and guard the **gates** in order to keep the Sabbath day holy.
Est 2:19 assembled a second time, Mordecai was sitting at the king's **gate**.
2:21 During the time Mordecai was sitting at the king's **gate**, Bigthana
3: 2 All the royal officials at the king's **gate** knelt down and paid honor
3: 3 Then the royal officials at the king's **gate** asked Mordecai,
4: 2 he went only as far as the king's **gate**, because no one clothed in
4: 2 no one clothed in sackcloth was allowed to enter **it**[s] [+2021+4889].
4: 6 Mordecai in the open square of the city in front of the king's **gate**.
5: 9 when he saw Mordecai at the king's **gate** and observed that he
5:13 as long as I see that Jew Mordecai sitting at the king's **gate**."
6:10 have suggested for Mordecai the Jew, who sits at the king's **gate**.
6:12 Afterward Mordecai returned to the king's **gate**. But Haman
Job 5: 4 children are far from safety, crushed in **court** without a defender.
29: 7 "When I went to the **gate** of the city and took my seat in the public
31:21 hand against the fatherless, knowing that I had influence in **court**,
38:17 Have the **gates** *of* death been shown to you? Have you seen the
38:17 shown to you? Have you seen the **gates** *of* the shadow of death?
Ps 9:13 [9:14] Have mercy and lift me up from the **gates** *of* death,
9:14 [9:15] that I may declare your praises in the **gates** *of* the Daughter
24: 7 Lift up your heads, O you **gates**; be lifted up, you ancient doors,
24: 9 Lift up your heads, O you **gates**; lift them up, you ancient doors,
69:12 [69:13] Those who sit at the **gate** mock me, and I am the song of
87: 2 the LORD loves the **gates** *of* Zion more than all the dwellings of
100: 4 Enter his **gates** with thanksgiving and his courts with praise;
107:18 They loathed all food and drew near the **gates** *of* death.
118:19 Open for me the **gates** *of* righteousness; I will enter and give
118:20 This is the **gate** of the LORD through which the righteous may
122: 2 Our feet are standing in your **gates**, O Jerusalem.
127: 5 be put to shame when they contend with their enemies in the **gate**.
147:13 for he strengthens the bars of your **gates** and blesses your people
Pr 1:21 in the **gateways** [+7339] of the city she makes her speech:
8: 3 beside the **gates** leading into the city, at the entrances, she cries
14:19 presence of the good, and the wicked at the **gates** *of* the righteous.
22:22 because they are poor and do not crush the needy in **court**,
24: 7 high for a fool; in the **assembly at the gate** he has nothing to say.
31:23 Her husband is respected at the **city gate**, where he takes his seat
31:31 she has earned, and let her works bring her praise at the **city gate**.
SS 7: 4 [7:5] Your eyes are the pools of Heshbon by the **gate** *of* Bath
Isa 14:31 Wail, O **gate**! Howl, O city! Melt away, all you Philistines!
22: 7 are full of chariots, and horsemen are posted at the **city gates**;
24:12 The city is left in ruins, its **gate** is battered to pieces.
26: 2 Open the **gates** that the righteous nation may enter, the nation that
28: 6 a source of strength to those who turn back the battle at the **gate**.
29:21 who ensnare the defender in **court** and with false testimony
38:10 "In the prime of my life must I go through the **gates** *of* death
45: 1 to open doors before him so that **gates** will not be shut:
54:12 your **gates** of sparkling jewels, and all your walls of precious
60:11 Your **gates** will always stand open, they will never be shut,
60:18 but you will call your walls Salvation and your **gates** Praise.
62:10 Pass through, pass through the **gates**! Prepare the way for the
Jer 1:15 and set up their thrones in the entrance of the **gates** *of* Jerusalem;
7: 2 "Stand at the **gate** *of* the LORD's house and there proclaim this
7: 2 all you people of Judah who come through these **gates** to worship
14: 2 "Judah mourns, her **cities** languish; they wail for the land,
15: 7 I will winnow them with a winnowing fork at the **city gates** *of* the
17:19 "Go and stand at the **gate** *of* the people, through which the kings of
17:19 Judah go in and out; stand also at all the other **gates** *of* Jerusalem.
17:20 and everyone living in Jerusalem who come through these **gates**.
17:21 load on the Sabbath day or bring it through the **gates** *of* Jerusalem.
17:24 and bring no load through the **gates** *of* this city on the Sabbath,
17:25 kings who sit on David's throne will come through the **gates** *of*
17:27 as you come through the **gates** *of* Jerusalem on the Sabbath day,
17:27 I will kindle an unquenchable fire in the **gates** *of* Jerusalem that
19: 2 the Valley of Ben Hinnom, near the entrance of the Potsherd **Gate**.
20: 2 put in the stocks at the Upper **Gate** *of* Benjamin at the LORD's
22: 2 your officials and your people who come through these **gates**.
22: 4 kings who sit on David's throne will come through the **gates** *of*
22:19 dragged away and thrown outside the **gates** *of* Jerusalem."
26:10 took their places at the entrance of the New **Gate** *of* the LORD's
31:38 be rebuilt for me from the Tower of Hananel to the Corner **Gate**.
31:40 Kidron Valley on the east as far as the corner of the Horse **Gate**,
36:10 the upper courtyard at the entrance of the New **Gate** *of* the temple,
37:13 But when he reached the Benjamin **Gate**, the captain of the guard,
38: 7 into the cistern. While the king was sitting in the Benjamin **Gate**,
39: 3 of the king of Babylon came and took seats in the Middle **Gate**:
39: 4 through the **gate** between the two walls, and headed toward the
51:58 thick wall will be leveled and her high **gates** set on fire;
52: 7 They left the city at night through the **gate** between the two walls
La 1: 4 All her **gateways** are desolate, her priests groan, her maidens
2: 9 Her **gates** have sunk into the ground; their bars he has broken
4:12 that enemies and foes could enter the **gates** *of* Jerusalem.
5:14 The elders are gone from the **city gate**; the young men have
Eze 8: 3 to the entrance to the north **gate** *of* the inner court, where the idol
8: 5 in the entrance north of the **gate** *of* the altar I saw this idol of
8:14 he brought me to the entrance to the north **gate** *of* the house of the
9: 2 And I saw six men coming from the direction of the upper **gate**,
10:19 They stopped at the entrance to the east **gate** *of* the LORD's
11: 1 brought me to the **gate** *of* the house of the LORD that faces east.
11: 1 There at the entrance to the **gate** were twenty-five men, and I saw
21:15 [21:20] I have stationed the sword for slaughter at all their **gates**.
21:22 [21:27] to set battering rams against the **gates**, to build a ramp
26:10 chariots when he enters your **gates** as men enter a city whose walls
40: 3 he was standing in the **gateway** with a linen cord and a measuring
40: 6 Then he went to the **gate** facing east. He climbed its steps
40: 6 He climbed its steps and measured the threshold of the **gate**;
40: 7 the threshold of the **gate** next to the portico facing the temple was
40: 7 the threshold of the gate next to the portico **[RPH]** facing the
40: 8 Then he measured the portico of the **gateway**;
40: 9 [BHS+ *Then he measured the portico of the* ***gateway***;] it was eight
40: 9 two cubits thick. The portico of the **gateway** faced the temple.
40:10 Inside the east **gate** were three alcoves on each side; the three had
40:11 Then he measured the width of the entrance to the **gateway**;
40:11 it was ten cubits and **its**[s] [+2021] length was thirteen cubits.
40:13 he measured the **gateway** from the top of the rear wall of one
40:14 faces of the projecting walls all around the inside of the **gateway**—
40:15 The distance from the entrance of the **gateway** to the far end of its
40:15 the gateway to the far end of **its**[s] [+2021] portico was fifty cubits.
40:16 the projecting walls inside the **gateway** were surmounted by
40:18 It abutted the sides of the **gateways** and was as wide as they were
40:18 sides of the gateways and was as wide as **they**[s] [+2021] were long;
40:19 he measured the distance from the inside of the lower **gateway** to
40:20 Then he measured the length and width of the **gate** facing north,
40:21 portico had the same measurements as those of the first **gateway**.
40:22 had the same measurements as those of the **gate** facing east.
40:23 There was a **gate** to the inner court facing the north gate, just as
40:23 There was a gate to the inner court facing the north **gate**, just as
40:23 He measured from one **gate** to the opposite one; it was a hundred
40:23 He measured from one gate to the **opposite**[s] *one*; it was a hundred
40:24 Then he led me to the south side and I saw a **gate** facing south.
40:27 The inner court also had a **gate** facing south, and he measured from
40:27 and he measured from this **gate** to the outer gate on the south side;
40:27 and he measured from this gate to the outer **gate** *on* the south side;
40:28 Then he brought me into the inner court through the south **gate**,
40:28 inner court through the south gate, and he measured the south **gate**;
40:32 to the inner court on the east side, and he measured the **gateway**;
40:35 he brought me to the north **gate** and measured it. It had the same
40:38 with a doorway was by the portico in each of the inner **gateways**,
40:39 In the portico of the **gateway** were two tables on each side,
40:40 By the outside wall of the portico of the **gateway**, near the steps at
40:40 near the steps at the entrance to the north **gateway** were two tables,
40:41 So there were four tables on one side of the **gateway** and four on
40:44 Outside the inner **gate**, within the inner court, were two rooms,
40:44 were two rooms, one at the side of the north **gate** and facing south,
40:44 and another at the side of the south **gate** and facing north.
40:48 The width of the **entrance** was fourteen cubits and its projecting
42:15 he led me out by the east **gate** and measured the area all around:

Eze 43: 1 Then the man brought me to the **gate** facing east,
43: 1 Then the man brought me to the gate **[RPH]** facing east,
43: 4 The glory of the LORD entered the temple through the **gate**
44: 1 Then the man brought me back to the outer **gate** *of* the sanctuary,
44: 2 The LORD said to me, "This **gate** is to remain shut. It must not
44: 3 He is to enter by way of the portico of the **gateway** and go out the
44: 4 the man brought me by way of the north **gate** to the front of the
44: 11 having charge of the **gates** *of* the temple and serving in it;
44: 17 " 'When they enter the **gates** *of* the inner court, they are to wear
44: 17 woolen garment while ministering at the **gates** *of* the inner court
45: 19 ledge of the altar and on the **gateposts of** [+4647] the inner court.
46: 1 The **gate** *of* the inner court facing east is to be shut on the six
46: 2 is to enter from the outside through the portico of the **gateway**
46: 2 the portico of the gateway and stand by the **gatepost** [+4647].
46: 2 He is to worship at the threshold of the **gateway** and then go out,
46: 2 and then go out, but the **gate** will not be shut until evening.
46: 3 in the presence of the LORD at the entrance to that **gateway**.
46: 8 the prince enters, he is to go in through the portico of the **gateway**,
46: 9 whoever enters by the north **gate** to worship is to go out the south
46: 9 enters by the north gate to worship is to go out the south **gate**;
46: 9 and whoever enters by the south **gate** is to go out the north gate.
46: 9 and whoever enters by the south gate is to go out the north **gate**.
46: 9 No one is to return through the **gate** by which he entered, but each
46: 12 fellowship offerings—the **gate** facing east is to be opened for him.
46: 12 he shall go out, and after he has gone out, the **gate** will be shut.
46: 19 the man brought me through the entrance at the side of the **gate** to
47: 2 He then brought me out through the north **gate** and led me around
47: 2 and led me around the outside to the outer **gate** facing east,
48: 31 the **gates** *of* the city will be named after the tribes of Israel.
48: 31 The three **gates** on the north side will be the gate of Reuben,
48: 31 The three gates on the north side will be the **gate** *of* Reuben,
48: 31 will be the gate of Reuben, the **gate** *of* Judah and the gate of Levi.
48: 31 will be the gate of Reuben, the gate of Judah and the **gate** *of* Levi.
48: 32 "On the east side, which is 4,500 cubits long, will be three **gates**:
48: 32 the **gate** *of* Joseph, the gate of Benjamin and the gate of Dan.
48: 32 the gate of Joseph, the **gate** *of* Benjamin and the gate of Dan.
48: 32 the gate of Joseph, the gate of Benjamin and the **gate** *of* Dan.
48: 33 the south side, which measures 4,500 cubits, will be three **gates**:
48: 33 the **gate** *of* Simeon, the gate of Issachar and the gate of Zebulun.
48: 33 the gate of Simeon, the **gate** *of* Issachar and the gate of Zebulun.
48: 33 the gate of Simeon, the gate of Issachar and the **gate** *of* Zebulun.
48: 34 "On the west side, which is 4,500 cubits long, will be three **gates**:
48: 34 the **gate** *of* Gad, the gate of Asher and the gate of Naphtali.
48: 34 the gate of Gad, the **gate** *of* Asher and the gate of Naphtali.
48: 34 the gate of Gad, the gate of Asher and the **gate** *of* Naphtali.
Am 5: 10 you hate the one who reproves in **court** and despise him who tells
5: 12 and take bribes and you deprive the poor of justice in the **courts**.
5: 15 Hate evil, love good; maintain justice in the **courts**.
Ob 1: 11 and foreigners entered his **gates** and cast lots for Jerusalem,
1: 13 You should not march through the **gates** *of* my people in the day of
Mic 1: 9 It has reached the very **gate** *of* my people, even to Jerusalem itself.
1: 12 disaster has come from the LORD, even to the **gate** *of* Jerusalem.
2: 13 go up before them; they will break through the **gate** and go out.
Na 2: 6 [2:7] The river **gates** are thrown open and the palace collapses.
3: 13 The **gates** *of* your land are wide open to your enemies; fire has
Zep 1: 10 declares the LORD, "a cry will go up from the Fish **Gate**,
Zec 8: 16 to each other, and render true and sound judgment in your **courts**;
14: 10 from the Benjamin **Gate** to the site of the First Gate, to the Corner
14: 10 from the Benjamin Gate to the site of the First **Gate**, to the Corner
14: 10 the Benjamin Gate to the site of the First Gate, to the Corner **Gate**,

9134 ²שַׂעַר ša'ar², n.[m.]. [1] [√ 9132]

hundredfold [+4395] [1]

Ge 26: 12 in that land and the same year reaped a **hundredfold** [+4395],

9135 שֹׁעָר šō'ār, a. [1] [√ 9133]

poor [1]

Jer 29: 17 plague against them and I will make them like **poor** figs that are

9136 שַׁעֲרוּר ša'ărûr, n.f. [2] [→ 9137]

shocking thing [1], something horrible [1]

Jer 5: 30 "A horrible and **shocking thing** has happened in the land:
23: 14 among the prophets of Jerusalem I have seen **something horrible**:

9137 שַׁעֲרוּרִי ša'ărûrî, n.f. [2] [√ 9136]

horrible thing [2]

Jer 18: 13 like this? A most **horrible thing** has been done by Virgin Israel.
Hos 6: 10 I have seen a **horrible thing** in the house of Israel. There Ephraim

9138 שְׁעַרְיָה še'aryâ, n.pr.m. [2] [√ 3378]

Sheariah [2]

1Ch 8: 38 Azrikam, Bokeru, Ishmael, **Sheariah**, Obadiah and Hanan.
9: 44 Azrikam, Bokeru, Ishmael, **Sheariah**, Obadiah and Hanan.

9139 שַׁעֲרַיִם ša'ărayim, n.pr.loc. [3] [√ 9133]

Shaaraim [3]

Jos 15: 36 **Shaaraim**, Adithaim and Gederah (or Gederothaim)—
1Sa 17: 52 Their dead were strewn along the **Shaaraim** road to Gath
1Ch 4: 31 Beth Marcaboth, Hazar Susim, Beth Biri and **Shaaraim**.

9140 שַׁעַשְׁגַז ša'ašgaz, n.pr.m. [1]

Shaashgaz [1]

Est 2: 14 return to another part of the harem to the care of **Shaashgaz**,

9141 שַׁעֲשׁוּעִים ša'ăšû'îm, n.[m.]pl.intens. [9] [√ 9130]

delight [7], delighting [1], filled with delight [1]

Ps 119: 24 Your statutes are my **delight**; they are my counselors.
119: 77 compassion come to me that I may live, for your law is my **delight**.
119: 92 If your law had not been my **delight**, I would have perished in my
119: 143 distress have come upon me, but your commands are my **delight**.
119: 174 I long for your salvation, O LORD, and your law is my **delight**.
Pr 8: 30 I was **filled with delight** day after day, rejoicing always in his
8: 31 rejoicing in his whole world and **delighting** in mankind.
Isa 5: 7 house of Israel, and the men of Judah are the garden of his **delight**.
Jer 31: 20 Is not Ephraim my dear son, the child in whom I **delight**?

9142 שָׁפָה šāpâ, v. [2] [→ 3834, 3836?, 9143?, 9147?, 9155, 9156]

bare [1], stick out [1]

Job 33: 21 [E] and his bones, once hidden, now **stick** [K 9155] **out**.
Isa 13: 2 [C] Raise a banner on a **bare** hilltop, shout to them; beckon to

9143 שְׁפוֹ šepô, n.pr.m. [1 / 2] [√ 9142?; cf. 9156]

Shepho [2]

Ge 36: 23 The sons of Shobal: Alvan, Manahath, Ebal, **Shepho** and Onam.
1Ch 1: 40 Alvan, Manahath, Ebal, **Shepho** [BHS 9156] and Onam.

9144 שְׁפוֹט šepôṭ, n.m. [2] [√ 9149]

judgment [1], punishment [1]

2Ch 20: 9 upon us, whether the sword of **judgment**, or plague or famine,
Eze 23: 10 a byword among women, and **punishment** was inflicted on her.

9145 שְׁפוּפָם šepûpām, n.pr.m. [1 / 0] [cf. 8792]

Nu 26: 39 through Shupham, [BHS *Shephupham*; NIV 8792] the Shuphamite

9146 שְׁפוּפָן šepûpān, n.pr.m. [1] [√ 9159?]

Shephuphan [1]

1Ch 8: 5 Gera, **Shephuphan** and Huram.

9147 שְׁפוֹת šepôt, n.f. [1] [√ 9142?]

cheese [1]

2Sa 17: 29 and **cheese** *from* cows' milk for David and his people to eat.

9148 שִׁפְחָה šipḥâ, n.f. [63] [→ 5476; cf. 6202, 6203]

servant [19], maidservant [12], maidservants [11], female slaves [7], servant girl [3], maid [2], slave girl [2], slaves [+2256+6269] [2], enslaved [+2256+3899+4200+4200+6269] [1], servant girls [1], serve [1], women [1], women servants [1]

Ge 12: 16 and female donkeys, menservants and **maidservants**, and camels.
16: 1 no children. But she had an Egyptian **maidservant** named Hagar;
16: 2 Go, sleep with my **maidservant**; perhaps I can build a family
16: 3 Sarai his wife took her Egyptian **maidservant** Hagar and gave her
16: 5 I put my **servant** in your arms, and now that she knows she is
16: 6 "Your **servant** is in your hands," Abram said. "Do with her
16: 8 And he said, "Hagar, **servant** *of* Sarai, where have you come from,
20: 14 and cattle and male and **female slaves** and gave them to Abraham,
24: 35 and cattle, silver and gold, menservants and **maidservants**,
25: 12 whom Sarah's **maidservant**, Hagar the Egyptian, bore to
29: 24 Laban gave his **servant girl** Zilpah to his daughter as her
29: 24 gave his servant girl Zilpah to his daughter as her **maidservant**.
29: 29 Laban gave his **servant girl** Bilhah to his daughter Rachel as her
29: 29 his servant girl Bilhah to his daughter Rachel as her **maidservant**.
30: 4 So she gave him her **servant** Bilhah as a wife. Jacob slept with her,
30: 7 Rachel's **servant** Bilhah conceived again and bore Jacob a second
30: 9 she took her **maidservant** Zilpah and gave her to Jacob as a wife.

Ge 30: 10 Leah's **servant** Zilpah bore Jacob a son.
30: 12 Leah's **servant** Zilpah bore Jacob a second son.
30: 18 "God has rewarded me for giving my **maidservant** to my
30: 43 and **maidservants** and menservants, and camels and donkeys.
32: 5 [32:6] sheep and goats, menservants and **maidservants**.
32: 22 [32:23] his two **maidservants** and his eleven sons and crossed the
33: 1 the children among Leah, Rachel and the two **maidservants**.
33: 2 He put the **maidservants** and their children in front, Leah
33: 6 the **maidservants** and their children approached and bowed down.
35: 25 The sons of Rachel's **maidservant** Bilhah: Dan and Naphtali.
35: 26 The sons of Leah's **maidservant** Zilpah: Gad and Asher.
Ex 11: 5 who sits on the throne, to the firstborn son of the **slave girl**,
Lev 19: 20 " 'If a man sleeps with a woman who is a **slave girl** promised to
Dt 28: 68 yourselves for sale to your enemies as male and **female slaves**,
Ru 2: 13 have given me comfort and have spoken kindly to your **servant**—
2: 13 though I do not have the standing of one of your **servant girls**."
1Sa 1: 18 She said, "May your **servant** find favor in your eyes." Then she
8: 16 Your menservants and **maidservants** and the best of your cattle
25: 27 And let this gift, which your **servant** has brought to my master,
25: 41 ready to **serve** you and wash the feet of my master's servants."
28: 21 she said, "Look, your **maidservant** has obeyed you.
28: 22 Now please listen to your **servant** and let me give you some food
2Sa 14: 6 I your **servant** had two sons. They got into a fight with each other
14: 7 Now the whole clan has risen up against your **servant**; they say,
14: 12 woman said, "Let your **servant** speak a word to my lord the king."
14: 15 Your **servant** thought, 'I will speak to the king; perhaps he will do
14: 17 "And now your **servant** says, 'May the word of my lord the king
14: 19 and who put all these words into the mouth of your **servant**.
17: 17 A **servant girl** was to go and inform them, and they were to go
2Ki 4: 2 "Your **servant** has nothing there at all," she said, "except a little
4: 16 she objected. "Don't mislead your **servant**, O man of God!"
5: 26 vineyards, flocks, herds, or menservants and **maidservants**?
2Ch 28: 10 to make the men and **women** of Judah and Jerusalem your slaves.
Est 7: 4 If we had merely been sold as male and **female slaves**, I would
Ps 123: 2 as the eyes of a **maid** look to the hand of her mistress, so our eyes
Pr 30: 23 who is married, and a **maidservant** who displaces her mistress.
Ecc 2: 7 I bought male and **female slaves** and had other slaves who were
Isa 14: 2 nations as menservants and **maidservants** in the LORD's land.
24: 2 as for servant, for mistress as for **maid**, for seller as for buyer,
Jer 34: 9 Everyone was to free his Hebrew **slaves**, both male and **female**;
34: 10 their male and **female slaves** and no longer hold them in bondage.
34: 11 took back the **slaves** [+2256+6269] they had freed and enslaved
34: 11 and **enslaved** [+2256+3899+4200+4200+6269] them again.
34: 16 and **female slaves** you had set free to go where they wished.
34: 16 You have forced them to become your **slaves** [+2256+6269] again.
Joel 2: 29 [3:2] Even on my **servants**, both men and **women**, I will pour out

9149 שָׁפַט ***šāpaṭ***, v. [203] [→ 5477, 9143, 9144, 9150, 9151, 9154; Ar 10735; *also used with compound proper names*]

judge [69], judges [26], led [12], rulers [8], execute judgment [6], govern [5], decide [4], judged [4], judging [4], vindicate [4], defend [3], lead [3], leaders [3], *untranslated* [2], defend the cause [2], delivered [2], governed [2], play the judge [+9149] [2], rule [2], ruler [2], sentence [2], administer [1], argue [1], be judged [1], bring judgment [1], bring justice [1], bring to judgment [1], brought to trial [1], condemn [1], confront with evidence [1], decide dispute [1], decided [1], defend cause [1], defending [1], enter into judgment [1], executing judgment [1], given[s] [1], gives judgment [1], goes to court [1], is tried [1], judge [+906+5477] [1], judge in office [1], judges decide [1], judges in office [1], leader [1], leading [1], pass judgment [1], pleads case [1], punish [1], render judgment [+5477] [1], ruled [1], serve as judge [1], serve as judges [1], served as judges [1], served [1], them[s] [+2021] [1], uphold [1]

Ge 16: 5 [A] despises me. *May* the LORD **judge** between you and me."
18: 25 [A] be it from you! Will not the **Judge** *of* all the earth do right?"
19: 9 [A] as an alien, and now *he wants to* **play the judge** [+9149]!
19: 9 [A] as an alien, and now *he wants to* **play the judge** [+9149]!
31: 53 [A] and the God of Nahor, the God of their father, **judge**
Ex 2: 14 [A] The man said, "Who made you ruler and **judge** over us? Are
5: 21 [A] they said, "May the LORD look upon you and **judge** you!
18: 13 [A] The next day Moses took his seat to **serve as judge** *for* the
18: 16 [A] *I* **decide** between the parties and inform them of God's
18: 22 [A] *Have them* **serve as judges** *for* the people at all times,
18: 22 [A] case to you; the simple cases *they can* **decide** themselves.
18: 26 [A] *They* **served as judges** *for* the people at all times.
18: 26 [A] to Moses, but the simple ones *they* **decided** themselves.
Lev 19: 15 [A] or favoritism to the great, but **judge** your neighbor fairly.
Nu 25: 5 [A] So Moses said to Israel's **judges**, "Each of you must put to
35: 24 [A] the assembly *must* **judge** between him and the avenger of
Dt 1: 16 [A] I charged your **judges** at that time: Hear the disputes between
1: 16 [A] Hear the disputes between your brothers and **judge** fairly,
16: 18 [A] Appoint **judges** and officials for each of your tribes in every
16: 18 [A] and *they shall* **judge** [+906+5477] the people fairly.
17: 9 [A] are Levites, and to the **judge** who is **in office** at that time.
17: 12 [A] The man who shows contempt for the **judge** or for the priest
19: 17 [A] the priests and the **judges** who are **in office** at the time.
19: 18 [A] The **judges** must make a thorough investigation, and if the
21: 2 [A] your elders and **judges** shall go out and measure the distance
25: 1 [A] are to take it to court and *the* **judges** *will* **decide** the case,
25: 2 [A] the **judge** shall make him lie down and have him flogged in
Jos 8: 33 [A] and citizens alike, with their elders, officials and **judges**,
23: 2 [A] their elders, leaders, **judges** and officials—and said to them:
24: 1 [A] summoned the elders, leaders, **judges** and officials of Israel,
Jdg 2: 16 [A] the LORD raised up **judges**, who saved them out of the
2: 17 [A] Yet they would not listen to their **judges** but prostituted
2: 18 [A] Whenever the LORD raised up a **judge** for them, he was
2: 18 [A] he was with the **judge** and saved them out of the hands of
2: 18 [A] out of the hands of their enemies as long as the **judge** lived;
2: 19 [A] when the **judge** died, the people returned to ways even more
3: 10 [A] upon him, so that *he became* Israel's **judge** and went to war.
4: 4 [A] the wife of Lappidoth, *was* **leading** Israel at that time.
10: 2 [A] *He* **led** Israel twenty-three years; then he died, and was
10: 3 [A] followed by Jair of Gilead, *who* **led** Israel twenty-two years.
11: 27 [A] Let the LORD, the **Judge**, decide the dispute this day
11: 27 [A] *Let* the LORD, the Judge, **decide** *the* **dispute** this day
12: 7 [A] Jephthah **led** Israel six years. Then Jephthah the Gileadite
12: 8 [A] After him, Ibzan of Bethlehem **led** Israel.
12: 9 [A] as wives from outside his clan. Ibzan **led** Israel seven years.
12: 11 [A] After him, Elon the Zebulunite **led** Israel ten years.
12: 11 [A] After him, Elon the Zebulunite led Israel **[RPH]** ten years.
12: 13 [A] After him, Abdon son of Hillel, from Pirathon, **led** Israel.
12: 14 [A] who rode on seventy donkeys. *He* **led** Israel eight years.
15: 20 [A] Samson **led** Israel for twenty years in the days of the
16: 31 [A] tomb of Manoah his father. He *had* **led** Israel twenty years.
Ru 1: 1 [A] In the days when the **judges** ruled, there was a famine in the
1: 1 [A] In the days when the judges **ruled**, there was a famine in the
1Sa 3: 13 [A] For I told him that I *would* **judge** his family forever
4: 18 [A] he was an old man and heavy. He *had* **led** Israel forty years.
7: 6 [A] the LORD." And Samuel *was* **leader** *of* Israel at Mizpah.
7: 15 [A] Samuel *continued as* **judge** *over* Israel all the days of his
7: 16 [A] Bethel to Gilgal to Mizpah, **judging** Israel in all those places.
7: 17 [A] where his home was, and there *he* also **judged** Israel.
8: 1 [A] Samuel grew old, he appointed his sons as **judges** for Israel.
8: 2 [A] of his second was Abijah, and *they* **served** at Beersheba.
8: 5 [A] now appoint a king to **lead** us, such as all the other nations
8: 6 [A] when they said, "Give us a king to **lead** us," this displeased
8: 20 [A] with a king *to* **lead** us and to go out before us and fight our
12: 7 [C] *I am going to* **confront** you **with evidence** before the LORD
24: 12 [24:13] [A] *May* the LORD **judge** between you and me.
24: 15 [24:16] [A] May the LORD be our judge and **decide** between
24: 15 [24:16] [A] *may he* **vindicate** me by delivering me from your
2Sa 7: 11 [A] have done ever since the time I appointed **leaders** over my
15: 4 [A] would add, "If only I were appointed **judge** in the land!
18: 19 [A] take the news to the king that the LORD *has* **delivered** him
18: 31 [A] The LORD *has* **delivered** you today from all who rose up
1Ki 3: 9 [A] So give your servant a discerning heart to **govern** your
3: 9 [A] For who is able to **govern** this great people of yours?"
3: 28 [A] When all Israel heard the verdict the king *had* **given**[s], they
7: 7 [A] the throne hall, the Hall of Justice, where *he was to* **judge**,
8: 32 [A] **Judge** *between* your servants, condemning the guilty
2Ki 15: 5 [A] charge of the palace and **governed** the people of the land.
23: 22 [A] Not since the days of the **judges** who led Israel,
23: 22 [A] Not since the days of the judges who **led** Israel,
1Ch 16: 33 [A] for joy before the LORD, for he comes to **judge** the earth.
17: 6 [A] did I ever say to any of their **leaders** whom I commanded to
17: 10 [A] have done ever since the time I appointed **leaders** over my
23: 4 [A] the LORD and six thousand are to be officials and **judges**.
26: 29 [A] away from the temple, as officials and **judges** over Israel.
2Ch 1: 2 [A] to the **judges** and to all the leaders in Israel, the heads of
1: 10 [A] for who *is able to* **govern** this great people of yours?"
1: 11 [A] knowledge *to* **govern** my people over whom I have made
6: 23 [A] **Judge** *between* your servants, repaying the guilty by
19: 5 [A] He appointed **judges** in the land, in each of the fortified cities
19: 6 [A] He told **them**[s] [+2021], "Consider carefully what you do,
19: 6 [A] because *you are* not **judging** for man but for the LORD,
20: 12 [A] O our God, *will you* not **judge** them? For we have no power
22: 8 [C] While Jehu was **executing judgment** on the house of Ahab,
26: 21 [A] charge of the palace and **governed** the people of the land.
Ezr 10: 14 [A] along with the elders and **judges** *of* each town, until the
Job 9: 15 [D] answer him; I could only plead with my **Judge** for mercy.
9: 24 [A] falls into the hands of the wicked, he blindfolds its **judges**.
12: 17 [A] leads counselors away stripped and makes fools of **judges**.
21: 22 [A] teach knowledge to God, since he **judges** even the highest?
22: 13 [A] does God know? *Does he* **judge** through such darkness?
23: 7 [A] before him, and I would be delivered forever from my **judge**.
Ps 2: 10 [A] you kings, be wise; be warned, you **rulers** *of* the earth.
7: 8 [7:9] [A] **Judge** me, O LORD, according to my righteousness,

Ps 7:11 [7:12] [A] God is a righteous **judge**, a God who expresses his
9: 4 [9:5] [A] you have sat on your throne, **judging** righteously.
9: 8 [9:9] [A] He *will* **judge** the world in righteousness; he will
9:19 [9:20] [C] *let* the nations **be judged** in your presence.
10:18 [A] **defending** the fatherless and the oppressed, in order that
26: 1 [A] **Vindicate** me, O LORD, for I have led a blameless life; I
35:24 [A] **Vindicate** me in your righteousness, O LORD my God; do
37:33 [C] their power or let them be condemned when **brought to trial**.
43: 1 [A] **Vindicate** me, O God, and plead my cause against an
50: 6 [A] proclaim his righteousness, for God himself *is* **judge**.
51: 4 [51:6] [A] right when you speak and justified when you **judge**.
58: 1 [58:2] [A] speak justly? *Do you* **judge** uprightly among men?
58:11 [58:12] [A] surely there is a God *who* **judges** the earth."
67: 4 [67:5] [A] for *you* **rule** the peoples justly and guide the nations
72: 4 [A] *He will* **defend** the afflicted among the people and save the
75: 2 [75:3] [A] the appointed time; it is I *who* **judge** uprightly.
75: 7 [75:8] [A] it is God *who* **judges**: He brings one down, he exalts
82: 1 [A] in the great assembly; *he* **gives judgment** among the "gods":
82: 2 [A] "How long *will you* **defend** the unjust and show partiality to
82: 3 [A] **Defend** *the* **cause** *of* the weak and fatherless;
82: 8 [A] Rise up, O God, **judge** the earth, for all the nations are your
94: 2 [A] Rise up, O **Judge** *of* the earth; pay back to the proud what
96:13 [A] the LORD, for he comes, he comes to **judge** the earth.
96:13 [A] *He will* **judge** the world in righteousness and the peoples in
98: 9 [A] sing before the LORD, for he comes to **judge** the earth.
98: 9 [A] *He will* **judge** the world in righteousness and the peoples
109: 7 [C] When he **is tried**, let him be found guilty, and may his
109:31 [A] needy one, to save his life from *those who* **condemn** him.
141: 6 [A] their **rulers** will be thrown down from the cliffs,
148:11 [A] the earth and all nations, you princes and all **rulers** *on* earth,
Pr 8:16 [A] by me princes govern, and all nobles *who* **rule** *on* earth.
29: 9 [C] If a wise man **goes to court** with a fool, the fool rages
29:14 [A] If a king **judges** the poor with fairness, his throne will always
31: 9 [A] Speak up and **judge** fairly; defend the rights of the poor
Ecc 3:17 [A] "God *will* **bring to judgment** both the righteous and the
Isa 1:17 [A] **Defend the cause** *of* the fatherless, plead the case of the
1:23 [A] *They do* not **defend the cause** *of* the fatherless; the widow's
1:26 [A] I will restore your **judges** as in days of old, your counselors
2: 4 [A] *He will* **judge** between the nations and will settle disputes for
3: 2 [A] the hero and warrior, the **judge** and prophet, the soothsayer
5: 3 [A] and men of Judah, **judge** between me and my vineyard.
11: 3 [A] *He will* not **judge** by what he sees with his eyes, or decide by
11: 4 [A] with righteousness *he will* **judge** the needy, with justice he
16: 5 [A] *one who in* **judging** seeks justice and speeds the cause of
33:22 [A] For the LORD *is* our **judge**, the LORD is our lawgiver,
40:23 [A] to naught and reduces the **rulers** *of* this world to nothing.
43:26 [C] Review the past for me, *let us* **argue** *the matter* together;
51: 5 [A] is on the way, and my arm *will* **bring justice** *to* the nations.
59: 4 [C] one calls for justice; no *one* **pleads** *his* **case** with integrity.
66:16 [C] with his sword the LORD *will* **execute judgment** *upon* all
Jer 2:35 [C] I *will* **pass judgment** *on* you because you say, 'I have not
5:28 [A] fatherless to win it, *they do* not **defend** the rights of the poor.
11:20 [A] you *who* **judge** righteously and test the heart and mind,
25:31 [C] he *will* **bring judgment** on all mankind and put the wicked
La 3:59 [A] O LORD, the wrong done to me. **Uphold** my cause!
Eze 7: 3 [A] *I will* **judge** you according to your conduct and repay you for
7: 8 [A] *I will* **judge** you according to your conduct and repay you for
7:27 [A] their conduct, and by their own standards *I will* **judge** them.
11:10 [A] and *I will* **execute judgment** *on* you at the borders of Israel.
11:11 [A] in it; *I will* **execute judgment** *on* you at the borders of Israel.
16:38 [A] *I will* **sentence** you *to* the punishment of women who
17:20 [C] bring him to Babylon and **execute judgment** upon him there
18:30 [A] "Therefore, O house of Israel, *I will* **judge** you, each one
20: 4 [A] "*Will you* **judge** them? Will you judge them, son of man?
20: 4 [A] "Will you judge them? *Will you* **judge** them, son of man?
20:35 [C] and there, face to face, *I will* **execute judgment** upon you.
20:36 [C] As *I* **judged** your fathers in the desert of the land of Egypt,
20:36 [C] so *I will* **judge** you, declares the Sovereign LORD.
21:30 [21:35] [A] in the land of your ancestry, *I will* **judge** you.
22: 2 [A] "Son of man, *will you* **judge** her? Will you judge this city of
22: 2 [A] will you judge her? *Will you* **judge** this city of bloodshed?
23:24 [A] and *they will* **punish** you according to their standards.
23:36 [A] to me: "Son of man, *will you* **judge** Oholah and Oholibah?
23:45 [A] righteous men *will* **sentence** them *to* the punishment of
24:14 [A] You *will be* **judged** according to your conduct and your
33:20 [A] But *I will* **judge** each of you according to his own ways."
34:17 [A] I *will* **judge** between one sheep and another, and between
34:20 [A] I myself *will* **judge** between the fat sheep and the lean sheep.
34:22 [A] be plundered. *I will* **judge** between one sheep and another.
35:11 [A] I will make myself known among them when *I* **judge** you.
36:19 [A] *I* **judged** them according to their conduct and their actions.
38:22 [C] *I will* **execute judgment** upon him with plague
44:24 [A] the priests are to serve as **judges** [Q 5477] and decide it
44:24 [A] to serve as judges and **decide** it according to my ordinances.
Da 9:12 [A] and against our **rulers** by bringing upon us great disaster.
9:12 [A] against our rulers **[RPH]** by bringing upon us great disaster.
Hos 7: 7 [A] All of them are hot as an oven; they devour their **rulers**.
13:10 [A] Where are your **rulers** in all your towns, of whom you said,
Joel 3: 2 [4:2] [C] There *I will* **enter into judgment** against them
3:12 [4:12] [A] there I will sit to **judge** all the nations on every side.
Am 2: 3 [A] I will destroy her **ruler** and kill all her officials with him,"
Ob 1:21 [A] Deliverers will go up on Mount Zion to **govern** the
Mic 3:11 [A] Her leaders **judge** for a bribe, her priests teach for a price,
4: 3 [A] *He will* **judge** between many peoples and will settle disputes
5: 1 [4:14] [A] will strike Israel's **ruler** on the cheek with a rod.
7: 3 [A] the ruler demands gifts, the **judge** accepts bribes,
Zep 3: 3 [A] Her officials are roaring lions, her **rulers** are evening wolves,
Zec 7: 9 [A] '**Administer** true justice; show mercy and compassion to one
8:16 [A] and **render** true and sound **judgment** [+5477] in your courts;

9150 שֶׁ֫בֶט *šepeṭ*, n.m. [16] [√ 9149]

punishment [9], judgment [3], acts of judgment [2], judgments [1], penalties [1]

Ex 6: 6 you with an outstretched arm and with mighty **acts of judgment**.
7: 4 and with mighty **acts of judgment** I will bring out my divisions,
12:12 and animals—and I will bring **judgment** on all the gods of Egypt.
Nu 33: 4 among them; for the LORD had brought **judgment** on their gods.
2Ch 24:24 the God of their fathers, **judgment** was executed on Joash.
Pr 19:29 **Penalties** are prepared for mockers, and beatings for the backs of
Eze 5:10 I will inflict **punishment** on you and will scatter all your survivors
5:15 the nations around you when I inflict **punishment** on you in anger
11: 9 and hand you over to foreigners and inflict **punishment** on you.
14:21 it be when I send against Jerusalem my four dreadful **judgments**—
16:41 and inflict **punishment** on you in the sight of many women.
25:11 I will inflict **punishment** on Moab. Then they will know that I am
28:22 when I inflict **punishment** on her and show myself holy within
28:26 they will live in safety when I inflict **punishment** on all their
30:14 Upper Egypt, set fire to Zoan and inflict **punishment** on Thebes.
30:19 So I will inflict **punishment** on Egypt, and they will know that I

9151 שָׁפָט *šāpāṭ*, n.pr.m. [8] [√ 9149]

Shaphat [8]

Nu 13: 5 from the tribe of Simeon, **Shaphat** son of Hori;
1Ki 19:16 anoint Elisha son of **Shaphat** from Abel Meholah to succeed you
19:19 So Elijah went from there and found Elisha son of **Shaphat**.
2Ki 3:11 of the king of Israel answered, "Elisha son of **Shaphat** is here.
6:31 if the head of Elisha son of **Shaphat** remains on his shoulders
1Ch 3:22 his sons: Hattush, Igal, Bariah, Neariah and **Shaphat**—six in all.
5:12 the chief, Shapham the second, then Janai and **Shaphat**, in Bashan.
27:29 **Shaphat** son of Adlai was in charge of the herds in the valleys.

9152 שְׁפַטְיָה *šᵉpaṭyâ*, n.pr.m. [10] [√ 9149 + 3378]

Shephatiah [10]

2Sa 3: 4 the son of Haggith; the fifth, **Shephatiah** the son of Abital;
1Ch 3: 3 the fifth, **Shephatiah** the son of Abital; and the sixth, Ithream,
9: 8 Meshullam son of **Shephatiah**, the son of Reuel, the son of
Ezr 2: 4 of **Shephatiah** 372
2:57 **Shephatiah**, Hattil, Pokereth-Hazzebaim and Ami
8: 8 of the descendants of **Shephatiah**, Zebadiah son of Michael,
Ne 7: 9 of **Shephatiah** 372
7:59 **Shephatiah**, Hattil, Pokereth-Hazzebaim and Amon
11: 4 the son of Zechariah, the son of Amariah, the son of **Shephatiah**,
Jer 38: 1 **Shephatiah** son of Mattan, Gedaliah son of Pashhur, Jehucal son

9153 שְׁפַטְיָהוּ *šᵉpaṭyāhû*, n.pr.m. [3] [√ 9149 + 3378]

Shephatiah [3]

1Ch 12: 5 [12:6] Shemariah and **Shephatiah** the Haruphite;
27:16 son of Zicri; over the Simeonites: **Shephatiah** son of Maacah;
2Ch 21: 2 Jehiel, Zechariah, Azariahu, Michael and **Shephatiah**.

9154 שִׁפְטָן *šipṭān*, n.pr.m. [1] [√ 9149]

Shiphtan [1]

Nu 34:24 Kemuel son of **Shiphtan**, the leader from the tribe of Ephraim son

9155 שְׁפִי *šᵉpî*[1], n.m. [9] [→ 9156; cf. 9142]

barren heights [7], barren height [1], barren hill [1]

Nu 23: 3 reveals to me I will tell you." Then he went off to a **barren height**.
Job 33:21 [and his bones, once hidden, now **stick** [K; see Q 9142] **out**.]
Isa 41:18 I will make rivers flow on **barren heights**, and springs within the
49: 9 will feed beside the roads and find pasture on every **barren hill**.
Jer 3: 2 "Look up to the **barren heights** and see. Is there any place where
3:21 A cry is heard on the **barren heights**, the weeping and pleading of
4:11 "A scorching wind from the **barren heights** in the desert blows

Jer 7:29 take up a lament on the **barren heights**, for the LORD has
12:12 Over all the **barren heights** in the desert destroyers will swarm,
14: 6 Wild donkeys stand on the **barren heights** and pant like jackals;

9156 ²שְׁפִי **šᵉpî²**, n.pr.m. [1 / 0] [√ 9155? compare 9143]

1Ch 1:40 Alvan, Manahath, Ebal, Shepho [BHS *Shephi*; NIV 9143]

9157 ¹שֻׁפִּים **šuppîm¹**, n.pr.m. [1]

Shuppim [1]

1Ch 26:16 and the Shalleketh Gate on the upper road fell to **Shuppim**

9158 ²שֻׁפִּים **šuppîm²**, a.g.[pl.]. [2] [√ 9172]

Shuppites [2]

1Ch 7:12 The **Shuppites** and Huppites were the descendants of Ir,
7:15 Makir took a wife from among the Huppites and **Shuppites**.

9159 שְׁפִיפֹן **šᵉpîpōn**, n.[m.]. [1] [→ 9146?]

viper [1]

Ge 49:17 a **viper** along the path, that bites the horse's heels so that its rider

9160 שָׁפִיר **šāpîr**, n.pr.loc. [1] [√ 9182]

Shaphir [1]

Mic 1:11 Pass on in nakedness and shame, you who live in **Shaphir**.

9161 שָׁפַךְ **šāpak**, v. [115] [→ 9162, 9163]

pour out [33], shed [25], poured out [11], build [6], shedding [4], outpoured [3], pours out [3], be poured out [2], be shed [2], built [2], pour [2], pours [2], sheds [2], am poured out [1], be poured [1], been shed [1], bloodshed [+1947] [1], build up [1], drain out [1], dumped [1], ebb away [1], ebbs away [1], flowed [1], lavished [1], lost [1], outpouring [1], poured out [+4946] [1], pouring out [1], scattered [1], spilled out [1], spills [1]

Ge 9: 6 [A] "*Whoever* **sheds** the blood of man, by man shall his blood
9: 6 [C] sheds the blood of man, by man *shall* his blood **be shed**;
37:22 [A] "Don't **shed** any blood. Throw him into this cistern here in
Ex 4: 9 [A] take some water from the Nile and **pour** it *on* the dry ground.
29:12 [A] and **pour out** the rest of it at the base of the altar.
Lev 4: 7 [A] of Meeting. The rest of the bull's blood *he shall* **pour out**
4:18 [A] the Tent of Meeting. The rest of the blood *he shall* **pour out**
4:25 [A] and **pour out** the rest of the blood at the base of the altar.
4:30 [A] and **pour out** the rest of the blood at the base of the altar.
4:34 [A] and **pour out** the rest of the blood at the base of the altar.
14:41 [A] the material that is scraped off **dumped** into an unclean place
17: 4 [A] *he has* **shed** blood and must be cut off from his people.
17:13 [A] or bird that may be eaten *must* **drain out** the blood
Nu 35:33 [E] cannot be made for the land on which blood *has* **been shed**,
35:33 [A] has been shed, except by the blood of the *one who* **shed** it.
Dt 12:16 [A] must not eat the blood; **pour** it **out** on the ground like water.
12:24 [A] must not eat the blood; **pour** it **out** on the ground like water.
12:27 [C] The blood of your sacrifices *must* **be poured** beside the altar
15:23 [A] must not eat the blood; **pour** it **out** on the ground like water.
19:10 [C] Do this so that innocent blood *will* not **be shed** in your land,
21: 7 [A] "Our hands *did* not **shed** this blood, nor did our eyes see it
Jdg 6:20 [A] place them on this rock, and **pour out** the broth."
1Sa 1:15 [A] or beer; *I was* **pouring out** my soul to the LORD.
7: 6 [A] they drew water and **poured** it **out** before the LORD.
25:31 [A] the staggering burden of needless **bloodshed** [+1947]
2Sa 20:10 [A] it into his belly, and his intestines **spilled out** on the ground.
20:15 [A] *They* **built** a siege ramp up to the city, and it stood against
1Ki 2:31 [A] house of the guilt of the innocent blood that Joab **shed**.
13: 3 [C] will be split apart and the ashes on it *will* **be poured out**."
13: 5 [C] its ashes **poured** [+4946] **out** according to the sign given by
18:28 [A] and spears, as was their custom, until their blood **flowed**.
2Ki 19:32 [A] come before it with shield or **build** a siege ramp against it.
21:16 [A] Manasseh also **shed** so much innocent blood that he filled
24: 4 [A] including the **shedding** *of* innocent blood. For he had filled
1Ch 22: 8 [A] '*You have* **shed** much blood and have fought many wars.
22: 8 [A] because *you have* **shed** much blood on the earth in my sight.
28: 3 [A] my Name, because you are a warrior and *have* **shed** blood.'
Job 12:21 [A] *He* **pours** contempt on nobles and disarms the mighty.
16:13 [A] he pierces my kidneys and **spills** my gall on the ground.
30:16 [F] "And now my life **ebbs away**; days of suffering grip me.
Ps 22:14 [22:15] [C] *I* **am poured out** like water, and all my bones are
42: 4 [42:5] [A] These things I remember as *I* **pour out** my soul:
62: 8 [62:9] [A] **pour out** your hearts to him, for God is our refuge.
69:24 [69:25] [A] **Pour out** your wrath on them; let your fierce anger
73: 2 [E] my feet had almost slipped; I *had* nearly **lost** my foothold.
79: 3 [A] *They have* **poured out** blood like water all around
79: 6 [A] **Pour out** your wrath on the nations that do not acknowledge
79:10 [B] that you avenge the **outpoured** blood of your servants.
102: T [102:1] [A] and **pours out** his lament before the LORD.
106:38 [A] *They* **shed** innocent blood, the blood of their sons
107:40 [A] *he who* **pours** contempt on nobles made them wander in a
142: 2 [142:3] [A] *I* **pour out** my complaint before him; before him I
Pr 1:16 [A] for their feet rush into sin, they are swift to **shed** blood.
6:17 [A] a lying tongue, hands *that* **shed** innocent blood,
Isa 37:33 [A] come before it with shield or **build** a siege ramp against it.
42:25 [A] So *he* **poured out** on them his burning anger, the violence of
57: 6 [A] to them *you have* **poured out** drink offerings and offered
59: 7 [A] feet rush into sin; they are swift to **shed** innocent blood.
Jer 6: 6 [A] down the trees and **build** siege ramps against Jerusalem.
6:11 [A] "**Pour** it **out** on the children in the street and on the young
7: 6 [A] or the widow and *do* not **shed** innocent blood in this place,
10:25 [A] **Pour out** your wrath on the nations that do not acknowledge
14:16 [A] *I will* **pour out** on them the calamity they deserve.
22: 3 [A] or the widow, and *do* not **shed** innocent blood in this place.
22:17 [A] on **shedding** innocent blood and on oppression
La 2: 4 [A] *he has* **poured out** his wrath like fire on the tent of the
2:11 [C] my heart *is* **poured out** on the ground because my people are
2:12 [F] of the city, as their lives **ebb away** in their mothers' arms.
2:19 [A] **pour out** your heart like water in the presence of the Lord.
4: 1 [F] The sacred gems *are* **scattered** at the head of every street.
4:11 [A] full vent to his wrath; *he has* **poured out** his fierce anger.
4:13 [A] her priests, who **shed** within her the blood of the righteous.
Eze 4: 2 [A] **build** a ramp up to it, set up camps against it and put
7: 8 [A] *I am* about to **pour out** my wrath on you and spend my
9: 8 [A] of Israel in this **outpouring** *of* your wrath on Jerusalem?"
14:19 [A] that land and **pour out** my wrath upon it through bloodshed,
16:15 [A] *You* **lavished** your favors on anyone who passed by and your
16:36 [C] Because you **poured out** your wealth and exposed your
16:38 [A] of women who commit adultery and *who* **shed** blood;
17:17 [A] when ramps *are* **built** and siege works erected to destroy
18:10 [A] *who* **sheds** blood or does any of these other things
20: 8 [A] So I said I *would* **pour out** my wrath on them and spend my
20:13 [A] So I said *I would* **pour out** my wrath on them and destroy
20:21 [A] So I said I *would* **pour out** my wrath on them and spend my
20:33 [B] and an outstretched arm and with **outpoured** wrath.
20:34 [B] and an outstretched arm and with **outpoured** wrath.
21:22 [21:27] [A] the gates, to **build** a ramp and to erect siege works.
21:31 [21:36] [A] *I will* **pour out** my wrath upon you and breathe out
22: 3 [A] O city that brings on herself doom by **shedding** blood in her
22: 4 [A] you have become guilty because of the blood *you have* **shed**
22: 6 [A] of Israel who are in you uses his power to **shed** blood.
22: 9 [A] In you are slanderous men bent on **shedding** blood; in you
22:12 [A] In you men accept bribes to **shed** blood; you take usury
22:22 [A] you will know that I the LORD *have* **poured out** my wrath
22:27 [A] they **shed** blood and kill people to make unjust gain.
22:31 [A] So *I will* **pour out** my wrath on them and consume them
23: 8 [A] her virgin bosom and **poured out** their lust upon her.
23:45 [A] punishment of women who commit adultery and **shed** blood,
24: 7 [A] *she did* not **pour** it on the ground, where the dust would
26: 8 [A] **build** a ramp up to your walls and raise his shields against
30:15 [A] *I will* **pour out** my wrath on Pelusium, the stronghold of
33:25 [A] the blood still in it and look to your idols and **shed** blood,
36:18 [A] So *I* **poured out** my wrath on them because they had shed
36:18 [A] wrath on them because *they had* **shed** blood in the land and
39:29 [A] for *I will* **pour out** my Spirit on the house of Israel,
Da 11:15 [A] and **build up** siege ramps and will capture a fortified city.
Hos 5:10 [A] *I will* **pour out** my wrath on them like a flood of water.
Joel 2:28 [3:1] [A] "And afterward, *I will* **pour out** my Spirit on all
2:29 [3:2] [A] and women, *I will* **pour out** my Spirit in those days.
3:19 [4:19] [A] of Judah, in whose land *they* **shed** innocent blood.
Am 5: 8 [A] of the sea and **pours** them **out** over the face of the land—
9: 6 [A] of the sea and **pours** them **out** over the face of the land—
Zep 1:17 [E] Their blood *will* **be poured out** like dust and their entrails
3: 8 [A] to gather the kingdoms and to **pour out** my wrath on them—
Zec 12:10 [A] "And *I will* **pour out** on the house of David and the

9162 שֶׁפֶךְ **šepek**, n.[m.]. [2] [√ 9161]

heap [1], where thrown [1]

Lev 4:12 **where** the ashes are **thrown**, and burn it in a wood fire on the ash
4:12 the ashes are thrown, and burn it in a wood fire on the ash **heap**.

9163 שָׁפְכָה **šopkâ**, n.f. [1] [√ 9161]

cutting [+4162] [1]

Dt 23: 1 [23:2] or **cutting** [+4162] may enter the assembly of the LORD.

9164 ¹שָׁפֵל **šāpēl¹**, v. [30] [→ 9165, 9166, 9167, 9168, 9169, 9170; Ar 10737, 10738]

humbled [6], brought low [4], bring low [3], bring down [2], brings down [1], brings low [1], casts [1], come down [1], descended [1],

[F] Hitpael (hitpoel, hitpoal, hitpolel, hitpolal, hitpalel, hitpalal, hitpalpel, hitpalpal, hotpael, hotpaal) [G] Hiphil (hiphtil) [H] Hophal [I] Hishtaphel

fades [1], humble [1], humbles [1], humiliate [1], lay low [1], lays low [1], leveled completely [+928+2021+9168] [1], levels [1], low [1], stoops down [1]

1Sa 2: 7 [G] sends poverty and wealth; *he* **humbles** and he exalts.
2Sa 22: 28 [G] but your eyes are on the haughty *to* **bring** them **low**.
Job 22: 29 [G] When *men are* **brought low** and you say, 'Lift them up!'
40: 11 [G] of your wrath, look at every proud man and **bring** him **low**,
Ps 18: 27 [18:28] [G] but **bring low** those whose eyes are haughty.
75: 7 [75:8] [G] who judges: *He* **brings** one **down**, he exalts another.
113: 6 [G] who **stoops down** to look on the heavens and the earth?
147: 6 [G] sustains the humble but **casts** the wicked to the ground.
Pr 25: 7 [G] up here," than for him *to* **humiliate** you before a nobleman.
29: 23 [G] A man's pride **brings** him **low**, but a man of lowly spirit
Ecc 12: 4 [A] doors to the street are closed and the sound of grinding **fades**;
Isa 2: 9 [A] So man will be brought low and mankind **humbled**—do not
2: 11 [A] The eyes of the arrogant man *will be* **humbled** and the pride
2: 12 [A] and lofty, for all that is exalted (and *they will be* **humbled**),
2: 17 [A] of man will be brought low and the pride of men **humbled**;
5: 15 [A] So man will be brought low and mankind **humbled**, the eyes
5: 15 [A] and mankind humbled, the eyes of the arrogant **humbled**.
10: 33 [A] lofty trees will be felled, the tall ones *will be* **brought low**.
13: 11 [G] of the haughty and *will* **humble** the pride of the ruthless.
25: 11 [G] God *will* **bring down** their pride despite the cleverness of
25: 12 [G] will bring down your high fortified walls and **lay** *them* **low**;
26: 5 [G] humbles those who dwell on high, *he* **lays** the lofty city **low**;
26: 5 [G] *he* **levels** it to the ground and casts it down to the dust.
29: 4 [A] **Brought low**, you will speak from the ground; your speech
32: 19 [A] and the city *is* **leveled** [+928+2021+9168] **completely**,
40: 4 [A] valley shall be raised up, every mountain and hill *made* **low**;
57: 9 [G] ambassadors far away; *you* **descended** to the grave itself!
Jer 13: 18 [G] and to the queen mother, "**Come down** from your thrones,
Eze 17: 24 [G] field will know that I the LORD **bring down** the tall tree
21: 26 [21:31] [G] will be exalted and the exalted *will be* **brought low**.

9165 שֵׁפֶל šēpel, n.[m.]. [2] [√ 9164]

low estate [1], low [1]

Ps 136: 23 to the One who remembered us in our **low estate** *His love*
Ecc 10: 6 are put in many high positions, while the rich occupy the **low** *ones*.

9166 שָׁפָל šāpāl, a. [18] [√ 9164]

lowly [8], deep [3], humiliated [2], low [2], deeper [1], low [+7757] [1], lowliest [1]

Lev 13: 20 if it appears to be more than skin **deep** and the hair in it has turned
13: 21 no white hair in it and it is not more than skin **deep** and has faded,
13: 26 hair in the spot and if it is not more than skin **deep** and has faded,
14: 37 or reddish depressions that appear to be **deeper** than the surface of
2Sa 6: 22 undignified than this, and I will be **humiliated** in my own eyes.
Job 5: 11 The **lowly** he sets on high, and those who mourn are lifted to
Ps 138: 6 Though the LORD is on high, he looks upon the **lowly**,
Pr 16: 19 Better to be **lowly** *in* spirit and among the oppressed than to share
29: 23 man's pride brings him low, but a *man of* **lowly** spirit gains honor.
Isa 57: 15 holy place, but also with him who is contrite and **lowly** *in* spirit,
57: 15 to revive the spirit of the **lowly** and to revive the heart of the
Eze 17: 6 and it sprouted and became a **low** [+7757], spreading vine.
17: 14 so that the kingdom would be *brought* **low**, unable to rise again,
17: 24 LORD bring down the tall tree and make the **low** tree grow tall.
21: 26 [21:31] The **lowly** will be exalted and the exalted will be brought
29: 14 the land of their ancestry. There they will be a **lowly** kingdom.
29: 15 It will be the **lowliest** of kingdoms and will never again exalt itself
Mal 2: 9 caused you to be despised and **humiliated** before all the people,

9167 ²שָׁפֵל šāpēl[2], a. Not used in NIV/BHS [√ 9164]

9168 שִׁפְלָה šiplâ, n.f. [1] [√ 9164]

leveled completely [+928+2021+9164] [1]

Isa 32: 19 Though hail flattens the forest and the city *is* **leveled completely** [+928+2021+9164],

9169 שְׁפֵלָה šᵉpēlâ, n.f. [20] [√ 9164]

western foothills [13], foothills [7]

Dt 1: 7 in the **western foothills**, in the Negev and along the coast,
Jos 9: 1 those in the hill country, in the **western foothills**, and along the
10: 40 the Negev, the **western foothills** and the mountain slopes,
11: 2 in the **western foothills** and in Naphoth Dor on the west;
11: 16 the **western foothills**, the Arabah and the mountains of Israel with
11: 16 the Arabah and the mountains of Israel with their **foothills**,
12: 8 the hill country, the **western foothills**, the Arabah, the mountain
15: 33 In the **western foothills**: Eshtaol, Zorah, Ashnah,
Jdg 1: 9 living in the hill country, the Negev and the **western foothills**.
1Ki 10: 27 and cedar as plentiful as sycamore-fig trees in the **foothills**.
1Ch 27: 28 charge of the olive and sycamore-fig trees in the **western foothills**.
2Ch 1: 15 and cedar as plentiful as sycamore-fig trees in the **foothills**.
9: 27 and cedar as plentiful as sycamore-fig trees in the **foothills**.
26: 10 because he had much livestock in the **foothills** and in the plain.
28: 18 while the Philistines had raided towns in the **foothills** and in the
Jer 17: 26 from the territory of Benjamin and the **western foothills**, from the
32: 44 of the hill country, of the **western foothills** and of the Negev,
33: 13 of the **western foothills** and of the Negev, in the territory of
Ob 1: 19 people from the **foothills** will possess the land of the Philistines.
Zec 7: 7 and the Negev and the **western foothills** were settled?' "

9170 שִׁפְלוּת šiplût, n.f. [1] [√ 9164]

idle [1]

Ecc 10: 18 a man is lazy, the rafters sag; if his hands are **idle**, the house leaks.

9171 שָׁפָם šāpām, n.pr.m. [1]

Shapham [1]

1Ch 5: 12 the chief, **Shapham** the second, then Janai and Shaphat, in Bashan.

9172 שְׁפָם šᵉpām, n.pr.loc. [2] [→ 9175?]

Shepham [2]

Nu 34: 10 your eastern boundary, run a line from Hazar Enan to **Shepham**.
34: 11 The boundary will go down from **Shepham** to Riblah on the east

9173 שְׁפִּם šuppim, n.pr.m. Not used in NIV/BHS [√ 9158]

9174 שִׁפְמוֹת šipᵃmôt, n.pr.loc. Not used in NIV/BHS [cf. 8560]

9175 שִׁפְמִי šipmî, a.g. [1] [√ 9172?]

Shiphmite [1]

1Ch 27: 27 Zabdi the **Shiphmite** was in charge of the produce of the vineyards

9176 ¹שָׁפָן šāpān[1], n.m. [4] [→ 9177]

coney [2], coneys [2]

Lev 11: 5 The **coney**, though it chews the cud, does not have a split hoof;
Dt 14: 7 divided you may not eat the camel, the rabbit or the **coney**.
Ps 104: 18 belong to the wild goats; the crags are a refuge for the **coneys**.
Pr 30: 26 **coneys** are creatures of little power, yet they make their home in

9177 ²שָׁפָן šāpān[2], n.pr.m. [30] [√ 9176]

Shaphan [30]

2Ki 22: 3 **Shaphan** son of Azaliah, the son of Meshullam, to the temple of
22: 8 Hilkiah the high priest said to **Shaphan** the secretary, "I have
22: 8 in the temple of the LORD." He gave it to **Shaphan**, who read it.
22: 9 Then **Shaphan** the secretary went to the king and reported to him:
22: 10 **Shaphan** the secretary informed the king, "Hilkiah the priest has
22: 10 me a book." And **Shaphan** read from it in the presence of the king.
22: 12 Ahikam son of **Shaphan**, Acbor son of Micaiah, Shaphan the
22: 12 **Shaphan** the secretary and Asaiah the king's attendant:
22: 14 **Shaphan** and Asaiah went to speak to the prophetess Huldah,
25: 22 the son of **Shaphan**, to be over the people he had left behind in
2Ch 34: 8 he sent **Shaphan** son of Azaliah and Maaseiah the ruler of the city,
34: 15 Hilkiah said to **Shaphan** the secretary, "I have found the Book of
34: 15 of the Law in the temple of the LORD." He gave it to **Shaphan**.
34: 16 Then **Shaphan** took the book to the king and reported to him:
34: 18 **Shaphan** the secretary informed the king, "Hilkiah the priest has
34: 18 me a book." And **Shaphan** read from it in the presence of the king.
34: 20 Ahikam son of **Shaphan**, Abdon son of Micah, Shaphan the
34: 20 of Micah, **Shaphan** the secretary and Asaiah the king's attendant:
Jer 26: 24 Ahikam son of **Shaphan** supported Jeremiah, and so he was not
29: 3 He entrusted the letter to Elasah son of **Shaphan** and to Gemariah
36: 10 From the room of Gemariah son of **Shaphan** the secretary,
36: 11 When Micaiah son of Gemariah, the son of **Shaphan**, heard all the
36: 12 of Shemaiah, Elnathan son of Acbor, Gemariah son of **Shaphan**,
39: 14 son of Ahikam, the son of **Shaphan**, to take him back to his home.
40: 5 "Go back to Gedaliah son of Ahikam, the son of **Shaphan**,
40: 9 Gedaliah son of Ahikam, the son of **Shaphan**, took an oath to
40: 11 son of Ahikam, the son of **Shaphan**, as governor over them,
41: 2 Gedaliah son of Ahikam, the son of **Shaphan**, with the sword,
43: 6 the son of **Shaphan**, and Jeremiah the prophet and Baruch son of
Eze 8: 11 and Jaazaniah son of **Shaphan** was standing among them.

9178 שָׁפַע šāpaʿ, v. Not used in NIV/BHS [→ 9179, 9180, 9181]

9179 שֶׁפַע šepaʿ, n.[m.]. [1] [√ 9178]

abundance [1]

Dt 33: 19 they will feast on the **abundance** *of* the seas, on the treasures

9180 שִׁפְעָה ***šip'â***, n.f. [6] [√ 9178]
flood [2], troops [2], herds [1], many [1]

2Ki 9:17 standing on the tower in Jezreel saw Jehu's **troops** approaching,
9:17 troops approaching, he called out, "I see *some* **troops** coming."
Job 22:11 so dark you cannot see, and why a **flood** *of* water covers you.
38:34 your voice to the clouds and cover yourself with a **flood** *of* water?
Isa 60:6 **Herds** *of* camels will cover your land, young camels of Midian
Eze 26:10 His horses will be so **many** that they will cover you with dust.

9181 שִׁפְעִי ***šip'î***, n.pr.m. [1] [√ 9178]
Shiphi [1]

1Ch 4:37 and Ziza son of **Shiphi**, the son of Allon, the son of Jedaiah,

9182 שָׁפַר ***šāpar***, v. [1] [→ 9160, 9183, 9185, 9186, 9188; cf. 8795; Ar 10739]
delightful [1]

Ps 16:6 [A] me in pleasant places; surely I have a **delightful** inheritance.

9183 ¹שֶׁפֶר ***šeper¹***, n.m. [1] [√ 9182]
beautiful [1]

Ge 49:21 "Naphtali is a doe set free that bears **beautiful** fawns.

9184 ²שֶׁפֶר ***šeper²***, n.pr.loc. [2] [cf. 6223]
Shepher [2]

Nu 33:23 They left Kehelathah and camped at Mount **Shepher**.
33:24 They left Mount **Shepher** and camped at Haradah.

9185 ¹שִׁפְרָה ***šiprâ¹***, n.f. [1] [√ 9182]
fair [1]

Job 26:13 By his breath the skies became **fair**; his hand pierced the gliding

9186 ²שִׁפְרָה ***šiprâ²***, n.pr.f. [1] [√ 9182]
Shiphrah [1]

Ex 1:15 to the Hebrew midwives, whose names were **Shiphrah** and Puah,

9187 שַׁפְרוּר ***šaprûr***, n.[m.]. [0] [cf. 9188]

Jer 43:10 [he will spread his **royal canopy** [K; see Q 9188] above them.]

9188 שַׁפְרִיר ***šaprîr***, n.[m.]. [1] [√ 9182; cf. 9187]
royal canopy [1]

Jer 43:10 he will spread his **royal canopy** [K 9187] above them.

9189 שָׁפַת ***šāpat***, v.den. [5] [→ 883, 5478, 9190, 9191]
put on [3], establish [1], lay [1]

2Ki 4:38 [A] "**Put on** the large pot and cook some stew for these men."
Ps 22:15 [22:16] [A] roof of my mouth; *you* **lay** me in the dust of death.
Isa 26:12 [A] LORD, *you* **establish** peace for us; all that we have
Eze 24:3 [A] " '**Put on** the cooking pot; put it on and pour water into it.
24:3 [A] " 'Put on the cooking pot; **put it on** and pour water into it.

9190 ¹שְׁפַתַּיִם ***šᵉpattayim¹***, n.[m.]du. [1] [√ 9189]
campfires [1]

Ps 68:13 [68:14] Even while you sleep among the **campfires**, the wings of

9191 ²שְׁפַתַּיִם ***šᵉpattayim²***, n.[m.]du. [1] [√ 9189]
double-pronged hooks [1]

Eze 40:43 **double-pronged hooks**, each a handbreadth long, were attached to

9192 שֶׁצֶף ***šeṣep***, n.m. [1] [cf. 8851, 8852]
surge [1]

Isa 54:8 In a **surge** *of* anger I hid my face from you for a moment,

9193 ¹שָׁקַד ***šāqad¹***, v. [12] [→ 5481, 9195, 9196]
watching [3], did not hesitate [1], guard [1], have an eye for [1], lie awake [1], lie in wait [1], stand guard [1], watch kept [1], watch [1], watched [1]

Ezr 8:29 [A] **Guard** them carefully until you weigh them out in the
Job 21:32 [A] He is carried to the grave, and **watch** *is* **kept** over his tomb.
Ps 102:7 [102:8] [A] *I* **lie awake**; I have become like a bird alone on a
127:1 [A] watches over the city, the watchmen **stand guard** in vain.
Pr 8:34 [A] to me, **watching** daily at my doors, waiting at my doorway.
Isa 29:20 [A] and all *who* **have an eye for** evil will be cut down—
Jer 1:12 [A] for I *am* **watching** to see that my word is fulfilled."
5:6 [A] a leopard *will* **lie in wait** near their towns to tear to pieces
31:28 [A] Just as *I* **watched** over them to uproot and tear down, and to
31:28 [A] so *I will* **watch** over them to build and to plant,"
44:27 [A] For I *am* **watching** over them for harm, not for good; the
Da 9:14 [A] The LORD **did not hesitate** to bring the disaster upon us,

9194 ²שָׁקַד ***šāqad²***, v. Not used in NIV/BHS

9195 ³שָׁקַד ***šāqad³***, v.den. Not used in NIV/BHS [→ 5481, 9196; cf. 9193]

9196 שָׁקֵד ***šāqēd***, n.[m.]. [4] [√ 9195; cf. 9193]
almond tree [2], almonds [2]

Ge 43:11 some spices and myrrh, some pistachio nuts and **almonds**.
Nu 17:8 [17:23] but had budded, blossomed and produced **almonds**.
Ecc 12:5 when the **almond tree** blossoms and the grasshopper drags himself
Jer 1:11 Jeremiah?" "I see the branch of an **almond tree**," I replied.

9197 שָׁקָה ***šāqâ***, v. [61] [→ 5482, 5483, 9198, 9216; cf. 9272]
water [10], watered [6], drink [5], made drink [4], gave a drink [3], give to drink [3], gave [2], get a drink [2], get to drink [2], give drink [2], got to drink [2], have drink [2], drench [1], gave water [1], give a drink [+906+3926] [1], give a drink [1], give water [1], give [1], given a drink [1], given to drink [1], given [1], gives drink [1], irrigated [1], let drink [1], made to drink [1], make drink [1], rich [1], watering [1], waters [1], wine served [1]

Ge 2:6 [G] the earth and **watered** the whole surface of the ground—
2:10 [G] A river **watering** the garden flowed from Eden; from there it
19:32 [G] *Let's* **get** our father **to drink** wine and then lie with him
19:33 [G] That night *they* **got** their father **to drink** wine, and the older
19:34 [G] *Let's* **get** him **to drink** wine again tonight, and you go in
19:35 [G] So *they* **got** their father **to drink** wine that night also,
21:19 [G] and filled the skin with water and **gave** the boy **a drink**.
24:14 [G] and she says, 'Drink, and *I'll* **water** your camels too'—
24:18 [G] quickly lowered the jar to her hands and **gave** him **a drink**.
24:19 [G] After *she had* **given** him **a drink**, she said, "I'll draw water
24:43 [G] say to her, "Please **let** me **drink** a little water from your jar,"
24:45 [G] and drew water, and I said to her, 'Please **give** me **a drink**.'
24:46 [G] and said, 'Drink, and *I'll* **water** your camels too.'
24:46 [G] camels too.' So I drank, and *she* **watered** the camels also.
29:2 [G] lying near it because the flocks *were* **watered** from that well.
29:3 [G] the stone away from the well's mouth and **water** the sheep.
29:7 [G] **Water** the sheep and take them back to pasture."
29:8 [G] from the mouth of the well. Then *we will* **water** the sheep."
29:10 [G] from the mouth of the well and **watered** his uncle's sheep.
Ex 2:16 [G] draw water and fill the troughs to **water** their father's flock.
2:17 [G] got up and came to their rescue and **watered** their flock.
2:19 [G] He even drew water for us and **watered** the flock."
32:20 [G] scattered it on the water and **made** the Israelites **drink** it.
Nu 5:24 [G] *He shall* **have** the woman **drink** the bitter water that brings a
5:26 [G] the altar; after that, *he is to* **have** the woman **drink** the water.
5:27 [G] then when she *is* **made to drink** the water that brings a curse,
20:8 [G] for the community so they and their livestock *can* **drink**."
Dt 11:10 [G] your seed and **irrigated** it by foot as in a vegetable garden.
Jdg 4:19 [G] "I'm thirsty," he said. "Please **give** me some water." She
4:19 [G] a skin of milk, **gave** him **a drink**, and covered him up.
1Sa 30:11 [G] to David. They gave him water *to* **drink** and food to eat—
2Sa 23:15 [G] that someone *would* **get** me **a drink** *of* water from the well
1Ch 11:17 [G] that someone *would* **get** me **a drink** *of* water from the well
2Ch 28:15 [G] provided them with clothes and sandals, food and **drink**,
Est 1:7 [G] **Wine** *was* **served** in goblets of gold, each one different from
Job 21:24 [E] his body well nourished, his bones **rich** *with* marrow.
22:7 [G] *You* **gave** no water *to* the weary and you withheld food from
Ps 36:8 [36:9] [G] *you* **give** them **drink** *from* your river of delights.
60:3 [60:5] [G] *you have* **given** us wine that makes us stagger.
69:21 [69:22] [G] gall in my food and **gave** me vinegar for my thirst.
78:15 [G] in the desert and **gave** them **water** as abundant as the seas;
80:5 [80:6] [G] *you have* **made** them **drink** tears by the bowlful.
104:11 [G] *They* **give water** *to* all the beasts of the field; the wild
104:13 [G] *He* **waters** the mountains from his upper chambers; the earth
Pr 25:21 [G] give him food to eat; if he is thirsty, **give** him water **to drink**.
Ecc 2:6 [G] I made reservoirs to **water** groves of flourishing trees.
SS 8:2 [G] *I would* **give** you spiced wine **to drink**, the nectar of my
Isa 27:3 [G] I, the LORD, watch over it; *I* **water** it continually. I guard it
43:20 [G] in the wasteland, to **give drink** *to* my people, my chosen,
Jer 8:14 [G] doomed us to perish and **given** us poisoned water **to drink**,
9:15 [9:14] [G] this people eat bitter food and **drink** poisoned water.
16:7 [G] nor *will anyone* **give** them **a drink** [+906+3926] to console
23:15 [G] "I will make them eat bitter food and **drink** poisoned water,
25:15 [G] and **make** all the nations to whom I send you **drink** it.
25:17 [G] and **made** all the nations to whom he sent me **drink** it:
35:2 [G] of the house of the LORD and **give** them wine **to drink**."
Eze 17:7 [G] was planted and stretched out its branches to him for **water**.

Eze 32: 6 [G] *I will* **drench** the land *with* your flowing blood all the way to
Joel 3: 18 [4:18] [G] LORD's house and *will* **water** the valley of acacias.
Am 2: 12 [G] "But *you* **made** the Nazirites **drink** wine and commanded
8: 8 [c] [and then **sink** [K; see Q 9205] like the river of Egypt.]
Hab 2: 15 [G] "Woe to *him who* **gives drink** *to* his neighbors, pouring it

9198 שִׁקּוּי ***šiqqûy***, n.[m.]. [3] [√ 9197]

drink [2], nourishment [1]

Ps 102: 9 [102:10] I eat ashes as my food and mingle my **drink** with tears
Pr 3: 8 will bring health to your body and **nourishment** to your bones.
Hos 2: 5 [2:7] and my water, my wool and my linen, my oil and my **drink**.'

9199 שִׁקּוּץ ***šiqqûṣ***, n.m. [28] [√ 9210]

vile images [9], abomination [3], detestable god [3], detestable idols [3], abominable idols [1], abominations [1], detestable acts [1], detestable images [1], detestable things [1], filth [1], forbidden food [1], vile god [1], vile goddess [1], vile [1]

Dt 29: 17 [29:16] You saw among them their **detestable images** and idols
1Ki 11: 5 the Sidonians, and Molech the **detestable god** *of* the Ammonites.
11: 7 Solomon built a high place for Chemosh the **detestable god** *of*
11: 7 of Moab, and for Molech the **detestable god** *of* the Ammonites.
2Ki 23: 13 of Israel had built for Ashtoreth the **vile goddess** *of* the Sidonians,
23: 13 for Chemosh the **vile god** *of* Moab, and for Molech the detestable
23: 24 the idols and all the other **detestable things** seen in Judah
2Ch 15: 8 He removed the **detestable idols** from the whole land of Judah
Isa 66: 3 their own ways, and their souls delight in their **abominations**;
Jer 4: 1 "If you put your **detestable idols** out of my sight and no longer go
7: 30 They have set up their **detestable idols** in the house that bears my
13: 27 I have seen your **detestable acts** on the hills and in the fields.
16: 18 have defiled my land with the lifeless forms of their **vile images**
32: 34 They set up their **abominable idols** in the house that bears my
Eze 5: 11 because you have defiled my sanctuary with all your **vile images**
7: 20 and used it to make their detestable idols and **vile images**.
11: 18 will return to it and remove all its **vile images** and detestable idols.
11: 21 But as for those whose hearts are devoted to their **vile images**
20: 7 "Each of you, get rid of the **vile images** you have set your eyes on,
20: 8 they did not get rid of the **vile images** they had set their eyes on,
20: 30 the way your fathers did and lust after their **vile images**?
37: 23 with their idols and **vile images** or with any of their offenses,
Da 9: 27 on a wing ⌞of the temple⌟ he will set up an **abomination** that
11: 31 Then they will set up the **abomination** that causes desolation.
12: 11 is abolished and the **abomination** that causes desolation is set up,
Hos 9: 10 to that shameful idol and became as **vile** as the thing they loved.
Na 3: 6 I will pelt you with **filth**, I will treat you with contempt and make
Zec 9: 7 from their mouths, the **forbidden food** from between their teeth.

9200 שָׁקַט ***šāqaṭ***, v. [41] [→ 9201; cf. 9284]

at peace [5], quiet [5], rest [4], had peace [3], peaceful [3], quietness [3], calm [2], had rest [2], have peace [2], in peace [2], calms [1], enjoyed peace [1], grant relief [1], left [1], lies hushed [1], silent [1], still [1], troubled [+3523+4202] [1], unconcerned [+8932] [1], unsuspecting [1]

Jos 11: 23 [A] to their tribal divisions. Then the land **had rest** from war.
14: 15 [A] man among the Anakites.) Then the land **had rest** from war.
Jdg 3: 11 [A] So the land **had peace** for forty years, until Othniel son of
3: 30 [A] subject to Israel, and the land **had peace** for eighty years.
5: 31 [A] it rises in its strength." Then the land **had peace** forty years.
8: 28 [A] Gideon's lifetime, the land **enjoyed peace** forty years.
18: 7 [A] living in safety, like the Sidonians, **unsuspecting** and secure.
18: 27 [A] on to Laish, against a **peaceful** and unsuspecting people.
Ru 3: 18 [A] For the man *will* not **rest** until the matter is settled today."
2Ki 11: 20 [A] the city *was* **quiet**, because Athaliah had been slain with the
1Ch 4: 40 [A] good pasture, and the land was spacious, **peaceful** and quiet.
2Ch 14: 1 [13:23] [A] in his days the country *was* **at peace** for ten years.
14: 5 [14:4] [A] in Judah, and the kingdom *was* **at peace** under him.
14: 6 [14:5] [A] fortified cities of Judah, since the land *was* **at peace**.
20: 30 [A] the kingdom of Jehoshaphat *was* **at peace**, for his God had
23: 21 [A] the city *was* **quiet**, because Athaliah had been slain with the
Job 3: 13 [A] For now I would be lying down **in peace**; I would be asleep
3: 26 [A] I have no peace, no **quietness**; I have no rest, but only
34: 29 [G] if he *remains* **silent**, who can condemn him? If he hides his
37: 17 [G] You who swelter in your clothes when the land **lies hushed**
Ps 76: 8 [76:9] [A] and the land feared and *was* **quiet**—
83: 1 [83:2] [A] do not keep silent; be not quiet, O God, *be* not **still**.
94: 13 [G] you **grant** him **relief** from days of trouble, till a pit is dug for
Pr 15: 18 [G] man stirs up dissension, but a patient man **calms** a quarrel.
Isa 7: 4 [G] Say to him, 'Be careful, *keep* **calm** and don't be afraid. Do
14: 7 [A] All the lands are at rest and **at peace**; they break into singing.
18: 4 [A] "*I will remain* **quiet** and will look on from my dwelling
30: 15 [G] rest is your salvation, in **quietness** and trust is your strength,
32: 17 [G] the effect of righteousness *will be* **quietness** and confidence
57: 20 [G] which cannot **rest**, whose waves cast up mire and mud.
62: 1 [A] not keep silent, for Jerusalem's sake *I will* not *remain* **quiet**,
Jer 30: 10 [A] Jacob will again **have peace** and security, and no one will
46: 27 [A] Jacob will again **have peace** and security, and no one will
47: 6 [A] sword of the LORD,' ⌞you cry,⌟ 'how long till *you* **rest**?
47: 7 [A] But how *can it* **rest** when the LORD has commanded it,
48: 11 [A] has been at rest from youth, like wine **left** on its dregs,
49: 23 [G] They are disheartened, **troubled** [+3523+4202] like the
Eze 16: 42 [A] will turn away from you; *I will be* **calm** and no longer angry.
16: 49 [G] daughters were arrogant, overfed and **unconcerned** [+8932];
38: 11 [A] I will attack a **peaceful** and unsuspecting people—all of them
Zec 1: 11 [A] the earth and found the whole world at rest and **in peace**."

9201 שֶׁקֶט ***šeqeṭ***, n.[m.]. [1] [√ 9200]

quiet [1]

1Ch 22: 9 and I will grant Israel peace and **quiet** during his reign.

9202 שָׁקַל ***šāqal***, v. [22] [→ 5484, 5486, 5487?, 9203; Ar 10769]

weighed out [7], be weighed [+9202] [2], pay [2], weigh out [2], weigh [2], be weighed [1], paid [+906+8510] [1], pay [+4084] [1], put [+995+4200] [1], spend [1], took revenue [1], weighed [1]

Ge 23: 16 [A] **weighed out** for him the price he had named in the hearing
Ex 22: 17 [22:16] [A] *he must still* **pay** [+4084] the bride-price for
2Sa 14: 26 [A] *he would* **weigh** it, and its weight was two hundred shekels
18: 12 [A] "Even if a thousand shekels *were* **weighed out** into my
1Ki 20: 39 [A] be your life for his life, or *you must* **pay** a talent of silver.'
Ezr 8: 25 [A] *I* **weighed out** to them the offering of silver and gold and the
8: 26 [A] *I* **weighed out** to them 650 talents of silver, silver articles
8: 29 [A] Guard them carefully until *you* **weigh** them **out** in the
8: 33 [C] we **weighed out** the silver and gold and the sacred articles
Est 3: 9 [A] *I will* **put** [+995+4200] ten thousand talents of silver into the
4: 7 [A] to **pay** into the royal treasury for the destruction of the Jews.
Job 6: 2 [C] "If only my anguish *could* **be weighed** [+9202] and all my
6: 2 [A] "If only my anguish *could* **be weighed** [+9202] and all my
28: 15 [C] with the finest gold, nor *can* its price **be weighed** *in* silver.
31: 6 [A] *let* God **weigh** me in honest scales and he will know that I
Isa 33: 18 [A] that chief officer? Where is the *one who* **took** *the* **revenue**?
40: 12 [A] or **weighed** the mountains on the scales and the hills in a
46: 6 [A] out gold from their bags and **weigh out** silver on the scales;
55: 2 [A] Why **spend** money on what is not bread, and your labor on
Jer 32: 9 [A] and **weighed out** for him seventeen shekels of silver.
32: 10 [A] had it witnessed, and **weighed out** the silver on the scales.
Zec 11: 12 [A] So *they* **paid** [+906+8510] me thirty pieces of silver.

9203 שֶׁקֶל ***šeqel***, n.m. [88] [√ 9202; Ar 10770]

shekels [45], shekel [39], *untranslated* [1], price [1], weighs [1], which[s] [1]

Ge 23: 15 the land is worth four hundred **shekels** *of* silver, but what is that
23: 16 four hundred **shekels** *of* silver, according to the weight current
Ex 21: 32 the owner must pay thirty **shekels** of silver to the master of the
30: 13 who crosses over to those already counted is to give a half **shekel**,
30: 13 according to the sanctuary **shekel**, which weighs twenty gerahs.
30: 13 according to the sanctuary shekel, which **weighs** twenty gerahs.
30: 13 twenty gerahs. This half **shekel** is an offering to the LORD.
30: 15 The rich are not to give more than a half **shekel** and the poor are
30: 24 all according to the sanctuary **shekel**—and a hin of olive oil.
38: 24 for all the work on the sanctuary was 29 talents and 730 **shekels**,
38: 24 was 29 talents and 730 shekels, according to the sanctuary **shekel**.
38: 25 who were counted in the census was 100 talents and 1,775 **shekels**,
38: 25 100 talents and 1,775 shekels, according to the sanctuary **shekel**—
38: 26 one beka per person, that is, half a **shekel**, according to the
38: 26 per person, that is, half a shekel, according to the sanctuary **shekel**,
38: 29 bronze from the wave offering was 70 talents and 2,400 **shekels**.
Lev 5: 15 and of the proper value in silver, according to the sanctuary **shekel**.
5: 15 according to the sanctuary shekel. **[RPH]** It is a guilt offering.
27: 3 male between the ages of twenty and sixty at fifty **shekels** *of* silver,
27: 3 sixty at fifty shekels of silver, according to the sanctuary **shekel**;
27: 4 and if it is a female, set her value at thirty **shekels**.
27: 5 set the value of a male at twenty **shekels** and of a female at ten
27: 5 value of a male at twenty shekels and of a female at ten **shekels**.
27: 6 set the value of a male at five **shekels** *of* silver and that of a female
27: 6 five shekels of silver and that of a female at three **shekels** *of* silver.
27: 7 set the value of a male at fifteen **shekels** and of a female at ten
27: 7 value of a male at fifteen shekels and of a female at ten **shekels**.
27: 16 required for it—fifty **shekels** *of* silver to a homer of barley seed.
27: 25 Every value is to be set according to the sanctuary **shekel**,
27: 25 set according to the sanctuary shekel, twenty gerahs to the **shekel**.
Nu 3: 47 collect five **shekels** for each one, according to the sanctuary
3: 47 according to the sanctuary **shekel**, which weighs twenty gerahs.
3: 47 according to the sanctuary shekel, **which**[s] weighs twenty gerahs.

Nu 3:50 silver weighing 1,365 shekels, according to the sanctuary **shekel**.
7:13 and one silver sprinkling bowl weighing seventy **shekels**,
7:13 weighing seventy shekels, both according to the sanctuary **shekel**,
7:19 and one silver sprinkling bowl weighing seventy **shekels**,
7:19 weighing seventy shekels, both according to the sanctuary **shekel**,
7:25 and one silver sprinkling bowl weighing seventy **shekels**,
7:25 weighing seventy shekels, both according to the sanctuary **shekel**,
7:31 and one silver sprinkling bowl weighing seventy **shekels**,
7:31 weighing seventy shekels, both according to the sanctuary **shekel**,
7:37 and one silver sprinkling bowl weighing seventy **shekels**,
7:37 weighing seventy shekels, both according to the sanctuary **shekel**,
7:43 and one silver sprinkling bowl weighing seventy **shekels**,
7:43 weighing seventy shekels, both according to the sanctuary **shekel**,
7:49 and one silver sprinkling bowl weighing seventy **shekels**,
7:49 weighing seventy shekels, both according to the sanctuary **shekel**,
7:55 and one silver sprinkling bowl weighing seventy **shekels**,
7:55 weighing seventy shekels, both according to the sanctuary **shekel**,
7:61 and one silver sprinkling bowl weighing seventy **shekels**,
7:61 weighing seventy shekels, both according to the sanctuary **shekel**,
7:67 and one silver sprinkling bowl weighing seventy **shekels**,
7:67 weighing seventy shekels, both according to the sanctuary **shekel**,
7:73 and one silver sprinkling bowl weighing seventy **shekels**,
7:73 weighing seventy shekels, both according to the sanctuary **shekel**,
7:79 and one silver sprinkling bowl weighing seventy **shekels**,
7:79 weighing seventy shekels, both according to the sanctuary **shekel**,
7:85 thousand four hundred shekels, according to the sanctuary **shekel**.
7:86 weighed ten shekels each, according to the sanctuary **shekel**.
18:16 you must redeem them at the redemption price set at five **shekels**
18:16 according to the sanctuary **shekel**, which weighs twenty gerahs.
31:52 Eleazar presented as a gift to the LORD weighed 16,750 **shekels**.
Jos 7:21 two hundred **shekels** *of* silver and a wedge of gold weighing fifty
7:21 shekels of silver and a wedge of gold weighing fifty **shekels**,
1Sa 9:8 "Look," he said, "I have a quarter of a **shekel** *of* silver. I will give
17:5 a coat of scale armor of bronze weighing five thousand **shekels**;
17:7 a weaver's rod, and its iron point weighed six hundred **shekels**.
2Sa 14:26 and its weight was two hundred **shekels** by the royal standard.
24:24 and the oxen and paid fifty **shekels** of silver for them.
2Ki 7:1 a seah of flour will sell for a **shekel** and two seahs of barley for a
7:1 and two seahs of barley for a **shekel** at the gate of Samaria."
7:16 So a seah of flour sold for a **shekel**, and two seahs of barley sold
7:16 and two seahs of barley sold for a **shekel**, as the LORD had said.
7:18 a seah of flour will sell for a **shekel** and two seahs of barley for a
7:18 and two seahs of barley for a **shekel** at the gate of Samaria."
15:20 Every wealthy man had to contribute fifty **shekels** of silver to be
1Ch 21:25 So David paid Araunah six hundred **shekels** *of* gold for the site.
2Ch 3:9 The gold nails weighed fifty **shekels**. He also overlaid the upper
Ne 5:15 and took forty **shekels** of silver from them in addition to food
10:32 [10:33] **shekel** each year for the service of the house of our God:
Jer 32:9 and weighed out for him seventeen **shekels** of silver.
Eze 4:10 Weigh out twenty **shekels** of food to eat each day and eat it at set
45:12 The **shekel** is to consist of twenty gerahs. Twenty shekels plus
45:12 Twenty **shekels** plus twenty-five shekels plus fifteen shekels equal
45:12 Twenty shekels plus twenty-five **shekels** plus fifteen shekels equal
45:12 Twenty shekels plus twenty-five shekels plus fifteen **shekels** equal
Am 8:5 the measure, boosting the **price** and cheating with dishonest scales,

9204 שִׁקְמָה *šiqmâ*, n.f. [7]

sycamore-fig trees [5], fig trees [1], sycamore-figs [1]

1Ki 10:27 and cedar as plentiful as **sycamore-fig trees** in the foothills.
1Ch 27:28 charge of the olive and **sycamore-fig trees** in the western foothills.
2Ch 1:15 and cedar as plentiful as **sycamore-fig trees** in the foothills.
9:27 and cedar as plentiful as **sycamore-fig trees** in the foothills.
Ps 78:47 destroyed their vines with hail and their **sycamore-figs** with sleet.
Isa 9:10 [9:9] the **fig trees** have been felled, but we will replace them with
Am 7:14 but I was a shepherd, and I also took care of **sycamore-fig trees**.

9205 שָׁקַע *šāqaʿ*, v. [6] [→ 5488]

sink [2], died down [1], let settle [1], sinks [1], tie down [1]

Nu 11:2 [A] to Moses, he prayed to the LORD and the fire **died down**.
Job 41:1 [40:25] [G] with a fishhook or **tie down** his tongue with a rope?
Jer 51:64 [A] 'So *will* Babylon **sink** to rise no more because of the disaster
Eze 32:14 [G] *I will* **let** her waters **settle** and make her streams flow like oil,
Am 8:8 [C] be stirred up and then **sink** [K 9197] like the river of Egypt.
9:5 [A] land rises like the Nile, then **sinks** like the river of Egypt—

9206 שְׁקַעֲרוּרָה *šᵉqaʿărûrâ*, n.f. [1] [→ 7883]

depressions [1]

Lev 14:37 or reddish **depressions** that appear to be deeper than the surface of

9207 שָׁקַף *šāqap*, v. [22] [→ 5485, 9208?, 9209]

looked down [6], looks down [4], looked out [2], overlooking [2], watched [2], appears [1], look down [1], looked [1], looms [1], overlooks [1], peered [1]

Ge 18:16 [G] the men got up to leave, *they* **looked down** toward Sodom,
19:28 [G] *He* **looked down** toward Sodom and Gomorrah, toward all
26:8 [G] Abimelech king of the Philistines **looked down** from a
Ex 14:24 [G] During the last watch of the night the LORD **looked down**
Nu 21:20 [C] in Moab where the top of Pisgah **overlooks** the wasteland.
23:28 [C] took Balaam to the top of Peor, **overlooking** the wasteland.
Dt 26:15 [G] **Look down** from heaven, your holy dwelling place,
Jdg 5:28 [C] "Through the window **peered** Sisera's mother; behind the
1Sa 13:18 [C] the third toward the borderland **overlooking** the Valley of
2Sa 6:16 [C] of David, Michal daughter of Saul **watched** from a window.
24:20 [G] When Araunah **looked** and saw the king and his men coming
2Ki 9:30 [G] her eyes, arranged her hair and **looked out** of a window.
9:32 [G] my side? Who?" Two or three eunuchs **looked down** at him.
1Ch 15:29 [C] of David, Michal daughter of Saul **watched** from a window.
Ps 14:2 [G] The LORD **looks down** from heaven on the sons of men to
53:2 [53:3] [G] God **looks down** from heaven on the sons of men to
85:11 [85:12] [C] and righteousness **looks down** from heaven.
102:19 [102:20] [G] "The LORD **looked down** from his sanctuary on
Pr 7:6 [C] At the window of my house *I* **looked out** through the lattice.
SS 6:10 [C] Who is this that **appears** like the dawn, fair as the moon,
Jer 6:1 [C] For disaster **looms** out of the north, even terrible destruction.
La 3:50 [G] until the LORD **looks down** from heaven and sees.

9208 שֶׁקֶף *šāqep*, n.[m.]. [1] [√ 9207?]

frames [1]

1Ki 7:5 All the doorways had rectangular **frames**; they were in the front

9209 שְׁקֻפִים *šᵉqupîm*, n.m. [2] [√ 9207]

clerestory [1], windows placed high [1]

1Ki 6:4 He made narrow **clerestory** windows in the temple.
7:4 Its **windows** were **placed high** in sets of three, facing each other.

9210 שָׁקַץ *šāqaṣ*, v. [7] [→ 9199, 9211; cf. 7752, 7762]

defile [2], detest [2], utterly abhor [+9210] [2], disdained [1]

Lev 11:11 [D] must not eat their meat and *you must* **detest** their carcasses.
11:13 [D] " 'These are the birds *you are to* **detest** and not eat because
11:43 [D] *Do* not **defile** yourselves by any of these creatures. Do not
20:25 [D] *Do* not **defile** yourselves by any animal or bird or anything
Dt 7:26 [D] **Utterly abhor** [+9210] and detest it, for it is set apart for
7:26 [D] **Utterly abhor** [+9210] and detest it, for it is set apart for
Ps 22:24 [22:25] [D] or **disdained** the suffering of the afflicted one;

9211 שֶׁקֶץ *šeqeṣ*, n.m. [11] [√ 9210]

detestable [7], detest [3], abominable things [1]

Lev 7:21 or an unclean animal or any unclean, **detestable** *thing*—
11:10 all the other living creatures in the water—you are to **detest**.
11:11 And since you are to **detest** them, you must not eat their meat
11:12 water that does not have fins and scales is to be **detestable** to you.
11:13 the birds you are to detest and not eat because they are **detestable**:
11:20 " 'All flying insects that walk on all fours are to be **detestable** to
11:23 But all other winged creatures that have four legs you are to **detest**.
11:41 " 'Every creature that moves about on the ground is **detestable**;
11:42 on its belly or walks on all fours or on many feet; it is **detestable**.
Isa 66:17 who eat the flesh of pigs and rats and other **abominable things**—
Eze 8:10 and **detestable** animals and all the idols of the house of Israel.

9212 שָׁקַק *šāqaq*, v. [4] [→ 5480; cf. 8796?]

charging [1], pounce [1], rush [1], rushing back and forth [1]

Pr 28:15 [A] or a **charging** bear is a wicked man ruling over a helpless
Isa 33:4 [A] by young locusts; like a swarm of locusts *men* **pounce** on it.
Joel 2:9 [A] *They* **rush** upon the city; they run along the wall. They climb
Na 2:4 [2:5] [F] **rushing back and forth** through the squares.

9213 שָׁקַר *šāqar*, v.den. [6] [→ 9214, 9215]

false [2], betray [1], deal falsely [1], deceive [1], lie [1]

Ge 21:23 [A] to me here before God that *you will* not **deal falsely** with me
Lev 19:11 [D] " 'Do not steal. " 'Do not lie. " '*Do* not **deceive** one another.
1Sa 15:29 [D] He who is the Glory of Israel *does* not **lie** or change his
Ps 44:17 [44:18] [D] not forgotten you or *been* **false** to your covenant.
89:33 [89:34] [D] from him, nor *will I ever* **betray** my faithfulness.
Isa 63:8 [D] they are my people, sons *who will* not *be* **false** to me";

9214 שֶׁקֶר *šeqer*, n.m. [113] [√ 9213]

lies [21], lying [16], false [14], deceptive [4], falsely [+2021+4200] [4], lie [4], without cause [4], deceit [3], deceitful [3], falsehood [3], falsely [3], fraud [3], lies [+1821] [3], not true [3], false gods [2], liar [2], liars [+1819] [2], wrong [2], deceiver [1], deception [1], disillusionment [1], falsely [+6584] [1], gifts he does not give [+5522] [1], in vain [1], liars [1], lie [+1819] [1], lies [+609] [1], lying [+1819] [1], perjurers [+2021+4200+8678] [1], perjury [+2021+4200+8678] [1], pretense [1], put in jeopardy [+928+6913] [1], useless [+2021+4200] [1], vain hope [1], without reason [1]

Ex 5: 9 so that they keep working and pay no attention to **lies** [+1821]."
20: 16 "You shall not give **false** testimony against your neighbor.
23: 7 Have nothing to do with a **false** charge and do not put an innocent
Lev 6: 3 [5:22] and lies about it, or if he swears **falsely** [+6584],
6: 5 [5:24] or whatever it was he swore **falsely** [+2021+4200] about.
19: 12 " 'Do not swear **falsely** [+2021+4200] by my name and so profane
Dt 19: 18 if the witness proves to be a **liar**, giving false testimony against his
19: 18 proves to be a liar, giving **false** testimony against his brother,
1Sa 25: 21 David had just said, "It's been **useless** [+2021+4200]—all my
2Sa 18: 13 if *I had* **put** my life **in jeopardy** [+928+6913]—and nothing is
1Ki 22: 22 will go out and be a **lying** spirit in the mouths of all his prophets,'
22: 23 "So now the LORD has put a **lying** spirit in the mouths of all
2Ki 9: 12 "That's **not true**!" they said. "Tell us." Jehu said, "Here is what he
2Ch 18: 21 " 'I will go and be a **lying** spirit in the mouths of all his prophets,'
18: 22 "So now the LORD has put a **lying** spirit in the mouths of these
Job 13: 4 You, however, smear me with **lies**; you are worthless physicians,
36: 4 Be assured that my words are not **false**; one perfect in knowledge
Ps 7: 14 [7:15] and conceives trouble gives birth to **disillusionment**.
27: 12 for **false** witnesses rise up against me, breathing out violence.
31: 18 [31:19] Let their **lying** lips be silenced, for with pride
33: 17 A horse is a **vain hope** for deliverance; despite all its great strength
35: 19 Let not those gloat over me who are my enemies **without cause**;
38: 19 [38:20] those who hate me **without reason** are numerous.
52: 3 [52:5] rather than good, **falsehood** rather than speaking the truth.
63: 11 [63:12] while the mouths of **liars** [+1819] will be silenced.
69: 4 [69:5] many are my enemies **without cause**, those who seek to
101: 7 in my house; no one who speaks **falsely** will stand in my presence.
109: 2 against me; they have spoken against me with **lying** tongues.
119: 29 Keep me from **deceitful** ways; be gracious to me through your law.
119: 69 Though the arrogant have smeared me with **lies**, I keep your
119: 78 May the arrogant be put to shame for wronging me **without cause**;
119: 86 are trustworthy; help me, for men persecute me **without cause**.
119:104 from your precepts; therefore I hate every **wrong** path.
119:118 all who stray from your decrees, for their deceitfulness is **in vain**.
119:128 because I consider all your precepts right, I hate every **wrong** path.
119:163 I hate and abhor **falsehood** but I love your law.
120: 2 Save me, O LORD, from **lying** lips and from deceitful tongues.
144: 8 whose mouths are full of lies, whose right hands are **deceitful**.
144: 11 whose mouths are full of lies, whose right hands are **deceitful**.
Pr 6: 17 haughty eyes, a **lying** tongue, hands that shed innocent blood,
6: 19 a **false** witness who pours out lies and a man who stirs up
10: 18 He who conceals his hatred has **lying** lips, and whoever spreads
11: 18 The wicked man earns **deceptive** wages, but he who sows
12: 17 witness gives honest testimony, but a **false** witness tells lies.
12: 19 lips endure forever, but a **lying** tongue lasts only a moment.
12: 22 The LORD detests **lying** lips, but he delights in men who are
13: 5 The righteous hate what is **false**, but the wicked bring shame
14: 5 truthful witness does not deceive, but a **false** witness pours out lies.
17: 4 man listens to evil lips; a **liar** pays attention to a malicious tongue.
17: 7 lips are unsuited to a fool—how much worse **lying** lips to a ruler!
19: 5 A **false** witness will not go unpunished, and he who pours out lies
19: 9 A **false** witness will not go unpunished, and he who pours out lies
20: 17 Food gained by **fraud** tastes sweet to a man, but he ends up with a
21: 6 A fortune made by a **lying** tongue is a fleeting vapor and a deadly
25: 14 rain is a man who boasts of **gifts he does not give** [+5522].
25: 18 or a sharp arrow is the man who gives **false** testimony against his
26: 28 A **lying** tongue hates those it hurts, and a flattering mouth works
29: 12 If a ruler listens to **lies** [+1821], all his officials become wicked.
31: 30 Charm is **deceptive**, and beauty is fleeting; but a woman who fears
Isa 9: 15 [9:14] men are the head, the prophets who teach **lies** are the tail.
28: 15 for we have made a lie our refuge and **falsehood** our hiding place."
32: 7 he makes up evil schemes to destroy the poor with **lies** [+609],
44: 20 save himself, or say, "Is not this thing in my right hand a **lie**?"
57: 4 your tongue? Are you not a brood of rebels, the offspring of **liars**?
59: 3 Your lips have spoken **lies**, and your tongue mutters wicked things.
59: 13 and revolt, uttering **lies** [+1821] our hearts have conceived.
Jer 3: 10 me with all her heart, but only in **pretense**," declares the LORD.
3: 23 ⌊idolatrous⌋ commotion on the hills and mountains is a **deception**;
5: 2 the LORD lives,' still they are swearing **falsely** [+2021+4200]."
5: 31 The prophets prophesy **lies**, the priests rule by their own authority,
6: 13 are greedy for gain; prophets and priests alike, all practice **deceit**.
7: 4 Do not trust in **deceptive** words and say, "This is the temple of the
7: 8 But look, you are trusting in **deceptive** words that are worthless.
7: 9 and murder, commit adultery and **perjury** [+2021+4200+8678],
8: 8 when actually the **lying** pen of the scribes has handled it falsely?
8: 8 the lying pen of the scribes has handled it **falsely** [+2021+4200]?
8: 10 are greedy for gain; prophets and priests alike, all practice **deceit**.
9: 3 [9:2] "They make ready their tongue like a bow, to shoot **lies**; it is
9: 5 [9:4] They have taught their tongues *to* **lie** [+1819]; they weary
10: 14 by his idols. His images are a **fraud**; they have no breath in them.
13: 25 "because you have forgotten me and trusted in **false gods**.
14: 14 said to me, "The prophets are prophesying **lies** in my name.
14: 14 They are prophesying to you **false** visions, divinations, idolatries
16: 19 of the earth and say, "Our fathers possessed nothing but **false gods**,
20: 6 and all your friends to whom you have prophesied **lies**.' "
23: 14 They commit adultery and live a **lie**. They strengthen the hands of
23: 25 "I have heard what the prophets say who prophesy **lies** in my
23: 26 How long will this continue in the hearts of these **lying** prophets,
23: 32 Indeed, I am against those who prophesy **false** dreams,"
23: 32 "They tell them and lead my people astray with their reckless **lies**,
27: 10 They prophesy **lies** to you that will only serve to remove you far
27: 14 not serve the king of Babylon,' for they are prophesying **lies** to you.
27: 15 'They are prophesying **lies** in my name. Therefore, I will banish
27: 16 be brought back from Babylon.' They are prophesying **lies** to you.
28: 15 has not sent you, yet you have persuaded this nation to trust in **lies**.
29: 9 They are prophesying **lies** to you in my name. I have not sent
29: 21 son of Maaseiah, who are prophesying **lies** to you in my name:
29: 23 with their neighbors' wives and in my name have spoken **lies**,
29: 31 even though I did not send him, and has led you to believe a **lie**,
37: 14 "That's **not true**!" Jeremiah said. "I am not deserting to the
40: 16 do such a thing! What you are saying about Ishmael is **not true**."
43: 2 and all the arrogant men said to Jeremiah, "You *are* **lying** [+1819]!
51: 17 by his idols. His images are a **fraud**; they have no breath in them.
Eze 13: 22 Because you disheartened the righteous with your **lies**, when I had
Hos 7: 1 They practice **deceit**, thieves break into houses, bandits rob in the
Mic 2: 11 If a liar and **deceiver** comes and says, 'I will prophesy for you
6: 12 her people *are* **liars** [+1819] and their tongues speak deceitfully.
Hab 2: 18 is an idol, since a man has carved it? Or an image that teaches **lies**?
Zec 5: 4 of the thief and the house of him who swears **falsely** by my name.
8: 17 plot evil against your neighbor, and do not love to swear **falsely**.
10: 2 The idols speak deceit, diviners see visions that **lie**; they tell
13: 3 'You must die, because you have told **lies** in the LORD's name.'
Mal 3: 5 against sorcerers, adulterers and **perjurers** [+2021+4200+8678],

9215 שַׁקָּר *šaqqār*, n.m. Not used in NIV/BHS [√ 9213]

9216 שֹׁקֶת *šōqet*, n.f. [2] [√ 9197]

trough [1], troughs [+8110] [1]

Ge 24: 20 So she quickly emptied her jar into the **trough**, ran back to the well
30: 38 he placed the peeled branches in all the watering **troughs** [+8110],

9217 שֵׁר *šēr¹*, n.[f.]. [1] [→ 9225]

bracelets [1]

Isa 3: 19 the earrings and **bracelets** and veils,

9218 שֵׁר² *šēr²*, n.[m.]. Not used in NIV/BHS [cf. 9219]

9219 שֹׁר *šōr*, n.[m.]. [3] [√ 9242; cf. 9218]

body [1], cord [1], navel [1]

Pr 3: 8 This will bring health to your **body** and nourishment to your bones.
SS 7: 2 [7:3] Your **navel** is a rounded goblet that never lacks blended
Eze 16: 4 On the day you were born your **cord** was not cut, nor were you

9220 שָׁרָב *šārāb*, n.m. [2] [→ 9221?]

burning sand [1], desert heat [1]

Isa 35: 7 The **burning sand** will become a pool, the thirsty ground bubbling
49: 10 nor thirst, nor will the **desert heat** or the sun beat upon them.

9221 שֵׁרֵבְיָה *šērēbyâ*, n.pr.m. [8] [√ 9220? + 3378]

Sherebiah [8]

Ezr 8: 18 they brought us **Sherebiah**, a capable man, from the descendants
8: 24 together with **Sherebiah**, Hashabiah and ten of their brothers,
Ne 8: 7 Jeshua, Bani, **Sherebiah**, Jamin, Akkub, Shabbethai, Hodiah,
9: 4 Kadmiel, Shebaniah, Bunni, **Sherebiah**, Bani and Kenani—
9: 5 Hashabneiah, **Sherebiah**, Hodiah, Shebaniah and Pethahiah—
10: 12 [10:13] Zaccur, **Sherebiah**, Shebaniah,
12: 8 Binnui, Kadmiel, **Sherebiah**, Judah, and also Mattaniah, who,
12: 24 **Sherebiah**, Jeshua son of Kadmiel, and their associates, who stood

9222 שַׁרְבִיט *šarbîṭ*, n.m. [4] [√ 8657]

scepter [4]

Est 4: 11 The only exception to this is for the king to extend the gold **scepter**

Est 5: 2 with her and held out to her the gold **scepter** that was in his hand.
5: 2 his hand. So Esther approached and touched the tip of the **scepter**.
8: 4 Then the king extended the gold **scepter** to Esther and she arose

9223 ¹שָׂרָה **šārā¹**, v. [2] [→ 5489, 9233; Ar 10742]

deliver [1], unleashes [1]

Job 37: 3 [A] *He* **unleashes** his lightning beneath the whole heaven
Jer 15:11 [D] "Surely *I will* **deliver** [K 9250] you for a good purpose;

9224 ²שָׂרָה **šārâ²**, n.[m.]. [1] [√ 8805; cf. 8800]

vineyards [1]

Jer 5:10 "Go through her **vineyards** and ravage them, but do not destroy

9225 שֵׂרָה **šērâ**, n.[f.]. Not used in NIV/BHS [√ 9217]

9226 שָׂרוּחֶן **šārûḥen**, n.pr.loc. [1]

Sharuhen [1]

Jos 19: 6 Beth Lebaoth and **Sharuhen**—thirteen towns and their villages;

9227 שָׂרוֹן **šārôn**, n.pr.loc. [6] [→ 9228; cf. 3837, 4389]

Sharon [6]

1Ch 5:16 and on all the pasturelands of **Sharon** as far as they extended.
27:29 Shitrai the Sharonite was in charge of the herds grazing in **Sharon**.
SS 2: 1 I am a rose of **Sharon**, a lily of the valleys.
Isa 33: 9 **Sharon** is like the Arabah, and Bashan and Carmel drop their
35: 2 of Lebanon will be given to it, the splendor of Carmel and **Sharon**;
65:10 **Sharon** will become a pasture for flocks, and the Valley of Achor

9228 שָׂרוֹנִי **šārônî**, a.g. [1] [√ 9227; cf. 3837]

Sharonite [1]

1Ch 27:29 Shitrai the **Sharonite** was in charge of the herds grazing in Sharon.

9229 שְׂרוּקָה **šᵉrûqâ**, n.[f.]. [0] [cf. 9239?, 9240]

Jer 18:16 [will be laid waste, an **object of** lasting **scorn**; [K; see Q 9241]]

9230 שֵׂרוּת **šērût**, var. Not used in NIV/BHS [cf. 9223]

9231 שִׂרְטַי **širṭay**, n.pr.m. [0] [cf. 8855]

1Ch 27:29 [**Shitrai** [Q; see K 8855] the Sharonite was in charge of the herds]

9232 שָׂרַי **šāray**, n.pr.m. [1]

Sharai [1]

Ezr 10:40 Macnadebai, Shashai, **Sharai**,

9233 שִׂרְיָה **širyâ**, n.f. [1] [√ 9223]

javelin [1]

Job 41:26 [41:18] has no effect, nor does the spear or the dart or the **javelin**.

9234 שִׂרְיוֹן **širyôn**, n.[m.]. [8] [cf. 6246]

armor [3], *untranslated* [1], breastplate [1], coat of armor [1], coat of scale armor [+7989] [1], coats of armor [1]

1Sa 17: 5 wore a **coat of scale armor** [+7989] *of* bronze weighing five
17: 5 wore a coat of scale armor of bronze weighing **[RPH]** five
17:38 He put a **coat of armor** on him and a bronze helmet on his head.
1Ki 22:34 and hit the king of Israel between the sections of his **armor**.
2Ch 18:33 and hit the king of Israel between the sections of his **armor**.
26:14 **coats of armor**, bows and slingstones for the entire army.
Ne 4:16 [4:10] half were equipped with spears, shields, bows and **armor**.
Isa 59:17 He put on righteousness as his **breastplate**, and the helmet of

9235 שָׂרִיר **šārîr**, n.[m.]. [1] [√ 9242]

muscles [1]

Job 40:16 strength he has in his loins, what power in the **muscles** *of* his belly!

9236 שְׂרֵמוֹת **šᵉrēmôt**, n.f. [0]

Jer 31:40 [and all the **terraces** [K; see Q 8727] out to the Kidron Valley on]

9237 שָׂרַץ **šāraṣ**, v. [14] [→ 9238]

moves about [3], multiply [2], *untranslated* [1], move about [1], multiplied [1], swarm [1], swarms [1], teem [+9238] [1], teem [1], teemed [1], teems [1]

Ge 1:20 [A] God said, "*Let* the water **teem** [+9238] *with* living creatures,
1:21 [A] every living and moving thing with which the water **teems**,
7:21 [A] wild animals, all the creatures that **swarm** over the earth,
8:17 [A] so *they can* **multiply** on the earth and be fruitful
9: 7 [A] in number; **multiply** on the earth and increase upon it."
Ex 1: 7 [A] the Israelites were fruitful and **multiplied** greatly
8: 3 [7:28] [A] The Nile *will* **teem** *with* frogs. They will come up
Lev 11:29 [A] " 'Of the animals that **move about** on the ground, these are
11:41 [A] " 'Every creature that **moves about** on the ground is
11:42 [A] You are not to eat any creature that **moves about** on the
11:43 [A] **[RPH]** Do not make yourselves unclean by means of them
11:46 [A] and every creature that **moves about** on the ground.
Ps 105:30 [A] Their land **teemed** *with* frogs, which went up into the
Eze 47: 9 [A] **Swarms** of living creatures will live wherever the river

9238 שֶׁרֶץ **šereṣ**, n.m. [15] [√ 9237]

creatures [4], creature [3], animals [1], crawling thing [1], creatures that move along the ground [1], insects that swarm [1], insects [1], move along [1], swarming things [1], teem [+9237] [1]

Ge 1:20 And God said, "*Let* the water **teem with** [+9237] living creatures,
7:21 wild animals, all the **creatures** that swarm over the earth,
Lev 5: 2 or of unclean **creatures that move along the ground**—
11:10 whether among all the **swarming things** or among all the other
11:20 " 'All flying **insects** that walk on all fours are to be detestable to
11:21 some winged **creatures** that walk on all fours that you may eat:
11:23 all other winged **creatures** that have four legs you are to detest.
11:29 " 'Of the **animals** that move about on the ground, these are unclean
11:31 Of all those *that* **move along** the ground, these are unclean for
11:41 " 'Every **creature** that moves about on the ground is detestable;
11:42 You are not to eat any **creature** that moves about on the ground,
11:43 Do not defile yourselves by any of these **creatures**. Do not make
11:44 Do not make yourselves unclean by any **creature** that moves about
22: 5 or if he touches any **crawling thing** that makes him unclean,
Dt 14:19 All flying **insects that swarm** are unclean to you; do not eat them.

9239 שָׁרַק **šāraq**, v. [12] [→ 9240, 9241; cf. 9229?]

scoff [7], hiss [1], hisses [1], signal [1], whistle [1], whistles [1]

1Ki 9: 8 [A] all who pass by will be appalled and *will* **scoff** and say,
Job 27:23 [A] It claps its hands in derision and **hisses** him out of his place.
Isa 5:26 [A] distant nations, *he* **whistles** for those at the ends of the earth.
7:18 [A] In that day the LORD *will* **whistle** for flies from the distant
Jer 19: 8 [A] by will be appalled and *will* **scoff** because of all its wounds.
49:17 [A] by will be appalled and *will* **scoff** because of all its wounds.
50:13 [A] will be horrified and **scoff** because of all her wounds.
La 2:15 [A] *they* **scoff** and shake their heads at the Daughter of
2:16 [A] *they* **scoff** and gnash their teeth and say, "We have
Eze 27:36 [A] The merchants among the nations **hiss** at you; you have come
Zep 2:15 [A] wild beasts! All who pass by her **scoff** and shake their fists.
Zec 10: 8 [A] *I will* **signal** for them and gather them in. Surely I will

9240 שְׁרֵקָה **šᵉrēqâ**, n.f. [7] [√ 9239; cf. 9229]

scorn [5], derision [1], object of scorn [1]

2Ch 29: 8 he has made them an object of dread and horror and **scorn**,
Jer 19: 8 I will devastate this city and make it an **object of scorn**; all who
25: 9 destroy them and make them an object of horror and **scorn**,
25:18 to make them a ruin and an object of horror and **scorn** and cursing,
29:18 and an object of cursing and horror, of **scorn** and reproach,
51:37 a haunt of jackals, an object of horror and **scorn**, a place where no
Mic 6:16 Therefore I will give you over to ruin and your people to **derision**;

9241 שְׁרִקָה **šᵉriqâ**, n.[f.]. [2] [√ 9239]

object of scorn [1], whistling [1]

Jdg 5:16 Why did you stay among the campfires to hear the **whistling** *for*
Jer 18:16 Their land will be laid waste, an **object of** lasting **scorn**; [K 9229]

9242 שָׁרַר **šārar**, v. Not used in NIV/BHS [→ 9219, 9235, 9243, 9244]

9243 שָׁרָר **šārār**, n.pr.m. [1] [√ 9242]

Sharar [1]

2Sa 23:33 son of Shammah the Hararite, Ahiam son of **Sharar** the Hararite,

9244 שְׁרִרוּת **šᵉrirût**, n.f. [10] [√ 9242]

stubbornness [7], stubborn [2], persist in own way [+4213] [1]

Dt 29:19 [29:18] even though I **persist** [+4213] **in** going my **own way**."
Ps 81:12 [81:13] So I gave them over to their **stubborn** hearts to follow
Jer 3:17 No longer will they follow the **stubbornness** *of* their evil hearts.
7:24 they followed the **stubborn** inclinations of their evil hearts.
9:14 [9:13] they have followed the **stubbornness** *of* their hearts;
11: 8 instead, they followed the **stubbornness** *of* their evil hearts.
13:10 who follow the **stubbornness** *of* their hearts and go after other
16:12 See how each of you is following the **stubbornness** *of* his evil
18:12 each of us will follow the **stubbornness** *of* his evil heart.' "

Jer 23: 17 And to all who follow the **stubbornness** *of* their hearts they say,

9245 שָׁרַשׁ šāraš, v.den. [8] [√ 9247]

be uprooted [1], take root [+1614] [1], take root [1], taken root [1], taking root [1], took root [+9247] [1], uproot [1], uprooted [1]

Job 5: 3 [G] I myself have seen a fool **taking root**, but suddenly his house
31: 8 [E] others eat what I have sown, and *may* my crops **be uprooted**.
31: 12 [D] burns to Destruction; *it would have* **uprooted** my harvest.
Ps 52: 5 [52:7] [D] *he will* **uproot** you from the land of the living.
80: 9 [80:10] [G] for it, and *it* **took root** [+9247] and filled the land.
Isa 27: 6 [G] In days to come Jacob *will* **take root**, Israel will bud
40: 24 [D] no sooner *do they* **take root** [+1614] in the ground, than he
Jer 12: 2 [D] You have planted them, and *they have* **taken root**; they

9246 שֶׁרֶשׁ šereš, n.pr.m. [1] [√ 9247]

Sheresh [1]

1Ch 7: 16 His brother was named **Sheresh**, and his sons were Ulam

9247 שֹׁרֶשׁ šōreš, n.m. [33] [→ 9245, 9246; Ar 10743]

roots [15], root [12], be uprooted [+4572] [1], depths [1], family line [+5916] [1], soles [1], took root [+9245] [1], uprooted [+906+5998] [1]

Dt 29: 18 [29:17] make sure there is no **root** among you that produces such
Jdg 5: 14 Some came from Ephraim, whose **roots** were in Amalek;
2Ki 19: 30 Once more a remnant of the house of Judah will take **root** below
Job 8: 17 it entwines its **roots** around a pile of rocks and looks for a place
13: 27 watch on all my paths by putting marks on the **soles** *of* my feet.
14: 8 Its **roots** may grow old in the ground and its stump die in the soil,
18: 16 His **roots** dry up below and his branches wither above.
19: 28 'How we will hound him, since the **root** *of* the trouble lies in him,'
28: 9 assaults the flinty rock and lays bare the **roots** *of* the mountains.
29: 19 My **roots** will reach to the water, and the dew will lie all night on
30: 4 gathered salt herbs, and their food was the **root** *of* the broom tree.
36: 30 he scatters his lightning about him, bathing the **depths** *of* the sea.
Ps 80: 9 [80:10] ground for it, and *it* **took root** [+9245] and filled the land.
Pr 12: 3 but the righteous cannot **be uprooted** [+4572].
12: 12 the plunder of evil men, but the **root** *of* the righteous flourishes.
Isa 5: 24 so their **roots** will decay and their flowers blow away like dust;
11: 1 up from the stump of Jesse; from his **roots** a Branch will bear fruit.
11: 10 In that day the **Root** *of* Jesse will stand as a banner for the peoples;
14: 29 from the **root** *of* that snake will spring up a viper, its fruit will be a
14: 30 But your **root** I will destroy by famine; it will slay your survivors.
37: 31 Once more a remnant of the house of Judah will take **root** below
53: 2 before him like a tender shoot, and like a **root** out of dry ground.
Jer 17: 8 He will be like a tree planted by the water that sends out its **roots**
Eze 17: 6 Its branches turned toward him, but its **roots** remained under it.
17: 7 The vine now sent out its **roots** toward him from the plot where it
17: 9 *Will* it not *be* **uprooted** [+906+5998] and stripped of its fruit
17: 9 will not take a strong arm or many people to pull it up by the **roots**.
31: 7 its spreading boughs, for its **roots** went down to abundant waters.
Da 11: 7 "One from her **family** [+5916] **line** will arise to take her place.
Hos 9: 16 Ephraim is blighted, their **root** is withered, they yield no fruit.
14: 5 [14:6] Like a cedar of Lebanon he will send down his **roots**;
Am 2: 9 strong as the oaks. I destroyed his fruit above and his **roots** below.
Mal 4: 1 [3:19] "Not a **root** or a branch will be left to them.

9248 שַׁרְשָׁה šaršā, n.f. Not used in NIV/BHS [√ 9249]

9249 שַׁרְשְׁרָה šaršᵉrâ, n.f. [8] [→ 9248]

chains [5], chain [1], chains [+6310] [1], interwoven chains [+5126] [1]

Ex 28: 14 two braided **chains** *of* pure gold, like a rope, and attach the chains
28: 14 like a rope, and attach the **chains** [+6310] to the settings.
28: 22 "For the breastpiece make braided **chains** *of* pure gold, like a rope.
39: 15 For the breastpiece they made braided **chains** of pure gold,
1Ki 7: 17 A network of **interwoven chains** [+5126] festooned the capitals on
2Ch 3: 5 it with fine gold and decorated it with palm tree and **chain** designs.
3: 16 He made interwoven **chains** and put them on top of the pillars.
3: 16 made a hundred pomegranates and attached them to the **chains**.

9250 שָׁרַת šārat, v. [97] [→ 9251]

minister [29], ministering [14], serve [8], service [5], aide [4], assist [4], servants [4], served [4], ministered [3], servant [3], attendant [2], attending [2], ministers [2], *untranslated* [1], attendants [+5853] [1], attendants [1], attended [1], ministering [+9251] [1], officials [1], on duty [1], personal attendants [+5853] [1], personal servant [+5853] [1], serving [1], supply [1], take care of [1], waited on [1]

Ge 39: 4 [D] Joseph found favor in his eyes and *became* his **attendant**.
40: 4 [D] of the guard assigned them to Joseph, and *he* **attended** them.
Ex 24: 13 [D] Moses set out with Joshua his **aide**, and Moses went up on
28: 35 [D] Aaron must wear it when *he* **ministers**. The sound of the
28: 43 [D] or approach the altar to **minister** in the Holy Place,
29: 30 [D] comes to the Tent of Meeting to **minister** in the Holy Place
30: 20 [D] when they approach the altar to **minister** by presenting an
33: 11 [D] but his young **aide** Joshua son of Nun did not leave the tent.
35: 19 [D] the woven garments worn for **ministering** in the sanctuary—
39: 1 [D] scarlet yarn they made woven garments for **ministering** in
39: 26 [D] around the hem of the robe to be worn for **ministering**,
39: 41 [D] the woven garments worn for **ministering** in the sanctuary,
Nu 1: 50 [D] they *are to* **take care of** it and encamp around it.
3: 6 [D] of Levi and present them to Aaron the priest *to* **assist** him.
3: 31 [D] the altars, the articles of the sanctuary used in **ministering**,
4: 9 [D] and trays, and all its jars for the oil used *to* **supply** it.
4: 12 [D] are to take all the articles used for **ministering** [+9251]
4: 14 [D] they are to place on it all the utensils used *for* **ministering** at
8: 26 [D] *They may* **assist** their brothers in performing their duties at
11: 28 [D] *who had been* Moses' **aide** since youth, spoke up and said,
16: 9 [D] and to stand before the community and **minister** *to* them?
18: 2 [D] **assist** you when you and your sons minister before the Tent
Dt 10: 8 [D] to stand before the LORD to **minister** and to pronounce
17: 12 [D] or for the priest who stands **ministering** there *to* the LORD
18: 5 [D] tribes to stand and **minister** in the LORD's name always.
18: 7 [D] *he may* **minister** in the name of the LORD his God like all
21: 5 [D] for the LORD your God has chosen them to **minister** and to
Jos 1: 1 [D] the LORD said to Joshua son of Nun, Moses' **aide**:
1Sa 2: 11 [D] the boy **ministered** before the LORD under Eli the priest.
2: 18 [D] Samuel *was* **ministering** before the LORD—a boy wearing
3: 1 [D] The boy Samuel **ministered** before the LORD under Eli.
2Sa 13: 17 [D] He called his **personal servant** [+5853] and said, "Get this
13: 18 [D] So his **servant** put her out and bolted the door after her. She
1Ki 1: 4 [D] she took care of the king and **waited on** him, but the king
1: 15 [D] where Abishag the Shunammite *was* **attending** him.
8: 11 [D] the priests could not perform their **service** because of the
10: 5 [D] the attending **servants** in their robes, his cupbearers,
19: 21 [D] Then he set out to follow Elijah and *became* his **attendant**.
2Ki 4: 43 [D] his **servant** asked. But Elisha answered, "Give it to the
6: 15 [D] When the **servant** *of* the man of God got up and went out
25: 14 [D] dishes and all the bronze articles used *in* the temple **service**.
1Ch 6: 32 [6:17] [D] *They* **ministered** with music before the tabernacle,
15: 2 [D] the ark of the LORD and to **minister** *before* him forever."
16: 4 [D] He appointed some of the Levites *to* **minister** before the ark
16: 37 [D] of the covenant of the LORD to **minister** there regularly,
23: 13 [D] to **minister** *before* him and to pronounce blessings in his
26: 12 [D] had duties for **ministering** in the temple of the LORD,
27: 1 [D] who **served** the king in all that concerned the army divisions
28: 1 [D] the commanders of the divisions *in* the **service** *of* the king,
2Ch 5: 14 [D] the priests could not perform their **service** because of the
8: 14 [D] and to **assist** the priests according to each day's requirement.
9: 4 [D] seating of his officials, the attending **servants** in their robes,
13: 10 [D] The priests *who* **serve** the LORD are sons of Aaron,
17: 19 [D] These were the *men who* **served** the king, besides those he
22: 8 [D] *who had been* **attending** Ahaziah, and he killed them.
23: 6 [D] temple of the LORD except the priests and Levites **on duty**;
29: 11 [D] LORD has chosen you to stand before him and **serve** him,
29: 11 [D] and serve him, to **minister** before him and to burn incense."
31: 2 [D] to **minister**, to give thanks and to sing praises at the gates of
Ezr 8: 17 [D] so that they might bring **attendants** to us for the house of our
Ne 10: 36 [10:37] [D] house of our God, to the priests **ministering** there.
10: 39 [10:40] [D] are kept and where the **ministering** priests,
Est 1: 10 [D] he commanded the seven eunuchs who **served** him—
2: 2 [D] the king's **personal attendants** [+5853] proposed, "Let a
6: 3 [D] has been done for him," his **attendants** [+5853] answered.
Ps 101: 6 [D] with me; he whose walk is blameless *will* **minister** *to* me.
103: 21 [D] all his heavenly hosts, you his **servants** who do his will.
104: 4 [D] He makes winds his messengers, flames of fire his **servants**.
Pr 29: 12 [D] If a ruler listens to lies, all his **officials** become wicked.
Isa 56: 6 [D] foreigners who bind themselves to the LORD to **serve** him,
60: 7 [D] will be gathered to you, the rams of Nebaioth *will* **serve** you;
60: 10 [D] will rebuild your walls, and their kings *will* **serve** you.
61: 6 [D] of the LORD, you will be named **ministers** *of* our God.
Jer 15: 11 [d] ["Surely *I will* **deliver** [K; see Q 9223] you for a good]
33: 21 [D] with the Levites who are priests **ministering** *before* me—
33: 22 [D] the Levites *who* **minister** *before* me as countless as the stars
52: 18 [D] dishes and all the bronze articles used *in* the temple **service**.
Eze 20: 32 [D] like the peoples of the world, *who* **serve** wood and stone."
40: 46 [D] who may draw near to the LORD to **minister** *before* him."
42: 14 [D] until they leave behind the garments in which *they* **minister**,
43: 19 [D] the family of Zadok, who come near to **minister** *before* me,
44: 11 [D] **[RPH]** having charge of the gates of the temple and serving
44: 11 [D] having charge of the gates of the temple and **serving** *in* it;
44: 11 [D] for the people and stand before the people and **serve** them.
44: 12 [D] But because *they* **served** them in the presence of their idols
44: 15 [D] astray from me, are to come near to **minister** *before* me;
44: 16 [D] they alone are to come near my table to **minister** *before* me
44: 17 [D] they must not wear any woolen garment while **ministering** at
44: 19 [D] they are to take off the clothes they *have been* **ministering**

Eze 44:27 [D] the inner court of the sanctuary to **minister** in the sanctuary,
45:4 [D] *who* **minister** *in* the sanctuary and who draw near to minister
45:4 [D] and who draw near to **minister** *before* the LORD.
45:5 [D] *who* **serve** *in* the temple, as their possession for towns to live
46:24 [D] "These are the kitchens where *those who* **minister** *at* the
Joel 1:9 [D] are in mourning, *those who* **minister** *before* the LORD.
1:13 [D] and mourn; wail, *you who* **minister** *before* the altar.
1:13 [D] the night in sackcloth, *you who* **minister** *before* my God;
2:17 [D] Let the priests, *who* **minister** *before* the LORD,

9251 שָׁרֵת *šārēt*, n.m. [2] [√ 9250]

ministering [+9250] [1], service [1]

Nu 4:12 "They are to take all the articles used for **ministering** [+9250] in
2Ch 24:14 articles for the **service** and for the burnt offerings, and also dishes

9252 ¹שֵׁשׁ *šēš¹*, n.m. [274 / 275] [→ 9261, 9262; Ar 10747]

six [116], sixty [23], sixteen [+6926] [14], 666 [+2256+4395+9252 +9252] [6], sixteen [+6925] [4], sixty-six [+2256+9252] [4], 36,000 [+547+2256+8993] [3], 603,550 [+547+547+2256+2256+2256+2822 +2822+4395+4395+8993] [3], 666 [+2256+2256+4395+9252+9252] [3], *untranslated* [3], sixteenth [+6925] [3], 16,000 [+547+6925] [2], 4,600 [+547+752+2256+4395] [2], 45,650 [+547+752+2256+2256 +2256+2822+2822+4395] [2], 46,500 [+547+752+2256+2256+2822 +4395] [2], 6,720 [+547+2256+4395+6929+8679] [2], 62,700 [+547+2256+2256+4395+8679+9109] [2], 621 [+285+2256+4395 +6929] [2], 65 [+2256+2822] [2], 652 [+2256+2822+4395+9109] [2], 667 [+2256+4395+8679+9252] [2], 736 [+2256+4395+8679+8993] [2], 74,600 [+547+752+2256+2256+4395+8679] [2], 760 [+2256 +4395+8679] [2], ninety-six [+2256+9596] [2], sixty-two [+2256 +9109] [2], 1,365 [+547+2256+2256+2256+2822+4395+8993] [1], 1,760 [+547+2256+2256+4395+8679] [1], 153,600 [+547+547+2256 +2256+2256+2822+4395+4395+8993] [1], 156 [+2256+2822+4395] [1], 157,600 [+547+547+2256+2256+2256+2822+4395+4395+8679] [1], 16,750 [+547+2256+2822+4395+6925+8679] [1], 160 [+2256+4395] [1], 162 [+2256+2256+4395+9109] [1], 186,400 [+547+547+547+752+2256+2256+2256+4395+4395+9046] [1], 2,056 [+547+2256+2822] [1], 2,067 [+547+2256+8679] [1], 2,600 [+547+2256+4395] [1], 2,630 [+547+2256+2256+4395+8993] [1], 22,600 [+547+2256+2256+4395+6929+9109] [1], 26,000 [+547 +2256+6929] [1], 28,600 [+547+2256+2256+4395+6929+9046] [1], 3,600 [+547+2256+4395+8993] [1], 3,630 [+547+2256+2256+4395 +8993+8993] [1], 365 [+2256+2256+2822+4395+8993] [1], 42,360 [+547+752+2256+4395+8052+8993] [1], 42,360 [+547+752+4395 +8052+8993] [1], 44,760 [+547+752+752+2256+2256+2256 +4395+8679] [1], 45,600 [+547+752+2256+2256+2822+4395] [1], 468 [+752+2256+4395+9046] [1], 56 [+2256+2822] [1], 6,200 [+547+2256+4395] [1], 6,800 [+547+2256+4395+9046] [1], 60 [1], 60,500 [+547+2256+2822+4395] [1], 601,730 [+547+547+2256 +2256+4395+4395+8679+8993] [1], 61 [+285+2256] [1], 61,000 [+285+547+2256] [1], 61,000 [+547+2256+8052] [1], 62 [+2256 +9109] [1], 623 [+2256+4395+6929+8993] [1], 628 [+2256+4395 +6929+9046] [1], 64,300 [+547+752+2256+2256+4395+8993] [1], 64,400 [+547+752+752+2256+2256+4395] [1], 642 [+752+2256 +2256+4395+9109] [1], 642 [+752+2256+4395+9109] [1], 648 [+752+2256+4395+9046] [1], 650 [+2256+2822+4395] [1], 655 [+2256+2822+2822+4395] [1], 67 [+2256+8679] [1], 675 [+2256+2822+4395+8679] [1], 675,000 [+547+547+547+2256+2256 +2822+4395+8679] [1], 690 [+2256+4395+9596] [1], 76,500 [+547 +2256+2256+2822+4395+8679] [1], 8,600 [+547+2256+4395+9046] [1], 956 [+2256+2256+2822+4395+9596] [1], 962 [+2256+2256 +4395+9109+9596] [1], 969 [+2256+2256+4395+9596+9596] [1], eighty-six [+2256+9046] [1], over nine feet [+564+2256+2455] [1], sixth [1], sixty-eight [+2256+9046] [1], sixty-five [+2256+2822] [1], thirty-six [+2256+8993] [1], thirty-six hundred [+547+2256+4395 +8993] [1], thirty-sixth [+2256+8993] [1], twenty-six [+2256+6929] [1], twenty-six hundred [+547+2256+4395] [1], twenty-sixth [+2256+6929] [1]

Ge 5:15 When Mahalalel had lived **65** [+2256+2822] years, he became the
5:18 When Jared had lived **162** [+2256+2256+4395+9109] years, he
5:20 Jared lived **962** [+2256+2256+4395+9109+9596] years, and then
5:21 When Enoch had lived **65** [+2256+2822] years, he became the
5:23 Enoch lived **365** [+2256+2256+2822+4395+8993] years.
5:27 Methuselah lived **969** [+2256+2256+4395+9596+9596] years, and
7:6 Noah was **six** hundred years old when the floodwaters came on the
7:11 In the **six** hundredth year of Noah's life, on the seventeenth day of
8:13 By the first day of the first month of Noah's **six** hundred and first
16:16 Abram was **eighty-six** [+2256+9046] years old when Hagar bore
25:26 Isaac was **sixty** years old when Rebekah gave birth to them.
30:20 will treat me with honor, because I have borne him **six** sons."
31:41 fourteen years for your two daughters and **six** years for your flocks,
46:18 Laban had given to his daughter Leah—**sixteen** [+6926] in all.
46:26 his sons' wives—numbered **sixty-six** [+2256+9252] persons.
46:26 his sons' wives—numbered **sixty-six** [+2256+9252] persons.
Ex 12:37 There were about **six** hundred thousand men on foot, besides
14:7 He took **six** hundred of the best chariots, along with all the other
16:26 **Six** days you are to gather it, but on the seventh day, the Sabbath,
20:9 **Six** days you shall labor and do all your work,
20:11 For in **six** days the LORD made the heavens and the earth,
21:2 "If you buy a Hebrew servant, he is to serve you for **six** years.
23:10 "For **six** years you are to sow your fields and harvest the crops,
23:12 "**Six** days do your work, but on the seventh day do not work,
24:16 For **six** days the cloud covered the mountain, and on the seventh
25:32 **Six** branches are to extend from the sides of the lampstand—
25:33 and the same for all **six** branches extending from the lampstand.
25:35 and a third bud under the third pair—**six** branches in all.
26:9 the curtains together into one set and the other **six** into another set.
26:22 Make **six** frames for the far end, that is, the west end of the
26:25 So there will be eight frames and **sixteen** [+6925] silver bases—
28:10 **six** names on one stone and the remaining six on the other.
28:10 six names on one stone and the remaining **six** on the other.
31:15 For **six** days, work is to be done, but the seventh day is a Sabbath
31:17 for in **six** days the LORD made the heavens and the earth,
34:21 "**Six** days you shall labor, but on the seventh day you shall rest;
35:2 For **six** days, work is to be done, but the seventh day shall be your
36:16 five of the curtains into one set and the other **six** into another set.
36:27 They made **six** frames for the far end, that is, the west end of the
36:30 So there were eight frames and **sixteen** [+6925] silver bases—
37:18 **Six** branches extended from the sides of the lampstand—three on
37:19 and the same for all **six** branches extending from the lampstand.
37:21 and a third bud under the third pair—**six** branches in all.
38:26 those counted, twenty years old or more, a total of **603,550** [+547 +547+2256+2256+2256+2822+2822+4395+4395+8993] men.
Lev 12:5 she must wait **sixty-six** [+2256+9252] days to be purified from her
12:5 she must wait **sixty-six** [+2256+9252] days to be purified from her
23:3 " 'There are **six** days when you may work, but the seventh day is a
24:6 Set them in two rows, **six** *in* each row, on the table of pure gold
25:3 For **six** years sow your fields, and for six years prune your
25:3 and for **six** years prune your vineyards and gather their crops.
27:3 male between the ages of twenty and **sixty** at fifty shekels of silver,
27:7 If it is a person **sixty** years old or more, set the value of a male at
Nu 1:21 tribe of Reuben was **46,500** [+547+752+2256+2256+2822+4395].
1:25 Gad was **45,650** [+547+752+2256+2256+2256+2822+2822+4395].
1:27 tribe of Judah was **74,600** [+547+752+2256+2256+4395+8679].
1:39 tribe of Dan was **62,700** [+547+2256+2256+4395+8679+9109].
1:46 The total number was **603,550** [+547+547+2256+2256+2256 +2822+2822+4395+4395+8993].
2:4 His division numbers **74,600** [+547+752+2256+2256+4395+8679].
2:9 to the camp of Judah, according to their divisions, number **186,400** [+547+547+547+752+2256+2256+2256+4395+4395+9046].
2:11 His division numbers **46,500** [+547+752+2256+2256+2822+4395].
2:15 numbers **45,650** [+547+752+2256+2256+2256+2822+2822+4395].
2:26 division numbers **62,700** [+547+2256+2256+4395+8679+9109].
2:31 **157,600** [+547+547+2256+2256+2256+2822+4395+4395+8679].
2:32 All those in the camps, by their divisions, number **603,550** [+547+547+2256+2256+2256+2822+2822+4395+4395+8993].
3:28 males a month old or more was **8,600** [+547+2256+4395+9046].
3:34 or more who were counted was **6,200** [+547+2256+4395].
3:50 **1,365** [+547+2256+2256+2256+2822+4395+8993] shekels,
4:40 clans and families, were **2,630** [+547+2256+2256+4395+8993].
7:3 They brought as their gifts before the LORD **six** covered carts
7:88 **sixty** rams, sixty male goats and sixty male lambs a year old.
7:88 sixty rams, **sixty** male goats and sixty male lambs a year old.
7:88 sixty rams, sixty male goats and **sixty** male lambs a year old.
11:21 "Here I am among **six** hundred thousand men on foot, and you say,
26:22 numbered were **76,500** [+547+2256+2256+2822+4395+8679].
26:25 those numbered were **64,300** [+547+752+2256+2256+4395+8993].
26:27 Zebulun; those numbered were **60,500** [+547+2256+2822+4395].
26:41 those numbered were **45,600** [+547+752+2256+2256+2822+4395].
26:43 those numbered were **64,400** [+547+752+752+2256+2256+4395].
26:51 was **601,730** [+547+547+2256+2256+4395+4395+8679+8993].
31:32 **675,000** [+547+547+547+2256+2256+2822+4395+8679] sheep,
31:34 **61,000** [+285+547+2256] donkeys
31:37 the tribute for the LORD was **675** [+2256+2822+4395+8679];
31:38 **36,000** [+547+2256+8993] cattle, of which the tribute for the
31:39 of which the tribute for the LORD was **61** [+285+2256];
31:40 **16,000** [+547+6925] people, of which the tribute for the LORD
31:44 **36,000** [+547+2256+8993] cattle,
31:46 and **16,000** [+547+6925] people.
31:52 weighed **16,750** [+547+2256+2822+4395+6925+8679] shekels.
35:6 "**Six** *of* the towns you give the Levites will be cities of refuge,
35:13 These **six** towns you give will be your cities of refuge.
35:15 These **six** towns will be a place of refuge for Israelites, aliens
Dt 3:4 There was not one of the **sixty** cities that we did not take from
5:13 **Six** days you shall labor and do all your work,
15:12 or a woman, sells himself to you and serves you **six** years,
15:18 because his service to you these **six** years has been worth twice as

Dt 16: 8 For **six** days eat unleavened bread and on the seventh day hold an
Jos 6: 3 around the city once with all the armed men. Do this for **six** days.
6: 14 the city once and returned to the camp. They did this for **six** days.
7: 5 who killed about **thirty-six** [+2256+8993] of them. They chased
13: 30 king of Bashan—all the settlements of Jair in Bashan, **sixty** towns,
15: 41 and Makkedah—**sixteen** [+6926] towns and their villages.
15: 59 Maarath, Beth Anoth and Eltekon—**six** towns and their villages.
15: 62 the City of Salt and En Gedi—**six** towns and their villages.
19: 22 at the Jordan. There were **sixteen** [+6926] towns and their villages.
Jdg 3: 31 of Anath, who struck down **six** hundred Philistines with an oxgoad.
12: 7 Jephthah led Israel **six** years. Then Jephthah the Gileadite died,
18: 11 **six** hundred men from the clan of the Danites, armed for battle,
18: 16 The **six** hundred Danites, armed for battle, stood at the entrance to
18: 17 and the **six** hundred armed men stood at the entrance to the gate.
20: 15 mobilized **twenty-six** [+2256+6929] thousand swordsmen from
20: 47 **six** hundred men turned and fled into the desert to the rock of
Ru 3: 15 did so, he poured into it **six** measures of barley and put it on her.
3: 17 and added, "He gave me these **six** measures of barley, saying,
1Sa 13: 5 fight Israel, with three thousand chariots, **six** thousand charioteers,
13: 15 the men who were with him. They numbered about **six** hundred.
14: 2 tree in Migron. With him were about **six** hundred men,
17: 4 Philistine camp. He was **over nine feet** [+564+2256+2455] tall.
17: 7 like a weaver's rod, and its iron point weighed **six** hundred shekels.
23: 13 about **six** hundred in number, left Keilah and kept moving from
27: 2 So David and the **six** hundred men with him left and went over to
30: 9 and the **six** hundred men with him came to the Besor Ravine,
2Sa 2: 11 in Hebron over the house of Judah was seven years and **six** months.
2: 31 killed three hundred and **sixty** Benjamites who were with Abner.
5: 5 In Hebron he reigned over Judah seven years and **six** months,
6: 13 those who were carrying the ark of the LORD had taken **six** steps,
15: 18 all the **six** hundred Gittites who had accompanied him from Gath
21: 20 there was a huge man with **six** fingers on each hand and six toes on
21: 20 huge man with six fingers on each hand and **six** toes on each foot—
1Ki 4: 13 in Bashan and its **sixty** large walled cities with bronze gate bars);
4: 22 [5:2] were thirty cors of fine flour and **sixty** cors of meal,
6: 2 The temple that King Solomon built for the LORD was **sixty**
6: 6 cubits wide, the middle floor **six** cubits and the third floor seven.
10: 14 received yearly was **666** [+2256+4395+9252+9252] talents,
10: 14 received yearly was **666** [+2256+4395+9252+9252] talents,
10: 14 received yearly was **666** [+2256+4395+9252+9252] talents,
10: 16 hammered gold; **six** hundred bekas of gold went into each shield.
10: 19 The throne had **six** steps, and its back had a rounded top. On both
10: 20 Twelve lions stood on the **six** steps, one at either end of each step.
10: 29 They imported a chariot from Egypt for **six** hundred shekels of
11: 16 Joab and all the Israelites stayed there for **six** months, until they
16: 8 In the **twenty-sixth** [+2256+6929] year of Asa king of Judah, Elah
16: 23 king of Israel, and he reigned twelve years, **six** *of* them in Tirzah.
2Ki 5: 5 of silver, **six** thousand shekels of gold and ten sets of clothing.
11: 3 temple of the LORD for **six** years while Athaliah ruled the land.
13: 10 king of Israel in Samaria, and he reigned **sixteen** [+6926] years.
13: 19 and said, "You should have struck the ground five or **six** times;
14: 21 people of Judah took Azariah, who was **sixteen** [+6926] years old,
15: 2 He was **sixteen** [+6926] years old when he became king, and he
15: 8 became king of Israel in Samaria, and he reigned **six** months.
15: 33 became king, and he reigned in Jerusalem **sixteen** [+6926] years.
16: 2 became king, and he reigned in Jerusalem **sixteen** [+6926] years.
18: 10 So Samaria was captured in Hezekiah's **sixth** year, which was the
25: 19 people of the land and **sixty** of his men who were found in the city.
1Ch 2: 21 father of Gilead (he had married her when he was **sixty** years old),
2: 23 as well as Kenath with its surrounding settlements—**sixty** towns.)
3: 4 These **six** were born to David in Hebron, where he reigned seven
3: 4 to David in Hebron, where he reigned seven years and **six** months.
3: 22 his sons: Hattush, Igal, Bariah, Neariah and Shaphat—**six** in all.
4: 27 Shimei had **sixteen** [+6925] sons and six daughters, but his
4: 27 Shimei had sixteen sons and **six** daughters, but his brothers did not
5: 18 had **44,760** [+547+752+752+2256+2256+2256+4395+8679] men
7: 2 numbered **22,600** [+547+2256+2256+4395+6929+9109].
7: 4 they had **36,000** [+547+2256+8993] men ready for battle, for they
7: 40 as listed in their genealogy, was **26,000** [+547+2256+6929].
8: 38 Azel had **six** sons, and these were their names: Azrikam, Bokeru,
9: 6 The people from Judah numbered **690** [+2256+4395+9596].
9: 9 their genealogy, numbered **956** [+2256+2256+2822+4395+9596].
9: 13 of families, numbered **1,760** [+547+2256+2256+4395+8679].
9: 44 Azel had **six** sons, and these were their names: Azrikam, Bokeru,
12: 24 [12:25] spear—**6,800** [+547+2256+4395+9046] armed for battle;
12: 26 [12:27] men of Levi—**4,600** [+547+752+2256+4395],
12: 35 [12:36] for battle—**28,600** [+547+2256+2256+4395+6929+9046];
16: 38 and his **sixty-eight** [+2256+9046] associates to minister with them.
20: 6 there was a huge man with **six** fingers on each hand and six toes on
20: 6 huge man with six fingers on each hand and **six** toes on each foot—
21: 25 So David paid Araunah **six** hundred shekels of gold for the site.
23: 4 of the LORD and **six** thousand are to be officials and judges.
24: 4 **sixteen** [+6925] heads of families from Eleazar's descendants
24: 14 the fifteenth to Bilgah, the **sixteenth** [+6925] to Immer,
25: 3 Zeri, Jeshaiah, Shimei, Hashabiah and Mattithiah, **six** in all,
25: 23 the **sixteenth** [+6925] to Hananiah, his sons and relatives,
26: 8 do the work—descendants of Obed-Edom, **62** [+2256+9109] in all.
26: 17 There were **six** Levites a day on the east, four a day on the north,
2Ch 1: 17 They imported a chariot from Egypt for **six** hundred shekels of
2: 2 [2:1] and **thirty-six hundred** [+547+2256+4395+8993] as foremen
2: 17 [2:16] his father David had taken; and they were found to be
153,600 [+547+547+2256+2256+2256+2822+4395+4395+8993].
2: 18 [2:17] with **3,600** [+547+2256+4395+8993] foremen over them to
3: 3 Solomon laid for building the temple of God was **sixty** cubits long
3: 8 He overlaid the inside with **six** hundred talents of fine gold.
9: 13 received yearly was **666** [+2256+2256+4395+9252+9252] talents,
9: 13 received yearly was **666** [+2256+2256+4395+9252+9252] talents,
9: 13 received yearly was **666** [+2256+2256+4395+9252+9252] talents,
9: 15 **six** hundred bekas of hammered gold went into each shield.
9: 18 The throne had **six** steps, and a footstool of gold was attached to it.
9: 19 Twelve lions stood on the **six** steps, one at either end of each step.
11: 21 In all, he had eighteen wives and **sixty** concubines, twenty-eight
11: 21 and sixty concubines, twenty-eight sons and **sixty** daughters.
12: 3 With twelve hundred chariots and **sixty** thousand horsemen
13: 21 and had twenty-two sons and **sixteen** [+6926] daughters.
16: 1 In the **thirty-sixth** [+2256+8993] year of Asa's reign Baasha king
22: 12 He remained hidden with them at the temple of God for **six** years
26: 1 people of Judah took Uzziah, who was **sixteen** [+6926] years old,
26: 3 Uzziah was **sixteen** [+6926] years old when he became king,
26: 12 family leaders over the fighting men was **2,600** [+547+2256+4395].
27: 1 became king, and he reigned in Jerusalem **sixteen** [+6926] years.
27: 8 became king, and he reigned in Jerusalem **sixteen** [+6926] years.
28: 1 became king, and he reigned in Jerusalem **sixteen** [+6926] years.
29: 17 finishing on the **sixteenth** [+6925] day of the first month.
29: 33 The animals consecrated as sacrifices amounted to **six** hundred
35: 8 gave the priests **twenty-six hundred** [+547+2256+4395] Passover
Ezr 2: 9 of Zaccai **760** [+2256+4395+8679]
2: 10 of Bani **642** [+752+2256+4395+9109]
2: 11 of Bebai **623** [+2256+4395+6929+8993]
2: 13 of Adonikam **666** [+2256+4395+9252+9252]
2: 13 of Adonikam **666** [+2256+4395+9252+9252]
2: 13 of Adonikam **666** [+2256+4395+9252+9252]
2: 14 of Bigvai **2,056** [+547+2256+2822]
2: 22 of Netophah **56** [+2256+2822]
2: 26 of Ramah and Geba **621** [+285+2256+4395+6929]
2: 30 of Magbish **156** [+2256+2822+4395]
2: 35 of Senaah **3,630** [+547+2256+2256+4395+8993+8993]
2: 60 Delaiah, Tobiah and Nekoda **652** [+2256+2822+4395+9109]
2: 64 whole company numbered **42,360** [+547+752+4395+8052+8993],
2: 66 They had **736** [+2256+4395+8679+8993] horses, 245 mules,
2: 67 435 camels and **6,720** [+547+2256+4395+6929+8679] donkeys.
2: 69 for this work **61,000** [+547+2256+8052] drachmas of gold, 5,000
8: 10 Shelomith son of Josiphiah, and with him **160** [+2256+4395] men;
8: 13 names were Eliphelet, Jeuel and Shemaiah, and with them **60** men;
8: 26 I weighed out to them **650** [+2256+2822+4395] talents of silver,
8: 35 twelve bulls for all Israel, **ninety-six** [+2256+9596] rams,
Ne 5: 18 one ox, **six** choice sheep and some poultry were prepared for me,
7: 10 of Arah **652** [+2256+2822+4395+9109]
7: 14 of Zaccai **760** [+2256+4395+8679]
7: 15 of Binnui **648** [+752+2256+4395+9046]
7: 16 of Bebai **628** [+2256+4395+6929+9046]
7: 18 of Adonikam **667** [+2256+4395+8679+9252]
7: 18 of Adonikam **667** [+2256+4395+8679+9252]
7: 19 of Bigvai **2,067** [+547+2256+8679]
7: 20 of Adin **655** [+2256+2822+2822+4395]
7: 30 of Ramah and Geba **621** [+285+2256+4395+6929]
7: 62 Delaiah, Tobiah and Nekoda **642** [+752+2256+2256+4395+9109]
7: 66 company numbered **42,360** [+547+752+2256+4395+8052+8993],
7: 68 [7:67] There were **736** [+2256+4395+8679+8993] [BHS-] horses,
7: 69 [7:68] camels and **6,720** [+547+2256+4395+6929+8679] donkeys.
7: 72 [7:71] minas of silver and **67** [+2256+8679] garments for priests.
11: 6 in Jerusalem totaled **468** [+752+2256+4395+9046] able men.
Est 2: 12 **six** months with oil of myrrh and six with perfumes and cosmetics.
2: 12 six months with oil of myrrh and **six** with perfumes and cosmetics.
Job 5: 19 From **six** calamities he will rescue you; in seven no harm will
42: 12 **six** thousand camels, a thousand yoke of oxen and a thousand
Pr 6: 16 There are **six** things the LORD hates, seven that are detestable to
SS 3: 7 escorted by **sixty** warriors, the noblest of Israel,
6: 8 **Sixty** queens there may be, and eighty concubines, and virgins
Isa 6: 2 Above him were seraphs, each with **six** wings: With two wings
6: 2 **[RPH]** With two wings they covered their faces, with two they
7: 8 Within **sixty-five** [+2256+2822] years Ephraim will be too
Jer 34: 14 After he has served you **six** years, you must let him go free.'
52: 23 There were **ninety-six** [+2256+9596] pomegranates on the sides;
52: 25 people of the land and **sixty** of his men who were found in the city.
52: 30 There were **4,600** [+547+752+2256+4395] people in all.
Eze 9: 2 And I saw **six** men coming from the direction of the upper gate,
40: 5 The length of the measuring rod in the man's hand was **six** long

Eze 40:12 was a wall one cubit high, and the alcoves were **six** cubits square.
40:12 one cubit high, and the alcoves were six cubits square. **[RPH]**
40:14 projecting walls all around the inside of the gateway—**sixty** cubits.
41: 1 the jambs; the width of the jambs was **six** cubits on each side.
41: 1 the width of the jambs was six cubits on each side. **[RPH]**
41: 3 The entrance was **six** cubits wide, and the projecting walls on each
41: 5 it was **six** cubits thick, and each side room around the temple was
41: 8 of the side rooms. It was the length of the rod, **six** long cubits.
46: 1 The gate of the inner court facing east is to be shut on the **six**
46: 4 brings to the LORD on the Sabbath day is to be **six** male lambs
46: 6 he is to offer a young bull, **six** lambs and a ram, all without defect.
Da 9:25 there will be seven 'sevens,' and **sixty-two** [+2256+9109] 'sevens.'
9:26 After the **sixty-two** [+2256+9109] 'sevens,' the Anointed One will

9253 ²שֵׁשׁ ***šēš²***, n.m. [3] [→ 8880, 9254, 9260]

marble [3]

Est 1: 6 of white linen and purple material to silver rings on **marble** pillars.
1: 6 of porphyry, **marble**, mother-of-pearl and other costly stones.
SS 5:15 His legs are pillars of **marble** set on bases of pure gold.

9254 ³שֵׁשׁ ***šēš³***, n.m. [38] [→ 9260; cf. 9253]

linen [21], fine linen [17]

Ge 41:42 He dressed him in robes of **fine linen** and put a gold chain around
Ex 25: 4 blue, purple and scarlet yarn and **fine linen**; goat hair;
26: 1 "Make the tabernacle with ten curtains of finely twisted **linen**
26:31 a curtain of blue, purple and scarlet yarn and finely twisted **linen**,
26:36 a curtain of blue, purple and scarlet yarn and finely twisted **linen**—
27: 9 hundred cubits long and is to have curtains of finely twisted **linen**,
27:16 of blue, purple and scarlet yarn and finely twisted **linen**—
27:18 cubits wide, with curtains of finely twisted **linen** five cubits high,
28: 5 them use gold, and blue, purple and scarlet yarn, and **fine linen**.
28: 6 and of blue, purple and scarlet yarn, and of finely twisted **linen**—
28: 8 with blue, purple and scarlet yarn, and with finely twisted **linen**.
28:15 and of blue, purple and scarlet yarn, and of finely twisted **linen**.
28:39 "Weave the tunic of **fine linen** and make the turban of fine linen.
28:39 "Weave the tunic of fine linen and make the turban of **fine linen**.
35: 6 blue, purple and scarlet yarn and **fine linen**; goat hair;
35:23 purple or scarlet yarn or **fine linen**, or goat hair, ram skins dyed red
35:25 what she had spun—blue, purple or scarlet yarn or **fine linen**.
35:35 in blue, purple and scarlet yarn and **fine linen**, and weavers—
36: 8 made the tabernacle with ten curtains of finely twisted **linen**
36:35 the curtain of blue, purple and scarlet yarn and finely twisted **linen**,
36:37 a curtain of blue, purple and scarlet yarn and finely twisted **linen**—
38: 9 was a hundred cubits long and had curtains of finely twisted **linen**,
38:16 All the curtains around the courtyard were of finely twisted **linen**.
38:18 was of blue, purple and scarlet yarn and finely twisted **linen**—
38:23 and an embroiderer in blue, purple and scarlet yarn and **fine linen**.)
39: 2 and of blue, purple and scarlet yarn, and of finely twisted **linen**.
39: 3 to be worked into the blue, purple and scarlet yarn and **fine linen**—
39: 5 with blue, purple and scarlet yarn, and with finely twisted **linen**,
39: 8 and of blue, purple and scarlet yarn, and of finely twisted **linen**.
39:27 For Aaron and his sons, they made tunics of **fine linen**—the work
39:28 the turban of **fine linen**, the linen headbands and the
39:28 the **linen** headbands and the undergarments of finely twisted linen.
39:28 the linen headbands and the undergarments of finely twisted **linen**.
39:29 The sash was of finely twisted **linen** and blue, purple and scarlet
Pr 31:22 coverings for her bed; she is clothed in **fine linen** and purple.
Eze 16:10 I dressed you in **fine linen** and covered you with costly garments.
16:13 your clothes were of **fine linen** and costly fabric and embroidered
27: 7 **Fine** embroidered **linen** from Egypt was your sail and served as

9255 שָׁשָׁא ***šāšā'***, v.intens. [1]

drag along [1]

Eze 39: 2 [D] I will turn you around and **drag** you **along**. I will bring you

9256 שֵׁשְׁבַּצַּר ***šēšbaṣṣar***, n.pr.m. [2] [cf. 9256]

Sheshbazzar [2]

Ezr 1: 8 who counted them out to **Sheshbazzar** the prince of Judah.
1:11 **Sheshbazzar** brought all these along when the exiles came up

9257 שָׁשָׁה ***šāšâ***, v.den. [1]

sixth [1]

Eze 45:13 [D] of wheat and a **sixth** *of* an ephah from each homer of barley.

9258 שָׁשַׁי ***šāšay***, n.pr.m. [1]

Shashai [1]

Ezr 10:40 Macnadebai, **Shashai**, Sharai,

9259 שֵׁשַׁי ***šēšay***, n.pr.m. [3]

Sheshai [3]

Nu 13:22 and came to Hebron, where Ahiman, **Sheshai** and Talmai,
Jos 15:14 **Sheshai**, Ahiman and Talmai—descendants of Anak.
Jdg 1:10 called Kiriath Arba) and defeated **Sheshai**, Ahiman and Talmai.

9260 שֵׁשִׁי ***šēšî***, n.m. Not used in NIV/BHS [√ 9254; cf. 9253]

9261 שִׁשִּׁי ***šiššî***, a.num.ord. [28] [√ 9252]

sixth [28]

Ge 1:31 And there was evening, and there was morning—the **sixth** day.
30:19 Leah conceived again and bore Jacob a **sixth** son.
Ex 16: 5 On the **sixth** day they are to prepare what they bring in, and that is
16:22 On the **sixth** day, they gathered twice as much—two omers for
16:29 that is why on the **sixth** day he gives you bread for two days.
26: 9 another set. Fold the **sixth** curtain double at the front of the tent.
Lev 25:21 I will send you such a blessing in the **sixth** year that the land will
Nu 7:42 On the **sixth** day Eliasaph son of Deuel, the leader of the people of
29:29 " 'On the **sixth** day prepare eight bulls, two rams and fourteen male
Jos 19:32 The **sixth** lot came out for Naphtali, clan by clan:
2Sa 3: 5 the **sixth**, Ithream the son of David's wife Eglah. These were born
1Ch 2:15 the **sixth** Ozem and the seventh David.
3: 3 the son of Abital; and the **sixth**, Ithream, by his wife Eglah.
12:11 [12:12] Attai the **sixth**, Eliel the seventh,
24: 9 the fifth to Malkijah, the **sixth** to Mijamin,
25:13 the **sixth** to Bukkiah, his sons and relatives, 12
26: 3 Elam the fifth, Jehohanan the **sixth** and Eliehoenai the seventh.
26: 5 Ammiel the **sixth**, Issachar the seventh and Peullethai the eighth.
27: 9 The **sixth**, for the sixth month, was Ira the son of Ikkesh the
27: 9 The sixth, for the **sixth** month, was Ira the son of Ikkesh the
Ne 3:30 and Hanun, the **sixth** son of Zalaph, repaired another section.
Eze 4:11 Also measure out a **sixth** *of* a hin of water and drink it at set times.
8: 1 In the **sixth** year, in the sixth month on the fifth day, while I was
8: 1 In the sixth year, in the **sixth** month on the fifth day, while I was
45:13 a **sixth** *of* an ephah from each homer of wheat and a sixth of an
46:14 consisting of a **sixth** *of* an ephah with a third of a hin of oil to
Hag 1: 1 the second year of King Darius, on the first day of the **sixth** month,
1:15 on the twenty-fourth day of the **sixth** month in the second year of

9262 שִׁשִּׁים ***šiššîm***, n.indecl. Not used in NIV/BHS [√ 9252; Ar 10749]

9263 שֵׁשַׁךְ ***šēšak***, n.pr.loc. [2]

Sheshach [2]

Jer 25:26 And after all of them, the king of **Sheshach** will drink it too.
51:41 "How **Sheshach** will be captured, the boast of the whole earth

9264 שֵׁשָׁן ***šēšān***, n.pr.m. [5]

Sheshan [4], he[s] [1]

1Ch 2:31 The son of Appaim: Ishi, who was the father of **Sheshan**.
2:31 who was the father of Sheshan. **Sheshan** was the father of Ahlai.
2:34 **Sheshan** had no sons—only daughters. He had an Egyptian servant
2:34 only daughters. **He**[s] had an Egyptian servant named Jarha.
2:35 **Sheshan** gave his daughter in marriage to his servant Jarha,

9265 שָׁשָׁק ***šāšaq***, n.pr.m. [2]

Shashak [2]

1Ch 8:14 Ahio, **Shashak**, Jeremoth,
8:25 Iphdeiah and Penuel were the sons of **Shashak**.

9266 שָׁשַׁר ***šāšar***, n.[m.]. [2]

red [2]

Jer 22:14 large windows in it, panels it with cedar and decorates it in **red**.
Eze 23:14 men portrayed on a wall, figures of Chaldeans portrayed in **red**,

9267 שָׁת ***šāt***, n.m. Not used in NIV/BHS [√ 9268]

9268 ¹שֵׁת ***šēt¹***, n.[m.]. [3] [→ 9267, 9273]

buttocks [2], foundations [1]

2Sa 10: 4 cut off their garments in the middle at the **buttocks**, and sent them
Ps 11: 3 When the **foundations** are being destroyed, what can the righteous
Isa 20: 4 and Cushite exiles, young and old, with **buttocks** bared—

9269 ²שֵׁת ***šēt²***, n.pr.m. [9] [√ 8883]

Seth [8], Sheth [1]

Ge 4:25 and she gave birth to a son and named him **Seth**, saying,
4:26 **Seth** also had a son, and he named him Enosh. At that time men

Ge 5: 3 son in his own likeness, in his own image; and he named him **Seth**.
5: 4 After **Seth** was born, Adam lived 800 years and had other sons
5: 6 When **Seth** had lived 105 years, he became the father of Enosh.
5: 7 of Enosh, **Seth** lived 807 years and had other sons and daughters.
5: 8 Altogether, **Seth** lived 912 years, and then he died.
Nu 24: 17 crush the foreheads of Moab, the skulls of all the sons of **Sheth**.
1Ch 1: 1 Adam, **Seth**, Enosh,

9270 ³שֵׁת *šēt*³, n.pr.m. Not used in NIV/BHS

9271 ¹שָׁתָה *šātâ*¹, n.m. [0 / 1] [→ 9272?, 9274]

workers in cloth [1]

Isa 19: 10 [A] The **workers in cloth** [BHS-] will be dejected,

9272 ²שָׁתָה *šātâ*², v. [217] [→ 5492, 9275, 9276; cf. 9197; Ar 10748]

drink [127], drank [28], drinking [23], drinks [8], drunk [6], must drink [+9272] [6], *untranslated* [2], drinkers [2], getting drunk [+8893] [2], well-watered [+4784] [2], be drunk [1], dine [1], drained to dregs [+906+5172] [1], drinks in [1], drinks up [1], drunkards [+8911] [1], feasted [1], feasting [+430+2256] [1], get a drink [1], have a drink [1], refresh [1]

Ge 9: 21 [A] When *he* **drank** some of its wine, he became drunk and lay
24: 14 [A] 'Please let down your jar that *I may* **have a drink**,' and she
24: 14 [A] and she says, '**Drink**, and I'll water your camels too'—
24: 18 [A] "**Drink**, my lord," she said, and quickly lowered the jar to
24: 19 [A] for your camels too, until they have finished **drinking**."
24: 22 [A] When the camels had finished **drinking**, the man took out a
24: 44 [A] if she says to me, "**Drink**, and I'll draw water for your
24: 46 [A] quickly lowered her jar from her shoulder and said, '**Drink**,
24: 46 [A] camels too.' So *I* **drank**, and she watered the camels also.
24: 54 [A] who were with him ate and **drank** and spent the night there.
25: 34 [A] some lentil stew. He ate and **drank**, and then got up and left.
26: 30 [A] Isaac then made a feast for them, and they ate and **drank**.
27: 25 [A] to him and he ate; and he brought some wine and *he* **drank**.
30: 38 [A] be directly in front of the flocks when they came to **drink**.
30: 38 [A] to drink. When the flocks were in heat and came to **drink**,
43: 34 [A] as anyone else's. So *they* **feasted** and drank freely with him.
44: 5 [A] Isn't this the cup my master **drinks** from and also uses for
Ex 7: 18 [A] the Egyptians will not be able to **drink** its water.' "
7: 21 [A] so bad that the Egyptians could not **drink** its water.
7: 24 [A] all the Egyptians dug along the Nile to *get* **drinking** water,
7: 24 [A] because they could not **drink** the water of the river.
15: 23 [A] they could not **drink** its water because it was bitter.
15: 24 [A] grumbled against Moses, saying, "What *are we to* **drink**?"
17: 1 [A] at Rephidim, but there was no water *for* the people to **drink**.
17: 2 [A] quarreled with Moses and said, "Give us water *to* **drink**."
17: 6 [A] and water will come out of it *for* the people *to* **drink**."
24: 11 [A] of the Israelites; they saw God, and they ate and **drank**.
32: 6 [A] Afterward they sat down to eat and **drink** and got up to
34: 28 [A] and forty nights without eating bread or **drinking** water.
Lev 10: 9 [A] "You and your sons *are* not *to* **drink** wine or other
11: 34 [C] and any liquid that *could* **be drunk** from it is unclean.
Nu 6: 3 [A] fermented drink and *must* not **drink** vinegar made from wine
6: 3 [A] *He must* not **drink** grape juice or eat grapes or raisins.
6: 20 [A] that was presented. After that, the Nazirite *may* **drink** wine.
20: 5 [A] or pomegranates. And there is no water to **drink**!"
20: 11 [A] gushed out, and the community and their livestock **drank**.
20: 17 [A] through any field or vineyard, or **drink** water from any well.
20: 19 [A] if we or our livestock **drink** any of your water, we will pay
21: 22 [A] into any field or vineyard, or **drink** water from any well.
23: 24 [A] till he devours his prey and **drinks** the blood of his victims."
33: 14 [A] where there was no water for the people to **drink**.
Dt 2: 6 [A] in silver for the food you eat and the water *you* **drink**.' "
2: 28 [A] Sell us food to eat and water *to* **drink** for their price in silver.
9: 9 [A] and forty nights; I ate no bread and **drank** no water.
9: 18 [A] I ate no bread and **drank** no water, because of all the sin you
11: 11 [A] land of mountains and valleys that **drinks** rain from heaven.
28: 39 [A] cultivate them but *you will* not **drink** the wine or gather the
29: 6 [29:5] [A] You ate no bread and **drank** no wine or other
32: 14 [A] kernels of wheat. *You* **drank** the foaming blood of the grape.
32: 38 [A] their sacrifices and **drank** the wine of their drink offerings?
Jdg 7: 5 [A] tongues like a dog from those who kneel down to **drink**."
7: 6 [A] their mouths. All the rest got down on their knees to **drink**.
9: 27 [A] While they were eating and **drinking**, they cursed
13: 4 [A] Now see to it that *you* **drink** no wine or other fermented
13: 7 [A] **drink** no wine or other fermented drink and do not eat
13: 14 [A] nor **drink** any wine or other fermented drink nor eat anything
15: 19 [A] When Samson **drank**, his strength returned and he revived.
19: 4 [A] with him three days, eating and **drinking**, and sleeping there.
19: 6 [A] So the two of them sat down to eat and **drink** together.
19: 21 [A] had washed their feet, they had something to eat and **drink**.
Ru 2: 9 [A] go and **get a drink** from the water jars the men have filled."
3: 3 [A] know you are there until he has finished eating and **drinking**.
3: 7 [A] had finished eating and **drinking** and was in good spirits,
1Sa 1: 9 [A] Once when they had finished eating and **drinking** in Shiloh,
1: 15 [A] *I have* not *been* **drinking** wine or beer; I was pouring out
30: 12 [A] any food or **drunk** any water for three days and three nights.
30: 16 [A] **drinking** and reveling because of the great amount of
2Sa 11: 11 [A] I go to my house to eat and **drink** and lie with my wife?
11: 13 [A] At David's invitation, he ate and **drank** with him, and David
12: 3 [A] his food, **drank** from his cup and even slept in his arms.
16: 2 [A] the wine is to **refresh** those who become exhausted in the
19: 35 [19:36] [A] Can your servant taste what he eats and **drinks**?
23: 16 [A] he refused to **drink** it; instead, he poured it out before the
23: 17 [A] David would not **drink** it. Such were the exploits of the three
1Ki 1: 25 [A] Right now they are eating and **drinking** with him and saying,
4: 20 [A] on the seashore; they ate, *they* **drank** and they were happy.
13: 8 [A] not go with you, nor would I eat bread or **drink** water here.
13: 9 [A] 'You must not eat bread or **drink** water or return by the way
13: 16 [A] nor can I eat bread or **drink** water with you in this place.
13: 17 [A] 'You must not eat bread or **drink** water there or return by the
13: 18 [A] may eat bread and **drink** water.' " (But he was lying to him.)
13: 19 [A] of God returned with him and ate and **drank** in his house.
13: 22 [A] and **drank** water in the place where he told you not to eat
13: 22 [A] water in the place where he told you not to eat or **drink**.
13: 23 [A] When the man of God had finished eating and **drinking**, the
16: 9 [A] Elah was in Tirzah at the time, **getting drunk** [+8893] in the
17: 4 [A] *You will* **drink** from the brook, and I have ordered the
17: 6 [A] and meat in the evening, and *he* **drank** from the brook.
17: 10 [A] you bring me a little water in a jar so *I may have a* **drink**?"
18: 41 [A] Elijah said to Ahab, "Go, eat and **drink**, for there is the
18: 42 [A] So Ahab went off to eat and **drink**, but Elijah climbed to the
19: 6 [A] a jar of water. He ate and **drank** and then lay down again.
19: 8 [A] So he got up and ate and **drank**. Strengthened by that food,
20: 12 [A] message while he and the kings *were* **drinking** in their tents,
20: 16 [A] allied with him were in their tents **getting drunk** [+8893].
2Ki 3: 17 [A] and you, your cattle and your other animals *will* **drink**.
6: 22 [A] and water before them so that they may eat and **drink** and
6: 23 [A] after they had finished eating and **drinking**, he sent them
7: 8 [A] They ate and **drank**, and carried away silver, gold
9: 34 [A] Jehu went in and ate and **drank**. "Take care of that cursed
18: 27 [A] will have to eat their own filth and **drink** their own urine?"
18: 31 [A] own vine and fig tree and **drink** water from his own cistern,
19: 24 [A] I have dug wells in foreign lands and **drunk** the water there.
1Ch 11: 18 [A] he refused to **drink** it; instead, he poured it out before the
11: 19 [A] "*Should I* **drink** the blood of these men who went at the risk
11: 19 [A] risked their lives to bring it back, David would not **drink** it.
12: 39 [12:40] [A] three days there with David, eating and **drinking**,
29: 22 [A] **drank** with great joy in the presence of the LORD that day.
Ezr 10: 6 [A] While he was there, he ate no food and **drank** no water,
Ne 8: 10 [A] "Go and enjoy choice food and sweet **drinks**,
8: 12 [A] all the people went away to eat and **drink**, to send portions of
Est 3: 15 [A] The king and Haman sat down to **drink**, but the city of Susa
4: 16 [A] Do not eat or **drink** for three days, night or day. I and my
7: 1 [A] So the king and Haman went to **dine** with Queen Esther,
Job 1: 4 [A] would invite their three sisters to eat and **drink** with them.
1: 13 [A] and **drinking** wine at the oldest brother's house,
1: 18 [A] and **drinking** wine at the oldest brother's house,
6: 4 [A] of the Almighty are in me, my spirit **drinks in** their poison;
15: 16 [A] who is vile and corrupt, *who* **drinks up** evil like water!
21: 20 [A] his destruction; *let him* **drink** of the wrath of the Almighty.
34: 7 [A] What man is like Job, *who* **drinks** scorn like water?
Ps 50: 13 [A] Do I eat the flesh of bulls or **drink** the blood of goats?
69: 12 [69:13] [A] and I am the song of the **drunkards** [+8911].
75: 8 [75:9] [A] all the wicked of the earth drink it down **[RPH]** to
78: 44 [A] rivers to blood; *they could* not **drink** *from* their streams.
110: 7 [A] *He will* **drink** from a brook beside the way; therefore he will
Pr 4: 17 [A] eat the bread of wickedness and **drink** the wine of violence.
5: 15 [A] **Drink** water from your own cistern, running water from your
9: 5 [A] "Come, eat my food and **drink** the wine I have mixed.
23: 7 [A] "Eat and **drink**," he says to you, but his heart is not with you.
26: 6 [A] or **drinking** violence is the sending of a message by the hand
31: 4 [A] not for kings *to* **drink** wine, not for rulers to crave beer,
31: 5 [A] lest *they* **drink** and forget what the law decrees, and deprive
31: 7 [A] *let them* **drink** and forget their poverty and remember their
Ecc 2: 24 [A] better than to eat and **drink** and find satisfaction in his work.
3: 13 [A] That everyone may eat and **drink**, and find satisfaction in all
5: 18 [5:17] [A] that it is good and proper for a man to eat and **drink**,
8: 15 [A] for a man under the sun than to eat and **drink** and be glad.
9: 7 [A] food with gladness, and **drink** your wine with a joyful heart,
SS 5: 1 [A] and my honey; *I have* **drunk** my wine and my milk.
5: 1 [A] my milk. Eat, O friends, and **drink**; drink your fill, O lovers.
Isa 5: 22 [A] Woe to those who are heroes at **drinking** wine
21: 5 [A] set the tables, they spread the rugs, they eat, they **drink**!
22: 13 [A] and killing of sheep, eating of meat and **drinking** *of* wine!

Isa 22: 13 [A] "Let us eat and **drink**," you say, "for tomorrow we die!"
24: 9 [A] No longer *do they* **drink** wine with a song; the beer is bitter
24: 9 [A] they drink wine with a song; the beer is bitter to its **drinkers**.
29: 8 [A] as when a thirsty man dreams that *he is* **drinking**, but he
36: 12 [A] will have to eat their own filth and **drink** their own urine?"
36: 16 [A] own vine and fig tree and **drink** water from his own cistern,
37: 25 [A] I have dug wells in foreign lands and **drunk** the water there.
44: 12 [A] and loses his strength; *he* **drinks** no water and grows faint.
51: 17 [A] *you who have* **drunk** from the hand of the LORD the cup
51: 17 [A] *you who have* **drained** [+906+5172] **to** its **dregs** the goblet
51: 22 [A] *from* that cup, the goblet of my wrath, *you will* never **drink**
62: 8 [A] never again *will* foreigners **drink** the new wine for which
62: 9 [A] those who gather the grapes *will* **drink** it in the courts of my
65: 13 [A] go hungry; my servants *will* **drink**, but you will go thirsty;
Jer 2: 18 [A] Now why go to Egypt to **drink** water from the Shihor?
2: 18 [A] And why go to Assyria to **drink** water from the River?
16: 8 [A] a house where there is feasting and sit down to eat and **drink**.
22: 15 [A] and more cedar? Did not your father have food and **drink**?
25: 16 [A] When *they* **drink** it, they will stagger and go mad because of
25: 26 [A] And after all of them, the king of Sheshach *will* **drink** it too.
25: 27 [A] **Drink**, get drunk and vomit, and fall to rise no more
25: 28 [A] But if they refuse to take the cup from your hand and **drink**,
25: 28 [A] the LORD Almighty says: *You* **must drink** [+9272] it!
25: 28 [A] the LORD Almighty says: *You* **must drink** [+9272] it!
35: 5 [A] of the Recabite family and said to them, "**Drink** some wine."
35: 6 [A] they replied, "*We do* not **drink** wine, because our forefather
35: 6 [A] 'Neither you nor your descendants *must* ever **drink** wine.
35: 8 [A] our wives nor our sons and daughters *have* ever **drunk** wine
35: 14 [A] 'Jonadab son of Recab ordered his sons not *to* **drink** wine
35: 14 [A] To this day *they do* not **drink** wine, because they obey their
49: 12 [A] "If those who do not deserve to **drink** the cup must drink it,
49: 12 [A] who do not deserve to drink the cup **must drink** [+9272] it,
49: 12 [A] who do not deserve to drink the cup **must drink** [+9272] it,
49: 12 [A] You will not go unpunished, but **must drink** [+9272] it.
49: 12 [A] You will not go unpunished, but **must drink** [+9272] it.
51: 7 [A] The nations **drank** her wine; therefore they have now gone
La 5: 4 [A] We must buy the water *we* **drink**; our wood can be had only
Eze 4: 11 [A] out a sixth of a hin of water and **drink** it at set times.
4: 11 [A] out a sixth of a hin of water and drink it at set times. **[RPH]**
4: 16 [A] rationed food in anxiety and **drink** rationed water in despair,
12: 18 [A] eat your food, and shudder in fear *as you* **drink** your water.
12: 19 [A] will eat their food in anxiety and **drink** their water in despair,
23: 32 [A] "*You will* **drink** your sister's cup, a cup large and deep;
23: 34 [A] *You will* **drink** it and drain it dry; you will dash it to pieces
25: 4 [A] among you; they will eat your fruit and **drink** your milk.
31: 14 [A] No other trees *so* **well-watered** [+4784] are ever to reach
31: 16 [A] of Lebanon, all the trees *that were* **well-watered** [+4784],
34: 18 [A] Is it not enough for *you to* **drink** clear water? Must you also
34: 19 [A] and **drink** what you have muddied with your feet?
39: 17 [A] of Israel. There you will eat flesh and **drink** blood.
39: 18 [A] **drink** the blood of the princes of the earth as if they were
39: 19 [A] eat fat till you are glutted and **drink** blood till you are drunk.
44: 21 [A] No priest *is to* **drink** wine when he enters the inner court.
Da 1: 12 [A] Give us nothing but vegetables to eat and water *to* **drink**.
Joel 1: 5 [A] Wail, all you **drinkers** *of* wine; wail because of the new
3: 3 [4:3] [A] they sold girls for wine that *they might* **drink**.
Am 2: 8 [A] In the house of their god *they* **drink** wine taken as fines.
4: 1 [A] and say to your husbands, "Bring us *some* **drinks**!"
4: 8 [A] from town to town for water but did not get enough *to* **drink**,
5: 11 [A] have planted lush vineyards, *you will* not **drink** their wine.
6: 6 [A] *You* **drink** wine by the bowlful and use the finest lotions,
9: 14 [A] They will plant vineyards and **drink** their wine; they will
Ob 1: 16 [A] Just as *you* **drank** on my holy hill, so all the nations will
1: 16 [A] on my holy hill, so all the nations *will* **drink** continually;
1: 16 [A] *they will* **drink** and drink and be as if they had never been.
Jnh 3: 7 [A] herd or flock, taste anything; do not let them eat or **drink**.
Mic 6: 15 [A] on yourselves, you will crush grapes but not **drink** the wine.
Hab 2: 16 [A] instead of glory. Now it is your turn! **Drink** and be exposed!
Zep 1: 13 [A] in them; they will plant vineyards but not **drink** the wine.
Hag 1: 6 [A] *You* **drink**, but never have your fill. You put on clothes,
Zec 7: 6 [A] when you were eating and **drinking**, were you not just
7: 6 [A] *were* you not *just* **feasting for** [+430+2256] yourselves?
9: 15 [A] *They will* **drink** and roar as with wine; they will be full like

9273 שָׁתוֹת **šātôt**, n.m. Not used in NIV/BHS [√ 9268 & 9272]

9274 שְׁתִי ***šᵉtî***[1], n.m. [9] [√ 9271]

woven [9]

Lev 13: 48 any **woven** or knitted material of linen or wool, any leather
13: 49 or leather, or **woven** or knitted material, or any leather article,
13: 51 or the **woven** or knitted material, or the leather, whatever its use,
13: 52 up the clothing, or the **woven** or knitted material of wool or linen,
13: 53 the clothing, or the **woven** or knitted material, or the leather article,
13: 56 out of the clothing, or the leather, or the **woven** or knitted material.
13: 57 or in the **woven** or knitted material, or in the leather article,
13: 58 The clothing, or the **woven** or knitted material, or any leather
13: 59 by mildew in woolen or linen clothing, **woven** or knitted material,

9275 [2]שְׁתִי ***šᵉtî***[2], n.[m.]. [1] [√ 9272]

drunkenness [1]

Ecc 10: 17 eat at a proper time—for strength and not for **drunkenness**.

9276 שְׁתִיָּה ***šᵉtiyyâ***, n.f. [1] [√ 9272]

drink in own way [1]

Est 1: 8 king's command each guest was allowed to **drink in** his **own way**,

9277 שָׁתִיל **šātîl**, n.[m.]. [1] [√ 9278]

shoots [1]

Ps 128: 3 your house; your sons will be like olive **shoots** around your table.

9278 שָׁתַל **šātal**, v. [10] [→ 9277]

planted [5], plant [2], been planted [1], is planted [1], is transplanted [1]

Ps 1: 3 [B] He is like a tree **planted** by streams of water, which yields its
92: 13 [92:14] [B] **planted** in the house of the LORD, they will
Jer 17: 8 [B] He will be like a tree **planted** by the water that sends out its
Eze 17: 8 [B] It *had* **been planted** in good soil by abundant water so that it
17: 10 [B] Even if *it* **is transplanted**, will it thrive? Will it not wither
17: 22 [A] its topmost shoots and **plant** it on a high and lofty mountain.
17: 23 [A] On the mountain heights of Israel *I will* **plant** it; it will
19: 10 [B] " 'Your mother was like a vine in your vineyard **planted** by
19: 13 [B] Now *it* **is planted** in the desert, in a dry and thirsty land.
Hos 9: 13 [B] I have seen Ephraim, like Tyre, **planted** in a pleasant place.

9279 שֻׁתַלְחִי ***šutalḥî***, a.g. [1] [√ 8811]

Shuthelahite [1]

Nu 26: 35 through Shuthelah, the **Shuthelahite** clan; through Beker,

9280 שָׁתַם **šātam**, v. [2] [→ 9281]

sees clearly [2]

Nu 24: 3 [B] son of Beor, the oracle of one whose eye **sees clearly**,
24: 15 [B] son of Beor, the oracle of one whose eye **sees clearly**,

9281 שְׁתֻם ***šᵉtum***, a. *or* v.ptcp. Not used in NIV/BHS [√ 9280]

9282 שָׁתַן **šātan**, v. Not used in NIV/BHS [cf. 8874]

9283 שָׁתַע **šāta'**, v. [2] [cf. 9120]

dismayed [2]

Isa 41: 10 [A] for I am with you; *do* not *be* **dismayed**, for I am your God.
41: 23 [A] or bad, so that *we will be* **dismayed** and filled with fear.

9284 שָׁתַק **šātaq**, v. [4] [cf. 9200]

calm [2], calm down [1], dies down [1]

Ps 107: 30 [A] They were glad when *it grew* **calm**, and he guided them to
Pr 26: 20 [A] wood a fire goes out; without gossip a quarrel **dies down**.
Jnh 1: 11 [A] "What should we do to you *to make* the sea **calm down** for
1: 12 [A] throw me into the sea," he replied, "and it *will become* **calm**.

9285 שֵׁתָר **šētār**, n.pr.m. [1]

Shethar [1]

Est 1: 14 **Shethar**, Admatha, Tarshish, Meres, Marsena and Memucan,

9286 שָׁתַת **šātat**, v. [2] [cf. 8883]

destined [1], lay claim [1]

Ps 49: 14 [49:15] [A] Like sheep *they are* **destined** for the grave,
73: 9 [A] Their mouths **lay claim** to heaven, and their tongues take

ת, t

9287 ת **t**, letter. Not used in NIV/BHS [→ Ar 10751]

9288 תָּא **tā'**, n.m. [13]

alcoves [8], alcove [2], guardroom [+8132] [2], alcoves for the guards [1]

1Ki 14: 28 and afterward they returned them to the **guardroom** [+8132].
2Ch 12: 11 and afterward they returned them to the **guardroom** [+8132].
Eze 40: 7 The **alcoves for the guards** were one rod long and one rod wide,

Eze 40: 7 the projecting walls between the **alcoves** were five cubits thick.
40: 10 Inside the east gate were three **alcoves** on each side; the three had
40: 12 In front of each **alcove** was a wall one cubit high, and the alcoves
40: 12 was a wall one cubit high, and the **alcoves** were six cubits square.
40: 13 the top of the rear wall of one **alcove** to the top of the opposite one;
40: 16 The **alcoves** and the projecting walls inside the gateway were
40: 21 Its **alcoves**—three on each side—its projecting walls and its
40: 29 Its **alcoves**, its projecting walls and its portico had the same
40: 33 Its **alcoves**, its projecting walls and its portico had the same
40: 36 as did its **alcoves**, its projecting walls and its portico, and it had

9289 ¹תָּאַב *tā'ab*[1], v. [2] [→ 9291; cf. 14? *or* 3277?]

long for [2]

Ps 119: 40 [A] How *I* **long for** your precepts! Preserve my life in your
119: 174 [A] *I* **long for** your salvation, O LORD, and your law is my

9290 ²תָּאַב *tā'ab*[2], v. [1] [cf. 9493]

abhor [1]

Am 6: 8 [D] "I **abhor** the pride of Jacob and detest his fortresses; I will

9291 תַּאֲבָה *ta'^{a}bâ*, n.f. [1] [√ 9289]

longing [1]

Ps 119: 20 My soul is consumed with **longing** for your laws at all times.

9292 תָּאָה *tā'â*, v. [2] [cf. 204, 9344]

untranslated [1], run a line [1]

Nu 34: 7 [D] **run a line** from the Great Sea to Mount Hor
34: 8 [D] from Mount Hor **[RPH]** to Lebo Hamath. Then the

9293 תְּאוֹ *t^{e}'ô*, n.m. [2]

antelope [2]

Dt 14: 5 the wild goat, the ibex, the **antelope** and the mountain sheep.
Isa 51: 20 they lie at the head of every street, like **antelope** *caught in* a net.

9294 ¹תַּאֲוָה *ta'^{a}wâ*[1], n.f. [21] [√ 203]

desire [5], longing [2], longings [2], bounty [1], choicest [1], crave other food [+203] [1], craved [1], craves for more [+203] [1], craving [1], cravings [1], desires [1], gave in to craving [+203] [1], pleasing [1], selfish ends [1], what craved [1]

Ge 3: 6 that the fruit of the tree was good for food and **pleasing** to the eye,
49: 26 of the ancient mountains, than the **bounty** *of* the age-old hills.
Nu 11: 4 The rabble with them *began to* **crave other food** [+203],
Job 33: 20 being finds food repulsive and his soul loathes the **choicest** meal.
Ps 10: 3 He boasts of the **cravings** *of* his heart; he blesses the greedy
10: 17 You hear, O LORD, the **desire** *of* the afflicted; you encourage
21: 2 [21:3] You have granted him the **desire** *of* his heart and have not
38: 9 [38:10] All my **longings** lie open before you, O Lord; my sighing
78: 29 had more than enough, for he had given them **what** they **craved**.
78: 30 before they turned from the food they **craved**, even while it was
106: 14 In the desert *they* **gave in to** *their* **craving** [+203]; in the
112: 10 and waste away; the **longings** *of* the wicked will come to nothing.
Pr 10: 24 will overtake him; *what* the righteous **desire** will be granted.
11: 23 The **desire** *of* the righteous ends only in good, but the hope of the
13: 12 makes the heart sick, but a **longing** fulfilled is a tree of life.
13: 19 A **longing** fulfilled is sweet to the soul, but fools detest turning
18: 1 An unfriendly man pursues **selfish ends**; he defies all sound
19: 22 *What* a man **desires** is unfailing love; better to be poor than a liar.
21: 25 The sluggard's **craving** will be the death of him, because his hands
21: 26 All day long *he* **craves for more** [+203], but the righteous give
Isa 26: 8 wait for you; your name and renown are the **desire** *of* our hearts.

9295 ²תַּאֲוָה *ta'^{a}wâ*[2], n.f. Not used in NIV/BHS [√ 9344]

9296 תְּאוֹמִים *t^{e}'ômîm*, n.m. Not used in NIV/BHS [√ 9339]

9297 תַּאֲלָה *ta'^{a}lâ*, n.f. [1] [√ 457]

curse [1]

La 3: 65 Put a veil over their hearts, and may your **curse** be on them!

9298 תָּאַם *tā'am*, v.den. [2] [√ 9339]

has twin [2]

SS 4: 2 [G] the washing. Each **has** *its* **twin**; not one of them is alone.
6: 6 [G] the washing. Each **has** its **twin**, not one of them is alone.

9299 תַּאֲנָה *ta'^{a}nâ*, n.f. [1] [√ 628]

in heat [1]

Jer 2: 24 sniffing the wind in her craving—**in** her **heat** who can restrain her?

9300 תְּאֵנָה *t^{e}'ēnâ*, n.f. [39]

fig tree [15], figs [13], fig trees [6], fig [2], ones[s] [1], those[s] [1], tree [1]

Ge 3: 7 so they sewed **fig** leaves together and made coverings for
Nu 13: 23 it on a pole between them, along with some pomegranates and **figs**.
20: 5 It has no grain or **figs**, grapevines or pomegranates. And there is no
Dt 8: 8 a land with wheat and barley, vines and **fig trees**, pomegranates,
Jdg 9: 10 "Next, the trees said to the **fig tree**, 'Come and be our king.'
9: 11 "But the **fig tree** replied, 'Should I give up my fruit, so good
1Ki 4: 25 [5:5] lived in safety, each man under his own vine and **fig tree**.
2Ki 18: 31 his own vine and **fig tree** and drink water from his own cistern,
20: 7 Then Isaiah said, "Prepare a poultice *of* **figs**." They did so
Ne 13: 15 together with wine, grapes, **figs** and all other kinds of loads.
Ps 105: 33 he struck down their vines and **fig trees** and shattered the trees of
Pr 27: 18 He who tends a **fig tree** will eat its fruit, and he who looks after his
SS 2: 13 The **fig tree** forms its early fruit; the blossoming vines spread their
Isa 34: 4 withered leaves from the vine, like shriveled figs from the **fig tree**.
36: 16 his own vine and **fig tree** and drink water from his own cistern,
38: 21 Isaiah had said, "Prepare a poultice of **figs** and apply it to the boil,
Jer 5: 17 will devour your flocks and herds, devour your vines and **fig trees**.
8: 13 There will be no **figs** on the tree, and their leaves will wither.
8: 13 There will be no figs on the **tree**, and their leaves will wither.
24: 1 the LORD showed me two baskets of **figs** placed in front of the
24: 2 One basket had very good **figs**, like those that ripen early;
24: 2 One basket had very good figs, like **those**[s] that ripen early;
24: 2 the other basket had very poor **figs**, so bad they could not be eaten.
24: 3 asked me, "What do you see, Jeremiah?" "**Figs**," I answered.
24: 3 "The good **ones**[s] are very good, but the poor ones are so bad they
24: 5 'Like these good **figs**, I regard as good the exiles from Judah,
24: 8 " 'But like the poor **figs**, which are so bad they cannot be eaten,'
29: 17 plague against them and I will make them like poor **figs** that are
Hos 2: 12 [2:14] I will ruin her vines and her **fig trees**, which she said were
9: 10 I saw your fathers, it was like seeing the early fruit on the **fig tree**.
Joel 1: 7 It has laid waste my vines and ruined my **fig trees**. It has stripped
1: 12 The vine is dried up and the **fig tree** is withered; the pomegranate,
2: 22 are bearing their fruit; the **fig tree** and the vine yield their riches.
Am 4: 9 Locusts devoured your **fig** and olive trees, yet you have not
Mic 4: 4 Every man will sit under his own vine and under his own **fig tree**,
Na 3: 12 All your fortresses are like **fig trees** with their first ripe fruit;
Hab 3: 17 Though the **fig tree** does not bud and there are no grapes on the
Hag 2: 19 Until now, the vine and the **fig tree**, the pomegranate and the olive
Zec 3: 10 of you will invite his neighbor to sit under his vine and **fig tree**,'

9301 תֹּאֲנָה *tō'^{a}nâ*, n.f. [1] [√ 628]

occasion [1]

Jdg 14: 4 who was seeking an **occasion** to confront the Philistines;

9302 תַּאֲנִיָּה *ta'^{a}niyyâ*, n.f. [2] [√ 627]

mourn [1], mourning [1]

Isa 29: 2 she will **mourn** and lament, she will be to me like an altar hearth.
La 2: 5 He has multiplied **mourning** and lamentation for the Daughter of

9303 תְּאֻנִים *t^{e}'unîm*, n.[m.]. [1] [√ 224?]

efforts [1]

Eze 24: 12 It has frustrated *all* **efforts**; its heavy deposit has not been

9304 תַּאֲנַת שִׁלֹה *ta'^{a}nat šilōh*, n.pr.loc. [1] [cf. 8926]

Taanath Shiloh [1]

Jos 16: 6 Micmethath on the north it curved eastward to **Taanath Shiloh**,

9305 ¹תָּאַר *tā'ar*[1], v. [6] [cf. 9306, 9365?]

turned [3], curved [1], headed [1], went down [1]

Jos 15: 9 [A] From the hilltop the boundary **headed** toward the spring of
15: 9 [A] of Mount Ephron and **went down** *toward* Baalah (that is,
15: 11 [A] **turned** toward Shikkeron, passed along to Mount Baalah
18: 14 [A] the south the boundary **turned** south along the western side
18: 17 [A] *It* then **curved** north, went to En Shemesh, continued to
19: 13 [E] Eth Kazin; it came out at Rimmon and **turned** *toward* Neah.

9306 ²תָּאַר *tā'ar*[2], v.den. [2] [→ 9307; cf. 9305]

makes an outline [1], marks [1]

Isa 44: 13 [D] measures with a line and **makes an outline** with a marker;
44: 13 [D] he roughs it out with chisels and **marks** it with compasses.

9307 תֹּאַר *tō'ar*, n.m. [15] [√ 9306]

form [4], beautiful [+3637] [2], bearing [1], beauty [1], fine-looking [1], handsome [+3202] [1], look like [1], sleek [+3637] [1], they [+4392] [1], ugly [+8273] [1], well-built [+3637] [1]

Ge 29: 17 Leah had weak eyes, but Rachel was lovely **in form**, and beautiful.

[A] Qal [B] Qal passive [C] Niphal [D] Piel (poel, polel, pilel, pilal, pealal, pilpel) [E] Pual (poal, polal, poaal, pulal, pualal)

Ge 39: 6 food he ate. Now Joseph was **well-built** [+3637] and handsome,
41: 18 fat and **sleek** [+3637], and they grazed among the reeds.
41: 19 other cows came up—scrawny and very **ugly** [+8273] and lean.
Dt 21: 11 if you notice among the captives a **beautiful** [+3637] woman
Jdg 8: 18 like you," they answered, "each one with the **bearing** *of* a prince."
1Sa 16: 18 and a warrior. He speaks well and is a **fine-looking** man.
25: 3 She was an intelligent and **beautiful** [+3637] woman, but her
28: 14 "What does he **look like**?" he asked. "An old man wearing a robe
1Ki 1: 6 He was also very **handsome** [+3202] and was born next after
Est 2: 7 who was also known as Esther, was lovely in **form** and features,
Isa 52: 14 that of any man and his **form** marred beyond human likeness—
53: 2 He had no **beauty** or majesty to attract us to him, nothing in his
Jer 11: 16 called you a thriving olive tree with fruit beautiful in **form**.
La 4: 8 now **they** [+4392] are blacker than soot; they are not recognized in

9308 תַּאְרֵעַ ta'rēa', n.pr.m. [1] [cf. 9390]

Tarea [1]

1Ch 8: 35 The sons of Micah: Pithon, Melech, **Tarea** and Ahaz.

9309 תְּאַשּׁוּר te'aššûr, n.f. [2 / 3] [→ 898]

cypress [2], cypress wood [1]

Isa 41: 19 I will set pines in the wasteland, the fir and the **cypress** together,
60: 13 the pine, the fir and the **cypress** together, to adorn the place of my
Eze 27: 6 of **cypress** [BHS 855] **wood** from the coasts of Cyprus they made

9310 תֵּבָה tēbâ, n.f. [28]

ark [25], basket [2], it[s] [+2021] [1]

Ge 6: 14 So make yourself an **ark** *of* cypress wood; make rooms in it
6: 14 make rooms in **it**[s] [+2021] and coat it with pitch inside and out.
6: 15 The **ark** is to be 450 feet long, 75 feet wide and 45 feet high.
6: 16 Make a roof for it and finish the **ark** to within 18 inches of the top.
6: 16 Put a door in the side of the **ark** and make lower, middle and upper
6: 18 I will establish my covenant with you, and you will enter the **ark**—
6: 19 You are to bring into the **ark** two of all living creatures, male
7: 1 then said to Noah, "Go into the **ark**, you and your whole family,
7: 7 his sons' wives entered the **ark** to escape the waters of the flood.
7: 9 male and female, came to Noah and entered the **ark**, as God had
7: 13 with his wife and the wives of his three sons, entered the **ark**.
7: 15 have the breath of life in them came to Noah and entered the **ark**.
7: 17 as the waters increased they lifted the **ark** high above the earth.
7: 18 on the earth, and the **ark** floated on the surface of the water.
7: 23 from the earth. Only Noah was left, and those with him in the **ark**.
8: 1 the wild animals and the livestock that were with him in the **ark**,
8: 4 on the seventeenth day of the seventh month the **ark** came to rest
8: 6 After forty days Noah opened the window he had made in the **ark**
8: 9 over all the surface of the earth; so it returned to Noah in the **ark**.
8: 9 and took the dove and brought it back to himself in the **ark**.
8: 10 waited seven more days and again sent out the dove from the **ark**.
8: 13 Noah then removed the covering from the **ark** and saw that the
8: 16 "Come out of the **ark**, you and your wife and your sons and their
8: 19 moves on the earth—came out of the **ark**, one kind after another.
9: 10 all the wild animals, all those that came out of the **ark** with you—
9: 18 The sons of Noah who came out of the **ark** were Shem, Ham
Ex 2: 3 she got a papyrus **basket** for him and coated it with tar and pitch.
2: 5 She saw the **basket** among the reeds and sent her slave girl to get

9311 תְּבוּאָה tebû'â, n.f. [42] [√ 995]

harvest [11], crops [6], income [4], produce [4], *untranslated* [1], brings forth [1], comes [1], crop comes in [1], crop [1], enough [1], fruit [1], gain [1], harvesting crops [1], produce [+2446+3655] [1], produced [1], produces [1], product [1], revenue [1], what is taken [1], yield [1], yields returns [1]

Ge 47: 24 But when the **crop comes in**, give a fifth of it to Pharaoh.
Ex 23: 10 "For six years you are to sow your fields and harvest the **crops**,
Lev 19: 25 In this way your **harvest** will be increased. I am the LORD your
23: 39 after you have gathered the **crops** *of* the land, celebrate the festival
25: 3 and for six years prune your vineyards and gather their **crops**.
25: 7 animals in your land. Whatever the land **produces** may be eaten.
25: 12 to be holy for you; eat only **what is taken** directly from the fields.
25: 15 you on the basis of the number of years left for **harvesting crops**.
25: 16 because what he is really selling you is the number of **crops**.
25: 20 we eat in the seventh year if we do not plant or harvest our **crops**?"
25: 21 in the sixth year that the land will yield **enough** for three years.
25: 22 you will eat from the old **crop** and will continue to eat from it until
25: 22 will continue to eat from it until the **harvest** of the ninth year
Nu 18: 30 it will be reckoned to you as the **product** *of* the threshing floor
18: 30 you as the product of the threshing floor or **[RPH]** the winepress.
Dt 14: 22 a tenth of all that your fields **produce** [+2446+3655] each year.
14: 28 bring all the tithes of that year's **produce** and store it in your
16: 15 For the LORD your God will bless you in all your **harvest**
22: 9 crops you plant but also the **fruit** *of* the vineyard will be defiled.
26: 12 When you have finished setting aside a tenth of all your **produce**
33: 14 with the best the sun **brings forth** and the finest the moon can
Jos 5: 12 for the Israelites, but that year they ate of the **produce** *of* Canaan.
2Ki 8: 6 including all the **income** *from* her land from the day she left the
2Ch 31: 5 new wine, oil and honey and all *that* the fields **produced**.
32: 28 He also made buildings to store the **harvest** *of* grain, new wine
Ne 9: 37 its abundant **harvest** goes to the kings you have placed over us.
Job 31: 12 fire that burns to Destruction; it would have uprooted my **harvest**.
Ps 107: 37 sowed fields and planted vineyards that yielded a fruitful **harvest**;
Pr 3: 9 the LORD with your wealth, with the firstfruits of all your **crops**;
3: 14 is more profitable than silver and **yields** better **returns** than gold.
8: 19 fruit is better than fine gold; *what* I **yield** surpasses choice silver.
10: 16 them life, but the **income** *of* the wicked brings them punishment.
14: 4 but from the strength of an ox comes an abundant **harvest**.
15: 6 great treasure, but the **income** *of* the wicked brings them trouble.
16: 8 Better a little with righteousness than much **gain** with injustice.
18: 20 stomach is filled; with the **harvest** *from* his lips he is satisfied.
Ecc 5: 10 [5:9] whoever loves wealth is never satisfied with his **income**.
Isa 23: 3 the harvest of the Nile was the **revenue** *of* Tyre, and she became
30: 23 and the food *that* **comes** *from* the land will be rich and plentiful.
Jer 2: 3 Israel was holy to the LORD, the firstfruits of his **harvest**;
12: 13 So bear the shame of your **harvest** because of the LORD's fierce
Eze 48: 18 west side. Its **produce** will supply food for the workers of the city.

9312 תְּבוּנָה tebûnâ, n.f. [42] [→ 9341; cf. 1067]

understanding [28], ability [3], insight [2], cleverly fashioned [1], detect [1], discernment [1], experienced [+1981+2256] [1], judgment [1], reasoning [1], skillful [1], wisdom [1], words of insight [1]

Ex 31: 3 of God, with skill, **ability** and knowledge in all kinds of crafts—
35: 31 of God, with skill, **ability** and knowledge in all kinds of crafts—
36: 1 **ability** to know how to carry out all the work of constructing the
Dt 32: 28 They are a nation without sense, there is no **discernment** in them.
1Ki 4: 29 [5:9] God gave Solomon wisdom and very great **insight**, and a
7: 14 skilled and **experienced** [+1981+2256] in all kinds of bronze work.
Job 12: 12 found among the aged? Does not long life bring **understanding**?
12: 13 belong wisdom and power; counsel and **understanding** are his.
26: 12 up the sea; by his **wisdom** [K 9341] he cut Rahab to pieces.
32: 11 I waited while you spoke, I listened to your **reasoning**; while you
Ps 49: 3 [49:4] the utterance from my heart will give **understanding**.
78: 72 them with integrity of heart; with **skillful** hands he led them.
136: 5 who by his **understanding** made the heavens, *His love*
147: 5 is our Lord and mighty in power; his **understanding** has no limit.
Pr 2: 2 your ear to wisdom and applying your heart to **understanding**,
2: 3 and if you call out for insight and cry aloud for **understanding**,
2: 6 and from his mouth come knowledge and **understanding**.
2: 11 Discretion will protect you, and **understanding** will guard you.
3: 13 is the man who finds wisdom, the man who gains **understanding**,
3: 19 earth's foundations, by **understanding** he set the heavens in place;
5: 1 pay attention to my wisdom, listen well to my **words of insight**,
8: 1 not wisdom call out? Does not **understanding** raise her voice?
10: 23 in evil conduct, but a man of **understanding** delights in wisdom.
11: 12 his neighbor, but a man of **understanding** holds his tongue.
14: 29 A patient man has great **understanding**, but a quick-tempered man
15: 21 but a man of **understanding** keeps a straight course.
17: 27 with restraint, and a man of **understanding** is even-tempered.
18: 2 A fool finds no pleasure in **understanding** but delights in airing
19: 8 loves his own soul; he who cherishes **understanding** prospers.
20: 5 are deep waters, but a man of **understanding** draws them out.
21: 30 There is no wisdom, no **insight**, no plan that can succeed against
24: 3 a house is built, and through **understanding** it is established;
28: 16 A tyrannical ruler lacks **judgment**, but he who hates ill-gotten gain
Isa 40: 14 taught him knowledge or showed him the path of **understanding**?
40: 28 grow tired or weary, and his **understanding** no one can fathom.
44: 19 stops to think, no one has the knowledge or **understanding** to say,
Jer 10: 12 his wisdom and stretched out the heavens by his **understanding**.
51: 15 his wisdom and stretched out the heavens by his **understanding**.
Eze 28: 4 and **understanding** you have gained wealth for yourself
Hos 13: 2 **cleverly fashioned** images, all of them the work of craftsmen.
Ob 1: 7 eat your bread will set a trap for you, but you will not **detect** it.
1: 8 men of Edom, *men of* **understanding** in the mountains of Esau?

9313 תְּבוּסָה tebûsâ, n.f. [1] [√ 1008]

downfall [1]

2Ch 22: 7 Ahaziah's visit to Joram, God brought about Ahaziah's **downfall**.

9314 תָּבוֹר tābôr, n.pr.loc. [10] [→ 4079; cf. 268]

Tabor [10]

Jos 19: 22 The boundary touched **Tabor**, Shahazumah and Beth Shemesh,
Jdg 4: 6 men of Naphtali and Zebulun and lead the way to Mount **Tabor**.
4: 12 Sisera that Barak son of Abinoam had gone up to Mount **Tabor**,
4: 14 So Barak went down Mount **Tabor**, followed by ten thousand

Jdg 8:18 and Zalmunna, "What kind of men did you kill at **Tabor**?"
1Sa 10: 3 you will go on from there until you reach the great tree of **Tabor**.
1Ch 6:77 [6:62] Kartah, Rimmono and **Tabor**, together with their
Ps 89:12 [89:13] the south; **Tabor** and Hermon sing for joy at your name.
Jer 46:18 "one will come who is like **Tabor** among the mountains, like
Hos 5: 1 You have been a snare at Mizpah, a net spread out on **Tabor**.

9315 תֵּבֵל *tēbēl*, n.f. & m. [36] [√ 1006?]

world [30], earth [3], whole earth [+824] [1], whole world [+824] [1], world's [1]

1Sa 2: 8 of the earth are the LORD's; upon them he has set the **world**.
2Sa 22:16 the foundations of the **earth** laid bare at the rebuke of the LORD,
1Ch 16:30 all the earth! The **world** is firmly established; it cannot be moved.
Job 18:18 is driven from light into darkness and is banished from the **world**.
34:13 him over the earth? Who put him in charge of the whole **world**?
37:12 face of the **whole earth** [+824] to do whatever he commands them.
Ps 9: 8 [9:9] He will judge the **world** in righteousness; he will govern the
18:15 [18:16] and the foundations of the **earth** laid bare at your rebuke,
19: 4 [19:5] out into all the earth, their words to the ends of the **world**.
24: 1 and everything in it, the **world**, and all who live in it;
33: 8 earth fear the LORD; let all the people of the **world** revere him.
50:12 I would not tell you, for the **world** is mine, and all that is in it.
77:18 [77:19] heard in the whirlwind, your lightning lit up the **world**;
89:11 [89:12] also the earth; you founded the **world** and all that is in it.
90: 2 mountains were born or you brought forth the earth and the **world**,
93: 1 with strength. The **world** is firmly established; it cannot be moved.
96:10 The **world** is firmly established, it cannot be moved; he will judge
96:13 He will judge the **world** in righteousness and the peoples in his
97: 4 His lightning lights up the **world**; the earth sees and trembles.
98: 7 Let the sea resound, and everything in it, the **world**, and all who
98: 9 He will judge the **world** in righteousness and the peoples with
Pr 8:26 he made the earth or its fields or any of the dust of the **world**.
8:31 rejoicing in his **whole world** [+824] and delighting in mankind.
Isa 13:11 I will punish the **world** for its evil, the wicked for their sins.
14:17 the man who made the **world** a desert, who overthrew its cities
14:21 not to rise to inherit the land and cover the **earth** with their cities.
18: 3 All you people of the **world**, you who live on the earth, when a
24: 4 The earth dries up and withers, the **world** languishes and withers,
26: 9 come upon the earth, the people of the **world** learn righteousness.
26:18 to the earth; we have not given birth to people of the **world**.
27: 6 Israel will bud and blossom and fill all the **world** with fruit.
34: 1 Let the earth hear, and all that is in it, the **world**, and all that comes
Jer 10:12 he founded the **world** by his wisdom and stretched out the heavens
51:15 he founded the **world** by his wisdom and stretched out the heavens
La 4:12 nor did any of the **world's** people, that enemies and foes could
Na 1: 5 The earth trembles at his presence, the **world** and all who live in it.

9316 תֶּבֶל *tebel*, n.[m.]. [2] [√ 1176]

perversion [2]

Lev 18:23 to an animal to have sexual relations with it; that is a **perversion**.
20:12 What they have done is a **perversion**; their blood will be on their

9317 תֻּבַל *tubal*, n.pr.loc. [8]

Tubal [8]

Ge 10: 2 Gomer, Magog, Madai, Javan, **Tubal**, Meshech and Tiras.
1Ch 1: 5 Gomer, Magog, Madai, Javan, **Tubal**, Meshech and Tiras.
Isa 66:19 and Lydians (famous as archers), to **Tubal** and Greece,
Eze 27:13 " 'Greece, **Tubal** and Meshech traded with you; they exchanged
32:26 "Meshech and **Tubal** are there, with all their hordes around their
38: 2 of the land of Magog, the chief prince of Meshech and **Tubal**;
38: 3 I am against you, O Gog, chief prince of Meshech and **Tubal**.
39: 1 I am against you, O Gog, chief prince of Meshech and **Tubal**.

9318 תַּבְלִית *tablît*, n.f. [1] [√ 1162]

destruction [1]

Isa 10:25 you will end and my wrath will be directed to their **destruction**."

9319 תְּבַלֻּל *tᵉballul*, n.[m.]. [1] [√ 1176]

defect [1]

Lev 21:20 or who is hunchbacked or dwarfed, or who has any eye **defect**,

9320 תֶּבֶן *teben*, n.m. [17] [→ 5495]

straw [17]

Ge 24:25 she added, "We have plenty of **straw** and fodder, as well as room
24:32 **Straw** and fodder were brought for the camels, and water for him
Ex 5: 7 "You are no longer to supply the people with **straw** for making
5: 7 straw for making bricks; let them go and gather their own **straw**.
5:10 "This is what Pharaoh says: 'I will not give you any more **straw**.
5:11 Go and get your own **straw** wherever you can find it, but your
5:12 people scattered all over Egypt to gather stubble to use for **straw**.
5:13 work required of you for each day, just as when you had **straw**."
5:16 Your servants are given no **straw**, yet we are told, 'Make bricks!'
5:18 You will not be given any **straw**, yet you must produce your full
Jdg 19:19 We have both **straw** and fodder for our donkeys and bread
1Ki 4:28 [5:8] and **straw** for the chariot horses and the other horses.
Job 21:18 How often are they like **straw** before the wind, like chaff swept
41:27 [41:19] Iron he treats like **straw** and bronze like rotten wood.
Isa 11: 7 will lie down together, and the lion will eat **straw** like the ox.
65:25 the lamb will feed together, and the lion will eat **straw** like the ox,
Jer 23:28 For what has **straw** to do with grain?" declares the LORD.

9321 תִּבְנִי *tibnî*, n.pr.m. [3]

Tibni [3]

1Ki 16:21 half supported **Tibni** son of Ginath for king, and the other half
16:22 Omri's followers proved stronger than those of **Tibni** son of
16:22 of Tibni son of Ginath. So **Tibni** died and Omri became king.

9322 תַּבְנִית *tabnît*, n.f. [20] [√ 1215]

untranslated [5], plans [3], looked like [2], pattern [2], plan [2], adorn [1], form [1], formed [1], image [1], kinds [1], replica [1]

Ex 25: 9 all **[RPH]** its furnishings exactly like the pattern I will show you.
25: 9 and all its furnishings exactly like the **pattern** I will show you.
25:40 See that you make them according to the **pattern** shown you on
Dt 4:16 an image of any shape, whether **formed** *like* a man or a woman,
4:17 **[RPH]** or like any animal on earth or any bird that flies in the air,
4:17 or like any animal on earth **[RPH]** or any bird that flies in the air,
4:18 **[RPH]** or like any creature that moves along the ground or any
4:18 moves along the ground **[RPH]** or any fish in the waters below.
Jos 22:28 Look at the **replica** *of* the LORD's altar, which our fathers built,
2Ki 16:10 priest a sketch of the altar, with detailed **plans** for its construction.
1Ch 28:11 David gave his son Solomon the **plans** *for* the portico of the
28:12 He gave him the **plans** *of* all that the Spirit had put in his mind for
28:18 He also gave him the **plan** *for* the chariot, that is, the cherubim of
28:19 and he gave me understanding in all the details of the **plan**."
Ps 106:20 They exchanged their Glory for an **image** *of* a bull, which eats
144:12 and our daughters will be like pillars carved to **adorn** a palace.
Isa 44:13 He shapes it in the **form** *of* man, of man in all his glory, that it may
Eze 8: 3 He stretched out *what* **looked like** a hand and took me by the hair
8:10 and I saw portrayed all over the walls all **kinds** *of* crawling things
10: 8 (Under the wings of the cherubim could be seen *what* **looked like**

9323 תַּבְעֵרָה *tab'ērâ*, n.pr.loc. [2] [√ 1277]

Taberah [2]

Nu 11: 3 So that place was called **Taberah**, because fire from the LORD
Dt 9:22 You also made the LORD angry at **Taberah**, at Massah and at

9324 תֵּבֵץ *tēbēṣ*, n.pr.loc. [3] [√ 1288?]

Thebez [2], it[s] [1]

Jdg 9:50 Next Abimelech went to **Thebez** and besieged it and captured it.
9:50 Next Abimelech went to Thebez and besieged **it**[s] and captured it.
2Sa 11:21 upper millstone on him from the wall, so that he died in **Thebez**?

9325 תִּגְלַת פִּלְאֶסֶר *tiglat pil'eser*, n.pr.m. [3] [cf. 9433]

Tiglath-Pileser [3]

2Ki 15:29 **Tiglath-Pileser** king of Assyria came and took Ijon, Abel Beth
16: 7 Ahaz sent messengers to say to **Tiglath-Pileser** king of Assyria,
16:10 King Ahaz went to Damascus to meet **Tiglath-Pileser** king of

9326 תַּגְמוּל *tagmûl*, n.m. [1] [√ 1694]

goodness [1]

Ps 116:12 How can I repay the LORD for all his **goodness** to me?

9327 תִּגְרָה *tigrâ*, n.f. [1] [√ 1741]

blow [1]

Ps 39:10 [39:11] from me; I am overcome by the **blow** *of* your hand.

9328 תֹּגַרְמָה *tōgarmâ*, n.pr.loc. [2]

Togarmah [2]

Ge 10: 3 The sons of Gomer: Ashkenaz, Riphath and **Togarmah**.
1Ch 1: 6 The sons of Gomer: Ashkenaz, Riphath and **Togarmah**.

9329 תִּדְהָר *tidhār*, n.[m.]. [2]

fir [2]

Isa 41:19 I will set pines in the wasteland, the **fir** and the cypress together,
60:13 the pine, the **fir** and the cypress together, to adorn the place of my

9330 תַּדְמֹר tadmōr, n.pr.loc. [2]

Tadmor [2]

1Ki 9:18 Baalath, and **Tadmor** [K 9471] in the desert, within his land,
2Ch 8:4 He also built up **Tadmor** in the desert and all the store cities he

9331 תִּדְעָל tid'āl, n.pr.m. [2]

Tidal [2]

Ge 14:1 of Ellasar, Kedorlaomer king of Elam and **Tidal** king of Goiim
14:9 **Tidal** king of Goiim, Amraphel king of Shinar and Arioch king of

9332 תֹּהוּ tōhû, n.m. [20]

nothing [3], empty [2], formless [2], waste [2], barren [1], chaos [1], confusion [1], empty space [1], false [1], in vain [1], ruined [1], useless idols [1], useless [1], wasteland [1], worthless [1]

Ge 1:2 Now the earth was **formless** and empty, darkness was over the
Dt 32:10 In a desert land he found him, in a **barren** and howling waste.
1Sa 12:21 Do not turn away after **useless idols**. They can do you no good,
12:21 do you no good, nor can they rescue you, because they are **useless**.
Job 6:18 aside from their routes; they go up into the **wasteland** and perish.
12:24 their reason; he sends them wandering through a trackless **waste**.
26:7 He spreads out the northern ⌞skies⌟ over **empty space**; he suspends
Ps 107:40 pours contempt on nobles made them wander in a trackless **waste**.
Isa 24:10 The **ruined** city lies desolate; the entrance to every house is barred.
29:21 in court and with **false** testimony deprive the innocent of justice.
34:11 God will stretch out over Edom the measuring line of **chaos**
40:17 they are regarded by him as **worthless** and less than nothing.
40:23 princes to naught and reduces the rulers of this world to **nothing**.
41:29 deeds amount to nothing; their images are but wind and **confusion**.
44:9 All who make idols are **nothing**, and the things they treasure are
45:18 he did not create it to be **empty**, but formed it to be inhabited—
45:19 I have not said to Jacob's descendants, 'Seek me **in vain**.'
49:4 to no purpose; I have spent my strength in vain and for **nothing**.
59:4 They rely on **empty** arguments and speak lies; they conceive
Jer 4:23 I looked at the earth, and it was **formless** and empty; and at the

9333 תְּהוֹם tᵉhôm, n.f. & m. [36]

deep [19], depths [6], deep waters [3], deep springs [2], ocean depths [2], deeps [1], oceans [1], seas [1], springs [1]

Ge 1:2 and empty, darkness was over the surface of the **deep**,
7:11 on that day all the springs of the great **deep** burst forth,
8:2 Now the springs of the **deep** and the floodgates of the heavens had
49:25 blessings of the **deep** that lies below, blessings of the breast
Ex 15:5 The **deep waters** have covered them; they sank to the depths like a
15:8 firm like a wall; the **deep waters** congealed in the heart of the sea.
Dt 8:7 and pools of water, with **springs** flowing in the valleys and hills;
33:13 dew from heaven above and with the **deep waters** that lie below;
Job 28:14 The **deep** says, 'It is not in me'; the sea says, 'It is not with me.'
38:16 to the springs of the sea or walked in the recesses of the **deep**?
38:30 become hard as stone, when the surface of the **deep** is frozen?
41:32 [41:24] glistening wake; one would think the **deep** had white hair.
Ps 33:7 the waters of the sea into jars; he puts the **deep** into storehouses.
36:6 [36:7] like the mighty mountains, your justice like the great **deep**.
42:7 [42:8] **Deep** calls to deep in the roar of your waterfalls; all your
42:7 [42:8] Deep calls to **deep** in the roar of your waterfalls; all your
71:20 life again; from the **depths** *of* the earth you will again bring me up.
77:16 [77:17] saw you and writhed; the very **depths** were convulsed.
78:15 rocks in the desert and gave them water as abundant as the **seas**;
104:6 You covered it with the **deep** as with a garment; the waters stood
106:9 and it dried up; he led them through the **depths** as through a desert.
107:26 They mounted up to the heavens and went down to the **depths**;
135:6 in the heavens and on the earth, in the seas and all their **depths**.
148:7 from the earth, you great sea creatures and all **ocean depths**,
Pr 3:20 by his knowledge the **deeps** were divided, and the clouds let drop
8:24 When there were no **oceans**, I was given birth, when there were no
8:27 in place, when he marked out the horizon on the face of the **deep**,
8:28 the clouds above and fixed securely the fountains of the **deep**,
Isa 51:10 Was it not you who dried up the sea, the waters of the great **deep**,
63:13 who led them through the **depths**? Like a horse in open country,
Eze 26:19 when I bring the **ocean depths** over you and its vast waters cover
31:4 The waters nourished it, **deep springs** made it grow tall; their
31:15 down to the grave I covered the **deep springs** with mourning for it;
Am 7:4 judgment by fire; it dried up the great **deep** and devoured the land.
Jnh 2:5 [2:6] engulfing waters threatened me, *the* **deep** surrounded me;
Hab 3:10 of water swept by; the **deep** roared and lifted its waves on high.

9334 תָּהֳלָה tohºlâ, n.f. [1]

error [1]

Job 4:18 places no trust in his servants, if he charges his angels with **error**,

9335 תְּהִלָּה tᵉhillâ, n.f. [57] [√ 2146]

praise [46], praised [2], praises [2], boast [1], glory [1], hymn of praise [1], praiseworthy deeds [1], psalm of praise [1], renown [1], theme of praise [1]

Ex 15:11 majestic in holiness, awesome in **glory**, working wonders?
Dt 10:21 He is your **praise**; he is your God, who performed for you those
26:19 He has declared that he will set you in **praise**, fame and honor high
1Ch 16:35 give thanks to your holy name, that we may glory in your **praise**."
2Ch 20:22 As they began to sing and **praise**, the LORD set ambushes
Ne 9:5 glorious name, and may it be exalted above all blessing and **praise**.
12:46 the singers and for the songs of **praise** and thanksgiving to God.
Ps 9:14 [9:15] that I may declare your **praises** in the gates of the Daughter
22:3 [22:4] are enthroned as the Holy One; you are the **praise** *of* Israel.
22:25 [22:26] From you comes the **theme of** my **praise** in the great
33:1 you righteous; it is fitting for the upright to **praise** him.
34:1 [34:2] LORD at all times; his **praise** will always be on my lips.
35:28 will speak of your righteousness and of your **praises** all day long.
40:3 [40:4] put a new song in my mouth, a **hymn of praise** to our God.
48:10 [48:11] O God, your **praise** reaches to the ends of the earth;
51:15 [51:17] open my lips, and my mouth will declare your **praise**.
65:1 [65:2] **Praise** awaits you, O God, in Zion; to you our vows will be
66:2 Sing the glory of his name; make his **praise** glorious!
66:8 Praise our God, O peoples, let the sound of his **praise** be heard;
71:6 brought me forth from my mother's womb. I will ever **praise** you.
71:8 My mouth is filled with your **praise**, declaring your splendor all
71:14 I will always have hope; I will **praise** you more and more.
78:4 we will tell the next generation the **praiseworthy deeds** *of* the
79:13 from generation to generation we will recount your **praise**.
100:4 Enter his gates with thanksgiving and his courts with **praise**;
102:21 [102:22] will be declared in Zion and his **praise** in Jerusalem
106:2 proclaim the mighty acts of the LORD or fully declare his **praise**?
106:12 Then they believed his promises and sang his **praise**.
106:47 we may give thanks to your holy name and glory in your **praise**.
109:1 O God, whom I **praise**, do not remain silent,
111:10 precepts have good understanding. *To* him *belongs* eternal **praise**.
119:171 May my lips overflow with **praise**, for you teach me your decrees.
145:T [145:1] A **psalm of praise**. Of David.
145:21 My mouth will speak *in* **praise** *of* the LORD. Let every creature
147:1 to sing praises to our God, how pleasant and fitting to **praise** him!
148:14 the **praise** of all his saints, of Israel, the people close to his heart.
149:1 to the LORD a new song, his **praise** in the assembly of the saints.
Isa 42:8 my name! I will not give my glory to another or my **praise** to idols.
42:10 his **praise** from the ends of the earth, you who go down to the sea,
42:12 give glory to the LORD and proclaim his **praise** in the islands.
43:21 the people I formed for myself that they may proclaim my **praise**.
48:9 for the sake of my **praise** I hold it back from you, so as not to cut
60:6 and incense and proclaiming the **praise** *of* the LORD.
60:18 but you will call your walls Salvation and your gates **Praise**.
61:3 of mourning, and a garment of **praise** instead of a spirit of despair.
61:11 will make righteousness and **praise** spring up before all nations.
62:7 till he establishes Jerusalem and makes her the **praise** of the earth.
63:7 of the LORD, the *deeds for which* he is to be **praised**,
Jer 13:11 'to be my people for my renown and **praise** and honor.
17:14 save me and I will be saved, for you are the *one* I **praise**.
33:9 **praise** and honor before all nations on earth that hear of all the
48:2 Moab will be **praised** no more; in Heshbon men will plot her
49:25 Why has the city of **renown** not been abandoned, the town in
51:41 Sheshach will be captured, the **boast** *of* the whole earth seized!
Hab 3:3 His glory covered the heavens and his **praise** filled the earth.
Zep 3:19 I will give them **praise** and honor in every land where they were
3:20 **praise** among all the peoples of the earth when I restore your

9336 תַּהֲלוּכָה tahªlûkâ, n.f. [1 / 0] [√ 2143]

Ne 12:31 One *was to* proceed [BHS ***processions***; NIV 2143] on top of the

9337 תַּהְפֻּכוֹת tahpukôt, n.f. [10] [√ 2200]

perverse [6], confusing things [1], deceit [1], perverseness [1], perversity [1]

Dt 32:20 for they are a **perverse** generation, children who are unfaithful.
Pr 2:12 the ways of wicked men, from men whose words are **perverse**,
2:14 delight in doing wrong and rejoice in the **perverseness** *of* evil,
6:14 who plots evil with **deceit** in his heart—he always stirs up
8:13 I hate pride and arrogance, evil behavior and **perverse** speech.
10:31 brings forth wisdom, but a **perverse** tongue will be cut out.
10:32 what is fitting, but the mouth of the wicked only *what* is **perverse**.
16:28 A **perverse** man stirs up dissension, and a gossip separates close
16:30 He who winks with his eye is plotting **perversity**; he who purses
23:33 will see strange sights and your mind imagine **confusing things**.

9338 תָּו *tāw*, n.m. [3] [√ 9344]
mark [1], put a mark [+9344] [1], sign [1]
Job 31:35 **I sign** now my defense—let the Almighty answer me; let my
Eze 9: 4 and **put a mark** [+9344] on the foreheads of those who grieve
9: 6 and children, but do not touch anyone who has the **mark**.

9339 תּוֹאֲמִים *tôʾamîm*, n.m. [6] [→ 9296, 9298]
twin [3], double [2], twins [1]
Ge 25:24 time came for her to give birth, there were **twin** *boys* in her womb.
38:27 time came for her to give birth, there were **twin** *boys* in her womb.
Ex 26:24 At these two corners they must be **double** from the bottom all the
36:29 At these two corners the frames were **double** from the bottom all
SS 4: 5 like **twin** fawns *of* a gazelle that browse among the lilies.
7: 3 [7:4] Your breasts are like two fawns, **twins** *of* a gazelle.

9340 תּוּבַל קַיִן *tûbal qayin*, n.pr.m. [2] [√ 7803]
Tubal-Cain [1], Tubal-Cain's [1]
Ge 4:22 Zillah also had a son, **Tubal-Cain**, who forged all kinds of tools
4:22 of tools out of bronze and iron. **Tubal-Cain's** sister was Naamah.

9341 תּוּבָנָה *tûbnâ*, n.f. [0] [√ 9312; cf. 1067]
Job 26:12 [by his **wisdom** [K; see Q 9312] he cut Rahab to pieces.]

9342 תּוּגָה *tûgâ*, n.f. [4] [√ 3324]
grief [3], sorrow [1]
Ps 119:28 My soul is weary with **sorrow**; strengthen me according to your
Pr 10: 1 son brings joy to his father, but a foolish son **grief** *to* his mother.
14:13 Even in laughter the heart may ache, and joy may end in **grief**.
17:21 To have a fool for a son brings **grief**; there is no joy for the father

9343 תּוֹדָה *tôdâ*, n.f. [32] [√ 3344]
thanksgiving [9], thank offerings [8], thank [4], praise [2], songs of thanksgiving [2], choir [1], choirs that gave thanks [1], choirs to give thanks [1], confession [1], expression of thankfulness [1], giving thanks [1], thank offering [1]
Lev 7:12 " 'If he offers it as an **expression of thankfulness**, then along with
7:12 along with this **thank** offering he is to offer cakes of bread made
7:13 Along with his fellowship offering of **thanksgiving** he is to present
7:15 The meat of his fellowship offering of **thanksgiving** must be eaten
22:29 "When you sacrifice a **thank** offering to the LORD, sacrifice it in
Jos 7:19 glory to the LORD, the God of Israel, and give him the **praise**.
2Ch 29:31 bring sacrifices and **thank offerings** to the temple of the LORD."
29:31 So the assembly brought sacrifices and **thank offerings**, and all
33:16 and sacrificed fellowship offerings and **thank offerings** on it,
Ezr 10:11 Now make **confession** to the LORD, the God of your fathers,
Ne 12:27 to celebrate joyfully the dedication with **songs of thanksgiving**
12:31 I also assigned two large **choirs to give thanks**. One was to
12:38 The second **choir** proceeded in the opposite direction. I followed
12:40 The two **choirs that gave thanks** then took their places in the
Ps 26: 7 proclaiming aloud your **praise** and telling of all your wonderful
42: 4 [42:5] shouts of joy and **thanksgiving** among the festive throng.
50:14 Sacrifice **thank offerings** to God, fulfill your vows to the Most
50:23 He who sacrifices **thank offerings** honors me, and he prepares the
56:12 [56:13] to you, O God; I will present my **thank offerings** to you.
69:30 [69:31] God's name in song and glorify him with **thanksgiving**.
95: 2 Let us come before him with **thanksgiving** and extol him with
100: T [100:1] A psalm. For **giving thanks**.
100: 4 Enter his gates with **thanksgiving** and his courts with praise;
107:22 Let them sacrifice **thank** offerings and tell of his works with songs
116:17 I will sacrifice a **thank** offering to you and call on the name of the
147: 7 Sing to the LORD with **thanksgiving**; make music to our God on
Isa 51: 3 will be found in her, **thanksgiving** and the sound of singing.
Jer 17:26 incense and **thank offerings** to the house of the LORD.
30:19 From them will come **songs of thanksgiving** and the sound of
33:11 the voices of those who bring **thank offerings** to the house of the
Am 4: 5 Burn leavened bread as a **thank offering** and brag about your
Jnh 2: 9 [2:10] I, with a song of **thanksgiving**, will sacrifice to you.

9344 תָּוָה *tāwâ*[1], v.den. [2] [→ 9295, 9338; cf. 204, 9292]
making marks [1], put a mark [+9338] [1]
1Sa 21:13 [21:14] [D] **making marks** on the doors of the gate and letting
Eze 9: 4 [G] **put a mark** [+9338] on the foreheads of those who grieve

9345 [2]תָּוָה *tāwâ*[2], v. [1]
vexed [1]
Ps 78:41 [G] they put God to the test; *they* **vexed** the Holy One of Israel.

9346 תּוֹחַ *tôaḥ*, n.pr.m. [1] [cf. 9375]
Toah [1]
1Ch 6:34 [6:19] the son of Jeroham, the son of Eliel, the son of **Toah**,

9347 תּוֹחֶלֶת *tôḥelet*, n.f. [5] [√ 3498]
hope [2], expected [1], hoped [1], prospect [1]
Job 41: 9 [41:1] Any **hope** *of* subduing him is false; the mere sight of him is
Pr 10:28 The **prospect** *of* the righteous is joy, but the hopes of the wicked
11: 7 hope perishes; *all* he **expected** *from* his power comes to nothing.
13:12 **Hope** deferred makes the heart sick, but a longing fulfilled is a tree
La 3:18 "My splendor is gone and *all that* I had **hoped** from the LORD."

9348 תָּוֶךְ *tāwek*, subst. [418] [→ 2250, 9399] See Select Index
among [+928] [111], in [+928] [45], middle [27], *untranslated* [23], with [+928] [17], from [+4946] [16], inside [+928] [15], within [+928] [15], midst [13], out of [+4946] [13], among [12], center [11], into [+448] [11], into [+928] [9], through [+928] [8], along with [+928] [6], within [5], of [+4946] [4], there[s] [+928+2023] [4], between [+928] [3], from [+928] [2], from out of [+4946] [2], heart [2], inside [+448] [2], intersecting [+928] [2], presence [2], throughout [+928] [2], along [+928] [1], among [+448] [1], as one [+928] [1], at [+928] [1], branch of [+4946] [1], by [+4946] [1], by [+928] [1], central [1], centrally located in [+928] [1], do away with [+4946+6073] [1], entered [+928+995] [1], entering [+928+995] [1], flashed back and forth [+928+4374] [1], for [+928] [1], gone from [+4946] [1], in [+4946] [1], include [+928] [1], inner part [1], interior [1], joined in [+928] [1], leave [+3718+4946] [1], left [+4946+7756] [1], like [+928] [1], of [+928] [1], of all [+4946] [1], on [+928] [1], on board [+928] [1], onto [+448] [1], over [+928] [1], ranks [1], surrounded by [+928] [1], there[s] [+928+2257] [1], there[s] [+928+4392] [1], to [+448] [1], two [1], within [+928+5055] [1]

9349 תּוֹכֵחָה *tôkēḥâ*, n.f. [4] [√ 3519]
rebuke [2], punishment [1], reckoning [1]
2Ki 19: 3 This day is a day of distress and **rebuke** and disgrace, as when
Ps 149: 7 to inflict vengeance on the nations and **punishment** on the peoples,
Isa 37: 3 This day is a day of distress and **rebuke** and disgrace, as when
Hos 5: 9 Ephraim will be laid waste on the day of **reckoning**.

9350 תּוֹכַחַת *tôkaḥat*, n.f. [24] [√ 3519]
correction [8], rebuke [8], argument [1], arguments [1], complaint [1], corrections [1], punish [1], punished [1], rebukes [1], reply [1]
Job 13: 6 Hear now my **argument**; listen to the plea of my lips.
23: 4 state my case before him and fill my mouth with **arguments**.
Ps 38:14 [38:15] man who does not hear, whose mouth can offer no **reply**.
39:11 [39:12] You **rebuke** and discipline men for their sin; you
73:14 long I have been plagued; I have been **punished** every morning.
Pr 1:23 If you had responded to my **rebuke**, I would have poured out my
1:25 since you ignored all my advice and would not accept my **rebuke**,
1:30 since they would not accept my advice and spurned my **rebuke**,
3:11 not despise the LORD's discipline and do not resent his **rebuke**,
5:12 "How I hated discipline! How my heart spurned **correction**!
6:23 is a light, and the **corrections** *of* discipline are the way to life,
10:17 the way to life, but whoever ignores **correction** leads others astray.
12: 1 discipline loves knowledge, but he who hates **correction** is stupid.
13:18 to poverty and shame, but whoever heeds **correction** is honored.
15: 5 father's discipline, but whoever heeds **correction** shows prudence.
15:10 awaits him who leaves the path; he who hates **correction** will die.
15:31 He who listens to a life-giving **rebuke** will be at home among the
15:32 but whoever heeds **correction** gains understanding.
27: 5 Better is open **rebuke** than hidden love.
29: 1 A man who remains stiff-necked after many **rebukes** will suddenly
29:15 The rod of **correction** imparts wisdom, but a child left to himself
Eze 5:15 on you in anger and in wrath and with stinging **rebuke**.
25:17 carry out great vengeance on them and **punish** them in my wrath.
Hab 2: 1 he will say to me, and what answer I am to give to this **complaint**.

9351 תּוֹלָד *tôlād*, n.pr.loc. [1] [√ 3528?; cf. 557]
Tolad [1]
1Ch 4:29 Bilhah, Ezem, **Tolad**,

9352 תּוֹלְדוֹת *tôlēdôt*, n.f.pl. [39] [√ 3528]
records [14], account [10], listed genealogy [3], genealogical records [2], genealogy [2], account of line [1], account of the family [1], birth [1], descendants [1], family line [1], genealogical record [1], lines of descent [1], order of birth [1]
Ge 2: 4 This is the **account** *of* the heavens and the earth when they were
5: 1 This is the written **account of** Adam's **line**. When God created
6: 9 This is the **account** *of* Noah. Noah was a righteous man,

Ge 10: 1 This is the **account** *of* Shem, Ham and Japheth, Noah's sons,
10: 32 according to their **lines of descent**, within their nations.
11: 10 This is the **account** *of* Shem. Two years after the flood,
11: 27 This is the **account** *of* Terah. Terah became the father of Abram,
25: 12 This is the **account** *of* Abraham's son Ishmael, whom Sarah's
25: 13 the names of the sons of Ishmael, listed in the **order of** their **birth**:
25: 19 This is the **account** *of* Abraham's son Isaac. Abraham became the
36: 1 This is the **account** *of* Esau (that is, Edom).
36: 9 This is the **account** *of* Esau the father of the Edomites in the hill
37: 2 This is the **account** *of* Jacob. Joseph, a young man of seventeen,
Ex 6: 16 were the names of the sons of Levi according to their **records**:
6: 19 These were the clans of Levi according to their **records**.
28: 10 in the order of their **birth**—six names on one stone and the
Nu 1: 20 one by one, according to the **records** *of* their clans and families.
1: 22 one by one, according to the **records** *of* their clans and families.
1: 24 by name, according to the **records** *of* their clans and families.
1: 26 by name, according to the **records** *of* their clans and families.
1: 28 by name, according to the **records** *of* their clans and families.
1: 30 by name, according to the **records** *of* their clans and families.
1: 32 by name, according to the **records** *of* their clans and families.
1: 34 by name, according to the **records** *of* their clans and families.
1: 36 by name, according to the **records** *of* their clans and families.
1: 38 by name, according to the **records** *of* their clans and families.
1: 40 by name, according to the **records** *of* their clans and families.
1: 42 by name, according to the **records** *of* their clans and families.
3: 1 This is the **account of the family** *of* Aaron and Moses at the time
Ru 4: 18 This, then, is the **family line** *of* Perez: Perez was the father of
1Ch 1: 29 These were their **descendants**: Nebaioth the firstborn of Ishmael,
5: 7 relatives by clans, listed according to their **genealogical records**:
7: 2 the descendants of Tola listed as fighting men in their **genealogy**
7: 4 According to their family **genealogy**, they had 36,000 men ready
7: 9 Their **genealogical record** listed the heads of families and 20,200
8: 28 chiefs as **listed** in their **genealogy**, and they lived in Jerusalem.
9: 9 people from Benjamin, as **listed** in their **genealogy**, numbered 956.
9: 34 chiefs as **listed** in their **genealogy**, and they lived in Jerusalem.
26: 31 Jeriah was their chief according to the **genealogical records** of

9353 תּוֹלוֹן *tôlôn*, n.pr.m. [0] [cf. 9400]

1Ch 4: 20 [Amnon, Rinnah, Ben-Hanan and **Tilon**. [K; see Q 9400]]

9354 תּוֹלָל *tôlāl*, n.m. [1] [√ 2143]

tormentors [1]

Ps 137: 3 [A] asked us for songs, our **tormentors** demanded songs of joy;

9355 תּוֹלָע¹ *tôlā'*¹, n.[m.]. [2] [→ 9356, 9357, 9358, 9443]

crimson [1], purple [1]

Isa 1: 18 as snow; though they are red as **crimson**, they shall be like wool.
La 4: 5 in the streets. Those nurtured in **purple** now lie on ash heaps.

9356 תּוֹלָע² *tôlā'*², n.pr.m. [6] [→ 9358; cf. 9355]

Tola [6]

Ge 46: 13 The sons of Issachar: **Tola**, Puah, Jashub and Shimron.
Nu 26: 23 through **Tola**, the Tolaite clan; through Puah, the Puite clan;
Jdg 10: 1 of Issachar, **Tola** son of Puah, the son of Dodo, rose to save Israel.
1Ch 7: 1 The sons of Issachar: **Tola**, Puah, Jashub and Shimron—four in all.
7: 2 The sons of **Tola**: Uzzi, Rephaiah, Jeriel, Jahmai, Ibsam
7: 2 the descendants of **Tola** listed as fighting men in their genealogy

9357 תּוֹלֵעָה *tôlē'â*, n.f. [41] [√ 9355]

scarlet yarn [+9106] [31], worm [5], worms [2], maggots [1], scarlet [+9106] [1], scarlet wool [+9106] [1]

Ex 16: 20 of it until morning, but it was full of **maggots** and began to smell.
25: 4 blue, purple and **scarlet** [+9106] **yarn** and fine linen; goat hair;
26: 1 of finely twisted linen and blue, purple and **scarlet** [+9106] **yarn**,
26: 31 of blue, purple and **scarlet** [+9106] **yarn** and finely twisted linen,
26: 36 purple and **scarlet** [+9106] **yarn** and finely twisted linen—
27: 16 purple and **scarlet** [+9106] **yarn** and finely twisted linen—
28: 5 and blue, purple and **scarlet** [+9106] **yarn**, and fine linen.
28: 6 the ephod of gold, and of blue, purple and **scarlet** [+9106] **yarn**,
28: 8 made with gold, and with blue, purple and **scarlet** [+9106] **yarn**,
28: 15 of gold, and of blue, purple and **scarlet** [+9106] **yarn**, and of finely
28: 33 purple and **scarlet** [+9106] **yarn** around the hem of the robe,
35: 6 blue, purple and **scarlet** [+9106] **yarn** and fine linen; goat hair;
35: 23 purple or **scarlet** [+9106] **yarn** or fine linen, or goat hair, ram
35: 25 she had spun—blue, purple or **scarlet** [+9106] **yarn** or fine linen.
35: 35 purple and **scarlet** [+9106] **yarn** and fine linen, and weavers—
36: 8 of finely twisted linen and blue, purple and **scarlet** [+9106] **yarn**,
36: 35 of blue, purple and **scarlet** [+9106] **yarn** and finely twisted linen,
36: 37 purple and **scarlet** [+9106] **yarn** and finely twisted linen—
38: 18 purple and **scarlet** [+9106] **yarn** and finely twisted linen—
38: 23 in blue, purple and **scarlet** [+9106] **yarn** and fine linen.)
39: 1 **scarlet** [+9106] **yarn** they made woven garments for ministering in
39: 2 of blue, purple and **scarlet** [+9106] **yarn**, and of finely twisted
39: 3 into the blue, purple and **scarlet** [+9106] **yarn** and fine linen—
39: 5 made with gold, and with blue, purple and **scarlet** [+9106] **yarn**,
39: 8 of gold, and of blue, purple and **scarlet** [+9106] **yarn**, and of finely
39: 24 purple and **scarlet** [+9106] **yarn** and finely twisted linen around
39: 29 of finely twisted linen and blue, purple and **scarlet** [+9106] **yarn**—
Lev 14: 4 **scarlet** [+9106] **yarn** and hyssop be brought for the one to be
14: 6 with the cedar wood, the **scarlet** [+9106] **yarn** and the hyssop,
14: 49 two birds and some cedar wood, **scarlet** [+9106] **yarn** and hyssop.
14: 51 cedar wood, the hyssop, the **scarlet** [+9106] **yarn** and the live bird,
14: 52 the cedar wood, the hyssop and the **scarlet** [+9106] **yarn**.
Nu 4: 8 Over these they are to spread a **scarlet** [+9106] cloth, cover that
19: 6 hyssop and **scarlet** [+9106] **wool** and throw them onto the burning
Dt 28: 39 drink the wine or gather the grapes, because **worms** will eat them.
Job 25: 6 who is but a maggot—a son of man, who is only a **worm**!"
Ps 22: 6 [22:7] I am a **worm** and not a man, scorned by men and despised
Isa 14: 11 maggots are spread out beneath you and **worms** cover you.
41: 14 Do not be afraid, O **worm** Jacob, O little Israel, for I myself will
66: 24 their **worm** will not die, nor will their fire be quenched, and they
Jnh 4: 7 at dawn the next day God provided a **worm**, which chewed the

9358 תּוֹלָעִי *tôlā'î*, a.g. [1] [√ 9356; cf. 9355]

Tolaite [1]

Nu 26: 23 through Tola, the **Tolaite** clan; through Puah, the Puite clan;

9359 תּוֹעֵבָה *tô'ēbâ*, n.f. [117] [√ 9493?]

detestable practices [30], detestable [19], detestable things [18], detests [13], detestable thing [7], detest [6], detestable idols [6], detestable ways [3], things detestable [3], loathsome [2], things[s] [2], abhors [1], abominations [1], detestable god [1], detestable offense [1], detestable sins [1], repulsive [1], thing detestable [1], what detestable [1]

Ge 43: 32 could not eat with Hebrews, for that is **detestable** to Egyptians.
46: 34 of Goshen, for all shepherds are **detestable** *to* the Egyptians."
Ex 8: 26 [8:22] the LORD our God would be **detestable** *to* the Egyptians.
8: 26 [8:22] And if we offer sacrifices that are **detestable** in their eyes,
Lev 18: 22 not lie with a man as one lies with a woman; that is **detestable**.
18: 26 living among you must not do any of these **detestable things**,
18: 27 for all these **things**[s] were done by the people who lived in the land
18: 29 " 'Everyone who does any of these **detestable things**—such
18: 30 do not follow any of the **detestable** customs that were practiced
20: 13 one lies with a woman, both of them have done **what is detestable**.
Dt 7: 25 will be ensnared by it, for it is **detestable** *to* the LORD your God.
7: 26 Do not bring a **detestable thing** into your house or you, like it,
12: 31 they do all kinds of **detestable things** the LORD hates.
13: 14 [13:15] it has been proved that this **detestable thing** has been
14: 3 Do not eat any **detestable thing**.
17: 1 has any defect or flaw in it, for that would be **detestable** *to* him.
17: 4 it has been proved that this **detestable thing** has been done in
18: 9 do not learn to imitate the **detestable ways** *of* the nations there.
18: 12 Anyone who does these things is **detestable** *to* the LORD,
18: 12 because of these **detestable practices** the LORD your God will
20: 18 they will teach you to follow all the **detestable things** they do in
22: 5 for the LORD your God **detests** anyone who does this.
23: 18 [23:19] because the LORD your God **detests** them both.
24: 4 been defiled. That would be **detestable** in the eyes of the LORD.
25: 16 For the LORD your God **detests** anyone who does these things,
27: 15 a **thing detestable** *to* the LORD, the work of the craftsman's
32: 16 their foreign gods and angered him with their **detestable idols**.
1Ki 14: 24 the people engaged in all the **detestable practices** *of* the nations
2Ki 16: 3 following the **detestable ways** *of* the nations the LORD had
21: 2 following the **detestable practices** *of* the nations the LORD had
21: 11 "Manasseh king of Judah has committed these **detestable sins**.
23: 13 and for Molech the **detestable god** *of* the people of Ammon.
2Ch 28: 3 following the **detestable ways** *of* the nations the LORD had
33: 2 following the **detestable practices** *of* the nations the LORD had
34: 33 Josiah removed all the **detestable idols** from all the territory
36: 8 the **detestable things** he did and all that was found against him,
36: 14 following all the **detestable practices** *of* the nations and defiling
Ezr 9: 1 from the neighboring peoples with their **detestable practices**,
9: 11 By their **detestable practices** they have filled it with their impurity
9: 14 with the peoples who commit such **detestable practices**?
Ps 88: 8 [88:9] my closest friends and have made me **repulsive** to them.
Pr 3: 32 for the LORD **detests** a perverse man but takes the upright into
6: 16 are six things the LORD hates, seven that are **detestable** *to* him:
8: 7 My mouth speaks what is true, for my lips **detest** wickedness.
11: 1 The LORD **abhors** dishonest scales, but accurate weights are his
11: 20 The LORD **detests** men of perverse heart but he delights in those
12: 22 The LORD **detests** lying lips, but he delights in men who are
13: 19 fulfilled is sweet to the soul, but fools **detest** turning from evil.

Pr 15: 8 The LORD **detests** the sacrifice of the wicked, but the prayer of
15: 9 The LORD **detests** the way of the wicked but he loves those who
15:26 The LORD **detests** the thoughts of the wicked, but those of the
16: 5 The LORD **detests** all the proud of heart. Be sure of this:
16:12 Kings **detest** wrongdoing, for a throne is established through
17:15 and condemning the innocent—the LORD **detests** them both.
20:10 and differing measures—the LORD **detests** them both.
20:23 The LORD **detests** differing weights, and dishonest scales do not
21:27 The sacrifice of the wicked is **detestable**—how much more
24: 9 The schemes of folly are sin, and men **detest** a mocker.
26:25 do not believe him, for seven **abominations** fill his heart.
28: 9 anyone turns a deaf ear to the law, even his prayers are **detestable**.
29:27 The righteous **detest** the dishonest; the wicked detest the upright.
29:27 The righteous detest the dishonest; the wicked **detest** the upright.
Isa 1:13 Your incense is **detestable** to me. New Moons, Sabbaths
41:24 works are utterly worthless; he who chooses you is **detestable**.
44:19 and I ate. Shall I make a **detestable thing** from what is left?
Jer 2: 7 and defiled my land and made my inheritance **detestable**.
6:15 Are they ashamed of their **loathsome** conduct? No, they have no
7:10 and say, "We are safe"—safe to do all these **detestable things**?
8:12 Are they ashamed of their **loathsome** conduct? No, they have no
16:18 and have filled my inheritance with their **detestable idols**."
32:35 that they should do such a **detestable thing** and so make Judah sin.
44: 4 the prophets, who said, 'Do not do this **detestable** thing that I hate!'
44:22 endure your wicked actions and the **detestable things** you did,
Eze 5: 9 Because of all your **detestable idols**, I will do to you what I have
5:11 my sanctuary with all your vile images and **detestable practices**,
6: 9 for the evil they have done and for all their **detestable practices**.
6:11 of all the wicked and **detestable practices** *of* the house of Israel,
7: 3 to your conduct and repay you for all your **detestable practices**.
7: 4 you for your conduct and the **detestable practices** among you.
7: 8 to your conduct and repay you for all your **detestable practices**.
7: 9 with your conduct and the **detestable practices** among you.
7:20 and used it to make their **detestable** idols and vile images.
8: 6 the utterly **detestable things** the house of Israel is doing here,
8: 6 But you will see **things** *that* are even more **detestable**."
8: 9 and see the wicked and **detestable things** they are doing here."
8:13 "You will see them doing **things** *that* are even more **detestable**."
8:15 You will see **things** *that* are even more **detestable** than this."
8:17 the house of Judah to do the **detestable things** they are doing here?
9: 4 and lament over all the **detestable things** that are done in it."
11:18 will return to it and remove all its vile images and **detestable idols**.
11:21 whose hearts are devoted to their vile images and **detestable idols**,
12:16 they go they may acknowledge all their **detestable practices**.
14: 6 Turn from your idols and renounce all your **detestable practices**!
16: 2 "Son of man, confront Jerusalem with her **detestable practices**
16:22 In all your **detestable practices** and your prostitution you did not
16:36 because of all your **detestable** idols, and because you gave them
16:43 Did you not add lewdness to all your other **detestable practices**?
16:47 only walked in their ways and copied their **detestable practices**,
16:50 They were haughty and did **detestable things** before me.
16:51 You have done more **detestable things** than they, and have made
16:51 have made your sisters seem righteous by all these **things**[s] you
16:58 the consequences of your lewdness and your **detestable practices**,
18:12 took in pledge. He looks to the idols. He does **detestable things**.
18:13 Because he has done all these **detestable things**, he will surely be
18:24 and does the same **detestable things** the wicked man does,
20: 4 Then confront them with the **detestable practices** *of* their fathers
22: 2 of bloodshed? Then confront her with all her **detestable practices**
22:11 In you one man commits a **detestable offense** with his neighbor's
23:36 and Oholibah? Then confront them with their **detestable practices**,
33:26 You rely on your sword, you do **detestable things**, and each of
33:29 because of all the **detestable things** they have done.'
36:31 you will loathe yourselves for your sins and **detestable practices**.
43: 8 they defiled my holy name by their **detestable practices**.
44: 6 Enough of your **detestable practices**, O house of Israel!
44: 7 In addition to all your other **detestable practices**, you brought
44:13 they must bear the shame of their **detestable practices**.
Mal 2:11 A **detestable thing** has been committed in Israel and in Jerusalem:

9360 תּוֹעָה *tô'â*, n.f. [2] [√ 9494]

error [1], trouble [1]

Ne 4: 8 [4:2] and fight against Jerusalem and stir up **trouble** against it.
Isa 32: 6 practices ungodliness and spreads **error** concerning the LORD;

9361 תּוֹעָפוֹת *tô'āpôt*, n.f. [4]

strength [2], choicest [1], peaks [1]

Nu 23:22 brought them out of Egypt; they have the **strength** *of* a wild ox.
24: 8 brought them out of Egypt; they have the **strength** *of* a wild ox.
Job 22:25 then the Almighty will be your gold, the **choicest** silver for you.
Ps 95: 4 are the depths of the earth, and the mountain **peaks** belong to him.

9362 תּוֹצָאוֹת *tôṣā'ôt*, n.f. [23] [√ 3655]

ended [+2118] [5], out [5], end [+2118] [3], ending [+2118] [3], *untranslated* [2], escape [1], exits [1], extended [1], farthest limits [1], wellspring [1]

Nu 34: 4 continue on to Zin and go **[RPH]** south of Kadesh Barnea.
34: 5 it will turn, join the Wadi of Egypt and **end** [+2118] at the Sea.
34: 8 Hor to Lebo Hamath. Then the boundary will go **[RPH]** to Zedad,
34: 9 continue to Ziphron and **end** [+2118] *at* Hazar Enan. This will be
34:12 will go down along the Jordan and **end** [+2118] *at* the Salt Sea.
Jos 15: 4 and joined the Wadi of Egypt, **ending** [+2118] at the sea.
15: 7 along to the waters of En Shemesh and came **out** at En Rogel.
15:11 and reached Jabneel. The boundary **ended** [+2118] at the sea.
16: 3 of Lower Beth Horon and on to Gezer, **ending** [+2118] at the sea.
16: 8 went west to the Kanah Ravine and **ended** [+2118] at the sea.
17: 9 was the northern side of the ravine and **ended** [+2118] at the sea.
17:18 Clear it, and its **farthest limits** will be yours;
18:12 west into the hill country, coming **out** at the desert of Beth Aven.
18:14 south along the western side and came **out** at Kiriath Baal (that is,
18:19 and came **out** at the northern bay of the Salt Sea, at the mouth of
19:14 north to Hannathon and **ended** [+2118] at the Valley of Iphtah El.
19:22 Shahazumah and Beth Shemesh, and **ended** [+2118] at the Jordan.
19:29 toward Hosah and came **out** at the sea in the region of Aczib,
19:33 and Jabneel to Lakkum and **ending at** [+2118] the Jordan.
1Ch 5:16 and on all the pasturelands of Sharon as far as they **extended**.
Ps 68:20 [68:21] from the Sovereign LORD comes **escape** from death.
Pr 4:23 Above all else, guard your heart, for it is the **wellspring** *of* life.
Eze 48:30 "These will be the **exits** *of* the city: Beginning on the north side,

9363 תָּוֹקְהַת *towqᵉhat*, n.pr.m. [0] [cf. 9534]

2Ch 34:22 [the wife of Shallum son of **Tokhath**, [K; see Q 9534] the son of]

9364 תּוֹקְעִים *tôqᵉ'îm*, n.m.[pl.] *or* v.ptcp. [1] [√ 9546]

strike hands in pledge [1]

Pr 11:15 but whoever refuses to **strike hands in pledge** is safe.

9365 תּוּר *tûr*, v. [24] [cf. 3847, 9305?]

explore [6], explored [5], merchants [+408] [2], cautious [1], explored [+906+928+6296] [1], exploring [1], find [1], going [1], investigate [1], ranges [1], search out [1], searched out [1], sent to spy out [1], tried [+928+4213] [1]

Nu 10:33 [A] them during those three days to **find** them a place to rest.
13: 2 [A] "Send some men *to* **explore** the land of Canaan, which I am
13:16 [A] These are the names of the men Moses sent to **explore** the
13:17 [A] When Moses sent them to **explore** Canaan, he said, "Go up
13:21 [A] **explored** the land from the Desert of Zin as far as Rehob,
13:25 [A] At the end of forty days they returned from **exploring** the
13:32 [A] the Israelites a bad report about the land *they had* **explored**.
13:32 [A] They said, "The land *we* **explored** [+906+928+6296] devours
14: 6 [A] who were among those *who had* **explored** the land,
14: 7 [A] land we passed through and **explored** is exceedingly good.
14:34 [A] one year for each of the forty days *you* **explored** the land—
14:36 [A] So the men Moses had sent to **explore** the land, who returned
14:38 [A] Of the men who went to **explore** the land, only Joshua son of
15:39 [A] not prostitute yourselves by **going** after the lusts of your own
Dt 1:33 [A] to **search out** places for you to camp and to show you the
Jdg 1:23 [G] When they **sent** *men* **to spy out** Bethel (formerly called
1Ki 10:15 [A] not including the revenues from **merchants** [+408]
2Ch 9:14 [A] not including the revenues brought in by **merchants** [+408]
Job 39: 8 [A] *He* **ranges** the hills *for* his pasture and searches for any
Pr 12:26 [G] A righteous man *is* **cautious** in friendship, but the way of the
Ecc 1:13 [A] and to **explore** by wisdom all that is done under heaven.
2: 3 [A] *I* **tried** [+928+4213] cheering myself with wine,
7:25 [A] to **investigate** and to search out wisdom and the scheme of
Eze 20: 6 [A] them out of Egypt into a land *I had* **searched out** for them,

9366 ¹תּוֹר *tôr¹*, n.m. [5]

earrings [2], turn [2], most exalted [+5092] [1]

1Ch 17:17 looked on me as though I were the **most exalted of** [+5092] men,
Est 2:12 Before a girl's **turn** came to go in to King Xerxes, she had to
2:15 When the **turn** came for Esther (the girl Mordecai had adopted,
SS 1:10 Your cheeks are beautiful with **earrings**, your neck with strings of
1:11 We will make you **earrings** *of* gold, studded with silver.

9367 ²תּוֹר *tôr²*, n.f. & m. [14]

doves [9], dove [5]

Ge 15: 9 each three years old, along with a **dove** and a young pigeon."
Lev 1:14 is a burnt offering of birds, he is to offer a **dove** or a young pigeon.
5: 7 he is to bring two **doves** or two young pigeons to the LORD as a
5:11 however, he cannot afford two **doves** or two young pigeons,
12: 6 a burnt offering and a young pigeon or a **dove** for a sin offering.

Lev 12: 8 she is to bring two **doves** or two young pigeons, one for a burnt
14: 22 and two **doves** or two young pigeons, which he can afford,
14: 30 he shall sacrifice the **doves** or the young pigeons, which the person
15: 14 On the eighth day he must take two **doves** or two young pigeons
15: 29 On the eighth day she must take two **doves** or two young pigeons
Nu 6: 10 on the eighth day he must bring two **doves** or two young pigeons to
Ps 74: 19 Do not hand over the life of your **dove** to wild beasts; do not forget
SS 2: 12 of singing has come, the cooing of **doves** is heard in our land.
Jer 8: 7 the **dove**, the swift and the thrush observe the time of their

9368 תּוֹרָה *tôrâ*, n.f. [220] [√ 3723]

law [168], laws [16], regulations [15], teaching [8], instruction [5], instructions [2], *untranslated* [1], matters of law [1], teaching of law [1], teaching of the law [1], teachings [1], usual way of dealing [1]

Ge 26: 5 kept my requirements, my commands, my decrees and my **laws**."
Ex 12: 49 The same **law** applies to the native-born and to the alien living
13: 9 a reminder on your forehead that the **law** *of* the LORD is to be on
16: 4 I will test them and see whether they will follow my **instructions**.
16: 28 long will you refuse to keep my commands and my **instructions**?
18: 16 between the parties and inform them of God's decrees and **laws**."
18: 20 Teach them the decrees and **laws**, and show them the way to live
24: 12 with the **law** and commands I have written for their instruction."
Lev 6: 9 [6:2] 'These are the **regulations** *for* the burnt offering:
6: 14 [6:7] " 'These are the **regulations** *for* the grain offering:
6: 25 [6:18] his sons: 'These are the **regulations** *for* the sin offering:
7: 1 " 'These are the **regulations** *for* the guilt offering, which is most
7: 7 " 'The same **law** applies to both the sin offering and the guilt
7: 11 " 'These are the **regulations** *for* the fellowship offering a person
7: 37 These, then, are the **regulations** for the burnt offering, the grain
11: 46 " 'These are the **regulations** *concerning* animals, birds, every
12: 7 " 'These are the **regulations** *for* the woman who gives birth to a
13: 59 These are the **regulations** *concerning* contamination by mildew in
14: 2 "These are the **regulations** *for* the diseased person at the time of
14: 32 These are the **regulations** *for* anyone who has an infectious skin
14: 54 These are the **regulations** for any infectious skin disease, for an
14: 57 These are the **regulations** *for* infectious skin diseases and mildew.
15: 32 These are the **regulations** *for* a man with a discharge, for anyone
26: 46 the **regulations** that the LORD established on Mount Sinai
Nu 5: 29 is the **law** *of* jealousy when a woman goes astray and defiles
5: 30 her stand before the LORD and is to apply this entire **law** to her.
6: 13 " 'Now this is the **law** *for* the Nazirite when the period of his
6: 21 " 'This is the **law** *of* the Nazirite who vows his offering to the
6: 21 fulfill the vow he has made, according to the **law** *of* the Nazirite.' "
15: 16 The same **laws** and regulations will apply both to you and to the
15: 29 and the same **law** applies to everyone who sins unintentionally,
19: 2 "This is a requirement of the **law** that the LORD has commanded:
19: 14 "This is the **law** that applies when a person dies in a tent:
31: 21 "This is the requirement of the **law** that the LORD gave Moses:
Dt 1: 5 in the territory of Moab, Moses began to expound this **law**, saying:
4: 8 and laws as this body of **laws** I am setting before you today?
4: 44 This is the **law** Moses set before the Israelites.
17: 11 Act according to the **law** they teach you and the decisions they
17: 18 he is to write for himself on a scroll a copy of this **law**, taken from
17: 19 and follow carefully all the words of this **law** and these decrees
27: 3 Write on them all the words of this **law** when you have crossed
27: 8 you shall write very clearly all the words of this **law** on these
27: 26 "Cursed is the man who does not uphold the words of this **law** by
28: 58 If you do not carefully follow all the words of this **law**, which are
28: 61 kind of sickness and disaster not recorded in this Book of the **Law**,
29: 21 [29:20] curses of the covenant written in this Book of the **Law**.
29: 29 [29:28] that we may follow all the words of this **law**.
30: 10 his commands and decrees that are written in this Book of the **Law**
31: 9 So Moses wrote down this **law** and gave it to the priests, the sons
31: 11 he will choose, you shall read this **law** before them in their hearing.
31: 12 LORD your God and follow carefully all the words of this **law**.
31: 24 After Moses finished writing in a book the words of this **law** from
31: 26 "Take this Book of the **Law** and place it beside the ark of the
32: 46 command your children to obey carefully all the words of this **law**.
33: 4 the **law** that Moses gave us, the possession of the assembly of
33: 10 He teaches your precepts to Jacob and your **law** to Israel. He offers
Jos 1: 7 Be careful to obey all the **law** my servant Moses gave you;
1: 8 Do not let this Book of the **Law** depart from your mouth; meditate
8: 31 He built it according to what is written in the Book of the **Law** *of*
8: 32 Joshua copied on stones the **law** *of* Moses, which he had written.
8: 34 Afterward, Joshua read all the words of the **law**—the blessings
8: 34 and the curses—just as it is written in the Book of the **Law**.
22: 5 and the **law** that Moses the servant of the LORD gave you:
23: 6 be careful to obey all that is written in the Book of the **Law** *of*
24: 26 And Joshua recorded these things in the Book of the **Law** *of* God.
2Sa 7: 19 Is this your **usual way of dealing** *with* man, O Sovereign LORD?
1Ki 2: 3 his laws and requirements, as written in the **Law** *of* Moses,
2Ki 10: 31 Yet Jehu was not careful to keep the **law** *of* the LORD, the God
14: 6 in accordance with what is written in the Book of the **Law** *of*
17: 13 in accordance with the entire **Law** that I commanded your fathers
17: 34 the **laws** and commands that the LORD gave the descendants of
17: 37 and ordinances, the **laws** and commands he wrote for you.
21: 8 and will keep the whole **Law** that my servant Moses gave them."
22: 8 "I have found the Book of the **Law** in the temple of the LORD."
22: 11 When the king heard the words of the Book of the **Law**, he tore his
23: 24 This he did to fulfill the requirements of the **law** written in the
23: 25 and with all his strength, in accordance with all the **Law** *of* Moses.
1Ch 16: 40 in accordance with everything written in the **Law** *of* the LORD,
22: 12 over Israel, so that you may keep the **law** *of* the LORD your God.
2Ch 6: 16 are careful in all they do to walk before me according to my **law**,
12: 1 and all Israel with him abandoned the **law** *of* the LORD.
14: 4 [14:3] God of their fathers, and to obey his **laws** and commands.
15: 3 without the true God, without a priest to teach and without the **law**.
17: 9 taking with them the Book of the **Law** *of* the LORD;
19: 10 whether bloodshed or other concerns of the **law**, commands,
23: 18 the burnt offerings of the LORD as written in the **Law** *of* Moses,
25: 4 acted in accordance with what is written in the **Law**, in the Book of
30: 16 they took up their regular positions as prescribed in the **Law** *of*
31: 3 and appointed feasts as written in the **Law** *of* the LORD.
31: 4 so they could devote themselves to the **Law** *of* the LORD.
31: 21 of God's temple and in obedience to the **law** and the commands,
33: 8 to do everything I commanded them concerning all the **laws**,
34: 14 Hilkiah the priest found the Book of the **Law** *of* the LORD that
34: 15 "I have found the Book of the **Law** in the temple of the LORD."
34: 19 When the king heard the words of the **Law**, he tore his robes.
35: 26 according to what is written in the **Law** *of* the LORD—
Ezr 3: 2 in accordance with what is written in the **Law** *of* Moses the man of
7: 6 He was a teacher well versed in the **Law** *of* Moses,
7: 10 himself to the study and observance of the **Law** *of* the LORD,
10: 3 the commands of our God. Let it be done according to the **Law**.
Ne 8: 1 They told Ezra the scribe to bring out the Book of the **Law** *of*
8: 2 month Ezra the priest brought the **Law** before the assembly,
8: 3 And all the people listened attentively to the Book of the **Law**.
8: 7 instructed the people in the **Law** while the people were standing
8: 8 They read from the Book of the **Law** *of* God, making it clear
8: 9 people had been weeping as they listened to the words of the **Law**.
8: 13 around Ezra the scribe to give attention to the words of the **Law**.
8: 14 They found written in the **Law**, which the LORD had
8: 18 first day to the last, Ezra read from the Book of the **Law** *of* God.
9: 3 read from the Book of the **Law** *of* the LORD their God for a
9: 13 You gave them regulations and **laws** that are just and right,
9: 14 them commands, decrees and **laws** through your servant Moses.
9: 26 and rebelled against you; they put your **law** behind their backs.
9: 29 "You warned them to return to your **law**, but they became arrogant
9: 34 our leaders, our priests and our fathers did not follow your **law**;
10: 28 [10:29] the neighboring peoples for the sake of the **Law** *of* God,
10: 29 [10:30] an oath to follow the **Law** *of* God given through Moses
10: 34 [10:35] altar of the LORD our God, as it is written in the **Law**.
10: 36 [10:37] "As it is also written in the **Law**, we will bring the
12: 44 into the storerooms the portions required by the **Law** for the priests
13: 3 When the people heard this **law**, they excluded from Israel all who
Job 22: 22 Accept **instruction** from his mouth and lay up his words in your
Ps 1: 2 his delight is in the **law** *of* the LORD, and on his law he meditates
1: 2 the law of the LORD, and on his **law** he meditates day and night.
19: 7 [19:8] The **law** *of* the LORD is perfect, reviving the soul.
37: 31 The **law** *of* his God is in his heart; his feet do not slip.
40: 8 [40:9] to do your will, O my God; your **law** is within my heart."
78: 1 O my people, hear my **teaching**; listen to the words of my mouth.
78: 5 He decreed statutes for Jacob and established the **law** in Israel,
78: 10 they did not keep God's covenant and refused to live by his **law**.
89: 30 [89:31] "If his sons forsake my **law** and do not follow my statutes,
94: 12 man you discipline, O LORD, the man you teach from your **law**;
105: 45 that they might keep his precepts and observe his **laws**.
119: 1 ways are blameless, who walk according to the **law** *of* the LORD.
119: 18 Open my eyes that I may see wonderful things in your **law**.
119: 29 Keep me from deceitful ways; be gracious to me through your **law**.
119: 34 and I will keep your **law** and obey it with all my heart.
119: 44 I will always obey your **law**, for ever and ever.
119: 51 mock me without restraint, but I do not turn from your **law**.
119: 53 grips me because of the wicked, who have forsaken your **law**.
119: 55 night I remember your name, O LORD, and I will keep your **law**.
119: 61 Though the wicked bind me with ropes, I will not forget your **law**.
119: 70 Their hearts are callous and unfeeling, but I delight in your **law**.
119: 72 The **law** *from* your mouth is more precious to me than thousands
119: 77 compassion come to me that I may live, for your **law** is my delight.
119: 85 The arrogant dig pitfalls for me, contrary to your **law**.
119: 92 If your **law** had not been my delight, I would have perished in my
119: 97 Oh, how I love your **law**! I meditate on it all day long.
119:109 I constantly take my life in my hands, I will not forget your **law**.
119:113 I hate double-minded men, but I love your **law**.
119:126 It is time for you to act, O LORD; your **law** is being broken.
119:136 Streams of tears flow from my eyes, for your **law** is not obeyed.
119:142 Your righteousness is everlasting and your **law** is true.

Ps 119:150 devise wicked schemes are near, but they are far from your **law**.
119:153 my suffering and deliver me, for I have not forgotten your **law**.
119:163 I hate and abhor falsehood but I love your **law**.
119:165 Great peace have they who love your **law**, and nothing can make
119:174 I long for your salvation, O LORD, and your **law** is my delight.
Pr 1: 8 father's instruction and do not forsake your mother's **teaching**.
3: 1 My son, do not forget my **teaching**, but keep my commands in
4: 2 I give you sound learning, so do not forsake my **teaching**.
6: 20 father's commands and do not forsake your mother's **teaching**.
6: 23 For these commands are a lamp, this **teaching** is a light,
7: 2 and you will live; guard my **teachings** as the apple of your eye.
13: 14 The **teaching** *of* the wise is a fountain of life, turning a man from
28: 4 Those who forsake the **law** praise the wicked, but those who keep
28: 4 the law praise the wicked, but those who keep the **law** resist them.
28: 7 He who keeps the **law** is a discerning son, but a companion of
28: 9 If anyone turns a deaf ear to the **law**, even his prayers are
29: 18 the people cast off restraint; but blessed is he who keeps the **law**.
31: 26 She speaks with wisdom, and faithful **instruction** is on her tongue.
Isa 1: 10 of Sodom; listen to the **law** *of* our God, you people of Gomorrah!
2: 3 The **law** will go out from Zion, the word of the LORD from
5: 24 for they have rejected the **law** *of* the LORD Almighty
8: 16 Bind up the testimony and seal up the **law** among my disciples.
8: 20 To the **law** and to the testimony! If they do not speak according to
24: 5 they have disobeyed the **laws**, violated the statutes and broken the
30: 9 children unwilling to listen to the LORD's **instruction**.
42: 4 justice on earth. In his **law** the islands will put their hope."
42: 21 the LORD for the sake of his righteousness to make his **law** great
42: 24 For they would not follow his ways; they did not obey his **law**.
51: 4 The **law** will go out from me; my justice will become a light to the
51: 7 know what is right, you people who have my **law** in your hearts:
Jer 2: 8 Those who deal with the **law** did not know me; the leaders rebelled
6: 19 they have not listened to my words and have rejected my **law**.
8: 8 can you say, "We are wise, for we have the **law** *of* the LORD,"
9: 13 [9:12] LORD said, "It is because they have forsaken my **law**,
16: 11 and worshiped them. They forsook me and did not keep my **law**.
18: 18 for the **teaching of** the **law** by the priest will not be lost, nor will
26: 4 If you do not listen to me and follow my **law**, which I have set
31: 33 "I will put my **law** in their minds and write it on their hearts.
32: 23 took possession of it, but they did not obey you or follow your **law**;
44: 10 nor have they followed my **law** and the decrees I set before you
44: 23 obeyed him or followed his **law** or his decrees or his stipulations,
La 2: 9 and her princes are exiled among the nations, the **law** is no more,
Eze 7: 26 the **teaching of the law** by the priest will be lost, as will the
22: 26 Her priests do violence to my **law** and profane my holy things;
43: 11 and entrances—its whole design and all its regulations and **laws**.
43: 12 "This is the **law** *of* the temple: All the surrounding area on top of
43: 12 of the mountain will be most holy. Such is the **law** *of* the temple.
44: 5 **[RPH]** Give attention to the entrance of the temple and all the
44: 24 They are to keep my **laws** and my decrees for all my appointed
Da 9: 10 or kept the **laws** he gave us through his servants the prophets.
9: 11 All Israel has transgressed your **law** and turned away, refusing to
9: 11 the curses and sworn judgments written in the **Law** *of* Moses,
9: 13 Just as it is written in the **Law** *of* Moses, all this disaster has come
Hos 4: 6 because you have ignored the **law** *of* your God, I also will ignore
8: 1 the people have broken my covenant and rebelled against my **law**.
8: 12 I wrote for them the many things of my **law**, but they regarded
Am 2: 4 Because they have rejected the **law** *of* the LORD and have not
Mic 4: 2 The **law** will go out from Zion, the word of the LORD from
Hab 1: 4 Therefore the **law** is paralyzed, and justice never prevails.
Zep 3: 4 Her priests profane the sanctuary and do violence to the **law**.
Hag 2: 11 the LORD Almighty says: 'Ask the priests what the **law** says:
Zec 7: 12 made their hearts as hard as flint and would not listen to the **law**
Mal 2: 6 True **instruction** was in his mouth and nothing false was found on
2: 7 and from his mouth men should seek **instruction**—
2: 8 from the way and by your **teaching** have caused many to stumble;
2: 9 my ways but have shown partiality in **matters of** the **law**."
4: 4 [3:22] "Remember the **law** *of* my servant Moses, the decrees

9369 תּוֹשָׁב *tôšāb*, n.m. [14 / 13] [√ 3782]

temporary resident [5], stranger [2], guest [1], living [1], people living [1], strangers [1], temporary residents [1], tenants [1]

Ge 23: 4 "I am an alien and a **stranger** among you. Sell me some property
Ex 12: 45 but a **temporary resident** and a hired worker may not eat of it.
Lev 22: 10 nor may the **guest** *of* a priest or his hired worker eat it.
25: 6 the hired worker and **temporary resident** who live among you,
25: 23 because the land is mine and you are but aliens and my **tenants**.
25: 35 help him as you would an alien or a **temporary resident**,
25: 40 be treated as a hired worker or a **temporary resident** among you;
25: 45 You may also buy some of the **temporary residents** living among
25: 47 " 'If an alien or a **temporary resident** among you becomes rich
25: 47 sells himself to the alien **living** among you or to a member of the
Nu 35: 15 for Israelites, aliens and any *other* **people living** among them,
1Ki 17: 1 Elijah the Tishbite, from Tishbe [BHS *of the settlers*; NIV 9586] *in*
1Ch 29: 15 We are aliens and **strangers** in your sight, as were all our
Ps 39: 12 [39:13] with you as an alien, a **stranger**, as all my fathers were.

9370 תּוּשִׁיָּה *tûšiyyâ*, n.f. [11] [cf. 3780]

sound judgment [3], success [2], victory [2], wisdom [2], insight [1], true wisdom [1]

Job 5: 12 the plans of the crafty, so that their hands achieve no **success**.
6: 13 power to help myself, now that **success** has been driven from me?
11: 6 to you the secrets of wisdom, for **true wisdom** has two sides.
12: 16 To him belong strength and **victory**; both deceived and deceiver
26: 3 one without wisdom! And what great **insight** you have displayed!
30: 22 you toss me about in the **storm**. [BHS *wisdom*; Q 9370; NIV 9583]
Pr 2: 7 He holds **victory** in store for the upright, he is a shield to those
3: 21 My son, preserve **sound judgment** and discernment, do not let
8: 14 Counsel and **sound judgment** are mine; I have understanding
18: 1 man pursues selfish ends; he defies all **sound judgment**.
Isa 28: 29 wonderful in counsel and magnificent in **wisdom**.
Mic 6: 9 to fear your name is **wisdom**—"Heed the rod and the One who

9371 תּוֹתָח *tôtāḥ*, n.m. [1]

club [1]

Job 41: 29 [41:21] A **club** seems to him but a piece of straw; he laughs at the

9372 תָּזַז *tāzaz*, v. [1]

cut down [1]

Isa 18: 5 [G] and **cut down** and take away the spreading branches.

9373 תַּזְנוּת *taznût*, n.f.abst. [20] [√ 2388]

prostitution [8], promiscuity [5], lust [2], favors [1], illicit favors [1], promiscuous [1], prostitute [1], use as a prostitute [+2388] [1]

Eze 16: 15 You lavished your **favors** on anyone who passed by and your
16: 20 them as food to the idols. Was your **prostitution** not enough?
16: 22 your **prostitution** you did not remember the days of your youth,
16: 25 offering your body with increasing **promiscuity** to anyone who
16: 26 and provoked me to anger with your increasing **promiscuity**.
16: 29 Then you increased your **promiscuity** to include Babylonia,
16: 33 them to come to you from everywhere for your **illicit favors**.
16: 34 So in your **prostitution** you are the opposite of others; no one runs
16: 36 and exposed your nakedness in your **promiscuity** with your lovers,
23: 7 She gave herself as a **prostitute** to all the elite of the Assyrians
23: 8 She did not give up the **prostitution** she began in Egypt,
23: 8 caressed her virgin bosom and poured out their **lust** upon her.
23: 11 in her lust and **prostitution** she was more depraved than her sister.
23: 14 "But she carried her **prostitution** still further. She saw men
23: 17 came to her, to the bed of love, and in their **lust** they defiled her.
23: 18 When she carried on her **prostitution** openly and exposed her
23: 19 and more **promiscuous** as she recalled the days of her youth,
23: 29 your prostitution will be exposed. Your lewdness and **promiscuity**
23: 35 must bear the consequences of your lewdness and **prostitution**."
23: 43 'Now *let them* **use** her **as a prostitute** [+2388], for that is all she

9374 תַּחְבֻּלוֹת *taḥbulôt*, n.f. [6]

guidance [4], advice [1], direction [1]

Job 37: 12 At his **direction** they swirl around over the face of the whole earth
Pr 1: 5 and add to their learning, and let the discerning get **guidance**—
11: 14 For lack of **guidance** a nation falls, but many advisers make
12: 5 of the righteous are just, but the **advice** *of* the wicked is deceitful.
20: 18 Make plans by seeking advice; if you wage war, obtain **guidance**.
24: 6 for waging war you need **guidance**, and for victory many advisers.

9375 תֹּחוּ *tōḥû*, n.pr.m. [1] [cf. 9346]

Tohu [1]

1Sa 1: 1 the son of Elihu, the son of **Tohu**, the son of Zuph, an Ephraimite.

9376 תַּחְכְּמֹנִי *taḥk^{e}mōnî*, a.g. [1]

Tahkemonite [1]

2Sa 23: 8 Josheb-Basshebeth, a **Tahkemonite**, was chief of the Three;

9377 תַּחֲלֻאִים *taḥ^{a}lu'îm*, n.pl.m. [5] [√ 2688]

diseases [3], pain [1], ravages [1]

Dt 29: 22 [29:21] and the **diseases** with which the LORD has afflicted it.
2Ch 21: 19 bowels came out because of the disease, and he died in great **pain**.
Ps 103: 3 who forgives all your sins and heals all your **diseases**,
Jer 14: 18 slain by the sword; if I go into the city, I see the **ravages** *of* famine.
16: 4 "They will die of deadly **diseases**. They will not be mourned

9378 תְּחִלָּה ***tᵉḥillâ***, n.f. [22] [√ 2725]

beginning [7], first [+928+2021] [3], began [2], earlier [+928+2021] [2], first time [2], first [2], *untranslated* [1], already [+928+2021] [1], before [+928+2021] [1], led in thanksgiving [+3344+4200] [1]

Ge 13: 3 and Ai where his tent had been **earlier** [+928+2021]
41: 21 they had done so; they looked just as ugly as **before** [+928+2021].
43: 18 of the silver that was put back into our sacks the **first time**.
43: 20 they said, "we came down here the **first time** to buy food.
Jdg 1: 1 "Who will be the **first** to go up and fight for us against the
20: 18 "Who of us shall go **first** [+928+2021] to fight against the
20: 18 The LORD replied, "Judah shall go **first** [+928+2021]."
Ru 1: 22 arriving in Bethlehem as the barley harvest was **beginning**.
2Sa 17: 9 If he should attack your troops **first** [+928+2021], whoever hears
21: 9 first days of the harvest, just as the barley harvest was **beginning**.
21: 10 From the **beginning** *of* the harvest till the rain poured down from
2Ki 17: 25 When they **first** lived there, they did not worship the LORD;
Ezr 4: 6 At the **beginning** *of* the reign of Xerxes, they lodged an accusation
Ne 11: 17 the director *who* **led in thanksgiving** [+3344+4200] and prayer;
Pr 9: 10 "The fear of the LORD is the **beginning** *of* wisdom,
Ecc 10: 13 At the **beginning** his words are folly; at the end they are wicked
Isa 1: 26 your judges as in days of old, your counselors as at the **beginning**.
Da 8: 1 after the one that had **already** [+928+2021] appeared to me.
9: 21 Gabriel, the man I had seen in the **earlier** [+928+2021] vision,
9: 23 As soon as you **began** to pray, an answer was given, which I have
Hos 1: 2 *When* the LORD **began** to speak through Hosea, the LORD said
Am 7: 1 been harvested and just as **[NIE]** the second crop was coming up.

9379 תַּחְמָס ***taḥmās***, n.[m.]. [2] [√ 2803?]

screech owl [2]

Lev 11: 16 the horned owl, the **screech owl**, the gull, any kind of hawk,
Dt 14: 15 the horned owl, the **screech owl**, the gull, any kind of hawk,

9380 תַּ֫חַן ***taḥan***, n.pr.m. [2] [→ 9385; cf. 2858?]

Tahan [2]

Nu 26: 35 the Bekerite clan; through **Tahan**, the Tahanite clan.
1Ch 7: 25 was his son, Resheph his son, Telah his son, **Tahan** his son,

9381 תַּחֲנָה ***taḥᵃnâ***, n.f. [1] [√ 2837; cf. 9386]

set up camp [1]

2Ki 6: 8 he said, "I will **set up** my **camp** in such and such a place."

9382 תְּחִנָּה¹ ***tᵉḥinnâ¹***, n.f. [25] [→ 9383; cf. 2858]

plea [10], petition [4], plea for mercy [2], supplication [2], cry for mercy [1], gracious [1], mercy [1], pleading [+5877] [1], pleas [1], request [1], supplications [1]

Jos 11: 20 he might destroy them totally, exterminating them without **mercy**,
1Ki 8: 28 Yet give attention to your servant's prayer and his **plea for mercy**,
8: 30 Hear the **supplication** *of* your servant and of your people Israel
8: 38 and when a prayer or **plea** is made by any of your people Israel—
8: 45 hear from heaven their prayer and their **plea**, and uphold their
8: 49 from heaven, your dwelling place, hear their prayer and their **plea**,
8: 52 "May your eyes be open to your servant's **plea** and to the plea of
8: 52 open to your servant's plea and to the **plea** *of* your people Israel,
8: 54 had finished all these prayers and **supplications** to the LORD,
9: 3 "I have heard the prayer and **plea** you have made before me;
2Ch 6: 19 Yet give attention to your servant's prayer and his **plea for mercy**,
6: 29 and when a prayer or **plea** is made by any of your people Israel—
6: 35 hear from heaven their prayer and their **plea**, and uphold their
6: 39 from heaven, your dwelling place, hear their prayer and their **pleas**,
33: 13 the LORD was moved by his entreaty and listened to his **plea**;
Ezr 9: 8 the LORD our God has been **gracious** in leaving us a remnant
Ps 6: 9 [6:10] The LORD has heard my **cry for mercy**; the LORD
55: 1 [55:2] Listen to my prayer, O God, do not ignore my **plea**;
119:170 May my **supplication** come before you; deliver me according to
Jer 36: 7 Perhaps they will bring their **petition** before the LORD, and each
37: 20 lord the king, please listen. Let me bring my **petition** before you:
38: 26 'I *was* **pleading** [+5877] with the king not to send me back to
42: 2 "Please hear our **petition** and pray to the LORD your God for this
42: 9 God of Israel, to whom you sent me to present your **petition**, says:
Da 9: 20 and making my **request** to the LORD my God for his holy hill—

9383 תְּחִנָּה² ***tᵉḥinnâ²***, n.pr.m. [1] [√ 9382; cf. 2858]

Tehinnah [1]

1Ch 4: 12 of Beth Rapha, Paseah and **Tehinnah** the father of Ir Nahash.

9384 תַּחֲנוּן ***taḥᵃnûn***, n.[m.]pl.abst. [18] [√ 2858]

cry for mercy [+7754] [6], cry for mercy [2], pray [2], begging for mercy [1], mercy [1], petition [1], petitions [1], pleading [1], requests [1], supplication [1], supplications [1]

2Ch 6: 21 Hear the **supplications** *of* your servant and of your people Israel
Job 41: 3 [40:27] Will he keep **begging** you **for mercy**? Will he speak to
Ps 28: 2 Hear my **cry for mercy** [+7754] as I call to you for help, as I lift
28: 6 be to the LORD, for he has heard my **cry for mercy** [+7754].
31: 22 [31:23] Yet you heard my **cry for mercy** [+7754] when I called
86: 6 Hear my prayer, O LORD; listen to my **cry for mercy** [+7754].
116: 1 the LORD, for he heard my voice; he heard my **cry for mercy**.
130: 2 my voice. Let your ears be attentive to my **cry for mercy** [+7754].
140: 6 [140:7] my God." Hear, O LORD, my **cry for mercy** [+7754].
143: 1 O LORD, hear my prayer, listen to my **cry for mercy**; in your
Pr 18: 23 A poor man pleads for **mercy**, but a rich man answers harshly.
Jer 3: 21 barren heights, the weeping and **pleading** *of* the people of Israel,
31: 9 They will come with weeping; they will **pray** as I bring them back.
Da 9: 3 to the Lord God and pleaded with him in prayer and **petition**,
9: 17 "Now, our God, hear the prayers and **petitions** *of* your servant.
9: 18 We do not make **requests** of you because we are righteous,
9: 23 As soon as you began to **pray**, an answer was given, which I have
Zec 12: 10 and the inhabitants of Jerusalem a spirit of grace and **supplication**.

9385 תַּחֲנִי ***taḥᵃnî***, a.g. [1] [√ 9380; cf. 2858?]

Tahanite [1]

Nu 26: 35 the Bekerite clan; through Tahan, the **Tahanite** clan.

9386 תַּחֲנֹתִי ***taḥᵃnōtî***, n.f. Not used in NIV/BHS [√ 2837?]

9387 תַּחְפַּנְחֵס ***taḥpanḥēs***, n.pr.loc. [7] [cf. 7090]

Tahpanhes [7]

Jer 2: 16 of Memphis and **Tahpanhes** have shaved the crown of your head.
43: 7 in disobedience to the LORD and went as far as **Tahpanhes**.
43: 8 In **Tahpanhes** the word of the LORD came to Jeremiah:
43: 9 brick pavement at the entrance to Pharaoh's palace in **Tahpanhes**.
44: 1 in Migdol, **Tahpanhes** and Memphis—and in Upper Egypt:
46: 14 it in Migdol; proclaim it also in Memphis and **Tahpanhes**:
Eze 30: 18 Dark will be the day at **Tahpanhes** when I break the yoke of

9388 תַּחְפְּנֵיס ***taḥpᵉnês***, n.pr.f. [3]

Tahpenes [3]

1Ki 11: 19 gave him a sister of his own wife, Queen **Tahpenes**, in marriage.
11: 20 The sister of **Tahpenes** bore him a son named Genubath, whom
11: 20 named Genubath, whom **Tahpenes** brought up in the royal palace.

9389 תַּחְרָא ***taḥrā'***, n.[m.]. [2]

collar [+7023] [1], collar [1]

Ex 28: 32 There shall be a woven edge like a **collar** [+7023] around this
39: 23 an opening in the center of the robe like the opening of a **collar**,

9390 תַּחְרֵעַ ***taḥrēa'***, n.pr.m. [1] [cf. 9308]

Tahrea [1]

1Ch 9: 41 The sons of Micah: Pithon, Melech, **Tahrea** and Ahaz.

9391 תַּחַשׁ¹ ***taḥaš¹***, n.m. [14] [→ 9392]

sea cows [12], hides of sea cows [1], leather [1]

Ex 25: 5 ram skins dyed red and hides of **sea cows**; acacia wood;
26: 14 ram skins dyed red, and over that a covering of hides of **sea cows**.
35: 7 ram skins dyed red and hides of **sea cows**; acacia wood;
35: 23 or goat hair, ram skins dyed red or hides of **sea cows** brought them.
36: 19 ram skins dyed red, and over that a covering of hides of **sea cows**.
39: 34 the covering of hides of **sea cows** and the shielding curtain;
Nu 4: 6 they are to cover this with hides of **sea cows**, spread a cloth of
4: 8 cover that with hides of **sea cows** and put its poles in place.
4: 10 to wrap it and all its accessories in a covering of hides of **sea cows**
4: 11 and cover that with hides of **sea cows** and put its poles in place.
4: 12 cover that with hides of **sea cows** and put them on a carrying
4: 14 Over it they are to spread a covering of hides of **sea cows**
4: 25 its covering and the outer covering of **hides of sea cows**,
Eze 16: 10 you with an embroidered dress and put **leather** sandals on you.

9392 תַּחַשׁ² ***taḥaš²***, n.pr.m. [1] [√ 9391]

Tahash [1]

Ge 22: 24 was Reumah, also had sons: Tebah, Gaham, **Tahash** and Maacah.

9393 ¹תַּחַת ***taḥat¹***, n.[m.] & adv. & pp. [505] [→ 9394, 9395, 9396, 9397; cf. 5737; Ar 10757] See Select Index

under [150], succeeded [65], for [33], in place of [24], in place [23], *untranslated* [20], instead of [18], below [+4946] [16], beneath [15], below [10], under [+4946] [7], because [+889] [6], succeed [5], against [+3338+4946] [4], beneath [+4946] [4], instead [4], where [4], with [4], at feet [3], for [+889] [3], in return for [3], in [3], place [3], replace [3], while married to [3], among [2], at the foot of [2], from [+4946] [2], have a home [+8905] [2], in exchange for [2], on [2], succeeded [+7756] [2], to compensate for [2], to [2], unchanged [+6641] [2], underneath [2], although [1], amid [1], as a direct result [+3338] [1], at foot of [1], at the spot [1], because [+3954] [1], below [+4200+4946] [1], by [1], from [1], have [+3338+3780] [1], have on hand [+3338+3780] [1], have on hand [+448+3338] [1], homes [1], in exchange [1], in position [1], in stead [1], in the place of [1], instead of [+889] [1], land[s] [1], legs [1], lower [+4946] [1], made subject to [+3338+4044] [1], mine [+3276] [1], on behalf [1], on the spot [1], pad [+4946] [1], position [1], replace [+448+995] [1], replace [+8492] [1], replaced [+6641] [1], replaced [+906+5989] [1], resting on [+4946] [1], riding [1], since [+3954] [1], since [+889] [1], submission [1], succeeds [1], successor [+6641] [1], supported [1], take charge of [+3338] [1], take the place of [+2118] [1], take the place of [1], to [+3338] [1], to [+4946] [1], underfoot [+8079] [1], underneath [+4946] [1], undersides [1], when [1], where stand [1], why [+4537] [1]

9394 ²תַּחַת ***taḥat²***, n.pr.m. [4] [√ 9393]

Tahath [4]

1Ch 6: 24 [6:9] **Tahath** his son, Uriel his son, Uzziah his son and Shaul his
6: 37 [6:22] the son of **Tahath**, the son of Assir, the son of Ebiasaph,
7: 20 Shuthelah, Bered his son, **Tahath** his son, Eleadah his son,
7: 20 Bered his son, Tahath his son, Eleadah his son, **Tahath** his son,

9395 ³תַּחַת ***taḥat³***, n.pr.loc. [2] [√ 9393]

Tahath [2]

Nu 33: 26 They left Makheloth and camped at **Tahath**.
33: 27 They left **Tahath** and camped at Terah.

9396 תַּחְתּוֹן ***taḥtôn***, a. [13 / 14] [√ 9393]

lower [11], lowest [3]

Jos 16: 3 of the Japhletites as far as the region of **Lower** Beth Horon
18: 13 went down to Ataroth Addar on the hill south of **Lower** Beth
1Ki 6: 6 The **lowest** floor was five cubits wide, the middle floor six cubits
6: 8 The entrance to the **lowest** [BHS 9399] floor was on the south side
9: 17 And Solomon rebuilt Gezer.) He built up **Lower** Beth Horon,
1Ch 7: 24 who built **Lower** and Upper Beth Horon as well as Uzzen Sheerah.
2Ch 8: 5 Upper Beth Horon and **Lower** Beth Horon as fortified cities,
Isa 22: 9 breaches in its defenses; you stored up water in the **Lower** Pool.
Eze 40: 18 and was as wide as they were long; this was the **lower** pavement.
40: 19 he measured the distance from the inside of the **lower** gateway to
41: 7 A stairway went up from the **lowest** *floor* to the top floor through
42: 5 took more space from them than from the rooms on the **lower**
42: 6 so they were smaller in floor space than those *on* the **lower**
43: 14 From the gutter on the ground up to the **lower** ledge it is two cubits

9397 תַּחְתִּי ***taḥtî***, a. & subst. [19] [√ 9393]

below [7], depths [4], lower [4], lowest [2], beneath [1], foot [1]

Ge 6: 16 Put a door in the side of the ark and make **lower**, middle and upper
Ex 19: 17 camp to meet with God, and they stood at the **foot** *of* the mountain.
Dt 32: 22 kindled by my wrath, one that burns to the realm of death **below**.
Jos 15: 19 springs of water." So Caleb gave her the upper and **lower** springs.
Jdg 1: 15 of water." Then Caleb gave her the upper and **lower** springs.
Ne 4: 13 [4:7] Therefore I stationed some of the people behind the **lowest**
Job 41: 24 [41:16] His chest is hard as rock, hard as a **lower** millstone.
Ps 63: 9 [63:10] they will go down to the **depths** *of* the earth.
86: 13 toward me; you have delivered me from the **depths** of the grave.
88: 6 [88:7] You have put me in the **lowest** pit, in the darkest depths.
139: 15 When I was woven together in the **depths** *of* the earth,
Isa 44: 23 for the LORD has done this; shout aloud, O earth **beneath**.
La 3: 55 I called on your name, O LORD, from the **depths** of the pit.
Eze 26: 20 I will make you dwell in the earth **below**, as in ancient ruins,
31: 14 are all destined for death, for the earth **below**, among mortal men,
31: 16 the trees that were well-watered, were consoled in the earth **below**.
31: 18 will be brought down with the trees of Eden to the earth **below**;
32: 18 for the hordes of Egypt and consign to the earth **below** both her
32: 24 the land of the living went down uncircumcised to the earth **below**.

9398 תַּחְתִּים חָדְשִׁי ***taḥtîm ḥodšî***, n.pr.loc. [1] [cf. 2547]

Tahtim Hodshi [1]

2Sa 24: 6 They went to Gilead and the region of **Tahtim Hodshi**, and on to

9399 תִּיכוֹן ***tîkôn***, a. [11 / 10] [√ 9348]

middle [7], center [2], there[s] [+2021] [1]

Ex 26: 28 The **center** crossbar is to extend from end to end at the middle of
36: 33 They made the **center** crossbar so that it extended from end to end
Jdg 7: 19 reached the edge of the camp at the beginning of the **middle** watch,
1Ki 6: 6 cubits wide, the **middle** floor six cubits and the third floor seven.
6: 8 The entrance to the lowest [BHS *middle*; NIV 9396] floor
6: 8 a stairway led up to the **middle** *level* and from there to the third.
6: 8 led up to the middle level and from **there**[s] [+2021] to the third.
2Ki 20: 4 Before Isaiah had left the **middle** court, the word of the LORD
Eze 41: 7 up from the lowest floor to the top floor through the **middle** *floor*.
42: 5 from the rooms on the lower and **middle** *floors of* the building.
42: 6 smaller in floor space than those on the lower and **middle** *floors*.

9400 תִּילוֹן ***tîlôn***, n.pr.m. [1] [cf. 9353]

Tilon [1]

1Ch 4: 20 sons of Shimon: Amnon, Rinnah, Ben-Hanan and **Tilon**. [K 9353]

9401 תֵּימָא ***têmā'***, n.pr.loc. [& m.?]. [5]

Tema [4], Tema [+824] [1]

Ge 25: 15 Hadad, **Tema**, Jetur, Naphish and Kedemah.
1Ch 1: 30 Mishma, Dumah, Massa, Hadad, **Tema**,
Job 6: 19 The caravans of **Tema** look for water, the traveling merchants of
Isa 21: 14 you who live in **Tema** [+824], bring food for the fugitives.
Jer 25: 23 Dedan, **Tema**, Buz and all who are in distant places;

9402 ¹תֵּימָן ***têmān¹***, n.f. [23] [→ 9403; cf. 3545]

south [8], south [+2025] [5], south [+2025+5582] [3], south [+2025+2025+5582] [2], south [+5582] [2], south wind [2], southward [+4946] [1]

Ex 26: 18 Make twenty frames for the **south** [+2025+2025+5582] side of the tabernacle
26: 35 and put the lampstand opposite it on the **south** [+2025] side.
27: 9 The **south** [+2025+5582] side shall be a hundred cubits long
36: 23 They made twenty frames for the **south** [+2025+5582] side of the
38: 9 The **south** [+2025+5582] side was a hundred cubits long and had
Nu 2: 10 On the **south** will be the divisions of the camp of Reuben under
3: 29 The Kohathite clans were to camp on the **south** [+2025] side of the
10: 6 sounding of a second blast, the camps on the **south** are to set out.
Dt 3: 27 top of Pisgah and look west and north and **south** [+2025] and east.
Jos 12: 3 then **southward** [+4946] below the slopes of Pisgah.
13: 4 from the **south**, all the land of the Canaanites, from Arah of the
15: 1 of Edom, to the Desert of Zin in the extreme **south** [+5582].
Job 9: 9 and Orion, the Pleiades and the constellations of the **south**.
39: 26 take flight by your wisdom and spread his wings toward the **south**?
Ps 78: 26 wind from the heavens and led forth the **south wind** by his power.
SS 4: 16 Awake, north wind, and come, **south wind**! Blow on my garden,
Isa 43: 6 'Give them up!' and to the **south**, 'Do not hold them back.'
Eze 20: 46 [21:2] "Son of man, set your face toward the **south** [+2025];
47: 19 "On the **south** [+5582] side it will run from Tamar as far as the
47: 19 This will be the **south** [+2025+2025+5582] boundary.
48: 28 "The southern boundary of Gad will run **south** [+2025] from
Zec 6: 6 the west, and the one with the dappled horses toward the **south**."
9: 14 will sound the trumpet; he will march in the storms of the **south**,

9403 ²תֵּימָן ***têmān²***, n.pr.loc. [11] [→ 9404; cf. 3545, 9402]

Teman [11]

Ge 36: 11 The sons of Eliphaz: **Teman**, Omar, Zepho, Gatam and Kenaz.
36: 15 Eliphaz the firstborn of Esau: Chiefs **Teman**, Omar, Zepho, Kenaz,
36: 42 Kenaz, **Teman**, Mibzar,
1Ch 1: 36 **Teman**, Omar, Zepho, Gatam and Kenaz; by Timna: Amalek.
1: 53 Kenaz, **Teman**, Mibzar,
Jer 49: 7 "Is there no longer wisdom in **Teman**? Has counsel perished from
49: 20 what he has purposed against those who live in **Teman**:
Eze 25: 13 lay it waste, and from **Teman** to Dedan they will fall by the sword.
Am 1: 12 I will send fire upon **Teman** that will consume the fortresses of
Ob 1: 9 Your warriors, O **Teman**, will be terrified, and everyone in Esau's
Hab 3: 3 God came from **Teman**, the Holy One from Mount Paran.

9404 תֵּימָנִי ***têmānî***, a.g. [8] [√ 9403]

Temanite [6], Temanites [2]

Ge 36: 34 Husham from the land of the **Temanites** succeeded him as king.
1Ch 1: 45 Husham from the land of the **Temanites** succeeded him as king.
Job 2: 11 Eliphaz the **Temanite**, Bildad the Shuhite and Zophar the
4: 1 Then Eliphaz the **Temanite** replied:
15: 1 Then Eliphaz the **Temanite** replied:
22: 1 Then Eliphaz the **Temanite** replied:
42: 7 he said to Eliphaz the **Temanite**, "I am angry with you and your
42: 9 So Eliphaz the **Temanite**, Bildad the Shuhite and Zophar the

9405 תֵּימְנִי têmᵉnî, n.pr.m. [1] [√ 3545]

Temeni [1]

1Ch 4: 6 Naarah bore him Ahuzzam, Hepher, **Temeni** and Haahashtari.

9406 תִּימָרָה tîmārâ, n.f. [2] [→ 9473?, 9477; cf. 9469]

billows [1], column [1]

SS 3: 6 Who is this coming up from the desert like a **column** *of* smoke,
Joel 2: 30 [3:3] and on the earth, blood and fire and **billows** *of* smoke.

9407 תִּיצִי tîṣî, a.g. [1]

Tizite [1]

1Ch 11: 45 Jediael son of Shimri, his brother Joha the **Tizite**,

9408 תִּירוֹשׁ tîrôš, n.m. [38] [√ 3769]

new wine [34], grapes [1], juice [1], new [1], wine [1]

Ge 27: 28 and of earth's richness—an abundance of grain and **new wine**.
27: 37 his servants, and I have sustained him with grain and **new wine**.
Nu 18: 12 "I give you all the finest olive oil and all the finest **new wine**
Dt 7: 13 the crops of your land—your grain, **new wine** and oil—
11: 14 so that you may gather in your grain, **new wine** and oil.
12: 17 eat in your own towns the tithe of your grain and **new wine** and oil,
14: 23 Eat the tithe of your grain, **new wine** and oil, and the firstborn of
18: 4 are to give them the firstfruits of your grain, **new wine** and oil,
28: 51 **new wine** or oil, nor any calves of your herds or lambs of your
33: 28 Jacob's spring is secure in a land of grain and **new wine**, where the
Jdg 9: 13 'Should I give up my **wine**, which cheers both gods and men,
2Ki 18: 32 a land of grain and **new wine**, a land of bread and vineyards,
2Ch 31: 5 **new wine**, oil and honey and all that the fields produced.
32: 28 also made buildings to store the harvest of grain, **new wine** and oil;
Ne 5: 11 the hundredth part of the money, grain, **new wine** and oil."
10: 37 [10:38] of the fruit of all our trees and of our **new wine** and oil.
10: 39 [10:40] **new wine** and oil to the storerooms where the articles for
13: 5 **new wine** and oil prescribed for the Levites, singers
13: 12 brought the tithes of grain, **new wine** and oil into the storerooms.
Ps 4: 7 [4:8] greater joy than when their grain and **new wine** abound.
Pr 3: 10 filled to overflowing, and your vats will brim over with **new wine**.
Isa 24: 7 The **new wine** dries up and the vine withers; all the merrymakers
36: 17 a land of grain and **new wine**, a land of bread and vineyards.
62: 8 never again will foreigners drink the **new wine** for which you have
65: 8 "As when **juice** is still found in a cluster of grapes and men say,
Jer 31: 12 the grain, the **new wine** and the oil, the young of the flocks
Hos 2: 8 [2:10] the **new wine** and oil, who lavished on her the silver
2: 9 [2:11] grain when it ripens, and my **new wine** when it is ready.
2: 22 [2:24] the **new wine** and oil, and they will respond to Jezreel.
4: 11 to prostitution, to old wine and **new**, which take away the
7: 14 gather together for grain and **new wine** but turn away from me.
9: 2 winepresses will not feed the people; the **new wine** will fail them.
Joel 1: 10 the grain is destroyed, the **new wine** is dried up, the oil fails.
2: 19 "I am sending you grain, **new wine** and oil, enough to satisfy you
2: 24 be filled with grain; the vats will overflow with **new wine** and oil.
Mic 6: 15 the oil on yourselves, you will crush **grapes** but not drink the wine.
Hag 1: 11 the **new wine**, the oil and whatever the ground produces, on men
Zec 9: 17 will make the young men thrive, and **new wine** the young women.

9409 תִּירְיָא tîrᵉyā', n.pr.m. [1]

Tiria [1]

1Ch 4: 16 The sons of Jehallelel: Ziph, Ziphah, **Tiria** and Asarel.

9410 תִּירָס tîrās, n.pr.loc. [& m.?]. [2]

Tiras [2]

Ge 10: 2 Gomer, Magog, Madai, Javan, Tubal, Meshech and **Tiras**.
1Ch 1: 5 Gomer, Magog, Madai, Javan, Tubal, Meshech and **Tiras**.

9411 תַּיִשׁ tayiš, n.m. [4]

male goats [2], goats [1], he-goat [1]

Ge 30: 35 That same day he removed all the **male goats** that were streaked
32: 14 [32:15] two hundred female goats and twenty **male goats**,
2Ch 17: 11 seven hundred rams and seven thousand seven hundred **goats**.
Pr 30: 31 a strutting rooster, a **he-goat**, and a king with his army around him.

9412 תֹּךְ tōk, n.m. [4]

threats [2], oppression [1], oppressor [+408] [1]

Ps 10: 7 His mouth is full of curses and lies and **threats**; trouble and evil
55: 11 [55:12] at work in the city; **threats** and lies never leave its streets.
72: 14 He will rescue them from **oppression** and violence, for precious is
Pr 29: 13 The poor man and the **oppressor** [+408] have this in common:

9413 תָּכָה tākâ, v. [1]

bow down [1]

Dt 33: 3 [E] At your feet they all **bow down**, and from you receive

9414 תְּכוּנָה tᵉkûnâ, n.f. [3] [√ 3922]

arrangement [1], dwelling [1], supply [1]

Job 23: 3 only I knew where to find him; if only I could go to his **dwelling**!
Eze 43: 11 its **arrangement**, its exits and entrances—its whole design
Na 2: 9 [2:10] The **supply** is endless, the wealth from all its treasures!

9415 תֻּכִּיִּים tukkiyyîm, n.m.[pl.]. [2]

baboons [2]

1Ki 10: 22 it returned, carrying gold, silver and ivory, and apes and **baboons**.
2Ch 9: 21 it returned, carrying gold, silver and ivory, and apes and **baboons**.

9416 תִּכְלָה tiklâ, n.f. [1] [√ 3983]

perfection [1]

Ps 119: 96 To all **perfection** I see a limit; but your commands are boundless.

9417 תַּכְלִית taklît, n.f. [5] [√ 3983]

boundary [1], end [1], farthest recesses [+3972] [1], limits [1], nothing but [1]

Ne 3: 21 from the entrance of Eliashib's house to the **end** *of* it.
Job 11: 7 the mysteries of God? Can you probe the **limits** *of* the Almighty?
26: 10 the horizon on the face of the waters for a **boundary** *between* light
28: 3 he searches the **farthest recesses** [+3972] for ore in the blackest
Ps 139: 22 I have **nothing but** hatred for them; I count them my enemies.

9418 תְּכֵלֶת tᵉkēlet, n.f. [49]

blue [42], blue yarn [3], blue cloth [2], blue material [2]

Ex 25: 4 **blue**, purple and scarlet yarn and fine linen; goat hair;
26: 1 the tabernacle with ten curtains of finely twisted linen and **blue**,
26: 4 Make loops of **blue material** along the edge of the end curtain in
26: 31 "Make a curtain of **blue**, purple and scarlet yarn and finely twisted
26: 36 "For the entrance to the tent make a curtain of **blue**, purple
27: 16 of **blue**, purple and scarlet yarn and finely twisted linen—
28: 5 them use gold, and **blue**, purple and scarlet yarn, and fine linen.
28: 6 "Make the ephod of gold, and of **blue**, purple and scarlet yarn,
28: 8 and made with gold, and with **blue**, purple and scarlet yarn,
28: 15 of gold, and of **blue**, purple and scarlet yarn, and of finely twisted
28: 28 breastpiece are to be tied to the rings of the ephod with **blue** cord,
28: 31 "Make the robe of the ephod entirely of **blue cloth**,
28: 33 Make pomegranates of **blue**, purple and scarlet yarn around the
28: 37 Fasten a **blue** cord to it to attach it to the turban; it is to be on the
35: 6 **blue**, purple and scarlet yarn and fine linen; goat hair;
35: 23 Everyone who had **blue**, purple or scarlet yarn or fine linen,
35: 25 what she had spun—**blue**, purple or scarlet yarn or fine linen.
35: 35 embroiderers in **blue**, purple and scarlet yarn and fine linen,
36: 8 the tabernacle with ten curtains of finely twisted linen and **blue**,
36: 11 they made loops of **blue material** along the edge of the end curtain
36: 35 They made the curtain of **blue**, purple and scarlet yarn and finely
36: 37 For the entrance to the tent they made a curtain of **blue**, purple
38: 18 The curtain for the entrance to the courtyard was of **blue**, purple
38: 23 and an embroiderer in **blue**, purple and scarlet yarn and fine linen.)
39: 1 From the **blue**, purple and scarlet yarn they made woven garments
39: 2 and of **blue**, purple and scarlet yarn, and of finely twisted linen.
39: 3 out thin sheets of gold and cut strands to be worked into the **blue**,
39: 5 and made with gold, and with **blue**, purple and scarlet yarn,
39: 8 of gold, and of **blue**, purple and scarlet yarn, and of finely twisted
39: 21 rings of the breastpiece to the rings of the ephod with **blue** cord,
39: 22 They made the robe of the ephod entirely of **blue cloth**—the work
39: 24 They made pomegranates of **blue**, purple and scarlet yarn
39: 29 The sash was of finely twisted linen and **blue**, purple and scarlet
39: 31 Then they fastened a **blue** cord to it to attach it to the turban,
Nu 4: 6 spread a cloth of solid **blue** over that and put the poles in place.
4: 7 "Over the table of the Presence they are to spread a **blue** cloth
4: 9 "They are to take a **blue** cloth and cover the lampstand that is for
4: 11 "Over the gold altar they are to spread a **blue** cloth and cover that
4: 12 wrap them in a **blue** cloth, cover that with hides of sea cows
15: 38 on the corners of your garments, with a **blue** cord on each tassel.
2Ch 2: 7 [2:6] and iron, and in purple, crimson and **blue yarn**,
2: 14 [2:13] and with purple and **blue** and crimson **yarn** and fine linen.
3: 14 He made the curtain of **blue**, purple and crimson **yarn** and fine
Est 1: 6 The garden had hangings of white and **blue** linen, fastened with
8: 15 Mordecai left the king's presence wearing royal garments of **blue**
Jer 10: 9 and goldsmith have made is then dressed in **blue** and purple—
Eze 23: 6 clothed in **blue**, governors and commanders, all of them handsome
27: 7 your awnings were of **blue** and purple from the coasts of Elishah.
27: 24 **blue** fabric, embroidered work and multicolored rugs with cords

[F] Hitpael (hitpoel, hitpoal, hitpolel, hitpolal, hitpalel, hitpalal, hitpalpel, hitpalpal, hotpael, hotpaal) [G] Hiphil (hiphtil) [H] Hophal [I] Hishtaphel

9419 תָּכַן **tākan**, v. [18] [→ 5504, 9420, 9422; cf. 9545; Ar 10771]

just [5], unjust [+4202] [4], weighs [2], amount been determined [1], are weighed [1], hold firm [1], marked off [1], measured out [+928+4500] [1], understood [1], weighed [1]

1Sa 2: 3 [C] is a God who knows, and by him deeds **are weighed**.
2Ki 12: 11 [12:12] [E] When the **amount** *had* **been determined**, they gave
Job 28: 25 [D] of the wind and **measured out** [+928+4500] the waters,
Ps 75: 3 [75:4] [D] all its people quake, it is I *who* **hold** its pillars **firm**.
Pr 16: 2 [A] innocent to him, but motives are **weighed** *by* the LORD.
21: 2 [A] ways seem right to him, but the LORD **weighs** the heart.
24: 12 [A] about this," does not he *who* **weighs** the heart perceive it?
Isa 40: 12 [D] or with the breadth of his hand **marked off** the heavens?
40: 13 [D] Who *has* **understood** the mind of the LORD, or instructed
Eze 18: 25 [C] "Yet you say, 'The way of the Lord *is* not **just**.' Hear,
18: 25 [C] not just.' Hear, O house of Israel: *Is* my way **unjust** [+4202]?
18: 25 [C] my way unjust? Is it not your ways *that are* **unjust** [+4202]?
18: 29 [C] Yet the house of Israel says, 'The way of the Lord *is* not **just**.'
18: 29 [C] is not just.' *Are* my ways **unjust** [+4202], O house of Israel?
18: 29 [C] house of Israel? Is it not your ways *that are* **unjust** [+4202]?
33: 17 [C] "Yet your countrymen say, 'The way of the Lord *is* not **just**.'
33: 17 [C] way of the Lord is not just.' But it is their way that *is* not **just**.
33: 20 [C] O house of Israel, you say, 'The way of the Lord *is* not **just**.'

9420 ¹תֹּכֶן **tōken¹**, n.m. [2] [√ 9419]

full quota [1], size [1]

Ex 5: 18 given any straw, yet you must produce your **full quota** *of* bricks."
Eze 45: 11 The ephah and the bath are to be the same **size**, the bath containing

9421 ²תֹּכֶן **tōken²**, n.pr.loc. [1]

Token [1]

1Ch 4: 32 villages were Etam, Ain, Rimmon, **Token** and Ashan—

9422 תָּכְנִית **toknît**, n.f. [2] [√ 9419]

perfection [1], plan [1]

Eze 28: 12 " 'You were the model of **perfection**, full of wisdom and perfect in
43: 10 that they may be ashamed of their sins. Let them consider the **plan**,

9423 תַּכְרִיךְ **takrîk**, n.m. [1]

robe [1]

Est 8: 15 and white, a large crown of gold and a purple **robe** *of* fine linen.

9424 תֵּל **tēl**, n.[m.]. [5] [→ 9425, 9426, 9427, 9435, 9446?]

heap of ruins [1], mound [1], mounds [1], ruin [1], ruins [1]

Dt 13: 16 [13:17] It is to remain a **ruin** forever, never to be rebuilt.
Jos 8: 28 So Joshua burned Ai and made it a permanent **heap of ruins**,
11: 13 Yet Israel did not burn any of the cities built on their **mounds**—
Jer 30: 18 the city will be rebuilt on her **ruins**, and the palace will stand in its
49: 2 it will become a **mound** *of* ruins, and its surrounding villages will

9425 תֵּל אָבִיב **tēl 'ābîb**, n.pr.loc. [1] [√ 9424 + 26]

Tel Abib [1]

Eze 3: 15 I came to the exiles who lived at **Tel Abib** near the Kebar River.

9426 תֵּל חַרְשָׁא **tēl ḥaršā'**, n.pr.loc. [2] [√ 9424 + 3091 *or* 3093]

Tel Harsha [2]

Ezr 2: 59 the towns of Tel Melah, **Tel Harsha**, Kerub, Addon and Immer,
Ne 7: 61 the towns of Tel Melah, **Tel Harsha**, Kerub, Addon and Immer,

9427 תֵּל מֶלַח **tēl melaḥ**, n.pr.loc. [2] [√ 9424 + 4875]

Tel Melah [2]

Ezr 2: 59 The following came up from the towns of **Tel Melah**, Tel Harsha,
Ne 7: 61 The following came up from the towns of **Tel Melah**, Tel Harsha,

9428 תָּלָא **tālā'**, v. [3] [cf. 9434]

determined [1], hung [1], suspense [1]

Dt 28: 66 [B] You will live *in* constant **suspense**, filled with dread both
2Sa 21: 12 [A] where the Philistines *had* **hung** [K 9434] them after they
Hos 11: 7 [B] My people *are* **determined** to turn from me. Even if they call

9429 תַּלְאֻבוֹת **tal'ubôt**, n.f. [1]

burning heat [1]

Hos 13: 5 I cared for you in the desert, in the land of **burning heat**.

9430 תְּלָאָה **tᵉlā'â**, n.f. [5] [→ 5505; cf. 4206]

hardship [2], hardships [2], burden [1]

Ex 18: 8 and about all the **hardships** they had met along the way
Nu 20: 14 You know about all the **hardships** that have come upon us.
Ne 9: 32 of love, do not let all this **hardship** seem trifling in your eyes—
La 3: 5 has besieged me and surrounded me with bitterness and **hardship**.
Mal 1: 13 you say, 'What a **burden**!' and you sniff at it contemptuously,"

9431 תְּלַאשָּׂר **tᵉla'śśār**, n.pr.loc. [2] [√ 9445]

Tel Assar [2]

2Ki 19: 12 Haran, Rezeph and the people of Eden who were in **Tel Assar**?
Isa 37: 12 Haran, Rezeph and the people of Eden who were in **Tel Assar**?

9432 תִּלְבֹּשֶׁת **tilbōšet**, n.f. [1] [√ 4252]

put on [+4252] [1]

Isa 59: 17 *he* **put on** [+4252] the garments of vengeance and wrapped

9433 תִּלְגַת פִּלְנְאֶסֶר **tillᵉgat pilnᵉ'eser**, תִּלְגַת פִּלְנֶסֶר **tillᵉgat pilneser**, n.pr.m. [3] [cf. 9325]

Tiglath-Pileser [3]

1Ch 5: 6 his son, whom **Tiglath-Pileser** king of Assyria took into exile.
5: 26 **Tiglath-Pileser** king of Assyria), who took the Reubenites,
2Ch 28: 20 **Tiglath-Pileser** king of Assyria came to him, but he gave him

9434 תָּלָה **tālâ**, v. [27] [→ 3849, 9002, 9437; cf. 9428]

hanged [8], hung [7], hang [5], hanging [3], been hung up [1], is hung [1], suspends [1], were hanged [1]

Ge 40: 19 [A] days Pharaoh will lift off your head and **hang** you on a tree.
40: 22 [A] *he* **hanged** the chief baker, just as Joseph had said to them in
41: 13 [A] was restored to my position, and the other man *was* **hanged**."
Dt 21: 22 [A] capital offense is put to death and his body *is* **hung** on a tree,
21: 23 [B] because *anyone who* **is hung** on a tree is under God's curse.
Jos 8: 29 [A] *He* **hung** the king of Ai on a tree and left him there until
10: 26 [A] and killed the kings and **hung** them on five trees,
10: 26 [B] and they were *left* **hanging** on the trees until evening.
2Sa 4: 12 [A] and feet and **hung** the bodies by the pool in Hebron.
18: 10 [B] he told Joab, "I just saw Absalom **hanging** in an oak tree."
21: 12 [a] [where the Philistines *had* **hung** [K; see Q 9428] them after]
Est 2: 23 [C] found to be true, the two officials **were hanged** on a gallows.
5: 14 [A] ask the king in the morning *to have* Mordecai **hanged** on it.
6: 4 [A] **hanging** Mordecai on the gallows he had erected for him.
7: 9 [A] spoke up to help the king." The king said, "**Hang** him on it!"
7: 10 [A] So *they* **hanged** Haman on the gallows he had prepared for
8: 7 [A] estate to Esther, and *they have* **hanged** him on the gallows.
9: 13 [A] and *let* Haman's ten sons *be* **hanged** on gallows."
9: 14 [A] was issued in Susa, and *they* **hanged** the ten sons of Haman.
9: 25 [A] and that he and his sons *should be* **hanged** on the gallows.
Job 26: 7 [A] over empty space; *he* **suspends** the earth over nothing.
Ps 137: 2 [A] There on the poplars *we* **hung** our harps,
SS 4: 4 [B] on it **hang** a thousand shields, all of them shields of warriors.
Isa 22: 24 [A] All the glory of his family *will* **hang** on him: its offspring
La 5: 12 [C] Princes *have* **been hung up** by their hands; elders are shown
Eze 15: 3 [A] Do they make pegs from it to **hang** things on?
27: 10 [D] *They* **hung** their shields and helmets on your walls, bringing
27: 11 [D] *They* **hung** their shields around your walls; they brought

9435 תָּלוּל **tālûl**, a. [1] [√ 9424]

lofty [1]

Eze 17: 22 from its topmost shoots and plant it on a high and **lofty** mountain.

9436 תֶּלַח **telaḥ**, n.pr.m. [1]

Telah [1]

1Ch 7: 25 was his son, Resheph his son, **Telah** his son, Tahan his son,

9437 תְּלִי **tᵉlî**, n.[m.]. [1] [√ 9434]

quiver [1]

Ge 27: 3 Now then, get your weapons—your **quiver** and bow—and go out

9438 תָּלַל **tālal**, v. [9] [→ 4562; cf. 2252]

deceive [2], made a fool of [2], act deceitfully [1], cheated [1], deceives [1], deluded [1], making a fool of [1]

Ge 31: 7 [G] yet your father *has* **cheated** me by changing my wages ten
Ex 8: 29 [8:25] [G] Only *be sure that* Pharaoh *does* not **act deceitfully**
Jdg 16: 10 [G] Then Delilah said to Samson, "*You have* **made a fool of** me;
16: 13 [G] *you have been* **making a fool of** me and lying to me.
16: 15 [G] This is the third time *you have* **made a fool of** me
Job 13: 9 [G] *Could you* **deceive** him as you might deceive men?

Job 13: 9 [G] Could you deceive him as you *might* **deceive** men?
Isa 44:20 [H] He feeds on ashes, a **deluded** heart misleads him; he cannot
Jer 9: 5 [9:4] [G] Friend **deceives** friend, and no one speaks the truth.

9439 תֶּלֶם telem, n.m. [5] [→ 9440]

furrows [2], plowed [2], furrow [1]

Job 31:38 my land cries out against me and all its **furrows** are wet with tears,
39:10 Can you hold him to the **furrow** with a harness? Will he till the
Ps 65:10 [65:11] You drench its **furrows** and level its ridges; you soften it
Hos 10: 4 therefore lawsuits spring up like poisonous weeds in a **plowed**
12:11 [12:12] Their altars will be like piles of stones on a **plowed** field.

9440 תַּלְמַי talmay, n.pr.m. [6] [√ 9439]

Talmai [6]

Nu 13:22 and came to Hebron, where Ahiman, Sheshai and **Talmai**,
Jos 15:14 Sheshai, Ahiman and **Talmai**—descendants of Anak.
Jdg 1:10 called Kiriath Arba) and defeated Sheshai, Ahiman and **Talmai**.
2Sa 3: 3 Absalom the son of Maacah daughter of **Talmai** king of Geshur;
13:37 Absalom fled and went to **Talmai** son of Ammihud, the king of
1Ch 3: 2 Absalom the son of Maacah daughter of **Talmai** king of Geshur;

9441 תַּלְמִיד talmîd, n.[m.]. [1] [√ 4340]

student [1]

1Ch 25: 8 Young and old alike, teacher as well as **student**, cast lots for their

9442 תְּלֻנּוֹת tᵉlunnôt, n.f. [8] [√ 4296]

grumbling [5], complaints [1], constant grumbling [+4296] [1], grumbling [+4296] [1]

Ex 16: 7 of the LORD, because he has heard your **grumbling** against him.
16: 8 because he has heard your **grumbling** [+4296] against him.
16: 8 You are not **grumbling** against us, but against the LORD."
16: 9 'Come before the LORD, for he has heard your **grumbling**.'"
16:12 "I have heard the **grumbling** *of* the Israelites. Tell them, 'At
Nu 14:27 I have heard the **complaints** *of* these grumbling Israelites.
17: 5 [17:20] **constant grumbling** [+4296] against you *by* the
17:10 [17:25] This will put an end to their **grumbling** against me,

9443 תָּלַע tāla', v.den. [1] [√ 9355]

clad in scarlet [1]

Na 2: 3 [2:4] [E] of his soldiers are red; the warriors *are* **clad in scarlet**.

9444 תַּלְפִּיּוֹת talpiyyôt, n.f.pl. [1]

elegance [1]

SS 4: 4 Your neck is like the tower of David, built with **elegance**;

9445 תְּלַשָּׂר tᵉlaśśār, n.pr.loc. Not used in NIV/BHS [√ 9431]

9446 תַּלְתַּל taltāl, n.f.?. [1] [√ 9424?]

wavy [1]

SS 5:11 His head is purest gold; his hair is **wavy** and black as a raven.

9447 תָּם tām, a. [15 / 16] [→ 3462; cf. 9462]

blameless [8], fitted [+3481] [2], flawless [1], healthy [1], innocent [1], integrity [1], perfect [1], quiet [1]

Ge 25:27 while Jacob was a **quiet** man, staying among the tents.
Ex 26:24 bottom all the way to the top, and **fitted** [+3481] into a single ring;
36:29 bottom all the way to the top and **fitted** [+3481] into a single ring;
Job 1: 1 This man was **blameless** and upright; he feared God and shunned
1: 8 he is **blameless** and upright, a man who fears God and shuns evil."
2: 3 he is **blameless** and upright, a man who fears God and shuns evil.
8:20 "Surely God does not reject a **blameless** *man* or strengthen the
9:20 condemn me; if I were **blameless**, it would pronounce me guilty.
9:21 "Although I am **blameless**, I have no concern for myself; I despise
9:22 that is why I say, 'He destroys both the **blameless** and the wicked.'
Ps 37:37 Consider the **blameless**, observe the upright; there is a future for
64: 4 [64:5] They shoot from ambush at the **innocent** *man*; they shoot
73: 4 no struggles; their bodies are **healthy** [BHS 4392] and strong.
Pr 29:10 Bloodthirsty men hate a *man of* **integrity** and seek to kill the
SS 5: 2 "Open to me, my sister, my darling, my dove, my **flawless** *one*.
6: 9 my dove, my **perfect** *one*, is unique, the only daughter of her

9448 תֹּם tōm, n.[m.]. [23] [→ 9460; cf. 9462]

blameless [8], integrity [6], at random [+4200] [2], clear [2], full measure [1], full [1], man of integrity [+2006] [1], quite innocently [+4200] [1], righteous [1]

Ge 20: 5 I have done this with a **clear** conscience and clean hands."
20: 6 I know you did this with a **clear** conscience, and so I have kept you
2Sa 15:11 had been invited as guests and went **quite innocently** [+4200],
1Ki 9: 4 if you walk before me in **integrity** *of* heart and uprightness,
22:34 someone drew his bow **at random** [+4200] and hit the king of
2Ch 18:33 someone drew his bow **at random** [+4200] and hit the king of
Job 4: 6 piety be your confidence and your **blameless** ways your hope?
21:23 One man dies in **full** vigor, completely secure and at ease,
Ps 7: 8 [7:9] my righteousness, according to my **integrity**, O Most High.
25:21 May **integrity** and uprightness protect me, because my hope is in
26: 1 Vindicate me, O LORD, for I have led a **blameless** life; I have
26:11 But I lead a **blameless** life; redeem me and be merciful to me.
41:12 [41:13] In my **integrity** you uphold me and set me in your
78:72 David shepherded them with **integrity** *of* heart; with skillful hands
101: 2 you come to me? I will walk in my house with **blameless** heart.
Pr 2: 7 for the upright, he is a shield to those whose walk is **blameless**,
10: 9 The man of **integrity** walks securely, but he who takes crooked
10:29 The way of the LORD is a refuge for the **righteous**, but it is the
13: 6 Righteousness guards the **man of integrity** [+2006], but
19: 1 Better a poor man whose walk is **blameless** than a fool whose lips
20: 7 The righteous man leads a **blameless** life; blessed are his children
28: 6 Better a poor man whose walk is **blameless** than a rich man whose
Isa 47: 9 They will come upon you in **full measure**, in spite of your many

9449 תָּמַהּ tāmah, v. [10] [→ 9451; Ar 10755, 10763]

utterly amazed [+9449] [2], aghast [1], amazed [1], appalled [1], astounded [1], look aghast [1], looked in astonishment [1], stunned [1], surprised [1]

Ge 43:33 [A] and they **looked** at each other **in astonishment**.
Job 26:11 [A] The pillars of the heavens quake, **aghast** at his rebuke.
Ps 48: 5 [48:6] [A] they saw ⌞her⌟ and *were* **astounded**; they fled in
Ecc 5: 8 [5:7] [A] and rights denied, *do* not *be* **surprised** at such things;
Isa 13: 8 [A] *They will* **look aghast** at each other, their faces aflame.
29: 9 [F] *Be* **stunned** and amazed, blind yourselves and be sightless;
29: 9 [A] Be stunned and **amazed**, blind yourselves and be sightless;
Jer 4: 9 [A] priests will be horrified, and the prophets *will be* **appalled**."
Hab 1: 5 [F] at the nations and watch—and *be* **utterly amazed** [+9449].
1: 5 [A] at the nations and watch—and *be* **utterly amazed** [+9449].

9450 תֻּמָּה tummâ, n.f. [5] [√ 9462]

integrity [4], blameless [1]

Job 2: 3 he still maintains his **integrity**, though you incited me against him
2: 9 His wife said to him, "Are you still holding on to your **integrity**?
27: 5 admit you are in the right; till I die, I will not deny my **integrity**.
31: 6 weigh me in honest scales and he will know that I am **blameless**—
Pr 11: 3 The **integrity** *of* the upright guides them, but the unfaithful are

9451 תִּמָּהוֹן timmāhôn, n.[m.]. [2] [√ 9449]

confusion [1], panic [1]

Dt 28:28 will afflict you with madness, blindness and **confusion** *of* mind.
Zec 12: 4 On that day I will strike every horse with **panic** and its rider with

9452 תַּמּוּז tammûz, n.pr.[m.]. [1]

Tammuz [1]

Eze 8:14 and I saw women sitting there, mourning for **Tammuz**.

9453 תְּמוֹל tᵉmôl, subst.adv. [23] [→ 919]

before [+8997] [6], yesterday [4], malice aforethought [+4200+4946+8533+8997] [3], had the habit [+4946+8997] [2], *untranslated* [1], as usual [+3869+8997] [1], before [+4946+8997] [1], for some time [+1685+1685+8997] [1], had been [+8997] [1], in the past [+8997] [1], malice aforethought [+4946+8533+8997] [1], past [+8997] [1]

Ge 31: 2 Laban's attitude toward him was not what *it* **had been** [+8997].
31: 5 your father's attitude toward me is not what it was **before** [+8997],
Ex 4:10 neither in the **past** [+8997] nor since you have spoken to your
5: 7 for making bricks; let them go and gather their own straw. **[RPH]**
5: 8 them to make the same number of bricks as **before** [+8997];
5:14 "Why didn't you meet your quota of bricks **yesterday** or today,
5:14 meet your quota of bricks yesterday or today, as **before** [+8997]?"
21:29 the bull has **had the habit** [+4946+8997] of goring and the owner
21:36 if it was known that the bull **had the habit** [+4946+8997] of
Dt 4:42 neighbor without **malice aforethought** [+4200+4946+8533+8997].
19: 4 without **malice aforethought** [+4200+4946+8533+8997].
19: 6 to his neighbor without **malice aforethought** [+4946+8533+8997].
Jos 3: 4 since you have never been this way **before** [+4946+8997].
4:18 returned to their place and ran at flood stage as **before** [+8997].
20: 5 and without **malice aforethought** [+4200+4946+8533+8997].
Ru 2:11 and came to live with a people you did not know **before** [+8997].
1Sa 20:27 the son of Jesse come to the meal, either **yesterday** or today?"
21: 5 [21:6] kept from us, **as usual** [+3869+8997] whenever I set out.
2Sa 3:17 "**For some time** [+1685+1685+8997] you have wanted to make
15:20 You came only **yesterday**. And today shall I make you wander

2Ki 13: 5 the Israelites lived in their own homes as they had **before** [+8997].
1Ch 11: 2 **In the past** [+8997], even while Saul was king, you were the one
Job 8: 9 for we were born only **yesterday** and know nothing, and our days

9454 תְּמוּנָה t^{e}mûnâ, n.f. [10] [√ 4786]

form [7], image [1], kind [1], likeness [1]

Ex 20: 4 "You shall not make for yourself an idol in the **form** of anything in
Nu 12: 8 clearly and not in riddles; he sees the **form** *of* the LORD.
Dt 4: 12 You heard the sound of words but saw no **form**; there was only a
4: 15 You saw no **form** of any kind the day the LORD spoke to you at
4: 16 an **image** *of* any shape, whether formed like a man or a woman,
4: 23 do not make for yourselves an idol in the **form** *of* anything the
4: 25 if you then become corrupt and make any **kind** *of* idol, doing evil
5: 8 "You shall not make for yourself an idol in the **form** of anything in
Job 4: 16 A **form** stood before my eyes, and I heard a hushed voice:
Ps 17: 15 when I awake, I will be satisfied with seeing your **likeness**.

9455 תְּמוּרָה t^{e}mûrâ, n.f. [6] [√ 4614]

substitute [2], had for [1], return [1], trading [1], transfer of property [+1821+3972] [1]

Lev 27: 10 one animal for another, both it and the **substitute** become holy.
27: 33 both the animal and its **substitute** become holy and cannot be
Ru 4: 7 and **transfer** [+1821+3972] **of property** to become final,
Job 15: 31 by trusting what is worthless, for he will get nothing *in* **return**.
20: 18 give back uneaten; he will not enjoy the profit from his **trading**.
28: 17 crystal can compare with it, nor can it be **had for** jewels of gold.

9456 תְּמוּתָה t^{e}mûtâ, n.f. [2] [√ 4637]

death [1], die [1]

Ps 79: 11 by the strength of your arm preserve those condemned to **die**.
102: 20 [102:21] of the prisoners and release those condemned to **death**."

9457 תֶּמַח temaḥ, n.pr.m. [2] [√ 4681?]

Temah [2]

Ezr 2: 53 Barkos, Sisera, **Temah**,
Ne 7: 55 Barkos, Sisera, **Temah**,

9458 תָּמִיד tāmîd, n.m. (used as adv.). [104]

always [23], regular [23], continually [12], regularly [12], ever [8], daily sacrifice [5], forever [3], constantly [2], *untranslated* [1], at all times [1], constant [1], continual [1], continued [1], continuing [1], continuously [1], daily [1], day after day [+3429] [1], endless [1], keep on [1], kept [1], lasting [+6409] [1], long [1], never [+4202] [1], often [1]

Ex 25: 30 the bread of the Presence on this table to be before me **at all times**.
27: 20 pressed olives for the light so that the lamps may be **kept** burning.
28: 29 of decision as a **continuing** memorial before the LORD.
28: 30 Thus Aaron will **always** bear the means of making decisions for
28: 38 It will be on Aaron's forehead **continually** so that they will be
29: 38 "This is what you are to offer on the altar **regularly** each day:
29: 42 **regularly** at the entrance to the Tent of Meeting before the
30: 8 so incense will burn **regularly** before the LORD for the
Lev 6: 13 [6:6] The fire must be kept burning on the altar **continuously**;
6: 20 [6:13] a tenth of an ephah of fine flour as a **regular** grain
24: 2 for the light so that the lamps may be kept burning **continually**.
24: 3 lamps before the LORD from evening till morning, **continually**.
24: 4 gold lampstand before the LORD must be tended **continually**.
24: 8 This bread is to be set out before the LORD **regularly**, Sabbath
Nu 4: 7 the bread that is **continually** there is to remain on it.
4: 16 fragrant incense, the **regular** grain offering and the anointing oil.
9: 16 That is how it **continued** to be; the cloud covered it, and at night it
28: 3 a year old without defect, as a **regular** burnt offering each day.
28: 6 This is the **regular** burnt offering instituted at Mount Sinai as a
28: 10 in addition to the **regular** burnt offering and its drink offering.
28: 15 Besides the **regular** burnt offering with its drink offering,
28: 23 Prepare these in addition to the **regular** morning burnt offering.
28: 24 it is to be prepared in addition to the **regular** burnt offering
28: 31 in addition to the **regular** burnt offering and its grain offering.
29: 6 **daily** burnt offerings with their grain offerings and drink offerings
29: 11 and the **regular** burnt offering with its grain offering,
29: 16 in addition to the **regular** burnt offering with its grain offering
29: 19 in addition to the **regular** burnt offering with its grain offering,
29: 22 in addition to the **regular** burnt offering with its grain offering
29: 25 in addition to the **regular** burnt offering with its grain offering
29: 28 in addition to the **regular** burnt offering with its grain offering
29: 31 in addition to the **regular** burnt offering with its grain offering
29: 34 in addition to the **regular** burnt offering with its grain offering
29: 38 in addition to the **regular** burnt offering with its grain offering
Dt 11: 12 the eyes of the LORD your God are **continually** on it from the
2Sa 9: 7 to your grandfather Saul, and you will **always** eat at my table."
9: 10 grandson of your master, will **always** eat at my table."
9: 13 because he **always** ate at the king's table, and he was crippled in
1Ki 10: 8 who **continually** stand before you and hear your wisdom!
2Ki 4: 9 "I know that this man who **often** comes our way is a holy man of
25: 29 and for the rest of his life ate **regularly** at the king's table.
25: 30 Day by day the king gave Jehoiachin a **regular** allowance as long
1Ch 16: 6 Jahaziel the priests were to blow the trumpets **regularly** before the
16: 11 Look to the LORD and his strength; seek his face **always**.
16: 37 the ark of the covenant of the LORD to minister there **regularly**,
16: 40 offerings to the LORD on the altar of burnt offering **regularly**,
23: 31 They were to serve before the LORD **regularly** in the proper
2Ch 2: 4 [2:3] for setting out the consecrated bread **regularly**, and for
9: 7 who **continually** stand before you and hear your wisdom!
24: 14 burnt offerings were presented **continually** in the temple of the
Ezr 3: 5 After that, they presented the **regular** burnt offerings, the New
Ne 10: 33 [10:34] for the **regular** grain offerings and burnt offerings;
10: 33 [10:34] **[RPH]** for the offerings on the Sabbaths, New Moon
Ps 16: 8 I have set the LORD **always** before me. Because he is at my right
25: 15 My eyes are **ever** on the LORD, for only he will release my feet
34: 1 [34:2] LORD at all times; his praise will **always** be on my lips.
35: 27 may they **always** say, "The LORD be exalted, who delights in the
38: 17 [38:18] For I am about to fall, and my pain is **ever** with me.
40: 11 [40:12] may your love and your truth **always** protect me.
40: 16 [40:17] may those who love your salvation **always** say,
50: 8 your sacrifices or your burnt offerings, which are **ever** before me.
51: 3 [51:5] I know my transgressions, and my sin is **always** before me.
69: 23 [69:24] so they cannot see, and their backs be bent **forever**.
70: 4 [70:5] may those who love your salvation **always** say, "Let God
71: 3 Be my rock of refuge, to which I can **always** go; give the
71: 6 brought me forth from my mother's womb. I will **ever** praise you.
71: 14 But as for me, I will **always** have hope; I will praise you more
72: 15 May people **ever** pray for him and bless him all day long.
73: 23 Yet I am **always** with you; you hold me by my right hand.
74: 23 the uproar of your enemies, which rises **continually**.
105: 4 Look to the LORD and his strength; seek his face **always**.
109: 15 May their sins **always** remain before the LORD, that he may cut
109: 19 a cloak wrapped about him, like a belt tied **forever** around him.
119: 44 I will **always** obey your law, for ever and ever.
119: 109 Though I **constantly** take my life in my hands, I will not forget
119: 117 and I will be delivered; I will **always** have regard for your decrees.
Pr 5: 19 breasts satisfy you always, may you **ever** be captivated by her love.
6: 21 Bind them upon your heart **forever**; fasten them around your neck.
15: 15 are wretched, but the cheerful heart has a **continual** feast.
28: 14 Blessed is the man who **always** fears the LORD, but he who
Isa 21: 8 And the lookout shouted, "**Day after day** [+3429], my lord,
49: 16 you on the palms of my hands; your walls are **ever** before me.
51: 13 that you live in **constant** terror every day because of the wrath of
52: 5 "And all day long my name is **constantly** blasphemed.
58: 11 The LORD will guide you **always**; he will satisfy your needs in a
60: 11 Your gates will **always** stand open, they will never be shut,
62: 6 O Jerusalem; they will **never** [+4202] be silent day or night.
65: 3 a people who **continually** provoke me to my very face,
Jer 6: 7 resound in her; her sickness and wounds are **ever** before me.
52: 33 and for the rest of his life ate **regularly** at the king's table.
52: 34 Day by day the king of Babylon gave Jehoiachin a **regular**
Eze 38: 8 nations to the mountains of Israel, which had **long** been desolate.
39: 14 " 'Men will be **regularly** employed to cleanse the land. Some will
46: 14 of this grain offering to the LORD is a **lasting** [+6409] ordinance.
46: 15 the oil shall be provided morning by morning for a **regular** burnt
Da 8: 11 it took away the **daily sacrifice** from him, and the place of his
8: 12 the host ⌞of the saints⌟ and the **daily sacrifice** were given over to it.
8: 13 the vision concerning the **daily sacrifice**, the rebellion that causes
11: 31 to desecrate the temple fortress and will abolish the **daily sacrifice**.
12: 11 "From the time that the **daily sacrifice** is abolished
Hos 12: 6 [12:7] maintain love and justice, and wait for your God **always**.
Ob 1: 16 drank on my holy hill, so all the nations will drink **continually**;
Na 3: 19 his hands at your fall, for who has not felt your **endless** cruelty?
Hab 1: 17 Is he to **keep on** emptying his net, destroying nations without

9459 תָּמִים tāmîm, a. [91] [√ 9462]

without defect [47], blameless [19], perfect [8], *untranslated* [4], full [3], good faith [2], whole [2], all [1], blameless [+1475] [1], blameless [+1505] [1], entire [1], right answer [1], truth [1]

Ge 6: 9 **blameless** among the people of his time, and he walked with God.
17: 1 and said, "I am God Almighty; walk before me and be **blameless**.
Ex 12: 5 The animals you choose must be year-old males **without defect**,
29: 1 me as priests: Take a young bull and two rams **without defect**.
Lev 1: 3 a burnt offering from the herd, he is to offer a male **without defect**.
1: 10 either the sheep or the goats, he is to offer a male **without defect**.
3: 1 he is to present before the LORD an animal **without defect**.

Lev 3: 6 to the LORD, he is to offer a male or female **without defect**.
3: 9 its fat, the **entire** fat tail cut off close to the backbone, all the fat
4: 3 he must bring to the LORD a young bull **without defect** as a sin
4: 23 he must bring as his offering a male goat **without defect**.
4: 28 his offering for the sin he committed a female goat **without defect**.
4: 32 a lamb as his sin offering, he is to bring a female **without defect**.
5: 15 one **without defect** and of the proper value in silver, according to
5: 18 a ram from the flock, one **without defect** and of the proper value.
6: 6 [5:25] from the flock, one **without defect** and of the proper value.
9: 2 and a ram for your burnt offering, *both* **without defect**,
9: 3 a calf and a lamb—both a year old and **without defect**—
14: 10 two male lambs and one ewe lamb a year old, each **without defect**,
14: 10 **[RPH]** along with three-tenths of an ephah of fine flour mixed
22: 19 you must present a male **without defect** from the cattle, sheep
22: 21 it must be **without defect** or blemish to be acceptable.
23: 12 a burnt offering to the LORD a lamb a year old **without defect**,
23: 15 brought the sheaf of the wave offering, count off seven **full** weeks.
23: 18 each a year old and **without defect**, one young bull and two rams.
25: 30 If it is not redeemed before a **full** year has passed, the house in the
Nu 6: 14 a year-old male lamb **without defect** for a burnt offering,
6: 14 a year-old ewe lamb **without defect** for a sin offering, a ram
6: 14 for a sin offering, a ram **without defect** for a fellowship offering,
19: 2 Tell the Israelites to bring you a red heifer **without defect**
28: 3 two lambs a year old **without defect**, as a regular burnt offering
28: 9 make an offering of two lambs a year old **without defect**,
28: 11 one ram and seven male lambs a year old, *all* **without defect**.
28: 19 one ram and seven male lambs a year old, *all* **without defect**.
28: 31 and its grain offering. Be sure the animals are **without defect**.
29: 2 one ram and seven male lambs a year old, *all* **without defect**.
29: 8 one ram and seven male lambs a year old, *all* **without defect**.
29: 13 two rams and fourteen male lambs a year old, *all* **without defect**.
29: 17 two rams and fourteen male lambs a year old, *all* **without defect**.
29: 20 two rams and fourteen male lambs a year old, *all* **without defect**.
29: 23 two rams and fourteen male lambs a year old, *all* **without defect**.
29: 26 two rams and fourteen male lambs a year old, *all* **without defect**.
29: 29 two rams and fourteen male lambs a year old, *all* **without defect**.
29: 32 two rams and fourteen male lambs a year old, *all* **without defect**.
29: 36 one ram and seven male lambs a year old, *all* **without defect**.
Dt 18: 13 You must be **blameless** before the LORD your God.
32: 4 He is the Rock, his works are **perfect**, and all his ways are just.
Jos 10: 13 in the middle of the sky and delayed going down about a **full** day.
24: 14 "Now fear the LORD and serve him with **all** faithfulness.
Jdg 9: 16 and in **good faith** when you made Abimelech king,
9: 19 and in **good faith** toward Jerub-Baal and his family today,
1Sa 14: 41 to the LORD, the God of Israel, "Give me the **right answer**."
2Sa 22: 24 I have been **blameless** before him and have kept myself from sin.
22: 26 to the **blameless** [+1475] you show yourself blameless,
22: 31 "As for God, his way is **perfect**; the word of the LORD is
22: 33 It is God who arms me with strength and makes my way **perfect**.
Job 12: 4 a mere laughingstock, though righteous and **blameless**!
36: 4 that my words are not false; *one* **perfect** *in* knowledge is with you.
37: 16 hang poised, those wonders of *him who* is **perfect** *in* knowledge?
Ps 15: 2 He whose walk is **blameless** and who does what is righteous,
18: 23 [18:24] I have been **blameless** before him and have kept myself
18: 25 [18:26] to the **blameless** [+1505] you show yourself blameless,
18: 30 [18:31] As for God, his way is **perfect**; the word of the LORD is
18: 32 [18:33] who arms me with strength and makes my way **perfect**.
19: 7 [19:8] The law of the LORD is **perfect**, reviving the soul.
37: 18 The days of the **blameless** are known to the LORD, and their
84: 11 [84:12] does he withhold from those whose walk is **blameless**.
101: 2 I will be careful to lead a **blameless** life—when will you come to
101: 6 dwell with me; he whose walk is **blameless** will minister to me.
119: 1 Blessed are *they* whose ways are **blameless**, who walk according
119: 80 May my heart be **blameless** toward your decrees, that I may not be
Pr 1: 12 let's swallow them alive, like the grave, and **whole**, like those who
2: 21 upright will live in the land, and the **blameless** will remain in it;
11: 5 The righteousness of the **blameless** makes a straight way for them,
11: 20 perverse heart but he delights in *those whose* ways are **blameless**.
28: 10 his own trap, but the **blameless** will receive a good inheritance.
28: 18 He whose walk is **blameless** is kept safe, but he whose ways are
Eze 15: 5 If it was not useful for anything when it was **whole**, how much less
28: 15 You were **blameless** in your ways from the day you were created
43: 22 "On the second day you are to offer a male goat **without defect** for
43: 23 you are to offer a young bull **[RPH]** and a ram from the flock,
43: 23 offer a young bull and a ram from the flock, both **without defect**.
43: 25 a young bull and a ram from the flock, *both* **without defect**.
45: 18 month on the first day you are to take a young bull **without defect**
45: 23 and seven rams **without defect** as a burnt offering to the LORD,
46: 4 on the Sabbath day is to be six male lambs **[RPH]** and a ram,
46: 4 Sabbath day is to be six male lambs and a ram, *all* **without defect**.
46: 6 he is to offer a young bull, six lambs and a ram, *all* **without defect**.
46: 6 a young bull, six lambs and a ram, all without defect. **[RPH]**
46: 13 " 'Every day you are to provide a year-old lamb **without defect** for
Am 5: 10 the one who reproves in court and despise him who tells the **truth**.

9460 תֻּמִּים *tummîm*, n.m.[pl.]. [5] [√ 9448; cf. 9462]

Thummim [5]

Ex 28: 30 Also put the Urim and the **Thummim** in the breastpiece, so they
Lev 8: 8 on him and put the Urim and **Thummim** in the breastpiece.
Dt 33: 8 "Your **Thummim** and Urim belong to the man you favored.
Ezr 2: 63 until there was a priest ministering with the Urim and **Thummim**.
Ne 7: 65 there should be a priest ministering with the Urim and **Thummim**.

9461 תָּמַךְ *tāmak*, v. [21]

uphold [3], gains [2], holds [2], lay hold [2], accepting [1], gain [1], grasps [1], held up [1], held [1], hold fast [1], lead straight [1], made secure [1], support [1], taken hold [1], took hold [1], upholds [1]

Ge 48: 17 [A] so *he* **took hold** *of* his father's hand to move it from
Ex 17: 12 [A] Aaron and Hur **held** his hands **up**—one on one side, one on
Job 36: 17 [A] the wicked; judgment and justice *have* **taken hold** of you.
Ps 16: 5 [A] me my portion and my cup; you *have* **made** my lot **secure**.
17: 5 [A] My steps *have* **held** to your paths; my feet have not slipped.
41: 12 [41:13] [A] In my integrity *you* **uphold** me and set me in your
63: 8 [63:9] [A] My soul clings to you; your right hand **upholds** me.
Pr 3: 18 [A] who embrace her; *those who* **lay hold** *of* her will be blessed.
4: 4 [A] and said, "**Lay hold** *of* my words *with* all your heart;
5: 5 [A] feet go down to death; her steps **lead straight** *to* the grave.
5: 22 [C] wicked man ensnare him; the cords of his sin **hold** *him* **fast**.
11: 16 [A] A kindhearted woman **gains** respect, but ruthless men gain
11: 16 [A] woman gains respect, but ruthless men **gain** only wealth.
28: 17 [A] murder will be a fugitive till death; *let* no *one* **support** him.
29: 23 [A] pride brings him low, but a man of lowly spirit **gains** honor.
31: 19 [A] she holds the distaff and **grasps** the spindle *with* her fingers.
Isa 33: 15 [A] from extortion and keeps his hand from **accepting** bribes,
41: 10 [A] help you; *I will* **uphold** you with my righteous right hand.
42: 1 [A] "Here is my servant, whom *I* **uphold**, my chosen one in
Am 1: 5 [A] of Aven and the *one who* **holds** the scepter in Beth Eden.
1: 8 [A] of Ashdod and the *one who* **holds** the scepter in Ashkelon.

9462 תָּמַם *tāmam*, v. [64] [→ 3462, 5507, 9447, 9448, 9450, 9459, 9460]

gone [5], *untranslated* [4], completely [4], end [4], perish [3], all [2], blameless [2], completed [2], finished [2], last [2], over [2], put an end [2], show yourself blameless [2], vanish [2], all gone [1], almost to a man [+4392+6330] [1], burn away [1], burned away [1], burned [1], consumed [1], cook well [1], destroy [1], destroyed [1], die [1], died [1], done [1], doomed [1], down to [+6330] [1], ended [1], fail [1], full [1], have get ready [1], meet end [1], overtaken [1], perfect [1], perished [1], perishing [1], settled [1], spent [1], stop [1]

Ge 47: 15 [A] the money of the people of Egypt and Canaan *was* **gone**,
47: 18 [A] When that year *was* **over**, they came to him the following
47: 18 [A] hide from our lord the fact that since our money *is* **gone**
Lev 25: 29 [A] he retains the right of redemption a **full** year after its sale.
26: 20 [A] Your strength *will be* **spent** in vain, because your soil will
Nu 14: 33 [A] until the **last** *of* your bodies lies in the desert.
14: 35 [A] *They will* **meet** their **end** in this desert; here they will die."
17: 13 [17:28] [A] of the LORD will die. *Are we* **all** going to die?"
32: 13 [A] generation of those who had done evil in his sight *was* **gone**.
Dt 2: 14 [A] that entire generation of fighting men *had* **perished** from the
2: 15 [A] LORD's hand was against them until he had **completely**
2: 16 [A] Now when the **last** *of* these fighting men among the people
31: 24 [A] in a book the words of this law from beginning to **end**,
31: 30 [A] Moses recited the words of this song from beginning to **end**
34: 8 [A] until the time of weeping and mourning *was* **over**.
Jos 3: 16 [A] the Sea of the Arabah (the Salt Sea) was **completely** cut off.
3: 17 [A] all Israel passed by until the whole nation *had* **completed**
4: 1 [A] When the whole nation *had* **finished** crossing the Jordan,
4: 10 [A] the LORD had commanded Joshua *was* **done** by the people,
4: 11 [A] as soon as all of them **[RPH]** had crossed, the ark of the
5: 6 [A] who were of military age when they left Egypt *had* **died**,
5: 8 [A] And after **[RPH]** the whole nation had been circumcised,
8: 24 [A] **[NIE]** all the Israelites returned to Ai and killed those who
10: 20 [A] them completely—**almost to a man** [+4392+6330]—
1Sa 16: 11 [A] So he asked Jesse, "*Are these* **all** the sons you have?" "There
2Sa 15: 24 [A] Abiathar offered sacrifices until all the people *had* **finished**
20: 18 [G] used to say, 'Get your answer at Abel,' and that **settled** *it*.
22: 26 [F] to the blameless *you* **show yourself blameless**,
1Ki 6: 22 [A] **[NIE]** He also overlaid with gold the altar that belonged to
7: 22 [A] of lilies. And so the work on the pillars *was* **completed**.
14: 10 [A] the house of Jeroboam as one burns dung, until it *is* **all gone**.
2Ki 7: 13 [A] they will only be like all these Israelites who *are* **doomed**.
22: 4 [G] **have** *him* **get ready** the money that has been brought into the
Job 22: 3 [G] What would he gain if your ways *were* **blameless**?
31: 40 [A] and weeds instead of barley." The words of Job *are* **ended**.
Ps 9: 6 [9:7] [A] Endless ruin *has* **overtaken** the enemy, you have
18: 25 [18:26] [F] to the blameless *you* **show yourself blameless**,

Ps 19:13 [19:14] [A] *will I be* **blameless**, innocent of great transgression.
64: 6 [64:7] [A] and say, "*We have* devised *a* **perfect** plan!"
73:19 [A] are they destroyed, **completely** swept away by terrors!
102:27 [102:28] [A] remain the same, and your years *will* never **end**.
104:35 [A] *may* sinners **vanish** from the earth and the wicked be no
Isa 16: 4 [A] will cease; the aggressor *will* **vanish** from the land.
18: 5 [A] when the blossom *is* **gone** and the flower becomes a ripening
33: 1 [G] When you **stop** destroying, you will be destroyed; when you
Jer 1: 3 [A] **down to** [+6330] the fifth month of the eleventh year of
6:29 [A] The bellows blow fiercely *to* **burn away** the lead with fire,
14:15 [A] Those same prophets *will* **perish** by sword and famine.
24:10 [A] plague against them until they *are* **destroyed** from the land I
27: 8 [A] declares the LORD, until I **destroy** it by his hand.
36:23 [A] into the firepot, until the entire scroll *was* **burned** in the fire.
37:21 [A] the bakers each day until all the bread in the city *was* **gone**.
44:12 [A] *They will* all **perish** in Egypt; they will fall by the sword
44:12 [A] in Egypt; they will fall by the sword or **die** from famine.
44:18 [A] had nothing and *have been* **perishing** by sword and famine."
44:27 [A] the Jews in Egypt *will* **perish** by sword and famine until they
La 3:22 [A] Because of the LORD's great love *we are* not **consumed**,
4:22 [A] O Daughter of Zion, your punishment *will* **end**; he will not
Eze 22:15 [G] the countries; and *I will* **put an end** *to* your uncleanness.
24:10 [G] **Cook** the meat **well**, mixing in the spices; and let the bones
24:11 [A] so its impurities may be melted and its deposit **burned away**.
47:12 [A] Their leaves will not wither, nor *will* their fruit **fail**.
Da 8:23 [G] when rebels *have become* **completely** wicked, a stern-faced
9:24 [G] to **put an end** [K 3159] *to* sin, to atone for wickedness, to

9463 תִּמְנָה *timnâ*, n.pr.loc. [12] [→ 9464; cf. 4948?]

Timnah [11], there[s] [+928+2025] [1]

Ge 38:12 he went up to **Timnah**, to the men who were shearing his sheep,
38:13 "Your father-in-law is on his way to **Timnah** to shear his sheep,"
38:14 down at the entrance to Enaim, which is on the road to **Timnah**.
Jos 15:10 continued down to Beth Shemesh and crossed to **Timnah**.
15:57 Kain, Gibeah and **Timnah**—ten towns and their villages.
19:43 Elon, **Timnah**, Ekron,
Jdg 14: 1 Samson went down to **Timnah** and saw there a young Philistine
14: 1 to Timnah and saw **there**[s] [+928+2025] a young Philistine woman.
14: 2 his father and mother, "I have seen a Philistine woman in **Timnah**;
14: 5 Samson went down to **Timnah** together with his father
14: 5 As they approached the vineyards of **Timnah**, suddenly a young
2Ch 28:18 Aijalon and Gederoth, as well as Soco, **Timnah** and Gimzo,

9464 תִּמְנִי *timnî*, a.g. [1] [√ 9463; cf. 4948?]

Timnite's [1]

Jdg 15: 6 they were told, "Samson, the **Timnite's** son-in-law, because his

9465 תִּמְנַע *timna'*, n.pr.m. & f. [6]

Timna [6]

Ge 36:12 Esau's son Eliphaz also had a concubine named **Timna**, who bore
36:22 The sons of Lotan: Hori and Homam. **Timna** was Lotan's sister.
36:40 according to their clans and regions: **Timna**, Alvah, Jetheth,
1Ch 1:36 Teman, Omar, Zepho, Gatam and Kenaz; *by* **Timna**: Amalek.
1:39 The sons of Lotan: Hori and Homam. **Timna** was Lotan's sister.
1:51 Hadad also died. The chiefs of Edom were: **Timna**, Alvah, Jetheth,

9466 תִּמְנַת־חֶרֶס *timnat-ḥeres*, n.pr.loc. [1] [√ 4948? + 3065]

Timnath Heres [1]

Jdg 2: 9 at **Timnath Heres** in the hill country of Ephraim, north of Mount

9467 תִּמְנַת־סֶרַח *timnat-seraḥ*, n.pr.loc. [2] [√ 4948? + 3064]

Timnath Serah [2]

Jos 19:50 town he asked for—**Timnath Serah** in the hill country of Ephraim.
24:30 at **Timnath Serah** in the hill country of Ephraim, north of Mount

9468 תֶּמֶס *temes*, n.m. [1] [√ 5022]

melting away [1]

Ps 58: 8 [58:9] Like a slug **melting away** as it moves along, like a stillborn

9469 תָּמָר[1] *tāmār*[1], n.m. [12] [→ 1265, 2954, 6559, 9470, 9471, 9472, 9474; cf. 9406]

palms [5], palm [3], palm tree [2], palm trees [2]

Ex 15:27 to Elim, where there were twelve springs and seventy **palm trees**,
Lev 23:40 **palm** fronds, leafy branches and poplars, and rejoice before the
Nu 33: 9 to Elim, where there were twelve springs and seventy **palm trees**,
Dt 34: 3 from the Valley of Jericho, the City of **Palms**, as far as Zoar.
Jdg 1:16 went up from the City of **Palms** with the men of Judah to live
3:13 and attacked Israel, and they took possession of the City of **Palms**.
2Ch 28:15 countrymen at Jericho, the City of **Palms**, and returned to Samaria.
Ne 8:15 and from myrtles, **palms** and shade trees, to make booths"—
Ps 92:12 [92:13] The righteous will flourish like a **palm tree**, they will
SS 7: 7 [7:8] Your stature is like that of the **palm**, and your breasts like
7: 8 [7:9] I said, "I will climb the **palm tree**; I will take hold of its
Joel 1:12 the pomegranate, the **palm** and the apple tree—all the trees of the

9470 תָּמָר[2] *tāmār*[2], n.pr.f. [22] [√ 9469]

Tamar [22]

Ge 38: 6 Judah got a wife for Er, his firstborn, and her name was **Tamar**.
38:11 Judah then said to his daughter-in-law **Tamar**, "Live as a widow in
38:11 just like his brothers." So **Tamar** went to live in her father's house.
38:13 When **Tamar** was told, "Your father-in-law is on his way to
38:24 "Your daughter-in-law **Tamar** is guilty of prostitution, and as a
Ru 4:12 your family be like that of Perez, whom **Tamar** bore to Judah."
2Sa 13: 1 the course of time, Amnon son of David fell in love with **Tamar**,
13: 2 frustrated to the point of illness on account of his sister **Tamar**,
13: 4 Amnon said to him, "I'm in love with **Tamar**, my brother
13: 5 'I would like my sister **Tamar** to come and give me something to
13: 6 "I would like my sister **Tamar** to come and make some special
13: 7 David sent word to **Tamar** at the palace: "Go to the house of your
13: 8 So **Tamar** went to the house of her brother Amnon, who was lying
13:10 Amnon said to **Tamar**, "Bring the food here into my bedroom
13:10 **Tamar** took the bread she had prepared and brought it to her
13:19 **Tamar** put ashes on her head and tore the ornamented robe she
13:20 **Tamar** lived in her brother Absalom's house, a desolate woman.
13:22 he hated Amnon because he had disgraced his sister **Tamar**.
13:32 intention ever since the day Amnon raped his sister **Tamar**.
14:27 The daughter's name was **Tamar**, and she became a beautiful
1Ch 2: 4 **Tamar**, Judah's daughter-in-law, bore him Perez and Zerah.
3: 9 besides his sons by his concubines. And **Tamar** was their sister.

9471 תָּמָר[3] *tāmār*[3], n.pr.loc. [2 / 3] [√ 9469]

Tamar [3]

1Ki 9:18 [and **Tadmor** [K; see Q 9330] in the desert, within his land,]
Eze 47:18 land of Israel, to the eastern sea and as far as **Tamar**. [BHS 4499]
47:19 "On the south side it will run from **Tamar** as far as the waters of
48:28 "The southern boundary of Gad will run south from **Tamar** to the

9472 תֹּמֶר[1] *tōmer*[1], n.m.loc. [1] [√ 9469]

palm [1]

Jdg 4: 5 She held court under the **Palm** *of* Deborah between Ramah

9473 תֹּמֶר[2] *tōmer*[2], n.m. [1] [√ 607, 9406?]

scarecrow [1]

Jer 10: 5 Like a **scarecrow** *in* a melon patch, their idols cannot speak;

9474 תִּמֹרָה *timōrâ*, n.f. [19] [√ 9469]

palm trees [14], palm tree decorations [2], palm tree [2], palm tree designs [1]

1Ki 6:29 outer rooms, he carved cherubim, **palm trees** and open flowers.
6:32 **palm trees** and open flowers, and overlaid the cherubim and palm
6:32 and overlaid the cherubim and **palm trees** with beaten gold.
6:35 **palm trees** and open flowers on them and overlaid them with gold
7:36 lions and **palm trees** on the surfaces of the supports and on the
2Ch 3: 5 with fine gold and decorated it with **palm tree** and chain **designs**.
Eze 40:16 The faces of the projecting walls were decorated with **palm trees**.
40:22 its **palm tree decorations** had the same measurements as those of
40:26 it had **palm tree decorations** on the faces of the projecting walls
40:31 **palm trees** decorated its jambs, and eight steps led up to it.
40:34 **palm trees** decorated the jambs on either side, and eight steps led
40:37 **palm trees** decorated the jambs on either side, and eight steps led
41:18 were carved cherubim and **palm trees**. Palm trees alternated with
41:18 and palm trees. **Palm trees** alternated with cherubim.
41:19 the face of a man toward the **palm tree** on one side and the face of
41:19 one side and the face of a lion toward the **palm tree** on the other.
41:20 and **palm trees** were carved on the wall of the outer sanctuary.
41:25 carved cherubim and **palm trees** like those carved on the walls,
41:26 were narrow windows with **palm trees** carved on each side.

9475 תַּמְרוּק *tamrûq*, n.[m.]. [4] [√ 5347]

beauty treatments [2], cleanse away [1], cosmetics [1]

Est 2: 3 charge of the women; and let **beauty treatments** be given to them.
2: 9 Immediately he provided her with her **beauty treatments**
2:12 six months with oil of myrrh and six with perfumes and **cosmetics**.
Pr 20:30 Blows and wounds **cleanse** [K 5347] **away** evil, and beatings

9476 תַּמְרוּרִים¹ ***tamrûrîm¹***, n.m. [3] [√ 5352]

bitter [1], bitterly [1], great [1]

Jer 6:26 mourn with **bitter** wailing as for an only son, for suddenly the
31:15 "A voice is heard in Ramah, mourning and **great** weeping,
Hos 12:14 [12:15] Ephraim has **bitterly** provoked him to anger; his Lord

9477 ²תַּמְרוּרִים ***tamrûrîm²***, n.m. [1] [√ 9406]

guideposts [1]

Jer 31:21 "Set up road signs; put up **guideposts**. Take note of the highway,

9478 תַּן ***tan***, n.[m. & f.]. [14] [√ 9490]

jackals [13], jackal [1]

Job 30:29 I have become a brother of **jackals**, a companion of owls.
Ps 44:19 [44:20] you crushed us and made us a haunt for **jackals**
Isa 13:22 will howl in her strongholds, **jackals** in her luxurious palaces.
34:13 She will become a haunt for **jackals**, a home for owls.
35:7 In the haunts where **jackals** once lay, grass and reeds and papyrus
43:20 The wild animals honor me, the **jackals** and the owls, because I
Jer 9:11 [9:10] "I will make Jerusalem a heap of ruins, a haunt of **jackals**;
10:22 It will make the towns of Judah desolate, a haunt of **jackals**.
14:6 Wild donkeys stand on the barren heights and pant like **jackals**;
49:33 "Hazor will become a haunt of **jackals**, a desolate place forever.
51:37 a haunt of **jackals**, an object of horror and scorn, a place where no
La 4:3 Even **jackals** offer their breasts to nurse their young, but my
Mic 1:8 and naked. I will howl like a **jackal** and moan like an owl.
Mal 1:3 into a wasteland and left his inheritance to the desert **jackals**."

9479 תָּנָה¹ ***tānâ¹***, v. [2] [√ 924]

sold [2]

Hos 8:9 [G] donkey wandering alone. Ephraim *has* **sold** *herself to* lovers.
8:10 [A] Although *they have* **sold** *themselves* among the nations,

9480 ²תָּנָה ***tānâ²***, v. [2]

commemorate [1], recite [1]

Jdg 5:11 [D] *They* **recite** the righteous acts of the LORD, the righteous
11:40 [D] to **commemorate** the daughter of Jephthah the Gileadite.

9481 תְּנוּאָה ***tᵉnû'â***, n.f. [2] [√ 5648]

against [1], fault [1]

Nu 14:34 for your sins and know what it is like to have me **against** you.'
Job 33:10 Yet God has found **fault** with me; he considers me his enemy.

9482 תְּנוּבָה ***tᵉnûbâ***, n.f. [5] [√ 5649]

fruit [3], crops [1], food [1]

Dt 32:13 on the heights of the land and fed him with the **fruit** *of* the fields.
Jdg 9:11 the fig tree replied, 'Should I give up my **fruit**, so good and sweet,
Isa 27:6 Israel will bud and blossom and fill all the world with **fruit**.
La 4:9 with hunger, they waste away for lack of **food** *from* the field.
Eze 36:30 I will increase the fruit of the trees and the **crops** *of* the field,

9483 תְּנוּךְ ***tᵉnûk***, n.[m.]. [8]

lobe [5], lobes [2], *untranslated* [1]

Ex 29:20 and put it on the **lobes** *of* the right ears of Aaron and his sons,
29:20 put it on the lobes of the right ears of Aaron and **[RPH]** his sons,
Lev 8:23 took some of its blood and put it on the **lobe** *of* Aaron's right ear,
8:24 and put some of the blood on the **lobes** *of* their right ears,
14:14 and put it on the **lobe** *of* the right ear of the one to be cleansed,
14:17 in his palm on the **lobe** *of* the right ear of the one to be cleansed,
14:25 and put it on the **lobe** *of* the right ear of the one to be cleansed,
14:28 on the **lobe** *of* the right ear of the one to be cleansed, on the thumb

9484 תְּנוּמָה ***tᵉnûmâ***, n.f. [5] [√ 5670]

slumber [5]

Job 33:15 when deep sleep falls on men as they **slumber** in their beds,
Ps 132:4 I will allow no sleep to my eyes, no **slumber** to my eyelids,
Pr 6:4 Allow no sleep to your eyes, no **slumber** to your eyelids.
6:10 A little sleep, a little **slumber**, a little folding of the hands to rest—
24:33 A little sleep, a little **slumber**, a little folding of the hands to rest—

9485 תְּנוּפָה ***tᵉnûpâ***, n.f. [30] [√ 5677]

wave offering [21], waved [5], blows [1], uplifted [1], was waved [+5677] [1], wave offerings [1]

Ex 29:24 and his sons and wave them before the LORD as a **wave offering**.
29:26 wave it before the LORD as a **wave offering**, and it will be your
29:27 the breast that **was waved** [+5677] and the thigh that was
35:22 They all presented their gold as a **wave offering** to the LORD.
38:24 The total amount of the gold from the **wave offering** used for all
38:29 The bronze from the **wave offering** was 70 talents and 2,400
Lev 7:30 and wave the breast before the LORD as a **wave offering**.
7:34 I have taken the breast that is **waved** and the thigh that is presented
8:27 his sons and waved them before the LORD as a **wave offering**.
8:29 waved it before the LORD as a **wave offering**, as the LORD
9:21 and the right thigh before the LORD as a **wave offering**,
10:14 your sons and your daughters may eat the breast that was **waved**
10:15 the breast that was **waved** must be brought with the fat portions of
10:15 made by fire, to be waved before the LORD as a **wave offering**.
14:12 he shall wave them before the LORD as a **wave offering**.
14:21 he must take one male lamb as a guilt offering to be **waved** to
14:24 log of oil, and wave them before the LORD as a **wave offering**.
23:15 the day you brought the sheaf of the **wave offering**, count off
23:17 baked with yeast, as a **wave offering** of firstfruits to the LORD.
23:20 is to wave the two lambs before the LORD as a **wave offering**,
Nu 6:20 priest shall then wave them before the LORD as a **wave offering**;
6:20 together with the breast that was **waved** and the thigh that was
8:11 Levites before the LORD as a **wave offering** from the Israelites,
8:13 his sons and then present them as a **wave offering** to the LORD.
8:15 have purified the Levites and presented them as a **wave offering**,
8:21 Then Aaron presented them as a **wave offering** before the LORD
18:11 whatever is set aside from the gifts of all the **wave offerings** *of* the
18:18 just as the breast of the **wave offering** and the right thigh are
Isa 19:16 They will shudder with fear at the **uplifted** hand that the LORD
30:32 and harps, as he fights them in battle with the **blows** of his arm.

9486 תַּנּוּר ***tannûr***, n.m. [15]

oven [8], furnace [3], ovens [3], firepot [1]

Ge 15:17 a smoking **firepot** with a blazing torch appeared and passed
Ex 8:3 [7:28] on your people, and into your **ovens** and kneading troughs.
Lev 2:4 " 'If you bring a grain offering baked in an **oven**, it is to consist of
7:9 Every grain offering baked in an **oven** or cooked in a pan or on a
11:35 on becomes unclean; an **oven** or cooking pot must be broken up.
26:26 of bread, ten women will be able to bake your bread in one **oven**,
Ne 3:11 Pahath-Moab repaired another section and the Tower of the **Ovens**.
12:38 half the people—past the Tower of the **Ovens** to the Broad Wall,
Ps 21:9 [21:10] your appearing you will make them like a fiery **furnace**.
Isa 31:9 the LORD, whose fire is in Zion, whose **furnace** is in Jerusalem.
La 5:10 Our skin is hot as an **oven**, feverish from hunger.
Hos 7:4 burning like an **oven** whose fire the baker need not stir from the
7:6 Their hearts are like an **oven**; they approach him with intrigue.
7:7 All of them are hot as an **oven**; they devour their rulers. All their
Mal 4:1 [3:19] "Surely the day is coming; it will burn like a **furnace**. All

9487 תַּנְחוּמוֹת ***tanḥûmôt***, n.[m.pl.]. [2] [√ 5714]

consolation [1], consolations [1]

Job 15:11 Are God's **consolations** not enough for you, words spoken gently
21:2 carefully to my words; let this be the **consolation** you give me.

9488 תַּנְחוּמִים ***tanḥûmîm***, n.m.[pl.]. [3] [√ 5714]

comforting [1], consolation [1], console [1]

Ps 94:19 was great within me, your **consolation** brought joy to my soul.
Isa 66:11 For you will nurse and be satisfied at her **comforting** breasts;
Jer 16:7 or a mother—nor will anyone give them a drink to **console** them.

9489 תַּנְחֻמֶת ***tanḥumet***, n.pr.m. [2] [√ 5714]

Tanhumeth [2]

2Ki 25:23 son of Kareah, Seraiah son of **Tanhumeth** the Netophathite,
Jer 40:8 and Jonathan the sons of Kareah, Seraiah son of **Tanhumeth**,

9490 תַּנִּין ***tannîn***, n.m. [15] [→ 6531, 9478]

monster [5], snake [3], serpent [2], creatures of the sea [1], great sea creatures [1], jackal [1], monster of the deep [1], serpents [1]

Ge 1:21 So God created the great **creatures of the sea** and every living
Ex 7:9 and throw it down before Pharaoh,' and it will become a **snake**."
7:10 down in front of Pharaoh and his officials, and it became a **snake**.
7:12 Each one threw down his staff and it became a **snake**. But Aaron's
Dt 32:33 Their wine is the venom of **serpents**, the deadly poison of cobras.
Ne 2:13 By night I went out through the Valley Gate toward the **Jackal**
Job 7:12 Am I the sea, or the **monster of the deep**, that you put me under
Ps 74:13 by your power; you broke the heads of the **monster** in the waters.
91:13 and the cobra; you will trample the great lion and the **serpent**.
148:7 from the earth, you **great sea creatures** and all ocean depths,
Isa 27:1 Leviathan the coiling serpent; he will slay the **monster** of the sea.
51:9 you who cut Rahab to pieces, who pierced that **monster** through?
Jer 51:34 Like a **serpent** he has swallowed us and filled his stomach with
Eze 29:3 king of Egypt, you great **monster** lying among your streams.
32:2 you are like a **monster** in the seas thrashing about in your streams,

9491 [1]תִּנְשֶׁמֶת **tinšemet**[1], n.f. [1] [√ 5971]
chameleon [1]

Lev 11:30 the monitor lizard, the wall lizard, the skink and the **chameleon**.

9492 [2]תִּנְשֶׁמֶת **tinšemet**[2], n.f. [2] [√ 5971]
white owl [2]

Lev 11:18 the **white owl**, the desert owl, the osprey,
Dt 14:16 the little owl, the great owl, the **white owl**,

9493 תָּעַב **tā'ab**, v.den. [22] [→ 9359?; cf. 9290]
vile [4], abhor [3], detest [3], abhorred [2], despise [2], detest [+9493] [2], abhors [1], behaved in the vilest manner [+4394] [1], degraded [1], loathed [1], rejected [1], repulsive [1]

Dt 7:26 [D] Utterly abhor and **detest** [+9493] it, for it is set apart for
7:26 [D] Utterly abhor and **detest** [+9493] it, for it is set apart for
23:7 [23:8] [D] *Do* not **abhor** an Edomite, for he is your brother.
23:7 [23:8] [D] *Do* not **abhor** an Egyptian, because you lived as an
1Ki 21:26 [G] *He* **behaved in the vilest** [+4394] **manner** by going after
1Ch 21:6 [C] because the king's command *was* **repulsive** *to* him.
Job 9:31 [D] me into a slime pit so that even my clothes *would* **detest** me.
15:16 [C] how much less man, *who is* **vile** and corrupt, who drinks up
19:19 [D] All my intimate friends **detest** me; those I love have turned
30:10 [D] *They* **detest** me and keep their distance; they do not hesitate
Ps 5:6 [5:7] [D] bloodthirsty and deceitful men the LORD **abhors**.
14:1 [G] They are corrupt, their deeds *are* **vile**; there is no one who
53:1 [53:2] [G] They are corrupt, and *their* ways *are* **vile**; there is no
106:40 [D] was angry with his people and **abhorred** his inheritance.
107:18 [D] They **loathed** all food and drew near the gates of death.
119:163 [D] I hate and **abhor** falsehood but I love your law.
Isa 14:19 [C] you are cast out of your tomb like a **rejected** branch; you are
49:7 [D] to him who was despised and **abhorred** *by* the nation,
Eze 16:25 [D] street you built your lofty shrines and **degraded** your beauty,
16:52 [G] Because your sins *were* more **vile** than theirs, they appear
Am 5:10 [D] who reproves in court and **despise** him who tells the truth.
Mic 3:9 [D] of Israel, who **despise** justice and distort all that is right;

9494 תָּעָה **tā'â**, v. [50] [→ 9360; cf. 3246]
led astray [6], leads astray [4], go astray [3], lead astray [3], wandered [3], went astray [3], reel [2], stray [2], strayed [2], wayward [2], deceive himself [1], did[s] [1], error [1], falters [1], go about [1], gone astray [1], had wander [1], made a fatal mistake [+928+5883] [1], made wander [1], make stagger [1], make wander [1], makes stagger [1], mislead [1], sends wandering [1], spread [1], staggers around [1], strays [1], wander about [1], wandering around [1], wandering off [1]

Ge 20:13 [G] And when God **had** me **wander** from my father's household,
21:14 [A] went on her way and **wandered** in the desert of Beersheba.
37:15 [A] a man found him **wandering around** in the fields and asked
Ex 23:4 [A] you come across your enemy's ox or donkey **wandering off**,
2Ki 21:9 [G] Manasseh **led** them **astray**, so that they did more evil than
2Ch 33:9 [G] But Manasseh **led** Judah and the people of Jerusalem **astray**,
Job 12:24 [G] *he* **sends** them **wandering** through a trackless waste.
12:25 [G] with no light; *he* **makes** them **stagger** like drunkards.
15:31 [C] *Let him* not **deceive himself** by trusting what is worthless,
38:41 [A] its young cry out to God and **wander about** for lack of food?
Ps 58:3 [58:4] [A] from the womb *they are* **wayward** and speak lies.
95:10 [A] I said, "They are a people whose hearts **go astray**, and they
107:4 [A] *Some* **wandered** in desert wastelands, finding no way to a
107:40 [G] he who pours contempt on nobles **made** them **wander** in a
119:110 [A] a snare for me, but *I have* not **strayed** from your precepts.
119:176 [A] *I have* **strayed** like a lost sheep. Seek your servant, for I
Pr 7:25 [A] Do not let your heart turn to her ways or **stray** into her paths.
10:17 [G] to life, but whoever ignores correction **leads** others **astray**.
12:26 [G] in friendship, but the way of the wicked **leads** them **astray**.
14:22 [A] *Do* not those who plot evil **go astray**? But those who plan
21:16 [A] A man *who* **strays** from the path of understanding comes to
Isa 3:12 [G] O my people, your guides **lead** you **astray**; they turn you
9:16 [9:15] [G] Those who guide this people **mislead** them,
16:8 [A] which once reached Jazer and **spread** *toward* the desert.
19:13 [G] the cornerstones of her peoples *have* **led** Egypt **astray**.
19:14 [G] *they* **make** Egypt **stagger** in all that she does, as a drunkard
19:14 [C] all that she does, as a drunkard **staggers around** in his vomit.
21:4 [A] My heart **falters**, fear makes me tremble; the twilight I
28:7 [A] And these also stagger from wine and **reel** from beer: Priests
28:7 [A] *they* **reel** from beer, they stagger when seeing visions,
29:24 [A] *Those who are* **wayward** *in* spirit will gain understanding;
30:28 [G] in the jaws of the peoples a bit *that* **leads** them **astray**.
35:8 [A] who walk in that Way; wicked fools *will* not **go about** on it.
47:15 [A] Each of them goes on in his **error**; there is not one that can
53:6 [A] We all, like sheep, *have* **gone astray**, each of us has turned
63:17 [G] *do you* **make** us **wander** from your ways and harden our
Jer 23:13 [G] They prophesied by Baal and **led** my people Israel **astray**.
23:32 [G] tell them and **lead** my people **astray** with their reckless lies,
42:20 [G] that *you* **made a fatal mistake** [+928+5883] when you sent
50:6 [G] their shepherds *have* **led** them **astray** and caused them to
Eze 14:11 [A] the people of Israel *will* no longer **stray** from me, nor will
44:10 [A] Levites who went far from me when Israel **went astray**
44:10 [A] who **wandered** from me after their idols must bear the
44:15 [A] of my sanctuary when the Israelites **went astray** from me,
48:11 [A] *did* not **go astray** as the Levites did when the Israelites went
48:11 [A] did not go astray as the Levites **did**[s] when the Israelites went
48:11 [A] go astray as the Levites did when the Israelites **went astray**.
Hos 4:12 [G] A spirit of prostitution **leads** them **astray**; they are unfaithful
Am 2:4 [G] because they *have been* **led astray** *by* false gods,
Mic 3:5 [G] "As for the prophets *who* **lead** my people **astray**, if one

9495 תֹּעוּ **tō'û**, n.pr.m. [2] [cf. 9497]
Tou [2]

1Ch 18:9 When **Tou** king of Hamath heard that David had defeated the
18:10 victory in battle over Hadadezer, who had been at war with **Tou**.

9496 תְּעוּדָה **tᵉ'ûdâ**, n.f. [3] [√ 6386]
testimony [2], method of legalizing transactions [1]

Ru 4:7 This was the **method of legalizing transactions** in Israel.)
Isa 8:16 Bind up the **testimony** and seal up the law among my disciples.
8:20 To the law and to the **testimony**! If they do not speak according to

9497 תֹּעִי **tō'î**, n.pr.m. [3] [cf. 9495]
Tou [2], he[s] [1]

2Sa 8:9 When **Tou** king of Hamath heard that David had defeated the
8:10 **he**[s] sent his son Joram to King David to greet him and congratulate
8:10 victory in battle over Hadadezer, who had been at war with **Tou**.

9498 [1]תְּעָלָה **tᵉ'ālâ**[1], n.f. [9] [√ 6590?]
aqueduct [3], trench [3], channel [1], channels [1], tunnel [1]

1Ki 18:32 he dug a **trench** around it large enough to hold two seahs of seed.
18:35 The water ran down around the altar and even filled the **trench**.
18:38 the stones and the soil, and also licked up the water in the **trench**.
2Ki 18:17 up to Jerusalem and stopped at the **aqueduct** *of* the Upper Pool,
20:20 the pool and the **tunnel** by which he brought water into the city,
Job 38:25 Who cuts a **channel** for the torrents of rain, and a path for the
Isa 7:3 to meet Ahaz at the end of the **aqueduct** *of* the Upper Pool,
36:2 When the commander stopped at the **aqueduct** *of* the Upper Pool,
Eze 31:4 around its base and sent their **channels** to all the trees of the field.

9499 [2]תְּעָלָה **tᵉ'ālâ**[2], n.f. [2] [√ 6590]
healing [2]

Jer 30:13 to plead your cause, no remedy for your sore, no **healing** for you.
46:11 But you multiply remedies in vain; there is no **healing** for you.

9500 תַּעֲלוּלִים **taᵃlûlîm**, n.m.pl.abst. [2] [√ 6618]
harsh treatment [1], mere children [1]

Isa 3:4 I will make boys their officials; **mere children** will govern them.
66:4 so I also will choose **harsh treatment** *for* them and will bring

9501 תַּעְלֻם **taᵃlum**, n.f. Not used in NIV/BHS [√ 6623]

9502 תַּעֲלֻמָה **taᵃlumâ**, n.f. [3] [√ 6623]
secrets [2], hidden things [1]

Job 11:6 disclose to you the **secrets** *of* wisdom, for true wisdom has two
28:11 the sources of the rivers and brings **hidden things** to light.
Ps 44:21 [44:22] discovered it, since he knows the **secrets** *of* the heart?

9503 תַּעֲנוּג **taᵃnûg**, n.[m.]. [5] [√ 6695]
delight [1], delights of the heart [1], delights [1], live in luxury [1], pleasant [1]

Pr 19:10 It is not fitting for a fool to **live in luxury**—how much worse for a
Ecc 2:8 and a harem as well—the **delights of the heart** *of* man.
SS 7:6 [7:7] you are and how pleasing, O love, with your **delights**!
Mic 1:16 your heads in mourning for the children in whom you **delight**;
2:9 You drive the women of my people from their **pleasant** homes.

9504 תַּעֲנִית **taᵃnît**, n.f. [1] [√ 6700]
self-abasement [1]

Ezr 9:5 I rose from my **self-abasement**, with my tunic and cloak torn,

9505 תַּעְנָךְ ***ta'anak***, n.pr.loc. [7]

Taanach [7]

Jos 12:21 the king of **Taanach** one the king of Megiddo one
17:11 Ibleam and the people of Dor, Endor, **Taanach** and Megiddo,
21:25 From half the tribe of Manasseh they received **Taanach** and Gath
Jdg 1:27 or **Taanach** or Dor or Ibleam or Megiddo and their surrounding
5:19 the kings of Canaan fought at **Taanach** by the waters of Megiddo,
1Ki 4:12 in **Taanach** and Megiddo, and in all of Beth Shan next to Zarethan
1Ch 7:29 **Taanach**, Megiddo and Dor, together with their villages.

9506 תָּעַע ***tā'a'***, v. [2] [→ 9511]

scoffed [1], tricking [1]

Ge 27:12 [D] I would appear *to be* **tricking** him and would bring down a
2Ch 36:16 [F] **scoffed** at his prophets until the wrath of the LORD was

9507 תְּעֻפָה ***te'upâ***, n.f. [1] [√ 6415]

darkness [1]

Job 11:17 be brighter than noonday, and **darkness** will become like morning.

9508 תַּעֲצֻמוֹת ***ta'aṣumôt***, n.f.[pl.]. [1] [√ 6793]

strength [1]

Ps 68:35 [68:36] the God of Israel gives power and **strength** to his people.

9509 תַּעַר ***ta'ar***, n.m. [13] [√ 6867]

scabbard [5], razor [4], have shave [+6296+6584] [1], knife [1], sheath [1], unsheathed [+3655+4946] [1]

Nu 6:5 " 'During the entire period of his vow of separation no **razor** may
8:7 **have** *them* **shave** [+6296+6584] their whole bodies and wash their
1Sa 17:51 took hold of the Philistine's sword and drew it from the **scabbard**.
2Sa 20:8 strapped over it at his waist was a belt with a dagger in its **sheath**.
Ps 52:2 [52:4] it is like a sharpened **razor**, you who practice deceit.
Isa 7:20 In that day the Lord will use a **razor** hired from beyond the River—
Jer 36:23 the king cut them off with a scribe's **knife** and threw them into the
47:6 long till you rest? Return to your **scabbard**; cease and be still.'
Eze 5:1 and use it as a barber's **razor** to shave your head and your beard.
21:3 [21:8] I will draw my sword from its **scabbard** and cut off from
21:4 [21:9] my sword *will be* **unsheathed** [+3655+4946] against
21:5 [21:10] I the LORD have drawn my sword from its **scabbard**;
21:30 [21:35] Return the sword to its **scabbard**. In the place where you

9510 תַּעֲרֻבוֹת ***ta'arûbôt***, n.f.[pl.]. [2] [√ 6842]

hostages [+1201] [2]

2Ki 14:14 He also took **hostages** [+1201] and returned to Samaria.
2Ch 25:24 together with the palace treasures and the **hostages** [+1201],

9511 תַּעְתֻּעִים ***ta'tu'îm***, n.[m.]pl.abst. [2] [√ 9506]

mockery [2]

Jer 10:15 They are worthless, the objects of **mockery**; when their judgment
51:18 They are worthless, the objects of **mockery**; when their judgment

9512 [1]תֹּף ***tōp[1]***, n.m. [16] [→ 4191, 9528; cf. 9513]

tambourines [9], tambourine [4], music of tambourines [2], music of tambourine [1]

Ge 31:27 with joy and singing to the **music of tambourines** and harps?
Ex 15:20 the prophetess, Aaron's sister, took a **tambourine** in her hand,
15:20 and all the women followed her, with **tambourines** and dancing.
Jdg 11:34 meet him but his daughter, dancing to the sound of **tambourines**!
1Sa 10:5 **tambourines**, flutes and harps being played before them, and they
18:6 and dancing, with joyful songs and with **tambourines** and lutes.
2Sa 6:5 and with harps, lyres, **tambourines**, sistrums and cymbals.
1Ch 13:8 and with harps, lyres, **tambourines**, cymbals and trumpets.
Job 21:12 They sing to the **music of tambourine** and harp; they make merry
Ps 81:2 [81:3] Begin the music, strike the **tambourine**,
149:3 with dancing and make music to him with **tambourine** and harp.
150:4 praise him with **tambourine** and dancing, praise him with the
Isa 5:12 and lyres at their banquets, **tambourines** and flutes and wine,
24:8 The gaiety of the **tambourines** is stilled, the noise of the revelers
30:32 them with his punishing rod will be to the **music of tambourines**
Jer 31:4 Again you will take up your **tambourines** and go out to dance with

9513 [2]תֹּף ***tōp[2]***, n.m. [1] [cf. 9512]

settings [+4856] [1]

Eze 28:13 Your **settings** [+4856] and mountings were made of gold;

9514 תִּפְאֶרֶת ***tip'eret***, n.f. [51] [√ 6995]

glorious [11], glory [11], splendor [9], honor [7], fine [3], beautiful [2], boasted [2], *untranslated* [1], adorned [+906+4200+7596] [1], elation [1], finery [1], look [1], pride [1]

Ex 28:2 garments for your brother Aaron, to give him dignity and **honor**.
28:40 and headbands for Aaron's sons, to give them dignity and **honor**.
Dt 26:19 fame and **honor** high above all the nations he has made and that
Jdg 4:9 of the way you are going about this, the **honor** will not be yours,
1Ch 22:5 and fame and **splendor** in the sight of all the nations.
29:11 is the greatness and the power and the **glory** and the majesty
29:13 our God, we give you thanks, and praise your **glorious** name.
2Ch 3:6 *He* **adorned** the temple **with** [+906+4200+7596] precious stones.
Est 1:4 wealth of his kingdom and the splendor and **glory** *of* his majesty.
Ps 71:8 is filled with your praise, declaring your **splendor** all day long.
78:61 his might into captivity, his **splendor** into the hands of the enemy.
89:17 [89:18] For you are their **glory** and strength, and by your favor
96:6 majesty are before him; strength and **glory** are in his sanctuary.
Pr 4:9 of grace on your head and present you with a crown of **splendor**."
16:31 Gray hair is a crown of **splendor**; it is attained by a righteous life.
17:6 are a crown to the aged, and parents are the **pride** *of* their children.
19:11 gives him patience; it is to his **glory** to overlook an offense.
20:29 The **glory** *of* young men is their strength, gray hair the splendor of
28:12 When the righteous triumph, there is great **elation**; but when the
Isa 3:18 In that day the Lord will snatch away their **finery**: the bangles
4:2 of the land will be the pride and **glory** of the survivors in Israel.
10:12 for the willful pride of his heart and the haughty **look** *in* his eyes.
13:19 the jewel of kingdoms, the **glory** *of* the Babylonians' pride,
20:5 in Cush and **boasted** *in* Egypt will be afraid and put to shame.
28:1 of Ephraim's drunkards, to the fading flower, his **glorious** beauty,
28:4 That fading flower, his **glorious** beauty, set on the head of a fertile
28:5 In that day the LORD Almighty will be a **glorious** crown,
44:13 form of man, of man in all his **glory**, that it may dwell in a shrine.
46:13 be delayed. I will grant salvation to Zion, my **splendor** to Israel.
52:1 Put on your garments of **splendor**, O Jerusalem, the holy city.
60:7 as offerings on my altar, and I will adorn my **glorious** temple.
60:19 will be your everlasting light, and your God will be your **glory**.
62:3 You will be a crown of **splendor** in the LORD's hand, a royal
63:12 who sent his **glorious** arm of power to be at Moses' right hand,
63:14 how you guided your people to make for yourself a **glorious** name.
63:15 from heaven and see from your lofty throne, holy and **glorious**.
64:11 [64:10] Our holy and **glorious** temple, where our fathers praised
Jer 13:11 'to be my people for my renown and praise and **honor**.
13:18 your thrones, for your **glorious** crowns will fall from your heads."
13:20 flock that was entrusted to you, the sheep of which you **boasted**?
33:9 **honor** before all nations on earth that hear of all the good things I
48:17 'How broken is the mighty scepter, how broken the **glorious** staff!'
La 2:1 He has hurled down the **splendor** *of* Israel from heaven to earth;
Eze 16:12 earrings on your ears and a **beautiful** crown on your head.
16:17 You also took the **fine** jewelry I gave you, the jewelry made of my
16:39 and take your **fine** jewelry and leave you naked and bare.
23:26 They will also strip you of your clothes and take your **fine** jewelry.
23:42 of the woman and her sister and **beautiful** crowns on their heads.
24:25 their joy and **glory**, the delight of their eyes, their heart's desire,
Zec 12:7 so that the **honor** *of* the house of David and of Jerusalem's
12:7 **[RPH]** of Jerusalem's inhabitants may not be greater than that of

9515 [1]תַּפּוּחַ ***tappûaḥ[1]***, n.[m.]. [6] [→ 1130, 9516, 9517; cf. 5870]

apple tree [3], apples [3]

Pr 25:11 A word aptly spoken is like **apples** *of* gold in settings of silver.
SS 2:3 Like an **apple tree** among the trees of the forest is my lover among
2:5 me with raisins, refresh me with **apples**, for I am faint with love.
7:8 [7:9] clusters of the vine, the fragrance of your breath like **apples**,
8:5 Under the **apple tree** I roused you; there your mother conceived
Joel 1:12 the pomegranate, the palm and the **apple tree**—all the trees of the

9516 [2]תַּפּוּחַ ***tappûaḥ[2]***, n.pr.m. [1] [√ 9515; cf. 5870]

Tappuah [1]

1Ch 2:43 The sons of Hebron: Korah, **Tappuah**, Rekem and Shema.

9517 [3]תַּפּוּחַ ***tappûaḥ[3]***, n.pr.loc. [5] [→ 6540; cf. 5870, 9515]

Tappuah [5]

Jos 12:17 the king of **Tappuah** one the king of Hepher one
15:34 Zanoah, En Gannim, **Tappuah**, Enam,
16:8 From **Tappuah** the border went west to the Kanah Ravine
17:8 (Manasseh had the land of **Tappuah**, but Tappuah itself,
17:8 **Tappuah** itself, on the boundary of Manasseh, belonged to the

9518 תְּפוּצָה t^e*pûṣâ*, n.f.pl. [1] [√ 7046]
shattered [1]

Jer 25:34 has come; you will fall and *be* **shattered** like fine pottery.

9519 תֻּפִּינִים *tupînîm*, n.[m.]pl. [1] [cf. 684?]
broken [1]

Lev 6:21 [6:14] present the grain offering **broken** *in* pieces as an aroma

9520 תָּפַל *tāpal*, v. [1 / 0] [→ 9522, 9524]

2Sa 22:27 [f] *you* show yourself shrewd. [BHS *unsavory* ?; NIV 7349]

9521 ¹תָּפֵל *tāpēl¹*, n.[m.]. [5] [cf. 3260]
whitewash [4], whitewash [+3212] [1]

Eze 13:10 when a flimsy wall is built, they cover it with **whitewash**,
13:11 therefore tell those who cover it with **whitewash** that it is going to
13:14 I will tear down the wall you have covered with **whitewash**
13:15 against the wall and against those who covered it with **whitewash**.
22:28 Her prophets **whitewash** [+3212] these deeds for them by false

9522 ²תָּפֵל *tāpēl²*, a. [2] [→ 9524; cf. 9520]
tasteless [1], worthless [1]

Job 6:6 Is **tasteless** *food* eaten without salt, or is there flavor in the white
La 2:14 The visions of your prophets were false and **worthless**; they did

9523 תֹּפֶל *tōpel*, n.pr.loc. [1] [→ 330?]
Tophel [1]

Dt 1:1 between Paran and **Tophel**, Laban, Hazeroth and Dizahab.

9524 תִּפְלָה *tiplâ*, n.f. [3] [√ 9522; cf. 9520]
wrongdoing [2], repulsive thing [1]

Job 1:22 In all this, Job did not sin by charging God with **wrongdoing**.
24:12 cry out for help. But God charges no one with **wrongdoing**.
Jer 23:13 "Among the prophets of Samaria I saw this **repulsive thing**:

9525 תְּפִלָּה t^e*pillâ*, n.f. [77] [√ 7137]
prayer [60], prayers [10], petition [2], pray [+5951] [2], offer prayer [+448+906+7137] [1], plea [1], pray [1]

2Sa 7:27 has found courage to **offer** you this **prayer** [+448+906+7137].
1Ki 8:28 Yet give attention to your servant's **prayer** and his plea for mercy,
8:28 the **prayer** that your servant is praying in your presence this day.
8:29 so that you will hear the **prayer** your servant prays toward this
8:38 and when a **prayer** or plea is made by any of your people Israel—
8:45 hear from heaven their **prayer** and their plea, and uphold their
8:49 from heaven, your dwelling place, hear their **prayer** and their plea,
8:54 When Solomon had finished all these **prayers** and supplications to
9:3 "I have heard the **prayer** and plea you have made before me;
2Ki 19:4 Therefore **pray** [+5951] for the remnant that still survives."
20:5 I have heard your **prayer** and seen your tears; I will heal you.
2Ch 6:19 Yet give attention to your servant's **prayer** and his plea for mercy,
6:19 and the **prayer** that your servant is praying in your presence.
6:20 May you hear the **prayer** your servant prays toward this place.
6:29 and when a **prayer** or plea is made by any of your people Israel—
6:35 hear from heaven their **prayer** and their plea, and uphold their
6:39 your dwelling place, hear their **prayer** and their pleas,
6:40 and your ears attentive to the **prayers** *offered in* this place.
7:12 "I have heard your **prayer** and have chosen this place for myself as
7:15 and my ears attentive to the **prayers** *offered in* this place.
30:27 God heard them, for their **prayer** reached heaven, his holy
33:18 including his **prayer** to his God and the words the seers spoke to
33:19 His **prayer** and how God was moved by his entreaty, as well as all
Ne 1:6 your eyes open to hear the **prayer** your servant is praying before
1:11 let your ear be attentive to the **prayer** *of* this your servant
1:11 to the **prayer** *of* your servants who delight in revering your name.
11:17 the son of Asaph, the director who led in thanksgiving and **prayer**;
Job 16:17 yet my hands have been free of violence and my **prayer** is pure.
Ps 4:1 [4:2] from my distress; be merciful to me and hear my **prayer**.
6:9 [6:10] heard my cry for mercy; the LORD accepts my **prayer**.
17:T [17:1] A **prayer** of David.
17:1 Give ear to my **prayer**—it does not rise from deceitful lips.
35:13 myself with fasting. When my **prayers** returned to me unanswered,
39:12 [39:13] "Hear my **prayer**, O LORD, listen to my cry for help;
42:8 [42:9] night his song is with me—a **prayer** to the God of my life.
54:2 [54:4] Hear my **prayer**, O God; listen to the words of my mouth.
55:1 [55:2] Listen to my **prayer**, O God, do not ignore my plea;
61:1 [61:2] Hear my cry, O God; listen to my **prayer**.
65:2 [65:3] O you who hear **prayer**, to you all men will come.
66:19 but God has surely listened and heard my voice in **prayer**.
66:20 who has not rejected my **prayer** or withheld his love from me!
69:13 [69:14] I **pray** to you, O LORD, in the time of your favor;
72:20 This concludes the **prayers** *of* David son of Jesse.
80:4 [80:5] how long will your anger smolder against the **prayers** *of*
84:8 [84:9] Hear my **prayer**, O LORD God Almighty; listen to me,
86:T [86:1] A **prayer** of David.
86:6 Hear my **prayer**, O LORD; listen to my cry for mercy.
88:2 [88:3] May my **prayer** come before you; turn your ear to my cry.
88:13 [88:14] O LORD; in the morning my **prayer** comes before you.
90:T [90:1] A **prayer** of Moses the man of God.
102:T [102:1] A **prayer** of an afflicted man. When he is faint and pours
102:1 [102:2] Hear my **prayer**, O LORD; let my cry for help come to
102:17 [102:18] He will respond to the **prayer** *of* the destitute; he will
102:17 [102:18] the prayer of the destitute; he will not despise their **plea**.
109:4 return for my friendship they accuse me, but I am a man of **prayer**.
109:7 let him be found guilty, and may his **prayers** condemn him.
141:2 May my **prayer** be set before you like incense; may the lifting up
141:5 not refuse it. Yet my **prayer** is ever against the deeds of evildoers;
142:T [142:1] *maskil* of David. When he was in the cave. A **prayer**.
143:1 O LORD, hear my **prayer**, listen to my cry for mercy; in your
Pr 15:8 sacrifice of the wicked, but the **prayer** *of* the upright pleases him.
15:29 is far from the wicked but he hears the **prayer** *of* the righteous.
28:9 anyone turns a deaf ear to the law, even his **prayers** are detestable.
Isa 1:15 eyes from you; even if you offer many **prayers**, I will not listen.
37:4 Therefore **pray** [+5951] for the remnant that still survives."
38:5 I have heard your **prayer** and seen your tears; I will add fifteen
56:7 to my holy mountain and give them joy in my house of **prayer**.
56:7 for my house will be called a house of **prayer** for all nations."
Jer 7:16 do not pray for this people nor offer any plea or **petition** for them;
11:14 not pray for this people nor offer any plea or **petition** for them,
La 3:8 Even when I call out or cry for help, he shuts out my **prayer**.
3:44 covered yourself with a cloud so that no **prayer** can get through.
Da 9:3 to the Lord God and pleaded with him in **prayer** and petition,
9:17 "Now, our God, hear the **prayers** and petitions of your servant.
9:21 while I was still in **prayer**, Gabriel, the man I had seen in the
Jnh 2:7 [2:8] I remembered you, LORD, and my **prayer** rose to you,
Hab 3:1 A **prayer** of Habakkuk the prophet. On *shigionoth*.

9526 תִּפְלֶצֶת *tipleṣet*, n.f. [1] [√ 7145]
terror [1]

Jer 49:16 The **terror** you inspire and the pride of your heart have deceived

9527 תִּפְסַח *tipsaḥ*, n.pr.loc. [2] [√ 7173]
Tiphsah [2]

1Ki 4:24 [5:4] the River, from **Tiphsah** to Gaza, and had peace on all sides.
2Ki 15:16 attacked **Tiphsah** and everyone in the city and its vicinity,

9528 תָּפַף *tāpap*, v.den. [2] [√ 9512]
beat [1], playing tambourines [1]

Ps 68:25 [68:26] [A] with them are the maidens **playing tambourines**.
Na 2:7 [2:8] [D] girls moan like doves and **beat** upon their breasts.

9529 תָּפַר *tāpar*, v. [4]
mend [1], sew [1], sewed together [1], sewed [1]

Ge 3:7 [A] so *they* **sewed** fig leaves **together** and made coverings for
Job 16:15 [A] "*I have* **sewed** sackcloth over my skin and buried my brow
Ecc 3:7 [A] a time to tear and a time to **mend**, a time to be silent and a
Eze 13:18 [D] Woe to *the women who* **sew** magic charms on all their wrists

9530 תָּפַשׂ *tāpaś*, v. [65]
captured [8], seize [4], seized [4], take [4], took [4], capture [3], arrested [2], be caught [2], caught [2], grasped [2], surely be captured [+9530] [2], taken [2], was trapped [2], *untranslated* [1], archer [+8008] [1], are caught [1], be captured [1], be taken captive [+928+2021+4090] [1], been caught in the act [1], brandishing [1], capturing [1], carry [1], covered [1], deal with [1], dishonor [1], handle [1], hold [1], occupy [1], play [1], rapes [+2256+6640+8886] [1], reaper [1], recapture [1], soldiers [+4878] [1], take captive [1], take hold [1], taken over [1], took hold [1]

Ge 4:21 [A] he was the father of all *who* **play** the harp and flute.
39:12 [A] *She* **caught** him by his cloak and said, "Come to bed with
Nu 5:13 [C] witness against her and she *has* not **been caught in the act**),
31:27 [A] Divide the spoils between the **soldiers** [+4878] who took part
Dt 9:17 [A] So *I* **took** the two tablets and threw them out of my hands,
20:19 [A] to a city for a long time, fighting against it to **capture** it,
21:19 [A] his father and mother *shall* **take hold** of him and bring him
22:28 [A] and **rapes** [+2256+6640+8886] her and they are discovered,
Jos 8:8 [A] When you *have* **taken** the city, set it on fire. Do what the
8:23 [A] *they* **took** the king of Ai alive and brought him to Joshua.
1Sa 15:8 [A] *He* **took** Agag king of the Amalekites alive, and all his
23:26 [A] were closing in on David and his men to **capture** them,

1Ki 11:30 [A] Ahijah **took hold** of the new cloak he was wearing and tore it
13: 4 [A] stretched out his hand from the altar and said, "**Seize** him!"
18:40 [A] Then Elijah commanded them, "**Seize** the prophets of Baal.
18:40 [A] *They* **seized** them, and Elijah had them brought down to the
20:18 [A] He said, "If they have come out for peace, **take** them alive;
20:18 [A] them alive; if they have come out for war, **take** them alive."
2Ki 7:12 [A] and then *we will* **take** them alive and get into the city.' "
10:14 [A] "**Take** them alive!" he ordered. So they took them alive
10:14 [A] So *they* **took** them alive and slaughtered them by the well of
14: 7 [A] Edomites in the Valley of Salt and **captured** Sela in battle,
14:13 [A] Jehoash king of Israel **captured** Amaziah king of Judah,
16: 9 [A] Assyria complied by attacking Damascus and **capturing** it.
18:13 [A] attacked all the fortified cities of Judah and **captured** them.
25: 6 [A] he *was* **captured**. He was taken to the king of Babylon at
2Ch 25:23 [A] Jehoash king of Israel **captured** Amaziah king of Judah,
Ps 10: 2 [C] down the weak, *who* **are caught** in the schemes he devises.
71:11 [A] pursue him and **seize** him, for no one will rescue him."
Pr 30: 9 [A] and steal, and so **dishonor** the name of my God.
30:28 [D] a lizard *can be* **caught** with the hand, yet it is found in kings'
Isa 3: 6 [A] A man *will* **seize** one of his brothers at his father's home,
36: 1 [A] attacked all the fortified cities of Judah and **captured** them.
Jer 2: 8 [A] *Those who* **deal with** the law did not know me; the leaders
26: 8 [A] the prophets and all the people **seized** him and said,
34: 3 [C] but *will* **surely be captured** [+9530] and handed over to him.
34: 3 [A] but *will* **surely be captured** [+9530] and handed over to him.
37:13 [A] the son of Hananiah, **arrested** him and said, "You are
37:14 [A] *he* **arrested** Jeremiah and brought him to the officials.
38:23 [C] their hands but *will* **be captured** by the king of Babylon;
40:10 [A] storage jars, and live in the towns *you have* **taken over**."
46: 9 [A] men of Cush and Put *who* **carry** shields, men of Lydia who
46: 9 [A] who carry shields, men of Lydia **[RPH]** who draw the bow.
48:41 [C] Kerioth will be captured and the strongholds **taken**. In that
49:16 [A] in the clefts of the rocks, *who* **occupy** the heights of the hill.
50:16 [A] Babylon the sower, and the **reaper** with his sickle at harvest.
50:24 [C] you were found and **captured** because you opposed the
50:46 [C] At the sound of Babylon's **capture** the earth will tremble;
51:32 [C] the river crossings **seized**, the marshes set on fire, and the
51:41 [C] will be captured, the boast of the whole earth **seized**!
52: 9 [A] he *was* **captured**. He was taken to the king of Babylon at
Eze 12:13 [C] spread my net for him, and *he will* **be caught** in my snare;
14: 5 [A] I will do this to **recapture** the hearts of the people of Israel,
17:20 [C] spread my net for him, and *he will* **be caught** in my snare.
19: 4 [C] nations heard about him, and *he* **was trapped** in their pit.
19: 8 [C] spread their net for him, and *he* **was trapped** in their pit.
21:11 [21:16] [A] to be polished, to *be* **grasped** with the hand;
21:23 [21:28] [C] remind them of their guilt and **take** them **captive**.
21:24 [21:29] [C] *you will* **be taken captive** [+928+2021+4090].
27:29 [A] All *who* **handle** the oars will abandon their ships;
29: 7 [A] When they **grasped** you with their hands, you splintered
30:21 [A] in a splint so as to become strong enough to **hold** a sword.
38: 4 [A] and small shields, all of them **brandishing** their swords.
Am 2:15 [A] The **archer** [+8008] will not stand his ground,
Hab 2:19 [B] It *is* **covered** *with* gold and silver; there is no breath in it.

9531 ¹תֹּפֶת tōpet¹, n.f. [1]

spit [1]

Job 17: 6 made me a byword to everyone, a man in whose face people **spit**.

9532 ²תֹּפֶת tōpet², n.pr.loc. [9]

Topheth [9]

2Ki 23:10 He desecrated **Topheth**, which was in the Valley of Ben Hinnom,
Jer 7:31 They have built the high places of **Topheth** in the Valley of Ben
7:32 when people will no longer call it **Topheth** or the Valley of Ben
7:32 for they will bury the dead in **Topheth** until there is no more room.
19: 6 when people will no longer call this place **Topheth** or the Valley
19:11 They will bury the dead in **Topheth** until there is no more room.
19:12 live here, declares the LORD. I will make this city like **Topheth**.
19:13 of the kings of Judah will be defiled like this place, **Topheth**—
19:14 Jeremiah then returned from **Topheth**, where the LORD had sent

9533 תָּפְתֶּה topteh, n.pr.loc. [1]

Topheth [1]

Isa 30:33 **Topheth** has long been prepared; it has been made ready for the

9534 תָּקְהַת toqhat, n.pr.m. [1] [cf. 9363]

Tokhath [1]

2Ch 34:22 who was the wife of Shallum son of **Tokhath**, [K 9363] the son of

9535 ¹תִּקְוָה tiqwâ¹, n.f. [2] [√ 7747]

cord [+2562] [1], cord [1]

Jos 2:18 you have tied this scarlet **cord** [+2562] in the window through
2:21 and they departed. And she tied the scarlet **cord** in the window.

9536 ²תִּקְוָה tiqwâ², n.f. [32] [→ 9537; cf. 7747]

hope [30], expectation [1], hopes [1]

Ru 1:12 Even if I thought there was still **hope** for me—even if I had a
Job 4: 6 piety be your confidence and your blameless ways your **hope**?
5:16 So the poor have **hope**, and injustice shuts its mouth.
6: 8 I might have my request, that God would grant *what* I **hope** *for*,
7: 6 than a weaver's shuttle, and they come to an end without **hope**.
8:13 destiny of all who forget God; so perishes the **hope** *of* the godless.
11:18 You will be secure, because there is **hope**; you will look about you
11:20 and escape will elude them; their **hope** will become a dying gasp."
14: 7 "At least there is **hope** for a tree: If it is cut down, it will sprout
14:19 and torrents wash away the soil, so you destroy man's **hope**.
17:15 where then is my **hope**? Who can see any hope for me?
17:15 where then is my hope? Who can see any **hope** *for* me?
19:10 down on every side till I am gone; he uproots my **hope** like a tree.
27: 8 For what **hope** has the godless when he is cut off, when God takes
Ps 9:18 [9:19] be forgotten, nor the **hope** *of* the afflicted ever perish.
62: 5 [62:6] O my soul, in God alone; my **hope** comes from him.
71: 5 For you have been my **hope**, O Sovereign LORD, my confidence
Pr 10:28 the righteous is joy, but the **hopes** *of* the wicked come to nothing.
11: 7 When a wicked man dies, his **hope** perishes; all he expected from
11:23 ends only in good, but the **hope** *of* the wicked only in wrath.
19:18 Discipline your son, for in that there is **hope**; do not be a willing
23:18 is surely a future hope for you, and your **hope** will not be cut off.
24:14 there is a future hope for you, and your **hope** will not be cut off.
26:12 wise in his own eyes? There is more **hope** for a fool than for him.
29:20 who speaks in haste? There is more **hope** for a fool than for him.
Jer 29:11 and not to harm you, plans to give you **hope** and a future.
31:17 So there is **hope** for your future," declares the LORD. "Your
La 3:29 Let him bury his face in the dust—there may yet be **hope**.
Eze 19: 5 her **expectation** gone, she took another of her cubs and made him a
37:11 They say, 'Our bones are dried up and our **hope** is gone; we are cut
Hos 2:15 [2:17] and will make the Valley of Achor a door of **hope**.
Zec 9:12 Return to your fortress, O prisoners of **hope**; even now I announce

9537 ³תִּקְוָה tiqwâ³, n.pr.m. [2] [√ 9536; cf. 7747]

Tikvah [2]

2Ki 22:14 who was the wife of Shallum son of **Tikvah**, the son of Harhas,
Ezr 10:15 Only Jonathan son of Asahel and Jahzeiah son of **Tikvah**,

9538 תְּקוּמָה t^eqûmâ, n.f. [1] [√ 7756]

able to stand [1]

Lev 26:37 So you will not be **able to stand** before your enemies.

9539 תְּקוֹמֵם t^eqômēm, v. [1 / 0] [√ 7756]

Ps 139:21 and abhor *those who* rise up [BHS ?; NIV 7756] *against* you?

9540 תָּקוֹעַ tāqôa', n.[m.]. [1] [√ 9546]

trumpet [1]

Eze 7:14 Though they blow the **trumpet** and get everything ready, no one

9541 תְּקוֹעַ t^eqôa', n.pr.loc. [7] [→ 9542; cf. 9546]

Tekoa [7]

2Sa 14: 2 So Joab sent someone to **Tekoa** and had a wise woman brought
1Ch 2:24 Abijah the wife of Hezron bore him Ashhur the father of **Tekoa**.
4: 5 Ashhur the father of **Tekoa** had two wives, Helah and Naarah.
2Ch 11: 6 Bethlehem, Etam, **Tekoa**,
20:20 Early in the morning they left for the Desert of **Tekoa**. As they set
Jer 6: 1 of Benjamin! Flee from Jerusalem! Sound the trumpet in **Tekoa**!
Am 1: 1 The words of Amos, one of the shepherds of **Tekoa**—what he saw

9542 תְּקוֹעִי t^eqô'î, a.g. [7] [√ 9541]

from Tekoa [4], men of Tekoa [2], Tekoite [1]

2Sa 14: 4 When the woman **from Tekoa** went to the king, she fell with her
14: 9 But the woman **from Tekoa** said to him, "My lord the king,
23:26 Helez the Paltite, Ira son of Ikkesh **from Tekoa**,
1Ch 11:28 Ira son of Ikkesh **from Tekoa**, Abiezer from Anathoth,
27: 9 for the sixth month, was Ira the son of Ikkesh the **Tekoite**.
Ne 3: 5 The next section was repaired by the **men of Tekoa**, but their
3:27 Next to them, the **men of Tekoa** repaired another section,

9543 תְּקוּפָה *teqûpâ*, n.f. [4] [cf. 5938]
turn [2], circuit [1], course [1]

Ex 34:22 wheat harvest, and the Feast of Ingathering at the **turn** *of* the year.
1Sa 1:20 So in the **course** *of* time Hannah conceived and gave birth to a son.
2Ch 24:23 At the **turn** *of* the year, the army of Aram marched against Joash;
Ps 19:6 [19:7] one end of the heavens and makes its **circuit** to the other;

9544 תַּקִּיף *taqqîp*, a. [1] [√ 9548; Ar 10768]
stronger [1]

Ecc 6:10 no man can contend with one who is **stronger** than he.

9545 תָּקַן *tāqan*, v. [3] [cf. 9419; Ar 10771]
set in order [1], straighten [1], straightened [1]

Ecc 1:15 [A] What is twisted cannot *be* **straightened**; what is lacking
7:13 [D] has done: Who can **straighten** what he has made crooked?
12:9 [D] and searched out and **set in order** many proverbs.

9546 תָּקַע *tāqa'*, v. [67 / 68] [→ 9364, 9540, 9541, 9542, 9547]
blow [10], sounded [10], blew [7], sound [7], blowing [5], sounding [3], plunged [2], sounds [2], strikes in pledge [2], blow trumpets [1], blows [1], camped [1], carried [1], clap [1], claps [1], drive [1], driven [1], drove [1], fastened [1], had blown [1], hung up [1], pitch [1], pitched [1], put up security [+3338+4200] [1], signal [1], sounded blast [1], struck in pledge [1], tighten [1], tightened [1]

Ge 31:25 [A] Jacob *had* **pitched** his tent in the hill country of Gilead when
31:25 [A] overtook him, and Laban and his relatives **camped** there too.
Ex 10:19 [A] caught up the locusts and **carried** them into the Red Sea.
Nu 10:3 [A] When both *are* **sounded**, the whole community is to
10:4 [A] If only one *is* **sounded**, the leaders—the heads of the clans of
10:5 [A] When a trumpet blast *is* **sounded**, the tribes camping on the
10:6 [A] At the **sounding** *of* a second blast, the camps on the south are
10:6 [A] are to set out. The blast *will be the* **signal** for setting out.
10:7 [A] To gather the assembly, **blow** *the* **trumpets**, but not with the
10:8 [A] "The sons of Aaron, the priests, *are to* **blow** the trumpets.
10:10 [A] *you are to* **sound** the trumpets over your burnt offerings
Jos 6:4 [A] the city seven times, with the priests **blowing** the trumpets.
6:8 [A] **blowing** their trumpets, and the ark of the LORD's
6:9 [A] The armed guard marched ahead of the priests *who* **blew** the
6:9 [A] followed the ark. All this time the trumpets *were* **sounding**.
6:13 [A] before the ark of the LORD and **blowing** the trumpets.
6:13 [A] the ark of the LORD, while the trumpets kept **sounding**.
6:16 [A] time around, when the priests **sounded** the trumpet **blast**,
6:20 [A] When the trumpets **sounded**, the people shouted, and at the
Jdg 3:21 [A] from his right thigh and **plunged** it into the king's belly.
3:27 [A] *he* **blew** a trumpet in the hill country of Ephraim,
4:21 [A] *She* **drove** the peg through his temple into the ground, and he
6:34 [A] *he* **blew** a trumpet, summoning the Abiezrites to follow him.
7:18 [A] When I and all who are with me **blow** our trumpets,
7:18 [A] from all around the camp **blow** yours and shout, 'For the
7:19 [A] *They* **blew** their trumpets and broke the jars that were in their
7:20 [A] The three companies **blew** the trumpets and smashed the jars.
7:20 [A] holding in their right hands the trumpets *they were to* **blow**,
7:22 [A] When the three hundred trumpets **sounded**, the LORD
16:13 [A] the fabric ⌞on the loom⌟ and **tighten** [BHS-] it with the pin,
16:14 [A] **tightened** it with the pin. Again she called to him, "Samson,
1Sa 13:3 [A] Saul **had** the trumpet **blown** throughout the land and said,
31:10 [A] and **fastened** his body to the wall of Beth Shan.
2Sa 2:28 [A] So Joab **blew** the trumpet, and all the men came to a halt;
18:14 [A] **plunged** them into Absalom's heart while Absalom was still
18:16 [A] Joab **sounded** the trumpet, and the troops stopped pursuing
20:1 [A] *He* **sounded** the trumpet and shouted, "We have no share in
20:22 [A] So *he* **sounded** the trumpet, and his men dispersed from the
1Ki 1:34 [A] **Blow** the trumpet and shout, 'Long live King Solomon!'
1:39 [A] Then *they* **sounded** the trumpet and all the people shouted,
2Ki 9:13 [A] Then *they* **blew** the trumpet and shouted, "Jehu is king!"
11:14 [A] all the people of the land *were* rejoicing and **blowing**
1Ch 10:10 [A] of their gods and **hung up** his head *in* the temple of Dagon.
2Ch 23:13 [A] all the people of the land *were* rejoicing and **blowing**
Ne 4:18 [4:12] [A] the *man who* **sounded** the trumpet stayed with me.
Job 17:3 [C] Who else *will* **put** [+3338+4200] **up security** *for* me?
Ps 47:1 [47:2] [A] **Clap** your hands, all you nations; shout to God with
81:3 [81:4] [A] **Sound** the ram's horn at the New Moon, and when
Pr 6:1 [A] if *you have* **struck** hands **in pledge** for another,
17:18 [A] A man lacking in judgment **strikes** hands **in pledge** and puts
22:26 [A] Do not be a *man who* **strikes** hands **in pledge** or puts up
Isa 18:3 [A] you will see it, and when a trumpet **sounds**, you will hear it.
22:23 [A] *I will* **drive** him like a peg into a firm place; he will be a seat
22:25 [B] "the peg **driven** into the firm place will give way;
27:13 [C] in that day a great trumpet *will* **sound**. Those who were
Jer 4:5 [A] and say: '**Sound** the trumpet throughout the land!'
6:1 [A] Flee from Jerusalem! **Sound** the trumpet in Tekoa!
6:3 [A] *they will* **pitch** their tents around her, each tending his own
51:27 [A] up a banner in the land! **Blow** the trumpet among the nations!
Eze 7:14 [A] Though *they* **blow** the trumpet and get everything ready, no
33:3 [A] against the land and **blows** the trumpet to warn the people,
33:6 [A] *does* not **blow** the trumpet to warn the people and the sword
Hos 5:8 [A] "**Sound** the trumpet in Gibeah, the horn in Ramah.
Joel 2:1 [A] **Blow** the trumpet in Zion; sound the alarm on my holy hill.
2:15 [A] **Blow** the trumpet in Zion, declare a holy fast, call a sacred
Am 3:6 [C] When a trumpet **sounds** in a city, do not the people tremble?
Na 3:19 [A] Everyone who hears the news about you **claps** his hands at
Zec 9:14 [A] The Sovereign LORD *will* **sound** the trumpet; he will

9547 תֵּקַע *tēqa'*, n.[m.]. [1] [√ 9546]
sounding [1]

Ps 150:3 Praise him with the **sounding** *of* the trumpet, praise him with the

9548 תָּקַף *tāqap*, v. [3] [→ 9544, 9549; Ar 10772]
overpower [1], overpowered [1], overwhelm [1]

Job 14:20 [A] *You* **overpower** him once for all, and he is gone; you change
15:24 [A] *they* **overwhelm** him, like a king poised to attack,
Ecc 4:12 [A] Though one *may be* **overpowered**, two can defend

9549 תֹּקֶף *tōqep*, n.m. [3] [→ 9548; Ar 10773]
authority [1], might [1], power [1]

Est 9:29 wrote with full **authority** to confirm this second letter concerning
10:2 all his acts of **power** and might, together with a full account of the
Da 11:17 He will determine to come with the **might** *of* his entire kingdom

9550 תַּרְאֲלָה *tar'ălâ*, n.pr.loc. [1] [→ 739?, 740?]
Taralah [1]

Jos 18:27 Rekem, Irpeel, **Taralah**,

9551 תַּרְבּוּת *tarbût*, n.f. [1] [√ 8049]
brood [1]

Nu 32:14 "And here you are, a **brood** *of* sinners, standing in the place of

9552 תַּרְבִּית *tarbît*, n.f. [6] [√ 8049]
excessive interest [4], exorbitant interest [+2256+5968] [1], interest of any kind [+2256+5968] [1]

Lev 25:36 Do not take **interest of any kind** [+2256+5968] from him,
Pr 28:8 He who increases his wealth by **exorbitant interest** [+2256+5968]
Eze 18:8 He does not lend at usury or take **excessive interest**. He withholds
18:13 He lends at usury and takes **excessive interest**. Will such a man
18:17 his hand from sin and takes no usury or **excessive interest**.
22:12 you take usury and **excessive interest** and make unjust gain from

9553 תִּרְגֵּם *tirgēm*, v. [1] [→ 8084]
language [1]

Ezr 4:7 [E] was written in Aramaic script and in the Aramaic **language**.

9554 תַּרְדֵּמָה *tardēmâ*, n.f. [7] [√ 8101]
deep sleep [6], deep sleep [+8120] [1]

Ge 2:21 So the LORD God caused the man to fall into a **deep sleep**;
15:12 Abram fell into a **deep sleep**, and a thick and dreadful darkness
1Sa 26:12 all sleeping, because the LORD had put them into a **deep sleep**.
Job 4:13 disquieting dreams in the night, when **deep sleep** falls on men,
33:15 when **deep sleep** falls on men as they slumber in their beds,
Pr 19:15 Laziness brings on **deep sleep**, and the shiftless man goes hungry.
Isa 29:10 The LORD has brought over you a **deep sleep** [+8120]: He has

9555 תִּרְהָקָה *tirhāqâ*, n.pr.m. [2]
Tirhakah [2]

2Ki 19:9 Now Sennacherib received a report that **Tirhakah**, the Cushite
Isa 37:9 Now Sennacherib received a report that **Tirhakah**, the Cushite

9556 תְּרוּמָה *terûmâ*, n.f. [76] [√ 8123]
offering [19], portion [12], contributions [8], offerings [7], *untranslated* [5], presented [4], contribution [3], special gifts [+3338] [3], part [2], set aside [2], special gift [2], bribes [1], district [1], gift [1], portion as a special gift [1], present [+8123] [1], present an offering [1], special gifts [1], special portion [1], was presented [+8123] [1]

Ex 25:2 "Tell the Israelites to bring me an **offering**. You are to receive the
25:2 You are to receive the **offering** *for* me from each man whose heart
25:3 These are the **offerings** you are to receive from them: gold,
29:27 breast that was waved and the thigh that **was presented** [+8123].

Ex 29: 28 It is the **contribution** the Israelites are to make to the LORD from
29: 28 It is the contribution the Israelites are to make **[RPH]** to the
29: 28 to make to the LORD from their fellowship offerings. **[RPH]**
30: 13 twenty gerahs. This half shekel is an **offering** to the LORD.
30: 14 twenty years old or more, are to give an **offering** *to* the LORD.
30: 15 the poor are not to give less when you make the **offering** *to* the
35: 5 From what you have, take an **offering** for the LORD.
35: 5 Everyone who is willing is to bring *to* the LORD an **offering** *of*
35: 21 brought an **offering** *to* the LORD for the work on the Tent of
35: 24 Those presenting an **offering** *of* silver or bronze brought it as an
35: 24 of silver or bronze brought it as an **offering** *to* the LORD,
36: 3 They received from Moses all the **offerings** the Israelites had
36: 6 or woman is to make anything else as an **offering** *for* the
Lev 7: 14 one of each kind as an offering, a **contribution** to the LORD;
7: 32 thigh of your fellowship offerings to the priest as a **contribution**.
7: 34 have taken the breast that is waved and the thigh that is **presented**
10: 14 eat the breast that was waved and the thigh that was **presented**.
10: 15 The thigh that was **presented** and the breast that was waved must
22: 12 than a priest, she may not eat any of the sacred **contributions**.
Nu 5: 9 All the sacred **contributions** the Israelites bring to a priest will
6: 20 with the breast that was waved and the thigh that was **presented**.
15: 19 food of the land, present a portion as an **offering** to the LORD.
15: 20 **Present** [+8123] a cake from the first of your ground meal
15: 20 ground meal and present it as an **offering** *from* the threshing floor.
15: 21 Throughout the generations to come you are to give this **offering**
18: 8 "I myself have put you in charge of the **offerings** *presented to* me;
18: 11 *whatever* is **set aside** *from* the gifts of all the wave offerings of
18: 19 Whatever is **set aside** *from* the holy offerings the Israelites present
18: 24 the tithes that the Israelites present as an **offering** to the LORD.
18: 26 you must present a tenth of that tithe as the LORD's **offering**.
18: 27 Your **offering** will be reckoned to you as grain from the threshing
18: 28 In this way you also will present an **offering** *to* the LORD from
18: 28 From these tithes you must give the LORD's **portion** to Aaron
18: 29 You must present as the LORD's **portion** the best and holiest part
31: 29 half share and give it to Eleazar the priest as the LORD's **part**.
31: 41 Moses gave the tribute to Eleazar the priest as the LORD's **part**,
31: 52 Eleazar presented as a **gift** to the LORD weighed 16,750 shekels.
Dt 12: 6 and sacrifices, your tithes and **special gifts** [+3338],
12: 11 and sacrifices, your tithes and **special gifts** [+3338],
12: 17 vowed to give, or your freewill offerings or **special gifts** [+3338].
2Sa 1: 21 have neither dew nor rain, nor fields that yield **offerings** ⌊of grain⌋.
2Ch 31: 10 "Since the people began to bring their **contributions** to the temple
31: 12 they faithfully brought in the **contributions**, tithes and dedicated
31: 14 distributing the **contributions** *made to* the LORD and also the
Ezr 8: 25 I weighed out to them the **offering** *of* silver and gold and the
Ne 10: 37 [10:38] of our ⌊grain⌋ **offerings**, of the fruit of all our trees and of
10: 39 [10:40] are to bring their **contributions** *of* grain, new wine
12: 44 appointed to be in charge of the storerooms for the **contributions**,
13: 5 and gatekeepers, as well as the **contributions** *for* the priests.
Pr 29: 4 a country stability, but one who is greedy for **bribes** tears it down.
Isa 40: 20 A man too poor to **present** *such* **an offering** selects wood that will
Eze 20: 40 There I will require your **offerings** and your choice gifts,
44: 30 the firstfruits of all and of all your **special gifts** will belong to the priests.
44: 30 and of all your special gifts **[RPH]** will belong to the priests.
45: 1 you are to present to the LORD a **portion** of the land as a sacred
45: 6 cubits wide and 25,000 cubits long, adjoining the sacred **portion**;
45: 7 land bordering each side of the area formed by the sacred **district**
45: 7 **[RPH]** It will extend westward from the west side and eastward
45: 13 " 'This is the **special gift** you are to offer: a sixth of an ephah from
45: 16 All the people of the land will participate in this **special gift** for the
48: 8 east to west will be the **portion** you are to present **as a special gift**.
48: 9 "The **special portion** you are to offer to the LORD will be 25,000
48: 10 This will be the sacred **portion** for the priests. It will be 25,000
48: 12 It will be a special gift to them from the sacred **portion** *of* the land,
48: 18 bordering on the sacred **portion** and running the length of it,
48: 18 **[RPH]** Its produce will supply food for the workers of the city.
48: 20 The entire **portion** will be a square, 25,000 cubits on each side.
48: 20 As a special gift you will set aside the sacred **portion**, along with
48: 21 remains on both sides of the area formed by the sacred **portion**
48: 21 from the 25,000 cubits of the sacred **portion** to the eastern border,
48: 21 the sacred **portion** with the temple sanctuary will be in the center
Mal 3: 8 "But you ask, 'How do we rob you?' "In tithes and **offerings**.

9557 תרומיה תְּרוּמִיָּה *terûmiyyâ*, n.f.den. [1] [√ 8123]

special gift [1]

Eze 48: 12 It will be a **special gift** to them from the sacred portion of the land,

9558 תרועה תְּרוּעָה *terû'â*, n.f. [36] [√ 8131]

battle cry [5], shouts of joy [3], shouts [3], blast [2], cry [2], gave a shout [+8131] [2], war cries [2], acclaim [1], give a shout [+8131] [1], made noise [+8131] [1], raised a shout [+8131] [1], resounding [1], shout for joy [1], shout [1], shouted [+928+7754+8123] [1], shouting [+7754] [1], shouting [1], shouts for joy [1], signaling [1], sound the trumpets [1], trumpet [+8795] [1], trumpet blast [1], trumpet blasts [1], uproar [+7754] [1]

Lev 23: 24 of rest, a sacred assembly commemorated with **trumpet blasts**.
25: 9 have the **trumpet** [+8795] sounded everywhere on the tenth day of
Nu 10: 5 When a **trumpet blast** is sounded, the tribes camping on the east
10: 6 At the sounding of a second **blast**, the camps on the south are to set
10: 6 the south are to set out. The **blast** will be the signal for setting out.
23: 21 their God is with them; the **shout** *of* the King is among them.
29: 1 and do no regular work. It is a day for you to **sound the trumpets**.
31: 6 him articles from the sanctuary and the trumpets for **signaling**.
Jos 6: 5 on the trumpets, *have* all the people **give a** loud **shout** [+8131];
6: 20 when the people **gave a** loud **shout** [+8131], the wall collapsed;
1Sa 4: 5 all Israel **raised** such a great **shout** [+8131] that the ground shook.
4: 6 Hearing the **uproar** [+7754], the Philistines asked, "What's all this
4: 6 "What's all this **shouting** [+7754] in the Hebrew camp?"
2Sa 6: 15 house of Israel brought up the ark of the LORD with **shouts**
1Ch 15: 28 brought up the ark of the covenant of the LORD with **shouts**,
2Ch 13: 12 His priests with their trumpets will sound the **battle cry** against
15: 14 with loud acclamation, with **shouting** and with trumpets and horns.
Ezr 3: 11 all the people **gave a** great **shout** [+8131] of praise to the LORD,
3: 12 while many others **shouted** [+928+7754+8123] for joy.
3: 13 No one could distinguish the sound of the **shouts** *of* joy from the
3: 13 of weeping, because the people **made** so much **noise** [+8131].
Job 8: 21 yet fill your mouth with laughter and your lips with **shouts of joy**.
33: 26 and finds favor with him, he sees God's face and **shouts for joy**;
39: 25 of battle from afar, the shout of commanders and the **battle cry**.
Ps 27: 6 at his tabernacle will I sacrifice with **shouts of joy**; I will sing
33: 3 Sing to him a new song; play skillfully, and **shout for joy**.
47: 5 [47:6] God has ascended amid **shouts of joy**, the LORD amid
89: 15 [89:16] Blessed are those who have learned to **acclaim** you,
150: 5 with the clash of cymbals, praise him with **resounding** cymbals.
Jer 4: 19 I have heard the sound of the trumpet; I have heard the battle **cry**.
20: 16 May he hear wailing in the morning, a **battle cry** at noon.
49: 2 "when I will sound the battle **cry** against Rabbah of the
Eze 21: 22 [21:27] to give the command to slaughter, to sound the **battle cry**,
Am 1: 14 will consume her fortresses amid **war cries** on the day of battle,
2: 2 Moab will go down in great tumult amid **war cries** and the blast of
Zep 1: 16 a day of trumpet and **battle cry** against the fortified cities

9559 תרופה תְּרוּפָה *terûpâ*, n.f. [1] [√ 8324]

healing [1]

Eze 47: 12 Their fruit will serve for food and their leaves for **healing**."

9560 תרזה תִּרְזָה *tirzâ*, n.f. [1]

cypress [1]

Isa 44: 14 He cut down cedars, or perhaps took a **cypress** or oak. He let it

9561 תרח תֶּרַח *teraḥ*, n.pr.m. [11] [√ 9562]

Terah [10], he[s] [1]

Ge 11: 24 When Nahor had lived 29 years, he became the father of **Terah**.
11: 25 And after he became the father of **Terah**, Nahor lived 119 years
11: 26 After **Terah** had lived 70 years, he became the father of Abram,
11: 27 This is the account of **Terah**. Terah became the father of Abram,
11: 27 of Terah. **Terah** became the father of Abram, Nahor and Haran.
11: 28 While his father **Terah** was still alive, Haran died in Ur of the
11: 31 **Terah** took his son Abram, his grandson Lot son of Haran,
11: 32 **Terah** lived 205 years, and he died in Haran.
11: 32 Terah lived 205 years, and **he**[s] died in Haran.
Jos 24: 2 including **Terah** the father of Abraham and Nahor, lived beyond
1Ch 1: 26 Serug, Nahor, **Terah**

9562 תרח תָּרַח *tāraḥ*, n.pr.loc. [2] [√ 9561]

Terah [2]

Nu 33: 27 They left Tahath and camped at **Terah**.
33: 28 They left **Terah** and camped at Mithcah.

9563 תרחנה תִּרְחֲנָה *tirḥanâ*, n.pr.[f.?]. [1]

Tirhanah [1]

1Ch 2: 48 concubine Maacah was the mother of Sheber and **Tirhanah**.

9564 תרמה תָּרְמָה *tormâ*, n.[f.]. [1] [√ 8228]

under cover [+928] [1]

Jdg 9: 31 **Under cover** [+928] he sent messengers to Abimelech, saying,

9565 תרמוק תַּרְמוּק *tarmûq*, n.m. Not used in NIV/BHS

9566 תרמות תַּרְמוּת *tarmût*, n.f. [0] [√ 9567; cf. 8228]

Jer 14: 14 [idolatries and the **delusions** [K; see Q 9567] *of* their own minds.]

9567 תַּרְמִית tarmît, n.f. [5] [→ 9566; cf. 8228]

delusions [2], deceit [+4383] [1], deceit [1], deceitfulness [1]

Ps 119:118 all who stray from your decrees, for their **deceitfulness** is in vain.
Jer 8: 5 always turn away? They cling to **deceit**; they refuse to return.
14: 14 idolatries and the **delusions** [K 9566] *of* their own minds.
23: 26 lying prophets, who prophesy the **delusions** *of* their own minds?
Zep 3: 13 speak no lies, nor will **deceit** [+4383] be found in their mouths.

9568 תֹּרֶן tōren, n.m. [3]

flagstaff [1], mast [+4029] [1], mast [1]

Isa 30: 17 till you are left like a **flagstaff** on a mountaintop, like a banner on a
33: 23 The **mast** [+4029] is not held secure, the sail is not spread.
Eze 27: 5 they took a cedar from Lebanon to make a **mast** for you.

9569 תַּרְעִית tar'ît, n.f. Not used in NIV/BHS [√ 8290]

9570 תַּרְעֵלָה tar'ēlâ, n.f. [3] [√ 8302]

makes stagger [2], made stagger [1]

Ps 60: 3 [60:5] you have given us wine *that* **makes** us **stagger**.
Isa 51: 17 who have drained to its dregs the goblet that **makes** men **stagger**.
51: 22 I have taken out of your hand the cup that **made** you **stagger**;

9571 תִּרְעָתִים tir'ātîm, n.pr.m.pl. [1]

Tirathites [1]

1Ch 2: 55 who lived at Jabez: the **Tirathites**, Shimeathites and Sucathites.

9572 תְּרָפִים tᵉrāpîm, n.m.pl. [15]

household gods [8], idol [3], idols [3], idolatry [1]

Ge 31: 19 gone to shear his sheep, Rachel stole her father's **household gods**.
31: 34 Now Rachel had taken the **household gods** and put them inside her
31: 35 my period." So he searched but could not find the **household gods**.
Jdg 17: 5 he made an ephod and *some* **idols** and installed one of his sons as
18: 14 an ephod, other **household gods**, a carved image and a cast idol?
18: 17 the other **household gods** and the cast idol while the priest
18: 18 the ephod, the other **household gods** and the cast idol, the priest
18: 20 the other **household gods** and the carved image and went along
1Sa 15: 23 is like the sin of divination, and arrogance like the evil of **idolatry**.
19: 13 Michal took an **idol** and laid it on the bed, covering it with a
19: 16 when the men entered, there was the **idol** in the bed, and at the
2Ki 23: 24 the **household gods**, the idols and all the other detestable things
Eze 21: 21 [21:26] he will consult his **idols**, he will examine the liver.
Hos 3: 4 or prince, without sacrifice or sacred stones, without ephod or **idol**.
Zec 10: 2 The **idols** speak deceit, diviners see visions that lie; they tell

9573 תִּרְצָה tirṣâ¹, n.pr.f. [4] [√ 8354]

Tirzah [4]

Nu 26: 33 whose names were Mahlah, Noah, Hoglah, Milcah and **Tirzah**.)
27: 1 of the daughters were Mahlah, Noah, Hoglah, Milcah and **Tirzah**.
36: 11 Mahlah, **Tirzah**, Hoglah, Milcah and Noah—
Jos 17: 3 whose names were Mahlah, Noah, Hoglah, Milcah and **Tirzah**.

9574 ²תִּרְצָה tirṣâ², n.pr.loc. [14] [√ 8354]

Tirzah [14]

Jos 12: 24 the king of **Tirzah** one thirty-one kings in all.
1Ki 14: 17 Then Jeroboam's wife got up and left and went to **Tirzah**.
15: 21 heard this, he stopped building Ramah and withdrew to **Tirzah**.
15: 33 Baasha son of Ahijah became king of all Israel in **Tirzah**,
16: 6 Baasha rested with his fathers and was buried in **Tirzah**. And Elah
16: 8 Baasha became king of Israel, and he reigned in **Tirzah** two years.
16: 9 Elah was in **Tirzah** at the time, getting drunk in the home of Arza,
16: 9 in the home of Arza, the man in charge of the palace at **Tirzah**.
16: 15 year of Asa king of Judah, Zimri reigned in **Tirzah** seven days.
16: 17 with him withdrew from Gibbethon and laid siege to **Tirzah**.
16: 23 king of Israel, and he reigned twelve years, six of them in **Tirzah**.
2Ki 15: 14 Then Menahem son of Gadi went from **Tirzah** up to Samaria.
15: 16 starting out from **Tirzah**, attacked Tiphsah and everyone in the city
SS 6: 4 You are beautiful, my darling, as **Tirzah**, lovely as Jerusalem,

9575 תֶּרֶשׁ tereš, n.pr.m. [2]

Teresh [2]

Est 2: 21 Bigthana and **Teresh**, two of the king's officers who guarded the
6: 2 recorded there that Mordecai had exposed Bigthana and **Teresh**,

9576 תַּרְשִׁישׁ taršîš¹, n.pr.loc. [24] [√ 8406?]

Tarshish [15], fleet of trading ships [+639] [1], fleet of trading ships [+641] [1], fleet of trading ships [+641+2143] [1], fleet of trading ships [+641+2143+4200] [1], it^s [+639] [1], it^s [+641] [1], that port^s [1], trade [1], trading ship [+641] [1]

1Ki 10: 22 The king had a **fleet of trading ships** [+639] at sea along with the
10: 22 Once every three years **it**^s [+639] returned, carrying gold,
22: 48 [22:49] Now Jehoshaphat built a **fleet of trading ships** [+641] to
2Ch 9: 21 The king had a **fleet of trading ships** [+641+2143] manned by
9: 21 Once every three years **it**^s [+641] returned, carrying gold,
20: 36 with him to construct a **fleet of trading ships** [+641+2143+4200].
20: 37 The ships were wrecked and were not able to set sail to **trade**.
Ps 48: 7 [48:8] You destroyed them like ships of **Tarshish** shattered by an
72: 10 The kings of **Tarshish** and of distant shores will bring tribute to
Isa 2: 16 for every **trading ship** [+641] and every stately vessel.
23: 1 Wail, O ships of **Tarshish**! For Tyre is destroyed and left without
23: 6 Cross over to **Tarshish**; wail, you people of the island.
23: 10 Till your land as along the Nile, O Daughter of **Tarshish**,
23: 14 Wail, you ships of **Tarshish**; your fortress is destroyed!
60: 9 in the lead are the ships of **Tarshish**, bringing your sons from afar,
66: 19 to **Tarshish**, to the Libyans and Lydians (famous as archers),
Jer 10: 9 Hammered silver is brought from **Tarshish** and gold from Uphaz.
Eze 27: 12 " '**Tarshish** did business with you because of your great wealth of
27: 25 " 'The ships of **Tarshish** serve as carriers for your wares. You are
38: 13 Sheba and Dedan and the merchants of **Tarshish** and all her
Jnh 1: 3 But Jonah ran away from the LORD and headed for **Tarshish**.
1: 3 went down to Joppa, where he found a ship bound for **that port**^s.
1: 3 he went aboard and sailed for **Tarshish** to flee from the LORD.
4: 2 That is why I was so quick to flee to **Tarshish**. I knew that you are

9577 ²תַּרְשִׁישׁ taršîš², n.m. [7] [√ 8406?]

chrysolite [6], chrysolite [+74] [1]

Ex 28: 20 in the fourth row a **chrysolite**, an onyx and a jasper. Mount them in
39: 13 in the fourth row a **chrysolite**, an onyx and a jasper. They were
SS 5: 14 His arms are rods of gold set with **chrysolite**. His body is like
Eze 1: 16 They sparkled like **chrysolite**, and all four looked alike.
10: 9 each of the cherubim; the wheels sparkled like **chrysolite** [+74].
28: 13 **chrysolite**, onyx and jasper, sapphire, turquoise and beryl.
Da 10: 6 His body was like **chrysolite**, his face like lightning, his eyes like

9578 ³תַּרְשִׁישׁ taršîš³, n.pr.m. [4] [√ 8406?]

Tarshish [4]

Ge 10: 4 The sons of Javan: Elishah, **Tarshish**, the Kittim and the Rodanim.
1Ch 1: 7 The sons of Javan: Elishah, **Tarshish**, the Kittim and the Rodanim.
7: 10 Benjamin, Ehud, Kenaanah, Zethan, **Tarshish** and Ahishahar.
Est 1: 14 Shethar, Admatha, **Tarshish**, Meres, Marsena and Memucan,

9579 תִּרְשָׁתָא tiršātā', n.m. [5]

governor [5]

Ezr 2: 63 The **governor** ordered them not to eat any of the most sacred food
Ne 7: 65 The **governor**, therefore, ordered them not to eat any of the most
7: 70 [7:69] The **governor** gave to the treasury 1,000 drachmas of gold,
8: 9 Nehemiah the **governor**, Ezra the priest and scribe, and the Levites
10: 1 [10:2] Nehemiah the **governor**, the son of Hacaliah. Zedekiah,

9580 תַּרְתָּן tartān, n.m. [2] [→ Ar 10775, 10778]

supreme commander [2]

2Ki 18: 17 The king of Assyria sent his **supreme commander**, his chief
Isa 20: 1 In the year that the **supreme commander**, sent by Sargon king of

9581 תַּרְתָּק tartāq, n.pr.[m.]. [1]

Tartak [1]

2Ki 17: 31 the Avvites made Nibhaz and **Tartak**, and the Sepharvites burned

9582 תְּשׂוּמֶת tᵉśûmâ, n.f. [1] [√ 8492]

left [1]

Lev 6: 2 [5:21] something entrusted to him or **left** *in* his care or stolen,

9583 תְּשֻׁאָה tᵉšu'â, n.f. [4 / 5] [√ 8616; cf. 9589, 9594]

commotion [1], shout [1], shouts [1], storm [1], thunders [1]

Job 30: 22 the wind; you toss me about in the **storm**. [BHS Q 9370; K 9589]
36: 29 he spreads out the clouds, how he **thunders** *from* his pavilion?
39: 7 at the commotion in the town; he does not hear a driver's **shout**.
Isa 22: 2 O town full of **commotion**, O city of tumult and revelry?
Zec 4: 7 Then he will bring out the capstone to **shouts** *of* 'God bless it!

9584 תִּשְׁבֶּה tišbeh, n.pr.loc. Not used in NIV/BHS [√ 9586]

9585 תִּשְׁבִּי tišbî, a.g. [6] [√ 9586]

Tishbite [6]

1Ki 17: 1 Now Elijah the **Tishbite**, from Tishbe in Gilead, said to Ahab,

1Ki 21: 17 Then the word of the LORD came to Elijah the **Tishbite**:
21: 28 Then the word of the LORD came to Elijah the **Tishbite**:
2Ki 1: 3 But the angel of the LORD said to Elijah the **Tishbite**, "Go up
1: 8 around his waist." The king said, "That was Elijah the **Tishbite**."
9: 36 the LORD that he spoke through his servant Elijah the **Tishbite**:

9586 תִּשְׁבֵּי **tišbê**, n.pr.loc. [0 / 1] [→ 9584, 9585]

Tishbe [1]

1Ki 17: 1 from **Tishbe** [BHS 9369] *in* Gilead, said to Ahab,

9587 תַּשְׁבֵּץ **tašbēṣ**, n.[m.]. [1] [√ 8687]

woven [1]

Ex 28: 4 a breastpiece, an ephod, a robe, a **woven** tunic, a turban and a sash.

9588 תְּשׁוּבָה **tešûbâ**, n.f. [8] [√ 8740]

spring [+9102] [3], answering [1], answers [1], spring [+2021+9102] [1], spring [+6961+9102] [1], went back [1]

1Sa 7: 17 But he always **went back** to Ramah, where his home was,
2Sa 11: 1 In the **spring** [+9102], at the time when kings go off to war,
1Ki 20: 22 because next **spring** [+2021+9102] the king of Aram will attack
20: 26 The next **spring** [+9102] Ben-Hadad mustered the Arameans
1Ch 20: 1 In the **spring** [+6961+9102], at the time when kings go off to war,
2Ch 36: 10 In the **spring** [+9102], King Nebuchadnezzar sent for him
Job 21: 34 your nonsense? Nothing is left of your **answers** but falsehood!"
34: 36 that Job might be tested to the utmost for **answering** like a wicked

9589 תְּשֻׁוָּה **tešuwwâ**, n.f. [1 / 0] [√ 8616; cf. 9594]

Job 30: 22 [you toss me about in the storm. [K; Q 9370; NIV 9583]]

9590 תַּשְׁוִית **tašwît**, n.f. Not used in NIV/BHS [√ 8750]

9591 תְּשׁוּעָה **tešû'â**, n.f. [34] [√ 3828]

salvation [12], victory [12], help [2], brought about victory [+3828] [1], deliverance [1], delivered [1], rescue [1], rescued [+928+6913] [1], save [1], saves [1], Savior [1]

Jdg 15: 18 to the LORD, "You have given your servant this great **victory**.
1Sa 11: 9 you will be **delivered**.' " When the messengers went and reported
11: 13 for this day the LORD *has* **rescued** [+928+6913] Israel."
19: 5 The LORD won a great **victory** for all Israel, and you saw it
2Sa 19: 2 [19:3] for the whole army the **victory** that day was turned into
23: 10 to the sword. The LORD brought about a great **victory** that day.
23: 12 Philistines down, and the LORD brought about a great **victory**.
2Ki 5: 1 because through him the LORD had given **victory** to Aram.
13: 17 "The LORD's arrow of **victory**, the arrow of victory over Aram!"
13: 17 "The LORD's arrow of victory, the arrow of **victory** over Aram!"
1Ch 11: 14 and the LORD **brought about** a great **victory** [+3828].
19: 12 "If the Arameans are too strong for me, then you are to **rescue** me;
2Ch 6: 41 May your priests, O LORD God, be clothed with **salvation**,
Ps 33: 17 A horse is a vain hope for **deliverance**; despite all its great strength
37: 39 The **salvation** *of* the righteous comes from the LORD; he is their
38: 22 [38:23] Come quickly to help me, O Lord my **Savior**.
40: 10 [40:11] in my heart; I speak of your faithfulness and **salvation**.
40: 16 [40:17] may those who love your **salvation** always say,
51: 14 [51:16] Save me from bloodguilt, O God, the God who **saves** me,
60: 11 [60:13] us aid against the enemy, for the **help** *of* man is worthless.
71: 15 of your **salvation** all day long, though I know not its measure.
108: 12 [108:13] aid against the enemy, for the **help** *of* man is worthless.
119: 41 come to me, O LORD, your **salvation** according to your promise;
119: 81 My soul faints with longing for your **salvation**, but I have put my
144: 10 to the One who gives **victory** to kings, who delivers his servant
146: 3 Do not put your trust in princes, in mortal men, who cannot **save**.
Pr 11: 14 of guidance a nation falls, but many advisers make **victory** sure.
21: 31 ready for the day of battle, but **victory** rests with the LORD.
24: 6 for waging war you need guidance, and for **victory** many advisers.
Isa 45: 17 Israel will be saved by the LORD with an everlasting **salvation**;
46: 13 it is not far away; and my **salvation** will not be delayed.
46: 13 be delayed. I will grant **salvation** to Zion, my splendor to Israel.
Jer 3: 23 surely in the LORD our God is the **salvation** *of* Israel.
La 3: 26 it is good to wait quietly for the **salvation** *of* the LORD.

9592 תְּשׁוּקָה **tešûqâ**, n.f. [3]

desire [2], desires [1]

Ge 3: 16 Your **desire** will be for your husband, and he will rule over you."
4: 7 at your door; it **desires** to have you, but you must master it."
SS 7: 10 [7:11] I belong to my lover, and his **desire** is for me.

9593 תְּשׁוּרָה **tešûrâ**, n.f. [1] [√ 8802]

gift [1]

1Sa 9: 7 We have no **gift** to take to the man of God. What do we have?"

9594 תֻּשִׁיָּה **tušiyyâ**, n.f. Not used in NIV/BHS [√ 8616; cf. 9589]

9595 תְּשִׁיעִי **tešî'î**, a.num.ord. [18] [√ 9596]

ninth [18]

Lev 25: 22 will continue to eat from it until the harvest of the **ninth** year
Nu 7: 60 On the **ninth** day Abidan son of Gideoni, the leader of the people
2Ki 17: 6 In the **ninth** year of Hoshea, the king of Assyria captured Samaria
25: 1 So in the **ninth** year of Zedekiah's reign, on the tenth day of the
1Ch 12: 12 [12:13] Johanan the eighth, Elzabad the **ninth**,
24: 11 the **ninth** to Jeshua, the tenth to Shecaniah,
25: 16 the **ninth** to Mattaniah, his sons and relatives, 12
27: 12 The **ninth**, for the ninth month, was Abiezer the Anathothite,
27: 12 The ninth, for the **ninth** month, was Abiezer the Anathothite,
Ezr 10: 9 on the twentieth day of the **ninth** month, all the people were sitting
Jer 36: 9 In the **ninth** month of the fifth year of Jehoiakim son of Josiah
36: 22 It was the **ninth** month and the king was sitting in the winter
39: 1 In the **ninth** year of Zedekiah king of Judah, in the tenth month,
52: 4 So in the **ninth** year of Zedekiah's reign, on the tenth day of the
Eze 24: 1 In the **ninth** year, in the tenth month on the tenth day, the word of
Hag 2: 10 On the twenty-fourth day of the **ninth** month, in the second year of
2: 18 'From this day on, from this twenty-fourth day of the **ninth** month,
Zec 7: 1 LORD came to Zechariah on the fourth day of the **ninth** month,

9596 תֵּשַׁע **tēša'**, n.m. & f. [78] [→ 9595, 9597]

nine [12], ninth [5], twenty-nine [+2256+6929] [5], ninety-nine [+2256+9596] [4], 29 [+2256+6929] [3], thirty-ninth [+2256+8993] [3], 390 [+2256+4395+8993] [2], 392 [+2256+4395+8993+9109] [2], 59,300 [+547+2256+2256+2822+4395+8993] [2], 95 [+2256+2822] [2], 969 [+2256+2256+4395+9252+9596] [2], 973 [+2256+4395 +8679+8993] [2], 98 [+2256+9046] [2], nineteenth [+6925] [2], nineteenth [+6926] [2], ninety [2], ninety-six [+2256+9252] [2], 1,290 [+547+2256+4395] [1], 119 [+2256+4395+6926] [1], 139 [+2256 +4395+8993] [1], 209 [+2256+4395] [1], 3,930 [+547+2256+4395 +8993+8993] [1], 595 [+2256+2256+2822+2822+4395] [1], 690 [+2256+4395+9252] [1], 895 [+2256+2256+2822+4395+9046] [1], 90 [1], 905 [+2256+2822+4395] [1], 910 [+2256+4395+6924] [1], 912 [+2256+4395+6926+9109] [1], 928 [+2256+4395+6929+9046] [1], 930 [+2256+4395+8993] [1], 945 [+752+2256+2256+2822+4395] [1], 950 [+2256+2822+4395] [1], 956 [+2256+2256+2822+4395 +9252] [1], 962 [+2256+2256+4395+9109+9252] [1], forty-nine [+752+2256] [1], more than thirteen feet [+564] [1], nine-and-a-half [+2256+2942] [1], nineteen [+6925] [1], nineteen [+6926] [1], ninety-eight [+2256+9046] [1]

Ge 5: 5 Adam lived **930** [+2256+4395+8993] years, and then he died.
5: 8 Seth lived **912** [+2256+4395+6926+9109] years, and then he died.
5: 9 When Enosh had lived **90** years, he became the father of Kenan.
5: 11 Enosh lived **905** [+2256+2822+4395] years, and then he died.
5: 14 Kenan lived **910** [+2256+4395+6924] years, and then he died.
5: 17 Mahalalel lived **895** [+2256+2256+2822+4395+9046] years, and
5: 20 Jared lived **962** [+2256+2256+4395+9109+9252] years, and then
5: 27 Methuselah lived **969** [+2256+2256+4395+9252+9596] years, and
5: 27 Methuselah lived **969** [+2256+2256+4395+9252+9596] years, and
5: 30 Lamech lived **595** [+2256+2256+2822+2822+4395] years and had
9: 29 Noah lived **950** [+2256+2822+4395] years, and then he died.
11: 19 Peleg lived **209** [+2256+4395] years and had other sons
11: 24 When Nahor had lived **29** [+2256+6929] years, he became the
11: 25 Nahor lived **119** [+2256+4395+6926] years and had other sons and
17: 1 When Abram was **ninety-nine** [+2256+9596] years old, the LORD
17: 1 When Abram was **ninety-nine** [+2256+9596] years old, the LORD
17: 17 a hundred years old? Will Sarah bear a child at the age of **ninety**?"
17: 24 was **ninety-nine** [+2256+9596] years old when he was circumcised,
17: 24 was **ninety-nine** [+2256+9596] years old when he was circumcised,
Ex 38: 24 used for all the work on the sanctuary was **29** [+2256+6929] talents
Lev 23: 32 From the evening of the **ninth** day of the month until the following
25: 8 of years amount to a period of **forty-nine** [+752+2256] years.
Nu 1: 23 tribe of Simeon was **59,300** [+547+2256+2256+2822+4395+8993].
2: 13 division numbers **59,300** [+547+2256+2256+2822+4395+8993].
29: 26 " 'On the fifth day prepare **nine** bulls, two rams and fourteen male
34: 13 The LORD has ordered that it be given to the **nine** and a half
Dt 3: 11 and was **more than thirteen feet** [+564] long and six feet wide.
Jos 13: 7 divide it as an inheritance among the **nine** tribes and half of the
14: 2 were assigned by lot to the **nine-and-a-half** [+2256+2942] tribes,
15: 32 a total of **twenty-nine** [+2256+6929] towns and their villages.
15: 44 Keilah, Aczib and Mareshah—**nine** towns and their villages.
15: 54 Arba (that is, Hebron) and Zior—**nine** towns and their villages.
19: 38 There were **nineteen** [+6926] towns and their villages.
21: 16 with their pasturelands—**nine** towns from these two tribes.
Jdg 4: 3 Because he had **nine** hundred iron chariots and had cruelly
4: 13 Sisera gathered together his **nine** hundred iron chariots and all the
1Sa 4: 15 who was **ninety-eight** [+2256+9046] years old and whose eyes
2Sa 2: 30 **nineteen** [+6925] of David's men were found missing.

2Sa 24: 8 they came back to Jerusalem at the end of **nine** months and twenty
2Ki 14: 2 and he reigned in Jerusalem **twenty-nine** [+2256+6929] years.
15: 13 became king in the **thirty-ninth** [+2256+8993] year of Uzziah king
15: 17 In the **thirty-ninth** [+2256+8993] year of Azariah king of Judah,
17: 1 Elah became king of Israel in Samaria, and he reigned **nine** years.
18: 2 and he reigned in Jerusalem **twenty-nine** [+2256+6929] years.
18: 10 sixth year, which was the **ninth** year of Hoshea king of Israel.
25: 3 By the **ninth** day of the ⌞fourth⌟ month the famine in the city had
25: 8 in the **nineteenth** [+6926] year of Nebuchadnezzar king of
1Ch 3: 8 Elishama, Eliada and Eliphelet—**nine** in all.
9: 6 The people from Judah numbered **690** [+2256+4395+9252].
9: 9 their genealogy, numbered **956** [+2256+2256+2822+4395+9252].
24: 16 the **nineteenth** [+6925] to Pethahiah, the twentieth to Jehezkel,
25: 26 the **nineteenth** [+6925] to Mallothi, his sons and relatives,
2Ch 16: 12 In the **thirty-ninth** [+2256+8993] year of his reign Asa was
25: 1 and he reigned in Jerusalem **twenty-nine** [+2256+6929] years.
29: 1 and he reigned in Jerusalem **twenty-nine** [+2256+6929] years.
Ezr 1: 9 gold dishes 30 silver dishes 1,000 silver pans **29** [+2256+6929]
2: 8 of Zattu **945** [+752+2256+2256+2822+4395]
2: 16 of Ater (through Hezekiah) **98** [+2256+9046]
2: 20 of Gibbar **95** [+2256+2822]
2: 36 (through the family of Jeshua) **973** [+2256+4395+8679+8993]
2: 42 Ater, Talmon, Akkub, Hatita and Shobai **139** [+2256+4395+8993]
2: 58 of the servants of Solomon **392** [+2256+4395+8993+9109]
8: 35 twelve bulls for all Israel, **ninety-six** [+2256+9252] rams,
Ne 7: 21 of Ater (through Hezekiah) **98** [+2256+9046]
7: 25 of Gibeon **95** [+2256+2822]
7: 38 of Senaah **3,930** [+547+2256+4395+8993+8993]
7: 39 (through the family of Jeshua) **973** [+2256+4395+8679+8993]
7: 60 of the servants of Solomon **392** [+2256+4395+8993+9109]
11: 1 while the remaining **nine** were to stay in their own towns.
11: 8 followers, Gabbai and Sallai—**928** [+2256+4395+6929+9046] men.
Jer 39: 2 on the **ninth** day of the fourth month of Zedekiah's eleventh year,
52: 6 By the **ninth** day of the fourth month the famine in the city had
52: 12 in the **nineteenth** [+6926] year of Nebuchadnezzar king of
52: 23 There were **ninety-six** [+2256+9252] pomegranates on the sides;
Eze 4: 5 So for **390** [+2256+4395+8993] days you will bear the sin of the
4: 9 You are to eat it during the **390** [+2256+4395+8993] days you lie
41: 12 was five cubits thick all around, and its length was **ninety** cubits.
Da 12: 11 desolation is set up, there will be **1,290** [+547+2256+4395] days.

9597 תִּשְׁעִים *tiš'îm*, n.indecl. Not used in NIV/BHS √ 9596

The Aramaic-English Concordance to the Old Testament

א, ’

10001 א ’, letter. Not used in NIV/BHS [√ Hb 1]

10002 א-ָ -ā’, art.suf. [814 / 815] [√ 10191] Not indexed

the [412], *untranslated* [298], O [26], a [15], this [7], his[s] [4], these [4], he[s] [+10421] [3], him[s] [+10421] [3], that [3], an [2], continually [+10089+10753] [2], cordial greetings [+10002+10353+10720] [2], ever [+10550] [2], he[s] [+10421+10453] [2], his[s] [+10421] [2], immediately [+10734] [2], my[s] [2], as soon as [+10089+10168+10530] [1], as soon as [+10168+10232+10341] [1], certainly [+10327] [1], ever [+10527+10550] [1], forever [+10378+10550] [1], forever [+10509+10527] [1], forever [+10527+10550] [1], forever [+10550] [1], it[s] [+10418] [1], it[s] [+10424] [1], it[s] [+10614] [1], it[s] [1], its[s] [1], never end [+10509+10527] [1], order [+10302+10427+10682] [1], she[s] [+10423] [1], sundown [+10436+10728] [1], them[s] [+10038] [1], they[s] [+10353+10553] [1], this[s] [+10418] [1], Trans-Euphrates [+10468+10526] [1], what [+10418] [1], when [+10089+10530] [1], who[s] [+10131] [1]

10003 אַב *’ab*, n.m. [9] [√ Hb 3]

father [6], fathers [2], predecessors [1]

Ezr 4: 15 so that a search may be made in the archives of your **predecessors**.
5: 12 because our **fathers** angered the God of heaven, he handed them
Da 2: 23 I thank and praise you, O God of my **fathers**: You have given me
5: 2 silver goblets that Nebuchadnezzar his **father** had taken from the
5: 11 In the time of your **father** he was found to have insight
5: 11 King Nebuchadnezzar your **father**—your father the king,
5: 11 King Nebuchadnezzar your father—your **father** the king, I say—
5: 13 one of the exiles my **father** the king brought from Judah?
5: 18 the Most High God gave your **father** Nebuchadnezzar sovereignty

10004 אֵב *’ēb*, n.m. [3] [√ Hb 4]

fruit [3]

Da 4: 12 [4:9] Its leaves were beautiful, its **fruit** abundant, and on it was
4: 14 [4:11] off its branches; strip off its leaves and scatter its **fruit**.
4: 21 [4:18] with beautiful leaves and abundant **fruit**, providing food

10005 אֲבַד *’ăbad*, v. [7] [√ Hb 6]

execute [2], completely destroyed [+10221+10722] [1], destroyed [1], executed [1], execution [1], perish [1]

Jer 10: 11 [J] *will* **perish** from the earth and from under the heavens.’ ”
Da 2: 12 [P] furious that he ordered the **execution** of all the wise men of
2: 18 [P] his friends *might* not *be* **executed** with the rest of the wise
2: 24 [P] whom the king had appointed to **execute** the wise men of
2: 24 [P] and said to him, “*Do* not **execute** the wise men of Babylon.
7: 11 [Q] and its body **destroyed** and thrown into the blazing fire.
7: 26 [P] away and **completely destroyed** [+10221+10722] forever.

10006 אֶבֶן *’eben*, n.f. [8] [√ Hb 74]

rock [3], stone [3], large stones [+10146] [2]

Ezr 5: 8 The people are building it with **large stones** [+10146] and placing
6: 4 with three courses of **large stones** [+10146] and one of timbers.
Da 2: 34 you were watching, a **rock** was cut out, but not by human hands.
2: 35 But the **rock** that struck the statue became a huge mountain
2: 45 This is the meaning of the vision of the **rock** cut out of a mountain,
5: 4 the gods of gold and silver, of bronze, iron, wood and **stone**.
5: 23 the gods of silver and gold, of bronze, iron, wood and **stone**,
6: 17 [6:18] A **stone** was brought and placed over the mouth of the den,

10007 אִגְּרָה *’iggerâ*, n.f. [3] [√ Hb 115]

letter [3]

Ezr 4: 8 Shimshai the secretary wrote a **letter** against Jerusalem to
4: 11 (This is a copy of the **letter** they sent him.) To King Artaxerxes,
5: 6 This is a copy of the **letter** that Tattenai, governor of

10008 אֱדַיִן *’edayin*, adv. [57] [√ Hb 255]

then [+10089] [13], *untranslated* [11], then [11], so [+10089] [8], so [3], when [+10089] [2], also [+10358] [1], and [+10221] [1], as soon as [+10168+10427] [1], at this [1], finally [1], now [1], that day[s] [1], therefore [+10089] [1], thus [+10089] [1]

Ezr 4: 9 **[NIE]** Rehum the commanding officer and Shimshai the
4: 23 **As** [+10168+10427] **soon as** the copy of the letter of King
4: 24 **Thus** [+10089] the work on the house of God in Jerusalem came to
5: 2 **Then** [+10089] Zerubbabel son of Shealtiel and Jeshua son of
5: 4 They **also** [+10358] asked, “What are the names of the men
5: 5 could go to Darius **and** [+10221] his written reply be received.
5: 9 **[NIE]** We questioned the elders and asked them,
5: 16 **So** this Sheshbazzar came and laid the foundations of the house of
5: 16 From **that day**[s] to the present it has been under construction
6: 1 King Darius **then** [+10089] issued an order, and they searched in
6: 13 **Then**, because of the decree King Darius had sent, Tattenai,
Da 2: 14 **When** [+10089] Arioch, the commander of the king’s guard,
2: 15 such a harsh decree?” Arioch **then** explained the matter to Daniel.
2: 17 **Then** Daniel returned to his house and explained the matter to his
2: 19 **[NIE]** During the night the mystery was revealed to Daniel in a
2: 19 to Daniel in a vision. **Then** Daniel praised the God of heaven
2: 25 **[NIE]** Arioch took Daniel to the king at once and said, “I have
2: 35 **Then** [+10089] the iron, the clay, the bronze, the silver
2: 46 **Then** [+10089] King Nebuchadnezzar fell prostrate before Daniel
2: 48 **Then** the king placed Daniel in a high position and lavished many
3: 3 **So** [+10089] the satraps, prefects, governors, advisers, treasurers,
3: 13 **[NIE]** Furious with rage, Nebuchadnezzar summoned Shadrach,
3: 13 Abednego. **So** [+10089] these men were brought before the king,
3: 19 **Then** [+10089] Nebuchadnezzar was furious with Shadrach,
3: 21 **So** [+10089] these men, wearing their robes, trousers, turbans
3: 24 **Then** King Nebuchadnezzar leaped to his feet in amazement
3: 26 Nebuchadnezzar **then** [+10089] approached the opening of the
3: 26 Come here!” **So** [+10089] Shadrach, Meshach and Abednego came
3: 30 **Then** [+10089] the king promoted Shadrach, Meshach
4: 7 [4:4] **When** [+10089] the magicians, enchanters, astrologers and
4: 19 [4:16] **Then** Daniel (also called Belteshazzar) was greatly

Da 5: 3 So [+10089] they brought in the gold goblets that had been taken
5: 6 [NIE] His face turned pale and he was so frightened that his
5: 8 **Then** all the king's wise men came in, but they could not read the
5: 9 **So** King Belshazzar became even more terrified and his face grew
5:13 **So** [+10089] Daniel was brought before the king, and the king said
5:17 **Then** [+10089] Daniel answered the king, "You may keep your
5:24 **Therefore** [+10089] he sent the hand that wrote the inscription.
5:29 **Then** [+10089] at Belshazzar's command, Daniel was clothed in
6: 3 [6:4] **Now** Daniel so distinguished himself among the
6: 4 [6:5] **At this**, the administrators and the satraps tried to find
6: 5 [6:6] **Finally** these men said, "We will never find any basis for
6: 6 [6:7] **So** the administrators and the satraps went as a group to the
6:11 [6:12] **Then** these men went as a group and found Daniel praying
6:12 [6:13] **So** [+10089] they went to the king and spoke to him about
6:13 [6:14] **Then** [+10089] they said to the king, "Daniel, who is one
6:14 [6:15] **[NIE]** When the king heard this, he was greatly
6:15 [6:16] **Then** [+10089] the men went as a group to the king
6:16 [6:17] **So** [+10089] the king gave the order, and they brought
6:18 [6:19] **Then** the king returned to his palace and spent the night
6:19 [6:20] **[NIE]** At the first light of dawn, the king got up
6:21 [6:22] **[NIE]** Daniel answered, "O king, live forever!
6:23 [6:24] **[NIE]** The king was overjoyed and gave orders to lift
6:25 [6:26] **Then** [+10089] King Darius wrote to all the peoples,
7: 1 on his bed. **[NIE]** He wrote down the substance of his dream.
7:11 "**Then** [+10089] I continued to watch because of the boastful
7:19 "**Then** I wanted to know the true meaning of the fourth beast,

10009 אֲדָר '^{a}dār, n.pr.month. [1] [√ Hb 160]

Adar [1]

Ezr 6:15 The temple was completed on the third day of the month **Adar**,

10010 אִדַּר 'iddar, n.m. [1]

threshing floor [1]

Da 2:35 and became like chaff on a **threshing floor** *in* the summer.

10011 אֲדַרְגָּזַר '^{a}dargāzar, n.m. [2]

advisers [2]

Da 3: 2 prefects, governors, **advisers**, treasurers, judges, magistrates
3: 3 prefects, governors, **advisers**, treasurers, judges, magistrates

10012 אַדְרַזְדָּא 'adrazdā', adv. [1]

with diligence [1]

Ezr 7:23 let it be done **with diligence** for the temple of the God of heaven.

10013 אֶדְרָע 'edrā', n.[f.]. [1] [√ 10185; Hb 274, 2432]

force [1]

Ezr 4:23 to the Jews in Jerusalem and compelled them by **force** to stop.

10014 אַזְדָּא 'azdā', a. [2]

firmly [2]

Da 2: 5 replied to the astrologers, "This is what I have **firmly** decided:
2: 8 because you realize that this is what I have **firmly** decided:

10015 אֵזָה '^{a}zâ, v. [3]

heated [1], hot [1], hotter [1]

Da 3:19 [J] He ordered the furnace **heated** seven times hotter than usual
3:19 [J] He ordered the furnace heated seven times **hotter** than usual
3:22 [Jp] so **hot** that the flames of the fire killed the soldiers who took

10016 אֲזַל '^{a}zal, v. [7] [√ Hb 261]

untranslated [2], returned [2], went [2], go [1]

Ezr 4:23 [J] *they* **went** immediately to the Jews in Jerusalem
5: 8 [J] The king should know that *we* **went** to the district of Judah,
5:15 [J] 'Take these articles and **go** and deposit them in the temple in
Da 2:17 [J] Daniel **returned** to his house and explained the matter to his
2:24 [J] **[NIE]** and said to him, "Do not execute the wise men of
6:18 [6:19] [J] the king **returned** to his palace and spent the night
6:19 [6:20] [J] the king got up and hurried to the lions' den. **[NIE]**

10017 אַח 'aḥ, n.m. [1] [√ Hb 278]

brother Jews [1]

Ezr 7:18 You and your **brother Jews** may then do whatever seems best with

10018 אַחֲוָיָה 'aḥ^{a}wāyâ, n.f. Not used in NIV/BHS [√ 10252]

10019 אֲחִידָה '^{a}ḥîdâ, n.f. [1] [√ Hb 2648]

riddles [1]

Da 5:12 to interpret dreams, explain **riddles** and solve difficult problems.

10020 אַחְמְתָא 'aḥm^{e}tā', n.pr.loc. [1]

Ecbatana [1]

Ezr 6: 2 A scroll was found in the citadel of **Ecbatana** in the province of

10021 אַחַר 'aḥar, pp. [3] [→ 10022, 10024; Hb 339]

after [1], in the future [+10180] [1], to come [+10180+10201] [1]

Da 2:29 O king, your mind turned to things **to come** [+10180+10201],
2:45 has shown the king what will take place **in the future** [+10180].
7:24 **After** them another king will arise, different from the earlier ones;

10022 אַחֲרִי 'aḥ^{a}rî, n.f.constr. [1] [√ 10021; Hb 344]

to come [1]

Da 2:28 shown King Nebuchadnezzar what will happen in days **to come**.

10023 אָחֳרִי 'oḥ^{o}rî, a.f. [6] [√ 10025]

another [3], a^{s} [1], one [1], other [1]

Da 2:39 "After you, **another** kingdom will rise, inferior to yours. Next,
2:39 Next, a third kingdom, **one** of bronze, will rule over the whole
7: 5 "And there before me was **a**^{s} second beast, which looked like a
7: 6 "After that, I looked, and there before me was **another** beast,
7: 8 there before me was **another** horn, a little one, which came up
7:20 the ten horns on its head and about the **other** horn that came up,

10024 אָחֳרֵין 'oḥ^{o}rên, adv. [1] [√ 10021]

finally [+10221+10527] [1]

Da 4: 8 [4:5] **Finally** [+10221+10527], Daniel came into my presence and I

10025 אָחֳרָן 'oḥ^{o}rān, a.m. [5] [→ 10023]

another [2], one [1], other [1], someone else [1]

Da 2:11 No **one** can reveal it to the king except the gods, and they do not
2:44 that will never be destroyed, nor will it be left to **another** people.
3:29 turned into piles of rubble, for no **other** god can save in this way."
5:17 your gifts for yourself and give your rewards to **someone else**.
7:24 After them **another** king will arise, different from the earlier ones;

10026 אֲחַשְׁדַּרְפַּן '^{a}ḥašdarpan, n.m. [9] [√ Hb 346]

satraps [9]

Da 3: 2 He then summoned the **satraps**, prefects, governors, advisers,
3: 3 So the **satraps**, prefects, governors, advisers, treasurers, judges,
3:27 the **satraps**, prefects, governors and royal advisers crowded around
6: 1 [6:2] It pleased Darius to appoint 120 **satraps** to rule throughout
6: 2 [6:3] The **satraps** were made accountable to them so that the king
6: 3 [6:4] the **satraps** by his exceptional qualities that the king
6: 4 [6:5] the **satraps** tried to find grounds for charges against Daniel
6: 6 [6:7] and the **satraps** went as a group to the king and said:
6: 7 [6:8] **satraps**, advisers and governors have all agreed that the king

10027 אִילָן 'îlān, n.m. [6] [√ Hb 471]

tree [6]

Da 4:10 [4:7] and there before me stood a **tree** in the middle of the land.
4:11 [4:8] The **tree** grew large and strong and its top touched the sky;
4:14 [4:11] 'Cut down the **tree** and trim off its branches; strip off its
4:20 [4:17] The **tree** you saw, which grew large and strong, with its
4:23 [4:20] from heaven and saying, 'Cut down the **tree** and destroy it,
4:26 [4:23] The command to leave the stump of the **tree** with its roots

10028 אֵימְתָן 'êm^{e}tān, a. [1]

frightening [1]

Da 7: 7 was a fourth beast—terrifying and **frightening** and very powerful.

10029 אִיתַי 'îtay, pt. [17] [√ Hb 3780]

untranslated [6], there is [3], are [2], do [1], have [+10089] [1], in fact [1], there are [1], unharmed [+10089+10244+10379] [1], will be left with [+10378] [1]

Ezr 4:16 you **will be left** [+10378] **with** nothing in Trans-Euphrates.
5:17 did **in fact** issue a decree to rebuild this house of God in Jerusalem.
Da 2:10 "**There is** not a man on earth who can do what the king asks!
2:11 No one **[NIE]** can reveal it to the king except the gods, and they
2:11 it to the king except the gods, and they **do** not live among men."
2:26 "**Are** you able to tell me what I saw in my dream and interpret it?"
2:28 **there is** a God in heaven who reveals mysteries. He has shown
2:30 because I **have** [+10089] greater wisdom than other living men,

Da 3:12 **there are** some Jews whom you have set over the affairs of the
3:14 that **[NIE]** you do not serve my gods or worship the image of gold
3:15 if you **are** ready to fall down and worship the image I made,
3:17 **[NIE]** the God we serve is able to save us from it, and he will
3:18 that **[NIE]** we will not serve your gods or worship the image of
3:25 in the fire, unbound and **unharmed** [+10089+10244+10379],
3:29 into piles of rubble, for no **[NIE]** other god can save in this way."
4:35 [4:32] No **[NIE]** one can hold back his hand or say to him:
5:11 **There is** a man in your kingdom who has the spirit of the holy

10030 אֲכַל *'akal*, v. [7] [√ Hb 430]

devoured [2], ate [1], denounced [+10642] [1], devour [1], eat [1], falsely accused [+10642] [1]

Da 3:8 [J] astrologers came forward and **denounced** [+10642] the Jews.
4:33 [4:30] [J] was driven away from people and **ate** grass like cattle.
6:24 [6:25] [J] the men who *had* **falsely accused** [+10642] Daniel
7:5 [J] its teeth. It was told, 'Get up and **eat** your fill of flesh!'
7:7 [J] it crushed and **devoured** its victims and trampled underfoot
7:19 [J] the beast that crushed and **devoured** its victims and trampled
7:23 [J] from all the other kingdoms and *will* **devour** the whole earth,

10031 אַל *'al*, neg.adv. [4] [√ Hb 440]

don't [2], not [2]

Da 2:24 and said to him, "Do **not** execute the wise men of Babylon.
4:19 [4:16] do **not** let the dream or its meaning alarm you."
5:10 live forever!" she said. "**Don't** be alarmed! Don't look so pale!
5:10 live forever!" she said. "Don't be alarmed! **Don't** look so pale!

10032 אֵל *'ēl*, p.demo.pl. [1] [√ 10180; Hb 447]

these [1]

Ezr 5:15 'Take **these** [K 10034] articles and go and deposit them in the

10033 אֱלָהּ *'elāh*, n.m. [95] [√ Hb 468]

god [79], gods [15], *untranslated* [1]

Ezr 4:24 Thus the work on the house of **God** in Jerusalem came to a
5:1 the Jews in Judah and Jerusalem in the name of the **God** *of* Israel,
5:2 Jeshua son of Jozadak set to work to rebuild the house of **God** in
5:2 And the prophets of **God** were with them, helping them.
5:5 But the eye of their **God** was watching over the elders of the Jews,
5:8 we went to the district of Judah, to the temple of the great **God**.
5:11 "We are the servants of the **God** *of* heaven and earth, and we are
5:12 because our fathers angered the **God** *of* heaven, he handed them
5:13 King Cyrus issued a decree to rebuild this house of **God**.
5:14 temple of Babylon the gold and silver articles of the house of **God**,
5:15 the temple in Jerusalem. And rebuild the house of **God** on its site.'
5:16 and laid the foundations of the house of **God** in Jerusalem.
5:17 did in fact issue a decree to rebuild this house of **God** in Jerusalem.
6:3 the king issued a decree concerning the temple of **God** in
6:5 Also, the gold and silver articles of the house of **God**, which
6:5 temple in Jerusalem; they are to be deposited in the house of **God**.
6:7 Do not interfere with the work on this temple of **God**. Let the
6:7 and the Jewish elders rebuild this house of **God** on its site.
6:8 these elders of the Jews in the construction of this house of **God**:
6:9 rams, male lambs for burnt offerings to the **God** *of* heaven,
6:10 so that they may offer sacrifices pleasing to the **God** *of* heaven
6:12 May **God**, who has caused his Name to dwell there, overthrow any
6:12 change this decree or to destroy this temple **[RPH]** in Jerusalem.
6:14 building the temple according to the command of the **God** *of* Israel
6:16 the exiles—celebrated the dedication of the house of **God** with joy.
6:17 For the dedication of this house of **God** they offered a hundred
6:18 and the Levites in their groups for the service of **God** at Jerusalem,
7:12 To Ezra the priest, a teacher of the Law of the **God** *of* heaven:
7:14 about Judah and Jerusalem with regard to the Law of your **God**,
7:15 the king and his advisers have freely given to the **God** *of* Israel,
7:16 of the people and priests for the temple of their **God** in Jerusalem.
7:17 sacrifice them on the altar of the temple of your **God** in Jerusalem.
7:18 rest of the silver and gold, in accordance with the will of your **God**.
7:19 Deliver to the **God** *of* Jerusalem all the articles entrusted to you for
7:19 the articles entrusted to you for worship in the temple of your **God**.
7:20 anything else needed for the temple of your **God** that you may
7:21 a teacher of the Law of the **God** *of* heaven, may ask of you—
7:23 Whatever the **God** *of* heaven has prescribed, let it be done with
7:23 let it be done with diligence for the temple of the **God** *of* heaven.
7:24 gatekeepers, temple servants or other workers at this house of **God**.
7:25 And you, Ezra, in accordance with the wisdom of your **God**,
7:25 people of Trans-Euphrates—all who know the laws of your **God**.
7:26 Whoever does not obey the law of your **God** and the law of the
Jer 10:11 'These **gods**, who did not make the heavens and the earth,
Da 2:11 No one can reveal it to the king except the **gods**, and they do not
2:18 He urged them to plead for mercy from the **God** *of* heaven
2:19 to Daniel in a vision. Then Daniel praised the **God** *of* heaven
2:20 "Praise be to the name of **God** for ever and ever; wisdom and
2:23 I thank and praise you, O **God** *of* my fathers: You have given me
2:28 there is a **God** in heaven who reveals mysteries. He has shown
2:37 The **God** *of* heaven has given you dominion and power and might
2:44 the **God** *of* heaven will set up a kingdom that will never be
2:45 "The great **God** has shown the king what will take place in the
2:47 "Surely your **God** is the God of gods and the Lord of kings
2:47 "Surely your God is the **God** *of* gods and the Lord of kings
2:47 "Surely your God is the God of **gods** and the Lord of kings
3:12 They neither serve your **gods** nor worship the image of gold you
3:14 that you do not serve my **gods** or worship the image of gold I have
3:15 Then what **god** will be able to rescue you from my hand?"
3:17 the **God** we serve is able to save us from it, and he will rescue us
3:18 that we will not serve your **gods** or worship the image of gold you
3:25 and unharmed, and the fourth looks like a son of the **gods**."
3:26 and Abednego, servants of the Most High **God**, come out!
3:28 "Praise be to the **God** of Shadrach, Meshach and Abednego,
3:28 lives rather than serve or worship any **god** except their own God.
3:28 lives rather than serve or worship any god except their own **God**.
3:29 or language who say anything against the **God** of Shadrach,
3:29 turned into piles of rubble, for no other **god** can save in this way."
4:2 [3:32] wonders that the Most High **God** has performed for me.
4:8 [4:5] (He is called Belteshazzar, after the name of my **god**,
4:8 [4:5] name of my god, and the spirit of the holy **gods** is in him.)
4:9 [4:6] I know that the spirit of the holy **gods** is in you,
4:18 [4:15] But you can, because the spirit of the holy **gods** is in you."
5:3 goblets that had been taken from the temple of **God** in Jerusalem,
5:4 they praised the **gods** *of* gold and silver, of bronze, iron, wood
5:11 There is a man in your kingdom who has the spirit of the holy **gods**
5:11 to have insight and intelligence and wisdom like that of the **gods**.
5:14 I have heard that the spirit of the **gods** is in you and that you have
5:18 the Most High **God** gave your father Nebuchadnezzar sovereignty
5:21 until he acknowledged that the Most High **God** is sovereign over
5:23 You praised the **gods** *of* silver and gold, of bronze, iron, wood
5:23 But you did not honor the **God** who holds in his hand your life
5:26 **God** has numbered the days of your reign and brought it to an end.
6:5 [6:6] unless it has something to do with the law of his **God**."
6:7 [6:8] enforce the decree that anyone who prays to any **god** or man
6:10 [6:11] down on his knees and prayed, giving thanks to his **God**,
6:11 [6:12] a group and found Daniel praying and asking **God** for help.
6:12 [6:13] during the next thirty days anyone who prays to any **god**
6:16 [6:17] The king said to Daniel, "May your **God**, whom you serve
6:20 [6:21] "Daniel, servant of the living **God**, has your God,
6:20 [6:21] "Daniel, servant of the living God, has your **God**,
6:22 [6:23] My **God** sent his angel, and he shut the mouths of the lions.
6:23 [6:24] was found on him, because he had trusted in his **God**.
6:26 [6:27] people must fear and reverence the **God** of Daniel.
6:26 [6:27] "For he is the living **God** and he endures forever; his

10034 אֵלֶּה *'ēlleh*, p.demo.pl. [1] [√ 10180; Hb 465] Not indexed

untranslated [1]

10035 אֲלוּ *'alû*, interj. [5] [√ 10067]

there [4], *untranslated* [1]

Da 2:31 "You looked, O king, and **there** before you stood a large statue—
4:10 [4:7] and **there** before me stood a tree in the middle of the land.
4:13 [4:10] I looked, and **there** before me was a messenger, a holy one,
7:8 **there** before me was another horn, a little one, which came up
7:8 **[RPH]** This horn had eyes like the eyes of a man and a mouth that

10036 אִלֵּין *'illên*, p.demo.pl. [5] [√ 10180]

untranslated [3], the others[s] [1], those [1]

Da 2:40 breaks things to pieces, so it will crush and break all **the others**[s].
2:44 It will crush all **those** kingdoms and bring them to an end,
6:2 [6:3] The satraps **[RPR]** were made accountable to them so that
6:6 [6:7] and the satraps **[RPR]** went as a group to the king and said:
7:17 'The four great **[RPR]** beasts are four kingdoms that will rise from

10037 אִלֵּךְ *'illēk*, p.demo.pl. [14] [√ 10180]

these [8], *untranslated* [6]

Ezr 4:21 Now issue an order to **these** men to stop work, so that this city will
5:9 We questioned the elders **[RPR]** and asked them,
6:8 I hereby decree what you are to do for **these** elders of the Jews in
6:8 The expenses of **these** men are to be fully paid out of the royal
Da 3:12 and Abednego—who **[RPR]** pay no attention to you, O king.
3:13 and Abednego. So **these** men were brought before the king,
3:21 So **these** men, wearing their robes, trousers, turbans and other
3:22 so hot that the flames of the fire killed the soldiers **[NIE]** who
3:23 and **these** three men, firmly tied, fell into the blazing furnace.
3:27 They saw **[RPR]** that the fire had not harmed their bodies,

Da 6: 5 [6:6] Finally **these** men said, "We will never find any basis for
6: 11 [6:12] Then **these** men went as a group and found Daniel praying
6: 15 [6:16] the men **[RPR]** went as a group to the king and said to
6: 24 [6:25] the men **[RPR]** who had falsely accused Daniel were

10038 אֲלַף *ᵃlap*, n.m. [4] [√ Hb 547]

thousands [2], them[s] [+10002] [1], thousand [1]

Da 5: 1 King Belshazzar gave a great banquet for a **thousand** of his nobles
5: 1 for a thousand of his nobles and drank wine with **them**[s] [+10002].
7: 10 **Thousands** *upon* thousands attended him; ten thousand times ten
7: 10 Thousands upon **thousands** attended him; ten thousand times ten

10039 אַמָּה *'ammâ*, n.f. [4] [√ Hb 564]

ninety feet [+10749] [3], nine feet [+10747] [1]

Ezr 6: 3 It is to be **ninety feet** [+10749] high and ninety feet wide,
6: 3 It is to be ninety feet high and **ninety feet** [+10749] wide,
Da 3: 1 Nebuchadnezzar made an image of gold, **ninety feet** [+10749]
3: 1 an image of gold, ninety feet high and **nine feet** [+10747] wide,

10040 אֻמָּה *'ummâ*, n.f. [8] [√ Hb 569]

nations [6], nation [1], people [1]

Ezr 4: 10 the other **people** whom the great and honorable Ashurbanipal
Da 3: 4 commanded to do, O peoples, **nations** and men of every language:
3: 7 **nations** and men of every language fell down and worshiped the
3: 29 Therefore I decree that the people of any **nation** or language who
4: 1 [3:31] To the peoples, **nations** and men of every language,
5: 19 all the peoples and **nations** and men of every language dreaded
6: 25 [6:26] **nations** and men of every language throughout the land:
7: 14 all peoples, **nations** and men of every language worshiped him.

10041 אֲמַן *ᵃman*, v. [3] [√ Hb 586]

trustworthy [2], trusted [1]

Da 2: 45 [Pp] The dream is true and the interpretation *is* **trustworthy**."
6: 4 [6:5] [Pp] because he *was* **trustworthy** and neither corrupt nor
6: 23 [6:24] [P] found on him, because *he had* **trusted** in his God.

10042 אֲמַר *ᵃmar*, v. [71] [→ 10397; Hb 606]

untranslated [32], said [6], tell [6], told [5], asked [3], command [3], commanded [2], gave orders [2], interpret [+10600] [2], ordered [2], say [2], decreed [1], gave explanation [1], gave the order [1], saying [1], spoke [1], summoned [+10085+10378+10378] [1]

Ezr 5: 3 [J] and their associates went to them and **asked**,
5: 4 [J] *They* also **asked**, "What are the names of the men
5: 9 [J] We questioned the elders and **asked** them, "Who authorized
5: 11 [J] **[NIE]** "We are the servants of the God of heaven and earth,
5: 15 [J] *he* **told** him, 'Take these articles and go and deposit them in
Jer 10: 11 [J] "**Tell** them this: 'These gods, who did not make the heavens
Da 2: 4 [J] **Tell** your servants the dream, and we will interpret it."
2: 5 [J] The king replied **[NIE]** to the astrologers, "This is what I
2: 7 [J] they replied, **[NIE]** "Let the king tell his servants the dream,
2: 7 [J] more they replied, "*Let* the king **tell** his servants the dream,
2: 8 [J] **[NIE]** "I am certain that you are trying to gain time,
2: 9 [J] You have conspired to **tell** me misleading and wicked things,
2: 9 [J] So then, **tell** me the dream, and I will know that you can
2: 10 [J] **[NIE]** "There is not a man on earth who can do what the
2: 12 [J] furious that *he* **ordered** the execution of all the wise men of
2: 15 [J] He asked **[NIE]** the king's officer, "Why did the king issue
2: 20 [J] and **said**: "Praise be to the name of God for ever and ever;
2: 24 [J] and **said** to him, "Do not execute the wise men of Babylon.
2: 25 [J] Arioch took Daniel to the king at once and **said**, "I have found
2: 26 [J] The king asked **[NIE]** Daniel (also called Belteshazzar),
2: 27 [J] **[NIE]** "No wise man, enchanter, magician or diviner can
2: 36 [J] the dream, and now *we will* **interpret** [+10600] it to the king.
2: 46 [J] paid him honor and **ordered** that an offering and incense be
2: 47 [J] **[NIE]** "Surely your God is the God of gods and the Lord of
3: 4 [J] "This is what you *are* **commanded** to do, O peoples, nations
3: 9 [J] They said **[NIE]** to King Nebuchadnezzar, "O king,
3: 13 [J] Nebuchadnezzar **summoned** [+10085+10378+10378] Shadrach,
3: 14 [J] Nebuchadnezzar said **[NIE]** to them, "Is it true, Shadrach,
3: 16 [J] Shadrach, Meshach and Abednego replied **[NIE]** to the king,
3: 19 [J] He ordered **[NIE]** the furnace heated seven times hotter than
3: 20 [J] **commanded** some of the strongest soldiers in his army to tie
3: 24 [J] to his feet in amazement and asked **[NIE]** his advisers,
3: 24 [J] into the fire?" They replied, **[NIE]** "Certainly, O king."
3: 25 [J] He said, **[NIE]** "Look! I see four men walking around in the
3: 26 [J] and shouted, **[NIE]** "Shadrach, Meshach and Abednego,
3: 28 [J] **[NIE]** "Praise be to the God of Shadrach, Meshach
3: 29 [J] or language who **say** anything against the God of Shadrach,
4: 7 [4:4] [J] and diviners came, **I told** them the dream,
4: 8 [4:5] [J] came into my presence and *I* **told** him the dream.
4: 9 [4:6] [J] Here is my dream; **interpret** [+10600] it for me.
4: 14 [4:11] [J] **[NIE]** 'Cut down the tree and trim off its branches;
4: 18 [4:15] [J] Now, Belteshazzar, **tell** me what it means, for none of
4: 19 [4:16] [J] So the king said, **[NIE]** "Belteshazzar, do not let the
4: 19 [4:16] [J] Belteshazzar answered, **[NIE]** "My lord, if only the
4: 23 [4:20] [J] a holy one, coming down from heaven and **saying**,
4: 26 [4:23] [J] *The* **command** to leave the stump of the tree with its
4: 30 [4:27] [J] **[NIE]** "Is not this the great Babylon I have built as
4: 31 [4:28] [J] is what *is* **decreed** for you, King Nebuchadnezzar:
4: 35 [4:32] [J] No one can hold back his hand or **say** to him:
5: 2 [J] *he* **gave orders** to bring in the gold and silver goblets that
5: 7 [J] to be brought and said **[NIE]** to these wise men of Babylon,
5: 10 [J] she said. **[NIE]** "Don't be alarmed! Don't look so pale!
5: 13 [J] the king, and the king said **[NIE]** to him, "Are you Daniel,
5: 17 [J] Daniel answered **[NIE]** the king, "You may keep your gifts
5: 29 [J] *at* Belshazzar's **command**, Daniel was clothed in purple,
6: 5 [6:6] [J] Finally these men **said**, "We will never find any basis
6: 6 [6:7] [J] and the satraps went as a group to the king and **said**:
6: 12 [6:13] [J] to the king and **spoke** to him about his royal decree:
6: 12 [6:13] [J] The king answered, **[NIE]** "The decree stands—
6: 13 [6:14] [J] they said **[NIE]** to the king, "Daniel, who is one of
6: 15 [6:16] [J] the men went as a group to the king and **said** to him,
6: 16 [6:17] [J] So the king **gave the order**, and they brought Daniel
6: 16 [6:17] [J] The king said **[NIE]** to Daniel, "May your God,
6: 20 [6:21] [J] he called **[NIE]** to Daniel in an anguished voice,
6: 23 [6:24] [J] and **gave orders** to lift Daniel out of the den.
6: 24 [6:25] [J] *At* the king's **command**, the men who had falsely
7: 1 [J] his bed. He wrote down the substance of his dream. **[RPH]**
7: 2 [J] **[NIE]** "In my vision at night I looked, and there before me
7: 5 [J] its teeth. It *was* **told**, 'Get up and eat your fill of flesh!'
7: 16 [J] "So *he* **told** me and gave me the interpretation of these things:
7: 23 [J] "*He* **gave** me this **explanation**: 'The fourth beast is a fourth

10043 אִמַּר *'immar*, n.m. [3]

male lambs [3]

Ezr 6: 9 rams, **male lambs** for burnt offerings to the God of heaven,
6: 17 two hundred rams, four hundred **male lambs** and, as a sin offering
7: 17 rams and **male lambs**, together with their grain offerings and drink

10044 אֲנָה *ᵃnâ*, p.1.com.s. [16] [√ Hb 638] Not indexed

I [15], me [1]

10045 אִנּוּן *'innûn*, p.3.m.pl. [4] [√ 10200] Not indexed

untranslated [3], those [1]

10046 אֱנוֹשׁ *ᵉnôš*, n.m. [0] [√ 10050; Hb 632]

Da 4: 16 [4:13] [his mind be changed from that of a **man** [K; see Q 10050]]
4: 17 [4:14] [is sovereign over the kingdoms of **men** [K; see Q 10050]]

10047 אֲנַחְנָא *ᵃnaḥnā'*, p.1.com.pl. [4] [√ Hb 636] Not indexed

we [4]

10048 אֲנַס *ᵃnas*, v. [1] [√ Hb 646]

difficult [1]

Da 4: 9 [4:6] [J] gods is in you, and no mystery is *too* **difficult** for you.

10049 אַנַף *ᵃnap*, n.m. [2] [√ Hb 647]

attitude [+10614] [1], prostrate [+10542] [1]

Da 2: 46 Then King Nebuchadnezzar fell **prostrate** [+10542] before Daniel
3: 19 and Abednego, and his **attitude** [+10614] toward them changed.

10050 אֱנָשׁ *ᵉnāš*, n.m. [25] [→ 10046; Hb 632]

man [8], men [6], people [3], anyone [+10353] [2], everyone [+10353] [1], human [1], mankind [+10120] [1], people [+10120] [1], people [+10240] [1], whoever [+10168+10353] [1]

Ezr 4: 11 King Artaxerxes, From your servants, the **men** *of* Trans-Euphrates:
6: 11 Furthermore, I decree that if **anyone** [+10353] changes this edict,
Da 2: 10 "There is not a **man** on earth who can do what the king asks!
2: 38 in your hands he has placed **mankind** [+10120] and the beasts of
2: 43 so the **people** [+10240] will be a mixture and will not remain
3: 10 that **everyone** [+10353] who hears the sound of the horn, flute,
4: 16 [4:13] Let his mind be changed from that of a **man** [K 10046]
4: 17 [4:14] High is sovereign over the kingdoms of **men** [K 10046]
4: 17 [4:14] anyone he wishes and sets over them the lowliest of **men**.'
4: 25 [4:22] You will be driven away from **people** and will live with the
4: 25 [4:22] that the Most High is sovereign over the kingdoms of **men**
4: 32 [4:29] You will be driven away from **people** and will live with the
4: 32 [4:29] that the Most High is sovereign over the kingdoms of **men**

Da 4: 33 [4:30] He was driven away from **people** and ate grass like cattle.
5: 5 Suddenly the fingers of a **human** hand appeared and wrote on the
5: 7 "**Whoever** [+10168+10353] reads this writing and tells me what it
5: 21 He was driven away from **people** [+10120] and given the mind of
5: 21 that the Most High God is sovereign over the kingdoms of **men**
6: 7 [6:8] who prays to any god or **man** during the next thirty days,
6: 12 [6:13] the next thirty days **anyone** [+10353] who prays to any god
6: 12 [6:13] days anyone who prays to any god or **man** except to you,
7: 4 was lifted from the ground so that it stood on two feet like a **man**,
7: 4 on two feet like a man, and the heart of a **man** was given to it.
7: 8 This horn had eyes like the eyes of a **man** and a mouth that spoke
7: 13 at night I looked, and there before me was one like a son of **man**,

10051 אַנְתְּ 'ant, p.2.s.m. Not used in NIV/BHS [cf. 10052; Hb 911]

10052 אַנְתָּה 'antâ, p.2.m.s. [15] [cf. 10051; Hb 911] Not indexed

you [13], *untranslated* [2]

10053 אַנְתּוּן 'antûn, p.2.m.pl. [1] [√ Hb 917]

you [1]

Da 2: 8 the king answered, "I am certain that **you** are trying to gain time,

10054 אֱסוּר 'esûr, n.[m.]. [3] [→ 10057; Hb 657]

bound [2], imprisonment [1]

Ezr 7: 26 by death, banishment, confiscation of property, or **imprisonment**.
Da 4: 15 [4:12] let the stump and its roots, **bound** with iron and bronze,
4: 23 [4:20] but leave the stump, **bound** with iron and bronze,

10055 אָסְנַפַּר 'āsᵉnappar, n.pr.m. [1]

Ashurbanipal [1]

Ezr 4: 10 honorable **Ashurbanipal** deported and settled in the city of

10056 אָסְפַּרְנָא 'osparnā', adv. [7]

with diligence [3], be sure [1], diligence [1], fully [1], surely [1]

Ezr 5: 8 The work is being carried on *with* **diligence** and is making rapid
6: 8 The expenses of these men are to be **fully** paid out of the royal
6: 12 I Darius have decreed it. Let it be carried out **with diligence**.
6: 13 and their associates carried it out **with diligence**.
7: 17 With this money **be sure** to buy bulls, rams and male lambs,
7: 21 to provide **with diligence** whatever Ezra the priest,
7: 26 and the law of the king must **surely** be punished by death,

10057 אֱסָר 'esār, n.m. [7] [√ 10054; Hb 674]

decree [7]

Da 6: 7 [6:8] enforce the **decree** that anyone who prays to any god or man
6: 8 [6:9] issue the **decree** and put it in writing so that it cannot be
6: 9 [6:10] So King Darius put the **decree** in writing.
6: 12 [6:13] went to the king and spoke to him about his royal **decree**:
6: 12 [6:13] "Did you not publish a **decree** that during the next thirty
6: 13 [6:14] to you, O king, or to the **decree** you put in writing.
6: 15 [6:16] according to the law of the Medes and Persians no **decree**

10058 אָע 'ā', n.m. [5] [√ Hb 6770]

timbers [2], wood [2], beam [1]

Ezr 5: 8 building it with large stones and placing the **timbers** in the walls.
6: 4 with three courses of large stones and one of **timbers**. The costs
6: 11 a **beam** is to be pulled from his house and he is to be lifted up
Da 5: 4 the gods of gold and silver, of bronze, iron, **wood** and stone.
5: 23 the gods of silver and gold, of bronze, iron, **wood** and stone,

10059 אַף 'ap, c. [4] [√ Hb 677]

also [+10221] [2], even [+10221] [1], nor [+10221+10379] [1]

Ezr 5: 10 We **also** [+10221] asked them their names, so that we could write
5: 14 He **even** [+10221] removed from the temple of Babylon the gold
6: 5 **Also** [+10221], the gold and silver articles of the house of God,
Da 6: 22 [6:23] I was found innocent in his sight. **Nor** [+10221+10379]

10060 אֲפָרְסָי 'ᵃpārᵉsāy, n.pr.pl.g. [1] [√ Hb 7273?]

Persia [1]

Ezr 4: 9 from Tripolis, **Persia**, Erech and Babylon, the Elamites of Susa,

10061 אֲפַרְסְכָי 'ᵃparsᵉkāy, n.m.pl.[pr.g.?]. [2]

officials [2]

Ezr 5: 6 and their associates, the **officials** of Trans-Euphrates,
6: 6 and you, their fellow **officials** of that province,

10062 אֲפַרְסַתְכָי 'ᵃparsatkāy, n.pr.m.pl.[pr.g.?]. [1]

officials [1]

Ezr 4: 9 the judges and **officials** over the men from Tripolis, Persia,

10063 אַפְּתֹם 'appᵉtōm, n.m. [1]

revenues [1]

Ezr 4: 13 tribute or duty will be paid, and the royal **revenues** will suffer.

10064 אֶצְבַּע 'eṣba', n.f. [3] [√ Hb 720]

fingers [1], toes [+10655] [1], toes [1]

Da 2: 41 that the feet and **toes** were partly of baked clay and partly of iron,
2: 42 As the **toes** [+10655] were partly iron and partly clay, so this
5: 5 Suddenly the **fingers** of a human hand appeared and wrote on the

10065 אַרְבַּע 'arba', n.m. & f. [8] [√ 10651; Hb 752]

four [8]

Ezr 6: 17 two hundred rams, **four** hundred male lambs and, as a sin offering
Da 3: 25 I see **four** men walking around in the fire, unbound and unharmed,
7: 2 there before me were the **four** winds of heaven churning up the
7: 3 **Four** great beasts, each different from the others, came up out of
7: 6 on its back it had **four** wings like those of a bird. This beast had
7: 6 This beast had **four** heads, and it was given authority to rule.
7: 17 'The **four** great beasts are four kingdoms that will rise from the
7: 17 'The four great beasts are **four** kingdoms that will rise from the

10066 אַרְגְּוָן 'argᵉwān, n.m. [3] [√ Hb 763]

purple [3]

Da 5: 7 this writing and tells me what it means will be clothed in **purple**
5: 16 you will be clothed in **purple** and have a gold chain placed around
5: 29 Then at Belshazzar's command, Daniel was clothed in **purple**,

10067 אֲרוּ 'ᵃrû, interj. [5] [√ 10035]

there [5]

Da 7: 2 **there** before me were the four winds of heaven churning up the
7: 5 "And **there** before me was a second beast, which looked like a
7: 6 "After that, I looked, and **there** before me was another beast,
7: 7 vision at night I looked, and **there** before me was a fourth beast—
7: 13 at night I looked, and **there** before me was one like a son of man,

10068 אֲרַח 'ᵃraḥ, n.[m.?]. [2] [√ Hb 784]

ways [2]

Da 4: 37 [4:34] everything he does is right and all his **ways** are just.
5: 23 honor the God who holds in his hand your life and all your **ways**.

10069 אַרְיֵה 'aryēh, n.m. [10] [√ Hb 793]

lions [9], lion [1]

Da 6: 7 [6:8] except to you, O king, shall be thrown into the **lions**' den.
6: 12 [6:13] to you, O king, would be thrown into the **lions**' den?"
6: 16 [6:17] and they brought Daniel and threw him into the **lions**' den.
6: 19 [6:20] light of dawn, the king got up and hurried to the **lions**' den.
6: 20 [6:21] serve continually, been able to rescue you from the **lions**?"
6: 22 [6:23] My God sent his angel, and he shut the mouths of the **lions**.
6: 24 [6:25] Daniel were brought in and thrown into the **lions**' den,
6: 24 [6:25] the **lions** overpowered them and crushed all their bones.
6: 27 [6:28] He has rescued Daniel from the power of the **lions**."
7: 4 "The first was like a **lion**, and it had the wings of an eagle.

10070 אַרְיוֹךְ 'aryôk, n.pr.m. [5] [√ Hb 796]

Arioch [4], *untranslated* [1]

Da 2: 14 When **Arioch**, the commander of the king's guard, had gone out to
2: 15 He asked **[RPH]** the king's officer, "Why did the king issue such
2: 15 such a harsh decree?" **Arioch** then explained the matter to Daniel.
2: 24 Daniel went to **Arioch**, whom the king had appointed to execute
2: 25 **Arioch** took Daniel to the king at once and said, "I have found a

10071 אֲרִיךְ 'ᵃrîk, a.vbl. [1]

proper [1]

Ezr 4: 14 to the palace and it is not **proper** for us to see the king dishonored,

10072 אַרְכֻבָּה 'arkubbâ, n.f. [1] [√ Hb 1384]

knees [1]

Da 5: 6 and he was so frightened that his **knees** knocked together

10073 אַרְכָה 'arkâ, n.f. [2] [√ Hb 801]

continue [1], live [+10089+10261] [1]

Da 4:27 [4:24] It may be that then your prosperity will **continue**."
7:12 but were allowed to **live** [+10089+10261] for a period of time.)

10074 אַרְכְוָי 'arkᵉwāy, n.pr.g. [1] [√ Hb 804]

Erech [1]

Ezr 4: 9 from Tripolis, Persia, **Erech** and Babylon, the Elamites of Susa,

10075 אֲרַע 'ᵃra', n.[f.]. [21] [→ 10076, 10077; Hb 824]

earth [14], ground [3], land [2], inferior [1], world [1]

Ezr 5:11 "We are the servants of the God of heaven and **earth**, and we are
Jer 10:11 will perish from the **earth** and from under the heavens.' "
Da 2:35 the statue became a huge mountain and filled the whole **earth**.
2:39 "After you, another kingdom will rise, **inferior** to yours. Next,
2:39 a third kingdom, one of bronze, will rule over the whole **earth**.
4: 1 [3:31] and men of every language, who live in all the **world**:
4:10 [4:7] and there before me stood a tree in the middle of the **land**.
4:11 [4:8] top touched the sky; it was visible to the ends of the **earth**.
4:15 [4:12] bound with iron and bronze, remain in the **ground**,
4:15 [4:12] let him live with the animals among the plants of the **earth**.
4:20 [4:17] with its top touching the sky, visible to the whole **earth**,
4:22 [4:19] and your dominion extends to distant parts of the **earth**.
4:23 [4:20] the grass of the field, while its roots remain in the **ground**.
4:35 [4:32] All the peoples of the **earth** are regarded as nothing. He
4:35 [4:32] with the powers of heaven and the peoples of the **earth**.
6:25 [6:26] nations and men of every language throughout the **land**:
6:27 [6:28] and wonders in the heavens and on the **earth**.
7: 4 it was lifted from the **ground** so that it stood on two feet like a
7:17 four great beasts are four kingdoms that will rise from the **earth**.
7:23 'The fourth beast is a fourth kingdom that will appear on **earth**.
7:23 from all the other kingdoms and will devour the whole **earth**,

10076 אַרְעִי 'ar'î, n.f.den. [1] [√ 10075]

floor [1]

Da 6:24 [6:25] before they reached the **floor** *of* the den, the lions

10077 אֲרַק 'ᵃraq, n.[f.]. [1] [√ 10075; Hb 824]

earth [1]

Jer 10:11 'These gods, who did not make the heavens and the **earth**,

10078 אַרְתַּחְשַׁשְׂתְּא 'artaḥšast', אַרְתַּחְשַׁסְתְּא 'artaḥšast', אַרְתַּחְשַׁשְׂתְּ 'artaḥšast, n.pr.m. [6] [√ Hb 831]

Artaxerxes [6]

Ezr 4: 8 wrote a letter against Jerusalem to **Artaxerxes** the king as follows:
4:11 To King **Artaxerxes**, From your servants, the men of
4:23 As soon as the copy of the letter of King **Artaxerxes** was read to
6:14 and the decrees of Cyrus, Darius and **Artaxerxes**, kings of Persia.
7:12 **Artaxerxes**, king of kings, To Ezra the priest, a teacher of the Law
7:21 Now I, King **Artaxerxes**, order all the treasurers of

10079 אֹשׁ 'ōš, n.m. [3] [√ Hb 9268]

foundations [3]

Ezr 4:12 They are restoring the walls and repairing the **foundations**.
5:16 and laid the **foundations** of the house of God in Jerusalem.
6: 3 as a place to present sacrifices, and let its **foundations** be laid.

10080 אֶשָּׁא 'eššā', n.[f.]. [1] [√ Hb 836, 852]

fire [1]

Da 7:11 was slain and its body destroyed and thrown into the blazing **fire**.

10081 אָשַׁף 'āšap, n.m. [6] [√ Hb 879]

enchanters [4], enchanter [2]

Da 2:10 asked such a thing of any magician or **enchanter** or astrologer.
2:27 **enchanter**, magician or diviner can explain to the king the mystery
4: 7 [4:4] the magicians, **enchanters**, astrologers and diviners came,
5: 7 The king called out for the **enchanters**, astrologers and diviners to
5:11 him chief of the magicians, **enchanters**, astrologers and diviners.
5:15 and **enchanters** were brought before me to read this writing

10082 אֻשַּׁרְנָא 'uššarnā', n.m. [2]

structure [2]

Ezr 5: 3 authorized you to rebuild this temple and restore this **structure**?"
5: 9 authorized you to rebuild this temple and restore this **structure**?"

10083 אֶשְׁתַּדּוּר 'eštaddûr, n.m. [2] [√ 10700]

rebellion [1], sedition [1]

Ezr 4:15 to kings and provinces, a place of **rebellion** from ancient times.
4:19 revolt against kings and has been a place of rebellion and **sedition**.

10084 אָת 'āt, n.m. [3] [√ Hb 253]

signs [2], miraculous signs [1]

Da 4: 2 [3:32] It is my pleasure to tell you about the **miraculous signs**
4: 3 [3:33] How great are his **signs**, how mighty his wonders!
6:27 [6:28] he performs **signs** and wonders in the heavens and on the

10085 אֲתָה 'ᵃtâ, v. [16] [√ Hb 910]

brought [3], brought in [2], came [2], come [2], bring in [1], coming [1], gone [1], summoned [+10042+10378+10378] [1], was brought [1], went [1], were brought [1]

Ezr 4:12 [J] the Jews who came up to us from you *have* **gone** to Jerusalem
5: 3 [J] and their associates **went** to them and asked,
5:16 [J] So this Sheshbazzar **came** and laid the foundations of the
Da 3: 2 [J] all the other provincial officials to **come** to the dedication of
3:13 [P] Nebuchadnezzar **summoned** [+10042+10378+10378] Shadrach,
3:13 [Pp] and Abednego. So these men **were brought** before the king,
3:26 [J] servants of the Most High God, come out! **Come** here!"
5: 2 [P] he gave orders to **bring in** the gold and silver goblets that
5: 3 [P] So *they* **brought in** the gold goblets that had been taken from
5:13 [P] one of the exiles my father the king **brought** from Judah?
5:23 [P] You had the goblets from his temple **brought** to you, and you
6:16 [6:17] [P] *they* **brought** Daniel and threw him into the lions'
6:17 [6:18] [Pp] A stone **was brought** and placed over the mouth of
6:24 [6:25] [P] men who had falsely accused Daniel *were* **brought in**
7:13 [J] was one like a son of man, **coming** with the clouds of heaven.
7:22 [J] until the Ancient of Days **came** and pronounced judgment in

10086 אַתּוּן 'attûn, n.m. [& f.?]. [10]

furnace [10]

Da 3: 6 and worship will immediately be thrown into a blazing **furnace**."
3:11 not fall down and worship will be thrown into a blazing **furnace**.
3:15 worship it, you will be thrown immediately into a blazing **furnace**.
3:17 If we are thrown into the blazing **furnace**, the God we serve is able
3:19 He ordered the **furnace** heated seven times hotter than usual
3:20 Meshach and Abednego and throw them into the blazing **furnace**.
3:21 other clothes, were bound and thrown into the blazing **furnace**.
3:22 The king's command was so urgent and the **furnace** so hot that the
3:23 and these three men, firmly tied, fell into the blazing **furnace**.
3:26 then approached the opening of the blazing **furnace** and shouted,

10087 אֲתַר 'ᵃtar, n.m. [5] [→ 10092; Hb 889]

site [2], place [1], places [1], trace [1]

Ezr 5:15 the temple in Jerusalem. And rebuild the house of God on its **site**.'
6: 3 Let the temple be rebuilt as a **place** to present sacrifices, and let its
6: 5 are to be returned to their **places** in the temple in Jerusalem;
6: 7 and the Jewish elders rebuild this house of God on its **site**.
Da 2:35 the summer. The wind swept them away without leaving a **trace**.

ב, b

10088 ב b, letter. Not used in NIV/BHS [√ Hb 927]

10089 בְּ- bᵉ-, pp.pref. [226] [→ 10092; Hb 928] Not indexed

in [79], *untranslated* [31], then [+10008] [13], with [11], on [9], at [8], so [+10008] [8], over [7], by [6], of [6], from [4], have [3], continually [+10002+10753] [2], throughout [+10353] [2], to [2], under [2], underfoot [+10655] [2], when [+10008] [2], about [1], among [1], as soon as [+10002+10168+10530] [1], be handed over [+10311+10314] [1], because [1], daily [+10317+10317] [1], Daniel's [+10181] [1], during [1], had [1], handed over [+10311+10314] [1], have [+10029] [1], his [+10192] [1], immediately [+10096] [1], in [+10135] [1], in [+10135+10464] [1], live [+10073+10261] [1], loudly [+10264] [1], on [+10135] [1], place[s] [+10135+10193] [1], place[s] [+10193] [1], possess [+10311] [1], something to do with [1], therefore [+10008] [1], thus [+10008] [1], wearing [1], when [+10002+10530] [1], wherever [+10168+10353] [1], while [1], with regard to [1]

10090 בִּאישׁ bi'yš, a. [1] [√ 10091]

wicked [1]

Ezr 4:12 to Jerusalem and are rebuilding that rebellious and **wicked** city.

10091 בְּאֵשׁ bᵉʼēš, v. [1] [→ 10090; Hb 944]

distressed [1]

Da 6: 14 [6:15] [J] When the king heard this, he *was* greatly **distressed**;

10092 בָּאתַר bāʼtar, pp. + n.m. [3] [√ 10089 & 10087]

after [3]

Da 2: 39 "**After** you, another kingdom will rise, inferior to yours. Next,
7: 6 "**After** that, I looked, and there before me was another beast,
7: 7 "**After** that, in my vision at night I looked, and there before me

10093 בָּבֶל bābel, n.pr.loc. [25] [→ 10094; Hb 951]

Babylon [24], its[s] [1]

Ezr 5: 12 king of **Babylon**, who destroyed this temple and deported the
5: 12 who destroyed this temple and deported the people to **Babylon**.
5: 13 "However, in the first year of Cyrus king of **Babylon**, King Cyrus
5: 14 He even removed from the temple of **Babylon** the gold and silver
5: 14 the temple in Jerusalem and brought to the temple in **Babylon**.
5: 17 let a search be made in the royal archives of **Babylon** to see if
6: 1 and they searched in the archives stored in the treasury at **Babylon**.
6: 5 took from the temple in Jerusalem and brought to **Babylon**,
7: 16 the silver and gold you may obtain from the province of **Babylon**,
Da 2: 12 that he ordered the execution of all the wise men of **Babylon**.
2: 14 had gone out to put to death the wise men of **Babylon**,
2: 18 might not be executed with the rest of the wise men of **Babylon**.
2: 24 whom the king had appointed to execute the wise men of **Babylon**,
2: 24 and said to him, "Do not execute the wise men of **Babylon**.
2: 48 He made him ruler over the entire province of **Babylon** and placed
2: 48 province of Babylon and placed him in charge of all **its**[s] wise men.
2: 49 and Abednego administrators over the province of **Babylon**,
3: 1 and set it up on the plain of Dura in the province of **Babylon**.
3: 12 whom you have set over the affairs of the province of **Babylon**—
3: 30 Meshach and Abednego in the province of **Babylon**.
4: 6 [4:3] So I commanded that all the wise men of **Babylon** be
4: 29 [4:26] was walking on the roof of the royal palace of **Babylon**,
4: 30 [4:27] "Is not this the great **Babylon** I have built as the royal
5: 7 and diviners to be brought and said to these wise men of **Babylon**,
7: 1 In the first year of Belshazzar king of **Babylon**, Daniel had a

10094 בָּבְלִי bābᵉlî, a.g. [1] [√ 10093]

Babylon [1]

Ezr 4: 9 from Tripolis, Persia, Erech and **Babylon**, the Elamites of Susa,

10095 בְּדַר bᵉdar, v. [1] [√ Hb 1029, 7061]

scatter [1]

Da 4: 14 [4:11] [M] its branches; strip off its leaves and **scatter** its fruit.

10096 בְּהִילוּ bᵉhîlû, n.f. [1] [√ 10097; Hb 987]

immediately [+10089] [1]

Ezr 4: 23 they went **immediately** [+10089] to the Jews in Jerusalem

10097 בְּהַל bᵉhal, v. [11] [→ 10096, 10218; Hb 987]

terrified [3], alarm [1], alarmed [1], amazement [+10755] [1], at once [1], disturbed [1], frightened [1], hurried [1], troubled [1]

Da 2: 25 [L] Arioch took Daniel to the king **at once** and said, "I have
3: 24 [L] Nebuchadnezzar leaped to his feet in **amazement** [+10755]
4: 5 [4:2] [M] visions that passed through my mind **terrified** me.
4: 19 [4:16] [M] perplexed for a time, and his thoughts **terrified** him.
4: 19 [4:16] [M] *do* not *let* the dream or its meaning **alarm** you."
5: 6 [M] and he *was so* **frightened** that his knees knocked together
5: 9 [O] So King Belshazzar *became* even more **terrified** and his face
5: 10 [M] she said. "Don't *be* **alarmed**! Don't look so pale!
6: 19 [6:20] [L] the king got up and **hurried** to the lions' den.
7: 15 [M] and the visions that passed through my mind **disturbed** me.
7: 28 [M] I, Daniel, *was* deeply **troubled** *by* my thoughts, and my face

10098 בְּטֵל bᵉṭal, v. [6] [√ Hb 1060]

stop [2], *untranslated* [1], came to a standstill [1], stop work [1], stopped [1]

Ezr 4: 21 [M] Now issue an order to these men to **stop work**, so that this
4: 23 [M] the Jews in Jerusalem and compelled them by force *to* **stop**.
4: 24 [J] **came to a standstill** until the second year of the reign of
4: 24 [J] **[RPH]** until the second year of the reign of Darius king of
5: 5 [M] and they *were* not **stopped** until a report could go to Darius
6: 8 [M] revenues of Trans-Euphrates, so that the work *will* not **stop**.

10099 בֵּין bên, pp. [2] [√ Hb 1068]

among [1], between [1]

Da 7: 5 one of its sides, and it had three ribs in its mouth **between** its teeth.
7: 8 me was another horn, a little one, which came up **among** them;

10100 בִּינָה bînâ, n.f. [1] [√ Hb 1069]

discerning [+10313] [1]

Da 2: 21 wisdom to the wise and knowledge to the **discerning** [+10313].

10101 בִּירָה bîrâ, n.f. [1] [√ Hb 1072]

citadel [1]

Ezr 6: 2 A scroll was found in the **citadel** of Ecbatana in the province of

10102 בִּית bît, v.den. [1] [√ 10103]

spent the night [1]

Da 6: 18 [6:19] [J] to his palace and **spent the night** without eating

10103 בַּיִת bayit, n.m. [44] [→ 10102; Hb 1074]

house [17], temple [16], home [2], houses [2], *untranslated* [1], archives [+10148] [1], archives [+10515] [1], hall [1], residence [1], treasury [+10148] [1], treasury [1]

Ezr 4: 24 Thus the work on the **house** *of* God in Jerusalem came to a
5: 2 Jeshua son of Jozadak set to work to rebuild the **house** *of* God in
5: 3 "Who authorized you to rebuild this **temple** and restore this
5: 8 we went to the district of Judah, to the **temple** *of* the great God.
5: 9 "Who authorized you to rebuild this **temple** and restore this
5: 11 and we are rebuilding the **temple** that was built many years ago,
5: 12 who destroyed this **temple** and deported the people to Babylon.
5: 13 King Cyrus issued a decree to rebuild this **house** *of* God.
5: 14 temple of Babylon the gold and silver articles of the **house** *of* God,
5: 15 the temple in Jerusalem. And rebuild the **house** *of* God on its site.'
5: 16 and laid the foundations of the **house** *of* God in Jerusalem.
5: 17 let a search be made in the royal **archives** [+10148] of Babylon to
5: 17 did in fact issue a decree to rebuild this **house** *of* God in Jerusalem.
6: 1 they searched in the **archives** [+10515] stored in the treasury at
6: 3 the king issued a decree concerning the **temple** *of* God in
6: 3 Let the **temple** be rebuilt as a place to present sacrifices, and let its
6: 4 and one of timbers. The costs are to be paid by the royal **treasury**.
6: 5 Also, the gold and silver articles of the **house** *of* God, which
6: 5 temple in Jerusalem; they are to be deposited in the **house** *of* God.
6: 7 Do not interfere with the work on this **temple** *of* God. Let the
6: 7 and the Jewish elders rebuild this **house** *of* God on its site.
6: 8 these elders of the Jews in the construction of this **house** *of* God:
6: 11 a beam is to be pulled from his **house** and he is to be lifted up
6: 11 And for this crime his **house** is to be made a pile of rubble.
6: 12 a hand to change this decree or to destroy this **temple** in Jerusalem.
6: 15 The **temple** was completed on the third day of the month Adar,
6: 16 the exiles—celebrated the dedication of the **house** *of* God with joy.
6: 17 For the dedication of this **house** *of* God they offered a hundred
7: 16 of the people and priests for the **temple** *of* their God in Jerusalem.
7: 17 sacrifice them on the altar of the **temple** *of* your God in Jerusalem.
7: 19 the articles entrusted to you for worship in the **temple** *of* your God.
7: 20 anything else needed for the **temple** *of* your God that you may
7: 20 to supply, you may provide from the royal **treasury** [+10148].
7: 23 let it be done with diligence for the **temple** *of* the God of heaven.
7: 24 gatekeepers, temple servants or other workers at this **house** *of* God.
Da 2: 5 you cut into pieces and your **houses** turned into piles of rubble.
2: 17 Daniel returned to his **house** and explained the matter to his friends
3: 29 be cut into pieces and their **houses** be turned into piles of rubble,
4: 4 [4:1] was at **home** in my palace, contented and prosperous.
4: 30 [4:27] this the great Babylon I have built as the royal **residence**,
5: 3 that had been taken from the temple of **[RPH]** God in Jerusalem,
5: 10 the voices of the king and his nobles, came into the banquet **hall**.
5: 23 You had the goblets from his **temple** brought to you, and you
6: 10 [6:11] he went **home** to his upstairs room where the windows

10104 בָּל bāl, n.[m.] [1]

determined [+10542+10682] [1]

Da 6: 14 [6:15] *he was* **determined** [+10542+10682] to rescue Daniel and

10105 בֵּלְשַׁאצַּר bēlʼšaṣṣar, n.pr.m. [2] [√ 10109; Hb 1157]

Belshazzar [2]

Da 5: 30 That very night **Belshazzar**, king of the Babylonians, was slain,
7: 1 In the first year of **Belshazzar** king of Babylon, Daniel had a

10106 בְּלָה bᵉlâ, v. [1] [√ Hb 1162]

oppress [1]

Da 7: 25 [M] **oppress** his saints and try to change the set times

10107 בְּלוֹ *b*ᵉ*lô*, n.[m.]. [3]

tribute [3]

Ezr 4: 13 its walls are restored, no more taxes, **tribute** or duty will be paid,
4: 20 of Trans-Euphrates, and taxes, **tribute** and duty were paid to them.
7: 24 **tribute** or duty on any of the priests, Levites, singers, gatekeepers,

10108 בֵּלְטְשַׁאצַּר *bēlṭ*ᵉ*ša'ṣṣar*, n.pr.m. [8] [cf. 10109; Hb 1171]

Belteshazzar [8]

Da 2: 26 The king asked Daniel (also called **Belteshazzar**), "Are you able to
4: 8 [4:5] (He is called **Belteshazzar**, after the name of my god,
4: 9 [4:6] I said, "**Belteshazzar**, chief of the magicians, I know that
4: 18 [4:15] Now, **Belteshazzar**, tell me what it means, for none of the
4: 19 [4:16] Daniel (also called **Belteshazzar**) was greatly perplexed
4: 19 [4:16] So the king said, "**Belteshazzar**, do not let the dream or its
4: 19 [4:16] **Belteshazzar** answered, "My lord, if only the dream
5: 12 This man Daniel, whom the king called **Belteshazzar**, was found

10109 בֵּלְשַׁאצַּר *bēlša'ṣṣar*, n.pr.m. [5] [√ 10105; Hb 1157]

Belshazzar [4], Belshazzar's [1]

Da 5: 1 King **Belshazzar** gave a great banquet for a thousand of his nobles
5: 2 While **Belshazzar** was drinking his wine, he gave orders to bring
5: 9 So King **Belshazzar** became even more terrified and his face grew
5: 22 "But you his son, O **Belshazzar**, have not humbled yourself,
5: 29 Then at **Belshazzar's** command, Daniel was clothed in purple,

10110 בֵּן *bēn*, n.m. Not used in NIV/BHS

10111 בְּנָה *b*ᵉ*nâ*, v. [22] [→ 10112; Hb 1215]

rebuild [7], built [3], be rebuilt [2], building [2], is built [2], rebuilding [2], build [1], constructing [1], construction [1], under construction [1]

Ezr 4: 12 [J] and *are* **rebuilding** that rebellious and wicked city.
4: 13 [L] the king should know that if this city **is built** and its walls are
4: 16 [L] We inform the king that if this city **is built** and its walls are
4: 21 [L] stop work, so that this city *will* not **be rebuilt** until I so order.
5: 2 [J] Jeshua son of Jozadak set to work to **rebuild** the house of
5: 3 [J] "Who authorized you to **rebuild** this temple and restore this
5: 4 [J] "What are the names of the men **constructing** this building?"
5: 8 [L] The people *are* **building** it *with* large stones and placing the
5: 9 [J] "Who authorized you to **rebuild** this temple and restore this
5: 11 [J] we *are* **rebuilding** the temple that was built many years ago,
5: 11 [Jp] we are rebuilding the temple that was **built** many years ago,
5: 11 [J] years ago, one that a great king of Israel **built** and finished.
5: 13 [J] King Cyrus issued a decree to **rebuild** this house of God.
5: 15 [L] in Jerusalem. And **rebuild** the house of God on its site.'
5: 16 [L] From that day to the present *it has been* **under construction**
5: 17 [J] fact issue a decree to **rebuild** this house of God in Jerusalem.
6: 3 [L] *Let* the temple **be rebuilt** as a place to present sacrifices,
6: 7 [J] *Let* the governor of the Jews and the Jewish elders **rebuild**
6: 8 [J] elders of the Jews in the **construction** *of* this house of God:
6: 14 [J] So the elders of the Jews *continued to* **build** and prosper
6: 14 [J] They finished **building** the temple according to the command
Da 4: 30 [4:27] [J] "Is not this the great Babylon I *have* **built** as the royal

10112 בִּנְיָן *binyān*, n.[m.]. [1] [√ 10111; Hb 1230]

building [1]

Ezr 5: 4 "What are the names of the men constructing this **building**?"

10113 בְּנַס *b*ᵉ*nas*, v. [1]

angry [1]

Da 2: 12 [J] This made the king so **angry** and furious that he ordered the

10114 בְּעָה *b*ᵉ*'â*, v. [12] [→ 10115; Hb 1239]

asked [2], prays [+10115] [2], asked for [1], look for [1], plead [1], praying [1], prays [1], request [1], sought out [1], tried [1]

Da 2: 13 [J] *men were sent to* **look for** Daniel and his friends to put them
2: 16 [J] At this, Daniel went in to the king and **asked for** time, so that
2: 18 [J] He urged them to **plead** *for* mercy from the God of heaven
2: 23 [J] you have made known to me what *we* **asked** of you,
2: 49 [J] *at* Daniel's **request** the king appointed Shadrach, Meshach
4: 36 [4:33] [M] My advisers and nobles **sought** me **out**, and I was
6: 4 [6:5] [J] the satraps **tried** to find grounds for charges against
6: 7 [6:8] [J] enforce the decree that anyone who **prays** [+10115] to
6: 11 [6:12] [J] and found Daniel **praying** and asking God for help.
6: 12 [6:13] [J] the next thirty days anyone who **prays** to any god
6: 13 [6:14] [J] in writing. *He still* **prays** [+10115] three times a day."
7: 16 [J] standing there and **asked** him the true meaning of all this.

10115 בָּעוּ *bā'û*, n.f. [2] [√ 10114]

prays [+10114] [2]

Da 6: 7 [6:8] enforce the decree that anyone who **prays** [+10114] to any
6: 13 [6:14] put in writing. *He still* **prays** [+10114] three times a day."

10116 בְּעֵל *b*ᵉ*'ēl*, n.m. [3] [√ Hb 1251]

commanding officer [+10302] [3]

Ezr 4: 8 Rehum the **commanding officer** [+10302] and Shimshai the
4: 9 Rehum the **commanding officer** [+10302] and Shimshai the
4: 17 To Rehum the **commanding officer** [+10302], Shimshai the

10117 בִּקְעָה *biq'â*, n.f. [1] [√ Hb 1326]

plain [1]

Da 3: 1 and set it up on the **plain** *of* Dura in the province of Babylon.

10118 בְּקַר *b*ᵉ*qar*, v. [5] [√ Hb 1329]

a search made [2], a search be made [1], inquire [1], searched [1]

Ezr 4: 15 [M] so that **a search** *may be* **made** in the archives of your
4: 19 [M] I issued an order and **a search** *was* **made**, and it was found
5: 17 [O] *let* **a search be made** in the royal archives of Babylon to see
6: 1 [M] *they* **searched** in the archives stored in the treasury at
7: 14 [M] by the king and his seven advisers to **inquire** about Judah

10119 ¹בַּר *bar*¹, n.[m.]. [8] [√ Hb 1340]

field [5], wild [3]

Da 2: 38 placed mankind and the beasts of the **field** and the birds of the air.
4: 12 [4:9] Under it the beasts of the **field** found shelter, and the birds
4: 15 [4:12] and bronze, remain in the ground, in the grass of the **field**.
4: 21 [4:18] food for all, giving shelter to the beasts of the **field**,
4: 23 [4:20] bound with iron and bronze, in the grass of the **field**,
4: 23 [4:20] let him live like the **wild** animals, until seven times pass by
4: 25 [4:22] away from people and will live with the **wild** animals;
4: 32 [4:29] away from people and will live with the **wild** animals;

10120 ²בַּר *bar*², n.m. [19] [√ Hb 1337, 1201]

son [5], exiles [+10145] [4], descendant [2], sons [2], age [+10732] [1], children [1], mankind [+10050] [1], people [+10050] [1], people [1], young [1]

Ezr 5: 1 the prophet and Zechariah the prophet, a **descendant** *of* Iddo,
5: 2 Zerubbabel **son** *of* Shealtiel and Jeshua son of Jozadak set to work
5: 2 Jeshua **son** *of* Jozadak set to work to rebuild the house of God in
6: 9 **young** bulls, rams, male lambs for burnt offerings to the God of
6: 10 of heaven and pray for the well-being of the king and his **sons**.
6: 14 of Haggai the prophet and Zechariah, a **descendant** *of* Iddo.
6: 16 the **people** *of* Israel—the priests, the Levites and the rest of the
6: 16 the priests, the Levites and the rest of the **exiles** [+10145]—
7: 23 should there be wrath against the realm of the king and of his **sons**?
Da 2: 25 "I have found a man among the **exiles** [+10145] from Judah who
2: 38 in your hands he has placed **mankind** [+10050] and the beasts of
3: 25 and unharmed, and the fourth looks like a **son** *of* the gods."
5: 13 one of the **exiles** [+10145] my father the king brought from Judah?
5: 21 He was driven away from **people** [+10050] and given the mind of
5: 22 "But you his **son**, O Belshazzar, have not humbled yourself,
5: 31 [6:1] took over the kingdom, at the **age** [+10732] of sixty-two.
6: 13 [6:14] "Daniel, who is one of the **exiles** [+10145] from Judah,
6: 24 [6:25] into the lions' den, along with their wives and **children**.
7: 13 at night I looked, and there before me was one like a **son** *of* man,

10121 ¹בְּרַךְ *b*ᵉ*rak*¹, v. [1] [→ 10123; Hb 1384]

got down [1]

Da 6: 10 [6:11] [J] Three times a day he **got down** on his knees

10122 ²בְּרַךְ *b*ᵉ*rak*², v. [4] [√ Hb 1385]

praise [2], praised [2]

Da 2: 19 [M] Daniel in a vision. Then Daniel **praised** the God of heaven
2: 20 [N] "**Praise** be to the name of God for ever and ever; wisdom
3: 28 [Jp] "**Praise** *be to* the God of Shadrach, Meshach and Abednego,
4: 34 [4:31] [M] *I* **praised** the Most High; I honored and glorified

10123 בְּרֵךְ *b*ᵉ*rēk*, n.[f.]. [1] [√ 10121; Hb 1386]

knees [1]

Da 6: 10 [6:11] Three times a day he got down on his **knees** and prayed,

10124 בְּרַם *b*ᵉ*ram*, adv.advers. [5]

but [3], however [1], nevertheless [1]

Ezr 5: 13 "**However**, in the first year of Cyrus king of Babylon, King Cyrus

Da 2:28 **but** there is a God in heaven who reveals mysteries. He has shown
4:15 [4:12] **But** let the stump and its roots, bound with iron
4:23 [4:20] 'Cut down the tree and destroy it, **but** leave the stump,
5:17 **Nevertheless**, I will read the writing for the king and tell him what

10125 בְּשַׂר *beśar*, n.m. [3] [√ Hb 1414]

creature [1], flesh [1], men [1]

Da 2:11 it to the king except the gods, and they do not live among **men**."
4:12 [4:9] the air lived in its branches; from it every **creature** was fed.
7:5 between its teeth. It was told, 'Get up and eat your fill of **flesh**!'

10126 בַּת *bat*, n.[m.]. [2] [√ Hb 1427]

baths [2]

Ezr 7:22 a hundred cors of wheat, a hundred **baths** of wine, a hundred baths
7:22 baths of wine, a hundred **baths** of olive oil, and salt without limit.

ג, *g*

10127 ג *g*, letter. Not used in NIV/BHS [√ Hb 1446]

10128 גַּב *gab*, n.[m.]. [1] [√ 10129?]

back [1]

Da 7:6 on its **back** it had four wings like those of a bird. This beast had

10129 גֹּב *gōb*, n.m. [10] [√ 10128?; Hb 1463]

den [10]

Da 6:7 [6:8] except to you, O king, shall be thrown into the lions' **den**.
6:12 [6:13] to you, O king, would be thrown into the lions' **den**?"
6:16 [6:17] and they brought Daniel and threw him into the lions' **den**.
6:17 [6:18] A stone was brought and placed over the mouth of the **den**,
6:19 [6:20] light of dawn, the king got up and hurried to the lions' **den**.
6:20 [6:21] When he came near the **den**, he called to Daniel in an
6:23 [6:24] was overjoyed and gave orders to lift Daniel out of the **den**.
6:23 [6:24] when Daniel was lifted from the **den**, no wound was found
6:24 [6:25] Daniel were brought in and thrown into the lions' **den**,
6:24 [6:25] before they reached the floor of the **den**, the lions

10130 גְּבוּרָה *gebûrâ*, n.f. [2] [√ 10131; Hb 1476]

power [2]

Da 2:20 to the name of God for ever and ever; wisdom and **power** are his.
2:23 You have given me wisdom and **power**, you have made known to

10131 גְּבַר *gebar*, n.m. [21] [→ 10130, 10132; Hb 1505]

men [12], some[s] [3], *untranslated* [2], man [2], soldiers [1], who[s] [+10002] [1]

Ezr 4:21 Now issue an order to these **men** to stop work, so that this city will
5:4 "What are the names of the **men** constructing this building?"
5:10 so that we could write down the names of **[RPH]** their leaders for
6:8 The expenses of these **men** are to be fully paid out of the royal
Da 2:25 "I have found a **man** among the exiles from Judah who can tell the
3:8 At this time **some**[s] astrologers came forward and denounced the
3:12 there are **some**[s] Jews whom you have set over the affairs of the
3:12 and Abednego—**who**[s] [+10002] pay no attention to you, O king.
3:13 and Abednego. So these **men** were brought before the king,
3:20 commanded **some**[s] *of* the strongest soldiers in his army to tie up
3:21 So these **men**, wearing their robes, trousers, turbans and other
3:22 so hot that the flames of the fire killed the **soldiers** who took up
3:23 and these three **men**, firmly tied, fell into the blazing furnace.
3:24 "Weren't there three **men** that we tied up and threw into the fire?"
3:25 I see four **men** walking around in the fire, unbound and unharmed,
3:27 They saw **[RPH]** that the fire had not harmed their bodies,
5:11 There is a **man** in your kingdom who has the spirit of the holy
6:5 [6:6] Finally these **men** said, "We will never find any basis for
6:11 [6:12] Then these **men** went as a group and found Daniel praying
6:15 [6:16] Then the **men** went as a group to the king and said to him,
6:24 [6:25] the **men** who had falsely accused Daniel were brought in

10132 גִּבַּר *gibbar*, n.m. [1] [√ 10131; Hb 1475]

strongest soldiers [+10264] [1]

Da 3:20 commanded some of the **strongest** [+10264] **soldiers** in his army

10133 גְּדָבַר *gedābar*, n.m. [2] [cf. 10139; Hb 1601]

treasurers [2]

Da 3:2 prefects, governors, advisers, **treasurers**, judges, magistrates
3:3 prefects, governors, advisers, **treasurers**, judges, magistrates

10134 גְּדַד *gedad*, v. [2] [√ Hb 1517]

cut down [2]

Da 4:14 [4:11] [J] '**Cut down** the tree and trim off its branches; strip off
4:23 [4:20] [J] and saying, '**Cut down** the tree and destroy it,

10135 גַּו *gaw*, n.m. [13] [√ Hb 1569]

into [+10378] [6], *untranslated* [1], in [+10089] [1], in [+10089+10464] [1], middle [1], of [+10427] [1], on [+10089] [1], place[s] [+10089+10193] [1]

Ezr 4:15 a **place**[s] [+10089+10193] of rebellion from ancient times.
5:7 him read as follows: **[NIE]** To King Darius: Cordial greetings.
6:2 in the province of Media, and this was written **on** [+10089] it:
Da 3:6 worship will immediately be thrown **into** [+10378] a blazing
3:11 and worship will be thrown **into** [+10378] a blazing furnace.
3:15 you will be thrown immediately **into** [+10378] a blazing furnace.
3:21 were bound and thrown **into** [+10378] the blazing furnace.
3:23 these three men, firmly tied, fell **into** [+10378] the blazing furnace.
3:24 there three men that we tied up and threw **into** [+10378] the fire?"
3:25 I see four men walking around **in** [+10089] the fire, unbound
3:26 Meshach and Abednego came out **of** [+10427] the fire,
4:10 [4:7] and there before me stood a tree in the **middle** *of* the land.
7:15 "I, Daniel, was troubled **in** [+10089+10464] spirit, and the visions

10136 גֵּוָה *gēwâ*, n.f. [1] [√ Hb 1575]

pride [1]

Da 4:37 [4:34] are just. And those who walk in **pride** he is able to humble.

10137 גּוּחַ *gûaḥ*, v. [1] [√ Hb 1631]

churning up [1]

Da 7:2 [P] there before me were the four winds of heaven **churning up**

10138 גּוֹן *gôn*, var. Not used in NIV/BHS

10139 גִּזְבַּר *gizbar*, n.m. [1] [cf. 10133; Hb 1601]

treasurers [1]

Ezr 7:21 order all the **treasurers** of Trans-Euphrates to provide with

10140 גְּזַר *gezar*, v. [6] [→ 10141; Hb 1615]

diviners [3], cut out [1], diviner [1], was cut out [1]

Da 2:27 [J] or **diviner** can explain to the king the mystery he has asked
2:34 [L] were watching, a rock **was cut out**, but not by human hands.
2:45 [L] This is the meaning of the vision of the rock **cut out** of a
4:7 [4:4] [J] enchanters, astrologers and **diviners** came,
5:7 [J] astrologers and **diviners** to be brought and said to these wise
5:11 [J] chief of the magicians, enchanters, astrologers and **diviners**.

10141 גְּזֵרָה *gezērâ*, n.f. Not used in NIV/BHS [√ 10140; Hb 1620]

10142 גִּיר *gîr*, n.[m.]. [1] [√ Hb 1732]

plaster [1]

Da 5:5 of a human hand appeared and wrote on the **plaster** of the wall,

10143 גַּלְגַּל *galgal*, n.m. [1] [√ 10146; Hb 1649, 1651]

wheels [1]

Da 7:9 His throne was flaming with fire, and its **wheels** were all ablaze.

10144 גְּלָה *gelâ*, v. [9] [√ Hb 1655]

deported [2], revealer [2], reveals [2], been revealed [1], reveal [1], was revealed [1]

Ezr 4:10 [P] honorable Ashurbanipal **deported** and settled in the city of
5:12 [P] destroyed this temple and **deported** the people to Babylon.
Da 2:19 [K] During the night the mystery **was revealed** to Daniel in a
2:22 [J] He **reveals** deep and hidden things; he knows what lies in
2:28 [J] there is a God in heaven *who* **reveals** mysteries. He has
2:29 [J] the **revealer** *of* mysteries showed you what is going to
2:30 [K] this mystery *has* **been revealed** to me, not because I have
2:47 [J] of gods and the Lord of kings and a **revealer** *of* mysteries,
2:47 [J] of mysteries, for you were able to **reveal** this mystery."

10145 גָּלוּ *gālû*, n.f. [4] [√ Hb 1661]

exiles [+10120] [4]

Ezr 6:16 the priests, the Levites and the rest of the **exiles** [+10120]—
Da 2:25 "I have found a man among the **exiles** [+10120] from Judah who
5:13 one of the **exiles** [+10120] my father the king brought from Judah?
6:13 [6:14] "Daniel, who is one of the **exiles** [+10120] from Judah,

10146 גְּלָל gelāl, n.[m.]. [2] [→ 10143, 10399; Hb 1670]
large stones [+10006] [2]
Ezr 5: 8 The people are building it with **large stones** [+10006] and placing
6: 4 with three courses of **large stones** [+10006] and one of timbers.

10147 גְּמַר gemar, v. [1] [√ Hb 1698]
greetings [1]
Ezr 7: 12 [Jp] a teacher of the Law of the God of heaven: **Greetings**.

10148 גְּנַז genaz, n.m. [3] [√ Hb 1709]
archives [+10103] [1], treasury [+10103] [1], treasury [1]
Ezr 5: 17 let a search be made in the royal **archives** [+10103] of Babylon to
6: 1 they searched in the archives stored in the **treasury** at Babylon.
7: 20 to supply, you may provide from the royal **treasury** [+10103].

10149 גַּף gap, n.f. [3]
wings [3]
Da 7: 4 "The first was like a lion, and it had the **wings** of an eagle.
7: 4 I watched until its **wings** were torn off and it was lifted from the
7: 6 on its back it had four **wings** like those of a bird. This beast had

10150 גְּרַם geram, n.[m.]. [1] [√ Hb 1752]
bones [1]
Da 6: 24 [6:25] the lions overpowered them and crushed all their **bones**.

10151 גְּשֵׁם gešēm, n.m. [5]
body [3], bodies [1], lives [1]
Da 3: 27 They saw that the fire had not harmed their **bodies**, nor was a hair
3: 28 and were willing to give up their **lives** rather than serve
4: 33 [4:30] His **body** was drenched with the dew of heaven until his
5: 21 his **body** was drenched with the dew of heaven, until he
7: 11 was slain and its **body** destroyed and thrown into the blazing fire.

ד, d

10152 ד d, letter. Not used in NIV/BHS [√ Hb 1789]

10153 דְּ- de-, pt.rel. Not used in NIV/BHS [√ 10168]

10154 דָּא dā', p.demo.f. [6] [√ Hb 2297, 2305, 2296]
this [2], together [+10154+10378] [2], each [1], others[s] [1]
Da 4: 30 [4:27] "Is not **this** the great Babylon I have built as the royal
5: 6 knees knocked **together** [+10154+10378] and his legs gave way.
5: 6 His face turned pale and he was so frightened that his knees
knocked **together** [+10154+10378] and his legs gave way.
7: 3 Four great beasts, **each** different from the others, came up out of
7: 3 Four great beasts, each different from the **others**[s], came up out of
7: 8 **This** horn had eyes like the eyes of a man and a mouth that spoke

10155 דֹּב dōb, n.[m.]. [1] [√ Hb 1800]
bear [1]
Da 7: 5 there before me was a second beast, which looked like a **bear**.

10156 דְּבַח debaḥ[1], v. [1] [→ 10157, 10401; Hb 2284]
present [1]
Ezr 6: 3 [J] Let the temple be rebuilt as a place *to* **present** sacrifices,

10157 ²דְּבַח debaḥ[2], n.[m.]. [1] [√ 10156; Hb 2285]
sacrifices [1]
Ezr 6: 3 Let the temple be rebuilt as a place to present **sacrifices**, and let its

10158 דְּבַק debaq, v. [1] [√ Hb 1815]
united [+10180+10180+10554] [1]
Da 2: 43 [J] so the people will be a mixture and will not remain **united**
[+10180+10180+10554], any more than iron mixes with clay.

10159 דִּבְרָה dibrâ, n.f. [2] [√ Hb 1826]
so that [+10168+10527] [1], so that [+10168+10542] [1]
Da 2: 30 **so that** [+10168+10542] you, O king, may know the interpretation
4: 17 [4:14] **so that** [+10168+10527] the living may know that the

10160 דְּהַב dehab, n.m. [23] [√ Hb 2298]
gold [23]
Ezr 5: 14 He even removed from the temple of Babylon the **gold** and silver
6: 5 Also, the **gold** and silver articles of the house of God, which
7: 15 you are to take with you the silver and **gold** that the king and his
7: 16 the silver and **gold** you may obtain from the province of Babylon,
7: 18 then do whatever seems best with the rest of the silver and **gold**,
Da 2: 32 The head of the statue was made of pure **gold**, its chest and arms of
2: 35 the silver and the **gold** were broken to pieces at the same time
2: 38 he has made you ruler over them all. You are that head of **gold**.
2: 45 the iron, the bronze, the clay, the silver and the **gold** to pieces.
3: 1 King Nebuchadnezzar made an image of **gold**, ninety feet high
3: 5 worship the image of **gold** that King Nebuchadnezzar has set up.
3: 7 worshiped the image of **gold** that King Nebuchadnezzar had set up.
3: 10 all kinds of music must fall down and worship the image of **gold**,
3: 12 They neither serve your gods nor worship the image of **gold** you
3: 14 do not serve my gods or worship the image of **gold** I have set up?
3: 18 not serve your gods or worship the image of **gold** you have set up."
5: 2 he gave orders to bring in the **gold** and silver goblets that
5: 3 So they brought in the **gold** goblets that had been taken from the
5: 4 they praised the gods of **gold** and silver, of bronze, iron, wood
5: 7 be clothed in purple and have a **gold** chain placed around his neck,
5: 16 clothed in purple and have a **gold** chain placed around your neck,
5: 23 You praised the gods of silver and **gold**, of bronze, iron, wood
5: 29 was clothed in purple, a **gold** chain was placed around his neck,

10161 דְּהוּא dehû', pt. + pr. Not used in NIV/BHS [√ 10168 + 10200]

10162 דֶּהָיֵא dehāyē', pt. + pr. Not used in NIV/BHS [√ 10168 + 10200]

10163 דּוּר dûr, v. [7] [→ 10183, 10403, 10407, 10753; Hb 1884]
live [2], peoples [2], *untranslated* [1], lived [1], shelter [1]
Da 2: 38 [J] Wherever *they* **live**, he has made you ruler over them all.
4: 1 [3:31] [J] and men of every language, who **live** in all the world:
4: 12 [4:9] [J] and the birds of the air **lived** in its branches;
4: 21 [4:18] [J] food for all, *giving* **shelter** to the beasts of the field,
4: 35 [4:32] [J] All the **peoples** *of* the earth are regarded as nothing.
4: 35 [4:32] [J] the powers of heaven and the **peoples** *of* the earth.
6: 25 [6:26] [J] men of every language **[NIE]** throughout the land:

10164 דּוּרָא dûrā', n.pr.loc. [1]
Dura [1]
Da 3: 1 and set it up on the plain of **Dura** in the province of Babylon.

10165 דּוּשׁ dûš, v. [1] [√ Hb 1889]
trampling down [1]
Da 7: 23 [J] devour the whole earth, **trampling** it **down** and crushing it.

10166 דַּחֲוָה daḥ^a^wâ, n.f. [1]
entertainment [1]
Da 6: 18 [6:19] and without any **entertainment** being brought to him.

10167 דְּחַל deḥal, v. [6] [√ Hb 2324]
terrifying [2], awesome [1], feared [1], made afraid [1], reverence [1]
Da 2: 31 [Jp] an enormous, dazzling statue, **awesome** in appearance.
4: 5 [4:2] [M] I had a dream *that* **made** me **afraid**. As I was lying in
5: 19 [J] and men of every language dreaded and **feared** him.
6: 26 [6:27] [J] people must fear and **reverence** the God of Daniel.
7: 7 [Jp] fourth beast—**terrifying** and frightening and very powerful.
7: 19 [Jp] which was different from all the others and most **terrifying**,

10168 דִּי dî, pt.rel. & c. [345 / 346] [→ 10153; Hb 2296, 2306] Not indexed
untranslated [133], of [46], that [46], who [18], which [9], until [+10527] [8], whom [8], so that [6], those [5], anyone [+10426] [4], from [4], because [+10353+10619] [3], because [3], for [+10353+10619] [3], in [3], when [+10341] [3], with [3], but [2], for [2], just as [2], what [2], whatever [+10353] [2], whoever [+10426] [2], any more than [+10195+10341] [1], as [+10527] [1], as soon as [+10002+10089+10530] [1], as soon as [+10002+10232+10341] [1], as soon as [+10008+10427] [1], as [1], because [+10427] [1], because of [+10378+10619] [1], by [+10353+10619] [1], during [1], even as [+10353+10619] [1], hoping [+10527] [1], if [1], just as [+10353+10619] [1], one [1], over [1], since [+10353+10619] [1], so

that [+10159+10527] [1], so that [+10159+10542] [1], surely [+10427+10643] [1], this is the meaning [+10353+10619] [1], though [+10353+10619] [1], whatever [+10408] [1], when [+10427] [1], wherever [+10089+10353] [1], while [+10527] [1], whoever [+10050+10353] [1], whoever [+10353] [1], whose [1]

10169 דִּין[1] ***dîn***[1], v. [1] [→ 10170, 10171, 10172, 10406; Hb 1906]

administer justice [1]

Ezr 7:25 [J] judges to **administer justice** to all the people of

10170 דִּין[2] ***dîn***[2], n.m. [5] [√ 10169; Hb 1907]

court [2], judgment [1], just [1], punished [+10191+10427+10522] [1]

Ezr 7:26 must surely be **punished** [+10191+10427+10522] by death,
Da 4:37 [4:34] everything he does is right and all his ways are **just**.
7:10 before him. The **court** was seated, and the books were opened.
7:22 and pronounced **judgment** in favor of the saints of the Most High,
7:26 " 'But the **court** will sit, and his power will be taken away

10171 דַּיָּן ***dayyān***, n.m. [1 / 2] [√ 10169; Hb 1908]

judges [2]

Ezr 4:9 the **judges** [BHS 10172] and officials over the men from Tripolis,
7:25 **judges** to administer justice to all the people of Trans-Euphrates—

10172 דִּינָיֵא ***dînāyē'***, n.pr.g. [1 / 0] [√ 10169]

Ezr 4:9 the judges [BHS ?; NIV 10171] and officials over the men

10173 דֵּךְ ***dēk***, p.demo.com. [13] [→ 10174]

this [12], *untranslated* [1]

Ezr 4:13 the king should know that if **this** city is built and its walls are
4:15 In these records you will find that **this** city is a rebellious city,
4:15 rebellion from ancient times. That is why **this** city was destroyed.
4:16 We inform the king that if **this** city is built and its walls are
4:19 it was found that **this** city has a long history of revolt against kings
4:21 to stop work, so that **this** city will not be rebuilt until I so order.
5:8 The work is being carried on **[RPR]** with diligence and is making
5:16 So **this** Sheshbazzar came and laid the foundations of the house of
5:17 did in fact issue a decree to rebuild **this** house of God in Jerusalem.
6:7 Do not interfere with the work on **this** temple of God. Let the
6:7 and the Jewish elders rebuild **this** house of God on its site.
6:8 these elders of the Jews in the construction of **this** house of God:
6:12 a hand to change this decree or to destroy **this** temple in Jerusalem.

10174 דִּכֵּן ***dikkēn***, p.demo.com. [3] [√ 10173] Not indexed

untranslated [1], that [1], this [1]

10175 דְּכַר ***dekar***, n.m. [3] [√ Hb 2351]

rams [3]

Ezr 6:9 young bulls, **rams**, male lambs for burnt offerings to the God of
6:17 two hundred **rams**, four hundred male lambs and, as a sin offering
7:17 **rams** and male lambs, together with their grain offerings and drink

10176 דִּכְרוֹן ***dikrôn***, n.[m.]. [1] [→ 10177; Hb 2355]

memorandum [1]

Ezr 6:2 the province of Media, and this was written on it: **Memorandum**:

10177 דָּכְרָן ***dokrān***, n.[m.]. [2] [√ 10176; Hb 2355]

archives [+10515] [1], records [+10515] [1]

Ezr 4:15 so that a search may be made in the **archives** [+10515] of your
4:15 In these **records** [+10515] you will find that this city is a rebellious

10178 דְּלַק ***delaq***, v. [1] [√ Hb 1944]

all ablaze [+10471] [1]

Da 7:9 [J] flaming with fire, and its wheels were **all ablaze** [+10471].

10179 דְּמָה ***demâ***, v. [2] [√ Hb 1948]

like [1], looked like [1]

Da 3:25 [J] and unharmed, and the fourth looks **like** a son of the gods."
7:5 [J] there before me was a second beast, which **looked like** a bear.

10180 דְּנָה ***denâ***, p.demo.com. [58] [→ 10032, 10034, 10036, 10037] Not indexed

this [30], *untranslated* [10], that [2], united [+10158+10180+10554] [2], ago [+10427+10622] [1], as follows [+10341] [1], before [+10427+10622] [1], in the future [+10021] [1], so [+10353+10619] [1], such [+10341] [1], that is why [+10542] [1], the [1], then [+10353+10619] [1], therefore [+10353+10619] [1], these [1], this [+10341] [1], this made [+10353+10619] [1], to come [+10021+10201] [1]

10181 דָּנִיֵּאל ***dāniyyē'l***, n.pr.m. [52] [√ Hb 1975]

Daniel [46], *untranslated* [2], Daniel's [+10089] [1], Daniel's [1], he[s] [1], him[s] [1]

Da 2:13 men were sent to look for **Daniel** and his friends to put them to
2:14 wise men of Babylon, **Daniel** spoke to him with wisdom and tact.
2:15 such a harsh decree?" Arioch then explained the matter to **Daniel**.
2:16 At this, **Daniel** went in to the king and asked for time, so that he
2:17 **Daniel** returned to his house and explained the matter to his friends
2:18 so that **he**[s] and his friends might not be executed with the rest of
2:19 During the night the mystery was revealed to **Daniel** in a vision.
2:19 to Daniel in a vision. Then **Daniel** praised the God of heaven
2:20 **[RPH]** and said: "Praise be to the name of God for ever and ever;
2:24 **Daniel** went to Arioch, whom the king had appointed to execute
2:25 Arioch took **Daniel** to the king at once and said, "I have found a
2:26 The king asked **Daniel** (also called Belteshazzar), "Are you able to
2:27 **Daniel** replied, "No wise man, enchanter, magician or diviner can
2:46 King Nebuchadnezzar fell prostrate before **Daniel** and paid him
2:47 The king said to **Daniel**, "Surely your God is the God of gods
2:48 the king placed **Daniel** in a high position and lavished many gifts
2:49 at **Daniel's** request the king appointed Shadrach, Meshach
2:49 of Babylon, while **Daniel** himself remained at the royal court.
4:8 [4:5] **Daniel** came into my presence and I told him the dream.
4:19 [4:16] **Daniel** (also called Belteshazzar) was greatly perplexed for
5:12 This man **Daniel**, whom the king called Belteshazzar, was found to
5:12 Call for **Daniel**, and he will tell you what the writing means."
5:13 So **Daniel** was brought before the king, and the king said to him,
5:13 before the king, and the king said to **him**[s], "Are you Daniel,
5:13 brought before the king, and the king said to him, "Are you **Daniel**,
5:17 **Daniel** answered the king, "You may keep your gifts for yourself
5:29 Then at Belshazzar's command, **Daniel** was clothed in purple,
6:2 [6:3] three administrators over them, one of whom was **Daniel**.
6:3 [6:4] Now **Daniel** so distinguished himself among the
6:4 [6:5] the satraps tried to find grounds for charges against **Daniel**
6:5 [6:6] **Daniel** unless it has something to do with the law of his
6:10 [6:11] Now when **Daniel** learned that the decree had been
6:11 [6:12] a group and found **Daniel** praying and asking God for help.
6:13 [6:14] they said to the king, "**Daniel**, who is one of the exiles
6:14 [6:15] he was determined to rescue **Daniel** and made every effort
6:16 [6:17] and they brought **Daniel** and threw him into the lions' den.
6:16 [6:17] The king said to **Daniel**, "May your God, whom you serve
6:17 [6:18] so that **Daniel's** [+10089] situation might not be changed.
6:20 [6:21] he called to **Daniel** in an anguished voice, "Daniel,
6:20 [6:21] **[RPH]** "Daniel, servant of the living God, has your God,
6:20 [6:21] "**Daniel**, servant of the living God, has your God,
6:21 [6:22] **Daniel** answered, "O king, live forever!
6:23 [6:24] was overjoyed and gave orders to lift **Daniel** out of the den.
6:23 [6:24] when **Daniel** was lifted from the den, no wound was found
6:24 [6:25] the men who had falsely accused **Daniel** were brought in
6:26 [6:27] people must fear and reverence the God of **Daniel**.
6:27 [6:28] He has rescued **Daniel** from the power of the lions."
6:28 [6:29] So **Daniel** prospered during the reign of Darius and the
7:1 the first year of Belshazzar king of Babylon, **Daniel** had a dream,
7:2 **Daniel** said: "In my vision at night I looked, and there before me
7:15 "I, **Daniel**, was troubled in spirit, and the visions that passed
7:28 I, **Daniel**, was deeply troubled by my thoughts, and my face turned

10182 דְּקַק ***deqaq***, v. [10] [√ Hb 1990]

crushed [3], crush [2], breaks [1], broke to pieces [1], broken to pieces [1], crushing [1], smashed [1]

Da 2:34 [P] the statue on its feet of iron and clay and **smashed** them.
2:35 [J] and the gold *were* **broken to pieces** at the same time
2:40 [P] strong as iron—for iron **breaks** and smashes everything—
2:40 [P] things to pieces, so *it will* **crush** and break all the others.
2:44 [P] *It will* **crush** all those kingdoms and bring them to an end,
2:45 [P] *that* **broke** the iron, the bronze, ... silver and the gold **to pieces**.
6:24 [6:25] [P] lions overpowered them and **crushed** all their bones.
7:7 [P] *it* **crushed** and devoured its victims and trampled underfoot
7:19 [P] the beast *that* **crushed** and devoured its victims and trampled
7:23 [P] devour the whole earth, trampling it down and **crushing** it.

10183 דָּר ***dār***, n.[m.]. [4] [√ 10163; Hb 1887]

generation [4]

Da 4:3 [3:33] his dominion endures from **generation** to generation.
4:3 [3:33] his dominion endures from generation to **generation**.
4:34 [4:31] his kingdom endures from **generation** to generation.
4:34 [4:31] his kingdom endures from generation to **generation**.

10184 דָּרְיָוֶשׁ dārᵉyāweš, n.pr.m. [15] [√ Hb 2003]
Darius [15]
Ezr 4: 24 until the second year of the reign of **Darius** king of Persia.
5: 5 and they were not stopped until a report could go to **Darius**
5: 6 the officials of Trans-Euphrates, sent to King **Darius**.
5: 7 they sent him read as follows: To King **Darius**: Cordial greetings.
6: 1 King **Darius** then issued an order, and they searched in the
6: 12 I **Darius** have decreed it. Let it be carried out with diligence.
6: 13 Then, because of the decree King **Darius** had sent, Tattenai,
6: 14 and the decrees of Cyrus, **Darius** and Artaxerxes, kings of Persia.
6: 15 of the month Adar, in the sixth year of the reign of King **Darius**.
Da 5: 31 [6:1] **Darius** the Mede took over the kingdom, at the age of
6: 1 [6:2] It pleased **Darius** to appoint 120 satraps to rule throughout
6: 6 [6:7] a group to the king and said: "O King **Darius**, live forever!
6: 9 [6:10] So King **Darius** put the decree in writing.
6: 25 [6:26] King **Darius** wrote to all the peoples, nations and men of
6: 28 [6:29] So Daniel prospered during the reign of **Darius** and the

10185 דְּרָע dᵉrā', n.[f.]. [1] [→ 10013; Hb 2432]
arms [1]
Da 2: 32 its chest and **arms** of silver, its belly and thighs of bronze,

10186 דָּת dāt, n.f. [14] [√ Hb 2017]
law [7], laws [4], decree [2], penalty [1]
Ezr 7: 12 To Ezra the priest, a teacher of the **Law** of the God of heaven:
7: 14 about Judah and Jerusalem with regard to the **Law** *of* your God,
7: 21 a teacher of the **Law** of the God of heaven, may ask of you—
7: 25 people of Trans-Euphrates—all who know the **laws** *of* your God.
7: 26 Whoever does not obey the **law** of your God and the law of the
7: 26 and the **law** of the king must surely be punished by death,
Da 2: 9 If you do not tell me the dream, there is just one **penalty** *for* you.
2: 13 So the **decree** was issued to put the wise men to death, and men
2: 15 the king's officer, "Why did the king issue such a harsh **decree**?"
6: 5 [6:6] unless it has something to do with the **law** *of* his God."
6: 8 [6:9] in accordance with the **laws** *of* the Medes and Persians,
6: 12 [6:13] in accordance with the **laws** *of* the Medes and Persians,
6: 15 [6:16] that according to the **law** of the Medes and Persians no
7: 25 and oppress his saints and try to change the set times and the **laws**.

10187 דְּתֵא dete', n.[m.]. [2] [√ Hb 2013]
grass [2]
Da 4: 15 [4:12] and bronze, remain in the ground, in the **grass** of the field.
4: 23 [4:20] bound with iron and bronze, in the **grass** of the field,

10188 דְּתָבַר dᵉtābar, n.m. [2] [√ Hb 2017]
judges [2]
Da 3: 2 prefects, governors, advisers, treasurers, **judges**, magistrates
3: 3 prefects, governors, advisers, treasurers, **judges**, magistrates

ה, h

10189 ה h, letter. Not used in NIV/BHS [√ Hb 2020]

10190 הֲ- hª-, inter.pt. [6] [→ cf. 10216; Hb 2022] Not indexed
untranslated [5], is it true [+10609] [1]

10191 הָ- -â, art.suf. [50] [√ 10002] Not indexed
the [15], *untranslated* [13], Trans-Euphrates [+10468+10526] [12], its[s] [2], immediately [+10734] [1], it[s] [+10424] [1], punished [+10170+10427+10522] [1], suddenly [+10734] [1], that province[s] [+10468+10526] [1], that [1], this [1], your[s] [1]

10192 הֵ- -ēh, p.suf.3.m.s. [159] [√ 10204; Hb 2024] Not indexed
his [47], *untranslated* [41], him [24], it [16], its [10], he [7], the[s] [5], their [3], a[s] [1], his [+10089] [1], his [+10378] [1], his own [1], man[s] [1], same[s] [1]

10193 הַּ- -ah, p.suf.3.f.s. [44] [√ Hb 2023] Not indexed
it [15], *untranslated* [13], its [7], them [5], place[s] [+10089] [1], place[s] [+10089+10135] [1], the[s] [1], which [1]

10194 הָא hā', demo.pt. [1] [√ Hb 2026]
look [1]
Da 3: 25 He said, "**Look**! I see four men walking around in the fire,

10195 הֵא hē', demo.pt. [1] [√ Hb 2026]
any more than [+10168+10341] [1]
Da 2: 43 **any more than** [+10168+10341] iron mixes with clay.

10196 הַדָּבַר haddābar, n.m. [4]
advisers [4]
Da 3: 24 leaped to his feet in amazement and asked his **advisers**,
3: 27 prefects, governors and royal **advisers** crowded around them.
4: 36 [4:33] My **advisers** and nobles sought me out, and I was restored
6: 7 [6:8] **advisers** and governors have all agreed that the king should

10197 הַדָּם haddām, n.[m.]. [2]
pieces [2]
Da 2: 5 I will have you cut into **pieces** and your houses turned into piles of
3: 29 Meshach and Abednego be cut into **pieces** and their houses be

10198 הדר¹ hᵃdar¹, v. [3] [→ 10199; Hb 2075]
glorified [1], glorify [1], honor [1]
Da 4: 34 [4:31] [M] I honored and **glorified** him who lives forever.
4: 37 [4:34] [M] praise and exalt and **glorify** the King of heaven,
5: 23 [M] *you did* not **honor** the God who holds in his hand your life

10199 הֲדַר² hᵃdar², n.[m.]. [3] [√ 10198; Hb 2077, 2078]
honor [1], majesty [1], splendor [1]
Da 4: 30 [4:27] by my mighty power and for the glory of my **majesty**?"
4: 36 [4:33] my **honor** and splendor were returned to me for the glory
5: 18 and greatness and glory and **splendor**.

10200 הוּא hû', p.3.m.s. [16] [→ 10045, 10205; Hb 2085] Not indexed
untranslated [8], he [5], it [1], that tree[s] [1], that [1]

10201 הֲוָה hᵃwâ, v. [71] [√ Hb 2118, 2093]
untranslated [36], be [11], was [7], became [2], happen [2], were [2], appear [1], continued [1], had [+10542] [1], have [1], keep [1], kept [1], must [1], remain [1], stay [1], take place [1], to come [+10021+10180] [1]
Ezr 4: 12 [J] The king should know **[NIE]** that the Jews who came up to
4: 13 [J] the king should know **[NIE]** that if this city is built and its
4: 20 [J] Jerusalem *has* **had** [+10542] powerful kings ruling over the
4: 22 [J] **Be** careful not to neglect this matter. Why let this threat grow,
4: 24 [J] **[NIE]** until the second year of the reign of Darius king of
5: 5 [J] the eye of their God **was** watching over the elders of the Jews,
5: 8 [J] The king should know **[NIE]** that we went to the district of
5: 11 [J] we are rebuilding the temple that **was** built many years ago,
6: 6 [J] their fellow officials of that province, **stay** away from there.
6: 8 [J] The expenses of these men *are to* **be** fully paid out of the
6: 9 [J] priests in Jerusalem—*must* **be** given them daily without fail,
6: 10 [J] so that **[NIE]** they may offer sacrifices pleasing to the God
7: 23 [J] Why *should there* **be** wrath against the realm of the king
7: 25 [J] judges **[NIE]** to administer justice to all the people of
7: 26 [J] Whoever **[NIE]** does not obey the law of your God
7: 26 [J] and the law of the king *must* surely **be** punished by death,
Da 2: 20 [J] "Praise **be** *to* the name of God for ever and ever; wisdom and
2: 28 [J] He has shown King Nebuchadnezzar what *will* **happen** in
2: 29 [J] O king, your mind turned to things **to come** [+10021+10180],
2: 29 [J] revealer of mysteries showed you what *is going to* **happen**.
2: 31 [J] "You looked, **[NIE]** O king, and there before you stood a
2: 34 [J] While *you* **were** watching, a rock was cut out, but not by
2: 35 [J] and **became** like chaff on a threshing floor in the summer.
2: 35 [J] But the rock that struck the statue **became** a huge mountain
2: 40 [J] Finally, *there will* **be** a fourth kingdom, strong as iron—for
2: 41 [J] and partly of iron, so *this will* **be** a divided kingdom;
2: 41 [J] yet *it will* **have** some of the strength of iron in it, even as you
2: 42 [J] so this kingdom *will* **be** partly strong and partly brittle.
2: 42 [J] this kingdom will be partly strong and partly **[RPH]** brittle.
2: 43 [J] so the people *will* **be** a mixture and will not remain united,
2: 43 [J] so the people will be a mixture and *will* not **remain** united,
2: 45 [J] "The great God has shown the king what *will* **take place** in
3: 18 [J] But even if he does not, we want you to know, **[NIE]** O king,
4: 4 [4:1] [J] **was** at home in my palace, contented and prosperous.
4: 10 [4:7] [J] **[NIE]** and there before me stood a tree in the middle
4: 13 [4:10] [J] I looked, **[NIE]** and there before me was a
4: 25 [4:22] [J] and will **[NIE]** live with the wild animals;

Da 4:27 [4:24] [J] *It may* **be** that then your prosperity will continue."
4:29 [4:26] [J] *as* the king **was** walking on the roof of the royal
5:17 [J] "You *may* **keep** your gifts for yourself and give your rewards
5:19 [J] and nations and men of every language **[NIE]** dreaded
5:19 [J] Those the king **[NIE]** wanted to put to death, he put to death;
5:19 [J] Those the king wanted to put to death, **[NIE]** he put to death;
5:19 [J] he put to death; those **[NIE]** he wanted to spare, he spared;
5:19 [J] he put to death; those he wanted to spare, **[NIE]** he spared;
5:19 [J] he spared; those **[NIE]** he wanted to promote, he promoted;
5:19 [J] he spared; those he wanted to promote, **[NIE]** he promoted;
5:19 [J] and those **[NIE]** he wanted to humble, he humbled.
5:19 [J] and those he wanted to humble, **[NIE]** he humbled.
5:29 [J] he was proclaimed **[NIE]** the third highest ruler in the
6:1 [6:2] [J] It pleased Darius to appoint 120 satraps to rule **[NIE]**
6:2 [6:3] [J] The satraps **were** made accountable to them so that the
6:2 [6:3] [J] to them so that the king might not suffer loss. **[NIE]**
6:3 [6:4] [J] **[NIE]** so distinguished himself among the
6:4 [6:5] [J] the satraps **[NIE]** tried to find grounds for charges
6:10 [6:11] [J] thanks to his God, just as **[NIE]** he had done before.
6:14 [6:15] [J] **[NIE]** made every effort until sundown to save him.
6:26 [6:27] [J] that in every part of my kingdom *people* **must** fear
7:2 [J] **[NIE]** and there before me were the four winds of heaven
7:4 [J] I watched **[NIE]** until its wings were torn off and it was
7:6 [J] I looked, **[NIE]** and there before me was another beast,
7:7 [J] I looked, **[NIE]** and there before me was a fourth beast—
7:8 [J] "*While I* **was** thinking about the horns, there before me was
7:9 [J] "As I looked, **[RPH]** "thrones were set in place,
7:11 [J] "Then *I* **continued** to watch because of the boastful words the
7:11 [J] *I* **kept** looking until the beast was slain and its body destroyed
7:13 [J] **[NIE]** and there before me was one like a son of man,
7:13 [J] night I looked, and there before me **was** one like a son of man,
7:19 [J] which **was** different from all the others and most terrifying,
7:21 [J] **[NIE]** this horn was waging war against the saints
7:23 [J] 'The fourth beast is a fourth kingdom *that will* **appear** on

10202 הוּךְ ***hûk***, v. Not used in NIV/BHS [√ 10207]

10203 ־הוֹן ***-hôn***, p.suf.3.m.pl. [51] [√ Hb 2157] Not indexed
their [17], them [17], *untranslated* [12], the[s] [3], their own [1], they [1]

10204 ־הִי ***-hî***, p.suf.3.m.s. [76] [√ 10192; Hb 2114] Not indexed
his [26], *untranslated* [14], its [14], him [11], he [5], it [4], one [1], the[s] [1]

10205 הִיא ***hî'***, p.3.f.s. [7] [√ 10200; Hb 2085] Not indexed
untranslated [3], it [1], itself [1], there [1], this [1]

10206 הֵיכַל ***hêkal***, n.m. [13] [√ Hb 2121]
temple [8], palace [5]

Ezr 4:14 Now since we are under obligation to the **palace** and it is not
5:14 He even removed from the **temple** of Babylon the gold and silver
5:14 which Nebuchadnezzar had taken from the **temple** in Jerusalem
5:14 the temple in Jerusalem and brought to the **temple** in Babylon.
5:15 these articles and go and deposit them in the **temple** in Jerusalem.
6:5 which Nebuchadnezzar took from the **temple** in Jerusalem
6:5 are to be returned to their places in the **temple** in Jerusalem;
Da 4:4 [4:1] was at home in my **palace**, contented and prosperous.
4:29 [4:26] as the king was walking on the roof of the royal **palace** of
5:2 his father had taken from the **temple** in Jerusalem,
5:3 goblets that had been taken from the **temple** of God in Jerusalem,
5:5 on the plaster of the wall, near the lampstand in the royal **palace**.
6:18 [6:19] the king returned to his **palace** and spent the night without

10207 הֲלַךְ ***hᵃlak***, v. [7] [→ 10208; cf. 10202; Hb 2143]
go [3], *untranslated* [1], walk [1], walking around [1], walking [1]

Ezr 5:5 [J] and they were not stopped until a report *could* **go** to Darius
6:5 [J] are to be returned **[NIE]** to their places in the temple in
7:13 [J] and Levites, who wish to **go** to Jerusalem with you, may go.
7:13 [J] and Levites, who wish to go to Jerusalem with you, *may* **go**.
Da 3:25 [P] I see four men **walking around** in the fire, unbound
4:29 [4:26] [M] as the king was **walking** on the roof of the royal
4:37 [4:34] [P] And those *who* **walk** in pride he is able to humble.

10208 הֲלָךְ ***hᵃlāk***, n.[m.]. [3] [√ 10207]
duty [3]

Ezr 4:13 its walls are restored, no more taxes, tribute or **duty** will be paid,
4:20 of Trans-Euphrates, and taxes, tribute and **duty** were paid to them.
7:24 tribute or **duty** on any of the priests, Levites, singers, gatekeepers,

10209 ־הֹם ***-hōm***, p.suf.3.m.pl. [12] [√ 10214; Hb 2157] Not indexed
their [5], them [4], *untranslated* [3]

10210 הִמּוֹ ***himmô***, p.3.pl. [12] [√ Hb 2156, 2160] Not indexed
them [6], *untranslated* [5], they [1]

10211 המונכא ***hmwnk***, n.[m.]. [0]

Da 5:7 [and have a gold **chain** [K; see Q 10212] placed around his neck,]
5:16 [and have a gold **chain** [K; see Q 10212] placed around your neck,]
5:29 [a gold **chain** [K; see Q 10212] was placed around his neck,]

10212 הַמְיָנֵךְ ***hamyānak***, n.[m.]. [3]
chain [3]

Da 5:7 and have a gold **chain** [K 10211] placed around his neck,
5:16 and have a gold **chain** [K 10211] placed around your neck,
5:29 in purple, a gold **chain** [K 10211] was placed around his neck,

10213 הֵן ***hēn***, c. [16] [√ Hb 2176, 561?]
if [11], *untranslated* [3], even if [1], then [1]

Ezr 4:13 the king should know that **if** this city is built and its walls are
4:16 We inform the king that **if** this city is built and its walls are
5:17 Now **if** it pleases the king, let a search be made in the royal
5:17 let a search be made in the royal archives of Babylon to see **if** King
7:26 and the law of the king must surely be punished **[RPH]** by death,
7:26 **[RPH]** banishment, confiscation of property, or imprisonment.
7:26 banishment, **[RPH]** confiscation of property, or imprisonment.
Da 2:5 **If** you do not tell me what my dream was and interpret it, I will
2:6 **if** you tell me the dream and explain it, you will receive from me
2:9 **If** you do not tell me the dream, there is just one penalty for you.
3:15 **if** you are ready to fall down and worship the image I made,
3:15 **if** you do not worship it, you will be thrown immediately into a
3:17 **If** we are thrown into the blazing furnace, the God we serve is able
3:18 **even if** he does not, we want you to know, O king, that we will not
4:27 [4:24] It may be that **then** your prosperity will continue."
5:16 **If** you can read this writing and tell me what it means, you will be

10214 ־הֵן ***-hēn***, p.suf.3.f.pl. [8] [√ 10209, 10386; Hb 2157] Not indexed
untranslated [6], the others[s] [1], them [1]

10215 הַנְזָקָה ***hanzāqâ***, n.[f.] *or* v.inf. Not used in NIV/BHS [√ 10472]

10216 הַצְדָּא ***haṣdā'***, inter. [+ n.?]. Not used in NIV/BHS [√ 10190 + 10609]

10217 הַרְהֹר ***harhōr***, n.[m.]. [1]
images [1]

Da 4:5 [4:2] the **images** and visions that passed through my mind

10218 הִתְבְּהָלָה ***hitbᵉhālâ***, n. *or* v. Not used in NIV/BHS [√ 10097]

10219 התנדבו ***hitnaddābû***, n.m. *or* v. Not used in NIV/BHS [√ 10461]

ו, *w*

10220 ו ***w***, letter. Not used in NIV/BHS [√ Hb 2255]

10221 ־וְ ***wᵉ-***, c.pref. [731] [√ Hb 2256] Not indexed
and [400], *untranslated* [221], or [20], but [19], then [9], now [5], so that [5], so [5], moreover [3], nor [+10379] [3], that [3], together with [3], with [3], also [+10059] [2], also [2], 120 [+10395+10574] [1], and [+10008] [1], and now [1], and that [1], and when [1], as for [1], as [1], at this [1], completely destroyed [+10005+10722] [1], even [+10059] [1], finally [+10024+10527] [1], finally [1], furthermore [1], including [1], instead [1], next [1], nor [+10059+10379] [1], nor [1], period of time [+10232+10530] [1], set to work [+10624+10742] [1], sixty-two [+10749+10775] [1], therefore [1], till [1], until [1], when [1], while [1], yes [1], yet [1]

ז, z

10222 ז z, letter. Not used in NIV/BHS [√ Hb 2268]

10223 זְבַן zeban, v. [1]

gain [1]

Da 2: 8 [J] king answered, "I am certain that you *are trying to* **gain** time,

10224 זְהִיר zehîr, v. [1] [√ Hb 2302]

careful [1]

Ezr 4: 22 Be **careful** not to neglect this matter. Why let this threat grow,

10225 זוּד zûd, v. [1] [√ Hb 2326]

pride [1]

Da 5: 20 [P] when his heart became arrogant and hardened *with* **pride**,

10226 זוּן zûn, v. [1] [→ 10410; Hb 2315]

was fed [1]

Da 4: 12 [4:9] [L] lived in its branches; from it every creature **was fed**.

10227 זוּעַ zûa', v. [2] [√ Hb 2316]

dreaded [1], fear [1]

Da 5: 19 [J] the peoples and nations and men of every language **dreaded**
6: 26 [6:27] [J] that in every part of my kingdom people must **fear**

10228 זִיו zîw, n.m. [6]

face pale [3], dazzling [1], look so pale [+10731] [1], splendor [1]

Da 2: 31 an enormous, **dazzling** statue, awesome in appearance.
4: 36 [4:33] **splendor** were returned to me for the glory of my
5: 6 His **face** turned **pale** and he was so frightened that his knees
5: 9 became even more terrified and his **face** grew more **pale**.
5: 10 she said. "Don't be alarmed! Don't **look so pale** [+10731]!
7: 28 and my **face** turned **pale**, but I kept the matter to myself."

10229 זָכוּ zākû, n.f. [1] [√ Hb 2342]

innocent [1]

Da 6: 22 [6:23] not hurt me, because I was found **innocent** in his sight.

10230 זְכַרְיָה zekaryâ, n.pr.m. [2] [√ Hb 2357]

Zechariah [2]

Ezr 5: 1 Now Haggai the prophet and **Zechariah** the prophet, a descendant
6: 14 prosper under the preaching of Haggai the prophet and **Zechariah**,

10231 זְמַן zeman[1], v.den. [1] [√ 10232; Hb 2374]

conspired [1]

Da 2: 9 [L] *You have* **conspired** to tell me misleading and wicked

10232 זְמָן[2] zeman[2], n.m. [11] [→ 10232; Hb 2375]

time [5], times [2], as soon as [+10002+10168+10341] [1], period of time [+10221+10530] [1], seasons [1], set times [1]

Ezr 5: 3 At that **time** Tattenai, governor of Trans-Euphrates, and
Da 2: 16 At this, Daniel went in to the king and asked for **time**, so that he
2: 21 He changes times and **seasons**; he sets up kings and deposes them.
3: 7 Therefore, **as soon as** [+10002+10168+10341] they heard the
3: 8 At this **time** some astrologers came forward and denounced the
4: 36 [4:33] At the same **time** that my sanity was restored, my honor
6: 10 [6:11] Three **times** a day he got down on his knees and prayed,
6: 13 [6:14] decree you put in writing. He still prays three **times** a day."
7: 12 but were allowed to live for a **period of time** [+10221+10530].)
7: 22 Most High, and the **time** came when they possessed the kingdom.
7: 25 and oppress his saints and try to change the **set times** and the laws.

10233 זְמָר zemār, n.[m.]. [4] [→ 10234; Hb 2376]

music [4]

Da 3: 5 flute, zither, lyre, harp, pipes and all kinds of **music**, you must fall
3: 7 flute, zither, lyre, harp and all kinds of **music**, all the peoples,
3: 10 pipes and all kinds of **music** must fall down and worship the image
3: 15 flute, zither, lyre, harp, pipes and all kinds of **music**, if you are

10234 זַמָּר zammār, n.m. [1] [√ 10233; Hb 2376]

singers [1]

Ezr 7: 24 Levites, **singers**, gatekeepers, temple servants or other workers at

10235 זַן zan, n.[m.]. [4] [√ Hb 2385]

kinds [4]

Da 3: 5 flute, zither, lyre, harp, pipes and all **kinds** *of* music, you must fall
3: 7 flute, zither, lyre, harp and all **kinds** *of* music, all the peoples,
3: 10 pipes and all **kinds** *of* music must fall down and worship the image
3: 15 flute, zither, lyre, harp, pipes and all **kinds** *of* music, if you are

10236 זְעֵיר ze'êr, a. Not used in NIV/BHS [√ Hb 2402]

10237 זְעִק ze'iq, v. [1] [√ Hb 4210, 7590]

called [1]

Da 6: 20 [6:21] [J] he **called** to Daniel in an anguished voice, "Daniel,

10238 זְקַף zeqap, v. [1] [√ Hb 2422]

be lifted up [1]

Ezr 6: 11 [Jp] from his house and *he is to* **be lifted up** and impaled on it.

10239 זְרֻבָּבֶל zerubbābel, n.pr.m. [1] [√ Hb 2428]

Zerubbabel [1]

Ezr 5: 2 **Zerubbabel** son of Shealtiel and Jeshua son of Jozadak set to work

10240 זְרַע zera', n.[m.]. [1] [√ Hb 2446]

people [+10050] [1]

Da 2: 43 so the **people** [+10050] will be a mixture and will not remain

---

ח, ḥ

10241 ח ḥ, letter. Not used in NIV/BHS [√ Hb 2459]

10242 חֲבוּלָה ḥabûlâ, n.f. [1] [√ 10243]

wrong [1]

Da 6: 22 [6:23] Nor have I ever done any **wrong** before you, O king."

10243 חֲבַל ḥabal, v. [6] [→ 10242, 10244; Hb 2472]

be destroyed [3], destroy [2], hurt [1]

Ezr 6: 12 [M] to change this decree or to **destroy** this temple in Jerusalem.
Da 2: 44 [O] heaven will set up a kingdom that *will* never **be destroyed**,
4: 23 [4:20] [M] and saying, 'Cut down the tree and **destroy** it,
6: 22 [6:23] [M] *They have* not **hurt** me, because I was found
6: 26 [6:27] [O] his kingdom *will* not **be destroyed**, his dominion will
7: 14 [O] and his kingdom is one that *will* never **be destroyed**.

10244 חֲבָל ḥabāl, n.m. [3] [√ 10243]

threat [1], unharmed [+10029+10089+10379] [1], wound [1]

Ezr 4: 22 Why let this **threat** grow, to the detriment of the royal interests?
Da 3: 25 in the fire, unbound and **unharmed** [+10029+10089+10379], and
6: 23 [6:24] no **wound** was found on him, because he had trusted in his

10245 חֲבַר ḥabar, n.m. [3] [→ 10246; Hb 2492]

friends [3]

Da 2: 13 were sent to look for Daniel and his **friends** to put them to death.
2: 17 to his house and explained the matter to his **friends** Hananiah,
2: 18 his **friends** might not be executed with the rest of the wise men of

10246 חַבְרָה ḥabrâ, n.f. [1] [√ 10245; Hb 2492]

others [1]

Da 7: 20 the horn that looked more imposing than the **others** and that had

10247 חַגַּי ḥaggay, n.pr.m. [2] [√ Hb 2516]

Haggai [2]

Ezr 5: 1 Now **Haggai** the prophet and Zechariah the prophet, a descendant
6: 14 prosper under the preaching of **Haggai** the prophet and Zechariah,

10248 חַד ḥad, a. & subst. [14 / 15] [√ Hb 285]

a [5], one [5], first [3], same [1], times [1]

Ezr 4: 8 Shimshai the secretary wrote **a** letter against Jerusalem to
5: 13 "However, in the **first** year of Cyrus king of Babylon, King Cyrus
6: 2 **A** scroll was found in the citadel of Ecbatana in the province of
6: 3 In the **first** year of King Cyrus, the king issued a decree concerning
6: 4 three courses of large stones and **one** [BHS 10251] of timbers.
Da 2: 9 If you do not tell me the dream, there is just **one** penalty for you.
2: 31 "You looked, O king, and there before you stood **a** large statue—

Da 2:35 the silver and the gold were broken to pieces at the **same** *time*
3:19 He ordered the furnace heated seven **times** hotter than usual
4:19 [4:16] was greatly perplexed for **a** time, and his thoughts terrified
6: 2 [6:3] three administrators over them, **one** of whom was Daniel.
6:17 [6:18] **A** stone was brought and placed over the mouth of the den,
7: 1 In the **first** year of Belshazzar king of Babylon, Daniel had a
7: 5 It was raised up on **one** of its sides, and it had three ribs in its
7:16 I approached **one** of those standing there and asked him the true

10249 חֲדֵה ḥ^{a}dēh, n.m. [1] [√ Hb 2601]

chest [1]

Da 2:32 its **chest** and arms of silver, its belly and thighs of bronze,

10250 חֶדְוָה ḥedwâ, n.f. [1] [√ Hb 2530]

joy [1]

Ezr 6:16 the exiles—celebrated the dedication of the house of God with **joy**.

10251 חֲדַת ḥ^{a}dat, a. [1 / 0] [√ Hb 2543]

Ezr 6: 4 courses of large stones and one [BHS *new*; NIV 10248] of timbers.

10252 חֲוָה ḥ^{a}wâ, v. [15] [→ 10018; Hb 2555]

interpret [+10600] [5], tell [4], explain [2], do[s] [1], explain [+10600] [1], reveal [1], tells [1]

Da 2: 4 [M] your servants the dream, and *we will* **interpret** [+10600] it."
2: 6 [P] if *you* **tell** me the dream and explain it, you will receive from
2: 6 [P] and great honor. So **tell** me the dream and interpret it for me."
2: 7 [P] his servants the dream, and *we will* **interpret** [+10600] it."
2: 9 [P] and I will know that *you can* **interpret** it **for** [+10600] me."
2:10 [P] "There is not a man on earth who can **do**[s] what the king asks!
2:11 [M] No one *can* **reveal** it to the king except the gods, and they do
2:16 [P] so that he *might* **interpret** [+10600] the dream for him.
2:24 [M] the king, and *I will* **interpret** [+10600] his dream for him."
2:27 [P] or diviner can **explain** to the king the mystery he has asked
4: 2 [3:32] [P] It is my pleasure to **tell** you *about* the miraculous
5: 7 [M] and **tells** me what it means will be clothed in purple
5:12 [P] interpret dreams, **explain** riddles and solve difficult problems.
5:12 [P] Call for Daniel, and *he will* **tell** you what the writing means."
5:15 [P] tell me what it means, but they could not **explain** [+10600] it.

10253 חוט ḥûṭ, v. [1]

repairing [1]

Ezr 4:12 [P] They are restoring the walls and **repairing** the foundations.

10254 חִוָּר ḥiwwār, a. [1]

white [1]

Da 7: 9 His clothing was as **white** as snow; the hair of his head was white

10255 חֲזָה ḥ^{a}zâ, v. [31] [→ 10256, 10257; Hb 2600]

looked [8], saw [7], had[s] [3], see [3], watched [3], *untranslated* [1], looking [1], realize [1], usual [1], vision [1], watch [1], watching [1]

Ezr 4:14 [J] and it is not proper for us to **see** the king dishonored,
Da 2: 8 [J] because *you* **realize** that this is what I have firmly decided:
2:26 [J] "Are you able to tell me what *I* **saw** in my dream and interpret
2:31 [J] "You **looked**, O king, and there before you stood a large
2:34 [J] While you were **watching**, a rock was cut out, but not by
2:41 [J] Just as *you* **saw** that the feet and toes were partly of baked
2:41 [J] strength of iron in it, even as *you* **saw** iron mixed with clay.
2:43 [J] just as *you* **saw** the iron mixed with baked clay, so the people
2:45 [J] This is the meaning of *the* **vision** of the rock cut out of a
3:19 [Jp] He ordered the furnace heated seven times hotter than **usual**
3:25 [J] I **see** four men walking around in the fire, unbound
3:27 [J] *They* **saw** that the fire had not harmed their bodies, nor was a
4: 5 [4:2] [J] *I* **had**[s] a dream that made me afraid. As I was lying in
4: 9 [4:6] [J] for you. Here is my dream; **[RPH]** interpret it for me.
4:10 [4:7] [J] I **looked**, and there before me stood a tree in the middle
4:13 [4:10] [J] I **looked**, and there before me was a messenger, a holy
4:18 [4:15] [J] "This is the dream that I, King Nebuchadnezzar, **had**[s].
4:20 [4:17] [J] The tree *you* **saw**, which grew large and strong,
4:23 [4:20] [J] "*You*, O king, **saw** a messenger, a holy one,
5: 5 [J] in the royal palace. The king **watched** the hand as it wrote.
5:23 [J] iron, wood and stone, which cannot **see** or hear or understand.
7: 1 [J] year of Belshazzar king of Babylon, Daniel **had**[s] a dream,
7: 2 [J] "In my vision at night *I* **looked**, and there before me were the
7: 4 [J] I **watched** until its wings were torn off and it was lifted from
7: 6 [J] "After that, I **looked**, and there before me was another beast,
7: 7 [J] "After that, in my vision at night I **looked**, and there before
7: 9 [J] "As I **looked**, "thrones were set in place, and the Ancient of
7:11 [J] "Then I continued *to* **watch** because of the boastful words the
7:11 [J] I kept **looking** until the beast was slain and its body destroyed
7:13 [J] "In my vision at night I **looked**, and there before me was one
7:21 [J] *As* I **watched**, this horn was waging war against the saints

10256 חֵזוּ ḥ^{e}zû, n.m. [12] [√ 10255]

visions [6], vision [4], dream [+10267] [1], looked [1]

Da 2:19 During the night the mystery was revealed to Daniel in a **vision**.
2:28 the **visions** *that passed through* your mind as you lay on your bed
4: 5 [4:2] and **visions** *that passed through* my mind terrified me.
4: 9 [4:6] for you. Here is my **dream** [+10267]; interpret it for me.
4:10 [4:7] These are the **visions** I saw while lying in my bed: I looked,
4:13 [4:10] "In the **visions** I saw while lying in my bed, I looked, and
7: 1 and **visions** *passed through* his mind as he was lying on his bed.
7: 2 "In my **vision** at night I looked, and there before me were the four
7: 7 "After that, in my **vision** *at* night I looked, and there before me
7:13 "In my **vision** *at* night I looked, and there before me was one like a
7:15 and the **visions** *that passed through* my mind disturbed me.
7:20 the horn that **looked** more imposing than the others and that had

10257 חָזוֹת ḥ^{a}zôt, n.f. [2] [√ 10255]

visible [2]

Da 4:11 [4:8] top touched the sky; it was **visible** to the ends of the earth.
4:20 [4:17] with its top touching the sky, **visible** to the whole earth,

10258 חַטָּאָה ḥaṭṭā'â, n.f. Not used in NIV/BHS [√ 10259; Hb 2633]

10259 חֲטָי ḥ^{a}ṭāy, n.[m.]. [1] [→ 10258, 10260; Hb 2628]

sins [1]

Da 4:27 [4:24] Renounce your **sins** by doing what is right, and your

10260 חַטָּיָא ḥaṭṭāyā', n.f. [1] [√ 10259; Hb 2633]

sin offering [1]

Ezr 6:17 as a **sin** [Q 2632] **offering** for all Israel, twelve male goats,

10261 חַי ḥay, a. [7] [√ 10262; Hb 2644, 2645]

living [4], live [+10073+10089] [1], lives [1], well-being [1]

Ezr 6:10 of heaven and pray for the **well-being** *of* the king and his sons.
Da 2:30 not because I have greater wisdom than other **living** *men*,
4:17 [4:14] so that the **living** may know that the Most High is
4:34 [4:31] Most High; I honored and glorified *him who* **lives** forever.
6:20 [6:21] "Daniel, servant of the **living** God, has your God,
6:26 [6:27] "For he is the **living** God and he endures forever; his
7:12 but were allowed to **live** [+10073+10089] for a period of time.)

10262 חֲיָה ḥ^{a}yâ, v. [6] [→ 10261, 10263; Hb 2649]

live [5], spared [1]

Da 2: 4 [J] answered the king in Aramaic, "O king, **live** forever!
3: 9 [J] They said to King Nebuchadnezzar, "O king, **live** forever!
5:10 [J] "O king, **live** forever!" she said. "Don't be alarmed! Don't
5:19 [P] he put to death; those he wanted to spare, *he* **spared**;
6: 6 [6:7] [J] to the king and said: "O King Darius, **live** forever!
6:21 [6:22] [J] Daniel answered, "O king, **live** forever!

10263 חֵיוָה ḥêwâ, n.f. [20] [√ 10262; Hb 2651]

beasts [7], beast [6], animals [5], animal [2]

Da 2:38 placed mankind and the **beasts** *of* the field and the birds of the air.
4:12 [4:9] Under it the **beasts** *of* the field found shelter, and the birds
4:14 [4:11] Let the **animals** flee from under it and the birds from its
4:15 [4:12] let him live with the **animals** among the plants of the earth.
4:16 [4:13] that of a man and let him be given the mind of an **animal**,
4:21 [4:18] food for all, giving shelter to the **beasts** *of* the field,
4:23 [4:20] let him live like the wild **animals**, until seven times pass by
4:25 [4:22] away from people and will live with the wild **animals**;
4:32 [4:29] away from people and will live with the wild **animals**;
5:21 He was driven away from people and given the mind of an **animal**;
7: 3 Four great **beasts**, each different from the others, came up out of
7: 5 "And there before me was a second **beast**, which looked like a
7: 6 This **beast** had four heads, and it was given authority to rule.
7: 7 vision at night I looked, and there before me was a fourth **beast**—
7: 7 It was different from all the former **beasts**, and it had ten horns.
7:11 I kept looking until the **beast** was slain and its body destroyed
7:12 (The other **beasts** had been stripped of their authority, but were
7:17 'The four great **beasts** are four kingdoms that will rise from the
7:19 "Then I wanted to know the true meaning of the fourth **beast**,
7:23 'The fourth **beast** is a fourth kingdom that will appear on earth.

10264 חֲיִל **ḥayil**, n.m. [7] [√ Hb 2657]

untranslated [1], army [1], compelled [1], loud [1], loudly [+10089] [1], powers [1], strongest soldiers [+10132] [1]

Ezr 4: 23 to the Jews in Jerusalem and **compelled** them by force to stop.
Da 3: 4 the herald **loudly** [+10089] proclaimed, "This is what you are
3: 20 commanded some of the **strongest soldiers** [+10132] in his army
3: 20 commanded some of the strongest soldiers in his **army** to tie up
4: 14 [4:11] He called in a **loud** *voice*: 'Cut down the tree and trim off
4: 35 [4:32] He does as he pleases with the **powers** *of* heaven and the
5: 7 The king called out **[NIE]** for the enchanters, astrologers

10265 חַכִּים **ḥakkîm**, n.m. [14] [√ 10266; Hb 2682]

wise [14]

Da 2: 12 furious that he ordered the execution of all the **wise** *men of*
2: 13 So the decree was issued to put the **wise** *men* to death, and men
2: 14 had gone out to put to death the **wise** *men of* Babylon,
2: 18 his friends might not be executed with the rest of the **wise** *men of*
2: 21 He gives wisdom to the **wise** and knowledge to the discerning.
2: 24 whom the king had appointed to execute the **wise** *men of* Babylon,
2: 24 and said to him, "Do not execute the **wise** *men of* Babylon.
2: 27 "No **wise** *man*, enchanter, magician or diviner can explain to the
2: 48 province of Babylon and placed him in charge of all its **wise** *men*.
4: 6 [4:3] So I commanded that all the **wise** *men of* Babylon be
4: 18 [4:15] for none of the **wise** *men in* my kingdom can interpret it
5: 7 and diviners to be brought and said to these **wise** *men of* Babylon,
5: 8 all the king's **wise** *men* came in, but they could not read the
5: 15 The **wise** *men* and enchanters were brought before me to read this

10266 חָכְמָה **ḥokmâ**, n.f. [8] [→ 10265; Hb 2683]

wisdom [7], that[s] [1]

Ezr 7: 25 And you, Ezra, in accordance with the **wisdom** *of* your God,
Da 2: 20 to the name of God for ever and ever; **wisdom** and power are his.
2: 21 He gives **wisdom** to the wise and knowledge to the discerning.
2: 23 You have given me **wisdom** and power, you have made known to
2: 30 not because I have greater **wisdom** than other living men,
5: 11 to have insight and intelligence and **wisdom** like that of the gods.
5: 11 to have insight and intelligence and wisdom like **that**[s] *of* the gods.
5: 14 and that you have insight, intelligence and outstanding **wisdom**.

10267 חֵלֶם **ḥēlem**, n.m. [22] [√ Hb 2706]

dream [20], dream [+10256] [1], dreams [1]

Da 2: 4 Tell your servants the **dream**, and we will interpret it."
2: 5 If you do not tell me what my **dream** was and interpret it,
2: 6 if you tell me the **dream** and explain it, you will receive from me
2: 6 and great honor. So tell me the **dream** and interpret it for me."
2: 7 Once more they replied, "Let the king tell his servants the **dream**,
2: 9 If you do not tell me the **dream**, there is just one penalty for you.
2: 9 So then, tell me the **dream**, and I will know that you can interpret
2: 26 "Are you able to tell me what I saw in my **dream** and interpret it?"
2: 28 Your **dream** and the visions that passed through your mind as you
2: 36 "This was the **dream**, and now we will interpret it to the king.
2: 45 the future. The **dream** is true and the interpretation is trustworthy."
4: 5 [4:2] I had a **dream** that made me afraid. As I was lying in my
4: 6 [4:3] be brought before me to interpret the **dream** for me.
4: 7 [4:4] and diviners came, I told them the **dream**,
4: 8 [4:5] Daniel came into my presence and I told him the **dream**.
4: 9 [4:6] for you. Here is my **dream** [+10256]; interpret it for me.
4: 18 [4:15] "This is the **dream** that I, King Nebuchadnezzar, had.
4: 19 [4:16] do not let the **dream** or its meaning alarm you."
4: 19 [4:16] if only the **dream** applied to your enemies and its meaning
5: 12 also the ability to interpret **dreams**, explain riddles and solve
7: 1 the first year of Belshazzar king of Babylon, Daniel had a **dream**,
7: 1 was lying on his bed. He wrote down the substance of his **dream**.

10268 חֲלַף **ḥ**[a]**lap**, v. [4] [√ Hb 2736]

pass by [4]

Da 4: 16 [4:13] [J] mind of an animal, till seven times **pass by** for him.
4: 23 [4:20] [J] the wild animals, until seven times **pass by** for him.'
4: 25 [4:22] [J] Seven times *will* **pass by** for you until you
4: 32 [4:29] [J] Seven times *will* **pass by** for you until you

10269 חֲלָק **ḥ**[a]**lāq**, n.[m.]. [3] [→ 10412; Hb 2750]

live [2], nothing [+10379] [1]

Ezr 4: 16 you will be left with **nothing** [+10379] in Trans-Euphrates.
Da 4: 15 [4:12] let him **live** with the animals among the plants of the earth.
4: 23 [4:20] let him **live** like the wild animals, until seven times pass by

10270 חֲמָה **ḥ**[a]**mâ**, n.f. [2] [√ Hb 2779]

furious [+10416] [1], furious [1]

Da 3: 13 **Furious** with rage, Nebuchadnezzar summoned Shadrach,
3: 19 Then Nebuchadnezzar *was* **furious** [+10416] *with* Shadrach,

10271 חֲמַר **ḥ**[a]**mar**, n.m. [6] [√ Hb 2815]

wine [6]

Ezr 6: 9 wheat, salt, **wine** and oil, as requested by the priests in Jerusalem—
7: 22 a hundred cors of wheat, a hundred baths of **wine**, a hundred baths
Da 5: 1 banquet for a thousand of his nobles and drank **wine** with them.
5: 2 While Belshazzar was drinking his **wine**, he gave orders to bring in
5: 4 As they drank the **wine**, they praised the gods of gold and silver,
5: 23 your wives and your concubines drank **wine** from them.

10272 חִנְטָה **ḥinṭâ**, n.f. [2] [√ Hb 2636]

wheat [2]

Ezr 6: 9 **wheat**, salt, wine and oil, as requested by the priests in Jerusalem—
7: 22 a hundred cors of **wheat**, a hundred baths of wine, a hundred baths

10273 חֲנֻכָּה **ḥ**[a]**nukkâ**, n.f. [4] [√ Hb 2853]

dedication [4]

Ezr 6: 16 celebrated the **dedication** *of* the house of God with joy.
6: 17 For the **dedication** *of* this house of God they offered a hundred
Da 3: 2 all the other provincial officials to come to the **dedication** *of* the
3: 3 all the other provincial officials assembled for the **dedication** *of*

10274 חֲנַן **ḥ**[a]**nan**, v. [2] [√ Hb 2858]

asking for help [1], kind [1]

Da 4: 27 [4:24] [J] and your wickedness by *being* **kind** *to* the oppressed.
6: 11 [6:12] [O] and found Daniel praying and **asking** God **for help**.

10275 חֲנַנְיָה **ḥ**[a]**nanyâ**, n.pr.m. [1] [√ Hb 2863]

Hananiah [1]

Da 2: 17 to his house and explained the matter to his friends **Hananiah**,

10276 חַסִּיר **ḥassîr**, a. [1] [√ Hb 2894]

wanting [1]

Da 5: 27 You have been weighed on the scales and found **wanting**.

10277 חֲסַן **ḥ**[a]**san**, v. [2] [→ 10278; Hb 2889]

possess [1], possessed [1]

Da 7: 18 [P] High will receive the kingdom and *will* **possess** it forever—
7: 22 [P] and the time came when they **possessed** the kingdom.

10278 חֱסֵן **ḥ**[e]**sēn**, n.m. [2] [√ 10277; Hb 2890]

mighty [1], power [1]

Da 2: 37 of heaven has given you dominion and **power** and might and glory;
4: 30 [4:27] by my **mighty** power and for the glory of my majesty?"

10279 חֲסַף **ḥ**[a]**sap**, n.[m.]. [9]

clay [5], baked clay [2], baked clay [+10298] [1], clay [+10298] [1]

Da 2: 33 its legs of iron, its feet partly of iron and partly of **baked clay**.
2: 34 It struck the statue on its feet of iron and **clay** and smashed them.
2: 35 the **clay**, the bronze, the silver and the gold were broken to pieces
2: 41 that the feet and toes were partly of **baked clay** and partly of iron,
2: 41 of iron in it, even as you saw iron mixed with **clay** [+10298].
2: 42 As the toes were partly iron and partly **clay**, so this kingdom will
2: 43 And just as you saw the iron mixed with **baked clay** [+10298],
2: 43 and will not remain united, any more than iron mixes with **clay**.
2: 45 the iron, the bronze, the **clay**, the silver and the gold to pieces.

10280 חֲצַף **ḥ**[a]**ṣap**, v. [2]

harsh [1], urgent [1]

Da 2: 15 [P] "Why did the king issue *such* a **harsh** decree?"
3: 22 [P] The king's command *was* so **urgent** and the furnace so hot

10281 חֲרַב **ḥ**[a]**rab**, v. [1] [√ Hb 2990]

was destroyed [1]

Ezr 4: 15 [Q] from ancient times. That is why this city **was destroyed**.

10282 חַרְטֹם **ḥarṭōm**, n.m. [5] [√ Hb 3033]

magicians [3], magician [2]

Da 2: 10 has ever asked such a thing of any **magician** or enchanter
2: 27 **magician** or diviner can explain to the king the mystery he has

Da 4: 7 [4:4] When the **magicians**, enchanters, astrologers and diviners
4: 9 [4:6] I said, "Belteshazzar, chief of the **magicians**, I know that the
5: 11 appointed him chief of the **magicians**, enchanters, astrologers

10283 חֲרַךְ ḥ^{a}rak, v. [1]
was singed [1]
Da 3: 27 [O] not harmed their bodies, nor **was** a hair of their heads **singed**;

10284 חֲרַץ ḥ^{a}raṣ, n.[m.]. [1] [√ Hb 2743]
legs [+10626] [1]
Da 5: 6 that his knees knocked together and his **legs** [+10626] gave way.

10285 חֲשַׁב ḥ^{a}šab, v. [1] [√ Hb 3108]
are regarded [1]
Da 4: 35 [4:32] [Jp] All the peoples of the earth **are regarded** as nothing.

10286 חֲשׁוֹךְ ḥ^{a}šôk, n.[m.]. [1] [√ Hb 3125]
darkness [1]
Da 2: 22 he knows what lies in **darkness**, and light dwells with him.

10287 חֲשַׁח ḥ^{a}šaḥ, v. [1] [→ 10288, 10289]
need [1]
Da 3: 16 [J] we *do* not **need** to defend ourselves before you in this matter.

10288 חַשְׁחָה ḥašḥâ, n.f. [1] [√ 10287]
needed [1]
Ezr 6: 9 Whatever is **needed**—young bulls, rams, male lambs for burnt

10289 חַשְׁחוּ ḥašḥû, n.f.col. [1] [√ 10287]
needed [1]
Ezr 7: 20 anything else **needed** *for* the temple of your God that you may

10290 חֲשַׁל ḥ^{a}šal, v. [1]
smashes [1]
Da 2: 40 [J] strong as iron—for iron breaks and **smashes** everything—

10291 חֲתַם ḥ^{a}tam, v. [1] [√ Hb 3159]
sealed [1]
Da 6: 17 [6:18] [J] the king **sealed** it with his own signet ring and with

ט, ṭ

10292 ט ṭ, letter. Not used in NIV/BHS [√ Hb 3172]

10293 טְאֵב ṭ^e'ēb, v. [1] [→ 10294; cf. 10320; Hb 3201, 3512]
overjoyed [+10542+10678] [1]
Da 6: 23 [6:24] [J] The king *was* **overjoyed** [+10542+10678] and gave orders to lift Daniel out of the den. And when Daniel was lifted from

10294 טָב ṭāb, a. [2] [√ 10293; Hb 3202]
pleases [1], pure [1]
Ezr 5: 17 Now if it **pleases** the king, let a search be made in the royal
Da 2: 32 The head of the statue was made of **pure** gold, its chest and arms

10295 טַבָּח ṭabbāḥ, n.m. [1] [√ Hb 3184]
guard [1]
Da 2: 14 When Arioch, the commander of the king's **guard**, had gone out to

10296 טוּר ṭûr, n.m. [2] [√ Hb 7446]
mountain [2]
Da 2: 35 But the rock that struck the statue became a huge **mountain**
2: 45 is the meaning of the vision of the rock cut out of a **mountain**,

10297 טְוָת ṭ^{e}wāt, adv. [1]
without eating [1]
Da 6: 18 [6:19] returned to his palace and spent the night **without eating**

10298 טִין ṭîn, n.[m.]. [2] [√ Hb 3226]
baked clay [+10279] [1], clay [+10279] [1]
Da 2: 41 of iron in it, even as you saw iron mixed with **clay** [+10279].
2: 43 And just as you saw the iron mixed with **baked clay** [+10279],

10299 טַל ṭal, n.[m.]. [5] [√ Hb 3228]
dew [5]
Da 4: 15 [4:12] " 'Let him be drenched with the **dew** *of* heaven, and let him
4: 23 [4:20] Let him be drenched with the **dew** *of* heaven; let him live
4: 25 [4:22] grass like cattle and be drenched with the **dew** *of* heaven.
4: 33 [4:30] His body was drenched with the **dew** *of* heaven until his
5: 21 his body was drenched with the **dew** *of* heaven, until he

10300 טְלַל ṭ^{e}lal, v. [1] [√ Hb 7511]
found shelter [1]
Da 4: 12 [4:9] [P] Under it the beasts of the field **found shelter**,

10301 [1]טְעֵם ṭ^e'ēm[1], v. [3] [→ 10302; Hb 3247]
eat [2], ate [1]
Da 4: 25 [4:22] [M] you *will* **eat** grass like cattle and be drenched with
4: 32 [4:29] [M] with the wild animals; you *will* **eat** grass like cattle.
5: 21 [M] he lived with the wild donkeys and **ate** grass like cattle;

10302 [2]טְעֵם ṭ^e'ēm[2], n.m. [30] [√ 10301; Hb 3248]
decree [5], decree [+10427+10682] [4], commanding officer [+10116] [3], order [3], attention [2], authorized [+10378+10682] [2], accountable [1], command [1], commanded [+10427+10682] [1], decreed [+10682] [1], decrees [1], drinking [1], order [+10002+10427+10682] [1], order [+10378+10427+10682] [1], prescribed [+10427] [1], report [1], tact [1]
Ezr 4: 8 Rehum the **commanding officer** [+10116] and Shimshai the
4: 9 Rehum the **commanding officer** [+10116] and Shimshai the
4: 17 To Rehum the **commanding officer** [+10116], Shimshai the
4: 19 I issued an **order** and a search was made, and it was found that this
4: 21 Now issue an **order** to these men to stop work, so that this city will
4: 21 city will not be rebuilt until I so **order** [+10002+10427+10682].
5: 3 "Who **authorized** [+10378+10682] you to rebuild this temple and
5: 5 and they were not stopped until a **report** could go to Darius
5: 9 "Who **authorized** [+10378+10682] you to rebuild this temple and
5: 13 King Cyrus issued a **decree** to rebuild this house of God.
5: 17 did in fact issue a **decree** to rebuild this house of God in Jerusalem.
6: 1 King Darius then issued an **order**, and they searched in the
6: 3 the king issued a **decree** *concerning* the temple of God in
6: 8 Moreover, I hereby **decree** [+10427+10682] what you are to do for
6: 11 Furthermore, I **decree** [+10427+10682] that if anyone changes this
6: 12 I Darius *have* **decreed** [+10682] it. Let it be carried out with
6: 14 They finished building the temple according to the **command** *of*
6: 14 to the command of the God of Israel and the **decrees** *of* Cyrus,
7: 13 Now I **decree** [+10427+10682] that any of the Israelites in my
7: 21 Now I, King Artaxerxes, **order** [+10378+10427+10682] all the
7: 23 Whatever the God of heaven has **prescribed** [+10427], let it be
Da 2: 14 wise men of Babylon, Daniel spoke to him with wisdom and **tact**.
3: 10 You have issued a **decree**, O king, that everyone who hears the
3: 12 Meshach and Abednego—who pay no **attention** to you, O king.
3: 29 Therefore I **decree** [+10427+10682] that the people of any nation
4: 6 [4:3] So I **commanded** [+10427+10682] that all the wise men of
5: 2 While Belshazzar was **drinking** his wine, he gave orders to bring
6: 2 [6:3] The satraps were made **accountable** to them so that the king
6: 13 [6:14] pays no **attention** to you, O king, or to the decree you put
6: 26 [6:27] "I issue a **decree** that in every part of my kingdom people

10303 טְפַר ṭ^{e}par, n.m. [2] [√ Hb 7632]
claws [1], nails [1]
Da 4: 33 [4:30] feathers of an eagle and his **nails** like the claws of a bird.
7: 19 and most terrifying, with its iron teeth and bronze **claws**—

10304 טְרַד ṭ^{e}rad, v. [4] [√ Hb 3265]
driven away [2], was driven away [2]
Da 4: 25 [4:22] [J] You *will be* **driven away** from people and will live
4: 32 [4:29] [J] You *will be* **driven away** from people and will live
4: 33 [4:30] [K] *He* **was driven away** from people and ate grass like
5: 21 [K] *He* **was driven away** from people and given the mind of an

10305 טַרְפְּלָי ṭarp^{e}lāy, n.pr.g. [1]
men from Tripolis [1]
Ezr 4: 9 the judges and officials over the **men from Tripolis**, Persia,

י, y

10306 י *y*, letter. Not used in NIV/BHS [√ Hb 3275]

10307 ־ִי *-î*, p.suf.1.com.s. [70] [√ 10477; Hb 3276] Not indexed

my [33], I [14], me [12], *untranslated* [9], my [+10621] [1], myself [+10380] [1]

10308 יְבַל *yᵉbal*, v. [3] [√ Hb 3297]

brought [2], take [1]

Ezr 5:14 [P] temple in Jerusalem and **brought** to the temple in Babylon.
6:5 [P] took from the temple in Jerusalem and **brought** to Babylon,
7:15 [P] you are to **take** with you the silver and gold that the king

10309 יַבֶּשָׁה *yabbᵉšâ*, n.f. [1] [√ Hb 3317]

earth [1]

Da 2:10 "There is not a man on **earth** who can do what the king asks!

10310 יְגַר *yᵉgar*, n.[m.]. Not used in NIV/BHS [√ Hb 1681, 337]

10311 יַד *yad*, n.f. [17] [√ Hb 3338]

hand [7], hands [3], hand [+10589] [2], be handed over [+10089+10314] [1], direction [1], handed over [+10089+10314] [1], possess [+10089] [1], power [1]

Ezr 5:8 with diligence and is making rapid progress under their **direction**.
5:12 *he* **handed** [+10089+10314] them **over** *to* Nebuchadnezzar the
6:12 any king or people who lifts a **hand** to change this decree
7:14 with regard to the Law of your God, which is in your **hand**.
7:25 which you **possess** [+10089], appoint magistrates and judges to
Da 2:34 you were watching, a rock was cut out, but not by human **hands**.
2:38 in your **hands** he has placed mankind and the beasts of the field
2:45 vision of the rock cut out of a mountain, but not by human **hands**—
3:15 Then what god will be able to rescue you from my **hand**?"
3:17 to save us from it, and he will rescue us from your **hand**, O king.
4:35 [4:32] No one can hold back his **hand** or say to him: "What have
5:5 Suddenly the fingers of a human **hand** appeared and wrote on the
5:5 the royal palace. The king watched the **hand** [+10589] as it wrote.
5:23 But you did not honor the God who holds in his **hand** your life
5:24 Therefore he sent the **hand** [+10589] that wrote the inscription.
6:27 [6:28] He has rescued Daniel from the **power** *of* the lions."
7:25 The saints *will* **be handed** [+10089+10314] **over** *to* him for a time,

10312 יְדָה *yᵉdâ*, v. [2] [√ Hb 3344]

giving thanks [1], thank [1]

Da 2:23 [P] I **thank** and praise you, O God of my fathers: You have given
6:10 [6:11] [P] on his knees and prayed, **giving thanks** to his God,

10313 יְדַע *yᵉdaʿ*, v. [47] [→ 10430; Hb 3359]

know [11], tell [8], acknowledge [3], interpret [+10600] [3], explained [2], inform [2], made known [2], shown [2], understand [2], *untranslated* [1], acknowledged [1], certain [+10327+10427] [1], discerning [+10100] [1], gave [1], information [1], knew [1], knows [1], learned [1], remember [1], showed [1], teach [1]

Ezr 4:12 [Jp] The king *should* **know** that the Jews who came up to us from
4:13 [Jp] Furthermore, the king *should* **know** that if this city is built
4:14 [P] we are sending this message *to* **inform** the king,
4:15 [J] In these records you will find **[RPH]** that this city is a
4:16 [P] We **inform** the king that if this city is built and its walls are
5:8 [Jp] The king *should* **know** that we went to the district of Judah,
5:10 [P] write down the names of their leaders *for* your **information**.
7:24 [P] You *are* also *to* **know** that you have no authority to impose
7:25 [J] of Trans-Euphrates—all *who* **know** the laws of your God.
7:25 [P] your God. And *you are to* **teach** any who do not know them.
7:25 [J] your God. And you are to teach any who *do* not **know** them.
Da 2:5 [P] If *you do* not **tell** me what my dream was and interpret it,
2:8 [J] "I *am* **certain** [+10327+10427] that you are trying to gain time,
2:9 [P] If *you do* not **tell** me the dream, there is just one penalty for
2:9 [J] the dream, and *I will* **know** that you can interpret it for me."
2:15 [P] a harsh decree?" Arioch then **explained** the matter to Daniel.
2:17 [P] his house and **explained** the matter to his friends Hananiah,
2:21 [J] to the wise and knowledge to the **discerning** [+10100].
2:22 [J] *he* **knows** what lies in darkness, and light dwells with him.
2:23 [P] *you have* **made known** *to* me what we asked of you,
2:23 [P] of you, *you have* **made known** *to* us the dream of the king."
2:25 [P] from Judah who *can* **tell** the king what his dream means."
2:26 [P] "Are you able to **tell** me what I saw in my dream
2:28 [P] *He has* **shown** King Nebuchadnezzar what will happen in
2:29 [P] the revealer of mysteries **showed** you what is going to
2:30 [P] so that *you*, O king, *may* **know** the interpretation and that
2:30 [J] and that *you may* **understand** what went through your mind.
2:45 [P] "The great God *has* **shown** the king what will take place in
3:18 [Jp] even if he does not, we *want* you *to* **know**, O king, that we
4:6 [4:3] [P] before me *to* **interpret** the dream **for** [+10600] me.
4:7 [4:4] [P] but *they could* not **interpret** [+10600] it for me.
4:9 [4:6] [J] I **know** that the spirit of the holy gods is in you,
4:17 [4:14] [J] so that the living *may* **know** that the Most High is
4:18 [4:15] [P] in my kingdom can **interpret** it **for** [+10600] me.
4:25 [4:22] [J] *you* **acknowledge** that the Most High is sovereign
4:26 [4:23] [J] to you when *you* **acknowledge** that Heaven rules.
4:32 [4:29] [J] *you* **acknowledge** that the Most High is sovereign
5:8 [P] they could not read the writing or **tell** the king what it meant.
5:15 [P] before me to read this writing and **tell** me what it means,
5:16 [P] If you can read this writing and **tell** me what it means,
5:17 [P] I will read the writing for the king and **tell** him what it means.
5:21 [J] until *he* **acknowledged** that the Most High God is sovereign
5:22 [J] have not humbled yourself, though *you* **knew** all this.
5:23 [J] wood and stone, which cannot see or hear or **understand**.
6:10 [6:11] [J] Now when Daniel **learned** that the decree had been
6:15 [6:16] [J] to the king and said to him, "**Remember**, O king,
7:16 [P] "So he told me and **gave** me the interpretation of these things:

10314 יְהַב *yᵉhab*, v. [28] [→ cf. 10498; Hb 3364]

given [4], gave [3], was given [3], be given [1], be handed over [+10089+10311] [1], be handed over [1], be paid [1], entrusted [1], give up [1], give [1], gives [1], handed over [+10089+10311] [1], laid [1], lavished [1], made [1], paid [1], placed [1], pronounced [1], thrown [1], were allowed [1], were paid [1]

Ezr 4:20 [L] and taxes, tribute and duty **were paid** to them.
5:12 [J] the God of heaven, *he* **handed** them **over to** [+10089+10311]
5:14 [Jp] "Then King Cyrus **gave** *them* to a man named Sheshbazzar,
5:16 [J] and **laid** the foundations of the house of God in Jerusalem.
6:4 [L] of timbers. The costs *are to* **be paid** by the royal treasury.
6:8 [L] The expenses of these men are to be fully **paid** out of the
6:9 [L] priests in Jerusalem—must be **given** them daily without fail,
7:19 [L] Deliver to the God of Jerusalem all the articles **entrusted** to
Da 2:21 [J] *He* **gives** wisdom to the wise and knowledge to the
2:23 [J] *You have* **given** me wisdom and power, you have made
2:37 [J] The God of heaven *has* **given** you dominion and power and
2:38 [J] in your hands *he has* **placed** mankind and the beasts of the
2:48 [J] Daniel in a high position and **lavished** many gifts on him.
3:28 [J] and *were willing to* **give up** their lives rather than serve
4:16 [4:13] [L] of a man and *let* him **be given** the mind of an animal,
5:17 [J] your gifts for yourself and **give** your rewards to someone else.
5:18 [J] the Most High God **gave** your father Nebuchadnezzar
5:19 [J] Because of the high position *he* **gave** him, all the peoples
5:28 [Jp] kingdom is divided and **given** to the Medes and Persians."
6:2 [6:3] [J] The satraps were **made** accountable to them so that the
7:4 [Jp] two feet like a man, and the heart of a man **was given** to it.
7:6 [Jp] This beast had four heads, and it **was given** authority to rule.
7:11 [Jp] and its body destroyed and **thrown** into the blazing fire.
7:12 [Jp] their authority, but **were allowed** to live for a period of time.)
7:14 [Jp] He **was given** authority, glory and sovereign power; all
7:22 [Jp] **pronounced** judgment in favor of the saints of the Most
7:25 [L] The saints *will* **be handed over to** [+10089+10311] him for a
7:27 [Jp] under the whole heaven *will* **be handed over** to the saints,

10315 יְהוּד *yᵉhûd*, n.pr.loc. [7] [→ 10316; Hb 3373]

Judah [6], *untranslated* [1]

Ezr 5:1 prophesied to the Jews in **Judah** and Jerusalem in the name of the
5:8 The king should know that we went to the district of **Judah**,
7:14 are sent by the king and his seven advisers to inquire about **Judah**
Da 2:25 "I have found a man among the exiles from **Judah** who can tell the
5:13 one of the exiles **[RPH]** my father the king brought from Judah?
5:13 one of the exiles my father the king brought from **Judah**?
6:13 [6:14] "Daniel, who is one of the exiles from **Judah**, pays no

10316 יְהוּדָי *yᵉhûdāy*, n.g. [10] [√ 10315; Hb 3374]

Jews [9], Jewish [1]

Ezr 4:12 The king should know that the **Jews** who came up to us from you
4:23 they went immediately to the **Jews** in Jerusalem and compelled
5:1 prophesied to the **Jews** in Judah and Jerusalem in the name of the
5:5 But the eye of their God was watching over the elders of the **Jews**,
6:7 Let the governor of the **Jews** and the Jewish elders rebuild this
6:7 and the **Jewish** elders rebuild this house of God on its site.
6:8 I hereby decree what you are to do for these elders of the **Jews** in

Ezr 6:14 So the elders of the **Jews** continued to build and prosper under the
Da 3: 8 this time some astrologers came forward and denounced the **Jews**.
3:12 there are some **Jews** whom you have set over the affairs of the

10317 יוֹם yôm, n.m. [16] [√ Hb 3427]

days [6], day [3], time [3], daily [+10089+10317] [2], long history [+10427+10550] [1], times [1]

Ezr 4:15 to kings and provinces, a place of rebellion from ancient **times**.
4:19 this city has a **long history** [+10427+10550] of revolt against kings
6: 9 must be given them **daily** [+10089+10317] without fail,
6: 9 must be given them **daily** [+10089+10317] without fail,
6:15 The temple was completed on the third **day** of the month Adar,
Da 2:28 He has shown King Nebuchadnezzar what will happen in **days** to
2:44 "In the **time** of those kings, the God of heaven will set up a
4:34 [4:31] At the end of that **time**, I, Nebuchadnezzar, raised my eyes
5:11 In the **time** *of* your father he was found to have insight
6: 7 [6:8] who prays to any god or man during the next thirty **days**,
6:10 [6:11] Three times a **day** he got down on his knees and prayed,
6:12 [6:13] during the next thirty **days** anyone who prays to any god
6:13 [6:14] decree you put in writing. He still prays three times a **day**."
7: 9 "thrones were set in place, and the Ancient of **Days** took his seat.
7:13 He approached the Ancient of **Days** and was led into his presence.
7:22 until the Ancient of **Days** came and pronounced judgment in favor

10318 יוֹצָדָק yôṣādāq, n.pr.m. [1] [√ Hb 3392]

Jozadak [1]

Ezr 5: 2 Jeshua son of **Jozadak** set to work to rebuild the house of God in

10319 יְחַת yeḥat, v. Not used in NIV/BHS

10320 יְטַב yeṭab, v. [1] [cf. 10293; Hb 3512]

seems best [1]

Ezr 7:18 [J] do whatever **seems best** with the rest of the silver and gold,

10321 יְכִל yekil, v. [12] [cf. 10346; Hb 3523]

able [5], can [5], defeating [1], unable [+10379] [1]

Da 2:10 [J] "There is not a man on earth who **can** do what the king asks!
2:27 [J] or diviner **can** explain to the king the mystery he has asked
2:47 [J] of mysteries, for *you were* **able** to reveal this mystery."
3:17 [J] the God we serve *is* **able** to save us from it, and he will rescue
3:29 [J] into piles of rubble, for no other god **can** save in this way."
4:18 [4:15] [J] for none of the wise men in my kingdom **can** interpret
4:37 [4:34] [J] And those who walk in pride *he is* **able** to humble.
5:16 [J] Now I have heard that *you are* **able** to give interpretations
5:16 [J] If *you* **can** read this writing and tell me what it means,
6: 4 [6:5] [J] but *they were* **unable** [+10379] to do so.
6:20 [6:21] [J] *has* your God, whom you serve continually, *been* **able**
7:21 [J] horn was waging war against the saints and **defeating** them,

10322 יָם yam, n.m. [2] [√ Hb 3542]

sea [2]

Da 7: 2 before me were the four winds of heaven churning up the great **sea**.
7: 3 great beasts, each different from the others, came up out of the **sea**.

10323 יְסַף yesap, v. [1] [√ Hb 3578]

became even greater [+10339+10378+10650] [1]

Da 4:36 [4:33] [Q] nobles sought me out, and I was restored to my throne and **became even greater** [+10339+10378+10650] than before.

10324 יְעַט ye'aṭ, v. [1] [→ 10325, 10539; Hb 3619]

agreed [1]

Da 6: 7 [6:8] [O] governors *have* all **agreed** that the king should issue

10325 יָעֵט yā'ēṭ, n.m. *or* v.ptcp. [2] [√ 10324; Hb 3619]

advisers [2]

Ezr 7:14 are sent by the king and his seven **advisers** to inquire about Judah
7:15 the king and his **advisers** have freely given to the God of Israel,

10326 יְצַב yeṣab, v. [1] [→ 10327; Hb 3656]

know the true meaning [1]

Da 7:19 [M] "Then I wanted to **know the true meaning** of the fourth

10327 יַצִּיב yaṣṣîb, a. [5] [√ 10326]

certain [+10313+10427] [1], certainly [+10002] [1], stands [1], true meaning [1], true [1]

Da 2: 8 "I *am* **certain** [+10313+10427] that you are trying to gain time,
2:45 the future. The dream is **true** and the interpretation is trustworthy."
3:24 threw into the fire?" They replied, "**Certainly** [+10002], O king."
6:12 [6:13] The king answered, "The decree **stands**—in accordance
7:16 of those standing there and asked him the **true meaning** of all this.

10328 יְקַד yeqad, v. [8] [→ 10329; Hb 3678]

blazing [+10471] [8]

Da 3: 6 [J] worship will immediately be thrown into a **blazing** [+10471]
3:11 [J] and worship will be thrown into a **blazing** [+10471] furnace.
3:15 [J] you will be thrown immediately into a **blazing** [+10471]
3:17 [J] If we are thrown into the **blazing** [+10471] furnace, the God
3:20 [J] and throw them into the **blazing** [+10471] furnace.
3:21 [J] were bound and thrown into the **blazing** [+10471] furnace.
3:23 [J] three men, firmly tied, fell into the **blazing** [+10471] furnace.
3:26 [J] then approached the opening of the **blazing** [+10471] furnace

10329 יְקֵדָה yeqēdâ, n.f. [1] [√ 10328]

blazing [1]

Da 7:11 was slain and its body destroyed and thrown into the **blazing** fire.

10330 יַקִּיר yaqqîr, a. [2] [√ 10331; Hb 3692]

honorable [1], too difficult [1]

Ezr 4:10 **honorable** Ashurbanipal deported and settled in the city of
Da 2:11 What the king asks is **too difficult**. No one can reveal it to the king

10331 יְקָר yeqār, n.m. [7] [→ 10330; Hb 3702]

glory [6], honor [1]

Da 2: 6 you will receive from me gifts and rewards and great **honor**.
2:37 of heaven has given you dominion and power and might and **glory**;
4:30 [4:27] by my mighty power and for the **glory** *of* my majesty?"
4:36 [4:33] splendor were returned to me for the **glory** *of* my kingdom.
5:18 and greatness and **glory** and splendor.
5:20 he was deposed from his royal throne and stripped of his **glory**.
7:14 He was given authority, **glory** and sovereign power; all peoples,

10332 יְרוּשְׁלֶם yerûšelem, n.pr.loc. [26] [√ Hb 3731]

Jerusalem [26]

Ezr 4: 8 Shimshai the secretary wrote a letter against **Jerusalem** to
4:12 that the Jews who came up to us from you have gone to **Jerusalem**
4:20 **Jerusalem** has had powerful kings ruling over the whole of
4:23 they went immediately to the Jews in **Jerusalem** and compelled
4:24 Thus the work on the house of God in **Jerusalem** came to a
5: 1 the Jews in Judah and **Jerusalem** in the name of the God of Israel,
5: 2 of Jozadak set to work to rebuild the house of God in **Jerusalem**.
5:14 which Nebuchadnezzar had taken from the temple in **Jerusalem**
5:15 these articles and go and deposit them in the temple in **Jerusalem**.
5:16 and laid the foundations of the house of God in **Jerusalem**.
5:17 in fact issue a decree to rebuild this house of God in **Jerusalem**.
6: 3 king issued a decree concerning the temple of God in **Jerusalem**:
6: 5 which Nebuchadnezzar took from the temple in **Jerusalem**
6: 5 are to be returned to their places in the temple in **Jerusalem**;
6: 9 salt, wine and oil, as requested by the priests in **Jerusalem**—
6:12 hand to change this decree or to destroy this temple in **Jerusalem**.
6:18 the Levites in their groups for the service of God at **Jerusalem**,
7:13 and Levites, who wish to go to **Jerusalem** with you, may go.
7:14 about Judah and **Jerusalem** with regard to the Law of your God,
7:15 freely given to the God of Israel, whose dwelling is in **Jerusalem**,
7:16 of the people and priests for the temple of their God in **Jerusalem**.
7:17 sacrifice them on the altar of the temple of your God in **Jerusalem**.
7:19 Deliver to the God of **Jerusalem** all the articles entrusted to you
Da 5: 2 his father had taken from the temple in **Jerusalem**,
5: 3 goblets that had been taken from the temple of God in **Jerusalem**,
6:10 [6:11] room where the windows opened toward **Jerusalem**.

10333 יְרַח yeraḥ, n.m. [2] [√ Hb 3732]

month [1], months [1]

Ezr 6:15 The temple was completed on the third day of the **month** Adar,
Da 4:29 [4:26] Twelve **months** later, as the king was walking on the roof

10334 יַרְכָה yarkâ, n.f. [1] [√ Hb 3751]

thighs [1]

Da 2:32 its chest and arms of silver, its belly and **thighs** of bronze,

10335 יִשְׂרָאֵל yiśrā'ēl, n.pr.g. [8] [√ Hb 3776]

Israel [7], Israelites [+10553] [1]

Ezr 5: 1 the Jews in Judah and Jerusalem in the name of the God of **Israel**,
5:11 many years ago, one that a great king of **Israel** built and finished.
6:14 building the temple according to the command of the God of **Israel**

Ezr 6:16 the people of **Israel**—the priests, the Levites and the rest of the
6:17 male lambs and, as a sin offering for all **Israel**, twelve male goats,
6:17 all Israel, twelve male goats, one for each of the tribes of **Israel**.
7:13 Now I decree that any of the **Israelites** [+10553] in my kingdom,
7:15 the king and his advisers have freely given to the God of **Israel**,

10336 יֵשׁוּעַ ***yēšûaʿ***, n.pr.m. [1] [√ Hb 3800]

Jeshua [1]

Ezr 5:2 **Jeshua** son of Jozadak set to work to rebuild the house of God in

10337 יָת ***yāt***, pt. [1] [√ Hb 906]

untranslated [1]

Da 3:12 there are some Jews whom you have set **[OBJ]** over the affairs of

10338 יְתִב ***yᵉtib***, v. [5] [√ Hb 3782]

living [1], seated [1], settled [1], sit [1], took seat [1]

Ezr 4:10 [P] **settled** in the city of Samaria and elsewhere in
4:17 [J] the secretary and the rest of their associates **living** in Samaria
Da 7:9 [J] were set in place, and the Ancient of Days **took** *his* **seat**.
7:10 [J] The court *was* **seated**, and the books were opened.
7:26 [J] " 'But the court *will* **sit**, and his power will be taken away

10339 יַתִּיר ***yattîr***, a. [8] [√ Hb 3835]

untranslated [1], became even greater [+10323+10378+10650] [1], exceptional [1], keen [1], most [1], outstanding [1], so [1], very [1]

Da 2:31 an enormous, dazzling statue, **[RPH]** awesome in appearance.
3:22 **so** hot that the flames of the fire killed the soldiers who took up
4:36 [4:33] **became even greater** [+10323+10378+10650] than before.
5:12 was found to have a **keen** mind and knowledge and understanding,
5:14 and that you have insight, intelligence and **outstanding** wisdom.
6:3 [6:4] the satraps by his **exceptional** qualities that the king planned
7:7 was a fourth beast—terrifying and frightening and **very** powerful.
7:19 which was different from all the others and **most** terrifying,

כ, *k*

10340 כ ***k***, letter. Not used in NIV/BHS [√ Hb 3868]

10341 -כְּ ***kᵉ-***, pp.pref. [41] [√ Hb 3869] Not indexed

like [14], as [6], in accordance with [4], when [+10168] [3], at [2], how [+10408] [2], according to [1], after [1], any more than [+10168+10195] [1], as follows [+10180] [1], as soon as [+10002+10168+10232] [1], for [1], in way [1], such [+10180] [1], this [+10180] [1], when [1]

10342 ךְ- ***-k***, p.suf.2.m.s. [99] [√ Hb 3870] Not indexed

your [46], you [40], *untranslated* [9], there[s] [+10444] [1], yours [1], yourself [+10381] [1], yourself [1]

10343 כְּדַב ***kᵉdab***, a. [1] [→ 10344; Hb 3942]

misleading [1]

Da 2:9 You have conspired to tell me **misleading** and wicked things,

10344 כִּדְבָה ***kidbâ***, a. Not used in NIV/BHS [√ 10323; Hb 3942]

10345 כָּה ***kâ***, adv. [1] [√ Hb 3907]

this [+10527] [1]

Da 7:28 "**This** [+10527] is the end of the matter. I, Daniel, was deeply

10346 כְּהַל ***kᵉhal***, v. [4] [cf. 10321]

could [2], able [1], can [1]

Da 2:26 [J] "Are you **able** to tell me what I saw in my dream and interpret
4:18 [4:15] [J] you **can**, because the spirit of the holy gods is in you."
5:8 [J] *they* **could** not read the writing or tell the king what it meant.
5:15 [J] and tell me what it means, but *they* **could** not explain it.

10347 כָּהֵן ***kāhēn***, n.m. [8] [√ Hb 3913]

priests [6], priest [2]

Ezr 6:9 salt, wine and oil, as requested by the **priests** in Jerusalem—
6:16 of Israel—the **priests**, the Levites and the rest of the exiles—
6:18 they installed the **priests** in their divisions and the Levites in their
7:12 Artaxerxes, king of kings, To Ezra the **priest**, a teacher of the Law
7:13 including **priests** and Levites, who wish to go to Jerusalem with
7:16 of the people and **priests** for the temple of their God in Jerusalem.
7:21 to provide with diligence whatever Ezra the **priest**,
7:24 tribute or duty on any of the **priests**, Levites, singers, gatekeepers,

10348 כַּוָּה ***kawwâ***, n.f. [1]

windows [1]

Da 6:10 [6:11] he went home to his upstairs room where the **windows**

10349 כוֹן- ***-kôn***, p.suf.2.m.pl. [10] [√ 10355; Hb 4013] Not indexed

you [8], your [2]

10350 כּוֹרֶשׁ ***kôreš***, n.pr.m. [8] [√ Hb 3931]

Cyrus [7], *untranslated* [1]

Ezr 5:13 "However, in the first year of **Cyrus** king of Babylon, King Cyrus
5:13 King **Cyrus** issued a decree to rebuild this house of God.
5:14 "Then King **Cyrus** gave them to a man named Sheshbazzar,
5:17 **Cyrus** did in fact issue a decree to rebuild this house of God in
6:3 In the first year of King **Cyrus**, the king issued a decree
6:3 **[RPH]** the king issued a decree concerning the temple of God in
6:14 to the command of the God of Israel and the decrees of **Cyrus**,
Da 6:28 [6:29] the reign of Darius and the reign of **Cyrus** the Persian.

10351 כִּיל ***kîl***, v. Not used in NIV/BHS [√ Hb 3920?]

10352 כַּכַּר ***kakkar***, n.[f.]. [1] [√ Hb 3971]

talents [1]

Ezr 7:22 up to a hundred **talents** of silver, a hundred cors of wheat,

10353 כֹּל ***kōl***, n.m. [104] [√ 10354; Hb 3972]

all [36], *untranslated* [10], any [9], whole [7], no [+10379] [4], because [+10168+10619] [3], for [+10168+10619] [3], anyone [+10050] [2], every [2], everything [2], throughout [+10089] [2], whatever [+10168] [2], a[s] [1], anyone [1], by [+10168+10619] [1], cordial greetings [+10002+10002+10720] [1], do so[s] [+10544+10708] [1], entire [1], even as [+10168+10619] [1], everyone [+10050] [1], just as [+10168+10619] [1], none [+10379] [1], other[s] [1], since [+10168+10619] [1], so [+10180+10619] [1], then [+10180+10619] [1], therefore [+10180+10619] [1], they[s] [+10002+10553] [1], this is the meaning [+10168+10619] [1], this made [+10180+10619] [1], though [+10168+10619] [1], wherever [+10089+10168] [1], whoever [+10050+10168] [1], whoever [+10168] [1]

Ezr 4:14 Now **since** [+10168+10619] we are under obligation to the palace
4:20 Jerusalem has had powerful kings ruling over the **whole** *of*
5:7 To King Darius: **Cordial greetings** [+10002+10002+10720].
6:11 Furthermore, I decree that if **anyone** [+10050] changes this edict,
6:12 overthrow **any** king or people who lifts a hand to change this
6:17 male lambs and, as a sin offering for **all** Israel, twelve male goats,
7:13 Now I decree that **any** of the Israelites in my kingdom,
7:14 **[NIE]** You are sent by the king and his seven advisers to inquire
7:16 together with **all** the silver and gold you may obtain from the
7:16 and gold you may obtain from **[RPH]** the province of Babylon,
7:17 **[NIE]** With this money be sure to buy bulls, rams and male
7:21 order **all** the treasurers of Trans-Euphrates to provide with
7:21 to provide with diligence **whatever** [+10168] Ezra the priest,
7:23 **Whatever** [+10168] the God of heaven has prescribed, let it be
7:24 tribute or duty on **any** *of* the priests, Levites, singers, gatekeepers,
7:25 judges to administer justice to **all** the people of Trans-Euphrates—
7:25 people of Trans-Euphrates—**all** who know the laws of your God.
7:26 **Whoever** [+10168] does not obey the law of your God and the law
Da 2:8 you are trying to gain time, **because** [+10168+10619] you realize
2:10 **[NIE]** No king, however great and mighty, has ever asked such a
2:10 **No** [+10379] king, however great and mighty, has ever asked such
2:10 has ever asked such a thing of **any** magician or enchanter
2:12 **This made** [+10180+10619] the king so angry and furious that he
2:12 furious that he ordered the execution of **all** the wise men of
2:24 **Then** [+10180+10619] Daniel went to Arioch, whom the king had
2:30 not because I have greater wisdom than **other**[s] living men,
2:35 the summer. The wind swept them away without leaving **a**[s] trace.
2:35 the statue became a huge mountain and filled the **whole** earth.
2:38 **Wherever** [+10089+10168] they live, he has made you ruler over
2:38 of the air. Wherever they live, he has made you ruler over them **all**.
2:39 a third kingdom, one of bronze, will rule over the **whole** earth.
2:40 strong as iron—**for** [+10168+10619] iron breaks and smashes
2:40 strong as iron—for iron breaks and smashes **everything**—
2:40 breaks things to pieces, so it will crush and break **all** the others.
2:41 have some of the strength of iron in it, **even as** [+10168+10619]
2:44 It will crush **all** those kingdoms and bring them to an end,
2:45 **This is the meaning of** [+10168+10619] the vision of the rock cut
2:48 He made him ruler over the **entire** province of Babylon and placed

Da 2:48 province of Babylon and placed him in charge of **all** its wise men.
3: 2 **all** the other provincial officials to come to the dedication of the
3: 3 **all** the other provincial officials assembled for the dedication of the
3: 5 flute, zither, lyre, harp, pipes and **all** kinds of music, you must fall
3: 7 **Therefore** [+10180+10619], as soon as they heard the sound of the
3: 7 as soon as **they**ˢ [+10002+10553] heard the sound of the horn,
3: 7 flute, zither, lyre, harp and **all** kinds of music, all the peoples,
3: 7 **all** the peoples, nations and men of every language fell down
3: 8 **[NIE]** At this time some astrologers came forward and denounced
3:10 that **everyone** [+10050] who hears the sound of the horn, flute,
3:10 pipes and **all** kinds of music must fall down and worship the image
3:15 flute, zither, lyre, harp, pipes and **all** kinds of music, if you are
3:22 **[NIE]** The king's command was so urgent and the furnace
3:28 lives rather than serve or worship **any** god except their own God.
3:29 Therefore I decree that the people of **any** nation or language who
3:29 their houses be turned into piles of rubble, **for** [+10168+10619] no
4: 1 [3:31] To **[RPH]** the peoples, nations and men of every
4: 1 [3:31] and men of every language, who live in **all** the world:
4: 6 [4:3] So I commanded that **all** the wise men of Babylon be
4: 9 [4:6] is in you, and **no** [+10379] mystery is too difficult for you.
4:11 [4:8] the sky; it was visible to the ends of **[NIE]** the earth.
4:12 [4:9] were beautiful, its fruit abundant, and on it was food for **all**.
4:12 [4:9] the air lived in its branches; from it **every** creature was fed.
4:18 [4:15] tell me what it means, **for** [+10168+10619] none of the
4:18 [4:15] for **none of** [+10379] the wise men in my kingdom can
4:20 [4:17] with its top touching the sky, visible to the **whole** earth,
4:21 [4:18] beautiful leaves and abundant fruit, providing food for **all**,
4:28 [4:25] **All** this happened to King Nebuchadnezzar.
4:35 [4:32] **All** the peoples of the earth are regarded as nothing. He
4:37 [4:34] because **everything** he does is right and all his ways are
5: 7 "**Whoever** [+10050+10168] reads this writing and tells me what it
5: 8 **all** the king's wise men came in, but they could not read the
5:12 **[NIE]** This man Daniel, whom the king called Belteshazzar,
5:19 **all** the peoples and nations and men of every language dreaded
5:22 not humbled yourself, **though** [+10168+10619] you knew all this.
5:22 have not humbled yourself, though you knew **all** this.
5:23 honor the God who holds in his hand your life and **all** your ways.
6: 1 [6:2] 120 satraps to rule **throughout** [+10089] the kingdom,
6: 3 [6:4] the satraps **by** [+10168+10619] his exceptional qualities that
6: 3 [6:4] that the king planned to set him over the **whole** kingdom.
6: 4 [6:5] but they were unable to **do so**ˢ [+10544+10708].
6: 4 [6:5] **because** [+10168+10619] he was trustworthy and neither
6: 4 [6:5] was trustworthy and neither corrupt nor **[NIE]** negligent.
6: 5 [6:6] "We will never find **any** basis for charges against this man
6: 7 [6:8] governors have **all** agreed that the king should issue an edict
6: 7 [6:8] enforce the decree that **anyone** who prays to any god or man
6: 7 [6:8] enforce the decree that anyone who prays to **any** god or man
6: 9 [6:10] **So** [+10180+10619] King Darius put the decree in writing.
6:10 [6:11] giving thanks to his God, **just as** [+10168+10619] he had
6:12 [6:13] the next thirty days **anyone** [+10050] who prays to any god
6:12 [6:13] during the next thirty days anyone who prays to **any** god
6:15 [6:16] to the law of the Medes and Persians **no** [+10379] decree
6:22 [6:23] not hurt me, **because** [+10168+10619] I was found innocent
6:23 [6:24] when Daniel was lifted from the den, **no** [+10379] wound
6:24 [6:25] the lions overpowered them and crushed **all** their bones.
6:25 [6:26] King Darius wrote to **all** the peoples, nations and men of
6:25 [6:26] and men of every language **throughout** [+10089] the land:
6:26 [6:27] "I issue a decree that in **every** part of my kingdom people
7: 7 It was different from **all** the former beasts, and it had ten horns.
7:14 **all** peoples, nations and men of every language worshiped him.
7:16 of those standing there and asked him the true meaning of **all** this.
7:19 which was different from **all** the others and most terrifying,
7:23 It will be different from **all** the other kingdoms and will devour the
7:23 from all the other kingdoms and will devour the **whole** earth,
7:27 greatness of the kingdoms under the **whole** heaven will be handed
7:27 an everlasting kingdom, and **all** rulers will worship and obey him.'

10354 כְּלַל k^elal, v. [7] [→ 10353; Hb 4005]

are restored [2], finished [2], restore [2], restoring [1]

Ezr 4:12 [P] *They are* **restoring** the walls and repairing the foundations.
4:13 [R] know that if this city is built and its walls **are restored**,
4:16 [R] the king that if this city is built and its walls **are restored**,
5: 3 [P] you to rebuild this temple and **restore** this structure?"
5: 9 [P] you to rebuild this temple and **restore** this structure?"
5:11 [P] years ago, one that a great king of Israel built and **finished**.
6:14 [P] *They* **finished** building the temple according to the command

10355 -כֹם -kōm, p.suf.2.m.pl. [5] [√ 10349; Hb 4013] Not indexed

you [3], your [2]

10356 כְּמָה k^emâ, pp. & p.inter. Not used in NIV/BHS [√ 10341 + 10408]

10357 כֵּן kēn, adv. [8] [√ Hb 4027] Not indexed

untranslated [6], this [2]

10358 כְּנֵמָא k^enēmā', adv. [5]

untranslated [2], also [+10008] [1], as follows [1], this [1]

Ezr 4: 8 wrote a letter against Jerusalem to Artaxerxes the king **as follows**:
5: 4 They **also** [+10008] asked, "What are the names of the men
5: 9 We questioned the elders **[NIE]** and asked them,
5:11 **This** is the answer they gave us: "We are the servants of the God
6:13 and their associates carried it out **[NIE]** with diligence.

10359 כְּנַשׁ k^enaš, v. [3] [√ Hb 4043]

assembled [1], crowded around [1], summoned [+10378+10378+10714] [1]

Da 3: 2 [J] He then **summoned** [+10378+10378+10714] the satraps,
3: 3 [O] all the other provincial officials **assembled** for the dedication
3:27 [O] and royal advisers **crowded around** them.

10360 כְּנָת k^enāt, n.m. [7] [√ Hb 4056]

associates [6], fellow [1]

Ezr 4: 9 Shimshai the secretary, together with the rest of their **associates**—
4:17 the secretary and the rest of their **associates** living in Samaria
4:23 read to Rehum and Shimshai the secretary and their **associates**,
5: 3 and Shethar-Bozenai and their **associates** went to them and asked,
5: 6 of Trans-Euphrates, and Shethar-Bozenai and their **associates**,
6: 6 and you, their **fellow** officials of that province,
6:13 and their **associates** carried it out with diligence.

10361 כַּשְׂדַּי kasdāy, n.pr.g. Not used in NIV/BHS [cf. 10373]

10362 כְּסַף k^esap, n.m. [13] [√ Hb 4084]

silver [12], money [1]

Ezr 5:14 temple of Babylon the gold and **silver** articles of the house of God,
6: 5 Also, the gold and **silver** articles of the house of God, which
7:15 you are to take with you the **silver** and gold that the king and his
7:16 together with all the **silver** and gold you may obtain from the
7:17 With this **money** be sure to buy bulls, rams and male lambs,
7:18 then do whatever seems best with the rest of the **silver** and gold,
7:22 up to a hundred talents of **silver**, a hundred cors of wheat,
Da 2:32 its chest and arms of **silver**, its belly and thighs of bronze,
2:35 the **silver** and the gold were broken to pieces at the same time
2:45 the iron, the bronze, the clay, the **silver** and the gold to pieces.
5: 2 **silver** goblets that Nebuchadnezzar his father had taken from the
5: 4 they praised the gods of gold and **silver**, of bronze, iron, wood
5:23 You praised the gods of **silver** and gold, of bronze, iron, wood

10363 כְּעַן k^e'an, adv. [13] [→ 10364, 10365]

now [6], *untranslated* [4], furthermore [1], now then [1], the present [1]

Ezr 4:13 **Furthermore**, the king should know that if this city is built
4:14 **Now** since we are under obligation to the palace and it is not
4:21 **Now** issue an order to these men to stop work, so that this city will
5:16 From that day to **the present** it has been under construction
5:17 **Now** if it pleases the king, let a search be made in the royal
6: 6 **Now then**, Tattenai, governor of Trans-Euphrates, and
Da 2:23 **[NIE]** you have made known to me what we asked of you,
3:15 **Now** when you hear the sound of the horn, flute, zither, lyre,
4:37 [4:34] **Now** I, Nebuchadnezzar, praise and exalt and glorify the
5:12 **[NIE]** Call for Daniel, and he will tell you what the writing
5:15 **[NIE]** The wise men and enchanters were brought before me to
5:16 **[NIE]** If you can read this writing and tell me what it means,
6: 8 [6:9] **Now**, O king, issue the decree and put it in writing so that it

10364 כְּעֶנֶת k^e'enet, adv. [3] [√ 10363]

untranslated [2], now [1]

Ezr 4:10 in the city of Samaria and elsewhere in Trans-Euphrates. **[NIE]**
4:11 From your servants, the men of Trans-Euphrates: **[NIE]**
7:13 [7:12] **Now** I decree that any of the Israelites in my kingdom,

10365 כְּעֶת k^e'et, adv. [1] [√ 10363]

untranslated [1]

Ezr 4:17 in Samaria and elsewhere in Trans-Euphrates: Greetings. **[NIE]**

10366 כְּפַת k^{e}pat, v. [4]

firmly tied [1], tie up [1], tied up [1], were bound [1]

Da 3:20 [M] of the strongest soldiers in his army to **tie up** Shadrach,
3:21 [K] **were bound** and thrown into the blazing furnace.
3:23 [N] these three men, **firmly tied**, fell into the blazing furnace.
3:24 [N] "Weren't there three men that we **tied up** and threw into the

10367 כֹּר kōr, n.[m.]. [1] [√ Hb 4123]

cors [1]

Ezr 7:22 a hundred **cors** of wheat, a hundred baths of wine, a hundred baths

10368 כַּרְבְּלָה karb^{e}lâ, n.f. [1]

turbans [1]

Da 3:21 trousers, **turbans** and other clothes, were bound and thrown into

10369 כְּרָה k^{e}râ, v. [1]

troubled [1]

Da 7:15 [L] "I, Daniel, *was* **troubled** in spirit, and the visions that passed

10370 כָּרוֹז kārôz, n.m. [1] [→ 10371]

herald [1]

Da 3:4 the **herald** loudly proclaimed, "This is what you are commanded to

10371 כְּרַז k^{e}raz, v.den. [1] [→ 10370]

proclaimed [1]

Da 5:29 [P] he *was* **proclaimed** the third highest ruler in the kingdom.

10372 כָּרְסֵא korsē', n.m. [3] [√ Hb 4058]

throne [2], thrones [1]

Da 5:20 he was deposed from his royal **throne** and stripped of his glory.
7:9 "As I looked, "**thrones** were set in place, and the Ancient of Days
7:9 His **throne** was flaming with fire, and its wheels were all ablaze.

10373 כַּשְׂדָּי kaśdāy, n.pr.g. [9] [cf. 10361; Hb 4169]

astrologers [6], astrologer [1], Babylonians [1], Chaldean [1]

Ezr 5:12 he handed them over to Nebuchadnezzar the **Chaldean**, king of
Da 2:5 The king replied to the **astrologers**, "This is what I have firmly
2:10 The **astrologers** answered the king, "There is not a man on earth
2:10 asked such a thing of any magician or enchanter or **astrologer**.
3:8 At this time some **astrologers** came forward and denounced the
4:7 [4:4] the magicians, enchanters, **astrologers** and diviners came,
5:7 **astrologers** and diviners to be brought and said to these wise men
5:11 him chief of the magicians, enchanters, **astrologers** and diviners.
5:30 That very night Belshazzar, king of the **Babylonians**, was slain,

10374 כְּתַב k^{e}tab, v. [8] [→ 10375; Hb 4180]

wrote [4], read [1], was written [1], write down [1], wrote down [1]

Ezr 4:8 [J] Shimshai the secretary **wrote** a letter against Jerusalem to
5:7 [K] The report they sent him **read** as follows: To King Darius:
5:10 [J] so that *we could* **write down** the names of their leaders for
6:2 [K] in the province of Media, and this **was written** on it:
Da 5:5 [J] a human hand appeared and **wrote** on the plaster of the wall,
5:5 [J] in the royal palace. The king watched the hand as *it* **wrote**.
6:25 [6:26] [J] King Darius **wrote** to all the peoples, nations and men
7:1 [J] lying on his bed. *He* **wrote down** the substance of his dream.

10375 כְּתָב k^{e}tāb, n.m. [12] [√ 10374; Hb 4181]

writing [5], inscription [2], put in writing [+10673] [2], decree [1], limit [1], what written [1]

Ezr 6:18 at Jerusalem, according to **what** is **written** *in* the Book of Moses.
7:22 baths of wine, a hundred baths of olive oil, and salt without **limit**.
Da 5:7 "Whoever reads this **writing** and tells me what it means will be
5:8 but they could not read the **writing** or tell the king what it meant.
5:15 and enchanters were brought before me to read this **writing**
5:16 If you can read this **writing** and tell me what it means, you will be
5:17 I will read the **writing** for the king and tell him what it means.
5:24 Therefore he sent the hand that wrote the **inscription**.
5:25 "This is the **inscription** that was written: MENE, MENE,
6:8 [6:9] issue the decree and **put** it **in writing** [+10673] so that it
6:9 [6:10] So King Darius **put** the decree **in writing** [+10673].
6:10 [6:11] Now when Daniel learned that the **decree** had been

10376 כְּתַל k^{e}tal, n.[m.]. [2]

wall [1], walls [1]

Ezr 5:8 building it with large stones and placing the timbers in the **walls**.
Da 5:5 of a human hand appeared and wrote on the plaster of the **wall**,

ל, l

10377 ל l, letter. Not used in NIV/BHS [√ Hb 4199]

10378 -לְ l^e-, pp.pref. [356] [√ Hb 4200] Not indexed

untranslated [162], to [102], for [22], of [11], into [7], forever [+10550] [6], had [6], into [+10135] [6], in [3], against [2], as [2], before [+10619] [2], on [2], why [+10408] [2], against [+10608] [1], applied to [1], at [1], because of [+10168+10619] [1], by [1], extends to [1], forever [+10002+10550] [1], his [+10192] [1], in favor of [1], later [+10636] [1], near [+10619] [1], never [+10379+10550] [1], so that [1], summoned [+10042+10085+10378] [1], summoned [+10359+10378+10714] [1], together [+10154+10154] [1], toward [1], what [+10408] [1], will be left with [+10029] [1], with [+10619] [1], with [1]

10379 לָא lā', adv.neg. [82] [cf. 10384; Hb 4202]

not [38], no [10], *untranslated* [6], cannot [4], no [+10353] [4], without [4], nor [+10221] [3], never [2], before [1], neither [1], never [+10378+10550] [1], none [+10353] [1], nor [+10059+10221] [1], nothing [+10269] [1], nothing [1], rather than [1], unable [+10321] [1], unharmed [+10029+10089+10244] [1], weren't [1]

Ezr 4:13 its walls are restored, **no** *more* taxes, tribute or duty will be paid,
4:14 to the palace and it is **not** proper for us to see the king dishonored,
4:16 you will be left with **nothing** [+10269] in Trans-Euphrates.
4:21 to stop work, so that this city will **not** be rebuilt until I so order.
5:5 and they were **not** stopped until a report could go to Darius
5:16 the present it has been under construction but is **not** *yet* finished."
6:8 the revenues of Trans-Euphrates, so that the work will **not** stop.
6:9 the priests in Jerusalem—must be given them daily **without** fail,
7:22 baths of wine, a hundred baths of olive oil, and salt **without** limit.
7:24 You are also to know that you have **no** authority to impose taxes,
7:25 of your God. And you are to teach any who do **not** know them.
7:26 Whoever does **not** obey the law of your God and the law of the
Jer 10:11 'These gods, who did **not** make the heavens and the earth,
Da 2:5 If you do **not** tell me what my dream was and interpret it, I will
2:9 If you do **not** tell me the dream, there is just one penalty for you.
2:10 "There is **not** a man on earth who can do what the king asks!
2:10 **No** [+10353] king, however great and mighty, has ever asked such
2:11 **No** one can reveal it to the king except the gods, and they do not
2:11 it to the king except the gods, and they do **not** live among men."
2:18 his friends might **not** be executed with the rest of the wise men of
2:27 "**No** wise man, enchanter, magician or diviner can explain to the
2:30 **not** because I have greater wisdom than other living men,
2:34 you were watching, a rock was cut out, but **not** by human hands.
2:35 the summer. The wind swept them away **without** leaving a trace.
2:43 so the people will be a mixture and will **not** remain united,
2:43 not remain united, any more than iron **[RPH]** mixes with clay.
2:44 set up a kingdom that will **never** [+10378+10550] be destroyed,
2:44 will set up a kingdom that will never be destroyed, **nor** [+10221]
2:45 vision of the rock cut out of a mountain, but **not** by human hands—
3:6 Whoever does **not** fall down and worship will immediately be
3:11 that whoever does **not** fall down and worship will be thrown into a
3:12 Meshach and Abednego—who pay **no** attention to you, O king.
3:12 They **neither** serve your gods nor worship the image of gold you
3:12 They neither serve your gods **nor** [+10221] worship the image of
3:14 that you do **not** serve my gods or worship the image of gold I have
3:14 serve my gods or **[RPH]** worship the image of gold I have set up?
3:15 if you do **not** worship it, you will be thrown immediately into a
3:16 we do **not** need to defend ourselves before you in this matter.
3:18 even if he does **not**, we want you to know, O king, that we will not
3:18 that we will **not** serve your gods or worship the image of gold you
3:18 your gods or **[RPH]** worship the image of gold you have set up."
3:24 "**Weren't** there three men that we tied up and threw into the fire?"
3:25 in the fire, unbound and **unharmed** [+10029+10089+10244], and
3:27 They saw that the fire had **not** harmed their bodies, nor was a hair
3:27 They saw that the fire had not harmed their bodies, **nor** [+10221]
3:27 their robes were **not** scorched, and there was no smell of fire on
3:27 robes were not scorched, and there was **no** smell of fire on them.
3:28 and were willing to give up their lives **rather than** serve
3:28 than serve or **[RPH]** worship any god except their own God.
3:29 turned into piles of rubble, for **no** other god can save in this way."
4:7 [4:4] I told them the dream, but they could **not** interpret it for me.
4:9 [4:6] is in you, and **no** [+10353] mystery is too difficult for you.
4:18 [4:15] for **none** [+10353] *of* the wise men in my kingdom can
4:30 [4:27] "Is **not** this the great Babylon I have built as the royal
4:35 [4:32] All the peoples of the earth are regarded as **nothing**. He
4:35 [4:32] **No** one can hold back his hand or say to him: "What have
5:8 but they could **not** read the writing or tell the king what it meant.
5:15 and tell me what it means, but they could **not** explain it.

Da 5:22 "But you his son, O Belshazzar, have **not** humbled yourself,
5:23 iron, wood and stone, which **cannot** see or hear or understand.
5:23 and stone, which cannot see or **[RPH]** hear or understand.
5:23 and stone, which cannot see or hear or **[RPH]** understand.
5:23 But you did **not** honor the God who holds in his hand your life
6:2 [6:3] accountable to them so that the king might **not** suffer loss.
6:4 [6:5] but *they were* **unable** [+10321] to do so.
6:4 [6:5] They could find **no** corruption in him, because he was
6:5 [6:6] "We will **never** find any basis for charges against this man
6:8 [6:9] the decree and put it in writing so that it **cannot** be altered—
6:8 [6:9] laws of the Medes and Persians, which **cannot** be repealed."
6:12 [6:13] "Did you **not** publish a decree that during the next thirty
6:12 [6:13] of the Medes and Persians, which **cannot** be repealed."
6:13 [6:14] pays **no** attention to you, O king, or to the decree you put
6:15 [6:16] to the law of the Medes and Persians **no** [+10353] decree
6:17 [6:18] his nobles, so that Daniel's situation might **not** be changed.
6:18 [6:19] and **without** any entertainment being brought to him.
6:22 [6:23] They have **not** hurt me, because I was found innocent in
6:22 [6:23] I was found innocent in his sight. **Nor** [+10059+10221]
6:23 [6:24] when Daniel was lifted from the den, **no** [+10353] wound
6:24 [6:25] **before** they reached the floor of the den, the lions
6:26 [6:27] his kingdom will **not** be destroyed, his dominion will never
7:14 His dominion is an everlasting dominion that will **not** pass away,
7:14 pass away, and his kingdom is one that will **never** be destroyed.

10380 לֵב ***lēb***, n.m.]. [1] [√ 10381; Hb 4213]
myself [+10307] [1]

Da 7:28 and my face turned pale, but I kept the matter to **myself** [+10307]."

10381 לְבַב ***lᵉbab***, n.m. [7] [→ 10380; Hb 4222]
mind [3], heart [2], mind [+10669] [1], yourself [+10342] [1]

Da 2:30 that you may understand what went through your **mind** [+10669].
4:16 [4:13] Let his **mind** be changed from that of a man and let him be
4:16 [4:13] that of a man and let him be given the **mind** *of* an animal,
5:20 But when his **heart** became arrogant and hardened with pride,
5:21 He was driven away from people and given the **mind** of an animal;
5:22 you his son, O Belshazzar, have not humbled **yourself** [+10342],
7:4 on two feet like a man, and the **heart** *of* a man was given to it.

10382 לְבוּשׁ ***lᵉbûš***, n.m. [2] [√ 10383; Hb 4230]
clothes [1], clothing [1]

Da 3:21 trousers, turbans and other **clothes**, were bound and thrown into
7:9 His **clothing** was as white as snow; the hair of his head was white

10383 לְבַשׁ ***lᵉbaš***, v. [3] [→ 10382; Hb 4252]
clothed [3]

Da 5:7 [J] and tells me what it means *will be* **clothed** *in* purple
5:16 [J] *you will be* **clothed** *in* purple and have a gold chain placed
5:29 [P] at Belshazzar's command, Daniel *was* **clothed** *in* purple,

10384 לָה ***lâ***, adv.neg. Not used in NIV/BHS [cf. 10379; Hb 4202]

10385 לָהֵן ***lāhēn¹***, c. [3] [√ Hb 4270]
so then [1], so [1], therefore [1]

Da 2:6 and great honor. **So** tell me the dream and interpret it for me."
2:9 **So then**, tell me the dream, and I will know that you can interpret
4:27 [4:24] **Therefore**, O king, be pleased to accept my advice:

10386 ²לָהֵן ***lāhēn²***, c. [7] [√ 10379 & 10214]
except [4], but [2], unless [1]

Ezr 5:12 **But** because our fathers angered the God of heaven, he handed
Da 2:11 No one can reveal it to the king **except** the gods, and they do not
2:30 **but** so that you, O king, may know the interpretation and that you
3:28 lives rather than serve or worship any god **except** their own God.
6:5 [6:6] **unless** it has something to do with the law of his God."
6:7 [6:8] **except** to you, O king, shall be thrown into the lions' den.
6:12 [6:13] days anyone who prays to any god or man **except** to you,

10387 לֵוָי ***lēwāy***, n.g. [4] [√ Hb 4290, 4291]
Levites [4]

Ezr 6:16 of Israel—the priests, the **Levites** and the rest of the exiles—
6:18 and the **Levites** in their groups for the service of God at Jerusalem,
7:13 including priests and **Levites**, who wish to go to Jerusalem with
7:24 **Levites**, singers, gatekeepers, temple servants or other workers at

10388 לְוָת ***lᵉwāt***, pp. [1] [cf. 10378 + 10337]
from [+10427] [1]

Ezr 4:12 who came up to us **from** [+10427] you have gone to Jerusalem

10389 לְחֶם ***lᵉḥem***, n.m. [1] [√ Hb 4312]
banquet [1]

Da 5:1 King Belshazzar gave a great **banquet** for a thousand of his nobles

10390 לְחֵנָה ***lᵉḥēnâ***, n.f. [3]
concubines [3]

Da 5:2 his nobles, his wives and his **concubines** might drink from them.
5:3 and his nobles, his wives and his **concubines** drank from them.
5:23 your wives and your **concubines** drank wine from them.

10391 לֵילֵי ***lêlê***, n.[m.]. [5] [√ Hb 4325]
night [5]

Da 2:19 During the **night** the mystery was revealed to Daniel in a vision.
5:30 That very **night** Belshazzar, king of the Babylonians, was slain,
7:2 "In my vision at **night** I looked, and there before me were the four
7:7 "After that, in my vision at **night** I looked, and there before me
7:13 "In my vision at **night** I looked, and there before me was one like a

10392 לִשָּׁן ***liššān***, n.m. [7] [√ Hb 4383]
men of every language [6], language [1]

Da 3:4 commanded to do, O peoples, nations and **men of every language**:
3:7 nations and **men of every language** fell down and worshiped the
3:29 or **language** who say anything against the God of Shadrach,
4:1 [3:31] To the peoples, nations and **men of every language**,
5:19 all the peoples and nations and **men of every language** dreaded
6:25 [6:26] nations and **men of every language** throughout the land:
7:14 all peoples, nations and **men of every language** worshiped him.

מ, m

10393 מ ***m***, letter. Not used in NIV/BHS [√ Hb 4391]

10394 מָא ***mā'***, p.inter. & indef. Not used in NIV/BHS [√ 10408; Hb 4537]

10395 מְאָה ***mᵉ'â***, n.f. [8] [√ Hb 4395, 4396]
hundred [7], 120 [+10221+10574] [1]

Ezr 6:17 For the dedication of this house of God they offered a **hundred**
6:17 *two* **hundred** rams, four hundred male lambs and, as a sin offering
6:17 two hundred rams, four **hundred** male lambs and, as a sin offering
7:22 up to a **hundred** talents of silver, a hundred cors of wheat,
7:22 a **hundred** cors of wheat, a hundred baths of wine, a hundred baths
7:22 a hundred cors of wheat, a **hundred** baths of wine, a hundred baths
7:22 baths of wine, a **hundred** baths of olive oil, and salt without limit.
Da 6:1 [6:2] It pleased Darius to appoint **120** [+10221+10574] satraps to

10396 מֹאזְנֵא ***mō'znē'***, n.m.emph. [1] [√ Hb 4404]
scales [1]

Da 5:27 You have been weighed on the **scales** and found wanting.

10397 מֵאמַר ***mē'mar***, n.[m.]. [2] [√ 10042; Hb 4411]
declare [1], requested [1]

Ezr 6:9 salt, wine and oil, as **requested** *by* the priests in Jerusalem—
Da 4:17 [4:14] by messengers, the holy ones **declare** the verdict,

10398 מָאן ***mā'n***, n.m. [7]
articles [4], goblets [3]

Ezr 5:14 temple of Babylon the gold and silver **articles** of the house of God,
5:15 'Take these **articles** and go and deposit them in the temple in
6:5 Also, the gold and silver **articles** *of* the house of God, which
7:19 Deliver to the God of Jerusalem *all* the **articles** entrusted to you
Da 5:2 silver **goblets** that Nebuchadnezzar his father had taken from the
5:3 So they brought in the gold **goblets** that had been taken from the
5:23 You had the **goblets** from his temple brought to you, and you

10399 מְגִלָּה ***mᵉgillâ***, n.f. [1] [√ 10146; Hb 4479]
scroll [1]

Ezr 6:2 A **scroll** was found in the citadel of Ecbatana in the province of

10400 מְגַר mᵉgar, v. [1] [√ Hb 4489]

overthrow [1]

Ezr 6:12 [M] *May* God, who has caused his Name to dwell there, **overthrow**

10401 מַדְבַּח madbaḥ, n.[m.]. [1] [√ 10156; Hb 4640]

altar [1]

Ezr 7:17 sacrifice them on the **altar** of the temple of your God in Jerusalem.

10402 מִדָּה middâ, n.f. [4] [cf. 10429; Hb 4501]

taxes [3], revenues [1]

Ezr 4:13 its walls are restored, no more **taxes**, tribute or duty will be paid,
4:20 of Trans-Euphrates, and **taxes**, tribute and duty were paid to them.
6:8 from the **revenues** *of* Trans-Euphrates, so that the work will not
7:24 You are also to know that you have no authority to impose **taxes**,

10403 מְדוֹר mᵉdôr, n.[m.]. [3] [√ 10163]

live [2], lived [1]

Da 4:25 [4:22] away from people and will **live** with the wild animals;
4:32 [4:29] away from people and will **live** with the wild animals;
5:21 an animal; he **lived** with the wild donkeys and ate grass like cattle;

10404 מָדַי māday, n.pr.g. [6] [→ 10405; Hb 4512]

Medes [4], Mede [1], Media [1]

Ezr 6:2 was found in the citadel of Ecbatana in the province of **Media**,
Da 5:28 Your kingdom is divided and given to the **Medes** and Persians."
5:31 [6:1] Darius the **Mede** took over the kingdom, at the age of
6:8 [6:9] in accordance with the laws of the **Medes** and Persians,
6:12 [6:13] in accordance with the laws of the **Medes** and Persians,
6:15 [6:16] that according to the law of the **Medes** and Persians no

10405 מָדָיָא mādāyā', n.g. Not used in NIV/BHS [√ 10404; Hb 4512]

10406 מְדִינָה mᵉdînâ, n.f. [11] [√ 10169; Hb 4519]

province [7], provincial [2], district [1], provinces [1]

Ezr 4:15 troublesome to kings and **provinces**, a place of rebellion from
5:8 The king should know that we went to the **district** of Judah,
6:2 A scroll was found in the citadel of Ecbatana in the **province** of
7:16 the silver and gold you may obtain from the **province** *of* Babylon,
Da 2:48 He made him ruler over the entire **province** *of* Babylon and placed
2:49 and Abednego administrators over the **province** *of* Babylon,
3:1 and set it up on the plain of Dura in the **province** *of* Babylon.
3:2 all the other **provincial** officials to come to the dedication of
3:3 all the other **provincial** officials assembled for the dedication of
3:12 whom you have set over the affairs of the **province** *of* Babylon—
3:30 Meshach and Abednego in the **province** *of* Babylon.

10407 מְדָר mᵉdār, n.m. [1] [√ 10163]

live [1]

Da 2:11 it to the king except the gods, and they do not **live** among men."

10408 מָה mâ, p.inter. & indef. [14] [→ 10308; cf. 10426; Hb 4537]

what [5], how [+10341] [2], why [+10378] [2], things [1], what [+10378] [1], whatever [+10168] [1], whatever [1], why [+10542] [1]

Ezr 4:22 Be careful not to neglect this matter. **Why** [+10378] let this threat
6:8 I hereby decree **what** [+10378] you are to do for these elders of the
6:9 **Whatever** is needed—young bulls, rams, male lambs for burnt
7:18 then do **whatever** [+10168] seems best with the rest of the silver
7:23 with diligence for the temple of the God of heaven. **Why** [+10378]
Da 2:15 He asked the king's officer, "**Why** [+10542] did the king issue
2:22 he knows **what** lies in darkness, and light dwells with him.
2:28 He has shown King Nebuchadnezzar **what** will happen in days to
2:29 you were lying there, O king, your mind turned to **things** to come,
2:29 and the revealer of mysteries showed you **what** is going to happen.
2:45 "The great God has shown the king **what** will take place in the
4:3 [3:33] **How** [+10341] great are his signs, how mighty his
4:3 [3:33] How great are his signs, **how** [+10341] mighty his
4:35 [4:32] hold back his hand or say to him: "**What** have you done?"

10409 מוֹת môt, n.[m.]. [1] [√ Hb 4638]

death [1]

Ezr 7:26 and the law of the king must surely be punished by **death**,

10410 מָזוֹן māzôn, n.[m.]. [2] [√ 10226; Hb 2315]

food [2]

Da 4:12 [4:9] were beautiful, its fruit abundant, and on it was **food** for all.
4:21 [4:18] beautiful leaves and abundant fruit, providing **food** for all,

10411 מְחָא mᵉḥā', v. [4] [√ Hb 4730]

struck [2], hold back [1], impaled [1]

Ezr 6:11 [L] from his house and he is to be lifted up and **impaled** on it.
Da 2:34 [J] *It* **struck** the statue on its feet of iron and clay and smashed
2:35 [J] But the rock that **struck** the statue became a huge mountain
4:35 [4:32] [M] No one *can* **hold back** his hand or say to him:

10412 מַחְלְקָה maḥlᵉqâ, n.f. [1] [√ 10269; Hb 4713]

groups [1]

Ezr 6:18 and the Levites in their **groups** for the service of God at Jerusalem,

10413 מְטָא mᵉṭā', v. [8] [→]

approached [1], came [1], happened [1], issued [1], reached [1], reaches [1], touched [1], touching [1]

Da 4:11 [4:8] [J] tree grew large and strong and its top **touched** the sky;
4:20 [4:17] [J] grew large and strong, with its top **touching** the sky,
4:22 [4:19] [J] your greatness has grown until *it* **reaches** the sky,
4:24 [4:21] [J] this is the decree the Most High *has* **issued** against my
4:28 [4:25] [J] All this **happened** to King Nebuchadnezzar.
6:24 [6:25] [J] before *they* **reached** the floor of the den, the lions
7:13 [J] *He* **approached** the Ancient of Days and was led into his
7:22 [J] and the time **came** when they possessed the kingdom.

10414 מִישָׁאֵל mîšā'ēl, n.pr.m. [1] [√ Hb 4792]

Mishael [1]

Da 2:17 explained the matter to his friends Hananiah, **Mishael** and Azariah.

10415 מֵישַׁךְ mêšak, n.pr.m. [14] [√ Hb 4794]

Meshach [13], *untranslated* [1]

Da 2:49 **Meshach** and Abednego administrators over the province of
3:12 Shadrach, **Meshach** and Abednego—who pay no attention to you,
3:13 Nebuchadnezzar summoned Shadrach, **Meshach** and Abednego.
3:14 "Is it true, Shadrach, **Meshach** and Abednego, that you do not
3:16 Shadrach, **Meshach** and Abednego replied to the king,
3:19 **Meshach** and Abednego, and his attitude toward them changed.
3:20 **Meshach** and Abednego and throw them into the blazing furnace.
3:22 killed the soldiers who took up Shadrach, **Meshach** and Abednego,
3:23 these three men, **[RPH]** firmly tied, fell into the blazing furnace.
3:26 blazing furnace and shouted, "Shadrach, **Meshach** and Abednego,
3:26 So Shadrach, **Meshach** and Abednego came out of the fire,
3:28 **Meshach** and Abednego, who has sent his angel and rescued his
3:29 **Meshach** and Abednego be cut into pieces and their houses be
3:30 **Meshach** and Abednego in the province of Babylon.

10416 מְלָא mᵉlā', v. [2] [√ Hb 4848]

filled [1], furious [+10270] [1]

Da 2:35 [J] the statue became a huge mountain and **filled** the whole earth.
3:19 [L] Then Nebuchadnezzar *was* **furious with** [+10270] Shadrach,

10417 מַלְאַךְ mal'ak, n.m. [2] [√ Hb 4855]

angel [2]

Da 3:28 and Abednego, who has sent his **angel** and rescued his servants!
6:22 [6:23] My God sent his **angel**, and he shut the mouths of the lions.

10418 מִלָּה millâ, n.f. [24] [√ 10425; Hb 4863]

matter [4], words [3], command [2], decided [2], things [2], decree [1], dream[s] [1], it[s] [+10002] [1], speak [+10425] [1], substance [+10646] [1], thing [1], this[s] [+10002] [1], voices [1], what asks [1], what said [1], what[s] [+10002] [1]

Da 2:5 replied to the astrologers, "This is what I have firmly **decided**:
2:8 because you realize that this is what I have firmly **decided**:
2:9 You have conspired to tell me misleading and wicked **things**,
2:10 "There is not a man on earth who can do **what** the king **asks**!
2:10 has ever asked such a **thing** of any magician or enchanter
2:11 **What**[s] [+10002] the king asks is too difficult. No one can reveal it
2:15 such a harsh decree?" Arioch then explained the **matter** to Daniel.
2:17 to his house and explained the **matter** to his friends Hananiah,
2:23 asked of you, you have made known to us the **dream**[s] *of* the king."
3:22 The king's **command** was so urgent and the furnace so hot that the
3:28 They trusted in him and defied the king's **command** and were
4:31 [4:28] The **words** were still on his lips when a voice came from
4:33 [4:30] Immediately **what** had been **said** about Nebuchadnezzar

Da 5:10 The queen, hearing the **voices** *of* the king and his nobles, came into
5:15 and tell me what it means, but they could not explain **it**[s] [+10002].
5:26 "This is *what* these **words** mean: *Mene*: God has numbered the
6:12 [6:13] The king answered, "The **decree** stands—in accordance
6:14 [6:15] When the king heard **this**[s] [+10002], he was greatly
7:1 on his bed. He wrote down the **substance** [+10646] of his dream.
7:11 to watch because of the boastful **words** the horn was speaking.
7:16 "So he told me and gave me the interpretation of these **things**:
7:25 *He will* **speak** [+10425] against the Most High and oppress his
7:28 "This is the end of the **matter**. I, Daniel, was deeply troubled by
7:28 and my face turned pale, but I kept the **matter** to myself."

10419 ¹מְלַח ***m[e]laḥ[1]***, v.den. [1] [→ 10420; Hb 4873]
under obligation [+10420] [1]

Ezr 4:14 [J] Now since *we are* **under obligation** [+10420] *to* the palace

10420 ²מְלַח ***m[e]laḥ[2]***, n.m. [3] [√ 10419; Hb 4875]
salt [2], under obligation [+10419] [1]

Ezr 4:14 Now since *we are* **under obligation to** [+10419] the palace
6:9 wheat, **salt**, wine and oil, as requested by the priests in Jerusalem—
7:22 baths of wine, a hundred baths of olive oil, and **salt** without limit.

10421 מֶ֫לֶךְ ***melek***, n.m. [180] [→ 10423, 10424; Hb 4889]
king [137], kings [11], royal [9], king's [6], *untranslated* [4], he[s] [+10002] [3], him[s] [+10002] [3], he[s] [+10002+10453] [2], his[s] [+10002] [2], kingdoms [1], royal interests [1], them[s] [1]

Ezr 4:8 wrote a letter against Jerusalem to Artaxerxes the **king** as follows:
4:11 To **King** Artaxerxes, From your servants, the men of
4:12 The **king** should know that the Jews who came up to us from you
4:13 the **king** should know that if this city is built and its walls are
4:13 tribute or duty will be paid, and the **royal** revenues will suffer.
4:14 to the palace and it is not proper for us to see the **king** dishonored,
4:14 king dishonored, we are sending this message to inform the **king**,
4:15 troublesome to **kings** and provinces, a place of rebellion from
4:16 We inform the **king** that if this city is built and its walls are
4:17 The **king** sent this reply: To Rehum the commanding officer,
4:19 it was found that this city has a long history of revolt against **kings**
4:20 Jerusalem has had powerful **kings** ruling over the whole of
4:22 Why let this threat grow, to the detriment of the **royal interests**?
4:23 As soon as the copy of the letter of **King** Artaxerxes was read to
4:24 until the second year of the reign of Darius **king** *of* Persia.
5:6 the officials of Trans-Euphrates, sent to **King** Darius.
5:7 they sent him read as follows: To **King** Darius: Cordial greetings.
5:8 The **king** should know that we went to the district of Judah,
5:11 many years ago, one that a great **king** of Israel built and finished.
5:12 **king** *of* Babylon, who destroyed this temple and deported the
5:13 "However, in the first year of Cyrus **king** of Babylon, King Cyrus
5:13 **King** Cyrus issued a decree to rebuild this house of God.
5:14 "Then **King** Cyrus gave them to a man named Sheshbazzar,
5:17 Now if it pleases the **king**, let a search be made in the royal
5:17 let a search be made in the **royal** archives of Babylon to see if
5:17 let a search be made in the royal archives of Babylon to see if **King**
5:17 in Jerusalem. Then let the **king** send us his decision in this matter.
6:1 **King** Darius then issued an order, and they searched in the
6:3 In the first year of **King** Cyrus, the king issued a decree concerning
6:3 the **king** issued a decree concerning the temple of God in
6:4 and one of timbers. The costs are to be paid by the **royal** treasury.
6:8 The expenses of these men are to be fully paid out of the **royal**
6:10 of heaven and pray for the well-being of the **king** and his sons.
6:12 overthrow any **king** or people who lifts a hand to change this
6:13 Then, because of the decree **King** Darius had sent, Tattenai,
6:14 and the decrees of Cyrus, Darius and Artaxerxes, **kings** *of* Persia.
6:15 of the month Adar, in the sixth year of the reign of **King** Darius.
7:12 Artaxerxes, **king** *of* kings, To Ezra the priest, a teacher of the Law
7:12 Artaxerxes, king of **kings**, To Ezra the priest, a teacher of the Law
7:14 You are sent by the **king** and his seven advisers to inquire about
7:15 you are to take with you the silver and gold that the **king** and his
7:20 have occasion to supply, you may provide from the **royal** treasury.
7:21 Now I, **King** Artaxerxes, order all the treasurers of
7:23 Why should there be wrath against the realm of the **king** and of his
7:26 and the law of the **king** must surely be punished by death,
Da 2:4 astrologers answered the king in Aramaic, "O **king**, live forever!
2:5 The **king** replied to the astrologers, "This is what I have firmly
2:7 Once more they replied, "Let the **king** tell his servants the dream,
2:8 the **king** answered, "I am certain that you are trying to gain time,
2:10 The astrologers answered the **king**, "There is not a man on earth
2:10 "There is not a man on earth who can do what the **king** asks!
2:10 No **king**, however great and mighty, has ever asked such a thing of
2:11 What the **king** asks is too difficult. No one can reveal it to the king
2:11 No one can reveal it to the **king** except the gods, and they do not
2:12 This made the **king** so angry and furious that he ordered the
2:14 When Arioch, the commander of the **king's** guard, had gone out to
2:15 He asked the **king's** officer, "Why did the king issue such a harsh
2:15 the king's officer, "Why did the **king** issue such a harsh decree?"
2:16 At this, Daniel went in to the **king** and asked for time, so that he
2:16 for time, so that he might interpret the dream for **him**[s] [+10002].
2:21 He changes times and seasons; he sets up **kings** and deposes them.
2:21 changes times and seasons; he sets up kings and deposes **them**[s].
2:23 asked of you, you have made known to us the dream of the **king**."
2:24 whom the **king** had appointed to execute the wise men of Babylon,
2:24 Take me to the **king**, and I will interpret his dream for him."
2:24 me to the king, and I will interpret his dream for **him**[s] [+10002]."
2:25 Arioch took Daniel to the **king** at once and said, "I have found a
2:25 exiles from Judah who can tell the **king** what his dream means."
2:26 The **king** asked Daniel (also called Belteshazzar), "Are you able to
2:27 **[RPH]** "No wise man, enchanter, magician or diviner can explain
2:27 or diviner can explain to the **king** the mystery he has asked about,
2:27 or diviner can explain to the king the mystery **he**[s] [+10002] has
2:28 He has shown **King** Nebuchadnezzar what will happen in days to
2:29 "As you were lying there, O **king**, your mind turned to things to
2:30 so that you, O **king**, may know the interpretation and that you may
2:31 "You looked, O **king**, and there before you stood a large statue—
2:36 "This was the dream, and now we will interpret it to the **king**.
2:37 You, O **king**, are the king of kings. The God of heaven has given
2:37 You, O king, are the **king** *of* kings. The God of heaven has given
2:37 You, O king, are the king of **kings**. The God of heaven has given
2:44 "In the time of those **kings**, the God of heaven will set up a
2:45 "The great God has shown the **king** what will take place in the
2:46 **King** Nebuchadnezzar fell prostrate before Daniel and paid him
2:47 The **king** said to Daniel, "Surely your God is the God of gods
2:47 the God of gods and the Lord of **kings** and a revealer of mysteries,
2:48 the **king** placed Daniel in a high position and lavished many gifts
2:49 at Daniel's request the **king** appointed Shadrach, Meshach
2:49 of Babylon, while Daniel himself remained at the **royal** court.
3:1 **King** Nebuchadnezzar made an image of gold, ninety feet high
3:2 **He**[s] [+10002+10453] then summoned the satraps, prefects,
3:2 to the dedication of the image **he**[s] [+10002+10453] had set up.
3:3 the dedication of the image that **King** Nebuchadnezzar had set up,
3:5 worship the image of gold that **King** Nebuchadnezzar has set up.
3:7 worshiped the image of gold that **King** Nebuchadnezzar had set up.
3:9 They said to **King** Nebuchadnezzar, "O king, live forever!
3:9 They said to King Nebuchadnezzar, "O **king**, live forever!
3:10 You have issued a decree, O **king**, that everyone who hears the
3:12 Meshach and Abednego—who pay no attention to you, O **king**.
3:13 and Abednego. So these men were brought before the **king**,
3:16 Shadrach, Meshach and Abednego replied to the **king**,
3:17 to save us from it, and he will rescue us from your hand, O **king**.
3:18 even if he does not, we want you to know, O **king**, that we will not
3:22 The **king's** command was so urgent and the furnace so hot that the
3:24 Then **King** Nebuchadnezzar leaped to his feet in amazement
3:24 threw into the fire?" They replied, **[RPH]** "Certainly, O king."
3:24 and threw into the fire?" They replied, "Certainly, O **king**."
3:27 prefects, governors and **royal** advisers crowded around them.
3:28 They trusted in him and defied the **king's** command and were
3:30 the **king** promoted Shadrach, Meshach and Abednego in the
4:1 [3:31] **King** Nebuchadnezzar, To the peoples, nations and men of
4:18 [4:15] "This is the dream that I, **King** Nebuchadnezzar, had. Now,
4:19 [4:16] So the **king** said, "Belteshazzar, do not let the dream or its
4:22 [4:19] you, O **king**, are that tree! You have become great
4:23 [4:20] "You, O **king**, saw a messenger, a holy one, coming down
4:24 [4:21] "This is the interpretation, O **king**, and this is the decree
4:24 [4:21] decree the Most High has issued against my lord the **king**:
4:27 [4:24] Therefore, O **king**, be pleased to accept my advice:
4:28 [4:25] All this happened to **King** Nebuchadnezzar.
4:30 [4:27] **he**[s] [+10002] said, "Is not this the great Babylon I have
4:31 [4:28] The words were still on **his**[s] [+10002] lips when a voice
4:31 [4:28] "This is what is decreed for you, **King** Nebuchadnezzar:
4:37 [4:34] praise and exalt and glorify the **King** *of* heaven,
5:1 **King** Belshazzar gave a great banquet for a thousand of his nobles
5:2 so that the **king** and his nobles, his wives and his concubines might
5:3 the **king** and his nobles, his wives and his concubines drank from
5:5 on the plaster of the wall, near the lampstand in the **royal** palace.
5:5 in the royal palace. The **king** watched the hand as it wrote.
5:6 **His**[s] [+10002] face turned pale and he was so frightened that his
5:7 The **king** called out for the enchanters, astrologers and diviners to
5:7 to be brought and said **[RPH]** to these wise men of Babylon,
5:8 all the **king's** wise men came in, but they could not read the
5:8 but they could not read the writing or tell the **king** what it meant.
5:9 So **King** Belshazzar became even more terrified and his face grew
5:10 The queen, hearing the voices of the **king** and his nobles,
5:10 "O **king**, live forever!" she said. "Don't be alarmed! Don't look
5:11 **King** Nebuchadnezzar your father—your father the king, I say—
5:11 King Nebuchadnezzar your father—your father the **king**, I say—
5:12 This man Daniel, whom the **king** called Belteshazzar, was found to
5:13 So Daniel was brought before the **king**, and the king said to him,

Da 5: 13 brought before the king, and the **king** said to him, "Are you Daniel,
5: 13 one of the exiles my father the **king** brought from Judah?
5: 17 Daniel answered the **king**, "You may keep your gifts for yourself
5: 17 I will read the writing for the **king** and tell him what it means.
5: 18 "O **king**, the Most High God gave your father Nebuchadnezzar
5: 30 That very night Belshazzar, **king** *of* the Babylonians, was slain,
6: 2 [6:3] accountable to them so that the **king** might not suffer loss.
6: 3 [6:4] the satraps by his exceptional qualities that the **king** planned
6: 6 [6:7] and the satraps went as a group to the **king** and said:
6: 6 [6:7] a group to the king and said: "O **King** Darius, live forever!
6: 7 [6:8] governors have all agreed that the **king** should issue an edict
6: 7 [6:8] except to you, O **king**, shall be thrown into the lions' den.
6: 8 [6:9] Now, O **king**, issue the decree and put it in writing so that it
6: 9 [6:10] So **King** Darius put the decree in writing.
6: 12 [6:13] So they went to the **king** and spoke to him about his royal
6: 12 [6:13] went to the king and spoke to him about his **royal** decree:
6: 12 [6:13] who prays to any god or man except to you, O **king**,
6: 12 [6:13] The **king** answered, "The decree stands—in accordance
6: 13 [6:14] they said to the **king**, "Daniel, who is one of the exiles
6: 13 [6:14] pays no attention to you, O **king**, or to the decree you put
6: 14 [6:15] When the **king** heard this, he was greatly distressed; he
6: 15 [6:16] Then the men went as a group to the **king** and said to him,
6: 15 [6:16] went as a group to the king and said to **him**[s] [+10002],
6: 15 [6:16] a group to the king and said to him, "Remember, O **king**,
6: 15 [6:16] no decree or edict that the **king** issues can be changed."
6: 16 [6:17] So the **king** gave the order, and they brought Daniel
6: 16 [6:17] The **king** said to Daniel, "May your God, whom you serve
6: 17 [6:18] the **king** sealed it with his own signet ring and with the
6: 18 [6:19] the **king** returned to his palace and spent the night without
6: 19 [6:20] light of dawn, the **king** got up and hurried to the lions' den.
6: 20 [6:21] **he**[s] [+10002] called to Daniel in an anguished voice,
6: 21 [6:22] Daniel answered, **[RPH]** "O king, live forever!
6: 21 [6:22] Daniel answered, "O **king**, live forever!
6: 22 [6:23] Nor have I ever done any wrong before you, O **king**."
6: 23 [6:24] The **king** was overjoyed and gave orders to lift Daniel out
6: 24 [6:25] At the **king's** command, the men who had falsely accused
6: 25 [6:26] **King** Darius wrote to all the peoples, nations and men of
7: 1 In the first year of Belshazzar **king** *of* Babylon, Daniel had a
7: 17 'The four great beasts are four **kingdoms** that will rise from the
7: 24 The ten horns are ten **kings** who will come from this kingdom.
7: 24 different from the earlier ones; he will subdue three **kings**.

10422 מְלַךְ m^e lak, n.m. [1] [√ Hb 4888]

advice [1]

Da 4: 27 [4:24] Therefore, O king, be pleased to accept my **advice**:

10423 מַלְכָּה malkâ, n.f. [2] [√ 10421; Hb 4893]

queen [1], she[s] [+10002] [1]

Da 5: 10 The **queen**, hearing the voices of the king and his nobles,
5: 10 "O king, live forever!" **she**[s] [+10002] said. "Don't be alarmed!

10424 מַלְכוּ malkû, n.f. [57] [√ 10421; Hb 4895]

kingdom [30], kingdoms [7], reign [5], royal [4], sovereignty [2], *untranslated* [1], dominion [1], government affairs [1], it[s] [+10002] [1], it[s] [+10191] [1], realm [1], royal authority [1], sovereign power [1], throne [1]

Ezr 4: 24 until the second year of the **reign** *of* Darius king of Persia.
6: 15 of the month Adar, in the sixth year of the **reign** *of* King Darius.
7: 13 Now I decree that any of the Israelites in my **kingdom**,
7: 23 Why should there be wrath against the **realm** *of* the king and of his
Da 2: 37 The God of heaven has given you **dominion** and power and might
2: 39 "After you, another **kingdom** will rise, inferior to yours. Next,
2: 39 Next, a third **kingdom**, one of bronze, will rule over the whole
2: 40 Finally, there will be a fourth **kingdom**, strong as iron—for iron
2: 41 of baked clay and partly of iron, so this will be a divided **kingdom**;
2: 42 partly clay, so this **kingdom** will be partly strong and partly brittle.
2: 44 the God of heaven will set up a **kingdom** that will never be
2: 44 never be destroyed, nor will **it**[s] [+10191] be left to another people.
2: 44 It will crush all those **kingdoms** and bring them to an end,
4: 3 [3:33] His **kingdom** is an eternal kingdom; his dominion endures
4: 3 [3:33] His kingdom is an eternal **kingdom**; his dominion endures
4: 17 [4:14] that the Most High is sovereign over the **kingdoms** *of* men
4: 18 [4:15] for none of the wise men in my **kingdom** can interpret it
4: 25 [4:22] that the Most High is sovereign over the **kingdoms** *of* men
4: 26 [4:23] **kingdom** will be restored to you when you acknowledge
4: 29 [4:26] as the king was walking on the roof of the **royal** palace of
4: 30 [4:27] "Is not this the great Babylon I have built as the **royal**
4: 31 [4:28] Your **royal authority** has been taken from you.
4: 32 [4:29] that the Most High is sovereign over the **kingdoms** *of* men
4: 34 [4:31] his **kingdom** endures from generation to generation.
4: 36 [4:33] splendor were returned to me for the glory of my **kingdom**.
4: 36 [4:33] I was restored to my **throne** and became even greater than
5: 7 and he will be made the third highest ruler in the **kingdom**."
5: 11 There is a man in your **kingdom** who has the spirit of the holy
5: 16 and you will be made the third highest ruler in the **kingdom**."
5: 18 the Most High God gave your father Nebuchadnezzar **sovereignty**
5: 20 he was deposed from his **royal** throne and stripped of his glory.
5: 21 that the Most High God is sovereign over the **kingdoms** *of* men
5: 26 God has numbered the days of your **reign** and brought it to an end.
5: 28 Your **kingdom** is divided and given to the Medes and Persians."
5: 29 and he was proclaimed the third highest ruler in the **kingdom**.
5: 31 [6:1] Darius the Mede took over the **kingdom**, at the age of
6: 1 [6:2] It pleased Darius to appoint 120 satraps to rule **[RPH]**
6: 1 [6:2] to appoint 120 satraps to rule throughout the **kingdom**,
6: 3 [6:4] that the king planned to set him over the whole **kingdom**.
6: 4 [6:5] against Daniel in his conduct of **government affairs**,
6: 7 [6:8] The **royal** administrators, prefects, satraps, advisers and
6: 26 [6:27] "I issue a decree that in every part of my **kingdom** people
6: 26 [6:27] his **kingdom** will not be destroyed, his dominion will never
6: 28 [6:29] So Daniel prospered during the **reign** *of* Darius and the
6: 28 [6:29] the reign of Darius and the **reign** *of* Cyrus the Persian.
7: 14 He was given authority, glory and **sovereign power**; all peoples,
7: 14 pass away, and his **kingdom** is one that will never be destroyed.
7: 18 But the saints of the Most High will receive the **kingdom**
7: 18 will receive the kingdom and will possess **it**[s] [+10002] forever—
7: 22 Most High, and the time came when they possessed the **kingdom**.
7: 23 'The fourth beast is a fourth **kingdom** that will appear on earth.
7: 23 It will be different from all the other **kingdoms** and will devour the
7: 24 The ten horns are ten kings who will come from this **kingdom**.
7: 27 the **sovereignty**, power and greatness of the kingdoms under the
7: 27 greatness of the **kingdoms** under the whole heaven will be handed
7: 27 His **kingdom** will be an everlasting kingdom, and all rulers will
7: 27 His kingdom will be an everlasting **kingdom**, and all rulers will

10425 מַלֵּל m^e lal, v. [5] [→ 10418; Hb 4910]

spoke [2], answered [1], speak [+10418] [1], speaking [1]

Da 6: 21 [6:22] [M] Daniel **answered**, "O king, live forever!
7: 8 [M] like the eyes of a man and a mouth *that* **spoke** boastfully.
7: 11 [M] because of the boastful words the horn *was* **speaking**.
7: 20 [M] and that had eyes and a mouth *that* **spoke** boastfully.
7: 25 [M] *He will* **speak** [+10418] against the Most High and oppress

10426 מַן man, p.inter. & indef. [10] [cf. 10408; Hb 4943]

anyone [+10168] [4], what [2], who [2], whoever [+10168] [2]

Ezr 5: 3 "**Who** authorized you to rebuild this temple and restore this
5: 4 "**What** are the names of the men constructing this building?"
5: 9 "**Who** authorized you to rebuild this temple and restore this
Da 3: 6 **Whoever** [+10168] does not fall down and worship will
3: 11 that **whoever** [+10168] does not fall down and worship will be
3: 15 Then **what** god will be able to rescue you from my hand?"
4: 17 [4:14] gives them to **anyone** [+10168] he wishes and sets over
4: 25 [4:22] of men and gives them to **anyone** [+10168] he wishes.
4: 32 [4:29] of men and gives them to **anyone** [+10168] he wishes."
5: 21 kingdoms of men and sets over them **anyone** [+10168] he wishes.

10427 מִן min, pp. [119] [√ Hb 4946] See Select Index

from [41], *untranslated* [21], of [8], partly [7], to [5], with [3], because of [2], before [+10621] [2], from [+10621] [2], one [2], out of [2], according to [1], ago [+10180+10622] [1], among [1], as soon as [+10008+10168] [1], because [+10168] [1], before [+10180+10622] [1], by [+10621] [1], by [1], certain [+10313+10327] [1], for [1], from [+10388] [1], greater than [1], in [+10608] [1], issue [+10621] [1], long history [+10317+10550] [1], more than [1], of [+10135] [1], on [1], over [+10543] [1], partly [+10636] [1], prescribed [+10302] [1], some [1], surely [+10168+10643] [1], when [+10168] [1]

10428 מְנֵא m^e nē', n.[m.]. [3] [√ 10431; Hb 4948]

mene [3]

Da 5: 25 inscription that was written: **MENE**, MENE, TEKEL, PARSIN
5: 25 inscription that was written: MENE, **MENE**, TEKEL, PARSIN
5: 26 "This is what these words mean: ***Mene***: God has numbered the

10429 מִנְדָּה mindâ, n.f. Not used in NIV/BHS [cf. 10402]

10430 מַנְדַּע manda', n.[m.]. [4] [√ 10313; Hb 4529]

knowledge [2], sanity [2]

Da 2: 21 He gives wisdom to the wise and **knowledge** to the discerning.
4: 34 [4:31] raised my eyes toward heaven, and my **sanity** was restored.
4: 36 [4:33] At the same time that my **sanity** was restored, my honor
5: 12 was found to have a keen mind and **knowledge** and understanding,

10431 מְנָה *m^{e}nâ*, v. [5] [→ 10428, 10433; Hb 4948]

appointed [2], appoint [1], numbered [1], set [1]

Ezr 7:25 [M] **appoint** magistrates and judges to administer justice to all
Da 2:24 [M] whom the king *had* **appointed** to execute the wise men of
2:49 [M] the king **appointed** Shadrach, Meshach and Abednego
3:12 [M] there are some Jews whom *you have* **set** over the affairs of
5:26 [J] God *has* **numbered** the days of your reign and brought it to

10432 מִנְחָה *minḥâ*, n.f. [2] [√ Hb 4966]

grain offerings [1], offering [1]

Ezr 7:17 together with their **grain offerings** and drink offerings,
Da 2:46 paid him honor and ordered that an **offering** and incense be

10433 מִנְיָן *minyān*, n.[m.]. [1] [√ 10431]

each [1]

Ezr 6:17 for all Israel, twelve male goats, one for **each** of the tribes of Israel.

10434 מַעֲבָד *ma'ᵃbād*, n.[m.]. [1] [√ 10522; Hb 5042]

does [1]

Da 4:37 [4:34] because everything he **does** is right and all his ways are

10435 מְעֵה *m^{e}'ēh*, n.[m.]pl. [1] [√ Hb 5055]

belly [1]

Da 2:32 its chest and arms of silver, its **belly** and thighs of bronze,

10436 מֶעָל *me'āl*, n.[m.]. [1] [√ 10549]

sundown [+10002+10728] [1]

Da 6:14 [6:15] every effort until **sundown** [+10002+10728] to save him.

10437 מָרֵא *mārē'*, n.m. [4]

lord [4]

Da 2:47 the God of gods and the **Lord** *of* kings and a revealer of mysteries,
4:19 [4:16] Belteshazzar answered, "My **lord**, if only the dream
4:24 [4:21] this is the decree the Most High has issued against my **lord**
5:23 Instead, you have set yourself up against the **Lord** *of* heaven.

10438 מְרַד *m^{e}rad*, n.[m.]. [1] [→ 10439; Hb 5278]

rebellion [1]

Ezr 4:19 revolt against kings and has been a place of **rebellion** and sedition.

10439 מָרָד *mārād*, a. [2] [√ 10438]

rebellious [2]

Ezr 4:12 to Jerusalem and are rebuilding that **rebellious** and wicked city.
4:15 In these records you will find that this city is a **rebellious** city,

10440 מְרַט *m^{e}raṭ*, v. [1] [√ Hb 5307]

were torn off [1]

Da 7:4 [K] I watched until its wings **were torn off** and it was lifted from

10441 מֹשֶׁה *mōšeh*, n.pr.m. [1] [√ Hb 5407]

Moses [1]

Ezr 6:18 at Jerusalem, according to what is written in the Book of **Moses**.

10442 מְשַׁח *m^{e}šaḥ[1]*, n.[m.]. [2] [√ Hb 5418]

oil [1], olive oil [1]

Ezr 6:9 wheat, salt, wine and **oil**, as requested by the priests in Jerusalem—
7:22 baths of wine, a hundred baths of **olive oil**, and salt without limit.

10443 ²מְשַׁח *m^{e}šaḥ[2]*, n.[m.]. Not used in NIV/BHS [√ Hb 5419]

10444 מִשְׁכַּב *miškab*, n.[m.]. [6] [√ Hb 5435]

bed [5], there^{s} [+10342] [1]

Da 2:28 the visions that passed through your mind as you lay on your **bed**
2:29 "As you were lying **there**^{s} [+10342], O king, your mind turned to
4:5 [4:2] As I was lying in my **bed**, the images and visions that
4:10 [4:7] These are the visions I saw while lying in my **bed**: I looked,
4:13 [4:10] "In the visions I saw while lying in my **bed**, I looked, and
7:1 and visions passed through his mind as he was lying on his **bed**.

10445 מִשְׁכַּן *miškan*, n.[m.]. [1] [√ 10709; Hb 5438]

dwelling [1]

Ezr 7:15 freely given to the God of Israel, whose **dwelling** is in Jerusalem,

10446 מַשְׁרוֹקִי *mašrôqî*, n.f. [4]

flute [4]

Da 3:5 **flute**, zither, lyre, harp, pipes and all kinds of music, you must fall
3:7 **flute**, zither, lyre, harp and all kinds of music, all the peoples,
3:10 **flute**, zither, lyre, harp, pipes and all kinds of music must fall down
3:15 **flute**, zither, lyre, harp, pipes and all kinds of music, if you are

10447 מִשְׁתֵּא *mištē'*, n.m. [1] [√ 10748; Hb 5492]

banquet [1]

Da 5:10 the voices of the king and his nobles, came into the **banquet** hall.

10448 מַתְּנָה *matt^{e}nâ*, n.f. [3] [√ 10498; Hb 5508]

gifts [3]

Da 2:6 you will receive from me **gifts** and rewards and great honor.
2:48 placed Daniel in a high position and lavished many **gifts** on him.
5:17 "You may keep your **gifts** for yourself and give your rewards to

נ, *n*

10449 נ *n*, letter. Not used in NIV/BHS [√ Hb 5526]

10450 -נָא *-nā'*, p.suf.1.com.pl. [10] [√ Hb 5646] Not indexed

us [7], our [1], the^{s} [1], we [1]

10451 נְבָא *n^{e}bā'*, v. [1] [→ 10452, 10455; Hb 5547]

prophesied [1]

Ezr 5:1 [O] **prophesied** to the Jews in Judah and Jerusalem in the name

10452 נְבוּאָה *n^{e}bû'â*, n.f. [1] [√ 10451; Hb 5553]

preaching [1]

Ezr 6:14 prosper under the **preaching** *of* Haggai the prophet and Zechariah,

10453 נְבוּכַדְנֶצַּר *n^{e}bûkadneṣṣar*, n.pr.m. [31] [√ Hb 5556, 5557]

Nebuchadnezzar [28], he^{s} [+10002+10421] [2], *untranslated* [1]

Ezr 5:12 he handed them over to **Nebuchadnezzar** the Chaldean, king of
5:14 which **Nebuchadnezzar** had taken from the temple in Jerusalem
6:5 which **Nebuchadnezzar** took from the temple in Jerusalem
Da 2:28 He has shown King **Nebuchadnezzar** what will happen in days to
2:46 King **Nebuchadnezzar** fell prostrate before Daniel and paid him
3:1 King **Nebuchadnezzar** made an image of gold, ninety feet high
3:2 **He**^{s} [+10002+10421] then summoned the satraps, prefects,
3:2 to the dedication of the image **he**^{s} [+10002+10421] had set up.
3:3 the dedication of the image that King **Nebuchadnezzar** had set up,
3:3 Nebuchadnezzar had set up, and they stood before it. **[RPH]**
3:5 worship the image of gold that King **Nebuchadnezzar** has set up.
3:7 worshiped the image of gold that King **Nebuchadnezzar** had set
3:9 They said to King **Nebuchadnezzar**, "O king, live forever!
3:13 **Nebuchadnezzar** summoned Shadrach, Meshach and Abednego.
3:14 and **Nebuchadnezzar** said to them, "Is it true, Shadrach, Meshach
3:16 Meshach and Abednego replied to the king, "O **Nebuchadnezzar**,
3:19 Then **Nebuchadnezzar** was furious with Shadrach, Meshach
3:24 Then King **Nebuchadnezzar** leaped to his feet in amazement
3:26 **Nebuchadnezzar** then approached the opening of the blazing
3:28 Then **Nebuchadnezzar** said, "Praise be to the God of Shadrach,
4:1 [3:31] King **Nebuchadnezzar**, To the peoples, nations and men
4:4 [4:1] I, **Nebuchadnezzar**, was at home in my palace, contented
4:18 [4:15] "This is the dream that I, King **Nebuchadnezzar**, had.
4:28 [4:25] All this happened to King **Nebuchadnezzar**.
4:31 [4:28] "This is what is decreed for you, King **Nebuchadnezzar**:
4:33 [4:30] Immediately what had been said about **Nebuchadnezzar**
4:34 [4:31] At the end of that time, I, **Nebuchadnezzar**, raised my
4:37 [4:34] **Nebuchadnezzar**, praise and exalt and glorify the King of
5:2 silver goblets that **Nebuchadnezzar** his father had taken from the
5:11 King **Nebuchadnezzar** your father—your father the king,
5:18 the Most High God gave your father **Nebuchadnezzar** sovereignty

10454 נְבִזְבָּה *n^{e}bizbâ*, n.f. [2]

rewards [2]

Da 2:6 you will receive from me gifts and **rewards** and great honor.
5:17 your gifts for yourself and give your **rewards** to someone else.

10455 נְבִיא *nebî’*, n.m. [4] [√ 10451; Hb 5566]

prophet [3], prophets [1]

Ezr 5: 1 Now Haggai the **prophet** and Zechariah the prophet, a descendant
5: 1 Now Haggai the prophet and Zechariah the **prophet**, a descendant
5: 2 And the **prophets** of God were with them, helping them.
6: 14 prosper under the preaching of Haggai the **prophet** and Zechariah,

10456 נֶבְרְשָׁה *nebrešâ*, n.f.emph. [1]

lampstand [1]

Da 5: 5 on the plaster of the wall, near the **lampstand** in the royal palace.

10457 נְגַד *negad*, v. [1] [→ 10458; Hb 5583]

flowing [1]

Da 7: 10 [J] A river of fire *was* **flowing**, coming out from before him.

10458 נֶגֶד *neged*, pp. [1] [√ 10457; Hb 5584]

toward [1]

Da 6: 10 [6:11] room where the windows opened **toward** Jerusalem.

10459 נְגַה *negah*, n.[f.]. [1] [√ Hb 5586]

first light [1]

Da 6: 19 [6:20] At the **first light** of dawn, the king got up and hurried to

10460 נְגוֹ *negô*, n.pr.m. Not used in NIV/BHS [cf. 10524]

10461 נְדַב *nedab*, v. [4] [→ 10219; Hb 5605]

untranslated [1], freely given [1], freewill offerings [1], wish [1]

Ezr 7: 13 [O] and Levites, *who* **wish** to go to Jerusalem with you, may go.
7: 15 [O] and his advisers *have* **freely given** to the God of Israel,
7: 16 [O] as well as the **freewill offerings** *of* the people and priests for
7: 16 [O] and priests **[RPH]** for the temple of their God in Jerusalem.

10462 נִדְבָּךְ *nidbāk*, n.m. [2]

untranslated [1], courses [1]

Ezr 6: 4 with three **courses** of large stones and one of timbers. The costs are
6: 4 with three courses of large stones and **[RPH]** one of timbers.

10463 נְדַד *nedad*, v. [1] [cf. 10469; Hb 5610]

could not [1]

Da 6: 18 [6:19] [J] being brought to him. And he **could not** sleep.

10464 נִדְנֶה *nidneh*, n.[m.]. [1]

in [+10089+10135] [1]

Da 7: 15 "I, Daniel, was troubled **in** [+10089+10135] spirit, and the visions

10465 נְהוֹר *nehôr*, n.m. [0] [→ 10466, 10467; Hb 5644]

Da 2: 22 [what lies in darkness, and **light** [Q; see K 10466] dwells with him.]

10466 נְהִיר *nehîr*, n.m. [1] [√ 10465; Hb 5644]

light [1]

Da 2: 22 knows what lies in darkness, and **light** [Q 10465] dwells with him.

10467 נַהִירוּ *nahîrû*, n.f. [2] [√ 10465; Hb 5644]

insight [2]

Da 5: 11 In the time of your father he was found to have **insight**
5: 14 heard that the spirit of the gods is in you and that you have **insight**,

10468 נְהַר *nehar*, n.m. [15] [√ Hb 5643]

Trans-Euphrates [+10191+10526] [12], river [1], that province[s] [+10191+10526] [1], Trans-Euphrates [+10002+10526] [1]

Ezr 4: 10 of Samaria and elsewhere in **Trans-Euphrates** [+10191+10526].
4: 11 your servants, the men of **Trans-Euphrates** [+10191+10526]:
4: 16 you will be left with nothing in **Trans-Euphrates** [+10002+10526].
4: 17 in Samaria and elsewhere in **Trans-Euphrates** [+10191+10526]:
4: 20 kings ruling over the whole of **Trans-Euphrates** [+10191+10526],
5: 3 that time Tattenai, governor of **Trans-Euphrates** [+10191+10526],
5: 6 governor of **Trans-Euphrates** [+10191+10526], and
5: 6 the officials of **Trans-Euphrates** [+10191+10526], sent to King
6: 6 Tattenai, governor of **Trans-Euphrates** [+10191+10526], and
6: 6 officials of **that province**[s] [+10191+10526], stay away from there.
6: 8 from the revenues of **Trans-Euphrates** [+10191+10526], so that
6: 13 Tattenai, governor of **Trans-Euphrates** [+10191+10526], and
7: 21 order all the treasurers of **Trans-Euphrates** [+10191+10526] to
7: 25 justice to all the people of **Trans-Euphrates** [+10191+10526]—

Da 7: 10 A **river** of fire was flowing, coming out from before him.

10469 נוּד *nûd*, v. [1] [cf. 10463; Hb 5653]

flee [1]

Da 4: 14 [4:11] [J] *Let* the animals **flee** from under it and the birds from

10470 נְוָלוּ *newālû*, n.f. [3]

piles of rubble [2], pile of rubble [1]

Ezr 6: 11 And for this crime his house is to be made a **pile of rubble**.
Da 2: 5 you cut into pieces and your houses turned into **piles of rubble**.
3: 29 be cut into pieces and their houses be turned into **piles of rubble**,

10471 נוּר *nûr*, n.f. & m. [17] [√ Hb 5775]

blazing [+10328] [8], fire [8], all ablaze [+10178] [1]

Da 3: 6 worship will immediately be thrown into a **blazing** [+10328]
3: 11 and worship will be thrown into a **blazing** [+10328] furnace.
3: 15 you will be thrown immediately into a **blazing** [+10328] furnace.
3: 17 If we are thrown into the **blazing** [+10328] furnace, the God we
3: 20 and Abednego and throw them into the **blazing** [+10328] furnace.
3: 21 were bound and thrown into the **blazing** [+10328] furnace.
3: 22 so hot that the flames of the **fire** killed the soldiers who took up
3: 23 these three men, firmly tied, fell into the **blazing** [+10328] furnace.
3: 24 "Weren't there three men that we tied up and threw into the **fire**?"
3: 25 I see four men walking around in the **fire**, unbound and unharmed,
3: 26 then approached the opening of the **blazing** [+10328] furnace
3: 26 So Shadrach, Meshach and Abednego came out of the **fire**,
3: 27 They saw that the **fire** had not harmed their bodies, nor was a hair
3: 27 robes were not scorched, and there was no smell of **fire** on them.
7: 9 His throne was flaming with **fire**, and its wheels were all ablaze.
7: 9 was flaming with fire, and its wheels were **all ablaze** [+10178].
7: 10 A river of **fire** was flowing, coming out from before him.

10472 נְזַק *nezaq*, v. [4] [→ 10215; Hb 5691]

detriment [1], suffer loss [1], suffer [1], troublesome [1]

Ezr 4: 13 [P] or duty will be paid, and the royal revenues *will* **suffer**.
4: 15 [P] **troublesome** *to* kings and provinces, a place of rebellion
4: 22 [P] let this threat grow, to the **detriment** *of* the royal interests?
Da 6: 2 [6:3] [J] to them so that the king *might* not **suffer loss**.

10473 נְחָשׁ *nehāš*, n.m. [9] [√ Hb 5703, 5733]

bronze [9]

Da 2: 32 its chest and arms of silver, its belly and thighs of **bronze**,
2: 35 the clay, the **bronze**, the silver and the gold were broken to pieces
2: 39 Next, a third kingdom, one of **bronze**, will rule over the whole
2: 45 the iron, the **bronze**, the clay, the silver and the gold to pieces.
4: 15 [4:12] let the stump and its roots, bound with iron and **bronze**,
4: 23 [4:20] but leave the stump, bound with iron and **bronze**,
5: 4 the gods of gold and silver, of **bronze**, iron, wood and stone.
5: 23 the gods of silver and gold, of **bronze**, iron, wood and stone,
7: 19 and most terrifying, with its iron teeth and **bronze** claws—

10474 נְחַת *nehat*, v. [6] [√ Hb 5737]

coming down [2], deposit [1], deposited [1], stored [1], was deposed [1]

Ezr 5: 15 [P] and go and **deposit** them in the temple in Jerusalem.
6: 1 [P] they searched in the archives **stored** in the treasury at
6: 5 [P] in Jerusalem; they *are to be* **deposited** in the house of God.
Da 4: 13 [4:10] [J] a messenger, a holy one, **coming down** from heaven.
4: 23 [4:20] [J] a holy one, **coming down** from heaven and saying,
5: 20 [Q] *he* **was deposed** from his royal throne and stripped of his

10475 נְטַל *neṭal*, v. [2] [√ Hb 5747]

raised [1], was lifted [1]

Da 4: 34 [4:31] [J] I, Nebuchadnezzar, **raised** my eyes toward heaven,
7: 4 [K] *it* **was lifted** from the ground so that it stood on two feet like

10476 נְטַר *neṭar*, v. [1] [√ Hb 5915]

kept [1]

Da 7: 28 [J] and my face turned pale, but *I* **kept** the matter to myself."

10477 נִי- *-nî*, p.suf.1.com.s. [18] [√ 10307; Hb 5761] Not indexed

me [17], *untranslated* [1]

10478 נִיחֹחַ *nîhoah*, n.[m.]. [2] [√ Hb 5767]

incense [1], pleasing [1]

Ezr 6: 10 so that they may offer sacrifices **pleasing** to the God of heaven
Da 2: 46 and ordered that an offering and **incense** be presented to him.

10479 נְכַס ***n^e^kas***, n.[m.]. [2] [√ Hb 5794]

property [1], treasury [1]

Ezr 6: 8 of these men are to be fully paid out of the royal **treasury**,
7: 26 by death, banishment, confiscation of **property**, or imprisonment.

10480 נְמַר ***n^e^mar***, n.[m.]. [1] [√ Hb 5807]

leopard [1]

Da 7: 6 there before me was another beast, one that looked like a **leopard**.

10481 נְסַח ***n^e^saḥ***, v. [1] [√ Hb 5815]

be pulled [1]

Ezr 6: 11 [L] a beam *is to* **be pulled** from his house and he is to be lifted

10482 נְסַךְ¹ ***n^e^sak¹***, v. [1] [→ 10483; Hb 5818]

presented [1]

Da 2: 46 [M] ordered that an offering and incense *be* **presented** to him.

10483 ²נְסַךְ ***n^e^sak²***, n.[m.]. [1] [√ 10482; Hb 5821]

drink offerings [1]

Ezr 7: 17 together with their grain offerings and **drink offerings**,

10484 נְפַל ***n^e^pal***, v. [11] [√ Hb 5877]

fall down [5], fell [3], came [1], fell down [1], have occasion [1]

Ezr 7: 20 [J] temple of your God that you *may* **have occasion** to supply,
Da 2: 46 [J] King Nebuchadnezzar **fell** prostrate before Daniel and paid
3: 5 [J] *you must* **fall down** and worship the image of gold that King
3: 6 [J] Whoever *does* not **fall down** and worship will immediately be
3: 7 [J] nations and men of every language **fell down** and worshiped
3: 10 [J] pipes and all kinds of music *must* **fall down** and worship the
3: 11 [J] that whoever *does* not **fall down** and worship will be thrown
3: 15 [J] if you are ready *to* **fall down** and worship the image I made,
3: 23 [J] and these three men, firmly tied, **fell** into the blazing furnace.
4: 31 [4:28] [J] The words were still on his lips *when* a voice **came**
7: 20 [J] the other horn that came up, before which three of *them* **fell**—

10485 נְפַק ***n^e^paq***, v. [11] [→ 10486]

taken [3], appeared [1], came out [1], come out [1], coming out [1], gone out [1], issued [1], removed [1], took [1]

Ezr 5: 14 [P] *He* even **removed** from the temple of Babylon the gold and
5: 14 [P] which Nebuchadnezzar *had* **taken** from the temple in
6: 5 [P] which Nebuchadnezzar **took** from the temple in Jerusalem
Da 2: 13 [J] So the decree *was* **issued** to put the wise men to death,
2: 14 [J] *had* **gone out** to put to death the wise men of Babylon,
3: 26 [J] and Abednego, servants of the Most High God, **come out**!
3: 26 [J] So Shadrach, Meshach and Abednego **came out** of the fire,
5: 2 [P] silver goblets that Nebuchadnezzar his father *had* **taken** from
5: 3 [P] So they brought in the gold goblets that *had been* **taken** from
5: 5 [J] Suddenly the fingers of a human hand **appeared** and wrote on
7: 10 [J] A river of fire was flowing, **coming out** from before him.

10486 נִפְקָה ***nipqâ***, n.f. [2] [√ 10485]

costs [1], expenses [1]

Ezr 6: 4 and one of timbers. The **costs** are to be paid by the royal treasury.
6: 8 The **expenses** of these men are to be fully paid out of the royal

10487 נִצְבָּה ***niṣbâ***, n.f. [1]

strength [1]

Da 2: 41 yet it will have some of the **strength** of iron in it, even as you saw

10488 נְצַח ***n^e^ṣaḥ***, v. [1] [√ Hb 5904]

distinguished himself [1]

Da 6: 3 [6:4] [O] so **distinguished himself** among the administrators

10489 נְצַל ***n^e^ṣal***, v. [3] [√ Hb 5911]

save [2], saves [1]

Da 3: 29 [P] into piles of rubble, for no other god can **save** in this way."
6: 14 [6:15] [P] and made every effort until sundown to **save** him.
6: 27 [6:28] [P] He rescues and *he* **saves**; he performs signs

10490 נְקֵא ***n^e^qē'***, a. [1] [√ Hb 5929]

white [1]

Da 7: 9 was as white as snow; the hair of his head was **white** like wool.

10491 נְקַשׁ ***n^e^qaš***, v. [1] [√ Hb 5943]

knocked [1]

Da 5: 6 [J] and he was so frightened that his knees **knocked** together

10492 נְשָׂא ***n^e^śā'***, v. [3] [√ Hb 5951]

revolt [1], swept away [1], take [1]

Ezr 4: 19 [O] it was found that this city has a long history of **revolt** against
5: 15 [J] '**Take** these articles and go and deposit them in the temple in
Da 2: 35 [J] The wind **swept** them **away** without leaving a trace.

10493 נְשִׁין ***n^e^šîn***, n.f.pl. [1] [√ Hb 851]

wives [1]

Da 6: 24 [6:25] into the lions' den, along with their **wives** and children.

10494 נִשְׁמָה ***nišmâ***, n.f. [1] [√ Hb 5972]

life [1]

Da 5: 23 But you did not honor the God who holds in his hand your **life**

10495 נְשַׁר ***n^e^šar***, n.m. [2] [√ Hb 5979]

eagle [2]

Da 4: 33 [4:30] of heaven until his hair grew like the feathers of an **eagle**
7: 4 "The first was like a lion, and it had the wings of an **eagle**.

10496 נִשְׁתְּוָן ***ništ^e^wān***, n.m. Not used in NIV/BHS [√ Hb 5981]

10497 נְתִין ***n^e^tîn***, n.m.pl. [1] [√ 10498; Hb 5987]

temple servants [1]

Ezr 7: 24 **temple servants** or other workers at this house of God.

10498 נְתַן ***n^e^tan***, v. [7] [→ 10448, 10497; cf. 10314; Hb 5989]

gives [3], *untranslated* [1], paid [1], provide [1], supply [1]

Ezr 4: 13 [J] walls are restored, no more taxes, tribute or duty *will be* **paid**,
7: 20 [J] temple of your God that you may have occasion to **supply**,
7: 20 [J] occasion to supply, *you may* **provide** from the royal treasury.
Da 2: 16 [J] for time, **[NIE]** so that he might interpret the dream for him.
4: 17 [4:14] [J] **gives** them to anyone he wishes and sets over them the
4: 25 [4:22] [J] kingdoms of men and **gives** them to anyone he wishes.
4: 32 [4:29] [J] of men and **gives** them to anyone he wishes."

10499 נְתַר ***n^e^tar***, v. [1]

strip off [1]

Da 4: 14 [4:11] [P] its branches; **strip off** its leaves and scatter its fruit.

ס, *s*

10500 ס ***s***, letter. Not used in NIV/BHS [√ Hb 6005]

10501 סַבְּכָא ***sabb^e^kā'***, n.[f.]. Not used in NIV/BHS [cf. 10676]

10502 סְבַל ***s^e^bal***, v. [1] [√ Hb 6022]

be laid [1]

Ezr 6: 3 [N] a place to present sacrifices, and *let* its foundations **be laid**.

10503 סְבַר ***s^e^bar***, v. [1] [√ Hb 8431, 8432]

try [1]

Da 7: 25 [J] his saints and **try** to change the set times and the laws.

10504 סְגִד ***s^e^gid***, v. [12] [√ Hb 6032]

worship [10], paid honor [1], worshiped [1]

Da 2: 46 [J] **paid** him **honor** and ordered that an offering and incense be
3: 5 [J] **worship** the image of gold that King Nebuchadnezzar has set
3: 6 [J] **worship** will immediately be thrown into a blazing furnace."
3: 7 [J] **worshiped** the image of gold that King Nebuchadnezzar had
3: 10 [J] of music must fall down and **worship** the image of gold,
3: 11 [J] fall down and **worship** will be thrown into a blazing furnace.
3: 12 [J] They neither serve your gods nor **worship** the image of gold
3: 14 [J] serve my gods or **worship** the image of gold I have set up?
3: 15 [J] if you are ready to fall down and **worship** the image I made,
3: 15 [J] if *you do* not **worship** it, you will be thrown immediately into
3: 18 [J] your gods or **worship** the image of gold you have set up."
3: 28 [J] rather than serve or **worship** any god except their own God.

10505 סְגַן se**gan**, n.m. [5] [√ Hb 6036]

prefects [4], in charge [+10647] [1]

Da 2:48 of Babylon and placed him **in charge** [+10647] of all its wise men.
3: 2 **prefects**, governors, advisers, treasurers, judges, magistrates
3: 3 **prefects**, governors, advisers, treasurers, judges, magistrates
3:27 **prefects**, governors and royal advisers crowded around them.
6: 7 [6:8] **prefects**, satraps, advisers and governors have all agreed

10506 סְגַר se**gar**, v. [1] [√ Hb 6037]

shut [1]

Da 6:22 [6:23] [J] sent his angel, and *he* **shut** the mouths of the lions.

10507 סוּמְפֹּנְיָה sûmpōne**yâ**, n.f. [3] [cf. 10510, cf. 10512]

pipes [3]

Da 3: 5 flute, zither, lyre, harp, **pipes** and all kinds of music, you must fall
3:10 **pipes** and all kinds of music must fall down and worship the image
3:15 flute, zither, lyre, harp, **pipes** and all kinds of music, if you are

10508 סוּף sûp, v. [2] [→ 10509; Hb 6066]

bring to an end [1], fulfilled [1]

Da 2:44 [P] It will crush all those kingdoms and **bring** them **to an end**,
4:33 [4:30] [J] had been said about Nebuchadnezzar *was* **fulfilled**.

10509 סוֹף sôp, n.[m.]. [5] [√ 10508; Hb 6067]

distant parts [1], end [1], ends [1], forever [+10002+10527] [1], never end [+10002+10527] [1]

Da 4:11 [4:8] top touched the sky; it was visible to the **ends** *of* the earth.
4:22 [4:19] and your dominion extends to **distant parts** *of* the earth.
6:26 [6:27] his dominion will **never end** [+10002+10527].
7:26 away and completely destroyed **forever** [+10002+10527].
7:28 "This is the **end** of the matter. I, Daniel, was deeply troubled by

10510 סִיפֹּנְיָא sîppōne**yā'**, n.f. Not used in NIV/BHS [cf. 10507]

10511 סְטַר se**ṭar**, n.m. Not used in NIV/BHS [cf. 10680]

10512 סִיפֹּנְיָא sîppōne**yā'**, n.f. Not used in NIV/BHS [cf. 10507]

10513 סְלַק se**laq**, v. [8] [√ Hb 6158]

came up [4], lift out [1], took up [1], turned [1], was lifted [1]

Ezr 4:12 [J] The king should know that the Jews who **came up** to us from
Da 2:29 [J] were lying there, O king, your mind **turned** *to* things to come,
3:22 [P] flames of the fire killed the soldiers who **took up** Shadrach,
6:23 [6:24] [P] and gave orders to **lift** Daniel **out** of the den.
6:23 [6:24] [Q] when Daniel **was lifted** from the den, no wound was
7: 3 [J] each different from the others, **came up** out of the sea.
7: 8 [J] was another horn, a little one, *which* **came up** among them;
7:20 [J] ten horns on its head and about the other horn that **came up**,

10514 סְעַד se**'ad**, v. [1] [√ Hb 6184]

helping [1]

Ezr 5: 2 [M] And the prophets of God were with them, **helping** them.

10515 סְפַר se**par**, n.m. [5] [→ 10516; Hb 6219]

archives [+10103] [1], archives [+10177] [1], book [1], books [1], records [+10177] [1]

Ezr 4:15 so that a search may be made in the **archives** [+10177] of your
4:15 In these **records** [+10177] you will find that this city is a rebellious
6: 1 they searched in the **archives** [+10103] stored in the treasury at
6:18 at Jerusalem, according to what is written in the **Book** *of* Moses.
Da 7:10 before him. The court was seated, and the **books** were opened.

10516 סָפַר sāpar, n.m. [6] [√ 10515; Hb 6221]

secretary [4], teacher [2]

Ezr 4: 8 Shimshai the **secretary** wrote a letter against Jerusalem to
4: 9 Rehum the commanding officer and Shimshai the **secretary**,
4:17 Shimshai the **secretary** and the rest of their associates living in
4:23 read to Rehum and Shimshai the **secretary** and their associates,
7:12 To Ezra the priest, a **teacher** *of* the Law of the God of heaven:
7:21 a **teacher** *of* the Law of the God of heaven, may ask of you—

10517 סַרְבָּל sarbāl, n.[m.]. [2]

robes [2]

Da 3:21 wearing their **robes**, trousers, turbans and other clothes, were
3:27 their **robes** were not scorched, and there was no smell of fire on

10518 סָרַךְ sārak, n.m. [5]

administrators [5]

Da 6: 2 [6:3] with three **administrators** over them, one of whom was
6: 3 [6:4] so distinguished himself among the **administrators**
6: 4 [6:5] the **administrators** and the satraps tried to find grounds for
6: 6 [6:7] So the **administrators** and the satraps went as a group to the
6: 7 [6:8] The royal **administrators**, prefects, satraps, advisers and

10519 סְתַר¹ se**tar**[1], v. [1] [√ Hb 6259]

hidden [1]

Da 2:22 [N] He reveals deep and **hidden** *things*; he knows what lies in

10520 סְתַר² se**tar**[2], v. [1] [√ Hb 8609]

destroyed [1]

Ezr 5:12 [J] *who* **destroyed** this temple and deported the people to

---

ע, ʿ

10521 ע ʿ, letter. Not used in NIV/BHS [√ Hb 6263]

10522 עֲבַד ʿa**bad**, v. [28] [→ 10434, 10523, 10525; Hb 6268]

untranslated [3], done [3], do [2], made [2], be carried out [1], be cut into [1], be done [1], be made [1], being carried on [1], carried out [1], celebrated [1], cut into [1], does [1], gave [1], make [1], neglect [+10542+10712] [1], obey [1], performed [1], performs [1], provide [1], punished [+10170+10191+10427] [1], waging [1]

Ezr 4:15 [J] and provinces, a place of rebellion **[NIE]** from ancient times.
4:19 [L] and has been a place of rebellion and sedition. **[NIE]**
4:22 [J] Be careful not to **neglect** [+10542+10712] this matter. Why let this threat grow, to the detriment of the royal interests?
5: 8 [L] The work *is* **being carried on** with diligence and is making
6: 8 [J] I hereby decree what *you are to* **do** for these elders of the
6:11 [L] And for this crime his house *is to* **be made** a pile of rubble.
6:12 [L] I Darius have decreed it. *Let it* **be carried out** with diligence.
6:13 [J] and their associates **carried** it **out** with diligence.
6:16 [J] **celebrated** the dedication of the house of God with joy.
7:18 [J] your brother Jews *may* then **do** whatever seems best with the
7:18 [J] and gold, **[RPH]** in accordance with the will of your God.
7:21 [L] order all the treasurers of Trans-Euphrates *to* **provide** with
7:23 [L] *let it* **be done** with diligence for the temple of the God of
7:26 [J] Whoever *does* not **obey** the law of your God and the law of
7:26 [L] must surely be **punished** [+10170+10191+10427] by death,
Jer 10:11 [J] 'These gods, who *did* not **make** the heavens and the earth,
Da 2: 5 [L] I *will have you* **cut into** pieces and your houses turned into
3: 1 [J] King Nebuchadnezzar **made** an image of gold, ninety feet
3:15 [J] if you are ready to fall down and worship the image *I* **made**,
3:29 [L] Meshach and Abednego **be cut into** pieces and their houses
4: 2 [3:32] [J] wonders that the Most High God *has* **performed** for
4:35 [4:32] [J] *He* **does** as he pleases with the powers of heaven
4:35 [4:32] [J] back his hand or say to him: "What *have you* **done**?"
5: 1 [J] King Belshazzar **gave** a great banquet for a thousand of his
6:10 [6:11] [J] giving thanks to his God, just as *he had* **done** before.
6:22 [6:23] [J] Nor *have I ever* **done** any wrong before you, O king."
6:27 [6:28] [J] *he* **performs** signs and wonders in the heavens and on
7:21 [J] this horn *was* **waging** war against the saints and defeating

10523 עֲבֵד ʿa**bēd**, n.m. [7] [√ 10522; Hb 6269]

servants [6], servant [1]

Ezr 4:11 To King Artaxerxes, From your **servants**, the men of
5:11 "We are the **servants** of the God of heaven and earth, and we are
Da 2: 4 Tell your **servants** the dream, and we will interpret it."
2: 7 Once more they replied, "Let the king tell his **servants** the dream,
3:26 and Abednego, **servants** *of* the Most High God, come out!
3:28 and Abednego, who has sent his angel and rescued his **servants**!
6:20 [6:21] "Daniel, **servant** *of* the living God, has your God,

10524 עֲבֵד נְגוֹ ʿa**bēd n**e**gô**, n.pr.m. [14] [√ 10523 & ?; Hb 6284]

Abednego [13], *untranslated* [1]

Da 2:49 and **Abednego** administrators over the province of Babylon,

Da 3:12 Shadrach, Meshach and **Abednego**—who pay no attention to you,
3:13 Nebuchadnezzar summoned Shadrach, Meshach and **Abednego**.
3:14 "Is it true, Shadrach, Meshach and **Abednego**, that you do not
3:16 Shadrach, Meshach and **Abednego** replied to the king,
3:19 Meshach and **Abednego**, and his attitude toward them changed.
3:20 Meshach and **Abednego** and throw them into the blazing furnace.
3:22 killed the soldiers who took up Shadrach, Meshach and **Abednego**,
3:23 these three men, **[RPH]** firmly tied, fell into the blazing furnace.
3:26 blazing furnace and shouted, "Shadrach, Meshach and **Abednego**,
3:26 So Shadrach, Meshach and **Abednego** came out of the fire,
3:28 Meshach and **Abednego**, who has sent his angel and rescued his
3:29 Meshach and **Abednego** be cut into pieces and their houses be
3:30 Meshach and **Abednego** in the province of Babylon.

10525 עֲבִידָה *ᵃbîdâ*, n.f. [6] [√ 10522; Hb 6275]

work [3], administrators [1], affairs [1], service [1]

Ezr 4:24 Thus the **work** *on* the house of God in Jerusalem came to a
5:8 The **work** is being carried on with diligence and is making rapid
6:7 Do not interfere with the **work** *on* this temple of God. Let the
6:18 and the Levites in their groups for the **service** *of* God at Jerusalem,
Da 2:49 and Abednego **administrators** over the province of Babylon,
3:12 there are some Jews whom you have set over the **affairs** *of* the

10526 עֲבַר *ᵃbar*, n.m. [14] [√ Hb 6298]

Trans-Euphrates [+10191+10468] [12], that province[s] [+10191+10468] [1], Trans-Euphrates [+10002+10468] [1]

Ezr 4:10 of Samaria and elsewhere in **Trans-Euphrates** [+10191+10468].
4:11 your servants, the men of **Trans-Euphrates** [+10191+10468]:
4:16 will be left with nothing in **Trans-Euphrates** [+10002+10468].
4:17 in Samaria and elsewhere in **Trans-Euphrates** [+10191+10468]:
4:20 kings ruling over the whole of **Trans-Euphrates** [+10191+10468],
5:3 Tattenai, governor of **Trans-Euphrates** [+10191+10468], and
5:6 governor of **Trans-Euphrates** [+10191+10468], and
5:6 the officials of **Trans-Euphrates** [+10191+10468], sent to King
6:6 Tattenai, governor of **Trans-Euphrates** [+10191+10468], and
6:6 officials of **that province**[s] [+10191+10468], stay away from there.
6:8 **Trans-Euphrates** [+10191+10468], so that the work will not stop.
6:13 Tattenai, governor of **Trans-Euphrates** [+10191+10468], and
7:21 order all the treasurers of **Trans-Euphrates** [+10191+10468] to
7:25 justice to all the people of **Trans-Euphrates** [+10191+10468]—

10527 עַד *ʿad*, pp. & c. [35] [√ 10528?; Hb 6330] See Select Index

until [+10168] [8], *untranslated* [5], until [4], for [3], during [2], as [+10168] [1], ever [+10002+10550] [1], finally [+10024+10221] [1], forever [+10002+10509] [1], forever [+10002+10550] [1], hoping [+10168] [1], never end [+10002+10509] [1], on [1], so that [+10159 +10168] [1], this [+10345] [1], to [1], up to [1], while [+10168] [1]

10528 עֲדָה *ᵃdâ*, v. [9] [→ 10527?; Hb 6334]

repealed [2], stripped [2], deposes [1], pass away [1], taken away [1], taken [1], was [1]

Da 2:21 [P] and seasons; he sets up kings and **deposes** them.
3:27 [J] were not scorched, and *there* **was** no smell of fire on them.
4:31 [4:28] [J] Your royal authority *has been* **taken** from you.
5:20 [P] was deposed from his royal throne and **stripped** of his glory.
6:8 [6:9] [J] of the Medes and Persians, which cannot *be* **repealed**."—
6:12 [6:13] [J] the Medes and Persians, which cannot *be* **repealed**."
7:12 [P] (The other beasts *had been* **stripped** *of* their authority,
7:14 [P] dominion is an everlasting dominion that *will* not **pass away**,
7:26 [P] his power *will be* **taken away** and completely destroyed

10529 עִדּוֹא *ʿiddôʾ*, n.pr.m. [2] [√ Hb 6341, 6342]

Iddo [2]

Ezr 5:1 the prophet and Zechariah the prophet, a descendant of **Iddo**,
6:14 of Haggai the prophet and Zechariah, a descendant of **Iddo**.

10530 עִדָּן *ʿiddān*, n.m. [13]

times [6], time [3], as soon as [+10002+10089+10168] [1], period of time [+10221+10232] [1], situation [1], when [+10002+10089] [1]

Da 2:8 the king answered, "I am certain that you are trying to gain **time**,
2:9 and wicked things, hoping the **situation** will change.
2:21 He changes **times** and seasons; he sets up kings and deposes them.
3:5 **As soon as** [+10002+10089+10168] you hear the sound of the
3:15 Now **when** [+10002+10089] you hear the sound of the horn,
4:16 [4:13] the mind of an animal, till seven **times** pass by for him.
4:23 [4:20] like the wild animals, until seven **times** pass by for him.'
4:25 [4:22] Seven **times** will pass by for you until you acknowledge
4:32 [4:29] Seven **times** will pass by for you until you acknowledge
7:12 but were allowed to live for a **period of time** [+10221+10232].)
7:25 The saints will be handed over to him for a **time**, times and half a
7:25 saints will be handed over to him for a time, **times** and half a time.
7:25 saints will be handed over to him for a time, times and half a **time**.

10531 עוֹד *ʿôd*, adv. [1] [√ Hb 6388]

still [1]

Da 4:31 [4:28] The words were **still** on his lips when a voice came from

10532 עֲוָיָה *ᵃwāyâ*, n.f. [1]

wickedness [1]

Da 4:27 [4:24] and your **wickedness** by being kind to the oppressed.

10533 עוֹף *ʿôp*, n.[m.]. [2] [√ Hb 6416]

bird [1], birds [1]

Da 2:38 placed mankind and the beasts of the field and the **birds** *of* the air.
7:6 on its back it had four wings like those of a **bird**. This beast had

10534 עוּר *ʿûr*, n.[m.]. [1]

chaff [1]

Da 2:35 and became like **chaff** on a threshing floor in the summer.

10535 עֵז *ʿēz*, n.[f.]. [1]

male goats [+10615] [1]

Ezr 6:17 as a sin offering for all Israel, twelve **male goats** [+10615],

10536 עִזְקָה *ʿizqâ*, n.f. [2]

rings [1], signet ring [1]

Da 6:17 [6:18] the king sealed it with his own **signet ring** and with the
6:17 [6:18] it with his own signet ring and with the **rings** *of* his nobles,

10537 עֶזְרָא *ʿezrāʾ*, n.pr.m. [3] [√ Hb 6474]

Ezra [3]

Ezr 7:12 Artaxerxes, king of kings, To **Ezra** the priest, a teacher of the Law
7:21 to provide with diligence whatever **Ezra** the priest,
7:25 And you, **Ezra**, in accordance with the wisdom of your God,

10538 עֲזַרְיָה *ᵃzaryâ*, n.pr.m. [1] [√ Hb 6481]

Azariah [1]

Da 2:17 the matter to his friends Hananiah, Mishael and **Azariah**.

10539 עֵטָה *ʿēṭâ*, n.f. [1] [√ 10324; Hb 6783]

wisdom [1]

Da 2:14 wise men of Babylon, Daniel spoke to him with **wisdom** and tact.

10540 עַיִן *ʿayin*, n.f. [5] [√ Hb 6524]

eyes [4], eye [1]

Ezr 5:5 But the **eye** *of* their God was watching over the elders of the Jews,
Da 4:34 [4:31] I, Nebuchadnezzar, raised my **eyes** toward heaven,
7:8 This horn had **eyes** like the eyes of a man and a mouth that spoke
7:8 This horn had eyes like the **eyes** *of* a man and a mouth that spoke
7:20 the others and that had **eyes** and a mouth that spoke boastfully.

10541 עִיר *ʿîr*, n.m. [3] [√ Hb 6424]

messenger [2], messengers [1]

Da 4:13 [4:10] I looked, and there before me was a **messenger**, a holy one,
4:17 [4:14] " 'The decision is announced by **messengers**, the holy ones
4:23 [4:20] "You, O king, saw a **messenger**, a holy one, coming down

10542 עַל *ʿal*, pp. [104] [→ 10543, 10545, 10546, 10547, 10548; Hb 6584] See Select Index

untranslated [25], to [16], on [13], over [8], for [7], against [6], about [4], in [4], around [3], lying in [3], of [3], among [1], concerning [1], had [+10201] [1], lying on [1], lying [1], prostrate [+10049] [1], rule [1], so that [+10159+10168] [1], than [1], that is why [+10180] [1], toward [1], why [+10408] [1]

10543 עֵלָּא *ʿēllāʾ*, adv. [1] [√ 10542; Hb 6584]

over [+10427] [1]

Da 6:2 [6:3] with three administrators **over** [+10427] them, one of whom

10544 עִלָּה *ʿillâ*, n.f. [3] [√ Hb 6618]

basis for charges [1], do so[s] [+10353+10708] [1], grounds for charges [1]

Da 6:4 [6:5] the satraps tried to find **grounds for charges** against Daniel

Da 6: 4 [6:5] but they were unable to **do so**ˢ [+10353+10708].
6: 5 [6:6] "We will never find any **basis for charges** against this man

10545 עֲלָוָה ᵃlāwâ, n.f. [1] [√ 10542; Hb 6592]

burnt offerings [1]

Ezr 6: 9 rams, male lambs for **burnt offerings** to the God of heaven,

10546 עִלָּי ʿillāy, a. [10] [√ 10542; Hb 6604]

Most High [10]

Da 3: 26 and Abednego, servants of the **Most High** God, come out!
4: 2 [3:32] wonders that the **Most High** God has performed for me.
4: 17 [4:14] so that the living may know that the **Most High** is
4: 24 [4:21] this is the decree the **Most High** has issued against my lord
4: 25 [4:22] that the **Most High** is sovereign over the kingdoms of men
4: 32 [4:29] that the **Most High** is sovereign over the kingdoms of men
4: 34 [4:31] I praised the **Most High**; I honored and glorified him who
5: 18 the **Most High** God gave your father Nebuchadnezzar sovereignty
5: 21 until he acknowledged that the **Most High** God is sovereign over
7: 25 He will speak against the **Most High** and oppress his saints

10547 עִלִּי ʿillî, n.f. [1] [√ 10542; Hb 6606]

upstairs room [1]

Da 6: 10 [6:11] he went home to his **upstairs room** where the windows

10548 עֶלְיוֹן ʿelyôn, a. [4] [√ 10542; Hb 6610]

Most High [3], hisˢ [1]

Da 7: 18 But the saints of the **Most High** will receive the kingdom
7: 22 and pronounced judgment in favor of the saints of the **Most High**,
7: 25 oppress **his**ˢ saints and try to change the set times and the laws.
7: 27 will be handed over to the saints, the people of the **Most High**.

10549 עֲלַל ᵃlal, v. [14] [→ 10436; Hb 6619]

brought [3], came [3], went [2], came in [1], take [1], took [1], was brought [1], went in [1], were brought [1]

Da 2: 16 [J] At this, Daniel **went in** *to* the king and asked for time, so that
2: 24 [J] Daniel **went** to Arioch, whom the king had appointed to
2: 24 [P] **Take** me to the king, and I will interpret his dream for him."
2: 25 [P] Arioch **took** Daniel to the king at once and said, "I have
4: 6 [4:3] [P] *be* **brought** before me to interpret the dream for me.
4: 7 [4:4] [J] enchanters, astrologers and diviners **came**,
4: 8 [4:5] [J] **came** into my presence and I told him the dream.
5: 7 [P] astrologers and diviners to *be* **brought** and said to these wise
5: 8 [J] all the king's wise men **came in**, but they could not read the
5: 10 [J] voices of the king and his nobles, **came** into the banquet hall.
5: 13 [Q] So Daniel **was brought** before the king, and the king said to
5: 15 [Q] and enchanters **were brought** before me to read this writing
6: 10 [6:11] [J] *he* **went** home to his upstairs room where the
6: 18 [6:19] [P] and without any entertainment *being* **brought** to him.

10550 עָלַם ʿālam, n.[m.]. [20] [√ Hb 6409]

forever [+10378] [6], eternal [2], ever [+10002] [2], everlasting [2], ancient [1], ever [+10002+10527] [1], ever [1], forever [+10002] [1], forever [+10002+10378] [1], forever [+10002+10527] [1], long history [+10317+10427] [1], never [+10378+10379] [1]

Ezr 4: 15 to kings and provinces, a place of rebellion from **ancient** times.
4: 19 it was found that this city has a **long** [+10317+10427] **history** of
Da 2: 4 answered the king in Aramaic, "O king, live **forever** [+10378]!
2: 20 "Praise be to the name of God for **ever** [+10002] and ever;
2: 20 "Praise be to the name of God for ever and **ever** [+10002+10527];
2: 44 set up a kingdom that will **never** [+10378+10379] be destroyed,
2: 44 to an end, but it will itself endure **forever** [+10002+10378].
3: 9 said to King Nebuchadnezzar, "O king, live **forever** [+10378]!
4: 3 [3:33] His kingdom is an **eternal** kingdom; his dominion endures
4: 34 [4:31] I honored and glorified him who lives **forever** [+10002].
4: 34 [4:31] His dominion is an **eternal** dominion; his kingdom endures
5: 10 "O king, live **forever** [+10378]!" she said. "Don't be alarmed!
6: 6 [6:7] to the king and said: "O King Darius, live **forever** [+10378]!
6: 21 [6:22] Daniel answered, "O king, live **forever** [+10378]!
6: 26 [6:27] "For he is the living God and he endures **forever** [+10378];
7: 14 His dominion is an **everlasting** dominion that will not pass away,
7: 18 will possess it **forever** [+10002+10527]—yes, for ever and ever.'
7: 18 the kingdom and will possess it forever—yes, for **ever** and ever.'
7: 18 and will possess it forever—yes, for ever and **ever** [+10002].'
7: 27 His kingdom will be an **everlasting** kingdom, and all rulers will

10551 עֵלְמָי ʿēlmāy, n.g.pl. [1] [√ Hb 6520]

Elamites [1]

Ezr 4: 9 from Tripolis, Persia, Erech and Babylon, the **Elamites** of Susa,

10552 עֲלַע ᵃlaʿ, n.f. [1] [√ Hb 7521]

ribs [1]

Da 7: 5 one of its sides, and it had three **ribs** in its mouth between its teeth.

10553 עַם ʿam, n.m. [15] [√ Hb 6639]

people [7], peoples [6], Israelites [+10335] [1], theyˢ [+10002+10353] [1]

Ezr 5: 12 who destroyed this temple and deported the **people** to Babylon.
6: 12 any king or **people** who lifts a hand to change this decree
7: 13 Now I decree that any of the **Israelites** [+10335] in my kingdom,
7: 16 as well as the freewill offerings of the **people** and priests for the
7: 25 judges to administer justice to all the **people** of Trans-Euphrates—
Da 2: 44 that will never be destroyed, nor will it be left to another **people**.
3: 4 commanded to do, O **peoples**, nations and men of every language:
3: 7 as soon as **they**ˢ [+10002+10353] heard the sound of the horn,
3: 7 all the **peoples**, nations and men of every language fell down
3: 29 Therefore I decree that the **people** *of* any nation or language who
4: 1 [3:31] To the **peoples**, nations and men of every language,
5: 19 all the **peoples** and nations and men of every language dreaded
6: 25 [6:26] King Darius wrote to all the **peoples**, nations and men of
7: 14 all **peoples**, nations and men of every language worshiped him.
7: 27 will be handed over to the saints, the **people** *of* the Most High.

10554 עִם ʿim, pp. [22] [√ Hb 6640] See Select Index

with [10], for [2], to [2], *untranslated* [1], against [1], among [1], as well as [1], at [1], like [1], of [1], united [+10158+10180+10180] [1]

10555 עַמִּיק ʿammîq, a. [1] [√ Hb 6678]

deep [1]

Da 2: 22 He reveals **deep** and hidden things; he knows what lies in

10556 עֲמַר ᵃmar, n.m. [1] [√ Hb 7547]

wool [1]

Da 7: 9 was as white as snow; the hair of his head was white like **wool**.

10557 עַן ʿan, adv. Not used in NIV/BHS [cf. 10363]

10558 עֲנָה ᵃnâ, v. [30] [√ Hb 6699]

said [13], answered [5], replied [5], asked [3], *untranslated* [2], ordered [1], shouted [1]

Da 2: 5 [J] The king **replied** to the astrologers, "This is what I have
2: 7 [J] Once more *they* **replied**, "Let the king tell his servants the
2: 8 [J] the king **answered**, "I am certain that you are trying to gain
2: 10 [J] The astrologers **answered** the king, "There is not a man on
2: 15 [J] *He* **asked** the king's officer, "Why did the king issue such a
2: 20 [J] **[NIE]** and said: "Praise be to the name of God for ever and
2: 26 [J] The king **asked** Daniel (also called Belteshazzar), "Are you
2: 27 [J] Daniel **replied**, "No wise man, enchanter, magician or diviner
2: 47 [J] The king **said** to Daniel, "Surely your God is the God of gods
3: 9 [J] *They* **said** to King Nebuchadnezzar, "O king, live forever!
3: 14 [J] Nebuchadnezzar **said** to them, "Is it true, Shadrach, Meshach
3: 16 [J] Shadrach, Meshach and Abednego **replied** to the king,
3: 19 [J] *He* **ordered** the furnace heated seven times hotter than usual
3: 24 [J] leaped to his feet in amazement and **asked** his advisers,
3: 24 [J] and threw into the fire?" *They* **replied**, "Certainly, O king."
3: 25 [J] *He* **said**, "Look! I see four men walking around in the fire,
3: 26 [J] approached the opening of the blazing furnace and **shouted**,
3: 28 [J] Nebuchadnezzar **said**, "Praise be to the God of Shadrach,
4: 19 [4:16] [J] So the king **said**, "Belteshazzar, do not let the dream
4: 19 [4:16] [J] Belteshazzar **answered**, "My lord, if only the dream
4: 30 [4:27] [J] he **said**, "Is not this the great Babylon I have built as
5: 7 [J] diviners to be brought and **said** to these wise men of Babylon,
5: 10 [J] "O king, live forever!" she **said**. "Don't be alarmed! Don't
5: 13 [J] before the king, and the king **said** to him, "Are you Daniel,
5: 17 [J] Daniel **answered** the king, "You may keep your gifts for
6: 12 [6:13] [J] The king **answered**, "The decree stands—
6: 13 [6:14] [J] *they* **said** to the king, "Daniel, who is one of the
6: 16 [6:17] [J] The king **said** to Daniel, "May your God, whom you
6: 20 [6:21] [J] he called **[NIE]** to Daniel in an anguished voice,
7: 2 [J] Daniel **said**: "In my vision at night I looked, and there before

10559 עֲנֵה ᵃnēh, a. [1] [√ Hb 6714, 6705]

oppressed [1]

Da 4: 27 [4:24] and your wickedness by being kind to the **oppressed**.

10560 עֲנָן ᵃnān, n.[m.]. [1] [√ Hb 6727]

clouds [1]

Da 7: 13 me was one like a son of man, coming with the **clouds** *of* heaven.

10561 עֲנַף **ʿanap**, n.[m.]. [4] [√ Hb 6733]

branches [4]

Da 4: 12 [4:9] found shelter, and the birds of the air lived in its **branches**;
4: 14 [4:11] 'Cut down the tree and trim off its **branches**; strip off its
4: 14 [4:11] animals flee from under it and the birds from its **branches**.
4: 21 [4:18] having nesting places in its **branches** for the birds of the

10562 עֲנָשׁ **ʿnāš**, n.[m.]. [1] [√ Hb 6741]

confiscation [1]

Ezr 7: 26 by death, banishment, **confiscation** *of* property, or imprisonment.

10563 עֶנֶת **ʿenet**, adv. Not used in NIV/BHS [cf. 10364]

10564 עֳפִי **ʿpî**, n.m. [3] [√ Hb 6751]

leaves [3]

Da 4: 12 [4:9] Its **leaves** were beautiful, its fruit abundant, and on it was
4: 14 [4:11] trim off its branches; strip off its **leaves** and scatter its fruit.
4: 21 [4:18] with beautiful **leaves** and abundant fruit, providing food for

10565 עֲצִיב **ʿṣib**, v. [1]

anguished [1]

Da 6: 20 [6:21] he called to Daniel in an **anguished** voice, "Daniel,

10566 עֲקַר **ʿqar**, v.den. [1] [→ 10567; Hb 6827]

were uprooted [1]

Da 7: 8 [L] and three of the first horns **were uprooted** before it.

10567 עִקַּר **ʿiqqar**, n.[m.]. [3] [√ 10566]

stump [3]

Da 4: 15 [4:12] let the **stump** and its roots, bound with iron and bronze,
4: 23 [4:20] 'Cut down the tree and destroy it, but leave the **stump**,
4: 26 [4:23] The command to leave the **stump** of the tree with its roots

10568 עָר **ʿār**, n.m. [1] [√ Hb 7640]

adversaries [1]

Da 4: 19 [4:16] to your enemies and its meaning to your **adversaries**!

10569 עֲרַב **ʿrab**, v. [4] [√ Hb 6843]

mixed [2], mixes [1], mixture [1]

Da 2: 41 [N] strength of iron in it, even as you saw iron **mixed** with clay.
2: 43 [N] just as you saw the iron **mixed** with baked clay, so the people
2: 43 [O] so the people will be a **mixture** and will not remain united,
2: 43 [O] will not remain united, any more than iron **mixes** with clay.

10570 עֲרָד **ʿrād**, n.m. [1] [√ Hb 6871]

wild donkeys [1]

Da 5: 21 an animal; he lived with the **wild donkeys** and ate grass like cattle;

10571 עַרְוָה **ʿarwā**, n.f. [1] [√ Hb 6872]

dishonored [1]

Ezr 4: 14 to the palace and it is not proper for us to see the king **dishonored**,

10572 עֲשַׂב **ʿśab**, n.[m.]. [5] [√ Hb 6912]

grass [4], plants [1]

Da 4: 15 [4:12] let him live with the animals among the **plants** *of* the earth.
4: 25 [4:22] you will eat **grass** like cattle and be drenched with the dew
4: 32 [4:29] live with the wild animals; you will eat **grass** like cattle.
4: 33 [4:30] He was driven away from people and ate **grass** like cattle.
5: 21 an animal; he lived with the wild donkeys and ate **grass** like cattle;

10573 עֲשַׂר **ʿśar**, n.m. & f. [6] [→ 10574; Hb 6924, 6927]

ten [4], twelve [+10775] [2]

Ezr 6: 17 as a sin offering for all Israel, **twelve** [+10775] male goats,
Da 4: 29 [4:26] **Twelve** [+10775] months later, as the king was walking on
7: 7 It was different from all the former beasts, and it had **ten** horns.
7: 20 I also wanted to know about the **ten** horns on its head and about
7: 24 The **ten** horns are ten kings who will come from this kingdom.
7: 24 The ten horns are **ten** kings who will come from this kingdom.

10574 עֶשְׂרִין **ʿeśrîn**, n.pl.indecl. [1] [√ 10573; Hb 6929]

120 [+10221+10395] [1]

Da 6: 1 [6:2] It pleased Darius to appoint **120** [+10221+10395] satraps to

10575 עֲשַׁת **ʿšat**, v. [1] [√ Hb 6951]

planned [1]

Da 6: 3 [6:4] [J] the king **planned** to set him over the whole kingdom.

10576 עֵת **ʿet**, adv. Not used in NIV/BHS [cf. 10365]

10577 עֲתִיד **ʿtîd**, a. [1] [√ Hb 6969]

ready [1]

Da 3: 15 if you are **ready** to fall down and worship the image I made,

10578 עַתִּיק **ʿattîq**, a. [3]

Ancient [3]

Da 7: 9 "thrones were set in place, and the **Ancient** *of* Days took his seat.
7: 13 He approached the **Ancient** *of* Days and was led into his presence.
7: 22 until the **Ancient** *of* Days came and pronounced judgment in favor

פ, *p*

10579 פ **p**, letter. Not used in NIV/BHS [√ Hb 6989]

10580 פֶּחָה **peḥâ**, n.m. [10] [√ Hb 7068]

governor [6], governors [4]

Ezr 5: 3 **governor** *of* Trans-Euphrates, and Shethar-Bozenai and their
5: 6 **governor** *of* Trans-Euphrates, and Shethar-Bozenai and their
5: 14 to a man named Sheshbazzar, whom he had appointed **governor**,
6: 6 Now then, Tattenai, **governor** *of* Trans-Euphrates, and
6: 7 Let the **governor** *of* the Jews and the Jewish elders rebuild this
6: 13 Tattenai, **governor** *of* Trans-Euphrates, and Shethar-Bozenai
Da 3: 2 prefects, **governors**, advisers, treasurers, judges, magistrates
3: 3 prefects, **governors**, advisers, treasurers, judges, magistrates
3: 27 prefects, **governors** and royal advisers crowded around them.
6: 7 [6:8] **governors** have all agreed that the king should issue an edict

10581 פֶּחָר **peḥār**, n.m. [1]

untranslated [1]

Da 2: 41 and toes were partly of baked clay **[NIE]** and partly of iron,

10582 פַּטִּישׁ **paṭṭîš**, n.[m.]. [1]

trousers [1]

Da 3: 21 **trousers**, turbans and other clothes, were bound and thrown into

10583 פְּלַג **pᵉlag¹**, v. [1] [→ 10584, 10585; Hb 7103]

divided [1]

Da 2: 41 [Jp] and partly of iron, so this will be a **divided** kingdom;

10584 פְּלַג **pᵉlag²**, n.[m.]. [1] [√ 10583; Hb 7104]

half [1]

Da 7: 25 saints will be handed over to him for a time, times and **half** a time.

10585 פְּלֻגָּה **pᵉluggâ**, n.f. [1] [√ 10583; Hb 7107]

divisions [1]

Ezr 6: 18 they installed the priests in their **divisions** and the Levites in their

10586 פְּלַח **pᵉlaḥ**, v. [10] [→ 10587; Hb 7114?]

serve [7], workers [1], worship [1], worshiped [1]

Ezr 7: 24 [J] temple servants or other **workers** *at* this house of God.
Da 3: 12 [J] *They* neither **serve** your gods nor worship the image of gold
3: 14 [J] that you *do* not **serve** my gods or worship the image of gold I
3: 17 [J] the God we **serve** is able to save us from it, and he will rescue
3: 18 [J] that we *will* not **serve** your gods or worship the image of gold
3: 28 [J] and were willing to give up their lives rather than **serve**
6: 16 [6:17] [J] your God, whom you **serve** continually, rescue you!"
6: 20 [6:21] [J] whom you **serve** continually, been able to rescue you
7: 14 [J] nations and men of every language **worshiped** him.
7: 27 [J] and all rulers *will* **worship** and obey him.'

10587 פָּלְחָן **polḥān**, n.[m.]. [1] [√ 10586]

worship [1]

Ezr 7: 19 articles entrusted to you for **worship** *in* the temple of your God.

10588 פֻּם *pum*, n.m. [6]
mouth [4], lips [1], mouths [1]

Da 4: 31 [4:28] The words were still on his **lips** when a voice came from
6: 17 [6:18] A stone was brought and placed over the **mouth** *of* the den,
6: 22 [6:23] God sent his angel, and he shut the **mouths** *of* the lions.
7: 5 one of its sides, and it had three ribs in its **mouth** between its teeth.
7: 8 had eyes like the eyes of a man and a **mouth** that spoke boastfully.
7: 20 the others and that had eyes and a **mouth** that spoke boastfully.

10589 פַּס *pas*, n.m. [2] [√ Hb 7168]
hand [+10311] [2]

Da 5: 5 the royal palace. The king watched the **hand** [+10311] as it wrote.
5: 24 Therefore he sent the **hand** [+10311] that wrote the inscription.

10590 פְּסַנְתֵּרִין *p^{e}santērîn*, n.[m.]. [4]
harp [4]

Da 3: 5 flute, zither, lyre, **harp**, pipes and all kinds of music, you must fall
3: 7 flute, zither, lyre, **harp** and all kinds of music, all the peoples,
3: 10 lyre, **harp**, pipes and all kinds of music must fall down
3: 15 flute, zither, lyre, **harp**, pipes and all kinds of music, if you are

10591 פַּרְזֶל *parzel*, n.m. [20] [√ Hb 1366]
iron [20]

Da 2: 33 its legs of **iron**, its feet partly of iron and partly of baked clay.
2: 33 its legs of iron, its feet partly of **iron** and partly of baked clay.
2: 34 It struck the statue on its feet of **iron** and clay and smashed them.
2: 35 the **iron**, the clay, the bronze, the silver and the gold were broken
2: 40 Finally, there will be a fourth kingdom, strong as **iron**—for iron
2: 40 strong as iron—for **iron** breaks and smashes everything—
2: 40 as **iron** breaks things to pieces, so it will crush and break all the
2: 41 that the feet and toes were partly of baked clay and partly of **iron**,
2: 41 yet it will have some of the strength of **iron** in it, even as you saw
2: 41 of the strength of iron in it, even as you saw **iron** mixed with clay.
2: 42 As the toes were partly **iron** and partly clay, so this kingdom will
2: 43 just as you saw the **iron** mixed with baked clay, so the people will
2: 43 and will not remain united, any more than **iron** mixes with clay.
2: 45 a rock that broke the **iron**, the bronze, the clay, the silver
4: 15 [4:12] let the stump and its roots, bound with **iron** and bronze,
4: 23 [4:20] but leave the stump, bound with **iron** and bronze,
5: 4 the gods of gold and silver, of bronze, **iron**, wood and stone.
5: 23 the gods of silver and gold, of bronze, **iron**, wood and stone,
7: 7 It had large **iron** teeth; it crushed and devoured its victims
7: 19 and most terrifying, with its **iron** teeth and bronze claws—

10592 פְּרַס *p^{e}ras*, v. [1] [→ 10593; Hb 7271]
is divided [1]

Da 5: 28 [K] Your kingdom **is divided** and given to the Medes

10593 פְּרֵס *p^{e}rēs*, n.[m.]. [2] [√ 10592]
parsin [1], peres [1]

Da 5: 25 inscription that was written: MENE, MENE, TEKEL, **PARSIN**
5: 28 ***Peres***: Your kingdom is divided and given to the Medes

10594 פָּרַס *pāras*, n.pr.loc. & g. [6] [→ 10595; Hb 7273]
Persians [4], Persia [2]

Ezr 4: 24 until the second year of the reign of Darius king of **Persia**.
6: 14 and the decrees of Cyrus, Darius and Artaxerxes, kings of **Persia**.
Da 5: 28 Your kingdom is divided and given to the Medes and **Persians**."
6: 8 [6:9] in accordance with the laws of the Medes and **Persians**,
6: 12 [6:13] in accordance with the laws of the Medes and **Persians**,
6: 15 [6:16] according to the law of the Medes and **Persians** no decree

10595 פָּרְסָי *parsāy*, a.g. [1] [√ 10594; Hb 7275]
Persian [1]

Da 6: 28 [6:29] the reign of Darius and the reign of Cyrus the **Persian**.

10596 פְּרַק *p^{e}raq*, v. [1] [√ Hb 7293]
renounce [1]

Da 4: 27 [4:24] [J] **Renounce** your sins by doing what is right, and your

10597 פְּרַשׁ *p^{e}raš*, v. [1] [√ Hb 7298]
translated [1]

Ezr 4: 18 [N] you sent us has been read and **translated** in my presence.

10598 פַּרְשֶׁגֶן *paršegen*, n.m. [3] [√ Hb 7358]
copy [3]

Ezr 4: 11 (This is a **copy** *of* the letter they sent him.) To King Artaxerxes,
4: 23 As soon as the **copy** *of* the letter of King Artaxerxes was read to
5: 6 This is a **copy** *of* the letter that Tattenai, governor of

10599 פְּשַׁר[1] *p^{e}šar[1]*, v. [2] [→ 10600; Hb 7323, 7354]
give interpretations [+10600] [1], interpret [1]

Da 5: 12 [M] also the *ability to* **interpret** dreams, explain riddles
5: 16 [J] I have heard that you are able to **give interpretations** [+10600]

10600 פְּשַׁר[2] *p^{e}šar[2]*, n.m. [31] [√ 10599; Hb 7323]
means [7], interpret [+10252] [5], interpretation [4], interpret [+10313] [3], interpret [3], interpret [+10042] [2], meaning [2], explain [+10252] [1], explain [1], give interpretations [+10599] [1], mean [1], meant [1]

Da 2: 4 Tell your servants the dream, and *we will* **interpret** [+10252] it."
2: 5 If you do not tell me what my dream was and **interpret** it,
2: 6 if you tell me the dream and **explain** it, you will receive from me
2: 6 and great honor. So tell me the dream and **interpret** it for me."
2: 7 tell his servants the dream, and *we will* **interpret** [+10252] it."
2: 9 and I will know that *you can* **interpret** [+10252] it *for* me."
2: 16 for time, so that he *might* **interpret** [+10252] the dream for him.
2: 24 me to the king, and *I will* **interpret** [+10252] his dream for him."
2: 25 exiles from Judah who can tell the king *what* his dream **means**."
2: 26 "Are you able to tell me what I saw in my dream and **interpret** it?"
2: 30 may know the **interpretation** and that you may understand what
2: 36 was the dream, and now *we will* **interpret** [+10042] it to the king.
2: 45 The dream is true and the **interpretation** is trustworthy."
4: 6 [4:3] brought before me *to* **interpret** [+10313] the dream *for* me.
4: 7 [4:4] the dream, but *they could* not **interpret** [+10313] it for me.
4: 9 [4:6] for you. Here is my dream; **interpret** [+10042] it for me.
4: 18 [4:15] Now, Belteshazzar, tell me *what* it **means**, for none of the
4: 18 [4:15] men in my kingdom can **interpret** [+10313] it *for* me.
4: 19 [4:16] do not let the dream or its **meaning** alarm you."
4: 19 [4:16] to your enemies and its **meaning** to your adversaries!
4: 24 [4:21] "This is the **interpretation**, O king, and this is the decree
5: 7 this writing and tells me *what* it **means** will be clothed in purple
5: 8 but they could not read the writing or tell the king *what* it **meant**.
5: 12 Call for Daniel, and he will tell you *what* the writing **means**."
5: 15 brought before me to read this writing and tell me *what* it **means**,
5: 15 and tell me what it means, but they could not **explain** [+10252] it.
5: 16 I have heard that you are able to **give interpretations** [+10599] and
5: 16 If you can read this writing and tell me *what* it **means**, you will be
5: 17 I will read the writing for the king and tell him *what* it **means**.
5: 26 "This is what these words **mean**: *Mene*: God has numbered the
7: 16 "So he told me and gave me the **interpretation** *of* these things:

10601 פִּתְגָם *pitgām*, n.m. [6] [√ Hb 7330]
answer [1], decision [1], defend [+10754] [1], edict [1], reply [1], report [1]

Ezr 4: 17 The king sent this **reply**: To Rehum the commanding officer,
5: 7 The **report** they sent him read as follows: To King Darius:
5: 11 This is the **answer** they gave us: "We are the servants of the God
6: 11 Furthermore, I decree that if anyone changes this **edict**, a beam is
Da 3: 16 we do not need to **defend** [+10754] ourselves *before* you in this
4: 17 [4:14] " 'The **decision** is announced by messengers, the holy ones

10602 פְּתַח *p^{e}taḥ*, v. [2] [√ Hb 7337]
opened [1], were opened [1]

Da 6: 10 [6:11] [Jp] room where the windows **opened** toward Jerusalem.
7: 10 [Jp] The court was seated, and the books **were opened**.

10603 פְּתָי *p^{e}tāy*, n.[m.]. [2]
wide [2]

Ezr 6: 3 be laid. It is to be ninety feet high and ninety feet **wide**,
Da 3: 1 made an image of gold, ninety feet high and nine feet **wide**,

צ, ṣ

10604 צ *ṣ*, letter. Not used in NIV/BHS [√ Hb 7360]

10605 צְבָה *ṣ^{e}bâ*, v. [10] [→ 10606]
wanted to [4], wishes [4], pleases [1], wanted [1]

Da 4: 17 [4:14] [J] gives them to anyone *he* **wishes** and sets over them
4: 25 [4:22] [J] of men and gives them to anyone *he* **wishes**.
4: 32 [4:29] [J] of men and gives them to anyone *he* **wishes**."

[J] Peal [Jp] Peal passive [K] Peil [L] Hithpeel (Hitpolel, Itpeel) [M] Pael [Mp] Pael passive [N] Pual (Poel)

Da 4: 35 [4:32] [J] He does as he **pleases** with the powers of heaven
5: 19 [J] Those the king **wanted to** put to death, he put to death; those
5: 19 [J] to death, he put to death; those *he* **wanted to** spare, he spared;
5: 19 [J] he spared; those *he* **wanted to** promote, he promoted;
5: 19 [J] he promoted; and those *he* **wanted to** humble, he humbled.
5: 21 [J] the kingdoms of men and sets over them anyone *he* **wishes**.
7: 19 [J] "Then *I* **wanted** to know the true meaning of the fourth beast,

10606 צְבוּ ṣebû, n.f. [1] [√ 10605]

situation [1]

Da 6: 17 [6:18] so that Daniel's **situation** might not be changed.

10607 צְבַע ṣeba', v. [5] [√ Hb 7388]

be drenched [2], was drenched [2], drenched [1]

Da 4: 15 [4:12] [O] " '*Let him* **be drenched** with the dew of heaven,
4: 23 [4:20] [O] *Let him* **be drenched** with the dew of heaven; let
4: 25 [4:22] [M] like cattle and *be* **drenched** with the dew of heaven.
4: 33 [4:30] [O] His body **was drenched** with the dew of heaven until
5: 21 [O] his body **was drenched** with the dew of heaven, until he

10608 צַד ṣad, n.[m.]. [2] [√ Hb 7396]

against [+10378] [1], in [+10427] [1]

Da 6: 4 [6:5] Daniel **in** [+10427] his conduct of government affairs,
7: 25 He will speak **against** [+10378] the Most High and oppress his

10609 צְדָא ṣedā', n.[m.]. [1] [cf. 10216]

is it true [+10190] [1]

Da 3: 14 and Nebuchadnezzar said to them, "**Is it true** [+10190], Shadrach,

10610 צִדְקָה ṣidqâ, n.f. [1] [√ Hb 7407]

right [1]

Da 4: 27 [4:24] Renounce your sins by doing *what* is **right**, and your

10611 צַוַּאר ṣawwa'r, n.m. [3] [√ Hb 7418]

neck [3]

Da 5: 7 be clothed in purple and have a gold chain placed around his **neck**,
5: 16 clothed in purple and have a gold chain placed around your **neck**,
5: 29 was clothed in purple, a gold chain was placed around his **neck**,

10612 צְלָה ṣelâ, v. [2]

pray [1], prayed [1]

Ezr 6: 10 [M] and **pray** for the well-being of the king and his sons.
Da 6: 10 [6:11] [M] times a day he got down on his knees and **prayed**,

10613 צְלַח ṣelaḥ, v. [4] [√ Hb 7503]

making rapid progress [1], promoted [1], prosper [1], prospered [1]

Ezr 5: 8 [P] and *is* **making rapid progress** under their direction.
6: 14 [P] **prosper** under the preaching of Haggai the prophet and
Da 3: 30 [P] the king **promoted** Shadrach, Meshach and Abednego in the
6: 28 [6:29] [P] So Daniel **prospered** during the reign of Darius

10614 צְלֵם ṣelēm, n.m. [17] [√ Hb 7512]

image [10], statue [5], attitude [+10049] [1], it[s] [+10002] [1]

Da 2: 31 "You looked, O king, and there before you stood a large **statue**—
2: 31 an enormous, dazzling **statue**, awesome in appearance.
2: 32 The head of the **statue** was made of pure gold, its chest and arms
2: 34 It struck the **statue** on its feet of iron and clay and smashed them.
2: 35 But the rock that struck the **statue** became a huge mountain
3: 1 King Nebuchadnezzar made an **image** of gold, ninety feet high
3: 2 officials to come to the dedication of the **image** he had set up.
3: 3 the dedication of the **image** that King Nebuchadnezzar had set up,
3: 3 Nebuchadnezzar had set up, and they stood before **it**[s] [+10002].
3: 5 worship the **image** *of* gold that King Nebuchadnezzar has set up.
3: 7 worshiped the **image** *of* gold that King Nebuchadnezzar had set up.
3: 10 all kinds of music must fall down and worship the **image** *of* gold,
3: 12 They neither serve your gods nor worship the **image** *of* gold you
3: 14 do not serve my gods or worship the **image** *of* gold I have set up?
3: 15 if you are ready to fall down and worship the **image** I made,
3: 18 not serve your gods or worship the **image** *of* gold you have set up."
3: 19 and Abednego, and his **attitude** [+10049] toward them changed.

10615 צְפִיר ṣepîr, n.m. [1] [√ Hb 7618]

male goats [+10535] [1]

Ezr 6: 17 as a sin offering for all Israel, twelve **male goats** [+10535],

10616 צִפַּר ṣippar, n.f. [4] [√ Hb 7607]

birds [3], bird [1]

Da 4: 12 [4:9] found shelter, and the **birds** *of* the air lived in its branches;
4: 14 [4:11] animals flee from under it and the **birds** from its branches.
4: 21 [4:18] having nesting places in its branches for the **birds** *of* the
4: 33 [4:30] feathers of an eagle and his nails like the claws of a **bird**.

ק, q

10617 ק q, letter. Not used in NIV/BHS [√ Hb 7682]

10618 קְבַל qebal, v.den. [3] [→ 10619; Hb 7691]

receive [2], took over [1]

Da 2: 6 [M] *you will* **receive** from me gifts and rewards and great honor.
5: 31 [6:1] [M] Darius the Mede **took over** the kingdom, at the age of
7: 18 [M] the saints of the Most High *will* **receive** the kingdom

10619 קֳבֵל qobēl, subst. & pp. & c. [29] [√ 10618]

untranslated [8], because [+10168+10353] [3], for [+10168+10353] [3], before [+10378] [2], because of [+10168+10378] [1], by [+10168+10353] [1], even as [+10168+10353] [1], just as [+10168 +10353] [1], near [+10378] [1], since [+10168+10353] [1], so [+10180+10353] [1], then [+10180+10353] [1], therefore [+10180+ 10353] [1], this is the meaning [+10168+10353] [1], this made [+10180+10353] [1], though [+10168+10353] [1], with [+10378] [1]

Ezr 4: 14 Now **since** [+10168+10353] we are under obligation to the palace
4: 16 **[NIE]** you will be left with nothing in Trans-Euphrates.
6: 13 Then, **because** [+10168+10378] **of** the decree King Darius had
7: 14 **[NIE]** You are sent by the king and his seven advisers to inquire
7: 17 **[NIE]** With this money be sure to buy bulls, rams and male
Da 2: 8 you are trying to gain time, **because** [+10168+10353] you realize
2: 10 **[NIE]** No king, however great and mighty, has ever asked such a
2: 12 **This made** [+10180+10353] the king so angry and furious that he
2: 24 **Then** [+10180+10353] Daniel went to Arioch, whom the king had
2: 31 O king, and there **before** [+10378] you stood a large statue—
2: 40 strong as iron—**for** [+10168+10353] iron breaks and smashes
2: 41 have some of the strength of iron in it, **even as** [+10168+10353]
2: 45 **This is the meaning** [+10168+10353] *of* the vision of the rock cut
3: 3 Nebuchadnezzar had set up, and they stood **before** [+10378] it.
3: 7 **Therefore** [+10180+10353], as soon as they heard the sound of the
3: 8 **[NIE]** At this time some astrologers came forward and denounced
3: 22 **[NIE]** The king's command was so urgent and the furnace
3: 29 their houses be turned into piles of rubble, **for** [+10168+10353] no
4: 18 [4:15] tell me what it means, **for** [+10168+10353] none of the
5: 1 for a thousand of his nobles and drank wine **with** [+10378] them.
5: 5 of the wall, **near** [+10378] the lampstand in the royal palace.
5: 10 The queen, **[NIE]** hearing the voices of the king and his nobles,
5: 12 **[NIE]** This man Daniel, whom the king called Belteshazzar,
5: 22 not humbled yourself, **though** [+10168+10353] you knew all this.
6: 3 [6:4] the satraps **by** [+10168+10353] his exceptional qualities that
6: 4 [6:5] **because** [+10168+10353] he was trustworthy and neither
6: 9 [6:10] **So** [+10180+10353] King Darius put the decree in writing.
6: 10 [6:11] giving thanks to his God, **just as** [+10168+10353] he had
6: 22 [6:23] not hurt me, **because** [+10168+10353] I was found innocent

10620 קַדִּישׁ qaddîš, a. [13] [√ Hb 7705]

holy [7], saints [5], they[s] [1]

Da 4: 8 [4:5] name of my god, and the spirit of the **holy** gods is in him.)
4: 9 [4:6] I know that the spirit of the **holy** gods is in you,
4: 13 [4:10] was a messenger, a **holy** *one*, coming down from heaven.
4: 17 [4:14] by messengers, the **holy** *ones* declare the verdict,
4: 18 [4:15] But you can, because the spirit of the **holy** gods is in you."
4: 23 [4:20] "You, O king, saw a messenger, a **holy** *one*, coming down
5: 11 There is a man in your kingdom who has the spirit of the **holy** gods
7: 18 the **saints** *of* the Most High will receive the kingdom and will
7: 21 this horn was waging war against the **saints** and defeating them,
7: 22 and pronounced judgment in favor of the **saints** *of* the Most High,
7: 22 Most High, and the time came when **they**[s] possessed the kingdom.
7: 25 and oppress his **saints** and try to change the set times and the laws.
7: 27 under the whole heaven will be handed over to the **saints**,

10621 קֳדָם qodām, pp. [42] [→ 10622, 10623; Hb 7710]

untranslated [12], to [11], before [7], before [+10427] [2], from [+10427] [2], into presence [2], by [+10427] [1], former [1], in presence [1], in sight [1], issue [+10427] [1], my [+10307] [1]

Ezr 4: 18 The letter you sent us has been read and translated **in my presence**.
4: 23 As soon as the copy of the letter of King Artaxerxes was read **to**

Ezr 7:14 You are sent **by** [+10427] the king and his seven advisers to
7:19 Deliver **to** the God of Jerusalem all the articles entrusted to you for
Da 2: 6 you will receive **from** [+10427] me gifts and rewards and great
2: 9 You have conspired to tell **[OBJ]** me misleading and wicked
2:10 The astrologers answered **[OBJ]** the king, "There is not a man on
2:11 No one can reveal it **to** the king except the gods, and they do not
2:15 "Why did the king **issue** [+10427] such a harsh decree?"
2:18 He urged them to plead for mercy **from** [+10427] the God of
2:24 Take me **to** the king, and I will interpret his dream for him."
2:25 Arioch took Daniel **to** the king at once and said, "I have found a
2:27 **[OBJ]** "No wise man, enchanter, magician or diviner can explain
2:36 "This was the dream, and now we will interpret it **to** the king.
3:13 and Abednego. So these men were brought **before** the king,
4: 2 [3:32] It is **my** [+10307] pleasure to tell you about the miraculous
4: 6 [4:3] be brought **before** me to interpret the dream for me.
4: 7 [4:4] and diviners came, I told **[OBJ]** them the dream,
4: 8 [4:5] Daniel came **into** my **presence** and I told him the dream.
4: 8 [4:5] came into my presence and I told **[OBJ]** him the dream.
5:13 So Daniel was brought **before** the king, and the king said to him,
5:15 and enchanters were brought **before** me to read this writing
5:17 Daniel answered **[OBJ]** the king, "You may keep your gifts for
5:19 and men of every language dreaded and feared **[OBJ]** him.
5:23 You had the goblets from his temple brought **to** you, and you
5:24 Therefore he sent **[OBJ]** the hand that wrote the inscription.
6: 1 [6:2] It pleased **[OBJ]** Darius to appoint 120 satraps to rule
6:10 [6:11] down on his knees and prayed, giving thanks **to** his God,
6:11 [6:12] found Daniel praying and asking God for help. **[OBJ]**
6:12 [6:13] went to the king and spoke **to** him about his royal decree:
6:13 [6:14] they said **to** the king, "Daniel, who is one of the exiles
6:18 [6:19] and without any entertainment being brought **to** him.
6:22 [6:23] not hurt me, because I was found innocent **in** his **sight**.
6:22 [6:23] Nor have I ever done any wrong **before** you, O king."
6:26 [6:27] "I issue **[OBJ]** a decree that in every part of my kingdom
6:26 [6:27] people must fear and reverence **[OBJ]** the God of Daniel.
7: 7 It was different from all the **former** beasts, and it had ten horns.
7: 8 and three of the first horns were uprooted **before** [+10427] it.
7:10 A river of fire was flowing, coming out from **before** him.
7:10 attended him; ten thousand times ten thousand stood **before** him.
7:13 He approached the Ancient of Days and was led **into** his **presence**.
7:20 about the other horn that came up, **before** [+10427] which three of

10622 קַדְמָה *qadmâ*, n.f. [2] [√ 10621; Hb 7712]

ago [+10180+10427] [1], before [+10180+10427] [1]

Ezr 5:11 the temple that was built many years **ago** [+10180+10427],
Da 6:10 [6:11] to his God, just as he had done **before** [+10180+10427].

10623 קַדְמָי *qadmāy*, a. [3] [√ 10621; Hb 7710]

first [2], earlier [1]

Da 7: 4 "The **first** was like a lion, and it had the wings of an eagle.
7: 8 among them; and three of the **first** horns were uprooted before it.
7:24 After them another king will arise, different from the **earlier** *ones*;

10624 קוּם *qûm*, v. [35] [→ 10628?, 10629; Hb 7756]

set up [9], stood [4], issue [2], rise [2], sets [2], *untranslated* [1], appoint [1], appointed [1], arise [1], come [1], endure [1], get up [1], got up [1], installed [1], issues [1], leaped to feet [1], set to work [+10221+10742] [1], set [1], sets up [1], standing [1], was raised up [1]

Ezr 5: 2 [J] Jeshua son of Jozadak **set** [+10221+10742] **to work** to rebuild
6:18 [P] *they* **installed** the priests in their divisions and the Levites in
Da 2:21 [P] and seasons; *he* **sets up** kings and deposes them.
2:31 [J] O king, and there before you **stood** a large statue—
2:39 [J] "After you, another kingdom *will* **rise**, inferior to yours. Next,
2:44 [P] the God of heaven *will* **set up** a kingdom that will never be
2:44 [J] and bring them to an end, but *it will* itself **endure** forever.
3: 1 [P] and **set** it **up** on the plain of Dura in the province of Babylon.
3: 2 [P] to come to the dedication of the image he *had* **set up**.
3: 3 [P] of the image that King Nebuchadnezzar *had* **set up**,
3: 3 [J] King Nebuchadnezzar had set up, and *they* **stood** before it.
3: 3 [P] had set up, and they stood before it. **[RPH]**
3: 5 [P] the image of gold that King Nebuchadnezzar *has* **set up**.
3: 7 [P] the image of gold that King Nebuchadnezzar *had* **set up**.
3:12 [P] your gods nor worship the image of gold *you have* **set up**."
3:14 [P] serve my gods or worship the image of gold *I have* **set up**?
3:18 [P] your gods or worship the image of gold *you have* **set up**."
3:24 [J] Then King Nebuchadnezzar **leaped to** *his* **feet** in amazement
4:17 [4:14] [P] he wishes and **sets** over them the lowliest of men.'
5:11 [P] **appointed** him chief of the magicians, enchanters, astrologers
5:21 [P] the kingdoms of men and **sets** over them anyone he wishes.
6: 1 [6:2] [P] It pleased Darius *to* **appoint** 120 satraps to rule
6: 3 [6:4] [P] the king planned to **set** him over the whole kingdom.
6: 7 [6:8] [M] governors have all agreed that the king *should* **issue**
6: 8 [6:9] [P] **issue** the decree and put it in writing so that it cannot
6:15 [6:16] [P] or edict that the king **issues** can be changed."
6:19 [6:20] [J] of dawn, the king **got up** and hurried to the lions' den.
7: 4 [Q] lifted from the ground so that *it* **stood** on two feet like a man,
7: 5 [Q] *It* **was raised up** on one of its sides, and it had three ribs in
7: 5 [J] its teeth. It was told, '**Get up** and eat your fill of flesh!'
7:10 [J] ten thousand times ten thousand **stood** before him.
7:16 [J] I approached one of *those* **standing** there and asked him the
7:17 [J] 'The four great beasts are four kingdoms *that will* **rise** from
7:24 [J] The ten horns are ten kings *who will* **come** from this
7:24 [J] After them another king *will* **arise**, different from the earlier

10625 קְטַל *qᵉṭal*, v. [7] [√ Hb 7779]

put to death [4], was slain [2], killed [1]

Da 2:13 [O] So the decree was issued *to* **put** the wise men **to death**,
2:13 [L] sent to look for Daniel and his friends to **put** them **to death**.
2:14 [M] had gone out to **put to death** the wise men of Babylon,
3:22 [M] so hot that the flames of the fire **killed** the soldiers who took
5:19 [J] Those the king wanted to put to death, *he* **put to death**; those
5:30 [K] very night Belshazzar, king of the Babylonians, **was slain**,
7:11 [K] I kept looking until the beast **was slain** and its body

10626 קְטַר *qᵉṭar*, n.m. [3]

difficult problems [2], legs [+10284] [1]

Da 5: 6 that his knees knocked together and his **legs** [+10284] gave way.
5:12 to interpret dreams, explain riddles and solve **difficult problems**.
5:16 are able to give interpretations and to solve **difficult problems**.

10627 קַיִט *qayiṭ*, n.[m.]. Not used in NIV/BHS [√ Hb 7811]

10628 קְיָם *qᵉyām*, n.[m.]. [2] [√ 10624?]

edict [2]

Da 6: 7 [6:8] governors have all agreed that the king should issue an **edict**
6:15 [6:16] no decree or **edict** that the king issues can be changed."

10629 קַיָּם *qayyām*, a. [2] [√ 10624]

endures [1], restored [1]

Da 4:26 [4:23] **restored** to you when you acknowledge that Heaven rules.
6:26 [6:27] "For he is the living God and he **endures** forever; his

10630 קִיתָרֹס *qîᵗᵉrōs*, n.[m.]. [4]

zither [4]

Da 3: 5 flute, **zither**, [Q 10644] lyre, harp, pipes and all kinds of music,
3: 7 flute, **zither**, [Q 10644] lyre, harp and all kinds of music,
3:10 flute, **zither**, [Q 10644] lyre, harp, pipes and all kinds of music
3:15 flute, **zither**, [Q 10644] lyre, harp, pipes and all kinds of music,

10631 קָל *qāl*, n.m. [7] [√ Hb 7754]

sound [4], voice [2], *untranslated* [1]

Da 3: 5 As soon as you hear the **sound** *of* the horn, flute, zither, lyre,
3: 7 as soon as they heard the **sound** *of* the horn, flute, zither, lyre,
3:10 that everyone who hears the **sound** *of* the horn, flute, zither,
3:15 Now when you hear the **sound** *of* the horn, flute, zither, lyre,
4:31 [4:28] The words were still on his lips when a **voice** came from
6:20 [6:21] he called to Daniel in an anguished **voice**, "Daniel,
7:11 because of **[NIE]** the boastful words the horn was speaking.

10632 קְנָה *qᵉnâ*, v. [1] [√ Hb 7864]

buy [1]

Ezr 7:17 [J] With this money be sure *to* **buy** bulls, rams and male lambs,

10633 קְצַף¹ *qᵉṣap¹*, v. [1] [→ 10634; Hb 7911]

furious [1]

Da 2:12 [J] **furious** that he ordered the execution of all the wise men of

10634 קְצַף² *qᵉṣap²*, n.[m.]. [1] [√ 10633; Hb 7912]

wrath [1]

Ezr 7:23 Why should there be **wrath** against the realm of the king and of his

10635 קְצַץ *qᵉṣaṣ*, v. [1] [√ Hb 7915]

trim off [1]

Da 4:14 [4:11] [M] 'Cut down the tree and **trim off** its branches; strip off

10636 קְצָת *qᵉṣāt*, n.f. [3] [√ Hb 7921]

end [1], later [+10378] [1], partly [+10427] [1]

Da 2:42 so this kingdom will be **partly** [+10427] strong and partly brittle.

Da 4:29 [4:26] Twelve months **later** [+10378], as the king was walking on
4:34 [4:31] At the **end** *of* that time, I, Nebuchadnezzar, raised my eyes

10637 קְרָא qerā', v. [11] [√ Hb 7924]

read [4], been read [1], call [1], called out [1], called [1], proclaimed [1], reads [1], was read [1]

Ezr 4:18 [K] The letter you sent us *has* **been read** and translated in my
4:23 [K] the copy of the letter of King Artaxerxes **was read** to Rehum
Da 3:4 [J] the herald loudly **proclaimed**, "This is what you are
4:14 [4:11] [J] *He* **called** in a loud voice: 'Cut down the tree and trim
5:7 [J] The king **called out** for the enchanters, astrologers and
5:7 [J] "Whoever **reads** this writing and tells me what it means will
5:8 [J] they could not **read** the writing or tell the king what it meant.
5:12 [L] **Call** *for* Daniel, and he will tell you what the writing means."
5:15 [J] and enchanters were brought before me *to* **read** this writing
5:16 [J] If you can **read** this writing and tell me what it means,
5:17 [J] *I will* **read** the writing for the king and tell him what it means.

10638 קְרֵב qerēb, v. [9] [→ 10639; Hb 7928]

approached [2], came forward [1], came near [1], led [1], offer sacrifices [1], offered [1], sacrifice [1], went [1]

Ezr 6:10 [P] so that *they may* **offer sacrifices** pleasing to the God of
6:17 [P] For the dedication of this house of God *they* **offered** a
7:17 [M] **sacrifice** them on the altar of the temple of your God in
Da 3:8 [J] At this time some astrologers **came forward** and denounced
3:26 [J] **approached** the opening of the blazing furnace and shouted,
6:12 [6:13] [J] So *they* **went** *to* the king and spoke to him about his
6:20 [6:21] [J] When he **came near** the den, he called to Daniel in an
7:13 [P] the Ancient of Days and *was* **led** into his presence.
7:16 [J] *I* **approached** one of those standing there and asked him the

10639 קְרָב qerāb, n.[m.]. [1] [√ 10638; Hb 7930]

war [1]

Da 7:21 this horn was waging **war** against the saints and defeating them,

10640 קִרְיָה qiryâ, n.f. [9] [√ Hb 7953]

city [9]

Ezr 4:10 settled in the **city** of Samaria and elsewhere in Trans-Euphrates.
4:12 to Jerusalem and are rebuilding that rebellious and wicked **city**.
4:13 the king should know that if this **city** is built and its walls are
4:15 In these records you will find that this **city** is a rebellious city,
4:15 In these records you will find that this city is a rebellious **city**,
4:15 rebellion from ancient times. That is why this **city** was destroyed.
4:16 We inform the king that if this **city** is built and its walls are
4:19 it was found that this **city** has a long history of revolt against kings
4:21 to stop work, so that this **city** will not be rebuilt until I so order.

10641 קֶרֶן qeren, n.f. [14] [√ Hb 7967]

horn [9], horns [5]

Da 3:5 As soon as you hear the sound of the **horn**, flute, zither, lyre,
3:7 as soon as they heard the sound of the **horn**, flute, zither, lyre,
3:10 that everyone who hears the sound of the **horn**, flute, zither,
3:15 Now when you hear the sound of the **horn**, flute, zither, lyre,
7:7 It was different from all the former beasts, and it had ten **horns**.
7:8 "While I was thinking about the **horns**, there before me was
7:8 there before me was another **horn**, a little one, which came up
7:8 among them; and three of the first **horns** were uprooted before it.
7:8 This **horn** had eyes like the eyes of a man and a mouth that spoke
7:11 to watch because of the boastful words the **horn** was speaking.
7:20 I also wanted to know about the ten **horns** on its head and about
7:20 the **horn** that looked more imposing than the others and that had
7:21 this **horn** was waging war against the saints and defeating them,
7:24 The ten **horns** are ten kings who will come from this kingdom.

10642 קְרַץ qeraṣ, n.[m.]. [2]

denounced [+10030] [1], falsely accused [+10030] [1]

Da 3:8 some astrologers came forward and **denounced** [+10030] the Jews.
6:24 [6:25] the men who *had* **falsely accused** [+10030] Daniel were

10643 קְשֹׁט qešōṭ, n.[m.]. [2] [√ Hb 7999]

right [1], surely [+10168+10427] [1]

Da 2:47 "**Surely** [+10168+10427] your God is the God of gods and the
4:37 [4:34] because everything he does is **right** and all his ways are

10644 קַתְרוֹס qatrôs, n.[m.]. [0] [cf. 10630]

Da 3:5 [flute, **zither**, [Q; see K 10630] lyre, harp, pipes and all kinds of]
3:7 [flute, **zither**, [Q; see K 10630] lyre, harp and all kinds of music,]
3:10 [of the horn, flute, **zither**, [Q; see K 10630] lyre, harp, pipes and]
3:15 [flute, **zither**, [Q; see K 10630] lyre, harp, pipes and all kinds of]

ר, r

10645 ר r, letter. Not used in NIV/BHS [√ Hb 8010]

10646 רֵאשׁ rēš, n.m. [14] [√ Hb 8031]

head [4], mind [4], heads [2], saw [2], leaders [1], substance [+10418] [1]

Ezr 5:10 so that we could write down the names of their **leaders** for your
Da 2:28 the visions that passed through your **mind** as you lay on your bed
2:32 The **head** *of* the statue was made of pure gold, its chest and arms
2:38 he has made you ruler over them all. You are that **head** of gold.
3:27 had not harmed their bodies, nor was a hair of their **heads** singed;
4:5 [4:2] and visions that passed through my **mind** terrified me.
4:10 [4:7] These are the visions I **saw** while lying in my bed: I looked,
4:13 [4:10] "In the visions I **saw** while lying in my bed, I looked, and
7:1 and visions passed through his **mind** as he was lying on his bed.
7:1 on his bed. He wrote down the **substance** [+10418] of his dream.
7:6 This beast had four **heads**, and it was given authority to rule.
7:9 was as white as snow; the hair of his **head** was white like wool.
7:15 and the visions that passed through my **mind** disturbed me.
7:20 I also wanted to know about the ten horns on its **head** and about

10647 רַב rab, a. [23] [√ 10648; Hb 8041]

great [11], boastfully [2], chief [2], boastful [1], commander [1], enormous [1], huge [1], imposing [1], in charge [+10505] [1], large [1], many [+10678] [1]

Ezr 4:10 the other people whom the **great** and honorable Ashurbanipal
5:8 we went to the district of Judah, to the temple of the **great** God.
5:11 many years ago, one that a **great** king of Israel built and finished.
Da 2:10 No king, however **great** and mighty, has ever asked such a thing of
2:14 When Arioch, the **commander** *of* the king's guard, had gone out to
2:31 an **enormous**, dazzling statue, awesome in appearance.
2:35 But the rock that struck the statue became a **huge** mountain
2:45 "The **great** God has shown the king what will take place in the
2:48 in a high position and lavished **many** [+10678] gifts on him.
2:48 of Babylon and placed him **in charge** [+10505] of all its wise men.
4:3 [3:33] How **great** are his signs, how mighty his wonders!
4:9 [4:6] I said, "Belteshazzar, **chief** *of* the magicians, I know that the
4:30 [4:27] "Is not this the **great** Babylon I have built as the royal
5:1 King Belshazzar gave a **great** banquet for a thousand of his nobles
5:11 appointed him **chief** *of* the magicians, enchanters, astrologers
7:2 me were the four winds of heaven churning up the **great** sea.
7:3 Four **great** beasts, each different from the others, came up out of
7:7 It had **large** iron teeth; it crushed and devoured its victims
7:8 had eyes like the eyes of a man and a mouth that spoke **boastfully**.
7:11 to watch because of the **boastful** words the horn was speaking.
7:17 'The four **great** beasts are four kingdoms that will rise from the
7:20 the horn that looked more **imposing** than the others and that had
7:20 the others and that had eyes and a mouth that spoke **boastfully**.

10648 רְבָה rebâ, v. [6] [→ 10647, 10649?, 10650, 10652; Hb 8049]

grew large [2], great [1], grew [1], grown [1], placed in a high position [1]

Da 2:48 [M] the king **placed** Daniel **in a high position** and lavished
4:11 [4:8] [J] The tree **grew large** and strong and its top touched the
4:20 [4:17] [J] The tree you saw, which **grew large** and strong,
4:22 [4:19] [J] *You have become* **great** and strong; your greatness
4:22 [4:19] [J] your greatness *has* **grown** until it reaches the sky,
4:33 [4:30] [J] heaven until his hair **grew** like the feathers of an eagle

10649 רִבּוֹ ribbô, n.f. [2] [√ 10648?; Hb 8052]

ten thousand [2]

Da 7:10 attended him; **ten thousand** *times* ten thousand stood before him.
7:10 attended him; ten thousand times **ten thousand** stood before him.

10650 רְבוּ rebû, n.f. [5] [√ 10648]

greatness [3], became even greater [+10323+10339+10378] [1], high position [1]

Da 4:22 [4:19] your **greatness** has grown until it reaches the sky, and your
4:36 [4:33] **became even greater** [+10323+10339+10378] than before.
5:18 and **greatness** and glory and splendor.
5:19 Because of the **high position** he gave him, all the peoples
7:27 **greatness** of the kingdoms under the whole heaven will be handed

10651 רְבִיעָי *rebî'āy*, a.num.ord. [6] [√ 10065; Hb 8055]

fourth [6]

Da 2: 40 Finally, there will be a **fourth** kingdom, strong as iron—for iron
3: 25 and unharmed, and the **fourth** looks like a son of the gods."
7: 7 vision at night I looked, and there before me was a **fourth** beast—
7: 19 "Then I wanted to know the true meaning of the **fourth** beast,
7: 23 'The **fourth** beast is a fourth kingdom that will appear on earth.
7: 23 'The fourth beast is a **fourth** kingdom that will appear on earth.

10652 רַבְרְבָנִין *rabrebānîn*, n.m.pl. [8] [√ 10648]

nobles [8]

Da 4: 36 [4:33] My advisers and **nobles** sought me out, and I was restored
5: 1 King Belshazzar gave a great banquet for a thousand of his **nobles**
5: 2 so that the king and his **nobles**, his wives and his concubines might
5: 3 the king and his **nobles**, his wives and his concubines drank from
5: 9 and his face grew more pale. His **nobles** were baffled.
5: 10 The queen, hearing the voices of the king and his **nobles**,
5: 23 you and your **nobles**, your wives and your concubines drank wine
6: 17 [6:18] it with his own signet ring and with the rings of his **nobles**,

10653 רְגַז *regaz[1]*, v. [1] [→ 10654; Hb 8074]

angered [1]

Ezr 5: 12 [P] because our fathers **angered** the God of heaven, he handed

10654 ²רְגַז *regaz[2]*, n.m. [1] [√ 10653; Hb 8075]

rage [1]

Da 3: 13 Furious with **rage**, Nebuchadnezzar summoned Shadrach,

10655 רְגַל *regal*, n.[f.]. [7] [√ Hb 8079]

feet [4], underfoot [+10089] [2], toes [+10064] [1]

Da 2: 33 its legs of iron, its **feet** partly of iron and partly of baked clay.
2: 34 It struck the statue on its **feet** of iron and clay and smashed them.
2: 41 Just as you saw that the **feet** and toes were partly of baked clay
2: 42 As the **toes** [+10064] were partly iron and partly clay, so this
7: 4 was lifted from the ground so that it stood on *two* **feet** like a man,
7: 7 its victims and trampled **underfoot** [+10089] whatever was left.
7: 19 its victims and trampled **underfoot** [+10089] whatever was left.

10656 רְגַשׁ *regaš*, v. [3] [√ Hb 8093]

went as a group [3]

Da 6: 6 [6:7] [P] and the satraps **went as a group** to the king and said:
6: 11 [6:12] [P] these men **went as a group** and found Daniel praying
6: 15 [6:16] [P] the men **went as a group** to the king and said to him,

10657 רֵו *rēw*, n.m. [2]

appearance [1], looks [1]

Da 2: 31 an enormous, dazzling statue, awesome in **appearance**.
3: 25 and unharmed, and the fourth **looks** like a son of the gods."

10658 רוּחַ *rûaḥ*, n.f. [11] [cf. 10666; Hb 8120]

spirit [6], *untranslated* [1], mind [1], qualities [1], wind [1], winds [1]

Da 2: 35 in the summer. The **wind** swept them away without leaving a trace.
4: 8 [4:5] name of my god, and the **spirit** *of* the holy gods is in him.)
4: 9 [4:6] I know that the **spirit** *of* the holy gods is in you,
4: 18 [4:15] But you can, because the **spirit** *of* the holy gods is in you."
5: 11 There is a man in your kingdom who has the **spirit** *of* the holy
5: 12 was found to have a keen **mind** and knowledge and understanding,
5: 14 I have heard that the **spirit** *of* the gods is in you and that you have
5: 20 when his heart became arrogant and **[RPH]** hardened with pride,
6: 3 [6:4] the satraps by his exceptional **qualities** that the king planned
7: 2 there before me were the four **winds** *of* heaven churning up the
7: 15 "I, Daniel, was troubled in **spirit**, and the visions that passed

10659 ¹רוּם *rûm[1]*, v. [4] [→ 10660; Hb 8123]

arrogant [1], exalt [1], promoted [1], set up [1]

Da 4: 37 [4:34] [M] praise and **exalt** and glorify the King of heaven,
5: 19 [P] he spared; those he wanted to promote, *he* **promoted**;
5: 20 [J] when his heart *became* **arrogant** and hardened with pride,
5: 23 [L] *you have* **set** *yourself* **up** against the Lord of heaven.

10660 ²רוּם *rûm[2]*, n.m. [5] [√ 10659; Hb 8124?]

high [2], top [2], height [1]

Ezr 6: 3 be laid. It is to be ninety feet **high** and ninety feet wide,
Da 3: 1 made an image of gold, ninety feet **high** and nine feet wide,
4: 10 [4:7] a tree in the middle of the land. Its **height** was enormous.
4: 11 [4:8] The tree grew large and strong and its **top** touched the sky;
4: 20 [4:17] which grew large and strong, with its **top** touching the sky,

10661 רָז *rāz*, n.m. [9]

mystery [6], mysteries [3]

Da 2: 18 plead for mercy from the God of heaven concerning this **mystery**,
2: 19 During the night the **mystery** was revealed to Daniel in a vision.
2: 27 or diviner can explain to the king the **mystery** he has asked about,
2: 28 there is a God in heaven who reveals **mysteries**. He has shown
2: 29 and the revealer of **mysteries** showed you what is going to happen.
2: 30 this **mystery** has been revealed to me, not because I have greater
2: 47 the God of gods and the Lord of kings and a revealer of **mysteries**,
2: 47 a revealer of mysteries, for you were able to reveal this **mystery**."
4: 9 [4:6] holy gods is in you, and no **mystery** is too difficult for you.

10662 רְחוּם *reḥûm*, n.pr.m. [4] [cf. 10664; Hb 8156]

Rehum [4]

Ezr 4: 8 **Rehum** the commanding officer and Shimshai the secretary wrote
4: 9 **Rehum** the commanding officer and Shimshai the secretary,
4: 17 To **Rehum** the commanding officer, Shimshai the secretary
4: 23 as the copy of the letter of King Artaxerxes was read to **Rehum**

10663 רַחִיק *raḥîq*, a. [1] [√ Hb 8158]

away [1]

Ezr 6: 6 their fellow officials of that province, stay **away** from there.

10664 רַחֲמִין *raḥamîn*, n.[m.]pl.intens. [1] [cf. 10662; Hb 8171]

mercy [1]

Da 2: 18 He urged them to plead for **mercy** from the God of heaven

10665 רְחַץ *reḥaṣ*, v. [1]

trusted [1]

Da 3: 28 [L] *They* **trusted** in him and defied the king's command

10666 רֵיחַ *rêaḥ*, n.f. [1] [cf. 10658; Hb 8194]

smell [1]

Da 3: 27 robes were not scorched, and there was no **smell** *of* fire on them.

10667 רְמָה *remâ*, v. [12] [√ Hb 8227]

be thrown [5], threw [2], thrown [2], impose [1], throw [1], were set in place [1]

Ezr 7: 24 [J] You are also to know that you have no authority to **impose**
Da 3: 6 [L] worship *will* immediately **be thrown** into a blazing furnace."
3: 11 [L] fall down and worship will **be thrown** into a blazing furnace.
3: 15 [L] *you will* **be thrown** immediately into a blazing furnace.
3: 20 [J] and Abednego and **throw** them into the blazing furnace.
3: 21 [K] were bound and **thrown** into the blazing furnace.
3: 24 [J] "Weren't there three men that *we* tied up and **threw** into the
6: 7 [6:8] [L] to you, O king, *shall* **be thrown** into the lions' den.
6: 12 [6:13] [L] O king, *would* **be thrown** into the lions' den?"
6: 16 [6:17] [J] they brought Daniel and **threw** him into the lions' den.
6: 24 [6:25] [J] Daniel were brought in and **thrown** into the lions' den,
7: 9 [K] "As I looked, "thrones **were set in place**, and the Ancient of

10668 רְעוּ *re'û*, n.f. [2] [→ 10669; Hb 8296]

decision [1], will [1]

Ezr 5: 17 in Jerusalem. Then let the king send us his **decision** in this matter.
7: 18 rest of the silver and gold, in accordance with the **will** *of* your God.

10669 רַעְיוֹן *ra'yôn*, n.m. [6] [√ 10668; Hb 8301]

untranslated [2], thoughts [2], mind [+10381] [1], mind [1]

Da 2: 29 you were lying there, O king, your **mind** turned to things to come,
2: 30 that you may understand what went through your **mind** [+10381].
4: 19 [4:16] perplexed for a time, and his **thoughts** terrified him.
5: 6 His face turned pale and **[NIE]** he was so frightened that his
5: 10 she said. "Don't be alarmed! **[NIE]** Don't look so pale!
7: 28 I, Daniel, was deeply troubled by my **thoughts**, and my face turned

10670 רַעֲנַן *ra'anan*, a. [1] [√ Hb 8316?]

prosperous [1]

Da 4: 4 [4:1] was at home in my palace, contented and **prosperous**.

10671 רְעַע *re'a'*, v. [2] [√ Hb 8368]

break [1], breaks to pieces [1]

Da 2: 40 [M] as iron **breaks** things **to pieces**, so it will crush and break all
2: 40 [J] things to pieces, so it will crush and **break** all the others.

[J] Peal [Jp] Peal passive [K] Peil [L] Hithpeel (Hitpolel, Itpeel) [M] Pael [Mp] Pael passive [N] Pual (Poel)

10672 רְפַס ***rᵉpas***, v. [2] [√ Hb 8346]

trampled [2]

Da 7: 7 [J] its victims and **trampled** underfoot whatever was left.
7: 19 [J] its victims and **trampled** underfoot whatever was left.

10673 רְשַׁם ***rᵉšam***, v. [7] [√ Hb 8398]

put in writing [+10375] [2], been published [1], publish [1], put in writing [1], was written [1], wrote [1]

Da 5: 24 [K] Therefore he sent the hand that **wrote** the inscription.
5: 25 [K] "This is the inscription that **was written**: MENE, MENE,
6: 8 [6:9] [J] issue the decree and **put** it **in writing** [+10375] so that
6: 9 [6:10] [J] So King Darius **put** the decree **in writing** [+10375].
6: 10 [6:11] [K] Daniel learned that the decree *had* **been published**,
6: 12 [6:13] [J] "*Did you* not **publish** a decree that during the next
6: 13 [6:14] [J] to you, O king, or to the decree *you* **put in writing**.

שׂ, *ś*

10674 שׂ ***ś***, letter. Not used in NIV/BHS [√ Hb 8418]

10675 שָׂב ***śāb***, n.m. *or* v.ptcp. [5] [√ 10681]

elders [5]

Ezr 5: 5 But the eye of their God was watching over the **elders** *of* the Jews,
5: 9 We questioned the **elders** and asked them, "Who authorized you to
6: 7 and the Jewish **elders** rebuild this house of God on its site.
6: 8 I hereby decree what you are to do for these **elders** *of* the Jews in
6: 14 So the **elders** *of* the Jews continued to build and prosper under the

10676 שַׂבְּכָא ***śabbᵉkāʾ***, n.[f.]. [4] [cf. 10501; Hb 8422]

lyre [4]

Da 3: 5 flute, zither, **lyre**, harp, pipes and all kinds of music, you must fall
3: 7 flute, zither, **lyre**, harp and all kinds of music, all the peoples,
3: 10 **lyre**, harp, pipes and all kinds of music must fall down
3: 15 flute, zither, **lyre**, harp, pipes and all kinds of music, if you are

10677 שְׂגָא ***śᵉgāʾ***, v. [3] [→ 10678; Hb 8434, 8436]

greatly [2], grow [1]

Ezr 4: 22 [J] Why *let* this threat **grow**, to the detriment of the royal
Da 4: 1 [3:31] [J] who live in all the world: *May* you prosper **greatly**!
6: 25 [6:26] [J] throughout the land: "*May* you prosper **greatly**!

10678 שַׂגִּיא ***śaggîʾ***, a. [13] [√ 10677; Hb 8438]

abundant [2], deeply [1], enormous [1], even more [1], fill [1], great [1], greatly [1], large [1], many [+10647] [1], many [1], overjoyed [+10293+10542] [1], so [1]

Ezr 5: 11 and we are rebuilding the temple that was built **many** years ago,
Da 2: 6 you will receive from me gifts and rewards and **great** honor.
2: 12 This made the king **so** angry and furious that he ordered the
2: 31 "You looked, O king, and there before you stood a **large** statue—
2: 48 in a high position and lavished **many** [+10647] gifts on him.
4: 10 [4:7] a tree in the middle of the land. Its height was **enormous**.
4: 12 [4:9] Its leaves were beautiful, its fruit **abundant**, and on it was
4: 21 [4:18] with beautiful leaves and **abundant** fruit, providing food
5: 9 So King Belshazzar became **even more** terrified and his face grew
6: 14 [6:15] When the king heard this, he was **greatly** distressed; he
6: 23 [6:24] The king *was* **overjoyed** [+10293+10542] and gave orders
7: 5 between its teeth. It was told, 'Get up and eat your **fill** of flesh!'
7: 28 I, Daniel, was **deeply** troubled by my thoughts, and my face turned

10679 שַׂהֲדוּ ***śāhᵃdû***, n.f. Not used in NIV/BHS [√ Hb 3337, 8447]

10680 שְׂטַר ***śᵉṭar***, n.m. [1] [cf. 10511]

sides [1]

Da 7: 5 It was raised up on one of its **sides**, and it had three ribs in its

10681 שִׂיב ***śîb***, v. Not used in NIV/BHS [→ 10675; Hb 8482]

10682 שִׂים ***śîm***, v. [26] [√ Hb 8492]

issued [5], decree [+10302+10427] [4], issue [3], authorized [+10302+10378] [2], appointed [1], called [+10721] [1], commanded [+10302+10427] [1], decreed [+10302] [1], determined [+10104+10542] [1], order [+10002+10302+10427] [1], order [+10302+10378+10427] [1], pay [1], pays [1], placed [1], placing [1], turned into [1]

Ezr 4: 19 [K] I **issued** an order and a search was made, and it was found
4: 21 [J] Now **issue** an order *to* these men to stop work, so that this city
4: 21 [L] city will not be rebuilt until I so **order** [+10002+10302+10427].
5: 3 [J] "Who **authorized** [+10302+10378] you to rebuild this temple
5: 8 [L] it with large stones and **placing** the timbers in the walls.
5: 9 [J] "Who **authorized** [+10302+10378] you to rebuild this temple
5: 13 [J] King Cyrus **issued** a decree to rebuild this house of God.
5: 14 [J] man named Sheshbazzar, whom *he had* **appointed** governor,
5: 17 [K] *did* in fact **issue** a decree to rebuild this house of God in
6: 1 [J] King Darius then **issued** an order, and they searched in the
6: 3 [J] the king **issued** a decree concerning the temple of God in
6: 8 [K] Moreover, I hereby **decree** [+10302+10427] what you are to
6: 11 [K] Furthermore, I **decree** [+10302+10427] that if anyone
6: 12 [J] I Darius *have* **decreed** [+10302] it. Let it be carried out with
7: 13 [K] Now I **decree** [+10302+10427] that any of the Israelites in
7: 21 [K] Now I, King Artaxerxes, **order** [+10302+10378+10427] all the
Da 2: 5 [L] cut into pieces and your houses **turned into** piles of rubble.
3: 10 [J] You *have* **issued** a decree, O king, that everyone who hears
3: 12 [J] and Abednego—who **pay** no attention to you, O king.
3: 29 [K] Therefore I **decree** [+10302+10427] that the people of any
4: 6 [4:3] [K] So I **commanded** [+10302+10427] that all the wise men
5: 12 [J] man Daniel, whom the king **called** [+10721] Belteshazzar,
6: 13 [6:14] [J] **pays** no attention to you, O king, or to the decree you
6: 14 [6:15] [J] *he was* **determined** [+10104+10542] to rescue Daniel
6: 17 [6:18] [K] was brought and **placed** over the mouth of the den,
6: 26 [6:27] [K] "I **issue** a decree that in every part of my kingdom

10683 שְׂכַל ***śᵉkal***, v. [1] [→ 10684; Hb 8505]

thinking [1]

Da 7: 8 [O] "While I was **thinking** about the horns, there before me was

10684 שָׂכְלְתָנוּ ***śoklᵉtānû***, n.f. [3] [√ 10683]

intelligence [2], understanding [1]

Da 5: 11 to have insight and **intelligence** and wisdom like that of the gods.
5: 12 found to have a keen mind and knowledge and **understanding**,
5: 14 and that you have insight, **intelligence** and outstanding wisdom.

10685 שִׂלָּה ***śillâ***, n.f. Not used in NIV/BHS [√ Hb 6136]

10686 שְׂנָא ***śᵉnāʾ***, v. [1] [√ Hb 8533]

enemies [1]

Da 4: 19 [4:16] [J] if only the dream applied to your **enemies** and its

10687 שְׂעַר ***śᵉʿar***, n.m. [3] [√ Hb 8552]

hair [3]

Da 3: 27 had not harmed their bodies, nor was a **hair** *of* their heads singed;
4: 33 [4:30] of heaven until his **hair** grew like the feathers of an eagle
7: 9 was as white as snow; the **hair** *of* his head was white like wool.

שׁ, *š*

10688 שׁ ***š***, letter. Not used in NIV/BHS [√ Hb 8610]

10689 שְׁאֵל ***šᵉʾēl***, v. [6] [→ 10690; Hb 8626]

asked [3], ask [1], asks [1], questioned [1]

Ezr 5: 9 [J] *We* **questioned** the elders and asked them, "Who authorized
5: 10 [J] *We* also **asked** them their names, so that we could write down
7: 21 [J] a teacher of the Law of the God of heaven, *may* **ask** *of* you—
Da 2: 10 [J] *has ever* **asked** such a thing of any magician or enchanter
2: 11 [J] What the king **asks** is too difficult. No one can reveal it to the
2: 27 [J] can explain to the king the mystery he *has* **asked** *about*,

10690 שְׁאֵלָה ***šᵉʾēlâ***, n.f. [1] [√ 10689; Hb 8629]

verdict [1]

Da 3: 29 [or language who say **anything** [Q 10712] against the God of Shadrach,]
4: 17 [4:14] by messengers, the holy ones declare the **verdict**,

10691 שְׁאַלְתִּיאֵל ***šᵉʾaltîʾēl***, n.pr.m. [1] [√ Hb 8630]

Shealtiel [1]

Ezr 5: 2 Zerubbabel son of **Shealtiel** and Jeshua son of Jozadak set to work

10692 שְׁאָר ***šeʾār***, n.m. [12] [√ Hb 8637]

rest [5], elsewhere [2], left [2], other [2], anything else [1]

Ezr 4: 9 Shimshai the secretary, together with the **rest** *of* their associates—
4: 10 the **other** people whom the great and honorable Ashurbanipal
4: 10 settled in the city of Samaria and **elsewhere** *in* Trans-Euphrates.
4: 17 the secretary and the **rest** *of* their associates living in Samaria
4: 17 associates living in Samaria and **elsewhere** *in* Trans-Euphrates:
6: 16 of Israel—the priests, the Levites and the **rest** *of* the exiles—
7: 18 then do whatever seems best with the **rest** *of* the silver and gold,
7: 20 **anything else** needed for the temple of your God that you may
Da 2: 18 his friends might not be executed with the **rest** *of* the wise men of
7: 7 devoured its victims and trampled underfoot *whatever* was **left**.
7: 12 (The **other** beasts had been stripped of their authority, but were
7: 19 devoured its victims and trampled underfoot *whatever* was **left**.

10693 שְׁבַח ***šebaḥ***, v. [5] [√ Hb 8655]

praise [2], praised [2], honored [1]

Da 2: 23 [M] I thank and **praise** you, O God of my fathers: You have
4: 34 [4:31] [M] *I* **honored** and glorified him who lives forever.
4: 37 [4:34] [M] **praise** and exalt and glorify the King of heaven,
5: 4 [M] *they* **praised** the gods of gold and silver, of bronze, iron,
5: 23 [M] *You* **praised** the gods of silver and gold, of bronze, iron,

10694 שְׁבַט ***šebaṭ***, n.m. [1] [√ Hb 8657]

tribes [1]

Ezr 6: 17 all Israel, twelve male goats, one for each of the **tribes** *of* Israel.

10695 שְׁבִיב ***šebîb***, n.[m.]. [2] [√ Hb 8663]

flames [1], flaming [1]

Da 3: 22 so hot that the **flames** of the fire killed the soldiers who took up
7: 9 His throne was **flaming** with fire, and its wheels were all ablaze.

10696 שְׁבַע ***šebaʿ***, n.m. & f. [6] [√ Hb 8679]

seven [6]

Ezr 7: 14 are sent by the king and his **seven** advisers to inquire about Judah
Da 3: 19 He ordered the furnace heated **seven** times hotter than usual
4: 16 [4:13] the mind of an animal, till **seven** times pass by for him.
4: 23 [4:20] like the wild animals, until **seven** times pass by for him.'
4: 25 [4:22] **Seven** times will pass by for you until you acknowledge
4: 32 [4:29] **Seven** times will pass by for you until you acknowledge

10697 שְׁבַק ***šebaq***, v. [5]

leave [2], be left [1], not interfere [1], remain [1]

Ezr 6: 7 [J] *Do* **not interfere** with the work on this temple of God. Let the
Da 2: 44 [L] will never be destroyed, nor *will* it **be left** to another people.
4: 15 [4:12] [J] stump and its roots, bound with iron and bronze, **remain**
4: 23 [4:20] [J] 'Cut down the tree and destroy it, but **leave** the stump,
4: 26 [4:23] [J] The command to **leave** the stump of the tree with its

10698 שְׁבַשׁ ***šebaš***, v. [1]

baffled [1]

Da 5: 9 [O] and his face grew more pale. His nobles *were* **baffled**.

10699 שֵׁגַל ***šēgal***, n.f. [3] [√ Hb 8712?]

wives [3]

Da 5: 2 his nobles, his **wives** and his concubines might drink from them.
5: 3 and his nobles, his **wives** and his concubines drank from them.
5: 23 your **wives** and your concubines drank wine from them.

10700 שְׁדַר ***šedar***, v. [1] [→ 10083]

made every effort [1]

Da 6: 14 [6:15] [O] and **made every effort** until sundown to save him.

10701 שַׁדְרַךְ ***šadrak***, n.pr.m. [14] [√ Hb 8731]

Shadrach [13], *untranslated* [1]

Da 2: 49 at Daniel's request the king appointed **Shadrach**, Meshach
3: 12 **Shadrach**, Meshach and Abednego—who pay no attention to you,
3: 13 Nebuchadnezzar summoned **Shadrach**, Meshach and Abednego.
3: 14 "Is it true, **Shadrach**, Meshach and Abednego, that you do not
3: 16 **Shadrach**, Meshach and Abednego replied to the king,
3: 19 Then Nebuchadnezzar was furious with **Shadrach**, Meshach
3: 20 some of the strongest soldiers in his army to tie up **Shadrach**,
3: 22 the flames of the fire killed the soldiers who took up **Shadrach**,
3: 23 these three men, **[RPH]** firmly tied, fell into the blazing furnace.
3: 26 blazing furnace and shouted, "**Shadrach**, Meshach and Abednego,
3: 26 So **Shadrach**, Meshach and Abednego came out of the fire,
3: 28 "Praise be to the God of **Shadrach**, Meshach and Abednego,
3: 29 or language who say anything against the God of **Shadrach**,
3: 30 the king promoted **Shadrach**, Meshach and Abednego in the

10702 שְׁוָה ***šewâ***, v. [2] [√ Hb 8750]

be turned into [1], given [1]

Da 3: 29 [O] into pieces and their houses **be turned into** piles of rubble,
5: 21 [M] driven away from people and **given** the mind of an animal;

10703 שׁוּר ***šûr***, n.m. [3] [√ Hb 8803]

walls [3]

Ezr 4: 12 They are restoring the **walls** and repairing the foundations.
4: 13 king should know that if this city is built and its **walls** are restored,
4: 16 inform the king that if this city is built and its **walls** are restored,

10704 שׁוּשַׁנְכָי ***šûšankāy***, n.pr.g. & loc. [1] [√ Hb 8809]

of Susa [1]

Ezr 4: 9 from Tripolis, Persia, Erech and Babylon, the Elamites **of Susa**,

10705 שְׁחַת ***šeḥat***, v. [3] [√ Hb 8845]

corrupt [1], corruption [1], wicked [1]

Da 2: 9 [Jp] You have conspired to tell me misleading and **wicked** things,
6: 4 [6:5] [Jp] They could find no **corruption** in him, because he was
6: 4 [6:5] [Jp] he was trustworthy and neither **corrupt** nor negligent.

10706 שֵׁיזִב ***šêzib***, v. [9]

rescue [5], rescued [2], rescues [1], save [1]

Da 3: 15 [P] Then what god *will be able to* **rescue** you from my hand?"
3: 17 [P] the God we serve is able to **save** us from it, and he will rescue
3: 17 [P] us from it, and *he will* **rescue** us from your hand, O king.
3: 28 [P] who has sent his angel and **rescued** his servants!
6: 14 [6:15] [P] he was determined to **rescue** Daniel and made every
6: 16 [6:17] [P] "*May* your God, whom you serve continually, **rescue**
6: 20 [6:21] [P] been able to **rescue** you from the lions?"
6: 27 [6:28] [P] *He* **rescues** and he saves; he performs signs
6: 27 [6:28] [P] *He has* **rescued** Daniel from the power of the lions."

10707 שֵׁיצִיא ***šêṣîʾ***, v. [1]

completed [1]

Ezr 6: 15 [P] The temple *was* **completed** on the third day of the month

10708 שְׁכַח ***šekaḥ***, v. [18] [√ Hb 8894]

was found [5], find [4], found [4], *untranslated* [2], do so[s] [+10353+10544] [1], leaving [1], obtain [1]

Ezr 4: 15 [P] In these records *you will* **find** that this city is a rebellious
4: 19 [P] *it was* **found** that this city has a long history of revolt against
6: 2 [L] A scroll **was found** in the citadel of Ecbatana in the province
7: 16 [P] and gold *you may* **obtain** from the province of Babylon,
Da 2: 25 [P] "*I have* **found** a man among the exiles from Judah who can
2: 35 [L] The wind swept them away without **leaving** a trace.
5: 11 [L] In the time of your father he **was found** to have insight
5: 12 [L] **was found** to have a keen mind and knowledge
5: 14 [L] have insight, intelligence and outstanding wisdom. **[RPH]**
5: 27 [L] You have been weighed on the scales and **found** wanting.
6: 4 [6:5] [P] the satraps tried to **find** grounds for charges against
6: 4 [6:5] [P] but they were unable to **do so**[s] [+10353+10544].
6: 4 [6:5] [L] *They could* **find** no corruption in him, because he was
6: 5 [6:6] [P] "*We will* never **find** any basis for charges against this
6: 5 [6:6] [P] **[RPH]** it has something to do with the law of his
6: 11 [6:12] [P] and **found** Daniel praying and asking God for help.
6: 22 [6:23] [L] hurt me, because I **was found** innocent in his sight.
6: 23 [6:24] [L] no wound **was found** on him, because he had trusted

10709 שְׁכַן ***šekan***, v. [2] [→ 10445; Hb 8905]

caused to dwell [1], nesting places [1]

Ezr 6: 12 [M] May God, who *has* **caused** his Name **to dwell** there,
Da 4: 21 [4:18] [J] *having* **nesting places** in its branches for the birds of

10710 שְׁלֵה ***šelēh***, a. [1] [→ 10711, 10712, 10713; Hb 8929]

contented [1]

Da 4: 4 [4:1] was at home in my palace, **contented** and prosperous.

10711 שָׁלֻה ***šāluh***, n.f. Not used in NIV/BHS [√ 10710]

10712 שְׁלוּ šālû, n.f. [4] [√ 10710; Hb 8930]

anything [1], fail [1], neglect [+10522+10542] [1], negligent [1]

Ezr 4:22 Be careful not to **neglect** [+10522+10542] this matter. Why let this
6:9 by the priests in Jerusalem—must be given them daily without **fail**,
Da 3:29 who say **anything** [K 10690?] against the God of Shadrach,
6:4 [6:5] he was trustworthy and neither corrupt nor **negligent**.

10713 שְׁלֵוָה šᵉlēwâ, n.f. [1] [√ 10710; Hb 8932]

prosperity [1]

Da 4:27 [4:24] It may be that then your **prosperity** will continue."

10714 שְׁלַח šᵉlaḥ, v. [14] [√ Hb 8938]

sent [9], are sent [1], lifts [1], send [1], sending message [1], summoned [+10359+10378+10378] [1]

Ezr 4:11 [J] (This is a copy of the letter *they* **sent** him.) To King
4:14 [J] *we are* **sending** *this* **message** to inform the king,
4:17 [J] The king **sent** this reply: To Rehum the commanding officer,
4:18 [J] The letter *you* **sent** us has been read and translated in my
5:6 [J] the officials of Trans-Euphrates, **sent** to King Darius.
5:7 [J] The report *they* **sent** him read as follows: To King Darius:
5:17 [J] Then *let* the king **send** us his decision in this matter.
6:12 [J] any king or people who **lifts** a hand to change this decree
6:13 [J] Then, because of the decree King Darius *had* **sent**, Tattenai,
7:14 [Jp] You **are sent** by the king and his seven advisers to inquire
Da 3:2 [J] He then **summoned** [+10359+10378+10378] the satraps,
3:28 [J] who *has* **sent** his angel and rescued his servants!
5:24 [Jp] Therefore he **sent** the hand that wrote the inscription.
6:22 [6:23] [J] My God **sent** his angel, and he shut the mouths of the

10715 שְׁלֵט šᵉlēṭ, v. [7] [→ 10716, 10717, 10718; Hb 8948]

made ruler [2], ruler [2], harmed [1], overpowered [1], rule [1]

Da 2:38 [P] Wherever they live, *he has* **made** you **ruler** over them all.
2:39 [J] third kingdom, one of bronze, *will* **rule** over the whole earth.
2:48 [P] *He* **made** him **ruler** over the entire province of Babylon
3:27 [J] They saw that the fire *had* not **harmed** their bodies, nor was a
5:7 [J] and *he will be made* the third highest **ruler** in the kingdom."
5:16 [J] *you will be made* the third highest **ruler** in the kingdom."
6:24 [6:25] [J] lions **overpowered** them and crushed all their bones.

10716 שִׁלְטוֹן šilṭōn, n.m. [2] [√ 10715; Hb 8950]

officials [2]

Da 3:2 all the other provincial **officials** to come to the dedication of the
3:3 all the other provincial **officials** assembled for the dedication of the

10717 שָׁלְטָן šolṭān, n.m. [14] [√ 10715; Hb 8950?]

dominion [7], authority [2], power [2], authority to rule [1], part [1], rulers [1]

Da 4:3 [3:33] his **dominion** endures from generation to generation.
4:22 [4:19] and your **dominion** extends to distant parts of the earth.
4:34 [4:31] His **dominion** is an eternal dominion; his kingdom endures
4:34 [4:31] His dominion is an eternal **dominion**; his kingdom endures
6:26 [6:27] "I issue a decree that in every **part** *of* my kingdom people
6:26 [6:27] will not be destroyed, his **dominion** will never end.
7:6 This beast had four heads, and it was given **authority to rule**.
7:12 (The other beasts had been stripped of their **authority**, but were
7:14 He was given **authority**, glory and sovereign power; all peoples,
7:14 His **dominion** is an everlasting dominion that will not pass away,
7:14 His dominion is an everlasting **dominion** that will not pass away,
7:26 his **power** will be taken away and completely destroyed forever.
7:27 **power** and greatness of the kingdoms under the whole heaven will
7:27 an everlasting kingdom, and all **rulers** will worship and obey him.'

10718 שַׁלִּיט šallîṭ, a. [10] [√ 10715; Hb 8954]

sovereign [4], authority [1], mighty [1], officer [1], ruler [1], rules [1], ruling [1]

Ezr 4:20 Jerusalem has had powerful kings **ruling** over the whole of
7:24 You are also to know that you have no **authority** to impose taxes,
Da 2:10 No king, however great and **mighty**, has ever asked such a thing of
2:15 He asked the king's **officer**, "Why did the king issue such a harsh
4:17 [4:14] that the living may know that the Most High is **sovereign**
4:25 [4:22] that the Most High is **sovereign** over the kingdoms of men
4:26 [4:23] restored to you when you acknowledge that Heaven **rules**.
4:32 [4:29] that the Most High is **sovereign** over the kingdoms of men
5:21 until he acknowledged that the Most High God is **sovereign** over
5:29 and he was proclaimed the third highest **ruler** in the kingdom.

10719 שְׁלִם šᵉlim, v. [3] [→ 10720; Hb 8966]

brought to an end [1], deliver [1], finished [1]

Ezr 5:16 [J] present it has been under construction but *is* not yet **finished**."
7:19 [P] **Deliver** to the God of Jerusalem all the articles entrusted to
Da 5:26 [P] numbered the days of your reign and **brought it to an end**.

10720 שְׁלָם šᵉlām, n.m. [4] [√ 10719; Hb 8934]

prosper [2], cordial greetings [+10002+10002+10353] [1], greetings [1]

Ezr 4:17 living in Samaria and elsewhere in Trans-Euphrates: **Greetings**.
5:7 To King Darius: **Cordial greetings** [+10002+10002+10353].
Da 4:1 [3:31] who live in all the world: May you **prosper** greatly!
6:25 [6:26] language throughout the land: "May you **prosper** greatly!

10721 שֻׁם šum, n.m. [12] [√ Hb 9005]

name [4], called [3], names [3], called [+10682] [1], named [1]

Ezr 5:1 the Jews in Judah and Jerusalem in the **name** *of* the God of Israel,
5:4 "What are the **names** *of* the men constructing this building?"
5:10 We also asked them their **names**, so that we could write down the
5:10 so that we could write down the **names** *of* their leaders for your
5:14 "Then King Cyrus gave them to a man **named** Sheshbazzar,
6:12 May God, who has caused his **Name** to dwell there, overthrow any
Da 2:20 "Praise be to the **name** of God for ever and ever; wisdom and
2:26 The king asked Daniel (also **called** Belteshazzar), "Are you able to
4:8 [4:5] (He is **called** Belteshazzar, after the name of my god,
4:8 [4:5] (He is called Belteshazzar, after the **name** *of* my god,
4:19 [4:16] Daniel (also **called** Belteshazzar) was greatly perplexed for
5:12 This man Daniel, whom the king **called** [+10682] Belteshazzar,

10722 שְׁמַד šᵉmad, v. [1] [√ Hb 9012]

completely destroyed [+10005+10221] [1]

Da 7:26 [P] away and **completely destroyed** [+10005+10221] forever.

10723 שְׁמַיִן šᵉmayin, n.m.pl. [38] [√ Hb 9028]

heaven [29], air [3], heavens [3], sky [3]

Ezr 5:11 "We are the servants of the God of **heaven** and earth, and we are
5:12 because our fathers angered the God of **heaven**, he handed them
6:9 rams, male lambs for burnt offerings to the God of **heaven**,
6:10 so that they may offer sacrifices pleasing to the God of **heaven**
7:12 To Ezra the priest, a teacher of the Law of the God of **heaven**:
7:21 a teacher of the Law of the God of **heaven**, may ask of you—
7:23 Whatever the God of **heaven** has prescribed, let it be done with
7:23 let it be done with diligence for the temple of the God of **heaven**.
Jer 10:11 'These gods, who did not make the **heavens** and the earth,
10:11 will perish from the earth and from under the **heavens**.' "
Da 2:18 He urged them to plead for mercy from the God of **heaven**
2:19 to Daniel in a vision. Then Daniel praised the God of **heaven**
2:28 there is a God in **heaven** who reveals mysteries. He has shown
2:37 The God of **heaven** has given you dominion and power and might
2:38 placed mankind and the beasts of the field and the birds of the **air**.
2:44 the God of **heaven** will set up a kingdom that will never be
4:11 [4:8] The tree grew large and strong and its top touched the **sky**;
4:12 [4:9] found shelter, and the birds of the **air** lived in its branches;
4:13 [4:10] was a messenger, a holy one, coming down from **heaven**.
4:15 [4:12] " 'Let him be drenched with the dew of **heaven**, and let him
4:20 [4:17] which grew large and strong, with its top touching the **sky**,
4:21 [4:18] nesting places in its branches for the birds of the **air**—
4:22 [4:19] your greatness has grown until it reaches the **sky**, and your
4:23 [4:20] a holy one, coming down from **heaven** and saying,
4:23 [4:20] Let him be drenched with the dew of **heaven**; let him live
4:25 [4:22] grass like cattle and be drenched with the dew of **heaven**.
4:26 [4:23] restored to you when you acknowledge that **Heaven** rules.
4:31 [4:28] were still on his lips when a voice came from **heaven**,
4:33 [4:30] His body was drenched with the dew of **heaven** until his
4:34 [4:31] I, Nebuchadnezzar, raised my eyes toward **heaven**,
4:35 [4:32] He does as he pleases with the powers of **heaven** and the
4:37 [4:34] praise and exalt and glorify the King of **heaven**,
5:21 his body was drenched with the dew of **heaven**, until he
5:23 Instead, you have set yourself up against the Lord of **heaven**.
6:27 [6:28] and wonders in the **heavens** and on the earth.
7:2 there before me were the four winds of **heaven** churning up the
7:13 me was one like a son of man, coming with the clouds of **heaven**.
7:27 greatness of the kingdoms under the whole **heaven** will be handed

10724 שְׁמַם šᵉmam, v. [1] [√ Hb 9037]

greatly perplexed [1]

Da 4:19 [4:16] [O] *was* **greatly perplexed** for a time, and his thoughts

10725 שְׁמַע šᵉmaʿ, v. [9] [√ Hb 9048]
heard [4], hear [3], hears [1], obey [1]
Da 3: 5 [J] As soon as *you* **hear** the sound of the horn, flute, zither, lyre,
3: 7 [J] as soon as they **heard** the sound of the horn, flute, zither, lyre,
3: 10 [J] that everyone who **hears** the sound of the horn, flute, zither,
3: 15 [J] Now when *you* **hear** the sound of the horn, flute, zither, lyre,
5: 14 [J] *I have* **heard** that the spirit of the gods is in you and that you
5: 16 [J] Now I *have* **heard** that you are able to give interpretations
5: 23 [J] iron, wood and stone, which cannot see or **hear** or understand.
6: 14 [6:15] [J] When the king **heard** this, he was greatly distressed;
7: 27 [O] and all rulers will worship and **obey** him.'

10726 שָׁמְרַיִן šāmᵉrayin, n.pr.loc. [2] [√ Hb 9076]
Samaria [2]
Ezr 4: 10 settled in the city of **Samaria** and elsewhere in Trans-Euphrates.
4: 17 the secretary and the rest of their associates living in **Samaria**

10727 [1]שְׁמַשׁ šᵉmaš[1], v. [1] [→ 10728?]
attended [1]
Da 7: 10 [M] Thousands upon thousands **attended** him; ten thousand

10728 [2]שְׁמַשׁ šᵉmaš[2], n.[m.]. [1] [√ 10727?, 10728; Hb 9087]
sundown [+10002+10436] [1]
Da 6: 14 [6:15] was greatly distressed; he was determined to rescue Daniel and made every effort until **sundown** [+10002+10436] to save him.

10729 שִׁמְשַׁי šimšay, n.pr.m. Not used in NIV/BHS [√ 10728]

10730 שֵׁן šēn, n.[f.]. [3] [√ Hb 9094]
teeth [3]
Da 7: 5 one of its sides, and it had three ribs in its mouth between its **teeth**.
7: 7 It had large iron **teeth**; it crushed and devoured its victims
7: 19 and most terrifying, with its iron **teeth** and bronze claws—

10731 [1]שְׁנָה šᵉnâ[1], v. [21] [→ 10732; Hb 9101]
different [5], changed [4], change [3], changes [2], turned [2], altered [1], defied [1], grew [1], look so pale [+10228] [1], scorched [1]
Ezr 6: 11 [P] Furthermore, I decree that if anyone **changes** this edict, a
6: 12 [P] any king or people who lifts a hand to **change** this decree
Da 2: 9 [O] and wicked things, hoping the situation *will* **change**.
2: 21 [P] He **changes** times and seasons; he sets up kings and deposes
3: 19 [O] and Abednego, and his attitude toward them **changed**.
3: 27 [J] their robes *were* not **scorched**, and there was no smell of fire
3: 28 [M] They trusted in him and **defied** the king's command
4: 16 [4:13] [M] *Let* his mind *be* **changed** from that of a man and let
5: 6 [J] His face **turned** pale and he was so frightened that his knees
5: 9 [J] became even more terrified and his face **grew** more pale.
5: 10 [O] she said. "Don't be alarmed! Don't **look so pale** [+10228]!
6: 8 [6:9] [P] and put it in writing so that *it* cannot *be* **altered**—
6: 15 [6:16] [P] or edict that the king issues *can be* **changed**."
6: 17 [6:18] [J] so that Daniel's situation *might* not *be* **changed**.
7: 3 [J] Four great beasts, each **different** from the others, came up out
7: 7 [M] It *was* **different** from all the former beasts, and it had ten
7: 19 [J] which was **different** from all the others and most terrifying,
7: 23 [J] *It will be* **different** from all the other kingdoms and will
7: 24 [J] them another king will arise, **different** from the earlier ones;
7: 25 [P] his saints and try to **change** the set times and the laws.
7: 28 [O] and my face **turned** pale, but I kept the matter to myself."

10732 [2]שְׁנָה šᵉnâ[2], n.f. [7] [√ 10731; Hb 9102]
year [5], age [+10120] [1], years [1]
Ezr 4: 24 until the second **year** of the reign of Darius king of Persia.
5: 11 and we are rebuilding the temple that was built many **years** ago,
5: 13 "However, in the first **year** of Cyrus king of Babylon, King Cyrus
6: 3 In the first **year** of King Cyrus, the king issued a decree concerning
6: 15 of the month Adar, in the sixth **year** of the reign of King Darius.
Da 5: 31 [6:1] took over the kingdom, at the **age** [+10120] of sixty-two.
7: 1 In the first **year** of Belshazzar king of Babylon, Daniel had a

10733 [3]שְׁנָה šᵉnâ[3], n.f. [1] [√ Hb 9104]
sleep [1]
Da 6: 18 [6:19] being brought to him. And he could not **sleep**.

10734 שָׁעָה šāʿâ, n.f. [5]
immediately [+10002] [2], immediately [+10191] [1], suddenly [+10191] [1], time [1]
Da 3: 6 worship will **immediately** [+10002] be thrown into a blazing
3: 15 you will be thrown **immediately** [+10191] into a blazing furnace.
4: 19 [4:16] was greatly perplexed for a **time**, and his thoughts terrified
4: 33 [4:30] **Immediately** [+10002] what had been said about
5: 5 **Suddenly** [+10191] the fingers of a human hand appeared

10735 שְׁפַט šᵉpaṭ, v. [1] [√ Hb 9149]
magistrates [1]
Ezr 7: 25 [J] appoint **magistrates** and judges to administer justice to all the

10736 שַׁפִּיר šappîr, a. [2] [√ 10739]
beautiful [2]
Da 4: 12 [4:9] Its leaves were **beautiful**, its fruit abundant, and on it was
4: 21 [4:18] with **beautiful** leaves and abundant fruit, providing food

10737 [1]שְׁפַל šᵉpal[1], v. [4] [→ 10738; Hb 9164]
humbled [2], humble [1], subdue [1]
Da 4: 37 [4:34] [P] And those who walk in pride he is able to **humble**.
5: 19 [P] he promoted; and those he wanted to humble, *he* **humbled**.
5: 22 [P] "But you his son, O Belshazzar, *have* not **humbled** yourself,
7: 24 [P] different from the earlier ones; *he will* **subdue** three kings.

10738 [2]שְׁפַל šᵉpal[2], a. [1] [√ 10737; Hb 9166]
lowliest [1]
Da 4: 17 [4:14] anyone he wishes and sets over them the **lowliest** *of* men.'

10739 שְׁפַר šᵉpar, v. [3] [→ 10736, 10740?; Hb 9182]
pleased [2], pleasure [1]
Da 4: 2 [3:32] [J] *It is* my **pleasure** to tell you about the miraculous
4: 27 [4:24] [J] Therefore, O king, *be* **pleased** to accept my advice:
6: 1 [6:2] [J] *It* **pleased** Darius to appoint 120 satraps to rule

10740 שְׁפַרְפָּר šᵉparpār, n.[m.]. [1] [√ 10739?]
dawn [1]
Da 6: 19 [6:20] At the first light of **dawn**, the king got up and hurried to

10741 שָׁק šāq, n.[m.]. [1] [√ Hb 8797]
legs [1]
Da 2: 33 its **legs** of iron, its feet partly of iron and partly of baked clay.

10742 שְׁרָה šᵉrâ, v. [6] [√ Hb 9223]
solve [2], dwells [1], gave way [1], set to work [+10221+10624] [1], unbound [1]
Ezr 5: 2 [M] Jeshua son of Jozadak **set to work** [+10221+10624] to
Da 2: 22 [Jp] he knows what lies in darkness, and light **dwells** with him.
3: 25 [Jp] men walking around in the fire, **unbound** and unharmed,
5: 6 [O] that his knees knocked together and his legs **gave way**.
5: 12 [J] interpret dreams, explain riddles and **solve** difficult problems.
5: 16 [J] are able to give interpretations and to **solve** difficult problems.

10743 שְׁרֹשׁ šᵉrōš, n.m. [3] [→ 10744, 10745; Hb 9247]
roots [3]
Da 4: 15 [4:12] let the stump and its **roots**, bound with iron and bronze,
4: 23 [4:20] the grass of the field, while its **roots** remain in the ground.
4: 26 [4:23] The command to leave the stump of the tree with its **roots**

10744 שְׁרֹשׁוּ šᵉrōšû, n.f. [1] [√ 10743]
banishment [1]
Ezr 7: 26 **banishment**, [Q 10745] confiscation of property,

10745 שְׁרֹשִׁי šᵉrōšî, n.f. [0] [√ 10743]
Ezr 7: 26 [must surely be punished by death, **banishment**, [Q; see K 10744]]

10746 שֵׁשְׁבַּצַּר šēšbaṣṣar, n.pr.m. [2] [√ Hb 9256]
Sheshbazzar [2]
Ezr 5: 14 "Then King Cyrus gave them to a man named **Sheshbazzar**,
5: 16 So this **Sheshbazzar** came and laid the foundations of the house of

10747 שֵׁת šēt, n.m. & f. [2] [→ 10749; Hb 9252]
nine feet [+10039] [1], sixth [1]
Ezr 6: 15 of the month Adar, in the **sixth** year of the reign of King Darius.
Da 3: 1 an image of gold, ninety feet high and **nine feet** [+10039] wide,

10748 שְׁתָה *šetâ*, v. [5] [→ 10447; Hb 9272]

drank [4], drink [1]

Da 5: 1 [J] for a thousand of his nobles and **drank** wine with them.
5: 2 [J] his wives and his concubines *might* **drink** from them.
5: 3 [J] his nobles, his wives and his concubines **drank** from them.
5: 4 [J] *As they* **drank** the wine, they praised the gods of gold
5: 23 [J] your wives and your concubines **drank** wine from them.

10749 שִׁתִּין *šittîn*, n.indecl. [4] [√ 10747; Hb 9262]

ninety feet [+10039] [3], sixty-two [+10221+10775] [1]

Ezr 6: 3 It is to be **ninety feet** [+10039] high and ninety feet wide,
6: 3 It is to be ninety feet high and **ninety feet** [+10039] wide,
Da 3: 1 Nebuchadnezzar made an image of gold, **ninety feet** [+10039]
5: 31 [6:1] the kingdom, at the age of **sixty-two** [+10221+10775].

10750 שְׁתַר בּוֹזְנַי *šetar bôzenay*, n.pr.m. [4]

Shethar-Bozenai [4]

Ezr 5: 3 and **Shethar-Bozenai** and their associates went to them and asked,
5: 6 of Trans-Euphrates, and **Shethar-Bozenai** and their associates,
6: 6 governor of Trans-Euphrates, and **Shethar-Bozenai** and you,
6: 13 **Shethar-Bozenai** and their associates carried it out with diligence.

ת, t

10751 ת *t*, letter. Not used in NIV/BHS [√ Hb 9287]

10752 תְּבַר *tebar*, v. [1] [√ Hb 8689]

brittle [1]

Da 2: 42 [Jp] so this kingdom will be partly strong and partly **brittle**.

10753 תְּדִיר *tedîr*, n.f. [2] [√ 10163]

continually [+10002+10089] [2]

Da 6: 16 [6:17] him into the lions' den. The king said to Daniel, "May your God, whom you serve **continually** [+10002+10089], rescue you!"
6: 20 [6:21] "Daniel, servant of the living God, has your God, whom you serve **continually** [+10002+10089], been able to rescue you from

10754 תּוּב *tûb*, v. [8] [√ Hb 8740]

restored [2], returned [2], defend [+10601] [1], gave [1], received [1], spoke [1]

Ezr 5: 5 [P] a report could go to Darius and his written reply *be* **received**.
5: 11 [P] This is the answer *they* **gave** us: "We are the servants of the
6: 5 [P] *are to be* **returned** to their places in the temple in Jerusalem;
Da 2: 14 [P] men of Babylon, Daniel **spoke** to him *with* wisdom and tact.
3: 16 [P] we do not need to **defend** ourselves **before** [+10601] you in
4: 34 [4:31] [J] my eyes toward heaven, and my sanity *was* **restored**.
4: 36 [4:33] [J] At the same time that my sanity *was* **restored**, my
4: 36 [4:33] [J] splendor *were* **returned** to me for the glory of my

10755 תְּוַה *tewah*, v. [1] [√ Hb 9449]

amazement [+10097] [1]

Da 3: 24 [J] Nebuchadnezzar leaped to his feet in **amazement** [+10097]

10756 תּוֹר *tôr*, n.m. [7] [√ Hb 8802]

cattle [4], bulls [3]

Ezr 6: 9 young **bulls**, rams, male lambs for burnt offerings to the God of
6: 17 the dedication of this house of God they offered a hundred **bulls**,
7: 17 With this money be sure to buy **bulls**, rams and male lambs,
Da 4: 25 [4:22] you will eat grass like **cattle** and be drenched with the dew
4: 32 [4:29] live with the wild animals; you will eat grass like **cattle**.
4: 33 [4:30] He was driven away from people and ate grass like **cattle**.
5: 21 an animal; he lived with the wild donkeys and ate grass like **cattle**;

10757 תְּחוֹת *teḥôt*, pp. [5] [√ Hb 9393]

under [4], *untranslated* [1]

Jer 10: 11 will perish from the earth and from **under** the heavens.' "
Da 4: 12 [4:9] **Under** it the beasts of the field found shelter, and the birds
4: 14 [4:11] Let the animals flee from **under** it and the birds from its
4: 21 [4:18] **[NIE]** and having nesting places in its branches for the
7: 27 greatness of the kingdoms **under** the whole heaven will be handed

10758 תְּלַג *telag*, n.[m.]. [1] [√ Hb 8920]

snow [1]

Da 7: 9 His clothing was as white as **snow**; the hair of his head was white

10759 תְּלִיתָי *telîtāy*, a. [1] [√ 10760; Hb 8958]

third [1]

Da 2: 39 Next, a **third** kingdom, one of bronze, will rule over the whole

10760 תְּלָת *telāt*, n.m. [11] [→ 10759, 10761, 10762; Hb 8993]

three [10], third [1]

Ezr 6: 4 with **three** courses of large stones and one of timbers. The costs
6: 15 The temple was completed on the **third** day of the month Adar,
Da 3: 23 and these **three** men, firmly tied, fell into the blazing furnace.
3: 24 "Weren't there **three** men that we tied up and threw into the fire?"
6: 2 [6:3] with **three** administrators over them, one of whom was
6: 10 [6:11] **Three** times a day he got down on his knees and prayed,
6: 13 [6:14] decree you put in writing. He still prays **three** times a day."
7: 5 one of its sides, and it had **three** ribs in its mouth between its teeth.
7: 8 among them; and **three** of the first horns were uprooted before it.
7: 20 the other horn that came up, before which **three** of them fell—
7: 24 different from the earlier ones; he will subdue **three** kings.

10761 תַּלְתָּא *taltā'*, a.den. [3] [√ 10760; 8958]

third highest [3]

Da 5: 7 and he will be made the **third highest** ruler in the kingdom."
5: 16 and you will be made the **third highest** ruler in the kingdom."
5: 29 and he was proclaimed the **third highest** ruler in the kingdom.

10762 תְּלָתִין *telātîn*, n.indecl. [2] [√ 10760; Hb 9001]

thirty [2]

Da 6: 7 [6:8] who prays to any god or man during the next **thirty** days,
6: 12 [6:13] "Did you not publish a decree that during the next **thirty**

10763 תְּמַהּ *temah*, n.m. [3]

wonders [3]

Da 4: 2 [3:32] **wonders** that the Most High God has performed for me.
4: 3 [3:33] How great are his signs, how mighty his **wonders**!
6: 27 [6:28] and **wonders** in the heavens and on the earth.

10764 תַּמָּה *tammâ*, adv. [4] [√ Hb 9004]

untranslated [2], there [2]

Ezr 5: 17 let a search be made in the royal archives **[NIE]** of Babylon to see
6: 1 they searched in the archives stored in the treasury **[NIE]** at
6: 6 their fellow officials of that province, stay away from **there**.
6: 12 May God, who has caused his Name to dwell **there**, overthrow any

10765 תִּנְיָן *tinyān*, a. [1] [√ 10775]

second [1]

Da 7: 5 "And there before me was a **second** beast, which looked like a

10766 תִּנְיָנוּת *tinyānût*, adv. [1] [√ 10775]

once more [1]

Da 2: 7 **Once more** they replied, "Let the king tell his servants the dream,

10767 תִּפְתָּי *tiptāy*, n.m.pl. [2]

magistrates [2]

Da 3: 2 **magistrates** and all the other provincial officials to come to the
3: 3 **magistrates** and all the other provincial officials assembled for the

10768 תַּקִּיף *taqqîp*, a. [5] [√ 10772; Hb 9544]

powerful [2], strong [2], mighty [1]

Ezr 4: 20 Jerusalem has had **powerful** kings ruling over the whole of
Da 2: 40 Finally, there will be a fourth kingdom, **strong** as iron—for iron
2: 42 partly clay, so this kingdom will be partly **strong** and partly brittle.
4: 3 [3:33] How great are his signs, how **mighty** his wonders!
7: 7 was a fourth beast—terrifying and frightening and very **powerful**.

10769 תְּקַל *teqal*, v. [1] [→ 10770; Hb 9202]

been weighed [1]

Da 5: 27 [K] *You have* **been weighed** on the scales and found wanting.

10770 תְּקֵל *teqēl*, n.[m.]. [2] [√ 10769; Hb 9203]

tekel [2]

Da 5: 25 inscription that was written: MENE, MENE, **TEKEL**, PARSIN

Da 5:27 *Tekel*: You have been weighed on the scales and found wanting.

10771 תְּקַן tᵉqan, v. [1] [√ Hb 9545, 9419]

was restored [1]

Da 4:36 [4:33] [Q] *I* **was restored** to my throne and became even

10772 תְּקִף tᵉqip, v. [5] [→ 10768, 10773, 10774; Hb 9548]

strong [3], enforce [1], hardened [1]

Da 4:11 [4:8] [J] The tree grew large and **strong** and its top touched the
4:20 [4:17] [J] The tree you saw, which grew large and **strong**,
4:22 [4:19] [J] You have become great and **strong**; your greatness
5:20 [J] But when his heart became arrogant and **hardened** with pride,
6:7 [6:8] [M] **enforce** the decree that anyone who prays to any god

10773 תְּקֹף tᵉqōp, n.[m.]. [1] [√ 10772; Hb 9549]

might [1]

Da 2:37 of heaven has given you dominion and power and **might** and glory;

10774 תְּקָף tᵉqāp, n.[m.]. [1] [√ 10772]

power [1]

Da 4:30 [4:27] by my mighty **power** and for the glory of my majesty?"

10775 תְּרֵין tᵉrên, n.m. & f. [4] [→ 10765, 10766, 10778; Hb 9109]

twelve [+10573] [2], second [1], sixty-two [+10221+10749] [1]

Ezr 4:24 until the **second** year of the reign of Darius king of Persia.
6:17 as a sin offering for all Israel, **twelve** [+10573] male goats,
Da 4:29 [4:26] **Twelve** [+10573] months later, as the king was walking on
5:31 [6:1] the kingdom, at the age of **sixty-two** [+10221+10749].

10776 תְּרַע tᵉraʿ, n.[m.]. [2] [→ 10777; Hb 9133]

court [1], opening [1]

Da 2:49 of Babylon, while Daniel himself remained at the royal **court**.
3:26 then approached the **opening** *of* the blazing furnace and shouted,

10777 תָּרָע tārāʿ, n.m. [1] [√ 10776; Hb 8788]

gatekeepers [1]

Ezr 7:24 Levites, singers, **gatekeepers**, temple servants or other workers at

10778 תַּרְתֵּין tartên, n.m. & f. Not used in NIV/BHS [√ 10775]

10779 תַּתְּנַי tattᵉnay, n.pr.m. [4]

Tattenai [4]

Ezr 5:3 At that time **Tattenai**, governor of Trans-Euphrates, and
5:6 This is a copy of the letter that **Tattenai**, governor of
6:6 Now then, **Tattenai**, governor of Trans-Euphrates, and
6:13 **Tattenai**, governor of Trans-Euphrates, and Shethar-Bozenai

Select Index of Adverbs, Conjunctions, Particles, and Prepositions

448 אֶל 'el, pp. [5513]

32:14, 21; 33:13, 26; 34:14, 14, 18, 23, 31; 36:21; 38:20, 22, 41; 39:11; 40:23; 41:3, 3, 9; 42:7, 7, 7, 8, 8, 9, 11; Ps 2:5, 7, 7; 3:4; 4:3, 5; 5:T, 2, 7; 18:6; 22:5, 8, 24, 27; 25:1, 15, 16; 27:14, 14; 28:1, 2, 2, 5, 5; 30:2, 8, 8, 9; 31:2, 6, 22; 32:6, 6, 9; 33:14, 15, 18; 34:5, 15, 15; 36:2; 37:34; 39:12; 40:1, 4, 5, 5; 41:1; 42:1, 3, 7, 10; 43:3, 3, 4, 4; 50:4, 4; 51:T, T, 13; 52:T; 55:16; 56:3; 59:9, 17; 61:2; 62:1; 66:17; 69:16, 18, 26, 33; 71:2; 73:17; 77:1, 1, 1; 78:54; 79:6, 12; 80:T, 11; 84:2, 7, 7; 85:8, 8; 86:2, 3, 4, 16; 88:9, 13; 90:16; 91:7, 10; 95:11; 99:6, 7; 101:2; 102:1, 2, 17, 19; 104:8, 22, 27, 29; 105:13, 13; 107:6, 7, 13, 19, 28, 30; 109:14; 119:6, 20, 36, 36, 48, 59, 132; 120:1; 121:1; 123:1, 2, 2, 2; 129:8; 130:7; 131:3; 137:9; 138:2; 141:8; 142:1, 1, 5, 6; 143:1, 6, 8, 9; 144:13; 145:15; Pr 2:18, 18; 3:5, 5; 5:8; 6:6, 29; 7:22, 22, 23, 25, 27; 8:4, 4; 15:12; 16:3; 17:8; 19:18, 24; 26:15, 27; 30:10; 31:8; Ecc 1:5, 6, 6, 7, 7; 3:20, 20; 5:1; 6:6; 7:2, 2, 2; 8:14, 14; 9:1, 3, 4, 13, 14; 10:15; 12:5, 6, 7; SS 2:4; 3:4, 4; 4:6, 6; 6:11; 8:2; Isa 1:23; 2:2, 3, 3, 4; 3:8; 6:3, 6; 7:3, 3, 3, 4, 6, 10; 8:1, 3, 3, 5, 11, 19, 19, 19, 19, 19, 22; 9:19; 10:21; 11:10; 13:8, 14, 14; 14:2, 10, 10, 15, 15, 16, 16, 19; 16:1, 12, 13; 17:7, 8; 18:2, 2, 4, 7; 19:3, 3, 3, 11, 17, 20; 21:6, 11, 16; 22:5, 8, 11, 15, 18; 23:11; 24:18; 28:11, 12; 29:11, 22; 30:29; 31:4; 32:6; 36:2, 3, 4, 4, 7, 7, 10, 10, 11, 11, 11, 12, 12, 15, 16, 16, 17, 22; 37:2, 3, 5, 6, 6, 7, 9, 10, 15, 21, 21, 21, 23, 28, 29, 33, 33, 34; 38:1, 1, 2, 2, 4, 5, 18, 19; 39:1, 3, 3, 3, 3, 5, 8; 40:2, 18, 25; 41:1; 44:17, 19, 22; 45:14, 14, 20, 22; 46:3, 7, 12; 48:12, 13, 16; 49:1, 5, 22, 22; 50:8; 51:1, 1, 1, 2, 2, 4, 4, 5, 5, 6, 7; 54:14; 55:2, 3, 5, 7, 7, 11; 56:3, 7; 60:8, 11, 13, 14; 62:11; 63:15; 65:1, 2, 5, 7; 66:2, 2, 5, 12, 17, 19; Jer 1:2, 4, 7, 9, 11, 12, 13, 14, 17, 19; 2:1, 3, 7, 19, 27, 29, 31; 3:1, 1, 6, 6, 7, 8, 10, 11, 17; 4:1, 3, 5, 23; 5:5, 8, 19; 6:3, 19, 21; 7:1, 4, 12, 13, 20, 25, 26, 27, 27, 27, 28; 8:4, 14; 9:3, 12, 17; 10:2; 11:1, 2, 3, 6, 9, 11, 11, 11, 12, 14, 20, 23; 12:1, 6; 13:1, 3, 6, 8, 11, 11, 12, 12, 13, 14; 14:1, 11, 12, 14, 14, 17, 18; 15:1, 1, 2, 2, 19, 19, 20; 16:1, 10, 11, 12, 19; 17:15, 19, 20, 24, 27; 18:1, 5, 11, 18, 19; 19:2, 2, 11, 14, 15; 20:3, 12; 21:1, 1, 3, 3, 4, 8, 13; 22:8, 11, 18, 21; 23:21, 33, 35, 37, 38; 24:3, 4, 7; 25:2, 3, 3, 4, 7, 9, 15, 15, 17, 26, 27, 28, 30, 30, 30, 32; 26:2, 3, 4, 4, 5, 8, 9, 11, 11, 11, 12, 12, 12, 12, 13, 15, 15, 16, 16, 16, 17, 18, 19, 22, 23, 23; 27:1, 2, 3, 3, 3, 3, 3, 3, 4, 4, 9, 9, 9, 9, 9, 9, 12, 13, 14, 14, 16, 16, 16, 17, 19, 22; 28:1, 3, 4, 5, 6, 8, 12, 13, 15, 16; 29:1, 1, 1, 1, 3, 7, 8, 10, 12, 12, 14, 16, 16, 16, 19, 19, 21, 21, 24, 25, 25, 25, 26, 26, 28, 30, 31; 30:1, 2, 2, 3, 4, 4, 21, 21; 31:6, 9, 12, 21; 32:1, 6, 7, 8, 8, 8, 12, 16, 16, 18, 25, 26, 33, 36, 37, 42; 33:1, 3, 4, 4, 14, 19, 23, 26; 34:1, 2, 2, 6, 7, 7, 8, 12, 14, 17, 17, 17, 17, 22; 35:1, 2, 2, 4, 5, 11, 12, 13, 14, 14, 15, 15, 15, 16, 17, 17, 17; 36:1, 2, 2, 2, 4, 7, 14, 14, 15, 16, 16, 18, 19, 20, 23, 23, 25, 27, 31, 31, 32; 37:2, 3, 3, 6, 7, 7, 13, 14, 14, 16, 16, 18, 18; 38:1, 2, 4, 4, 6, 7, 8, 9, 11, 11, 11, 12, 14, 14, 14, 15, 15, 16, 17, 17, 18, 19, 19, 20, 22, 23, 24, 25, 25, 25, 25, 26, 27; 39:1, 5, 12, 14, 14, 15, 16; 40:1, 2, 2, 4, 4, 5, 5, 6, 8, 10, 12, 13, 14, 15, 15, 16, 16; 41:1, 6, 6, 7, 7, 8, 10, 12, 14, 15; 42:2, 2, 4, 4, 5, 5, 6, 7, 8, 8, 9, 9, 10, 12, 20, 20, 21; 43:1, 1, 2, 8, 10; 44:1, 1, 4, 7, 16, 16, 20, 24, 24; 45:1, 4; 46:1, 10, 13, 16, 16, 16, 25; 47:1, 1, 3, 5, 6, 7, 7; 48:1, 8, 11, 11, 19, 21, 21, 21, 31, 36, 40, 44, 44, 44; 49:2, 4, 19, 19, 20, 20, 28, 31, 34, 34, 36; 50:1, 1, 5, 6, 14, 14, 16, 18, 18, 18, 19, 21, 29, 29, 29, 31, 35, 35, 35, 36, 36, 37, 37, 37, 37, 38, 44, 44, 45, 45; 51:1, 3, 9, 12, 12, 25, 35, 44, 60, 60, 60, 61, 62, 63; 52:9, 15, 26; La 1:12; 2:12, 18, 19; 3:21, 41, 41; 4:4, 17, 17; 5:21; Eze 1:3, 9, 9, 10, 12, 12, 23; 2:1, 2, 2, 3, 3, 3, 4, 4, 6, 7, 8, 8, 9, 10; 3:1, 1, 3, 3, 4, 4, 4, 5, 5, 6, 6, 6, 7, 7, 10, 10, 11, 11, 11, 11, 13, 15, 15, 16, 22, 22, 23, 24, 26, 27; 4:3, 7, 8, 15, 16; 5:4, 4; 6:1, 2, 2, 9, 10, 11, 13; 7:1, 6, 7, 12, 13, 13, 14, 16, 18, 26; 8:3, 5, 6, 7, 8, 9, 12, 13, 14, 14, 15, 16, 16, 17, 17; 9:3, 3, 4, 7, 9; 10:1, 2, 2, 2, 7, 7, 11, 22; 11:1, 2, 5, 11, 14, 21, 24, 25; 12:1, 3, 8, 9, 10, 12, 17, 19, 19, 21, 23, 23, 26, 28; 13:1, 2, 8, 9, 9, 11, 12, 14, 16, 17, 19, 20; 14:1, 2, 4, 4, 4, 6, 7, 7, 12, 19, 21, 22; 15:1; 16:1, 5, 25, 26, 28, 29, 33, 37, 61; 17:1, 2, 3, 4, 6, 8, 8, 11, 12; 18:1, 6, 6, 6, 11, 12, 15; 19:1, 4, 4, 9, 9, 11; 20:2, 3, 5, 6, 7, 8, 9, 10, 15, 18, 27, 27, 28, 29, 30, 35, 35, 38, 39, 42, 42, 45, 46, 46; 21:1, 2, 2, 2, 3, 4, 7, 7, 8, 12, 12, 14, 17, 18, 21, 28, 28, 29, 30; 22:1, 9, 13, 17, 19, 20, 23; 23:1, 5, 12, 14, 16, 17, 27, 36, 39, 40, 42, 42, 44, 44, 44, 44; 24:1, 2, 3, 3, 4, 15, 18, 19, 20, 20, 23, 26; 25:1, 2, 3, 3, 3, 6; 26:1, 2, 7, 20; 27:1, 3, 29, 31, 31, 32; 28:1, 11, 20, 21; 29:1, 10, 10, 17, 18; 30:1, 20, 22, 25; 31:1, 2, 2, 2, 4, 7, 8, 8, 10, 12, 13, 14, 14, 14, 14, 17, 18, 18; 32:1, 2, 6, 17, 18, 24; 33:1, 2, 2, 10, 11, 12, 21, 22, 22, 23, 25, 25, 27, 31; 34:1, 2, 10, 13, 13, 14, 20, 21; 35:1, 3; 36:1, 9, 9, 15, 16, 20, 24, 29; 37:3, 4, 4, 7, 9, 9, 9, 11, 12, 12, 15, 17, 18, 19, 21, 21; 38:1, 2, 3, 8, 12; 39:1, 15, 28; 40:2, 2, 4, 6, 14, 16, 16, 16, 17, 17, 18, 23, 26, 27, 28, 31, 31, 32, 34, 35, 37, 39, 40, 40, 41, 42, 43, 44, 44, 45, 46, 48, 49, 49; 41:1, 4, 4, 6, 9, 12, 15, 17, 19, 19, 19, 22, 25, 25, 25, 26; 42:1, 1, 1, 2, 3, 4, 7, 10, 10, 13, 13, 14, 14, 19; 43:1, 3, 3, 4, 5, 6, 7, 13, 16, 17, 18, 19, 19, 20, 20; 44:2, 4, 4, 5, 6, 6, 7, 9, 11, 13, 13, 15, 16, 16, 17, 19, 19, 19, 21, 25, 27, 27, 30; 45:2, 7, 7, 7, 11, 16, 19, 19; 46:19, 19, 20, 20, 21, 21, 24; 47:1, 2, 6, 7, 8, 8, 8, 9, 16, 19; 48:1, 1, 12, 20, 21, 28, 32; Da 1:11; 8:1, 1, 6, 7, 9, 9, 9, 14, 17; 9:2, 3, 6, 6, 6, 17, 17, 21; 10:3, 11, 11, 11, 12, 16, 20; 11:6, 7, 9, 16, 23; 12:7; Hos 1:1, 2, 4; 2:7; 3:1, 1, 3, 3, 5, 5; 4:8; 5:4, 13, 13, 15; 6:1; 7:7, 10, 14, 15; 8:1; 9:1, 13; 11:4, 5, 7; 12:4, 6; 14:2, 2; Joel 1:1, 14, 19, 20; 2:13, 20, 20, 20; 3:2, 3, 8, 12; Am 2:7; 3:7; 4:8; 5:16, 16; 7:8, 10, 12, 12, 14, 15, 15; 8:2, 2; Jnh 1:1, 2, 4, 5, 5, 5, 6, 6, 7, 8, 9, 10, 11, 12, 12, 13, 14, 15; 2:1, 2, 4, 7, 7, 10; 3:1, 2, 2, 2, 3, 6, 8; 4:1, 2, 9; Mic 1:1; 3:4; 4:2, 2, 3; 7:10, 17; Na 1:9; 2:13; 3:5; Hab 1:2, 13; 2:5, 5; Zep 1:1; 3:2, 9; Hag 1:1, 1, 6, 9; 2:2, 2, 2, 10, 12, 12, 12, 12, 12, 15, 16, 16, 17, 20, 21; Zec 1:1, 3, 3, 3, 4, 4, 7, 9, 14, 19, 19, 21; 2:2, 4, 4, 8, 11, 11; 3:2, 4, 4, 10, 10; 4:2, 4, 5, 6, 6, 8, 9, 11, 12, 13; 5:2, 3, 4, 4, 5, 8, 8, 10, 11; 6:4, 5, 6, 6, 6, 8, 8, 9, 12, 15; 7:1, 3, 3, 4, 5, 5, 8; 8:3, 18, 21; 10:10; 11:12, 13, 13, 13, 15; 12:10; 13:3, 6; 14:2, 5, 8, 8, 17; Mal 1:2; 2:1, 3, 4, 13; 3:1, 5, 7, 7, 10

561 אִם *'im*, c. & pt.inter. [1070]

Ge 4:7, 7; 13:9, 9, 16; 14:23, 23; 15:4, 5; 17:17; 18:3, 21, 26, 28, 30; 20:7; 21:23; 23:8, 13; 24:8, 19, 21, 33, 38, 41, 42, 49, 49; 25:22; 26:29; 27:21, 46; 28:15, 17, 20; 30:1, 27, 31; 31:8, 8, 50, 50, 52, 52; 32:8, 26, 28; 33:10; 34:15, 17; 35:10; 37:8, 32; 38:9, 17; 39:6, 9; 40:14; 42:15, 15, 16, 19, 37; 43:4, 5, 9, 11; 44:23, 26, 32; 47:6, 16, 18, 18, 29; 50:4; Ex 1:16, 16; 4:8, 9; 8:2, 21; 9:2; 10:4; 12:4, 9; 13:13; 15:26; 16:4; 17:7; 18:23; 19:5, 13, 13; 20:25; 21:3, 3, 4, 5, 8, 9, 10, 11, 19, 21, 23, 27, 29, 30, 32; 22:2, 3, 3, 4, 7, 8, 8, 11, 12, 13, 15, 15, 17, 23, 23, 25, 26; 23:22; 29:34; 32:32, 32; 33:13, 15; 34:9, 20; 40:37; Lev 1:3, 10, 14; 2:5, 7, 14; 3:1, 1, 1, 6, 7, 12; 4:3, 13, 27, 32; 5:1, 7, 11, 17; 6:28; 7:12, 16, 18; 12:5, 8; 13:4, 7, 12, 21, 22, 23, 26, 27, 28, 35, 37, 41, 53, 56, 57; 14:21, 43, 48; 15:23, 24, 28; 17:16; 19:7; 20:4; 21:2, 14; 22:6; 25:28, 30, 51, 52, 54; 26:3, 14, 15, 15, 18, 21, 23, 27; 27:4, 5, 6, 7, 7, 8, 9, 10, 11, 13, 15, 16, 17, 18, 19, 20, 20, 22, 26, 26, 27, 27, 31, 33; Nu 5:8, 19, 19, 27, 28; 10:4, 30; 11:12, 15, 15, 22, 23; 12:6; 13:18, 19, 19, 20, 20; 14:8, 23, 28, 30, 30, 35; 15:24, 27; 16:29, 30; 17:13; 19:12; 20:19; 21:2, 9; 22:18, 20, 34; 24:13, 22; 26:33, 65; 27:9, 10, 11; 30:5, 6, 8, 10, 12, 14, 15; 32:5, 11, 17, 20, 20, 23, 29, 30; 33:55; 35:16, 17, 20, 22, 26, 33; 36:4; Dt 1:35; 5:25; 7:5; 8:2, 19; 10:12; 11:13, 22, 28; 12:5, 14, 18; 15:5; 16:6; 18:3, 3; 19:8; 20:11, 12; 21:14; 22:2, 20, 25; 24:1, 12; 25:2, 7; 28:1, 15, 58; 30:4, 17; 32:30, 41; Jos 2:14, 19, 20; 5:13; 7:12; 14:4, 9; 17:3, 15; 22:19, 22, 22, 23, 23, 24; 23:8, 12; 24:15, 15, 15; Jdg 2:22; 4:8, 8, 20; 5:8; 6:3, 17, 31, 31, 36, 37; 7:10, 14; 9:2, 15, 15, 16, 16, 16, 19, 20; 11:9, 10, 25, 30; 13:16, 16; 14:12, 13; 15:7, 7; 16:7, 11, 13, 17; 20:28; 21:21; Ru 2:21; 3:10, 10, 12, 13, 13, 18; 4:4, 4; 1Sa 1:11; 2:15, 16, 25, 25; 3:9, 14, 17; 6:3, 9, 9; 7:3; 8:19; 11:3; 12:14, 15, 25; 14:9, 10, 39, 45; 15:17; 17:9, 9, 55; 19:6, 11; 20:6, 7, 7, 8, 9, 14, 21, 22, 29; 21:4, 4, 5, 6, 9; 23:23; 24:6, 21, 21; 25:22, 34; 26:10, 19, 19; 27:5; 28:10; 30:15, 15, 17, 22; 2Sa 3:13, 35; 5:6; 10:11, 11; 11:11, 20; 12:3, 8; 13:33; 14:11, 19, 32; 15:8, 21, 21, 21, 25, 26, 33, 34; 17:6, 13; 18:3, 3, 25; 19:7, 13, 28, 35, 35, 42; 20:20, 20; 21:2; 24:13, 13; 1Ki 1:27, 51, 52, 52; 2:4, 8; 3:14; 6:12; 8:19, 25; 9:4, 6; 11:38; 12:7, 27; 13:8; 17:1, 1, 12, 12; 18:10, 18, 21, 21; 20:6, 10, 18, 18, 23, 25, 39; 21:2, 6; 22:6, 8, 15, 18, 28, 31; 2Ki 1:2, 10, 12; 2:2, 4, 6, 10, 10; 3:14, 14; 4:2, 24, 30; 5:15, 16, 17, 20; 6:31; 7:4, 4, 4, 4, 10; 9:15, 26, 35; 10:6, 23; 13:7; 14:6; 17:36, 39, 40; 18:23; 19:18; 20:9, 19; 21:8; 23:9, 23; 1Ch 2:34; 4:10; 12:17, 17; 13:2; 15:2; 19:12, 12; 21:12, 12, 12; 22:13; 23:22; 28:7, 9, 9; 2Ch 2:6; 6:16, 22, 24; 7:13, 17, 19; 10:7; 15:2, 2; 18:5, 14, 17, 27, 30; 20:9; 21:17; 23:6; 25:8; 30:9; 33:8; Ezr 2:59; Ne 1:9; 2:2, 5, 5, 7, 12; 4:3; 7:61; 13:21, 25, 25; Est 1:19; 2:14, 15; 3:9; 4:14, 14; 5:4, 8, 8, 12; 6:13; 7:3, 3; 8:5, 5; 9:13; Job 1:11; 2:5; 4:17; 6:5, 6, 12, 12, 13, 28, 30; 7:4, 12; 8:3, 4, 5, 6, 18; 9:3, 15, 16, 19, 19, 20, 23, 24, 27, 30; 10:4, 5, 14, 15; 11:2, 7, 10, 13, 14; 13:8, 9, 10; 14:5, 7, 8, 14; 16:6; 17:2, 13, 16; 19:5; 20:6, 12; 21:4, 6; 22:3, 20, 23; 24:25; 27:4, 4, 5, 10, 14, 16; 30:24, 25; 31:5, 7, 9, 13, 16, 19, 20, 21, 24, 25, 26, 29, 31, 33, 36, 38, 39; 33:5, 23, 32, 33; 34:14, 16, 17, 32; 35:6, 7; 36:8, 11, 12, 29; 37:13, 13, 13, 20; 38:4, 18, 33; 39:9, 10, 13, 27; 40:9; 41:3; 42:8; Ps 1:2, 4; 7:3, 3, 4, 12; 27:3, 3; 41:6; 44:20; 50:12, 18; 59:15; 63:6; 66:18; 68:13; 73:15; 77:9; 78:20, 34; 81:8; 88:10; 89:30, 31, 35; 90:10; 94:9, 18; 95:7, 11; 127:1, 1; 130:3; 131:2; 132:3, 3, 4, 12; 137:5, 6, 6; 138:7; 139:8, 19, 24; Pr 1:10, 11; 2:1, 3, 4; 3:24, 30, 34; 4:12, 16, 16; 6:1, 28; 9:12; 19:19; 20:11, 11; 22:27; 23:2, 15, 17, 18; 24:11, 14; 25:21, 21; 27:22, 24; 30:32, 32; Ecc 3:12; 4:10, 11, 12; 5:8, 11, 12, 12; 6:3; 8:15, 17; 10:4, 10, 11; 11:3, 3, 6, 8; 12:14, 14; SS 1:8; 2:7, 7; 3:5, 5; 5:8; 7:12; 8:7, 9, 9; Isa 1:18, 18, 19, 20; 4:4; 5:9; 6:11; 7:9; 8:20; 10:9, 9, 15, 22; 14:24; 21:12; 22:14; 24:13; 27:7; 28:25; 29:16; 30:17; 33:21; 36:8; 37:19; 40:28; 42:19; 49:24; 50:2; 53:10; 55:10, 11; 58:9, 13; 59:2; 62:8, 8; 65:6, 18; 66:8, 9; Jer 2:14, 22, 28, 31; 3:5, 10; 4:1, 1; 5:1, 1, 2, 9, 22, 29; 7:5, 5, 23, 32; 8:4, 19, 22; 9:9, 24; 12:16, 17; 13:17; 14:7, 18, 18, 19, 22; 15:1, 11, 11, 19, 19; 16:15; 17:24, 27; 18:14; 19:6; 20:3; 22:4, 5, 6, 17, 24, 28; 23:8, 22, 24, 38; 26:4, 15; 27:18, 18; 30:6; 31:20, 30, 36, 37; 33:20, 25; 37:10; 38:4, 6, 16, 16, 17, 18, 21; 39:12; 40:4, 4; 42:5, 6, 6, 10, 13, 15; 44:14, 26; 48:27, 27; 49:1, 9, 9, 20, 20; 50:45, 45; 51:14; La 1:12; 2:20, 20; 3:32; 5:22; Eze 2:5, 5, 7, 7; 3:6, 11, 11; 5:11; 12:23; 14:16, 16, 20, 20; 15:3; 16:48; 17:16, 19; 18:3; 20:3, 31, 33, 39; 21:13; 22:14; 33:11, 11, 27; 34:8; 35:6; 36:5, 7, 22; 38:19; 43:11; 44:10, 22, 25; Da 10:21; Hos 4:15; 9:12; 12:11; Joel 1:2; 3:4; Am 3:3, 4, 6, 6, 7; 5:22; 6:2, 9, 12; 7:2; 8:7, 11; 9:2, 2, 3, 3, 4; Ob 1:4, 4, 5, 5, 5; Mic 2:7; 4:9; 5:8; 6:8; Na 1:12; 3:12; Hab 2:3; 3:8, 8; Hag 2:13; Zec 3:7, 7; 4:6; 6:15; 11:12, 12; 14:18; Mal 1:6, 6; 2:2, 2; 3:10

677 ^{1}אַף *'ap*^{1}, c. [134]

Ge 3:1; 18:13, 23, 24; 40:16; Lev 26:16, 24, 28, 39, 40, 41, 42, 42, 44; Nu 16:14; Dt 2:11, 20; 15:17; 31:27; 33:3, 20, 28; Jdg 5:29; 1Sa 2:7; 14:30; 21:5; 23:3; 2Sa 4:11; 16:11; 20:14; 1Ki 8:27; 2Ki 2:14; 5:13; 1Ch 8:32; 9:38; 16:30; 2Ch 6:18; 12:5; 32:15; Ne 2:18; 9:18; 13:15; Est 5:12; Job 4:19; 6:27; 9:14; 14:3; 15:4, 16; 19:4; 25:6; 32:10, 17, 17; 34:12, 17; 35:14; 36:16, 29, 33; 37:1, 11; 40:8; Ps 16:6, 7, 9; 18:48; 44:9; 58:2; 65:13; 68:8, 16, 18; 74:16; 77:16, 17; 89:5, 11, 21, 27, 43; 93:1; 96:10; 108:1; 119:3; 135:17; Pr 9:2; 11:31; 15:11; 17:7; 19:7, 10; 21:27; 22:19; 23:28; Ecc 2:9; SS 1:16, 16; Isa 26:8, 9, 11; 33:2; 35:2; 40:24, 24, 24; 41:10, 10, 23, 26, 26, 26; 42:13; 43:7, 19; 44:15, 15, 16, 19; 45:21; 46:6, 7, 11, 11, 11; 48:12, 13, 15; Eze 14:21; 15:5; 23:40; Am 2:11; Hab 2:5, 15

725 ^{1}אֵצֶל *'ēṣel*^{1}, subst.pp. [61]

Ge 39:10, 15, 16, 18; 41:3; Lev 1:16; 6:10; 10:12; Dt 11:30; 16:21; Jdg 19:14; 1Sa 5:2; 17:30; 20:19, 41; 1Ki 1:9; 2:29; 3:20; 4:12; 10:19; 13:24, 25, 28, 31; 20:36; 21:1, 2; 2Ki 12:9; 2Ch 9:18; 28:15; Ne 2:6; 3:23; 4:3, 12, 18; 8:4; Pr 7:8, 12; 8:30; Isa 19:19; Jer 35:4; 41:17; Eze 1:15, 19; 9:2; 10:6, 9, 9, 9, 16, 16; 33:30; 39:15; 40:7; 43:6, 8; Da 8:7, 17; 10:13; Am 2:8

907 ^{2}אֵת *'ēt*^{2}, pp. [934]

Ge 4:1; 5:22, 24; 6:9, 13, 18, 18, 19; 7:7, 13, 23; 8:1, 8, 16, 17, 17, 18; 9:8, 9, 9, 10, 10, 10, 11, 12; 11:31; 12:4; 13:5; 14:5, 8, 9, 9, 17, 24; 15:18; 17:3, 4, 19, 21, 22, 23, 27, 27; 19:13, 24, 27, 33, 34; 20:16; 21:20; 22:3; 23:8, 8, 20; 24:32, 40, 49, 55; 25:10; 26:10, 24, 27, 31; 27:15, 30; 28:4; 30:29, 33; 31:25; 32:7; 33:15, 18; 34:5, 6, 7, 8, 10, 16, 21, 22, 23; 35:13, 14, 15, 22; 37:2, 2; 38:1; 39:2, 3, 6, 8, 21, 23; 40:4, 7, 14; 41:9, 12; 42:4, 7, 13, 16, 24, 30, 32, 33; 43:3, 4, 5, 8, 16, 16, 32, 32, 34; 44:9, 10, 23, 26, 26, 28, 30, 34; 45:1, 15; 46:6, 7, 7; 47:22; 49:25, 30, 32; 50:7, 13, 13, 14; Ex 1:1; 2:21, 24, 24, 24; 5:20; 6:4; 10:11; 11:2, 2; 12:38, 48; 13:19; 17:5; 18:22; 20:23; 25:2, 3, 22; 27:21; 28:1, 41; 29:21, 21, 28, 28; 30:16; 31:6, 18; 33:21; 34:23, 24, 27, 27, 29, 32, 33, 34, 35; 35:5, 23, 24; 38:23; Lev 4:6, 17; 6:4; 7:34, 34, 36; 8:2, 30, 30; 10:4, 9, 14, 15; 15:18, 24; 16:5, 15, 16; 18:22; 19:13, 20, 33, 34; 20:10, 10, 11, 12, 13, 18, 20; 24:8; 25:15, 36, 44; 26:9, 39, 44; 27:24; Nu 1:4, 5; 3:1, 9, 49, 50; 5:13, 19; 7:5, 84, 89; 8:11; 9:14; 10:29; 11:17, 31; 14:9; 15:14, 16; 16:10, 35; 17:2, 2; 18:1, 1, 2, 2, 7, 11, 19, 19, 26, 26, 28; 20:13, 24; 22:20, 40; 23:13, 17; 25:11, 14; 26:3; 27:21; 31:2, 3, 28, 51, 52, 52, 54; 32:19, 29, 30, 32; 35:8, 8; Dt 1:26, 30, 43; 2:6, 6, 8; 3:4; 5:3, 3, 24; 9:23; 10:21; 12:12; 16:16, 16; 18:3, 3; 19:5; 28:8; 29:1, 14, 15, 15, 19; 31:7, 11, 16; Jos 1:18; 2:19; 6:17, 27; 8:5, 11; 10:1, 4, 4, 24, 25; 11:18, 20; 14:12; 15:18, 63; 17:11, 14; 21:16, 34; 22:9, 15, 19, 30, 32, 32; 23:7, 12; 24:8, 32; Jdg 1:3, 3, 3, 14, 16, 16, 17, 19, 21; 2:1; 3:19; 4:11, 13; 7:1, 2, 4, 4, 18, 19; 8:1, 4, 7, 7; 9:32, 33, 35, 48; 11:27; 12:4; 14:11; 16:15; 17:2, 11; 19:2, 4; 20:20; Ru 1:10, 18; 2:23; 3:2; 4:5; 1Sa 1:22; 2:11, 11, 13, 17, 18, 19, 22, 23; 3:1; 6:15; 7:14; 8:10; 9:3, 7; 12:2, 7, 7, 7, 14, 15; 13:22, 22; 14:17, 20; 16:5, 14; 17:9; 20:41; 21:1; 22:3, 4, 6, 23; 23:23; 24:18; 25:15, 29; 26:2, 6; 28:1; 29:3, 6, 10; 30:4, 9, 21, 21, 23; 31:9; 2Sa 1:11; 2:6; 3:12, 13, 13, 16, 20, 20, 21, 23, 27, 31; 6:2; 7:12; 10:19; 11:9, 17; 12:17; 13:26, 27; 14:19; 15:3, 11, 12, 14, 19, 22, 24, 27, 30, 33; 16:14, 15, 17, 17, 18, 21, 21; 17:2, 8, 10, 12, 16, 22, 29; 18:1; 19:7, 17, 26, 31, 33, 34, 36, 38; 20:15; 21:12, 15, 17; 24:2, 24; 1Ki 1:27, 41, 44; 2:16, 20; 3:1, 18; 4:34; 6:12, 33; 8:5; 9:25, 26; 11:15, 17, 23, 25; 12:6, 8, 10, 24; 13:7, 15, 16, 16, 16, 18, 19, 26; 15:19; 16:24; 18:12; 20:1, 23, 25, 34, 36; 21:8; 22:4, 7, 8, 24; 2Ki 1:15, 15; 2:10, 16; 3:7, 11, 12, 26; 4:3,

1068 בַּ֫יִן ***bayin***, subst. & pp. [408]

1172 בְּלִי ***b^{e}lî***, subst. [57]

1237 בַּ֫עַד ***ba'ad[1]***, subst.pp. [104]

1685 גַּם ***gam***, adv. [769]

2176 הֵן ***hēn[1]***, adv.demo. *or* interj. [99]

2180 הִנֵּה ***hinnēh***, pt.demo. [1060]

3610 יַ֫עַן ***ya'an[1]***, subst.pp.c. [99]

3780 יֵשׁ *yēš*, subst. [138]

3907 כֹּה *kōh*, adv.demo. [576]

3954 כִּי *kî²*, c. [4483]

118:1, 1, 2, 3, 4, 10, 11, 12, 17, 21, 29, 29; 119:22, 32, 35, 39, 42, 43, 45, 50, 56, 66, 71, 74, 75, 77, 78, 83, 91, 93, 94, 98, 99, 100, 102, 111, 118, 131, 139, 152, 153, 155, 159, 168, 171, 172, 173, 176; 120:5, 7; 122:5; 123:3; 125:3; 127:5; 128:2, 4; 130:4, 7; 132:13, 14; 133:3; 135:3, 3, 4, 5, 5, 14; 136:1, 1, 2, 3, 4, 5, 6, 7, 8, 9, 10, 11, 12, 13, 14, 15, 16, 17, 18, 19, 20, 21, 22, 23, 24, 25, 26; 137:3; 138:2, 4, 5, 6; 139:4, 13, 14; 140:12; 141:5, 6, 8; 142:6, 6, 7; 143:2, 3, 8, 8, 10, 12; 147:1, 1, 13; 148:5, 13; 149:4; Pr 1:9, 16, 17, 29, 32; 2:3, 6, 10, 18, 21; 3:2, 12, 14, 25, 26, 32; 4:2, 3, 8, 13, 16, 17, 22, 23; 5:3, 21; 6:3, 23, 26, 30, 30, 34, 35; 7:6, 19, 23, 26; 8:6, 7, 11, 35; 9:11, 18; 11:15, 31; 15:11; 16:12, 26; 17:7; 18:2; 19:7, 10, 18, 19; 20:16; 21:7, 25, 27; 22:6, 9, 18, 18, 22, 23; 23:1, 5, 7, 9, 11, 13, 17, 18, 21, 22, 27, 31, 31; 24:2, 6, 12, 13, 16, 20, 22; 25:7, 22; 26:25, 25; 27:1, 13, 24; 28:22; 29:19; 30:2, 4, 22, 22, 23, 23, 33; 31:18, 21; Ecc 1:18; 2:10, 12, 16, 17, 17, 21, 22, 23, 24, 25, 26; 3:12, 12, 14, 17, 19, 19, 22, 22, 22; 4:4, 10, 14, 14, 16; 5:1, 2, 3, 4, 6, 7, 7, 8, 11, 18, 20, 20; 6:2, 4, 8, 11, 12; 7:3, 6, 7, 9, 10, 12, 13, 18, 20, 22; 8:3, 6, 6, 7, 7, 12, 15, 16, 17; 9:1, 3, 4, 4, 5, 5, 7, 9, 10, 11, 11, 12; 10:4, 20; 11:1, 2, 6, 8, 8, 9, 10; 12:3, 5, 13, 14; SS 1:2; 2:5, 11, 14; 8:6; Isa 1:2, 12, 15, 20, 29, 30; 2:3, 6, 6, 12, 22; 3:1, 6, 8, 8, 9, 10, 10, 11, 16; 4:5; 5:7, 10, 24; 6:5, 5, 5; 7:5, 8, 9, 13, 16, 22, 24; 8:4, 6, 10, 11, 19, 21; 9:1, 4, 5, 6, 17, 18; 10:7, 8, 12, 13, 13, 22, 23, 25; 11:9; 12:1, 2, 4, 5, 6; 13:6, 10; 14:1, 20, 27, 29, 29, 31, 32; 15:1, 1, 5, 5, 6, 6, 8, 9, 9; 16:4, 8, 9, 12, 12; 17:10; 18:4, 5; 19:20; 21:6, 15, 16, 17; 22:1, 5, 9, 13, 16, 25; 23:1, 4, 14, 18; 24:3, 5, 13, 18, 23; 25:1, 2, 4, 4, 8, 10; 26:3, 4, 5, 9, 12, 19, 21; 27:10, 11; 28:8, 10, 11, 15, 15, 15, 18, 19, 20, 21, 22, 27, 27, 28; 29:10, 11, 13, 16, 20, 23; 30:4, 5, 9, 15, 16, 18, 19, 21, 21, 31, 33; 31:1, 1, 4, 7; 32:6, 10, 13, 14; 33:5, 21, 22; 34:2, 5, 6, 8, 16; 35:6; 36:5, 7, 11, 14, 16, 19, 20, 21; 37:3, 8, 8, 19, 19, 20, 32; 38:1, 17, 18, 22; 39:1, 8; 40:2, 2, 2, 5, 7; 41:10, 10, 13, 20, 23; 42:19; 43:1, 2, 2, 3, 5, 10, 20, 22; 44:3, 17, 18, 21, 22, 23, 23; 45:3, 6, 18, 22, 23; 46:9; 47:1, 5; 48:2, 4, 8, 11; 49:10, 13, 18, 19, 19, 23, 25, 26; 50:7; 51:2, 3, 4, 6, 8; 52:1, 3, 4, 5, 6, 8, 9, 12, 12, 15; 53:8; 54:1, 3, 4, 4, 4, 5, 6, 6, 10, 14, 14; 55:5, 7, 8, 9, 10, 10, 11, 12; 56:1, 4, 7; 57:1, 8, 11, 15, 16, 16, 20; 58:7, 14; 59:2, 3, 12, 12, 14, 15, 16, 16, 19; 60:1, 2, 5, 9, 9, 10, 12, 16, 20; 61:8, 9, 10, 11; 62:4, 4, 5, 9; 63:4, 16, 16; 64:7; 65:5, 6, 8, 16, 16, 17, 18, 18, 20, 22, 23; 66:8, 12, 15, 16, 22, 24; Jer 1:6, 7, 8, 12, 15, 19; 2:5, 10, 13, 19, 20, 20, 22, 25, 26, 27, 28, 34, 35, 37; 3:8, 10, 12, 13, 14, 16, 21, 22, 25; 4:3, 6, 8, 13, 15, 17, 18, 18, 19, 20, 22, 27, 28, 30, 30, 30, 31, 31; 5:4, 5, 6, 10, 11, 19, 26; 6:1, 4, 4, 6, 11, 12, 13, 15, 19, 25, 26, 30; 7:5, 12, 16, 22, 23, 29, 30, 32, 34; 8:10, 12, 14, 14, 17, 22; 9:2, 3, 4, 7, 10, 19, 19, 19, 20, 21, 24, 24, 24, 26; 10:2, 3, 3, 5, 5, 7, 7, 14, 16, 18, 21, 23, 25; 11:7, 13, 14, 15, 19, 20, 23; 12:1, 4, 5, 6, 6, 11, 12; 13:11, 12, 15, 17, 18, 21, 22; 14:4, 5, 5, 6, 7, 12, 12, 12, 13, 17, 18, 20, 22; 15:2, 5, 10, 14, 16, 17, 20; 16:3, 5, 5, 9, 10, 15, 17, 21; 17:4, 6, 8, 13, 14; 18:12, 15, 18, 20, 22, 22; 19:6, 15; 20:3, 4, 8, 8, 10, 11, 12, 13; 21:2, 10; 22:4, 5, 6, 10, 11, 12, 15, 17, 17, 20, 21, 22, 24, 24, 30; 23:8, 10, 10, 11, 12, 15, 18, 33, 36; 24:7, 7, 8; 25:14, 15, 28, 29, 29, 31, 34, 36, 38; 26:11, 15, 15, 15, 16; 27:10, 14, 15, 16, 19, 21; 28:4, 14, 16; 29:7, 8, 9, 10, 10, 11, 13, 15, 16, 28, 32; 30:3, 5, 7, 10, 11, 11, 12, 14, 17, 17, 21; 31:6, 7, 9, 11, 15, 16, 18, 19, 19, 20, 22, 25, 30, 33, 34, 34; 32:4, 5, 7, 8, 8, 15, 30, 30, 31, 42, 44; 33:4, 11, 11, 11, 17, 26; 34:3, 5, 7; 35:6, 7, 14, 16; 36:7; 37:9, 10, 15, 16, 18; 38:4, 4, 4, 5, 6, 7, 9, 15, 15, 23, 25, 25, 27; 39:12, 18, 18; 40:3, 7, 7, 11, 11, 14, 16; 41:8, 18, 18; 42:2, 6, 10, 11, 14, 18, 19, 20, 20, 22; 43:2, 7; 44:14, 14, 15, 17, 19, 29, 29; 45:3, 5; 46:10, 12, 14, 15, 18, 19, 21, 21, 22, 23, 23, 27, 28, 28; 47:4; 48:1, 5, 5, 7, 9, 18, 20, 20, 26, 27, 34, 37, 38, 40, 42, 44, 45, 46; 49:3, 3, 8, 10, 12, 12, 13, 13, 15, 16, 19, 19, 23, 30; 50:3, 9, 11, 11, 11, 14, 15, 20, 24, 25, 27, 29, 31, 38, 44, 44; 51:2, 5, 5, 6, 9, 11, 11, 12, 14, 17, 19, 26, 29, 31, 33, 48, 51, 51, 53, 53, 55, 56, 56, 62; 52:3; La 1:5, 8, 9, 10, 11, 16, 16, 18, 19, 20, 20, 21, 21, 22; 2:13; 3:8, 22, 22, 27, 28, 31, 32, 33; 4:12, 15, 18; 5:16, 22; Eze 1:20, 21; 2:5, 5, 6, 6, 7; 3:5, 7, 7, 9, 19, 20, 21, 21, 26, 27; 5:6, 13; 6:7, 10, 13, 14; 7:4, 4, 9, 12, 13, 13, 14, 19, 23, 27; 8:12, 17; 9:9; 10:11, 17, 20; 11:10, 12, 16, 16; 12:2, 3, 6, 15, 16, 20, 23, 24, 25, 25; 13:9, 14, 21, 23; 14:7, 8, 9, 13, 18, 21, 21, 23, 23; 15:5, 7; 16:14, 59, 62; 17:21, 24; 18:5, 11, 18, 21, 32; 19:5; 20:12, 16, 20, 38, 40, 42, 44, 48; 21:5, 7, 7, 12, 13, 21, 32; 22:16, 22; 23:8, 13, 28, 34, 37, 40, 45, 46, 49; 24:7, 19, 24, 27; 25:3, 3, 3, 5, 6, 7, 11, 17; 26:5, 6, 7, 14, 19; 28:10, 22, 23, 24, 26; 29:6, 9, 13, 16, 21; 30:3, 8, 9, 19, 25, 26; 31:7, 14; 32:11, 15, 25, 26, 27, 32; 33:2, 6, 9, 10, 11, 29, 31, 33; 34:11, 27, 30; 35:4, 6, 9, 12, 15; 36:8, 9, 11, 22, 23, 36, 38; 37:6, 13, 14, 28; 38:23; 39:5, 6, 7, 10, 22, 23, 28; 40:4; 41:7; 42:5, 6, 8, 13, 14; 44:2, 10, 22, 25; 45:14; 46:9, 12, 16, 17; 47:1, 5, 9, 12; 48:14; Da 8:17, 19, 26; 9:9, 11, 14, 16, 18, 18, 19, 23; 10:11, 12, 14, 19, 21; 11:4, 25, 27, 35, 36, 37; 12:7, 9; Hos 1:2, 4, 6, 6, 9, 11; 2:2, 4, 5, 5, 7, 8; 3:4; 4:1, 1, 6, 10, 12, 13, 14, 14, 14, 16; 5:1, 1, 3, 4, 7, 11, 14; 6:1, 6, 9; 7:1, 6, 13, 13, 14; 8:6, 7, 9, 10, 11; 9:1, 4, 6, 12, 12, 15, 16, 17; 10:3, 3, 5, 5, 13; 11:1, 3, 5, 9, 10; 13:9, 13, 15, 16; 14:1, 4, 9; Joel 1:5, 6, 10, 11, 12, 13, 15, 17, 18, 19, 20; 2:1, 1, 11, 11, 11, 13, 20, 21, 22, 22, 23, 27, 32; 3:1, 8, 12, 13, 13, 13, 14, 17; Am 3:7, 7, 14; 4:2, 5, 12, 13; 5:3, 4, 5, 12, 13, 17, 22; 6:10, 11, 12, 14; 7:2, 5, 11, 13, 14; 8:11; 9:8, 9; Ob 1:15, 16, 18; Jnh 1:2, 10, 10, 10, 11, 12, 12, 13, 14; 3:10; 4:2, 2, 3; Mic 1:3, 7, 9, 9, 12, 12, 13, 16; 2:1, 3, 10; 3:7; 4:2, 4, 5, 9, 10, 12, 13; 5:4, 5, 5, 6, 6; 6:2, 4, 8; 7:1, 6, 8, 8, 9, 18; Na 1:10, 14, 15; 2:2, 2; 3:19; Hab 1:4, 5, 5, 6, 16; 2:3, 3, 5, 8, 11, 14, 17, 18, 18; 3:8, 17; Zep 1:7, 7, 11, 17, 18; 2:4, 7, 9, 10, 11, 14; 3:8, 8, 9, 11, 13, 20; Hag 2:4, 6, 23; Zec 2:6, 8, 8, 9, 9, 10, 11, 13; 3:8, 8, 9; 4:6, 9, 10; 5:3; 6:15; 7:5, 6, 6; 8:6, 10, 12, 14, 17, 23; 9:1, 2, 5, 8, 13, 16, 17; 10:2, 2, 3, 5, 6, 6, 8; 11:2, 2, 3, 3, 6, 11, 16; 13:3, 3, 5; 14:5; Mal 1:4, 8, 8, 11, 11, 14; 2:2, 4, 7, 7, 11, 14, 16; 3:2, 6, 8, 12, 14, 14; 4:1, 3

4017 כְּמוֹ *kemô*, adv. & c. [141]

Ge 19:15; 34:15; 41:39; 44:15, 18; Ex 9:14, 18, 24; 10:14; 11:6, 6; 15:5, 8, 11, 11; 30:32, 33, 38; Lev 19:18, 34; Nu 23:10; Dt 4:32; 5:14, 26; 7:26; 18:15, 18; 33:29; Jdg 8:18, 18; 9:48; 1Sa 10:24; 21:9; 26:15; 2Sa 7:22; 9:8; 18:3; 1Ki 3:12, 12, 13; 8:23; 13:18; 22:4, 4; 2Ki 3:7, 7; 18:5; 23:25, 25; 1Ch 17:20; 2Ch 6:14; 18:3, 3; 35:18; Ne 6:11, 11; 9:11; 13:26; Job 1:8; 2:3; 6:15; 9:32; 10:22, 22; 12:3, 3; 14:9; 19:22; 28:5; 31:37; 35:8; 36:22; 38:14; 40:9, 17; 41:24; Ps 29:6, 6; 35:10; 50:21; 58:4, 7, 7, 8, 9, 9; 61:6; 63:5; 71:19; 73:15; 78:13, 69; 79:5; 86:8; 88:5; 89:8, 46; 90:9; 92:7; 115:8; 135:18; 140:3; 141:7; Pr 23:7; SS 6:10; 7:1; Isa 14:10; 26:17, 18; 30:22; 38:19; 41:25, 25; 44:7; 46:9; 51:6; Jer 10:6, 7; 13:21; 15:18; 30:7; 49:19; 50:26, 44; La 1:21; 4:6; Eze 5:9; 16:57; Hos 7:4; 8:12; 13:7; Joel 2:2; Mic 7:18; Hab 3:14; Hag 2:3; Zec 5:3, 3; 9:15; 10:2, 7, 8

4027 כֵּן² *kēn*[2], adv. [753]

Ge 1:7, 9, 11, 15, 24, 30; 2:24; 4:15; 6:4, 22; 10:9; 11:9; 15:14; 16:14; 18:5, 5; 19:8, 22; 20:6; 21:31; 23:19; 25:22, 26, 30; 26:33; 29:26, 28, 34, 35; 30:6, 15; 31:48; 32:20, 32; 33:10, 17; 34:7; 38:26; 41:13, 31; 42:20, 21, 25; 43:11; 44:10; 45:15, 21; 47:22; 48:18; 50:3, 11, 12; Ex 1:12, 12; 3:20; 5:8, 17; 6:6, 9; 7:6, 10, 11, 20, 22; 8:7, 17, 18, 24, 26; 10:10, 11, 14, 14, 29; 11:1, 8; 12:28, 50; 13:15; 14:4; 15:23; 16:17, 29; 17:6; 20:11; 22:30; 23:11; 25:9, 33; 26:4, 17, 24; 27:8, 11; 34:32; 36:11, 22, 29; 37:19; 39:32, 42, 43; 40:16; Lev 4:20; 8:35; 10:13; 14:36; 16:16, 26, 28; 17:12; 24:19, 20; 27:12, 14; Nu 1:54; 2:17, 34, 34; 4:15; 5:4, 4; 6:21; 8:3, 4, 15, 20, 22, 22; 9:5, 14, 16, 17; 10:31; 12:7; 13:33; 14:28, 43; 15:14, 20; 16:11; 17:11; 18:24, 28; 20:12; 21:14, 27; 25:12; 32:23, 31; 36:10; Dt 3:21; 4:5; 5:15; 7:19; 8:20; 10:9; 12:4, 22, 30, 31; 15:11, 15, 17; 18:14; 19:7; 20:15; 21:13; 22:3, 3, 3, 26; 24:18, 22; 28:63; Jos 1:17; 4:8; 5:15; 7:26; 8:34; 9:26; 10:1, 23, 26, 39; 11:15, 15; 14:5, 14; 21:42; 23:15; Jdg 1:7; 2:17; 5:15, 31; 6:20, 22, 38, 40; 7:17, 17; 8:7; 10:13; 11:8, 10; 14:10; 15:11, 19; 16:4; 18:12; 21:14, 23; 1Sa 1:7, 7; 2:30; 3:14; 5:5, 7; 6:10; 8:8; 9:13, 13; 10:5, 12; 15:33; 19:24; 20:29; 23:17, 28; 24:5, 8; 25:25; 26:24; 27:6; 28:2, 2, 18; 30:23; 2Sa 2:1; 3:9, 28; 5:8, 20, 25; 7:17, 22, 27; 8:1; 9:11; 10:1; 12:31; 13:1, 12, 18, 35; 14:17; 15:1; 16:10, 19, 23; 18:14, 20; 20:18, 21; 21:14, 18; 22:50; 24:10; 1Ki 1:30, 36, 37; 2:7, 38; 6:26, 33; 7:18, 29; 9:9; 10:12, 20, 29; 11:8; 12:32; 13:9; 14:4, 10; 20:23, 25, 40; 22:8, 12, 19, 22; 2Ki 1:4, 6, 16; 2:10; 6:24; 7:20; 15:12; 16:11; 18:21; 19:32; 21:12; 22:20; 1Ch 11:7; 13:4; 14:11; 17:15, 25; 18:1; 19:1; 20:3, 4; 23:30; 2Ch 1:12, 12, 17; 7:22; 8:14; 9:19; 16:7; 18:7, 11, 18, 21; 20:1, 26, 35; 24:4; 32:17, 23, 31; 33:14; 35:12; Ezr 3:5; 10:16; Ne 2:16; 5:12, 15; 6:6, 13; 8:17; Est 1:8, 13; 2:4, 12; 3:2; 4:16, 16; 6:10; 7:5; 9:14, 19, 26, 26; Job 3:1; 5:27; 6:3; 7:3, 9; 8:13; 9:2, 22, 35; 17:4; 20:2, 21; 22:10; 23:15; 32:6, 10; 34:10, 25, 27; 37:24; 42:3, 6; Ps 1:4, 5; 16:9; 18:49; 25:8; 42:1, 6; 45:2, 7, 17; 46:2; 48:5, 8, 10; 61:8; 63:2, 4; 65:9; 73:6, 10; 78:21; 83:15; 103:15; 110:7; 119:104, 119, 127, 128, 129; 123:2; 127:2, 4; 128:4; 147:20; Pr 1:19; 6:15, 29; 7:15; 10:26; 15:7; 23:7; 24:14, 29; 26:1, 2, 8, 19; 27:8, 19; 30:20; Ecc 3:19; 5:2, 16; 7:6; 8:10, 10, 11; SS 1:3; 2:2, 3; Isa 1:24, 26; 5:13, 14, 24, 25; 7:14; 8:7; 9:17; 10:7, 7, 11, 16, 24; 13:7, 13; 14:24; 15:4, 7; 16:6, 7, 9, 11; 17:10; 20:2, 4; 21:3; 22:4; 24:6, 6, 15; 25:3; 26:14, 17; 27:9, 11; 28:14, 16; 29:8, 14, 22; 30:7, 12, 13, 16, 16, 18, 18; 31:4, 5; 36:6; 37:33; 38:13, 14; 47:15; 50:7, 7; 51:21; 52:6, 6, 14, 15; 53:12; 54:9; 55:9, 11; 57:10; 59:9; 61:7, 11; 63:14; 65:8, 13; 66:13, 22; Jer 2:9, 26, 33; 3:20; 5:2, 6, 14, 19, 27, 27, 31; 6:7, 15, 18, 21; 7:20, 32; 8:10, 12; 9:7, 15; 10:21; 11:11, 21, 22; 12:8; 13:11; 14:10, 15; 15:19; 16:14, 16, 21; 18:6, 13, 21; 19:6, 12; 20:11; 21:7; 22:18; 23:2, 7, 12, 15, 30, 38, 39; 24:5, 8; 25:8; 28:6, 16; 29:28, 32; 30:16; 31:3, 20, 28; 32:28, 36, 42; 33:22; 34:5, 11, 17; 35:17, 19; 36:30; 38:4, 12; 39:12; 42:5, 15, 18, 20; 44:11, 23, 26; 46:26; 48:11, 12, 30, 30, 31, 36, 36; 49:2, 6, 20, 26; 50:18, 30, 39, 45; 51:7, 36, 47, 52; La 1:8; 3:21, 24; Eze 1:28; 5:7, 8, 10, 11; 7:20; 11:4, 5, 7, 16, 17; 12:7, 11, 23, 28; 13:8, 8, 13, 20, 23; 14:4, 6; 15:6, 6; 16:35, 37; 17:19; 18:30; 20:27, 30, 36; 21:4, 12, 24; 22:4, 19, 19, 20, 22; 23:9, 22, 35, 44; 24:6, 9; 25:4, 7, 9, 13, 16; 26:3; 28:6, 7; 29:8, 10, 19; 30:22; 31:5, 10; 33:10, 25; 34:7, 9, 12, 20; 35:6, 11, 15; 36:3, 4, 5, 6, 7, 14, 22, 38; 37:12; 38:14; 39:25; 40:16; 41:7, 7; 42:6, 11; 44:12; 45:20; Hos 2:6, 9, 14; 4:3, 7, 13; 6:5; 11:2; 13:3, 6; Joel 2:4, 28; Am 3:2, 11, 12; 4:5, 12; 5:11, 13, 14, 16; 6:7; 7:17; Jnh 4:2; Mic 1:14; 2:3, 5; 3:6, 12; 5:3; Na 1:12, 12; Hab 1:4, 4, 15, 16, 17; Zep 2:9; 3:8; Hag 1:10; 2:14, 14, 14; Zec 1:6, 16; 7:13; 8:13, 15; 10:2; 11:7, 11; 14:15

4202 לֹא *lō'*, adv. [5172]

Ge 2:5, 17, 18, 20, 25; 3:1, 3, 3, 4, 17; 4:5, 7, 7, 9, 12, 15; 6:3; 7:2; 8:9, 12, 21, 21, 22; 9:4, 11, 11, 15, 23; 11:6, 7; 12:18; 13:6, 6, 9; 14:23; 15:3, 4, 10, 13, 16; 16:1, 10; 17:5, 12, 14, 15; 18:15, 15, 21, 24, 25, 28, 29, 30, 31, 32; 19:2, 8, 19, 20, 22, 33, 35; 20:4, 5, 6, 9, 12; 21:10, 26, 26, 26; 22:12, 16; 23:6, 11; 24:3, 5, 8, 8, 16, 21, 27, 33, 37, 38, 39, 41, 49, 50; 26:22, 29; 27:2, 12, 21, 23, 36; 28:1, 6, 15, 16; 29:7, 8, 25, 26; 30:1, 31, 40, 42; 31:7, 15, 27, 28, 32, 32, 33, 34, 35, 35, 38, 38, 39, 52, 52; 32:12, 25, 26, 28, 32; 34:7, 14, 17, 19, 23; 35:5, 10; 36:7; 37:4, 13, 21, 32; 38:9, 14, 16, 20, 21, 22, 22, 23, 26, 26; 39:6, 8, 9, 10; 40:8, 15, 23; 41:19, 21, 31, 36, 44; 42:2, 4, 8, 10, 11, 12, 16, 20, 21, 22, 22, 23, 31, 34, 37, 38; 43:3, 5, 5, 8, 9, 22, 32; 44:4, 5, 15, 22, 23, 23, 26, 26, 28, 32; 45:1, 1, 3, 8, 26; 47:9, 18, 18, 19, 19, 22, 22, 26; 48:10, 11, 18; 49:10; Ex 1:8, 17, 19; 2:3; 3:3, 19, 19, 21; 4:1, 1, 1, 8, 8, 9, 9, 10, 11, 14, 21; 5:2, 2, 7, 8, 14, 18, 19, 23; 6:3, 9, 12; 7:4, 13, 16, 21, 22, 23, 24; 8:15, 18, 19, 26, 26, 28, 31, 32; 9:4, 6, 7, 7, 11, 12, 18, 19, 21, 24, 26, 28, 29, 32, 33, 35; 10:5, 6, 11, 14, 14, 15, 19, 20, 23, 23, 26, 26, 27, 29; 11:6, 6, 7, 9, 10; 12:10, 13, 16, 19, 20, 22, 23, 39, 39, 39, 43, 45, 46, 46, 48; 13:3, 7, 7, 13, 17, 22; 14:12, 13, 20, 28; 15:22, 23, 26; 16:4, 8, 15, 18, 18, 20, 24, 24, 25, 26, 27; 18:17, 18; 19:13, 13, 23; 20:3, 4, 5, 5, 7, 7, 10, 13, 14, 15, 16, 17, 17, 23, 23, 25, 26, 26; 21:5, 7, 8, 10, 11, 13, 18, 21, 22, 28, 29, 33, 36; 22:8, 8, 11, 11, 13, 15, 16, 18, 21, 21, 22, 25, 25, 28, 28, 29, 31; 23:1, 2, 2, 3, 6, 7, 8, 9, 13, 13, 15, 18, 18, 19, 21, 24, 24, 24, 26, 29, 32, 33; 24:2, 2, 11; 25:15; 28:28, 32, 35, 43; 29:33, 34; 30:9, 9, 12, 15, 15, 20, 21, 32, 32, 37; 32:1, 23; 33:3, 4, 11, 12, 16, 20, 20, 23; 34:3, 7, 10, 14, 17, 20, 20, 24, 25, 25, 26, 28, 28, 29; 35:3; 39:21, 23; 40:35, 37, 37; Lev 1:17; 2:11, 11, 12, 13; 3:17; 4:2, 13, 22, 27; 5:1, 7, 8, 11, 11, 11, 17, 17, 18; 6:12, 13, 17, 23, 30; 7:15, 18, 18, 19, 23, 24, 26; 8:33, 35; 10:1, 6, 6, 7, 9, 17, 18; 11:4, 5, 6, 7, 8, 8, 11, 13, 41, 42, 43, 44, 47; 12:4, 4, 8; 13:4, 5, 6, 11, 23, 28, 32, 32, 33, 34, 36, 53, 55, 55; 14:32, 36, 48; 15:11, 25, 31; 16:2, 13, 17, 29; 17:4, 7, 9, 12, 12, 14, 16, 16; 18:3, 3, 3, 6, 7, 7, 8, 9, 10, 11, 12, 13, 14, 14, 15, 15, 16, 17, 17, 18, 19, 20, 21, 21, 22, 23, 23, 26, 28, 30; 19:4, 7, 9, 9, 10, 10, 11, 11, 11, 12, 13, 13, 13, 14, 14, 15, 15, 15, 16, 16, 17, 17, 18, 18, 19, 19, 19, 20, 20, 20, 20, 23, 26, 26, 26, 27, 27, 28, 28, 29, 33, 35; 20:14, 19, 22, 23, 25; 21:1, 3, 4, 5, 5, 5, 6, 7, 7, 10, 10, 11, 11, 12, 12, 14, 15, 17, 18, 21, 21, 23, 23, 23; 22:2, 4, 6, 8, 9, 10, 10, 12, 13, 15, 20, 20, 21, 22, 22, 23, 24, 24, 25, 25, 28, 30, 32; 23:3, 7, 8, 14, 21, 22, 22, 25, 28, 29, 31, 35, 36; 25:4, 4, 5, 5, 11, 11, 11, 17, 20, 20, 23, 26, 28, 30, 30, 34, 37, 37, 39, 42, 43, 46, 53, 54; 26:1, 1, 1, 6, 11, 14, 14, 18, 20, 20, 21, 23, 26, 27, 31, 35, 37, 44, 44; 27:10, 10, 11, 20, 20, 22, 26, 27, 28, 28, 29, 33, 33, 33; Nu 1:47, 49, 49, 53; 2:33; 3:4; 4:15, 19, 20; 5:3, 13, 14, 15, 15, 19, 19, 28; 6:3, 3, 3, 4, 5, 6, 7; 7:9; 8:19, 25, 26; 9:6, 12, 12, 13, 13, 19, 22; 10:7, 30; 11:11, 14, 17, 19, 19, 19, 19, 19, 23, 25, 26; 12:2, 7, 8, 8, 14, 15; 13:31; 14:3, 11, 18, 22, 23, 28, 35, 41, 42, 43, 44; 15:22, 34, 39; 16:12, 14, 14, 15, 15, 28, 29, 40, 40, 40; 17:10; 18:3, 3, 4, 5, 17, 20, 20, 22, 23, 24, 32, 32, 32; 19:2, 12, 12, 13, 13, 20, 20; 20:2, 5, 12, 12, 17, 17, 17, 18, 20, 24; 21:22, 22, 23; 22:12, 12, 18, 30, 30, 34, 37, 37, 37; 23:8, 8, 9, 12, 13, 19, 19, 19, 20, 21, 21, 23, 23, 24, 25, 25, 26; 24:1, 12, 13, 17, 17; 25:11; 26:11, 33, 62, 62, 64, 65; 27:3, 3, 17; 28:18, 25, 26; 29:1, 7, 12, 35; 30:2, 5, 11, 12; 31:18, 23, 35, 49; 32:11, 18, 19, 23, 30; 33:14, 55; 35:12, 22, 22, 23, 23, 23, 30, 31, 32, 33, 33, 34; 36:7, 9; Dt 1:9, 17, 17, 26, 29, 29, 37, 39, 42, 42, 42, 43, 45, 45; 2:5, 7, 9, 19, 27, 30, 34, 36, 37; 3:4, 4, 22, 26, 27; 4:2, 2, 15, 26, 28, 28, 28, 28, 31, 31, 31, 42; 5:3, 5, 7, 8, 9, 9, 11, 11, 14, 17, 18, 19, 20, 21, 21, 22, 32; 6:10, 11, 11, 11, 14, 16; 7:2, 2, 3, 3, 3, 7, 10, 14, 15, 16, 16, 18, 21, 22, 24, 25, 26; 8:2, 3, 3, 3, 4, 4, 9, 9, 16, 20; 9:5, 6, 9, 9, 18, 18, 23, 23; 10:9, 10, 16, 17, 17; 11:2, 2, 2, 10, 17, 17, 25, 28, 28, 30; 12:4, 8, 9, 16, 17, 23, 24, 25, 31, 32, 32; 13:2, 3, 6, 8, 8, 8, 8, 8, 11, 13, 16, 17; 14:1, 1, 3, 7, 7, 8, 8, 8, 10, 12, 19, 21, 21, 24, 27; 15:2, 4, 6, 6, 7, 7, 9, 10, 11, 13, 16, 18, 19, 19, 21, 23; 16:3, 4, 4, 5, 8, 16, 19, 19, 19, 21, 22; 17:1, 3, 6, 11, 13, 15, 15, 16, 16, 16, 17, 17, 17; 18:1, 2,

4537 מָה ***mâ***, p.inter. & indef. [752]

10:12; 29:24, 24; 32:20; Jos 4:6, 21; 5:14; 7:7, 8, 9, 10, 19, 25; 9:22; 15:18; 22:16, 24; Jdg 1:14; 2:2; 5:16, 17; 6:13, 15; 7:11; 8:1, 2, 3; 9:2, 48; 11:12; 12:3; 13:8, 12, 18; 14:18, 18; 15:10, 11; 16:5, 5, 6, 6, 10, 13, 15; 18:3, 3, 8, 14, 18, 23, 24, 24, 24; 20:12; 21:3, 7, 16; Ru 1:11, 21; 1Sa 1:8, 8, 8; 2:23, 29; 3:17; 4:3, 6, 14, 16; 5:8; 6:2, 2, 3, 4, 6; 9:7, 7, 21; 10:2, 11, 15, 27; 11:5; 13:11; 14:38, 43; 15:14, 19; 17:8, 26, 28, 29; 19:3, 5, 17, 17; 20:1, 1, 1, 4, 8, 10, 32, 32; 21:3, 14; 22:3, 13; 24:9; 25:17; 26:15, 18, 18, 18; 27:5; 28:9, 12, 13, 14, 15, 15, 16; 29:3, 4, 8, 8; 2Sa 1:4; 2:22; 3:24, 24; 6:20; 7:7, 20; 9:8; 11:21; 12:21, 23; 13:26; 14:5, 13, 31, 32; 15:19; 16:2, 9, 10, 17, 20; 17:5; 18:22, 22, 23, 29; 19:10, 11, 12, 22, 25, 28, 29, 34, 35, 36, 42; 20:19; 21:3, 3, 4; 24:3, 13, 17; 1Ki 1:16; 2:22; 3:5; 9:8, 13; 11:22; 12:9, 16; 14:3, 6, 14; 17:18; 18:9; 19:9, 13, 20; 21:5; 22:16, 22; 2Ki 1:5, 7; 2:9; 3:13; 4:2, 2, 13, 14, 43; 5:8; 6:28, 33; 7:3; 8:13, 14; 9:18, 19, 22; 14:10; 18:19; 20:8, 14, 15; 23:17; 1Ch 12:32; 15:13; 17:6, 18; 21:3, 3, 12, 17; 2Ch 1:7; 7:21; 10:9, 16; 18:15, 20; 19:6; 20:12; 24:20; 25:9, 15, 16, 19; 30:3; 32:4, 10, 13; 35:21; Ezr 9:10; Ne 2:4, 12, 16, 19; 4:2; 6:3; 13:17; Est 1:15; 2:11; 4:5, 5; 5:3, 3, 6, 6; 6:3, 6; 7:2, 2; 8:1; 9:12, 12, 12, 26, 26; Job 3:11, 12, 20; 6:11, 11, 24, 25, 25; 7:17, 19, 20, 20, 21; 9:2, 12, 29; 10:2, 18; 11:8, 8; 13:13, 14, 23, 24; 15:9, 12, 12, 14; 16:3, 6; 19:22, 28; 21:15, 15, 17, 21; 22:13, 17; 23:5; 25:4, 4; 26:2, 3, 7, 14; 27:8, 12; 30:2; 31:1, 2, 14, 14; 34:4, 33; 35:3, 3, 6, 6, 7, 7; 37:19; 38:6; 40:4; Ps 2:1; 3:1; 4:2; 8:1, 4, 9; 10:1, 13; 11:3; 21:1; 22:1; 30:9; 31:19; 35:17; 36:7; 39:4, 4, 7; 42:5, 9, 9, 11, 11; 43:2, 2, 5, 5; 44:23, 24; 49:5; 50:16; 52:1; 56:4, 11; 66:3; 68:16; 74:1, 9, 11; 78:40; 79:5, 10; 80:12; 84:1; 85:8; 88:14; 89:46, 47, 47; 92:5; 104:24; 114:5; 115:2; 116:12; 118:6; 119:9, 84, 97, 103; 120:3, 3; 133:1, 1; 139:17, 17; 144:3; Pr 4:19; 5:20; 9:13; 15:23; 16:16; 17:16; 20:24; 22:27; 25:8; 27:1; 30:4, 4, 13; 31:2, 2, 2; Ecc 1:3, 9, 9; 2:2, 12, 15, 22; 3:9, 15, 22; 5:6, 11, 16; 6:8, 8, 10, 11, 12, 12; 7:10, 16, 17, 24; 8:4, 7; 10:14; 11:2, 5; SS 1:7; 4:10, 10; 5:8, 9, 9; 6:13; 7:1, 6, 6; 8:4, 4, 8; Isa 1:5, 11; 2:22; 3:15; 5:4; 10:3; 14:32; 19:12; 21:11, 11; 22:1, 16; 36:4; 38:15, 22; 39:3, 4; 40:6, 18, 27; 41:22; 45:9, 10, 10; 52:5, 7; 55:2; 58:3; 63:17; Jer 1:11, 13; 2:5, 18, 18, 23, 29, 33, 36; 4:30; 5:15, 19, 31; 6:20; 7:17; 8:6, 9, 14; 9:12; 11:15; 13:21; 14:8, 9; 15:18; 16:10, 10, 10; 20:18; 22:8, 23; 23:28, 33, 33, 35, 35, 37, 37; 24:3; 27:13, 17; 29:27; 30:15; 33:24; 37:18; 38:25, 25; 40:15; 44:7; 48:19; 49:4; La 2:13, 13, 13; 3:39; 5:1, 20; Eze 8:6; 12:9, 22; 15:2; 16:30; 17:12; 18:2, 31; 19:2; 20:29; 21:7, 13; 24:19; 33:11, 30; 37:18; Da 1:10; 10:20; 12:8; Hos 6:4, 4; 9:5, 14; 10:3; 14:8; Joel 1:18; 2:17; 3:4; Am 4:13; 5:18; 7:8; 8:2; Jnh 1:6, 8, 8, 10, 11; 4:5; Mic 4:9; 6:3, 3, 5, 5, 6, 8, 8; Na 1:9; Hab 1:3, 13; 2:1, 1, 18; Hag 1:9; 2:3; Zec 1:9, 9, 19, 21; 2:2, 2; 4:2, 4, 5, 11, 12, 13; 5:2, 5, 6; 6:4; 7:3; 9:17, 17; 13:6; Mal 1:2, 6, 7, 13; 2:14, 15, 17; 3:7, 8, 13, 14

4769 מִי *mî*, p.inter. [422]

Ge 3:11; 19:12; 21:7, 26; 24:23, 47, 65; 27:18, 32, 33; 32:17, 17; 33:5, 8; 38:25; 43:22; 48:8; 49:9; Ex 2:14; 3:11; 4:11, 11; 5:2; 10:8, 8; 15:11, 11; 16:3; 24:14; 32:24, 26, 33; Nu 11:4, 18, 29; 22:9; 23:10; 24:9, 23; Dt 3:24; 4:7, 8; 5:26, 29; 9:2; 20:5, 6, 7, 8; 21:1; 28:67, 67; 30:12, 13; 33:29; Jos 9:8; 24:15; Jdg 1:1; 6:29; 7:3; 9:28, 28, 29, 38; 10:18; 13:17; 15:6; 18:3; 20:18; 21:5, 8; Ru 2:5; 3:9, 16; 1Sa 2:25; 4:8; 6:20, 20; 9:20; 10:12; 11:12; 12:3, 3, 3, 3, 3; 14:17; 17:26, 28, 55, 56, 58; 18:18, 18; 20:10; 22:14; 23:22; 24:14, 14; 25:10, 10; 26:6, 9, 14, 15; 28:11; 30:13, 24; 2Sa 1:8; 3:12; 7:18, 18, 23; 11:21; 12:22; 15:4; 16:10, 19; 18:33; 20:11, 11; 22:32, 32; 23:15; 1Ki 1:20, 27; 3:9; 20:14, 14; 22:20; 2Ki 6:11; 9:5, 32, 32; 10:9, 13; 18:20, 35; 19:22, 22; 1Ch 11:17; 17:16, 16, 21; 29:5, 14, 14; 2Ch 1:10; 2:6, 6; 18:19; 32:14; 36:23; Ezr 1:3; Ne 6:11; Est 4:14; 6:4, 6; 7:5; Job 4:2, 7; 5:1; 6:8; 9:4, 12, 12, 19, 24; 11:5, 10; 12:3, 9; 13:5, 19; 14:4, 13; 17:3, 15; 19:23, 23; 21:31, 31; 23:3, 13; 24:25; 25:3; 26:4, 4, 14; 29:2; 31:31, 35; 34:7, 13, 13, 29, 29; 36:22, 23, 23; 38:2, 5, 5, 6, 25, 28, 29, 29, 36, 36, 37, 37, 41; 39:5, 5; 41:10, 11, 13, 13, 14; 42:3; Ps 4:6; 6:5; 12:4; 14:7; 15:1, 1; 18:31, 31; 19:12; 24:3, 3, 8, 10; 25:12; 27:1, 1; 34:12; 35:10; 39:6; 53:6; 55:6; 59:7; 60:9, 9; 64:5; 71:19; 73:25; 76:7; 77:13; 89:6, 8, 48; 90:11; 94:16, 16; 106:2; 107:43; 108:10, 10; 113:5; 130:3; 147:17; Pr 9:4, 16; 18:14; 20:6, 9; 23:29, 29, 29, 29, 29, 29; 24:22; 27:4; 30:4, 4, 4, 4, 9; 31:10; Ecc 2:19, 25, 25; 3:21, 22; 4:8; 5:10; 6:12, 12; 7:13, 24; 8:1, 1, 4, 7; 9:4; 10:14; SS 3:6; 6:10; 8:1, 5; Isa 1:12; 6:8, 8; 10:3; 14:27, 27; 22:16; 23:8; 27:4; 28:9, 9; 29:15, 15; 33:14, 14; 36:5, 20; 37:23, 23; 40:12, 13, 14, 18, 25, 26; 41:2, 4, 26; 42:19, 19, 23, 24; 43:9, 13; 44:7, 10; 45:21; 46:5; 48:14; 49:21, 21; 50:1, 8, 8, 9, 10; 51:12, 19, 19; 53:1, 1, 8; 54:15; 57:4, 4, 11; 60:8; 63:1; 66:8, 8; Jer 2:24; 6:10; 9:1, 2, 12; 10:7; 15:5, 5, 5; 17:9; 18:13; 21:13, 13; 23:18, 18; 30:21; 44:28; 46:7; 49:4, 19, 19, 19, 19; 50:44, 44, 44, 44; La 2:13, 20; 3:37; Eze 27:32; 31:2, 18; 32:19; Hos 14:9; Joel 2:11, 14; Am 3:8, 8; 7:2, 5; Ob 1:3; Jnh 1:7, 8; 3:9; Mic 1:5, 5; 6:9; 7:18; Na 1:6, 6; 3:7, 19; Hag 2:3; Zec 4:7, 10; Mal 1:10; 3:2, 2

4946 מִן *min*, pp. [7521]

Ge 1:7, 7, 9; 2:2, 3, 6, 7, 8, 9, 10, 10, 16, 17, 17, 17, 19, 21, 22, 23, 23, 23; 3:1, 1, 2, 3, 3, 5, 6, 8, 11, 11, 12, 14, 14, 17, 17, 19, 22, 22, 23, 23, 24; 4:3, 3, 4, 4, 10, 11, 11, 13, 14, 14, 16; 5:29, 29, 29; 6:2, 4, 7, 7, 13, 14, 14, 16, 17, 19, 19, 19, 20, 20, 20, 20, 21; 7:2, 2, 3, 4, 7, 8, 8, 8, 15, 16, 17, 20, 22, 23, 23; 8:2, 3, 3, 6, 7, 8, 8, 10, 11, 13, 16, 17, 19, 20, 20, 21; 9:5, 5, 5, 10, 11, 18, 19, 21, 24; 10:5, 11, 14, 19, 30, 32; 11:2, 6, 8, 9, 31; 12:1, 1, 1, 4, 8, 8, 8, 8; 13:1, 3, 9, 11, 11, 14, 14; 14:15, 17, 20, 23, 23; 15:4, 7, 18; 16:2, 2, 3, 6, 8, 8, 10; 17:6, 12, 12, 14, 16, 16, 22, 27; 18:2, 3, 14, 16, 17, 22, 25; 19:4, 4, 9, 11, 12, 14, 16, 24, 24, 26, 29, 30, 32, 34, 34, 36; 20:1, 6, 13; 21:15, 16, 16, 17, 21, 30; 22:4, 9, 11, 12, 15; 23:3, 4, 6, 6, 6, 8, 13, 20; 24:3, 5, 7, 7, 7, 8, 10, 11, 17, 27, 37, 40, 40, 41, 41, 43, 46, 50, 62, 64; 25:6, 10, 18, 20, 23, 23, 29, 30; 26:1, 16, 16, 17, 22, 23, 26, 27, 31; 27:1, 9, 19, 25, 28, 28, 30, 30, 31, 33, 39, 39, 39, 40, 45, 45, 46, 46, 46; 28:1, 2, 2, 6, 6, 10, 11, 16; 29:2, 3, 4, 4, 8, 10, 19, 30, 35; 30:2, 3, 9, 14, 16, 32; 31:1, 13, 16, 24, 29, 29, 31, 33, 35, 37, 39, 40, 49; 32:10, 10, 11, 11, 12, 13; 33:10, 15, 18, 19; 34:7, 19, 26; 35:1, 7, 8, 9, 11, 11, 13, 16, 21; 36:2, 6, 7, 7, 33, 34, 36, 37; 37:3, 4, 14, 17, 18, 21, 22, 25, 28; 38:1, 14, 17, 19, 20, 24, 26; 39:1, 5, 9, 9, 11; 40:14, 15, 17, 17, 17, 19, 19; 41:1, 2, 3, 14, 18, 31, 32, 40, 42, 46; 42:2, 3, 7, 7, 15, 16, 24, 24, 26; 43:2, 9, 11, 34, 34; 44:7, 8, 8, 9, 17, 28, 29, 32; 45:1, 3, 19, 23, 25; 46:3, 5, 26, 34; 47:1, 2, 10, 13, 15, 15, 18, 21, 22, 30; 48:7, 10, 12, 13, 13, 15, 16, 17, 19, 22; 49:9, 10, 10, 12, 12, 20, 24, 24, 25, 25, 30, 32; 50:13, 24, 25; Ex 1:9, 10, 12; 2:1, 4, 6, 7, 10, 11, 15, 19, 23, 23; 3:2, 4, 5, 6, 7, 8, 8, 10, 11, 12, 17, 22, 22; 4:3, 7, 9, 9, 10, 10, 10, 26; 5:4, 5, 8, 11, 11, 19, 20, 23; 6:1, 6, 6, 7, 9, 9, 11, 13, 25, 26, 27; 7:2, 4, 5, 18, 21, 24; 8:8, 8, 9, 9, 11, 11, 11, 11, 12, 13, 13, 13, 24, 29, 29, 29, 29, 30, 31, 31, 31; 9:4, 6, 6, 7, 11, 15, 18, 20, 24, 25, 28, 30, 33; 10:3, 5, 5, 6, 6, 11, 17, 18, 23, 26, 28; 11:1, 1, 2, 2, 5, 7, 8, 10; 12:4, 4, 5, 5, 7, 9, 10, 10, 12, 15, 15, 15, 17, 19, 22, 22, 29, 31, 33, 35, 37, 37, 39, 39, 41, 41, 42, 46, 46, 51; 13:3, 3, 3, 8, 9, 10, 14, 14, 15, 16, 18, 19, 20; 14:5, 11, 11, 12, 12, 19, 19, 19, 22, 22, 25, 29, 29, 30; 15:22, 23; 16:1, 1, 4, 6, 16, 19, 20, 27, 29, 32, 32; 17:1, 3, 5, 6, 12, 12, 14, 16; 18:1, 4, 9, 10, 10, 10, 11, 13, 13, 14, 18, 21, 22, 25; 19:1, 2, 3, 5, 14, 17, 18, 21; 20:2, 2, 4, 4, 4, 18, 21, 22; 21:14, 29, 36; 22:4, 7, 12, 14; 23:5, 7, 15, 16, 21, 25, 28, 29, 30, 31, 31, 31; 24:1, 1, 9, 16; 25:2, 3, 11, 11, 15, 18, 19, 19, 19, 19, 21, 22, 22, 31, 32, 32, 32, 33, 35, 35, 35, 35, 36; 26:4, 13, 13, 13, 13, 14, 24, 28, 33, 35; 27:2, 5, 21, 21, 21; 28:1, 8, 10, 27, 27, 27, 28, 28, 42; 29:12, 14, 20, 21, 21, 22, 23, 25, 26, 27, 27, 27, 28, 28, 28, 30, 34, 34, 46; 30:2, 4, 10, 14, 15, 16, 19, 33, 33, 36, 36, 38; 31:14; 32:1, 1, 4, 4, 6, 7, 8, 8, 11, 12, 12, 15, 15, 15, 15, 19, 23, 27, 28, 30, 32, 33; 33:1, 1, 5, 6, 7, 7, 7, 11, 15, 16; 34:11, 15, 16, 18, 24, 29, 29, 30, 33; 35:5, 20; 36:3, 4, 5, 6, 11, 19, 29, 33; 37:2, 2, 7, 8, 8, 8, 8, 8, 8, 17, 18, 18, 18, 19, 21, 21, 21, 21, 22, 25, 27; 38:2, 4, 15, 15, 26; 39:1, 5, 20, 20, 20, 21, 21, 31; 40:19, 20, 22, 31, 36; Lev 1:1, 2, 2, 2, 2, 3, 10, 10, 10, 14, 14, 14; 2:2, 2, 2, 3, 3, 8, 9, 10, 10, 11, 13, 16, 16; 3:1, 3, 6, 9, 14; 4:2, 2, 2, 5, 6, 7, 8, 10, 12, 13, 13, 16, 17, 18, 19, 21, 22, 25, 26, 27, 27, 30, 31, 34, 35; 5:2, 3, 4, 4, 5, 6, 6, 8, 9, 10, 12, 13, 13, 15, 15, 16, 17, 18; 6:3, 5, 6, 7, 11, 15, 15, 15, 16, 17, 18, 22, 27, 30; 7:3, 14, 14, 15, 16, 16, 17, 18, 18, 20, 20, 21, 21, 25, 25, 25, 27, 29, 32, 33, 34, 34, 34, 35, 36; 8:11, 12, 17, 23, 24, 26, 28, 29, 30, 30, 33; 9:10, 10, 11, 17, 17, 19, 19, 22, 24; 10:2, 4, 4, 5, 7, 12, 13, 14; 11:2, 4, 4, 8, 9, 10, 10, 11, 13, 21, 21, 22, 25, 32, 32, 33, 34, 35, 37, 38, 39, 40, 45; 12:7; 13:2, 3, 4, 12, 20, 21, 25, 26, 30, 31, 32, 34, 41, 46, 56, 56, 56, 56, 58; 14:3, 3, 7, 8, 14, 15, 16, 16, 17, 19, 25, 26, 27, 28, 29, 30, 30, 30, 37, 38, 40, 41, 41, 45, 53; 15:2, 3, 13, 15, 16, 28, 30, 31, 32; 16:2, 5, 12, 12, 12, 14, 14, 15, 16, 16, 18, 18, 19, 19, 20, 27, 30, 34; 17:3, 3, 4, 8, 8, 9, 10, 10, 10, 12, 13, 13; 18:21, 24, 26, 29, 29, 30; 19:6, 8, 14, 22, 32, 32, 34, 36; 20:2, 2, 3, 3, 4, 4, 5, 6, 18, 23, 24, 26; 21:7, 10, 12, 14, 17, 21, 22, 22; 22:2, 3, 3, 4, 4, 6, 7, 13, 18, 18, 22, 25, 25, 27, 30, 33; 23:11, 15, 15, 16, 17, 29, 30, 32, 38, 38, 38, 38, 43; 24:3, 3, 8, 9, 14, 23; 25:12, 14, 15, 17, 22, 25, 33, 36, 36, 38, 41, 42, 43, 44, 44, 45, 45, 45, 48, 49, 49, 50, 51, 55; 26:6, 8, 8, 10, 13, 13, 37, 43, 43, 45; 27:3, 5, 6, 7, 8, 9, 11, 16, 17, 18, 22, 24, 28, 28, 28, 29, 30, 30, 31; Nu 1:1, 3, 18, 20, 22, 24, 26, 28, 30, 32, 34, 36, 38, 40, 42, 45; 2:2; 3:9, 12, 12, 13, 15, 22, 28, 34, 39, 40, 43, 46, 49, 50; 4:2, 3, 6, 18, 23, 25, 30, 35, 39, 43, 47; 5:2, 3, 3, 4, 6, 8, 13, 17, 19, 20, 25, 26, 31; 6:3, 4, 4, 4, 11, 19, 19, 21; 7:5, 84, 89, 89; 8:6, 11, 14, 16, 16, 19, 24, 25, 25; 9:1, 12, 13, 17, 21; 10:9, 11, 12, 33, 34, 35; 11:13, 14, 16, 17, 20, 20, 24, 25, 28, 31, 31, 35; 12:3, 10, 12, 14, 15, 16; 13:3, 20, 21, 23, 23, 23, 24, 25, 25, 31, 33; 14:6, 9, 12, 13, 16, 19, 29, 38, 43, 44; 15:3, 3, 19, 21, 23, 24, 30, 30, 30, 35, 36, 41; 16:2, 9, 9, 13, 15, 15, 21, 24, 26, 27, 27, 28, 33, 35, 37, 40, 41, 45, 46, 46, 49; 17:2, 2, 5, 8, 9, 10; 18:6, 7, 9, 9, 16, 26, 26, 26, 26, 27, 27, 28, 28, 28, 29, 29, 29, 30, 32; 19:3, 4, 4, 9, 13, 17, 20; 20:5, 6, 8, 9, 10, 14, 16, 21, 22, 28; 21:1, 4, 5, 6, 7, 11, 11, 12, 13, 13, 13, 16, 18, 19, 19, 20, 24, 26, 28, 28; 22:1, 3, 3, 5, 5, 6, 6, 11, 15, 16, 23, 24, 24, 30, 33, 41; 23:7, 7, 9, 9, 13, 13, 22, 27; 24:7, 7, 8, 11, 13, 17, 17, 19, 19, 23, 24; 25:4, 6, 7, 8, 11; 26:2, 4, 4, 62, 64, 65; 27:4, 11, 20; 28:23, 31; 29:6, 11, 16, 19, 22, 25, 28, 31, 34, 38, 39; 30:2, 14; 31:2, 3, 5, 13, 14, 19, 28, 28, 28, 28, 28, 29, 30, 30, 30, 30, 30, 30, 30, 35, 37, 42, 42, 43, 47, 47, 47, 49, 51, 52, 52, 54; 32:7, 8, 11, 11, 15, 17, 19, 19, 21, 22, 22, 24, 32; 33:1, 3, 3, 5, 6, 7, 8, 9, 10, 11, 12, 13, 14, 15, 16, 17, 18, 19, 20, 21, 22, 23, 24, 25, 26, 27, 28, 29, 30, 31, 32, 33, 34, 35, 36, 37, 38, 41, 42, 43, 44, 45, 46, 47, 48, 49, 52, 55, 55; 34:3, 3, 4, 4, 5, 7, 8, 10, 11, 11, 15, 18; 35:2, 4, 5, 8, 8, 8, 8, 12, 14, 25, 27; 36:1, 3, 3, 3, 4, 7, 8, 8, 9, 12; Dt 1:2, 17, 17, 19, 23, 25, 27, 28, 29; 2:4, 5, 6, 6, 8, 8, 8, 8, 9, 12, 14, 14, 15, 16, 19, 21, 22, 23, 25, 26, 36, 36; 3:4, 5, 8, 8, 11, 12, 16, 17; 4:2, 3, 9, 12, 15, 18, 20, 20, 26, 29, 32, 32, 32, 33, 34, 35, 36, 36, 37, 38, 38, 39, 39, 42, 42, 45, 46, 48; 5:4, 5, 6, 6, 8, 8, 8, 15, 22, 23, 24, 26; 6:12, 12, 14, 15, 19, 21, 23; 7:1, 1, 4, 6, 7, 7, 7, 8, 8, 8, 8, 14, 15, 17, 18, 19, 20, 21, 22, 24; 8:4, 9, 14, 14, 15, 20; 9:1, 4, 4, 5, 7, 7, 10, 11, 12, 12, 12, 14, 14, 14, 15, 16, 17, 19, 21, 23, 24, 26, 28, 28, 28; 10:4, 5, 6, 7, 7, 12, 15; 11:10, 12, 17, 23, 23, 24, 24, 28; 12:3, 5, 10, 10, 21, 21, 21, 29, 30, 32; 13:5, 5, 5, 5, 7, 7, 7, 10, 10, 10, 13, 17, 17; 14:2, 7, 7, 8, 9, 12, 24, 24, 28; 15:1, 7, 7, 11, 12, 13, 14, 14, 14, 16, 18; 16:1, 3, 3, 4, 6, 9, 13, 13; 17:7, 8, 10, 11, 12, 15, 18, 20, 20; 18:3, 3, 5, 6, 6, 12, 15, 15, 16, 18, 19, 22; 19:4, 5, 6, 12, 13, 19; 20:1, 1, 1, 3, 15, 15, 16, 19, 19; 21:9, 13, 21; 22:1, 3, 4, 8, 21, 22, 24; 23:4, 4, 9, 10, 10, 12, 14, 15, 17, 17, 21; 24:1, 2, 3, 7, 7, 7, 9, 14, 14, 18; 25:5, 6, 9, 11, 17, 19, 19, 19; 26:2, 2, 4, 8, 13, 13, 13, 14, 14, 14, 15, 15; 28:10, 14, 20, 21, 24, 31, 31, 34, 35, 47, 49, 49, 55, 55, 55, 55, 56, 56, 57, 60, 63, 64, 66, 67, 67; 29:1, 5, 5, 11, 18, 20, 21, 22, 22, 25, 28; 30:3, 4, 4, 5, 11, 13; 31:3, 6, 10, 17, 21, 26, 29; 32:13, 13, 17, 19, 20, 25, 25, 26, 32, 32, 39, 42, 42, 42, 47, 52; 33:2, 2, 2, 2, 2, 3, 7, 11, 13, 13, 13, 14, 14, 15, 15, 16, 22, 24, 27, 27; 34:1; Jos 1:4, 7, 8; 2:1, 2, 4, 9, 10, 10, 11, 11, 13, 17, 19, 20, 23, 24; 3:1, 2, 3, 4, 10, 12, 13, 14, 16, 16; 4:2, 2, 3, 3, 3, 4, 4, 7, 8, 16, 17, 18, 19, 20, 23, 23; 5:1, 1, 4, 4, 5, 6, 9, 11, 11, 12, 12, 12, 15; 6:1, 10, 18, 18, 21, 21, 22, 23; 7:1, 2, 2, 4, 5, 9, 11, 12, 13, 19, 23, 26; 8:2, 4, 4, 6, 7, 9, 11, 12, 13, 13, 14, 16, 19, 22, 22, 22, 25, 29, 33, 33, 35; 9:6, 8, 9, 12, 13, 14, 16, 22, 23, 24, 24, 26; 10:2, 6, 7, 8, 8, 9, 11, 11, 11, 20, 22, 23, 27, 29, 31, 34, 36, 41; 11:2, 2, 3, 3, 6, 15, 17, 20, 21, 21, 21, 21, 21, 21, 23; 12:1, 2, 3, 4, 7, 9; 13:3, 4, 4, 5, 6, 6, 9, 12, 16, 26, 26, 30, 32; 14:3, 7, 10, 15; 15:1, 2, 2, 3, 3, 5, 5, 6, 7, 7, 8, 9, 10, 10, 14, 15, 18, 18, 21, 46; 16:1, 1, 2, 6, 6, 7, 8; 17:5, 5, 7, 9, 10, 10; 18:5, 5, 7, 12, 12, 13, 13, 14, 15, 17; 19:9, 9, 12, 13, 14, 27, 29, 33, 33, 34, 34, 34, 47, 51; 20:3, 4, 5, 6, 8, 8, 8, 8; 21:3, 4, 4, 4, 4, 5, 5, 5, 6, 6, 6, 6, 7, 7, 7, 9, 9, 10, 10, 16, 17, 20, 20, 23, 25, 27, 27, 28, 30, 32, 34, 36, 38, 40, 44, 44, 45; 22:9, 9, 16, 17, 18, 19, 23, 24, 24, 29, 29, 29, 31, 32, 32, 32; 23:1, 1, 1, 3, 4, 5, 5, 6, 9, 10, 13, 13, 14, 14, 15, 16; 24:2, 3, 6, 8, 10, 12, 16, 17, 17, 18, 30, 32, 32; Jdg 1:11, 13, 14, 14, 16, 20, 24, 36, 36; 2:1, 1, 3, 9, 12, 12, 14, 16, 17, 18, 18, 18, 19, 19, 19, 21, 21; 3:3, 9, 16, 19, 19, 20, 21, 22, 27; 4:6, 6, 6, 11, 11, 13, 14, 15; 5:4, 4, 5, 5, 11, 14, 20, 20, 22, 24, 24; 6:2, 6, 8, 8, 9, 9, 9, 11, 13, 14, 18, 21, 21, 27, 27, 38, 38; 7:1, 1, 2, 3, 3, 5, 8, 17, 23, 23, 23, 25; 8:2, 3, 8, 10, 11, 13, 13, 14, 22, 24, 26, 26, 34, 34; 9:4, 15, 17, 17, 20, 20, 20, 21, 35, 36, 37, 37, 40, 41, 42, 43; 10:11, 11, 11, 11, 12, 16; 11:3, 4, 5, 7, 13, 13, 16, 18, 22, 22, 23, 24, 25, 29, 31, 31, 33, 33, 34, 36, 36, 36, 37, 39, 40; 12:2, 6, 8, 9; 13:2, 2, 5, 5, 6, 7, 13, 14, 14, 20, 23; 14:1, 2, 3, 4, 4, 8, 9, 14, 14, 18, 18, 19; 15:1, 2, 3, 5, 11, 13, 14, 17, 19; 16:12, 14, 17, 17, 19, 20, 20, 25, 28, 28, 30; 17:1, 3, 5, 7, 7, 8, 8, 9, 9, 11; 18:2, 2, 2, 2, 7, 11, 11, 11, 11, 13, 16, 22, 26, 28; 19:1, 2, 12, 16, 16, 16, 17, 18, 18, 30, 30; 20:1, 13, 14, 15, 15, 16, 17, 21, 25, 31, 31, 32, 33, 33, 33, 34, 34, 38, 40, 42, 43, 44, 45, 46, 48; 21:1, 3, 4, 5, 6, 7, 8, 8, 9, 10, 12, 14, 16, 17, 18, 19, 19, 19, 21, 21, 23, 24, 24; Ru 1:1, 2, 5, 5, 6, 7, 12, 13, 16, 22; 2:1, 3, 4, 6, 7, 8, 9, 12, 14, 14, 16, 18, 20; 3:10, 12; 4:2, 3, 5, 5, 9, 10, 10, 12, 12, 15; 1Sa 1:1, 1, 3, 3, 7, 8, 14, 16, 17, 20, 27; 2:3, 8, 8, 15, 19, 20, 23, 28, 29, 29, 31, 33; 3:15, 17, 17, 17, 18, 19, 20; 4:3, 3, 4, 8, 10, 12, 16, 16, 18, 21, 22; 5:1, 3, 4, 9; 6:3, 5, 5, 5, 7, 8, 18, 20; 7:2, 3, 3, 7, 8, 8, 8, 11, 11, 14, 14, 14, 16; 8:7, 8, 8, 10, 18; 9:1, 2, 2, 2, 2, 3, 5, 7, 16, 16, 21, 21, 25; 10:2, 3, 4, 5, 9, 11, 12, 13, 18, 18, 18, 19, 23, 23, 23; 11:5, 11; 12:2, 3, 4, 6, 8, 10, 11, 11, 20, 23, 23; 13:2, 8, 11, 15, 17; 14:1, 4, 4, 4, 4, 5, 5, 11, 17, 24, 28, 30, 31, 39, 45, 46, 48; 15:2, 3, 3, 3, 3, 6, 6, 6, 7, 11, 15, 21, 22, 22, 23, 26, 28, 28, 33; 16:1, 13, 14, 14, 18, 23; 17:3, 3, 4, 4, 12, 15, 22, 23, 23, 24, 26, 30, 33, 34, 35, 36, 37, 37, 37, 39, 39, 40, 46, 49, 50, 51, 53, 57; 18:6, 6, 9, 10, 11, 12, 12, 13, 15, 29, 30,

7, 7, 8, 15; Ob 1:1, 4, 8, 8, 9, 9, 10, 11, 11; Jnh 1:3, 3, 5, 8, 8, 10, 11, 12, 15; 2:1, 2, 2, 4, 6; 3:5, 6, 6, 7, 8, 8, 9, 10; 4:3, 3, 5, 5, 6, 6, 8, 11; Mic 1:2, 3, 4, 7, 11, 12, 16; 2:3, 8, 8, 9, 9, 12; 3:2, 2, 3, 4, 6, 6; 4:1, 2, 2, 2, 7, 10, 10; 5:2, 2, 2, 6, 7, 10, 12, 13, 14; 6:4, 4, 5, 8; 7:2, 4, 5, 12, 13, 15, 16, 17, 17, 20; Na 1:5, 5, 6, 11, 13, 14, 14; 2:9, 13; 3:4, 7, 7, 8, 11, 16; Hab 1:7, 8, 8, 8, 12, 13, 13; 2:8, 9, 11, 11, 13, 16, 17, 20; 3:3, 3, 4, 13, 17; Zep 1:2, 3, 4, 6, 7, 10, 10, 10; 2:5, 11; 3:6, 6, 6, 10, 11, 11, 18, 18; Hag 1:10, 12; 2:5, 9, 15, 15, 16, 18, 18, 18, 19; Zec 1:4, 17; 2:4, 6, 13, 13; 3:2, 4, 4; 4:1, 3, 12; 5:3, 3; 6:1, 5, 10, 10, 10, 10, 10, 12; 7:11, 12, 12, 14, 14; 8:4, 7, 7, 9, 10, 23; 9:5, 7, 7, 8, 8, 8, 10, 10, 10, 10, 11; 10:1, 4, 4, 4, 4, 10, 10; 11:6, 13; 13:2, 2, 4, 5; 14:2, 4, 4, 5, 8, 10, 10, 16, 16, 17, 21; Mal 1:5, 9, 9, 10, 11, 13; 2:5, 6, 7, 8, 12, 13, 13; 3:7, 7, 14

5087 ²מַעַל *ma'al²*, subst.adv. & pp. [140]

Ge 6:16; 7:20; 22:9; Ex 20:4; 25:20, 21; 26:14; 28:27; 30:14; 36:19; 37:9; 38:26; 39:20, 31; 40:19, 20; Lev 11:21; 27:7; Nu 1:3, 18, 20, 22, 24, 26, 28, 30, 32, 34, 36, 38, 40, 42, 45; 3:15, 22, 28, 34, 39, 40, 43; 4:3, 6, 23, 25, 30, 35, 39, 43, 47; 8:24; 14:29; 26:2, 4, 62; 32:11; Dt 4:39; 5:8; 28:13, 43, 43; Jos 2:11; 3:13, 16; Jdg 1:36; 7:13; 1Sa 9:2; 10:23; 16:13; 30:25; 1Ki 7:3, 11, 20, 25, 29, 31; 8:7, 23; 2Ki 3:21; 19:30; 1Ch 14:2; 22:5; 23:3, 17, 24, 27; 29:3, 25; 2Ch 1:1; 4:4; 5:8; 16:12; 17:12; 20:19; 25:5; 26:8; 31:16, 17; 34:4; Ezr 3:8; 9:6; Job 3:4; 18:16; 31:2, 28; Ps 74:5; 78:23; Pr 8:28; 15:24; Ecc 3:21; Isa 6:2; 7:11; 8:21; 14:13; 37:31; 45:8; Jer 4:28; 31:37; 35:4; 43:10; 52:32; Eze 1:11, 22, 26, 26, 27; 8:2; 10:19; 11:22; 37:8; 41:7, 7, 7, 7, 7; 43:15; Da 12:6, 7; Am 2:9; Hag 2:15, 18

5528 ¹נָא *nā'¹*, pt. [405]

Ge 12:11, 13; 13:8, 9, 14; 15:5; 16:2, 2; 18:3, 3, 4, 21, 27, 30, 31, 32; 19:2, 2, 7, 8, 8, 18, 19, 20, 20; 22:2; 24:2, 12, 14, 17, 23, 42, 43, 45; 25:30; 26:28; 27:2, 3, 9, 19, 21, 26; 30:14, 27; 31:12; 32:11, 29; 33:10, 10, 11, 14, 15; 34:8; 37:6, 14, 16, 32; 38:16, 25; 40:8, 14; 44:18, 33; 45:4; 47:4, 29, 29, 29; 48:9; 50:4, 4, 5, 17, 17; Ex 3:3, 18; 4:6, 13, 18; 5:3; 10:11, 17; 11:2; 32:32; 33:13, 13, 18; 34:9, 9; Nu 10:31; 11:15; 12:6, 11, 12, 13, 13; 14:17, 19; 16:8, 26; 20:10, 17; 22:6, 16, 17, 19; 23:13, 27; Dt 3:25; 4:32; Jos 2:12; 7:19, 19; 22:26; Jdg 1:24; 4:19; 6:17, 18, 39, 39; 7:3; 8:5; 9:2, 38; 10:15; 11:17, 19; 12:6; 13:3, 4, 8, 15; 14:12; 15:2; 16:6, 10, 28, 28; 18:5; 19:6, 8, 9, 9, 11, 23, 24; Ru 2:2, 7; 1Sa 2:36; 3:17; 9:3, 6, 18; 10:15; 14:17, 29; 15:25, 30; 16:15, 16, 17, 22; 17:17; 19:2; 20:29, 29, 36; 22:3, 7, 12; 23:11, 22; 25:8, 24, 25, 28; 26:8, 11, 19; 27:5; 28:8, 22; 30:7; 2Sa 1:4, 9; 2:14; 7:2; 13:5, 6, 7, 13, 17, 24, 24, 25, 26, 28; 14:2, 2, 11, 12, 15, 17, 18, 18, 21; 15:7, 31; 16:9; 17:1, 5; 18:19, 22; 19:37; 20:16; 24:2, 10, 14, 17; 1Ki 1:12; 2:17; 8:26; 13:6; 14:2; 17:10, 11, 21; 18:43; 19:20; 20:7, 31, 31, 32, 35, 37; 22:5, 13, 13; 2Ki 1:13; 2:2, 4, 6, 9, 16, 16, 19; 4:9, 10, 13, 22, 26; 5:7, 8, 15, 15, 17, 18, 22; 6:1, 2, 3, 17, 18; 7:12, 13; 8:4; 9:12, 34; 18:19, 23, 26; 19:19; 20:3; 1Ch 21:8, 13, 17; 22:5; 29:20; 2Ch 6:40; 18:4, 12; Ezr 10:14; Ne 1:6, 8, 11, 11; 5:10, 11; Job 1:11; 2:5; 4:7; 5:1; 6:29; 8:8; 10:9; 12:7; 13:6, 18; 17:3, 10; 22:21, 22; 32:21; 33:1, 2; 38:3; 40:7, 10, 15, 16; 42:4; Ps 7:9; 50:22; 80:14; 115:2; 116:14, 18; 118:2, 3, 4, 25, 25; 119:76, 108; 122:8; 124:1; 129:1; Ecc 2:1; SS 3:2; 7:8; Isa 1:18; 5:1, 3, 5; 7:3, 13; 19:12; 29:11, 12; 36:4, 8, 11; 38:3; 47:12, 13; 51:21; 64:9; Jer 4:31; 5:1, 21, 24; 7:12; 17:15; 18:11, 11, 13; 21:2; 25:5; 27:18; 28:7, 15; 30:6; 32:8; 35:15; 36:15, 17; 37:3, 20, 20; 38:4, 12, 20, 25; 40:15; 42:2; 44:4; 45:3; La 1:18; 5:16; Eze 8:5, 8; 17:12; 18:25; 33:30; Da 1:12; 9:16; Am 7:2, 5; Jnh 1:8, 14; 4:3; Mic 3:1, 9; 6:1, 5; Hag 2:2, 11, 15, 18; Zec 1:4; 3:8; 5:5; Mal 1:8, 9; 3:10

6330 ²עַד *'ad²*, pp. [1261]

Ge 3:19; 6:7, 7, 7; 7:23, 23, 23; 8:5, 7; 10:19, 19; 11:31; 12:6, 6; 13:3, 3, 12, 15; 14:6, 14, 15, 23; 15:16, 18; 19:4, 11, 22, 37, 38; 22:5; 24:19, 33; 25:18; 26:13, 33; 27:33, 34, 44, 45; 28:15; 29:8; 31:24, 29; 32:4, 24, 32; 33:3, 3, 14; 34:5; 35:20; 38:1, 11, 17; 39:16; 41:49; 43:25; 44:28; 46:34; 47:21, 26; 48:5, 15; 49:10; 50:10; Ex 7:16; 9:7, 18, 25; 10:3, 6, 7, 26; 11:5, 7; 12:6, 10, 10, 12, 15, 18, 22, 24, 29; 13:15; 14:13, 28; 15:16, 16; 16:19, 20, 23, 24, 28, 35, 35; 17:12; 18:13, 14; 22:4, 4, 9, 26; 23:18, 30, 31, 31; 24:14; 27:5, 21; 28:42; 29:34; 32:20; 33:8, 22; 34:34, 35; 38:4; 40:37; Lev 6:9; 7:15; 8:33; 11:24, 25, 27, 28, 31, 32, 39, 40, 40, 42; 12:4; 13:12; 14:46; 15:5, 6, 7, 8, 10, 10, 11, 16, 17, 18, 19, 21, 22, 23, 27; 16:17; 17:15; 19:6, 13; 22:4, 6, 30; 23:14, 14, 16, 32; 24:3; 25:22, 22, 28, 29, 30, 40, 50, 52; 26:18; 27:3, 5, 6, 18, 23; Nu 3:13; 4:3, 23, 30, 35, 39, 43, 47; 5:3; 6:4, 5; 8:4, 4; 9:12, 15, 21; 10:21; 11:20, 20; 12:15; 13:21, 22, 23; 14:11, 11, 19, 27, 33, 45; 19:7, 8, 10, 21, 22; 20:17; 21:22, 24, 24, 26, 30, 30, 30, 35; 22:30; 23:18, 24; 24:20, 22, 24; 32:9, 13, 17, 18, 21; 33:49; 35:12, 25, 28, 32; Dt 1:2, 7, 19, 20, 24, 31, 31, 44; 2:5, 14, 14, 15, 22, 23, 29, 36; 3:3, 8, 10, 14, 14, 16, 16, 17, 20; 4:11, 30, 32, 48, 49; 7:20, 23, 24; 9:7, 7, 21; 10:8; 11:4, 5, 5, 12, 24; 12:9, 28; 13:7; 20:20; 22:2; 23:3; 28:20, 20, 21, 22, 24, 35, 45, 46, 48, 51, 51, 52, 61, 64; 29:4, 11, 29; 30:2; 31:24, 30; 32:22; 34:1, 2, 3, 6; Jos 1:4, 4, 15; 2:16, 22; 3:1, 8, 15, 17; 4:7, 9, 10, 23, 23; 5:1, 6, 8, 9; 6:10, 21, 21, 21, 25; 7:5, 6, 13, 26, 26; 8:6, 22, 24, 25, 26, 28, 29, 29; 9:27; 10:10, 10, 11, 13, 20, 26, 27, 33, 41, 41; 11:8, 8, 8, 8, 14, 17; 12:1, 2, 3, 3, 5, 7; 13:3, 4, 4, 5, 6, 9, 10, 11, 13, 25, 26, 26, 27; 14:9, 14; 15:5, 47, 63; 16:3, 3, 5, 10; 17:14, 14; 18:3; 19:8, 10, 28, 29, 33; 20:6, 6, 9; 22:3, 17; 23:8, 9, 13, 15; Jdg 1:21, 26; 3:3, 25, 26; 4:11, 16, 16, 24; 5:7; 6:4, 18, 18, 24, 31; 7:13, 22, 22, 24, 24; 9:40, 52, 52; 10:4; 11:13, 13, 16, 19, 22, 22, 33, 33; 13:7; 14:5; 15:5, 5, 14, 19; 16:2, 3, 13; 17:8; 18:1, 2, 12, 13, 30; 19:8, 10, 12, 18, 18, 25, 26, 30; 20:1, 23, 26, 43, 45, 48, 48; 21:2; Ru 1:13, 19; 2:7, 17, 21, 23; 3:3, 13, 14, 18; 1Sa 1:14, 16, 22, 22, 23, 23; 2:5, 30; 3:13, 14, 15, 20; 5:5, 9; 6:12, 18, 18; 7:11, 12, 14; 8:8; 9:9, 13; 10:3, 8; 11:11, 15; 12:2; 13:13; 14:9, 19, 20, 24, 36; 15:3, 3, 3, 3, 5, 18, 35; 16:1, 11; 17:52, 52, 52, 52; 18:4, 4, 4; 19:22, 23; 20:5, 8, 15, 23, 28, 37, 41, 42; 22:3, 19, 19; 25:22, 34, 36, 36; 27:6, 8; 29:3, 6, 8; 30:2, 4, 9, 17, 19, 19, 19, 25; 2Sa 1:12; 2:17, 24, 26; 3:10, 16, 28; 4:3, 6; 5:25; 6:6, 8, 19, 23; 7:6, 13, 16, 16, 18, 24, 25, 26; 10:4, 5; 11:23; 12:10; 13:22; 14:25; 15:24, 28, 32; 16:5; 17:11, 13, 13, 22, 22; 18:18; 19:7, 15, 24; 20:2, 3, 16; 21:10; 22:38, 51; 23:10, 19; 24:2, 15, 15; 1Ki 1:4; 2:28, 33, 45; 3:1, 2; 4:12, 12, 21, 24, 25, 33; 5:3, 9; 6:15, 16, 22, 24; 7:7, 9, 9, 23; 8:8; 8:65; 9:3, 13, 21; 10:7, 12; 11:16, 40; 12:19, 30; 14:10; 15:29; 17:14, 17; 18:21, 26, 28, 29, 45, 45, 46; 19:8; 22:11, 16, 27; 2Ki 2:2, 17, 22; 3:25; 4:20, 22, 35; 6:2, 25; 7:3, 5, 8, 9, 15; 8:6, 7, 11, 22; 9:18, 20, 22; 10:8, 11, 17, 25, 27; 11:11; 13:17, 19, 23; 14:7, 13, 25; 15:5; 16:6, 11; 17:9, 20, 23, 23, 34, 41; 18:4, 8, 8, 32; 19:3; 20:17; 21:15, 16; 23:2, 8; 24:7, 20; 25:2, 26; 1Ch 4:27, 31, 33, 39, 41, 43; 5:8, 9, 11, 22, 23, 26; 6:32; 7:28; 9:18; 11:8, 21; 12:16, 22, 29, 40; 13:5, 9, 11; 14:16; 15:2, 29; 16:3, 36; 17:5, 12, 14, 14, 16, 22, 23, 24; 19:4, 5; 21:2, 21; 22:10; 23:13, 13, 25; 28:7, 8, 20; 29:10; 2Ch 5:9; 7:8, 16; 8:8, 16, 16; 9:6, 26, 26; 10:19; 12:4; 14:9, 13; 15:13, 13, 19; 16:12, 14; 17:12; 18:10, 15, 26, 34; 19:4; 20:26; 21:10, 15; 23:10; 24:10; 25:13, 23; 26:8, 8, 15, 15, 16, 21; 28:9; 29:28, 30, 34, 34; 30:5, 10; 31:1, 10; 32:24; 34:6, 30; 35:14, 25; 36:16, 16, 20, 21; Ezr 2:63; 3:13; 4:5; 8:29; 9:4, 6, 7, 12, 12, 14; 10:14, 14, 17; Ne 2:6, 7, 16; 3:1, 1, 8, 13, 15, 16, 16, 16, 20, 21, 24, 24, 26, 27, 31, 31; 4:6, 11, 21; 5:14; 6:1; 7:3, 3, 65; 8:2, 3, 17, 18; 9:5, 32; 11:30; 12:23, 37, 38, 39; 13:1, 19; Est 1:1, 5, 20; 2:13; 3:13; 4:2; 5:3, 6; 7:2; 8:9; Job 1:18; 2:7, 7; 4:5; 5:9; 6:20; 7:4, 19; 8:2, 21; 9:10, 10; 11:7; 14:6, 12, 13, 14; 18:2; 19:2; 20:5; 22:23; 23:3; 25:5; 26:10; 27:5; 31:12; 32:11, 11, 12; 34:36; 38:11, 16, 18; Ps 4:2; 6:3; 13:1, 1, 2, 2; 18:37, 50; 28:9; 36:5; 38:6, 8; 40:12; 41:13; 42:4; 46:9; 48:8; 49:19, 19; 50:1; 57:1, 10, 10; 60:9; 62:3; 65:2; 69:1; 71:17, 18, 18, 19; 72:7, 8, 8; 73:17; 74:9, 10; 79:5; 80:4, 11; 82:2; 83:17; 89:4, 46; 90:2, 3, 13; 92:7; 94:3, 3, 13, 15; 100:5; 103:17; 104:23; 105:19; 106:31, 48; 107:18; 108:4, 10; 110:1; 112:8; 113:2, 3; 115:18; 118:27; 119:8, 43, 51, 107; 121:8; 123:2; 125:2; 131:3; 132:5, 12, 14; 133:3; 135:8; 137:7; 141:10; 147:6, 15; Pr 1:22; 4:18; 6:9, 26; 7:18, 23; 8:26; 12:19; 28:17; Ecc 2:3; 3:11; 12:1, 2, 6; SS 1:12; 2:7, 17; 3:4, 4, 5; 4:6; 8:4; Isa 1:6; 5:8; 6:11, 11; 8:8; 9:7, 13; 10:18; 13:20; 15:4, 5, 8; 16:8; 19:22; 22:14, 24; 25:12; 26:4, 5, 5, 20; 27:12; 30:8, 17, 28; 32:14, 15, 17; 33:23; 34:17; 36:17; 37:3; 38:12, 13, 13; 39:6; 42:4; 45:17, 24; 46:4, 4; 48:20; 49:6; 57:9, 9; 59:21; 62:1, 7, 7; 64:9, 12; 65:18; Jer 1:3, 3; 3:25; 4:10, 14, 18, 21; 6:13, 13; 7:7, 25; 8:10, 10; 9:10, 16; 11:7; 12:4, 12; 17:4; 23:20, 20, 26; 24:10; 25:3, 5, 31, 33; 27:7, 8, 22; 30:24, 24; 31:22, 34, 40, 40; 32:5, 20, 31; 33:12; 35:6, 14; 36:2, 23; 37:21; 38:28; 42:1, 8; 43:7; 44:10, 12, 27; 47:5, 6; 48:32, 34, 34, 34, 47; 49:33, 37; 50:3, 39; 51:9, 62, 64; 52:3, 5, 11, 34; La 3:40, 50; 5:22; Eze 2:3; 4:8, 10, 11, 14; 10:5; 20:29, 31; 21:27; 24:13; 27:36; 28:15, 19; 29:10; 33:22; 34:21; 37:25; 39:15; 41:16, 17, 20; 43:14, 14; 46:2, 17; 47:10, 19, 20; 48:2, 3, 4, 5, 6, 7, 8, 8, 21, 23, 24, 25, 26, 27; Da 1:21; 8:6, 8, 10, 11, 13, 14; 9:25, 26, 27; 10:3; 11:10, 24, 25, 35, 36, 45; 12:1, 4, 6, 9; Hos 5:15; 7:4; 8:5; 10:12; 14:1; Joel 2:12, 12; Am 4:6, 8, 9, 10, 11; 6:14; 8:12, 12; Ob 1:7, 20; Jnh 2:5; 3:5; 4:2, 5, 9; Mic 1:7, 9, 9, 9, 15; 4:3, 7, 8, 10; 5:3, 4; 6:5; 7:9, 12, 12; Na 1:10; Hab 1:2; 2:6; 3:13; Zep 2:9; Hag 2:19; Zec 1:12; 9:10, 10; 14:10, 10, 10; Mal 1:4, 11; 3:10

6584 ²עַל *'al²*, pp. & c. [5771]

Ge 1:2, 2, 7, 11, 15, 17, 20, 20, 26, 28, 29, 30; 2:5, 16, 21, 24; 3:14; 4:14; 6:1, 7, 12, 17; 7:3, 4, 4, 6, 8, 10, 12, 14, 17, 17, 18, 18, 19, 21, 21, 23, 24; 8:1, 3, 4, 7, 8, 9, 11, 13, 17, 17, 19; 9:2, 2, 14, 16, 17, 23; 10:9; 11:4, 8, 9, 9, 28; 12:17, 20; 13:9, 11; 14:6, 15; 15:11, 12, 12; 16:5, 7, 7, 12, 14; 17:3, 17, 22; 18:2, 3, 5, 5, 8, 16, 19, 19; 19:4, 8, 16, 17, 22, 23, 24, 24, 28, 28, 31; 20:3, 6, 9, 9, 11, 18; 21:11, 12, 12, 14, 25, 31; 22:2, 6, 9, 17; 23:3, 19; 24:9, 13, 15, 18, 22, 30, 30, 30, 42, 43, 45, 46, 47, 47, 49, 49, 61, 64; 25:6, 9, 18, 18, 30; 26:7, 9, 10, 21, 22, 32, 33; 27:12, 13, 16, 16, 39, 40, 40, 41; 28:6, 9, 13, 13, 18; 29:2, 2, 3, 3, 8, 10, 34, 35; 30:3, 6, 28, 33, 37, 40; 31:10, 12, 17, 20, 34, 46, 48, 50; 32:11, 21, 31, 32, 32; 33:1, 1, 1, 4, 10, 13, 17; 34:3, 12, 25, 27, 30; 35:5, 13, 14, 14, 20; 37:8, 8, 8, 23, 34; 38:12, 14, 14, 19, 21, 26, 28, 29, 30; 39:4, 5; 40:2, 2, 2, 11, 13, 16, 17, 19, 19, 19, 21, 21; 41:1, 3, 10, 13, 15, 17, 32, 33, 34, 40, 40, 41, 42, 42, 43, 45, 56; 42:6, 21, 21, 24, 26, 36, 37; 43:7, 16, 18, 18, 18, 19; 44:1, 4, 13, 21; 45:1, 1, 14, 14, 15, 20, 21; 46:4, 29, 29; 47:6, 20, 22, 26, 31; 48:2, 6, 7, 14, 14, 17, 17, 17, 18, 22; 49:13, 17, 17, 22, 22, 25, 26, 30; 50:1, 1, 11, 13, 20, 21, 23; Ex 1:8, 10, 11, 16; 2:3, 5, 5, 6, 14, 15; 3:5, 5, 12, 18, 22, 22; 4:20; 5:3, 8, 8, 9, 14, 17, 21; 6:26; 7:5, 15, 17, 19, 19, 19, 19, 19; 8:3, 5, 5, 5, 5, 6, 7, 9, 12, 21, 22; 9:9, 9, 9, 19, 22, 22, 22, 23, 23; 10:6, 12, 13, 14, 17, 21, 21, 22, 28; 11:1, 1, 5; 12:4, 7, 7, 7, 8, 9, 9, 13, 13, 23, 23, 27, 29, 33, 34, 51; 13:9, 15, 16; 14:2, 3, 7, 9, 9, 16, 21, 26, 26, 26, 26, 27, 30; 15:16, 19, 23, 24, 26, 27; 16:2, 2, 3, 5, 7, 7, 8, 8, 8, 14, 20, 29; 17:1, 3, 6, 7, 7, 9, 12, 16; 18:8, 9, 11, 13, 14, 21, 22, 23, 25; 19:4, 11, 16, 18, 20; 20:3, 5, 5, 5, 11, 12, 20, 24, 25, 26, 26; 21:14, 19, 22, 30, 30; 22:3, 9, 9, 9, 9, 9, 9, 25; 23:2, 13, 18, 29; 24:6, 8, 8, 16; 25:11, 12, 12, 12, 14, 19, 20, 21, 22, 22, 26, 30, 37; 26:4, 7, 10, 10, 12, 13, 24, 32, 32, 34, 35, 35; 27:2, 4, 4, 7, 21; 28:8, 9, 10, 10, 11, 12, 12, 14, 21, 21, 21, 22, 23, 23, 24, 25, 25, 26, 26, 27, 28, 28, 29, 30, 30, 33, 33, 34, 35, 36, 37, 37, 38, 38, 43, 43; 29:3, 6, 6, 7, 10, 12, 13, 13, 15, 16, 17, 17, 19, 20, 20, 20, 20, 21, 21, 21, 21, 22, 24, 24, 25, 36, 36, 36, 37, 38; 30:4, 4, 6, 7, 9, 9, 10, 10, 13, 14, 15, 15, 16, 32, 33; 31:7; 32:1, 12, 12, 14, 16, 20, 21, 27, 29, 34, 35; 33:4, 5, 16, 19, 21, 22; 34:1, 1, 2, 6, 7, 7, 7, 7, 12, 25, 27, 28, 33, 35; 35:22; 36:11, 14, 17, 17; 37:3, 3, 3, 5, 9, 13, 16, 27, 27; 38:2, 7, 21, 26; 39:4, 5, 6, 7, 14, 14, 14, 15, 16, 17, 17, 18, 18, 19, 19, 20, 21, 21, 24, 25, 26, 30, 31, 31; 40:3, 19, 19, 20, 20, 21, 22, 23, 24, 27, 29, 35, 36, 38; Lev 1:4, 4, 5, 7, 7, 8, 8, 11, 11, 12, 12, 12, 15, 17, 17; 2:1, 1, 2, 5, 6, 13, 13, 15, 15, 16; 3:2, 2, 3, 4, 4, 4, 4, 5, 5, 8, 8, 9, 10, 10, 10, 10, 13, 13, 14, 15, 15, 15, 15; 4:3, 4, 7, 8, 8, 9, 9, 9, 9, 10, 11, 11, 12, 12, 14, 15, 18, 20, 24, 25, 26, 28, 29, 30, 31, 31, 33, 34, 35, 35, 35; 5:5, 6, 6, 9, 10, 11, 11, 12, 13, 13, 16, 16, 18, 18; 6:3, 3, 5, 5, 7, 7, 9, 9, 10, 10, 12, 12, 12, 12, 13, 15, 21, 27, 27, 27; 7:2, 4, 4, 4, 9, 12, 12, 13, 13, 20, 30; 8:7, 7, 8, 9, 9, 11, 12, 14, 15, 15, 16, 18, 19, 22, 23, 23, 23, 24, 24, 24, 25, 26, 26, 27, 27, 28, 28, 30, 30, 30, 30, 30, 34; 9:9, 12, 13, 14, 17, 18, 20, 24, 24; 10:1, 3, 6, 7, 15, 16, 16, 17; 11:2, 20, 21, 21, 27, 27, 29, 32, 34, 35, 37, 38, 38, 41, 42, 42, 42, 44, 46; 12:5, 7, 8; 13:45; 14:5, 6, 7, 7, 14, 14, 14, 15, 16, 17, 17, 17, 17, 18, 18, 18, 19, 20, 21, 25, 25, 25, 26, 27, 28, 28, 28, 28, 28, 29, 29, 29, 31, 31, 50, 53; 15:4, 4, 6, 6, 9, 15, 17, 20, 20, 22, 23, 23, 23, 24, 24, 25, 26, 26, 30; 16:2, 2, 4, 8, 9, 10, 10, 12, 13, 13, 14, 15, 16, 18, 18, 19, 21, 21, 21, 22, 30, 33, 33, 34; 17:5, 6, 11, 11, 12; 18:18, 25; 19:16, 17, 19, 22, 22, 26; 21:10, 11, 12; 22:3, 9, 14, 22; 23:18, 20, 20, 28; 24:4, 6, 7, 12, 14; 25:18, 19, 31; 26:1, 16, 18, 21, 24, 25, 28, 30, 32, 35; 27:8, 13, 15, 18, 19, 27, 31; Nu 1:18, 50, 50, 50, 52, 52, 53; 2:2, 5, 12, 17, 20, 27, 34; 3:4, 16, 26, 26, 29, 35, 39, 46, 49, 51; 4:6, 7, 7, 7, 8, 10, 11, 12, 13, 14, 14, 14, 19, 25, 26, 26, 27, 27, 37, 41, 45, 49, 49, 49; 5:7, 8, 14, 14, 15, 15, 15, 18, 30; 6:5, 6, 7, 9, 11, 11, 17, 18, 19, 20, 20, 21, 21, 27; 7:2, 3, 9, 89, 89; 8:7, 7, 10, 12, 12, 19, 21, 22; 9:11, 15, 17, 18, 18, 18, 19, 20, 20, 20, 22, 22, 23, 23, 23; 10:9, 10, 10, 11, 13, 14, 15, 16, 18, 19, 20, 22, 23, 24, 25, 26, 27, 29, 31, 34; 11:9, 9, 11, 12, 13, 17, 17, 25, 25, 25, 26, 29, 31, 31; 12:1, 3, 10, 11; 13:3, 18, 24, 29, 29; 14:2, 2, 5, 9, 14, 18, 18, 18, 27, 27, 29, 35, 36, 36, 43; 15:5, 9, 25, 25, 28, 28, 38, 38; 16:3, 3, 3, 4, 7, 11, 11, 13, 17, 18, 18, 19, 22, 22, 26, 27, 29, 33, 41, 41, 42, 42, 45, 46, 46, 47, 49; 17:2, 3, 5, 5, 10; 18:2, 4, 5, 17, 24, 32; 19:2, 5, 13, 15, 16, 17, 18, 18, 18, 18, 19, 20; 20:2, 2, 6, 21, 23, 24; 21:7, 8, 9, 11, 14, 20, 27; 22:5, 22, 30, 32, 36; 23:3, 6, 15, 17, 28; 24:2, 6, 6; 25:8, 11, 13, 18, 18, 18; 26:3, 9, 9, 9, 56, 63; 27:3, 16, 18, 20, 21, 21, 23; 28:10, 15, 22, 24, 30; 29:5; 30:2, 4, 4, 5, 6, 6, 7, 8, 8, 9, 9, 10, 11, 14; 31:3, 7, 8, 12, 14, 16, 50; 32:14; 33:2, 7, 7, 10, 38, 48, 49, 50, 55; 34:3,

11; 35:1, 6, 20, 22, 23, 24; 36:3, 4, 5, 12, 13; Dt 1:11, 15; 2:25, 36; 3:12, 14; 4:2, 10, 13, 21, 26, 26, 32, 36, 39, 40, 48; 5:7, 9, 9, 9, 15, 16, 22; 6:6, 8, 9, 15; 7:6, 13, 16, 22, 25; 8:3, 3, 4, 10; 9:10, 15, 17, 18, 19; 10:2, 2, 4, 9; 11:4, 9, 17, 18, 18, 20, 21, 21, 25, 29, 29; 12:1, 2, 2, 16, 19, 24, 27, 27, 32; 13:5, 8, 8, 10; 14:2; 15:9, 11, 15, 23; 16:3, 3; 17:6, 6, 10, 11, 11, 14, 15, 15, 15, 18, 18, 20; 18:8; 19:7, 9, 10, 11, 13, 15, 15; 20:1, 3, 10, 12, 19, 19, 20; 21:5, 6, 10, 13, 16, 22, 23; 22:5, 6, 6, 6, 6, 12, 14, 19, 24, 24, 26; 23:4, 4, 9, 13, 20, 25; 24:5, 15, 15, 16, 16, 18, 22; 25:3, 5, 6, 9, 15; 26:6, 19; 27:3, 5, 6, 8, 12, 13; 28:1, 2, 7, 10, 11, 15, 21, 23, 24, 35, 35, 36, 43, 45, 48, 49, 56, 61, 63, 63, 63; 29:5, 5, 24, 25, 27, 28; 30:1, 7, 7, 9, 9, 18, 20; 31:13, 15, 17, 18, 24; 32:2, 2, 11, 11, 13, 23, 36, 38, 47, 49, 51, 51; 33:8, 10, 12, 12, 29; 34:1, 5, 9; Jos 2:6, 7, 8, 8, 9, 11; 3:15, 16; 4:5, 18; 5:1, 9, 15, 15; 7:6, 6, 9, 10, 26, 26; 8:29, 29, 31, 31, 32; 9:5, 18, 20, 20; 10:5, 5, 11, 13, 18, 24, 24, 26, 26, 27, 27, 31, 34, 34, 36, 38; 11:4, 7, 7, 13; 12:2; 13:3, 9, 16, 16, 25; 14:6, 6, 14; 15:8, 18, 46; 17:7; 18:5, 5, 9, 13, 14, 16; 19:11, 12, 50; 22:9, 10, 12, 20, 23, 23, 33; 23:13, 14, 15, 15, 15, 16; 24:7; Jdg 1:14; 3:10, 10, 12, 12, 16, 19, 19, 20, 21; 4:9, 15, 24; 5:10, 10, 17, 18, 19; 6:2, 3, 4, 7, 22, 25, 26, 28, 28, 30, 31, 37, 37, 39, 40; 7:1, 2, 5, 6, 12, 22; 8:3, 26; 9:3, 5, 8, 8, 9, 10, 11, 12, 13, 14, 15, 17, 18, 18, 18, 22, 24, 24, 25, 25, 31, 33, 34, 43, 44, 48, 49, 49, 51, 53; 10:4; 11:11, 26, 29, 37, 37, 38, 38; 12:1, 14; 13:5, 19, 20, 20; 14:6, 16, 17, 19; 15:8, 10, 14, 14, 14, 19; 16:3, 3, 9, 12, 12, 14, 17, 19, 19, 20, 20, 26, 26, 27, 29, 29, 30, 30; 18:5, 9, 12, 19, 27, 27; 19:2, 3, 20, 22, 27, 28, 30; 20:5, 5, 9, 19, 34, 41; Ru 1:19; 2:5, 6, 10, 13; 3:3, 9, 15, 15; 4:5, 7, 7, 10; 1Sa 1:9, 9, 10, 11, 13, 14; 2:1, 8, 10, 11, 28; 4:1, 12, 13, 13, 18, 19, 20; 5:4, 5, 5, 7, 7; 6:5, 5, 5, 7, 12, 18, 20; 7:10; 8:7, 9, 11, 19; 9:6, 16, 24, 25; 10:1, 1, 6, 10, 12, 19; 11:1, 2, 6, 7, 12; 12:1, 12, 12, 13, 14, 19; 13:1, 5, 8, 11, 14, 18; 14:4, 10, 13, 13, 25, 32, 33, 47, 52; 15:1, 1, 3, 7, 9, 9, 9, 9, 15, 17, 26, 28, 35; 16:1, 16, 23; 17:5, 6, 15, 20, 22, 22, 26, 28, 32, 35, 38, 39, 39, 46, 49; 18:4, 5; 19:20, 20, 23, 24; 20:8, 9, 13, 15, 25, 29, 31, 33; 21:13, 15; 22:2, 6, 7, 8, 8, 8, 9, 13, 17; 23:9, 17, 21, 27, 28; 24:2, 3, 5, 10, 22; 25:8, 13, 16, 17, 18, 20, 23, 23, 24, 25, 30, 30, 36, 42; 26:1, 3, 3, 12, 13, 16, 16; 27:10, 10, 11; 28:15, 16, 18; 29:4; 30:6, 6, 14, 14, 16, 17, 23, 24; 31:4, 5; 2Sa 1:2, 6, 9, 10, 10, 10, 12, 12, 12, 12, 16, 17, 17, 18, 19, 21, 24, 25, 26; 2:4, 7, 9, 9, 9, 10, 11, 13, 13, 13, 19, 19, 21, 21, 24, 25; 3:8, 8, 10, 10, 17, 29, 30, 34; 4:2, 7, 11, 12; 5:2, 2, 3, 5, 5, 8, 12, 17, 20; 6:2, 7, 8, 10, 21, 21; 7:8, 8, 11, 22, 25, 25, 26, 27; 8:10, 15, 16; 9:6, 7, 10, 11, 13; 10:14; 11:1, 2, 2, 2, 11, 20, 21, 21, 23, 23, 24, 26; 12:6, 7, 11, 17, 28, 28, 30, 30; 13:5, 9, 9, 17, 18, 19, 19, 22, 25, 29, 32, 37, 39; 14:1, 2, 4, 7, 7, 8, 9, 9, 13, 26, 33; 15:2, 4, 14, 18, 18, 20, 23, 32, 33; 16:1, 8, 22; 17:2, 11, 11, 12, 12, 19, 19, 21, 25; 18:1, 5, 8, 9, 11, 12, 17, 18, 20, 31, 32, 33; 19:1, 2, 7, 7, 9, 10, 22, 26, 38, 42, 42; 20:8, 8, 11, 12, 12, 15, 21, 22, 23, 23, 24; 21:1, 7, 7, 10, 10; 22:11, 11, 28, 34, 50; 23:2, 8, 18; 24:4, 12, 20, 21, 25; 1Ki 1:13, 17, 20, 20, 23, 24, 27, 30, 33, 34, 35, 35, 35, 38, 38, 44, 46, 47, 48, 53; 2:4, 4, 11, 12, 15, 18, 19, 19, 24, 26, 27, 31, 31, 32, 35, 43; 3:4, 6, 19, 26; 4:1, 4, 5, 6, 6, 7, 7, 20, 29, 33, 33, 33, 33, 33; 5:5, 7, 14, 16; 6:1, 3, 3, 3, 5, 8, 10, 32, 32, 32, 35; 7:2, 2, 3, 3, 6, 6, 16, 17, 18, 18, 19, 20, 20, 22, 25, 25, 29, 29, 31, 35, 36, 36, 38, 39, 39, 41, 41, 42, 43, 48; 8:5, 7, 7, 8, 16, 20, 23, 25, 27, 36, 40, 43, 44, 54, 66; 9:5, 5, 5, 7, 7, 8, 8, 9, 9, 9, 23, 25, 26; 10:6, 6, 9, 16, 17, 20; 11:7, 10, 11, 11, 24, 25, 30, 37, 41, 42; 12:4, 9, 10, 11, 11, 14, 17, 18, 20, 32, 33, 33; 13:1, 2, 2, 2, 3, 4, 4, 4, 13, 30, 32, 32, 34; 14:2, 2, 7, 14, 15, 19, 23, 25, 27, 29; 15:1, 7, 17, 19, 20, 20, 23, 25, 25, 27, 27, 30, 31, 33; 16:1, 2, 5, 7, 7, 8, 9, 9, 11, 14, 15, 16, 17, 18, 19, 20, 23, 24, 27, 29, 29; 17:3, 5, 14, 19, 20, 21, 21, 22; 18:1, 3, 7, 12, 21, 23, 23, 26, 28, 33, 33, 33, 39; 19:15, 16; 20:1, 12, 20, 22, 23, 30, 33, 38, 38, 41, 43; 21:4, 4, 7, 27, 29; 22:6, 8, 10, 18, 19, 19, 23, 24, 32, 38, 39, 41, 45, 51, 51; 2Ki 1:9, 13, 18; 2:3, 5, 7, 13, 13, 14, 15; 3:1, 11, 15, 21, 22, 27, 27, 27; 4:4, 9, 20, 21, 29, 31, 32, 34, 34, 34, 34, 34, 35, 37; 5:18, 21, 26; 6:11, 14, 24, 25, 26, 30, 30, 31; 7:2, 6, 6, 17, 17; 8:5, 5, 13, 15, 20, 23; 9:3, 17, 25, 29, 37; 10:3, 3, 5, 5, 9, 10, 22, 24, 30, 31, 33, 34, 36; 11:3, 8, 11, 12, 14, 18, 19; 12:4, 11, 12, 15, 17, 17, 18, 19; 13:1, 8, 10, 12, 13, 14, 16, 16, 19, 21, 23; 14:6, 6, 15, 18, 19, 20, 28; 15:5, 6, 8, 10, 11, 12, 15, 17, 18, 19, 20, 20, 21, 23, 25, 26, 27, 30, 31, 36; 16:4, 5, 7, 12, 12, 13, 14, 15, 15, 17, 17, 17, 19; 17:1, 3, 5, 9, 10, 18, 21, 23, 23; 18:9, 9, 12, 13, 14, 14, 14, 18, 20, 21, 21, 21, 21, 23, 24, 25, 25, 26, 27, 27, 27, 37; 19:2, 8, 21, 22, 22, 32; 20:6, 6, 7, 13, 20; 21:12, 13, 13, 17, 23, 24, 25; 22:5, 7, 8, 9, 13, 13, 13, 13, 16, 19, 19, 20, 20; 23:3, 3, 6, 8, 12, 13, 16, 17, 20, 20, 21, 24, 26, 27, 28, 29, 29, 33, 35; 24:3, 3, 5, 11, 11, 12, 20, 20; 25:1, 1, 1, 4, 4, 5, 11, 17, 17, 17, 19, 20, 21, 22, 28; 1Ch 5:10, 16, 20; 6:31, 32, 39, 44, 49, 49, 49; 7:4, 29; 9:1, 19, 19, 20, 23, 26, 26, 27, 27, 28, 29, 29, 31, 32, 33; 10:3, 4, 5, 13; 11:2, 3, 7, 10, 11, 15, 20, 25, 42; 12:4, 8, 15, 17, 19, 19, 20, 21, 22, 23, 32, 38; 13:2, 2, 7, 10, 10; 14:2, 8, 10, 11, 14, 17; 15:15, 20, 21, 27; 16:21, 25, 40, 40; 17:7, 10, 17, 23, 23, 25, 26; 18:7, 10, 14, 15, 17; 19:2, 5; 20:2, 2; 21:1, 3, 4, 7, 10, 15, 16, 16, 22, 26; 22:8, 9, 10, 11, 12, 13, 14; 23:1, 4, 14, 28, 28, 28, 31; 25:2, 2, 3, 3, 6, 6; 26:20, 22, 24, 26, 28, 29, 30, 32; 27:2, 2, 4, 4, 5, 6, 7, 8, 9, 10, 11, 12, 13, 14, 15, 16, 24, 25, 25, 26, 27, 27, 28, 28, 29, 29, 30, 30, 31; 28:2, 4, 4, 5, 5, 18, 19; 29:8, 9, 15, 23, 25, 25, 25, 26, 27, 29, 29, 29, 30, 30, 30; 2Ch 1:1, 6, 6, 9, 11, 13; 2:2, 4, 11, 16; 3:4, 4, 5, 7, 8, 13, 14, 15, 16, 17; 4:4, 4, 12, 12, 13, 14, 19; 5:6, 8, 8, 8, 9; 6:5, 6, 10, 13, 13, 16, 18, 27, 31, 33, 34; 7:3, 3, 6, 10, 11, 13, 14, 20, 20, 21, 22, 22, 22; 8:3, 12, 14, 14, 15, 17; 9:5, 5, 6, 8, 8, 15, 16, 18, 19, 29, 29, 29, 30; 10:4, 9, 10, 11, 11, 14, 17, 18; 11:13; 12:2, 9, 10; 13:1, 4, 5, 6, 7, 7, 11, 12, 18; 14:11, 11, 14; 15:1, 4, 5, 9, 15; 16:1, 3, 7, 7, 7, 8, 9, 10, 11; 17:1, 10, 15, 16, 18; 18:7, 9, 16, 17, 18, 18, 22, 23, 31; 19:2, 7, 9, 10, 10, 10, 11; 20:1, 2, 3, 9, 10, 11, 12, 12, 14, 16, 22, 23, 24, 26, 29, 31, 34, 37; 21:4, 8, 15, 16, 16; 22:5, 12; 23:3, 10, 11, 13, 13, 18, 18, 19, 20; 24:6, 9, 13, 18, 20, 21, 23, 25, 25, 26, 27, 27; 25:3, 4, 4, 26, 27, 28; 26:7, 7, 9, 9, 9, 11, 13, 13, 15, 15, 16, 18, 19, 21; 27:5, 7; 28:4, 9, 11, 12, 13, 13, 13, 13, 16, 20, 26; 29:8, 9, 21, 21, 21, 21, 23, 24, 27, 36; 30:1, 1, 9, 10, 16, 17, 18, 22; 31:2, 9, 9, 12, 14, 15; 32:1, 2, 5, 6, 6, 8, 9, 9, 9, 10, 12, 16, 16, 17, 18, 18, 19, 20, 25, 25, 25, 26, 31, 32; 33:8, 11, 16, 18, 19, 24, 25; 34:4, 4, 5, 10, 12, 13, 17, 17, 21, 21, 21, 24, 24, 24, 27, 27, 28, 28, 31, 31; 35:2, 10, 10, 15, 15, 16, 20, 21, 24, 24, 25, 25, 25, 25, 27; 36:4, 6, 8, 8, 10, 15, 15, 15, 17, 17, 23; Ezr 1:2, 6, 8; 2:61, 68; 3:2, 3, 3, 3, 7, 8, 9, 10, 11, 11; 4:5, 6, 7; 6:22; 7:6, 9, 11, 28, 28; 8:17, 18, 21, 22, 22, 23, 26, 31, 31, 33, 35; 9:4, 5, 9, 13, 15; 10:2, 4, 6, 9, 10, 12, 15, 19; Ne 1:2, 2, 6, 6; 2:4, 5, 7, 7, 8, 18, 19, 19; 3:2, 2, 4, 4, 4, 5, 7, 8, 8, 9, 10, 10, 12, 17, 19, 28; 4:1, 5, 9, 12, 14, 18, 19; 5:7, 7, 15, 15, 16, 17, 18, 19; 6:3, 6, 7, 12, 17; 7:2, 63; 8:4, 4, 5, 7, 16; 9:1, 2, 3, 4, 5, 6, 9, 10, 13, 19, 30, 33, 33, 36, 37, 37, 38; 10:1, 29, 32, 32, 33, 34, 34; 11:9, 9, 14, 16, 21, 23, 23; 12:8, 22, 23, 31, 31, 37, 37, 37, 38, 38, 39, 39, 39, 44, 44, 44; 13:2, 11, 13, 13, 13, 14, 15, 18, 18, 18, 19, 22, 26, 26, 28, 29; Est 1:2, 6, 6, 8, 15, 16, 16, 16, 17, 19; 2:1, 10, 20, 23; 3:1, 9, 9, 10, 12; 4:4, 5, 5, 7, 8, 8, 16, 17; 5:1, 4, 8, 9, 11, 14; 6:2, 3, 4, 8, 9, 9; 7:3, 7, 8, 8, 9, 9, 10; 8:2, 3, 5, 7, 7, 8, 11, 17; 9:2, 3, 13, 13, 16, 19, 21, 24, 25, 25, 25, 26, 26, 26, 26, 26, 27, 27, 27, 27, 31, 31, 31; 10:1, 2; Job 1:6, 8, 11, 14, 17, 19; 2:1, 1, 11, 12; 3:4, 5; 4:13, 15; 5:10, 10; 6:3, 5, 5, 16, 27, 27, 28; 7:1, 12, 20; 8:6, 9, 15, 16, 17; 9:8, 11, 22, 26, 33, 34; 10:1, 2, 3, 7; 12:14, 21; 13:11, 13, 14, 21, 26, 27; 14:3, 6, 16, 17, 22, 22; 15:27; 16:4, 4, 9, 10, 10, 11, 13, 14, 14, 15, 16, 17; 17:4, 8, 8, 16; 18:6, 8, 9, 10, 15, 17, 20; 19:5, 5, 6, 8, 9, 11, 12, 13, 25; 20:4, 11, 13, 21, 23, 25; 21:5, 9, 17, 26, 26, 27, 31, 32; 22:2, 10, 24, 26, 28; 23:2, 15; 24:18, 23; 25:3; 26:7, 7, 9, 10; 27:9, 10, 22, 23, 23; 28:8; 29:3, 4, 7, 13, 22; 30:1, 2, 4, 5, 12, 12, 15, 16, 17, 30; 31:1, 5, 9, 9, 10, 21, 36, 38; 32:2, 3, 6; 33:7, 10, 15, 15, 19, 23, 27; 34:6, 13, 15, 21, 23, 27, 28, 29, 29, 36, 37; 36:21, 23, 28, 30, 32, 32, 33, 33; 37:3, 12, 15, 16, 22; 38:5, 6, 10, 24, 26, 32; 39:9, 14, 23, 27, 28; 41:6, 8, 23, 30, 33, 34; 42:6, 6, 8, 11, 11; Ps 1:3, 5; 2:2, 2, 6; 3:1, 6, 8; 4:4, 6; 5:11; 6:T; 7:T, 7, 16; 8:T, 1; 9:T, 19; 10:3, 13, 14; 11:2, 6; 12:T; 13:2, 6; 14:2; 15:3, 3, 5; 16:2, 4, 6; 17:9; 18:10, 10, 33, 41, 42, 49; 19:6; 21:5, 11, 12; 22:T, 9, 10, 13, 18; 23:2; 24:2, 2; 25:8; 27:2, 3, 3, 6; 29:3, 3; 31:13, 14, 16, 18, 23; 32:4, 5, 6, 8; 33:22; 35:13, 15, 16, 20, 21, 26; 36:4, 4; 37:4, 5, 5, 10, 11, 12, 29; 38:2, 16; 39:10, 11; 40:2, 7, 12, 15; 41:3, 7, 7, 9, 11; 42:1, 4, 5, 6, 6, 7, 11; 43:5; 44:19, 22; 45:T, 2, 3, 4, 7, 17; 46:T, 2; 47:2, 8, 8; 48:10, 14; 49:6, 11; 50:4, 5, 8, 16; 51:19; 52:6; 53:T, 2; 54:3; 55:3, 4, 10, 12, 15, 22; 56:T, 5, 7, 12; 57:2, 5, 5, 11, 11; 59:3; 60:T, 8, 8; 61:T, 6; 62:T, 3, 7; 63:6, 10; 64:8; 66:5; 68:29, 34; 69:T, 7, 9, 15, 24, 27; 70:3; 71:6, 14; 72:6, 13; 74:13; 77:T; 78:24, 27; 79:6, 9, 9; 80:15, 17, 17; 81:T, 5, 7, 14; 83:3, 3, 5, 18; 84:T; 86:13, 14; 88:T, 7, 16, 17; 89:7, 19, 45, 47; 90:13, 16, 17, 17; 91:12, 13; 92:3, 3, 3, 11; 94:2, 20, 21, 23; 95:3; 96:4; 97:9, 9; 99:2, 8; 102:7; 103:10, 11, 11, 13, 13, 17; 104:3, 5, 6, 12, 34; 105:14, 16, 38; 106:7, 17, 22, 32; 107:40; 108:4, 5, 5, 9, 9; 109:2, 5, 6, 6, 20; 110:4, 5, 6, 7; 113:4, 4; 115:1, 1, 14, 14, 14; 116:7, 12; 117:2; 119:14, 17, 22, 49, 62, 69, 104, 127, 128, 129, 136, 162, 164; 121:5; 124:2, 4, 5; 125:3, 5; 128:6; 129:3; 131:2, 2; 132:3, 18; 133:2, 2, 2, 3; 135:14; 136:6; 137:1, 2, 4, 6; 138:2, 2, 2, 7; 139:5, 14, 16; 140:10; 141:3; 142:3, 7; 143:4; 145:9; 146:5; 148:4, 13; 149:5; Pr 1:27; 2:11; 3:3, 3, 29; 4:15; 5:8; 6:15, 21, 21, 22, 28; 7:3, 3, 14, 15; 8:2, 27, 34; 9:3, 14; 10:12; 13:11; 14:14, 19; 16:10, 20, 23, 26, 27; 17:4, 4, 26; 19:3, 11, 12; 20:8, 26; 21:1, 9; 22:6, 18; 23:30; 24:13, 18, 25, 30, 30; 25:11, 12, 20, 20, 22, 24, 25; 26:11, 14, 14, 17, 23; 27:22; 28:15, 21, 25; 29:5, 5, 12; 30:6, 19; 31:26, 29; Ecc 1:6, 12, 13, 16, 16; 2:17, 20; 3:14, 17, 18; 5:2, 2, 2, 6, 8, 8, 8; 6:1; 7:10, 14; 8:2, 6, 11, 14, 16; 9:8, 12, 14; 10:4, 7, 7; 11:1, 2, 3, 9; 12:6, 7, 14; SS 1:3, 7, 8; 2:4, 8, 8, 17; 3:1, 8; 4:4; 5:4, 5, 7, 12, 12, 15; 7:4, 5, 10, 13; 8:5, 6, 6, 9, 9, 14; Isa 1:1, 5, 14, 25; 2:1, 12, 12, 13, 13, 14, 14, 15, 15, 16, 16; 4:1, 5, 5, 5; 5:6, 6, 25, 25, 30; 6:1, 6, 7, 7; 7:1, 1, 2, 5, 17, 17, 17, 17; 8:1, 7, 7, 7; 9:2, 6, 7, 7, 11, 17, 17, 20, 20, 21; 10:3, 6, 12, 12, 15, 15, 20, 20, 24, 25, 26, 26, 27, 27, 28; 11:2, 8, 8, 15; 13:2, 7, 11, 11, 13, 17, 18; 14:1, 1, 1, 2, 4, 8, 12, 14, 22, 25, 25, 25, 26, 26; 15:2, 2, 3, 4, 7, 7, 9; 16:5, 9, 9, 9, 11, 12; 17:7, 10; 18:2, 4, 6, 6; 19:1, 7, 7, 8, 12, 16, 17; 20:2, 2, 3, 3; 21:3, 8, 8; 22:4, 4, 15, 15, 22, 24, 25; 23:8, 11, 17; 24:6, 6, 11, 15, 17, 20, 21, 21, 21, 22, 22; 25:3, 7, 7, 8, 8; 26:21, 21; 27:1, 1, 3, 11; 28:1, 4, 6, 22, 27; 29:1, 3, 3, 3, 7, 8, 10, 12; 30:1, 5, 6, 6, 6, 8, 8, 12, 16, 16, 16, 17, 17, 25, 25, 28, 32; 31:1, 1, 1, 2, 2, 4, 4, 4, 4, 5; 32:8, 10, 11, 12, 12, 12, 13, 13, 15, 20; 34:2, 2, 5, 5, 11, 14, 16; 35:10; 36:1, 3, 5, 6, 6, 6, 6, 8, 9, 10, 11, 12, 12, 22; 37:2, 8, 9, 22, 23, 33, 35; 38:5, 6, 15, 16, 20, 21; 39:2; 40:2, 9, 22; 41:18; 42:1, 5, 13, 25, 25; 44:3, 3, 3, 3, 4, 16, 19; 45:11, 11, 12, 14; 46:7, 8; 47:1, 6, 6, 7, 9, 11, 11, 11, 13; 48:2; 49:9, 10, 16, 22; 50:7, 7; 51:11; 52:7, 14, 15; 53:1, 5, 9; 54:9, 9, 15, 17; 56:3, 6, 7, 8; 57:1, 2, 4, 4, 6, 7, 10, 11; 58:14, 14; 59:4, 9, 18, 18, 21; 60:1, 2, 2, 4, 5, 7, 14; 61:1; 62:5, 5, 6, 10; 63:3, 7, 19; 64:12; 65:3, 3, 6, 7, 7, 17; 66:2, 10, 12, 12, 20; Jer 1:7, 9, 10, 10, 12, 14, 15, 15, 16, 18; 2:5, 12, 15, 20, 34, 35, 37; 3:2, 2, 6, 8, 16, 18, 18, 21; 4:8, 16, 16, 17, 20, 28, 28; 5:6, 6, 9, 12, 15, 27, 29, 31; 6:1, 3, 4, 6, 7, 9, 10, 11, 11, 12, 14, 16, 17, 19, 23, 23, 26; 7:8, 10, 11, 14, 15, 20, 20, 20, 21, 22, 29, 30, 31; 8:2, 6, 11, 14, 18, 18, 21; 9:4, 9, 10, 10, 12, 13, 18, 22, 25, 26, 26, 26, 26, 26, 26; 10:1, 19, 21, 25, 25; 11:2, 8, 10, 15, 16, 17, 19, 21, 22; 12:8, 8, 9, 11, 11, 12, 14, 14; 13:1, 2, 4, 13, 16, 21, 21, 26, 27; 14:1, 3, 6, 9, 15, 16; 15:1, 3, 4, 5, 6, 8, 8, 14, 15, 16; 16:3, 3, 3, 3, 4, 7, 7, 7, 7, 10, 10, 11, 13, 13, 15, 16, 16, 17, 18; 17:1, 2, 2, 8, 8, 18, 25; 18:3, 7, 7, 8, 8, 9, 9, 10, 11, 11, 11, 16, 18, 20, 21, 22, 23, 23; 19:3, 5, 8, 8, 13, 15, 15; 20:2, 11; 21:2, 2, 4, 7, 9, 9, 13, 14; 22:2, 4, 6, 7, 7, 8, 8, 9, 17, 17, 17, 17, 24, 26, 27, 28, 30; 23:2, 2, 3, 4, 8, 12, 15, 16, 17, 19, 30, 31, 32, 34, 34, 35, 39, 40; 24:6, 6, 10; 25:1, 1, 2, 5, 9, 9, 9, 12, 12, 12, 13, 13, 13, 26, 29, 29, 30, 33; 26:2, 5, 13, 15, 15, 19, 19, 20, 20; 27:2, 5, 8, 10, 11, 19, 19, 19, 21; 28:8, 10, 11, 12, 14, 15, 16; 29:10, 11, 28, 31, 31, 32, 32, 32; 30:6, 8, 14, 15, 15, 18, 18, 20, 23; 31:3, 12, 12, 12, 12, 15, 15, 19, 20, 26, 28, 28, 33, 37, 39; 32:2, 19, 24, 29, 29, 31, 31, 31, 32, 34, 35, 40, 41, 42, 42; 33:4, 4, 5, 9, 9, 13, 14, 17, 21; 34:1, 4, 7, 7, 15, 21, 22; 35:6, 7, 17, 18; 36:2, 2, 2, 4, 11, 12, 18, 21, 23, 23, 28, 28, 29, 29, 30, 30, 31, 31, 31, 31, 31, 32, 32; 37:5, 5, 8, 9, 11, 14, 15, 19, 19; 38:4; 39:1, 9, 11, 12; 40:4, 4, 11; 42:17, 18, 18, 19; 43:10; 44:2, 2, 13, 13, 20, 20, 20, 21, 23, 27, 29, 29; 45:1, 2, 3, 5, 5; 46:1, 2, 2, 6, 21, 25, 25, 25, 25, 25, 25; 47:4; 48:2, 11, 21, 22, 22, 22, 23, 23, 23, 24, 24, 24, 26, 31, 31, 32, 32, 36, 37, 37, 38, 42, 43; 49:5, 8, 11, 14, 17, 17, 19, 20, 22, 29, 30, 30, 37; 50:3, 9, 13, 13, 14, 15, 21, 21, 27, 29, 35, 42, 42, 44, 45; 51:1, 2, 7, 8, 11, 13, 14, 25, 27, 27, 27, 28, 29, 35, 42, 44, 46, 47, 48, 50, 51, 52, 56, 56, 63, 64; 52:3, 3, 4, 4, 4, 7, 7, 8, 22, 22, 23, 25, 27; La 1:2, 5, 7, 8, 10, 14, 15, 16, 22; 2:10, 11, 14, 15, 15, 16, 17, 19; 3:5, 20, 21, 24, 28, 39, 46, 48, 54, 61, 62; 4:5, 8, 19, 21, 22; 5:5, 17, 17, 18, 22; Eze 1:1, 3, 3, 8, 17, 19, 20, 21, 22, 22, 25, 25, 26, 26, 26, 28; 2:1, 2; 3:14, 22, 23, 23, 24, 25; 4:1, 2, 2, 2, 2, 2, 3, 4, 4, 4, 6, 7, 8, 9, 15; 5:1, 1, 8, 16, 17, 17; 6:3, 9, 14; 7:2, 3, 3, 4, 4, 8, 8, 9, 20, 26; 8:1, 6, 10; 9:3, 3, 4, 4, 6, 6, 8, 8; 10:1, 1, 2, 4, 4, 16, 18, 18, 19, 22; 11:4, 5, 8, 10, 13, 15, 22, 23, 23, 24; 12:6, 7, 13, 22; 13:3, 5, 17, 18, 18, 20; 14:3, 5, 6, 6, 9, 13, 17, 19, 22, 22, 22; 15:3; 16:5, 5, 6, 8, 8, 9, 11, 11, 12, 12, 14, 15, 15, 16, 27, 36, 36, 37, 37, 37, 40, 43, 44, 46; 17:5, 7, 10, 20, 22; 18:2, 15, 20, 20, 26, 31; 19:8, 8, 10, 11; 20:8, 13, 17, 21, 32, 33; 21:7, 15, 22, 31, 31; 22:3, 4, 13, 20, 21, 22, 31; 23:5, 7, 8, 9, 14, 16, 18, 18, 20, 22, 22, 24, 24, 30, 41, 41, 42, 46, 47, 49; 24:6, 7, 7, 7, 8, 11, 17, 17, 22, 23; 25:2, 7, 10, 13, 16; 26:2, 3, 3, 8, 8, 8, 16, 16, 16, 17, 19; 27:2, 3, 5, 11, 11, 30, 30, 32, 35, 36; 28:7, 7, 12, 17, 17, 18, 19, 21, 22, 23, 25, 26; 29:2, 2, 2, 3, 5, 7, 8, 14, 15, 18, 18; 30:11, 15; 31:5, 13, 15, 15, 15; 32:2, 3, 4, 4, 5, 8, 8, 9, 10, 10, 10, 13, 16, 16, 18, 27, 31; 33:2, 3, 10, 13, 19, 24, 25, 26, 27, 29; 34:2, 6, 6, 23, 27; 35:2, 2, 3, 5, 12, 13, 13, 15; 36:2, 3, 5, 5, 6, 10, 11, 12, 17, 18, 18, 18, 21, 25, 29, 31, 31; 37:1, 2, 2, 4, 6, 6, 6, 8, 8, 10, 14, 16, 16, 19, 20, 24, 25, 25, 27; 38:2, 7, 8, 10, 11, 12, 12, 16, 16, 17, 18, 19, 20, 20, 21, 22, 22, 22; 39:1, 2, 4, 5, 14, 17, 17, 20, 23, 26, 28, 29; 40:1, 2, 15, 15, 44; 41:7, 7, 15, 17, 17, 20; 42:6, 8; 43:12, 18, 18, 20, 24, 27; 44:10, 10, 12, 12, 13, 15, 17, 18, 18, 24; 45:9, 15, 17, 19; 46:2, 2, 14, 19; 47:8, 10, 12, 12, 18; 48:2, 3, 4, 5, 6, 7, 8, 15, 21, 21, 24, 25, 26, 27, 28, 28, 31; Da 1:1, 8, 11, 20; 2:1; 8:2, 5, 12, 17, 18, 18, 25, 25, 27; 9:1, 11, 12, 12, 12, 13, 14, 14, 14, 17, 18, 18, 18, 19, 19, 20, 24, 24, 27, 27; 10:4, 7, 8, 9, 10, 11, 16, 16, 21; 11:5, 14, 20, 21, 21, 24, 25, 25, 27, 28, 30, 30, 34, 36, 36, 37, 37, 37, 38, 40; 12:1; Hos 1:4; 2:13, 14; 4:3, 9, 13, 13, 13, 14, 14; 5:1, 10; 6:5; 7:12, 13, 14, 14; 8:1, 1; 9:1, 1, 7, 8, 15; 10:4, 5, 5, 5, 7, 8, 8, 9, 10, 11, 14; 11:3, 4, 8, 11; 12:2, 10, 11, 14; 13:6, 7; 14:3; Joel 1:3, 5, 6, 8, 11, 11; 2:2, 5, 13, 17, 18, 20, 28, 29, 29; 3:2, 4, 4, 6; Am 1:1, 3, 3, 3, 6, 6, 6, 8, 9, 9, 9, 11, 11, 11, 13, 13, 13; 2:1, 1, 1, 4, 4, 4, 6, 6, 6, 7, 8, 12; 3:1, 1, 2, 2, 5, 9, 9, 9, 14, 14, 15; 4:2, 7, 7, 7, 13; 5:1, 2, 8, 9, 9, 11, 19, 23; 6:4, 4, 5, 6, 14; 7:3, 6, 7, 9, 10, 11, 16, 16, 17, 17; 8:8, 10, 10; 9:1, 4, 6, 6, 8, 12, 15, 15; Ob 1:1, 11, 14, 15, 16; Jnh 1:2, 5, 7, 11, 12, 12, 13, 14; 2:3, 7; 3:6, 6, 10; 4:2, 2, 2, 6, 6, 6, 8, 9, 10, 11; Mic 1:1, 3, 8, 14, 16; 2:1, 3, 4, 9; 3:2, 2, 3, 5, 5, 5, 6, 6, 7, 11, 11; 4:1, 7, 11; 5:1, 1, 3, 5, 7, 9; 6:13; 7:3, 13, 16, 18; Na 1:11, 13, 14, 15; 2:1, 7; 3:5, 6, 10, 12, 18, 19, 19; Hab 1:4, 4, 15, 16, 17; 2:1, 1, 1, 2, 6, 6, 14, 15, 16, 16, 18; 3:1, 8, 19; Zep 1:2, 3, 4, 4, 5, 8, 8, 8, 9, 9, 12,

12, 16, 16; 2:2, 2, 5, 7, 8, 10, 11, 13, 15; 3:7, 8, 17, 17, 18; Hag 1:5, 7, 10, 10, 11, 11, 11, 11, 11, 11, 11, 11, 11, 12; Zec 1:2, 8, 15, 16; 2:9, 12; 3:1, 4, 4, 5, 5, 9; 4:2, 2, 2, 3, 3, 11, 11, 12, 14; 5:3, 11; 6:5, 13, 13; 7:14; 9:8, 9, 9, 13, 14, 15, 16; 10:2, 3, 3; 11:5, 6, 13, 17, 17; 12:1, 2, 2, 3, 4, 6, 6, 7, 9, 10, 10, 10, 10, 10, 10; 13:7, 7, 7; 14:4, 4, 9, 12, 12, 13, 16, 17, 18, 20; Mal 1:5, 7; 2:2, 2, 3, 14, 14, 16; 3:13, 13, 17, 17; 4:4, 6, 6

6640 עִם *ʿim*, pp. [1049]

Ge 3:6; 13:1, 14; 18:16, 23, 25; 19:30, 32, 34, 35; 21:10, 10, 22, 23, 23; 22:5; 23:4, 4; 24:12, 14, 25, 27, 54, 58; 25:11; 26:3, 16, 20, 20, 28, 28, 29, 29; 27:44; 28:15; 29:6, 9, 9, 14, 25, 30; 30:8, 15, 16; 31:2, 3, 23, 24, 29, 29, 31, 32, 38, 50; 32:4, 6, 9, 12, 24, 25, 28, 28; 33:1, 15; 35:2, 4, 6; 39:7, 10, 12, 14; 41:32; 42:38; 43:34; 44:29, 32, 33; 46:4; 47:30; 48:1, 12, 21; 50:9; Ex 3:12; 4:12, 15, 15; 8:12, 29, 30; 9:33; 10:6, 10, 18, 24, 26; 11:8; 13:19; 14:6; 17:2, 8; 18:6, 12, 18, 19; 19:9, 24; 20:19, 19, 22; 21:3, 14; 22:12, 14, 14, 15, 16, 19, 25, 30; 23:1, 5; 24:2, 8, 14; 33:9, 12, 16; 34:3, 5, 10, 28; Lev 15:33; 25:6, 35, 35, 36, 39, 40, 40, 41, 41, 45, 45, 47, 47, 47, 50, 50, 53, 54; 26:21, 23, 24, 27, 28, 40, 41; Nu 10:32, 32; 11:16, 17; 13:31; 14:24, 43; 20:3; 22:8, 9, 12, 13, 14, 19, 21, 22, 35, 35, 39; 23:21; Dt 2:7; 4:23; 5:2, 4; 8:5; 9:7, 9, 10, 24; 10:9, 12; 12:23; 14:27, 29; 15:9, 12, 13, 16, 16, 18; 17:19; 18:1, 13, 16, 19; 20:1, 4, 4, 12, 12, 20; 22:2, 4, 22, 22, 23, 25, 25, 28, 29; 23:15, 16, 21; 27:20, 21, 22, 23; 29:12, 15, 15, 17, 18, 25; 31:6, 8, 16, 23, 27, 27; 32:12, 14, 14, 24, 25; 33:21; Jos 1:5, 5, 9, 17, 17; 2:12, 12, 14; 3:7, 7; 4:3, 8; 7:2, 12, 24; 8:1; 9:2, 2; 10:7, 15, 29, 29, 31, 34, 36, 38, 43; 11:4, 5, 7, 21; 13:8; 14:7, 8; 19:46, 47; 20:4; 22:7, 8, 14; 24:27; Jdg 1:22, 24; 2:18; 3:27; 4:6, 8, 8, 9, 9, 10; 5:15, 20; 6:12, 13, 16, 17; 7:4; 8:10, 35, 35; 9:6, 16, 16, 19, 19, 34, 37, 44, 48; 11:3, 4, 5, 8, 11, 20, 25; 12:1; 13:9; 15:3; 16:3, 13, 13, 30; 18:3, 7, 19, 22, 25, 28; 19:3, 10, 10, 11, 19; 20:14, 18, 20, 23, 28, 38; Ru 1:7, 8, 8, 11, 22; 2:4, 6, 8, 12, 19, 19, 21, 22; 4:10; 1Sa 1:17, 24, 26, 27; 2:8, 21, 26, 26, 33; 3:19; 4:4; 5:7; 9:5, 19, 23, 24, 25; 10:2, 6, 7, 9, 11, 26; 12:24; 13:2, 2, 5, 15, 16; 14:2, 7, 17, 21, 21, 21, 45; 15:6, 6, 25, 26, 30; 16:12, 14, 18; 17:19, 23, 26, 32, 33, 37, 42; 18:12, 12, 13, 14, 28; 20:5, 7, 8, 9, 13, 13, 15, 16, 33, 34, 35; 22:2, 4, 8, 17; 23:19; 25:7, 16, 25; 26:6; 27:2, 3, 5; 28:8, 19, 19; 29:2, 4, 9; 30:22, 22; 31:5; 2Sa 1:2, 24; 2:3, 5, 5, 6; 3:8, 12, 15, 15, 17, 22, 22, 26, 28; 5:10; 6:4, 7, 22, 22; 7:3, 9, 15; 8:11; 9:1, 3, 7; 10:2, 13, 17; 11:1, 4, 11, 13; 12:3, 3, 11, 24; 13:11, 16, 20, 22, 23, 24, 26; 14:17; 15:19, 20, 28, 31, 35, 36; 17:24; 18:2; 19:16, 17, 25, 37, 37, 40, 41; 20:8; 21:4, 4, 15, 18, 19; 22:26, 26, 27, 27; 23:5, 9; 24:16, 21; 1Ki 1:7, 7, 8, 9, 14, 21, 22, 33, 37, 37; 2:8, 10, 33; 3:6, 6, 17; 5:6; 8:9, 17, 18, 18, 21, 57, 57, 61, 62, 65; 9:27; 10:2, 22, 26; 11:4, 9, 11, 18, 21, 22, 38, 43; 12:15, 21, 24; 13:8; 14:5, 20, 31, 31; 15:3, 8, 14, 24, 24; 16:6, 17, 28; 17:20; 20:26; 22:40, 44, 49, 50, 50; 2Ki 2:9; 6:33; 8:21, 24, 24, 28; 9:28; 10:15, 23, 35; 11:9; 12:21; 13:9, 12, 13, 13; 14:10, 15, 16, 16, 20, 22, 29, 29; 15:7, 7, 22, 25, 38, 38; 16:20, 20; 18:7, 26, 27; 20:21; 21:18; 24:6; 1Ch 4:10, 23; 5:10, 19, 20; 8:32; 9:20, 25, 38; 11:9, 10, 10, 13; 12:18, 19, 21, 27, 34, 39; 13:1, 2, 14; 15:18; 16:41, 42; 17:2, 8, 11, 13; 18:11; 19:2, 2, 6, 14, 17, 19; 20:4; 21:15, 20; 22:7, 11, 15, 16, 18; 24:5; 25:7, 8; 26:16; 27:32; 28:1, 2, 12, 20, 21; 29:30; 2Ch 1:1, 3, 8, 9, 11, 14; 2:3, 7, 7, 8, 14; 5:10, 12; 6:7, 8, 8, 11; 7:8; 8:18; 9:1, 1, 21, 25, 31; 10:15; 11:1, 4; 12:1, 3, 16; 13:3, 8, 12, 12; 14:1, 6, 11, 11, 13; 15:2, 2, 9, 9; 16:9, 9, 10, 13; 17:3, 8, 8, 9, 10, 14, 15, 16, 17, 18; 18:2, 3, 3; 19:3, 6, 7, 11; 20:1, 6, 17, 17, 29, 35, 36, 37; 21:1, 1, 3, 9, 9, 19; 22:7, 8; 23:1, 3, 8; 24:4, 16, 16, 22; 25:7, 7, 13, 19, 24, 28; 26:2, 17, 19, 23, 23; 27:5, 9; 28:10, 27; 29:10; 32:3, 7, 7, 7, 8, 8, 9, 33; 33:20; 35:21; 36:10, 23; Ezr 1:3, 4, 11; 2:2; 4:2; 7:28; 8:1, 3, 4, 5, 6, 7, 8, 9, 10, 11, 12, 13, 14, 24, 33, 33; 10:4, 14; Ne 2:9, 12, 12; 4:13; 5:18; 7:7; 9:8, 13, 17; 10:38; 12:1, 40; 13:25; Est 2:6, 6, 13; 5:12, 12, 14; 6:3, 14; 7:1, 8; 9:25; Job 1:4, 12; 3:14, 15; 5:23; 9:2, 3, 14, 26; 10:13, 17; 11:5; 12:2, 13, 16; 14:3; 15:9, 11; 16:21; 17:3; 20:11; 21:8; 22:4, 21; 23:7, 14; 25:2, 4; 26:10; 27:11, 13; 28:4; 29:18; 30:1; 31:5; 33:29; 34:8, 8, 9, 33; 35:4; 36:4; 37:18; 40:2, 15; 41:4; 42:8, 11; Ps 18:23, 25, 25, 26, 26; 26:4, 5, 9, 9; 28:1, 3, 3, 3; 36:9; 39:12; 42:8; 46:7, 11; 50:18, 18; 54:T; 66:15, 15; 69:28; 72:5; 73:5, 22, 23, 25; 77:6; 78:37; 81:2; 83:7, 8; 85:4; 86:17; 87:4; 88:4; 89:13, 21, 24, 33, 38; 91:15; 94:16, 16; 104:25; 106:5, 6; 113:8, 8; 115:13; 119:65, 124; 120:4, 5, 6; 121:2; 126:2, 3; 130:4, 7, 7; 139:18; 143:7; 148:12; Pr 3:30; 10:22; 18:3; 23:7; 24:21; 29:24; 30:31; 31:23; Ecc 1:11, 16; 2:16, 16; 4:15; 6:10; 7:11; 9:9; SS 1:11; 4:13, 13, 14, 14; 5:1, 1, 1; 6:1; Isa 3:14; 7:11; 8:10, 18; 11:6, 6; 25:11; 28:15, 29; 29:6; 34:7, 7; 36:12; 38:11; 41:10; Jer 6:11, 11; 32:4; 34:14; 39:12; 41:12; 51:40; Da 1:13; 8:18; 9:22; 10:7, 11, 15, 17, 19, 20, 21; 11:8, 8, 11, 11, 17, 39, 40; Hos 2:18, 18; 4:1, 5, 14, 14; 5:5; 9:8; 11:12, 12; 12:1, 2, 4; 14:2; Joel 2:26; 3:2; Am 2:3; 4:10; 6:10; Jnh 1:3; Mic 2:7; 6:2, 2, 8; Na 3:12; Zep 1:4; Zec 8:23, 23; 10:5; 14:5

6643 עִמָּד *ʿimmād*, pp. [45]

Ge 3:12; 19:19; 20:9, 13; 21:23; 28:20; 29:19, 27; 31:5, 7, 32; 35:3; 40:14; 47:29; Ex 17:2; Lev 25:23; Dt 5:31; 32:34, 39; Jdg 17:10; Ru 1:8; 1Sa 10:2; 20:14, 28; 22:23; 2Sa 10:2; 19:33; Job 6:4; 9:35; 10:12, 17; 13:19, 20; 17:2; 23:6, 10; 28:14; 29:5, 6, 20; 31:13; Ps 23:4; 50:11; 55:18; 101:6

6964 עַתָּה *ʿattâ*, adv. [432]

Ge 3:22; 4:11; 11:6; 12:19; 19:9; 20:7; 21:23; 22:12; 24:49; 26:22, 29; 27:3, 8, 36, 43; 29:32, 34; 30:30; 31:13, 16, 28, 30, 42, 44; 32:4, 10; 37:20; 41:33; 43:10; 44:10, 30, 33; 45:5, 8; 46:34; 47:4; 48:5; 50:5, 17, 21; Ex 3:9, 10, 18; 4:12; 5:5, 18; 6:1; 9:15, 18, 19; 10:17; 18:11, 19; 19:5; 32:10, 30, 32, 34; 33:5, 13; Nu 11:6, 23; 14:17; 22:4, 6, 11, 19, 29, 33, 34, 38; 24:11, 14, 17; 31:17; Dt 2:13; 4:1; 5:25; 10:12, 22; 12:9; 26:10; 31:19; 32:39; Jos 1:2; 2:12; 3:12; 5:14; 9:6, 11, 12, 19, 23, 25; 13:7; 14:10, 10, 11, 12; 22:4, 4; 24:14, 23; Jdg 6:13; 7:3; 8:2, 6, 15; 9:16, 32, 38; 11:7, 8, 13, 23, 25; 13:4, 7, 12; 14:2; 15:18; 16:10; 17:3, 13; 18:14; 20:9, 13; Ru 2:7; 3:2, 11, 12; 1Sa 2:16, 30; 6:7; 8:5, 9; 9:6, 12, 13; 10:19; 12:2, 7, 10, 13, 16; 13:12, 13, 14; 14:30; 15:1, 3, 25, 30; 17:29; 18:22; 19:2; 20:29, 31; 21:3; 23:20; 24:20, 21; 25:7, 7, 17, 26, 26, 27; 26:8, 11, 16, 19, 20; 27:1; 28:22; 29:7, 10; 2Sa 2:6, 7; 3:18; 4:11; 7:8, 25, 28, 29; 12:10, 23, 28; 13:13, 20, 33; 14:15, 32; 15:34; 16:11; 17:9, 16; 18:3; 19:7, 7, 9, 10; 20:6; 24:10, 13, 16; 1Ki 1:12, 18, 18; 2:9, 16, 24; 3:7; 5:4, 6; 8:25, 26; 12:4, 11, 16, 26; 14:14; 17:24; 18:11, 14, 19; 19:4; 21:7; 22:23; 2Ki 1:14; 3:15, 23; 4:26; 5:6, 15, 22; 7:4, 9; 8:6; 9:26; 10:2, 19; 12:7; 13:19, 23; 18:20, 21, 23, 25; 19:19, 25; 1Ch 17:7, 23, 26, 27; 21:8, 12, 15; 22:11, 19; 28:8, 10; 29:13, 17; 2Ch 1:9, 10; 2:7, 13, 15; 6:16, 17, 40, 41; 7:15, 16; 10:4, 11, 16; 13:8; 16:9; 18:22; 19:7; 20:10; 25:19; 28:10, 11; 29:5, 10, 11, 31; 30:8; 32:15; 35:3; Ezr 9:8, 10, 12; 10:2, 3, 11; Ne 5:5; 6:7, 7, 9; 9:32; Job 3:13; 4:5; 6:3, 21, 28; 7:21; 8:6; 13:19; 14:16; 16:7, 19; 30:1, 9, 16; 35:15; 37:21; 42:5, 8; Ps 2:10; 12:5; 17:11; 20:6; 27:6; 39:7; 74:6, 6; 113:2; 115:18; 119:67; 121:8; 125:2; 131:3; Pr 5:7; 7:24; 8:32; Isa 1:21; 5:3, 5; 9:7; 16:14; 28:22; 29:22, 22; 30:8; 33:10, 10, 10; 36:5, 8, 10; 37:20, 26; 43:1, 19; 44:1; 47:8; 48:6, 7, 16; 49:5, 19; 52:5; 59:21; 64:8; Jer 2:18; 3:4; 4:12; 7:13; 14:10; 18:11; 26:13; 27:6, 16; 29:27; 32:36; 37:20; 40:4; 42:15, 22; 44:7; Eze 4:14; 7:3, 8; 19:13; 23:43, 43; 26:18; 39:25; 43:9; Da 9:15, 17, 22; 10:11, 17, 20; 11:2; Hos 2:7, 10; 4:16; 5:3, 7; 7:2; 8:8, 10, 13; 10:2, 3; 13:2; Joel 2:12; Am 6:7; 7:16; Jnh 4:3; Mic 4:7, 9, 10, 11; 5:1, 4; 7:4, 10; Na 1:13; Hag 1:5; 2:3, 4, 15; Zec 8:11; 9:8; Mal 1:9; 2:1; 3:15

8370 רַק[2] *raq*[2], adv. [109]

Ge 6:5; 14:24; 19:8; 20:11; 24:8; 26:29; 41:40; 47:22, 26; 50:8; Ex 8:9, 11, 28, 29; 9:26; 10:17, 24; 21:19; Nu 12:2; 20:19; Dt 2:28, 35, 37; 3:11, 19; 4:6, 9; 10:15; 12:15, 16, 23, 26; 15:5, 23; 17:16; 20:14, 16, 20; 28:13, 33; Jos 1:7, 17, 18; 6:15, 17, 18, 24; 8:2, 27; 11:13, 14, 22; 13:6, 14; 22:5; Jdg 3:2, 2; 6:39; 11:34; 14:16; 19:20, 20; 1Sa 1:13; 5:4; 1Ki 3:2, 3; 8:9, 19, 25; 11:13; 14:8; 15:5, 14, 23; 21:25; 22:16; 2Ki 3:2, 3; 10:29; 12:3; 14:3, 4; 15:4, 35; 17:2, 18; 21:8; 2Ch 5:10; 6:9, 16; 15:17; 18:15; 25:2; 27:2; 28:10; 29:34; 33:8, 17; Job 1:12, 15, 16, 17, 19; Ps 32:6; 91:8; Pr 13:10; Isa 4:1; 28:19; Am 3:2

8611 -שֶׁ *ša-*, pt.rel.pref. [140]

Ge 6:3; 49:10; Jdg 5:7, 7; 6:17; 7:12; 8:26; 2Ki 6:11; 1Ch 5:20; 27:27; Ezr 8:20; Job 19:29; Ps 122:3, 4; 123:2; 124:1, 2, 6; 129:6, 7; 133:2, 3; 135:2, 8, 10; 136:23; 137:8, 8, 9; 144:15, 15; 146:3, 5; Ecc 1:3, 7, 9, 9, 9, 9, 10, 11, 11, 14, 17; 2:7, 9, 11, 11, 12, 13, 14, 15, 16, 17, 18, 18, 18, 19, 19, 20, 21, 21, 22, 24, 26; 3:13, 14, 15, 18, 22; 4:2, 10; 5:5, 15, 15, 16, 16, 18; 6:3, 10, 10; 7:10, 14, 24; 8:7, 14, 14, 17; 9:5, 12, 12; 10:3, 5, 14, 16, 17; 11:3, 8; 12:3, 7, 9; SS 1:6, 6, 6, 7, 7, 12; 2:7, 17; 3:1, 2, 3, 4, 4, 4, 4, 5, 7, 11; 4:1, 2, 2, 6; 5:2, 8, 9; 6:5, 5, 6, 6; 8:4, 8, 12; La 2:15, 16; 4:9; 5:18; Jnh 1:7, 12; 4:10

9004 שָׁם *šām*, adv. [835]

Ge 2:8, 10, 11, 12; 3:23; 10:14; 11:2, 7, 8, 9, 9, 31; 12:7, 8, 8, 10; 13:3, 4, 4, 14, 18; 14:10; 18:16, 22, 28, 29, 30, 30, 31, 32; 19:20, 20, 22, 22, 27; 20:1, 13; 21:17, 31, 33; 22:2, 9; 23:13; 24:5, 6, 7, 8; 25:10; 26:8, 17, 17, 19, 22, 23, 25, 25, 25; 27:9, 45; 28:2, 6, 11; 29:2, 3; 30:32; 31:13, 13, 46; 32:13, 29; 33:19, 20; 35:1, 1, 3, 7, 7, 15, 27; 38:2; 39:1, 11, 20, 22; 40:3; 41:12; 42:2, 2, 26; 43:25, 30; 44:14; 45:11; 46:3; 48:7; 49:24, 31, 31, 31; 50:5, 10; Ex 8:22; 9:26; 10:26; 12:13, 30; 15:25, 25, 27, 27; 16:33; 17:3, 6; 18:5; 19:2; 20:21; 21:13, 33; 24:12; 25:22; 26:33; 29:42, 42, 43; 30:6, 18, 36; 34:2, 5, 28; 40:3, 7, 30; Lev 2:2; 8:31; 16:23; 18:3; 20:22; Nu 9:17, 17; 11:16, 17, 34; 13:22, 23, 24, 28, 33; 14:24, 35, 43; 15:18; 17:4; 19:18; 20:1, 1, 4, 26, 28; 21:12, 13, 16, 32; 22:41; 23:13, 13, 27; 32:26; 33:9, 14, 38, 54; 35:6, 11, 15, 25, 26; Dt 1:28, 37, 38, 39; 3:21; 4:5, 14, 26, 27, 28, 29, 42; 5:15; 6:1, 23; 7:1; 9:28; 10:5, 6, 6, 7; 11:8, 10, 10, 11, 29; 12:2, 5, 5, 6, 7, 11, 11, 14, 14, 21, 29; 13:12; 14:23, 24, 26; 16:2, 6, 11; 17:12; 18:6, 7; 19:3, 4, 12; 21:4; 23:12, 20; 24:18; 26:2, 5, 5; 27:5, 7; 28:21, 36, 37, 63, 64, 65, 68; 30:1, 3, 4, 4, 16, 18; 31:13, 16, 26; 32:47, 50, 52; 33:19, 21; 34:4, 5; Jos 2:1, 16, 22; 3:1; 4:8, 9; 6:22; 7:3, 4; 8:32; 10:27; 14:12; 15:14, 15; 17:15; 18:1, 10, 13; 19:13, 34; 20:3, 6, 9; 22:10, 19; 24:26; Jdg 1:7, 11, 20; 2:5; 5:11, 27; 6:24; 7:4; 8:8, 25, 27; 9:21, 51; 14:10; 16:1, 27; 17:7; 18:2, 3, 10, 11, 13, 15, 17; 19:2, 4, 7, 15, 18, 26; 20:22, 26, 27; 21:2, 4, 9, 10, 24, 24; Ru 1:2, 4, 7, 17; 3:4; 4:1; 1Sa 1:3, 22, 28; 2:14; 3:3; 4:4, 4; 5:11; 6:14, 14; 7:6, 17, 17, 17; 9:6, 10; 10:3, 3, 5, 5, 10, 12, 23; 11:14, 15, 15, 15; 14:11, 34; 17:49; 19:3, 23; 20:6, 19; 21:6, 7; 22:1, 1, 3, 22; 23:22, 23, 29; 24:3; 26:5, 5; 27:5; 29:4; 30:31; 31:12; 2Sa 1:21; 2:2, 4, 18, 23, 23; 3:27; 4:3; 5:20, 21; 6:2, 7, 7; 10:18; 11:16; 13:38; 14:2, 30, 32; 15:21, 21, 29, 32, 35, 36; 16:5, 14; 17:12, 13, 18; 18:7, 7, 8, 11; 20:1; 21:12, 13; 23:9, 11; 24:25; 1Ki 1:14, 34, 45; 2:3, 36, 36; 3:4; 4:28; 5:9; 6:19; 7:7, 8; 8:8, 9, 16, 21, 21, 29, 47, 64; 9:3, 3, 28; 10:20; 11:16, 36; 12:25; 13:17; 14:2, 21; 17:4, 9, 9, 10, 13, 19; 18:10, 40; 19:3, 9, 9, 19; 21:18; 2Ki 1:4, 6, 16; 2:20, 21, 21, 23, 25, 25; 4:8, 8, 10, 10, 11, 11; 5:18; 6:1, 2, 2, 2, 6, 9, 10, 14; 7:2, 4, 5, 8, 8, 10, 19; 9:2, 2, 16, 27; 10:15; 11:16; 12:5, 9; 14:19; 15:20; 16:6; 17:11, 25, 27, 27, 27, 29, 33; 19:32; 23:7, 8, 12, 16, 20, 27, 34; 24:13; 1Ch 1:12; 3:4; 4:23, 40, 41, 41, 43; 11:4, 13; 12:39; 13:6, 10; 14:11, 12; 16:37; 21:26, 28; 2Ch 1:3, 5, 6; 5:9; 6:5, 6, 11, 11, 20, 37; 7:7, 16, 16; 8:2, 18; 9:19; 12:13; 20:26; 23:15; 25:27; 26:20; 28:9, 18; 32:21; Ezr 1:4; 8:15, 15, 21, 32; 10:6; Ne 1:3, 9, 9; 2:11; 4:20; 5:16; 10:39; 13:5, 9; Job 1:21; 3:17, 17, 19; 23:7; 34:22; 35:12; 39:29, 30; 40:20; Ps 14:5; 36:12; 48:6; 53:5; 66:6; 68:27; 69:35; 76:3; 87:4, 6; 104:17, 25, 26; 107:36; 122:4, 5; 132:17; 133:3; 137:1, 3; 139:8, 10; Pr 8:27; 9:18; 15:17; 22:14; Ecc 1:5, 7; 3:16, 16, 17; 9:10; 11:3; SS 7:12; 8:5, 5; Isa 7:23, 24, 25; 13:20, 20, 21, 21, 21; 20:6; 22:18, 18; 23:12; 27:10, 10; 28:10, 10, 13, 13; 33:21; 34:12, 14, 15, 15; 35:8, 9, 9; 37:33; 48:16; 52:4, 11; 55:10; 57:7; 65:9, 20; Jer 2:6; 3:6; 7:2, 12; 8:3, 14, 22; 13:4, 6, 6, 7; 16:13, 15; 18:2; 19:2, 14; 20:6, 6; 22:1, 11, 12, 24, 26, 26, 27, 27; 23:3, 8; 24:9; 27:22; 29:6, 7, 14, 14, 18; 30:11; 32:5, 37; 35:7; 36:12; 37:12, 13, 16, 20; 38:11, 26; 40:4, 12; 41:1, 3, 9; 42:14, 15, 16, 16, 16, 17, 22; 43:2, 5, 12; 44:8, 12, 14, 14, 28; 45:5; 46:17, 28; 47:7; 49:16, 18, 33, 36, 38; 50:9, 40; Eze 1:3, 12, 20, 20; 3:15, 15, 22, 22, 23; 4:13; 5:3; 6:9, 13; 8:1, 3, 4, 14; 11:16, 18; 12:13, 16; 13:20; 17:20; 20:28, 28, 28, 28, 29, 35, 40, 40, 40, 43; 23:3, 3; 29:13, 14; 30:18; 32:22, 24, 26, 29, 30; 34:12, 14; 35:10; 36:20, 21, 22; 37:21; 39:11, 11, 28; 40:1, 3, 38; 42:13, 13, 14; 43:7; 46:19, 20, 24; 47:9, 9, 23; 48:35; Da 9:7; 10:13; Hos 2:15, 15; 6:7, 10; 9:15; 10:9; 12:4; 13:8; Joel 3:2, 7, 11, 12; Am 6:2; 7:12, 12; 9:2, 2, 3, 3, 4; Ob 1:4; Jnh 4:5; Mic 2:3; 4:10, 10; Na 2:11; 3:15; Hab 3:4; Zep 1:14; Hag 2:14; Zec 5:11

9348 תָּוֶךְ *tāwek*, subst. [418]

Ge 1:6; 2:9; 3:3, 8; 9:21; 15:10; 18:24, 26; 19:29; 23:6, 9, 10; 35:2; 37:7; 40:20; 41:48; 42:5; Ex 2:5; 3:2, 4; 7:5; 9:24; 11:4; 12:31, 49; 14:16, 22, 23, 27, 29; 15:19; 24:16, 18; 25:8; 26:28; 28:1, 32, 33; 29:45, 46; 33:11; 36:33; 39:3, 3, 3, 23, 25, 25; Lev 11:33, 33; 15:31; 16:16, 29; 17:8, 10, 12, 13; 18:26; 20:14; 22:32; 24:10; 25:33; 26:11, 12, 25; Nu 1:47, 49; 2:17, 33; 3:12; 4:2, 18; 5:3, 21; 8:6, 14, 16, 19; 9:7; 13:32; 15:14, 26, 29; 16:3, 21, 33, 45, 47; 17:6; 18:6, 20, 20, 23, 24; 19:6, 10, 20; 25:7, 11; 26:62, 62; 27:3, 4, 4, 7; 32:30; 33:8; 35:5, 15, 34, 34; Dt 3:16; 4:12, 15, 33, 36; 5:4, 22, 23, 24, 26; 9:10; 10:4; 11:3; 13:16; 19:2; 21:12; 22:2; 23:10, 11; 32:51, 51; Jos 3:17; 4:3, 5, 8, 9, 10, 18; 7:21, 23; 8:9, 13, 22; 12:2; 13:9, 16; 14:3; 15:13; 16:9; 17:4, 4, 6, 9; 19:1, 9, 49; 20:9; 21:41; 22:19, 31; Jdg 7:16; 9:51; 12:4, 4; 15:4; 16:29; 18:1; 20:42; 1Sa 7:3; 9:14, 18; 10:10, 23; 11:11; 15:6, 6; 18:10; 25:29; 2Sa 1:25; 3:27; 4:6; 6:17; 7:2; 20:12; 23:12, 20; 24:5; 1Ki 3:8, 20; 6:13, 19, 27, 27; 8:51, 64; 11:20, 20; 14:7; 2Ki 4:13; 6:20; 9:2; 11:2; 23:9; 1Ch 11:14, 22; 16:1; 21:6; 2Ch 6:13; 7:7; 20:14; 22:11; 23:20; 32:4; Ne 4:11, 22; 6:10; 7:4; 9:11; Est 4:1; 9:28; Job 1:6; 2:1, 8; 15:19; 20:13; 42:15; Ps 22:14, 22; 40:8, 10; 57:4, 6; 68:25; 109:30; 116:19; 135:9; 136:11, 14; 137:2; 143:4; Pr 1:14; 4:21; 5:14, 15; 8:20; 17:2; 22:13; 27:22; SS 3:10; Isa 5:2; 6:5; 7:6; 16:3; 19:19; 24:13, 18; 41:18; 52:11; 58:9; 61:9; 66:17; Jer 9:6; 12:14, 16; 21:4; 29:32;

KEY FEATURES OF THE NIV ENGLISH INDEX

NIV WORD
The indexed word exactly as it is spelled in the NIV. See the introduction, page xii.

NIV FREQUENCY
The total number of times this word occurs in the NIV Old Testament. See the introduction, page xii.

SLAVE [55]

slave, 6269, *'ebed*[1] [15]

HEBREW FREQUENCY
The total number of times this word is translated by the entry word in the NIV Old Testament. See the introduction, page xii.

HEBREW TRANSLATIONS
The Hebrew or Aramaic word or phrase translated by the entry word is indicated by G/K number and transliteration. See the introduction, pages viii-x, xii.

ABBREVIATIONS
NIV words that do not directly translate a Hebrew or Aramaic word are indicated by special codes. See the introduction, pages ix-x, xii.

slave, *NIH/RPE* [3]

slave by birth, 3535+1074, *yālîd+bayit*[1] [1]

MULTIPLE WORD TRANSLATIONS
When more than one NIV word is used to translate a Hebrew or Aramaic word or phrase, all words in the NIV phrase appear on the index line. When more than one Hebrew or Aramaic word is translated by a word or phrase, all words in the Hebrew or Aramaic phrase are indicated by G/K number and transliteration. See the introduction, pages ix, xii.

female [slave], 563, *'āmâ* [2]

BRACKETS
When an NIV word is used more than once in a multiple word translation, it is in brackets to indicate it was counted only once in the NIV total frequency. See the introduction, page xii.

The NIV English–Hebrew & Aramaic Index to the NIV Old Testament

12 [24]
12, 9109+6925, *š^{e}nayim+ʿāśār* [24]

13 [1]
13, 8993+6925, *šālōš+ʿāśār* [1]

18 [3]
18, 9046+6925, *š^{e}mōneh+ʿāśār* [2]
18 inches, 564, *ʾammâ^{1}* [1]

20 [2]
20, 6929, *ʿeśrîm* [2]

22 [1]
22, 6929+2256+9109, *ʿeśrîm+w^{e}-+š^{e}nayim* [1]

28 [1]
28, 6929+2256+9046, *ʿeśrîm+w^{e}-+š^{e}mōneh* [1]

29 [3]
29, 9596+2256+6929, *tēšaʿ+w^{e}-+ʿeśrîm* [3]

30 [5]
30, 8993, *šālōš* [5]

32 [3]
32, 9109+2256+8993, *š^{e}nayim+w^{e}-+šālōš* [2]
32, 8993+2256+9109, *šālōš+w^{e}-+š^{e}nayim* [1]

34 [1]
34, 752+2256+8993, *ʾarbaʿ^{1}+w^{e}-+šālōš* [1]

35 [1]
35, 2822+2256+8993, *ḥāmēš+w^{e}-+šālōš* [1]

40 [1]
40, 752, *ʾarbaʿ^{1}* [1]

42 [2]
42, 752+2256+9109, *ʾarbaʿ^{1}+w^{e}-+š^{e}nayim* [2]

45 [1]
45 feet, 8993+564, *šālōš+ʾammâ^{1}* [1]

50 [3]
50, 2822, *ḥāmēš* [3]

52 [2]
52, 2822+2256+9109, *ḥāmēš+w^{e}-+š^{e}nayim* [2]

56 [1]
56, 2822+2256+9252, *ḥāmēš+w^{e}-+šēš^{1}* [1]

60 [1]
60, 9252, *šēš^{1}* [1]

61 [1]
61, 285+2256+9252, *ʾeḥād+w^{e}-+šēš^{1}* [1]

62 [1]
62, 9252+2256+9109, *šēš^{1}+w^{e}-+š^{e}nayim* [1]

65 [2]
65, 2822+2256+9252, *ḥāmēš+w^{e}-+šēš^{1}* [2]

67 [1]
67, 9252+2256+8679, *šēš^{1}+w^{e}-+šebaʿ^{1}* [1]

70 [5]
70, 8679, *šebaʿ^{1}* [5]

72 [1]
72, 9109+2256+8679, *š^{e}nayim+w^{e}-+šebaʿ^{1}* [1]

74 [2]
74, 8679+2256+752, *šebaʿ^{1}+w^{e}-+ʾarbaʿ^{1}* [2]

75 [1]
75 feet, 2822+564, *ḥāmēš+ʾammâ^{1}* [1]

80 [2]
80, 9046, *š^{e}mōneh* [2]

90 [1]
90, 9596, *tēšaʿ* [1]

95 [2]
95, 9596+2256+2822, *tēšaʿ+w^{e}-+ḥāmēš* [2]

98 [2]
98, 9596+2256+9046, *tēšaʿ+w^{e}-+š^{e}mōneh* [2]

100 [8]
100, 4395, *mēʾâ^{1}* [8]

105 [1]
105, 2822+2256+4395, *ḥāmēš+w^{e}-+mēʾâ^{1}* [1]

110 [1]
110, 4395+2256+6927, *mēʾâ^{1}+w^{e}-+ʿ^{a}śārâ* [1]

112 [3]
112, 4395+2256+9109+6925,
mēʾâ^{1}+w^{e}-+š^{e}nayim+ʿāśār [2]
112, 4395+9109+6925,
mēʾâ^{1}+š^{e}nayim+ʿāśār [1]

119 [1]
119, 9596+6926+2256+4395,
tēšaʿ+ʿeśrēh+w^{e}-+mēʾâ^{1} [1]

120 [6]
120, 4395+2256+6929, *mēʾâ^{1}+w^{e}-+ʿeśrîm* [5]
120, 10395+10221+10574, *m^{e}ʾâ+w^{e}-+ʿeśrîn* [1]

122 [2]
122, 4395+2256+6929+2256+9109,
mēʾâ^{1}+w^{e}-+ʿeśrîm+w^{e}-+š^{e}nayim [1]
122, 4395+6929+2256+9109,
mēʾâ^{1}+ʿeśrîm+w^{e}-+š^{e}nayim [1]

123 [2]
123, 4395+6929+2256+8993,
mēʾâ^{1}+ʿeśrîm+w^{e}-+šālōš [2]

127 [3]
127, 8679+2256+6929+2256+4395,
šebaʿ^{1}+w^{e}-+ʿeśrîm+w^{e}-+mēʾâ^{1} [3]

128 [4]
128, 4395+6929+2256+9046,
mēʾâ^{1}+ʿeśrîm+w^{e}-+š^{e}mōneh [4]

130 [2]
130, 4395+2256+8993, *mēʾâ^{1}+w^{e}-+šālōš* [1]
130, 8993+2256+4395, *šālōš+w^{e}-+mēʾâ^{1}* [1]

133 [1]
133, 8993+2256+8993+2256+4395,
šālōš+w^{e}-+šālōš+w^{e}-+mēʾâ^{1} [1]

137 [2]
137, 8679+2256+8993+2256+4395,
šebaʿ^{1}+w^{e}-+šālōš+w^{e}-+mēʾâ^{1} [2]

138 [1]
138, 4395+8993+2256+9046,
mēʾâ^{1}+šālōš+w^{e}-+š^{e}mōneh [1]

139 [1]
139, 4395+8993+2256+9596,
mēʾâ^{1}+šālōš+w^{e}-+tēšaʿ [1]

148 [1]
148, 4395+752+2256+9046,
mēʾâ^{1}+ʾarbaʿ^{1}+w^{e}-+š^{e}mōneh [1]

150 [2]
150, 4395+2256+2822, *mēʾâ^{1}+w^{e}-+ḥāmēš* [2]

156 [1]
156, 4395+2822+2256+9252,
mēʾâ^{1}+ḥāmēš+w^{e}-+šēš^{1} [1]

160 [1]
160, 4395+2256+9252, *mēʾâ^{1}+w^{e}-+šēš^{1}* [1]

162 [1]
162, 9109+2256+9252+2256+4395,
š^{e}nayim+w^{e}-+šēš^{1}+w^{e}-+mēʾâ^{1} [1]

172 [1]
172, 4395+8679+2256+9109,
mēʾâ^{1}+šebaʿ^{1}+w^{e}-+š^{e}nayim [1]

180 [1]
180, 9046+2256+4395,
š^{e}mōneh+w^{e}-+mēʾâ^{1} [1]

182 [1]
182, 9109+2256+9046+2256+4395, *š^{e}nayim+w^{e}-+š^{e}mōneh+w^{e}-+mē’â^{1}* [1]

187 [1]
187, 8679+2256+9046+2256+4395, *šeba‘^{1}+w^{e}-+š^{e}mōneh+w^{e}-+mē’â^{1}* [1]

188 [1]
188, 4395+9046+2256+9046, *mē’â^{1}+š^{e}mōneh+w^{e}-+š^{e}mōneh* [1]

200 [5]
200, 4395, *mē’â^{1}* [5]

205 [1]
205, 2822+2256+4395, *ḥāmēš+w^{e}-+mē’â^{1}* [1]

207 [1]
207, 8679+2256+4395, *šeba‘^{1}+w^{e}-+mē’â^{1}* [1]

209 [1]
209, 9596+2256+4395, *tēša‘+w^{e}-+mē’â^{1}* [1]

212 [1]
212, 4395+2256+9109+6925, *mē’â^{1}+w^{e}-+š^{e}nayim+‘āśār* [1]

218 [1]
218, 4395+2256+9046+6925, *mē’â^{1}+w^{e}-+š^{e}mōneh+‘āśār* [1]

220 [2]
220, 4395+2256+6929, *mē’â^{1}+w^{e}-+‘eśrîm* [2]

223 [2]
223, 4395+6929+2256+8993, *mē’â^{1}+‘eśrîm+w^{e}-+šālōš* [2]

232 [1]
232, 4395+9109+2256+8993, *mē’â^{1}+š^{e}nayim+w^{e}-+šālōš* [1]

242 [1]
242, 4395+752+2256+9109, *mē’â^{1}+’arba‘^{1}+w^{e}-+š^{e}nayim* [1]

245 [3]
245, 4395+752+2256+2822, *mē’â^{1}+’arba‘^{1}+w^{e}-+ḥāmēš* [2]
245, 4395+2256+752+2256+2822, *mē’â^{1}+w^{e}-+’arba‘^{1}+w^{e}-+ḥāmēš* [1]

250 [10]
250, 2822+2256+4395, *ḥāmēš+w^{e}-+mē’â^{1}* [10]

273 [1]
273, 8993+2256+8679+2256+4395, *šālōš+w^{e}-+šeba‘^{1}+w^{e}-+mē’â^{1}* [1]

284 [1]
284, 4395+9046+2256+752, *mē’â^{1}+š^{e}mōneh+w^{e}-+’arba‘^{1}* [1]

288 [1]
288, 4395+9046+2256+9046, *mē’â^{1}+š^{e}mōneh+w^{e}-+š^{e}mōneh* [1]

300 [2]
300, 8993+4395, *šālōš+mē’â^{1}* [2]

318 [1]
318, 9046+6925+2256+8993+4395, *š^{e}mōneh+‘āśār+w^{e}-+šālōš+mē’â^{1}* [1]

320 [2]
320, 8993+4395+2256+6929, *šālōš+mē’â^{1}+w^{e}-+‘eśrîm* [2]

323 [1]
323, 8993+4395+6929+2256+8993, *šālōš+mē’â^{1}+‘eśrîm+w^{e}-+šālōš* [1]

324 [1]
324, 8993+4395+6929+2256+752, *šālōš+mē’â^{1}+‘eśrîm+w^{e}-+’arba‘^{1}* [1]

328 [1]
328, 8993+4395+6929+2256+9046, *šālōš+mē’â^{1}+‘eśrîm+w^{e}-+š^{e}mōneh* [1]

345 [2]
345, 8993+4395+752+2256+2822, *šālōš+mē’â^{1}+’arba‘^{1}+w^{e}-+ḥāmēš* [2]

350 [1]
350, 8993+4395+2256+2822, *šālōš+mē’â^{1}+w^{e}-+ḥāmēš* [1]

365 [1]
365, 2822+2256+9252+2256+8993+4395, *ḥāmēš+w^{e}-+šēš^{1}+w^{e}-+šālōš+mē’â^{1}* [1]

372 [2]
372, 8993+4395+8679+2256+9109, *šālōš+mē’â^{1}+šeba‘^{1}+w^{e}-+š^{e}nayim* [2]

390 [2]
390, 8993+4395+2256+9596, *šālōš+mē’â^{1}+w^{e}-+tēša‘* [2]

392 [2]
392, 8993+4395+9596+2256+9109, *šālōš+mē’â^{1}+tēša‘+w^{e}-+š^{e}nayim* [2]

403 [2]
403, 8993+2256+752+4395, *šālōš+w^{e}-+’arba‘^{1}+mē’â^{1}* [2]

410 [1]
410, 752+4395+2256+6927, *’arba‘^{1}+mē’â^{1}+w^{e}-+‘^{a}śārâ* [1]

420 [1]
420, 752+4395+2256+6929, *’arba‘^{1}+mē’â^{1}+w^{e}-+‘eśrîm* [1]

430 [3]
430, 8993+2256+752+4395, *šālōš+w^{e}-+’arba‘^{1}+mē’â^{1}* [3]

435 [2]
435, 752+4395+8993+2256+2822, *’arba‘^{1}+mē’â^{1}+šālōš+w^{e}-+ḥāmēš* [2]

450 [1]
450 feet, 8993+4395+564, *šālōš+mē’â^{1}+’ammâ^{1}* [1]

454 [1]
454, 752+4395+2822+2256+752, *’arba‘^{1}+mē’â^{1}+ḥāmēš+w^{e}-+’arba‘^{1}* [1]

468 [1]
468, 752+4395+9252+2256+9046, *’arba‘^{1}+mē’â^{1}+šēš^{1}+w^{e}-+š^{e}mōneh* [1]

500 [5]
500, 2822+4395, *ḥāmēš+mē’â^{1}* [5]

530 [1]
530, 8993+2256+2822+4395, *šālōš+w^{e}-+ḥāmēš+mē’â^{1}* [1]

550 [1]
550, 2822+2256+2822+4395, *ḥāmēš+w^{e}-+ḥāmēš+mē’â^{1}* [1]

595 [1]
595, 2822+2256+9596+2256+2822+4395, *ḥāmēš+w^{e}-+tēša‘+w^{e}-+ḥāmēš+mē’â^{1}* [1]

621 [2]
621, 9252+4395+6929+2256+285, *šēš^{1}+mē’â^{1}+‘eśrîm+w^{e}-+’eḥād* [2]

623 [1]
623, 9252+4395+6929+2256+8993, *šēš^{1}+mē’â^{1}+‘eśrîm+w^{e}-+šālōš* [1]

628 [1]
628, 9252+4395+6929+2256+9046, *šēš^{1}+mē’â^{1}+‘eśrîm+w^{e}-+š^{e}mōneh* [1]

642 [2]
642, 9252+4395+2256+752+2256+9109, *šēš^{1}+mē’â^{1}+w^{e}-+’arba‘^{1}+w^{e}-+š^{e}nayim* [1]
642, 9252+4395+752+2256+9109, *šēš^{1}+mē’â^{1}+’arba‘^{1}+w^{e}-+š^{e}nayim* [1]

648 [1]
648, 9252+4395+752+2256+9046, *šēš^{1}+mē’â^{1}+’arba‘^{1}+w^{e}-+š^{e}mōneh* [1]

650 [1]
650, 9252+4395+2256+2822, *šēš^{1}+mē’â^{1}+w^{e}-+ḥāmēš* [1]

652 [2]
652, 9252+4395+2822+2256+9109, *šēš^{1}+mē’â^{1}+ḥāmēš+w^{e}-+š^{e}nayim* [2]

655 [1]
655, 9252+4395+2822+2256+2822, *šēš^{1}+mē’â^{1}+ḥāmēš+w^{e}-+ḥāmēš* [1]

666 [3]
666, 9252+4395+9252+2256+9252, *šēš^{1}+mē’â^{1}+šēš^{1}+w^{e}-+šēš^{1}* [2]
666, 9252+4395+2256+9252+2256+9252, *šēš^{1}+mē’â^{1}+w^{e}-+šēš^{1}+w^{e}-+šēš^{1}* [1]

667 [1]
667, 9252+4395+9252+2256+8679, *šēš^{1}+mē’â^{1}+šēš^{1}+w^{e}-+šeba‘^{1}* [1]

675 [1]
675, 9252+4395+2822+2256+8679, *šēš^{1}+mē’â^{1}+ḥāmēš+w^{e}-+šeba‘^{1}* [1]

690 [1]
690, 9252+4395+2256+9596, *šēš^{1}+mē’â^{1}+w^{e}-+tēša‘* [1]

721 [1]
721, 8679+4395+2256+6929+2256+285, *šeba‘^{1}+mē’â^{1}+w^{e}-+‘eśrîm+w^{e}-+’eḥād* [1]

725 [1]
725, 8679+4395+6929+2256+2822, *šeba‘^{1}+mē’â^{1}+‘eśrîm+w^{e}-+ḥāmēš* [1]

730 [1]
730, 8679+4395+2256+8993, *šeba‘^{1}+mē’â^{1}+w^{e}-+šālōš* [1]

736 [2]
736, 8679+4395+8993+2256+9252, *šeba‘^{1}+mē’â^{1}+šālōš+w^{e}-+šēš^{1}* [2]

743 [2]
743, 8679+4395+2256+752+2256+8993, *šeba‘^{1}+mē’â^{1}+w^{e}-+’arba‘^{1}+w^{e}-+šālōš* [1]
743, 8679+4395+752+2256+8993, *šeba‘^{1}+mē’â^{1}+’arba‘^{1}+w^{e}-+šālōš* [1]

745 [1]
745, 8679+4395+752+2256+2822, *šeba‘^{1}+mē’â^{1}+’arba‘^{1}+w^{e}-+ḥāmēš* [1]

760 [2]
760, 8679+4395+2256+9252, *šeba‘^{1}+mē’â^{1}+w^{e}-+šēš^{1}* [2]

775 [1]
775, 8679+4395+2822+2256+8679, *šeba‘^{1}+mē’â^{1}+ḥāmēš+w^{e}-+šeba‘^{1}* [1]

777 [1]
777, 8679+2256+8679+2256+8679+4395, *šeba‘^{1}+w^{e}-+šeba‘^{1}+w^{e}-+šeba‘^{1}+mē’â^{1}* [1]

782 [1]
782, 9109+2256+9046+2256+8679+4395, *š^{e}nayim+w^{e}-+š^{e}mōneh+w^{e}-+šeba‘^{1} +mē’â^{1}* [1]

800 [2]
800, 9046+4395, *š^{e}mōneh+mē’â^{1}* [2]

807 [1]
807, 8679+2256+9046+4395, *šeba‘^{1}+w^{e}-+š^{e}mōneh+mē’â^{1}* [1]

815 [1]
815, 2822+6926+2256+9046+4395, *ḥāmēš+‘eśrēh+w^{e}-+š^{e}mōneh+mē’â^{1}* [1]

17,200 [1]
17,200, 8679+6925+547+2256+4395, *šeba'^{1}+'āśār+'elep^{2}+w^{e}-+mē'â^{1}* [1]

18,000 [2]
18,000, 9046+6925+547, *š^{e}mōneh+'āśār+'elep^{2}* [2]

20,000 [3]
20,000, 9109+8052, *š^{e}nayim+ribbô'* [2]
20,000, 6929+547, *'eśrîm+'elep^{2}* [1]

20,200 [1]
20,200, 6929+547+2256+4395, *'eśrîm+'elep^{2}+w^{e}-+mē'â^{1}* [1]

20,800 [1]
20,800, 6929+547+2256+9046+4395, *'eśrîm+'elep^{2}+w^{e}-+š^{e}mōneh+mē'â^{1}* [1]

22,000 [1]
22,000, 9109+2256+6929+547, *š^{e}nayim+w^{e}-+'eśrîm+'elep^{2}* [1]

22,034 [1]
22,034, 6929+2256+9109+547+2256+8993 +2256+752, *'eśrîm+w^{e}-+š^{e}nayim+'elep^{2} +w^{e}-+šālōš+w^{e}-+'arba'^{1}* [1]

22,200 [1]
22,200, 9109+2256+6929+547+2256+4395, *š^{e}nayim+w^{e}-+'eśrîm+'elep^{2}+w^{e}-+mē'â^{1}* [1]

22,273 [1]
22,273, 9109+2256+6929+547+8993+2256 +8679+2256+4395, *š^{e}nayim+w^{e}-+'eśrîm +'elep^{2}+šālōš+w^{e}-+šeba'^{1}+w^{e}-+mē'â^{1}* [1]

22,600 [1]
22,600, 6929+2256+9109+547+2256+9252 +4395, *'eśrîm+w^{e}-+š^{e}nayim+'elep^{2}+w^{e}- +šēš^{1}+mē'â^{1}* [1]

23,000 [1]
23,000, 8993+2256+6929+547, *šālōš+w^{e}-+'eśrîm+'elep^{2}* [1]

24,000 [14]
24,000, 6929+2256+752+547, *'eśrîm+w^{e}-+'arba'^{1}+'elep^{2}* [13]
24,000, 752+2256+6929+547, *'arba'^{1}+w^{e}-+'eśrîm+'elep^{2}* [1]

25,000 [14]
25,000, 2822+2256+6929+547, *ḥāmēš+w^{e}-+'eśrîm+'elep^{2}* [14]

25,100 [1]
25,100, 6929+2256+2822+547+2256+4395, *'eśrîm+w^{e}-+ḥāmēš+'elep^{2}+w^{e}-+mē'â^{1}* [1]

26,000 [1]
26,000, 6929+2256+9252+547, *'eśrîm+w^{e}-+šēš^{1}+'elep^{2}* [1]

28,600 [1]
28,600, 6929+2256+9046+547+2256+9252 +4395, *'eśrîm+w^{e}-+š^{e}mōneh+'elep^{2}+w^{e}- +šēš^{1}+mē'â^{1}* [1]

30,500 [2]
30,500, 8993+547+2256+2822+4395, *šālōš+'elep^{2}+w^{e}-+ḥāmēš+mē'â^{1}* [2]

32,000 [1]
32,000, 9109+2256+8993+547, *š^{e}nayim+w^{e}-+šālōš+'elep^{2}* [1]

32,200 [2]
32,200, 9109+2256+8993+547+2256+4395, *š^{e}nayim+w^{e}-+šālōš+'elep^{2}+w^{e}-+mē'â^{1}* [2]

32,500 [1]
32,500, 9109+2256+8993+547+2256+2822 +4395, *š^{e}nayim+w^{e}-+šālōš+'elep^{2}+w^{e}- +ḥāmēš+mē'â^{1}* [1]

35,400 [2]
35,400, 2822+2256+8993+547+2256+752+4395, *ḥāmēš+w^{e}-+šālōš+'elep^{2}+w^{e}-+'arba'^{1} +mē'â^{1}* [2]

36,000 [3]
36,000, 9252+2256+8993+547, *šēš^{1}+w^{e}-+šālōš+'elep^{2}* [2]
36,000, 8993+2256+9252+547, *šālōš+w^{e}-+šēš^{1}+'elep^{2}* [1]

37,000 [1]
37,000, 8993+2256+8679+547, *šālōš+w^{e}-+šeba'^{1}+'elep^{2}* [1]

40,000 [1]
40,000, 752+547, *'arba'^{1}+'elep^{2}* [1]

40,500 [3]
40,500, 752+547+2256+2822+4395, *'arba'^{1}+'elep^{2}+w^{e}-+ḥāmēš+mē'â^{1}* [3]

41,500 [2]
41,500, 285+2256+752+547+2256+2822+4395, *'eḥād+w^{e}-+'arba'^{1}+'elep^{2}+w^{e}-+ḥāmēš +mē'â^{1}* [2]

42,360 [2]
42,360, 752+8052+547+8993+4395+2256 +9252, *'arba'^{1}+ribbô'+'elep^{2}+šālōš +mē'â^{1}+w^{e}-+šēš^{1}* [1]
42,360, 752+8052+547+8993+4395+9252, *'arba'^{1}+ribbô'+'elep^{2}+šālōš+mē'â^{1}+šēš^{1}* [1]

43,730 [1]
43,730, 8993+2256+752+547+2256+8679 +4395+2256+8993, *šālōš+w^{e}-+'arba'^{1} +'elep^{2}+w^{e}-+šeba'^{1}+mē'â^{1}+w^{e}-+šālōš* [1]

44,760 [1]
44,760, 752+2256+752+547+2256+8679+4395 +2256+9252, *'arba'^{1}+w^{e}-+'arba'^{1}+'elep^{2} +w^{e}-+šeba'^{1}+mē'â^{1}+w^{e}-+šēš^{1}* [1]

45,400 [1]
45,400, 2822+2256+752+547+2256+752+4395, *ḥāmēš+w^{e}-+'arba'^{1}+'elep^{2}+w^{e}-+'arba'^{1} +mē'â^{1}* [1]

45,600 [1]
45,600, 2822+2256+752+547+2256+9252 +4395, *ḥāmēš+w^{e}-+'arba'^{1}+'elep^{2}+w^{e}- +šēš^{1}+mē'â^{1}* [1]

45,650 [2]
45,650, 2822+2256+752+547+2256+9252 +4395+2256+2822, *ḥāmēš+w^{e}-+'arba'^{1} +'elep^{2}+w^{e}-+šēš^{1}+mē'â^{1}+w^{e}-+ḥāmēš* [2]

46,500 [2]
46,500, 9252+2256+752+547+2256+2822 +4395, *šēš^{1}+w^{e}-+'arba'^{1}+'elep^{2}+w^{e}- +ḥāmēš+mē'â^{1}* [2]

50,000 [1]
50,000, 2822+547, *ḥāmēš+'elep^{2}* [1]

52,700 [1]
52,700, 9109+2256+2822+547+2256+8679 +4395, *š^{e}nayim+w^{e}-+ḥāmēš+'elep^{2} +w^{e}-+šeba'^{1} +mē'â^{1}* [1]

53,400 [3]
53,400, 8993+2256+2822+547+2256+752 +4395, *šālōš+w^{e}-+ḥāmēš+'elep^{2}+w^{e}- +'arba'^{1}+mē'â^{1}* [3]

54,400 [2]
54,400, 752+2256+2822+547+2256+752+4395, *'arba'^{1}+w^{e}-+ḥāmēš+'elep^{2}+w^{e}-+'arba'^{1} +mē'â^{1}* [2]

57,400 [2]
57,400, 8679+2256+2822+547+2256+752 +4395, *šeba'^{1}+w^{e}-+ḥāmēš+'elep^{2}+w^{e}- +'arba'^{1} +mē'â^{1}* [2]

59,300 [2]
59,300, 9596+2256+2822+547+2256+8993 +4395, *tēša'+w^{e}-+ḥāmēš+'elep^{2}+w^{e}- +šālōš+mē'â^{1}* [2]

60,500 [1]
60,500, 9252+547+2256+2822+4395, *šēš^{1}+'elep^{2}+w^{e}-+ḥāmēš+mē'â^{1}* [1]

61,000 [2]
61,000, 285+2256+9252+547, *'eḥād+w^{e}-+šēš^{1}+'elep^{2}* [1]
61,000, 9252+8052+2256+547, *šēš^{1}+ribbô'+w^{e}-+'elep^{2}* [1]

62,700 [2]
62,700, 9109+2256+9252+547+2256+8679 +4395, *š^{e}nayim+w^{e}-+šēš^{1}+'elep^{2}+w^{e}- +šeba'^{1}+mē'â^{1}* [2]

64,300 [1]
64,300, 752+2256+9252+547+2256+8993 +4395, *'arba'^{1}+w^{e}-+šēš^{1}+'elep^{2}+w^{e}-+šālōš +mē'â^{1}* [1]

64,400 [1]
64,400, 752+2256+9252+547+2256+752+4395, *'arba'^{1}+w^{e}-+šēš^{1}+'elep^{2}+w^{e}-+'arba'^{1} +mē'â^{1}* [1]

70,000 [1]
70,000, 8679+547, *šeba'^{1}+'elep^{2}* [1]

72,000 [1]
72,000, 9109+2256+8679+547, *š^{e}nayim+w^{e}-+šeba'^{1}+'elep^{2}* [1]

74,600 [2]
74,600, 752+2256+8679+547+2256+9252 +4395, *'arba'^{1}+w^{e}-+šeba'^{1}+'elep^{2}+w^{e}- +šēš^{1}+mē'â^{1}* [2]

76,500 [1]
76,500, 9252+2256+8679+547+2256+2822 +4395, *šēš^{1}+w^{e}-+šeba'^{1}+'elep^{2}+w^{e}- +ḥāmēš+mē'â^{1}* [1]

80,000 [1]
80,000, 9046+547, *š^{e}mōneh+'elep^{2}* [1]

87,000 [1]
87,000, 9046+2256+8679+547, *š^{e}mōneh+w^{e}-+šeba'^{1}+'elep^{2}* [1]

108,100 [1]
108,100, 4395+547+2256+9046+547+2256 +4395, *mē'â^{1}+'elep^{2}+w^{e}-+š^{e}mōneh +'elep^{2}+w^{e}-+mē'â^{1}* [1]

120,000 [1]
120,000, 4395+2256+6929+547, *mē'â^{1}+w^{e}-+'eśrîm+'elep^{2}* [1]

151,450 [1]
151,450, 4395+547+2256+285+2256+2822 +547+2256+752+4395+2256+2822, *mē'â^{1} +'elep^{2}+w^{e}-+'eḥād+w^{e}-+ḥāmēš+'elep^{2} +w^{e}-+'arba'^{1}+mē'â^{1}+w^{e}-+ḥāmēš* [1]

153,600 [1]
153,600, 4395+2256+2822+547+2256+8993 +547+2256+9252+4395, *mē'â^{1}+w^{e}-+ḥāmēš +'elep^{2}+w^{e}-+šālōš+'elep^{2}+w^{e}-+šēš^{1}+mē'â^{1}* [1]

157,600 [1]
157,600, 4395+547+2256+8679+2256+2822 +547+2256+9252+4395, *mē'â^{1}+'elep^{2}+w^{e}-+šeba'^{1}+w^{e}-+ḥāmēš+'elep^{2}+w^{e}-+šēš^{1}+mē'â^{1}* [1]

180,000 [1]
180,000, 4395+2256+9046+547, *mē'â^{1}+w^{e}-+š^{e}mōneh+'elep^{2}* [1]

186,400 [1]
186,400, 4395+547+2256+9046+547+2256 +9252+547+2256+752+4395, *mē'â^{1}+'elep^{2}*

Abishai^{s}, 2257, *-ô* [1]

ABISHALOM [2]
Abishalom, 58, *'ᵃbîšālôm* [2]

ABISHUA [5]
Abishua, 55, *'ᵃbîšûa'* [5]

ABISHUR [1]
Abishur, 56, *'ᵃbîšûr* [1]

ABISHUR'S [1]
Abishur's, 56, *'ᵃbîšûr* [1]

ABITAL [2]
Abital, 40, *'ᵃbîṭāl* [2]

ABITUB [1]
Abitub, 39, *'ᵃbîṭûb* [1]

ABLAZE [11]
ablaze, 1277, *bā'ar*^{1} [2]
set ablaze, 1277, *bā'ar*^{1} [2]
sets ablaze, 4265, *lāhaṭ*^{1} [2]
set ablaze, 928+2021+836+3675, *b^{e}-+ha-+'ēš^{1}+yāṣat* [1]
sets ablaze, 1277, *bā'ar*^{1} [1]
sets ablaze, 3675, *yāṣat* [1]
sets ablaze, 7706, *qādaḥ* [1]
all ablaze, 10471+10178, *nûr+d^{e}laq* [1]

ABLE [84]
able, *AIT* [33]
able, 3523, *yākōl* [23]
able, 10321, *y^{e}kil* [5]
able men, 1201+2657, *bēn^{1}+ḥayil* [4]
able, 1033, *bāḥûr*^{1} [3]
able men, 1475+2657, *gibbôr+ḥayil* [2]
able, 6806+3946, *'āṣar+kōaḥ*^{1} [2]
able, *NIH/RPE* [2]
able, 1067, *bîn* [1]
able, 1201+2657, *bēn^{1}+ḥayil* [1]
be able to have children, 2445+2446, *zāra'+zera'* [1]
able, 2657, *ḥayil* [1]
able, 3359, *yāda'* [1]
ever able, 3523+3523, *yākōl+yākōl* [1]
not be able, 4206, *lā'â* [1]
able, 6806, *'āṣar* [1]
able to stand, 9538, *t^{e}qûmâ* [1]
able, 10346, *k^{e}hal* [1]

ABLE-BODIED [3]
able-bodied, 2657, *ḥayil* [2]
able-bodied, 1201+2657, *bēn^{1}+ḥayil* [1]

ABNER [56]
Abner, 79, *'abnēr* [55]
Abner, 46, *'ᵃbînēr* [1]

ABNER'S [3]
Abner's, 79, *'abnēr* [3]

ABOARD [2]
aboard, 928, *b^{e}-* [1]
went aboard, 3718+928, *yārad+b^{e}-* [1]

ABODE [2]
abode, 5659, *nāweh*^{1} [1]
abode, 8905, *šākan* [1]

ABOLISH [2]
abolish, 6073, *sûr*^{1} [1]
abolish, 8689, *šābar*^{1} [1]

ABOLISHED [1]
is abolished, 6073, *sûr*^{1} [1]

ABOMINABLE [2]
abominable idols, 9199, *šiqqûṣ* [1]
abominable things, 9211, *šeqeṣ* [1]

ABOMINATION [3]
abomination, 9199, *šiqqûṣ* [3]

ABOMINATIONS [2]
abominations, 9199, *šiqqûṣ* [1]
abominations, 9359, *tô'ēbâ* [1]

ABOUND [4]
abound, 2118+7172, *hāyâ+pissâ* [1]
all abound, 8041, *rab*^{1} [1]
abound, 8044, *rōb* [1]
abound, 8045, *rābab*^{1} [1]

ABOUNDING [10]
abounding, 8041, *rab*^{1} [8]
abounding, 3877, *kābēd*^{1} [1]
abounding, 8428, *śāba'* [1]

ABOUNDS [1]
abounds, 5951, *nāśā'* [1]

ABOUT [477]
about, *AIT* [156]
about, 6584, *'al*^{2} [53]
about, 4200, *l^{e}-*^{1} [42]
about, 3869, *k^{e}-* [41]
about, 928, *b^{e}-* [20]
about, 448, *'el* [16]
about, *NIH/RPE* [12]
go about, 2143, *hālak* [7]
know about, 3359, *yāda'* [6]
knew about, 3359, *yāda'* [5]
about, 10542, *'al* [4]
bring about, 995, *bô'* [3]
going about, 2143, *hālak* [3]
go about, 6015, *sābab* [3]
prowl about, 6015, *sābab* [3]
about, 6584+128, *'al^{2}+'ōdôt* [3]
brought about, 6913, *'āśâ*^{1} [3]
moves about, 9237, *šāraṣ* [3]
about six hundred feet, 752+4395+564, *'arba'^{1}+mē'â^{1}+'ammâ*^{1} [2]
kicking about, 1008, *bûs* [2]
goes about, 2143, *hālak* [2]
moved about, 2143, *hālak* [2]
walk about, 2143, *hālak* [2]
concerned about, 3359, *yāda'* [2]
about, 4946, *min* [2]
make wander about, 5675, *nûa'* [2]
wander about, 5675, *nûa'* [2]
turn about, 6015, *sābab* [2]
about, 6017, *sābîb* [2]
about, 6584+1821, *'al^{2}+dābār* [2]
about, 7928, *qārab* [2]
about this time, 255, *'āz* [1]
go about, 261, *'āzal* [1]
swirled about, 705, *'āpap* [1]
about, 907, *'ēt*^{2} [1]
brought about, 995, *bô'* [1]
mill about, 1003, *bûk* [1]
about to, 1335, *bāqaš* [1]
brings about, 1343, *bārā'*^{1} [1]
thrashing about, 1631, *gîaḥ*^{1} [1]
about a foot and a half, 1688, *gōmed* [1]
care about, 2011, *dāraš* [1]
inquired about, 2011+2011, *dāraš+dāraš* [1]
what about, 2022+4202, *h^{a}-+lō'* [1]
bring about, 2118+928, *hāyâ+b^{e}-* [1]
about, 2143, *hālak* [1]
moves about, 2143, *hālak* [1]
moving about, 2143, *hālak* [1]
went about, 2143, *hālak* [1]
bustles about, 2159, *hāmâ* [1]
turned about, 2200+3338, *hāpak+yād* [1]
and what about, 2256, *w^{e}-* [1]
what about, 2256, *w^{e}-* [1]
think about, 2349, *zākar*^{1} [1]
sets about work, 2520+5516, *ḥāgar+motnayim* [1]
look about, 2916, *ḥāpar*^{1} [1]
bring about destruction, 3049, *ḥāram*^{1} [1]
care about, 3359, *yāda'* [1]
know all about, 3359, *yāda'* [1]
knowing about, 3359, *yāda'* [1]
learned about, 3359, *yāda'* [1]
go about business, 3655+2256+995, *yāṣā'+w^{e}-+bô'* [1]
go about, 3655, *yāṣā'* [1]
travel about, 3655+2256+995, *yāṣā'+w^{e}-+bô'* [1]
brought about victory, 3828+9591, *yāša'+t^{e}šû'â* [1]
about to, 3922, *kûn*^{1} [1]
brought about, 3922, *kûn*^{1} [1]
gather about, 4193, *kātar*^{2} [1]
what do I care about, 4200+4537+2296+4200+3276, *l^{e}-^{1}+mâ+zeh+l^{e}-^{1}+-î* [1]
what about, 4537, *mâ* [1]
toss about, 4570, *mûg* [1]
bring about death, 4637, *mût* [1]
brought about, 4946+2118, *min+hāyâ* [1]
carried about, 5362, *maśśā'*^{1} [1]
grope about, 5491, *māšaš* [1]
been told about, 5583+5583, *nāgad+nāgad* [1]
wanders about, 5610, *nādad* [1]
move about, 5825, *nāsa'* [1]
carry about, 5951, *nāśā'* [1]
looked about, 5951+6524, *nāśā'+'ayin*^{1} [1]
images that are carried about, 5953, *n^{e}śû'â* [1]
walk about, 6015, *sābab* [1]
swirled about, 6015, *sābab* [1]
ringed about, 6017, *sābîb* [1]
round about, 6017, *sābîb* [1]
think about, 6590+6584+4213, *'ālâ+'al^{2}+lēb* [1]
went about, 6913, *'āśâ*^{1} [1]
about to, 6964+4946+7940, *'attâ+min+qārôb* [1]
concerned about, 7212, *pāqad* [1]
dart about, 8132, *rûṣ* [1]
moves about, 8253, *rāmaś* [1]
dance about, 8376, *rāqad* [1]
leap about, 8376, *rāqad* [1]
care about, 8492+448+4213, *śîm+'el+lēb* [1]
concerned about, 8492+448+4213, *śîm+'el+lēb* [1]
move about, 9237, *šāraṣ* [1]
go about, 9494, *tā'â* [1]
wander about, 9494, *tā'â* [1]
about, 10089, *b^{e}-* [1]

ABOVE [119]
above, 6584, *'al*^{2} [45]
above, 4946+5087, *min+ma'al*^{2} [19]
above, 4946+6584, *min+'al*^{2} [13]
above, 4946, *min* [11]
above, 4946+4200+5087+2025, *min+l^{e}-^{1}+ma'al^{2}+-â*^{2} [4]
above, *AIT* [3]
above, 4200+5087+2025, *l^{e}-^{1}+ma'al^{2}+-â*^{2} [3]
above, 448+1068, *'el+bayin* [2]
above, 448, *'el* [2]
just above, 4946+5087, *min+ma'al*^{2} [2]
room above, 6608, *'ᵃliyyâ* [2]
above, *NIH/RPE* [1]
above, 928+2021+5294, *b^{e}-+ha-+mārôm* [1]
above, 1068, *bayin* [1]
above, 4200, *l^{e}-*^{1} [1]
over and above, 4200+5087+2025, *l^{e}-^{1}+ma'al^{2}+-â*^{2} [1]
above, 4946+5087+4946+4200+6645, *min+ma'al^{2}+min+l^{e}-^{1}+'ummâ*^{1} [1]
above, 4946+5087+6584, *min+ma'al^{2}+'al*^{2} [1]
high above, 4946+4200+5087+2025, *min+l^{e}-^{1}+ma'al^{2}+-â*^{2} [1]
heights above, 5294, *mārôm* [1]
above, 6584+1068, *'al^{2}+bayin* [1]
above, 6584+7156, *'al^{2}+pāneh* [1]
skies above, 8836, *šaḥaq* [1]
skies above, 9028+9028, *šāmayim+šāmayim* [1]

ABRAHAM [158]
Abraham, 90, *'abrāhām* [153]
Abraham, *NIH/RPE* [3]
Abraham^{s}, 2257, *-ô* [2]

ABRAHAM'S [12]
Abraham's, 90, *'abrāhām* [11]
Abraham's^{s}, 2257, *-ô* [1]

ABRAM [60]
Abram, 92, *'abrām* [50]
Abram, *NIH/RPE* [4]
Abram^{s}, 2257, *-ô* [3]
Abram^{s}, 2085, *hû'* [2]
Abram^{s}, 2084, *-hû* [1]

ABRAM'S [5]
Abram's, 92, *'abrām* [5]

ABROAD [3]
abroad, 4200+2021+2575, *le-1+ha-+ḥûṣ* [1]
spread abroad, 5688, *nāzal* [1]
scattered abroad, 7061, *pāzar* [1]

ABRONAH [2]
Abronah, 6307, *'abrōnâ* [2]

ABSALOM [92]
Absalom, 94, *'abšālôm* [88]
Absalom, *NIH/RPE* [3]
Absalom[s], 5647, *-nû[2]* [1]

ABSALOM'S [12]
Absalom's, 94, *'abšālôm* [10]
Absalom's[s], 2257, *-ô* [1]
Absalom's, 4200+94, *le-1+'abšālôm* [1]

ABSENT [1]
absent, 2532, *ḥādal[1]* [1]

ABSOLUTELY [1]
absolutely refuses, 4412+4412, *mā'an+mā'an* [1]

ABSTAIN [2]
abstain from sexual relations, 440+5602+448+851, *'al[1]+nāgaš+'el+'iššâ* [1]
abstain, 5693, *nāzar[2]* [1]

ABSTAINED [1]
abstained from work, 8697, *šābat[1]* [1]

ABUNDANCE [27]
abundance, 8426, *śābā'* [7]
abundance, 2016, *dešen* [3]
in abundance, 4200+8044, *le-1+rōb* [3]
abundance, 8044, *rōb* [2]
abundance, *NIH/RPE* [1]
abundance, 2162, *hāmôn* [1]
abundance, 2221+4394, *harbēh+me'ōd* [1]
abundance, 2221, *harbēh* [1]
abundance, 3883, *kābôd[1]* [1]
abundance, 3892, *kābar* [1]
abundance, 4849, *mālē'[2]* [1]
abundance, 5269, *marbeh* [1]
in abundance, 8044, *rōb* [1]
use an abundance, 8049, *rābâ[1]* [1]
place of abundance, 8122, *rewāyâ* [1]
abundance, 9179, *šepa'* [1]

ABUNDANT [30]
abundant, 8041, *rab[1]* [12]
abundant, 8044, *rōb* [3]
have abundant, 8425, *śāba'* [2]
abundant, 10678, *śaggî'* [2]
bless abundant, 1385+1385, *bārak[2]+bārak[2]* [1]
abundant showers, 1773, *gešem[1]* [1]
abundant supply, 2221, *harbēh* [1]
grant abundant, 3855, *yātar* [1]
abundant, 3972, *kōl* [1]
abundant, 4200+8044, *le-1+rōb* [1]
abundant, 5607, *nedābâ* [1]
abundant, 6988, *'ateret* [1]
abundant, 8049, *rābâ[1]* [1]
abundant rain, 8053, *rebîbîm* [1]
abundant, 8429, *śob'â* [1]

ABUNDANTLY [4]
abundantly, 4394, *me'ōd* [1]
abundantly, 6330+889+6330+3907, *'ad[2]+'ašer+'ad[2]+kōh* [1]
abundantly, 8041, *rab[1]* [1]
flowed abundantly, 8851, *šāṭap* [1]

ABUSE [4]
abuse, 6618, *'ālal[1]* [2]
abuse, 4583, *mûm* [1]
abuse, 6662, *'āmāl[1]* [1]

ABUSED [1]
abused, 6618, *'ālal[1]* [1]

ABUTTED [1]
abutted, 448, *'el* [1]

ACACIA [28]
acacia, 8847, *šiṭṭâ* [25]
acacia wood, 8847, *šiṭṭâ* [3]

ACACIAS [1]
acacias, 8847, *šiṭṭâ* [1]

ACBOR [7]
Acbor, 6570, *'akbôr* [7]

ACCEPT [55]
accept, 4374, *lāqaḥ* [23]
accept, 8354, *rāṣâ[1]* [10]
accept, *NIH/RPE* [4]
accept, 5951+7156, *nāśā'+pāneh* [3]
accept, 7691, *qābal* [3]
accept, 14, *'ābâ* [2]
accept possession, 296, *'āḥaz[1]* [1]
accept, 2014, *dāšēn[1]* [1]
accept correction, 3579, *yāsar[1]* [1]
accept atonement, 4105, *kāpar[1]* [1]
accept, 4340, *lāmad* [1]
accept, 5951, *nāśā'* [1]
accept, 6699, *'ānâ[1]* [1]
accept, 7155, *pānâ* [1]
accept, 7156+5951, *pāneh+nāśā'* [1]
accept, 8193, *rîaḥ* [1]

ACCEPTABLE [12]
acceptable, 8356, *rāṣôn* [5]
acceptable, *NIH/RPE* [2]
acceptable, 7928, *qārab* [2]
acceptable, 1047, *bāhar[1]* [1]
acceptable, 6844, *'ārab[3]* [1]
be acceptable, 8354, *rāṣâ[1]* [1]

ACCEPTED [21]
accepted, 4374, *lāqaḥ* [7]
accepted, 8356, *rāṣôn* [7]
be accepted, 8354, *rāṣâ[1]* [5]
accepted, 5951+906+7156, *nāśā'+'ēt[1]+pāneh* [1]
accepted, 8420, *śe'ēt[1]* [1]

ACCEPTING [2]
accepting, 4374, *lāqaḥ* [1]
accepting, 9461, *tāmak* [1]

ACCEPTS [7]
accepts, 4374, *lāqaḥ* [6]
accepts, *NIH/RPE* [1]

ACCESS [1]
had special access to, 8011+7156, *rā'â[1]+pāneh* [1]

ACCESSORIES [7]
accessories, 3998, *kelî* [7]

ACCIDENTALLY [4]
accidentally, 928+8705, *be-+šegāgâ* [4]

ACCLAIM [2]
acclaim, 7412, *ṣāhal[1]* [1]
acclaim, 9558, *terû'â* [1]

ACCLAMATION [1]
acclamation, 7754, *qôl* [1]

ACCO [1]
Acco, 6573, *'akkô* [1]

ACCOMPANIED [15]
accompanied by, 928, *be-* [4]
accompanied by, 6640, *'im* [2]
accompanied, *NIH/RPE* [1]
accompanied by, 907, *'ēt[2]* [1]
accompanied, 907+2143, *'ēt[2]+hālak* [1]
accompanied, 995+8079, *bô'+regel* [1]
accompanied by, 2143+6640, *hālak+'im* [1]
accompanied by, 2256, *we-* [1]
accompanied, 4200, *le-1* [1]
accompanied by, 6584+3338, *'al[2]+yād* [1]
accompanied, 6590+907, *'ālâ+'ēt[2]* [1]

ACCOMPANIES [2]
accompanies, 4200+7156, *le-1+pāneh* [2]

ACCOMPANY [6]
accompany, 6640, *'im* [2]
accompany, 907+3655, *'ēt[2]+yāṣā'* [1]
accompany, 2143+4200+5584, *hālak+le-1+neged* [1]
accompany, 4277, *lāwâ[1]* [1]
accompany, 5952, *nāśag* [1]

ACCOMPANYING [1]
accompanying, *NIH/RPE* [1]

ACCOMPLICE [1]
accomplice, 2745+6640, *ḥālaq[2]+'im* [1]

ACCOMPLISH [10]
accomplish, 6913, *'āśâ[1]* [8]
accomplish, 7756, *qûm* [1]
accomplish, 8966, *šālēm[1]* [1]

ACCOMPLISHED [2]
accomplished, 5126, *ma'aśeh* [1]
accomplished, 6913, *'āśâ[1]* [1]

ACCOMPLISHES [2]
fully accomplishes, 6913+2256+7756, *'āśâ[1]+we-+qûm* [2]

ACCOMPLISHING [1]
accomplishing, 6913, *'āśâ[1]* [1]

ACCORD [3]
with one accord, 3481, *yaḥdāw* [1]
accord, 4213, *lēb* [1]
in accord with, 4222+3838, *lēbāb+yāšār[1]* [1]

ACCORDANCE [47]
in accordance with, 3869, *ke-* [30]
in accordance with, 6584, *'al[2]* [4]
in accordance with, 10341, *ke-* [4]
in accordance with, 4200, *le-1* [2]
in accordance with, 448, *'el* [1]
in accordance with, 928, *be-* [1]
in accordance with, 3869+4027, *ke-+kēn[2]* [1]
in accordance with, 3869+889, *ke-+'ašer* [1]
in accordance with, 3972+889, *kōl+'ašer* [1]
in accordance with, 4200+7023, *le-1+peh* [1]
in accordance with, 6584+7023, *'al[2]+peh* [1]

ACCORDED [1]
accorded, *AIT* [1]

ACCORDING [239]
according to, 3869, *ke-* [86]
according to, 4200, *le-1* [61]
according to, 928, *be-* [50]
according to, 6584, *'al[2]* [18]
according, *NIH/RPE* [5]
according to, 6584+7023, *'al[2]+peh* [3]
according to, 3869+6584, *ke-+'al[2]* [2]
according to, 4017, *kemô* [2]
according to, 4200+7023, *le-1+peh* [2]
according to, 448, *'el* [1]
according to, 889, *'ašer* [1]
according to, 907, *'ēt[2]* [1]
according to the rules, 3869, *ke-* [1]
according to, 3869+7023, *ke-+peh* [1]
according to, 3869+889, *ke-+'ašer* [1]
according to, 4946, *min* [1]
according to the weight current, 6296, *'ābar[1]* [1]
according to, 10341, *ke-* [1]
according to, 10427, *min* [1]

ACCORDINGLY [3]
accordingly, *AIT* [1]
accordingly, 3869+7023, *ke-+peh* [1]
accordingly, 4027, *kēn[2]* [1]

ACCOUNT [46]
account, 9352, *tôlēdôt* [10]
on account of, 928, *be-* [5]
account, 1821, *dābār* [4]
call to account, 2011, *dāraš* [3]
on account of, 6584, *'al[2]* [3]
on account of, 928+6288, *be-+'abūr[1]* [2]

call to account, 1335, *bāqaš* [2]
on account of, 4200, *le-1* [2]
account, *NIH/RPE* [1]
no account, 224, *ʾāwen1* [1]
on account of, 448, *ʾel* [1]
taken into account, 928, *be-* [1]
call to account, 1335+4946+3338, *bāqaš+min+yād* [1]
call to account, 2011+4946+6640, *dāraš+min+ʿim* [1]
account for, 3108+907, *ḥāšab+ʾēt2* [1]
account, 3108, *ḥāšab* [1]
of no account, 4202, *lōʾ* [1]
account, 5031, *mispār1* [1]
gave account, 6218, *sāpar* [1]
called to account, 7212, *pāqad* [1]
full account, 7308, *pārāšâ* [1]
account of line, 9352, *tôlēdôt* [1]
account of the family, 9352, *tôlēdôt* [1]

ACCOUNTABLE [7]
hold accountable, 4946+3338+1335, *min+yād+bāqaš* [3]
hold accountable, 2011+4946+3338, *dāraš+min+yād* [1]
hold accountable, 4946+3338+2011, *min+yād+dāraš* [1]
hold accountable, 5989+6584, *nātan+ʿal2* [1]
accountable, 10302, *ṭeʿēm2* [1]

ACCOUNTED [1]
accounted, *NIH/RPE* [1]

ACCOUNTING [5]
demand an accounting, 2011, *dāraš* [3]
give an accounting, 928, *dāraš* [1]
require an accounting, 3108, *ḥāšab* [1]

ACCOUNTS [1]
accounts, 253, *ʾôt1* [1]

ACCUMULATE [1]
accumulate large amounts, 8049+4394, *rābâ1+meʾōd* [1]

ACCUMULATED [4]
accumulated, 665, *ʾāsap* [2]
accumulated, 8223, *rākaš* [2]

ACCURATE [5]
accurate, 7406, *ṣedeq* [3]
accurate, 8969, *šālēm2* [2]

ACCURSED [4]
accursed, 460, *ʾālâ4* [1]
accursed, 2404, *zāʿam* [1]
be considered accursed, 7837, *qālal* [1]
accursed, 7839, *qelālâ* [1]

ACCUSATION [2]
accusation, 8190, *rîb2* [1]
accusation, 8478, *śiṭnâ1* [1]

ACCUSATIONS [1]
accusations, 1821, *dābār* [1]

ACCUSE [10]
accuse, 8189, *rîb1* [3]
accuse, 8476, *śāṭan* [2]
accuse, 3519, *yākaḥ* [1]
accuse, 6699, *ʿānâ1* [1]
accuse, 6885, *ʿārak* [1]
accuse, 7212+6584, *pāqad+ʿal2* [1]
accuse, 8492+928+1821, *śîm+be-+dābār* [1]

ACCUSED [14]
accused of murder, 8357, *rāṣaḥ* [7]
accused, 8357, *rāṣaḥ* [3]
accused, *NIH/RPE* [1]
accused of, 4200, *le-1* [1]
accused, 8189, *rîb1* [1]
falsely accused, 10030+10642, *ʾakal+qeraṣ* [1]

ACCUSER [3]
accuser, 408+8190, *ʾîš1+rîb2* [1]
accuser, 1251+5477, *baʿal1+mišpāṭ* [1]
accuser, 8477, *śāṭān* [1]

ACCUSERS [5]
accusers, 8476, *śāṭan* [3]
my accusers[s], 2157, *-hem* [1]
accusers, 3742, *yārîb1* [1]

ACCUSES [2]
accuses, 3519, *yākaḥ* [1]
accuses, 7756+4200+2021+5477, *qûm+le-1+ha-+mišpāṭ* [1]

ACCUSING [1]
accusing, 8190, *rîb2* [1]

ACCUSTOMED [2]
accustomed to, 4341, *limmud* [2]

ACHAN [7]
Achan, 6575, *ʿākān* [6]
Achan[s], 2257, *-ô* [1]

ACHAR [1]
Achar, 6580, *ʿākār* [1]

ACHE [1]
ache, 3872, *kāʾab* [1]

ACHIEVE [4]
achieve, 6913, *ʿāśâ1* [3]
achieve purpose, 7503, *ṣālaḥ2* [1]

ACHIEVED [3]
achieved, 6913, *ʿāśâ1* [2]
achieved, *NIH/RPE* [1]

ACHIEVEMENT [1]
achievement, 4179+5126, *kišrôn+maʿăśeh* [1]

ACHIEVEMENTS [10]
achievements, 1476, *gebûrâ* [8]
achievements, 1821, *dābār* [2]

ACHISH [19]
Achish, 429, *ʾākîš* [19]

ACHOR [5]
Achor, 6574, *ʿākôr* [5]

ACKNOWLEDGE [30]
acknowledge, 3359, *yādaʿ* [21]
acknowledge, 5795, *nākar1* [4]
acknowledge, 10313, *yedaʿ* [3]
acknowledge, 6218, *sāpar* [1]
acknowledge holiness, 7727, *qādaš* [1]

ACKNOWLEDGED [6]
acknowledged, 3359, *yādaʿ* [3]
acknowledged as king, 4887, *mālak1* [1]
be acknowledged as holy, 7727, *qādaš* [1]
acknowledged, 10313, *yedaʿ* [1]

ACKNOWLEDGES [1]
acknowledges, 3359, *yādaʿ* [1]

ACKNOWLEDGMENT [2]
acknowledgment, 1981, *daʿat1* [2]

ACQUAINTANCES [1]
acquaintances, 3359, *yādaʿ* [1]

ACQUIRE [5]
acquire, 7864, *qānâ1* [2]
acquire property, 296, *ʾāḥaz1* [1]
acquire, 5162, *māṣāʾ* [1]
acquire great numbers, 8049, *rābâ1* [1]

ACQUIRED [12]
acquired, 6913, *ʿāśâ1* [4]
acquired, 8223, *rākaš* [2]
acquired property, 296, *ʾāḥaz1* [1]
acquired, 296, *ʾāḥaz1* [1]
acquired, 2118+4200, *hāyâ+le-1* [1]
acquired, 5162, *māṣāʾ* [1]
acquired, 5238, *miqneh* [1]
acquired, 7864, *qānâ1* [1]

ACQUIRES [2]
acquires, 5162, *māṣāʾ* [1]
acquires, 7864, *qānâ1* [1]

ACQUIRING [1]
acquiring, 4374, *lāqaḥ* [1]

ACQUIT [3]
acquit, 7405, *ṣādaq* [2]
acquit, 2342, *zākâ* [1]

ACQUITTING [2]
acquitting, 7405, *ṣādaq* [2]

ACRE [1]
acre, 5103+7538, *maʿănâ+ṣemed* [1]

ACROSS [40]
across, *AIT* [8]
across, 928+6298, *be-+ʿēber1* [4]
across, 6584, *ʿal2* [4]
across, 4946+6298, *min+ʿēber1* [3]
across, 4200, *le-1* [2]
bring across, 6296, *ʿābar1* [2]
across from, 6584+7156, *ʿal2+pāneh* [2]
across, 6584+7156, *ʿal2+pāneh* [2]
across, *NIH/RPE* [1]
across, 448, *ʾel* [1]
across, 928, *be-* [1]
across, 2025, *-â2* [1]
across from, 4946+6298, *min+ʿēber1* [1]
across the way, 4946+5584, *min+neged* [1]
came across, 5162, *māṣāʾ* [1]
bring across, 6296+6296, *ʿābar1+ʿābar1* [1]
goes across, 6296, *ʿābar1* [1]
lead across, 6296+4200+7156, *ʿābar1+le-1+pāneh* [1]
sent across, 6296, *ʿābar1* [1]
come across, 7003, *pāgaʿ* [1]
come across, 7925+4200+7156, *qārāʾ2+le-1+pāneh* [1]

ACSAH [5]
Acsah, 6578, *ʿaksâ* [5]

ACSHAPH [3]
Acshaph, 439, *ʾakšāp* [3]

ACT [30]
act, 6913, *ʿāśâ1* [17]
act corruptly, 8845, *šāḥat* [2]
act, 2118, *hāyâ* [1]
lewd act, 2365, *zimmâ1* [1]
act at once, 4554, *māhar1* [1]
act of impurity, 5614, *niddâ* [1]
act, 6641, *ʿāmad* [1]
act, 7188, *pāʿal* [1]
righteous act, 7407, *ṣedāqâ* [1]
act wisely, 8505, *śākal1* [1]
irreverent act, 8915, *šal* [1]
act deceitfully, 9438, *tālal* [1]
been caught in the act, 9530, *tāpaś* [1]

ACTED [25]
acted, 6913, *ʿāśâ1* [10]
acted wickedly, 8399, *rāšaʿ* [3]
acted unfaithfully, 5085+5086, *māʿal+maʿal1* [2]
acted, *NIH/RPE* [1]
acted treacherously, 953, *bāgad* [1]
acted wisely, 1067, *bîn* [1]
acted like a madman, 2147, *hālal3* [1]
acted very wickedly, 2472+2472, *ḥābal2+ḥābal2* [1]
acted unfaithfully, 5085, *māʿal* [1]
acted foolishly, 6118, *sākal* [1]
acted like a fool, 6118, *sākal* [1]
acted wickedly, 8317, *rāʿaʿ1* [1]
acted corruptly, 8845, *šāḥat* [1]

ACTING [5]
acting, 6913, *ʿāśâ1* [3]
acting, 5126, *maʿăśeh* [1]
acting as witness, 6386, *ʿûd1* [1]

ACTION [2]
action, 2006, *derek* [1]
take action, 6913, *ʿāśâ1* [1]

ACTIONS [16]
actions, 5095, *maʿălāl* [8]
actions, 6613, *ʿălîlâ* [6]

actions, 3338, *yād* [1]
actions, 5126, *maʿ^{a}śeh* [1]

ACTIVITY [3]
activity, 2914, *ḥēpeṣ* [2]
activity, 1821, *dābār* [1]

ACTS [26]
righteous acts, 7407, *ṣ^{e}dāqâ* [7]
mighty acts, 1476, *g^{e}bûrâ* [4]
acts, *AIT* [2]
acts of devotion, 2876, *ḥesed*[2] [2]
acts, 6913, *ʿāśâ*[1] [2]
acts of judgment, 9150, *šepeṭ* [2]
acts of power, 1476, *g^{e}bûrâ* [1]
lewd acts, 2365, *zimmâ*[1] [1]
acts, 5126, *maʿ^{a}śeh* [1]
acts like a prophet, 5547, *nābāʾ* [1]
acts, 7189, *pōʿal* [1]
kindest acts, 8171, *raḥ^{a}mîm* [1]
detestable acts, 9199, *šiqqûṣ* [1]

ACTUAL [1]
actual, *NIH/RPE* [1]

ACTUALLY [4]
actually, *NIH/RPE* [1]
actually, 434, *ʾākēn*[1] [1]
actually come, 995+995, *bôʾ+bôʾ* [1]
actually rule, 5440+5440, *māšal*[2]*+māšal*[2] [1]

ACZIB [4]
Aczib, 424, *ʾakzîb* [4]

ADADAH [1]
Adadah, 6368, *ʿadʿādâ* [1]

ADAH [8]
Adah, 6336, *ʿādâ*[3] [8]

ADAIAH [9]
Adaiah, 6347, *ʿ^{a}dāyâ* [8]
Adaiah, 6348, *ʿ^{a}dāyāhû* [1]

ADALIA [1]
Adalia, 130, *ʾ^{a}dalyāʾ* [1]

ADAM [12]
Adam, 134, *ʾādām*[3] [11]
Adam, 136, *ʾādām*[5] [1]

ADAM'S [1]
Adam's, 134, *ʾādām*[3] [1]

ADAMAH [1]
Adamah, 142, *ʾ^{a}dāmâ*[2] [1]

ADAMI NEKEB [1]
Adami Nekeb, 146, *ʾ^{a}dāmî hanneqeb* [1]

ADAR [9]
Adar, 160, *ʾ^{a}dār* [8]
Adar, 10009, *ʾ^{a}dār* [1]

ADBEEL [2]
Adbeel, 118, *ʾadb^{e}ʾēl* [2]

ADD [27]
add, 3578, *yāsap* [21]
add, 606, *ʾāmar*[1] [1]
add, 5595, *nāgaʿ* [1]
add, 6584, *ʿal*[2] [1]
add, 6913, *ʿāśâ*[1] [1]
add, 7928, *qārab* [1]
add to numbers, 8049, *rābâ*[1] [1]

ADDAR [2]
Addar, 161, *ʾaddār*[1] [1]
Addar, 162, *ʾaddār*[2] [1]

ADDED [29]
added, 606, *ʾāmar*[1] [15]
added, 3578, *yāsap* [6]
added, *NIH/RPE* [2]
yeast added, 2806, *ḥāmēṣ*[1] [1]
be added, 3578, *yāsap* [1]
added, 6388, *ʿôd* [1]
were added, 6388+3578, *ʿôd+yāsap* [1]
added, 6468, *ʿāzar* [1]
added, 8492, *śîm* [1]

ADDER [2]
adder, 704, *ʾepʿeh* [2]

ADDERS [1]
adders, 704, *ʾepʿeh* [1]

ADDING [5]
adding, 3578, *yāsap* [2]
adding, *NIH/RPE* [1]
adding to, 2256+907, *w^{e}-+ʾēt*[2] [1]
adding, 8049, *rābâ*[1] [1]

ADDITION [34]
in addition to, 4946+4200+963, *min+l^{e}-*[1]*+bad*[1] [18]
in addition to, 6584, *ʿal*[2] [4]
in addition to, 339, *ʾaḥar* [2]
in addition to, 448, *ʾel* [2]
in addition to, 4200+963, *l^{e}-*[1]*+bad*[1] [2]
in addition to, 907, *ʾēt*[2] [1]
in addition, 2256, *w^{e}-* [1]
in addition to, 2256, *w^{e}-* [1]
anything in addition, 3463, *yôtēr* [1]
in addition, 4200+963, *l^{e}-*[1]*+bad*[1] [1]
in addition, 4946+4200+963, *min+l^{e}-*[1]*+bad*[1] [1]

ADDITIONAL [3]
additional, 6369, *ʿādap* [2]
additional, 337, *ʾaḥēr*[1] [1]

ADDON [2]
Addon, 124, *ʾaddôn* [1]
Addon, 150, *ʾaddān* [1]

ADDRESS [1]
address, 1819, *dābar*[2] [1]

ADDS [3]
adds, 3578, *yāsap* [2]
adds length, 3578, *yāsap* [1]

ADHERE [1]
adhere to, 6913+3869, *ʿāśâ*[1]*+k^{e}-* [1]

ADIEL [3]
Adiel, 6346, *ʿ^{a}dîʾēl* [3]

ADIN [4]
Adin, 6350, *ʿādîn*[2] [4]

ADINA [1]
Adina, 6351, *ʿ^{a}dînāʾ* [1]

ADITHAIM [1]
Adithaim, 6353, *ʿ^{a}dîtayim* [1]

ADJOINING [5]
adjoining, *AIT* [1]
adjoining, 448+7156, *ʾel+pāneh* [1]
adjoining, 4200+6645, *l^{e}-*[1]*+ʿummâ*[1] [1]
adjoining, 6584+3338, *ʿal*[2]*+yād* [1]
adjoining section, 6584+3338, *ʿal*[2]*+yād* [1]

ADLAI [1]
Adlai, 6354, *ʿadlay* [1]

ADMAH [5]
Admah, 144, *ʾadmâ* [5]

ADMATHA [1]
Admatha, 148, *ʾadmātāʾ* [1]

ADMINISTER [5]
administer, *NIH/RPE* [1]
administer, 1906, *dîn*[1] [1]
administer, 6913, *ʿāśâ*[1] [1]
administer, 9149, *šāpaṭ* [1]
administer justice, 10169, *dîn*[1] [1]

ADMINISTERING [1]
administering, 9048, *šāmaʿ* [1]

ADMINISTRATOR [7]
administrator^{s}, 889+6584, *ʾ^{a}šer+ʿal*[2] [7]

ADMINISTRATORS [8]
administrators, 10518, *sārak* [5]
administrators, 5592, *nāgîd* [1]
administrators, 6913+4856, *ʿāśâ*[1]*+m^{e}lāʾkâ* [1]
administrators, 10525, *ʿ^{a}bîdâ* [1]

ADMIT [5]
admit, 665, *ʾāsap* [1]
admit guilt, 870, *ʾāšam* [1]
admit, 3344, *yādâ*[2] [1]
admit, 5583, *nāgad* [1]
admit in the right, 7405, *ṣādaq* [1]

ADMITTED [1]
admitted, 995, *bôʾ* [1]

ADMONISHED [2]
admonished, 6386, *ʿûd*[1] [2]

ADMONITION [2]
admonition, 5184, *miṣwâ* [2]

ADNA [2]
Adna, 6363, *ʿadnāʾ* [2]

ADNAH [2]
Adnah, 6365, *ʿadnâ* [1]
Adnah, 6367, *ʿadnaḥ* [1]

ADONI-BEZEK [3]
Adoni-Bezek, 152, *ʾ^{a}dōnî bezeq* [3]

ADONI-ZEDEK [2]
Adoni-Zedek, 155, *ʾ^{a}dōnî-ṣedeq* [2]

ADONIJAH [26]
Adonijah, 154, *ʾ^{a}dōniyyāhû* [17]
Adonijah, 153, *ʾ^{a}dōniyyâ* [7]
Adonijah, *NIH/RPE* [1]
Adonijah^{s}, 2257, *-ō* [1]

ADONIJAH'S [1]
Adonijah's, 4200+154, *l^{e}-*[1]*+ʾ^{a}dōniyyāhû* [1]

ADONIKAM [3]
Adonikam, 156, *ʾ^{a}dōnîqām* [3]

ADONIRAM [5]
Adoniram, 157, *ʾ^{a}dōnîrām* [4]
Adoniram, 2067, *h^{a}dôrām*[2] [1]

ADOPT [1]
adopt, 1047, *bāḥar*[1] [1]

ADOPTED [2]
adopted, 4340, *lāmad* [1]
adopted, 4374+4200+1426, *lāqaḥ+l^{e}-*[1]*+bat*[1] [1]

ADORAIM [1]
Adoraim, 126, *ʾ^{a}dôrayim* [1]

ADORE [1]
adore, 170, *ʾāhab* [1]

ADORN [7]
adorn, 6995, *pāʾar*[2] [2]
adorn, *NIH/RPE* [1]
adorn yourself, 3636, *yāpâ* [1]
adorn, 3636, *yāpâ* [1]
adorn, 6335, *ʿādâ*[2] [1]
adorn, 9322, *tabnît* [1]

ADORNED [8]
adorned, *AIT* [2]
adorned, 6335, *ʿādâ*[2] [2]
adorned, 3512, *yāṭab* [1]
adorned, 5010, *m^{e}sukâ* [1]
adorned, 6590+6584, *ʿālâ+ʿal*[2] [1]
adorned, 7596+4200+9514, *ṣāpâ*[2]*+l^{e}-*[1]*+tipʾeret* [1]

ADORNS [3]
adorns, 5533, *nāʾâ* [1]
adorns, 6335, *ʿādâ*[2] [1]
adorns head, 6996, *p^{e}ʾēr* [1]

ADRAMMELECH [3]
Adrammelech, 166, *ʾadrammelek*[2] [2]
Adrammelech, 165, *ʾadrammelek*[1] [1]

ADRIEL [2]
Adriel, 6377, ʿadrîʾēl [2]
ADULLAM [9]
Adullam, 6355, ʿ[a]dullām [8]
of Adullam, 6356, ʿ[a]dullāmî [1]
ADULLAMITE [2]
Adullamite, 6356, ʿ[a]dullāmî [2]
ADULTERER [2]
adulterer, 5537, nāʾap [2]
ADULTERERS [6]
adulterers, 5537, nāʾap [6]
ADULTERESS [9]
adulteress, 2424, zār [3]
adulteress, 5537, nāʾap [3]
adulteress, 851+2424, ʾiššâ+zār [2]
adulteress, 851+408, ʾiššâ+ʾîš[1] [1]
ADULTERIES [2]
adulteries, 5537, nāʾap [1]
adulteries, 5539, niʾupîm [1]
ADULTEROUS [5]
adulterous, 5537, nāʾap [2]
adulterous, 2388, zānâ[1] [1]
adulterous look, 2393, z[e]nûnîm [1]
adulterous, 2393, z[e]nûnîm [1]
ADULTERY [23]
commit adultery, 5537, nāʾap [7]
committed adultery, 5537, nāʾap [5]
committed adultery, 2388, zānâ[1] [2]
adultery, 5537, nāʾap [2]
commits adultery, 5537, nāʾap [2]
committed adultery with, 995+448, bôʾ+ʾel [1]
commit adultery, 2388, zānâ[1] [1]
guilty of the vilest adultery, 2388+2388, zānâ[1]+zānâ[1] [1]
adultery, 2393, z[e]nûnîm [1]
adultery, 5539, niʾupîm [1]
ADUMMIM [2]
Adummim, 147, ʾ[a]dummîm [2]
ADVANCE [15]
advance, 6590, ʿālâ [2]
advance, 7928, qārab [2]
advance, 8132, rûṣ [2]
advance, 910, ʾātâ [1]
advance, 995+995, bôʾ+bôʾ [1]
advance, 995, bôʾ [1]
advance, 3655, yāṣāʾ [1]
at advance, 4200+7156, l[e]-[1]+pāneh [1]
advance, 5825, nāsaʿ [1]
advance, 6296, ʿābar[1] [1]
advance, 7156+2025, pāneh+-â[2] [1]
advance, 7320, pāšaṭ [1]
ADVANCED [18]
well advanced, 995, bôʾ [7]
advanced, 6296, ʿābar[1] [3]
advanced, 2143, hālak [2]
advanced, 5602, nāgaš [2]
advanced, 995, bôʾ [1]
advanced, 3655, yāṣāʾ [1]
advanced, 6590, ʿālâ [1]
advanced, 8044, rōb [1]
ADVANCES [3]
advances, 6590, ʿālâ [2]
advances, 2143, hālak [1]
ADVANCING [2]
advancing, 995, bôʾ [1]
advancing, 3655, yāṣāʾ [1]
ADVANTAGE [8]
take advantage of, 3561, yānâ [2]
advantage, 3463, yôtēr [1]
advantage, 3603, yāʿal [1]
advantage, 3862, yitrôn [1]
advantage, 4639, môtār [1]
take advantage of, 6700, ʿānâ[2] [1]
take advantage, 6943, ʿāšaq [1]
ADVENTURERS [2]
adventurers, 7069, pāḥaz [1]
adventurers, 8199, rêq [1]
ADVERSARIES [13]
adversaries, 7756, qûm [3]
adversaries, 8533, śānēʾ [3]
adversaries, 7640, ṣar[2] [2]
adversaries, 6839, ʿār[1] [1]
adversaries, 7675, ṣārar[2] [1]
adversaries, 8477, śāṭān [1]
adversaries, 8806, šôrēr [1]
adversaries, 10568, ʿār [1]
ADVERSARY [6]
adversary, 8477, śāṭān [4]
adversary, 7640, ṣar[2] [2]
ADVERSITY [2]
adversity, 7639, ṣar[1] [1]
adversity, 7650, ṣārâ[1] [1]
ADVICE [34]
advice, 6783, ʿēṣâ[1] [15]
advice, 1821, dābār [4]
advice gave, 6783+3619, ʿēṣâ[1]+yāʿaṣ [3]
advice, 3619, yāʿaṣ [2]
advice given, 6783+3619, ʿēṣâ[1]+yāʿaṣ [2]
wise advice, 2683, ḥokmâ [1]
advice offered, 3619, yāʿaṣ [1]
give advice, 3619, yāʿaṣ [1]
giving advice, 3619+6783, yāʿaṣ+ʿēṣâ[1] [1]
seeking advice, 3619, yāʿaṣ [1]
take advice, 3619, yāʿaṣ [1]
advice, 9374, taḥbulôt [1]
advice, 10422, m[e]lak [1]
ADVISE [4]
advise, 3619, yāʿaṣ [3]
advise, 3619+6783, yāʿaṣ+ʿēṣâ[1] [1]
ADVISED [4]
advised, 3619, yāʿaṣ [3]
advised, 606, ʾāmar[1] [1]
ADVISER [3]
adviser, 3446, yôʿēṣ [1]
personal adviser, 5335, mērēaʿ[1] [1]
personal adviser, 8291, rēʿeh [1]
ADVISERS [20]
advisers, 3446, yôʿēṣ [6]
advisers, 10196, haddābar [4]
advisers, 8011+7156, rāʾâ[1]+pāneh [2]
advisers, 10011, ʾ[a]dargāzar [2]
advisers, 10325, yāʿēṭ [2]
trusted advisers, 586, ʾāman[1] [1]
advisers, 2682, ḥākām [1]
consulted advisers, 3619, yāʿaṣ [1]
royal advisers, 3913, kōhēn [1]
ADVOCATE [1]
advocate, 8446, śāhēd [1]
AFAR [16]
afar, 8158, rāḥôq [10]
afar, 5305, merḥāq [4]
stretches afar, 5305, merḥāq [1]
afar, 7891, qēṣ [1]
AFFAIR [2]
affair, 1821, dābār [2]
AFFAIRS [6]
affairs, 1821, dābār [3]
affairs, 2142, h[a]lîkâ [1]
government affairs, 10424, malkû [1]
affairs, 10525, ʿ[a]bîdâ [1]
AFFECT [1]
affect, 7188, pāʿal [1]
AFFECTED [3]
affected article, 5596, negaʿ [2]
affected, 928, b[e]- [1]
AFFECTION [3]
set affection, 3137, ḥāšaq[1] [2]
affection, 5883, nepeš [1]
AFFECTS [1]
affects, 4200, l[e]-[1] [1]
AFFIXING [1]
affixing seals, 3159, ḥatam [1]
AFFLICT [6]
afflict, 5782, nākâ [4]
afflict, 6700, ʿānâ[2] [2]
AFFLICTED [45]
afflicted, 6714, ʿānî [15]
afflicted, 6700, ʿānâ[2] [12]
afflicted, 5782, nākâ [4]
afflicted, 6705, ʿānāw [4]
afflicted, 5595, nāgaʿ [2]
afflicted, 5597, nāgap [2]
afflicted, 1868, dawwāy [1]
afflicted, 1895, dāḥaq [1]
afflicted with a disease, 2688, ḥālāʾ [1]
afflicted, 2703, ḥālâ[1] [1]
were afflicted, 5782, nākâ [1]
be afflicted, 6700, ʿānâ[2] [1]
AFFLICTING [1]
afflicting, 8845, šāḥat [1]
AFFLICTION [20]
affliction, 6715, ʿ[o]nî [14]
affliction, 4316, laḥaṣ [2]
affliction, 2716, ḥ[o]lî [1]
affliction, 6411, ʿāwōn [1]
bring affliction, 6700, ʿānâ[2] [1]
suffered affliction, 6700, ʿānâ[2] [1]
AFFLICTIONS [3]
afflictions, 5596, negaʿ [2]
afflictions, 4804, makkâ [1]
AFFORD [9]
afford, 5952+3338, nāśag+yād [6]
afford, 3338+5952, yād+nāśag [1]
afford, 5162+3338+1896, māṣāʾ+yād+day [1]
afford, 5595+3338+1896, nāgaʿ+yād+day [1]
AFIRE [1]
set afire, 4265, lāhaṭ[1] [1]
AFLAME [1]
aflame, 4258, lahab [1]
AFORETHOUGHT [5]
malice aforethought, 8533+4946+9453+8997, śānēʾ+min+t[e]môl+šilšōm [4]
malice aforethought, 8534, śinʾâ [1]
AFRAID [149]
afraid, 3707, yārēʾ[1] [118]
make afraid, 3006, ḥārad [9]
afraid, 3710, yārēʾ[4] [4]
afraid, 1593, gûr[3] [3]
afraid, 7064, pāḥad [3]
make afraid, 987, bāhal [2]
afraid, 3169, ḥātat [2]
afraid, *NIH/RPE* [1]
afraid[s], 606, ʾāmar[1] [1]
afraid, 1286, bāʿat [1]
afraid, 1793, dāʾag [1]
made afraid, 3707, yārēʾ[1] [1]
afraid, 3724, yārah [1]
afraid, 5877+7065+6584, nāpal+paḥad[1]+ʿal[2] [1]
made afraid, 10167, d[e]ḥal [1]
AFTER [510]
after, 339, ʾaḥar [205]
after, 2256, w[e]- [78]
after, 928, b[e]- [27]
after, 3869+889, k[e]+ʾ[a]šer [14]
after, 3869, k[e]- [12]
after, *NIH/RPE* [12]
after, 4200, l[e]-[1] [11]
after, 4946, min [11]
after that, 339, ʾaḥar [10]
after, *AIT* [8]
after, 6584, ʿal[2] [8]

chasing after, 8296, *reʿût*[2] [7]
day after, 4740, *moḥorāt* [6]
after, 339+4027, *ʾaḥar+kēn*[2] [4]
and after, 2256, *we-* [4]
after, 3954, *kî*[2] [4]
day after day, 3972+2021+3427,
kōl+ha-+yôm[1] [4]
after, 6330, *ʿad*[2] [4]
after, 448, *ʾel* [3]
after that, 2256, *we-* [3]
after, 4946+7891, *min+qēṣ* [3]
lusted after, 6311+6584, *ʿāgab+ʿal*[2] [3]
after, 10092, *bāʾtar* [3]
after this, 339, *ʾaḥar* [2]
look after, 1329, *bāqar* [2]
after, 2025, *-â*[2] [2]
after all, 3954, *kî*[2] [2]
after, 4200+7891, *le-*[1]*+qēṣ* [2]
look after, 8011, *rāʾâ*[1] [2]
chase after, 8103, *rādap* [2]
chasing after, 8301, *raʿyôn* [2]
after, 255, *ʾāz* [1]
after the time of, 339, *ʾaḥar* [1]
shortly after, 339, *ʾaḥar* [1]
after a while, 339+2021+1821+2021+465,
ʾaḥar+ha-+dābār+ha-+ʾēlleh [1]
lust after, 339+2388, *ʾaḥar+zānâ*[1] [1]
next after, 339, *ʾaḥar* [1]
runs after for favors, 339+2388, *ʾaḥar+zānâ*[1] [1]
some time after, 339, *ʾaḥar* [1]
after, 421, *ʾak* [1]
just after, 421, *ʾak* [1]
lusted after, 448+6311, *ʾel+ʿāgab* [1]
after, 561+3983, *ʿim+kālâ*[1] [1]
Sabbath after Sabbath, 928+3427+2021+8701
+928+3427+2021+8701, *be-+yôm*[1]*+ha-*
+šabbāt+be-+yôm[1]*+ha-+šabbāt* [1]
after, 928+3427, *be-+yôm*[1] [1]
after, 928+8079, *be-+regel* [1]
after, 928+9005, *be-+šēm*[1] [1]
even after, 928, *be-* [1]
go after ill-gotten gain, 1298+1299,
bāṣaʿ+beṣaʿ [1]
looks after, 1333, *baqqārâ* [1]
pressed hard after, 1815, *dābaq* [1]
after, 1821+928, *dābār+be-* [1]
sought after, 2011, *dāraš* [1]
after all, 2180, *hinnēh* [1]
after this, 2256, *we-* [1]
after, 2256+1685, *we-+gam* [1]
and even after, 2256, *we-* [1]
lusted after, 2388+339, *zānâ*[1]*+ʾaḥar* [1]
lust after, 2773, *ḥāmad* [1]
day after day, 3427, *yôm*[1] [1]
after, 3869+9005, *ke-+šēm*[1] [1]
after, 3983, *kālâ*[1] [1]
one kind after another, 4200+5476+2157,
le-[1]*+mišpāḥâ+-hem* [1]
after, 4946+7895, *min+qāṣeh* [1]
after, 4946+1896+928, *min+day+be-* [1]
after, 4946+339, *min+ʾaḥar* [1]
after, 4946+7921, *min+qeṣāt* [1]
lusted after, 6311, *ʿāgab* [1]
look after, 6524+8492+6584, *ʿayin*[1]*+śîm+ʿal*[2]
[1]
time after time, 8041+6961, *rab*[1]*+ʿēt* [1]
time after time, 8049, *rābâ*[1] [1]
run after, 8103, *rādap* [1]
look after, 8492+6524+6584,
śîm+ʿayin[1]*+ʿal*[2] [1]
day after tomorrow, 8958, *šelîšî* [1]
day after, 8958, *šelîšî* [1]
the day after tomorrow, 8992, *šālaš* [1]
looks after, 9068, *šāmar* [1]
after, 9108, *šēnî* [1]
day after day, 9458+3429, *tāmîd+yômām* [1]
after, 10021, *ʾaḥar* [1]
after, 10341, *ke-* [1]

AFTERBIRTH [1]
afterbirth, 8953, *šilyâ* [1]

AFTERNOON [1]
afternoon, 5742+2021+3427,
nāṭâ+ha-+yôm[1] [1]

AFTERWARD [29]
afterward, 339+4027, *ʾaḥar+kēn*[2] [15]
afterward, 339, *ʾaḥar* [7]
afterward, 2256, *we-* [4]
and afterward, 2256, *we-* [3]

AGAG [7]
Agag, 97, *ʾagag* [7]

AGAGITE [5]
Agagite, 98, *ʾagāgî* [5]

AGAIN [290]
again, 6388, *ʿôd* [72]
again, 8740, *šûb*[1] [34]
again, 3578, *yāsap* [26]
again, 3578+6388, *yāsap+ʿôd* [22]
again and again, 8899, *šākam* [22]
again, *NIH/RPE* [21]
again, 2256, *we-* [20]
again, *AIT* [13]
again, 9108, *šēnî* [5]
once again, 6388, *ʿôd* [4]
again and again, 8740, *šûb*[1] [4]
again, 1685, *gam* [3]
do again, 3578, *yāsap* [3]
blessed again and again, 1385+1385,
bārak[2]*+bārak*[2] [2]
once again, 3578+6388, *yāsap+ʿôd* [2]
once again, 3578, *yāsap* [2]
never again, 4202+4200+6409, *lōʾ+le-*[1]*+ʿôlām*
[2]
again and again bursts, 7287+7288+7288,
pāraṣ+pereṣ[1]*+pereṣ*[1] [2]
again and again, 8899+2256+8938,
šākam+we-+šālaḥ [2]
do again, 9101, *šānâ*[1] [2]
again, 339, *ʾaḥar* [1]
again, 1685+928+2021+7193+2021+2085,
gam+be-+ha-+paʿam+ha-+hûʾ [1]
and again, 2256, *we-* [1]
live again, 2649, *ḥāyâ* [1]
make again, 3578+6388, *yāsap+ʿôd* [1]
once again, 3869+2021+8037, *ke-+ha-+riʾšôn*
[1]
again, 4200+6409, *le-*[1]*+ʿôlām* [1]
ever again, 4200+5905+5905,
le-[1]*+nēṣaḥ*[1]*+nēṣaḥ*[1] [1]
time and again, 4202+285+2256+4202+9109,
lōʾ+ʾeḥād+we-+lōʾ+šenayim [1]
rise again, 5951, *nāśāʾ* [1]
once again, 6015, *sābab* [1]
do again, 6388+3578, *ʿôd+yāsap* [1]
ever again, 6388, *ʿôd* [1]
go over the vines again, 6618+339,
ʿālal[1]*+ʾaḥar* [1]
restore again, 8740, *šûb*[1] [1]
again be used, 8740, *šûb*[1] [1]
again give allegiance, 8740+4213, *šûb*[1]*+lēb* [1]
again, 8740+9108, *šûb*[1]*+šēnî* [1]
back again, 8740, *šûb*[1] [1]
came again, 8740, *šûb*[1] [1]
made prosperous again, 8740+8654,
šûb[1]*+šebût* [1]
pass again, 8740, *šûb*[1] [1]
try again, 8740, *šûb*[1] [1]
turn again, 8740, *šûb*[1] [1]
turned again, 8740, *šûb*[1] [1]
again, 9101, *šānâ*[1] [1]
did again, 9101, *šānâ*[1] [1]

AGAINST [1095]
against, 6584, *ʿal*[2] [400]
against, 928, *be-* [260]
against, 448, *ʾel* [128]
against, 4200, *le-*[1] [91]
against, *AIT* [46]
against, 6640, *ʿim* [42]
against, 907, *ʾēt*[2] [34]
against, 4200+7156, *le-*[1]*+pāneh* [13]
against, 7925, *qārāʾ*[2] [13]
against, 4946, *min* [9]
against, *NIH/RPE* [7]
against, 10542, *ʿal* [6]
against, 928+7156, *be-+pāneh* [5]
against, 4946+9393+3338, *min+taḥat*[1]*+yād* [4]
against, 4946+6584, *min+ʿal*[2] [3]
against, 4946+7156, *min+pāneh* [3]
against, 339, *ʾaḥar* [2]
against, 6643, *ʿimmād* [2]
against, 10378, *le-* [2]
against, 928+6330, *be-+ʿad*[2] [1]
against, 1068, *bayin* [1]
against, 2025, *-â*[2] [1]
turn against, 2118+4200+8477,
hāyâ+le-[1]*+śāṭān* [1]
plot against, 3108+928+4222,
ḥāšab+be-+lēbāb [1]
succeed against, 4200+5584, *le-*[1]*+neged* [1]
against, 4202+3869, *lōʾ+ke-* [1]
against, 4946+3338, *min+yād* [1]
defense against, 4946+7156, *min+pāneh* [1]
against, 5584, *neged* [1]
bear a grudge against, 5757, *nāṭar*[1] [1]
turn against, 6015, *sābab* [1]
waged against from all sides, 6015, *sābab* [1]
revolted against, 6240, *sārâ*[2] [1]
brought charges against, 6386, *ʿûd*[1] [1]
against side, 6584, *ʿal*[2] [1]
against, 6584+7156, *ʿal*[2]*+pāneh* [1]
charged against, 6584, *ʿal*[2] [1]
set against, 6584, *ʿal*[2] [1]
has a claim against, 7709, *qādam* [1]
held a grudge against, 8475, *śāṭam* [1]
holds a grudge against, 8475, *śāṭam* [1]
against, 9481, *tenûʾâ* [1]
against, 10378+10608, *le-+ṣad* [1]
against, 10554, *ʿim* [1]

AGATE [2]
agate, 8648, *šebô* [2]

AGE [38]
age, 1201, *bēn*[1] [10]
old age, 8484, *śêbâ* [6]
age, 1201+9102, *bēn*[1]*+šānâ*[2] [4]
old age, 2421, *zequnîm* [4]
old age, 2420, *ziqnâ* [3]
military age, 4878, *milḥāmâ* [2]
age of childbearing, 784+3869+2021+851,
ʾōraḥ+ke-+ha-+ʾiššâ [1]
age, 1426+9102, *bat*[1]*+šānâ*[2] [1]
age, 1636, *gîl*[2] [1]
of ripe old age, 2418, *zāqēn*[2] [1]
old age, 2419, *zōqen* [1]
age, 3427, *yôm*[1] [1]
age, 8044+3427, *rōb+yôm*[1] [1]
age, 8483, *śêb* [1]
age, 10120+10732, *bar*[2]*+šenâ*[2] [1]

AGE-OLD [4]
age-old, 6409, *ʿôlām* [2]
age-old, 1887+2256+1887, *dôr*[2]*+we-+dôr*[2] [1]
age-old, 7704, *qedûmîm* [1]

AGED [11]
aged, 2418, *zāqēn*[2] [5]
aged, 3813, *yāšîš* [2]
aged, 2416+4394, *zāqēn*[1]*+meʾōd* [1]
aged, 3844, *yāšēš* [1]
aged, 8484, *śêbâ* [1]
aged wine, 9069, *šemer*[1] [1]

AGEE [1]
Agee, 96, *ʾāgēʾ* [1]

AGENT [1]
agent, 4200+3338, *le-*[1]*+yād* [1]

AGES [5]
ages, 1201+9102, *bēn*[1]*+šānâ*[2] [2]
ages, 1148+7584, *bekōrâ+seʿîrâ* [1]
ages, 6409, *ʿôlām* [1]
ages, 9102, *šānâ*[2] [1]

AGGRESSION [1]
aggression, 5284, *murdāp* [1]

AGGRESSIVE [2]
aggressive, 4431, *mebûšâ* [2]

AGGRESSOR [1]
- aggressor, 8252, *rāmas* [1]

AGHAST [2]
- aghast, 9449, *tāmah* [1]
- look aghast, 9449, *tāmah* [1]

AGO [28]
- long ago, 4946+255, *min+ʾāz* [5]
- long ago, 7710, *qedem* [5]
- long ago, 6409, *ʿôlām* [4]
- long ago, 4200+4946+8158, *lᵉ-[1]+min+rāḥôq* [2]
- long ago, 4946+6409, *min+ʿôlām* [2]
- long ago, 4946+7710, *min+qedem* [2]
- long ago, 4946+8158, *min+rāḥôq* [2]
- ago, *AIT* [1]
- long ago, 928+2021+8037, *bᵉ-+ha-+riʾšôn* [1]
- ago, 2021+3427, *ha-+yôm[1]* [1]
- long ago, 4200+6409, *lᵉ-[1]+ʿôlām* [1]
- long ago, 4946+3427+7710, *min+yôm[1]+qedem* [1]
- ago, 10427+10622+10180, *min+qadmâ+dᵉnâ* [1]

AGONY [6]
- in agony, 987, *bāhal* [1]
- in agony, 1631, *gîaḥ[1]* [1]
- writhe in agony, 2655+2655, *ḥîl[1]+ḥîl[1]* [1]
- writhe in agony, 2655+4394, *ḥîl[1]+mᵉʿōd* [1]
- agony, 7815, *qîr[1]* [1]
- mortal agony, 8358, *reṣaḥ* [1]

AGREE [5]
- agree, 2118+3869+285, *hāyâ+kᵉ-+ʾeḥād* [2]
- agree, 9048, *šāmaʿ* [2]
- agree to demands, 14, *ʾābâ* [1]

AGREED [22]
- agreed, 9048, *šāmaʿ* [9]
- agreed, 3283, *yāʾal[2]* [2]
- agreed, 252, *ʾût* [1]
- agreed, 606, *ʾāmar[1]* [1]
- agreed, 2176, *hēn[1]* [1]
- agreed, 2489, *ḥābar[2]* [1]
- agreed, 3359, *yādaʿ* [1]
- agreed, 3619, *yāʿaṣ* [1]
- agreed, 4026, *kēn[1]* [1]
- agreed, 4202, *lōʾ* [1]
- agreed, 7691, *qābal* [1]
- agreed with, 9048+4200+7754, *šāmaʿ+lᵉ-[1]+qôl* [1]
- agreed, 10324, *yᵉʿaṭ* [1]

AGREEMENT [9]
- agreement, 1382, *bᵉrît* [3]
- sworn agreement, 460, *ʾālâ[1]* [1]
- binding agreement, 591, *ʾᵃmānâ[1]* [1]
- coming to an agreement, 2489, *ḥābar[2]* [1]
- agreement, 2603, *ḥōzeh[2]* [1]
- agreement, 2607, *ḥāzût* [1]
- met by agreement, 3585, *yāʿad* [1]

AGREEMENTS [1]
- agreements, 1382, *bᵉrît* [1]

AGUR [1]
- Agur, 101, *ʾāgûr* [1]

AH [15]
- ah, 177, *ʾᵃhāh* [9]
- ah, 2098, *hôy* [3]
- ah, 208, *ʾôy* [1]
- ah, 2027, *heʾāḥ* [1]
- ah, 8011, *rāʾâ[1]* [1]

AHA [11]
- aha, 2027, *heʾāḥ* [11]

AHAB [85]
- Ahab, 281, *ʾaḥʾāb* [79]
- Ahab, *NIH/RPE* [3]
- Ahab[s], 2257, *-ô* [2]
- Ahab, 282, *ʾeḥāb* [1]

AHAB'S [8]
- Ahab's, 281, *ʾaḥʾāb* [7]
- Ahab's[s], 2257, *-ô* [1]

AHARAH [1]
- Aharah, 341, *ʾaḥraḥ* [1]

AHARHEL [1]
- Aharhel, 342, *ʾᵃḥarḥēl* [1]

AHASBAI [1]
- Ahasbai, 335, *ʾᵃḥasbay* [1]

AHAVA [3]
- Ahava, 178, *ʾahᵃwāʾ* [3]

AHAZ [42]
- Ahaz, 298, *ʾāḥāz* [41]
- Ahaz[s], 2257, *-ô* [1]

AHAZIAH [39]
- Ahaziah, 302, *ʾᵃḥazyāhû* [27]
- Ahaziah, 301, *ʾᵃḥazyâ* [7]
- Ahaziah[s], 2257, *-ô* [2]
- Ahaziah, 3370, *yᵉhôʾāḥāz* [2]
- Ahaziah, *NIH/RPE* [1]

AHAZIAH'S [5]
- Ahaziah's, 302, *ʾᵃḥazyāhû* [4]
- Ahaziah's, *NIH/RPE* [1]

AHBAN [1]
- Ahban, 283, *ʾaḥbān* [1]

AHEAD [62]
- ahead, 4200+7156, *lᵉ-[1]+pāneh* [45]
- straight ahead, 448+6298+7156, *ʾel+ʿēber[1]+pāneh* [3]
- go ahead, 2143, *hālak* [3]
- ahead, *AIT* [2]
- ahead, 4200, *lᵉ-[1]* [1]
- straight ahead, 4200+5790, *lᵉ-[1]+nōkaḥ* [1]
- ahead, 4946+4200+7156, *min+lᵉ-[1]+pāneh* [1]
- straight ahead, 5019, *mᵉsillâ* [1]
- drove ahead, 5627, *nāhag[1]* [1]
- go ahead, 5742, *nāṭâ* [1]
- moved on ahead, 6296, *ʿābar[1]* [1]
- ahead, 6584+7156, *ʿal[2]+pāneh* [1]
- gone ahead, 6590, *ʿālâ* [1]

AHER [1]
- Aher, 338, *ʾaḥēr[2]* [1]

AHI [2]
- Ahi, 306, *ʾᵃḥî* [2]

AHIAH [1]
- Ahiah, 308, *ʾᵃḥiyyâ* [1]

AHIAM [2]
- Ahiam, 307, *ʾᵃḥîʾām* [2]

AHIAN [1]
- Ahian, 319, *ʾaḥyān* [1]

AHIEZER [6]
- Ahiezer, 323, *ʾᵃḥîʿezer* [6]

AHIHUD [2]
- Ahihud, 310, *ʾᵃḥîhûd* [1]
- Ahihud, 312, *ʾᵃḥîḥud* [1]

AHIJAH [21]
- Ahijah, 308, *ʾᵃḥiyyâ* [16]
- Ahijah, 309, *ʾᵃḥiyyāhû* [5]

AHIJAH'S [1]
- Ahijah's, 308, *ʾᵃḥiyyâ* [1]

AHIKAM [20]
- Ahikam, 324, *ʾᵃḥîqām* [20]

AHILUD [5]
- Ahilud, 314, *ʾᵃḥîlûd* [5]

AHIMAAZ [15]
- Ahimaaz, 318, *ʾᵃḥîmaʿaṣ* [15]

AHIMAN [4]
- Ahiman, 317, *ʾᵃḥîman* [4]

AHIMELECH [19]
- Ahimelech, 316, *ʾᵃḥîmelek* [18]
- Ahimelech, *NIH/RPE* [1]

AHIMOTH [1]
- Ahimoth, 315, *ʾᵃḥîmôt* [1]

AHINADAB [1]
- Ahinadab, 320, *ʾᵃḥînādāb* [1]

AHINOAM [7]
- Ahinoam, 321, *ʾᵃḥînōʿam* [7]

AHIO [6]
- Ahio, 311, *ʾaḥyô* [6]

AHIRA [5]
- Ahira, 327, *ʾᵃḥîraʿ* [5]

AHIRAM [1]
- Ahiram, 325, *ʾᵃḥîrām* [1]

AHIRAMITE [1]
- Ahiramite, 326, *ʾᵃḥîrāmî* [1]

AHISAMACH [3]
- Ahisamach, 322, *ʾᵃḥîsāmāk* [3]

AHISHAHAR [1]
- Ahishahar, 328, *ʾᵃḥîšāḥar* [1]

AHISHAR [1]
- Ahishar, 329, *ʾᵃḥîšār* [1]

AHITHOPHEL [17]
- Ahithophel, 330, *ʾᵃḥîtōpel* [17]

AHITHOPHEL'S [3]
- Ahithophel's, 330, *ʾᵃḥîtōpel* [3]

AHITUB [15]
- Ahitub, 313, *ʾᵃḥîṭûb* [15]

AHLAB [1]
- Ahlab, 331, *ʾaḥlāb* [1]

AHLAI [2]
- Ahlai, 333, *ʾaḥlāy* [2]

AHOAH [1]
- Ahoah, 291, *ʾᵃḥôaḥ* [1]

AHOHITE [5]
- Ahohite, 292, *ʾᵃḥôḥî* [4]
- Ahohite, 1201+292, *bēn[1]+ʾᵃḥôḥî* [1]

AHUMAI [1]
- Ahumai, 293, *ʾᵃḥûmay* [1]

AHUZZAM [1]
- Ahuzzam, 303, *ʾᵃḥuzzām* [1]

AHUZZATH [1]
- Ahuzzath, 304, *ʾᵃḥuzzat* [1]

AHZAI [1]
- Ahzai, 300, *ʾaḥzay* [1]

AI [37]
- Ai, 6504, *ʿay* [36]
- Ai[s], 2021+6551, *ha-+ʿîr[1]* [1]

AIAH [4]
- Aiah, 371, *ʾayyâ[2]* [4]

AIAH'S [2]
- Aiah's, 371, *ʾayyâ[2]* [2]

AIATH [1]
- Aiath, 6569, *ʿayyat* [1]

AID [9]
- aid, 6476, *ʿezrâ[1]* [3]
- surely come to aid, 7212+7212, *pāqad+pāqad* [3]
- come to aid, 6842, *ʿārab[1]* [1]
- come to aid, 7212, *pāqad* [1]
- come to the aid of, 7212, *pāqad* [1]

AIDE [5]
- aide, 9250, *šārat* [4]
- aide, 5853, *naʿar[2]* [1]

AIJA [1]

Aija, 6509, *ʿayyâ* [1]

AIJALON [10]

Aijalon, 389, *ʾayyālôn* [10]

AILS [1]

ails, 5344, *māraṣ* [1]

AIM [2]

aim, 2005, *dārak* [1]

aim, 3922, *kûn*^{1} [1]

AIN [5]

Ain, 6526, *ʿayin*^{3} [5]

AIR [44]

air, 9028, *šāmayim* [40]

air, 10723, *š*^{e}*mayin* [3]

air, 8120, *rûaḥ* [1]

AIRING [1]

airing, 1655, *gālâ* [1]

AKAN [2]

Akan, 6826, *ʿ*^{a}*qān* [2]

AKKAD [1]

Akkad, 422, *ʾakkad* [1]

AKKUB [8]

Akkub, 6822, *ʿaqqûb* [8]

ALAMOTH [2]

alamoth, 6628, *ʿ*^{a}*lāmôt* [2]

ALARM [6]

alarm, 987, *bāhal* [1]

alarm, 1286, *bāʿat* [1]

alarm, 2905, *ḥāpaz* [1]

alarm, 3006, *ḥārad* [1]

sound alarm, 8131, *rûaʿ* [1]

alarm, 10097, *b*^{e}*hal* [1]

ALARMED [5]

alarmed, 3707, *yārēʾ*^{1} [2]

alarmed, 987, *bāhal* [1]

alarmed, 2905, *ḥāpaz* [1]

alarmed, 10097, *b*^{e}*hal* [1]

ALAS [11]

alas, 2098, *hôy* [5]

alas, 208, *ʾôy* [3]

alas, 177, *ʾ*^{a}*hāh* [1]

alas, 277, *ʾāḥ*^{1} [1]

alas, 2081, *hāh* [1]

ALCOVE [2]

alcove, 9288, *tāʾ* [2]

ALCOVES [9]

alcoves, 9288, *tāʾ* [8]

alcoves for the guards, 9288, *tāʾ* [1]

ALEMETH [4]

Alemeth, 6631, *ʿālemet*^{2} [3]

Alemeth, 6630, *ʿālemet*^{1} [1]

ALERT [4]

on the alert, 3922, *kûn*^{1} [1]

alert, 7992+7993, *qāšab+qešeb* [1]

alert, 7993, *qešeb* [1]

alert, 8883, *šît*^{1} [1]

ALGUM [1]

algum, 454, *ʾalgûmmîm* [1]

ALGUMWOOD [2]

algumwood, 6770+454, *ʿēṣ+ʾalgûmmîm* [2]

ALIEN [73]

alien, 1731, *gēr* [61]

alien, 5799, *nokrî* [4]

alien, 2424, *zār* [2]

alien, 1591, *gûr*^{1} [1]

lived as an alien, 1591, *gûr*^{1} [1]

living as an alien, 1591, *gûr*^{1} [1]

alien, 4472, *māgôr*^{2} [1]

live as an alien, 4472, *māgôr*^{2} [1]

alien, 5797, *nēkār* [1]

ALIEN'S [1]

alien's, 1731, *gēr* [1]

ALIENATED [1]

alienated, 8178, *rāḥaq* [1]

ALIENS [30]

aliens, 1731, *gēr* [26]

aliens, 1591, *gûr*^{1} [2]

aliens, 2424, *zār* [2]

ALIKE [22]

alike, 3869, *k*^{e}*-* [4]

alike, 3480, *yaḥad* [3]

alike, 3481, *yaḥdāw* [3]

and alike, 6330, *ʿad*^{2} [3]

alike, 285, *ʾeḥād* [2]

alike, *AIT* [1]

and alike, 2256, *w*^{e}*-* [1]

both alike, 3869, *k*^{e}*-* [1]

alike, 4027, *kēn*^{2} [1]

alike, 4200+6645, *l*^{e}*-*^{1}*+ʿummâ*^{1} [1]

and alike, 6584, *ʿal*^{2} [1]

and alike, 6640, *ʿim* [1]

ALIVE [57]

alive, 2645, *ḥay*^{2} [34]

keep alive, 2649, *ḥāyâ* [7]

kept alive, 2649, *ḥāyâ* [3]

leave alive, 2649, *ḥāyâ* [3]

leave alive, 8636, *šāʾar* [2]

makes alive, 2649, *ḥāyâ* [1]

stay alive, 2649, *ḥāyâ* [1]

be left alive, 3855, *yātar* [1]

been left alive, 3855, *yātar* [1]

alive, 5883+928, *nepeš+b*^{e}*-* [1]

while still alive, 6584+7156, *ʿal*^{2}*+pāneh* [1]

keep themselves alive, 8740+5883, *šûb*^{1}*+nepeš* [1]

keep themselves alive, 8740+906+5883+4392, *šûb*^{1}*+ʾēt*^{1}*+nepeš+-ām* [1]

ALL [3748]*

all, 3972, *kōl* [3246]

all, *NIH/RPE* [102]

all, *AIT* [89]

all, 10353, *kōl* [36]

all around, 6017, *sābîb* [23]

all around, 6017+6017, *sābîb+sābîb* [17]

all generations, 1887+2256+1887, *dôr*^{2}*+w*^{e}*-+dôr*^{2} [14]

on all sides, 6017, *sābîb* [13]

all, 3480, *yaḥad* [8]

all, 3481, *yaḥdāw* [7]

all, 6017, *sābîb* [5]

all, 8044, *rōb* [5]

all, 408, *ʾîš*^{1} [4]

ALL-NIGHT [1]

all-night, 3972+2021+4326, *kōl+ha-+laylâ* [1]

ALLAMMELECH [1]

Allammelech, 526, *ʾallammelek* [1]

ALLEGIANCE [3]

swear allegiance, 8678, *šābaʿ* [1]

sworn allegiance, 8678+8652, *šābaʿ+š*^{e}*bûʿâ* [1]

again give allegiance, 8740+4213, *šûb*^{1}*+lēb* [1]

ALLEGORY [1]

allegory, 2648, *ḥîdâ* [1]

ALLIANCE [8]

made an alliance, 2489, *ḥābar*^{2} [2]

alliance, 1382, *b*^{e}*rît* [1]

made an alliance, 3161, *ḥātan* [1]

alliance, 3838, *yāšār*^{1} [1]

alliance, 4797, *mêšārîm* [1]

forming an alliance, 5818+5011, *nāsak*^{1}*+massēkâ*^{1} [1]

alliance, 7736, *qāhāl* [1]

ALLIED [8]

allied with, 907, *ʾēt*^{2} [2]

allied, *AIT* [1]

allied, 1251+1382, *baʿal*^{1}*+b*^{e}*rît* [1]

allied with, 2489, *ḥābar*^{2} [1]

allied himself by marriage, 3161, *ḥātan* [1]

allied, 5663, *nûaḥ*^{1} [1]

allied with, 6468, *ʿāzar* [1]

ALLIES [13]

allies, 170, *ʾāhab* [4]

allies, 408+1382, *ʾîš*^{1}*+b*^{e}*rît* [1]

allies, 476, *ʾallûp*^{1} [1]

allies, 2432, *z*^{e}*rôaʿ* [1]

allies, 2489, *ḥābar*^{2} [1]

allies, 6164, *sāmak* [1]

allies, 6468, *ʿāzar* [1]

allies, 6476, *ʿezrâ*^{1} [1]

allies^{s}, 8611+6640, *ša-+ʿim* [1]

allies, 8969, *šālēm*^{2} [1]

ALLOCATE [1]

allocate, 5877, *nāpal* [1]

ALLON [1]

Allon, 474, *ʾallôn*^{2} [1]

ALLON BACUTH [1]

Allon Bacuth, 475, *ʾallôn bākût* [1]

ALLOT [3]

allot, 5877, *nāpal* [3]

ALLOTMENT [13]

allotment, 1598, *gôrāl* [5]

allotment, 2750, *ḥēleq*^{2} [4]

allotment, *NIH/RPE* [2]

allotment, 2976, *ḥōq* [1]

regular allotment, 2976, *ḥōq* [1]

ALLOTS [4]

allots, 2745, *ḥālaq*^{2} [1]

allots, 4946, *min* [1]

allots, 5877, *nāpal* [1]

allots to, 6640, *ʿim* [1]

ALLOTTED [32]

allotted, 928+2021+1598, *b*^{e}*-+ha-+gôrāl* [4]

allotted, 5877, *nāpal* [4]

allotted, *AIT* [3]

allotted, 1598, *gôrāl* [3]

allotted, 2118+1598, *hāyâ+gôrāl* [2]

allotted, 5989+928+2021+1598, *nātan+b*^{e}*-+ha-+gôrāl* [2]

allotted territory, 1473, *g*^{e}*bûl* [1]

allotted portions, 1474, *g*^{e}*bûlâ* [1]

allotted inheritance, 1598, *gôrāl* [1]

territory allotted, 1598, *gôrāl* [1]

allotted, 2118+928+2021+1598, *hāyâ+b*^{e}*-+ha-+gôrāl* [1]

allotted, 2475, *ḥebel*^{2} [1]

be allotted, 2745, *ḥālaq*^{2} [1]

allotted time, 3427, *yôm*^{1} [1]

allotted, 4200, *l*^{e}*-*^{1} [1]

allotted, 5031, *mispār*^{1} [1]

allotted, 5706, *nāḥal* [1]

been allotted, 5706, *nāḥal* [1]

allotted, 5989, *nātan* [1]

been allotted, 5989, *nātan* [1]

ALLOTTING [1]

allotting, 2745, *ḥālaq*^{2} [1]

ALLOW [13]

allow, 5989, *nātan* [5]

allow, *AIT* [3]

allow to live, 2649, *ḥāyâ* [1]

allow pity, 2798, *ḥāmal* [1]

allow to remain, 3855, *yātar* [1]

allow to possess, 5989, *nātan* [1]

allow to dwell, 8905, *šākan* [1]

ALLOWANCE [2]

allowance, 786, *ʾ*^{a}*ruḥâ* [2]

ALLOWED [21]

allowed, 5989, *nātan* [4]

allowed, *AIT* [2]

allowed to live, 2649, *ḥāyâ* [2]

allowed, 3523, *yākōl* [2]

allowed, 5663, *nûaḥ*[1] [2]
allowed, *NIH/RPE* [1]
allowed, 401+646, *'ayin*[1]*+'ānas* [1]
allowed to, 3523, *yākōl* [1]
allowed, 4200, *l*[e]*-*[1] [1]
allowed to remain, 5663, *nûaḥ*[1] [1]
not be allowed, 7153, *pen* [1]
allowed to see, 8011, *rā'â*[1] [1]
allowed to fall into ruin, 8845, *šāḥat* [1]
were allowed, 10314, *y*[e]*hab* [1]

ALLOWING [2]
allowing, *AIT* [1]
allowing, 5989, *nātan* [1]

ALLOWS [1]
allows, 5989, *nātan* [1]

ALLURE [1]
allure, 7331, *pātā*[1] [1]

ALLURING [1]
alluring, 3202+2834, *ṭôb*[2]*+ḥēn*[1] [1]

ALLY [2]
chosen ally, 170, *'āhab* [1]
ally, 1815, *dābaq* [1]

ALMIGHTY [333]
Almighty, 7372, *ṣābā'*[2] [285]
Almighty, 8724, *šadday* [48]

ALMODAD [2]
Almodad, 525, *'almôdād* [2]

ALMON [1]
Almon, 6626, *'almôn* [1]

ALMON DIBLATHAIM [2]
Almon Diblathaim, 6627, *'almôn diblātayim* [2]

ALMOND [7]
shaped like almond flowers, 5481, *m*[e]*šuqqād* [4]
almond tree, 9196, *šāqēd* [2]
almond, 4280, *lûz*[2] [1]

ALMONDS [2]
almonds, 9196, *šāqēd* [2]

ALMOST [8]
almost, 3869+5071, *k*[e]*-+m*[e]*'aṭ* [2]
almost, *AIT* [1]
almost upon, 1815, *dābaq* [1]
almost, 4394, *m*[e]*'ōd* [1]
almost to a man, 6330+9462+4392, *'ad*[2]*+tāmam+-ām* [1]
almost, 6388+5071, *'ôd+m*[e]*'aṭ* [1]
almost, 8332, *rāpâ*[1] [1]

ALMUGWOOD [3]
almugwood, 6770+523, *'ēṣ+'almuggîm* [3]

ALOES [4]
aloes, 189, *'*[a]*hālôt* [2]
aloes, 193, *'*[a]*hālîm*[1] [2]

ALONE [90]
alone, 4200+963, *l*[e]*-*[1]*+bad*[1] [40]
alone, *AIT* [6]
alone, 970, *bādād* [6]
alone, 421, *'ak* [4]
leave alone, 5663, *nûaḥ*[1] [4]
alone, *NIH/RPE* [3]
let alone, 2532, *ḥādal*[1] [3]
let alone, 8332, *rāpâ*[1] [3]
alone, 928+1727+2257, *b*[e]*-+gap*[2]*+-ô* [2]
leave alone, 6073+4946, *sûr*[1]*+min* [2]
alone, 8891, *šakkûl* [2]
all alone, 401+9108, *'ayin*[1]*+šēnî* [1]
you alone, 911+911, *'attâ+'attâ* [1]
alone, 928+285, *b*[e]*-+'eḥād* [1]
alone, 969, *bādad* [1]
wandering alone, 969, *bādad* [1]
he alone, 2085, *hû'* [1]
leave alone, 2532+4946, *ḥādal*[1]*+min* [1]
me alone, 3276+638, *-î+'*[a]*nî* [1]
alone, 3480, *yaḥad* [1]
alone, 3481, *yaḥdāw* [1]
all alone, 4200+963, *l*[e]*-*[1]*+bad*[1] [1]
alone, 4200+970, *l*[e]*-*[1]*+bādād* [1]
leave alone, 6641+4946, *'āmad+min* [1]
leave alone, 8332, *rāpâ*[1] [1]
left alone, 8636, *šā'ar* [1]

ALONG [242]
along with, 2256, *w*[e]*-* [48]
along, 6584, *'al*[2] [29]
along, 928, *b*[e]*-* [25]
along, *NIH/RPE* [17]
along, *AIT* [15]
along with, 907, *'ēt*[2] [13]
along with, 6640, *'im* [11]
along with, 6584, *'al*[2] [8]
along with, 928+9348, *b*[e]*-+tāwek* [6]
along, 448, *'el* [4]
along, 4200, *l*[e]*-*[1] [3]
came along, 6296, *'ābar*[1] [3]
along with, 448, *'el* [2]
along with, 928, *b*[e]*-* [2]
along with, 4200+6645, *l*[e]*-*[1]*+'ummâ*[1] [2]
along, 4946, *min* [2]
passed along, 6296, *'ābar*[1] [2]
along, 6584+3338, *'al*[2]*+yād* [2]
moves along, 8253, *rāmaś* [2]
along with, 928+3338, *b*[e]*-+yād* [1]
along with, 928+7931, *b*[e]*-+qereb* [1]
along, 928+6298, *b*[e]*-+'ēber*[1] [1]
along, 928+9348, *b*[e]*-+tāwek* [1]
walking along, 928+2021+2006, *b*[e]*-+ha-+derek* [1]
take along, 995, *bô'* [1]
came along, 995, *bô'* [1]
grope along, 1779, *gāšaš* [1]
along, 2006, *derek* [1]
along, 2025, *-â*[2] [1]
follow along, 2143, *hālak* [1]
moves along, 2143, *hālak* [1]
runs along, 2143, *hālak* [1]
travel along, 2143, *hālak* [1]
tripping along with mincing steps, 2143+2256+3262, *hālak+w*[e]*+ṭāpap* [1]
walked along, 2143+2143, *hālak+hālak* [1]
walked along, 2143, *hālak* [1]
walking along, 2143+2143, *hālak+hālak* [1]
walking along, 2143, *hālak* [1]
went along, 2143+2143, *hālak+hālak* [1]
along with, 2256+1685, *w*[e]*-+gam* [1]
comes along, 2736, *ḥālap*[1] [1]
along, 3338, *yād* [1]
along with, 3480, *yaḥad* [1]
along with, 4200, *l*[e]*-*[1] [1]
along, 4200+3338, *l*[e]*-*[1]*+yād* [1]
along with, 4946+4200+963, *min+l*[e]*-*[1]*+bad*[1] [1]
along, 4946+6298, *min+'ēber*[1] [1]
draw along, 5432, *māšak* [1]
move along, 5633, *nāhal* [1]
drives along, 5674, *nûs* [1]
echoes along, 5938, *nāqap*[2] [1]
along, 6017, *sābîb* [1]
drags himself along, 6022, *sābal* [1]
continued along, 6296, *'ābar*[1] [1]
traveled along, 6296, *'ābar*[1] [1]
along, 6298, *'ēber*[1] [1]
fly along, 6414, *'ûp*[1] [1]
brought along, 6590, *'ālâ* [1]
walking along, 7575, *ṣā'ad* [1]
gallop along, 8132, *rûṣ* [1]
had ride along, 8206, *rākab* [1]
creatures that move along the ground, 8254, *remeś* [1]
creatures that move along the ground, 9238, *šereṣ* [1]
move along, 9238, *šereṣ* [1]
drag along, 9255, *šāšā'* [1]

ALONGSIDE [5]
alongside, 907, *'ēt*[2] [1]
alongside, 928, *b*[e]*-* [1]
Alongside, 4200+6645, *l*[e]*-*[1]*+'ummâ*[1] [1]
alongside of, 4200+6645, *l*[e]*-*[1]*+'ummâ*[1] [1]
alongside, 4946+6298, *min+'ēber*[1] [1]

ALOOF [3]
stand aloof, 8178, *rāḥaq* [2]
aloof, 4946+5584, *min+neged* [1]

ALOTH [1]
Aloth, 6599, *'ālôt* [1]

ALOUD [32]
aloud, 5951+906+7754, *nāśā'+'ēt*[1]*+qôl* [5]
aloud, 5951+7754, *nāśā'+qôl* [4]
shout aloud, 8131, *rûa'* [4]
aloud, 7754+1524, *qôl+gādôl* [2]
aloud, 7754, *qôl* [2]
read aloud, 7924, *qārā'*[1] [2]
aloud, 928+7754+1524, *b*[e]*-+qôl+gādôl* [1]
aloud, 928+7754, *b*[e]*-+qôl* [1]
wept aloud, 1134, *bākâ* [1]
weeping aloud, 2410, *zā'aq* [1]
aloud, 4848, *mālē'*[1] [1]
cry aloud, 5989+7754, *nātan+qôl* [1]
shout aloud, 7412, *ṣāhal*[1] [1]
cry aloud, 7590, *ṣā'aq* [1]
shout aloud, 7924+928+1744, *qārā'*[1]*+b*[e]*-+gārôn* [1]
was read aloud, 7924, *qārā'*[1] [1]
cry aloud, 8131+8275, *rûa'+rēa'*[1] [1]
calls aloud, 8264, *rānan* [1]
cries aloud, 8264, *rānan* [1]

ALREADY [34]
already, *AIT* [17]
already, 3893, *k*[e]*bār*[1] [5]
already, *NIH/RPE* [4]
already, 2180, *hinnēh* [2]
already, 6964, *'attâ* [2]
already, 255, *'āz* [1]
already, 928+2021+9378, *b*[e]*-+ha-+t*[e]*ḥillâ* [1]
already, 4946+255, *min+'āz* [1]
already dead, 5577, *n*[e]*bēlâ* [1]

ALSO [525]
also, 2256, *w*[e]*-* [251]
also, 1685, *gam* [106]
and also, 2256, *w*[e]*-* [56]
also, *NIH/RPE* [40]
also, 2256+1685, *w*[e]*-+gam* [26]
but also, 2256, *w*[e]*-* [10]
also, 677, *'ap*[1] [4]
also, 6388, *'ôd* [4]
also, 421, *'ak* [2]
and also, 677, *'ap*[1] [2]
but also, 1685, *gam* [2]
and also, 1685, *gam* [2]
also, 6640, *'im* [2]
also, 10221+10059, *w*[e]*-+'ap* [2]
also, 10221, *w*[e]*-* [2]
also, 196, *'ô* [1]
but also, 421, *'ak* [1]
but also, 677, *'ap*[1] [1]
when also, 2256, *w*[e]*-* [1]
yet also, 2256, *w*[e]*-* [1]
also included, 2256, *w*[e]*-* [1]
also, 2256+677, *w*[e]*-+'ap*[1] [1]
also, 3480, *yaḥad* [1]
also sweets, 4027, *kēn*[2] [1]
also, 4027, *kēn*[2] [1]
also, 4200+963, *l*[e]*-*[1]*+bad*[1] [1]
but also, 6388, *'ôd* [1]
but also, 8370, *raq*[2] [1]
also, 10008+10358, *'*[e]*dayin+k*[e]*nēmā'* [1]

ALTAR [357]
altar, 4640, *mizbēaḥ* [337]
the altars, 2257, *-ô* [11]
altar hearth, 789, *'*[a]*rî'ēl*[1] [2]
the altars, 5647, *-nû*[2] [2]
altar, *AIT* [1]
the altars, 2084, *-hû* [1]
altar hearth, 2219, *har'ēl* [1]
this altars, 2257, *-ô* [1]
altar, 10401, *madbaḥ* [1]

ALTARS [60]
altars, 4640, *mizbēaḥ* [50]
incense altars, 2802, *ḥammān* [8]
altars of brick, 4246, *l*[e]*bēnâ* [1]

incense altars, 5232, meqaṭṭeret [1]

ALTER [1]
alter, 9101, šānâ[1] [1]

ALTERED [1]
altered, 10731, šenâ[1] [1]

ALTERNATE [1]
alternate[s], 7194+2298+2256+8232, paʿamôn+zāhāb+we-+rimmôn[1] [1]

ALTERNATED [2]
alternated with, 1068, bayin [1]
alternated[s], 7194+2256+8232, paʿamôn+we-+rimmôn[1] [1]

ALTHOUGH [47]
although, 3954, kî[2] [12]
although, 2256, we- [11]
although, *NIH/RPE* [8]
although, 561, ʾim [5]
although, 889, ʾašer [2]
although, *AIT* [1]
although, 421, ʾak [1]
although, 928+3972+889, be-+kōl+ʾašer [1]
although, 1685+3954, gam+kî[2] [1]
although, 3954+561, kî[2]+ʾim [1]
although, 6584, ʿal[2] [1]
although, 6964, ʿattâ [1]
although, 8370, raq[2] [1]
although, 9393, taḥat[1] [1]

ALTOGETHER [21]
altogether, 3972, kōl [14]
altogether, *NIH/RPE* [2]
altogether, 2256+465, we-+ʾēlleh [2]
was altogether, 2118+2118, hāyâ+hāyâ [1]
altogether silent, 3087+3087, ḥārēš[2]+ḥārēš[2] [1]
altogether, 3481, yaḥdāw [1]

ALUSH [2]
Alush, 478, ʾālûš [2]

ALVAH [2]
Alvah, 6595, ʿalwâ[2] [2]

ALVAN [2]
Alvan, 6597, ʿalwān [2]

ALWAYS [78]
always, 9458, tāmîd [23]
always, 3972+2021+3427, kōl+ha-+yôm[1] [18]
always, 928+3972+6961, be-+kōl+ʿēt [5]
always, 4200+5905, le-[1]+nēṣaḥ[1] [4]
always, *AIT* [3]
always, *NIH/RPE* [3]
always, 6330+6409, ʿad[2]+ʿôlām [3]
always, 6409, ʿôlām [3]
always, 3972+3427, kōl+yôm[1] [2]
always, 4200+6409, le-[1]+ʿôlām [2]
always, 8370, raq[2] [2]
always, 440+2893, ʾal[1]+ḥāsēr[1] [1]
always, 3972, kōl [1]
always, 4200+1887+2256+1887, le-[1]+dôr[2]+we-+dôr[2] [1]
always, 4200+6329, le-[1]+ʿad[1] [1]
always be, 4202+2532, lōʾ+ḥādal[1] [1]
always, 4946+6388, min+ʿôd [1]
always do, 5477, mišpāṭ [1]
does always, 5904, nāṣaḥ [1]
always, 6964, ʿattâ [1]
always, 7940, qārôb [1]

AM [762]*
am, *NIH/RPE* [439]
am, *AIT* [279]
am, 2118, hāyâ [17]
am, 3780, yēš [3]

AMAD [1]
Amad, 6675, ʿamʿād [1]

AMAL [1]
Amal, 6663, ʿāmāl[2] [1]

AMALEK [12]
Amalek, 6667, ʿamālēq [12]

AMALEKITE [4]
Amalekite, 6668, ʿamālēqî [3]
Amalekite, 6667, ʿamālēq [1]

AMALEKITES [34]
Amalekites, 6667, ʿamālēq [25]
Amalekites, 6668, ʿamālēqî [9]

AMAM [1]
Amam, 585, ʾamām [1]

AMANA [1]
Amana, 592, ʾamānâ[2] [1]

AMARIAH [15]
Amariah, 618, ʾamaryâ [12]
Amariah, 619, ʾamaryāhû [3]

AMARIAH'S [1]
Amariah's, 618, ʾamaryâ [1]

AMASA [18]
Amasa, 6690, ʿamāśāʾ [15]
Amasa, *NIH/RPE* [2]
Amasa[s], 2257, -ô [1]

AMASAI [5]
Amasai, 6691, ʿamāśay [5]

AMASHSAI [1]
Amashsai, 6692, ʿamaššay [1]

AMASIAH [1]
Amasiah, 6674, ʿamasyâ [1]

AMASSED [2]
amassed, 4043, kānas [1]
amassed, 6913, ʿāśâ[1] [1]

AMASSES [1]
amasses, 7695, qābaṣ [1]

AMAZED [2]
amazed, 9449, tāmah [1]
utterly amazed, 9449+9449, tāmah+tāmah [1]

AMAZEMENT [1]
amazement, 10755+10097, tewah+behal [1]

AMAZIAH [40]
Amaziah, 605, ʾamaṣyāhû [29]
Amaziah, 604, ʾamaṣyâ [9]
Amaziah[s], 2021+4889, ha-+melek[1] [2]

AMAZIAH'S [2]
Amaziah's, 605, ʾamaṣyāhû [2]

AMAZING [3]
amazing, 7098, pālāʾ [3]

AMBASSADORS [1]
ambassadors, 7495, ṣîr[3] [1]

AMBUSH [23]
ambush, 741, ʾārab [9]
in ambush, 741, ʾārab [3]
set an ambush, 741, ʾārab [3]
ambush, 5041, mistār [2]
the men of the ambush[s], 465, ʾēlleh [1]
ambush set, 741, ʾārab [1]
lie in ambush, 2675, ḥākâ [1]
ambush, 4422, maʾarāb [1]
place of ambush, 4422, maʾarāb [1]
ambush, 6811, ʿāqēb[1] [1]

AMBUSHES [1]
ambushes, 741, ʾārab [1]

AMEN [27]
amen, 589, ʾāmēn [26]
amen so be it, 589+589, ʾāmēn+ʾāmēn [1]

AMENDS [3]
making amends for sin, 871, ʾāšām [1]
make amends, 4105, kāpar[1] [1]
make amends, 8355, rāṣâ[2] [1]

AMETHYST [2]
amethyst, 334, ʾaḥlāmâ [2]

AMI [1]
Ami, 577, ʾāmî [1]

AMID [7]
amid, 928, be- [6]
amid, 9393, taḥat[1] [1]

AMITTAI [2]
Amittai, 624, ʾamittay [2]

AMMAH [1]
Ammah, 565, ʾammâ[2] [1]

AMMIEL [6]
Ammiel, 6653, ʿammîʾēl [6]

AMMIHUD [10]
Ammihud, 6654, ʿammîhûd [10]

AMMINADAB [13]
Amminadab, 6657, ʿammînādāb [13]

AMMISHADDAI [5]
Ammishaddai, 6659, ʿammîšaddāy [5]

AMMIZABAD [1]
Ammizabad, 6655, ʿammîzābād [1]

AMMON [15]
Ammon, 1201+6648, bēn[1]+ʿammôn [9]
Ammon, 6648, ʿammôn [5]
Ammon, 6649, ʿammônî [1]

AMMONITE [21]
Ammonite, 6649, ʿammônî [13]
Ammonite, 1201+6648, bēn[1]+ʿammôn [8]

AMMONITES [88]
Ammonites, 1201+6648, bēn[1]+ʿammôn [79]
Ammonites, 6649, ʿammônî [6]
Ammonites, *NIH/RPE* [1]
the Ammonites[s], 2157, -hem [1]
Ammonites, 6648, ʿammôn [1]

AMNON [28]
Amnon, 596, ʾamnôn [25]
Amnon[s], 2257, -ô [2]
Amnon, 578, ʾamînôn [1]

AMNON'S [1]
Amnon's, 596, ʾamnôn [1]

AMOK [1]
Amok, 6651, ʿāmôq [1]

AMOK'S [1]
Amok's, 6651, ʿāmôq [1]

AMON [16]
Amon, 571, ʾāmôn[2] [15]
Amon, 572, ʾāmôn[3] [1]

AMON'S [3]
Amon's, 571, ʾāmôn[2] [2]
Amon's[s], 2257, -ô [1]

AMONG [642]
among, 928, be- [241]
among, 928+9348, be-+tāwek [111]
among, 928+7931, be-+qereb [52]
among, 1068, bayin [31]
among, *AIT* [28]
among, 6640, ʿim [24]
among, 4946, min [23]
among, 4200, le-[1] [20]
among, 7931, qereb [18]
among, 907, ʾēt[2] [14]
among, 448, ʾel [12]
among, 9348, tāwek [12]
from among, 4946, min [11]
among, *NIH/RPE* [9]
among, 6584, ʿal[2] [5]
among, 4946+7931, min+qereb [4]
among, 6330, ʿad[2] [3]
among, 9393, taḥat[1] [2]
among yourselves, 408+448+278, ʾîš[1]+ʾel+ʾāḥ[2] [1]
equally among them, 408+3869+278+2257, ʾîš[1]+ke-+ʾāḥ[2]+-ô [1]

among, 448+9348, *ʾel+tāwek* [1]
distributed among, 928, *be-* [1]
among, 1075, *bayit*[2] [1]
low among men, 1201+132, *bēn*[1]*+ʾādām*[1] [1]
among, 2025, *-â*[2] [1]
among, 2489, *ḥābar*[2] [1]
among, 3869, *ke-* [1]
among, 4200+3972, *le-*[1]*+kōl* [1]
from among, 4200, *le-*[1] [1]
whispering among themselves, 4317, *lāḥaš* [1]
among, 4946+1068, *min+bayin* [1]
among, 4946+907, *min+ʾēt*[2] [1]
spreading among, 6296, *ʿābar*[1] [1]
among, 8905+907, *šākan+ʾēt*[2] [1]
among which[s], 9004, *šām* [1]
among, 10089, *be-* [1]
among, 10099, *bên* [1]
among, 10427, *min* [1]
among, 10542, *ʿal* [1]
among, 10554, *ʿim* [1]

AMORITE [10]
Amorite, 616, *ʾemōrî* [10]

AMORITES [76]
Amorites, 616, *ʾemōrî* [76]

AMOS [7]
Amos, 6650, *ʿāmôs* [7]

AMOUNT [21]
amount, *AIT* [3]
great amount, 4200+8044, *le-*[1]*+rōb* [3]
large amount, 8041, *rab*[1] [2]
amount to nothing, 700, *ʾepes* [1]
great amount, 1524, *gādôl* [1]
amount, 1821, *dābār* [1]
amount to, 2118, *hāyâ* [1]
great amount, 2162, *hāmôn* [1]
large amount, 2221+4394, *harbēh+meʾōd* [1]
same amount[s], 2296, *zeh* [1]
determine amount needed, 4082, *kāsas* [1]
large amount, 4200+8044, *le-*[1]*+rōb* [1]
specified amount, 6886, *ʿērek* [1]
amount, 7023, *peh* [1]
exact amount, 7308, *pārāšâ* [1]
amount been determined, 9419, *tākan* [1]

AMOUNTED [3]
amounted, *NIH/RPE* [2]
amounted to, 2118, *hāyâ* [1]

AMOUNTS [3]
in equal amounts, 963+928+963, *bad*[1]*+be-+bad*[1] [1]
amounts, 7217, *pequdîm* [1]
accumulate large amounts, 8049+4394, *rābâ*[1]*+meʾōd* [1]

AMOZ [13]
Amoz, 576, *ʾāmôṣ* [13]

AMRAM [13]
Amram, 6688, *ʿamrām* [13]

AMRAM'S [1]
Amram's, 6688, *ʿamrām* [1]

AMRAMITES [2]
Amramites, 6689, *ʿamrāmî* [2]

AMRAPHEL [2]
Amraphel, 620, *ʾamrāpel* [2]

AMZI [2]
Amzi, 603, *ʾamṣî* [2]

AN [951]*
an, *NIH/RPE* [715]
an, 2021, *ha-* [78]
an, *AIT* [12]
an, 285, *ʾeḥād* [4]
an[s], 2257, *-ô* [4]
an[s], 3870, *-kā* [2]
an, 3972, *kōl* [2]
an, 10002, *-āʾ* [2]
an[s], 3276, *-î* [1]
an[s], 3972, *kōl* [1]
an[s], 4013, *-kem* [1]
an[s], 4392, *-ām* [1]

ANAB [2]
Anab, 6693, *ʿanāb* [2]

ANAH [12]
Anah, 6704, *ʿanâ* [12]

ANAHARATH [1]
Anaharath, 637, *ʾanāḥarat* [1]

ANAIAH [2]
Anaiah, 6717, *ʿanāyâ* [2]

ANAK [7]
Anak, 6737, *ʿanāq*[2] [6]
Anak, 6710, *ʿanôq* [1]

ANAKITES [11]
Anakites, 6737, *ʿanāq*[2] [7]
Anakites, 1201+6737, *bēn*[1]*+ʿanāq*[2] [4]

ANAMITES [2]
Anamites, 6723, *ʿanāmîm* [2]

ANAMMELECH [1]
Anammelech, 6724, *ʿanammelek* [1]

ANAN [1]
Anan, 6728, *ʿānān*[2] [1]

ANANI [1]
Anani, 6730, *ʿanānî* [1]

ANANIAH [2]
Ananiah, 6731, *ʿanāneyâ*[1] [1]
Ananiah, 6732, *ʿanāneyâ*[2] [1]

ANATH [2]
Anath, 6742, *ʿanāt* [2]

ANATHOTH [18]
Anathoth, 6743, *ʿanātôt*[1] [13]
from Anathoth, 6745, *ʿannetōtî* [3]
Anathoth, 6744, *ʿanātôt*[2] [2]

ANATHOTHITE [2]
Anathothite, 6745, *ʿannetōtî* [2]

ANCESTOR [2]
ancestor, 3, *ʾāb* [2]

ANCESTORS [3]
ancestors, 3, *ʾāb* [2]
ancestors, 8037, *riʾšôn* [1]

ANCESTRAL [10]
ancestral, 3, *ʾāb* [9]
ancestral property, 5709, *naḥalâ*[1] [1]

ANCESTRY [4]
ancestry, 4808, *mekûrâ* [3]
indicated ancestry, 3528, *yālad* [1]

ANCIENT [30]
ancient, 6409, *ʿôlām* [13]
ancient, 4946+6409, *min+ʿôlām* [3]
ancient, 7710, *qedem* [3]
ancient, 10578, *ʿattîq* [3]
ancient, 6329, *ʿad*[1] [2]
ancient times, 6409, *ʿôlām* [2]
ancient, *NIH/RPE* [1]
from ancient times, 6972, *ʿattîq* [1]
ancient times, 7710, *qedem* [1]
ancient, 10550, *ʿālam* [1]

AND [22881]*
and, 2256, *we-* [19276]
and, *NIH/RPE* [2387]
and, 10221, *we-* [400]
and then, 2256, *we-* [91]
both and, 2256, *we-* [76]
and when, 2256, *we-* [64]
and also, 2256, *we-* [56]
and, 2256+1685, *we+gam* [53]
and, 1685, *gam* [49]
and so, 2256, *we-* [44]
and, 6640, *ʿim* [25]
and, 3954, *kî*[2] [20]
and, 4200, *le-*[1] [18]
and, 6330, *ʿad*[2] [13]
and now, 2256, *we-* [11]
and yet, 2256, *we-* [10]
and, 677, *ʾap*[1] [8]
and, 907, *ʾēt*[2] [8]
and, 928, *be-* [8]

ANEM [1]
Anem, 6722, *ʿānēm* [1]

ANER [3]
Aner, 6738, *ʿānēr*[1] [2]
Aner, 6739, *ʿānēr*[2] [1]

ANGEL [104]
angel, 4855, *malʾāk* [98]
angel, *NIH/RPE* [2]
angel, 10417, *malʾak* [2]
the angel[s], 2257, *-ô* [1]
the angel, 4855+3378, *malʾāk+yhwh* [1]

ANGELS [13]
angels, 4855, *malʾāk* [9]
angels, 1201+2021+466, *bēn*[1]*+ha-+ʾelōhîm* [2]
angels, 52, *ʾabbîr* [1]
angels, 1201+466, *bēn*[1]*+ʾelōhîm* [1]

ANGER [250]
anger, 678, *ʾap*[2] [173]
provoked to anger, 4087, *kāʿas* [19]
anger, 2779, *ḥēmâ* [12]
provoke to anger, 4087, *kāʿas* [7]
anger, 7912, *qeṣep*[1] [7]
provoking to anger, 4087, *kāʿas* [6]
anger, 6301, *ʿebrâ* [4]
jealous anger, 7863, *qinʾâ* [4]
provoked to anger, 4088+4087, *kaʿas+kāʿas* [2]
anger, 8120, *rûaḥ* [2]
anger, 2405, *zaʿam* [1]
anger, 3013+678, *ḥārâ*[1]*+ʾap*[2] [1]
burning anger, 3019, *ḥārôn* [1]
anger, 4088, *kaʿas* [1]
provoke to anger, 4088+4087, *kaʿas+kāʿas* [1]
provoked to anger, 4088, *kaʿas* [1]
anger, 4089, *kaʿaś* [1]
harbor anger, 5757, *nāṭar*[1] [1]
anger smolder, 6939, *ʿāšan* [1]
broke out in anger, 7287, *pāraṣ* [1]
stirred up jealous anger, 7861, *qānāʾ* [1]
anger, 7911, *qāṣap* [1]
provoked to anger, 7911, *qāṣap* [1]
anger, 8074, *rāgaz* [1]

ANGERED [8]
angered, 4087, *kāʿas* [3]
angered, 7911, *qāṣap* [2]
easily angered, 2779, *ḥēmâ* [1]
angered, 4088, *kaʿas* [1]
angered, 10653, *regaz*[1] [1]

ANGERS [1]
angers, 6297, *ʿābar*[2] [1]

ANGLE [5]
angle, 5243, *miqṣōaʿ* [4]
angle of the wall, 5243, *miqṣōaʿ* [1]

ANGRY [108]
angry, 7911, *qāṣap* [23]
angry, 3013, *ḥārâ*[1] [22]
angry, 647, *ʾānap* [14]
angry, 3013+678, *ḥārâ*[1]*+ʾap*[2] [11]
angry, 678, *ʾap*[2] [4]
very angry, 3013+678, *ḥārâ*[1]*+ʾap*[2] [4]
very angry, 6297, *ʿābar*[2] [4]
angry, 7912, *qeṣep*[1] [3]
angry, 2404, *zāʿam* [2]
angry, 2409, *zāʿēp* [2]
angry, 2779, *ḥēmâ* [2]
angry, 4087, *kāʿas* [2]
angry, 5757, *nāṭar*[1] [2]
angry, 2406, *zāʿap*[1] [1]
angry, 3013+928+6524, *ḥārâ*[1]*+be-+ʿayin*[1] [1]
angry, 3019+678, *ḥārôn+ʾap*[2] [1]
make angry, 4087, *kāʿas* [1]

angry, 5723, *nāhar* [1]
angry, 6297, *ʿābar*^{2} [1]
angry, 7752, *qûṭ* [1]
made angry, 7911+2118, *qāṣap+hāyâ* [1]
very angry, 7911+7912, *qāṣap+qeṣep*^{1} [1]
angry, 7912+7911, *qeṣep*^{1}*+qāṣap* [1]
angry, 7918, *qāṣar*^{2} [1]
not angry, 8740+678, *šûb*^{1}*+ʾap*^{2} [1]
angry, 10113, *b*^{e}*nas* [1]

ANGUISH [37]
in anguish, 2655, *ḥîl*^{1} [4]
anguish, 7650, *ṣārâ*^{1} [4]
anguish, 5188, *m*^{e}*ṣûqâ* [3]
anguish, 5253, *mar*^{1} [3]
anguish, 2714, *ḥalḥālâ* [2]
anguish, 3873, *kʾēb* [2]
anguish, 5055, *mēʿeh* [2]
anguish, 5210, *mēṣar* [2]
in anguish, 987+4394, *bāhal+m*^{e}*ʾōd* [1]
anguish, 2082+2082, *hô+hô* [1]
anguish, 2477, *ḥebel* [1]
in deep anguish, 2655, *ḥîl*^{1} [1]
anguish, 2659, *ḥîl*^{3} [1]
anguish, 3326, *yāgôn* [1]
anguish, 4089, *kaʿaś* [1]
in anguish, 5253+5883, *mar*^{1}*+nepeš* [1]
bitter anguish, 5352, *mārar* [1]
anguish, 5639, *n*^{e}*hāmâ* [1]
anguish, 6552, *ʿîr*^{2} [1]
anguish, 7496, *ṣîr*^{4} [1]
anguish, 7639, *ṣar*^{1} [1]
in anguish, 8074, *rāgaz* [1]
anguish, 8490, *śîaḥ*^{3} [1]

ANGUISHED [2]
anguished, 7639, *ṣar*^{1} [1]
anguished, 10565, *ʿ*^{a}*ṣîb* [1]

ANIAM [1]
Aniam, 642, *ʾ*^{a}*nîʿām* [1]

ANIM [1]
Anim, 6719, *ʿānîm* [1]

ANIMAL [83]
animal, 989, *b*^{e}*hēmâ* [44]
animal, *NIH/RPE* [7]
animal, 2651, *ḥayyâ*^{1} [7]
animal, *AIT* [5]
the animal^s, 2085, *hûʾ* [2]
animal^s, 5647, *-nû*^{2} [2]
animal, 8802, *šôr* [2]
animal, 10263, *ḥêwâ* [2]
animal^s, 1821, *dābār* [1]
animal^s, 2257, *-ô* [1]
the animal^s, 2257, *-ô* [1]
wild animal, 2651, *ḥayyâ*^{1} [1]
animal, 3181, *ṭebaḥ*^{1} [1]
was torn to pieces by a wild animal, 3271+3271, *ṭārap+ṭārap* [1]
animal torn by beasts, 3274, *ṭ*^{e}*rēpâ* [1]
animal, 5238, *miqneh* [1]
animal found dead, 5577, *n*^{e}*bēlâ* [1]
the animal^s, 5626, *-nâ* [1]
animal from flock, 7366, *ṣōʾn* [1]
animal, 7473+2651, *ṣayid*^{1}*+ḥayyâ*^{1} [1]

ANIMALS [134]
animals, 989, *b*^{e}*hēmâ* [63]
animals, 2651, *ḥayyâ*^{1} [25]
animals, *AIT* [6]
animals, *NIH/RPE* [6]
wild animals, 2651, *ḥayyâ*^{1} [6]
animals, 7366, *ṣōʾn* [6]
torn by wild animals, 3274, *ṭ*^{e}*rēpâ* [5]
animals, 10263, *ḥêwâ* [5]
animals, 1330, *bāqār* [2]
fattened animals, 5309, *m*^{e}*rîʾ* [2]
animals^s, 465, *ʾēlleh* [1]
animals, 1248, *b*^{e}*ʿîr* [1]
animals torn by wild beasts, 3274, *ṭ*^{e}*rēpâ* [1]
fat animals, 4671, *mēaḥ* [1]
animals, 5238, *miqneh* [1]
Passover animals, 7175, *pesaḥ* [1]
animals, 8445, *śeh* [1]
animals, 9238, *šereṣ* [1]

ANKLE [1]
ankle chains, 7578, *ṣ*^{e}*ʿādâ*^{2} [1]

ANKLE-DEEP [1]
ankle-deep, 701, *ʾōpes* [1]

ANKLES [3]
ankles, 7972, *qarsōl* [2]
ankles, 8079, *regel* [1]

ANNALS [40]
annals, 1821+3427, *dābār+yôm*^{1} [37]
annals, 1821, *dābār* [3]

ANNIHILATE [6]
annihilate, 6, *ʾābad* [3]
annihilate, 3049, *ḥāram*^{1} [1]
annihilate, 5782, *nākâ* [1]
annihilate, 9012, *šāmad* [1]

ANNIHILATED [1]
annihilated, 3948, *kāḥad* [1]

ANNIHILATION [2]
annihilation, 6, *ʾābad* [1]
annihilation, 9012, *šāmad* [1]

ANNIVERSARY [1]
anniversary, 4595, *môʿēd* [1]

ANNOTATIONS [2]
annotations, 4535, *midrāš* [2]

ANNOUNCE [12]
announce, 5583, *nāgad* [8]
announce, 1819, *dābar*^{2} [2]
announce, 7924, *qārāʾ*^{1} [1]
announce, 9048, *šāmaʿ* [1]

ANNOUNCED [9]
announced, 606, *ʾāmar*^{1} [2]
announced, 7924, *qārāʾ*^{1} [2]
announced, 1620, *g*^{e}*zērâ* [1]
announced, 1819, *dābar*^{2} [1]
announced, 3655, *yāṣāʾ* [1]
announced, 5989, *nātan* [1]
announced, 9048, *šāmaʿ* [1]

ANNOUNCEMENT [1]
announcement, *NIH/RPE* [1]

ANNOUNCES [2]
announces, 5583, *nāgad* [1]
announces, 5989, *nātan* [1]

ANNOUNCING [1]
announcing, 5583, *nāgad* [1]

ANNOYANCE [1]
annoyance, 4088, *kaʿas* [1]

ANNUAL [6]
annual, 3427, *yôm*^{1} [3]
annual, 285+928+2021+9102, *ʾeḥād+b*^{e}*-+ha-+šānâ*^{2} [1]
annual, 4946+3427+3427+2025, *min+yôm*^{1}*+yôm*^{1}*+-â*^{2} [1]
annual, 7193+928+2021+9102, *paʿam+b*^{e}*+ha+šānâ*^{2} [1]

ANNUALLY [2]
annually, 928+3972+9102+2256+9102, *b*^{e}*-+kōl+šānâ*^{2}*+w*^{e}*-+šānâ*^{2} [1]
due annually, 4946+1896+9102+928+9102, *min+day+šānâ*^{2}*+b*^{e}*-+šānâ*^{2} [1]

ANNULLED [1]
be annulled, 4105, *kāpar*^{1} [1]

ANOINT [26]
anoint, 5417, *māšaḥ* [24]
anoint, 2014, *dāšēn*^{1} [1]
anoint, 6584, *ʿal*^{2} [1]

ANOINTED [77]
anointed, 5431, *māšîaḥ* [38]
anointed, 5417, *māšaḥ* [33]
was anointed, 5417, *māšaḥ* [2]
anointed, 1201+2021+3658, *bēn*^{1}*+ha-+yiṣhār*^{1} [1]
been anointed, 3668, *yāṣaq* [1]
anointed, 4937, *mimšaḥ* [1]
been anointed, 5417, *māšaḥ* [1]

ANOINTING [25]
anointing, 5418, *mišḥâ*^{1} [21]
anointing, 5417, *māšaḥ* [3]
anointing, 5420, *mošḥâ*^{1} [1]

ANOTHER [196]
another, 337, *ʾaḥēr*^{1} [39]
another, *NIH/RPE* [26]
another^s, 285, *ʾeḥād* [12]
another^s, 8276, *rēaʿ*^{2} [12]
another, 9108, *šēnî* [12]
another, 6388, *ʿôd* [9]
another^s, 278, *ʾāḥ*^{2} [7]
another^s, 2296, *zeh* [7]
another, *AIT* [5]
another, 2424, *zār* [4]
another^s, 408, *ʾîš*^{1} [3]
another, 6388+337, *ʿôd+ʾaḥēr*^{1} [3]
another, 10023, *ʾoḥ*^{o}*rî* [3]
another, 1685, *gam* [2]
another messenger^s, 2296, *zeh* [2]
still another, 6388, *ʿôd* [2]
another man's, 8276, *rēaʿ*^{2} [2]
another^s, 8445, *śeh* [2]
another, 10025, *ʾoḥ*^{o}*rān* [2]
another^s, 74, *ʾeben* [1]
another^s, 185, *ʾōhel*^{1} [1]
another, 285, *ʾeḥad* [1]
another^s, 295, *ʾāḥôt* [1]
another creature^s, 408, *ʾîš*^{1} [1]
another^s, 989, *b*^{e}*hēmâ* [1]
another^s, 1475, *gibbôr* [1]
another^s, 1580, *gôy* [1]
another^s, 1887, *dôr*^{2} [1]
another^s, 2021+132, *ha-+ʾādām*^{1} [1]
another^s, 2021+2215+4946+2296, *ha-+har+min+zeh* [1]
another^s, 2021+9019, *ha-+š*^{e}*mûʿâ* [1]
another^s, 2021, *ha-* [1]
one another, 2021+6639, *ha-+ʿam*^{2} [1]
another^s, 2023, *-āh* [1]
another^s, 2257, *-ô* [1]
another messenger, 2296, *zeh* [1]
another^s, 2544, *ḥōdeš*^{1} [1]
another^s, 2754, *ḥelqâ*^{2} [1]
another, 3578+6388, *yāsap+ʿôd* [1]
another, 3578, *yāsap* [1]
still another, 3578+6388, *yāsap+ʿôd* [1]
another^s, 3998, *k*^{e}*lî* [1]
into another set, 4200+963, *l*^{e}*-*^{1}*+bad*^{1} [1]
one kind after another, 4200+5476+2157, *l*^{e}*-*^{1}*+mišpāḥâ+-hem* [1]
another^s, 5246+7731, *miqrāʾ+qōdeš* [1]
another^s, 5647, *-nû*^{2} [1]
another man's, 5799, *nokrî* [1]
another, 5799, *nokrî* [1]
another^s, 5883, *nepeš* [1]
another^s, 6551, *ʿîr*^{1} [1]
another^s, 6660, *ʿāmît* [1]
another^s, 7521, *ṣēlāʿ*^{1} [1]
at another time, 8092, *regaʿ* [1]
another^s, 8132, *rûš* [1]
another^s, 8288, *rāʿâ*^{3} [1]
another^s, 8295, *r*^{e}*ʿût*^{1} [1]
kills another, 8357, *rāṣaḥ* [1]
another^s, 8701, *šabbāt* [1]
another, 8740, *šûb*^{1} [1]
another part, 9108, *šēnî* [1]
another, 9109, *š*^{e}*nayim* [1]

ANOTHER'S [2]
another's^s, 8276, *rēaʿ*^{2} [1]
another's^s, 8295, *r*^{e}*ʿût*^{1} [1]

ANSWER [131]
answer, 6699, *ʿānâ*^{1} [73]
answer, 606, *ʾāmar*^{1} [12]
answer, 1821, *dābār* [9]
answer, 8740+1821, *šûb*^{1}*+dābār* [8]

answer, 8740, *šûb1* [5]
answer, 3359, *yāda'* [3]
give answer, 1819+1821, *dābar2+dābār* [2]
answer, 5101, *ma'aneh1* [2]
give an answer, 1819, *dābar2* [1]
answer, 2648, *ḥîdâ* [1]
give an answer, 5583, *nāgad* [1]
give answer, 5583+5583, *nāgad+nāgad* [1]
tell answer, 5583, *nāgad* [1]
told answer, 5583, *nāgad* [1]
answer given, 6699, *'ānâ1* [1]
answer, 6699+1821, *'ānâ1+dābār* [1]
give answer, 6699, *'ānâ1* [1]
gives back answer, 6699, *'ānâ1* [1]
have answer, 6699, *'ānâ1* [1]
answer, 6913, *'āśâ1* [1]
get answer, 8626+8626, *šā'al+šā'al* [1]
answer give, 8740, *šûb1* [1]
prompt to answer, 8740, *šûb1* [1]
right answer, 9459, *tāmîm* [1]
answer, 10601, *pitgām* [1]

ANSWERED [257]
answered, 606, *'āmar1* [161]
answered, 6699, *'ānâ1* [74]
answered, 10558, *'anâ* [5]
answered, 5583, *nāgad* [4]
answered prayer, 6983, *'ātar1* [4]
answered, 8740+1821, *šûb1+dābār* [3]
answered, 1819, *dābar2* [2]
be answered, 6699, *'ānâ1* [1]
answered prayers, 6983, *'ātar1* [1]
answered, 8740, *šûb1* [1]
answered, 10425, *melal* [1]

ANSWERING [3]
answering, 6699, *'ānâ1* [2]
answering, 9588, *tešûbâ* [1]

ANSWERS [12]
answers, 6699, *'ānâ1* [9]
answers, 609, *'ēmer1* [1]
answers, 8740+1821, *šûb1+dābār* [1]
answers, 9588, *tešûbâ* [1]

ANT [1]
ant, 5805, *nemālâ* [1]

ANTELOPE [2]
antelope, 9293, *te'ô* [2]

ANTHOTHIJAH [1]
Anthothijah, 6746, *'antōtiyy al* [1]

ANTS [1]
ants, 5805, *nemālâ* [1]

ANUB [1]
Anub, 6707, *'ānûb* [1]

ANVIL [1]
anvil, 7193, *pa'am* [1]

ANXIETY [4]
anxiety, 1796, *de'āgâ* [2]
anxiety, 4088, *ka'as* [1]
anxiety, 8595, *śar'appîm* [1]

ANXIOUS [4]
anxious, 1796, *de'āgâ* [1]
anxious, 8076, *raggāz* [1]
anxious striving, 8301+4213, *ra'yôn+lēb* [1]
anxious thoughts, 8595, *śar'appîm* [1]

ANY [456]
any, 3972, *kōl* [155]
any, *NIH/RPE* [120]
any, 4946, *min* [40]
any, *AIT* [34]
any, 2021, *ha-* [21]
any, 285, *'eḥād* [16]
any, 408, *'îš1* [11]
any, 10353, *kōl* [9]
any, 928, *be-* [6]
any, 285+3972, *'eḥād+kōl* [3]
anys, 2257, *-ô* [3]
any longer, 6388, *'ôd* [3]
any more, 6388, *'ôd* [3]
any, 4200, *le-1* [2]
any, 132, *'ādām1* [1]
anys, 401, *'ayin1* [1]
any man, 408+408, *'îš1+'îš1* [1]
any, 408+408, *'îš1+'îš1* [1]
any, 889, *'ašer* [1]
anys, 1505, *geber1* [1]
anys, 2085, *hû'* [1]
in any direction, 2178+2256+2178, *hēnnâ1+we-+hēnnâ1* [1]
any such things, 2257, *-ô* [1]
without any payment, 2855+401, *ḥinnām+'ayin1* [1]
without any reason, 2855, *ḥinnām* [1]
take any pleasure in, 2911+2911, *ḥāpēṣ1+ḥāpēṣ1* [1]
have any right, 3512, *yāṭab* [1]
any longer, 3578+6388, *yāsap+'ôd* [1]
any longer, 3578, *yāsap* [1]
anys, 3870, *-kā* [1]
in any direction, 3907+2256+3907, *kōh+we-+kōh* [1]
any, 3972+408, *kōl+'îš1* [1]
any kind, 4399, *me'ûmâ* [1]
any man, 4769+2021+408, *mî+ha-+'îš1* [1]
any of, 4946+907, *min+'ēt2* [1]
any, 5031, *mispār1* [1]
anys, 5647, *-nû2* [1]
paid any attention, 5742+265+4200+9048, *nāṭâ+'ōzen+le-1+šāma'* [1]
interest of any kind, 5968+2256+9552, *nešek+we-+tarbît* [1]
any, 6388+4946, *'ôd+min* [1]
any time, 6409, *'ôlām* [1]
any, 8031, *rō'š1* [1]
at any time, 8092, *rega'* [1]
any more than, 10195+10341+10168, *hē'+ke-+dî* [1]

ANYMORE [15]
anymore, 6388, *'ôd* [8]
anymore, 3578+6388, *yāsap+'ôd* [4]
anymore, 3578, *yāsap* [3]

ANYONE [194]
anyone, 3972, *kōl* [38]
anyone, *AIT* [34]
anyone, 408, *'îš1* [29]
anyone, 2021, *ha-* [18]
anyone, 132, *'ādām1* [9]
anyone, *NIH/RPE* [8]
anyone, 4769, *mî* [7]
anyone, 5883, *nepeš* [7]
anyone, 889, *'ašer* [6]
anyone else, 2424, *zār* [4]
anyone, 10426+10168, *man+dî* [4]
anyone, 2257, *-ô* [3]
anyone, 4769+2021+408, *mî+ha-+'îš1* [3]
anyone, 408+408, *'îš1+'îš1* [2]
anyone other than a priest, 2424, *zār* [2]
anyone, 3972+2021+5883, *kōl+ha-+nepeš* [2]
anyone, 3972+408, *kōl+'îš1* [2]
anyone, 3972+5883, *kōl+nepeš* [2]
anyone, 10353+10050, *kōl+'enāš* [2]
anyone elses, 278, *'āḥ2* [1]
anyones, 2021+4637, *ha-+mût* [1]
anyone, 2021+408, *ha-+'îš1* [1]
anyone, 2085, *hû'* [1]
anyone, 3972+132, *kōl+'ādām1* [1]
anyone, 3972+2021+408, *kōl+ha-+'îš1* [1]
anyone, 4200+963, *le-1+bad1* [1]
anyone, 4392, *-ām* [1]
anyone elses, 6639, *'am2* [1]
anyones, 7127, *pālîṭ* [1]
anyones, 8357, *rāṣaḥ* [1]
anyone, 10353, *kōl* [1]

ANYONE'S [2]
anyone's, *AIT* [1]
anyone's, 408, *'îš1* [1]

ANYTHING [124]
anything, 3972, *kōl* [37]
anything, 1821, *dābār* [14]
anything, *NIH/RPE* [11]
anything, 4399, *me'ûmâ* [10]
anything, *AIT* [9]
anything, 3972+1821, *kōl+dābār* [7]
anything, 4856, *melā'kâ* [3]
anything found dead, 5577, *nebēlâ* [3]
anything, 2021, *ha-* [2]
anything containing yeast, 2809, *ḥāmēṣ4* [2]
anything, 3972+2021+3998, *kōl+ha-+kelî* [2]
anything, 3972+4399, *kōl+me'ûmâ* [2]
anything, 3998, *kelî* [2]
anything, 1821+4946+3972+2021+1821, *dābār+min+kōl+ha-+dābār* [1]
anything, 1821+4946+3972, *dābār+min+kōl* [1]
anythings, 2021, *ha-* [1]
anything with yeast in it, 2809, *ḥāmēṣ4* [1]
without paying anything, 2855, *ḥinnām* [1]
anything with warts, 3301, *yabbelet* [1]
anything in addition, 3463, *yôtēr* [1]
if anything but, 3954, *kî2* [1]
anything, 3972+889, *kōl+'ašer* [1]
anything, 3972+2021+1821, *kōl+ha-+dābār* [1]
anything, 3972+3998, *kōl+kelî* [1]
anythings, 4202, *lō'* [1]
anything, 4537, *mâ* [1]
anything with yeast in it, 4721, *maḥmeṣet* [1]
anything useful, 4856, *melā'kâ* [1]
anything to say, 4863, *millâ* [1]
taken anything, 5951+5951, *nāśā'+nāśā'* [1]
do anything that endangers life, 6641+6584+1947, *'āmad+'al2+dām* [1]
anything else, 10692, *še'ār* [1]
anything, 10712, *šālû* [1]

ANYWHERE [14]
anywhere, 3972, *kōl* [7]
anywhere else, 625+2025+2256+625+2025, *'ān+-â2+we-+'ān+-â2* [2]
anywhere, 928+3972+5226, *be-+kōl+māqôm* [2]
anywhere, 625+2025+2256+625+2025, *'ān+-â2+we-+'ān+-â2* [1]
anywhere in, 928+3972+1473, *be-+kōl+gebûl* [1]
anywhere, 3972+1473, *kōl+gebûl* [1]

APART [45]
set apart, 976, *bādal* [7]
set apart, 7727, *qādaš* [6]
apart, 4200+963, *le-1+bad1* [3]
apart from, 4946+1187, *min+bal'adê* [3]
apart, *AIT* [2]
split apart, 1324, *bāqa'* [2]
set apart for destruction, 3051, *ḥērem1* [2]
was set apart, 976, *bādal* [1]
tear apart, 1324, *bāqa'* [1]
apart from, 2314, *zûlâ* [1]
set apart, 2930, *ḥopšî* [1]
set apart, 2936, *ḥāśâ* [1]
apart, 4200+970, *le-1+bādād* [1]
set apart, 4848+3338, *mālē'1+yād* [1]
apart from, 6584, *'al2* [1]
set apart, 7111, *pālâ* [1]
keeps apart, 7233, *pārad* [1]
set apart by themselves, 7233, *pārad* [1]
tore apart, 7293, *pāraq* [1]
set apart as holy, 7727, *qādaš* [1]
set apart, 7731, *qōdeš* [1]
tear apart, 7763, *qûṣ2* [1]
be split apart, 7973, *qāra'* [1]
tore apart, 7973+4200+9109+7974, *qāra'+le-1+šenayim+qerā'îm* [1]
was split apart, 7973, *qāra'* [1]
set apart, 8123, *rûm1* [1]
tore apart, 9117, *šāsa'* [1]

APARTMENT [1]
apartment, 1074, *bayit1* [1]

APES [2]
apes, 7761, *qôp* [2]

APHEK [9]
Aphek, 707, *'apēq* [9]

APHEKAH [1]
Aphekah, 708, *'apēqâ* [1]

APHIAH [1]
Aphiah, 688, *'ᵃpîaḥ* [1]

APPAIM [2]
Appaim, 691, *'appayim*[2] [2]

APPALLED [22]
appalled, 9037, *šāmēm*[1] [19]
are appalled, 9037, *šāmēm*[1] [1]
cause to be appalled, 9037, *šāmēm*[1] [1]
appalled, 9449, *tāmah* [1]

APPEAL [3]
appeal, 2011, *dāraš* [1]
appeal, 2704, *ḥālâ*[2] [1]
appeal, 7924, *qārā'*[1] [1]

APPEALED [3]
appealed to, 3512+928+6524, *yāṭab+bᵉ-+'ayin*[1] [1]
appealed, 7590, *ṣā'aq* [1]
appealed, 8938, *šālaḥ* [1]

APPEALS [1]
make appeals, 2410, *zā'aq* [1]

APPEAR [37]
appear, 8011, *rā'â*[1] [20]
appear, 5260, *mar'eh* [3]
appear, 6641, *'āmad* [2]
appear, *NIH/RPE* [1]
appear, 995, *bô'* [1]
appear, 2118+928+6524+3869, *hāyâ+bᵉ-+'ayin*[1]*+kᵉ-* [1]
appear, 2118, *hāyâ* [1]
appear, 3922+4604, *kûn*[1]*+môṣā'*[1] [1]
appear righteous, 7405, *ṣādaq* [1]
made appear righteous, 7405, *ṣādaq* [1]
appear, 7541, *ṣāmaḥ* [1]
appear, 7756, *qûm* [1]
appear, 7928, *qārab* [1]
appear before, 8011+7156, *rā'â*[1]*+pāneh* [1]
appear, 10201, *hᵃwâ* [1]

APPEARANCE [22]
appearance, 5260, *mar'eh* [14]
appearance, 6524, *'ayin*[1] [2]
appearance, 1619, *gizrâ* [1]
appearance, 1952, *dᵉmût* [1]
handsome appearance, 3637, *yāpeh* [1]
outward appearance, 6524, *'ayin*[1] [1]
appearance, 7156, *pāneh* [1]
appearance, 10657, *rēw* [1]

APPEARED [44]
appeared, 8011, *rā'â*[1] [33]
appeared, 5260, *mar'eh* [3]
appeared, 2180, *hinnēh* [2]
appeared, 995, *bô'* [1]
appeared, 2118, *hāyâ* [1]
suddenly appeared, 2180, *hinnēh* [1]
appeared, 6590, *'ālâ* [1]
appeared, 6641, *'āmad* [1]
appeared, 10485, *nᵉpaq* [1]

APPEARING [3]
appearing, 3655, *yāṣā'* [1]
appearing, 7156, *pāneh* [1]
appearing, 8011, *rā'â*[1] [1]

APPEARS [18]
appears, 8011, *rā'â*[1] [7]
appears, 5260, *mar'eh* [5]
appears, 2118, *hāyâ* [3]
appears, 2436, *zāraḥ* [1]
appears, 7756, *qûm* [1]
appears, 9207, *šāqap* [1]

APPEASE [1]
appease, 4105, *kāpar*[1] [1]

APPETITE [6]
appetite, 5883, *nepeš* [6]

APPETITES [1]
appetites, 5883, *nepeš* [1]

APPLE [7]
apple tree, 9515, *tappûaḥ*[1] [3]
apple, 413, *'îšôn* [2]
apple, 413+1426, *'îšôn+bat*[1] [1]
apple, 949, *bābâ* [1]

APPLES [3]
apples, 9515, *tappûaḥ*[1] [3]

APPLIED [6]
applied, 5989, *nātan* [3]
applied, 8492, *śîm* [1]
applied, 8883, *šît*[1] [1]
applied to, 10378, *lᵉ-* [1]

APPLIES [6]
applies, 2118, *hāyâ* [2]
applies to, 4200, *lᵉ-*[1] [2]
applies, *NIH/RPE* [1]
applies, 6913, *'āśâ*[1] [1]

APPLY [6]
apply, 995, *bô'* [1]
apply, 2118, *hāyâ* [1]
apply, 3359, *yāda'* [1]
apply, 5302, *māraḥ* [1]
apply, 6913, *'āśâ*[1] [1]
apply, 8883, *šît*[1] [1]

APPLYING [1]
applying, 5742, *nāṭâ* [1]

APPOINT [27]
appoint, 7212, *pāqad* [11]
appoint, 8492, *śîm* [3]
appoint, 5989, *nātan* [2]
appoint, 6641, *'āmad* [2]
appoint, 2035, *hab*[1] [1]
appoint, 4374, *lāqaḥ* [1]
appoint as king, 4887, *mālak*[1] [1]
appoint, 4948, *mānâ*[1] [1]
appoint, 6202, *sāpaḥ*[1] [1]
appoint, 7422, *ṣāwâ* [1]
be sure to appoint, 8492+8492, *śîm+śîm* [1]
appoint, 10431, *mᵉnâ* [1]
appoint, 10624, *qûm* [1]

APPOINTED [123]
appointed feasts, 4595, *mô'ēd* [24]
appointed time, 4595, *mô'ēd* [15]
appointed, 5989, *nātan* [10]
appointed, 6641, *'āmad* [10]
appointed, 7212, *pāqad* [9]
appointed, 7422, *ṣāwâ* [8]
appointed, 8492, *śîm* [8]
appointed as governor, 7212, *pāqad* [5]
appointed, 6913, *'āśâ*[1] [4]
appointed, 4595, *mô'ēd* [2]
were appointed, 7212, *pāqad* [2]
appointed order, 7213, *pᵉquddâ* [2]
appointed, 7213, *pᵉquddâ* [2]
appointed, 10431, *mᵉnâ* [2]
appointed, *NIH/RPE* [1]
appointed, 285, *'eḥād* [1]
appointed, 609, *'ēmer*[1] [1]
time appointed, 2375, *zᵉmān* [1]
appointed time, 2976, *ḥōq* [1]
appointed, 3585, *yā'ad* [1]
appointed, 3922, *kûn*[1] [1]
appointed feast, 4595, *mô'ēd* [1]
appointed seasons, 4595, *mô'ēd* [1]
appointed times, 4595, *mô'ēd* [1]
appointed, 4948, *mānâ*[1] [1]
was appointed, 5820, *nāsak*[3] [1]
appointed time, 6961, *'ēt* [1]
appointed for the task, 6967, *'ittî* [1]
appointed, 7756, *qûm* [1]
were appointed, 7924, *qārā'*[1] [1]
appointed, 7951, *qārî* [1]
appointed, 8883, *šît*[1] [1]
appointed, 10624, *qûm* [1]
appointed, 10682, *śîm* [1]

APPOINTING [1]
appointing, 6641, *'āmad* [1]

APPOINTMENT [1]
appointment, 5152, *mipqād* [1]

APPOINTS [1]
appoints, 5989, *nātan* [1]

APPORTIONED [1]
apportioned, 2745, *ḥālaq*[2] [1]

APPRAISED [1]
appraised, 6218, *sāpar* [1]

APPROACH [19]
approach, 5602, *nāgaš* [6]
approach, 7928, *qārab* [6]
approach, 995, *bô'* [2]
approach, 7940, *qārôb* [2]
approach, 5595, *nāga'* [1]
approach, 6590, *'ālâ* [1]
approach, 7156, *pāneh* [1]

APPROACHED [31]
approached, 5602, *nāgaš* [12]
approached, 7928, *qārab* [9]
approached, 995+6330, *bô'+'ad*[2] [4]
approached, 10638, *qᵉrēb* [2]
approached, 995+448, *bô'+'el* [1]
approached, 995, *bô'* [1]
approached, 7929, *qārēb* [1]
approached, 10413, *mᵉṭā'* [1]

APPROACHES [5]
approaches, 995+448, *bô'+'el* [2]
approaches, 7155, *pānâ* [1]
approaches, 7928, *qārab* [1]
approaches, 7929, *qārēb* [1]

APPROACHING [3]
approaching, 995, *bô'* [2]
approaching, 7928, *qārab* [1]

APPROPRIATE [1]
appropriate, 3869, *kᵉ-* [1]

APPROVAL [3]
approval, 2876, *ḥesed*[2] [1]
approval, 3359, *yāda'* [1]
approval, 5790, *nōkaḥ* [1]

APPROVE [2]
approve of, 928+6524+3202, *bᵉ-+'ayin*[1]*+ṭôb*[2] [1]
approve, 8354, *rāṣâ*[1] [1]

APT [1]
giving an apt reply, 5101+7023, *ma'ᵃneh*[1]*+peh* [1]

APTITUDE [1]
showing aptitude, 8505, *śākal*[1] [1]

APTLY [1]
aptly, 6584+698, *'al*[2]*+'ōpen* [1]

AQUEDUCT [3]
aqueduct, 9498, *tᵉ'ālâ*[1] [3]

AR [6]
Ar, 6840, *'ār*[2] [6]

ARA [1]
Ara, 736, *'ᵃrā'* [1]

ARAB [4]
Arab, 6861, *'arbî* [2]
Arab, 742, *'ᵃrāb* [1]
Arab, 6862, *'ᵃrābî* [1]

ARABAH [28]
Arabah, 6858, *'ᵃrābâ*[2] [28]

ARABIA [6]
Arabia, 6851, *'ᵃrab*[1] [6]

ARABIAN [1]
Arabian, 6851, *'ᵃrab*[1] [1]

ARABS [5]
Arabs, 6861, *'arbî* [5]

ARAD [5]
Arad, 6866, 'ᵃrād^{2} [4]
Arad, 6865, 'ᵃrād^{1} [1]

ARAH [5]
Arah, 783, 'āraḥ^{2} [4]
Arah, 6869, 'ārā'^{3} [1]

ARAM [69]
Aram, 806, 'ᵃrām [69]

ARAM MAACAH [1]
Aram Maacah, 807, 'ᵃram maʿᵃkâ [1]

ARAM NAHARAIM [5]
Aram Naharaim, 808, 'ᵃram nahᵃrayim [5]

ARAM ZOBAH [1]
Aram Zobah, 809, 'ᵃram ṣôbâ [1]

ARAMAIC [5]
in Aramaic, 811, 'ᵃrāmî [5]

ARAMEAN [17]
Aramean, 812, 'ᵃrammî [8]
Aramean, 806, 'ᵃrām [7]
Aramean kingdom, 806, 'ᵃrām [2]

ARAMEANS [48]
Arameans, 806, 'ᵃrām [42]
Arameans, 812, 'ᵃrammî [4]
Arameans, *NIH/RPE* [1]
the Arameans^{s}, 4392, -ām [1]

ARAN [2]
Aran, 814, 'ᵃrān [2]

ARARAT [4]
Ararat, 827, 'ᵃrāraṭ [4]

ARAUNAH [17]
Araunah, 821, 'ornān [9]
Araunah, 779, 'ᵃrawnâ [8]

ARBA [3]
Arba, *NIH/RPE* [3]

ARBATHITE [2]
Arbathite, 6863, ʿarbātî [2]

ARBITE [1]
Arbite, 750, 'arbî [1]

ARBITRATE [1]
arbitrate, 3519, yākaḥ [1]

ARCHER [4]
archer, 2005, dārak [1]
archer, 8043, rab^{3} [1]
archer, 8050+8009, rābâ^{2}+qaššāt [1]
archer, 9530+8008, tāpaś+qešet [1]

ARCHERS [9]
archers, 8043, rab^{3} [2]
archers, 1251+2932, baʿal^{1}+ḥēṣ [1]
archers, 3452, yôreh^{1} [1]
archers, 4619+408+928+2021+8008, môreh^{1}+'îš^{1}+bᵉ+ha-+qešet [1]
archers, 4619+928+2021+8008, môreh^{1}+bᵉ-+ha-+qešet [1]
archers, 4619, môreh^{1} [1]
archers, 5432+8008, māšak+qešet [1]
archers, 8227+8008, rāmâ^{1}+qešet [1]

ARCHIVES [3]
archives, 10103+10148, bayit+gᵉnaz [1]
archives, 10103+10515, bayit+sᵉpar [1]
archives, 10515+10177, sᵉpar+dokrān [1]

ARD [3]
Ard, 764, 'ard [3]

ARDITE [1]
Ardite, 766, 'ardî [1]

ARDON [1]
Ardon, 765, 'ardôn [1]

ARE [2749]*
are, *NIH/RPE* [1298]
are, *AIT* [1198]
are, 2118, hāyâ [76]
are no more, 401, 'ayin^{1} [5]
are, 3780, yēš [4]
there are, 3780, yēš [3]
are, 10029, 'îtay [2]

AREA [39]
area, *NIH/RPE* [12]
area, 824, 'ereṣ [5]
area, 1473, gᵉbûl [4]
open area, 4965, munnāḥ [3]
area, *AIT* [2]
temple area, 1074, bayit^{1} [2]
the area^{s}, 2257, -ô [2]
remote area, 3752, yᵉrēkâ [2]
area, 8441, śādeh [2]
area, 4946+2575, min+ḥûṣ [1]
area, 5226, māqôm [1]
diseased area, 5999, neteq [1]
area around, 6017, sābîb [1]
sanctuary area, 7731, qōdeš [1]

AREAS [6]
areas, *NIH/RPE* [1]
areas of land, 824, 'ereṣ [1]
the areas^{s}, 889, 'ašer [1]
areas, 1473, gᵉbûl [1]
market areas, 2575, ḥûṣ [1]
wooded areas, 3091, ḥōreš^{1} [1]

ARELI [2]
Areli, 739, 'ar'ēlî^{1} [2]

ARELITE [1]
Arelite, 740, 'ar'ēlî^{2} [1]

AREN'T [8]
aren't, 4202, lō' [5]
aren't, 401, 'ayin^{1} [1]
aren't, 2022, hᵃ- [1]
aren't do something, 3120, ḥāšâ [1]

ARGOB [5]
Argob, 758, 'argōb^{1} [4]
Argob, 759, 'argōb^{2} [1]

ARGUE [7]
argue, *NIH/RPE* [1]
argue case, 3519, yākaḥ [1]
argue, 3519, yākaḥ [1]
argue the case, 8189, rîb [1]
argue, 8189, rîb^{1} [1]
argue, 9048+7754, šāmaʿ+qôl [1]
argue, 9149, šāpaṭ [1]

ARGUED [1]
argued, 1819, dābar^{2} [1]

ARGUING [2]
arguing with each other, 1906, dîn^{1} [1]
arguing, 6699, ʿānâ^{1} [1]

ARGUMENT [1]
argument, 9350, tôkaḥat [1]

ARGUMENTS [6]
arguments, 609, 'ēmer^{1} [2]
arguments, *NIH/RPE* [1]
arguments, 3519, yākaḥ [1]
arguments, 6802, ʿᵃṣumôt [1]
arguments, 9350, tôkaḥat [1]

ARIDAI [1]
Aridai, 767, 'ᵃriday [1]

ARIDATHA [1]
Aridatha, 792, 'ᵃrîdātā' [1]

ARIEH [1]
Arieh, 794, 'aryēh^{2} [1]

ARIEL [5]
Ariel, 790, 'ᵃrî'ēl^{2} [4]
Ariel, 791, 'ᵃrî'ēl^{3} [1]

ARIGHT [1]
aright, 4026, kēn^{1} [1]

ARIOCH [6]
Arioch, 10070, 'aryôk [4]
Arioch, 796, 'aryôk [2]

ARISAI [1]
Arisai, 798, 'ᵃrîsay [1]

ARISE [31]
arise, 7756, qûm [22]
arise, 6641, ʿāmad [4]
arise, 6424, ʿûr^{3} [2]
arise, 3655, yāṣā' [1]
arise and come, 7756, qûm [1]
arise, 10624, qûm [1]

ARISEN [1]
arisen, 3655, yāṣā' [1]

ARISES [1]
arises, 3655, yāṣā' [1]

ARK [211]
ark, 778, 'ᵃrôn [181]
ark, 9310, tēbâ [25]
ark, *NIH/RPE* [3]
the ark^{s}, 2257, -ô [2]

ARKITE [5]
Arkite, 805, 'arkî [5]

ARKITES [3]
Arkites, 6909, ʿarqî [2]
Arkites, 805, 'arkî [1]

ARM [74]
arm, 2432, zᵉrôaʿ [53]
arm, 3338, yād [7]
arm, *NIH/RPE* [6]
arm, 7396, ṣad^{1} [2]
arm, 274, 'ezrôaʿ [1]
arm of power, 2432, zᵉrôaʿ [1]
arm, 2741, ḥālaṣ^{2} [1]
arm ourselves, 2741, ḥālaṣ^{2} [1]
arm yourselves, 2741, ḥālaṣ^{2} [1]
arm, 4190, kātēp [1]

ARMED [45]
armed, 2741, ḥālaṣ^{2} [12]
armed, 273, 'āzar [4]
armed, 2520+3998, ḥāgar+kᵉlî [3]
armed, 8990, šālap [3]
armed, 2616, ḥāzaq [2]
armed guard, 2741, ḥālaṣ^{2} [2]
armed, 4482, māgēn^{1} [2]
armed, 5976, nāšaq^{2} [2]
armed, *AIT* [1]
armed yourself, 273, 'āzar [1]
armed forces, 2432, zᵉrôaʿ [1]
was armed, 2520, ḥāgar [1]
armed forces, 2657+7372, ḥayil+ṣābā'^{2} [1]
armed force, 2657, ḥayil [1]
armed for battle, 2741, ḥālaṣ^{2} [1]
armed for battle, 2821, ḥāmaš [1]
armed, 2821, ḥāmaš [1]
fully armed, 2821, ḥāmaš [1]
armed, 4229, lābûš [1]
armed, 4878, milḥāmâ [1]
armed, 5951, nāśā' [1]
armed, 5976+8227, nāšaq^{2}+rāmâ^{1} [1]
men armed with slings, 7847, qallāʿ [1]

ARMIES [12]
armies, 7372, ṣābā'^{2} [6]
armies, 5120, maʿᵃrākâ [3]
armies, 4722, maḥᵃneh [2]
armies, 2657, ḥayil [1]

ARMLETS [1]
armlets, 731, 'eṣʿādâ [1]

ARMONI [1]
Armoni, 813, 'armōnî [1]

ARMOR [15]
armor, 3998, kᵉlî [5]

armor, 9234, *širyôn* [3]
armor, 6246, *siryôn* [2]
puts on armor, 2520, *ḥāgar* [1]
armor, 5516, *motnayim* [1]
coat of armor, 9234, *širyôn* [1]
coat of scale armor, 9234+7989, *širyôn+qaśqešet* [1]
coats of armor, 9234, *širyôn* [1]

ARMOR-BEARER [18]
armor-bearer, 5951+3998, *nāśā'+k^{e}lî* [18]

ARMOR-BEARERS [2]
armor-bearers, 5951+3998, *nāśā'+k^{e}lî* [2]

ARMORY [3]
armory, 1074+3998, *bayit^{1}+k^{e}lî* [2]
armory, 5977, *nešeq^{1}* [1]

ARMRESTS [2]
armrests, 3338, *yād* [2]

ARMS [43]
arms, 2432, *z^{e}rôa'* [15]
arms, 2668, *ḥêq* [6]
arms, 3338, *yād* [6]
arms, 273, *'āzar* [2]
arms, 2950, *ḥōṣen* [2]
threw arms around, 5877+6584+7418, *nāpal+'al^{2}+ṣawwā'r* [2]
arms, 723+3338, *'aṣṣîl+yād* [1]
calling to arms, 2410+339, *zā'aq+'aḥar* [1]
strong arms, 2432+3338, *z^{e}rôa'+yād* [1]
hold in arms, 2485, *ḥābaq* [1]
bear arms, 2520+2514, *ḥāgar+h^{a}gôrâ* [1]
arms, 4090, *kap* [1]
threw arms around, 5877+6584, *nāpal+'al^{2}* [1]
be called to arms, 7212, *pāqad* [1]
were called to arms, 7590, *ṣā'aq* [1]
arms, 10185, *d^{e}rā'* [1]

ARMY [248]
army, 2657, *ḥayil* [77]
army, 7372, *ṣābā'^{2}* [59]
army, 6639, *'am^{2}* [48]
army, 4722, *maḥ^{a}neh* [23]
army, 2162, *hāmôn* [11]
army, 408+4878, *'îš^{1}+milḥāmâ* [4]
army, 6639+4878, *'am^{2}+milḥāmâ* [4]
army, *AIT* [3]
army, *NIH/RPE* [2]
vast army, 2162, *hāmôn* [2]
army, 7736, *qāhāl* [2]
army, 408, *'îš^{1}* [1]
army, 554, *'alqûm* [1]
army, 824, *'ereṣ* [1]
army, 1201, *bēn^{1}* [1]
army, 2162+2657, *hāmôn+ḥayil* [1]
army, 2432, *z^{e}rôa'* [1]
army, 2657+7372, *ḥayil+ṣābā'^{2}* [1]
army, 2741, *ḥālaṣ^{2}* [1]
the army^{s}, 4392, *-ām* [1]
army, 4595, *mô'ēd* [1]
army divisions, 4713, *maḥ^{a}lōqet* [1]
army, 7736+2256+6639, *qāhāl+w^{e}-+'am^{2}* [1]
army, 10264, *ḥayil* [1]

ARNAN [1]
Arnan, 820, *'arnān* [1]

ARNON [24]
Arnon, 818, *'arnôn* [24]

ARNON'S [1]
Arnon's, 818, *'arnôn* [1]

ARODI [2]
Arodi, 771, *'^{a}rôdî^{1}* [2]

ARODITE [1]
Arodite, 772, *'^{a}rôdî^{2}* [1]

AROER [16]
Aroer, 6876, *'^{a}rô'ēr^{2}* [16]

AROERITE [1]
Aroerite, 6901, *'^{a}rō'ērî* [1]

AROMA [40]
aroma, 8194, *rêaḥ* [40]

AROMATIC [1]
aromatic resin, 978, *b^{e}dōlaḥ* [1]

AROSE [7]
arose, 7756, *qûm* [4]
arose, 2118, *hāyâ* [2]
early arose, 8899, *šākam* [1]

AROUND [323]
around, 6017, *sābîb* [108]
around, 6584, *'al^{2}* [27]
all around, 6017, *sābîb* [23]
all around, 6017+6017, *sābîb+sābîb* [17]
around, 448, *'el* [10]
around, 928, *b^{e}-* [10]
around, *AIT* [9]
around, 4946+6017, *min+sābîb* [7]
around^{s}, 824, *'ereṣ* [6]
around, *NIH/RPE* [3]
tied around, 2520, *ḥāgar* [3]
around, 6017+6017, *sābîb+sābîb* [3]
turned around, 8740, *šûb^{1}* [3]
around, 10542, *'al* [3]
around, 339, *'aḥar* [2]
around, 1237, *ba'ad^{1}* [2]
wheel around, 2200+3338, *hāpak+yād* [2]
around, 4059, *kāsâ* [2]
around, 4990, *mēsab* [2]
threw arms around, 5877+6584+7418, *nāpal+'al^{2}+ṣawwā'r* [2]
circle around, 6015, *sābab* [2]
coiled around, 6015, *sābab* [2]
led around, 6015, *sābab* [2]
made way around, 6015, *sābab* [2]
march around, 6015, *sābab* [2]
marched around, 6015, *sābab* [2]
measure around, 6015+6017, *sābab+sābîb* [2]
turned around, 6015, *sābab* [2]
went around, 6015, *sābab* [2]
around, 6640, *'im* [2]
look around, 8011, *rā'â^{1}* [2]
turn around, 8740, *šûb^{1}* [2]
gather around, 665, *'āsap* [1]
all around, 907, *'ēt^{2}* [1]
wandering around in confusion, 1003, *bûk* [1]
around, 1237+4946+6017, *ba'ad^{1}+min+sābîb* [1]
put limits around, 1487, *gābal* [1]
going around, 2143, *hālak* [1]
walked around, 2143, *hālak* [1]
walking around, 2143, *hālak* [1]
walks around, 2143, *hālak* [1]
went around, 2143, *hālak* [1]
turned around, 2200, *hāpak* [1]
wrapped around, 2502, *ḥābaš* [1]
put sackcloth around, 2520, *ḥāgar* [1]
tie around, 2520, *ḥāgar* [1]
look around, 2924, *ḥāpaś* [1]
all around, 3869+2021+1885, *k^{e}+ha-+dûr^{3}* [1]
around, 3972, *kōl* [1]
wrap around, 4043, *kānas* [1]
around, 4200, *l^{e}-^{1}* [1]
all around, 4946+6017, *min+sābîb* [1]
around, 4946+2021+2575, *min+ha-+ḥûṣ* [1]
around, 4991, *m^{e}sibbâ* [1]
look around, 5564, *nābaṭ* [1]
looked around, 5564, *nābaṭ* [1]
threw arms around, 5877+6584, *nāpal+'al^{2}* [1]
go around, 5938, *nāqap^{2}* [1]
march around, 6015+5938, *sābab+nāqap^{2}* [1]
all around, 6015, *sābab* [1]
around, 6015, *sābab* [1]
brought around, 6015, *sābab* [1]
carried around, 6015, *sābab* [1]
coming around, 6015, *sābab* [1]
curved around, 6015, *sābab* [1]
gather around, 6015, *sābab* [1]
gathered around, 6015, *sābab* [1]
go around, 6015, *sābab* [1]
put around, 6015, *sābab* [1]
sent around, 6015, *sābab* [1]
swarmed around, 6015, *sābab* [1]
area around, 6017, *sābîb* [1]
everything around, 6017, *sābîb* [1]
stationed around, 6017, *sābîb* [1]
led around, 6296, *'ābar^{1}* [1]
wrap around himself, 6486, *'āṭâ^{1}* [1]
wraps around him, 6486, *'āṭâ^{1}* [1]
wearing around, 6584, *'al^{2}* [1]
looked around, 7155, *pānâ* [1]
turn around, 7155, *pānâ* [1]
turned around, 7155, *pānâ* [1]
went around, 8763, *šûṭ^{1}* [1]
lie around, 8886, *šākab* [1]
staggers around, 9494, *tā'â* [1]
wandering around, 9494, *tā'â* [1]
walking around, 10207, *h^{a}lak* [1]
crowded around, 10359, *k^{e}naš* [1]

AROUSE [3]
arouse, 6424, *'ûr^{3}* [3]

AROUSED [13]
aroused, 3013, *ḥārâ^{1}* [4]
aroused, 6424, *'ûr^{3}* [2]
aroused, 6590, *'ālâ* [2]
aroused, 2801, *ḥāmam* [1]
aroused, 4023, *kāmar* [1]
aroused, 6584+2118, *'al^{2}+hāyâ* [1]
aroused jealousy, 7861, *qānā'* [1]
aroused wrath, 7911, *qāṣap* [1]

AROUSES [1]
arouses, *NIH/RPE* [1]

ARPAD [6]
Arpad, 822, *'arpād* [6]

ARPHAXAD [9]
Arphaxad, 823, *'arpakšad* [9]

ARRANGE [4]
arrange, 6885, *'ārak* [4]

ARRANGED [7]
arranged, 6885, *'ārak* [3]
arranged, 3512, *yāṭab* [1]
was arranged, 3922, *kûn^{1}* [1]
arranged, 4595+2118, *mô'ēd+hāyâ* [1]
arranged, 5989, *nātan* [1]

ARRANGEMENT [1]
arrangement, 9414, *t^{e}kûnâ* [1]

ARRAY [2]
array, 7372, *ṣābā'^{2}* [1]
vast array, 7372, *ṣābā'^{2}* [1]

ARRAYED [2]
arrayed in, 928, *b^{e}-* [1]
arrayed, 3598, *yā'aṭ* [1]

ARREST [1]
arrest, 4374, *lāqaḥ* [1]

ARRESTED [2]
arrested, 9530, *tāpaś* [2]

ARRIVAL [2]
arrival, 995, *bô'* [2]

ARRIVE [3]
arrive, 995+448, *bô'+'el* [1]
arrive, 995+6330, *bô'+'ad^{2}* [1]
arrive, 995, *bô'* [1]

ARRIVED [58]
arrived, 995, *bô'* [48]
arrived, 995+448, *bô'+'el* [4]
arrived, 5595, *nāga'* [3]
arrived, *NIH/RPE* [1]
arrived, 995+6330, *bô'+'ad^{2}* [1]
arrived, 8740, *šûb^{1}* [1]

ARRIVES [5]
arrives, 995, *bô'* [2]
arrives, *NIH/RPE* [1]
arrives, 995+7024, *bô'+pōh* [1]
arrives, 3528, *yālad* [1]

ARRIVING [4]
arriving, 995, bôʾ [3]
arriving, NIH/RPE [1]

ARROGANCE [15]
arrogance, 1454, gāʾôn [5]
arrogance, 1452, gaʾᵃwâ [2]
arrogance, 1455, gēʾût [1]
arrogance, 1471, gabhût [1]
arrogance, 1542, gōdel [1]
arrogance, 2295, zādôn [1]
arrogance, 2326, zîd [1]
arrogance, 5294, mārôm [1]
arrogance, 6981, ʿātāq [1]
arrogance, 7210, pāšar [1]

ARROGANT [31]
arrogant, 2294, zēd [10]
arrogant, 2147, hālal^{3} [3]
arrogant, 2295, zādôn [2]
arrogant, 2326, zîd [2]
arrogant, 3400, yāhîr [2]
arrogant, 5951+4213, nāśāʾ+lēb [2]
arrogant, 1454, gāʾôn [1]
arrogant, 1456, gaʾᵃyôn [1]
arrogant, 1467, gābah [1]
arrogant, 1469, gābōah [1]
arrogant, 1471, gabhût [1]
arrogant, 3594, yāʾaz [1]
arrogant, 3856, yeter^{1} [1]
arrogant, 6981, ʿātāq [1]
arrogant, 7069, pāḥaz [1]
arrogant, 10659, rûm^{1} [1]

ARROGANTLY [4]
arrogantly, 1504, gābar [1]
arrogantly treated, 2326, zîd [1]
treated arrogantly, 2326, zîd [1]
arrogantly, 6981, ʿātāq [1]

ARROW [18]
arrow, 2932, ḥēṣ [12]
arrow, 2943, ḥēṣî^{1} [5]
arrow, 8008, qešet [1]

ARROWS [45]
arrows, 2932, ḥēṣ [38]
arrows, 1201+8008, bēn^{1}+qešet [1]
arrows^{s}, 1201, bēn^{1} [1]
shoot arrows, 3721, yārâ^{1} [1]
shot arrows, 3721, yārâ^{1} [1]
shot with arrows, 3721+3721, yārâ^{1}+yārâ^{1} [1]
arrows, 4751, maṭṭeh [1]
arrows, 8008, qešet [1]

ARSENAL [1]
arsenal, 238, ʾôṣār [1]

ART [1]
art of engraving, 7338+7334, pātaḥ^{2}+pittûaḥ [1]

ARTAXERXES [15]
Artaxerxes, 831, ʾartaḥšastʾ [9]
Artaxerxes, 10078, ʾartaḥšaśtʾ [6]

ARTICLE [14]
article, 3998, kᵉlî [8]
affected article, 5596, negaʿ [2]
article, NIH/RPE [1]
the article^{s}, 2257, -ô [1]
article^{s}, 5596, negaʿ [1]
contaminated article, 5596, negaʿ [1]

ARTICLES [77]
articles, 3998, kᵉlî [67]
articles, 10398, māʾn [4]
household articles, 3998, kᵉlî [2]
these articles^{s}, 4392, -ām [2]
articles of clothing, 955, beged^{2} [1]
articles of value, 4458, meged [1]

ARTIFICIAL [1]
artificial, 6913, ʿāśâ^{1} [1]

ARTISANS [4]
artisans, 4994, masgēr^{2} [4]

ARTISTIC [3]
artistic designs, 4742, maḥᵃšābâ [2]
artistic craftsmanship, 4742, maḥᵃšābâ [1]

ARTS [4]
secret arts, 4319, lāṭ [3]
secret arts, 4268, lᵉhāṭîm [1]

ARUBBOTH [1]
Arubboth, 749, ʾᵃrubbôt [1]

ARUMAH [1]
Arumah, 777, ʾᵃrûmâ [1]

ARVAD [2]
Arvad, 770, ʾarwād [2]

ARVADITES [2]
Arvadites, 773, ʾarwādî [2]

ARZA [1]
Arza, 825, ʾarṣāʾ [1]

AS [3005]*
as, NIH/RPE [492]
as, 3869, kᵉ- [425]
as, 3869+889, kᵉ-+ʾᵃšer [270]
as, 4200, lᵉ-^{1} [210]
as, AIT [176]
as far as, 6330, ʿad^{2} [140]
as surely as lives, 2644, ḥay^{1} [92]
as, 2256, wᵉ- [89]
as well as, 2256, wᵉ- [82]
as, 928, bᵉ- [80]
as for, 2256, wᵉ- [61]
just as, 3869+889, kᵉ-+ʾᵃšer [58]
as soon as, 3869, kᵉ- [48]
as surely as live, 2644, ḥay^{1} [46]
as, 4017, kᵉmô [25]
just as, 3869+3972+889, kᵉ-+kōl+ʾᵃšer [24]
as, 889, ʾᵃšer [18]
as long as, 3972+3427, kōl+yôm^{1} [18]
just as, 3869, kᵉ- [16]
just as, 3869+889+4027, kᵉ-+ʾᵃšer+kēn^{2} [14]
as, 4946, min [14]
but as for, 2256, wᵉ- [12]
as for, 4200, lᵉ-^{1} [12]
as if, 3869, kᵉ- [11]
same as, 3869, kᵉ- [11]
as though, 3869, kᵉ- [8]
such as, 3869, kᵉ- [8]
as, 3954, kî^{2} [8]
as, 6584, ʿal^{2} [8]
and as well, 2256, wᵉ- [7]
as, 3869+889+4027, kᵉ-+ʾᵃšer+kēn^{2} [7]
as, 6330, ʿad^{2} [7]
as soon as, 2256, wᵉ- [6]
as well as, 2256+1685, wᵉ-+gam [6]
as live, 2644, ḥay^{1} [6]
as common as, 3869, kᵉ- [6]
as long as lived, 3972+3427, kōl+yôm^{1} [6]
as, 4027, kēn^{2} [6]
as soon as, 4200, lᵉ-^{1} [6]
as, 10341, kᵉ- [6]
just as, 2256, wᵉ- [5]
as, 3869+3972+889, kᵉ-+kōl+ʾᵃšer [5]
as, 4027+3869+889, kēn^{2}+kᵉ-+ʾᵃšer [5]
as soon as, 928, bᵉ- [4]
as long as, 928, bᵉ- [4]
as well, 1685, gam [4]
as surely as, 2256, wᵉ- [4]

ASA [50]
Asa, 654, ʾāsāʾ [50]

ASA'S [7]
Asa's, 654, ʾāsāʾ [7]

ASAHEL [18]
Asahel, 6915, ʿᵃśāhʾēl [17]
Asahel, NIH/RPE [1]

ASAHEL'S [1]
Asahel's^{s}, 2084, -hû [1]

ASAIAH [8]
Asaiah, 6919, ʿᵃśāyâ [8]

ASAPH [45]
Asaph, 666, ʾāsāp [45]

ASAPH'S [1]
Asaph's, 666, ʾāsāp [1]

ASAREL [1]
Asarel, 832, ʾᵃśarʾēl [1]

ASARELAH [1]
Asarelah, 833, ʾᵃśarʾēlâ [1]

ASCEND [4]
ascend, 6590, ʿālâ [4]

ASCENDED [5]
ascended, 6590, ʿālâ [5]

ASCENDING [2]
in ascending stages,
4200+5087+2025+4200+5087+2025,
lᵉ-^{1}+maʿal^{2}+-â^{2}+lᵉ-^{1}+maʿal^{2}+-â^{2} [1]
ascending, 6590, ʿālâ [1]

ASCENT [2]
ascent, 5090, maʿᵃleh [1]
ascent, 6590, ʿālâ [1]

ASCENTS [15]
ascents, 5092, maʿᵃlâ^{2} [15]

ASCRIBE [10]
ascribe, 2035, hab^{1} [9]
ascribe, 5989, nātan [1]

ASENATH [3]
Asenath, 664, ʾāsᵉnat [3]

ASH [4]
ash heap, 883, ʾašpōt [2]
ash heaps, 883, ʾašpōt [1]
ash, 2016, dešen [1]

ASHAMED [32]
ashamed, 1017, bôš^{1} [24]
ashamed, 4007, kālam [6]
felt ashamed, 1017, bôš^{1} [1]
ashamed, 2917, ḥāpar^{2} [1]

ASHAN [4]
Ashan, 6941, ʿāšān^{2} [4]

ASHBEL [3]
Ashbel, 839, ʾašbēl [3]

ASHBELITE [1]
Ashbelite, 840, ʾašbēlî [1]

ASHDOD [21]
Ashdod, 846, ʾašdôd [15]
people of Ashdod, 847, ʾašdôdî [2]
Ashdod, 847, ʾašdôdî [1]
from Ashdod, 847, ʾašdôdî [1]
men of Ashdod, 847, ʾašdôdî [1]
language of Ashdod, 848, ʾašdôdît [1]

ASHER [43]
Asher, 888, ʾāšēr [37]
Asher, 1201+888, bēn^{1}+ʾāšēr [5]
people of Asher, 896, ʾāšērî [1]

ASHER'S [1]
Asher's, 4946+888, min+ʾāšēr [1]

ASHERAH [39]
Asherah poles, 895, ʾᵃšērâ [22]
Asherah pole, 895, ʾᵃšērâ [14]
Asherah, 895, ʾᵃšērâ [3]

ASHERAHS [1]
Asherahs, 895, ʾᵃšērâ [1]

ASHES [31]
ashes, 709, ʾēper [20]
ashes, 2016, dešen [7]
remove ashes, 2014, dāšēn^{1} [2]
ashes, 6760, ʿāpār [2]

ASHHUR [2]
Ashhur, 858, *'ašḥûr* [2]

ASHIMA [1]
Ashima, 860, *'ašîmā'* [1]

ASHKELON [13]
Ashkelon, 884, *'ašqelôn* [12]
Ashkelon, 885, *'ešqelônî* [1]

ASHKENAZ [3]
Ashkenaz, 867, *'aškenaz* [3]

ASHNAH [2]
Ashnah, 877, *'ašnâ* [2]

ASHPENAZ [1]
Ashpenaz, 881, *'ašpenaz* [1]

ASHTAROTH [6]
Ashtaroth, 6958, *'aštārōt* [6]

ASHTERATHITE [1]
Ashterathite, 6960, *'ašterātî* [1]

ASHTEROTH KARNAIM [1]
Ashteroth Karnaim, 6959, *'ašterōt qarnayim* [1]

ASHTORETH [3]
Ashtoreth, 6956, *'aštōret* [3]

ASHTORETHS [6]
Ashtoreths, 6956, *'aštōret* [6]

ASHURBANIPAL [1]
Ashurbanipal, 10055, *'āsenappar* [1]

ASHURI [1]
Ashuri, 856, *'ašûrî* [1]

ASHVATH [1]
Ashvath, 6937, *'ašwāt* [1]

ASIDE [51]
turn aside, 6073, *sûr*[1] [6]
turned aside, 6073, *sûr*[1] [4]
set aside, 976, *bādal* [3]
took aside, 5742, *nāṭâ* [3]
turn aside, 5742, *nāṭâ* [3]
turning aside, 6073, *sûr*[1] [3]
set aside, 7727, *qādaš* [2]
put aside, 9101, *šānâ*[1] [2]
set aside, 9556, *terûmâ* [2]
aside, *NIH/RPE* [1]
set aside, 665, *'āsap* [1]
cast aside, 1763, *gāraš*[1] [1]
go aside, 2143, *hālak* [1]
stepped aside, 2461, *ḥābā'* [1]
turn aside, 4369, *lāpat* [1]
set aside, 4426, *mibdālôt* [1]
be cast aside, 5610, *nādad* [1]
turned aside, 5742, *nāṭâ* [1]
turning aside, 5742, *nāṭâ* [1]
stand aside, 6015, *sābab* [1]
stepped aside, 6015, *sābab* [1]
lay aside, 6073, *sûr*[1] [1]
put aside, 6073, *sûr*[1] [1]
set aside, 6073, *sûr*[1] [1]
turned aside, 6296, *'ābar*[1] [1]
aside, 6640, *'im* [1]
be sure to set aside a tenth, 6923+6923, *'āśar+'āśar* [1]
setting aside a tenth, 6923+5130, *'āśar+ma'aśēr* [1]
as a special gift set aside, 8123, *rûm*[1] [1]
turn aside, 8454, *śûṭ* [1]
thrown aside, 8959, *šālak* [1]
was set aside, 9068, *šāmar* [1]

ASIEL [1]
Asiel, 6918, *'aśî'ēl* [1]

ASK [101]
ask, 606, *'āmar*[1] [45]
ask, 8626, *šā'al* [39]
ask, *NIH/RPE* [4]
ask, 1819, *dābar*[2] [3]
ask, 1239, *bā'â*[1] [2]
ask, 1741, *gārâ* [2]
I ask, 626, *'onnā'* [1]
ask for, 1335, *bāqaš* [1]
ask, 2011+1821, *dāraš+dābār* [1]
ask, 2011, *dāraš* [1]
ask, 8626+907, *šā'al+'ēt*[2] [1]
ask, 10689, *še'ēl* [1]

ASKED [292]
asked, 606, *'āmar*[1] [215]
asked, 8626, *šā'al* [36]
asked, 6699, *'ānâ*[1] [7]
asked, 1821, *dābār* [5]
asked, 1819, *dābar*[2] [4]
asked, *NIH/RPE* [3]
asked, 10042, *'amar* [3]
asked, 10558, *'anâ* [3]
asked, 10689, *še'ēl* [3]
asked, 10114, *be'â* [2]
asked for permission, 1335, *bāqaš* [1]
asked for, 1335, *bāqaš* [1]
asked, 1335, *bāqaš* [1]
asked, 1336, *baqqāšâ* [1]
asked, 2011, *dāraš* [1]
asked how they were, 8626+4200+8934, *šā'al+le-[1]+šālôm* [1]
earnestly asked for permission, 8626+8626, *šā'al+šā'al* [1]
earnestly asked permission, 8626+8626, *šā'al+šā'al* [1]
gave what asked for, 8626, *šā'al* [1]
what asked for, 8629, *še'ēlâ* [1]
asked for, 10114, *be'â* [1]

ASKING [10]
asking, 606, *'āmar*[1] [4]
asking, 8626, *šā'al* [2]
asking, *NIH/RPE* [1]
asking for, 1335, *bāqaš* [1]
asking, 1819, *dābar*[2] [1]
asking for help, 10274, *ḥanan* [1]

ASKS [15]
asks, 8626, *šā'al* [4]
asks, 606, *'āmar*[1] [3]
what asks, 1821, *dābār* [2]
asks, 7924, *qārā'*[1] [2]
asks, *NIH/RPE* [1]
asks, 1819, *dābar*[2] [1]
what asks, 10418, *millâ* [1]
asks, 10689, *še'ēl* [1]

ASLEEP [6]
fell asleep, 3822, *yāšēn*[1] [2]
asleep, 3825, *yāšēn*[3] [2]
asleep, 3822, *yāšēn*[1] [1]
lay fast asleep, 8101, *rādam* [1]

ASNAH [1]
Asnah, 663, *'asnâ* [1]

ASPATHA [1]
Aspatha, 672, *'aspātā'* [1]

ASRIEL [3]
Asriel, 835, *'aśrî'ēl* [3]

ASRIELITE [1]
Asrielite, 834, *'aśrî'ēlî* [1]

ASSAIL [2]
assail, 5877+6584, *nāpal+'al*[2] [1]
assail, 8720, *šādad* [1]

ASSAILANT [1]
assailant, 5782, *nākâ* [1]

ASSAILS [1]
assails, 8475, *śāṭam* [1]

ASSASSINATE [2]
assassinate, 8938+3338+928, *šālaḥ+yād+be-* [2]

ASSASSINATED [9]
assassinated, 4637, *mût* [5]
assassinated, 5782, *nākâ* [3]
assassinated, 5782+2256+4637, *nākâ+we-+mût* [1]

ASSASSINATION [1]
assassination, 4637, *mût* [1]

ASSASSINS [1]
assassins, 5782, *nākâ* [1]

ASSAULT [2]
assault, 2109, *hût* [1]
assault, 5596, *nega'* [1]

ASSAULTS [3]
assaults, 928+8938, *be-+šālaḥ* [1]
assaults, 5596+4200+5596, *nega'+le-[1]+nega'* [1]
assaults, 7756+6584, *qûm+'al*[2] [1]

ASSEMBLE [32]
assemble, 7695, *qābaṣ* [10]
assemble, 665, *'āsap* [6]
assemble, 7735, *qāhal* [5]
assemble, 3585, *yā'ad* [2]
assemble, 6590, *'ālâ* [2]
assemble, 4043, *kānas* [1]
assemble, 5246, *miqrā'* [1]
assemble, 5602+3481, *nāgaš+yaḥdāw* [1]
assemble, 6590+928+2021+7736, *'ālâ+be-+ha-+qāhāl* [1]
assemble yourselves, 7695, *qābaṣ* [1]
assemble, 7695+3481, *qābaṣ+yaḥdāw* [1]
summoned to assemble, 7735, *qāhal* [1]

ASSEMBLED [42]
assembled, 665, *'āsap* [14]
assembled, 7695, *qābaṣ* [12]
assembled, 7735, *qāhal* [8]
were assembled, 7695, *qābaṣ* [2]
assembled, 910, *'ātâ* [1]
assembled, 2410, *zā'aq* [1]
assembled, 6337, *'ēdâ*[1] [1]
assembled, 7212, *pāqad* [1]
assembled, 7736+995, *qāhāl+bô'* [1]
assembled, 10359, *kenaš* [1]

ASSEMBLIES [5]
assemblies, 5246, *miqrā'* [3]
assemblies, 6809, *'aṣārâ* [2]

ASSEMBLING [1]
assembling, 665, *'āsap* [1]

ASSEMBLY [151]
assembly, 7736, *qāhāl* [72]
assembly, 6337, *'ēdâ*[1] [50]
assembly, 5246, *miqrā'* [15]
assembly, 6809, *'aṣārâ* [5]
sacred assembly, 6809, *'aṣārâ* [2]
assembly, 4595, *mô'ēd* [1]
great assembly, 5220, *maqhēl* [1]
assembly, 5227, *māqôr* [1]
closing assembly, 6809, *'aṣārâ* [1]
whole assembly, 7736+2256+6337, *qāhāl+we-+'ēdâ*[1] [1]
assembly, 7737, *qehillâ* [1]
assembly at the gate, 9133, *ša'ar*[1] [1]

ASSESSMENTS [1]
assessments, 6886, *'ērek* [1]

ASSHUR [7]
Asshur, 855, *'aššûr* [7]

ASSHURITES [1]
Asshurites, 857, *'aššûrim* [1]

ASSIGN [10]
assign as an inheritance, 5706, *nāḥal* [2]
assign, 7212, *pāqad* [2]
assign, 8492, *śîm* [2]
assign inheritance, 5706, *nāḥal* [1]
help assign, 5706, *nāḥal* [1]
assign, 6913, *'āśâ*[1] [1]
assign, 8883, *šît*[1] [1]

ASSIGNED [42]
assigned, 7212, *pāqad* [9]
assigned, 5989, *nātan* [8]
assigned, 6641, *'āmad* [6]

assigned, 4948, *mānâ*^{1} [3]
assigned, *AIT* [2]
assigned to, 4200, *l*^{e}-^{1} [2]
assigned, *NIH/RPE* [1]
assigned to positions, 3569, *yāsad*^{1} [1]
assigned, 3569, *yāsad*^{1} [1]
assigned, 4200, *l*^{e}-^{1} [1]
assigned portion, 4595, *mô'ēd* [1]
were assigned, 4948, *mānâ*^{1} [1]
assigned, 4987, *m*^{e}*nāt* [1]
assigned, 5466, *mišmeret* [1]
assigned, 5706, *nāḥal* [1]
were assigned, 5989, *nātan* [1]
assigned, 6913, *'āśâ*^{1} [1]
assigned, 8938, *šālaḥ* [1]

ASSIGNMENT [1]
assignment, 7213, *p*^{e}*quddâ* [1]

ASSIGNMENTS [1]
made assignments, 2745, *ḥālaq*^{2} [1]

ASSIGNS [1]
assigns, 2745, *ḥālaq*^{2} [1]

ASSIR [4]
Assir, 661, *'assîr*^{2} [4]

ASSIST [8]
assist, 9250, *šārat* [4]
assist, 4856, *m*^{e}*lā'kâ* [1]
assist, 6275, *'*^{a}*bōdâ* [1]
assist, 6468, *'āzar* [1]
assist, 6641+907, *'āmad+'ēt*^{2} [1]

ASSISTANCE [1]
gave assistance, 5951, *nāśā'* [1]

ASSISTANT [2]
assistant, 6584+3338, *'al*^{2}*+yād* [1]
assistant, 6641+4200+7156, *'āmad+l*^{e}-^{1}*+pāneh* [1]

ASSISTANTS [1]
assistants, 5853, *na'ar*^{2} [1]

ASSISTED [3]
assisted, 2616+3338, *ḥāzaq+yād* [1]
assisted, 2616+928+3338, *ḥāzaq+b*^{e}*-+yād* [1]
assisted, 6584+3338, *'al*^{2}*+yād* [1]

ASSOCIATE [4]
associate with, 995+928, *bô'+b*^{e}*-* [2]
associate, 278, *'āḥ*^{2} [1]
associate, 995, *bô'* [1]

ASSOCIATED [4]
associated with, 2492, *ḥābēr* [3]
closely associated, 7940, *qārôb* [1]

ASSOCIATES [26]
associates, 278, *'āḥ*^{2} [17]
associates, 10360, *k*^{e}*nāt* [6]
associates, 2143, *hālak* [1]
associates, 4056, *k*^{e}*nāt* [1]
associates, 8276, *rēa'*^{2} [1]

ASSUME [2]
assume, *NIH/RPE* [1]
assume the responsibility for carrying out, 6641+6584, *'āmad+'al*^{2} [1]

ASSUMED [1]
assumed, 4334, *lākad* [1]

ASSURANCE [3]
have assurance, 586, *'āman*^{1} [1]
assurance, 622, *'*^{e}*met* [1]
assurance, 6859, *'*^{a}*rubbâ* [1]

ASSURED [5]
be assured, 597, *'omnām* [1]
assured, 606, *'āmar*^{1} [1]
assured, 3359+3359, *yāda'+yāda'* [1]
assured, 3359, *yāda'* [1]
assured, 5583+5583, *nāgad+nāgad* [1]

ASSUREDLY [1]
assuredly, 928+622, *b*^{e}*-+'*^{e}*met* [1]

ASSURES [1]
assures, 9068, *šāmar* [1]

ASSYRIA [122]
Assyria, 855, *'aššûr* [120]
Assyria, 824+855, *'ereṣ+'aššûr* [2]

ASSYRIA'S [1]
Assyria's, 855, *'aššûr* [1]

ASSYRIAN [9]
Assyrian, 855, *'aššûr* [9]

ASSYRIANS [11]
Assyrians, 855, *'aššûr* [5]
Assyrians, 1201+855, *bēn*^{1}*+'aššûr* [5]
Assyrians, *NIH/RPE* [1]

ASTIR [2]
astir, 2159, *hāmâ* [1]
all astir, 8074, *rāgaz* [1]

ASTONISHED [1]
astonished, 9037, *šāmēm*^{1} [1]

ASTONISHING [1]
astonishing things, 7099, *pele'* [1]

ASTONISHMENT [1]
looked in astonishment, 9449, *tāmah* [1]

ASTOUND [1]
astound, 7098, *pālā'* [1]

ASTOUNDED [1]
astounded, 9449, *tāmah* [1]

ASTOUNDING [2]
astounding, 7098, *pālā'* [1]
astounding, 7099, *pele'* [1]

ASTRAY [38]
led astray, 9494, *tā'â* [6]
leads astray, 9494, *tā'â* [4]
go astray, 9494, *tā'â* [3]
lead astray, 9494, *tā'â* [3]
went astray, 9494, *tā'â* [3]
led astray, 5615, *nādaḥ*^{1} [2]
goes astray, 8474, *śāṭâ* [2]
gone astray, 8474, *śāṭâ* [2]
led astray, 8706, *šāgâ* [2]
are led astray, 1182, *bāla'*^{3} [1]
go astray, 2319, *zûr*^{2} [1]
lead astray, 3246, *ṭā'â* [1]
go astray, 5653, *nûd* [1]
led astray, 5742+4213, *nāṭâ+lēb* [1]
led astray, 5742, *nāṭâ* [1]
led astray, 6073, *sûr*^{1} [1]
went astray, 8704, *šāgag* [1]
gone astray, 8706, *šāgâ* [1]
leads astray, 8706, *šāgâ* [1]
gone astray, 9494, *tā'â* [1]

ASTROLOGER [1]
astrologer, 10373, *kaśdāy* [1]

ASTROLOGERS [9]
astrologers, 10373, *kaśdāy* [6]
astrologers, 4169, *kaśdîm* [2]
astrologers, 2042+9028, *hābar+šāmayim* [1]

ASUNDER [2]
asunder, 1617, *gezer*^{1} [1]
is split asunder, 7297+7297, *pārar*^{2}*+pārar*^{2} [1]

ASWAN [3]
Aswan, 6059, *s*^{e}*wēnēh* [3]

AT [1638]*
at, 928, *b*^{e}*-* [580]
at, *AIT* [161]
at, *NIH/RPE* [142]
at, 6584, *'al*^{2} [128]
at, 4200, *l*^{e}-^{1} [102]
at, 4946, *min* [94]
at, 448, *'el* [91]
at, 2025, *-â*^{2} [58]
at this, 2256, *w*^{e}*-* [14]
at, 3869, *k*^{e}*-* [13]
at that time, 255, *'āz* [11]
at, 6330, *'ad*^{2} [8]
at once, 7756, *qûm* [8]
at, 10089, *b*^{e}*-* [8]
at, 6640, *'im* [7]
at once, 4554, *māhar*^{1} [4]
at, 4946+7156, *min+pāneh* [4]
at, 448+4578, *'el+mûl*^{3} [3]
at, 889, *'*^{a}*šer* [3]
at, 1068, *bayin* [3]
at, 725, *'ēṣel*^{1} [2]
at, 928+6961, *b*^{e}*-+'ēt* [2]
at, 4200+7156, *l*^{e}-^{1}*+pāneh* [2]
at, 10341, *k*^{e}*-* [2]
at, 10378, *l*^{e}*-* [1]
at, 10554, *'im* [1]

ATAD [2]
Atad, 354, *'āṭād*^{2} [2]

ATARAH [1]
Atarah, 6499, *'aṭārâ*^{2} [1]

ATAROTH [4]
Ataroth, 6500, *'*^{a}*ṭārôt* [4]

ATAROTH ADDAR [2]
Ataroth Addar, 6501, *'aṭrôt 'addār* [2]

ATE [78]
ate, 430, *'ākal* [70]
ate up, 430, *'ākal* [4]
ate, *NIH/RPE* [1]
ate, 995+448+7931, *bô'+'el+qereb* [1]
ate, 10030, *'*^{a}*kal* [1]
ate, 10301, *ṭ*^{e}*'ēm*^{1} [1]

ATER [5]
Ater, 359, *'āṭēr* [5]

ATHACH [1]
Athach, 6973, *'*^{a}*tāk* [1]

ATHAIAH [1]
Athaiah, 6970, *'*^{a}*tāyâ* [1]

ATHALIAH [17]
Athaliah, 6976, *'*^{a}*talyāhû* [10]
Athaliah, 6975, *'*^{a}*talyâ* [7]

ATHARIM [1]
Atharim, 926, *'*^{a}*tārîm* [1]

ATHLAI [1]
Athlai, 6974, *'atlāy* [1]

ATONE [3]
atone, 4105, *kāpar*^{1} [3]

ATONED [6]
be atoned for, 4105, *kāpar*^{1} [3]
atoned for, 4105, *kāpar*^{1} [1]
be atoned, 4105, *kāpar*^{1} [1]
is atoned for, 4105, *kāpar*^{1} [1]

ATONEMENT [102]
make atonement, 4105, *kāpar*^{1} [58]
atonement cover, 4114, *kappōret* [15]
making atonement, 4105, *kāpar*^{1} [6]
atonement, 4113, *kippurîm* [6]
atonement made, 4105, *kāpar*^{1} [5]
made atonement, 4105, *kāpar*^{1} [4]
makes atonement, 4105, *kāpar*^{1} [2]
accept atonement, 4105, *kāpar*^{1} [1]
atonement be made, 4105, *kāpar*^{1} [1]
atonement was made, 4105, *kāpar*^{1} [1]
atonement, 4105, *kāpar*^{1} [1]
atonement made, 4113+4105, *kippurîm+kāpar*^{1} [1]
atonement, 4114, *kappōret* [1]

ATONING [1]
atoning, 4113, *kippurîm* [1]

ATROTH BETH JOAB [1]
Atroth Beth Joab, 6502, *'aṭrôt bêt yô'āb* [1]

ATROTH SHOPHAN [1]
Atroth Shophan, 6503, ʿaṭrôt šôpān [1]

ATTACH [7]
attach, 5989, nātan [5]
attach, 2118, hāyâ [1]
attach, 8492, śîm [1]

ATTACHED [15]
attached, 5989, nātan [3]
attached, 2489, ḥābar^{2} [2]
attached to, 6584, ʿal^{2} [2]
attached, 8492, śîm [2]
attached to, 297, ʾāḥaz^{2} [1]
was attached, 297, ʾāḥaz^{2} [1]
attached to, 928, b^{e}- [1]
attached to, 1068, bayin [1]
were attached, 3922, kûn^{1} [1]
attached, 4277, lāwâ^{1} [1]

ATTACHING [2]
attaching, 5989, nātan [2]

ATTACK [96]
attack, 5782, nākâ [13]
attack, 6590, ʿālâ [11]
attack, 6584, ʿal^{2} [10]
attack, 4309, lāḥam^{1} [7]
attack, 995+6584, bôʾ+ʿal^{2} [5]
attack, 448, ʾel [4]
attack, 6590+448, ʿālâ+ʾel [4]
attack, 6590+6584, ʿālâ+ʿal^{2} [4]
attack, 995+4200, bôʾ+l^{e}-^{1} [3]
attack, 995+448, bôʾ+ʾel [3]
attack, 995, bôʾ [2]
attack, 7925, qārāʾ^{2} [2]
attack, *NIH/RPE* [1]
made attack, 995, bôʾ [1]
attack, 1574, gûd [1]
attack, 1592+1592, gûr^{2}+gûr^{2} [1]
attack, 1670, gālal^{1} [1]
attack from the rear, 2386, zānab [1]
attack, 2686, ḥākar [1]
attack, 3718+928, yārad+b^{e}- [1]
attack, 3718, yārad [1]
attack, 3960, kîdôr [1]
attack, 4200, l^{e}-^{1} [1]
pressed attack, 4309, lāḥam^{1} [1]
attack, 4804, makkâ [1]
attack, 4878, milḥāmâ [1]
attack, 5595, nāgaʿ [1]
attack, 5877+928, nāpal+b^{e}- [1]
attack, 6584+6590, ʿal^{2}+ʿālâ [1]
attack, 6590+3338+6584, ʿālâ+yād+ʿal^{2} [1]
attack, 6913+4200, ʿāśâ^{1}+l^{e}-^{1} [1]
attack, 7003, pāgaʿ [1]
attack, 7008, pāgaš [1]
attack, 7371, ṣābāʾ^{1} [1]
attack, 7444, ṣûr^{2} [1]
attack, 7756+448, qûm+ʾel [1]
attack, 7756, qûm [1]
attack, 8132, rûṣ [1]
attack, 8475, śāṭam [1]
attack, 8938+3338+928, šālaḥ+yād+b^{e}- [1]

ATTACKED [61]
attacked, 5782, nākâ [21]
attacked, 4309, lāḥam^{1} [15]
attacked, 6590+6584, ʿālâ+ʿal^{2} [5]
attacked, 6590, ʿālâ [5]
attacked, 995+6584, bôʾ+ʿal^{2} [2]
attacked, 1574, gûd [1]
attacked, 2837, ḥānâ^{1} [1]
attacked, 4878, milḥāmâ [1]
bitterness attacked, 5352, mārar [1]
attacked viciously, 5782+8797+6584+3751, nākâ+šôq+ʿal^{2}+yārēk [1]
attacked, 5877+928, nāpal+b^{e}- [1]
attacked, 5877, nāpal [1]
attacked, 6584+6590, ʿal^{2}+ʿālâ [1]
attacked, 6590+928, ʿālâ+b^{e}- [1]
attacked, 7003, pāgaʿ [1]
attacked, 7756+448, qûm+ʾel [1]
attacked, 7756+6584, qûm+ʿal^{2} [1]
attacked, 8938+3338+928, šālaḥ+yād+b^{e}- [1]

ATTACKER [1]
attacker, 7046, pûṣ^{1} [1]

ATTACKERS [1]
attackers, 5782, nākâ [1]

ATTACKING [13]
attacking, 4309, lāḥam^{1} [5]
attacking, 7756+6584, qûm+ʿal^{2} [3]
attacking, 6590, ʿālâ [2]
attacking, 995+6584, bôʾ+ʿal^{2} [1]
attacking, 6584, ʿal^{2} [1]
attacking, 6590+448, ʿālâ+ʾel [1]

ATTACKS [12]
attacks, 5782, nākâ [4]
attacks, 8190, rîb^{2} [2]
attacks, 995+6584, bôʾ+ʿal^{2} [1]
attacks, 1592, gûr^{2} [1]
attacks, 6590, ʿālâ [1]
attacks, 7756+6584, qûm+ʿal^{2} [1]
attacks, 7756, qûm [1]
attacks, 8938+3338+928, šālaḥ+yād+b^{e}- [1]

ATTAI [4]
Attai, 6968, ʿattay [4]

ATTAIN [2]
attain, 3523, yākōl [1]
attain, 5952, nāśag [1]

ATTAINED [1]
is attained, 5162, māṣāʾ [1]

ATTAINING [1]
attaining, 3359, yādaʿ [1]

ATTAINS [1]
attains, 4200, l^{e}-^{1} [1]

ATTEND [3]
attend, 4200+7156, l^{e}-^{1}+pāneh [1]
attend, 6641+4200+7156, ʿāmad+l^{e}-^{1}+pāneh [1]
attend to, 6913, ʿāśâ^{1} [1]

ATTENDANCE [1]
attendance, 7992, qāšab [1]

ATTENDANT [4]
attendant, 6269, ʿebed^{1} [2]
attendant, 9250, šārat [2]

ATTENDANTS [23]
attendants, 6269, ʿebed^{1} [14]
attendants, 4722, maḥ^{a}neh [1]
attendants, 5853+9250, naʿar^{2}+šārat [1]
attendants, 5853, naʿar^{2} [1]
personal attendants, 5853+9250, naʿar^{2}+šārat [1]
attendants, 5855, naʿ^{a}râ^{1} [1]
attendants, 5893, nāṣab^{1} [1]
attendants, 6247, sārîs [1]
attendants, 6641+6584, ʿāmad+ʿal^{2} [1]
attendants, 9250, šārat [1]

ATTENDED [4]
attended by, 2143+4200+8079, hālak+l^{e}-^{1}+regel [1]
attended at wedding, 8287, rāʿâ^{2} [1]
attended, 9250, šārat [1]
attended, 10727, ^{š}emaš^{1} [1]

ATTENDING [6]
attending, 5096, maʿ^{a}mād [2]
attending, 9250, šārat [2]
attending, 4200+7156, l^{e}-^{1}+pāneh [1]
attending, 5893, nāṣab^{1} [1]

ATTENTION [63]
pay attention, 7992, qāšab [12]
attention, 4213, lēb [7]
pay attention, 5742+265, nāṭâ+ʾōzen [7]
paid attention, 9048, šāmaʿ [4]
pay attention, 263, ʾāzan^{1} [3]
pay attention, 9048, šāmaʿ [3]
give attention, 7155, pānâ [2]
paid attention, 7992, qāšab [2]
attention, 10302, ṭ^{e}ʿēm^{2} [2]
paid attention, 263, ʾāzan^{1} [1]
pays attention, 263, ʾāzan^{1} [1]
gave full attention, 1067, bîn [1]
bring to attention, 1655+265, gālâ+ʾōzen [1]
draw attention to, 2349, zākar^{1} [1]
attention, 4200+7156, l^{e}-^{1}+pāneh [1]
careful attention, 4213, lēb [1]
been brought to attention, 5583+2256+9048, nāgad+w^{e}-+šāmaʿ [1]
paid any attention, 5742+265+4200+9048, nāṭâ+ʾōzen+l^{e}-^{1}+šāmaʿ [1]
paid attention, 5742+265, nāṭâ+ʾōzen [1]
pays attention, 7155, pānâ [1]
attention, 7156, pāneh [1]
pay close attention, 7992+2256+9048, qāšab+w^{e}-+šāmaʿ [1]
paid attention, 7993, qešeb [1]
paid attention, 8011, rāʾâ^{1} [1]
give attention, 8505, śākal^{1} [1]
giving attention, 8505, śākal^{1} [1]
pays attention, 8800, šûr^{1} [1]
pay attention, 9068, šāmar [1]
paid attention, 9068, šāmar [1]
pay attention, 9120, šāʿâ [1]

ATTENTIVE [6]
attentive, 7995, qaššub [3]
attentive, 7994, qaššāb [2]
attentive to, 448, ʾel [1]

ATTENTIVELY [2]
listened attentively to, 265+448, ʾōzen+ʾel [1]
attentively, 7992, qāšab [1]

ATTESTED [1]
was attested, 586, ʾāman^{1} [1]

ATTITUDE [5]
attitude, 7156, pāneh [2]
attitude, 4213, lēb [1]
attitude, 6640, ʿim [1]
attitude, 10614+10049, ṣ^{e}lēm+ʾ^{a}nap [1]

ATTRACT [1]
attract, 8011, rāʾâ^{1} [1]

ATTRACTED [2]
attracted to, 170, ʾāhab [1]
attracted, 3137, ḥāšaq^{1} [1]

ATTRACTIVE [2]
attractive, 3202, ṭôb^{2} [1]
attractive, 3206, ṭûb [1]

AUDIENCE [3]
audience, 7156, pāneh [2]
seek an audience with, 1335+7156, bāqaš+pāneh [1]

AUNT [2]
aunt, 1860, dôdâ [2]

AUTHORITY [12]
authority, 3338, yād [2]
authority, 10717, šolṭān [2]
authority, 2086, hôd^{1} [1]
authority, 4058, kisseʾ [1]
authority, 4939, memšālâ [1]
authority, 8031, rōʾš^{1} [1]
authority, 9549, tōqep [1]
royal authority, 10424, malkû [1]
authority to rule, 10717, šolṭān [1]
authority, 10718, šallîṭ [1]

AUTHORIZED [3]
authorized, 10682+10302, śîm+ṭ^{e}ʿēm^{2} [2]
authorized, 8397, rišyôn [1]

AUTUMN [5]
autumn, 3453, yôreh^{2} [2]
autumn rains, 4620, môreh^{2} [2]
autumn, 4620, môreh^{2} [1]

AVAIL [2]
avail, 3523, yākōl [1]
avail, 7503, ṣālaḥ^{2} [1]

AVAILABLE [1]
available space, 5113, *ma'ar* [1]

AVEN [1]
Aven, 225, *'āwen*^{2} [1]

AVENGE [14]
avenge, 5933, *nāqam* [6]
to avenge, 928, *b*^{e}*-* [1]
avenge myself, 5933, *nāqam* [1]
avenge themselves, 5933, *nāqam* [1]
avenge wrongs, 5933, *nāqam* [1]
avenge, 5933+5934, *nāqam+nāqām* [1]
avenge, 5933+5935, *nāqam+n*^{e}*qāmâ* [1]
avenge, 5934, *nāqām* [1]
avenge, 5935, *n*^{e}*qāmâ* [1]

AVENGED [9]
avenged, 3828, *yāša'* [1]
be avenged, 5714, *nāḥam* [1]
avenged myself, 5933, *nāqam* [1]
avenged, 5933, *nāqam* [1]
is avenged, 5933, *nāqam* [1]
avenged, 5934, *nāqām* [1]
avenged, 5989+5935, *nātan+n*^{e}*qāmâ* [1]
avenged, 6913+5935, *'āśâ*^{1}*+n*^{e}*qāmâ* [1]
avenged, 8492, *śîm* [1]

AVENGER [14]
avenger, 1457, *gā'al*^{1} [13]
avenger, 5933, *nāqam* [1]

AVENGES [5]
avenges, 5935, *n*^{e}*qāmâ* [2]
avenges, 5989+5935, *nātan+n*^{e}*qāmâ* [2]
avenges, 2011, *dāraš* [1]

AVENGING [3]
avenging, 3828, *yāša'* [2]
avenging, 5933, *nāqam* [1]

AVERT [1]
avert, 6296+4946+6584, *'ābar*^{1}*+min+'al*^{2} [1]

AVITH [2]
Avith, 6400, *'*^{a}*wît* [2]

AVOID [9]
avoid, 1194, *biltî* [1]
avoid stepping, 1925, *dālag* [1]
avoid, 3655, *yāṣā'* [1]
avoid, 3782+4946, *yāšab+min* [1]
avoid, 4200+4202+6843, *l*$^{e-1}$*+lō'+'ārab*^{2} [1]
avoid, 4946, *min* [1]
avoid, 6641, *'āmad* [1]
avoid, 7277, *pāra'*^{2} [1]
avoid, 8178, *rāḥaq* [1]

AVOIDS [2]
avoids, 6073, *sûr*^{1} [2]

AVVA [1]
Avva, 6379, *'awwā'* [1]

AVVIM [1]
Avvim, 6399, *'awwîm*^{2} [1]

AVVITES [3]
Avvites, 6398, *'awwîm*^{1} [3]

AWAIT [3]
await, 6584, *'al*^{2} [2]
await, *NIH/RPE* [1]

AWAITS [8]
awaits, 4200, *l*$^{e-1}$ [3]
awaits, 995, *bô'* [1]
awaits, 1875, *dûmiyyâ* [1]
disaster awaits, 1950, *dāmâ*^{3} [1]
awaits, 4200+7156, *l*$^{e-1}$*+pāneh* [1]
awaits, 6388, *'ôd* [1]

AWAKE [25]
awake, 6424, *'ûr*^{3} [16]
awake, 7810, *qîṣ* [7]
stay awake, 7219+6524, *pāqaḥ+'ayin*^{1} [1]
lie awake, 9193, *šāqad*^{1} [1]

AWAKEN [6]
awaken, 6424, *'ûr*^{3} [6]

AWAKENED [2]
awakened, 3699, *yāqaṣ* [1]
awakened, 7810, *qîṣ* [1]

AWAKENS [2]
awakens, 7810, *qîṣ* [2]

AWAKES [1]
awakes, 7810, *qîṣ* [1]

AWARE [12]
aware, 3359, *yāda'* [8]
is made aware, 3359, *yāda'* [2]
become aware, 3359, *yāda'* [1]
without being aware, 4946+6524, *min+'ayin*^{1} [1]

AWAY [591]
turn away, 6073, *sûr*^{1} [22]
sent away, 8938, *šālaḥ* [22]
turn away, 8740, *šûb*^{1} [15]
turned away, 8740, *šûb*^{1} [13]
take away, 4374, *lāqaḥ* [12]
went away, 2143, *hālak* [11]
took away, 4374, *lāqaḥ* [10]
away from, 4946+6584, *min+'al*^{2} [10]
away from, 4946, *min* [10]
turned away, 6073, *sûr*^{1} [10]
far away, 8158, *rāḥôq* [9]
send away, 8938, *šālaḥ* [9]
away, 6073, *sûr*^{1} [7]
take away, 6073, *sûr*^{1} [7]
far away, 8178, *rāḥaq* [7]
turns away, 8740, *šûb*^{1} [7]
far away, 4946+8158, *min+rāḥôq* [5]
take away, 5951, *nāśā'* [5]
take away, 665, *'āsap* [4]
go away, 2143, *hālak* [4]
taken away, 4374, *lāqaḥ* [4]
waste away, 5245, *māqaq* [4]
be swept away, 6200, *sāpâ* [4]
take away, 6296, *'ābar*^{1} [4]
fly away, 6414, *'ûp*^{1} [4]
away, *NIH/RPE* [3]
are taken away, 665, *'āsap* [3]
running away, 1368, *bāraḥ*^{1} [3]
drove away, 1763, *gāraš*^{1} [3]
carried away, 4374, *lāqaḥ* [3]
melt away, 4570, *mûg* [3]
away from, 4946+6640, *min+'im* [3]
away, 4946, *min* [3]
flee away, 5674, *nûs* [3]
turned away, 5742, *nāṭā* [3]
taken away, 6073, *sûr*^{1} [3]
dragged away, 6079, *sāḥab* [3]
pass away, 6296, *'ābar*^{1} [3]
took away, 7915, *qāṣaṣ*^{1} [3]
throw away, 8959, *šālak* [3]
stole away, 1704, *gānab* [2]
away, 2143, *hālak* [2]
leads away, 2143, *hālak* [2]
frighten away, 3006, *ḥārad* [2]
wither away, 3312, *yābēš*^{1} [2]
turned away in disgust, 3697, *yāqa'* [2]
carry away, 4374, *lāqaḥ* [2]
led away, 4374, *lāqaḥ* [2]
takes away, 4374, *lāqaḥ* [2]
was taken away, 4374, *lāqaḥ* [2]
got away, 4880, *mālaṭ*^{1} [2]
let get away, 4880, *mālaṭ*^{1} [2]
away from, 4946+339, *min+'aḥar* [2]
away from, 4946+907, *min+'ēt*^{2} [2]
away, 4946+725, *min+'ēṣel*^{1} [2]
away, 4946+9004, *min+šām* [2]
melted away, 5022, *māsas* [2]
far away, 5305, *merḥāq* [2]
blow away, 5622, *nādap* [2]
waste away, 5877, *nāpal* [2]
turned away in disgust, 5936, *nāqa'* [2]
carried away, 5951, *nāśā'* [2]
turned away, 6015, *sābab* [2]
sweep away, 6066, *sûp*^{1} [2]
put away, 6073, *sûr*^{1} [2]
throw away, 6073, *sûr*^{1} [2]
took away, 6073, *sûr*^{1} [2]
sweep away, 6200, *sāpâ* [2]
taken away, 6296, *'ābar*^{1} [2]
as far away as, 6330, *'ad*^{2} [2]
turns away, 7155, *pānâ* [2]
tore away, 7973, *qāra'* [2]
waste away, 8140, *rāzî* [2]
put away, 8178, *rāḥaq* [2]
sent far away, 8178, *rāḥaq* [2]
turn away, 8740+8740, *šûb*^{1}*+šûb*^{1} [2]
wash away, 8851, *šāṭap* [2]
thrown away, 8959, *šālak* [2]
driven away, 10304, *ṭ*^{e}*rad* [2]
was driven away, 10304, *ṭ*^{e}*rad* [2]
away, 294, *'āḥôr* [1]
eat away, 430, *'ākal* [1]
eaten away, 430, *'ākal* [1]
eats away, 430, *'ākal* [1]
away, 448+2021+2575+2025, *'el+ha-+ḥûṣ+-â*^{2} [1]
pine away, 581, *'āmal*^{1} [1]
pines away, 581, *'āmal*^{1} [1]
waste away, 581, *'āmal*^{1} [1]
wasted away, 581, *'āmal*^{1} [1]
wastes away, 581, *'āmal*^{1} [1]
steal away, 665, *'āsap* [1]
store away, 665, *'āsap* [1]
sweep away, 665+6066, *'āsap+sûp*^{1} [1]
taken away, 665, *'āsap* [1]
vanish away, 700, *'epes* [1]
away, 995, *bô'* [1]
carried away, 995, *bô'* [1]
wasted away, 1162, *bālâ*^{1} [1]
wastes away, 1162, *bālâ*^{1} [1]
come away, 1368, *bāraḥ*^{1} [1]
drove away, 1368, *bāraḥ*^{1} [1]
fly away, 1368, *bāraḥ*^{1} [1]
ran away, 1368, *bāraḥ*^{1} [1]
run away, 1368, *bāraḥ*^{1} [1]
snatch away, 1608, *gāzal* [1]
carried away, 1655, *gālâ* [1]
carry away, 1655, *gālâ* [1]
stripped away, 1655, *gālâ* [1]
rolled away, 1670, *gālal*^{1} [1]
snatches away, 1704, *gānab* [1]
steal away, 1704, *gānab* [1]
swept away, 1704, *gānab* [1]
be taken away, 1757, *gāra'*^{1} [1]
take away, 1757, *gāra'*^{1} [1]
swept away, 1759, *gārap* [1]
drag away, 1760, *gārar* [1]
drive away, 1763, *gāraš*^{1} [1]
drain away, 1853, *dûb* [1]
driving away, 1890, *dāḥâ* [1]
float away, 1950, *dāmâ*^{3} [1]
push away, 2074, *hādap* [1]
driven away, 2133, *hālā'* [1]
some distance away, 2134, *hāl*$^{e'}$*â* [1]
fade away, 2143, *hālak* [1]
flows away, 2143, *hālak* [1]
get away, 2143, *hālak* [1]
gone away, 2143, *hālak* [1]
passed away, 2143, *hālak* [1]
waste away, 2307, *zûb* [1]
throw away, 2430, *zārâ*^{1} [1]
sweep away, 2442, *zāram*^{2} [1]
hidden away, 2461, *ḥābā'* [1]
gone away, 2532, *ḥādal*^{1} [1]
away from, 2667, *ḥîṣôn* [1]
snatches away, 3166, *ḥātap* [1]
hurl away, 3214+3232, *ṭûl+ṭalṭēlâ* [1]
withered away, 3312, *yābēš*^{1} [1]
wasted away, 3532, *yālah* [1]
sweep away, 3589, *yā'â* [1]
away, 3655, *yāṣā'* [1]
carried away, 3655, *yāṣā'* [1]
put away, 3655, *yāṣā'* [1]
send away, 3655, *yāṣā'* [1]
went away, 3655, *yāṣā'* [1]
washed away, 3668, *yāṣaq* [1]
turn away, 3697, *yāqa'* [1]
take away possessions, 3769, *yāraš*^{1} [1]
wash away, 3891, *kābas* [1]
wastes away, 3983, *kālâ*^{1} [1]

barter away, 4126, *kārā*^{2} [1]
take away, 4162, *kārat* [1]
stayed away, 4202+995, *lō'+bô'* [1]
be taken away, 4374, *lāqaḥ* [1]
been taken away, 4374, *lāqaḥ* [1]
being led away, 4374, *lāqaḥ* [1]
blow away, 4374, *lāqaḥ* [1]
are swept away, 4554, *māhar*^{1} [1]
made waste away, 4570, *mûg* [1]
melted away, 4570, *mûg* [1]
melting away, 4570+2256+2143, *mûg+w*^{e}*-+hālak* [1]
go away, 4631, *mûš*^{2} [1]
be wiped away, 4681, *māḥâ*^{1} [1]
swept away, 4681, *māḥâ*^{1} [1]
wipe away, 4681, *māḥâ*^{1} [1]
wasted away, 4812, *mākak* [1]
get away, 4880, *mālaṭ*^{1} [1]
slipped away, 4880, *mālaṭ*^{1} [1]
withers away, 4908, *mālal*^{1} [1]
away from, 4946+5584, *min+neged* [1]
away from, 4946+7156, *min+pāneh* [1]
away, 4946+6584, *min+'al*^{2} [1]
away, 4946+6640, *min+'im* [1]
away, 4946+907, *min+'ēt*^{2} [1]
far away, 4946+5305, *min+merḥāq* [1]
some distance away, 4946+8158, *min+rāḥôq* [1]
tilting away from, 4946+7156, *min+pāneh* [1]
waste away, 5022, *māsas* [1]
wastes away, 5022, *māsas* [1]
dwindles away, 5070, *mā'aṭ* [1]
waste away, 5071, *m*^{e}*'aṭ* [1]
turning away, 5086, *ma'al*^{1} [1]
wasting away, 5245, *māqaq* [1]
some distance away, 5305, *merḥāq* [1]
withers away, 5376, *māśôś*^{2} [1]
turn away, 5412, *m*^{e}*šûbâ* [1]
take away, 5432, *māšak* [1]
drag away, 5432, *māšak* [1]
drags away, 5432, *māšak* [1]
die away, 5570, *nābēl*^{1} [1]
flown away, 5610, *nādad* [1]
fly away, 5610, *nādad* [1]
are drawn away, 5615, *nādaḥ*^{1} [1]
be driven away, 5615, *nādaḥ*^{1} [1]
chased away, 5615, *nādaḥ*^{1} [1]
driven away, 5615, *nādaḥ*^{1} [1]
turn away, 5615, *nādaḥ*^{1} [1]
blows away, 5622, *nādap* [1]
is blown away, 5622, *nādap* [1]
drive away, 5627, *nāhag*^{1} [1]
driven away, 5627, *nāhag*^{1} [1]
lead away, 5627, *nāhag*^{1} [1]
away, 5653, *nûd* [1]
drive away, 5653, *nûd* [1]
draining away, 5674, *nûs* [1]
get away, 5674+5674, *nûs+nûs* [1]
get away, 5674, *nûs* [1]
running away, 5674, *nûs* [1]
kept away, 5742, *nāṭâ* [1]
turn away, 5742, *nāṭâ* [1]
blew away, 5870, *nāpaḥ* [1]
wastes away, 5877, *nāpal* [1]
take away, 5911+5362, *nāṣal+maśśā'*^{1} [1]
taken away, 5911, *nāṣal* [1]
took away, 5911, *nāṣal* [1]
turned away, 5936, *nāqa'* [1]
carry away, 5951, *nāśā'* [1]
sweep away, 5951, *nāśā'* [1]
sweeps away, 5951, *nāśā'* [1]
taken away, 5951, *nāśā'* [1]
took away, 5951, *nāśā'* [1]
drove away, 5959, *nāšab* [1]
give away, 5989, *nātan* [1]
broke away, 5998, *nātaq* [1]
draw away, 5998, *nātaq* [1]
lured away, 5998, *nātaq* [1]
tear away, 5998, *nātaq* [1]
were drawn away, 5998, *nātaq* [1]
were lured away, 5998, *nātaq* [1]
took away, 6015, *sābab* [1]
turn away, 6015+7156, *sābab+pāneh* [1]
turn away, 6047, *sûg*^{1} [1]
turned away, 6047, *sûg*^{1} [1]
go away, 6073, *sûr*^{1} [1]
broke away, 6073, *sûr*^{1} [1]
carry away, 6073, *sûr*^{1} [1]
cleared away, 6073, *sûr*^{1} [1]
did away with, 6073, *sûr*^{1} [1]
do away with, 6073+4946+9348, *sûr*^{1}*+min+tāwek* [1]
moved away, 6073, *sûr*^{1} [1]
pass away, 6073, *sûr*^{1} [1]
sent away, 6073, *sûr*^{1} [1]
snatch away, 6073, *sûr*^{1} [1]
turns away, 6073, *sûr*^{1} [1]
drew away, 6077, *sût*^{1} [1]
drag away, 6079, *sāḥab* [1]
scrape away, 6081, *sāḥâ* [1]
being swept away, 6200, *sāpâ* [1]
sweeps away, 6200, *sāpâ* [1]
swept away, 6200, *sāpâ* [1]
away, 6259, *sātar* [1]
turn away, 6296, *'ābar*^{1} [1]
go away, 6296, *'ābar*^{1} [1]
passed away, 6296, *'ābar*^{1} [1]
swept away, 6296, *'ābar*^{1} [1]
went away, 6296, *'ābar*^{1} [1]
far away, 6330+4200+4946+8158, *'ad*^{2}*+l*^{e}*-1+min+rāḥôq* [1]
takes away, 6334, *'ādâ*^{1} [1]
flies away, 6414, *'ûp*^{1} [1]
ebbed away, 6494, *'āṭap*^{2} [1]
ebbing away, 6494, *'āṭap*^{2} [1]
move away, 6590, *'ālâ* [1]
blow away, 6590, *'ālâ* [1]
carried away, 6590, *'ālâ* [1]
drag away, 6590, *'ālâ* [1]
moved away, 6590, *'ālâ* [1]
take away, 6590, *'ālâ* [1]
turn away, 6623, *'ālam* [1]
withered away, 6634, *'ālap* [1]
blow away, 7046, *pûš*^{1} [1]
pass away, 7155, *pānâ* [1]
turned away, 7155, *pānâ* [1]
put away, 7212, *pāqad* [1]
strum away, 7260, *pāraṭ* [1]
taking away, 7277, *pāra'*^{2} [1]
breaking away, 7287, *pāraṣ* [1]
put away, 7296, *pārar*^{1} [1]
tuck away, 7443, *ṣûr*^{1} [1]
thoroughly purge away, 7671+3869+2021+1342, *ṣārap+k*^{e}*-+ha-+bōr*^{2} [1]
sweep away, 7674+928+4053, *ṣārar*^{1}*+b*^{e}*-+kānāp* [1]
get away, 7756, *qûm* [1]
hurl away, 7843, *qāla'*^{1} [1]
far away, 7921, *q*^{e}*ṣāt* [1]
keep away, 7928+448+3870, *qārab+'el+-kā* [1]
most certainly tear away, 7973+7973, *qāra'+qāra'* [1]
driven away, 8103, *rādap* [1]
took away, 8123, *rûm*^{1} [1]
waste away, 8135, *rāzâ* [1]
away, 8158, *rāḥôq* [1]
wash away, 8175, *rāḥaṣ* [1]
away, 8178, *rāḥaq* [1]
distance away, 8178, *rāḥaq* [1]
some distance away, 8178+4946, *rāḥaq+min* [1]
get away, 8250, *rāmam*^{2} [1]
drive away, 8286, *rā'â*^{1} [1]
swept away, 8548, *śā'ar*^{2} [1]
carried away, 8647, *šābâ* [1]
is taken away, 8647, *šābâ* [1]
did away with, 8697, *šābat*^{1} [1]
do away with, 8697, *šābat*^{1} [1]
shy away, 8740, *šûb*^{1} [1]
take away, 8740, *šûb*^{1} [1]
turning away, 8740, *šûb*^{1} [1]
wears away, 8835, *šāḥaq* [1]
conjure away, 8838, *šāḥar*^{2} [1]
be swept away, 8851, *šāṭap* [1]
swept away, 8851, *šāṭap* [1]
takes away, 8923, *šālâ*^{2} [1]
sent away, 8933, *šillûḥîm* [1]
let get away, 8938, *šālaḥ* [1]
sending away, 8938, *šālaḥ* [1]
gave away in marriage, 8938, *šālaḥ* [1]
let get away, 8938+928+2006, *šālaḥ+b*^{e}*-+derek* [1]
was sent away, 8938, *šālaḥ* [1]
cast away, 8959, *šālak* [1]
threw away, 8959, *šālak* [1]
keep away, 9068, *šāmar* [1]
turn away, 9120, *šā'â* [1]
ebb away, 9161, *šāpak* [1]
ebbs away, 9161, *šāpak* [1]
burn away, 9462, *tāmam* [1]
burned away, 9462, *tāmam* [1]
melting away, 9468, *temes* [1]
cleanse away, 9475, *tamrûq* [1]
swept away, 10492, *n*^{e}*šā'* [1]
pass away, 10528, *'adâ* [1]
taken away, 10528, *'adâ* [1]
away, 10663, *raḥîq* [1]

AWE [10]
stand in awe, 3707, *yārē'*^{1} [3]
stood in awe, 3169, *ḥātat* [1]
held in awe, 3707, *yārē'*^{1} [1]
stood in awe, 3707+4394, *yārē'*^{1}*+m*^{e}*'ōd* [1]
stand in awe, 6907, *'āraṣ* [1]
in awe, 7064, *pāḥad* [1]
awe, 7065, *paḥad*^{1} [1]
awe, 7067, *paḥdâ* [1]

AWESOME [34]
awesome, 3707, *yārē'*^{1} [24]
awesome wonders, 3707, *yārē'*^{1} [3]
awesome deeds, 3707, *yārē'*^{1} [1]
awesome works, 3707, *yārē'*^{1} [1]
awesome, 3711, *yir'â* [1]
awesome deeds, 4616, *môrā'* [1]
awesome, 4616, *môrā'* [1]
display awesome power, 7098, *pālā'* [1]
awesome, 10167, *d*^{e}*ḥal* [1]

AWFUL [5]
awful, 1524, *gādôl* [2]
awful, 2098+1524, *hôy+gādôl* [1]
awful crime, 8288, *rā'â*^{3} [1]
awful thing, 8288, *rā'â*^{3} [1]

AWHILE [2]
live awhile, 1591, *gûr*^{1} [1]
awhile, 3869+2021+3427, *k*^{e}*-+ha-+yôm*^{1} [1]

AWL [2]
awl, 5345, *marṣēa'* [2]

AWNINGS [1]
awnings, 4833, *m*^{e}*kasseh* [1]

AWOKE [7]
awoke, 3699, *yāqaṣ* [6]
awoke, 7810, *qîṣ* [1]

AX [6]
ax, 1749, *garzen* [3]
ax, 1366, *barzel* [2]
ax, 7935, *qardōm* [1]

AXES [7]
axes, 7935, *qardōm* [4]
axes, 4172, *kaššîl* [1]
axes, 4477, *magzērâ* [1]
axes, 4490, *m*^{e}*gērâ* [1]

AXHEAD [1]
iron axhead, 1366, *barzel* [1]

AXLES [3]
axles, 3338, *yād* [2]
axles, 6248, *seren*^{1} [1]

AYYAH [1]
Ayyah, 6509, *'ayyâ* [1]

AZALIAH [2]
Azaliah, 729, *'aṣalyāhû* [2]

AZANIAH [1]
Azaniah, 271, *'*^{a}*zanyâ* [1]

AZAREL [6]
Azarel, 6475, *'*^{a}*zar'ēl* [6]

AZARIAH [46]
Azariah, 6481, *ʿaᵃzaryâ* [31]
Azariah, 6482, *ʿaᵃzaryāhû* [14]
Azariah, 10538, *ʿaᵃzaryâ* [1]

AZARIAH'S [2]
Azariah's, 6481, *ʿaᵃzaryâ* [1]
Azariah's, 6482, *ʿaᵃzaryāhû* [1]

AZARIAHU [1]
Azariahu, 6482, *ʿaᵃzaryāhû* [1]

AZAZ [1]
Azaz, 6452, *ʿāzāz* [1]

AZAZIAH [3]
Azaziah, 6453, *ʿaᵃzazyāhû* [3]

AZBUK [1]
Azbuk, 6443, *ʿazbûq* [1]

AZEKAH [7]
Azekah, 6467, *ʿaᵃzēqâ* [7]

AZEL [7]
Azel, 727, *ʾāṣēl¹* [6]
Azel, 728, *ʾāṣēl²* [1]

AZGAD [4]
Azgad, 6444, *ʿazgād* [4]

AZIEL [1]
Aziel, 6456, *ʿaᵃzîʾēl* [1]

AZIZA [1]
Aziza, 6461, *ʿaᵃzîzāʾ* [1]

AZMAVETH [8]
Azmaveth, 6462, *ʿazmāwet¹* [6]
Azmaveth, 6463, *ʿazmāwet²* [2]

AZMON [2]
Azmon, 6801, *ʿaṣmôn* [2]

AZNOTH TABOR [1]
Aznoth Tabor, 268, *ʾaznôt tābôr* [1]

AZRIEL [3]
Azriel, 6480, *ʿazrîʾēl* [3]

AZRIKAM [6]
Azrikam, 6483, *ʿazrîqām* [6]

AZUBAH [4]
Azubah, 6448, *ʿaᵃzûbâ²* [4]

AZZAN [1]
Azzan, 6464, *ʿazzān* [1]

AZZUR [3]
Azzur, 6473, *ʿazzur* [3]

BAAL [62]
Baal, 1251, *baʿal¹* [55]
Baal worship, 1251, *baʿal¹* [3]
Baal, 1252, *baʿal²* [3]
Baalˢ, 2085, *hûʾ* [1]

BAAL GAD [3]
Baal Gad, 1254, *baʿal gād* [3]

BAAL HAMON [1]
Baal Hamon, 1255, *baʿal hāmôn* [1]

BAAL HAZOR [1]
Baal Hazor, 1258, *baʿal ḥāṣôr* [1]

BAAL HERMON [2]
Baal Hermon, 1259, *baʿal ḥermôn* [2]

BAAL MEON [3]
Baal Meon, 1260, *baʿal meʿôn* [3]

BAAL PEOR [2]
Baal Peor, 1261, *baʿal peʿôr* [2]

BAAL PERAZIM [4]
Baal Perazim, 1262, *baʿal-perāṣîm* [4]

BAAL SHALISHAH [1]
Baal Shalishah, 1264, *baʿal šālišâ* [1]

BAAL TAMAR [1]
Baal Tamar, 1265, *baʿal tāmār* [1]

BAAL ZEPHON [3]
Baal Zephon, 1263, *baʿal ṣepōn* [3]

BAAL'S [4]
Baal's, 1251, *baʿal¹* [3]
Baal'sˢ, 2257, *-ô* [1]

BAAL-BERITH [2]
Baal-Berith, 1253, *baʿal berît* [2]

BAAL-HANAN [5]
Baal-Hanan, 1257, *baʿal ḥānān* [5]

BAAL-ZEBUB [4]
Baal-Zebub, 1256, *baʿal zebûb* [4]

BAALAH [6]
Baalah, 1267, *baʿᵃlâ²* [6]

BAALATH [4]
Baalath, 1272, *baʿᵃlāt* [4]

BAALATH BEER [1]
Baalath Beer, 1273, *baʿᵃlat beʾēr* [1]

BAALIS [1]
Baalis, 1271, *baʿᵃlîs* [1]

BAALS [18]
Baals, 1251, *baʿal¹* [18]

BAANA [3]
Baana, 1275, *baʿᵃnāʾ* [3]

BAANAH [9]
Baanah, 1276, *baʿᵃnâ* [9]

BAARA [1]
Baara, 1281, *baʿᵃrāʾ* [1]

BAASEIAH [1]
Baaseiah, 1283, *baʿᵃśēyâ* [1]

BAASHA [25]
Baasha, 1284, *baʿšāʾ* [25]

BAASHA'S [2]
Baasha's, 1284, *baʿšāʾ* [2]

BABEL [1]
Babel, 951, *bābel* [1]

BABIES [2]
babies, 1201, *bēn¹* [1]
babies, 3529, *yeled* [1]

BABOONS [2]
baboons, 9415, *tukkiyyîm* [2]

BABY [9]
baby, 3529, *yeled* [4]
baby, 3528, *yālad* [2]
had a baby, 3528, *yālad* [2]
baby at breast, 6403, *ʿûl³* [1]

BABY'S [1]
baby's, 3529, *yeled* [1]

BABYLON [270]
Babylon, 951, *bābel* [242]
Babylon, 10093, *bābel* [24]
Babylon, 824+4169, *ʾereṣ+kaśdîm* [1]
Babylon, 824+951, *ʾereṣ+bābel* [1]
Babylonˢ, 4392, *-ām* [1]
Babylon, 10094, *bābelî* [1]

BABYLON'S [3]
Babylon's, 951, *bābel* [3]

BABYLONIA [10]
Babylonia, 4169, *kaśdîm* [5]
Babylonia, 9114, *šinʿār* [3]
Babylonia, 824+9114, *ʾereṣ+šinʿār* [1]
Babylonia, 951, *bābel* [1]

BABYLONIAN [13]
Babylonian, 4169, *kaśdîm* [12]
Babylonian, 1201+951, *bēn¹+bābel* [1]

BABYLONIANS [54]
Babylonians, 4169, *kaśdîm* [50]
Babylonians, 1201+951, *bēn¹+bābel* [2]
Babylonians, *NIH/RPE* [1]
Babylonians, 10373, *kaśdāy* [1]

BACA [1]
Baca, 1133, *bākāʾ²* [1]

BACK [508]
bring back, 8740, *šûb¹* [39]
go back, 8740, *šûb¹* [37]
turn back, 8740, *šûb¹* [34]
come back, 8740, *šûb¹* [23]
brought back, 8740, *šûb¹* [21]
went back, 8740, *šûb¹* [21]
back, 8740, *šûb¹* [20]
back, 294, *ʾāḥôr* [14]
bring back, 995, *bôʾ* [10]
put back, 8740, *šûb¹* [10]
turned back, 8740, *šûb¹* [10]
give back, 8740, *šûb¹* [9]
send back, 8740, *šûb¹* [9]
brought back, 995, *bôʾ* [7]
go back, 2143, *hālak* [7]
came back, 8740, *šûb¹* [7]
take back, 8740, *šûb¹* [7]
back, 339, *ʾaḥar* [6]
went back, 995, *bôʾ* [6]
pay back, 8966, *šālēm¹* [6]
took back, 8740, *šûb¹* [5]
back, 995, *bôʾ* [4]
came back, 995, *bôʾ* [4]
back, 1568, *gēw¹* [5]
bring back, 4374, *lāqaḥ* [4]
pay back, 8740, *šûb¹* [4]
hold back, 3104, *ḥāśak* [3]
back, 4946+9004, *min+šām* [3]
give back, 5989, *nātan* [3]
bringing back, 8740, *šûb¹* [3]
started back, 8740, *šûb¹* [3]
sent back, 8938, *šālaḥ* [3]
back, *AIT* [2]
back, *NIH/RPE* [2]
back, 345, *ʾᵃḥōrannît* [2]
go back, 995, *bôʾ* [2]
back, 1567, *gaw* [2]
going back and forth, 2143, *hālak* [2]
going back, 2143, *hālak* [2]
turned back, 2200, *hāpak* [2]
bring back to life, 2649, *ḥāyâ* [2]
back, 4946+339, *min+ʾaḥar* [2]
brought back, 5951, *nāśāʾ* [2]
go back, 6590, *ʿālâ* [2]
back, 6902, *ʿōrep* [2]
turned back, 7155, *pānâ* [2]
be sure to take back, 8740+8740, *šûb¹+šûb¹* [2]
coming back, 8740, *šûb¹* [2]
sent back, 8740, *šûb¹* [2]
send back, 8938, *šālaḥ* [2]
back and forth, 285+2178+2256+285+2178, *ʾeḥād+hēnnâ¹+we-+ʾeḥād+hēnnâ¹* [1]
drawn back, 294+6047, *ʾāḥôr+sûg¹* [1]
hold back, 336, *ʾāḥar* [1]
called back, 606, *ʾāmar¹* [1]
be brought back, 665, *ʾāsap* [1]
bring back, 665, *ʾāsap* [1]
brought back, 665, *ʾāsap* [1]
held myself back, 706, *ʾāpaq* [1]
hold yourself back, 706, *ʾāpaq* [1]
far back in, 928+3752, *be-+yerēkâ* [1]
carried back, 995, *bôʾ* [1]
carry back, 995, *bôʾ* [1]
come back, 995, *bôʾ* [1]
pulled back, 995, *bôʾ* [1]
report back, 995, *bôʾ* [1]
take back, 995, *bôʾ* [1]
took back, 995, *bôʾ* [1]
slung on back, 1068+4190, *bayin+kātēp* [1]
go back, 1368, *bāraḥ¹* [1]
gone back, 1368, *bāraḥ¹* [1]
back, 1452, *gaʾᵃwâ* [1]
back, 1461, *gab¹* [1]

back, 1576, *gēwâ*^{2} [1]
paying back, 1694, *gāmal* [1]
was pushed back, 1890+1890, *dāḥâ+dāḥâ* [1]
drove back, 2118+6584, *hāyâ+ʿal*^{2} [1]
get back, 2143, *hālak* [1]
came back, 2143+2256+995, *hālak+w*^{e}*+bôʾ* [1]
drove back, 2143, *hālak* [1]
flashed back and forth, 2143, *hālak* [1]
moved back and forth, 2143, *hālak* [1]
take back, 2143, *hālak* [1]
walked back and forth, 2143, *hālak* [1]
went back, 2143, *hālak* [1]
flashing back and forth, 2200, *hāpak* [1]
back^{s}, 2296, *zeh* [1]
hold back, 2616, *ḥāzaq* [1]
hold back, 2641, *ḥāṭam* [1]
brought back to life, 2649, *ḥāyâ* [1]
set farther back, 2958+2021+337,
ḥāṣēr^{1}*+ha-+ʾaḥēr*^{1} [1]
bring back, 3297, *yābal* [1]
back, 3578+6388, *yāsap+ʿôd* [1]
take back, 3655, *yāṣāʾ* [1]
keep back, 3948, *kāḥad* [1]
hold back, 3973, *kālāʾ*^{1} [1]
back, 4072, *kesel*^{1} [1]
hold back overnight, 4328+6330+1332,
lîn+ʿad^{2}*+bōqer*^{2} [1]
come back, 4374, *lāqaḥ* [1]
flashed back and forth, 4374+928+9348,
lāqaḥ+b^{e}*-+tāwek* [1]
get back, 4374, *lāqaḥ* [1]
be sold back, 4835, *mākar* [1]
held back, 4979, *mānaʿ* [1]
keep back, 4979, *mānaʿ* [1]
report came back, 5583, *nāgad* [1]
push back, 5590, *nāgaḥ* [1]
let themselves be driven back, 5595, *nāgaʿ* [1]
fled back, 5674, *nûs* [1]
get back on, 5742, *nāṭâ* [1]
take back, 5911, *nāṣal* [1]
carry back, 5951, *nāśāʾ* [1]
bring back, 6015, *sābab* [1]
back and forth, 6017+6017, *sābîb+sābîb* [1]
is driven back, 6047+294, *sûg*^{1}*+ʾāḥôr* [1]
turn back, 6047, *sûg*^{1} [1]
move back, 6073, *sûr*^{1} [1]
take back, 6073, *sûr*^{1} [1]
back, 6388, *ʿôd* [1]
come back, 6590, *ʿālâ* [1]
back, 6590, *ʿālâ* [1]
bring back, 6590, *ʿālâ* [1]
brought back, 6590, *ʿālâ* [1]
surely bring back, 6590+6590, *ʿālâ+ʿālâ* [1]
went back, 6590, *ʿālâ* [1]
gives back answer, 6699, *ʿānâ*^{1} [1]
holds back, 6806, *ʿāṣar* [1]
holds back, 6810, *ʿāqab* [1]
be paid back, 6913, *ʿāśâ*^{1} [1]
buy back, 7009, *pādâ* [1]
back, 7155+339, *pānâ+ʾaḥar* [1]
back, 7155, *pānâ* [1]
looking back, 7155, *pānâ* [1]
turn back, 7155, *pānâ* [1]
turns back, 7155, *pānâ* [1]
hold back, 7277, *pāraʿ*^{2} [1]
back, 7307, *paršᵉdōn* [1]
bring back, 7695, *qābaṣ* [1]
bought back, 7864, *qānâ*^{1} [1]
call back, 7924, *qārāʾ*^{1} [1]
from front to back, 8145, *rōḥab* [1]
hurries back, 8634, *šāʾap*^{1} [1]
back again, 8740, *šûb*^{1} [1]
be brought back, 8740, *šûb*^{1} [1]
draw back, 8740, *šûb*^{1} [1]
drew back, 8740, *šûb*^{1} [1]
flow back, 8740, *šûb*^{1} [1]
flowed back, 8740, *šûb*^{1} [1]
get back, 8740, *šûb*^{1} [1]
gives back, 8740, *šûb*^{1} [1]
go back, 8740+345, *šûb*^{1}*+ʾ*^{a}*ḥōrannît* [1]
going back, 8740, *šûb*^{1} [1]
hold back, 8740, *šûb*^{1} [1]
made go back, 8740, *šûb*^{1} [1]
paid back, 8740, *šûb*^{1} [1]
pays back, 8740+8740, *šûb*^{1}*+šûb*^{1} [1]
pays back, 8740, *šûb*^{1} [1]
pull back, 8740, *šûb*^{1} [1]
roll back, 8740, *šûb*^{1} [1]
sending back, 8740, *šûb*^{1} [1]
take back, 8740+8740, *šûb*^{1}*+šûb*^{1} [1]
taken back, 8740, *šûb*^{1} [1]
takes back, 8740+8740, *šûb*^{1}*+šûb*^{1} [1]
were brought back, 8740, *šûb*^{1} [1]
come back, 8938, *šālaḥ* [1]
took back, 8938+2256+995, *šālaḥ+w*^{e}*+bôʾ* [1]
pushed back, 8959, *šālak* [1]
paid back, 8966, *šālēm*^{1} [1]
pay back in full, 8966, *šālēm*^{1} [1]
pays back, 8966, *šālēm*^{1} [1]
back^{s}, 9004+2025, *šām+-â*^{2} [1]
back, 9004, *šām* [1]
get back to, 9048, *šāmaʿ* [1]
rushing back and forth, 9212, *šāqaq* [1]
went back, 9588, *t*^{e}*šûbâ* [1]
back, 10128, *gab* [1]
hold back, 10411, *m*^{e}*ḥāʾ* [1]

BACKBONE [1]
backbone, 6782, *ʿāṣeh* [1]

BACKGROUND [2]
family background, 4580, *môledet* [2]

BACKS [22]
backs, 6902, *ʿōrep* [7]
backs, 4190, *kātēp* [3]
backs, 5516, *motnayim* [3]
backs, 294, *ʾāḥôr* [2]
backs, 1568, *gēw*^{1} [2]
backs, 339, *ʾaḥar* [1]
backs, 1461, *gab*^{1} [1]
backs, 1567, *gaw* [1]
backs, 7396, *ṣad*^{1} [1]
backs, 8900, *š*^{e}*kem*^{1} [1]

BACKSLIDING [5]
backsliding, 5412, *m*^{e}*šûbâ* [4]
backsliding, 294, *ʾāḥôr* [1]

BACKSLIDINGS [1]
backslidings, 5412, *m*^{e}*šûbâ* [1]

BACKWARD [5]
backward, 294, *ʾāḥôr* [2]
backward, 345, *ʾ*^{a}*ḥōrannît* [2]
backward, 4200+294, *l*^{e}*-*^{1}*+ʾāḥôr* [1]

BAD [42]
bad, 8273, *raʿ*^{1} [23]
bad, 8278, *rōaʿ* [4]
bad, 8288, *rāʿâ*^{3} [3]
bad, 8317, *rāʿaʿ*^{1} [3]
bad report, 1804, *dibbâ* [2]
give a bad smell, 944+5580, *bāʾaš+nābaʿ* [1]
smelled bad, 944, *bāʾaš* [1]
bad fruit, 946, *b*^{e}*ʾuš* [1]
bad, 946, *b*^{e}*ʾuš* [1]
bad reputation, 1804, *dibbâ* [1]
bad, 3986, *kālâ*^{3} [1]
bad news, 7997, *qāšeh* [1]

BADLY [3]
badly, 8288, *rāʿâ*^{3} [2]
badly, 4394, *m*^{e}*ʾōd* [1]

BAFFLED [1]
baffled, 10698, *š*^{e}*baš* [1]

BAG [6]
bag, 3967, *kîs* [3]
bag, 3998, *k*^{e}*lî* [2]
bag, 7655, *s*^{e}*rôr*^{1} [1]

BAGGAGE [1]
baggage, 3998, *k*^{e}*lî* [1]

BAGS [5]
bags, 3998, *k*^{e}*lî* [2]
bags, 3038, *ḥārîṭ* [1]
bags, 3967, *kîs* [1]
put into bags, 7443, *ṣûr*^{1} [1]

BAHARUMITE [1]
Baharumite, 1049, *baḥ*^{a}*rûmî* [1]

BAHURIM [5]
Bahurim, 1038, *baḥûrîm*^{2} [5]

BAKBAKKAR [1]
Bakbakkar, 1320, *baqbaqqar* [1]

BAKBUK [2]
Bakbuk, 1317, *baqbûq* [2]

BAKBUKIAH [3]
Bakbukiah, 1319, *baqbuqyâ* [3]

BAKE [9]
bake, 684, *ʾāpâ* [5]
bake, 6913, *ʿāśâ*^{1} [2]
bake, 6383, *ʿûg* [1]
bake thoroughly, 8596+4200+8599,
śārap+l^{e}*-*^{1}*+ś*^{e}*rēpâ* [1]

BAKED [14]
baked, 684, *ʾāpâ* [5]
baked clay, 10279, *h*^{a}*sap* [2]
be baked, 684, *ʾāpâ* [1]
baked, 1418, *bāšal* [1]
baked, 4312, *leḥem* [1]
baked goods, 4407+5126+685,
maʾ^{a}*kāl+maʿ*^{a}*śeh+ʾōpeh* [1]
baked, 4418, *maʾ*^{a}*peh* [1]
baked over hot coals, 8363, *reṣep*^{1} [1]
baked clay, 10279+10298, *h*^{a}*sap+ṭîn* [1]

BAKER [8]
baker, 685, *ʾōpeh* [8]

BAKERS [2]
bakers, 685, *ʾōpeh* [2]

BAKES [1]
bakes, 684, *ʾāpâ* [1]

BAKING [3]
baking, 684, *ʾāpâ* [1]
baking, 4679, *maḥ*^{a}*bat* [1]
baking, 5126, *maʿ*^{a}*śeh* [1]

BALAAM [57]
Balaam, 1189, *bilʿām*^{1} [53]
Balaam, *NIH/RPE* [3]
Balaam^{s}, 2085, *hûʾ* [1]

BALAAM'S [4]
Balaam's, 1189, *bilʿām*^{1} [4]

BALADAN [2]
Baladan, 1156, *balʾ*^{a}*dān* [2]

BALAH [1]
Balah, 1163, *bālâ*^{2} [1]

BALAK [35]
Balak, 1192, *bālāq* [34]
Balak, *NIH/RPE* [1]

BALAK'S [2]
Balak's, 1192, *bālāq* [2]

BALANCE [3]
balance, 4404, *mōʾznayim* [2]
balance, 6369, *ʿādap* [1]

BALANCES [1]
balances, 7144, *peles* [1]

BALD [5]
bald forehead, 1477, *gibbēaḥ* [1]
make bald, 6867, *ʿārâ*^{1} [1]
bald, 7944, *qērēaḥ* [1]
bald head, 7949, *qāraḥat* [1]
make bald, 8143+7947, *rāḥab+qorḥâ* [1]

BALDHEAD [2]
baldhead, 7944, *qērēaḥ* [2]

BALDNESS [1]
baldness, 7947, *qorḥâ* [1]

BALL [1]
ball, 1885, *dûr*[3] [1]

BALM [7]
balm, 7661, *ṣorî* [6]
healing balm, 6057, *sûk*[2] [1]

BALSAM [4]
balsam trees, 1132, *bākā'*[1] [4]

BAMAH [1]
Bamah, 1196, *bāmâ*[2] [1]

BAMOTH [2]
Bamoth, 1199, *bāmôt* [2]

BAMOTH BAAL [2]
Bamoth Baal, 1200, *bāmôt ba'al* [2]

BAN [1]
violating the ban, 5085, *mā'al* [1]

BAND [15]
band of raiders, 1522, *gedûd*[2] [2]
band, 6337, *'ēdâ*[1] [2]
band of survivors, 7129, *pelêṭâ* [2]
band, 731, *'eṣ'ādâ* [1]
band together, 1518, *gādad*[2] [1]
band of rebels, 1522, *gedûd*[2] [1]
band, 2653, *ḥayyâ*[3] [1]
band, 4722, *maḥaneh* [1]
whole band, 4850, *melō'* [1]
band, 5449, *mišlaḥat* [1]
circular band, 6318+6017, *'āgōl+sābîb* [1]
band, 8557, *śāpâ* [1]

BANDAGED [1]
bandaged, 2502, *ḥābaš* [1]

BANDED [4]
banded together, 3585, *yā'ad* [3]
banded together, 665+4200+2021+2653, *'āsap+le-[1]+ha-+ḥayyâ*[3] [1]

BANDIT [3]
bandit, 2143, *hālak* [2]
bandit, 3167, *ḥetep* [1]

BANDITS [2]
bandits, 741, *'ārab* [1]
bandits, 1522, *gedûd*[2] [1]

BANDS [17]
bands, 3122, *ḥăšûq* [8]
raiding bands, 1522, *gedûd*[2] [3]
bands, 1522, *gedûd*[2] [2]
bands, 3138, *ḥāšaq*[2] [2]
bands, 2490, *ḥeber*[1] [1]
make bands, 3138, *ḥāšaq*[2] [1]

BANGLES [1]
bangles, 6577, *'ekes* [1]

BANI [14]
Bani, 1220, *bānî* [14]

BANISH [11]
banish, 5615, *nādaḥ*[1] [6]
banish, 6, *'ābad* [1]
banish, 2143, *hālak* [1]
banish, 4162, *kārat* [1]
banish, 6073, *sûr*[1] [1]
banish, 8959, *šālak* [1]

BANISHED [16]
banished, 5615, *nādaḥ*[1] [5]
banished, 5610, *nādad* [2]
be banished, 5927, *nāqâ* [2]
banished, 1655, *gālâ* [1]
been banished, 1763, *gāraš*[1] [1]
were banished, 1763, *gāraš*[1] [1]
be banished, 1890, *dāḥâ* [1]
been banished, 5615, *nādaḥ*[1] [1]
was banished, 6806, *'āṣar* [1]
banished, 8938, *šālaḥ* [1]

BANISHMENT [1]
banishment, 10744, *šerōšû* [1]

BANK [10]
bank, 8557, *śāpâ* [7]
bank, 3338, *yād* [2]
bank, 1473, *gebûl* [1]

BANKS [3]
banks, 1536, *gidyâ* [2]
banks, 8557, *śāpâ* [1]

BANNER [15]
banner, 5812, *nēs* [14]
banner, 1840, *degel* [1]

BANNERS [3]
banners, 253, *'ôt*[1] [1]
lift up banners, 1839, *dāgal*[2] [1]
troops with banners, 1839, *dāgal*[2] [1]

BANQUET [16]
banquet, 5492, *mišteh* [12]
banquet hall, 1074+3516, *bayit*[1]*+yayin* [1]
banquet, 5492+3516, *mišteh+yayin* [1]
banquet, 10389, *leḥem* [1]
banquet, 10447, *mištē'* [1]

BANQUETS [1]
banquets, 5492, *mišteh* [1]

BAR [3]
bar, 296, *'āḥaz*[1] [1]
bar, 1378, *berîaḥ* [1]
bar, 4751, *maṭṭeh* [1]

BARAK [12]
Barak, 1399, *bārāq*[2] [12]

BARAK'S [1]
Barak's, 1399, *bārāq*[2] [1]

BARAKEL [2]
Barakel, 1387, *barak'ēl* [2]

BARBER'S [1]
barber's, 1647, *gallāb* [1]

BARBS [1]
barbs, 8493, *śēk* [1]

BARE [25]
bare, 6880, *'eryâ* [4]
bare, 7460, *ṣāḥîaḥ* [4]
laid bare, 1655, *gālâ* [2]
bare, 1655, *gālâ* [1]
be laid bare, 1655, *gālâ* [1]
lay bare, 1655, *gālâ* [1]
bare, 1752, *gerem* [1]
lays bare, 2200, *hāpak* [1]
lay bare, 3106, *ḥāśap*[1] [1]
strip bare, 3106, *ḥāśap*[1] [1]
strips bare, 3106, *ḥāśap*[1] [1]
bare, 3504, *yāḥēp* [1]
make bare, 3657, *yāṣag* [1]
strip bare, 3983, *kālâ*[1] [1]
bare, 4399+401+928, *me'ûmâ+'ayin*[1]*+be-* [1]
stripped bare, 6910, *'ārar* [1]
was rubbed bare, 7942, *qāraḥ* [1]
bare, 9142, *šāpâ* [1]

BARED [2]
bared, 3106, *ḥāśap*[1] [2]

BAREFOOT [5]
barefoot, 3504, *yāḥēp* [4]
barefoot, 8768, *šôlāl* [1]

BARELY [2]
barely, 4202, *lō'* [1]
barely whisper a prayer, 7440+4318, *ṣûq*[2]*+laḥaš* [1]

BARGAIN [2]
make a bargain, 6842, *'ārab*[1] [2]

BARHUMITE [1]
Barhumite, 1372, *barḥumî* [1]

BARIAH [1]
Bariah, 1377, *bārîaḥ* [1]

BARK [4]
bark, *AIT* [1]
bark, 3076+4383, *ḥāraṣ*[1]*+lāšôn* [1]
stripped off bark, 3106+3106, *ḥāśap*[1]*+ḥāśap*[1] [1]
bark, 5560, *nābaḥ* [1]

BARKOS [2]
Barkos, 1401, *barqôs* [2]

BARLEY [33]
barley, 8555, *śe'ōrâ* [33]

BARN [1]
barn, 4476, *megûrâ* [1]

BARNS [3]
barns, 662, *'āsām* [2]
barns, 4646, *māzû* [1]

BARRED [4]
barred gates, 1378, *berîaḥ* [1]
barred in, 1378+1237, *berîaḥ+ba'ad*[1] [1]
barred, 1553, *gādar* [1]
is barred, 6037, *sāgar* [1]

BARREN [24]
barren, 6829, *'āqār* [8]
barren heights, 9155, *šepî*[1] [7]
barren, 1678, *galmûd* [3]
barren wilderness, 4497, *midbār*[1] [1]
barren, 6808, *'ōṣer* [1]
barren, 9039, *šemāmâ* [1]
barren height, 9155, *šepî*[1] [1]
barren hill, 9155, *šepî*[1] [1]
barren, 9332, *tōhû* [1]

BARRIER [1]
barrier, 2976, *ḥōq* [1]

BARS [23]
bars, 1378, *berîaḥ* [17]
bars, 4574, *môṭâ* [2]
bars of gates, 964, *bad*[2] [1]
bars of gates, 1378, *berîaḥ* [1]
gate bars, 1378, *berîaḥ* [1]
bars, 8349, *raṣ* [1]

BARTER [3]
barter away, 4126, *kārâ*[2] [1]
barter, 4126, *kārâ*[2] [1]
barter, 5989, *nātan* [1]

BARUCH [28]
Baruch, 1358, *bārûk* [26]
Baruch, *NIH/RPE* [1]
Baruch[s], 2257, *-ô* [1]

BARZILLAI [13]
Barzillai, 1367, *barzillay* [12]
Barzillai, *NIH/RPE* [1]

BASE [21]
base, 3572, *yesôd* [9]
base, 3751, *yārēk* [3]
base, 149, *'eden* [2]
base, *AIT* [1]
base, 4760, *maṭṭā'* [1]
base, 5226, *māqôm* [1]
base, 5346, *marṣepet* [1]
base, 5572, *nābāl*[1] [1]
base, 7829, *qālâ*[2] [1]
base, 8339, *repîdâ* [1]

BASED [2]
based on, 928, *be-* [1]
based on the rate paid, 3869+3427, *ke-+yôm*[1] [1]

BASEMATH [7]
Basemath, 1412, *bāśemat* [7]

BASES [41]
bases, 149, *'eden* [41]

BASEWORK [1]
basework, 5126+4029, *ma'aśeh+kēn*[4] [1]

BASHAN [60]
Bashan, 1421, bāšān[1] [59]
Bashan, 824+1421, ʾereṣ+bāšān[1] [1]

BASIN [13]
basin, 3963, kiyyôr [12]
basin, 6195, sap[1] [1]

BASING [3]
on basing, 1053, bāṭaḥ[1] [2]
basing confidence, 1053, bāṭaḥ[1] [1]

BASINS [9]
basins, 3963, kiyyôr [6]
basins, 6195, sap[1] [3]

BASIS [5]
on the basis of, 928, b[e]- [3]
on the basis of, 4946, min [1]
basis for charges, 10544, ʿillâ [1]

BASKET [32]
basket, 6130, sal [12]
basket, 406, ʾêpâ [4]
basket, 3244, ṭeneʾ [4]
basket, 1857, dûd [3]
basket, 3990, k[e]lûb[1] [2]
basket, 9310, tēbâ [2]
basket, *NIH/RPE* [1]
measuring basket, 406, ʾêpâ [1]
the basket[s], 2257, -ô [1]
basket, 3998, k[e]lî [1]
basket, 8955, šālîš[1] [1]

BASKETS [4]
baskets, 1857, dûd [2]
baskets, 6130, sal [2]

BAT [2]
bat, 6491, ʿ[a]ṭallēp [2]

BATH [6]
bath, 1427, bat[2] [6]

BATH RABBIM [1]
Bath Rabbim, 1442, bat-rabbîm [1]

BATHE [26]
bathe, 8175, rāḥaṣ [25]
bathe, 3188, ṭābal [1]

BATHED [5]
bathed, 8175, rāḥaṣ [4]
bathed in, 4848, mālēʾ[1] [1]

BATHING [2]
bathing, 4059, kāsâ [1]
bathing, 8175, rāḥaṣ [1]

BATHS [10]
baths, 1427, bat[2] [8]
baths, 10126, bat [2]

BATHSHEBA [13]
Bathsheba, 1444, bat-šebaʿ [12]
Bathsheba, *NIH/RPE* [1]

BATS [1]
bats, 6491, ʿ[a]ṭallēp [1]

BATTERED [1]
battered to pieces, 8625+4198, š[e]ʿiyyâ+kātat [1]

BATTERING [6]
battering rams, 4119, kar[1] [3]
battering rams, 7692, q[e]bōl [1]
battering down, 7982, qārar[2] [1]
battering, 8845, šāḥat [1]

BATTLE [203]
battle, 4878, milḥāmâ [135]
battle, 7372, ṣābāʾ[2] [12]
battle, 4309, lāḥam[1] [5]
battle cry, 9558, t[e]rûʿâ [5]
battle, 7930, q[e]rāb [4]
battle, *NIH/RPE* [3]
battle line, 5120, maʿ[a]rākâ [3]
prepare for battle, 273, ʾāzar [2]
battle formation, 4878, milḥāmâ [2]
battle lines, 4878, milḥāmâ [2]
battle standard, 5812, nēs [2]
formed battle lines, 6885, ʿārak [2]
meet in battle, 7925, qārāʾ[2] [2]
ready for battle, 408+7372+4200+2021+4878, ʾîš[1]+ṣābāʾ[2]+l[e]-[1]+ha-+milḥāmâ [1]
men ready for battle, 1522+7372+4878, g[e]dûd[2]+ṣābāʾ[2]+milḥāmâ [1]
battle, 2657, ḥayil [1]
slain in battle, 2728, ḥālāl[1] [1]
armed for battle, 2741, ḥālaṣ[2] [1]
armed for battle, 2821, ḥāmaš [1]
engage in battle, 4309, lāḥam[1] [1]
fight battle, 4309, lāḥam[1] [1]
battle[s], 4392, -ām [1]
battle lines, 5120, maʿ[a]rākâ [1]
battle positions, 5120, maʿ[a]rākâ [1]
engage in battle, 5590, nāgaḥ [1]
fall in battle, 5877+2728, nāpal+ḥālāl[1] [1]
battle, 5977, nešeq[1] [1]
do battle, 7371, ṣābāʾ[1] [1]
battle, 7372+4878, ṣābāʾ[2]+milḥāmâ [1]
ready for battle, 7372+928+2021+4878, ṣābāʾ[2]+b[e]-+ha-+milḥāmâ [1]
raise the battle cry, 7658, ṣāraḥ [1]
raise the battle cry, 8131, rûaʿ [1]
raised the battle cry, 8131, rûaʿ [1]
sound of battle cry, 8131, rûaʿ [1]
battle, 8323, raʿaš [1]
roar of battle, 8623, šāʾôn[2] [1]
carry the battle, 8740+2256+1741, šûb[1]+w[e]-+gārâ [1]

BATTLEFIELD [2]
battlefield, 824, ʾereṣ [1]
battlefield, 5120+8441, maʿ[a]rākâ+śādeh [1]

BATTLEMENTS [1]
battlements, 9087, šemeš [1]

BATTLES [4]
battles, 4878, milḥāmâ [4]

BAY [3]
bay, 4383, lāšôn [3]

BAZLUTH [2]
Bazluth, 1296, baṣlût [2]

BE [3742]*
be, *AIT* [1325]
be, 2118, hāyâ [715]
be, *NIH/RPE* [518]
far be it, 2721, ḥālîl[2] [12]
be, 10201, h[a]wâ [11]
be, 3780, yēš [5]
be no, 401, ʾayin[1] [4]
be, 3782, yāšab [3]

BE ESHTARAH [1]
Be Eshtarah, 1285, b[e]ʿešt[e]râ [1]

BEAK [1]
beak, 7023, peh [1]

BEALIAH [1]
Bealiah, 1270, b[e]ʿalyâ [1]

BEALOTH [1]
Bealoth, 1268, b[e]ʿālôt [1]

BEAM [1]
beam, 10058, ʾāʿ [1]

BEAMS [18]
trimmed beams, 4164, k[e]rutôt [3]
beams, *AIT* [2]
laid beams, 7936, qārâ[1] [2]
beams, *NIH/RPE* [1]
beams of cedar, 781, ʾarzâ [1]
beams, 1464, gēb[2] [1]
beams, 4096, kāpîs [1]
beams, 6770, ʿēṣ [1]
beams, 7521, ṣēlāʿ[1] [1]
beams, 7771, qôrâ [1]
ceiling beams, 7771, qôrâ [1]
beams, 7936, qārâ[1] [1]
lays beams, 7936, qārâ[1] [1]
make beams, 7936, qārâ[1] [1]

BEANS [2]
beans, 7038, pôl [2]

BEAR [93]
bear, 5951, nāśāʾ [35]
bear, 1800, dōb [10]
bear, 6913, ʿāśâ[1] [6]
bear children, 3528, yālad [4]
bear guilt, 870, ʾāšam [3]
bear, 3528, yālad [3]
bear, 7924+6584, qārāʾ[1]+ʿal[2] [3]
bear, *NIH/RPE* [2]
bear the blame, 2627, ḥāṭāʾ [2]
bear, 3523, yākōl [2]
bear, 6022, sābal [2]
bear shame, 1017, bôš[1] [1]
bear, 1144, bākar [1]
bear arms, 2520+2514, ḥāgar+ḥ[a]gôrâ [1]
bear, 2798, ḥāmal [1]
bear a child, 3528, yālad [1]
bear, 3920, kûl [1]
bear, 4192, kātar[1] [1]
cannot bear, 4202+3523, lōʾ+yākōl [1]
bear, 4848, mālēʾ[1] [1]
bear, 5432, māšak [1]
bear fruit, 5649, nûb [1]
bear a grudge against, 5757, nāṭar[1] [1]
bear with, 5951, nāśāʾ [1]
bear up, 5951, nāśāʾ [1]
bear, 6568, ʿayiš [1]
bear, 6584+7924, ʿal[2]+qārāʾ[1] [1]
bear, 6933, ʿāš[3] [1]
bear fruit, 7238, pārâ[1] [1]
bear no longer, 7918, qāṣar[2] [1]
bear in mind, 8011, rāʾâ[1] [1]
bear, 10155, dōb [1]

BEARD [12]
beard, 2417, zāqān [11]
pulled out beard, 5307, māraṭ [1]

BEARDS [5]
beards, 2417, zāqān [5]

BEARER [2]
bearer, 5951, nāśāʾ [2]

BEARING [12]
bearing, 5951, nāśāʾ [5]
bearing first child, 1144, bākar [1]
bearing, 2256, w[e]- [1]
bearing, 2445, zāraʿ [1]
stately bearing, 3512, yāṭab [1]
bearing children, 3528, yālad [1]
bearing, 6913, ʿāśâ[1] [1]
bearing, 9307, tōʾar [1]

BEARS [19]
bears, 7924+6584, qārāʾ[1]+ʿal[2] [10]
bears, 3528, yālad [3]
bears, 1800, dōb [2]
bears, 928, b[e]- [1]
bears, 2655, ḥîl[1] [1]
bears, 5989, nātan [1]
bears burdens, 6673, ʿāmas [1]

BEAST [18]
beast, 10263, ḥêwâ [6]
beast, 989, b[e]hēmâ [5]
beast, 2651, ḥayyâ[1] [4]
beast, *NIH/RPE* [2]
brute beast, 989, b[e]hēmâ [1]

BEASTS [53]
beasts, 2651, ḥayyâ[1] [25]
beasts, 989, b[e]hēmâ [13]
beasts, 10263, ḥêwâ [7]
wild beasts, 2651, ḥayyâ[1] [2]
wild beasts, 989, b[e]hēmâ [2]
proud beasts, 1201+8832, bēn[1]+šaḥaṣ [1]
beasts of burden, 2651+2256+989, ḥayyâ[1]+w[e]-+b[e]hēmâ [1]
animal torn by beasts, 3274, ṭ[e]rēpâ [1]
animals torn by wild beasts, 3274, ṭ[e]rēpâ [1]

ravenous beasts, 4266, *lāhaṭ*[2] [1]

BEAT [24]
beat, 5782, *nākâ* [10]
beat, 4198, *kātat* [3]
beat down, 4198, *kātat* [2]
beat, 6215, *sāpaq*[1] [2]
beat fine, 8835, *šāḥaq* [2]
beat, 2150, *hālam* [1]
beat, 2468, *ḥābaṭ* [1]
beat down, 5782, *nākâ* [1]
beat, 6199, *sāpad* [1]
beat, 9528, *tāpap* [1]

BEATEN [13]
beaten, 5782, *nākâ* [2]
had beaten, 5782, *nākâ* [2]
beaten, 5939, *nōqep* [2]
is beaten out, 2468, *ḥābaṭ* [1]
beaten down, 5330, *mirmās* [1]
were beaten, 5597, *nāgap* [1]
be beaten, 5782, *nākâ* [1]
being beaten, 5782, *nākâ* [1]
were beaten, 5782, *nākâ* [1]
beaten, 8096, *rādad* [1]

BEATING [2]
beating, 4547, *mahalumôt* [1]
beating, 5782, *nākâ* [1]

BEATINGS [2]
beatings, 4547, *mahalumôt* [1]
beatings, 4804, *makkâ* [1]

BEATS [1]
beats, 5782, *nākâ* [1]

BEAUTIFUL [63]
beautiful, 3637, *yāpeh* [23]
beautiful, 7382, *ṣebî*[1] [6]
beautiful, 3202+5260, *ṭôb*[2]*+mar'eh* [5]
beautiful, 3636, *yāpâ* [3]
beautiful, 3637+5260, *yāpeh+mar'eh* [3]
beautiful, 3202, *ṭôb*[2] [2]
beautiful, 3637+9307, *yāpeh+tō'ar* [2]
beautiful, 5533, *nā'â* [2]
most beautiful, 7382, *ṣebî*[1] [2]
beautiful, 9514, *tip'eret* [2]
beautiful, 10736, *šappîr* [2]
beautiful, 3201, *ṭôb*[1] [1]
beautiful, 3642, *yopî* [1]
beautiful, 3645, *yepêpiyyâ* [1]
beautiful garments, 4815, *maklûl* [1]
beautiful, 5051, *ma'adannôt* [1]
beautiful, 5534, *nā'weh* [1]
beautiful, 5833, *nā'îm*[1] [1]
most beautiful of jewels, 6344+6344, *'adî+'adî* [1]
beautiful jewelry, 7382+6344, *ṣebî*[1]*+'adî* [1]
most beautiful, 7382+7382, *ṣebî*[1]*+ṣebî*[1] [1]
beautiful, 9183, *šeper*[1] [1]

BEAUTY [30]
beauty, 3642, *yopî* [18]
beauty, *NIH/RPE* [2]
beauty, 7382, *ṣebî*[1] [2]
beauty treatments, 9475, *tamrûq* [2]
beauty, 1542, *gōdel* [1]
beauty, 3701, *yāqār* [1]
beauty treatments, 5299, *merûqîm* [1]
beauty, 5840, *nō'am* [1]
crown of beauty, 6996, *pe'ēr* [1]
beauty, 9307, *tō'ar* [1]

BEBAI [6]
Bebai, 950, *bēbay* [6]

BECAME [265]
became, *AIT* [185]
became, 2118, *hāyâ* [59]
became, *NIH/RPE* [4]
became more and more powerful, 2143+2143+2256+1524, *hālak+hālak+we-+gādôl* [2]
became, 10201, *hawâ* [2]
became, 995, *bô'* [1]
became more and more powerful, 2143+2256+1524, *hālak+we-+gādôl* [1]
turned and became, 2200, *hāpak* [1]
became powerful, 2621, *ḥezqâ* [1]
became defiled, 3237, *ṭāmē'*[1] [1]
became Jews, 3366, *yāhad* [1]
became, 4200, *le-*[1] [1]
became king, 4895, *malkût* [1]
became, 5989, *nātan* [1]
became famous, 6913+9005, *'āśâ*[1]*+šēm*[1] [1]
became crippled, 7174, *pāsaḥ*[2] [1]
became one with, 8003, *qāšar* [1]
became even greater, 10650+10339+10323, *rebû+yattîr+yesap* [1]

BECAUSE [1140]
because, 3954, *kî*[2] [531]
because of, 928, *be-* [59]
because of, 6584, *'al*[2] [57]
because of, 4946+7156, *min+pāneh* [54]
because of, 4946, *min* [43]
because, 2256, *we-* [41]
because, 3610, *ya'an*[1] [34]
because, 6584, *'al*[2] [29]
because, 889, *'ašer* [28]
because, *NIH/RPE* [27]
because, 3610+889, *ya'an*[1]*+'ašer* [21]
because of, 4200+5100, *le-*[1]*+ma'an* [17]
because, 928, *be-* [16]
because, 4946, *min* [16]
because, 6584+889, *'al*[2]*+'ašer* [14]
because of, 928+1673, *be-+gālāl*[2] [9]
because, 4946+7156, *min+pāneh* [8]
because of, 448, *'el* [6]
because of, 928+6288, *be-+'abûr*[1] [6]
because, 3869, *ke-* [6]
because of, 3954, *kî*[2] [6]
because of, 4200, *le-*[1] [6]
because of, 6584+1821, *'al*[2]*+dābār* [6]
because, 9393+889, *taḥat*[1]*+'ašer* [6]
because, 3869+889, *ke-+'ašer* [5]
because, 6584+3954, *'al*[2]*+kî*[2] [5]
because, 6584+4027, *'al*[2]*+kēn*[2] [5]
because of, 6584+128, *'al*[2]*+'ōdôt* [4]
because, 928+6288, *be-+'abûr*[1] [3]
because of, 3610, *ya'an*[1] [3]
because, 3610+3954, *ya'an*[1]*+kî*[2] [3]
because, 6584+1821, *'al*[2]*+dābār* [3]
because, 6813+889, *'ēqeb+'ašer* [3]
because, 8611, *ša-* [3]
because, 10168, *dî* [3]
because, 10353+10619+10168, *kōl+qobēl+dî* [3]
because, 928+889, *be-+'ašer* [2]
and because, 2256, *we-* [2]
because of, 3869, *ke-* [2]
because, 3954+6584+4027, *kî*[2]*+'al*[2]*+kēn*[2] [2]
because, 6813+3954, *'ēqeb+kî*[2] [2]
because, 7153, *pen* [2]
because of, 10427, *min* [2]
because, *AIT* [1]
because surely, 434, *'ākēn*[1] [1]
because, 448, *'el* [1]
because, 561+4202+3610, *'im+lō'+ya'an*[1] [1]
because, 561, *'im* [1]
because of, 907, *'ēt*[2] [1]
because of, 928+3338, *be-+yād* [1]
because, 928+1673, *be-+gālāl*[2] [1]
because of, 928+3610, *be-+ya'an*[1] [1]
because, 2256+4202, *we-+lō'* [1]
because of, 2549, *ḥûb* [1]
because, 3610+928+3610, *ya'an*[1]*+be-+ya'an*[1] [1]
because, 3610+2256+928+3610, *ya'an*[1]*+we-+be-+ya'an*[1] [1]
because of, 3869+889, *ke-+'ašer* [1]
because, 3869+7023+889, *ke-+peh+'ašer* [1]
just because, 3954, *kî*[2] [1]
because of, 3954+4946+7156, *kî*[2]*+min+pāneh* [1]
because that will mean, 3954, *kî*[2] [1]
because, 3954+4200+4537, *kî*[2]*+le-*[1]*+mâ* [1]
because of this, 4200+4027, *le-*[1]*+kēn*[2] [1]
because, 4200+4027, *le-*[1]*+kēn*[2] [1]
because, 4200, *le-*[1] [1]
because of, 4946+5584, *min+neged* [1]
because of, 4946+6584, *min+'al*[2] [1]
because of, 4946+9004, *min+šām* [1]
because, 4946+889, *min+'ašer* [1]
because of this, 6584+4027, *'al*[2]*+kēn*[2] [1]
because of, 6584+4027, *'al*[2]*+kēn*[2] [1]
because of, 6584+3970, *'al*[2]*+kākâ* [1]
because of, 6584+6813, *'al*[2]*+'ēqeb* [1]
because, 6584+1826, *'al*[2]*+dibrâ* [1]
because of, 6640, *'im* [1]
because, 6813, *'ēqeb* [1]
because, 9393+3954, *taḥat*[1]*+kî*[2] [1]
because, 10089, *be-* [1]
because of, 10378+10619+10168, *le-+qobēl+dî* [1]
because, 10427+10168, *min+dî* [1]

BECKON [2]
beckon, 5677+3338, *nûp*[1]*+yād* [1]
beckon, 5951+3338, *nāśā'+yād* [1]

BECOME [300]
become, 2118, *hāyâ* [164]
become, *AIT* [85]
become, *NIH/RPE* [25]
become, 4200, *le-*[1] [3]
become fools, 3282, *yā'al*[1] [2]
become, 2093, *hāwâ*[2] [1]
become, 2118+4200, *hāyâ+le-*[1] [1]
surely become, 2118+2118, *hāyâ+hāyâ* [1]
become hard, 2461, *ḥābā'* [1]
become strong, 2621, *ḥezqâ* [1]
let become defiled, 3237, *ṭāmē'*[1] [1]
become aware, 3359, *yāda'* [1]
become known, 3359, *yāda'* [1]
become known, 3655, *yāṣā'* [1]
become poor, 3769, *yāraš*[1] [1]
become wise, 4220, *lābab*[1] [1]
become wife, 4374+4200+851, *lāqaḥ+le-*[1]*+'iššâ* [1]
become, 5162, *māṣā'* [1]
become like, 5439, *māšal*[1] [1]
become, 5877, *nāpal* [1]
become guilty, 5951+6584+2628, *nāśā'+'al*[2]*+ḥēṭ'* [1]
become, 6015, *sābab* [1]
become, 7756, *qûm* [1]
become undignified, 7837, *qālal* [1]
become, 8492, *śîm* [1]
sure to become utterly corrupt, 8845+8845, *šāḥat+šāḥat* [1]

BECOMES [28]
becomes, *AIT* [17]
becomes, 2118, *hāyâ* [9]
becomes like, 2924, *ḥāpaś* [1]
becomes prey, 8964, *šālal*[2] [1]

BECOMING [4]
becoming, *AIT* [2]
becoming, 2118, *hāyâ* [1]
becoming, 2725, *ḥālal*[1] [1]

BECORATH [1]
Becorath, 1138, *bekôrat* [1]

BED [66]
bed, 5435, *miškāb* [23]
bed, 4753, *miṭṭâ* [17]
bed, 10444, *miškab* [5]
bed, 6911, *'ereś* [4]
bed, *NIH/RPE* [2]
bed, 3661, *yāṣûa'*[1] [2]
come to bed with, 8886+6640, *šākab+'im* [2]
dishonor bed, 1655+4053, *gālâ+kānāp* [1]
dishonors bed, 1655+4053, *gālâ+kānāp* [1]
marriage bed, 3661, *yāṣûa'*[1] [1]
make bed, 3667, *yāṣa'* [1]
bed, 5201, *maṣṣā'* [1]
coverings bed, 5267, *marbad* [1]
dishonor bed, 6872+1655, *'erwâ+gālâ* [1]
bed, 6911+3661, *'ereś+yāṣûa'*[1] [1]
bed with, 8886+6640, *šākab+'im* [1]
go to bed with, 8886+725, *šākab+'ēṣel*[1] [1]
gone to bed, 8886, *šākab* [1]

BEDAD [2]
Bedad, 971, *b^{e}dad* [2]

BEDAN [1]
Bedan, 979, *b^{e}dān* [1]

BEDDING [1]
bedding, 5435, *miškāb* [1]

BEDEIAH [1]
Bedeiah, 973, *bēd^{e}yâ* [1]

BEDROOM [8]
bedroom, 2540+5435, *ḥeder+miškāb* [4]
bedroom, 2540+4753, *ḥeder+miṭṭâ* [2]
bedroom, 2540, *ḥeder* [2]

BEDROOMS [1]
bedrooms, 2540, *ḥeder* [1]

BEDS [11]
beds, 5435, *miškāb* [6]
beds, 4753, *miṭṭâ* [2]
beds, 6870, *ʿ^{a}rûgâ* [2]
stream beds, 5707, *naḥal^{1}* [1]

BEELIADA [1]
Beeliada, 1269, *b^{e}ʿelyādāʿ* [1]

BEEN [542]*
been, *AIT* [176]
been, 2118, *hāyâ* [77]

BEER [13]
beer, 8911, *šēkār* [11]
Beer, 932, *b^{e}ʾēr^{2}* [2]

BEER ELIM [1]
Beer Elim, 935, *b^{e}ʾēr ʾêlîm* [1]

BEER LAHAI ROI [3]
Beer Lahai Roi, 936, *b^{e}ʾēr laḥay rōʾî* [3]

BEERA [1]
Beera, 938, *b^{e}ʾērāʾ* [1]

BEERAH [2]
Beerah, 939, *b^{e}ʾērâ* [1]
Beerah^{s}, 2085, *hûʾ* [1]

BEERI [2]
Beeri, 941, *b^{e}ʾērî* [2]

BEEROTH [6]
Beeroth, 940, *b^{e}ʾērôt* [5]
people of Beeroth, 943, *b^{e}ʾērōtî* [1]

BEEROTHITE [4]
Beerothite, 943, *b^{e}ʾērōtî* [4]

BEERSHEBA [34]
Beersheba, 937, *b^{e}ʾēr šebaʿ* [34]

BEES [4]
bees, 1805, *d^{e}bôrâ^{1}* [3]
swarm of bees, 1805, *d^{e}bôrâ^{1}* [1]

BEFALL [2]
befall, 628+448, *ʾānâ^{2}+ʾel* [1]
befall, 5595, *nāgaʿ* [1]

BEFALLS [1]
befalls, 628+4200, *ʾānâ^{2}+l^{e-1}* [1]

BEFORE [1072]
before, 4200+7156, *l^{e-1}+pāneh* [542]
before, 4946+7156, *min+pāneh* [82]
before, 4200, *l^{e-1}* [71]
before, 928+3270, *b^{e}+ṭerem* [36]
before, *NIH/RPE* [31]
before, 448, *ʾel* [30]
before, 5584, *neged* [29]
before, *AIT* [25]
before, 4946+4200+7156, *min+l^{e-1}+pāneh* [24]
before, 7156, *pāneh* [19]
before, 4200+5584, *l^{e-1}+neged* [13]
before, 4202, *lōʾ* [12]
before, 907+7156, *ʾēt^{2}+pāneh* [9]
before, 3270, *ṭerem* [9]
before, 6330, *ʿad^{2}* [9]
before, 6584, *ʿal^{2}* [8]
before, 928, *b^{e}-* [7]
before, 6640, *ʿim* [7]
before, 10621, *q^{o}dām* [7]
before, 928+2021+8037, *b^{e}+ha+riʾšôn* [6]
before, 9453+8997, *t^{e}môl+šilšôm* [6]
before, 4200+6524, *l^{e-1}+ʿayin^{1}* [5]
before, 4946, *min* [5]
before, 6584+7156, *ʿal^{2}+pāneh* [5]
before, 2256, *w^{e}-* [4]
come before, 7709, *qādam* [4]
before, 8037, *riʾšôn* [4]
before, 928+4202, *b^{e}+lōʾ* [3]
before, 5790, *nōkaḥ* [3]
before, 6330+889+4202, *ʿad^{2}+ʾ^{a}šer+lōʾ* [3]
before, 7712, *qadmâ* [3]
before, 907, *ʾēt^{2}* [2]
before, 919+8997, *ʾetmôl+šilšôm* [2]
before, 928+265, *b^{e}+ʾōzen* [2]
before, 928+3270+4202, *b^{e}+ṭerem+lōʾ* [2]
as before, 3869+7193+928+7193, *k^{e}+paʿam+b^{e}+paʿam* [2]
before, 4946+6584, *min+ʿal^{2}* [2]
before, 5584+7156, *neged+pāneh* [2]
before, 7710, *qedem* [2]
before, 10378+10619, *l^{e}+q^{o}bēl* [2]
before, 10427+10621, *min+q^{o}dām* [2]
before, 448+7156, *ʾel+pāneh* [1]
before, 928+2021+9378, *b^{e}+ha+t^{e}hillâ* [1]
before, 928+678, *b^{e}+ʾap^{2}* [1]
just before, 928+3270, *b^{e}+ṭerem* [1]
as done before, 3869+7193+928+7193, *k^{e}+paʿam+b^{e}+paʿam* [1]
before, 3893, *k^{e}bār^{1}* [1]
before, 3954+401, *kî^{2}+ʾayin^{1}* [1]
before eyes, 4200+7156, *l^{e-1}+pāneh* [1]
before, 4200+5584+6524, *l^{e-1}+neged+ʿayin^{1}* [1]
before, 4200+678, *l^{e-1}+ʾap^{2}* [1]
right before, 4200+5584, *l^{e-1}+neged* [1]
right before, 4200, *l^{e-1}* [1]
before elapsed, 4202+4848, *lōʾ+mālēʾ^{1}* [1]
before, 4578, *mûl^{3}* [1]
before time, 4946+4200+7156, *min+l^{e-1}+pāneh* [1]
before, 4946+3270, *min+ṭerem* [1]
before, 4946+6640, *min+ʿim* [1]
before, 4946+9453+8997, *min+t^{e}môl+šilšôm* [1]
before, 4974, *minnî^{2}* [1]
before, 5162, *māṣāʾ* [1]
open before, 5790+7156, *nōkaḥ+pāneh* [1]
before, 6330+4202, *ʿad^{2}+lōʾ* [1]
before, 6388+4202, *ʿôd+lōʾ* [1]
comes before, 7709, *qādam* [1]
go before, 7709, *qādam* [1]
before began, 7710, *qedem* [1]
appear before, 8011+7156, *rāʾâ^{1}+pāneh* [1]
before, 8035, *riʾšâ* [1]
before^{s}, 8049, *rābâ^{1}* [1]
before, 10379, *lāʾ* [1]
before, 10427+10622+10180, *min+qadmâ+d^{e}nâ* [1]

BEFOREHAND [1]
beforehand, 4946+4200+7156, *min+l^{e-1}+pāneh* [1]

BEFUDDLED [1]
befuddled, 1182, *bālaʿ^{3}* [1]

BEG [11]
I beg you, 5528, *nāʾ^{1}* [5]
beg, 7590, *ṣāʿaq* [2]
beg, 1335, *bāqaš* [1]
beg for mercy, 2858, *ḥānan^{1}* [1]
beg, 2858, *ḥānan^{1}* [1]
beg, 8626, *šāʾal* [1]

BEGAN [74]
began, *AIT* [32]
began, 2725, *ḥālal^{1}* [25]
began, *NIH/RPE* [2]
began, 2143, *hālak* [2]
began, 3655, *yāṣāʾ* [2]
began, 9378, *t^{e}hillâ* [2]
when began, 928+3427, *b^{e}+yôm^{1}* [1]
began, 2118, *hāyâ* [1]
began, 2616+3338, *ḥāzaq+yād* [1]
began, 3283, *yāʾal^{2}* [1]
began, 5951+906+7754, *nāśāʾ+ʾēt^{1}+qôl* [1]
began, 6015, *sābab* [1]
began, 6913, *ʿāśâ^{1}* [1]
before began, 7710, *qedem* [1]
began, 7756, *qûm* [1]

BEGGARS [1]
beggars, 8626, *šāʾal* [1]

BEGGED [3]
begged, 2858, *ḥānan^{1}* [2]
begged for favor, 2858, *ḥānan^{1}* [1]

BEGGING [2]
begging, 1335, *bāqaš* [1]
begging for mercy, 9384, *taḥ^{a}nûn* [1]

BEGIN [16]
begin, 2725, *ḥālal^{1}* [8]
begin, *AIT* [3]
begin, 7756, *qûm* [2]
begin, 995, *bôʾ* [1]
begin, 5951, *nāśāʾ* [1]
begin, 8031, *rōʾš^{1}* [1]

BEGINNING [45]
beginning, 8037, *riʾšôn* [13]
beginning, 8031, *rōʾš^{1}* [8]
beginning, 8040, *rēʾšît* [7]
beginning, 9378, *t^{e}hillâ* [7]
beginning, 2725, *ḥālal^{1}* [3]
beginning, *NIH/RPE* [2]
from beginning to, 6330, *ʿad^{2}* [2]
beginning with, 928, *b^{e}-* [1]
beginning, 2118, *hāyâ* [1]
beginning, 7156, *pāneh* [1]

BEGINNINGS [1]
beginnings, 8040, *rēʾšît* [1]

BEGINS [4]
begins, *NIH/RPE* [4]

BEGOTTEN [1]
begotten, 3528, *yālad* [1]

BEGRUDGE [1]
begrudge, 8317+6524, *rāʿaʿ^{1}+ʿayin^{1}* [1]

BEGUN [8]
begun, 2725, *ḥālal^{1}* [6]
begun, *AIT* [1]
begun, 3569, *yāsad^{1}* [1]

BEHALF [35]
on behalf, 4200, *l^{e-1}* [7]
behalf, *AIT* [5]
in behalf of, 4200, *l^{e-1}* [3]
on behalf of, 1237, *baʿad^{1}* [2]
in behalf, 4200, *l^{e-1}* [2]
on behalf of, 4200, *l^{e-1}* [2]
in behalf, 6584, *ʿal^{2}* [2]
on behalf, 6584, *ʿal^{2}* [2]
on behalf, 1237, *baʿad^{1}* [1]
in behalf of, 4200+5100, *l^{e-1}+maʿan* [1]
on behalf of, 4200+5466, *l^{e-1}+mišmeret* [1]
on behalf of, 4200+5790, *l^{e-1}+nōkaḥ* [1]
on behalf of, 4946+907, *min+ʾēt^{2}* [1]
in behalf of, 6584+1821, *ʿal^{2}+dābār* [1]
in behalf of, 6584, *ʿal^{2}* [1]
in behalf, 6584+3208, *ʿal^{2}+ṭôbâ* [1]
on behalf of, 6584, *ʿal^{2}* [1]
on behalf, 9393, *taḥat^{1}* [1]

BEHAVE [1]
behave, 6913, *ʿāśâ^{1}* [1]

BEHAVED [5]
behaved, 6913, *ʿāśâ^{1}* [2]
how behaved, 2006, *derek* [1]
behaved, 3359, *yādaʿ* [1]
behaved in the vilest manner, 9493+4394, *tāʿab+m^{e}ʾōd* [1]

BEHAVES [1]
behaves, 6913, ʿāśâ[1] [1]

BEHAVIOR [2]
behavior, 1821, *dābār* [1]
behavior, 2006, *derek* [1]

BEHELD [1]
beheld, 8011, *rāʾâ*[1] [1]

BEHEMOTH [1]
behemoth, 990, *bᵉhēmôt* [1]

BEHIND [83]
behind, 339, *ʾaḥar* [42]
behind, 4946+339, *min+ʾaḥar* [9]
left behind, 8636, *šāʾar* [6]
behind, 1237, *baʿad*[1] [5]
behind, 4946+1074, *min+bayit*[1] [4]
behind, 4946+1237, *min+baʿad*[1] [3]
behind, 294, *ʾāḥôr* [2]
stayed behind, 6641, *ʿāmad* [2]
behind, 9004, *šām* [2]
behind, *AIT* [1]
leaves behind, 339, *ʾaḥar* [1]
right behind, 339, *ʾaḥar* [1]
behind, 928, *bᵉ-* [1]
leave behind, 3657, *yāṣag* [1]
left behind, 3782, *yāšab* [1]
behind, 4946+294, *min+ʾāḥôr* [1]
left behind, 6440, *ʿāzab*[1] [1]

BEHOLD [2]
behold, 2180, *hinnēh* [1]
behold, 8800, *šûr*[1] [1]

BEING [71]
being, *NIH/RPE* [21]
being, *AIT* [17]
being profaned, 2725, *ḥālal*[1] [3]
inmost being, 2540+1061, *ḥeder+beṭen*[1] [2]
inmost being, 4000, *kilyâ* [2]
inmost being, 7931, *qereb* [2]
human being, 132, *ʾādām*[1] [1]
being taken, 296, *ʾāḥaz*[1] [1]
being carried into exile, 1655, *gālâ* [1]
being, 2118, *hāyâ* [1]
came into being, 2118, *hāyâ* [1]
come into being, 2118+2118, *hāyâ+hāyâ* [1]
being destroyed, 2238, *hāras* [1]
very being, 2652, *ḥayyâ*[2] [1]
being scorched, 3917, *kāwâ* [1]
being led away, 4374, *lāqaḥ* [1]
without being aware, 4946+6524, *min+ʿayin*[1] [1]
being beaten, 5782, *nākâ* [1]
being, 5883, *nepeš* [1]
being swept away, 6200, *sāpâ* [1]
being closed, 6258, *sātam* [1]
being stirred up, 6424, *ʿûr*[3] [1]
being, 6795, *ʿeṣem*[1] [1]
spring into being, 7541, *ṣāmaḥ* [1]
being called, 7924, *qārāʾ*[1] [1]
being summoned, 7924, *qārāʾ*[1] [1]
being seen, 8011, *rāʾâ*[1] [1]
being burned, 8596, *śārap* [1]
being sent, 8938, *šālaḥ* [1]
being carried on, 10522, *ʿᵃbad* [1]

BEINGS [2]
heavenly beings, 466, *ʾᵉlōhîm* [1]
heavenly beings, 1201+446, *bēn*[1]*+ʾēl*[5] [1]

BEKA [2]
beka, 1325, *beqaʿ* [2]

BEKAS [3]
bekas, *NIH/RPE* [3]

BEKER [5]
Beker, 1146, *beker* [5]

BEKERITE [1]
Bekerite, 1151, *bakrî* [1]

BEL [3]
Bel, 1155, *bēl* [3]

BELA [14]
Bela, 1185, *belaʿ*[3] [12]
Bela, 1186, *belaʿ*[4] [2]

BELAITE [1]
Belaite, 1188, *balʿî* [1]

BELIEFS [1]
beliefs, 4375, *leqaḥ* [1]

BELIEVE [21]
believe, 586, *ʾāman*[1] [20]
led to believe, 1053, *bāṭaḥ*[1] [1]

BELIEVED [7]
believed, 586, *ʾāman*[1] [7]

BELIEVER [1]
believer, 3707, *yārēʾ*[1] [1]

BELIEVES [1]
believes, 586, *ʾāman*[1] [1]

BELLOW [1]
bellow, 1716, *gāʿâ* [1]

BELLOWS [1]
bellows, 5135, *mappuaḥ* [1]

BELLS [6]
bells, 7194, *paʿᵃmôn* [4]
the bells[s], 2257, *-ô* [1]
bells, 5197, *mᵉṣillâ* [1]

BELLY [8]
belly, 1061, *beṭen*[1] [4]
belly, 1623, *gāḥôn* [2]
belly, 2824, *ḥōmeš*[2] [1]
belly, 10435, *mᵉʿēh* [1]

BELONG [49]
belong to, 4200, *lᵉ-*[1] [25]
belong to, 4200+2118, *lᵉ-*[1]*+hāyâ* [7]
belong to, 2118+4200, *hāyâ+lᵉ-*[1] [4]
to belong, 4200, *lᵉ-*[1] [4]
belong to, 4946, *min* [3]
to belong, 6640, *ʿim* [2]
belong to, 928+2118, *bᵉ-+hāyâ* [1]
belong, 2118, *hāyâ* [1]
belong to, 6640, *ʿim* [1]
belong, 7756, *qûm* [1]

BELONGED [36]
belonged to, 4200, *lᵉ-*[1] [16]
belonged, *AIT* [8]
belonged to, 2118+4200, *hāyâ+lᵉ-*[1] [4]
to belonged, 4200, *lᵉ-*[1] [3]
belonged to, 448, *ʾel* [1]
belonged to, 928+8079, *bᵉ-+regel* [1]
belonged to, 2118+448, *hāyâ+ʾel* [1]
belonged, 3769, *yārāš*[1] [1]
belonged to, 4200+2118, *lᵉ-*[1]*+hāyâ* [1]

BELONGING [34]
belonging to, 4200, *lᵉ-*[1] [25]
belonging, *AIT* [7]
belonging to, 2118+4200, *hāyâ+lᵉ-*[1] [1]
belonging to, 4946, *min* [1]

BELONGINGS [8]
belongings, 3998, *kᵉlî* [4]
belongings, *NIH/RPE* [2]
belongings, 2723, *ḥᵃlîṣâ* [1]
belongings, 4045, *kinʿâ* [1]

BELONGS [42]
belongs to, 4200, *lᵉ-*[1] [28]
belongs, *AIT* [2]
belongs to, 2118+4200, *hāyâ+lᵉ-*[1] [2]
belongs to, 4200+2118, *lᵉ-*[1]*+hāyâ* [2]
to belongs, 4200, *lᵉ-*[1] [2]
belongs, *NIH/RPE* [1]
belongs to, 448, *ʾel* [1]
firstborn belongs to, 1144+4200, *bākar+lᵉ-*[1] [1]
belongs, 2118, *hāyâ* [1]
belongs to, 4946, *min* [1]
what belongs, 6886, *ʿērek* [1]

BELOVED [4]
beloved, 1856, *dôd* [2]
beloved, 3351, *yādîd* [2]

BELOW [39]
below, 4946+9393, *min+taḥat*[1] [17]
below, 9393, *taḥat*[1] [10]
below, 9397, *taḥtî* [7]
below, 4200+4752, *lᵉ-*[1]*+maṭṭâ* [3]
below deck, 3752+2021+6208, *yᵉrēkâ+ha+sᵉpînâ* [1]
below, 6584+2021+141, *ʿal*[2]*+ha+ʾᵃdāmâ*[1] [1]

BELSHAZZAR [6]
Belshazzar, 10109, *bēlšaʾṣṣar* [4]
Belshazzar, 10105, *bēlʾšaṣṣar* [2]

BELSHAZZAR'S [2]
Belshazzar's, 1157, *bēlʾšaṣṣar* [1]
Belshazzar's, 10109, *bēlšaʾṣṣar* [1]

BELT [20]
belt, 258, *ʾēzôr* [9]
belt, 2512, *ḥᵃgôr* [2]
tuck cloak into belt, 2520+5516, *ḥāgar+motnayim* [2]
belt, 258+5516, *ʾēzôr+motnayim* [1]
belt, 2514, *ḥᵃgôrâ* [1]
warrior's belt, 2514, *ḥᵃgôrâ* [1]
belt, 2520, *ḥāgar* [1]
belt, 4652, *mēzaḥ*[2] [1]
cloak tucked into belt, 5516+2520, *motnayim+ḥāgar* [1]
tucking cloak into belt, 9113+5516, *šānas+motnayim* [1]

BELTESHAZZAR [10]
Belteshazzar, 10108, *bēlṭᵉšaʾṣṣar* [8]
Belteshazzar, 1171, *bēlṭᵉšaʾṣṣar* [2]

BELTS [1]
belts, 2513+258, *ḥāgôr+ʾēzôr* [1]

BEN HINNOM [10]
Ben Hinnom, 1208, *ben-hinnōm* [10]

BEN-ABINADAB [1]
Ben-Abinadab, 1203, *ben-ʾᵃbînādāb* [1]

BEN-AMMI [1]
Ben-Ammi, 1214, *ben-ʿammî* [1]

BEN-DEKER [1]
Ben-Deker, 1206, *ben-deqer* [1]

BEN-GEBER [1]
Ben-Geber, 1205, *ben-geber* [1]

BEN-HADAD [28]
Ben-Hadad, 1207, *ben-hᵃdad* [24]
Ben-Hadad, *NIH/RPE* [3]
Ben-Hadad[s], 2084, *-hû* [1]

BEN-HADAD'S [1]
Ben-Hadad's, 1207, *ben-hᵃdad* [1]

BEN-HAIL [1]
Ben-Hail, 1211, *ben-ḥayil* [1]

BEN-HANAN [1]
Ben-Hanan, 1212, *ben-ḥānān* [1]

BEN-HESED [1]
Ben-Hesed, 1213, *ben-ḥesed* [1]

BEN-HUR [1]
Ben-Hur, 1210, *ben-ḥûr* [1]

BEN-ONI [1]
Ben-Oni, 1204, *ben-ʾônî* [1]

BEN-ZOHETH [1]
Ben-Zoheth, 1209, *ben-zôḥēt* [1]

BENAIAH [45]
Benaiah, 1226, *bᵉnāyāhû* [31]
Benaiah, 1225, *bᵉnāyâ* [11]
Benaiah, *NIH/RPE* [2]
Benaiah[s], 2257, *-ô* [1]

BEND [9]
bend, 2005, *dārak* [4]
bend, 5737, *nāḥat* [2]
bend, *NIH/RPE* [1]
bend down, 4156, *kāraʿ* [1]
bend, 5742, *nāṭâ* [1]

BENE BERAK [1]
Bene Berak, 1222, *bᵉnê-bᵉraq* [1]

BENE JAAKAN [2]
Bene Jaakan, 1223, *bᵉnê yaʿᵃqān* [2]

BENEATH [22]
beneath, 9393, *taḥat*^{1} [15]
beneath, 4946+9393, *min+taḥat*^{1} [4]
beneath, *AIT* [1]
beneath, *NIH/RPE* [1]
beneath, 9397, *taḥtî* [1]

BENEFIT [6]
benefit in the least, 3603+3603, *yāʿal+yāʿal* [1]
benefit, 3603, *yāʿal* [1]
benefit, 4179, *kišrôn* [1]
be of benefit, 6122, *sākan*^{1} [1]
benefit, 6122, *sākan*^{1} [1]
benefit, 8934, *šālôm* [1]

BENEFITED [1]
benefited, 3202, *ṭôb*^{2} [1]

BENEFITS [4]
benefits, 1691, *gᵉmûl* [1]
benefits, 1694, *gāmal* [1]
benefits, 2750, *ḥēleq*^{2} [1]
benefits, 3463, *yôtēr* [1]

BENINU [1]
Beninu, 1231, *bᵉnînû* [1]

BENJAMIN [132]
Benjamin, 1228, *binyāmîn* [111]
Benjamin, 1201+1228, *bēn*^{1}*+binyāmîn* [13]
tribe of Benjamin, 1228, *binyāmîn* [2]
people from Benjamin, 278+2157, *ʾāḥ*^{2}*+-hem* [1]
tribe of Benjamin, 408+3549, *ʾîš*^{1}*+yᵉmînî* [1]
Benjamin, 824+1228, *ʾereṣ+binyāmîn* [1]
Benjamin, 1201+408+3549, *bēn*^{1}*+ʾîš*^{1}*+yᵉmînî* [1]
men of Benjamin, 1229, *ben-yᵉmînî* [1]
Benjamin, 3549, *yᵉmînî* [1]

BENJAMIN'S [2]
Benjamin's, 1228, *binyāmîn* [2]

BENJAMITE [14]
Benjamite, 1229, *ben-yᵉmînî* [7]
Benjamite, 1228, *binyāmîn* [4]
Benjamite, 408+1228, *ʾîš*^{1}*+binyāmîn* [1]
Benjamite, 408+3549, *ʾîš*^{1}*+yᵉmînî* [1]
Benjamite, 4946+1228, *min+binyāmîn* [1]

BENJAMITES [33]
Benjamites, 1201+1228, *bēn*^{1}*+binyāmîn* [17]
Benjamites, 1228, *binyāmîn* [11]
Benjamites, 1229, *ben-yᵉmînî* [1]
the Benjamites^{s}, 2156, *hēm* [1]
the Benjamites^{s}, 2257, *-ô* [1]
Benjamites, 4946+1228+408, *min+binyāmîn+ʾîš*^{1} [1]
Benjamites, 4946+1228, *min+binyāmîn* [1]

BENO [2]
Beno, 1217, *bᵉnô* [2]

BENT [14]
bent on, 1335, *bāqaš* [2]
bent on, 4200, *lᵉ-*^{1} [2]
bent on, 928+6783, *bᵉ-+ʿēṣâ*^{1} [1]
bent down, 1566, *gāhar* [1]
bent, 2005, *dārak* [1]
bent on, 3922, *kûn*^{1} [1]
bent on, 3983, *kālâ*^{1} [1]
bent on, 4200+5100, *lᵉ-*^{1}*+maʿan* [1]
bent, 5048, *māʿad* [1]
bent on, 5584+7156, *neged+pāneh* [1]
bent down, 5742, *nāṭâ* [1]
bent on revenge, 5933, *nāqam* [1]

BEON [1]
Beon, 1274, *bᵉʿōn* [1]

BEOR [10]
Beor, 1242, *bᵉʿôr* [10]

BERA [1]
Bera, 1396, *beraʿ* [1]

BERACAH [3]
Beracah, 1390, *bᵉrākâ*^{3} [2]
Beracah, 1389, *bᵉrākâ*^{2} [1]

BERAIAH [1]
Beraiah, 1349, *bᵉrāʾyâ* [1]

BEREAVE [1]
bereave, 8897, *šākal* [1]

BEREAVED [3]
bereaved, 8897, *šākal* [2]
bereaved, 8892, *šᵉkûlâ* [1]

BEREAVEMENT [2]
bring bereavement, 8897, *šākal* [1]
bereavement, 8898, *šikkulîm* [1]

BEREAVES [1]
bereaves, 8897, *šākal* [1]

BERED [2]
Bered, 1354, *bered*^{1} [1]
Bered, 1355, *bered*^{2} [1]

BEREKIAH [11]
Berekiah, 1392, *berekyâ* [7]
Berekiah, 1393, *berekyāhû* [4]

BERI [1]
Beri, 1373, *bērî* [1]

BERIAH [11]
Beriah, 1380, *bᵉrîʿâ* [11]

BERIITE [1]
Beriite, 1381, *bᵉrîʿî* [1]

BERITES [1]
Berites, 1379, *bērîm* [1]

BEROTHAH [1]
Berothah, 1363, *bērôtâ* [1]

BEROTHAI [1]
Berothai, 1408, *bērōtay* [1]

BEROTHITE [1]
Berothite, 1409, *bērōtî* [1]

BERYL [3]
beryl, 1403, *bāreqet* [2]
beryl, 1404, *bārᵉqat* [1]

BESAI [2]
Besai, 1234, *bēsay* [2]

BESET [2]
beset, 995+928, *bôʾ+bᵉ-* [1]
beset, 3668, *yāṣaq* [1]

BESIDE [78]
beside, 725, *ʾēṣel*^{1} [30]
beside, 6584, *ʿal*^{2} [25]
beside, 928, *bᵉ-* [4]
beside, 6640, *ʿim* [3]
beside, 448, *ʾel* [2]
beside, 4200+6645, *lᵉ-*^{1}*+ʿummâ*^{1} [2]
beside, 4200+7156, *lᵉ-*^{1}*+pāneh* [2]
beside, 4946+7396, *min+ṣad*^{1} [2]
beside, 448+3338, *ʾel+yād* [1]
beside, 928+2668, *bᵉ-+ḥêq* [1]
beside, 928+3338, *bᵉ-+yād* [1]
beside, 4200+3338, *lᵉ-*^{1}*+yād* [1]
beside, 4946+6584, *min+ʿal*^{2} [1]
beside, 6584+3338, *ʿal*^{2}*+yād* [1]
beside, 6584+7156, *ʿal*^{2}*+pāneh* [1]
beside, 9004, *šām* [1]

BESIDES [36]
besides, 4946+4200+963, *min+lᵉ-*^{1}*+bad*^{1} [7]
besides, 2256, *wᵉ-* [6]
besides, 6388, *ʿôd* [4]
besides, 4946+1187, *min+balʿᵃdê* [3]
besides, 2256+1685, *wᵉ-+gam* [2]
besides, 2314, *zûlâ* [2]
besides, 4200+963+4946, *lᵉ-*^{1}*+bad*^{1}*+min* [2]
besides, 6584, *ʿal*^{2} [2]
besides, 1187, *balʿᵃdê* [1]
besides, 1194, *biltî* [1]
besides, 1685, *gam* [1]
more besides, 3578, *yāsap* [1]
besides, 4200+963, *lᵉ-*^{1}*+bad*^{1} [1]
besides, 4200, *lᵉ-*^{1} [1]
besides, 6640, *ʿim* [1]
besides, 6643, *ʿimmād* [1]

BESIEGE [9]
besiege, 7443, *ṣûr*^{1} [3]
besiege, 2837+6584, *ḥānâ*^{1}*+ʿal*^{2} [2]
besiege, 7439, *ṣûq*^{1} [2]
besiege, 995+928+2021+5189, *bôʾ+bᵉ-+ha-+māṣôr*^{1} [1]
besiege, 7674, *ṣārar*^{1} [1]

BESIEGED [11]
besieged, 7443, *ṣûr*^{1} [6]
besieged, 5189, *māṣôr*^{1} [2]
besieged, 1215+6584, *bānâ+ʿal*^{2} [1]
besieged, 2837+6584, *ḥānâ*^{1}*+ʿal*^{2} [1]
besieged, 2837+928, *ḥānâ*^{1}*+bᵉ-* [1]

BESIEGES [1]
besieges, 7443, *ṣûr*^{1} [1]

BESIEGING [7]
besieging, 7443, *ṣûr*^{1} [7]

BESODEIAH [1]
Besodeiah, 1233, *bᵉsôdᵉyâ* [1]

BESOR [2]
Besor, 1410, *bᵉśôr* [2]

BEST [59]
best, 3202, *ṭôb*^{2} [17]
best, 8040, *rēʾšît* [6]
best, 4774, *mêṭāb* [5]
best, 1047, *bāḥar*^{1} [3]
best, 2693, *ḥēleb*^{1} [3]
best, 3206, *ṭûb* [3]
best, 4436, *mibḥār*^{1} [3]
best men, 738, *ʾᵃrîʾēl* [2]
best fighting men, 1475+2657, *gibbôr+ḥayil* [2]
best, 4458, *meged* [2]
best, *AIT* [1]
best strength, 2086, *hôd*^{1} [1]
best products, 2380, *zimrâ*^{2} [1]
do best, 2616, *ḥāzaq* [1]
best, 2776, *ḥᵃmudôt* [1]
best things, 3206, *ṭûb* [1]
best, 3512, *yāṭab* [1]
best, 3603, *yāʿal* [1]
best, 3837, *yāšar* [1]
best clothes, 8529, *śimlâ* [1]
in best interest, 8750, *šāwâ*^{1} [1]
best, 9043, *šemen* [1]
seems best, 10320, *yᵉṭab* [1]

BESTOW [6]
bestow, *NIH/RPE* [1]
bestow a title of honor, 4033, *kānâ* [1]
bestow, 5918, *nāqab*^{1} [1]
bestow, 5989, *nātan* [1]
bestow, 7188, *pāʿal* [1]
bestow punishment, 7212, *pāqad* [1]

BESTOWED [4]
bestowed, 8751, *šāwâ*^{2} [2]
bestowed, 5989, *nātan* [1]
bestowed care on, 7212, *pāqad* [1]

BESTOWER [1]
bestower of crowns, 6497, *ʿāṭar*^{2} [1]

BESTOWING [1]
bestowing, 5706, *nāḥal* [1]

BESTOWS [3]
bestows, 5989, *nātan* [2]
bestows, 7422, *ṣāwâ* [1]

BETEN [1]
Beten, 1062, *beṭen*^{2} [1]

BETH ANATH [3]
Beth Anath, 1117, *bêt-ʿ*^{a}*nāt* [3]

BETH ANOTH [1]
Beth Anoth, 1116, *bêt-ʿ*^{a}*nôt* [1]

BETH ARABAH [4]
Beth Arabah, 1098, *bêt hāʿ*^{a}*rābâ* [4]

BETH ARBEL [1]
Beth Arbel, 1079, *bêt ʾarbēʾl* [1]

BETH ASHBEA [1]
Beth Ashbea, 1080, *bêt ʾašbēaʿ* [1]

BETH AVEN [7]
Beth Aven, 1077, *bêt ʾāwen* [7]

BETH AZMAVETH [1]
Beth Azmaveth, 1115, *bêt-ʿazmāwet* [1]

BETH BAAL MEON [1]
Beth Baal Meon, 1081, *bêt baʿal m*^{e}*ʿôn* [1]

BETH BARAH [2]
Beth Barah, 1083, *bêt bārâ* [2]

BETH BIRI [1]
Beth Biri, 1082, *bêt birʾî* [1]

BETH CAR [1]
Beth Car, 1105, *bêt kār* [1]

BETH DAGON [2]
Beth Dagon, 1087, *bêt-dāgôn* [2]

BETH DIBLATHAIM [1]
Beth Diblathaim, 1086, *bêt diblātayim* [1]

BETH EDEN [1]
Beth Eden, 1114, *bêt ʿeden* [1]

BETH EKED [2]
Beth Eked, 1118, *bêt-ʿēqed* [2]

BETH EMEK [1]
Beth Emek, 1097, *bêt hāʿēmeq* [1]

BETH EZEL [1]
Beth Ezel, 1089, *bêt hāʾēṣel* [1]

BETH GADER [1]
Beth Gader, 1084, *bêt-gādēr* [1]

BETH GAMUL [1]
Beth Gamul, 1085, *bêt gāmûl* [1]

BETH GILGAL [1]
Beth Gilgal, 1090, *bêt haggilgāl* [1]

BETH HAGGAN [1]
Beth Haggan, 1091, *bêt haggān* [1]

BETH HAKKEREM [2]
Beth Hakkerem, 1094, *bêt-hakkerem* [2]

BETH HARAM [1]
Beth Haram, 1099, *bêt hārām* [1]

BETH HARAN [1]
Beth Haran, 1100, *bêt hārān* [1]

BETH HOGLAH [3]
Beth Hoglah, 1102, *bêt-ḥoglâ* [3]

BETH HORON [14]
Beth Horon, 1103, *bêt-ḥôrôn* [14]

BETH JESHIMOTH [4]
Beth Jeshimoth, 1093, *bêt hay*^{e}*šîmôt* [4]

BETH LEBAOTH [1]
Beth Lebaoth, 1106, *bêt l*^{e}*bāʾôt* [1]

BETH MARCABOTH [2]
Beth Marcaboth, 1096, *bêt-hammarkābôt* [1]
Beth Marcaboth, 1112, *bêt markābôt* [1]

BETH MEON [1]
Beth Meon, 1110, *bêt m*^{e}*ʿôn* [1]

BETH MILLO [4]
Beth Millo, 1109, *bêt millôʾ* [4]

BETH NIMRAH [2]
Beth Nimrah, 1113, *bêt nimrâ* [2]

BETH OPHRAH [1]
Beth Ophrah, 1108, *bêt l*^{e}*ʿaprâ* [1]

BETH PAZZEZ [1]
Beth Pazzez, 1122, *bêt paṣṣēṣ* [1]

BETH PELET [2]
Beth Pelet, 1120, *bêt peleṭ* [2]

BETH PEOR [4]
Beth Peor, 1121, *bêt p*^{e}*ʿôr* [4]

BETH RAPHA [1]
Beth Rapha, 1125, *bêt rāpāʾ* [1]

BETH REHOB [2]
Beth Rehob, 1124, *bêt-r*^{e}*ḥôb* [2]

BETH SHAN [10]
Beth Shan, 1126, *bêt-šᵉʾān* [9]
Beth Shan, *NIH/RPE* [1]

BETH SHEMESH [20]
Beth Shemesh, 1127, *bêt šemeš* [20]

BETH SHITTAH [1]
Beth Shittah, 1101, *bêt haššiṭṭâ* [1]

BETH TAPPUAH [1]
Beth Tappuah, 1130, *bêt-tappûaḥ* [1]

BETH TOGARMAH [2]
Beth Togarmah, 1129, *bêt tôgarmâ* [2]

BETH ZUR [4]
Beth Zur, 1123, *bêt-ṣûr* [4]

BETHEL [71]
Bethel, 1078, *bêt-ʾēl* [70]
of Bethel, 1088, *bêt hāʾ*^{e}*lî* [1]

BETHLEHEM [43]
Bethlehem, 1107, *bêt leḥem* [40]
of Bethlehem, 1095, *bêt-hallaḥmî* [3]

BETHLEHEMITE [1]
the Bethlehemite, 1095, *bêt-hallaḥmî* [1]

BETHUEL [10]
Bethuel, 1432, *b*^{e}*tûʾēl*^{1} [9]
Bethuel, 1433, *b*^{e}*tûʾēl*^{2} [1]

BETHUL [1]
Bethul, 1434, *b*^{e}*tûl* [1]

BETONIM [1]
Betonim, 1064, *b*^{e}*ṭōnîm* [1]

BETRAY [7]
betray, 953, *bāgad* [2]
betray, 1655, *gālâ* [2]
betray, 5085, *māʿal* [1]
betray, 8228, *rāmâ*^{2} [1]
betray, 9213, *šāqar* [1]

BETRAYED [7]
betrayed, 953, *bāgad* [5]
betrayed, 8228, *rāmâ*^{2} [2]

BETRAYING [1]
betraying, 953, *bāgad* [1]

BETRAYS [4]
betrays, 953, *bāgad* [2]
betrays, 1655, *gālâ* [2]

BETROTH [3]
betroth, 829, *ʾāraś* [3]

BETROTHED [2]
betrothed, 829, *ʾāraś* [2]

BETTER [90]
better, 3202, *ṭôb*^{2} [64]
better than, 4946, *min* [7]
better off, 3202, *ṭôb*^{2} [6]
feel better, 3201, *ṭôb*^{1} [2]
better, 3862, *yitrôn* [2]
better than, 440, *ʾal*^{1} [1]
how much better, 677+3954, *ʾap*^{1}*+kî*^{2} [1]
better, 1524, *gādôl* [1]
better, 3201+3201, *ṭôb*^{1}*+ṭôb*^{1} [1]
better, 3202+4946, *ṭôb*^{2}*+min* [1]
better, 3512, *yāṭab* [1]
better than, 4202, *lōʾ* [1]
better than, 6584, *ʿal*^{2} [1]
consider better, 8123+4222, *rûm*^{1}*+lēbāb* [1]

BETWEEN [202]
between, 1068, *bayin* [164]
between, *AIT* [13]
between, 928+9348, *b*^{e}*-+tāwek* [3]
between, 4200, *l*$^{e-1}$ [3]
between, 4946+1068, *min+bayin* [3]
between, 4946+2256+6330, *min+w*^{e}*-+ʿad*^{2} [3]
between, 4946, *min* [2]
between, *NIH/RPE* [1]
between, 928, *b*^{e}*-* [1]
difference between, 1068, *bayin* [1]
distinction between, 1068, *bayin* [1]
relationships between, 1068, *bayin* [1]
the difference between, 1068, *bayin* [1]
between, 1075, *bayit*^{2} [1]
learn the difference between, 3359, *yādaʿ* [1]
quarrel between, 4200, *l*$^{e-1}$ [1]
between, 6584, *ʿal*^{2} [1]
between, 10099, *bên* [1]

BEULAH [1]
Beulah, 1241, *b*^{e}*ʿûlâ* [1]

BEWARE [6]
beware, 2180, *hinnēh* [3]
beware, 9068, *šāmar* [2]
beware, 9068+440, *šāmar+ʾal*^{1} [1]

BEWILDERED [2]
am bewildered, 987, *bāhal* [1]
bewildered, 1003, *bûk* [1]

BEYOND [48]
beyond, 401, *ʾayin*^{1} [5]
beyond, 928+6298, *b*^{e}*-+ʿēber*^{1} [5]
beyond, 4946, *min* [4]
beyond, 6298, *ʿēber*^{1} [4]
beyond, 4202, *lōʾ* [3]
beyond measure, 6330+4394, *ʿad*^{2}*+m*^{e}*ʾōd* [3]
beyond, 339, *ʾaḥar* [2]
beyond, 4946+2256+2134, *min+w*^{e}*-+hālᵉʾâ* [2]
beyond, 4946+6298, *min+ʿēber*^{1} [2]
go beyond, 6296, *ʿābar*^{1} [2]
beyond cure, 631, *ʾānûš* [1]
beyond healing, 2703, *ḥālâ*^{1} [1]
beyond, 4946+2134+4200, *min+hālᵉʾâ+l*$^{e-1}$ [1]
beyond, 4946+2134, *min+hālᵉʾâ* [1]
even beyond, 4946+6584, *min+ʿal*^{2} [1]
beyond, 5087+2025, *maʿal*^{2}*+-â*^{2} [1]
beyond all remedy, 5344, *māraṣ* [1]
beyond, 5584, *neged* [1]
beyond, 6296, *ʿābar*^{1} [1]
moved on beyond, 6296, *ʿābar*^{1} [1]
land beyond, 6298, *ʿēber*^{1} [1]
beyond, 6584, *ʿal*^{2} [1]
beyond understanding, 7100, *pilʾî* [1]
beyond number, 8041+4394, *rab*^{1}*+m*^{e}*ʾōd* [1]
beyond reach, 8158, *rāḥôq* [1]
beyond, 8158, *rāḥôq* [1]

BEZAI [3]
Bezai, 1291, *bēṣay* [3]

BEZALEL [9]
Bezalel, 1295, *bᵉṣal'ēl* [9]
BEZEK [2]
Bezek, 1028, *bezeq* [2]
BEZER [5]
Bezer, 1311, *beṣer*[3] [4]
Bezer, 1310, *beṣer*[2] [1]
BICRI [8]
Bicri, 1152, *bikrî* [8]
BIDDING [2]
bidding, 1821, *dābār* [2]
BIDKAR [1]
Bidkar, 982, *bidqar* [1]
BIER [2]
bier, 4753, *miṭṭâ* [1]
bier, 5435, *miškāb* [1]
BIG [11]
big toe, 991, *bōhen* [5]
big toes, 991, *bōhen* [2]
big toes, 8079, *regel* [2]
big, 1524, *gādôl* [1]
big talk, 7023, *peh* [1]
BIGTHA [1]
Bigtha, 960, *bigtā'* [1]
BIGTHANA [2]
Bigthana, 961, *bigtān* [1]
Bigthana, 962, *bigtānā'* [1]
BIGVAI [6]
Bigvai, 958, *bigway* [6]
BILDAD [5]
Bildad, 1161, *bildad* [5]
BILEAM [1]
Bileam, 1190, *bil'ām*[2] [1]
BILGAH [2]
Bilgah, 1159, *bilgâ* [2]
BILGAH'S [1]
Bilgah's, 1159, *bilgâ* [1]
BILGAI [1]
Bilgai, 1160, *bilgay* [1]
BILHAH [10]
Bilhah, 1167, *bilhâ*[1] [9]
Bilhah, 1168, *bilhâ*[2] [1]
BILHAN [4]
Bilhan, 1169, *bilhān* [4]
BILLOWED [1]
billowed up, 6590, *'ālâ* [1]
BILLOWS [1]
billows, 9406, *tîmārâ* [1]
BILSHAN [2]
Bilshan, 1193, *bilšān* [2]
BIMHAL [1]
Bimhal, 1197, *bimhāl* [1]
BIND [15]
bind, 8003, *qāšar* [4]
bind up, 2502, *ḥābaš* [3]
bind, 2118+4200+3213, *hāyâ+lᵉ-*[1]*+ṭôṭāpōt* [2]
bind themselves, 4277, *lāwâ*[1] [2]
bind, 673, *'āsar* [1]
bind themselves with, 995+928, *bô'+bᵉ-* [1]
bind, 6386, *'ûd*[1] [1]
bind up, 7674, *ṣārar*[1] [1]
BINDING [6]
binding, 520, *'ālam*[2] [1]
binding agreement, 591, *'ᵃmānâ*[1] [1]
binding, 673, *'āsar* [1]
not binding, 5929, *nāqî* [1]
binding on, 6584, *'al*[2] [1]
binding, 7756, *qûm* [1]
BINDINGS [1]
bindings, 657, *'ēsûr* [1]
BINDS [4]
binds up, 2502, *ḥābaš* [3]
binds, 273, *'āzar* [1]
BINEA [2]
Binea, 1232, *bin'ā'* [2]
BINNUI [8]
Binnui, 1218, *binnûy* [8]
BIRD [37]
bird, 7606, *ṣippôr*[1] [18]
bird, 6416, *'ôp* [12]
bird of prey, 6514, *'ayiṭ* [3]
bird on the wing, 1251+4053, *ba'al*[1]*+kānāp* [1]
bird, 7606+4053, *ṣippôr*[1]*+kānāp* [1]
bird, 10533, *'ôp* [1]
bird, 10616, *ṣippar* [1]
BIRD'S [2]
bird's, 7606, *ṣippôr*[1] [2]
BIRDS [80]
birds, 6416, *'ôp* [54]
birds, 7606, *ṣippôr*[1] [12]
birds of prey, 6514, *'ayiṭ* [3]
birds, 10616, *ṣippar* [3]
birds, 7256, *pārah*[2] [2]
birds, 1251+4053, *ba'al*[1]*+kānāp* [1]
men who snare birds, 3687, *yāqûš* [1]
birds, 6514, *'ayiṭ* [1]
carrion birds, 6514+7606, *'ayiṭ+ṣippôr*[1] [1]
birds, 7606+4053, *ṣippôr*[1]*+kānāp* [1]
birds, 10533, *'ôp* [1]
BIRSHA [1]
Birsha, 1407, *birša'* [1]
BIRTH [110]
gave birth, 3528, *yālad* [46]
give birth, 3528, *yālad* [16]
gives birth, 3528, *yālad* [8]
birth, 1061, *beṭen*[1] [4]
birth, 8167, *reḥem* [4]
given birth, 3528, *yālad* [3]
birth, 1061+562, *beṭen*[1]*+'ēm* [2]
gave birth, 2655, *ḥîl*[1] [2]
was given birth, 2655, *ḥîl*[1] [2]
birth, 3528, *yālad* [2]
birth, 4580, *môledet* [2]
point of birth, 5402, *mašbēr* [2]
birth, *NIH/RPE* [1]
birth, 1201, *bēn*[1] [1]
gave birth, 2225, *hārâ* [1]
at birth, 2655, *ḥîl*[1] [1]
brought to birth, 2655, *ḥîl*[1] [1]
giving birth, 3528, *yālad* [1]
placed at birth, 3528, *yālad* [1]
slave by birth, 3535+1074, *yālîd+bayit*[1] [1]
gives birth prematurely, 3655+3529, *yāṣā'+yeled* [1]
birth, 4256, *lēdâ* [1]
birth, 5055+562, *mē'eh+'ēm* [1]
give birth, 5877, *nāpal* [1]
given birth, 5877, *nāpal* [1]
of royal birth, 8576, *śārâ*[2] [1]
bring to the moment of birth, 8689, *šābar*[1] [1]
birth, 9352, *tôlēdôt* [1]
order of birth, 9352, *tôlēdôt* [1]
BIRTHDAY [1]
birthday, 3427+3528, *yôm*[1]*+yālad* [1]
BIRTHRIGHT [6]
birthright, 1148, *bᵉkōrâ* [6]
BIRZAITH [1]
Birzaith, 1365, *birzāyit* [1]
BISHLAM [1]
Bishlam, 1420, *bišlām* [1]
BIT [5]
bit, 5496, *meteg* [3]
bit, 5966, *nāšak*[1] [1]
bit, 8270, *resen*[1] [1]
BITE [3]
bite, 5966, *nāšak*[1] [3]
BITES [3]
bites, 5966, *nāšak*[1] [3]
BITHIAH [1]
Bithiah, 1437, *bityâ* [1]
BITHRON [1]
Bithron, 1443, *bitrôn* [1]
BITS [1]
bits, 1323, *bāqîa'* [1]
BITTEN [3]
bitten, 5966, *nāšak*[1] [2]
is bitten, 5966, *nāšak*[1] [1]
BITTER [40]
bitter, 5253, *mar*[1] [16]
bitter, 5352, *mārar* [4]
bitter, 4360, *la'ᵃnâ* [3]
bitter herbs, 5353, *mārōr* [3]
bitter suffering, 5253, *mar*[1] [2]
made bitter, 5352, *mārar* [2]
bitter, 2617, *ḥāzāq* [1]
bitter, 5308, *mᵉrî* [1]
bitter grief, 5320, *mᵉrîrût* [1]
bitter, 5344, *māraṣ* [1]
bitter anguish, 5352, *mārar* [1]
in bitter distress, 5352, *mārar* [1]
bitter things, 5353, *mārōr* [1]
bitter labor, 6662, *'āmāl*[1] [1]
bitter, 8273, *ra'*[1] [1]
bitter, 9476, *tamrûrîm*[1] [1]
BITTERLY [19]
bitterly, 1524, *gādôl* [4]
bitterly, 5253, *mar*[1] [4]
curse bitterly, 826+826, *'ārar+'ārar* [1]
bitterly weeps, 1134+1134, *bākâ+bākâ* [1]
weep bitterly, 1134+1134, *bākâ+bākâ* [1]
wept bitterly, 1134+2221+1135, *bākâ+harbēh+bekeh* [1]
weeping bitterly, 1140+1140, *bᵉkî+bᵉkî* [1]
weep bitterly, 1963+1963, *dāma'+dāma'* [1]
bitterly, 3878+4394, *kābēd*[2]*+mᵉ'ōd* [1]
bitterly, 4394, *mᵉ'ōd* [1]
bitterly, 5352, *mārar* [1]
grieve bitterly, 5352, *mārar* [1]
bitterly, 9476, *tamrûrîm*[1] [1]
BITTERNESS [16]
bitterness, 5253, *mar*[1] [7]
bitterness, 4360, *la'ᵃnâ* [2]
bitterness, 8032, *rō'š*[2] [2]
bitterness, 4933, *memer* [1]
bitterness, 5289, *mōrâ* [1]
bitterness attacked, 5352, *mārar* [1]
made taste bitterness, 5352, *mārar* [1]
bitterness, 5353, *mārōr* [1]
BIZIOTHIAH [1]
Biziothiah, 1026, *bizyôtᵉyâ* [1]
BIZTHA [1]
Biztha, 1030, *bizzᵉtā'* [1]
BLACK [13]
black, 8839, *šāḥōr* [5]
black kite, 370, *'ayyâ*[1] [2]
black vulture, 6465, *'ozniyyâ* [2]
black, 3124, *ḥāšak* [1]
black, 3125, *ḥōšek* [1]
black, 7722, *qādar* [1]
grows black, 8837, *šāḥar*[1] [1]
BLACKENED [1]
blackened, 7722, *qādar* [1]
BLACKER [1]
blacker, 3124, *ḥāšak* [1]

BLACKEST [1]
- blackest, 7516, *ṣalmāwet* [1]

BLACKNESS [4]
- blackness, 6906, *ʿ[a]rāpel* [2]
- blackness, 4025, *kamrîr* [1]
- blackness, 7516, *ṣalmāwet* [1]

BLACKSMITH [3]
- blacksmith, 3093, *ḥārāš* [2]
- blacksmith, 3093+1366, *ḥārāš+barzel* [1]

BLADE [2]
- blade, 4258, *lahab* [1]
- blade, 7156, *pāneh* [1]

BLAME [5]
- bear the blame, 2627, *ḥāṭāʾ* [2]
- blame, 6411, *ʿāwōn* [2]
- free from blame, 5929, *nāqî* [1]

BLAMELESS [42]
- blameless, 9459, *tāmîm* [19]
- blameless, 9447, *tām* [8]
- blameless, 9448, *tōm* [8]
- blameless, 9462, *tāmam* [2]
- show yourself blameless, 9462, *tāmam* [2]
- blameless, 1475+9459, *gibbôr+tāmîm* [1]
- blameless, 1505+9459, *geber[1]+tāmîm* [1]
- blameless, 9450, *tummâ* [1]

BLANKET [1]
- blanket, 5012, *massēkâ[2]* [1]

BLANKETS [2]
- blankets, 955+2927, *beged[2]+ḥōpeš* [1]
- saddle blankets, 4496, *mad* [1]

BLASPHEME [1]
- blaspheme, 7837, *qālal* [1]

BLASPHEMED [7]
- blasphemed, 1552, *gādap* [5]
- is blasphemed, 5540, *nāʾaṣ* [1]
- blasphemed, 5919, *nāqab[2]* [1]

BLASPHEMER [2]
- blasphemer, 7837, *qālal* [2]

BLASPHEMES [3]
- blasphemes, 5919, *nāqab[2]* [2]
- blasphemes, 1552, *gādap* [1]

BLASPHEMIES [2]
- blasphemies, 5542, *neʾāṣâ* [2]

BLAST [18]
- blast, 7754, *qôl* [3]
- blast, 8120, *rûaḥ* [3]
- blast, 5972, *n[e]šāmâ* [2]
- blast, 9558, *t[e]rûʿâ* [2]
- at the blast, 928+1896, *b[e]-+day* [1]
- sounds a long blast, 5432, *māšak* [1]
- blast, 5870, *nāpaḥ* [1]
- blast, 7754+8795, *qôl+šôpār* [1]
- icy blast, 7938, *qārâ[2]* [1]
- sound a blast, 8131, *rûaʿ* [1]
- sounded blast, 9546, *tāqaʿ* [1]
- trumpet blast, 9558, *t[e]rûʿâ* [1]

BLASTS [1]
- trumpet blasts, 9558, *t[e]rûʿâ* [1]

BLAZE [2]
- blaze, 4259, *lehābâ* [2]

BLAZED [7]
- blazed, 1277, *bāʿar[1]* [4]
- blazed forth, 1277, *bāʿar[1]* [1]
- blazed, 5782, *nākâ* [1]
- blazed up, 6590, *ʿālâ* [1]

BLAZES [2]
- blazes, 1277, *bāʿar[1]* [1]
- blazes, 4265, *lāhaṭ[1]* [1]

BLAZING [15]
- blazing, 10471+10328, *nûr+y[e]qad* [8]
- blazing, 1277, *bāʿar[1]* [2]
- blazing, 836, *ʾēš[1]* [1]
- blazing, 3679, *y[e]qōd* [1]
- blazing, 4259, *lehābâ* [1]
- blazing, 8404, *rešep[1]* [1]
- blazing, 10329, *y[e]qēdâ* [1]

BLEAT [1]
- bleat, 7924, *qārāʾ[1]* [1]

BLEATING [1]
- bleating, 7754, *qôl* [1]

BLEEDING [2]
- bleeding, 1947, *dām* [2]

BLEMISH [3]
- blemish, 4583, *mûm* [3]

BLEMISHED [1]
- blemished, 8845, *šāḥat* [1]

BLEND [2]
- blend, 8381, *rōqaḥ* [1]
- fragrant blend, 8381, *rōqaḥ* [1]

BLENDED [2]
- blended wine, 4641, *mezeg* [1]
- blended, 8379, *rāqaḥ* [1]

BLESS [89]
- bless, 1385, *bārak[2]* [79]
- bless, 2834, *ḥēn[1]* [2]
- bless, 887, *ʾāšar[2]* [1]
- bless abundant, 1385+1385, *bārak[2]+bārak[2]* [1]
- bless at all, 1385+1385, *bārak[2]+bārak[2]* [1]
- bless, 1385+1385, *bārak[2]+bārak[2]* [1]
- done nothing but bless, 1385+1385, *bārak[2]+bārak[2]* [1]
- richly bless, 1385+1385, *bārak[2]+bārak[2]* [1]
- surely bless, 1385+1385, *bārak[2]+bārak[2]* [1]
- bless, 5989+1388, *nātan+b[e]rākâ[1]* [1]

BLESSED [163]
- blessed, 1385, *bārak[2]* [86]
- blessed, 897, *ʾašrê* [37]
- be blessed, 1385, *bārak[2]* [23]
- call blessed, 887, *ʾāšar[2]* [4]
- blessed, 1388, *b[e]rākâ[1]* [2]
- be blessed, 887, *ʾāšar[2]* [1]
- called blessed, 887, *ʾāšar[2]* [1]
- blessed, 890, *ʾešer* [1]
- blessed again and again, 1385+1385, *bārak[2]+bārak[2]* [1]
- blessed, 1385+1385, *bārak[2]+bārak[2]* [1]
- counted blessed, 1385, *bārak[2]* [1]
- is blessed, 1385, *bārak[2]* [1]
- blessed, 1388+5989, *b[e]rākâ[1]+nātan* [1]
- blessed, 1388+995, *b[e]rākâ[1]+bôʾ* [1]
- blessed, 5989+1388, *nātan+b[e]rākâ[1]* [1]
- blessed, 6584, *ʿal[2]* [1]

BLESSES [7]
- blesses, 1385, *bārak[2]* [7]

BLESSING [54]
- blessing, 1388, *b[e]rākâ[1]* [37]
- give blessing, 1385, *bārak[2]* [6]
- blessing, 1385, *bārak[2]* [2]
- gave blessing, 1385, *bārak[2]* [2]
- invokes a blessing on himself, 1385, *bārak[2]* [1]
- invokes a blessing, 1385, *bārak[2]* [1]
- pronounce blessing, 1385, *bārak[2]* [1]
- giving blessing, 1388+1385, *b[e]rākâ[1]+bārak[2]* [1]
- blessing, 2077, *hādār* [1]
- under blessing, 4200+7156, *l[e]-[1]+pāneh* [1]
- blessing, 8934, *šālôm* [1]

BLESSINGS [20]
- blessings, 1388, *b[e]rākâ[1]* [14]
- pronounce blessings, 1385, *bārak[2]* [3]
- blessings, 897, *ʾašrê* [1]
- blessings given, 1385, *bārak[2]* [1]
- blessings, 3206, *ṭûb* [1]

BLEW [11]
- blew, 9546, *tāqaʿ* [7]
- blew trumpets, 2955, *ḥaṣṣar* [1]
- blew, 2955, *ḥaṣṣar* [1]
- blew away, 5870, *nāpaḥ* [1]
- blew, 5973, *nāšap* [1]

BLIGHT [5]
- blight, 8730, *šiddāpôn* [5]

BLIGHTED [2]
- blighted, 5782, *nākâ* [1]
- is blighted, 5782, *nākâ* [1]

BLIND [31]
- blind, 6426, *ʿiwwēr* [26]
- blind, 1153+8011, *bal[1]+rāʾâ[1]* [1]
- blind, 3983, *kālâ[1]* [1]
- blind, 5782+928+2021+6427, *nākâ+b[e]-+ha-+ʿiwwārôn* [1]
- blind, 6428, *ʿawweret* [1]
- blind yourselves, 9129, *šāʿaʿ[1]* [1]

BLINDED [1]
- totally blinded, 3908+3908, *kāhâ[1]+kāhâ[1]* [1]

BLINDFOLDS [1]
- blindfolds, 7156+4059, *pāneh+kāsâ* [1]

BLINDNESS [4]
- blindness, 6177, *sanwērîm* [3]
- blindness, 6427, *ʿiwwārôn* [1]

BLINDS [2]
- blinds, 6422, *ʿāwar[1]* [2]

BLOCK [7]
- stumbling block, 4842, *mikšôl* [4]
- block, 1005, *bûl[2]* [1]
- block the way, 2888, *ḥāsam* [1]
- block, 8455, *śûk* [1]

BLOCKED [5]
- blocked, 6258, *sātam* [2]
- blocked, 1553, *gādar* [1]
- blocked, 3159, *ḥātam* [1]
- blocked, 5379, *m[e]śukâ* [1]

BLOCKING [1]
- blocking off, 6258, *sātam* [1]

BLOCKS [5]
- blocks, 74, *ʾeben* [2]
- blocks, *AIT* [1]
- blocks of stone, 1607, *gāzît* [1]
- stumbling blocks, 4842, *mikšôl* [1]

BLOOD [313]
- blood, 1947, *dām* [282]
- blood, 6795, *ʿeṣem[1]* [6]
- flesh and blood, 1414, *bāśār* [3]
- guilt of blood, 1947, *dām* [3]
- blood, *NIH/RPE* [2]
- guilt of shedding blood, 1947, *dām* [2]
- blood, 2446, *zeraʿ* [2]
- flesh and blood, 3655+4946+2743, *yāṣāʾ+min+ḥ[a]lāṣayim* [2]
- your own flesh and blood, 3655+4946+3870, *yāṣāʾ+min+-kā* [2]
- blood, 5906, *nēṣaḥ[2]* [2]
- blood relatives, 408+1460, *ʾîš[1]+g[e]ʾullâ* [1]
- blood shed, 1947, *dām* [1]
- blood vengeance, 1947, *dām* [1]
- guilty of blood, 1947, *dām* [1]
- shedding of blood, 1947, *dām* [1]
- the blood[s], 5647, *-nû[2]* [1]
- blood relative, 8638+1414, *š[e]ʾēr+bāśār* [1]

BLOOD-STAINED [1]
- blood-stained, 1947, *dām* [1]

BLOODGUILT [2]
- bloodguilt, 1947, *dām* [2]

BLOODSHED [30]
- bloodshed, 1947, *dām* [17]
- guilty of bloodshed, 1947, *dām* [4]
- bloodshed, 995+928+1947, *bôʾ+b[e]-+dām* [2]
- bloodshed, 1947+4200+1947, *dām+l[e]-[1]+dām* [2]
- guilt of bloodshed, 1947, *dām* [2]
- bloodshed, 5384, *mišpāḥ* [1]

bloodshed, 5477+1947, *mišpāṭ+dām* [1]
bloodshed, 9161+1947, *šāpak+dām* [1]

BLOODSHOT [1]
bloodshot, 2680, *ḥaklilût* [1]

BLOODSTAINS [1]
bloodstains, 1947, *dām* [1]

BLOODTHIRSTY [6]
bloodthirsty, 1947, *dām* [6]

BLOOM [5]
in bloom, 5914, *nāṣaṣ*^{2} [2]
in bloom, 1499, *gib'ōl* [1]
in bloom, 6163, *s*^{e}*mādar* [1]
burst into bloom, 7255+7255, *pāraḥ*^{1}*+pāraḥ*^{1} [1]

BLOSSOM [7]
blossom, 7255, *pāraḥ*^{1} [4]
blossom, 7258, *peraḥ* [3]

BLOSSOMED [3]
blossomed, 6590+5890, *'ālâ+nēṣ*^{1} [1]
blossomed, 7255, *pāraḥ*^{1} [1]
blossomed, 7437+7488, *ṣûṣ*^{1}*+ṣîṣ*^{1} [1]

BLOSSOMING [1]
blossoming, 6163, *s*^{e}*mādar* [1]

BLOSSOMS [12]
blossoms, 7258, *peraḥ* [8]
henna blossoms, 4110, *kōper*^{3} [1]
blossoms, 5900, *niṣṣâ* [1]
blossoms, 5914, *nāṣaṣ*^{2} [1]
blossoms, 6163, *s*^{e}*mādar* [1]

BLOT [13]
blot out, 4681, *māḥâ*^{1} [11]
completely blot out, 4681+4681, *māḥâ*^{1}*+māḥâ*^{1} [1]
blot out, 8697, *šābat*^{1} [1]

BLOTS [1]
blots out, 4681, *māḥâ*^{1} [1]

BLOTTED [5]
be blotted out, 4681, *māḥâ*^{1} [3]
blotted out, 4681, *māḥâ*^{1} [2]

BLOW [30]
blow, 9546, *tāqa'* [10]
blow, 4487, *maggēpâ* [2]
blow, 4804, *makkâ* [2]
blow away, 5622, *nādap* [2]
blow, *AIT* [1]
blow, *NIH/RPE* [1]
blow, 2955, *ḥaṣṣar* [1]
blow away, 4374, *lāqaḥ* [1]
made blow, 5627, *nāhag*^{1} [1]
blow fiercely, 5723, *nāḥar* [1]
strikes the blow, 5782, *nākâ* [1]
struck the blow, 5782, *nākâ* [1]
blow, 5870, *nāpaḥ* [1]
blow away, 6590, *'ālâ* [1]
blow, 7031, *pûaḥ*^{1} [1]
blow away, 7046, *pûṣ*^{1} [1]
blow, 9327, *tigrâ* [1]
blow trumpets, 9546, *tāqa'* [1]

BLOWING [6]
blowing, 9546, *tāqa'* [5]
blowing in, 6590, *'ālâ* [1]

BLOWN [3]
is blown away, 5622, *nādap* [1]
blown, 6296, *'ābar*^{1} [1]
had blown, 9546, *tāqa'* [1]

BLOWS [14]
blows, *NIH/RPE* [2]
blows, 2143, *hālak* [1]
blows, 2467, *ḥabbûrâ* [1]
blows, 4303, *l*^{e}*ḥûm*^{2} [1]
blows, 4693, *m*^{e}*ḥî* [1]
blows, 4804, *makkâ* [1]
blows, 5596, *nega'* [1]
blows away, 5622, *nādap* [1]
blows, 5959, *nāšab* [1]
blows, 5973, *nāšap* [1]
blows, 6296, *'ābar*^{1} [1]
blows, 9485, *t*^{e}*nûpâ* [1]
blows, 9546, *tāqa'* [1]

BLUE [49]
blue, 9418, *t*^{e}*kēlet* [42]
blue yarn, 9418, *t*^{e}*kēlet* [3]
blue cloth, 9418, *t*^{e}*kēlet* [2]
blue material, 9418, *t*^{e}*kēlet* [2]

BLUNTED [1]
be blunted, 4908, *mālal*^{1} [1]

BLURTS [1]
blurts out, 7924, *qārā'*^{1} [1]

BLUSH [3]
blush, 4007, *kālam* [2]
blush with shame, 4007, *kālam* [1]

BLUSTERING [1]
blustering, 3888, *kabbîr* [1]

BOARD [2]
on board, 928+9348, *b*^{e}*-+tāwek* [1]
on board, 928, *b*^{e}*-* [1]

BOARDS [4]
boards, 4283, *lûaḥ* [2]
boards, 7521, *ṣēlā'*^{1} [2]

BOARS [1]
boars, 2614, *ḥ*^{a}*zîr* [1]

BOAST [22]
boast, 2146, *hālal*^{2} [11]
boast, *NIH/RPE* [2]
boast, 606, *'āmar*^{1} [1]
boast, 607, *'āmar*^{2} [1]
boast so much, 1540+7023+3870, *gādal+peh+-kā* [1]
boast, 1540, *gādal* [1]
make boast, 2146, *hālal*^{2} [1]
boast, 2147, *hālal*^{3} [1]
boast, 6995, *pā'ar*^{2} [1]
boast, 9048, *šāma'* [1]
boast, 9335, *t*^{e}*hillâ* [1]

BOASTED [5]
boasted, 9514, *tip'eret* [2]
boasted, 606, *'āmar*^{1} [1]
boasted, 1540+928+7023, *gādal+b*^{e}*-+peh* [1]
boasted, 6218, *sāpar* [1]

BOASTERS [1]
noisy boasters, 1201+8623, *bēn*^{1}*+šā'ôn*^{2} [1]

BOASTFUL [2]
boastful, 1819+1524, *dābār*^{2}*+gādôl* [1]
boastful, 10647, *rab* [1]

BOASTFULLY [2]
boastfully, 10647, *rab* [2]

BOASTING [1]
full of boasting, 607, *'āmar*^{2} [1]

BOASTS [8]
boasts, 2146, *hālal*^{2} [4]
boasts, 966, *bad*^{4} [2]
boasts, 606, *'āmar*^{1} [1]
boasts, 8143, *rāhab* [1]

BOATS [2]
boats, 641, *'*^{o}*niyyâ* [1]
boats, 3998, *k*^{e}*lî* [1]

BOAZ [26]
Boaz, 1244, *bō'az*^{1} [22]
Boaz, 1245, *bō'az*^{2} [2]
Boaz, *NIH/RPE* [1]
Boaz^{s}, 2021+408, *ha-+'îš*^{1} [1]

BODIES [42]
bodies, 7007, *peger* [7]
dead bodies, 7007, *peger* [7]
bodies, 1414, *bāśār* [5]
dead bodies, 5577, *n*^{e}*bēlâ* [5]
bodies, 1581, *g*^{e}*wiyyâ* [4]
bodies, *NIH/RPE* [2]
bodies, 6795, *'eṣem*^{1} [2]
bodies, 214, *'ûl*^{1} [1]
bodies, 1061, *beṭen*^{1} [1]
bodies, 1590, *gûpâ* [1]
the bodies^{s}, 2157, *-hem* [1]
bodies, 2728, *ḥālāl*^{1} [1]
dead bodies, 2728, *ḥālāl*^{1} [1]
naked bodies, 5067, *mā'ôr* [1]
bodies, 5516, *motnayim* [1]
bodies, 5577, *n*^{e}*bēlâ* [1]
bodies, 10151, *g*^{e}*šēm* [1]

BODILY [2]
bodily discharge, 2307, *zûb* [1]
bodily, 4946+1414, *min+bāśār* [1]

BODY [85]
body, 1414, *bāśār* [21]
body, 5577, *n*^{e}*bēlâ* [13]
body, 1581, *g*^{e}*wiyyâ* [4]
body, 5055, *mē'eh* [4]
body, 5883, *nepeš* [4]
dead body, 5883, *nepeš* [4]
body, 2728, *ḥālāl*^{1} [3]
body, 6795, *'eṣem*^{1} [3]
body, 10151, *g*^{e}*šēm* [3]
body, 132, *'ādām*^{1} [2]
body, 1061, *beṭen*^{1} [2]
body, 5516, *motnayim* [2]
body, *AIT* [1]
body, *NIH/RPE* [1]
man's body, 408, *'îš*^{1} [1]
body, 1414+6872, *bāśār+'erwâ* [1]
unformed body, 1677, *gōlem* [1]
his body^{s}, 1837, *dāgôn* [1]
his body^{s}, 2257, *-ô* [1]
body, 2743, *ḥ*^{a}*lāṣayim* [1]
body, 3338, *yād* [1]
body, 3972, *kōl* [1]
body, 4637, *mût* [1]
body, 6425, *'ôr* [1]
body, 6489, *'*^{a}*ṭîn* [1]
body, 6811, *'āqēb*^{1} [1]
offering body, 7316+906+8079, *pāśaq+'ēt*^{1}*+regel* [1]
body, 7687, *qēbâ* [1]
body, 7931, *qereb* [1]
body^{s}, 8611, *ša-* [1]
body, 8638, *še'ēr* [1]
body, 9219, *šōr* [1]

BODYGUARD [4]
bodyguard, 5463, *mišma'at* [3]
bodyguard, 9068+4200+8031, *šāmar+l*^{e}*-*$_{1}$*+rō'š*^{1} [1]

BOHAN [2]
Bohan, 992, *bōhan* [2]

BOIL [10]
boil, 8825, *š*^{e}*ḥîn* [6]
boil, 1418, *bāšal* [2]
causes to boil, 1240, *bā'â*^{2} [1]
bring to a boil, 8409+8410, *rātaḥ+retaḥ* [1]

BOILED [4]
boiled, 1418, *bāšal* [3]
boiled, 1419, *bāšēl* [1]

BOILING [3]
boiling, 5870, *nāpaḥ* [2]
boiling, *NIH/RPE* [1]

BOILS [5]
boils, 8825, *š*^{e}*ḥîn* [5]

BOKERU [2]
Bokeru, 1150, *bōk*^{e}*rû* [2]

BOKIM [2]
Bokim, 1141, *bōkîm* [2]

BOLD [5]
bold, 3283, *yāʿal*[2] [2]
bold, 1053, *bāṭaḥ*[1] [1]
puts up a bold front, 6451+928+7156, *ʿāzaz+b*[e]*-+pāneh* [1]
made bold, 8104, *rāhab* [1]

BOLDLY [2]
boldly, 928+3338+8123, *b*[e]*-+yād+rûm*[1] [2]

BOLT [1]
bolt, 5835, *nāʿal*[1] [1]

BOLTED [1]
bolted, 5835, *nāʿal*[1] [1]

BOLTS [12]
bolts, 4980, *manʿûl* [5]
bolts of lightning, 1398, *bārāq*[1] [2]
bolts, 1624, *gaḥal* [2]
lightning bolts, 1398, *bārāq*[1] [1]
bolts of gates, 4981, *minʿāl* [1]
bolts of lightning, 8404, *rešep*[1] [1]

BOND [1]
bond, 5037, *māsōret* [1]

BONDAGE [8]
hold in bondage, 6268, *ʿābad* [2]
in bondage, 6269, *ʿebed*[1] [2]
bondage, 6285, *ʿabdut* [2]
bondage, 6275+6268, *ʿ*[a]*bōdâ+ʿābad* [1]
bondage, 6275, *ʿ*[a]*bōdâ* [1]

BONDS [4]
bonds, 4593, *môsērâ*[1] [3]
put in bonds, 673, *ʾāsar* [1]

BONE [7]
bone, 6795, *ʿeṣem*[1] [6]
bone, 1752, *gerem* [1]

BONES [86]
bones, 6795, *ʿeṣem*[1] [80]
bones, *NIH/RPE* [2]
bones, 1752, *gerem* [1]
leg bones, 4157, *keraʿ* [1]
crush bones, 6793, *ʿāṣam*[1] [1]
bones, 10150, *g*[e]*ram* [1]

BOOK [106]
book, 6219, *sēper*[1] [104]
book, 4181, *k*[e]*tāb* [1]
book, 10515, *s*[e]*par* [1]

BOOKS [2]
books, 6219, *sēper*[1] [1]
books, 10515, *s*[e]*par* [1]

BOOSTING [1]
boosting, 1540, *gādal* [1]

BOOT [1]
boot, 6007, *s*[e]*ʾôn* [1]

BOOTHS [7]
booths, 6109, *sukkâ* [7]

BOOTY [2]
booty, 1023, *bizzâ* [1]
booty, 8965, *šālāl* [1]

BOR ASHAN [1]
Bor Ashan, 1016, *bôr-ʿāšān* [1]

BORDER [57]
border, 1473, *g*[e]*bûl* [36]
border, 6584, *ʿal*[2] [10]
border, 7895, *qāṣeh* [3]
border, *NIH/RPE* [1]
border, 995, *bōʾ* [1]
border, 3338, *yād* [1]
border, 3752, *y*[e]*rēkâ* [1]
border, 4578, *mûl*[3] [1]
border, 6991, *pēʾâ*[1] [1]
border, 7156, *pāneh* [1]
border, 8557, *śāpâ* [1]

BORDERED [1]
bordered, 7003, *pāgaʿ* [1]

BORDERING [4]
bordering, 448, *ʾel* [1]
bordering, 4200+6645, *l*[e]*-*[1]*+ʿummâ*[1] [1]
bordering each sides[s], 4946+2296+2256+4946+2296, *min+zeh+w*[e]*-+min+zeh* [1]
bordering, 6584, *ʿal*[2] [1]

BORDERLAND [1]
borderland, 1473, *g*[e]*bûl* [1]

BORDERS [14]
borders, 1473, *g*[e]*bûl* [10]
the borders, 1473, *g*[e]*bûl* [1]
borders, 1487, *gābal* [1]
borders, 3338, *yād* [1]
borders, 7898, *qāṣû* [1]

BORE [56]
bore, 3528, *yālad* [49]
bore, 5951, *nāśāʾ* [3]
bore, *AIT* [1]
bore the loss, 2627, *ḥāṭāʾ* [1]
bore a child, 3528, *yālad* [1]
bore young, 3528, *yālad* [1]

BORED [1]
bored, 5918, *nāqab*[1] [1]

BORN [91]
born, 3528, *yālad* [24]
were born, 3528, *yālad* [20]
was born, 3528, *yālad* [7]
is born, 3528, *yālad* [5]
be born, 3528, *yālad* [4]
born, 3533, *yillôd* [4]
born, *AIT* [3]
born, 3535, *yālîd* [3]
those born, 3535, *yālîd* [3]
born, 1201, *bēn*[1] [2]
been born, 3528, *yālad* [2]
born, *NIH/RPE* [1]
born, 275, *ʾezrāḥ* [1]
born, 1061, *beṭen*[1] [1]
slave born in household, 1201+563, *bēn*[1]*+ʾāmâ* [1]
is born, 2225, *hārâ* [1]
be born, 2655, *ḥîl*[1] [1]
child was born, 3528, *yālad* [1]
children born, 3528, *yālad* [1]
son be born, 3528, *yālad* [1]
children born, 3533, *yillôd* [1]
born, 3655+4946+8167, *yāṣāʾ+min+reḥem* [1]
born in the same home, 4580+1074, *môledet+bayit*[1] [1]
born, 4580, *môledet* [1]
one born of a forbidden marriage, 4927, *mamzēr* [1]

BORNE [19]
borne, 3528, *yālad* [13]
borne children, 3528, *yālad* [2]
borne, 1061, *beṭen*[1] [1]
borne by, 4200, *l*[e]*-*[1] [1]
borne fruit, 5951, *nāśāʾ* [1]
borne on, 6584+7156, *ʿal*[2]*+pāneh* [1]

BORROW [4]
borrow, 4278, *lāwâ*[2] [3]
borrow, 6292, *ʿābaṭ*[1] [1]

BORROWED [2]
borrowed, 5957+928, *nāšāʾ*[1]*+b*[e]*-* [1]
was borrowed, 8626, *šāʾal* [1]

BORROWER [3]
borrower, 4278, *lāwâ*[2] [2]
borrower, *NIH/RPE* [1]

BORROWS [1]
borrows, 8626, *šāʾal* [1]

BOSOM [3]
bosom, 1843, *dad* [2]
bosom, 2668, *ḥêq* [1]

BOSOMS [1]
bosoms, 1843, *dad* [1]

BOTH [230]
both and, 2256, *w*[e]*-* [76]
both, 9109, *š*[e]*nayim* [52]
both, *AIT* [22]
both, *NIH/RPE* [17]
both, 1685, *gam* [13]
both, 2256, *w*[e]*-* [12]
on both sides[s], 4946+2296+2256+4946+2296, *min+zeh+w*[e]*-+min+zeh* [6]
both, 3481, *yaḥdāw* [4]
both, 3972, *kōl* [4]
both, 4946, *min* [4]
both, 421, *ʾak* [1]
both and, 448, *ʾel* [1]
both and, 907, *ʾēt*[2] [1]
both[s], 2021+170+2256+2021+8533, *ha-+ʾāhab+w*[e]*-+ha-+śānēʾ* [1]
both[s], 2157, *-hem* [1]
both[s], 2177, *-hēn*[2] [1]
both, 2179, *hēnnâ*[2] [1]
with both, 2256, *w*[e]*-* [1]
both[s], 2257, *-ô* [1]
both outer, 2667, *ḥîṣôn* [1]
both, 3480, *yaḥad* [1]
both alike, 3869, *k*[e]*-* [1]
both and, 3869, *k*[e]*-* [1]
both of you, 3870+2256+2084, *-kā+w*[e]*-+-hû* [1]
on both sides[s], 4946+2296+2256+2296, *min+zeh+w*[e]*-+zeh* [1]
on both, 4946+2296+2256+4946+2296, *min+zeh+w*[e]*-+min+zeh* [1]
both and, 6640, *ʿim* [1]
on both sides, 7156+2256+294, *pāneh+w*[e]*-+ʾāḥôr* [1]
both sides, 9109, *š*[e]*nayim* [1]

BOTHER [1]
bother, 5595, *nāgaʿ* [1]

BOTTLED-UP [1]
bottled-up, 4202+7337, *lōʾ+pātaḥ*[1] [1]

BOTTLES [1]
bottles, 1074, *bayit*[1] [1]

BOTTOM [6]
bottom, 4752, *maṭṭâ* [3]
bottom, 4946+4200+4752, *min+l*[e]*-*[1]*+maṭṭâ* [2]
bottom, 7977, *qarqaʿ*[1] [1]

BOUGHS [10]
boughs, 1936, *dālît* [2]
boughs, 6190, *s*[e]*ʿappâ* [2]
boughs, 6187, *sāʿîp*[2] [1]
boughs, 6250, *sarʿappâ* [1]
boughs, 6291, *ʿābōt*[2] [1]
leafy boughs, 6997, *pōʾrâ* [1]
boughs, 6998, *puʾrâ* [1]
boughs, 7908, *qāṣîr*[2] [1]

BOUGHT [35]
bought, 7864, *qānâ*[1] [19]
bought, 5239, *miqnâ* [4]
bought, 5239+4084, *miqnâ+kesep* [2]
be bought, 6137, *sālâ*[2] [2]
be bought, 7864, *qānâ*[1] [2]
bought, *NIH/RPE* [1]
bought, 4126, *kārâ*[2] [1]
bought, 5238, *miqneh* [1]
be bought, 5989, *nātan* [1]
bought back, 7864, *qānâ*[1] [1]
bought, 7864+928+2021+4084, *qānâ*[1]*+b*[e]*-+ha-+kesep* [1]

BOUND [32]
bound, 673, *ʾāsar* [9]
bound, 1815, *dābaq* [2]
servant bound by contract, 8502, *śākîr* [2]
bound, 10054, *ʾ*[e]*sûr* [2]
bound, *AIT* [1]
bound under an oath, 457, *ʾālâ*[1] [1]

are bound, 673, *'āsar* [1]
were bound, 673, *'āsar* [1]
bound, 995, *bô'* [1]
been bound up, 2502, *ḥābaš* [1]
bound up, 2502, *ḥābaš* [1]
bound himself, 4277, *lāwâ1* [1]
bound, 6818, *'āqad* [1]
bound securely, 7674, *ṣārar1* [1]
bound, 7855, *qāmaṭ* [1]
closely bound up, 8003, *qāšar* [1]
is bound up, 8003, *qāšar* [1]
been bound, 8567, *śāqad* [1]
bound under a strict oath, 8678+8678, *šāba'+šāba'* [1]
bound with the oath, 8678, *šāba'* [1]
were bound, 10366, *kepat* [1]

BOUNDARIES [11]
boundaries, 1474, *gebûlâ* [6]
boundaries, 1473, *gebûl* [4]
boundaries, 2976, *ḥōq* [1]

BOUNDARY [59]
boundary, 1473, *gebûl* [44]
boundary stone, 1473, *gebûl* [4]
boundary, 6991, *pē'â1* [4]
boundary, *NIH/RPE* [1]
boundary stones, 1473, *gebûl* [1]
boundary stones, 1474, *gebûlâ* [1]
formed the boundary, 1487, *gābal* [1]
boundary lines, 2475, *ḥebel2* [1]
boundary, 2976, *ḥōq* [1]
boundary, 9417, *taklît* [1]

BOUNDING [1]
bounding, 7890, *qāpaṣ* [1]

BOUNDLESS [2]
boundless, 401+7897, *'ayin1+qēṣeh* [1]
boundless, 8146+4394, *rāḥāb1+me'ōd* [1]

BOUNDS [1]
break all bounds, 7287, *pāraṣ* [1]

BOUNTY [7]
bounty, 3206, *ṭûb* [2]
bounty, 3208, *ṭôbâ* [2]
bounty, 3202, *ṭôb2* [1]
bounty, 3338, *yād* [1]
bounty, 9294, *ta'awâ1* [1]

BOW [99]
bow, 8008, *qešet* [45]
bow down, 2556, *ḥāwâ2* [33]
bow, 995, *bô'* [2]
bow down, 4156, *kāra'* [2]
bow, 4156, *kāra'* [2]
made bow, 4156, *kāra'* [2]
bow down, 6032, *sāgad* [2]
draw the bow, 2005, *dārak* [1]
bow down to worship, 2556, *ḥāwâ2* [1]
bow, 2556, *ḥāwâ2* [1]
humbly bow, 2556, *ḥāwâ2* [1]
bow, 3857, *yeter2* [1]
bow down, 4104, *kāpap* [1]
drawn bow, 4798, *mētār* [1]
bow, 5989, *nātan* [1]
bow, 8000, *qōšeṭ* [1]
bow down, 8820, *šāḥaḥ* [1]
bow down, 9413, *tākâ* [1]

BOWED [64]
bowed down, 2556, *ḥāwâ2* [30]
bowed down, 7702, *qādad* [7]
bowed, 2556, *ḥāwâ2* [6]
bowed low, 7702, *qādad* [5]
bowed in worship, 2556, *ḥāwâ2* [2]
are bowed down, 4104, *kāpap* [2]
bowed, 7702, *qādad* [2]
bowed low, 2556, *ḥāwâ2* [1]
bowed, 3718, *yārad* [1]
bowed down in distress, 4104, *kāpap* [1]
bowed down, 4156, *kāra'* [1]
bowed down to the ground, 5877+6584+7156, *nāpal+'al2+pāneh* [1]
bowed down, 5877+6584+7156, *nāpal+'al2+pāneh* [1]
bowed, 5989, *nātan* [1]
bowed down, 6390, *'āwâ1* [1]
bowed heads, 7702, *qādad* [1]
bowed head, 8820, *šāḥaḥ* [1]

BOWELS [4]
bowels, 5055, *mē'eh* [4]

BOWING [7]
bowing down, 2556, *ḥāwâ2* [5]
bowing, 4104, *kāpap* [1]
bowing, 8820, *šāḥaḥ* [1]

BOWL [19]
sprinkling bowl, 4670, *mizrāq* [13]
bowl, 1657, *gullâ* [3]
bowl used for sprinkling, 4670, *mizrāq* [1]
bowl, 6210, *sēpel* [1]
bowl, 7504, *ṣelōḥît* [1]

BOWL-SHAPED [7]
bowl-shaped, 1657, *gullâ* [6]
bowl-shaped part, 1061, *beṭen1* [1]

BOWLFUL [3]
bowlful, 4670, *mizrāq* [1]
bowlful, 4850+6210, *melō'+sēpel* [1]
bowlful, 8955, *šālîš1* [1]

BOWLS [30]
sprinkling bowls, 4670, *mizrāq* [15]
bowls, 4094, *kepôr1* [3]
bowls, 4984, *menaqqît* [3]
bowls, 110, *'aggān* [2]
bowls of mixed wine, 4932, *mimsāk* [2]
bowls, 1483, *gābîa'* [1]
bowls, 4670, *mizrāq* [1]
sacred bowls, 4670, *mizrāq* [1]
bowls used for drink offerings, 4984, *menaqqît* [1]
bowls, 6195, *sap1* [1]

BOWMEN [1]
bowmen, 5031+8008, *mispār1+qešet* [1]

BOWS [19]
bows, 8008, *qešet* [14]
bows down, 6032, *sāgad* [2]
with bows, 2005+8008, *dārak+qešet* [1]
bows down, 2556, *ḥāwâ2* [1]
bows down, 4156, *kāra'* [1]

BOWSHOT [1]
bowshot, 3217+8008, *ṭāḥâ+qešet* [1]

BOY [67]
boy, 5853, *na'ar2* [48]
boy, 3529, *yeled* [8]
boy, 1201, *bēn1* [5]
boy, *NIH/RPE* [1]
boy, 1505, *geber1* [1]
the boys, 2257, *-ô* [1]
boy, 2351, *zākār* [1]
boy, 5853+7783, *na'ar2+qāṭān1* [1]
boy, 6624, *'elem* [1]

BOY'S [8]
boy's, 5853, *na'ar2* [4]
boy's, 3529, *yeled* [3]
the boy'ss, 2257, *-ô* [1]

BOYHOOD [1]
boyhood, 5830, *ne'ûrîm* [1]

BOYS [13]
boys, 3529, *yeled* [5]
boys, 5853, *na'ar2* [4]
boys, *AIT* [2]
boys, 2351+3251, *zākār+ṭap1* [1]
little boys, 6396, *'awîl1* [1]

BOZEZ [1]
Bozez, 1010, *bôṣēṣ* [1]

BOZKATH [2]
Bozkath, 1304, *boṣqat* [2]

BOZRAH [8]
Bozrah, 1313, *boṣrâ2* [8]

BRACE [3]
brace, 273+2743, *'āzar+ḥalāṣayim* [2]
brace yourselves, 2616+5516, *ḥāzaq+motnayim* [1]

BRACELETS [7]
bracelets, 7543, *ṣāmîd1* [5]
bracelets, 7543+6584+3338, *ṣāmîd1+'al2+yād* [1]
bracelets, 9217, *šēr1* [1]

BRACING [1]
bracing, 6164, *sāmak* [1]

BRAG [1]
brag, 7924, *qārā'1* [1]

BRAIDED [3]
braided, 1491, *gablut* [2]
braided, 4456, *migbālôt* [1]

BRAIDS [3]
braids, 4710, *maḥalāpâ* [3]

BRAMBLES [1]
brambles, 2560, *ḥôaḥ1* [1]

BRANCH [22]
branch, 7542, *ṣemaḥ* [5]
branch, 7866, *qāneh* [4]
branch, 2367, *zemôrâ* [3]
palm branch, 4093, *kippâ* [2]
branch, 5916, *nēṣer* [2]
branch, 4751, *maṭṭeh* [1]
branch of, 4946+9348, *min+tāwek* [1]
branch, 5234, *maqqēl* [1]
branch, 6733, *'ānāp* [1]
branch out, 7541, *ṣāmaḥ* [1]
choicest branch, 8605, *śerēqâ* [1]

BRANCHES [64]
branches, 7866, *qāneh* [10]
branches, 1936, *dālît* [6]
branches, 5234, *maqqēl* [6]
branches, 6733, *'ānāp* [6]
branches, 6997, *pō'râ* [5]
branches, 10561, *'anap* [4]
branches, 8585, *śārîg* [3]
branches, 4751, *maṭṭeh* [2]
branches, 5746, *neṭîšôt* [2]
branches, 7908, *qāṣîr2* [2]
branches, *NIH/RPE* [1]
branches, 580, *'āmîr* [1]
branches, 964, *bad2* [1]
branches, 1426, *bat1* [1]
branches, 4093, *kippâ* [1]
main branches, 4751+964, *maṭṭeh+bad2* [1]
spreading branches, 5746, *neṭîšôt* [1]
branches, 6151, *salsillâ* [1]
branches, 6187, *sā'îp2* [1]
branches, 6591, *'āleh* [1]
full of branches, 6734, *'ānēp* [1]
branches, 6751, *'opî* [1]
go over the branches a second time, 6994+339, *pā'ar1+'aḥar* [1]
branches off, 8031, *rō'š1* [1]
thick branches, 8449, *śôbek* [1]
branches, 8456, *śôk* [1]
branches, 8457+6770, *śôkâ+'ēṣ* [1]
branches, 8672, *šibbōlet1* [1]

BRANDING [1]
branding, 3953, *kî1* [1]

BRANDISH [3]
brandish, 6758, *'āpap* [1]
brandish, 8123, *rûm1* [1]
brandish, 8197, *rîq1* [1]

BRANDISHED [1]
brandished, 8302, *rā'al* [1]

BRANDISHES [1]
brandishes, 5742, *nāṭâ* [1]

BRANDISHING [1]
brandishing, 9530, *tāpaś* [1]

BRAVE [15]
brave warriors, 1475+2657, *gibbôr+ḥayil* [6]
brave, 1201+2657, *bēn^{1}+ḥayil* [4]
brave men, 737, *'er'ēl* [1]
brave fighting men, 1475+2657, *gibbôr+ḥayil* [1]
brave man, 1475+2657, *gibbôr+ḥayil* [1]
brave warrior, 1475+2657, *gibbôr+ḥayil* [1]
brave, 2657, *ḥayil* [1]

BRAVELY [3]
fight bravely, 2616, *ḥāzaq* [2]
bravely, 4200+1201+2657, *l^{e-1}+bēn^{1}+ḥayil* [1]

BRAVEST [2]
bravest, 579+4213, *'ammîṣ+lēb* [1]
bravest soldier, 1201+2657, *bēn^{1}+ḥayil* [1]

BRAWLER [1]
brawler, 2159, *hāmâ* [1]

BRAWLERS [1]
brawlers, 8623, *šā'ôn^{2}* [1]

BRAY [1]
bray, 5640, *nāhaq* [1]

BRAYED [1]
brayed, 5640, *nāhaq* [1]

BRAZEN [3]
brazen look, 5195, *mēṣaḥ* [1]
brazen, 6451, *'āzaz* [1]
brazen, 8951, *šalleṭet* [1]

BREACH [2]
breach, 7288, *pereṣ^{1}* [2]

BREACHES [1]
breaches in defenses, 1323, *bāqîa'* [1]

BREACHING [2]
breaching, 7080, *pāṭar* [1]
breaching of walls, 7288, *pereṣ^{1}* [1]

BREAD [188]
bread, 4312, *leḥem* [116]
unleavened bread, 5174, *maṣṣâ^{1}* [20]
bread made without yeast, 5174, *maṣṣâ^{1}* [14]
loaves of bread, 4312, *leḥem* [6]
bread without yeast, 5174, *maṣṣâ^{1}* [3]
bread, *NIH/RPE* [2]
bread, 3971+4312, *kikkār+leḥem* [2]
consecrated bread, 5121, *ma'^{a}reket* [2]
bread, 5174, *maṣṣâ^{1}* [2]
cake of bread, 6314, *'ugâ* [2]
bread, 1841, *dāgān* [1]
the bread^{s}, 2257, *-ô* [1]
offering bread, 2503, *ḥ^{a}bittîm* [1]
loaves of bread, 2705, *ḥallâ* [1]
bread made with yeast, 2809, *ḥāmēṣ^{4}* [1]
leavened bread, 2809, *ḥāmēṣ^{4}* [1]
daily bread, 2976, *ḥōq* [1]
bread, 3035, *ḥōrî^{1}* [1]
cakes of bread, 3924, *kawwān* [1]
made bread, 4221, *lābab^{2}* [1]
make special bread, 4221+4223, *lābab^{2}+l^{e}bibâ* [1]
bread, 4223, *l^{e}bibâ* [1]
daily bread, 4312+2976, *leḥem+ḥōq* [1]
bread, 5056, *mā'ôg* [1]
setting out the consecrated bread, 5121, *ma'^{a}reket* [1]
Feast of Unleavened Bread, 5174, *maṣṣâ^{1}* [1]
this bread^{s}, 5647, *-nû^{2}* [1]
bread, 6314, *'ugâ* [1]
bread, 7326, *pat* [1]

BREADTH [4]
breadth, 8145, *rōḥab* [3]
breadth of hand, 2455, *zeret* [1]

BREAK [83]
break, 8689, *šābar^{1}* [19]
break, 7296, *pārar^{1}* [8]
break down, 5997, *nātaṣ* [4]
break down, 8689, *šābar^{1}* [4]
break neck, 6904, *'ārap^{2}* [3]
break faith, 953, *bāgad* [2]
break out, 3655, *yāṣā'* [2]
break up, 5774, *nîr^{1}* [2]
break, 5998, *nātaq* [2]
break down, 7287, *pāraṣ* [2]
break out, 7287, *pāraṣ* [2]
break out, 7288, *pereṣ^{1}* [2]
break into, 995, *bô'* [1]
break forth, 1324, *bāqa'* [1]
break through, 1324, *bāqa'* [1]
break in pieces, 1751, *gāram^{2}* [1]
break out, 1819, *dābar^{2}* [1]
break to pieces, 1990, *dāqaq* [1]
break, 2238, *hāras* [1]
break down, 2238, *hāras* [1]
break, 2725, *ḥālal^{1}* [1]
break into, 3168, *ḥātar* [1]
break faith, 5086+5085, *ma'al^{1}+mā'al* [1]
break up, 5782, *nākâ* [1]
break up, 5995, *nātas* [1]
break camp, 7155, *pānâ* [1]
break of day, 7155+1332, *pānâ+bōqer^{2}* [1]
break in pieces, 7200, *pāṣaḥ^{2}* [1]
break, 7200, *pāṣaḥ^{2}* [1]
break out, 7255, *pāraḥ^{1}* [1]
break all bounds, 7287, *pāraṣ* [1]
break, 7287, *pāraṣ* [1]
break open, 7337, *pātaḥ^{1}* [1]
break out, 7756, *qûm* [1]
break off, 7786, *qāṭap* [1]
break, 8318, *rā'a'^{2}* [1]
break up the ground, 8440, *śādad* [1]
break to pieces, 8689+8689, *šābar^{1}+šābar^{1}* [1]
break to pieces, 8689, *šābar^{1}* [1]
break up, 8689, *šābar^{1}* [1]
break in pieces, 8691, *šeber^{1}* [1]
break, 8740, *šûb^{1}* [1]
break, 10671, *r^{e}'a'* [1]

BREAKERS [3]
breakers, 5403, *mišbār* [2]
breakers, 1644, *gal^{2}* [1]

BREAKING [17]
breaking, 7296, *pārar^{1}* [5]
breaking, *NIH/RPE* [3]
breaking in, 4747, *maḥteret* [2]
breaking to pieces, 8689, *šābar^{1}* [2]
breaking faith, 953, *bāgad* [1]
breaking ranks, 1298, *bāṣa'* [1]
breaking out, 7255, *pāraḥ^{1}* [1]
breaking away, 7287, *pāraṣ* [1]
breaking up, 7337, *pātaḥ^{1}* [1]

BREAKS [21]
breaks, 7031, *pûaḥ^{1}* [2]
breaks, 8689, *šābar^{1}* [2]
breaks, 1306, *bāṣar^{2}* [1]
breaks up, 1324, *bāqa'* [1]
breaks out, 1679, *gāla'* [1]
breaks out, 3655, *yāṣā'* [1]
breaks down, 5997, *nātaṣ* [1]
breaks neck, 6904, *'ārap^{2}* [1]
breaks in pieces, 7207, *pāṣaṣ* [1]
breaks out all over, 7255+7255, *pāraḥ^{1}+pāraḥ^{1}* [1]
breaks open, 7287, *pāraṣ* [1]
breaks through, 7287, *pāraṣ* [1]
breaks in the wall, 7288, *pereṣ^{1}* [1]
breaks, 7288, *pereṣ^{1}* [1]
breaks out, 7925, *qārā'^{2}* [1]
breaks down, 8689, *šābar^{1}* [1]
breaks in pieces, 8689, *šābar^{1}* [1]
breaks, 10182, *d^{e}qaq* [1]
breaks to pieces, 10671, *r^{e}'a'* [1]

BREAST [21]
breast, 2601, *ḥāzeh* [11]
breast, 8716, *šad* [4]
breast, 2668, *ḥêq* [2]
breast, 3751, *yārēk* [2]
baby at breast, 6403, *'ûl^{3}* [1]
breast, 8718, *šōd^{1}* [1]

BREASTPIECE [23]
breastpiece, 3136, *ḥōšen* [23]

BREASTPLATE [1]
breastplate, 9234, *širyôn* [1]

BREASTS [23]
breasts, 8716, *šad* [17]
breasts, 2601, *ḥāzeh* [2]
breasts, 8718, *šōd^{1}* [2]
breasts, 1843, *dad* [1]
breasts, 4222, *lēbāb* [1]

BREATH [55]
breath, 8120, *rûaḥ* [31]
breath, 5972, *n^{e}šāmâ* [11]
breath, 2039, *hebel^{1}* [5]
breath, 5883, *nepeš* [3]
breath, 678, *'ap^{2}* [1]
mere breath, 2039, *hebel^{1}* [1]
gasping for breath, 3640, *yāpaḥ* [1]
breath, 5972+8120, *n^{e}šāmâ+rûaḥ* [1]
life breath, 8120+678, *rûaḥ+'ap^{2}* [1]

BREATHE [4]
breathe last, 5870+5883, *nāpaḥ+nepeš* [1]
breathe, 5870, *nāpaḥ* [1]
can hardly breathe, 5972+4202+8636, *n^{e}šāmâ+lō'+šā'ar* [1]
breathe out, 7032, *pûaḥ^{2}* [1]

BREATHED [10]
breathed his last, 1588, *gāwa'* [4]
breathed, 5972, *n^{e}šāmâ* [4]
breathed her last, 3655+5883, *yāṣā'+nepeš* [1]
breathed, 5870, *nāpaḥ* [1]

BREATHES [2]
breathes his last, 1588, *gāwa'* [1]
breathes, 5972, *n^{e}šāmâ* [1]

BREATHING [2]
breathing out, 3641, *yāpēaḥ* [1]
breathing, 5972, *n^{e}šāmâ* [1]

BRED [1]
especially bred, 1201+2021+8247, *bēn^{1}+ha-+rammākâ* [1]

BREED [1]
breed, 6296, *'ābar^{1}* [1]

BREEDING [1]
breeding, 3501+2021+7366, *yāḥam+ha-+ṣō'n* [1]

BREEDS [1]
breeds, 5989, *nātan* [1]

BREEZE [1]
breeze, 8120, *rûaḥ* [1]

BREEZES [1]
breezes, 8120, *rûaḥ* [1]

BRIBE [15]
bribe, 8816, *šōḥad* [12]
bribe, 4111, *kōper^{4}* [2]
bribe, 5510, *mattānâ^{1}* [1]

BRIBERY [1]
bribery, 5228+8816, *miqqāḥ+šōḥad* [1]

BRIBES [11]
bribes, 8816, *šōḥad* [6]
bribes, 4111, *kōper^{4}* [1]
bribes, 5510, *mattānâ^{1}* [1]
those who love bribes, 8816, *šōḥad* [1]
bribes, 8936, *šillûm* [1]
bribes, 9556, *t^{e}rûmâ* [1]

BRIBING [1]
bribing, 8815, *šāḥad* [1]

BRICK [4]
brick, 4246, *l^{e}bēnâ* [2]
altars of brick, 4246, *l^{e}bēnâ* [1]
brick pavement, 4861, *malbēn* [1]

BRICKMAKING [1]
brickmaking, 4861, *malbēn* [1]

BRICKS [8]
bricks, 4246, *l*^{e}*bēnâ* [5]
bricks, 4236, *lāban*^{2} [1]
make bricks, 4236+4246, *lāban*^{2}*+l*^{e}*bēnâ* [1]
making bricks, 4236+4246, *lāban*^{2}*+l*^{e}*bēnâ* [1]

BRICKWORK [1]
brickwork, 4861, *malbēn* [1]

BRIDAL [1]
bridal week, 8651, *šābûaʿ* [1]

BRIDE [19]
bride, 3987, *kallâ* [15]
bride, 3994, *k*^{e}*lûlōt* [1]
price for bride, 4558, *mōhar* [1]
price for the bride, 4558, *mōhar* [1]
royal bride, 8712, *šēgal* [1]

BRIDE-PRICE [2]
must pay bride-price, 4555+4555, *māhar*^{2}*+māhar*^{2} [1]
bride-price, 4558, *mōhar* [1]

BRIDEGROOM [10]
bridegroom, 3163, *ḥātān* [10]

BRIDEGROOMS [1]
bridegrooms, 1033, *bāḥûr*^{1} [1]

BRIDLE [2]
bridle, 4101+8270, *kepel+resen*^{1} [1]
bridle, 8270+6344, *resen*^{1}*+ʿ*^{a}*dî* [1]

BRIEF [3]
brief, 4946+7940, *min+qārôb* [1]
brief, 5071, *m*^{e}*ʿaṭ* [1]
brief, 7785, *qāṭōn*^{2} [1]

BRIER [1]
brier, 2537, *ḥēdeq* [1]

BRIERS [15]
briers, 9031, *šāmîr*^{1} [8]
briers, 1402, *barqōn* [2]
briers, 2560, *ḥôaḥ*^{1} [1]
briers, 6141, *sillôn* [1]
briers, 6235, *sārāb* [1]
briers, 6252, *sirpād* [1]
briers, 7853, *qimmôś* [1]

BRIGHT [7]
bright spot, 994, *baheret* [2]
bright, 183, *ʾāhal*^{2} [1]
bright, 986, *bāhîr* [1]
bright, 1338, *bar*^{2} [1]
bright, 2303, *zōhar* [1]
bright, 5586, *nōgah*^{1} [1]

BRIGHTENED [2]
brightened, 239, *ʾôr*^{1} [2]

BRIGHTENS [2]
brightens, 239, *ʾôr*^{1} [1]
brightens, 240, *ʾôr*^{2} [1]

BRIGHTER [4]
brighter, *AIT* [1]
shining ever brighter, 2143+2256+239, *hālak+w*^{e}*-+ʾôr*^{1} [1]
brighter, 2348, *zākak* [1]
brighter, 7756, *qûm* [1]

BRIGHTLY [1]
shines brightly, 8523, *śāmaḥ* [1]

BRIGHTNESS [8]
brightness, 5586, *nōgah*^{1} [5]
brightness, 2303, *zōhar* [1]
ray of brightness, 5586, *nōgah*^{1} [1]
brightness, 5588, *n*^{e}*gōhâ* [1]

BRILLIANT [3]
brilliant light, 5586, *nōgah*^{1} [2]
brilliant, 1067, *bîn* [1]

BRIM [1]
brim over, 7287, *pāraṣ* [1]

BRING [640]
bring, 995, *bôʾ* [177]
bring back, 8740, *šûb*^{1} [39]
bring, 7928, *qārab* [36]
bring out, 3655, *yāṣāʾ* [35]
bring up, 6590, *ʿālâ* [23]
bring, 4374, *lāqaḥ* [20]
bring down, 3718, *yārad* [19]
bring, *NIH/RPE* [16]
bring in, 995, *bôʾ* [13]
bring, 5989, *nātan* [12]
bring, 5602, *nāgaš* [11]
bring back, 995, *bôʾ* [10]
bring, 6913, *ʿāśâ*^{1} [10]
bring, 6590, *ʿālâ* [9]
bring, 3655, *yāṣāʾ* [8]
bring, 2118, *hāyâ* [6]
bring, 5951, *nāśāʾ* [6]
bring charges, 8189, *rîb*^{1} [6]
bring, 2118+4200, *hāyâ+l*^{e}*-*^{1} [5]
bring, 3297, *yābal* [5]
bring, 8740, *šûb*^{1} [5]
bring forth, 3655, *yāṣāʾ* [4]
bring back, 4374, *lāqaḥ* [4]
bring down, 5989, *nātan* [4]
bring disaster, 8317, *rāʿaʿ*^{1} [4]
bring, 8492, *śîm* [4]
bring about, 995, *bôʾ* [3]
bring into, 995, *bôʾ* [3]
bring at once, 4554, *māhar*^{1} [3]
bring down, 5877, *nāpal* [3]
bring joy, 8523, *śāmaḥ* [3]
bring low, 9164, *šāpēl*^{1} [3]
bring, *AIT* [2]
bring, 910, *ʾātâ* [2]
bring down, 995, *bôʾ* [2]
bring good tidings, 1413, *bāśar* [2]
bring, 2035, *hab*^{1} [2]
bring back to life, 2649, *ḥāyâ* [2]
bring victory, 3828, *yāšaʿ* [2]
bring, 5877, *nāpal* [2]
bring across, 6296, *ʿābar*^{1} [2]
bring trouble, 6579, *ʿākar* [2]
bring distress, 7674, *ṣārar*^{1} [2]
bring, 7695, *qābaṣ* [2]
bring near, 7928, *qārab* [2]
bring an end, 8697, *šābat*^{1} [2]
bring down, 8740, *šûb*^{1} [2]
bring, 8883, *šît*^{1} [2]
bring down, 9164, *šāpēl*^{1} [2]
bring, 665, *ʾāsap* [1]
bring back, 665, *ʾāsap* [1]
bring shame, 944, *bāʾaš* [1]
bring home, 995, *bôʾ* [1]
bring out, 995, *bôʾ* [1]
bring, 995+907, *bôʾ+ʾēt*^{2} [1]
bring shame, 1017, *bôš*^{1} [1]
bring to nothing, 1182, *bālaʿ*^{3} [1]
bring down, 1298, *bāṣaʿ* [1]
bring good news, 1413, *bāśar* [1]
bring tidings, 1413, *bāśar* [1]
bring to attention, 1655+265, *gālâ+ʾōzen* [1]
bring to an end, 1698, *gāmar* [1]
bring rain, 1772, *gāšam* [1]
bring about, 2118+928, *hāyâ+b*^{e}*-* [1]
bring praise, 2146, *hālal*^{2} [1]
bring new, 2542, *ḥādaš* [1]
bring sin, 2627, *ḥāṭāʾ* [1]
bring to life, 2649, *ḥāyâ* [1]
bring low, 2725, *ḥālal*^{1} [1]
bring about destruction, 3049, *ḥāram*^{1} [1]
bring relief, 3104, *ḥāśak* [1]
bring back, 3297, *yābal* [1]
bring forth, 3528, *yālad* [1]
bring to delivery, 3528, *yālad* [1]
bring more and more, 3578, *yāsap* [1]
bring, 3578, *yāsap* [1]
bring glory, 3877, *kābēd*^{1} [1]
bring honor, 3877, *kābēd*^{1} [1]
bring, 4043, *kānas* [1]
bring down, 4156, *kāraʿ* [1]
bring to ruin, 4173, *kāšal* [1]
bring, 4178, *kāšēr* [1]
bring, 4200, *l*^{e}*-*^{1} [1]
bring, 4374+2256+3655, *lāqaḥ+w*^{e}*-+yāṣāʾ* [1]
bring down, 4572, *môṭ*^{1} [1]
bring about death, 4637, *mût* [1]
bring a reward, 5162, *māṣāʾ* [1]
bring down, 5595, *nāgaʿ* [1]
bring defeat upon, 5597, *nāgap* [1]
bring in, 5602, *nāgaš* [1]
bring near, 5602, *nāgaš* [1]
bring, 5616, *nādaḥ*^{2} [1]
hurried to bring, 5674, *nûs* [1]
relent and do not bring, 5714, *nāḥam* [1]
relent and not bring, 5714, *nāḥam* [1]
relent so that not bring, 5714, *nāḥam* [1]
bring down, 5737, *nāḥat* [1]
bring upon, 5951, *nāśāʾ* [1]
bring down to ruin, 5997, *nātaṣ* [1]
bring back, 6015, *sābab* [1]
bring over, 6015, *sābab* [1]
bring disaster, 6200, *sāpâ* [1]
bring across, 6296+6296, *ʿābar*^{1}*+ʿābar*^{1} [1]
bring to a place of shelter, 6395, *ʿûz* [1]
bring back, 6590, *ʿālâ* [1]
surely bring back, 6590+6590, *ʿālâ+ʿālâ* [1]
bring, 6623, *ʿālam* [1]
bring affliction, 6700, *ʿānâ*^{2} [1]
bring clouds, 6725+6727, *ʿānan*^{1}*+ʿānān*^{1} [1]
bring, 6813, *ʿēqeb* [1]
bring up, 6913, *ʿāśâ*^{1} [1]
bring wealth, 6947, *ʿāšar* [1]
bring honor, 6995, *pāʾar*^{2} [1]
bring forth, 7114, *pālaḥ* [1]
bring, 7188, *pāʿal* [1]
bring punishment, 7212, *pāqad* [1]
bring, 7212, *pāqad* [1]
bring to bud, 7255, *pāraḥ*^{1} [1]
bring to fruition, 7541, *ṣāmaḥ* [1]
bring back, 7695, *qābaṣ* [1]
bring together, 7695, *qābaṣ* [1]
surely bring together, 7695+7695, *qābaṣ+qābaṣ* [1]
bring, 7709, *qādam* [1]
bring, 7756, *qûm* [1]
bring out, 7924, *qārāʾ*^{1} [1]
bring here, 7928, *qārab* [1]
bring forward, 7928, *qārab* [1]
bring rest, 8089, *rāgaʿ*^{2} [1]
bring a case, 8189, *rîb*^{1} [1]
bring a charge, 8189, *rîb*^{1} [1]
bring trouble, 8317, *rāʿaʿ*^{1} [1]
bring to a boil, 8409+8410, *rātaḥ+retaḥ* [1]
bring happiness, 8523, *śāmaḥ* [1]
bring sores on, 8558, *śāpaḥ* [1]
bring to the moment of birth, 8689, *šābar*^{1} [1]
bring to an end, 8697, *šābat*^{1} [1]
bring in, 8740, *šûb*^{1} [1]
bring down, 8820, *šāḥaḥ* [1]
bring bereavement, 8897, *šākal* [1]
bring punishment, 8966, *šālēm*^{1} [1]
bring word, 9048, *šāmaʿ* [1]
bring judgment, 9149, *šāpaṭ* [1]
bring justice, 9149, *šāpaṭ* [1]
bring to judgment, 9149, *šāpaṭ* [1]
bring in, 10085, *ʾ*^{a}*tâ* [1]
bring to an end, 10508, *sûp* [1]

BRINGING [47]
bringing, 995, *bôʾ* [19]
bringing out, 3655, *yāṣāʾ* [4]
bringing down, 5989, *nātan* [3]
bringing back, 8740, *šûb*^{1} [3]
bringing in, 995, *bôʾ* [2]
bringing good news, 1413, *bāśar* [2]
bringing, 3655, *yāṣāʾ* [2]
bringing, *NIH/RPE* [1]
bringing up, 594, *ʾomnâ*^{2} [1]
bringing into, 995, *bôʾ* [1]
came bringing, 995, *bôʾ* [1]
bringing news, 1413, *bāśar* [1]
bringing forth, 3655, *yāṣāʾ* [1]
bringing, 4200, *l*^{e}*-*^{1} [1]
bringing, 5989, *nātan* [1]
bringing up, 6590, *ʿālâ* [1]

kept bringing pressure, 7210+4394,
pāṣar+m[e]ʿōd [1]
bringing near, 7928, *qārab* [1]
bringing, 7928, *qārab* [1]

BRINGS [71]
brings, *NIH/RPE* [8]
brings, 995, *bôʾ* [8]
brings, 7928, *qārab* [7]
brings a curse, 826, *ʾārar* [5]
brings out, 3655, *yāṣāʾ* [4]
brings trouble, 6579, *ʿākar* [4]
brings joy, 8523, *śāmaḥ* [4]
brings, 3655, *yāṣāʾ* [2]
brings, 4200, *l[e]-[1]* [2]
brings death, 4637, *mût* [2]
brings, 928, *b[e]-* [1]
brings shame, 1017, *bôš[1]* [1]
brings about, 1343, *bārāʾ[1]* [1]
brings good news, 1413, *bāśar* [1]
brings, 1694, *gāmal* [1]
brings, 2118, *hāyâ* [1]
brings, 2655, *ḥîl[1]* [1]
brings darkness, 3124, *ḥāšak* [1]
brings grief, 3324, *yāgâ[1]* [1]
brings praise, 3344, *yādâ[2]* [1]
brings, 3578, *yāsap* [1]
brings on, 3670, *yāṣar* [1]
brings down, 3718, *yārad* [1]
brings upon, 5162, *māṣāʾ* [1]
brings, 5162, *māṣāʾ* [1]
brings, 5602, *nāgaš* [1]
brings forth, 5649, *nûb* [1]
brings on, 5877, *nāpal* [1]
brings, 5989, *nātan* [1]
brings to ruin, 6156+4200+2021+8273,
sālap+l[e]-[1]+ha+raʿ[1] [1]
brings grief, 6618, *ʿālal[1]* [1]
brings wealth, 6947, *ʿāšar* [1]
brings down, 9164, *šāpēl[1]* [1]
brings low, 9164, *šāpēl[1]* [1]
brings forth, 9311, *t[e]bûʾâ* [1]

BRINK [1]
brink, 5071, *m[e]ʿaṭ* [1]

BRITTLE [1]
brittle, 10752, *t[e]bar* [1]

BROAD [9]
broad, 8146, *rāḥāb[1]* [2]
broad daylight, 3427+240, *yôm[1]+ʾôr[2]* [1]
in broad daylight,
4200+6524+2021+9087+2021+2296,
l[e]-[1]+ʿayin[1]+ha+šemeš+ha+zeh [1]
in broad daylight, 5584+2021+9087,
neged+ha+šemeš [1]
broad, 8143, *rāḥab* [1]
broad, 8145, *rōḥab* [1]
broad, 8146+3338, *rāḥāb[1]+yād* [1]
broad daylight, 9087, *šemeš* [1]

BROADEN [2]
broaden, 8143, *rāḥab* [2]

BROKE [56]
broke, 8689, *šābar[1]* [9]
broke down, 5997, *nātaṣ* [6]
broke, 7296, *pārar[1]* [4]
broke down, 7287, *pāraṣ* [3]
broke, 1324, *bāqaʿ* [2]
broke, 1548, *gādaʿ* [2]
broke through, 5782, *nākâ* [2]
broke camp, 5825, *nāsaʿ* [2]
broke up, 8689, *šābar[1]* [2]
broke, 995, *bôʾ* [1]
broke down, 1548, *gādaʿ* [1]
broke, 1917, *dākāʾ* [1]
broke to pieces, 1990, *dāqaq* [1]
broke up, 1990, *dāqaq* [1]
broke out, 2118, *hāyâ* [1]
broke out, 2436, *zāraḥ* [1]
broke into pieces, 4198, *kātat* [1]
broke faith, 5085, *māʿal* [1]
broke camp, 5825+4946+185,
nāsaʿ+min+ʾōhel[1] [1]
broke, 5879, *nāpaṣ[1]* [1]
fight broke out, 5897, *nāṣâ[1]* [1]
broke out, 5956, *nāśaq* [1]
broke away, 5998, *nātaq* [1]
broke away, 6073, *sûr[1]* [1]
broke out, 6641, *ʿāmad* [1]
broke, 6700, *ʿānâ[2]* [1]
broke out, 7255, *pāraḥ[1]* [1]
broke out in anger, 7287, *pāraṣ* [1]
broke out, 7287, *pāraṣ* [1]
broke off, 7786, *qāṭap* [1]
broke off, 8689, *šābar[1]* [1]
broke off, 8740+4946, *šûb[1]+min* [1]
broke to pieces, 10182, *d[e]qaq* [1]

BROKEN [111]
broken, 8689, *šābar[1]* [16]
be broken, 8689, *šābar[1]* [9]
broken, 7296, *pārar[1]* [6]
broken faith, 953, *bāgad* [4]
broken out, 7287, *pāraṣ* [4]
was broken through, 1324, *bāqaʿ* [3]
broken out, 7255, *pāraḥ[1]* [3]
broken down, 7287, *pāraṣ* [3]
is broken, 8689, *šābar[1]* [3]
broken down, 2238, *hāras* [2]
broken, 5879, *nāpaṣ[1]* [2]
broken, 5998, *nātaq* [2]
broken, 6296, *ʿābar[1]* [2]
broken, 8368, *rāṣaṣ* [2]
are broken, 8689, *šābar[1]* [2]
was broken off, 8689, *šābar[1]* [2]
broken, *NIH/RPE* [1]
broken, 6, *ʾābad* [1]
been broken through, 1324, *bāqaʿ* [1]
broken down, 1548, *gādaʿ* [1]
broken, 1548, *gādaʿ* [1]
broken, 1756, *gāras* [1]
been broken down, 2238, *hāras* [1]
broken, 2318, *zûr[1]* [1]
be broken, 2472, *ḥābal[2]* [1]
is broken, 2472, *ḥābal[2]* [1]
piece of broken pottery, 3084, *ḥereś* [1]
broken, 3146, *ḥat[2]* [1]
broken, 3169, *ḥātat* [1]
be broken, 4162, *kārat* [1]
been broken off, 4162, *kārat* [1]
are broken to pieces, 4198, *kātat* [1]
be broken to pieces, 4198, *kātat* [1]
broken, 5870, *nāpaḥ* [1]
are broken, 5996, *nātaʿ* [1]
be broken up, 5997, *nātaṣ* [1]
broken down, 5997, *nātaṣ* [1]
is broken, 5998, *nātaq* [1]
broken man, 6505, *ʿî* [1]
neck was broken, 6904, *ʿārap[2]* [1]
are broken down, 7287, *pāraṣ* [1]
broken into, 7287, *pāraṣ* [1]
broken out, 7287+7288, *pāraṣ+pereṣ[1]* [1]
broken through, 7287, *pāraṣ* [1]
broken, 7287, *pāraṣ* [1]
broken, 7288, *pereṣ[1]* [1]
broken places, 7288, *pereṣ[1]* [1]
be broken, 7296, *pārar[1]* [1]
broken, 8090, *rāgaʿ[3]* [1]
broken, 8318, *rāʿaʿ[2]* [1]
is broken up, 8318+8318, *rāʿaʿ[2]+rāʿaʿ[2]* [1]
broken in pieces, 8646, *š[e]bābîm* [1]
are broken off, 8689, *šābar[1]* [1]
be broken off, 8689, *šābar[1]* [1]
be broken up, 8689, *šābar[1]* [1]
been broken, 8689, *šābar[1]* [1]
broken off, 8689, *šābar[1]* [1]
was broken, 8689, *šābar[1]* [1]
broken, 8691, *šeber[1]* [1]
broken, 8695, *šibbārôn* [1]
broken, 9519, *tupînîm* [1]
broken to pieces, 10182, *d[e]qaq* [1]

BROKENHEARTED [4]
brokenhearted, 8689+4213, *šābar[1]+lēb* [3]
brokenhearted, 3874+4222, *kāʾâ+lēbāb* [1]

BROKENNESS [1]
brokenness, 8691, *šeber[1]* [1]

BRONZE [155]
bronze, 5733, *n[e]ḥōšet[1]* [128]
bronze, 10473, *n[e]ḥāš* [9]
bronze, 5703, *n[e]ḥûšâ* [8]
bronze shackles, 5733, *n[e]ḥōšet[1]* [5]
bronze, *NIH/RPE* [3]
cast bronze, 4607, *mûṣāq[1]* [1]
bronze, 5702, *nāḥûš* [1]

BRONZE-TIPPED [1]
bronze-tipped, 5703, *n[e]ḥûšâ* [1]

BROOCHES [1]
brooches, 2626, *ḥāḥ* [1]

BROOD [4]
brood, 1201, *bēn[1]* [1]
brood, 2446, *zeraʿ* [1]
brood, 3529, *yeled* [1]
brood, 9551, *tarbût* [1]

BROOK [7]
brook, 5707, *naḥal[1]* [5]
brook, *NIH/RPE* [1]
brook, 4782+4784, *mîkāl+mayim* [1]

BROOM [4]
broom tree, 8413, *rōtem* [3]
broom, 4748, *maṭʾ[a]ṭēʾ* [1]

BROTH [3]
broth, 5348, *mārāq* [3]

BROTHER [219]
brother, 278, *ʾāḥ[2]* [210]
brother Israelite, 278, *ʾāḥ[2]* [2]
husband's brother, 3303, *yābām* [2]
have brother, 278, *ʾāḥ[2]* [1]
brother Israelites, 278, *ʾāḥ[2]* [1]
very own brother, 278+1201+562+3870,
ʾāḥ[2]+bēn[1]+ʾēm+-kā [1]
brother, 408, *ʾîš[1]* [1]
brother Jews, 10017, *ʾaḥ* [1]

BROTHER'S [20]
brother's, 278, *ʾāḥ[2]* [17]
your brother's[s], 2257, *-ô* [1]
brother's widow, 3304, *y[e]bāmâ* [1]
brother's wife, 3304, *y[e]bāmâ* [1]

BROTHER-IN-LAW [4]
fulfill the duty of a brother-in-law, 3302, *yābam* [2]
brother-in-law, 3162, *ḥōtēn* [1]
fulfill duty as a brother-in-law, 3302, *yābam* [1]

BROTHERHOOD [2]
brotherhood, 278, *ʾāḥ[2]* [1]
brotherhood, 288, *ʾaḥ[a]wâ[1]* [1]

BROTHERS [206]
brothers, 278, *ʾāḥ[2]* [201]
brothers, *NIH/RPE* [1]
brothers, 278+562, *ʾāḥ[2]+ʾēm* [1]
brothers, 1201+1061, *bēn[1]+beṭen[1]* [1]
the brothers[s], 2157, *-hem* [1]
your brothers[s], 4392, *-ām* [1]

BROUGHT [649]
brought, 995, *bôʾ* [165]
brought out, 3655, *yāṣāʾ* [100]
brought up, 6590, *ʿālâ* [46]
brought back, 8740, *šûb[1]* [21]
brought, *NIH/RPE* [20]
brought, 4374, *lāqaḥ* [20]
brought, 7928, *qārab* [16]
brought in, 995, *bôʾ* [11]
brought, 3655, *yāṣāʾ* [8]
brought down, 3718, *yārad* [8]
brought, 5951, *nāśāʾ* [8]
brought back, 995, *bôʾ* [7]
brought, 5602, *nāgaš* [7]
brought, 6913, *ʿāśâ[1]* [7]
brought together, 665, *ʾāsap* [4]
brought, 2143, *hālak* [4]
brought, 6590, *ʿālâ* [4]
brought forward, 7928, *qārab* [4]

brought low, 9164, *šāpēl*^{1} [4]
brought, *AIT* [3]
brought into, 995, *bô'* [3]
is brought, 995, *bô'* [3]
was brought, 995, *bô'* [3]
had brought, 3655, *yāṣā'* [3]
brought, 5989, *nātan* [3]
brought trouble, 6579, *ʿākar* [3]
brought about, 6913, *ʿāśâ*^{1} [3]
brought together, 7695, *qābaṣ* [3]
brought near, 7928, *qārab* [3]
brought trouble, 8317, *rāʿaʿ*^{1} [3]
brought, 8492, *śîm* [3]
brought low, 8820, *šāḥaḥ* [3]
brought, 10085, *'ᵃtâ* [3]
brought, 10549, *ʿᵃlal* [3]
be brought, 995, *bô'* [2]
been brought into, 995, *bô'* [2]
brought to pass, 995, *bô'* [2]
were brought, 995, *bô'* [2]
brought the news, 1413, *bāśar* [2]
brought, 2118, *hāyâ* [2]
be brought out, 3655, *yāṣā'* [2]
be brought down, 3718, *yārad* [2]
brought to perfection, 4005, *kālal* [2]
be brought down, 4173, *kāšal* [2]
brought report, 5583, *nāgad* [2]
brought close, 5602, *nāgaš* [2]
brought out, 5825, *nāsaʿ* [2]
brought down, 5877, *nāpal* [2]
brought back, 5951, *nāśā'* [2]
brought forth, 7865, *qānâ*^{2} [2]
brought up, 8123, *rûm*^{1} [2]
brought, 8740, *šûb*^{1} [2]
be brought low, 8820, *šāḥaḥ* [2]
brought in, 10085, *'ᵃtâ* [2]
brought, 10308, *yᵉbal* [2]
brought ruin, 6, *'ābad* [1]
brought up, 587, *'āman*^{2} [1]
brought up, 606, *'āmar*^{1} [1]
be brought back, 665, *'āsap* [1]
been brought, 665, *'āsap* [1]
brought back, 665, *'āsap* [1]
brought, 665, *'āsap* [1]
had brought, 665, *'āsap* [1]
were brought together, 665, *'āsap* [1]
brought with, 928+3338+2118, *bᵉ-+yād+hāyâ* [1]
brought, 928+3338, *bᵉ-+yād* [1]
are brought, 995, *bô'* [1]
be brought in, 995, *bô'* [1]
been brought, 995, *bô'* [1]
brought about, 995, *bô'* [1]
brought in as wives, 995, *bô'* [1]
had brought in, 995, *bô'* [1]
had brought, 995, *bô'* [1]
was brought into, 995, *bô'* [1]
brought up, 1540, *gādal* [1]
brought forth, 1602, *gāzâ* [1]
brought, 1631, *gîaḥ*^{1} [1]
brought, 1655, *gālâ* [1]
brought up, 1694, *gāmal* [1]
brought, 1694, *gāmal* [1]
was secretly brought, 1704, *gānab* [1]
are brought down, 1890, *dāḥâ* [1]
be brought, 2200, *hāpak* [1]
brought to mind, 2349, *zākar*^{1} [1]
brought back to life, 2649, *ḥāyâ* [1]
were brought forth, 2655, *ḥîl*^{1} [1]
brought forth, 2655, *ḥîl*^{1} [1]
brought to birth, 2655, *ḥîl*^{1} [1]
be brought, 3297, *yābal* [1]
brought grief, 3324, *yāgâ*^{1} [1]
brought, 3324, *yāgâ*^{1} [1]
brought success, 3512, *yāṭab* [1]
be brought forth, 3528, *yālad* [1]
been brought out, 3655, *yāṣā'* [1]
was brought out, 3655, *yāṣā'* [1]
are brought down, 3718, *yārad* [1]
been brought down, 3718, *yārad* [1]
brought, 3718, *yārad* [1]
brought to live, 3782, *yāšab* [1]
brought about victory, 3828+9591, *yāšaʿ+tᵉšûʿâ* [1]
brought grief, 3872, *kāʿab* [1]
was brought under control, 3899, *kābaš* [1]
brought about, 3922, *kûn*^{1} [1]
brought to knees, 4156, *kāraʿ* [1]
are brought down, 4173, *kāšal* [1]
brought, 4200, *lᵉ-*^{1} [1]
be brought, 4374, *lāqaḥ* [1]
had brought, 4374, *lāqaḥ* [1]
are brought low, 4812, *mākak* [1]
brought about, 4946+2118, *min+hāyâ* [1]
been brought, 5162, *māṣā'* [1]
been brought to attention, 5583+2256+9048, *nāgad+wᵉ-+šāmaʿ* [1]
brought down, 5595, *nāgaʿ* [1]
be brought, 5602, *nāgaš* [1]
brought as freewill offerings, 5605+5607, *nādab+nᵉdābâ* [1]
brought, 5633, *nāhal* [1]
brought, 5697, *nāḥâ*^{1} [1]
brought down, 5759, *nātaš* [1]
brought, 5818, *nāsak*^{1} [1]
brought around, 6015, *sābab* [1]
brought over, 6296, *ʿābar*^{1} [1]
brought, 6296, *ʿābar*^{1} [1]
brought charges against, 6386, *ʿûd*^{1} [1]
brought along, 6590, *ʿālâ* [1]
brought back, 6590, *ʿālâ* [1]
brought down to terror, 7064, *pāḥad* [1]
brought low, 7592, *ṣāʿar* [1]
were brought, 7695, *qābaṣ* [1]
brought upon, 7925, *qārā'*^{2} [1]
brought offering, 7928, *qārab* [1]
brought to a close, 7928, *qārab* [1]
quickly brought, 8132, *rûṣ* [1]
brought misfortune, 8317, *rāʿaʿ*^{1} [1]
brought to grief, 8317, *rāʿaʿ*^{1} [1]
brought tragedy, 8317, *rāʿaʿ*^{1} [1]
destruction brought, 8317, *rāʿaʿ*^{1} [1]
had brought, 8492, *śîm* [1]
be brought back, 8740, *šûb*^{1} [1]
brought down, 8740, *šûb*^{1} [1]
were brought back, 8740, *šûb*^{1} [1]
brought forth, 8751, *šāwâ*^{2} [1]
brought, 8938, *šālaḥ* [1]
had brought, 8938+2256+4374, *šālaḥ+wᵉ-+lāqaḥ* [1]
was brought low, 8959, *šālak* [1]
brought to ruin, 9012, *šāmad* [1]
brought devastation, 9037, *šāmēm*^{1} [1]
brought joy, 9130, *šāʿaʿ*^{2} [1]
brought to trial, 9149, *šāpaṭ* [1]
was brought, 10085, *'ᵃtâ* [1]
were brought, 10085, *'ᵃtâ* [1]
was brought, 10549, *ʿᵃlal* [1]
were brought, 10549, *ʿᵃlal* [1]
brought to an end, 10719, *šᵉlim* [1]

BROW [4]
brow, 7721, *qodqōd* [2]
brow, 678, *'ap*^{2} [1]
brow, 7967, *qeren* [1]

BROWN [1]
brown, 8601, *śārōq*^{1} [1]

BROWSE [2]
browse, 8286, *rāʿâ*^{1} [2]

BROWSES [2]
browses, 8286, *rāʿâ*^{1} [2]

BRUISE [2]
bruise, 2467, *ḥabbûrâ* [2]

BRUISED [4]
bruised, 5080, *māʿak* [1]
bruised, 6700, *ʿānâ*^{2} [1]
bruised, 7205, *pāṣaʿ* [1]
bruised, 8368, *rāṣaṣ* [1]

BRUISES [2]
bruises, 7206, *peṣaʿ* [1]
bruises, 8691, *šeber*^{1} [1]

BRUSH [1]
brush, 8489, *śîaḥ*^{2} [1]

BRUSHING [1]
brushing, 5976, *nāšaq*^{2} [1]

BRUTAL [1]
brutal, 1279, *bāʿar*^{3} [1]

BRUTALLY [2]
brutally, 928+7266, *bᵉ-+perek* [1]
brutally oppressed, 8368, *rāṣaṣ* [1]

BRUTE [1]
brute beast, 989, *bᵉhēmâ* [1]

BUBASTIS [1]
Bubastis, 7083, *pî-beset* [1]

BUBBLING [2]
bubbling springs, 4432+4784, *mabbûaʿ+mayim* [1]
bubbling, 5580, *nābaʿ* [1]

BUCKET [1]
bucket, 1932, *dᵉlî* [1]

BUCKETS [2]
buckets, *AIT* [1]
buckets, 1932, *dᵉlî* [1]

BUCKLER [1]
buckler, 7558, *ṣinnâ*^{2} [1]

BUD [11]
bud, 4117, *kaptôr*^{2} [6]
bud, 7255, *pāraḥ*^{1} [2]
making bud, 3528, *yālad* [1]
bring to bud, 7255, *pāraḥ*^{1} [1]
bud, 7437, *ṣûṣ*^{1} [1]

BUDDED [5]
budded, 7255, *pāraḥ*^{1} [3]
budded, 3655+7258, *yāṣā'+peraḥ* [1]
budded, 7437, *ṣûṣ*^{1} [1]

BUDS [8]
buds, 4117, *kaptôr*^{2} [8]

BUILD [133]
build, 1215, *bānâ* [96]
build up, 1215, *bānâ* [7]
build, 6913, *ʿāśâ*^{1} [6]
build, 9161, *šāpak* [6]
build up, 6148, *sālal*^{2} [4]
build a family, 1215, *bānâ* [2]
build, 6148, *sālal*^{2} [2]
build, 7756, *qûm* [2]
build high, 1467, *gābah* [1]
build up, 1553, *gādar* [1]
build, 3922, *kûn*^{1} [1]
build, 7392, *ṣābar* [1]
build, 8069, *rābaṣ* [1]
build on high, 8123, *rûm*^{1} [1]
build up, 9161, *šāpak* [1]
build, 10111, *bᵉnâ* [1]

BUILDERS [9]
builders, 1215, *bānâ* [9]

BUILDING [40]
building, 1215, *bānâ* [24]
building, 1074, *bayit*^{1} [4]
building, 1230, *binyān* [4]
building, *NIH/RPE* [2]
building, 10111, *bᵉnâ* [2]
building, 1224, *binyâ* [1]
building, 4856, *mᵉlā'kâ* [1]
building, 6590, *ʿālâ* [1]
building, 10112, *binyān* [1]

BUILDINGS [9]
buildings, 1074, *bayit*^{1} [6]
buildings, *NIH/RPE* [1]
buildings, 4445, *mibneh* [1]
buildings to store, 5016, *miskᵉnôt* [1]

BUILDS [9]
builds, 1215, *bānâ* [6]
builds up, 1215, *bānâ* [1]
builds, 1298, *bāṣaʿ* [1]
builds high, 1467, *gābah* [1]

BUILT [179]
built, 1215, *bānâ* [114]
built, 6913, *'āśâ*[1] [22]
built up, 1215, *bānâ* [12]
built, *NIH/RPE* [6]
be built, 1215, *bānâ* [4]
built, 10111, *b^{e}nâ* [3]
been built, 1215, *bānâ* [2]
is built, 1215, *bānâ* [2]
built, 9161, *šāpak* [2]
is built, 10111, *b^{e}nâ* [2]
built up, 995, *bô'* [1]
indeed built, 1215+1215, *bānâ+bānâ* [1]
newly built, 1215, *bānâ* [1]
was built, 1215, *bānâ* [1]
built, 3922, *kûn*[1] [1]
built up, 6148, *sālal*[2] [1]
built, 6641, *'āmad* [1]
is built, 6913, *'āśâ*[1] [1]
built many, 8049, *rābâ*[1] [1]
built more, 8049, *rābâ*[1] [1]

BUKKI [5]
Bukki, 1321, *buqqî* [5]

BUKKIAH [2]
Bukkiah, 1322, *buqqiyyāhû* [2]

BUL [1]
Bul, 1004, *bûl*[1] [1]

BULGES [1]
bulges with flesh, 6913+7089, *'āśâ*[1]*+pîmâ* [1]

BULGING [1]
bulging, 1240, *bā'â*[2] [1]

BULL [98]
bull, 7228, *par* [47]
bull, 7228+1330, *par+bāqār* [27]
bull, 8802, *šôr* [16]
bull, 1330, *bāqār* [4]
bull, *NIH/RPE* [2]
bull, 1201+1330, *bēn*[1]*+bāqār* [1]
bull calves, 7228, *par* [1]

BULL'S [9]
bull's, 7228, *par* [9]

BULLS [61]
bulls, 7228, *par* [30]
bulls, 1330, *bāqār* [14]
bulls, 7228+1330, *par+bāqār* [5]
young bulls, 7228, *par* [3]
bulls, 10756, *tôr* [3]
bulls, *NIH/RPE* [2]
bulls, 52, *'abbîr* [2]
bulls, 8802, *šôr* [2]

BUNAH [1]
Bunah, 1007, *bûnâ* [1]

BUNCH [1]
bunch, 99, *'^{a}guddâ* [1]

BUNDLE [1]
bundle, 7655, *ṣ^{e}rôr*[1] [1]

BUNDLES [1]
bundles, 7395, *ṣebet* [1]

BUNNI [3]
Bunni, 1221, *bunnî* [3]

BURDEN [24]
burden, 5362, *maśśā'*[1] [8]
burden, 6024, *sōbel* [2]
burden, 6721+6701, *'inyān+'ānâ*[3] [2]
burden, *NIH/RPE* [1]
beasts of burden, 2651+2256+989, *ḥayyâ*[1]*+w^{e}+b^{e}hēmâ* [1]
burden, 3268, *ṭōraḥ* [1]
burden, 3877, *kābēd*[1] [1]
placed a heavy burden, 3877, *kābēd*[1] [1]
too heavy a burden to carry, 4202+3523+5951, *lō'+yākōl+nāśā'* [1]
burden, 5368, *maś'ēt* [1]
burden, 5748, *nēṭel* [1]
burden, 6022, *sābal* [1]
burden, 6023, *sēbel* [1]
staggering burden, 7050+2256+4842, *pûqâ+w^{e}+mikšôl* [1]
burden, 9430, *t^{e}lā'â* [1]

BURDENED [3]
burdened, 6268, *'ābad* [2]
burdened, 4206, *lā'â* [1]

BURDENS [6]
burdens, 5362, *maśśā'*[1] [2]
burdens, 4601, *mû'āqâ* [1]
burdens, 6024, *sōbel* [1]
burdens, 6662, *'āmāl*[1] [1]
bears burdens, 6673, *'āmas* [1]

BURDENSOME [1]
burdensome, 6673, *'āmas* [1]

BURIAL [11]
burial, 7700, *qeber* [5]
burial, 7690, *q^{e}bûrâ* [2]
have burial, 7690+7699, *q^{e}bûrâ+qābar* [1]
proper burial, 7690, *q^{e}bûrâ* [1]
burial place, 7700, *qeber* [1]
burial site, 7700, *qeber* [1]

BURIED [101]
buried, 7699, *qābar* [54]
was buried, 7699, *qābar* [31]
be buried, 7699, *qābar* [4]
be buried, 665+448+7700, *'āsap+'el+qeber* [2]
buried, 3243, *ṭāman* [2]
buried, 7700, *qeber* [2]
buried, 995+448+7700, *bô'+'el+qeber* [1]
buried, 995, *bô'* [1]
buried, 4059, *kāsâ* [1]
buried, 6619, *'ālal*[2] [1]
buried, 7690, *q^{e}bûrâ* [1]
is buried, 7699, *qābar* [1]

BURIES [2]
buries, 3243, *ṭāman* [2]

BURN [131]
burn, 7787, *qāṭar*[1] [35]
burn incense, 7787, *qāṭar*[1] [18]
burn, 8596, *śārap* [13]
burn, 1277, *bā'ar*[1] [11]
burn down, 8596+928+2021+836, *śārap+b^{e}+ha+'ēš*[1] [8]
burn, 3013, *ḥārâ*[1] [6]
burn, 4805, *mikwâ* [4]
burn, *NIH/RPE* [3]
burn up, 1277, *bā'ar*[1] [3]
burn sacrifices, 7787, *qāṭar*[1] [3]
burn, 8596+928+2021+836, *śārap+b^{e}+ha+'ēš*[1] [3]
burn, 3678, *yāqad* [2]
burn, 3918, *k^{e}wiyyâ* [2]
burn up, 8596+928+2021+836, *śārap+b^{e}+ha+'ēš*[1] [2]
burn up, 8596, *śārap* [2]
burn up, 430, *'ākal* [1]
burn down, 928+2021+836+8596, *b^{e}+ha+'ēš*[1]*+śārap* [1]
burn up, 928+2021+836+8596, *b^{e}+ha+'ēš*[1]*+śārap* [1]
burn, 928+2021+836+8596, *b^{e}+ha+'ēš*[1]*+śārap* [1]
burn with lust, 2801, *ḥāmam* [1]
burn, 3081, *ḥārar*[1] [1]
burn, 3675, *yāṣat* [1]
burn, 4805+836, *mikwâ+'ēš*[1] [1]
burn up, 5956, *nāśaq* [1]
burn, 6251, *sārap* [1]
burn, 6939, *'āšan* [1]
burn offerings, 7787, *qāṭar*[1] [1]
burn as sacrifices, 8596, *śārap* [1]
burn down, 8596, *śārap* [1]
burn to death, 8596+928+2021+836, *śārap+b^{e}+ha+'ēš*[1] [1]
burn away, 9462, *tāmam* [1]

BURNED [138]
burned, 8596, *śārap* [27]
burned, 3013, *ḥārâ*[1] [18]
burned incense, 7787, *qāṭar*[1] [14]
burned, 7787, *qāṭar*[1] [12]
burned, 8596+928+2021+836, *śārap+b^{e}+ha+'ēš*[1] [8]
burned, 1277, *bā'ar*[1] [5]
be burned up, 928+2021+836+8596, *b^{e}+ha+'ēš*[1]*+śārap* [4]
burned sacrifices, 7787, *qāṭar*[1] [4]
burned up, 8596+928+2021+836, *śārap+b^{e}+ha+'ēš*[1] [4]
burned down, 8596+928+2021+836, *śārap+b^{e}+ha+'ēš*[1] [3]
burned, *NIH/RPE* [2]
burned up, 1277, *bā'ar*[1] [2]
burned, 3013+4394, *ḥārâ*[1]*+m^{e}'ōd* [2]
been burned, 3675, *yāṣat* [2]
be burned, 8596, *śārap* [2]
been burned up, 8596, *śārap* [2]
burned, 8599, *ś^{e}rēpâ* [2]
burned up, 430, *'ākal* [1]
burned, 430, *'ākal* [1]
are burned up, 928+2021+836+8596+8596, *b^{e}+ha+'ēš*[1]*+śārap+śārap* [1]
be burned, 928+2021+836+8596, *b^{e}+ha+'ēš*[1]*+śārap* [1]
burned to cook, 1418, *bāšal* [1]
burned up, 3081, *ḥārar*[1] [1]
are burned, 3675, *yāṣat* [1]
be burned, 3917, *kāwâ* [1]
burned, 4259, *lehābâ* [1]
burned up, 4265, *lāhaṭ*[1] [1]
burned, 5386, *miśrāpôt* [1]
be burned, 7787, *qāṭar*[1] [1]
burned up, 7787+7787, *qāṭar*[1]*+qāṭar*[1] [1]
burned, 7828, *qālâ*[1] [1]
be burned down, 8596+928+2021+836, *śārap+b^{e}+ha+'ēš*[1] [1]
being burned, 8596, *śārap* [1]
burned as sacrifices, 8596, *śārap* [1]
burned down, 8596+2021+836, *śārap+ha+'ēš*[1] [1]
burned to death, 8596+928+2021+836, *śārap+b^{e}+ha+'ēš*[1] [1]
burned to death, 8596, *śārap* [1]
burned up, 8596, *śārap* [1]
is burned, 8596, *śārap* [1]
burned, 8938+928+2021+836, *šālaḥ+b^{e}+ha+'ēš*[1] [1]
burned away, 9462, *tāmam* [1]
burned, 9462, *tāmam* [1]

BURNED-OUT [1]
burned-out, 8599, *ś^{e}rēpâ* [1]

BURNING [62]
burning incense, 7787, *qāṭar*[1] [11]
burning, 836, *'ēš*[1] [6]
burning, 1277, *bā'ar*[1] [5]
burning coals, 1624, *gaḥal* [5]
burning sulfur, 1730, *goprît* [4]
be kept burning, 3678, *yāqad* [3]
burning, 6584+2021+836, *'al*[2]*+ha+'ēš*[1] [3]
burning, *NIH/RPE* [2]
burning stick, 202, *'ûd* [2]
burning, 2779, *ḥēmâ* [2]
burning, 3019, *ḥārôn* [2]
burning, 8599, *ś^{e}rēpâ* [2]
keep burning, 239, *'ôr*[1] [1]
burning coal, 1625, *gaḥelet* [1]
burning, 3013, *ḥārâ*[1] [1]
burning anger, 3019, *ḥārôn* [1]
burning, 3034, *ḥ^{o}rî* [1]
burning, 3678, *yāqad* [1]
burning, 4611, *môqēd* [1]
burning, 5230, *miqṭār* [1]
burning, 5585, *nāgah* [1]
burning, 6590, *'ālâ* [1]
kept burning, 6590, *'ālâ* [1]
burning, 7787, *qāṭar*[1] [1]
burning waste, 8599, *ś^{e}rēpâ* [1]
burning sand, 9220, *šārāb* [1]
burning heat, 9429, *tal'ubôt* [1]

BURNISHED [3]
- burnished, 7838, *qālāl* [2]
- burnished, 5307, *māraṭ* [1]

BURNS [20]
- burns, 430, *ʾākal* [4]
- burns, 3013, *ḥārâ*[1] [4]
- burns, 8596, *śārap* [4]
- burns, 1277, *bāʿar*[1] [2]
- burns memorial, 2349, *zākar*[1] [1]
- burns, 3081, *ḥarar*[1] [1]
- burns, 3675, *yāṣat* [1]
- burns, 3678, *yāqad* [1]
- burns incense, 7787, *qāṭar*[1] [1]
- burns, 8404, *rešep*[1] [1]

BURNT [272]
- burnt offering, 6592, *ʿōlâ*[1] [159]
- burnt offerings, 6592, *ʿōlâ*[1] [108]
- whole burnt offerings, 4003, *kālîl* [1]
- whole burnt offering, 4003, *kālîl* [1]
- burnt offerings, 6590, *ʿālâ* [1]
- burnt, 6592, *ʿōlâ*[1] [1]
- burnt offerings, 10545, *ʿ[a]lāwâ* [1]

BURST [17]
- burst, 7200, *pāsaḥ*[2] [6]
- burst forth, 1324, *bāqaʿ* [2]
- burst out, 3655, *yāṣāʾ* [2]
- burst, 1324, *bāqaʿ* [1]
- ready to burst, 1324, *bāqaʿ* [1]
- burst, 1631, *gîaḥ*[1] [1]
- burst forth, 3655, *yāṣāʾ* [1]
- burst into bloom, 7255+7255, *pāraḥ*[1]*+pāraḥ*[1] [1]
- burst forth, 7287, *pāraṣ* [1]
- burst out, 7590, *ṣāʿaq* [1]

BURSTS [1]
- again and again bursts, 7287+7288+7288, *pāraṣ+pereṣ*[1]*+pereṣ*[1] [1]

BURY [34]
- bury, 7699, *qābar* [30]
- bury, 3243, *ṭāman* [2]
- bury, 5989, *nātan* [1]
- be sure to bury, 7699+7699, *qābar+qābar* [1]

BURYING [7]
- burying, 7699, *qābar* [7]

BUSH [7]
- bush, 6174, *s[e]neh* [5]
- bush, 6899, *ʿarʿār* [2]

BUSHES [2]
- bushes, 8489, *śîaḥ*[2] [2]

BUSINESS [9]
- did business with, 6086, *sāḥar* [4]
- business, 4856, *m[e]lāʾkâ* [2]
- business, 1821, *dābār* [1]
- go about business, 3655+2256+995, *yāṣāʾ+w[e]+bôʾ* [1]
- business, 6721, *ʿinyān* [1]

BUSTLES [1]
- bustles about, 2159, *hāmâ* [1]

BUSY [4]
- busy, 6913, *ʿāśâ*[1] [2]
- busy, 8132, *rûṣ* [1]
- busy, 8485, *śîg* [1]

BUT [2560]
- but, 2256, *w[e]-* [1877]
- but, *NIH/RPE* [270]
- but, 3954, *kî*[2] [108]
- but, 3954+561, *kî*[2]*+ʾim* [39]
- but, 421, *ʾak* [31]
- but when, 2256, *w[e]-* [25]
- but, 8370, *raq*[2] [22]
- but, 10221, *w[e]-* [19]
- but as for, 2256, *w[e]-* [12]
- but also, 2256, *w[e]-* [10]
- but, 219, *ʾûlām*[1] [9]
- but, 2176, *hēn*[1] [7]
- but if, 561, *ʾim* [6]
- but, 1685, *gam* [6]
- but now, 2256, *w[e]-* [6]
- but then, 2256, *w[e]-* [6]
- but, 2314, *zûlâ* [6]
- but only, 421, *ʾak* [5]
- but, 2180, *hinnēh* [5]
- but, 4200+4027, *l[e]-*[1]*+kēn*[2] [5]
- nothing but, 421, *ʾak* [4]
- but, 434, *ʾākēn*[1] [4]
- but, 66, *ʾ[a]bāl* [3]
- but, 6330, *ʿad*[2] [3]
- but, 10124, *b[e]ram* [3]
- but, *AIT* [2]
- but, 561+4202, *ʾim+lōʾ* [2]
- but, 700+3954, *ʾepes+kî*[2] [2]
- but, 1065, *bî* [2]
- but also, 1685, *gam* [2]
- but even, 2256, *w[e]-* [2]
- but, 2256+1685, *w[e]+gam* [2]
- but, 3869, *k[e]-* [2]
- but only, 3954+561, *kî*[2]*+ʾim* [2]
- but only, 3954, *kî*[2] [2]
- nothing but, 4316, *lahaṣ* [2]
- nothing but, 4946, *min* [2]
- but, 6964, *ʿattâ* [2]
- but, 10168, *dî* [2]
- but, 10386, *lāhēn*[2] [2]
- yes but, 66, *ʾ[a]bāl* [1]
- but perhaps, 218, *ʾûlay*[2] [1]
- but, 218, *ʾûlay*[2] [1]
- but if, 219, *ʾûlām*[1] [1]
- but how, 377, *ʾêkâ* [1]
- but also, 421, *ʾak* [1]
- but too, 421, *ʾak* [1]
- but, 421+3954, *ʾak+kî*[2] [1]
- but, 561, *ʾim* [1]
- but also, 677, *ʾap*[1] [1]
- but even, 677, *ʾap*[1] [1]
- but now, 677, *ʾap*[1] [1]
- but, 700, *ʾepes* [1]
- but, 889, *ʾ[a]šer* [1]
- but, 1194, *biltî* [1]
- done nothing but bless, 1385+1385, *bārak*[2]*+bārak*[2] [1]
- but even, 1685, *gam* [1]
- but if, 2176, *hēn*[1] [1]
- but while, 2256, *w[e]-* [1]
- but, 2256+8370, *w[e]+raq*[2] [1]
- but even, 2256+1685, *w[e]+gam* [1]
- but too, 2256, *w[e]-* [1]
- but, 2256+3463, *w[e]+yôtēr* [1]
- but since, 3610, *yaʿan*[1] [1]
- nothing but, 3869, *k[e]-* [1]
- if anything but, 3954, *kî*[2] [1]
- nothing but, 3972, *kōl* [1]
- but, 4017, *k[e]mô* [1]
- but why, 4200+4537, *l[e]-*[1]*+mâ* [1]
- but, 4200, *l[e]-*[1] [1]
- but, 4202, *lōʾ* [1]
- but, 4295, *lûlēʾ* [1]
- but, 5528, *nāʾ*[1] [1]
- but also, 6388, *ʿôd* [1]
- nothing but skin, 6425+2256+1414, *ʿôr+w[e]+bāśār* [1]
- but also, 8370, *raq*[2] [1]
- but only, 8370, *raq*[2] [1]
- nothing but, 8370, *raq*[2] [1]
- nothing but, 9417, *taklît* [1]

BUTCHERED [3]
- butchered, 2284, *zābaḥ* [1]
- butchered, 3186, *ṭibḥâ* [1]
- butchered, 8821, *šāḥaṭ*[1] [1]

BUTT [1]
- butt, 339, *ʾaḥar* [1]

BUTTER [2]
- butter, 2772, *ḥemʾâ* [1]
- butter, 4717, *maḥmāʾōt* [1]

BUTTING [1]
- butting, 5590, *nāgaḥ* [1]

BUTTOCKS [3]
- buttocks, 9268, *šēt*[1] [2]
- buttocks, 5156, *mipśāʿâ* [1]

BUY [38]
- buy, 7864, *qānâ*[1] [20]
- buy, 8690, *šābar*[2] [11]
- buy grain, 8690, *šābar*[2] [2]
- buy, 928+4084, *b[e]+kesep* [1]
- buy, 4374, *lāqaḥ* [1]
- buy, 5989, *nātan* [1]
- buy back, 7009, *pādâ* [1]
- buy, 10632, *q[e]nâ* [1]

BUYER [6]
- buyer, 7864, *qānâ*[1] [6]

BUYERS [1]
- buyers, 7864, *qānâ*[1] [1]

BUYING [2]
- buying, 7864, *qānâ*[1] [1]
- buying, 8690, *šābar*[2] [1]

BUYS [2]
- buys, 4374, *lāqaḥ* [1]
- buys, 7864+7871, *qānâ*[1]*+qinyān* [1]

BUZ [3]
- Buz, 998, *bûz*[3] [3]

BUZI [1]
- Buzi, 1001, *bûzî*[2] [1]

BUZITE [2]
- Buzite, 1000, *bûzî*[1] [2]

BY [1618]*
- by, 928, *b[e]-* [501]
- by, *AIT* [314]
- by, 4200, *l[e]-*[1] [209]
- by, 6584, *ʿal*[2] [92]
- by, *NIH/RPE* [77]
- by, 4946, *min* [50]
- by, 4200+7156, *l[e]-*[1]*+pāneh* [21]
- by, 928+3338, *b[e]-+yād* [18]
- by, 448, *ʾel* [12]
- by, 3869, *k[e]-* [8]
- by, 4946+7156, *min+pāneh* [7]
- by, 6330, *ʿad*[2] [7]
- by, 3954, *kî*[2] [6]
- by, 10089, *b[e]-* [6]
- by, 907, *ʾēt*[2] [4]
- by, 2006, *derek* [3]
- by, 4200+7023, *l[e]-*[1]*+peh* [3]
- by, 6640, *ʿim* [3]
- by, 725, *ʾēṣel*[1] [2]
- by, 928+6524, *b[e]-+ʿayin*[1] [2]
- by, 4946+6640, *min+ʿim* [2]
- by, 4974, *minnî*[2] [2]
- by, 5584, *neged* [2]
- by, 10378, *l[e]-* [1]
- by, 10427+10621, *min+q[o]dām* [1]
- by, 10427, *min* [1]

BYPATHS [1]
- bypaths, 5986, *n[e]tîbâ* [1]

BYWORD [9]
- byword, 5442, *māšāl*[1] [6]
- byword, 4863, *millâ* [1]
- byword, 5439, *māšal*[1] [1]
- byword, 9005, *šēm*[1] [1]

CAB [1]
- cab, 7685, *qab* [1]

CABBON [1]
- Cabbon, 3887, *kabbôn* [1]

CABUL [2]
- Cabul, 3886, *kābûl* [2]

CAGE [1]
- cage, 6050, *sûgar* [1]

CAGES [1]
- cages, 3990, *k[e]lûb*[1] [1]

came forward, 3655, *yāṣāʾ* [3]
came upon, 4252, *lābaš* [3]
came upon, 5162, *māṣāʾ* [3]
came, 5877, *nāpal* [3]
came along, 6296, *ʿābar*[1] [3]
came together, 7735, *qāhal* [3]
came near, 7928, *qārab* [3]
came, 10549, *ʿ[a]lal* [3]
came home, 995, *bôʾ* [2]
came to pass, 995, *bôʾ* [2]
came to life, 2649, *ḥāyâ* [2]
came, 5162, *māṣāʾ* [2]
came up, 5602, *nāgaš* [2]
came to rest, 5663, *nûaḥ*[1] [2]
came by, 6296, *ʿābar*[1] [2]
came to a halt, 6641, *ʿāmad* [2]
came together, 7695, *qābaṣ* [2]
came, 7756, *qûm* [2]
came toward, 7925, *qārāʾ*[2] [2]
came forward, 7928, *qārab* [2]
came, 10085, *ʾ[a]tā* [2]
came, 606, *ʾāmar*[1] [1]
came together, 665, *ʾāsap* [1]
came, 910, *ʾātā* [1]
came along, 995, *bôʾ* [1]
came bringing, 995, *bôʾ* [1]
came up, 995, *bôʾ* [1]
came with, 995, *bôʾ* [1]
rash words came, 1051, *bāṭāʾ* [1]
message came, 1819, *dābar*[2] [1]
came into being, 2118, *hāyâ* [1]
came on, 2118, *hāyâ* [1]
came to be, 2118, *hāyâ* [1]
came to, 2118, *hāyâ* [1]
came, 2118+2118, *hāyâ+hāyâ* [1]
came back, 2143+2256+995, *hālak+w[e]-+bôʾ* [1]
came tumbling, 2200, *hāpak* [1]
came out, 3655+3655, *yāṣāʾ+yāṣāʾ* [1]
out came, 3655, *yāṣāʾ* [1]
came down, 3718+3718, *yārad+yārad* [1]
came out, 3718, *yārad* [1]
came, 3718, *yārad* [1]
came to rescue, 3828, *yāšaʿ* [1]
came to an end, 3983, *kālâ*[1] [1]
came from, 4604, *môṣāʾ*[1] [1]
came, 4848, *mālēʾ*[1] [1]
came to power, 4887, *mālak*[1] [1]
came to rest, 4955, *mānôaḥ*[1] [1]
came across, 5162, *māṣāʾ* [1]
word came, 5583, *nāgad* [1]
report came back, 5583, *nāgad* [1]
came forward, 5602, *nāgaš* [1]
came near, 5602, *nāgaš* [1]
came over, 5602, *nāgaš* [1]
down came, 5877, *nāpal* [1]
came, 5989, *nātan* [1]
came to the other side, 6296, *ʿābar*[1] [1]
came to rescue, 6468, *ʿāzar* [1]
came, 7212, *pāqad* [1]
came forcefully, 7502, *ṣālaḥ*[1] [1]
came together, 7695+3481, *qābaṣ+yaḥdāw* [1]
came as a group, 7735, *qāhal* [1]
came out, 7756, *qûm* [1]
came to power, 7756, *qûm* [1]
out came to meet, 7925, *qārāʾ*[2] [1]
came together, 7928, *qārab* [1]
came, 7929, *qārēb* [1]
came by in pursuit, 8103, *rādap* [1]
came riding, 8206, *rākab* [1]
trouble came, 8317, *rāʿaʿ*[1] [1]
came again, 8740, *šûb*[1] [1]
came to rest, 8905, *šākan* [1]
word came, 9048, *šāmaʿ* [1]
came to a standstill, 10098, *b[e]ṭal* [1]
came, 10413, *m[e]tāʾ* [1]
came, 10484, *n[e]pal* [1]
came out, 10485, *n[e]paq* [1]
came in, 10549, *ʿ[a]lal* [1]
came forward, 10638, *q[e]rēb* [1]
came near, 10638, *q[e]rēb* [1]

CAMEL [3]
camel, 1695, *gāmāl* [3]

CAMEL'S [1]
camel's, 1695, *gāmāl* [1]

CAMEL-LOADS [1]
camel-loads, 5362+1695, *maśśāʾ*[1]*+gāmāl* [1]

CAMELS [50]
camels, 1695, *gāmāl* [48]
young camels, 1145, *bēker* [1]
camels, 4140, *kirkārâ* [1]

CAMP [177]
camp, 4722, *maḥ[a]neh* [144]
camp, 2837, *ḥānâ*[1] [11]
set up camp, 2837, *ḥānâ*[1] [4]
camp, 5046, *maʿgāl*[1] [3]
made camp, 2837, *ḥānâ*[1] [2]
pitched camp, 2837, *ḥānâ*[1] [2]
broke camp, 5825, *nāsaʿ* [2]
remain in camp, 2837, *ḥānâ*[1] [1]
remained in camp, 2837, *ḥānâ*[1] [1]
camp, 4328, *lîn* [1]
camp overnight, 4869, *mālôn* [1]
camp, 4869, *mālôn* [1]
broke camp, 5825+4946+185, *nāsaʿ+min+ʾōhel*[1] [1]
break camp, 7155, *pānâ* [1]
camp, 8905, *šākan* [1]
set up camp, 9381, *taḥ[a]nâ* [1]

CAMPAIGN [3]
campaign, 6275, *ʿ[a]bōdâ* [2]
campaign, 7193, *paʿam* [1]

CAMPAIGNS [4]
led in campaigns, 3655+2256+995+4200+7156, *yāṣāʾ+w[e]-+bôʾ+l[e]-*[1]*+pāneh* [2]
led on military campaigns, 3655+2256+995, *yāṣāʾ+w[e]-+bôʾ* [2]

CAMPED [79]
camped, 2837, *ḥānâ*[1] [77]
camped, 4328, *lîn* [1]
camped, 9546, *tāqaʿ* [1]

CAMPFIRES [2]
campfires, 5478, *mišp[e]tayim* [1]
campfires, 9190, *š[e]pattayim*[1] [1]

CAMPING [1]
camping, 2837, *ḥānâ*[1] [1]

CAMPS [13]
camps, 4722, *maḥ[a]neh* [8]
camps, 3227, *ṭîrâ* [3]
camps, 185, *ʾōhel*[1] [1]
camps, 5661+1074, *nāwâ*[3]*+bayit*[1] [1]

CAN [509]
can, *AIT* [445]
can, *NIH/RPE* [25]
can, 3523, *yākōl* [22]
can, 10321, *y[e]kil* [5]
can do, 3523, *yākōl* [2]
can[s], 1591, *gûr*[1] [1]
what can do, 2180, *hinnēh* [1]
can read, 3359+6219, *yādaʿ+sēper*[1] [1]
can, 3359, *yādaʿ* [1]
can certainly do, 3523+3523, *yākōl+yākōl* [1]
can, 3523+3523, *yākōl+yākōl* [1]
can no longer, 4206, *lāʾâ* [1]
can hardly breathe, 5972+4202+8636, *n[e]šāmâ+lōʾ+šāʾar* [1]
can[s], 6641, *ʿāmad* [1]
can, 10346, *k[e]hal* [1]

CAN'T [11]
can't, 4202+3523, *lōʾ+yākōl* [7]
can't, 4202, *lōʾ* [2]
can't, *NIH/RPE* [1]
can't, 7153, *pen* [1]

CANAAN [82]
Canaan, 4046, *k[e]naʿan*[1] [51]
Canaan, 824+4046, *ʾereṣ+k[e]naʿan*[1] [29]
Canaan, 4050, *k[e]naʿ[a]nî*[1] [1]
in Canaan, 4050, *k[e]naʿ[a]nî*[1] [1]

CANAANITE [18]
Canaanite, 4050, *k[e]naʿ[a]nî*[1] [13]
Canaanite, 4046, *k[e]naʿan*[1] [5]

CANAANITES [57]
Canaanites, 4050, *k[e]naʿ[a]nî*[1] [56]
the Canaanites[s], 4392, *-ām* [1]

CANAL [6]
canal, 67, *ʾubāl* [3]
canal, 5643, *nāhār* [3]

CANALS [3]
canals, 3284, *y[e]ʾōr* [2]
canals, 5643, *nāhār* [1]

CANCEL [4]
cancel, *NIH/RPE* [1]
cancel debts, 6913+9024, *ʿāśâ*[1]*+š[e]miṭṭâ* [1]
cancel debt, 9023, *šāmaṭ* [1]
cancel, 9023, *šāmaṭ* [1]

CANCELING [3]
canceling debts, 9024, *š[e]miṭṭâ* [2]
time for canceling debts, 9024, *š[e]miṭṭâ* [1]

CANE [2]
cane, 5475, *mišʿenet* [1]
cane, 7866, *qāneh* [1]

CANNEH [1]
Canneh, 4034, *kannēh* [1]

CANNOT [182]
cannot, 4202, *lōʾ* [101]
cannot, 4202+3523, *lōʾ+yākōl* [45]
cannot, 401, *ʾayin*[1] [9]
cannot, 1153, *bal*[1] [6]
cannot, 10379, *lāʾ* [4]
cannot, 440, *ʾal*[1] [2]
cannot, 1187, *balʿ[a]dê* [2]
cannot, 4946, *min* [2]
cannot, *NIH/RPE* [1]
cannot, 401+3946, *ʾayin*[1]*+kōaḥ*[1] [1]
that cannot speak, 522, *ʾillēm* [1]
those who cannot speak, 522, *ʾillēm* [1]
cannot, 561, *ʾim* [1]
cannot bear, 4202+3523, *lōʾ+yākōl* [1]
cannot read, 4202+3359+6219, *lōʾ+yādaʿ+sēper*[1] [1]
cannot stand, 4202+3523, *lōʾ+yākōl* [1]
cannot, 4206, *lāʾâ* [1]
so cannot, 4946, *min* [1]
so cannot, 7153, *pen* [1]

CANOPY [6]
canopy, 6109, *sukkâ* [2]
canopy, 1988, *dōq* [1]
canopy, 2903, *ḥuppâ*[1] [1]
canopy, 4590, *mûsāk* [1]
royal canopy, 9188, *šaprîr* [1]

CAPABLE [6]
capable, 2657, *ḥayil* [3]
capable men, 1475+2657, *gibbôr+ḥayil* [1]
very capable men, 1475+2657, *gibbôr+ḥayil* [1]
capable, 8507, *śekel* [1]

CAPES [1]
capes, 5074, *maʿ[a]ṭepet* [1]

CAPHTOR [3]
Caphtor, 4116, *kaptôr*[1] [3]

CAPHTORITES [3]
Caphtorites, 4118, *kaptōrî* [3]

CAPITAL [7]
capital, 4196, *kōteret* [5]
capital offense, 5477+4638, *mišpāṭ+māwet* [1]
capital, 7633, *ṣepet* [1]

CAPITALS [12]
capitals, 4196, *kōteret* [11]
capitals, *NIH/RPE* [1]

CAPSTONE [2]
capstone, 74+8036, *ʾeben+rōʾšâ* [1]

capstone, 8031+7157, *rō'š^{1}+pinnâ* [1]

CAPTAIN [18]

captain, 8569, *śar* [7]
captain, 8569+2822, *śar+ḥămēš* [5]
captain, *NIH/RPE* [2]
captain, 1251, *ba'al^{1}* [1]
the captain^{s}, 2257, *-ô* [1]
captain, 6233, *sār* [1]
captain, 8042+2021+2480, *rab^{2}+ha+ḥōbēl* [1]

CAPTAINS [4]

captains, 8957, *šālîš^{3}* [2]
captains, 2980, *ḥāqaq* [1]
captains, 8569+2822, *śar+ḥămēš* [1]

CAPTIVATE [1]

captivate, 4374, *lāqaḥ* [1]

CAPTIVATED [2]

captivated, 8706, *šāgâ* [2]

CAPTIVE [39]

taken captive, 8647, *šābâ* [4]
taken captive, 1655, *gālâ* [3]
took captive, 8647, *šābâ* [3]
captive, *NIH/RPE* [2]
took captive, 1655, *gālâ* [2]
are held captive, 8647, *šābâ* [2]
take captive, 8647, *šābâ* [2]
takes captive, 8647+8647, *šābâ+šābâ* [2]
captive, 408, *'îš^{1}* [1]
captive, 659, *'āsîr* [1]
captive, 660, *'assîr^{1}* [1]
is held captive, 673, *'āsar* [1]
be taken captive, 928+2021+4090+9530,
b^{e}-+ha-+kap+tāpaś [1]
taken captive, 1020, *baz* [1]
captive, 1583, *gôlâ* [1]
captive, 1655, *gālâ* [1]
led captive, 1655, *gālâ* [1]
were taken captive, 1655, *gālâ* [1]
be taken captive, 4334, *lākad* [1]
takes captive, 7695, *qābaṣ* [1]
be taken captive, 8647, *šābâ* [1]
been carried captive, 8647, *šābâ* [1]
been taken captive, 8647, *šābâ* [1]
held captive, 8647, *šābâ* [1]
takes captive, 8647, *šābâ* [1]
captive, 8665, *š^{e}biyyâ* [1]
take captive, 9530, *tāpaś* [1]

CAPTIVES [24]

captives, 8660, *š^{e}bî* [8]
captives, 659, *'āsîr* [2]
captives, 660, *'assîr^{1}* [2]
captives, 8647, *šābâ* [2]
captives, 8664, *šibyâ* [2]
captives, 673, *'āsar* [1]
captives, 1661, *gālût* [1]
communities of captives, 1661, *gālût* [1]
made captives of, 8647, *šābâ* [1]
make captives, 8647, *šābâ* [1]
take captives, 8647+8660, *šābâ+š^{e}bî* [1]
captives, 8669, *š^{e}bît* [1]
captives, 8860, *šîbâ^{2}* [1]

CAPTIVITY [30]

captivity, 8660, *š^{e}bî* [17]
captivity, 8654, *š^{e}bût* [7]
went into captivity, 1655, *gālâ* [2]
captivity, 8664, *šibyâ* [2]
captivity, 1655, *gālâ* [1]
going into captivity, 3448, *yôṣē't* [1]

CAPTORS [4]

captors, 8647, *šābâ* [4]

CAPTURE [17]

capture, 4334, *lākad* [9]
capture, 4374, *lāqaḥ* [5]
capture, 9530, *tāpaś* [3]

CAPTURED [74]

captured, 4334, *lākad* [33]
captured, 9530, *tāpaś* [8]
be captured, 4334, *lākad* [6]
captured, 4374, *lāqaḥ* [5]
captured, 8660, *š^{e}bî* [4]
been captured, 4374, *lāqaḥ* [3]
captured, 8647, *šābâ* [3]
was captured, 4334, *lākad* [2]
been captured, 673, *'āsar* [1]
captured, 2616, *ḥāzaq* [1]
is captured, 4334, *lākad* [1]
was captured, 4374, *lāqaḥ* [1]
captured, 5162, *māṣā'* [1]
is captured, 5162, *māṣā'* [1]
been captured, 8647, *šābâ* [1]
captured, 8647+8660, *šābâ+š^{e}bî* [1]
be captured, 9530, *tāpaś* [1]
surely be captured, 9530+9530, *tāpaś+tāpaś* [1]

CAPTURES [2]

captures, 4334, *lākad* [2]

CAPTURING [2]

capturing, 3769, *yāraš^{1}* [1]
capturing, 9530, *tāpaś* [1]

CARAVAN [3]

caravan, 2657, *ḥayil* [2]
caravan, 785, *'ōrḥâ* [1]

CARAVANS [3]

caravans, 785, *'ōrḥâ* [3]

CARAWAY [3]

caraway, 7902, *qeṣaḥ* [3]

CARCAS [1]

Carcas, 4139, *karkas* [1]

CARCASS [8]

carcass, 5577, *n^{e}bēlâ* [5]
carcass, *NIH/RPE* [1]
carcass, 1581, *g^{e}wiyyâ* [1]
carcass, 5147, *mappelet* [1]

CARCASSES [15]

carcasses, 5577, *n^{e}bēlâ* [13]
carcasses, 7007, *peger* [2]

CARCHEMISH [3]

Carchemish, 4138, *kark^{e}mîš* [3]

CARE [71]

care, 3338, *yād* [14]
care for, 7212, *pāqad* [6]
care, 5466, *mišmeret* [5]
take care of, 9068, *šāmar* [5]
take care of, 8286, *rā'â^{1}* [3]
care, 9068, *šāmar* [3]
care, *NIH/RPE* [2]
responsible for care, 5466, *mišmeret* [2]
under care, 907, *'ēt^{2}* [1]
without a care, 1055, *beṭaḥ^{1}* [1]
took care of, 1179, *bālas* [1]
care for young, 1842, *dāgar* [1]
care about, 2011, *dāraš* [1]
care for, 2011, *dāraš* [1]
take care of, 2118+4200+5466,
hāyâ+l^{e}-^{1}+mišmeret [1]
take care of, 2118+6125, *hāyâ+sōkēn* [1]
took care of, 2118+6125, *hāyâ+sōkēn* [1]
care, 2914, *ḥēpeṣ* [1]
care for, 3108, *ḥāšab* [1]
under care, 3338, *yād* [1]
care about, 3359, *yāda'* [1]
care for, 3359, *yāda'* [1]
what do I care about, 4200+4537+2296+4200
+3276, *l^{e}-^{1}+mâ+zeh+l^{e}-^{1}+-î* [1]
take care of, 5466, *mišmeret* [1]
took care of, 5633, *nāhal* [1]
take care of, 5757, *nāṭar^{1}* [1]
care for, 6584, *'al^{2}* [1]
take care of, 6584, *'al^{2}* [1]
in the care of, 6640, *'im* [1]
took care of, 6640, *'im* [1]
taken care of, 6913, *'āśâ^{1}* [1]
take care of, 7212, *pāqad* [1]
bestowed care on, 7212, *pāqad* [1]
took care of mixing, 8379+5351,
rāqaḥ+mirqaḥat [1]
care about, 8492+448+4213, *śîm+'el+lēb* [1]
care, 8492+448+4213, *śîm+'el+lēb* [1]
care for, 8800, *šûr^{1}* [1]
take care, 9068, *šāmar* [1]
take care of, 9250, *šārat* [1]

CARED [7]

cared, 587, *'āman^{2}* [1]
cared for, 1067, *bîn* [1]
cared for, 3254, *ṭāpaḥ^{2}* [1]
cared for, 3259, *ṭippuḥîm* [1]
cared for, 3359, *yāda'* [1]
cared for, 8286, *rā'â^{1}* [1]
cared for, 9068, *šāmar* [1]

CAREFREE [3]

carefree, 8929, *šālēw* [2]
carefree, 6611, *'allîz* [1]

CAREFUL [63]

careful, 9068, *šāmar* [46]
give careful thought, 8492+4222, *śîm+lēbāb* [5]
be careful, 9068, *šāmar* [2]
careful, *NIH/RPE* [1]
careful, 2778, *ḥāmâ* [1]
careful attention, 4213, *lēb* [1]
careful to carry out, 6913+6913, *'āśâ^{1}+'āśâ^{1}* [1]
careful, 8505, *śākal^{1}* [1]
careful, 8838, *šāḥar^{2}* [1]
careful to obey, 9048+9048, *šāma'+šāma'* [1]
careful to do, 9068, *šāmar* [1]
careful, 9068+9068, *šāmar+šāmar* [1]
careful, 10224, *z^{e}hîr* [1]

CAREFULLY [29]

carefully, 9068, *šāmar* [16]
listen carefully, 9048+9048, *šāma'+šāma'* [4]
listen carefully, 928+265+9048,
b^{e}-+'ōzen+šāma' [1]
consider carefully, 1067, *bîn* [1]
carefully investigated, 2011+2256+1335,
dāraš+w^{e}-+bāqaš [1]
consider carefully, 8011, *rā'â^{1}* [1]
listen carefully, 8011, *rā'â^{1}* [1]
look carefully, 8011+928+6524,
rā'â^{1}+b^{e}-+'ayin^{1} [1]
listen carefully, 9048+928+7754,
šāma'+b^{e}-+qôl [1]
carefully observe, 9068+9068, *šāmar+šāmar* [1]
watch carefully, 9068, *šāmar* [1]

CARELESSLY [1]

carelessly, 1051, *bāṭā'* [1]

CARES [9]

cares for, 2011, *dāraš* [2]
cares for, 3359, *yāda'* [2]
cares, 2011, *dāraš* [1]
cares, 3365, *y^{e}hāb* [1]
cares, 6721, *'inyān* [1]
cares, 7065, *paḥad^{1}* [1]
cares, 8492+6584+4213, *śîm+'al^{2}+lēb* [1]

CARESSED [3]

caressed, 6914, *'āśâ^{2}* [3]

CARESSING [1]

caressing, 7464, *ṣāḥaq* [1]

CARGO [2]

cargo, *AIT* [1]
cargo, 3998+889+928+2021+641,
k^{e}lî+'ašer+b^{e}-+ha-+'oniyyâ [1]

CARGOES [1]

cargoes, *AIT* [1]

CARITES [2]

Carites, 4133, *kārî* [2]

CARMEL [27]

Carmel, 4151, *karmel^{3}* [15]
Carmel, 4150, *karmel^{2}* [7]
of Carmel, 4153, *karm^{e}lî* [5]

CARMELITE [2]

Carmelite, 4153, *karm^{e}lî* [2]

CARMI [8]
Carmi, 4145, *karmî*[1] [8]

CARMITE [1]
Carmite, 4146, *karmî*[2] [1]

CARPENTER [1]
carpenter, 3093+6770, *ḥārāš+ʿēṣ* [1]

CARPENTERS [8]
carpenters, 3093, *ḥārāš* [4]
carpenters, 3093+6770, *ḥārāš+ʿēṣ* [3]
carpenters, 6770, *ʿēṣ* [1]

CARRIAGE [2]
carriage, 712, *ʾappiryôn* [1]
carriage, 4753, *miṭṭâ* [1]

CARRIED [138]
carried, 5951, *nāśāʾ* [26]
carried into exile, 1655, *gālâ* [11]
carried off, 4374, *lāqaḥ* [6]
carried off, 5951, *nāśāʾ* [6]
carried off, 995, *bôʾ* [4]
carried off, 1024, *bāzaz* [4]
carried out, 6913, *ʿāśâ*[1] [4]
carried off, 8647, *šābâ* [4]
carried away, 4374, *lāqaḥ* [3]
carried, 4374, *lāqaḥ* [3]
carried off, 5627, *nāhag*[1] [3]
be carried off, 5951, *nāśāʾ* [3]
carried out, 7756, *qûm* [3]
carried, 995, *bôʾ* [2]
been carried into exile, 1655, *gālâ* [2]
was carried out, 3922, *kûn*[1] [2]
carried away, 5951, *nāśāʾ* [2]
carried up, 6590, *ʿālâ* [2]
carried, 6590, *ʿālâ* [2]
carried out, 9068, *šāmar* [2]
carried, *NIH/RPE* [1]
are carried, 587, *ʾāman*[2] [1]
carried away, 995, *bôʾ* [1]
carried back, 995, *bôʾ* [1]
be carried into exile, 1655, *gālâ* [1]
being carried into exile, 1655, *gālâ* [1]
carried away, 1655, *gālâ* [1]
carried into exile, 1655+1655, *gālâ+gālâ* [1]
carried on openly, 1655, *gālâ* [1]
was forcibly carried off, 1704+1704, *gānab+gānab* [1]
carried by, 2118+6584, *hāyâ+ʿal*[2] [1]
carried on prostitution, 2388, *zānâ*[1] [1]
carried out repairs, 2616, *ḥāzaq* [1]
be carried, 3297, *yābal* [1]
been carried, 3297, *yābal* [1]
is carried, 3297, *yābal* [1]
carried still further, 3578, *yāsap* [1]
carried away, 3655, *yāṣāʾ* [1]
carried out, 3655, *yāṣāʾ* [1]
carried down, 3718, *yārad* [1]
carried, 4374+928+3338, *lāqaḥ+b*[e]*-+yād* [1]
carried about, 5362, *maśśāʾ*[1] [1]
be carried, 5951, *nāśāʾ* [1]
carried, 5951+6673, *nāśāʾ+ʿāmas* [1]
is carried off, 5951, *nāśāʾ* [1]
must be carried, 5951+5951, *nāśāʾ+nāśāʾ* [1]
images that are carried about, 5953, *n*[e]*śûʾâ* [1]
carried around, 6015, *sābab* [1]
carried, 6022, *sābal* [1]
carried over, 6296, *ʿābar*[1] [1]
carried away, 6590, *ʿālâ* [1]
be carried out, 6913, *ʿāśâ*[1] [1]
carried on, 6913, *ʿāśâ*[1] [1]
carried through, 6913, *ʿāśâ*[1] [1]
is carried out, 6913, *ʿāśâ*[1] [1]
were carried off, 7855, *qāmaṭ* [1]
carried out, 8003, *qāšar* [1]
been carried captive, 8647, *šābâ* [1]
carried away, 8647, *šābâ* [1]
faithfully carried out, 9068, *šāmar* [1]
carried, 9546, *tāqaʿ* [1]
be carried out, 10522, *ʿ*[a]*bad* [1]
being carried on, 10522, *ʿ*[a]*bad* [1]
carried out, 10522, *ʿ*[a]*bad* [1]

CARRIERS [7]
carriers, 8612, *šāʾab* [3]
carriers, 6025, *sabbāl* [2]
carriers, 5951+6025, *nāśāʾ+sabbāl* [1]
carriers, 8801, *šûr*[2] [1]

CARRIES [8]
carries, 5951, *nāśāʾ* [5]
carries off, 5951, *nāśāʾ* [1]
carries out, 7756, *qûm* [1]
carries out, 8966, *šālēm*[1] [1]

CARRION [1]
carrion birds, 6514+7606, *ʿayiṭ+ṣippôr*[1] [1]

CARRY [110]
carry, 5951, *nāśāʾ* [36]
carry out, 6913, *ʿāśâ*[1] [20]
carry, 5362, *maśśāʾ*[1] [5]
carry off, 1024, *bāzaz* [4]
carry off, 5951, *nāśāʾ* [4]
carry, *NIH/RPE* [2]
carry, 995, *bôʾ* [2]
carry, 2143, *hālak* [2]
carry away, 4374, *lāqaḥ* [2]
what to carry, 5362, *maśśāʾ*[1] [2]
carry up, 6590, *ʿālâ* [2]
carry off, 928+2021+8660+995, *b*[e]*-+ha-+š*[e]*bî+bôʾ* [1]
carry back, 995, *bôʾ* [1]
carry off, 995, *bôʾ* [1]
carry away, 1655, *gālâ* [1]
carry into exile, 1655, *gālâ* [1]
carry off, 1655, *gālâ* [1]
carry on the memory, 2349, *zākar*[1] [1]
carry out purpose, 2372, *zāmam* [1]
carry out duties, 3655+2256+995, *yāṣāʾ+w*[e]*-+bôʾ* [1]
carry out, 3655, *yāṣāʾ* [1]
carry, 3655, *yāṣāʾ* [1]
too heavy a burden to carry, 4202+3523+5951, *lōʾ+yākōl+nāśāʾ* [1]
carry about, 5951, *nāśāʾ* [1]
carry away, 5951, *nāśāʾ* [1]
carry back, 5951, *nāśāʾ* [1]
carry out, 5989, *nātan* [1]
carry, 6022, *sābal* [1]
carry away, 6073, *sûr*[1] [1]
carry over, 6296, *ʿābar*[1] [1]
careful to carry out, 6913+6913, *ʿāśâ*[1]*+ʿāśâ*[1] [1]
certainly carry out, 6913+6913, *ʿāśâ*[1]*+ʿāśâ*[1] [1]
carry off, 7117, *pālaṭ* [1]
carry on, 7756+6584, *qûm+ʿal*[2] [1]
carry on, 7756, *qûm* [1]
carry out, 7756, *qûm* [1]
carry, 8612, *šāʾab* [1]
carry on, 8713, *šāgaʿ* [1]
carry the battle, 8740+2256+1741, *šûb*[1]*+w*[e]*-+gārâ* [1]
carry, 9530, *tāpaś* [1]

CARRYING [40]
carrying, 5951, *nāśāʾ* [26]
carrying poles, 964, *bad*[2] [2]
carrying frame, 4573, *môṭ*[2] [2]
carrying, 5362, *maśśāʾ*[1] [2]
carrying out, 6913, *ʿāśâ*[1] [2]
carrying out, 9068, *šāmar* [2]
carrying, 928, *b*[e]*-* [1]
assume the responsibility for carrying out, 6641+6584, *ʿāmad+ʿal*[2] [1]
carrying on, 6913, *ʿāśâ*[1] [1]
succeeded in carrying out, 7503, *ṣālaḥ*[2] [1]

CARSHENA [1]
Carshena, 4161, *karš*[e]*nāʾ* [1]

CART [14]
cart, 6322, *ʿ*[a]*gālâ* [13]
threshing cart, 6322, *ʿ*[a]*gālâ* [1]

CARTS [9]
carts, 6322, *ʿ*[a]*gālâ* [8]
carts, 5047, *maʿgāl*[2] [1]

CARTWHEEL [1]
cartwheel, 236+6322, *ʾôpan+ʿ*[a]*gālâ* [1]

CARVED [26]
carved image, 7181, *pesel* [5]
were carved, 6913, *ʿāśâ*[1] [3]
carved, 6913, *ʿāśâ*[1] [2]
carved, 7181, *pesel* [2]
carved, 7844+5237, *qālaʿ*[2]*+miqlaʿat* [2]
carved, *NIH/RPE* [1]
carved, 2634, *ḥāṭab* [1]
carved, 5237, *miqlaʿat* [1]
carved images, 5381, *maśkît* [1]
carved, 5381, *maśkît* [1]
carved idols, 7178, *pāsîl* [1]
carved images, 7178, *pāsîl* [1]
carved, 7180, *pāsal* [1]
carved images, 7181, *pesel* [1]
carved paneling, 7334, *pittûaḥ* [1]
carved, 7338, *pātaḥ*[2] [1]
carved, 7844, *qālaʿ*[2] [1]

CARVES [1]
carves, 6913, *ʿāśâ*[1] [1]

CARVINGS [1]
carvings, 2977, *ḥāqâ* [1]

CASE [38]
case, 8190, *rîb*[2] [11]
case, 1821, *dābār* [6]
case, 5477, *mišpāṭ* [4]
case, *NIH/RPE* [2]
case, 1907, *dîn*[2] [2]
case, *AIT* [1]
case[s], 465, *ʾēlleh* [1]
argue case, 3519, *yākaḥ* [1]
present case, 3519, *yākaḥ* [1]
as in the case of, 3869, *k*[e]*-* [1]
as is the case, 3869, *k*[e]*-* [1]
the case[s], 4392, *-ām* [1]
draw up case, 6885, *ʿārak* [1]
argue the case, 8189, *rîb*[1] [1]
bring a case, 8189, *rîb*[1] [1]
plead case, 8189, *rîb*[1] [1]
plead the case, 8189, *rîb*[1] [1]
pleads case, 9149, *šāpaṭ* [1]

CASES [8]
cases, 1821, *dābār* [5]
cases, *NIH/RPE* [1]
cases, 1821+8191, *dābār+rîbâ* [1]
cases of dispute, 8190, *rîb*[2] [1]

CASIPHIA [2]
Casiphia, 4085, *kāsipyāʾ* [2]

CASLUHITES [2]
Casluhites, 4078, *kasluḥîm* [2]

CASSIA [3]
cassia, 7703, *qiddâ* [2]
cassia, 7904, *q*[e]*ṣîʿâ* [1]

CAST [84]
cast, 5877, *nāpal* [13]
cast, 3668, *yāṣaq* [10]
cast, 8959, *šālak* [8]
cast idol, 5011, *massēkâ*[1] [5]
cast, 3341, *yādad* [3]
cast metal, 4607, *mûṣāq*[1] [3]
idol cast, 5011, *massēkâ*[1] [3]
were cast, 3668, *yāṣaq* [2]
cast idols, 5011, *massēkâ*[1] [2]
cast, 5011, *massēkâ*[1] [2]
cast, *NIH/RPE* [1]
been cast down, 1548, *gādaʿ* [1]
cast aside, 1763, *gāraš*[1] [1]
cast up, 1764, *gāraš*[2] [1]
cast off, 2396, *zānaḥ*[2] [1]
is cast, 3214, *ṭûl* [1]
cast, 3721, *yārâ*[1] [1]
cast, 4489, *māgar* [1]
cast bronze, 4607, *mûṣāq*[1] [1]
cast in molds, 4607, *mûṣāq*[1] [1]
cast, 4607, *mûṣāq*[1] [1]
cast images, 5011, *massēkâ*[1] [1]

cast metal, 5011, *massēkâ*^{1} [1]
idol cast from metal, 5011, *massēkâ*^{1} [1]
idols cast, 5011, *massēkâ*^{1} [1]
be cast aside, 5610, *nādad* [1]
cast, 5663, *nûaḥ*^{1} [1]
cast out, 5759, *nāṭaš* [1]
cast down, 5877, *nāpal* [1]
cast, 5989, *nātan* [1]
cast off, 6296, *ʿābar*^{1} [1]
cast, 6414, *ʿûp*^{1} [1]
cast spells, 6726, *ʿānan*^{2} [1]
cast, 6913, *ʿāśâ*^{1} [1]
cast off restraint, 7277, *pāraʿ*^{2} [1]
cast, 7298, *pāraś* [1]
cast, 7445, *ṣûr*^{3} [1]
cast lots, 7837, *qālal* [1]
cast fruit, 8897, *šākal* [1]
cast, 8938, *šālaḥ* [1]
are cast, 8959, *šālak* [1]
cast away, 8959, *šālak* [1]
cast out, 8959, *šālak* [1]

CASTING [3]
casting, *NIH/RPE* [1]
casting, 5877, *nāpal* [1]
casting up, 6590, *ʿālâ* [1]

CASTS [7]
casts, 5818, *nāsak*^{1} [2]
casts, *NIH/RPE* [1]
casts spells, 2489+2490, *ḥābar*^{2}*+ḥeber*^{1} [1]
casts down, 5595, *nāgaʿ* [1]
casts, 5951, *nāśāʾ* [1]
casts, 9164, *šāpēl*^{1} [1]

CASUALTIES [7]
casualties, 2728, *ḥālāl*^{1} [4]
casualties, 4487, *maggēpâ* [1]
casualties, 4804, *makkâ* [1]
inflicted casualties, 5782, *nākâ* [1]

CATASTROPHE [2]
catastrophe, 2202, *hăpēkâ* [1]
catastrophe, 8739, *šōʾâ* [1]

CATCH [12]
catch up, 5952, *nāśag* [2]
catch, 296, *ʾāḥaz*^{1} [1]
catch, 1899, *dîg* [1]
catch, 2642, *ḥāṭap* [1]
catch, 3579, *yāsar*^{1} [1]
catch, 4334+4334, *lākad+lākad* [1]
catch, 4334, *lākad* [1]
catch, 4374, *lāqaḥ* [1]
catch, 5162, *māṣāʾ* [1]
catch, 5952, *nāśag* [1]
catch glimpse, 8011, *rāʾâ*^{1} [1]

CATCHES [4]
catches, 1760, *gārar* [1]
catches, 2642, *ḥāṭap* [1]
catches, 4334, *lākad* [1]
catches the scent, 8193, *rîaḥ* [1]

CATTLE [81]
cattle, 1330, *bāqār* [40]
cattle, 989, *bᵉhēmâ* [17]
cattle, 8802, *šôr* [13]
cattle, 5238, *miqneh* [4]
cattle, 10756, *tôr* [4]
kinds of cattle, 989+2256+989, *bᵉhēmâ+wᵉ-+bᵉhēmâ* [1]
cattle, 1248, *bᵉʿîr* [1]
cattle, 5238+1330, *miqneh+bāqār* [1]

CAUGHT [42]
is caught, 5162, *māṣāʾ* [6]
be caught, 4334, *lākad* [4]
caught, 4334, *lākad* [3]
caught, 296, *ʾāḥaz*^{1} [2]
be caught, 9530, *tāpaś* [2]
caught, 9530, *tāpaś* [2]
caught, *AIT* [1]
are caught, 296, *ʾāḥaz*^{1} [1]
were caught, 665, *ʾāsap* [1]
caught, 1608, *gāzal* [1]
caught up, 1815, *dābaq* [1]
caught, 2118, *hāyâ* [1]
caught hold, 2616, *ḥāzaq* [1]
caught, 2616, *ḥāzaq* [1]
are caught, 4334, *lākad* [1]
is caught, 4334, *lākad* [1]
was caught, 4334, *lākad* [1]
were caught, 4334, *lākad* [1]
caught, 4374, *lāqaḥ* [1]
was caught, 5162, *māṣāʾ* [1]
caught up, 5162, *māṣāʾ* [1]
were caught, 5162, *māṣāʾ* [1]
caught up, 5951, *nāśāʾ* [1]
caught up, 5952, *nāśag* [1]
are caught, 6200, *sāpâ* [1]
caught sight of, 8011, *rāʾâ*^{1} [1]
caught the smell, 8193+8194, *rîaḥ+rêaḥ* [1]
are caught, 9530, *tāpaś* [1]
been caught in the act, 9530, *tāpaś* [1]

CAULK [1]
caulk, 2616, *ḥāzaq* [1]

CAUSE [74]
cause, 5477, *mišpāṭ* [11]
cause, 8190, *rîb*^{2} [9]
without cause, 2855, *ḥinnām* [7]
cause, *AIT* [5]
without cause, 9214, *šeqer* [4]
cause, 1907, *dîn*^{2} [3]
cause, 5989, *nātan* [3]
cause, 4200, *lᵉ-*^{1} [2]
defend the cause, 9149, *šāpaṭ* [2]
cause, *NIH/RPE* [1]
cause, 928+3338, *bᵉ-+yād* [1]
cause, 1821, *dābār* [1]
cause, 1826, *dibrâ* [1]
cause, 2118+4946, *hāyâ+min* [1]
cause to walk, 2143, *hālak* [1]
cause to be honored, 2349, *zākar*^{1} [1]
cause to sin, 2627, *ḥāṭāʾ* [1]
cause to suffer, 2703, *ḥālâ*^{1} [1]
cause to fall, 4173, *kāšal* [1]
justice of cause, 5477, *mišpāṭ* [1]
cause to inherit, 5706, *nāḥal* [1]
cause to fall, 5877, *nāpal* [1]
cause to pass, 6296, *ʿābar*^{1} [1]
cause terror, 6907, *ʿāraṣ* [1]
cause to come near, 7928, *qārab* [1]
defends cause, 8189, *rîb*^{1} [1]
plead cause, 8189, *rîb*^{1} [1]
uphold cause, 8189, *rîb*^{1} [1]
without cause, 8200, *rêqām* [1]
cause to ride, 8206, *rākab* [1]
given cause to rejoice, 8523, *śāmaḥ* [1]
cause to stop, 8697, *šābat*^{1} [1]
cause devastation, 8845, *šāḥat* [1]
cause of destruction, 8845, *šāḥat* [1]
cause to be appalled, 9037, *šāmēm*^{1} [1]
cause to hear, 9048, *šāmaʿ* [1]
defend cause, 9149, *šāpaṭ* [1]

CAUSED [42]
caused to commit, 2627, *ḥāṭāʾ* [20]
caused to sin, 2627, *ḥāṭāʾ* [4]
caused, 5989, *nātan* [3]
caused, 6913, *ʿāśâ*^{1} [3]
caused by, 4946, *min* [2]
caused, *AIT* [1]
caused, *NIH/RPE* [1]
caused to come, 995, *bôʾ* [1]
caused to prostitute themselves, 2388, *zānâ*^{1} [1]
caused to stumble, 4173, *kāšal* [1]
caused to fall, 5877, *nāpal* [1]
caused to turn, 8492, *śîm* [1]
caused to roam, 8740, *šûb*^{1} [1]
caused to hear, 9048, *šāmaʿ* [1]
caused to dwell, 10709, *šᵉkan* [1]

CAUSES [11]
causes desolation, 9037, *šāmēm*^{1} [4]
causes, 5989, *nātan* [2]
causes, *AIT* [1]
causes to boil, 1240, *bāʿâ*^{2} [1]
causes, 4946, *min* [1]
causes to stumble, 5598, *negep* [1]
causes to grow, 7541, *ṣāmaḥ* [1]

CAUSING [3]
causing to die, 4637, *mût* [2]
causing to hunger, 8279, *rāʿēb*^{1} [1]

CAUTIOUS [1]
cautious, 9365, *tûr* [1]

CAVALRY [5]
cavalry, 7305, *pārāš*^{2} [5]

CAVE [34]
cave, 5117, *mᵉʿārâ*^{1} [30]
cave, 6186, *sāʿîp*^{1} [2]
cave, 7074, *paḥat* [2]

CAVERNS [1]
caverns, 5942, *nᵉqārâ* [1]

CAVES [8]
caves, 5117, *mᵉʿārâ*^{1} [6]
caves, *NIH/RPE* [2]

CEASE [14]
cease, 3983, *kālâ*^{1} [2]
cease, 6073, *sûr*^{1} [2]
cease, 8697, *šābat*^{1} [2]
cease, 1060, *bāṭal* [1]
cease, 2532, *ḥādal*^{1} [1]
cease, 4162, *kārat* [1]
cease, 5980, *nāšat* [1]
cease, 6296, *ʿābar*^{1} [1]
cease to flow, 7551, *ṣāmat* [1]
cease, 8089, *rāgaʿ*^{2} [1]
makes cease, 8697, *šābat*^{1} [1]

CEASED [3]
ceased, 2532, *ḥādal*^{1} [3]

CEASING [2]
ceasing, 1949, *dāmâ*^{2} [1]
ceasing, 1957, *dāmam*^{1} [1]

CEDAR [57]
cedar, 780, *ʾerez* [53]
cedar of Lebanon, 4248, *lᵉbānôn* [2]
cedar, *NIH/RPE* [1]
beams of cedar, 781, *ʾarzâ* [1]

CEDARS [19]
cedars, 780, *ʾerez* [19]

CEILING [4]
ceiling, 7815, *qîr*^{1} [2]
ceiling, 6212, *sippun* [1]
ceiling beams, 7771, *qôrâ* [1]

CELEBRATE [47]
celebrate, 6913, *ʿāśâ*^{1} [25]
celebrate, 2510, *ḥāgag* [9]
celebrate, 9068, *šāmar* [4]
celebrate, *NIH/RPE* [3]
celebrate, 2352+5580, *zēker+nābaʿ* [1]
celebrate a festival, 2510, *ḥāgag* [1]
celebrate the Feast, 2510, *ḥāgag* [1]
celebrate holy, 7727, *qādaš* [1]
celebrate, 8471, *śāḥaq* [1]
celebrate, 8525, *śimḥâ* [1]

CELEBRATED [18]
celebrated, 6913, *ʿāśâ*^{1} [13]
celebrated, *NIH/RPE* [2]
was celebrated, 6913, *ʿāśâ*^{1} [2]
celebrated, 10522, *ʿăbad* [1]

CELEBRATING [5]
celebrating, 8471, *śāḥaq* [3]
celebrating, 3427+3202, *yôm*^{1}*+ṭôb*^{2} [1]
celebrating, 6913, *ʿāśâ*^{1} [1]

CELEBRATION [5]
the celebration^s, 889, *ʾăšer* [1]
celebration, 3202, *ṭôb*^{2} [1]
celebration, 6913, *ʿāśâ*^{1} [1]
held a celebration, 7412, *ṣāhal*^{1} [1]
held a celebration, 8523, *śāmaḥ* [1]

CELEBRATIONS [1]
celebrations, 5375, *māśôś*^{1} [1]

CELL [1]
vaulted cell, 2844, *ḥānût* [1]

CENSER [6]
censer, 4746, *maḥtâ* [4]
censer, 5233, *miqṭeret* [2]

CENSERS [13]
censers, 4746, *maḥtâ* [11]
censers, *NIH/RPE* [1]
the censers^{s}, 4392, *-ām* [1]

CENSUS [14]
take a census, 5951+906+8031, *nāśā'+'ēt*^{1}*+rō'š*^{1} [3]
take a census, 4948, *mānâ*^{1} [2]
take a census, 5951+8031, *nāśā'+rō'š*^{1} [2]
census, *NIH/RPE* [1]
include in the census, 906+8031+5951, *'ēt*^{1}*+rō'š*^{1}*+nāśā'* [1]
census, 5031, *mispār*^{1} [1]
took a census, 6218, *sāpar* [1]
census taken, 6222+6218, *s*^{e}*pār*^{1}*+sāpar* [1]
census, 6296+408, *'ābar*^{1}*+'îš*^{1} [1]
were counted in the census, 7212, *pāqad* [1]

CENTER [17]
center, 9348, *tāwek* [11]
center, 1074, *bayit*^{1} [2]
center, 3179, *ṭabbûr* [2]
center, 9399, *tîkôn* [2]

CENTERS [1]
centers, *AIT* [1]

CENTRAL [1]
central, 9348, *tāwek* [1]

CENTRALLY [1]
centrally located in, 928+9348, *b*^{e}*-+tāwek* [1]

CEREMONIAL [2]
ceremonial cleansing, 3200, *ṭoh*^{o}*râ* [2]

CEREMONIALLY [38]
ceremonially clean, 3196, *ṭāhôr* [13]
ceremonially unclean, 3238, *ṭāmē'*^{2} [12]
ceremonially clean, 3197, *ṭāhēr* [3]
ceremonially unclean, 3237, *ṭāmē'*^{1} [3]
make himself ceremonially unclean, 3237, *ṭāmē'*^{1} [2]
ceremonially unclean, 1194+3196, *biltî+ṭāhôr* [1]
make ceremonially clean, 3197, *ṭāhēr* [1]
purified themselves ceremonially, 3197, *ṭāhēr* [1]
pronounce ceremonially unclean, 3237, *ṭāmē'*^{1} [1]
ceremonially unclean, 3240, *ṭum'â* [1]

CEREMONY [4]
ceremony, 6275, *'*^{a}*bōdâ* [3]
ceremony of mourning, 65, *'ēbel* [1]

CERTAIN [18]
certain, 285, *'eḥād* [5]
certain, *NIH/RPE* [4]
certain, 2021, *ha-* [2]
certain, *AIT* [1]
certain, 586, *'āman*^{1} [1]
know for certain, 3359+3359, *yāda'+yāda'* [1]
certain place, 4595, *mô'ēd* [1]
certain, 4946, *min* [1]
certain, 7141+532, *p*^{e}*lōnî+'almōnî* [1]
certain, 10427+10327+10313, *min+yaṣṣîb+y*^{e}*da'* [1]

CERTAINLY [34]
certainly die, 4637+4637, *mût+mût* [3]
certainly come, 995+995, *bô'+bô'* [2]
certainly recover, 2649+2649, *ḥāyâ+ḥāyâ* [2]
certainly, 3954, *kî*^{2} [2]
certainly be handed over, 5989+5989+928+3338, *nātan+nātan+b*^{e}*-+yād* [2]
certainly be destroyed, 6+6, *'ābad+'ābad* [1]
certainly, 561+4202, *'im+lō'* [1]
certainly go into exile, 1655+1655, *gālâ+gālâ* [1]
certainly, 1685, *gam* [1]
certainly demand, 2011+2011, *dāraš+dāraš* [1]
certainly come true, 2118+2118, *hāyâ+hāyâ* [1]
certainly, 2180, *hinnēh* [1]
must certainly put to death, 2222+2222, *hārag+hārag* [1]
can certainly do, 3523+3523, *yākōl+yākōl* [1]
certainly drive out, 3769+3769, *yāraš*^{1}*+yāraš*^{1} [1]
certainly be put to death, 4637+4637, *mût+mût* [1]
must certainly put, 5782+5782, *nākâ+nākâ* [1]
certainly overtake, 5952+5952, *nāśag+nāśag* [1]
must certainly give, 5989+5989, *nātan+nātan* [1]
certainly hide, 6259+6259, *sātar+sātar* [1]
certainly carry out, 6913+6913, *'āśâ*^{1}*+'āśâ*^{1} [1]
certainly do, 6913+6913, *'āśâ*^{1}*+'āśâ*^{1} [1]
certainly make, 6913+6913, *'āśâ*^{1}*+'āśâ*^{1} [1]
most certainly tear away, 7973+7973, *qāra'+qāra'* [1]
must certainly make restitution, 8966+8966, *šālēm*^{1}*+šālēm*^{1} [1]
certainly be destroyed, 9012+9012, *šāmad+šāmad* [1]
certainly hear, 9048+9048, *šāma'+šāma'* [1]
certainly, 10327+10002, *yaṣṣîb+-ā'* [1]

CERTIFICATE [4]
certificate, 6219, *sēper*^{1} [4]

CHAFF [16]
chaff, 5161, *mōṣ* [8]
chaff, 7990, *qaš* [6]
chaff, 3143, *ḥ*^{a}*šaš* [1]
chaff, 10534, *'ûr* [1]

CHAIN [6]
chain, 10212, *hamyānak* [3]
chain, 6736, *'*^{a}*nāq*^{1} [1]
chain, 8054, *rābîd* [1]
chain, 9249, *šarš*^{e}*râ* [1]

CHAINS [31]
chains, 9249, *šarš*^{e}*râ* [5]
chains, 6310, *'*^{a}*bōt* [4]
chains, 4591, *môsēr* [3]
chains, 272, *'*^{a}*ziqqîm* [2]
chains, 2414, *zēq*^{1} [2]
chains, 4593, *môsērâ*^{1} [2]
chains, 657, *'ēsûr* [1]
put in chains, 673, *'āsar* [1]
iron chains, 1366, *barzel* [1]
chains, 3078, *ḥarṣōb* [1]
interwoven chains, 5126+9249, *ma'*^{a}*śeh+šarš*^{e}*râ* [1]
chains, 5733, *n*^{e}*ḥōšet*^{1} [1]
chains, 6736, *'*^{a}*nāq*^{1} [1]
ankle chains, 7578, *ṣ*^{e}*'ādâ*^{2} [1]
chains, 8408, *rattôq* [1]
chains, 8411, *rattîqâ* [1]
were put in chains, 8415+928+2414, *rātaq+b*^{e}*-+zēq*^{1} [1]
chains, 8416, *r*^{e}*tuqôt* [1]
chains, 9249+6310, *šarš*^{e}*râ+'*^{a}*bōt* [1]

CHAIR [4]
chair, 4058, *kissē'* [4]

CHALDEA [2]
Chaldea, 4169, *kaśdîm* [2]

CHALDEAN [1]
Chaldean, 10373, *kaśdāy* [1]

CHALDEANS [8]
Chaldeans, 4169, *kaśdîm* [8]

CHALK [1]
chalk, 1732, *gir* [1]

CHALLENGE [5]
challenge, 606, *'āmar*^{1} [2]
challenge, 3585, *yā'ad* [2]
challenge, 1043, *bāḥan* [1]

CHAMBER [3]
chamber, *NIH/RPE* [1]
chamber, 2540, *ḥeder* [1]
chamber, 2903, *ḥuppâ*^{1} [1]

CHAMBERS [5]
chambers, 2540, *ḥeder* [2]
upper chambers, 6608, *'*^{a}*liyyâ* [2]
chambers, 4384, *liškâ* [1]

CHAMELEON [1]
chameleon, 9491, *tinšemet*^{1} [1]

CHAMPION [3]
champion, 408+2021+1227, *'îš*^{1}*+ha-+bēnayim* [2]
champion, 1475, *gibbôr* [1]

CHAMPIONS [1]
champions, 408+2657, *'îš*^{1}*+ḥayil* [1]

CHANCE [4]
looking for a chance, 1335, *bāqaš* [1]
had chance, 2118+928+3338, *hāyâ+b*^{e}*-+yād* [1]
by chance, 5247, *miqreh* [1]
chance, 7004, *pega'* [1]

CHANGE [23]
change, 8740, *šûb*^{1} [5]
change mind, 5714, *nāḥam* [4]
change, 10731, *š*^{e}*nâ*^{1} [3]
change, 2736, *ḥālap*^{1} [2]
change, 9101, *šānâ*^{1} [2]
change, 2200, *hāpak* [1]
change, 2722, *ḥ*^{a}*lîpâ* [1]
really change, 3512+3512, *yāṭab+yāṭab* [1]
change minds, 5714, *nāḥam* [1]
change, 6015, *sābab* [1]
change, 6440, *'āzab*^{1} [1]
change, 8883, *šît*^{1} [1]

CHANGED [26]
changed, 2200, *hāpak* [4]
changed, 6015, *sābab* [4]
changed, 10731, *š*^{e}*nâ*^{1} [4]
changed, 2736, *ḥālap*^{1} [3]
be changed, 2200, *hāpak* [2]
was changed, 2200, *hāpak* [2]
changed, 2200+337, *hāpak+'aḥēr*^{1} [1]
changed, 3558, *yāmar* [1]
were changed, 6015, *sābab* [1]
changed, 7756+7756, *qûm+qûm* [1]
changed minds, 8740, *šûb*^{1} [1]
changed mind, 8740, *šûb*^{1} [1]
changed, 8740, *šûb*^{1} [1]

CHANGES [3]
changes, 10731, *š*^{e}*nâ*^{1} [2]
changes, 9101, *šānâ*^{1} [1]

CHANGING [3]
changing, 2736, *ḥālap*^{1} [1]
changing, 6015, *sābab* [1]
changing, 9101, *šānâ*^{1} [1]

CHANNEL [1]
channel, 9498, *t*^{e}*'ālâ*^{1} [1]

CHANNELED [1]
channeled, 3837, *yāšar* [1]

CHANNELS [4]
channels, 692, *'āpîq*^{1} [1]
channels, 4609, *mûṣāqâ* [1]
channels, 5226, *māqôm* [1]
channels, 9498, *t*^{e}*'ālâ*^{1} [1]

CHANT [3]
chant, 7801, *qîn* [3]

CHAOS [1]
chaos, 9332, *tōhû* [1]

CHARACTER [3]
noble character, 2657, *ḥayil* [3]

CHARCOAL [1]
charcoal, 7073, *peḥām* [1]

CHARGE [125]
in charge of, 6584, *ʿal*[2] [43]
charge, *NIH/RPE* [6]
put in charge, 7212, *pāqad* [6]
had charge of, 6584, *ʿal*[2] [5]
charge, 8678, *šābaʿ* [5]
in charge, 9068, *šāmar* [5]
in charge, 7224, *pāqîd* [3]
officials in charge, 8569, *śar* [3]
in charge of, 928, *be-* [2]
charge, 1821, *dābār* [2]
in charge, 5592, *nāgîd* [2]
official in charge, 5592, *nāgîd* [2]
charge, 8190, *rîb*[2] [2]
in charge, 8569, *śar* [2]
have charge of, 9068+5466, *šāmar+mišmeret* [2]
in charge of, 448, *ʾel* [1]
public charge, 460, *ʾālâ*[4] [1]
put in charge of the storerooms, 732+6584+238, *ʾāṣar+ʿal*[2]*+ʾôṣār* [1]
in charge of, 928+3338, *be-+yād* [1]
lodging a charge, 3519, *yākaḥ* [1]
in charge of, 4200, *le-*[1] [1]
charge, 4697, *meḥîr*[1] [1]
in charge, 5440, *māšal*[2] [1]
in charge, 5466, *mišmeret* [1]
officer in charge, 5592, *nāgîd* [1]
charge interest, 5967+5968, *nāšak*[2]*+nešek* [1]
charge interest, 5967, *nāšak*[2] [1]
charge, 5989, *nātan* [1]
officer in charge, 6221, *sōpēr* [1]
in charge, 6254, *sārar*[2] [1]
gave charge, 6386, *ʿûd*[1] [1]
charge, 6590, *ʿālâ* [1]
in charge, 6641+6584, *ʿāmad+ʿal*[2] [1]
put in charge, 6641+6584+3338, *ʿāmad+ʿal*[2]*+yād* [1]
in charge, 6913, *ʿāśâ*[1] [1]
in charge of, 7212, *pāqad* [1]
in charge, 7212, *pāqad* [1]
charge, 7213, *pequddâ* [1]
having charge, 7213, *pequddâ* [1]
in charge, 7213, *pequddâ* [1]
gave a charge, 7422, *ṣāwâ* [1]
put in charge, 7422, *ṣāwâ* [1]
charge, 8132, *rûṣ* [1]
bring a charge, 8189, *rîb*[1] [1]
charge, 8492, *śîm* [1]
put in charge, 8492, *śîm* [1]
had charge of, 9068, *šāmar* [1]
have charge of, 9068, *šāmar* [1]
take charge of, 9393+3338, *taḥat*[1]*+yād* [1]
in charge, 10647+10505, *rab+segan* [1]

CHARGED [8]
charged, 7422, *ṣāwâ* [3]
charged out, 1631, *gîaḥ*[1] [1]
charged, 5590, *nāgaḥ* [1]
charged against, 6584, *ʿal*[2] [1]
charged, 6590, *ʿālâ* [1]
charged, 8132, *rûṣ* [1]

CHARGES [17]
bring charges, 8189, *rîb*[1] [6]
charges, 8492, *śîm* [2]
charges, 1821, *dābār* [1]
charges, 3655, *yāṣāʾ* [1]
charges, 5477, *mišpāṭ* [1]
brought charges against, 6386, *ʿûd*[1] [1]
charges, 8189, *rîb*[1] [1]
charges, 8190, *rîb*[2] [1]
press charges, 8492, *śîm* [1]
basis for charges, 10544, *ʿillâ* [1]
grounds for charges, 10544, *ʿillâ* [1]

CHARGING [6]
usury charging, 5957, *nāšāʾ*[1] [1]
charging, 5989, *nātan* [1]
charging, 6590, *ʿālâ* [1]
charging, 8132, *rûṣ* [1]
charging, 8851, *šāṭap* [1]
charging, 9212, *šāqaq* [1]

CHARIOT [61]
chariot, 8207, *rekeb* [26]
chariot, 5324, *merkābâ* [20]
chariot horses, 8207, *rekeb* [2]
chariot driver, 8208, *rakkāb* [2]
chariot officers, 8957, *šālîš*[3] [2]
chariot, *NIH/RPE* [1]
chariot wheels, 1649, *galgal*[1] [1]
chariot, 5323, *merkāb* [1]
got into chariot, 8206, *rākab* [1]
in a chariot, 8206, *rākab* [1]
took by chariot, 8206, *rākab* [1]
chariot, 8213, *rekûb* [1]
chariot horses, 8224, *rekeš* [1]
chariot officer, 8957, *šālîš*[3] [1]

CHARIOTEERS [11]
charioteers, 7305, *pārāš*[2] [6]
charioteers, 8207, *rekeb* [3]
charioteers, 8207+132, *rekeb+ʾādām*[1] [1]
chariots and charioteers, 8207, *rekeb* [1]

CHARIOTS [101]
chariots, 8207, *rekeb* [78]
chariots, 5324, *merkābâ* [21]
riding in chariots, 8206, *rākab* [1]
chariots and charioteers, 8207, *rekeb* [1]

CHARM [2]
charm, 74+2834, *ʾeben+ḥēn*[1] [1]
charm, 2834, *ḥēn*[1] [1]

CHARMED [2]
charmed, 4318, *laḥaš* [2]

CHARMER [2]
charmer, 1251+4383, *baʿal*[1]*+lāšôn* [1]
charmer, 4317, *lāḥaš* [1]

CHARMING [2]
charming, 2858, *ḥānan*[1] [1]
charming, 5833, *nāʿîm*[1] [1]

CHARMS [3]
magic charms, 4086, *keset* [2]
charms, 4318, *laḥaš* [1]

CHARRED [3]
charred, 1277+928+2021+836, *bāʿar*[1]*+be-+ha-+ʾēš*[1] [1]
be charred, 3081, *ḥārar*[1] [1]
is charred, 3081, *ḥārar*[1] [1]

CHARS [1]
chars, 3081, *ḥārar*[1] [1]

CHASE [8]
chase, 8103, *rādap* [4]
chase after, 8103, *rādap* [2]
chase, 8132, *rûṣ* [2]

CHASED [10]
chased, 8103, *rādap* [8]
chased, 1944, *dālaq* [1]
chased away, 5615, *nādaḥ*[1] [1]

CHASES [2]
chases, 8103, *rādap* [2]

CHASING [12]
chasing after, 8296, *reʿût*[2] [7]
chasing, 339, *ʾaḥar* [2]
chasing after, 8301, *raʿyôn* [2]
chasing, 1944+339, *dālaq+ʾaḥar* [1]

CHASTENED [2]
be chastened, 3519, *yākaḥ* [1]
chastened severely, 3579+3579, *yāsar*[1]*+yāsar*[1] [1]

CHATTERING [2]
chattering, 8557, *śāpâ* [2]

CHEAT [1]
cheat, 5792, *nākal* [1]

CHEATED [3]
cheated, 6943, *ʿāšaq* [2]
cheated, 9438, *tālal* [1]

CHEATING [1]
cheating, 6430, *ʿāwat* [1]

CHEATS [1]
cheats, 6943, *ʿāšaq* [1]

CHECK [1]
check, 995+4200+7156, *bôʾ+le-*[1]*+pāneh* [1]

CHECKED [3]
checked, 1067, *bîn* [1]
was checked, 6806, *ʿāṣar* [1]
checked on, 8938+448, *šālaḥ+ʾel* [1]

CHEEK [3]
cheek, 4305, *leḥî*[1] [3]

CHEEKS [4]
cheeks, 4305, *leḥî*[1] [4]

CHEER [1]
cheer up, 3512+4213, *yāṭab+lēb* [1]

CHEERFUL [4]
cheerful, 3202, *ṭôb*[2] [1]
makes cheerful, 3512, *yāṭab* [1]
cheerful, 4401, *māʾôr* [1]
cheerful, 8524, *śāmēaḥ* [1]

CHEERING [3]
cheering, 2146, *hālal*[2] [1]
cheering, 5432, *māšak* [1]
cheering, 8524, *śāmēaḥ* [1]

CHEERS [2]
cheers up, 8523, *śāmaḥ* [1]
cheers, 8523, *śāmaḥ* [1]

CHEESE [2]
cheese, 1482, *gebînâ* [1]
cheese, 9147, *šepôt* [1]

CHEESES [1]
cheeses, 3043+2692, *ḥārîṣ*[1]*+ḥālāb* [1]

CHEMOSH [8]
Chemosh, 4019, *kemôš* [8]

CHERISH [2]
cherish, 7621, *ṣāpan* [2]

CHERISHED [2]
cherished, 4718, *maḥmād* [1]
cherished, 8011, *rāʿâ*[1] [1]

CHERISHES [1]
cherishes, 9068, *šāmar* [1]

CHERUB [16]
cherub, 4131, *kerûb*[1] [15]
cherub, *NIH/RPE* [1]

CHERUBIM [72]
cherubim, 4131, *kerûb*[1] [66]
the cherubims, 4392, *-ām* [3]
cherubim, *NIH/RPE* [2]
the cherubims, 2157, *-hem* [1]

CHEST [16]
chest, 778, *ʾarôn* [10]
chest, 761, *ʾargaz* [3]
chest, 4213, *lēb* [1]
the chests, 9004, *šām* [1]
chest, 10249, *ḥadēh* [1]

CHEW [6]
chew, 6590, *ʿālâ* [4]
chew, *NIH/RPE* [1]
chew, 1760, *gārar* [1]

CHEWED [1]
chewed, 5782, *nākâ* [1]

CHEWS [5]
chews, 6590, *ʿālâ* [5]

CHIEF [74]
chief, 8031, *rō'š*[1] [33]
chief, 8569, *śar* [17]
chief officer, 7224, *pāqîd* [3]
chief, 8042, *rab*[2] [3]
chief officer, 8569+2021+7372, *śar+ha-+ṣābā'*[2] [2]
chief, 10647, *rab* [2]
chief, 1524, *gādôl* [1]
chief, 2418, *zāqēn*[2] [1]
chief, 5592, *nāgîd* [1]
chief leader, 5954+5954, *nāśî'*[1]*+nāśî'*[1] [1]
chief, 5954, *nāśî'*[1] [1]
chief officer, 6221, *sōpēr* [1]
commander in chief, 6584+2021+7372, *'al*[2]*+ha-+ṣābā'*[2] [1]
chief officials, 8037, *ri'šôn* [1]
chief, 8037, *ri'šôn* [1]
chief, 8041, *rab*[1] [1]
chief men, 8569, *śar* [1]
chief officials, 8569, *śar* [1]
chief men, 8657, *šēbeṭ* [1]
chief officers, 8957, *šālîš*[3] [1]

CHIEFS [25]
chiefs, 477, *'allûp*[2] [16]
chiefs, 8031, *rō'š*[1] [6]
chiefs, 5954, *nāśî'*[1] [3]

CHILD [60]
child, 3529, *yeled* [21]
child, 5853, *na'ar*[2] [13]
child, *AIT* [3]
child, 1201, *bēn*[1] [3]
only child, 3495, *yāḥîd* [3]
with child, 2225, *hārâ* [2]
with child, 2226, *hāreh* [2]
stillborn child, 5878, *nēpel* [2]
child, 408, *'îš*[1] [1]
bearing first child, 1144, *bākar* [1]
young child, 1694, *gāmal* [1]
the child[s], 2084, *-hû* [1]
child, 2446, *zera'* [1]
bear a child, 3528, *yālad* [1]
bore a child, 3528, *yālad* [1]
child was born, 3528, *yālad* [1]
have a child, 3528, *yālad* [1]
fatherless child, 3846, *yātôm* [1]
stillborn child, 5878+851, *nēpel+'iššâ* [1]

CHILD'S [2]
child's, 5853, *na'ar*[2] [1]
child's, 5854, *nō'ar* [1]

CHILDBEARING [2]
age of childbearing, 784+3869+2021+851, *'ōraḥ+kᵉ-+ha-+'iššâ* [1]
childbearing, 2228, *hērôn* [1]

CHILDBIRTH [4]
in childbirth, 3528, *yālad* [2]
childbirth, 3528, *yālad* [1]
help in childbirth, 3528, *yālad* [1]

CHILDHOOD [3]
childhood, 5830, *nᵉ'ûrîm* [3]

CHILDLESS [15]
childless, 6884, *'ᵃrîrî* [4]
childless, 4202+3528, *lō'+yālad* [2]
leave childless, 8897, *šākal* [2]
make childless, 8897, *šākal* [2]
remained childless, 4202+3528, *lō'+yālad* [1]
childless, 6829, *'āqār* [1]
childless, 8891, *šakkûl* [1]
childless, 8897, *šākal* [1]
made childless, 8897, *šākal* [1]

CHILDREN [307]
children, 1201, *bēn*[1] [175]
children, 3251, *ṭap*[1] [27]
children, 2446, *zera'* [20]
children, 3529, *yeled* [20]
children, 6407, *'ôlēl* [7]
children, 6408, *'ôlāl* [7]
women and children, 3251, *ṭap*[1] [6]
bear children, 3528, *yālad* [4]
having children, 3528, *yālad* [3]
children, 5853, *na'ar*[2] [3]
children, *AIT* [2]
little children, 3251, *ṭap*[1] [2]
borne children, 3528, *yālad* [2]
had children, 3528, *yālad* [2]
have children, 3528, *yālad* [2]
loss of children, 8890, *šᵉkôl* [2]
deprive of children, 8897, *šākal* [2]
children, *NIH/RPE* [1]
guardians of children, 587, *'āman*[2] [1]
children, 1887+1201, *dôr*[2]*+bēn*[1] [1]
children, 2263, *wālād* [1]
be able to have children, 2445+2446, *zāra'+zera'* [1]
bearing children, 3528, *yālad* [1]
children born, 3528, *yālad* [1]
children, 3528, *yālad* [1]
children born, 3533, *yillôd* [1]
fatherless children, 3846, *yātôm* [1]
children, 4580, *môledet* [1]
children, 5769, *nîn*[2] [1]
children, 6396, *'ᵃwîl*[1] [1]
little children, 6407, *'ôlēl* [1]
children, 7262+1061, *pᵉrî+beṭen*[1] [1]
children, 7262+2021+1061, *pᵉrî+ha-+beṭen*[1] [1]
children, 7368+5055, *ṣe'ᵉṣā'îm+mē'eh* [1]
deprived of children, 8897, *šākal* [1]
rob of children, 8897, *šākal* [1]
mere children, 9500, *ta'ᵃlûlîm* [1]
children, 10120, *bar*[2] [1]

CHILDREN'S [10]
children's, 1201, *bēn*[1] [9]
children's, 4200+1201, *lᵉ-*[1]*+bēn*[1] [1]

CHIN [2]
chin, 2417, *zāqān* [2]

CHIRP [1]
chirp, 7627, *ṣāpap* [1]

CHISEL [4]
chisel out, 7180, *pāsal* [2]
chisel, 1749, *garzen* [1]
chisel, 5108, *ma'ᵃṣād* [1]

CHISELED [2]
chiseled out, 7180, *pāsal* [2]

CHISELING [1]
chiseling, 2980, *ḥāqaq* [1]

CHISELS [1]
chisels, 5244, *maqṣu'â* [1]

CHOICE [31]
choice, 1047, *bāḥar*[1] [4]
choice, 3202, *ṭôb*[2] [3]
choice, 1405, *bārar*[1] [2]
choice morsels, 4269, *lāham* [2]
choice, 4458, *meged* [2]
choice, 80, *'ābas* [1]
choice, 1201, *bēn*[1] [1]
choice sheep, 1374, *bārî'* [1]
choice, 1374, *bārî'* [1]
choice food, 2016, *dešen* [1]
choice, 2077, *hādār* [1]
choice, 2773, *ḥāmad* [1]
choice, 2776, *ḥᵃmudôt* [1]
choice lambs, 4119+4946+7366, *kar*[1]*+min+ṣō'n* [1]
choice possessions, 4436, *mibḥār*[1] [1]
choice, 5309, *mᵉrî'* [1]
choice food, 5460, *mašmannîm* [1]
choice wine, 6011, *sōbe'* [1]
choice food, 7329, *pat-bag* [1]
take choice, 7691, *qābal* [1]
choice parts, 8040, *rē'šît* [1]
choice, 8040, *rē'šît* [1]
choice vine, 8603, *śōrēq*[1] [1]

CHOICEST [12]
choicest, 4436, *mibḥār*[1] [4]
choicest, 1374, *bārî'* [1]
choicest, 4435, *mibḥôr* [1]
choicest gifts, 8031, *rō'š*[1] [1]
choicest vines, 8602, *śārōq*[2] [1]
choicest vines, 8603, *śōrēq*[1] [1]
choicest branch, 8605, *śᵉrēqâ* [1]
choicest, 9294, *ta'ᵃwâ*[1] [1]
choicest, 9361, *tô'āpôt* [1]

CHOIR [1]
choir, 9343, *tôdâ* [1]

CHOIRS [4]
choirs, 8876, *šîr*[1] [2]
choirs that gave thanks, 9343, *tôdâ* [1]
choirs to give thanks, 9343, *tôdâ* [1]

CHOOSE [58]
choose, 1047, *bāḥar*[1] [42]
choose, 4374, *lāqaḥ* [7]
choose, 1405, *bārar*[1] [1]
choose, 2035, *hab*[1] [1]
choose life, 2649, *ḥāyâ* [1]
choose, 4200, *lᵉ-*[1] [1]
choose as wives, 4374, *lāqaḥ* [1]
choose, 5989, *nātan* [1]
choose, 7864+1047, *qānâ*[1]*+bāḥar*[1] [1]
choose, 8011, *rā'â*[1] [1]
choose princes, 8606, *śārar* [1]

CHOOSES [9]
chooses, 1047, *bāḥar*[1] [7]
chooses, *NIH/RPE* [1]
chooses, 2773, *ḥāmad* [1]

CHOOSING [1]
choosing, 968, *bādā'* [1]

CHOP [3]
chop, 2634, *ḥāṭab* [1]
chop down, 4162, *kārat* [1]
chop up, 7298, *pāraś* [1]

CHOPPED [1]
chopped up, 1324, *bāqa'* [1]

CHOSE [31]
chose, 1047, *bāḥar*[1] [27]
chose, *NIH/RPE* [1]
chose, 4374, *lāqaḥ* [1]
chose, 5951, *nāśā'* [1]
chose, 8011, *rā'â*[1] [1]

CHOSEN [90]
chosen, 1047, *bāḥar*[1] [63]
chosen, 1040, *bāḥîr* [13]
was chosen, 4334, *lākad* [3]
chosen, 1405, *bārar*[1] [2]
chosen, 3359, *yāda'* [2]
chosen, 3519, *yākaḥ* [2]
chosen, 7924+928+9005, *qārā'*[1]*+bᵉ-+šēm*[1] [2]
chosen ally, 170, *'āhab* [1]
chosen, 6590, *'ālâ* [1]
chosen, 8011, *rā'â*[1] [1]

CHRONIC [1]
chronic, 3823, *yāšēn*[2] [1]

CHRONICLES [1]
chronicles, 2355, *zikkārôn* [1]

CHRYSOLITE [7]
chrysolite, 9577, *taršîš*[2] [6]
chrysolite, 74+9577, *'eben+taršîš*[2] [1]

CHURN [1]
makes churn, 8409, *rātaḥ* [1]

CHURNED [1]
churned up, 8088, *rāga'*[1] [1]

CHURNING [5]
churning, 1931, *dālaḥ* [1]
churning, 2816, *ḥōmer*[1] [1]
churning, 4790, *mîṣ* [1]
churning, 8409, *rātaḥ* [1]
churning up, 10137, *gûaḥ* [1]

CHURNS [1]
churns up, 8088, *rāga'*[1] [1]

CINNAMON [3]
cinnamon, 7872, qinnāmôn [3]

CIRCLE [3]
circle around, 6015, sābab [2]
circle, 2553, ḥûg[2] [1]

CIRCLED [1]
circled, 6015, sābab [1]

CIRCLING [1]
circling, 5938, nāqap[2] [1]

CIRCUIT [2]
circuit, 6015, sābab [1]
circuit, 9543, tᵉqûpâ [1]

CIRCULAR [4]
circular in shape, 6318+6017, ʿāgōl+sābîb [2]
circular frame, 4196, kōteret [1]
circular band, 6318+6017, ʿāgōl+sābîb [1]

CIRCUMCISE [5]
circumcise yourselves, 4576, mûl[1] [1]
circumcise, 4576+6889, mûl[1]+ʿorlâ [1]
circumcise, 4576, mûl[1] [1]
circumcise, 4909, mālal[2] [1]
circumcise, 6073+6889, sûr[1]+ʿorlâ [1]

CIRCUMCISED [22]
circumcised, 4576, mûl[1] [7]
be circumcised, 4576, mûl[1] [4]
been circumcised, 4576, mûl[1] [2]
was circumcised, 4576, mûl[1] [2]
not circumcised, 4200+2257+6889, lᵉ-[1]+-ô+ʿorlâ [1]
be circumcised, 4576+1414+6889, mûl[1]+bāśār+ʿorlâ [1]
been circumcised, 4576+6889, mûl[1]+ʿorlâ [1]
circumcised, 4576+1414+6889, mûl[1]+bāśār+ʿorlâ [1]
must be circumcised, 4576+4576, mûl[1]+mûl[1] [1]
was circumcised, 4576+1414+6889, mûl[1]+bāśār+ʿorlâ [1]
were circumcised, 4576, mûl[1] [1]

CIRCUMCISING [1]
circumcising, 4576, mûl[1] [1]

CIRCUMCISION [2]
undergo circumcision, 4576+906+1414+6889, mûl[1]+ʾēt[1]+bāśār+ʿorlâ [1]
circumcision, 4581, mûlâ [1]

CIRCUMFERENCE [1]
circumference, 2562+6015, ḥûṭ+sābab [1]

CIRCUMSTANCES [1]
circumstances, 6961, ʿēt [1]

CISTERN [20]
cistern, 1014, bôr [19]
cistern, 1465, gebeʾ [1]

CISTERNS [6]
cisterns, 1014, bôr [5]
cisterns, 1463, gēb[1] [1]

CITADEL [20]
citadel, 1072, bîrâ [14]
citadel, 810, ʾarmôn [3]
citadel, 6551, ʿîr[1] [1]
citadel, 6755, ʿōpel[2] [1]
citadel, 10101, bîrâ [1]

CITADELS [4]
citadels, 810, ʾarmôn [4]

CITIES [142]
cities, 6551, ʿîr[1] [126]
cities, 9133, šaʿar[1] [6]
cities, 7953, qiryâ [3]
cities, NIH/RPE [2]
cities, 824+9133, ʾereṣ+šaʿar[1] [2]
fortified cities, 4448, mibṣār[1] [2]
cities, 6551+2256+6551, ʿîr[1]+wᵉ-+ʿîr[1] [1]

CITIZENS [21]
citizens, 1251, baʿal[1] [18]
citizens, 275, ʾezrāḥ [1]
citizens, 3782, yāšab [1]
citizens of[s], 4946, min [1]

CITY [613]
city, 6551, ʿîr[1] [512]
city, 7953, qiryâ [20]
city, NIH/RPE [14]
the city[s], 2023, -āh [12]
city gate, 9133, šaʿar[1] [11]
city, 10640, qiryâ [9]
city, 7984, qeret [5]
city gates, 9133, šaʿar[1] [4]
that city[s], 2023, -āh [3]
this city[s], 2085, hûʾ [3]
city, AIT [2]
city wall, 2570, ḥômâ [2]
the city[s], 9076, šōmᵉrôn [2]
city, 1426, bat[1] [1]
city[s], 2023, -āh [1]
this city[s], 2023, -āh [1]
the city[s], 2085, hûʾ [1]
the city[s], 3731, yᵉrûšālaim [1]
this city[s], 3871, -k [1]
fortified city, 4448, mibṣār[1] [1]
the city[s], 5626, -nâ [1]
the city[s], 6042, sᵉdōm [1]
city[s], 6504, ʿay [1]
every city, 6551+2256+6551, ʿîr[1]+wᵉ-+ʿîr[1] [1]
city without walls, 7252, pᵉrāzôt [1]
city, 7815, qîr[1] [1]
the city[s], 9004, šām [1]

CLAD [2]
clad, 4252, lābaš [1]
clad in scarlet, 9443, tālaʿ [1]

CLAIM [8]
claim, 606, ʾāmar[1] [2]
have a claim on, 928, bᵉ- [1]
claim, 1457, gāʾal[1] [1]
claim, 6641, ʿāmad [1]
claim, 7407, ṣᵉdāqâ [1]
has a claim against, 7709, qādam [1]
lay claim, 9286, šātat [1]

CLAIMED [2]
claimed, 430, ʾākal [1]
claimed, 606, ʾāmar[1] [1]

CLAIMS [4]
claims, 606, ʾāmar[1] [2]
claims, 1821, dābār [1]
claims, 7924, qārāʾ[1] [1]

CLAMOR [2]
clamor, 2162, hāmôn [1]
clamor, 7754, qôl [1]

CLAN [170]
clan, 5476, mišpāḥâ [131]
clan, NIH/RPE [29]
clan by clan, 4200+5476, lᵉ-[1]+mišpāḥâ [4]
clan, AIT [2]
clan, 548, ʾelep[3] [1]
clan, 1074, bayit[1] [1]
clan, 5476+1074+3, mišpāḥâ+bayit[1]+ʾāb [1]
each clan, 5476+5476, mišpāḥâ+mišpāḥâ [1]

CLANS [137]
clans, 5476, mišpāḥâ [124]
clans, 548, ʾelep[3] [9]
clans, 3, ʾāb [2]
clans, 1074+3, bayit[1]+ʾāb [1]
clans, 1201, bēn[1] [1]

CLAP [6]
clap, 4673, māḥāʾ [2]
clap, NIH/RPE [1]
clap, 6215, sāpaq[1] [1]
clap, 8492, śîm [1]
clap, 9546, tāqaʿ [1]

CLAPPED [2]
clapped, 4673, māḥāʾ [1]
clapped, 5782, nākâ [1]

CLAPS [3]
scornfully claps hands, 6215, sāpaq[1] [1]
claps in derision, 8562, śāpaq[1] [1]
claps, 9546, tāqaʿ [1]

CLASH [1]
clash, 9049, šemaʿ[1] [1]

CLASP [1]
clasp hands, 8562, śāpaq[1] [1]

CLASPS [7]
clasps, 7971, qeres [7]

CLATTER [2]
clatter, 7193, paʿam [1]
clatter, 7754+8323, qôl+raʿaš [1]

CLAWS [2]
claws, NIH/RPE [1]
claws, 10303, ṭᵉpar [1]

CLAY [37]
clay, 2817, ḥōmer[2] [11]
clay, 3084, ḥereś [9]
clay, 10279, ḥᵃsap [5]
clay, 141, ʾᵃdāmâ[1] [2]
clay, 3226, ṭîṭ [2]
baked clay, 10279, ḥᵃsap [2]
clay, 824, ʾereṣ [1]
clay tablet, 4246, lᵉbēnâ [1]
clay, 4879, meleṭ [1]
clay, 6760, ʿāpār [1]
baked clay, 10279+10298, ḥᵃsap+ṭîn [1]
clay, 10279+10298, ḥᵃsap+ṭîn [1]

CLEAN [93]
clean, 3196, ṭāhôr [33]
clean, 3197, ṭāhēr [23]
ceremonially clean, 3196, ṭāhôr [13]
pronounce clean, 3197, ṭāhēr [9]
ceremonially clean, 3197, ṭāhēr [3]
pronounced clean, 3200, ṭohᵒrâ [2]
stripped clean, 430, ʾākal [1]
make yourselves clean, 2342, zākâ [1]
clean, 2899, ḥap[1] [1]
make ceremonially clean, 3197, ṭāhēr [1]
pronounces clean, 3197, ṭāhēr [1]
pronouncing clean, 3197, ṭāhēr [1]
clean, 3200, ṭohᵒrâ [1]
make clean, 5470, mišʿî [1]
clean, 5929, nāqî [1]
clean, 5931, niqqāyôn [1]

CLEANNESS [5]
cleanness, 1341, bōr[1] [5]

CLEANSE [17]
cleanse, 3197, ṭāhēr [12]
cleanse, NIH/RPE [1]
cleanse, 1405, bārar[1] [1]
cleanse, 1866, dûaḥ [1]
cleanse, 2627, ḥāṭāʾ [1]
cleanse away, 9475, tamrûq [1]

CLEANSED [24]
be cleansed, 3197, ṭāhēr [12]
cleansed, 3197, ṭāhēr [8]
cleansed, NIH/RPE [1]
cleansed, 2318, zûr[1] [1]
cleansed, 3200, ṭohᵒrâ [1]
are cleansed, 8175, rāḥaṣ [1]

CLEANSING [12]
cleansing, 5614, niddâ [6]
cleansing, 3200, ṭohᵒrâ [3]
ceremonial cleansing, 3200, ṭohᵒrâ [2]
cleansing, 2633, ḥaṭṭāʾt [1]

CLEAR [14]
clear, 2341, zak [2]
clear, 9448, tōm [2]
clear, 1345, bārāʾ[3] [1]
clear land, 1345, bārāʾ[3] [1]
clear, 3198, ṭōhar [1]
clear, 5488, mišqāʾ [1]

made clear, 5583, *nāgad* [1]
clear, 6073, *sûr*[1] [1]
clear, 7300, *pāraš*[1] [1]
made clear, 7300, *pāraš*[1] [1]
making clear, 7300, *pāraš*[1] [1]
clear, 7456, *ṣaḥ* [1]

CLEARED [7]
cleared, 3655, *yāṣāʾ* [1]
be cleared of guilt, 5927, *nāqâ* [1]
cleared away, 6073, *sûr*[1] [1]
cleared of stones, 6232, *sāqal* [1]
cleared ground, 7155, *pānâ* [1]
cleared, 7405, *ṣādaq* [1]
cleared, 7406, *ṣedeq* [1]

CLEARLY [9]
sees clearly, 9280, *šātam* [2]
clearly, 930, *bāʿar* [1]
understand clearly, 1067+1069, *bîn+bînâ* [1]
clearly reveal myself, 1655+1655, *gālâ+gālâ* [1]
clearly, 5260, *marʾeh* [1]
were clearly told, 5583+5583, *nāgad+nāgad* [1]
clearly, 8011+3954, *rāʾâ*[1]*+kî*[2] [1]
saw clearly, 8011+8011, *rāʾâ*[1]*+rāʾâ*[1] [1]

CLEFT [1]
cleft, 5942, *n^{e}qārâ* [1]

CLEFTS [4]
clefts, 2511, *ḥāgû* [3]
mountain clefts, 2215, *har* [1]

CLERESTORY [1]
clerestory, 9209, *š^{e}qupîm* [1]

CLEVER [2]
clever, 1067, *bîn* [2]

CLEVERLY [1]
cleverly fashioned, 9312, *t^{e}bûnâ* [1]

CLEVERNESS [1]
cleverness, 747, *ʿorbâ* [1]

CLIFF [4]
cliff, 6152, *selaʿ*[1] [2]
cliff, 9094+6152, *šēn*[1]*+selaʿ*[1] [1]
cliff, 9094, *šēn*[1] [1]

CLIFFS [3]
cliffs, 6152, *selaʿ*[1] [2]
cliffs, 4533, *madrēgâ* [1]

CLIMAX [3]
climax, 7891, *qēṣ* [3]

CLIMB [7]
climb up, 6590, *ʿālâ* [4]
climb, 6590, *ʿālâ* [2]
climb, 7575, *ṣāʿad* [1]

CLIMBED [13]
climbed, 6590, *ʿālâ* [7]
climbed up, 6590, *ʿālâ* [3]
climbed up, 2143, *hālak* [1]
climbed down, 3718, *yārad* [1]
climbed in, 6590, *ʿālâ* [1]

CLIMBING [1]
climbing up, 6590, *ʿālâ* [1]

CLIMBS [2]
climbs, 6590, *ʿālâ* [2]

CLING [9]
cling, 1815, *dābaq* [5]
cling, 9068, *šāmar* [2]
cling, 2616, *ḥāzaq* [1]
cling together, 4334, *lākad* [1]

CLINGING [1]
clinging, 296, *ʾāḥaz*[1] [1]

CLINGS [2]
clings, 1815, *dābaq* [1]
clings, 2616, *ḥāzaq* [1]

CLIP [1]
clip off, 8845, *šāḥat* [1]

CLOAK [37]
cloak, 955, *beged*[2] [8]
cloak, 168, *ʾadderet* [5]
cloak, 2668, *ḥêq* [5]
cloak, 5077, *m^{e}ʿîl* [4]
cloak, 8515, *śalmâ*[1] [4]
cloak, 8529, *śimlâ* [4]
tuck cloak into belt, 2520+5516,
ḥāgar+motnayim [2]
fold of cloak, 955, *beged*[2] [1]
cloak, 4064, *k^{e}sût* [1]
cloak tucked into belt, 5516+2520,
motnayim+ḥāgar [1]
cloak, 8100, *r^{e}dîd* [1]
tucking cloak into belt, 9113+5516,
šānas+motnayim [1]

CLOAKS [2]
cloaks, 955, *beged*[2] [1]
cloaks, 4762, *miṭpaḥat* [1]

CLODS [2]
clods, 4493, *megrāpâ* [1]
clods of earth, 8073, *regeb* [1]

CLOSE [57]
close to, 4200+6645, *l^{e}-*[1]*+ʿummâ*[1] [5]
close relative, 8638, *šeʾēr* [3]
close friends, 476, *ʾallûp*[1] [2]
close to, 907, *ʾēt*[2] [2]
brought close, 5602, *nāgaš* [2]
close, 5602, *nāgaš* [2]
come close, 5602, *nāgaš* [2]
get so close, 5602, *nāgaš* [2]
close up, 6037, *sāgar* [2]
close, 6037, *sāgar* [2]
close, 7940, *qārôb* [2]
close, 358, *ʾāṭar* [1]
close friend, 408+8934, *ʾîš*[1]*+šālôm* [1]
close to, 725, *ʾēṣel*[1] [1]
close to, 928, *b^{e}-* [1]
close relative, 1457, *gāʾal*[1] [1]
close to death, 1588, *gāwaʿ* [1]
stayed close, 1815, *dābaq* [1]
close friends, 3359, *yādaʿ* [1]
close friend, 3359, *yādaʿ* [1]
pressed close, 4315, *lāḥaṣ* [1]
went close, 5602, *nāgaš* [1]
close up, 6258, *sātam* [1]
close, 6623+6623, *ʿālam+ʿālam* [1]
close, 6623, *ʿālam* [1]
close, 6660, *ʿāmît* [1]
close up, 6806, *ʿāṣar* [1]
brought to a close, 7928, *qārab* [1]
close at hand, 7940, *qārôb* [1]
close relative, 7940, *qārôb* [1]
close to heart, 7940, *qārôb* [1]
close to, 7940+725, *qārôb+ʾēṣel*[1] [1]
pay close attention, 7992+2256+9048,
qāšab+w^{e}-+šāmaʿ [1]
comes close, 8193, *rîaḥ* [1]
one who is close, 8291, *rēʿeh* [1]
close relative, 8638+1414, *šeʾēr+bāśār* [1]
close relative, 8638+7940, *šeʾēr+qārôb* [1]
close relatives, 8640, *šaʾarâ* [1]
close, 8883, *šît*[1] [1]
keep close watch on, 9068, *šāmar* [1]
keeps close watch, 9068, *šāmar* [1]
close, 9129, *šāʿaʿ*[1] [1]

CLOSE-KNIT [1]
close-knit, 8571, *śārag* [1]

CLOSED [16]
closed up, 6037, *sāgar* [2]
closed, 6037, *sāgar* [2]
closed, *NIH/RPE* [1]
closed, 4059, *kāsâ* [1]
are closed, 6037, *sāgar* [1]
closed in, 6037, *sāgar* [1]
been closed, 6126, *sākar*[1] [1]
being closed, 6258, *sātam* [1]
closed up, 6258, *sātam* [1]
closed up, 6806+6806, *ʿāṣar+ʿāṣar* [1]
closed, 6888, *ʿārēl* [1]
closed, 7429, *ṣûp*[1] [1]
closed, 7621, *ṣāpan* [1]
closed, 9129, *šāʿaʿ*[1] [1]

CLOSELY [12]
closely, 4394, *m^{e}ʾōd* [2]
closely followed, 296, *ʾāḥaz*[1] [1]
listen closely, 928+265+9048,
b^{e}-+ʾōzen+šāmaʿ [1]
looked closely, 1067, *bîn* [1]
is closely compacted, 2489, *ḥābar*[2] [1]
listen closely, 5742+265, *nāṭâ+ʾōzen* [1]
closely associated, 7940, *qārôb* [1]
closely related, 7940, *qārôb* [1]
closely bound up, 8003, *qāšar* [1]
watched closely, 8617, *šāʿâ*[3] [1]
questioned closely, 8626+8626, *šāʾal+šāʾal* [1]

CLOSER [6]
closer and closer, 2143+2256+7929,
hālak+w^{e}-+qārēb [2]
sticks closer, 1816, *dābēq* [1]
closer, 7928, *qārab* [1]
come closer, 7928, *qārab* [1]
closer, 7929, *qārēb* [1]

CLOSES [1]
closes, 6623, *ʿālam* [1]

CLOSEST [4]
closest friends, 3359, *yādaʿ* [1]
closest friend, 3359, *yādaʿ* [1]
closest, 7940, *qārôb* [1]
closest friend, 8276+889+3869+5883+3870,
rēaʿ[2]*+ʾ^{a}šer+k^{e}-+nepeš+-kā* [1]

CLOSING [4]
kept from closing, 296+9073, *ʾāḥaz*[1]*+š^{e}murâ* [1]
closing in from every side, 2539, *ḥādar* [1]
closing in, 6496, *ʿāṭar*[1] [1]
closing assembly, 6809, *ʿ^{a}ṣārâ* [1]

CLOTH [16]
cloth, 955, *beged*[2] [8]
cloth, 8529, *śimlâ* [2]
blue cloth, 9418, *t^{e}kēlet* [2]
menstrual cloth, 1865, *dāweh* [1]
thick cloth, 4802, *makbēr* [1]
embroidered cloth, 8391, *riqmâ* [1]
workers in cloth, 9271, *šātâ*[1] [1]

CLOTHE [13]
clothe, 4252, *lābaš* [10]
clothe, *NIH/RPE* [1]
clothe, 4059, *kāsâ* [1]
clothe, 6493+8884, *ʿāṭap*[1]*+šît*[2] [1]

CLOTHED [37]
clothed, 4252, *lābaš* [15]
clothed, 4229, *lābûš* [7]
clothed, 4230, *l^{e}bûš* [3]
clothed, 10383, *l^{e}baš* [3]
clothed, 4059, *kāsâ* [2]
clothed, 273, *ʾāzar* [1]
clothed, 955, *beged*[2] [1]
clothed, 2520, *ḥāgar* [1]
was clothed, 4124, *kirbēl* [1]
clothed, 4252+955, *lābaš+beged*[2] [1]
clothed with, 5951, *nāśāʾ* [1]
clothed with gloom, 7722, *qādar* [1]

CLOTHES [118]
clothes, 955, *beged*[2] [79]
clothes, 8529, *śimlâ* [12]
clothes, 8515, *śalmâ*[1] [5]
clothes, 4860, *malbûš* [3]
clothes, 4230, *l^{e}bûš* [2]
clothes, 4496, *mad* [2]
clothes, 4874, *melaḥ*[1] [2]
clothes, *NIH/RPE* [1]
clothes, 2722, *ḥ^{a}lîpâ* [1]
clothes, 4053, *kānāp* [1]
clothes, 4252, *lābaš* [1]
provided with clothes, 4252, *lābaš* [1]
put clothes on, 4252, *lābaš* [1]

put on clothes, 4252, *lābaš* [1]
wear clothes, 4252, *lābaš* [1]
clothes, 4833, *m^{e}kasseh* [1]
clothes, 6886+955, *'ērek+beged*[2] [1]
strip off clothes, 7320+2256+6910, *pāšaṭ+w^{e}-+'ārar* [1]
best clothes, 8529, *śimlâ* [1]
clothes, 10382, *l^{e}bûš* [1]

CLOTHING [44]
clothing, 955, *beged*[2] [23]
clothing, 8529, *śimlâ* [7]
clothing, 4230, *l^{e}bûš* [5]
articles of clothing, 955, *beged*[2] [1]
clothing, 3998, *k^{e}lî* [1]
clothing, 4064, *k^{e}sût* [1]
put on as clothing, 4252, *lābaš* [1]
clothing, 4496, *mad* [1]
clothing, 4860, *malbûš* [1]
fine clothing, 7345, *p^{e}tîgîl* [1]
clothing, 8515, *śalmâ*[1] [1]
clothing, 10382, *l^{e}bûš* [1]

CLOTHS [1]
wrapped in cloths, 3156+3156, *ḥātal+ḥātal* [1]

CLOUD [78]
cloud, 6727, *'ānān*[1] [63]
cloud, 6265, *'āb*[2] [7]
dark cloud, 6906, *'^{a}rāpel* [2]
cloud, *NIH/RPE* [1]
the clouds[s], 2257, *-ô* [1]
cloud, 5368, *maś'ēt* [1]
covered with the cloud, 6380, *'ûb* [1]
cloud, 6729, *'^{a}nānâ* [1]
cloud of smoke, 6940, *'āšān*[1] [1]

CLOUDBURST [1]
cloudburst, 5881, *nepeṣ* [1]

CLOUDLESS [1]
cloudless, 4202+6265, *lō'+'āb*[2] [1]

CLOUDS [60]
clouds, 6265, *'āb*[2] [19]
clouds, 6727, *'ānān*[1] [17]
clouds, 8836, *šaḥaq* [8]
clouds, 5955, *nāśî'*[2] [4]
clouds of the sky, 6265+8836, *'āb*[2]*+šaḥaq* [2]
dark clouds, 6906, *'^{a}rāpel* [2]
the clouds[s], 2084, *-hû* [1]
storm clouds, 2613, *ḥ^{a}zîz* [1]
clouds of smoke, 5366, *maśśā'â* [1]
thick clouds, 6265, *'āb*[2] [1]
bring clouds, 6725+6727, *'ānan*[1]*+'ānān*[1] [1]
clouds, 6882, *'^{a}rîpîm* [1]
clouds, 7798, *qîṭôr* [1]
clouds, 10560, *'^{a}nān* [1]

CLUB [8]
club, 4751, *maṭṭeh* [3]
club, 8657, *šēbeṭ* [2]
club, 5138, *mēpîṣ* [1]
war club, 5151, *mappēṣ* [1]
club, 9371, *tôtāḥ* [1]

CLUBS [1]
war clubs, 5234+3338, *maqqēl+yād* [1]

CLUNG [3]
clung, 1815, *dābaq* [2]
clung to, 928, *b^{e}-* [1]

CLUSTER [5]
cluster of grapes, 864, *'eškôl*[1] [3]
cluster, 864, *'eškôl*[1] [2]

CLUSTERS [4]
clusters, 864, *'eškôl*[1] [3]
clusters of fruit, 864, *'eškôl*[1] [1]

CLUTCHES [4]
clutches, 3338, *yād* [3]
clutches, 4090, *kap* [1]

COAL [2]
burning coal, 1625, *gaḥelet* [1]
live coal, 8365, *riṣpâ*[1] [1]

COALS [19]
coals, 1624, *gaḥal* [6]
burning coals, 1624, *gaḥal* [5]
coals, 7073, *peḥām* [3]
coals, 836, *'ēš*[1] [2]
hot coals, 1624, *gaḥal* [1]
coals, 1625, *gaḥelet* [1]
baked over hot coals, 8363, *reṣep*[1] [1]

COAST [10]
coast, 2572+3542, *ḥôp+yām* [4]
coast, 3542, *yām* [2]
coast, 362, *'î*[1] [1]
coast, 1473, *g^{e}bûl* [1]
coast, 2572, *ḥôp* [1]
coast, 8557+3542, *śāpâ+yām* [1]

COASTLANDS [9]
coastlands, 362, *'î*[1] [8]
western coastlands, 4183, *kittiyyîm* [1]

COASTLINE [2]
coastline, 1473, *g^{e}bûl* [2]

COASTS [5]
coasts, 362, *'î*[1] [5]

COAT [6]
coat, 8486, *šîd*[1] [2]
coat, 4106, *kāpar*[2] [1]
coat, 4230, *l^{e}bûš* [1]
coat of armor, 9234, *širyôn* [1]
coat of scale armor, 9234+7989, *širyôn+qaśqeśet* [1]

COATED [1]
coated, 2814, *ḥāmar*[3] [1]

COATING [1]
coating, 7596, *ṣāpâ*[2] [1]

COATS [1]
coats of armor, 9234, *širyôn* [1]

COAX [1]
coax, 7331, *pātâ*[1] [1]

COBRA [3]
cobra, 7352, *peten* [3]

COBRAS [1]
cobras, 7352, *peten* [1]

COBWEBS [1]
cobwebs, 7770, *qûr*[2] [1]

COCOON [1]
moth's cocoon, 6931, *'āš*[1] [1]

COFFIN [1]
coffin, 778, *'^{a}rôn* [1]

COHORTS [1]
cohorts, 6468, *'āzar* [1]

COILED [2]
coiled around, 6015, *sābab* [2]

COILING [1]
coiling, 6825, *'^{a}qallātôn* [1]

COL-HOZEH [2]
Col-Hozeh, 3997, *kol-ḥōzeh* [2]

COLD [8]
cold, 7938, *qārâ*[2] [5]
cold, 7922, *qar* [1]
cold, 7923, *qōr* [1]
cold, 7943, *qeraḥ* [1]

COLLAPSE [3]
collapse, 3655, *yāṣā'* [1]
collapse, 5877, *nāpal* [1]
collapse, 8820, *šāḥaḥ* [1]

COLLAPSED [5]
collapsed, 5877, *nāpal* [4]
collapsed, 8820, *šāḥaḥ* [1]

COLLAPSES [3]
collapses, 995+8691, *bô'+šeber*[1] [1]
collapses, 4570, *mûg* [1]
collapses, 5877, *nāpal* [1]

COLLAR [3]
collar, 7023+9389, *peh+taḥrā'* [1]
collar, 7023, *peh* [1]
collar, 9389, *taḥrā'* [1]

COLLECT [7]
collect, 4374, *lāqaḥ* [2]
collect, 7695, *qābaṣ* [2]
collect, *NIH/RPE* [1]
collect, 1024, *bāzaz* [1]
collect tithes, 6923, *'āśar* [1]

COLLECTED [11]
collected, 665, *'āsap* [3]
collected, 4374, *lāqaḥ* [3]
collected, *AIT* [1]
be collected, 665, *'āsap* [1]
collected sayings, 1251+670, *ba'al*[1]*+'^{a}suppâ* [1]
collected, 4377, *lāqaṭ* [1]
collected, 7695, *qābaṣ* [1]

COLLECTING [1]
collecting, 5224, *miqweh*[2] [1]

COLLECTION [1]
collection, 7689, *qibbûṣ* [1]

COLLECTOR [1]
tax collector, 5601, *nāgaś* [1]

COLONNADE [1]
colonnade, 395+6647, *'êlām+'ammûd* [1]

COLORED [1]
colored, 2635, *ḥ^{a}ṭubôt* [1]

COLORFUL [2]
colorful garments, 7389, *ṣeba'* [2]

COLORS [2]
varied colors, 8391, *riqmâ* [1]
various colors, 8391, *riqmâ* [1]

COLT [3]
colt, 6555, *'ayir* [2]
colt, 1201+912, *bēn*[1]*+'ātôn* [1]

COLUMN [3]
column, 1455, *gē'ût* [1]
column, 6647, *'ammûd* [1]
column, 9406, *tîmārâ* [1]

COLUMNS [5]
columns, 6647, *'ammûd* [2]
columns, 1946, *delet* [1]
columns, 4117, *kaptôr*[2] [1]
front columns, 7156, *pāneh* [1]

COMB [2]
honey from the comb, 5885, *nōpet* [1]
comb, 7430, *ṣûp*[2] [1]

COMBED [1]
combed, 8591, *śārîq* [1]

COME [1020]
come, 995, *bô'* [374]
come, 2143, *hālak* [94]
come, *NIH/RPE* [52]
come out, 3655, *yāṣā'* [39]
generations to come, 1887, *dôr*[2] [37]
come down, 3718, *yārad* [28]
come, 2118, *hāyâ* [26]
come up, 6590, *'ālâ* [23]
come back, 8740, *šûb*[1] [23]
come, 3655, *yāṣā'* [21]
come, 6590, *'ālâ* [13]
come in, 995, *bô'* [12]
come near, 5602, *nāgaš* [11]
come near, 7928, *qārab* [11]
come, 7756, *qûm* [9]
come, 7928, *qārab* [9]
to come, 344, *'aḥ^{a}rît* [8]

come, 910, ʾātâ [7]
come quickly, 2590, ḥûš[1] [7]
come upon, 5162, māṣāʾ [7]
come, *AIT* [6]
come, 2035, hab[1] [5]
come, 6296, ʿābar[1] [5]
come in peace, 8934, šālôm [5]
come, 2098, hôy [4]
come, 5595, nāgaʿ [4]
come, 5602, nāgaš [4]
come before, 7709, qādam [4]
come to nothing, 6, ʾābad [3]
come, 3718, yārad [3]
come over, 6296, ʿābar[1] [3]
come now, 6964+5528, ʿattâ+nāʾ[1] [3]
come, 7212, pāqad [3]
surely come to aid, 7212+7212, pāqad+pāqad [3]
come forward, 7928, qārab [3]
had come forward, 7928, qārab [3]
come to an end, 8697, šābat[1] [3]
to come, 340, ʾaḥarôn [2]
come true, 586, ʾāman[1] [2]
certainly come, 995+995, bôʾ+bôʾ [2]
come into, 995, bôʾ [2]
come true, 995, bôʾ [2]
come what may, 2118+4537, hāyâ+mâ [2]
come to life, 2649, ḥāyâ [2]
come trembling, 3006, ḥārad [2]
come forth, 3655, yāṣāʾ [2]
come up, 3655, yāṣāʾ [2]
come to an end, 3983, kālâ[1] [2]
come here, 5602, nāgaš [2]
come close, 5602, nāgaš [2]
come forward, 5602, nāgaš [2]
come in, 6073, sûr[1] [2]
come, 6073, sûr[1] [2]
come to, 6330, ʿad[2] [2]
come together, 7695, qābaṣ [2]
come to meet, 7709, qādam [2]
come upon, 7925, qārāʾ[2] [2]
come here, 7928, qārab [2]
come, 8740, šûb[1] [2]
come to bed with, 8886+6640, šākab+ʿim [2]
come, 10085, ʾatâ [2]
come to ruin, 6, ʾābad [1]
time to come, 294, ʾāḥôr [1]
yet to come, 340, ʾaḥarôn [1]
come to an end, 699, ʾāpēs [1]
come forward, 910, ʾātâ [1]
things to come, 910, ʾātâ [1]
actually come, 995+995, bôʾ+bôʾ [1]
caused to come, 995, bôʾ [1]
come back, 995, bôʾ [1]
come home, 995, bôʾ [1]
come on, 995, bôʾ [1]
come to rest, 995, bôʾ [1]
come away, 1368, bāraḥ[1] [1]
word come, 1655, gālâ [1]
come rolling in, 1670, gālal[1] [1]
generations to come, 1887+2256+1887, dôr[2]+we-+dôr[2] [1]
to come, 1887+2256+1887, dôr[2]+we-+dôr[2] [1]
come, 2005, dārak [1]
certainly come true, 2118+2118, hāyâ+hāyâ [1]
come into being, 2118+2118, hāyâ+hāyâ [1]
come then, 2180, hinnēh [1]
come, 2180, hinnēh [1]
come trembling, 2520, ḥāgar [1]
come, 2616, ḥāzaq [1]
come to an end, 2951, ḥāṣaṣ[1] [1]
come trembling, 3004, ḥārag [1]
come to, 3359, yādaʿ [1]
made come out, 3655, yāṣāʾ [1]
makes come up, 3655, yāṣāʾ [1]
surely come out, 3655+3655, yāṣāʾ+yāṣāʾ [1]
come cringing, 3950, kāḥaš [1]
still to come, 4202+6913, lōʾ+ʿāśâ[1] [1]
come to ruin, 4231, lābaṭ [1]
have come, 4374, lāqaḥ [1]
come back, 4374, lāqaḥ [1]
come quickly, 4554+4394, māhar[1]+meʾōd [1]
come quickly, 4554, māhar[1] [1]
symbolic of things to come, 4603, môpēt [1]
days to come, 4737, māḥār [1]
come to an end, 4848, mālēʾ[1] [1]
come, 4848, mālēʾ[1] [1]
come down, 5737, nāḥat [1]
come, 5737, nāḥat [1]
come into, 5877+928, nāpal+be- [1]
come over, 5877, nāpal [1]
made come down, 5877, nāpal [1]
surely come to ruin, 5877+5877, nāpal+nāpal [1]
come to rescue, 5911, nāṣal [1]
come over, 6073, sûr[1] [1]
made come off, 6073, sûr[1] [1]
yet to come, 6388, ʿôd [1]
to come, 6409, ʿôlām [1]
come back, 6590, ʿālâ [1]
had come up, 6590, ʿālâ [1]
made come up, 6590, ʿālâ [1]
make come up, 6590, ʿālâ [1]
make come, 6590, ʿālâ [1]
come forward, 6641, ʿāmad [1]
come, 6641, ʿāmad [1]
come to relief, 6699, ʿānâ[1] [1]
come to aid, 6842, ʿārab[1] [1]
come across, 7003, pāgaʿ [1]
come to the help of, 7003, pāgaʿ [1]
come trembling, 7064, pāḥad [1]
come to aid, 7212, pāqad [1]
come to the aid of, 7212, pāqad [1]
fails to come, 7212, pāqad [1]
punishments come, 7212, pāqad [1]
come in power, 7502, ṣālaḥ[1] [1]
come and join, 7695, qābaṣ [1]
come, 7709, qādam [1]
come on, 7756, qûm [1]
arise and come, 7756, qûm [1]
come forward, 7756, qûm [1]
come out, 7756, qûm [1]
come to life, 7810, qîṣ [1]
come across, 7925+4200+7156, qārāʾ[2]+le-[1]+pāneh [1]
come, 7925, qārāʾ[2] [1]
cause to come near, 7928, qārab [1]
come closer, 7928, qārab [1]
have come near, 7928, qārab [1]
come near, 7932, qirbâ [1]
come true, 7936, qārâ[1] [1]
come, 7936, qārâ[1] [1]
come near, 7940, qārôb [1]
come into presence, 8011+906+7156, rāʾâ[1]+ʾēt[1]+pāneh [1]
come into view, 8011, rāʾâ[1] [1]
come trembling, 8074, rāgaz [1]
relief come, 8118, rāwaḥ [1]
come to ruin, 8318, rāʿaʿ[2] [1]
come to dwell, 8905, šākan [1]
come back, 8938, šālaḥ [1]
come down, 9164, šāpēl[1] [1]
to come, 10022, ʾaḥarî [1]
to come, 10201+10021+10180, hawâ+ʾaḥar+denâ [1]
come out, 10485, nepaq [1]
come, 10624, qûm [1]

COMES [169]

comes, 995, bôʾ [67]
comes, *NIH/RPE* [37]
comes, 2118, hāyâ [8]
comes, 3655, yāṣāʾ [7]
comes out, 3655, yāṣāʾ [5]
comes true, 995, bôʾ [3]
comes down, 3718, yārad [3]
comes to nothing, 6, ʾābad [2]
comes, 910, ʾātâ [2]
comes to ruin, 4231, lābaṭ [2]
comes, 6296, ʿābar[1] [2]
comes by, 995, bôʾ [1]
comes in, 995, bôʾ [1]
comes true, 995+995, bôʾ+bôʾ [1]
comes, 995+995, bôʾ+bôʾ [1]
comes looking for, 2011, dāraš [1]
comes of, 2118, hāyâ [1]
comes, 2143, hālak [1]
comes along, 2736, ḥālap[1] [1]
out comes, 3655, yāṣāʾ [1]
word that comes from, 4604, môṣāʾ[1] [1]
comes, 5162, māṣāʾ [1]
comes to rest, 5663, nûaḥ[1] [1]
comes out, 6590, ʿālâ [1]
comes, 6590, ʿālâ [1]
comes, 6913, ʿāśâ[1] [1]
comes, 7008, pāgaš [1]
all that comes out, 7368, ṣeʾeṣāʾîm [1]
that comes out, 7368, ṣeʾeṣāʾîm [1]
comes before, 7709, qādam [1]
comes easily, 7837, qālal [1]
comes, 7925, qārāʾ[2] [1]
comes near, 7928, qārab [1]
comes, 7928, qārab [1]
comes near, 7929, qārēb [1]
even comes near, 7929+7929, qārēb+qārēb [1]
comes, 7936, qārâ[1] [1]
comes close, 8193, rîaḥ [1]
comes roar, 8613, šāʾag [1]
comes, 8801, šûr[2] [1]
comes, 9311, tebûʾâ [1]
crop comes in, 9311, tebûʾâ [1]

COMFORT [33]

comfort, 5714, nāḥam [23]
give comfort, 5714, nāḥam [2]
comfort, 5653, nûd [1]
find comfort, 5714, nāḥam [1]
given comfort, 5714, nāḥam [1]
giving comfort, 5714, nāḥam [1]
comfort, 5717, neḥāmâ [1]
comfort, 5719, niḥumîm [1]
comfort, 5739, naḥat[2] [1]
comfort, 5764, nîd [1]

COMFORTED [11]

comforted, 5714, nāḥam [5]
be comforted, 5714, nāḥam [4]
comforted, 5653, nûd [1]
was comforted, 5714, nāḥam [1]

COMFORTER [3]

comforter, 5714, nāḥam [2]
Comforter, 4443, mablîgît [1]

COMFORTERS [2]

comforters, 5714, nāḥam [2]

COMFORTING [2]

comforting, 5719, niḥumîm [1]
comforting, 9488, tanḥûmîm [1]

COMFORTS [4]

comforts, 5714, nāḥam [4]

COMING [127]

coming, 995, bôʾ [71]
coming up, 6590, ʿālâ [9]
coming out, 3655, yāṣāʾ [8]
coming down, 3718, yārad [6]
coming, *NIH/RPE* [4]
coming, 2143, hālak [4]
coming, 3655, yāṣāʾ [4]
coming, 2118, hāyâ [3]
coming back, 8740, šûb[1] [2]
coming down, 10474, neḥat [2]
coming, 910, ʾātâ [1]
kept coming, 2143+2143, hālak+hālak [1]
the coming storm[s], 2257, -ô [1]
coming to an agreement, 2489, ḥābar[2] [1]
coming forth, 3655, yāṣāʾ [1]
coming quickly, 4554+4394, māhar[1]+meʾōd [1]
coming down, 5738, naḥat[1] [1]
coming around, 6015, sābab [1]
coming over, 6296, ʿābar[1] [1]
coming, 6296, ʿābar[1] [1]
coming out, 6590, ʿālâ [1]
coming, 6590, ʿālâ [1]
coming, 10085, ʾatâ [1]
coming out, 10485, nepaq [1]

COMMAND [148]

command, 7422, ṣāwâ [45]
command, 7023, peh [39]
command, 1821, dābār [11]
command, 5184, miṣwâ [11]
command, 3338, yād [6]

gave command, 7422, *ṣāwâ* [5]
in command, 6584+7372, *'al^{2}+ṣābā'^{2}* [4]
give command, 7422, *ṣāwâ* [4]
command, 10042, *'^{a}mar* [3]
command, 606, *'āmar^{1}* [2]
command, 8569, *śar* [2]
command, 10418, *millâ* [2]
command, *NIH/RPE* [1]
under the command of, 339, *'aḥar* [1]
command, 614, *'imrâ* [1]
command, 2017, *dāt* [1]
take command, 2118+4200+5464, *hāyâ+l^{e-1}+mišmār^{1}* [1]
command, 4411, *ma'^{a}mār* [1]
give command, 7337+7023, *pātaḥ^{1}+peh* [1]
given a command, 7422, *ṣāwâ* [1]
given the command, 7422, *ṣāwâ* [1]
puts in command, 7422, *ṣāwâ* [1]
command, 7754, *qôl* [1]
command, 8031, *rō'š^{1}* [1]
second in command, 9108, *šēnî* [1]
command, 10302, *ṭ^{e}'ēm^{2}* [1]

COMMANDED [249]
commanded, 7422, *ṣāwâ* [210]
commanded, 606, *'āmar^{1}* [13]
commanded, 1821, *dābār* [4]
commanded, 5184, *miṣwâ* [4]
commanded, 7023, *peh* [4]
been commanded, 7422, *ṣāwâ* [4]
was commanded, 7422, *ṣāwâ* [3]
commanded, 5184+7422, *miṣwâ+ṣāwâ* [2]
commanded, 10042, *'^{a}mar* [2]
commanded, 1819, *dābar^{2}* [1]
commanded, 3338, *yād* [1]
commanded, 10682+10302, *śîm+ṭ^{e}'ēm^{2}* [1]

COMMANDER [86]
commander, 8569, *śar* [36]
commander, 8042, *rab^{2}* [23]
field commander, 8072, *rab-šāqēh* [12]
commander, 7903, *qāṣîn* [4]
commander, 8072, *rab-šāqēh* [4]
supreme commander, 9580, *tartān* [2]
commander, *NIH/RPE* [1]
commander, 3261, *ṭipsār* [1]
commander in chief, 6584+2021+7372, *'al^{2}+ha–+ṣābā'^{2}* [1]
commander, 7422, *ṣāwâ* [1]
commander, 10647, *rab* [1]

COMMANDER'S [1]
commander's, 6221, *sōpēr* [1]

COMMANDER-IN-CHIEF [1]
commander-in-chief, 8031+2256+8569, *rō'š^{1}+w^{e}-+śar* [1]

COMMANDERS [87]
commanders, 8569, *śar* [74]
commanders, *NIH/RPE* [6]
commanders, 6036, *segen* [3]
commanders, 5592, *nāgîd* [1]
commanders, 7903, *qāṣîn* [1]
commanders, 8031, *rō'š^{1}* [1]
commanders, 8569+7372, *śar+ṣābā'^{2}* [1]

COMMANDING [4]
commanding officer, 10116+10302, *b^{e}'ēl+ṭ^{e}'ēm^{2}* [3]
commanding, 7422, *ṣāwâ* [1]

COMMANDMENT [1]
commandment, 5184, *miṣwâ* [1]

COMMANDMENTS [9]
commandments, 1821, *dābār* [6]
commandments, 5184, *miṣwâ* [3]

COMMANDS [164]
commands, 5184, *miṣwâ* [138]
commands, 7422, *ṣāwâ* [13]
commands, 1821, *dābār* [3]
commands, 606, *'āmar^{1}* [2]
commands, 5477, *mišpāṭ* [2]
commands, 7023, *peh* [2]
commands, *NIH/RPE* [1]
commands, 5226, *māqôm* [1]
gave commands, 7422, *ṣāwâ* [1]
give commands, 7422, *ṣāwâ* [1]

COMMEMORATE [4]
commemorate, 606, *'āmar^{1}* [1]
commemorate, 2349, *zākar^{1}* [1]
commemorate, 2355, *zikkārôn* [1]
commemorate, 9480, *tānâ^{2}* [1]

COMMEMORATED [1]
commemorated, 2355, *zikkārôn* [1]

COMMEND [2]
commend, 8655, *šābaḥ^{1}* [2]

COMMENDED [2]
commended, 1385, *bārak^{2}* [1]
commended, 6386, *'ûd^{1}* [1]

COMMENDS [1]
commends, 3512, *yāṭab* [1]

COMMISSION [3]
commission, 7422, *ṣāwâ* [3]

COMMISSIONED [1]
commissioned, 7422, *ṣāwâ* [1]

COMMISSIONERS [2]
commissioners, 7224, *pāqîd* [2]

COMMIT [40]
caused to commit, 2627, *ḥāṭā'* [20]
commit adultery, 5537, *nā'ap* [7]
commit robbery, 1611+1608, *g^{e}zēlâ+gāzal* [2]
commit, 1670, *gālal^{1}* [2]
commit, *AIT* [1]
commit robbery, 1608+1610, *gāzal+gāzēl* [1]
commit, 2143+928, *hālak+b^{e}-* [1]
commit adultery, 2388, *zānâ^{1}* [1]
commit a sin, 2627, *ḥāṭā'* [1]
commit, 2627, *ḥāṭā'* [1]
commit, 3922, *kûn^{1}* [1]
commit, 6913, *'āśâ^{1}* [1]
commit, 7212, *pāqad* [1]

COMMITS [13]
commits, 6913, *'āśâ^{1}* [5]
commits adultery, 5537, *nā'ap* [2]
commits, *NIH/RPE* [1]
commits robbery, 1611+1608, *g^{e}zēlâ+gāzal* [1]
commits sin, 2627, *ḥāṭā'* [1]
commits himself, 3656, *yāṣab* [1]
commits a violation, 5085+5086, *mā'al+ma'al^{1}* [1]
commits, 6440, *'āzab^{1}* [1]

COMMITTED [70]
committed, 2627, *ḥāṭā'* [23]
committed, 6913, *'āśâ^{1}* [14]
committed adultery, 5537, *nā'ap* [5]
fully committed, 8969, *šālēm^{2}* [4]
committed, *NIH/RPE* [2]
committed, 1655, *gālâ* [2]
committed adultery, 2388, *zānâ^{1}* [2]
committed, 7321, *pāša'* [2]
committed, *AIT* [1]
committed adultery with, 995+448, *bô'+'el* [1]
committed, 1694, *gāmal* [1]
committed, 2118, *hāyâ* [1]
was committed, 2118, *hāyâ* [1]
committed, 2143+928, *hālak+b^{e}-* [1]
a sin committed, 2627+2631, *ḥāṭā'+ḥ^{a}ṭā'â* [1]
committed a sin, 2627+2631, *ḥāṭā'+ḥ^{a}ṭā'â* [1]
crime committed, 2627, *ḥāṭā'* [1]
committed, 2628+2627, *ḥēṭ'+ḥāṭā'* [1]
committed, 4200, *l^{e-1}* [1]
been committed, 5989, *nātan* [1]
committed, 5989, *nātan* [1]
been committed, 6913, *'āśâ^{1}* [1]
wrong committed unintentionally, 8705+8704, *š^{e}gāgâ+šāgag* [1]
committed, 8966, *šālēm^{1}* [1]

COMMITTING [1]
committing, 6913, *'āśâ^{1}* [1]

COMMON [19]
common, 2687, *ḥōl* [4]
common, 285, *'eḥād* [3]
as common as, 3869, *k^{e}-* [3]
common people, 1201+6639, *bēn^{1}+'am^{2}* [2]
have in common, 4200, *l^{e-1}* [2]
have in common, 7008, *pāgaš* [2]
common, *AIT* [1]
common use, 2687, *ḥōl* [1]
common people, 6639, *'am^{2}* [1]

COMMOTION [4]
commotion, 2162, *hāmôn* [2]
commotion, 8323, *ra'aš* [1]
commotion, 9583, *t^{e}šu'â* [1]

COMMUNITIES [2]
communities of captives, 1661, *gālût* [1]
communities, 1661, *gālût* [1]

COMMUNITY [85]
community, 6337, *'ēdâ^{1}* [69]
community, 7736, *qāhāl* [13]
community, 824, *'ereṣ* [2]
community, 6639+2021+824, *'am^{2}+ha–+'ereṣ* [1]

COMMUNITY'S [1]
community's, 6337, *'ēdâ^{1}* [1]

COMPACT [3]
compact, 1382, *b^{e}rît* [3]

COMPACTED [1]
is closely compacted, 2489, *ḥābar^{2}* [1]

COMPANIES [8]
companies, 8031, *rō'š^{1}* [6]
companies, *NIH/RPE* [1]
companies, 3338, *yād* [1]

COMPANION [7]
companion, 8287, *rā'â^{2}* [3]
companion, 8276, *rēa'^{2}* [2]
companion, 476, *'allûp^{1}* [1]
my companion^{s}, 2257, *-ô* [1]

COMPANIONS [8]
companions, 8276, *rēa'^{2}* [3]
companions, 2492, *ḥābēr* [2]
companions, 278, *'āḥ^{2}* [1]
companions, 5335, *mērēa'^{1}* [1]
companions, 8292, *rē'â* [1]

COMPANY [29]
company, 1201, *bēn^{1}* [9]
company, 7736, *qāhāl* [5]
company, 6337, *'ēdâ^{1}* [2]
in company with, 6640, *'im* [2]
company, *AIT* [1]
keeps company, 782+4200+2495, *'āraḥ^{1}+l^{e-1}+ḥebrâ* [1]
company, 1887, *dôr^{2}* [1]
company, 2118+907, *hāyâ+'ēt^{2}* [1]
company, 2657, *ḥayil* [1]
company, 4722, *maḥ^{a}neh* [1]
company, 6051, *sôd* [1]
part company, 7233, *pārad* [1]
parted company, 7233, *pārad* [1]
company, 7372, *ṣābā'^{2}* [1]
company, 8031, *rō'š^{1}* [1]

COMPARE [14]
compare, 1948, *dāmâ^{1}* [4]
compare, 6885, *'ārak* [3]
compare, 8750, *šāwâ^{1}* [2]
compare, *NIH/RPE* [1]
compare with, 2118+3869, *hāyâ+k^{e}-* [1]
compare with, 3869, *k^{e}-* [1]
compare with, 6885, *'ārak* [1]
compare, 8011, *rā'â^{1}* [1]

COMPARED [5]
compared, 1948, *dāmâ^{1}* [3]
compared to, 3869, *k^{e}-* [2]

COMPASSES [1]
compasses, 4684, *meḥûgâ* [1]

COMPASSION [63]
compassion, 8171, *raḥamîm* [18]
have compassion, 8163, *rāḥam* [15]
compassion, 8163, *rāḥam* [4]
has compassion, 8163, *rāḥam* [4]
have compassion, 5714, *nāḥam* [3]
show compassion, 8163, *rāḥam* [3]
compassion, 5714, *nāḥam* [2]
look with compassion, 2571+6524, *ḥûs+ʿayin*[1] [1]
compassion, 2798, *ḥāmal* [1]
had compassion, 2798, *ḥāmal* [1]
in compassion spares, 2798, *ḥāmal* [1]
had compassion, 5714, *nāḥam* [1]
look with compassion, 5714, *nāḥam* [1]
show compassion, 5714, *nāḥam* [1]
compassion, 5716, *nōḥam* [1]
compassion, 5719, *niḥumîm* [1]
find compassion, 8163, *rāḥam* [1]
full of compassion, 8163, *rāḥam* [1]
had compassion, 8163, *rāḥam* [1]
have great compassion, 8163+8163, *rāḥam+rāḥam* [1]
have no compassion, 8317+6524, *rāʿaʿ*[1]*+ʿayin*[1] [1]

COMPASSIONATE [12]
compassionate, 8157, *raḥûm* [10]
compassionate, 2843, *ḥannûn* [1]
compassionate, 8172, *raḥamānî* [1]

COMPASSIONS [1]
compassions, 8171, *raḥamîm* [1]

COMPELLED [2]
felt compelled, 706, *ʾāpaq* [1]
compelled, 10264, *ḥayil* [1]

COMPELS [2]
compels, 928, *be-* [1]
compels, 7439, *ṣûq*[1] [1]

COMPENSATE [2]
to compensate for, 9393, *taḥat*[1] [2]

COMPENSATION [1]
compensation, 4111, *kōper*[4] [1]

COMPETE [1]
compete, 3013, *ḥārâ*[1] [1]

COMPLACENCY [2]
complacency, 1055, *beṭaḥ*[1] [1]
complacency, 8932, *šalwâ* [1]

COMPLACENT [4]
complacent, 8633, *šaʾanān* [3]
complacent, 7884, *qāpāʾ* [1]

COMPLAIN [7]
complain, 8189, *rîb*[1] [2]
complain, 606, *ʾāmar*[1] [1]
complain, 645, *ʾānan* [1]
complain, 1819, *dābar*[2] [1]
complain, 8087, *rāgan* [1]
complain, 8488, *śîaḥ*[1] [1]

COMPLAINED [2]
complained, 645, *ʾānan* [1]
complained, 3519, *yākaḥ* [1]

COMPLAINT [10]
complaint, 8490, *śîaḥ*[3] [7]
complaint, 8190, *rîb*[2] [2]
complaint, 9350, *tôkaḥat* [1]

COMPLAINTS [2]
complaints, 8490, *śîaḥ*[3] [1]
complaints, 9442, *telunnôt* [1]

COMPLETE [6]
complete, 3983, *kālâ*[1] [2]
complete, 421, *ʾak* [1]
complete honesty, 575, *ʾemûnâ* [1]
complete, 1298, *bāṣaʿ* [1]
complete, 4946+7891+2118, *min+qēṣ+hāyâ* [1]

COMPLETED [17]
completed, 3983, *kālâ*[1] [6]
completed, 4848, *mālēʾ*[1] [5]
completed, 9462, *tāmam* [2]
were completed, 3983, *kālâ*[1] [1]
be completed, 6913, *ʿāśâ*[1] [1]
completed, 8966, *šālēm*[1] [1]
completed, 10707, *šēṣîʾ* [1]

COMPLETELY [79]
completely destroyed, 3049, *ḥāram*[1] [6]
completely destroy, 3049, *ḥāram*[1] [5]
completely, 3972, *kōl* [5]
completely destroy, 6913+3986, *ʿāśâ*[1]*+kālâ*[3] [4]
completely, 9462, *tāmam* [4]
severing completely, 976, *bādal* [2]
destroy completely, 3049, *ḥāram*[1] [2]
destroying completely, 3049, *ḥāram*[1] [2]
completely, 3480, *yaḥad* [2]
completely, 3983, *kālâ*[1] [2]
destroy completely, 3986+6913, *kālâ*[3]*+ʿāśâ*[1] [2]
completely, 4003, *kālîl* [2]
completely, 4200+2021+3972, *le-*[1]*+ha-+kōl* [2]
completely destroy, 9037, *šāmēm*[1] [2]
completely divided, 9117+9118, *šāsaʿ+šesaʿ* [2]
completely, *NIH/RPE* [1]
destroy completely, 6+6, *ʾābad+ʾābad* [1]
completely, 421, *ʾak* [1]
crushed completely, 430+2256+4730, *ʾākal+we-+māḥaṣ* [1]
leveled completely, 928+2021+9168+9164, *be-+ha-+šiplâ+šāpēl*[1] [1]
be completely laid waste, 1327+1327, *bāqaq*[1]*+bāqaq*[1] [1]
be completely destroyed, 1950+1950, *dāmâ*[3]*+dāmâ*[3] [1]
completely defiled, 2866+2866, *ḥānēp*[1]*+ḥānēp*[1] [1]
completely destroy, 3049+3049, *ḥāram*[1]*+ḥāram*[1] [1]
completely dry, 3312, *yābēš*[1] [1]
completely withered, 3312+3312, *yābēš*[1]*+yābēš*[1] [1]
wither completely, 3312+3312, *yābēš*[1]*+yābēš*[1] [1]
drive out completely, 3769+3769, *yāraš*[1]*+yāraš*[1] [1]
drove out completely, 3769+3769, *yāraš*[1]*+yāraš*[1] [1]
destroy completely, 3983, *kālâ*[1] [1]
completely destroy, 3986+6913, *kālâ*[3]*+ʿāśâ*[1] [1]
completely, 3986, *kālâ*[3] [1]
completely, 4394, *meʾōd* [1]
rejected completely, 4415+4415, *māʾas*[1]*+māʾas*[1] [1]
completely blot out, 4681+4681, *māḥâ*[1]*+māḥâ*[1] [1]
did completely, 4848, *mālēʾ*[1] [1]
completely, 4946+5883+2256+6330+1414, *min+nepeš+we-+ʿad*[2]*+bāśār* [1]
completely deceived, 5958+5958, *nāšāʾ*[2]*+nāšāʾ*[2] [1]
completely uproot, 6004+6004, *nātaš+nātaš* [1]
completely surrounding, 6017+6017, *sābîb+sābîb* [1]
completely, 6017, *sābîb* [1]
completely destroyed, 6330+3983, *ʿad*[2]*+kālâ*[1] [1]
completely, 6330+3983, *ʿad*[2]*+kālâ*[1] [1]
destroy completely, 6913+3986, *ʿāśâ*[1]*+kālâ*[3] [1]
see that is completely healed, 8324+8324, *rāpāʾ*[1]*+rāpāʾ*[1] [1]
completely, 8934, *šālôm* [1]
completely destroyed, 9012, *šāmad* [1]
completely divided, 9117, *šāsaʿ* [1]
completely divided, 9118+9117, *šesaʿ+šāsaʿ* [1]
completely destroyed, 10722+10221+10005, *šemad+we-+ʾabad* [1]

COMPLETION [1]
completion, 3983, *kālâ*[1] [1]

COMPLIED [1]
complied, 9048, *šāmaʿ* [1]

COMPLIMENTS [1]
compliments, 1821+5833, *dābār+naʿîm*[1] [1]

COMPLY [1]
comply, 9048, *šāmaʿ* [1]

COMPOSED [1]
composed laments, 7801, *qîn* [1]

COMPREHEND [3]
comprehend, 5162, *māṣāʾ* [2]
comprehend, 3359, *yādaʿ* [1]

COMPREHENDED [1]
comprehended, 1067, *bîn* [1]

COMPUTE [1]
compute, 3108, *ḥāšab* [1]

CONANIAH [3]
Conaniah, 4042, *kānanyāhû* [3]

CONCEAL [8]
conceal, 3948, *kāḥad* [2]
conceal, 4059, *kāsâ* [2]
conceal, 6259, *sātar* [2]
conceal himself, 2464, *ḥābâ* [1]
conceal, 6114, *sākak*[1] [1]

CONCEALED [9]
concealed, 4059, *kāsâ* [2]
concealed, 6259, *sātar* [2]
took up concealed positions, 741, *ʾārab* [1]
concealed in, 928, *be-* [1]
concealed, 6260, *sēter* [1]
concealed, 7621, *ṣāpan* [1]
is concealed, 7621, *ṣāpan* [1]

CONCEALS [2]
conceals, 4059, *kāsâ* [2]

CONCEDE [1]
concede, 7130, *pālîl* [1]

CONCEIT [2]
conceit, 1452, *gaʾawâ* [1]
conceit, 1470, *gōbah* [1]

CONCEITED [1]
conceited, 2295, *zādôn* [1]

CONCEITS [1]
evil conceits, 5381, *maśkît* [1]

CONCEIVE [8]
conceive, 2225, *hārâ* [7]
conceive, 2231, *hērāyôn* [1]

CONCEIVED [19]
conceived, 2225, *hārâ* [16]
conceived, 1061, *beṭen*[1] [1]
conceived, 2473, *ḥābal*[3] [1]
conceived, 3501, *yāḥam* [1]

CONCEIVES [1]
conceives, 2225, *hārâ* [1]

CONCEPTION [1]
conception, 2231, *hērāyôn* [1]

CONCERN [9]
concern, 3359, *yādaʿ* [2]
concern, 907, *ʾēt*[2] [1]
have concern, 1067+1981, *bîn+daʿat*[1] [1]
concern, 2143, *hālak* [1]
concern, 2798, *ḥāmal* [1]
had concern, 2798, *ḥāmal* [1]
have concern for, 3359, *yādaʿ* [1]
showed concern for, 7155+448, *pānâ+ʾel* [1]

CONCERNED [12]
concerned, 2571, *ḥûs* [2]
concerned about, 3359, *yādaʿ* [2]
concerned, *NIH/RPE* [1]
concerned, 128, *ʾōdôt* [1]
concerned for, 448, *ʾel* [1]
concerned, 1821, *dābār* [1]
concerned, 2703, *hālâ*[1] [1]
concerned, 5795, *nākar*[1] [1]

concerned about, 7212, *pāqad* [1]
concerned about, 8492+448+4213, *śîm+ʾel+lēb* [1]

CONCERNING [95]
concerning, 6584, *ʿal*^{2} [31]
concerning, *AIT* [19]
concerning, 448, *ʾel* [17]
concerning, 4200, *l*^{e}*-*^{1} [16]
concerning, *NIH/RPE* [5]
concerning, 6584+1821, *ʿal*^{2}*+dābār* [3]
concerning, 928, *b*^{e}*-* [1]
concerning, 4946, *min* [1]
concerning, 6640, *ʿim* [1]
concerning, 10542, *ʿal* [1]

CONCERNS [6]
concerns, 4200, *l*^{e}*-*^{1} [4]
concerns, *AIT* [1]
concerns, *NIH/RPE* [1]

CONCLUDED [1]
concluded, 1013, *bûr* [1]

CONCLUDES [1]
concludes, 3983, *kālâ*^{1} [1]

CONCLUSION [1]
conclusion, 6067, *sôp* [1]

CONCUBINE [21]
concubine, 7108, *pilegeš* [21]

CONCUBINES [17]
concubines, 7108, *pilegeš* [14]
concubines, 10390, *l*^{e}*hēnâ* [3]

CONDEMN [9]
condemn, 8399, *rāšaʿ* [7]
condemn, 2118+4200+2631, *hāyâ+l*^{e}*-*^{1}*+ḥ*^{a}*ṭāʾâ* [1]
condemn, 9149, *šāpaṭ* [1]

CONDEMNATION [2]
condemnation, 7839, *q*^{e}*lālâ* [2]

CONDEMNED [7]
condemned, 870, *ʾāšam* [2]
condemned to, 1201, *bēn*^{1} [2]
condemned things, 3051, *ḥērem*^{1} [1]
condemned, 8399, *rāšaʿ* [1]
let be condemned, 8399, *rāšaʿ* [1]

CONDEMNING [3]
condemning, 8399, *rāšaʿ* [3]

CONDEMNS [2]
condemns, 8399, *rāšaʿ* [2]

CONDITION [4]
on the condition that, 928+2296, *b*^{e}*-+zeh* [1]
one condition^{s}, 2296, *zeh* [1]
the condition^{s}, 2296, *zeh* [1]
condition, 7156, *pāneh* [1]

CONDITIONS [1]
conditions, 2976, *ḥōq* [1]

CONDUCT [28]
conduct, 2006, *derek* [18]
conduct, 6913, *ʿāśâ*^{1} [3]
conduct, 1821, *dābār* [2]
conduct, 7189, *pōʿal* [2]
conduct, *NIH/RPE* [1]
conduct, 784, *ʾōraḥ* [1]
conduct, 2143, *hālak* [1]

CONDUCTS [1]
conducts, 3920, *kûl* [1]

CONEY [2]
coney, 9176, *šāpān*^{1} [2]

CONEYS [2]
coneys, 9176, *šāpān*^{1} [2]

CONFECTIONS [1]
confections, 7154, *pannag* [1]

CONFER [1]
confer, 3619, *yāʿaṣ* [1]

CONFERRED [3]
conferred, 1821, *dābār* [1]
conferred, 2118+1821, *hāyâ+dābār* [1]
conferred, 3619, *yāʿaṣ* [1]

CONFERRING [1]
conferring, 3619, *yāʿaṣ* [1]

CONFESS [11]
confess, 3344, *yādâ*^{2} [10]
confess, 5583, *nāgad* [1]

CONFESSED [3]
confessed, 3344, *yādâ*^{2} [2]
confessed, 606, *ʾāmar*^{1} [1]

CONFESSES [1]
confesses, 3344, *yādâ*^{2} [1]

CONFESSING [2]
confessing, 3344, *yādâ*^{2} [2]

CONFESSION [2]
confession, 3344, *yādâ*^{2} [1]
confession, 9343, *tôdâ* [1]

CONFIDE [1]
confide in, 4213+907, *lēb+ʾēt*^{2} [1]

CONFIDENCE [18]
confidence, 6051, *sôd* [4]
put confidence, 1053, *bāṭaḥ*^{1} [2]
confidence, 1055, *beṭaḥ*^{1} [2]
confidence, 1059, *biṭṭāḥôn* [2]
confidence, 4440, *mibṭāḥ* [2]
basing confidence, 1053, *bāṭaḥ*^{1} [1]
has full confidence, 1053+4213, *bāṭaḥ*^{1}*+lēb* [1]
confidence, 4073, *kesel*^{2} [1]
confidence, 4074, *kislâ* [1]
source of confidence, 4440, *mibṭāḥ* [1]
gained confidence, 6164, *sāmak* [1]

CONFIDENT [3]
confident, 1053, *bāṭaḥ*^{1} [2]
confident, 586, *ʾāman*^{1} [1]

CONFIDENTLY [1]
confidently, 5051, *maʿ*^{a}*dannôt* [1]

CONFIDES [1]
confides, 6051, *sôd* [1]

CONFIDING [1]
confiding in, 1655+906+265, *gālâ+ʾēt*^{1}*+ʾōzen* [1]

CONFINE [1]
confine, 6037, *sāgar* [1]

CONFINED [9]
was confined, 673, *ʾāsar* [1]
were confined, 673, *ʾāsar* [1]
am confined, 3973, *kālāʾ*^{1} [1]
confined, 3973, *kālāʾ*^{1} [1]
confined, 4315, *lāḥaṣ* [1]
confined, 5877, *nāpal* [1]
confined, 6037, *sāgar* [1]
confined, 6806, *ʿāṣar* [1]
was confined, 6806, *ʿāṣar* [1]

CONFINEMENT [1]
kept in confinement, 7674, *ṣārar*^{1} [1]

CONFINES [1]
confines in prison, 6037, *sāgar* [1]

CONFIRM [7]
confirm, 7756, *qûm* [4]
confirm, 1504, *gābar* [1]
confirm, 4848, *mālēʾ*^{1} [1]
confirm, 5989, *nātan* [1]

CONFIRMED [8]
confirmed, 6641, *ʿāmad* [2]
confirmed, 7756, *qûm* [2]
be confirmed, 586, *ʾāman*^{1} [1]
confirmed, 3922, *kûn*^{1} [1]
confirmed as king, 4887, *mālak*^{1} [1]
confirmed by oath, 8678, *šābaʿ* [1]

CONFIRMING [1]
confirming, 7756, *qûm* [1]

CONFIRMS [3]
confirms, 7756, *qûm* [3]

CONFISCATION [1]
confiscation, 10562, *ʿ*^{a}*nāš* [1]

CONFLICT [1]
conflict, 4506, *mādôn*^{1} [1]

CONFORMED [2]
conformed to, 3869+6913, *k*^{e}*-+ʿāśâ*^{1} [2]

CONFOUND [1]
confound, 7103, *pālag* [1]

CONFRONT [13]
confront, 3359, *yādaʿ* [3]
confront, 3656, *yāṣab* [3]
confront, 7709, *qādam* [2]
confront, 995, *bôʾ* [1]
confront, 4946, *min* [1]
confront, 5583, *nāgad* [1]
confront, 5602, *nāgaš* [1]
confront with evidence, 9149, *šāpaṭ* [1]

CONFRONTED [6]
confronted, 7709, *qādam* [4]
confronted, 6641+6584, *ʿāmad+ʿal*^{2} [1]
confronted, 7756+6584, *qûm+ʿal*^{2} [1]

CONFRONTING [2]
confronting, *NIH/RPE* [1]
confronting, 4946+7156, *min+pāneh* [1]

CONFRONTS [1]
confronts, 7756, *qûm* [1]

CONFUSE [2]
confuse, 1176, *bālal*^{1} [1]
confuse, 1182, *bālaʿ*^{3} [1]

CONFUSED [1]
confused, 1176, *bālal*^{1} [1]

CONFUSING [1]
confusing things, 9337, *tahpukôt* [1]

CONFUSION [16]
confusion, 2917, *ḥāpar*^{2} [4]
threw into confusion, 2169, *hāmam*^{1} [2]
confusion, 4539, *m*^{e}*hûmâ* [2]
wandering around in confusion, 1003, *bûk* [1]
confusion, 2162, *hāmôn* [1]
throw into confusion, 2169, *hāmam*^{1} [1]
throwing into confusion, 2169+4539, *hāmam*^{1}*+m*^{e}*hûmâ* [1]
thrown into confusion, 2169, *hāmam*^{1} [1]
confusion, 4428, *m*^{e}*bûkâ* [1]
confusion, 9332, *tōhû* [1]
confusion, 9451, *timmāhôn* [1]

CONGEALED [1]
congealed, 7884, *qāpāʾ* [1]

CONGRATULATE [3]
congratulate, 1385, *bārak*^{2} [3]

CONGREGATION [2]
great congregation, 5220, *maqhēl* [1]
congregation, 7736, *qāhāl* [1]

CONJURE [1]
conjure away, 8838, *šāḥar*^{2} [1]

CONNECTED [4]
connected to, 6584, *ʿal*^{2} [4]

CONNECTING [2]
connecting, 2118, *hāyâ* [2]

CONNECTION [2]
in connection with, 4200, *l*^{e}*-*^{1} [2]

CONQUER [2]
conquer, 1324, *bāqaʿ* [1]
conquer, 3769, *yārāš1* [1]

CONQUERED [10]
conquered, 5782, *nākâ* [5]
conquered, 3771, *yerēšâ* [2]
conquered, 2616+6584, *ḥāzaq+ʿal2* [1]
conquered, 4162, *kārat* [1]
conquered, 4334, *lākad* [1]

CONQUEROR [1]
conqueror, 3769, *yārāš1* [1]

CONQUERORS [2]
conquerors, 8647, *šābâ* [2]

CONQUERS [1]
conquers, 5782, *nākâ* [1]

CONQUEST [1]
conquest, *NIH/RPE* [1]

CONSCIENCE [4]
conscience, 4222, *lēbāb* [3]
conscience, 4213, *lēb* [1]

CONSCIENCE-STRICKEN [2]
conscience-stricken, 5782+4213, *nākâ+lēb* [2]

CONSCIENTIOUS [1]
conscientious, 3838+4222, *yāšār1+lēbāb* [1]

CONSCRIPTED [5]
conscripted, 6590, *ʿālâ* [4]
conscripted, 6218, *sāpar* [1]

CONSCRIPTING [2]
conscripting, 7371, *ṣābāʾ1* [2]

CONSECRATE [43]
consecrate, 7727, *qādaš* [30]
consecrate yourselves, 7727, *qādaš* [9]
consecrate himself, 4848+3338+2257, *mālēʾ1+yād+-ô* [1]
consecrate himself, 4848+3338, *mālēʾ1+yād* [1]
consecrate themselves, 7727, *qādaš* [1]
solemnly consecrate, 7727+7727, *qādaš+qādaš* [1]

CONSECRATED [51]
consecrated, 7727, *qādaš* [22]
consecrated themselves, 7727, *qādaš* [7]
consecrated, 7731, *qōdeš* [7]
consecrated, 7705, *qādôš* [4]
consecrated bread, 5121, *maʿareket* [2]
been consecrated, 7727, *qādaš* [2]
consecrated, 2883, *ḥāsîd* [1]
consecrated, 4848+906+3338, *mālēʾ1+ʾēt1+yād* [1]
setting out the consecrated bread, 5121, *maʿareket* [1]
consecrated themselves, 5692, *nāzar1* [1]
be consecrated, 7727, *qādaš* [1]
consecrated gifts, 7731+7731, *qōdeš+qōdeš* [1]
consecrated things, 7731, *qōdeš* [1]

CONSECRATING [3]
consecrating themselves, 7727+7731, *qādaš+qōdeš* [1]
consecrating themselves, 7727, *qādaš* [1]
consecrating, 7727, *qādaš* [1]

CONSECRATION [3]
consecration, 7727, *qādaš* [3]

CONSENT [5]
give consent, 252, *ʾût* [2]
consent, 14, *ʾābâ* [1]
consent, 252, *ʾût* [1]
consent, 4946, *min* [1]

CONSEQUENCES [8]
consequences of sin, 6411, *ʿāwōn* [3]
consequences of lewdness, 2365, *zimmâ1* [2]
consequences of sin, 2628, *ḥēṭʾ* [2]
consequences of sins, 2628, *ḥēṭʾ* [1]

CONSIDER [57]
consider, 8011, *rāʾâ1* [10]
consider, 1067, *bîn* [8]
consider, 5564, *nābaṭ* [6]
consider, 2118+4200, *hāyâ+le-1* [5]
consider, 3359, *yādaʿ* [3]
consider, 8488, *śîaḥ1* [3]
consider, 2349, *zākar1* [2]
consider, *NIH/RPE* [1]
consider, 928+4222, *be-+lēbāb* [1]
consider, 928+6524, *be-+ʿayin1* [1]
consider carefully, 1067, *bîn* [1]
consider, 1329, *bāqar* [1]
consider, 2180, *hinnēh* [1]
consider themselves, 3108, *ḥāšab* [1]
consider, 3108, *ḥāšab* [1]
consider right, 3837, *yāšar* [1]
consider, 4499, *mādad* [1]
consider innocent, 5927, *nāqâ* [1]
consider, 6418, *ʿûš1* [1]
consider, 6590, *ʿālâ* [1]
consider carefully, 8011, *rāʾâ1* [1]
consider better, 8123+4222, *rûm1+lēbāb* [1]
consider, 8492+4213, *śîm+lēb* [1]
consider, 8492+6584+4213, *śîm+ʿal2+lēb* [1]
consider, 8492, *śîm* [1]
consider well, 8883+4213, *šît1+lēb* [1]
consider, 9068, *šāmar* [1]

CONSIDERED [21]
was considered, 3108, *ḥāšab* [3]
are considered, 3108, *ḥāšab* [2]
be considered, 3108, *ḥāšab* [2]
considered, 3108, *ḥāšab* [2]
were considered, 3108, *ḥāšab* [2]
considered, 8492+4213, *śîm+lēb* [2]
considered, *NIH/RPE* [1]
considered, 928+6524, *be-+ʿayin1* [1]
be considered stolen, 1704, *gānab* [1]
is considered, 3108, *ḥāšab* [1]
considered stupid, 3241, *ṭāmâ* [1]
considered a liar, 3941, *kāzab* [1]
be considered accursed, 7837, *qālal* [1]
considered trivial, 7837, *qālal* [1]

CONSIDERS [4]
considers, 1067, *bîn* [1]
considers, 2372, *zāmam* [1]
considers, 3108, *ḥāšab* [1]
considers, 8011, *rāʾâ1* [1]

CONSIGN [2]
consign, 3718, *yārad* [1]
consign, 5989, *nātan* [1]

CONSIGNING [2]
consigning to labor, 8492, *śîm* [2]

CONSIST [2]
consist, *NIH/RPE* [1]
consist of, 2118, *hāyâ* [1]

CONSISTED [2]
consisted, *NIH/RPE* [1]
consisted of, 5877, *nāpal* [1]

CONSISTING [1]
consisting, *NIH/RPE* [1]

CONSISTS [1]
consists, *NIH/RPE* [1]

CONSOLATION [3]
consolation, 5717, *neḥāmâ* [1]
consolation, 9487, *tanḥûmôt* [1]
consolation, 9488, *tanḥûmîm* [1]

CONSOLATIONS [1]
consolations, 9487, *tanḥûmôt* [1]

CONSOLE [4]
console, 5714, *nāḥam* [3]
console, 9488, *tanḥûmîm* [1]

CONSOLED [6]
be consoled, 5714, *nāḥam* [2]
consoled, 5714, *nāḥam* [2]
was consoled, 5714, *nāḥam* [1]
were consoled, 5714, *nāḥam* [1]

CONSOLING [1]
consoling himself, 5714, *nāḥam* [1]

CONSORT [2]
consort, 995, *bōʾ* [1]
consort, 7233, *pārad* [1]

CONSPICUOUS [1]
conspicuous, 8011, *rāʾâ1* [1]

CONSPIRACY [8]
conspiracy, 8004, *qešer* [5]
conspiracy, 6051, *sôd* [1]
raising a conspiracy, 8003, *qāšar* [1]
conspiracy led, 8004+8003, *qešer+qāšar* [1]

CONSPIRATORS [1]
conspirators, 8003, *qāšar* [1]

CONSPIRE [8]
conspire, 1592, *gûr2* [2]
conspire, 3570, *yāsad2* [1]
conspire, 3619, *yāʿaṣ* [1]
conspire, 5792, *nākal* [1]
conspire, 6051, *sôd* [1]
conspire, 6309, *ʿābat* [1]
conspire, 8093, *rāgaš* [1]

CONSPIRED [18]
conspired, 8003, *qāšar* [10]
conspired, 8003+8004, *qāšar+qešer* [4]
conspired, 1335, *bāqaš* [2]
conspired, 5742, *nāṭâ* [1]
conspired, 10231, *zeman1* [1]

CONSTANT [7]
constant dripping, 1942+3265, *delep+ṭārad* [2]
constant, 419, *ʾêtān1* [1]
constant, 3429, *yômām* [1]
constant, 4946+5584, *min+neged* [1]
constant grumbling, 9442+4296, *telunnôt+lûn* [1]
constant, 9458, *tāmîd* [1]

CONSTANTLY [3]
constantly, 9458, *tāmîd* [2]
constantly, 928+3972+6961, *be-+kōl+ʿēt* [1]

CONSTELLATIONS [4]
constellations, 2540, *ḥeder* [1]
constellations, 4068, *kesîl2* [1]
constellations, 4655, *mazzāl* [1]
constellations, 4666, *mazzārôt* [1]

CONSTRUCT [1]
construct, 6913, *ʿāśâ1* [1]

CONSTRUCTED [3]
constructed, 1215, *bānâ* [1]
been constructed, 6913, *ʿāśâ1* [1]
constructed, 6913, *ʿāśâ1* [1]

CONSTRUCTING [3]
constructing, 6275, *ʿabōdâ* [2]
constructing, 10111, *benâ* [1]

CONSTRUCTION [4]
construction, 1215, *bānâ* [1]
construction, 5126, *maʿaśeh* [1]
construction, 10111, *benâ* [1]
under construction, 10111, *benâ* [1]

CONSULT [18]
consult, 2011, *dāraš* [5]
consult, 2011+928, *dāraš+be-* [4]
consult, 8626, *šāʾal* [3]
consult, 448+2143, *ʾel+hālak* [1]
consult, 448, *ʾel* [1]
consult, 2011+928+1821, *dāraš+be-+dābār* [1]
consult, 3619, *yāʿaṣ* [1]
consult, 4200+7156, *le-1+pāneh* [1]
consult, 7876, *qāsam* [1]

CONSULTATION [1]
consultation, 6783, *ʿēṣâ1* [1]

CONSULTED [10]
consulted, 3619, yāʿaṣ [5]
consulted, 6913, ʿāśâ[1] [2]
consulted, 2011, dāraš [1]
consulted advisers, 3619, yāʿaṣ [1]
consulted, 8626, šāʾal [1]

CONSULTING [2]
consulting, 3619, yāʿaṣ [1]
consulting, 7023+8626, peh+šāʾal [1]

CONSULTS [2]
consults, 2011, dāraš [2]

CONSUME [37]
consume, 430, ʾākal [30]
consume, 3983, kālâ[1] [3]
consume, 1277, bāʿar[1] [2]
consume, 3920, kûl [1]
consume, 4998, māsâ [1]

CONSUMED [32]
consumed, 430, ʾākal [19]
be consumed, 430, ʾākal [5]
consumed, 3983, kālâ[1] [2]
consumed, 1180, bālaʿ[1] [1]
consumed, 1277, bāʿar[1] [1]
consumed, 1756, gāras [1]
be consumed, 4162, kārat [1]
consumed, 4265, lāhaṭ[1] [1]
consumed, 9462, tāmam [1]

CONSUMES [8]
consumes, 430, ʾākal [6]
consumes, 1277, bāʿar[1] [1]
consumes, 4265, lāhaṭ[1] [1]

CONSUMING [10]
consuming, 430, ʾākal [9]
consuming, 4310, lāham[2] [1]

CONTACT [1]
contact, AIT [1]

CONTAIN [4]
contain, 3920, kûl [3]
contain, 3973, kālāʾ[1] [1]

CONTAINER [1]
container, 3998, kᵉlî [1]

CONTAINING [9]
containing, NIH/RPE [3]
anything containing yeast, 2809, ḥāmēṣ[4] [2]
containing, AIT [1]
containing, 928, bᵉ- [1]
containing yeast, 2809, ḥāmēṣ[4] [1]
containing, 5951, nāśāʾ [1]

CONTAINS [2]
contains, NIH/RPE [1]
contains, 4200, lᵉ-[1] [1]

CONTAMINATED [4]
contaminated, 5596, negaʿ [2]
the contaminated part[s], 2257, -ô [1]
contaminated article, 5596, negaʿ [1]

CONTAMINATION [3]
contamination, 5596, negaʿ [3]

CONTEMPLATING [1]
contemplating, 8011, rāʾâ[1] [1]

CONTEMPT [28]
contempt, 997, bûz[2] [9]
contempt, 3075, ḥerpâ [3]
shows contempt, 3070, ḥārap[2] [2]
treated with contempt, 5540, nāʾaṣ [2]
show contempt, 1022, bāzâ [1]
shown contempt, 1022, bāzâ [1]
contempt, 1994, dērāʾôn [1]
contempt, 2295, zādôn [1]
treating with contempt, 2725, ḥālal[1] [1]
treats with contempt, 3070, ḥārap[2] [1]
made show utter contempt, 5540+5540, nāʾaṣ+nāʾaṣ [1]
treat with contempt, 5540, nāʾaṣ [1]
treating with contempt, 5540, nāʾaṣ [1]
treat with contempt, 5571, nābal[2] [1]
treat with contempt, 7837, qālal [1]
treated with contempt, 7837, qālal [1]

CONTEMPTIBLE [5]
contemptible, 1022, bāzâ [3]
contemptible things, 5542, neʾāṣâ [1]
made contemptible, 7837, qālal [1]

CONTEMPTUOUS [2]
contemptuous, 1022, bāzâ [1]
contemptuous, 2326, zîd [1]

CONTEMPTUOUSLY [1]
sniff contemptuously, 5870, nāpaḥ [1]

CONTEND [10]
contend, 8189, rîb[1] [4]
contend, 1906, dîn[1] [2]
contend, 3742, yārîb[1] [2]
contend, 1819, dābar[2] [1]
contend, 8190, rîb[2] [1]

CONTENDED [1]
contended, 8189, rîb[1] [1]

CONTENDS [2]
contends, 4506, mādôn[1] [1]
contends, 8189, rîb[1] [1]

CONTENT [4]
content, 3283, yāʾal[2] [1]
content, 8425, śābaʿ [1]
content, 8427, śōbaʿ [1]
content, 8428, śābēaʿ [1]

CONTENTED [1]
contented, 10710, šᵉlēh [1]

CONTENTION [1]
source of contention, 4506, mādôn[1] [1]

CONTENTMENT [2]
contentment, 5833, nāʿîm[1] [1]
contentment, 8934, šālôm [1]

CONTENTS [1]
contents, 5901, nōṣâ[1] [1]

CONTINUAL [3]
continual, 3972+2021+3427, kōl+ha-+yôm[1] [2]
continual, 9458, tāmîd [1]

CONTINUALLY [21]
continually, 9458, tāmîd [12]
continually, 3972+2021+3427, kōl+ha-+yôm[1] [2]
continually, 10089+10753+10002, bᵉ-+tᵉdîr+-āʾ [2]
walk continually, 2143, hālak [1]
continually, 3782, yāšab [1]
continually, 4200+6329, lᵉ-[1]+ʿad[1] [1]
continually, 4200+8092, lᵉ-[1]+regaʿ [1]
continually, 8740, šûb[1] [1]

CONTINUE [37]
continue, AIT [10]
continue, 2118, hāyâ [6]
continue, 2143, hālak [6]
continue until, 5952, nāśag [2]
continue, NIH/RPE [1]
continue prostitution, 2388+2388, zānâ[1]+zānâ[1] [1]
continue, 3655, yāṣāʾ [1]
continue, 3780, yēš [1]
continue, 4682, māḥâ[2] [1]
continue, 5432, māšak [1]
continue, 5672, nûn[1] [1]
continue on, 6296, ʿābar[1] [1]
continue, 6388, ʿôd [1]
continue, 6409, ʿôlām [1]
continue, 6913, ʿāśâ[1] [1]
continue, 9068, šāmar [1]
continue, 10073, ʾarkâ [1]

CONTINUED [64]
continued, AIT [14]
continued, 606, ʾāmar[1] [8]
continued, 6388, ʿôd [8]
continued, 2143, hālak [6]
continued, 3578, yāsap [4]
continued, NIH/RPE [3]
continued, 6296, ʿābar[1] [3]
continued, 3655, yāṣāʾ [2]
continued down, 3718, yārad [2]
continued, 2118+2143, hāyâ+hālak [1]
continued to grow, 2143, hālak [1]
continued, 3578+6388, yāsap+ʿôd [1]
continued, 3718, yārad [1]
continued on journey, 5951+8079, nāśāʾ+regel [1]
continued along, 6296, ʿābar[1] [1]
continued on, 6296, ʿābar[1] [1]
continued, 6409, ʿôlām [1]
continued up, 6590, ʿālâ [1]
continued, 6590, ʿālâ [1]
continued, 6913, ʿāśâ[1] [1]
continued, 9068, šāmar [1]
continued, 9458, tāmîd [1]
continued, 10201, hᵃwâ [1]

CONTINUES [5]
continues, NIH/RPE [3]
continues, AIT [1]
while continues, 3972+3427, kōl+yôm[1] [1]

CONTINUING [2]
continuing, 2134, hālēʾâ [1]
continuing, 9458, tāmîd [1]

CONTINUOUSLY [1]
continuously, 9458, tāmîd [1]

CONTRACT [2]
servant bound by contract, 8502, śākîr [2]

CONTRARY [5]
contrary to, 928+4202+3869, bᵉ-+lōʾ+kᵉ- [1]
on the contrary, 3954, kî[2] [1]
contrary to, 4202+3869, lōʾ+kᵉ- [1]
contrary to, 4202, lōʾ [1]
contrary, 4202, lōʾ [1]

CONTRIBUTE [1]
contribute, 6584, ʿal[2] [1]

CONTRIBUTED [4]
contributed, 5989, nātan [2]
contributed, 4987, mᵉnāt [1]
contributed, 8123, rûm[1] [1]

CONTRIBUTION [4]
contribution, 9556, tᵉrûmâ [3]
contribution, 7934, qurbān [1]

CONTRIBUTIONS [10]
contributions, 9556, tᵉrûmâ [8]
contributions, NIH/RPE [1]
contributions, 7934, qurbān [1]

CONTRITE [4]
contrite, 1917, dākāʾ [1]
contrite, 1918, dakkāʾ[1] [1]
contrite, 1920, dākâ [1]
contrite, 5783, nākeh [1]

CONTROL [14]
control, 3338, yād [5]
control, NIH/RPE [1]
control himself, 706, ʾāpaq [1]
under control, 928+294, bᵉ-+ʾāḥôr [1]
was brought under control, 3899, kābaš [1]
took control, 4887, mālak[1] [1]
gain control, 5440, māšal[2] [1]
in control, 6584, ʿal[2] [1]
get out of control, 7277, pāraʿ[2] [1]
have control, 8948, šālaṭ [1]

CONTROLLED [3]
controlled, 1178, bālam [1]
controlled, 2118+4200, hāyâ+lᵉ-[1] [1]
controlled, 4200, lᵉ-[1] [1]

CONTROLLING [1]
controlling himself, 706, ʾāpaq [1]

CONTROLS [2]
controls, 5440, *māšal*^{2} [1]
controls, 8492, *śîm* [1]

CONVENES [1]
convenes a court, 7735, *qāhal* [1]

CONVERSATION [3]
conversation, 1821, *dābār* [3]

CONVICT [3]
convict, 872, *'āšēm* [1]
convict, 3519, *yākaḥ* [1]
convict, 7756, *qûm* [1]

CONVICTIONS [1]
convictions, 6640+4222, *'im+lēbāb* [1]

CONVINCED [1]
convinced, 8041, *rab*^{1} [1]

CONVOCATIONS [1]
convocations, 7924+5246, *qārā'*^{1}*+miqrā'* [1]

CONVULSED [1]
convulsed, 8074, *rāgaz* [1]

COOING [1]
cooing, 7754, *qôl* [1]

COOK [14]
cook, 1418, *bāšal* [10]
cook, 3184, *ṭabbāḥ* [2]
burned to cook, 1418, *bāšal* [1]
cook well, 9462, *tāmam* [1]

COOKED [8]
cooked, 1418, *bāšal* [5]
cooked, *NIH/RPE* [1]
cooked, 1419+1418, *bāšēl+bāšal* [1]
cooked, 6913, *'āśâ*^{1} [1]

COOKING [5]
cooking pot, 6105, *sîr* [2]
cooking, 2326, *zîd* [1]
cooking pot, 3968, *kîr* [1]
cooking pots, 6105, *sîr* [1]

COOKS [1]
cooks, 3185, *ṭabbāḥâ* [1]

COOL [2]
cool, 7922, *qar* [1]
cool, 8120, *rûaḥ* [1]

COOLNESS [1]
coolness, 7557, *ṣinnâ*^{1} [1]

COPIED [3]
copied, 4180+5467, *kātab+mišneh* [1]
copied, 6913, *'āśâ*^{1} [1]
copied, 6980, *'ātaq* [1]

COPIES [1]
copies, *AIT* [1]

COPPER [5]
copper, 5733, *n*^{e}*ḥōšet*^{1} [4]
copper, 5703, *n*^{e}*ḥûšâ* [1]

COPY [12]
copy, 7358, *patšegen* [3]
copy, 10598, *paršegen* [3]
copy, *AIT* [2]
copy of covenant, 6343, *'ēdût* [2]
copy, 5467, *mišneh* [1]
copy, 7306, *paršegen* [1]

COR [1]
cor, 4123, *kōr* [1]

CORAL [2]
coral, 8029, *rā'môt*^{1} [2]

CORD [15]
cord, 7348, *pātîl* [8]
cord, 109, *'agmôn* [1]
cord, 2475, *ḥebel*^{2} [1]
length of cord, 2475, *ḥebel*^{2} [1]
cord, 2562, *ḥûṭ* [1]
cord, 9219, *šōr* [1]
cord, 9535+2562, *tiqwâ*^{1}*+ḥûṭ* [1]
cord, 9535, *tiqwâ*^{1} [1]

CORDIAL [1]
cordial greetings, 10720+10002+10353+10002, *š*^{e}*lām+-ā'+kōl+-ā'* [1]

CORDIALLY [2]
cordially, 8934, *šālôm* [2]

CORDS [16]
cords, 2475, *ḥebel*^{2} [11]
cords, 99, *'*^{a}*guddâ* [1]
cords of tent, 3857, *yeter*^{2} [1]
cords, 4798, *mêtār* [1]
cords, 5436, *mōš*^{e}*kôt* [1]
cords, 6310, *'*^{a}*bōt* [1]

CORIANDER [2]
coriander, 1512, *gad*^{1} [2]

CORMORANT [2]
cormorant, 8960, *šālāk* [2]

CORNER [25]
corner, 7157, *pinnâ* [15]
corner, 4053, *kānāp* [3]
corner of garment, 4053, *kānāp* [2]
corner, 4578, *mûl*^{3} [2]
in each corner, 928+5243+928+5243, *b*^{e}*-+miqṣôa'+b*^{e}*-+miqṣôa'* [1]
corner defenses, 7157, *pinnâ* [1]
street corner, 7157, *pinnâ* [1]

CORNERS [30]
corners, 7896, *qāṣâ*^{2} [9]
corners, 5243, *miqṣôa'* [5]
corners, 7157, *pinnâ* [5]
corners, 4053, *kānāp* [3]
corners, 7910, *qāṣā'*^{2} [3]
corners, 6991, *pē'â*^{1} [2]
farthest corners, 721, *'āṣîl*^{1} [1]
corners, 2312, *zāwît* [1]
corners, 7921, *q*^{e}*ṣāt* [1]

CORNERSTONE [4]
cornerstone, 7157, *pinnâ* [3]
cornerstone, 74+7157, *'eben+pinnâ* [1]

CORNERSTONES [1]
cornerstones, 7157, *pinnâ* [1]

CORPSE [2]
corpse, 5883, *nepeš* [1]
corpse, 7007, *peger* [1]

CORPSES [1]
corpses, 1581, *g*^{e}*wiyyâ* [1]

CORRECT [3]
correct, 3519, *yākaḥ* [1]
correct, 3574, *yissôr* [1]
correct, 3579, *yāsar*^{1} [1]

CORRECTED [1]
be corrected, 3579, *yāsar*^{1} [1]

CORRECTION [16]
correction, 9350, *tôkaḥat* [8]
correction, 4592, *mûsār* [6]
correction, 3519, *yākaḥ* [1]
accept correction, 3579, *yāsar*^{1} [1]

CORRECTIONS [1]
corrections, 9350, *tôkaḥat* [1]

CORRECTLY [2]
correctly, 3512, *yāṭab* [1]
correctly, 4026, *kēn*^{1} [1]

CORRECTS [2]
corrects, 3519, *yākaḥ* [1]
corrects, 3579, *yāsar*^{1} [1]

CORRESPONDING [3]
corresponding, 2054, *hāgîn* [1]
corresponding to, 4200, *l*^{e}*-*^{1} [1]
corresponding to, 6584+7156, *'al*^{2}*+pāneh* [1]

CORRUPT [23]
corrupt, 8845, *šāḥat* [10]
corrupt, 480, *'ālaḥ* [3]
corrupt, 1175, *b*^{e}*liyya'al* [1]
corrupt, 2095, *hawwâ*^{2} [1]
corrupt, 2866, *ḥānēp*^{1} [1]
corrupt, 3237, *ṭāmē'*^{1} [1]
corrupt talk, 4299, *lāzût* [1]
corrupt, 6074, *sûr*^{2} [1]
corrupt, 6838, *'iqq*^{e}*šût* [1]
corrupt practices, 8845, *šāḥat* [1]
sure to become utterly corrupt, 8845+8845, *šāḥat+šāḥat* [1]
corrupt, 10705, *š*^{e}*ḥat* [1]

CORRUPTED [2]
corrupted, 8845, *šāḥat* [2]

CORRUPTION [7]
corruption, 8846, *šaḥat* [2]
corruption, 5422, *mašḥît* [1]
corruption, 5614, *niddâ* [1]
corruption, 8845, *šāḥat* [1]
given to corruption, 8845, *šāḥat* [1]
corruption, 10705, *š*^{e}*ḥat* [1]

CORRUPTLY [3]
act corruptly, 8845, *šāḥat* [2]
acted corruptly, 8845, *šāḥat* [1]

CORRUPTS [1]
corrupts, 6, *'ābad* [1]

CORS [8]
cors, 4123, *kōr* [6]
cors, *NIH/RPE* [1]
cors, 10367, *kōr* [1]

COSMETIC [1]
cosmetic lotions, 9043, *šemen* [1]

COSMETICS [1]
cosmetics, 9475, *tamrûq* [1]

COST [12]
at the cost of, 928, *b*^{e}*-* [5]
cost, 928, *b*^{e}*-* [3]
at no cost, 2855, *ḥinnām* [1]
cost nothing, 2855, *ḥinnām* [1]
cost, 4697, *m*^{e}*ḥîr*^{1} [1]
cost, 5883, *nepeš* [1]

COSTLY [6]
costly gifts, 2776, *ḥ*^{a}*mudôt* [1]
costly, 3700, *yāqar* [1]
costly gifts, 4458, *meged* [1]
costly fabric, 5429, *mešî* [1]
costly garments, 5429, *mešî* [1]
costly stones, 6090, *sōḥeret* [1]

COSTS [3]
costs nothing, 2855, *ḥinnām* [1]
costs, 5989, *nātan* [1]
costs, 10486, *nipqâ* [1]

COUCH [7]
couch, 4753, *miṭṭâ* [4]
couch, 3661, *yāṣûa'*^{1} [1]
couch, 5435, *miškāb* [1]
couch, 6911, *'ereś* [1]

COUCHES [3]
couches, 6911, *'ereś* [2]
couches, 4753, *miṭṭâ* [1]

COULD [190]
could, *AIT* [130]
could, 3523, *yākōl* [38]
could, *NIH/RPE* [12]
could, 10346, *k*^{e}*hal* [2]
could not, 2118+6584, *hāyâ+'al*^{2} [1]
could do, 3523, *yākōl* [1]
could risk, 3523, *yākōl* [1]
could, 3922, *kûn*^{1} [1]
could not, 4206, *lā'â* [1]
could not, 5610, *nādad* [1]

all could eat, 8427, *śōba'* [1]
could not, 10463, *n^{e}dad* [1]

COULDN'T [1]
couldn't, 4202, *lō'* [1]

COUNCIL [9]
council, 6051, *sôd* [7]
council, 4595, *mô'ēd* [1]
council, 4632, *môšāb* [1]

COUNSEL [31]
counsel, 6783, *'ēṣâ^1* [23]
counsel, 1821, *dābār* [2]
one to give counsel, 3446, *yô'ēṣ* [1]
counsel, 3619, *yā'aṣ* [1]
give counsel, 3619, *yā'aṣ* [1]
take counsel, 3619, *yā'aṣ* [1]
counsel, 4600, *mô'ēṣâ* [1]
counsel, 6051, *sôd* [1]

COUNSELED [1]
counseled, 3619, *yā'aṣ* [1]

COUNSELOR [8]
counselor, 3446, *yô'ēṣ* [7]
counselor, 408+6783, *'îš^1+'ēṣâ^1* [1]

COUNSELORS [6]
counselors, 3446, *yô'ēṣ* [5]
counselors, 408+6783, *'îš^1+'ēṣâ^1* [1]

COUNSELS [2]
counsels, 3619, *yā'aṣ* [2]

COUNT [40]
count, 6218, *sāpar* [12]
count, 7212, *pāqad* [8]
count off, 6218, *sāpar* [6]
count, *NIH/RPE* [3]
count, 3108, *ḥāšab* [3]
count, 4948, *mānâ^1* [3]
count, 2118+4200, *hāyâ+l^e-^{1}* [1]
count, 5031, *mispār^1* [1]
do not count, 5877, *nāpal* [1]
count, 5951+906+8031, *nāśā'+'ēt^1+rō'š^1* [1]
count equal, 8750, *šāwâ^1* [1]

COUNTED [64]
counted, 7212, *pāqad* [23]
were counted, 7212, *pāqad* [11]
counted, 5031, *mispār^1* [8]
counted, 4948, *mānâ^1* [4]
counted, 6218, *sāpar* [3]
be counted, 4948, *mānâ^1* [2]
counted, *NIH/RPE* [1]
counted blessed, 1385, *bārak^2* [1]
am counted, 3108, *ḥāšab* [1]
counted, 3108, *ḥāšab* [1]
counted, 5951+906+8031, *nāśā'+'ēt^1+rō'š^1* [1]
be counted, 6218, *sāpar* [1]
counted out, 6218, *sāpar* [1]
were counted, 6218, *sāpar* [1]
counted off, 6296+928+5031,
'ābar^1+b^e-+mispār^1 [1]
counted, 7212+7212, *pāqad+pāqad* [1]
was counted, 7212, *pāqad* [1]
were counted in the census, 7212, *pāqad* [1]
were counted, 7924, *qārā'^{1}* [1]

COUNTENANCE [1]
countenance, 7156, *pāneh* [1]

COUNTING [3]
counting on, 448+5951+906+5883,
'el+nāśā'+'ēt^1+nepeš [1]
not counting, 4200+963+4946,
l^e-^{1}+bad^1+min [1]
not counting, 4946+4200+963, *min+l^e-^{1}+bad^1* [1]

COUNTLESS [3]
countless, 401+5031, *'ayin^1+mispār^1* [1]
make countless, 889+4202+6218+8049,
'ašer+lō'+sāpar+rābâ^1 [1]
countless, 8047, *r^{e}bābâ* [1]

COUNTRIES [43]
countries, 824, *'ereṣ* [39]
countries, *AIT* [1]
countries, *NIH/RPE* [1]
countries, 1580, *gôy* [1]
countries, 5226, *māqôm* [1]

COUNTRY [213]
country, 824, *'ereṣ* [92]
hill country, 2215, *har* [82]
country, 8441, *śādeh* [17]
open country, 8441, *śādeh* [8]
country, 1473, *g^{e}bûl* [7]
country, 141, *'^{a}dāmâ^1* [2]
country, *NIH/RPE* [1]
the country^s, 2257, *-ô* [1]
open country, 4497, *midbār^1* [1]
country, 5213, *miṣrayim* [1]
country, 7253, *p^{e}rāzî* [1]

COUNTRYMAN [3]
countryman, 278, *'āḥ^2* [2]
countryman, 6660, *'āmît* [1]

COUNTRYMEN [25]
countrymen, 278, *'āḥ^2* [10]
countrymen, 1201+6639, *bēn^1+'am^2* [6]
fellow countrymen, 278, *'āḥ^2* [5]
countrymen, 8276, *rēa'^{2}* [3]
countrymen, 6660, *'āmît* [1]

COUNTRYSIDE [7]
countryside, 824, *ereṣ* [4]
countryside, 8441, *śādeh* [2]
countryside, 2575, *ḥûṣ* [1]

COUNTS [2]
counts, 3108, *ḥāšab* [1]
counts, 4948, *mānâ^1* [1]

COURAGE [12]
took courage, 2616, *ḥāzaq* [2]
courage, 4213, *lēb* [2]
courage, 8120, *rûaḥ* [2]
courage, 2616, *ḥāzaq* [1]
take courage, 2616, *ḥāzaq* [1]
courage, 4222, *lēbāb* [1]
found courage, 5162, *māṣā'* [1]
courage, 5883, *nepeš* [1]
lost courage, 8332+3338, *rāpâ^1+yād* [1]

COURAGEOUS [12]
courageous, 599, *'āmēṣ* [11]
courageous, 1201+2657, *bēn^1+ḥayil* [1]

COURAGEOUSLY [1]
courageously, 2616, *ḥāzaq* [1]

COURIER [1]
courier, 8132, *rûṣ* [1]

COURIERS [6]
couriers, 8132, *rûṣ* [6]

COURSE [28]
in the course of time, 339+4027, *'aḥar+kēn^2* [8]
course, 784, *'ōraḥ* [4]
course, 2006, *derek* [2]
course, 3215, *ṭûr* [2]
course, 5297, *m^{e}rûṣâ^1* [2]
course of life, 2006, *derek* [1]
course, 2143, *hālak* [1]
of course not, 2721, *ḥālîl^2* [1]
in the course of time, 4200+3427+4946+3427,
l^e-^{1}+yôm^1+min+yôm^1 [1]
in the course of time, 4946+339+4027,
min+'aḥar+kēn^2 [1]
course, 5707, *naḥal^1* [1]
run course, 5938, *nāqap^2* [1]
course, 6017, *sābîb* [1]
course, 7891, *qēṣ* [1]
course, 9543, *t^{e}qûpâ* [1]

COURSES [4]
courses, 3215, *ṭûr* [2]
courses, 5019, *m^{e}sillâ* [1]
courses, 10462, *nidbāk* [1]

COURT [80]
court, 2958, *ḥāṣēr^1* [48]
court, 9133, *ša'ar^1* [5]
court officials, 6247, *sārîs* [4]
court, *NIH/RPE* [2]
court, 1074, *bayit^1* [2]
court, 5477, *mišpāṭ* [2]
court, 6478, *'^{a}zārâ* [2]
court, 7232, *parbār* [2]
court, 10170, *dîn^2* [2]
court favor, 2704+7156, *ḥālâ^2+pāneh* [1]
held court, 3782, *yāšab* [1]
court, 6269, *'ebed^1* [1]
outer court, 6478, *'^{a}zārâ* [1]
court, 7130, *pālîl* [1]
court, 7247, *parwār* [1]
convenes a court, 7735, *qāhal* [1]
in court, 8189, *rîb^1* [1]
court, 8190, *rîb^2* [1]
goes to court, 9149, *šāpaṭ* [1]
court, 10776, *t^{e}ra'* [1]

COURTS [27]
courts, 2958, *ḥāṣēr^1* [21]
courts, 9133, *ša'ar^1* [4]
courts^s, 4392, *-ām* [2]

COURTYARD [67]
courtyard, 2958, *ḥāṣēr^1* [59]
courtyard, 1619, *gizrâ* [7]
the courtyard^s, 2023, *-āh* [1]

COURTYARDS [4]
courtyards, 2958, *ḥāṣēr^1* [4]

COUSIN [5]
cousin, 1201+1856, *bēn^1+dôd* [3]
cousin, 1201, *bēn^1* [1]
cousin, 1426+1856, *bat^1+dôd* [1]

COUSINS [3]
cousins, 278, *'āḥ^2* [2]
cousins on their father's side, 1201+1856,
bēn^1+dôd [1]

COVENANT [264]
covenant, 1382, *b^{e}rît* [246]
covenant, *NIH/RPE* [4]
the covenant^s, 889, *'^{a}šer* [4]
made a covenant, 4162, *kārat* [3]
covenant, 6343, *'ēdût* [2]
copy of covenant, 6343, *'ēdût* [2]
covenant^s, 889, *'^{a}šer* [1]
marriage covenant, 1382, *b^{e}rît* [1]
makes a covenant, 4162, *kārat* [1]

COVENANTED [2]
covenanted, 4162, *kārat* [2]

COVER [90]
cover, 4059, *kāsâ* [26]
atonement cover, 4114, *kappōret* [15]
cover, 4114, *kappōret* [10]
cover, 6486, *'āṭâ^1* [5]
cover up, 4059, *kāsâ* [3]
cover, 4059+4832, *kāsâ+mikseh* [3]
cover, 2902, *ḥāpâ* [2]
cover, 3212, *ṭûaḥ* [2]
cover, 6584, *'al^2* [2]
cover, 74, *'eben* [1]
cover, 743, *'ereb* [1]
under cover, 928+9564, *b^e-+tormâ* [1]
cover, 3260, *ṭāpal* [1]
cover, 3971, *kikkār* [1]
cover themselves, 4059, *kāsâ* [1]
cover the offense, 4064+6524, *k^{e}sût+'ayin^1* [1]
cover, 4064, *k^{e}sût* [1]
cover, 4833, *m^{e}kasseh* [1]
cover, 4848, *mālē'^{1}* [1]
cover, 4848+7156, *mālē'^{1}+pāneh* [1]
cover, 4850, *m^{e}lō'* [1]
cover, 5041, *mistār* [1]
cover, 5989+4062, *nātan+kāsûy* [1]
cover, 6108, *sōk* [1]
cover, 6114, *sākak^1* [1]
cover, 6296+6584, *'ābar^1+'al^2* [1]

cover, 6296, ʿābar[1] [1]
take cover, 6395, ʿûz [1]
cover, 7965, qāram [1]
cover, 8503, śākak[1] [1]
cover up, 8740+2256+4059, šûb[1]+wᵉ-+kāsâ [1]

COVERED [92]
covered, 4059, kāsâ [37]
covered, 4848, mālēʾ[1] [5]
covered, 2902, ḥāpâ [4]
covered, 7596, ṣāpâ[2] [4]
covered, 3212, ṭûaḥ [3]
be covered, 4059, kāsâ [3]
were covered, 4059, kāsâ [3]
covered with, 6584, ʿal[2] [3]
covered with, 4200+7156, lᵉ-[1]+pāneh [2]
covered, 4252, lābaš [2]
covered, 6114, sākak[1] [2]
covered, 448, ʾel [1]
covered, 682, ʾᵃpuddâ [1]
is covered, 2014, dāšēn[1] [1]
covered, 2118+928, hāyâ+bᵉ- [1]
was covered, 2902, ḥāpâ [1]
covered with shame, 2917, ḥāpar[2] [1]
covered with, 3972, kōl [1]
are covered, 4059, kāsâ [1]
covered herself, 4059, kāsâ [1]
covered up, 4059, kāsâ [1]
was covered, 4059, kāsâ [1]
covered, 4229, lābûš [1]
covered, 4286, lûṭ [1]
covered, 5267+8048, marbad+rābad [1]
covered, 6211, sāpan [1]
covered with the cloud, 6380, ʿûb [1]
covered with a mantle, 6486, ʿāṭā[1] [1]
covered, 6486, ʿāṭā[1] [1]
covered with smoke, 6939, ʿāšan [1]
covered, 7369, ṣāb[1] [1]
covered, 7965, qāram [1]
covered with, 8470+6017+6017, śāḥîp+sābîb+sābîb [1]
covered, 8492+4200, śîm+lᵉ-[1] [1]
covered, 9530, tāpaś [1]

COVERING [37]
covering, 4832, mikseh [12]
covering, 3866, yōteret [11]
covering, 4059, kāsâ [7]
covering, 4064, kᵉsût [2]
covering, 5009, māsāk [2]
covering, 4062, kāsûy [1]
covering, 6260, sēter [1]
covering, 8526, śᵉmîkâ [1]

COVERINGS [3]
coverings, 2514, hᵃgôrâ [1]
coverings, 4832, mikseh [1]
coverings bed, 5267, marbad [1]

COVERS [21]
covers, 4059, kāsâ [15]
covers, 297, ʾāḥaz[2] [1]
covers, 955, beged[2] [1]
covers, 995+928, bôʾ+bᵉ- [1]
covers over, 4059, kāsâ [1]
covers, 5819, nāsak[2] [1]
covers, 6259, sātar [1]

COVES [1]
coves, 5153, miprāṣ [1]

COVET [6]
covet, 2773, ḥāmad [6]

COVETED [1]
coveted, 2773, ḥāmad [1]

COW [4]
cow, 1330, bāqār [1]
young cow, 6320+1330, ʿeglâ+bāqār [1]
cow, 7239, pārâ[2] [1]
cow, 8802, šôr [1]

COWER [1]
cower, 3950, kāḥaš [1]

COWERED [1]
cowered, 8820, šāḥaḥ [1]

COWERING [1]
cowering prisoners, 7579, ṣāʿâ [1]

COWS [34]
cows, 7239, pārâ[2] [18]
sea cows, 9391, taḥaš[1] [12]
cows, 1330, bāqār [2]
cows[s], 2179, hēnnâ[2] [1]
hides of sea cows, 9391, taḥaš[1] [1]

COZBI [2]
Cozbi, 3944, kozbî [2]

COZEBA [1]
Cozeba, 3943, kōzēbāʾ [1]

CRACK [1]
crack, 7754, qôl [1]

CRACKED [5]
cracked, 1324, bāqaʿ [2]
cracked, 3169, ḥātat [1]
cracked, 7288+5877, pereṣ[1]+nāpal [1]
cracked, 8368, rāṣaṣ [1]

CRACKLING [2]
crackling, 7754, qôl [2]

CRAFT [1]
craft, 6275, ʿᵃbōdâ [1]

CRAFTED [1]
crafted, 5126, maʿᵃśeh [1]

CRAFTINESS [1]
craftiness, 6891, ʿāram[2] [1]

CRAFTS [2]
crafts, 4856, mᵉlāʾkâ [2]

CRAFTSMAN [18]
craftsman, 3093, ḥārāš [8]
skilled craftsman, 3110, ḥōšēb [8]
craftsman, 570, ʾāmôn[1] [1]
craftsman, 3086, ḥārāš[1] [1]

CRAFTSMAN'S [2]
craftsman's, 588, ʾommān [1]
craftsman's, 3093, ḥārāš [1]

CRAFTSMANSHIP [2]
artistic craftsmanship, 4742, maḥᵃšābâ [1]
craftsmanship, 4856, mᵉlāʾkâ [1]

CRAFTSMEN [21]
craftsmen, 3093, ḥārāš [11]
craftsmen, 2682, ḥākām [2]
skilled craftsmen, 2682, ḥākām [2]
craftsmen, NIH/RPE [1]
the craftsmen[s], 465, ʾēlleh [1]
craftsmen, 570, ʾāmôn[1] [1]
craftsmen, 1215, bānâ [1]
craftsmen, 2682+4213, ḥākām+lēb [1]
master craftsmen, 6913+4856, ʿāśâ[1]+mᵉlāʾkâ [1]

CRAFTY [7]
crafty, 6874, ʿārûm [3]
crafty, 4659, mᵉzimmâ [2]
crafty, 5915, nāṣar [1]
very crafty, 6891+6891, ʿāram[2]+ʿāram[2] [1]

CRAG [3]
rocky crag, 6152, selaʿ[1] [1]
crag, 7446, ṣûr[4] [1]
crag, 9094, šēn[1] [1]

CRAGS [6]
crags, 6152, selaʿ[1] [4]
rocky crags, 6152, selaʿ[1] [1]
crags, 7446, ṣûr[4] [1]

CRASH [1]
crash, 8691, šeber[1] [1]

CRAVE [6]
crave, 203, ʾāwâ[1] [4]
crave, 197, ʾaw [1]
crave other food, 203+9294, ʾāwâ[1]+taʾᵃwâ[1] [1]

CRAVED [4]
craved other food, 203, ʾāwâ[1] [1]
craved, 5883, nepeš [1]
craved, 9294, taʾᵃwâ[1] [1]
what craved, 9294, taʾᵃwâ[1] [1]

CRAVES [3]
craves, 203, ʾāwâ[1] [2]
craves for more, 203+9294, ʾāwâ[1]+taʾᵃwâ[1] [1]

CRAVING [6]
gave in to craving, 203+9294, ʾāwâ[1]+taʾᵃwâ[1] [1]
craving, 205+5883, ʾawwâ+nepeš [1]
craving, 1061, beṭen[1] [1]
craving, 2094, hawwâ[1] [1]
craving, 5883, nepeš [1]
craving, 9294, taʾᵃwâ[1] [1]

CRAVINGS [1]
cravings, 9294, taʾᵃwâ[1] [1]

CRAWL [2]
crawl, 2143, hālak [1]
crawl, 2323, zāḥal[1] [1]

CRAWLING [3]
crawling out, 3655, yāṣāʾ [1]
crawling things, 8254, remeś [1]
crawling thing, 9238, šereṣ [1]

CREAM [2]
cream, 2772, ḥemʾâ [2]

CREATE [10]
create, 1343, bārāʾ[1] [10]

CREATED [32]
created, 1343, bārāʾ[1] [21]
were created, 1343, bārāʾ[1] [6]
are created, 1343, bārāʾ[1] [2]
not yet created, 1343, bārāʾ[1] [1]
created, 6913, ʿāśâ[1] [1]
created, 7865, qānâ[2] [1]

CREATES [1]
creates, 1343, bārāʾ[1] [1]

CREATING [2]
creating, 1343, bārāʾ[1] [2]

CREATION [1]
creation, 3671, yēṣer[1] [1]

CREATOR [7]
Creator, 1343, bārāʾ[1] [3]
Creator, 7865, qānâ[2] [3]
Creator, 3670, yāṣar [1]

CREATURE [31]
creature, 1414, bāśār [7]
creature, 5883, nepeš [4]
creature, 9238, šereṣ [3]
living creature, 2651, ḥayyâ[1] [2]
creature, 8254, remeś [2]
creature, AIT [1]
creature, NIH/RPE [1]
another creature[s], 408, ʾîš[1] [1]
creature[s], 889, ʾᵃšer [1]
creature, 2644, ḥay[1] [1]
creature, 2651, ḥayyâ[1] [1]
living creature, 3685, yᵉqûm [1]
creature made, 5126, maʿᵃśeh [1]
winged creature, 6416, ʿôp [1]
creature, 6913, ʿāśâ[1] [1]
creature that moves, 8253, rāmaś [1]
creature that moves, 8254, remeś [1]
creature, 10125, bᵉśar [1]

CREATURES [66]
living creatures, 2651, ḥayyâ[1] [13]
creatures, 5883, nepeš [6]
creatures that move, 8254, remeś [5]
the creatures[s], 4392, -ām [4]
desert creatures, 7470, ṣî[2] [4]
creatures, 9238, šereṣ [4]

creatures, 2651, *ḥayyâ*[1] [3]
creatures, *NIH/RPE* [2]
the creatures[s], 889, *'^{a}šer* [2]
creatures, 1414, *bāśār* [2]
creatures, 2328, *zîz*[1] [2]
creatures, 6639, *'am*[2] [2]
creatures, 8254, *remeś* [2]
creatures, *AIT* [1]
creatures[s], 889, *'^{a}šer* [1]
living creatures, 2645, *ḥay*[2] [1]
night creatures, 4327, *lîlît* [1]
the creatures[s], 5527, *-ān* [1]
creatures of the desert, 7470, *ṣî*[2] [1]
creatures, 7871, *qinyān* [1]
creatures that move, 8253, *rāmaś* [1]
creatures that move along the ground, 8254, *remeś* [1]
sea creatures, 8254, *remeś* [1]
small creatures, 8254, *remeś* [1]
teeming creatures, 8254, *remeś* [1]
creatures that move along the ground, 9238, *šereṣ* [1]
creatures of the sea, 9490, *tannîn* [1]
great sea creatures, 9490, *tannîn* [1]

CREDIT [1]
giving credit to, 928+9005, *b^{e}-+šēm*[1] [1]

CREDITED [5]
be credited, 3108, *ḥāšab* [1]
credited, 3108, *ḥāšab* [1]
was credited, 3108, *ḥāšab* [1]
credited, 5989, *nātan* [1]
credited to, 6584, *'al*[2] [1]

CREDITOR [4]
creditor, 5957, *nāšā'*[1] [3]
creditor, 1251+5408+3338+2257, *ba'al*[1]*+maššeh+yād+-ô* [1]

CREDITORS [1]
creditors, 5957, *nāšā'*[1] [1]

CREPT [2]
crept, 995, *bô'* [1]
crept up, 7756, *qûm* [1]

CRESCENT [1]
crescent necklaces, 8448, *śah^{a}rōnîm* [1]

CREST [2]
crest, 4195, *keter* [1]
crest, 8031, *rō'š*[1] [1]

CREVICE [1]
crevice, 5932, *nāqîq* [1]

CREVICES [2]
crevices, 5932, *nāqîq* [2]

CRICKET [1]
cricket, 3005, *ḥargōl* [1]

CRIED [75]
cried out, 2410, *zā'aq* [16]
cried out, 7590, *ṣā'aq* [16]
cried out, 7924, *qārā'*[1] [9]
cried, 606, *'āmar*[1] [6]
cried, 2410, *zā'aq* [5]
cried for help, 8775, *šāwa'* [4]
cried out, 606, *'āmar*[1] [3]
cried for help, 7590, *ṣā'aq* [3]
cried, 7924, *qārā'*[1] [3]
cried, 7590, *ṣā'aq* [2]
cried, 1134, *bākâ* [1]
cried for help, 2410, *zā'aq* [1]
cried out for help, 2410, *zā'aq* [1]
cried for mercy, 2858, *ḥānan*[1] [1]
cried out, 3291, *yābab* [1]
cried, 7627, *ṣāpap* [1]
cried out for help, 7754+7590, *qôl+ṣā'aq* [1]
cried out, 7754, *qôl* [1]

CRIES [22]
cries out, 2410, *zā'aq* [4]
cries out, 7590, *ṣā'aq* [3]
cries, 7754, *qôl* [3]
cries, *NIH/RPE* [2]
cries, 7591, *ṣ^{e}'āqâ* [2]
war cries, 9558, *t^{e}rû'â* [2]
cries, 606, *'āmar*[1] [1]
cries, 7424, *ṣ^{e}wāḥâ* [1]
cries of distress, 7591, *ṣ^{e}'āqâ* [1]
cries out, 7924, *qārā'*[1] [1]
cries aloud, 8264, *rānan* [1]
cries for help, 8780, *šûa'*[1] [1]

CRIME [13]
crime, 6411, *'āwōn* [4]
crime, *AIT* [1]
crime committed, 2627, *ḥāṭā'* [1]
crime, 2805, *ḥāmās* [1]
crime, 5126+8288, *ma'^{a}śeh+rā'â*[3] [1]
crime, 6240, *sārâ*[2] [1]
crime, 6406, *'awlâ* [1]
crime, 7322, *peša'* [1]
awful crime, 8288, *rā'â*[3] [1]
crime, 8402, *riš'â* [1]

CRIMES [5]
crimes, 8288, *rā'â*[3] [2]
shameful crimes, 2365, *zimmâ*[1] [1]
crimes, 6411, *'āwōn* [1]
crimes, 8273, *ra'*[1] [1]

CRIMINALS [1]
criminals, 2629, *ḥaṭṭā'* [1]

CRIMSON [5]
crimson, 4147, *karmîl* [3]
stained crimson, 2808, *ḥāmēṣ*[3] [1]
crimson, 9355, *tôlā'*[1] [1]

CRINGE [4]
cringe, 3950, *kāḥaš* [3]
cringe, 4156, *kāra'* [1]

CRINGING [1]
come cringing, 3950, *kāḥaš* [1]

CRIPPLED [6]
crippled, 7177, *pissēaḥ* [3]
crippled, 5783, *nākeh* [1]
became crippled, 7174, *pāsaḥ*[2] [1]
crippled, 8691, *šeber*[1] [1]

CRITICAL [1]
critical, 7639, *ṣar*[1] [1]

CRITICALLY [1]
critically, 4394, *m^{e}'ōd* [1]

CRITICIZED [1]
criticized, 8189, *rîb*[1] [1]

CROCUS [1]
crocus, 2483, *ḥ^{a}baṣṣelet* [1]

CROOKED [11]
crooked, 6836, *'iqqēš*[1] [3]
crooked, 5675, *nûa'* [1]
made crooked, 6390, *'āwâ*[1] [1]
made crooked, 6430, *'āwat* [1]
crooked ways, 6824, *'^{a}qalqāl* [1]
takes crooked, 6835, *'āqaš* [1]
turned crooked, 6835, *'āqaš* [1]
crooked, 7349, *pātal* [1]
crooked, 7350, *p^{e}taltōl* [1]

CROP [6]
second crop, 4381, *leqeš* [1]
crop, 5126, *ma'^{a}śeh* [1]
crop, 5263, *mur'â* [1]
crop, 6913, *'āsâ*[1] [1]
crop comes in, 9311, *t^{e}bû'â* [1]
crop, 9311, *t^{e}bû'â* [1]

CROPS [38]
crops, 3292, *y^{e}bûl* [7]
crops, 7262, *p^{e}rî* [7]
crops, 9311, *t^{e}bû'â* [6]
crops, 141, *'^{a}dāmâ*[1] [2]
planted crops, 2445, *zāra'* [2]
crops, 5126, *ma'^{a}śeh* [2]
crops, *NIH/RPE* [1]
gathers crops, 112, *'āgar* [1]
crops, 2446, *zera'* [1]
crops, 3946, *kōaḥ*[1] [1]
crops, 4312, *leḥem* [1]
land for crops, 4760, *maṭṭā'* [1]
crops, 4852, *m^{e}lē'â* [1]
crops, 7262+2021+141, *p^{e}rî+ha-+'^{a}dāmâ*[1] [1]
crops, 7368, *ṣe'^{e}ṣā'îm* [1]
crops, 7542, *ṣemaḥ* [1]
harvesting crops, 9311, *t^{e}bû'â* [1]
crops, 9482, *t^{e}nûbâ* [1]

CROSS [55]
cross, 6296, *'ābar*[1] [28]
cross over, 6296, *'ābar*[1] [23]
cross over, 2005, *dārak* [1]
cross, 6015, *sābab* [1]
cross over without fail, 6296+6296, *'ābar*[1]*+'ābar*[1] [1]
make cross, 6296, *'ābar*[1] [1]

CROSSBAR [2]
crossbar, 1378, *b^{e}rîaḥ* [2]

CROSSBARS [12]
crossbars, 1378, *b^{e}rîaḥ* [11]
crossbars, 4574, *môṭâ* [1]

CROSSED [49]
crossed, 6296, *'ābar*[1] [31]
crossed over, 6296, *'ābar*[1] [17]
crossed, 3655, *yāṣā'* [1]

CROSSES [1]
crosses over, 6296, *'ābar*[1] [1]

CROSSING [15]
crossing, 6296, *'ābar*[1] [12]
crossing over, 6296, *'ābar*[1] [1]
crossing, 6584+7156, *'al*[2]*+pāneh* [1]
crossing, 8506, *śākal*[2] [1]

CROSSINGS [1]
river crossings, 5045, *ma'bārâ* [1]

CROSSROADS [2]
crossroads, 2006, *derek* [1]
crossroads, 7294, *pereq* [1]

CROUCH [3]
crouch down, 4156, *kāra'* [1]
crouch, 4156, *kāra'* [1]
crouch, 8820, *šāḥaḥ* [1]

CROUCHES [1]
crouches, 4156, *kāra'* [1]

CROUCHING [2]
crouching, 3782, *yāšab* [1]
crouching, 8069, *rābaṣ* [1]

CROWD [15]
crowd, 2162, *hāmôn* [7]
crowd, 7736, *qāhāl* [3]
crowd, 8041, *rab*[1] [2]
crowd, 3972+889+6641, *kōl+'^{a}šer+'āmad* [1]
crowd, 6809, *'^{a}ṣārâ* [1]
noisy crowd, 8095, *rigšâ* [1]

CROWDED [4]
crowded into, 995, *bô'* [1]
crowded, 4848, *mālē'*[1] [1]
crowded, 7735, *qāhal* [1]
crowded around, 10359, *k^{e}naš* [1]

CROWN [36]
crown, 6498, *'^{a}ṭārâ*[1] [18]
crown, 5694, *nēzer* [7]
crown, 4195, *keter* [2]
crown, 6584, *'al*[2] [2]
crown, *NIH/RPE* [1]
crown, 4200, *l^{e}-*[1] [1]
crown, 4887, *mālak*[1] [1]
crown, 6497, *'āṭar*[2] [1]
crown of beauty, 6996, *p^{e}'ēr* [1]
crown, 7619, *ṣ^{e}pîrâ* [1]
crown of head, 7721, *qodqōd* [1]

CROWNED [3]
crowned, 6497, *ʿāṭar*[2] [2]
crowned, 4194, *kātar*[3] [1]

CROWNS [8]
crowns, 6498, *ʿaṭārâ*[1] [2]
crowns, 4200+8031, *le-*[1]*+rōʾš*[1] [1]
bestower of crowns, 6497, *ʿāṭar*[2] [1]
crowns, 6497, *ʿāṭar*[2] [1]
crowns, 6584, *ʿal*[2] [1]
crowns, 6995, *pāʾar*[2] [1]
crowns, 7721, *qodqōd* [1]

CRUCIBLE [2]
crucible, 5214, *maṣrēp* [2]

CRUEL [16]
cruel, 426, *ʾakzārî* [7]
cruel, 7997, *qāšeh* [3]
cruel, 427, *ʾakzeriyyût* [1]
cruel, 2807, *ḥāmēṣ*[2] [1]
cruel, 6883, *ʿārîṣ* [1]
cruel, 7996, *qāšâ* [1]
cruel, 8273, *raʿ*[1] [1]
cruel, 8368, *rāṣaṣ* [1]

CRUELLY [1]
cruelly, 928+2622, *be-+ḥozqâ* [1]

CRUELTY [1]
cruelty, 8288, *rāʿâ*[3] [1]

CRUMBLE [2]
crumble, 5877, *nāpal* [1]
crumble, 7359+7326, *pātat+pat* [1]

CRUMBLED [1]
crumbled, 7207, *pāṣaṣ* [1]

CRUMBLES [1]
crumbles, 5570, *nābēl*[1] [1]

CRUMBLING [1]
crumbling, 6963, *ʿātad* [1]

CRUSH [26]
crush, 1917, *dākāʾ* [7]
crush, 4730, *māḥaṣ* [3]
crush, 8689, *šābar*[1] [2]
crush, 8789, *šûp*[1] [2]
crush, 10182, *deqaq* [2]
crush, *NIH/RPE* [1]
crush, 1990, *dāqaq* [1]
crush, 2070, *hādak* [1]
crush, 2318, *zûr*[1] [1]
crush, 3561, *yānâ* [1]
crush, 4198, *kātat* [1]
crush, 6421, *ʿûq* [1]
crush bones, 6793, *ʿāṣam*[1] [1]
crush olives, 7414, *ṣāhar* [1]
crush, 8368, *rāṣaṣ* [1]

CRUSHED [41]
crushed, 1917, *dākāʾ* [4]
crushed, 1920, *dākâ* [4]
crushed, 4198, *kātat* [3]
crushed, 10182, *deqaq* [3]
crushed, 4730, *māḥaṣ* [2]
crushed, 5779, *nākēʾ* [2]
crushed, 8368, *rāṣaṣ* [2]
are crushed, 8689, *šābar*[1] [2]
crushed completely, 430+2256+4730, *ʾākal+we-+māḥaṣ* [1]
crushed grain, 1762, *gereś* [1]
crushed, 1762, *gereś* [1]
crushed, 1870, *dûk* [1]
was crushed, 1917, *dākāʾ* [1]
crushed, 1918, *dakkāʾ*[1] [1]
crushed, 3983, *kālâ*[1] [1]
was crushed, 4198, *kātat* [1]
crushed, 4536, *medušâ* [1]
crushed, 4735, *māḥaq* [1]
crushed to pieces, 5879, *nāpaṣ*[1] [1]
crushed, 6943, *ʿāšaq* [1]
crushed, 7207, *pāṣaṣ* [1]
crushed, 8317, *rāʿaʿ*[1] [1]
been crushed, 8406, *rāšaš* [1]
crushed, 8689, *šābar*[1] [1]
were crushed, 8689, *šābar*[1] [1]
crushed, 8691, *šeber*[1] [1]
crushed, 9012, *šāmad* [1]

CRUSHES [4]
crushes, 1917, *dākāʾ* [1]
crushes, 5779, *nākēʾ* [1]
crushes, 6421, *ʿûq* [1]
crushes, 8691, *šeber*[1] [1]

CRUSHING [6]
crushing, 1917, *dākāʾ* [1]
crushing, 1918, *dakkāʾ*[1] [1]
crushing, 2703+4394, *ḥālâ*[1]*+meʾōd* [1]
crushing, 4315, *lāḥaṣ* [1]
crushing, 4730, *māḥaṣ* [1]
crushing, 10182, *deqaq* [1]

CRUST [2]
crust, 3971, *kikkār* [1]
crust, 7326, *pat* [1]

CRUTCH [1]
crutch, 7134, *pelek*[1] [1]

CRY [154]
cry out, 2410, *zāʿaq* [18]
cry, 8262, *rinnâ*[1] [10]
cry out, 7590, *ṣāʿaq* [9]
cry, 7591, *ṣeʿāqâ* [9]
cry, 7754, *qôl* [8]
cry, 2411, *zeʿāqâ* [7]
cry out, 7924, *qārāʾ*[1] [7]
cry for help, 8775, *šāwaʿ* [7]
cry, 8784, *šawʿâ* [7]
cry for mercy, 7754+9384, *qôl+taḥanûn* [6]
cry, 7924, *qārāʾ*[1] [6]
battle cry, 9558, *terûʿâ* [5]
cry, *NIH/RPE* [4]
cry, 2410, *zāʿaq* [3]
cry out, 8775, *šāwaʿ* [3]
cry for help, 8784, *šawʿâ* [3]
cry out, 606, *ʾāmar*[1] [2]
cry out, 8264, *rānan* [2]
cry for mercy, 9384, *taḥanûn* [2]
cry, 9558, *terûʿâ* [2]
cry, 606, *ʾāmar*[1] [1]
cry out, 2159, *hāmâ* [1]
cry out for help, 2410, *zāʿaq* [1]
sent up a cry, 2410, *zāʿaq* [1]
war cry, 4878, *milḥāmâ* [1]
cry out, 5951+4200+606, *nāśāʾ+le-*[1]*+ʾāmar*[1] [1]
cry aloud, 5989+7754, *nātan+qôl* [1]
cry out, 7184, *pāʿâ* [1]
cry out, 7412+7754, *ṣāhal*[1]*+qôl* [1]
cry of distress, 7424, *ṣewāḥâ* [1]
cry out, 7424, *ṣewāḥâ* [1]
cry, 7424, *ṣewāḥâ* [1]
cry aloud, 7590, *ṣāʿaq* [1]
cry out, 7590+7590, *ṣāʿaq+ṣāʿaq* [1]
cry, 7590, *ṣāʿaq* [1]
cry, 7591+7754, *ṣeʿāqâ+qôl* [1]
raise the battle cry, 7658, *ṣāraḥ* [1]
cry for help, 7754+2410, *qôl+zāʿaq* [1]
cry for help, 7754+8776, *qôl+šewaʿ* [1]
cry out, 7754+2411, *qôl+zeʿāqâ* [1]
cry, 7754+7591, *qôl+ṣeʿāqâ* [1]
war cry, 7754, *qôl* [1]
raised a cry, 7924, *qārāʾ*[1] [1]
raise the battle cry, 8131, *rûaʿ* [1]
raise the war cry, 8131, *rûaʿ* [1]
cry aloud, 8131+8275, *rûaʿ+rēaʿ*[1] [1]
cry out, 8131, *rûaʿ* [1]
give a war cry, 8131, *rûaʿ* [1]
raised the battle cry, 8131, *rûaʿ* [1]
sound of battle cry, 8131, *rûaʿ* [1]
cry out for help, 8775, *šāwaʿ* [1]
cry out, 9048+2411, *šāmaʿ+zeʿāqâ* [1]
cry out, 9048, *šāmaʿ* [1]
cry for mercy, 9382, *teḥinnâ*[1] [1]

CRYING [11]
crying out, 2410, *zāʿaq* [2]
crying out, 7590, *ṣāʿaq* [2]
crying, 7754, *qôl* [2]
crying, 1134, *bākâ* [1]
crying, 2411, *zeʿāqâ* [1]
crying out, 7591, *ṣeʿāqâ* [1]
crying out, 8131, *rûaʿ* [1]
crying out, 8779, *šôaʿ*[3] [1]

CRYSTAL [1]
crystal, 2343, *zekôkît* [1]

CUB [2]
cub, 1594, *gûr*[4] [2]

CUBIT [37]
cubit, 564, *ʾammâ*[1] [37]

CUBITS [219]
cubits, 564, *ʾammâ*[1] [164]
cubits, *NIH/RPE* [53]
long cubits, 564, *ʾammâ*[1] [2]

CUBS [11]
cubs, 1594, *gûr*[4] [3]
cubs, 1201, *bēn*[1] [2]
cubs, 1596, *gôr* [2]
robbed of cubs, 8891, *šakkûl* [2]
cubs, 408, *ʾîš*[1] [1]
cubs, 1594+793, *gûr*[4]*+ʾaryēh*[1] [1]

CUCUMBERS [1]
cucumbers, 7991, *qiššuʾâ* [1]

CUD [11]
cud, 1742, *gērâ*[1] [11]

CULTIVATE [2]
cultivate, 6268, *ʿābad* [1]
cultivate, 6275, *ʿabōdâ* [1]

CULTIVATED [4]
cultivated, 6371, *ʿādar*[2] [2]
cultivated, 4340, *lāmad* [1]
be cultivated, 6268, *ʿābad* [1]

CUMMIN [3]
cummin, 4021, *kammōn* [3]

CUN [1]
Cun, 3923, *kûn*[2] [1]

CUNNING [2]
cunning, 6678, *ʿāmōq* [1]
cunning, 6891, *ʿāram*[2] [1]

CUP [34]
cup, 3926, *kôs*[1] [26]
cup, 1483, *gābîaʿ* [4]
cup, *NIH/RPE* [2]
the cup[s], 889, *ʾašer* [1]
cup, 6195, *sap*[1] [1]

CUPBEARER [10]
cupbearer, 5482, *mašqeh*[1] [10]

CUPBEARERS [2]
cupbearers, 5482, *mašqeh*[1] [2]

CUPS [7]
cups, 1483, *gābîaʿ* [6]
cups, 3926, *kôs*[1] [1]

CURDLE [1]
curdle, 7884, *qāpāʾ* [1]

CURDLED [1]
curdled milk, 2772, *ḥemʾâ* [1]

CURDS [7]
curds, 2772, *ḥemʾâ* [6]
curds, 2692, *ḥālāb* [1]

CURE [7]
cure, 665, *ʾāsap* [3]
cure, 8324, *rāpāʾ*[1] [2]
beyond cure, 631, *ʾānûš* [1]
no cure, 631, *ʾānûš* [1]

CURED [3]
be cured, 8324, *rāpāʾ*[1] [2]
cured, 665, *ʾāsap* [1]

CURRENT [1]
according to the weight current, 6296, ʿābar[1] [1]

CURRENTS [1]
currents, 5643, nāhār [1]

CURRY [1]
curry favor with, 2704+7156, ḥālâ[2]+pāneh [1]

CURSE [78]
curse, 7837, qālal [12]
curse, 7839, qᵉlālâ [12]
curse, 826, ʾārar [11]
curse, 7686, qābab [8]
curse, 460, ʾālâ[4] [7]
brings a curse, 826, ʾārar [5]
curse, 1385, bārak[2] [3]
put a curse on, 826, ʾārar [2]
under a curse, 826, ʾārar [2]
curse, 4423, mᵉʾērâ [2]
put a curse on, 7686, qābab [2]
utter a curse, 457, ʾālâ[1] [2]
curse bitterly, 826+826, ʾārar+ʾārar [1]
use name as a curse, 928+8678, bᵉ-+šābaʿ [1]
curse, 3051, ḥērem[1] [1]
curse, 4423+826, mᵉʾērâ+ʾārar [1]
curse at all, 7686+7686, qābab+qābab [1]
call a curse down, 7837, qālal [1]
called down a curse, 7837, qālal [1]
pronounce a curse on, 7837, qālal [1]
put a curse on, 7837, qālal [1]
curse, 8652, šᵉbûʿâ [1]
curse, 9297, taʾᵃlâ [1]

CURSED [53]
cursed, 826, ʾārar [32]
cursed, 7837, qālal [8]
be cursed, 826, ʾārar [7]
cursed, 1385, bārak[2] [3]
cursed, 7686, qābab [2]
is cursed, 7837, qālal [1]

CURSES [28]
curses, 460, ʾālâ[4] [8]
curses, 7837, qālal [7]
curses, 7839, qᵉlālâ [7]
curses, 4423, mᵉʾērâ [2]
curses, 1821, dābār [1]
called curses down, 7837, qālal [1]
called down curses, 7837+7839, qālal+qᵉlālâ [1]
pronounce curses, 7839, qᵉlālâ [1]

CURSING [16]
cursing, 7839, qᵉlālâ [5]
object of cursing, 7839, qᵉlālâ [4]
object of cursing, 460, ʾālâ[4] [3]
cursing, 7837, qālal [3]
cursing, 457, ʾālâ[1] [1]

CURTAIN [56]
curtain, 7267, pārōket [25]
curtain, 5009, māsāk [17]
curtain, 3749, yᵉrîʿâ [14]

CURTAINS [36]
curtains, 3749, yᵉrîʿâ [18]
curtains, 7846, qelaʿ[2] [15]
curtains, NIH/RPE [1]
tent curtains, 3749, yᵉrîʿâ [1]
curtains, 5009, māsāk [1]

CURVED [4]
curved, 6015, sābab [2]
curved around, 6015, sābab [1]
curved, 9305, tāʾar[1] [1]

CUSH [27]
Cush, 3932, kûš[1] [26]
Cush, 3933, kûš[2] [1]

CUSHAN [1]
Cushan, 3936, kûšān [1]

CUSHAN-RISHATHAIM [2]
Cushan-Rishathaim, 3937, kûšan rišʿātayim [2]

CUSHI [2]
Cushi, 3935, kûšî[2] [2]

CUSHITE [17]
Cushite, 3934, kûšî[1] [14]
Cushite, 3932, kûš[1] [3]

CUSHITES [8]
Cushites, 3934, kûšî[1] [7]
Cushites, 1201+3934, bēn[1]+kûšî[1] [1]

CUSTODY [7]
custody, 5464, mišmār[1] [6]
custody, 3338, yād [1]

CUSTOM [8]
custom, 5477, mišpāṭ [2]
custom, 2006, derek [1]
custom, 2976, ḥōq [1]
it was the custom of, 3954, kî[2] [1]
custom, 6913+4027, ʿāśâ[1]+kēn[2] [1]
custom, 6913, ʿāśâ[1] [1]
establish the custom, 7756, qûm [1]

CUSTOMARY [5]
customary, NIH/RPE [2]
customary, 3869+7193+928+7193, kᵉ-+paʿam+bᵉ-+paʿam [1]
customary, 4027+1821, kēn[2]+dābār [1]
customary, 6913, ʿāśâ[1] [1]

CUSTOMERS [2]
customers, 6086+3338, sāḥar+yād [1]
customers, 6088+3338, sᵉḥōrâ+yād [1]

CUSTOMS [6]
customs, 2978, ḥuqqâ [3]
customs, 2017, dāt [1]
customs, 5126, maʿᵃśeh [1]
customs, 5477, mišpāṭ [1]

CUT [257]
cut off, 4162, kārat [56]
be cut off, 4162, kārat [37]
cut down, 4162, kārat [20]
cut, 4162, kārat [7]
cut off, 6073, sûr[1] [6]
cut down, 5782, nākâ [5]
cut down, 1548, gādaʿ [4]
cut into pieces, 5983, nātaḥ [4]
cut, 5983, nātaḥ [4]
cut off, 7915, qāṣaṣ[1] [4]
cut off, 8689, šābar[1] [4]
cut off, 1298, bāṣaʿ [3]
cut off, 1548, gādaʿ [3]
be cut down, 4162, kārat [3]
cut off, 4577, mûl[2] [3]
cut down, 5877, nāpal [3]
cut short, 7918, qāṣar[2] [3]
cut down, 8845, šāḥat [3]
cut yourselves, 1517, gādad[1] [2]
cut to pieces, 1548, gādaʿ [2]
cut, 1607, gāzît [2]
are cut off, 1615, gāzar[1] [2]
cut hair, 1662, gālaḥ [2]
cut off, 1757, gāraʿ[1] [2]
cut, 2634, ḥāṭab [2]
cut out, 2933, ḥāṣēb[1] [2]
cut, 3098, ḥᵃrōšet[1] [2]
was cut off, 4162, kārat [2]
have cut down, 5877, nāpal [2]
cut down, 10134, gᵉdad [2]
cut, NIH/RPE [1]
cut off, 1299, beṣaʿ [1]
cut, 1324, bāqaʿ [1]
cut down, 1345, bārā[3] [1]
cut in half, 1439, bātar [1]
cut, 1439, bātar [1]
cut himself, 1517, gādad[1] [1]
cut themselves, 1517, gādad[1] [1]
be cut off, 1548, gādaʿ [1]
cut short, 1548, gādaʿ [1]
cut through, 1548, gādaʿ [1]
is cut off, 1548, gādaʿ [1]
cut off, 1605, gāzaz [1]
be cut off, 1605, gāzaz [1]
cut in two, 1615, gāzar[1] [1]
cut, 1615, gāzar[1] [1]
be cut off, 1615, gāzar[1] [1]
cut down, 1615, gāzar[1] [1]
was cut off, 1615, gāzar[1] [1]
am cut off, 1746, gāraz [1]
cut off, 2386, zānab [1]
are cut short, 2403, zāʿak [1]
cut down, 2634, ḥāṭab [1]
cut in pieces, 2933, ḥāṣēb[1] [1]
cut to pieces, 2933, ḥāṣēb[1] [1]
were cut, 2933, ḥāṣēb[1] [1]
cut down, 3718, yārad [1]
cut, 4065, kāsaḥ [1]
is cut down, 4065, kāsaḥ [1]
cut out, 4125, kārâ[1] [1]
are cut off, 4162, kārat [1]
be cut out, 4162, kārat [1]
been cut off, 4162, kārat [1]
cut up, 4162, kārat [1]
is cut down, 4162, kārat [1]
must surely be cut off, 4162+4162, kārat+kārat [1]
was cut, 4162, kārat [1]
were cut off, 4162, kārat [1]
cut to pieces, 4730, māḥaṣ [1]
are cut off, 4909, mālal[2] [1]
cut down, 5937, nāqap[1] [1]
cut hair, 5938, nāqap[2] [1]
cut up, 5983, nātaḥ [1]
cut down, 6618, ʿālal[1] [1]
cut grain, 6658, ʿāmîr [1]
cut up, 7114, pālaḥ [1]
cut, 7180, pāsal [1]
cut, 7892, qāṣab [1]
cut free, 7915, qāṣaṣ[1] [1]
cut, 7915, qāṣaṣ[1] [1]
cut off, 7973, qāraʿ [1]
cut, 8581+8583, śāraṭ+śāreṭet [1]
cut, 8582+5989, śereṭ+nātan [1]
cut off, 8697, šābat[1] [1]
cut down, 8961, šalleket[1] [1]
cut off, 9012, šāmad [1]
cut down, 9372, tāzaz [1]
cut out, 10140, gᵉzar [1]
was cut out, 10140, gᵉzar [1]
be cut into, 10522, ʿᵃbad [1]
cut into, 10522, ʿᵃbad [1]

CUTHAH [2]
Cuthah, 3939, kût [1]
Cuthah, 3940, kûtâ [1]

CUTS [3]
cuts through, 1548, gādaʿ [1]
cuts, 7103, pālag [1]
cuts, 7287, pāraṣ [1]

CUTTER [1]
cutter, 3093, ḥārāš [1]

CUTTING [6]
cutting down, 4156, kāraʿ [1]
cutting off, 4162, kārat [1]
cutting, 4162+9163, kārat+šopkâ [1]
cutting, 4162, kārat [1]
cutting down, 5877, nāpal [1]
cutting off, 7894, qāṣâ[1] [1]

CYCLE [1]
cycle go on, 5938, nāqap[2] [1]

CYMBALS [16]
cymbals, 5199, mᵉṣiltayim [13]
cymbals, 7529, ṣelṣelîm [3]

CYPRESS [5]
cypress, 9309, tᵉʾaššûr [2]
cypress, 1729, gōper [1]
cypress wood, 9309, tᵉʾaššûr [1]
cypress, 9560, tirzâ [1]

CYPRUS [3]
Cyprus, 4183, kittiyyîm [3]

CYRUS [23]
Cyrus, 3931, kôreš [15]

Cyrus, 10350, *kôreš* [7]
Cyrus^{s}, 2084, *-hû* [1]

DABBESHETH [1]
Dabbesheth, 1833, *dabbešet*^{2} [1]

DABERATH [3]
Daberath, 1829, *dāb^{e}rat* [3]

DAGGER [3]
dagger, 2995, *ḥereb* [3]

DAGON [8]
Dagon, 1837, *dāgôn* [8]

DAGON'S [2]
Dagon's, 1837, *dāgôn* [2]

DAILY [18]
daily sacrifice, 9458, *tāmîd* [5]
daily, 3427+928+3427, *yôm*^{1}*+b^{e}-+yôm*^{1} [3]
daily, 3427+3427, *yôm*^{1}*+yôm*^{1} [2]
daily, 1821+3427+928+3427,
dābār+yôm^{1}*+b^{e}-+yôm*^{1} [1]
daily bread, 2976, *ḥōq* [1]
daily, 3427+928+3427+2257,
yôm^{1}*+b^{e}-+yôm*^{1}*+-ô* [1]
daily, 4200+2021+3427, *l^{e}-*^{1}*+ha-+yôm*^{1} [1]
daily, 4200+3427+285, *l^{e}-*^{1}*+yôm*^{1}*+'eḥād* [1]
daily bread, 4312+2976, *leḥem+ḥōq* [1]
daily, 9458, *tāmîd* [1]
daily, 10317+10089+10317, *yôm+b^{e}-+yôm* [1]

DALPHON [1]
Dalphon, 1943, *dalpôn* [1]

DAM [1]
dam, 4784, *mayim* [1]

DAMAGE [2]
damage, 981, *bedeq* [2]

DAMAGED [1]
damaged, 5293, *mārôaḥ* [1]

DAMASCUS [44]
Damascus, 1966, *dammeśeq* [37]
Damascus, 2008, *darmeśeq* [6]
Damascus, 1877, *dûmmeśeq* [1]

DAMPNESS [1]
dampness, 8268, *rāsîs*^{1} [1]

DAN [59]
Dan, 1968, *dān*^{1} [33]
Dan, 1969, *dān*^{2} [20]
Dan, 1201+1968, *bēn*^{1}*+dān*^{1} [4]
Dan, 1974, *dānî* [1]
men of Dan, 1974, *dānî* [1]

DAN JAAN [1]
Dan Jaan, 1970, *dān ya'an* [1]

DANCE [5]
dance, 4688, *māḥôl*^{1} [2]
dance, 4703, *m^{e}ḥōlâ* [1]
dance about, 8376, *rāqad* [1]
dance, 8376, *rāqad* [1]

DANCED [3]
danced, 4159, *kārar* [1]
danced, 7174, *pāsaḥ*^{2} [1]
danced, 8471, *śāḥaq* [1]

DANCES [2]
dances, 4703, *m^{e}ḥōlâ* [2]

DANCING [12]
dancing, 4703, *m^{e}ḥōlâ* [5]
dancing, 4688, *māḥôl*^{1} [4]
dancing, 2565, *ḥûl*^{1} [1]
dancing, 4159, *kārar* [1]
dancing, 8376, *rāqad* [1]

DANDLED [1]
dandled, 9130, *šā'a'*^{2} [1]

DANGER [3]
danger, 8288, *rā'â*^{3} [2]
danger, 1821, *dābār* [1]

DANGERS [1]
dangers, 3152, *ḥatḥat* [1]

DANGLES [1]
dangles, 1938, *dālal*^{2} [1]

DANIEL [75]
Daniel, 10181, *dāniyyē'l* [46]
Daniel, 1975, *dāniyyē'l* [29]

DANIEL'S [2]
Daniel's, 10089+10181, *b^{e}-+dāniyyē'l* [1]
Daniel's, 10181, *dāniyyē'l* [1]

DANITE [1]
Danite, 4200+4751+1968, *l^{e}-*^{1}*+maṭṭeh+dān*^{1} [1]

DANITES [14]
Danites, 1201+1968, *bēn*^{1}*+dān*^{1} [9]
Danites, 1974, *dānî* [3]
Danites, *NIH/RPE* [1]
Danites, 1968, *dān*^{1} [1]

DANNAH [1]
Dannah, 1972, *dannâ* [1]

DAPPLED [2]
dappled, 1353, *bārōd* [2]

DARDA [2]
Darda, 1997, *darda'* [2]

DARE [3]
dare, *AIT* [2]
dare, 3523, *yākōl* [1]

DARED [1]
dared, 4848+4213, *mālē'*^{1}*+lēb* [1]

DARES [4]
dares, *AIT* [3]
dares, 3523, *yākōl* [1]

DARICS [2]
darics, 163, *'^{a}darkōnîm* [2]

DARING [1]
not daring, 3707, *yārē'*^{1} [1]

DARIUS [25]
Darius, 10184, *dār^{e}yāweš* [15]
Darius, 2003, *dār^{e}yāweš* [10]

DARK [27]
dark, 3124, *ḥāšak* [5]
dark, 3125, *ḥōšek* [4]
dark, 3128, *ḥ^{a}šēkâ* [3]
dark clouds, 6906, *'^{a}rāpel* [2]
dark cloud, 6906, *'^{a}rāpel* [2]
dark, *NIH/RPE* [1]
dark, 413+696, *'îšôn+'^{a}pēlâ* [1]
dark, 696, *'^{a}pēlâ* [1]
made dark, 3124, *ḥāšak* [1]
dark place, 3125, *ḥōšek* [1]
dark, 4326, *laylâ* [1]
dark places, 4743, *maḥšāk* [1]
dark, 7722, *qādar* [1]
go dark, 7722, *qādar* [1]
dark, 8839, *šāḥōr* [1]
dark, 8842, *š^{e}ḥarḥōr* [1]

DARK-COLORED [4]
dark-colored, 2569, *ḥûm* [4]

DARKEN [3]
darken, 7722, *qādar* [2]
darken, 3124, *ḥāšak* [1]

DARKENED [7]
darkened, 3124, *ḥāšak* [3]
darkened, 7722, *qādar* [3]
darkened, 8812, *šāzap* [1]

DARKENING [1]
darkening, 5974, *nešep* [1]

DARKENS [2]
darkens, 3124, *ḥāšak* [2]

DARKER [1]
darker, 2679, *ḥaklîlî* [1]

DARKEST [1]
darkest, 4743, *maḥšāk* [1]

DARKNESS [113]
darkness, 3125, *ḥōšek* [70]
darkness, 4743, *maḥšāk* [5]
darkness, 694, *'ōpel* [4]
darkness, 3128, *ḥ^{a}šēkâ* [4]
thick darkness, 6906, *'^{a}rāpel* [4]
thick darkness, 694, *'ōpel* [2]
darkness, 6906, *'^{a}rāpel* [2]
deep darkness, 6906, *'^{a}rāpel* [2]
darkness, 7516, *ṣalmāwet* [2]
deep darkness, 7516, *ṣalmāwet* [2]
release from darkness, 7223, *p^{e}qaḥ-qôaḥ* [1]
darkness, 696, *'^{a}pēlâ* [1]
deep darkness, 696, *'^{a}pēlâ* [1]
utter darkness, 696, *'^{a}pēlâ* [1]
pitch darkness, 854+3125, *'^{e}šûn+ḥōšek* [1]
brings darkness, 3124, *ḥāšak* [1]
total darkness, 3125+696, *ḥōšek+'^{a}pēlâ* [1]
darkness, 3127, *ḥoškâ* [1]
darkness, 4419, *ma'^{a}pēl* [1]
great darkness, 4420, *ma'pēlyâ* [1]
darkness, 6547, *'êpâ*^{1} [1]
darkness, 6602, *'^{a}lāṭâ* [1]
thick darkness, 7516, *ṣalmāwet* [1]
darkness, 7725, *qadrût* [1]
darkness, 9507, *t^{e}'upâ* [1]
darkness, 10286, *ḥ^{a}šōk* [1]

DARKON [2]
Darkon, 2010, *darqôn* [2]

DARLING [9]
darling, 8299, *ra'yâ* [9]

DART [3]
dart, 3655, *yāṣā'* [1]
dart, 5025, *massā'*^{2} [1]
dart about, 8132, *rûṣ* [1]

DARTING [4]
darting, 6414, *'ûp*^{1} [3]
darting, 4554, *māhar*^{1} [1]

DASH [5]
dash, 1751, *gāram*^{2} [1]
dash, 4554, *māhar*^{1} [1]
dash to pieces, 5879, *nāpaṣ*^{1} [1]
made a dash, 7320, *pāšaṭ* [1]
dash to the ground, 8187, *rāṭaš* [1]

DASHED [6]
let be dashed, 1017, *bôš*^{1} [1]
were dashed to pieces, 1324, *bāqa'* [1]
be dashed to pieces, 8187, *rāṭaš* [1]
be dashed to the ground, 8187, *rāṭaš* [1]
were dashed to pieces, 8187, *rāṭaš* [1]
were dashed to the ground, 8187, *rāṭaš* [1]

DASHES [1]
dashes, 5879, *nāpaṣ*^{1} [1]

DATE [2]
date, 3427, *yôm*^{1} [2]

DATES [2]
cake of dates, 882, *'ešpār* [2]

DATHAN [10]
Dathan, 2018, *dātān* [10]

DAUGHTER [256]
daughter, 1426, *bat*^{1} [245]
daughter, *AIT* [7]
daughter, *NIH/RPE* [1]
daughter^{s}, 2085, *hû'* [1]
daughter, 3528, *yālad* [1]
daughter, 5922, *n^{e}qēbâ* [1]

DAUGHTER'S [5]
daughter's, 1426, *bat*^{1} [3]
daughter's, *AIT* [1]
the daughter's^s, 2023, *-āh* [1]

DAUGHTER-IN-LAW [14]
daughter-in-law, 3987, *kallâ* [14]

DAUGHTERS [209]
daughters, 1426, *bat*^{1} [204]
daughters, *NIH/RPE* [3]
daughters in marriage, 1426, *bat*^{1} [1]
daughters, 1435, *b*^{e}*tûlâ* [1]

DAUGHTERS-IN-LAW [5]
daughters-in-law, 3987, *kallâ* [5]

DAVID [947]
David, 1858, *dāwid* [906]
David, *NIH/RPE* [25]
David^s, 2257, *-ô* [11]
David^s, 2084, *-hû* [4]
David^s, 2085, *hû'* [1]

DAVID'S [83]
David's, 1858, *dāwid* [69]
David's, 4200+1858, *l*$^{e-1}$*+dāwid* [8]
David's^s, 2257, *-ô* [4]
David's line, 1858, *dāwid* [1]
David's^s, 2021, *ha-* [1]

DAWN [29]
dawn, 8840, *šaḥar* [14]
dawn, 1332, *bōqer*^{2} [3]
dawn, 240+2021+1332, *'ôr*^{2}*+ha-+bōqer*^{2} [2]
dawn, 5586, *nōgah*^{1} [2]
dawn, 5974, *nešep* [2]
dawn, 240, *'ôr*^{2} [1]
dawn, 2437, *zeraḥ*^{1} [1]
dawn, 5423, *mišḥār* [1]
first light of dawn, 6590+8840, *'ālâ+šaḥar* [1]
light of dawn, 8840, *šaḥar* [1]
dawn, 10740, *š*^{e}*parpār* [1]

DAWNED [3]
dawned, 239, *'ôr*^{1} [1]
dawned, 2436, *zāraḥ* [1]
dawned, 5585, *nāgah* [1]

DAWNS [3]
dawns, 2436, *zāraḥ* [1]
where dawns, 4604, *môṣā'*^{1} [1]
day dawns, 8840, *šaḥar* [1]

DAY [1159]
day, 3427, *yôm*^{1} [950]
day, *NIH/RPE* [71]
day, 3429, *yômām* [23]
next day, 4740, *moḥ*^{o}*rāt* [22]
by day, 3429, *yômām* [19]
day after day, 3972+2021+3427, *kōl+ha-+yôm*^{1} [8]
day after, 4740, *moḥ*^{o}*rāt* [6]
one day, 2256+2118, *w*^{e}*-+hāyâ* [4]
one day, 2256, *w*^{e}*-* [4]
day of rest, 8702, *šabbātôn* [4]
day, 10317, *yôm* [3]
the day^s, 889, *'ašer* [2]
all day long, 928+2021+3427+2021+2085, *b*^{e}*+ha-+yôm*^{1}*+ha-+hû'* [2]
day by day, 1821+3427+928+3427+2257, *dābār+yôm*^{1}*+b*^{e}*-+yôm*^{1}*+-ô* [2]
day by day, 1821+3427+928+3427, *dābār+yôm*^{1}*+b*^{e}*-+yôm*^{1} [2]
for each day, 1821+3427+928+3427, *dābār+yôm*^{1}*+b*^{e}*-+yôm*^{1} [2]
day after day, 3427, *yôm*^{1} [2]
each day, 3427+928+3427, *yôm*^{1}*+b*^{e}*-+yôm*^{1} [2]
day after day, 9458+3429, *tāmîd+yômām* [2]
day, *AIT* [1]
light of day, 240, *'ôr*^{2} [1]
new day, 240, *'ôr*^{2} [1]
by day, 928+3429, *b*^{e}*-+yômām* [1]
that day^s, 2023, *-āh* [1]
that day^s, 2084, *-hû* [1]
this day^s, 2178, *hēnnâ*^{1} [1]
day, 3427+919, *yôm*^{1}*+'etmôl* [1]
every day, 3427+928+3427, *yôm*^{1}*+b*^{e}*-+yôm*^{1} [1]
every day, 3427, *yôm*^{1} [1]
that day, 3427+3427, *yôm*^{1}*+yôm*^{1} [1]
during the day, 3429, *yômām* [1]
every day, 3429, *yômām* [1]
every day, 3972+3427+2256+3427, *kōl+yôm*^{1}*+w*^{e}*-+yôm*^{1} [1]
each day, 4200+2021+3427+4200+2021+3427, *l*$^{e-1}$*+ha-+yôm*^{1}*+l*$^{e-1}$*+ha-+yôm*^{1} [1]
every day, 4200+2021+3427, *l*$^{e-1}$*+ha-+yôm*^{1} [1]
each day, 4200+2021+3427, *l*$^{e-1}$*+ha-+yôm*^{1} [1]
some day, 4737, *māḥār* [1]
select a day, 4946+3427+4200+3427, *min+yôm*^{1}*+l*$^{e-1}$*+yôm*^{1} [1]
that day, 6964, *'attâ* [1]
this day, 6964, *'attâ* [1]
break of day, 7155+1332, *pānâ+bōqer*^{2} [1]
day of fasting, 7427, *ṣôm* [1]
day dawns, 8840, *šaḥar* [1]
day after tomorrow, 8958, *š*^{e}*lîšî* [1]
day after, 8958, *š*^{e}*lîšî* [1]
the day after tomorrow, 8992, *šālaš* [1]
day, 9102, *šānâ*^{2} [1]
that day^s, 10008, *'*^{e}*dayin* [1]

DAY'S [6]
day's, 3427, *yôm*^{1} [3]
each day's, 3427+3427, *yôm*^{1}*+yôm*^{1} [1]
each day's, 3427+928+3427+2257, *yôm*^{1}*+b*^{e}*-+yôm*^{1}*+-ô* [1]
each day's, 3427+928+3427, *yôm*^{1}*+b*^{e}*-+yôm*^{1} [1]

DAYBREAK [11]
daybreak, 240+2021+1332, *'ôr*^{2}*+ha-+bōqer*^{2} [3]
daybreak, 6590+2021+8840, *'ālâ+ha-+šaḥar* [2]
daybreak, 8840, *šaḥar* [2]
daybreak, 239, *'ôr*^{1} [1]
daybreak, 240, *'ôr*^{2} [1]
daybreak, 7155+1332, *pānâ+bōqer*^{2} [1]
daybreak, 7155+2021+1332, *pānâ+ha-+bōqer*^{2} [1]

DAYLIGHT [9]
daylight, 240, *'ôr*^{2} [3]
daylight, 240+2021+1332, *'ôr*^{2}*+ha-+bōqer*^{2} [1]
broad daylight, 3427+240, *yôm*^{1}*+'ôr*^{2} [1]
daylight, 3427, *yôm*^{1} [1]
in broad daylight, 4200+6524+2021+9087+2021+2296, *l*$^{e-1}$*+'ayin*^{1}*+ha-+šemeš+ha-+zeh* [1]
in broad daylight, 5584+2021+9087, *neged+ha-+šemeš* [1]
broad daylight, 9087, *šemeš* [1]

DAYS [497]
days, 3427, *yôm*^{1} [474]
days, 10317, *yôm* [6]
days, *NIH/RPE* [4]
days, 6961, *'ēt* [2]
these days^s, 2157, *-hem* [1]
days as, 3427, *yôm*^{1} [1]
days of life, 3427, *yôm*^{1} [1]
length of days, 3427+9102, *yôm*^{1}*+šānâ*^{2} [1]
other days, 3427+3427, *yôm*^{1}*+yôm*^{1} [1]
spend days, 4328, *lîn* [1]
the days^s, 4392, *-ām* [1]
days to come, 4737, *māḥār* [1]
days of old, 7710, *qedem* [1]
days of old, 8037, *ri'šôn* [1]
Sabbath days, 8701, *šabbāt* [1]

DAYTIME [6]
daytime, 3427, *yôm*^{1} [2]
in the daytime, 3429, *yômām* [2]
during the daytime, 3429, *yômām* [1]
in daytime, 3429, *yômām* [1]

DAZZLING [1]
dazzling, 10228, *zîw* [1]

DEAD [158]
dead, 4637, *mût* [103]
dead bodies, 7007, *peger* [7]
dead, 2728, *ḥālāl*^{1} [6]
dead bodies, 5577, *n*^{e}*bēlâ* [5]
dead, 8327, *r*^{e}*pā'îm*^{1} [5]
dead, *NIH/RPE* [4]
dead body, 5883, *nepeš* [4]
anything found dead, 5577, *n*^{e}*bēlâ* [3]
dead, 5883, *nepeš* [3]
dead, 4638, *māwet* [2]
dead, 6, *'ābad* [1]
spirits of the dead, 356, *'iṭṭîm* [1]
dead, 1581, *g*^{e}*wiyyâ* [1]
fell dead, 1588, *gāwa'* [1]
dead bodies, 2728, *ḥālāl*^{1} [1]
as good as dead, 4637, *mût* [1]
fell dead, 4637, *mût* [1]
already dead, 5577, *n*^{e}*bēlâ* [1]
animal found dead, 5577, *n*^{e}*bēlâ* [1]
found dead, 5577, *n*^{e}*bēlâ* [1]
fell dead, 5877, *nāpal* [1]
dead, 7007, *peger* [1]
strip the dead, 7320, *pāšaṭ* [1]
spirits of the dead, 8327, *r*^{e}*pā'îm*^{1} [1]
dead, 8720, *šādad* [1]
dead, 8821, *šāḥaṭ*^{1} [1]

DEADLY [13]
deadly, 4638, *māwet* [3]
deadly, 8273, *ra'*^{1} [2]
deadly, 425, *'akzār* [1]
deadly, 2095, *hawwâ*^{2} [1]
deadly plague, 4638, *māwet* [1]
deadly, 4926, *māmôt* [1]
deadly, 5150, *mappāṣ* [1]
deadly, 5253, *mar*^{1} [1]
deadly, 5321, *m*^{e}*rîrî* [1]
deadly, 8821, *šāḥaṭ*^{1} [1]

DEAF [13]
deaf, 3094, *ḥērēš* [8]
deaf, 3087, *ḥārēš*^{2} [2]
turn a deaf ear, 3087, *ḥārēš*^{2} [1]
turned a deaf ear, 4202+263, *lō'+'āzan*^{1} [1]
deaf, 4946+9048, *min+šāma'* [1]

DEAL [46]
deal, 6913, *'āśâ*^{1} [24]
deal with, 6913, *'āśâ*^{1} [5]
deal, 5989, *nātan* [3]
deal, 6913+6913, *'āśâ*^{1}*+'āśâ*^{1} [2]
deal, 7212, *pāqad* [2]
great deal, 8041, *rab*^{1} [2]
deal, *NIH/RPE* [1]
deal shrewdly, 2681, *ḥākam* [1]
deal with genealogies, 3509, *yāḥaś* [1]
deal with, 6584, *'al*^{2} [1]
deal, 6618, *'ālal*^{1} [1]
deal differently, 7111, *pālâ* [1]
deal falsely, 9213, *šāqar* [1]
deal with, 9530, *tāpaś* [1]

DEALING [2]
dealing with, 928, *b*^{e}*-* [1]
usual way of dealing, 9368, *tôrâ* [1]

DEALINGS [1]
dealings, 5095, *ma'*^{a}*lāl* [1]

DEALS [2]
deals, 6913, *'āśâ*^{1} [2]

DEALT [7]
dealt with, 1694, *gāmal* [2]
dealt, 6913, *'āśâ*^{1} [2]
dealt, 5782, *nākâ* [1]
dealt harshly, 6618, *'ālal*^{1} [1]
dealt, 6618, *'ālal*^{1} [1]

DEAR [3]
dear, 3692, *yaqqîr* [1]
dear, 5838, *nā'ēm* [1]
dear to, 8354, *rāṣâ*^{1} [1]

DEARLY [1]
dearly, 170, *'āhab* [1]

DEATH [309]
death, 4638, *māwet* [109]
put to death, 4637, *mût* [43]

death, 4637, *mût* [30]
be put to death, 4637, *mût* [26]
must be put to death, 4637+4637, *mût+mût* [18]
put to death, 2222, *hārag* [7]
death, 8619, *šeʾôl* [6]
shall be put to death, 4637+4637, *mût+mût* [4]
surely be put to death, 4637+4637, *mût+mût* [4]
death, 5883, *nepeš* [4]
put to death, 10625, *q^{e}ṭal* [4]
putting to death, 4637, *mût* [3]
put to death, 5782, *nākâ* [3]
shadow of death, 7516, *ṣalmāwet* [3]
death, *NIH/RPE* [2]
brings death, 4637, *mût* [2]
died a natural death, 4637, *mût* [2]
going to death, 5877, *nāpal* [2]
death, *AIT* [1]
death, 1014, *bôr* [1]
close to death, 1588, *gāwaʿ* [1]
silence of death, 1872, *dûmâ^{1}* [1]
death, 1947, *dām* [1]
death^{s}, 2085, *hûʾ* [1]
face death, 2222, *hārag* [1]
must certainly put to death, 2222+2222, *hārag+hārag* [1]
put to death, 2222+2222, *hārag+hārag* [1]
put to death, 2222+4638, *hārag+māwet* [1]
bring about death, 4637, *mût* [1]
certainly be put to death, 4637+4637, *mût+mût* [1]
is put to death, 4637, *mût* [1]
messengers of death, 4637, *mût* [1]
must be put to death, 4637, *mût* [1]
must put to death, 4637+4637, *mût+mût* [1]
put death, 4637, *mût* [1]
put to death, 4637+4637, *mût+mût* [1]
was put to death, 4637, *mût* [1]
were put to death, 4637, *mût* [1]
death, 4926, *māmôt* [1]
lie in death, 5435, *miškāb* [1]
putting to death, 5782, *nākâ* [1]
was put to death, 5782, *nākâ* [1]
must be stoned to death, 6232+6232, *sāqal+sāqal* [1]
give over to death, 6867, *ʿārâ^{1}* [1]
stoned to death, 8083+74, *rāgam+ʾeben* [1]
put to death, 8357, *rāṣaḥ* [1]
burn to death, 8596+928+2021+836, *śārap+b^{e}-+ha-+ʾēš^{1}* [1]
burned to death, 8596+928+2021+836, *śārap+b^{e}-+ha-+ʾēš^{1}* [1]
burned to death, 8596, *śārap* [1]
realm of death, 8619, *šeʾôl* [1]
throes of death, 8688, *šābāṣ* [1]
sleep of death, 9104, *šēnâ* [1]
put to death, 9119, *šāsap* [1]
death, 9456, *t^{e}mûtâ* [1]
death, 10409, *môt* [1]

DEATH'S [1]
death's, 4638, *māwet* [1]

DEATHLY [2]
deathly pale, 3766, *yērāqôn* [1]
deathly pale, 5422, *mašḥît* [1]

DEATHS [1]
deaths, *NIH/RPE* [1]

DEBIR [12]
Debir, 1810, *d^{e}bîr^{3}* [11]
Debir, 1809, *d^{e}bîr^{2}* [1]

DEBORAH [11]
Deborah, 1806, *d^{e}bôrâ^{2}* [10]
Deborah, *NIH/RPE* [1]

DEBT [4]
seized for a debt, 2471, *ḥābal^{1}* [1]
take as security for a debt, 2471, *ḥābal^{1}* [1]
in debt, 4200+5957, *l^{e}-^{1}+nāšāʾ^{1}* [1]
cancel debt, 9023, *šāmaṭ* [1]

DEBTOR [1]
debtor, 5957+928, *nāšāʾ^{1}+b^{e}-* [1]

DEBTORS [1]
debtors, 5967, *nāšak^{2}* [1]

DEBTS [7]
canceling debts, 9024, *š^{e}miṭṭâ* [2]
debts, 5391+3338, *maššāʾ+yād* [1]
debts, 5394, *maššāʾâ* [1]
debts, 5963, *n^{e}šî* [1]
cancel debts, 6913+9024, *ʿāśâ^{1}+š^{e}miṭṭâ* [1]
time for canceling debts, 9024, *š^{e}miṭṭâ* [1]

DECAY [6]
decay, 8373, *rāqāb* [2]
decay, 8846, *šaḥat* [2]
decay, 1162, *bālâ^{1}* [1]
decay, 5215, *maq* [1]

DECAYED [1]
decayed, 6244, *sāraḥ^{2}* [1]

DECEIT [26]
deceit, 5327, *mirmâ^{1}* [12]
deceit, 8245, *r^{e}miyyâ^{2}* [4]
deceit, 9214, *šeqer* [3]
deceit, 224, *ʾāwen^{1}* [1]
speak deceit, 2744, *ḥālaq^{1}* [1]
deceit, 4279, *lûz^{1}* [1]
deceit, 4383+9567, *lāšôn+tarmît* [1]
deceit, 8736, *šāwʾ* [1]
deceit, 9337, *tahpukôt* [1]
deceit, 9567, *tarmît* [1]

DECEITFUL [21]
deceitful, 5327, *mirmâ^{1}* [9]
deceitful, 9214, *šeqer* [3]
deceitful, 8245, *r^{e}miyyâ^{2}* [2]
deceitful, 8736, *šāwʾ* [2]
deceitful, 2200, *hāpak* [1]
deceitful, 2744, *ḥālaq^{1}* [1]
deceitful, 3952, *keḥāš* [1]
deceitful, 6157, *selep* [1]
deceitful, 6815, *ʿāqōb^{2}* [1]

DECEITFULLY [6]
deceitfully, 928+5327, *b^{e}-+mirmâ^{1}* [2]
deceitfully, 8245, *r^{e}miyyâ^{2}* [2]
deceitfully, 5327, *mirmâ^{1}* [1]
act deceitfully, 9438, *tālal* [1]

DECEITFULNESS [1]
deceitfulness, 9567, *tarmît* [1]

DECEIVE [19]
deceive, 5958, *nāšāʾ^{2}* [5]
let deceive, 5958, *nāšāʾ^{2}* [3]
deceive, 7331, *pātâ^{1}* [2]
deceive, 8228, *rāmâ^{2}* [2]
deceive, 9438, *tālal* [2]
deceive, 1704, *gānab* [1]
deceive, 3941, *kāzab* [1]
deceive, 3950, *kāḥaš* [1]
deceive, 9213, *šāqar* [1]
deceive himself, 9494, *tāʿâ* [1]

DECEIVED [16]
deceived, 5958, *nāšāʾ^{2}* [3]
deceived, 8228, *rāmâ^{2}* [2]
deceived, 928+5793+5792, *b^{e}-+nēkel+nākal* [1]
deceived, 1704+4213, *gānab+lēb* [1]
deceived, 1704+4222, *gānab+lēbāb* [1]
are deceived, 5958, *nāšāʾ^{2}* [1]
completely deceived, 5958+5958, *nāšāʾ^{2}+nāšāʾ^{2}* [1]
deceived, 6810, *ʿāqab* [1]
be deceived, 7331, *pātâ^{1}* [1]
deceived, 7331, *pātâ^{1}* [1]
easily deceived, 7331, *pātâ^{1}* [1]
was deceived, 7331, *pātâ^{1}* [1]
deceived, 8704, *šāgag* [1]

DECEIVER [3]
deceiver, 6810+6810, *ʿāqab+ʿāqab* [1]
deceiver, 8706, *šāgâ* [1]
deceiver, 9214, *šeqer* [1]

DECEIVERS [1]
deceivers, 6812, *ʿāqēb^{2}* [1]

DECEIVES [2]
deceives, 8228, *rāmâ^{2}* [1]
deceives, 9438, *tālal* [1]

DECEIVING [1]
deceiving, 3950, *kāḥaš* [1]

DECEPTION [7]
deception, 5327, *mirmâ^{1}* [3]
deception, 3951, *kaḥaš* [1]
deception, 4213+2256+4213, *lēb+w^{e}-+lēb* [1]
deception, 5396, *maššāʾôn* [1]
deception, 9214, *šeqer* [1]

DECEPTIVE [7]
deceptive, 9214, *šeqer* [4]
deceptive, 423, *ʾakzāb* [2]
deceptive, 3942, *kāzāb* [1]

DECEPTIVELY [1]
deceptively, 928+6817, *b^{e}-+ʿoqbâ* [1]

DECIDE [13]
decide, 9149, *šāpaṭ* [4]
decide, 8011, *rāʾâ^{1}* [2]
decide, 1047, *bāḥar^{1}* [1]
decide, 1615, *gāzar^{1}* [1]
decide, 3359, *yādaʿ* [1]
decide, 3519, *yākaḥ* [1]
decide, 6584+7023+2118, *ʿal^{2}+peh+hāyâ* [1]
decide dispute, 9149, *šāpaṭ* [1]
judges decide, 9149, *šāpaṭ* [1]

DECIDED [11]
decided, 10418, *millâ* [2]
decided, 2118+6640+4213, *hāyâ+ʿim+lēb* [1]
decided, 2372, *zāmam* [1]
decided, 3619, *yāʿaṣ* [1]
been firmly decided, 3922, *kûn^{1}* [1]
decided, 3983, *kālâ^{1}* [1]
decided, 5477, *mišpāṭ* [1]
disputes decided, 5477, *mišpāṭ* [1]
decided, 6641+1821, *ʿāmad+dābār* [1]
decided, 9149, *šāpaṭ* [1]

DECIMATED [1]
been decimated, 9012, *šāmad* [1]

DECISION [9]
decision, 5477, *mišpāṭ* [3]
decision, 3025, *ḥārûṣ^{5}* [2]
decision, 6783, *ʿēṣâ^{1}* [1]
decision, 7131, *p^{e}lîlâ* [1]
decision, 10601, *pitgām* [1]
decision, 10668, *r^{e}ʿû* [1]

DECISIONS [8]
decisions, 5477, *mišpāṭ* [2]
decisions, 1821, *dābār* [1]
give decisions, 3519, *yākaḥ* [1]
making decisions, 5477, *mišpāṭ* [1]
means of making decisions, 5477, *mišpāṭ* [1]
rendering decisions, 7133, *p^{e}lîliyyâ* [1]
obtain decisions, 8626, *šāʾal* [1]

DECK [2]
below deck, 3752+2021+6208, *y^{e}rēkâ+ha-+s^{e}pînâ* [1]
deck, 7983, *qereš* [1]

DECKED [1]
decked, 6335, *ʿādâ^{2}* [1]

DECKS [1]
decks, *AIT* [1]

DECLARE [39]
declare, 5583, *nāgad* [14]
declare, 6218, *sāpar* [6]
declare, 606, *ʾāmar^{1}* [4]
declare, 1819, *dābar^{2}* [2]
declare, 6699, *ʿānâ^{1}* [2]
declare not guilty, 7405, *ṣādaq* [2]
declare holy, 7727, *qādaš* [2]
declare, 9048, *šāmaʿ* [2]
declare, *NIH/RPE* [1]
declare guilty, 870, *ʾāšam* [1]

declare, 5535, *nā'am* [1]
declare guilty, 8399, *rāša'* [1]
declare, 10397, *mē'mar* [1]

DECLARED [27]
declared, 606, *'āmar*[1] [9]
declared, 1819, *dābar*[2] [5]
declared, 5583, *nāgad* [3]
declared, *NIH/RPE* [2]
declared, 7924, *qārā'*[1] [2]
declared, 5536, *nᵉ'um* [1]
is declared, 6218, *sāpar* [1]
declared, 6218, *sāpar* [1]
solemnly declared, 6386, *'ûd*[1] [1]
declared, 8655, *šābaḥ*[1] [1]
declared on oath, 8678, *šāba'* [1]

DECLARES [365]
declares, 5536, *nᵉ'um* [363]
declares, 606+606, *'āmar*[1]*+'āmar*[1] [1]
declares, 5583, *nāgad* [1]

DECLARING [2]
declaring, *NIH/RPE* [1]
declaring, 5583, *nāgad* [1]

DECORATE [1]
decorate, 4059, *kāsâ* [1]

DECORATED [8]
decorated, 448, *'el* [3]
decorated with, 6584, *'al*[2] [2]
decorated with, 448, *'el* [1]
decorated, 6590, *'ālâ* [1]
decorated, 6634, *'ālap* [1]

DECORATES [1]
decorates, 5417, *māšaḥ* [1]

DECORATING [4]
decorating, 4059, *kāsâ* [4]

DECORATIONS [2]
palm tree decorations, 9474, *timōrâ* [2]

DECREASE [2]
decrease, 5070, *mā'aṭ* [2]

DECREASED [2]
decreased, 5070, *mā'aṭ* [1]
numbers decreased, 5070, *mā'aṭ* [1]

DECREE [39]
decree, 2976, *ḥōq* [8]
decree, 10057, *'ᵉsār* [7]
decree, 10302, *ṭᵉ'ēm*[2] [5]
decree, 10682+10302, *śîm+ṭᵉ'ēm*[2] [4]
decree, *NIH/RPE* [3]
decree, 1821, *dābār* [2]
decree, 10186, *dāt* [2]
decree, 1620, *gᵉzērâ* [1]
decree, 1819, *dābar*[2] [1]
decree, 3248, *ṭa'am* [1]
decree be issued, 4180, *kātab* [1]
decree, 4411, *ma'ᵃmār* [1]
decree, 7422, *ṣāwâ* [1]
decree, 10375, *kᵉtāb* [1]
decree, 10418, *millâ* [1]

DECREED [23]
decreed, 1819, *dābar*[2] [5]
decreed, 7422, *ṣāwâ* [3]
been decreed, 3076, *ḥāraṣ*[1] [2]
decreed, 3076, *ḥāraṣ*[1] [2]
decreed, 7756, *qûm* [2]
decreed, 907, *'ēt*[2] [1]
decreed, 1615, *gāzar*[1] [1]
is decreed, 3076, *ḥāraṣ*[1] [1]
are decreed, 3155, *ḥātak* [1]
decreed, 4496, *mad* [1]
decreed, 5893, *nāṣab*[1] [1]
decreed, 7924, *qārā'*[1] [1]
decreed, 10042, *'ᵃmar* [1]
decreed, 10682+10302, *śîm+ṭᵉ'ēm*[2] [1]

DECREES [131]
decrees, 2976, *ḥōq* [75]
decrees, 2978, *ḥuqqâ* [52]
decrees, 2980, *ḥāqaq* [1]
issue decrees, 4180+4180, *kātab+kātab* [1]
decrees, 7422, *ṣāwâ* [1]
decrees, 10302, *ṭᵉ'ēm*[2] [1]

DEDAN [10]
Dedan, 1847, *dᵉdān* [10]

DEDANITES [1]
Dedanites, 1848, *dᵉdānî* [1]

DEDICATE [7]
dedicate, 7727, *qādaš* [2]
dedicate, *NIH/RPE* [1]
dedicate, 2852, *ḥānak* [1]
dedicate, 4848+3338, *mālē'*[1]*+yād* [1]
dedicate, 5693, *nāzar*[2] [1]
dedicate, 7731, *qōdeš* [1]

DEDICATED [29]
dedicated, 7727, *qādaš* [10]
dedicated, 2852, *ḥānak* [3]
dedicated, 5694, *nēzer* [3]
dedicated, 5989, *nātan* [2]
dedicated things, 7731, *qōdeš* [2]
dedicated, 7731, *qōdeš* [2]
things dedicated, 7731, *qōdeš* [2]
dedicated, *AIT* [1]
dedicated, *NIH/RPE* [1]
dedicated, 4848+3338, *mālē'*[1]*+yād* [1]
dedicated gifts, 7731, *qōdeš* [1]
gifts dedicated, 7731, *qōdeš* [1]

DEDICATES [7]
dedicates, 7727, *qādaš* [7]

DEDICATION [13]
dedication, 2853, *ḥᵃnukkâ* [6]
dedication, 10273, *ḥᵃnukkâ* [4]
offerings for dedication, 2853, *ḥᵃnukkâ* [2]
dedication, 5694, *nēzer* [1]

DEED [9]
deed, 6219, *sēper*[1] [6]
deed, 5126, *ma'ᵃśeh* [2]
deed, 1821, *dābār* [1]

DEEDED [2]
deeded, 7756, *qûm* [2]

DEEDS [78]
deeds, *AIT* [16]
deeds, 5095, *ma'ᵃlāl* [16]
deeds, 5126, *ma'ᵃśeh* [8]
deeds, 7189, *pō'al* [8]
deeds, 6613, *'ᵃlîlâ* [4]
deeds, 1821, *dābār* [2]
deeds, 7190, *pᵉ'ullâ* [2]
evil deeds, 8288, *rā'â*[3] [2]
deeds, *NIH/RPE* [1]
deeds, 1524, *gādôl* [1]
great deeds, 1525, *gᵉdûllâ* [1]
deeds, 1691, *gᵉmûl* [1]
good deeds, 3208, *ṭôbâ* [1]
awesome deeds, 3707, *yārē'*[1] [1]
awesome deeds, 4616, *môrā'* [1]
deeds, 4856, *mᵉlā'kâ* [1]
deeds, 5042, *ma'ᵃbād* [1]
wicked deeds, 5095, *ma'ᵃlāl* [1]
deeds, 5148, *mip'āl* [1]
deeds, 6219, *sēper*[1] [1]
evil deeds, 6411, *'āwōn* [1]
mighty deeds, 6613, *'ᵃlîlâ* [1]
deeds, 6614, *'ᵃlîliyyâ* [1]
deeds, 6913, *'āśâ*[1] [1]
righteous deeds, 7407, *ṣᵉdāqâ* [1]
deeds of evildoers, 8288, *rā'â*[3] [1]
evil deeds, 8400, *reša'* [1]
praiseworthy deeds, 9335, *tᵉhillâ* [1]

DEEP [93]
deep, 9333, *tᵉhôm* [19]
deep, 6678, *'āmōq* [13]
deep sleep, 9554, *tardēmâ* [6]
deep shadow, 7516, *ṣalmāwet* [4]
deep, *NIH/RPE* [3]
deep, 6676, *'āmaq* [3]
deep, 9166, *šāpāl* [3]
deep waters, 9333, *tᵉhôm* [3]
deep, 1524, *gādôl* [2]
deep, 4394, *mᵉ'ōd* [2]
deep, 5099, *ma'ᵃmaqqîm* [2]
deep, 5185, *mᵉṣôlâ* [2]
deep darkness, 6906, *'ᵃrāpel* [2]
deep darkness, 7516, *ṣalmāwet* [2]
deep shadows, 7516, *ṣalmāwet* [2]
deep, 8041, *rab*[1] [2]
fell into a deep sleep, 8101, *rādam* [2]
deep, 8145, *rōḥab* [2]
deep springs, 9333, *tᵉhôm* [2]
deep darkness, 696, *'ᵃpēlâ* [1]
deep shadows, 696, *'ᵃpēlâ* [1]
in deep anguish, 2655, *ḥîl*[1] [1]
deep, 5087+2025, *ma'al*[2]*+-â*[2] [1]
made deep, 6676, *'āmaq* [1]
sunk deep, 6676, *'āmaq* [1]
deep, 6679, *'ōmeq* [1]
deep gloom, 6906, *'ᵃrāpel* [1]
watery deep, 7425, *ṣûlâ* [1]
deep, 7757, *qômâ* [1]
in a deep sleep, 8101, *rādam* [1]
drink deep, 8115, *rāwâ* [1]
deep sleep, 8120+9554, *rûaḥ+tardēmâ* [1]
deep enough to swim in, 8467, *śāḥû* [1]
deep in thought, 8490, *śîaḥ*[3] [1]
monster of the deep, 9490, *tannîn* [1]
deep, 10555, *'ammîq* [1]

DEEPER [2]
deeper, 6678, *'āmōq* [1]
deeper, 9166, *šāpāl* [1]

DEEPEST [4]
deepest gloom, 7516, *ṣalmāwet* [2]
deepest night, 6547+4017+694, *'êpâ*[1]*+kᵉmô+'ōpel* [1]
deepest, 6676, *'āmaq* [1]

DEEPLY [4]
deeply moved, 4023+8171, *kāmar+raḥᵃmîm* [1]
drink deeply, 5209, *māṣaṣ* [1]
deeply troubled, 7997+8120, *qāšeh+rûaḥ* [1]
deeply, 10678, *śaggî'* [1]

DEEPS [1]
deeps, 9333, *tᵉhôm* [1]

DEER [14]
deer, 385, *'ayyāl* [9]
deer, 387, *'ayyālâ* [3]
roe deer, 3502, *yaḥmûr* [1]
deer, 3607, *ya'ᵃlâ*[1] [1]

DEFAMED [1]
be defamed, 2725, *ḥālal*[1] [1]

DEFEAT [8]
defeat, 5782, *nākâ* [3]
defeat, *NIH/RPE* [2]
defeat, 2711, *ḥᵃlûšâ* [1]
bring defeat upon, 5597, *nāgap* [1]
defeat, 8288, *rā'â*[3] [1]

DEFEATED [52]
defeated, 5782, *nākâ* [32]
be defeated, 5597, *nāgap* [5]
been defeated, 5597, *nāgap* [4]
were defeated, 5597, *nāgap* [3]
was defeated, 5597, *nāgap* [2]
defeated, *NIH/RPE* [1]
are defeated, 4198, *kātat* [1]
defeated, 5597, *nāgap* [1]
indeed defeated, 5782+5782, *nākâ+nākâ* [1]
defeated, 5877, *nāpal* [1]
be defeated, 5989+928+3338, *nātan+bᵉ-+yād* [1]

DEFEATING [5]
defeating, 5782, *nākâ* [2]
defeating, 5597+5597, *nāgap+nāgap* [1]
defeating, 5597, *nāgap* [1]
defeating, 10321, *yᵉkil* [1]

DEFECT [57]
without defect, 9459, *tāmîm* [47]
defect, 4583, *mûm* [8]
physical defect, 4583, *mûm* [1]
defect, 9319, *teballul* [1]

DEFECTED [3]
defected, 5877, *nāpal* [2]
defected, 976, *bādal* [1]

DEFECTS [1]
defects, 4583, *mûm* [1]

DEFEND [20]
defend, 1713, *gānan* [4]
defend, 8189, *rîb*[1] [4]
defend, 9149, *šāpaṭ* [3]
defend the cause, 9149, *šāpaṭ* [2]
defend rights, 1906, *dîn*[1] [1]
defend, 2837, *ḥānâ*[1] [1]
defend, 3519, *yākaḥ* [1]
defend, 6641+5584, *ʿāmad+neged* [1]
vigorously defend, 8189+8189, *rîb*[1]*+rîb*[1] [1]
defend cause, 9149, *šāpaṭ* [1]
defend, 10601+10754, *pitgām+tûb* [1]

DEFENDED [3]
defended, 5911, *nāṣal* [2]
defended, 1906, *dîn*[1] [1]

DEFENDER [6]
defender, 1457, *gāʾal*[1] [1]
defender, 1908, *dayyān* [1]
the defender[s], 2257, *-ô* [1]
defender, 3519, *yākaḥ* [1]
defender, 5911, *nāṣal* [1]
defender, 8189, *rîb*[1] [1]

DEFENDERS [1]
strongest defenders, 408+2657, *ʾîš*[1]*+ḥayil* [1]

DEFENDING [2]
defending, 9068, *šāmar* [1]
defending, 9149, *šāpaṭ* [1]

DEFENDS [3]
defends, 6913, *ʿāśâ*[1] [1]
defends cause, 8189, *rîb*[1] [1]
defends, 8189, *rîb*[1] [1]

DEFENSE [5]
defense, *NIH/RPE* [1]
defense, 2658, *ḥêl* [1]
defense against, 4946+7156, *min+pāneh* [1]
defense, 5190, *māṣôr*[2] [1]
defense, 5477, *mišpāṭ* [1]

DEFENSES [8]
defenses, 1462, *gab*[2] [2]
breaches in defenses, 1323, *bāqîaʿ* [1]
defenses, 4448, *mibṣār*[1] [1]
defenses, 5009, *māsāk* [1]
defenses, 5193, *meṣûrâ* [1]
corner defenses, 7157, *pinnâ* [1]
defenses, 8939, *šelaḥ*[1] [1]

DEFERENCE [1]
in deference to, 4946+7156, *min+pāneh* [1]

DEFERRED [1]
deferred, 5432, *māšak* [1]

DEFIANCE [1]
defiance, 1821, *dābār* [1]

DEFIANT [1]
defiant, 6253, *sārar*[1] [1]

DEFIANTLY [2]
defiantly, 928+7418, *be-+ṣawwāʾr* [1]
sins defiantly, 6913+928+3338+8123, *ʿāśâ*[1]*+be-+yād+rûm*[1] [1]

DEFIED [9]
defied, 3070, *ḥārap*[2] [3]
defied, 5286, *mārâ*[1] [2]
defied, 6584+1540, *ʿal*[2]*+gādal* [2]
defied, 2326, *zîd* [1]
defied, 10731, *šenâ*[1] [1]

DEFIES [1]
defies, 1679, *gālaʿ* [1]

DEFILE [30]
defile, 3237, *ṭāmēʾ*[1] [12]
defile yourselves, 3237, *ṭāmēʾ*[1] [6]
defile, 2725, *ḥālal*[1] [5]
defile himself, 1458, *gāʾal*[2] [2]
defile themselves, 3237, *ṭāmēʾ*[1] [2]
defile, 9210, *šāqaṣ* [2]
defile himself, 3237, *ṭāmēʾ*[1] [1]

DEFILED [68]
defiled, 3237, *ṭāmēʾ*[1] [28]
defiled, 3238, *ṭāmēʾ*[2] [7]
defiled, 2725, *ḥālal*[1] [5]
defiled, 1458, *gāʾal*[2] [4]
defiled, 2866, *ḥānēp*[1] [4]
defiled herself, 3237, *ṭāmēʾ*[1] [4]
defiled, 2729, *ḥālāl*[2] [2]
defiled yourself, 3237, *ṭāmēʾ*[1] [2]
are defiled, 1458, *gāʾal*[2] [1]
defiled, 1459, *gōʾal* [1]
was defiled, 1718, *gāʿal* [1]
defiled, 1815+4583, *dābaq+mûm* [1]
been defiled, 2725, *ḥālal*[1] [1]
completely defiled, 2866+2866, *ḥānēp*[1]*+ḥānēp*[1] [1]
became defiled, 3237, *ṭāmēʾ*[1] [1]
been defiled, 3237, *ṭāmēʾ*[1] [1]
defiled yourselves, 3237, *ṭāmēʾ*[1] [1]
let become defiled, 3237, *ṭāmēʾ*[1] [1]
defiled[s], 6913, *ʿāśâ*[1] [1]
defiled, 7727, *qādaš* [1]

DEFILEMENT [1]
defilement, 5614, *niddâ* [1]

DEFILES [7]
defiles, 3237, *ṭāmēʾ*[1] [5]
defiles herself, 2725, *ḥālal*[1] [1]
defiles herself, 3237, *ṭāmēʾ*[1] [1]

DEFILING [3]
defiling, 3237, *ṭāmēʾ*[1] [3]

DEFINITE [1]
definite information, 3922, *kûn*[1] [1]

DEFINITELY [2]
definitely, 448+3922, *ʾel+kûn*[1] [1]
heard definitely, 9048+9048, *šāmaʿ+šāmaʿ* [1]

DEFORMED [3]
deformed, 8594, *śāraʿ* [2]
deformed, 5426, *mošḥāt* [1]

DEFRAUD [4]
defraud, 6943, *ʿāšaq* [4]

DEFY [3]
defy, 3070, *ḥārap*[2] [3]

DEFYING [1]
defying, 5286, *mārâ*[1] [1]

DEGRADE [1]
degrade, 2725, *ḥālal*[1] [1]

DEGRADED [2]
be degraded, 7829, *qālâ*[2] [1]
degraded, 9493, *tāʿab* [1]

DEJECTED [2]
dejected, 1917, *dākāʾ* [1]
dejected, 2407, *zāʿap*[2] [1]

DELAIAH [7]
Delaiah, 1933, *delāyâ* [4]
Delaiah, 1934, *delāyāhû* [3]

DELAY [11]
delay, 336, *ʾāḥar* [5]
delay, 6641, *ʿāmad* [2]
delay, 799, *ʾārak* [1]
delay, 2675, *ḥākâ* [1]
delay, 4538, *māhah* [1]
delay, 5432, *māšak* [1]

DELAYED [5]
delayed, 336, *ʾāḥar* [2]
delayed, 4202+237, *lōʾ+ʾûṣ* [1]
delayed, 4538, *māhah* [1]
be delayed, 5432, *māšak* [1]

DELEGATION [3]
delegation, 928+3338+6269, *be-+yād+ʿebed*[1] [1]
delegation, 4855, *malʾāk* [1]
delegation, 7493, *ṣîr*[1] [1]

DELIBERATELY [1]
deliberately, 928+6893, *be-+ʿormâ* [1]

DELICACIES [6]
delicacies, 4761, *maṭʿam* [2]
delicacies, 5052, *maʿadannîm* [2]
delicacies, 4982, *manʿammîm* [1]
delicacies, 6358, *ʿēden*[1] [1]

DELICACY [1]
delicacy, 4458, *meged* [1]

DELICATE [2]
delicate, 6695, *ʿānag* [1]
delicate, 6697, *ʿānōg* [1]

DELICIOUS [1]
delicious, 5838, *nāʿēm* [1]

DELIGHT [62]
delight, 9141, *šaʿašûʿîm* [7]
delight, 2911, *ḥāpēṣ*[1] [4]
delight, 2914, *ḥēpeṣ* [3]
delight, 4718, *maḥmād* [3]
delight, 8523, *śāmaḥ* [3]
delight, 9130, *šāʿaʿ*[2] [3]
delight in, 2911, *ḥāpēṣ*[1] [2]
delight, 2913, *ḥāpēṣ*[3] [2]
delight, 5375, *māśôś*[1] [2]
delight, 6695, *ʿānag* [2]
find delight, 6695, *ʿānag* [1]
delight, 8464, *śûś* [2]
delight, 1637, *gîl*[3] [1]
delight, 1638, *gîlâ* [1]
delight in, 2773, *ḥāmad* [1]
delight, 2773, *ḥāmad* [1]
find delight, 2911, *ḥāpēṣ*[1] [1]
finds delight, 2911, *ḥāpēṣ*[1] [1]
have delight, 2911, *ḥāpēṣ*[1] [1]
take delight, 2911, *ḥāpēṣ*[1] [1]
delight in, 2913, *ḥāpēṣ*[3] [1]
delight, 5052, *maʿadannîm* [1]
delight yourself, 6695, *ʿānag* [1]
delight, 6696, *ʿōneg* [1]
delight, 8193, *rîaḥ* [1]
take delight, 8193, *rîaḥ* [1]
delight, 8354, *rāṣâ*[1] [1]
in delight, 8354, *rāṣâ*[1] [1]
take delight in, 8354, *rāṣâ*[1] [1]
takes delight, 8354, *rāṣâ*[1] [1]
delight, 8356, *rāṣôn* [1]
delight greatly, 8464+8464, *śûś+śûś* [1]
take delight, 8464, *śûś* [1]
take great delight, 8464+928+8525, *śûś+be-+śimḥâ* [1]
delight in, 8524, *śāmēaḥ* [1]
delight, 8524, *śāmēaḥ* [1]
delight, 8525, *śimḥâ* [1]
filled with delight, 9141, *šaʿašûʿîm* [1]
delight, 9503, *taʿanûg* [1]

DELIGHTED [9]
delighted, 2911, *ḥāpēṣ*[1] [5]
delighted, 2525, *ḥādâ*[1] [1]
delighted, 2773, *ḥāmad* [1]
delighted, 3512, *yāṭab* [1]
delighted, 8464, *śûś* [1]

DELIGHTFUL [4]
delightful, 2914, *ḥēpeṣ* [1]
delightful, 3202, *ṭôb*[2] [1]
delightful, 3636, *yāpâ* [1]
delightful, 9182, *šāpar* [1]

DELIGHTING [1]
delighting, 9141, *šaʿᵃšûʿîm* [1]

DELIGHTS [20]
delights, 2911, *ḥāpēṣ*[1] [6]
delights, 8356, *rāṣôn* [3]
delights, *NIH/RPE* [2]
delights in, 8354, *rāṣâ*[1] [2]
delights in, 2911, *ḥāpēṣ*[1] [1]
delights in, 2913, *ḥāpēṣ*[3] [1]
delights, 6358, *ʿēden*[1] [1]
delights, 8523, *śāmaḥ* [1]
delights, 8525, *śimḥâ* [1]
delights of the heart, 9503, *taʿᵃnûg* [1]
delights, 9503, *taʿᵃnûg* [1]

DELILAH [7]
Delilah, 1935, *dᵉlîlâ* [6]
Delilah, *NIH/RPE* [1]

DELIVER [75]
deliver, 5911, *nāṣal* [40]
deliver, 5989, *nātan* [7]
deliver, 3828, *yāšaʿ* [5]
deliver, 2740, *ḥālaṣ*[1] [4]
deliver, 7117, *pālaṭ* [3]
deliver, 4256, *lēdâ* [2]
deliver, 4880, *mālaṭ*[1] [2]
surely deliver, 5911+5911, *nāṣal+nāṣal* [2]
deliver over, 5989, *nātan* [2]
deliver, 7198, *pāṣâ* [2]
deliver, 3802, *yᵉšûʿâ* [1]
deliver, 3829, *yēšaʿ* [1]
deliver, 5989+5989, *nātan+nātan* [1]
deliver up, 6037, *sāgar* [1]
deliver, 9223, *šārâ*[1] [1]
deliver, 10719, *šᵉlim* [1]

DELIVERANCE [18]
deliverance, 3802, *yᵉšûʿâ* [9]
deliverance, 7129, *pᵉlêṭâ* [4]
deliverance, 2208, *haṣṣālâ* [1]
deliverance, 3828, *yāšaʿ* [1]
deliverance, 5911, *nāṣal* [1]
deliverance, 7119, *pallēṭ* [1]
deliverance, 9591, *tᵉšûʿâ* [1]

DELIVERED [61]
delivered, 5911, *nāṣal* [17]
delivered, 5989, *nātan* [12]
delivered, 7117, *pālaṭ* [4]
be delivered, 4880, *mālaṭ*[1] [3]
delivered, 995, *bôʾ* [2]
be delivered, 2740, *ḥālaṣ*[1] [2]
be delivered, 5911, *nāṣal* [2]
delivered over, 5989, *nātan* [2]
delivered, 6037, *sāgar* [2]
delivered, 7009, *pādâ* [2]
delivered, 9149, *šāpaṭ* [2]
delivered, 928+3338, *bᵉ+yād* [1]
delivered, 1457, *gāʾal*[1] [1]
delivered, 2740, *ḥālaṣ*[1] [1]
is delivered, 3297, *yābal* [1]
be delivered, 3828, *yāšaʿ* [1]
delivered, 4481, *māgan* [1]
delivered over, 5599, *nāgar* [1]
ever delivered, 5911+5911, *nāṣal+nāṣal* [1]
delivered up, 6037, *sāgar* [1]
delivered, 8938, *šālaḥ* [1]
delivered, 9591, *tᵉšûʿâ* [1]

DELIVERER [9]
deliverer, 7117, *pālaṭ* [5]
deliverer, 4635, *môšîaʿ* [3]
deliverer, 3802, *yᵉšûʿâ* [1]

DELIVERERS [2]
deliverers, 4635, *môšîaʿ* [2]

DELIVERING [2]
delivering, *NIH/RPE* [1]
delivering, 5911, *nāṣal* [1]

DELIVERS [15]
delivers, 5911, *nāṣal* [6]
delivers, 2740, *ḥālaṣ*[1] [2]
delivers, 4880, *mālaṭ*[1] [2]
delivers, 5989, *nātan* [2]
delivers, 7117, *pālaṭ* [2]
delivers, 7198, *pāṣâ* [1]

DELIVERY [4]
delivery stool, 78, *ʾobnayim* [1]
bring to delivery, 3528, *yālad* [1]
give delivery, 3528, *yālad* [1]
near the time of delivery, 3528, *yālad* [1]

DELUDED [1]
deluded, 9438, *tālal* [1]

DELUSIONS [3]
delusions, 9567, *tarmît* [2]
delusions, 8198, *rîq*[2] [1]

DEMAND [12]
demand an accounting, 2011, *dāraš* [3]
demand, 1335, *bāqaš* [2]
demand, *NIH/RPE* [1]
demand, 606, *ʾāmar*[1] [1]
demand, 1821, *dābār* [1]
certainly demand, 2011+2011, *dāraš+dāraš* [1]
demand, 5989, *nātan* [1]
demand, 6640, *ʿim* [1]
demand, 8626, *šāʾal* [1]

DEMANDED [10]
demanded, 606, *ʾāmar*[1] [2]
is demanded, 8883, *šît*[1] [2]
demanded, *NIH/RPE* [1]
demanded payment, 1335, *bāqaš* [1]
demanded, 1335, *bāqaš* [1]
demanded security, 2471, *ḥābal*[1] [1]
demanded, 6584+7023, *ʿal*[2]*+peh* [1]
demanded, 8938, *šālaḥ* [1]

DEMANDING [2]
demanding, 606, *ʾāmar*[1] [1]
demanding, 8626, *šāʾal* [1]

DEMANDS [6]
demands, *NIH/RPE* [1]
agree to demands, 14, *ʾābâ* [1]
demands, 6275, *ʿᵃbōdâ* [1]
demands, 6343, *ʿēdût* [1]
demands, 8626, *šāʾal* [1]
demands, 8883, *šît*[1] [1]

DEMOLISH [9]
demolish, 5997, *nātaṣ* [2]
demolish, 9012, *šāmad* [2]
demolish, 6, *ʾābad* [1]
demolish, 2238, *hāras* [1]
must demolish, 2238+2238, *hāras+hāras* [1]
demolish, 6904, *ʿārap*[2] [1]
demolish, 8689, *šābar*[1] [1]

DEMOLISHED [11]
demolished, 5997, *nātaṣ* [4]
demolished, 9037, *šāmēm*[1] [2]
demolished, 2238, *hāras* [1]
demolished, 6066, *sûp*[1] [1]
are demolished, 9037, *šāmēm*[1] [1]
be demolished, 9037, *šāmēm*[1] [1]
demolished, 9039, *šᵉmāmâ* [1]

DEMONS [2]
demons, 8717, *šēd* [2]

DEN [13]
den, 10129, *gōb* [10]
den, 5061, *māʿôn*[2] [1]
den, 5104, *mᵉʿōnâ* [1]
den, 5117, *mᵉʾārâ*[1] [1]

DENIED [7]
denied, 724, *ʾāṣal* [1]
denied, 1609, *gēzel* [1]
denied, 3948, *kāḥad* [1]
denied, 4415, *māʾas*[1] [1]
are denied, 4979, *mānaʿ* [1]
denied, 4979, *mānaʿ* [1]
denied, 6073, *sûr*[1] [1]

DENIES [1]
denies, 6073, *sûr*[1] [1]

DENOUNCE [4]
denounce, 2404, *zāʿam* [3]
denounce, 8652, *šᵉbûʿâ* [1]

DENOUNCED [2]
denounced, 2404, *zāʿam* [1]
denounced, 10030+10642, *ʾᵃkal+qᵉraṣ* [1]

DENOUNCES [2]
denounces, 5583, *nāgad* [2]

DENS [6]
dens, 5104, *mᵉʿōnâ* [5]
dens, 4995, *misgeret* [1]

DENSE [6]
dense, 1293, *bāṣîr*[2] [1]
dense, 3878, *kābēd*[2] [1]
dense, 3880, *kōbed* [1]
dense, 4202+2983, *lōʾ+ḥāqar* [1]
dense, 6265, *ʿāb*[2] [1]
dense smoke, 7798, *qîṭôr* [1]

DENY [12]
deny, 6700, *ʿānâ*[2] [6]
deny, 5742, *nāṭâ* [3]
deny, 6073, *sûr*[1] [2]
deny himself, 6700, *ʿānâ*[2] [1]

DENYING [1]
denying, 4202, *lōʾ* [1]

DEPART [10]
depart, 6073, *sûr*[1] [4]
depart, 3655, *yāṣāʾ* [2]
depart, 4631, *mûš*[2] [2]
depart, 2143, *hālak* [1]
depart, 8740, *šûb*[1] [1]

DEPARTED [10]
departed, 1655, *gālâ* [2]
departed, 3655, *yāṣāʾ* [2]
departed, 6073, *sûr*[1] [2]
departed, 2143, *hālak* [1]
departed, 4631, *mûš*[2] [1]
departed spirits, 8327, *rᵉpāʾîm*[1] [1]
spirits of the departed, 8327, *rᵉpāʾîm*[1] [1]

DEPARTING [1]
departing from, 4946+339, *min+ʾaḥar* [1]

DEPARTS [4]
departs, 2143, *hālak* [2]
departs, 3655, *yāṣāʾ* [1]
departs, 8740, *šûb*[1] [1]

DEPARTURE [3]
departure, 3655, *yāṣāʾ* [2]
departure, 1818, *dābar*[1] [1]

DEPEND [5]
depend, 1053, *bāṭaḥ*[1] [3]
let depend, 1053, *bāṭaḥ*[1] [1]
depend on, 6584, *ʿal*[2] [1]

DEPENDED [2]
depended, 1053, *bāṭaḥ*[1] [1]
depended, 9128, *šāʿan* [1]

DEPENDENT [1]
dependent, 7940, *qārôb* [1]

DEPENDING [8]
depending, 1053, *bāṭaḥ*[1] [8]

DEPENDS [1]
depends on, 8492, *śîm* [1]

DEPLOYED [5]
deployed, 6885, *ʿārak* [4]
deployed forces, 6885, *ʿārak* [1]

DEPORTED [11]
deported, 1655, *gālâ* [7]
deported, 10144, *gᵉlâ* [2]
deported, 995+1583, *bôʾ+gôlâ* [1]
deported, 2143, *hālak* [1]

DEPOSE [1]
depose, 2074, *hādap* [1]

DEPOSED [3]
deposed, 6073, *sûr*[1] [2]
was deposed, 10474, *nehat* [1]

DEPOSES [1]
deposes, 10528, *'adâ* [1]

DEPOSIT [4]
deposit, 2689, *ḥel'â'* [3]
deposit, 10474, *neḥat* [1]

DEPOSITED [2]
deposited, 5663, *nûaḥ*[1] [1]
deposited, 10474, *neḥat* [1]

DEPRAVED [2]
depraved, 8845, *šāḥat* [2]

DEPRESSIONS [1]
depressions, 9206, *šeqa'arûrâ* [1]

DEPRIVE [11]
deprive, 5742, *nāṭâ* [4]
deprive of justice, 5742, *nāṭâ* [2]
deprive of children, 8897, *šākal* [2]
deprive, 1757, *gāra'*[1] [1]
deprive, 6430, *'āwat* [1]
deprive, 9101, *šānâ*[1] [1]

DEPRIVED [4]
deprived, 2396, *zānaḥ*[2] [1]
deprived of, 4946, *min* [1]
deprived, 4979, *māna'* [1]
deprived of children, 8897, *šākal* [1]

DEPRIVES [1]
deprives, 6073, *sûr*[1] [1]

DEPRIVING [1]
depriving, 2893, *ḥāsēr*[1] [1]

DEPTH [2]
depth, 3972, *kōl* [1]
depth, 4200+5087+2025, *le-1+ma'al2+-â2* [1]

DEPTHS [36]
depths, 5185, *meṣôlâ* [9]
depths, 9333, *tehôm* [6]
depths, 9397, *taḥtî* [4]
depths, 5099, *ma'amaqqîm* [3]
depths, 3752, *yerēkâ* [2]
depths, 8619, *še'ôl* [2]
depths of the grave, 8619, *še'ôl* [2]
ocean depths, 9333, *tehôm* [2]
depths, 1061, *beṭen*[1] [1]
lifted out of the depths, 1926, *dālâ*[1] [1]
depths, 4736, *meḥqār* [1]
go to great depths, 6676, *'āmaq* [1]
depths, 6679, *'ōmeq* [1]
depths, 9247, *šōreš* [1]

DEPUTY [2]
deputy, 5893, *nāṣab*[1] [1]
deputy, 7224, *pāqîd* [1]

DERIDE [1]
deride, 7840, *qālas* [1]

DERIDES [1]
derides, 996, *bûz*[1] [1]

DERISION [5]
derision, 7841, *qeles* [2]
derision, 4353, *la'ag* [1]
claps in derision, 8562, *śāpaq*[1] [1]
derision, 9240, *šerēqâ* [1]

DESCEND [6]
descend, 3718, *yārad* [3]
descend, 5688, *nāzal* [1]
descend, 5737, *nāḥat* [1]
descend, 8801, *šûr*[1] [1]

DESCENDANT [21]
descendant, 1201, *bēn*[1] [12]
descendant, 2446, *zera'* [2]
descendant, 10120, *bar*[2] [2]
descendant, *NIH/RPE* [1]
descendant, 408+4946+2446, *'îš1+min+zera'* [1]
descendant, 1426, *bat*[1] [1]
descendant, 3528, *yālad* [1]
descendant, 8642, *še'ērît* [1]

DESCENDANTS [348]
descendants, 1201, *bēn*[1] [229]
descendants, 2446, *zera'* [82]
descendants, 1887, *dôr*[2] [6]
descendants, 3535, *yālîd* [6]
descendants, *NIH/RPE* [4]
descendants, 5781, *neked* [3]
descendants, 7368, *ṣe'eṣā'îm* [3]
descendants, 344, *'aḥarît* [2]
descendants, 3528, *yālad* [2]
descendants, 339, *'aḥar* [1]
descendants, 1074, *bayit*[1] [1]
his descendants^s, 2157, *-hem* [1]
his descendants^s, 2257, *-ô* [1]
have descendants, 2445, *zāra'* [1]
direct descendants, 3655+3751, *yāṣā'+yārēk* [1]
descendants, 5270+1074, *marbît+bayit*[1] [1]
descendants, 5883+3655+3751, *nepeš+yāṣā'+yārēk* [1]
descendants, 7262+1061, *perî+beṭen*[1] [1]
descendants, 7262, *perî* [1]
descendants, 9352, *tôlēdôt* [1]

DESCENDED [17]
descended, *AIT* [4]
descended, 1201, *bēn*[1] [4]
descended, 3718, *yārad* [3]
descended, 2446, *zera'* [2]
was descended, 3528, *yālad* [2]
descended, 3655, *yāṣā'* [1]
descended, 9164, *šāpēl*[1] [1]

DESCENDING [4]
descending, 1683, *gālaš* [2]
descending, 3718, *yārad* [2]

DESCENDS [1]
descends, 3718, *yārad* [1]

DESCENT [5]
descent, 2446, *zera'* [3]
of foreign descent, 6850, *'ēreb*[2] [1]
lines of descent, 9352, *tôlēdôt* [1]

DESCRIBE [1]
describe, 5583, *nāgad* [1]

DESCRIBED [1]
described, 1819, *dābar*[2] [1]

DESCRIPTION [3]
write a description, 4180, *kātab* [2]
wrote description, 4180, *kātab* [1]

DESCRIPTIONS [1]
written descriptions, 4180, *kātab* [1]

DESECRATE [8]
desecrate, 2725, *ḥālal*[1] [7]
desecrate, 3237, *ṭāmē'*[1] [1]

DESECRATED [17]
desecrated, 2725, *ḥālal*[1] [11]
desecrated, 3237, *ṭāmē'*[1] [3]
be desecrated, 2725, *ḥālal*[1] [1]
was desecrated, 2725, *ḥālal*[1] [1]
desecrated, 2866, *ḥānēp*[1] [1]

DESECRATES [1]
desecrates, 2725, *ḥālal*[1] [1]

DESECRATING [5]
desecrating, 2725, *ḥālal*[1] [5]

DESERT [279]
desert, 4497, *midbār*[1] [256]
desert, 6858, *'arābâ*[2] [4]
desert creatures, 7470, *ṣî*[2] [4]
desert owl, 7684, *qā'at* [4]
desert, 6440, *'āzab*[1] [2]
desert, 7480, *ṣiyyâ* [2]
desert, 7481, *ṣāyôn* [2]
desert, 824+4497, *'ereṣ+midbār1* [1]
creatures of the desert, 7470, *ṣî*[2] [1]
desert tribes, 7470, *ṣî*[2] [1]
desert wind, 7708, *qādîm* [1]
desert heat, 9220, *šārāb* [1]

DESERTED [27]
deserted, 6440, *'āzab*[1] [11]
deserted, 9037, *šāmēm*[1] [4]
deserted, 401+3782, *'ayin1+yāšab* [1]
deserted, 970, *bādād* [1]
deserted, 2319, *zûr*[2] [1]
left deserted, 2990, *ḥārēb*[1] [1]
deserted, 4202+3782, *lō'+yāšab* [1]
deserted, 4946+1172+3782, *min+belî+yāšab* [1]
deserted, 4946+401+132, *min+'ayin1+'ādām1* [1]
deserted, 4946+401+3782, *min+'ayin1+yāšab* [1]
deserted, 5759, *nāṭaš* [1]
deserted, 6047+294, *sûg1+'āḥôr* [1]
deserted, 6590+4946+339, *'ālâ+min+'aḥar* [1]
deserted, 8861, *šāyâ* [1]

DESERTING [2]
deserting, 5877, *nāpal* [2]

DESERTS [7]
deserts, 6440, *'āzab*[1] [2]
deserts, 2999, *ḥorbâ* [1]
deserts, 4497, *midbār*[1] [1]
deserts, 5877, *nāpal* [1]
deserts, 6858, *'arābâ*[2] [1]
deserts, 7233, *pārad* [1]

DESERVE [20]
what deserve, 1691, *gemûl* [3]
deserve, *AIT* [2]
what deserve, 3869+5126, *ke-+ma'aśeh* [2]
deserve, 7262, *perî* [2]
deserve to, 408, *'îš*[1] [1]
deserve to, 1201, *bēn*[1] [1]
those who deserve, 1251, *ba'al*[1] [1]
deserve, 1691, *gemûl* [1]
as deserve, 3869, *ke-* [1]
what deserve for, 3869, *ke-* [1]
what deserve, 3869, *ke-* [1]
deserve, 5477, *mišpāṭ* [1]
us deserve, 5646, *-nû*[1] [1]
deserve, 6913, *'āśâ*[1] [1]
what deserve, 7262, *perî* [1]

DESERVED [3]
deserved, 408, *'îš*[1] [1]
than deserved, 4946, *min* [1]
get what deserved, 8750, *šāwâ*[1] [1]

DESERVES [7]
deserves to, 1201, *bēn*[1] [1]
deserves, 1201, *bēn*[1] [1]
deserves, 1691+3338, *gemûl+yād* [1]
what deserves, 1691, *gemûl* [1]
deserves, 3869+1896, *ke-+day* [1]
what deserves, 3869, *ke-* [1]
deserves, 8401, *rāšā'* [1]

DESERVING [2]
deserving, *AIT* [1]
deserving, 5477, *mišpāṭ* [1]

DESIGN [6]
design, 7451, *ṣûrâ* [3]
design, 4742, *maḥašābâ* [1]
design, 5126, *ma'aśeh* [1]
original design, 5504, *matkōnet* [1]

DESIGNATE [3]
designate, 2118, *hāyâ* [1]
designate, 5989, *nātan* [1]
designate, 8492, *śîm* [1]

DESIGNATED [12]
designated, 5918, *nāqab*[1] [3]
designated, *NIH/RPE* [2]
designated, 2374, *zāman* [1]

designated times, 2375, zemān [1]
designated, 4595, mô'ēd [1]
designated, 4597, mû'ādâ [1]
designated part, 5152, mipqād [1]
were designated, 5918, nāqab[1] [1]
designated, 5989, nātan [1]

DESIGNED [1]
designed, 4742, maḥašābâ [1]

DESIGNER [1]
designer, 3110, ḥōšēb [1]

DESIGNERS [2]
designers, 3110+4742, ḥōšēb+maḥašābâ [1]
designers, 3110, ḥōšēb [1]

DESIGNS [3]
artistic designs, 4742, maḥašābâ [2]
palm tree designs, 9474, timōrâ [1]

DESIRABLE [3]
desirable, 1047, bāḥar[1] [1]
desirable, 2773, ḥāmad [1]
desirable, 2775, ḥemdâ [1]

DESIRE [38]
desire, 2911, ḥāpēṣ[1] [7]
desire, 9294, ta'awâ[1] [5]
desire, 2913, ḥāpēṣ[3] [3]
desire, 2914, ḥēpeṣ [3]
desire, 5883, nepeš [3]
desire, 2773, ḥāmad [2]
desire, 9592, tešûqâ [2]
desire, NIH/RPE [1]
desire, 37, 'abiyyônâ [1]
desire, 203, 'āwâ[1] [1]
set desire on, 203, 'āwâ[1] [1]
desire, 1047, bāḥar[1] [1]
desire, 2094, hawwâ[1] [1]
desire, 2775, ḥemdâ [1]
have desire, 2911, ḥāpēṣ[1] [1]
desire, 3671+4742, yēṣer[1]+maḥašābâ [1]
desire, 3869, ke- [1]
desire, 4213, lēb [1]
desire, 5362, maśśā'[1] [1]
desire, 6640, 'im [1]

DESIRED [12]
desired, 203, 'āwâ[1] [3]
desired, 2914, ḥēpeṣ [3]
desired, 2775, ḥemdâ [2]
desired, 3139+3137, ḥēšeq+ḥāšaq[1] [2]
desired, 3139+2911, ḥēšeq+ḥāpēṣ[1] [1]
desired, 8626, šā'al [1]

DESIRES [20]
desires, 203, 'āwâ[1] [3]
desires, 2911, ḥāpēṣ[1] [3]
desires, 5883, nepeš [2]
desires, 8356, rāṣôn [2]
desires, 170, 'āhab [1]
evil desires, 2094, hawwâ[1] [1]
desires, 2914, ḥēpeṣ [1]
desires, 4397, ma'awiyyîm [1]
desires, 4626, môrāš[2] [1]
desires, 5399, miš'ālâ [1]
desires, 6344, 'adî [1]
desires, 8934, šālôm [1]
desires, 9294, ta'awâ[1] [1]
desires, 9592, tešûqâ [1]

DESOLATE [80]
desolate, 9039, šemāmâ [30]
desolate, 9037, šāmēm[1] [15]
desolate, 9014, šammâ[1] [7]
desolate, 2999, ḥorbâ [5]
lies desolate, 9037, šāmēm[1] [4]
desolate, 2990, ḥārēb[1] [3]
desolate, 8739, šô'â [2]
desolate, 9038, šāmēm[2] [2]
desolate place, 9039, šemāmâ [2]
desolate, 970, bādād [1]
desolate waste, 2992, ḥārēb[3] [1]
desolate, 2992, ḥārēb[3] [1]
desolate, 5898, nāṣâ[2] [1]
desolate, 8689, šābar[1] [1]
made desolate, 9037, šāmēm[1] [1]
was left so desolate, 9037, šāmēm[1] [1]
desolate waste, 9039, šemāmâ [1]
utterly desolate, 9039, šemāmâ [1]
desolate, 9040, šimemâ [1]

DESOLATION [11]
causes desolation, 9037, šāmēm[1] [4]
desolation, 9039, šemāmâ [3]
desolation, 983, bōhû [1]
desolation, 2999, ḥorbâ [1]
desolation, 9014, šammâ[1] [1]
desolation, 9037, šāmēm[1] [1]

DESOLATIONS [2]
desolations, 9014, šammâ[1] [1]
desolations, 9037, šāmēm[1] [1]

DESPAIR [11]
despair, 1017, bôš[1] [2]
despair, 9041, šimmāmôn [2]
despair, 631, 'ānûš [1]
despair, 3286, yā'aš [1]
despair, 3707, yārē'[1] [1]
despair, 3910, kēheh [1]
despair, 5000, massâ[2] [1]
in despair, 7041, pûn [1]
despair, 9039, šemāmâ [1]

DESPAIRING [4]
despairing, 1792, de'ābôn [1]
despairing, 3286, yā'aš [1]
despairing, 4007, kālam [1]
despairing man, 4988, mās [1]

DESPAIRS [1]
despairs, 4202+586, lō'+'āman[1] [1]

DESPERATE [4]
desperate, 4394, me'ōd [2]
desperate times, 7997, qāšeh [1]
something desperate, 8288, rā'â[3] [1]

DESPISE [29]
despise, 4415, mā'as[1] [8]
despise, 1022, bāzâ [6]
despise, 996, bûz[1] [4]
despise, 5540, nā'aṣ [4]
despise, 9493, tā'ab [2]
despise, 1022+928+6524, bāzâ+be-+'ayin[1] [1]
despise, 1718, gā'al [1]
despise, 2361, zālal[1] [1]
despise, 7837+928+6524, qālal+be-+'ayin[1] [1]
despise, 8764, šûṭ[2] [1]

DESPISED [36]
despised, 1022, bāzâ [20]
was despised, 1022, bāzâ [3]
despised, 4415, mā'as[1] [3]
be despised, 1022, bāzâ [2]
despised, 1718, gā'al [2]
despised, 997, bûz[2] [1]
despised, 999, bûzâ [1]
despised, 1719, gō'al [1]
despised, 2361, zālal[1] [1]
despised, 5540, nā'aṣ [1]
be despised, 7829, qālâ[2] [1]

DESPISES [11]
despises, 996, bûz[1] [4]
despises, 4415, mā'as[1] [3]
despises, 1022, bāzâ [2]
despises, 1022+928+6524, bāzâ+be-+'ayin[1] [1]
despises, 7837+928+6524, qālal+be-+'ayin[1] [1]

DESPITE [9]
despite, 928, be- [6]
despite, 928+8611+4200, be-+ša-+le-[1] [1]
despite, 3954, kî[2] [1]
despite, 6640, 'im [1]

DESPOIL [1]
despoil, 5989+4200+1020, nātan+le-[1]+baz [1]

DESTINATION [1]
destination, NIH/RPE [1]

DESTINE [1]
destine, 4948, mānâ[1] [1]

DESTINED [7]
destined for, 4200, le-[1] [5]
destined, 5989, nātan [1]
destined, 9286, šātat [1]

DESTINY [6]
destiny, 5247, miqreh [2]
final destiny, 344, 'aḥarît [1]
destiny, 784, 'ōraḥ [1]
destiny, 4972, menî [1]
destiny, 6067, sôp [1]

DESTITUTE [7]
destitute, 9037, šāmēm[1] [2]
destitute, 1201+2710, bēn[1]+ḥalôp [1]
destitute, 3769, yāraš[1] [1]
destitute, 5927, nāqâ [1]
left destitute, 6440, 'āzab[1] [1]
destitute, 6899, 'ar'ār [1]

DESTROY [218]
destroy, 8845, šāḥat [60]
destroy, 9012, šāmad [31]
destroy, 6, 'ābad [28]
destroy, 4162, kārat [14]
destroy, 3983, kālâ[1] [11]
completely destroy, 3049, ḥāram[1] [5]
destroy, 5782, nākâ [5]
destroy, 8720, šādad [5]
completely destroy, 6913+3986, 'āśâ[1]+kālâ[3] [4]
destroy, 7551, ṣāmat [4]
destroy, 2472, ḥābal[2] [3]
totally destroy, 3049, ḥāram[1] [3]
destroy, 430, 'ākal [2]
destroy, 1180, bāla'[1] [2]
destroy, 1950, dāmâ[3] [2]
destroy completely, 3049, ḥāram[1] [2]
destroy, 3769, yāraš[1] [2]
destroy completely, 3986+6913, kālâ[3]+'āśâ[1] [2]
destroy, 4637, mût [2]
destroy, 8689, šābar[1] [2]
completely destroy, 9037, šāmēm[1] [2]
destroy, 10243, ḥabal [2]
destroy completely, 6+6, 'ābad+'ābad [1]
destroy, 665, 'āsap [1]
destroy, 1818, dābar[1] [1]
destroy, 2222, hārag [1]
destroy, 2238, hāras [1]
completely destroy, 3049+3049, ḥāram[1]+ḥāram[1] [1]
destroy totally, 3049, ḥāram[1] [1]
destroy, 3049, ḥāram[1] [1]
must destroy totally, 3049+3049, ḥāram[1]+ḥāram[1] [1]
destroy, 3948, kāḥad [1]
destroy completely, 3983, kālâ[1] [1]
completely destroy, 3986+6913, kālâ[3]+'āśâ[1] [1]
power to destroy, 3986, kālâ[3] [1]
destroy, 5422, mašḥît [1]
destroy, 5997, nātaṣ [1]
destroy completely, 6913+3986, 'āśâ[1]+kālâ[3] [1]
destroy, 7212, pāqad [1]
destroy, 7287, pāraṣ [1]
seek to destroy, 7551, ṣāmat [1]
destroy, 8406, rāšaš [1]
destroy, 8492+9039, śîm+šemāmâ [1]
destroy, 8596, śārap [1]
totally destroy, 9012+9012, šāmad+šāmad [1]
destroy yourself, 9037, šāmēm[1] [1]
destroy, 9462, tāmam [1]

DESTROYED [192]
destroyed, 9012, šāmad [24]
destroyed, 6, 'ābad [18]
destroyed, 3983, kālâ[1] [14]
totally destroyed, 3049, ḥāram[1] [13]
destroyed, 8845, šāḥat [11]
completely destroyed, 3049, ḥāram[1] [6]
destroyed, 8720, šādad [6]
be destroyed, 9012, šāmad [6]
be destroyed, 8689, šābar[1] [5]
are destroyed, 9012, šāmad [5]
be destroyed, 4162, kārat [4]

destroyed, 4162, *kārat* [4]
destroyed, 7551, *ṣāmat* [3]
destroyed, 8691, *šeber*[1] [3]
is destroyed, 8720, *šādad* [3]
be destroyed, 10243, *ḥabal* [3]
been destroyed, 430, *'ākal* [2]
destroyed, 430, *'ākal* [2]
destroyed, 1278, *bā'ar*[2] [2]
destroyed, 2222, *hārag* [2]
destroyed, 2238, *hāras* [2]
destroyed, 2805, *ḥāmās* [2]
destroyed, 3049, *ḥāram*[1] [2]
destroyed, 5782, *nākâ* [2]
were destroyed, 5782, *nākâ* [2]
destroyed, 5997, *nātaṣ* [2]
destroyed, 8689, *šābar*[1] [2]
are destroyed, 8720, *šādad* [2]
be destroyed, 8720, *šādad* [2]
destroyed, 9037, *šāmēm*[1] [2]
be destroyed, 6, *'ābad* [1]
certainly be destroyed, 6+6, *'ābad+'ābad* [1]
surely be destroyed, 6+6, *'ābad+'ābad* [1]
destroyed, 1818, *dābar*[1] [1]
are destroyed, 1950, *dāmâ*[3] [1]
be completely destroyed, 1950+1950, *dāmâ[3]+dāmâ[3]* [1]
be destroyed, 1959, *dāmam*[3] [1]
being destroyed, 2238, *hāras* [1]
is destroyed, 2238, *hāras* [1]
was destroyed, 2238, *hāras* [1]
be destroyed, 3049, *ḥāram*[1] [1]
devoted and destroyed, 3049, *ḥāram*[1] [1]
destroyed, 3051, *ḥērem*[1] [1]
totally destroyed, 3051, *ḥērem*[1] [1]
are destroyed, 3948, *kāḥad* [1]
were destroyed, 3948, *kāḥad* [1]
destroyed, 5782+4804+1524+4394, *nākâ+makkâ+gādôl+me'ōd* [1]
destroyed, 5937, *nāqap*[1] [1]
be destroyed, 6200, *sāpâ* [1]
completely destroyed, 6330+3983, *'ad[2]+kālâ[1]* [1]
are destroyed, 7400, *ṣādâ*[2] [1]
be destroyed, 8596, *śārap* [1]
destroyed by fire, 8596, *śārap* [1]
destroyed, 8596, *śārap* [1]
been destroyed, 8720, *šādad* [1]
destroyed, 8739, *šō'â* [1]
been destroyed, 9012, *šāmad* [1]
certainly be destroyed, 9012+9012, *šāmad+šāmad* [1]
completely destroyed, 9012, *šāmad* [1]
destroyed, 9014, *šammâ*[1] [1]
be destroyed, 9037, *šāmēm*[1] [1]
destroyed, 9462, *tāmam* [1]
destroyed, 10005, *'abad* [1]
was destroyed, 10281, *ḥarab* [1]
destroyed, 10520, *setar*[2] [1]
completely destroyed, 10722+10221+10005, *šemad+we-+'abad* [1]

DESTROYER [11]

destroyer, 8720, *šādad* [7]
destroyer, 5422, *mašḥît* [4]

DESTROYERS [6]

destroyers, 8720, *šādad* [3]
destroyers, *NIH/RPE* [1]
destroyers, 1327, *bāqaq*[1] [1]
destroyers, 5422, *mašḥît* [1]

DESTROYING [17]

destroying, 8845, *šāḥat* [5]
destroying, 2095, *hawwâ*[2] [2]
destroying completely, 3049, *ḥāram*[1] [2]
destroying, 8720, *šādad* [2]
destroying, 6, *'ābad* [1]
destroying, 12, *'abdān* [1]
destroying, 1180, *bāla'*[1] [1]
destroying, 2222, *hārag* [1]
destroying, 3049, *ḥāram*[1] [1]
destroying, 8273, *ra'*[1] [1]

DESTROYS [11]

destroys, 8845, *šāḥat* [3]
destroys, 6, *'ābad* [2]
destroys, 8720, *šādad* [2]
one who destroys, 1251+5422, *ba'al[1]+mašḥît* [1]
destroys, 3983, *kālâ*[1] [1]
destroys, 5422, *mašḥît* [1]
destroys, 8135, *rāzâ* [1]

DESTRUCTION [79]

destruction, 8691, *šeber*[1] [14]
destruction, 8719, *šōd*[2] [13]
destruction, 6, *'ābad* [5]
destruction, 11, *'abaddôn* [5]
destruction, 3051, *ḥērem*[1] [3]
destruction, 9012, *šāmad* [3]
destruction, 369, *'êd* [2]
destruction, 1175, *beliyya'al* [2]
destruction, 2095, *hawwâ*[2] [2]
set apart for destruction, 3051, *ḥērem*[1] [2]
destruction, 3986, *kālâ*[3] [2]
destruction, 8288, *rā'â*[3] [2]
destruction, 8845, *šāḥat* [2]
destruction, 9, *'abaddōh* [1]
destruction, 13, *'obdān* [1]
destruction, 1172, *belî* [1]
destruction, 1947, *dām* [1]
destruction, 2239, *heres* [1]
bring about destruction, 3049, *ḥāram*[1] [1]
devoted to destruction, 3051+3049, *ḥērem[1]+ḥāram[1]* [1]
devoted to destruction, 3051, *ḥērem*[1] [1]
destruction, 3957, *kîd* [1]
destruction, 4001, *killāyôn* [1]
destruction, 4162, *kārat* [1]
destruction, 4550, *mahpēkâ* [1]
destruction, 5404, *mišbāt* [1]
destruction, 5422, *mašḥît* [1]
destruction, 7776, *qeṭeb* [1]
destruction, 8273, *ra'*[1] [1]
destruction brought, 8317, *rā'a'*[1] [1]
destruction, 8695, *šibbārôn* [1]
doomed to destruction, 8720, *šādad* [1]
destruction, 8736, *šāw'* [1]
cause of destruction, 8845, *šāḥat* [1]
destruction, 9318, *tablît* [1]

DESTRUCTIVE [8]

destructive, 4421, *mā'ar* [3]
destructive, 5422, *mašḥît* [2]
destructive forces, 2095, *hawwâ*[2] [1]
destructive, 3986, *kālâ*[3] [1]
destructive, 7776, *qeṭeb* [1]

DETACHMENT [1]

detachment, 5163, *maṣṣāb* [1]

DETACHMENTS [1]

detachments, 8031, *rō'š*[1] [1]

DETAILED [1]

detailed, 3972, *kōl* [1]

DETAILS [3]

details, 1821, *dābār* [1]
details, 3972, *kōl* [1]
details, 4856, *melā'kâ* [1]

DETAIN [2]

detain, 336, *'āḥar* [1]
detain, 6806, *'āṣar* [1]

DETAINED [2]

was detained, 3855, *yātar* [1]
detained, 6806, *'āṣar* [1]

DETECT [3]

detect, 5162, *māṣā'* [1]
detect, 5564, *nābaṭ* [1]
detect, 9312, *tebûnâ* [1]

DETERMINE [8]

determine, *NIH/RPE* [2]
determine, 3108, *ḥāšab* [2]
determine the value, 3108, *ḥāšab* [1]
determine, 3723, *yārâ*[3] [1]
determine amount needed, 4082, *kāsas* [1]
determine, 8492+7156, *śîm+pāneh* [1]

DETERMINED [29]

determined, 8492+7156, *śîm+pāneh* [4]
determined, 2372, *zāmam* [3]
determined, 3283, *yā'al*[2] [3]
was determined, 2983, *ḥāqar* [2]
determined, 3619, *yā'aṣ* [2]
determined, 3983, *kālâ*[1] [2]
determined, *AIT* [1]
determined, 599, *'āmēṣ* [1]
fully determined, 928+4222+8969, *be-+lēbāb+šālēm[2]* [1]
determined should die, 3051, *ḥērem*[1] [1]
been determined, 3076, *ḥāraṣ*[1] [1]
determined, 3076, *ḥāraṣ*[1] [1]
determined, 3108, *ḥāšab* [1]
determined, 4946+907, *min+'ēt[2]* [1]
determined, 7422, *ṣāwâ* [1]
determined, 8492+8492+7156, *śîm+śîm+pāneh* [1]
amount been determined, 9419, *tākan* [1]
determined, 9428, *tālā'* [1]
determined, 10682+10104, *śîm+bāl* [1]

DETERMINES [2]

determines, 3922, *kûn*[1] [1]
determines, 4948, *mānâ*[1] [1]

DETEST [17]

detest, 9359, *tô'ēbâ* [6]
detest, 9211, *šeqeṣ* [3]
detest, 9493, *tā'ab* [3]
detest, 9210, *šāqaṣ* [2]
detest, 7762, *qûṣ*[1] [1]
detest, 8533, *śānē'* [1]
detest, 9493+9493, *tā'ab+tā'ab* [1]

DETESTABLE [107]

detestable practices, 9359, *tô'ēbâ* [30]
detestable, 9359, *tô'ēbâ* [19]
detestable things, 9359, *tô'ēbâ* [18]
detestable, 9211, *šeqeṣ* [7]
detestable thing, 9359, *tô'ēbâ* [7]
detestable idols, 9359, *tô'ēbâ* [6]
detestable god, 9199, *šiqqûṣ* [3]
detestable idols, 9199, *šiqqûṣ* [3]
detestable ways, 9359, *tô'ēbâ* [3]
things detestable, 9359, *tô'ēbâ* [3]
detestable acts, 9199, *šiqqûṣ* [1]
detestable images, 9199, *šiqqûṣ* [1]
detestable things, 9199, *šiqqûṣ* [1]
detestable god, 9359, *tô'ēbâ* [1]
detestable offense, 9359, *tô'ēbâ* [1]
detestable sins, 9359, *tô'ēbâ* [1]
thing detestable, 9359, *tô'ēbâ* [1]
what detestable, 9359, *tô'ēbâ* [1]

DETESTED [1]

detested, 1041, *bāḥal*[1] [1]

DETESTS [13]

detests, 9359, *tô'ēbâ* [13]

DETHRONED [1]

dethroned, 6073, *sûr*[1] [1]

DETRIMENT [1]

detriment, 10472, *nezaq* [1]

DEUEL [5]

Deuel, 1979, *de'û'ēl* [5]

DEVASTATE [6]

devastate, 8845, *šāḥat* [2]
devastate, 1191, *bālaq* [1]
devastate, 1327, *bāqaq*[1] [1]
devastate, 2200, *hāpak* [1]
devastate, 9014, *šammâ*[1] [1]

DEVASTATED [11]

devastated, 9037, *šāmēm*[1] [4]
devastated, 8720, *šādad* [2]
devastated, 870, *'āšam* [1]
devastated, 2990, *ḥārēb*[1] [1]
devastated, 5782+4804+1524+4394, *nākâ+makkâ+gādôl+me'ōd* [1]
be devastated, 8720, *šādad* [1]
devastated, 8845, *šāḥat* [1]

DEVASTATION [2]
cause devastation, 8845, *šāḥat* [1]
brought devastation, 9037, *šāmēm*[1] [1]

DEVELOPED [1]
developed, 1540, *gādal* [1]

DEVIATE [1]
deviate, 6073, *sûr*[1] [1]

DEVICES [1]
devices, 4600, *mōʿēṣâ* [1]

DEVIOUS [3]
devious, 4279, *lûz*[1] [2]
devious, 2203, *hᵃpakpak* [1]

DEVISE [7]
devise, 3108, *ḥāšab* [3]
devise plans, 3108, *ḥāšab* [1]
devise, 6418, *ʿûṣ*[1] [1]
devise, 7188, *pāʿal* [1]
devise, 8103, *rādap* [1]

DEVISED [7]
devised, 3108, *ḥāšab* [5]
devised, 2924, *ḥāpaś* [1]
devised, 4742, *maḥᵃšābâ* [1]

DEVISES [3]
devises, 3108, *ḥāšab* [2]
devises, 3086, *ḥāraš*[1] [1]

DEVISING [1]
devising, 3108, *ḥāšab* [1]

DEVOTE [5]
devote, 2616, *ḥāzaq* [1]
devote, 3049, *ḥāram*[1] [1]
devote, 3922, *kûn*[1] [1]
devote, 5989, *nātan* [1]
devote, 6842, *ʿārab*[1] [1]

DEVOTED [25]
devoted things, 3051, *ḥērem*[1] [6]
devoted, 3051, *ḥērem*[1] [4]
fully devoted, 8969, *šālēm*[2] [2]
devoted to, 339+2143, *ʾaḥar+hālak* [1]
devoted, 1467, *gābah* [1]
devoted to, 2143, *hālak* [1]
devoted, 2616, *ḥāzaq* [1]
devoted, 2883, *ḥāsîd* [1]
devoted and destroyed, 3049, *ḥāram*[1] [1]
that which is devoted, 3051, *ḥērem*[1] [1]
devoted to God, 3051, *ḥērem*[1] [1]
devoted to destruction, 3051+3049, *ḥērem*[1]*+ḥāram*[1] [1]
devoted to destruction, 3051, *ḥērem*[1] [1]
devoted to the LORD, 3051, *ḥērem*[1] [1]
devoted, 3922, *kûn*[1] [1]
devoted, 5989, *nātan* [1]

DEVOTES [1]
devotes, 3049, *ḥāram*[1] [1]

DEVOTION [11]
acts of devotion, 2876, *ḥesed*[2] [2]
devotion, 2876, *ḥesed*[2] [2]
wholehearted devotion, 4213+8969, *lēb+šālēm*[2] [2]
wholehearted devotion, 4222+8969, *lēbāb+šālēm*[2] [2]
devotion, 6313, *ʿᵃgābîm* [1]
devotion, 8354, *rāṣâ*[1] [1]
devotion, 8491, *śîḥâ* [1]

DEVOUR [49]
devour, 430, *ʾākal* [43]
devour, 433, *ʾoklâ* [2]
devour, 1616, *gāzar*[2] [1]
devour, 2887, *ḥāsal* [1]
devour, 8286, *rāʿâ*[1] [1]
devour, 10030, *ʾᵃkal* [1]

DEVOURED [28]
devoured, 430, *ʾākal* [22]
be devoured, 430, *ʾākal* [2]
devoured, 10030, *ʾᵃkal* [2]
devoured, 1180, *bālaʿ*[1] [1]
devoured, 4407, *maʾᵃkāl* [1]

DEVOURING [3]
devouring, 430, *ʾākal* [2]
devouring, 8845, *šāḥat* [1]

DEVOURS [11]
devours, 430, *ʾākal* [10]
devours, 1180, *bālaʿ*[1] [1]

DEVOUT [2]
devout, 2876, *ḥesed*[2] [1]
devout, 4394, *mᵉʾōd* [1]

DEW [36]
dew, 3228, *ṭal* [31]
dew, 10299, *ṭal* [5]

DIADEM [4]
diadem, 5694, *nēzer* [3]
diadem, 7565, *ṣānîp* [1]

DIAMETER [1]
diameter, 7757, *qômâ* [1]

DIBLAH [1]
Diblah, 1812, *diblâ* [1]

DIBLAIM [1]
Diblaim, 1813, *diblayim* [1]

DIBON [9]
Dibon, 1897, *dîbôn* [9]

DIBON GAD [2]
Dibon Gad, 1898, *dîbôn gād* [2]

DIBRI [1]
Dibri, 1828, *dibrî* [1]

DICTATE [2]
dictate, 1819, *dābar*[2] [1]
dictate, 4946+7023, *min+peh* [1]

DICTATED [4]
dictated, 4946+7023, *min+peh* [2]
dictated, 4946+7023+7924, *min+peh+qārāʾ*[1] [1]
dictated, 7023, *peh* [1]

DICTATING [1]
dictating, 4946+7023, *min+peh* [1]

DICTATION [1]
dictation, 4946+7023, *min+peh* [1]

DID [937]
did, *AIT* [522]
did, 6913, *ʿāśâ*[1] [286]
did, *NIH/RPE* [63]
did business with, 6086, *sāḥar* [4]
did[s], 2143, *hālak* [3]
did, 2118, *hāyâ* [2]
did well, 3201, *ṭôb*[1] [2]
did[s], 3655, *yāṣāʾ* [2]
what did, 5126, *maʿᵃśeh* [2]
did so[s], 296, *ʾāḥaz*[1] [1]
did weaving, 755+1428, *ʾārag+bat*[3] [1]
did[s], 1162, *bālâ*[1] [1]
did work, 1215, *bānâ* [1]
did, 1694, *gāmal* [1]
did, 2006, *derek* [1]
things did, 2006, *derek* [1]
what did, 2006, *derek* [1]
did[s], 2388, *zānâ*[1] [1]
did the same[s], 2489+285+448+285, *ḥābar*[2]*+ʾeḥād+ʾel+ʾeḥād* [1]
did so[s], 2502, *ḥābaš* [1]
secretly did, 2901, *ḥāpāʾ* [1]
did good, 3603, *yāʿal* [1]
did so[s], 3782, *yāšab* [1]
as usually did, 3869+3427+928+3427, *kᵉ+yôm*[1]*+bᵉ+yôm*[1] [1]
did[s], 3877+906+4213+4392, *kābēd*[1]*+ʾēt*[1]*+lēb+-ām* [1]
did so[s], 4374+8008+2256+2932, *lāqaḥ+qešet+wᵉ+ḥēṣ* [1]
did so[s], 4374, *lāqaḥ* [1]
did[s], 4374, *lāqaḥ* [1]
did so[s], 4576, *mûl*[1] [1]
how did it go, 4769+905, *mî+ʾatt* [1]
did completely, 4848, *mālēʾ*[1] [1]
things did, 5126+3338, *maʿᵃśeh+yād* [1]
things did, 5126, *maʿᵃśeh* [1]
relented and did not, 5714, *nāḥam* [1]
did this[s], 5742+3338+2257, *nāṭâ+yād+-ô* [1]
did[s], 5814, *nāśâ* [1]
did[s], 5989+3338+2257, *nātan+yād+-ô* [1]
did away with, 6073, *sûr*[1] [1]
did so[s], 6296, *ʿābar*[1] [1]
did wrong, 6390, *ʿāwâ*[1] [1]
did, 6613, *ʿālîlâ* [1]
as did[s], 6641, *ʿāmad* [1]
did so[s], 6913+906+2021+7175, *ʿāśâ*[1]*+ʾēt*[1]*+ha+pesaḥ* [1]
did, 7188, *pāʿal* [1]
did, 7189, *pōʿal* [1]
what did, 7189, *pōʿal* [1]
did[s], 7212, *pāqad* [1]
did[s], 7924, *qārāʾ*[1] [1]
did evil, 8317, *rāʿaʿ*[1] [1]
did wrong, 8399, *rāšaʿ* [1]
did[s], 8492, *śîm* [1]
did away with, 8697, *šābat*[1] [1]
did[s], 8740, *šûb*[1] [1]
did[s], 8959, *šālak* [1]
did the third time, 8992, *šālaš* [1]
did, 9048, *šāmaʿ* [1]
did[s], 9068, *šāmar* [1]
did again, 9101, *šānâ*[1] [1]
did not hesitate, 9193, *šāqad*[1] [1]
did[s], 9494, *tāʿâ* [1]

DIDN'T [32]
didn't, 4202, *lōʾ* [30]
didn't, *AIT* [1]
didn't, 1194, *biltî* [1]

DIE [255]
die, 4637, *mût* [200]
die, 4638, *māwet* [11]
die, 1588, *gāwaʿ* [8]
surely die, 4637+4637, *mût+mût* [7]
die, 4637+4637, *mût+mût* [5]
must die, 4637+4637, *mût+mût* [4]
certainly die, 4637+4637, *mût+mût* [3]
causing to die, 4637, *mût* [2]
die, 6, *ʾābad* [1]
must die, 1201+4638, *bēn*[1]*+māwet* [1]
die, 2728, *ḥālāl*[1] [1]
determined should die, 3051, *ḥērem*[1] [1]
die, 4202+2649, *lōʾ+ḥāyâ* [1]
die out, 4637, *mût* [1]
doomed to die, 4637+4637, *mût+mût* [1]
in fact die, 4637+4637, *mût+mût* [1]
make die, 4637, *mût* [1]
ready to die, 4637, *mût* [1]
die away, 5570, *nābēl*[1] [1]
die, 5883, *nepeš* [1]
die out, 6066, *sûp*[1] [1]
die, 9456, *tᵉmûtâ* [1]
die, 9462, *tāmam* [1]

DIED [185]
died, 4637, *mût* [162]
died, 4638, *māwet* [11]
died, 1588, *gāwaʿ* [4]
died a natural death, 4637, *mût* [2]
died, 6, *ʾābad* [1]
died out, 1980, *dāʿak* [1]
struck down and died, 4637, *mût* [1]
died, 5877, *nāpal* [1]
died down, 9205, *šāqaʿ* [1]
died, 9462, *tāmam* [1]

DIES [31]
dies, 4637, *mût* [25]
dies, 4638, *māwet* [5]
dies down, 9284, *šātaq* [1]

DIFFERENCE [4]
difference between, 1068, *bayin* [1]
the difference between, 1068, *bayin* [1]
learn the difference between, 3359, *yādaʿ* [1]

tell the difference, 3359, *yāda'* [1]

DIFFERENT [11]
different, 10731, *š^{e}nâ^{1}* [5]
different, 337, *'aḥēr^{1}* [2]
different, 9101, *šānâ^{1}* [2]
different kinds, 3977, *kil'ayim* [1]
outcome different, 4202+3869, *lō'+k^{e}-* [1]

DIFFERENTLY [1]
deal differently, 7111, *pālâ* [1]

DIFFERING [5]
differing weights, 74+2256+74, *'eben+w^{e}-+'eben* [2]
two differing weights, 74+2256+74, *'eben+w^{e}-+'eben* [1]
differing measures, 406+2256+406, *'ēpâ+w^{e}-+'ēpâ* [1]
two differing measures, 406+2256+406, *'ēpâ+w^{e}-+'ēpâ* [1]

DIFFICULT [12]
difficult, 3878, *kābēd^{2}* [2]
difficult, 7098, *pālā'* [2]
difficult problems, 10626, *q^{e}ṭar* [2]
difficult, 1524, *gādôl* [1]
difficult, 7996, *qāšâ* [1]
difficult, 7997, *qāšeh* [1]
difficult, 8273, *ra'^{1}* [1]
difficult, 10048, *'^{a}nas* [1]
too difficult, 10330, *yaqqîr* [1]

DIFFICULTIES [2]
difficulties, 7650, *ṣārâ^{1}* [2]

DIFFICULTY [4]
had difficulty taking possession of, 3655+4946, *yāṣā'+min* [1]
difficulty, 3881, *k^{e}bēdut* [1]
great difficulty, 7996, *qāšâ* [1]
having great difficulty, 7996, *qāšâ* [1]

DIG [8]
dig, 2933, *ḥāṣēb^{1}* [2]
dig, 3168, *ḥātar* [2]
dig a hole, 2916, *ḥāpar^{1}* [1]
dig down, 3168, *ḥātar* [1]
something to dig with, 3845, *yātēd* [1]
dig, 4125, *kārâ^{1}* [1]

DIGNITARIES [3]
dignitaries, 2418, *zāqēn^{2}* [2]
dignitaries, 8569, *śar* [1]

DIGNITY [4]
dignity, 3883, *kābôd^{1}* [2]
dignity, 2077, *hādār* [1]
dignity, 5619, *n^{e}dîbâ* [1]

DIGS [4]
digs, 4125, *kārâ^{1}* [3]
digs, 2916, *ḥāpar^{1}* [1]

DIKLAH [2]
Diklah, 1989, *diqlâ* [2]

DILEAN [1]
Dilean, 1939, *dil'ān* [1]

DILIGENCE [5]
with diligence, 10056, *'osparnā'* [3]
with diligence, 10012, *'adrazdā'* [1]
diligence, 10056, *'osparnā'* [1]

DILIGENT [6]
diligent, 3026, *ḥārûṣ^{6}* [5]
diligent, 6913, *'āśâ^{1}* [1]

DILIGENTLY [1]
diligently obey, 9048+9048+928+7754, *šāma'+šāma'+b^{e}+qôl* [1]

DILUTED [1]
diluted, 4543, *māhal* [1]

DIM [4]
dim, 3124, *ḥāšak* [2]
dim, 1790, *dā'ab* [1]
grown dim, 3908, *kāhâ^{1}* [1]

DIMENSIONS [2]
dimensions, 4924, *mēmād* [1]
dimensions, 5477, *mišpāṭ* [1]

DIMINISH [1]
let diminish, 5070, *mā'aṭ* [1]

DIMNAH [1]
Dimnah, 1962, *dimnâ* [1]

DIMON [1]
Dimon, 1904, *dîmôn* [1]

DIMON'S [1]
Dimon's, 1904, *dîmôn* [1]

DIMONAH [1]
Dimonah, 1905, *dîmônâ* [1]

DIN [1]
noisy din, 7754+1524, *qôl+gādôl* [1]

DINAH [7]
Dinah, 1909, *dînâ* [7]

DINAH'S [2]
Dinah's, 1909, *dînâ* [1]
Dinah's^{s}, 2023, *-āh* [1]

DINE [4]
dine on, 430, *'ākal* [1]
supposed to dine, 3782+3782+430, *yāšab+yāšab+'ākal* [1]
dine, 4310, *lāḥam^{2}* [1]
dine, 9272, *šātâ^{2}* [1]

DINED [1]
dined, 430, *'ākal* [1]

DINHABAH [2]
Dinhabah, 1973, *dinhābâ* [2]

DINNER [2]
dinner, *NIH/RPE* [1]
dinner, 5492, *mišteh* [1]

DIP [8]
dip, 3188, *ṭābal* [8]

DIPPED [4]
dipped, 3188, *ṭābal* [4]

DIRE [2]
dire, 3972, *kōl* [1]
dire, 7997, *qāšeh* [1]

DIRECT [10]
direct, 3922, *kûn^{1}* [2]
direct, 5989, *nātan* [2]
direct, 2005, *dārak* [1]
direct descendants, 3655+3751, *yāṣā'+yārēk* [1]
direct, 3723, *yārâ^{3}* [1]
direct, 5904, *nāṣaḥ* [1]
direct, 7422, *ṣāwâ* [1]
as a direct result, 9393+3338, *taḥat^{1}+yād* [1]

DIRECTED [19]
directed, 7422, *ṣāwâ* [6]
directed, 1819, *dābar^{2}* [5]
directed, 606, *'āmar^{1}* [1]
directed, 1821, *dābār* [1]
directed to, 4200, *l^{e}-^{1}* [1]
directed by, 4946, *min* [1]
directed to, 6584, *'al^{2}* [1]
are directed, 7422, *ṣāwâ* [1]
directed, 8097, *rādâ^{1}* [1]
directed, 8938, *šālaḥ* [1]

DIRECTING [1]
directing, 5904, *nāṣaḥ* [1]

DIRECTION [23]
direction, 2006, *derek* [9]
direction, 3338, *yād* [5]
in any direction, 2178+2256+2178, *hēnnâ^{1}+w^{e}-+hēnnâ^{1}* [1]
in any direction, 3907+2256+3907, *kōh+w^{e}-+kōh* [1]
under direction, 4200+7156, *l^{e}-^{1}+pāneh* [1]
opposite direction, 4578, *mûl^{3}* [1]
direction, 5226, *māqôm* [1]
direction, 7023, *peh* [1]
direction, 7224, *pāqîd* [1]
direction, 9374, *taḥbulôt* [1]
direction, 10311, *yad* [1]

DIRECTIONS [5]
directions, 8063, *reba'^{1}* [2]
in all directions, 2151, *h^{a}lōm* [1]
get directions, 3723, *yārâ^{3}* [1]
directions written, 4181, *k^{e}tāb* [1]

DIRECTLY [5]
fix directly, 3837, *yāšar* [1]
directly in front of, 4200+5790, *l^{e}-^{1}+nōkaḥ* [1]
directly opposite, 4200+7156+5790, *l^{e}-^{1}+pāneh+nōkaḥ* [1]
directly from, 4946, *min* [1]
directly, 5584, *neged* [1]

DIRECTOR [57]
director of music, 5904, *nāṣaḥ* [56]
director, 8031, *rō'š^{1}* [1]

DIRECTORS [1]
directors, 8031, *rō'š^{1}* [1]

DIRECTS [4]
as directs, 928, *b^{e}-* [1]
directs, 2005, *dārak* [1]
directs, 5742, *nāṭâ* [1]
directs, 7422, *ṣāwâ* [1]

DIRT [2]
dirt, 3226, *ṭîṭ* [1]
dirt, 6760, *'āpār* [1]

DISAPPEAR [5]
disappear, 1757, *gāra'^{1}* [1]
disappear, 2736, *ḥālap^{1}* [1]
disappear, 3983, *kālâ^{1}* [1]
disappear, 4162, *kārat* [1]
disappear, 8697, *šābat^{1}* [1]

DISAPPEARED [2]
disappeared, 401, *'ayin^{1}* [1]
disappeared, 2143+4946+6524, *hālak+min+'ayin^{1}* [1]

DISAPPEARS [3]
disappears, 2143, *hālak* [2]
disappears, 261, *'āzal* [1]

DISAPPOINTED [4]
disappointed, 1017, *bôš^{1}* [3]
disappointed, 2917, *ḥāpar^{2}* [1]

DISAPPROVE [1]
disapprove, 8317+928+6524, *rā'a'^{1}+b^{e}-+'ayin^{1}* [1]

DISARMS [1]
disarms, 4653+8332, *māzîaḥ+rāpâ^{1}* [1]

DISASTER [119]
disaster, 8288, *rā'â^{3}* [79]
disaster, 369, *'êd* [16]
disaster, 8273, *ra'^{1}* [5]
bring disaster, 8317, *rā'a'^{1}* [4]
disaster, 5596, *nega'* [3]
disaster, 8691, *šeber^{1}* [2]
disaster, 224, *'āwen^{1}* [1]
disaster^{s}, 889, *'^{a}šer* [1]
disaster awaits, 1950, *dāmâ^{3}* [1]
disaster, 2095, *hawwâ^{2}* [1]
disaster, 4804, *makkâ* [1]
disaster, 5798, *nēker* [1]
bring disaster, 6200, *sāpâ* [1]
disaster, 7004+8273, *pega'+ra'^{1}* [1]
disaster, 7065, *paḥad^{1}* [1]
disaster, 8739, *šô'â* [1]

DISASTERS [5]
disasters, 8288, *rā'â^{3}* [4]

disasters, 4804, *makkâ* [1]

DISCARD [1]
discard, 8697, *šābat*[1] [1]

DISCARDED [1]
discarded, 2736, *ḥālap*[1] [1]

DISCERN [5]
discern, 1067, *bîn* [3]
discern, 1047, *bāhar*[1] [1]
discern, 2431, *zārâ*[2] [1]

DISCERNING [19]
discerning, 1067, *bîn* [16]
discerning, 9048, *šāma'* [2]
discerning, 10313+10100, *y[e]da'+bînâ* [1]

DISCERNMENT [8]
discernment, 1067, *bîn* [3]
give discernment, 1067, *bîn* [1]
discernment, 1069, *bînâ* [1]
discernment, 3248, *ṭa'am* [1]
discernment, 4659, *m[e]zimmâ* [1]
discernment, 9312, *t[e]bûnâ* [1]

DISCHARGE [20]
discharge, 2307, *zûb* [9]
discharge, 2308, *zôb* [7]
bodily discharge, 2307, *zûb* [1]
discharge, 2307+2308, *zûb+zôb* [1]
has a discharge, 2307+2308, *zûb+zôb* [1]
discharge, 2308+3240, *zôb+ṭum'â* [1]

DISCHARGED [1]
discharged, 5449, *mišlaḥat* [1]

DISCIPLE [1]
disciple, 1201, *bēn*[1] [1]

DISCIPLES [1]
disciples, 4341, *limmud* [1]

DISCIPLINE [31]
discipline, 4592, *mûsār* [21]
discipline, 3579, *yāsar*[1] [10]

DISCIPLINED [4]
disciplined, 4592, *mûsār* [2]
been disciplined, 3579, *yāsar*[1] [1]
disciplined, 3579, *yāsar*[1] [1]

DISCIPLINES [4]
disciplines, 3579, *yāsar*[1] [3]
disciplines, 3519, *yākaḥ* [1]

DISCLOSE [2]
disclose, 1655, *gālâ* [1]
disclose, 5583, *nāgad* [1]

DISCOMFORT [1]
discomfort, 8288, *rā'â*[3] [1]

DISCONTENTED [1]
discontented, 5253+5883, *mar*[1]*+nepeš* [1]

DISCORD [1]
discord, 7912, *qeṣep*[1] [1]

DISCOURAGE [2]
discourage, 5648+4213, *nû'+lēb* [1]
discourage, 8332+3338, *rāpâ*[1]*+yād* [1]

DISCOURAGED [13]
discouraged, 3169, *ḥātat* [10]
discouraged, 4206, *lā'â* [1]
discouraged, 5648+4213, *nû'+lēb* [1]
discouraged, 8368, *rāṣaṣ* [1]

DISCOURAGEMENT [1]
discouragement, 7919+8120, *qōṣer+rûaḥ* [1]

DISCOURAGING [1]
discouraging, 8332+3338, *rāpâ*[1]*+yād* [1]

DISCOURSE [2]
discourse, 5442, *māšāl*[1] [2]

DISCOVER [4]
discover, 5162, *māṣā'* [3]
discover meaning, 5162, *māṣā'* [1]

DISCOVERED [11]
discovered, 5162, *māṣā'* [6]
discovered, 2180, *hinnēh* [2]
discovered, 2983, *ḥāqar* [1]
been discovered, 3359, *yāda'* [1]
was discovered, 3359, *yāda'* [1]

DISCREDIT [2]
discredit, 3070, *ḥārap*[2] [1]
discredit, 7296, *pārar*[1] [1]

DISCREETLY [1]
discreetly, 3248, *ṭa'am* [1]

DISCRETION [6]
discretion, 4659, *m[e]zimmâ* [4]
discretion, 3248, *ṭa'am* [1]
discretion, 8507, *śekel* [1]

DISCUSSED [1]
discussed, 1819, *dābar*[2] [1]

DISDAINED [4]
disdained, 4415, *mā'as*[1] [1]
disdained, 7592, *ṣā'ar* [1]
disdained, 7837, *qālal* [1]
disdained, 9210, *šāqaṣ* [1]

DISDAINFUL [1]
disdainful, 5951, *nāśā'* [1]

DISEASE [36]
skin disease, 7669, *ṣāra'at* [10]
infectious disease, 7669, *ṣāra'at* [7]
disease, 2716, *ḥ[o]lî* [5]
disease, 4701, *mah[a]lâ* [2]
disease, 7669, *ṣāra'at* [2]
wasting disease, 8137, *rāzôn*[1] [2]
disease, 1821, *dābār* [1]
afflicted with a disease, 2688, *ḥālā'* [1]
disease, 4700, *mah[a]leh* [1]
disease, 5710, *naḥ[a]lâ*[2] [1]
disease, 7665, *ṣāra'* [1]
has an infectious skin disease, 7665, *ṣāra'* [1]
infectious skin disease, 7665, *ṣāra'* [1]
wasting disease, 8831, *šaḥepet* [1]

DISEASED [6]
diseased, 2703, *ḥālâ*[1] [3]
diseased, 7665, *ṣāra'* [2]
diseased area, 5999, *neteq* [1]

DISEASES [11]
diseases, 9377, *taḥ[a]lu'îm* [3]
diseases, 4504, *madweh*[2] [2]
diseases, 5596, *nega'* [2]
diseases, 1822, *deber*[1] [1]
diseases, 4701, *maḥ[a]lâ* [1]
infectious skin diseases and mildew, 7669, *ṣāra'at* [1]
wasting diseases, 8831, *šaḥepet* [1]

DISFIGURED [2]
disfigured, 3050, *ḥāram*[2] [1]
disfigured, 5425, *mišḥat* [1]

DISGRACE [52]
disgrace, 3075, *ḥerpâ* [17]
disgrace, 4009, *k[e]limmâ* [12]
disgrace, 1017, *bôš*[1] [3]
disgrace, 2875, *ḥesed*[1] [3]
disgrace, 2917, *ḥāpar*[2] [3]
disgrace, 7830, *qālôn* [3]
disgrace, 4007, *kālam* [2]
disgrace, 5541, *n[e]'āṣâ* [2]
disgrace, 1425+7156, *bōšet+pāneh* [1]
disgrace, 2725, *ḥālal*[1] [1]
drove in disgrace, 2725, *ḥālal*[1] [1]
been in disgrace, 4007, *kālam* [1]
fear disgrace, 4007, *kālam* [1]
in disgrace, 4007, *kālam* [1]
disgrace, 7814, *qîqālôn* [1]

DISGRACED [24]
disgraced, 1017, *bôš*[1] [8]
disgraced, 4007, *kālam* [6]
disgraced, 2917, *ḥāpar*[2] [3]
be disgraced, 1017, *bôš*[1] [2]
disgraced, 1425, *bōšet* [2]
disgraced, 1423+4374, *bošnâ+lāqaḥ* [1]
be disgraced, 4007, *kālam* [1]
disgraced, 6700, *'ānâ*[2] [1]

DISGRACEFUL [10]
disgraceful thing, 5576, *n[e]bālâ* [4]
disgraceful, 1017, *bôš*[1] [3]
disgraceful, 5576, *n[e]bālâ* [2]
disgraceful, 7830, *qālôn* [1]

DISGRACES [3]
disgraces, 1017, *bôš*[1] [1]
disgraces, 2725, *ḥālal*[1] [1]
disgraces, 4007, *kālam* [1]

DISGUISE [4]
in disguise, 2924, *ḥāpaś* [2]
disguise herself, 6634, *'ālap* [1]
disguise yourself, 9101, *šānâ*[1] [1]

DISGUISED [5]
disguised himself, 2924, *ḥāpaś* [5]

DISGUISES [1]
disguises himself, 5795, *nākar*[1] [1]

DISGUST [4]
turned away in disgust, 3697, *yāqa'* [2]
turned away in disgust, 5936, *nāqa'* [2]

DISGUSTED [1]
disgusted, 7762, *qûṣ*[1] [1]

DISH [17]
dish, 4090, *kap* [12]
dish, 7505, *ṣallaḥat* [3]
each dish, 4094+2256+4094, *k[e]pôr*[1]*+w[e]-+k[e]pôr*[1] [2]

DISHAN [5]
Dishan, 1915, *dîšān* [4]
Dishan, 1914, *dîšôn*[2] [1]

DISHEARTENED [3]
disheartened, 3874+4213, *kā'â+lēb* [1]
disheartened, 4570, *mûg* [1]
disheartened, 5022+906+4222, *māsas+'ēt*[1]*+lēbāb* [1]

DISHES [15]
dishes, 4090, *kap* [12]
dishes, 113, *'[a]garṭāl* [2]
dishes, 3998, *k[e]lî* [1]

DISHON [7]
Dishon, 1914, *dîšôn*[2] [7]

DISHONEST [12]
dishonest, 5327, *mirmâ*[1] [4]
dishonest gain, 1299, *beṣa'* [3]
dishonest, 6404, *'āwel* [3]
dishonest, 2039, *hebel*[1] [1]
dishonest, 8400, *reša'* [1]

DISHONESTLY [1]
dishonestly, 6404, *'āwel* [1]

DISHONOR [12]
dishonor, 6872, *'erwâ* [3]
dishonor bed, 1655+4053, *gālâ+kānāp* [1]
dishonor, 2725, *ḥālal*[1] [1]
dishonor, 4009, *k[e]limmâ* [1]
dishonor, 5571, *nābal*[2] [1]
dishonor, 6867, *'ārâ*[1] [1]
dishonor bed, 6872+1655, *'erwâ+gālâ* [1]
dishonor by having sexual relations with, 6872+1655, *'erwâ+gālâ* [1]
dishonor by to have sexual relations, 6872+1655, *'erwâ+gālâ* [1]
dishonor, 9530, *tāpaś* [1]

DISHONORED [6]
dishonored, 6872+1655, *'erwâ+gālâ* [4]
dishonored, 6700, *'ānâ*[2] [1]
dishonored, 10571, *'arwâ* [1]

DISHONORS [4]
dishonors bed, 1655+4053, *gālâ+kānāp* [1]
dishonors, 4009, *k^{e}limmâ* [1]
dishonors, 5571, *nābal*^{2} [1]
dishonors, 7829, *qālâ*^{2} [1]

DISILLUSIONMENT [1]
disillusionment, 9214, *šeqer* [1]

DISLIKES [3]
dislikes, 8533, *śānē'* [3]

DISLODGE [3]
dislodge, 3769, *yāraš*^{1} [3]

DISLOYAL [1]
disloyal, 6047, *sûg*^{1} [1]

DISMAY [3]
dismay, 1791, *d^{e}'ābâ* [1]
dismay, 2905, *ḥāpaz* [1]
dismay, 2917, *ḥāpar*^{2} [1]

DISMAYED [18]
dismayed, 3169, *ḥātat* [7]
dismayed, 987, *bāhal* [3]
dismayed, 1017, *bôš*^{1} [3]
dismayed, 9283, *šāta'* [2]
dismayed, 987+4394, *bāhal+m^{e}'ōd* [1]
dismayed, 2591, *hûš*^{2} [1]
dismayed, 9037, *šāmēm*^{1} [1]

DISMISSED [3]
dismissed, 8938, *šālaḥ* [2]
dismissed, 976, *bādal* [1]

DISOBEDIENCE [2]
disobedience, 4202+9048+928+7754, *lō'+šāma'+b^{e}-+qôl* [1]
disobedience, 5086, *ma'al*^{1} [1]

DISOBEDIENT [1]
disobedient, 5286, *mārâ*^{1} [1]

DISOBEY [4]
disobey, 6296, *'ābar*^{1} [2]
disobey, 1194+9048+928+7754, *biltî+šāma'+b^{e}-+qôl* [1]
disobey, 4202+9048, *lō'+šāma'* [1]

DISOBEYED [6]
disobeyed, 4202+9048+928+7754, *lō'+šāma'+b^{e}-+qôl* [2]
disobeyed, 4202+9048, *lō'+šāma'* [2]
disobeyed, 5286, *mārâ*^{1} [1]
disobeyed, 6296, *'ābar*^{1} [1]

DISOBEYING [1]
disobeying, 6296, *'ābar*^{1} [1]

DISOBEYS [1]
disobeys, 7322, *peša'* [1]

DISORDER [1]
disorder, 4202+6043, *lō'+sēder* [1]

DISOWN [1]
disown, 3950, *kāḥaš* [1]

DISOWNS [1]
disowns, 3950, *kāḥaš* [1]

DISPATCH [1]
dispatch, 7422, *ṣāwâ* [1]

DISPATCHED [1]
dispatched, 8938, *šālaḥ* [1]

DISPATCHES [4]
dispatches, 6219, *sēper*^{1} [4]

DISPENSES [1]
dispenses, 5989, *nātan* [1]

DISPERSE [7]
disperse, 7046, *pûṣ*^{1} [7]

DISPERSED [5]
dispersed, 7046, *pûṣ*^{1} [2]
dispersed, 2143+4200+2006, *hālak+l^{e-1}+derek* [1]
is dispersed, 2745, *ḥālaq*^{2} [1]
dispersed, 7061, *pāzar* [1]

DISPERSES [2]
disperses, 5615, *nādaḥ*^{1} [1]
disperses, 5697, *nāḥâ*^{1} [1]

DISPERSING [1]
dispersing, 7287, *pāraṣ* [1]

DISPLACES [1]
displaces, 3769, *yāraš*^{1} [1]

DISPLAY [10]
display splendor, 6995, *pā'ar*^{2} [3]
display, 2555, *ḥāwâ*^{1} [1]
display, 3359, *yāda'* [1]
display, 3723, *yārā*^{3} [1]
display, 5989, *nātan* [1]
display awesome power, 7098, *pālā'* [1]
display, 7298, *pāraś* [1]
display, 8011, *rā'â*^{1} [1]

DISPLAYED [6]
displayed, *NIH/RPE* [1]
displayed, 1540, *gādal* [1]
displayed, 3359, *yāda'* [1]
displayed, 6913, *'āśâ*^{1} [1]
displayed, 8011, *rā'â*^{1} [1]
displayed, 8492, *śîm* [1]

DISPLAYS [2]
displays glory, 6995, *pā'ar*^{2} [1]
displays, 8123, *rûm*^{1} [1]

DISPLEASE [2]
displease, 4202+5162+2834+928+6524, *lō'+māṣā'+ḥēn^{1}+b^{e}-+'ayin^{1}* [1]
displease, 8273+928+6524, *ra'^{1}+b^{e}-+'ayin^{1}* [1]

DISPLEASED [7]
displeased, 8317+928+6524, *rā'a'^{1}+b^{e}-+'ayin^{1}* [5]
displeased, 8317+8288, *rā'a'^{1}+rā'â^{3}* [1]
displeased, 8317, *rā'a'^{1}* [1]

DISPLEASES [2]
displeases, 4202+2911, *lō'+ḥāpēṣ*^{1} [2]

DISPLEASING [2]
displeasing, 4202+5162+2834+928+6524, *lō'+māṣā'+ḥēn^{1}+b^{e}-+'ayin^{1}* [1]
displeasing, 8273+928+6524, *ra'^{1}+b^{e}-+'ayin^{1}* [1]

DISPLEASURE [1]
displeasure, 4088, *ka'as* [1]

DISPOSED [5]
favorably disposed toward, 2834+928+6524, *ḥēn^{1}+b^{e}-+'ayin^{1}* [3]
favorably disposed, 3201, *tôb*^{1} [1]
disposed, 3671, *yēṣer*^{1} [1]

DISPOSSESS [5]
dispossess, 3769, *yāraš*^{1} [5]

DISPOSSESSING [2]
dispossessing, 1766, *g^{e}rušâ* [1]
dispossessing, 3769, *yāraš*^{1} [1]

DISPUTE [10]
dispute, 8190, *rîb*^{2} [4]
dispute, 1821, *dābār* [2]
dispute, 6699, *'ānâ*^{1} [1]
dispute, 8189, *rîb*^{1} [1]
cases of dispute, 8190, *rîb*^{2} [1]
decide dispute, 9149, *šāpaṭ* [1]

DISPUTED [1]
disputed, 6921, *'āśaq* [1]

DISPUTES [9]
settle disputes, 3519, *yākaḥ* [2]
disputes, 4506, *mādôn*^{1} [2]
disputes, 8190, *rîb*^{2} [2]
disputes, *NIH/RPE* [1]
disputes, 1821, *dābār* [1]
disputes decided, 5477, *mišpāṭ* [1]

DISQUIETING [1]
disquieting, 8546, *śe'ippîm* [1]

DISREGARDED [2]
disregarded, 6296, *'ābar*^{1} [1]
disregarded, 6440, *'āzab*^{1} [1]

DISREGARDING [1]
disregarding, 4202+2349, *lō'+zākar*^{1} [1]

DISRESPECT [1]
disrespect, 1025, *bizzāyôn* [1]

DISROBING [1]
disrobing, 1655, *gālâ* [1]

DISSENSION [7]
dissension, 4506, *mādôn*^{1} [7]

DISSOLVED [1]
be dissolved, 5245, *māqaq* [1]

DISSUADE [2]
dissuade, 2302, *zāhar*^{2} [2]

DISTAFF [1]
distaff, 3969, *kîšôr* [1]

DISTANCE [35]
distance, 8158, *rāḥôq* [10]
distance, *NIH/RPE* [2]
distance, 2006, *derek* [2]
short distance, 5071, *m^{e}'aṭ* [2]
distance, 5584, *neged* [2]
distance, 8145, *rōḥab* [2]
some distance away, 2134, *hāl^{e}'â* [1]
kept distance, 3656+4946+5584, *yāṣab+min+neged* [1]
little distance, 3896+824, *k^{e}bārâ^{2}+'ereṣ* [1]
some distance, 3896+2021+824, *k^{e}bārâ^{2}+ha-+'ereṣ* [1]
some distance, 3896+824, *k^{e}bārâ^{2}+'ereṣ* [1]
measure distance, 4499, *mādad* [1]
some distance away, 4946+8158, *min+rāḥôq* [1]
some distance from, 4946+7156, *min+pāneh* [1]
some distance away, 5305, *merḥāq* [1]
some distance, 5584, *neged* [1]
at a distance, 8158+4394, *rāḥôq+m^{e}'ōd* [1]
distance away, 8178, *rāḥaq* [1]
gone some distance, 8178, *rāḥaq* [1]
keep distance, 8178, *rāḥaq* [1]
some distance away, 8178+4946, *rāḥaq+min* [1]

DISTANT [35]
distant, 8158, *rāḥôq* [11]
distant, 5305, *merḥāq* [4]
distant, 7916, *qāṣaṣ*^{2} [3]
distant, 4946+5305, *min+merḥāq* [2]
distant, 4946+8158, *min+rāḥôq* [2]
distant place, 8158, *rāḥôq* [2]
distant past, 255, *'āz* [1]
distant shores, 362+3542, *'î^{1}+yām* [1]
distant shores, 362, *'î*^{1} [1]
distant sources, 2424, *zār* [1]
distant future, 3427+8041, *yôm^{1}+rab^{1}* [1]
distant lands, 5305, *merḥāq* [1]
distant, 7895, *qāṣeh* [1]
most distant land, 7895, *qāṣeh* [1]
distant, 8041, *rab*^{1} [1]
distant, 8049+2021+2006, *rābâ^{1}+ha-+derek* [1]
distant parts, 10509, *sôp* [1]

DISTILL [1]
distill, 2423, *zāqaq* [1]

DISTINCTION [5]
make a distinction, 976, *bādal* [1]
distinction between, 1068, *bayin* [1]
make a distinction, 7111, *pālâ* [1]
makes a distinction, 7111, *pālâ* [1]
distinction, 7151, *p^{e}lut* [1]

DISTINGUISH [7]
distinguish, 976, *bādal* [3]
distinguish, 1067, *bîn* [1]

show how to distinguish, 3359, *yāda'* [1]
distinguish, 5795, *nākar*[1] [1]
distinguish, 7111, *pālâ* [1]

DISTINGUISHED [3]
distinguished himself, 3877, *kābēd*[1] [1]
distinguished, 3877, *kābēd*[1] [1]
distinguished himself, 10488, *nᵉṣaḥ* [1]

DISTORT [2]
distort, 2200, *hāpak* [1]
distort, 6835, *'āqaš* [1]

DISTORTED [1]
distorted with fear, 8307, *rā'am*[2] [1]

DISTRAUGHT [1]
distraught, 2101, *hûm* [1]

DISTRESS [75]
distress, 7650, *ṣārâ*[1] [22]
distress, 7639, *ṣar*[1] [20]
distress, 5188, *mᵉṣûqâ* [4]
distress, 5186, *māṣôq* [3]
distress, 7674, *ṣārar*[1] [3]
distress, 8288, *rā'â*[3] [3]
bring distress, 7674, *ṣārar*[1] [2]
in distress, 7674, *ṣārar*[1] [2]
distress, 224, *'āwen*[1] [1]
in distress, 2655, *ḥîl*[1] [1]
bowed down in distress, 4104, *kāpap* [1]
distress, 4608, *mûṣāq*[2] [1]
distress, 5210, *mēṣar* [1]
in bitter distress, 5352, *mārar* [1]
in distress, 5601, *nāgaś* [1]
distress, 6662, *'āmāl*[1] [1]
distress, 6714, *'ānî* [1]
distress, 6715, *'ᵒnî* [1]
distress, 7085, *pîd* [1]
cry of distress, 7424, *ṣᵉwāḥâ* [1]
distress, 7442, *ṣûqâ* [1]
cries of distress, 7591, *ṣᵉ'āqâ* [1]
distress, 8190, *rîb*[2] [1]
in distress, 8488, *śîaḥ*[1] [1]

DISTRESSED [12]
distressed, 6772, *'āṣab*[2] [2]
distressed, 7639, *ṣar*[1] [2]
distressed, 8317+928+6524, *rā'a'*[1]*+bᵉ+'ayin*[1] [2]
distressed, 1017, *bôš*[1] [1]
distressed, 7650, *ṣārâ*[1] [1]
distressed, 7674, *ṣārar*[1] [1]
distressed, 7996, *qāšâ* [1]
greatly distressed, 8283, *rā'ad* [1]
distressed, 10091, *bᵉ'ēš* [1]

DISTRESSES [1]
distresses, 7650, *ṣārâ*[1] [1]

DISTRESSING [1]
distressing, 8273, *ra'*[1] [1]

DISTRIBUTE [6]
distribute, 2745, *ḥālaq*[2] [2]
distribute, 5706, *nāḥal* [2]
distribute, 1029, *bāzar* [1]
distribute, 5989, *nātan* [1]

DISTRIBUTED [7]
distributed, *NIH/RPE* [2]
distributed among, 928, *bᵉ-* [1]
be distributed, 2745, *ḥālaq*[2] [1]
distributed, 2745, *ḥālaq*[2] [1]
is distributed, 2745, *ḥālaq*[2] [1]
distributed, 5989, *nātan* [1]

DISTRIBUTES [1]
distributes, 2745, *ḥālaq*[2] [1]

DISTRIBUTING [3]
distributing, 5989, *nātan* [2]
distributing supplies, 2745, *ḥālaq*[2] [1]

DISTRICT [21]
district, 824, *'ereṣ* [4]
district, 7135, *pelek*[2] [4]
Second District, 5467, *mišneh* [3]
district officers, 5893, *nāṣab*[1] [2]
district, *AIT* [1]
district, 2475, *ḥebel*[2] [1]
district, 4500, *middâ*[1] [1]
district, 4519, *mᵉdînâ* [1]
market district, 4847, *maktēš* [1]
district governors, 5893, *nāṣab*[1] [1]
district, 9556, *tᵉrûmâ* [1]
district, 10406, *mᵉdînâ* [1]

DISTRICTS [5]
districts, 7106, *pᵉlaggâ* [2]
districts, 824, *'ereṣ* [1]
districts, 1473, *gᵉbûl* [1]
outlying districts, 8441, *śādeh* [1]

DISTURB [1]
disturb, 5675, *nûa'* [1]

DISTURBED [11]
disturbed, 2159, *hāmâ* [3]
disturbed, 8074, *rāgaz* [3]
disturbed, 2200, *hāpak* [1]
greatly disturbed, 2591, *ḥûš*[2] [1]
disturbed, 6700, *'ānâ*[2] [1]
very disturbed, 8317+8288, *rā'a'*[1]*+rā'â*[3] [1]
disturbed, 10097, *bᵉhal* [1]

DISTURBING [1]
disturbing, 5691, *nēzeq* [1]

DITCHES [1]
full of ditches, 1463+1463, *gēb*[1]*+gēb*[1] [1]

DIVIDE [20]
divide, 2745, *ḥālaq*[2] [9]
divide, 1324, *bāqa'* [2]
divide up, 2745, *ḥālaq*[2] [1]
divide, 2936, *ḥāṣâ* [1]
divide equally, 2936, *ḥāṣâ* [1]
divide up, 2936, *ḥāṣâ* [1]
divide as inheritance, 5706, *nāḥal* [1]
divide for an inheritance, 5706, *nāḥal* [1]
divide, 5706, *nāḥal* [1]
divide, 8959, *šālak* [1]
divide into three, 8992, *šālaš* [1]

DIVIDED [35]
divided, 2745, *ḥālaq*[2] [6]
divided, 2936, *ḥāṣâ* [5]
divided, 1324, *bāqa'* [3]
divided, 1021, *bāzā'* [2]
were divided, 1324, *bāqa'* [2]
be divided, 2745, *ḥālaq*[2] [2]
was divided, 7103, *pālag* [2]
completely divided, 9117+9118, *šāsa'+šesa'* [2]
divided, 1615, *gāzar*[1] [1]
be divided up, 2745, *ḥālaq*[2] [1]
divided up, 2745, *ḥālaq*[2] [1]
be divided, 2936, *ḥāṣâ* [1]
divided up, 4614, *mûr*[1] [1]
divided, 7233, *pārad* [1]
completely divided, 9117, *šāsa'* [1]
divided, 9117+9118, *šāsa'+šesa'* [1]
completely divided, 9118+9117, *šesa'+šāsa'* [1]
divided, 10583, *pᵉlag*[1] [1]
is divided, 10592, *pᵉras* [1]

DIVIDES [1]
divides, 2745, *ḥālaq*[2] [1]

DIVIDING [5]
dividing, 2745, *ḥālaq*[2] [3]
dividing, 2936, *ḥāṣâ* [1]
dividing, 5706, *nāḥal* [1]

DIVINATION [16]
divination, 5727, *nāḥaš* [2]
divination, 7876, *qāsam* [2]
divination, 7877, *qesem* [2]
find things out by divination, 5727+5727, *nāḥaš+nāḥaš* [1]
learned by divination, 5727, *nāḥaš* [1]
practice divination, 5727, *nāḥaš* [1]
uses for divination, 5727+5727, *nāḥaš+nāḥaš* [1]
practice divination, 6726, *'ānan*[2] [1]
practiced divination, 7876+7877, *qāsam+qesem* [1]
practiced divination, 7876, *qāsam* [1]
practices divination, 7876+7877, *qāsam+qesem* [1]
fee for divination, 7877, *qesem* [1]
practice divination, 7877+7876, *qesem+qāsam* [1]

DIVINATIONS [7]
divinations, 5241, *miqsām* [2]
divinations, 7876, *qāsam* [2]
divinations, 7877, *qesem* [2]
utter divinations, 7876, *qāsam* [1]

DIVINE [1]
divine, 466, *'ᵉlōhîm* [1]

DIVINER [1]
diviner, 10140, *gᵉzar* [1]

DIVINERS [9]
diviners, 7876, *qāsam* [6]
diviners, 10140, *gᵉzar* [3]

DIVISION [39]
division, 7372, *ṣābā'*[2] [20]
division, 4713, *maḥᵃlōqet* [17]
division, 1074, *bayit*[1] [2]

DIVISIONS [48]
divisions, 7372, *ṣābā'*[2] [21]
divisions, 4713, *maḥᵃlōqet* [19]
tribal divisions, 4713, *maḥᵃlōqet* [2]
divisions, 477, *'allûp*[2] [1]
divisions, 1522, *gᵉdûd*[2] [1]
separated into divisions, 2745, *ḥālaq*[2] [1]
army divisions, 4713, *maḥᵃlōqet* [1]
divisions, 8031, *rō'š*[1] [1]
divisions, 10585, *pᵉluggâ* [1]

DIVORCE [7]
divorce, 4135, *kᵉrîtût* [4]
divorce, 8938, *šālaḥ* [3]

DIVORCED [7]
divorced, 1763, *gāraš*[1] [5]
divorced, 8938, *šālaḥ* [2]

DIVORCES [1]
divorces, 8938, *šālaḥ* [1]

DIZAHAB [1]
Dizahab, 1903, *dî zāhāb* [1]

DIZZINESS [1]
dizziness, 6413, *'iw'îm* [1]

DO [1804]
do, *AIT* [1090]
do, 6913, *'āśâ*[1] [405]
do, *NIH/RPE* [127]
do, 7188, *pā'al* [12]
do, 6268, *'ābad* [11]
do good, 3512, *yāṭab* [10]
do, 7422, *ṣāwâ* [8]
have to do with, 4200, *lᵉ-*[1] [5]
do again, 3578, *yāsap* [3]
do, 5126, *ma'ᵃśeh* [3]
do work, 6913, *'āśâ*[1] [3]
do harm, 8317, *rā'a'*[1] [3]
do, 9048, *šāma'* [3]
do, 9068, *šāmar* [3]
do, 928, *bᵉ-* [2]
do it[s], 1457, *gā'al*[1] [2]
all do, 2006, *derek* [2]
do, 2118, *hāyâ* [2]
do wrong, 2627, *ḥāṭā'* [2]
do violence, 2803, *ḥāmas*[1] [2]
do what is right, 3512, *yāṭab* [2]
can do, 3523, *yākōl* [2]
do for, 4200, *lᵉ-*[1] [2]
what do[s], 5477, *mišpāṭ* [2]
do so[s], 5989, *nātan* [2]
do, 5989, *nātan* [2]
do again, 9101, *šānâ*[1] [2]
do, 10522, *'ᵃbad* [2]

done, 1821, *dābār* [1]
done, 2006, *derek* [1]
done this[s], 2349, *zākar*[1] [1]
done well, 3201, *ṭôb*[1] [1]
good done, 3512, *yāṭab* [1]
as done before, 3869+7193+928+7193, *kᵉ-+paʿam+bᵉ-+paʿam* [1]
done[s], 3922, *kûn*[1] [1]
done, 3983, *kālâ*[1] [1]
done, 4856, *mᵉlāʾkâ* [1]
is done, 5126+6913, *maʿᵃśeh+ʿāśâ*[1] [1]
that done, 5126, *maʿᵃśeh* [1]
what done, 5149, *mipʿālâ* [1]
done so[s], 5602, *nāgaš* [1]
done, 6268, *ʿābad* [1]
wrong done, 6432, *ʿawwātâ* [1]
done, 6613, *ʿᵃlîlâ* [1]
done[s], 7727, *qādaš* [1]
done, 7756, *qûm* [1]
done more, 8049, *rābâ*[1] [1]
done evil, 8317, *rāʿaʿ*[1] [1]
done wrong, 8317+8317, *rāʿaʿ*[1]*+rāʿaʿ*[1] [1]
done wrong, 8399, *rāšaʿ* [1]
done this[s], 8886+6640, *šākab+ʿim* [1]
done, 9068, *šāmar* [1]
done, 9462, *tāmam* [1]
be done, 10522, *ʿᵃbad* [1]

DONKEY [66]
donkey, 2789, *ḥᵃmôr*[1] [47]
donkey, 912, *ʾātôn* [13]
wild donkey, 7230, *pereʾ* [4]
donkey, 6554, *ʿîr*[4] [1]
wild donkey, 7241, *pereh* [1]

DONKEY'S [5]
donkey's, 2789, *ḥᵃmôr*[1] [3]
donkey's, 912, *ʾātôn* [1]
wild donkey's, 7230, *pereʾ* [1]

DONKEYS [72]
donkeys, 2789, *ḥᵃmôr*[1] [45]
donkeys, 912, *ʾātôn* [12]
donkeys, 6555, *ʿayir* [4]
wild donkeys, 7230, *pereʾ* [3]
female donkeys, 912, *ʾātôn* [2]
donkeys, *NIH/RPE* [1]
donkeys, 2789+2789, *ḥᵃmôr*[1]*+ḥᵃmôr*[1] [1]
male donkeys, 2789, *ḥᵃmôr*[1] [1]
male donkeys, 6555, *ʿayir* [1]
donkeys, 7230, *pereʾ* [1]
wild donkeys, 10570, *ʿᵃrād* [1]

DOOM [6]
doom, *NIH/RPE* [2]
doom, 7619, *ṣᵉpîrâ* [2]
doom, 6961, *ʿēt* [1]
doom, 6969, *ʿātîd* [1]

DOOMED [5]
doomed to perish, 1959, *dāmam*[3] [1]
doomed to, 4200, *lᵉ-*[1] [1]
doomed to die, 4637+4637, *mût+mût* [1]
doomed to destruction, 8720, *šādad* [1]
doomed, 9462, *tāmam* [1]

DOOR [38]
door, 1946, *delet* [21]
door, 7339, *petaḥ* [15]
door, *NIH/RPE* [1]
door, 1923, *dal*[1] [1]

DOORFRAME [3]
doorframe, 4647, *mᵉzûzâ* [3]

DOORFRAMES [4]
doorframes, 4647, *mᵉzûzâ* [3]
doorframes, 6197, *sap*[3] [1]

DOORKEEPER [2]
doorkeeper, 6214, *sāpap* [1]
doorkeeper, 9068+6197, *šāmar+sap*[3] [1]

DOORKEEPERS [9]
doorkeepers, 9068+6197, *šāmar+sap*[3] [5]
doorkeepers, 8788, *šōʿēr* [4]

DOORPOST [2]
doorpost, 4647, *mᵉzûzâ* [2]

DOORPOSTS [6]
doorposts, 4647, *mᵉzûzâ* [4]
doorposts, 564, *ʾammâ*[1] [1]
doorposts, 595, *ʾōmᵉnâ* [1]

DOORS [53]
doors, 1946, *delet* [46]
doors, 7339, *petaḥ* [5]
doors, *NIH/RPE* [1]
doors, 6197, *sap*[3] [1]

DOORWAY [12]
doorway, 7339, *petaḥ* [9]
doorway, 6197, *sap*[3] [2]
doorway, 4647+7339, *mᵉzûzâ+petaḥ* [1]

DOORWAYS [4]
doorways, 7339, *petaḥ* [2]
doorways, 6197, *sap*[3] [1]
doorways, 7339+4647, *petaḥ+mᵉzûzâ* [1]

DOPHKAH [2]
Dophkah, 1986, *dopqâ* [2]

DOR [4]
Dor, 1888, *dôr*[3] [3]
Dor, 1799, *dōʾr* [1]

DOTHAN [3]
Dothan, 2019, *dōtān* [3]

DOUBLE [21]
double, 9109, *šᵉnayim* [8]
double, 5467, *mišneh* [4]
folded double, 4100, *kāpal* [2]
double portion, 5467, *mišneh* [2]
double, 9339, *tôʾᵃmîm* [2]
double, 678, *ʾap*[2] [1]
fold double, 4100, *kāpal* [1]
double, 4101, *kepel* [1]

DOUBLE-EDGED [3]
double-edged, 7023, *peh* [1]
double-edged, 7092, *pîpiyyôt* [1]
double-edged, 9109+7023, *šᵉnayim+peh* [1]

DOUBLE-MINDED [1]
double-minded, 6189, *sēʿēp* [1]

DOUBLE-PRONGED [1]
double-pronged hooks, 9191, *šᵉpattayim*[2] [1]

DOUBLY [1]
doubly, 928+2021+9109, *bᵉ-+ha-+šᵉnayim* [1]

DOUBTLESS [1]
doubtless, 597, *ʾomnām* [1]

DOUGH [6]
dough, 1302, *bāṣēq*[2] [5]
dough, *NIH/RPE* [1]

DOVE [20]
dove, 3433, *yônâ*[1] [14]
dove, 9367, *tôr*[2] [5]
the dove[s], 2023, *-āh* [1]

DOVES [17]
doves, 9367, *tôr*[2] [9]
doves, 3433, *yônâ*[1] [8]

DOWN [988]
went down, 3718, *yārad* [63]
go down, 3718, *yārad* [61]
struck down, 5782, *nākâ* [57]
bow down, 2556, *ḥāwâ*[2] [33]
bowed down, 2556, *ḥāwâ*[2] [30]
come down, 3718, *yārad* [28]
came down, 3718, *yārad* [24]
sat down, 3782, *yāšab* [22]
cut down, 4162, *kārat* [20]
lie down, 8886, *šākab* [20]
bring down, 3718, *yārad* [19]
down, 3718, *yārad* [13]
lay down, 8886, *šākab* [13]
lie down, 8069, *rābaṣ* [11]
strike down, 5782, *nākâ* [9]
brought down, 3718, *yārad* [8]
gone down, 3718, *yārad* [8]
burn down, 8596+928+2021+836, *śārap+bᵉ-+ha-+ʾēš*[1] [8]
tear down, 2238, *hāras* [7]
take down, 3718, *yārad* [7]
bowed down, 7702, *qādad* [7]
coming down, 3718, *yārad* [6]
write down, 4180, *kātab* [6]
broke down, 5997, *nātaṣ* [6]
tore down, 5997, *nātaṣ* [6]
looked down, 9207, *šāqap* [6]
down, *NIH/RPE* [5]
bowing down, 2556, *ḥāwâ*[2] [5]
going down, 3718, *yārad* [5]
settle down, 3782, *yāšab* [5]
wrote down, 4180, *kātab* [5]
cut down, 5782, *nākâ* [5]
fall down, 10484, *nᵉpal* [5]
trample down, 1008, *bûs* [4]
cut down, 1548, *gādaʿ* [4]
took down, 3718, *yārad* [4]
down, 5877, *nāpal* [4]
bring down, 5989, *nātan* [4]
break down, 5997, *nātaṣ* [4]
strike down, 7003, *pāgaʿ* [4]
struck down, 7003, *pāgaʿ* [4]
break down, 8689, *šābar*[1] [4]
lying down, 8886, *šākab* [4]
looks down, 9207, *šāqap* [4]
down, *AIT* [3]
tears down, 2238, *hāras* [3]
comes down, 3718, *yārad* [3]
let down, 3718, *yārad* [3]
sit down, 3782, *yāšab* [3]
be cut down, 4162, *kārat* [3]
down, 4200+4752, *lᵉ-*[1]*+maṭṭâ* [3]
rained down, 4763, *māṭar* [3]
struck down, 4804, *makkâ* [3]
strike down, 5597, *nāgap* [3]
struck down, 5597, *nāgap* [3]
bring down, 5877, *nāpal* [3]
cut down, 5877, *nāpal* [3]
fall down, 5877, *nāpal* [3]
fell down, 5877, *nāpal* [3]
bringing down, 5989, *nātan* [3]
tear down, 5997, *nātaṣ* [3]
torn down, 5997, *nātaṣ* [3]
broke down, 7287, *pāraṣ* [3]
broken down, 7287, *pāraṣ* [3]
laid down, 7422, *ṣāwâ* [3]
burned down, 8596+928+2021+836, *śārap+bᵉ-+ha-+ʾēš*[1] [3]
cut down, 8845, *šāḥaṭ* [3]
lies down, 8886, *šākab* [3]
throw down, 8959, *šālak* [3]
thrown down, 8959, *šālak* [3]
down to, 448, *ʾel* [2]
down, 928, *bᵉ-* [2]
bring down, 995, *bôʾ* [2]
goes down, 995, *bôʾ* [2]
swooping down, 1797, *dāʾâ*[1] [2]
broken down, 2238, *hāras* [2]
torn down, 2238, *hāras* [2]
swirling down, 2565, *ḥûl*[1] [2]
be brought down, 3718, *yārad* [2]
continued down, 3718, *yārad* [2]
goes down, 3718, *yārad* [2]
lead down, 3718, *yārad* [2]
pull down, 3718, *yārad* [2]
are bowed down, 4104, *kāpap* [2]
bow down, 4156, *kāraʿ* [2]
kneel down, 4156, *kāraʿ* [2]
knelt down, 4156, *kāraʿ* [2]
be brought down, 4173, *kāšal* [2]
beat down, 4198, *kātat* [2]
road down, 4618, *môrād* [2]
rain down, 4763, *māṭar* [2]
look down, 5564, *nābaṭ* [2]
put down, 5663, *nûaḥ*[1] [2]
striking down, 5782, *nākâ* [2]
brought down, 5877, *nāpal* [2]
got down, 5877, *nāpal* [2]

have cut down, 5877, *nāpal* [2]
threw down, 5877, *nāpal* [2]
poured down, 5988, *nātak* [2]
pulled down, 5997, *nātaṣ* [2]
bow down, 6032, *sāgad* [2]
bows down, 6032, *sāgad* [2]
going down, 6296, *ʿābar^{1}* [2]
down to, 6330, *ʿad^{2}* [2]
tear down, 6867, *ʿārâ^{1}* [2]
break down, 7287, *pāraṣ* [2]
look down on, 8011, *rāʾâ^{1}* [2]
lay down, 8069, *rābaṣ* [2]
bring down, 8740, *šûb^{1}* [2]
reached down, 8938, *šālaḥ* [2]
hurled down, 8959, *šālak* [2]
threw down, 8959, *šālak* [2]
bring down, 9164, *šāpēl^{1}* [2]
cut down, 10134, *g^{e}dad* [2]
coming down, 10474, *n^{e}ḥat* [2]
down, 824+2025, *ʾereṣ+-â^{2}* [1]
tracked down, 892, *ʾāšur* [1]
burn down, 928+2021+836+8596,
b^{e}-+ha-+ʾēš^{1}+śārap [1]
go down, 995, *bôʾ* [1]
going down, 995, *bôʾ* [1]
make go down, 995, *bôʾ* [1]
trampled down, 1008, *bûs* [1]
gulps down, 1180, *bālaʿ^{1}* [1]
bring down, 1298, *bāṣaʿ* [1]
cut down, 1345, *bārāʾ^{3}* [1]
had kneel down, 1384, *bārak^{1}* [1]
knelt down, 1384+6584+1386,
bārak^{1}+ʿal^{2}+berek [1]
been cast down, 1548, *gādaʿ* [1]
broken down, 1548, *gādaʿ* [1]
bent down, 1566, *gāhar* [1]
cut down, 1615, *gāzar^{1}* [1]
swoop down, 1797, *dāʾâ^{1}* [1]
is trampled down, 1889, *dûš* [1]
are brought down, 1890, *dāḥâ* [1]
thrown down, 1890, *dāḥâ* [1]
hunt down, 1944, *dālaq* [1]
hunts down, 1944, *dālaq* [1]
trample down, 2005, *dārak* [1]
push down, 2074, *hādap* [1]
flashed down, 2143, *hālak* [1]
goes down, 2143, *hālak* [1]
ran down, 2143, *hālak* [1]
went down, 2143, *hālak* [1]
trampled down, 2150, *hālam* [1]
got down, 2200, *hāpak* [1]
turn upside down, 2201, *hēpek* [1]
are torn down, 2238, *hāras* [1]
been broken down, 2238, *hāras* [1]
break down, 2238, *hāras* [1]
pull down, 2238, *hāras* [1]
threw down, 2238, *hāras* [1]
poured down, 2442, *zāram^{2}* [1]
bow down to worship, 2556, *ḥāwâ^{2}* [1]
bows down, 2556, *ḥāwâ^{2}* [1]
nails down, 2616+928+5021,
ḥāzaq+b^{e}-+masmēr [1]
cut down, 2634, *ḥāṭab* [1]
gone down, 2893, *ḥāsēr^{1}* [1]
hunt down, 2924, *ḥāpaś* [1]
track down, 2924, *ḥāpaś* [1]
dig down, 3168, *ḥātar* [1]
sank down, 3190, *ṭābaʿ* [1]
swooping down, 3216, *ṭûś* [1]
throw down, 3343, *yādâ^{1}* [1]
broke down, 3359, *yādaʿ* [1]
set down, 3668, *yāṣaq* [1]
are brought down, 3718, *yārad* [1]
been brought down, 3718, *yārad* [1]
been taken down, 3718, *yārad* [1]
brings down, 3718, *yārad* [1]
came down, 3718+3718, *yārad+yārad* [1]
carried down, 3718, *yārad* [1]
climbed down, 3718, *yārad* [1]
cut down, 3718, *yārad* [1]
fall down, 3718, *yārad* [1]
flowed down, 3718, *yārad* [1]
flowing down, 3718, *yārad* [1]
goes down, 3718+4200+4752,
yārad+l^{e}-^{1}+maṭṭâ [1]
gone down, 3718+345, *yārad+ʾ^{a}ḥōrannît* [1]
haul down, 3718, *yārad* [1]
leading down, 3718, *yārad* [1]
led down, 3718, *yārad* [1]
let go down, 3718, *yārad* [1]
letting run down, 3718, *yārad* [1]
made flow down, 3718, *yārad* [1]
march down, 3718, *yārad* [1]
moved down, 3718, *yārad* [1]
pulls down, 3718, *yārad* [1]
ran down, 3718, *yārad* [1]
road down, 3718, *yārad* [1]
running down, 3718, *yārad* [1]
sank down, 3718, *yārad* [1]
send down, 3718, *yārad* [1]
sent down, 3718, *yārad* [1]
step down, 3718, *yārad* [1]
stepped down, 3718, *yārad* [1]
was taken down, 3718, *yārad* [1]
weighed down, 3877, *kābēd^{1}* [1]
is cut down, 4065, *kāsaḥ* [1]
bow down, 4104, *kāpap* [1]
bowed down in distress, 4104, *kāpap* [1]
bend down, 4156, *kāraʿ* [1]
bowed down, 4156, *kāraʿ* [1]
bows down, 4156, *kāraʿ* [1]
bring down, 4156, *kāraʿ* [1]
crouch down, 4156, *kāraʿ* [1]
cutting down, 4156, *kāraʿ* [1]
down, 4156, *kāraʿ* [1]
got down, 4156, *kāraʿ* [1]
slumped down, 4156, *kāraʿ* [1]
be struck down, 4162, *kārat* [1]
chop down, 4162, *kārat* [1]
is cut down, 4162, *kārat* [1]
are brought down, 4173, *kāšal* [1]
was written down, 4180, *kātab* [1]
took down, 4374, *lāqaḥ* [1]
go down, 4427, *mābôʾ* [1]
bring down, 4572, *môṭ^{1}* [1]
go down, 4637, *mût* [1]
struck down and died, 4637, *mût* [1]
going down to, 4752, *maṭṭâ* [1]
pour down, 4763, *māṭar* [1]
weighed down, 4849, *mālēʾ^{2}* [1]
down, 4946+8031, *min+rōʾš^{1}* [1]
down, 4946, *min* [1]
drink down, 5172, *māṣâ* [1]
beaten down, 5330, *mirmās* [1]
looks down, 5564, *nābaṭ* [1]
bring down, 5595, *nāgaʿ* [1]
brought down, 5595, *nāgaʿ* [1]
casts down, 5595, *nāgaʿ* [1]
set down, 5663, *nûaḥ^{1}* [1]
settled down, 5663, *nûaḥ^{1}* [1]
pour down moisture, 5688, *nāzal* [1]
shower down, 5688, *nāzal* [1]
streaming down, 5688, *nāzal* [1]
bring down, 5737, *nāḥat* [1]
come down, 5737, *nāḥat* [1]
go down, 5737, *nāḥat* [1]
coming down, 5738, *naḥat^{1}* [1]
going down, 5741, *nāḥēt* [1]
bent down, 5742, *nāṭâ* [1]
let down, 5742, *nāṭâ* [1]
lie down, 5742, *nāṭâ* [1]
poured down rain, 5752, *nāṭap* [1]
poured down, 5752, *nāṭap* [1]
brought down, 5759, *nāṭaš* [1]
be struck down, 5782, *nākâ* [1]
beat down, 5782, *nākâ* [1]
had struck down, 5782, *nākâ* [1]
send down, 5782, *nākâ* [1]
strikes down, 5782, *nākâ* [1]
struck down, 5782+4804, *nākâ+makkâ* [1]
tear down, 5782, *nākâ* [1]
tears down, 5815, *nāsaḥ* [1]
been pulled down, 5825, *nāsaʿ* [1]
bowed down to the ground, 5877+6584+7156,
nāpal+ʿal^{2}+pāneh [1]
bowed down, 5877+6584+7156,
nāpal+ʿal^{2}+pāneh [1]
cast down, 5877, *nāpal* [1]
cutting down, 5877, *nāpal* [1]
down came, 5877, *nāpal* [1]
fallen down, 5877, *nāpal* [1]
falls down, 5877, *nāpal* [1]
gone down, 5877, *nāpal* [1]
hurtling down, 5877, *nāpal* [1]
made come down, 5877, *nāpal* [1]
make lie down, 5877, *nāpal* [1]
throwing himself down, 5877, *nāpal* [1]
cut down, 5937, *nāqap^{1}* [1]
send down, 5989, *nātan* [1]
been torn down, 5997, *nātaṣ* [1]
breaks down, 5997, *nātaṣ* [1]
bring down to ruin, 5997, *nātaṣ* [1]
broken down, 5997, *nātaṣ* [1]
tears down, 5997, *nātaṣ* [1]
sit down, 6015, *sābab* [1]
drag down, 6079, *sāḥab* [1]
hang down, 6243, *sāraḥ^{1}* [1]
down to, 6330+9462, *ʿad^{2}+tāmam* [1]
bowed down, 6390, *ʿāwâ^{1}* [1]
swoop down, 6414, *ʿûp^{1}* [1]
upside down, 6584+7156, *ʿal^{2}+pāneh* [1]
weigh down, 6584, *ʿal^{2}* [1]
cut down, 6618, *ʿālal^{1}* [1]
stoop down, 6700, *ʿānâ^{2}* [1]
stoop down, 6708, *ʿ^{a}nāwâ* [1]
trample down, 6748, *ʿāsas* [1]
slow down, 6806+4200+8206,
ʿāṣar+l^{e}-^{1}+rākab [1]
brought down to terror, 7064, *pāḥad* [1]
are broken down, 7287, *pāraṣ* [1]
tear down, 7287, *pāraṣ* [1]
swept down, 7320, *pāšaṭ* [1]
hunting down, 7399, *ṣādâ^{1}* [1]
hunt down, 7421+4200+4511,
ṣûd+l^{e}-^{1}+madḥēpâ [1]
hunt down, 7421, *ṣûd* [1]
lay down, 7579, *ṣāʿâ* [1]
call a curse down, 7837, *qālal* [1]
called curses down, 7837, *qālal* [1]
called down a curse, 7837, *qālal* [1]
called down curses, 7837+7839, *qālal+q^{e}lālâ* [1]
called down, 7924, *qārāʾ^{1}* [1]
calling down, 7924, *qārāʾ^{1}* [1]
battering down, 7982, *qārar^{2}* [1]
looks down on, 8011, *rāʾâ^{1}* [1]
lying down, 8061, *rābaʿ^{1}* [1]
fallen down, 8069, *rābaṣ* [1]
have lie down, 8069, *rābaṣ* [1]
lies down, 8069, *rābaṣ* [1]
lying down, 8069, *rābaṣ* [1]
makes lie down, 8069, *rābaṣ* [1]
strike down, 8187, *rāṭaš* [1]
trample down, 8252, *rāmas* [1]
trod down, 8252, *rāmas* [1]
rain down, 8319, *rāʿap* [1]
sinks down, 8332, *rāpâ^{1}* [1]
throw down, 8357, *rāṣaḥ* [1]
trample down, 8492+5330, *śîm+mirmās* [1]
be burned down, 8596+928+2021+836,
śārap+b^{e}-+ha-+ʾēš^{1} [1]
burn down, 8596, *śārap* [1]
burned down, 8596+2021+836, *śārap+ha-+ʾēš^{1}* [1]
breaks down, 8689, *šābar^{1}* [1]
brought down, 8740, *šûb^{1}* [1]
leads down, 8755, *šûaḥ^{1}* [1]
go up and down, 8763, *šûṭ^{1}* [1]
weighs down, 8817, *šāḥâ* [1]
bow down, 8820, *šāḥaḥ* [1]
bring down, 8820, *šāḥaḥ* [1]
struck down, 8845, *šāḥat* [1]
tear down, 8845, *šāḥat* [1]
down, 8863, *šîaḥ* [1]
lain down, 8886, *šākab* [1]
lay down to sleep, 8886, *šākab* [1]
made lie down, 8886, *šākab* [1]
lie down to rest, 8905, *šākan* [1]
reach down, 8938, *šālaḥ* [1]
let down, 8938, *šālaḥ* [1]
hurls down, 8959, *šālak* [1]
pushed down, 8959, *šālak* [1]
set down, 8959, *šālak* [1]
cut down, 8961, *šalleket^{1}* [1]
throw down, 9023, *šāmaṭ* [1]
be thrown down, 9023, *šāmaṭ* [1]

threw down, 9023, šāmaṭ [1]
come down, 9164, šāpēl^{1} [1]
brings down, 9164, šāpēl^{1} [1]
stoops down, 9164, šāpēl^{1} [1]
died down, 9205, šāqaʿ [1]
tie down, 9205, šāqaʿ [1]
look down, 9207, šāqap [1]
calm down, 9284, šātaq [1]
dies down, 9284, šātaq [1]
went down, 9305, tāʿar^{1} [1]
cut down, 9372, tāzaz [1]
bow down, 9413, tākâ [1]
got down, 10121, b^{e}rak^{1} [1]
trampling down, 10165, dûš [1]
write down, 10374, k^{e}tab [1]
wrote down, 10374, k^{e}tab [1]
fell down, 10484, n^{e}pal [1]

DOWNCAST [9]
downcast, 8863, šîaḥ [4]
downcast, 5877, nāpal [2]
downcast, 2118+4200, hāyâ+l^{e}-^{1} [1]
downcast, 8814+6524, šaḥ+ʿayin^{1} [1]
downcast, 8820, šāḥaḥ [1]

DOWNFALL [16]
downfall, 5877, nāpal [4]
downfall, NIH/RPE [2]
downfall, 4173, kāšal [2]
downfall, 5147, mappelet [2]
led to downfall, 3948, kāḥad [1]
downfall, 4842, mikšôl [1]
downfall, 8288, rāʿâ^{3} [1]
downfall, 8691, šeber^{1} [1]
downfall, 8845, šāḥat [1]
downfall, 9313, t^{e}bûsâ [1]

DOWNHEARTED [1]
downhearted, 8317+4222, rāʿaʿ+lēbāb [1]

DOWNPOUR [2]
downpour, 1773+4764, gešem^{1}+māṭār [1]
flooding downpour, 3888+8851, kabbîr+šāṭap [1]

DOWNSTREAM [1]
downstream, 4946+4200+5087+2025, min+l^{e}-^{1}+maʿal^{2}+-â^{2} [1]

DRACHMAS [4]
drachmas, 2007, dark^{e}mônîm [4]

DRAG [7]
drag away, 1760, gārar [1]
drag away, 5432, māšak [1]
drag off, 5998, nātaq [1]
drag away, 6079, sāḥab [1]
drag down, 6079, sāḥab [1]
drag away, 6590, ʿālâ [1]
drag along, 9255, šāšāʾ [1]

DRAGGED [6]
dragged away, 6079, sāḥab [3]
dragged off, 5432, māšak [1]
dragged, 6015, sābab [1]
dragged, 6073, sûr^{1} [1]

DRAGNET [2]
dragnet, 4823, mikmeret [2]

DRAGS [4]
drags on, 4499, mādad [1]
drags away, 5432, māšak [1]
drags off, 5432, māšak [1]
drags himself along, 6022, sābal [1]

DRAIN [3]
drain away, 1853, dûb [1]
drain dry, 5172, māṣâ [1]
drain out, 9161, šāpak [1]

DRAINED [5]
be drained out, 5172, māṣâ [2]
drained, 7920, qāṣēr [2]
drained to dregs, 9272+5172, šātâ^{2}+māṣâ [1]

DRAINING [1]
draining away, 5674, nûs [1]

DRANK [34]
drank, 9272, šātâ^{2} [28]
drank, 10748, š^{e}tâ [4]
drank in, 7023+7196, peh+pāʿar [1]
drank freely, 8910, šākar [1]

DRAW [36]
draw water, 8612, šāʾab [5]
draw, 8612, šāʾab [4]
draw, 8990, šālap [4]
draw, 2005, dārak [3]
draw, 8197, rîq^{1} [3]
draw near, 7929, qārēb [2]
draw water, 1926, dālâ^{1} [1]
draw the bow, 2005, dārak [1]
draw attention to, 2349, zākar^{1} [1]
draw, 2980, ḥāqaq [1]
draw, 3106, ḥāśap^{1} [1]
draw, 3655, yāṣāʾ [1]
draw along, 5432, māšak [1]
draw near, 5602, nāgaš [1]
draw away, 5998, nātaq [1]
draw heavy loads, 6022, sābal [1]
draw up case, 6885, ʿārak [1]
draw, 7337, pātaḥ^{1} [1]
draw near, 7928, qārab [1]
draw out, 8197, rîq^{1} [1]
draw back, 8740, šûb^{1} [1]

DRAWING [2]
drawing lots, 1598, gôrāl [1]
drawing up, 6885, ʿārak [1]

DRAWN [23]
drawn, 8990, šālap [4]
drawn, 8197, rîq^{1} [3]
drawn back, 294+6047, ʾāḥôr+sûg^{1} [1]
drawn, 1815, dābaq [1]
drawn, 3655, yāṣāʾ [1]
drawn bow, 4798, mêtār [1]
drawn, 5432, māšak [1]
are drawn away, 5615, nādaḥ^{1} [1]
let be drawn, 5742, nāṭâ [1]
drawn, 5759, nāṭaš [1]
drawn, 5938, nāqap^{2} [1]
is drawn, 5989, nātan [1]
were drawn away, 5998, nātaq [1]
drawn up, 6885, ʿārak [1]
drawn, 7337, pātaḥ^{1} [1]
drawn sword, 7347, p^{e}tîḥâ [1]
drawn swords, 7347, p^{e}tîḥâ [1]
drawn up, 8883, šît^{1} [1]

DRAWS [5]
draws, AIT [1]
draws up, 1758, gāraʾ^{2} [1]
draws out, 1926, dālâ^{1} [1]
draws near, 5595, nāgaʿ [1]
draws near, 7928, qārab [1]

DREAD [22]
dread, 7065, paḥad^{1} [8]
dread, 3336, yāgōr [2]
dread, 6907, ʿāraṣ [2]
overwhelmed with dread, 7064+7065, pāḥad+paḥad^{1} [2]
dread, 7762, qûṣ^{1} [2]
dread, 1793, dāʾag [1]
object of dread, 2317, z^{e}wāʿâ [1]
dread, 3145, ḥat^{1} [1]
dread, 4475, m^{e}gôrâ [1]
filled with dread, 7064, pāḥad [1]
filled with dread, 7762, qûṣ^{1} [1]

DREADED [8]
dreaded, 3336, yāgōr [2]
dreaded, 1593, gûr^{3} [1]
dreaded, 1793, dāʾag [1]
dreaded, 3169, ḥātat [1]
dreaded, 3707, yārēʾ^{1} [1]
dreaded, 7065, paḥad^{1} [1]
dreaded, 10227, zûaʿ [1]

DREADFUL [8]
dreadful, 3707, yārēʾ^{1} [4]
dreadful, 399, ʾêmâ [1]
something dreadful, 3170, ḥ^{a}tat^{1} [1]
dreadful, 3707+4394, yārēʾ^{1}+m^{e}ʾōd [1]
dreadful, 8273, raʿ^{1} [1]

DREADS [1]
dreads, 4475, m^{e}gôrâ [1]

DREAM [70]
dream, 2706, ḥ^{a}lôm [28]
dream, 10267, ḥēlem [20]
had a dream, 2731, ḥālam^{2} [5]
dream, NIH/RPE [3]
had a dream, 2706+2731, ḥ^{a}lôm+ḥālam^{2} [3]
had a dream, 2731+2706, ḥālam^{2}+ḥ^{a}lôm [3]
dream had, 2706+2731, ḥ^{a}lôm+ḥālam^{2} [2]
had dream, 2731+2706, ḥālam^{2}+ḥ^{a}lôm [2]
dream, 2111, hāzâ [1]
dream, 2731, ḥālam^{2} [1]
dream, 10256+10267, ḥ^{e}zû+ḥēlem [1]
dreams, 10418, millâ [1]

DREAMED [2]
dreamed, 2706, ḥ^{a}lôm [1]
dreamed, 2731, ḥālam^{2} [1]

DREAMER [3]
dreamer, 2731+2706, ḥālam^{2}+ḥ^{a}lôm [2]
dreamer, 1251+2021+2706, baʿal^{1}+ha-+ḥ^{a}lôm [1]

DREAMING [1]
dreaming, 2706, ḥ^{a}lôm [1]

DREAMS [25]
dreams, 2706, ḥ^{a}lôm [14]
dreams, 2731, ḥālam^{2} [2]
dreams, NIH/RPE [1]
dreams, 2612, ḥizzāyôn [1]
dreams encourage to have, 2706+2731, ḥ^{a}lôm+ḥālam^{2} [1]
dreams, 2706+2731, ḥ^{a}lôm+ḥālam^{2} [1]
had dreams, 2706+2731, ḥ^{a}lôm+ḥālam^{2} [1]
interpreters of dreams, 2706, ḥ^{a}lôm [1]
foretells by dreams, 2731+2706, ḥālam^{2}+ḥ^{a}lôm [1]
had dreams, 2731+2706, ḥālam^{2}+ḥ^{a}lôm [1]
dreams, 10267, ḥēlem [1]

DREGS [4]
dregs, 9069, šemer^{1} [3]
drained to dregs, 9272+5172, šātâ^{2}+māṣâ [1]

DRENCH [4]
drench, 8115, rāwâ [2]
drench, 4998, māsâ [1]
drench, 9197, šāqâ [1]

DRENCHED [9]
be drenched, 10607, ṣ^{e}baʿ [2]
was drenched, 10607, ṣ^{e}baʿ [2]
drenched, 4848, mālēʾ^{1} [1]
drenched, 8115, rāwâ [1]
drenched, 8175, rāḥaṣ [1]
drenched, 8182, rāṭab [1]
drenched, 10607, ṣ^{e}baʿ [1]

DRESS [10]
dress, 4252, lābaš [5]
dress, 8324, rāpāʾ^{1} [2]
dress, 4229, lābûš [1]
dress in, 4252, lābaš [1]
embroidered dress, 8391, riqmâ [1]

DRESSED [22]
dressed stone, 1607, gāzît [3]
dressed, 1607, gāzît [3]
dressed in, 4252, lābaš [3]
dressed, 4252, lābaš [3]
dressed, 4732, maḥṣēb [3]
dressed stones, 1607, gāzît [1]
dressed, 2502, ḥābaš [1]
dressed, 4229, lābûš [1]
dressed, 4230, l^{e}bûš [1]
dressed, 6913, ʿāśâ^{1} [1]
dressed, 8884, šît^{2} [1]
dressed, 8969, šālēm^{2} [1]

DREW [30]
drew, 8612, *šāʾab* [4]
drew near, 7928, *qārab* [3]
drew out, 5406, *māšâ* [2]
drew, 5432, *māšak* [2]
drew up line, 6885, *ʿārak* [2]
drew up, 6885, *ʿārak* [2]
drew up, 665, *ʾāsap* [1]
drew water, 1926+1926, *dālâ[1]+dālâ[1]* [1]
drew, 2005, *dārak* [1]
drew out, 3655, *yāṣāʾ* [1]
drew, 4374, *lāqaḥ* [1]
drew, 4848+3338+928, *mālēʾ[1]+yād+b[e]-* [1]
drew, 5406, *māšâ* [1]
drew near, 5595, *nāgaʿ* [1]
drew near, 5602, *nāgaš* [1]
drew away, 6077, *sût[1]* [1]
drew up lines, 6885, *ʿārak* [1]
drew up, 8492, *śîm* [1]
drew water, 8612, *šāʾab* [1]
drew back, 8740, *šûb[1]* [1]
drew, 8990, *šālap* [1]

DRIED [26]
dried up, 3312, *yābēš[1]* [15]
dried up, 2990, *ḥārēb[1]* [5]
been dried, 2990, *ḥārēb[1]* [2]
dried up, 5457, *m[e]ṣammâ* [2]
dried up, 62, *ʾābal[2]* [1]
dried up, 430, *ʾākal* [1]

DRIES [4]
dries up, 62, *ʾābal[2]* [2]
dries up, 3312, *yābēš[1]* [2]

DRINK [254]
drink, 9272, *šātâ[2]* [127]
drink offerings, 5821, *nesek[1]* [32]
drink offering, 5821, *nesek[1]* [27]
fermented drink, 8911, *šēkār* [9]
drink, 9197, *šāqâ* [5]
made drink, 9197, *šāqâ* [4]
drink, 5492, *mišteh* [3]
gave a drink, 9197, *šāqâ* [3]
give to drink, 9197, *šāqâ* [3]
must drink, 9272+9272, *šātâ[2]+šātâ[2]* [3]
get a drink, 9197, *šāqâ* [2]
get to drink, 9197, *šāqâ* [2]
give drink, 9197, *šāqâ* [2]
got to drink, 9197, *šāqâ* [2]
have drink, 9197, *šāqâ* [2]
drink, 9198, *šiqqûy* [2]
drink, 3567, *yānaq* [1]
drink, 4363, *lāʿaʿ[2]* [1]
bowls used for drink offerings, 4984, *m[e]naqqît* [1]
drink down, 5172, *māṣâ* [1]
drink up, 5172, *māṣâ* [1]
drink deeply, 5209, *māṣaṣ* [1]
drink[s], 5647, *-nû[2]* [1]
drink offerings, 5816, *nāsîk[1]* [1]
pouring out of drink offerings, 5818, *nāsak[1]* [1]
drink fill, 6010, *sābāʾ[1]* [1]
drink too much, 6010, *sābāʾ[1]* [1]
drink deep, 8115, *rāwâ* [1]
drink fill, 8910, *šākar* [1]
give a drink, 9197+3926, *šāqâ+kôs[1]* [1]
give a drink, 9197, *šāqâ* [1]
given a drink, 9197, *šāqâ* [1]
given to drink, 9197, *šāqâ* [1]
gives drink, 9197, *šāqâ* [1]
let drink, 9197, *šāqâ* [1]
made to drink, 9197, *šāqâ* [1]
make drink, 9197, *šāqâ* [1]
get a drink, 9272, *šātâ[2]* [1]
have a drink, 9272, *šātâ[2]* [1]
drink in own way, 9276, *š[e]tiyyâ* [1]
drink offerings, 10483, *n[e]sak[2]* [1]
drink, 10748, *š[e]tâ* [1]

DRINKERS [2]
drinkers, 9272, *šātâ[2]* [2]

DRINKING [27]
drinking, 9272, *šātâ[2]* [23]
drinking, 5492, *mišteh* [2]
drinking, *NIH/RPE* [1]
drinking, 10302, *ṭ[e]ʿēm[2]* [1]

DRINKS [13]
drinks, 9272, *šātâ[2]* [8]
drinks, 8911, *šēkār* [2]
drinks, 6011, *sōbeʾ* [1]
drinks in, 9272, *šātâ[2]* [1]
drinks up, 9272, *šātâ[2]* [1]

DRIP [3]
drip, 5752, *nāṭap* [3]

DRIPPED [1]
dripped, 5752, *nāṭap* [1]

DRIPPING [3]
constant dripping, 1942+3265, *delep+ṭārad* [2]
dripping, 5752, *nāṭap* [1]

DRIVE [67]
drive out, 3769, *yāraš[1]* [24]
drive out, 1763, *gāraš[1]* [8]
drive, 1763, *gāraš[1]* [7]
drive far, 8178, *rāḥaq* [3]
drive out, 3655, *yāṣāʾ* [2]
drive, 5615, *nādaḥ[1]* [2]
drive, 5627, *nāhag[1]* [2]
drive, 8206, *rākab* [2]
drive out, 8938, *šālaḥ* [2]
drive away, 1763, *gāraš[1]* [1]
drive out, 1763+1763, *gāraš[1]+gāraš[1]* [1]
drive out, 2074, *hādap* [1]
drive, 2143, *hālak* [1]
drive furiously, 2147, *hālal[3]* [1]
certainly drive out, 3769+3769, *yāraš[1]+yāraš[1]* [1]
drive from, 3769, *yāraš[1]* [1]
drive out completely, 3769+3769, *yāraš[1]+yāraš[1]* [1]
drive out, 5615, *nādaḥ[1]* [1]
drive away, 5627, *nāhag[1]* [1]
drive away, 5653, *nûd* [1]
drive out, 5970, *nāšal* [1]
drive away, 8286, *rāʿaʿ[1]* [1]
drive mad, 8713, *šāgaʿ* [1]
drive, 9546, *tāqaʿ* [1]

DRIVEN [39]
driven out, 3769, *yāraš[1]* [11]
driven, 1763, *gāraš[1]* [2]
driven away, 10304, *ṭ[e]rad* [2]
was driven away, 10304, *ṭ[e]rad* [2]
driven out, 1655, *gālâ* [1]
be driven, 1763, *gāraš[1]* [1]
been driven out, 1763, *gāraš[1]* [1]
driven hard, 1985, *dāpaq* [1]
driven out, 2074, *hādap* [1]
driven, 2074, *hādap* [1]
driven away, 2133, *hālāʾ* [1]
driven, 2143, *hālak* [1]
driven from, 4946, *min* [1]
let themselves be driven back, 5595, *nāgaʿ* [1]
be driven away, 5615, *nādaḥ[1]* [1]
been driven, 5615, *nādaḥ[1]* [1]
driven away, 5615, *nādaḥ[1]* [1]
driven, 5615, *nādaḥ[1]* [1]
driven away, 5627, *nāhag[1]* [1]
were driven out, 5777, *nākāʾ[1]* [1]
is driven back, 6047+294, *sûg[1]+ʾāḥôr* [1]
driven, 6296, *ʿābar[1]* [1]
driven, 7046, *pûṣ[1]* [1]
driven away, 8103, *rādap* [1]
driven, 8103, *rādap* [1]
driven, 9546, *tāqaʿ* [1]

DRIVER [3]
chariot driver, 8208, *rakkāb* [2]
driver, 8206, *rākab* [1]

DRIVER'S [2]
driver's, 5601, *nāgaś* [1]
slave driver's, 5601, *nāgaś* [1]

DRIVERS [7]
slave drivers, 5601, *nāgaś* [5]
drivers, *NIH/RPE* [1]
drivers, 8206, *rākab* [1]

DRIVES [8]
drives on, 436, *ʾākap* [1]
drives out, 1368, *bāraḥ[1]* [1]
drives out, 2048, *hāgâ[2]* [1]
drives over, 2169, *hāmam[1]* [1]
drives, 5627, *nāhag[1]* [1]
drives along, 5674, *nûs* [1]
drives out, 5970, *nāšal* [1]
drives, 8740, *šûb[1]* [1]

DRIVING [14]
driving out, 1763, *gāraš[1]* [2]
driving, *AIT* [1]
driving, 928, *b[e]-* [1]
driving, 1760, *gārar* [1]
driving, 1763, *gāraš[1]* [1]
driving away, 1890, *dāḥâ* [1]
driving rain, 2443+4784, *zerem+mayim* [1]
driving, 3561, *yānâ* [1]
driving winds, 4668, *m[e]zārîm* [1]
driving, 4952, *minhāg* [1]
driving, 5627, *nāhag[1]* [1]
driving out, 5970, *nāšal* [1]
driving, 6085, *sāḥap* [1]

DROP [9]
drop, 5254, *mar[2]* [1]
drop, 5752, *nāṭap* [1]
drop, 5759, *nāṭaš* [1]
drop leaves, 5850, *nāʿar[2]* [1]
make drop, 5877, *nāpal* [1]
drop off, 5970, *nāšal* [1]
drop, 5989, *nātan* [1]
drop, 6903, *ʿārap[1]* [1]
let drop, 8319, *rāʿap* [1]

DROPPED [3]
dropped, 5022, *māsas* [1]
dropped out, 5877, *nāpal* [1]
dropped, 8959, *šālak* [1]

DROPPING [1]
dropping, 8959, *šālak* [1]

DROPS [3]
drops, 103, *ʾēgel* [1]
drops, 5754, *neṭep* [1]
drops, 5877, *nāpal* [1]

DROSS [7]
dross, 6092, *sîg* [7]

DROUGHT [8]
drought, 2996, *ḥōreb[1]* [3]
drought, 7480, *ṣiyyâ* [2]
drought, 1314, *baṣṣārâ* [1]
drought, 1316, *baṣṣōret* [1]
drought, 3312, *yābēš[1]* [1]

DROVE [34]
drove out, 3769, *yāraš[1]* [9]
drove out, 1763, *gāraš[1]* [5]
drove away, 1763, *gāraš[1]* [3]
drove, 1763, *gāraš[1]* [2]
drove away, 1368, *bāraḥ[1]* [1]
drove out, 1368, *bāraḥ[1]* [1]
drove in, 1577, *gûz* [1]
drove through, 1991, *dāqar* [1]
drove back, 2118+6584, *hāyâ+ʿal[2]* [1]
drove back, 2143, *hālak* [1]
drove in disgrace, 2725, *ḥālal[1]* [1]
drove out completely, 3769+3769, *yāraš[1]+yāraš[1]* [1]
drove, 3769, *yāraš[1]* [1]
drove ahead, 5627, *nāhag[1]* [1]
drove, 5627, *nāhag[1]* [1]
drove, 5782, *nākâ* [1]
drove away, 5959, *nāšab* [1]
drove, 6268, *ʿābad* [1]
drove, 9546, *tāqaʿ* [1]

DROVES [4]
droves, 4200+8044, *l[e]-[1]+rōb* [1]
droves, 4722, *maḥ[a]neh* [1]
droves, 4856, *m[e]lāʾkâ* [1]

droves of livestock, 5238, *miqneh* [1]

DROWNED [2]
are drowned, 3190, *ṭāba'* [1]
drowned, 8116, *rāweh* [1]

DROWSINESS [1]
drowsiness, 5671, *nûmâ* [1]

DRUNK [30]
drunk, 8910, *šākar* [6]
drunk, 9272, *šātâ*^{2} [6]
make drunk, 8910, *šākar* [4]
made drunk, 8910, *šākar* [3]
drunk, 8893, *šikkôr* [2]
getting drunk, 9272+8893, *šātâ*^{2}*+šikkôr* [2]
drunk, 6010, *sābā'*^{1} [1]
drunk its fill, 8115, *rāwâ* [1]
get drunk, 8910, *šākar* [1]
keep on getting drunk, 8910, *šākar* [1]
made drunk, 8912, *šākur* [1]
drunk, 8913, *šikkārôn*^{1} [1]
be drunk, 9272, *šātâ*^{2} [1]

DRUNKARD [3]
drunkard, 8893, *šikkôr* [2]
drunkard, 6010, *sābā'*^{1} [1]

DRUNKARD'S [1]
drunkard's, 8893, *šikkôr* [1]

DRUNKARDS [6]
drunkards, 8893, *šikkôr* [4]
drunkards, 6010, *sābā'*^{1} [1]
drunkards, 9272+8911, *šātâ*^{2}*+šēkār* [1]

DRUNKEN [2]
drunken men, 8893, *šikkôr* [1]
drunken, 8893, *šikkôr* [1]

DRUNKENNESS [3]
drunkenness, 8913, *šikkārôn*^{1} [2]
drunkenness, 9275, *š^{e}tî*^{2} [1]

DRY [75]
dry ground, 3317, *yabbāšâ* [10]
dry, 3313, *yābēš*^{2} [8]
dry up, 3312, *yābēš*^{1} [7]
dry up, 2990, *ḥārēb*^{1} [5]
dry, 3312, *yābēš*^{1} [5]
dry, 7480, *ṣiyyâ* [5]
dry ground, 3000, *ḥārābâ* [4]
dry, 2996, *ḥōreb*^{1} [3]
dry land, 3000, *ḥārābâ* [3]
run dry, 2893, *ḥāsēr*^{1} [2]
dry, 2990, *ḥārēb*^{1} [2]
dry, 2992, *ḥārēb*^{3} [2]
dry land, 3317, *yabbāšâ* [2]
dry up, 62, *'ābal*^{2} [1]
dry, 2427, *zārab* [1]
makes run dry, 2990, *ḥārēb*^{1} [1]
dry, 3019, *ḥārôn* [1]
dry grass, 3143, *ḥ^{a}šaš* [1]
completely dry, 3312, *yābēš*^{1} [1]
make dry, 3312, *yābēš*^{1} [1]
dry land, 3318, *yabbešet* [1]
dry, 4908, *mālal*^{1} [1]
drain dry, 5172, *māṣâ* [1]
dry up, 5980, *nāšat* [1]
dry up, 5989+3000, *nātan+ḥārābâ* [1]
dry, 6877, *'ārûṣ* [1]
dry land, 7480, *ṣiyyâ* [1]
dry, 7534, *ṣāmē'*^{2} [1]
dry, 7535, *ṣim'â* [1]
dry, 7546, *ṣāmaq* [1]

DUE [16]
due, *AIT* [9]
due punishment, 1334, *biqqōret* [1]
due, 1691, *g^{e}mûl* [1]
due, 3278, *yā'â* [1]
due annually, 4946+1896+9102+928+9102, *min+day+šānâ*^{2}*+b^{e}-+šānâ*^{2} [1]
due, 5477, *mišpāṭ* [1]
due time, 6961, *'ēt* [1]
receive due, 8966, *šālēm*^{1} [1]

DUG [28]
dug, 2916, *ḥāpar*^{1} [10]
dug, 4125, *kārâ*^{1} [5]
dug, 2933, *ḥāṣēb*^{1} [3]
dug, 3168, *ḥātar* [3]
dug, 6913, *'āśâ*^{1} [2]
dug wells, 7769, *qûr*^{1} [2]
dug up, 2916, *ḥāpar*^{1} [1]
is dug, 4125, *kārâ*^{1} [1]
dug up, 6466, *'āzaq* [1]

DULL [5]
dull, 3877, *kābēd*^{1} [1]
make dull, 3877, *kābēd*^{1} [1]
dull, 3910, *kēheh* [1]
dull, 7733, *qāhâ* [1]
dull, 9096, *šānā'* [1]

DUMAH [4]
Dumah, 1874, *dûmâ*^{3} [3]
Dumah, 1873, *dûmâ*^{2} [1]

DUMPED [1]
dumped, 9161, *šāpak* [1]

DUNG [6]
dung, 883, *'ašpōt* [4]
dung, 1645, *gēl* [1]
dung, 1672, *gālāl*^{1} [1]

DUNGEON [7]
dungeon, 1014, *bôr* [3]
dungeon, 1074+1014, *bayit*^{1}*+bôr* [2]
dungeon, 1074+3975, *bayit*^{1}*+kele'* [1]
dungeon, 8846, *šaḥat* [1]

DUPLICITY [1]
duplicity, 6157, *selep* [1]

DURA [1]
Dura, 10164, *dûrā'* [1]

DURING [112]
during, 928, *b^{e}-* [59]
during, *AIT* [20]
during, *NIH/RPE* [15]
during, 3427, *yôm*^{1} [2]
during, 3972, *kōl* [2]
during, 4200, *l^{e}-*^{1} [2]
during, 10527, *'ad* [2]
during, 448, *'el* [1]
during, 928+3427, *b^{e}-+yôm*^{1} [1]
during that time, 3427, *yôm*^{1} [1]
during the daytime, 3429, *yômām* [1]
during the day, 3429, *yômām* [1]
during, 4946, *min* [1]
during, 5031, *mispār*^{1} [1]
during, 6584, *'al*^{2} [1]
during, 10089, *b^{e}-* [1]
during, 10168, *dî* [1]

DUSK [10]
dusk, 5974, *nešep* [4]
dusk, 6602, *'^{a}lāṭâ* [3]
dusk, 6847, *'ereb*^{2} [2]
dusk, 3125, *ḥōšek* [1]

DUST [101]
dust, 6760, *'āpār* [81]
dust, *NIH/RPE* [4]
dust, 85, *'ābāq* [4]
dust, 141, *'^{a}dāmâ*^{1} [4]
dust, 824, *'ereṣ* [3]
dust, 709, *'ēper* [2]
fine dust, 85, *'ābāq* [1]
dust, 1919, *dakkā'*^{2} [1]
dust, 8836, *šaḥaq* [1]

DUTIES [23]
duties, 5466, *mišmeret* [10]
duties, 6275, *'^{a}bōdâ* [5]
duties, 4856, *m^{e}lā'kâ* [3]
duties, 1821, *dābār* [1]
carry out duties, 3655+2256+995, *yāṣā'+w^{e}-+bô'* [1]
duties, 5126, *ma'^{a}śeh* [1]
share their duties, 6640+465, *'im+'ēlleh* [1]
were exempt from duties, 7080, *pāṭar* [1]

DUTY [25]
going on duty, 995, *bô'* [4]
duty, 10208, *h^{a}lāk* [3]
fulfill the duty of a brother-in-law, 3302, *yābam* [2]
going off duty, 3655, *yāṣā'* [2]
duty, 5466, *mišmeret* [2]
duty, *NIH/RPE* [1]
on duty, 995+2256+3655, *bô'+w^{e}-+yāṣā'* [1]
as nearest relative duty, 1460, *g^{e}'ullâ* [1]
duty, 1821, *dābār* [1]
fulfill duty as a brother-in-law, 3302, *yābam* [1]
go off duty, 3655, *yāṣā'* [1]
duty, 5096, *ma'^{a}mād* [1]
the duty of, 6584, *'al*^{2} [1]
on duty, 6641, *'āmad* [1]
on duty at, 9068, *šāmar* [1]
on duty, 9068, *šāmar* [1]
on duty, 9250, *šārat* [1]

DWARFED [1]
dwarfed, 1987, *daq* [1]

DWELL [73]
dwell, 8905, *šākan* [21]
dwell, 3782, *yāšab* [14]
dwell, 1591, *gûr*^{1} [10]
dwell in, 3782, *yāšab* [8]
dwell in, 8905, *šākan* [4]
make dwell, 3782, *yāšab* [2]
dwell, 4328, *lîn* [2]
dwell, 5226, *māqôm* [2]
dwell on, 1067, *bîn* [1]
dwell, 1884, *dûr*^{2} [1]
made dwell, 3782, *yāšab* [1]
makes dwell, 3782, *yāšab* [1]
place where dwell, 5438, *miškān* [1]
dwell, 5661, *nāwâ*^{3} [1]
dwell with, 6640, *'im* [1]
allow to dwell, 8905, *šākan* [1]
come to dwell, 8905, *šākan* [1]
caused to dwell, 10709, *š^{e}kan* [1]

DWELLERS [1]
dwellers, 3782, *yāšab* [1]

DWELLING [65]
dwelling, 3782, *yāšab* [10]
dwelling place, 5438, *miškān* [8]
dwelling, 8905, *šākan* [8]
dwelling, 5061, *mā'ôn*^{2} [7]
dwelling place, 5061, *mā'ôn*^{2} [4]
dwelling place, 5226, *māqôm* [3]
dwelling, 5438, *miškān* [3]
dwelling, 5659, *nāweh*^{1} [3]
dwelling, 4632, *môšāb* [2]
dwelling, 4722, *maḥ^{a}neh* [2]
dwelling places, 5438, *miškān* [2]
dwelling place, 4632, *môšāb* [1]
dwelling place, 4806, *mākôn* [1]
dwelling place, 5104, *m^{e}'ōnâ* [1]
dwelling, 5226, *māqôm* [1]
dwelling places, 5659, *nāweh*^{1} [1]
dwelling place, 5659, *nāweh*^{1} [1]
dwelling, 6108, *sōk* [1]
dwelling, 6109, *sukkâ* [1]
dwelling place, 8070, *rēbeṣ* [1]
dwelling, 8494, *śōk* [1]
made a dwelling, 8905, *šākan* [1]
dwelling, 9414, *t^{e}kûnâ* [1]
dwelling, 10445, *miškan* [1]

DWELLINGS [12]
dwellings, 5438, *miškān* [4]
dwellings, 185, *'ōhel*^{1} [3]
dwellings, 1074, *bayit*^{1} [1]
dwellings, 3749, *y^{e}rî'â* [1]
dwellings, 3782, *yāšab* [1]
dwellings, 4632, *môšāb* [1]
dwellings, 5661, *nāwâ*^{3} [1]

DWELLS [11]
dwells, 8905, *šākan* [4]
dwells, 3782, *yāšab* [2]

where dwells, 5438, *miškān* [2]
where dwells, 5226, *māqôm* [1]
dwells in, 8905, *šākan* [1]
dwells, 10742, *šᵉrâ* [1]

DWELT [6]
dwelt, 3782, *yāšab* [2]
dwelt in, 8905, *šākan* [2]
dwelt, 8905, *šākan* [2]

DWINDLE [1]
dwindle, 1937, *dālal*[1] [1]

DWINDLES [1]
dwindles away, 5070, *mā'aṭ* [1]

DYED [6]
dyed red, 131, *'ādēm* [6]

DYING [9]
dying, 4637, *mût* [5]
dying, 6, *'ābad* [1]
dying, 665, *'āsap* [1]
dying, 4638, *māwet* [1]
dying, 5883, *nepeš* [1]

DYNASTY [3]
dynasty, 1074, *bayit*[1] [3]

EACH [501]
each, 408, *'îš*[1] [160]
each, 285, *'eḥād* [58]
each, *AIT* [42]
each, 2021, *ha-* [40]
each, *NIH/RPE* [38]
each, 3972, *kōl* [26]
each, 9109, *šᵉnayim* [16]
on each side, 4946+7024+2256+4946+7024, *min+pōh+wᵉ-+min+pōh* [10]
each, 2257, *-ô* [9]
each, 851, *'iššâ* [7]
each, 4392, *-ām* [3]
each province, 4519+2256+4519, *mᵉdînâ+wᵉ-+mᵉdînâ* [3]
each people, 6639+2256+6639, *'am*[2]*+wᵉ-+'am*[2] [3]
each year, 9102+928+9102, *šānâ*[2]*+bᵉ-+šānâ*[2] [3]
each, 408+408, *'îš*[1]*+'îš*[1] [2]
each, 928, *bᵉ-* [2]
for each day, 1821+3427+928+3427, *dābār+yôm*[1]*+bᵉ-+yôm*[1] [2]
each, 2084, *-hû* [2]
each, 2157, *-hem* [2]
each day, 3427+928+3427, *yôm*[1]*+bᵉ-+yôm*[1] [2]
each other, 3480, *yaḥad* [2]
each dish, 4094+2256+4094, *kᵉpôr*[1]*+wᵉ-+kᵉpôr*[1] [2]
each, 4200, *lᵉ-*[1] [2]
facing each other, 4691+448+4691, *meḥᵉzâ+'el+meḥᵉzâ* [2]
each year, 4946+3427+3427+2025, *min+yôm*[1]*+yôm*[1]*+-â*[2] [2]
each lampstand, 4963+2256+4963, *mᵉnôrâ+wᵉ-+mᵉnôrâ* [2]
each, 5527, *-ān* [2]
faced each other, 8011+7156, *rā'â*[1]*+pāneh* [2]
each gate, 9133+2256+9133, *ša'ar*[1]*+wᵉ-+ša'ar*[1] [2]
each one, 285, *'eḥād* [1]
each, 408+278+2257, *'îš*[1]*+'āḥ*[2]*+-ô* [1]
each other, 465, *'ēlleh* [1]
each of us, 638+2256+2085, *'ᵃnî+wᵉ-+hû'* [1]
each[s], 752, *'arba'*[1] [1]
each morning, 928+2021+1332+928+2021+1332, *bᵉ-+ha-+bōqer*[2]*+bᵉ-+ha-+bōqer*[2] [1]
in each corner, 928+5243+928+5243, *bᵉ-+miqṣôa'+bᵉ-+miqṣôa'* [1]
on each side, 928, *bᵉ-* [1]
to each man, 928+9005, *bᵉ-+šēm*[1] [1]
each[s], 1505, *geber*[1] [1]
each national group, 1580+1580, *gôy+gôy* [1]
each one, 1653, *gulgōlet* [1]
each, 1653+5031, *gulgōlet+mispār*[1] [1]
arguing with each other, 1906, *dîn*[1] [1]
each[s], 2021+4090, *ha-+kap* [1]
each, 2522, *ḥad*[2] [1]
each day's, 3427+3427, *yôm*[1]*+yôm*[1] [1]
each day's, 3427+928+3427+2257, *yôm*[1]*+bᵉ-+yôm*[1]*+-ô* [1]
each day's, 3427+928+3427, *yôm*[1]*+bᵉ-+yôm*[1] [1]
each[s], 3427, *yôm*[1] [1]
each other, 3481, *yaḥdāw* [1]
one for each, 3869+5031, *kᵉ-+mispār*[1] [1]
each other[s], 3870, *-kā* [1]
each[s], 4053, *kānāp* [1]
each day, 4200+2021+3427+4200+2021+3427, *lᵉ-*[1]*+ha-+yôm*[1]*+lᵉ-*[1]*+ha-+yôm*[1] [1]
at each successive level, 4200+5087+2025+4200+5087+2025, *lᵉ-*[1]*+ma'al*[2]*+-â*[2]*+lᵉ-*[1]*+ma'al*[2]*+-â*[2] [1]
each day, 4200+2021+3427, *lᵉ-*[1]*+ha-+yôm*[1] [1]
each morning, 4200+2021+1332+4200+2021+1332, *lᵉ-*[1]*+ha-+bōqer*[2]*+lᵉ-*[1]*+ha-+bōqer*[2] [1]
each[s], 4200+5031, *lᵉ-*[1]*+mispār*[1] [1]
each[s], 4392, *-ām* [1]
each other[s], 4564, *-mô* [1]
on each side, 4946+2021+6298+4946+2296+4946+2021+6298+4946+2296, *min+ha-+'ēber*[1]*+min+zeh+min+ha-+'ēber*[1]*+min+zeh* [1]
bordering each side[s], 4946+2296+2256+4946+2296, *min+zeh+wᵉ-+min+zeh* [1]
on each side[s], 4946+2296+2256+4946+2296, *min+zeh+wᵉ-+min+zeh* [1]
each lampstand, 4963+4963, *mᵉnôrâ+mᵉnôrâ* [1]
each clan, 5476+5476, *mišpāḥâ+mišpāḥâ* [1]
oppress each other, 5601, *nāgaś* [1]
each herd, 6373+6373, *'ēder*[1]*+'ēder*[1] [1]
each towns, 6551+6551, *'îr*[1]*+'îr*[1] [1]
each town, 6551+2256+6551, *'îr*[1]*+wᵉ-+'îr*[1] [1]
facing each other, 7925+5120, *qārā'*[2]*+ma'ᵃrākâ* [1]
looking at each other, 8011, *rā'â*[1] [1]
each, 8031, *rō'š*[1] [1]
each other[s], 8276, *rēa'*[2] [1]
jostled each other, 8368, *rāṣaṣ* [1]
each table, 8947+2256+8947, *šulḥān+wᵉ-+šulḥān* [1]
each year, 9102+9102, *šānâ*[2]*+šānâ*[2] [1]
each, 9108, *šēnî* [1]
each[s], 9109, *šᵉnayim* [1]
each other[s], 9109+2157, *šᵉnayim+-hem* [1]
each other, 9109+5646, *šᵉnayim+-nû*[1] [1]
each, 10154, *dā'* [1]
each, 10433, *minyān* [1]

EAGER [8]
eager, 2911, *ḥāpēṣ*[1] [2]
eager, 237, *'ûṣ* [1]
eager, 987, *bāhal* [1]
eager, 1894, *dāḥap* [1]
eager, 2914, *ḥēpeṣ* [1]
eager, 7747, *qāwâ*[1] [1]
eager, 8899, *šākam* [1]

EAGERLY [3]
eagerly, 928+3972+8356, *bᵉ-+kōl+rāṣôn* [1]
waiting eagerly, 7747, *qāwâ*[1] [1]
eagerly, 8838, *šāḥar*[2] [1]

EAGLE [17]
eagle, 5979, *nešer* [15]
eagle, 10495, *nᵉšar* [2]

EAGLE'S [2]
eagle's, 5979, *nešer* [2]

EAGLES [6]
eagles, 5979, *nešer* [6]

EAR [37]
ear, 265, *'ōzen* [25]
give ear, 5742+265, *nāṭâ+'ōzen* [6]
give ear, 263, *'āzan*[1] [2]
ear perceived, 263, *'āzan*[1] [1]
ear lobe, 265, *'ōzen* [1]
turn a deaf ear, 3087, *ḥārēš*[2] [1]
turned a deaf ear, 4202+263, *lō'+'āzan*[1] [1]

EARLIER [12]
earlier, 8037, *ri'šôn* [6]
earlier, 928+2021+9378, *bᵉ-+ha-+tᵉḥillâ* [2]
earlier, 2118, *hāyâ* [1]
in earlier times, 4200+7156, *lᵉ-*[1]*+pāneh* [1]
earlier times, 7156, *pāneh* [1]
earlier, 10623, *qadmāy* [1]

EARLY [53]
early, 8899, *šākam* [18]
got up early, 8899, *šākam* [5]
get up early, 8899, *šākam* [4]
early, 928+8040, *bᵉ-+rē'šît* [3]
early got up, 8899, *šākam* [3]
early in the morning, 8899, *šākam* [3]
rose early, 8899, *šākam* [3]
early the next morning, 8899, *šākam* [2]
early figs, 1136, *bikkûrâ* [1]
early fruit, 1136, *bikkûrâ* [1]
ripen early, 1136, *bikkûrâ* [1]
early, 4554, *māhar*[1] [1]
early times, 6409, *'ôlām* [1]
early fruit, 7001, *pag* [1]
early, 8037, *ri'šôn* [1]
early, 8040, *rē'šît* [1]
early arose, 8899, *šākam* [1]
early morning get up, 8899, *šākam* [1]
go early, 8899, *šākam* [1]
rise early, 8899, *šākam* [1]

EARN [3]
earn, 430, *'ākal* [1]
earn interest, 5967, *nāšak*[2] [1]
earn wages, 8509+8509, *śākar+śākar* [1]

EARNED [1]
reward earned, 7262+3338, *pᵉrî+yād* [1]

EARNERS [1]
earners, 6913, *'āśâ*[1] [1]

EARNEST [1]
earnest, 5883, *nepeš* [1]

EARNESTLY [4]
earnestly seek, 8838, *šāḥar*[2] [2]
earnestly asked for permission, 8626+8626, *šā'al+šā'al* [1]
earnestly asked permission, 8626+8626, *šā'al+šā'al* [1]

EARNESTNESS [1]
earnestness, 205+5883, *'awwâ+nepeš* [1]

EARNINGS [3]
earnings, 924, *'etnan* [2]
earnings, 7262+4090, *pᵉrî+kap* [1]

EARNS [1]
earns, 6913, *'āśâ*[1] [1]

EARRING [2]
earring, 5690, *nezem* [2]

EARRINGS [9]
earrings, 5690, *nezem* [4]
earrings, 6316, *'āgîl* [2]
earrings, 9366, *tôr*[1] [2]
earrings, 5755, *nᵉṭipâ* [1]

EARS [59]
ears, 265, *'ōzen* [58]
ears, *NIH/RPE* [1]

EARTH [582]
earth, 824, *'ereṣ* [524]
earth, 141, *'ᵃdāmâ*[1] [30]
earth, 10075, *'ᵃra'* [14]
earth, 6760, *'āpār* [5]
earth, 9315, *tēbēl* [3]
earth, *NIH/RPE* [1]
the earth[s], 2023, *-āh* [1]
clods of earth, 8073, *regeb* [1]
whole earth, 9315+824, *tēbēl+'ereṣ* [1]

earth, 10077, *'ᵃraq* [1]
earth, 10309, *yabbᵉšâ* [1]

EARTH'S [5]
earth's, 824, *'ereṣ* [5]

EARTHEN [1]
earthen ramps, 6760, *'āpār* [1]

EARTHENWARE [1]
earthenware, 3084, *ḥereś* [1]

EARTHQUAKE [7]
earthquake, 8323, *ra'aš* [7]

EASE [9]
at ease, 8929, *šālēw* [2]
ease, 5911, *nāṣal* [1]
ease, 5951, *nāšā'* [1]
at ease, 8631, *šā'an* [1]
enjoy ease, 8631, *šā'an* [1]
at ease, 8633, *ša'ᵃnān* [1]
at ease, 8922, *šālâ*[1] [1]
live at ease, 8922, *šālâ*[1] [1]

EASILY [5]
easily angered, 2779, *ḥēmâ* [1]
as easily as, 3869+889, *kᵉ+'ᵃšer* [1]
easily, 4957, *mᵉnûḥâ* [1]
easily deceived, 7331, *pātâ*[1] [1]
comes easily, 7837, *qālal* [1]

EAST [179]
east, 7708, *qādîm* [38]
east, 4667, *mizrāḥ* [34]
east, 7710, *qedem* [17]
east, 7708+2025, *qādîm+-â*[2] [13]
east, 7711, *qēdem* [10]
east, 928+6298, *bᵉ-+'ēber*[1] [9]
east, 4667+2025, *mizrāḥ+-â*[2] [7]
east wind, 7708, *qādîm* [7]
east, 7711+2025, *qēdem+-â*[2] [7]
east, 6584+7156, *'al*[2]*+pāneh* [5]
east, 7713, *qidmâ* [4]
east, 4667+2021+9087, *mizrāḥ+ha-+šemeš* [3]
east, 4946+7710, *min+qedem* [3]
east, 7156, *pāneh* [3]
east, 4667+2025+2021+9087, *mizrāḥ+-â*[2]*+ha-+šemeš* [2]
east, 4667+9087, *mizrāḥ+šemeš* [2]
east, 4946+6298, *min+'ēber*[1] [2]
east, 7719, *qadmōnî*[1] [2]
east, 241, *'ûr*[1] [1]
east, 928+6298+4667+2025+9087, *bᵉ-+'ēber*[1]*+mizrāḥ+-â*[2]*+šemeš* [1]
east, 928+6298+4667+2025, *bᵉ-+'ēber*[1]*+mizrāḥ+-â*[2] [1]
east, 928+6298+4667+9087, *bᵉ-+'ēber*[1]*+mizrāḥ+šemeš* [1]
east, 4604, *môṣā'*[1] [1]
east side, 6298, *'ēber*[1] [1]
east, 6298+4667+2025, *'ēber*[1]*+mizrāḥ+-â*[2] [1]
east, 6298, *'ēber*[1] [1]
east, 6584+7156+7710, *'al*[2]*+pāneh+qedem* [1]
east winds, 7708, *qādîm* [1]
hot east wind, 7708, *qādîm* [1]

EASTERN [20]
eastern, 7710, *qedem* [7]
eastern, 7711+2025, *qēdem+-â*[2] [3]
eastern, 7719, *qadmōnî*[1] [3]
eastern, 4667+2025, *mizrāḥ+-â*[2] [2]
eastern, *NIH/RPE* [1]
eastern, 4667+9087, *mizrāḥ+šemeš* [1]
eastern, 4667, *mizrāḥ* [1]
eastern, 7708+2025, *qādîm+-â*[2] [1]
eastern, 7716, *qadmôn* [1]

EASTWARD [8]
eastward, 7708, *qādîm* [2]
eastward, 4667+2025, *mizrāḥ+-â*[2] [1]
eastward, 4946+7710, *min+qedem* [1]
eastward, 7708+2025, *qādîm+-â*[2] [1]
extend eastward, 7708+2025, *qādîm+-â*[2] [1]
eastward, 7711+2025+4667+2025, *qēdem+-â*[2]*+mizrāḥ+-â*[2] [1]
eastward, 7711+2025, *qēdem+-â*[2] [1]

EASY [3]
thinking it easy, 2103, *hûn* [1]
too easy on, 3104, *ḥāśak* [1]
easy, 7837, *qālal* [1]

EAT [405]
eat, 430, *'ākal* [359]
eat, *NIH/RPE* [5]
gave to eat, 430, *'ākal* [4]
eat, 4310, *lāḥam*[2] [4]
eat, 1356, *bārâ*[1] [3]
eat up, 430, *'ākal* [2]
had to eat, 430, *'ākal* [2]
make eat food, 430, *'ākal* [2]
make eat, 430, *'ākal* [2]
eat, 433, *'oklâ* [2]
something to eat, 7326+4312, *pat+leḥem* [2]
eat, 8286, *rā'â*[1] [2]
eat, 10301, *ṭᵉ'ēm*[1] [2]
eat away, 430, *'ākal* [1]
free to eat, 430+430, *'ākal+'ākal* [1]
give to eat, 430, *'ākal* [1]
have plenty to eat, 430+430, *'ākal+'ākal* [1]
must eat, 430+430, *'ākal+'ākal* [1]
prepare food to eat, 430, *'ākal* [1]
give to eat, 1356, *bārâ*[1] [1]
urged to eat, 1356, *bārâ*[1] [1]
eat, 4312, *leḥem* [1]
something to eat, 4407, *ma'ᵃkāl* [1]
have something to eat, 6184, *sā'ad* [1]
eat fill, 8425, *śāba'* [1]
all could eat, 8427, *śōba'* [1]
eat, 10030, *'ᵃkal* [1]

EATEN [57]
be eaten, 430, *'ākal* [25]
eaten, 430, *'ākal* [23]
eaten, 430+430, *'ākal+'ākal* [3]
eaten, *NIH/RPE* [1]
is eaten, 430, *'ākal* [1]
eaten away, 430, *'ākal* [1]
eaten provisions, 430+430, *'ākal+'ākal* [1]
is eaten, 430+430, *'ākal+'ākal* [1]
eaten enough, 8427, *śōba'* [1]

EATER [3]
eater, 430, *'ākal* [3]

EATING [23]
eating, 430, *'ākal* [22]
without eating, 10297, *ṭᵉwāt* [1]

EATS [28]
eats, 430, *'ākal* [25]
eats away, 430, *'ākal* [1]
eats up, 1686, *gāmā'* [1]
eats fill, 8425, *śāba'* [1]

EAVES [1]
eaves, 3258, *ṭapḥâ*[2] [1]

EBAL [7]
Ebal, 6506, *'êbāl*[1] [4]
Ebal, 6507, *'êbāl*[2] [3]

EBB [1]
ebb away, 9161, *šāpak* [1]

EBBED [1]
ebbed away, 6494, *'āṭap*[2] [1]

EBBING [1]
ebbing away, 6494, *'āṭap*[2] [1]

EBBS [1]
ebbs away, 9161, *šāpak* [1]

EBED [6]
Ebed, 6270, *'ebed*[2] [6]

EBED-MELECH [6]
Ebed-Melech, 6283, *'ebed-melek* [6]

EBENEZER [3]
Ebenezer, 75, *'eben hā'ēzer* [3]

EBER [15]
Eber, 6299, *'ēber*[2] [15]

EBEZ [1]
Ebez, 82, *'ebeṣ* [1]

EBIASAPH [3]
Ebiasaph, 47, *'ebyāsāp* [3]

EBONY [1]
ebony, 2041, *hobnîm* [1]

ECBATANA [1]
Ecbatana, 10020, *'aḥmᵉtā'* [1]

ECHO [2]
echo, 6699, *'ānâ*[1] [1]
echo, 8876, *šîr*[1] [1]

ECHOES [1]
echoes along, 5938, *nāqap*[2] [1]

EDEN [19]
Eden, 6359, *'ēden*[2] [14]
Eden, 6361, *'eden* [3]
Eden, 6360, *'ēden*[3] [2]

EDER [4]
Eder, 6374, *'ēder*[2] [2]
Eder, 6375, *'ēder*[3] [1]
Eder, 6376, *'eder* [1]

EDGE [28]
edge, 7895, *qāṣeh* [11]
edge, 8557, *śāpâ* [10]
set on edge, 7733, *qāhâ* [3]
edge, 995, *bō'* [1]
edge, 6991, *pē'â*[1] [1]
edge, 7156, *pāneh* [1]
edge, 7644, *ṣōr*[1] [1]

EDGES [5]
edges, 6991, *pē'â*[1] [4]
edges, 4053, *kānāp* [1]

EDICT [16]
edict, 2017, *dāt* [8]
edict, *NIH/RPE* [2]
edict, 10628, *qᵉyām* [2]
edict[s], 889, *'ᵃšer* [1]
edict, 1821, *dābār* [1]
edict, 7330, *pitgām* [1]
edict, 10601, *pitgām* [1]

EDOM [92]
Edom, 121, *'ᵉdôm* [79]
Edom, 824+121, *'ereṣ+'ᵉdôm* [11]
Edom[s], 2023, *-āh* [1]
Edom[s], 5647, *-nû*[2] [1]

EDOM'S [3]
Edom's, 121, *'ᵉdôm* [2]
Edom's[s], 2023, *-āh* [1]

EDOMITE [8]
Edomite, 122, *'ᵃdômî* [8]

EDOMITES [15]
Edomites, 121, *'ᵉdôm* [10]
Edomites, 122, *'ᵃdômî* [4]
Edomites, 1201+121, *bēn*[1]*+'ᵉdôm* [1]

EDREI [8]
Edrei, 167, *'edre'î* [8]

EFFECT [2]
effect, 6275, *'ᵃbōdâ* [1]
has effect, 7756, *qûm* [1]

EFFORT [2]
poured effort, 6661, *'āmal* [1]
made every effort, 10700, *šᵉdar* [1]

EFFORTS [5]
efforts, 4410, *ma'ᵃmāṣ* [1]
efforts, 6268, *'ābad* [1]
efforts, 6661, *'āmal* [1]
efforts, 6662, *'āmāl*[1] [1]
efforts, 9303, *tᵉ'unîm* [1]

EGG [1]
egg, 2733, *ḥallāmût* [1]

EGGS [7]
eggs, 1070, *bêṣâ* [5]
hatches eggs, 1842, *dāgar* [1]
lay eggs, 4880, *mālaṭ*[1] [1]

EGLAH [2]
Eglah, 6321, *ʿeglâ*[2] [2]

EGLAIM [1]
Eglaim, 104, *ʾeglayim* [1]

EGLATH SHELISHIYAH [2]
Eglath Shelishiyah, 6326, *ʿeglat šᵉlišiyyâ* [2]

EGLON [13]
Eglon, 6324, *ʿeglôn*[2] [8]
Eglon, 6323, *ʿeglôn*[1] [4]
Eglon, *NIH/RPE* [1]

EGYPT [582]
Egypt, 5213, *miṣrayim* [374]
Egypt, 824+5213, *ʾereṣ+miṣrayim* [184]
Egypt, *NIH/RPE* [7]
Egypt, 5191, *māṣôr*[3] [5]
Upper [Egypt], 7356, *patrôs* [3]
Lower Egypt, 824+5213, *ʾereṣ+miṣrayim* [2]
Upper Egypt, 824+7356, *ʾereṣ+patrôs* [2]
Egypt, 1426+5213, *bat*[1]*+miṣrayim* [1]
Egypt, 1473+5213, *gᵉbûl+miṣrayim* [1]
Egypt[s], 2023, *-āh* [1]
Egypt[s], 2257, *-ô* [1]
Egypt[s], 4392, *-ām* [1]
Lower Egypt, 5213, *miṣrayim* [1]

EGYPT'S [5]
Egypt's, 5213, *miṣrayim* [5]

EGYPTIAN [31]
Egyptian, 5212, *miṣrî* [21]
Egyptian, 5213, *miṣrayim* [10]

EGYPTIAN'S [2]
Egyptian's, 5212, *miṣrî* [2]

EGYPTIANS [89]
Egyptians, 5213, *miṣrayim* [82]
Egyptians, *NIH/RPE* [3]
Egyptians, 1201+5213, *bēn*[1]*+miṣrayim* [1]
the Egyptians[s], 2157, *-hem* [1]
Egyptians, 5212, *miṣrî* [1]
the Egyptians, 5213, *miṣrayim* [1]

EHI [1]
Ehi, 305, *ʾēḥî* [1]

EHUD [12]
Ehud, 179, *ʾēhûd* [8]
Ehud, *NIH/RPE* [2]
Ehud, 287, *ʾēḥûd* [1]
Ehud[s], 2257, *-ô* [1]

EIGHT [29]
eight, 9046, *šᵉmōneh* [29]

EIGHTEEN [12]
eighteen, 9046+6926, *šᵉmōneh+ʿeśrēh* [7]
eighteen, 9046+6925, *šᵉmōneh+ʿāśār* [4]
eighteen thousand, 8052+2256+9046+547, *ribbôʾ+wᵉ-+šᵉmōneh+ʾelep*[2] [1]

EIGHTEENTH [11]
eighteenth, 9046+6926, *šᵉmōneh+ʿeśrēh* [9]
eighteenth, 9046+6925, *šᵉmōneh+ʿāśār* [2]

EIGHTH [30]
eighth, 9029, *šᵉmînî* [27]
eighth, 9046, *šᵉmōneh* [3]

EIGHTIETH [1]
eightieth, 9046, *šᵉmōneh* [1]

EIGHTY [16]
eighty, 9046, *šᵉmōneh* [16]

EIGHTY-FIVE [4]
eighty-five, 9046+2256+2822, *šᵉmōneh+wᵉ-+ḥāmēš* [3]
eighty-five, 2822+2256+9046, *ḥāmēš+wᵉ-+šᵉmōneh* [1]

EIGHTY-SIX [1]
eighty-six, 9046+2256+9252, *šᵉmōneh+wᵉ-+šēš*[1] [1]

EIGHTY-THREE [1]
eighty-three, 8993+2256+9046, *šālōš+wᵉ-+šᵉmōneh* [1]

EITHER [31]
either or, 2256, *wᵉ-* [7]
either, 1685, *gam* [5]
either or, 196, *ʾô* [4]
on either side, 4946+7024+2256+4946+7024, *min+pōh+wᵉ-+min+pōh* [4]
either, *NIH/RPE* [3]
either, 4946, *min* [3]
at either ends[s], 4946+2296+2256+4946+2296, *min+zeh+wᵉ-+min+zeh* [2]
either, 196, *ʾô* [1]
and either, 2256, *wᵉ-* [1]
either, 4202, *lōʾ* [1]

EKER [1]
Eker, 6831, *ʿēqer*[2] [1]

EKRON [24]
Ekron, 6833, *ʿeqrôn* [22]
Ekron, 6834, *ʿeqrônî* [1]
people of Ekron, 6834, *ʿeqrônî* [1]

EL BETHEL [1]
El Bethel, 450, *ʾēl bêt-ʾēl* [1]

EL ELOHE ISRAEL [1]
El Elohe Israel, 449, *ʾēl ʾᵉlōhê yiśrāʾēl* [1]

EL PARAN [1]
El Paran, 386, *ʾêl pāʾrān* [1]

EL-BERITH [1]
El-Berith, 451, *ʾēl bᵉrît* [1]

ELA [1]
Ela, 452, *ʾēlāʾ* [1]

ELAH [16]
Elah, 462, *ʾēlâ*[2] [12]
Elah, 463, *ʾēlâ*[3] [3]
Elah[s], 2085, *hûʾ* [1]

ELAH'S [1]
Elah's, 462, *ʾēlâ*[2] [1]

ELAM [27]
Elam, 6520, *ʿêlām*[1] [14]
Elam, 6521, *ʿêlām*[2] [13]

ELAM'S [1]
Elam's, 6520, *ʿêlām*[1] [1]

ELAMITES [1]
Elamites, 10551, *ʿēlmāy* [1]

ELAPSED [1]
before elapsed, 4202+4848, *lōʾ+mālēʾ* [1]

ELASAH [2]
Elasah, 543, *ʾelʿāśâ* [2]

ELATED [1]
elated, 8523, *śāmaḥ* [1]

ELATH [7]
Elath, 397, *ʾēlat* [4]
Elath, 393, *ʾēlôt* [3]

ELATION [1]
elation, 9514, *tipʾeret* [1]

ELDAAH [2]
Eldaah, 456, *ʾeldāʿâ* [2]

ELDAD [2]
Eldad, 455, *ʾeldād* [2]

ELDER [1]
elder, 2418, *zāqēn*[2] [1]

ELDERLY [1]
elderly, 2418, *zāqēn*[2] [1]

ELDERS [129]
elders, 2418, *zāqēn*[2] [122]
elders, 10675, *śāb* [5]
elders, *NIH/RPE* [2]

ELEAD [1]
Elead, 537, *ʾelʿād* [1]

ELEADAH [1]
Eleadah, 538, *ʾelʿādâ* [1]

ELEALEH [5]
Elealeh, 542, *ʾelʿālēh* [4]
Elealeh, 541, *ʾelʿālēʾ* [1]

ELEASAH [4]
Eleasah, 543, *ʾelʿāśâ* [4]

ELEAZAR [72]
Eleazar, 540, *ʾelʿāzār* [70]
Eleazar, *NIH/RPE* [1]
Eleazar[s], 2257, *-ô* [1]

ELEAZAR'S [2]
Eleazar's, 540, *ʾelʿāzār* [2]

ELEGANCE [1]
elegance, 9444, *talpiyyôt* [1]

ELEGANT [1]
elegant, 3884, *kābôd*[2] [1]

ELEVATED [1]
elevated, 5951, *nāśāʾ* [1]

ELEVATING [1]
elevating, 5951, *nāśāʾ* [1]

ELEVEN [17]
eleven, 285+6926, *ʾeḥād+ʿeśrēh* [6]
eleven, 6954+6926, *ʿaštê+ʿeśrēh* [4]
eleven, 285+6925, *ʾeḥād+ʿāśār* [3]
eleven hundred, 547+2256+4395, *ʾelep*[2]*+wᵉ-+mēʾâ* [3]
eleven, 6954+6925, *ʿaštê+ʿāśār* [1]

ELEVENTH [17]
eleventh, 6954+6925, *ʿaštê+ʿāśār* [8]
eleventh, 6954+6926, *ʿaštê+ʿeśrēh* [5]
eleventh, 285+6926, *ʾeḥād+ʿeśrēh* [4]

ELHANAN [4]
Elhanan, 481, *ʾelḥānān* [4]

ELI [33]
Eli, 6603, *ʿēlî*[1] [27]
Eli, *NIH/RPE* [6]

ELI'S [4]
Eli's, 6603, *ʿēlî*[1] [4]

ELIAB [20]
Eliab, 482, *ʾᵉlîʾāb* [20]

ELIADA [4]
Eliada, 486, *ʾelyādāʿ* [4]

ELIAHBA [2]
Eliahba, 494, *ʾelyaḥbāʾ* [2]

ELIAKIM [12]
Eliakim, 509, *ʾelyāqîm* [12]

ELIAKIM'S [3]
Eliakim's[s], 2257, *-ô* [3]

ELIAM [2]
Eliam, 500, *ʾᵉlîʿām* [2]

ELIASAPH [6]
Eliasaph, 498, *ʾelyāsāp* [6]

ELIASHIB [15]
Eliashib, 513, *ʾelyāšîb* [15]

ELIASHIB'S [1]
Eliashib's, 513, *ʾelyāšîb* [1]

ELIATHAH [2]
Eliath[illegible]484, *ʾᵉlîʾātâ* [1]

Eliathah, 517, *'^{e}liyyātâ* [1]

ELIDAD [1]
Elidad, 485, *'^{e}lîdād* [1]

ELIEHOENAI [2]
Eliehoenai, 492, *'ely^{e}hô'ênay* [2]

ELIEL [10]
Eliel, 483, *'^{e}lî'ēl* [10]

ELIENAI [1]
Elienai, 501, *'^{e}lî'ēnay* [1]

ELIEZER [14]
Eliezer, 499, *'^{e}lî'ezer* [14]

ELIHOREPH [1]
Elihoreph, 495, *'^{e}lîḥōrep* [1]

ELIHU [10]
Elihu, 491, *'^{e}lîhû'* [6]
Elihu, 490, *'^{e}lîhû* [4]

ELIJAH [83]
Elijah, 489, *'ēliyyāhû* [60]
Elijah, *NIH/RPE* [9]
Elijah, 488, *'ēliyyâ* [8]
Elijah^{s}, 2257, *-ô* [4]
Elijah^{s}, 2085, *hû'* [1]
Elijah and Elisha^{s}, 9109+2157, *š^{e}nayim+-hem* [1]

ELIJAH'S [1]
Elijah's, 489, *'ēliyyāhû* [1]

ELIKA [1]
Elika, 508, *'^{e}lîqā'* [1]

ELIM [5]
Elim, 396, *'êlim* [5]

ELIMELECH [6]
Elimelech, 497, *'^{e}lîmelek* [6]

ELIMINATE [1]
eliminate, 3983, *kālâ^{1}* [1]

ELIMINATED [1]
eliminated, 2169, *hāmam^{1}* [1]

ELIOENAI [7]
Elioenai, 493, *'elyô'ênay* [7]

ELIPHAL [1]
Eliphal, 503, *'^{e}lîpal* [1]

ELIPHAZ [14]
Eliphaz, 502, *'^{e}lîpaz* [14]

ELIPHELEHU [2]
Eliphelehu, 504, *'^{e}lîp^{e}lēhû* [2]

ELIPHELET [8]
Eliphelet, 505, *'^{e}lîpeleṭ* [8]

ELISHA [89]
Elisha, 515, *'^{e}lîšā'* [54]
Elisha, *NIH/RPE* [29]
Elisha^{s}, 2257, *-ô* [4]
Elisha^{s}, 2085, *hû'* [1]
Elijah and Elisha^{s}, 9109+2157, *š^{e}nayim+-hem* [1]

ELISHA'S [4]
Elisha's, 515, *'^{e}lîšā'* [3]
Elisha's^{s}, 2257, *-ô* [1]

ELISHAH [3]
Elishah, 511, *'^{e}lîšâ* [3]

ELISHAMA [16]
Elishama, 514, *'^{e}lîšāmā'* [16]

ELISHAPHAT [1]
Elishaphat, 516, *'^{e}lîšāpāṭ* [1]

ELISHEBA [1]
Elisheba, 510, *'^{e}lîšeba'* [1]

ELISHUA [3]
Elishua, 512, *'^{e}lîšûa'* [3]

ELITE [1]
elite, 4436, *mibḥār^{1}* [1]

ELIZAPHAN [4]
Elizaphan, 507, *'^{e}lîṣāpān* [4]

ELIZUR [5]
Elizur, 506, *'^{e}lîṣûr* [5]

ELKANAH [20]
Elkanah, 555, *'elqānâ* [20]

ELKOSHITE [1]
Elkoshite, 556, *'elqōšî* [1]

ELLASAR [2]
Ellasar, 536, *'ellāsār* [2]

ELNAAM [1]
Elnaam, 534, *'elnā'am* [1]

ELNATHAN [7]
Elnathan, 535, *'elnātān* [7]

ELON [7]
Elon, 390, *'êlôn^{1}* [4]
Elon, 472, *'ēlōn^{2}* [2]
Elon, 391, *'êlôn^{2}* [1]

ELON BETHHANAN [1]
Elon Bethhanan, 392, *'êlôn bêt ḥānān* [1]

ELONITE [1]
Elonite, 533, *'ēlōnî* [1]

ELOQUENT [1]
eloquent, 408+1821, *'îš^{1}+dābār* [1]

ELPAAL [3]
Elpaal, 551, *'elpa'al* [3]

ELPELET [1]
Elpelet, 550, *'elpeleṭ* [1]

ELSE [54]
else, *NIH/RPE* [8]
else, *AIT* [7]
else, 337, *'aḥēr^{1}* [4]
anyone else, 2424, *zār* [4]
else, 2424, *zār* [3]
else, 6388, *'ôd* [3]
anywhere else, 625+2025+2256+625+2025, *'ān+-â^{2}+w^{e}-+'ān+-â^{2}* [2]
else^{s}, 132, *'ādām^{1}* [1]
or else, 196, *'ô* [1]
anyone else^{s}, 278, *'āḥ^{2}* [1]
someone else, 337, *'aḥēr^{1}* [1]
what else, 375, *'êk* [1]
else^{s}, 889, *'^{a}šer* [1]
everything else, 889, *'^{a}šer* [1]
someone else^{s}, 928+3338, *b^{e}-+yād* [1]
else, 1821, *dābār* [1]
else, 2085, *hû'* [1]
else, 3578, *yāsap* [1]
everyone else, 3972+7736, *kōl+qāhāl* [1]
else, 4202, *lō'* [1]
else^{s}, 5464, *mišmār^{1}* [1]
pretend to be someone else, 5796, *nākar^{2}* [1]
someone else, 5799, *nokrî* [1]
something else, 6388, *'ôd* [1]
anyone else^{s}, 6639, *'am^{2}* [1]
or else, 7153, *pen* [1]
someone else, 8295, *r^{e}'ût^{1}* [1]
something else, 8740, *šûb^{1}* [1]
someone else, 10025, *'oḥ^{o}rān* [1]
anything else, 10692, *š^{e}'ār* [1]

ELSE'S [2]
someone else's, 337, *'aḥēr^{1}* [1]
else's, 4392, *-ām* [1]

ELSEWHERE [5]
elsewhere, *NIH/RPE* [2]
elsewhere, 10692, *š^{e}'ār* [2]
elsewhere, 2575, *ḥûṣ* [1]

ELTEKEH [2]
Eltekeh, 558, *'elt^{e}qē'* [1]
Eltekeh, 559, *'elt^{e}qēh* [1]

ELTEKON [1]
Eltekon, 560, *'elt^{e}qôn* [1]

ELTOLAD [2]
Eltolad, 557, *'eltôlad* [2]

ELUDE [1]
elude, 6, *'ābad* [1]

ELUDED [2]
eluded, 6015+4946+7156, *sābab+min+pāneh* [1]
eluded, 7080, *pāṭar* [1]

ELUL [1]
Elul, 469, *'^{e}lûl^{1}* [1]

ELUZAI [1]
Eluzai, 539, *'el'ûzay* [1]

ELZABAD [2]
Elzabad, 479, *'elzābād* [2]

ELZAPHAN [2]
Elzaphan, 553, *'elṣāpān* [2]

EMASCULATED [1]
been emasculated, 7205, *pāṣa'* [1]

EMBALM [1]
embalm, 2846, *ḥānaṭ^{2}* [1]

EMBALMED [2]
embalmed, 2846, *ḥānaṭ^{2}* [2]

EMBALMING [1]
embalming, 2847, *ḥ^{a}nuṭîm* [1]

EMBARRASS [1]
embarrass, 4007, *kālam* [1]

EMBARRASSMENT [1]
embarrassment, 1017, *bôš^{1}* [1]

EMBEDDED [1]
firmly embedded, 5749, *nāṭa'* [1]

EMBERS [2]
embers, 1624, *gaḥal* [1]
glowing embers, 4611, *môqēd* [1]

EMBITTERED [1]
embittered, 9111, *šānan^{1}* [1]

EMBRACE [5]
embrace, 2485, *ḥābaq* [3]
embrace, 2616, *ḥāzaq* [1]
embrace, 2668, *ḥêq* [1]

EMBRACED [6]
embraced, 2485, *ḥābaq* [3]
embraced, 2616, *ḥāzaq* [2]
embraced, 6584+7418, *'al^{2}+ṣawwā'r* [1]

EMBRACES [2]
embraces, 2485, *ḥābaq* [2]

EMBRACING [1]
embracing, 296, *'āḥaz^{1}* [1]

EMBROIDERED [10]
embroidered, 8391, *riqmâ* [4]
embroidered work, 8391, *riqmâ* [2]
embroidered cloth, 8391, *riqmâ* [1]
embroidered dress, 8391, *riqmâ* [1]
embroidered garments, 8391, *riqmâ* [1]
highly embroidered, 8391, *riqmâ* [1]

EMBROIDERER [7]
embroiderer, 8387, *rāqam* [7]

EMBROIDERERS [1]
embroiderers, 8387, *rāqam* [1]

EMEK KEZIZ [1]
Emek Keziz, 6681, *'ēmeq q^{e}ṣîṣ* [1]

EMERALD [3]
emerald, 3402, *yāh^{a}lōm* [3]

EMERGE [1]
emerge, 6641, *ʿāmad* [1]

EMISSION [6]
emission, 8887, *šikbâ* [4]
emission, 2444, *zirmâ* [1]
emission, 7937, *qāreh* [1]

EMITES [3]
Emites, 400, *ʾêmîm* [3]

EMPIRE [4]
empire, 824, *ʾereṣ* [2]
empire, 4895, *malkût* [2]

EMPLOYED [1]
employed, 976, *bādal* [1]

EMPTIED [4]
emptied, 1763, *gāraš*[1] [1]
emptied, 6867, *ʿārâ*[1] [1]
emptied, 7155, *pānâ* [1]
emptied, 8199, *rêq* [1]

EMPTIES [1]
empties, 3655, *yāṣāʾ* [1]

EMPTY [29]
empty, 8199, *rêq* [4]
empty, 7212, *pāqad* [3]
empty, 8200, *rêqām* [3]
empty, 983, *bōhû* [2]
empty words, 1821+8557, *dābār+śāpâ* [2]
empty, 9332, *tōhû* [2]
empty, 1338, *bar*[2] [1]
empty talk, 2039, *hebel*[1] [1]
empty, 3655, *yāṣāʾ* [1]
empty, 3803, *yešaḥ* [1]
empty, 4202+4027, *lōʾ+kēn*[2] [1]
empty stomachs, 5931+9094,
niqqāyôn+šēn[1] [1]
empty, 6867, *ʿārâ*[1] [1]
empty, 8120, *rûaḥ* [1]
empty, 8197, *rîq*[1] [1]
leaves empty, 8197, *rîq*[1] [1]
empty, 8198, *rîq*[2] [1]
empty plea, 8736, *šāwʾ* [1]
empty space, 9332, *tōhû* [1]

EMPTY-HANDED [9]
empty-handed, 8200, *rêqām* [9]

EMPTYING [2]
emptying, 8197, *rîq*[1] [2]

EN EGLAIM [1]
En Eglaim, 6536, *ʿên ʿeglayim* [1]

EN GANNIM [3]
En Gannim, 6528, *ʿên gannîm* [3]

EN GEDI [6]
En Gedi, 6527, *ʿên gedî* [6]

EN HADDAH [1]
En Haddah, 6532, *ʿên ḥaddâ* [1]

EN HAKKORE [1]
En Hakkore, 6530, *ʿên haqqōrēʾ* [1]

EN HAZOR [1]
En Hazor, 6533, *ʿên ḥāṣôr* [1]

EN MISHPAT [1]
En Mishpat, 6535, *ʿên mišpāṭ* [1]

EN RIMMON [1]
En Rimmon, 6538, *ʿên rimmôn* [1]

EN ROGEL [4]
En Rogel, 6537, *ʿên rōgēl* [4]

EN SHEMESH [2]
En Shemesh, 6539, *ʿên šemeš* [2]

EN TAPPUAH [1]
En Tappuah, 6540, *ʿên tappûaḥ* [1]

ENABLE [1]
enable, 8948, *šālaṭ* [1]

ENABLED [2]
enabled to walk, 2143, *hālak* [1]
enabled, 5989, *nātan* [1]

ENABLES [4]
enables to stand, 6641, *ʿāmad* [2]
enables to go, 2005, *dārak* [1]
enables, 8948, *šālaṭ* [1]

ENAIM [2]
Enaim, 6542, *ʿênayim* [2]

ENAM [1]
Enam, 6543, *ʿênām* [1]

ENAN [5]
Enan, 6544, *ʿênān* [5]

ENCAMP [9]
encamp, 2837, *ḥānâ*[1] [9]

ENCAMPED [14]
encamped, 2837, *ḥānâ*[1] [12]
encamped, 3655+4722, *yāṣāʾ+maḥ^{a}neh* [1]
encamped, 8905, *šākan* [1]

ENCAMPS [1]
encamps, 2837, *ḥānâ*[1] [1]

ENCHANTER [4]
enchanter, 10081, *ʾāšap* [2]
enchanter, 2489+2490, *ḥābar*[2]*+ḥeber*[1] [1]
enchanter, 4318, *laḥaš* [1]

ENCHANTERS [6]
enchanters, 10081, *ʾāšap* [4]
enchanters, 879, *ʾaššāp* [2]

ENCIRCLE [2]
encircle, 4193, *kātar*[2] [1]
encircle, 7443+6584, *ṣûr*[1]*+ʿal*[2] [1]

ENCIRCLED [4]
encircled, 5938, *nāqap*[2] [1]
encircled, 6017+6015, *sābîb+sābab* [1]
encircled, 6017+6017+6015,
sābîb+sābîb+sābab [1]
encircled, 6048, *sûg*[2] [1]

ENCIRCLING [2]
encircling, 6015, *sābab* [1]
encircling, 6017, *sābîb* [1]

ENCLOSE [1]
enclose, 7443, *ṣûr*[1] [1]

ENCLOSED [3]
enclosed, 2958, *ḥāṣēr*[1] [1]
enclosed, 3159, *ḥātam* [1]
enclosed, 7788, *qāṭar*[2] [1]

ENCOUNTER [3]
encounter, 7193, *paʿam* [2]
encounter, 995+928, *bôʾ+b^{e}-* [1]

ENCOURAGE [9]
encourage, 2616, *ḥāzaq* [4]
encourage, 599, *ʾāmēṣ* [1]
encourage, 887, *ʾāšar*[2] [1]
encourage, 1819+6584+4213,
dābar[2]*+ʿal*[2]*+lēb* [1]
dreams encourage to have, 2706+2731,
ḥ^{a}lôm+ḥālam[2] [1]
encourage, 3922+4213, *kûn*[1]*+lēb* [1]

ENCOURAGED [6]
encouraged, 2616+3338, *ḥāzaq+yād* [2]
encouraged, 2616, *ḥāzaq* [2]
encouraged, 1819+6584+4222,
dābar[2]*+ʿal*[2]*+lēbāb* [1]
encouraged, 3446, *yōʿēṣ* [1]

ENCOURAGES [1]
encourages, 2616, *ḥāzaq* [1]

ENCOURAGINGLY [1]
encouragingly, 6584+4213, *ʿal*[2]*+lēb* [1]

ENCROACH [2]
encroach, 995, *bôʾ* [1]
encroach, 7928, *qārab* [1]

ENCRUSTED [1]
encrusted, 2689, *ḥelʾâ*[1] [1]

END [229]
end, 7891, *qēṣ* [40]
end, 7895, *qāṣeh* [28]
end, 344, *ʾaḥ^{a}rît* [20]
put an end, 8697, *šābat*[1] [14]
end, 340, *ʾaḥ^{a}rôn* [10]
far end, 3752, *y^{e}rēkâ* [6]
end, 3986, *kālâ*[3] [6]
end, *NIH/RPE* [5]
end, 3983, *kālâ*[1] [4]
put an end, 3983, *kālâ*[1] [4]
end, 6991, *pēʾâ*[1] [4]
end, 7023, *peh* [4]
end, 7812, *qîṣôn* [4]
end, 7896, *qāṣā*[2] [4]
end, 9462, *tāmam* [4]
horrible end, 1166, *ballāhâ* [3]
end, 2118+9362, *hāyâ+tôṣāʾôt* [3]
come to an end, 8697, *šābat*[1] [3]
come to an end, 3983, *kālâ*[1] [2]
put an end, 4162, *kārat* [2]
at either ends, 4946+2296+2256+4946+2296,
min+zeh+w^{e}-+min+zeh [2]
end, 6067, *sôp* [2]
in the end, 6330, *ʿad*[2] [2]
end, 7897, *qēṣeh* [2]
end, 7921, *q^{e}ṣāt* [2]
bring an end, 8697, *šābat*[1] [2]
made an end, 8966, *šālēm*[1] [2]
put an end, 9462, *tāmam* [2]
in the end, 343, *ʾaḥ^{a}ray* [1]
end of life, 344, *ʾaḥ^{a}rît* [1]
put an end, 430, *ʾākal* [1]
come to an end, 699, *ʾāpēs* [1]
end, 784, *ʾōraḥ* [1]
bring to an end, 1698, *gāmar* [1]
end, 2118+928+2021+340,
hāyâ+b^{e}-+ha-+ʾaḥ^{a}rôn [1]
come to an end, 2951, *ḥāṣas*[1] [1]
end, 3655, *yāṣāʾ* [1]
end, 3752, *y^{e}rēkâ* [1]
no end, 3869+1896, *k^{e}-+day* [1]
at wits end, 3972+2683+1182,
kōl+ḥokmâ+bālaʿ[3] [1]
came to an end, 3983, *kālâ*[1] [1]
made an end, 3983, *kālâ*[1] [1]
make an end, 3983, *kālâ*[1] [1]
to the very end, 4200+6409+6813,
l^{e}-[1]*+ʿôlām+ʿēqeb* [1]
end, 4637, *mût* [1]
come to an end, 4848, *mālēʾ*[1] [1]
meet end, 6066, *sûp*[1] [1]
end, 6073, *sûr*[1] [1]
stood on end, 6169, *sāmar* [1]
put an end, 6296, *ʿābar*[1] [1]
end, 6330, *ʿad*[2] [1]
in the end, 6330+889, *ʿad*[2]*+ʾ^{a}šer* [1]
until the end of, 6330, *ʿad*[2] [1]
to the end, 6813, *ʿēqeb* [1]
end, 6961, *ʿēt* [1]
end, 7156, *pāneh* [1]
far end, 7164, *p^{e}nîmî* [1]
end, 7551, *ṣāmat* [1]
end, 7895+1473, *qāṣeh+g^{e}bûl* [1]
far end, 7895, *qāṣeh* [1]
end, 8492+7874, *śîm+qeneṣ* [1]
bring to an end, 8697, *šābat*[1] [1]
end, 8966, *šālēm*[1] [1]
ends, 9133, *šaʿar*[1] [1]
end, 9417, *taklît* [1]
meet end, 9462, *tāmam* [1]
bring to an end, 10508, *sûp* [1]

end, 10509, *sôp* [1]
never end, 10527+10509+10002, *ʿad+sôp+-āʾ* [1]
end, 10636, *qeṣāt* [1]
brought to an end, 10719, *šelim* [1]

ENDANGER [1]
endanger, 8845, *šāḥat* [1]

ENDANGERED [1]
be endangered, 6124, *sākan[3]* [1]

ENDANGERS [1]
do anything that endangers life, 6641+6584+1947, *ʿāmad+ʿal[2]+dām* [1]

ENDED [13]
ended, 2118+9362, *hāyâ+tôṣāʾôt* [5]
ended, 3983, *kālâ[1]* [3]
ended, 8697, *šābat[1]* [2]
ended, *NIH/RPE* [1]
ended, 8938, *šālaḥ* [1]
ended, 9462, *tāmam* [1]

ENDING [4]
ending, 2118+9362, *hāyâ+tôṣāʾôt* [3]
ending, 3983, *kālâ[1]* [1]

ENDLESS [7]
endless, 401+7891, *ʾayin[1]+qēṣ* [1]
endless, 401+7897, *ʾayin[1]+qēṣeh* [1]
endless, 802, *ʾōrek* [1]
endless generations, 1887+2256+1887, *dôr[2]+we-+dôr[2]* [1]
endless, 4200+5905, *le-[1]+nēṣaḥ[1]* [1]
endless, 6330+6409, *ʿad[2]+ʿôlām* [1]
endless, 9458, *tāmîd* [1]

ENDOR [3]
Endor, 6529, *ʿên-dōʾr* [3]

ENDOW [2]
not endow, 5960, *nāšâ[1]* [1]
endow, 5989, *nātan* [1]

ENDOWED [4]
endowed with splendor, 6995, *pāʾar[2]* [2]
endowed with, 3359, *yādaʿ* [1]
endowed, 8883, *šît[1]* [1]

ENDS [59]
ends, 7895, *qāṣeh* [16]
ends, 700, *ʾepes* [14]
ends, 7896, *qāṣâ[2]* [11]
ends, 3752, *yerēkâ* [4]
ends, *NIH/RPE* [2]
ends, 4053, *kānāp* [2]
ends, 7898, *qāṣû* [2]
ends, 8031, *rōʾš[1]* [2]
ends up, 339, *ʾaḥar* [1]
ends, 2118, *hāyâ* [1]
ends, 5102, *maʿaneh[2]* [1]
ends, 6330, *ʿad[2]* [1]
selfish ends, 9294, *taʾawâ[1]* [1]
ends, 10509, *sôp* [1]

ENDUED [1]
endued with, 6640, *ʿim* [1]

ENDURE [30]
endure, 6641, *ʿāmad* [5]
endure, 2118, *hāyâ* [4]
endure, 5951, *nāśāʾ* [4]
endure, 3920, *kûl* [3]
endure, 7756, *qûm* [3]
endure, *NIH/RPE* [2]
endure, 586, *ʾāman[1]* [1]
endure, 799, *ʾārak* [1]
endure, 2118+4200, *hāyâ+le-[1]* [1]
endure, 2656, *ḥîl[2]* [1]
endure, 3523, *yākōl* [1]
as long as endure, 3869+3427, *ke-+yôm[1]* [1]
endure, 3922, *kûn[1]* [1]
endure, 4328, *lîn* [1]
endure, 10624, *qûm* [1]

ENDURED [3]
endured, 8425, *śābaʿ* [2]
hardships endured, 6700, *ʿānâ[2]* [1]

ENDURES [58]
endures, *NIH/RPE* [51]
endures, 6641, *ʿāmad* [4]
endures, 3427, *yôm[1]* [1]
endures, 3782, *yāšab* [1]
endures, 10629, *qayyām* [1]

ENDURING [4]
enduring, 419, *ʾêtān[1]* [1]
enduring, 586, *ʾāman[1]* [1]
enduring, 6641, *ʿāmad* [1]
enduring, 6982, *ʿātēq* [1]

ENEMIES [252]
enemies, 367, *ʾōyēb* [191]
enemies, 7640, *ṣar[2]* [28]
enemies, 8533, *śānēʾ* [9]
enemies, 7675, *ṣārar[2]* [7]
enemies, 7756, *qûm* [3]
the enemies[s], 4392, *-ām* [2]
enemies, 408+5194, *ʾîš[1]+maṣṣût* [1]
enemies[s], 2157, *-hem* [1]
enemies, 2424, *zār* [1]
his enemies[s], 4392, *-ām* [1]
the enemies, 4392, *-ām* [1]
their enemies[s], 4392, *-ām* [1]
my enemies[s], 4564, *-mô* [1]
treat as enemies, 7675, *ṣārar[2]* [1]
treated as enemies, 7675, *ṣārar[2]* [1]
enemies, 8533+5883, *śānēʾ+nepeš* [1]
enemies, 8806, *šōrēr* [1]
enemies, 10686, *śenāʾ* [1]

ENEMY [94]
enemy, 367, *ʾōyēb* [70]
enemy, 7640, *ṣar[2]* [11]
enemy, 7675, *ṣārar[2]* [4]
enemy, *NIH/RPE* [3]
enemy, 8533, *śānēʾ* [3]
enemy, 366, *ʾāyab* [1]
enemy[s], 2257, *-ô* [1]
enemy, 6839, *ʿār[1]* [1]

ENEMY'S [3]
enemy's, 367, *ʾōyēb* [1]
the enemy's[s], 2257, *-ô* [1]
enemy's, 8533, *śānēʾ* [1]

ENFOLDS [1]
enfolds, 4286, *lûṭ* [1]

ENFORCE [1]
enforce, 10772, *teqip* [1]

ENGAGE [9]
engage, 6913, *ʿāśâ[1]* [3]
engage, *NIH/RPE* [2]
engage, 1741, *gārâ* [1]
engage in prostitution, 2388, *zānâ[1]* [1]
engage in battle, 4309, *lāḥam[1]* [1]
engage in battle, 5590, *nāgaḥ* [1]

ENGAGED [6]
engaged in prostitution, 2388, *zānâ[1]* [4]
engaged in, 2118, *hāyâ* [1]
engaged in, 6913, *ʿāśâ[1]* [1]

ENGAGES [1]
engages in witchcraft, 4175, *kāšap* [1]

ENGAGING [1]
engaging in prostitution, 2388, *zānâ[1]* [1]

ENGRAVE [4]
engrave, 7338, *pātaḥ[2]* [3]
engrave, 7338+7334, *pātaḥ[2]+pittûaḥ* [1]

ENGRAVED [9]
engraved, 4180, *kātab* [2]
engraved, 7334, *pittûaḥ* [2]
engraved, 2933, *ḥāšēb[1]* [1]
engraved, 2980, *ḥāqaq* [1]
engraved, 3100, *ḥārat* [1]
engraved, 7338+7334, *pātaḥ[2]+pittûaḥ* [1]
engraved, 7338, *pātaḥ[2]* [1]

ENGRAVES [1]
engraves, 7334, *pittûaḥ* [1]

ENGRAVING [3]
engraving, 5237, *miqlaʿat* [1]
art of engraving, 7338+7334, *pātaḥ[2]+pittûaḥ* [1]
experienced in engraving, 7338+7334, *pātaḥ[2]+pittûaḥ* [1]

ENGULF [3]
engulf, 8851, *šāṭap* [2]
engulf, 6015, *sābab* [1]

ENGULFED [3]
engulfed, 4059, *kāsâ* [1]
engulfed, 5938, *nāqap[2]* [1]
engulfed, 8851, *šāṭap* [1]

ENGULFING [1]
engulfing, 705, *ʾāpap* [1]

ENJOY [34]
enjoy, 430, *ʾākal* [5]
enjoy, 8011, *rāʾâ[1]* [5]
enjoy, 2725, *ḥālal[1]* [4]
enjoy, 8354, *rāṣâ[1]* [3]
enjoy, 3512, *yāṭab* [2]
enjoy, 8523, *śāmaḥ* [2]
enjoy a long life, 799+3427, *ʾārak+yôm[1]* [1]
enjoy long life, 799+3427, *ʾārak+yôm[1]* [1]
long enjoy, 1162, *bālâ[1]* [1]
let enjoy, 1655, *gālâ* [1]
enjoy, 3359, *yādaʿ* [1]
enjoy ourselves, 6632, *ʿālas* [1]
enjoy, 6632, *ʿālas* [1]
enjoy, 6695, *ʿānag* [1]
enjoy fragrance, 8193, *rîaḥ* [1]
enjoy pasture, 8286, *rāʿâ[1]* [1]
enjoy plenty, 8425, *śābaʿ* [1]
enjoy, 8425, *śābaʿ* [1]
enjoy ease, 8631, *šāʾan* [1]

ENJOYED [5]
enjoyed, 430, *ʾākal* [1]
enjoyed sweet, 5517, *mātaq* [1]
enjoyed, 8354, *rāṣâ[1]* [1]
enjoyed long life, 8428+3427, *śābēaʿ+yôm[1]* [1]
enjoyed peace, 9200, *šāqaṭ* [1]

ENJOYING [2]
enjoying, *NIH/RPE* [1]
enjoying, 3512, *yāṭab* [1]

ENJOYMENT [3]
find enjoyment, 2591, *ḥûš[2]* [1]
enjoyment, 3208, *ṭôbâ* [1]
enjoyment, 8525, *śimḥâ* [1]

ENJOYS [3]
enjoys, 430, *ʾākal* [2]
enjoys, *NIH/RPE* [1]

ENLARGE [3]
enlarge, 8143, *rāḥab* [2]
enlarge, 8049, *rābâ[1]* [1]

ENLARGED [5]
enlarged, 3578, *yāsap* [2]
enlarged, 2226, *hāreh* [1]
enlarged, 8049, *rābâ[1]* [1]
enlarged, 8143, *rāḥab* [1]

ENLARGES [4]
enlarges, 8143, *rāḥab* [3]
enlarges, 8848, *šāṭaḥ* [1]

ENLIGHTEN [1]
enlighten, 1067, *bîn* [1]

ENMITY [1]
enmity, 368, *ʾêbâ* [1]

ENOCH [10]
Enoch, 2840, *ḥanôk[1]* [10]

ENORMOUS [2]
enormous, 10647, *rab* [1]
enormous, 10678, *śaggîʾ* [1]

ENOSH [7]
Enosh, 633, *ʾ^{e}nôš^{2}* [7]

ENOUGH [77]
enough, *AIT* [17]
enough, 8041, *rab^{1}* [6]
not enough, 5071, *m^{e}ʿaṭ* [5]
enough, 1896, *day* [4]
enough, *NIH/RPE* [3]
get enough, 8425, *śābaʿ* [3]
have enough, 8425, *śābaʿ* [3]
enough, 2104, *hôn* [2]
isn't enough, 5071, *m^{e}ʿaṭ* [2]
have enough, 5162, *māṣāʾ* [2]
enough, 6330, *ʿad^{2}* [2]
long enough, 8041, *rab^{1}* [2]
had enough, 8425, *śābaʿ* [2]
has enough, 8425, *śābaʿ* [2]
had food enough, 430, *ʾākal* [1]
enough, 1821, *dābār* [1]
just enough, 1896, *day* [1]
room enough, 1896, *day* [1]
no enough, 2532, *ḥādal^{1}* [1]
large enough, 3869, *k^{e}-* [1]
enough, 4027, *kēn^{2}* [1]
enough, 4200+4537+1896, *l^{e-1}+mâ+day* [1]
enough, 4394, *m^{e}ʾōd* [1]
wasn't enough, 5071, *m^{e}ʿaṭ* [1]
be room enough, 5162, *māṣāʾ* [1]
enough, 5162, *māṣāʾ* [1]
even enough, 6330, *ʿad^{2}* [1]
not enough, 7781+6388, *qāṭōn^{1}+ʿôd* [1]
not enough, 7781, *qāṭōn^{1}* [1]
gone far enough, 8041, *rab^{1}* [1]
have more than enough, 8425, *śābaʿ* [1]
eaten enough, 8427, *śōbaʿ* [1]
enough, 8429, *śobʿâ* [1]
deep enough to swim in, 8467, *śāḥû* [1]
enough, 8563, *śāpaq^{2}* [1]
enough, 9311, *t^{e}bûʾâ* [1]

ENRAGED [6]
enraged, 7911, *qāṣap* [2]
enraged, 2408, *zaʿap* [1]
enraged, 4848+2779, *mālēʾ^{1}+ḥēmâ* [1]
enraged, 6192+4213, *sāʿar+lēb* [1]
enraged, 8074, *rāgaz* [1]

ENRICH [2]
enrich, *NIH/RPE* [1]
enrich, 6947, *ʿāšar* [1]

ENRICHED [2]
enriched, 4848, *mālēʾ^{1}* [1]
enriched, 6947, *ʿāšar* [1]

ENROLL [2]
enroll, 7212, *pāqad* [2]

ENROLLED [1]
enrolled in the genealogical records, 3509, *yāḥaś* [1]

ENROLLMENT [1]
enrollment, 7213, *p^{e}quddâ* [1]

ENSLAVE [3]
enslave, 6268, *ʿābad* [3]

ENSLAVED [6]
enslaved, 6268, *ʿābad* [3]
been enslaved, 3899, *kābaš* [1]
enslaved, 3899+4200+6269+2256+4200+9148, *kābaš+l^{e-1}+ʿebed^{1}+w^{e}-+l^{e-1}+šipḥâ* [1]
enslaved, 4835, *mākar* [1]

ENSLAVING [1]
enslaving, 6268, *ʿābad* [1]

ENSNARE [7]
ensnare, 7421, *ṣûd* [4]
ensnare, 4334, *lākad* [2]
ensnare, 7772, *qûš* [1]

ENSNARED [5]
are ensnared, 3704, *yāqaš* [1]
be ensnared, 3704, *yāqaš* [1]
ensnared, 4334, *lākad* [1]
ensnared, 4613, *môqēš* [1]
be ensnared, 5943, *nāqaš* [1]

ENSURE [1]
ensure, 6842, *ʿārab^{1}* [1]

ENTANGLE [1]
entangle, 4334, *lākad* [1]

ENTANGLED [3]
entangled, 705, *ʾāpap* [2]
entangled, 6018, *sābak* [1]

ENTER [105]
enter, 995+448, *bôʾ+ʾel* [32]
enter, 995, *bôʾ* [31]
enter, 995+928, *bôʾ+b^{e}-* [24]
enter, 448+995, *ʾel+bôʾ* [4]
enter, 6590+6584, *ʿālâ+ʿal^{2}* [4]
enter, 4427, *mābôʾ* [2]
enter, 928+995, *b^{e}-+bôʾ* [1]
enter, 995+4200, *bôʾ+l^{e-1}* [1]
enter, 995+6584, *bôʾ+ʿal^{2}* [1]
make enter, 995+928, *bôʾ+b^{e}-* [1]
enter, 6296, *ʿābar^{1}* [1]
enter, 6584+995, *ʿal^{2}+bôʾ* [1]
enter service, 6641+4200+7156, *ʿāmad+l^{e-1}+pāneh* [1]
enter into judgment, 9149, *šāpaṭ* [1]

ENTERED [61]
entered, 995, *bôʾ* [19]
entered, 995+448, *bôʾ+ʾel* [17]
entered, 995+928, *bôʾ+b^{e}-* [8]
entered, 995+4200, *bôʾ+l^{e-1}* [3]
entered, *NIH/RPE* [2]
entered service, 6641+4200+7156, *ʿāmad+l^{e-1}+pāneh* [2]
entered and went, 995, *bôʾ* [1]
entered, 995+2025, *bôʾ+-â^{2}* [1]
entered, 995+6584, *bôʾ+ʿal^{2}* [1]
entered, 995+928+9348, *bôʾ+b^{e}-+tāwek* [1]
entered, 2143+6330, *hālak+ʿad^{2}* [1]
were entered in the genealogical records, 3509, *yāḥaś* [1]
entered, 4162, *kārat* [1]
entered, 6073+448, *sûr^{1}+ʾel* [1]
entered, 6590, *ʿālâ* [1]
entered the service, 6641+4200+7156, *ʿāmad+l^{e-1}+pāneh* [1]

ENTERING [21]
entering, 995, *bôʾ* [12]
entering, 995+4200, *bôʾ+l^{e-1}* [2]
entering, *NIH/RPE* [1]
entering, 995+2025, *bôʾ+-â^{2}* [1]
entering, 995+448, *bôʾ+ʾel* [1]
entering, 995+6330, *bôʾ+ʿad^{2}* [1]
entering, 995+928+7931, *bôʾ+b^{e}-+qereb* [1]
entering, 995+928+9348, *bôʾ+b^{e}-+tāwek* [1]
entering, 995+928, *bôʾ+b^{e}-* [1]

ENTERS [16]
enters, 995, *bôʾ* [8]
enters, 995+448, *bôʾ+ʾel* [5]
enters, 995+2025, *bôʾ+-â^{2}* [1]
enters, 995+4200, *bôʾ+l^{e-1}* [1]
enters, 995+928, *bôʾ+b^{e}-* [1]

ENTERTAIN [1]
entertain, 8471, *śāḥaq* [1]

ENTERTAINMENT [1]
entertainment, 10166, *dah^{a}wâ* [1]

ENTHRALLED [1]
enthralled, 203, *ʾāwâ^{1}* [1]

ENTHRONED [20]
enthroned, 3782, *yāšab* [11]
sit enthroned, 3782, *yāšab* [5]
sits enthroned, 3782, *yāšab* [4]

ENTHRONES [1]
enthrones, 4200+2021+4058+3782, *l^{e-1}+ha-+kissēʾ+yāšab* [1]

ENTICE [5]
entice, 7331, *pātâ^{1}* [5]

ENTICED [7]
enticed, 7331, *pātâ^{1}* [2]
be enticed, 5615, *nādaḥ^{1}* [1]
enticed, 5615, *nādaḥ^{1}* [1]
been enticed, 7331, *pātâ^{1}* [1]
enticed, 7331+4222, *pātâ^{1}+lēbāb* [1]
is enticed, 7331, *pātâ^{1}* [1]

ENTICES [3]
entices, 6077, *sût^{1}* [2]
entices, 7331, *pātâ^{1}* [1]

ENTICING [2]
enticing, 7331, *pātâ^{1}* [2]

ENTIRE [85]
entire, 3972, *kōl* [82]
entire, 4946+7895, *min+qāṣeh* [1]
entire, 9459, *tāmîm* [1]
entire, 10353, *kōl* [1]

ENTIRELY [4]
entirely, 4003, *kālîl* [2]
let go entirely unpunished, 5927+5927, *nāqâ+nāqâ* [2]

ENTRAILS [1]
entrails, 4302, *l^{e}ḥûm^{1}* [1]

ENTRANCE [137]
entrance, 7339, *petaḥ* [110]
entrance, 9133, *šaʿar^{1}* [10]
entrance, 4427, *mābôʾ* [7]
entrance, 995, *bôʾ* [4]
entrance, *NIH/RPE* [2]
entrance, 415, *ʾîtôn* [1]
entrance, 929, *biʾâ* [1]
entrance, 6197, *sap^{3}* [1]
entrance, 7339+9133, *petaḥ+šaʿar^{1}* [1]

ENTRANCES [5]
entrances, 7339, *petaḥ* [3]
entrances, 4427+7339, *mābôʾ+petaḥ* [1]
entrances, 4569, *môbāʾ* [1]

ENTREAT [3]
entreat, 2704+906+7156, *ḥālâ^{2}+ʾēt^{1}+pāneh* [3]

ENTREATY [2]
was moved by entreaty, 6983, *ʿātar^{1}* [2]

ENTRUST [2]
entrust, 5989, *nātan* [2]

ENTRUSTED [16]
entrusted, 5989, *nātan* [8]
entrusted with, 928+575, *b^{e}-+ʾ^{e}mûnâ* [2]
entrusted to, 448+3338, *ʾel+yād* [1]
entrusted to, 928+3338, *b^{e}-+yād* [1]
was entrusted, 5989, *nātan* [1]
something entrusted, 7214, *piqqādôn* [1]
was entrusted, 7214+7212, *piqqādôn+pāqad* [1]
entrusted, 10314, *y^{e}hab* [1]

ENTRYWAY [1]
entryway, 4427, *mābôʾ* [1]

ENTWINES [1]
entwines, 6018, *sābak* [1]

ENVELOPED [1]
enveloped, 4946+6017, *min+sābîb* [1]

ENVIED [2]
envied, 7861, *qānāʾ* [2]

ENVIOUS [4]
envious, 7861, *qānāʾ* [3]
make envious, 7861, *qānāʾ* [1]

ENVOY [3]
envoy, 7495, *ṣîr^{3}* [3]

ENVOYS [12]
envoys, 4855, *malʾāk* [6]
envoys, *NIH/RPE* [1]

the envoys[s], 2157, *-hem* [1]
envoys, 3134, *ḥašman* [1]
envoys, 4885, *mēlîṣ* [1]
envoys, 6269, *ʿebed[1]* [1]
envoys, 7495, *ṣîr[3]* [1]

ENVY [8]
envy, 7861, *qānāʾ* [4]
envy, 7863, *qinʾâ* [3]
gaze in envy, 8353, *rāṣad* [1]

EPHAH [52]
ephah, 406, *ʾêpâ* [29]
ephah, *NIH/RPE* [18]
Ephah, 6549, *ʿêpâ[3]* [4]
Ephah, 6548, *ʿêpâ[2]* [1]

EPHAI [1]
Ephai, 6550, *ʿêpay* [1]

EPHER [4]
Epher, 6761, *ʿēper* [4]

EPHES DAMMIM [1]
Ephes Dammim, 702, *ʾepes dammîm* [1]

EPHLAL [2]
Ephlal, 697, *ʾeplāl* [2]

EPHOD [50]
ephod, 680, *ʾēpōd[1]* [46]
the ephod[s], 5647, *-nû[2]* [2]
ephod, 681, *ʾēpōd[2]* [1]
the ephod[s], 2257, *-ô* [1]

EPHRAIM [156]
Ephraim, 713, *ʾeprayim* [148]
Ephraim, 1201+713, *bēn[1]+ʾeprayim* [6]
Ephraim, 824+713, *ʾereṣ+ʾeprayim* [2]

EPHRAIM'S [12]
Ephraim's, 713, *ʾeprayim* [12]

EPHRAIMITE [6]
Ephraimite, 718, *ʾeprātî* [3]
Ephraimite, 1201+713, *bēn[1]+ʾeprayim* [2]
Ephraimite, 713, *ʾeprayim* [1]

EPHRAIMITES [8]
Ephraimites, 1201+713, *bēn[1]+ʾeprayim* [4]
Ephraimites, 713, *ʾeprayim* [2]
Ephraimites, 408+713, *ʾîš[1]+ʾeprayim* [1]
Ephraimites, 4946+713, *min+ʾeprayim* [1]

EPHRATH [5]
Ephrath, 714, *ʾeprāt[1]* [4]
Ephrath, 715, *ʾeprāt[2]* [1]

EPHRATHAH [5]
Ephrathah, 716, *ʾeprātâ[1]* [3]
Ephrathah, 717, *ʾeprātâ[2]* [2]

EPHRATHITE [1]
Ephrathite, 718, *ʾeprātî* [1]

EPHRATHITES [1]
Ephrathites, 718, *ʾeprātî* [1]

EPHRON [10]
Ephron, 6766, *ʿeprôn[1]* [8]
Ephron, 6767, *ʿeprôn[2]* [2]

EPHRON'S [2]
Ephron's, 6766, *ʿeprôn[1]* [2]

EQUAL [13]
equal, 3869, *k[e]-* [2]
equal, *NIH/RPE* [1]
without equal, 401+3202+4946, *ʾayin[1]+ṭôb[2]+min* [1]
in equal amounts, 963+928+963, *bad[1]+b[e]-+bad[1]* [1]
equal, 1948, *dāmâ[1]* [1]
equal to, 3869, *k[e]-* [1]
equal to, 4017, *k[e]mô* [1]
equal, 4017, *k[e]mô* [1]
equal, 5444, *mōšel[1]* [1]
equal, 5952, *nāśag* [1]
count equal, 8750, *šāwâ[1]* [1]
equal, 8750, *šāwâ[1]* [1]

EQUALLY [5]
equally among them, 408+3869+278+2257, *ʾîš[1]+k[e]-+ʾāḥ[2]+-ô* [1]
equally, 408+3869+278+2257, *ʾîš[1]+k[e]-+ʾāḥ[2]+-ô* [1]
divide equally, 2936, *ḥāṣâ* [1]
equally, 3869+285, *k[e]-+ʾeḥād* [1]
equally, 3869, *k[e]-* [1]

EQUIPMENT [10]
equipment, 3998, *k[e]lî* [8]
equipment, 266, *ʾāzēn* [1]
equipment, 8214, *r[e]kûš* [1]

EQUIPPED [3]
equipped, 2616, *ḥāzaq* [1]
equipped, 5951, *nāśāʾ* [1]
equipped, 8214, *r[e]kûš* [1]

EQUITY [3]
equity, 4797, *mêšārîm* [3]

EQUIVALENT [2]
equivalent, *NIH/RPE* [1]
equivalent values, 6886, *ʿērek* [1]

ER [9]
Er, 6841, *ʿēr* [9]

ERAN [1]
Eran, 6896, *ʿērān* [1]

ERANITE [1]
Eranite, 6897, *ʿērānî* [1]

ERECH [2]
Erech, 804, *ʾerek[2]* [1]
Erech, 10074, *ʾark[e]wāy* [1]

ERECT [3]
erect, 1215, *bānâ* [2]
erect, 7756, *qûm* [1]

ERECTED [9]
erected, 7756, *qûm* [4]
erected, 1215, *bānâ* [1]
erected, 3922, *kûn[1]* [1]
erected as a monument, 5893, *nāṣab[1]* [1]
erected, 6913, *ʿāśâ[1]* [1]
erected, 8492, *śîm* [1]

ERI [2]
Eri, 6878, *ʿērî[1]* [2]

ERITE [1]
Erite, 6879, *ʿērî[2]* [1]

ERODES [1]
erodes, 5877, *nāpal* [1]

ERRED [2]
erred, 8704, *šāgag* [1]
erred, 8706, *šāgâ* [1]

ERROR [5]
error, 5413, *m[e]šûgâ* [1]
error, 8705, *š[e]gāgâ* [1]
error, 9334, *toh[o]lâ* [1]
error, 9360, *tōʿâ* [1]
error, 9494, *tāʿâ* [1]

ERRORS [2]
errors, 2628, *ḥēṭʾ* [1]
errors, 8709, *š[e]gîʾâ* [1]

ESARHADDON [3]
Esarhaddon, 675, *ʾēsar-ḥaddōn* [3]

ESAU [84]
Esau, 6916, *ʿēśāw* [79]
Esau, *NIH/RPE* [5]

ESAU'S [14]
Esau's, 6916, *ʿēśāw* [14]

ESCAPE [56]
escape, 4880, *mālaṭ[1]* [17]
escape, 7127, *pālîṭ* [6]
escape, 3655, *yāṣāʾ* [4]
escape with, 4200+8965, *l[e]-[1]+šālāl* [4]
escape, 7129, *p[e]lēṭâ* [4]
escape, 4946+7156, *min+pāneh* [3]
escape, 5674, *nûs* [3]
escape, 5911, *nāṣal* [2]
not escape, 6+4960, *ʾābad+mānôs* [1]
not escape, 1815, *dābaq* [1]
escape, 2143, *hālak* [1]
escape, 2740, *ḥālaṣ[1]* [1]
escape, 4880+4880, *mālaṭ[1]+mālaṭ[1]* [1]
escape, 4880+7127, *mālaṭ[1]+pālîṭ* [1]
made escape, 4880, *mālaṭ[1]* [1]
escape, 4960, *mānôs* [1]
made good escape, 5674+2256+4880, *nûs+w[e]-+mālaṭ[1]* [1]
escape, 6073, *sûr[1]* [1]
let escape, 7117, *pālaṭ* [1]
place to escape, 7129, *p[e]lēṭâ* [1]
escape, 9362, *tôṣāʾôt* [1]

ESCAPED [32]
escaped, 4880, *mālaṭ[1]* [20]
escaped, 7129, *p[e]lēṭâ* [3]
escaped, 5674, *nûs* [2]
escaped, 7127, *pālîṭ* [2]
escaped, 3655, *yāṣāʾ* [1]
escaped, 3855, *yātar* [1]
escaped from, 4946, *min* [1]
man who escaped, 7127, *pālîṭ* [1]
escaped, 7128, *pālēṭ* [1]

ESCAPES [3]
escapes, 3655, *yāṣāʾ* [1]
escapes, 5911, *nāṣal* [1]
escapes, 7129+2118, *p[e]lēṭâ+hāyâ* [1]

ESCAPING [4]
escaping, *NIH/RPE* [1]
escaping, 1368, *bāraḥ[1]* [1]
escaping, 4880, *mālaṭ[1]* [1]
escaping, 8740, *šûb[1]* [1]

ESCORT [1]
escort, 995, *bôʾ* [1]

ESCORTED [2]
escorted, 2143, *hālak* [1]
escorted by, 6017, *sābîb* [1]

ESEK [1]
Esek, 6922, *ʿēśeq* [1]

ESH-BAAL [2]
Esh-Baal, 843, *ʾešbaʿal* [2]

ESHAN [1]
Eshan, 878, *ʾešʿān* [1]

ESHBAN [2]
Eshban, 841, *ʾešbān* [2]

ESHCOL [6]
Eshcol, 865, *ʾeškôl[2]* [4]
Eshcol, 866, *ʾeškōl[3]* [2]

ESHEK [1]
Eshek, 6944, *ʿēšeq* [1]

ESHTAOL [7]
Eshtaol, 900, *ʾeštāʾôl* [7]

ESHTAOLITES [1]
Eshtaolites, 901, *ʾeštāʾulî* [1]

ESHTEMOA [5]
Eshtemoa, 904, *ʾešt[e]mōaʿ* [5]

ESHTEMOH [1]
Eshtemoh, 903, *ʾešt[e]mōh* [1]

ESHTON [2]
Eshton, 902, *ʾeštôn* [2]

ESPECIALLY [2]
especially bred, 1201+2021+8247, *bēn[1]+ha-+rammākâ* [1]
especially, 2256, *w[e]-* [1]

ESTABLISH [34]
establish, 7756, *qûm* [13]
establish, 3922, *kûn*^{1} [10]
establish, 5989, *nātan* [3]
establish, 1215, *bānâ* [1]
establish, 5893, *nāṣab*^{1} [1]
establish, 6641, *ʿāmad* [1]
establish, 6913, *ʿāśâ*^{1} [1]
establish the custom, 7756, *qûm* [1]
establish, 8492, *śîm* [1]
establish, 8883, *šît*^{1} [1]
establish, 9189, *šāpat* [1]

ESTABLISHED [66]
established, 3922, *kûn*^{1} [22]
be established, 3922, *kûn*^{1} [10]
established, 7756, *qûm* [8]
established, 8492, *śîm* [5]
established, 3569, *yāsad*^{1} [3]
is firmly established, 3922, *kûn*^{1} [3]
be established, 586, *ʾāman*^{1} [2]
established himself firmly, 2616, *ḥāzaq* [2]
is established, 3922, *kûn*^{1} [2]
was established, 3922, *kûn*^{1} [2]
established, 5989, *nātan* [2]
long established, 419, *ʾêtān*^{1} [1]
established, 599, *ʾāmēṣ* [1]
be established, 1215, *bānâ* [1]
was firmly established, 3922, *kûn*^{1} [1]
established, 6913, *ʿāśâ*^{1} [1]

ESTABLISHES [5]
establishes, 3922, *kûn*^{1} [2]
establishes, 6913, *ʿāśâ*^{1} [2]
establishes, 8492, *śîm* [1]

ESTABLISHING [1]
establishing, 3922, *kûn*^{1} [1]

ESTATE [7]
estate, 1074, *bayit*^{1} [5]
estate, 5709, *naḥ*^{a}*lâ*^{1} [1]
low estate, 9165, *šēpel* [1]

ESTEEM [3]
esteem, 5564, *nābaṭ* [1]
Esteem, 6147, *sālal*^{1} [1]
held in high esteem, 8354, *rāṣâ*^{1} [1]

ESTEEMED [5]
highly esteemed, 2776, *ḥ*^{a}*mudôt* [3]
esteemed, 2834, *ḥēn*^{1} [1]
esteemed, 3108, *ḥāšab* [1]

ESTHER [42]
Esther, 676, *ʾestēr* [42]

ESTHER'S [5]
Esther's, 676, *ʾestēr* [5]

ESTRANGED [2]
estranged, 2319, *zûr*^{2} [1]
estranged, 5615, *nādaḥ*^{1} [1]

ETAM [5]
Etam, 6515, *ʿêṭām* [5]

ETERNAL [15]
eternal, 6409, *ʿôlām* [5]
eternal, 4200+6409, *l*$^{e-1}$*+ʿôlām* [3]
eternal, 4200+6329, *l*$^{e-1}$*+ʿad*^{1} [2]
eternal, 10550, *ʿālam* [2]
eternal, 5905, *nēṣaḥ*^{1} [1]
eternal, 6329, *ʿad*^{1} [1]
eternal, 7710, *qedem* [1]

ETERNITY [3]
eternity, 6409, *ʿôlām* [2]
all eternity, 6409, *ʿôlām* [1]

ETH KAZIN [1]
Eth Kazin, 6962, *ʿēt qāṣîn* [1]

ETHAM [4]
Etham, 918, *ʾētām* [4]

ETHAN [8]
Ethan, 420, *ʾêtān*^{2} [8]

ETHANIM [1]
Ethanim, 923, *ʾētānîm* [1]

ETHBAAL [1]
Ethbaal, 909, *ʾetbaʿal* [1]

ETHER [2]
Ether, 6987, *ʿeter* [2]

ETHIOPIAN [1]
Ethiopian, 3934, *kûšî*^{1} [1]

ETHNAN [1]
Ethnan, 925, *ʾetnān* [1]

ETHNI [1]
Ethni, 922, *ʾetnî* [1]

EUNUCH [4]
eunuch, 6247, *sārîs* [4]

EUNUCHS [10]
eunuchs, 6247, *sārîs* [10]

EUPHRATES [18]
Euphrates, 7310, *p*^{e}*rāt* [15]
Euphrates^{s}, 5643, *nāhār* [2]
Euphrates, *NIH/RPE* [1]

EVE [2]
Eve, 2558, *ḥawwâ*^{2} [2]

EVEN [342]
even, 1685, *gam* [64]
even, *NIH/RPE* [56]
even, 2256, *w*^{e}*-* [56]
even though, 2256, *w*^{e}*-* [22]
even, 2256+1685, *w*^{e}*+gam* [15]
even, 3954, *kî*^{2} [14]
even, *AIT* [11]
even if, 561, *ʾim* [9]
even, 677, *ʾap*^{1} [6]
even though, 3954, *kî*^{2} [6]
even if, 2256, *w*^{e}*-* [5]
make even heavier, 3578, *yāsap* [4]
even, 6330, *ʿad*^{2} [4]
even more, 1524, *gādôl* [3]
even, 2180, *hinnēh* [3]
and even, 2256, *w*^{e}*-* [3]
even if, 3954, *kî*^{2} [3]
even though, 889, *ʾ*^{a}*šer* [2]
but even, 2256, *w*^{e}*-* [2]
even when, 2256, *w*^{e}*-* [2]
even as, 3869+889, *k*^{e}*-+ʾ*^{a}*šer* [2]
even, 3954+1685, *kî*^{2}*+gam* [2]
even, 3972, *kōl* [2]
even more than, 4946, *min* [2]
even, 6388, *ʿôd* [2]
even though, 561, *ʾim* [1]
if even, 561, *ʾim* [1]
not even, 561, *ʾim* [1]
but even, 677, *ʾap*^{1} [1]
even if, 928, *b*^{e}*-* [1]
even after, 928, *b*^{e}*-* [1]
even if, 1685, *gam* [1]
and even, 1685, *gam* [1]
but even, 1685, *gam* [1]
grew even wilder, 2143+2256+6192,
hālak+w^{e}*-+sāʿar* [1]
even, 2176, *hēn*^{1} [1]
and even though, 2256, *w*^{e}*-* [1]
even while, 2256, *w*^{e}*-* [1]
and even after, 2256, *w*^{e}*-* [1]
but even, 2256+1685, *w*^{e}*+gam* [1]
even then, 2256, *w*^{e}*-* [1]
even, 2256+677+3954, *w*^{e}*-+ʾap*^{1}*+kî*^{2} [1]
even, 2256+677, *w*^{e}*-+ʾap*^{1} [1]
or even, 2256, *w*^{e}*-* [1]
even, 3481, *yaḥdāw* [1]
given even more,
3578+3869+2179+2256+3869+2179,
yāsap+k^{e}*-+hēnnâ*^{2}*+w*^{e}*+k*^{e}*-+hēnnâ*^{2} [1]
even far, 3856+4394, *yeter*^{1}*+m*^{e}*ʾōd* [1]
even, 3869, *k*^{e}*-* [1]
even for, 3869, *k*^{e}*-* [1]
even when, 3954, *kî*^{2} [1]
even, 3954+561, *kî*^{2}*+ʾim* [1]
even so, 4017, *k*^{e}*mô* [1]
even though, 4200+963, *l*$^{e-1}$*+bad*^{1} [1]
even more, 4394, *m*^{e}*ʾōd* [1]
even beyond, 4946+6584, *min+ʿal*^{2} [1]
have a right to get even, 5927, *nāqâ* [1]
even as far as, 6330, *ʿad*^{2} [1]
even enough, 6330, *ʿad*^{2} [1]
even as, 6388, *ʿôd* [1]
even more, 6388, *ʿôd* [1]
even as, 6640, *ʿim* [1]
even comes near, 7929+7929, *qārēb+qārēb* [1]
even if, 10213, *hēn* [1]
even, 10221+10059, *w*^{e}*-+ʾap* [1]
even as, 10353+10619+10168, *kōl+q*^{o}*bēl+dî* [1]
became even greater, 10650+10339+10323,
r^{e}*bû+yattîr+y*^{e}*sap* [1]
even more, 10678, *śaggî*^{1} [1]

EVEN-TEMPERED [1]
even-tempered, 7922+8120, *qar+rûaḥ* [1]

EVENING [121]
evening, 6847, *ʿereb*^{2} [110]
evening, 5742, *nāṭâ* [2]
evening, 6845, *ʿārab*^{4} [2]
evening, 928+2021+6847+928+2021+6847,
b^{e}*-+ha-+ʿereb*^{2}*+b*^{e}*-+ha-+ʿereb*^{2} [1]
every evening,
928+2021+6847+928+2021+6847,
b^{e}*-+ha-+ʿereb*^{2}*+b*^{e}*-+ha-+ʿereb*^{2} [1]
toward evening, 3718+4394, *yārad+m*^{e}*ʾōd* [1]
evening sacrifice, 6590+4966, *ʿālâ+minḥâ* [1]
evening, 6961+2021+6847, *ʿēt+ha-+ʿereb*^{2} [1]
evening shadows, 7498, *ṣēl* [1]
evening shadows fell, 7511, *ṣālal*^{3} [1]

EVENINGS [2]
evenings, 6847, *ʿereb*^{2} [2]

EVENLY [1]
hammered evenly, 3837, *yāšar* [1]

EVENTS [53]
events, 1821, *dābār* [51]
turn of events, 5813, *n*^{e}*sibbâ* [1]
turn of events, 6016, *sibbâ* [1]

EVER [167]
ever, *AIT* [50]
ever, 6329, *ʿad*^{1} [16]
ever so, 3907, *kōh* [12]
ever, 6409, *ʿôlām* [9]
ever, 9458, *tāmîd* [8]
ever, 4200+6409, *l*$^{e-1}$*+ʿôlām* [5]
ever, 6330+6409, *ʿad*^{2}*+ʿôlām* [5]
for ever, 6409, *ʿôlām* [5]
ever, *NIH/RPE* [4]
ever and ever, 6329, *ʿad*^{1} [4]
ever since, 4946, *min* [3]
ever since, 6330+2021+3427+2021+2296,
ʿad^{2}*+ha-+yôm*^{1}*+ha-+zeh* [3]
ever, 3972, *kōl* [2]
ever, 4200+6329, *l*$^{e-1}$*+ʿad*^{1} [2]
ever since, 4946+255, *min+ʾāz* [2]
ever, 4946+6409, *min+ʿôlām* [2]
ever, 6388, *ʿôd* [2]
ever return, 8740+8740, *šûb*^{1}*+šûb*^{1} [2]
ever, 10550+10002, *ʿālam+-ā* [2]
ever, 339, *ʾaḥar* [1]
ever flowing, 419, *ʾêtān*^{1} [1]
ever, 1685, *gam* [1]
ever say, 1821+1819, *dābār+dābar*^{2} [1]
shining ever brighter, 2143+2256+239,
hālak+w^{e}*-+ʾôr*^{1} [1]
ever able, 3523+3523, *yākōl+yākōl* [1]
ever, 3578, *yāsap* [1]
ever goes outside, 3655+3655, *yāṣāʾ+yāṣāʾ* [1]
ever, 3954, *kî*^{2} [1]
ever, 3972+2021+3427, *kōl+ha-+yôm*^{1} [1]
ever, 3972+3427, *kōl+yôm*^{1} [1]
ever since, 4200+4946, *l*$^{e-1}$*+min* [1]
ever again, 4200+5905+5905,
l^{e-1}*+nēṣaḥ*^{1}*+nēṣaḥ*^{1} [1]
ever, 4200+7156, *l*$^{e-1}$*+pāneh* [1]
ever, 4202, *lōʾ* [1]
ever so, 4537, *mâ* [1]

exalted yourself, 5951, *nāśā'* [1]
is exalted, 5951, *nāśā'* [1]
are exalted, 6590, *'ālâ* [1]
exalted, 6590, *'ālâ* [1]
most exalted, 6609, *'elyôn¹* [1]
exalted, 7756, *qûm* [1]
exalted, 8250, *rāmam²* [1]
exalted, 8438, *śaggî'* [1]
most exalted, 9366+5092, *tôr¹+ma'alâ²* [1]

EXALTS [4]
exalts, 8123, *rûm¹* [3]
exalts, 1467, *gābah* [1]

EXAMINE [34]
examine, 8011, *rā'â¹* [25]
examine, 1043, *bāḥan* [3]
examine, 7212, *pāqad* [2]
examine, 2924, *ḥāpaś* [1]
examine to see, 5795, *nākar¹* [1]
examine, 7671, *ṣārap* [1]
examine, 8492, *śîm* [1]

EXAMINED [2]
examined, 2983, *ḥāqar* [2]

EXAMINES [8]
examines, 8011, *rā'â¹* [6]
examines, 1043, *bāḥan* [1]
examines, 7143, *pālas²* [1]

EXAMINING [2]
examining, 8431, *śābar¹* [2]

EXAMPLE [3]
example, *AIT* [1]
example, 253, *'ôt¹* [1]
followed the example, 3869+6913+6913, *kᵉ-+'āśâ¹+'āśâ¹* [1]

EXCEED [2]
exceed, 6296, *'ābar¹* [1]
exceed number, 6369, *'ādap* [1]

EXCEEDED [3]
far exceeded, 3578, *yāsap* [2]
exceeded number, 6369, *'ādap* [1]

EXCEEDINGLY [6]
exceedingly, 928+4394+4394, *bᵉ-+mᵉ'ōd+mᵉ'ōd* [2]
exceedingly, 4394+4394, *mᵉ'ōd+mᵉ'ōd* [2]
exceedingly, 4200+5087+2025, *lᵉ-¹+ma'al²+-â²* [1]
exceedingly, 4394, *mᵉ'ōd* [1]

EXCEL [1]
excel, 3855, *yātar* [1]

EXCELLED [1]
excelled, 4946, *min* [1]

EXCELLENT [1]
most excellent, 3636, *yāpâ* [1]

EXCELLING [2]
excelling, 3856, *yeter¹* [2]

EXCEPT [49]
except, 3954+561, *kî²+'im* [24]
except, 8370, *raq²* [5]
except, 2314, *zûlâ* [4]
except, 10386, *lāhēn²* [4]
except, 1194, *biltî* [2]
except that, 8370, *raq²* [2]
except, 421, *'ak* [1]
except, 889+4202, *'ašer+lō'* [1]
except for, 1194, *biltî* [1]
except, 1194+561, *biltî+'im* [1]
except for, 2256+4202, *wᵉ-+lō'* [1]
except for, 2296, *zeh* [1]
except for, 4946, *min* [1]
except, 4946+1187, *min+bal'adê* [1]

EXCEPTION [1]
only exception, 4200+963, *lᵉ-¹+bad¹* [1]

EXCEPTIONAL [1]
exceptional, 10339, *yattîr* [1]

EXCESSIVE [4]
excessive interest, 9552, *tarbît* [4]

EXCHANGE [10]
in exchange for, 928, *bᵉ-* [4]
in exchange for, 9393, *taḥat¹* [2]
exchange, 2736, *ḥālap¹* [1]
exchange, 4614, *mûr¹* [1]
exchange, 5989, *nātan* [1]
in exchange, 9393, *taḥat¹* [1]

EXCHANGED [10]
exchanged, 5989, *nātan* [7]
exchanged, 4614, *mûr¹* [3]

EXCITEMENT [1]
excitement, 8075, *rōgez* [1]

EXCLAIM [2]
exclaim, 606, *'āmar¹* [1]
exclaim, 7924, *qārā'¹* [1]

EXCLAIMED [5]
exclaimed, 606, *'āmar¹* [5]

EXCLUDE [2]
surely exclude, 976+976, *bādal+bādal* [1]
exclude, 5612, *nādâ* [1]

EXCLUDED [4]
excluded from, 4946, *min* [2]
excluded, 976, *bādal* [1]
excluded, 1615, *gāzar¹* [1]

EXCREMENT [3]
excrement, 1645+7362, *gēl+ṣē'â* [1]
excrement, 1645, *gēl* [1]
excrement, 7362, *ṣē'â* [1]

EXCUSE [1]
without excuse, 8200, *rêqām* [1]

EXECUTE [10]
execute judgment, 9149, *šāpaṭ* [6]
execute, 10005, *'abad* [2]
execute, *NIH/RPE* [1]
execute, 3108, *ḥāšab* [1]

EXECUTED [6]
executed, 2222, *hārag* [1]
executed, 5782+2256+4637, *nākâ+wᵉ-+mût* [1]
executed, 5782, *nākâ* [1]
had executed, 5782+2256+4637, *nākâ+wᵉ-+mût* [1]
executed, 6913, *'āśâ¹* [1]
executed, 10005, *'abad* [1]

EXECUTING [1]
executing judgment, 9149, *šāpaṭ* [1]

EXECUTION [1]
execution, 10005, *'abad* [1]

EXEMPT [3]
exempt, 5929, *nāqî* [1]
exempt from taxes, 6913+2930, *'āśâ¹+ḥopšî* [1]
were exempt from duties, 7080, *pāṭar* [1]

EXERCISED [1]
exercised, 5440, *māšal²* [1]

EXERCISES [1]
exercises, 6913, *'āśâ¹* [1]

EXHAUST [2]
exhaust, 3333, *yāga'* [1]
exhaust, 3615, *yā'ēp¹* [1]

EXHAUSTED [11]
exhausted, 3617, *yā'ēp³* [2]
exhausted, 6545, *'îp* [2]
exhausted, 6546, *'āyēp* [2]
exhausted, 7006, *pāgar* [2]
exhausted, 2118, *hāyâ* [1]
exhausted, 5980, *nāšat* [1]
exhausted, 6545+4394, *'îp+mᵉ'ōd* [1]

EXILE [73]
exile, 1583, *gôlâ* [16]
exile, 8660, *šᵉbî* [13]
carried into exile, 1655, *gālâ* [11]
exile, 1661, *gālût* [5]
go into exile, 1655, *gālâ* [3]
taken into exile, 1655, *gālâ* [3]
been carried into exile, 1655, *gālâ* [2]
exile, 1655, *gālâ* [2]
sent into exile, 1655, *gālâ* [2]
surely go into exile, 1655+1655, *gālâ+gālâ* [2]
took into exile, 1655, *gālâ* [2]
went into exile, 1655, *gālâ* [2]
exile, *NIH/RPE* [1]
be carried into exile, 1655, *gālâ* [1]
being carried into exile, 1655, *gālâ* [1]
carried into exile, 1655+1655, *gālâ+gālâ* [1]
carry into exile, 1655, *gālâ* [1]
certainly go into exile, 1655+1655, *gālâ+gālâ* [1]
go into exile, 1655+1655, *gālâ+gālâ* [1]
gone into exile, 1655, *gālâ* [1]
send into exile, 1655, *gālâ* [1]
exile, 8938, *šālaḥ* [1]

EXILED [8]
exiled, 1655, *gālâ* [2]
exiled, *NIH/RPE* [1]
be exiled, 1655, *gālâ* [1]
exiled, 2143, *hālak* [1]
exiled, 5615, *nādaḥ¹* [1]
were exiled, 5615, *nādaḥ¹* [1]
exiled, 8654, *šᵉbût* [1]

EXILES [38]
exiles, 1583, *gôlâ* [15]
exiles, 1661, *gālût* [7]
exiles, 1201+1583, *bēn¹+gôlâ* [6]
exiles, 5615, *nādaḥ¹* [5]
exiles, 10120+10145, *bar²+gālû* [4]
exiles, *NIH/RPE* [1]

EXISTS [1]
exists, 2118, *hāyâ* [1]

EXITS [4]
exits, 4604, *môṣā'¹* [3]
exits, 9362, *tôṣā'ôt* [1]

EXORBITANT [1]
exorbitant interest, 5968+2256+9552, *nešek+wᵉ-+tarbît* [1]

EXPANSE [13]
expanse, 8385, *rāqîa'* [13]

EXPANSES [1]
vast expanses, 8144, *raḥab* [1]

EXPECT [3]
expect, 3498, *yāḥal* [1]
expect, 7747, *qāwâ¹* [1]
expect to be heard, 9048, *šāma'* [1]

EXPECTANT [1]
expectant mothers, 2226, *hāreh* [1]

EXPECTANTLY [1]
expectantly, 3498, *yāḥal* [1]

EXPECTATION [2]
wait in expectation, 7595, *ṣāpâ¹* [1]
expectation, 9536, *tiqwâ²* [1]

EXPECTED [3]
expected, 7136, *pālal¹* [1]
expected, 7155, *pānâ* [1]
expected, 9347, *tôḥelet* [1]

EXPELLED [4]
expelled, 6, *'ābad* [1]
be expelled, 976, *bādal* [1]
expelled, 6073, *sûr¹* [1]
expelled, 6296, *'ābar¹* [1]

EXPENSES [2]
met expenses, 3655, *yāṣā'* [1]
expenses, 10486, *nipqâ* [1]

EXPERIENCE [2]
had experience, 3359, *yādaʿ* [1]
experience, 7212, *pāqad* [1]

EXPERIENCED [12]
experienced, 3359, *yādaʿ* [4]
experienced soldiers, 3655+7372, *yāṣāʾ+ṣābāʾ*[2] [2]
experienced fighter, 408+4878, *ʾîš*[1]*+milḥāmâ* [1]
experienced fighting men, 408+4878+1475+2657, *ʾîš*[1]*+milḥāmâ+gibbôr+ḥayil* [1]
experienced, 4340, *lāmad* [1]
experienced in engraving, 7338+7334, *pātaḥ*[2]*+pittûaḥ* [1]
experienced, 8011, *rāʾâ*[1] [1]
experienced, 9312+2256+1981, *tᵉbûnâ+wᵉ-+daʿat*[1] [1]

EXPERTS [1]
experts, 3359, *yādaʿ* [1]

EXPLAIN [13]
explain, 5583, *nāgad* [6]
explain, 10252, *ḥᵃwâ* [2]
explain, 606, *ʾāmar*[1] [1]
explain, 1067, *bîn* [1]
explain, 2555, *ḥāwâ*[1] [1]
explain, 10600+10252, *pᵉšar*[2]*+ḥᵃwâ* [1]
explain, 10600, *pᵉšar*[2] [1]

EXPLAINED [7]
explained, 5583, *nāgad* [3]
explained, 10313, *yᵉdaʿ* [2]
explained, 1819, *dābar*[2] [1]
explained, 6699, *ʿānâ*[1] [1]

EXPLAINING [2]
explaining, 1067, *bîn* [1]
explaining, 5583, *nāgad* [1]

EXPLANATION [2]
explanation, 7323, *pēšer* [1]
gave explanation, 10042, *ʾᵃmar* [1]

EXPLOIT [2]
exploit, 1608, *gāzal* [1]
exploit, 5601, *nāgaś* [1]

EXPLOITS [7]
exploits, 6913, *ʿāśâ*[1] [4]
military exploits, 4309, *lāḥam*[1] [1]
exploits, 7189, *pōʿal* [1]
performed exploits, 7189, *pōʿal* [1]

EXPLORE [11]
explore, 9365, *tûr* [6]
explore, 2983, *ḥāqar* [4]
explore, 8078, *rāgal* [1]

EXPLORED [7]
explored, 9365, *tûr* [5]
explored, 6296+9365, *ʿābar*[1]*+tûr* [1]
explored, 8078, *rāgal* [1]

EXPLORING [1]
exploring, 9365, *tûr* [1]

EXPORTED [2]
exported, 3655, *yāṣāʾ* [2]

EXPOSE [7]
expose, 1655, *gālâ* [4]
kill and expose, 3697, *yāqaʿ* [1]
expose, 5583, *nāgad* [1]
expose, 7337, *pātaḥ*[1] [1]

EXPOSED [19]
be exposed, 1655, *gālâ* [4]
exposed, 1655, *gālâ* [3]
killed and exposed, 3697, *yāqaʿ* [2]
exposed, 6867, *ʿārâ*[1] [2]
were exposed, 8011, *rāʾâ*[1] [2]
exposed, *NIH/RPE* [1]
been killed and exposed, 3697, *yāqaʿ* [1]
exposed, 5583, *nāgad* [1]
be exposed, 6887, *ʿāral* [1]
exposed places, 7460, *ṣāḥîaḥ* [1]
exposed, 8848, *šāṭaḥ* [1]

EXPOSES [1]
exposes, 7298, *pāraś* [1]

EXPOSING [1]
exposing, 4741, *maḥśōp* [1]

EXPOUND [2]
expound, 930, *bāʾar* [1]
expound, 7337, *pātaḥ*[1] [1]

EXPRESS [6]
express sympathy, 5714, *nāḥam* [5]
express, 6913, *ʿāśâ*[1] [1]

EXPRESSED [1]
expressed, 6584+7023, *ʿal*[2]*+peh* [1]

EXPRESSES [1]
expresses wrath, 2404, *zāʿam* [1]

EXPRESSION [2]
expression, 7156, *pāneh* [1]
expression of thankfulness, 9343, *tôdâ* [1]

EXTEND [20]
extend, 2118, *hāyâ* [3]
extend from, 4946, *min* [2]
extend, 8938, *šālaḥ* [2]
extend, 1368, *bāraḥ*[1] [1]
extend out, 2575+2025, *ḥûṣ+-â*[2] [1]
extend westward, 3542+2025, *yām+-â*[2] [1]
extend, 3655, *yāṣāʾ* [1]
extend, 3804, *yāšaṭ* [1]
extend, 4887, *mālak*[1] [1]
extend, 5432, *māšak* [1]
extend, 5595, *nāgaʿ* [1]
extend, 5742, *nāṭâ* [1]
extend toward, 6584, *ʿal*[2] [1]
extend the territory, 7332, *pātâ*[2] [1]
extend eastward, 7708+2025, *qādîm+-â*[2] [1]
extend, 8143, *rāḥab* [1]

EXTENDED [16]
extended, 2118, *hāyâ* [2]
extended from, 4946, *min* [2]
extended, 5742, *nāṭâ* [2]
extended, 802, *ʾōrek* [1]
extended, 1368, *bāraḥ*[1] [1]
extended, 3655, *yāṣāʾ* [1]
extended, 3804, *yāšaṭ* [1]
extended, 6296, *ʿābar*[1] [1]
extended, 6584+7156, *ʿal*[2]*+pāneh* [1]
extended, 7003, *pāgaʿ* [1]
extended, 7298, *pāraś* [1]
extended, 8178, *rāḥaq* [1]
extended, 9362, *tôṣāʾôt* [1]

EXTENDING [11]
extending, 3655, *yāṣāʾ* [5]
extending from, 4946, *min* [2]
extending, 995, *bôʾ* [1]
extending, 2006, *derek* [1]
extending, 2118, *hāyâ* [1]
extending, 8178, *rāḥaq* [1]

EXTENDS [4]
extends to, 4200+4946, *lᵉ-*[1]*+min* [1]
extends to, 6330, *ʿad*[2] [1]
extends, 8938, *šālaḥ* [1]
extends to, 10378, *lᵉ-* [1]

EXTENSIVE [3]
extensive, 4200+8044, *lᵉ-*[1]*+rōb* [2]
extensive, 2221, *harbēh* [1]

EXTERMINATE [2]
exterminate, 6, *ʾābad* [1]
exterminate, 3049, *ḥāram*[1] [1]

EXTERMINATING [1]
exterminating, 9012, *šāmad* [1]

EXTINGUISHED [2]
extinguished, 1980, *dāʿak* [1]
extinguished, 3882, *kābâ* [1]

EXTOL [11]
extol, 1385, *bārak*[2] [3]
extol, 3344, *yādâ*[2] [2]
extol, 8655, *šābaḥ*[1] [2]
extol, 2146, *hālal*[2] [1]
extol, 6148, *sālal*[2] [1]
extol, 8131, *rûaʿ* [1]
extol, 8434, *śāgāʾ* [1]

EXTORTION [9]
extortion, 6945, *ʿōšeq* [3]
extortion, 5131, *maʿᵃšaqqôt* [1]
extortion, 5298, *mᵉrûṣâ*[2] [1]
extortion, 6294, *ʿabṭîṭ* [1]
practice extortion, 6943+6945, *ʿāšaq+ʿōšeq* [1]
practiced extortion, 6943+6945, *ʿāšaq+ʿōšeq* [1]
taken by extortion, 6945+6943, *ʿōšeq+ʿāšaq* [1]

EXTREME [1]
extreme, 7895, *qāṣeh* [1]

EXTREMELY [1]
extremely wise, 2682+2681, *ḥākām+ḥākam* [1]

EXTREMES [1]
extremes[s], 4392, *-ām* [1]

EXULT [3]
exult, 2146, *hālal*[2] [1]
exult, 8123, *rûm*[1] [1]
exult, 8523, *śāmaḥ* [1]

EYE [40]
eye, 6524, *ʿayin*[1] [36]
eye, 5260, *marʾeh* [1]
kept jealous eye on, 6523, *ʿāyan* [1]
have an eye for, 9193, *šāqad*[1] [1]
eye, 10540, *ʿayin* [1]

EYEBROWS [1]
eyebrows, 1461+6524, *gab*[1]*+ʿayin*[1] [1]

EYED [1]
eyed, 9068, *šāmar* [1]

EYELIDS [3]
eyelids, 6757, *ʿapʿappayim* [3]

EYES [450]
eyes, 6524, *ʿayin*[1] [437]
eyes, 10540, *ʿayin* [4]
eyes, 6757, *ʿapʿappayim* [3]
eyes, *AIT* [1]
eyes, *NIH/RPE* [1]
eyes, 1426+6524, *bat*[1]*+ʿayin*[1] [1]
before eyes, 4200+7156, *lᵉ-*[1]*+pāneh* [1]
in eyes, 4200+7156, *lᵉ-*[1]*+pāneh* [1]
in the eyes of, 4200+7156, *lᵉ-*[1]*+pāneh* [1]

EYESIGHT [1]
eyesight, 6524, *ʿayin*[1] [1]

EZBAI [1]
Ezbai, 256, *ʾezbāy* [1]

EZBON [2]
Ezbon, 719, *ʾeṣbōn* [2]

EZEKIEL [2]
Ezekiel, 3489, *yᵉḥezqēʾl* [2]

EZEL [1]
Ezel, 262, *ʾezel* [1]

EZEM [3]
Ezem, 6796, *ʿeṣem*[2] [3]

EZER [10]
Ezer, 733, *ʾēṣer* [5]
Ezer, 6470, *ʿēzer*[2] [4]
Ezer, 6472, *ʿezer*[2] [1]

EZION GEBER [7]
Ezion Geber, 6787, *ʿeṣyôn geber* [7]

EZRA [26]
Ezra, 6474, *ʿezrāʾ* [21]
Ezra, 10537, *ʿezrāʾ* [3]
Ezra, *NIH/RPE* [2]

EZRA'S [1]
Ezra's, 6474, *ʿezrāʾ* [1]
EZRAH [1]
Ezrah, 6477, *ʿezrā^{2}* [1]
EZRAHITE [3]
Ezrahite, 276, *ʾezrāḥî* [3]
EZRI [1]
Ezri, 6479, *ʿezrî* [1]
FABRIC [6]
fabric, 5018, *masseket* [3]
fabric, *NIH/RPE* [1]
fabric, 1659, *g^{e}lôm* [1]
costly fabric, 5429, *mešî* [1]
FACE [270]
face, 7156, *pāneh* [211]
face, 678, *ʾap^{2}* [14]
face, 7023, *peh* [7]
face, 6524, *ʿayin^{1}* [6]
face to face, 7156, *pāneh* [4]
face, 4200+7156, *l^{e}-^{1}+pāneh* [3]
face, 6425+7156, *ʿôr+pāneh* [3]
lower part of face, 8559, *śāpām* [3]
face pale, 10228, *zîw* [3]
face, 4305, *l^{e}ḥî^{1}* [2]
face, 5260, *marʾeh* [2]
face, 8011, *rāʾâ^{1}* [2]
face, *NIH/RPE* [1]
reflects a face, 2021+7156+4200+2021+7156, *ha-+pāneh+l^{e}-^{1}+ha-+pāneh* [1]
face, 2086, *hôd^{1}* [1]
face death, 2222, *hārag* [1]
in the face of, 4200+5584, *l^{e}-^{1}+neged* [1]
face, 4946+7156, *min+pāneh* [1]
look in the face, 5951+7156+448, *nāśāʾ+pāneh+ʾel* [1]
made face, 5989+7156, *nātan+pāneh* [1]
face, 6641, *ʿāmad* [1]
face, 7155, *pānâ* [1]
FACED [17]
faced, 4200, *l^{e}-^{1}* [3]
faced, *NIH/RPE* [2]
faced, 448+7156, *ʾel+pāneh* [2]
faced, 7156, *pāneh* [2]
faced each other, 8011+7156, *rāʾâ^{1}+pāneh* [2]
faced forward, 448+4578+7156, *ʾel+mûl^{3}+pāneh* [1]
faced, 448, *ʾel* [1]
faced, 4200+7156, *l^{e}-^{1}+pāneh* [1]
faced, 4946, *min* [1]
faced, 7155, *pānâ* [1]
faced, 8011, *rāʾâ^{1}* [1]
FACEDOWN [19]
facedown, 6584+7156, *ʿal^{2}+pāneh* [15]
facedown, 448+7156, *ʾel+pāneh* [3]
fell facedown, 2556+4200+678, *ḥāwâ^{2}+l^{e}-^{1}+ʾap^{2}* [1]
FACES [52]
faces, 7156, *pāneh* [35]
faces, 678, *ʾap^{2}* [4]
faces, *NIH/RPE* [3]
faces, 6584+7156, *ʿal^{2}+pāneh* [3]
faces, 5790, *nōkaḥ* [2]
faces, 7155, *pānâ* [2]
faces, *AIT* [1]
on the faces of, 448, *ʾel* [1]
faces, 8559, *śāpām* [1]
FACING [46]
facing, 7155, *pānâ* [14]
facing, 7156, *pāneh* [9]
facing, 448+7156, *ʾel+pāneh* [3]
facing, 5584, *neged* [3]
facing, 5790, *nōkaḥ* [3]
facing, 6584+7156, *ʿal^{2}+pāneh* [3]
facing, *AIT* [2]
facing, 2006, *derek* [2]
facing each other, 4691+448+4691, *meḥ^{e}zâ+ʾel+meḥ^{e}zâ* [2]
facing, 2025, *-â^{2}* [1]
facing, 4578, *mûl^{3}* [1]
facing, 4946+5584, *min+neged* [1]
facing, 4946, *min* [1]
facing each other, 7925+5120, *qārāʾ^{2}+maʿ^{a}rākâ* [1]
FACT [5]
in fact, 3954, *kî^{2}* [2]
fact, *AIT* [1]
in fact die, 4637+4637, *mût+mût* [1]
in fact, 10029, *ʾîtay* [1]
FACTIONS [1]
factions, *AIT* [1]
FADE [3]
fade, 581, *ʾāmal^{1}* [1]
fade, 1937, *dālal^{1}* [1]
fade away, 2143, *hālak* [1]
FADED [5]
faded, 3910, *kēheh* [3]
faded, 3908, *kāhâ^{1}* [2]
FADES [2]
fades, *NIH/RPE* [1]
fades, 9164, *šāpēl^{1}* [1]
FADING [5]
fading, 5570, *nābēl^{1}* [3]
fading, 6847, *ʿereb^{2}* [1]
fading, 7155, *pānâ* [1]
FAIL [46]
fail, 3983, *kālâ^{1}* [9]
fail to have, 4162+4200, *kārat+l^{e}-^{1}* [7]
fail, 2532, *ḥādal^{1}* [4]
fail, 4202, *lōʾ* [3]
fail, 1194, *biltî* [2]
never fail, 586, *ʾāman^{1}* [1]
not fail, 586, *ʾāman^{1}* [1]
fail, 1718, *gāʿal* [1]
fail to speak, 3087, *ḥārēš^{2}* [1]
fail, 3169, *ḥātat* [1]
fail, 3312, *yābēš^{1}* [1]
fail, 3718, *yārad* [1]
fail, 3941, *kāzab* [1]
fail, 3950, *kāḥaš* [1]
fail to have, 4200+4162, *l^{e}-^{1}+kārat* [1]
fail, 4202+8505, *lōʾ+śākal^{1}* [1]
fail, 5877+824+2025, *nāpal+ʾereṣ+-â^{2}* [1]
fail, 6073+4946, *sûr^{1}+min* [1]
cross over without fail, 6296+6296, *ʿābar^{1}+ʿābar^{1}* [1]
fail, 6296, *ʿābar^{1}* [1]
fail, 6372, *ʿādar^{3}* [1]
fail, 6980, *ʿātaq* [1]
fail, 7296, *pārar^{1}* [1]
fail, 8332, *rāpâ^{1}* [1]
fail, 9462, *tāmam* [1]
fail, 10712, *šālû* [1]
FAILED [20]
failed, 4202, *lōʾ* [8]
failed, 5877, *nāpal* [4]
failed, 1698, *gāmar* [1]
failed to do, 2627, *ḥāṭāʾ* [1]
failed, 3983, *kālâ^{1}* [1]
failed, 4202+3523, *lōʾ+yākōl* [1]
failed, 4202+7756+6388, *lōʾ+qûm+ʿōd* [1]
failed, 4637, *mût* [1]
failed to keep, 6073+4946, *sûr^{1}+min* [1]
failed, 6980+4946, *ʿātaq+min* [1]
FAILING [3]
failing, 1194, *biltî* [1]
failing, 2532, *ḥādal^{1}* [1]
failing, 3877, *kābēd^{1}* [1]
FAILS [16]
fails, 4202, *lōʾ* [3]
fails, 3983, *kālâ^{1}* [2]
fails, 6440, *ʿāzab^{1}* [2]
fails, 581, *ʾāmal^{1}* [1]
fails, 2532, *ḥādal^{1}* [1]
fails to find, 2627, *ḥāṭāʾ* [1]
fails to reach, 2627, *ḥāṭāʾ* [1]
fails, 3950, *kāḥaš* [1]
fails, 4173, *kāšal* [1]
fails, 4202+586, *lōʾ+ʾāman^{1}* [1]
fails, 4631, *mûš^{2}* [1]
fails to come, 7212, *pāqad* [1]
FAINT [30]
faint, 6494, *ʿāṭap^{2}* [8]
faint, 2703, *ḥālâ^{1}* [3]
faint, 1865, *dāweh* [2]
faint, 1868, *dawwāy* [2]
faint, 3615, *yāʿēp^{1}* [2]
faint, 6634, *ʿālap* [2]
faint, 581, *ʾāmal^{1}* [1]
faint, 583, *ʾumlal* [1]
faint, 3760, *yāraʿ* [1]
faint, 3908, *kāhâ^{1}* [1]
faint, 5883+1790, *nepeš+dāʾab* [1]
faint, 6488, *ʿāṭûp* [1]
faint, 6545, *ʿîp* [1]
faint, 6546, *ʿāyēp* [1]
made faint, 8216, *rākak* [1]
faint, 8820, *šāḥaḥ* [1]
faint, 9066, *šēmeṣ* [1]
FAINTED [1]
fainted, 6634, *ʿālap* [1]
FAINTHEARTED [2]
fainthearted, 8205+4222, *rak+lēbāb* [1]
fainthearted, 8216+4222, *rākak+lēbāb* [1]
FAINTING [1]
fainting, 6545, *ʿîp* [1]
FAINTS [2]
faints with longing, 3983, *kālâ^{1}* [1]
faints, 3983, *kālâ^{1}* [1]
FAIR [6]
fair, 4797, *mêšārîm* [2]
fair, 3206, *ṭûb* [1]
fair, 3208, *ṭôbâ* [1]
fair, 3637, *yāpeh* [1]
fair, 9185, *šiprâ^{1}* [1]
FAIRLY [5]
fairly, 7406, *ṣedeq* [3]
fairly, 622, *ʾ^{e}met* [1]
fairly, 928+7406, *b^{e}-+ṣedeq* [1]
FAIRNESS [1]
fairness, 622, *ʾ^{e}met* [1]
FAITH [16]
broken faith, 953, *bāgad* [4]
have faith, 586, *ʾāman^{1}* [2]
break faith, 953, *bāgad* [2]
good faith, 9459, *tāmîm* [2]
faith, 574, *ʾēmûn^{2}* [1]
faith, 575, *ʾ^{e}mûnâ* [1]
stand firm in faith, 586, *ʾāman^{1}* [1]
breaking faith, 953, *bāgad* [1]
broke faith, 5085, *māʿal* [1]
break faith, 5086+5085, *maʿal^{1}+māʿal* [1]
FAITHFUL [41]
faithful, 586, *ʾāman^{1}* [15]
faithful, 2883, *ḥāsîd* [6]
faithful, 575, *ʾ^{e}mûnâ* [5]
faithful, 622, *ʾ^{e}met* [5]
faithful, 573, *ʾēmûn^{1}* [2]
faithful, 574, *ʾēmûn^{2}* [2]
show yourself faithful, 2874, *ḥāsad^{2}* [2]
faithful, 9068, *šāmar* [2]
faithful, 2143+928+622, *hālak+b^{e}-+ʾ^{e}met* [1]
faithful, 2876, *ḥesed^{2}* [1]
FAITHFULLY [17]
faithfully, 928+575, *b^{e}-+ʾ^{e}mûnâ* [5]
faithfully, 622, *ʾ^{e}met* [4]
faithfully, 928+622, *b^{e}-+ʾ^{e}met* [4]
faithfully, 2876, *ḥesed^{2}* [1]
faithfully, 6913+622, *ʿāśâ^{1}+ʾ^{e}met* [1]
faithfully obey, 9048+9048, *šāmaʿ+šāmaʿ* [1]
faithfully carried out, 9068, *šāmar* [1]

FAITHFULNESS [54]
faithfulness, 622, 'emet [34]
faithfulness, 575, 'emûnâ [20]

FAITHLESS [11]
faithless, 5412, mešûbâ [4]
faithless, 953, bāgad [2]
faithless, 8743, šôbāb[1] [2]
faithless, 953+954, bāgad+beged[1] [1]
faithless, 6047+4213, sûg[1]+lēb [1]
faithless, 6091, sēṭ [1]

FALCON [1]
falcon, 1901, dayyâ [1]

FALCON'S [1]
falcon's, 370, 'ayyâ[1] [1]

FALCONS [1]
falcons, 1901, dayyâ [1]

FALL [180]
fall, 5877, nāpal [102]
fall, 2118, hāyâ [9]
fall, 3718, yārad [6]
fall, 4173, kāšal [5]
fall, 4572, môṭ[1] [5]
fall down, 10484, nepal [5]
fall, NIH/RPE [4]
make fall, 5877, nāpal [4]
fall, 5147, mappelet [3]
fall, 5570, nābēl[1] [3]
fall down, 5877, nāpal [3]
fall in, 6015+448, sābab+'el [2]
fall, 369, 'ēd [1]
fall, 2092, hāwâ[1] [1]
made fall, 2118+4200+4842, hāyâ+le-1+mikšôl [1]
fall, 2565, ḥûl[1] [1]
fall, 3214, ṭûl [1]
fall, 3615, yā'ēp[1] [1]
fall down, 3718, yārad [1]
cause to fall, 4173, kāšal [1]
make fall, 4173, kāšal [1]
stumble and fall, 4173+4173, kāšal+kāšal [1]
fall, 4174, kiššālôn [1]
let fall, 4572, môṭ[1] [1]
makes fall, 4842, mikšôl [1]
fall on, 5162, māšā' [1]
fall, 5782, nākâ [1]
cause to fall, 5877, nāpal [1]
caused to fall, 5877, nāpal [1]
fall in battle, 5877+2728, nāpal+ḥālāl[1] [1]
fall limp, 5877, nāpal [1]
have fall, 5877, nāpal [1]
let fall, 5877, nāpal [1]
fall, 6296, 'ābar[1] [1]
fall, 6903, 'ārap[1] [1]
fall, 7520, ṣela' [1]
fall upon, 7925, qārā'[2] [1]
fall, 8069, rābaṣ [1]
showers fall, 8319, rā'ap [1]
fall prostrate, 8817, šāḥâ [1]
allowed to fall into ruin, 8845, šāḥat [1]

FALLEN [59]
fallen, 5877, nāpal [40]
fallen, 2118, hāyâ [5]
lie fallen, 5877, nāpal [2]
fallen, NIH/RPE [1]
fallen, 995, bô' [1]
fallen, 3190, ṭāba' [1]
fallen, 3718, yārad [1]
fallen, 3721, yārâ[1] [1]
fallen, 4842, mikšôl [1]
fallen, 5147, mappelet [1]
fallen, 5782, nākâ [1]
fallen down, 5877, nāpal [1]
grapes that have fallen, 7261, pereṭ [1]
fallen down, 8069, rābaṣ [1]
snow fallen, 8919, šālag [1]

FALLING [6]
falling, 5877, nāpal [3]
falling, 3718, yārad [2]
stopped falling, 3973, kālā'[1] [1]

FALLS [31]
falls, 5877, nāpal [23]
falls prostrate, 5877, nāpal [2]
falls, 3655, yāṣā' [1]
falls, 3718, yārad [1]
falls down, 5877, nāpal [1]
falls, 5989, nātan [1]
falls, 6590, 'ālâ [1]
falls, 7520, ṣela' [1]

FALSE [51]
false, 8736, šāw' [15]
false, 9214, šeqer [14]
false gods, 3942, kāzāb [3]
false, 5327, mirmâ[1] [3]
false prophets, 967, bad[5] [2]
false, 3941, kāzab [2]
prove false, 3941, kāzab [2]
false, 3942, kāzāb [2]
false, 9213, šāqar [2]
false gods, 9214, šeqer [2]
false, 224, 'āwen[1] [1]
fill with false hopes, 2038, hābal [1]
false, 6406, 'awlâ [1]
false, 9332, tōhû [1]

FALSEHOOD [6]
falsehood, 9214, šeqer [3]
falsehood, 8736, šāw' [2]
falsehood, 5086, ma'al[1] [1]

FALSELY [12]
falsely, 4200+2021+9214, le-1+ha-+šeqer [4]
falsely, 9214, šeqer [3]
falsely, 6584+9214, 'al[2]+šeqer [1]
swears falsely, 8678, šāba' [1]
falsely, 8736, šāw' [1]
deal falsely, 9213, šāqar [1]
falsely accused, 10030+10642, 'akal+qeraṣ [1]

FALTER [2]
falter, 3908, kāhâ[1] [1]
falter, 8332, rāpâ[1] [1]

FALTERED [1]
faltered, 4173, kāšal [1]

FALTERING [3]
faltering, 6888, 'ārēl [2]
faltering, 4156, kāra' [1]

FALTERS [1]
falters, 9494, tā'â [1]

FAME [16]
fame, 9005, šēm[1] [10]
fame, 9051, šēma' [4]
fame, 2352, zēker [1]
fame, 9053, šōma' [1]

FAMILIAR [2]
familiar with, 3359, yāda' [1]
familiar with, 6122, sākan[1] [1]

FAMILIES [109]
families, 1074+3, bayit[1]+'āb [57]
families, 3, 'āb [36]
families, 5476, mišpāḥâ [7]
families, 1074, bayit[1] [4]
families, 278, 'āḥ[2] [1]
families, 1201, bēn[1] [1]
families, 1505, geber[1] [1]
families, 3251, ṭap[1] [1]
registration by families, 3509, yāḥaś [1]

FAMILY [155]
family, 1074, bayit[1] [67]
family, 1074+3, bayit[1]+'āb [25]
family, 3, 'āb [14]
family, 5476, mišpāḥâ [7]
family, NIH/RPE [6]
family, 2446, zera' [5]
family line, 1074, bayit[1] [4]
family, 278, 'āḥ[2] [3]
family land, 8441+299, śādeh+'aḥuzzâ [3]
build a family, 1215, bānâ [2]
family line, 2446, zera' [2]
family, 3509, yāḥaś [2]
family background, 4580, môledet [2]
family, 4580, môledet [2]
family possessions, 3, 'āb [1]
family of Aaron, 195, 'aharôn [1]
family property, 299, 'aḥuzzâ [1]
outside the family, 2021+2575+2025+2424, ha-+ḥûṣ+-â[2]+zār [1]
outside a priest's family, 2424, zār [1]
family, 2646, ḥay[3] [1]
family, 4751, maṭṭeh [1]
every family, 5476+2256+5476, mišpāḥâ+we-+mišpāḥâ [1]
family line, 5916+9247, nēṣer+šōreš [1]
account of the family, 9352, tôlēdôt [1]
family line, 9352, tôlēdôt [1]

FAMINE [95]
famine, 8280, rā'āb [91]
famine, NIH/RPE [1]
famine, 4103, kāpān [1]
feel the famine, 8279, rā'ēb[1] [1]
famine, 8282, re'ābôn [1]

FAMISHED [3]
famished, 6546, 'āyēp [2]
famished, 8279, rā'ēb[1] [1]

FAMOUS [11]
famous, 9005, šēm[1] [5]
famous, 7924+9005, qārā'[1]+šēm[1] [2]
famous, NIH/RPE [1]
famous, 408+9005, 'îš[1]+šēm[1] [1]
make famous, 3512, yāṭab [1]
became famous, 6913+9005, 'āśâ[1]+šēm[1] [1]

FANGS [5]
fangs, 5506, metalle'ôt [2]
fangs, 4383, lāšôn [1]
fangs, 4922, maltā'ôt [1]
fangs, 9094, šēn[1] [1]

FANS [1]
fans, 5870, nāpaḥ [1]

FANTASIES [3]
fantasies, 8199, rêq [2]
fantasies, 7513, ṣelem[2] [1]

FAR [214]
as far as, 6330, 'ad[2] [70]
far be it, 2721, ḥālîl[2] [12]
far, 8158, rāḥôq [12]
far, 8178, rāḥaq [12]
far away, 8158, rāḥôq [9]
far, NIH/RPE [8]
far away, 8178, rāḥaq [7]
far end, 3752, yerēkâ [6]
far away, 4946+8158, min+rāḥôq [5]
far from, 4946, min [4]
far, 3752, yerēkâ [3]
drive far, 8178, rāḥaq [3]
keep far, 8178, rāḥaq [3]
as far as, 2025, -â[2] [2]
far exceeded, 3578, yāsap [2]
far and wide, 4946+2085+2256+2134, min+hû'+we-+hāle'â [2]
far from, 4946+5584, min+neged [2]
far away, 5305, merḥāq [2]
as far away as, 6330, 'ad[2] [2]
this far, 6330+2151, 'ad[2]+halōm [2]
gone too far, 8041, rab[1] [2]
remove far, 8178, rāḥaq [2]
sent far away, 8178, rāḥaq [2]
far side, 339, 'aḥar [1]
far side, 344, 'aḥarît [1]
as far as, 448+4578, 'el+mûl[3] [1]
as far as, 448, 'el [1]
far back in, 928+3752, be-+yerēkâ [1]
far off, 928+8158, be-+rāḥôq [1]
far, 1524, gādôl [1]
as far as, 2256, we- [1]
by far, 3578, yāsap [1]
even far, 3856+4394, yeter[1]+me'ōd [1]
as far as possible, 3869+1896, ke-+day [1]
as far as, 3869, ke- [1]

so far as, 4200+3972, *l^{e}-^{1}+kōl* [1]
far, 4394, *m^{e}'ōd* [1]
far away, 4946+5305, *min+merḥāq* [1]
far, 6073, *sûr^{1}* [1]
went as far as, 6296, *'ābar^{1}* [1]
this far, 6330+7024, *'ad^{2}+pōh* [1]
thus far, 6330+2178, *'ad^{2}+hēnnā^{1}* [1]
even as far as, 6330, *'ad^{2}* [1]
far and wide, 6330+4200+4946+8158, *'ad^{2}+l^{e}-^{1}+min+rāḥôq* [1]
far and wide, 6330+8158, *'ad^{2}+rāḥôq* [1]
far away, 6330+4200+4946+8158, *'ad^{2}+l^{e}-^{1}+min+rāḥôq* [1]
as far as, 6584, *'al^{2}* [1]
far end, 7164, *p^{e}nîmî* [1]
far and wide, 7287, *pāraṣ* [1]
far end, 7895, *qāṣeh* [1]
far away, 7921, *q^{e}ṣāt* [1]
gone far enough, 8041, *rab^{1}* [1]
far off, 8158, *rāḥôq* [1]
withdraw far, 8178, *rāḥaq* [1]
far off, 8178, *rāḥaq* [1]
far removed, 8178, *rāḥaq* [1]
go far, 8178, *rāḥaq* [1]
must very far, 8178+8178, *rāḥaq+rāḥaq* [1]
send far, 8178, *rāḥaq* [1]
stays far, 8178, *rāḥaq* [1]
strayed far, 8178, *rāḥaq* [1]
went far, 8178, *rāḥaq* [1]
far, 8179, *rāḥēq* [1]

FAR-OFF [2]
far-off, 5305, *merḥāq* [1]
far-off, 8158, *rāḥôq* [1]

FARAWAY [1]
faraway, 5305, *merḥāq* [1]

FARE [2]
richest of fare, 2016, *dešen* [1]
fare, 8510, *śākār^{1}* [1]

FARED [2]
fared, 2118, *hāyâ* [1]
fared like, 3869, *k^{e}-* [1]

FARM [3]
farm, 6268, *'ābad* [2]
farm, 4494, *migrāš* [1]

FARMED [1]
farmed, 6275, *'^{a}bōdâ* [1]

FARMER [3]
farmer, 408+6268+141, *'îš^{1}+'ābad+'^{a}dāmâ^{1}* [1]
farmer, 438, *'ikkār* [1]
farmer, 3086, *ḥārāš^{1}* [1]

FARMERS [5]
farmers, 438, *'ikkār* [4]
farmers, 5749, *nāṭa'* [1]

FARTHER [2]
set farther back, 2958+2021+337, *ḥāṣēr^{1}+ha-+'aḥēr^{1}* [1]
farther, 3578, *yāsap* [1]

FARTHEST [5]
farthest corners, 721, *'āṣîl^{1}* [1]
farthest recesses, 3972+9417, *kōl+taklît* [1]
farthest, 7895, *qāṣeh* [1]
farthest, 8158, *rāḥôq* [1]
farthest limits, 9362, *tôṣā'ôt* [1]

FASHION [1]
fashion, 6913, *'āśâ^{1}* [1]

FASHIONED [5]
fashioned, 5126, *ma'^{a}śeh* [2]
fashioned, 3670, *yāṣar* [1]
fashioned, 6913, *'āśâ^{1}* [1]
cleverly fashioned, 9312, *t^{e}bûnâ* [1]

FASHIONING [1]
fashioning, 7445, *ṣûr^{3}* [1]

FASHIONS [3]
fashions, 3922, *kûn^{1}* [1]
fashions, 7188, *pā'al* [1]
fashions, 7671, *ṣārap* [1]

FAST [36]
fast, 7427, *ṣôm* [9]
hold fast, 1815, *dābaq* [7]
fast, 7426, *ṣûm* [5]
hold fast, 2616, *ḥāzaq* [3]
held fast, 1815, *dābaq* [2]
holds fast, 2616, *ḥāzaq* [2]
hold fast, 296, *'āḥaz^{1}* [1]
are joined fast, 1815, *dābaq* [1]
held fast, 1816, *dābēq* [1]
held fast, 4334, *lākad* [1]
fast, 5692, *nāzar^{1}* [1]
lay fast asleep, 8101, *rādam* [1]
fast horses, 8224, *rekeš* [1]
hold fast, 9461, *tāmak* [1]

FASTED [14]
fasted, 7426, *ṣûm* [12]
fasted, 7426+7426, *ṣûm+ṣûm* [1]
fasted, 7426+7427, *ṣûm+ṣôm* [1]

FASTEN [15]
fasten, 5989, *nātan* [4]
fasten, 8492, *śîm* [3]
fasten together, 2489, *ḥābar^{2}* [2]
fasten, 2489, *ḥābar^{2}* [2]
fasten, 2616, *ḥāzaq* [2]
fasten, 679, *'āpad* [1]
fasten, 6698, *'ānad* [1]

FASTENED [15]
fastened, 5989, *nātan* [4]
be fastened, 2489, *ḥābar^{2}* [2]
fastened, 8492, *śîm* [2]
fastened, *NIH/RPE* [1]
fastened, 296, *'āḥaz^{1}* [1]
fastened, 679, *'āpad* [1]
fastened, 2502, *ḥābaš* [1]
fastened on, 2520, *ḥāgar* [1]
fastened, 7348, *pātîl* [1]
fastened, 9546, *tāqa'* [1]

FASTENS [2]
fastens piercing, 4323, *lāṭaš* [1]
fastens, 8492, *śîm* [1]

FASTING [13]
fasting, 7427, *ṣôm* [10]
fasting, 7426, *ṣûm* [1]
day of fasting, 7427, *ṣôm* [1]
time of fasting, 7427, *ṣôm* [1]

FASTS [1]
fasts, 7427, *ṣôm* [1]

FAT [93]
fat, 2693, *ḥēleb^{1}* [64]
fat portions, 2693, *ḥēleb^{1}* [7]
fat tail, 487, *'alyâ* [5]
fat, 1374, *bārî'* [4]
fat, 7022, *peder* [3]
fat, 1374+1414, *bārî'+bāśār* [2]
fat, 5458, *mišmān* [2]
fat, *NIH/RPE* [1]
fat animals, 4671, *mēaḥ* [1]
layer of fat, 4833, *m^{e}kasseh* [1]
fat, 9042, *šāmēn^{1}* [1]
grew fat, 9042, *šāmēn^{1}* [1]
fat, 9043, *šemen* [1]

FATAL [2]
fatal, 2703, *ḥālâ^{1}* [1]
made a fatal mistake, 9494+928+5883, *tā'â+b^{e}-+nepeš* [1]

FATALLY [1]
fatally wounded, 1991, *dāqar* [1]

FATE [13]
fate, 5247, *miqreh* [4]
fate, *NIH/RPE* [2]
fate, 2750, *ḥēleq^{2}* [2]
fate, 2006, *derek* [1]
fate, 2475, *hebel^{2}* [1]
fate, 3427, *yôm^{1}* [1]
fate, 5787, *nākôn^{1}* [1]
fate, 8288, *rā'â^{3}* [1]

FATHER [692]
father, 3, *'āb* [528]
father, 3528, *yālad* [147]
father, 10003, *'ab* [6]
father, *NIH/RPE* [4]
father, 408, *'îš^{1}* [2]
father^{s}, 1201, *bēn^{1}* [2]
the father^{s}, 2085, *hû'* [1]
his father^{s}, 2257, *-ô* [1]
your father^{s}, 2257, *-ô* [1]

FATHER'S [128]
father's, 3, *'āb* [121]
father's, 4200+3, *l^{e}-^{1}+'āb* [4]
cousins on their father's side, 1201+1856, *bēn^{1}+dôd* [1]
father's sister, 1860, *dôdâ* [1]
his father's^{s}, 2257, *-ô* [1]

FATHER-IN-LAW [23]
father-in-law, 3162, *ḥōtēn* [19]
father-in-law, 2767, *ḥām^{1}* [4]

FATHERED [1]
fathered, 3528, *yālad* [1]

FATHERLESS [39]
fatherless, 3846, *yātôm* [36]
fatherless, 401+3, *'ayin^{1}+'āb* [1]
fatherless children, 3846, *yātôm* [1]
fatherless child, 3846, *yātôm* [1]

FATHERS [277]
fathers, 3, *'āb* [269]
our fathers^{s}, 4392, *-ām* [2]
fathers, 10003, *'ab* [2]
fathers, *NIH/RPE* [1]
foster fathers, 587, *'āman^{2}* [1]
fathers, 3528, *yālad* [1]
fathers, 8037, *ri'šôn* [1]

FATHOM [4]
fathom, 2984, *ḥēqer* [2]
fathom, 5162, *māṣā'* [2]

FATHOMED [2]
fathomed, 2984, *ḥēqer* [2]

FATTENED [11]
fattened, 5272, *marbēq* [3]
fattened calves, 5309, *m^{e}rî'* [3]
fattened animals, 5309, *m^{e}rî'* [2]
fattened, 80, *'ābas* [1]
fattened, 2693, *ḥēleb^{1}* [1]
fattened calf, 5309, *m^{e}rî'* [1]

FATTENING [1]
fattening, 1344, *bārā'^{2}* [1]

FAULT [7]
through fault, 928, *b^{e}-* [1]
fault, 928+8611+4200, *b^{e}-+ša-+l^{e}-^{1}* [1]
fault, 2627, *ḥāṭā'* [1]
fault, 4399, *m^{e}'ûmâ* [1]
fault, 6404, *'āwel* [1]
fault, 8288, *rā'â^{3}* [1]
fault, 9481, *t^{e}nû'â* [1]

FAULTLESS [1]
faultless, 3838, *yāšār^{1}* [1]

FAULTS [2]
faults, *AIT* [1]
faults, 6411, *'āwōn* [1]

FAULTY [2]
faulty, 8244, *r^{e}miyyâ^{1}* [2]

FAVOR [98]
favor, 2834, *ḥēn^{1}* [41]
favor, 8356, *rāṣôn* [15]
sought the favor of, 2704+906+7156, *ḥālâ^{2}+'ēt^{1}+pāneh* [3]
favor, 3208, *ṭôbâ* [3]

favor, 5840, *nō'am* [3]
special favor, 1388, *berākâ*[1] [2]
favor, 2876, *ḥesed*[2] [2]
look with favor, 7155, *pānâ* [2]
look with favor, 239+7156, *'ôr*[1]*+pāneh* [1]
show favor, 1067, *bîn* [1]
withdraw favor, 1757, *gāra'*[1] [1]
court favor, 2704+7156, *ḥālâ*[2]*+pāneh* [1]
curry favor with, 2704+7156, *ḥālâ*[2]*+pāneh* [1]
seek favor, 2704+906+7156, *ḥālâ*[2]*+'ēt*[1]*+pāneh* [1]
sought favor, 2704+906+7156, *ḥālâ*[2]*+'ēt*[1]*+pāneh* [1]
favor, 2850, *ḥanînâ* [1]
begged for favor, 2858, *ḥānan*[1] [1]
favor, 2858, *ḥānan*[1] [1]
show favor, 2858, *ḥānan*[1] [1]
shows favor, 2858, *ḥānan*[1] [1]
good favor, 2876, *ḥesed*[2] [1]
favor, 3202, *ṭôb*[2] [1]
found favor, 3512, *yāṭab* [1]
look with favor, 5564+7156, *nābaṭ+pāneh* [1]
favor, 5795, *nākar*[1] [1]
seek favor, 7156+2704, *pāneh+ḥālâ*[2] [1]
sought favor, 7156+2704, *pāneh+ḥālâ*[2] [1]
favor, 8171, *raḥamîm* [1]
finds favor with, 8354, *rāṣâ*[1] [1]
regain favor, 8354, *rāṣâ*[1] [1]
show favor, 8354, *rāṣâ*[1] [1]
showed favor, 8354, *rāṣâ*[1] [1]
look with favor, 9120, *šā'â* [1]
looked with favor, 9120, *šā'â* [1]
in favor of, 10378, *le-* [1]

FAVORABLE [5]
favorable, 3202, *ṭôb*[2] [4]
favorable toward, 5162+2834+928+6524, *māṣā'+ḥēn*[1]*+be-+'ayin*[1] [1]

FAVORABLY [7]
favorably disposed toward, 2834+928+6524, *ḥēn*[1]*+be-+'ayin*[1] [3]
favorably, 3202, *ṭôb*[2] [2]
favorably disposed, 3201, *ṭôb*[1] [1]
received favorably, 8354, *rāṣâ*[1] [1]

FAVORED [4]
favored, 2883, *ḥāsîd* [1]
more favored, 5838, *nā'ēm* [1]
favored, 8354, *rāṣâ*[1] [1]
favored, 8356, *rāṣôn* [1]

FAVORITE [1]
favorite, 1338, *bar*[2] [1]

FAVORITISM [2]
favoritism, 2075+7156, *hādar+pāneh* [1]
show favoritism, 2075, *hādar* [1]

FAVORS [6]
runs after for favors, 339+2388, *'aḥar+zānâ*[1] [1]
favors, 2006, *derek* [1]
favors, 2911, *ḥāpēṣ*[1] [1]
favors, 8354, *rāṣâ*[1] [1]
favors, 9373, *taznût* [1]
illicit favors, 9373, *taznût* [1]

FAWN [2]
fawn, *AIT* [1]
fawn, *NIH/RPE* [1]

FAWNS [4]
fawns, 6762, *'ōper* [2]
fawns, *NIH/RPE* [1]
fawns, 611, *'immēr*[1] [1]

FEAR [210]
fear, 3707, *yārē'*[1] [91]
fear, 3711, *yir'â* [34]
fear, 3710, *yārē'*[4] [32]
fear, 7065, *paḥad*[1] [14]
fear, 4616, *môrā'* [4]
fear, 399, *'êmâ* [2]
fear, 1593, *gûr*[3] [2]
fear, 1796, *de'āgâ* [2]
fear, 3010, *ḥarādâ*[1] [2]
fear, 3328, *yāgôr* [2]
have fear, 3707, *yārē'*[1] [2]
melting in fear, 4570, *mûg* [2]
fear, 7064, *pāḥad* [2]
great fear, 399, *'êmâ* [1]
showed fear, 2316, *zûa'* [1]
fear, 3006, *ḥārad* [1]
quaking with fear, 3006, *ḥārad* [1]
fear, 3007, *ḥārēd* [1]
fear, 3145, *ḥat*[1] [1]
filled with fear, 3707+4394, *yārē'*[1]*+me'ōd* [1]
fear disgrace, 4007, *kālam* [1]
for fear of, 4946+7156, *min+pāneh* [1]
for fear of, 4946, *min* [1]
made melt with fear, 4998, *māsâ* [1]
melt with fear, 5022+5022, *māsas+māsas* [1]
looked in fear, 7064, *pāḥad* [1]
showed fear, 7064, *pāḥad* [1]
turn in fear, 7064, *pāḥad* [1]
fear, 7146, *pallāṣût* [1]
distorted with fear, 8307, *rā'am*[2] [1]
fear, 8549, *śā'ar*[3] [1]
fear, 10227, *zûa'* [1]

FEARED [31]
feared, 3707, *yārē'*[1] [12]
be feared, 3707, *yārē'*[1] [4]
feared, 3710, *yārē'*[4] [3]
feared, 398, *'āyōm* [1]
feared, 2118+3007, *hāyâ+ḥārēd* [1]
feared, 3336, *yāgōr* [1]
are feared, 3707, *yārē'*[1] [1]
feared, 3707+3711, *yārē'*[1]*+yir'â* [1]
is feared, 3707, *yārē'*[1] [1]
feared, 3711, *yir'â* [1]
feared, 4616, *môrā'* [1]
feared, 6907, *'āraṣ* [1]
is feared, 6907, *'āraṣ* [1]
feared, 7064, *pāḥad* [1]
feared, 10167, *deḥal* [1]

FEARFUL [5]
fearful, 2324, *zāḥal*[2] [1]
fearful, 4554, *māhar*[1] [1]
fearful, 5322, *mōrek* [1]
send fearful, 7098, *pālā'* [1]
fearful, 7442, *ṣûqâ* [1]

FEARFULLY [1]
fearfully, 3707, *yārē'*[1] [1]

FEARING [1]
fearing, 3707, *yārē'*[1] [1]

FEARS [13]
fears, 3710, *yārē'*[4] [7]
fears, 3707, *yārē'*[1] [3]
fears, 3711, *yir'â* [1]
fears, 4475, *megôrâ* [1]
fears, 7064, *pāḥad* [1]

FEARSOME [1]
fearsome, 399, *'êmâ* [1]

FEAST [61]
feast, 2504, *ḥag* [33]
feast, 5492, *mišteh* [12]
feast, 430, *'ākal* [3]
feast on, 430, *'ākal* [1]
celebrate the Feast, 2510, *ḥāgag* [1]
feast on, 3567, *yānaq* [1]
prepared a feast, 4127+4130, *kārâ*[3]*+kērâ* [1]
feast, 4312, *leḥem* [1]
appointed feast, 4595, *mô'ēd* [1]
feast, 4595, *mô'ēd* [1]
Feast of Unleavened Bread, 5174, *maṣṣâ*[1] [1]
feast on, 6633, *'āla'* [1]
feast on, 8021, *re'ût* [1]
feast, 8115, *rāwâ* [1]
feast on, 8425, *śāba'* [1]
Feast of Weeks, 8651, *šābûa'* [1]

FEASTED [1]
feasted, 9272, *šātâ*[2] [1]

FEASTING [13]
feasting, 5492, *mišteh* [8]
feasting, 430, *'ākal* [2]
feasting, 430+2256+9272, *'ākal+we-+šātâ*[2] [1]
feasting, 2285, *zebaḥ*[1] [1]
feasting, 5301, *marzēaḥ* [1]

FEASTS [29]
appointed feasts, 4595, *mô'ēd* [24]
religious feasts, 2504, *ḥag* [2]
feasts, 4595, *mô'ēd* [1]
feasts, 5492, *mišteh* [1]
feasts on, 5517, *mātaq* [1]

FEAT [1]
feat, 1821+1524, *dābār+gādôl* [1]

FEATHERS [6]
feathers, 89, *'ebrâ* [2]
feathers, *NIH/RPE* [1]
feathers, 88, *'ēber* [1]
spreads feathers to run, 928+2021+5294+5257, *be-+ha-+mārôm+mārā'*[2] [1]
feathers, 5681, *nôṣâ* [1]

FEATURES [3]
features, *NIH/RPE* [1]
features, 5260, *mar'eh* [1]
features, 8024, *ro'î* [1]

FED [7]
fed, 430, *'ākal* [3]
fed, 1176, *bālal*[1] [1]
place where fed, 5337, *mir'eh* [1]
fed, 5338, *mar'ît* [1]
was fed, 10226, *zûn* [1]

FEE [2]
fee, 5613, *nēdeh* [1]
fee for divination, 7877, *qesem* [1]

FEEBLE [7]
feeble, 8333, *rāpeh* [2]
feeble, 584, *'amēlāl* [1]
feeble, 4202+3888, *lō'+kabbîr* [1]
feeble, 4202+6437, *lō'+'ōz* [1]
feeble, 7028, *pûg* [1]
feeble, 8332, *rāpâ*[1] [1]

FEEBLEST [1]
feeblest, 4173, *kāšal* [1]

FEED [25]
feed, 8286, *rā'â*[1] [7]
feed on, 430, *'ākal* [6]
feed on, 8286, *rā'â*[1] [4]
feed, 430, *'ākal* [2]
feed, 3920, *kûl* [2]
feed, *NIH/RPE* [1]
feed, 4312, *leḥem* [1]
feed, 5028, *mispô'* [1]
feed on, 6584, *'al*[2] [1]

FEEDING [1]
feeding, 430, *'ākal* [1]

FEEDS [5]
feeds on, 8286, *rā'â*[1] [3]
feeds on, 430, *'ākal* [1]
feeds, 5966+928+9094, *nāšak*[1]*+be-+šēn*[1] [1]

FEEL [16]
feel secure, 1053, *bāṭaḥ*[1] [4]
feel secure, 8932, *šalwâ* [3]
feel better, 3201, *ṭôb*[1] [2]
feel, 4630, *mûš*[1] [2]
feel, 1067, *bîn* [1]
feel, 3359, *yāda'* [1]
feel, 5883, *nepeš* [1]
feel the famine, 8279, *rā'ēb*[1] [1]
feel secure, 8633, *ša'anān* [1]

FEELING [2]
feeling of security, 1055, *beṭaḥ*[1] [1]
feeling way, 1779, *gāšaš* [1]

FEELINGS [2]
feelings, 8120, *rûaḥ* [2]

FEELS [2]
feels pain, 3872, *kā'ab* [1]

how it feels, 5883, *nepeš* [1]

FEET [191]
feet, 8079, *regel* [131]
feet, 7193, *pa'am* [10]
feet, 4090+8079, *kap+regel* [5]
feet, *NIH/RPE* [4]
feet, 5274, *marg^{e}lôt* [4]
feet, 10655, *r^{e}gal* [4]
at feet, 9393, *taḥat^{1}* [3]
ninety feet, 10039+10749, *'ammâ+šittîn* [3]
about six hundred feet, 752+4395+564, *'arba'^{1}+mē'â^{1}+'ammâ^{1}* [2]
feet, 892, *'āšur* [2]
seventy-five feet, 2822+564, *ḥāmēš+'ammâ^{1}* [2]
fifteen hundred feet, 547+564, *'elep^{2}+'ammâ^{1}* [1]
three thousand feet, 547+564, *'elep^{2}+'ammâ^{1}* [1]
three feet, 564, *'ammâ^{1}* [1]
six feet, 752+564, *'arba'^{1}+'ammâ^{1}* [1]
set feet, 2005, *dārak* [1]
75 feet, 2822+564, *ḥāmēš+'ammâ^{1}* [1]
seven and a half feet, 2822+928+2021+564, *ḥāmēš+b^{e}-+ha-+'ammâ^{1}* [1]
twenty feet, 2822+6926+564, *ḥāmēš+'eśrēh+'ammâ^{1}* [1]
to feet, 6641, *'āmad* [1]
feet, 6642, *'ōmed* [1]
fifteen feet, 6924+928+2021+564, *'eśer+b^{e}-+ha-+'ammâ^{1}* [1]
thirty feet, 6929+928+2021+564, *'eśrîm+b^{e}-+ha-+'ammâ^{1}* [1]
get it to its feet, 7756+7756, *qûm+qûm* [1]
45 feet, 8993+564, *šālōš+'ammâ^{1}* [1]
450 feet, 8993+4395+564, *šālōš+mē'â^{1}+'ammâ^{1}* [1]
four and a half feet, 8993+564, *šālōš+'ammâ^{1}* [1]
twenty-seven feet, 9046+6926+564, *š^{e}mōneh+'eśrēh+'ammâ^{1}* [1]
over nine feet, 9252+564+2256+2455, *šēš^{1}+'ammâ^{1}+w^{e}-+zeret* [1]
more than thirteen feet, 9596+564, *tēša'+'ammâ^{1}* [1]
nine feet, 10039+10747, *'ammâ+šēt* [1]
leaped to feet, 10624, *qûm* [1]

FELL [111]
fell, 5877, *nāpal* [67]
fell, *NIH/RPE* [6]
fell, 2118, *hāyâ* [6]
fell, 3655, *yāṣā'* [3]
fell down, 5877, *nāpal* [3]
fell, 10484, *n^{e}pal* [3]
fell in love with, 170, *'āhab* [2]
fell, 3718, *yārad* [2]
fell asleep, 3822, *yāšēn^{1}* [2]
fell, 4156, *kāra'* [2]
fell prostrate, 5877, *nāpal* [2]
fell into a deep sleep, 8101, *rādam* [2]
fell dead, 1588, *gāwa'* [1]
fell facedown, 2556+4200+678, *ḥāwâ^{2}+l^{e}-^{1}+'ap^{2}* [1]
fell prostrate, 2556, *ḥāwâ^{2}* [1]
fell heir, 3769, *yāraš^{1}* [1]
fell, 4162, *kārat* [1]
fell dead, 4637, *mût* [1]
fell gently, 5752, *nāṭap* [1]
fell upon, 5782, *nākâ* [1]
fell dead, 5877, *nāpal* [1]
evening shadows fell, 7511, *ṣālal^{3}* [1]
fell down, 10484, *n^{e}pal* [1]

FELLED [2]
be felled, 1548, *gāda'* [1]
been felled, 1548, *gāda'* [1]

FELLING [1]
felling, 4162, *kārat* [1]

FELLOW [44]
fellow, 278, *'āḥ^{2}* [19]
fellow, *AIT* [7]
fellow countrymen, 278, *'āḥ^{2}* [5]
fellow, 408, *'îš^{1}* [2]
fellow Israelite, 8276, *rēa'^{2}* [2]
fellow Jews, 278, *'āḥ^{2}* [1]
fellow Levites, 278, *'āḥ^{2}* [1]
fellow^{s}, 285, *'eḥād* [1]
fellow townsmen, 408+6551, *'îš^{1}+'îr^{1}* [1]
fellow men, 1569, *gēw^{2}* [1]
fellow officers, 6269+123, *'ebed^{1}+'ādôn* [1]
fellow, 8276, *rēa'^{2}* [1]
fellow townsmen, 9133+6639, *ša'ar^{1}+'am^{2}* [1]
fellow, 10360, *k^{e}nāt* [1]

FELLOW'S [1]
this fellow's^{s}, 4200+2296, *l^{e}-^{1}+zeh* [1]

FELLOWMAN [2]
fellowman, 408, *'îš^{1}* [1]
fellowman, 7940, *qārôb* [1]

FELLOWS [3]
fellows, *AIT* [3]

FELLOWSHIP [87]
fellowship, 8968, *šelem* [34]
fellowship offerings, 8968, *šelem* [32]
fellowship offering, 8968, *šelem* [20]
fellowship, 6051, *sôd* [1]

FELT [9]
felt compelled, 706, *'āpaq* [1]
felt ashamed, 1017, *bôš^{1}* [1]
felt shame, 1017, *bôš^{1}* [1]
felt pain, 2655, *ḥîl^{1}* [1]
felt sorry, 2798, *ḥāmal* [1]
felt, 5491, *māšaš* [1]
felt, 6296, *'ābar^{1}* [1]
felt secure, 8930, *šālû* [1]
felt secure, 8932, *šalwâ* [1]

FEMALE [34]
female, 5922, *n^{e}qēbâ* [16]
female slaves, 9148, *šipḥâ* [7]
female, *AIT* [3]
female slave, 563, *'āmâ* [2]
female donkeys, 912, *'ātôn* [3]
female, *NIH/RPE* [1]
female slaves, 563, *'āmâ* [1]
female, 3567, *yānaq* [1]

FEMALES [1]
females, *AIT* [1]

FENCE [1]
fence, 1555, *gādēr* [1]

FERMENTED [9]
fermented drink, 8911, *šēkār* [9]

FEROCIOUS [3]
ferocious, 8273, *ra'^{1}* [2]
ferocious, 7264, *pārîṣ^{1}* [1]

FERTILE [16]
fertile field, 4149, *karmel^{1}* [5]
fertile, 9045, *šāmēn^{2}* [3]
fertile, 9043, *šemen* [2]
fertile, 1201+9043, *bēn^{1}+šemen* [1]
fertile, 2446, *zera'* [1]
fertile fields, 4149, *karmel^{1}* [1]
fertile lands, 4149, *karmel^{1}* [1]
fertile pasturelands, 4149, *karmel^{1}* [1]
fertile, 4149, *karmel^{1}* [1]

FERVENT [1]
fervent, 1944, *dālaq* [1]

FESTAL [1]
festal procession, 2504, *ḥag* [1]

FESTER [1]
fester, 5245, *māqaq* [1]

FESTERING [6]
festering, 81, *'^{a}ba'bu'ōt* [2]
festering, 1734, *gārāb* [2]
festering sores, 1734, *gārāb* [1]
festering, 4416, *mā'as^{2}* [1]

FESTIVAL [30]
festival, 2504, *ḥag* [19]
New Moon festival, 2544, *ḥōdeš^{1}* [3]
festival, *NIH/RPE* [2]
festival, 2136, *hillûlîm* [1]
festival offerings, 2504, *ḥag* [1]
festival sacrifices, 2504, *ḥag* [1]
celebrate a festival, 2510, *ḥāgag* [1]
hold a festival, 2510, *ḥāgag* [1]
festival offerings, 4595, *mô'ēd* [1]

FESTIVALS [12]
festivals, 2504, *ḥag* [4]
New Moon festivals, 2544, *ḥōdeš^{1}* [4]
festivals, 4595, *mô'ēd* [2]
yearly festivals, 2504, *ḥag* [1]
New Moon festivals, 8031+2544, *rō'š^{1}+ḥōdeš^{1}* [1]

FESTIVE [2]
festive, 2510, *ḥāgag* [1]
festive, 3202, *ṭôb^{2}* [1]

FESTOONED [1]
festooned, 1544, *gādil* [1]

FETTERED [1]
were fettered, 4200+5733+5602, *l^{e}-^{1}+n^{e}ḥōšet^{1}+nāgaš* [1]

FETTERS [3]
fetters, 673, *'āsar* [1]
fetters, 2414, *zēq^{1}* [1]
fetters, 6310, *'^{a}bōt* [1]

FEVER [3]
fever, 7707, *qaddaḥat* [2]
fever, 2996, *ḥōreb^{1}* [1]

FEVERISH [1]
feverish, 2363, *zal'āpâ* [1]

FEW [55]
few, 5071, *m^{e}'aṭ* [12]
few, 5031, *mispār^{1}* [7]
only a few, 5071, *m^{e}'aṭ* [5]
few, *AIT* [4]
few, 5070, *mā'aṭ* [4]
few, 5493, *mōt^{1}* [3]
few grapes, 6622, *'ōlēlôt* [2]
few, 285, *'eḥād* [1]
only a few, 285, *'eḥād* [1]
very few, 632+4663, *'enôš^{1}+miz'ār* [1]
few, 3869+5071, *k^{e}-+m^{e}'aṭ* [1]
few, 4946, *min* [1]
only a few, 5031, *mispār^{1}* [1]
just a few, 5070, *mā'aṭ* [1]
make few in number, 5070, *mā'aṭ* [1]
few, 5071+928+5031, *m^{e}'aṭ+b^{e}-+mispār^{1}* [1]
too few, 5071, *m^{e}'aṭ* [1]
very few, 5071+4663, *m^{e}'aṭ+miz'ār* [1]
only a few, 5203, *miṣ'ār^{1}* [1]
few in number, 5493+5071, *mōt^{1}+m^{e}'aṭ* [1]
only a few, 5493+5031, *mōt^{1}+mispār^{1}* [1]
very few, 5493+5031, *mōt^{1}+mispār^{1}* [1]
few, 7920, *qāṣēr* [1]
few, 8586, *śārîd^{1}* [1]
few, 9109, *š^{e}nayim* [1]

FEWEST [1]
fewest, 5071, *m^{e}'aṭ* [1]

FIELD [185]
field, 8441, *śādeh* [128]
field commander, 8072, *rab-šāqēh* [12]
field, 2754, *ḥelqâ^{2}* [10]
field, 8442, *śāday* [9]
fertile field, 4149, *karmel^{1}* [5]
field, 10119, *bar^{1}* [5]
field, 2754+8441, *ḥelqâ^{2}+śādeh* [4]
field, *NIH/RPE* [3]
open field, 8441, *śādeh* [2]
field, 824, *'ereṣ* [1]
field, 1474, *g^{e}bûlâ* [1]
mown field, 1600, *gēz* [1]
sown field, 4669, *mizrā'* [1]
field of melons, 5252, *miqšâ^{2}* [1]

field, 5776, *nîr*[3] [1]
field, 7156, *pāneh* [1]

FIELDS [99]
fields, 8441, *śādeh* [76]
fields, 824, *'ereṣ* [5]
fields, 8727, *šedēmâ* [4]
fields, 141, *'adāmâ*[1] [2]
fields, 2575, *ḥûṣ* [2]
fields, 3320, *yāgab* [2]
fields, 8442, *śāday* [2]
work fields, 438, *'ikkār* [1]
fields, 2750, *ḥēleq*[2] [1]
fields, 3321, *yāgēb* [1]
fields, 4120, *kar*[2] [1]
working fields and vineyards, 4144, *kōrēm* [1]
fertile fields, 4149, *karmel*[1] [1]

FIELDSTONES [1]
fieldstones, 74+8969, *'eben+šālēm*[2] [1]

FIERCE [49]
fierce, 3019, *ḥārôn* [28]
fierce, 3034, *ḥorî* [3]
fierce, 6434, *'az* [3]
fierce, 7997, *qāšeh* [3]
fierce, 1524, *gādôl* [2]
fierce, 2779, *ḥēmâ* [2]
fierce, 6883, *'ārîṣ* [2]
fierce, 425, *'akzār* [1]
fierce lion, 787, *'arî* [1]
fierce, 2405, *za'am* [1]
fierce, 3877, *kābēd*[1] [1]
grew fierce, 3877, *kābēd*[1] [1]
fierce, 5253+5883, *mar*[1]*+nepeš* [1]

FIERCE-LOOKING [1]
fierce-looking, 6434+7156, *'az+pāneh* [1]

FIERCELY [3]
fiercely, 928+2021+6677, *be-+ha-+'ēmeq* [1]
fiercely, 2805, *ḥāmās* [1]
blow fiercely, 5723, *nāḥar* [1]

FIERCER [1]
fiercer, 2523, *ḥādad* [1]

FIERCEST [1]
fiercest, 2617, *ḥāzāq* [1]

FIERY [9]
fiery, 836, *'ēš*[1] [9]

FIFTEEN [17]
fifteen, 2822+6926, *ḥāmēš+'eśrēh* [8]
fifteen, 2822+6925, *ḥāmēš+'āśār* [6]
fifteen hundred feet, 547+564,
'elep[2]*+'ammâ*[1] [1]
fifteen feet, 6924+928+2021+564,
'eśer+be-+ha-+'ammâ[1] [1]
fifteen, 6927+2256+2822,
'aśārâ+we-+ḥāmēš [1]

FIFTEENTH [17]
fifteenth, 2822+6925, *ḥāmēš+'āśār* [15]
fifteenth, 2822+6926, *ḥāmēš+'eśrēh* [2]

FIFTH [51]
fifth, 2797, *ḥamîšî* [43]
fifth, 2822, *ḥāmēš* [5]
one fifth, 2797, *ḥamîšî* [1]
take a fifth, 2821, *ḥāmaš* [1]
fifth, 2823, *ḥōmeš*[1] [1]

FIFTIES [4]
fifties, 2822, *ḥāmēš* [4]

FIFTIETH [3]
fiftieth, 2822, *ḥāmēš* [3]

FIFTY [77]
fifty, 2822, *ḥāmēš* [77]

FIFTY-FIVE [2]
fifty-five, 2822+2256+2822,
ḥāmēš+we-+ḥāmēš [2]

FIFTY-SECOND [1]
fifty-second, 2822+2256+9109,
ḥāmēš+we-+šenayim [1]

FIFTY-TWO [3]
fifty-two, 2822+2256+9109,
ḥāmēš+we-+šenayim [3]

FIG [26]
fig tree, 9300, *te'ēnâ* [15]
fig trees, 9300, *te'ēnâ* [6]
fig, 9300, *te'ēnâ* [2]
fig ripe, 1136, *bikkûrâ* [1]
fig cakes, 1811, *debēlâ* [1]
fig trees, 9204, *šiqmâ* [1]

FIGHT [101]
fight, 4309, *lāḥam*[1] [70]
fight, 4878, *milḥāmâ* [14]
fight, *NIH/RPE* [2]
fight bravely, 2616, *ḥāzaq* [2]
fight, 6913, *'āśâ*[1] [2]
fight, 7371, *ṣābā'*[1] [2]
called out to fight, 2410, *zā'aq* [1]
fight, 3655+4200+2021+4878,
yāṣā'+le-[1]+ha-+milḥāmâ [1]
fight battle, 4309, *lāḥam*[1] [1]
fight, 4309+4309, *lāḥam*[1]*+lāḥam*[1] [1]
fight broke out, 5897, *nāṣâ*[1] [1]
got into a fight, 5897, *nāṣâ*[1] [1]
fight, 6584, *'al*[2] [1]
fight, 7925, *qārā'*[2] [1]
fight hand to hand, 8471, *śāḥaq* [1]

FIGHTER [4]
valiant fighter, 1201+408+2657,
bēn[1]*+'îš*[1]*+ḥayil* [2]
experienced fighter, 408+4878, *'îš*[1]*+milḥāmâ* [1]
fighter, 1475, *gibbôr* [1]

FIGHTERS [4]
valiant fighters, 408+2657, *'îš*[1]*+ḥayil* [2]
fighters, 1475, *gibbôr* [1]
good fighters, 1475, *gibbôr* [1]

FIGHTING [64]
fighting, 4878, *milḥāmâ* [16]
fighting men, 1475+2657, *gibbôr+ḥayil* [12]
fighting, 4309, *lāḥam*[1] [11]
fighting men, 6639, *'am*[2] [6]
fighting, 5897, *nāṣâ*[1] [3]
best fighting men, 1475+2657, *gibbôr+ḥayil* [2]
fighting men, 1475, *gibbôr* [2]
fighting, 4722, *maḥaneh* [2]
fighting, 6584, *'al*[2] [2]
fighting, 6913+4878, *'āśâ*[1]*+milḥāmâ* [2]
experienced fighting men,
408+4878+1475+2657,
'îš[1]*+milḥāmâ+gibbôr+ḥayil* [1]
fighting, 1201+2657, *bēn*[1]*+ḥayil* [1]
brave fighting men, 1475+2657,
gibbôr+ḥayil [1]
fighting with, 2118+907, *hāyâ+'ēt*[2] [1]
fighting, 2657, *ḥayil* [1]
fighting, 7371, *ṣābā'*[1] [1]

FIGHTS [5]
fights, 4309, *lāḥam*[1] [4]
fights, 8189, *rîb*[1] [1]

FIGS [19]
figs, 9300, *te'ēnâ* [13]
figs, *NIH/RPE* [2]
early figs, 1136, *bikkûrâ* [1]
cake of pressed figs, 1811, *debēlâ* [1]
cakes of pressed figs, 1811, *debēlâ* [1]
cakes of figs, 7811, *qayiṣ* [1]

FIGURE [2]
figure, 1952, *demût* [2]

FIGURES [2]
figures, 1952, *demût* [1]
figures, 7512, *ṣelem*[1] [1]

FILIGREE [6]
filigree, 5401, *mišbeṣôt* [3]
filigree settings, 5401, *mišbeṣôt* [2]
filigree settings, 8687, *šābaṣ* [1]

FILL [59]
fill, 4848, *mālē'*[1] [38]
fill, 928, *be-* [2]
fill, 8425, *śāba'* [2]
fill, 8427, *śōba'* [2]
fill, *NIH/RPE* [1]
fill with terror, 1286, *bā'at* [1]
fill with false hopes, 2038, *hābal* [1]
have fill, 4848, *mālē'*[1] [1]
drink fill, 6010, *sābā'*[1] [1]
fill, 7064, *pāḥad* [1]
drunk its fill, 8115, *rāwâ* [1]
eat fill, 8425, *śāba'* [1]
eats fill, 8425, *śāba'* [1]
had fill, 8425, *śāba'* [1]
have fill, 8425, *śāba'* [1]
drink fill, 8910, *šākar* [1]
have fill, 8910, *šākar* [1]
fill with horror, 9037, *šāmēm*[1] [1]
fill, 10678, *śaggî'* [1]

FILLED [134]
filled, 4848, *mālē'*[1] [45]
filled, 4849, *mālē'*[2] [32]
be filled, 4848, *mālē'*[1] [10]
filled, 8425, *śāba'* [9]
filled, *AIT* [4]
was filled, 4848, *mālē'*[1] [4]
filled with terror, 3169, *ḥātat* [3]
filled, 4850, *melō'* [3]
filled, *NIH/RPE* [1]
filled with, 928+7931, *be-+qereb* [1]
filled with, 1251, *ba'al*[1] [1]
filled, 2118+928+3972, *hāyâ+be-+kōl* [1]
terror filled, 3006+4394, *ḥārad+me'ōd* [1]
filled with fear, 3707+4394, *yārē'*[1]*+me'ōd* [1]
filled with, 4023, *kāmar* [1]
are filled, 4848, *mālē'*[1] [1]
were filled, 4848, *mālē'*[1] [1]
filled, 5989, *nātan* [1]
filled in, 6037, *sāgar* [1]
filled, 6590, *'ālâ* [1]
filled with grief, 6772, *'āṣab*[2] [1]
was filled with pain, 6772, *'āṣab*[2] [1]
filled with dread, 7064, *pāḥad* [1]
filled with dread, 7762, *qûṣ*[1] [1]
filled with pride, 8123+4222, *rûm*[1]*+lēbāb* [1]
filled with joy, 8523, *śāmaḥ* [1]
filled with gladness, 8524+448+1637,
śāmēaḥ+'el+gîl[3] [1]
filled with joy, 8524, *śāmēaḥ* [1]
filled, 8612, *šā'ab* [1]
filled with food, 9042, *šāmēn*[1] [1]
filled with delight, 9141, *ša'ašû'îm* [1]
filled, 10416, *melā'* [1]

FILLING [3]
filling, 4848, *mālē'*[1] [3]

FILLS [4]
fills, 4848, *mālē'*[1] [3]
fills, 4059, *kāsâ* [1]

FILTH [7]
filth, 7363, *ṣō'â* [3]
filth, 2989, *ḥarā'îm* [2]
filth, 1672, *gālāl*[1] [1]
filth, 9199, *šiqqûṣ* [1]

FILTHINESS [1]
filthiness, 3240, *ṭum'â* [1]

FILTHY [3]
filthy, 7364, *ṣō'î* [2]
filthy, 6340, *'iddâ* [1]

FINAL [3]
final destiny, 344, *'aḥarît* [1]
final outcome, 344, *'aḥarît* [1]
final, 7756, *qûm* [1]

FINALLY [14]
finally, 2256, *w^{e}-* [7]
finally, *NIH/RPE* [1]
finally, 2256+1685, *w^{e}-+gam* [1]
finally, 3983, *kālâ^{1}* [1]
finally, 6330+889, *ʿad^{2}+'ăšer* [1]
finally, 10008, *'^{e}dayin* [1]
finally, 10221+10527+10024, *w^{e}-+ʿad+'oh^{o}rên* [1]
finally, 10221, *w^{e}-* [1]

FIND [160]
find, 5162, *māṣā'* [85]
find out, 3359, *yādaʿ* [8]
find out, 8011, *rā'â^{1}* [8]
find, *NIH/RPE* [5]
find, 8011, *rā'â^{1}* [4]
find, 10708, *š^{e}kaḥ* [4]
find, 1335, *bāqaš* [3]
find refuge, 2879, *ḥāsâ* [3]
find rest, 5663, *nûaḥ^{1}* [3]
find out, 3359+2256+8011, *yādaʿ+w^{e}-+rā'â^{1}* [2]
find delight, 6695, *ʿānag* [2]
find pasture, 8286, *rāʿâ^{1}* [2]
find, 995+448, *bô'+'el* [1]
find, 1047, *bāḥar^{1}* [1]
find, 1067, *bîn* [1]
try to find, 1335, *bāqaš* [1]
find rest, 1957, *dāmam^{1}* [1]
find out, 2011, *dāraš* [1]
find, 2118, *hāyâ* [1]
find enjoyment, 2591, *ḥûš^{2}* [1]
helped find strength, 2616+906+3338, *ḥāzaq+'ēt^{1}+yād* [1]
fails to find, 2627, *ḥāṭā'* [1]
find missing, 2627, *ḥāṭā'* [1]
find delight, 2911, *ḥāpēṣ^{1}* [1]
find pleasure, 2911, *ḥāpēṣ^{1}* [1]
find, 3359, *yādaʿ* [1]
find out, 3922, *kûn^{1}* [1]
find, 4200, *l^{e}-^{1}* [1]
find, 4374, *lāqaḥ* [1]
how find things, 4537, *mâ* [1]
find out, 5162, *māṣā'* [1]
find comfort, 5714, *nāḥam* [1]
find things out by divination, 5727+5727, *nāḥaš+nāḥaš* [1]
find joy, 6695, *ʿānag* [1]
find, 7003, *pāgaʿ* [1]
find out, 8011+2256+3359, *rā'â^{1}+w^{e}+yādaʿ* [1]
find repose, 8089, *rāgaʿ^{2}* [1]
find relief, 8118, *rāwaḥ* [1]
find compassion, 8163, *rāḥam* [1]
find out, 8626, *šā'al* [1]
find shelter, 8905, *šākan* [1]
find out, 9048, *šāmaʿ* [1]
find, 9365, *tûr* [1]

FINDING [8]
finding, 5162, *māṣā'* [6]
finding, *NIH/RPE* [1]
finding out, 2984, *ḥēqer* [1]

FINDS [29]
finds, 5162, *māṣā'* [16]
finds, *NIH/RPE* [5]
finds, *AIT* [1]
finds, 1335, *bāqaš* [1]
finds repulsive, 2299, *zāham* [1]
finds delight, 2911, *ḥāpēṣ^{1}* [1]
finds pleasure, 2911, *ḥāpēṣ^{1}* [1]
finds, 4200, *l^{e}-^{1}* [1]
finds mercy, 8163, *rāḥam* [1]
finds favor with, 8354, *rāṣâ^{1}* [1]

FINE [106]
fine flour, 6159, *sōlet* [46]
fine linen, 9254, *šēš^{3}* [17]
fine, 3202, *ṭôb^{2}* [9]
fine linen, 1009, *bûṣ* [6]
fine, 9514, *tip'eret* [3]
fine, 1987, *daq* [2]
fine, 2775, *ḥemdâ* [2]
beat fine, 8835, *šāḥaq* [2]
fine dust, 85, *'ābāq* [1]
fine, 1524+2256+3202, *gādôl+w^{e}-+ṭôb^{2}* [1]
fine, 1990, *dāqaq* [1]
make fine speeches, 2488+928+4863, *ḥābar^{1}+b^{e}-+millâ* [1]
fine linen, 2583, *ḥôrāy* [1]
fine, 3637, *yāpeh* [1]
fine, 3701, *yāqār* [1]
fine gold, 4188, *ketem* [1]
fine, 4436, *mibḥār^{1}* [1]
fine robes, 4711, *maḥ^{a}lāṣôt* [1]
fine, 6159, *sōlet* [1]
fine, 6740, *ʿānaš* [1]
fine, 6971, *ʿātîq* [1]
fine gold, 7058, *paz* [1]
fine, 7059, *pāzaz^{1}* [1]
fine clothing, 7345, *p^{e}tîgîl* [1]
fine, 8031, *rō'š^{1}* [1]
fine, 8316, *ra'^{a}nān* [1]
fine perfume, 9043, *šemen* [1]

FINE-LOOKING [1]
fine-looking, 9307, *tō'ar* [1]

FINED [1]
must be fined, 6740+6740, *ʿānaš+ʿānaš* [1]

FINELY [22]
finely twisted, 8813, *šāzar* [21]
finely ground, 1987, *daq* [1]

FINERY [2]
finery, 6358, *ʿēden^{1}* [1]
finery, 9514, *tip'eret* [1]

FINES [1]
fines, 6711, *'^{a}nûšîm* [1]

FINEST [19]
finest, 2693, *ḥēleb^{1}* [5]
finest of forests, 3623+4149, *ya'ar^{1}+karmel^{1}* [2]
finest, 8031, *rō'š^{1}* [2]
finest, 1047, *bāḥar^{1}* [1]
finest, 2423, *zāqaq* [1]
finest, 3202, *ṭôb^{2}* [1]
finest wares, 3206, *ṭûb* [1]
finest gold, 4188+233, *ketem+'ûpāz* [1]
finest, 4436, *mibḥār^{1}* [1]
finest, 4458, *meged* [1]
finest, 5846, *na'^{a}mānîm* [1]
finest gold, 6033, *s^{e}gôr* [1]
finest, 8040, *rē'šît* [1]

FINGER [23]
finger, 720, *'eṣbaʿ* [17]
finger, 3338, *yād* [4]
little finger, 7782, *qōṭen* [2]

FINGERS [13]
fingers, 720, *'eṣbaʿ* [11]
fingers, 4090, *kap* [1]
fingers, 10064, *'eṣbaʿ* [1]

FINISH [9]
finish, 3983, *kālâ^{1}* [6]
finish, 3922, *kûn^{1}* [1]
finish, 3974, *kālā'^{2}* [1]
finish, 4848, *mālē'^{1}* [1]

FINISHED [70]
finished, 3983, *kālâ^{1}* [55]
finished, 8966, *šālēm^{1}* [3]
finished, *AIT* [2]
finished, 339, *'aḥar* [2]
finished, 9462, *tāmam* [2]
finished, 10354, *k^{e}lal* [2]
finished, 1298, *bāṣaʿ* [1]
finished, 4848, *mālē'^{1}* [1]
finished, 6913, *ʿāśâ^{1}* [1]
finished, 10719, *š^{e}lim* [1]

FINISHING [2]
finishing, 3983, *kālâ^{1}* [2]

FINS [5]
fins, 6181, *s^{e}nappîr* [5]

FIR [2]
fir, 9329, *tidhār* [2]

FIRE [388]
fire, 836, *'ēš^{1}* [259]
offering made by fire, 852, *'iššeh* [38]
offerings made by fire, 852, *'iššeh* [19]
fire, 10471, *nûr* [8]
set on fire, 3675+928+2021+836, *yāṣat+b^{e}+ha-+'ēš^{1}* [7]
fire, 241, *'ûr^{1}* [4]
set fire, 3675+836, *yāṣat+'ēš^{1}* [4]
set on fire, 8596+928+2021+836, *śārap+b^{e}-+ha-+'ēš^{1}* [4]
fire, 1277, *bāʿar^{1}* [3]
set fire to, 8596, *śārap* [3]
fire, 8599, *ś^{e}rēpâ* [3]
fire, *NIH/RPE* [2]
made by fire, 852, *'iššeh* [2]
offering by fire, 852, *'iššeh* [2]
sacrifice made by fire, 852, *'iššeh* [2]
set on fire, 928+2021+836+3675, *b^{e}-+ha-+'ēš^{1}+yāṣat* [2]
fire, 4258+836, *lahab+'ēš^{1}* [2]
offerings made with fire, 852, *'iššeh* [1]
fuel for fire, 928+1896+836, *b^{e}-+day+'ēš^{1}* [1]
on fire, 1277+928+2021+836, *bāʿar^{1}+b^{e}-+ha-+'ēš^{1}* [1]
fire, 1282, *b^{e}ʿērâ* [1]
set on fire, 1944, *dālaq* [1]
the fire^{s}, 2023, *-āh* [1]
fire^{s}, 2085, *hû'* [1]
set on fire, 3675+836, *yāṣat+'ēš^{1}* [1]
set on fire, 3675, *yāṣat* [1]
fire, 3679, *y^{e}qōd* [1]
quench fire, 3882, *kābâ* [1]
set on fire, 4265, *lāhaṭ^{1}* [1]
fire, 4442, *mabbēl* [1]
places for fire, 4453, *m^{e}bašš^{e}lôt* [1]
fire pit, 4509, *m^{e}dûrâ* [1]
funeral fire, 5386, *miśrāpôt* [1]
kindles a fire, 5956, *nāśaq* [1]
set on fire, 7455, *ṣût* [1]
offering made by fire, 7933+852, *qorbān+'iššeh* [1]
destroyed by fire, 8596, *śārap* [1]
make a fire, 8596, *śārap* [1]
set fire to, 8596+928+2021+836, *śārap+b^{e}-+ha-+'ēš^{1}* [1]
set fire to, 8938+928+2021+836, *šālaḥ+b^{e}-+ha-+'ēš^{1}* [1]
fire, 10080, *'eššā'* [1]

FIREBRANDS [2]
firebrands, 2415, *zēq^{2}* [1]
firebrands, 4365, *lappîd* [1]

FIREPANS [3]
firepans, 4746, *maḥtâ* [3]

FIREPOT [4]
firepot, 279, *'aḥ* [2]
firepot, 3963+836, *kiyyôr+'ēš^{1}* [1]
firepot, 9486, *tannûr* [1]

FIRES [5]
fires, 836, *'ēš^{1}* [2]
light fires, 239, *'ôr^{1}* [1]
make fires, 239, *'ôr^{1}* [1]
fires, 1277, *bāʿar^{1}* [1]

FIREWOOD [2]
firewood, 202, *'ûd* [1]
firewood, 6770, *ʿēṣ* [1]

FIRM [29]
stand firm, 6641, *ʿāmad* [3]
firm, 586, *'āman^{1}* [2]
firm, 3668, *yāṣaq* [2]
firm, 3922, *kûn^{1}* [2]
stand firm in faith, 586, *'āman^{1}* [1]
stand firm, 586+4394, *'āman^{1}+m^{e}'ōd* [1]
make firm, 1215, *bānâ* [1]
stands firm, 1215, *bānâ* [1]
take firm hold, 2616, *ḥāzaq* [1]
stand firm, 3572, *y^{e}sôd* [1]
stand firm, 3656, *yāṣab* [1]
firm place, 3845, *yātēd* [1]
gave a firm, 3922, *kûn^{1}* [1]

makes firm, 3922, *kûn*[1] [1]
firm, 3946, *kōaḥ*[1] [1]
made stand firm, 5893, *nāṣab*[1] [1]
stands firm, 5893, *nāṣab*[1] [1]
stood firm, 5893, *nāṣab*[1] [1]
stand firm, 6386, *ʿûd*[1] [1]
firm, 6437, *ʿōz* [1]
take firm hold, 6487+6487, *ʿāṭā*[2]*+ʿāṭā*[2] [1]
stands firm, 6641, *ʿāmad* [1]
stood firm, 6641, *ʿāmad* [1]
hold firm, 9419, *tākan* [1]

FIRMLY [17]
firmly, 2616, *ḥāzaq* [4]
is firmly established, 3922, *kûn*[1] [3]
established himself firmly, 2616, *ḥāzaq* [2]
firmly, 10014, *ʾazdāʾ* [2]
firmly, 586, *ʾāman*[1] [1]
been firmly decided, 3922, *kûn*[1] [1]
was firmly established, 3922, *kûn*[1] [1]
firmly, 4394, *m*[e]*ʾōd* [1]
firmly embedded, 5749, *nāṭaʿ* [1]
firmly tied, 10366, *k*[e]*pat* [1]

FIRS [1]
firs, 1361, *b*[e]*rôt* [1]

FIRST [216]
first, 8037, *riʾšôn* [100]
first, 285, *ʾeḥād* [39]
first, 8031, *rōʾš*[1] [16]
first, 8040, *rēʾšît* [13]
first, *NIH/RPE* [7]
first offspring, 7081, *peṭer* [5]
first, 3869+2021+3427, *k*[e]*-+ha-+yôm*[1] [4]
first, 928+2021+9378, *b*[e]*-+ha-+t*[e]*ḥillâ* [3]
first, 10248, *ḥad* [3]
first, 928+2021+8037, *b*[e]*-+ha-+riʾšôn* [2]
first time, 2725, *ḥālal*[1] [2]
first time, 9378, *t*[e]*ḥillâ* [2]
first, 9378, *t*[e]*ḥillâ* [2]
first, 10623, *qadmāy* [2]
first, *AIT* [1]
the first[s], 465, *ʾēlleh* [1]
first ripe fruit, 1137, *bikkûrîm* [1]
first ripe grain, 1137, *bikkûrîm* [1]
first ripe, 1137, *bikkûrîm* [1]
bearing first child, 1144, *bākar* [1]
first male offspring, 1147+7081+8167, *b*[e]*kōr+peṭer+reḥem* [1]
first male offspring, 1147, *b*[e]*kōr* [1]
first, 1147, *b*[e]*kōr* [1]
the first woman[s], 2023, *-āh* [1]
the first ones[s], 2296, *zeh* [1]
first, 3869+3427, *k*[e]*-+yôm*[1] [1]
first light of dawn, 6590+8840, *ʿālâ+šaḥar* [1]
first rays, 6757, *ʿapʿappayim* [1]
first, 8038, *riʾšōnî* [1]
first light, 10459, *n*[e]*gah* [1]

FIRSTBORN [122]
firstborn, 1147, *b*[e]*kōr* [108]
firstborn, 7081, *peṭer* [3]
firstborn male, 1147, *b*[e]*kōr* [2]
firstborn, *NIH/RPE* [1]
firstborn belongs to, 1144+4200, *bākar+l*[e]*-*[1] [1]
give the rights of the firstborn, 1144, *bākar* [1]
firstborn, 1148, *b*[e]*kōrâ* [1]
rights as firstborn, 1148, *b*[e]*kōrâ* [1]
rights of the firstborn, 1148, *b*[e]*kōrâ* [1]
firstborn, 7081+8167, *peṭer+reḥem* [1]
firstborn, 7081+8715, *peṭer+šeger* [1]
firstborn, 7082, *piṭrâ* [1]

FIRSTFRUITS [23]
firstfruits, 1137, *bikkûrîm* [12]
firstfruits, 8040, *rēʾšît* [8]
firstfruits, 8040+7262, *rēʾšît+p*[e]*rî* [2]
firstfruits of harvest, 8040, *rēʾšît* [1]

FISH [33]
fish, 1834, *dāg* [17]
fish, 1836, *dāgâ*[2] [15]
fish, 1794, *dāʾg* [1]

FISHERMEN [3]
fishermen, 1900, *dayyāg* [2]
fishermen, 1854, *dawwāg* [1]

FISHHOOK [1]
fishhook, 2676, *ḥakkâ* [1]

FISHHOOKS [1]
fishhooks, 6106+1855, *sîrâ+dûgâ* [1]

FISHING [1]
fishing, 1834, *dāg* [1]

FISHNETS [2]
fishnets, 3052, *ḥērem*[2] [2]

FIST [4]
fist, 3338, *yād* [3]
fist, 114, *ʾegrōp* [1]

FISTS [2]
fists, 114, *ʾegrōp* [1]
fists, 3338, *yād* [1]

FIT [9]
fit, 3838, *yāšār*[1] [3]
fit, *AIT* [2]
fit, *NIH/RPE* [1]
fit for, 448, *ʾel* [1]
fit for, 4200, *l*[e]*-*[1] [1]
fit for, 6913, *ʿāśâ*[1] [1]

FITTED [2]
fitted, 3481+9447, *yaḥdāw+tām* [2]

FITTING [5]
fitting, 5534, *nāʾweh* [4]
fitting, 8356, *rāṣôn* [1]

FITTINGS [1]
fittings, 4677, *m*[e]*ḥabb*[e]*rôt* [1]

FIVE [165]
five, 2822, *ḥāmēš* [164]
five hundred yards, 547+564, *ʾelep*[2]*+ʾammâ*[1] [1]

FIVE-SIDED [1]
five-sided, 2797, *ḥ*[a]*mîšî* [1]

FIX [5]
fix, 8492, *śîm* [2]
fix in mind, 899, *ʾāšaš* [1]
fix directly, 3837, *yāšar* [1]
fix, 7219, *pāqaḥ* [1]

FIXED [5]
fixed on, 448, *ʾel* [1]
fixed laws, 2978, *ḥuqqâ* [1]
fixed securely, 6451, *ʿāzaz* [1]
stared with a fixed gaze, 6641+906+7156+2256+8492, *ʿāmad+ʾēt*[1]*+pāneh+w*[e]*-+śîm* [1]
fixed, 8689, *šābar*[1] [1]

FLAGSTAFF [1]
flagstaff, 9568, *tōren* [1]

FLAKES [1]
flakes, 2892, *ḥaspas* [1]

FLAME [15]
flame, 4259, *lehābâ* [6]
flame, 836, *ʾēš*[1] [3]
flame, 4258, *lahab* [2]
flame, 8927, *šalhebet* [2]
flame, 8663, *šābîb* [1]
mighty flame, 8928, *šalhebetyâ* [1]

FLAMED [1]
flamed unchecked, 9068+5905, *šāmar+nēṣaḥ*[1] [1]

FLAMES [11]
flames, 4258, *lahab* [3]
flames, 4259, *lehābâ* [3]
fuel for flames, 928+1896+836, *b*[e]*-+day+ʾēš*[1] [1]
flames, 4225, *labbâ* [1]
flames, 4265, *lāhaṭ*[1] [1]
in flames, 4265, *lāhaṭ*[1] [1]
flames, 10695, *š*[e]*bîb* [1]

FLAMING [10]
flaming, 4259, *lehābâ* [3]
flaming, 836, *ʾēš*[1] [2]
flaming, 1944, *dālaq* [1]
flaming torches, 2338, *zîqôt* [1]
flaming, 4267, *lahaṭ* [1]
flaming torches, 4365, *lappîd* [1]
flaming, 10695, *š*[e]*bîb* [1]

FLANK [2]
flank, 4190, *kātēp* [1]
flank, 7396, *ṣad*[1] [1]

FLAP [1]
flap joyfully, 6632, *ʿālas* [1]

FLAPPED [1]
flapped, 5610, *nādad* [1]

FLARE [2]
flare up, 1277, *bāʿar*[1] [1]
flare up, 6590, *ʿālâ* [1]

FLARED [3]
flared up, 3013, *ḥārā*[1] [1]
flared, 3013, *ḥārā*[1] [1]
flared, 6590, *ʿālâ* [1]

FLASH [7]
flash like lightning, 1398, *bārāq*[1] [3]
flash, 2565, *ḥûl*[1] [1]
makes flash, 3649, *yāpaʿ* [1]
flash, 3655, *yāṣāʾ* [1]
flash, 8141, *rāzam* [1]

FLASHED [6]
flashed, *NIH/RPE* [1]
flashed back and forth, 2143, *hālak* [1]
flashed down, 2143, *hālak* [1]
flashed out, 3655, *yāṣāʾ* [1]
flashed, 3655, *yāṣāʾ* [1]
flashed back and forth, 4374+928+9348, *lāqaḥ+b*[e]*-+tāwek* [1]

FLASHES [5]
flashes, 928+836, *b*[e]*-+ʾēš*[1] [1]
flashes of lightning, 1027, *bāzāq* [1]
flashes, 1158, *bālag* [1]
throws out flashes, 2145, *hālal*[1] [1]
flashes, 4259, *lehābâ* [1]

FLASHING [7]
flashing, 4258, *lahab* [2]
flashing, 1398, *bārāq*[1] [1]
flashing back and forth, 2200, *hāpak* [1]
flashing, 4374, *lāqaḥ* [1]
flashing, 5586, *nōgah*[1] [1]
flashing, 8404, *rešep*[1] [1]

FLASK [3]
flask, 7095, *pak* [3]

FLAT [1]
flat cake, 6314, *ʿugâ* [1]

FLATS [1]
salt flats, 4877, *m*[e]*lēḥâ* [1]

FLATTENS [1]
flattens, 3718, *yārad* [1]

FLATTER [2]
flatter, 4033, *kānâ* [1]
flatter, 7331, *pātâ*[1] [1]

FLATTERING [5]
flattering, 2747, *ḥālāq*[1] [4]
flattering, 2744, *ḥālaq*[1] [1]

FLATTERS [2]
flatters, 2744, *ḥālaq*[1] [2]

FLATTERY [2]
flattery, 2747, *ḥālāq*[1] [1]
flattery, 4033, *kānâ* [1]

FLAVOR [1]
flavor, 3248, *ṭa'am* [1]

FLAW [3]
flaw, 4583, *mûm* [2]
flaw, 1821+8273, *dābār+ra'*[1] [1]

FLAWLESS [6]
flawless, 7671, *ṣārap* [3]
flawless, 2341, *zak* [1]
flawless, 3196, *ṭāhôr* [1]
flawless, 9447, *tām* [1]

FLAX [6]
flax, 7324, *pēšet* [4]
flax, 7325, *pištâ* [2]

FLEA [2]
flea, 7282, *par'ōš*[1] [2]

FLED [108]
fled, 5674, *nûs* [63]
fled, 1368, *bāraḥ*[1] [32]
fled, 2143, *hālak* [4]
fled, 5610, *nādad* [3]
fled, *NIH/RPE* [1]
fled, 995, *bô'* [1]
fled, 2905, *ḥāpaz* [1]
fled back, 5674, *nûs* [1]
fled up, 5674, *nûs* [1]
fled, 7155, *pānâ* [1]

FLEE [78]
flee, 5674, *nûs* [38]
flee, 1368, *bāraḥ*[1] [5]
flee, 4880, *mālaṭ*[1] [5]
flee, 5610, *nādad* [5]
flee, *NIH/RPE* [4]
flee, 995, *bô'* [4]
flee, 5653, *nûd* [3]
flee away, 5674, *nûs* [3]
flee, 339, *'aḥar* [2]
flee for safety, 6395, *'ûz* [2]
make flee, 1368, *bāraḥ*[1] [1]
flee in haste, 4960+5674, *mānôs+nûs* [1]
flee, 4960, *mānôs* [1]
flee in haste, 5610+5610, *nādad+nādad* [1]
forced to flee, 5674+5674, *nûs+nûs* [1]
flee, 5680, *nûṣ* [1]
flee, 10469, *nûd* [1]

FLEECE [7]
fleece, 1603, *gizzâ* [6]
fleece, 1600, *gēz* [1]

FLEEING [13]
fleeing, 5674, *nûs* [6]
fleeing, 1368, *bāraḥ*[1] [3]
fleeing, *NIH/RPE* [1]
fleeing, 2143, *hālak* [1]
fleeing, 4451, *mibrāḥ* [1]
fleeing, 4961, *menûsâ* [1]

FLEES [9]
flees, 5674, *nûs* [7]
flees headlong, 1368+1368, *bāraḥ*[1]*+bāraḥ*[1] [1]
flees, 1368, *bāraḥ*[1] [1]

FLEET [6]
fleet of trading ships, 639+9576, *'onî+taršîš*[1] [1]
fleet, 639, *'onî* [1]
fleet of ships, 641, *'oniyyâ* [1]
fleet of trading ships, 641+2143+9576, *'oniyyâ+hālak+taršîš*[1] [1]
fleet of trading ships, 641+4200+2143+9576, *'oniyyâ+le-*[1]*+hālak+taršîš*[1] [1]
fleet of trading ships, 641+9576, *'oniyyâ+taršîš*[1] [1]

FLEET-FOOTED [2]
fleet-footed, 7824+928+8079, *qal+be-+regel* [2]

FLEETING [6]
fleeting, 1368, *bāraḥ*[1] [1]
fleeting, 2039, *hebel*[1] [1]
fleeting, 2534, *ḥādēl* [1]
fleeting life, 2698, *ḥeled* [1]
fleeting, 5622, *nādap* [1]
fleeting, 6296, *'ābar*[1] [1]

FLESH [95]
flesh, 1414, *bāśār* [75]
flesh, 8638, *še'ēr* [5]
flesh and blood, 1414, *bāśār* [3]
flesh and blood, 3655+4946+2743, *yāṣā'+min+ḥalāṣayim* [2]
your own flesh and blood, 3655+4946+3870, *yāṣā'+min+-kā* [2]
flesh, *NIH/RPE* [1]
flesh, 2693, *ḥēleb*[1] [1]
raw flesh, 4695, *miḥyâ* [1]
flesh, 5055, *mē'eh* [1]
flesh, 6425, *'ôr* [1]
flesh, 6889, *'orlâ* [1]
bulges with flesh, 6913+7089, *'āśâ*[1]*+pîmâ* [1]
flesh, 10125, *beśar* [1]

FLEW [3]
flew, 6414, *'ûp*[1] [3]

FLIES [15]
swarms of flies, 6856, *'ārōb* [5]
flies, 6856, *'ārōb* [4]
flies, 2279, *zebûb* [2]
flies, 6414, *'ûp*[1] [2]
flies, 4031, *kēn*[6] [1]
flies away, 6414, *'ûp*[1] [1]

FLIGHT [14]
flight, *NIH/RPE* [2]
take flight, 87, *'ābar* [1]
put to flight, 1368, *bāraḥ*[1] [1]
takes to flight, 1368, *bāraḥ*[1] [1]
headlong flight, 2905, *ḥāpaz* [1]
took to flight, 2905, *ḥāpaz* [1]
swift flight, 3616+3618, *yā'ēp*[2]*+ye'āp* [1]
flight, 4961, *menûsâ* [1]
flight of stairs, 5092, *ma'alâ*[2] [1]
in flight, 5610, *nādad* [1]
flight, 5674, *nûs* [1]
put to flight, 5674, *nûs* [1]
put to flight, 8103, *rādap* [1]

FLIMSY [1]
flimsy wall, 2666, *ḥayiṣ* [1]

FLINT [8]
flint, 7644, *ṣōr*[1] [3]
flint, 2734, *ḥallāmîš* [1]
flint, 7641, *ṣar*[3] [1]
flint knife, 7644, *ṣōr*[1] [1]
as hard as flint, 9032, *šāmîr*[2] [1]
flint, 9032, *šāmîr*[2] [1]

FLINTY [2]
flinty rock, 2734, *ḥallāmîš* [1]
flinty, 2734, *ḥallāmîš* [1]

FLIRTING [1]
flirting, 8568, *śāqar* [1]

FLOAT [4]
float, 995, *bô'* [1]
float away, 1950, *dāmâ*[3] [1]
made float, 7429, *ṣûp*[1] [1]
float, 8492, *śîm* [1]

FLOATED [1]
floated, 2143, *hālak* [1]

FLOCK [90]
flock, 7366, *ṣō'n* [66]
flock, 6373, *'ēder*[1] [15]
flock, 8445, *śeh* [2]
young of the flock, 4166, *keśeb* [1]
flock, 5338, *mar'ît* [1]
the flock^s, 5626, *-nâ* [1]
the flock^s, 5883+4392, *nepeš+-ām* [1]
animal from flock, 7366, *ṣō'n* [1]
graze flock, 8286, *rā'â*[1] [1]
shepherd flock, 8286, *rā'â*[1] [1]

FLOCKING [1]
flocking together, 6337, *'ēdâ*[1] [1]

FLOCKS [98]
flocks, 7366, *ṣō'n* [69]
flocks, 6373, *'ēder*[1] [15]
flocks, 5238, *miqneh* [4]
small flocks, 3105, *ḥāśip* [1]
flocks and herds, 5238, *miqneh* [1]
flocks, 5238+7366, *miqneh+ṣō'n* [1]
herds and flocks, 5238, *miqneh* [1]
flocks and herds, 6373, *'ēder*[1] [1]
flocks, 7556, *ṣōneh* [1]
rest flocks, 8069, *rābaṣ* [1]
flocks, 8214, *rekûš* [1]
grazing flocks, 8286, *rā'â*[1] [1]
grazing the flocks, 8286, *rā'â*[1] [1]

FLOG [2]
flog, 5782, *nākâ* [2]

FLOGGED [2]
flogged, 5782+4804, *nākâ+makkâ* [1]
have flogged, 5782, *nākâ* [1]

FLOGGING [1]
flogging, 5596, *nega'* [1]

FLOGGINGS [1]
floggings, 5596, *nega'* [1]

FLOOD [27]
flood, 4429, *mabbûl* [10]
flood, 4784, *mayim* [3]
flood, 5643, *nāhār* [2]
flood, 8851, *šāṭap* [2]
flood, 8852, *šeṭep* [2]
flood, 9180, *šip'â* [2]
flood, *NIH/RPE* [1]
flood, 3298, *yābāl*[1] [1]
flood, 4059, *kāsâ* [1]
at flood stage, 4848+6584+3972+1536, *mālē'*[1]*+'al*[2]*+kōl+gidyâ* [1]
at flood stage, 6584+3972+1536, *'al*[2]*+kōl+gidyâ* [1]
flood, 8466, *śāḥâ* [1]

FLOODED [1]
flooded, 1504, *gābar* [1]

FLOODGATES [6]
floodgates, 748, *'arubbâ* [6]

FLOODING [2]
flooding downpour, 3888+8851, *kabbîr+šāṭap* [1]
flooding, 8851, *šāṭap* [1]

FLOODS [1]
floods, 8673, *šibbōlet*[2] [1]

FLOODWATERS [5]
floodwaters, 4429+4784, *mabbûl+mayim* [2]
floodwaters, 4784+4429, *mayim+mabbûl* [1]
floodwaters, 4784+8041, *mayim+rab*[1] [1]
floodwaters, 8673+4784, *šibbōlet*[2]*+mayim* [1]

FLOOR [55]
threshing floor, 1755, *gōren* [32]
floor, 7977, *qarqa'*[1] [5]
floor, *AIT* [4]
floor, 824, *'ereṣ* [3]
floor, *NIH/RPE* [2]
floor, 7156, *pāneh* [2]
floor space, 824, *'ereṣ* [1]
threshing floor, 1755+1841, *gōren+dāgān* [1]
floor, 2668, *ḥēq* [1]
floor, 3666, *yāṣîa'* [1]
floor, 7521, *ṣēlā'*[1] [1]
threshing floor, 10010, *'iddar* [1]
floor, 10076, *'ar'î* [1]

FLOORS [6]
threshing floors, 1755, *gōren* [3]
floors, *AIT* [2]
floors, 7977, *qarqa'*[1] [1]

FLORAL [2]
floral work, 7258, *peraḥ* [2]

FLOUR [65]
fine flour, 6159, *sōlet* [46]
flour, 7854, *qemaḥ* [13]
flour, 6159, *sōlet* [6]

FLOURISH [13]
flourish, 7255, *pāraḥ[1]* [5]
flourish, 7437, *ṣûṣ[1]* [2]
flourish, 2649, *ḥāyâ* [1]
flourish, 7238, *pārā[1]* [1]
make flourish, 7255, *pāraḥ[1]* [1]
flourish, 7541, *ṣāmaḥ* [1]
flourish, 8315, *rā‘an* [1]
made flourish, 8938, *šālaḥ* [1]

FLOURISHES [2]
flourishes, 5989, *nātan* [1]
flourishes, 7437, *ṣûṣ[1]* [1]

FLOURISHING [4]
flourishing, 3202, *ṭôb[2]* [1]
flourishing, 6867, *‘ārā[1]* [1]
flourishing, 7541, *ṣāmaḥ* [1]
flourishing, 8316, *ra‘[a]nān* [1]

FLOW [27]
flow, 5688, *nāzal* [3]
flow, *NIH/RPE* [2]
flow, 2143, *hālak* [2]
flow out, 3655, *yāṣā’* [2]
flow, 1947, *dām* [1]
make flow, 2143, *hālak* [1]
flow, 2307, *zûb* [1]
regular flow, 2307+928+1414, *zûb+b[e]-+bāśār* [1]
flow, 3298, *yābāl[1]* [1]
flow from, 3718, *yārad* [1]
flow, 3718, *yārad* [1]
let flow, 3718, *yārad* [1]
made flow down, 3718, *yārad* [1]
flow, 4570, *mûg* [1]
flow, 4784, *mayim* [1]
flow, 5227, *māqôr* [1]
flow, 5599, *nāgar* [1]
monthly flow, 5614, *niddâ* [1]
made flow, 5688, *nāzal* [1]
make flow, 7337, *pātaḥ[1]* [1]
cease to flow, 7551, *ṣāmat* [1]
flow back, 8740, *šûb[1]* [1]

FLOWED [9]
flowed, 2143, *hālak* [2]
flowed, 3655, *yāṣā’* [1]
flowed down, 3718, *yārad* [1]
flowed over, 6590, *‘ālâ* [1]
flowed back, 8740, *šûb[1]* [1]
flowed abundantly, 8851, *šāṭap* [1]
flowed, 8851, *šāṭap* [1]
flowed, 9161, *šāpak* [1]

FLOWER [5]
flower, 7488, *ṣîṣ[1]* [3]
flower, 5900, *niṣṣâ* [1]
flower, 7491, *ṣîṣâ* [1]

FLOWERLIKE [2]
flowerlike, *NIH/RPE* [2]

FLOWERS [13]
flowers, 7488, *ṣîṣ[1]* [7]
shaped like almond flowers, 5481, *m[e]šuqqād* [4]
flowers, 5890, *nēṣ[1]* [1]
flowers, 7258, *peraḥ* [1]

FLOWING [42]
flowing, 2307, *zûb* [19]
flowing, 3718, *yārad* [2]
flowing springs, 4604+4784, *môṣā’[1]+mayim* [2]
flowing, *AIT* [1]
flowing, *NIH/RPE* [1]
ever flowing, 419, *’êtān[1]* [1]
flowing stream, 419, *’êtān[1]* [1]
flowing, 995, *bô’* [1]
flowing gently, 1803, *dābab* [1]
flowing, 2143, *hālak* [1]
flowing, 2645, *ḥay[2]* [1]
flowing streams, 3298+4784, *yābāl[1]+mayim* [1]
flowing, 3655, *yāṣā’* [1]
flowing down, 3718, *yārad* [1]
flowing, 6242, *sārûaḥ* [1]
flowing, 6296, *‘ābar[1]* [1]
flowing, 7096, *pākâ* [1]
flowing, 7597, *ṣāpā[3]* [1]
flowing, 8201, *rîr[1]* [1]
flowing mane, 8310, *ra‘mâ[1]* [1]
flowing, 8673, *šibbōlet[2]* [1]
flowing, 10457, *n[e]gad* [1]

FLOWN [1]
flown away, 5610, *nādad* [1]

FLOWS [8]
flows, 995, *bô’* [4]
flows, 3655, *yāṣā’* [2]
flows away, 2143, *hālak* [1]
flows, 2143, *hālak* [1]

FLUENT [1]
fluent, 4554+4200+1819, *māhar[1]+l[e]-[1]+dābar[2]* [1]

FLUNG [1]
flung, 8959, *šālak* [1]

FLUTE [10]
flute, 6385, *‘ûgāb* [4]
flute, 10446, *mašrôqî* [4]
flute, 2720, *ḥālîl[1]* [2]

FLUTES [5]
flutes, 2720, *ḥālîl[1]* [4]
flutes, 5704, *n[e]ḥîlôt* [1]

FLUTTERING [2]
fluttering, 5610, *nādad* [1]
fluttering, 5653, *nûd* [1]

FLY [13]
fly away, 6414, *‘ûp[1]* [4]
fly, 6414, *‘ûp[1]* [3]
fly, *NIH/RPE* [1]
fly away, 1368, *bāraḥ[1]* [1]
fly away, 5610, *nādad* [1]
fly off, 5970, *nāšal* [1]
fly along, 6414, *‘ûp[1]* [1]
fly off, 6414, *‘ûp[1]* [1]

FLYING [9]
flying, 6414, *‘ûp[1]* [3]
flying, 4053, *kānāp* [2]
flying, 6416, *‘ôp* [2]
flying, 2143, *hālak* [1]
flying, 3655, *yāṣā’* [1]

FOAL [1]
foal, 1201, *bēn[1]* [1]

FOAM [2]
foam, 2812, *ḥāmar[1]* [1]
foam, 7824, *qal* [1]

FOAMING [2]
foaming, 2812, *ḥāmar[1]* [1]
foaming, 2815, *ḥemer* [1]

FODDER [7]
fodder, 5028, *mispô’* [4]
fodder, 1173, *b[e]lîl* [3]

FOE [10]
foe, 367, *’ōyēb* [3]
foe, 7640, *ṣar[2]* [3]
foe, 8533, *śānē’* [2]
foe, *NIH/RPE* [1]
foe, 7675, *ṣārar[2]* [1]

FOES [52]
foes, 7640, *ṣar[2]* [19]
foes, 367, *’ōyēb* [12]
foes, 8533, *śānē’* [11]
foes, 7756, *qûm* [5]
foes, 7675, *ṣārar[2]* [4]
foes, 7799, *qîm* [1]

FOILS [2]
foils, 7296, *pārar[1]* [2]

FOLD [4]
fold, 4053, *kānāp* [2]
fold of cloak, 955, *beged[2]* [1]
fold double, 4100, *kāpal* [1]

FOLDED [2]
folded double, 4100, *kāpal* [2]

FOLDING [2]
folding, 2486, *ḥibbuq* [2]

FOLDS [5]
folds, 2485, *ḥābaq* [1]
folds of robe, 2950, *ḥōṣen* [1]
folds of garment, 4053, *kānāp* [1]
folds, 5139, *mappāl* [1]
folds, 7931, *qereb* [1]

FOLIAGE [4]
thick foliage, 6291, *‘ābôt[2]* [4]

FOLLOW [124]
follow, 6913, *‘āśâ[1]* [39]
follow, 2143+339, *hālak+’aḥar* [17]
follow, 339, *’aḥar* [12]
follow, 928+2143, *b[e]-+hālak* [11]
follow, 2143+928, *hālak+b[e]-* [11]
follow, 339+2143, *’aḥar+hālak* [3]
follow, 2143, *hālak* [3]
follow, 8103, *rādap* [3]
follow, 2118+339, *hāyâ+’aḥar* [2]
follow, 6913+3869, *‘āśâ[1]+k[e]-* [2]
follow, 9068, *šāmar* [2]
follow, 339+995, *’aḥar+bô’* [1]
follow, 340, *’aḥ[a]rôn* [1]
follow, 448+3338, *’el+yād* [1]
follow, 928+8079, *b[e]-+regel* [1]
follow, 1815+339, *dābaq+’aḥar* [1]
follow, 2006, *derek* [1]
follow, 2011, *dāraš* [1]
follow, 2118, *hāyâ* [1]
follow along, 2143, *hālak* [1]
follow, 2143+928+8079, *hālak+b[e]-+regel* [1]
follow, 3655+339, *yāṣā’+’aḥar* [1]
follow, 3655, *yāṣā’* [1]
follow, 3869, *k[e]-* [1]
follow lead, 4027+6913, *kēn[2]+‘āśâ[1]* [1]
follow, 5432, *māšak* [1]
follow, 6296+339, *‘ābar[1]+’aḥar* [1]
follow, 6913+4027, *‘āśâ[1]+kēn[2]* [1]
follow, 7756+339, *qûm+’aḥar* [1]
follow, 7756+4946+339, *qûm+min+’aḥar* [1]

FOLLOWED [78]
followed, 2143+339, *hālak+’aḥar* [27]
followed, 339, *’aḥar* [11]
followed, 2143+928, *hālak+b[e]-* [7]
followed, 995+339, *bô’+’aḥar* [5]
followed, 928+2143, *b[e]-+hālak* [3]
followed, 2143, *hālak* [3]
followed, *NIH/RPE* [2]
followed by, 2256, *w[e]-* [2]
followed, 3869, *k[e]-* [2]
followed, 9068, *šāmar* [2]
closely followed, 296, *’āḥaz[1]* [1]
followed, 339+995, *’aḥar+bô’* [1]
followed, 928, *b[e]-* [1]
followed in, 995+339, *bô’+’aḥar* [1]
followed, 2118+339, *hāyâ+’aḥar* [1]
followed, 3655+339, *yāṣā’+’aḥar* [1]
followed, 3655+6640, *yāṣā’+‘im* [1]
followed, 3655, *yāṣā’* [1]
followed the example, 3869+6913+6913, *k[e]-+‘āśâ[1]+‘āśâ[1]* [1]
followed, 6590+928+8079, *‘ālâ+b[e]-+regel* [1]
followed, 6640, *‘im* [1]
been followed, 6913, *‘āśâ[1]* [1]
followed, 6913+4027, *‘āśâ[1]+kēn[2]* [1]
followed, 7756+339, *qûm+’aḥar* [1]

FOLLOWERS [16]
followers, 6337, *‘ēdâ[1]* [10]
followers, 339, *’aḥar* [2]

followers, 408+889+2143+6640, *ʼîš[1]+ʼᵃšer+hālak+ʻim* [1]
followers, 2021+6639+889+339, *ha-+ʻam[2]+ʼᵃšer+ʼaḥar* [1]
followers, 2143+339, *hālak+ʼaḥar* [1]
his followers[s], 2157, *-hem* [1]

FOLLOWING [41]
following, 339, *ʼaḥar* [11]
following, *NIH/RPE* [5]
following, 2143+339, *hālak+ʼaḥar* [5]
following, 3869, *kᵉ-* [5]
following[s], 465, *ʼēlleh* [4]
following, 928+8079, *bᵉ-+regel* [2]
following, 928, *bᵉ-* [2]
following, 339+2143, *ʼaḥar+hālak* [1]
following, 2006, *derek* [1]
following, 4740, *moḥᵒrāt* [1]
following, 5162, *māṣāʼ* [1]
following, 6639+907, *ʻam[2]+ʼēt[2]* [1]
following[s], 9029, *šᵉmînî* [1]
following, 9108, *šēnî* [1]

FOLLOWS [14]
follows, 928+2143, *bᵉ-+hālak* [3]
follows, 995+339, *bôʼ+ʼaḥar* [2]
follows, 7925, *qārāʼ[2]* [2]
follows, 339+4027, *ʼaḥar+kēn[2]* [1]
follows, 339, *ʼaḥar* [1]
as follows, 465, *ʼēlleh* [1]
follows, 5595, *nāgaʻ* [1]
follows, 6584+7925, *ʻal[2]+qārāʼ[2]* [1]
as follows, 10341+10180, *kᵉ+dᵉnâ* [1]
as follows, 10358, *kᵉnēmāʼ* [1]

FOLLY [35]
folly, 222, *ʼiwwelet* [22]
folly, 6121, *siklût* [6]
folly, 5576, *nᵉbālâ* [3]
sinful folly, 222, *ʼiwwelet* [1]
folly, 4070, *kᵉsîlût* [1]
folly, 4074, *kislâ* [1]
folly, 8508, *śiklût* [1]

FOMENTING [1]
fomenting, 1819, *dābar[2]* [1]

FOND [1]
fond, 2911, *ḥāpēṣ[1]* [1]

FONDLED [2]
fondled, 5080, *māʻak* [1]
were fondled, 5080, *māʻak* [1]

FOOD [263]
food, 4312, *leḥem* [124]
food, 431, *ʼōkel* [36]
food, 4407, *maʼᵃkāl* [21]
food, 433, *ʼoklâ* [11]
food, 430, *ʼākal* [8]
tasty food, 4761, *maṭʻām* [6]
food, *NIH/RPE* [4]
food, 3272, *ṭerep* [4]
food, 7329, *pat-bag* [4]
food, *AIT* [3]
food, 1376, *biryâ* [3]
make eat food, 430, *ʼākal* [2]
food, 7474, *ṣayid[2]* [2]
food, 7476, *ṣêdâ* [2]
food, 10410, *māzôn* [2]
crave other food, 203+9294, *ʼāwâ[1]+taʼᵃwâ[1]* [1]
craved other food, 203, *ʼāwâ[1]* [1]
food, 428, *ʼakîlâ* [1]
get food, 430, *ʼākal* [1]
had food enough, 430, *ʼākal* [1]
have food, 430, *ʼākal* [1]
prepare food to eat, 430, *ʼākal* [1]
food, 1356, *bārâ[1]* [1]
food, 1362, *bārût* [1]
choice food, 2016, *dešen* [1]
supply with food, 3920, *kûl* [1]
food, 4695, *miḥyâ* [1]
food, 4818, *makkōlet* [1]
portions of food, 4950, *mānâ[2]* [1]
presents of food, 4950, *mānâ[2]* [1]
special food, 4950, *mānâ[2]* [1]
food, 4987, *mᵉnāt* [1]
choice food, 5460, *mašmannîm* [1]
the food[s], 5626, *-nâ* [1]
food, 6289, *ʻᵃbûr[2]* [1]
offer food, 7271, *pāras[1]* [1]
food, 7326+4312, *pat+leḥem* [1]
food, 7326, *pat* [1]
choice food, 7329, *pat-bag* [1]
food supply, 7474, *ṣayid[2]* [1]
most sacred food, 7731+7731, *qōdeš+qōdeš* [1]
food, 8638, *šᵉʼēr* [1]
filled with food, 9042, *šāmēn[1]* [1]
rich food, 9043, *šemen* [1]
forbidden food, 9199, *šiqqûṣ* [1]
food, 9482, *tᵉnûbâ* [1]

FOODS [1]
richest of foods, 2693+2256+2016, *ḥēleb[1]+wᵉ-+dešen* [1]

FOOL [73]
fool, 4067, *kᵉsîl[1]* [36]
fool, 211, *ʼᵉwîl[1]* [16]
fool, 5572, *nābāl[1]* [9]
fool, 6119, *sākāl* [4]
made a fool of, 9438, *tālal* [2]
fool, *NIH/RPE* [1]
turns into a fool, 2147, *hālal[3]* [1]
played the fool, 5571, *nābal[2]* [1]
acted like a fool, 6118, *sākal* [1]
made a fool, 6618, *ʻālal[1]* [1]
making a fool of, 9438, *tālal* [1]

FOOL'S [5]
fool's, 4067, *kᵉsîl[1]* [4]
fool's, 211, *ʼᵉwîl[1]* [1]

FOOLISH [24]
foolish, 4067, *kᵉsîl[1]* [9]
foolish, 5572, *nābāl[1]* [4]
done a foolish thing, 6118, *sākal* [3]
foolish, 222, *ʼiwwelet* [2]
foolish, 216, *ʼᵉwilî* [1]
foolish, 2147, *hālal[3]* [1]
foolish, 3282, *yāʼal[1]* [1]
foolish, 4071, *kāsal* [1]
foolish, 6118, *sākal* [1]
foolish, 6119, *sākāl* [1]

FOOLISHLY [2]
foolishly, 3282, *yāʼal[1]* [1]
acted foolishly, 6118, *sākal* [1]

FOOLISHNESS [1]
turn into foolishness, 6118, *sākal* [1]

FOOLS [37]
fools, 4067, *kᵉsîl[1]* [21]
fools, 211, *ʼᵉwîl[1]* [7]
makes fools of, 2147, *hālal[3]* [2]
become fools, 3282, *yāʼal[1]* [2]
fools, 5572, *nābāl[1]* [2]
wicked fools, 211, *ʼᵉwîl[1]* [1]
wicked fools, 5572, *nābāl[1]* [1]
fools, 6120, *sekel* [1]

FOOT [70]
foot, 8079, *regel* [42]
foot soldiers, 8081, *raglî* [6]
foot, 4090+8079, *kap+regel* [4]
foot soldiers, 408+8081, *ʼîš[1]+raglî* [3]
foot, 7895, *qāṣeh* [2]
on foot, 8081, *raglî* [2]
at the foot of, 9393, *taḥat[1]* [2]
foot, *NIH/RPE* [1]
set foot, 995, *bôʼ* [1]
about a foot and a half, 1688, *gōmed* [1]
set foot on, 2005, *dārak* [1]
foot, 3572, *yᵉsôd* [1]
on foot, 6584+2021+824, *ʻal[2]+ha-+ʼereṣ* [1]
men on foot, 8081, *raglî* [1]
at foot of, 9393, *taḥat[1]* [1]
foot, 9397, *taḥtî* [1]

FOOTHILLS [20]
western foothills, 9169, *šᵉpēlâ* [13]
foothills, 9169, *šᵉpēlâ* [7]

FOOTHOLD [2]
foothold, 892, *ʼāšur* [1]
foothold, 5097, *moʻᵒmād* [1]

FOOTINGS [1]
footings, 149, *ʼeden* [1]

FOOTPRINTS [2]
footprints, 6811, *ʻāqēb[1]* [1]
footprints, 6814, *ʻāqōb[1]* [1]

FOOTSTEPS [4]
footsteps, 7193, *paʻam* [2]
footsteps, 8079, *regel* [2]

FOOTSTOOL [7]
footstool, 2071+8079, *hᵃdōm+regel* [5]
footstool, 2071, *hᵃdōm* [1]
footstool, 3900, *kebeš* [1]

FOR [5303]*
for, 4200, *lᵉ-[1]* [1684]
for, 3954, *kî[2]* [1059]
for, *AIT* [802]
for, 6584, *ʻal[2]* [250]
for, *NIH/RPE* [241]
for, 928, *bᵉ-* [160]
for, 2256, *wᵉ-* [88]
for, 448, *ʼel* [74]
as for, 2256, *wᵉ-* [61]
for, 1237, *baʻad[1]* [48]
for, 4946, *min* [39]
for, 9393, *taḥat[1]* [33]
for, 889, *ʼᵃšer* [28]
for the sake of, 4200+5100, *lᵉ-[1]+maʻan* [22]
for, 10378, *lᵉ-* [22]
for sake, 4200+5100, *lᵉ-[1]+maʻan* [21]
for, 3869, *kᵉ-* [20]
for, 6640, *ʻim* [13]
but as for, 2256, *wᵉ-* [12]
as for, 4200, *lᵉ-[1]* [12]
for the sake of, 928+6288, *bᵉ-+ʻᵃbûr[1]* [11]
for, 4200+7156, *lᵉ-[1]+pāneh* [10]
for, 2025, *-â[2]* [9]
for, 10542, *ʻal* [7]
for, 4200+5100, *lᵉ-[1]+maʻan* [6]
for, 6330, *ʻad[2]* [6]
for, 907, *ʼēt[2]* [5]
for nothing, 2855, *ḥinnām* [5]
for sake, 4200, *lᵉ-[1]* [5]
for ever, 6409, *ʻôlām* [5]
for sake, 6584, *ʻal[2]* [5]
for sake, 928+6288, *bᵉ-+ʻᵃbûr[1]* [4]
in exchange for, 928, *bᵉ-* [4]
for no reason, 2855, *ḥinnām* [4]
as for, 448, *ʼel* [3]
for, 3610+889, *yaʻan[1]+ʼᵃšer* [3]
for, 9393+889, *taḥat[1]+ʼᵃšer* [3]
for, 10527, *ʻad* [3]
for, 10168, *dî* [2]
for, 10554, *ʻim* [2
for, 10341, *kᵉ-* [1]
for, 10427, *min* [1]

FORAGING [1]
foraging, 8838, *šāḥar[2]* [1]

FORBID [5]
forbid, 2721, *ḥālîl[2]* [4]
forbid, 5648, *nûʼ* [1]

FORBIDDEN [15]
forbidden, 4202+6913, *lōʼ+ʻāśâ[1]* [5]
forbidden, 7422+4202, *ṣāwâ+lōʼ* [2]
forbidden, *NIH/RPE* [1]
one born of a forbidden marriage, 4927, *mamzēr* [1]
forbidden, 5648, *nûʼ* [1]
regard as forbidden, 6887+6889, *ʻāral+ʻorlâ* [1]
forbidden, 6888, *ʻārēl* [1]
forbidden, 7422+1194, *ṣāwâ+biltî* [1]
forbidden, 7422, *ṣāwâ* [1]
forbidden food, 9199, *šiqqûṣ* [1]

FORBIDS [2]
forbids, 5648, *nûʼ* [2]

FORCE [30]
force, 2657, *ḥayil* [4]
force way through, 2238, *hāras* [2]
in full force, 3972, *kōl* [2]
force, *AIT* [1]
take by force, 1608, *gāzal* [1]
force into hiding, 2461, *ḥābāʾ* [1]
force, 2622, *ḥozqâ* [1]
armed force, 2657, *ḥayil* [1]
force, 3338, *yād* [1]
in force, 3480, *yaḥad* [1]
full force, 3972, *kōl* [1]
force to give, 4374, *lāqaḥ* [1]
force, 4722, *mah^{a}neh* [1]
force, 4804, *makkâ* [1]
labor force, 4989, *mas* [1]
slave labor force, 4989, *mas* [1]
force, 5486, *mišqāl* [1]
such force^{s}, 5877, *nāpal* [1]
labor force, 6023, *sēbel* [1]
still in force, 6330, *ʿad^{2}* [1]
force of men, 6639, *ʿam^{2}* [1]
force, 6639+4878, *ʿam^{2}+milḥāmâ* [1]
force, 6700, *ʿānâ^{2}* [1]
force, 8938, *šālaḥ* [1]
force, 10013, *ʾedrāʿ* [1]

FORCED [20]
forced labor, 4989, *mas* [14]
forced, 3899, *kābaš* [1]
forced to, 4200, *l^{e}-^{1}* [1]
forced laborers, 4989, *mas* [1]
forced to flee, 5674+5674, *nûs+nûs* [1]
forced labor, 6026, *siblôt* [1]
forced to restore, 8740, *šûb^{1}* [1]

FORCEFULLY [2]
forcefully, 928+3338, *b^{e}-+yād* [1]
came forcefully, 7502, *ṣālaḥ^{1}* [1]

FORCES [34]
forces, 4722, *maḥ^{a}neh* [5]
forces, 7372, *ṣābāʾ^{2}* [5]
forces, 2657, *ḥayil* [3]
forces, 1522, *g^{e}dûd^{2}* [2]
joined forces, 3585, *yāʿad* [2]
forces, *NIH/RPE* [1]
forces, 408, *ʾîš^{1}* [1]
join forces, 665, *ʾāsap* [1]
joined forces, 665+3481, *ʾāsap+yaḥdāw* [1]
joined forces, 665, *ʾāsap* [1]
destructive forces, 2095, *hawwâ^{2}* [1]
armed forces, 2432, *z^{e}rôaʿ* [1]
forces, 2432, *z^{e}rôaʿ* [1]
joined forces, 2489, *ḥābar^{2}* [1]
armed forces, 2657+7372, *ḥayil+ṣābāʾ^{2}* [1]
the forces^{s}, 4392, *-ām* [1]
forces, 4939, *memšālâ* [1]
forces, 5120, *maʿ^{a}rākâ* [1]
forces, 6639, *ʿam^{2}* [1]
deployed forces, 6885, *ʿārak* [1]
muster forces, 7212, *pāqad* [1]
joined forces, 7695, *qābaṣ* [1]

FORCIBLY [2]
be forcibly taken, 1608, *gāzal* [1]
was forcibly carried off, 1704+1704, *gānab+gānab* [1]

FORD [2]
ford, 5044, *maʿ^{a}bār* [1]
ford, 6302, *ʿ^{a}bārâ* [1]

FORDED [1]
forded, 6296, *ʿābar^{1}* [1]

FORDS [7]
fords, 5045, *maʿbārâ* [5]
fords, 6302, *ʿ^{a}bārâ* [2]

FOREFATHER [12]
forefather, 3, *ʾāb* [11]
forefather, 3528, *yālad* [1]

FOREFATHER'S [1]
forefather's, 3, *ʾāb* [1]

FOREFATHERS [83]
forefathers, 3, *ʾāb* [80]
forefathers, 3+3, *ʾāb+ʾāb* [2]
forefathers, 3+8037, *ʾāb+riʾšôn* [1]

FOREFINGER [2]
forefinger, 720, *ʾeṣbaʿ* [2]

FOREHEAD [14]
forehead, 5195, *mēṣaḥ* [8]
forehead, 1478, *gabbaḥat* [3]
on forehead, 1068+6524, *bayin+ʿayin^{1}* [2]
bald forehead, 1477, *gibbēaḥ* [1]

FOREHEADS [5]
on foreheads, 1068+6524, *bayin+ʿayin^{1}* [2]
foreheads, 6991, *pēʾâ^{1}* [2]
foreheads, 5195, *mēṣaḥ* [1]

FOREIGN [47]
foreign, 5797, *nēkār* [16]
foreign, 5799, *nokrî* [14]
foreign, 2424, *zār* [9]
foreign people, 6850, *ʿēreb^{2}* [2]
foreign, 824, *ʾereṣ* [1]
foreign, 1580, *gôy* [1]
foreign, 4353, *laʿag* [1]
foreign tongue, 4357, *lāʿaz* [1]
made foreign, 5796, *nākar^{2}* [1]
of foreign descent, 6850, *ʿēreb^{2}* [1]

FOREIGNER [16]
foreigner, 5799, *nokrî* [10]
foreigner, 1201+5797, *bēn^{1}+nēkār* [5]
foreigner, 1201+2021+5797, *bēn^{1}+ha-+nēkār* [1]

FOREIGNERS [33]
foreigners, 2424, *zār* [15]
foreigners, 1201+5797, *bēn^{1}+nēkār* [10]
foreigners, 5799, *nokrî* [4]
foreigners, 1201+2021+5797, *bēn^{1}+ha-+nēkār* [1]
foreigners, 4927, *mamzēr* [1]
foreigners, 6639+5799, *ʿam^{2}+nokrî* [1]
foreigners, 6850, *ʿēreb^{2}* [1]

FOREMAN [2]
foreman, 5853+5893, *naʿar^{2}+nāṣab^{1}* [2]

FOREMEN [8]
foremen, 8853, *šōṭar* [5]
foremen, 5904, *nāṣaḥ* [2]
foremen, 8569+5893, *śar+nāṣab^{1}* [1]

FOREMOST [2]
foremost, 8031, *rōʾš^{1}* [1]
foremost, 8040, *rēʾšît* [1]

FORESEE [1]
foresee, 3359, *yādaʿ* [1]

FORESKIN [1]
foreskin, 6889, *ʿorlâ* [1]

FORESKINS [3]
foreskins, 6889, *ʿorlâ* [3]

FOREST [40]
forest, 3623, *yaʿar^{1}* [38]
forest, 3091, *ḥōreš^{1}* [1]
forest, 7236, *pardēs* [1]

FORESTED [1]
forested, 3623, *yaʿar^{1}* [1]

FORESTS [9]
forests, 3623, *yaʿar^{1}* [7]
finest of forests, 3623+4149, *yaʿar^{1}+karmel^{1}* [2]

FORETELL [2]
foretell, 5583, *nāgad* [2]

FORETELLS [1]
foretells by dreams, 2731+2706, *ḥālam^{2}+ḥ^{a}lôm* [1]

FORETOLD [9]
foretold, 5583, *nāgad* [3]
foretold, 1819, *dābar^{2}* [2]
foretold, 9048, *šāmaʿ* [2]
what foretold, 1821, *dābār* [1]
foretold, 7924, *qārāʾ^{1}* [1]

FOREVER [259]
forever, 4200+6409, *l^{e}-^{1}+ʿôlām* [136]
forever, 6330+6409, *ʿad^{2}+ʿôlām* [44]
forever, 6409, *ʿôlām* [22]
forever, 4200+5905, *l^{e}-^{1}+nēṣaḥ^{1}* [18]
forever, 4200+6329, *l^{e}-^{1}+ʿad^{1}* [12]
forever, 10378+10550, *l^{e}-+ʿālam* [6]
forever, 3972+2021+3427, *kōl+ha-+yôm^{1}* [3]
forever, 6330+6329, *ʿad^{2}+ʿad^{1}* [3]
forever, 9458, *tāmîd* [3]
forever, 6330+2021+6409, *ʿad^{2}+ha-+ʿôlām* [2]
forever, 6330+4200+6409, *ʿad^{2}+l^{e}-^{1}+ʿôlām* [2]
forever, 4200+802+3427, *l^{e}-^{1}+ʾōrek+yôm^{1}* [1]
forever, 5905, *nēṣaḥ^{1}* [1]
forever, 6329, *ʿad^{1}* [1]
forever, 7710, *qedem* [1]
forever, 10378+10550+10002, *l^{e}-+ʿālam+-āʾ* [1]
forever, 10527+10509+10002, *ʿad+sôp+-āʾ* [1]
forever, 10527+10550+10002, *ʿad+ʿālam+-āʾ* [1]
forever, 10550+10002, *ʿālam+-āʾ* [1]

FOREVERMORE [6]
forevermore, 6330+6409, *ʿad^{2}+ʿôlām* [5]
forevermore, 6330+2021+6409, *ʿad^{2}+ha-+ʿôlām* [1]

FORFEIT [2]
forfeit, 3049, *ḥaram^{1}* [1]
forfeit, 6440, *ʿāzab^{1}* [1]

FORFEITING [1]
forfeiting, 2627, *ḥāṭāʾ* [1]

FORFEITS [1]
forfeits, 2627, *ḥāṭāʾ* [1]

FORGAVE [4]
forgave, 4105, *kāpar^{1}* [2]
forgave, 5951, *nāśāʾ* [2]

FORGED [2]
forged, 3670, *yāṣar* [1]
forged, 4323, *lāṭaš* [1]

FORGES [2]
forges, 3655, *yāṣāʾ* [1]
forges, 7188, *pāʿal* [1]

FORGET [53]
forget, 8894, *šākaḥ* [42]
forget, 5960, *nāšâ^{1}* [3]
forget, 8895, *šākēaḥ* [2]
forget, 440+2349, *ʾal^{1}+zākar^{1}* [1]
made forget, 5960, *nāšâ^{1}* [1]
surely forget, 5960+5960, *nāšâ^{1}+nāšâ^{1}* [1]
ever forget, 8894+8894, *šākaḥ+šākaḥ* [1]
made forget, 8894, *šākaḥ* [1]
make forget, 8894, *šākaḥ* [1]

FORGETS [2]
forgets, 8894, *šākaḥ* [2]

FORGIVE [42]
forgive, 6142, *sālaḥ* [26]
forgive, 5951, *nāśāʾ* [10]
forgive, 4105, *kāpar^{1}* [2]
forgive, *NIH/RPE* [1]
forgive, 5927, *nāqâ* [1]
at all forgive, 5951+5951, *nāśāʾ+nāśāʾ* [1]
forgive, 6296, *ʿābar^{1}* [1]

FORGIVEN [17]
be forgiven, 6142, *sālaḥ* [13]
forgiven, 6142, *sālaḥ* [2]
are forgiven, 5951, *nāśāʾ* [1]
be forgiven, 5951, *nāśāʾ* [1]

FORGIVENESS [1]
forgiveness, 6145, *s^{e}lîḥâ* [1]

FORGIVES [2]
forgives, 6142, *sālaḥ* [1]

forgives, 6296, *ʿābar^{1}* [1]

FORGIVING [6]
forgiving, 5951, *nāśāʾ* [3]
forgiving, 6145, *s^{e}lîḥâ* [2]
forgiving, 6143, *sallāḥ* [1]

FORGO [1]
forgo, 5759, *nāṭaš* [1]

FORGOT [11]
forgot, 8894, *šākaḥ* [11]

FORGOTTEN [35]
forgotten, 8894, *šākaḥ* [22]
be forgotten, 8894, *šākaḥ* [9]
forgotten, 5960, *nāšāʾ^{1}* [2]
am forgotten, 8894+4946+4213, *šākaḥ+min+lēb* [1]
is forgotten, 8894, *šākaḥ* [1]

FORK [5]
fork, 4657, *mazlēg* [2]
fork, 562, *ʾēm* [1]
winnowing fork, 4665, *mizreh* [1]
fork, 8181, *raḥat* [1]

FORKS [6]
meat forks, 4657, *mazlēg* [4]
forks, 4657, *mazlēg* [1]
forks, 7849, *qill^{e}šôn* [1]

FORLORN [1]
forlorn, 8890, *š^{e}kôl* [1]

FORM [18]
form, 9454, *t^{e}mûnâ* [7]
form, 9307, *tōʾar* [4]
form, 1215, *bānâ* [1]
form, 1952, *d^{e}mût* [1]
form, 3670, *yāṣar* [1]
form, 3922, *kûn^{1}* [1]
form, 4162, *kārat* [1]
form, 6886, *ʿērek* [1]
form, 9322, *tabnît* [1]

FORMATION [4]
battle formation, 4878, *milḥāmâ* [2]
formation, 6885, *ʿārak* [1]
in formation, 6885, *ʿārak* [1]

FORMED [34]
formed, 3670, *yāṣar* [15]
formed, *NIH/RPE* [3]
formed, 3922, *kûn^{1}* [3]
formed battle lines, 6885, *ʿārak* [2]
formed, 6913, *ʿāśâ^{1}* [2]
formed the boundary, 1487, *gābal* [1]
formed, 2118, *hāyâ* [1]
was formed, 3670, *yāṣar* [1]
formed, 3671, *yēṣer^{1}* [1]
were formed, 3922, *kûn^{1}* [1]
what formed, 5126, *maʿ^{a}śeh* [1]
formed lines, 6885, *ʿārak* [1]
formed, 8492, *śîm* [1]
formed, 9322, *tabnît* [1]

FORMER [26]
former, 8037, *riʾšôn* [19]
former, *NIH/RPE* [2]
former, 7719, *qadmōnî^{1}* [2]
his former righteousness^{s}, 2023, *-āh* [1]
former, 4946+7710, *min+qedem* [1]
former, 10621, *q^{o}dām* [1]

FORMERLY [9]
formerly, 4200+7156, *l^{e}-^{1}+pāneh* [7]
formerly, 928+2021+8037, *b^{e}+ha+riʾšôn* [1]
formerly, 4946+919+8997, *min+ʾetmôl+šilšôm* [1]

FORMING [3]
forming, *NIH/RPE* [2]
forming an alliance, 5818+5011, *nāsak^{1}+massēkâ^{1}* [1]

FORMLESS [2]
formless, 9332, *tōhû* [2]

FORMS [8]
forms, 3670, *yāṣar* [3]
forms, 2845, *ḥānaṭ^{1}* [1]
lifeless forms, 5577, *n^{e}bēlâ* [1]
lifeless forms, 7007, *peger* [1]
forms, 7193, *paʿam* [1]
forms, 7497, *ṣîr^{5}* [1]

FORMULA [2]
formula, 5504, *matkōnet* [2]

FORSAKE [43]
forsake, 6440, *ʿāzab^{1}* [37]
forsake, 5759, *nāṭaš* [5]
forsake, 5663, *nûaḥ^{1}* [1]

FORSAKEN [36]
forsaken, 6440, *ʿāzab^{1}* [34]
forsaken, 527, *ʾalmān^{1}* [1]
is forsaken, 6440, *ʿāzab^{1}* [1]

FORSAKES [1]
forsakes, 6440, *ʿāzab^{1}* [1]

FORSAKING [7]
forsaking, 6440, *ʿāzab^{1}* [5]
forsaking, 4946+907, *min+ʾēt^{2}* [1]
forsaking, 5085+5086, *māʿal+maʿal^{1}* [1]

FORSOOK [8]
forsook, 6440, *ʿāzab^{1}* [8]

FORTH [61]
bring forth, 3655, *yāṣāʾ* [4]
burst forth, 1324, *bāqaʿ* [2]
going back and forth, 2143, *hālak* [2]
shine forth, 3649, *yāpaʿ* [2]
come forth, 3655, *yāṣāʾ* [2]
forth, 3655, *yāṣāʾ* [2]
brought forth, 7865, *qānâ^{2}* [2]
send forth, 8938, *šālaḥ* [2]
back and forth, 285+2178+2256+285+2178, *ʾeḥād+hēnnâ^{1}+w^{e}-+ʾeḥād+hēnnâ^{1}* [1]
blazed forth, 1277, *bāʿar^{1}* [1]
break forth, 1324, *bāqaʿ* [1]
gush forth, 1324, *bāqaʿ* [1]
send forth lightning, 1397+1398, *bāraq+bārāq^{1}* [1]
brought forth, 1602, *gāzâ* [1]
steals forth, 2118, *hāyâ* [1]
flashed back and forth, 2143, *hālak* [1]
moved back and forth, 2143, *hālak* [1]
walked back and forth, 2143, *hālak* [1]
went forth, 2143, *hālak* [1]
flashing back and forth, 2200, *hāpak* [1]
set forth, 2554, *ḥûd* [1]
were brought forth, 2655, *ḥîl^{1}* [1]
brought forth, 2655, *ḥîl^{1}* [1]
be led forth, 3297, *yābal* [1]
be brought forth, 3528, *yālad* [1]
bring forth, 3528, *yālad* [1]
shines forth, 3649, *yāpaʿ* [1]
shone forth, 3649, *yāpaʿ* [1]
bringing forth, 3655, *yāṣāʾ* [1]
burst forth, 3655, *yāṣāʾ* [1]
coming forth, 3655, *yāṣāʾ* [1]
leads forth, 3655, *yāṣāʾ* [1]
flashed back and forth, 4374+928+9348, *lāqaḥ+b^{e}+tāwek* [1]
pour forth, 5580, *nābaʿ* [1]
set forth, 5602, *nāgaš* [1]
led forth, 5627, *nāhag^{1}* [1]
brings forth, 5649, *nûb* [1]
back and forth, 6017+6017, *sābîb+sābîb* [1]
forth, 6296, *ʿābar^{1}* [1]
put forth, 6913, *ʿāśâ^{1}* [1]
bring forth, 7114, *pālaḥ* [1]
burst forth, 7287, *pāraṣ* [1]
springs forth, 7541, *ṣāmaḥ* [1]
calling forth, 7924, *qārāʾ^{1}* [1]
ride forth, 8206, *rākab* [1]
call forth songs of joy, 8264, *rānan* [1]
sped forth, 8351, *rāṣāʾ^{1}* [1]
brought forth, 8751, *šāwâ^{2}* [1]
sent forth, 8938, *šālaḥ* [1]
rushing back and forth, 9212, *šāqaq* [1]
brings forth, 9311, *t^{e}bûʾâ* [1]

FORTIETH [3]
fortieth, 752, *ʾarbaʿ^{1}* [3]

FORTIFICATIONS [1]
outer fortifications, 2658, *ḥêl* [1]

FORTIFIED [63]
fortified, 1290, *bāṣûr* [22]
fortified, 4448, *mibṣār^{1}* [21]
fortified, 5193, *m^{e}ṣûrâ* [5]
fortified, 1215, *bānâ* [4]
fortified, 6437, *ʿōz* [3]
fortified cities, 4448, *mibṣār^{1}* [2]
fortified, 5190, *māṣôr^{2}* [2]
fortified, 2616, *ḥāzaq* [1]
fortified city, 4448, *mibṣār^{1}* [1]
fortified places, 4448, *mibṣār^{1}* [1]
fortified, 6434, *ʿaz* [1]

FORTIFIES [1]
fortifies, 1307, *bāṣar^{3}* [1]

FORTRESS [35]
fortress, 5181, *m^{e}ṣûdâ^{2}* [9]
fortress, 5369, *miśgāb^{1}* [9]
fortress, 5057, *māʿôz* [8]
fortress, 5171, *m^{e}ṣād* [2]
fortress, 810, *ʾarmôn* [1]
strong fortress, 1074+5181, *bayit^{1}+m^{e}ṣûdâ^{2}* [1]
fortress, 1315, *biṣṣārôn* [1]
fortress, 4448, *mibṣār^{1}* [1]
fortress, 5183, *m^{e}ṣôdâ^{2}* [1]
fortress, 5193, *m^{e}ṣûrâ* [1]
fortress, 6437, *ʿōz* [1]

FORTRESSES [26]
fortresses, 810, *ʾarmôn* [19]
fortresses, 4448, *mibṣār^{1}* [3]
fortresses, 5057, *māʿôz* [2]
mightiest fortresses, 4448+5057, *mibṣār^{1}+māʿôz* [1]
fortresses, 5058, *māʿôzen* [1]

FORTS [2]
forts, 1072, *bîrâ* [2]

FORTUNE [4]
fortune, 238, *ʾōṣar* [1]
fortune, 1513, *gad^{2}* [1]
good fortune, 1513, *gad^{2}* [1]
fortune, 3888, *kabbîr* [1]

FORTUNES [19]
fortunes, 8654, *š^{e}bût* [14]
fortunes, 8669, *š^{e}bît* [4]
tell fortunes, 7876, *qāsam* [1]

FORTY [79]
forty, 752, *ʾarbaʿ^{1}* [79]

FORTY-EIGHT [2]
forty-eight, 752+2256+9046, *ʾarbaʿ^{1}+w^{e}-+š^{e}mōneh* [2]

FORTY-FIRST [1]
forty-first, 752+2256+285, *ʾarbaʿ^{1}+w^{e}-+ʾeḥād* [1]

FORTY-FIVE [3]
forty-five, 752+2256+2822, *ʾarbaʿ^{1}+w^{e}-+ḥāmēš* [3]

FORTY-NINE [1]
forty-nine, 9596+2256+752, *tēšaʿ+w^{e}-+ʾarbaʿ^{1}* [1]

FORTY-ONE [4]
forty-one, 752+2256+285, *ʾarbaʿ^{1}+w^{e}-+ʾeḥād* [4]

FORTY-SEVEN [1]
forty-seven, 8679+2256+752, *šebaʿ^{1}+w^{e}-+ʾarbaʿ^{1}* [1]

FORTY-TWO [4]
forty-two, 752+2256+9109, *ʾarbaʿ^{1}+w^{e}-+š^{e}nayim* [4]

FORWARD [43]
brought forward, 7928, *qārab* [4]
came forward, 3655, *yāṣāʾ* [3]
come forward, 7928, *qārab* [3]
had come forward, 7928, *qārab* [3]
stepped forward, 3655, *yāṣāʾ* [2]
come forward, 5602, *nāgaš* [2]
stepped forward, 7756, *qûm* [2]
came forward, 7928, *qārab* [2]
forward, *AIT* [1]
faced forward, 448+4578+7156, *ʾel+mûl*[3]*+pāneh* [1]
come forward, 910, *ʾātâ* [1]
forward, 2134, *hālᵉʾâ* [1]
go forward, 2143, *hālak* [1]
went forward, 2143, *hālak* [1]
forward, 4200+7156, *lᵉ-*[1]*+pāneh* [1]
came forward, 5602, *nāgaš* [1]
moved forward, 5602, *nāgaš* [1]
step forward, 5602, *nāgaš* [1]
stepped forward, 5602, *nāgaš* [1]
go forward, 5742, *nāṭâ* [1]
put himself forward, 5951, *nāśāʾ* [1]
went forward, 6296, *ʿābar*[1] [1]
come forward, 6641, *ʿāmad* [1]
rushed forward, 7320, *pāšaṭ* [1]
striding forward, 7579, *ṣāʿâ* [1]
come forward, 7756, *qûm* [1]
surged forward, 7756, *qûm* [1]
bring forward, 7928, *qārab* [1]
rushed forward, 8132, *rûṣ* [1]
came forward, 10638, *qᵉrēb* [1]

FOSTER [1]
foster fathers, 587, *ʾāman*[2] [1]

FOUGHT [42]
fought, 4309, *lāḥam*[1] [30]
fought, 5782, *nākâ* [4]
fought, 6913, *ʿāśâ*[1] [2]
fought, 7371, *ṣābāʾ*[1] [2]
must have fought, 2991+2991, *ḥārēb*[2]*+ḥārēb*[2] [1]
fought in, 3655+4200, *yāṣāʾ+lᵉ-*[1] [1]
fought in, 3655+928, *yāṣāʾ+bᵉ-* [1]
fought, 5897, *nāṣâ*[1] [1]

FOUND [232]
found, 5162, *māṣāʾ* [108]
be found, 5162, *māṣāʾ* [25]
found, 2180, *hinnēh* [12]
was found, 5162, *māṣāʾ* [12]
is found, 5162, *māṣāʾ* [11]
found, *NIH/RPE* [9]
been found, 5162, *māṣāʾ* [8]
were found, 5162, *māṣāʾ* [8]
was found, 10708, *šᵉkaḥ* [5]
found, 10708, *šᵉkaḥ* [4]
anything found dead, 5577, *nᵉbēlâ* [3]
found, *AIT* [2]
found out, 3359, *yādaʿ* [2]
found, 4374, *lāqaḥ* [2]
found, 1815, *dābaq* [1]
found strength, 2616, *ḥāzaq* [1]
found pleasure, 2911, *ḥāpēṣ*[1] [1]
be found out, 3359, *yādaʿ* [1]
found favor, 3512, *yāṭab* [1]
found, 3655, *yāṣāʾ* [1]
are found, 5162, *māṣāʾ* [1]
found courage, 5162, *māṣāʾ* [1]
found out, 5162, *māṣāʾ* [1]
found to be true, 5162, *māṣāʾ* [1]
is found, 5162+5162, *māṣāʾ+māṣāʾ* [1]
animal found dead, 5577, *nᵉbēlâ* [1]
found dead, 5577, *nᵉbēlâ* [1]
nowhere to be found, 6372, *ʿādar*[3] [1]
found pleasure, 6844, *ʿārab*[3] [1]
found, 7003, *pāgaʿ* [1]
were found missing, 7212, *pāqad* [1]
be found, 8011, *rāʾâ*[1] [1]
found, 8011+4200+7156, *rāʾâ*[1]*+lᵉ-*[1]*+pāneh* [1]
found, 8011, *rāʾâ*[1] [1]
found shelter, 10300, *ṭᵉlal* [1]

FOUNDATION [25]
the foundation was laid, 3569, *yāsad*[1] [4]
laid the foundation, 3569, *yāsad*[1] [3]
the foundation laid, 3569, *yāsad*[1] [2]
foundation, 3572, *yᵉsôd* [2]
foundation, 4806, *mākôn* [2]
foundation, 99, *ʾᵃguddâ* [1]
sure foundation, 575, *ʾᵉmûnâ* [1]
lays the foundation, 3569, *yāsad*[1] [1]
provide a foundation, 3569, *yāsad*[1] [1]
the foundation been laid, 3569, *yāsad*[1] [1]
foundation, 3573, *yᵉsûdâ* [1]
foundation laid, 4586, *mûsād* [1]
foundation, 4586, *mûsād* [1]
foundation, 4588, *mûsādâ* [1]
foundation, 4589, *môsādâ* [1]
foundation, 4807, *mᵉkônâ* [1]
foundation, 4996, *massad* [1]

FOUNDATIONS [33]
foundations, 4587, *môsād* [8]
foundations, 3572, *yᵉsôd* [6]
laid the foundations, 3569, *yāsad*[1] [5]
foundations, 4589, *môsādâ* [3]
foundations, 10079, *ʾōš* [3]
the foundations were laid, 3569, *yāsad*[1] [1]
foundations be laid, 3569, *yāsad*[1] [1]
foundations, 3569, *yāsad*[1] [1]
laid foundations, 3569, *yāsad*[1] [1]
lay foundations, 3569, *yāsad*[1] [1]
foundations, 4806, *mākôn* [1]
foundations, 5187, *māṣûq* [1]
foundations, 9268, *šēt*[1] [1]

FOUNDED [10]
founded, 3922, *kûn*[1] [4]
founded, 3569, *yāsad*[1] [2]
was founded, 3569, *yāsad*[1] [1]
founded, 4589, *môsādâ* [1]
founded on, 6330, *ʿad*[2] [1]
founded, 6913, *ʿāśâ*[1] [1]

FOUNTAIN [15]
fountain, 5227, *māqôr* [9]
fountain, 6524, *ʿayin*[1] [3]
fountain, 5078, *maʿyān* [2]
fountain, 1644, *gal*[2] [1]

FOUNTAINS [2]
fountains, 5078, *maʿyān* [1]
fountains, 6524, *ʿayin*[1] [1]

FOUR [183]
four, 752, *ʾarbaʿ*[1] [172]
four, 10065, *ʾarbaʿ* [8]
four, *NIH/RPE* [1]
four[s], 3972, *kōl* [1]
four and a half feet, 8993+564, *šālōš+ʾammâ*[1] [1]

FOUR-FIFTHS [1]
four-fifths, 752+3338, *ʾarbaʿ*[1]*+yād* [1]

FOUR-SIDED [1]
four-sided, 8055, *rᵉbîʿî* [1]

FOURS [4]
all fours, 752, *ʾarbaʿ*[1] [4]

FOURTEEN [21]
fourteen, 752+6925, *ʾarbaʿ*[1]*+ʿāśār* [12]
fourteen, 752+6926, *ʾarbaʿ*[1]*+ʿeśrēh* [6]
fourteen hundred, 547+2256+752+4395, *ʾelep*[2]*+wᵉ-+ʾarbaʿ*[1]*+mēʾâ*[1] [2]
fourteen, 752, *ʾarbaʿ*[1] [1]

FOURTEENTH [23]
fourteenth, 752+6925, *ʾarbaʿ*[1]*+ʿāśār* [19]
fourteenth, 752+6926, *ʾarbaʿ*[1]*+ʿeśrēh* [4]

FOURTH [63]
fourth, 8055, *rᵉbîʿî* [44]
fourth, 10651, *rᵉbîʿāy* [6]
fourth, 752, *ʾarbaʿ*[1] [5]
fourth generation, 8067, *ribbēaʿ* [4]
fourth generation, 8055, *rᵉbîʿî* [2]
fourth, *NIH/RPE* [1]
fourth part, 8065, *rōbaʿ*[1] [1]

FOWL [1]
fowl, 1350, *barbur* [1]

FOWLER [1]
fowler, 3687, *yāqûš* [1]

FOWLER'S [2]
fowler's, 3687, *yāqûš* [1]
fowler's, 3704, *yāqaš* [1]

FOX [1]
fox, 8785, *šûʿāl*[1] [1]

FOXES [4]
foxes, 8785, *šûʿāl*[1] [3]
foxes, *NIH/RPE* [1]

FRACTURE [2]
fracture, 8691, *šeber*[1] [2]

FRACTURES [1]
fractures, 8691, *šeber*[1] [1]

FRAGILE [1]
fragile, 3684, *yāqôṭ* [1]

FRAGMENT [1]
fragment, 3084, *ḥereś* [1]

FRAGRANCE [11]
fragrance, 8194, *rêaḥ* [8]
fragrance, 1411, *bōśem* [2]
enjoy fragrance, 8193, *rîaḥ* [1]

FRAGRANT [26]
fragrant, 6160, *sam* [14]
fragrant incense, 8194+5767, *rêaḥ+nîḥōaḥ* [4]
fragrant, 1411, *bōśem* [2]
fragrant, *NIH/RPE* [1]
fragrant, 5351, *mirqaḥat* [1]
fragrant spices, 6160, *sam* [1]
fragrant, 6986, *ʿātār*[2] [1]
fragrant calamus, 7866, *qāneh* [1]
fragrant blend, 8381, *rōqaḥ* [1]

FRAME [14]
frame, 7983, *qereš* [8]
carrying frame, 4573, *môṭ*[2] [2]
frame, 3674, *yᵉṣurîm* [1]
circular frame, 4196, *kōteret* [1]
frame, 6795, *ʿeṣem*[1] [1]
frame, 6798, *ʿōṣem*[2] [1]

FRAMES [29]
frames, 7983, *qereš* [27]
frames, *NIH/RPE* [1]
frames, 9208, *šāqep* [1]

FRANKINCENSE [1]
frankincense, 4247, *lᵉbōnâ* [1]

FRANKLY [1]
rebuke frankly, 3519+3519, *yākaḥ+yākaḥ* [1]

FRANTIC [1]
frantic prophesying, 5547, *nābāʾ* [1]

FRAUD [3]
fraud, 9214, *šeqer* [3]

FRAY [1]
fray, 5977, *nešeq*[1] [1]

FREE [67]
free, 2930, *ḥopšî* [9]
free, 6440, *ʿāzab*[1] [5]
set free, 8938, *šālaḥ* [5]
go free, 3655, *yāṣāʾ* [4]
free, 3655, *yāṣāʾ* [3]
free, *AIT* [2]
free from, 4202, *lōʾ* [2]
go free, 4880, *mālaṭ*[1] [2]
free yourself, 5911, *nāṣal* [2]
free, 8938+2930, *šālaḥ+ḥopšî* [2]
free, 8938, *šālaḥ* [2]
free from, 401, *ʾayin*[1] [1]
free to eat, 430+430, *ʾākal+ʾākal* [1]

free from, 1194, *biltî* [1]
free, 1655, *gālâ* [1]
free from impurity, 3196, *ṭāhôr* [1]
set free, 3655, *yāṣāʾ* [1]
sets free, 3655, *yāṣāʾ* [1]
free from, 4202+928, *lōʾ+be-* [1]
free of, 4202, *lōʾ* [1]
free from, 4946, *min* [1]
setting free, 5303, *merḥāb* [1]
shake myself free, 5850, *nāʿar*[2] [1]
free, 5911, *nāṣal* [1]
free from blame, 5929, *nāqî* [1]
free from obligation, 5929, *nāqî* [1]
free, 5929, *nāqî* [1]
sets free, 6002, *nātar*[3] [1]
keep free, 6073, *sûr*[1] [1]
set free, 6296, *ʿābar*[1] [1]
give free rein, 6440, *ʿāzab*[1] [1]
free, 7293, *pāraq* [1]
free yourself, 7337, *pātaḥ*[1] [1]
be set free, 7337, *pātaḥ*[1] [1]
set free, 7337, *pātaḥ*[1] [1]
cut free, 7915, *qāṣaṣ*[1] [1]
set free, 8143, *rāḥab* [1]
letting range free, 8938+8079, *šālaḥ+regel* [1]
set free, 8938+2930, *šālaḥ+ḥopšî* [1]
set free, 8938+4946+3338, *šālaḥ+min+yād* [1]

FREED [6]
been freed, 2926, *ḥāpaš* [1]
freed, 2930, *ḥopšî* [1]
freed, 3655, *yāṣāʾ* [1]
freed, 7293, *pāraq* [1]
freed, 7337, *pātaḥ*[1] [1]
freed, 8938+2930, *šālaḥ+ḥopšî* [1]

FREEDOM [9]
freedom, 2002, *derôr*[3] [5]
freedom, *NIH/RPE* [1]
freedom for slaves, 2002, *derôr*[3] [1]
freedom, 2928, *ḥupšâ* [1]
freedom, 8146, *rāḥāb*[1] [1]

FREEING [1]
freeing, 7337, *pātaḥ*[1] [1]

FREELY [11]
freely, 5607, *nedābâ* [2]
freely strut, 2143, *hālak* [1]
lend freely, 4278, *lāwâ*[2] [1]
lends freely, 4278, *lāwâ*[2] [1]
given freely, 5605, *nādab* [1]
freely lend, 6292+6292, *ʿābaṭ*[1]*+ʿābaṭ*[1] [1]
gives freely, 7061, *pāzar* [1]
freely, 8049, *rābâ* [1]
drank freely, 8910, *šākar* [1]
freely given, 10461, *nedab* [1]

FREEWILL [22]
freewill offerings, 5607, *nedābâ* [10]
freewill offering, 5607, *nedābâ* [7]
brought as freewill offerings, 5605+5607, *nādab+nedābâ* [1]
freewill offerings, 5605, *nādab* [1]
gave freewill offerings, 5605, *nādab* [1]
freewill, 5607, *nedābâ* [1]
freewill offerings, 10461, *nedab* [1]

FRENZIED [1]
frenzied, 8323, *raʿaš* [1]

FRESH [16]
fresh, 2645, *ḥay*[2] [8]
fresh, 4300, *laḥ* [2]
fresh, 8324, *rāpāʾ*[1] [2]
fresh, 2015, *dāšēn*[2] [1]
fresh, 2543, *ḥādāš* [1]
fresh, 3269, *ṭārî* [1]
makes fresh, 8324, *rāpāʾ*[1] [1]

FRESH-CUT [1]
fresh-cut, 4300, *laḥ* [1]

FRESHLY [1]
freshly plucked, 3273, *ṭārāp* [1]

FRET [4]
fret, 3013, *ḥārâ*[1] [4]

FRIEND [45]
friend, 8276, *rēaʿ*[2] [26]
friend, 170, *ʾāhab* [4]
friend, 5335, *mērēaʿ*[1] [3]
friend, 476, *ʾallûp*[1] [2]
friend, 2492, *ḥābēr* [2]
friend, 8291, *rēʿeh* [2]
friend[s], 408, *ʾîš*[1] [1]
close friend, 408+8934, *ʾîš*[1]*+šālôm* [1]
close friend, 3359, *yādaʿ* [1]
closest friend, 3359, *yādaʿ* [1]
friend, 7141+532, *pelōnî+ʾalmōnî* [1]
closest friend, 8276+889+3869+5883+3870, *rēaʿ*[2]*+ʾašer+ke-+nepeš+-kā* [1]

FRIENDLY [3]
on friendly terms, 170, *ʾāhab* [1]
friendly relations, 8934, *šālôm* [1]
friendly, 8969, *šālēm*[2] [1]

FRIENDS [48]
friends, 8276, *rēaʿ*[2] [15]
friends, 170, *ʾāhab* [8]
friends, 5335, *mērēaʿ*[1] [3]
friends, 10245, *ḥabar* [3]
friends, 278, *ʾāḥ*[2] [2]
close friends, 476, *ʾallûp*[1] [2]
friends, 2492, *ḥābēr* [2]
friends, 3359, *yādaʿ* [2]
friends, *NIH/RPE* [1]
friends, 408+8934, *ʾîš*[1]*+šālôm* [1]
trusted friends, 408+8934, *ʾîš*[1]*+šālôm* [1]
friends, 632+8934, *ʾenôš*[1]*+šālôm* [1]
close friends, 3359, *yādaʿ* [1]
closest friends, 3359, *yādaʿ* [1]
friends, 5493, *mōt*[1] [1]
make friends with, 5795, *nākar*[1] [1]
make friends, 8287, *rāʿâ*[2] [1]
friends, 8292, *rēʿâ* [1]
friends, 8934, *šālôm* [1]

FRIENDSHIP [7]
friendship, 173, *ʾahabâ*[1] [2]
treaty of friendship, 8934+2256+3208, *šālôm+we-+ṭôbâ* [2]
friendship, *NIH/RPE* [1]
intimate friendship, 6051, *sôd* [1]
friendship, 8276, *rēaʿ*[2] [1]

FRIGHTEN [6]
frighten away, 3006, *ḥārad* [2]
frighten, 1286, *bāʿat* [1]
frighten, 3006, *ḥārad* [1]
frighten, 3169, *ḥātat* [1]
frighten, 3707, *yārēʾ*[1] [1]

FRIGHTENED [4]
frightened, 3707, *yārēʾ*[1] [2]
frightened, 3169, *ḥātat* [1]
frightened, 10097, *behal* [1]

FRIGHTENING [2]
frightening, 1286, *bāʿat* [1]
frightening, 10028, *ʾêmetān* [1]

FRINGE [1]
outer fringe, 7896, *qāṣâ*[2] [1]

FRO [2]
go to and fro, 2143, *hālak* [1]
goes to and fro, 2143, *hālak* [1]

FROGS [13]
frogs, 7630, *ṣepardēaʿ* [13]

FROLIC [2]
frolic, 7055, *pûš*[1] [1]
frolic, 8471, *śāḥaq* [1]

FROM [3940]*
from, 4946, *min* [2541]
from, *AIT* [289]
from, 4200, *le-*[1] [157]
from, 4946+6584, *min+ʿal*[2] [155]
from, *NIH/RPE* [121]
from, 928, *be-* [98]
from, 4946+907, *min+ʾēt*[2] [93]
from, 4946+7156, *min+pāneh* [45]
from, 10427, *min* [41]
from, 4946+3338, *min+yād* [33]
from, 4946+6640, *min+ʿim* [25]
from, 6584, *ʿal*[2] [18]
from, 4946+7931, *min+qereb* [16]
from, 4946+9348, *min+tāwek* [16]
from, 4946+339, *min+ʾaḥar* [12]
from, 4974, *minnî*[2] [12]
from among, 4946, *min* [11]
from, 4946+4200+7156, *min+le-*[1]*+pāneh* [11]
away from, 4946+6584, *min+ʿal*[2] [10]
away from, 4946, *min* [10]
from, 4200+7156, *le-*[1]*+pāneh* [8]
from, 1068, *bayin* [6]
from, 4946+5584, *min+neged* [5]
from, 1237, *baʿad*[1] [4]
far from, 4946, *min* [4]
from, 6330, *ʿad*[2] [4]
from, 10089, *be-* [4]
from, 10168, *dî* [4]
from, 448, *ʾel* [3]
from, 2025, *-â*[2] [3]
apart from, 4946+1187, *min+balʿadê* [3]
away from, 4946+6640, *min+ʿim* [3]
from, 4946+1896, *min+day* [3]
from, 440, *ʾal*[1] [2]
from, 928+9348, *be-+tāwek* [2]
from, 2256, *we-* [2]
from, 4200+4974, *le-*[1]*+minnî*[2] [2]
from, 4202, *lōʾ* [2]
away from, 4946+339, *min+ʾaḥar* [2]
away from, 4946+907, *min+ʾēt*[2] [2]
far from, 4946+5584, *min+neged* [2]
from every side, 4946+6017, *min+sābîb* [2]
from out of, 4946+9348, *min+tāwek* [2]
from, 4946+6584+7156, *min+ʿal*[2]*+pāneh* [2]
from, 4946+9393, *min+taḥat*[1] [2]
out from, 4946, *min* [2]
separated from, 4946+6584, *min+ʿal*[2] [2]
turning from, 4946, *min* [2]
from beginning to, 6330, *ʿad*[2] [2]
across from, 6584+7156, *ʿal*[2]*+pāneh* [2]
from, 6584+7156, *ʿal*[2]*+pāneh* [2]
from, 10427+10621, *min+qodām* [2]
from, 448+7156, *ʾel+pāneh* [1]
from now, 928+6388, *be-+ʿôd* [1]
from, 928+3338, *be-+yād* [1]
from, 928+6524, *be-+ʿayin*[1] [1]
from, 928+889, *be-+ʾašer* [1]
from, 1194, *biltî* [1]
from, 1198, *bemô* [1]

FRONDS [1]
fronds, 4093, *kippâ* [1]

FRONT [139]
in front of, 4200+7156, *le-*[1]*+pāneh* [66]
front, 7156, *pāneh* [25]
in front of, 5584, *neged* [6]
in front of, 6584+7156, *ʿal*[2]*+pāneh* [6]
in front of, 448+7156, *ʾel+pāneh* [4]
in front of, 448+4578, *ʾel+mûl*[3] [3]
in front of, 448, *ʾel* [2]
in front of, 907+7156, *ʾēt*[2]*+pāneh* [2]
in front of, 4200+5584, *le-*[1]*+neged* [2]
in front of, 4946+4578, *min+mûl*[3] [2]
in front of, 6584, *ʿal*[2] [2]
in front of, 7156, *pāneh* [2]
in front of, 448+4578+7156, *ʾel+mûl*[3]*+pāneh* [1]
in the front line, 448+4578+7156, *ʾel+mûl*[3]*+pāneh* [1]
front of heads, 1068+6524, *bayin+ʿayin*[1] [1]
front[s], 2296, *zeh* [1]
directly in front of, 4200+5790, *le-*[1]*+nōkaḥ* [1]
in front of, 4200+6524, *le-*[1]*+ʿayin*[1] [1]
in the front part, 4578, *mûl*[3] [1]
in front of, 4946+7156, *min+pāneh* [1]
in front of, 5790, *nōkaḥ* [1]
puts up a bold front, 6451+928+7156, *ʿāzaz+be-+pāneh* [1]

front, 6991, *pē'â[1]* [1]
front columns, 7156, *pāneh* [1]
in front, 7156, *pāneh* [1]
in front of, 7692, *q[e]bōl* [1]
in front, 7709, *qādam* [1]
front, 8037, *ri'šōn* [1]
from front to back, 8145, *rōḥab* [1]

FRONTAL [1]
frontal, 4946+5584, *min+neged* [1]

FRONTIER [2]
frontier, 7895, *qāṣeh* [2]

FRONTIERS [1]
remotest frontiers, 6992, *pē'â[2]* [1]

FROST [5]
frost, 4095, *k[e]pôr[2]* [3]
frost, 7885, *qippā'ôn* [1]
frost, 7943, *qeraḥ* [1]

FROWN [1]
frown, 5877+7156, *nāpal+pāneh* [1]

FROZE [1]
froze, 1815, *dābaq* [1]

FROZEN [2]
frozen, 3668, *yāṣaq* [1]
frozen, 4334, *lākad* [1]

FRUIT [120]
fruit, 7262, *p[e]rî* [80]
fruit, *NIH/RPE* [6]
fruit, 4407, *ma'[a]kāl* [4]
summer fruit, 7811, *qayiṣ* [3]
fruit, 9482, *t[e]nûbâ* [3]
fruit, 10004, *'ēb* [3]
ripe fruit, 7811, *qayiṣ* [2]
ripened fruit, 7811, *qayiṣ* [2]
harvest of fruit, 668, *'ōsep* [1]
clusters of fruit, 864, *'eškôl[1]* [1]
bad fruit, 946, *b[e]'uš* [1]
early fruit, 1136, *bikkûrâ* [1]
first ripe fruit, 1137, *bikkûrîm* [1]
fruit of labor, 3330+4090, *y[e]gîa'+kap* [1]
fruit, 4312, *leḥem* [1]
fruit, 5126, *ma'[a]śeh* [1]
bear fruit, 5649, *nûb* [1]
borne fruit, 5951, *nāśā'* [1]
fruit, 6180, *sansinnâ* [1]
early fruit, 7001, *pag* [1]
fruit, 7023, *peh* [1]
bear fruit, 7238, *pārâ[1]* [1]
fruit, 7811, *qayiṣ* [1]
cast fruit, 8897, *šākal* [1]
fruit, 9311, *t[e]bû'â* [1]

FRUITAGE [1]
fruitage, 7262, *p[e]rî* [1]

FRUITFUL [28]
fruitful, 7238, *pārâ[1]* [14]
make fruitful, 7238, *pārâ[1]* [5]
fruitful vine, 1201+7238, *bēn[1]+pārâ[1]* [2]
made fruitful, 7238, *pārâ[1]* [2]
fruitful, 7262, *p[e]rî* [2]
fruitful, 2307, *zûb* [1]
fruitful, 2774, *ḥemed* [1]
fruitful land, 4149, *karmel[1]* [1]

FRUITFULNESS [2]
fruitfulness, 4458, *meged* [1]
fruitfulness, 7262, *p[e]rî* [1]

FRUITION [1]
bring to fruition, 7541, *ṣāmaḥ* [1]

FRUITS [5]
fruits, 7262, *p[e]rî* [3]
fruits of labor, 3330, *y[e]gîa'* [2]

FRUSTRATE [3]
frustrate, 7296, *pārar[1]* [2]
frustrate, 1017, *bôš[1]* [1]

FRUSTRATED [3]
frustrated, 4206, *lā'â* [1]
frustrated, 7296, *pārar[1]* [1]
frustrated, 7674, *ṣārar[1]* [1]

FRUSTRATES [2]
frustrates, 6156, *sālap* [1]
frustrates, 6430, *'āwat* [1]

FRUSTRATING [1]
frustrating, 7296, *pārar[1]* [1]

FRUSTRATION [1]
frustration, 4087, *ka'as* [1]

FUEL [13]
fuel, 433, *'oklâ* [3]
fuel, *NIH/RPE* [2]
use for fuel, 1277+836, *bā'ar[1]+'ēš[1]* [2]
fuel, 4409, *ma'[a]kōlet* [2]
fuel for fire, 928+1896+836, *b[e]-+day+'ēš[1]* [1]
fuel for flames, 928+1896+836, *b[e]-+day+'ēš[1]* [1]
use for fuel, 1277, *bā'ar[1]* [1]
used for fuel, 8596+1198+836, *śārap+b[e]mô+'ēš[1]* [1]

FUGITIVE [2]
fugitive, 5674, *nûs* [1]
fugitive, 7127, *pālîṭ* [1]

FUGITIVES [14]
fugitives, 7127, *pālîṭ* [3]
fugitives, 1371, *bāriaḥ* [2]
fugitives, 5610, *nādad* [2]
fugitives, 5615, *nādaḥ[1]* [2]
fugitives, 5674, *nûs* [2]
fugitives, 7128, *pālêṭ* [2]
fugitives, 7129, *p[e]lêṭâ* [1]

FULFILL [36]
fulfill, 8966, *šālēm[1]* [12]
fulfill, 7756, *qûm* [10]
fulfill the duty of a brother-in-law, 3302, *yābam* [2]
fulfill, 3983, *kālâ[1]* [2]
fulfill, 6913, *'āśâ[1]* [2]
fulfill, *AIT* [1]
fulfill, *NIH/RPE* [1]
fulfill, 995, *bô'* [1]
fulfill, 1698, *gāmar* [1]
fulfill duty as a brother-in-law, 3302, *yābam* [1]
fulfill, 3869+7023+4027+6913, *k[e]-+peh+kēn[2]+'āśâ[1]* [1]
to fulfill, 4200, *l[e]-[1]* [1]
fulfill a special vow, 7098+5624, *pālā'+nēder* [1]

FULFILLED [29]
fulfilled, 995, *bô'* [7]
fulfilled, 4848, *mālē'[1]* [5]
fulfilled, 7756, *qûm* [3]
fulfilled, 2118, *hāyâ* [2]
be fulfilled, 6913, *'āśâ[1]* [2]
fulfilled, *NIH/RPE* [1]
fulfilled, 1298, *bāṣa'* [1]
fulfilled, 1821, *dābār* [1]
fulfilled, 2118+4027, *hāyâ+kēn[2]* [1]
fulfilled, 6913, *'āśâ[1]* [1]
fulfilled, 7891, *qēṣ* [1]
be fulfilled, 8966, *šālēm[1]* [1]
fulfilled obligations, 8966, *šālēm[1]* [1]
fulfilled, 8966, *šālēm[1]* [1]
fulfilled, 10508, *sûp* [1]

FULFILLING [3]
fulfilling, 4848, *mālē'[1]* [1]
fulfilling by doing, 6268, *'ābad* [1]
fulfilling, 8966, *šālēm[1]* [1]

FULFILLMENT [3]
in fulfillment of, 4200, *l[e]-[1]* [1]
fulfillment, 4848, *mālē'[1]* [1]
fulfillment, 6641, *'āmad* [1]

FULFILLS [3]
fulfills, 1698, *gāmar* [1]
fulfills, 6913, *'āśâ[1]* [1]
fulfills, 8966, *šālēm[1]* [1]

FULL [135]
full, 4848, *mālē'[1]* [33]
full, 4849, *mālē'[2]* [23]
full, 3972, *kōl* [7]
full, 8428, *śābēa'* [7]
full, 8425, *śāba'* [6]
full, 8041, *rab[1]* [4]
full, 4850, *m[e]lō'* [3]
full, 9459, *tāmîm* [3]
full of, 1819, *dābar[2]* [2]
in full force, 3972, *kōl* [2]
full view, 6524, *'ayin[1]* [2]
full, *AIT* [1]
full of boasting, 607, *'āmar[2]* [1]
full of pits, 931+931, *b[e]'ēr[1]+b[e]'ēr[1]* [1]
has full confidence, 1053+4213, *bāṭaḥ[1]+lēb* [1]
gave full attention, 1067, *bîn* [1]
full, 1074+6017, *bayit[1]+sābîb* [1]
full grape harvest, 1292, *bāṣîr[1]* [1]
full of ditches, 1463+1463, *gēb[1]+gēb[1]* [1]
full well, 2176, *hēn[1]* [1]
full, 2221, *harbēh* [1]
full moon, 3427+4057, *yôm[1]+kese'* [1]
full, 3427, *yôm[1]* [1]
full, 3856, *yeter[1]* [1]
full, 3922, *kûn[1]* [1]
full force, 3972, *kōl* [1]
full, 3983, *kālâ[1]* [1]
given full vent, 3983, *kālâ[1]* [1]
full vigor, 3995, *kelaḥ[1]* [1]
moon full, 4057, *kese'* [1]
full moon, 4061, *kissēh* [1]
full well, 4394, *m[e]'ōd* [1]
measure the full payment, 4499, *mādad* [1]
full, 4814, *miklôl* [1]
be paid in full, 4848, *mālē'[1]* [1]
give full, 4848, *mālē'[1]* [1]
making full, 4848, *mālē'[1]* [1]
presented the full number, 4848, *mālē'[1]* [1]
taking full, 4848, *mālē'[1]* [1]
in full view, 5790+6524, *nōkaḥ+'ayin[1]* [1]
full of branches, 6734, *'ānēp* [1]
full account, 7308, *pārāšâ* [1]
full, 8031, *rō'š[1]* [1]
full of compassion, 8163, *rāḥam* [1]
full, 8249, *rāmam[1]* [1]
make full restitution, 8740+928+8031, *šûb[1]+b[e]-+rō'š[1]* [1]
pay back in full, 8966, *šālēm[1]* [1]
repay in full, 8966+8966, *šālēm[1]+šālēm[1]* [1]
full measure, 8969, *šālēm[2]* [1]
full years, 9102+3427, *šānâ[2]+yôm[1]* [1]
full quota, 9420, *tōken[1]* [1]
full measure, 9448, *tōm* [1]
full, 9448, *tōm* [1]
full, 9462, *tāmam* [1]

FULLNESS [1]
fullness, 4850, *m[e]lō'* [1]

FULLY [27]
fully committed, 8969, *šālēm[2]* [4]
fully, 3972, *kōl* [3]
fully, 4394, *m[e]'ōd* [2]
fully accomplishes, 6913+2256+7756, *'āśâ[1]+w[e]-+qûm* [2]
fully, 8041, *rab[1]* [2]
fully devoted, 8969, *šālēm[2]* [2]
fully obey, 9048+9048+928+7754, *šāma'+šāma'+b[e]-+qôl* [2]
fully, 421, *'ak* [1]
fully determined, 928+4222+8969, *b[e]-+lēbāb+šālēm[2]* [1]
are fully satisfied, 2014, *dāšēn[1]* [1]
fully armed, 2821, *ḥāmaš* [1]
fully, 4814, *miklôl* [1]
fully repaid, 8425, *śāba'* [1]
satisfy fully, 8425, *śāba'* [1]
fully obeyed, 9048+2256+6913, *šāma'+w[e]-+'āśâ[1]* [1]
obey fully, 9048+9048+928+7754, *šāma'+šāma'+b[e]-+qôl* [1]
fully, 10056, *'osparnā'* [1]

FUNCTION [1]
function, *NIH/RPE* [1]

FUNERAL [2]
funeral meal, 5301, *marzēaḥ* [1]
funeral fire, 5386, *miśrāpôt* [1]

FURIOUS [8]
furious, 2779, *ḥēmâ* [2]
furious, 3013+4394, *ḥārâ*[1]*+meʾōd* [1]
furious, 3013+678+4394, *ḥārâ*[1]*+ʾap*[2]*+meʾōd* [1]
furious, 7911+4394, *qāṣap+meʾōd* [1]
furious, 10270, *ḥamâ* [1]
furious, 10416+10270, *melāʾ+ḥamâ* [1]
furious, 10633, *qeṣap*[1] [1]

FURIOUSLY [2]
drive furiously, 2147, *hālal*[3] [1]
furiously, 5352, *mārar* [1]

FURNACE [27]
furnace, 10086, *ʾattûn* [10]
furnace, 3929, *kûr*[2] [9]
furnace, 3901, *kibšān* [4]
furnace, 9486, *tannûr* [3]
furnace, 6612, *ʿalîl* [1]

FURNISHED [1]
furnished justification, 7136, *pālal*[1] [1]

FURNISHINGS [23]
furnishings, 3998, *kelî* [21]
holy furnishings, 7731, *qōdeš* [2]

FURROW [1]
furrow, 9439, *telem* [1]

FURROWS [3]
furrows, 9439, *telem* [2]
furrows, 5103, *maʿanâ* [1]

FURTHER [9]
further, 6388, *ʿôd* [6]
carried still further, 3578, *yāsap* [1]
further, 4027, *kēn*[2] [1]
further, 6964, *ʿattâ* [1]

FURTHERMORE [11]
furthermore, 2256, *we-* [2]
furthermore, 421, *ʾak* [1]
furthermore, 1685, *gam* [1]
furthermore, 2256+1685, *we-+gam* [1]
furthermore, 2256+2021+9108, *we-+ha-+šēnî* [1]
furthermore, 2256+6964, *we-+ʿattâ* [1]
furthermore, 2256+6388, *we-+ʿôd* [1]
furthermore, 6964, *ʿattâ* [1]
furthermore, 10221, *we-* [1]
furthermore, 10363, *keʿan* [1]

FURY [19]
fury, 2779, *ḥēmâ* [8]
fury, 6301, *ʿebrâ* [4]
fury, 678, *ʾap*[2] [2]
fury shown, 2404, *zāʿam* [1]
vent fury, 2404, *zāʿam* [1]
fury, 3013+4394, *ḥārâ*[1]*+meʾōd* [1]
fury, 5290, *marhēbâ* [1]
fury, 7912, *qeṣep*[1] [1]

FUTILE [3]
futile, 2039, *hebel*[1] [1]
futile, 4202+4027, *lōʾ+kēn*[2] [1]
futile, 8736, *šāwʾ* [1]

FUTILITY [3]
futility, 8736, *šāwʾ* [2]
futility, 2039, *hebel*[1] [1]

FUTURE [27]
future, 344, *ʾaḥarît* [7]
in the future, 4737, *māḥār* [4]
future hope, 344, *ʾaḥarît* [3]
future, 340, *ʾaḥarôn* [2]
future, 4946+8158, *min+rāḥôq* [2]
future, 294, *ʾāḥōr* [1]
future, 339, *ʾaḥar* [1]
future, 344+3427, *ʾaḥarît+yôm*[1] [1]
future, 995, *bôʾ* [1]
distant future, 3427+8041, *yôm*[1]*+rab*[1] [1]
future, 3427+4737, *yôm*[1]*+māḥār* [1]
future, 4537+8611+2118, *mâ+ša-+hāyâ* [1]
future, 6961, *ʿēt* [1]
in the future, 10021+10180, *ʾaḥar+denâ* [1]

GAAL [10]
Gaal, 1720, *gaʿal* [9]
Gaal[s], 2085, *hûʾ* [1]

GAASH [4]
Gaash, 1724, *gaʿaš* [4]

GABBAI [1]
Gabbai, 1480, *gabbay* [1]

GABRIEL [2]
Gabriel, 1508, *gabrîʾēl* [2]

GAD [54]
Gad, 1514, *gād* [43]
Gad, 1201+1514, *bēn*[1]*+gād* [7]
Gad, *NIH/RPE* [1]
Gad, 1201+1532, *bēn*[1]*+gādî*[1] [1]
Gad, 1532, *gādî*[1] [1]
of Gad, 1532, *gādî*[1] [1]

GAD'S [1]
Gad's, 1514, *gād* [1]

GADDI [1]
Gaddi, 1534, *gaddî* [1]

GADDIEL [1]
Gaddiel, 1535, *gaddîʾēl* [1]

GADFLY [1]
gadfly, 7976, *qereṣ* [1]

GADI [2]
Gadi, 1533, *gādî*[2] [2]

GADITES [29]
Gadites, 1201+1514, *bēn*[1]*+gād* [16]
Gadites, 1532, *gādî*[1] [12]
Gadites, *NIH/RPE* [1]

GAHAM [1]
Gaham, 1626, *gaḥam* [1]

GAHAR [2]
Gahar, 1627, *gaḥar* [2]

GAIETY [2]
gaiety, 5375, *māśôś*[1] [2]

GAIN [50]
gain, 1299, *beṣaʿ* [9]
gain, 1067, *bîn* [3]
dishonest gain, 1299, *beṣaʿ* [3]
gain, 3603, *yāʿal* [3]
gain, 3862, *yitrôn* [3]
gain glory, 3877, *kābēd*[1] [3]
gain, 6913, *ʿāśâ*[1] [3]
gain understanding, 1067, *bîn* [2]
unjust gain, 1299, *beṣaʿ* [2]
gain, 3359, *yādaʿ* [2]
gain, *AIT* [1]
gain, 995, *bôʾ* [1]
go after ill-gotten gain, 1298+1299, *bāṣaʿ+beṣaʿ* [1]
make unjust gain, 1298+1299, *bāṣaʿ+beṣaʿ* [1]
make unjust gain, 1298, *bāṣaʿ* [1]
ill-gotten gain, 1299, *beṣaʿ* [1]
selfish gain, 1299, *beṣaʿ* [1]
gain support, 2118+3338+907, *hāyâ+yād+ʾēt*[2] [1]
gain, 3463, *yôtēr* [1]
gain possession, 3769, *yāraš*[1] [1]
gain glory for myself, 3877, *kābēd*[1] [1]
gain, 4200, *le-*[1] [1]
gain, 5162, *māṣāʾ* [1]
gain control, 5440, *māšal*[2] [1]
gain, 9311, *tebûʾâ* [1]
gain, 9461, *tāmak* [1]
gain, 10223, *zeban* [1]

GAINED [12]
gained, 6913, *ʿāśâ*[1] [3]
gained, *AIT* [1]
quickly gained, 987, *bāhal* [1]
gained, 2118, *hāyâ* [1]
gained power, 2621, *ḥezqâ* [1]
gained the victory, 3523, *yākōl* [1]
gained, 3862, *yitrôn* [1]
gained glory for yourself, 3877, *kābēd*[1] [1]
gained, 5162, *māṣāʾ* [1]
gained confidence, 6164, *sāmak* [1]

GAINING [2]
gaining, 8049, *rābâ*[1] [1]
gaining wisdom, 8505, *śākal*[1] [1]

GAINS [7]
gains, 9461, *tāmak* [2]
ill-gotten gains, 1299, *beṣaʿ* [1]
gains, 3578, *yāsap* [1]
gains, 6913, *ʿāśâ*[1] [1]
gains, 7049, *pûq*[2] [1]
gains, 7864, *qānâ*[1] [1]

GALAL [3]
Galal, 1674, *gālāl*[3] [3]

GALBANUM [1]
galbanum, 2697, *ḥelbenâ* [1]

GALE [3]
gale, 6070, *sûpâ*[1] [2]
gale, 6194, *seʿārâ* [1]

GALEED [2]
Galeed, 1681, *galʿēd* [2]

GALILEE [6]
Galilee, 1665, *gālîl*[2] [5]
Galilee, 824+1665, *ʾereṣ+gālîl*[2] [1]

GALL [5]
gall, 4360, *laʿanâ* [3]
gall, 5354, *merērâ* [1]
gall, 8032, *rōʾš*[2] [1]

GALLED [1]
galled, 8317+928+6524, *rāʿaʿ*[1]*+be-+ʿayin*[1] [1]

GALLERIES [3]
galleries, 916, *ʾattîq* [3]

GALLERY [2]
gallery, 916, *ʾattîq* [2]

GALLEY [1]
galley, 639, *ʾonî* [1]

GALLIM [2]
Gallim, 1668, *gallîm* [2]

GALLOP [1]
gallop along, 8132, *rûṣ* [1]

GALLOPING [4]
galloping, 1852, *daharâ* [2]
galloping, 1851, *dāhar* [1]
galloping, 9121, *šeʿāṭâ* [1]

GALLOPS [1]
gallops headlong, 7055, *pûš*[1] [1]

GALLOWS [9]
gallows, 6770, *ʿēṣ* [9]

GAMALIEL [5]
Gamaliel, 1697, *gamlîʾēl* [5]

GAME [10]
game, 7473, *ṣayid*[1] [7]
wild game, 7473, *ṣayid*[1] [2]
game, 3272, *ṭerep* [1]

GAMMAD [1]
men of Gammad, 1689, *gammādîm* [1]

GAMUL [1]
Gamul, 1690, *gāmûl* [1]

GAP [4]
gap, 7288, *pereṣ*[1] [3]
gap in the wall, 7288, *pereṣ*[1] [1]

GAPE [1]
gape, 8143+7023, *rāḥab+peh* [1]

GAPING [1]
gaping, 8146, *rāḥāb*[1] [1]

GAPS [1]
gaps, 7287, *pāraṣ* [1]

GARDEN [47]
garden, 1703, *gan* [39]
garden, 1708, *gannâ* [6]
garden, *NIH/RPE* [1]
garden, 5750, *neṭa'* [1]

GARDENS [11]
gardens, 1708, *gannâ* [9]
gardens, 1703, *gan* [2]

GAREB [3]
Gareb, 1735, *gārēb*[1] [2]
Gareb, 1736, *gārēb*[2] [1]

GARLAND [2]
garland, 4292, *liwyâ* [2]

GARLIC [1]
garlic, 8770, *šûmîm* [1]

GARMENT [36]
garment, 955, *beged*[2] [14]
garment, 4230, *l[e]bûš* [4]
garment, 8529, *śimlâ* [3]
corner of garment, 4053, *kānāp* [2]
garment, 8515, *śalmâ*[1] [2]
garment, 168, *'adderet* [1]
prophet's garment, 168, *'adderet* [1]
garment, 2668, *ḥēq* [1]
folds of garment, 4053, *kānāp* [1]
garment, 4064, *k[e]sût* [1]
garment, 4189, *kuttōnet* [1]
garment, 4496, *mad* [1]
garment, 5073, *ma'[a]ṭeh* [1]
garment, 5077, *m[e]'îl* [1]
woolen garment, 7547, *ṣemer* [1]
garment of hair, 8552, *śē'ār* [1]

GARMENTS [71]
garments, 955, *beged*[2] [48]
garments, 4230, *l[e]bûš* [5]
garments, 4189, *kuttōnet* [4]
linen garments, 6041, *sādîn* [4]
garments, 4503, *mādû* [2]
colorful garments, 7389, *ṣeba'* [2]
rich garments, 4711, *maḥ[a]lāṣôt* [1]
beautiful garments, 4815, *maklûl* [1]
costly garments, 5429, *mešî* [1]
garments, 7389, *ṣeba'* [1]
embroidered garments, 8391, *riqmâ* [1]
garments, 8515, *śalmâ*[1] [1]

GARMITE [1]
Garmite, 1753, *garmî* [1]

GARRISON [2]
garrison, 5163, *maṣṣāb* [1]
garrison, 5907, *n[e]ṣîb*[1] [1]

GARRISONS [5]
garrisons, 5907, *n[e]ṣîb*[1] [4]
garrisons, *NIH/RPE* [1]

GASP [2]
gasp, 5134, *mappāḥ* [1]
gasp, 5971, *nāšam* [1]

GASPING [1]
gasping for breath, 3640, *yāpaḥ* [1]

GATAM [3]
Gatam, 1725, *ga'tām* [3]

GATE [204]
gate, 9133, *ša'ar*[1] [177]
city gate, 9133, *ša'ar*[1] [11]
gate, *NIH/RPE* [5]
gate, 7339, *petaḥ* [2]
each gate, 9133+2256+9133, *ša'ar*[1]*+w[e]-+ša'ar*[1] [2]
town gate, 9133, *ša'ar*[1] [2]
gate bars, 1378, *b[e]rîaḥ* [1]
gate, 1378, *b[e]rîaḥ* [1]
gate, 1946, *delet* [1]
keeper of Gate, 8788, *šô'ēr* [1]
assembly at the gate, 9133, *ša'ar*[1] [1]

GATEKEEPER [2]
gatekeeper, 8788, *šô'ēr* [2]

GATEKEEPERS [34]
gatekeepers, 8788, *šô'ēr* [29]
the gatekeepers[s], 2156, *hēm* [2]
gatekeepers, *NIH/RPE* [1]
the gatekeepers[s], 2157, *-hem* [1]
gatekeepers, 10777, *tārā'* [1]

GATEPOST [1]
gatepost, 4647+9133, *m[e]zûzâ+ša'ar*[1] [1]

GATEPOSTS [1]
gateposts, 4647+9133, *m[e]zûzâ+ša'ar*[1] [1]

GATES [99]
gates, 9133, *ša'ar*[1] [75]
gates, 1946, *delet* [10]
city gates, 9133, *ša'ar*[1] [4]
gates, *NIH/RPE* [2]
gates, 7339, *petaḥ* [2]
bars of gates, 964, *bad*[2] [1]
gates, 964, *bad*[2] [1]
barred gates, 1378, *b[e]rîaḥ* [1]
bars of gates, 1378, *b[e]rîaḥ* [1]
bolts of gates, 4981, *min'āl* [1]
various gates, 9133+2256+9133, *ša'ar*[1]*+w[e]-+ša'ar*[1] [1]

GATEWAY [34]
gateway, 9133, *ša'ar*[1] [29]
the gateway[s], 2257, *-ô* [4]
gateway, 4427, *mābô'* [1]

GATEWAYS [6]
gateways, 9133, *ša'ar*[1] [4]
gateways, *NIH/RPE* [1]
gateways, 7339+9133, *petaḥ+ša'ar*[1] [1]

GATH [36]
Gath, 1781, *gat*[2] [34]
Gath, 1785, *gittî* [1]
Gath[s], 9004, *šām* [1]

GATH HEPHER [2]
Gath Hepher, 1783, *gat haḥēper* [2]

GATH RIMMON [4]
Gath Rimmon, 1784, *gat-rimmôn* [4]

GATHER [100]
gather, 7695, *qābaṣ* [38]
gather, 665, *'āsap* [17]
gather, 4377, *lāqaṭ* [11]
gather together, 665, *'āsap* [3]
gather, 4043, *kānas* [3]
gather together, 7695, *qābaṣ* [3]
gather in, 665, *'āsap* [2]
gather up, 665, *'āsap* [2]
gather, 7735, *qāhal* [2]
gather together, 8006, *qāšaš*[1] [2]
gather, 8006, *qāšaš*[1] [2]
gather grapes, 112, *'āgar* [1]
gather around, 665, *'āsap* [1]
surely gather, 665+665, *'āsap+'āsap* [1]
gather together, 1591, *gûr*[1] [1]
gather, 3570, *yāsad*[2] [1]
gather together, 4043, *kānas* [1]
gather about, 4193, *kātar*[2] [1]
gather up, 4377, *lāqaṭ* [1]
gather, 5951, *nāšā'* [1]
gather around, 6015, *sābab* [1]
gather in, 7695, *qābaṣ* [1]
gather, 7697, *q[e]buṣâ* [1]
gather together, 7735, *qāhal* [1]
gather, 7748, *qāwâ*[2] [1]
gather, 7917, *qāṣar*[1] [1]

GATHERED [100]
gathered, 665, *'āsap* [18]
gathered, 7695, *qābaṣ* [15]
be gathered, 665, *'āsap* [9]
gathered, 7735, *qāhal* [9]
gathered, 4377, *lāqaṭ* [8]
was gathered, 665, *'āsap* [5]
gathered together, 665, *'āsap* [4]
gathered up, 665, *'āsap* [3]
gathered, 3585, *yā'ad* [2]
gathered together, 7735, *qāhal* [2]
gathered, 7736, *qāhāl* [2]
are gathered, 665, *'āsap* [1]
be gathered up, 665, *'āsap* [1]
be gathered, 665+665, *'āsap+'āsap* [1]
been gathered, 665, *'āsap* [1]
is gathered in, 665, *'āsap* [1]
were gathered, 665, *'āsap* [1]
gathered, 768, *'ārâ* [1]
gathered, 1305, *bāṣar*[1] [1]
gathered together, 2410, *zā'aq* [1]
are gathered, 4374, *lāqaḥ* [1]
be gathered up, 4377, *lāqaṭ* [1]
gathered little, 5070, *mā'aṭ* [1]
gathered, 5224, *miqweh*[2] [1]
gathered around, 6015, *sābab* [1]
gathered, 6051, *sôd* [1]
gathered, 6590, *'ālâ* [1]
be gathered, 7695, *qābaṣ* [1]
gathered together, 7695, *qābaṣ* [1]
were gathered, 7695, *qābaṣ* [1]
be gathered, 7748, *qāwâ*[2] [1]
gathered, 7786, *qāṭap* [1]
gathered up, 7890, *qāpaṣ* [1]
gathered much, 8049, *rābâ*[1] [1]

GATHERING [7]
gathering, 8006, *qāšaš*[1] [4]
gathering, 665, *'āsap* [1]
gathering grapes, 1305, *bāṣar*[1] [1]
gathering, 4377, *lāqaṭ* [1]

GATHERS [16]
gathers, 7695, *qābaṣ* [5]
gathers up, 665, *'āsap* [2]
gathers, 665, *'āsap* [2]
gathers, 4043, *kānas* [2]
gathers crops, 112, *'āgar* [1]
gathers, 112, *'āgar* [1]
gathers, 668, *'ōsep* [1]
gathers, 4377, *lāqaṭ* [1]
gathers, 6682, *'āmar*[1] [1]

GAUDY [1]
gaudy, 3229, *ṭālā'* [1]

GAUNT [3]
gaunt, 1987+1414, *daq+bāśār* [2]
gaunt, 4946+9043, *min+šemen* [1]

GAUNTNESS [1]
gauntness, 3951, *kaḥaš* [1]

GAVE [493]
gave, 5989, *nātan* [231]
gave birth, 3528, *yālad* [46]
gave, 7422, *ṣāwâ* [25]
gave, *NIH/RPE* [11]
gave orders, 7422, *ṣāwâ* [10]
gave, 6913, *'āśâ*[1] [9]
gave order, 7422, *ṣāwâ* [7]
gave, 7924, *qārā'*[1] [7]
gave, 1819, *dābar*[2] [6]
gave orders, 606, *'āmar*[1] [5]
gave in marriage, 5989+4200+851, *nātan+l[e]-*[1]*+'iššâ* [5]
gave command, 7422, *ṣāwâ* [5]
gave, 8492, *śîm* [5]
gave to eat, 430, *'ākal* [4]
gave victory, 3828, *yāša'* [4]
gave over, 5989, *nātan* [4]
gave rest, 5663, *nûaḥ*[1] [3]

gave over, 6037, *sāgar* [3]
advice gave, 6783+3619, *ʿēṣâ*[1]*+yāʿaṣ* [3]
gave instructions, 7422, *ṣāwâ* [3]
gave success, 7503, *ṣālaḥ*[2] [3]
gave a drink, 9197, *šāqâ* [3]
gave, 10314, *y^{e}hab* [3]
gave blessing, 1385, *bārak*[2] [2]
gave birth, 2655, *ḥîl*[1] [2]
gave, 2745, *ḥālaq*[2] [2]
gave inheritance, 5706, *nāḥal* [2]
gave name, 7924, *qārāʾ*[1] [2]
gave many, 8049, *rābâ*[1] [2]
gave a shout, 8131+9558, *rûaʿ+t^{e}rûʿâ* [2]
gave orders, 8938, *šālaḥ* [2]
gave over, 8938, *šālaḥ* [2]
gave, 9197, *šāqâ* [2]
gave orders, 10042, *ʾ^{a}mar* [2]
gave in to craving, 203+9294, *ʾāwâ*[1]*+taʾ^{a}wâ*[1] [1]
gave an order, 606, *ʾāmar*[1] [1]
gave the order, 606, *ʾāmar*[1] [1]
gave, 606, *ʾāmar*[1] [1]
gave, 995, *bôʾ* [1]
gave full attention, 1067, *bîn* [1]
gave the message, 1819+3972+2021+1821+2021+465, *dābar*[2]*+kōl+ha-+dābār+ha-+ʾēlleh* [1]
gave thanks, 2146, *hālal*[2] [1]
gave birth, 2225, *hārâ* [1]
gave, 2600, *ḥāzâ* [1]
gave power, 2616, *ḥāzaq* [1]
gave strength, 2616, *ḥāzaq* [1]
gave strong support, 2616+6640, *ḥāzaq+ʿim* [1]
gave thanks, 3344, *yādâ*[2] [1]
gave life, 3528, *yālad* [1]
gave, 3578, *yāsap* [1]
gave as an inheritance, 3769, *yāraš*[1] [1]
gave a firm, 3922, *kûn*[1] [1]
gave permission, 4200, *l^{e}-*[1] [1]
gave, 5184, *miṣwâ* [1]
gave freewill offerings, 5605, *nādab* [1]
gave willingly, 5605, *nādab* [1]
gave, 5678, *nûp*[2] [1]
gave, 5706, *nāḥal* [1]
gave assistance, 5951, *nāśāʾ* [1]
gave in marriage, 5989+851, *nātan+ʾiššâ* [1]
gave in marriage, 5989, *nātan* [1]
gave in pledge, 5989, *nātan* [1]
gave up, 5989, *nātan* [1]
gave victory, 5989+928+3338, *nātan+b^{e}-+yād* [1]
gave support, 6164, *sāmak* [1]
gave account, 6218, *sāpar* [1]
warnings gave, 6343+6386, *ʿēdût+ʿûd*[1] [1]
gave charge, 6386, *ʿûd*[1] [1]
gave up, 6440, *ʿāzab*[1] [1]
gave support, 6468+339, *ʿāzar+ʾaḥar* [1]
gave ruling, 6699, *ʿānâ*[1] [1]
gave a charge, 7422, *ṣāwâ* [1]
gave an order, 7422, *ṣāwâ* [1]
gave commands, 7422, *ṣāwâ* [1]
gave the order, 7422, *ṣāwâ* [1]
gave trouble, 7674, *ṣārar*[1] [1]
gave, 7756, *qûm* [1]
gave success, 7936, *qārâ*[1] [1]
gave heed, 7992, *qāšab* [1]
generously gave, 8049, *rābâ*[1] [1]
gave a high rank in, 8492+6584, *śîm+ʿal*[2] [1]
gave thought, 8505, *śākal*[1] [1]
gave understanding, 8505, *śākal*[1] [1]
gave what asked for, 8626, *šāʾal* [1]
gave, 8626, *šāʾal* [1]
gave oath, 8678, *šābaʿ* [1]
gave solemn oath, 8678, *šābaʿ* [1]
gave, 8740, *šûb*[1] [1]
gave a place, 8883, *šît*[1] [1]
gave away in marriage, 8938, *šālaḥ* [1]
gave, 8938, *šālaḥ* [1]
gave in, 9048+928+7754, *šāmaʿ+b^{e}-+qôl* [1]
gave water, 9197, *šāqâ* [1]
choirs that gave thanks, 9343, *tôdâ* [1]
gave explanation, 10042, *ʾ^{a}mar* [1]
gave the order, 10042, *ʾ^{a}mar* [1]
gave, 10313, *y^{e}daʿ* [1]
gave, 10522, *ʿ^{a}bad* [1]
gave way, 10742, *š^{e}râ* [1]
gave, 10754, *tûb* [1]

GAZA [22]
Gaza, 6445, *ʿazzâ* [20]
Gaza, 6484, *ʿazzātî* [1]
people of Gaza, 6484, *ʿazzātî* [1]

GAZE [10]
gaze, 2600, *ḥāzâ* [3]
gaze, 5564, *nābaṭ* [2]
stared with a fixed gaze, 6641+906+7156+2256+8492, *ʿāmad+ʾēt*[1]*+pāneh+w^{e}-+śîm* [1]
gaze, 6757, *ʿapʿappayim* [1]
gaze, 8011, *rāʾâ*[1] [1]
gaze in envy, 8353, *rāṣad* [1]
gaze, 8800, *šûr*[1] [1]

GAZELLE [12]
gazelle, 7383, *ṣ^{e}bî*[2] [10]
gazelle, 7386, *ṣ^{e}biyyâ* [2]

GAZELLES [4]
gazelles, 7374, *ṣ^{e}bāʾâ* [2]
gazelles, 7373, *ṣābāʾ*[3] [1]
gazelles, 7383, *ṣ^{e}bî*[2] [1]

GAZEZ [2]
Gazez, 1606, *gāzēz* [2]

GAZING [2]
gazing, 8011, *rāʾâ*[1] [1]
gazing, 8708, *šāgaḥ* [1]

GAZZAM [2]
Gazzam, 1613, *gazzām* [2]

GE HARASHIM [1]
Ge Harashim, 1629, *gêʾ ḥ^{a}rāšîm* [1]

GEBA [15]
Geba, 1494, *gebaʿ* [15]

GEBAL [3]
Gebal, 1488, *g^{e}bal* [1]
Gebal, 1489, *g^{e}bāl* [1]
men of Gebal, 1490, *giblî* [1]

GEBALITES [1]
Gebalites, 1490, *giblî* [1]

GEBER [1]
Geber, 1506, *geber*[2] [1]

GEBIM [1]
Gebim, 1481, *gēbîm* [1]

GECKO [1]
gecko, 652, *ʾ^{a}nāqâ*[2] [1]

GEDALIAH [31]
Gedaliah, 1546, *g^{e}dalyāhû* [25]
Gedaliah, 1545, *g^{e}dalyâ* [6]

GEDALIAH'S [1]
Gedaliah's, 1546, *g^{e}dalyāhû* [1]

GEDER [1]
Geder, 1554, *geder* [1]

GEDERAH [2]
Gederah, 1557, *g^{e}dērâ*[2] [2]

GEDERATHITE [1]
Gederathite, 1561, *g^{e}dērātî* [1]

GEDERITE [1]
Gederite, 1559, *g^{e}dērî* [1]

GEDEROTH [2]
Gederoth, 1558, *g^{e}dērôt* [2]

GEDEROTHAIM [1]
Gederothaim, 1562, *g^{e}dērōtayim* [1]

GEDOR [7]
Gedor, 1529, *g^{e}dôr*[1] [4]
Gedor, 1530, *g^{e}dôr*[2] [3]

GEHAZI [20]
Gehazi, 1634, *gêḥ^{a}zî* [12]
Gehazi, *NIH/RPE* [5]
Gehazi[s], 2257, *-ô* [2]
Gehazi[s], 2085, *hûʾ* [1]

GELILOTH [3]
Geliloth, 1667, *g^{e}lîlôt* [3]

GEM [1]
gem, 74, *ʾeben* [1]

GEMALLI [1]
Gemalli, 1696, *g^{e}mallî* [1]

GEMARIAH [5]
Gemariah, 1702, *g^{e}maryāhû* [4]
Gemariah, 1701, *g^{e}maryâ* [1]

GEMS [4]
gems, 74, *ʾeben* [4]

GENEALOGICAL [11]
genealogical records, 9352, *tôlēdôt* [2]
be listed in the genealogical record, 3509, *yāḥaś* [1]
enrolled in the genealogical records, 3509, *yāḥaś* [1]
genealogical record listed, 3509, *yāḥaś* [1]
kept a genealogical record, 3509, *yāḥaś* [1]
listed in genealogical records, 3509, *yāḥaś* [1]
names in the genealogical records, 3509, *yāḥaś* [1]
were entered in the genealogical records, 3509, *yāḥaś* [1]
genealogical, 3510, *yaḥaś* [1]
genealogical record, 9352, *tôlēdôt* [1]

GENEALOGIES [3]
deal with genealogies, 3509, *yāḥaś* [1]
was listed in the genealogies, 3509, *yāḥaś* [1]
were recorded in the genealogies, 3509, *yāḥaś* [1]

GENEALOGY [8]
listed genealogy, 9352, *tôlēdôt* [3]
listed in genealogy, 3509, *yāḥaś* [2]
genealogy, 9352, *tôlēdôt* [1]
were registered by genealogy, 3509, *yāḥaś* [1]

GENERATION [55]
generation, 1887, *dôr*[2] [44]
fourth generation, 8067, *ribbēaʿ* [4]
generation, 10183, *dār* [4]
fourth generation, 8055, *r^{e}bîʿî* [2]
third generation, 9000, *šillēšîm* [1]

GENERATIONS [75]
generations to come, 1887, *dôr*[2] [37]
all generations, 1887+2256+1887, *dôr*[2]*+w^{e}-+dôr*[2] [14]
generations, 1887, *dôr*[2] [12]
generations, 1887+2256+1887, *dôr*[2]*+w^{e}-+dôr*[2] [3]
generations, *NIH/RPE* [2]
all generations, 1887+1887, *dôr*[2]*+dôr*[2] [2]
endless generations, 1887+2256+1887, *dôr*[2]*+w^{e}-+dôr*[2] [1]
generations to come, 1887+2256+1887, *dôr*[2]*+w^{e}-+dôr*[2] [1]
many generations, 1887+2256+1887, *dôr*[2]*+w^{e}-+dôr*[2] [1]
through all generations, 1887+1887, *dôr*[2]*+dôr*[2] [1]
generations long past, 9102+1887+2256+1887, *šānâ*[2]*+dôr*[2]*+w^{e}-+dôr*[2] [1]

GENEROUS [4]
generous, 2858, *ḥānan*[1] [2]
generous, 1388, *b^{e}rākâ*[1] [1]
generous man, 3202+6524, *ṭôb*[2]*+ʿayin*[1] [1]

GENEROUSLY [4]
generously, 2858, *ḥānan*[1] [1]
give generously, 5605, *nādab* [1]
give generously, 5989+5989, *nātan+nātan* [1]
generously gave, 8049, *rābâ*[1] [1]

GENITALS [1]
genitals, 1414, *bāśār* [1]

GENTILE [2]
Gentile, 1580, *gôy* [2]

GENTILES [5]
Gentiles, 1580, *gôy* [5]

GENTLE [10]
gentle, 8205, *rak* [5]
gentle, 351, *ʾaṭ^{1}* [1]
gentle, 476, *ʾallûp^{1}* [1]
gentle, 1987, *daq* [1]
gentle, 6714, *ʿānî* [1]
gentle, 8204, *rōk* [1]

GENTLY [5]
gently, 4200+351, *l^{e}-^{1}+ʾaṭ^{1}* [2]
flowing gently, 1803, *dābab* [1]
gently leads, 5633, *nāhal* [1]
fell gently, 5752, *nāṭap* [1]

GENUBATH [2]
Genubath, 1707, *g^{e}nubat* [2]

GERA [9]
Gera, 1733, *gērāʾ* [9]

GERAHS [5]
gerahs, 1743, *gērā^{2}* [5]

GERAR [10]
Gerar, 1761, *g^{e}rār* [10]

GERIZIM [4]
Gerizim, 1748, *g^{e}rizîm* [4]

GERSHOM [7]
Gershom, 1768, *gēršōm* [7]

GERSHON [15]
Gershon, 1767, *gēršôn* [9]
Gershon, 1768, *gēršōm* [6]

GERSHONITE [10]
Gershonite, 1769, *gēršunnî* [7]
Gershonite, 1201+1767, *bēn^{1}+gēršôn* [2]
Gershonite, 1201+1769, *bēn^{1}+gēršunnî* [1]

GERSHONITES [12]
Gershonites, 1201+1767, *bēn^{1}+gēršôn* [6]
Gershonites, 1769, *gēršunnî* [3]
Gershonites, *NIH/RPE* [1]
Gershonites, 1201+1768, *bēn^{1}+gēršōm* [1]
Gershonites, 1201+1769, *bēn^{1}+gēršunnî* [1]

GERUTH KIMHAM [1]
Geruth Kimham, 1745, *gērût kimhām* [1]

GESHAN [1]
Geshan, 1642, *gêšān* [1]

GESHEM [4]
Geshem, 1774, *gešem^{2}* [3]
Geshem, 1776, *gašmû* [1]

GESHUR [11]
Geshur, 1770, *g^{e}šûr* [8]
people of Geshur, 1771, *g^{e}šûrî* [3]

GESHURITES [3]
Geshurites, 1771, *g^{e}šûrî* [3]

GET [209]
get, 4374, *lāqaḥ* [46]
get up, 7756, *qûm* [24]
get out, 3655, *yāṣāʾ* [7]
get, 7864, *qānâ^{1}* [7]
get, 995, *bôʾ* [6]
get, 5989, *nātan* [5]
get ready, 3922, *kûn^{1}* [4]
get, 5951, *nāśāʾ* [4]
get up early, 8899, *šākam* [4]
get, *AIT* [3]
get, *NIH/RPE* [3]
get in, 995, *bôʾ* [3]
get, 4200, *l^{e}-^{1}* [3]
get rid of, 6073, *sûr^{1}* [3]
get enough, 8425, *śābaʿ* [3]
get there, 995, *bôʾ* [2]
get, 2118, *hāyâ* [2]
get out, 2143, *hālak* [2]
get, 2143, *hālak* [2]
let get away, 4880, *mālaṭ^{1}* [2]
get, 5595, *nāgaʿ* [2]
get so close, 5602, *nāgaš* [2]
get through, 6296, *ʿābar^{1}* [2]
get, 6590, *ʿālâ* [2]
get, 6913, *ʿāśâ^{1}* [2]
get ready, 7756, *qûm* [2]
get rid of, 8959, *šālak* [2]
get a drink, 9197, *šāqâ* [2]
get to drink, 9197, *šāqâ* [2]
get ready, 273+5516, *ʾāzar+motnayim* [1]
get food, 430, *ʾākal* [1]
get, 665, *ʾāsap* [1]
get, 928, *b^{e}-* [1]
to get, 928, *b^{e}-* [1]
those who get, 1251, *baʿal^{1}* [1]
try to get, 1335, *bāqaš* [1]
trying to get, 1335, *bāqaš* [1]
get rid of, 1763, *gāraš^{1}* [1]
get, 2093, *hāwâ^{2}* [1]
get back, 2143, *hālak* [1]
get away, 2143, *hālak* [1]
get rid of, 2143, *hālak* [1]
get share of property, 2745, *ḥālaq^{2}* [1]
get directions, 3723, *yārâ^{3}* [1]
get help for, 3828, *yāšaʿ* [1]
get back, 4374, *lāqaḥ* [1]
how to get into, 4427, *mābôʾ* [1]
get away, 4880, *mālaṭ^{1}* [1]
get, 5162, *māṣāʾ* [1]
get out, 5602, *nāgaš* [1]
get relief, 5663, *nûaḥ^{1}* [1]
get away, 5674+5674, *nûs+nûs* [1]
get away, 5674, *nûs* [1]
get inheritance, 5706, *nāḥal* [1]
get relief, 5714, *nāḥam* [1]
get back on, 5742, *nāṭâ* [1]
get off, 5742, *nāṭâ* [1]
have a right to get even, 5927, *nāqâ* [1]
get revenge, 5933+5934, *nāqam+nāqām* [1]
get revenge, 5933, *nāqam* [1]
get, 6292, *ʿābaṭ* [1]
get up, 6590, *ʿālâ* [1]
get response, 6699, *ʿānâ^{1}* [1]
get ready, 6913, *ʿāśâ^{1}* [1]
get rich, 6947, *ʿāšar* [1]
get ready, 6963, *ʿātad* [1]
get out of control, 7277, *pāraʿ^{2}* [1]
get away, 7756, *qûm* [1]
get it to its feet, 7756+7756, *qûm+qûm* [1]
get, 7924, *qārāʾ^{1}* [1]
get more, 8049, *rābâ^{1}* [1]
get away, 8250, *rāmam^{2}* [1]
get answer, 8626+8626, *šāʾal+šāʾal* [1]
get back, 8740, *šûb^{1}* [1]
get what deserved, 8750, *šāwâ^{1}* [1]
early morning get up, 8899, *šākam* [1]
get drunk, 8910, *šākar* [1]
get out of here, 8938+2021+2575+2025, *šālaḥ+ha-+ḥûṣ+-â^{2}* [1]
let get away, 8938, *šālaḥ* [1]
let get away, 8938+928+2006, *šālaḥ+b^{e}+derek* [1]
get rid of, 9012, *šāmad* [1]
get back to, 9048, *šāmaʿ* [1]
get a drink, 9272, *šātâ^{2}* [1]
have get ready, 9462, *tāmam* [1]
get up, 10624, *qûm* [1]

GETHER [2]
Gether, 1788, *geter* [2]

GETS [10]
gets, *AIT* [2]
gets up, 7756, *qûm* [2]
gets, *NIH/RPE* [1]
gets mercy, 2858, *ḥānan^{1}* [1]
gets, 4374, *lāqaḥ* [1]
gets up, 6641, *ʿāmad* [1]
see that gets justice, 7405, *ṣādaq* [1]
gets, 7864, *qānâ^{1}* [1]

GETTING [5]
getting, *AIT* [2]
getting drunk, 9272+8893, *šātâ^{2}+šikkôr* [2]
keep on getting drunk, 8910, *šākar* [1]

GEUEL [1]
Geuel, 1451, *g^{e}ʾûʾēl* [1]

GEZER [14]
Gezer, 1618, *gezer^{2}* [14]

GHOSTLIKE [1]
ghostlike, 3869+200, *k^{e}-+ʾôb^{2}* [1]

GIAH [1]
Giah, 1632, *gîaḥ^{2}* [1]

GIBBAR [1]
Gibbar, 1507, *gibbār* [1]

GIBBETHON [5]
Gibbethon, 1510, *gibb^{e}tôn* [5]

GIBEA [1]
Gibea, 1495, *gibʿāʾ* [1]

GIBEAH [48]
Gibeah, 1497, *gibʿâ^{2}* [48]

GIBEATH HAARALOTH [1]
Gibeath Haaraloth, 1502, *gibʿat hāʿ^{a}rālôt* [1]

GIBEATHITE [1]
Gibeathite, 1503, *gibʿātî* [1]

GIBEON [40]
Gibeon, 1500, *gibʿōn* [38]
Gibeon, *NIH/RPE* [1]
of Gibeon, 1498, *gibʿônî* [1]

GIBEONITE [1]
Gibeonite, 1498, *gibʿônî* [1]

GIBEONITES [10]
Gibeonites, 1498, *gibʿônî* [6]
the Gibeonites^{s}, 2157, *-hem* [2]
Gibeonites, 408+1500, *ʾîš^{1}+gibʿōn* [1]
the Gibeonites^{s}, 4392, *-ām* [1]

GIDDALTI [2]
Giddalti, 1547, *giddaltî* [2]

GIDDEL [4]
Giddel, 1543, *giddēl* [4]

GIDEON [46]
Gideon, 1549, *gidʿôn* [35]
Gideon, *NIH/RPE* [7]
Gideon^{s}, 2257, *-ô* [4]

GIDEON'S [1]
Gideon's, 1549, *gidʿôn* [1]

GIDEONI [5]
Gideoni, 1551, *gidʿōnî* [5]

GIDOM [1]
Gidom, 1550, *gidʿōm* [1]

GIFT [37]
gift, 4966, *minḥâ* [11]
gift, 5510, *mattānâ^{1}* [5]
gift, 5508, *mattān^{1}* [3]
gift, 5522, *mattat* [3]
gift, 1388, *b^{e}rākâ^{1}* [2]
gift, 8816, *šōḥad* [2]
special gift, 9556, *t^{e}rûmâ* [2]
gift, 2273, *zēbed* [1]
gift, 5368, *maśʾēt* [1]
gift, 7933, *qorbān* [1]
as a special gift set aside, 8123, *rûm^{1}* [1]
wedding gift, 8933, *šillûḥîm* [1]
gift, 9556, *t^{e}rûmâ* [1]
portion as a special gift, 9556, *t^{e}rûmâ* [1]
special gift, 9557, *t^{e}rûmiyyâ* [1]
gift, 9593, *t^{e}šûrâ* [1]

GIFTS [56]
gifts, 5510, *mattānâ^{1}* [9]
gifts, 4966, *minḥâ* [8]
gifts, *NIH/RPE* [4]
gifts, 8856, *šay* [3]
special gifts, 9556+3338, *t^{e}rûmâ+yād* [3]
gifts, 10448, *matt^{e}nâ* [3]
valuable gifts, 4458, *meged* [2]
gifts, 5368, *maś'ēt* [2]
gifts, 5508, *mattān^{1}* [2]
gifts, 5989, *nātan* [2]
sacred gifts, 7731, *qōdeš* [2]
gifts, 7933, *qorbān* [2]
gifts, 868, *'eškār* [1]
temple gifts, 924, *'etnan* [1]
costly gifts, 2776, *ḥ^{a}mudôt* [1]
costly gifts, 4458, *meged* [1]
gifts he does not give, 5522+9214, *mattat+šeqer* [1]
gifts, 5621, *nādān^{2}* [1]
gives gifts, 5989, *nātan* [1]
consecrated gifts, 7731+7731, *qōdeš+qōdeš* [1]
dedicated gifts, 7731, *qōdeš* [1]
gifts dedicated, 7731, *qōdeš* [1]
choicest gifts, 8031, *rō'š^{1}* [1]
parting gifts, 8933, *šillûḥîm* [1]
gifts, 8988, *šalmōnîm* [1]
special gifts, 9556, *t^{e}rûmâ* [1]

GIHON [6]
Gihon, 1633, *gîḥôn* [6]

GILALAI [1]
Gilalai, 1675, *gil^{a}lay* [1]

GILBOA [8]
Gilboa, 1648, *gilbōa'* [8]

GILEAD [97]
Gilead, 1680, *gil'ād* [85]
Gilead, 824+1680, *'ereṣ+gil'ād* [8]
of Gilead, 1682, *gil'ādî* [2]
Gilead, 1201+1680, *bēn^{1}+gil'ād* [1]
of Gilead, 1201+1682, *bēn^{1}+gil'ādî* [1]

GILEAD'S [1]
Gilead's, 1680, *gil'ād* [1]

GILEADITE [8]
Gileadite, 1682, *gil'ādî* [8]

GILEADITES [4]
Gileadites, 1680, *gil'ād* [3]
Gileadites, 408+1680, *'îš^{1}+gil'ād* [1]

GILGAL [39]
Gilgal, 1652, *gilgāl^{2}* [39]

GILOH [2]
Giloh, 1656, *gilōh* [2]

GILONITE [2]
Gilonite, 1639, *gîlōnî* [2]

GIMZO [1]
Gimzo, 1693, *gimzô* [1]

GINATH [2]
Ginath, 1640, *gînat* [2]

GINNETHON [2]
Ginnethon, 1715, *ginn^{e}tôn* [2]

GINNETHON'S [1]
Ginnethon's, 1715, *ginn^{e}tôn* [1]

GIRD [1]
gird, 2520, *ḥāgar* [1]

GIRGASHITES [7]
Girgashites, 1739, *girgāšî* [7]

GIRL [38]
girl, 5855, *na'^{a}râ^{1}* [19]
girl, 1426, *bat^{1}* [3]
servant girl, 9148, *šipḥâ* [3]
slave girl, 563, *'āmâ* [2]
slave girl, 9148, *šipḥâ* [2]
girl, *NIH/RPE* [1]
the girl^{s}, 889, *'ăšer* [1]
girl, 1435, *b^{e}tûlâ* [1]
the girl^{s}, 2023, *-āh* [1]
girl, 3251+851, *ṭap^{1}+'iššâ* [1]
girl, 3530, *yaldâ* [1]
girl, 5922, *n^{e}qēbâ* [1]
girl, 6625, *'almâ* [1]
girl, 8167, *reḥem* [1]

GIRL'S [11]
girl's, 5855, *na'^{a}râ^{1}* [10]
girl's, 4200+5855, *l^{e-1}+na'^{a}râ^{1}* [1]

GIRLS [23]
servant girls, 5855, *na'^{a}râ^{1}* [5]
slave girls, 563, *'āmâ* [4]
girls, 5855, *na'^{a}râ^{1}* [4]
girls, *AIT* [2]
girls, 1426, *bat^{1}* [2]
girls, 3530, *yaldâ* [2]
the girls^{s}, 2177, *-hēn^{2}* [1]
girls, 5855+1435, *na'^{a}râ^{1}+b^{e}tûlâ* [1]
girls, 8292, *rē'â* [1]
servant girls, 9148, *šipḥâ* [1]

GIRZITES [1]
Girzites, 1747, *girzî* [1]

GISHPA [1]
Gishpa, 1778, *gišpā'* [1]

GITTAIM [2]
Gittaim, 1786, *gittayim* [2]

GITTITE [8]
Gittite, 1785, *gittî* [8]

GITTITES [1]
Gittites, 1785, *gittî* [1]

GITTITH [3]
gittith, 1787, *gittît* [3]

GIVE [695]
give, 5989, *nātan* [344]
give thanks, 3344, *yādâ^{2}* [35]
give birth, 3528, *yālad* [16]
give, *NIH/RPE* [14]
give, 2035, *hab^{1}* [12]
give, 8492, *śîm* [11]
give, 7422, *ṣāwâ* [10]
give back, 8740, *šûb^{1}* [9]
give over, 5989, *nātan* [7]
give light, 239, *'ôr^{1}* [6]
give blessing, 1385, *bārak^{2}* [6]
give ear, 5742+265, *nāṭâ+'ōzen* [6]
give in marriage, 5989+4200+851, *nātan+l^{e-1}+'iššâ* [6]
give in marriage, 5989, *nātan* [5]
give up, 5989, *nātan* [5]
give careful thought, 8492+4222, *śîm+lēbāb* [5]
give understanding, 1067, *bîn* [4]
give, 5583, *nāgad* [4]
give rest, 5663, *nûaḥ^{1}* [4]
give, 6913, *'āśâ^{1}* [4]
give command, 7422, *ṣāwâ* [4]
give, 995, *bô'* [3]
give, 1819, *dābar^{2}* [3]
give praise, 2146, *hālal^{2}* [3]
give up, 2532, *ḥādal^{1}* [3]
give back, 5989, *nātan* [3]
give orders, 7422, *ṣāwâ* [3]
give to drink, 9197, *šāqâ* [3]
give, *AIT* [2]
give consent, 252, *'ût* [2]
give ear, 263, *'āzan^{1}* [2]
give^{s}, 430, *'ākal* [2]
give answer, 1819+1821, *dābar^{2}+dābār* [2]
give message, 1819, *dābar^{2}* [2]
give warning, 2302, *zāhar^{2}* [2]
give victory, 3828, *yāša'* [2]
give way, 4173, *kāšal* [2]
give, 4200, *l^{e-1}* [2]
give comfort, 5714, *nāḥam* [2]
give, 6699, *'ānâ^{1}* [2]
give attention, 7155, *pānâ* [2]
give success, 7503, *ṣālaḥ^{2}* [2]
give larger, 8049, *rābâ^{1}* [2]
give, 8332, *rāpâ^{1}* [2]
give, 8740, *šûb^{1}* [2]
give, 8883, *šît^{1}* [2]
give, 9048, *šāma'* [2]
give drink, 9197, *šāqâ* [2]
give up, 6, *'ābad* [1]
give light, 239+240, *'ôr^{1}+'ôr^{2}* [1]
give a hearing, 263+7754, *'āzan^{1}+qôl* [1]
give to eat, 430, *'ākal* [1]
give, 606, *'āmar^{1}* [1]
give long, 799, *'ārak* [1]
give a bad smell, 944+5580, *bā'aš+nāba'* [1]
give in, 995, *bô'* [1]
give discernment, 1067, *bîn* [1]
give thought, 1067, *bîn* [1]
give the rights of the firstborn, 1144, *bākar* [1]
give senseless, 1279, *bā'ar^{3}* [1]
give to eat, 1356, *bārâ^{1}* [1]
give greetings, 1385, *bārak^{2}* [1]
give, 1686, *gāmā'* [1]
give an answer, 1819, *dābar^{2}* [1]
give opinion, 1819, *dābar^{2}* [1]
give an accounting, 2011, *dāraš* [1]
give in marriage, 2021+851+5989, *ha-+'iššâ+nātan* [1]
give shelter, 2118+6261, *hāyâ+sitrâ* [1]
give, 2118+4200, *hāyâ+l^{e-1}* [1]
give, 2118, *hāyâ* [1]
give visions, 2600, *ḥāzâ* [1]
give strength, 2616, *ḥāzaq* [1]
give life, 2649, *ḥāyâ* [1]
give a portion, 2745, *ḥālaq^{2}* [1]
give a share, 2745, *ḥālaq^{2}* [1]
give, 3271, *ṭārap* [1]
give up, 3286, *yā'aš* [1]
one to give counsel, 3446, *yô'ēṣ* [1]
give undivided, 3479, *yāḥad* [1]
give joy, 3512, *yāṭab* [1]
give decisions, 3519, *yākaḥ* [1]
give delivery, 3528, *yālad* [1]
give advice, 3619, *yā'aṣ* [1]
give counsel, 3619, *yā'aṣ* [1]
give guidance, 3723, *yārâ^{3}* [1]
give, 3769, *yāraš^{1}* [1]
give, 3782, *yāšab* [1]
give glory, 3877, *kābēd^{1}* [1]
give, 4200+7156, *l^{e-1}+pāneh* [1]
force to give, 4374, *lāqaḥ* [1]
give way, 4614, *mûr^{1}* [1]
give way, 4631, *mûš^{2}* [1]
give full, 4848, *mālē'^{1}* [1]
give king, 4887+4889, *mālak^{1}+melek^{1}* [1]
give less, 5070, *mā'aṭ* [1]
gifts he does not give, 5522+9214, *mattat+šeqer* [1]
give an answer, 5583, *nāgad* [1]
give answer, 5583+5583, *nāgad+nāgad* [1]
give, 5585, *nāgah* [1]
give more space, 5602, *nāgaš* [1]
give generously, 5605, *nādab* [1]
prompts to give, 5605, *nādab* [1]
vows to give, 5623, *nādar* [1]
give peace, 5663, *nûaḥ^{1}* [1]
give as an inheritance, 5706, *nāḥal* [1]
give inheritance, 5706, *nāḥal* [1]
give lashes, 5782, *nākâ* [1]
give birth, 5877, *nāpal* [1]
give up, 5877, *nāpal* [1]
wants to give, 5952+3338, *nāśag+yād* [1]
give generously, 5989+5989, *nātan+nātan* [1]
give, 5989+928+3338, *nātan+b^{e}-+yād* [1]
give away, 5989, *nātan* [1]
give in marriage, 5989+4200+408, *nātan+l^{e-1}+'îš^{1}* [1]
give permission, 5989, *nātan* [1]
give, 5989+4200+851, *nātan+l^{e-1}+'iššâ* [1]
give, 5989+5989, *nātan+nātan* [1]
glad to give, 5989+5989, *nātan+nātan* [1]
must certainly give, 5989+5989, *nātan+nātan* [1]
give up, 6073, *sûr^{1}* [1]
give up pursuit, 6073, *sûr^{1}* [1]
give over, 6296, *'ābar^{1}* [1]

give warning, 6386, *ʿûd*^{1} [1]
give free rein, 6440, *ʿāzab*^{1} [1]
give up, 6440, *ʿāzab*^{1} [1]
give support, 6468, *ʿāzar* [1]
give, 6640, *ʿim* [1]
give answer, 6699, *ʿānâ*^{1} [1]
give testimony, 6699, *ʿānâ*^{1} [1]
give over to death, 6867, *ʿārâ*^{1} [1]
give way to panic, 6907, *ʿāraṣ* [1]
give over, 6913, *ʿāśâ*^{1} [1]
give a tenth, 6923+6923, *ʿāśar+ʿāśar* [1]
give wealth, 6947+6948, *ʿāšar+ʿōšer* [1]
give way, 7211, *piq* [1]
give command, 7337+7023, *pātaḥ*^{1}*+peh* [1]
give a message, 7422, *ṣāwâ* [1]
give commands, 7422, *ṣāwâ* [1]
give the order, 7422, *ṣāwâ* [1]
give trouble, 7675, *ṣārar*^{2} [1]
give, 7924, *qārāʾ*^{1} [1]
give success, 7936, *qārâ*^{1} [1]
give more, 8049, *rābâ*^{1} [1]
give rest, 8089, *rāgaʿ*^{2} [1]
give a shout, 8131+9558, *rûaʿ+t*^{e}*rûʿâ* [1]
give a war cry, 8131, *rûaʿ* [1]
give relief, 8143, *rāḥab* [1]
give up, 8332+3338, *rāpâ*^{1}*+yād* [1]
give attention, 8505, *śākal*^{1} [1]
give insight, 8505, *śākal*^{1} [1]
give joy, 8523, *śāmaḥ* [1]
give, 8626, *šāʾal* [1]
again give allegiance, 8740+4213, *šûb*^{1}*+lēb* [1]
answer give, 8740, *šûb*^{1} [1]
give up, 8740+4946, *šûb*^{1}*+min* [1]
give an order, 8938, *šālaḥ* [1]
give, 9068, *šāmar* [1]
give a drink, 9197+3926, *šāqâ+kôs*^{1} [1]
give a drink, 9197, *šāqâ* [1]
give water, 9197, *šāqâ* [1]
give, 9197, *šāqâ* [1]
choirs to give thanks, 9343, *tôdâ* [1]
give up, 10314, *y*^{e}*hab* [1]
give, 10314, *y*^{e}*hab* [1]
give interpretations, 10600+10599, *p*^{e}*šar*^{2}*+p*^{e}*šar*^{1} [1]

GIVEN [304]

given, 5989, *nātan* [147]
be given, 5989, *nātan* [18]
given, *NIH/RPE* [10]
given rest, 5663, *nûaḥ*^{1} [8]
given, 1819, *dābar*^{2} [4]
given to, 4200, *l*$^{e-1}$ [4]
been given, 5989, *nātan* [4]
was given, 5989, *nātan* [4]
given, 7422, *ṣāwâ* [4]
given, 10314, *y*^{e}*hab* [4]
given, 2118, *hāyâ* [3]
given birth, 3528, *yālad* [3]
was given, 10314, *y*^{e}*hab* [3]
given, *AIT* [2]
was given birth, 2655, *ḥîl*^{1} [2]
given, 3655, *yāṣāʾ* [2]
given, 4200, *l*$^{e-1}$ [2]
are given, 5989, *nātan* [2]
be given wholly, 5989+5989, *nātan+nātan* [2]
given over, 5989, *nātan* [2]
is given, 5989, *nātan* [2]
advice given, 6783+3619, *ʿēṣâ*^{1}*+yāʿaṣ* [2]
given orders, 7422, *ṣāwâ* [2]
given order, 7422, *ṣāwâ* [2]
given, 7924, *qārāʾ*^{1} [2]
given, 8492, *śîm* [2]
been given, 606, *ʾāmar*^{1} [1]
given to, 907, *ʾēt*^{2} [1]
given by, 928, *b*^{e}- [1]
given, 995, *bôʾ* [1]
given to gluttony, 1251+5883, *baʿal*^{1}*+nepeš* [1]
blessings given, 1385, *bārak*^{2} [1]
given, 1385, *bārak*^{2} [1]
was given, 1655, *gālâ* [1]
given, 2037, *habhab* [1]
given, 2554, *ḥûd* [1]
given strength, 2616, *ḥāzaq* [1]
given, 2745, *ḥālaq*^{2} [1]
graciously given, 2858, *ḥānan*^{1} [1]
given hope, 3498, *yāḥal* [1]
given even more, 3578+3869+2179+2256+3869+2179, *yāsap+k*^{e}*-+hēnnâ*^{2}*+w*^{e}*-+k*^{e}*-+hēnnâ*^{2} [1]
given, 3769, *yāraš*^{1} [1]
given provisions, 3920, *kûl* [1]
given full vent, 3983, *kālâ*^{1} [1]
given over to, 4200, *l*$^{e-1}$ [1]
given, 4374, *lāqaḥ* [1]
given, 4848, *mālēʾ*^{1} [1]
given, 5510, *mattānâ*^{1} [1]
given over, 5599+6584+3338, *nāgar+ʿal*^{2}*+yād* [1]
given freely, 5605, *nādab* [1]
given willingly, 5605, *nādab* [1]
willingly given, 5605, *nādab* [1]
inheritance given, 5706, *nāḥal* [1]
given comfort, 5714, *nāḥam* [1]
wounds was given, 5782, *nākâ* [1]
given birth, 5877, *nāpal* [1]
been given, 5918, *nāqab*^{1} [1]
be given in marriage, 5989+4200+851, *nātan+l*$^{e-1}$*+ʾiššâ* [1]
been given over, 5989, *nātan* [1]
given in pledge, 5989, *nātan* [1]
given up, 5989, *nātan* [1]
was given in marriage, 5989+4200+851, *nātan+l*$^{e-1}$*+ʾiššâ* [1]
were given over, 5989, *nātan* [1]
were given, 5989, *nātan* [1]
given up, 6037, *sāgar* [1]
warnings given, 6343+6386, *ʿēdût+ʿûd*^{1} [1]
answer given, 6699, *ʿānâ*^{1} [1]
given, 6913, *ʿāśâ*^{1} [1]
given word, 7198+906+7023, *pāṣâ+ʾēt*^{1}*+peh* [1]
given interpretation, 7354, *pātar* [1]
given a command, 7422, *ṣāwâ* [1]
given an order, 7422, *ṣāwâ* [1]
given the command, 7422, *ṣāwâ* [1]
are given, 8011, *rāʾâ*^{1} [1]
given room, 8143, *rāḥab* [1]
given cause to rejoice, 8523, *śāmaḥ* [1]
given joy, 8523+8525, *śāmaḥ+śimḥâ* [1]
be given over, 8626, *šāʾal* [1]
given oath, 8678, *šābaʿ* [1]
given to corruption, 8845, *šāḥat* [1]
was given, 9101, *šānâ*^{1} [1]
given^{s}, 9149, *šāpaṭ* [1]
given a drink, 9197, *šāqâ* [1]
given to drink, 9197, *šāqâ* [1]
given, 9197, *šāqâ* [1]
be given, 10314, *y*^{e}*hab* [1]
freely given, 10461, *n*^{e}*dab* [1]
given, 10702, *š*^{e}*wâ* [1]

GIVER [1]

giver^{s}, 132, *ʾādām*^{1} [1]

GIVES [100]

gives, 5989, *nātan* [45]
gives birth, 3528, *yālad* [8]
gives rest, 5663, *nûaḥ*^{1} [3]
gives, 10498, *n*^{e}*tan* [3]
gives, *NIH/RPE* [2]
gives light, 239, *ʾôr*^{1} [2]
gives thought, 1067, *bîn* [2]
gives understanding, 1067, *bîn* [2]
gives great, 1540, *gādal* [2]
gives, *AIT* [1]
gives sight, 239, *ʾôr*^{1} [1]
gives patience, 799+678, *ʾārak+ʾap*^{2} [1]
one who gives, 1251, *baʿal*^{1} [1]
gives, 1819, *dābar*^{2} [1]
gives health, 2014, *dāšēn*^{1} [1]
gives life, 2649, *ḥāyâ* [1]
gives, 3512, *yāṭab* [1]
gives birth prematurely, 3655+3529, *yāṣāʾ+yeled* [1]
gives vent to, 3655, *yāṣāʾ* [1]
gives, 3655, *yāṣāʾ* [1]
gives, 3769, *yāraš*^{1} [1]
gives way, 4202+6641, *lōʾ+ʿāmad* [1]
gives way, 4572, *môṭ*^{1} [1]
gives relief, 5663, *nûaḥ*^{1} [1]
gives gifts, 5989, *nātan* [1]
gives over, 5989, *nātan* [1]
gives stability, 6641, *ʿāmad* [1]
gives back answer, 6699, *ʿānâ*^{1} [1]
gives, 6699, *ʿānâ*^{1} [1]
gives, 7032, *pûaḥ*^{2} [1]
gives freely, 7061, *pāzar* [1]
gives thought, 7143, *pālas*^{2} [1]
gives sight, 7219, *pāqaḥ* [1]
gives, 7298, *pāraś* [1]
gives heed, 8505, *śākal*^{1} [1]
gives back, 8740, *šûb*^{1} [1]
gives satisfaction, 8750, *šāwâ*^{1} [1]
gives judgment, 9149, *šāpaṭ* [1]
gives drink, 9197, *šāqâ* [1]
gives, 10314, *y*^{e}*hab* [1]

GIVING [101]

giving, 5989, *nātan* [58]
giving, 7422, *ṣāwâ* [13]
giving, 5447, *mišlôaḥ* [2]
giving as an inheritance, 5706, *nāḥal* [2]
giving orders, 7422, *ṣāwâ* [2]
giving, 8492, *śîm* [2]
giving, *AIT* [1]
giving, *NIH/RPE* [1]
giving light, 239, *ʾôr*^{1} [1]
giving credit to, 928+9005, *b*^{e}*-+šēm*^{1} [1]
giving blessing, 1388+1385, *b*^{e}*rākâ*^{1}*+bārak*^{2} [1]
giving, 1819, *dābar*^{2} [1]
giving praise, 2146, *hālal*^{2} [1]
giving birth, 3528, *yālad* [1]
giving advice, 3619+6783, *yāʿaṣ+ʿēṣâ*^{1} [1]
giving out, 4173, *kāšal* [1]
giving an apt reply, 5101+7023, *maʿ*^{a}*neh*^{1}*+peh* [1]
giving rest, 5663, *nûaḥ*^{1} [1]
giving comfort, 5714, *nāḥam* [1]
giving, 5742, *nāṭâ* [1]
giving, 5747, *nāṭal* [1]
giving testimony, 6699, *ʿānâ*^{1} [1]
giving interpretation, 7354, *pātar* [1]
giving instructions, 7422, *ṣāwâ* [1]
giving attention, 8505, *śākal*^{1} [1]
giving joy, 8523, *śāmaḥ* [1]
giving thanks, 9343, *tôdâ* [1]
giving thanks, 10312, *y*^{e}*dâ* [1]

GIZONITE [1]

Gizonite, 1604, *gizônî* [1]

GLAD [56]

glad, 8523, *śāmaḥ* [30]
glad, 1635, *gîl*^{1} [11]
make glad, 8523, *śāmaḥ* [3]
glad, 3202, *ṭôb*^{2} [2]
glad, 8464, *śûś* [2]
made glad, 2525, *ḥādâ*^{1} [1]
glad, 3512+4213, *yāṭab+lēb* [1]
glad, 3512+928+6524, *yāṭab+b*^{e}*-+ʿayin*^{1} [1]
glad to give, 5989+5989, *nātan+nātan* [1]
glad, 6600, *ʿālaz* [1]
made very glad, 8523+8523, *śāmaḥ+śāmaḥ* [1]
makes glad, 8523, *śāmaḥ* [1]
glad occasions, 8525, *śimḥâ* [1]

GLADDENS [1]

gladdens, 8523, *śāmaḥ* [1]

GLADLY [6]

gladly, 8523, *śāmaḥ* [2]
how gladly, 375, *ʾēk* [1]
gladly, 928+3206+4222, *b*^{e}*-+ṭûb+lēbāb* [1]
gladly, 8464, *śûś* [1]
received gladly, 8523+6584, *śāmaḥ+ʿal*^{2} [1]

GLADNESS [23]

gladness, 8525, *śimḥâ* [10]
gladness, 8607, *śāśôn* [6]
gladness, 1637, *gîl*^{3} [5]
gladness, 8523, *śāmaḥ* [1]
filled with gladness, 8524+448+1637, *śāmēaḥ+ʾel+gîl*^{3} [1]

GLANCE [2]

glance, *NIH/RPE* [1]

glance, 6524, *ʿayin*[1] [1]

GLANCES [1]

glances, 6757, *ʿapʿappayim* [1]

GLANCING [1]

glancing, 7155, *pānâ* [1]

GLAZE [1]

glaze, 6213, *sapsîg* [1]

GLEAM [2]

gleam, 240, *ʾôr*[2] [1]
gleam, 6524, *ʿayin*[1] [1]

GLEAMED [1]

gleamed, 5913, *nāṣaṣ*[1] [1]

GLEAMING [1]

gleaming point, 1398, *bārāq*[1] [1]

GLEAN [8]

glean, 4377, *lāqaṭ* [6]
glean, 4380, *lāqaš* [1]
glean thoroughly, 6618+6618, *ʿālal*[1]*+ʿālal*[1] [1]

GLEANED [1]

gleaned, 4377, *lāqaṭ* [1]

GLEANING [1]

gleaning, 6622, *ʿōlēlôt* [1]

GLEANINGS [5]

gleanings, 4378, *leqeṭ* [2]
gleanings, 6622, *ʿōlēlôt* [2]
gleanings of grapes, 6622, *ʿōlēlôt* [1]

GLEANS [1]

gleans, 4377, *lāqaṭ* [1]

GLEE [2]

glee, 8523, *śāmaḥ* [1]
glee, 8525, *śimḥâ* [1]

GLIDE [1]

glide, 2323, *zāḥal*[1] [1]

GLIDED [1]

glided past, 2736, *ḥālap*[1] [1]

GLIDING [2]

gliding, 1371, *bārîaḥ* [2]

GLIMPSE [2]

catch glimpse, 8011, *rāʾâ*[1] [1]
glimpse, 8011, *rāʾâ*[1] [1]

GLINT [1]

glint, 240, *ʾôr*[2] [1]

GLISTENING [1]

leaves glistening, 239, *ʾôr*[1] [1]

GLITTERING [1]

glittering, 1398, *bārāq*[1] [1]

GLOAT [11]

gloat, 8523, *śāmaḥ* [5]
let gloat, 8523, *śāmaḥ* [2]
gloat, 2600, *ḥāzâ* [1]
gloat, 8011, *rāʾâ*[1] [1]
let gloat, 8011, *rāʾâ*[1] [1]
gloat, 8524, *śāmēaḥ* [1]

GLOATED [1]

gloated, 6424, *ʿûr*[3] [1]

GLOATING [1]

gloating, 6617, *ʿalîṣut* [1]

GLOATS [1]

gloats, 8524, *śāmēaḥ* [1]

GLOOM [11]

gloom, 696, *ʾᵃpēlâ* [2]
deepest gloom, 7516, *ṣalmāwet* [2]
gloom, 694, *ʾōpel* [1]
gloom, 3125, *ḥōšek* [1]
gloom, 4599, *mûʿāp* [1]
gloom, 5066, *māʿûp* [1]
turns to gloom, 6845, *ʿārab*[4] [1]
deep gloom, 6906, *ʿᵃrāpel* [1]
clothed with gloom, 7722, *qādar* [1]

GLORIFIED [3]

am glorified, 3877, *kābēd*[1] [1]
glorified, 3877, *kābēd*[1] [1]
glorified, 10198, *hᵃdar*[1] [1]

GLORIFY [6]

glorify, 1540, *gādal* [2]
glorify, 3877, *kābēd*[1] [2]
glorify, 8655, *šābaḥ*[1] [1]
glorify, 10198, *hᵃdar*[1] [1]

GLORIOUS [29]

glorious, 9514, *tipʾeret* [11]
glorious, 3883, *kābôd*[1] [10]
glorious, 3877, *kābēd*[1] [2]
glorious, 129, *ʾaddîr* [1]
glorious, 158, *ʾādar* [1]
glorious, 1452, *gaʾᵃwâ* [1]
glorious things, 1455, *gēʾût* [1]
glorious, 2086, *hôd*[1] [1]
glorious, 3884, *kābôd*[2] [1]

GLORIOUSLY [1]

gloriously, 3883, *kābôd*[1] [1]

GLORY [165]

glory, 3883, *kābôd*[1] [120]
glory, 9514, *tipʾeret* [11]
glory, 10331, *yᵉqār* [6]
glory, 2146, *hālal*[2] [4]
glory, 7382, *ṣᵉbî*[1] [4]
gain glory, 3877, *kābēd*[1] [3]
glory, 2086, *hôd*[1] [2]
glory, 8655, *šābaḥ*[1] [2]
glory, *NIH/RPE* [1]
glory, 1454, *gāʾôn* [1]
glory, 2077, *hādār* [1]
glory, 2079, *hᵃdārâ* [1]
glory, 2876, *ḥesed*[2] [1]
glory, 3877, *kābēd*[1] [1]
bring glory, 3877, *kābēd*[1] [1]
gain glory for myself, 3877, *kābēd*[1] [1]
gained glory for yourself, 3877, *kābēd*[1] [1]
give glory, 3877, *kābēd*[1] [1]
glory, 5905, *nēṣaḥ*[1] [1]
displays glory, 6995, *pāʾar*[2] [1]
glory, 9335, *tᵉhillâ* [1]

GLOW [1]

glow, 5586, *nōgah*[1] [1]

GLOWING [4]

glowing metal, 3133, *ḥašmal* [3]
glowing embers, 4611, *môqēd* [1]

GLOWS [1]

glows, 3081, *ḥārar*[1] [1]

GLUTTED [1]

glutted, 8429, *śobʿâ* [1]

GLUTTONS [2]

gluttons, 2361, *zālal*[1] [2]

GLUTTONY [1]

given to gluttony, 1251+5883, *baʿal*[1]*+nepeš* [1]

GNASH [3]

gnash, 3080, *ḥāraq* [3]

GNASHED [1]

gnashed, 3080, *ḥāraq* [1]

GNASHES [1]

gnashes, 3080, *ḥāraq* [1]

GNATS [6]

gnats, 4031, *kēn*[6] [4]
gnats, 4038, *kinnām* [2]

GNAWING [1]

gnawing pains, 6908, *ʿāraq* [1]

GO [1142]

go, 2143, *hālak* [327]
go, 995, *bôʾ* [105]
go up, 6590, *ʿālâ* [76]
go down, 3718, *yārad* [61]
go out, 3655, *yāṣāʾ* [57]
let go, 8938, *šālaḥ* [55]
go, 3655, *yāṣāʾ* [40]
go back, 8740, *šûb*[1] [37]
go, *NIH/RPE* [30]
go, 6590, *ʿālâ* [24]
go in, 995, *bôʾ* [19]
go, 6296, *ʿābar*[1] [17]
go well, 3512, *yāṭab* [14]
go unpunished, 5927, *nāqâ* [9]
go, 7756, *qûm* [9]
go, *AIT* [8]
go, 2118, *hāyâ* [7]
go about, 2143, *hālak* [7]
go back, 2143, *hālak* [7]
go, 3718, *yārad* [7]
go over, 6296, *ʿābar*[1] [7]
go near, 7928, *qārab* [7]
go into, 995, *bôʾ* [6]
go out, 2143, *hālak* [5]
go on, 6296, *ʿābar*[1] [5]
go, 8740, *šûb*[1] [5]
go away, 2143, *hālak* [4]
go off, 2143, *hālak* [4]
go, 2143+2256+8740, *hālak+wᵉ-+šûb*[1] [4]
go free, 3655, *yāṣāʾ* [4]
go into exile, 1655, *gālâ* [3]
go ahead, 2143, *hālak* [3]
go out, 3882, *kābâ* [3]
go about, 6015, *sābab* [3]
go limp, 8332, *rāpâ*[1] [3]
let go, 8332, *rāpâ*[1] [3]
go astray, 9494, *tāʿâ* [3]
go, 10207, *hᵃlak* [3]
go back, 995, *bôʾ* [2]
surely go into exile, 1655+1655, *gālâ+gālâ* [2]
go to, 2006, *derek* [2]
go now, 2143+995, *hālak+bôʾ* [2]
go way, 2143, *hālak* [2]
go, 2143+2143, *hālak+hālak* [2]
go mad, 2147, *hālal*[3] [2]
ready to go out, 3655+7372, *yāṣāʾ+ṣābāʾ*[2] [2]
go free, 4880, *mālaṭ*[1] [2]
go up, 5602, *nāgaš* [2]
go, 5602, *nāgaš* [2]
let go entirely unpunished, 5927+5927, *nāqâ+nāqâ* [2]
go, 6073, *sûr*[1] [2]
go beyond, 6296, *ʿābar*[1] [2]
go on way, 6296, *ʿābar*[1] [2]
go past, 6296, *ʿābar*[1] [2]
go on up, 6590, *ʿālâ* [2]
go back, 6590, *ʿālâ* [2]
go straight up, 6590, *ʿālâ* [2]
go, 8103, *rādap* [2]
go about, 261, *ʾāzal* [1]
go by, 799, *ʾārak* [1]
go home, 995, *bôʾ* [1]
go sleep with, 995+448, *bôʾ+ʾel* [1]
go down, 995, *bôʾ* [1]
make go down, 995, *bôʾ* [1]
go after ill-gotten gain, 1298+1299, *bāṣaʿ+beṣaʿ* [1]
go back, 1368, *bāraḥ*[1] [1]
certainly go into exile, 1655+1655, *gālâ+gālâ* [1]
go into exile, 1655+1655, *gālâ+gālâ* [1]
go, 1655, *gālâ* [1]
go on threshing, 1889+1889, *dûš+dûš* [1]
enables to go, 2005, *dārak* [1]
go, 2005, *dārak* [1]
by all means go, 2143+995, *hālak+bôʾ* [1]
go in, 2143+2256+995, *hālak+wᵉ-+bôʾ* [1]
go, 2143+995, *hālak+bôʾ* [1]
have go, 2143, *hālak* [1]
very well go, 2143+2143, *hālak+hālak* [1]
go aside, 2143, *hālak* [1]
go at once, 2143+2143, *hālak+hālak* [1]
go at once, 2143+2256+995, *hālak+wᵉ-+bôʾ* [1]
go forward, 2143, *hālak* [1]
go on way, 2143, *hālak* [1]
go on, 2143, *hālak* [1]
go over, 2143, *hālak* [1]

go to and fro, 2143, hālak [1]
go up, 2143, hālak [1]
go, 2143+928+2006, hālak+b^{e}-+derek [1]
go astray, 2319, zûr^{2} [1]
go quickly, 2590, ḥûš^{1} [1]
go, 2736, ḥālap^{1} [1]
go into hiding, 2924, ḥāpaś [1]
go well, 3201, ṭôb^{1} [1]
go to the right, 3554, yāman [1]
go about business, 3655+2256+995, yāṣā’+w^{e}-+bô’ [1]
go about, 3655, yāṣā’ [1]
go into, 3655, yāṣā’ [1]
go off duty, 3655, yāṣā’ [1]
go off to war, 3655, yāṣā’ [1]
go off, 3655, yāṣā’ [1]
go up, 3655, yāṣā’ [1]
let go down, 3718, yārad [1]
go, 3782, yāšab [1]
go straight, 3837, yāšar [1]
go unanswered, 4202+6699, lō’+‘ānâ^{1} [1]
go down, 4427, mābô’ [1]
go at once, 4554, māhar^{1} [1]
go, 4604, môṣā’^{1} [1]
go away, 4631, mûš^{2} [1]
go down, 4637, mûṭ [1]
how did it go, 4769+905, mî+’att [1]
go at once, 5432, māšak [1]
go near, 5602, nāgaš [1]
go astray, 5653, nûd [1]
let go, 5663+906+3338, nûaḥ^{1}+’ēt^{1}+yād [1]
go down, 5737, nāḥat [1]
go ahead, 5742, nāṭâ [1]
go forward, 5742, nāṭâ [1]
go well, 5838, nā‘ēm [1]
go unpunished, 5927+5927, nāqâ+nāqâ [1]
indeed go unpunished, 5927+5927, nāqâ+nāqâ [1]
let go unpunished, 5927, nāqâ [1]
cycle go on, 5938, nāqap^{2} [1]
go around, 5938, nāqap^{2} [1]
go around, 6015, sābab [1]
go, 6015, sābab [1]
go away, 6073, sûr^{1} [1]
go over, 6073, sûr^{1} [1]
go up, 6158, sālaq [1]
go into hiding, 6259, sātar [1]
go away, 6296, ‘ābar^{1} [1]
go, 6440, ‘āzab^{1} [1]
in the way should go, 6584+7023+2006, ‘al^{2}+peh+derek [1]
had go up, 6590, ‘ālâ [1]
should go up, 6590+6590, ‘ālâ+‘ālâ [1]
go over a second time, 6618, ‘ālal^{1} [1]
go over the vines again, 6618+339, ‘ālal^{1}+’aḥar [1]
go to great depths, 6676, ‘āmaq [1]
go over the branches a second time, 6994+339, pā’ar^{1}+’aḥar [1]
go out, 7046, pûṣ^{1} [1]
go, 7155, pānâ [1]
go raiding, 7320, pāšaṭ [1]
go, 7337, pātaḥ^{1} [1]
go before, 7709, qādam [1]
go, 7709, qādam [1]
go dark, 7722, qādar [1]
go up, 7756, qûm [1]
go, 7928, qārab [1]
go quickly, 8132, rûṣ [1]
go, 8132, rûṣ [1]
go far, 8178, rāḥaq [1]
let go hungry, 8279, rā‘ēb^{1} [1]
go to the left, 8521, śim’ēl [1]
go back, 8740+345, šûb^{1}+’^{a}ḥōrannît [1]
go on, 8740, šûb^{1} [1]
made go back, 8740, šûb^{1} [1]
make go, 8740, šûb^{1} [1]
turned to go, 8740, šûb^{1} [1]
go up and down, 8763, šûṭ^{1} [1]
go, 8763, šûṭ^{1} [1]
go here and there, 8763, šûṭ^{1} [1]
go, 8886, šākab [1]
go to bed with, 8886+725, šākab+’ēṣel^{1} [1]
go to sleep, 8886, šākab [1]
go early, 8899, šākam [1]
be sure to let go, 8938+8938, šālaḥ+šālaḥ [1]
do let go, 8938+8938, šālaḥ+šālaḥ [1]
letting go, 8938, šālaḥ [1]
go about, 9494, tā‘â [1]
go, 10016, ’^{a}zal [1]

GOADS [2]
goads, 1995, dorbān [1]
goads, 1996, dorbōnâ [1]

GOAH [1]
Goah, 1717, gō‘â [1]

GOAT [84]
male goat, 8538+6436, śā‘îr^{2}+‘ēz [24]
goat, 8538, śā‘îr^{2} [10]
goat, 6436, ‘ēz [8]
young goat, 1531+6436, g^{e}dî+‘ēz [7]
goat hair, 6436, ‘ēz [7]
male goat, 8538, śā‘îr^{2} [7]
young goat, 1531, g^{e}dî [5]
goat, NIH/RPE [2]
goat, 7618+6436, ṣāpîr+‘ēz [2]
goat, 8538+6436, śā‘îr^{2}+‘ēz [2]
goat idols, 8539, śā‘îr^{3} [2]
goat, 8544+6436, ś^{e}‘îrâ^{1}+‘ēz [2]
wild goat, 735, ’aqqô [1]
goat, 1531, g^{e}dî [1]
the goat^{s}, 2023, -āh [1]
young goat, 6436, ‘ēz [1]
goat, 7618, ṣāpîr [1]
goat, 8445+6436, śeh+‘ēz [1]

GOAT'S [3]
goat's, 8538, śā‘îr^{2} [3]

GOATS [77]
male goats, 6966, ‘attûd [15]
goats, 6436, ‘ēz [12]
goats, 6966, ‘attûd [12]
sheep and goats, 7366, ṣō’n [11]
goats, 8538, śā‘îr^{2} [3]
wild goats, 3604, yā‘ēl^{1} [2]
goats hair, 3889+6436, kābîr+‘ēz [2]
male goats, 8538+6436, śā‘îr^{2}+‘ēz [2]
wild goats, 8538, śā‘îr^{2} [2]
male goats, 9411, tayiš [2]
goats, 1201+6436, bēn^{1}+‘ēz [1]
young goats, 1531+6436, g^{e}dî+‘ēz [1]
young goats, 1531, g^{e}dî [1]
young goats, 1537, g^{e}diyyâ [1]
goats, 3604, yā‘ēl^{1} [1]
the goats^{s}, 4392, -ām [1]
sheep and goats, 5238+7366, miqneh+ṣō’n [1]
goats, 7366, ṣō’n [1]
sheep goats or, 7366, ṣō’n [1]
sheep or goats, 7366, ṣō’n [1]
male goats, 7618+6436, ṣāpîr+‘ēz [1]
male goats, 7618, ṣāpîr [1]
goats, 9411, tayiš [1]
male goats, 10615+10535, ṣ^{e}pîr+‘ēz [1]

GOATSKINS [1]
goatskins, 6425+1531+6436, ‘ôr+g^{e}dî+‘ēz [1]

GOB [2]
Gob, 1570, gôb^{1} [2]

GOBLET [3]
goblet, 7694+3926, qubba‘at+kôs^{1} [2]
goblet, 110, ’aggān [1]

GOBLETS [6]
goblets, 10398, mā’n [3]
goblets, 3998+5482, k^{e}lî+mašqeh^{1} [2]
goblets, 3998, k^{e}lî [1]

GOD [2725]
God, 466, ’^{e}lōhîm [2302]
God, 446, ’ēl^{5} [218]
God, 10033, ’^{e}lāh [79]
God, NIH/RPE [55]
God, 468, ’^{e}lôah [53]
God^{s}, 2257, -ô [8]
detestable god, 9199, šiqqûṣ [3]
shameful god, 1425, bōšet [1]
god, 2006, derek [1]
God^{s}, 2084, -hû [1]
devoted to God, 3051, ḥērem^{1} [1]
metal god, 5822, nesek^{2} [1]
vile god, 9199, šiqqûṣ [1]
detestable god, 9359, tô‘ēbâ [1]

GOD'S [45]
God's, 466, ’^{e}lōhîm [25]
God's^{s}, 2257, -ô [6]
God's, 446, ’ēl^{5} [5]
God's, 468, ’^{e}lôah [4]
God's, NIH/RPE [1]
God's name^{s}, 2257, -ô [1]
this god's^{s}, 2257, -ô [1]
God's, 4200+466, l^{e}-^{1}+’^{e}lōhîm [1]
God's, 4946+466, min+’^{e}lōhîm [1]

GOD-FEARING [1]
God-fearing, 3710+2021+466, yārē’^{4}+ha-+’^{e}lōhîm [1]

GODDESS [3]
goddess, 466, ’^{e}lōhîm [2]
vile goddess, 9199, šiqqûṣ [1]

GODLESS [11]
godless, 2868, ḥānēp^{3} [10]
godless, 2866, ḥānēp^{1} [1]

GODLY [5]
godly, 2883, ḥāsîd [4]
godly, 466, ’^{e}lōhîm [1]

GODS [260]
gods, 466, ’^{e}lōhîm [205]
gods, NIH/RPE [15]
gods, 10033, ’^{e}lāh [15]
household gods, 9572, t^{e}rāpîm [8]
gods, 446, ’ēl^{5} [3]
false gods, 3942, kāzāb [3]
gods^{s}, 4392, -ām [2]
false gods, 9214, šeqer [2]
gods, 123, ’ādôn [1]
other gods, 337, ’aḥēr^{1} [1]
gods^{s}, 889, ’^{a}šer [1]
the gods^{s}, 889, ’^{a}šer [1]
shameful gods, 1425, bōšet [1]
the gods^{s}, 4392, -ām [1]
their gods^{s}, 4392, -ām [1]

GOES [69]
goes, 2143, hālak [7]
goes out, 3655, yāṣā’ [6]
goes, NIH/RPE [5]
goes, 995, bô’ [5]
goes up, 6590, ‘ālâ [4]
goes down, 995, bô’ [2]
goes in, 995, bô’ [2]
goes about, 2143, hālak [2]
goes, 3655, yāṣā’ [2]
goes down, 3718, yārad [2]
goes astray, 8474, śāṭâ [2]
off goes, 261, ’āzal [1]
goes, 606, ’āmar^{1} [1]
wherever goes, 928+3655+2256+928+995, b^{e}-+yāṣā’+w^{e}-+b^{e}-+bô’ [1]
wherever goes, 928+995+2256+928+3655, b^{e}-+bô’+w^{e}-+b^{e}-+yāṣā’ [1]
goes, 1881, dûṣ [1]
goes out, 1980, dā‘ak [1]
goes, 2118+8079, hāyâ+regel [1]
goes down, 2143, hālak [1]
goes out, 2143+2143, hālak+hālak [1]
goes to and fro, 2143, hālak [1]
goes into labor, 2655, ḥîl^{1} [1]
goes by, 2736, ḥālap^{1} [1]
goes hungry, 2893, ḥāsēr^{1} [1]
goes well, 3512, yāṭab [1]
ever goes outside, 3655+3655, yāṣā’+yāṣā’ [1]
goes over, 3655, yāṣā’ [1]
out goes, 3655, yāṣā’ [1]
goes down, 3718+4200+4752, yārad+l^{e}-^{1}+maṭṭâ [1]
goes out, 3882, kābâ [1]
goes across, 6296, ‘ābar^{1} [1]
goes through, 6296, ‘ābar^{1} [1]

goes, 6296, ʿābar[1] [1]
goes on, 6298, ʿēber[1] [1]
goes, 6590, ʿālâ [1]
goes on, 6913, ʿāśâ[1] [1]
goes, 7155, pānâ [1]
refining goes on, 7671+7671, ṣārap+ṣārap [1]
goes near, 7929, qārēb [1]
goes hungry, 8279, rāʿēb[1] [1]
goes to court, 9149, šāpaṭ [1]

GOG [11]
Gog, 1573, gôg [10]
Gog^{s}, 2257, -ô [1]

GOIIM [2]
Goiim, 1582, gôyim [2]

GOING [169]
going, *AIT* [82]
going, 2143, hālak [15]
going out, 3655, yāṣāʾ [7]
going, *NIH/RPE* [5]
going down, 3718, yārad [5]
going on duty, 995, bôʾ [4]
going, 995, bôʾ [4]
going up, 6590, ʿālâ [4]
going in, 995, bôʾ [3]
going about, 2143, hālak [3]
going, 3655, yāṣāʾ [3]
going, 6296, ʿābar[1] [3]
going back and forth, 2143, hālak [2]
going back, 2143, hālak [2]
going off duty, 3655, yāṣāʾ [2]
going to death, 5877, nāpal [2]
going down, 6296, ʿābar[1] [2]
going out, 782, ʾāraḥ[1] [1]
going down, 995, bôʾ [1]
do not know where am going, 2143+6584+889 +2143, hālak+ʿal[2]+ʾ^{a}šer+hālak [1]
going around, 2143, hālak [1]
going off, 2143, hālak [1]
going into captivity, 3448, yôṣēʾt [1]
going, 4200, l^{e}-[1] [1]
how was going, 4200+8934, l^{e}-[1]+šālôm [1]
going down to, 4752, maṭṭâ [1]
going up, 5090, maʿ^{a}leh [1]
what is going through, 5091, maʿ^{a}lâ[1] [1]
going down, 5741, nāḥēt [1]
going over, 6296, ʿābar[1] [1]
kept on going, 6296, ʿābar[1] [1]
over going, 6296, ʿābar[1] [1]
going, 6590, ʿālâ [1]
going, 6913, ʿāśâ[1] [1]
going to, 6964, ʿattâ [1]
going, 7929, qārēb [1]
going back, 8740, šûb[1] [1]
going, 9365, tûr [1]

GOLAN [4]
Golan, 1584, gôlān [4]

GOLD [427]
gold, 2298, zāhāb [367]
gold, 10160, d^{e}hab [23]
gold, *NIH/RPE* [8]
gold, 3021, ḥārûṣ[1] [5]
gold, 4188, ketem [5]
pure gold, 7058, paz [5]
pure gold, 2298+2298, zāhāb+zāhāb [2]
gold, 7058, paz [2]
gold of Ophir, 234, ʾôpîr[1] [1]
gold, 1309, beṣer[1] [1]
the gold^{s}, 2257, -ô [1]
nuggets of gold, 2298, zāhāb [1]
fine gold, 4188, ketem [1]
finest gold, 4188+233, ketem+ʾûpāz [1]
pure gold, 4188, ketem [1]
purest gold, 4188+7058, ketem+paz [1]
finest gold, 6034, sāgûr [1]
fine gold, 7058, paz [1]

GOLDEN [9]
golden, 2298, zāhāb [9]

GOLDSMITH [6]
goldsmith, 7671, ṣārap [6]

GOLDSMITHS [3]
goldsmiths, 7671, ṣārap [2]
goldsmiths, 7672, ṣōr^{e}pî [1]

GOLIATH [7]
Goliath, 1669, golyāt [6]
Goliath, *NIH/RPE* [1]

GOMER [8]
Gomer, 1699, gōmer[1] [5]
Gomer, *NIH/RPE* [2]
Gomer, 1700, gōmer[2] [1]

GOMORRAH [19]
Gomorrah, 6686, ʿ^{a}mōrâ [19]

GONE [168]
gone, 2143, hālak [29]
gone, 995, bôʾ [13]
gone out, 3655, yāṣāʾ [11]
gone up, 6590, ʿālâ [10]
gone, 401, ʾayin[1] [8]
gone down, 3718, yārad [8]
gone, 6, ʾābad [5]
gone, 9462, tāmam [5]
gone, 3655, yāṣāʾ [4]
gone over, 5877, nāpal [4]
gone, *NIH/RPE* [3]
gone, 3718, yārad [3]
gone, 3983, kālâ[1] [3]
gone, 261, ʾāzal [2]
gone from, 3655, yāṣāʾ [2]
gone, 6073, sûr[1] [2]
gone by, 6296, ʿābar[1] [2]
gone, 6296, ʿābar[1] [2]
gone, 6590, ʿālâ [2]
gone by, 7710, qedem [2]
gone too far, 8041, rab[1] [2]
gone astray, 8474, śāṭâ [2]
gone, 8697, šābat[1] [2]
gone, *AIT* [1]
gone from, 401+907, ʾayin[1]+ʾēt[2] [1]
gone, 665, ʾāsap [1]
gone, 699, ʾāpēs [1]
gone into, 995, bôʾ [1]
gone in search of, 1335, bāqaš [1]
gone back, 1368, bāraḥ[1] [1]
gone into exile, 1655, gālâ [1]
gone, 2118, hāyâ [1]
gone away, 2143, hālak [1]
gone off, 2143+2143, hālak+hālak [1]
gone up, 2143, hālak [1]
gone, 2143+2143, hālak+hālak [1]
gone mad, 2147, hālal[3] [1]
gone away, 2532, ḥādal[1] [1]
gone^{s}, 2616, ḥāzaq [1]
gone down, 2893, ḥāsēr[1] [1]
gone to trouble, 3006+3010, ḥārad+ḥ^{a}rādâ[1] [1]
gone down, 3718+345, yārad+ʾ^{a}ḥōrannît [1]
gone out, 3882, kābâ [1]
gone, 4202+2118+928, lōʾ+hāyâ+b^{e}- [1]
gone, 4202+6641+928, lōʾ+ʿāmad+b^{e}- [1]
gone from, 4946+9348, min+tāwek [1]
gone, 5674, nûs [1]
gone down, 5877, nāpal [1]
gone over, 6073, sûr[1] [1]
gone, 6086, sāḥar [1]
gone on, 6296, ʿābar[1] [1]
gone by, 6409, ʿôlām [1]
gone ahead, 6590, ʿālâ [1]
gone, 7756, qûm [1]
gone near, 7928, qārab [1]
gone far enough, 8041, rab[1] [1]
gone some distance, 8178, rāḥaq [1]
gone, 8324, rāpāʾ[1] [1]
gone astray, 8706, šāgâ [1]
gone, 8763, šûṭ[1] [1]
gone to bed, 8886, šākab [1]
all gone, 9462, tāmam [1]
gone astray, 9494, tāʿâ [1]
gone, 10085, ʾ^{a}tâ [1]
gone out, 10485, n^{e}paq [1]

GOOD [354]
good, 3202, ṭôb[2] [241]
good, 3208, ṭôbâ [22]
do good, 3512, yāṭab [10]
good, 3512, yāṭab [10]
good things, 3206, ṭûb [7]
good things, 3208, ṭôbâ [7]
good, *NIH/RPE* [4]
bring good tidings, 1413, bāśar [2]
bringing good news, 1413, bāśar [2]
good news, 1415, b^{e}śōrâ [2]
good, 3206, ṭûb [2]
good thing, 3208, ṭôbâ [2]
good grapes, 6694, ʿēnāb [2]
no good, 8273, raʿ[1] [2]
good health, 8934, šālôm [2]
good faith, 9459, tāmîm [2]
good, *AIT* [1]
good sense, 1069, bînâ [1]
good, 1388, b^{e}rākâ[1] [1]
bring good news, 1413, bāśar [1]
brings good news, 1413, bāśar [1]
hear good news, 1413, bāśar [1]
messenger of good tidings, 1413, bāśar [1]
preach good news, 1413, bāśar [1]
good fighters, 1475, gibbôr [1]
good fortune, 1513, gad[2] [1]
do good, 1694, gāmal [1]
been good, 1694, gāmal [1]
good, 1694, gāmal [1]
good, 2617, ḥāzāq [1]
good favor, 2876, ḥesed[2] [1]
doing good, 3201, ṭôb[1] [1]
good deeds, 3208, ṭôbâ [1]
good do, 3208+3512, ṭôbâ+yāṭab [1]
good work, 3208, ṭôbâ [1]
good judgment, 3248, ṭaʿam [1]
doing good, 3512, yāṭab [1]
good done, 3512, yāṭab [1]
in good spirits, 3512+4213, yāṭab+lēb [1]
did good, 3603, yāʿal [1]
do good, 3603, yāʿal [1]
good quality, 3701, yāqār [1]
good, 3837, yāšar [1]
as good as, 3869, k^{e}- [1]
as good as dead, 4637, mût [1]
made good escape, 5674+2256+4880, nûs+w^{e}+mālaṭ[1] [1]
took as a good sign, 5727, nāḥaš [1]
make good, 7756, qûm [1]
good pleasure, 8356, rāṣôn [1]
good, 8934, šālôm [1]
make good, 8966, šālēm[1] [1]

GOOD-BY [3]
kiss good-by, 5975, nāšaq[1] [2]
kissed good-by, 5975, nāšaq[1] [1]

GOODNESS [13]
goodness, 3206, ṭûb [6]
goodness, 3202, ṭôb[2] [4]
goodness, 1694, gāmal [1]
goodness, 3208, ṭôbâ [1]
goodness, 9326, tagmûl [1]

GOODS [23]
goods, 8214, r^{e}kûš [7]
goods, 3998, k^{e}lî [4]
goods, 7871, qinyān [3]
wealth of goods, 2104, hôn [2]
stolen goods, 1610, gāzēl [1]
goods, 2657, ḥayil [1]
goods, 3208, ṭôbâ [1]
stolen goods, 4202+4200+2257, lōʾ+l^{e}-[1]+-ô [1]
baked goods, 4407+5126+685, maʾ^{a}kāl+maʿ^{a}śeh+ʾōpeh [1]
goods, 4928, mimkār [1]
goods, 8965, šālāl [1]

GOODWILL [3]
goodwill, 8356, rāṣôn [2]
goodwill, 8934, šālôm [1]

GORE [3]
gore, 5590, nāgaḥ [3]

GORES [3]
gores, 5590, nāgaḥ [3]

GORGE [22]
gorge, 5707, *naḥal^{1}* [19]
gorge, 2361, *zālal^{1}* [1]
gorge, 4848, *mālē'^{1}* [1]
gorge, 8425, *śāba'* [1]

GORING [2]
goring, 5591, *naggāḥ* [2]

GOSHEN [15]
Goshen, 1777, *gōšen* [11]
Goshen, 824+1777, *'ereṣ+gōšen* [4]

GOSSIP [6]
gossip, 8087, *rāgan* [4]
gossip, 2143+8215, *hālak+rākîl* [2]

GOT [101]
got up, 7756, *qûm* [50]
got, 4374, *lāqaḥ* [6]
got up early, 8899, *šākam* [5]
got rid of, 6073, *sûr^{1}* [4]
got up, 8899, *šākam* [4]
early got up, 8899, *šākam* [3]
got away, 4880, *mālaṭ^{1}* [2]
got down, 5877, *nāpal* [2]
got on, 6590, *'ālâ* [2]
got off, 7563+4946+6584, *ṣānaḥ+min+'al^{2}* [2]
got ready, 7756, *qûm* [2]
got to drink, 9197, *šāqâ* [2]
got, *AIT* [1]
got together, 665, *'āsap* [1]
got rid of, 1278, *bā'ar^{2}* [1]
got, 2118+4200, *hāyâ+l^{e}-^{1}* [1]
got down, 2200, *hāpak* [1]
got off, 3718+4946+6584, *yārad+min+'al^{2}* [1]
got rid of, 3948, *kāḥad* [1]
got down, 4156, *kāra'* [1]
got relief, 5663, *nûaḥ^{1}* [1]
got into a fight, 5897, *nāṣâ^{1}* [1]
got ready, 6913, *'āśâ^{1}* [1]
got, 7924, *qārā'^{1}* [1]
got into chariot, 8206, *rākab* [1]
got on, 8206, *rākab* [1]
got the upper hand, 8948, *šālaṭ* [1]
got down, 10121, *b^{e}rak^{1}* [1]
got up, 10624, *qûm* [1]

GOUGE [2]
gouge out, 5941, *nāqar* [2]

GOUGED [1]
gouged out, 5941, *nāqar* [1]

GOURDS [4]
gourds, 7225, *p^{e}qā'îm* [3]
gourds, 7226, *paqqu'ōt* [1]

GOVERN [16]
govern, 9149, *šāpaṭ* [5]
govern, 4939, *memšālâ* [4]
govern, 1906, *dîn^{1}* [2]
govern, 5440, *māšal^{2}* [2]
govern, 2502, *ḥābaš* [1]
govern, 6806, *'āṣar* [1]
govern, 8606, *śārar* [1]

GOVERNED [3]
governed, 9149, *šāpaṭ* [2]
governed, 8606, *śārar* [1]

GOVERNMENT [4]
government, 5385, *miśrâ* [2]
government officials, 6269, *'ebed^{1}* [1]
government affairs, 10424, *malkû* [1]

GOVERNOR [32]
governor, 7068, *peḥâ* [10]
governor, 10580, *peḥâ* [6]
appointed as governor, 7212, *pāqad* [5]
governor, 9579, *tiršātā'* [5]
governor, 8569, *śar* [2]
governor^{s}, 889+6584, *'^{a}šer+'al^{2}* [1]
governor, 5907, *n^{e}ṣîb^{1}* [1]
governor, 7213, *p^{e}quddâ* [1]
governor, 8954, *šallîṭ* [1]

GOVERNORS [20]
governors, 7068, *peḥâ* [15]
governors, 10580, *peḥâ* [4]
district governors, 5893, *nāṣab^{1}* [1]

GOVERNS [1]
governs, 1906, *dîn^{1}* [1]

GOWN [1]
gown, 4230, *l^{e}bûš* [1]

GOYIM [1]
Goyim, 1582, *gôyim* [1]

GOZAN [5]
Gozan, 1579, *gôzān* [5]

GRABBED [3]
grabbed, 2616, *ḥāzaq* [2]
grabbed, 4374, *lāqaḥ* [1]

GRACE [8]
grace, 2834, *ḥēn^{1}* [5]
ornament to grace, 2834, *ḥēn^{1}* [1]
grace is shown, 2858, *ḥānan^{1}* [1]
grace, 2876, *ḥesed^{2}* [1]

GRACEFUL [3]
graceful, 2665, *ḥîn* [1]
graceful, 2788, *ḥammûq* [1]
graceful, 2834, *ḥēn^{1}* [1]

GRACIOUS [39]
gracious, 2858, *ḥānan^{1}* [13]
gracious, 2843, *ḥannûn* [12]
gracious, 3202, *ṭôb^{2}* [6]
gracious, 2834, *ḥēn^{1}* [2]
gracious, 7212, *pāqad* [2]
gracious, 2858+2858, *ḥānan^{1}+ḥānan^{1}* [1]
gracious, 3208, *ṭôbâ* [1]
gracious, 5833, *nā'îm^{1}* [1]
gracious, 9382, *t^{e}ḥinnâ^{1}* [1]

GRACIOUSLY [2]
graciously given, 2858, *ḥānan^{1}* [1]
graciously, 3202, *ṭôb^{2}* [1]

GRAIN [253]
grain offering, 4966, *minḥâ* [92]
grain offerings, 4966, *minḥâ* [42]
grain, 1841, *dāgān* [38]
grain, 1339, *bar^{3}* [11]
grain, 8692, *šeber^{2}* [9]
heads of grain, 8672, *šibbōlet^{1}* [8]
grain, *NIH/RPE* [6]
standing grain, 7850, *qāmâ* [6]
grain, 2446, *zera'* [5]
roasted grain, 7833, *qālî* [4]
new grain, 4152, *karmel^{4}* [2]
grain, 4966, *minḥâ* [2]
offering of grain, 4966, *minḥâ* [2]
grain, 8195, *rîpôt* [2]
grain, 8672, *šibbōlet^{1}* [2]
buy grain, 8690, *šābar^{2}* [2]
sold grain, 8690, *šābar^{2}* [2]
sheaves of grain, 524, *'^{a}lummâ* [1]
first ripe grain, 1137, *bikkûrîm* [1]
shocks of grain, 1538, *gādîš^{1}* [1]
crushed grain, 1762, *gereś* [1]
threshing grain, 1889, *dûš* [1]
treading out grain, 1889, *dûš* [1]
grind grain, 3221, *ṭāḥan* [1]
heads of new grain, 4152, *karmel^{4}* [1]
cut grain, 6658, *'āmîr* [1]
grain, 6658, *'āmîr* [1]
sheaf of grain, 6684, *'ōmer^{1}* [1]
grain pile, 6894, *'^{a}rēmâ* [1]
grain, 6894, *'^{a}rēmâ* [1]
heaps of grain, 6894, *'^{a}rēmâ* [1]
roasted grain, 7828, *qālâ^{1}* [1]
harvesting grain, 7907, *qāṣîr^{1}* [1]
leftover grain, 8672, *šibbōlet^{1}* [1]
grain offerings, 10432, *minḥâ* [1]

GRAINFIELD [1]
grainfield, 7850, *qāmâ* [1]

GRAINS [3]
grains of sand, 2567, *ḥôl^{1}* [2]
grains, 5054, *mā'â* [1]

GRANARIES [3]
granaries, 4393, *ma'^{a}bûs* [1]
granaries, 4852, *m^{e}lē'â* [1]
granaries, 4923, *mamm^{e}gūrâ* [1]

GRANDCHILDREN [6]
grandchildren, 1201+1201, *bēn^{1}+bēn^{1}* [4]
grandchildren, 1201, *bēn^{1}* [2]

GRANDDAUGHTER [5]
granddaughter, 1426, *bat^{1}* [5]

GRANDDAUGHTERS [1]
granddaughters, 1426+1201, *bat^{1}+bēn^{1}* [1]

GRANDFATHER [1]
grandfather, 3, *'āb* [1]

GRANDFATHER'S [2]
grandfather's, 3, *'āb* [2]

GRANDMOTHER [2]
grandmother, 562, *'ēm* [2]

GRANDMOTHER'S [1]
grandmother's, 562, *'ēm* [1]

GRANDSON [9]
grandson, 1201, *bēn^{1}* [6]
grandson, 1201+1201, *bēn^{1}+bēn^{1}* [3]

GRANDSONS [7]
grandsons, 1201, *bēn^{1}* [4]
grandsons, 1201+1201, *bēn^{1}+bēn^{1}* [3]

GRANT [27]
grant, 5989, *nātan* [14]
grant, 6913, *'āśâ^{1}* [4]
grant, *NIH/RPE* [2]
grant success, 7503, *ṣālaḥ^{2}* [2]
grant abundant, 3855, *yātar* [1]
grant, 4848, *mālē'^{1}* [1]
grant, 5951+7156, *nāśā'+pāneh* [1]
grant support, 6184, *sā'ad* [1]
grant relief, 9200, *šāqaṭ* [1]

GRANTED [23]
granted, 5989, *nātan* [11]
be granted, 6913, *'āśâ^{1}* [3]
granted rest, 5663, *nûaḥ^{1}* [2]
granted, 8883, *šît^{1}* [2]
granted, 995, *bô'* [1]
granted request, 5951+7156, *nāśā'+pāneh* [1]
granted requests, 5989, *nātan* [1]
granted, 6913, *'āśâ^{1}* [1]
granted success, 7503, *ṣālaḥ^{2}* [1]

GRANTING [1]
granting, 5989, *nātan* [1]

GRANTS [2]
grants, 5989, *nātan* [1]
grants, 8492, *śîm* [1]

GRAPE [10]
grape harvest, 1292, *bāṣîr^{1}* [4]
grape pickers, 1305, *bāṣar^{1}* [2]
grape, 6694, *'ēnāb* [2]
grape, 1235, *bōser* [1]
full grape harvest, 1292, *bāṣîr^{1}* [1]

GRAPES [37]
grapes, 6694, *'ēnāb* [12]
cluster of grapes, 864, *'eškôl^{1}* [3]
sour grapes, 1235, *bōser* [3]
grapes, *NIH/RPE* [2]
few grapes, 6622, *'ōlēlôt* [2]
good grapes, 6694, *'ēnāb* [2]
gather grapes, 112, *'āgar* [1]
unripe grapes, 1235, *bōser* [1]
grapes, 1292, *bāṣîr^{1}* [1]
gathering grapes, 1305, *bāṣar^{1}* [1]
harvest grapes, 1305, *bāṣar^{1}* [1]
the grapes^{s}, 2257, *-ô* [1]

grapes, 3292, *y^{e}bûl* [1]
grapes, 4142, *kerem*[1] [1]
gleanings of grapes, 6622, *ʿōlēlôt* [1]
grapes or raisins, 6694+4300+2256+3313, *ʾēnāb+laḥ+w^{e}-+yābēš*[2] [1]
grapes that have fallen, 7261, *pereṭ* [1]
trample the grapes, 8097, *rādâ*[1] [1]
grapes, 9408, *tîrôš* [1]

GRAPEVINE [2]
grapevine, 1728+3516, *gepen+yayin* [2]

GRAPEVINES [1]
grapevines, 1728, *gepen* [1]

GRASP [5]
grasp, 3338, *yād* [2]
grasp, 4090, *kap* [2]
grasp, 296, *ʾāḥaz*[1] [1]

GRASPED [5]
grasped, 9530, *tāpaś* [2]
grasped, 2616, *ḥāzaq* [1]
is grasped, 6487, *ʿāṭā*[2] [1]
grasped heel, 6810, *ʿāqab* [1]

GRASPING [3]
grasping, 296, *ʾāḥaz*[1] [1]
grasping, 2616, *ḥāzaq* [1]
grasping, 7924, *qārāʾ*[1] [1]

GRASPS [2]
grasps, 296, *ʾāḥaz*[1] [1]
grasps, 9461, *tāmak* [1]

GRASS [44]
grass, 2945, *ḥāṣîr*[1] [19]
grass, 6912, *ʿēśeb* [11]
grass, 2013, *dešeʾ* [4]
grass, 10572, *ʿaśab* [4]
grass, 10187, *deteʾ* [2]
new grass, 2013, *dešeʾ* [1]
dry grass, 3143, *ḥ^{a}šaš* [1]
grass, 3764, *yereq* [1]
grass, 4604+2013, *môṣāʾ*[1]*+dešeʾ* [1]

GRASSHOPPER [3]
grasshopper, 2506, *ḥāgāb*[1] [2]
grasshopper, 2885, *ḥāsîl* [1]

GRASSHOPPERS [7]
grasshoppers, 3540, *yeleq* [3]
grasshoppers, 2506, *ḥāgāb*[1] [2]
grasshoppers, 2885, *ḥāsîl* [2]

GRASSLANDS [1]
grasslands, 5661, *nāwâ*[3] [1]

GRATING [6]
grating, 4803, *mikbār* [6]

GRAVE [81]
grave, 8619, *š^{e}ʾôl* [55]
grave, 7700, *qeber* [18]
grave, 7690, *q^{e}bûrâ* [4]
depths of the grave, 8619, *š^{e}ʾôl* [2]
grave, 3243, *ṭāman* [1]
grave, 8827, *š^{e}ḥît* [1]

GRAVEDIGGERS [1]
gravediggers, 7699, *qābar* [1]

GRAVEL [2]
gravel, 2953, *ḥāṣāṣ* [2]

GRAVES [10]
graves, 7700, *qeber* [10]

GRAY [11]
gray head, 8484, *śêbâ* [5]
gray hair, 8484, *śêbâ* [2]
gray, 8482, *śîb* [1]
gray hairs, 8484, *śêbâ* [1]
gray, 8484, *śêbâ* [1]
hair gray, 8484, *śêbâ* [1]

GRAY-HAIRED [2]
gray-haired, 8482, *śîb* [1]
gray-haired, 8484, *śêbâ* [1]

GRAZE [9]
graze, 8286, *rāʿâ*[1] [7]
graze, 1278, *bāʿar*[2] [1]
graze flock, 8286, *rāʿâ*[1] [1]

GRAZED [2]
grazed, 8286, *rāʿâ*[1] [2]

GRAZES [1]
grazes, 1278, *bāʿar* [1]

GRAZING [7]
grazing, 8286, *rāʿâ*[1] [3]
grazing land, 5659, *nāweh*[1] [2]
grazing flocks, 8286, *rāʿâ*[1] [1]
grazing the flocks, 8286, *rāʿâ*[1] [1]

GREAT [530]
great, 1524, *gādôl* [244]
great, 8041, *rab*[1] [73]
great, 8044, *rōb* [24]
great, 4394, *m^{e}ʾōd* [18]
great, 1540, *gādal* [17]
great, 10647, *rab* [11]
great love, 2876, *ḥesed*[2] [6]
great trees, 471, *ʾēlôn*[1] [4]
great tree, 471, *ʾēlôn*[1] [4]
great quantity, 2221+4394, *harbēh+m^{e}ʾōd* [4]
great, 2221, *harbēh* [4]
great, 3878, *kābēd*[2] [4]
great lion, 4097, *k^{e}pîr* [4]
great, 4200+8044, *l^{e}-*[1]*+rōb* [4]
great, 1525, *g^{e}dûllâ* [3]
great owl, 3568, *yanšûp* [3]
great amount, 4200+8044, *l^{e}-*[1]*+rōb* [3]
great, 8045, *rābab*[1] [3]
great, 8049, *rābâ*[1] [3]
great, *NIH/RPE* [2]
great locusts, 746, *ʾarbeh* [2]
great, 1504, *gābar* [2]
great, 1524+4394, *gādôl+m^{e}ʾōd* [2]
great thing, 1525, *g^{e}dûllâ* [2]
gives great, 1540, *gādal* [2]
make great, 1540, *gādal* [2]
great, 3714, *yārēb* [2]
great, 3972, *kōl* [2]
great deal, 8041, *rab*[1] [2]
so great, 8041, *rab*[1] [2]
great numbers, 8044, *rōb* [2]
great, 8044+3972, *rōb+kōl* [2]
make great, 8049, *rābâ*[1] [2]
great, 52, *ʾabbîr* [1]
great fear, 399, *ʾêmâ* [1]
great soldiers, 408+4878, *ʾîš*[1]*+milḥāmâ* [1]
great, 446, *ʾēl*[5] [1]
great tree, 461, *ʾēlâ*[1] [1]
great, 466, *ʾ^{e}lōhîm* [1]
great locust, 746, *ʾarbeh* [1]
taken great pains, 928+6715, *b^{e}-+ʿ^{o}nî* [1]
great amount, 1524, *gādôl* [1]
great deeds, 1525, *g^{e}dûllâ* [1]
great things done, 1540, *gādal* [1]
great, 1540+4394, *gādal+m^{e}ʾōd* [1]
made great, 1540, *gādal* [1]
set up to be great, 1540, *gādal* [1]
undertook great, 1540, *gādal* [1]
great power, 1542, *gōdel* [1]
great, 1542, *gōdel* [1]
great joy, 1635+1635, *gîl*[1]*+gîl*[1] [1]
in great need, 1937, *dālal*[1] [1]
great amount, 2162, *hāmôn* [1]
great numbers, 2221+4394, *harbēh+m^{e}ʾōd* [1]
great, 2221+4394, *harbēh+m^{e}ʾōd* [1]
great wrath, 2405+2256+7912, *zaʿam+w^{e}-+qeṣep*[1] [1]
great skill, 2682+3359+1069, *ḥākām+yādaʿ+bînâ* [1]
great rage, 3034+678, *ḥ^{o}rî+ʾap*[2] [1]
great numbers, 3878+4394, *kābēd*[2]*+m^{e}ʾōd* [1]
great, 3888, *kabbîr* [1]
great, 3946, *kōaḥ*[1] [1]
great lions, 4097, *k^{e}pîr* [1]
great numbers, 4200+8044, *l^{e}-*[1]*+rōb* [1]
great number, 4200+8044, *l^{e}-*[1]*+rōb* [1]
great quantities, 4200+8044+4394, *l^{e}-*[1]*+rōb+m^{e}ʾōd* [1]
great darkness, 4420, *maʾpēlyâ* [1]
great size, 4500, *middâ*[1] [1]
great, 4500, *middâ*[1] [1]
great power, 5124, *maʿ^{a}rāṣâ* [1]
great assembly, 5220, *maqhēl* [1]
great congregation, 5220, *maqhēl* [1]
great man's, 5618, *nādîb* [1]
great, 6434, *ʿaz* [1]
great power, 6437, *ʿōz* [1]
great, 6437, *ʿōz* [1]
go to great depths, 6676, *ʿāmaq* [1]
great, 6786, *ʿāṣûm* [1]
do great things, 6913+6913, *ʿāśâ*[1]*+ʿāśâ*[1] [1]
great lizard, 7370, *ṣāb*[2] [1]
great difficulty, 7996, *qāšâ* [1]
having great difficulty, 7996, *qāšâ* [1]
great quantities, 8041, *rab*[1] [1]
great number, 8044, *rōb* [1]
make as great as you like, 8049+4394, *rābâ*[1]*+m^{e}ʾōd* [1]
acquire great numbers, 8049, *rābâ*[1] [1]
great throng, 8086, *rigmâ* [1]
have great compassion, 8163+8163, *rāḥam+rāḥam* [1]
great mercy, 8171, *raḥ^{a}mîm* [1]
great, 8273, *raʿ*[1] [1]
wickedness is great, 8288+8288, *rāʿâ*[3]*+rāʿâ*[3] [1]
makes great, 8434, *śāgāʾ* [1]
great, 8438, *śaggîʾ* [1]
take great delight, 8464+928+8525, *śûś+b^{e}-+śimḥâ* [1]
had great success, 8505, *śākal*[1] [1]
great tumult, 8623, *šāʾôn*[2] [1]
great, 9476, *tamrûrîm*[1] [1]
great sea creatures, 9490, *tannîn* [1]
great, 10648, *r^{e}bâ* [1]
great, 10678, *śaggîʾ* [1]

GREATER [35]
greater, 1524, *gādôl* [9]
greater, 1540, *gādal* [8]
greater than, 4946, *min* [5]
greater, 8049, *rābâ*[1] [3]
greater, *NIH/RPE* [1]
greater, 1504, *gābar* [1]
make greater, 1540, *gādal* [1]
greater, 3512, *yāṭab* [1]
greater, 3954, *kî*[2] [1]
greater power, 8041, *rab*[1] [1]
greater, 8041, *rab*[1] [1]
greater, 8123, *rûm*[1] [1]
greater than, 10427, *min* [1]
became even greater, 10650+10339+10323, *r^{e}bû+yattîr+y^{e}sap* [1]

GREATER SIDON [2]
Greater Sidon, 7478, *ṣîdôn rabbâ* [2]

GREATEST [17]
greatest, 1524, *gādôl* [17]

GREATLY [56]
greatly, 4394, *m^{e}ʾōd* [22]
greatly, 1524, *gādôl* [5]
greatly, 4200+8044, *l^{e}-*[1]*+rōb* [3]
greatly, 8041, *rab*[1] [3]
greatly, 8049, *rābâ*[1] [3]
greatly, 928+4394+4394, *b^{e}-+m^{e}ʾōd+m^{e}ʾōd* [2]
greatly, 10677, *śegāʾ* [2]
rejoice greatly, 1635+677+1638, *gîl*[1]*+ʾap*[1]*+gîlâ* [1]
greatly, 2221+4394, *harbēh+m^{e}ʾōd* [1]
greatly, 2221, *harbēh* [1]
greatly disturbed, 2591, *hûš*[2] [1]
sinned greatly, 2628+2627, *ḥēṭʾ+ḥāṭāʾ* [1]
greatly, 4027, *kēn*[2] [1]
greatly, 4394+4394, *m^{e}ʾōd+m^{e}ʾōd* [1]
greatly, 6676, *ʿāmaq* [1]
greatly, 7098, *pālāʾ* [1]
greatly increase, 8049+8049, *rābâ*[1]*+rābâ*[1] [1]
numbers increased greatly, 8049+2256+7238, *rābâ*[1]*+w^{e}-+pārâ*[1] [1]
greatly distressed, 8283, *rāʿad* [1]
delight greatly, 8464+8464, *śûś+śûś* [1]

rejoice greatly, 8464+5375, śûś+māśôś[1] [1]
greatly, 10678, śaggîʾ [1]
greatly perplexed, 10724, šemam [1]

GREATNESS [14]
greatness, 1525, gedûllâ [3]
greatness, 1542, gōdel [3]
greatness, 10650, rebû [3]
greatness, 8044, rōb [2]
greatness, 1540, gādal [1]
show greatness, 1540, gādal [1]
greatness, 5270, marbît [1]

GREAVES [1]
greaves, 5196, miṣḥâ [1]

GREECE [6]
Greece, 3430, yāwān [6]

GREED [2]
greed, 1299, beṣaʿ [1]
greed, 5883, nepeš [1]

GREEDY [8]
greedy, 1298, bāṣaʿ [3]
greedy, *AIT* [1]
greedy, 339+2143, ʾaḥar+hālak [1]
greedy, 1298+1299, bāṣaʿ+beṣaʿ [1]
greedy, 8143, rāḥab [1]
greedy man, 8146+5883, rāḥāb[1]+nepeš [1]

GREEKS [2]
Greeks, 1201+3436, bēn[1]+yewānî [1]
Greeks, 3430, yāwān [1]

GREEN [19]
green, 2013, dešeʾ [4]
green, 3764, yereq [4]
green, 8316, raʿanān [3]
green, 4300, laḥ [2]
green, 2012, dāšāʾ [1]
green, 2645, ḥay[2] [1]
green thing, 3728, yārôq [1]
green leaf, 6591, ʿāleh [1]
green thing, 6912, ʿēśeb [1]
green tree, 8316, raʿanān [1]

GREENISH [2]
greenish, 3768, yeraqraq [2]

GREET [8]
greet, 8626+4200+8934, šāʾal+le-[1]+šālôm [4]
greet, *NIH/RPE* [1]
greet, 1385, bārak[2] [1]
greet, 7925+1385, qārāʾ[2]+bārak[2] [1]
greet, 8934, šālôm [1]

GREETED [6]
greeted, 8626+4200+8934, šāʾal+le-[1]+šālôm [4]
greeted, 606, ʾāmar[1] [1]
greeted, 1385, bārak[2] [1]

GREETINGS [4]
give greetings, 1385, bārak[2] [1]
greetings, 10147, gemar [1]
cordial greetings, 10720+10002+10353+10002, šelām+-āʾ+kōl+-āʾ [1]
greetings, 10720, šelām [1]

GREETS [1]
greets, 1385, bārak[2] [1]

GREW [56]
grew, *AIT* [18]
grew up, 1540, gādal [6]
grew, 1540, gādal [5]
grew up, 6590, ʿālâ [3]
grew, 2725, ḥālal[1] [2]
grew large, 10648, rebâ [2]
grew, *NIH/RPE* [1]
grew older, 1540, gādal [1]
grew worse and worse, 2118+2716+2617+4394, hāyâ+ḥolî+ḥāzāq+meʾōd [1]
grew even wilder, 2143+2256+6192, hālak+we-+sāʿar [1]
grew louder and louder, 2143+2256+2618+4394, hālak+we-+ḥāzēq+meʾōd [1]
grew stronger and stronger, 2143+2256+2618, hālak+we-+ḥāzēq [1]
grew stronger and stronger, 2143+2256+7997, hālak+we-+qāšeh [1]
grew weaker and weaker, 2143+2256+1924, hālak+we-+dal[2] [1]
grew old, 2416, zāqēn[1] [1]
grew old, 2420, ziqnâ [1]
grew in strength, 2616, ḥāzaq [1]
grew fierce, 3877, kābēd[1] [1]
grew, 7541, ṣāmaḥ [1]
grew, 7542, ṣemaḥ [1]
grew up, 7756, qûm [1]
grew weary, 7918, qāṣar[2] [1]
grew up, 8049, rābâ[1] [1]
grew fat, 9042, šāmēn[1] [1]
grew, 10648, rebâ [1]
grew, 10731, šenâ[1] [1]

GRIDDLE [3]
griddle, 4679, maḥabat [3]

GRIEF [25]
grief, 4088, kaʿas [4]
grief, 9342, tûgâ [3]
grief, *NIH/RPE* [1]
grief, 63, ʾābēl[1] [1]
brings grief, 3324, yāgâ[1] [1]
brought grief, 3324, yāgâ[1] [1]
grief, 3324, yāgâ[1] [1]
brought grief, 3872, kāʾab [1]
grief, 4089, kaʿaś [1]
grief, 4799, makʾōb [1]
grief, 4959, mānôn [1]
source of grief, 5289+8120, mōrâ+rûaḥ [1]
bitter grief, 5320, merîrût [1]
recovered from grief, 5714, nāḥam [1]
brings grief, 6618, ʿālal[1] [1]
grief, 6715, ʿonî [1]
filled with grief, 6772, ʿāṣab[2] [1]
grief, 6780, ʿaṣṣebet [1]
grief, 7722, qādar [1]
brought to grief, 8317, rāʿaʿ[1] [1]

GRIEVANCE [1]
grievance, 8190, rîb[2] [1]

GRIEVE [12]
grieve, 6772, ʿāṣab[2] [2]
grieve, *NIH/RPE* [1]
grieve, 61, ʾābal[1] [1]
grieve, 63, ʾābēl[1] [1]
grieve, 117, ʾādab [1]
grieve, 634, ʾānaḥ [1]
grieve, 2703, ḥālâ[1] [1]
grieve, 3324, yāgâ[1] [1]
grieve bitterly, 5352, mārar [1]
grieve, 5778, nākāʾ[2] [1]
grieve, 7639, ṣarʾ [1]

GRIEVED [17]
was grieved, 5714, nāḥam [4]
grieved, 5714, nāḥam [3]
am grieved, 5714, nāḥam [2]
grieved, 6772, ʿāṣab[2] [2]
grieved, 1134, bākâ [1]
was grieved, 2806, ḥāmēṣ[1] [1]
grieved, 6327, ʿāgam [1]
be grieved, 6772, ʿāṣab[2] [1]
was grieved, 6772, ʿāṣab[2] [1]
been grieved, 8689, šābar[1] [1]

GRIEVES [1]
grieves, 5352, mārar [1]

GRIEVING [3]
grieving, *NIH/RPE* [1]
grieving, 61, ʾābal[1] [1]
grieving, 6772, ʿāṣab[2] [1]

GRIEVOUS [7]
grievous, 2703, ḥālâ[1] [2]
grievous, 8273, raʿ[1] [2]
grievous, 631, ʾānûš [1]
grievous, 1524, gādôl [1]
grievous, 3877, kābēd[1] [1]

GRIND [5]
grind, 1990, dāqaq [1]
grind grain, 3221, ṭāḥan [1]
grind, 3221, ṭāḥan [1]
grind, 4197, kātaš [1]
grind, 8835, šāḥaq [1]

GRINDERS [1]
grinders, 3223, ṭōḥanâ [1]

GRINDING [4]
grinding, 3221, ṭāḥan [2]
grinding, *NIH/RPE* [1]
grinding, 3222, ṭaḥanâ [1]

GRIP [4]
grip, 296, ʾāḥaz[1] [4]

GRIPPED [3]
gripped, 2616, ḥāzaq [3]

GRIPS [3]
grips, 296, ʾāḥaz[1] [2]
grips, 2616, ḥāzaq [1]

GROAN [16]
groan, 634, ʾānaḥ [7]
groan, 650, ʾānaq [3]
groan, 5637, nāham [2]
groan, 627, ʾānâ[1] [1]
groan, 5543+5544, nāʾaq+neʾāqâ [1]
groan, 7650, ṣārâ[1] [1]
groan, 8613, šāʾag [1]

GROANED [3]
groaned, 634, ʾānaḥ [1]
groaned, 2159, hāmâ [1]
groaned, 5544, neʾāqâ [1]

GROANING [13]
groaning, 635, ʾanāḥâ [6]
groaning, 634, ʾānaḥ [2]
groaning, 5544, neʾāqâ [2]
groaning, 8614, šeʾāgâ [2]
groaning, 651, ʾanāqâ[1] [1]

GROANS [6]
groans, 651, ʾanāqâ[1] [2]
groans, 634, ʾānaḥ [1]
groans, 635, ʾanāḥâ [1]
groans, 5543, nāʾaq [1]
groans, 8614, šeʾāgâ [1]

GROPE [5]
grope, 5491, māšaš [2]
grope along, 1779, gāšaš [1]
grope about, 5491, māšaš [1]
grope, 5675, nûaʿ [1]

GROUND [271]
ground, 824, ʾereṣ [160]
ground, 141, ʾadāmâ[1] [42]
dry ground, 3317, yabbāšâ [10]
ground, *NIH/RPE* [6]
dry ground, 3000, ḥārābâ [4]
ground meal, 6881, ʿarîsâ [4]
ground, 8441, śādeh [4]
ground, 6760, ʿāpār [3]
ground, 10075, ʾaraʿ [3]
ground, *AIT* [2]
ground, 1990, dāqaq [2]
plot of ground, 2750, ḥēleq[2] [2]
plot of ground, 2754, ḥelqâ[2] [2]
ground, 3221, ṭāḥan [2]
level ground, 4793, mîšôr [2]
unplowed ground, 5776, nîr[3] [2]
stand ground, 6641, ʿāmad [2]
thirsty ground, 7536, ṣimmāʾôn [2]
finely ground, 1987, daq [1]
be ground, 1990, dāqaq [1]
ground, 3045, ḥārîš [1]
ground to powder, 3221+3512, ṭāḥan+yāṭab [1]
ground, 3318, yabbešet [1]
ground, 4804, makkâ [1]
bowed down to the ground, 5877+6584+7156, nāpal+ʿal[2]+pāneh [1]
cleared ground, 7155, pānâ [1]

ground, 7156, *pāneh* [1]
parched ground, 7533, *ṣāmā'* [1]
stood ground, 7756, *qûm* [1]
be dashed to the ground, 8187, *rāṭaš* [1]
dash to the ground, 8187, *rāṭaš* [1]
were dashed to the ground, 8187, *rāṭaš* [1]
creatures that move along the ground, 8254, *remeś* [1]
break up the ground, 8440, *śādad* [1]
creatures that move along the ground, 9238, *šereṣ* [1]

GROUNDS [3]
palace grounds, 1074+4889, *bayit[1]+melek[1]* [2]
grounds for charges, 10544, *'illā* [1]

GROUP [19]
group, *AIT* [4]
went as a group, 10656, *rᵉgaš* [3]
one group[s], 465, *'ēlleh* [2]
group, 4722, *maḥᵃneh* [2]
group, *NIH/RPE* [1]
group, 99, *'ᵃguddâ* [1]
group, 408, *'îš[1]* [1]
each national group, 1580+1580, *gôy+gôy* [1]
group, 2755+1074+3, *ḥᵃluqqâ+bayit[1]+'āb* [1]
group, 4272, *lahᵃqâ* [1]
group, 4850, *mᵉlō'* [1]
came as a group, 7735, *qāhal* [1]

GROUPS [5]
groups, 4722, *maḥᵃneh* [2]
groups, *NIH/RPE* [1]
groups, 4713, *maḥᵃlōqet* [1]
groups, 10412, *maḥlᵉqā* [1]

GROVE [2]
grove, 1708, *gannâ* [1]
olive grove, 2339, *zayit* [1]

GROVES [8]
olive groves, 2339, *zayit* [7]
groves, 3623, *ya'ar[1]* [1]

GROW [60]
grow, *AIT* [15]
grow, 6590, *'ālâ* [4]
grow, 2143, *hālak* [3]
grow, 7541, *ṣāmaḥ* [3]
make grow, 7541, *ṣāmaḥ* [2]
makes grow, 7541, *ṣāmaḥ* [2]
grow, *NIH/RPE* [1]
let grow, 599, *'āmēṣ* [1]
made grow old, 1162, *bālâ[1]* [1]
grow tall, 1448, *gā'â* [1]
make grow tall, 1467, *gābah* [1]
grow long, 1540, *gādal* [1]
made grow, 1540, *gādal* [1]
make grow, 1540, *gādal* [1]
continued to grow, 2143, *hālak* [1]
grow old, 2416, *zāqēn[1]* [1]
grow pale, 2578, *ḥāwar[1]* [1]
grow strong, 2730, *ḥālam[1]* [1]
grow stronger, 3578+601, *yāsap+'ōmeṣ* [1]
grow poor, 3769, *yāraš[1]* [1]
grow weary, 3983, *kālâ[1]* [1]
grow long, 5742, *nāṭâ* [1]
grow up, 6590, *'ālâ* [1]
made grow up, 6590, *'ālâ* [1]
grow, 6913, *'āśâ[1]* [1]
causes to grow, 7541, *ṣāmaḥ* [1]
made grow, 7541, *ṣāmaḥ* [1]
grow, 8047, *rᵉbābâ* [1]
grow large, 8049, *rābâ[1]* [1]
makes grow, 8049, *rābâ[1]* [1]
made grow tall, 8123, *rûm[1]* [1]
grow, 8436, *śāgâ* [1]
make grow, 8451, *śûg[2]* [1]
grow well, 8934, *šālôm* [1]
let grow, 8938, *šālaḥ* [1]
grow, 8990, *šālap* [1]
grow, 10677, *śᵉgā'* [1]

GROWERS [1]
vine growers, 4144, *kōrēm* [1]

GROWING [10]
growing, 6912, *'ēśeb* [4]
growing, 6590, *'ālâ* [3]
growing, 4, *'ēb* [1]
growing old, 6980, *'ātaq* [1]
growing, 7541, *ṣāmaḥ* [1]

GROWL [5]
growl, 2159, *hāmâ* [1]
growl, 5637, *nāham* [1]
growl, 5849, *nā'ar[1]* [1]
growl, 5989+7754, *nātan+qôl* [1]
growl, 7754, *qôl* [1]

GROWLED [1]
growled, 5989+7754, *nātan+qôl* [1]

GROWLS [1]
growls, 2047, *hāgâ[1]* [1]

GROWN [19]
grown up, 1540, *gādal* [7]
grown, *AIT* [3]
grown, 7541, *ṣāmaḥ* [3]
grown, *NIH/RPE* [2]
grown, 1540, *gādal* [1]
grown dim, 3908, *kāhâ[1]* [1]
grown, 7756, *qûm* [1]
grown, 10648, *rᵉbâ* [1]

GROWS [17]
grows, *AIT* [6]
what grows by itself, 6206, *sāpîaḥ[1]* [2]
what grows of itself, 6206, *sāpîaḥ[1]* [2]
grows up, 7850, *qāmâ* [2]
grows, *NIH/RPE* [1]
grows up, 1540, *gādal* [1]
grows out, 3655, *yāṣā'* [1]
grows pale, 7695+6999, *qābaṣ+pā'rûr* [1]
grows black, 8837, *šāḥar[1]* [1]

GROWTH [3]
new growth, 4, *'ēb* [1]
new growth, 2013, *deše'* [1]
growth, 7542, *ṣemaḥ* [1]

GRUDGE [3]
bear a grudge against, 5757, *nāṭar[1]* [1]
held a grudge against, 8475, *śāṭam* [1]
holds a grudge against, 8475, *śāṭam* [1]

GRUDGING [1]
grudging, 8317, *rā'a'[1]* [1]

GRUMBLE [4]
grumble, 4296, *lûn* [3]
made grumble, 4296, *lûn* [1]

GRUMBLED [9]
grumbled, 4296, *lûn* [7]
grumbled, 8087, *rāgan* [2]

GRUMBLING [8]
grumbling, 9442, *tᵉlunnôt* [5]
grumbling, 4296, *lûn* [1]
constant grumbling, 9442+4296, *tᵉlunnôt+lûn* [1]
grumbling, 9442+4296, *tᵉlunnôt+lûn* [1]

GUARANTEE [1]
guarantee safety, 6842, *'ārab[1]* [1]

GUARANTEED [1]
guaranteed safety, 6842, *'ārab[1]* [1]

GUARD [93]
guard, 9068, *šāmar* [16]
guard, 3184, *ṭabbāḥ* [13]
guard, 4766, *maṭṭārâ* [13]
imperial guard, 3184, *ṭabbāḥ* [12]
rear guard, 665, *'āsap* [5]
guard, 5464, *mišmār[1]* [4]
guard, 5915, *nāṣar* [4]
special guard, 1475, *gibbôr* [3]
guard, 8132, *rûṣ* [3]
on guard, 9068, *šāmar* [3]
armed guard, 2741, *ḥālaṣ[2]* [2]
guard, 4915, *melṣar* [2]
guard yourself, 9068, *šāmar* [2]
guard, *NIH/RPE* [1]
guard, 5466, *mišmeret* [1]
under guard, 5466, *mišmeret* [1]
guard well, 5915, *nāṣar* [1]
under guard, 6584+5464, *'al[2]+mišmār[1]* [1]
guard, 7215, *pᵉqidut* [1]
guard, 9068+5466, *šāmar+mišmeret* [1]
guard, 9072, *šomrâ* [1]
guard, 9193, *šāqad[1]* [1]
stand guard, 9193, *šāqad[1]* [1]
guard, 10295, *ṭabbāḥ* [1]

GUARDED [6]
guarded, 9068, *šāmar* [3]
guarded, 5915, *nāṣar* [2]
guarded, 9068+5464, *šāmar+mišmār[1]* [1]

GUARDIAN [2]
guardian, 6114, *sākak[1]* [2]

GUARDIANS [2]
guardians of children, 587, *'āman[2]* [1]
guardians, 587, *'āman[2]* [1]

GUARDING [6]
guarding, 9068, *šāmar* [3]
guarding, 9068+5466, *šāmar+mišmeret* [2]
guarding, 5466, *mišmeret* [1]

GUARDROOM [2]
guardroom, 9288+8132, *tā'+rûṣ* [2]

GUARDS [28]
guards, 8132, *rûṣ* [10]
guards, 9068, *šāmar* [6]
guards, 5915, *nāṣar* [5]
guards, 7213, *pᵉquddâ* [2]
guards, 408+5464, *'îš[1]+mišmār[1]* [1]
guards, 4964, *minnᵉzār* [1]
guards, 5464, *mišmār[1]* [1]
guards, 5466, *mišmeret* [1]
alcoves for the guards, 9288, *tā'* [1]

GUDGODAH [1]
Gudgodah, 1516, *gudgōdâ* [1]

GUEST [3]
guest, *NIH/RPE* [1]
guest, 995+448+1074, *bô'+'el+bayit[1]* [1]
guest, 9369, *tôšāb* [1]

GUESTS [6]
guests, 7924, *qārā'[1]* [3]
guests, 1591+1074, *gûr[1]+bayit[1]* [1]
guests, 6639, *'am[2]* [1]
been invited as guests, 7924, *qārā'[1]* [1]

GUIDANCE [7]
guidance, 9374, *taḥbulôt* [4]
seeking guidance, 1329, *bāqar* [1]
guidance, 2011, *dāraš* [1]
give guidance, 3723, *yārâ[3]* [1]

GUIDE [18]
guide, 5697, *nāḥâ[1]* [9]
guide, 5633, *nāhal* [3]
guide, 2005, *dārak* [2]
guide, 5627, *nāhag[1]* [2]
guide, 886, *'āšar[1]* [1]
guide, 3723, *yārâ[3]* [1]

GUIDED [6]
guided, 5697, *nāḥâ[1]* [4]
are guided, 886, *'āšar[1]* [1]
guided, 5627, *nāhag[1]* [1]

GUIDEPOSTS [1]
guideposts, 9477, *tamrûrîm[2]* [1]

GUIDES [5]
guides, 5697, *nāḥâ[1]* [2]
guides, 886, *'āšar[1]* [1]
guides, 2005, *dārak* [1]
guides, 8505, *śākal[1]* [1]

GUIDING [3]
guiding, 5627, *nāhag[1]* [3]

GUILT [103]
guilt, 6411, *'āwōn* [35]
guilt offering, 871, *'āšām* [29]
guilt, 873, *'ašmâ* [13]
guilt offerings, 871, *'āšām* [5]
bear guilt, 870, *'āšam* [3]
guilt of blood, 1947, *dām* [3]
guilt, 871, *'āšām* [2]
guilt of bloodshed, 1947, *dām* [2]
guilt of shedding blood, 1947, *dām* [2]
admit guilt, 870, *'āšam* [1]
guilt offering, 873, *'ašmâ* [1]
guilt of murder, 1947+5883, *dām+nepeš* [1]
guilt, 2628, *ḥēṭ'* [1]
guilt, 2631, *ḥ^{a}ṭā'â* [1]
be cleared of guilt, 5927, *nāqâ* [1]
without guilt, 5929, *nāqî* [1]
guilt, 6404, *'āwel* [1]
guilt of rebellion, 7322, *peša'* [1]

GUILTLESS [4]
hold guiltless, 5927, *nāqâ* [2]
guiltless, 1172+7322, *b^{e}lî+peša'* [1]
guiltless, 5927, *nāqâ* [1]

GUILTY [68]
guilty, 870, *'āšam* [15]
guilty, 8401, *rāšā'* [9]
guilty of bloodshed, 1947, *dām* [4]
guilty, 6411, *'āwōn* [4]
guilty of sin, 2628, *ḥēṭ'* [3]
leave the guilty unpunished, 5927+5927, *nāqâ+nāqâ* [3]
guilty, 8399, *rāša'* [3]
guilty, 873, *'ašmâ* [2]
guilty, 928+3338, *b^{e}-+yād* [2]
guilty, 2628, *ḥēṭ'* [2]
declare not guilty, 7405, *ṣādaq* [2]
guilty, *NIH/RPE* [1]
declare guilty, 870, *'āšam* [1]
guilty of wrongdoing, 870+870, *'āšam+'āšam* [1]
held guilty, 870, *'āšam* [1]
very guilty, 870+870, *'āšam+'āšam* [1]
guilty of sins, 873, *'ašmâ* [1]
guilty of blood, 1947, *dām* [1]
guilty of murder, 1947, *dām* [1]
guilty, 2261, *wāzār* [1]
guilty of prostitution, 2388, *zānâ^{1}* [1]
guilty of the vilest adultery, 2388+2388, *zānâ^{1}+zānâ^{1}* [1]
make out to be guilty, 2627, *ḥāṭā'* [1]
unfaithfulness guilty of, 5086+5085, *ma'al^{1}+mā'al* [1]
become guilty, 5951+6584+2628, *nāśā'+'al^{2}+ḥēṭ'* [1]
guilty, 5951+2628, *nāśā'+ḥēṭ'* [1]
guilty, 5951, *nāśā'* [1]
pronounce guilty, 6835, *'āqaš* [1]
declare guilty, 8399, *rāša'* [1]
guilty of wickedness, 8399, *rāša'* [1]

GULF [1]
gulf, 4383, *lāšôn* [1]

GULL [2]
gull, 8830, *šaḥap* [2]

GULPS [1]
gulps down, 1180, *bāla'^{1}* [1]

GUM [1]
gum resin, 5753, *nāṭāp* [1]

GUNI [4]
Guni, 1586, *gûnî^{1}* [4]

GUNITE [1]
Gunite, 1587, *gûnî^{2}* [1]

GUR [1]
Gur, 1595, *gûr^{5}* [1]

GUR BAAL [1]
Gur Baal, 1597, *gûr-ba'al* [1]

GUSH [1]
gush forth, 1324, *bāqa'* [1]

GUSHED [4]
gushed out, 2307, *zûb* [3]
gushed out, 3655+8041, *yāṣā'+rab^{1}* [1]

GUSHES [2]
gushes, 5580, *nāba'* [2]

GUTTER [3]
gutter, 2668, *ḥêq* [3]

HAAHASHTARI [1]
Haahashtari, 2028, *hā'^{a}ḥaštārî* [1]

HABAKKUK [2]
Habakkuk, 2487, *ḥ^{a}baqqûq* [2]

HABAZZINIAH [1]
Habazziniah, 2484, *ḥ^{a}baṣṣinyâ* [1]

HABIT [3]
had the habit, 4946+9453+8997, *min+t^{e}môl+šilšôm* [2]
been in the habit of, 6122+6122, *sākan^{1}+sākan^{1}* [1]

HABITAT [1]
habitat, 5438, *miškān* [1]

HABOR [3]
Habor, 2466, *ḥābôr* [3]

HACALIAH [2]
Hacaliah, 2678, *ḥ^{a}kalyâ* [2]

HACK [1]
hack to pieces, 1438, *bātaq* [1]

HACMONI [1]
Hacmoni, 2685, *ḥakmônî* [1]

HACMONITE [1]
Hacmonite, 1201+2685, *bēn^{1}+ḥakmônî* [1]

HAD [2060]
had, *AIT* [1508]
had, *NIH/RPE* [196]
had, 4200, *l^{e-1}* [90]
had, 2118+4200, *hāyâ+l^{e-1}* [42]
had, 3528, *yālad* [31]
had, 2118, *hāyâ* [16]
had, 928, *b^{e}-* [11]
had, 4200+2118, *l^{e-1}+hāyâ* [8]
had leprosy, 7665, *ṣāra'* [6]
had, 10378, *l^{e}-* [6]
had a dream, 2731, *ḥālam^{2}* [5]
had charge of, 6584, *'al^{2}* [5]
had a dream, 2706+2731, *ḥ^{a}lôm+ḥālam^{2}* [3]
had a dream, 2731+2706, *ḥālam^{2}+ḥ^{a}lôm* [3]
had brought, 3655, *yāṣā'* [3]
had, 5162+907, *māṣā'+'ēt^{2}* [3]
had to, 6584, *'al^{2}* [3]
had stand, 6641, *'āmad* [3]
had come forward, 7928, *qārab* [3]
had peace, 9200, *šāqaṭ* [3]
had^{s}, 10255, *h^{a}zâ* [3]
had to eat, 430, *'ākal* [2]
had, 928+3338, *b^{e}-+yād* [2]
dream had, 2706+2731, *ḥ^{a}lôm+ḥālam^{2}* [2]
had dream, 2731+2706, *ḥālam^{2}+ḥ^{a}lôm* [2]
had pity, 2798, *ḥāmal* [2]
had a baby, 3528, *yālad* [2]
had a son, 3528, *yālad* [2]
had children, 3528, *yālad* [2]
had left over, 3855, *yātar* [2]
had, 3869, *k^{e}-* [2]
had the habit, 4946+9453+8997, *min+t^{e}môl+šilšôm* [2]
had beaten, 5782, *nākâ* [2]
had pass, 6296, *'ābar^{1}* [2]
had^{s}, 8011, *rā'â^{1}* [2]
had many, 8049, *rābâ^{1}* [2]
had enough, 8425, *śāba'* [2]
had rest, 9200, *šāqaṭ* [2]
had food enough, 430, *'ākal* [1]
had brought, 665, *'āsap* [1]
had made ready, 673, *'āsar* [1]
had, 907, *'ēt^{2}* [1]
had, 928+7023, *b^{e}-+peh* [1]
had, 928+7931, *b^{e}-+qereb* [1]
had brought in, 995, *bô'* [1]
had brought, 995, *bô'* [1]
had^{s}, 995, *bô'* [1]
had, 995, *bô'* [1]
had kneel down, 1384, *bārak^{1}* [1]
had chance, 2118+928+3338, *hāyâ+b^{e}-+yād* [1]
had part in, 2118+4946, *hāyâ+min* [1]
had to, 2118+6584, *hāyâ+'al^{2}* [1]
had, 2118+6584, *hāyâ+'al^{2}* [1]
had, 2118+928, *hāyâ+b^{e}-* [1]
had wedding songs, 2146, *hālal^{2}* [1]
had dreams, 2706+2731, *ḥ^{a}lôm+ḥālam^{2}* [1]
had dreams, 2731+2706, *ḥālam^{2}+ḥ^{a}lôm* [1]
had compassion, 2798, *ḥāmal* [1]
had concern, 2798, *ḥāmal* [1]
had nothing, 2893+3972, *ḥāsēr^{1}+kōl* [1]
had rain, 3197, *ṭāhēr* [1]
had experience, 3359, *yāda'* [1]
had intimate relations with, 3359, *yāda'* [1]
had regard for, 3359, *yāda'* [1]
had the least inkling, 3359+3359, *yāda'+yāda'* [1]
had sons, 3528, *yālad* [1]
had reaffirm, 3578, *yāsap* [1]
had difficulty taking possession of, 3655+4946, *yāṣā'+min* [1]
had, 3780+4200, *yēš+l^{e-1}* [1]
had, 3780, *yēš* [1]
had live, 3782, *yāšab* [1]
had some left over, 3855, *yātar* [1]
had been, 4200+7156, *l^{e-1}+pāneh* [1]
had brought, 4374, *lāqaḥ* [1]
had^{s}, 4576, *mûl^{1}* [1]
had rain, 4763, *māṭar* [1]
had^{s}, 4763, *māṭar* [1]
had, 5162+4200, *māṣā'+l^{e-1}* [1]
had, 5162, *māṣā'* [1]
had compassion, 5714, *nāḥam* [1]
had executed, 5782+2256+4637, *nākâ+w^{e}-+mût* [1]
had struck down, 5782, *nākâ* [1]
had a struggle, 5887+7349, *naptûlîm+pātal* [1]
had, 5951, *nāśā'* [1]
had pass by, 6296, *'ābar^{1}* [1]
had witnessed, 6386+6332, *'ûd^{1}+'ēd* [1]
had, 6584, *'al^{2}* [1]
had come up, 6590, *'ālâ* [1]
had go up, 6590, *'ālâ* [1]
had pledge, 6641, *'āmad* [1]
had serve, 6641, *'āmad* [1]
had^{s}, 6699, *'ānâ^{1}* [1]
had a vision, 8011, *rā'â^{1}* [1]
had special access to, 8011+7156, *rā'â^{1}+pāneh* [1]
had compassion, 8163, *rāḥam* [1]
had ride along, 8206, *rākab* [1]
had ride, 8206, *rākab* [1]
had fill, 8425, *śāba'* [1]
had plenty, 8425, *śāba'* [1]
had brought, 8492, *śîm* [1]
had take up positions, 8492, *śîm* [1]
had, 8492, *śîm* [1]
had great success, 8505, *śākal^{1}* [1]
had regard for, 8505, *śākal^{1}* [1]
had brought, 8938+2256+4374, *šālaḥ+w^{e}-+lāqaḥ* [1]
had removed, 8938+2256+4374, *šālaḥ+w^{e}-+lāqaḥ* [1]
had charge of, 9068, *šāmar* [1]
had been, 9453+8997, *t^{e}môl+šilšôm* [1]
had for, 9455, *t^{e}mûrâ* [1]
had wander, 9494, *tā'â* [1]
had blown, 9546, *tāqa'* [1]
had, 10089, *b^{e}-* [1]
had, 10201+10542, *h^{a}wâ+'al* [1]

HADAD [17]
Hadad, 2060, *h^{a}dad* [12]
Hadad, 2524, *ḥ^{a}dad* [2]
Hadad, *NIH/RPE* [1]
Hadad, 119, *'^{a}dad* [1]

Hadad[s], 2257, *-ô* [1]

HADAD RIMMON [1]
Hadad Rimmon, 2062, *h[a]dad-rimmôn* [1]

HADADEZER [17]
Hadadezer, 2061, *h[a]dad'ezer* [17]

HADADEZER'S [2]
Hadadezer's, 2061, *h[a]dad'ezer* [2]

HADASHAH [1]
Hadashah, 2546, *ḥ[a]dāšâ* [1]

HADASSAH [1]
Hadassah, 2073, *h[a]dassâ* [1]

HADID [3]
Hadid, 2531, *ḥādîd* [3]

HADLAI [1]
Hadlai, 2536, *ḥadlāy* [1]

HADORAM [4]
Hadoram, 2066, *h[a]dôrām[1]* [2]
Hadoram, *NIH/RPE* [1]
Hadoram, 2067, *h[a]dôrām[2]* [1]

HADRACH [1]
Hadrach, 2541, *ḥadrāk* [1]

HAELEPH [1]
Haeleph, 2030, *hā'elep* [1]

HAGAB [1]
Hagab, 2507, *ḥāgāb[2]* [1]

HAGABA [1]
Hagaba, 2509, *ḥ[a]gābâ* [1]

HAGABAH [1]
Hagabah, 2509, *ḥ[a]gābâ* [1]

HAGAR [13]
Hagar, 2057, *hāgār* [11]
Hagar[s], 2023, *-āh* [2]

HAGGAI [11]
Haggai, 2516, *ḥaggay* [9]
Haggai, 10247, *ḥaggay* [2]

HAGGARD [2]
haggard, 1678, *galmûd* [1]
haggard, 1924, *dal[2]* [1]

HAGGEDOLIM [1]
Haggedolim, 2045, *hagg[e]dôlîm* [1]

HAGGI [2]
Haggi, 2515, *ḥaggî* [2]

HAGGIAH [1]
Haggiah, 2517, *ḥaggiyyâ* [1]

HAGGITE [1]
Haggite, 2515, *ḥaggî* [1]

HAGGITH [5]
Haggith, 2518, *ḥaggît* [5]

HAGRI [2]
Hagri, 2058, *hagrî* [2]

HAGRITE [1]
Hagrite, 2058, *hagrî* [1]

HAGRITES [6]
Hagrites, 2058, *hagrî* [4]
the Hagrites[s], 2157, *-hem* [2]

HAIL [24]
hail, 1352, *bārād* [21]
hail, 74+1352, *'eben+bārād* [1]
hail, 1351, *bārad* [1]
hail, 7943, *qeraḥ* [1]

HAILSTONES [6]
hailstones, 74+453, *'eben+'elgābîš* [3]
hailstones, 74+1352, *'eben+bārād* [1]
hailstones, 74, *'eben* [1]
hailstones, 1352, *bārād* [1]

HAILSTORM [2]
hailstorm, 1352, *bārād* [1]
hailstorm, 2443+1352, *zerem+bārād* [1]

HAIR [74]
hair, 8552, *śē'ār* [23]
hair, 8031, *rō'š[1]* [8]
goat hair, 6436, *'ēz* [7]
hair, *NIH/RPE* [3]
hair, 8553, *śa'[a]râ* [3]
hair, 10687, *ś[e]'ar* [3]
cut hair, 1662, *gālaḥ* [2]
goats hair, 3889+6436, *kābîr+'ēz* [2]
lost hair, 5307+8031, *māraṭ+rō'š[1]* [2]
hair, 7767, *q[e]wuṣṣôt* [2]
gray hair, 8484, *śêbâ* [2]
hair of head, 8553, *śa'[a]râ* [2]
hair, 1929+8031, *dallâ[1]+rō'š[1]* [1]
hair, 2417, *zāqān* [1]
keep hair trimmed, 4080+4080, *kāsam+kāsam* [1]
the hair[s], 4392, *-ām* [1]
well-dressed hair, 5126+5250, *ma'[a]śeh+miqšeh* [1]
pulled out hair, 5307, *māraṭ* [1]
hair, 5694, *nēzer* [1]
cut hair, 5938, *nāqap[2]* [1]
hair long, 7279, *pera'[2]* [1]
hair, 7279+8552, *pera'[2]+śē'ār* [1]
hair, 7492, *ṣîṣit* [1]
tear out hair, 7947, *qorḥâ* [1]
hair gray, 8484, *śêbâ* [1]
white hair, 8484, *śêbâ* [1]
garment of hair, 8552, *śē'ār* [1]

HAIRS [3]
hairs, 8553, *śa'[a]râ* [2]
gray hairs, 8484, *śêbâ* [1]

HAIRY [4]
hairy, 8537, *śā'îr[1]* [2]
hairy, 8552, *śē'ār* [2]

HAKILAH [3]
Hakilah, 2677, *ḥ[a]kîlâ* [3]

HAKKATAN [1]
Hakkatan, 2214, *haqqāṭān* [1]

HAKKOZ [5]
Hakkoz, 2212, *haqqôṣ* [5]

HAKUPHA [2]
Hakupha, 2979, *ḥ[a]qûpā'* [2]

HALAH [3]
Halah, 2712, *ḥ[a]laḥ* [3]

HALAK [2]
Halak, 2748, *ḥālāq[2]* [2]

HALF [103]
half, 2942, *ḥ[a]ṣî* [79]
half, 4734, *maḥ[a]ṣît* [13]
half, 4733, *meḥ[e]ṣâ* [2]
cut in half, 1439, *bātar* [1]
about a foot and a half, 1688, *gōmed* [1]
the other half of Manasseh[s], 2257, *-ô* [1]
seven and a half feet, 2822+928+2021+564, *ḥāmēš+b[e]+ha+'ammâ[1]* [1]
live out half, 2936, *ḥāṣâ* [1]
half as much, 4734, *maḥ[a]ṣît* [1]
half share, 4734, *maḥ[a]ṣît* [1]
four and a half feet, 8993+564, *šālōš+'ammâ[1]* [1]
half, 10584, *p[e]lag[2]* [1]

HALF-DISTRICT [4]
half-district, 2942+7135, *ḥ[a]ṣî+pelek[2]* [4]

HALF-TRIBE [24]
half-tribe, 2942+8657, *ḥ[a]ṣî+šēbeṭ* [18]
half-tribe, 2942+4751, *ḥ[a]ṣî+maṭṭeh* [5]
half-tribe, 2942, *ḥ[a]ṣî* [1]

HALFWAY [2]
halfway, 2942, *ḥ[a]ṣî* [2]

HALHUL [1]
Halhul, 2713, *ḥalḥûl* [1]

HALI [1]
Hali, 2718, *ḥ[a]lî[2]* [1]

HALL [17]
main hall, 2121, *hêkāl* [6]
hall, 1074, *bayit[1]* [4]
hall, 395, *'êlām* [3]
banquet hall, 1074+3516, *bayit[1]+yayin* [1]
main hall, 1074, *bayit[1]* [1]
hall, 4384, *liškâ* [1]
hall, 10103, *bayit* [1]

HALLOHESH [2]
Hallohesh, 2135, *hallôḥēš* [2]

HALT [4]
came to a halt, 6641, *'āmad* [2]
halt, 6641, *'āmad* [1]
halt, 8883, *šît[1]* [1]

HALTED [2]
halted, 3104, *ḥāśak* [1]
halted, 6641, *'āmad* [1]

HALTER [1]
halter, 5496, *meteg* [1]

HALVES [3]
halves, 7115, *pelaḥ* [2]
halves, 1440, *beter[1]* [1]

HAM [16]
Ham, 2769, *ḥām[3]* [15]
Ham, 2154, *hām[1]* [1]

HAMAN [44]
Haman, 2172, *hāmān* [43]
Haman[s], 2257, *-ô* [1]

HAMAN'S [5]
Haman's, 2172, *hāmān* [5]

HAMATH [24]
Hamath, 2828, *ḥ[a]māt* [24]

HAMATH ZOBAH [1]
Hamath Zobah, 2832, *ḥ[a]māt ṣôbâ* [1]

HAMATHITES [2]
Hamathites, 2833, *ḥ[a]mātî* [2]

HAMITES [2]
Hamites, *NIH/RPE* [1]
Hamites, 2769, *ḥām[3]* [1]

HAMMATH [2]
Hammath, 2829, *ḥammat[1]* [1]
Hammath, 2830, *ḥammat[2]* [1]

HAMMEDATHA [5]
Hammedatha, 2158, *hamm[e]dātā'* [5]

HAMMER [9]
hammer, 5216, *maqqebet[1]* [3]
hammer, 7079, *paṭṭîš* [3]
hammer, 2153, *halmût* [1]
hammer out, 5251+6913, *miqšâ[1]+'āśâ[1]* [1]
hammer, 6913+8393, *'āśâ[1]+riqqua'* [1]

HAMMERED [17]
hammered, 5251, *miqšâ[1]* [5]
hammered, 8822, *šāḥaṭ[2]* [5]
hammered out, 5251, *miqšâ[1]* [2]
hammered out, 8392, *rāqa'* [2]
hammered evenly, 3837, *yāšar* [1]
hammered, 4618, *môrād* [1]
hammered, 8392, *rāqa'* [1]

HAMMERS [1]
hammers, 5216, *maqqebet[1]* [1]

HAMMOLEKETH [1]
Hammoleketh, 2168, *hammōleket* [1]

HAMMON [2]
Hammon, 2785, *ḥammôn* [2]

HAMMOTH DOR [1]
Hammoth Dor, 2831, *ḥammōt dō'r* [1]

HAMMUEL [1]
Hammuel, 2781, *ḥammû'ēl* [1]

HAMON GOG [2]
Hamon Gog, 2163, *h^{a}môn gôg* [2]

HAMONAH [1]
Hamonah, 2164, *h^{a}mônâ* [1]

HAMOR [12]
Hamor, 2791, *ḥ^{a}môr^{3}* [12]

HAMPERED [1]
hampered, 7674, *ṣārar^{1}* [1]

HAMSTRING [1]
hamstring, 6828, *'āqar^{2}* [1]

HAMSTRUNG [4]
hamstrung, 6828, *'āqar^{2}* [4]

HAMUL [3]
Hamul, 2783, *ḥāmûl* [3]

HAMULITE [1]
Hamulite, 2784, *ḥāmûlî* [1]

HAMUTAL [3]
Hamutal, 2782, *ḥ^{a}mûṭal* [3]

HANAMEL [4]
Hanamel, 2856, *ḥ^{a}nam'ēl* [4]

HANAN [12]
Hanan, 2860, *ḥānān* [12]

HANANEL [4]
Hananel, 2861, *ḥ^{a}nan'ēl* [4]

HANANI [11]
Hanani, 2862, *ḥ^{a}nānî* [11]

HANANIAH [28]
Hananiah, 2863, *ḥ^{a}nanyâ* [24]
Hananiah, 2864, *ḥ^{a}nanyāhû* [3]
Hananiah, 10275, *ḥ^{a}nanyâ* [1]

HAND [719]
hand, 3338, *yād* [538]
hand, *NIH/RPE* [65]
hand over, 5989+928+3338, *nātan+b^{e}-+yād* [35]
hand, 4090, *kap* [32]
hand over, 5989, *nātan* [8]
hand, 10311, *yad* [7]
at hand, 995, *bô'* [2]
palm of hand, 4090, *kap* [2]
hand over, 6037+928+3338, *sāgar+b^{e}-+yād* [2]
hand over, 6037, *sāgar* [2]
fight hand to hand, 8471, *śāḥaq* [2]
hand, 10589+10311, *pas+yad* [2]
hand, 437, *'ekep* [1]
have on hand, 448+9393+3338, *'el+taḥat^{1}+yād* [1]
in hand, 907, *'ēt^{2}* [1]
with in hand, 928, *b^{e}-* [1]
hand over, 928+3338+4835, *b^{e}-+yād+mākar* [1]
hand over, 995, *bô'* [1]
breadth of hand, 2455, *zeret* [1]
hand, 3545, *yāmîn^{1}* [1]
have on hand, 3780+9393+3338, *yēš+taḥat^{1}+yād* [1]
hand over, 4481, *māgan* [1]
hand over, 5162+928+3338, *māṣā'+b^{e}-+yād* [1]
hand over, 5599, *nāgar* [1]
hand over to, 5989+928+3338, *nātan+b^{e}-+yād* [1]
surely hand over, 5989+5989+928+3338, *nātan+nātan+b^{e}-+yād* [1]
hand over, 6127, *sākar^{2}* [1]
at hand, 7940+4200+995, *qārôb+l^{e}-^{1}+bô'* [1]
at hand, 7940+995, *qārôb+bô'* [1]
close at hand, 7940, *qārôb* [1]
hand mill, 8160, *rēḥayim* [1]
hired hand, 8502, *śākîr* [1]
got the upper hand, 8948, *šālaṭ* [1]
hollow of hand, 9123, *šō'al* [1]

HANDBREADTH [8]
handbreadth, 3256, *ṭōpaḥ* [5]
handbreadth, 3255, *ṭepaḥ* [2]
handbreadth, 3257, *ṭapḥâ^{1}* [1]

HANDED [51]
handed over, 5989+928+3338, *nātan+b^{e}-+yād* [20]
be handed over, 5989+928+3338, *nātan+b^{e}-+yād* [7]
handed over, 928+3338+5989, *b^{e}-+yād+nātan* [3]
handed, 5162, *māṣā'* [3]
handed, 3338, *yād* [2]
certainly be handed over, 5989+5989+928+3338, *nātan+nātan+b^{e}-+yād* [2]
handed over, 5989, *nātan* [2]
handed over, 6037+928+3338, *sāgar+b^{e}-+yād* [2]
be handed over, 928+3338+5989, *b^{e}-+yād+nātan* [1]
handed, 4946+3338, *min+yād* [1]
handed over, 5162+928+3338, *māṣā'+b^{e}-+yād* [1]
handed over, 5796+928+3338, *nākar^{2}+b^{e}-+yād* [1]
be handed over, 5989, *nātan* [1]
been handed over, 5989+928+3338, *nātan+b^{e}-+yād* [1]
handed, 5989+928+3338, *nātan+b^{e}-+yād* [1]
be handed over, 10314+10089+10311, *y^{e}hab+b^{e}-+yad* [1]
be handed over, 10314, *y^{e}hab* [1]
handed over, 10314+10089+10311, *y^{e}hab+b^{e}-+yad* [1]

HANDFUL [8]
handful, 4850+4090, *m^{e}lō'+kap* [2]
take a handful, 7858+4850+7859, *qāmaṣ+m^{e}lō'+qōmeṣ* [2]
took a handful, 4848+4090, *mālē'^{1}+kap* [1]
take a handful, 7858, *qāmaṣ* [1]
handful, 7859, *qōmeṣ* [1]
handful, 9123, *šō'al* [1]

HANDFULS [4]
handfuls, 4850+2908, *m^{e}lō'+ḥōpen* [2]
two handfuls, 4850+2908, *m^{e}lō'+ḥōpen* [1]
handfuls, 9123, *šō'al* [1]

HANDING [2]
handing over, 5989+928+3338, *nātan+b^{e}-+yād* [1]
handing over, 6037+928+3338, *sāgar+b^{e}-+yād* [1]

HANDIWORK [1]
handiwork, 5126+3338, *ma'^{a}śeh+yād* [1]

HANDLE [9]
handle, 8990, *šālap* [2]
handle, 296, *'āḥaz^{1}* [1]
handle, 2005, *dārak* [1]
handle, 5896, *niṣṣāb^{2}* [1]
handle, 5951, *nāśā'* [1]
handle, 6885, *'ārak* [1]
handle, 6913, *'āśâ^{1}* [1]
handle, 9530, *tāpaś* [1]

HANDLED [1]
handled, 6913, *'āśâ^{1}* [1]

HANDLES [2]
handles, 4090, *kap* [1]
handles, 4190, *kātēp* [1]

HANDMILL [1]
handmill, 8160, *rēḥayim* [1]

HANDS [447]
hands, 3338, *yād* [349]
hands, 4090, *kap* [76]
hands, *NIH/RPE* [4]
hands, 4090+3338, *kap+yād* [3]
hands, 10311, *yad* [3]
hands, 2908, *ḥōpen* [2]
hands together, 4090+448+4090, *kap+'el+kap* [2]
hollow of hands, 2908, *ḥōpen* [1]
palms of hands, 4090, *kap* [1]
hands over, 5989, *nātan* [1]
scornfully claps hands, 6215, *sāpaq^{1}* [1]
pass into other hands, 6296, *'ābar^{1}* [1]
in hands, 6584, *'al^{2}* [1]
clasp hands, 8562, *śāpaq^{1}* [1]
strike hands in pledge, 9364, *tôq^{e}'îm* [1]

HANDSOME [11]
handsome, 2774, *ḥemed* [3]
handsome, 3637+5260, *yāpeh+mar'eh* [2]
handsome, 159, *'eder* [1]
handsome, 3202+5260, *ṭôb^{2}+mar'eh* [1]
handsome, 3202+9307, *ṭôb^{2}+tō'ar* [1]
handsome, 3202, *ṭôb^{2}* [1]
handsome appearance, 3637, *yāpeh* [1]
handsome, 3637, *yāpeh* [1]

HANDSOMELY [2]
reward handsomely, 3877+3877+4394, *kābēd^{1}+kābēd^{1}+m^{e}'ōd* [1]
reward handsomely, 3877+3877, *kābēd^{1}+kābēd^{1}* [1]

HANES [1]
Hanes, 2865, *ḥānēs* [1]

HANG [15]
hang, 9434, *tālâ* [5]
hang limp, 8332, *rāpâ^{1}* [3]
hang, 5989, *nātan* [2]
hang limp, 1927, *dālâ^{2}* [1]
hang poised, 5146, *miplāś* [1]
hang down, 6243, *sāraḥ^{1}* [1]
hang, 6243, *sāraḥ^{1}* [1]
hang limp, 8342, *rippāyôn* [1]

HANGED [10]
hanged, 9434, *tālâ* [8]
hanged himself, 2871, *ḥānaq* [1]
were hanged, 9434, *tālâ* [1]

HANGING [6]
hanging, 9434, *tālâ* [3]
hanging, 3983, *kālâ^{1}* [1]
was left hanging, 5989, *nātan* [1]
hanging on, 6584, *'al^{2}* [1]

HANGINGS [1]
hangings of linen, 4158, *karpas* [1]

HANGS [1]
hangs loose, 5759, *nāṭaš* [1]

HANNAH [14]
Hannah, 2839, *ḥannâ* [12]
Hannah^{s}, 2023, *-āh* [1]
Hannah^{s}, 2085, *hû'* [1]

HANNATHON [1]
Hannathon, 2872, *ḥannātôn* [1]

HANNIEL [2]
Hanniel, 2848, *ḥannî'ēl* [2]

HANOCH [6]
Hanoch, 2840, *ḥ^{a}nôk^{1}* [6]

HANOCHITE [1]
Hanochite, 2854, *ḥ^{a}nōkî* [1]

HANUN [13]
Hanun, 2842, *ḥānûn* [11]
Hanun, *NIH/RPE* [1]
Hanun^{s}, 2257, *-ô* [1]

HAPHARAIM [1]
Hapharaim, 2921, *ḥ^{a}pārayim* [1]

HAPPEN [28]
happen, 2118, *hāyâ* [16]
happen, 7936, *qārâ^{1}* [3]

happen, 6913, *ʿāśâ^{1}* [2]
happen, 10201, *h^{a}wâ* [2]
happen, *NIH/RPE* [1]
what might happen, 344, *ʾaḥ^{a}rît* [1]
lets happen, 628+4200+3338, *ʿānâ^{2}+l^{e}-^{1}+yād* [1]
happen, 995, *bôʾ* [1]
happen, 7925, *qārāʾ^{2}* [1]

HAPPENED [57]
happened, 2118, *hāyâ* [26]
happened, *NIH/RPE* [8]
happened, 995, *bôʾ* [5]
happened, 7925, *qārāʾ^{2}* [4]
happened, 7936, *qārâ^{1}* [3]
happened, 5162, *māṣāʾ* [2]
what happened, 1821, *dābār* [1]
that happened, 2021+1821+2021+465, *ha-+dābār+ha-+ʾēlleh* [1]
what happened^{s}, 2023, *-āh* [1]
what happened, 3907, *kōh* [1]
happened to, 5162, *māṣāʾ* [1]
something happened, 5247, *miqreh* [1]
happened, 5595, *nāgaʿ* [1]
happened to be, 7925+7936, *qārāʾ^{2}+qārâ^{1}* [1]
happened, 10413, *m^{e}ṭāʾ* [1]

HAPPENING [4]
happening, *NIH/RPE* [1]
happening, 2118, *hāyâ* [1]
happening^{s}, 4027, *kēn^{2}* [1]
was happening, 6913, *ʿāśâ^{1}* [1]

HAPPENS [13]
happens, *AIT* [3]
happens, *NIH/RPE* [2]
happens, 995, *bôʾ* [2]
happens, 6913, *ʿāśâ^{1}* [2]
what happens, 344, *ʾaḥ^{a}rît* [1]
happens, 2118, *hāyâ* [1]
happens, 5877, *nāpal* [1]
what usually happens, 7213, *p^{e}quddâ* [1]

HAPPIER [1]
happier, *NIH/RPE* [1]

HAPPINESS [4]
time of happiness, 245, *ʾôrâ^{1}* [1]
happiness, 3202, *ṭôb^{2}* [1]
bring happiness, 8523, *śāmaḥ* [1]
happiness, 8525, *śimḥâ* [1]

HAPPIZZEZ [1]
Happizzez, 2204, *happiṣṣēṣ* [1]

HAPPY [20]
happy, 8524, *śāmēaḥ* [5]
how happy, 897, *ʾašrê* [4]
happy, 8523, *śāmaḥ* [3]
happy, 3202, *ṭôb^{2}* [2]
call happy, 887, *ʾāšar^{2}* [1]
happy, 890, *ʾešer* [1]
happy, 891, *ʾōšer* [1]
happy, 897, *ʾašrê* [1]
happy, 8464, *śûś* [1]
happy, 8523+8525, *śāmaḥ+śimḥâ* [1]

HARA [1]
Hara, 2217, *hārāʾ* [1]

HARADAH [2]
Haradah, 3011, *ḥ^{a}rādâ^{2}* [2]

HARAN [19]
Haran, 3059, *ḥārān^{1}* [10]
Haran, 2237, *hārān* [7]
Haran, 3060, *ḥārān^{2}* [2]

HARARITE [5]
Hararite, 2240, *h^{a}rārî* [5]

HARASS [2]
harass, 7444, *ṣûr^{2}* [2]

HARBONA [2]
Harbona, 3002, *ḥarbônāʾ* [1]
Harbona, 3003, *ḥarbônâ* [1]

HARBOR [7]
harbor in, 928, *b^{e}-* [1]
harbor, 2118+6640+4222, *hāyâ+ʿim+lēbāb* [1]
harbor, 4328+928+7931, *lîn+b^{e}-+qereb* [1]
harbor, 4427, *mābôʾ* [1]
harbor, 4651, *mēzaḥ^{1}* [1]
harbor anger, 5757, *nāṭar^{1}* [1]
harbor, 8492, *śîm* [1]

HARBORED [1]
harbored, 2118+4200, *hāyâ+l^{e}-^{1}* [1]

HARBORS [1]
harbors, 8883, *šît^{1}* [1]

HARD [36]
hard, 2616, *ḥāzaq* [4]
hard, 7098, *pālāʾ* [3]
hard service, 7372, *ṣābāʾ^{2}* [3]
hard questions, 2648, *ḥîdâ* [2]
hard, 3668, *yāṣaq* [2]
hard, 6623, *ʿālam* [2]
hard, 7997, *qāšeh* [2]
hard, *NIH/RPE* [1]
hard, 419, *ʾêtān^{1}* [1]
hard, 1524, *gādôl* [1]
pressed hard after, 1815, *dābaq* [1]
pressed hard, 1815, *dābaq* [1]
driven hard, 1985, *dāpaq* [1]
become hard, 2461, *hābāʾ* [1]
worked hard, 2616, *ḥāzaq* [1]
hard, 2617, *ḥāzāq* [1]
hard rock, 2734, *ḥallāmîš* [1]
hard, 2734, *ḥallāmîš* [1]
hard, 3668+4200+2021+4607, *yāṣaq+l^{e}-^{1}+ha-+mûṣāq^{1}* [1]
hard pressed, 5601, *nāgaś* [1]
hard labor, 6026, *siblôt* [1]
hard, 6437, *ʿōz* [1]
hard work, 6776, *ʿeṣeb^{2}* [1]
hard, 7996, *qāšâ* [1]
as hard as flint, 9032, *šāmîr^{2}* [1]

HARDEN [7]
harden, 2616, *ḥāzaq* [3]
harden, 7996, *qāšâ* [2]
harden, 3877, *kābēd^{1}* [1]
harden, 7998, *qāšaḥ* [1]

HARDENED [15]
hardened, 2616, *ḥāzaq* [6]
hardened, 3877, *kābēd^{1}* [4]
hardened, 599, *ʾāmēṣ* [1]
hardened, 2617+5195, *ḥāzāq+mēṣaḥ* [1]
hardened, 5195+2617, *mēṣaḥ+ḥāzāq* [1]
hardened rebels, 6073+6253, *sûr^{1}+sārar^{1}* [1]
hardened, 10772, *t^{e}qip* [1]

HARDENS [1]
hardens, 7996, *qāšâ* [1]

HARDER [3]
made harder, 2616, *ḥāzaq* [1]
harder, 2617, *ḥāzāq* [1]
harder, 3877, *kābēd^{1}* [1]

HARDEST [1]
hardest stone, 9032, *šāmîr^{2}* [1]

HARDHEARTED [1]
hardhearted, 599+906+4222, *ʾāmēṣ+ʾēt^{1}+lēbāb* [1]

HARDLY [3]
hardly, 4202, *lōʾ* [2]
can hardly breathe, 5972+4202+8636, *n^{e}šāmâ+lōʾ+šāʾar* [1]

HARDSHIP [7]
hardship, 9430, *t^{e}lāʾâ* [2]
hardship, *NIH/RPE* [1]
hardship, 224, *ʾāwen^{1}* [1]
hardship, 6715, *ʿ^{o}nî* [1]
hardship, 7650, *ṣārâ^{1}* [1]
hardship, 7996, *qāšâ* [1]

HARDSHIPS [5]
hardships, 9430, *t^{e}lāʾâ* [2]
hardships endured, 6700, *ʿānâ^{2}* [1]
shared hardships, 6700+928+889+6700, *ʿānâ^{2}+b^{e}-+ʾ^{a}šer+ʿānâ^{2}* [1]
hardships, 8273, *raʿ^{1}* [1]

HAREM [8]
harem, 1074+851, *bayit^{1}+ʾiššâ* [5]
harem, 851, *ʾiššâ* [2]
harem, 8721+2256+8721, *šiddâ+w^{e}-+šiddâ* [1]

HAREPH [1]
Hareph, 3073, *ḥārēp* [1]

HARHAIAH [1]
Harhaiah, 3015, *ḥarh^{a}yâ* [1]

HARHAS [1]
Harhas, 3030, *ḥarḥas* [1]

HARHUR [2]
Harhur, 3028, *ḥarḥûr* [2]

HARIM [10]
Harim, 3053, *ḥārim* [10]

HARIM'S [1]
Harim's, 3053, *ḥārim* [1]

HARIPH [2]
Hariph, 3040, *ḥārîp* [2]

HARLOT [2]
harlot, 2390, *zōnâ* [2]

HARLOTS [1]
harlots, 2390, *zōnâ* [1]

HARM [57]
harm, 8288, *rāʿâ^{3}* [26]
harm, 8273, *raʿ^{1}* [8]
harm, 8317, *rāʿaʿ^{1}* [6]
harm, 656, *ʾāsôn* [3]
do harm, 8317, *rāʿaʿ^{1}* [3]
harm, 6913+8273, *ʿāśâ^{1}+raʿ^{1}* [2]
harm, 6913+8288, *ʿāśâ^{1}+rāʿâ^{3}* [2]
harm, *NIH/RPE* [1]
harm, 224, *ʾāwen^{1}* [1]
harm, 1821+8273, *dābār+raʿ^{1}* [1]
harm, 5782, *nākâ* [1]
not harm, 5927+4946, *nāqâ+min* [1]
harm, 7212, *pāqad* [1]
suffers harm, 8317, *rāʿaʿ^{1}* [1]

HARMED [2]
harmed, 7003, *pāgaʿ* [1]
harmed, 10715, *š^{e}lēṭ* [1]

HARMFUL [2]
harmful, 1184, *b^{e}laʿ^{2}* [1]
harmful, 8273, *raʿ^{1}* [1]

HARMING [3]
harming, *NIH/RPE* [1]
harming, 8288, *rāʿâ^{3}* [1]
harming, 8317, *rāʿaʿ^{1}* [1]

HARMLESS [2]
harmless rash, 993, *bōhaq* [1]
harmless soul, 5929+2855, *nāqî+ḥinnām* [1]

HARMON [1]
Harmon, 2236, *harmôn* [1]

HARMONY [1]
harmony, 6783+8934, *ʿēṣâ^{1}+šālôm* [1]

HARMS [1]
harms, 2803, *ḥāmas^{1}* [1]

HARNEPHER [1]
Harnepher, 3062, *ḥarneper* [1]

HARNESS [4]
harness, 673, *ʾāsar* [1]
harness, 6310, *ʿ^{a}bōt* [1]
harness, 7537, *ṣāmad* [1]
harness, 8412, *rātam* [1]

HARNESSED [1]
harnessed to, 928, *b[e]-* [1]

HAROD [1]
Harod, 3008, *ḥ[a]rōd[1]* [1]

HARODITE [2]
Harodite, 3012, *ḥ[a]rōdî* [2]

HAROEH [1]
Haroeh, 2218, *hārō'eh* [1]

HARORITE [1]
Harorite, 2229, *h[a]rôrî* [1]

HAROSHETH HAGGOYIM [3]
Harosheth Haggoyim, 3099, *ḥ[a]rōšet haggôyim* [3]

HARP [30]
harp, 4036, *kinnôr* [21]
harp, 10590, *p[e]santērîn* [4]
play the harp, 5594, *nāgan* [2]
playing the harp, 5594+928+3338, *nāgan+b[e]-+yād* [2]
harp, 5575, *nēbel[2]* [1]

HARPIST [2]
harpist, 5594, *nāgan* [2]

HARPOONS [1]
harpoons, 8496, *śukkâ* [1]

HARPS [23]
harps, 4036, *kinnôr* [19]
harps, 5575, *nēbel[2]* [4]

HARROWING [1]
harrowing, 8440, *śādad* [1]

HARSH [8]
harsh, 7997, *qāšeh* [2]
harsh, 1524, *gādôl* [1]
harsh, 2616, *ḥāzaq* [1]
harsh, 6776, *'eṣeb[2]* [1]
harsh, 8044, *rōb* [1]
harsh treatment, 9500, *ta'alûlîm* [1]
harsh, 10280, *ḥ[a]ṣap* [1]

HARSHA [2]
Harsha, 3095, *ḥaršā'* [2]

HARSHLY [11]
harshly, 7997, *qāšeh* [5]
harshly, 928+2622, *b[e]-+ḥozqâ* [1]
harshly, 6434, *'az* [1]
dealt harshly, 6618, *'ālal[1]* [1]
treated harshly, 6618, *'ālal[1]* [1]
harshly, 7996, *qāšâ* [1]
treats harshly, 7998, *qāšaḥ* [1]

HARUM [1]
Harum, 2227, *hārûm* [1]

HARUMAPH [1]
Harumaph, 3018, *ḥ[a]rûmap* [1]

HARUPHITE [1]
Haruphite, 3020, *ḥ[a]rûpî* [1]

HARUZ [1]
Haruz, 3027, *ḥārûṣ[7]* [1]

HARVEST [72]
harvest, 7907, *qāṣîr[1]* [37]
harvest, 9311, *t[e]bû'â* [11]
harvest, 665, *'āsap* [5]
grape harvest, 1292, *bāṣîr[1]* [4]
harvest, 1305, *bāṣar[1]* [2]
harvest, 3292, *y[e]bûl* [2]
harvest time, 7907, *qāṣîr[1]* [2]
harvest, *NIH/RPE* [1]
harvest, 658, *'āsîp* [1]
harvest of fruit, 668, *'ōsep* [1]
full grape harvest, 1292, *bāṣîr[1]* [1]
harvest grapes, 1305, *bāṣar[1]* [1]
last year's harvest, 3824+3823, *yāšān+yāšēn[2]* [1]
harvest, 7811, *qayiṣ* [1]
harvest, 7917, *qāṣar[1]* [1]
firstfruits of harvest, 8040, *rē'šît* [1]

HARVESTED [4]
harvested, 665, *'āsap* [1]
is harvested, 665, *'āsap* [1]
harvested, 995, *bô'* [1]
harvested, 1600, *gēz* [1]

HARVESTERS [5]
harvesters, 7917, *qāṣar[1]* [5]

HARVESTING [5]
harvesting, 7917+7907, *qāṣar[1]+qāṣîr[1]* [2]
harvesting grain, 7907, *qāṣîr[1]* [1]
harvesting, 7917, *qāṣar[1]* [1]
harvesting crops, 9311, *t[e]bû'â* [1]

HARVESTS [5]
harvests, 7907, *qāṣîr[1]* [3]
harvests, 3292, *y[e]bûl* [1]
harvests, 7917, *qāṣar[1]* [1]

HAS [1716]
has, *AIT* [1436]
has, *NIH/RPE* [145]
has, 4200, *l[e]-[1]* [50]
has, 928, *b[e]-* [15]
has, 2118, *hāyâ* [11]
has, 2118+4200, *hāyâ+l[e]-[1]* [6]
has, 2118+928, *hāyâ+b[e]-* [5]
has, 3528, *yālad* [4]
has compassion, 8163, *rāḥam* [4]
has, 3780+928, *yēš+b[e]-* [3]
has, 907, *'ēt[2]* [2]
has, 3655, *yāṣā'* [2]
has, 3780, *yēš* [2]
has enough, 8425, *śāba'* [2]
has sexual relations with, 8886+6640, *šākab+'im* [2]
has twin, 9298, *tā'am* [2]
has, 928+3338, *b[e]-+yād* [1]
has, 995, *bô'* [1]
has full confidence, 1053+4213, *bāṭaḥ[1]+lēb* [1]
has a husband, 1249, *ba'al[1]* [1]
has, 1251, *ba'al[1]* [1]
has the right to do it[s], 1457, *gā'al[1]* [1]
has sexual relations with, 1655+906+6872, *gālâ+'ēt[1]+'erwâ* [1]
has worries, 1793, *dā'ag* [1]
has, 2118+6640, *hāyâ+'im* [1]
has a discharge, 2307+2308, *zûb+zôb* [1]
has knowledge, 3359+1981, *yāda'+da'at[1]* [1]
has son, 3528, *yālad* [1]
has to do with, 4200, *l[e]-[1]* [1]
has in mind, 4222+3108, *lēbāb+ḥāšab* [1]
has, 5162+4200, *māṣā'+l[e]-[1]* [1]
has right, 5440, *māšal[2]* [1]
all he has[s], 5647, *-nû[2]* [1]
has inherit, 5706, *nāḥal* [1]
has sexual relations, 5989+8888, *nātan+š[e]kōbet* [1]
has, 6584, *'al[2]* [1]
has, 6640, *'im* [1]
has an infectious skin disease, 7665, *ṣāra'* [1]
has a claim against, 7709, *qādam* [1]
has effect, 7756, *qûm* [1]
has regard for, 8505, *śākal[1]* [1]

HASADIAH [1]
Hasadiah, 2878, *ḥ[a]sadyâ* [1]

HASHABIAH [15]
Hashabiah, 3116, *ḥ[a]šabyâ* [12]
Hashabiah, 3117, *ḥ[a]šabyāhû* [3]

HASHABNAH [1]
Hashabnah, 3118, *ḥ[a]šabnâ* [1]

HASHABNEIAH [2]
Hashabneiah, 3119, *ḥ[a]šabn[e]yâ* [2]

HASHBADDANAH [1]
Hashbaddanah, 3111, *ḥašbaddānâ* [1]

HASHEM [1]
Hashem, 2244, *hāšēm* [1]

HASHMONAH [2]
Hashmonah, 3135, *ḥašmōnâ* [2]

HASHUBAH [1]
Hashubah, 3112, *ḥ[a]šubâ* [1]

HASHUM [5]
Hashum, 3130, *ḥāšum* [5]

HASN'T [5]
hasn't, 4202, *lō'* [5]

HASRAH [1]
Hasrah, 2897, *ḥasrâ* [1]

HASSENAAH [1]
Hassenaah, 2189, *hass[e]nā'â* [1]

HASSENUAH [2]
Hassenuah, 2190, *hass[e]nu'â* [2]

HASSHUB [5]
Hasshub, 3121, *ḥaššûb* [5]

HASSOPHERETH [1]
Hassophereth, 2191, *hassōperet* [1]

HASTE [7]
haste, 2906, *ḥippāzôn* [3]
haste, 237, *'ûṣ* [1]
in haste, 237, *'ûṣ* [1]
flee in haste, 4960+5674, *mānôs+nûs* [1]
flee in haste, 5610+5610, *nādad+nādad* [1]

HASTEN [5]
hasten, 2590, *ḥûš[1]* [2]
hasten, *NIH/RPE* [1]
hasten, 4554, *māhar[1]* [1]
hasten, 8132, *rûṣ* [1]

HASTILY [1]
hastily, 4554, *māhar[1]* [1]

HASTY [2]
hasty, 237+928+8079, *'ûṣ+b[e]-+regel* [1]
hasty, 4554, *māhar[1]* [1]

HASUPHA [2]
Hasupha, 3102, *ḥ[a]śûpā'* [2]

HATCH [2]
hatch, 1324, *bāqa'* [2]

HATCHED [1]
is hatched, 1324, *bāqa'* [1]

HATCHES [1]
hatches eggs, 1842, *dāgar* [1]

HATCHETS [1]
hatchets, 3965, *kêlappôt* [1]

HATE [63]
hate, 8533, *śānē'* [59]
hate, 8534, *śin'â* [2]
hate, *NIH/RPE* [1]
hate, 8534+8533, *śin'â+śānē'* [1]

HATED [19]
hated, 8533, *śānē'* [16]
is hated, 8533, *śānē'* [1]
thoroughly hated, 8533+8533, *śānē'+śānē'* [1]
hated, 8534, *śin'â* [1]

HATES [15]
hates, 8533, *śānē'* [14]
hates, 8534, *śin'â* [1]

HATHACH [3]
Hathach, 2251, *h[a]tāk* [3]

HATHATH [1]
Hathath, 3171, *ḥ[a]tat[2]* [1]

HATIPHA [2]
Hatipha, 2640, *ḥ[a]ṭîpā'* [2]

HATITA [2]
Hatita, 2638, *ḥ[a]ṭîṭā'* [2]

HATRED [9]
hatred, 8534, śinʾâ [8]
have hatred, 8534+8533, śinʾâ+śānēʾ [1]

HATTIL [2]
Hattil, 2639, ḥaṭṭîl [2]

HATTUSH [5]
Hattush, 2637, ḥaṭṭûš [5]

HAUGHTINESS [1]
haughtiness, 8124, rûm^{2} [1]

HAUGHTY [15]
haughty, 8123, rûm^{1} [5]
haughty, 1467, gābah [3]
haughty, 8124, rûm^{2} [2]
haughty, 1468, gābēah [1]
haughty, 1469, gābōah [1]
haughty, 1470, gōbah [1]
haughty, 2294, zēd [1]
haughty, 5294, mārôm [1]

HAUL [2]
haul down, 3718, yārad [1]
haul up, 6590, ʿālâ [1]

HAUNT [6]
haunt, 5061, māʿôn^{2} [4]
haunt, 5226, māqôm [1]
haunt, 5659, nāweh^{1} [1]

HAUNTS [3]
mountain haunts, 2215, har [1]
haunts, 5659, nāweh^{1} [1]
haunts, 5661, nāwâ^{3} [1]

HAURAN [2]
Hauran, 2588, ḥawrān [2]

HAVE [3123]
have, *AIT* [2419]
have, *NIH/RPE* [225]
have, 4200, l^{e}-^{1} [94]
have, 2118+4200, hāyâ+l^{e}-^{1} [44]
have, 2118, hāyâ [16]
have compassion, 8163, rāḥam [15]
have mercy, 2858, ḥānan^{1} [14]
have, 928, b^{e}- [12]
have, 3780+4200, yēš+l^{e}-^{1} [12]
have sexual relations with, 6872+1655, ʿerwâ+gālâ [10]
have, 907, ʾēt^{2} [8]
have, 3528, yālad [7]
fail to have, 4162+4200, kārat+l^{e}-^{1} [7]
have to do with, 4200, l^{e}-^{1} [5]
have, 928+3338, b^{e}+yād [4]
have understanding, 1067, bîn [4]
have, 3780, yēš [4]
have, 4200+2118, l^{e}-^{1}+hāyâ [4]
have, 6584, ʿal^{2} [4]
have stand, 6641, ʿāmad [4]
have regard for, 8011, rāʾâ^{1} [4]
have sexual relations, 1655+6872, gālâ+ʿerwâ [3]
have compassion, 5714, nāḥam [3]
have, 6640, ʿim [3]
have enough, 8425, śābaʿ [3]
have, 10089, b^{e}- [3]
have faith, 586, ʾāman^{1} [2]
have shame at all, 1017+1017, bôš^{1}+bôš^{1} [2]
have relations with, 1655+6872, gālâ+ʿerwâ [2]
have pity, 2798, ḥāmal [2]
have pity, 2858, ḥānan^{1} [2]
have sex with, 3359, yādaʿ [2]
have, 3359, yādaʿ [2]
have children, 3528, yālad [2]
have respect for, 3700+928+6524, yāqar+b^{e}-+ʿayin^{1} [2]
have fear, 3707, yārēʾ^{1} [2]
have reverence, 3707, yārēʾ^{1} [2]
have, 3780+907, yēš+ʾēt^{2} [2]
have in common, 4200, l^{e}-^{1} [2]
have enough, 5162, māṣāʾ [2]
have regard for, 5564, nābaṭ [2]
have cut down, 5877, nāpal [2]
have in common, 7008, pāgaš [2]
have success, 7503, ṣālaḥ^{2} [2]
have sexual relations with, 8061, rābaʿ^{1} [2]
have mercy, 8163, rāḥam [2]
have abundant, 8425, śābaʿ [2]
have request to make, 8629+8626, š^{e}ʾēlâ+šāʾal [2]
have left, 8636, šāʾar [2]
have a home, 8905+9393, šākan+taḥat^{1} [2]
have charge of, 9068+5466, šāmar+mišmeret [2]
have drink, 9197, šāqâ [2]
have peace, 9200, šāqaṭ [2]
have nowhere, 6+4946, ʾābad+min [1]
have no, 6+4946, ʾābad+min [1]
would have, 14, ʾābâ [1]
have brother, 278, ʾāḥ^{2} [1]
have^{s}, 430, ʾākal [1]
have food, 430, ʾākal [1]
have plenty to eat, 430+430, ʾākal+ʾākal [1]
have on hand, 448+9393+3338, ʾel+taḥat^{1}+yād [1]
have, 448, ʾel [1]
have assurance, 586, ʾāman^{1} [1]
what have to say, 614, ʾimrâ [1]
have long, 799, ʾārak [1]
have a claim on, 928, b^{e}- [1]
have, 928+5055, b^{e}-+mēʿeh [1]
have, 928+7023, b^{e}-+peh [1]
have, 995, bôʾ [1]
have concern, 1067+1981, bîn+daʿat^{1} [1]
insights have, 1067, bîn [1]
have joy, 1158, bālag [1]
those who have, 1251, baʿal^{1} [1]
have sexual relations with, 1655+6872, gālâ+ʿerwâ [1]
what have to say, 1821, dābār [1]
have knowledge, 1981+3359, daʿat^{1}+yādaʿ [1]
have, 2118+1068, hāyâ+bayin [1]
have, 2118+928, hāyâ+b^{e}- [1]
have go, 2143, hālak [1]
be able to have children, 2445+2446, zāraʿ+zeraʿ [1]
have descendants, 2445, zāraʿ [1]
have saddled, 2502, ḥābaš [1]
have pity, 2571, ḥûs [1]
have strength, 2616, ḥāzaq [1]
dreams encourage to have, 2706+2731, ḥ^{a}lôm+ḥālam^{2} [1]
have a refuge, 2879, ḥāsâ [1]
have too little, 2893, ḥāsēr^{1} [1]
have no, 2894, ḥāsēr^{2} [1]
have delight, 2911, ḥāpēṣ^{1} [1]
have desire, 2911, ḥāpēṣ^{1} [1]
have pleasure, 2911, ḥāpēṣ [1]
must have fought, 2991+2991, ḥārēb^{2}+ḥārēb^{2} [1]
have more and more, 3013, ḥārâ^{1} [1]
have concern for, 3359, yādaʿ [1]
have to do with, 3359, yādaʿ [1]
have any right, 3512, yāṭab [1]
have a right, 3512, yāṭab [1]
have time, 3523+4538, yākōl+māhah [1]
have a child, 3528, yālad [1]
have a son, 3528, yālad [1]
have value, 3603, yāʿal [1]
have leave, 3655, yāṣāʾ [1]
have on hand, 3780+9393+3338, yēš+taḥat^{1}+yād [1]
have, 3780+928, yēš+b^{e}- [1]
have, 3780+9393+3338, yēš+taḥat^{1}+yād [1]
have a home, 3782, yāšab [1]
have left over, 3855, yātar [1]
might well have, 3869+5071, k^{e}-+m^{e}ʿaṭ [1]
have ready, 3922, kûn^{1} [1]
fail to have, 4200+4162, l^{e}-^{1}+kārat [1]
have part, 4200, l^{e}-^{1} [1]
have right, 4200, l^{e}-^{1} [1]
have the right, 4200, l^{e}-^{1} [1]
have to do with, 4200+2256+4200, l^{e}-^{1}+w^{e}-+l^{e}-^{1} [1]
have, 4200+889, l^{e}-^{1}+ʾ^{a}šer [1]
let have, 4358, lāʿaṭ [1]
have come, 4374, lāqaḥ [1]
have, 4374, lāqaḥ [1]
what right have you, 4537+4200+3870, mâ+l^{e}-^{1}+-kā [1]
plans have, 4742+3108, maḥ^{a}šābâ+ḥāšab [1]
have fill, 4848, mālēʾ^{1} [1]
have, 5162+928+3338, māṣāʾ+b^{e}-+yād [1]
have, 5162, māṣāʾ [1]
have regard for, 5564+4200, nābaṭ+l^{e}-^{1} [1]
have rest, 5663, nûaḥ^{1} [1]
have inheritance, 5706+5709, nāḥal+naḥ^{a}lâ^{1} [1]
have inheritance, 5706, nāḥal [1]
have pity, 5714, nāḥam [1]
have flogged, 5782, nākâ [1]
have fall, 5877, nāpal [1]
have a right to get even, 5927, nāqâ [1]
have respect for, 5951, nāśāʾ [1]
let have, 5989, nātan [1]
have sexual relations, 5989+8888+4200+2446, nātan+š^{e}kōbet+l^{e}-^{1}+zeraʿ [1]
have sexual relations, 5989+8888, nātan+š^{e}kōbet [1]
have, 5989+4200, nātan+l^{e}-^{1} [1]
have, 5989, nātan [1]
have something to eat, 6184, sāʿad [1]
have no, 6259+4946+6524, sātar+min+ʿayin^{1} [1]
have no limit, 6296, ʿābar^{1} [1]
have shave, 6296+9509, ʿābar^{1}+taʿar [1]
have sounded, 6296, ʿābar^{1} [1]
have too much, 6369, ʿādap [1]
have testify, 6386, ʿûd^{1} [1]
have the transaction witnessed, 6386+6332, ʿûd^{1}+ʿēd [1]
have young, 6402, ʿûl^{2} [1]
have, 6584+2118, ʿal^{2}+hāyâ [1]
have, 6590, ʿālâ [1]
have answer, 6699, ʿānâ^{1} [1]
have say, 6699+2750, ʿānâ^{1}+ḥēleq^{2} [1]
dishonor by to have sexual relations, 6872+1655, ʿerwâ+gālâ [1]
have^{s}, 6913, ʿāśâ^{1} [1]
have, 6913, ʿāśâ^{1} [1]
have, 6953, ʿaštût [1]
grapes that have fallen, 7261, pereṭ [1]
have burial, 7690+7699, q^{e}bûrâ+qābar [1]
have purified, 7727, qādaš [1]
what have to say, 7754, qôl [1]
have, 7756, qûm [1]
have, 7871, qinyān [1]
have scraped, 7909, qāṣaʿ^{1} [1]
have come near, 7928, qārab [1]
have sexual relations, 8011+906+6872, rāʾâ^{1}+ʾēt^{1}+ʿerwâ [1]
have many, 8049, rābâ^{1} [1]
have lie down, 8069, rābaṣ [1]
have great compassion, 8163+8163, rāḥam+rāḥam [1]
have nothing to do, 8178, rāḥaq [1]
have no compassion, 8317+6524, rāʿaʿ^{1}+ʿayin^{1} [1]
have fill, 8425, śābaʿ [1]
have more than enough, 8425, śābaʿ [1]
have plenty, 8425, śābaʿ [1]
have to spare, 8425, śābaʿ [1]
have too much, 8425, śābaʿ [1]
have insight, 8505, śākal^{1} [1]
have hatred, 8534+8533, śinʾâ+śānēʾ [1]
have request, 8626+8629, šāʾal+š^{e}ʾēlâ [1]
have rest, 8697, šābat^{1} [1]
have^{s}, 8697, šābat^{1} [1]
have, 8883, šît^{1} [1]
have fill, 8910, šākar [1]
have peace, 8922, šālâ^{1} [1]
have control, 8948, šālaṭ [1]
have^{s}, 9048, šāmaʿ [1]
have charge of, 9068, šāmar [1]
have regard, 9120, šāʿâ [1]
have an eye for, 9193, šāqad^{1} [1]
have a drink, 9272, šātâ^{2} [1]
have get ready, 9462, tāmam [1]
have, 10029+10089, ʾîtay+b^{e}- [1]
have, 10201, h^{a}wâ [1]
have occasion, 10484, n^{e}pal [1]

HAVEN [2]
haven, 2572, ḥôp [1]
haven, 4685, māḥôz [1]

HAVEN'T [11]
haven't, 4202, lō' [11]

HAVILAH [7]
Havilah, 2564, ḥᵃwîlâ [7]

HAVING [26]
having, AIT [12]
having, NIH/RPE [4]
having children, 3528, yālad [3]
having, 2118+4200, hāyâ+lᵉ-[1] [1]
having salvation, 3828, yāša' [1]
having, 4200, lᵉ-[1] [1]
having set out, 5023, massa' [1]
dishonor by having sexual relations with, 6872+1655, 'erwâ+gālâ [1]
having charge, 7213, pᵉquddâ [1]
having great difficulty, 7996, qāšâ [1]

HAVOC [2]
work havoc, 2472, ḥābal[2] [1]
havoc, 8719, šōd[2] [1]

HAVVOTH JAIR [4]
Havvoth Jair, 2596, ḥawwōt yā'îr [4]

HAWK [3]
hawk, 5891, nēṣ[2] [3]

HAY [1]
hay, 2945, ḥāṣîr[1] [1]

HAZAEL [24]
Hazael, 2599, ḥᵃzā'ēl [21]
Hazael, NIH/RPE [3]

HAZAIAH [1]
Hazaiah, 2610, ḥᵃzāyâ [1]

HAZAR ADDAR [1]
Hazar Addar, 2960, ḥᵃṣar-'addār [1]

HAZAR ENAN [4]
Hazar Enan, 2966, ḥᵃṣar 'ênān [3]
Hazar Enan, 2965, ḥᵃṣar 'ênôn [1]

HAZAR GADDAH [1]
Hazar Gaddah, 2961, ḥᵃṣar gaddâ [1]

HAZAR SHUAL [4]
Hazar Shual, 2967, ḥᵃṣar šû'āl [4]

HAZAR SUSAH [1]
Hazar Susah, 2963, ḥᵃṣar sûsâ [1]

HAZAR SUSIM [1]
Hazar Susim, 2964, ḥᵃṣar sûsîm [1]

HAZARMAVETH [2]
Hazarmaveth, 2975, ḥᵃṣarmāwet [2]

HAZAZON TAMAR [2]
Hazazon Tamar, 2954, ḥaṣᵉṣôn tāmār [2]

HAZER HATTICON [1]
Hazer Hatticon, 2962, ḥāṣēr hattîkôn [1]

HAZEROTH [5]
Hazeroth, 2972, ḥᵃṣērôt [5]

HAZIEL [1]
Haziel, 2609, ḥᵃzî'ēl [1]

HAZO [1]
Hazo, 2605, ḥᵃzô [1]

HAZOR [18]
Hazor, 2937, ḥāṣôr[1] [15]
Hazor, 2938, ḥāṣôr[2] [3]

HAZOR HADATTAH [1]
Hazor Hadattah, 2939, ḥāṣôr ḥᵃdattâ [1]

HAZZELELPONI [1]
Hazzelelponi, 2209, haṣṣᵉlelpônî [1]

HAZZOBEBAH [1]
Hazzobebah, 2206, haṣṣōbēbâ [1]

HE [6860]*
he, AIT [5007]
he, 2257, -ô [548]
he, 2085, hû' [438]
he, NIH/RPE [353]
he[s], 2021, ha- [44]
he, 5647, -nû[2] [24]
he, 2084, -hû [20]
he, 2296, zeh [9]
he, 5883+2257, nepeš+-ô [7]
he, 10192, -ēh [7]
he[s], 889, 'ᵃšer [6]
he[s], 2021+408, ha+'îš[1] [6]
he[s], 408, 'îš[1] [5]
he, 10200, hû' [5]
he, 10204, -hî [5]
he, 4392, -ām [4]
he[s], 2021+5883+2021+2085, ha-+nepeš+ha-+hû' [2]
he, 3338+2257, yād+-ô [2]
he[s], 8611, ša- [2]
he[s], 1505, geber[1] [1]
he alone, 2085, hû' [1]
he himself, 2085, hû' [1]
he himself, 2257, -ô [1]
he, 4564, -mô [1]
he[s], 5883, nepeš [1]

HE'S [4]
he's, NIH/RPE [2]
he's, AIT [1]
he's, 2296, zeh [1]

HE-GOAT [1]
he-goat, 9411, tayiš [1]

HEAD [274]
head, 8031, rō'š[1] [217]
head, NIH/RPE [6]
head, AIT [5]
near head, 5265, mᵉra'ᵃšôt [4]
gray head, 8484, śêbâ [5]
head, 10646, rē'š [4]
top of head, 7721, qodqōd [3]
head, 4946+8900+2256+5087+2025, min+šᵉkem[1]+wᵉ+ma'al[2]+-â[2] [2]
at head, 5265, mᵉra'ᵃšôt [2]
under head, 5265, mᵉra'ᵃšôt [2]
head, 7721, qodqōd [2]
head, 7949, qāraḥat [2]
hair of head, 8553, śa'ᵃrâ [2]
head, 52, 'abbîr [1]
shave head in mourning, 995+7947, bô'+qorḥâ [1]
head, 1366, barzel [1]
hold head high, 1448, gā'â [1]
head, 1653, gulgōlet [1]
at the head of, 4200+7156, lᵉ-[1]+pāneh [1]
head, 4213, lēb [1]
by head, 5265, mᵉra'ᵃšôt [1]
shake head in scorn, 5653, nûd [1]
adorns head, 6996, pᵉ'ēr [1]
head, 7156, pāneh [1]
head, 7418, ṣawwā'r [1]
head, 7542, ṣemaḥ [1]
crown of head, 7721, qodqōd [1]
shave head, 7942, qāraḥ [1]
bald head, 7949, qāraḥat [1]
head, 8569, śar [1]
bowed head, 8820, šāḥaḥ [1]

HEADBAND [2]
headband, 710, 'ᵃpēr [2]

HEADBANDS [5]
headbands, 4457, migbā'â [3]
headbands, 6996+4457, pᵉ'ēr+migbā'â [1]
headbands, 8667, šābîs [1]

HEADDRESSES [1]
headdresses, 6996, pᵉ'ēr [1]

HEADED [6]
headed, NIH/RPE [1]
headed, 26, 'ābîb [1]
headed, 3655, yāṣā' [1]
headed, 6590, 'ālâ [1]
headed for, 8492+7156, śîm+pāneh [1]
headed, 9305, tā'ar[1] [1]

HEADLONG [3]
flees headlong, 1368+1368, bāraḥ[1]+bāraḥ[1] [1]
headlong flight, 2905, ḥāpaz [1]
gallops headlong, 7055, pûš[1] [1]

HEADS [155]
heads, 8031, rō'š[1] [124]
heads of grain, 8672, šibbōlet[1] [8]
heads, NIH/RPE [7]
heads, 8672, šibbōlet[1] [3]
heads, 10646, rē'š [2]
heads, 26, 'ābîb [1]
front of heads, 1068+6524, bayin+'ayin[1] [1]
heads of new grain, 4152, karmel[4] [1]
heads, 5265, mᵉra'ᵃšôt [1]
shake heads in scorn, 5653, nûd [1]
bowed heads, 7702, qādad [1]
heads, 7721, qodqōd [1]
with heads held high, 7758, qômᵉmiyyût [1]
shave heads, 7942+1605, qāraḥ+gāzaz [1]
shave heads, 7942+7947, qāraḥ+qorḥâ [1]
heads, 8569, śar [1]

HEADWATERS [1]
headwaters, 8031, rō'š[1] [1]

HEAL [23]
heal, 8324, rāpā'[1] [21]
heal, 1564, gāhâ [1]
heal, 3911, kēhâ [1]

HEALED [19]
healed, 8324, rāpā'[1] [10]
be healed, 8324, rāpā'[1] [4]
healed, 2649, ḥāyâ [1]
healed, 5340, marpē'[1] [1]
are healed, 8324, rāpā'[1] [1]
been healed, 8324, rāpā'[1] [1]
see that is completely healed, 8324+8324, rāpā'[1]+rāpā'[1] [1]

HEALING [16]
healing, 5340, marpē'[1] [8]
healing, 9499, tᵉ'ālâ[2] [2]
healing for wound, 776, 'ᵃrûkâ [1]
healing, 776, 'ᵃrûkâ [1]
beyond healing, 2703, ḥālâ[1] [1]
healing, 5989+8337, nātan+rᵉpû'â [1]
healing balm, 6057, sûk[2] [1]
healing, 9559, tᵉrûpâ [1]

HEALS [5]
heals, 8324, rāpā'[1] [5]

HEALTH [10]
health, 776, 'ᵃrûkâ [2]
health, 5507, mᵉtōm [2]
good health, 8934, šālôm [2]
gives health, 2014, dāšēn[1] [1]
restored to health, 2730, ḥālam[1] [1]
health, 5340, marpē'[1] [1]
health, 8326, rip'ût [1]

HEALTHIER [1]
healthier, 3202, ṭôb[2] [1]

HEALTHY [4]
healthy, 1374, bārî' [2]
healthy, 5893, nāṣab[1] [1]
healthy, 9447, tām [1]

HEAP [26]
heap, 1643, gal[1] [8]
heap of rubble, 6505, 'î [3]
ash heap, 883, 'ašpōt [2]
heap of ruins, 1643, gal[1] [2]
heap, 5603, nēd [2]
heap of rubble, 1643, gal[1] [1]
heap, 3149, ḥāṭā [1]
heap, 3578, yāsap [1]
heap of ruins, 4843, makšēlâ [1]
heap, 5075, mᵉ'î [1]
heap, 6894, 'ᵃrēmâ [1]

heap, 8049, *rābâ*^{1} [1]
heap, 9162, *šepek* [1]
heap of ruins, 9424, *tēl* [1]

HEAPED [4]
heaped insults on, 3070, *ḥārap*^{2} [2]
heaped up, 7392, *ṣābar* [1]
heaped up, 7756, *qûm* [1]

HEAPING [2]
heaping, 3578, *yāsap* [1]
heaping up, 4848, *mālē'*^{1} [1]

HEAPS [10]
heaps, 6894, *'*^{a}*rēmâ* [3]
ash heaps, 883, *'ašpōt* [1]
heaps, 2818+2818, *ḥōmer*^{3}*+ḥōmer*^{3} [1]
heaps of rubble, 4843, *makšēlâ* [1]
heaps of grain, 6894, *'*^{a}*rēmâ* [1]
in heaps, 6894+6894, *'*^{a}*rēmâ+'*^{a}*rēmâ* [1]
heaps up wealth, 7392, *ṣābar* [1]
heaps up, 7392, *ṣābar* [1]

HEAR [274]
hear, 9048, *šāma'* [238]
hear, 263, *'āzan*^{1} [11]
hear, 7992, *qāšab* [4]
hear, *NIH/RPE* [3]
let hear, 9048, *šāma'* [3]
hear, 10725, *š*^{e}*ma'* [3]
hear, 7754, *qôl* [2]
hear, 9051, *šēma'* [2]
hear good news, 1413, *bāśar* [1]
hear, 5742+265, *nāṭâ+'ōzen* [1]
hear, 5877+4200+7156, *nāpal+l*$^{e-1}$*+pāneh* [1]
cause to hear, 9048, *šāma'* [1]
caused to hear, 9048, *šāma'* [1]
certainly hear, 9048+9048, *šāma'+šāma'* [1]
made hear, 9048, *šāma'* [1]
make hear, 9048, *šāma'* [1]

HEARD [345]
heard, 9048, *šāma'* [293]
be heard, 9048, *šāma'* [9]
is heard, 9048, *šāma'* [6]
was heard, 9048, *šāma'* [4]
heard, 10725, *š*^{e}*ma'* [4]
heard, 928+265, *b*^{e}*-+'ōzen* [3]
heard, *NIH/RPE* [2]
heard, 5583, *nāgad* [2]
heard, 7754, *qôl* [2]
are heard, 9048, *šāma'* [2]
heard, 9048+7754, *šāma'+qôl* [2]
heard, 265, *'ōzen* [1]
heard, 606+928+265, *'āmar*^{1}*+b*^{e}*-+'ōzen* [1]
be heard^{s}, 995, *bô'* [1]
heard, 2180, *hinnēh* [1]
let be heard, 5989, *nātan* [1]
heard, 7992, *qāšab* [1]
make heard, 9048, *šāma'* [1]
been heard of, 9048, *šāma'* [1]
been heard, 9048, *šāma'* [1]
expect to be heard, 9048, *šāma'* [1]
heard definitely, 9048+9048, *šāma'+šāma'* [1]
let be heard, 9048, *šāma'* [1]
sound be heard, 9048, *šāma'* [1]
surely heard, 9048+9048, *šāma'+šāma'* [1]
were heard, 9048, *šāma'* [1]
heard, 9051+9048, *šēma'+šāma'* [1]

HEARING [35]
hearing, 265, *'ōzen* [24]
hearing, 9048, *šāma'* [8]
hearing, *NIH/RPE* [1]
give a hearing, 263+7754, *'āzan*^{1}*+qôl* [1]
ever hearing, 9048+9048, *šāma'+šāma'* [1]

HEARS [33]
hears, 9048, *šāma'* [27]
what hears, 5461, *mišmā'*^{1} [1]
make sure hears, 8492+928+265, *śîm+b*^{e}*-+'ōzen* [1]
hears, 9048+7754, *šāma'+qôl* [1]
hears, 9048+9048+7754, *šāma'+šāma'+qôl* [1]
hears, 9048+9048, *šāma'+šāma'* [1]
hears, 10725, *š*^{e}*ma'* [1]

HEART [489]
heart, 4213, *lēb* [310]
heart, 4222, *lēbāb* [120]
heart, 5883, *nepeš* [16]
heart, 7931, *qereb* [5]
heart, 4000, *kilyâ* [4]
heart, 5055, *mē'eh* [4]
heart, 8120, *rûaḥ* [4]
heart, 1061, *beṭen*^{1} [2]
heart, 2668, *ḥêq* [2]
stolen heart, 4220, *lābab*^{1} [2]
lose heart, 5570, *nābēl*^{1} [2]
heart, 9348, *tāwek* [2]
heart, 10381, *l*^{e}*bab* [2]
take heart, 599+4213, *'āmēṣ+lēb* [1]
take heart, 599+4222, *'āmēṣ+lēbāb* [1]
lose heart, 1327+8120+928+7931, *bāqaq*^{1}*+rûaḥ+b*^{e}*-+qereb* [1]
heart, 2460, *ḥōb* [1]
heart, 2743, *ḥ*^{a}*lāṣayim* [1]
heart, 3219, *ṭuḥôt* [1]
heart and soul, 3869+4222, *k*^{e}*-+lēbāb* [1]
lose heart, 3874, *kā'â* [1]
heart, 3879, *kābēd*^{3} [1]
heart, 3883, *kābôd*^{1} [1]
heart, 5516, *motnayim* [1]
close to heart, 7940, *qārôb* [1]
set heart, 8751, *šāwâ*^{2} [1]
delights of the heart, 9503, *ta'*^{a}*nûg* [1]

HEART'S [3]
heart's, 4222, *lēbāb* [2]
heart's, 5883, *nepeš* [1]

HEARTACHE [1]
heartache, 6780+4213, *'aṣṣebet+lēb* [1]

HEARTH [6]
altar hearth, 789, *'*^{a}*rî'ēl*^{1} [2]
hearth, 789, *'*^{a}*rî'ēl*^{1} [1]
altar hearth, 2219, *har'ēl* [1]
hearth, 3683, *yāqûd* [1]
hearth, 4612, *môq*^{e}*dâ* [1]

HEARTLESS [1]
heartless, 425, *'akzār* [1]

HEARTS [128]
hearts, 4213, *lēb* [74]
hearts, 4222, *lēbāb* [46]
hearts, 5883, *nepeš* [4]
callous hearts, 2693, *ḥēleb*^{1} [2]
hearts, 4000, *kilyâ* [1]
hearts, 7931, *qereb* [1]

HEAT [26]
heat, 2770, *ḥōm* [8]
heat, 2996, *ḥōreb*^{1} [6]
in heat, 3501, *yāḥam* [2]
heat, *NIH/RPE* [1]
heat, 2780, *ḥammâ* [1]
heat, 2801, *ḥāmam* [1]
heat, 3001, *ḥ*^{a}*rābôn* [1]
heat, 3019, *ḥārôn* [1]
scorching heat, 3031, *ḥarḥur* [1]
heat, 3880, *kōbed* [1]
desert heat, 9220, *šārāb* [1]
in heat, 9299, *ta'*^{a}*nâ* [1]
burning heat, 9429, *tal'ubôt* [1]

HEATED [1]
heated, 10015, *'*^{a}*zâ* [1]

HEAVEN [186]
heaven, 9028, *šāmayim* [154]
heaven, 10723, *š*^{e}*mayin* [29]
heaven, 5294, *mārôm* [1]
heights of heaven, 5294, *mārôm* [1]
highest heaven, 9028+9028, *šāmayim+šāmayim* [1]

HEAVEN'S [1]
heaven's, 9028, *šāmayim* [1]

HEAVENLY [6]
heavenly hosts, 7372, *ṣābā'*^{2} [2]
heavenly, 9028, *šāmayim* [2]
heavenly beings, 466, *'*^{e}*lōhîm* [1]
heavenly beings, 1201+446, *bēn*^{1}*+'ēl*^{5} [1]

HEAVENS [158]
heavens, 9028, *šāmayim* [141]
highest heavens, 9028+9028, *šāmayim+šāmayim* [6]
heavens, 5294, *mārôm* [4]
heavens, 10723, *š*^{e}*mayin* [3]
heavens, 8385, *rāqîa'* [2]
the heavens^{s}, 2157, *-hem* [1]
heavens, 2292, *z*^{e}*bul*^{2} [1]

HEAVIER [6]
make even heavier, 3578, *yāsap* [4]
heavier, 2616, *ḥāzaq* [1]
heavier, 3878, *kābēd*^{2} [1]

HEAVILY [3]
weighs heavily, 8041, *rab*^{1} [2]
lies heavily, 6164, *sāmak* [1]

HEAVY [45]
heavy, 1524, *gādôl* [8]
heavy, 3877, *kābēd*^{1} [8]
heavy, 3878, *kābēd*^{2} [8]
made heavy, 3877, *kābēd*^{1} [2]
put heavy, 3877, *kābēd*^{1} [2]
put heavy, 7996, *qāšâ* [2]
heavy, 8041, *rab*^{1} [2]
heavy, 8273, *ra'*^{1} [2]
heavy, 2162, *hāmôn* [1]
heavy work, 3330, *y*^{e}*gîa'* [1]
heavy, 3877+4394, *kābēd*^{1}*+m*^{e}*'ōd* [1]
laid heavy, 3877, *kābēd*^{1} [1]
placed a heavy burden, 3877, *kābēd*^{1} [1]
heavy, 3878+3877, *kābēd*^{2}*+kābēd*^{1} [1]
heavy, 3880, *kōbed* [1]
too heavy a burden to carry, 4202+3523+5951, *lō'+yākōl+nāśā'* [1]
draw heavy loads, 6022, *sābal* [1]
heavy, 6286, *'ābâ* [1]
heavy, 7996, *qāšâ* [1]

HEBER [10]
Heber, 2491, *ḥeber*^{2} [10]

HEBER'S [1]
Heber's, 2491, *ḥeber*^{2} [1]

HEBERITE [1]
Heberite, 2499, *ḥebrî* [1]

HEBREW [22]
Hebrew, 6303, *'ibrî*^{1} [16]
in Hebrew, 3376, *y*^{e}*hûdît*^{1} [5]
Hebrew, *NIH/RPE* [1]

HEBREWS [16]
Hebrews, 6303, *'ibrî*^{1} [16]

HEBRON [74]
Hebron, 2496, *ḥebrôn*^{1} [62]
Hebron, 2497, *ḥebrôn*^{2} [10]
Hebron, *NIH/RPE* [1]
Hebron^{s}, 9004, *šām* [1]

HEBRONITE [1]
Hebronite, 2498, *ḥebrônî* [1]

HEBRONITES [5]
Hebronites, 2498, *ḥebrônî* [4]
the Hebronites^{s}, 2157, *-hem* [1]

HEDGE [3]
thorn hedge, 5004, *m*^{e}*sûkâ* [1]
hedge, 5372, *m*^{e}*śûkkâ* [1]
put a hedge, 8455, *śûk* [1]

HEDGED [1]
hedged in, 6114, *sākak*^{1} [1]

HEED [9]
heed, 9048, *šāma'* [3]
take heed, 1067, *bîn* [1]
pays heed, 1067, *bîn* [1]
gave heed, 7992, *qāšab* [1]
heed, 7992, *qāšab* [1]

gives heed, 8505, *śākal1* [1]
heed, 9068, *šāmar* [1]

HEEDED [2]
are heeded, 9048, *šāmaʿ* [1]
be heeded, 9048, *šāmaʿ* [1]

HEEDS [5]
heeds, 9068, *šāmar* [3]
heeds, *NIH/RPE* [1]
heeds, 9048, *šāmaʿ* [1]

HEEL [5]
heel, 6811, *ʿāqēb1* [4]
grasped heel, 6810, *ʿāqab* [1]

HEELS [3]
heels, 6811, *ʿāqēb1* [2]
at heels, 6584+7418, *ʿal2+ṣawwāʾr* [1]

HEGAI [4]
Hegai, 2051, *hēgay* [3]
Hegai, 2043, *hēgēʾ* [1]

HEIFER [14]
heifer, 6320, *ʿeglâ1* [6]
heifer, 7239, *pārâ2* [6]
heifer, 6320+1330, *ʿeglâ1+bāqār* [2]

HEIFER'S [1]
heifer's, 6320, *ʿeglâ1* [1]

HEIGHT [13]
height, 1470, *gōbah* [4]
height, 7757, *qômâ* [2]
height, 1469+7757, *gābōah+qômâ* [1]
height, 5057, *māʿôz* [1]
height, 5294, *mārôm* [1]
height of power, 6793, *ʿāṣam1* [1]
reached height, 8003+6330, *qāšar+ʿad2* [1]
barren height, 9155, *šepî1* [1]
height, 10660, *rûm2* [1]

HEIGHTS [40]
heights, 1195, *bāmâ1* [9]
heights, 5294, *mārôm* [9]
barren heights, 9155, *šepî1* [7]
utmost heights, 3752, *yerēkâ* [4]
heights, 1496, *gibʿâ1* [2]
heights, 1469, *gābōah* [1]
heights, 1470, *gōbah* [1]
heights of Hermon, 3056, *ḥermôn* [1]
heights, 4200+5087+2025, *le-1+maʿal2+-â2* [1]
heights above, 5294, *mārôm* [1]
heights of heaven, 5294, *mārôm* [1]
on heights, 5294, *mārôm* [1]
heights, 8031+5294, *rōʾš1+mārôm* [1]
heights, 8123, *rûm1* [1]

HEIR [5]
heir, 3769, *yāraš1* [4]
fell heir, 3769, *yāraš1* [1]

HEIRS [2]
heirs, 3769, *yāraš1* [1]
heirs, 3772, *yeruššâ* [1]

HELAH [2]
Helah, 2690, *ḥelʾâ2* [2]

HELAM [2]
Helam, 2663, *ḥêlām* [2]

HELBAH [1]
Helbah, 2695, *ḥelbâ* [1]

HELBON [1]
Helbon, 2696, *ḥelbôn* [1]

HELD [57]
held responsible, 6411+5951, *ʿāwōn+nāśāʾ* [4]
held, 3920, *kûl* [3]
held responsible, 5951+6411, *nāśāʾ+ʿāwōn* [3]
held, 6913, *ʿāśâ1* [3]
held, *NIH/RPE* [2]
held fast, 1815, *dābaq* [2]
held, 2616, *ḥāzaq* [2]
was held in honor, 3877, *kābēd1* [2]
held out, 5742, *nāṭâ* [2]
are held captive, 8647, *šābâ* [2]
held, *AIT* [1]
held, 296, *ʾāḥaz1* [1]
held, 659, *ʾāsîr* [1]
is held captive, 673, *ʾāsar* [1]
were held, 673, *ʾāsar* [1]
held myself back, 706, *ʾāpaq* [1]
held guilty, 870, *ʾāšam* [1]
held fast, 1816, *dābēq* [1]
held secure, 2616, *ḥāzaq* [1]
held responsible, 2628+5951, *ḥēṭʾ+nāśāʾ* [1]
held in awe, 3707, *yārēʾ1* [1]
held court, 3782, *yāšab* [1]
held out, 3804, *yāšaṭ* [1]
be held in honor, 3877, *kābēd1* [1]
held in honor, 3877, *kābēd1* [1]
held fast, 4334, *lākad* [1]
held back, 4979, *mānaʿ* [1]
not be held responsible, 5927, *nāqâ* [1]
not held responsible, 5929, *nāqî* [1]
held responsible, 5951+2628, *nāśāʾ+ḥēṭʾ* [1]
held, 6641, *ʿāmad* [1]
held in reserve, 7214, *piqqādôn* [1]
held out, 7298, *pāraś* [1]
held a celebration, 7412, *ṣāhal1* [1]
with heads held high, 7758, *qômemiyyût* [1]
held up, 8123, *rûm1* [1]
held in high esteem, 8354, *rāṣâ1* [1]
held a grudge against, 8475, *śāṭam* [1]
held a celebration, 8523, *śāmaḥ* [1]
held captive, 8647, *šābâ* [1]
held up, 9461, *tāmak* [1]
held, 9461, *tāmak* [1]

HELDAI [3]
Heldai, 2702, *ḥelday* [3]

HELECH [1]
Helech, 2662, *ḥêlēk* [1]

HELED [2]
Heled, 2699, *ḥēled* [2]

HELEK [2]
Helek, 2751, *ḥēleq3* [2]

HELEKITE [1]
Helekite, 2757, *ḥelqî* [1]

HELEM [1]
Helem, 2152, *hēlem* [1]

HELEPH [1]
Heleph, 2738, *ḥēlep1* [1]

HELEZ [5]
Helez, 2742, *ḥeleṣ* [5]

HELIOPOLIS [1]
Heliopolis, 225, *ʾāwen2* [1]

HELKAI [1]
Helkai, 2758, *ḥelqāy* [1]

HELKATH [2]
Helkath, 2762, *ḥelqat* [2]

HELKATH HAZZURIM [1]
Helkath Hazzurim, 2763, *ḥelqat haṣṣurîm* [1]

HELMET [5]
helmet, 3916, *kôbaʿ* [2]
helmet, 5057+8031, *māʿôz+rōʾš1* [2]
helmet, 7746, *qôbaʿ* [1]

HELMETS [5]
helmets, 3916, *kôbaʿ* [4]
helmets, 7746, *qôbaʿ* [1]

HELON [5]
Helon, 2735, *ḥēlōn* [5]

HELP [173]
help, 6468, *ʿāzar* [42]
help, 6476, *ʿezrâ1* [19]
help, 6469, *ʿēzer1* [13]
help, 3828, *yāšaʿ* [7]
cry for help, 8775, *šāwaʿ* [7]
help, *NIH/RPE* [3]
help, 6640, *ʿim* [3]
cried for help, 7590, *ṣāʿaq* [3]
help up, 7756, *qûm* [3]
call for help, 8775, *šāwaʿ* [3]
called for help, 8775, *šāwaʿ* [3]
cried for help, 8775, *šāwaʿ* [3]
cry for help, 8784, *šawʿâ* [3]
help, 907, *ʾēt2* [2]
with help, 928, *be-* [2]
seek help, 2011, *dāraš* [2]
help, 2118+6640, *hāyâ+ʿim* [2]
with the help of, 2256, *we-* [2]
help, 2616, *ḥāzaq* [2]
help, 6699, *ʿānâ1* [2]
help, 9591, *tešûʿâ* [2]
help, *AIT* [1]
with the help of, 907, *ʾēt2* [1]
help, 907+2118, *ʾēt2+hāyâ* [1]
seek help, 1335, *bāqaš* [1]
cried for help, 2410, *zāʿaq* [1]
cried out for help, 2410, *zāʿaq* [1]
cry out for help, 2410, *zāʿaq* [1]
help, 3202, *ṭôb2* [1]
help, 3338+2616, *yād+ḥāzaq* [1]
help, 3338+6640, *yād+ʿim* [1]
help in childbirth, 3528, *yālad* [1]
get help for, 3828, *yāšaʿ* [1]
help at all, 3828+3828, *yāšaʿ+yāšaʿ* [1]
help, 4200+2118, *le-1+hāyâ* [1]
help, 4200+3338, *le-1+yād* [1]
help, 4200, *le-1* [1]
with the help of, 4946+907, *min+ʾēt2* [1]
help assign, 5706, *nāḥal* [1]
help, 6370, *ʿādar1* [1]
look for help, 6395, *ʿûz* [1]
be sure help, 6441+6441, *ʿāzab2+ʿāzab2* [1]
receive help, 6468+6469, *ʿāzar+ʿēzer1* [1]
help, 6584, *ʿal2* [1]
with help, 6640, *ʿim* [1]
with the help of, 6640, *ʿim* [1]
help, 6913+4200, *ʿāśâ1+le-1* [1]
help, 6913, *ʿāśâ1* [1]
come to the help of, 7003, *pāgaʿ* [1]
turn to help, 7155, *pānâ* [1]
scream for help, 7590, *ṣāʿaq* [1]
cried out for help, 7754+7590, *qôl+ṣāʿaq* [1]
cry for help, 7754+2410, *qôl+zāʿaq* [1]
cry for help, 7754+8776, *qôl+šewaʿ* [1]
call for help, 7924, *qārāʾ1* [1]
calling for help, 7924, *qārāʾ1* [1]
help, 7925, *qārāʾ2* [1]
scream for help, 8123+7754+2256+7924, *rûm1+qôl+we-+qārāʾ1* [1]
screamed for help, 8123+7754+2256+7924, *rûm1+qôl+we-+qārāʾ1* [1]
cry out for help, 8775, *šāwaʿ* [1]
cries for help, 8780, *šûaʿ1* [1]
help, 8883+3338+6640, *šît1+yād+ʿim* [1]
sent for help, 8938, *šālaḥ* [1]
without help, 9037, *šāmēm1* [1]
cried for help, 9120, *šāʿâ* [1]
asking for help, 10274, *ḥanan* [1]

HELPED [23]
helped, 6468, *ʿāzar* [12]
helped, 907, *ʾēt2* [1]
helped find strength, 2616+906+3338, *ḥāzaq+ʾēt1+yād* [1]
helped, 2616+906+3338, *ḥāzaq+ʾēt1+yād* [1]
helped, 2616, *ḥāzaq* [1]
helped, 5951, *nāśāʾ* [1]
am helped, 6468, *ʿāzar* [1]
is helped, 6468, *ʿāzar* [1]
was helped, 6468, *ʿāzar* [1]
were helped, 6468, *ʿāzar* [1]
helped up, 6590, *ʿālâ* [1]
helped, 7503, *ṣālaḥ2* [1]

HELPER [9]
helper, 6469, *ʿēzer1* [5]
helper, 6468, *ʿāzar* [2]
helper, 5853, *naʿar2* [1]
helper, 6476, *ʿezrâ1* [1]

HELPERS [1]
helpers, 6468, *ʿāzar* [1]

HELPING [4]
helping, *NIH/RPE* [1]
helping, 907, *ʾēt²* [1]
helping, 6468, *ʿāzar* [1]
helping, 10514, *seʿad* [1]

HELPLESS [8]
helpless, 4202+6806+3946, *lōʾ+ʿāṣar+kōaḥ¹* [2]
helpless, 6714, *ʿānî* [2]
helpless, 1924, *dal²* [1]
helpless, 4946+3946, *min+kōaḥ¹* [1]
helpless, 5683, *nûš* [1]
helpless, 6705, *ʿānāw* [1]

HELPS [6]
helps, 6468, *ʿāzar* [6]

HEM [9]
hem, 8767, *šûl* [5]
hem of robe, 4053, *kānāp* [1]
hem, 4053, *kānāp* [1]
hem in, 4193, *kātar²* [1]
hem in, 7443, *ṣûr¹* [1]

HEMAN [16]
Heman, 2124, *hêmān* [16]

HEMAN'S [1]
Heman'sˢ, 2257, *-ô* [1]

HEMDAN [2]
Hemdan, 2777, *ḥemdān* [2]

HEMMED [1]
hemmed in, 6037, *sāgar* [1]

HEN [1]
Hen, 2835, *ḥēn²* [1]

HENA [3]
Hena, 2184, *hēnaʿ* [3]

HENADAD [4]
Henadad, 2836, *ḥēnādād* [4]

HENNA [2]
henna blossoms, 4110, *kōper³* [1]
henna, 4110, *kōper³* [1]

HEPHER [9]
Hepher, 2918, *ḥēper¹* [7]
Hepher, 2919, *ḥēper²* [2]

HEPHERITE [1]
Hepherite, 2920, *ḥeprî* [1]

HEPHZIBAH [2]
Hephzibah, 2915, *ḥepṣî-bāh* [2]

HER [1389]
her, 2023, *-āh* [1135]
her, *NIH/RPE* [80]
her, 2257, *-ô* [36]
her, *AIT* [33]
herˢ, 2021, *ha-* [22]
her, 5626, *-nā* [22]
herˢ, 2021+851, *ha+ʾiššā* [6]
her own, 2023, *-āh* [5]
her, 2157, *-hem* [5]
her, 4200+2023, *le-¹+-āh* [5]
her, 2084, *-hû* [4]
her, 4392, *-ām* [3]
herˢ, 851, *ʾiššā* [2]
herˢ, 2021+5855, *ha+naʿarâ¹* [2]
herˢ, 2021+912, *ha+ʾātôn* [2]
her, 2085, *hûʾ* [2]
her, 3276, *-î* [2]
her, 3871, *-k* [2]
herˢ, 141+3776, *ʾadāmâ¹+yiśrāʾēl* [1]
herˢ, 563+3870, *ʾāmâ+-kā* [1]
herˢ, 676, *ʾestēr* [1]
herˢ, 851+123+2257, *ʾiššā+ʾādôn+-ô* [1]
herˢ, 851+2257, *ʾiššâ+-ô* [1]
herˢ, 2021+6320, *ha+ʿeglâ¹* [1]
the woman and her sisterˢ, 2177, *-hēn²* [1]
her husbandˢ, 2257, *-ô* [1]
her sonˢ, 2257, *-ô* [1]
her, 2296, *zeh* [1]
ply her trade, 2388, *zānâ¹* [1]
herˢ, 2839, *ḥannâ* [1]
her own, 3276, *-î* [1]
herˢ, 3276, *-î* [1]
herˢ, 3304+3871, *yebāmâ+-k* [1]
breathed her last, 3655+5883, *yāṣāʾ+nepeš* [1]
herˢ, 3776, *yiśrāʾēl* [1]
her, 3870, *-kā* [1]
her, 4200+3276, *le-¹+-î* [1]
herˢ, 5319, *miryām* [1]
herˢ, 8162, *rāḥēl²* [1]

HERALD [2]
herald, 7924, *qārāʾ¹* [1]
herald, 10370, *kārôz* [1]

HERBS [5]
bitter herbs, 5353, *mārōr* [3]
herbs, 246, *ʾôrâ²* [1]
salt herbs, 4865, *mallûaḥ* [1]

HERD [14]
herd, 1330, *bāqār* [10]
herd, 8802, *šôr* [2]
herd, 6337, *ʿēdâ¹* [1]
each herd, 6373+6373, *ʿēder¹+ʿēder¹* [1]

HERDED [1]
be herded together, 665+669, *ʾāsap+ʾasēpâ* [1]

HERDING [1]
herding, 8286, *rāʿâ¹* [1]

HERDS [52]
herds, 1330, *bāqār* [32]
herds, 546, *ʾelep¹* [5]
herds, 989, *behēmâ* [3]
herds, 6373, *ʿēder¹* [3]
flocks and herds, 5238, *miqneh* [1]
herds and flocks, 5238, *miqneh* [1]
herds of livestock, 5238, *miqneh* [1]
herds, 5238+1330, *miqneh+bāqār* [1]
herds, 5238, *miqneh* [1]
flocks and herds, 6373, *ʿēder¹* [1]
herds, 6373+1330, *ʿēder¹+bāqār* [1]
herds, 7871, *qinyān* [1]
herds, 9180, *šipʿâ* [1]

HERDSMEN [6]
herdsmen, 8286, *rāʿâ¹* [3]
herdsmen, 8286+5238, *rāʿâ¹+miqneh* [2]
herdsmen, 5238, *miqneh* [1]

HERE [269]
here, 2180, *hinnēh* [57]
here, 7024, *pōh* [43]
here, *NIH/RPE* [41]
here, 2178, *hēnnâ¹* [25]
here, 2296, *zeh* [17]
here, 928+2296, *be-+zeh* [12]
here, 9004, *šām* [9]
here, *AIT* [6]
here, 2151, *halōm* [4]
here, 3907, *kōh* [4]
here, 465, *ʾēlleh* [3]
here, 889, *ʾašer* [2]
hereˢ, 2021+5226+2021+2296, *ha-+māqôm+ha-+zeh* [2]
here, 2256, *we-* [2]
hereˢ, 2257, *-ô* [2]
hereˢ, 3276, *-î* [2]
come here, 5602, *nāgaš* [2]
come here, 7928, *qārab* [2]
here, 8011, *rāʾâ¹* [2]
here are no, 401, *ʾayin¹* [1]
here, 448, *ʾel* [1]
hereˢ, 928+2021+4497, *be-+ha-+midbār¹* [1]
hereˢ, 928+2021+5226+2021+2296, *be-+ha-+māqôm+ha-+zeh* [1]
hereˢ, 928+2021+824, *be-+ha-+ʾereṣ* [1]
hereˢ, 928+2023, *be-+-āh* [1]
hereˢ, 928+5226, *be-+māqôm* [1]
out here, 928+2021+2575, *be-+ha-+ḥûṣ* [1]
here, 995, *bôʾ* [1]
hereˢ, 2021+5226, *ha-+māqôm* [1]
hereˢ, 2021+824, *ha-+ʾereṣ* [1]
here, 2026, *hēʾ* [1]
over here, 2151, *halōm* [1]
here, 2176, *hēn¹* [1]
here, 2178+2025, *hēnnâ¹+-â²* [1]
here now, 2180, *hinnēh* [1]
here is what, 3869+2296+2256+3869+2296, *ke-+zeh+we-+ke-+zeh* [1]
here, 4200+7156, *le-¹+pāneh* [1]
over here, 4200+6298+285, *le-¹+ʿēber¹+ʾeḥād* [1]
here, 5162, *māṣāʾ* [1]
hereˢ, 5213+2025, *miṣrayim+-â²* [1]
hereˢ, 5646, *-nû¹* [1]
here, 6330+2178, *ʿad²+hēnnâ¹* [1]
hereˢ, 6584+3276, *ʿal²+-î* [1]
hereˢ, 6584+3870, *ʿal²+-kā* [1]
hereˢ, 6640+3276, *ʿim+-î* [1]
here, 6640, *ʿim* [1]
bring here, 7928, *qārab* [1]
running here and there, 8592+2006, *śārak+derek* [1]
go here and there, 8763, *šûṭ¹* [1]
rush here and there, 8763, *šûṭ¹* [1]
get out of here, 8938+2021+2575+2025, *šālaḥ+ha-+ḥûṣ+-â²* [1]

HEREBY [2]
hereby, *AIT* [1]
hereby, *NIH/RPE* [1]

HERES [2]
Heres, 3065, *ḥeres³* [2]

HERESH [1]
Heresh, 3090, *ḥereš³* [1]

HERETH [1]
Hereth, 3101, *ḥeret* [1]

HERITAGE [7]
heritage, 5709, *naḥalâ¹* [5]
heritage, 3772, *yeruššâ* [1]
heritage, 5706, *nāḥal* [1]

HERMON [14]
Hermon, 3056, *ḥermôn* [13]
heights of Hermon, 3056, *ḥermôn* [1]

HERO [2]
hero, 1475, *gibbôr* [2]

HEROES [3]
heroes, 1475, *gibbôr* [3]

HERON [2]
heron, 649, *ʾanāpâ* [2]

HERS [4]
hers, 2023, *-āh* [2]
hers, 4200+2023, *le-¹+-āh* [1]
hers, 5647, *-nû²* [1]

HERSELF [38]
herself, 2023, *-āh* [8]
herself, 5883+2023, *nepeš+-āh* [7]
herself, *AIT* [6]
defiled herself, 3237, *ṭāmēʾ¹* [4]
herself, *NIH/RPE* [2]
herself, 2085, *hûʾ* [1]
herself, 2257, *-ô* [1]
defiles herself, 2725, *ḥālal¹* [1]
defiles herself, 3237, *ṭāmēʾ¹* [1]
covered herself, 4059, *kāsâ* [1]
wears herself out, 4206, *lāʾâ* [1]
herself, 4222+2023, *lēbāb+-āh* [1]
herself, 5883, *nepeš* [1]
disguise herself, 6634, *ʿālap* [1]
purified herself, 7727, *qādaš* [1]
herself, 7931+2023, *qereb+-āh* [1]

HESHBON [38]
Heshbon, 3114, *ḥešbôn²* [38]

HESHMON [1]
Heshmon, 3132, *ḥešmôn* [1]

HESITATE [3]
hesitate, 3104, *ḥāśak* [1]
hesitate, 6788, *ʿāṣal* [1]
did not hesitate, 9193, *šāqad*^{1} [1]

HESITATED [1]
hesitated, 4538, *māhah* [1]

HETHLON [2]
Hethlon, 3158, *ḥetlôn* [2]

HEWING [1]
hewing, 2933, *ḥāṣēb*^{1} [1]

HEWN [2]
hewn out, 2933, *ḥāṣēb*^{1} [1]
were hewn, 5941, *nāqar* [1]

HEZEKIAH [121]
Hezekiah, 2625, *ḥizqiyyāhû* [66]
Hezekiah, 3491, *yᵉḥizqiyyāhû* [37]
Hezekiah, 2624, *ḥizqiyyâ* [9]
Hezekiah, *NIH/RPE* [6]
Hezekiah, 3490, *yᵉḥizqiyyâ* [3]

HEZEKIAH'S [10]
Hezekiah's, 2625, *ḥizqiyyāhû* [5]
Hezekiah's, 3491, *yᵉḥizqiyyāhû* [2]
Hezekiah's, 2624, *ḥizqiyyâ* [1]
Hezekiah's, 4200+2624, *lᵉ-*^{1}*+ḥizqiyyâ* [1]
Hezekiah's, 4200+2625, *lᵉ-*^{1}*+ḥizqiyyāhû* [1]

HEZION [1]
Hezion, 2611, *ḥezyôn* [1]

HEZIR [2]
Hezir, 2615, *ḥēzîr* [2]

HEZRO [2]
Hezro, 2968, *ḥeṣrô* [2]

HEZRON [17]
Hezron, 2969, *ḥeṣrôn*^{1} [16]
Hezron, 2970, *ḥeṣrôn*^{2} [1]

HEZRONITE [2]
Hezronite, 2971, *ḥeṣrônî* [2]

HID [26]
hid, 6259, *sātar* [9]
hid, 2461, *ḥābāʾ* [7]
hid, 3243, *ṭāman* [6]
hid themselves, 2461, *ḥābāʾ* [2]
hid in, 995, *bôʾ* [1]
hid, 7621, *ṣāpan* [1]

HIDDAI [1]
Hiddai, 2068, *hidday* [1]

HIDDEN [59]
hidden, 3243, *ṭāman* [10]
hidden, 6259, *sātar* [10]
hidden, 2461, *ḥābāʾ* [7]
hidden, 6623, *ʿālam* [4]
hidden, 3948, *kāḥad* [3]
hidden, 741, *ʾārab* [2]
hidden treasure, 4759, *maṭmôn* [2]
is hidden, 6259, *sātar* [2]
hidden, 7621, *ṣāpan* [2]
hidden away, 2461, *ḥābāʾ* [1]
hidden himself, 2461, *ḥābāʾ* [1]
hidden, 2470, *ḥebyôn* [1]
hidden things, 2648, *ḥîdâ* [1]
was hidden, 3948, *kāḥad* [1]
hidden, 4052, *kānap* [1]
hidden, 4202+8011, *lōʾ+rāʾâ*^{1} [1]
hidden, 4759, *maṭmôn* [1]
hidden treasures, 5208, *maṣpôn* [1]
hidden, 5915, *nāṣar* [1]
hidden path, 5985, *nātîb* [1]
are hidden, 6259, *sātar* [1]
hidden, 6260, *sēter* [1]
hidden, 6670, *ʿāmam*^{2} [1]
treasures hidden, 8561+3243, *śāpan+ṭāman* [1]
hidden things, 9502, *taʿᵃlumâ* [1]
hidden, 10519, *sᵉtar*^{1} [1]

HIDE [73]
hide, 6259, *sātar* [35]
hide, 3948, *kāḥad* [8]
hide, 6425, *ʿôr* [8]
hide, 2464, *ḥābâ* [3]
hide, 3243, *ṭāman* [3]
hide, 4059, *kāsâ* [3]
hide, 6623, *ʿālam* [2]
hide, 7621, *ṣāpan* [2]
hide, 741, *ʾārab* [1]
hide yourselves, 2461, *ḥābāʾ* [1]
hide themselves, 2461, *ḥābāʾ* [1]
hide, 2461, *ḥābāʾ* [1]
hide in, 3782, *yāšab* [1]
hide, 5040, *mastēr* [1]
certainly hide, 6259+6259, *sātar+sātar* [1]
hide yourself, 6259, *sātar* [1]
hide, 8789, *šûp*^{1} [1]

HIDES [17]
hides, 6425, *ʿôr* [13]
hides, 3948, *kāḥad* [1]
hides himself, 6259, *sātar* [1]
hides, 6259, *sātar* [1]
hides of sea cows, 9391, *taḥaš*^{1} [1]

HIDING [29]
hiding, 2461, *ḥābāʾ* [5]
hiding, 6259, *sātar* [4]
hiding, 3243, *ṭāman* [2]
hiding, 3948, *kāḥad* [2]
hiding, 5041, *mistār* [2]
hiding place, 6260, *sēter* [2]
hiding, *NIH/RPE* [1]
force into hiding, 2461, *ḥābāʾ* [1]
go into hiding, 2924, *ḥāpaś* [1]
hiding place, 4422, *maʾᵃrāb* [1]
hiding places, 4676, *maḥᵃbōʾ* [1]
hiding place, 5039, *mistôr* [1]
hiding places, 5041, *mistār* [1]
go into hiding, 6259, *sātar* [1]
hiding place, 6259, *sātar* [1]
hiding places, 6260, *sēter* [1]
hiding, 6260, *sēter* [1]
hiding, 6623, *ʿālam* [1]

HIEL [1]
Hiel, 2647, *ḥîʾēl* [1]

HIGGAION [1]
Higgaion, 2053, *higgāyôn* [1]

HIGH [292]
high places, 1195, *bāmâ*^{1} [62]
Most High, 6610, *ʿelyôn*^{2} [31]
high, 7757, *qômâ* [28]
high, 1524, *gādôl* [23]
high place, 1195, *bāmâ*^{1} [20]
high, 1469, *gābōah* [19]
on high, 5294, *mārôm* [10]
Most High, 10546, *ʿillāy* [10]
high, 8123, *rûm*^{1} [9]
high, *NIH/RPE* [6]
lifted high, 8123, *rûm*^{1} [5]
in high spirits, 3201+4213, *ṭôb*^{1}*+lēb* [4]
Most High, 6583, *ʿal*^{1} [4]
on high, 928+2021+5294, *bᵉ-+ha-+mārôm* [3]
high, 1470, *gōbah* [3]
high seas, 4213+3542, *lēb+yām* [3]
high, 5294, *mārôm* [3]
Most High, 10548, *ʿelyôn* [3]
on high, 928+7757, *bᵉ-+qômâ* [2]
high, 1467, *gābah* [2]
high, 6609, *ʿelyôn*^{1} [2]
high, 8031, *rōʾš*^{1} [2]
high, 8042, *rab*^{2} [2]
high, 10660, *rûm*^{2} [2]
high, 466, *ʾᵉlōhîm* [1]
high, 1201+408, *bēn*^{1}*+ʾîš*^{1} [1]
hold head high, 1448, *gāʾâ* [1]
build high, 1467, *gābah* [1]
builds high, 1467, *gābah* [1]
pile high, 1540, *gādal* [1]
on high, 2021+5294, *ha-+mārôm* [1]
high priest, 3912, *kāhan* [1]
on high, 4200+2021+5294, *lᵉ-*^{1}*+ha-+mārôm* [1]
in high spirits, 4213+3201, *lēb+ṭôb*^{1} [1]
high platform, 4463, *migdāl*^{1} [1]
high above, 4946+4200+5087+2025, *min+lᵉ-*^{1}*+maʿal*^{2}*+-â*^{2} [1]
on high, 4946+5087, *min+maʿal*^{2} [1]
on high, 4946+5294, *min+mārôm* [1]
high positions, 5294, *mārôm* [1]
high, 5369, *miśgāb*^{1} [1]
high, 5951, *nāśāʾ* [1]
rises high, 5951, *nāśāʾ* [1]
Most High, 6604, *ʿēlî*^{2} [1]
high noon, 7416, *ṣohᵒrayim* [1]
on high, 7757, *qômâ* [1]
with heads held high, 7758, *qômᵉmiyyût* [1]
men of high rank, 7924, *qārāʾ*^{1} [1]
high, 8041, *rab*^{1} [1]
build on high, 8123, *rûm*^{1} [1]
set high, 8123, *rûm*^{1} [1]
high, 8124, *rûm*^{2} [1]
on high, 8125, *rôm* [1]
held in high esteem, 8354, *rāṣâ*^{1} [1]
high, 8435, *śāgab* [1]
gave a high rank in, 8492+6584, *śîm+ʿal*^{2} [1]
windows placed high, 9209, *šᵉqupîm* [1]
placed in a high position, 10648, *rᵉbâ* [1]
high position, 10650, *rᵉbû* [1]

HIGH-GRADE [2]
high-grade, 3701, *yāqār* [2]

HIGHBORN [1]
highborn, 1201+408, *bēn*^{1}*+ʾîš*^{1} [1]

HIGHER [15]
higher than, 4946+6584, *min+ʿal*^{2} [3]
higher, 1467, *gābah* [2]
higher, 5087+2025, *maʿal*^{2}*+-â*^{2} [2]
made higher, 1467, *gābah* [1]
higher, 1470, *gōbah* [1]
higher, 4946+5087, *min+maʿal*^{2} [1]
higher, 4946+6584, *min+ʿal*^{2} [1]
over higher, 6584, *ʿal*^{2} [1]
higher, 7757, *qômâ* [1]
higher than, 8049+4200+5087+2025, *rābâ*^{1}*+lᵉ-*^{1}*+maʿal*^{2}*+-â*^{2} [1]
higher, 8123, *rûm*^{1} [1]

HIGHEST [17]
highest heavens, 9028+9028, *šāmayim+šāmayim* [6]
third highest, 10761, *taltāʾ* [3]
highest, 1467, *gābah* [1]
highest point, 1726+5294, *gap*^{1}*+mārôm* [1]
highest point, 5294, *mārôm* [1]
highest, 6584+8031, *ʿal*^{2}*+rōʾš*^{1} [1]
highest, 8031, *rōʾš*^{1} [1]
highest, 8037, *riʾšôn* [1]
highest, 8123, *rûm*^{1} [1]
highest heaven, 9028+9028, *šāmayim+šāmayim* [1]

HIGHLY [17]
highly esteemed, 2776, *hᵃmudôt* [3]
highly exalted, 1448+1448, *gāʾâ+gāʾâ* [2]
highly respected, 3877, *kābēd*^{1} [2]
highly, 4200+5087+2025, *lᵉ-*^{1}*+maʿal*^{2}*+-â*^{2} [2]
highly regarded, 1524+4394, *gādôl+mᵉʾōd* [1]
highly, 4394, *mᵉʾōd* [1]
so highly, 4394, *mᵉʾōd* [1]
highly, 4848, *mālēʾ*^{1} [1]
highly regarded, 5951+7156, *nāśāʾ+pāneh* [1]
was highly regarded, 5951, *nāśāʾ* [1]
highly embroidered, 8391, *riqmâ* [1]
highly respected, 8777, *šôaʿ*^{1} [1]

HIGHWAY [11]
highway, 5019, *mᵉsillâ* [6]
highway, 2006, *derek* [3]
highway, 5020, *maslûl* [1]
is a highway, 6148, *sālal*^{2} [1]

HIGHWAYS [2]
highways, 5019, *mᵉsillâ* [2]

HILEN [1]
Hilen, 2664, *ḥilēn* [1]

HILKIAH [31]
Hilkiah, 2760, *ḥilqiyyāhû* [18]
Hilkiah, 2759, *ḥilqiyyâ* [13]

HILKIAH'S [1]
Hilkiah's, 2759, *ḥilqiyyâ* [1]

HILL [149]
hill country, 2215, *har* [82]
hill, 2215, *har* [32]
hill, 1496, *gibʿâ*[1] [26]
hill of Ophel, 6755, *ʿōpel*[2] [4]
hill, 5090, *maʿªleh* [2]
hill, 6755, *ʿōpel*[2] [1]
hill, 8229, *rāmâ*[3] [1]
barren hill, 9155, *šᵉpî*[1] [1]

HILLEL [2]
Hillel, 2148, *hillēl* [2]

HILLS [76]
hills, 2215, *har* [40]
hills, 1496, *gibʿâ*[1] [36]

HILLSIDE [3]
hillside, 2215, *har* [1]
hillside, 7521+2215, *ṣēlāʿ*[1]*+har* [1]
hillside, 7967, *qeren* [1]

HILLTOP [2]
hilltop, 2215, *har* [1]
hilltop, 8031+2215, *rōʾš*[1]*+har* [1]

HILLTOPS [3]
hilltops, 1496, *gibʿâ*[1] [2]
hilltops, 8031+2215, *rōʾš*[1]*+har* [1]

HIM [3499]*
him, 2257, *-ô* [2172]
him, 2084, *-hû* [484]
him, *NIH/RPE* [285]
him, 5647, *-nû*[2] [175]
him, *AIT* [101]
him, 10192, *-ēh* [24]
him, 10204, *-hî* [11]
him[s], 2021, *ha-* [10]
him, 3870, *-kā* [10]
him, 2085, *hûʾ* [7]
him[s], 889, *ʾªšer* [4]
him[s], 408, *ʾîš*[1] [3]
him[s], 2021+408, *ha-+ʾîš*[1] [3]
him, 2023, *-āh* [3]
him, 2157, *-hem* [3]
him, 4392, *-ām* [3]
him, 4564, *-mô* [3]
him, 3276, *-î* [2]
him, 5626, *-nâ* [2]
him[s], 1505, *geber*[1] [1]
him, 3338+2257, *yād+-ô* [1]
him, 5761, *-nî* [1]
him[s], 5883, *nepeš* [1]
him, 5883+2257, *nepeš+-ô* [1]

HIMSELF [263]*
himself, 2257, *-ô* [55]
himself, *AIT* [39]
himself, 2085, *hûʾ* [22]
himself, 5883+2257, *nepeš+-ô* [18]
himself, 1414+2257, *bāśār+-ô* [10]
himself, 4213+2257, *lēb+-ô* [10]
himself, *NIH/RPE* [9]
the man himself, 2257, *-ô* [2]
himself[s], 2021+408, *ha-+ʾîš*[1] [1]
he himself, 2085, *hûʾ* [1]
he himself, 2257, *-ô* [1]
by himself, 4200+963+2257, *lᵉ-*[1]*+bad*[1]*+-ô* [1]
himself, 4222+2257, *lēbāb+-ô* [1]
himself, 5626, *-nâ* [1]
himself, 8031+2257, *rōʾš*[1]*+-ô* [1]
himself, 9005+2257, *šēm*[1]*+-ô* [1]

HIN [22]
hin, 2125, *hîn* [22]

HINDER [2]
hinder, 1757, *gāraʿ*[1] [1]
hinder, 5109, *maʿṣôr* [1]

HINDQUARTERS [2]
hindquarters, 294, *ʾāḥôr* [2]

HINGED [1]
hinged, 6015, *sābab* [1]

HINGES [1]
hinges, 7494, *ṣîr*[2] [1]

HINNOM [3]
Hinnom, 2183, *hinnōm* [3]

HIP [5]
hip, 3751, *yārēk* [5]

HIRAH [2]
Hirah, 2669, *ḥîrâ* [2]

HIRAM [23]
Hiram, 2671, *ḥîrām* [15]
Hiram, 2586, *ḥûrām* [6]
Hiram, 2670, *ḥîrôm* [2]

HIRAM'S [2]
Hiram's, 2586, *ḥûrām* [1]
Hiram's, 2671, *ḥîrām* [1]

HIRE [6]
hire, 8509, *śākar* [3]
hire as a prostitute, 924, *ʾetnan* [1]
hire themselves out, 8509, *śākar* [1]
money paid for hire, 8510, *śākār*[1] [1]

HIRED [26]
hired, 8509, *śākar* [9]
hired man, 8502, *śākîr* [5]
hired worker, 8502, *śākîr* [4]
hired, 8502, *śākîr* [3]
hired, 6128, *sākar*[3] [1]
hired hand, 8502, *śākîr* [1]
man hired, 8502, *śākîr* [1]
been hired, 8509, *śākar* [1]
hired, 8509+8509, *śākar+śākar* [1]

HIRES [1]
hires, 8509, *śākar* [1]

HIS [5697]*
his, 2257, *-ô* [4456]
his, *NIH/RPE* [303]
his[s], 2021, *ha-* [157]
his own, 2257, *-ô* [140]
his, 2084, *-hû* [137]
his, *AIT* [121]
his, 4200+2257, *lᵉ-*[1]*+-ô* [81]
his, 10192, *-ēh* [47]
his, 10204, *-hî* [26]
his, 907+2257, *ʾēt*[2]*+-ô* [13]
his, 2023, *-āh* [13]
his, 2024, *-ōh* [10]
his, 5647, *-nû*[2] [10]
his own, 4200+2257, *lᵉ-*[1]*+-ô* [8]
his, 4392, *-ām* [7]
his own, 2084, *-hû* [6]
his, 2085, *hûʾ* [6]
his, 3870, *-kā* [6]
his, 2157, *-hem* [5]
his own[s], 2021, *ha-* [4]
his[s], 10002, *-āʾ* [4]
his, 3276, *-î* [3]
his, 4200+4564, *lᵉ-*[1]*+-mô* [2]
his[s], 5695, *nōaḥ* [2]
his, 6640+2257, *ʿim+-ô* [2]
his[s], 465, *ʾēlleh* [1]
his[s], 632, *ʾᵉnôš*[1] [1]
his, 928+2257, *bᵉ-+-ô* [1]
his[s], 2021+408, *ha-+ʾîš*[1] [1]
his, 2114, *-hî* [1]
his own, 4392, *-ām* [1]
his, 4564, *-mô* [1]
his[s], 4777, *mîkâ* [1]
his, 4946+5647, *min+-nû*[2] [1]
his own, 5647, *-nû*[2] [1]
his own, 5883+2257, *nepeš+-ô* [1]
his, 6584+2257, *ʿal*[2]*+-ô* [1]
his, 10089+10192, *bᵉ-+-ēh* [1]
his own, 10192, *-ēh* [1]
his, 10378+10192, *lᵉ-+-ēh* [1]

HISS [2]
hiss, 7754, *qôl* [1]
hiss, 9239, *šāraq* [1]

HISSES [1]
hisses, 9239, *šāraq* [1]

HISTORIC [1]
historic right, 2355, *zikkārôn* [1]

HISTORY [1]
long history, 10427+10317+10550, *min+yôm+ʿālam* [1]

HIT [5]
hit, 5782, *nākâ* [3]
hit, 5162, *māṣāʾ* [1]
hit, 5597, *nāgap* [1]

HITCH [3]
hitch up, 673, *ʾāsar* [2]
hitch, 673, *ʾāsar* [1]

HITCHED [2]
hitched up, 673, *ʾāsar* [1]
hitched, 673, *ʾāsar* [1]

HITS [4]
hits, 5782, *nākâ* [4]

HITTING [1]
hitting, 5782, *nākâ* [1]

HITTITE [25]
Hittite, 3153, *ḥittî* [23]
Hittite, 3147, *ḥēt* [2]

HITTITES [36]
Hittites, 3153, *ḥittî* [25]
Hittites, 1201+3147, *bēn*[1]*+ḥēt* [9]
Hittites, 3147, *ḥēt* [2]

HIVITE [2]
Hivite, 2563, *ḥiwwî* [2]

HIVITES [23]
Hivites, 2563, *ḥiwwî* [23]

HIZKI [1]
Hizki, 2623, *ḥizqî* [1]

HIZKIAH [1]
Hizkiah, 2624, *ḥizqiyyâ* [1]

HOARD [1]
hoard, 732, *ʾāṣar* [1]

HOARDED [2]
hoarded, 2889, *ḥāsan* [1]
hoarded, 9068, *šāmar* [1]

HOARDS [1]
hoards, 4979, *mānaʿ* [1]

HOBAB [2]
Hobab, 2463, *ḥōbāb* [2]

HOBAH [1]
Hobah, 2551, *ḥôbâ* [1]

HOBAIAH [2]
Hobaiah, 2469, *ḥᵒbayyâ* [2]

HOD [1]
Hod, 2087, *hôd*[2] [1]

HODAVIAH [6]
Hodaviah, 2089, *hôdawyâ* [3]
Hodaviah, 2088, *hôdᵉwâ* [2]
Hodaviah, 2090, *hôdawyāhû* [1]

HODESH [1]
Hodesh, 2545, *ḥōdeš*[2] [1]

HODIAH [5]
Hodiah, 2091, *hôdiyyâ* [5]

HODIAH'S [1]
Hodiah's, 2091, *hôdiyyâ* [1]

HOE [1]
hoe, 5053, *maʿdēr* [1]

HOGLAH [4]
Hoglah, 2519, *ḥoglâ* [4]

HOHAM [1]
Hoham, 2097, *hôhām* [1]

HOLD [122]
hold, 2118, *hāyâ* [10]
hold, 1074, *bayit*^{1} [8]
hold fast, 1815, *dābaq* [7]
took hold, 2616, *ḥāzaq* [7]
hold, *NIH/RPE* [5]
take hold, 2616, *ḥāzaq* [4]
hold fast, 2616, *ḥāzaq* [3]
hold back, 3104, *ḥāśak* [3]
hold, 3920, *kûl* [3]
took hold, 4374, *lāqaḥ* [3]
hold accountable, 4946+3338+1335, *min+yād+bāqaš* [3]
hold sway, 5675, *nûaʿ* [3]
hold, 296, *ʾāḥaz*^{1} [2]
took hold, 296, *ʾāḥaz*^{1} [2]
hold in pledge, 2471, *ḥābal*^{1} [2]
hold guiltless, 5927, *nāqâ* [2]
hold in bondage, 6268, *ʿābad* [2]
lay hold, 9461, *tāmak* [2]
hold fast, 296, *ʾāḥaz*^{1} [1]
hold out, 296, *ʾāḥaz*^{1} [1]
take hold, 296, *ʾāḥaz*^{1} [1]
hold as a possession, 299, *ʾ^{a}ḥuzzâ* [1]
hold, 299, *ʾ^{a}ḥuzzâ* [1]
hold back, 336, *ʾāḥar* [1]
hold yourself back, 706, *ʾāpaq* [1]
hold head high, 1448, *gāʾâ* [1]
hold accountable, 2011+4946+3338, *dāraš+min+yād* [1]
hold, 2118+928+3338, *hāyâ+b^{e}-+yād* [1]
take hold of, 2118+928, *hāyâ+b^{e}-* [1]
hold, 2349, *zākar*^{1} [1]
hold in arms, 2485, *ḥābaq* [1]
hold a festival, 2510, *ḥāgag* [1]
hold on, 2616, *ḥāzaq* [1]
caught hold, 2616, *ḥāzaq* [1]
hold back, 2616, *ḥāzaq* [1]
lay hold, 2616, *ḥāzaq* [1]
take firm hold, 2616, *ḥāzaq* [1]
takes hold, 2616, *ḥāzaq* [1]
hold back, 2641, *ḥāṭam* [1]
hold, 3108, *ḥāšab* [1]
hold, 3338, *yād* [1]
hold out, 3782, *yāšab* [1]
hold in, 3920, *kûl* [1]
hold back, 3973, *kālāʾ*^{1} [1]
hold, 4200, *l^{e}-*^{1} [1]
hold shut, 4315, *lāḥaṣ* [1]
hold back overnight, 4328+6330+1332, *lîn+ʿad*^{2}*+bōqer*^{2} [1]
taking hold, 4374, *lāqaḥ* [1]
hold accountable, 4946+3338+2011, *min+yād+dāraš* [1]
hold responsible, 4946+3338+1335, *min+yād+bāqaš* [1]
lay hold, 5162, *māṣāʾ* [1]
hold out, 5742, *nāṭâ* [1]
hold innocent, 5927, *nāqâ* [1]
hold accountable, 5989+6584, *nātan+ʿal*^{2} [1]
hold, 5989, *nātan* [1]
take firm hold, 6487+6487, *ʿāṭâ*^{2}*+ʿāṭâ*^{2} [1]
hold back, 7277, *pāraʿ*^{2} [1]
hold, 7756, *qûm* [1]
hold, 8003, *qāšar* [1]
hold back, 8740, *šûb*^{1} [1]
hold, 8883, *šît*^{1} [1]
hold firm, 9419, *tākan* [1]
hold fast, 9461, *tāmak* [1]
taken hold, 9461, *tāmak* [1]
took hold, 9461, *tāmak* [1]
hold, 9530, *tāpaś* [1]
take hold, 9530, *tāpaś* [1]
took hold, 9530, *tāpaś* [1]
hold back, 10411, *m^{e}ḥāʾ* [1]

HOLDING [10]
holding, 4200, *l^{e}-*^{1} [2]
holding, *NIH/RPE* [1]
holding, 928+3338, *b^{e}-+yād* [1]
holding on, 2616, *ḥāzaq* [1]
holding, 2616, *ḥāzaq* [1]
holding out, 3855, *yātar* [1]
holding in, 3920, *kûl* [1]
holding, 3920, *kûl* [1]
holding, 6913, *ʿāśâ*^{1} [1]

HOLDS [17]
holds fast, 2616, *ḥāzaq* [2]
holds, 9461, *tāmak* [2]
holds, *NIH/RPE* [1]
holds, 357, *ʾāṭam* [1]
holds, 910, *ʾātâ* [1]
holds, 928+3338+2118, *b^{e}-+yād+hāyâ* [1]
holds tongue, 3087, *ḥārēš*^{2} [1]
holds, 3104, *ḥāśak* [1]
holds, 3920, *kûl* [1]
holds back, 6806, *ʿāṣar* [1]
holds back, 6810, *ʿāqab* [1]
holds in store, 7621, *ṣāpan* [1]
holds up, 8123, *rûm*^{1} [1]
holds a grudge against, 8475, *śāṭam* [1]
holds, 8938, *šālaḥ* [1]

HOLE [6]
hole, 2986, *ḥōr*^{2} [2]
hole, *NIH/RPE* [1]
hole, 1014, *bôr* [1]
dig a hole, 2916, *ḥāpar*^{1} [1]
hole, 2987, *ḥur* [1]

HOLES [5]
holes, 2986, *ḥōr*^{2} [2]
holes, 4704, *m^{e}ḥillâ* [1]
water holes, 5635, *nah^{a}lōl*^{1} [1]
holes, 5918, *nāqab*^{1} [1]

HOLIDAY [1]
holiday, 2182, *h^{a}nāḥâ* [1]

HOLIEST [1]
holiest, 5219, *miqdāš* [1]

HOLINESS [13]
holiness, 7731, *qōdeš* [9]
acknowledge holiness, 7727, *qādaš* [1]
holiness, 7727, *qādaš* [1]
show holiness, 7727, *qādaš* [1]
uphold holiness, 7727, *qādaš* [1]

HOLLOW [6]
hollow, 5554, *nābûb* [3]
hollow of hands, 2908, *ḥōpen* [1]
hollow place, 4847, *maktēš* [1]
hollow of hand, 9123, *šōʿal* [1]

HOLON [3]
Holon, 2708, *ḥōlôn* [3]

HOLY [391]
holy, 7731, *qōdeš* [136]
holy, 7705, *qādôš* [62]
Holy One, 7705, *qādôš* [43]
most holy, 7731+7731, *qōdeš+qōdeš* [23]
holy place, 7731, *qōdeš* [14]
Most Holy Place, 7731+7731, *qōdeš+qōdeš* [11]
holy things, 7731, *qōdeš* [10]
Most Holy Place, 7731, *qōdeš* [8]
holy, 7727, *qādaš* [7]
keep holy, 7727, *qādaš* [7]
makes holy, 7727, *qādaš* [7]
show myself holy, 7727, *qādaš* [7]
holy, 10620, *qaddîš* [7]
holy offerings, 7731, *qōdeš* [5]
most holy offerings, 7731+7731, *qōdeš+qōdeš* [5]
made holy, 7727, *qādaš* [3]
most holy things, 7731+7731, *qōdeš+qōdeš* [3]
holy, *NIH/RPE* [2]
holy place, 5219, *miqdāš* [2]
declare holy, 7727, *qādaš* [2]
honor as holy, 7727, *qādaš* [2]
keeping holy, 7727, *qādaš* [2]
make holy, 7727, *qādaš* [2]
regard as holy, 7727, *qādaš* [2]
holy furnishings, 7731, *qōdeš* [2]
something holy, 7731, *qōdeš* [2]
Most Holy Place, 1808+7731, *d^{e}bîr*^{1}*+qōdeš* [1]
not holy, 2687, *ḥōl* [1]
holy, 2883, *ḥāsîd* [1]
Most Holy Place, 5219+7731, *miqdāš+qōdeš* [1]
holy places, 5219, *miqdāš* [1]
holy things, 5219, *miqdāš* [1]
be acknowledged as holy, 7727, *qādaš* [1]
celebrate holy, 7727, *qādaš* [1]
set apart as holy, 7727, *qādaš* [1]
show himself holy, 7727, *qādaš* [1]
showed himself holy, 7727, *qādaš* [1]
Holy One, 7731, *qōdeš* [1]
holy ones, 7731, *qōdeš* [1]
holy precincts, 7731, *qōdeš* [1]
what holy, 7731, *qōdeš* [1]

HOMAGE [2]
paid homage, 2556, *ḥāwâ*^{2} [1]
offered a kiss of homage, 5975+4200+7023, *nāšaq*^{1}*+l^{e}-*^{1}*+peh* [1]

HOMAM [2]
Homam, 2102, *hômām* [1]
Homam, 2123, *hêmām* [1]

HOME [127]
home, 1074, *bayit*^{1} [71]
home, 5226, *māqôm* [14]
home, 185, *ʾōhel*^{1} [10]
home, *NIH/RPE* [9]
came home, 995, *bôʾ* [2]
have a home, 8905+9393, *šākan+taḥat*^{1} [2]
home, 10103, *bayit* [2]
home, 141, *ʾ^{a}dāmâ*^{1} [1]
go home, 995, *bôʾ* [1]
bring home, 995, *bôʾ* [1]
come home, 995, *bôʾ* [1]
take home, 995, *bôʾ* [1]
went home, 2143, *hālak* [1]
home, 2948, *ḥāṣîr*^{4} [1]
have a home, 3782, *yāšab* [1]
stayed at home, 3782, *yāšab* [1]
at home, 4328, *lîn* [1]
born in the same home, 4580+1074, *môledet+bayit*^{1} [1]
home, 4632, *môšāb* [1]
home, 4955, *mānôaḥ*^{1} [1]
home, 5659, *nāweh*^{1} [1]
returned home, 6015, *sābab* [1]
home, 8699, *šebet*^{1} [1]
make home, 8905, *šākan* [1]

HOMELAND [7]
homeland, 5659, *nāweh*^{1} [2]
homeland, 141, *ʾ^{a}dāmâ*^{1} [1]
homeland, 824+4580, *ʾereṣ+môledet* [1]
homeland, 1473, *g^{e}bûl* [1]
homeland, 5226+824, *māqôm+ʾereṣ* [1]
homeland, 5226, *māqôm* [1]

HOMER [10]
homer, 2818, *ḥōmer*^{3} [10]

HOMERS [1]
homers, 2818, *ḥōmer*^{3} [1]

HOMES [24]
homes, 1074, *bayit*^{1} [10]
homes, 185, *ʾōhel*^{1} [9]
homes, 2540, *ḥeder* [1]
ruined homes, 2999, *ḥorbâ* [1]
homes, 5226, *māqôm* [1]
homes, 5438, *miškān* [1]
homes, 9393, *taḥat*^{1} [1]

HOMETOWN [3]
hometown, 6551, *ʿîr*^{1} [3]

HONEST [18]
honest, 7406, *ṣedeq* [8]
honest, 4026, *kēn*^{1} [5]

honest, 3841, *yōšer* [2]
honest, 5477, *mišpāṭ* [1]
honest, 5791, *nākōaḥ* [1]
honest, 7404, *ṣaddîq* [1]

HONESTLY [1]
honestly, 5477, *mišpāṭ* [1]

HONESTY [3]
complete honesty, 575, *ʼemûnâ* [1]
honesty, 5791, *nākōaḥ* [1]
honesty, 7407, *ṣedāqâ* [1]

HONEY [56]
honey, 1831, *debaš* [52]
honey, 5885, *nōpet* [3]
honey from the comb, 5885, *nōpet* [1]

HONEYCOMB [4]
honeycomb, 3624, *yaʻar*[2] [1]
honeycomb, 3626+1831, *yaʻarâ*[1]+*debaš* [1]
sweetness as the honeycomb, 5885, *nōpet* [1]
honeycomb, 7430+1831, *ṣûp*[2]+*debaš* [1]

HONOR [117]
honor, 3883, *kābôd*[1] [33]
honor, 3877, *kābēd*[1] [19]
pay honor, 2556, *ḥāwâ*[2] [7]
honor, 3702, *yeqār* [7]
honor, 9514, *tipʼeret* [7]
honor, *NIH/RPE* [4]
in honor, 4200, *le-*[1] [4]
seat of honor, 4058, *kissēʼ* [3]
honor, 9005, *šēm*[1] [3]
honor, 2086, *hôd*[1] [2]
was held in honor, 3877, *kābēd*[1] [2]
honor as holy, 7727, *qādaš* [2]
honor, 8420, *śeʼēt*[1] [2]
honor, *AIT* [1]
honor, 1525, *gedûllâ* [1]
honor, 2077, *hādār* [1]
treat with honor, 2290, *zābal* [1]
honor, 2349, *zākar*[1] [1]
honor, 2556, *ḥāwâ*[2] [1]
paid honor, 2556, *ḥāwâ*[2] [1]
be held in honor, 3877, *kābēd*[1] [1]
bring honor, 3877, *kābēd*[1] [1]
held in honor, 3877, *kābēd*[1] [1]
bestow a title of honor, 4033, *kānâ* [1]
to honor, 4200, *le-*[1] [1]
honor, 5989+3883, *nātan+kābôd*[1] [1]
honor, 6913+3702, *ʻāśâ*[1]+*yeqār* [1]
bring honor, 6995, *pāʼar*[2] [1]
leave the honor, 6995, *pāʼar*[2] [1]
shown honor, 7156+5951, *pāneh+nāśāʼ* [1]
call in honor of, 7727+4200, *qādaš+le-*[1] [1]
honor, 10198, *hedar*[1] [1]
honor, 10199, *hedar*[2] [1]
honor, 10331, *yeqār* [1]
paid honor, 10504, *segid* [1]

HONORABLE [5]
honorable, 3877, *kābēd*[1] [3]
honorable, 3883, *kābôd*[1] [1]
honorable, 10330, *yaqqîr* [1]

HONORABLY [2]
honorably, 928+622, *be-+ʼemet* [2]

HONORED [23]
honored, 3877, *kābēd*[1] [6]
be honored, 3877, *kābēd*[1] [3]
honored, 1540, *gādal* [2]
honored, 3883, *kābôd*[1] [2]
cause to be honored, 2349, *zākar*[1] [1]
honored, 3108, *ḥāšab* [1]
honored, 3701, *yāqār* [1]
am honored, 3877, *kābēd*[1] [1]
is honored, 3877, *kābēd*[1] [1]
was honored, 3877, *kābēd*[1] [1]
honored, 3883+6913, *kābôd*[1]+*ʻāśâ*[1] [1]
honored, 5951+7156, *nāśāʼ+pāneh* [1]
honored, 8123, *rûm*[1] [1]
honored, 10693, *šebaḥ* [1]

HONORING [3]
honoring, 3877, *kābēd*[1] [2]
honoring, 3883, *kābôd*[1] [1]

HONORS [4]
honors, 3877, *kābēd*[1] [4]

HOOF [12]
hoof, 7274, *parsâ* [12]

HOOFS [8]
hoofs, 7274, *parsâ* [6]
hoofs, 6811, *ʻāqēb*[1] [1]
hoofs, 7271, *pāras*[1] [1]

HOOK [4]
hook, 2560, *ḥôaḥ*[1] [2]
hook, 2626, *ḥāḥ* [2]

HOOKS [24]
hooks, 2260, *wāw* [13]
hooks, 2626, *ḥāḥ* [4]
pruning hooks, 4661, *mazmērâ* [3]
hooks, 2676, *ḥakkâ* [2]
hooks, 7553, *ṣēn* [1]
double-pronged hooks, 9191, *šepattayim*[2] [1]

HOOPOE [2]
hoopoe, 1871, *dûkîpat* [2]

HOPE [86]
hope, 9536, *tiqwâ*[2] [30]
put hope, 3498, *yāḥal* [14]
hope, 3498, *yāḥal* [7]
hope in, 7747, *qāwâ*[1] [7]
hope, 5223, *miqweh*[1] [5]
future hope, 344, *ʼaḥarît* [3]
hope, 7747, *qāwâ*[1] [3]
hope, 9347, *tôḥelet* [2]
hope, *NIH/RPE* [1]
hope, 1059, *biṭṭāḥôn* [1]
wait in hope, 2675, *ḥākâ* [1]
given hope, 3498, *yāḥal* [1]
hope unfulfilled, 3498, *yāḥal* [1]
wait in hope, 3498, *yāḥal* [1]
hope, 4438, *mabbāṭ* [1]
hope, 4440, *mibṭāḥ* [1]
watch in hope, 7595, *ṣāpâ*[1] [1]
hope for, 7747, *qāwâ*[1] [1]
in hope, 7747, *qāwâ*[1] [1]
look in hope, 7747, *qāwâ*[1] [1]
hope, 8432, *śābar*[2] [1]
hope, 8433, *śēber* [1]
vain hope, 9214, *šeqer* [1]

HOPED [5]
hoped, 7747, *qāwâ*[1] [2]
hoped for, 7747, *qāwâ*[1] [1]
hoped, 8432, *śābar*[2] [1]
hoped, 9347, *tôḥelet* [1]

HOPELESS [1]
hopeless, 3286, *yāʼaš* [1]

HOPES [4]
fill with false hopes, 2038, *hābal* [1]
hopes, 8433, *śēber* [1]
raise hopes, 8922, *šālâ*[1] [1]
hopes, 9536, *tiqwâ*[2] [1]

HOPHNI [5]
Hophni, 2909, *ḥopnî* [5]

HOPHRA [1]
Hophra, 2922, *ḥopraʻ* [1]

HOPING [1]
hoping, 10527+10168, *ʻad+dî* [1]

HOPPING [1]
hopping, 6001, *nātar*[2] [1]

HOR [12]
Hor, 2216, *hōr* [12]

HOR HAGGIDGAD [2]
Hor Haggidgad, 2988, *ḥōr haggidgād* [2]

HORAM [1]
Horam, 2235, *hōrām* [1]

HORDE [4]
horde, 7736, *qāhāl* [4]

HORDES [21]
hordes, 2162, *hāmôn* [18]
hordes, 7736, *qāhāl* [2]
hordes, 4480, *megammâ* [1]

HOREB [17]
Horeb, 2998, *ḥōrēb* [17]

HOREM [1]
Horem, 3054, *ḥorēm* [1]

HORESH [4]
Horesh, 3092, *ḥōreš*[2] [4]

HORI [3]
Hori, 3036, *ḥōrî*[2] [3]

HORITE [4]
Horite, 3037, *ḥōrî*[3] [4]

HORITES [4]
Horites, 3037, *ḥōrî*[3] [3]
the Horites[s], 4392, *-ām* [1]

HORIZON [3]
horizon, 2553, *ḥûg*[2] [1]
horizon, 2976, *ḥōq* [1]
horizon, 9028, *šāmayim* [1]

HORMAH [9]
Hormah, 3055, *ḥormâ* [9]

HORN [37]
horn, 7967, *qeren* [23]
horn, 10641, *qeren* [9]
ram's horn, 8795, *šôpār* [2]
horn, *NIH/RPE* [1]
horn, 2956, *ḥaṣōṣerâ* [1]
ram's horn, 3413, *yôbēl* [1]

HORNED [2]
horned owl, 1426+3613, *bat*[1]+*yaʻanâ* [2]

HORNET [3]
hornet, 7667, *ṣirʻâ* [3]

HORNS [56]
horns, 7967, *qeren* [44]
horns, 10641, *qeren* [5]
horns, *NIH/RPE* [3]
rams horns, 3413, *yôbēl* [1]
horns, 7966, *qāran* [1]
horns, 8795, *šôpār* [1]
rams horns, 8795, *šôpār* [1]

HORONAIM [5]
Horonaim, 2589, *ḥôrōnayim* [5]

HORONITE [3]
Horonite, 3061, *ḥōrōnî* [3]

HORRIBLE [8]
horrible end, 1166, *ballāhâ* [3]
horrible thing, 9137, *šaʻarûrî* [2]
horrible, 8273, *raʻ*[1] [1]
horrible, 9014, *šammâ*[1] [1]
something horrible, 9136, *šaʻarûr* [1]

HORRIFIED [2]
horrified, 9037, *šāmēm*[1] [2]

HORROR [23]
horror, 9014, *šammâ*[1] [6]
object of horror, 9014, *šammâ*[1] [5]
horror, 8550, *śaʻar*[1] [3]
thing of horror, 2400, *zaʻawâ* [1]
horror, 2990, *ḥārēb*[1] [1]
object of horror, 2997, *ḥōreb*[2] [1]
horror, 3010, *ḥarādâ*[1] [1]
object of horror, 4745, *meḥittâ* [1]
object of horror, 5457, *mešammâ* [1]
horror, 7146, *pallāṣût* [1]
thing of horror, 9014, *šammâ*[1] [1]
fill with horror, 9037, *šāmēm*[1] [1]

HORSE [30]
horse, 6061, *sûs*[1] [30]

HORSE'S [1]
horse's, 6061, *sûs*[1] [1]

HORSEBACK [3]
horseback, 6061, *sûs*[1] [2]
led on horseback, 8206, *rākab* [1]

HORSEMAN [4]
horseman, 8206+6061, *rākab+sûs*[1] [3]
horseman, 8208, *rakkāb* [1]

HORSEMEN [28]
horsemen, 7305, *pārāš*[2] [27]
horsemen, 8206+6061, *rākab+sûs*[1] [1]

HORSES [116]
horses, 6061, *sûs*[1] [90]
horses, 7304, *pārāš*[1] [14]
horses, *NIH/RPE* [4]
war horses, 7304, *pārāš*[1] [2]
chariot horses, 8207, *rekeb* [2]
work horses, 6061, *sûs*[1] [1]
chariot horses, 8224, *rekeš* [1]
fast horses, 8224, *rekeš* [1]
horses, 8224, *rekeš* [1]

HOSAH [5]
Hosah, 2880, *ḥōsâ*[1] [4]
Hosah, 2881, *ḥōsâ*[2] [1]

HOSEA [4]
Hosea, 2107, *hôšēaʿ* [2]
Hosea[s], 2257, *-ô* [2]

HOSHAIAH [3]
Hoshaiah, 2108, *hôšaʿyâ* [3]

HOSHAMA [1]
Hoshama, 2106, *hôšāmāʿ* [1]

HOSHEA [12]
Hoshea, 2107, *hôšēaʿ* [12]

HOST [12]
host, 7372, *ṣābāʾ*[2] [8]
starry host, 7372, *ṣābāʾ*[2] [4]

HOSTAGES [2]
hostages, 1201+9510, *bēn*[1]*+taʿ[a]rûbôt* [2]

HOSTILE [11]
hostile, 7950, *q[e]rî* [6]
hostile, *NIH/RPE* [1]
hostile, 7640, *ṣar*[2] [1]
hostile, 7675, *ṣārar*[2] [1]
hostile, 7762, *qûṣ*[1] [1]
hostile, 8533, *śānēʾ* [1]

HOSTILITY [13]
hostility, 368, *ʾêbâ* [4]
hostility, 5378, *maśṭēmâ* [2]
hostility, 5286, *mārâ*[1] [1]
in hostility toward, 6584+7156, *ʿal*[2]*+pāneh* [1]
lived in hostility toward, 6584+7156+5877, *ʿal*[2]*+pāneh+nāpal* [1]
hostility, 7650, *ṣārâ*[1] [1]
hostility, 7950, *q[e]rî* [1]
hostility, 8120, *rûaḥ* [1]
hostility, 8475, *śāṭam* [1]

HOSTS [11]
hosts, 7372, *ṣābāʾ*[2] [8]
heavenly hosts, 7372, *ṣābāʾ*[2] [2]
starry hosts, 7372, *ṣābāʾ*[2] [1]

HOT [17]
hot, 2801, *ḥāmam* [6]
in hot pursuit, 339, *ʾaḥar* [1]
hot coals, 1624, *gaḥal* [1]
hot, 2770, *ḥōm* [1]
hot, 2779, *ḥēmâ* [1]
hot, 3019, *ḥārôn* [1]
hot, 3034, *ḥ[o]rî* [1]
hot springs, 3553, *yēmim* [1]
hot, 4023, *kāmar* [1]
hot east wind, 7708, *qādîm* [1]
baked over hot coals, 8363, *reṣep*[1] [1]
hot, 10015, *ʾ[a]zâ* [1]

HOT-TEMPERED [5]
hot-tempered, 678, *ʾap*[2] [1]
hot-tempered, 1251+2779, *baʿal*[1]*+ḥēmâ* [1]
hot-tempered, 1524+2779, *gādôl+ḥēmâ* [1]
hot-tempered, 2779, *ḥēmâ* [1]
hot-tempered, 5253+5883, *mar*[1]*+nepeš* [1]

HOTHAM [2]
Hotham, 2598, *ḥôtām*[2] [2]

HOTHEADED [1]
hotheaded, 6297, *ʿābar*[2] [1]

HOTHIR [2]
Hothir, 2110, *hôtîr* [2]

HOTLY [2]
hotly pursue, 8634, *šāʾap*[1] [2]

HOTTER [1]
hotter, 10015, *ʾ[a]zâ* [1]

HOUND [1]
hound, 8103, *rādap* [1]

HOUNDED [2]
hounded, 8103, *rādap* [1]
hounded, 8635, *šāʾap*[2] [1]

HOUR [1]
hour, 6961, *ʿēt* [1]

HOUSE [812]
house, 1074, *bayit*[1] [770]
house, 10103, *bayit* [17]
house, *NIH/RPE* [14]
house, 5659, *nāweh*[1] [3]
house, 185, *ʾōhel*[1] [2]
house, 185+1074, *ʾōhel*[1]*+bayit*[1] [1]
house, 1074+4632, *bayit*[1]*+môšāb* [1]
roof of house, 1511, *gāg* [1]
house, 1886, *dôr*[1] [1]
house, 5249, *m[e]qērâ* [1]
house, 7860, *qēn* [1]

HOUSEHOLD [95]
household, 1074, *bayit*[1] [81]
household gods, 9572, *t[e]rāpîm* [8]
household articles, 3998, *k[e]lî* [2]
household, *NIH/RPE* [1]
household, 185, *ʾōhel*[1] [1]
slave born in household, 1201+563, *bēn*[1]*+ʾāmâ* [1]
household, 6337, *ʿēdâ*[1] [1]

HOUSEHOLDS [6]
households, 1074, *bayit*[1] [6]

HOUSES [88]
houses, 1074, *bayit*[1] [81]
houses, *NIH/RPE* [2]
houses, 10103, *bayit* [2]
houses[s], 889, *ʾ[a]šer* [1]
houses, 4632, *môšāb* [1]
houses, 5438, *miškān* [1]

HOVERING [2]
hovering overhead, 6414, *ʿûp*[1] [1]
hovering, 8173, *rāḥap*[1] [1]

HOVERS [1]
hovers, 8173, *rāḥap*[1] [1]

HOW [475]
how, 4537, *mâ* [69]
how, *NIH/RPE* [64]
how, 375, *ʾêk* [47]
how, 3954, *kî*[2] [39]
how, 889, *ʾ[a]šer* [28]
how long, 6330+5503, *ʿad*[2]*+mātay* [27]
how, 928+4537, *b[e]+mâ* [16]
how, *AIT* [15]
how, 377, *ʾêkâ* [12]
how long, 6330+625+2025, *ʿad*[2]*+ʾān+-â*[2] [12]
know how, 3359, *yādaʿ* [8]
how much less, 677+3954, *ʾap*[1]*+kî*[2] [6]
this is how, 928+2296, *b[e]+zeh* [6]
how, 2180, *hinnēh* [6]
how much more, 677+3954, *ʾap*[1]*+kî*[2] [4]
how much more, 677, *ʾap*[1] [4]
how happy, 897, *ʾašrê* [4]
knows how, 3359, *yādaʿ* [4]
this is how, 3970, *kākâ* [4]
how long, 6330+4537, *ʿad*[2]*+mâ* [4]
how much worse, 677+3954, *ʾap*[1]*+kî*[2] [3]
how, 3869+4537, *k[e]-+mâ* [3]
how, 4394, *m[e]ʾōd* [3]
how are, 8934, *šālôm* [3]
how, 379, *ʾêkākâ* [2]
how much more so, 677+3954, *ʾap*[1]*+kî*[2] [2]
how much, 889, *ʾ[a]šer* [2]
how, 2120, *hêk* [2]
how, 2256, *w[e]-* [2]
this is how, 2296, *zeh* [2]
how, 2296, *zeh* [2]
how often, 3869+4537, *k[e]-+mâ* [2]
this is how, 3907, *kōh* [2]
this is how, 4027, *kēn*[2] [2]
that is how, 4027, *kēn*[2] [2]
how, 4769, *mî* [2]
how many, 5031, *mispār*[1] [2]
how long, 5503, *mātay* [2]
how many, 6330+3869+4537, *ʿad*[2]*+k[e]-+mâ* [2]
how, 10341+10408, *k[e]-+mâ* [2]
how long, 339+5503+6388, *ʾaḥar+mātay+ʿôd* [1]
how gladly, 375, *ʾêk* [1]
but how, 377, *ʾêkâ* [1]
see how, 377, *ʾêkâ* [1]
how, 434, *ʾākēn*[1] [1]
how much better, 677+3954, *ʾap*[1]*+kî*[2] [1]
how much less, 677+3954+4202, *ʾap*[1]*+kî*[2]*+lōʾ* [1]
how, 677, *ʾap*[1] [1]
how, 928+4537+686, *b[e]-+mâ+ʾēpôʾ* [1]
how, 928, *b[e]-* [1]
this is how, 928+3972+465, *b[e]-+kōl+ʾēlleh* [1]
how treacherous, 953+953, *bāgad+bāgad* [1]
how, 1821, *dābār* [1]
how behaved, 2006, *derek* [1]
how live, 2006, *derek* [1]
this is how, 2180, *hinnēh* [1]
how much more, 2256+677+3954, *w[e]-+ʾap*[1]*+kî*[2] [1]
know how to read, 3359+6219, *yādaʿ+sēper*[1] [1]
knowing how, 3359, *yādaʿ* [1]
show how to distinguish, 3359, *yādaʿ* [1]
how long must wait, 3869+4537+3427, *k[e]-+mâ+yôm*[1] [1]
how many more, 3869+4537, *k[e]-+mâ* [1]
how many, 3869+4537, *k[e]-+mâ* [1]
this is how, 3869+2021+1821+2021+465, *k[e]-+ha-+dābār+ha-+ʾēlleh* [1]
this is how, 3869+889, *k[e]-+ʾ[a]šer* [1]
how long, 3869+4537, *k[e]-+mâ* [1]
how quickly, 3869+5071, *k[e]-+m[e]ʿaṭ* [1]
how, 3869, *k[e]-* [1]
how well, 3954, *kî*[2] [1]
that was how, 4027, *kēn*[2] [1]
how was going, 4200+8934, *l[e]-*[1]*+šālôm* [1]
how was, 4200+8934, *l[e]-*[1]*+šālôm* [1]
how were, 4200+8934, *l[e]-*[1]*+šālôm* [1]
how to get into, 4427, *mābôʾ* [1]
how find things, 4537, *mâ* [1]
how much, 4537, *mâ* [1]
how, 4537+2296, *mâ+zeh* [1]
this is how, 4537, *mâ* [1]
how I long for, 4769+5989+5761, *mî+nātan+-nî* [1]
how did it go, 4769+905, *mî+ʾatt* [1]
oh how I wish, 4769+5989, *mî+nātan* [1]
how made, 5126, *maʿ[a]śeh* [1]
know how, 5795, *nākar*[1] [1]
how it feels, 5883, *nepeš* [1]
for how long, 6330+5503, *ʿad*[2]*+mātay* [1]
how long, 6330+625, *ʿad*[2]*+ʾān* [1]
how, 6584+4027, *ʿal*[2]*+kēn*[2] [1]
how, 6584, *ʿal*[2] [1]
how, 8611, *ša-* [1]

asked how they were, 8626+4200+8934,
šā'al+l^{e-1}+šālôm [1]
how is, 8934, *šālôm* [1]
how was, 8934, *šālôm* [1]

HOWEVER [113]
however, 2256, *w^{e}-* [73]
however, 8370, *raq^{2}* [13]
however, 421, *'ak* [8]
however, *NIH/RPE* [5]
however, 3954, *kî^{2}* [4]
however, 3954+561, *kî^{2}+'im* [3]
however, 66, *'^{a}bāl* [2]
however, 219, *'ûlām^{1}* [1]
however, 561, *'im* [1]
however, 700+3954, *'epes+kî^{2}* [1]
however, 4200+4027, *l^{e-1}+kēn^{2}* [1]
however, 10124, *b^{e}ram* [1]

HOWL [4]
howl, 2410, *zā'aq* [1]
howl, 4296, *lûn* [1]
howl, 6702, *'ānâ^{4}* [1]
howl, 6913+5027, *'āśâ^{1}+mispēd* [1]

HOWLING [1]
howling, 3537, *y^{e}lēl* [1]

HUBBAH [1]
Hubbah, 2465, *ḥubbâ* [1]

HUBS [1]
hubs, 3141, *ḥiššur* [1]

HUDDLED [1]
huddled, 6202, *sāpaḥ^{1}* [1]

HUG [1]
hug, 2485, *ḥābaq* [1]

HUGE [9]
huge, 1524, *gādôl* [2]
huge, 4500, *middâ^{1}* [2]
huge, 1524+6330+4200+4394,
gādôl+'ad^{2}+l^{e-1}+m^{e}'ōd [1]
huge, 4394, *m^{e}'ōd* [1]
huge, 5260, *mar'eh* [1]
huge, 8041, *rab^{1}* [1]
huge, 10647, *rab* [1]

HUKKOK [1]
Hukkok, 2982, *ḥuqqōq* [1]

HUKOK [1]
Hukok, 2577, *ḥûqōq* [1]

HUL [2]
Hul, 2566, *ḥûl^{2}* [2]

HULDAH [2]
Huldah, 2701, *ḥuldâ* [2]

HUMAN [21]
human, 132, *'ādām^{1}* [13]
human, *NIH/RPE* [5]
human being, 132, *'ādām^{1}* [1]
human, 1201+132, *bēn^{1}+'ādām^{1}* [1]
human, 10050, *'^{e}nāš* [1]

HUMBLE [29]
humble, 6705, *'ānāw* [7]
humble, 6700, *'ānâ^{2}* [4]
humble, *NIH/RPE* [2]
humble himself, 4044, *kāna'* [2]
humble, 6639+6714, *'am^{2}+'ānî* [2]
humble yourself, 6700, *'ānâ^{2}* [2]
humble, 1924, *dal^{2}* [1]
humble themselves, 4044, *kāna'* [1]
humble, 4044, *kāna'* [1]
humble, 5203, *miṣ'ār^{1}* [1]
humble ourselves, 6700, *'ānâ^{2}* [1]
humble, 6714, *'ānî* [1]
humble, 7837, *qālal* [1]
humble yourself, 8346, *rāpaś* [1]
humble, 9164, *šāpēl^{1}* [1]
humble, 10737, *š^{e}pal^{1}* [1]

HUMBLED [30]
humbled, 9164, *šāpēl^{1}* [6]
humbled himself, 4044, *kāna'* [5]
humbled themselves, 4044, *kāna'* [4]
humbled yourself, 4044, *kāna'* [3]
humbled, 6700, *'ānâ^{2}* [3]
humbled, 10737, *š^{e}pal^{1}* [2]
humbled themselves, 1917, *dākā'* [1]
humbled, 4007, *kālam* [1]
are humbled, 4044, *kāna'* [1]
humbled, 4044, *kāna'* [1]
humbled, 7837, *qālal* [1]
humbled, 8346, *rāpaś* [1]
humbled, 8820, *šāḥaḥ* [1]

HUMBLES [2]
humbles, 8820, *šāḥaḥ* [1]
humbles, 9164, *šāpēl^{1}* [1]

HUMBLY [3]
walk humbly, 1844, *dādâ* [1]
humbly bow, 2556, *ḥāwâ^{2}* [1]
humbly, 7570, *ṣāna'* [1]

HUMILIATE [1]
humiliate, 9164, *šāpēl^{1}* [1]

HUMILIATED [8]
humiliated, 4007, *kālam* [3]
humiliated, 2917, *ḥāpar^{2}* [2]
humiliated, 9166, *šāpāl* [2]
humiliated, 1017, *bôš^{1}* [1]

HUMILIATION [3]
humiliation, 1425+7156, *bōšet+pāneh* [1]
humiliation, 3075, *ḥerpâ* [1]
humiliation, 4009, *k^{e}limmâ* [1]

HUMILITY [6]
humility, 6708, *'^{a}nāwâ* [5]
humility, 7560, *ṣānûa'* [1]

HUMPS [1]
humps, 1832, *dabbešet^{1}* [1]

HUMTAH [1]
Humtah, 2794, *ḥumṭâ* [1]

HUNCHBACKED [1]
hunchbacked, 1492, *gibbēn* [1]

HUNDRED [266]
hundred, 4395, *mē'â^{1}* [233]
hundred, 10395, *m^{e}'â* [7]
units of a hundred, 4395, *mē'â^{1}* [6]
eleven hundred, 547+2256+4395,
'elep^{2}+w^{e}-+mē'â^{1} [3]
fourteen hundred, 547+2256+752+4395,
'elep^{2}+w^{e}-+'arba'+mē'â^{1} [2]
seventeen hundred, 547+2256+8679+4395,
'elep^{2}+w^{e}-+šeba'^{1}+mē'â^{1} [2]
about six hundred feet, 752+4395+564,
'arba'^{1}+mē'â^{1}+'ammâ^{1} [2]
hundred, 4396, *mē'â^{2}* [2]
fifteen hundred feet, 547+564,
'elep^{2}+'ammâ^{1} [1]
five hundred yards, 547+564,
'elep^{2}+'ammâ^{1} [1]
twelve hundred, 547+2256+4395,
'elep^{2}+w^{e}-+mē'â^{1} [1]
twenty-seven hundred, 547+2256+8679+4395,
'elep^{2}+w^{e}-+šeba'^{1}+mē'â^{1} [1]
twenty-six hundred, 547+2256+9252+4395,
'elep^{2}+w^{e}-+šēš^{1}+mē'â^{1} [1]
two hundred, 4395, *mē'â^{1}* [1]
thirty-six hundred, 8993+547+2256+9252
+4395, *šālōš+'elep^{2}+w^{e}-+šēš^{1}+mē'â^{1}* [1]
thirty-three hundred, 8993+547+2256+8993
+4395, *šālōš+'elep^{2}+w^{e}-+šālōš+mē'â^{1}* [1]
hundred and twenty thousand, 9109+6926
+8052, *š^{e}nayim+'eśrēh+ribbô'* [1]

HUNDREDFOLD [1]
hundredfold, 4395+9134, *mē'â^{1}+ša'ar^{2}* [1]

HUNDREDS [20]
hundreds, 4395, *mē'â^{1}* [18]
units of hundreds, 4395, *mē'â^{1}* [2]

HUNDREDTH [2]
hundredth, 4395, *mē'â^{1}* [2]

HUNG [12]
hung, 9434, *tālâ* [7]
hung, 8492, *śîm* [1]
hung, 9428, *tālā'* [1]
been hung up, 9434, *tālâ* [1]
is hung, 9434, *tālâ* [1]
hung up, 9546, *tāqa'* [1]

HUNGER [17]
hunger, 8280, *rā'āb* [6]
hunger, 5883, *nepeš* [2]
hunger, *NIH/RPE* [1]
racked with hunger, 1991, *dāqar* [1]
hunger, 2652, *ḥayyâ^{2}* [1]
hunger, 4103, *kāpān* [1]
still hunger, 4848+1061, *mālē'^{1}+beṭen^{1}* [1]
hunger, 7023, *peh* [1]
hunger, 8199+5883, *rêq+nepeš* [1]
causing to hunger, 8279, *rā'ēb^{1}* [1]
hunger, 8279, *rā'ēb^{1}* [1]

HUNGRY [29]
hungry, 8281, *rā'ēb^{2}* [17]
hungry, 8279, *rā'ēb^{1}* [6]
hungry, 5883+8281, *nepeš+rā'ēb^{2}* [2]
goes hungry, 2893, *ḥāsēr^{1}* [1]
hungry, 4083, *kāsap* [1]
goes hungry, 8279, *rā'ēb^{1}* [1]
let go hungry, 8279, *rā'ēb^{1}* [1]

HUNT [7]
hunt, 7421, *ṣûd* [3]
hunt down, 1944, *dālaq* [1]
hunt down, 2924, *ḥāpaś* [1]
hunt down, 7421+4200+4511,
ṣûd+l^{e-1}+madḥēpâ [1]
hunt down, 7421, *ṣûd* [1]

HUNTED [3]
hunted, 5615, *nādaḥ^{1}* [1]
hunted, 7421+7421, *ṣûd+ṣûd* [1]
hunted, 7421, *ṣûd* [1]

HUNTER [4]
hunter, 7473, *ṣayid^{1}* [2]
hunter, *NIH/RPE* [1]
hunter, 408+7473, *'îš^{1}+ṣayid^{1}* [1]

HUNTERS [1]
hunters, 7475, *ṣayyād* [1]

HUNTING [2]
hunting down, 7399, *ṣādâ^{1}* [1]
hunting, 7473, *ṣayid^{1}* [1]

HUNTS [4]
hunts, 7421, *ṣûd* [2]
hunts down, 1944, *dālaq* [1]
hunts, 8103, *rādap* [1]

HUPHAM [1]
Hupham, 2573, *ḥûpām* [1]

HUPHAMITE [1]
Huphamite, 2574, *ḥûpāmî* [1]

HUPPAH [1]
Huppah, 2904, *ḥuppâ^{2}* [1]

HUPPIM [1]
Huppim, 2907, *ḥuppîm* [1]

HUPPITES [2]
Huppites, 2907, *ḥuppîm* [2]

HUR [15]
Hur, 2581, *ḥûr^{2}* [15]

HURAI [1]
Hurai, 2584, *ḥûray* [1]

HURAM [6]
Huram, 2671, *ḥîrām* [3]
Huram, 2586, *ḥûrām* [2]

Huram, *NIH/RPE* [1]

HURAM-ABI [2]
Huram-Abi, 2587, *ḥûrām 'ābî* [2]

HURI [1]
Huri, 2585, *ḥûrî* [1]

HURL [8]
hurl, 3214, *ṭûl* [2]
hurl, *NIH/RPE* [1]
hurl away, 3214+3232, *ṭûl+ṭalṭēlâ* [1]
hurl insults, 7080+928+8557, *pāṭar+b*e*-+śāpâ* [1]
hurl away, 7843, *qāla'*[1] [1]
hurl out, 7843, *qāla'*[1] [1]
hurl, 8959, *šālak* [1]

HURLED [12]
hurled, 3214, *ṭûl* [2]
hurled, 8227, *rāmâ*[1] [2]
hurled down, 8959, *šālak* [2]
hurled, 8959, *šālak* [2]
hurled, 3070, *ḥārap*[2] [1]
be hurled out, 3214, *ṭûl* [1]
hurled, 3721, *yārâ*[1] [1]
hurled insults, 6512, *'îṭ*[1] [1]

HURLS [2]
hurls down, 8959, *šālak* [1]
hurls, 8959, *šālak* [1]

HURRIED [21]
hurried, 4554, *māhar*[1] [9]
hurried, 8132, *rûṣ* [4]
hurried, 987, *bāhal* [2]
hurried, 2590, *ḥûš*[1] [1]
hurried, 2905, *ḥāpaz* [1]
hurried to bring, 5674, *nûs* [1]
hurried, 7756, *qûm* [1]
hurried, 8103, *rādap* [1]
hurried, 10097, *b*e*hal* [1]

HURRIEDLY [1]
hurriedly, 4559, *m*e*hērâ* [1]

HURRIES [1]
hurries back, 8634, *šā'ap*[1] [1]

HURRY [14]
hurry, 4554, *māhar*[1] [4]
hurry, 8132, *rûṣ* [3]
hurry, 7756, *qûm* [2]
hurry, 987, *bāhal* [1]
in a hurry, 987, *bāhal* [1]
hurry, 2143+4559, *hālak+m*e*hērâ* [1]
hurry, 2590, *ḥûš*[1] [1]
hurry, 4559, *m*e*hērâ* [1]

HURRYING [1]
hurrying, 2905, *ḥāpaz* [1]

HURT [4]
hurt, 2703, *ḥālâ*[1] [1]
hurt, 2728, *ḥālāl*[1] [1]
hurt, 8273, *ra'*[1] [1]
hurt, 10243, *ḥ*a*bal* [1]

HURTLING [1]
hurtling down, 5877, *nāpal* [1]

HURTS [2]
hurts, 1916, *dak* [1]
hurts, 8317, *rā'a'*[1] [1]

HUSBAND [77]
husband, 408, *'îš*[1] [64]
husband, 1251, *ba'al*[1] [6]
husband, 1249, *bā'al*[1] [4]
has a husband, 1249, *bā'al*[1] [1]
her husband[s], 2257, *-ô* [1]
husband, 8276, *rēa'*[2] [1]

HUSBAND'S [5]
husband's brother, 3303, *yābām* [2]
husband's, 408, *'îš*[1] [1]
husband's, 1251, *ba'al*[1] [1]
husband's, 1505, *geber*[1] [1]

HUSBANDS [7]
husbands, 408, *'îš*[1] [4]
husbands, 1251, *ba'al*[1] [2]
husbands, 123, *'ādôn* [1]

HUSH [1]
hush, 2187, *has* [1]

HUSHAH [1]
Hushah, 2592, *ḥûšâ* [1]

HUSHAI [12]
Hushai, 2593, *ḥûšay* [12]

HUSHAM [4]
Husham, 2595, *ḥûšām* [4]

HUSHATHITE [5]
Hushathite, 3144, *ḥušātî* [5]

HUSHED [4]
hushed, 1960, *d*e*māmâ* [1]
hushed, 2461, *ḥābā'* [1]
hushed, 3120, *ḥāšâ* [1]
lies hushed, 9200, *šāqaṭ* [1]

HUSHIM [3]
Hushim, 2594, *ḥûšîm* [2]
Hushim, 3123, *ḥušîm* [1]

HUSHITES [1]
Hushites, 3131, *ḥušîm* [1]

HUT [3]
hut, 4870, *m*e*lûnâ* [2]
hut, 6109, *sukkâ* [1]

HYENAS [3]
hyenas, 363, *'î*[2] [3]

HYMN [1]
hymn of praise, 9335, *t*e*hillâ* [1]

HYPOCRITES [1]
hypocrites, 6623, *'ālam* [1]

HYSSOP [10]
hyssop, 257, *'ēzôb* [10]

I [6494]
I, *AIT* [4512]
I, 638, *'*a*nî* [790]
I, 3276, *-î* [381]
I, 644, *'ānōkî* [326]
I, *NIH/RPE* [205]
I, 5761, *-nî* [203]
I, 5883+3276, *nepeš+-î* [29]
I, 10044, *'*a*nâ* [15]
I, 10307, *-î* [14]
I beg you, 5528, *nā'*[1] [5]
I would like, 5528, *nā'*[1] [2]
I[s], 466, *'*e*lōhîm* [1]
I ask, 626, *'onnā'* [1]
what do I care about, 4200+4537+2296+4200+3276, *l*e*-*[1]*+mâ+zeh+l*e*-*[1]*+-î* [1]
I, 4213+3276, *lēb+-î* [1]
how I long for, 4769+5989+5761, *mî+nātan+-nî* [1]
I wish, 4769+5989, *mî+nātan* [1]
oh how I wish, 4769+5989, *mî+nātan* [1]
I, 5055+3276, *mē'eh+-î* [1]
I pray, 5528, *nā'*[1] [1]
I[s], 6269+3870, *'ebed*[1]*+-kā* [1]
I, 7023+3276, *peh+-î* [1]
I, 8120+3276, *rûaḥ+-î* [1]

I'LL [33]
I'll, *AIT* [25]
I'll, 638, *'*a*nî* [3]
I'll, 644, *'ānōkî* [3]
I'll, *NIH/RPE* [1]
I'll, 5761, *-nî* [1]

I'M [19]
I'm, 644, *'ānōkî* [8]
I'm, *AIT* [5]
I'm, 3276, *-î* [4]
I'm, *NIH/RPE* [1]
I'm, 638, *'*a*nî* [1]

I'VE [7]
I've, *AIT* [4]
I've, 3276, *-î* [2]
I've, *NIH/RPE* [1]

IBEX [1]
ibex, 1913, *dîšôn*[1] [1]

IBHAR [3]
Ibhar, 3295, *yibḥar* [3]

IBLEAM [3]
Ibleam, 3300, *yibl*e*'ām* [3]

IBNEIAH [1]
Ibneiah, 3307, *yibn*e*yâ* [1]

IBNIJAH [1]
Ibnijah, 3308, *yibniyyâ* [1]

IBRI [1]
Ibri, 6304, *'ibrî*[2] [1]

IBSAM [1]
Ibsam, 3311, *yibśām* [1]

IBZAN [3]
Ibzan, 83, *'ibṣān* [2]
Ibzan, *NIH/RPE* [1]

ICE [4]
ice, 7943, *qeraḥ* [4]

ICHABOD [1]
Ichabod, 376, *'îkābôd* [1]

ICHABOD'S [1]
Ichabod's, 376, *'îkābôd* [1]

ICY [1]
icy blast, 7938, *qārâ*[2] [1]

IDALAH [1]
Idalah, 3339, *yid'*a*lâ* [1]

IDBASH [1]
Idbash, 3340, *yidbāš* [1]

IDDO [13]
Iddo, 6341, *'iddô* [4]
Iddo, 120, *'iddô* [2]
Iddo, 6342, *'iddô'* [2]
Iddo, 10529, *'iddô'* [2]
Iddo, 3346, *yiddô* [1]
Iddo, 3587, *ye'dô* [1]
Iddo, 6333, *'iddō'* [1]

IDDO'S [1]
Iddo's, 6342, *'iddô'* [1]

IDEA [3]
scorned the idea, 1022+928+6524, *bāzâ+b*e*-+'ayin*[1] [1]
idea, 1821, *dābār* [1]
idea, 4946+4213, *min+lēb* [1]

IDENTICAL [2]
identical, 285, *'eḥād* [2]

IDLE [5]
idle, *NIH/RPE* [1]
idle talk, 966, *bad*[4] [1]
let be idle, 5663, *nûaḥ*[1] [1]
idle, 8199, *rêq* [1]
idle, 9170, *šiplût* [1]

IDLENESS [1]
idleness, 6791, *'aṣlût* [1]

IDOL [34]
idol, 7181, *pesel* [11]
cast idol, 5011, *massēkâ*[1] [5]
idol cast, 5011, *massēkâ*[1] [3]
idol, 9572, *t*e*rāpîm* [3]
idol, 5011, *massēkâ*[1] [2]
idol, 6166, *semel* [2]
idol, 224, *'āwen*[1] [1]

shameful idol, 1425, *bōšet* [1]
idol^s, 2084, *-hû* [1]
the idol^s, 2084, *-hû* [1]
idol cast from metal, 5011, *massēkā^1* [1]
idol, 5381, *maśkît* [1]
wooden idol, 6770, *'ēṣ* [1]
idol, 8736, *šāw'* [1]

IDOLATRIES [1]
idolatries, 496, *'^{e}lîl* [1]

IDOLATROUS [3]
idolatrous, *NIH/RPE* [1]
idolatrous priests, 3913, *kōhēn* [1]
idolatrous priests, 4024, *kōmer* [1]

IDOLATRY [4]
idolatry, 1658, *gillûlîm* [2]
idolatry, 2393, *z^{e}nûnîm* [1]
idolatry, 9572, *t^{e}rāpîm* [1]

IDOLS [155]
idols, 1658, *gillûlîm* [46]
idols, 7178, *pāsîl* [16]
idols, 496, *'^{e}lîl* [15]
idols, 6773, *'āṣāb* [13]
worthless idols, 2039, *hebel^1* [9]
idols, 7181, *pesel* [7]
idols, 7512, *ṣelem^1* [6]
detestable idols, 9359, *tô'ēbâ* [6]
idols, *NIH/RPE* [4]
the idols^s, 2157, *-hem* [3]
detestable idols, 9199, *šiqqûṣ* [3]
idols, 9572, *t^{e}rāpîm* [3]
worthless idols, 4202+3603, *lō'+yā'al* [2]
cast idols, 5011, *massēkā^1* [2]
lifeless idols, 7007, *peger* [2]
goat idols, 8539, *śā'îr^3* [2]
idols, 466, *'^{e}lōhîm* [1]
worthless idols, 2039+8736, *hebel^1+šāw'* [1]
their idols^s, 2156, *hēm* [1]
idols cast, 5011, *massēkā^1* [1]
idols made of metal, 5011, *massēkā^1* [1]
idols, 5011, *massēkâ^1* [1]
idols made, 5126, *ma'^{a}śeh* [1]
idols, 6777, *'ōṣeb^1* [1]
wooden idols, 6785, *'ēṣâ^3* [1]
carved idols, 7178, *pāsîl* [1]
idols, 7417, *ṣaw* [1]
idols, 7497, *ṣîr^5* [1]
idols, 8736, *šāw'* [1]
worthless idols, 8736, *šāw'* [1]
abominable idols, 9199, *šiqqûṣ* [1]
useless idols, 9332, *tōhû* [1]

IEZER [1]
Iezer, 404, *'î'ezer* [1]

IEZERITE [1]
Iezerite, 405, *'î'ezrî* [1]

IF [1131]
if, 561, *'im* [522]
if, 3954, *kî^2* [149]
if, *NIH/RPE* [143]
if, 2256, *w^e-* [60]
if, 2180, *hinnēh* [28]
if, 928, *b^e-* [16]
if, 2176, *hēn^1* [15]
if, 889, *'^{a}šer* [13]
if, *AIT* [12]
if, 4273, *lû* [12]
if, 2022, *h^a-* [11]
as if, 3869, *k^e-* [11]
if, 10213, *hēn* [11]
if, 3954+561, *kî^2+'im* [10]
if only, 4769+5989, *mî+nātan* [10]
what if, 218, *'ûlay^2* [9]
even if, 561, *'im* [9]
if only, 4273, *lû* [8]
but if, 561, *'im* [6]
even if, 2256, *w^e-* [5]
if not, 4295, *lûlē'* [5]
yet if, 561, *'im* [4]
if not, 3954+4295, *kî^2+lûlē'* [4]
if, 7153, *pen* [4]
if, 196, *'ô* [3]
only if, 561, *'im* [3]
if, 3869+889, *k^e-+'^{a}šer* [3]
even if, 3954, *kî^2* [3]
if not, 3954, *kî^2* [3]
as if, 4200, *l^e-^{1}* [3]
if only, 4769, *mî* [3]
if, 467, *'illû* [2]
if, 561+3907, *'im+kōh* [2]
if, 196+4537, *'ô+mâ* [1]
if not, 218, *'ûlay^2* [1]
but if, 219, *'ûlām^1* [1]
if, 219, *'ûlām^1* [1]
if only, 332, *'aḥ^{a}lay* [1]
if only, 561, *'im* [1]
as if, 561, *'im* [1]
if even, 561, *'im* [1]
if indeed, 561, *'im* [1]
if, 677, *'ap^1* [1]
even if, 928, *b^e-* [1]
if, 928+3427, *b^e-+yôm^1* [1]
only if, 928, *b^e-* [1]
even if, 1685, *gam* [1]
but if, 2176, *hēn^1* [1]
what if, 2176, *hēn^1* [1]
if then, 2256, *w^e-* [1]
if only, 3869+889, *k^e-+'^{a}šer* [1]
if, 3869, *k^e-* [1]
if so, 3954+6964, *kî^2+'attâ* [1]
if anything but, 3954, *kî^2* [1]
that if, 3954, *kî^2* [1]
if, 4202, *lō'* [1]
what if, 4273, *lû* [1]
if you will, 5528, *nā'^{1}* [1]
if, 6813, *'ēqeb* [1]
for if, 7153, *pen* [1]
if, 10168, *dî* [1]
even if, 10213, *hēn* [1]

IGAL [3]
Igal, 3319, *yig'āl* [3]

IGDALIAH [1]
Igdaliah, 3323, *yigdalyāhû* [1]

IGNORANCE [1]
ignorance, 7344, *petî^2* [1]

IGNORANT [4]
ignorant, 4202+3359, *lō'+yāda'* [2]
ignorant, 1153+3359, *bal^1+yāda'* [1]
ignorant, 1280, *ba'ar* [1]

IGNORE [9]
ignore, 6623, *'ālam* [4]
ignore, 8894, *šākaḥ* [4]
ignore, 7277, *pāra'^{2}* [1]

IGNORED [4]
ignored, 8894, *šākaḥ* [2]
ignored, 4202+8492+4213, *lō'+śîm+lēb* [1]
ignored, 7277, *pāra'^{2}* [1]

IGNORES [3]
ignores, 7277, *pāra'^{2}* [2]
ignores, 6440, *'āzab^1* [1]

IIM [1]
Iim, 6517, *'iyyîm* [1]

IJON [3]
Ijon, 6510, *'iyyôn* [3]

IKKESH [3]
Ikkesh, 6837, *'iqqēš^2* [3]

ILAI [1]
Ilai, 6519, *'îlay* [1]

ILL [20]
ill, 2703, *ḥālâ^1* [13]
ill, 653, *'ānaš* [1]
ill, 1867, *d^{e}way* [1]
lay ill, 2703, *ḥālâ^1* [1]
pretend to be ill, 2703, *ḥālâ^1* [1]
pretended to be ill, 2703, *ḥālâ^1* [1]
ill, 2716, *ḥ^{o}lî* [1]
show ill will, 8317+6524, *rā'a'^{1}+'ayin^1* [1]

ILL-GOTTEN [5]
ill-gotten, 8400, *reša'* [2]
go after ill-gotten gain, 1298+1299, *bāṣa'+beṣa'* [1]
ill-gotten gains, 1299, *beṣa'* [1]
ill-gotten gain, 1299, *beṣa'* [1]

ILL-TEMPERED [1]
ill-tempered, 4088, *ka'as* [1]

ILLEGAL [1]
illegal possession, 7322, *peša'* [1]

ILLEGITIMATE [1]
illegitimate, 2424, *zār* [1]

ILLICIT [1]
illicit favors, 9373, *taznût* [1]

ILLNESS [9]
illness, 2716, *ḥ^{o}lî* [5]
illness, 2703, *ḥālâ^1* [4]

ILLNESSES [1]
illnesses, 2716, *ḥ^{o}lî* [1]

ILLS [1]
ills, *NIH/RPE* [1]

ILLUSIONS [1]
illusions, 4562, *mah^{a}tallâ* [1]

IMAGE [32]
image, 10614, *ṣ^{e}lēm* [10]
carved image, 7181, *pesel* [5]
image, 7512, *ṣelem^1* [5]
image, 7181, *pesel* [4]
image, 5011, *massēkâ^1* [2]
image, 6166, *semel* [2]
image, 1952, *d^{e}mût* [1]
like image, 6771, *'āṣab^1* [1]
image, 9322, *tabnît* [1]
image, 9454, *t^{e}mûnâ* [1]

IMAGES [34]
vile images, 9199, *šiqqûṣ* [9]
images, 7178, *pāsîl* [5]
images, 6773, *'āṣāb* [4]
images, 5011, *massēkā^1* [3]
images, 5822, *nesek^2* [3]
images, 496, *'^{e}lîl* [1]
cast images, 5011, *massēkā^1* [1]
carved images, 5381, *maśkît* [1]
metal images, 5816, *nāsîk^1* [1]
images that are carried about, 5953, *n^{e}śû'â* [1]
carved images, 7178, *pāsîl* [1]
carved images, 7181, *pesel* [1]
images, 7181, *pesel* [1]
detestable images, 9199, *šiqqûṣ* [1]
images, 10217, *harhōr* [1]

IMAGINATION [2]
imagination, 4213, *lēb* [2]

IMAGINATIONS [2]
imaginations, 4742, *mah^{a}šābâ* [2]

IMAGINE [3]
imagine, 928+5381, *b^e-+maśkît* [1]
imagine, 1819, *dābar^2* [1]
imagine, 3108, *ḥāšab* [1]

IMITATE [2]
imitate, 6913+3869, *'āśâ^1+k^e-* [2]

IMITATED [1]
imitated, 339, *'aḥar* [1]

IMLAH [4]
Imlah, 3550, *yimlā'* [2]
Imlah, 3551, *yimlâ* [2]

IMMANUEL [2]
Immanuel, 6672, *'immānû 'ēl* [2]

IMMEDIATELY [9]
immediately, 4554, *māhar^1* [2]

immediately, 10734+10002, *šāʿâ+-āʾ* [2]
immediately, 987, *bāhal* [1]
immediately, 3869+2021+3427, *k^{e}+ha+yôm^{1}* [1]
immediately, 4559, *m^{e}hērâ* [1]
immediately, 10089+10096, *b^{e}+b^{e}hîlû* [1]
immediately, 10734+10191, *šāʿâ+-â* [1]

IMMENSE [1]
immense, 1524, *gādôl* [1]

IMMER [10]
Immer, 612, *ʾimmēr^{2}* [8]
Immer, 613, *ʾimmēr^{3}* [2]

IMMORAL [1]
immoral, 8273, *raʿ^{1}* [1]

IMMORALITY [2]
indulge in sexual immorality, 2388, *zānâ^{1}* [1]
immorality, 2394, *z^{e}nût* [1]

IMMORTALITY [1]
immortality, 440+4638, *ʾal^{1}+māwet* [1]

IMMOVABLE [2]
immovable, 1153+4572, *bal^{1}+môṭ^{1}* [1]
immovable, 5098, *maʿ^{a}māsâ* [1]

IMNA [1]
Imna, 3557, *yimnāʿ* [1]

IMNAH [4]
Imnah, 3555, *yimnâ* [4]

IMNITE [1]
Imnite, 3555, *yimnâ* [1]

IMPALED [1]
impaled, 10411, *m^{e}ḥāʾ* [1]

IMPARTED [1]
imparted, 4340, *lāmad* [1]

IMPARTIALLY [1]
impartially, 465+6640+465, *ʾēlleh+ʿim+ʾēlleh* [1]

IMPARTS [1]
imparts, 5989, *nātan* [1]

IMPATIENT [3]
impatient, 4206, *lāʾâ* [1]
impatient, 7918+5883, *qāṣar^{2}+nepeš* [1]
impatient, 7918, *qāṣar^{2}* [1]

IMPERIAL [12]
imperial guard, 3184, *ṭabbāḥ* [12]

IMPETUOUS [2]
impetuous, 4362, *lāʿaʿ^{1}* [1]
impetuous, 4554, *māhar^{1}* [1]

IMPLANTED [1]
implanted, 5749, *nāṭaʿ* [1]

IMPLORE [1]
implore, 2704+7156, *ḥālâ^{2}+pāneh* [1]

IMPORTANT [5]
important, 1524, *gādôl* [4]
most important, 1524, *gādôl* [1]

IMPORTED [7]
imported, 4604, *môṣāʾ^{1}* [2]
imported, 6590+2256+3655, *ʿālâ+w^{e}-+yāṣāʾ* [2]
imported, 995, *bôʾ* [1]
imported, 2424, *zār* [1]
imported, 3655, *yāṣāʾ* [1]

IMPOSE [1]
impose, 10667, *r^{e}mâ* [1]

IMPOSED [5]
imposed, *AIT* [1]
imposed, 5989, *nātan* [1]
imposed a levy, 6740, *ʿānaš* [1]
imposed, 7439, *ṣûq^{1}* [1]
imposed, 8492, *śîm* [1]

IMPOSING [4]
imposing, 6609, *ʿelyôn^{1}* [2]
imposing, 1524+4200+5260, *gādôl+l^{e}-^{1}+marʾeh* [1]
imposing, 10647, *rab* [1]

IMPOSSIBLE [3]
it was impossible, 401, *ʾayin^{1}* [1]
impossible, 1307, *bāṣar^{3}* [1]
impossible, 7098, *pālāʾ* [1]

IMPOVERISHED [1]
impoverished, 1937, *dālal^{1}* [1]

IMPRESS [1]
impress, 9112, *šānan^{2}* [1]

IMPRESSED [1]
impressed, 448, *ʾel* [1]

IMPRESSES [1]
impresses, 5737, *nāḥat* [1]

IMPRESSIVE [1]
impressive, 3202, *ṭôb^{2}* [1]

IMPRISONED [4]
imprisoned, 3973, *kālāʾ^{1}* [1]
imprisoned, 5989+1074+2021+657, *nātan+bayit^{1}+ha+ʾēsûr* [1]
imprisoned, 5989+928+5464, *nātan+b^{e}-+mišmār^{1}* [1]
imprisoned himself, 6037, *sāgar* [1]

IMPRISONMENT [1]
imprisonment, 10054, *ʾ^{e}sûr* [1]

IMPRISONS [1]
imprisons, 6037, *sāgar* [1]

IMPROVISE [1]
improvise, 3108, *ḥāšab* [1]

IMPURE [7]
impure, 3237, *ṭāmēʾ^{1}* [2]
impure, 7002, *piggûl* [2]
impure, 3238, *ṭāmēʾ^{2}* [1]
impure, 3240, *ṭumʾâ* [1]
impure, 8273, *raʿ^{1}* [1]

IMPURITIES [3]
impurities, 3240, *ṭumʾâ* [2]
impurities, 975, *bādîl* [1]

IMPURITY [9]
impurity, 3240, *ṭumʾâ* [4]
free from impurity, 3196, *ṭāhôr* [1]
impurity, 3237, *ṭāmēʾ^{1}* [1]
act of impurity, 5614, *niddâ* [1]
impurity of monthly period, 5614, *niddâ* [1]
impurity, 5614, *niddâ* [1]

IMRAH [1]
Imrah, 3559, *yimrâ* [1]

IMRI [2]
Imri, 617, *ʾimrî* [2]

IN [8372]*
in, 928, *b^{e}-* [4676]
in, *AIT* [694]
in, *NIH/RPE* [376]
in, 4200, *l^{e}-^{1}* [366]
in, 6584, *ʿal^{2}* [248]
in, 4946, *min* [116]
in, 448, *ʾel* [102]
in, 10089, *b^{e}-* [79]
in front of, 4200+7156, *l^{e}-^{1}+pāneh* [66]
in, 928+9348, *b^{e}-+tāwek* [45]
in charge of, 6584, *ʿal^{2}* [43]
in, 2025, *-â^{2}* [37]
in accordance with, 3869, *k^{e}-* [30]
in, 3869, *k^{e}-* [30]
in, 928+7931, *b^{e}-+qereb* [24]
in place of, 9393, *taḥat^{1}* [24]
in place, 9393, *taḥat^{1}* [23]
in order to, 4200, *l^{e}-^{1}* [21]
in addition to, 4946+4200+963, *min+l^{e}-^{1}+bad^{1}* [18]
in this way, 2256, *w^{e}-* [17]
in, 6640, *ʿim* [15]
in spite of, 928, *b^{e}-* [8]
in front of, 5584, *neged* [6]
in front of, 6584+7156, *ʿal^{2}+pāneh* [6]
in, 6584+7156, *ʿal^{2}+pāneh* [6]
in, 907, *ʾēt^{2}* [5]
in vain, 2039, *hebel^{1}* [5]
in order to, 4200+5100, *l^{e}-^{1}+maʿan* [5]
in front of, 448+7156, *ʾel+pāneh* [4]
in exchange for, 928, *b^{e}-* [4]
in vain, 4200+2021+8736, *l^{e}-^{1}+ha+šāwʾ* [4]
in vain, 4200+8198, *l^{e}-^{1}+rîq^{2}* [4]
in accordance with, 6584, *ʿal^{2}* [4]
in addition to, 6584, *ʿal^{2}* [4]
in accordance with, 10341, *k^{e}-* [4]
in, 10542, *ʿal* [4]
in front of, 448+4578, *ʾel+mûl^{3}* [3]
in, 1237, *baʿad^{1}* [3]
in, 2256, *w^{e}-* [3]
in this way, 3970, *kākâ* [3]
in this way, 4027, *kēn^{2}* [3]
in behalf of, 4200, *l^{e}-^{1}* [3]
in, 5584, *neged* [3]
in opposition to, 6584, *ʿal^{2}* [3]
in spite of, 6584, *ʿal^{2}* [3]
in vain, 8736, *šāwʾ* [3]
in, 9393, *taḥat^{1}* [3]
in, 10168, *dî* [3]
in, 10378, *l^{e}-* [3]
in front of, 907+7156, *ʾēt^{2}+pāneh* [2]
in order to, 928+6288, *b^{e}-+ʿabûr^{1}* [2]
in return for, 928, *b^{e}-* [2]
in, 1198, *b^{e}mô* [2]
in the order of, 3869, *k^{e}-* [2]
in way, 3869, *k^{e}-* [2]
in, 4200+6961, *l^{e}-^{1}+ʿēt* [2]
have in common, 4200, *l^{e}-^{1}* [2]
in accordance with, 4200, *l^{e}-^{1}* [2]
in addition to, 4200+963, *l^{e}-^{1}+bad^{1}* [2]
in behalf, 4200, *l^{e}-^{1}* [2]
in connection with, 4200, *l^{e}-^{1}* [2]
in front of, 4200+5584, *l^{e}-^{1}+neged* [2]
in order that, 4200, *l^{e}-^{1}* [2]
in presence, 4200+5584+6524, *l^{e}-^{1}+neged+ʿayin^{1}* [2]
in such a way that, 4200, *l^{e}-^{1}* [2]
in way, 4200+7156, *l^{e}-^{1}+pāneh* [2]
in, 4200+5584, *l^{e}-^{1}+neged* [2]
in front of, 4946+4578, *min+mûl^{3}* [2]
in regard to, 4946, *min* [2]
in the presence of, 5584+2025, *neged+-â^{2}* [2]
in the sight of, 5584, *neged* [2]
straight in, 5584, *neged* [2]
in the end, 6330, *ʿad^{2}* [2]
in, 6330, *ʿad^{2}* [2]
in behalf, 6584, *ʿal^{2}* [2]
in front of, 6584, *ʿal^{2}* [2]
in company with, 6640, *ʿim* [2]
in, 6643, *ʿimmād* [2]

INCAPABLE [1]
incapable, 4202+3523, *lōʾ+yākōl* [1]

INCENSE [141]
incense, 7792, *q^{e}ṭōret* [59]
incense, 4247, *l^{e}bōnâ* [20]
burn incense, 7787, *qāṭar^{1}* [18]
burned incense, 7787, *qāṭar^{1}* [14]
burning incense, 7787, *qāṭar^{1}* [11]
incense altars, 2802, *ḥammān* [8]
fragrant incense, 8194+5767, *rêaḥ+nîḥōaḥ* [4]
incense, 5231, *muqṭār* [1]
incense altars, 5232, *m^{e}qaṭṭeret* [1]
incense^{s}, 5626, *-nâ* [1]
incense, 7777, *q^{e}ṭôrâ* [1]
burns incense, 7787, *qāṭar^{1}* [1]
incense, 7789, *qiṭṭēr* [1]
incense, 10478, *nîḥôaḥ* [1]

INCENSED [1]
incensed, 4087, *kāʿas* [1]

INCHES [1]
18 inches, 564, *'ammâ*[1] [1]

INCIDENT [1]
incident, *NIH/RPE* [1]

INCITED [5]
incited, 6077, *sût*[1] [4]
incited, 7756, *qûm* [1]

INCITING [1]
inciting, 6077, *sût*[1] [1]

INCLINATION [2]
inclination, 3671, *yēṣer*[1] [2]

INCLINATIONS [1]
inclinations, 4600, *mô'ēṣâ* [1]

INCLINED [3]
inclined, 2118+2296, *hāyâ+zeh* [1]
inclined, 3512, *yāṭab* [1]
inclined, 5742+4213, *nāṭâ+lēb* [1]

INCLINES [1]
inclines to, 4200, *l[e]-[1]* [1]

INCLUDE [17]
include, 2256, *w[e]-* [10]
include, *NIH/RPE* [2]
include, 448, *'el* [2]
include in the census, 906+8031+5951, *'ēt[1]+rō'š[1]+nāśā'* [1]
include, 928+9348, *b[e]-+tāwek* [1]
include, 2118, *hāyâ* [1]

INCLUDED [17]
included, 995, *bô'* [4]
included, 2118, *hāyâ* [4]
included, *NIH/RPE* [3]
and included, 2256, *w[e]-* [2]
included, 2256, *w[e]-* [1]
also included, 2256, *w[e]-* [1]
be included, 2526, *ḥādâ*[2] [1]

INCLUDING [61]
including, 2256, *w[e]-* [40]
including, *NIH/RPE* [9]
including, 928, *b[e]-* [3]
not including, 4200+963+4946, *l[e]-[1]+bad[1]+min* [2]
including, 889, *'ăšer* [1]
including and, 2256, *w[e]-* [1]
including, 2256+1685, *w[e]-+gam* [1]
including, 4946, *min* [1]
including, 6330, *'ad*[2] [1]
including, 6584, *'al*[2] [1]
including, 10221, *w[e]-* [1]

INCOME [4]
income, 9311, *t[e]bû'â* [4]

INCOMPREHENSIBLE [1]
incomprehensible, 401+1069, *'ayin[1]+bînâ* [1]

INCREASE [47]
increase, 8049, *rābâ*[1] [14]
increase in number, 8049, *rābâ*[1] [9]
increase numbers, 8049, *rābâ*[1] [8]
increase the number, 8049, *rābâ*[1] [2]
increase by thousands, 545, *'ālap*[2] [1]
increase, 1835, *dāgâ*[1] [1]
increase, 2118, *hāyâ* [1]
increase, 3578, *yāsap* [1]
increase, 3578+6584, *yāsap+'al*[2] [1]
make increase, 3578, *yāsap* [1]
increase, 3862, *yitrôn* [1]
increase, 5269, *marbeh* [1]
increase, 5649, *nûb* [1]
increase, 7287, *pāraṣ* [1]
increase in number, 8045, *rābab*[1] [1]
greatly increase, 8049+8049, *rābâ[1]+rābâ[1]* [1]
so increase, 8049+8049, *rābâ[1]+rābâ[1]* [1]
increase, 8436, *śāgâ* [1]

INCREASED [27]
increased, 8049, *rābâ*[1] [9]
increased, 3578, *yāsap* [2]
increased, 7287, *pāraṣ* [2]
increased, 8045, *rābab*[1] [2]
increased, 1540, *gādal* [1]
increased more and more, 2143+2143+2256+8041, *hālak+hālak+w[e]-+rab[1]* [1]
increased, 3877, *kābēd*[1] [1]
increased, 6579, *'ākar* [1]
increased, 7238, *pārā*[1] [1]
increased, 8044, *rōb* [1]
increased in number, 8049, *rābâ*[1] [1]
increased numbers, 8049, *rābâ*[1] [1]
increased number, 8049, *rābâ*[1] [1]
numbers increased greatly, 8049+2256+7238, *rābâ[1]+w[e]-+pārā[1]* [1]
numbers increased, 8049, *rābâ*[1] [1]
increased, 8492, *śîm* [1]

INCREASES [4]
increases, 8049, *rābâ*[1] [3]
increases, 599, *'āmēṣ* [1]

INCREASING [4]
increasing, 8049, *rābâ*[1] [2]
increasing, 1504, *gābar* [1]
increasing, 8041, *rab*[1] [1]

INCUR [1]
incur, 5951, *nāśā'* [1]

INCURABLE [7]
incurable, 631, *'ānûš* [3]
incurable, 401+5340, *'ayin[1]+marpē'[1]* [1]
incurable wound, 631, *'ānûš* [1]
incurable, 2703, *ḥālâ*[1] [1]
incurable, 4412+8324, *mā'an+rāpā'[1]* [1]

INCURS [2]
incurs, *NIH/RPE* [1]
incurs, 2118, *hāyâ* [1]

INDECENT [2]
indecent, 6872, *'erwâ* [2]

INDECISIVE [1]
indecisive, 8205+4222, *rak+lēbāb* [1]

INDEED [40]
indeed, 2180, *hinnēh* [6]
indeed, 2256, *w[e]-* [5]
indeed, 3954, *kî*[2] [5]
indeed, 1685, *gam* [3]
indeed, *NIH/RPE* [2]
indeed, 421, *'ak* [2]
indeed, 597, *'omnām* [2]
indeed, 2256+1685, *w[e]-+gam* [2]
indeed, 3869, *k[e]-* [2]
indeed, 66, *'[a]bāl* [1]
if indeed, 561, *'im* [1]
indeed, 598, *'umnām* [1]
indeed, 677, *'ap*[1] [1]
indeed built, 1215+1215, *bānâ+bānâ* [1]
and indeed, 1685, *gam* [1]
indeed, 2256+677+3954, *w[e]-+'ap[1]+kî[2]* [1]
indeed, 3954+561, *kî[2]+'im* [1]
indeed defeated, 5782+5782, *nākâ+nākâ* [1]
indeed go unpunished, 5927+5927, *nāqâ+nāqâ* [1]
indeed seen, 8011+8011, *rā'â[1]+rā'â[1]* [1]

INDIA [2]
India, 2064, *hōddû* [2]

INDICATE [1]
indicate, 606, *'āmar*[1] [1]

INDICATED [2]
indicated, 606, *'āmar*[1] [1]
indicated ancestry, 3528, *yālad* [1]

INDICTMENT [1]
indictment, 6219, *sēper*[1] [1]

INDIGNATION [5]
indignation, 2405, *za'am* [3]
indignation, 2363, *zal'āpâ* [1]
indignation, 2779, *ḥēmâ* [1]

INDIVIDUALLY [1]
individually, 4200+1653, *l[e]-[1]+gulgōlet* [1]

INDULGE [2]
indulge in sexual immorality, 2388, *zānâ*[1] [1]
indulge in revelry, 7464, *ṣāḥaq* [1]

INEXPERIENCED [2]
inexperienced, 8205, *rak* [2]

INFAMOUS [1]
infamous, 3238+2021+9005, *ṭāmē'[2]+ha-+šēm[1]* [1]

INFAMY [1]
infamy, 1017, *bôš*[1] [1]

INFANT [6]
infant, 3437, *yônēq* [2]
infant, 6403, *'ûl*[3] [2]
stillborn infant, 4637, *mût* [1]
infant, 6407, *'ôlēl* [1]

INFANT'S [1]
infant's, 3437, *yônēq* [1]

INFANTS [10]
infants, 3437, *yônēq* [6]
infants, 6408, *'ôlāl* [2]
infants, 6407, *'ôlēl* [1]
infants, 7262+1061, *p[e]rî+beṭen[1]* [1]

INFECTED [4]
infected person, 5596, *nega'* [3]
infected person, 5596+5999, *nega'+neteq* [1]

INFECTION [1]
infection, 5596, *nega'* [1]

INFECTIOUS [21]
infectious, 5596, *nega'* [11]
infectious disease, 7669, *ṣāra'at* [7]
has an infectious skin disease, 7665, *ṣāra'* [1]
infectious skin disease, 7665, *ṣāra'* [1]
infectious skin diseases and mildew, 7669, *ṣāra'at* [1]

INFERIOR [3]
inferior, 5877, *nāpal* [2]
inferior, 10075, *'[a]ra'* [1]

INFIRMITIES [1]
infirmities, 2716, *ḥ[o]lî* [1]

INFLAMED [2]
inflamed, 1944, *dālaq* [1]
inflamed, 2703+2779, *ḥālâ+ḥēmâ* [1]

INFLAMMATION [1]
inflammation, 1945, *dalleqet* [1]

INFLICT [21]
inflict, 6913, *'āśâ*[1] [14]
inflict, 7439, *ṣûq*[1] [3]
inflict, 5782, *nākâ* [2]
inflict, 5989, *nātan* [1]
inflict, 8492, *śîm* [1]

INFLICTED [15]
inflicted, 5782, *nākâ* [7]
inflicted, 6913, *'āśâ*[1] [2]
inflicted, *AIT* [1]
inflicted, 4804, *makkâ* [1]
inflicted, 5595, *nāga'* [1]
inflicted casualties, 5782, *nākâ* [1]
was inflicted, 6618, *'ālal*[1] [1]
inflicted punishment, 8399, *rāša'* [1]

INFLICTS [2]
inflicts, *NIH/RPE* [1]
inflicts, 5597, *nāgap* [1]

INFLUENCE [1]
influence, 6476, *'ezrâ*[1] [1]

INFORM [8]
inform, 5583, *nāgad* [4]
inform, 10313, *y[e]da'* [2]
inform, 3359, *yāda'* [1]

inform, 6218, *sāpar* [1]

INFORMATION [2]
definite information, 3922, *kûn*[1] [1]
information, 10313, *y[e]da'* [1]

INFORMED [3]
informed, 5583, *nāgad* [2]
well informed, 3359+1981, *yāda'+da'at*[1] [1]

INGATHERING [2]
Ingathering, 658, *'āsîp* [2]

INHABIT [1]
inhabit, 8905, *šākan* [1]

INHABITANT [3]
inhabitant, 3782, *yāšab* [3]

INHABITANTS [33]
inhabitants, 3782, *yāšab* [30]
inhabitants, *NIH/RPE* [1]
inhabitants, 1426, *bat*[1] [1]
its inhabitants[s], 2023, *-āh* [1]

INHABITED [16]
inhabited, 3782, *yāšab* [13]
be inhabited, 3782, *yāšab* [2]
inhabited, 8905, *šākan* [1]

INHERIT [29]
inherit, 3769, *yāraš*[1] [11]
inherit, 5706, *nāḥal* [6]
inherit, 5709, *naḥ[a]lâ*[1] [3]
lead to inherit, 5706, *nāḥal* [2]
one who will inherit, 1201+5479, *bēn*[1]*+mešeq* [1]
inherit, 2118+448, *hāyâ+'el* [1]
make inherit, 3769, *yāraš*[1] [1]
cause to inherit, 5706, *nāḥal* [1]
has inherit, 5706, *nāḥal* [1]
inherit land, 5706, *nāḥal* [1]
territory inherit, 5709, *naḥ[a]lâ*[1] [1]

INHERITANCE [219]
inheritance, 5709, *naḥ[a]lâ*[1] [185]
assign as an inheritance, 5706, *nāḥal* [2]
gave inheritance, 5706, *nāḥal* [2]
giving as an inheritance, 5706, *nāḥal* [2]
inheritance, 5706, *nāḥal* [2]
receive inheritance, 5706, *nāḥal* [2]
received inheritance, 5706, *nāḥal* [2]
allotted inheritance, 1598, *gôrāl* [1]
inheritance, 2750, *ḥēleq*[2] [1]
gave as an inheritance, 3769, *yāraš*[1] [1]
inheritance, 3769, *yāraš*[1] [1]
leave as an inheritance, 3769, *yāraš*[1] [1]
share in the inheritance, 3769, *yāraš*[1] [1]
inheritance, 3772, *y[e]ruššâ* [1]
inheritance, 4625, *môrāš*[1] [1]
assign inheritance, 5706, *nāḥal* [1]
divide as inheritance, 5706, *nāḥal* [1]
divide for an inheritance, 5706, *nāḥal* [1]
get inheritance, 5706, *nāḥal* [1]
give as an inheritance, 5706, *nāḥal* [1]
give inheritance, 5706, *nāḥal* [1]
have inheritance, 5706+5709, *nāḥal+naḥ[a]lâ*[1] [1]
have inheritance, 5706, *nāḥal* [1]
inheritance given, 5706, *nāḥal* [1]
leaves an inheritance, 5706, *nāḥal* [1]
pass on as an inheritance, 5706, *nāḥal* [1]
receive inheritance, 5706+5709, *nāḥal+naḥ[a]lâ*[1] [1]
received as an inheritance, 5706, *nāḥal* [1]
take as inheritance, 5706, *nāḥal* [1]

INHERITANCES [2]
inheritances, 5709, *naḥ[a]lâ*[1] [2]

INHERITED [3]
inherited, 3769, *yāraš*[1] [1]
inherited, 5709, *naḥ[a]lâ*[1] [1]
land inherited, 5709, *naḥ[a]lâ*[1] [1]

INHERITS [3]
inherits, 3769, *yāraš*[1] [1]
inherits, 5706, *nāḥal* [1]
land inherits, 5709, *naḥ[a]lâ*[1] [1]

INIQUITIES [11]
iniquities, 6411, *'āwōn* [10]
iniquities, 2633, *ḥaṭṭā't* [1]

INIQUITY [14]
iniquity, 6411, *'āwōn* [12]
iniquity, 224, *'āwen*[1] [1]
iniquity, 6406, *'awlâ* [1]

INJURE [1]
injure themselves, 8581+8581, *śāraṭ+śāraṭ* [1]

INJURED [15]
injured, 8689, *šābar*[1] [3]
is injured, 8689, *šābar*[1] [2]
injured, 1608, *gāzal* [1]
the injured man[s], 2257, *-ô* [1]
injured, 2703, *ḥālâ*[1] [1]
injured, 2716, *ḥ[o]lî* [1]
injured, 5782, *nākâ* [1]
be injured, 5989, *nātan* [1]
injured, 5989+4583, *nātan+mûm* [1]
be injured, 6772, *'āṣab*[2] [1]
injured, 8653, *šābûr* [1]
be injured, 8689, *šābar*[1] [1]

INJURES [3]
injures, 4730, *māḥaṣ* [1]
injures, 5597, *nāgap* [1]
injures, 5989+4583, *nātan+mûm* [1]

INJURING [1]
injuring, 2467, *ḥabbûrâ* [1]

INJURY [6]
serious injury, 656, *'āsôn* [2]
injury, 4804, *makkâ* [2]
injury, 2716, *ḥ[o]lî* [1]
injury, 8691, *šeber*[1] [1]

INJUSTICE [10]
injustice, 4202+5477, *lō'+mišpāṭ* [3]
injustice, 6406, *'awlâ* [3]
injustice, 224, *'āwen*[1] [1]
injustice, 4754, *muṭṭeh* [1]
injustice, 6637, *'ōlātâ* [1]
injustice, 8400, *reša'* [1]

INK [1]
ink, 1902, *d[e]yô* [1]

INKLING [1]
had the least inkling, 3359+3359, *yāda'+yāda'* [1]

INLAID [6]
inlaid, *AIT* [3]
inlaid, *NIH/RPE* [2]
inlaid, 8362, *rāṣap* [1]

INMOST [9]
inmost being, 2540+1061, *ḥeder+beṭen*[1] [2]
inmost parts, 2540+1061, *ḥeder+beṭen*[1] [2]
inmost being, 4000, *kilyâ* [2]
inmost being, 7931, *qereb* [2]
inmost place, 6258, *sātam* [1]

INNER [76]
inner, 7164, *p[e]nîmî* [25]
inner parts, 7931, *qereb* [16]
inner sanctuary, 1808, *d[e]bîr*[1] [14]
inner room, 2540+928+2540, *ḥeder+b[e]-+ḥeder* [4]
inner, *NIH/RPE* [2]
inner, 6584, *'al*[2] [2]
inner sanctuary, 7164, *p[e]nîmî* [2]
inner, 1074, *bayit*[1] [1]
inner sanctuary[s], 2257, *-ô* [1]
inner room, 2540, *ḥeder* [1]
inner parts, 3219, *ṭuḥôt* [1]
inner, 4200+7156, *l[e]-*[1]*+pāneh* [1]
inner, 4200+7163, *l[e]-*[1]*+p[e]nîmâ* [1]
inner shrine, 6551, *'îr*[1] [1]
inner sanctuary, 7163, *p[e]nîmâ* [1]
inner parts, 7687, *qēbâ* [1]
inner and outer[s], 9109, *š[e]nayim* [1]
inner part, 9348, *tāwek* [1]

INNERMOST [2]
innermost, 7164, *p[e]nîmî* [2]

INNOCENCE [6]
innocence, 5931, *niqqāyôn* [2]
innocence, 7407, *ṣ[e]dāqâ* [2]
innocence, 7405, *ṣādaq* [1]
prove innocence, 7405, *ṣādaq* [1]

INNOCENT [58]
innocent, 5929, *nāqî* [30]
innocent, 7404, *ṣaddîq* [12]
innocent, 7405, *ṣādaq* [4]
innocent, 5927, *nāqâ* [3]
innocent, 870, *'āšam* [1]
innocent man, 1947+5929, *dām+nāqî* [1]
innocent, 2341, *zak* [1]
innocent, 2855, *ḥinnām* [1]
innocent, 3838, *yāšār*[1] [1]
consider innocent, 5927, *nāqâ* [1]
hold innocent, 5927, *nāqâ* [1]
innocent, 9447, *tām* [1]
innocent, 10229, *zākû* [1]

INNOCENTLY [1]
quite innocently, 4200+9448, *l[e]-*[1]*+tōm* [1]

INNUMERABLE [1]
innumerable, 401+5031, *'ayin*[1]*+mispār*[1] [1]

INQUIRE [36]
inquire of, 2011, *dāraš* [19]
inquire of, 2011+928, *dāraš+b[e]-* [4]
let inquire of, 2011+4200, *dāraš+l[e]-*[1] [2]
inquire of, 448+2011, *'el+dāraš* [1]
inquire of, 906+7023+8626, *'ēt*[1]*+peh+šā'al* [1]
inquire of, 2011+4200, *dāraš+l[e]-*[1] [1]
inquire of, 2011+4946+907, *dāraš+min+'ēt*[2] [1]
inquire, 2011, *dāraš* [1]
let inquire of at all, 2011+2011+4200, *dāraš+dāraš+l[e]-*[1] [1]
let inquire of, 2011, *dāraš* [1]
inquire of, 7928+448, *qārab+'el* [1]
inquire, 8626, *šā'al* [1]
inquire of, 8626+928, *šā'al+b[e]-* [1]
inquire, 10118, *b[e]qar* [1]

INQUIRED [19]
inquired of, 8626+928, *šā'al+b[e]-* [15]
inquired of, 606+448, *'āmar*[1]*+'el* [1]
inquired about, 2011+2011, *dāraš+dāraš* [1]
inquired of, 2011, *dāraš* [1]
inquired, 2924, *ḥāpaś* [1]

INQUIRES [1]
inquires of, 8626+928+1821, *šā'al+b[e]-+dābār* [1]

INQUIRING [4]
inquiring of, 1335, *bāqaš* [1]
inquiring, 2011, *dāraš* [1]
inquiring, 5477, *mišpāṭ* [1]
inquiring of, 8626+928, *šā'al+b[e]-* [1]

INQUIRY [1]
inquiry, 2984, *ḥēqer* [1]

INSANE [3]
pretended to be insane, 9101+3248, *šānâ*[1]*+ṭa'am* [2]
insane, 8713, *šāga'* [1]

INSATIABLE [1]
insatiable, 1194+8429, *biltî+śob'â* [1]

INSCRIBE [1]
inscribe, 2980, *ḥāqaq* [1]

INSCRIBED [6]
inscribed, 4180, *kātab* [3]
inscribed, *AIT* [1]
inscribed, *NIH/RPE* [1]
inscribed, 3086, *ḥāraš*[1] [1]

INSCRIPTION [4]
inscription, 10375, *k[e]tāb* [2]

inscription, 4844+7334, *miktāb+pittûaḥ* [1]
inscription, 7334, *pittûaḥ* [1]

INSECTS [2]
insects that swarm, 9238, *šereṣ* [1]
insects, 9238, *šereṣ* [1]

INSERT [1]
insert, 995, *bô’* [1]

INSERTED [6]
inserted, 995, *bô’* [2]
inserted, 296, *’āḥaz*^{1} [1]
inserted into, 928, *b*^{e}*-* [1]
be inserted, 995, *bô’* [1]
inserted, 5989, *nātan* [1]

INSIDE [62]
inside, 928+9348, *b*^{e}*-+tāwek* [15]
inside, 928, *b*^{e}*-* [9]
inside, 4946+1074, *min+bayit*^{1} [5]
inside, *NIH/RPE* [4]
inside, 448+9348, *’el+tāwek* [2]
inside, 928+2021+1074, *b*^{e}*-+ha-+bayit*^{1} [2]
inside, 1074+2025, *bayit*^{1}*+-â*^{2} [2]
inside, 2025, *-â*^{2} [2]
inside, 4200+7156, *l*^{e}*-*^{1}*+pāneh* [2]
inside, 5055, *mē‘eh* [2]
inside, 7163, *p*^{e}*nîmâ* [2]
inside, *AIT* [1]
inside, 448+2021+1074, *’el+ha-+bayit*^{1} [1]
inside, 448, *’el* [1]
inside, 928+5055, *b*^{e}*-+mē‘eh* [1]
inside, 928+7931, *b*^{e}*-+qereb* [1]
went inside, 995, *bô’* [1]
inside, 1061, *beṭen*^{1} [1]
inside, 1074, *bayit*^{1} [1]
the inside^{s}, 2084, *-hû* [1]
inside, 4200+4946+1074, *l*^{e}*-*^{1}*+min+bayit*^{1} [1]
inside, 4200+7163, *l*^{e}*-*^{1}*+p*^{e}*nîmâ* [1]
from inside, 4946, *min* [1]
inside, 4946+7163, *min+p*^{e}*nîmâ* [1]
inside, 7164, *p*^{e}*nîmî* [1]
inside^{s}, 9004+2025, *šām+-â*^{2} [1]

INSIGHT [12]
insight, 1069, *bînâ* [2]
insight, 9312, *t*^{e}*bûnâ* [2]
insight, 10467, *nahîrû* [2]
insight, 1067, *bîn* [1]
give insight, 8505, *śākal*^{1} [1]
have insight, 8505, *śākal*^{1} [1]
insight, 8505, *śākal*^{1} [1]
words of insight, 9312, *t*^{e}*bûnâ* [1]
insight, 9370, *tûšiyyâ* [1]

INSIGHTS [1]
insights have, 1067, *bîn* [1]

INSIST [2]
insist on paying for, 7864+7864+928+4697, *qānâ*^{1}*+qānâ*^{1}*+b*^{e}*-+m*^{e}*ḥîr*^{1} [1]
insist on paying, 7864+7864, *qānâ*^{1}*+qānâ*^{1} [1]

INSISTED [3]
insisted, 7210, *pāṣar* [2]
insisted, 606, *’āmar*^{1} [1]

INSOLENCE [6]
insolence, 3075, *ḥerpâ* [2]
insolence, 6301, *‘ebrâ* [2]
insolence, 8633, *ša’ănān* [2]

INSOLENT [2]
insolent, 2405, *za‘am* [1]
insolent, 3689, *yāqaḥ* [1]

INSPECT [2]
inspect, 8011, *rā’â*^{1} [2]

INSPECTED [1]
inspected, 8011, *rā’â*^{1} [1]

INSPECTION [1]
Inspection, 5152, *mipqād* [1]

INSPIRE [2]
inspire, *NIH/RPE* [1]
inspire, 5989+928+4222, *nātan+b*^{e}*-+lēbāb* [1]

INSPIRED [1]
inspired, 8120, *rûaḥ* [1]

INSPIRES [1]
inspires, 8120, *rûaḥ* [1]

INSTALLED [5]
installed, 4848+906+3338, *mālē’*^{1}*+’ēt*^{1}*+yād* [2]
installed, 5820, *nāsak*^{3} [1]
installed, 6641, *‘āmad* [1]
installed, 10624, *qûm* [1]

INSTANCE [1]
for instance, 2256, *w*^{e}*-* [1]

INSTANT [8]
in an instant, 7328, *pit’ōm* [2]
instant, 7353, *peta‘* [2]
for an instant, 6330+1180+8371, *‘ad*^{2}*+bāla‘*^{1}*+rōq* [1]
in an instant, 8088, *rāga‘*^{1} [1]
instant, 8088, *rāga‘*^{1} [1]
in an instant, 8092, *rega‘* [1]

INSTEAD [61]
instead, 2256, *w*^{e}*-* [18]
instead of, 9393, *taḥat*^{1} [18]
instead, 9393, *taḥat*^{1} [4]
instead, 3954, *kî*^{2} [3]
instead of, 4202, *lō’* [3]
instead, *NIH/RPE* [2]
instead, 3954+561, *kî*^{2}*+’im* [2]
instead of, 4946, *min* [2]
instead of, 440, *’al*^{1} [1]
instead, 2256+1685, *w*^{e}*-+gam* [1]
instead of, 4200+1194, *l*^{e}*-*^{1}*+biltî* [1]
instead of, 4200+7156, *l*^{e}*-*^{1}*+pāneh* [1]
instead of, 4200, *l*^{e}*-*^{1} [1]
instead of, 6073, *sûr*^{1} [1]
instead of, 6584+4030, *‘al*^{2}*+kēn*^{5} [1]
instead of, 9393+889, *taḥat*^{1}*+’ăšer* [1]
instead, 10221, *w*^{e}*-* [1]

INSTITUTED [3]
instituted, 6913, *‘āśâ*^{1} [3]

INSTRUCT [8]
instruct, 3723, *yārâ*^{3} [3]
instruct, 8505, *śākal*^{1} [2]
instruct, 673, *’āsar* [1]
instruct, 1067, *bîn* [1]
instruct, 5989, *nātan* [1]

INSTRUCTED [25]
instructed, 7422, *ṣāwâ* [9]
instructed, 1067, *bîn* [4]
instructed, 1819, *dābar*^{2} [3]
instructed, 606, *’āmar*^{1} [1]
instructed, 1819+7023, *dābar*^{2}*+peh* [1]
instructed, 1821, *dābār* [1]
instructed, 3359, *yāda‘* [1]
instructed, 3569, *yāsad*^{1} [1]
instructed, 3579, *yāsar*^{1} [1]
instructed, 3723, *yārâ*^{3} [1]
instructed, 4341, *limmud* [1]
instructed, 8505, *śākal*^{1} [1]

INSTRUCTING [1]
instructing, 1067, *bîn* [1]

INSTRUCTION [23]
instruction, 4592, *mûsār* [10]
instruction, 9368, *tôrâ* [5]
instruction, 1821, *dābār* [3]
instruction, 4375, *leqaḥ* [3]
instruction, 1830, *dabberet* [1]
instruction, 3723, *yārâ*^{3} [1]

INSTRUCTIONS [20]
instructions, 1821, *dābār* [5]
gave instructions, 7422, *ṣāwâ* [3]
instructions, 7422, *ṣāwâ* [3]
instructions, *NIH/RPE* [2]
instructions, 5184, *miṣwâ* [2]
instructions, 9368, *tôrâ* [2]
instructions, 4411, *ma’ămār* [1]
giving instructions, 7422, *ṣāwâ* [1]
left instructions, 7422, *ṣāwâ* [1]

INSTRUCTORS [1]
instructors, 4340, *lāmad* [1]

INSTRUCTS [3]
instructs, 3579, *yāsar*^{1} [2]
instructs, 3723, *yārâ*^{3} [1]

INSTRUMENT [1]
plays an instrument, 5594, *nāgan* [1]

INSTRUMENTS [21]
instruments, 3998, *k*^{e}*lî* [11]
stringed instruments, 5593, *n*^{e}*gînâ* [9]
instruments, 3998+8877, *k*^{e}*lî+šîr*^{2} [1]

INSULT [6]
insult, 3070, *ḥārap*^{2} [3]
insult, 7830, *qālôn* [2]
insult, 3075, *ḥerpâ* [1]

INSULTED [4]
insulted, 3070, *ḥārap*^{2} [3]
insulted, 3075, *ḥerpâ* [1]

INSULTING [3]
insulting, 3070, *ḥārap*^{2} [3]

INSULTS [12]
insults, 3075, *ḥerpâ* [5]
heaped insults on, 3070, *ḥārap*^{2} [2]
insults, 1528, *giddûpâ* [1]
thrown insults, 4087, *kā‘as* [1]
hurled insults, 6512, *‘îṭ*^{1} [1]
hurl insults, 7080+928+8557, *pāṭar+b*^{e}*-+śāpâ* [1]
insults, 7830, *qālôn* [1]

INTACT [2]
intact, 3782, *yāšab* [1]
keeps intact, 5893, *nāṣab*^{1} [1]

INTEGRITY [19]
integrity, 9448, *tōm* [6]
integrity, 9450, *tummâ* [4]
integrity, 575, *’emûnâ* [1]
integrity, 622, *’emet* [1]
integrity, 3841+4222, *yōšer+lēbāb* [1]
integrity, 3841, *yōšer* [1]
integrity, 4797, *mêšārîm* [1]
integrity, 7406, *ṣedeq* [1]
integrity, 7407, *ṣ*^{e}*dāqâ* [1]
integrity, 9447, *tām* [1]
man of integrity, 9448+2006, *tōm+derek* [1]

INTELLIGENCE [4]
intelligence, 10684, *śokl*^{e}*tānû* [2]
intelligence, 1069, *bînâ* [1]
intelligence, 8507, *śekel* [1]

INTELLIGENT [2]
intelligent, 1067, *bîn* [1]
intelligent, 3202+8507, *ṭôb*^{2}*+śekel* [1]

INTEND [8]
intend, 606, *’āmar*^{1} [3]
intend, 1335, *bāqaš* [2]
intend, 3619, *yā‘aṣ* [1]
intend to reign, 4887+4887, *mālak*^{1}*+mālak*^{1} [1]
intend, 6640+4222, *‘im+lēbāb* [1]

INTENDED [8]
intended, 3108, *ḥāšab* [2]
intended, *NIH/RPE* [1]
intended, 606, *’āmar*^{1} [1]
intended, 1335, *bāqaš* [1]
intended, 2372, *zāmam* [1]
intended, 3983, *kālâ*^{1} [1]
intended, 7156, *pāneh* [1]

INTENDING [1]
intending, 1948, *dāmâ*^{1} [1]

INTENDS [2]
intends, *AIT* [1]

intends, 1948, *dāmâ^{1}* [1]

INTENSE [1]
intense, 1524+4394, *gādôl+m^{e}ʾōd* [1]

INTENT [6]
evil intent, 2365, *zimmâ^{1}* [1]
intent on, 3283, *yāʿal^{2}* [1]
intent, 4213, *lēb* [1]
intent, 4222, *lēbāb* [1]
evil intent, 4659, *m^{e}zimmâ* [1]
evil intent, 8288, *rāʿâ^{3}* [1]

INTENTION [2]
intention, 8461, *śûmâ* [1]
intention, 8492+4213, *śîm+lēb* [1]

INTENTIONAL [1]
not intentional, 8705, *š^{e}gāgâ* [1]

INTENTIONALLY [2]
intentionally, 928+7402, *b^{e}-+ṣ^{e}diyyâ* [1]
do intentionally, 7399, *ṣādâ^{1}* [1]

INTERCEDE [4]
intercede, 7137, *pālal^{2}* [2]
intercede with, 2704+906+7156, *ḥālâ^{2}+ʾēt^{1}+pāneh* [1]
intercede, 7003, *pāgaʿ* [1]

INTERCEDED [1]
interceded with, 2704+906+7156, *ḥālâ^{2}+ʾēt^{1}+pāneh* [1]

INTERCESSION [1]
made intercession, 7003, *pāgaʿ* [1]

INTERCESSOR [1]
intercessor, 4885, *mēlîṣ* [1]

INTEREST [12]
excessive interest, 9552, *tarbît* [4]
interest, 5968, *nešek* [2]
charge interest, 5967+5968, *nāšak^{2}+nešek* [1]
charge interest, 5967, *nāšak^{2}* [1]
earn interest, 5967, *nāšak^{2}* [1]
exorbitant interest, 5968+2256+9552, *nešek+w^{e}-+tarbît* [1]
interest of any kind, 5968+2256+9552, *nešek+w^{e}-+tarbît* [1]
in best interest, 8750, *šāwâ^{1}* [1]

INTERESTS [1]
royal interests, 10421, *melek* [1]

INTERFERE [1]
not interfere, 10697, *š^{e}baq* [1]

INTERFERED [1]
interfered with, 6772, *ʿāṣab^{2}* [1]

INTERIOR [3]
interior, 1074, *bayit^{1}* [1]
interior, 4946+1074+2025, *min+bayit^{1}+-â^{2}* [1]
interior, 9348, *tāwek* [1]

INTERMARRY [5]
intermarry, 3161, *ḥātan* [4]
intermarry, 995, *bôʾ* [1]

INTERMITTENT [1]
intermittent streams, 5707, *naḥal^{1}* [1]

INTERPRET [18]
interpret, 10600+10252, *p^{e}šar^{2}+h^{a}wâ* [5]
interpret, 7354, *pātar* [4]
interpret, 10600+10313, *p^{e}šar^{2}+y^{e}daʿ* [3]
interpret, 10600, *p^{e}šar^{2}* [3]
interpret, 10600+10042, *p^{e}šar^{2}+ʾ^{a}mar* [2]
interpret, 10599, *p^{e}šar^{1}* [1]

INTERPRETATION [8]
interpretation, 10600, *p^{e}šar^{2}* [4]
given interpretation, 7354, *pātar* [1]
giving interpretation, 7354, *pātar* [1]
said in interpretation, 7354, *pātar* [1]
interpretation, 8694, *šēber* [1]

INTERPRETATIONS [2]
interpretations, 7355, *pittārôn* [1]
give interpretations, 10600+10599, *p^{e}šar^{2}+p^{e}šar^{1}* [1]

INTERPRETED [2]
interpreted, 7354, *pātar* [2]

INTERPRETER [1]
interpreter, 4885, *mēlîṣ* [1]

INTERPRETERS [1]
interpreters of dreams, 2706, *ḥ^{a}lôm* [1]

INTERPRETS [1]
interprets omens, 5727, *nāḥaš* [1]

INTERSECTING [2]
intersecting, 928+9348, *b^{e}-+tāwek* [2]

INTERVALS [1]
at regular intervals, 4500, *middâ^{1}* [1]

INTERVENE [1]
intervene, 7003, *pāgaʿ* [1]

INTERVENED [1]
intervened, 7136, *pālal^{1}* [1]

INTERWOVEN [3]
interwoven chains, 5126+9249, *maʿ^{a}śeh+šarš^{e}râ* [1]
interwoven, 5401, *mišbeṣôt* [1]
interwoven, 8054, *rābîd* [1]

INTESTINES [1]
intestines, 5055, *mēʿeh* [1]

INTIMATE [4]
had intimate relations with, 3359, *yādaʿ* [1]
intimate with, 4200, *l^{e}-^{1}* [1]
intimate friendship, 6051, *sôd* [1]
intimate, 6051, *sôd* [1]

INTIMIDATE [3]
intimidate, 3707, *yārēʾ^{1}* [3]

INTO [910]*
into, 928, *b^{e}-* [274]
into, 448, *ʾel* [160]
into, 4200, *l^{e}-^{1}* [110]
into, *AIT* [71]
into, 2025, *-â^{2}* [51]
into, 6584, *ʿal^{2}* [24]
into, *NIH/RPE* [12]
into, 448+9348, *ʾel+tāwek* [11]
into, 928+9348, *b^{e}-+tāwek* [9]
into, 10378, *l^{e}-* [7]
into, 10378+10135, *l^{e}-+gaw* [6]
into, 3869, *k^{e}-* [3]
into, 4946, *min* [3]
into, 6640, *ʿim* [2]
into, 907, *ʾēt^{2}* [1]

INTRIGUE [3]
intrigue, 744, *ʾōreb* [1]
intrigue, 2648, *ḥîdâ* [1]
intrigue, 2761, *ḥ^{a}laqlaq* [1]

INTRIGUES [2]
intrigues, 4600, *môʿēṣâ* [1]
intrigues, 8222, *rōkes* [1]

INTRODUCED [2]
introduced, 6913, *ʿāśâ^{1}* [2]

INVADE [14]
invade, 995+928, *bôʾ+b^{e}-* [6]
invade, 995, *bôʾ* [2]
invade, 995+448, *bôʾ+ʾel* [1]
invade, 995+9004+2025, *bôʾ+šām+-â^{2}* [1]
invade, 6296+928, *ʿābar^{1}+b^{e}-* [1]
invade, 6296, *ʿābar^{1}* [1]
invade, 6590+6584, *ʿālâ+ʿal^{2}* [1]
invade, 6590+928, *ʿālâ+b^{e}-* [1]

INVADED [15]
invaded, 995+928, *bôʾ+b^{e}-* [4]
invaded, 6590+6584, *ʿālâ+ʿal^{2}* [3]
invaded, 6590, *ʿālâ* [2]
invaded, 995+448, *bôʾ+ʾel* [1]
invaded, 995+6584, *bôʾ+ʿal^{2}* [1]
invaded, 1324, *bāqaʿ* [1]
invaded, 2143+4200, *hālak+l^{e}-^{1}* [1]
invaded, 6590+448, *ʿālâ+ʾel* [1]
invaded, 6590+928, *ʿālâ+b^{e}-* [1]

INVADER [2]
invader, *AIT* [1]
invader, 995+448, *bôʾ+ʾel* [1]

INVADERS [1]
invaders, 1522, *g^{e}dûd^{2}* [1]

INVADES [2]
invades, 995+928, *bôʾ+b^{e}-* [2]

INVADING [2]
invading, 995+4200, *bôʾ+l^{e}-^{1}* [1]
invading, 1574, *gûd* [1]

INVENTORY [1]
inventory, 5031, *mispār^{1}* [1]

INVESTIGATE [5]
investigate, 2011, *dāraš* [2]
investigate, *NIH/RPE* [1]
investigate, 8626, *šāʾal* [1]
investigate, 9365, *tûr* [1]

INVESTIGATED [2]
was investigated, 1335, *bāqaš* [1]
carefully investigated, 2011+2256+1335, *dāraš+w^{e}-+bāqaš* [1]

INVESTIGATION [1]
make investigation, 2011, *dāraš* [1]

INVITATION [1]
invitation, 7924, *qārāʾ^{1}* [1]

INVITE [9]
invite, 7924, *qārāʾ^{1}* [7]
invite, 1819, *dābar^{2}* [1]
invite, 8938+2256+7924, *šālaḥ+w^{e}-+qārāʾ^{1}* [1]

INVITED [15]
invited, 7924, *qārāʾ^{1}* [12]
invited, 995, *bôʾ* [1]
been invited as guests, 7924, *qārāʾ^{1}* [1]
were invited, 7924, *qārāʾ^{1}* [1]

INVITES [4]
invites, 1335, *bāqaš* [1]
invites, 4374, *lāqaḥ* [1]
invites, 7924, *qārāʾ^{1}* [1]
invites, 7940, *qārôb* [1]

INVITING [1]
inviting, *NIH/RPE* [1]

INVOKE [5]
invoke, 2349, *zākar^{1}* [4]
invoke, 7924+928+7023, *qārāʾ^{1}+b^{e}-+peh* [1]

INVOKED [1]
be invoked, 2349, *zākar^{1}* [1]

INVOKES [2]
invokes a blessing on himself, 1385, *bārak^{2}* [1]
invokes a blessing, 1385, *bārak^{2}* [1]

INVOKING [1]
invoking, 8626, *šāʾal* [1]

INVOLVED [4]
involved, *AIT* [1]
involved in, 928, *b^{e}-* [1]
involved in, 1251, *baʿal^{1}* [1]
involved in, 4200, *l^{e}-^{1}* [1]

INVOLVING [2]
involving, *AIT* [1]
involving, *NIH/RPE* [1]

INWARD [2]
inward, 1074+2025, *bayit^{1}+-â^{2}* [1]
inward, 7163, *p^{e}nîmâ* [1]

IPHDEIAH [1]
Iphdeiah, 3635, *yipdeyâ* [1]

IPHTAH [1]
Iphtah, 3652, *yiptāḥ*[1] [1]

IPHTAH EL [2]
Iphtah El, 3654, *yiptaḥ-'ēl* [2]

IR [1]
Ir, 6553, *ʿîr*[3] [1]

IR NAHASH [1]
Ir Nahash, 6560, *ʿîr nāḥāš* [1]

IR SHEMESH [1]
Ir Shemesh, 6561, *ʿîr šemeš* [1]

IRA [6]
Ira, 6562, *ʿîrāʾ* [6]

IRAD [2]
Irad, 6563, *ʿîrād* [2]

IRAM [2]
Iram, 6566, *ʿîrām* [2]

IRI [1]
Iri, 6565, *ʿîrî* [1]

IRIJAH [2]
Irijah, 3713, *yirʾiyyāyh* [2]

IRON [88]
iron, 1366, *barzel* [62]
iron, 10591, *parzel* [20]
iron tool, 1366, *barzel* [2]
iron axhead, 1366, *barzel* [1]
iron chains, 1366, *barzel* [1]
tool of iron, 1366, *barzel* [1]
Iron, 3712, *yirʾôn* [1]

IRON-SMELTING [3]
iron-smelting, 1366, *barzel* [3]

IRONS [1]
irons, 1366, *barzel* [1]

IRPEEL [1]
Irpeel, 3761, *yirpeʾēl* [1]

IRRESISTIBLE [1]
irresistible, 6296, *ʿābar*[1] [1]

IRREVERENT [1]
irreverent act, 8915, *šal* [1]

IRRIGATED [1]
irrigated, 9197, *šāqâ* [1]

IRRITATE [1]
irritate, 8307, *rāʿam*[2] [1]

IRU [1]
Iru, 6564, *ʿîrû* [1]

IS [5020]*
is, *NIH/RPE* [2528]
is, *AIT* [1334]
this is what, 3907, *kōh* [471]
there is no, 401, *ʾayin*[1] [98]
is, 2118, *hāyâ* [97]
there is, 3780, *yēš* [27]
is not, 401, *ʾayin*[1] [20]
is, 3780, *yēš* [11]
is there, 3780, *yēš* [8]
there is none, 401, *ʾayin*[1] [6]

ISAAC [111]
Isaac, 3663, *yiṣḥāq* [100]
Isaac, *NIH/RPE* [5]
Isaac, 3773, *yiśḥāq* [4]
Isaac[s], 2257, *-ô* [2]

ISAAC'S [3]
Isaac's, 3663, *yiṣḥāq* [3]

ISAIAH [31]
Isaiah, 3833, *yešaʿyāhû* [30]
Isaiah, *NIH/RPE* [1]

ISCAH [1]
Iscah, 3576, *yiskâ* [1]

ISH-BOSHETH [14]
Ish-Bosheth, 410, *ʾîš-bōšet* [11]
Ish-Bosheth, *NIH/RPE* [3]

ISHBAH [1]
Ishbah, 3786, *yišbāḥ* [1]

ISHBAK [2]
Ishbak, 3791, *yišbāq* [2]

ISHBI-BENOB [1]
Ishbi-Benob, 3787, *yišbî benōb* [1]

ISHHOD [1]
Ishhod, 412, *ʾîšhôd* [1]

ISHI [4]
Ishi, 3831, *yišʿî* [4]

ISHIJAH [1]
Ishijah, 3807, *yiššiyyâ* [1]

ISHMA [1]
Ishma, 3816, *yišmāʾ* [1]

ISHMAEL [47]
Ishmael, 3817, *yišmāʿēʾl* [47]

ISHMAELITE [2]
Ishmaelite, 3818, *yišmeʿēʾlî* [2]

ISHMAELITES [6]
Ishmaelites, 3818, *yišmeʿēʾlî* [6]

ISHMAIAH [2]
Ishmaiah, 3819, *yišmaʿyâ* [1]
Ishmaiah, 3820, *yišmaʿyāhû* [1]

ISHMERAI [1]
Ishmerai, 3821, *yišmeray* [1]

ISHPAH [1]
Ishpah, 3834, *yišpâ* [1]

ISHPAN [1]
Ishpan, 3836, *yišpān* [1]

ISHVAH [2]
Ishvah, 3796, *yišwâ* [2]

ISHVI [4]
Ishvi, 3798, *yišwî*[1] [4]

ISHVITE [1]
Ishvite, 3799, *yišwî*[2] [1]

ISLAND [2]
island, 362, *ʾî*[1] [2]

ISLANDS [15]
islands, 362, *ʾî*[1] [15]

ISMAKIAH [1]
Ismakiah, 3577, *yismakyāhû* [1]

ISN'T [23]
isn't, 4202, *lōʾ* [14]
isn't, *NIH/RPE* [2]
isn't, 401, *ʾayin*[1] [2]
isn't enough, 5071, *meʿaṭ* [2]
isn't, *AIT* [1]
isn't there, 401, *ʾayin*[1] [1]
isn't, 2022, *ha-* [1]

ISOLATE [2]
isolate, 6037, *sāgar* [2]

ISOLATION [7]
put in isolation, 6037, *sāgar* [5]
keep in isolation, 6037, *sāgar* [2]

ISRAEL [1771]
Israel, 3776, *yiśrāʾēl* [1712]
Israel, 1201+3776, *bēn*[1]*+yiśrāʾēl* [21]
Israel, *NIH/RPE* [7]
Israel, 824+3776, *ʾereṣ+yiśrāʾēl* [7]
Israel, 10335, *yiśrāʾēl* [7]
Israel[s], 4392, *-ām* [6]
Israel, 1074+3776, *bayit*[1]*+yiśrāʾēl* [5]
Israel[s], 2157, *-hem* [3]
Israel, 408+3776, *ʾîš*[1]*+yiśrāʾēl* [1]
Israel[s], 2257, *-ô* [1]
Israel, 6639+3776, *ʿam*[2]*+yiśrāʾēl* [1]

ISRAEL'S [43]
Israel's, 3776, *yiśrāʾēl* [35]
Israel's, 4200+3776, *le-*[1]*+yiśrāʾēl* [3]
Israel's[s], 2257, *-ô* [2]
Israel's, 928+3776, *be-+yiśrāʾēl* [1]
Israel's[s], 2021, *ha-* [1]
Israel's[s], 2023, *-āh* [1]

ISRAELITE [94]
Israelite, 1201+3776, *bēn*[1]*+yiśrāʾēl* [50]
Israelite, 3776, *yiśrāʾēl* [16]
Israelite, 408+4946+1074+3776, *ʾîš*[1]*+min+bayit*[1]*+yiśrāʾēl* [6]
Israelite, 408+3776, *ʾîš*[1]*+yiśrāʾēl* [5]
Israelite, 3778, *yiśreʾēlî* [3]
brother Israelite, 278, *ʾāḥ*[2] [2]
Israelite, 408+4946+1201+3776, *ʾîš*[1]*+min+bēn*[1]*+yiśrāʾēl* [2]
fellow Israelite, 8276, *rēaʿ*[2] [2]
Israelite, 408+2021+3778, *ʾîš*[1]*+ha-+yiśreʾēlî* [1]
Israelite, 928+1201+3776, *be-+bēn*[1]*+yiśrāʾēl* [1]
Israelite, 928+3776, *be-+yiśrāʾēl* [1]
Israelite, 1074+3776, *bayit*[1]*+yiśrāʾēl* [1]
Israelite[s], 3870, *-kā* [1]
Israelite, 4200+1201+3776, *le-*[1]*+bēn*[1]*+yiśrāʾēl* [1]
Israelite, 4946+1201+3776, *min+bēn*[1]*+yiśrāʾēl* [1]
Israelite, 4946+3776, *min+yiśrāʾēl* [1]

ISRAELITES [603]
Israelites, 1201+3776, *bēn*[1]*+yiśrāʾēl* [486]
Israelites, 3776, *yiśrāʾēl* [72]
Israelites, 408+3776, *ʾîš*[1]*+yiśrāʾēl* [14]
Israelites, *NIH/RPE* [8]
the Israelites[s], 4392, *-ām* [5]
Israelites[s], 6639, *ʿam*[2] [4]
the Israelites[s], 2157, *-hem* [3]
Israelites, 4946+1201+3776, *min+bēn*[1]*+yiśrāʾēl* [2]
brother Israelites, 278, *ʾāḥ*[2] [1]
Israelites, 1074+3776, *bayit*[1]*+yiśrāʾēl* [1]
Israelites[s], 2156, *hēm* [1]
the Israelites[s], 2156, *hēm* [1]
Israelites[s], 2157, *-hem* [1]
those Israelites[s], 2157, *-hem* [1]
Israelites, 4946+3776, *min+yiśrāʾēl* [1]
Israelites, 6639+1201+3776, *ʿam*[2]*+bēn*[1]*+yiśrāʾēl* [1]
Israelites, 10553+10335, *ʿam+yiśrāʾēl* [1]

ISSACHAR [42]
Issachar, 3779, *yiśśāśkār* [38]
Issachar, 1201+3779, *bēn*[1]*+yiśśāśkār* [4]

ISSHIAH [6]
Isshiah, 3807, *yiššiyyâ* [5]
Isshiah, 3808, *yiššiyyāhû* [1]

ISSUE [10]
issue, 10682, *śîm* [3]
issue, 10624, *qûm* [2]
issue, *NIH/RPE* [1]
issue, 3655, *yāṣāʾ* [1]
issue decrees, 4180+4180, *kātab+kātab* [1]
issue an order, 7422, *ṣāwâ* [1]
issue, 10427+10621, *min+qodām* [1]

ISSUED [18]
issued, 10682, *śîm* [5]
was issued, 5989, *nātan* [3]
be issued, 5989, *nātan* [2]
issued orders, 606, *ʾāmar*[1] [1]
issued a proclamation, 2410, *zāʿaq* [1]
decree be issued, 4180, *kātab* [1]
issued, 5989, *nātan* [1]
issued, 6296, *ʿābar*[1] [1]
issued an order, 9048, *šāmaʿ* [1]
issued, 10413, *meṭāʾ* [1]

issued, 10485, *n^{e}paq* [1]

ISSUES [1]
issues, 10624, *qûm* [1]

ISSUING [1]
issuing, 4604, *môṣāʾ^{1}* [1]

IT [3799]*
it, *NIH/RPE* [1155]
it, *AIT* [687]
it, 2023, *-āh* [539]
it, 2257, *-ô* [499]
it, 2085, *hûʾ* [191]
it, 2084, *-hû* [147]
it, 5647, *-nû^{2}* [85]
it, 5626, *-nâ* [84]
it, 4392, *-ām* [31]
it^{s}, 9004, *šām* [17]
it, 10192, *-ēh* [16]
it, 10193, *-ah* [15]
it, 2296, *zeh* [13]
far be it, 2721, *ḥālîl^{2}* [12]
it, 2157, *-hem* [9]
it^{s}, 2021, *ha-* [7]
it, 2156, *hēm* [5]
it, 5646, *-nû^{1}* [5]
it, 10204, *-hî* [4]
it, 2177, *-hēn^{2}* [2]
it^{s}, 3972, *kōl* [2]
it, 4564, *-mô* [2]
it^{s}, 10002, *-āʾ* [1]
it, 10200, *hûʾ* [1]
it, 10205, *hîʾ* [1]

IT'S [12]
it's, *NIH/RPE* [7]
it's, *AIT* [2]
it's not, 401, *ʾayin^{1}* [2]
it's, 2021+3427, *ha-+yôm^{1}* [1]

ITCH [8]
itch, 5999, *neteq* [7]
itch, 3063, *ḥeres^{1}* [1]

ITHAI [2]
Ithai, 416, *ʾîtay* [1]
Ithai, 915, *ʾittay* [1]

ITHAMAR [19]
Ithamar, 418, *ʾîtāmār* [19]

ITHAMAR'S [2]
Ithamar's, 418, *ʾîtāmār* [2]

ITHIEL [3]
Ithiel, 417, *ʾîtîʾēl* [3]

ITHLAH [1]
Ithlah, 3849, *yitlâ* [1]

ITHMAH [1]
Ithmah, 3850, *yitmâ* [1]

ITHNAN [1]
Ithnan, 3854, *yitnān* [1]

ITHRAN [3]
Ithran, 3864, *yitrān* [3]

ITHREAM [2]
Ithream, 3865, *yitr^{e}ʿām* [2]

ITHRITE [4]
Ithrite, 3863, *yitrî* [4]

ITHRITES [1]
Ithrites, 3863, *yitrî* [1]

ITS [898]*
its, 2257, *-ô* [373]
its, 2023, *-āh* [257]
its, *NIH/RPE* [71]
its^{s}, 2021, *ha-* [25]
its, *AIT* [16]
its, 10204, *-hî* [14]
its, 2084, *-hû* [13]
its own, 2257, *ô* [10]
its, 4392, *-ām* [10]
its, 10192, *-ēh* [10]
its, 10193, *-ah* [7]
its, 5626, *-nâ* [6]
its, 2157, *-hem* [5]
its, 3870, *-kā* [4]
its, 4200+2257, *l^{e}-^{1}+-ô* [4]
its land^{s}, 2023, *-āh* [2]
its^{s}, 2023, *-āh* [2]
its, 2024, *-ōh* [2]
its, 2085, *hûʾ* [2]
its own, 2157, *-hem* [2]
its, 2177, *-hēn^{2}* [2]
its, 4200+2023, *l^{e}-^{1}+-āh* [2]
its, 5647, *-nû^{2}* [2]
its^{s}, 10191, *-â* [2]
its own, 2023, *-āh* [1]
its, 2181, *-h^{e}nâ* [1]
its^{s}, 2296, *zeh* [1]
its, 3276, *-î* [1]
its^{s}, 3870, *-kā* [1]
its, 4564, *-mô* [1]
its own, 5883+2257, *nepeš+-ô* [1]
its, 6584+2023, *ʿal^{2}+-āh* [1]
its^{s}, 10002, *-āʾ* [1]

ITSELF [27]
itself, *AIT* [8]
itself, *NIH/RPE* [6]
what grows by itself, 6206, *sāpîaḥ^{1}* [2]
what grows of itself, 6206, *sāpîaḥ^{1}* [2]
itself, 2157, *-hem* [1]
itself, 2257, *-ô* [1]
by itself, 4200+963+2257, *l^{e}-^{1}+bad^{1}+-ô* [1]
by itself, 4200+963, *l^{e}-^{1}+bad^{1}* [1]
by itself, 4200+970, *l^{e}-^{1}+bādād* [1]
exalt itself, 5951, *nāśāʾ* [1]
itself, 6795, *ʿeṣem^{1}* [1]
raise itself, 6995, *pāʿar^{2}* [1]
itself, 10205, *hîʾ* [1]

ITTAI [7]
Ittai, 915, *ʾittay* [7]

IVORY [12]
ivory, 9094, *šēn^{1}* [10]
ivory, 9105, *šenhabbîm* [2]

IVVAH [3]
Ivvah, 6394, *ʿiwwâ* [3]

IYE ABARIM [2]
Iye Abarim, 6516, *ʿiyyê hāʿ^{a}bārîm* [2]

IYIM [1]
Iyim, 6517, *ʿiyyîm* [1]

IZHAR [9]
Izhar, 3659, *yiṣhār^{2}* [9]

IZHARITES [4]
Izharites, 3660, *yiṣhārî* [4]

IZLIAH [1]
Izliah, 3468, *yizlîʾâ* [1]

IZRAHIAH [2]
Izrahiah, 3474, *yizraḥyâ* [2]

IZRAHITE [1]
Izrahite, 3473, *yizrāḥ* [1]

IZRI [1]
Izri, 3673, *yiṣrî* [1]

IZZIAH [1]
Izziah, 3466, *yizziyyâ* [1]

JAAKANITES [1]
Jaakanites, 1201+3622, *bēn^{1}+yaʿ^{a}qān* [1]

JAAKOBAH [1]
Jaakobah, 3621, *yaʿ^{a}qōbâ* [1]

JAALA [2]
Jaala, 3606, *yaʿ^{a}lāʾ* [1]
Jaala, 3608, *yaʿ^{a}lâ^{2}* [1]

JAAR [1]
Jaar, 3625, *yaʿar^{3}* [1]

JAARE-OREGIM [1]
Jaare-Oregim, 3629, *yaʿ^{a}rê ʾōr^{e}gîm* [1]

JAARESHIAH [1]
Jaareshiah, 3631, *yaʿ^{a}rešyâ* [1]

JAASIEL [2]
Jaasiel, 3634, *yaʿ^{a}śîʾēl* [2]

JAASU [1]
Jaasu, 3632, *yaʿ^{a}śû* [1]

JAAZANIAH [5]
Jaazaniah, 3279, *ya^{a}zanyâ* [2]
Jaazaniah, 3280, *ya^{a}zanyāhû* [2]
Jaazaniah, 3471, *y^{e}zanyāhû* [1]

JAAZIAH [2]
Jaaziah, 3596, *yaʿ^{a}ziyyāhû* [2]

JAAZIEL [1]
Jaaziel, 3595, *yaʿ^{a}zîʾēl* [1]

JABAL [1]
Jabal, 3299, *yābāl^{2}* [1]

JABBOK [7]
Jabbok, 3309, *yabbōq* [7]

JABESH [11]
Jabesh, 3315, *yābēš^{4}* [8]
Jabesh, 3314, *yābēš^{3}* [3]

JABESH GILEAD [12]
Jabesh Gilead, 3316, *yābēš gilʿād* [12]

JABEZ [4]
Jabez, 3584, *yaʿbēṣ^{2}* [3]
Jabez, 3583, *yaʿbēṣ^{1}* [1]

JABIN [6]
Jabin, 3296, *yābîn* [6]

JABIN'S [1]
Jabin's, 3296, *yābîn* [1]

JABNEEL [2]
Jabneel, 3305, *yabn^{e}ʾēl* [2]

JABNEH [1]
Jabneh, 3306, *yabnēh* [1]

JACAN [1]
Jacan, 3602, *yaʿkān* [1]

JACINTH [2]
jacinth, 4385, *lešem^{1}* [2]

JACKAL [2]
jackal, 9478, *tan* [1]
jackal, 9490, *tannîn* [1]

JACKALS [17]
jackals, 9478, *tan* [13]
jackals, 8785, *šûʿāl^{1}* [3]
jackals, 280, *ʾōaḥ* [1]

JACOB [337]
Jacob, 3620, *yaʿ^{a}qōb* [316]
Jacob, *NIH/RPE* [17]
Jacob^{s}, 2257, *-ô* [4]

JACOB'S [20]
Jacob's, 3620, *yaʿ^{a}qōb* [17]
Jacob's^{s}, 2021, *ha-* [1]
Jacob's^{s}, 2257, *-ô* [1]
Jacob's, 4200+3620, *l^{e}-^{1}+yaʿ^{a}qōb* [1]

JADA [2]
Jada, 3360, *yādāʿ* [2]

JADAH [2]
Jadah, 3586, *yaʿdâ* [2]

JADDAI [1]
Jaddai, 3350, *yadday* [1]

JADDUA [3]
Jaddua, 3348, *yaddûaʿ* [3]

JADON [1]
Jadon, 3347, *yādôn* [1]

JAEL [6]
Jael, 3605, *yāʿēl*^{2} [6]

JAGGED [1]
jagged, 2529, *ḥaddûd* [1]

JAGUR [1]
Jagur, 3327, *yāgûr* [1]

JAHATH [7]
Jahath, 3511, *yaḥat* [7]

JAHAZ [7]
Jahaz, 3403, *yahaṣ* [7]

JAHAZIEL [6]
Jahaziel, 3487, *yaḥazîʾēl* [6]

JAHDAI [1]
Jahdai, 3367, *yāhdāy* [1]

JAHDIEL [1]
Jahdiel, 3484, *yaḥdîʾēl* [1]

JAHDO [1]
Jahdo, 3482, *yaḥdô* [1]

JAHLEEL [2]
Jahleel, 3499, *yaḥleʾēl* [2]

JAHLEELITE [1]
Jahleelite, 3500, *yaḥleʾēlî* [1]

JAHMAI [1]
Jahmai, 3503, *yaḥmay* [1]

JAHZAH [2]
Jahzah, 3404, *yahṣâ* [2]

JAHZEEL [1]
Jahzeel, 3505, *yaḥṣeʾēl* [1]

JAHZEELITE [1]
Jahzeelite, 3506, *yaḥṣeʾēlî* [1]

JAHZEIAH [1]
Jahzeiah, 3488, *yaḥzeyâ* [1]

JAHZERAH [1]
Jahzerah, 3492, *yaḥzērâ* [1]

JAHZIEL [2]
Jahziel, 3505, *yaḥṣeʾēl* [1]
Jahziel, 3507, *yaḥasîʾēl* [1]

JAIR [9]
Jair, 3281, *yāʾîr* [8]
Jair, 3600, *yāʾîr* [1]

JAIRITE [1]
Jairite, 3285, *yāʾirî* [1]

JAKEH [1]
Jakeh, 3681, *yāqeh* [1]

JAKIM [2]
Jakim, 3691, *yāqîm* [2]

JAKIN [8]
Jakin, 3520, *yākîn*^{1} [6]
Jakin, 3521, *yākîn*^{2} [2]

JAKINITE [1]
Jakinite, 3522, *yākînî* [1]

JALAM [4]
Jalam, 3609, *yaʿlām* [4]

JALON [1]
Jalon, 3534, *yālôn* [1]

JAMBS [12]
jambs, 382, *ʾayil*^{3} [9]
jambs, *NIH/RPE* [1]
jambs, 382+4647, *ʾayil*^{3}*+mezûzâ* [1]
jambs, 4647, *mezûzâ* [1]

JAMIN [6]
Jamin, 3546, *yāmîn*^{2} [6]

JAMINITE [1]
Jaminite, 3547, *yāmînî* [1]

JAMLECH [1]
Jamlech, 3552, *yamlēk* [1]

JANAI [1]
Janai, 3614, *yaʿnay* [1]

JANIM [1]
Janim, 3565, *yānîm* [1]

JANOAH [3]
Janoah, 3562, *yānôaḥ* [3]

JAPHETH [12]
Japheth, 3651, *yepet* [11]
Japheth, *NIH/RPE* [1]

JAPHIA [5]
Japhia, 3644, *yāpîaʿ*^{2} [4]
Japhia, 3643, *yāpîaʿ*^{1} [1]

JAPHLET [2]
Japhlet, 3646, *yaplēṭ* [2]

JAPHLET'S [1]
Japhlet's, 3646, *yaplēṭ* [1]

JAPHLETITES [1]
Japhletites, 3647, *yaplēṭî* [1]

JAR [27]
jar, 3902, *kad* [12]
jar, 3998, *kelî* [9]
jar, 1318, *baqbuq* [3]
storage jar, 3998, *kelî* [1]
jar, 7573, *ṣinṣenet* [1]
jar, 7608, *ṣappaḥat* [1]

JARED [6]
Jared, 3719, *yered* [6]

JARHA [2]
Jarha, 3739, *yarḥāʿ* [2]

JARIB [3]
Jarib, 3743, *yārîb*^{2} [3]

JARMUTH [7]
Jarmuth, 3754, *yarmût* [7]

JAROAH [1]
Jaroah, 3726, *yārôaḥ* [1]

JARS [19]
jars, 3998, *kelî* [7]
jars, 3902, *kad* [3]
jars, *NIH/RPE* [2]
jars, *AIT* [1]
large jars, 3902, *kad* [1]
storage jars, 3998, *kelî* [1]
jars, 5532, *nōʾd* [1]
jars, 5574, *nēbel*^{1} [1]
water jars, 5574, *nēbel*^{1} [1]
jars, 7987, *qaśwâ* [1]

JASHAR [2]
Jashar, 3839, *yāšār*^{2} [2]

JASHEN [1]
Jashen, 3826, *yāšēn*^{4} [1]

JASHOBEAM [3]
Jashobeam, 3790, *yāšobʿām* [3]

JASHUB [4]
Jashub, 3793, *yāšûb*^{1} [4]

JASHUBI LEHEM [1]
Jashubi Lehem, 3788, *yāšubî leḥem* [1]

JASHUBITE [1]
Jashubite, 3795, *yāšûbî* [1]

JASPER [4]
jasper, 3835, *yāšepēh* [3]
jasper, 1486, *gābîš* [1]

JATHNIEL [1]
Jathniel, 3853, *yatnîʾēl* [1]

JATTIR [4]
Jattir, 3848, *yattîr* [4]

JAVAN [4]
Javan, 3430, *yāwān* [4]

JAVELIN [7]
javelin, 3959, *kîdôn* [5]
javelin, 6038, *sāgār* [1]
javelin, 9233, *širyâ* [1]

JAVELINS [1]
javelins, 8657, *šēbeṭ* [1]

JAW [2]
jaw, 4305, *leḥî*^{1} [2]

JAWBONE [4]
jawbone, 4305, *leḥî*^{1} [4]

JAWS [5]
jaws, 4305, *leḥî*^{1} [3]
jaws, 5506, *metalleʿôt* [1]
jaws, 7023, *peh* [1]

JAZER [13]
Jazer, 3597, *yaʿzēr* [13]

JAZIZ [1]
Jaziz, 3467, *yāzîz* [1]

JEALOUS [25]
jealous, 7862, *qannāʾ* [6]
jealous, 7861, *qānāʾ* [5]
jealous anger, 7863, *qinʾâ* [4]
jealous, 7861+7863, *qānāʾ+qinʾâ* [2]
made jealous, 7861, *qānāʾ* [2]
jealous, 7868, *qannôʾ* [2]
jealous, 6296+6584+8120+7863, *ʿābar*^{1}*+ʿal*^{2}*+rûaḥ+qinʾâ* [1]
kept jealous eye on, 6523, *ʿāyan* [1]
stirred up jealous anger, 7861, *qānāʾ* [1]
jealous, 7863, *qinʾâ* [1]

JEALOUSY [18]
jealousy, 7863, *qinʾâ* [15]
aroused jealousy, 7861, *qānāʾ* [1]
jealousy, 7861, *qānāʾ* [1]
provokes to jealousy, 7861, *qānāʾ* [1]

JEARIM [1]
Jearim, 3630, *yeʿārîm* [1]

JEATHERAI [1]
Jeatherai, 3290, *yeʾāteray* [1]

JEBEREKIAH [1]
Jeberekiah, 3310, *yeberekyāhû* [1]

JEBUS [3]
Jebus, 3293, *yebûs* [3]

JEBUSITE [9]
Jebusite, 3294, *yebûsî* [9]

JEBUSITES [33]
Jebusites, 3294, *yebûsî* [32]
Jebusites, *NIH/RPE* [1]

JECOLIAH [2]
Jecoliah, 3524, *yekolyâ* [1]
Jecoliah, 3525, *yekolyāhû* [1]

JEDAIAH [11]
Jedaiah, 3361, *yedaʿyâ* [9]
Jedaiah, 3355, *yedāyâ* [2]

JEDAIAH'S [2]
Jedaiah's, 3361, *yedaʿyâ* [2]

JEDIAEL [6]
Jediael, 3356, *yedîaʿʾēl* [6]

JEDIDAH [1]
Jedidah, 3352, *yedîdâ* [1]

JEDIDIAH [1]
Jedidiah, 3354, *y^{e}dîd^{e}yāh* [1]

JEDUTHUN [16]
Jeduthun, 3349, *y^{e}dûtûn* [15]
Jeduthun, 3357, *y^{e}dîtûn* [1]

JEER [1]
jeer, *NIH/RPE* [1]

JEERED [1]
jeered, 7840, *qālas* [1]

JEGAR SAHADUTHA [1]
Jegar Sahadutha, 3337, *y^{e}gar śāh^{a}dûtā'* [1]

JEHALLELEL [2]
Jehallelel, 3401, *y^{e}hallel'ēl* [2]

JEHATH [1]
Jehath, 3511, *yaḥat* [1]

JEHDEIAH [2]
Jehdeiah, 3485, *yeḥd^{e}yāhû* [2]

JEHEZKEL [1]
Jehezkel, 3489, *y^{e}ḥezqē'l* [1]

JEHIAH [1]
Jehiah, 3496, *y^{e}ḥiyyâ* [1]

JEHIEL [14]
Jehiel, 3493, *y^{e}ḥî'ēl* [14]

JEHIELI [2]
Jehieli, 3494, *y^{e}ḥî'ēlî* [2]

JEHIZKIAH [1]
Jehizkiah, 3491, *y^{e}ḥizqiyyāhû* [1]

JEHOADDAH [2]
Jehoaddah, 3389, *y^{e}hô'addâ* [2]

JEHOADDIN [2]
Jehoaddin, 3390, *y^{e}hô'addîn* [1]
Jehoaddin, 3391, *y^{e}hô'addān* [1]

JEHOAHAZ [22]
Jehoahaz, 3370, *y^{e}hô'āḥāz* [18]
Jehoahaz, 3407, *yô'āḥāz* [3]
Jehoahaz^{s}, 2257, *-ô* [1]

JEHOASH [28]
Jehoash, 3409, *yô'āš* [16]
Jehoash, 3371, *y^{e}hô'āš* [9]
Jehoash, *NIH/RPE* [3]

JEHOHANAN [9]
Jehohanan, 3380, *y^{e}hôḥānān* [9]

JEHOIACHIN [26]
Jehoiachin, 3382, *y^{e}hôyākîn* [10]
Jehoiachin, 3526, *y^{e}konyâ* [6]
Jehoiachin^{s}, 2257, *-ô* [3]
Jehoiachin, 4037, *konyāhû* [3]
Jehoiachin, *NIH/RPE* [2]
Jehoiachin, 3422, *yôyākîn* [1]
Jehoiachin, 3527, *y^{e}konyāhû* [1]

JEHOIACHIN'S [2]
Jehoiachin's^{s}, 2257, *-ô* [2]

JEHOIADA [53]
Jehoiada, 3381, *y^{e}hôyādā'* [50]
Jehoiada, *NIH/RPE* [3]

JEHOIAKIM [34]
Jehoiakim, 3383, *y^{e}hôyāqîm* [34]

JEHOIAKIM'S [3]
Jehoiakim's, 3383, *y^{e}hôyāqîm* [2]
Jehoiakim's^{s}, 2257, *-ô* [1]

JEHOIARIB [2]
Jehoiarib, 3384, *y^{e}hôyārîb* [2]

JEHONADAB [3]
Jehonadab, 3386, *y^{e}hônādāb* [3]

JEHONATHAN [2]
Jehonathan, 3387, *y^{e}hônātān* [2]

JEHORAM [27]
Jehoram, 3393, *y^{e}hôrām* [16]
Jehoram^{s}, 2257, *-ô* [4]
Jehoram, 3456, *yôrām* [4]
Jehoram, *NIH/RPE* [3]

JEHORAM'S [3]
Jehoram's^{s}, 2257, *-ô* [2]
Jehoram's, 3456, *yôrām* [1]

JEHOSHAPHAT [83]
Jehoshaphat, 3398, *y^{e}hôšāpāṭ^{1}* [79]
Jehoshaphat, *NIH/RPE* [2]
Jehoshaphat, 3399, *y^{e}hôšāpāṭ^{2}* [2]

JEHOSHAPHAT'S [2]
Jehoshaphat's, 3398, *y^{e}hôšāpāṭ^{1}* [2]

JEHOSHEBA [3]
Jehosheba, 3395, *y^{e}hôšab'at* [2]
Jehosheba, 3394, *y^{e}hôšeba'* [1]

JEHOZABAD [4]
Jehozabad, 3379, *y^{e}hôzābād* [4]

JEHOZADAK [8]
Jehozadak, 3392, *y^{e}hôṣādāq* [8]

JEHU [74]
Jehu, 3369, *yēhû'* [52]
Jehu, *NIH/RPE* [18]
Jehu^{s}, 2257, *-ô* [4]

JEHU'S [3]
Jehu's, 3369, *yēhû'* [2]
Jehu's^{s}, 2257, *-ô* [1]

JEHUCAL [2]
Jehucal, 3385, *y^{e}hûkal* [1]
Jehucal, 3426, *yûkal* [1]

JEHUD [1]
Jehud, 3372, *y^{e}hûd* [1]

JEHUDI [4]
Jehudi, 3375, *y^{e}hûdî^{2}* [4]

JEIEL [13]
Jeiel, 3599, *y^{e}'î'ēl* [13]

JEKABZEEL [1]
Jekabzeel, 3677, *y^{e}qabṣ^{e}'ēl* [1]

JEKAMEAM [2]
Jekameam, 3694, *y^{e}qam'ām* [2]

JEKAMIAH [3]
Jekamiah, 3693, *y^{e}qamyâ* [3]

JEKUTHIEL [1]
Jekuthiel, 3688, *y^{e}qûtî'ēl* [1]

JEMIMAH [1]
Jemimah, 3544, *y^{e}mîmâ* [1]

JEMUEL [2]
Jemuel, 3543, *y^{e}mû'ēl* [2]

JEOPARDY [2]
put in jeopardy, 5951+1414+928+9094, *nāśā'+bāśār+b^{e}-+šēn^{1}* [1]
put in jeopardy, 6913+9214, *'āśâ^{1}+šeqer* [1]

JEPHTHAH [22]
Jephthah, 3653, *yiptāḥ^{2}* [22]

JEPHTHAH'S [1]
Jephthah's, 3653, *yiptāḥ^{2}* [1]

JEPHUNNEH [16]
Jephunneh, 3648, *y^{e}punneh* [16]

JERAH [2]
Jerah, 3733, *yeraḥ^{2}* [2]

JERAHMEEL [9]
Jerahmeel, 3737, *y^{e}raḥm^{e}'ēl* [8]
Jerahmeel, 3738, *y^{e}raḥm^{e}'ēlî* [1]

JERAHMEELITES [1]
Jerahmeelites, 3738, *y^{e}raḥm^{e}'ēlî* [1]

JERED [1]
Jered, 3719, *yered* [1]

JEREMAI [1]
Jeremai, 3757, *y^{e}rēmay* [1]

JEREMIAH [142]
Jeremiah, 3759, *yirm^{e}yāhû* [123]
Jeremiah, 3758, *yirm^{e}yâ* [16]
Jeremiah^{s}, 2257, *-ô* [2]
Jeremiah^{s}, 5647, *-nû^{2}* [1]

JEREMIAH'S [2]
Jeremiah's, 3758, *yirm^{e}yâ* [1]
Jeremiah's, 3759, *yirm^{e}yāhû* [1]

JEREMOTH [5]
Jeremoth, 3756, *y^{e}rēmôt* [5]

JERIAH [4]
Jeriah, 3746, *y^{e}riyyāhû* [2]
Jeriah^{s}, 2257, *-ô* [1]
Jeriah, 3745, *y^{e}riyyâ* [1]

JERIBAI [1]
Jeribai, 3744, *y^{e}rîbay* [1]

JERICHO [56]
Jericho, 3735, *y^{e}rîḥô* [56]

JERIEL [1]
Jeriel, 3741, *y^{e}rî'ēl* [1]

JERIMOTH [9]
Jerimoth, 3748, *y^{e}rîmôt* [7]
Jerimoth, 3756, *y^{e}rēmôt* [2]

JERIOTH [1]
Jerioth, 3750, *y^{e}rî'ôt* [1]

JEROBOAM [95]
Jeroboam, 3716, *yārob'ām* [94]
Jeroboam, *NIH/RPE* [1]

JEROBOAM'S [6]
Jeroboam's, 3716, *yārob'ām* [6]

JEROHAM [10]
Jeroham, 3736, *y^{e}rōḥām* [10]

JERUB-BAAL [11]
Jerub-Baal, 3715, *y^{e}rubba'al* [11]

JERUB-BAAL'S [3]
Jerub-Baal's, 3715, *y^{e}rubba'al* [3]

JERUB-BESHETH [1]
Jerub-Besheth, 3717, *y^{e}rubbešet* [1]

JERUEL [1]
Jeruel, 3725, *y^{e}rû'ēl* [1]

JERUSALEM [662]
Jerusalem, 3731, *y^{e}rûšālaim* [631]
Jerusalem, 10332, *y^{e}rûš^{e}lem* [26]
Jerusalem, *NIH/RPE* [3]
Jerusalem^{s}, 2023, *-āh* [2]

JERUSALEM'S [3]
Jerusalem's, 3731, *y^{e}rûšālaim* [3]

JERUSHA [2]
Jerusha, 3729, *y^{e}rûšā'* [1]
Jerusha, 3730, *y^{e}rûšâ* [1]

JESARELAH [1]
Jesarelah, 3777, *y^{e}śar'ēlâ* [1]

JESHAIAH [7]
Jeshaiah, 3832, *y^{e}ša'yâ* [4]
Jeshaiah, 3833, *y^{e}ša'yāhû* [3]

JESHANAH [3]
Jeshanah, 3827, *y^{e}šānâ* [3]

JESHEBEAB [1]
Jeshebeab, 3784, *yešeb'āb* [1]

JESHER [1]
Jesher, 3840, *yēšer* [1]

JESHIMON [4]
Jeshimon, 3810, *y^{e}šîmôn* [4]

JESHISHAI [1]
Jeshishai, 3814, *y^{e}šîšay* [1]

JESHOHAIAH [1]
Jeshohaiah, 3797, *y^{e}šôḥāyâ* [1]

JESHUA [29]
Jeshua, 3800, *yēšûa'*[1] [27]
Jeshua, 3801, *yēšûa'*[2] [1]
Jeshua, 10336, *yēšûa'* [1]

JESHURUN [4]
Jeshurun, 3843, *y^{e}šurûn* [4]

JESIMIEL [1]
Jesimiel, 3774, *y^{e}śîmi'ēl* [1]

JESSE [37]
Jesse, 3805, *yišay* [34]
Jesse, *NIH/RPE* [1]
Jesse, 414, *'îšay* [1]
Jesse[s], 2257, *-ô* [1]

JESSE'S [5]
Jesse's, 3805, *yišay* [5]

JETHER [10]
Jether, 3858, *yeter*[3] [8]
Jether[s], 2021+5853, *ha-+na'ar*[2] [1]
Jether, 3859, *yitrā'* [1]

JETHETH [2]
Jetheth, 3867, *y^{e}tēt* [2]

JETHRO [11]
Jethro, 3861, *yitrô* [8]
Jethro, *NIH/RPE* [1]
Jethro[s], 2257, *-ô* [1]
Jethro, 3858, *yeter*[3] [1]

JETUR [3]
Jetur, 3515, *y^{e}ṭûr* [3]

JEUEL [2]
Jeuel, 3590, *y^{e}'û'ēl* [2]

JEUSH [9]
Jeush, 3593, *y^{e}'ûš* [9]

JEUZ [1]
Jeuz, 3591, *y^{e}'ûṣ* [1]

JEW [10]
Jew, 3374, *y^{e}hûdî*[1] [10]

JEWEL [3]
jewel, 3998, *k^{e}lî* [1]
jewel, 6736, *'^{a}nāq*[1] [1]
jewel, 7382, *ṣ^{e}bî*[1] [1]

JEWELRY [12]
jewelry, 3998, *k^{e}lî* [5]
jewelry, *NIH/RPE* [2]
jewelry, 6344, *'^{a}dî* [2]
jewelry, 2719, *ḥelyâ* [1]
put on jewelry, 6335+6344, *'ādâ*[2]*+'^{a}dî* [1]
beautiful jewelry, 7382+6344, *ṣ^{e}bî*[1]*+'^{a}dî* [1]

JEWELS [9]
jewels, 3998, *k^{e}lî* [2]
jewels, 74, *'eben* [1]
sparkling jewels, 74+734, *'eben+'eqdāḥ* [1]
jewels, 2717, *ḥ^{a}lî*[1] [1]
strings of jewels, 3016, *ḥ^{a}rûzîm* [1]
mounted like jewels, 3782+6584+4859, *yāšab+'al*[2]*+millē't* [1]
jewels, 6344, *'^{a}dî* [1]
most beautiful of jewels, 6344+6344, *'^{a}dî+'^{a}dî* [1]

JEWISH [5]
Jewish, 3374, *y^{e}hûdî*[1] [4]
Jewish, 10316, *y^{e}hûdāy* [1]

JEWS [74]
Jews, 3374, *y^{e}hûdî*[1] [57]
Jews, 10316, *y^{e}hûdāy* [9]
Jews, 3373, *y^{e}hûdâ* [3]
Jews, *NIH/RPE* [1]
fellow Jews, 278, *'āḥ*[2] [1]
Jews[s], 2446, *zera'* [1]
became Jews, 3366, *yāhad* [1]
brother Jews, 10017, *'aḥ* [1]

JEZANIAH [1]
Jezaniah, 3470, *y^{e}zanyâ* [1]

JEZEBEL [18]
Jezebel, 374, *'îzebel* [18]

JEZEBEL'S [3]
Jezebel's, 374, *'îzebel* [3]

JEZER [3]
Jezer, 3672, *yēṣer*[2] [3]

JEZERITE [1]
Jezerite, 3673, *yiṣrî* [1]

JEZIEL [1]
Jeziel, 3465, *y^{e}zî'ēl* [1]

JEZRAHIAH [1]
Jezrahiah, 3474, *yizraḥyâ* [1]

JEZREEL [41]
Jezreel, 3476, *yizr^{e}'e'l*[2] [34]
of Jezreel, 3477, *yizr^{e}'ē'lî* [5]
Jezreel, 3475, *yizr^{e}'e'l*[1] [2]

JEZREELITE [7]
Jezreelite, 3477, *yizr^{e}'ē'lî* [7]

JIDLAPH [1]
Jidlaph, 3358, *yidlāp* [1]

JINGLING [1]
ornaments jingling, 6576, *'ākas* [1]

JOAB [141]
Joab, 3405, *yô'āb* [132]
Joab, *NIH/RPE* [6]
Joab[s], 2257, *-ô* [2]
Joab[s], 2084, *-hû* [1]

JOAB'S [9]
Joab's, 3405, *yô'āb* [8]
Joab's[s], 2257, *-ô* [1]

JOAH [11]
Joah, 3406, *yô'āḥ* [11]

JOAHAZ [1]
Joahaz, 3407, *yô'āḥāz* [1]

JOASH [42]
Joash, 3409, *yô'āš* [30]
Joash, 3371, *y^{e}hô'āš* [8]
Joash[s], 2257, *-ô* [2]
Joash, 3447, *yô'āš* [2]

JOB [53]
Job, 373, *'iyyôb* [49]
job, 6275, *'^{a}bōdâ* [2]
job, *NIH/RPE* [1]
Job[s], 2257, *-ô* [1]

JOB'S [7]
Job's, 373, *'iyyôb* [5]
Job's[s], 2257, *-ô* [2]

JOBAB [9]
Jobab, 3412, *yôbāb*[2] [7]
Jobab, 3411, *yôbāb*[1] [2]

JOCHEBED [2]
Jochebed, 3425, *yôkebed* [2]

JOED [1]
Joed, 3444, *yô'ēd* [1]

JOEL [20]
Joel, 3408, *yô„èl%n.pr.m.%√ 3378 + 446 [20]*

JOELAH [1]
Joelah, 3443, *yô'ē'lâ* [1]

JOEZER [1]
Joezer, 3445, *yô'ezer* [1]

JOGBEHAH [2]
Jogbehah, 3322, *yogb^{e}hâ* [2]

JOGLI [1]
Jogli, 3332, *yoglî* [1]

JOHA [2]
Joha, 3418, *yôḥā'* [2]

JOHANAN [24]
Johanan, 3419, *yôḥānān* [24]

JOIADA [5]
Joiada, 3421, *yôyādā'* [5]

JOIAKIM [4]
Joiakim, 3423, *yôyāqîm* [4]

JOIARIB [4]
Joiarib, 3424, *yôyārîb* [4]

JOIARIB'S [1]
Joiarib's, 3424, *yôyārîb* [1]

JOIN [35]
join, 4277, *lāwâ*[1] [5]
join, 6640, *'im* [4]
join, 339, *'aḥar* [2]
join, 3479, *yāḥad* [2]
join, 7928, *qārab* [2]
join, *NIH/RPE* [1]
join, 448, *'el* [1]
join forces, 665, *'āsap* [1]
join, 665, *'āsap* [1]
join in, 673, *'āsar* [1]
join, 995+6330, *bô'+'ad*[2] [1]
join, 2025, *-â*[2] [1]
join, 2118+928, *hāyâ+b^{e}-* [1]
join, 2143+6584, *hālak+'al*[2] [1]
join, 2143+6640, *hālak+'im* [1]
join together, 2489, *ḥābar*[2] [1]
join, 2489, *ḥābar*[2] [1]
join, 2565, *ḥûl*[1] [1]
join, 2616+6584, *ḥāzaq+'al*[2] [1]
join, 3578, *yāsap* [1]
join, 5989, *nātan* [1]
join, 6843, *'ārab*[2] [1]
come and join, 7695, *qābaṣ* [1]
join, 7695, *qābaṣ* [1]
join, 8354, *rāṣâ*[1] [1]

JOINED [22]
joined, 2489, *ḥābar*[2] [2]
joined forces, 3585, *yā'ad* [2]
joined in worshiping, 7537, *ṣāmad* [2]
joined forces, 665+3481, *'āsap+yaḥdāw* [1]
joined forces, 665, *'āsap* [1]
joined in, 928+9348, *b^{e}-+tāwek* [1]
are joined fast, 1815, *dābaq* [1]
joined, 1815, *dābaq* [1]
tightly joined, 1815, *dābaq* [1]
joined, 2118, *hāyâ* [1]
joined, 2256+1685, *w^{e}-+gam* [1]
joined forces, 2489, *ḥābar*[2] [1]
joined to, 2489, *ḥābar*[2] [1]
joined, 3655, *yāṣā'* [1]
be joined, 4277, *lāwâ*[1] [1]
joined, 4277, *lāwâ*[1] [1]
joined together, 6641+3869+285, *'āmad+k^{e}-+'eḥād* [1]
joined forces, 7695, *qābaṣ* [1]
joined, 7928, *qārab* [1]

JOINING [1]
joining, 448, *'el* [1]

JOINS [1]
joins, 5432, *māšak* [1]
JOINT [2]
out of joint, 7233, *pārad* [1]
joint, 7866, *qāneh* [1]
JOINTED [1]
jointed, 4946+5087+4200+8079, *min+maʿal^{2}+l^{e}-^{1}+regel* [1]
JOISTS [1]
joists, 4677, *m^{e}ḥabb^{e}rôt* [1]
JOKDEAM [1]
Jokdeam, 3680, *yoqd^{e}ʿām* [1]
JOKIM [1]
Jokim, 3451, *yôqîm* [1]
JOKING [2]
joking, 7464, *ṣāḥaq* [1]
joking, 8471, *śāḥaq* [1]
JOKMEAM [2]
Jokmeam, 3695, *yoqm^{e}ʿām* [2]
JOKNEAM [4]
Jokneam, 3696, *yoqn^{e}ʿām* [4]
JOKSHAN [4]
Jokshan, 3705, *yoqšān* [4]
JOKTAN [6]
Joktan, 3690, *yoqṭān* [6]
JOKTHEEL [2]
Joktheel, 3706, *yoqt^{e}ʾēl* [2]
JOLTING [1]
jolting, 8376, *rāqad* [1]
JONADAB [12]
Jonadab, 3432, *yônādāb* [7]
Jonadab, 3386, *y^{e}hônādāb* [5]
JONAH [18]
Jonah, 3434, *yônâ^{2}* [18]
JONAH'S [1]
Jonah's, 3434, *yônâ^{2}* [1]
JONATHAN [112]
Jonathan, 3387, *y^{e}hônātān* [68]
Jonathan, 3440, *yônātān* [42]
Jonathan, *NIH/RPE* [2]
JONATHAN'S [3]
Jonathan's, 3387, *y^{e}hônātān* [3]
JOPPA [4]
Joppa, 3639, *yāpô* [4]
JORAH [1]
Jorah, 3454, *yôrâ* [1]
JORAI [1]
Jorai, 3455, *yôray* [1]
JORAM [28]
Joram, 3456, *yôrām* [14]
Joram, 3393, *y^{e}hôrām* [13]
Joram, *NIH/RPE* [1]
JORDAN [178]
Jordan, 3720, *yardēn* [172]
the Jordan^{s}, 9004+2025, *šām+-â^{2}* [4]
Jordan, *NIH/RPE* [2]
JORDAN'S [3]
Jordan's, 3720, *yardēn* [3]
JORKEAM [1]
Jorkeam, 3767, *yorq^{o}ʿām* [1]
JOSEPH [199]
Joseph, 3441, *yôsēp* [180]
Joseph, *NIH/RPE* [13]
Joseph^{s}, 2257, *-ô* [3]
Joseph, 1201+3441, *bēn^{1}+yôsēp* [2]
Joseph, 3388, *y^{e}hôsēp* [1]
JOSEPH'S [21]
Joseph's, 3441, *yôsēp* [19]
Joseph's^{s}, 2257, *-ô* [2]
JOSHAH [1]
Joshah, 3459, *yôšâ* [1]
JOSHAPHAT [2]
Joshaphat, 3461, *yôšāpāṭ* [2]
JOSHAVIAH [1]
Joshaviah, 3460, *yôšawyâ* [1]
JOSHBEKASHAH [2]
Joshbekashah, 3792, *yošb^{e}qāšâ* [2]
JOSHEB-BASSHEBETH [1]
Josheb-Basshebeth, 3783, *yōšēb baššebet* [1]
JOSHIBIAH [1]
Joshibiah, 3458, *yôšibyâ* [1]
JOSHUA [215]
Joshua, 3397, *y^{e}hôšuaʿ* [203]
Joshua, *NIH/RPE* [9]
Joshua, 2107, *hôšēaʿ* [1]
Joshua^{s}, 2257, *-ô* [1]
Joshua, 3800, *yēšûaʿ^{1}* [1]
JOSIAH [54]
Josiah, 3288, *yōʾšiyyāhû* [47]
Josiah, *NIH/RPE* [4]
Josiah^{s}, 2257, *-ô* [2]
Josiah, 3287, *yōʾšiyyâ* [1]
JOSIAH'S [5]
Josiah's, 3288, *yōʾšiyyāhû* [3]
Josiah's^{s}, 2257, *-ô* [2]
JOSIPHIAH [1]
Josiphiah, 3442, *yôsipyâ* [1]
JOSTLE [1]
jostle, 1895, *dāḥaq* [1]
JOSTLED [1]
jostled each other, 8368, *rāšaṣ* [1]
JOTBAH [1]
Jotbah, 3513, *yoṭbâ* [1]
JOTBATHAH [3]
Jotbathah, 3514, *yoṭbātâ* [3]
JOTHAM [25]
Jotham, 3462, *yôtām* [22]
Jotham^{s}, 2085, *hûʾ* [3]
JOTHAM'S [2]
Jotham's, 3462, *yôtām* [2]
JOURNEY [41]
journey, 2006, *derek* [30]
journey, 5023, *massaʿ* [2]
journey, 6296, *ʿābar^{1}* [2]
journey, *NIH/RPE* [1]
journey, 784, *ʾōraḥ* [1]
journey, 2143, *hālak* [1]
journey, 4544, *mah^{a}lāk* [1]
stages in journey, 5023, *massaʿ* [1]
journey, 5092, *maʿ^{a}lâ^{2}* [1]
continued on journey, 5951+8079, *nāśāʾ+regel* [1]
JOURNEYED [3]
journeyed, 995, *bôʾ* [1]
journeyed, 2143, *hālak* [1]
journeyed, 5825, *nāsaʿ* [1]
JOWLS [1]
jowls, 4305, *l^{e}ḥî^{1}* [1]
JOY [155]
joy, 8525, *śimḥâ* [46]
sing for joy, 8264, *rānan* [15]
joy, 8607, *śāśôn* [14]
shout for joy, 8264, *rānan* [11]
joy, 5375, *māśôś^{1}* [6]
shout for joy, 8131, *rûaʿ* [4]
songs of joy, 8262, *rinnâ^{1}* [4]
brings joy, 8523, *śāmaḥ* [4]
shouts of joy, 2116, *hêdād* [3]
shouts of joy, 8262, *rinnâ^{1}* [3]
bring joy, 8523, *śāmaḥ* [3]
joy, 8523, *śāmaḥ* [3]
shouts of joy, 9558, *t^{e}rûʿâ* [3]
joy, 2530, *ḥedwâ* [2]
shouts of joy, 7754+8262, *qôl+rinnâ^{1}* [2]
have joy, 1158, *bālag* [1]
great joy, 1635+1635, *gîl^{1}+gîl^{1}* [1]
joy, 1635, *gîl^{1}* [1]
joy, 2059, *hēd* [1]
joy^{s}, 2085, *hûʾ* [1]
joy, 3206, *ṭûb* [1]
joy, 3208, *ṭôbâ* [1]
give joy, 3512, *yāṭab* [1]
joy, 6134, *sālad* [1]
leaps for joy, 6600, *ʿālaz* [1]
find joy, 6695, *ʿānag* [1]
shout for joy, 7412, *ṣāhal^{1}* [1]
shout with joy, 8131, *rûaʿ* [1]
shouted for joy, 8131, *rûaʿ* [1]
swell with joy, 8143, *rāḥab* [1]
joy, 8262, *rinnâ^{1}* [1]
call forth songs of joy, 8264, *rānan* [1]
ever sing for joy, 8264+8264, *rānan+rānan* [1]
shouted for joy, 8264, *rānan* [1]
songs of joy, 8264, *rānan* [1]
shout of joy, 8265, *r^{e}nānâ* [1]
filled with joy, 8523, *śāmaḥ* [1]
give joy, 8523, *śāmaḥ* [1]
given joy, 8523+8525, *śāmaḥ+śimḥâ* [1]
giving joy, 8523, *śāmaḥ* [1]
share joy, 8523+8525, *śāmaḥ+śimḥâ* [1]
filled with joy, 8524, *śāmēaḥ* [1]
joy, 8524, *śāmēaḥ* [1]
brought joy, 9130, *šāʿaʿ^{2}* [1]
shout for joy, 9558, *t^{e}rûʿâ* [1]
shouts for joy, 9558, *t^{e}rûʿâ* [1]
joy, 10250, *ḥedwâ* [1]
JOYFUL [13]
joyful, 8523, *śāmaḥ* [2]
joyful, 8524, *śāmēaḥ* [2]
joyful, 8525, *śimḥâ* [2]
joyful, 1635, *gîl^{1}* [1]
joyful, 3202, *ṭôb^{2}* [1]
joyful, 5375, *māśôś^{1}* [1]
joyful songs, 8265, *r^{e}nānâ* [1]
joyful, 8471, *śāḥaq* [1]
joyful songs, 8525, *śimḥâ* [1]
joyful, 8607, *śāśôn* [1]
JOYFULLY [7]
joyfully, 928+8525, *b^{e}-+śimḥâ* [2]
joyfully, 8525, *śimḥâ* [2]
flap joyfully, 6632, *ʿālas* [1]
sing joyfully, 8264, *rānan* [1]
joyfully sing, 8264, *rānan* [1]
JOYOUS [1]
joyous, 8523, *śāmaḥ* [1]
JOZABAD [11]
Jozabad, 3416, *yôzābād* [11]
JOZADAK [5]
Jozadak, 3449, *yôṣādāq* [4]
Jozadak, 10318, *yôṣādāq* [1]
JUBAL [1]
Jubal, 3415, *yûbal^{2}* [1]
JUBILANT [5]
jubilant, 6600, *ʿālaz* [2]
jubilant, 1637, *gîl^{3}* [1]
jubilant, 6636, *ʿālaṣ* [1]
jubilant song, 8264, *rānan* [1]
JUBILEE [21]
jubilee, 3413, *yôbēl* [20]
Year of Jubilee, 3413, *yôbēl* [1]

JUDAH [818]
Judah, 3373, *yehûdâ* [772]
Judah, 1201+3373, *bēn[1]+yehûdâ* [11]
Judah, *NIH/RPE* [7]
Judah, 824+3373, *'ereṣ+yehûdâ* [6]
Judah, 10315, *yehûd* [6]
Judah, 1074+3373, *bayit[1]+yehûdâ* [4]
men of Judah, 3374, *yehûdî[1]* [3]
Judah[s], 2021+824, *ha-+'ereṣ* [2]
Judah[s], 4392, *-ām* [2]
people from Judah, 278+2157, *'āḥ[2]+-hem* [1]
of Judah, 1201+3373, *bēn[1]+yehûdâ* [1]
Judah[s], 2023, *-āh* [1]
language of Judah, 3376, *yehûdît[1]* [1]
Judah[s], 5647, *-nû[2]* [1]

JUDAH'S [13]
Judah's, 3373, *yehûdâ* [11]
Judah's, 1201+3373, *bēn[1]+yehûdâ* [1]
Judah's[s], 2257, *-ô* [1]

JUDEAN [3]
Judean, 3373, *yehûdâ* [2]
Judean, 3374, *yehûdî[1]* [1]

JUDGE [91]
judge, 9149, *šāpaṭ* [69]
judge, 1906, *dîn[1]* [8]
judge, 3519, *yākaḥ* [2]
judge, 5477, *mišpāṭ* [2]
judge quality, 6885, *'ārak* [2]
judge, 1907, *dîn[2]* [1]
judge, 1908, *dayyān* [1]
sit as judge, 3782, *yāšab* [1]
judges[s], 6913, *'āśâ[1]* [1]
judge in office, 9149, *šāpaṭ* [1]
judge, 9149+5477, *šāpaṭ+mišpāṭ* [1]
play the judge, 9149+9149, *šāpaṭ+šāpaṭ* [1]
serve as judge, 9149, *šāpaṭ* [1]

JUDGED [7]
judged, 9149, *šāpaṭ* [4]
to be judged, 7132, *pelîlî* [2]
be judged, 9149, *šāpaṭ* [1]

JUDGES [39]
judges, 9149, *šāpaṭ* [26]
judges, 466, *'elōhîm* [4]
judges, 10171, *dayyān* [2]
judges, 10188, *detābar* [2]
judges, 5477+6913, *mišpāṭ+'āśâ[1]* [1]
judges decide, 9149, *šāpaṭ* [1]
judges in office, 9149, *šāpaṭ* [1]
serve as judges, 9149, *šāpaṭ* [1]
served as judges, 9149, *šāpaṭ* [1]

JUDGING [6]
judging, 9149, *šāpaṭ* [4]
judging, 5477, *mišpāṭ* [2]

JUDGMENT [71]
judgment, 5477, *mišpāṭ* [24]
judgment, 4213, *lēb* [11]
execute judgment, 9149, *šāpaṭ* [6]
judgment, 1907, *dîn[2]* [4]
judgment, 9150, *šepeṭ* [3]
sound judgment, 9370, *tûšiyyâ* [3]
judgment, 7213, *pequddâ* [2]
acts of judgment, 9150, *šepeṭ* [2]
judgment, *NIH/RPE* [1]
good judgment, 3248, *ṭa'am* [1]
judgment, 3248, *ṭa'am* [1]
place of judgment, 5477, *mišpāṭ* [1]
render judgment, 5477+9149, *mišpāṭ+šāpaṭ* [1]
judgment, 6524, *'ayin[1]* [1]
judgment, 8189, *rîb[1]* [1]
judgment, 9144, *šepôṭ* [1]
bring judgment, 9149, *šāpaṭ* [1]
bring to judgment, 9149, *šāpaṭ* [1]
enter into judgment, 9149, *šāpaṭ* [1]
executing judgment, 9149, *šāpaṭ* [1]
gives judgment, 9149, *šāpaṭ* [1]
pass judgment, 9149, *šāpaṭ* [1]
judgment, 9312, *tebûnâ* [1]
judgment, 10170, *dîn[2]* [1]

JUDGMENTS [13]
judgments, 5477, *mišpāṭ* [11]
sworn judgments, 8652, *šebû'â* [1]
judgments, 9150, *šepeṭ* [1]

JUDITH [1]
Judith, 3377, *yehûdît[2]* [1]

JUG [6]
jug, 7608, *ṣappaḥat* [6]

JUGS [1]
jugs, 5574, *nēbel[1]* [1]

JUICE [3]
juice, 4852, *melē'â* [1]
juice, 5489, *mišrâ* [1]
juice, 9408, *tîrôš* [1]

JUNCTION [1]
junction, 8031, *rō'š[1]* [1]

JUSHAB-HESED [1]
Jushab-Hesed, 3457, *yûšab ḥesed* [1]

JUST [237]
just as, 3869+889, *ke-+'ašer* [58]
just, 5477, *mišpāṭ* [28]
just as, 3869+3972+889, *ke-+kōl+'ašer* [24]
just as, 3869, *ke-* [16]
just as, 3869+889+4027, *ke-+'ašer+kēn[2]* [14]
just, *AIT* [11]
just, *NIH/RPE* [9]
just as, 2256, *we-* [5]
just, 9419, *tākan* [5]
just, 421, *'ak* [4]
just as, 889, *'ašer* [3]
just as, 1685, *gam* [3]
just, 3954, *kî[2]* [3]
just as, 4027+3869+889, *kēn[2]+ke-+'ašer* [3]
just, 7404, *ṣaddîq* [3]
just, 7406, *ṣedeq* [3]
just as, 928, *be-* [2]
just, 2180, *hinnēh* [2]
just then, 2256+2180, *we-+hinnēh* [2]
just, 3838, *yāšār[1]* [2]
just the way, 3869+889, *ke-+'ašer* [2]
just what, 3869+889+4027, *ke-+'ašer+kēn[2]* [2]
just as, 4200+6645, *le-[1]+'ummâ[1]* [2]
just above, 4946+5087, *min+ma'al[2]* [2]
just as, 10168, *dî* [2]
just after, 421, *'ak* [1]
just before, 928+3270, *be-+ṭerem* [1]
just enough, 1896, *day* [1]
just now, 2021+3427, *ha-+yôm[1]* [1]
just, 2021+3427, *ha-+yôm[1]* [1]
just as, 2180, *hinnēh* [1]
just right, 2914, *ḥēpeṣ* [1]
just as, 3869+3972, *ke-+kōl* [1]
just as, 3869+3972+889+4027, *ke-+kōl+'ašer+kēn[2]* [1]
just as, 3869+4027, *ke-+kēn[2]* [1]
just like, 3869+4027, *ke-+kēn[2]* [1]
just like, 3869+7023, *ke-+peh* [1]
just like, 3869, *ke-* [1]
just what, 3869+889, *ke-+'ašer* [1]
just because, 3954, *kî[2]* [1]
just as, 4027, *kēn[2]* [1]
just for that, 4200+4027, *le-[1]+kēn[2]* [1]
just as, 4200+3972+889, *le-[1]+kōl+'ašer* [1]
just who, 4769+2256+4769, *mî+we-+mî* [1]
just, 4946+6964, *min+'attâ* [1]
just a few, 5070, *mā'aṭ* [1]
just what wanted, 5883, *nepeš* [1]
just, 6964+2296, *'attâ+zeh* [1]
just, 7407, *ṣedāqâ* [1]
sheep just shorn, 7892, *qāṣab* [1]
just, 10170, *dîn[2]* [1]
just as, 10353+10619+10168, *kōl+qebēl+dî* [1]

JUSTICE [118]
justice, 5477, *mišpāṭ* [94]
justice, 7406, *ṣedeq* [5]
justice, 1907, *dîn[2]* [3]
justice, *NIH/RPE* [2]
justice, 4793, *mîšôr* [2]
deprive of justice, 5742, *nāṭâ* [2]
justice, 7407, *ṣedāqâ* [2]
provide justice, 1906, *dîn[1]* [1]
justice, 2006, *derek* [1]
justice, 4797, *mêšārîm* [1]
justice of cause, 5477, *mišpāṭ* [1]
see that gets justice, 7405, *ṣādaq* [1]
justice, 8190, *rîb[2]* [1]
bring justice, 9149, *šāpaṭ* [1]
administer justice, 10169, *dîn[1]* [1]

JUSTIFICATION [1]
furnished justification, 7136, *pālal[1]* [1]

JUSTIFIED [1]
justified, 2342, *zākâ* [1]

JUSTIFY [3]
justify, 7405, *ṣādaq* [2]
justify, 8750, *šāwâ[1]* [1]

JUSTIFYING [1]
justifying, 7405, *ṣādaq* [1]

JUSTLY [4]
justly, 5477, *mišpāṭ* [2]
justly, 4793, *mîšôr* [1]
justly, 7406, *ṣedeq* [1]

JUTTAH [3]
Juttah, 3420, *yûṭṭâ* [3]

KABZEEL [3]
Kabzeel, 7696, *qabṣe'ēl* [3]

KADESH [14]
Kadesh, 7729, *qādēš[2]* [14]

KADESH BARNEA [10]
Kadesh Barnea, 7732, *qādēš barnēa'* [10]

KADMIEL [8]
Kadmiel, 7718, *qadmî'ēl* [8]

KADMONITES [1]
Kadmonites, 7720, *qadmōnî[2]* [1]

KAIN [1]
Kain, 7805, *qayin[4]* [1]

KALLAI [1]
Kallai, 7834, *qallāy* [1]

KAMON [1]
Kamon, 7852, *qāmôn* [1]

KANAH [3]
Kanah, 7867, *qānâ[3]* [3]

KAREAH [14]
Kareah, 7945, *qārēaḥ* [14]

KARKA [1]
Karka, 7978, *qarqa'[2]* [1]

KARKOR [1]
Karkor, 7980, *qarqōr* [1]

KARNAIM [1]
Karnaim, 7969, *qarnayim* [1]

KARTAH [2]
Kartah, 7985, *qartâ* [2]

KARTAN [1]
Kartan, 7986, *qartān* [1]

KATTATH [1]
Kattath, 7793, *qaṭṭāt* [1]

KATYDID [1]
katydid, 6155, *sol'ām* [1]

KEBAR [8]
Kebar, 3894, *kebār[2]* [8]

KEDAR [11]
Kedar, 7723, *qēdār* [10]
Kedar, 1201+7723, *bēn[1]+qēdār* [1]

KEDAR'S [1]
Kedar's, 7723, *qēdār* [1]

KEDEMAH [2]
Kedemah, 7715, *qēdᵉmâ*[2] [2]

KEDEMOTH [4]
Kedemoth, 7717, *qᵉdēmôt* [4]

KEDESH [11]
Kedesh, 7730, *qedeš* [11]

KEDORLAOMER [5]
Kedorlaomer, 3906, *kᵉdorlāʻōmer* [5]

KEEN [1]
keen, 10339, *yattîr* [1]

KEEP [242]
keep, 9068, *šāmar* [83]
keep, *AIT* [25]
keep, 5915, *nāṣar* [15]
keep, 6913, *ʻāśâ*[1] [11]
keep, *NIH/RPE* [7]
keep alive, 2649, *ḥāyâ* [7]
keep holy, 7727, *qādaš* [7]
keep from, 1194, *biltî* [5]
keep, 2118, *hāyâ* [4]
keep, 7756, *qûm* [4]
keep, 2118+4200, *hāyâ+lᵉ-*[1] [3]
keep, 6073, *sûr*[1] [3]
keep far, 8178, *rāḥaq* [3]
keep, 1815, *dābaq* [2]
keep, 4374, *lāqaḥ* [2]
keep, 4979, *mānaʻ* [2]
keep, 5466, *mišmeret* [2]
keep in isolation, 6037, *sāgar* [2]
keep safe, 7621, *ṣāpan* [2]
keep, 8049, *rābâ*[1] [2]
keep, 8740, *šûb*[1] [2]
keep safe, 9068, *šāmar* [2]
keep burning, 239, *ʼôr*[1] [1]
keep saying, 606+606, *ʼāmar*[1]*+ʼāmar*[1] [1]
keep right, 886, *ʼāšar*[1] [1]
keep on, 2143, *hālak* [1]
keep, 2143+928, *hālak+bᵉ-* [1]
keep pure, 2342, *zākâ* [1]
keep, 2532, *ḥādal*[1] [1]
keep, 3104, *ḥāśak* [1]
keep silent, 3104+7023, *ḥāśak+peh* [1]
keep, 3855, *yātar* [1]
keep loyal, 3922, *kûn*[1] [1]
keep back, 3948, *kāḥad* [1]
keep, 3948, *kāḥad* [1]
keep, 4059, *kāsâ* [1]
keep hair trimmed, 4080+4080, *kāsam+kāsam* [1]
keep, 4200, *lᵉ-*[1] [1]
keep from, 4946, *min* [1]
keep back, 4979, *mānaʻ* [1]
keep, 5674, *nûs* [1]
keep separate, 5692, *nāzar*[1] [1]
keep safe, 5915, *nāṣar* [1]
keep watch over, 5915, *nāṣar* [1]
keep, 5989, *nātan* [1]
failed to keep, 6073+4946, *sûr*[1]*+min* [1]
keep free, 6073, *sûr*[1] [1]
keep working, 6268, *ʻābad* [1]
keep on, 6641, *ʻāmad* [1]
keep, 6806, *ʻāṣar* [1]
keep, 6885, *ʻārak* [1]
keep watchful, 7219, *pāqaḥ* [1]
keep watch, 7595, *ṣāpâ*[1] [1]
keep, 7756+7756, *qûm+qûm* [1]
keep away, 7928+448+3870, *qārab+ʼel+-kā* [1]
keep distance, 8178, *rāḥaq* [1]
keep, 8492, *śîm* [1]
keep themselves alive, 8740+5883, *šûb*[1]*+nepeš* [1]
keep themselves alive, 8740+906+5883+4392, *šûb*[1]*+ʼēt*[1]*+nepeš+-ām* [1]
keep watch, 8788, *šōʻēr* [1]
keep on getting drunk, 8910, *šākar* [1]
keep, 8966, *šālēm*[1] [1]
be sure to keep, 9068+9068, *šāmar+šāmar* [1]
keep away, 9068, *šāmar* [1]
keep close watch on, 9068, *šāmar* [1]
keep penned up, 9068, *šāmar* [1]
keep track of, 9068, *šāmar* [1]
keep on, 9458, *tāmîd* [1]
keep, 10201, *hᵃwâ* [1]

KEEPER [7]
keeper, 9068, *šāmar* [5]
keeper*, 889+6584, *ʼᵃšer+ʻal*[2] [1]
keeper of Gate, 8788, *šōʻēr* [1]

KEEPERS [1]
keepers, 9068, *šāmar* [1]

KEEPING [25]
keeping, 9068, *šāmar* [7]
in keeping with, 3869, *kᵉ-* [4]
keeping holy, 7727, *qādaš* [2]
keeping, *AIT* [1]
keeping, *NIH/RPE* [1]
in keeping with, 928, *bᵉ-* [1]
keeping all the way, 2143+2143, *hālak+hālak* [1]
keeping it to ourselves, 3120, *ḥāšâ* [1]
keeping, 3973, *kālāʼ*[1] [1]
keeping secret vigil, 5915, *nāṣar* [1]
keeping records, 6218, *sāpar* [1]
keeping, 6913, *ʻāśâ*[1] [1]
keeping watch, 7595, *ṣāpâ*[1] [1]
keeping watch, 8011+928+6524, *rāʼâ*[1]*+bᵉ-+ʻayin*[1] [1]
keeping, 8286, *rāʻâ*[1] [1]

KEEPS [33]
keeps, 9068, *šāmar* [10]
keeps, *AIT* [3]
keeps, 4059, *kāsâ* [2]
keeps, 4979, *mānaʻ* [2]
keeps, *NIH/RPE* [1]
keeps company, 782+4200+2495, *ʼāraḥ*[1]*+lᵉ-*[1]*+ḥebrâ* [1]
keeps quiet, 1957, *dāmam*[1] [1]
keeps silent, 3087, *ḥārēš*[2] [1]
keeps straight, 3837, *yāšar* [1]
keeps, 4202+4614, *lōʼ+mûr*[1] [1]
keeps, 5850, *nāʻar*[2] [1]
keeps intact, 5893, *nāṣab*[1] [1]
keeps, 5915, *nāṣar* [1]
keeps occupied, 6701, *ʻānâ*[3] [1]
keeps, 6913, *ʻāśâ*[1] [1]
keeps apart, 7233, *pārad* [1]
keeps, 8492, *śîm* [1]
keeps, 8656, *šābaḥ*[2] [1]
keeps saying, 8740+609, *šûb*[1]*+ʼēmer*[1] [1]
keeps close watch, 9068, *šāmar* [1]

KEHELATHAH [2]
Kehelathah, 7739, *qᵉhēlātâ* [2]

KEILAH [18]
Keilah, 7881, *qᵉʻîlâ* [18]

KELAIAH [1]
Kelaiah, 7835, *qēlāyâ* [1]

KELAL [1]
Kelal, 4006, *kᵉlāl* [1]

KELITA [3]
Kelita, 7836, *qᵉlîṭāʼ* [3]

KELUB [2]
Kelub, 3991, *kᵉlûb*[2] [2]

KELUHI [1]
Keluhi, 3988, *kᵉluhî* [1]

KEMUEL [3]
Kemuel, 7851, *qᵉmûʼēl* [3]

KENAANAH [5]
Kenaanah, 4049, *kᵉnaʻᵃnâ* [5]

KENAN [6]
Kenan, 7809, *qênān* [6]

KENANI [1]
Kenani, 4039, *kᵉnānî* [1]

KENANIAH [3]
Kenaniah, 4041, *kᵉnanyāhû* [2]
Kenaniah, 4040, *kᵉnanyâ* [1]

KENATH [2]
Kenath, 7875, *qᵉnāt* [2]

KENAZ [11]
Kenaz, 7869, *qᵉnaz* [11]

KENITE [5]
Kenite, 7808, *qênî* [5]

KENITES [9]
Kenites, 7808, *qênî* [7]
Kenites, 7804, *qayin*[3] [2]

KENIZZITE [3]
Kenizzite, 7870, *qᵉnizzî* [3]

KENIZZITES [1]
Kenizzites, 7870, *qᵉnizzî* [1]

KEPHAR AMMONI [1]
Kephar Ammoni, 4112, *kᵉpar hāʻammōnî* [1]

KEPHIRAH [4]
Kephirah, 4098, *kᵉpîrâ* [4]

KEPT [125]
kept, 9068, *šāmar* [19]
kept, *AIT* [15]
kept, 4979, *mānaʻ* [4]
kept, 5663, *nûaḥ*[1] [4]
kept, *NIH/RPE* [3]
kept, 2118, *hāyâ* [3]
kept alive, 2649, *ḥāyâ* [3]
be kept burning, 3678, *yāqad* [3]
kept, 5466, *mišmeret* [3]
kept, 7756, *qûm* [3]
kept, 995, *bôʼ* [2]
kept pure, 2342, *zākâ* [2]
kept, 3104, *ḥāśak* [2]
kept, 5989, *nātan* [2]
kept, 6913, *ʻāśâ*[1] [2]
kept myself, 9068, *šāmar* [2]
kept from closing, 296+9073, *ʼāḥaz*[1]*+šᵉmurâ* [1]
kept secret, 401+5583, *ʼayin*[1]*+nāgad* [1]
kept, 430, *ʼākal* [1]
be kept in prison, 673, *ʼāsar* [1]
kept themselves separate, 976, *bādal* [1]
be kept from, 1757+4200+1194, *gāraʻ*[1]*+lᵉ-*[1]*+biltî* [1]
kept coming, 2143+2143, *hālak+hālak* [1]
kept on, 2143+8743, *hālak+šôbāb*[1] [1]
kept on, 2143, *hālak* [1]
kept, 2143+928, *hālak+bᵉ-* [1]
kept, 2143, *hālak* [1]
kept, 2616, *ḥāzaq* [1]
kept quiet, 3087, *ḥārēš*[2] [1]
in love kept, 3137, *ḥāšaq*[1] [1]
kept a genealogical record, 3509, *yāḥaś* [1]
kept distance, 3656+4946+5584, *yāṣab+min+neged* [1]
kept safe, 3828, *yāšaʻ* [1]
kept, 3855, *yātar* [1]
kept, 3973, *kālāʼ*[1] [1]
kept in reserve, 4022, *kāmas* [1]
kept provoking, 4087+1685+4088, *kāʻas+gam+kaʻas* [1]
kept, 4200, *lᵉ-*[1] [1]
kept, 4328, *lîn* [1]
kept, 4374, *lāqaḥ* [1]
is kept safe, 4880, *mālaṭ*[1] [1]
kept from, 4946, *min* [1]
kept, 5697, *nāḥâ*[1] [1]
kept away, 5742, *nāṭâ* [1]
kept, 5915, *nāṣar* [1]
was kept, 6211, *sāpan* [1]
kept on going, 6296, *ʻābar*[1] [1]
kept on, 6388, *ʻôd* [1]
kept jealous eye on, 6523, *ʻāyan* [1]
kept burning, 6590, *ʻālâ* [1]
been kept, 6806, *ʻāṣar* [1]
kept, 6806, *ʻāṣar* [1]
kept bringing pressure, 7210+4394, *pāṣar+mᵉʻōd* [1]

kept on record, 7621, *ṣāpan* [1]
kept in confinement, 7674, *ṣārar*^{1} [1]
been kept, 7756, *qûm* [1]
kept on, 8049, *rābâ*^{1} [1]
kept, 8286, *rā'â*^{1} [1]
is kept safe, 8435, *śāgab* [1]
been kept, 8636, *šā'ar* [1]
kept a record, 9068, *šāmar* [1]
kept in mind, 9068, *šāmar* [1]
kept penned up, 9068, *šāmar* [1]
kept themselves, 9068, *šāmar* [1]
kept watch, 9068, *šāmar* [1]
watch kept, 9193, *šāqad*^{1} [1]
kept, 9458, *tāmîd* [1]
kept, 10201, *h*^{a}*wâ* [1]
kept, 10476, *n*^{e}*ṭar* [1]

KERAN [2]
Keran, 4154, *k*^{e}*rān* [2]

KEREN-HAPPUCH [1]
Keren-Happuch, 7968, *qeren happûk* [1]

KERETHITE [1]
Kerethite, 4165, *k*^{e}*rētî* [1]

KERETHITES [10]
Kerethites, 4165, *k*^{e}*rētî* [10]

KERIOTH [3]
Kerioth, 7954, *q*^{e}*riyyôt* [3]

KERIOTH HEZRON [1]
Kerioth Hezron, 7955, *q*^{e}*riyyôt ḥeṣrôn* [1]

KERITH [2]
Kerith, 4134, *k*^{e}*rît* [2]

KERNELS [2]
kernels, 4000, *kilyâ* [1]
kernels, 4884, *m*^{e}*lîlâ* [1]

KEROS [2]
Keros, 7820, *qērōs* [2]

KERUB [2]
Kerub, 4132, *k*^{e}*rûb*^{2} [2]

KESALON [1]
Kesalon, 4076, *k*^{e}*sālôn* [1]

KESED [1]
Kesed, 4168, *keśed* [1]

KESIL [1]
Kesil, 4069, *k*^{e}*sîl*^{3} [1]

KESULLOTH [1]
Kesulloth, 4063, *k*^{e}*sûlôt* [1]

KETTLE [1]
kettle, 1857, *dûd* [1]

KETURAH [4]
Keturah, 7778, *q*^{e}*ṭûrâ* [4]

KEY [4]
key, 5158, *maptēaḥ* [2]
the key^{s}, 2085, *hû'* [1]
key for opening, 5158, *maptēaḥ* [1]

KEZIAH [1]
Keziah, 7905, *q*^{e}*ṣî'â* [1]

KEZIB [1]
Kezib, 3945, *k*^{e}*zîb* [1]

KIBROTH HATTAAVAH [5]
Kibroth Hattaavah, 7701, *qibrôt hatta'*^{a}*wâ* [5]

KIBZAIM [1]
Kibzaim, 7698, *qibṣayim* [1]

KICKED [1]
kicked, 1246, *bā'aṭ* [1]

KICKING [2]
kicking about, 1008, *bûs* [2]

KIDNAPPER [1]
kidnapper, 1705, *gannāb* [1]

KIDNAPPING [1]
kidnapping, 1704+5883, *gānab+nepeš* [1]

KIDNAPS [1]
kidnaps, 1704, *gānab* [1]

KIDNEYS [18]
kidneys, 4000, *kilyâ* [18]

KIDON [1]
Kidon, 3961, *kîdōn* [1]

KIDRON [10]
Kidron, 7724, *qidrôn* [10]

KILEAB [1]
Kileab, 3976, *kil'āb* [1]

KILION [3]
Kilion, 4002, *kilyôn* [3]

KILL [125]
kill, 2222, *hārag* [46]
kill, 4637, *mût* [36]
kill, 5782, *nākâ* [15]
kill, 4162, *kārat* [6]
kill, 4637+4637, *mût+mût* [4]
kill, 2991, *ḥārēb*^{2} [2]
kill, 5782+5883, *nākâ+nepeš* [2]
kill, 5883+4374, *nepeš+lāqaḥ* [2]
kill, 6, *'ābad* [1]
wanted to kill, 1335+906+5883, *bāqaš+'ēt*^{1}*+nepeš* [1]
kill, 3049, *ḥāram*^{1} [1]
kill, 3272, *ṭerep* [1]
kill and expose, 3697, *yāqa'* [1]
kill, 4638, *māwet* [1]
kill, 5883, *nepeš* [1]
kill, 7003, *pāga'* [1]
kill, 8357, *rāṣaḥ* [1]
kill, 8821, *šāḥaṭ*^{1} [1]
kill, 8824, *š*^{e}*ḥîṭâ* [1]
wait to kill, 9068+5883, *šāmar+nepeš* [1]

KILLED [171]
killed, 2222, *hārag* [53]
killed, 5782, *nākâ* [39]
killed, 4637, *mût* [31]
killed, 2728, *ḥālāl*^{1} [21]
killed, 8821, *šāḥaṭ*^{1} [5]
killed and exposed, 3697, *yāqa'* [2]
killed, 8357, *rāṣaḥ* [2]
be killed, 2222, *hārag* [1]
been killed, 2222, *hārag* [1]
killed, 2223, *hereg* [1]
killed, 2726, *ḥālal*^{2} [1]
killed, 3271, *ṭārap* [1]
been killed and exposed, 3697, *yāqa'* [1]
be killed, 4637, *mût* [1]
was killed, 4637, *mût* [1]
killed off, 5782, *nākâ* [1]
killed, 5782+4200+7023+2995, *nākâ+l*$^{e-1}$*+peh+ḥereb* [1]
killed, 5782+4637, *nākâ+mût* [1]
was killed, 5782, *nākâ* [1]
killed, 5877, *nāpal* [1]
killed a person, 8357, *rāṣaḥ* [1]
killed, 8357+5782, *rāṣaḥ+nākâ* [1]
was killed, 8821, *šāḥaṭ*^{1} [1]
killed, 8845, *šāḥat* [1]
killed, 10625, *q*^{e}*ṭal* [1]

KILLING [18]
killing, 2222, *hārag* [6]
killing, 5782, *nākâ* [3]
killing, 4637, *mût* [2]
killing, 1947, *dām* [1]
killing, 2223, *hereg* [1]
killing off, 4162, *kārat* [1]
killing, 4162, *kārat* [1]
killing off, 4637, *mût* [1]
killing, 8821, *šāḥaṭ*^{1} [1]
killing, 8938+3338+928, *šālaḥ+yād+b*^{e}*-* [1]

KILLS [19]
kills, 5782, *nākâ* [10]
kills, 2222, *hārag* [3]
kills, 4637, *mût* [2]
kills, 5782+5883+2256+4637, *nākâ+nepeš+w*^{e}*-+mût* [1]
kills, 7779, *qāṭal* [1]
kills a man, 8357, *rāṣaḥ* [1]
kills another, 8357, *rāṣaḥ* [1]

KILMAD [1]
Kilmad, 4008, *kilmad* [1]

KIMHAM [3]
Kimham, 4016, *kimhām* [3]

KIN [1]
near of kin, 1457, *gā'al*^{1} [1]

KINAH [1]
Kinah, 7807, *qînâ*^{2} [1]

KIND [70]
kind, 4786, *mîn* [18]
kind, *AIT* [17]
kind, *NIH/RPE* [5]
kind, 2858, *ḥānan*^{1} [4]
kind, 3202, *ṭôb*^{2} [3]
kind, 1414, *bāśār* [2]
kind, 1580, *gôy* [1]
kind, 2492, *ḥābēr* [1]
kind, 2876, *ḥesed*^{2} [1]
be so kind as, 3283, *yā'al*^{2} [1]
kind, 3512, *yāṭab* [1]
kind, 3869+889, *k*^{e}*-+'*^{a}*šer* [1]
kind, 3869, *k*^{e}*-* [1]
kind, 4017, *k*^{e}*mô* [1]
this was the kind, 4027, *kēn*^{2} [1]
kind^{s}, 4053, *kānāp* [1]
one kind after another, 4200+5476+2157, *l*$^{e-1}$*+mišpāḥâ+-hem* [1]
any kind, 4399, *m*^{e}*'ûmâ* [1]
what kind, 4537, *mâ* [1]
every kind, 4946+2385+448+2385, *min+zan+'el+zan* [1]
proper kind, 5120, *ma'*^{a}*rākâ* [1]
kind, 5477, *mišpāṭ* [1]
this kind of sore, 5596+2021+5999, *nega'+ha+neteq* [1]
interest of any kind, 5968+2256+9552, *nešek+w*^{e}*-+tarbît* [1]
kind, 8934, *šālôm* [1]
kind, 9454, *t*^{e}*mûnâ* [1]
kind, 10274, *ḥ*^{a}*nan* [1]

KINDEST [1]
kindest acts, 8171, *raḥ*^{a}*mîm* [1]

KINDHEARTED [1]
kindhearted, 2834, *ḥēn*^{1} [1]

KINDLE [5]
kindle, 3675, *yāṣat* [3]
kindle, 1944, *dālaq* [1]
kindle, 7706, *qādaḥ* [1]

KINDLED [5]
kindled, 836+7706, *'ēš*^{1}*+qādaḥ* [1]
kindled, 1277, *bā'ar*^{1} [1]
kindled, 3675, *yāṣat* [1]
kindled, 3678, *yāqad* [1]
kindled, 7706, *qādaḥ* [1]

KINDLES [1]
kindles a fire, 5956, *nāśaq* [1]

KINDLING [1]
kindling, 3081, *ḥārar*^{1} [1]

KINDLY [5]
kindly, 3208, *ṭôbâ* [2]
spoken kindly, 1819+6584+4213, *dābar*^{2}*+'al*^{2}*+lēb* [1]
kindly, 2876, *ḥesed*^{2} [1]
kindly, 4213, *lēb* [1]

KINDNESS [48]
kindness, 2876, *ḥesed^{2}* [41]
unfailing kindness, 2876, *ḥesed^{2}* [3]
kindness, *NIH/RPE* [1]
kindness, 1691, *g^{e}mûl* [1]
do a kindness, 2858, *ḥānan^{1}* [1]
show kindness, 3512, *yāṭab* [1]

KINDNESSES [3]
kindnesses, 2876, *ḥesed^{2}* [3]

KINDS [54]
kinds, *AIT* [26]
kinds, 4786, *mîn* [9]
kinds, 10235, *zan* [4]
two kinds, 3977, *kilʾayim* [3]
various kinds of service, 6275+2256+6275, *ʿ^{a}bōdâ+w^{e}-+ʿ^{a}bōdâ* [2]
kinds of cattle, 989+2256+989, *b^{e}hēmâ+w^{e}-+b^{e}hēmâ* [1]
various kinds, 2446, *zeraʿ* [1]
different kinds, 3977, *kilʾayim* [1]
kinds, 3998, *k^{e}lî* [1]
kinds^{s}, 4053, *kānāp* [1]
various kinds, 4786, *mîn* [1]
kinds, 4856, *m^{e}lāʾkâ* [1]
all kinds, 4946+3972, *min+kōl* [1]
kinds, 5476, *mišpāḥâ* [1]
kinds, 9322, *tabnît* [1]

KING [2225]
king, 4889, *melek^{1}* [1840]
king, 4887, *mālak^{1}* [151]
king, 10421, *melek* [137]
king, *NIH/RPE* [35]
made king, 4887, *mālak^{1}* [24]
the king^{s}, 2257, *-ô* [7]
make king, 4887, *mālak^{1}* [7]
proclaimed king, 4887, *mālak^{1}* [3]
the king of the South^{s}, 2257, *-ô* [2]
king, 3782, *yāšab* [2]
set up king, 4887+4889, *mālak^{1}+melek^{1}* [2]
for king, 350, *ʾ^{a}ḥaš^{t}^{e}rān* [1]
the king, 2257, *-ô* [1]
king, 4867, *m^{e}lûkâ* [1]
acknowledged as king, 4887, *mālak^{1}* [1]
appoint as king, 4887, *mālak^{1}* [1]
confirmed as king, 4887, *mālak^{1}* [1]
give king, 4887+4889, *mālak^{1}+melek^{1}* [1]
king, 4887+4889, *mālak^{1}+melek^{1}* [1]
made king, 4887+4889, *mālak^{1}+melek^{1}* [1]
make king, 4887+4889, *mālak^{1}+melek^{1}* [1]
set a king, 4887+4889, *mālak^{1}+melek^{1}* [1]
surely be king, 4887+4887, *mālak^{1}+mālak^{1}* [1]
became king, 4895, *malkût* [1]
king, 4895, *malkût* [1]
position as king, 4895, *malkût* [1]

KING'S [194]
king's, 4889, *melek^{1}* [172]
the king's^{s}, 2257, *-ô* [7]
king's, 10421, *melek* [6]
king's, 4200+4889, *l^{e}-^{1}+melek^{1}* [4]
king's, 928+4889, *b^{e}-+melek^{1}* [3]
king's, *NIH/RPE* [1]
the king's, 2257, *-ô* [1]

KINGDOM [145]
kingdom, 4930, *mamlākâ* [58]
kingdom, 4895, *malkût* [36]
kingdom, 10424, *malkû* [30]
kingdom, 4867, *m^{e}lûkâ* [10]
kingdom, 4931, *mamlākût* [4]
kingdom, 4939, *memšālâ* [3]
Aramean kingdom, 806, *ʾ^{a}rām* [2]
the kingdom^{s}, 2023, *-āh* [1]
kingdom, 4889, *melek^{1}* [1]

KINGDOMS [58]
kingdoms, 4930, *mamlākâ* [45]
kingdoms, 10424, *malkû* [7]
kingdoms, 4895, *malkût* [2]
kingdoms, *NIH/RPE* [1]
kingdoms, 4889, *melek^{1}* [1]
kingdoms, 5476, *mišpāḥâ* [1]
kingdoms, 10421, *melek* [1]

KINGS [293]
kings, 4889, *melek^{1}* [272]
kings, 10421, *melek* [11]
kings, *NIH/RPE* [3]
kings, 4930, *mamlākâ* [2]
kings^{s}, 408, *ʾîš^{1}* [1]
kings, 3782, *yāšab* [1]
the kings^{s}, 4392, *-ām* [1]
kings, 4482, *māgēn^{1}* [1]
set up kings, 4887, *mālak^{1}* [1]

KINGSHIP [7]
kingship, 4867, *m^{e}lûkâ* [3]
kingship, 4930, *mamlākâ* [2]
kingship, 4887, *mālak^{1}* [1]
kingship, 4895, *malkût* [1]

KINNERETH [7]
Kinnereth, 4055, *kinneret* [4]
Kinnereth, 4054, *kinrôt* [3]

KINSMAN [2]
kinsman, 4530, *mōdāʿ* [1]
kinsman, 4531, *mōdaʿat* [1]

KINSMAN-REDEEMER [7]
kinsman-redeemer, 1457, *gāʾal^{1}* [7]

KINSMAN-REDEEMERS [1]
kinsman-redeemers, 1457, *gāʾal^{1}* [1]

KINSMEN [6]
kinsmen, 278, *ʾāḥ^{2}* [5]
kinsmen, 7940, *qārôb* [1]

KIR [5]
Kir, 7817, *qîr^{3}* [4]
Kir, 7816, *qîr^{2}* [1]

KIR HARESETH [5]
Kir Hareseth, 7818, *qîr-ḥereś* [3]
Kir Hareseth, 7819, *qîr ḥ^{a}reśet* [2]

KIRIATH [1]
Kiriath, 7956, *qiryat* [1]

KIRIATH ARBA [9]
Kiriath Arba, 7957, *qiryat ʾarbaʿ* [7]
Kiriath Arba, 7959, *qiryat hāʾarbaʿ* [2]

KIRIATH BAAL [2]
Kiriath Baal, 7958, *qiryat-baʿal* [2]

KIRIATH HUZOTH [1]
Kiriath Huzoth, 7960, *qiryat ḥuṣôt* [1]

KIRIATH JEARIM [19]
Kiriath Jearim, 7961, *qiryat y^{e}ʿārîm* [19]

KIRIATH SANNAH [1]
Kiriath Sannah, 7962, *qiryat-sannâ* [1]

KIRIATH SEPHER [4]
Kiriath Sepher, 7963, *qiryat-sēper* [4]

KIRIATHAIM [6]
Kiriathaim, 7964, *qiryātayim* [6]

KISH [21]
Kish, 7821, *qîš* [21]

KISHI [1]
Kishi, 7823, *qîšî* [1]

KISHION [2]
Kishion, 8002, *qišyôn* [2]

KISHON [6]
Kishon, 7822, *qîšôn* [6]

KISLEV [2]
Kislev, 4075, *kislēw* [2]

KISLON [1]
Kislon, 4077, *kislôn* [1]

KISLOTH TABOR [1]
Kisloth Tabor, 4079, *kislōt tābôr* [1]

KISS [12]
kiss, 5975, *nāšaq^{1}* [9]
kiss good-by, 5975, *nāšaq^{1}* [2]
offered a kiss of homage, 5975+4200+7023, *nāšaq^{1}+l^{e}-^{1}+peh* [1]

KISSED [18]
kissed, 5975, *nāšaq^{1}* [17]
kissed good-by, 5975, *nāšaq^{1}* [1]

KISSES [2]
kisses, 5965, *n^{e}šîqâ* [2]

KIT [3]
kit, 7879, *qeset* [2]
writing kit, 7879, *qeset* [1]

KITCHENS [1]
kitchens, 1074+1418, *bayit^{1}+bāšal* [1]

KITE [4]
black kite, 370, *ʾayyâ^{1}* [2]
red kite, 1798, *dāʾâ^{2}* [1]
red kite, 8012, *rāʾâ^{2}* [1]

KITLISH [1]
Kitlish, 4186, *kitlîš* [1]

KITRON [1]
Kitron, 7790, *qiṭrôn* [1]

KITTIM [4]
Kittim, 4183, *kittiyyîm* [4]

KNEAD [2]
knead, 4297, *lûš* [2]

KNEADED [2]
kneaded, 4297, *lûš* [2]

KNEADING [5]
kneading troughs, 5400, *mišʾeret* [2]
kneading trough, 5400, *mišʾeret* [2]
kneading, 4297, *lûš* [1]

KNEE [3]
knee, 1386, *berek* [3]

KNEE-DEEP [1]
knee-deep, 1386, *berek* [1]

KNEEL [6]
kneel down, 4156, *kāraʿ* [2]
had kneel down, 1384, *bārak^{1}* [1]
kneel, 1384, *bārak^{1}* [1]
kneel, 1386, *berek* [1]
kneel, 4156, *kāraʿ* [1]

KNEELING [2]
kneeling, 2556, *ḥāwâ^{2}* [1]
kneeling, 4156+6584+1386, *kāraʿ+ʿal^{2}+berek* [1]

KNEES [18]
knees, 1386, *berek* [15]
brought to knees, 4156, *kāraʿ* [1]
knees, 10072, *ʾarkubbâ* [1]
knees, 10123, *b^{e}rēk* [1]

KNELT [5]
knelt down, 4156, *kāraʿ* [2]
knelt down, 1384+6584+1386, *bārak^{1}+ʿal^{2}+berek* [1]
knelt, 2556, *ḥāwâ^{2}* [1]
knelt, 4156, *kāraʿ* [1]

KNEW [46]
knew, 3359, *yādaʿ* [39]
knew about, 3359, *yādaʿ* [5]
knew, 8011, *rāʾâ^{1}* [1]
knew, 10313, *y^{e}daʿ* [1]

KNIFE [6]
knife, 4408, *maʾ^{a}kelet* [3]
flint knife, 7644, *ṣōr^{1}* [1]
knife, 8501, *śakkîn* [1]
knife, 9509, *taʿar* [1]

KNIT [2]
knit together, 6115, *sākak*[2] [2]

KNITTED [9]
knitted material, 6849, *'ēreb*[1] [9]

KNIVES [4]
knives, 2995, *ḥereb* [2]
knives, 4408, *ma'^{a}kelet* [1]
pruning knives, 4661, *mazmērâ* [1]

KNOCKED [2]
knocked, 8959, *šālak* [1]
knocked, 10491, *n^{e}qaš* [1]

KNOCKING [1]
knocking, 1985, *dāpaq* [1]

KNOCKS [1]
knocks out, 5877, *nāpal* [1]

KNOTTED [1]
tightly knotted, 775, *'ārûz* [1]

KNOW [487]
know, 3359, *yāda'* [422]
know, 10313, *y^{e}da'* [11]
know how, 3359, *yāda'* [8]
know about, 3359, *yāda'* [6]
know, *NIH/RPE* [5]
know, 1981, *da'at*[1] [5]
what know, 1976, *dēa'* [3]
know, 3359+3359, *yāda'+yāda'* [3]
let know, 1655+906+265, *gālâ+'ēt*[1]*+'ōzen* [2]
as you know, 2022+4202, *h^{a}-+lō'* [2]
let know, 3359, *yāda'* [2]
know, 5795, *nākar*[1] [2]
know, *AIT* [1]
know, 907, *'ēt*[2] [1]
know, 1067, *bîn* [1]
what know, 1981, *da'at*[1] [1]
do not know where am going, 2143+6584+889+2143, *hālak+'al*[2]*+'ašer+hālak* [1]
be sure know, 3359+3359, *yāda'+yāda'* [1]
know for certain, 3359+3359, *yāda'+yāda'* [1]
know all about, 3359, *yāda'* [1]
know how to read, 3359+6219, *yāda'+sēper*[1] [1]
know what it is like, 3359, *yāda'* [1]
know what means, 3359, *yāda'* [1]
letting know, 3359, *yāda'* [1]
let know, 5583, *nāgad* [1]
know how, 5795, *nākar*[1] [1]
know no limits, 6296, *'ābar*[1] [1]
know the true meaning, 10326, *y^{e}ṣab* [1]

KNOWING [9]
knowing, 3359, *yāda'* [6]
knowing about, 3359, *yāda'* [1]
knowing how, 3359, *yāda'* [1]
knowing, 8011, *rā'â*[1] [1]

KNOWLEDGE [88]
knowledge, 1981, *da'at*[1] [68]
knowledge, 3359, *yāda'* [5]
knowledge, 1978, *dēa'* [4]
knowledge, 4529, *maddā'* [4]
knowledge, 1976, *dēa'* [2]
knowledge, 10430, *manda'* [2]
have knowledge, 1981+3359, *da'at*[1]*+yāda'* [1]
has knowledge, 3359+1981, *yāda'+da'at*[1] [1]
man of knowledge, 3359+1981, *yāda'+da'at*[1] [1]

KNOWN [79]
known, 3359, *yāda'* [23]
make known, 3359, *yāda'* [11]
made known, 3359, *yāda'* [10]
be known, 3359, *yāda'* [4]
is known, 3359, *yāda'* [3]
make myself known, 3359, *yāda'* [3]
known, *NIH/RPE* [2]
made known, 1655, *gālâ* [2]
made known, 10313, *y^{e}da'* [2]
are known, 3359, *yāda'* [1]
be made known, 3359, *yāda'* [1]
become known, 3359, *yāda'* [1]
been known, 3359, *yāda'* [1]
lets be known, 3359, *yāda'* [1]
made himself known, 3359, *yāda'* [1]
make himself known, 3359, *yāda'* [1]
makes known, 3359, *yāda'* [1]
was known, 3359, *yāda'* [1]
become known, 3655, *yāṣā'* [1]
well known, 3700+4394, *yāqar+m^{e}'ōd* [1]
make known, 5583, *nāgad* [1]
known to, 5584, *neged* [1]
is known, 5795, *nākar*[1] [1]
little known, 7829, *qālâ*[2] [1]
be known as, 7924+9005, *qārā'*[1]*+šēm*[1] [1]
be known as, 7924, *qārā'*[1] [1]
known as, 7924, *qārā'*[1] [1]
made known, 9048, *šāma'* [1]

KNOWS [54]
knows, 3359, *yāda'* [43]
knows how, 3359, *yāda'* [4]
knows, 8011, *rā'â*[1] [2]
knows, *NIH/RPE* [1]
knows, 1067, *bîn* [1]
knows, 1978, *dēa'* [1]
knows very well, 3359+3359, *yāda'+yāda'* [1]
knows, 10313, *y^{e}da'* [1]

KOA [1]
Koa, 7760, *qôa'* [1]

KOHATH [19]
Kohath, 7740, *q^{e}hāt* [18]
Kohath, 7741, *q^{e}hātî* [1]

KOHATH'S [2]
Kohath's, 7740, *q^{e}hāt* [2]

KOHATHITE [16]
Kohathite, 1201+7740, *bēn*[1]*+q^{e}hāt* [7]
Kohathite, 7741, *q^{e}hātî* [7]
Kohathite, 1201+7741, *bēn*[1]*+q^{e}hātî* [1]
the Kohathite^{s}, 2157, *-hem* [1]

KOHATHITES [12]
Kohathites, 1201+7740, *bēn*[1]*+q^{e}hāt* [4]
Kohathites, 1201+7741, *bēn*[1]*+q^{e}hātî* [3]
Kohathites, 7741, *q^{e}hātî* [3]
Kohathites, *NIH/RPE* [2]

KOLAIAH [2]
Kolaiah, 7755, *qôlāyâ* [2]

KORAH [35]
Korah, 7946, *qōraḥ* [34]
Korah, 7948, *qorḥî* [1]

KORAH'S [3]
Korah's, 7946, *qōraḥ* [2]
Korah's, 4200+7946, *l^{e}-*[1]*+qōraḥ* [1]

KORAHITE [3]
Korahite, 7948, *qorḥî* [3]

KORAHITES [4]
Korahites, 7948, *qorḥî* [3]
Korahites, 1201+7948, *bēn*[1]*+qorḥî* [1]

KORE [3]
Kore, 7927, *qōrē'*[2] [3]

KOZ [1]
Koz, 7766, *qôṣ*[3] [1]

KUE [4]
Kue, 7745, *q^{e}wē'* [2]
Kue, 7750, *q^{e}wēh* [2]

KUSHAIAH [1]
Kushaiah, 7773, *qûšāyāhû* [1]

LAADAH [1]
Laadah, 4355, *la'dâ* [1]

LABAN [49]
Laban, 4238, *lābān*[2] [45]
Laban, *NIH/RPE* [2]
Laban^{s}, 2257, *-ô* [1]
Laban, 4239, *lābān*[3] [1]

LABAN'S [5]
Laban's, 4238, *lābān*[2] [5]

LABOR [80]
forced labor, 4989, *mas* [14]
in labor, 3528, *yālad* [12]
labor, 6275, *'^{a}bōdâ* [7]
labor, 6662, *'āmāl*[1] [5]
in labor, 2655, *ḥîl*[1] [4]
labor, 3330, *y^{e}gîa'* [4]
labor, 6268, *'ābad* [3]
labor, 6661, *'āmal* [3]
fruits of labor, 3330, *y^{e}gîa'* [2]
labor, 5126, *ma'^{a}śeh* [2]
labor, 7189, *pō'al* [2]
in labor, 7674, *ṣārar*[1] [2]
in labor, 2473, *ḥābal*[3] [1]
labor pains, 2477, *ḥēbel* [1]
goes into labor, 2655, *ḥîl*[1] [1]
fruit of labor, 3330+4090, *y^{e}gîa'+kap* [1]
labor, 3333, *yāga'* [1]
labor, 3338, *yād* [1]
labor, 3615, *yā'ēp*[1] [1]
went into labor, 4156, *kāra'* [1]
in labor, 4256, *lēdâ* [1]
labor force, 4989, *mas* [1]
slave labor force, 4989, *mas* [1]
slave labor, 4989, *mas* [1]
labor force, 6023, *sēbel* [1]
forced labor, 6026, *siblôt* [1]
hard labor, 6026, *siblôt* [1]
bitter labor, 6662, *'āmāl*[1] [1]
labor, 6721, *'inyān* [1]
labor pains, 7496, *ṣîr*[4] [1]
consigning to labor, 8462, *śûr* [1]
consigning to labor, 8492, *śîm* [1]

LABORED [3]
labored, 3333, *yāga'* [3]

LABORER [1]
laborer, 6268, *'ābad* [1]

LABORER'S [1]
laborer's, 6664, *'āmēl*[1] [1]

LABORERS [5]
laborers, 6025, *sabbāl* [2]
forced laborers, 4989, *mas* [1]
laborers, 4989, *mas* [1]
laborers, 8502, *śākîr* [1]

LABORS [1]
labors, 6665, *'āmēl*[2] [1]

LACHISH [24]
Lachish, 4337, *lākîš* [24]

LACK [29]
lack, 401, *'ayin*[1] [6]
lack, 1172, *b^{e}lî* [6]
lack, 2893, *ḥāsēr*[1] [3]
lack, 2894, *ḥāsēr*[2] [3]
lack, 4202, *lō'* [2]
lack, 4728, *maḥsôr* [2]
lack, *NIH/RPE* [1]
lack, 401+4200, *'ayin*[1]*+l^{e}-*[1] [1]
lack, 401+928, *'ayin*[1]*+b^{e}-* [1]
lack, 2896, *ḥōser* [1]
lack, 4202+928, *lō'+b^{e}-* [1]
for lack of, 4946, *min* [1]
lack, 7212, *pāqad* [1]

LACKED [5]
lacked, 2893, *ḥāsēr*[1] [2]
lacked, 2894, *ḥāsēr*[2] [2]
lacked, 4007, *kālam* [1]

LACKING [5]
lacking, 1172, *b^{e}lî* [1]
lacking, 2894, *ḥāsēr*[2] [1]
lacking, 2898, *ḥesrôn* [1]
lacking, 4946+1172, *min+b^{e}lî* [1]
saw to it that was lacking, 6372, *'ādar*[3] [1]

LACKS [15]
lacks, 2894, *ḥāsēr*[2] [9]

lacks, 2893, *ḥāsēr*[1] [3]
lacks, 401, *ʾayin*[1] [2]
lacks, 4728, *maḥsôr* [1]

LADAN [7]
Ladan, 4356, *laʿdān* [7]

LADEN [3]
laden with, 4848, *mālēʾ*[1] [2]
laden with, 928, *bᵉ-* [1]

LADIES [1]
ladies, 8576, *śārâ*[2] [1]

LAEL [1]
Lael, 4210, *lāʾēl* [1]

LAGGING [1]
lagging, 3129, *ḥāšal* [1]

LAHAD [1]
Lahad, 4262, *lāhad* [1]

LAHMAS [1]
Lahmas, 4314, *laḥmās* [1]

LAHMI [1]
Lahmi, 4313, *laḥmî* [1]

LAID [117]
laid, 8492, *śîm* [11]
laid waste, 2990, *ḥārēb*[1] [6]
laid, 6164, *sāmak* [6]
laid the foundations, 3569, *yāsad*[1] [5]
laid siege, 7443, *ṣûr*[1] [5]
the foundation was laid, 3569, *yāsad*[1] [4]
laid, *NIH/RPE* [3]
laid the foundation, 3569, *yāsad*[1] [3]
laid, 5989, *nātan* [3]
laid down, 7422, *ṣāwâ* [3]
laid, 8883, *šît*[1] [3]
laid, 8886, *šākab* [3]
laid waste, 9014, *šammâ*[1] [3]
laid bare, 1655, *gālâ* [2]
the foundation laid, 3569, *yāsad*[1] [2]
laid, 5663, *nûaḥ*[1] [2]
are laid, 5989, *nātan* [2]
laid, 6673, *ʿāmas* [2]
laid beams, 7936, *qārâ*[1] [2]
be laid, 8886, *šākab* [2]
was laid waste, 9037, *šāmēm*[1] [2]
laid waste, 9039, *šᵉmāmâ* [2]
laid, *AIT* [1]
laid siege, 995+928+2021+5189, *bôʾ+bᵉ+ha-+māṣôr*[1] [1]
laid waste, 1278, *bāʿar*[2] [1]
be completely laid waste, 1327+1327, *bāqaq*[1]*+bāqaq*[1] [1]
laid waste, 1327, *bāqaq*[1] [1]
be laid bare, 1655, *gālâ* [1]
laid low, 1815, *dābaq* [1]
will be laid waste, 1959, *dāmam*[3] [1]
laid low, 2150, *hālam* [1]
laid waste, 2238+2256+2990, *hāras+wᵉ-+ḥārēb*[1] [1]
laid low, 2764, *ḥālaš*[1] [1]
laid low, 2765, *ḥālaš*[2] [1]
laid waste, 2803, *ḥāmas*[1] [1]
laid siege to, 2837+6584, *ḥānâ*[1]*+ʿal*[2] [1]
the foundations were laid, 3569, *yāsad*[1] [1]
foundations be laid, 3569, *yāsad*[1] [1]
laid foundations, 3569, *yāsad*[1] [1]
the foundation been laid, 3569, *yāsad*[1] [1]
laid waste, 3655+3655, *yāṣāʾ+yāṣāʾ* [1]
laid, 3704, *yāqaš* [1]
laid, 3721, *yārâ*[1] [1]
laid heavy, 3877, *kābēd*[1] [1]
foundation laid, 4586, *mûsād* [1]
laid, 5595, *nāgaʿ* [1]
laid, 5747, *nāṭal* [1]
laid waste, 5898, *nāṣâ*[2] [1]
be laid low, 6085, *sāḥap* [1]
laid siege, 6164, *sāmak* [1]
laid, 6296, *ʿābar*[1] [1]
be laid waste, 6440, *ʿāzab*[1] [1]
laid out, 6885, *ʿārak* [1]
laid, 7003, *pāgaʿ* [1]
laid, 7298, *pāraś* [1]
laid waste, 8845, *šāḥat* [1]
laid low, 8886, *šākab* [1]
laid to rest, 8886, *šākab* [1]
laid, 8938, *šālaḥ* [1]
be laid waste, 9037, *šāmēm*[1] [1]
laid waste, 9037, *šāmēm*[1] [1]
laid, 10314, *yᵉhab* [1]
be laid, 10502, *sᵉbal* [1]

LAIN [2]
lain with, 3359, *yādaʿ* [1]
lain down, 8886, *šākab* [1]

LAIR [3]
lair, 5271, *marbēṣ* [1]
lair, 6020, *sᵉbōk* [1]
lair, 6108, *sōk* [1]

LAIRS [1]
lairs, 2986, *ḥōr*[2] [1]

LAISH [6]
Laish, 4332, *layiš*[3] [4]
Laish, 4331, *layiš*[2] [2]

LAISHAH [1]
Laishah, 4333, *layᵉšâ* [1]

LAKE [1]
lake, 3542, *yām* [1]

LAKKUM [1]
Lakkum, 4373, *laqqûm* [1]

LAMB [65]
lamb, 3897, *kebeś* [19]
male lamb, 3897, *kebeś* [15]
lamb, 8445, *śeh* [11]
lamb, 4166, *keśeb* [5]
ewe lamb, 3898, *kibśâ* [4]
Passover lamb, 7175, *pesaḥ* [4]
lamb, 3231, *ṭāleh* [2]
the lamb[s], 2084, *-hû* [1]
lamb, 3898, *kibśâ* [1]
lamb, 4167, *kiśbâ* [1]
lamb, 8445+928+2021+3897, *śeh+bᵉ+ha-+kebeś* [1]
lamb, 8445+928+2021+4166, *śeh+bᵉ+ha-+keśeb* [1]

LAMBS [90]
male lambs, 3897, *kebeś* [35]
lambs, 3897, *kebeś* [25]
lambs, 4119, *kar*[1] [8]
lambs, 6957, *ʿašteret* [4]
Passover lambs, 7175, *pesaḥ* [3]
male lambs, 10043, *ʾimmar* [3]
lambs, *NIH/RPE* [2]
lambs, 1201+7366, *bēn*[1]*+ṣōʾn* [2]
ewe lambs, 3898, *kibśâ* [2]
lambs, 1531, *gᵉdî* [1]
the lambs[s], 2257, *-ô* [1]
lambs, 3231, *ṭāleh* [1]
lambs, 3898, *kibśâ* [1]
choice lambs, 4119+4946+7366, *kar*[1]*+min+ṣōʾn* [1]
lambs, 4166, *keśeb* [1]

LAME [16]
lame, 7177, *pissēaḥ* [11]
lame, 7519, *ṣālaʿ* [3]
lame, 5048, *māʿad* [1]
lame, 5783, *nākeh* [1]

LAMECH [11]
Lamech, 4347, *lemek* [11]

LAMENT [29]
lament, 7806, *qînâ*[1] [13]
lament, 6199, *sāpad* [3]
lament, *NIH/RPE* [1]
lament, 61, *ʾābal*[1] [1]
made lament, 61, *ʾābal*[1] [1]
lament, 627, *ʾānâ*[1] [1]
lament, 640, *ʾᵃniyyâ* [1]
lament, 650, *ʾānaq* [1]
lament, 2047, *hāgâ*[1] [1]
lament, 2411+6424, *zᵉʿāqâ+ʿûr*[3] [1]
lament, 5654, *nôd*[1] [1]
sang lament, 7801, *qîn* [1]
take up a lament, 7801, *qîn* [1]
took up lament, 7801+7806, *qîn+qînâ*[1] [1]
lament, 8490, *śîaḥ*[3] [1]

LAMENTATION [3]
lamentation, 640, *ʾᵃniyyâ* [1]
lamentation, 2411, *zᵉʿāqâ* [1]
lamentation, 3538, *yᵉlālâ* [1]

LAMENTED [1]
lamented, 6199+5027, *sāpad+mispēd* [1]

LAMENTS [6]
laments, 2159, *hāmâ* [3]
laments, 7806, *qînâ*[1] [2]
composed laments, 7801, *qîn* [1]

LAMP [23]
lamp, 5944, *nēr*[1] [16]
lamp, 5775, *nîr*[2] [5]
lamp, 240, *ʾôr*[2] [1]
lamp, 4963, *mᵉnôrâ* [1]

LAMPS [25]
lamps, 5944, *nēr*[1] [23]
the lamps[s], 2257, *-ô* [2]

LAMPSTAND [35]
lampstand, 4963, *mᵉnôrâ* [26]
the lampstand[s], 5626, *-nâ* [3]
each lampstand, 4963+2256+4963, *mᵉnôrâ+wᵉ-+mᵉnôrâ* [2]
lampstand, *NIH/RPE* [1]
the lampstand[s], 2023, *-āh* [1]
each lampstand, 4963+4963, *mᵉnôrâ+mᵉnôrâ* [1]
lampstand, 10456, *nebrᵉšâ* [1]

LAMPSTANDS [5]
lampstands, 4963, *mᵉnôrâ* [5]

LANCE [2]
lance, 3959, *kîdôn* [2]

LAND [1422]
land, 824, *ʾereṣ* [1150]
land, 141, *ʾᵃdāmâ*[1] [120]
land, *NIH/RPE* [38]
land, 1074, *bayit*[1] [15]
the land[s], 2023, *-āh* [12]
land, 8441, *śādeh* [11]
land, 1473, *gᵉbûl* [7]
land, 5226, *māqôm* [5]
land, 824+299, *ʾereṣ+ʾᵃḥuzzâ* [3]
the land[s], 889, *ʾᵃšer* [3]
dry land, 3000, *ḥārābâ* [3]
family land, 8441+299, *śādeh+ʾᵃḥuzzâ* [3]
land, *AIT* [2]
native land, 141, *ʾᵃdāmâ*[1] [2]
its land[s], 2023, *-āh* [2]
land[s], 2023, *-āh* [2]
land, 2475, *ḥebel*[2] [2]
dry land, 3317, *yabbāšâ* [2]
land, 3317, *yabbāšâ* [2]
grazing land, 5659, *nāweh*[1] [2]
parched land, 7480, *ṣiyyâ* [2]
land, 10075, *ʾᵃraʿ* [2]
land, 299+824, *ʾᵃḥuzzâ+ʾereṣ* [1]
areas of land, 824, *ʾereṣ* [1]
native land, 824, *ʾereṣ* [1]
tracts of land, 824, *ʾereṣ* [1]
clear land, 1345, *bārāʾ*[3] [1]
their land[s], 2023, *-āh* [1]
this land[s], 2023, *-āh* [1]
land, 2575, *ḥûš* [1]
land, 2750, *ḥēleq*[2] [1]
dry land, 3318, *yabbešet* [1]
the whole land[s], 3776, *yiśrāʾēl* [1]
fruitful land, 4149, *karmel*[1] [1]
open land, 4494, *migrāš* [1]
land for crops, 4760, *maṭṭāʿ* [1]
sell land, 4835+4928, *mākar+mimkār* [1]
land sold, 4928, *mimkār* [1]

the lands^{s}, 5626, *-nâ* [1]
land, 5659, *nāweh^{1}* [1]
inherit land, 5706, *nāḥal* [1]
land inherited, 5709, *naḥ^{a}lâ^{1}* [1]
land inherits, 5709, *naḥ^{a}lâ^{1}* [1]
land, 5709, *naḥ^{a}lâ^{1}* [1]
land beyond, 6298, *ʿēber^{1}* [1]
sun-scorched land, 7461, *ṣ^{e}ḥîḥâ* [1]
sun-scorched land, 7463, *ṣaḥṣāḥôt* [1]
dry land, 7480, *ṣiyyâ* [1]
most distant land, 7895, *qāṣeh* [1]
watered land, 8116, *rāweh* [1]
ridge of land, 8900, *š^{e}kem^{1}* [1]
that land^{s}, 9004, *šām* [1]
the land^{s}, 9004+2025, *šām+-â^{2}* [1]
land^{s}, 9393, *taḥat^{1}* [1]

LAND'S [1]
land's, 928+824, *b^{e}-+'ereṣ* [1]

LANDS [49]
lands, 824, *'ereṣ* [34]
lands, *AIT* [3]
lands, 141, *'^{a}dāmâ^{1}* [3]
lands, *NIH/RPE* [2]
lands, 299, *'^{a}ḥuzzâ* [1]
their lands^{s}, 2023, *-āh* [1]
lands, 2475, *ḥebel^{2}* [1]
fertile lands, 4149, *karmel^{1}* [1]
distant lands, 5305, *merḥāq* [1]
lands, 5709, *naḥ^{a}lâ^{1}* [1]
lands, 8441, *śādeh* [1]

LANGUAGE [28]
language, 4383, *lāšôn* [11]
language, 8557, *śāpâ* [6]
men of every language, 10392, *liššān* [6]
language of Ashdod, 848, *'ašdôdît* [1]
language, 1821, *dābār* [1]
language of Judah, 3376, *y^{e}hûdît^{1}* [1]
language, 9553, *tirgēm* [1]
language, 10392, *liššān* [1]

LANGUAGES [3]
languages, 4383, *lāšôn* [3]

LANGUISH [2]
languish, 581, *'āmal^{1}* [2]

LANGUISHES [1]
languishes, 581, *'āmal^{1}* [1]

LAP [7]
lap, 2668, *ḥêq* [4]
lap, 1386, *berek* [2]
lap, 4379, *lāqaq* [1]

LAPPED [2]
lapped, 4379, *lāqaq* [2]

LAPPIDOTH [1]
Lappidoth, 4366, *lappîdôt* [1]

LAPS [4]
laps, 2668, *ḥêq* [4]

LARGE [100]
large, 1524, *gādôl* [41]
large, 8041, *rab^{1}* [8]
large shields, 7558, *ṣinnâ^{2}* [7]
large, 4394, *m^{e}'ōd* [6]
large, 3878, *kābēd^{2}* [4]
large numbers, 4200+8044, *l^{e}-^{1}+rōb* [3]
large quantities, 4200+8044, *l^{e}-^{1}+rōb* [2]
large amount, 8041, *rab^{1}* [2]
large, 8041+4394, *rab^{1}+m^{e}'ōd* [2]
large, 8044, *rōb* [2]
large stones, 10006+10146, *'eben+g^{e}lāl* [2]
grew large, 10648, *r^{e}bâ* [2]
large tree, 471, *'ēlôn^{1}* [1]
large, 1524+4394, *gādôl+m^{e}'ōd* [1]
large, 2162, *hāmôn* [1]
large amount, 2221+4394, *harbēh+m^{e}'ōd* [1]
large number, 2221, *harbēh* [1]
large, 2221, *harbēh* [1]
large enough, 3869, *k^{e}-* [1]
large, 3878+4394, *kābēd^{2}+m^{e}'ōd* [1]
large jars, 3902, *kad* [1]
in large numbers, 4200+8044, *l^{e}-^{1}+rōb* [1]
large amount, 4200+8044, *l^{e}-^{1}+rōb* [1]
large^{s}, 4482, *māgēn^{1}* [1]
makes large, 7973, *qāraʿ* [1]
accumulate large amounts, 8049+4394, *rābâ^{1}+m^{e}'ōd* [1]
grow large, 8049, *rābâ^{1}* [1]
large, 8146+3338, *rāḥāb^{1}+yād* [1]
large, 8146, *rāḥāb^{1}* [1]
large, 10647, *rab* [1]
large, 10678, *śaggî'* [1]

LARGER [14]
larger, 8041, *rab^{1}* [6]
larger, 1524, *gādôl* [3]
give larger, 8049, *rābâ^{1}* [2]
larger, 4200+8044, *l^{e}-^{1}+rōb* [1]
larger share of, 4946, *min* [1]
larger number, 8041, *rab^{1}* [1]

LASH [2]
lash, 6424, *ʿûr^{3}* [1]
lash, 8765, *šôṭ^{1}* [1]

LASHA [1]
Lasha, 4388, *lešaʿ* [1]

LASHARON [1]
Lasharon, 4389, *laššārôn* [1]

LASHED [1]
lashed by storms, 6192, *sāʿar* [1]

LASHES [3]
lashes, *NIH/RPE* [1]
give lashes, 5782, *nākâ* [1]
lashes, 5782, *nākâ* [1]

LAST [52]
last, 340, *'aḥ^{a}rôn* [11]
last, 344, *'aḥ^{a}rît* [4]
breathed his last, 1588, *gāwaʿ* [4]
last, 2118, *hāyâ* [4]
last, *NIH/RPE* [3]
last night, 621, *'emeš* [3]
every last male, 8874+928+7815, *šîn+b^{e}-+qîr^{1}* [3]
last, 3856, *yeter^{1}* [2]
last, 6641, *ʿāmad* [2]
last, 9462, *tāmam* [2]
last of all, 339, *'aḥar* [1]
at last, 344, *'aḥ^{a}rît* [1]
last watch of the night, 874+1332, *'ašmûrâ+bōqer^{2}* [1]
last watch of the night, 874+2021+1332, *'ašmûrâ+ha-+bōqer^{2}* [1]
last, 995, *bô'* [1]
breathes his last, 1588, *gāwaʿ* [1]
at last, 2021+7193, *ha-+paʿam* [1]
last night, 2021+4326, *ha-+laylâ* [1]
breathed her last, 3655+5883, *yāṣā'+nepeš* [1]
last year's harvest, 3824+3823, *yāšān+yāšēn^{2}* [1]
last, 4848, *mālē'^{1}* [1]
breathe last, 5870+5883, *nāpaḥ+nepeš* [1]
last, 8642, *š^{e}'ērît* [1]
last sleep, 9104, *šēnâ* [1]

LASTED [2]
lasted, 2118, *hāyâ* [1]
lasted so long, 6330, *ʿad^{2}* [1]

LASTING [34]
lasting, 6409, *ʿôlām* [26]
lasting, *AIT* [1]
lasting, *NIH/RPE* [1]
lasting, 586, *'āman^{1}* [1]
lasting, 622, *'^{e}met* [1]
lasting, 4200+6409, *l^{e}-^{1}+ʿôlām* [1]
lasting, 6330+2021+3427+2021+2296, *ʿad^{2}+ha-+yôm^{1}+ha-+zeh* [1]
lasting, 6330+6409, *ʿad^{2}+ʿôlām* [1]
lasting, 6409+9458, *ʿôlām+tāmîd* [1]

LASTS [5]
lasts, *NIH/RPE* [3]
lasts, 6330, *ʿad^{2}* [2]

LATCH-OPENING [1]
latch-opening, 2986, *ḥōr^{2}* [1]

LATE [2]
late, 336, *'āḥar* [1]
stay up late, 336, *'āḥar* [1]

LATELY [2]
lately, 919, *'etmôl* [1]
lately, 928+700, *b^{e}-+'epes* [1]

LATER [44]
some time later, 339+2021+1821+2021+465, *'aḥar+ha-+dābār+ha-+'ēlleh* [6]
later, 4946+7891, *min+qēṣ* [4]
some time later, 339+4027, *'aḥar+kēn^{2}* [3]
later, 339+4027, *'aḥar+kēn^{2}* [3]
later, 339, *'aḥar* [3]
later, 928, *b^{e}-* [3]
later, *NIH/RPE* [2]
later, 340, *'aḥ^{a}rôn* [2]
some time later, 4946+3427, *min+yôm^{1}* [2]
later, 339+2021+1821+2021+465, *'aḥar+ha-+dābār+ha-+'ēlleh* [1]
later, 339+2296, *'aḥar+zeh* [1]
some time later, 339, *'aḥar* [1]
later, 344, *'aḥ^{a}rît* [1]
ripen later, 689, *'āpîl* [1]
later in time, 928+344, *b^{e}-+'aḥ^{a}rît* [1]
later, 928+2021+340, *b^{e}-+ha-+'aḥ^{a}rôn* [1]
later, 2256, *w^{e}-* [1]
later, 3578, *yāsap* [1]
some years later, 4200+7891+9102, *l^{e}-^{1}+qēṣ+šānâ^{2}* [1]
later, 4200+7891, *l^{e}-^{1}+qēṣ* [1]
later, 4200, *l^{e}-^{1}* [1]
later on, 4946+3427, *min+yôm^{1}* [1]
later, 4946+339+4027, *min+'aḥar+kēn^{2}* [1]
later, 4946, *min* [1]
later, 10378+10636, *l^{e}-+q^{e}ṣāt* [1]

LATRINE [1]
latrine, 4738, *maḥ^{a}rā'â* [1]

LATTER [3]
latter, *NIH/RPE* [1]
latter part of life, 344, *'aḥ^{a}rît* [1]
latter part, 344, *'aḥ^{a}rît* [1]

LATTICE [4]
lattice, 876, *'ešnāb* [2]
lattice, 3048, *ḥ^{a}rakkîm* [1]
lattice, 8422, *ś^{e}bākâ* [1]

LAUGH [11]
laugh, 8471, *śāḥaq* [7]
laugh, 7464, *ṣāḥaq* [4]

LAUGHED [3]
laughed, 7464, *ṣāḥaq* [2]
laughed, 8471, *śāḥaq* [1]

LAUGHINGSTOCK [6]
laughingstock, 8468, *ś^{e}ḥôq* [3]
laughingstock, 997, *bûz^{2}* [1]
laughingstock, 7842, *qallāsâ* [1]
laughingstock, 9067, *šimṣâ* [1]

LAUGHS [6]
laughs, 8471, *śāḥaq* [6]

LAUGHTER [9]
laughter, 8468, *ś^{e}ḥôq* [7]
shout with laughter, 6600, *ʿālaz* [1]
laughter, 7465, *ṣ^{e}ḥôq* [1]

LAUNCH [1]
launch, 2725, *ḥālal^{1}* [1]

LAUNDERER'S [1]
launderer's, 3891, *kābas* [1]

LAVISHED [4]
lavished, 8049, *rābâ^{1}* [1]
lavished on, 8115, *rāwâ* [1]
lavished, 9161, *šāpak* [1]

lavished, 10314, yehab [1]

LAW [195]
law, 9368, tôrâ [168]
law, 10186, dāt [7]
law, 2017, dāt [6]
law, 5477, mišpāṭ [5]
law, *NIH/RPE* [2]
law, 5184, miṣwâ [2]
my law[s], 2023, -āh [1]
law, 2976, ḥōq [1]
matters of law, 9368, tôrâ [1]
teaching of law, 9368, tôrâ [1]
teaching of the law, 9368, tôrâ [1]

LAWGIVER [1]
lawgiver, 2980, ḥāqaq [1]

LAWLESS [1]
lawless, 5572, nābāl[1] [1]

LAWS [111]
laws, 5477, mišpāṭ [83]
laws, 9368, tôrâ [16]
laws, 10186, dāt [4]
laws, 2017, dāt [2]
laws, 2976, ḥōq [1]
fixed laws, 2978, ḥuqqâ [1]
laws, 2978, ḥuqqâ [1]
make laws, 2980+2976, ḥāqaq+ḥōq [1]
make laws, 2980, ḥāqaq [1]
laws, 5184, miṣwâ [1]

LAWSUIT [2]
lawsuit, 8190, rîb[2] [2]

LAWSUITS [3]
lawsuits, 1907+4200+1907, dîn[2]+le-[1]+dîn[2] [1]
lawsuits, 5477, mišpāṭ [1]
lawsuits, 8190, rîb[2] [1]

LAX [1]
lax, 8244, remiyyâ[1] [1]

LAY [142]
lay, 6164, sāmak [17]
lay down, 8886, šākab [13]
lay, 8938, šālaḥ [11]
lay, 8492, śîm [8]
lay, 8886, šākab [8]
lay with, 995+448, bô'+'el [7]
lay, 5989, nātan [6]
lay, *NIH/RPE* [5]
lay with, 3359, yāda' [4]
lay waste, 9037, šāmēm[1] [4]
lay, 2118, hāyâ [3]
lay siege, 7443, ṣûr[1] [3]
lay, *AIT* [2]
lay in wait, 741, 'ārab [2]
lay people, 1201+6639, bēn[1]+'am[2] [2]
lay, 5877, nāpal [2]
lay down, 8069, rābaṣ [2]
lay, 8883, šît[1] [2]
lay with, 8886+6640, šākab+'im [2]
lay with, 8886+907, šākab+'ēt[2] [2]
lay hold, 9461, tāmak [2]
lay waste, 1327, bāqaq[1] [1]
lay bare, 1655, gālâ [1]
lay wallowing, 1670, gālal[1] [1]
lay hold, 2616, ḥāzaq [1]
lay ill, 2703, ḥālâ[1] [1]
lay waste, 2990, ḥārēb[1] [1]
lay bare, 3106, ḥāśap[1] [1]
lay, 3528, yālad [1]
lay foundations, 3569, yāsad[1] [1]
lay, 3569, yāsad[1] [1]
lay, 3655, yāṣā' [1]
lay, 3667, yāṣa' [1]
lay in wait, 3782, yāšab [1]
lay eggs, 4880, mālaṭ[1] [1]
lay hold, 5162, māṣā' [1]
lay on, 5162, māṣā' [1]
lay, 5447, mišlôaḥ [1]
lay to rest, 5663, nûaḥ[1] [1]
lay, 5663, nûaḥ[1] [1]
lay, 5742, nāṭâ [1]
lay prostrate, 5877, nāpal [1]
lay in ruins, 5997, nātaṣ [1]
lay aside, 6073, sûr[1] [1]
lay out, 6885, 'ārak [1]
lay, 6885, 'ārak [1]
lay down, 7579, ṣā'â [1]
lay siege, 7674, ṣārar[1] [1]
where lay, 8070, rēbeṣ [1]
lay fast asleep, 8101, rādam [1]
lay up, 8492, śîm [1]
lay down to sleep, 8886, šākab [1]
lay snares, 8938, šālaḥ [1]
lay low, 9164, šāpēl[1] [1]
lay, 9189, šāpat [1]
lay claim, 9286, šātat [1]

LAYER [2]
layer of fat, 4833, mekasseh [1]
layer, 8887, šikbâ [1]

LAYING [2]
laying, *NIH/RPE* [2]

LAYS [8]
lays bare, 2200, hāpak [1]
lays the foundation, 3569, yāsad[1] [1]
lays up, 3922, kûn[1] [1]
lays, 5663, nûaḥ[1] [1]
lays, 6440, 'āzab[1] [1]
lays beams, 7936, qārâ[1] [1]
lays, 8938, šālaḥ [1]
lays low, 9164, šāpēl[1] [1]

LAZINESS [2]
laziness, 6790, 'aṣlâ [1]
laziness, 8244, remiyyâ[1] [1]

LAZY [7]
lazy, 8332, rāpâ[1] [3]
lazy, 8244, remiyyâ[1] [2]
lazy, 4206, lā'â [1]
lazy, 6792, 'aṣaltayim [1]

LEAD [71]
lead, 5697, nāḥâ[1] [11]
lead, 6769, 'ōperet [9]
lead, 2143, hālak [4]
lead out, 3655, yāṣā' [3]
lead, 5627, nāhag[1] [3]
lead, 9149, šāpaṭ [3]
lead astray, 9494, tā'â [3]
lead down, 3718, yārad [2]
lead to inherit, 5706, nāḥal [2]
lead, *NIH/RPE* [2]
lead on, 339+3870, 'aḥar+-kā [1]
lead life, 928+2143, be-+hālak [1]
lead, 995, bô' [1]
lead, 2005, dārak [1]
lead, 2143+4200+7156, hālak+le-[1]+pāneh [1]
lead to do the same[s], 2388+339+466+2177, zānâ[1]+'aḥar+'elōhîm+-hēn[2] [1]
lead into sin, 2627, ḥāṭā' [1]
lead astray, 3246, ṭā'â [1]
lead, 3655+2256+995, yāṣā'+we-+bô' [1]
lead, 3655+4200+7156+2256+995, yāṣā'+le-[1]+pāneh+we-+bô' [1]
follow lead, 4027+6913, kēn[2]+'āśâ[1] [1]
lead to, 4200, le-[1] [1]
lead, 4200+7156, le-[1]+pāneh [1]
lead the way, 5432, māšak [1]
lead, 5466, mišmeret [1]
lead on, 5627+2256+2143, nāhag[1]+we-+hālak [1]
lead away, 5627, nāhag[1] [1]
lead, 5633, nāhal [1]
lead out, 5697, nāḥâ[1] [1]
lead, 5742, nāṭâ [1]
lead across, 6296+4200+7156, 'ābar[1]+le-[1]+pāneh [1]
lead, 6590, 'ālâ [1]
lead, 7156, pāneh [1]
take the lead, 7276, pāra'[1] [1]
lead to righteousness, 7405, ṣādaq [1]
lead, 8037, ri'šôn [1]
one in the lead, 8037, ri'šôn [1]
lead, 8206, rākab [1]
lead, 8286, rā'â[1] [1]
lead straight, 9461, tāmak [1]

LEADER [79]
leader, 5954, nāśî'[1] [43]
leader, 5592, nāgîd [13]
leader, 8569, śar [8]
leader, 8031, rō'š[1] [6]
leader, 2143+4200+7156, hālak+le-[1]+pāneh [2]
leader, 7903, qāṣîn [2]
leader, 129, 'addîr [1]
leader, 5893, nāṣab[1] [1]
chief leader, 5954+5954, nāśî'[1]+nāśî'[1] [1]
leader, 6584, 'al[2] [1]
leader, 9149, šāpaṭ [1]

LEADER'S [1]
leader's, 2980, ḥāqaq [1]

LEADERS [109]
leaders, 5954, nāśî'[1] [30]
leaders, 8569, śar [29]
leaders, 8031, rō'š[1] [19]
leaders, 129, 'addîr [3]
leaders, 477, 'allûp[2] [3]
leaders, 9149, šāpaṭ [3]
leaders, 2418, zāqēn[2] [2]
leaders, 6966, 'attûd [2]
leaders, 7157, pinnâ [2]
leaders, 380, 'ayil[1] [1]
leaders, 408+8031, 'îš[1]+rō'š[1] [1]
leaders, 722, 'āṣîl[2] [1]
leaders, 1475, gibbôr [1]
leaders, 1524, gādôl [1]
military leaders, 2657, ḥayil [1]
their leaders[s], 4392, -ām [1]
leaders, 4938, mimšāl [1]
leaders, 5592, nāgîd [1]
leaders, 5817, nāsîk[2] [1]
leaders, 7278, pera'[1] [1]
leaders, 7903, qāṣîn [1]
leaders, 8031+6639, rō'š[1]+'am[2] [1]
leaders, 8040, rē'šît [1]
leaders, 8286, rā'â[1] [1]
leaders, 10646, rē'š [1]

LEADERSHIP [2]
leadership, 3338, yād [1]
place of leadership, 7213, pequddâ [1]

LEADING [25]
leading, 4200+7156, le-[1]+pāneh [3]
leading, 8569, śar [3]
leading men, 380, 'ayil[1] [2]
leading, 2418, zāqēn[2] [2]
leading, 8031, rō'š[1] [2]
leading, *AIT* [1]
leading, 1524, gādôl [1]
leading, 1844, dādâ [1]
leading, 2143, hālak [1]
leading, 3359, yāda' [1]
leading down, 3718, yārad [1]
leading into, 4200+7023, le-[1]+peh [1]
leading into, 4200, le-[1] [1]
leading to, 4200, le-[1] [1]
leading to, 6590, 'ālâ [1]
leading men, 8031, rō'š[1] [1]
leading, 8097, rādâ[1] [1]
leading, 9149, šāpaṭ [1]

LEADS [23]
leads astray, 9494, tā'â [4]
leads to, 4200, le-[1] [3]
leads away, 2143, hālak [2]
leads, *NIH/RPE* [1]
leads, 928+2021+8037, be-+ha-+ri'šôn [1]
leads to, 2006, derek [1]
leads, 2006, derek [1]
leads a life, 2143, hālak [1]
leads, 2143, hālak [1]
leads forth, 3655, yāṣā' [1]
gently leads, 5633, nāhal [1]
leads, 5633, nāhal [1]
leads to, 6584, 'al[2] [1]
leads to evil, 8317, rā'a'[1] [1]
leads astray, 8706, šāgâ [1]

leads, 8706, *šāgâ* [1]
leads down, 8755, *šûaḥ*^{1} [1]

LEAF [6]
leaf, 6591, *ʿāleh* [5]
green leaf, 6591, *ʿāleh* [1]

LEAFY [4]
leafy, 6290, *ʿābôt*^{1} [3]
leafy boughs, 6997, *pōʾrâ* [1]

LEAH [29]
Leah, 4207, *lēʾâ* [28]
Leah^{s}, 2296, *zeh* [1]

LEAH'S [5]
Leah's, 4207, *lēʾâ* [5]

LEAKS [1]
leaks, 1940, *dālap*^{1} [1]

LEAN [7]
lean, 9128, *šāʿan* [3]
lean, 8369, *raq*^{1} [2]
lean, 8136, *rāzeh* [1]
lean, 8369+1414, *raq*^{1}*+bāśār* [1]

LEANED [3]
leaned, 9128, *šāʿan* [2]
worshiped leaned, 2556, *ḥāwâ*^{2} [1]

LEANING [5]
leaning, 9128, *šāʿan* [3]
leaning, 5742, *nāṭâ* [1]
leaning, 8345, *rāpaq* [1]

LEANNOTH [1]
leannoth, 4361, *l*^{e}*ʿannôt* [1]

LEANS [4]
leans, 6164, *sāmak* [2]
leans, 2616, *ḥāzaq* [1]
leans, 9128, *šāʿan* [1]

LEAP [5]
leap, 1925, *dālag* [1]
leap, 7055, *pûš*^{1} [1]
make leap, 8321, *rāʿaš*^{1} [1]
leap about, 8376, *rāqad* [1]
leap, 8376, *rāqad* [1]

LEAPED [1]
leaped to feet, 10624, *qûm* [1]

LEAPING [2]
leaping, 1925, *dālag* [1]
leaping, 7060, *pāzaz*^{2} [1]

LEAPS [2]
leaps, 6001, *nātar*^{2} [1]
leaps for joy, 6600, *ʿālaz* [1]

LEARN [28]
learn, 4340, *lāmad* [15]
learn, 3359, *yādaʿ* [6]
learn, 544, *ʾālap*^{1} [1]
learn the difference between, 3359, *yādaʿ* [1]
learn well, 4340+4340, *lāmad+lāmad* [1]
learn, 4374, *lāqaḥ* [1]
learn, 5583, *nāgad* [1]
learn prudence, 6891, *ʿāram*^{2} [1]
learn, 9048, *šāmaʿ* [1]

LEARNED [24]
learned, 3359, *yādaʿ* [9]
learned, 8011, *rāʾâ*^{1} [4]
learned, 4340, *lāmad* [3]
learned, 1067, *bîn* [1]
what learned, 2984, *ḥēqer* [1]
learned about, 3359, *yādaʿ* [1]
learned, 4374, *lāqaḥ* [1]
learned, 5583+4200, *nāgad+l*$^{e-1}$ [1]
learned by divination, 5727, *nāḥaš* [1]
man learned, 6221, *sōpēr* [1]
learned, 10313, *y*^{e}*daʿ* [1]

LEARNING [8]
learning, 4375, *leqaḥ* [3]
learning, 2683, *ḥokmâ* [2]
learning, 1067, *bîn* [1]
learning, 1981, *daʿat*^{1} [1]
learning, 3359, *yādaʿ* [1]

LEARNS [2]
learns, 3359, *yādaʿ* [2]

LEASH [1]
put on a leash, 8003, *qāšar* [1]

LEAST [23]
least, 7783, *qāṭān*^{1} [9]
least, 7785, *qāṭōn*^{2} [7]
least, 7582, *ṣāʿîr*^{1} [2]
least, 344, *ʾaḥ*^{a}*rît* [1]
had the least inkling, 3359+3359,
yādaʿ+yādaʿ [1]
benefit in the least, 3603+3603, *yāʿal+yāʿal* [1]
at least, 3954, *kî*^{2} [1]
least, 4394, *m*^{e}*ʾōd* [1]

LEATHER [15]
leather, 6425, *ʿôr* [14]
leather, 9391, *taḥaš*^{1} [1]

LEAVE [157]
leave, 6440, *ʿāzab*^{1} [28]
leave, 3655, *yāṣāʾ* [24]
leave, 5663, *nûaḥ*^{1} [11]
leave, 2143, *hālak* [7]
leave, 8636, *šāʾar* [7]
leave, 6073, *sûr*^{1} [6]
leave, 2118, *hāyâ* [4]
leave alone, 5663, *nûaḥ*^{1} [4]
leave, 8332, *rāpâ*^{1} [4]
leave, 2143+4946, *hālak+min* [3]
leave alive, 2649, *ḥāyâ* [3]
leave, 3718+4946, *yārad+min* [3]
leave, 3855, *yātar* [3]
leave, 4631, *mûš*^{2} [3]
leave, 5759, *nāṭaš* [3]
leave the guilty unpunished, 5927+5927,
nāqâ+nāqâ [3]
leave, 2143+4946+907, *hālak+min+ʾēt*^{2} [2]
leave alone, 6073+4946, *sûr*^{1}*+min* [2]
leave alive, 8636, *šāʾar* [2]
leave childless, 8897, *šākal* [2]
leave, 10697, *š*^{e}*baq* [2]
leave, *NIH/RPE* [1]
leave, 928, *b*^{e}*-* [1]
leave at once, 1368, *bāraḥ*^{1} [1]
leave, 1750, *gāram*^{1} [1]
leave, 2143+4946+6640, *hālak+min+ʿim* [1]
leave, 2143+4946+6643,
hālak+min+ʿimmād [1]
surely leave, 2143+2143+4946+6584,
hālak+hālak+min+ʿal^{2} [1]
leave alone, 2532+4946, *ḥādal*^{1}*+min* [1]
have leave, 3655, *yāṣāʾ* [1]
leave behind, 3657, *yāṣag* [1]
leave, 3657, *yāṣag* [1]
leave, 3718+4946+9348, *yārad+min+tāwek* [1]
leave as an inheritance, 3769, *yāraš*^{1} [1]
leave, 3856, *yeter*^{1} [1]
leave no, 4162, *kārat* [1]
leave overnight, 4328, *lîn* [1]
leave, 4946+2143, *min+hālak* [1]
leave, 4946+9004, *min+šām* [1]
leave, 4946, *min* [1]
leave, 5674, *nûs* [1]
leave, 5989, *nātan* [1]
leave, 6015+4946, *sābab+min* [1]
make leave, 6073, *sûr*^{1} [1]
leave, 6590+4946, *ʿālâ+min* [1]
leave alone, 6641+4946, *ʿāmad+min* [1]
leave the honor, 6995, *pāʾar*^{2} [1]
leave, 7629, *ṣāpar* [1]
leave, 7756+4946, *qûm+min* [1]
leave alone, 8332, *rāpâ*^{1} [1]
leave, 8697, *šābat*^{1} [1]
leave, 8938, *šālaḥ* [1]

LEAVENED [1]
leavened bread, 2809, *ḥāmēṣ*^{4} [1]

LEAVES [24]
leaves, 6591, *ʿāleh* [7]
leaves, 10564, *ʿ*^{o}*pî* [3]
leaves, 1946, *delet* [2]
leaves, 6440, *ʿāzab*^{1} [2]
leaves, *NIH/RPE* [1]
leaves glistening, 239, *ʾôr*^{1} [1]
leaves behind, 339, *ʾaḥar* [1]
leaves, 2143+4946+907, *hālak+min+ʾēt*^{2} [1]
leaves, 3655, *yāṣāʾ* [1]
leaves, 4200, *l*$^{e-1}$ [1]
leaves an inheritance, 5706, *nāḥal* [1]
drop leaves, 5850, *nāʿar*^{2} [1]
leaves, 7521, *ṣēlāʿ*^{1} [1]
leaves empty, 8197, *rîq*^{1} [1]

LEAVING [21]
leaving, 8636, *šāʾar* [5]
leaving, 3655, *yāṣāʾ* [4]
leaving, *NIH/RPE* [3]
leaving, 8492, *śîm* [2]
leaving, 2143, *hālak* [1]
leaving, 3855, *yātar* [1]
leaving white, 4235, *lāban*^{1} [1]
leaving, 5825+4946, *nāsaʿ+min* [1]
leaving, 6296+4946, *ʿābar*^{1}*+min* [1]
leaving a trail, 8331, *rāpad* [1]
leaving, 10708, *š*^{e}*kaḥ* [1]

LEB KAMAI [1]
Leb Kamai, 4214, *lēb qāmāy* [1]

LEBANA [1]
Lebana, 4245, *l*^{e}*bānâ*^{2} [1]

LEBANAH [1]
Lebanah, 4245, *l*^{e}*bānâ*^{2} [1]

LEBANON [70]
Lebanon, 4248, *l*^{e}*bānôn* [68]
cedar of Lebanon, 4248, *l*^{e}*bānôn* [2]

LEBAOTH [1]
Lebaoth, 4219, *l*^{e}*bāʾôt* [1]

LEBO HAMATH [12]
Lebo Hamath, 4217, *l*^{e}*bōʾ ḥ*^{a}*māt* [12]

LEBONAH [1]
Lebonah, 4228, *l*^{e}*bônâ* [1]

LECAH [1]
Lecah, 4336, *lēkâ* [1]

LED [114]
led, 2143, *hālak* [14]
led, 9149, *šāpaṭ* [12]
led, 5697, *nāḥâ*^{1} [6]
led up, 6590, *ʿālâ* [6]
led astray, 9494, *tāʿâ* [6]
led out, 3655, *yāṣāʾ* [3]
led, 5627, *nāhag*^{1} [3]
led, 6296, *ʿābar*^{1} [3]
led, *NIH/RPE* [2]
led by, 928+8031, *b*^{e}*-+rōʾš*^{1} [2]
led, 995, *bôʾ* [2]
led into sin, 2627, *ḥāṭāʾ* [2]
led in campaigns, 3655+2256+995+4200+7156,
yāṣāʾ+w^{e}*-+bôʾ+l*$^{e-1}$*+pāneh* [2]
led on military campaigns, 3655+2256+995,
yāṣāʾ+w^{e}*-+bôʾ* [2]
led, 3655, *yāṣāʾ* [2]
led away, 4374, *lāqaḥ* [2]
led astray, 5615, *nādaḥ*^{1} [2]
led around, 6015, *sābab* [2]
led through, 6296, *ʿābar*^{1} [2]
led astray, 8706, *šāgâ* [2]
led, *AIT* [1]
led, 339+2143, *ʾaḥar+hālak* [1]
led life, 928+2143, *b*^{e}*-+hālak* [1]
led into, 995, *bôʾ* [1]
led to believe, 1053, *bāṭaḥ*^{1} [1]
are led astray, 1182, *bālaʿ*^{3} [1]
led captive, 1655, *gālâ* [1]
led, 2005, *dārak* [1]
led to prostitute themselves, 2388, *zānâ*^{1} [1]
are led in, 3297, *yābal* [1]

be led forth, 3297, *yābal* [1]
is led, 3297, *yābal* [1]
led, 3297, *yābal* [1]
was led, 3297, *yābal* [1]
led the way, 3338+2118+8037, *yād+hāyâ+riʾšōn* [1]
led out, 3655+4200+7156, *yāṣāʾ+l^{e}-[1]+pāneh* [1]
led down, 3718, *yārad* [1]
led to downfall, 3948, *kāḥad* [1]
led to, 4200, *l^{e}-[1]* [1]
led, 4200+7156, *l^{e}-[1]+pāneh* [1]
being led away, 4374, *lāqaḥ* [1]
led, 5432, *māšak* [1]
led forth, 5627, *nāhag[1]* [1]
led in triumphal procession, 5627, *nāhag[1]* [1]
led out, 5627, *nāhag[1]* [1]
led astray, 5742+4213, *nāṭâ+lēb* [1]
led astray, 5742, *nāṭâ* [1]
led, 5825, *nāsaʿ* [1]
led astray, 6073, *sûr[1]* [1]
led, 6268, *ʿābad* [1]
led around, 6296, *ʿābar[1]* [1]
led to, 6330, *ʿad[2]* [1]
conspiracy led, 8004+8003, *qešer+qāšar* [1]
led on horseback, 8206, *rākab* [1]
led in train, 8647, *šābâ* [1]
led in thanksgiving, 9378+3344, *t^{e}hillâ+yādâ[2]* [1]
led, 10638, *q^{e}rēb* [1]

LEDGE [10]
ledge, 6478, *ʿ^{a}zārâ* [6]
ledge, 4136, *karkōb* [2]
ledge of stone, 3215, *ṭûr* [1]
ledge, 3227, *ṭîrâ* [1]

LEDGES [2]
ledges, 995, *bôʾ* [1]
offset ledges, 4492, *migrāʿôt* [1]

LEECH [1]
leech, 6598, *ʿ^{a}lûqâ* [1]

LEEKS [1]
leeks, 2946, *ḥāṣîr[2]* [1]

LEFT [417]
left, 8636, *šāʾar* [52]
left, 8520, *ś^{e}mōʾl* [45]
left, 5825, *nāsaʿ* [43]
left, 3655, *yāṣāʾ* [38]
left, 2143, *hālak* [32]
left, 3855, *yātar* [24]
left, *NIH/RPE* [22]
left, 6440, *ʿāzab[1]* [19]
left over, 3855, *yātar* [6]
left behind, 8636, *šāʾar* [6]
left, 2118, *hāyâ* [5]
left, 2143+4946, *hālak+min* [5]
left, 3856, *yeter[1]* [5]
left, 5663, *nûaḥ[1]* [5]
left, *AIT* [4]
left, 2143+4946+907, *hālak+min+ʾēt[2]* [4]
left, 5759, *nāṭaš* [4]
left, 6073, *sûr[1]* [4]
left, 344, *ʾaḥ^{a}rît* [3]
left, 3782, *yāšab* [3]
be left, 3855, *yātar* [3]
left, 7756+4946, *qûm+min* [3]
to the left, 8521, *śimʾēl* [3]
left, 8522, *ś^{e}māʾlî* [3]
left, 995+4946, *bôʾ+min* [2]
left[s], 2178, *hēnnâ[1]* [2]
had left over, 3855, *yātar* [2]
left of, 4946, *min* [2]
left, 5989, *nātan* [2]
left, 6369, *ʿādap* [2]
left, 6388, *ʿôd* [2]
left, 7155, *pānâ* [2]
left, 8586, *śārîd[1]* [2]
have left, 8636, *šāʾar* [2]
left, 8740, *šûb[1]* [2]
left, 10692, *š^{e}ʾār* [2]
left, 2118+4200, *hāyâ+l^{e}-[1]* [1]
left, 2143+4946+6640, *hālak+min+ʿim* [1]
left, 2200, *hāpak* [1]
left in ruins, 2238, *hāras* [1]
left, 2811, *ḥāmaq* [1]
left deserted, 2990, *ḥārēb[1]* [1]
left, 3655+3655, *yāṣāʾ+yāṣāʾ* [1]
left behind, 3782, *yāšab* [1]
are left, 3855, *yātar* [1]
be left alive, 3855, *yātar* [1]
been left alive, 3855, *yātar* [1]
had some left over, 3855, *yātar* [1]
have left over, 3855, *yātar* [1]
was left, 3855, *yātar* [1]
little left, 3856+7129+8636, *yeter[1]+p^{e}lêṭâ+šāʾar* [1]
left, 4328, *lîn* [1]
left place, 4631, *mûš[2]* [1]
left, 4946+339, *min+ʾaḥar* [1]
left, 4946+907, *min+ʾēt[2]* [1]
left, 4946, *min* [1]
left unweighed, 5663, *nûaḥ[1]* [1]
left, 5697, *nāḥâ[1]* [1]
left, 5825+4946, *nāsaʿ+min* [1]
left, 5877, *nāpal* [1]
be left, 5989, *nātan* [1]
was left hanging, 5989, *nātan* [1]
left undone, 6073, *sûr[1]* [1]
left over, 6369, *ʿādap* [1]
left, 6372, *ʿādar[3]* [1]
left now, 6388, *ʿôd* [1]
be left, 6440, *ʿāzab[1]* [1]
left behind, 6440, *ʿāzab[1]* [1]
left destitute, 6440, *ʿāzab[1]* [1]
left, 6590+4946, *ʿālâ+min* [1]
left, 7233, *pārad* [1]
left instructions, 7422, *ṣāwâ* [1]
left, 7756+4946+9348, *qûm+min+tāwek* [1]
left, 7756, *qûm* [1]
left, 8492, *śîm* [1]
go to the left, 8521, *śimʾēl* [1]
left, 8572, *śārad* [1]
men who were left, 8586, *śārîd[1]* [1]
left alone, 8636, *šāʾar* [1]
left survivor, 8636, *šāʾar* [1]
left, 8642, *š^{e}ʾērît* [1]
left without, 8697, *šābat[1]* [1]
left to himself, 8938, *šālaḥ* [1]
was left so desolate, 9037, *šāmēm[1]* [1]
left, 9200, *šāqaṭ* [1]
left, 9582, *t^{e}šûmâ* [1]
will be left with, 10029+10378, *ʾîtay+l^{e}-* [1]
be left, 10697, *š^{e}baq* [1]

LEFT-HANDED [3]
left-handed, 360+3338+3545, *ʾiṭṭēr+yād+yāmîn[1]* [2]
left-handed, 8521, *śimʾēl* [1]

LEFTOVER [1]
leftover grain, 8672, *šibbōlet[1]* [1]

LEG [3]
leg, 3751, *yārēk* [1]
leg bones, 4157, *keraʿ* [1]
leg, 8797, *šôq* [1]

LEGAL [2]
legal, 5477, *mišpāṭ* [2]

LEGALIZING [1]
method of legalizing transactions, 9496, *t^{e}ʿûdâ* [1]

LEGS [24]
legs, 4157, *keraʿ* [8]
legs, 8079, *regel* [6]
legs, 8797, *šôq* [5]
legs, 3751, *yārēk* [1]
legs, 5274, *marg^{e}lôt* [1]
legs, 9393, *taḥat[1]* [1]
legs, 10626+10284, *q^{e}ṭar+ḥ^{a}raṣ* [1]
legs, 10741, *šāq* [1]

LEHABITES [2]
Lehabites, 4260, *l^{e}hābîm* [2]

LEHI [4]
Lehi, 4306, *leḥî[2]* [4]

LEMUEL [2]
Lemuel, 4345, *l^{e}mûʾēl* [2]

LEND [10]
lend, 4278, *lāwâ[2]* [4]
lend, 5989, *nātan* [2]
lend, 2118, *hāyâ* [1]
lend freely, 4278, *lāwâ[2]* [1]
freely lend, 6292+6292, *ʿābaṭ[1]+ʿābaṭ[1]* [1]
lend, 6292, *ʿābaṭ[1]* [1]

LENDER [2]
lender, 4278, *lāwâ[2]* [2]

LENDING [1]
lending, 5957, *nāšāʾ[1]* [1]

LENDS [4]
lends, 5989, *nātan* [2]
lends freely, 4278, *lāwâ[2]* [1]
lends, 4278, *lāwâ[2]* [1]

LENGTH [25]
length, 802, *ʾōrek* [12]
length, *NIH/RPE* [1]
length of cord, 2475, *ḥebel[2]* [1]
length, 2475, *ḥebel[2]* [1]
length of days, 3427+9102, *yôm[1]+šānâ[2]* [1]
adds length, 3578, *yāsap* [1]
length, 4200+6645, *l^{e}-[1]+ʿummâ[1]* [1]
length, 4500, *middâ[1]* [1]
length of time, 4632, *môšāb* [1]
length, 4850, *m^{e}lōʾ* [1]
length, 5031, *mispār[1]* [1]
length, 6245, *seraḥ* [1]
length, 7757, *qômâ* [1]
length, 8145, *rōḥab* [1]

LENGTHEN [2]
lengthen, 799, *ʾārak* [2]

LENGTHS [2]
lengths, 2475, *ḥebel[2]* [1]
lengths, 7757, *qômâ* [1]

LENGTHWISE [1]
lengthwise, 802, *ʾōrek* [1]

LENT [1]
lent, 5957, *nāšāʾ[1]* [1]

LENTIL [1]
lentil, 6378, *ʿ^{a}dāšîm* [1]

LENTILS [3]
lentils, 6378, *ʿ^{a}dāšîm* [3]

LEOPARD [5]
leopard, 5807, *nāmēr* [4]
leopard, 10480, *n^{e}mar* [1]

LEOPARDS [2]
leopards, 5807, *nāmēr* [2]

LEPROSY [15]
had leprosy, 7665, *ṣāraʿ* [6]
leprosy, 7669, *ṣāraʿat* [5]
leprosy, 7665, *ṣāraʿ* [4]

LEPROUS [5]
leprous, 7665, *ṣāraʿ* [4]
leprous, 7669, *ṣāraʿat* [1]

LESHEM [2]
Leshem, 4386, *lešem[2]* [2]

LESS [15]
how much less, 677+3954, *ʾap[1]+kî[2]* [6]
less than, 4946, *min* [2]
how much less, 677+3954+4202, *ʾap[1]+kî[2]+lōʾ* [1]
number is less than, 2893, *ḥāsēr[1]* [1]
punished less, 3104+4200+4752, *ḥāśak+l^{e}-[1]+maṭṭâ* [1]
less, 4752, *maṭṭâ* [1]
no less than, 5070, *māʿaṭ* [1]
give less, 5070, *māʿaṭ* [1]
less meaning, 8049+2039, *rābâ[1]+hebel[1]* [1]

LESSER [2]
lesser, 7783, *qāṭān*[1] [1]
lesser, 7785, *qāṭōn*[2] [1]

LESSON [4]
lesson, 4592, *mûsār* [2]
lesson, 1821, *dābār* [1]
taught a lesson, 3359, *yāda'* [1]

LEST [9]
lest, 7153, *pen* [8]
lest, 889+4202, *'a^{š}er+lō'* [1]

LET [839]*
let, *AIT* [635]
let, *NIH/RPE* [22]

LET'S [38]
let's, *AIT* [38]

LETHEK [1]
lethek, 4390, *lētek* [1]

LETS [6]
lets, *NIH/RPE* [1]
lets happen, 628+4200+3338, *'ānâ*[2]*+l^{e}*[-1]*+yād* [1]
lets warm, 2801, *ḥāmam* [1]
lets be known, 3359, *yāda'* [1]
lets loose, 8938, *šālaḥ* [1]
lets stray, 8938, *šālaḥ* [1]

LETTER [27]
letter, 6219, *sēper*[1] [12]
letter, 115, *'iggeret* [4]
letter, 5981, *nište^{w}ān* [4]
letter, 10007, *'igg^{e}râ* [3]
letter, *NIH/RPE* [2]
letter, 4181, *k^{e}tāb* [1]
letter, 4844, *miktāb* [1]

LETTERS [16]
letters, 6219, *sēper*[1] [10]
letters, 115, *'iggeret* [6]

LETTING [4]
letting know, 3359, *yāda'* [1]
letting run down, 3718, *yārad* [1]
letting go, 8938, *šālaḥ* [1]
letting range free, 8938+8079, *šālaḥ+regel* [1]

LETUSHITES [1]
Letushites, 4322, *l^{e}ṭûšîm* [1]

LEUMMITES [1]
Leummites, 4212, *l^{e}'ummîm* [1]

LEVEL [13]
level ground, 4793, *mîšôr* [2]
level, 4793, *mîšôr* [2]
level, *AIT* [1]
level, 3837, *yāšar* [1]
level, 3838, *yāšār*[1] [1]
at each successive level, 4200+5087+2025+4200+5087+2025, *l^{e}*[-1]*+ma'al*[2]*+-â*[2]*+l^{e}*[-1]*+ma'al*[2]*+-â*[2] [1]
level, 4797, *mêšārîm* [1]
level, 5595, *nāga'* [1]
level, 5737, *nāḥat* [1]
make level, 7142, *pālas*[1] [1]
level, 7193, *pa'am* [1]

LEVELED [3]
leveled completely, 928+2021+9168+9164, *b^{e}-+ha-+šiplâ+šāpēl*[1] [1]
be leveled, 6910+6910, *'ārar+'ārar* [1]
leveled, 8750, *šāwâ*[1] [1]

LEVELS [3]
levels, *AIT* [1]
levels, *NIH/RPE* [1]
levels, 9164, *šāpēl*[1] [1]

LEVI [47]
Levi, 4290, *lēwî*[1] [42]
Levi, 4291, *lēwî*[2] [5]

LEVIATHAN [6]
leviathan, 4293, *liwyātān* [6]

LEVITE [28]
Levite, 4291, *lēwî*[2] [26]
Levite, 4290, *lēwî*[1] [2]

LEVITES [281]
Levites, 4291, *lēwî*[2] [245]
Levites, 1201+4290, *bēn*[1]*+lēwî*[1] [15]
Levites, *NIH/RPE* [5]
Levites, 10387, *lēwāy* [4]
Levites, 1201+4291, *bēn*[1]*+lēwî*[2] [3]
the Levites[s], 4392, *-ām* [3]
Levites, 4290, *lēwî*[1] [2]
fellow Levites, 278, *'āḥ*[2] [1]
the Levites[s], 2157, *-hem* [1]
Levites, 4751+4290, *maṭṭeh+lēwî*[1] [1]
Levites, 5476+4291, *mišpāḥâ+lēwî*[2] [1]

LEVITICAL [2]
Levitical, 4291, *lēwî*[2] [2]

LEVY [2]
imposed a levy, 6740, *'ānaš* [1]
levy, 6741, *'ōneš* [1]

LEWD [4]
lewd, 2365, *zimmâ*[1] [2]
lewd acts, 2365, *zimmâ*[1] [1]
lewd act, 2365, *zimmâ*[1] [1]

LEWDNESS [10]
lewdness, 2365, *zimmâ*[1] [6]
consequences of lewdness, 2365, *zimmâ*[1] [2]
penalty for lewdness, 2365, *zimmâ*[1] [1]
lewdness, 5578, *nablût* [1]

LIABLE [2]
liable to, 4200, *l^{e}*[-1] [2]

LIAR [6]
liar, 9214, *šeqer* [2]
liar, 408+3942, *'îš*[1]*+kāzāb* [1]
considered a liar, 3941, *kāzab* [1]
prove a liar, 3941, *kāzab* [1]
liar, 8120+3941, *rûaḥ+kāzab* [1]

LIARS [4]
liars, 1819+9214, *dābar*[2]*+šeqer* [2]
liars, 3941, *kāzab* [1]
liars, 9214, *šeqer* [1]

LIBATIONS [1]
libations, 5821, *nesek*[1] [1]

LIBERALITY [2]
liberality, 3338, *yād* [2]

LIBERALLY [1]
supply liberally, 6735+6735, *'ānaq+'ānaq* [1]

LIBERTY [1]
liberty, 2002, *d^{e}rôr*[3] [1]

LIBNAH [17]
Libnah, 4243, *libnâ* [17]

LIBNI [5]
Libni, 4249, *libnî*[1] [5]

LIBNITE [1]
Libnite, 4250, *libnî*[2] [1]

LIBNITES [1]
Libnites, 4250, *libnî*[2] [1]

LIBYA [2]
Libya, 4275, *lûb* [2]

LIBYANS [4]
Libyans, 4275, *lûb* [3]
Libyans, 7033, *pûṭ* [1]

LICK [6]
lick, 4308, *lāḥak* [3]
lick up, 430, *'ākal* [1]
lick up, 4308, *lāḥak* [1]
lick up, 4379, *lāqaq* [1]

LICKED [3]
licked up, 4379, *lāqaq* [2]
licked up, 4308, *lāḥak* [1]

LICKS [1]
licks up, 4308, *lāḥak* [1]

LID [2]
lid, 1946, *delet* [1]
lid, 7544, *ṣāmîd*[2] [1]

LIE [129]
lie down, 8886, *šākab* [20]
lie, 8886, *šākab* [18]
lie down, 8069, *rābaṣ* [11]
lie in wait, 741, *'ārab* [8]
lie, *AIT* [6]
lie, 2118, *hāyâ* [6]
lie, 3942, *kāzāb* [4]
lie with, 8886+6640, *šākab+'im* [4]
lie, 9214, *šeqer* [4]
lie, *NIH/RPE* [3]
lie with, 995+448, *bô'+'el* [3]
lie, 3941, *kāzab* [3]
lie fallen, 5877, *nāpal* [2]
lie in ruins, 5898, *nāṣâ*[2] [2]
lie, 8069, *rābaṣ* [2]
lie with, 448+7928, *'el+qārab* [1]
lie with, 448+995, *'el+bô'* [1]
lie with, 907+8886, *'ēt*[2]*+šākab* [1]
lie with, 995+6584, *bô'+'al*[2] [1]
lie, 1819+9214, *dābar*[2]*+šeqer* [1]
lie, 2093, *hāwâ*[2] [1]
lie, 2485, *ḥābaq* [1]
lie in ambush, 2675, *ḥākâ* [1]
lie, 3782, *yāšab* [1]
lie, 3942+1819, *kāzāb+dābar*[2] [1]
lie, 3950, *kāḥaš* [1]
lie all night, 4328, *lîn* [1]
lie in death, 5435, *miškāb* [1]
lie down, 5742, *nāṭâ* [1]
lie, 5877, *nāpal* [1]
make lie down, 5877, *nāpal* [1]
lie in wait, 7595, *ṣāpâ*[1] [1]
have lie down, 8069, *rābaṣ* [1]
makes lie down, 8069, *rābaṣ* [1]
lie still, 8101, *rādam* [1]
lie ruined, 8615, *šā'â*[1] [1]
lie, 8699, *šebet*[1] [1]
lie in wait, 8800, *šûr*[1] [1]
lie around, 8886, *šākab* [1]
lie in state, 8886+928+3883, *šākab+b^{e}-+kābôd*[1] [1]
made lie down, 8886, *šākab* [1]
lie down to rest, 8905, *šākan* [1]
lie, 8905, *šākan* [1]
lie unplowed, 9023, *šāmaṭ* [1]
lie, 9128, *šā'an* [1]
lie awake, 9193, *šāqad*[1] [1]
lie in wait, 9193, *šāqad*[1] [1]
lie, 9213, *šāqar* [1]

LIED [4]
lied, 3950, *kāḥaš* [3]
lied, 1819+3942, *dābar*[2]*+kāzāb* [1]

LIES [102]
lies, 9214, *šeqer* [21]
lies, *NIH/RPE* [11]
lies, 3942, *kāzāb* [11]
lies, 8886, *šākab* [7]
lies in wait, 741, *'ārab* [5]
lies, 3951, *kaḥaš* [4]
lies, 5327, *mirmâ*[1] [4]
lies desolate, 9037, *šāmēm*[1] [4]
lies, 1821+9214, *dābār+šeqer* [3]
lies, 8736, *šāw'* [3]
lies down, 8886, *šākab* [3]
lies with, 8886+907, *šākab+'ēt*[2] [3]
lies, *AIT* [2]
lies, 2118, *hāyâ* [2]
lies, 3782, *yāšab* [2]
lies with, 5435, *miškāb* [2]
lies, 609+9214, *'ēmer*[1]*+šeqer* [1]
lies, 1821+3942, *dābār+kāzāb* [1]
lies in ruins, 2990, *ḥārēb*[1] [1]

lies in wait, 3243, *ṭāman* [1]
lies, 3780, *yēš* [1]
lies, 3950, *kāḥaš* [1]
lies, 5162, *māšā'* [1]
lies heavily, 6164, *sāmak* [1]
lies down, 8069, *rābaṣ* [1]
lies, 8069, *rābaṣ* [1]
lies in ruins, 8720, *šādad* [1]
lies, 8736+1819, *šāw'+dābār*^{2} [1]
lies with, 8886+6640, *šākab+'im* [1]
lies with, 8886+8886+907, *šākab+šākab+'ēt*^{2} [1]
lies hushed, 9200, *šāqaṭ* [1]

LIFE [355]
life, 5883, *nepeš* [129]
life, 2644, *ḥay*^{1} [108]
life, 3427, *yôm*^{1} [17]
preserve life, 2649, *ḥāyâ* [12]
life, *NIH/RPE* [7]
life, 2006, *derek* [5]
save life, 2649, *ḥāyâ* [5]
life, 1414, *bāśār* [4]
restored to life, 2649, *ḥāyâ* [3]
life, 2652, *ḥayyâ*^{2} [3]
life, 2645, *ḥay*^{2} [2]
bring back to life, 2649, *ḥāyâ* [2]
came to life, 2649, *ḥāyâ* [2]
come to life, 2649, *ḥāyâ* [2]
preserves life, 2649, *ḥāyâ* [2]
precious life, 3495, *yāḥîd* [2]
takes life, 5782+5883, *nākâ+nepeš* [2]
for life, 6409, *'ôlām* [2]
life, *AIT* [1]
end of life, 344, *'aḥ^{a}rît* [1]
latter part of life, 344, *'aḥ^{a}rît* [1]
in the prime of life, 408, *'îš*^{1} [1]
my life, 638, *'^{a}nî* [1]
enjoy a long life, 799+3427, *'ārak+yôm*^{1} [1]
enjoy long life, 799+3427, *'ārak+yôm*^{1} [1]
lead life, 928+2143, *b^{e}-+hālak* [1]
led life, 928+2143, *b^{e}-+hālak* [1]
course of life, 2006, *derek* [1]
leads a life, 2143, *hālak* [1]
choose life, 2649, *ḥāyâ* [1]
bring to life, 2649, *ḥāyâ* [1]
brought back to life, 2649, *ḥāyâ* [1]
give life, 2649, *ḥāyâ* [1]
gives life, 2649, *ḥāyâ* [1]
preserved life, 2649, *ḥāyâ* [1]
restore life, 2649, *ḥāyâ* [1]
spare life, 2649, *ḥāyâ* [1]
life, 2698, *ḥeled* [1]
fleeting life, 2698, *ḥeled* [1]
my life, 3276, *-î* [1]
days of life, 3427, *yôm*^{1} [1]
life, 3427+889+2118, *yôm*^{1}*+'^{a}šer+hāyâ* [1]
span of life, 3427, *yôm*^{1} [1]
gave life, 3528, *yālad* [1]
for life, 3972+2021+3427, *kōl+ha-+yôm*^{1} [1]
long life, 4200+2021+2644, *l^{e}-*^{1}*+ha-+ḥay*^{1} [1]
for life, 4200+6409, *l^{e}-*^{1}*+'ôlām* [1]
life will not be worth living, 4200+4537+2644, *l^{e}-*^{1}*+mâ+ḥay*^{1} [1]
takes life, 4374, *lāqaḥ* [1]
lose life, 4637, *mût* [1]
new life, 4695, *miḥyâ* [1]
all life, 4946+6388, *min+'ôd* [1]
life span, 5031+3427, *mispār*^{1}*+yôm*^{1} [1]
life, 5893, *nāṣab*^{1} [1]
life, 5972, *n^{e}šāmâ* [1]
life, 6409, *'ôlām* [1]
do anything that endangers life, 6641+6584+1947, *'āmad+'al*^{2}*+dām* [1]
plant life, 6770, *'ēś* [1]
village life, 7251, *p^{e}rāzôn* [1]
come to life, 7810, *qîṣ* [1]
life breath, 8120+678, *rûaḥ+'ap*^{2} [1]
life, 8120, *rûaḥ* [1]
enjoyed long life, 8428+3427, *śābēa'+yôm*^{1} [1]
life, 10494, *nišmâ* [1]

LIFE'S [1]
my life's, 3276, *-î* [1]

LIFE-GIVING [1]
life-giving, 2644, *ḥay*^{1} [1]

LIFEBLOOD [3]
lifeblood, 1947+5883, *dām+nepeš* [2]
lifeblood, 5883+1947, *nepeš+dām* [1]

LIFELESS [6]
lifeless idols, 7007, *peger* [2]
lifeless, 1876, *dûmām* [1]
lifeless, 4637, *mût* [1]
lifeless forms, 5577, *n^{e}bēlâ* [1]
lifeless forms, 7007, *peger* [1]

LIFETIME [16]
lifetime, 3427, *yôm*^{1} [9]
lifetime, 2644, *ḥay*^{1} [2]
lifetime, 2645, *ḥay*^{2} [2]
lifetime, 3427+2644, *yôm*^{1}*+ḥay*^{1} [1]
in lifetime, 3972+3427, *kōl+yôm*^{1} [1]
lifetime, 7156, *pāneh* [1]

LIFT [64]
lift up, 5951, *nāśā'* [32]
lift up, 8123, *rûm*^{1} [8]
lift, 5951, *nāśā'* [5]
lift, 8938, *šālaḥ* [4]
lift, 6590, *'ālâ* [2]
lift, 8123, *rûm*^{1} [2]
lift, *NIH/RPE* [1]
lift up, 1575, *gēwâ*^{1} [1]
lift, 1655, *gālâ* [1]
lift up banners, 1839, *dāgal*^{2} [1]
lift up for mercy, 2858, *ḥānan*^{1} [1]
lift up, 3106, *ḥāśap*^{1} [1]
lift, 5162, *māšā'* [1]
lift, 7756, *qûm* [1]
lift, 7837, *qālal* [1]
lift out, 8123, *rûm*^{1} [1]
lift out, 10513, *s^{e}laq* [1]

LIFTED [58]
lifted up, 5951, *nāśā'* [16]
lifted, 6590, *'ālâ* [9]
lifted, 5951, *nāśā'* [7]
lifted high, 8123, *rûm*^{1} [5]
lifted, 6073, *sûr*^{1} [3]
be lifted up, 5951, *nāśā'* [2]
lifted up, 8123, *rûm*^{1} [2]
lifted, 8123, *rûm*^{1} [2]
lifted, 8435, *śāgab* [2]
lifted, *NIH/RPE* [1]
lifted up, 1540, *gādal* [1]
lifted out of the depths, 1926, *dālâ*^{1} [1]
lifted, 5089, *mō'al* [1]
lifted up, 5747, *nāṭal* [1]
be lifted up, 8123, *rûm*^{1} [1]
lifted, 8492, *śîm* [1]
be lifted up, 10238, *z^{e}qap* [1]
was lifted, 10475, *n^{e}ṭal* [1]
was lifted, 10513, *s^{e}laq* [1]

LIFTING [3]
lifting, 5989, *nātan* [2]
lifting up, 5368, *maś'ēt* [1]

LIFTS [8]
lifts up, 2422, *zāqap* [2]
lifts, 8123, *rûm*^{1} [2]
lifts up, 5951, *nāśā'* [1]
lifts, 5989, *nātan* [1]
lifts up, 8123, *rûm*^{1} [1]
lifts, 10714, *šelaḥ* [1]

LIGHT [139]
light, 240, *'ôr*^{2} [84]
light, 4401, *mā'ôr* [13]
give light, 239, *'ôr*^{1} [6]
light, 239, *'ôr*^{1} [4]
light, 1277, *bā'ar*^{1} [3]
light, *NIH/RPE* [2]
gives light, 239, *'ôr*^{1} [2]
turns into light, 5585, *nāgah* [2]
brilliant light, 5586, *nōgah*^{1} [2]
give light, 239+240, *'ôr*^{1}*+'ôr*^{2} [1]
giving light, 239, *'ôr*^{1} [1]
light fires, 239, *'ôr*^{1} [1]
made light shine, 239, *'ôr*^{1} [1]
resplendent with light, 239, *'ôr*^{1} [1]
light of day, 240, *'ôr*^{2} [1]
light, 241, *'ûr*^{1} [1]
light, 245, *'ôrâ*^{1} [1]
morning light, 1332, *bōqer*^{2} [1]
light, 3427, *yôm*^{1} [1]
light, 3649, *yāpa'* [1]
light, 5586, *nōgah*^{1} [1]
light, 5644, *n^{e}hārâ* [1]
in the light of, 6584, *'al*^{2} [1]
first light of dawn, 6590+8840, *'ālâ+šaḥar* [1]
light, 7706, *qādaḥ* [1]
light, 7783, *qāṭān*^{1} [1]
light, 8492, *śîm* [1]
light of dawn, 8840, *šaḥar* [1]
first light, 10459, *n^{e}gah* [1]
light, 10466, *n^{e}hîr* [1]

LIGHTEN [5]
lighten, 7837, *qālal* [5]

LIGHTER [3]
make lighter, 7837, *qālal* [3]

LIGHTNING [36]
lightning, 1398, *bārāq*^{1} [11]
lightning, 240, *'ôr*^{2} [7]
lightning, 836, *'ēš*^{1} [7]
flash like lightning, 1398, *bārāq*^{1} [3]
bolts of lightning, 1398, *bārāq*^{1} [2]
lightning, 836+4259, *'ēš*^{1}*+lehābâ* [1]
flashes of lightning, 1027, *bāzāq* [1]
send forth lightning, 1397+1398, *bāraq+bārāq*^{1} [1]
lightning bolts, 1398, *bārāq*^{1} [1]
lightning, 4365, *lappîd* [1]
bolts of lightning, 8404, *rešep*^{1} [1]

LIGHTS [9]
lights, 4401, *mā'ôr* [4]
lights, 5944, *nēr*^{1} [2]
lights up, 239, *'ôr*^{1} [1]
lights, 240, *'ôr*^{2} [1]
lights, 6590, *'ālâ* [1]

LIKE [1272]
like, 3869, *k^{e}-* [899]
like, *NIH/RPE* [126]
like, 4017, *k^{e}mô* [80]
like, 4200, *l^{e}-*^{1} [19]
like, *AIT* [15]
like, 10341, *k^{e}-* [14]
like, 3869+889, *k^{e}-+'^{a}šer* [12]
like, 6640, *'im* [7]
like, 928, *b^{e}-* [6]
like, 3869+5126, *k^{e}-+ma'^{a}śeh* [6]
like, 1952, *d^{e}mût* [4]
looked like, 1952, *d^{e}mût* [4]
shaped like almond flowers, 5481, *m^{e}šuqqād* [4]
flash like lightning, 1398, *bārāq*^{1} [3]
is like, 1948, *dāmâ*^{1} [3]
like, 3202+928+6524, *ṭôb*^{2}*+b^{e}-+'ayin*^{1} [3]
like, 3869+5260, *k^{e}-+mar'eh* [3]
like, 5126, *ma'^{a}śeh* [3]
like, 170, *'āhab* [2]
be like, 1948, *dāmâ*^{1} [2]
like that, 4027, *kēn*^{2} [2]
like this, 4027, *kēn*^{2} [2]
like, 4027, *kēn*^{2} [2]
like, 4946, *min* [2]
be like, 5439, *māšal*^{1} [2]
is like, 5439, *māšal*^{1} [2]
I would like, 5528, *nā'*^{1} [2]
looked like, 9322, *tabnît* [2]
like, 203, *'āwâ*^{1} [1]
like, 430, *'ākal* [1]
like, 889, *'^{a}šer* [1]
like, 928+9348, *b^{e}-+tāwek* [1]
am like, 1948, *dāmâ*^{1} [1]
are like, 1948, *dāmâ*^{1} [1]
been like, 1948, *dāmâ*^{1} [1]
like, 1948, *dāmâ*^{1} [1]
make myself like, 1948, *dāmâ*^{1} [1]
like, 1955, *dimyôn* [1]

acted like a madman, 2147, *hālal^{3}* [1]
becomes like, 2924, *ḥāpaś* [1]
know what it is like, 3359, *yāda'* [1]
mounted like jewels, 3782+6584+4859, *yāšab+'al^{2}+millē't* [1]
exactly like, 3869+3972+889+4027, *k^{e}-+kōl+'^{a}šer+kēn^{2}* [1]
exactly like, 3869+4027, *k^{e}-+kēn^{2}* [1]
fared like, 3869, *k^{e}-* [1]
just like, 3869+4027, *k^{e}-+kēn^{2}* [1]
just like, 3869+7023, *k^{e}-+peh* [1]
just like, 3869, *k^{e}-* [1]
like, 3869+1952, *k^{e}-+d^{e}mût* [1]
like, 3869+3972+889, *k^{e}-+kōl+'^{a}šer* [1]
like, 3869+5477, *k^{e}-+mišpāṭ* [1]
like, 3869+6524, *k^{e}-+'ayin^{1}* [1]
like, 3869+6886, *k^{e}-+'ērek* [1]
like, 3869+889+4027, *k^{e}-+'^{a}šer+kēn^{2}* [1]
like this, 3907, *kōh* [1]
like this, 3970, *kākâ* [1]
like, 4200+6645, *l^{e}-^{1}+'ummâ^{1}* [1]
what like, 4537, *mâ* [1]
become like, 5439, *māšal^{1}* [1]
acts like a prophet, 5547, *nābā'* [1]
acted like a fool, 6118, *sākal* [1]
like image, 6771, *'āṣāb^{1}* [1]
make as great as you like, 8049+4394, *rābâ^{1}+m^{e}'ōd* [1]
be like, 8750, *šāwâ^{1}* [1]
is like, 8750, *šāwâ^{1}* [1]
look like, 9307, *tō'ar* [1]
like, 10179, *d^{e}mâ* [1]
looked like, 10179, *d^{e}mâ* [1]
like, 10554, *'im* [1]

LIKED [3]
liked, 170, *'āhab* [2]
liked, 3837+928+6524, *yāšar+b^{e}-+'ayin^{1}* [1]

LIKELY [1]
likely, *AIT* [1]

LIKEN [3]
liken, 1948, *dāmâ^{1}* [1]
liken, 5439, *māšal^{1}* [1]
liken, 8750, *šāwâ^{1}* [1]

LIKENESS [7]
likeness, 1952, *d^{e}mût* [5]
likeness, *NIH/RPE* [1]
likeness, 9454, *t^{e}mûnâ* [1]

LIKES [2]
likes, 170, *'āhab* [1]
likes, 928+2021+3202+4200, *b^{e}-+ha-+ṭôb^{2}+l^{e}-^{1}* [1]

LIKEWISE [2]
likewise, 2256, *w^{e}-* [1]
and likewise, 2256, *w^{e}-* [1]

LIKHI [1]
Likhi, 4376, *liqḥî* [1]

LILIES [11]
lilies, 8808, *šûšan^{1}* [11]

LILY [6]
lily, 8808, *šûšan^{1}* [6]

LIMB [2]
limb, *NIH/RPE* [1]
limb, 6795, *'eṣem^{1}* [1]

LIMBER [1]
limber, 7060, *pāzaz^{2}* [1]

LIMBS [3]
limbs, 963, *bad^{1}* [2]
limbs, 1752, *gerem* [1]

LIME [2]
lime, 8487, *śîd^{2}* [2]

LIMIT [6]
limit, 1757, *gāra'^{1}* [1]
limit, 2976, *ḥōq* [1]
limit, 5031, *mispār^{1}* [1]
have no limit, 6296, *'ābar^{1}* [1]
limit, 7891, *qēṣ* [1]
limit, 10375, *k^{e}tāb* [1]

LIMITS [8]
limits, 2976, *ḥōq* [2]
limits, 1473, *g^{e}bûl* [1]
put limits around, 1487, *gābal* [1]
put limits, 1487, *gābal* [1]
know no limits, 6296, *'ābar^{1}* [1]
farthest limits, 9362, *tôṣā'ôt* [1]
limits, 9417, *taklît* [1]

LIMP [9]
go limp, 8332, *rāpâ^{1}* [3]
hang limp, 8332, *rāpâ^{1}* [3]
hang limp, 1927, *dālâ^{2}* [1]
fall limp, 5877, *nāpal* [1]
hang limp, 8342, *rippāyôn* [1]

LIMPING [1]
limping, 7519, *ṣāla'* [1]

LINE [52]
measuring line, 7742, *qāw^{1}* [7]
line, 1201, *bēn^{1}* [5]
family line, 1074, *bayit^{1}* [4]
line, 2446, *zera'* [4]
line, 7742, *qāw^{1}* [4]
plumb line, 643, *'^{a}nāk* [3]
battle line, 5120, *ma'^{a}rākâ* [3]
family line, 2446, *zera'* [2]
plumb line, 5487, *mišqelet* [2]
drew up line, 6885, *'ārak* [2]
plumb line, 74+974, *'eben+b^{e}dîl* [1]
plumb line, 74, *'eben* [1]
run a line, 204, *'āwâ^{2}* [1]
next in line, 339, *'aḥar* [1]
in the front line, 448+4578+7156, *'el+mûl^{3}+pāneh* [1]
David's line, 1858, *dāwid* [1]
line, 2006, *derek* [1]
that man's line^{s}, 2257, *-ô* [1]
line, 2475, *hebel^{2}* [1]
line, 2562, *ḥûṭ* [1]
line, 5055, *mē'eh* [1]
family line, 5916+9247, *nēṣer+šōreš* [1]
line up, 6885, *'ārak* [1]
run a line, 9292, *tā'â* [1]
account of line, 9352, *tôlēdôt* [1]
family line, 9352, *tôlēdôt* [1]

LINED [1]
lined, 1215, *bānâ* [1]

LINEN [87]
linen, 965, *bad^{3}* [22]
linen, 9254, *šēš^{3}* [21]
fine linen, 9254, *šēš^{3}* [17]
linen, 7324, *pēšet* [12]
fine linen, 1009, *bûṣ* [6]
linen garments, 6041, *sādîn* [4]
linen, *NIH/RPE* [1]
linen, 1009, *bûṣ* [1]
white linen, 1009, *bûṣ* [1]
fine linen, 2583, *ḥōrāy* [1]
hangings of linen, 4158, *karpas* [1]

LINENS [1]
linens, 355, *'ēṭûn* [1]

LINES [13]
lines, 4722, *maḥ^{a}neh* [2]
battle lines, 4878, *milḥāmâ* [2]
lines, 5120, *ma'^{a}rākâ* [2]
formed battle lines, 6885, *'ārak* [2]
boundary lines, 2475, *hebel^{2}* [1]
battle lines, 5120, *ma'^{a}rākâ* [1]
drew up lines, 6885, *'ārak* [1]
formed lines, 6885, *'ārak* [1]
lines of descent, 9352, *tôlēdôt* [1]

LINGER [5]
linger, 336, *'āḥar* [1]
linger, 1591, *gûr^{1}* [1]
linger, 3498, *yāḥal* [1]
linger, 4538, *māhah* [1]
linger, 6641, *'āmad* [1]

LINGERING [2]
lingering, 586, *'āman^{1}* [1]
lingering, 3427+6584+3427, *yôm^{1}+'al^{2}+yôm^{1}* [1]

LION [81]
lion, 793, *'aryēh^{1}* [34]
lion, 787, *'^{a}rî* [17]
lion, 4097, *k^{e}pîr* [7]
lion, 8828, *šaḥal* [6]
great lion, 4097, *k^{e}pîr* [4]
strong lion, 4097, *k^{e}pîr* [3]
lion, 4233, *lābî'* [3]
lion, 4330, *layiš^{1}* [2]
fierce lion, 787, *'^{a}rî* [1]
the lion^{s}, 2084, *-hû* [1]
young lion, 4097+787, *k^{e}pîr+'^{a}rî* [1]
young lion, 4097, *k^{e}pîr* [1]
lion, 10069, *'aryēh* [1]

LION'S [5]
lion's, 793, *'aryēh^{1}* [4]
lion's, 787, *'^{a}rî* [1]

LIONESS [8]
lioness, 4233, *lābî'* [7]
lioness, 4234, *l^{e}biyyā'* [1]

LIONESSES [1]
lionesses, 4233, *lābî'* [1]

LIONS [41]
lions, 787, *'^{a}rî* [14]
lions, 10069, *'aryēh* [9]
lions, 4097, *k^{e}pîr* [7]
lions, 793, *'aryēh^{1}* [4]
young lions, 4097, *k^{e}pîr* [4]
great lions, 4097, *k^{e}pîr* [1]
lions, 4216, *lebe'* [1]
lions, 4330, *layiš^{1}* [1]

LIPS [113]
lips, 8557, *śāpâ* [97]
lips, 7023, *peh* [13]
lips, 2674, *ḥēk* [1]
lips, 4383, *lāšôn* [1]
lips, 10588, *pum* [1]

LIQUID [2]
liquid, 2001, *d^{e}rôr^{2}* [1]
liquid, 5482, *mašqeh^{1}* [1]

LIST [8]
list, 5031, *mispār^{1}* [6]
list, *NIH/RPE* [1]
list, 8492, *śîm* [1]

LISTED [35]
listed, 5031, *mispār^{1}* [15]
listed genealogy, 9352, *tôlēdôt* [3]
listed, *NIH/RPE* [2]
listed in genealogy, 3509, *yāḥaś* [2]
listed, 3509, *yāḥaś* [2]
be listed, 4180, *kātab* [2]
listed, *AIT* [1]
listed, 995, *bô'* [1]
be listed in the genealogical record, 3509, *yāḥaś* [1]
genealogical record listed, 3509, *yāḥaś* [1]
listed in genealogical records, 3509, *yāḥaś* [1]
was listed in the genealogies, 3509, *yāḥaś* [1]
listed, 4180, *kātab* [1]
were listed, 4180, *kātab* [1]
listed, 7212, *pāqad* [1]

LISTEN [300]
listen, 9048, *šāma'* [225]
listen, 263, *'āzan^{1}* [19]
listen, 7992, *qāšab* [14]
listen, 7754, *qôl* [12]
listen, *NIH/RPE* [7]
listen, 2180, *hinnēh* [6]
listen carefully, 9048+9048, *šāma'+šāma'* [4]
listen, 5742+265, *nāṭâ+'ōzen* [2]

listen carefully, 928+265+9048, b^{e}-+'ōzen+šāma' [1]
listen closely, 928+265+9048, b^{e}-+'ōzen+šāma' [1]
makes listen, 1655+265, gālâ+'ōzen [1]
listen closely, 5742+265, nāṭâ+'ōzen [1]
listen well, 5742+265, nāṭâ+'ōzen [1]
listen, 7992+265, qāšab+'ōzen [1]
listen carefully, 8011, rā'â^{1} [1]
listen, 8011, rā'â^{1} [1]
listen carefully, 9048+928+7754, šāma'+b^{e}-+qôl [1]
listen in, 9048, šāma' [1]
listen, 9048+7754, šāma'+qôl [1]

LISTENED [47]
listened, 9048, šāma' [40]
listened, 7992, qāšab [3]
listened, 263, 'āzan^{1} [1]
listened attentively to, 265+448, 'ōzen+'el [1]
listened, 928+265, b^{e}-+'ōzen [1]
listened to, 9048, šāma' [1]

LISTENING [8]
listening, 9048, šāma' [8]

LISTENS [7]
listens, 9048, šāma' [4]
listens, 7992, qāšab [2]
listens, 265+9048, 'ōzen+šāma' [1]

LISTING [1]
listing, 5031, mispār^{1} [1]

LIT [2]
lit up, 239, 'ôr^{1} [1]
lit, 1277+836, bā'ar^{1}+'ēš^{1} [1]

LITERATURE [2]
literature, 6219, sēper^{1} [2]

LITTLE [90]
little, 5071, m^{e}'aṭ [33]
little, 2402, z^{e}'êr [5]
little ones, 3251, ṭap^{1} [4]
little, 4202, lō' [4]
little while, 5071, m^{e}'aṭ [3]
little, 7785, qāṭōn^{2} [3]
little children, 3251, ṭap^{1} [2]
little owl, 3927, kôs^{2} [2]
little by little, 6584+3338, 'al^{2}+yād [2]
little, 7582, ṣā'îr^{1} [2]
little finger, 7782, qōṭen [2]
little, 7783, qāṭān^{1} [2]
little^{s}, 655, 'āsûk [1]
little longer, 2402, z^{e}'êr [1]
have too little, 2893, ḥāsēr^{1} [1]
in little more than, 3427+6584, yôm^{1}+'al^{2} [1]
little ones, 3529, yeled [1]
little left, 3856+7129+8636, yeter^{1}+p^{e}lêṭâ+šā'ar [1]
of little value, 3869+5071, k^{e}-+m^{e}'aṭ [1]
little distance, 3896+824, k^{e}bārâ^{2}+'ereṣ [1]
little value, 4202+4399, lō'+m^{e}'ûmâ [1]
little value, 4399, m^{e}'ûmâ [1]
gathered little, 5070, mā'aṭ [1]
little, 5070, mā'aṭ [1]
little more, 5071, m^{e}'aṭ [1]
little while, 5071+8092, m^{e}'aṭ+rega' [1]
only a little, 5071, m^{e}'aṭ [1]
too little, 5071, m^{e}'aṭ [1]
little while, 5203, miṣ'ār^{1} [1]
little, 5493, môṭ^{1} [1]
little while, 6388+5071, 'ôd+m^{e}'aṭ [1]
little boys, 6396, '^{a}wîl^{1} [1]
little children, 6407, 'ôlēl [1]
little ones, 6407, 'ôlēl [1]
little, 7326, pat [1]
little ones, 7592, ṣā'ar [1]
little, 7825, qōl^{1} [1]
little known, 7829, qālâ^{2} [1]

LIVE [515]
live, 3782, yāšab [141]
live, 2649, ḥāyâ [90]
live in, 3782, yāšab [68]
live, 8905, šākan [26]
as surely as live, 2644, ḥay^{1} [23]
live, 2645, ḥay^{2} [15]
live, NIH/RPE [14]
live, 2644, ḥay^{1} [12]
live, 4632, môšāb [12]
long live, 2649, ḥāyâ [9]
surely live, 2649+2649, ḥāyâ+ḥāyâ [9]
live long, 799+3427, 'ārak+yôm^{1} [8]
live, 1591, gûr^{1} [7]
let live, 2649, ḥāyâ [7]
live, 2143, hālak [6]
as live, 2644, ḥay^{1} [6]
live in, 8905, šākan [6]
live, 10262, ḥ^{a}yâ [5]
as long as live, 928+6388, b^{e}-+'ôd [2]
live for a while, 1591, gûr^{1} [2]
as surely as live, 2644+5883, ḥay^{1}+nepeš [2]
allowed to live, 2649, ḥāyâ [2]
live, 3427, yôm^{1} [2]
let live, 8905, šākan [2]
live, 10163, dûr [2]
live, 10269, ḥ^{a}lāq [2]
live, 10403, m^{e}dôr [2]
live on, 430, 'ākal [1]
live, 928+2021+2644, b^{e}-+ha-+ḥay^{1} [1]
live awhile, 1591, gûr^{1} [1]
how live, 2006, derek [1]
live, 2143+928, hālak+b^{e}- [1]
as surely as live, 2644+2256+2644+5883, ḥay^{1}+w^{e}-+ḥay^{1}+nepeš [1]
as surely as live, 2645, ḥay^{2} [1]
allow to live, 2649, ḥāyâ [1]
live again, 2649, ḥāyâ [1]
live on, 2649, ḥāyâ [1]
live, 2652, ḥayyâ^{2} [1]
live out half, 2936, ḥāṣâ [1]
brought to live, 3782, yāšab [1]
had live, 3782, yāšab [1]
let live, 3782, yāšab [1]
live securely, 3782, yāšab [1]
make live, 3782, yāšab [1]
as long as live, 3972+3427+4200+6409, kōl+yôm^{1}+l^{e-1}+'ôlām [1]
as long as live, 3972+3427, kōl+yôm^{1} [1]
live as an alien, 4472, māgôr^{2} [1]
live out, 4848, mālē'^{1} [1]
as long as live, 4946+3427, min+yôm^{1} [1]
where live, 5061, mā'ôn^{2} [1]
live, 6641, 'āmad [1]
live in terror, 7064, pāḥad [1]
live quietly, 8091, rāga' [1]
live coal, 8365, riṣpâ^{1} [1]
people who live in, 8907, šākēn [1]
live at ease, 8922, šālâ^{1} [1]
makes live at peace, 8966, šālēm^{1} [1]
live in luxury, 9503, ta'^{a}nûg [1]
live, 10073+10089+10261, 'arkâ+b^{e}-+ḥay [1]
live, 10407, m^{e}dār [1]

LIVED [217]
lived, 3782, yāšab [91]
lived, 2649, ḥāyâ [43]
lived, 2118+3427, hāyâ+yôm^{1} [12]
lived in, 3782, yāšab [12]
lived, NIH/RPE [10]
lived, 2644, ḥay^{1} [9]
lived, 2118, hāyâ [8]
lived, AIT [3]
lived at, 3782, yāšab [3]
as long as lived, 3972+3427, kōl+yôm^{1} [3]
lived, 1591, gûr^{1} [2]
lived, 5162, māšā' [2]
lived in, 8905, šākan [2]
lived, 928+2021+1074, b^{e}-+ha-+bayit^{1} [1]
lived as an alien, 1591, gûr^{1} [1]
lived, 2143, hālak [1]
lived, 2645, ḥay^{2} [1]
lived, 3427, yôm^{1} [1]
lived a long time, 3823, yāšēn^{2} [1]
lived, 4472, māgôr^{2} [1]
where lived, 4472, māgôr^{2} [1]
places where lived, 4632, môšāb [1]
region where lived, 4632, môšāb [1]
lived, 4946, min [1]
where lived, 5226, māqôm [1]
lived, 5438, miškān [1]
lived in hostility toward, 6584+7156+5877, 'al^{2}+pāneh+nāpal [1]
lived, 8905, šākan [1]
lived, 10163, dûr [1]
lived, 10403, m^{e}dôr [1]

LIVELIHOOD [2]
livelihood, 5883, nepeš [1]
livelihood, 7871, qinyān [1]

LIVER [14]
liver, 3879, kābēd^{3} [13]
liver, 5355, m^{e}rōrâ [1]

LIVES [132]
as surely as lives, 2644, ḥay^{1} [46]
lives, 5883, nepeš [36]
lives, 3782, yāšab [10]
lives, 2644, ḥay^{1} [6]
lives, NIH/RPE [5]
as lives, 2644, ḥay^{1} [3]
lives, 2645, ḥay^{2} [3]
save lives, 2649, ḥāyâ [2]
as long as lives, 3972+3427, kōl+yôm^{1} [2]
lives, 6639, 'am^{2} [2]
lives, 8905, šākan [2]
lives a long time, 799, 'ārak [1]
lives, 1591, gûr^{1} [1]
lives, 2649, ḥāyâ [1]
protect lives, 2649, ḥāyâ [1]
saved lives, 2649, ḥāyâ [1]
spare lives, 2649, ḥāyâ [1]
spared lives, 2649, ḥāyâ [1]
lives, 2652, ḥayyâ^{2} [1]
lives, 2750, ḥēleq^{2} [1]
lives, 3427+9102, yôm^{1}+šānâ^{2} [1]
lives, 4637, mût [1]
save lives, 4695, miḥyâ [1]
lives in, 8905, šākan [1]
lives, 10151, g^{e}šēm [1]
lives, 10261, ḥay [1]

LIVESTOCK [88]
livestock, 5238, miqneh [45]
livestock, 989, b^{e}hēmâ [33]
livestock, 1248, b^{e}'îr [4]
tend livestock, 408+5238+2118, 'îš^{1}+miqneh+hāyâ [1]
tended livestock, 408+5238+2118, 'îš^{1}+miqneh+hāyâ [1]
livestock, 2651, ḥayyâ^{1} [1]
droves of livestock, 5238, miqneh [1]
herds of livestock, 5238, miqneh [1]
livestock, 5238+989, miqneh+b^{e}hēmâ [1]

LIVING [235]
living, 2645, ḥay^{2} [62]
living, 3782, yāšab [39]
living in, 3782, yāšab [33]
living, 1591, gûr^{1} [24]
living, NIH/RPE [14]
living creatures, 2651, ḥayyâ^{1} [13]
living, 2651, ḥayyâ^{1} [8]
living, 10261, ḥay [4]
living, 2644, ḥay^{1} [3]
living, AIT [2]
living thing, 1414, bāśār [2]
living, 2118, hāyâ [2]
living creature, 2651, ḥayyâ^{1} [2]
living thing, 3685, y^{e}qûm [2]
living, 8905, šākan [2]
living long, 799, 'ārak [1]
living thing^{s}, 889, '^{a}šer [1]
living in, 928, b^{e}- [1]
living with, 1074, bayit^{1} [1]
living as an alien, 1591, gûr^{1} [1]
living creatures, 2645, ḥay^{2} [1]
living thing, 2645, ḥay^{2} [1]
living things, 2651, ḥayyâ^{1} [1]
living, 2654, ḥayyût [1]
living, 2837, ḥānâ^{1} [1]
living creature, 3685, y^{e}qûm [1]
living at, 3782, yāšab [1]

life will not be worth living, 4200+4537+2644, *l[e]-[1]+mâ+ḥay[1]* [1]
living, 4472, *māgôr[2]* [1]
living thing, 4695, *miḥyâ* [1]
living soul, 5883, *nepeš* [1]
living quarters, 5969, *niškâ* [1]
living, 8907, *šākēn* [1]
one living in, 8907, *šākēn* [1]
living, 9068, *šāmar* [1]
living, 9369, *tôšāb* [1]
people living, 9369, *tôšāb* [1]
living, 10338, *y[e]tib* [1]

LIZARD [4]
monitor lizard, 3947, *kōaḥ[2]* [1]
wall lizard, 4321, *l[e]ṭā'â* [1]
great lizard, 7370, *ṣāb[2]* [1]
lizard, 8532, *ś[e]māmît* [1]

LO DEBAR [4]
Lo Debar, 4203, *lō' dābār* [2]
Lo Debar, 4274, *lô d[e]bār* [2]

LO-AMMI [1]
Lo-Ammi, 4204, *lō' 'ammî* [1]

LO-RUHAMAH [2]
Lo-Ruhamah, 4205, *lō' ruḥāmâ* [2]

LOAD [10]
load, 5362, *maśśā'[1]* [7]
load, 3250, *ṭā'an[2]* [1]
load, 6584, *'al[2]* [1]
load, 8044, *rōb* [1]

LOADED [12]
loaded, 5951, *nāśā'* [4]
loaded, *AIT* [1]
loaded, 3878, *kābēd[2]* [1]
loaded, 4374, *lāqaḥ* [1]
loaded, 4849, *mālē'[2]* [1]
loaded up, 5951, *nāśā'* [1]
loaded with, 6584, *'al[2]* [1]
loaded, 6673, *'āmas* [1]
loaded, 8492, *śîm* [1]

LOADING [1]
loading, 6673, *'āmas* [1]

LOADS [4]
loads, 3267, *ṭāraḥ* [1]
loads, 5362, *maśśā'[1]* [1]
draw heavy loads, 6022, *sābal* [1]
loads of wood, 6770, *'ēṣ* [1]

LOAF [6]
loaf, 2705, *ḥallâ* [2]
loaf, 3971, *kikkār* [2]
loaf, 3971+4312, *kikkār+leḥem* [1]
round loaf, 7501, *ṣ[e]lûl* [1]

LOAN [6]
require a pledge for a loan, 2478+2471, *ḥ[a]bōl+ḥābal[1]* [1]
what took in pledge for a loan, 2478, *ḥ[a]bōl* [1]
loan, 2550, *ḥôb* [1]
loan made, 5957, *nāšā'[1]* [1]
make a loan, 5957+5394, *nāšā'[1]+maššā'â* [1]
making loan, 5957, *nāšā'[1]* [1]

LOATHE [5]
loathe, 7752, *qûṭ* [4]
loathe, 2426, *zārā'* [1]

LOATHED [1]
loathed, 9493, *tā'ab* [1]

LOATHES [2]
loathes, *NIH/RPE* [1]
loathes, 1008, *bûs* [1]

LOATHING [1]
loathing, 7752, *qûṭ* [1]

LOATHSOME [5]
loathsome, 9359, *tô'ēbâ* [2]
loathsome, 944, *bā'aš* [1]
loathsome, 1994, *dērā'ôn* [1]
loathsome, 2859, *ḥānan[2]* [1]

LOAVES [10]
loaves of bread, 4312, *leḥem* [6]
loaves, *NIH/RPE* [1]
loaves of bread, 2705, *ḥallâ* [1]
loaves, 3971, *kikkār* [1]
loaves, 4312, *leḥem* [1]

LOBE [6]
lobe, 9483, *t[e]nûk* [5]
ear lobe, 265, *'ōzen* [1]

LOBES [2]
lobes, 9483, *t[e]nûk* [2]

LOCATED [1]
centrally located in, 928+9348, *b[e]-+tāwek* [1]

LOCATIONS [1]
locations, 3227, *ṭîrâ* [1]

LOCK [1]
lock, 4980, *man'ûl* [1]

LOCKED [4]
locked, 5835, *nā'al[1]* [2]
locked up, 5835, *nā'al[1]* [1]
locked, 6037, *sāgar* [1]

LOCUST [9]
locust, 746, *'arbeh* [5]
locust swarm, 1612, *gāzām* [2]
great locust, 746, *'arbeh* [1]
young locust, 3540, *yeleq* [1]

LOCUSTS [32]
locusts, 746, *'arbeh* [15]
great locusts, 746, *'arbeh* [2]
locusts, 2885, *ḥāsîl* [2]
locusts, 3540, *yeleq* [2]
young locusts, 3540, *yeleq* [2]
locusts, *NIH/RPE* [1]
locusts, 1466, *gēbā* [1]
locusts, 1479, *gōbay* [1]
swarms of locusts, 1479, *gōbay* [1]
locusts, 1612, *gāzām* [1]
locusts, 2506, *ḥāgāb[1]* [1]
young locusts, 2885, *ḥāsîl* [1]
swarm of locusts, 3540, *yeleq* [1]
swarms of locusts, 7526, *ṣ[e]lāṣal* [1]

LOD [4]
Lod, 4254, *lōd* [4]

LODGE [1]
lodge, 1074+4472, *bayit[1]+māgôr[2]* [1]

LODGED [1]
lodged, 4180, *kātab* [1]

LODGING [4]
lodging place, 4869, *mālôn* [2]
lodging a charge, 3519, *yākaḥ* [1]
lodging, 4472, *māgôr[2]* [1]

LOFTINESS [1]
loftiness, 5679, *nôp* [1]

LOFTY [19]
lofty, 5951, *nāśā'* [4]
lofty shrines, 8229, *rāmâ[3]* [3]
lofty, 8123, *rûm[1]* [2]
lofty, 8435, *śāgab* [2]
lofty, 1469, *gābōah* [1]
lofty throne, 2292, *z[e]bul[2]* [1]
lofty palace, 5092, *ma'[a]lâ[2]* [1]
lofty, 5294, *mārôm* [1]
lofty trees, 8123+7757, *rûm[1]+qômâ* [1]
lofty shrine, 8229, *rāmâ[3]* [1]
lofty place, 8420, *śe'ēt[1]* [1]
lofty, 9435, *tālûl* [1]

LOG [5]
log, 4253, *lōg* [5]

LOGS [10]
logs, 6770, *'ēṣ* [9]
logs, *NIH/RPE* [1]

LOINCLOTH [1]
loincloth, 258, *'ēzôr* [1]

LOINS [7]
loins, 4072, *kesel[1]* [5]
loins, 5516, *motnayim* [2]

LONELY [2]
lonely, 3495, *yāḥîd* [2]

LONG [356]
long, 802, *'ōrek* [65]
long, *AIT* [39]
long, *NIH/RPE* [28]
how long, 6330+5503, *'ad[2]+mātay* [27]
long, 8041, *rab[1]* [18]
how long, 6330+625+2025, *'ad[2]+'ān+-â[2]* [12]
long live, 2649, *ḥāyâ* [9]
as long as, 3972+3427, *kōl+yôm[1]* [9]
live long, 799+3427, *'ārak+yôm[1]* [8]
as long as, 3972+2021+3427, *kōl+ha-+yôm[1]* [5]
long ago, 4946+255, *min+'āz* [5]
long ago, 7710, *qedem* [5]
how long, 6330+4537, *'ad[2]+mâ* [4]
long ago, 6409, *'ôlām* [4]
as long as lived, 3972+3427, *kōl+yôm[1]* [3]
long cubits, 564, *'ammâ[1]* [2]
long, 799, *'ārak* [2]
so long, 799, *'ārak* [2]
long time, 801, *'ārōk* [2]
all day long, 928+2021+3427+2021+2085, *b[e]-+ha-+yôm[1]+ha-+hû'* [2]
as long as live, 928+6388, *b[e]-+'ôd* [2]
as long as, 928, *b[e]-* [2]
so long, 1018, *bôš[2]* [2]
as long as lives, 3972+3427, *kōl+yôm[1]* [2]
long ago, 4200+4946+8158, *l[e]-[1]+min+rāḥôq* [2]
as long as, 4200+7156, *l[e]-[1]+pāneh* [2]
long ago, 4946+6409, *min+'ôlām* [2]
long ago, 4946+7710, *min+qedem* [2]
long ago, 4946+8158, *min+rāḥôq* [2]
how long, 5503, *mātay* [2]
long, 5951+5883, *nāśā'+nepeš* [2]
long, 6409, *'ôlām* [2]
long enough, 8041, *rab[1]* [2]
long, 8049, *rābâ[1]* [2]
long way, 8158, *rāḥôq* [2]
long for, 9289, *tā'ab[1]* [2]
long for, 203, *'āwâ[1]* [1]
how long, 339+5503+6388, *'aḥar+mātay+'ôd* [1]
long established, 419, *'êtān[1]* [1]
as long as, 421, *'ak* [1]
as long as, 561+6388, *'im+'ôd* [1]
long, 723, *'aṣṣîl* [1]
been long, 799, *'ārak* [1]
enjoy a long life, 799+3427, *'ārak+yôm[1]* [1]
enjoy long life, 799+3427, *'ārak+yôm[1]* [1]
give long, 799, *'ārak* [1]
have long, 799, *'ārak* [1]
lives a long time, 799, *'ārak* [1]
living long, 799, *'ārak* [1]
made long, 799, *'ārak* [1]
long, 800, *'ārēk* [1]
so long, 802+3427, *'ōrek+yôm[1]* [1]
all night long, 928+2021+4326, *b[e]-+ha-+laylâ* [1]
as long as, 928+3427, *b[e]-+yôm[1]* [1]
long ago, 928+2021+8037, *b[e]-+ha-+ri'šôn* [1]
as long as, 928+3972+6961, *b[e]-+kōl+'ēt* [1]
as long as, 928+6388, *b[e]-+'ôd* [1]
long enjoy, 1162, *bālâ[1]* [1]
long, 1469, *gābōah* [1]
grow long, 1540, *gādal* [1]
long, 2006, *derek* [1]
long for[s], 2296, *zeh* [1]
long for, 2675, *ḥākâ* [1]
lived a long time, 3823, *yāšēn[2]* [1]
as long as, 3869+889, *k[e]-+'ašer* [1]
how long must wait, 3869+4537+3427, *k[e]-+mâ+yôm[1]* [1]
as long as endure, 3869+3427, *k[e]-+yôm[1]* [1]
how long, 3869+4537, *k[e]-+mâ* [1]
long since, 3893, *k[e]bār[1]* [1]

as long as live, 3972+3427+4200+6409, kōl+yôm^1+lᵉ-^{1}+ʿôlām [1]
as long as live, 3972+3427, kōl+yôm^1 [1]
as long as, 3972+6388, kōl+ʿôd [1]
as long as, 3972, kōl [1]
long, 3972, kōl [1]
long for, 4083, kāsap [1]
long life, 4200+2021+2644, lᵉ-^{1}+ha–+ḥay^1 [1]
long ago, 4200+6409, lᵉ-^{1}+ʿôlām [1]
long, 4200+6409, lᵉ-^{1}+ʿôlām [1]
long, 4500, middâ^1 [1]
how I long for, 4769+5989+5761, mî+nātan+-nî [1]
as long as live, 4946+3427, min+yôm^1 [1]
as long as, 4946, min [1]
long ago, 4946+3427+7710, min+yôm^1+qedem [1]
long, 4946+6409, min+ʿôlām [1]
long, 4946+8158, min+rāḥôq [1]
long, 4946+919, min+ʾetmôl [1]
sound long, 5432, māšak [1]
sounds a long blast, 5432, māšak [1]
grow long, 5742, nāṭâ [1]
for how long, 6330+5503, ʿad^2+mātay [1]
how long, 6330+625, ʿad^2+ʾān [1]
as long as, 6330, ʿad^2 [1]
lasted so long, 6330, ʿad^2 [1]
as long as, 6388+3972, ʿôd+kōl [1]
as long as, 6388, ʿôd [1]
long time, 6388, ʿôd [1]
long time, 6409, ʿôlām [1]
as long as, 6640, ʿim [1]
hair long, 7279, peraʿ^2 [1]
long for, 7747, qāwâ^1 [1]
long, 8037, riʾšôn [1]
too long, 8041, rab^1 [1]
long, 8044, rōb [1]
long way, 8158+4394, rāḥôq+mᵉʾōd [1]
enjoyed long life, 8428+3427, śābēaʿ+yôm^1 [1]
long for, 8634, šāʾap^1 [1]
generations long past, 9102+1887+2256+1887, šānâ^2+dôr^2+wᵉ-+dôr^2 [1]
long, 9458, tāmîd [1]
long history, 10427+10317+10550, min+yôm+ʿālam [1]

LONG-SUFFERING [1]

long-suffering, 800+678, ʾārēk+ʾap^2 [1]

LONG-WINDED [1]

long-winded, 8120, rûaḥ [1]

LONGED [7]

longed for, 203, ʾāwâ^1 [2]
longed for, 3139, ḥēšeq [1]
longed, 3983, kālâ^1 [1]
longed, 4083+4083, kāsap+kāsap [1]
longed for, 6584, ʿal^2 [1]
longed for, 7212, pāqad [1]

LONGER [144]

longer, 6388, ʿôd [74]
longer, *AIT* [36]
longer, 3578, yāsap [8]
longer, 3578+6388, yāsap+ʿôd [5]
any longer, 6388, ʿôd [3]
no longer shine, 665+5586, ʾāsap+nōgah^1 [2]
longer, 6964, ʿattâ [2]
longer, *NIH/RPE* [1]
took longer, 336, ʾāḥar [1]
longer, 801, ʾārōk [1]
longer, 802, ʾōrek [1]
no longer, 1172, bᵉlî [1]
longer, 1469, gābōah [1]
little longer, 2402, zᵉʿêr [1]
any longer, 3578+6388, yāsap+ʿôd [1]
any longer, 3578, yāsap [1]
can no longer, 4206, lāʾâ [1]
no longer be, 6073+4946, sûr^1+min [1]
no longer stirred, 7296, pārar^1 [1]
bear no longer, 7918, qāṣar^2 [1]
no longer, 8740, šûb^1 [1]

LONGING [8]

longing, 9294, taʾᵃwâ^1 [2]
longing for, 3277, yāʾab [1]
faints with longing, 3983, kālâ^1 [1]
weary with longing, 4001, killāyôn [1]
look with longing, 5951+6524, nāśāʾ+ʿayin^1 [1]
longing for, 8634, šāʾap^1 [1]
longing, 9291, taʾᵃbâ [1]

LONGINGS [2]

longings, 9294, taʾᵃwâ^1 [2]

LONGS [3]

longs, 2675, ḥākâ [1]
longs for, 4014, kāmah [1]
longs for, 8838, šāḥar^2 [1]

LOOK [254]

look, 2180, hinnēh [61]
look, 8011, rāʾâ^1 [52]
look, 5564, nābaṭ [20]
look for, 1335, bāqaš [10]
look, *NIH/RPE* [6]
look with pity, 2571+6524, ḥûs+ʿayin^1 [6]
look, 6524, ʿayin^1 [6]
look, 9120, šāʿâ [6]
look, 7747, qāwâ^1 [5]
look, 2176, hēn^1 [4]
look, 2600, ḥāzâ [3]
look, 6524+5951, ʿayin^1+nāśāʾ [3]
look, 7155, pānâ [3]
look, 1067, bîn [2]
look after, 1329, bāqar [2]
look, 2011, dāraš [2]
look down, 5564, nābaṭ [2]
look up, 5564, nābaṭ [2]
look, 5951+6524, nāśāʾ+ʿayin^1 [2]
look with favor, 7155, pānâ [2]
look after, 8011, rāʾâ^1 [2]
look around, 8011, rāʾâ^1 [2]
look down on, 8011, rāʾâ^1 [2]
look for, 8011, rāʾâ^1 [2]
look over, 8011, rāʾâ^1 [2]
look, 8432, śābar^2 [2]
look with favor, 239+7156, ʾôr^1+pāneh [1]
look, 928+6524, bᵉ-+ʿayin^1 [1]
look lustfully, 1067, bîn [1]
look, 1329, bāqar [1]
look to, 2011, dāraš [1]
look for, 2011, dāraš [1]
look, 2129, hakkārâ [1]
adulterous look, 2393, zᵉnûnîm [1]
look with compassion, 2571+6524, ḥûs+ʿayin^1 [1]
look about, 2916, ḥāpar^1 [1]
look around, 2924, ḥāpaś [1]
brazen look, 5195, mēṣaḥ [1]
look at, 5260, marʾeh [1]
look, 5260, marʾeh [1]
let look, 5564, nābaṭ [1]
look around, 5564, nābaṭ [1]
look on, 5564, nābaṭ [1]
look with favor, 5564+7156, nābaṭ+pāneh [1]
look with compassion, 5714, nāḥam [1]
look in the face, 5951+7156+448, nāśāʾ+pāneh+ʾel [1]
look with longing, 5951+6524, nāśāʾ+ʿayin^1 [1]
look for help, 6395, ʿûz [1]
look after, 6524+8492+6584, ʿayin^1+śîm+ʿal^2 [1]
look, 7595, ṣāpâ^1 [1]
look for, 7747, qāwâ^1 [1]
look in hope, 7747, qāwâ^1 [1]
look carefully, 8011+928+6524, rāʾâ^1+bᵉ-+ʿayin^1 [1]
make look, 8011, rāʾâ^1 [1]
only look, 8011+8011, rāʾâ^1+rāʾâ^1 [1]
look sad, 8273, raʿ^1 [1]
look sad, 8317, rāʿaʿ^1 [1]
look after, 8492+6524+6584, śîm+ʿayin^1+ʿal^2 [1]
look, 8800, šûr^1 [1]
look for, 8838, šāḥar^2 [1]
look, 8838, šāḥar^2 [1]
look with favor, 9120, šāʿâ [1]
look down, 9207, šāqap [1]
look like, 9307, tōʾar [1]
look aghast, 9449, tāmah [1]
look, 9514, tipʾeret [1]
look for, 10114, bᵉʿâ [1]
look, 10194, hāʾ [1]
look so pale, 10228+10731, zîw+šᵉnâ^1 [1]

LOOKED [151]

looked, 8011, rāʾâ^1 [37]
looked, 6524, ʿayin^1 [25]
looked for, 1335, bāqaš [10]
looked, 5260, marʾeh [10]
looked, 10255, ḥᵃzâ [8]
looked, 5564, nābaṭ [7]
looked down, 9207, šāqap [6]
looked, *NIH/RPE* [4]
looked like, 1952, dᵉmût [4]
looked, 7155, pānâ [4]
looked for, 7747, qāwâ^1 [4]
looked, 1952, dᵉmût [3]
looked, 5951+6524, nāśāʾ+ʿayin^1 [3]
looked with pity, 2571+6524, ḥûs+ʿayin^1 [2]
looked out, 9207, šāqap [2]
looked like, 9322, tabnît [2]
looked, 906+6524, ʾēt^1+ʿayin^1 [1]
looked closely, 1067, bîn [1]
looked, 2118+928+6524, hāyâ+bᵉ-+ʿayin^1 [1]
looked, 2600, ḥāzâ [1]
looked, 3498, yāḥal [1]
looked around, 5564, nābaṭ [1]
looked over, 5564, nābaṭ [1]
looked about, 5951+6524, nāśāʾ+ʿayin^1 [1]
looked in fear, 7064, pāḥad [1]
looked around, 7155, pānâ [1]
looked, 7156, pāneh [1]
looked things over, 8011, rāʾâ^1 [1]
looked, 8011+5260, rāʾâ^1+marʾeh [1]
looked, 8492+7156, śîm+pāneh [1]
looked for, 8838, šāḥar^2 [1]
looked with favor, 9120, šāʿâ [1]
looked, 9207, šāqap [1]
looked in astonishment, 9449, tāmah [1]
looked like, 10179, dᵉmâ [1]
looked, 10256, ḥᵉzû [1]

LOOKING [24]

looking for, 1335, bāqaš [6]
looking, *NIH/RPE* [4]
looking, 7156, pāneh [2]
looking, 8011, rāʾâ^1 [2]
looking for a chance, 1335, bāqaš [1]
comes looking for, 2011, dāraš [1]
looking worse, 2407, zāʿap^2 [1]
looking, 3498, yāḥal [1]
looking for, 5162, māṣāʾ [1]
looking back, 7155, pānâ [1]
looking, 7155, pānâ [1]
looking, 7595, ṣāpâ^1 [1]
looking at each other, 8011, rāʾâ^1 [1]
looking, 10255, ḥᵃzâ [1]

LOOKOUT [5]

lookout, 7595, ṣāpâ^1 [4]
lookout, 8011, rāʾâ^1 [1]

LOOKOUTS [1]

lookouts, 7595, ṣāpâ^1 [1]

LOOKS [23]

looks, 8011, rāʾâ^1 [5]
looks down, 9207, šāqap [4]
looks, 5564, nābaṭ [2]
looks, *NIH/RPE* [1]
looks after, 1333, baqqārâ [1]
looks for, 1335, bāqaš [1]
looks to, 1335, bāqaš [1]
looks, 2600, ḥāzâ [1]
looks down, 5564, nābaṭ [1]
looks, 5951+6524, nāśāʾ+ʿayin^1 [1]
looks, 7156, pāneh [1]
looks down on, 8011, rāʾâ^1 [1]
looks, 8626, šāʾal [1]
looks after, 9068, šāmar [1]
looks, 10657, rēw [1]

LOOM [3]

loom, *NIH/RPE* [1]
loom, 756, ʾereg [1]

loom, 1929, *dallâ1* [1]

LOOMS [1]
looms, 9207, *šāqap* [1]

LOOPS [11]
loops, 4339, *lulā'ōt* [11]

LOOSE [9]
loose, 7337, *pātaḥ1* [2]
places where turned loose, 5448, *mišlāḥ* [1]
hangs loose, 5759, *nāṭaš* [1]
let loose, 5825, *nāsa'* [1]
tore loose, 5825, *nāsa'* [1]
let loose, 6000, *nātar1* [1]
let loose, 8938, *šālaḥ* [1]
lets loose, 8938, *šālaḥ* [1]

LOOSEN [1]
loosen, 7277, *pāra'2* [1]

LOOSENED [1]
loosened, 7337, *pātaḥ1* [1]

LOOT [13]
loot, 8965, *šālāl* [3]
loot, 1024+1020, *bāzaz+baz* [2]
loot, 1024, *bāzaz* [2]
loot, 5468, *mᵉšissâ* [2]
loot, 8719, *šōd2* [1]
takes loot, 8720, *šādad* [1]
loot, 8964+8965, *šālal2+šālāl* [1]
loot, 9115, *šāsâ* [1]

LOOTED [5]
looted, 1024, *bāzaz* [2]
looted, 1020, *baz* [1]
looted, 9115, *šāsâ* [1]
be looted, 9116, *šāsas* [1]

LOOTER [1]
looter, 8720, *šādad* [1]

LOOTING [1]
looting, 9115, *šāsâ* [1]

LOP [1]
lop off, 6188, *sā'ap* [1]

LORD [315]
Lord, 123, *'ādôn* [159]
the Lord, 151, *'ᵃdōnāy* [91]
Lord, 151, *'ᵃdōnāy* [57]
Lord, 10437, *mārē'* [4]
lord, 1484, *gᵉbîr* [2]
the Lord, 123, *'ādôn* [1]
lord it, 8606+8606, *śārar+śārar* [1]

LORD'S [9]
lord's, 4200+123, *lᵉ-1+'ādôn* [4]
the Lord's, 151, *'ᵃdōnāy* [3]
lord's, 123, *'ādôn* [2]

LORD'S* [278]
the LORD's, 3378, *yhwh* [242]
the LORD's, 4200+3378, *lᵉ-1+yhwh* [27]
the LORD's, 4946+907+3378,
min+'ēt2+yhwh [3]
LORD's, *NIH/RPE* [2]
the LORD'sˢ, 2257, *-ô* [2]
LORD's, 3378, *yhwh* [1]
the LORD's, 4946+6640+3378,
min+'im+yhwh [1]

LORD [6551]
the LORD, 3378, *yhwh* [6030]
LORD, 3378, *yhwh* [399]
LORD, *NIH/RPE* [64]
the LORD, 3363, *yāh* [44]
the LORDˢ, 2257, *-ô* [6]
LORD, 3363, *yāh* [4]
the LORDˢ, 2085, *hû'* [2]
devoted to the LORD, 3051, *ḥērem1* [1]
the LORD himself, 7156+3378,
pāneh+yhwh [1]

LORDED [1]
lorded it over, 8948, *šālaṭ* [1]

LORDS [6]
lords, 123, *'ādôn* [5]
lords it over, 8948, *šālaṭ* [1]

LOSE [16]
lose, 6, *'ābad* [2]
lose heart, 5570, *nābēl1* [2]
lose, 8216, *rākak* [2]
lose, *NIH/RPE* [1]
lose, 665, *'āsap* [1]
lose heart, 1327+8120+928+7931,
bāqaq1+rûaḥ+bᵉ-+qereb [1]
lose heart, 3874, *kā'â* [1]
lose life, 4637, *mût* [1]
made lose, 5022, *māsas* [1]
lose, 5877, *nāpal* [1]
lose, 8740, *šûb1* [1]
lose, 8897, *šākal* [1]
lose, 9023, *šāmaṭ* [1]

LOSES [3]
loses, 8+6, *'ᵃbēdâ+'ābad* [1]
loses, 401, *'ayin1* [1]
loses temper, 3013+3013, *ḥārâ1+ḥārâ1* [1]

LOSS [8]
loss of children, 8890, *šᵉkôl* [2]
loss, *NIH/RPE* [1]
bore the loss, 2627, *ḥāṭā'* [1]
mourn loss, 5653, *nûd* [1]
loss of time, 8700, *šebet2* [1]
pay for the loss, 8966, *šālēm1* [1]
suffer loss, 10472, *nᵉzaq* [1]

LOSSES [4]
losses, 4804, *makkâ* [3]
losses, 4487, *maggēpâ* [1]

LOST [27]
lost, 6, *'ābad* [11]
lost property, 8, *'ᵃbēdâ* [3]
lost hair, 5307+8031, *māraṭ+rō'š1* [2]
lost time, 336, *'āḥar* [1]
lost, 3313, *yābēš2* [1]
lost, 3948, *kāḥad* [1]
lost no time, 4554, *māhar1* [1]
lost, 4946, *min* [1]
lost self-confidence, 5877+4394+928+6524,
nāpal+mᵉ'ōd+bᵉ-+'ayin1 [1]
lost, 5877+4946+907, *nāpal+min+'ēt2* [1]
lost, 5877+4946, *nāpal+min* [1]
lost luster, 6670, *'āmam2* [1]
lost courage, 8332+3338, *rāpâ1+yād* [1]
lost, 9161, *šāpak* [1]

LOT [81]
lot, 1598, *gôrāl* [37]
Lot, 4288, *lôṭ2* [30]
lot, 2750, *ḥēleq2* [6]
lot, *NIH/RPE* [5]
lot, 4987+3926, *mᵉnāt+kôs1* [1]
lot, 5162, *māṣā'* [1]
lot, 7877, *qesem* [1]

LOT'S [2]
Lot'sˢ, 2257, *-ô* [1]
Lot's, 4288, *lôṭ2* [1]

LOTAN [5]
Lotan, 4289, *lôṭān* [5]

LOTAN'S [2]
Lotan's, 4289, *lôṭān* [2]

LOTIONS [4]
put on lotions, 6057, *sûk2* [1]
used lotions at all, 6057+6057, *sûk2+sûk2* [1]
cosmetic lotions, 9043, *šemen* [1]
lotions, 9043, *šemen* [1]

LOTS [21]
lots, 1598, *gôrāl* [17]
lots, *NIH/RPE* [2]
drawing lots, 1598, *gôrāl* [1]
cast lots, 7837, *qālal* [1]

LOTUS [1]
lotus plants, 7365, *ṣe'ᵉlîm* [1]

LOTUSES [1]
lotuses, 7365, *ṣe'ᵉlîm* [1]

LOUD [25]
loud, 1524, *gādôl* [16]
loud, 2159, *hāmâ* [2]
loud, 1524+6330+4394, *gādôl+'ad2+mᵉ'ōd* [1]
loud, 2617, *ḥāzāq* [1]
loud, 4849, *mālē'2* [1]
loud, 7754, *qôl* [1]
loud, 8123, *rûm1* [1]
loud noise, 8623, *šā'ôn2* [1]
loud, 10264, *ḥayil* [1]

LOUDER [4]
louder, 1524, *gādôl* [2]
grew louder and louder,
2143+2256+2618+4394,
hālak+wᵉ-+ḥāzēq+mᵉ'ōd [2]

LOUDLY [6]
loudly, 1524, *gādôl* [2]
loudly, 928+7754+1524, *bᵉ-+qôl+gādôl* [1]
loudly, 5951+7754, *nāśā'+qôl* [1]
wept so loudly, 5989+906+7754+928+1140,
nātan+'ēt1+qôl+bᵉ-+bᵉkî [1]
loudly, 10089+10264, *bᵉ-+ḥayil* [1]

LOUNGE [1]
lounge, 6243, *sāraḥ1* [1]

LOUNGING [2]
lounging, 3782, *yāšab* [1]
lounging, 6242, *sārûaḥ* [1]

LOVE [319]
love, 2876, *ḥesed2* [129]
love, 170, *'āhab* [93]
unfailing love, 2876, *ḥesed2* [32]
love, 173, *'ahᵃbâ1* [26]
love, 1856, *dôd* [8]
great love, 2876, *ḥesed2* [6]
show love, 8163, *rāḥam* [4]
in love with, 170, *'āhab* [3]
love, 3351, *yādîd* [3]
fell in love with, 170, *'āhab* [2]
love, *NIH/RPE* [1]
show love, 170, *'āhab* [1]
showed love, 170, *'āhab* [1]
love, 171, *'ōhab* [1]
love, 2462, *ḥābab* [1]
love, 2668, *ḥēq* [1]
in love kept, 3137, *ḥāšaq1* [1]
love, 3342, *yᵉdidût* [1]
love, 6313, *'ᵃgābîm* [1]
love, 8163, *rāḥam* [1]
not love, 8533, *śānē'* [1]
not love, 8535, *śānî'* [1]
those who love bribes, 8816, *šōḥad* [1]

LOVED [45]
loved, 170, *'āhab* [33]
loved, 173, *'ahᵃbâ1* [2]
loved, 8163, *rāḥam* [2]
loved, *NIH/RPE* [1]
was loved, 170, *'āhab* [1]
were loved, 170, *'āhab* [1]
thing loved, 171, *'ōhab* [1]
loved one, 3351, *yādîd* [1]
loved, 8354, *rāṣâ1* [1]
am not loved, 8533, *śānē'* [1]
not loved, 8533, *śānē'* [1]

LOVELY [10]
lovely, 5534, *nā'weh* [4]
lovely, 3637, *yāpeh* [3]
lovely, 3202, *ṭôb2* [1]
lovely, 3351, *yādîd* [1]
lovely, 4718, *maḥmād* [1]

LOVER [28]
lover, 1856, *dôd* [28]

LOVER'S [1]
lover's, 4200+1856, *lᵉ-*[1]*+dôd* [1]

LOVERS [20]
lovers, 170, *ʾāhab* [12]
lovers, *NIH/RPE* [1]
lovers, 172, *ʾahab* [1]
lovers, 1856, *dôd* [1]
lovers[s], 2157, *-hem* [1]
your lovers[s], 4392, *-ām* [1]
lovers, 6311, *ʿāgab* [1]
lovers, 7108, *pilegeš* [1]
lovers, 8276, *rēaʿ*[2] [1]

LOVES [44]
loves, 170, *ʾāhab* [38]
loves, 2668, *ḥêq* [2]
loves, *NIH/RPE* [1]
loves, 2913, *ḥāpēṣ*[3] [1]
loves, 3137, *ḥāšaq*[1] [1]
loves, 3351, *yādîd* [1]

LOVING [8]
loving, 2876, *ḥesed*[2] [5]
loving, 2883, *ḥāsîd* [2]
loving, 172, *ʾahab* [1]

LOVING-KINDNESS [1]
loving-kindness, 2876, *ḥesed*[2] [1]

LOVINGLY [1]
lovingly, 173, *ʾahᵃbâ*[1] [1]

LOW [41]
bowed low, 7702, *qādad* [5]
brought low, 9164, *šāpēl*[1] [4]
brought low, 8820, *šāḥaḥ* [3]
bring low, 9164, *šāpēl*[1] [3]
be brought low, 8820, *šāḥaḥ* [2]
low, 9166, *šāpāl* [2]
low among men, 1201+132, *bēn*[1]*+ʾādām*[1] [1]
low, 1201+132, *bēn*[1]*+ʾādām*[1] [1]
laid low, 1815, *dābaq* [1]
laid low, 2150, *hālam* [1]
bowed low, 2556, *ḥāwâ*[2] [1]
bring low, 2725, *ḥālal*[1] [1]
laid low, 2764, *ḥālaš*[1] [1]
laid low, 2765, *ḥālaš*[2] [1]
are brought low, 4812, *mākak* [1]
be laid low, 6085, *sāḥap* [1]
brought low, 7592, *ṣāʿar* [1]
low, 7783, *qāṭān*[1] [1]
stoops low, 7970, *qāras* [1]
laid low, 8886, *šākab* [1]
was brought low, 8959, *šālak* [1]
brings low, 9164, *šāpēl*[1] [1]
lay low, 9164, *šāpēl*[1] [1]
lays low, 9164, *šāpēl*[1] [1]
low, 9164, *šāpēl*[1] [1]
low estate, 9165, *šēpel* [1]
low, 9165, *šēpel* [1]
low, 9166+7757, *šāpāl+qômâ* [1]

LOWBORN [1]
lowborn men, 1201+132, *bēn*[1]*+ʾādām*[1] [1]

LOWER [25]
lower, 9396, *taḥtôn* [11]
lower, 9397, *taḥtî* [4]
lower part of face, 8559, *śāpām* [3]
Lower Egypt, 824+5213, *ʾereṣ+miṣrayim* [2]
lower, 4752, *maṭṭâ* [2]
made lower, 2893, *ḥāsēr*[1] [1]
lower, 4946+9393, *min+taḥat*[1] [1]
Lower Egypt, 5213, *miṣrayim* [1]

LOWERED [7]
lowered, 3718, *yārad* [3]
lowered, 8332, *rāpâ*[1] [2]
lowered, 5663, *nûaḥ*[1] [1]
lowered, 8938, *šālaḥ* [1]

LOWEST [6]
lowest, 9396, *taḥtôn* [3]
lowest, 9397, *taḥtî* [2]
lowest of slaves, 6269+6269, *ʿebed*[1]*+ʿebed*[1] [1]

LOWING [3]
lowing, 7754, *qôl* [2]
lowing, 1716, *gāʿâ* [1]

LOWLIEST [2]
lowliest, 9166, *šāpāl* [1]
lowliest, 10738, *šᵉpal*[2] [1]

LOWLY [9]
lowly, 9166, *šāpāl* [8]
lowly, 7582, *ṣāʿîr*[1] [1]

LOYAL [7]
loyal, 3922, *kûn*[1] [2]
loyal to, 339, *ʾaḥar* [1]
loyal, 586, *ʾāman*[1] [1]
loyal, 2876, *ḥesed*[2] [1]
keep loyal, 3922, *kûn*[1] [1]
loyal, 9068+5466, *šāmar+mišmeret* [1]

LOYALTY [1]
undivided loyalty, 4202+4213+2256+4213, *lōʾ+lēb+wᵉ-+lēb* [1]

LUD [2]
Lud, 4276, *lûd* [2]

LUDITES [2]
Ludites, 4276, *lûd* [2]

LUHITH [2]
Luhith, 4284, *lûḥît* [2]

LUMBER [1]
lumber, 6770, *ʿēṣ* [1]

LURE [2]
lure, 5432, *māšak* [1]
lure, 7331, *pātâ*[1] [1]

LURED [2]
lured away, 5998, *nātaq* [1]
were lured away, 5998, *nātaq* [1]

LURK [2]
lurk, 7621, *ṣāpan* [1]
lurk, 8800, *šûr*[1] [1]

LURKED [1]
lurked, 741, *ʾārab* [1]

LURKS [1]
lurks, 741, *ʾārab* [1]

LUSH [2]
lush thicket, 1454, *gāʾôn* [1]
lush, 2774, *ḥemed* [1]

LUST [7]
lust, 9373, *taznût* [2]
lust after, 339+2388, *ʾaḥar+zānâ*[1] [1]
wanton lust, 2393, *zᵉnûnîm* [1]
lust after, 2773, *ḥāmad* [1]
burn with lust, 2801, *ḥāmam* [1]
lust, 6312, *ʿᵃgābâ* [1]

LUSTED [9]
lusted after, 6311+6584, *ʿāgab+ʿal*[2] [3]
lusted, *NIH/RPE* [1]
lusted after, 448+6311, *ʾel+ʿāgab* [1]
lusted after, 2388+339, *zānâ*[1]*+ʾaḥar* [1]
lusted, 2388, *zānâ*[1] [1]
lusted after, 6311, *ʿāgab* [1]
lusted, 6311, *ʿāgab* [1]

LUSTER [1]
lost luster, 6670, *ʿāmam*[2] [1]

LUSTFUL [2]
lustful, 1541+1414, *gādēl+bāśār* [1]
lustful neighings, 5177, *miṣhālôt* [1]

LUSTFULLY [1]
look lustfully, 1067, *bîn* [1]

LUSTS [1]
lusts, *NIH/RPE* [1]

LUSTY [1]
lusty, 3469, *yāzan* [1]

LUTES [2]
lutes, 4036, *kinnôr* [1]
lutes, 8956, *šālîš*[2] [1]

LUXURIOUS [1]
luxurious, 6696, *ʿōneg* [1]

LUXURY [2]
luxury, 9045, *šāmēn*[2] [1]
live in luxury, 9503, *taʿᵃnûg* [1]

LUZ [7]
Luz, 4281, *lûz*[3] [7]

LYDIA [3]
Lydia, 4276, *lûd* [2]
men of Lydia, 4276, *lûd* [1]

LYDIANS [1]
Lydians, 4276, *lûd* [1]

LYING [68]
lying, 9214, *šeqer* [16]
lying, 8886, *šākab* [10]
lying, 3942, *kāzāb* [5]
lying down, 8886, *šākab* [4]
lying on, 6590, *ʿālâ* [3]
lying in, 10542, *ʿal* [3]
lying, *NIH/RPE* [2]
lying, 2118, *hāyâ* [2]
lying, 3941, *kāzab* [2]
lying, 3950, *kāḥaš* [2]
lying, 5877, *nāpal* [2]
lying on, 6584+7156, *ʿal*[2]*+pāneh* [2]
lying, 8069, *rābaṣ* [2]
lying, *AIT* [1]
lying on, 448, *ʾel* [1]
lying in wait, 741, *ʾārab* [1]
lying with, 995+448, *bôʾ+ʾel* [1]
lying, 1819+3942, *dābar*[2]*+kāzāb* [1]
places lying in ruins, 2999, *ḥorbâ* [1]
lying, 3667, *yāṣaʿ* [1]
lying down, 8061, *rābaʿ*[1] [1]
lying down, 8069, *rābaṣ* [1]
lying with, 8886+907, *šākab+ʾēt*[2] [1]
lying, 9214+1819, *šeqer+dābar*[2] [1]
lying on, 10542, *ʿal* [1]
lying, 10542, *ʿal* [1]

LYRE [12]
lyre, 5575, *nēbel*[2] [7]
lyre, 10676, *śabbᵉkāʾ* [4]
lyre, 4036, *kinnôr* [1]

LYRES [15]
lyres, 5575, *nēbel*[2] [15]

MAACAH [25]
Maacah, 5082, *maʿᵃkâ*[2] [19]
Maacah, 5081, *maʿᵃkâ*[1] [3]
Maacah, 5084, *maʿᵃkātî* [3]

MAACATHITE [4]
Maacathite, 5084, *maʿᵃkātî* [3]
Maacathite, 1201+5084, *bēn*[1]*+maʿᵃkātî* [1]

MAACATHITES [1]
Maacathites, 5084, *maʿᵃkātî* [1]

MAADAI [1]
Maadai, 5049, *maʿᵃday* [1]

MAAI [1]
Maai, 5076, *māʿay* [1]

MAARATH [1]
Maarath, 5125, *maʿᵃrāt* [1]

MAASAI [1]
Maasai, 5127, *maʿśay* [1]

MAASEIAH [23]
Maaseiah, 5128, *maʿᵃśēyâ* [16]
Maaseiah, 5129, *maʿᵃśēyāhû* [7]

MAAZ [1]
Maaz, 5106, *maʿaṣ* [1]
MAAZIAH [2]
Maaziah, 5068, *maʿazyâ* [1]
Maaziah, 5069, *maʿazyāhû* [1]
MACBANNAI [1]
Macbannai, 4801, *makbannay* [1]
MACBENAH [1]
Macbenah, 4800, *makbēnâ* [1]
MACHINES [1]
machines, 3115, *ḥiššābôn* [1]
MACHPELAH [6]
Machpelah, 4834, *makpēlâ* [6]
MACNADEBAI [1]
Macnadebai, 4827, *maknadbay* [1]
MAD [4]
go mad, 2147, *hālal*^{3} [2]
gone mad, 2147, *hālal*^{3} [1]
drive mad, 8713, *šāgaʿ* [1]
MADAI [2]
Madai, 4512, *māday* [2]
MADE [910]
made, 6913, *ʿāśâ*^{1} [270]
made, 4162, *kārat* [45]
made, *NIH/RPE* [38]
offering made by fire, 852, *ʾiššeh* [38]
made, 5989, *nātan* [37]
made, 8492, *śîm* [35]
made king, 4887, *mālak*^{1} [24]
made, *AIT* [19]
offerings made by fire, 852, *ʾiššeh* [19]
made repairs, 2616, *ḥāzaq* [14]
made, 5126, *maʿ*^{a}*śeh* [14]
bread made without yeast, 5174, *maṣṣâ*^{1} [14]
made known, 3359, *yādaʿ* [10]
what made, 5126, *maʿ*^{a}*śeh* [10]
made, 2118, *hāyâ* [6]
made, 8883, *šît*^{1} [6]
made, 1819, *dābar*^{2} [5]
atonement made, 4105, *kāpar*^{1} [5]
repairs made, 2616, *ḥāzaq* [4]
made preparations, 3922, *kûn*^{1} [4]
made atonement, 4105, *kāpar*^{1} [4]
made a vow, 5623+5624, *nādar+nēder* [4]
be made, 6913, *ʿāśâ*^{1} [4]
made swear, 8678, *šābaʿ* [4]
made drink, 9197, *šāqâ* [4]
made, 928, *b*^{e}*-* [3]
made a covenant, 4162, *kārat* [3]
made holy, 7727, *qādaš* [3]
made swear an oath, 8678, *šābaʿ* [3]
made take an oath, 8678, *šābaʿ* [3]
made drunk, 8910, *šākar* [3]
made peace, 8966, *šālēm*^{1} [3]
made by fire, 852, *ʾiššeh* [2]
sacrifice made by fire, 852, *ʾiššeh* [2]
made, 1215, *bānâ* [2]
made known, 1655, *gālâ* [2]
promises made, 1819, *dābar*^{2} [2]
made sacrifices, 2284+2285, *zābaḥ+zebaḥ*^{1} [2]
made an alliance, 2489, *ḥābar*^{2} [2]
made camp, 2837, *ḥānâ*^{1} [2]
is made aware, 3359, *yādaʿ* [2]
made, 3657, *yāṣag* [2]
made, 3670, *yāṣar* [2]
made heavy, 3877, *kābēd*^{1} [2]
made bow, 4156, *kāraʿ* [2]
made spotless, 4235, *lāban*^{1} [2]
made war, 4309, *lāḥam*^{1} [2]
made of, 4946, *min* [2]
made without yeast, 5174, *maṣṣâ*^{1} [2]
made bitter, 5352, *mārar* [2]
vow made, 5624+5623, *nēder+nādar* [2]
made turn, 5989, *nātan* [2]
made rounds, 6015, *sābab* [2]
made way around, 6015, *sābab* [2]
made trouble, 6579, *ʿākar* [2]
made, 6590, *ʿālâ* [2]
been made, 6913, *ʿāśâ*^{1} [2]
made, 7188, *pāʿal* [2]
made fruitful, 7238, *pārâ*^{1} [2]
made jealous, 7861, *qānāʾ* [2]
made an offering, 7928, *qārab* [2]
made tremble, 8321, *rāʿaš*^{1} [2]
made a treaty of peace, 8966, *šālēm*^{1} [2]
made an end, 8966, *šālēm*^{1} [2]
made a fool of, 9438, *tālal* [2]
a search made, 10118, *b*^{e}*qar* [2]
made known, 10313, *y*^{e}*daʿ* [2]
made, 10522, *ʿ*^{a}*bad* [2]
made ruler, 10715, *š*^{e}*lēṭ* [2]
made lament, 61, *ʾābal*^{1} [1]
made light shine, 239, *ʾôr*^{1} [1]
had made ready, 673, *ʾāsar* [1]
made ready, 673, *ʾāsar* [1]
made long, 799, *ʾārak* [1]
offerings made with fire, 852, *ʾiššeh* [1]
made with, 928, *b*^{e}*-* [1]
made stench, 944+8194, *bāʾaš+rêaḥ* [1]
made yourself a stench, 944, *bāʾaš* [1]
made attack, 995, *bôʾ* [1]
made trust, 1053, *bāṭaḥ*^{1} [1]
made grow old, 1162, *bālâ*^{1} [1]
search be made for, 1335, *bāqaš* [1]
search made for, 1335, *bāqaš* [1]
made higher, 1467, *gābah* [1]
made great, 1540, *gādal* [1]
made grow, 1540, *gādal* [1]
made threats, 1540, *gādal* [1]
made request, 1819, *dābar*^{2} [1]
search was made, 2011, *dāraš* [1]
made fall, 2118+4200+4842, *hāyâ+l*^{e}*-*^{1}*+mikšôl* [1]
made walk, 2143, *hālak* [1]
made way, 2143, *hālak* [1]
made mention of, 2349, *zākar*^{1} [1]
made glad, 2525, *ḥādâ*^{1} [1]
made harder, 2616, *ḥāzaq* [1]
made strong, 2616, *ḥāzaq* [1]
made assignments, 2745, *ḥālaq*^{2} [1]
bread made with yeast, 2809, *ḥāmēṣ*^{4} [1]
made with yeast, 2809, *ḥāmēṣ*^{4} [1]
made^{s}, 2858, *ḥānan*^{1} [1]
made lower, 2893, *ḥāsēr*^{1} [1]
made no move, 3087, *ḥārēš*^{2} [1]
made dark, 3124, *ḥāšak* [1]
made an alliance, 3161, *ḥātan* [1]
be made unclean, 3237, *ṭāmēʾ*^{1} [1]
made shrivel, 3312, *yābēš*^{1} [1]
be made known, 3359, *yādaʿ* [1]
made himself known, 3359, *yādaʿ* [1]
made a place, 3569, *yāsad*^{1} [1]
made come out, 3655, *yāṣāʾ* [1]
made afraid, 3707, *yārēʾ*^{1} [1]
made flow down, 3718, *yārad* [1]
made dwell, 3782, *yāšab* [1]
been made ready, 3922, *kûn*^{1} [1]
is made ready, 3922, *kûn*^{1} [1]
made plans, 3922, *kûn*^{1} [1]
made ready, 3922, *kûn*^{1} [1]
made an end, 3983, *kālâ*^{1} [1]
made subject to, 4044+9393+3338, *kānaʿ+taḥat*^{1}*+yād* [1]
atonement be made, 4105, *kāpar*^{1} [1]
atonement was made, 4105, *kāpar*^{1} [1]
atonement made, 4113+4105, *kippurîm+kāpar*^{1} [1]
made miserable, 4156+4156, *kāraʿ+kāraʿ* [1]
made a pact, 4162, *kārat* [1]
made stumble, 4173, *kāšal* [1]
made bread, 4221, *lābab*^{2} [1]
made grumble, 4296, *lûn* [1]
made, 4374+928, *lāqaḥ+b*^{e}*-* [1]
something made, 4382, *lāšad* [1]
made waste away, 4570, *mûg* [1]
made with yeast, 4721, *maḥmeṣet* [1]
made, 4856, *m*^{e}*lāʾkâ* [1]
made escape, 4880, *mālaṭ*^{1} [1]
made king, 4887+4889, *mālak*^{1}*+melek*^{1} [1]
made queen, 4887, *mālak*^{1} [1]
was made ruler, 4887, *mālak*^{1} [1]
made from, 4946, *min* [1]
made up of, 4946, *min* [1]
made melt with fear, 4998, *māsâ* [1]
idols made of metal, 5011, *massēkâ*^{1} [1]
made lose, 5022, *māsas* [1]
creature made, 5126, *maʿ*^{a}*śeh* [1]
how made, 5126, *maʿ*^{a}*śeh* [1]
idols made, 5126, *maʿ*^{a}*śeh* [1]
that made, 5126, *maʿ*^{a}*śeh* [1]
made raw, 5307, *māraṭ* [1]
made taste bitterness, 5352, *mārar* [1]
made ruler, 5440, *māšal*^{2} [1]
made show utter contempt, 5540+5540, *nāʾaṣ+nāʾaṣ* [1]
made clear, 5583, *nāgad* [1]
made a vow, 5623, *nādar* [1]
made vows, 5623+5624, *nādar+nēder* [1]
made vow, 5623+5624, *nādar+nēder* [1]
made vow, 5623, *nādar* [1]
made vow, 5624+5623, *nēder+nādar* [1]
vows made, 5624+5623, *nēder+nādar* [1]
made blow, 5627, *nāhag*^{1} [1]
made good escape, 5674+2256+4880, *nûs+w*^{e}*-+mālaṭ*^{1} [1]
made wander, 5675, *nûaʿ* [1]
made flow, 5688, *nāzal* [1]
made foreign, 5796, *nākar*^{2} [1]
made come down, 5877, *nāpal* [1]
made stand firm, 5893, *nāṣab*^{1} [1]
made, 5893, *nāṣab*^{1} [1]
made, 5951, *nāśāʾ* [1]
loan made, 5957, *nāšāʾ*^{1} [1]
made forget, 5960, *nāšâ*^{1} [1]
made face, 5989+7156, *nātan+pāneh* [1]
made ready, 5989, *nātan* [1]
made tremble, 6001, *nātar*^{2} [1]
made come off, 6073, *sûr*^{1} [1]
made secure, 6184, *sāʿad* [1]
made work, 6296, *ʿābar*^{1} [1]
made crooked, 6390, *ʿāwâ*^{1} [1]
made crooked, 6430, *ʿāwat* [1]
made come up, 6590, *ʿālâ* [1]
made grow up, 6590, *ʿālâ* [1]
made merry, 6600, *ʿālaz* [1]
made a fool, 6618, *ʿālal*^{1} [1]
made stand, 6641, *ʿāmad* [1]
made deep, 6676, *ʿāmaq* [1]
made suffer, 6700, *ʿānâ*^{2} [1]
made numerous, 6793, *ʿāṣam*^{1} [1]
is made, 6913, *ʿāśâ*^{1} [1]
was made, 6913, *ʿāśâ*^{1} [1]
were made, 6913, *ʿāśâ*^{1} [1]
made rich, 6947, *ʿāšar* [1]
made intercession, 7003, *pāgaʿ* [1]
made shake, 7064, *pāḥad* [1]
am wonderfully made, 7098, *pālâ* [1]
made, 7189, *pōʿal* [1]
made a vow, 7198+7023, *pāṣâ+peh* [1]
made clear, 7300, *pāraš*^{1} [1]
made a dash, 7320, *pāšaṭ* [1]
made appear righteous, 7405, *ṣādaq* [1]
made seem righteous, 7405, *ṣādaq* [1]
made float, 7429, *ṣûp*^{1} [1]
made successful, 7503, *ṣālaḥ*^{2} [1]
made grow, 7541, *ṣāmaḥ* [1]
made, 7756, *qûm* [1]
made contemptible, 7837, *qālal* [1]
made angry, 7911+2118, *qāṣap+hāyâ* [1]
made offerings, 7928, *qārab* [1]
made, 7928, *qārab* [1]
offering made by fire, 7933+852, *qorbān+ʾiššeh* [1]
made stubborn, 7996, *qāšâ* [1]
made see, 8011, *rāʾâ*^{1} [1]
made many, 8049, *rābâ*^{1} [1]
made numerous, 8049, *rābâ*^{1} [1]
made tremble, 8074, *rāgaz* [1]
made bold, 8104, *rāhab* [1]
made grow tall, 8123, *rûm*^{1} [1]
made noise, 8131+9558, *rûaʿ+t*^{e}*rûʿâ* [1]
made ride, 8206, *rākab* [1]
made faint, 8216, *rākak* [1]
made sing, 8264, *rānan* [1]
made rejoice, 8523, *śāmaḥ* [1]
made very glad, 8523+8523, *śāmaḥ+śāmaḥ* [1]
made, 8596, *śārap* [1]
made captives of, 8647, *šābâ* [1]

made swear an oath, 8678+8678, *šābaʿ+šābaʿ* [1]
made go back, 8740, *šûb*^{1} [1]
made pay for, 8740+928+8031, *šûb*^{1}*+b*^{e}*+rōʾš*^{1} [1]
made prosperous again, 8740+8654, *šûb*^{1}*+š*^{e}*bût* [1]
made retreat, 8740+294, *šûb*^{1}*+ʾāḥôr* [1]
restitution made, 8740, *šûb*^{1} [1]
made lie down, 8886, *šākab* [1]
made forget, 8894, *šākaḥ* [1]
made childless, 8897, *šākal* [1]
made a dwelling, 8905, *šākan* [1]
made drunk, 8912, *šākur* [1]
made flourish, 8938, *šālaḥ* [1]
made desolate, 9037, *šāmēm*^{1} [1]
made hear, 9048, *šāmaʿ* [1]
made known, 9048, *šāmaʿ* [1]
made proclamation, 9048, *šāmaʿ* [1]
made to drink, 9197, *šāqâ* [1]
made secure, 9461, *tāmak* [1]
made a fatal mistake, 9494+928+5883, *tāʿâ+b*^{e}*+nepeš* [1]
made wander, 9494, *tāʿâ* [1]
made stagger, 9570, *tarʿēlâ* [1]
a search be made, 10118, *b*^{e}*qar* [1]
made afraid, 10167, *d*^{e}*ḥal* [1]
made, 10314, *y*^{e}*hab* [1]
this made, 10353+10619+10180, *kōl+q*^{o}*bēl+d*^{e}*nâ* [1]
be made, 10522, *ʿ*^{a}*bad* [1]
made every effort, 10700, *š*^{e}*dar* [1]

MADMAN [5]
madman, 408+8713, *ʾîš*^{1}*+šāgaʿ* [1]
acted like a madman, 2147, *hālal*^{3} [1]
madman, 4263, *lāhah* [1]
madman, 8713, *šāgaʿ* [1]
madman, 8714, *šiggāʿôn* [1]

MADMANNAH [2]
Madmannah, 4525, *madmannâ*^{1} [1]
Madmannah, 4526, *madmannâ*^{2} [1]

MADMEN [2]
Madmen, 4522, *madmēn* [1]
madmen, 8713, *šāgaʿ* [1]

MADMENAH [1]
Madmenah, 4524, *madmēnâ*^{2} [1]

MADNESS [7]
madness, 2099, *hôlēlôt* [4]
madness, 8714, *šiggāʿôn* [2]
madness, 2100, *hôlēlût* [1]

MADON [2]
Madon, 4507, *mādôn*^{2} [2]

MAGBISH [1]
Magbish, 4455, *magbîš* [1]

MAGDIEL [2]
Magdiel, 4462, *magdîʾēl* [2]

MAGGOT [1]
maggot, 8231, *rimmâ* [1]

MAGGOTS [3]
maggots, 8231, *rimmâ* [2]
maggots, 9357, *tôlēʿâ* [1]

MAGIC [3]
magic charms, 4086, *keset* [2]
magic spells, 2490, *ḥeber*^{1} [1]

MAGICIAN [2]
magician, 10282, *ḥarṭōm* [2]

MAGICIANS [13]
magicians, 3033, *ḥarṭōm* [10]
magicians, 10282, *ḥarṭōm* [3]

MAGISTRATES [3]
magistrates, 10767, *tiptāy* [2]
magistrates, 10735, *š*^{e}*paṭ* [1]

MAGNIFICENCE [1]
magnificence, 5087+2025, *maʿal*^{2}*+-â*^{2} [1]

MAGNIFICENT [4]
magnificent, 2292, *z*^{e}*bul*^{2} [2]
magnificent, 1540, *gādal* [1]
magnificent, 7098, *pālāʾ* [1]

MAGNIFY [1]
magnify, 1540, *gādal* [1]

MAGOG [4]
Magog, 4470, *māgôg* [4]

MAGOR-MISSABIB [1]
Magor-Missabib, 4474, *māgôr missābîb* [1]

MAGPIASH [1]
Magpiash, 4488, *magpîʿāš* [1]

MAHALALEL [7]
Mahalalel, 4546, *mah*^{a}*lalʾēl* [7]

MAHALATH [4]
mahalath, 4714, *māḥ*^{a}*lat*^{1} [2]
Mahalath, 4715, *māḥ*^{a}*lat*^{2} [2]

MAHANAIM [14]
Mahanaim, 4724, *maḥ*^{a}*nayim* [14]

MAHANEH DAN [2]
Mahaneh Dan, 4723, *maḥ*^{a}*nēh-dān* [2]

MAHARAI [3]
Maharai, 4560, *mah*^{a}*ray* [3]

MAHATH [3]
Mahath, 4744, *maḥat* [3]

MAHAVITE [1]
Mahavite, 4687, *maḥ*^{a}*wîm* [1]

MAHAZIOTH [2]
Mahazioth, 4692, *maḥ*^{a}*zîʾôt* [2]

MAHER-SHALAL-HASH-BAZ [2]
Maher-Shalal-Hash-Baz, 4561, *mahēr šālāl ḥāš baz* [2]

MAHLAH [5]
Mahlah, 4702, *maḥlâ* [5]

MAHLI [12]
Mahli, 4706, *maḥlî*^{1} [12]

MAHLITE [1]
Mahlite, 4707, *maḥlî*^{2} [1]

MAHLITES [1]
Mahlites, 4707, *maḥlî*^{2} [1]

MAHLON [3]
Mahlon, 4705, *maḥlôn* [3]

MAHLON'S [1]
Mahlon's, 4705, *maḥlôn* [1]

MAHOL [1]
Mahol, 4689, *māḥôl*^{2} [1]

MAHSEIAH [2]
Mahseiah, 4729, *maḥsēyâ* [2]

MAID [2]
maid, 9148, *šipḥâ* [2]

MAIDEN [5]
maiden, 1435, *b*^{e}*tûlâ* [3]
maiden, 6625, *ʿalmâ* [2]

MAIDENS [11]
maidens, 1435, *b*^{e}*tûlâ* [7]
maidens, 1426, *bat*^{1} [2]
maidens, 6625, *ʿalmâ* [2]

MAIDS [7]
maids, 5855, *naʿ*^{a}*râ*^{1} [7]

MAIDSERVANT [28]
maidservant, 563, *ʾāmâ* [16]
maidservant, 9148, *šipḥâ* [12]

MAIDSERVANTS [20]
maidservants, 9148, *šipḥâ* [11]
maidservants, 563, *ʾāmâ* [9]

MAIMED [1]
maimed, 3024, *ḥārûṣ*^{4} [1]

MAIN [11]
main hall, 2121, *hêkāl* [6]
main hall, 1074, *bayit*^{1} [1]
main, 1524, *gādôl* [1]
main road, 2006+2006, *derek+derek* [1]
main branches, 4751+964, *maṭṭeh+bad*^{2} [1]
main road, 5019, *m*^{e}*sillâ* [1]

MAINLAND [2]
mainland, 8441, *śādeh* [2]

MAINSTAY [1]
mainstay, 8040, *rēʾšît* [1]

MAINTAIN [15]
maintain, 9068, *šāmar* [5]
maintain, 5989, *nātan* [2]
maintain, 6913, *ʿāśâ*^{1} [2]
maintain, 7756, *qûm* [2]
maintain, *NIH/RPE* [1]
maintain, 2616, *ḥāzaq* [1]
maintain, 3657, *yāṣag* [1]
maintain rights, 7405, *ṣādaq* [1]

MAINTAINING [1]
maintaining, 5915, *nāṣar* [1]

MAINTAINS [3]
maintains, 799, *ʾārak* [1]
maintains, 2616, *ḥāzaq* [1]
maintains wrath, 5757, *nāṭar*^{1} [1]

MAJESTIC [13]
majestic, 129, *ʾaddîr* [3]
majestic, 158, *ʾādar* [2]
majestic, 398, *ʾāyōm* [2]
majestic, 2077, *hādār* [2]
majestic, 466, *ʾ*^{e}*lōhîm* [1]
majestic, 1454, *gāʾôn* [1]
majestic, 2086, *hôd*^{1} [1]
majestic, 3636, *yāpâ* [1]

MAJESTY [32]
majesty, 2077, *hādār* [10]
majesty, 1454, *gāʾôn* [6]
majesty, 1542, *gōdel* [4]
majesty, 2086, *hôd*^{1} [3]
majesty, 1452, *gaʾ*^{a}*wâ* [2]
majesty, 1455, *gēʾût* [2]
majesty, *NIH/RPE* [1]
majesty, 1525, *g*^{e}*dûllâ* [1]
majesty, 4889, *melek*^{1} [1]
majesty, 5905, *nēṣaḥ*^{1} [1]
majesty, 10199, *h*^{a}*dar*^{2} [1]

MAJOR [1]
major, 4435, *mibḥôr* [1]

MAKAZ [1]
Makaz, 5242, *māqaṣ* [1]

MAKE [716]
make, 6913, *ʿāśâ*^{1} [161]
make atonement, 4105, *kāpar*^{1} [58]
make, 5989, *nātan* [55]
make, 8492, *śîm* [48]
make, 4162, *kārat* [27]
make, *NIH/RPE* [19]
make known, 3359, *yādaʿ* [11]
make, *AIT* [10]
make music, 2376, *zāmar*^{1} [10]
make afraid, 3006, *ḥārad* [9]
make, 8883, *šît*^{1} [9]
make king, 4887, *mālak*^{1} [7]
make shine, 239, *ʾôr*^{1} [6]
make restitution, 8966, *šālēm*^{1} [6]
make war, 4309, *lāḥam*^{1} [5]
make fruitful, 7238, *pārâ*^{1} [5]
make even heavier, 3578, *yāsap* [4]
make straight, 3837, *yāšar* [4]

make fall, 5877, *nāpal* [4]
make numerous, 8049, *rābâ^{1}* [4]
make drunk, 8910, *šākar* [4]
make, 2118, *hāyâ* [3]
make himself unclean, 3237, *ṭāmēʾ^{1}* [3]
make myself known, 3359, *yādaʿ* [3]
make prosper, 3512, *yāṭab* [3]
used to make, 6913, *ʿāśâ^{1}* [3]
make lighter, 7837, *qālal* [3]
make glad, 8523, *śāmaḥ* [3]
make swear, 8678, *šābaʿ* [3]
make return, 8740, *šûb^{1}* [3]
make eat food, 430, *ʾākal* [2]
make eat, 430, *ʾākal* [2]
make afraid, 987, *bāhal* [2]
make great, 1540, *gādal* [2]
make stick, 1815, *dābaq* [2]
make a survey of, 2143+928, *hālak+b^{e}-* [2]
make, 3108, *ḥāšab* [2]
make himself ceremonially unclean, 3237, *ṭāmēʾ^{1}* [2]
make yourselves unclean, 3237, *ṭāmēʾ^{1}* [2]
make dwell, 3782, *yāšab* [2]
make a vow, 5623+5624, *nādar+nēder* [2]
make wander about, 5675, *nûaʿ* [2]
make, 6296, *ʿābar^{1}* [2]
make a bargain, 6842, *ʿārab^{1}* [2]
make sport, 7464, *ṣāḥaq* [2]
make grow, 7541, *ṣāmaḥ* [2]
make sprout, 7541, *ṣāmaḥ* [2]
make holy, 7727, *qādaš* [2]
make offerings, 7787, *qāṭar^{1}* [2]
make great, 8049, *rābâ^{1}* [2]
have request to make, 8629+8626, *š^{e}ʾēlâ+šāʾal* [2]
make childless, 8897, *šākal* [2]
must make restitution, 8966+8966, *šālēm^{1}+šālēm^{1}* [2]
make sure, 9068, *šāmar* [2]
make way, 91, *ʾabrēk* [1]
make fires, 239, *ʾôr^{1}* [1]
make countless, 889+4202+6218+8049, *ʾ^{a}šer+lōʾ+sāpar+rābâ^{1}* [1]
make plain, 930, *bāʾar* [1]
make a distinction, 976, *bādal* [1]
make enter, 995+928, *bôʾ+b^{e}-* [1]
make go down, 995, *bôʾ* [1]
make, 995, *bôʾ* [1]
make spoil, 1024, *bāzaz* [1]
make firm, 1215, *bānâ* [1]
make unjust gain, 1298+1299, *bāṣaʿ+beṣaʿ* [1]
make unjust gain, 1298, *bāṣaʿ* [1]
wanted to make, 1335+4200, *bāqaš+l^{e}-^{1}* [1]
make, 1345, *bārāʾ^{3}* [1]
make flee, 1368, *bāraḥ^{1}* [1]
make grow tall, 1467, *gābah* [1]
make greater, 1540, *gādal* [1]
make grow, 1540, *gādal* [1]
make so much of, 1540, *gādal* [1]
make many promises, 1819+1821, *dābar^{2}+dābār* [1]
make request, 1819, *dābar^{2}* [1]
make, 1819, *dābar^{2}* [1]
make promise, 1821+1819, *dābār+dābar^{2}* [1]
make myself like, 1948, *dāmâ^{1}* [1]
make ready to shoot, 2005, *dārak* [1]
make investigation, 2011, *dāraš* [1]
make sport of, 2118+4200+5442, *hāyâ+l^{e}-^{1}+māšāl^{1}* [1]
make flow, 2143, *hālak* [1]
make boast, 2146, *hālal^{2}* [1]
make tremble, 2316, *zûaʿ* [1]
make yourselves clean, 2342, *zākâ* [1]
make petition, 2349, *zākar^{1}* [1]
make appeals, 2410, *zāʿaq* [1]
make fine speeches, 2488+928+4863, *ḥābar^{1}+b^{e}+millâ* [1]
make out to be guilty, 2627, *ḥāṭāʾ* [1]
make sin, 2627, *ḥāṭāʾ* [1]
make wiser, 2681, *ḥākam* [1]
make music, 2727, *ḥālal^{3}* [1]
make laws, 2980+2976, *ḥāqaq+ḥōq* [1]
make laws, 2980, *ḥāqaq* [1]
make plans, 3108+4742, *ḥāšab+maḥ^{a}šābâ* [1]
make bands, 3138, *ḥāšaq^{2}* [1]
make ceremonially clean, 3197, *ṭāhēr* [1]
make prosper, 3201, *ṭôb^{1}* [1]
make unclean, 3237, *ṭāmēʾ^{1}* [1]
things that make unclean, 3240, *ṭumʾâ* [1]
make dry, 3312, *yābēš^{1}* [1]
make himself known, 3359, *yādaʿ* [1]
make predictions, 3359, *yādaʿ* [1]
make famous, 3512, *yāṭab* [1]
make more prosperous, 3512, *yāṭab* [1]
surely make prosper, 3512+3512, *yāṭab+yāṭab* [1]
make again, 3578+6388, *yāsap+ʿôd* [1]
make increase, 3578, *yāsap* [1]
make shine, 3655, *yāṣāʾ* [1]
make spew out, 3655+4946+7023, *yāṣāʾ+min+peh* [1]
make bare, 3657, *yāṣag* [1]
make bed, 3667, *yāṣaʿ* [1]
make, 3670, *yāṣar* [1]
make scarcer, 3700, *yāqar* [1]
make inherit, 3769, *yāraš^{1}* [1]
make vomit up, 3769, *yāraš^{1}* [1]
make live, 3782, *yāšab* [1]
make dull, 3877, *kābēd^{1}* [1]
make men slaves, 3899+6269, *kābaš+ʿebed^{1}* [1]
make, 3922, *kûn^{1}* [1]
make preparations, 3922, *kûn^{1}* [1]
make preparation, 3922, *kûn^{1}* [1]
make secure, 3922, *kûn^{1}* [1]
make an end, 3983, *kālâ^{1}* [1]
make angry, 4087, *kāʿas* [1]
make amends, 4105, *kāpar^{1}* [1]
make a treaty, 4162, *kārat* [1]
make fall, 4173, *kāšal* [1]
make special bread, 4221+4223, *lābab^{2}+l^{e}bibâ* [1]
make bricks, 4236+4246, *lāban^{2}+l^{e}bēnâ* [1]
make, 4374, *lāqaḥ* [1]
make a substitution, 4614+4614, *mûr^{1}+mûr^{1}* [1]
make substitution, 4614, *mûr^{1}* [1]
make die, 4637, *mût* [1]
make stumble, 4842, *mikšôl* [1]
make succeed, 4848, *mālēʾ^{1}* [1]
make king, 4887+4889, *mālak^{1}+melek^{1}* [1]
make room for, 4946+7156, *min+pānеh* [1]
make few in number, 5070, *māʿaṭ* [1]
make weak, 5070, *māʿaṭ* [1]
what make, 5126, *maʿ^{a}śeh* [1]
make rulers, 5440, *māšal^{2}* [1]
make clean, 5470, *mišʿî* [1]
make known, 5583, *nāgad* [1]
make vows, 5623, *nādar* [1]
make a vow, 5623, *nādar* [1]
make vows, 5623+5624, *nādar+nēder* [1]
make thrive, 5649, *nûb* [1]
make wander, 5653, *nûd* [1]
make friends with, 5795, *nākar^{1}* [1]
make drop, 5877, *nāpal* [1]
make lie down, 5877, *nāpal* [1]
make, 5877, *nāpal* [1]
make, 5951, *nāśāʾ* [1]
make a loan, 5957+5394, *nāšāʾ^{1}+maššāʾâ* [1]
make restitution, 5989, *nātan* [1]
make turn, 5989+448, *nātan+ʾel* [1]
make leave, 6073, *sûr^{1}* [1]
make slaves, 6268, *ʿābad* [1]
make work, 6268, *ʿābad* [1]
make cross, 6296, *ʿābar^{1}* [1]
make come up, 6590, *ʿālâ* [1]
make come, 6590, *ʿālâ* [1]
make offerings, 6590, *ʿālâ* [1]
make wear, 6590+6584+5516, *ʿālâ+ʿal^{2}+motnayim* [1]
make shut, 6623, *ʿālam* [1]
make bald, 6867, *ʿārâ^{1}* [1]
certainly make, 6913+6913, *ʿāśâ^{1}+ʿāśâ^{1}* [1]
make provision, 6913, *ʿāśâ^{1}* [1]
make up, 6913, *ʿāśâ^{1}* [1]
use to make, 6913, *ʿāśâ^{1}* [1]
make plead, 7003, *pāgaʿ* [1]
make a special vow, 7098+5623, *pālāʾ+nādar* [1]
make a distinction, 7111, *pālâ* [1]
make level, 7142, *pālas^{1}* [1]
make smooth, 7142, *pālas^{1}* [1]
make flourish, 7255, *pāraḥ^{1}* [1]
make flow, 7337, *pātaḥ^{1}* [1]
make shine, 7413, *ṣāhal^{2}* [1]
make success, 7503, *ṣālaḥ^{2}* [1]
make tingle, 7509, *ṣālal^{1}* [1]
make spring up, 7541, *ṣāmaḥ* [1]
make good, 7756, *qûm* [1]
make offering, 7787, *qāṭar^{1}* [1]
make envious, 7861, *qānāʾ* [1]
make nests, 7873, *qānan* [1]
make an offer, 7924, *qārāʾ^{1}* [1]
make proclamation, 7924, *qārāʾ^{1}* [1]
make, 7928, *qārab* [1]
make beams, 7936, *qārâ^{1}* [1]
make look, 8011, *rāʾâ^{1}* [1]
make see, 8011, *rāʾâ^{1}* [1]
make as great as you like, 8049+4394, *rābâ^{1}+m^{e}ʾōd* [1]
make many, 8049, *rābâ^{1}* [1]
make numerous, 8049+8049, *rābâ^{1}+rābâ^{1}* [1]
make plentiful, 8049, *rābâ^{1}* [1]
make tremble, 8074, *rāgaz* [1]
make bald, 8143+7947, *rāḥab+qorḥâ* [1]
make friends, 8287, *rāʿâ^{2}* [1]
make leap, 8321, *rāʿaš^{1}* [1]
make amends, 8355, *rāṣâ^{2}* [1]
make grow, 8451, *śûg^{2}* [1]
make a pet, 8471, *śāḥaq* [1]
make serve, 8492+4200, *śîm+l^{e}-^{1}* [1]
make sure hears, 8492+928+265, *śîm+b^{e}+ʾōzen* [1]
make merry, 8523, *śāmaḥ* [1]
make a fire, 8596, *śārap* [1]
make^{s}, 8626, *šāʾal* [1]
make captives, 8647, *šābâ* [1]
make full restitution, 8740+928+8031, *šûb^{1}+b^{e}+rōʾš^{1}* [1]
make go, 8740, *šûb^{1}* [1]
make right, 8740, *šûb^{1}* [1]
make turn, 8883, *šît^{1}* [1]
make forget, 8894, *šākaḥ* [1]
make unproductive, 8897, *šākal* [1]
make home, 8905, *šākan* [1]
make sleep, 8905, *šākan* [1]
make good, 8966, *šālēm^{1}* [1]
make pay, 8966, *šālēm^{1}* [1]
make peace, 8966, *šālēm^{1}* [1]
must certainly make restitution, 8966+8966, *šālēm^{1}+šālēm^{1}* [1]
make calloused, 9042, *šāmēn^{1}* [1]
make heard, 9048, *šāmaʿ* [1]
make hear, 9048, *šāmaʿ* [1]
make sharp, 9111, *šānan^{1}* [1]
make drink, 9197, *šāqâ* [1]
make stagger, 9494, *tāʿâ* [1]
make wander, 9494, *tāʿâ* [1]
make, 10522, *ʿ^{a}bad* [1]

MAKER [26]
Maker, 6913, *ʿāśâ^{1}* [21]
Maker, 3670, *yāṣar* [4]
Maker, 7188, *pāʿal* [1]

MAKERS [1]
makers, 3093, *ḥārāš* [1]

MAKES [98]
makes, 6913, *ʿāśâ^{1}* [8]
makes holy, 7727, *qādaš* [7]
makes, 8492, *śîm* [7]
makes, *NIH/RPE* [5]
makes, 5989, *nātan* [4]
makes, *AIT* [3]
makes rise, 6590, *ʿālâ* [3]
makes fools of, 2147, *hālal^{3}* [2]
makes atonement, 4105, *kāpar^{1}* [2]
makes a vow, 5623+5624, *nādar+nēder* [2]
makes grow, 7541, *ṣāmaḥ* [2]
makes, 8751, *šāwâ^{2}* [2]
makes stagger, 9570, *tarʿēlâ* [2]
makes speech, 609+606, *ʾēmer^{1}+ʾāmar^{1}* [1]
makes, 928, *b^{e}-* [1]
makes tremble, 1286, *bāʿat* [1]
makes listen, 1655+265, *gālâ+ʾōzen* [1]
makes alive, 2649, *ḥāyâ* [1]

makes wiser, 2681, *ḥākam* [1]
makes sick, 2703, *ḥālâ*[1] [1]
makes refuge, 2879, *ḥāsâ* [1]
makes run dry, 2990, *ḥārēb*[1] [1]
makes known, 3359, *yāda'* [1]
makes cheerful, 3512, *yāṭab* [1]
makes plans, 3619, *yā'aṣ* [1]
makes up, 3619, *yā'aṣ* [1]
makes flash, 3649, *yāpa'* [1]
makes come up, 3655, *yāṣā'* [1]
makes, 3670, *yāṣar* [1]
makes dwell, 3782, *yāšab* [1]
makes straight, 3837, *yāšar* [1]
makes wealthy, 3877, *kābēd*[1] [1]
makes firm, 3922, *kûn*[1] [1]
makes secure, 3922, *kûn*[1] [1]
makes a covenant, 4162, *kārat* [1]
makes, 4162, *kārat* [1]
makes fall, 4842, *mikšôl* [1]
makes a vow, 5623, *nādar* [1]
makes powerful, 6451, *'āzaz* [1]
makes offering, 6590, *'ālâ* [1]
makes a special vow, 7098+5624, *pālā'+nēder* [1]
makes a distinction, 7111, *pālâ* [1]
makes tremble, 7145, *pālaṣ* [1]
makes ready, 7188, *pā'al* [1]
makes rise, 7756, *qûm* [1]
makes nest, 7873, *qānan* [1]
makes large, 7973, *qāra'* [1]
makes grow, 8049, *rābâ*[1] [1]
makes lie down, 8069, *rābaṣ* [1]
makes fresh, 8324, *rāpā'*[1] [1]
makes skip, 8376, *rāqad* [1]
makes perfume, 8379, *rāqaḥ* [1]
makes churn, 8409, *rātaḥ* [1]
makes great, 8434, *śāgā'* [1]
makes glad, 8523, *śāmaḥ* [1]
makes merry, 8523, *śāmaḥ* [1]
makes cease, 8697, *šābat*[1] [1]
makes, 8883, *šît*[1] [1]
makes pour, 8938, *šālaḥ* [1]
makes live at peace, 8966, *šālēm*[1] [1]
makes an outline, 9306, *tā'ar*[2] [1]
makes stagger, 9494, *tā'â* [1]

MAKHELOTH [2]
Makheloth, 5221, *maqhēlôt* [2]

MAKI [1]
Maki, 4809, *mākî* [1]

MAKING [52]
making, 6913, *'āśâ*[1] [7]
making atonement, 4105, *kāpar*[1] [6]
making, 4162, *kārat* [4]
making, *NIH/RPE* [3]
making supplication, 2858, *ḥānan*[1] [2]
making, 5989, *nātan* [2]
making amends for sin, 871, *'āšām* [1]
making a stench, 944, *bā'aš* [1]
making up, 968, *bādā'* [1]
making, 2118, *hāyâ* [1]
making, 2284, *zābaḥ* [1]
making a prostitute, 2388, *zānâ*[1] [1]
making wise, 2681, *ḥākam* [1]
making bud, 3528, *yālad* [1]
making more, 3578, *yāsap* [1]
making bricks, 4236+4246, *lāban*[2]*+lᵉbēnâ* [1]
making full, 4848, *mālē'*[1] [1]
making, 5126, *ma'ᵃśeh* [1]
making decisions, 5477, *mišpāṭ* [1]
means of making decisions, 5477, *mišpāṭ* [1]
making a vow, 5623, *nādar* [1]
making vow, 5623, *nādar* [1]
making, 5877, *nāpal* [1]
making loan, 5957, *nāšā'*[1] [1]
making work, 6268, *'ābad* [1]
making, 6590, *'ālâ* [1]
making strong, 6641, *'āmad* [1]
making trouble, 6662, *'āmāl*[1] [1]
was spent for making, 6913+4946, *'āśâ*[1]*+min* [1]
making clear, 7300, *pāraš*[1] [1]
making, 8492, *śîm* [1]
making marks, 9344, *tāwâ*[1] [1]
making a fool of, 9438, *tālal* [1]
making rapid progress, 10613, *ṣᵉlaḥ* [1]

MAKIR [21]
Makir, 4810, *mākîr* [20]
Makir, *NIH/RPE* [1]

MAKIR'S [1]
Makir's, 4810, *mākîr* [1]

MAKIRITE [1]
Makirite, 4811, *mākîrî* [1]

MAKIRITES [2]
the Makirites[s], 2085, *hû'* [1]
Makirites, 4810, *mākîr* [1]

MAKKEDAH [9]
Makkedah, 5218, *maqqēdâ* [9]

MALACHI [1]
Malachi, 4858, *mal'ākî* [1]

MALCAM [1]
Malcam, 4903, *malkām* [1]

MALE [177]
male, 2351, *zākār* [37]
male lambs, 3897, *kebeś* [35]
male goat, 8538+6436, *śā'îr*[2]*+'ēz* [24]
male lamb, 3897, *kebeś* [15]
male goats, 6966, *'attûd* [15]
male, *AIT* [7]
male slaves, 6269, *'ebed*[1] [7]
male goat, 8538, *śā'îr*[2] [7]
male, 408, *'îš*[1] [4]
every last male, 8874+928+7815, *šîn+bᵉ-+qîr*[1] [3]
male, 8874+928+7815, *šîn+bᵉ-+qîr*[1] [3]
male lambs, 10043, *'immar* [3]
firstborn male, 1147, *bᵉkōr* [2]
male slave, 6269, *'ebed*[1] [2]
male goats, 8538+6436, *śā'îr*[2]*+'ēz* [2]
male goats, 9411, *tayiš* [2]
first male offspring, 1147+7081+8167, *bᵉkōr+peṭer+reḥem* [1]
first male offspring, 1147, *bᵉkōr* [1]
male donkeys, 2789, *ḥᵃmôr*[1] [1]
male prostitute, 3978, *keleb* [1]
slaves male, 6269, *'ebed*[1] [1]
male donkeys, 6555, *'ayir* [1]
male goats, 7618+6436, *ṣāpîr+'ēz* [1]
male goats, 7618, *ṣāpîr* [1]
male goats, 10615+10535, *ṣᵉpîr+'ēz* [1]

MALES [13]
males, 2351, *zākār* [11]
males, *AIT* [1]
males, 2350, *zākar*[2] [1]

MALICE [14]
malice aforethought, 8533+4946+9453+8997, *śānē'+min+tᵉmôl+šilšōm* [4]
malice, 8624, *šᵉ'āṭ* [3]
malice, 8273, *ra'*[1] [2]
malice, 224, *'āwen*[1] [1]
malice, 2095, *hawwâ*[2] [1]
malice, 8288, *rā'â*[3] [1]
malice aforethought, 8534, *śin'â* [1]
malice, 8534, *śin'â* [1]

MALICIOUS [7]
malicious, 2805, *ḥāmās* [2]
malicious, 224, *'āwen*[1] [1]
malicious, 2095, *hawwâ*[2] [1]
object of malicious talk, 6590+6584+8557+4383, *'ālâ+'al*[2]*+śāpâ+lāšôn* [1]
malicious, 8533, *śānē'* [1]
malicious, 8764, *śûṭ*[2] [1]

MALICIOUSLY [3]
maliciously mocked, 4353+5056, *la'ag+mā'ôg* [1]
maliciously wink, 7975, *qāraṣ* [1]
winks maliciously, 7975+6524, *qāraṣ+'ayin*[1] [1]

MALIGN [1]
malign, 7032, *pûaḥ*[2] [1]

MALIGNED [1]
maligned, 8764, *śûṭ*[2] [1]

MALKI-SHUA [5]
Malki-Shua, 4902, *malkî-šûa'* [5]

MALKIEL [3]
Malkiel, 4896, *malkî'ēl* [3]

MALKIELITE [1]
Malkielite, 4897, *malkî'ēlî* [1]

MALKIJAH [16]
Malkijah, 4898, *malkiyyâ* [15]
Malkijah, 4899, *malkiyyāhû* [1]

MALKIRAM [1]
Malkiram, 4901, *malkîrām* [1]

MALLOTHI [2]
Mallothi, 4871, *mallôtî* [2]

MALLUCH [6]
Malluch, 4866, *mallûk* [6]

MALLUCH'S [1]
Malluch's, 4868, *mallûkî* [1]

MAMRE [10]
Mamre, 4934, *mamrē'*[1] [8]
Mamre, 4935, *mamrē'*[2] [2]

MAN [1418]
man, 408, *'îš*[1] [612]
man, 132, *'ādām*[1] [278]
man, *AIT* [248]
man, *NIH/RPE* [68]
man, 1505, *geber*[1] [39]
young man, 5853, *na'ar*[2] [23]
man, 632, *'ᵉnôš*[1] [20]
man, 1201+132, *bēn*[1]*+'ādām*[1] [10]
man, 2351, *zākār* [9]
man, 10050, *'ᵉnāš* [8]
young man, 1033, *bāḥûr*[1] [6]
the man[s], 2257, *-ô* [6]
hired man, 8502, *śākîr* [5]
man[s], 285, *'eḥād* [4]
man, 1201, *bēn*[1] [4]
mighty man, 1475, *gibbôr* [4]
man, 5883, *nepeš* [4]
man, 1475, *gibbôr* [3]
the man[s], 2085, *hû'* [3]
man[s], 2307, *zûb* [3]
the man[s], 889, *'ᵃšer* [2]
mortal man, 1414, *bāśār* [2]
that man[s], 2085, *hû'* [2]
man[s], 2257, *-ô* [2]
the man himself, 2257, *-ô* [2]
man[s], 2296, *zeh* [2]
man, 7023, *peh* [2]
man, 10131, *gᵉbar* [2]
man, 226, *'ôn*[1] [1]
any man, 408+408, *'îš*[1]*+'îš*[1] [1]
man, 408+2256+408, *'îš*[1]*+wᵉ-+'îš*[1] [1]
man[s], 889, *'ᵃšer* [1]
to each man, 928+9005, *bᵉ-+šēm*[1] [1]
man, 1251, *ba'al*[1] [1]
brave man, 1475+2657, *gibbôr+ḥayil* [1]
strong man, 1475, *gibbôr* [1]
mighty man, 1505, *geber*[1] [1]
strong man, 1505, *geber*[1] [1]
innocent man, 1947+5929, *dām+nāqî* [1]
man[s], 2085, *hû'* [1]
this man[s], 2085, *hû'* [1]
man[s], 2143, *hālak* [1]
the man and the woman[s], 2157, *-hem* [1]
the injured man[s], 2257, *-ô* [1]
the other man[s], 2257, *-ô* [1]
mortally wounded man, 2728, *ḥālāl*[1] [1]
generous man, 3202+6524, *ṭôb*[2]*+'ayin*[1] [1]
man of knowledge, 3359+1981, *yāda'+da'at*[1] [1]
young man, 3529, *yeled* [1]
man, 3670, *yāṣar* [1]

reflects the man, 4200+2021+132, *lᵉ-[1]+ha-+ʾādām[1]* [1]
man[s], 4392, *-ām* [1]
man[s], 4637, *mût* [1]
any man, 4769+2021+408, *mî+ha-+ʾîš[1]* [1]
despairing man, 4988, *mās* [1]
man[s], 5647, *-nû[2]* [1]
the man[s], 5647, *-nû[2]* [1]
man, 5853, *naʿar[2]* [1]
man of rank, 5951+7156, *nāśāʾ+pāneh* [1]
man learned, 6221, *sōpēr* [1]
almost to a man, 6330+9462+4392, *ʿad[2]+tāmam+-ām* [1]
evil man, 6405, *ʿawwāl* [1]
broken man, 6505, *ʿî* [1]
young man, 6624, *ʿelem* [1]
man, 6639, *ʿam[2]* [1]
man who escaped, 7127, *pālîṭ* [1]
man[s], 7127, *pālîṭ* [1]
greedy man, 8146+5883, *rāḥāb[1]+nepeš* [1]
stingy man, 8273+6524, *raʿ[1]+ʿayin[1]* [1]
kills a man, 8357, *rāṣaḥ* [1]
man hired, 8502, *śākîr* [1]
man of integrity, 9448+2006, *tōm+derek* [1]
man[s], 10192, *-ēh* [1]

MAN'S [93]
man's, 408, *ʾîš[1]* [32]
man's, *AIT* [18]
man's, 132, *ʾādām[1]* [13]
man's[s], 2257, *-ô* [6]
man's, *NIH/RPE* [4]
man's, 632, *ʾenôš[1]* [2]
man's, 1201+132, *bēn[1]+ʾādām[1]* [2]
man's, 1505, *geber[1]* [2]
the man's[s], 2257, *-ô* [2]
man's, 4200+132, *lᵉ-[1]+ʾādām[1]* [2]
another man's, 8276, *rēaʿ[2]* [2]
man's body, 408, *ʾîš[1]* [1]
man's, 1251, *baʿal[1]* [1]
man's[s], 2021, *ha-* [1]
man's[s], 2157, *-hem* [1]
that man's line[s], 2257, *-ô* [1]
man's[s], 4392, *-ām* [1]
great man's, 5618, *nādîb* [1]
another man's, 5799, *nokrî* [1]

MAN-MADE [1]
man-made, 5126+3338+132, *maʿaśeh+yād+ʾādām[1]* [1]

MANAGE [1]
manage, 6913, *ʿāśâ[1]* [1]

MANAGED [2]
managed, 599, *ʾāmēṣ* [2]

MANAHATH [3]
Manahath, 4969, *mānaḥat[1]* [2]
Manahath, 4970, *mānaḥat[2]* [1]

MANAHATHITES [2]
Manahathites, 4971, *mānaḥtî* [2]

MANASSEH [141]
Manasseh, 4985, *mᵉnaššeh* [130]
Manasseh, 1201+4985, *bēn[1]+mᵉnaššeh* [5]
Manasseh, 4986, *mᵉnaššî* [3]
Manasseh[s], 2257, *-ô* [1]
the other half of Manasseh[s], 2257, *-ô* [1]
tribe of Manasseh, 4985, *mᵉnaššeh* [1]

MANASSEH'S [6]
Manasseh's, 4985, *mᵉnaššeh* [6]

MANASSITES [3]
Manassites, 1201+4985, *bēn[1]+mᵉnaššeh* [2]
Manassites, 4986, *mᵉnaššî* [1]

MANDRAKE [1]
mandrake plants, 1859, *dûdāʾîm* [1]

MANDRAKES [5]
mandrakes, 1859, *dûdāʾîm* [5]

MANE [1]
flowing mane, 8310, *raʿmâ[1]* [1]

MANGER [3]
manger, 17, *ʾēbûs* [3]

MANGLED [1]
mangled, 7318, *pāšaḥ* [1]

MANGLES [1]
mangles, 3271, *ṭārap* [1]

MANHOOD [2]
manhood, 226, *ʾôn[1]* [2]

MANIAC [1]
maniac, 8713, *šāgaʿ* [1]

MANKIND [32]
mankind, 132, *ʾādām[1]* [10]
mankind, 1414, *bāśār* [10]
mankind, 1201+132, *bēn[1]+ʾādām[1]* [6]
mankind, 408, *ʾîš[1]* [2]
mankind, 632, *ʾenôš[1]* [1]
all mankind, 1201+132, *bēn[1]+ʾādām[1]* [1]
mankind, 1414+408, *bāśār+ʾîš[1]* [1]
mankind, 10120+10050, *bar[2]+ʾenāš* [1]

MANNA [15]
manna, 4942, *mān[1]* [13]
the manna[s], 2084, *-hû* [1]
manna[s], 5647, *-nû[2]* [1]

MANNED [2]
manned, 6584, *ʿal[2]* [1]
manned by, 6640, *ʿim* [1]

MANNER [3]
in this manner, 3970, *kākâ* [1]
manner, 5477, *mišpāṭ* [1]
behaved in the vilest manner, 9493+4394, *tāʿab+mᵉʾōd* [1]

MANOAH [15]
Manoah, 4956, *mānôaḥ[2]* [15]

MANSERVANT [8]
manservant, 6269, *ʿebed[1]* [8]

MANSIONS [4]
mansions, *NIH/RPE* [1]
mansions, 1074+8041, *bayit[1]+rab[1]* [1]
mansions, 1074, *bayit[1]* [1]
princely mansions, 2292, *zᵉbul[2]* [1]

MANTLE [1]
covered with a mantle, 6486, *ʿāṭâ[1]* [1]

MANTLED [1]
mantled, 6493, *ʿāṭap[1]* [1]

MANURE [2]
manure, 4523, *madmēnâ[1]* [1]
manure, 7616, *ṣāpîaʿ* [1]

MANY [288]
many, 8041, *rab[1]* [162]
many, 8044, *rōb* [31]
many, 8049, *rābâ[1]* [10]
many, 2221, *harbēh* [8]
many, 8045, *rābab[1]* [7]
many, *AIT* [6]
many, 6793, *ʿāṣam[1]* [6]
many, *NIH/RPE* [4]
many, 2162, *hāmôn* [4]
many, 1524, *gādôl* [3]
as many as, 5031, *mispār[1]* [3]
many, 4200+8044, *lᵉ-[1]+rōb* [2]
so many, 4946+8044, *min+rōb* [2]
how many, 5031, *mispār[1]* [2]
how many, 6330+3869+4537, *ʿad[2]+kᵉ-+mâ* [2]
so many, 8041, *rab[1]* [2]
gave many, 8049, *rābâ[1]* [2]
had many, 8049, *rābâ[1]* [2]
take many, 8049, *rābâ[1]* [2]
many years, 802+3427, *ʾōrek+yôm[1]* [1]
make many promises, 1819+1821, *dābar[2]+dābār* [1]
many generations, 1887+2256+1887, *dôr[2]+wᵉ-+dôr[2]* [1]
many years, 3427+2256+9102, *yôm[1]+wᵉ-+šānâ[2]* [1]
how many more, 3869+4537, *kᵉ-+mâ* [1]
how many, 3869+4537, *kᵉ-+mâ* [1]
as many as, 3869, *kᵉ-* [1]
as many, 3869, *kᵉ-* [1]
so many, 3869+4537, *kᵉ-+mâ* [1]
so many, 4200+8044, *lᵉ-[1]+rōb* [1]
many, 4202+5071, *lōʾ+mᵉʿaṭ* [1]
many, 5031, *mispār[1]* [1]
so many, 5031+8041, *mispār[1]+rab[1]* [1]
many teeth, 7092, *pîpiyyôt* [1]
many, 7287, *pāraṣ* [1]
many, 8041+4394, *rab[1]+mᵉʾōd* [1]
so many, 8044, *rōb* [1]
many times, 8049, *rābâ[1]* [1]
built many, 8049, *rābâ[1]* [1]
have many, 8049, *rābâ[1]* [1]
made many, 8049, *rābâ[1]* [1]
make many, 8049, *rābâ[1]* [1]
offer many, 8049, *rābâ[1]* [1]
many thousands, 8052, *ribbōʾ* [1]
many, 8679, *šebaʿ[1]* [1]
many, 9180, *šipʿâ* [1]
many, 10647+10678, *rab+śaggîʾ* [1]
many, 10678, *śaggîʾ* [1]

MAOCH [1]
Maoch, 5059, *māʿôk* [1]

MAON [8]
Maon, 5063, *māʿôn[4]* [6]
Maon, 5062, *māʿôn[3]* [2]

MAONITES [1]
Maonites, 5062, *māʿôn[3]* [1]

MAP [1]
map out, 4180, *kātab* [1]

MARA [1]
Mara, 5259, *mārāʾ[4]* [1]

MARAH [4]
Marah, 5288, *mārâ[3]* [4]

MARALAH [1]
Maralah, 5339, *marʿalâ* [1]

MARAUDERS [3]
marauders, 8720, *šādad* [2]
marauders, 1522, *gᵉdûd[2]* [1]

MARAUDING [1]
marauding, 6296+2256+8740, *ʿābar[1]+wᵉ-+šûb[1]* [1]

MARBLE [4]
marble, 9253, *šēš[2]* [3]
marble, 74+8880, *ʾeben+šayiš* [1]

MARCH [24]
march out, 3655, *yāṣāʾ* [4]
march, 6590, *ʿālâ* [3]
march, 995, *bôʾ* [2]
march, 2143, *hālak* [2]
march around, 6015, *sābab* [2]
march on, 2005, *dārak* [1]
march, 2006, *derek* [1]
march on, 3655, *yāṣāʾ* [1]
surely march out, 3655+3655, *yāṣāʾ+yāṣāʾ* [1]
march down, 3718, *yārad* [1]
order of march, 5023, *massaʿ* [1]
march out, 5602, *nāgaš* [1]
march around, 6015+5938, *sābab+nāqap[2]* [1]
march on, 6296, *ʿābar[1]* [1]
march, 7314, *pāśaʿ* [1]
march up, 7928, *qārab* [1]

MARCHED [43]
marched out, 3655, *yāṣāʾ* [12]
marched up, 6590, *ʿālâ* [6]
marched, 2143, *hālak* [5]
marched, 6590, *ʿālâ* [5]
marched, 995, *bôʾ* [3]
marched out, 2143, *hālak* [2]
marched around, 6015, *sābab* [2]

marched, 6296, *ʿābar*[1] [2]
marched, 7575, *ṣāʿad* [2]
marched into, 3655, *yāṣāʾ* [1]
marched on, 6296, *ʿābar*[1] [1]
marched past, 6296+6584+3338, *ʿābar*[1]*+ʿal*[2]*+yād* [1]
marched off, 7575, *ṣāʿad* [1]

MARCHES [5]
marches, 2005, *dārak* [2]
marches out, 3655, *yāṣāʾ* [2]
marches, 2143, *hālak* [1]

MARCHING [9]
marching out, 3655, *yāṣāʾ* [3]
marching, 2143, *hālak* [2]
marching, 7577, *ṣᵉʿādâ*[1] [2]
marching, 5825, *nāsaʿ* [1]
marching, 6296, *ʿābar*[1] [1]

MARDUK [1]
Marduk, 5281, *mᵉrōdāk* [1]

MARE [1]
mare, 6063, *sûsâ* [1]

MARESHAH [8]
Mareshah, 5358, *mārēšâ*[1] [6]
Mareshah, 5359, *mārēšâ*[2] [2]

MARINERS [2]
mariners, 4876, *mallāḥ* [2]

MARITAL [1]
marital rights, 6703, *ʿōnâ* [1]

MARITIME [1]
maritime, 362, *ʾî*[1] [1]

MARK [10]
mark out, 8492, *śîm* [2]
mark my words, 9048, *šāmaʿ* [2]
mark, *NIH/RPE* [1]
mark, 253, *ʾôt*[1] [1]
mark, 928, *bᵉ-* [1]
strike mark, 7003, *pāgaʿ* [1]
mark, 9338, *tāw* [1]
put a mark, 9344+9338, *tāwâ*[1]*+tāw* [1]

MARKED [8]
marked, *AIT* [2]
marked out, 2980, *ḥāqaq* [2]
marked, *NIH/RPE* [1]
marked, 7595, *ṣāpâ*[1] [1]
marked off, 8492, *śîm* [1]
marked off, 9419, *tākan* [1]

MARKER [2]
marker, 7483, *ṣiyyûn* [1]
marker, 8574, *śered* [1]

MARKET [3]
market areas, 2575, *ḥûṣ* [1]
market district, 4847, *maktēš* [1]
market, 7337, *pātaḥ*[1] [1]

MARKETPLACE [2]
marketplace, 5326, *markōlet* [1]
marketplace, 6087, *saḥar* [1]

MARKS [8]
marks, *NIH/RPE* [2]
marks out, 2552, *ḥûg*[1] [1]
putting marks, 2977, *ḥāqâ* [1]
marks, 4182, *kᵉtōbet* [1]
marks off, 6913, *ʿāśâ*[1] [1]
marks, 9306, *tāʾar*[2] [1]
making marks, 9344, *tāwâ*[1] [1]

MAROTH [1]
Maroth, 5300, *mārôt* [1]

MARRED [2]
marred, *NIH/RPE* [1]
was marred, 8845, *šāḥat* [1]

MARRIAGE [32]
give in marriage, 5989+4200+851, *nātan+lᵉ-*[1]*+ʾiššâ* [6]
gave in marriage, 5989+4200+851, *nātan+lᵉ-*[1]*+ʾiššâ* [5]
give in marriage, 5989, *nātan* [5]
related by marriage, 1251, *baʿal*[1] [1]
marriage covenant, 1382, *bᵉrît* [1]
daughters in marriage, 1426, *bat*[1] [1]
give in marriage, 2021+851+5989, *ha-+ʾiššâ+nātan* [1]
allied himself by marriage, 3161, *ḥātan* [1]
related by marriage, 3163, *ḥātān* [1]
marriage bed, 3661, *yāṣûaʿ*[1] [1]
took in marriage, 4374+4200+851, *lāqaḥ+lᵉ-*[1]*+ʾiššâ* [1]
one born of a forbidden marriage, 4927, *mamzēr* [1]
take in marriage, 5951, *nāśāʾ* [1]
be given in marriage, 5989+4200+851, *nātan+lᵉ-*[1]*+ʾiššâ* [1]
gave in marriage, 5989+851, *nātan+ʾiššâ* [1]
gave in marriage, 5989, *nātan* [1]
give in marriage, 5989+4200+408, *nātan+lᵉ-*[1]*+ʾîš*[1] [1]
was given in marriage, 5989+4200+851, *nātan+lᵉ-*[1]*+ʾiššâ* [1]
gave away in marriage, 8938, *šālaḥ* [1]

MARRIAGES [1]
marriages, *NIH/RPE* [1]

MARRIED [59]
married, 4374, *lāqaḥ* [16]
married, 4374+851, *lāqaḥ+ʾiššâ* [9]
married, 3782, *yāšab* [5]
pledged to be married, 829, *ʾāraś* [5]
married, 4374+4200+851, *lāqaḥ+lᵉ-*[1]*+ʾiššâ* [4]
married, 2118+4200+851, *hāyâ+lᵉ-*[1]*+ʾiššâ* [3]
married, 5951, *nāśāʾ* [3]
while married to, 9393, *taḥat*[1] [3]
married, *AIT* [1]
married, *NIH/RPE* [1]
married, 851+4374, *ʾiššâ+lāqaḥ* [1]
married, 995+448, *bôʾ+ʾel* [1]
be married, 1249, *bāʿal*[1] [1]
married, 1249+1251, *bāʿal*[1]*+baʿal*[1] [1]
married, 1249, *bāʿal*[1] [1]
married to, 2118+4200+851, *hāyâ+lᵉ-*[1]*+ʾiššâ* [1]
married, 2118+851, *hāyâ+ʾiššâ* [1]
married, 4374+4200+2257+4200+851, *lāqaḥ+lᵉ-*[1]*+-ô+lᵉ-*[1]*+ʾiššâ* [1]
married, 5951+851, *nāśāʾ+ʾiššâ* [1]

MARRIES [10]
marries, 4374, *lāqaḥ* [5]
marries, 1249, *bāʿal*[1] [1]
marries, 2118+2118+4200+408, *hāyâ+hāyâ+lᵉ-*[1]*+ʾîš*[1] [1]
marries, 2118+4200+408, *hāyâ+lᵉ-*[1]*+ʾîš*[1] [1]
marries, 2118+4200, *hāyâ+lᵉ-*[1] [1]
marries, 4374+2256+1249, *lāqaḥ+wᵉ-+bāʿal*[1] [1]

MARROW [1]
marrow, 4672, *mōaḥ* [1]

MARRY [29]
marry, 4374, *lāqaḥ* [8]
marry, 2118+4200+851, *hāyâ+lᵉ-*[1]*+ʾiššâ* [5]
marry, 4374+4200+851, *lāqaḥ+lᵉ-*[1]*+ʾiššâ* [4]
marry, 4374+851, *lāqaḥ+ʾiššâ* [4]
never marry, 1436, *bᵉtûlîm* [2]
marry, 1249, *bāʿal*[1] [1]
into marry, 2118+4200, *hāyâ+lᵉ-*[1] [1]
marry into, 2118+4200, *hāyâ+lᵉ-*[1] [1]
marry, 2118+4200+408, *hāyâ+lᵉ-*[1]*+ʾîš*[1] [1]
pledged to marry, 4374, *lāqaḥ* [1]
marry, 5989, *nātan* [1]

MARRYING [3]
marrying, 3782, *yāšab* [2]
marrying, 1249, *bāʿal*[1] [1]

MARSENA [1]
Marsena, 5333, *marsᵉnāʾ* [1]

MARSH [2]
marsh, 1289, *biṣṣâ* [2]

MARSHAL [2]
marshal, 599, *ʾāmēṣ* [1]
marshal troops, 1518, *gādad*[2] [1]

MARSHALED [4]
marshaled, 6885, *ʿārak* [2]
marshaled strength, 2616, *ḥāzaq* [1]
marshaled, 7422, *ṣāwâ* [1]

MARSHES [2]
marshes, 106, *ʾᵃgam*[1] [1]
marshes, 1465, *gebeʾ* [1]

MARVELOUS [11]
marvelous, 7098, *pālāʾ* [10]
marvelous things, 7099, *peleʾ* [1]

MASH [1]
mash, 2796, *ḥāmîṣ* [1]

MASHAL [1]
Mashal, 5443, *māšāl*[2] [1]

MASKIL [13]
maskil, 5380, *maśkîl* [13]

MASONS [5]
masons, 1553, *gādar* [2]
masons, 2935, *ḥōṣēb* [2]
masons, 3093+74, *ḥārāš+ʾeben* [1]

MASREKAH [2]
Masrekah, 5388, *maśrēqâ* [2]

MASSA [2]
Massa, 5364, *maśśāʾ*[3] [2]

MASSACRE [1]
massacre, 1947, *dām* [1]

MASSAH [5]
Massah, 5001, *massâ*[3] [5]

MASSES [2]
masses, 2162, *hāmôn* [2]

MASSING [1]
massing together, 665, *ʾāsap* [1]

MAST [2]
mast, 4029+9568, *kēn*[4]*+tōren* [1]
mast, 9568, *tōren* [1]

MASTER [111]
master, 123, *ʾādôn* [105]
master, *NIH/RPE* [1]
master, 1067, *bîn* [1]
master, 1251, *baʿal*[1] [1]
master, 5440, *māšal*[2] [1]
master craftsmen, 6913+4856, *ʿāśâ*[1]*+mᵉlāʾkâ* [1]
master, 7864, *qānâ*[1] [1]

MASTER'S [28]
master's, 123, *ʾādôn* [28]

MASTERS [6]
masters, 123, *ʾādôn* [4]
masters, 8031, *rōʾš*[1] [1]
masters, 8569, *śar* [1]

MAT [1]
mat, 5435, *miškāb* [1]

MATCH [2]
match, 1948, *dāmâ*[1] [1]
match for, 4200, *lᵉ-*[1] [1]

MATCHING [1]
matching, 5467, *mišneh* [1]

MATE [7]
mate, 851, *ʾiššâ* [2]
mate, 8295, *rᵉʿût*[1] [2]
mate, 3501, *yāḥam* [1]
mate, 4218, *libʾâ* [1]
mate, 8061, *rābaʿ*[1] [1]

MATED [1]
mated, 3501, *yāḥam* [1]

MATERIAL [15]
knitted material, 6849, *ʿēreb*[1] [9]
blue material, 9418, *tᵉkēlet* [2]
purple material, 763, *ʾargāmān* [1]
material, 3998, *kᵉlî* [1]
material, 6760, *ʿāpār* [1]
woven material, 9122, *šaʿaṭnēz* [1]

MATERIALS [2]
materials, *NIH/RPE* [1]
materials, 6023, *sēbel* [1]

MATING [3]
mating with, 6590+6584, *ʿālâ+ʿal*[2] [2]
mating time, 2544, *ḥōdeš*[1] [1]

MATRED [2]
Matred, 4765, *maṭrēd* [2]

MATRI'S [1]
Matri's, 4767, *maṭrî* [1]

MATTAN [3]
Mattan, 5509, *mattān*[2] [3]

MATTANAH [2]
Mattanah, 5511, *mattānâ*[2] [2]

MATTANIAH [16]
Mattaniah, 5514, *mattanyâ* [13]
Mattaniah, 5515, *mattanyāhû* [3]

MATTATTAH [1]
Mattattah, 5523, *mattattâ* [1]

MATTENAI [3]
Mattenai, 5513, *mattᵉnay* [3]

MATTER [49]
matter, 1821, *dābār* [24]
matter, *AIT* [7]
matter, 10418, *millâ* [4]
matter, *NIH/RPE* [3]
what's the matter, 4537, *mâ* [3]
a matter of, 4200, *lᵉ-*[1] [2]
matterˢ, 889, *ʾᵃšer* [1]
this matterˢ, 2257, *-ô* [1]
matter, 2914, *ḥēpeṣ* [1]
what is the matter, 4537+4200+3871, *mâ+lᵉ-*[1]*+-k* [1]
matter, 4856, *mᵉlāʾkâ* [1]
matter, 5086, *maʿal*[1] [1]

MATTERED [1]
mattered, 2118, *hāyâ* [1]

MATTERS [5]
matters, *AIT* [2]
matters, *NIH/RPE* [1]
matters, 1821, *dābār* [1]
matters of law, 9368, *tôrâ* [1]

MATTITHIAH [8]
Mattithiah, 5524, *mattityâ* [4]
Mattithiah, 5525, *mattityāhû* [4]

MATTOCKS [2]
mattocks, 908, *ʾēt*[3] [2]

MAULED [3]
mauled, 8689, *šābar*[1] [2]
mauled, 1324, *bāqaʿ* [1]

MAULS [1]
mauls, 8252, *rāmas* [1]

MAXIMS [1]
maxims, 2355, *zikkārôn* [1]

MAY [917]
may, *AIT* [876]
may, *NIH/RPE* [29]
it may be, 218, *ʾûlay*[2] [3]
may, 2118, *hāyâ* [3]
come what may, 2118+4537, *hāyâ+mâ* [2]
may yet, 218, *ʾûlay*[2] [1]
whoever he may be, 6424+2256+6699, *ʿûr*[3]*+wᵉ+ʿānâ*[1] [1]
may do, 6913, *ʿāśâ*[1] [1]
may, 7153, *pen* [1]

MAYBE [3]
maybe, 218, *ʾûlay*[2] [3]

ME [3169]
me, 3276, *-î* [1800]
me, 5761, *-nî* [1011]
me, *NIH/RPE* [161]
me, *AIT* [85]
me, 5883+3276, *nepeš+-î* [35]
me, 638, *ʾᵃnî* [26]
me, 10477, *-nî* [17]
me, 10307, *-î* [12]
me, 644, *ʾānōkî* [5]
me, 7156+3276, *pāneh+-î* [3]
meˢ, 3378, *yhwh* [2]
me, 3883+3276, *kābôd*[1]*+-î* [2]
me, 5646, *-nû*[1] [2]
meˢ, 563+3870, *ʾāmâ+-kā* [1]
me, 2652+3276, *ḥayyâ*[2]*+-î* [1]
me alone, 3276+638, *-î+ʾᵃnî* [1]
meˢ, 3387, *yᵉhônātān* [1]
me, 3870, *-kā* [1]
meˢ, 6269+3870, *ʿebed*[1]*+-kā* [1]
me, 8120+3276, *rûaḥ+-î* [1]
me, 10044, *ʾᵃnâ* [1]

ME JARKON [1]
Me Jarkon, 4770, *mê hayyarqôn* [1]

ME-ZAHAB [2]
Me-Zahab, 4771, *mê zāhāb* [2]

MEADOW [2]
meadow, *NIH/RPE* [1]
meadow, 5303, *merḥāb* [1]

MEADOWS [3]
meadows, 4120, *kar*[2] [2]
meadows, 5661, *nāwâ*[3] [1]

MEAL [16]
ground meal, 6881, *ʿᵃrîsâ* [4]
meal, 4312, *leḥem* [2]
meal, *NIH/RPE* [1]
meal, 430+4312, *ʾākal+leḥem* [1]
stay for a meal, 430+4312, *ʾākal+leḥem* [1]
meal, 786, *ʾᵃruḥâ* [1]
meal, 1414, *bāśār* [1]
mealˢ, 2084, *-hû* [1]
meal, 4407, *maʾᵃkāl* [1]
funeral meal, 5301, *marzēaḥ* [1]
meal, 5492, *mišteh* [1]
meal, 7854, *qemaḥ* [1]

MEALTIME [1]
mealtime, 6961+2021+431, *ʿēt+ha-+ʾōkel* [1]

MEAN [17]
what mean, 4537, *mâ* [4]
mean by, 4200, *lᵉ-*[1] [3]
mean to, 4200, *lᵉ-*[1] [2]
mean, *NIH/RPE* [2]
that will mean, 255, *ʾāz* [1]
mean, 3108, *ḥāšab* [1]
mean more, 3202, *ṭôb*[2] [1]
because that will mean, 3954, *kî*[2] [1]
what do you mean, 4537+4200+4013, *mâ+lᵉ-*[1]*+-kem* [1]
mean, 8273, *raʿ*[1] [1]
mean, 10600, *pᵉšar*[2] [1]

MEANING [17]
meaning, 7355, *pittārôn* [2]
meaning, 10600, *pᵉšar*[2] [2]
without meaning, 928+2021+2039, *bᵉ-+ha-+hebel*[1] [1]
tell the meaning, 1067, *bîn* [1]
no meaning, 2039, *hebel*[1] [1]
what's the meaning of, 4508, *maddûaʿ* [1]
what is the meaning of, 4537, *mâ* [1]
what is the meaning, 4537+2179, *mâ+hēnnâ*[2] [1]
what is the meaning, 4537, *mâ* [1]
discover meaning, 5162, *māṣāʾ* [1]
less meaning, 8049+2039, *rābâ*[1]*+hebel*[1] [1]
meaning, 8507, *śekel* [1]
know the true meaning, 10326, *yᵉṣab* [1]
true meaning, 10327, *yaṣṣîb* [1]
this is the meaning, 10353+10619+10168, *kōl+qᵒbēl+dî* [1]

MEANINGLESS [37]
meaningless, 2039, *hebel*[1] [34]
utterly meaningless, 2039+2039, *hebel*[1]*+hebel*[1] [1]
meaningless talk, 2039+2038, *hebel*[1]*+hābal* [1]
meaningless, 8736, *šāwʾ* [1]

MEANS [28]
means, 10600, *pᵉšar*[2] [7]
means, *NIH/RPE* [4]
by what means, 928+4537, *bᵉ-+mâ* [2]
by means of, 928, *bᵉ-* [2]
means, 7355, *pittārôn* [2]
by means, 928, *bᵉ-* [1]
means, 1896, *day* [1]
by all means go, 2143+995, *hālak+bôʾ* [1]
by all means, 3283, *yāʿal*[2] [1]
know what means, 3359, *yādaʿ* [1]
by no means, 3480+4202, *yaḥad+lōʾ* [1]
sufficient means, 3869+1896, *kᵉ-+day* [1]
it means, 4200, *lᵉ-*[1] [1]
the means of, 5034, *māsar* [1]
means of making decisions, 5477, *mišpāṭ* [1]
by all means send, 8740+8740, *šûb*[1]*+šûb*[1] [1]

MEANT [2]
meant, 2911, *ḥāpēṣ*[1] [1]
meant, 10600, *pᵉšar*[2] [1]

MEANWHILE [20]
meanwhile, 2256, *wᵉ-* [17]
meanwhile, 255, *ʾāz* [1]
meanwhile, 2180, *hinnēh* [1]
meanwhile, 6330+3907+2256+6330+3907, *ʿad*[2]*+kōh+wᵉ-+ʿad*[2]*+kōh* [1]

MEASURE [21]
measure off, 4499, *mādad* [3]
beyond measure, 6330+4394, *ʿad*[2]*+mᵉʾōd* [3]
measure, 4499, *mādad* [2]
measure around, 6015+6017, *sābab+sābîb* [2]
measure, 406, *ʾêpâ* [1]
measure distance, 4499, *mādad* [1]
measure the full payment, 4499, *mādad* [1]
measure, 4500, *middâ*[1] [1]
measure, 5031, *mispār*[1] [1]
measure out, 5374, *mᵉśûrâ* [1]
standard measure, 5504, *matkōnet* [1]
measure, 6228, *sᵉpōrōt* [1]
measure, 7742, *qāw*[1] [1]
full measure, 8969, *šālēm*[2] [1]
full measure, 9448, *tōm* [1]

MEASURED [43]
measured, 4499, *mādad* [30]
measured off, 4499, *mādad* [5]
measured, *NIH/RPE* [3]
be measured, 4499, *mādad* [2]
measured, 2475, *hebel*[2] [1]
measured, 6913, *ʿāśâ*[1] [1]
measured out, 9419+928+4500, *tākan+bᵉ-+middâ*[1] [1]

MEASURELESS [2]
as measureless as, 3869, *kᵉ-* [1]
measureless, 4202+4499, *lōʾ+mādad* [1]

MEASUREMENT [1]
measurement, *NIH/RPE* [1]

MEASUREMENTS [13]
measurements, 4500, *middâ*[1] [12]
measurements of quantity, 5374, *mᵉśûrâ* [1]

MEASURES [9]
measures, *NIH/RPE* [2]
differing measures, 406+2256+406, *ʾêpâ+wᵉ-+ʾêpâ* [1]
measures, 406, *ʾêpâ* [1]
two differing measures, 406+2256+406, *ʾêpâ+wᵉ-+ʾêpâ* [1]

poured into measures, 4499, *mādad* [1]
measures, 4500, *middâ*^{1} [1]
measures, 5742, *nāṭâ* [1]
measures, 7053, *pûrâ* [1]

MEASURING [24]
measuring, 4500, *middâ*^{1} [9]
measuring line, 7742, *qāw*^{1} [7]
measuring, *NIH/RPE* [5]
measuring basket, 406, *'êpâ* [1]
standards measuring, 5477, *mišpāṭ* [1]
measuring rod, 7866, *qāneh* [1]

MEAT [84]
meat, 1414, *bāśār* [64]
meat, *NIH/RPE* [6]
meat forks, 4657, *mazlēg* [4]
meat, 8638, *š^{e}'ēr* [2]
meat, 3181, *ṭebaḥ*^{1} [1]
meat, 3186, *ṭibḥâ* [1]
piece of meat, 4950, *mānâ*^{2} [1]
portions of meat, 4950, *mānâ*^{2} [1]
the meat^{s}, 5647, *-nû*^{2} [1]
pieces of meat, 5984, *nētaḥ* [1]
unclean meat, 7002, *piggûl* [1]
meat, 7507, *ṣālî* [1]

MEATS [1]
meats, 4683, *māḥâ*^{3} [1]

MEBUNNAI [1]
Mebunnai, 4446, *m^{e}bunnay* [1]

MECONAH [1]
Meconah, 4828, *m^{e}kōnâ* [1]

MEDAD [2]
Medad, 4773, *mêdād* [2]

MEDAN [2]
Medan, 4527, *m^{e}dān*^{1} [2]

MEDDLES [1]
meddles, 6297, *ʿābar*^{2} [1]

MEDE [3]
Mede, 4512, *māday* [1]
Mede, 4513, *mādî* [1]
Mede, 10404, *māday* [1]

MEDEBA [5]
Medeba, 4772, *mêd^{e}bā'* [5]

MEDES [9]
Medes, 4512, *māday* [5]
Medes, 10404, *māday* [4]

MEDIA [8]
Media, 4512, *māday* [7]
Media, 10404, *māday* [1]

MEDIAN [1]
Median, 4512, *māday* [1]

MEDIATE [1]
mediate, 7136, *pālal*^{1} [1]

MEDIATOR [1]
mediator, 4885, *mēlîṣ* [1]

MEDICINE [1]
medicine, 1565, *gēhâ* [1]

MEDITATE [14]
meditate, 8488, *śîaḥ*^{1} [7]
meditate, 2047, *hāgâ*^{1} [3]
meditate, 8491, *śîḥâ* [2]
meditate, 1948, *dāmâ*^{1} [1]
meditate, 8452, *śûaḥ* [1]

MEDITATED [1]
meditated, 2052, *hāgîg* [1]

MEDITATES [1]
meditates, 2047, *hāgâ*^{1} [1]

MEDITATION [2]
meditation, 2053, *higgāyôn* [1]
meditation, 8490, *śîaḥ*^{3} [1]

MEDIUM [4]
medium, 200, *'ôb*^{2} [2]
medium, 1266+200, *ba'^{a}lâ^{1}+'ôb^{2}* [1]
medium, 8626+200, *šā'al+'ôb^{2}* [1]

MEDIUMS [10]
mediums, 200, *'ôb*^{2} [9]
mediums, 6726, *ʿānan*^{2} [1]

MEEK [2]
meek, 6705, *ʿānāw* [1]
meek, 6714, *ʿānî* [1]

MEEKLY [1]
meekly, 351, *'aṭ*^{1} [1]

MEET [129]
meet, 7925, *qārā'*^{2} [78]
meet, 3585, *yāʿad* [8]
meet, 4200+7156, *l^{e}-^{1}+pāneh* [7]
meet, 5162, *māṣā'* [7]
meet, *NIH/RPE* [3]
meet, 7003, *pāgaʿ* [2]
meet, 7008, *pāgaš* [2]
come to meet, 7709, *qādam* [2]
meet in battle, 7925, *qārā'*^{2} [2]
meet, 8011, *rā'â*^{1} [2]
meet, 448+7156, *'el+pāneh* [1]
meet, 448, *'el* [1]
meet, 1075, *bayit*^{2} [1]
meet, 3782, *yāšab* [1]
meet, 3983, *kālâ*^{1} [1]
meet, 4946+7156, *min+pāneh* [1]
meet end, 6066, *sûp*^{1} [1]
meet, 6913, *ʿāśâ*^{1} [1]
meet together, 7008, *pāgaš* [1]
meet, 7709, *qādam* [1]
out came to meet, 7925, *qārā'*^{2} [1]
went to meet, 7925, *qārā'*^{2} [1]
meet, 7928, *qārab* [1]
meet, 7936, *qārâ*^{1} [1]
meet with, 8011+7156, *rā'â^{1}+pāneh* [1]
meet end, 9462, *tāmam* [1]

MEETING [151]
meeting, 4595, *môʿēd* [147]
meeting, *NIH/RPE* [1]
meeting, 3782, *yāšab* [1]
place of meeting, 4595, *môʿēd* [1]
meeting, 7737, *q^{e}hillâ* [1]

MEETS [3]
meets, 7003, *pāgaʿ* [2]
meets, 7008, *pāgaš* [1]

MEGIDDO [12]
Megiddo, 4459, *m^{e}giddô* [11]
Megiddo, 4461, *m^{e}giddôn* [1]

MEHETABEL [3]
Mehetabel, 4541, *m^{e}hêṭab'ēl* [3]

MEHIDA [2]
Mehida, 4694, *m^{e}ḥîdā'* [2]

MEHIR [1]
Mehir, 4698, *m^{e}ḥîr* [1]

MEHOLAH [1]
of Meholah, 4716, *m^{e}ḥōlātî* [1]

MEHOLATHITE [1]
Meholathite, 4716, *m^{e}ḥōlātî* [1]

MEHUJAEL [2]
Mehujael, 4686, *m^{e}ḥûyā'ēl* [2]

MEHUMAN [1]
Mehuman, 4540, *m^{e}hûmān* [1]

MEKERATHITE [1]
Mekerathite, 4841, *m^{e}kērātî* [1]

MELATIAH [1]
Melatiah, 4882, *m^{e}laṭyâ* [1]

MELCHIZEDEK [2]
Melchizedek, 4900, *malkî-ṣedeq* [2]

MELECH [2]
Melech, 4890, *melek*^{2} [2]

MELODIOUS [1]
melodious, 5834, *nāʿîm*^{2} [1]

MELODY [1]
melody, 2053, *higgāyôn* [1]

MELON [1]
melon patch, 5252, *miqšâ*^{2} [1]

MELONS [2]
melons, 19, *'^{a}baṭṭîaḥ* [1]
field of melons, 5252, *miqšâ*^{2} [1]

MELT [14]
melt, 5022, *māsas* [6]
melt away, 4570, *mûg* [3]
melt, 5988, *nātak* [2]
melt, 4570, *mûg* [1]
made melt with fear, 4998, *māsâ* [1]
melt with fear, 5022+5022, *māsas+māsas* [1]

MELTED [11]
melted, 5022, *māsas* [3]
be melted, 5988, *nātak* [3]
melted away, 5022, *māsas* [2]
melted, 2247, *hittûk* [1]
melted away, 4570, *mûg* [1]
melted, 4784, *mayim* [1]

MELTING [5]
melting in fear, 4570, *mûg* [2]
melting, *NIH/RPE* [1]
melting away, 4570+2256+2143,
mûg+w^{e}-+hālak [1]
melting away, 9468, *temes* [1]

MELTS [4]
melts, 4570, *mûg* [2]
melts, 4998, *māsâ* [1]
melts, 5022, *māsas* [1]

MEMBER [3]
member, 4946, *min* [1]
member, 5883, *nepeš* [1]
member, 6830, *ʿēqer*^{1} [1]

MEMBERS [8]
members, *AIT* [3]
members, 5883, *nepeš* [2]
members, 408, *'îš*^{1} [1]
members, 1201, *bēn*^{1} [1]
members, 4632, *môšāb* [1]

MEMORABLE [1]
memorable, 9005, *šēm*^{1} [1]

MEMORANDUM [1]
memorandum, 10176, *dikrôn* [1]

MEMORIAL [18]
memorial, 2355, *zikkārôn* [9]
memorial portion, 260, *'azkārâ* [6]
memorial offering, 260, *'azkārâ* [1]
burns memorial, 2349, *zākar*^{1} [1]
memorial, 3338, *yād* [1]

MEMORY [13]
memory, 2352, *zēker* [11]
carry on the memory, 2349, *zākar*^{1} [1]
perpetuate memory, 2349+9005,
zākar^{1}+šēm^{1} [1]

MEMPHIS [8]
Memphis, 5862, *nōp* [7]
Memphis, 5132, *mōp* [1]

MEMUCAN [3]
Memucan, 4925, *m^{e}mûkān* [3]

MEN [1451]
men, 408, *'îš*^{1} [523]
men, *AIT* [248]
men, *NIH/RPE* [107]
men, 132, *'ādām*^{1} [82]
men, 6639, *ʿam*^{2} [72]

men, 6269, ʿebed^{1} [48]
men, 1201, bēn^{1} [35]
young men, 1033, bāḥûr^{1} [34]
men, 1201+132, bēn^{1}+ʾādām^{1} [23]
men, 5853, naʿar^{2} [21]
mighty men, 1475, gibbôr [17]
men, 2351, zākār [17]
fighting men, 1475+2657, gibbôr+ḥayil [12]
men, 10131, g^{e}bar [12]
young men, 3529, yeled [11]
men, 5493, mōt^{1} [11]
young men, 5853, naʿar^{2} [11]
men, 632, ʾ^{e}nôš^{1} [9]
men, 4855, malʾāk [8]
men, 1505, geber^{1} [7]
men^{s}, 2157, -hem [6]
men^{s}, 4392, -ām [6]
fighting men, 6639, ʿam^{2} [6]
men, 10050, ʾ^{e}nāš [6]
men of every language, 10392, liššān [6]
able men, 1201+2657, bēn^{1}+ḥayil [4]
men, 2344, z^{e}kûr [4]
men, 3782, yāšab [4]
men, 1033, bāḥûr^{1} [3]
men, 1414, bāśār [3]
men^{s}, 2021, ha- [3]
men of Judah, 3374, y^{e}hûdî^{1} [3]
the men^{s}, 4392, -ām [3]
leading men, 380, ʾayil^{1} [2]
men^{s}, 465, ʾēlleh [2]
best men, 738, ʾ^{a}riʾēl [2]
the men^{s}, 889, ʾ^{a}šer [2]
mortal men, 1201+132, bēn^{1}+ʾādām^{1} [2]
young men, 1201, bēn^{1} [2]
able men, 1475+2657, gibbôr+ḥayil [2]
best fighting men, 1475+2657, gibbôr+ḥayil [2]
fighting men, 1475, gibbôr [2]
men^{s}, 2156, hēm [2]
men^{s}, 2822, ḥāmēš [2]
men of Tekoa, 9542, t^{e}qôʿî [2]
valiant men, 52+4213, ʾabbîr+lēb [1]
experienced fighting men,
 408+4878+1475+2657,
 ʾîš^{1}+milḥāmâ+gibbôr+ḥayil [1]
the men of the ambush^{s}, 465, ʾēlleh [1]
the men^{s}, 465, ʾēlleh [1]
brave men, 737, ʾerʾēl [1]
men of Ashdod, 847, ʾašdôdî [1]
men, 861, ʾăšîš [1]
men^{s}, 889, ʾ^{a}šer [1]
you and your men, 917, ʾattem [1]
strong young men, 1033, bāḥûr^{1} [1]
younger men, 1033, bāḥûr^{1} [1]
evil men, 1175, b^{e}liyyaʿal [1]
lowborn men, 1201+132, bēn^{1}+ʾādām^{1} [1]
all men, 1201+2021+132, bēn^{1}+ha-+ʾādām^{1} [1]
low among men, 1201+132, bēn^{1}+ʾādām^{1} [1]
men, 1201+2021+132, bēn^{1}+ha-+ʾādām^{1} [1]
men, 1201+408, bēn^{1}+ʾîš^{1} [1]
these men^{s}, 1201+2021+5566,
 bēn^{1}+ha-+nābîʾ [1]
men of Benjamin, 1229, ben-y^{e}mînî [1]
men, 1251, baʿal^{1} [1]
brave fighting men, 1475+2657,
 gibbôr+ḥayil [1]
capable men, 1475+2657, gibbôr+ḥayil [1]
men, 1475, gibbôr [1]
mighty men, 1475+2657, gibbôr+ḥayil [1]
very capable men, 1475+2657, gibbôr+ḥayil [1]
men of Gebal, 1490, giblî [1]
men ready for battle, 1522+7372+4878,
 g^{e}dûd^{2}+ṣābāʾ^{2}+milḥāmâ [1]
fellow men, 1569, gēw^{2} [1]
men of Gammad, 1689, gammādîm [1]
men of Dan, 1974, dānî [1]
the men^{s}, 2157, -hem [1]
these men^{s}, 2157, -hem [1]
trained men, 2849, ḥānîk [1]
skillful men, 3110, ḥōšēb [1]
two men, 3481+408+2256+278,
 yaḥdāw+ʾîš^{1}+w^{e}-+ʾāḥ^{2} [1]
men^{s}, 3528, yālad [1]
men who snare birds, 3687, yāqûš [1]
old men, 3813, yāšîš [1]
men of rank, 3883, kābôd^{1} [1]
make men slaves, 3899+6269, kābaš+ʿebed^{1} [1]
men^{s}, 3972, kōl [1]
men of Lydia, 4276, lûd [1]
men, 4392, -ām [1]
men^{s}, 4855, malʾāk [1]
servants men, 6269, ʿebed^{1} [1]
evil men, 6397, ʿ^{a}wîl^{2} [1]
force of men, 6639, ʿam^{2} [1]
these men^{s}, 6913+2021+4856,
 ʿāśâ^{1}+ha-+m^{e}lāʾkâ [1]
wicked men, 7188+224, pāʿal+ʾāwen^{1} [1]
men from Tyre, 7660, ṣōrî [1]
men armed with slings, 7847, qallāʿ [1]
men of high rank, 7924, qārāʾ^{1} [1]
men of Reuben, 8018, r^{e}ʾûbēnî [1]
leading men, 8031, rōʾš^{1} [1]
men, 8031, rōʾš^{1} [1]
men on foot, 8081, raglî [1]
chief men, 8569, śar [1]
men who were left, 8586, śārîd^{1} [1]
chief men, 8657, šēbeṭ [1]
drunken men, 8893, šikkôr [1]
men, 10125, b^{e}śar [1]
men from Tripolis, 10305, ṭarp^{e}lāy [1]

MEN'S [6]

men's, 132, ʾādām^{1} [3]
men's, 408, ʾîš^{1} [1]
men's, 1505, geber^{1} [1]
men's, 5853, naʿar^{2} [1]

MENAHEM [7]

Menahem, 4968, m^{e}naḥēm [7]

MENAHEM'S [1]

Menahem's, 4968, m^{e}naḥēm [1]

MEND [2]

mend, 8324, rāpāʾ^{1} [1]
mend, 9529, tāpar [1]

MENDED [1]

mended, 7674, ṣārar^{1} [1]

MENE [3]

mene, 10428, m^{e}nēʾ [3]

MENSERVANTS [15]

menservants, 6269, ʿebed^{1} [15]

MENSTRUAL [1]

menstrual cloth, 1865, dāweh [1]

MENTION [8]

mention, 2349, zākar^{1} [4]
mention, 1819, dābar^{2} [1]
made mention of, 2349, zākar^{1} [1]
worthy of mention, 2349, zākar^{1} [1]
mention, 9019+928+7023, š^{e}mûʿâ+b^{e}-+peh [1]

MENTIONED [4]

mentioned, 2349, zākar^{1} [2]
mentioned, 1819, dābar^{2} [1]
be mentioned, 7924, qārāʾ^{1} [1]

MEONOTHAI [2]

Meonothai, 5065, m^{e}ʿônōtay [2]

MEPHAATH [4]

Mephaath, 4789, mêpaʿat [4]

MEPHIBOSHETH [16]

Mephibosheth, 5136, m^{e}pîbōšet [15]
Mephibosheth, *NIH/RPE* [1]

MERAB [4]

Merab, 5266, mērab [4]

MERAIAH [1]

Meraiah, 5316, m^{e}rāyâ [1]

MERAIOTH [6]

Meraioth, 5318, m^{e}rāyôt [6]

MERARI [21]

Merari, 5356, m^{e}rārî^{1} [21]

MERARITE [10]

Merarite, 1201+5356, bēn^{1}+m^{e}rārî^{1} [7]
Merarite, 5356, m^{e}rārî^{1} [2]
Merarite, 5357, m^{e}rārî^{2} [1]

MERARITES [9]

Merarites, 1201+5356, bēn^{1}+m^{e}rārî^{1} [9]

MERATHAIM [1]

Merathaim, 5361, m^{e}rātayim [1]

MERCENARIES [1]

mercenaries, 8502, śākîr [1]

MERCHANDISE [11]

merchandise, 6442, ʿizbônîm [7]
merchandise, 4836, meker [1]
merchandise, 5229, maqqāḥôt [1]
merchandise, 6087, saḥar [1]
merchandise, 8219, r^{e}kullâ [1]

MERCHANT [4]

merchant, 8217, rākal [2]
merchant, 4047, k^{e}naʿan^{2} [1]
merchant, 6086, sāḥar [1]

MERCHANTS [24]

merchants, 6086, sāḥar [8]
merchants, 8217, rākal [6]
merchants, 408+9365, ʾîš^{1}+tûr [2]
merchants, 4047, k^{e}naʿan^{2} [2]
merchants, 4051, k^{e}naʿ^{a}nî^{2} [2]
traveling merchants, 2142, h^{a}lîkâ [1]
merchants, 6639+4047, ʿam^{2}+k^{e}naʿan^{2} [1]
merchants, 6842+5114, ʿărab^{1}+maʿ^{a}rāb^{1} [1]
merchants, 6913+4856, ʿāśâ^{1}+m^{e}lāʾkâ [1]

MERCIFUL [15]

merciful, 2858, ḥānan^{1} [8]
merciful, 8157, raḥûm [3]
merciful, 2799, ḥemlâ [1]
merciful, 2876, ḥesed^{2} [1]
merciful, 2883, ḥāsîd [1]
merciful, 8171, raḥ^{a}mîm [1]

MERCILESS [1]

merciless, 426, ʾakzārî [1]

MERCILESSLY [1]

mercilessly, 4202+2798, lōʾ+ḥāmal [1]

MERCY [70]

have mercy, 2858, ḥānan^{1} [14]
mercy, 8171, raḥ^{a}mîm [11]
mercy, 2876, ḥesed^{2} [6]
cry for mercy, 7754+9384, qôl+taḥ^{a}nûn [6]
mercy, 8163, rāḥam [3]
show mercy, 2571, ḥûs [2]
mercy, 2798, ḥāmal [2]
show mercy, 2858, ḥānan^{1} [2]
have mercy, 8163, rāḥam [2]
show mercy, 8163, rāḥam [2]
plea for mercy, 9382, t^{e}ḥinnâ^{1} [2]
cry for mercy, 9384, taḥ^{a}nûn [2]
mercy, 2571, ḥûs [1]
show mercy, 2798, ḥāmal [1]
mercy, 2799, ḥemlâ [1]
beg for mercy, 2858, ḥānan^{1} [1]
cried for mercy, 2858, ḥānan^{1} [1]
gets mercy, 2858, ḥānan^{1} [1]
lift up for mercy, 2858, ḥānan^{1} [1]
plead for mercy, 2858, ḥānan^{1} [1]
shows mercy, 2858, ḥānan^{1} [1]
finds mercy, 8163, rāḥam [1]
great mercy, 8171, raḥ^{a}mîm [1]
cry for mercy, 9382, t^{e}ḥinnâ^{1} [1]
mercy, 9382, t^{e}ḥinnâ^{1} [1]
begging for mercy, 9384, taḥ^{a}nûn [1]
mercy, 9384, taḥ^{a}nûn [1]
mercy, 10664, raḥ^{a}mîn [1]

MERE [12]

mere, *NIH/RPE* [6]
mere, *AIT* [1]
mere, 421, ʾak [1]
mere, 1685, gam [1]
mere talk, 1821+8557, dābār+śāpâ [1]
mere breath, 2039, hebel^{1} [1]
mere children, 9500, taʿ^{a}lûlîm [1]

MERED [2]
- Mered, 5279, *mered*[2] [2]

MERED'S [1]
- Mered's, *NIH/RPE* [1]

MERELY [4]
- merely, *NIH/RPE* [2]
- merely, *AIT* [1]
- merely tasted, 3247+3247, *ṭā'am+ṭā'am* [1]

MEREMOTH [6]
- Meremoth, 5329, *merēmôt* [6]

MEREMOTH'S [1]
- Meremoth's, 5329, *merēmôt* [1]

MERES [1]
- Meres, 5332, *meres* [1]

MERIB-BAAL [2]
- Merib-Baal, 5311, *merîb ba'al* [2]

MERIBAH [7]
- Meribah, 5313, *merîbâ*[2] [7]

MERIBAH KADESH [4]
- Meribah Kadesh, 5315, *merîbat qādēš* [4]

MERODACH-BALADAN [2]
- Merodach-Baladan, 5282, *merōdak-bal'adān* [2]

MEROM [2]
- Merom, 5295, *mērôm* [2]

MERONOTH [1]
- of Meronoth, 5331, *mērōnōtî* [1]

MERONOTHITE [1]
- Meronothite, 5331, *mērōnōtî* [1]

MEROZ [1]
- Meroz, 5292, *mērôz* [1]

MERRIMENT [1]
- merriment, 5375, *māśôś*[1] [1]

MERRY [3]
- made merry, 6600, *'ālaz* [1]
- make merry, 8523, *śāmaḥ* [1]
- makes merry, 8523, *śāmaḥ* [1]

MERRYMAKERS [1]
- merrymakers, 8524+4213, *śāmēaḥ+lēb* [1]

MESH [1]
- mesh, 8422, *śebākâ* [1]

MESHA [4]
- Mesha, 4791, *mêšā'* [1]
- Mesha, 4795, *mêšā'* [1]
- Mesha, 4796, *mêšā'* [1]
- Mesha, 5392, *mêšā'* [1]

MESHACH [14]
- Meshach, 10415, *mêšak* [13]
- Meshach, 4794, *mêšak* [1]

MESHECH [10]
- Meshech, 5434, *mešek*[2] [10]

MESHELEMIAH [4]
- Meshelemiah, 5453, *mešelemyāhû* [3]
- Meshelemiah, 5452, *mešelemyâ* [1]

MESHEZABEL [3]
- Meshezabel, 5430, *mešêzab'ēl* [3]

MESHILLEMITH [1]
- Meshillemith, 5454, *mešillēmît* [1]

MESHILLEMOTH [2]
- Meshillemoth, 5451, *mešillēmôt* [2]

MESHOBAB [1]
- Meshobab, 5411, *mešôbāb* [1]

MESHULLAM [25]
- Meshullam, 5450, *mešullām* [25]

MESHULLEMETH [1]
- Meshullemeth, 5455, *mešullemet* [1]

MESSAGE [71]
- message, 1821, *dābār* [31]
- message, 606, *'āmar*[1] [18]
- message, 9019, *šemû'â* [5]
- message, *NIH/RPE* [2]
- give message, 1819, *dābar*[2] [2]
- sent message, 8938, *šālaḥ* [2]
- gave the message, 1819+3972+2021+1821+2021+465, *dābar*[2]*+kōl+ha-+dābār+ha-+'ēlleh* [1]
- message came, 1819, *dābar*[2] [1]
- message, 1819, *dābar*[2] [1]
- message, 4857, *mal'ākût* [1]
- message, 5583, *nāgad* [1]
- give a message, 7422, *ṣāwâ* [1]
- message, 7952, *qerî'â* [1]
- send a message, 8938, *šālaḥ* [1]
- sent a message, 8938, *šālaḥ* [1]
- received message, 9048, *šāma'* [1]
- sending message, 10714, *šelaḥ* [1]

MESSENGER [33]
- messenger, 4855, *mal'āk* [23]
- another messenger[s], 2296, *zeh* [2]
- messenger, 5583, *nāgad* [2]
- messenger, 10541, *'îr* [2]
- messenger of good tidings, 1413, *bāśar* [1]
- another messenger, 2296, *zeh* [1]
- messenger[s], 5583, *nāgad* [1]
- messenger, 7495, *ṣîr*[3] [1]

MESSENGERS [69]
- messengers, 4855, *mal'āk* [60]
- messengers, *NIH/RPE* [3]
- the messengers[s], 2157, *-hem* [1]
- messengers of death, 4637, *mût* [1]
- messengers, 6269, *'ebed*[1] [1]
- secret messengers, 8078, *rāgal* [1]
- sent messengers, 8938, *šālaḥ* [1]
- messengers, 10541, *'îr* [1]

MET [28]
- met, 5162, *māṣā'* [6]
- met, 7008, *pāgaš* [6]
- met, 7925, *qārā'*[2] [5]
- met, 7936, *qārā*[1] [4]
- met by agreement, 3585, *yā'ad* [1]
- met expenses, 3655, *yāṣā'* [1]
- place where met, 4595, *mô'ēd* [1]
- met, 7003, *pāga'* [1]
- met, 7709, *qādam* [1]
- met, 8011, *rā'â*[1] [1]
- met with success, 8505, *śākal*[1] [1]

METAL [12]
- glowing metal, 3133, *ḥašmal* [3]
- cast metal, 4607, *mûṣāq*[1] [3]
- cast metal, 5011, *massēkâ*[1] [1]
- idol cast from metal, 5011, *massēkâ*[1] [1]
- idols made of metal, 5011, *massēkâ*[1] [1]
- metal images, 5816, *nāsîk*[1] [1]
- metal god, 5822, *nesek*[2] [1]
- metal, 7110, *pelādōt* [1]

METALS [1]
- tester of metals, 1031, *bāḥôn* [1]

METE [1]
- mete out, 7142, *pālas*[1] [1]

METHEG AMMAH [1]
- Metheg Ammah, 5497, *meteg hā'ammâ* [1]

METHOD [1]
- method of legalizing transactions, 9496, *te'ûdâ* [1]

METHODS [1]
- methods, 3998, *kelî* [1]

METHUSELAH [6]
- Methuselah, 5500, *metûšelaḥ* [6]

METHUSHAEL [2]
- Methushael, 5499, *metûšā'ēl* [2]

MEUNIM [2]
- Meunim, 5064, *me'ûnîm* [2]

MEUNITES [3]
- Meunites, 5064, *me'ûnîm* [3]

MEZOBAITE [1]
- Mezobaite, 5168, *meṣōbāyâ* [1]

MIBHAR [1]
- Mibhar, 4437, *mibḥār*[2] [1]

MIBSAM [3]
- Mibsam, 4452, *mibśām* [3]

MIBZAR [2]
- Mibzar, 4449, *mibṣār*[2] [2]

MICA [5]
- Mica, 4775, *mîkā'* [4]
- Mica, 4777, *mîkâ* [1]

MICAH [25]
- Micah, 4777, *mîkâ* [24]
- Micah, 4781, *mîkāyehû* [1]

MICAH'S [7]
- Micah's, 4777, *mîkâ* [6]
- Micah's, 4781, *mîkāyehû* [1]

MICAIAH [28]
- Micaiah, 4781, *mîkāyehû* [19]
- Micaiah, *NIH/RPE* [4]
- Micaiah, 4779, *mîkāyâ* [3]
- Micaiah, 4777, *mîkâ* [1]
- Micaiah, 4780, *mîkāyāhû* [1]

MICHAEL [13]
- Michael, 4776, *mîkā'ēl* [13]

MICHAL [18]
- Michal, 4783, *mîkal* [17]
- Michal, *NIH/RPE* [1]

MICMASH [11]
- Micmash, 4825, *mikmāś* [9]
- Micmash, 4820, *mikmās* [2]

MICMETHATH [2]
- Micmethath, 4826, *mikmetāt* [2]

MICRI [1]
- Micri, 4840, *mikrî* [1]

MIDAIR [1]
- in midair, 1068+2021+9028+2256+1068+2021+824, *bayin+ha-+šāmayim+we-+bayin+ha-+'ereṣ* [1]

MIDDAY [7]
- midday, 7416, *ṣohorayim* [7]

MIDDIN [1]
- Middin, 4516, *middîn* [1]

MIDDLE [44]
- middle, 9348, *tāwek* [27]
- middle, 9399, *tîkôn* [7]
- middle, 2942, *ḥeṣî* [6]
- middle, 2940, *ḥeṣôt* [1]
- middle, 7931, *qereb* [1]
- middle, 9108, *šēnî* [1]
- middle, 10135, *gaw* [1]

MIDIAN [34]
- Midian, 4518, *midyān*[2] [32]
- Midian, 824+4518, *'ereṣ+midyān*[2] [2]

MIDIAN'S [2]
- Midian's, 4518, *midyān*[2] [2]

MIDIANITE [14]
- Midianite, 4518, *midyān*[2] [8]
- Midianite, 4520, *midyānî* [5]
- the Midianites[s], 4392, *-ām* [1]

MIDIANITES [17]
Midianites, 4518, *midyān^{2}* [12]
Midianites, 4520, *midyānî* [3]
the Midianites^{s}, 4392, *-ām* [1]
Midianites^{s}, 4722, *maḥ^{a}neh* [1]

MIDNIGHT [3]
midnight, 2940+4326, *ḥ^{a}sôt+laylâ* [2]
midnight, 2942+2021+4326, *ḥ^{a}ṣî+ha-+laylâ* [1]

MIDST [23]
midst, 9348, *tāwek* [13]
midst, 7931, *qereb* [6]
in the midst of, 1068, *bayin* [1]
midst, 1068, *bayin* [1]
midst, 2942, *ḥ^{a}ṣî* [1]
midst, 4848, *mālē'^{1}* [1]

MIDWIFE [2]
midwife, 3528, *yālad* [2]

MIDWIVES [7]
midwives, 3528, *yālad* [7]

MIGDAL EDER [1]
Migdal Eder, 4468, *migdal-'ēder* [1]

MIGDAL EL [1]
Migdal El, 4466, *migdal-'ēl* [1]

MIGDAL GAD [1]
Migdal Gad, 4467, *migdal-gad* [1]

MIGDOL [6]
Migdol, 4465, *migdōl* [6]

MIGHT [91]
might, *AIT* [56]
might, 1476, *g^{e}bûrâ* [11]
might, 6437, *'ōz* [6]
might, 3946, *kōaḥ^{1}* [4]
might, 7153, *pen* [4]
might, *NIH/RPE* [3]
might, 2657, *ḥayil* [2]
what might happen, 344, *'aḥ^{a}rît* [1]
might well have, 3869+5071, *k^{e}-+m^{e}'aṭ* [1]
might, 6797, *'ōṣem^{1}* [1]
might, 9549, *tōqep* [1]
might, 10773, *t^{e}qōp* [1]

MIGHTIER [2]
mightier, *NIH/RPE* [1]
mightier, 129, *'addîr* [1]

MIGHTIEST [1]
mightiest fortresses, 4448+5057, *mibṣār^{1}+mā'ôz* [1]

MIGHTILY [1]
roar mightily, 8613+8613, *šā'ag+šā'ag* [1]

MIGHTY [171]
mighty, 2617, *ḥāzāq* [23]
mighty, 1475, *gibbôr* [22]
mighty men, 1475, *gibbôr* [17]
mighty, 8041, *rab^{1}* [10]
mighty, 1524, *gādôl* [9]
mighty, 6437, *'ōz* [8]
mighty, 6786, *'āṣûm* [8]
Mighty One, 51, *'ābîr* [6]
mighty, 129, *'addîr* [6]
mighty, 52, *'abbîr* [4]
mighty, 446, *'ēl^{5}* [4]
mighty man, 1475, *gibbôr* [4]
mighty acts, 1476, *g^{e}bûrâ* [4]
mighty, 3888, *kabbîr* [4]
mighty, 6434, *'az* [4]
Mighty One, 446, *'ēl^{5}* [3]
mighty, 2620, *ḥōzeq* [3]
Mighty One, 129, *'addîr* [2]
mighty, 579, *'ammîṣ* [2]
mighty warriors, 1475, *gibbôr* [2]
mighty warrior, 1475, *gibbôr* [2]
mighty things, 2657, *ḥayil* [2]
mighty, *NIH/RPE* [1]
mighty, 466, *'^{e}lōhîm* [1]
mighty, 693, *'āpîq^{2}* [1]
mighty, 1201+446, *bēn^{1}+'ēl^{5}* [1]
mighty men, 1475+2657, *gibbôr+ḥayil* [1]
mighty warrior, 1475+2657, *gibbôr+ḥayil* [1]
mighty, 1475+3946, *gibbôr+kōaḥ^{1}* [1]
mighty power, 1476, *g^{e}bûrâ* [1]
mighty works, 1476, *g^{e}bûrâ* [1]
mighty man, 1505, *geber^{1}* [1]
mighty, 2657, *ḥayil* [1]
mighty, 2886, *ḥ^{a}sîn* [1]
mighty, 2891, *ḥāsōn* [1]
mighty, 3946, *kōaḥ^{1}* [1]
mighty, 4200+8044, *l^{e-1}+rōb* [1]
mighty deeds, 6613, *'^{a}lîlâ* [1]
mighty, 6883, *'ārîṣ* [1]
mighty, 8569, *śar* [1]
mighty flame, 8928, *šalhebetyâ* [1]
mighty, 10278, *ḥ^{e}sēn* [1]
mighty, 10718, *šallîṭ* [1]
mighty, 10768, *taqqîp* [1]

MIGRATION [1]
migration, 995, *bô'* [1]

MIGRON [2]
Migron, 4491, *migrôn* [2]

MIJAMIN [4]
Mijamin, 4785, *miyyāmîn* [4]

MIKLOTH [4]
Mikloth, 5235, *miqlôt* [4]

MIKNEIAH [2]
Mikneiah, 5240, *miqnēyāhû* [2]

MIKTAM [6]
miktam, 4846, *miktām* [6]

MILALAI [1]
Milalai, 4912, *mil^{a}lay* [1]

MILCAH [11]
Milcah, 4894, *milkâ* [11]

MILDEW [30]
mildew, 5596, *nega'* [15]
mildew, 7669, *ṣāra'at* [6]
mildew, 3766, *yērāqôn* [5]
spreading mildew, 5596+7669, *nega'+ṣāra'at* [1]
mildew, 7076, *p^{e}ḥetet* [1]
infectious skin diseases and mildew, 7669, *ṣāra'at* [1]
spreading mildew, 7669, *ṣāra'at* [1]

MILITARY [15]
military, 4878, *milḥāmâ* [3]
led on military campaigns, 3655+2256+995, *yāṣā'+w^{e}-+bô'* [2]
ready for military service, 3655+7372, *yāṣā'+ṣābā'^{2}* [2]
military age, 4878, *milḥāmâ* [2]
military staff, 1475, *gibbôr* [1]
military leaders, 2657, *ḥayil* [1]
military, 2657, *ḥayil* [1]
military exploits, 4309, *lāḥam^{1}* [1]
military, 4309, *lāḥam^{1}* [1]
military tunic, 4496+4230, *mad+l^{e}bûš* [1]

MILK [43]
milk, 2692, *ḥālāb* [41]
milk, *NIH/RPE* [1]
curdled milk, 2772, *ḥem'â* [1]

MILL [2]
mill about, 1003, *bûk* [1]
hand mill, 8160, *rēḥayim* [1]

MILLET [1]
millet, 1893, *dōḥan* [1]

MILLION [2]
million, 547+547, *'elep^{2}+'elep^{2}* [2]

MILLSTONE [3]
millstone, 7115, *pelaḥ* [3]

MILLSTONES [4]
millstones, 8160, *rēḥayim* [2]
millstones, 3218, *ṭ^{e}ḥôn* [1]
pair of millstones, 8160, *rēḥayim* [1]

MINA [1]
mina, 4949, *māneh* [1]

MINAS [4]
minas, 4949, *māneh* [4]

MINCING [1]
tripping along with mincing steps, 2143+2256+3262, *hālak+w^{e}-+ṭāpap* [1]

MIND [68]
mind, 4213, *lēb* [21]
mind, 4222, *lēbāb* [10]
mind, 8120, *rûaḥ* [5]
change mind, 5714, *nāḥam* [4]
mind, 10646, *rē'š* [4]
mind, 4000, *kilyâ* [3]
mind, 10381, *l^{e}bab* [3]
mind, 5883, *nepeš* [2]
mind, *NIH/RPE* [1]
fix in mind, 899, *'āšaš* [1]
brought to mind, 2349, *zākar^{1}* [1]
mind, 2571, *ḥûs* [1]
mind, 3671, *yēṣer^{1}* [1]
has in mind, 4222+3108, *lēbāb+ḥāšab* [1]
in mind, 6640, *'im* [1]
mind, 7931, *qereb* [1]
bear in mind, 8011, *rā'â^{1}* [1]
mind, 8498, *śekwî* [1]
call to mind, 8740+448+4213, *šûb^{1}+'el+lēb* [1]
changed mind, 8740, *šûb^{1}* [1]
kept in mind, 9068, *šāmar* [1]
mind, 10658, *rûaḥ* [1]
mind, 10669+10381, *ra'yôn+l^{e}bab* [1]
mind, 10669, *ra'yôn* [1]

MINDFUL [1]
mindful, 2349, *zākar^{1}* [1]

MINDS [14]
minds, 4213, *lēb* [7]
minds, 4222, *lēbāb* [2]
minds, 4000, *kilyâ* [1]
change minds, 5714, *nāḥam* [1]
minds, 5883, *nepeš* [1]
minds, 7931, *qereb* [1]
changed minds, 8740, *šûb^{1}* [1]

MINE [58]
mine, 4200+3276, *l^{e-1}+-î* [33]
mine, 3276, *-î* [16]
mine, 4946+5761, *min+-nî* [2]
mine, *NIH/RPE* [1]
mine, 638, *'^{a}nî* [1]
mine, 2085, *hû'* [1]
mine, 4604, *môṣā'^{1}* [1]
mine, 6643+3276, *'immād+-î* [1]
mine, 8611+4200+3276, *ša-+l^{e-1}+-î* [1]
mine, 9393+3276, *taḥat^{1}+-î* [1]

MINGLE [1]
mingle, 5007, *māsak* [1]

MINGLED [2]
mingled, 6843, *'ārab^{2}* [2]

MINIAMIN [2]
Miniamin, 4975, *minyāmîn* [2]

MINIAMIN'S [1]
Miniamin's, 4975, *minyāmîn* [1]

MINISTER [35]
minister, 9250, *šārat* [29]
minister, *NIH/RPE* [2]
minister, 2143, *hālak* [2]
minister, 6641, *'āmad* [2]

MINISTERED [3]
ministered, 9250, *šārat* [3]

MINISTERING [22]
ministering, 9250, *šārat* [14]

ministering, 6641, *'āmad* [4]
ministering, 6275, *'*^{a}*bōdâ* [3]
ministering, 9251+9250, *šārēt+šārat* [1]

MINISTERS [8]
ministers, 6268, *'ābad* [6]
ministers, 9250, *šārat* [2]

MINISTRY [2]
ministry, 6275, *'*^{a}*bōdâ* [2]

MINNI [1]
Minni, 4973, *minnî*[1] [1]

MINNITH [2]
Minnith, 4976, *minnît*[1] [2]

MIRACLE [1]
miracle, 4603, *môpēt* [1]

MIRACLES [10]
miracles, 7098, *pālā'* [5]
miracles, 7099, *pele'* [3]
miracles, 4603, *môpēt* [2]

MIRACULOUS [23]
miraculous signs, 253, *'ôt*[1] [17]
miraculous sign, 253, *'ôt*[1] [3]
miraculous sign, 4603, *môpēt* [2]
miraculous signs, 10084, *'āt* [1]

MIRE [4]
mire, 3226, *ṭîṭ* [2]
mire, 3431, *yāwēn* [1]
mire, 8347, *repeš* [1]

MIRIAM [13]
Miriam, 5319, *miryām* [13]

MIRMAH [1]
Mirmah, 5328, *mirmâ*[2] [1]

MIRROR [1]
mirror, 8023, *r*^{e}*'î* [1]

MIRRORS [2]
mirrors, 1663, *gillāyôn* [1]
mirrors, 5262, *mar'â*[2] [1]

MIRTH [1]
mirth, 8265, *r*^{e}*nānâ* [1]

MIRY [2]
miry, 3431, *yāwēn* [1]
miry pits, 4549, *mah*^{a}*mōrôt* [1]

MISCARRIED [1]
miscarried, 8897, *šākal* [1]

MISCARRY [3]
miscarry, 8897, *šākal* [3]

MISDEEDS [1]
misdeeds, 6613, *'*^{a}*lîlâ* [1]

MISERABLE [4]
made miserable, 4156+4156, *kāra'+kāra'* [1]
miserable, 6662, *'āmāl*[1] [1]
miserable, 7848, *q*^{e}*lōqēl* [1]
miserable, 8273, *ra'*[1] [1]

MISERY [22]
misery, 6715, *'*^{o}*nî* [8]
misery, 6662, *'āmāl*[1] [5]
misery, 6664, *'āmēl*[1] [2]
misery, 8288, *rā'â*[3] [2]
what misery, 518, *'allay* [1]
misery, 2095, *hawwâ*[2] [1]
misery, 4936, *mamm*^{e}*rōrîm* [1]
misery, 7639, *ṣar*[1] [1]
misery, 8273, *ra'*[1] [1]

MISFORTUNE [10]
misfortune, 8288, *rā'â*[3] [3]
misfortune, 7085, *pîd* [2]
misfortune, 224, *'āwen*[1] [1]
misfortune, 988, *behālâ* [1]
misfortune, 5798, *nēker* [1]
misfortune, 6721+8273, *'inyān+ra'*[1] [1]
brought misfortune, 8317, *rā'a'*[1] [1]

MISHAEL [8]
Mishael, 4792, *mîšā'ēl* [7]
Mishael, 10414, *mîšā'ēl* [1]

MISHAL [2]
Mishal, 5398, *miš'āl* [2]

MISHAM [1]
Misham, 5471, *miš'ām* [1]

MISHMA [4]
Mishma, 5462, *mišmā'*[2] [4]

MISHMANNAH [1]
Mishmannah, 5459, *mišmannâ* [1]

MISHRAITES [1]
Mishraites, 5490, *mišrā'î* [1]

MISLEAD [5]
mislead, 3941, *kāzab* [1]
let mislead, 6077, *sût*[1] [1]
mislead, 6077, *sût*[1] [1]
mislead, 8740, *šûb*[1] [1]
mislead, 9494, *tā'â* [1]

MISLEADING [4]
misleading, 6077, *sût*[1] [2]
misleading, 4505, *maddûḥîm* [1]
misleading, 10343, *k*^{e}*dab* [1]

MISLEADS [1]
misleads, 5742, *nāṭâ* [1]

MISLED [1]
misled, 6077, *sût*[1] [1]

MISPAR [1]
Mispar, 5032, *mispār*[2] [1]

MISPERETH [1]
Mispereth, 5033, *misperet* [1]

MISREPHOTH MAIM [2]
Misrephoth Maim, 5387, *miśr*^{e}*pôt mayim* [2]

MISS [2]
miss the way, 2627, *ḥāṭā'* [1]
miss, 2627, *ḥāṭā'* [1]

MISSED [3]
missed, 6296, *'ābar*[1] [1]
be missed, 7212, *pāqad* [1]
missed, 7212, *pāqad* [1]

MISSES [1]
misses at all, 7212+7212, *pāqad+pāqad* [1]

MISSING [13]
missing, 7212, *pāqad* [6]
missing, 6372, *'ādar*[3] [3]
find missing, 2627, *ḥāṭā'* [1]
be missing, 7212, *pāqad* [1]
missing, 7212+7212, *pāqad+pāqad* [1]
were found missing, 7212, *pāqad* [1]

MISSION [5]
mission, 2006, *derek* [3]
mission, 1821+889+8938, *dābār+'*^{a}*šer+šālaḥ* [1]
mission, 5466, *mišmeret* [1]

MISSIONS [1]
missions, 2006, *derek* [1]

MIST [3]
mist, 6727, *'ānān*[1] [2]
morning mist, 6727, *'ānān*[1] [1]

MISTAKE [5]
mistake, 8705, *š*^{e}*gāgâ* [2]
mistake, 5405, *mišgeh* [1]
mistake for, 8011+3869, *rā'â*[1]*+k*^{e}*-* [1]
made a fatal mistake, 9494+928+5883, *tā'â+b*^{e}*-+nepeš* [1]

MISTREAT [7]
mistreat, 3561, *yānâ* [2]
mistreat, 4007, *kālam* [2]
mistreat, 6618, *'ālal*[1] [1]
mistreat, 6700, *'ānâ*[2] [1]
mistreat, 6943, *'āšaq* [1]

MISTREATED [6]
mistreated, 6700, *'ānâ*[2] [1]
mistreated, 8317, *rā'a'*[1] [1]
mistreated, 2803, *ḥāmas*[1] [1]
mistreated, 3561, *yānâ* [1]

MISTRESS [8]
mistress, 1485, *g*^{e}*bîrâ* [7]
mistress, 1266, *ba'*^{a}*lâ*[1] [1]

MISUNDERSTAND [1]
misunderstand, 5795, *nākar*[1] [1]

MISUSE [3]
misuse, 5951+4200+2021+8736, *nāśā'+l*^{e}*-*[1]*+ha-+šāw'* [3]

MISUSES [2]
misuses, 5951+4200+2021+8736, *nāśā'+l*^{e}*-*[1]*+ha-+šāw'* [2]

MITHCAH [2]
Mithcah, 5520, *mitqâ* [2]

MITHNITE [1]
Mithnite, 5512, *mitnî* [1]

MITHREDATH [2]
Mithredath, 5521, *mitr*^{e}*dāt* [2]

MIXED [45]
mixed, 1176, *bālal*[1] [38]
bowls of mixed wine, 4932, *mimsāk* [2]
mixed, 5007, *māsak* [2]
mixed, 10569, *'*^{a}*rab* [2]
mixed with spices, 5008, *mesek* [1]

MIXES [2]
mixes, 1176, *bālal*[1] [1]
mixes, 10569, *'*^{a}*rab* [1]

MIXING [4]
mixing, 5007, *māsak* [1]
mixing, 8057, *rābak* [1]
mixing in, 8379, *rāqaḥ* [1]
took care of mixing, 8379+5351, *rāqaḥ+mirqaḥat* [1]

MIXTURE [1]
mixture, 10569, *'*^{a}*rab* [1]

MIZAR [1]
Mizar, 5204, *miṣ'ār*[2] [1]

MIZPAH [43]
Mizpah, 5207, *miṣpâ* [39]
Mizpah, 5206, *miṣpeh*[2] [4]

MIZRAIM [4]
Mizraim, 5213, *miṣrayim* [4]

MIZZAH [3]
Mizzah, 4645, *mizzâ* [3]

MOAB [152]
Moab, 4566, *mô'āb*[2] [136]
Moab, 8441+4566, *śādeh+mô'āb*[2] [7]
Moab, 824+4566, *'ereṣ+mô'āb*[2] [5]
Moab, 4565, *mô'āb*[1] [2]
Moab^{s}, 2023, *-āh* [1]
Moab, 4567, *mô'ābî* [1]

MOAB'S [7]
Moab's, 4566, *mô'āb*[2] [7]

MOABITE [12]
Moabite, 4566, *mô'āb*[2] [7]
Moabite, 4567, *mô'ābî* [5]

MOABITES [18]
Moabites, 4566, *mô'āb*[2] [12]
Moabites, 4567, *mô'ābî* [4]
Moabites, 1201+4566, *bēn*[1]*+mô'āb*[2] [1]
Moabites, 4566+408, *mô'āb*[2]*+'îš*[1] [1]

MOABITESS [6]
Moabitess, 4567, *môʾābî* [6]

MOADIAH [1]
Moadiah, 5050, *maʿadyâ* [1]

MOADIAH'S [1]
Moadiah's, 4598, *môʿadyâ* [1]

MOAN [6]
moan, 65, *ʾēbel* [1]
moan, 634, *ʾānaḥ* [1]
moan mournfully, 2047+2047, *hāgâ*[1]*+hāgâ*[1] [1]
moan, 2047, *hāgâ*[1] [1]
moan, 2049, *hegeh* [1]
moan, 5628, *nāhag*[2] [1]

MOANED [1]
moaned, 2047, *hāgâ*[1] [1]

MOANING [2]
moaning, 2159, *hāmâ* [1]
moaning, 5653, *nûd* [1]

MOB [3]
mob, 7736, *qāhāl* [3]

MOBILIZED [3]
mobilized, 7212, *pāqad* [2]
mobilized, 7695, *qābaṣ* [1]

MOCK [17]
mock, 4352, *lāʿag* [6]
mock, 4329, *lîṣ* [2]
mock in song, 5593, *n^{e}gînâ* [2]
mock, 2147, *hālal*[3] [1]
mock, 3070, *ḥārap*[2] [1]
mock, 3075, *ḥerpâ* [1]
mock in songs, 4947, *mangînâ* [1]
mock, 7840, *qālas* [1]
mock, 8471, *śāḥaq* [1]
mock, 8488, *śîaḥ*[1] [1]

MOCKED [7]
mocked, 3070, *ḥārap*[2] [3]
mocked, 3075, *ḥerpâ* [1]
mocked, 4351, *lāʿab* [1]
mocked, 4352, *lāʿag* [1]
maliciously mocked, 4352+4353, *lāʿag+laʿag* [1]

MOCKER [12]
mocker, 4370, *lēṣ* [11]
mocker, 4329, *lîṣ* [1]

MOCKERS [8]
mockers, 4370, *lēṣ* [4]
mockers, 408+4371, *ʾîš*[1]*+lāṣôn* [1]
mockers, 2253, *h^{a}tulîm* [1]
proud mockers, 4370, *lēṣ* [1]
mockers, 4372, *lāṣaṣ* [1]

MOCKERY [3]
mockery, 9511, *taʿtuʿîm* [2]
mockery, 4371, *lāṣôn* [1]

MOCKING [5]
mocking, 1540, *gādal* [1]
mocking, 4009, *k^{e}limmâ* [1]
mocking, 4329, *lîṣ* [1]
mocking, 6695, *ʿānag* [1]
mocking, 7464, *ṣāḥaq* [1]

MOCKS [8]
mocks, 4352, *lāʿag* [6]
mocks, 4329, *lîṣ* [2]

MODEL [1]
model, 3159, *ḥātam* [1]

MODELS [2]
models, 7512, *ṣelem*[1] [2]

MOISTEN [1]
moisten, 8272, *rāsas* [1]

MOISTURE [2]
pour down moisture, 5688, *nāzal* [1]
moisture, 8188, *rî* [1]

MOLADAH [4]
Moladah, 4579, *môlādâ* [4]

MOLDED [1]
molded, 6913, *ʿāśâ*[1] [1]

MOLDING [10]
molding, 2425, *zēr* [10]

MOLDS [3]
cast in molds, 4607, *mûṣāq*[1] [1]
molds, 5043, *maʿ^{a}beh* [1]
molds, 6295, *ʿ^{a}bî* [1]

MOLDY [2]
moldy, 5926, *niqqudîm* [2]

MOLECH [15]
Molech, 4891, *mōlek* [9]
Molech, 4903, *malkām* [3]
Molech, 4904, *milkōm* [3]

MOLEST [2]
molest, 3899, *kābaš* [1]
molest, 5595, *nāgaʿ* [1]

MOLESTS [1]
molests, 5595, *nāgaʿ* [1]

MOLID [1]
Molid, 4582, *môlîd* [1]

MOMENT [17]
moment, 8092, *regaʿ* [9]
in a moment, 8092, *regaʿ* [2]
moment, 1180, *bālaʿ*[1] [1]
in a moment, 3869+5071, *k^{e}-+m^{e}ʿaṭ* [1]
in a moment, 4017+8092, *k^{e}mô+regaʿ* [1]
moment, 7193, *paʿam* [1]
moment, 8088, *rāgaʿ*[1] [1]
bring to the moment of birth, 8689, *šābar*[1] [1]

MOMENT'S [1]
moment's, 5071, *m^{e}ʿaṭ* [1]

MONEY [69]
money, 4084, *kesep* [61]
money, *NIH/RPE* [3]
money, 2104, *hôn* [1]
money, 4697, *m^{e}ḥîr*[1] [1]
money from sale, 4928, *mimkār* [1]
money paid for hire, 8510, *śākār*[1] [1]
money, 10362, *k^{e}sap* [1]

MONEYLENDER [1]
moneylender, 5957, *nāšāʾ*[1] [1]

MONITOR [1]
monitor lizard, 3947, *kōaḥ*[2] [1]

MONSTER [6]
monster, 9490, *tannîn* [5]
monster of the deep, 9490, *tannîn* [1]

MONTH [207]
month, 2544, *ḥōdeš*[1] [193]
month, *NIH/RPE* [5]
month, 3732, *yeraḥ*[1] [5]
that month[s], 2257, *-ô* [1]
whole month, 2544+3427, *ḥōdeš*[1]*+yôm*[1] [1]
one month, 3732+3427, *yeraḥ*[1]*+yôm*[1] [1]
month, 10333, *y^{e}raḥ* [1]

MONTHLY [11]
monthly period, 5614, *niddâ* [3]
monthly period, 1865+5614, *dāweh+niddâ* [1]
monthly period, 1865, *dāweh* [1]
monthly, 2544+928+2544, *ḥōdeš*[1]*+b^{e}-+ḥōdeš*[1] [1]
monthly, 2544, *ḥōdeš*[1] [1]
woman's monthly uncleanness, 3240+2021+5614, *ṭumʾâ+ha-+niddâ* [1]
impurity of monthly period, 5614, *niddâ* [1]
monthly flow, 5614, *niddâ* [1]
monthly period, 5614+1864, *niddâ+dāwâ* [1]

MONTHS [38]
months, 2544, *ḥōdeš*[1] [30]
months, 3732, *yeraḥ*[1] [5]
months, *NIH/RPE* [2]
months, 10333, *y^{e}raḥ* [1]

MONUMENT [4]
monument, 3338, *yād* [2]
monument, 5167, *maṣṣēbâ* [1]
erected as a monument, 5893, *nāṣab*[1] [1]

MOON [51]
moon, 3734, *yārēaḥ* [27]
new moon, 2544, *ḥōdeš*[1] [8]
New Moon festivals, 2544, *ḥōdeš*[1] [4]
New Moon festival, 2544, *ḥōdeš*[1] [3]
moon, 4244, *l^{e}bānâ* [3]
full moon, 3427+4057, *yôm*[1]*+keseʾ* [1]
moon, 3732, *yeraḥ*[1] [1]
full moon, 4057, *keseʾ* [1]
moon full, 4057, *keseʾ* [1]
moon, 4401, *māʾôr* [1]
New Moon festivals, 8031+2544, *rōʾš*[1]*+ḥōdeš*[1] [1]

MOONS [7]
New Moons, 2544, *ḥōdeš*[1] [7]

MORDECAI [53]
Mordecai, 5283, *mord^{o}kay* [49]
Mordecai, *NIH/RPE* [4]

MORDECAI'S [5]
Mordecai's, 5283, *mord^{o}kay* [5]

MORE [390]
more than, 4946, *min* [93]
more, 5087+2025, *maʿal*[2]*+-â*[2] [36]
more, 6388, *ʿôd* [35]
more, *AIT* [28]
more, *NIH/RPE* [18]
more, 3578, *yāsap* [9]
be no more, 401, *ʾayin*[1] [7]
more, 3578+6388, *yāsap+ʿôd* [7]
are no more, 401, *ʾayin*[1] [5]
is no more, 401, *ʾayin*[1] [5]
once more, 3578, *yāsap* [5]
how much more, 677+3954, *ʾap*[1]*+kî*[2] [4]
how much more, 677, *ʾap*[1] [4]
became more and more powerful, 2143+2143+2256+1524, *hālak+hālak+w^{e}-+gādôl* [4]
more, 8041, *rab*[1] [4]
even more, 1524, *gādôl* [3]
more, 2221, *harbēh* [3]
more than, 4202, *lōʾ* [3]
any more, 6388, *ʿôd* [3]
once more, 7193, *paʿam* [3]
more, 337, *ʾaḥēr*[1] [2]
was no more, 401, *ʾayin*[1] [2]
how much more so, 677+3954, *ʾap*[1]*+kî*[2] [2]
more, 1524, *gādôl* [2]
more, 1685, *gam* [2]
became more and more powerful, 2143+2256+1524, *hālak+w^{e}-+gādôl* [2]
increased more and more, 2143+2143+2256+8041, *hālak+hālak+w^{e}-+rab*[1] [2]
more and more powerful, 2143+2256+1541+6330+4200+5087+2025, *hālak+w^{e}-+gādēl+ʿad*[2]*+l^{e}-*[1]*+maʿal*[2]*+-â*[2] [2]
have more and more, 3013, *ḥārâ*[1] [2]
once more, 3578+6388, *yāsap+ʿôd* [2]
all the more, 3578+6388, *yāsap+ʿôd* [2]
bring more and more, 3578, *yāsap* [2]
more and more, 3578+6584+3972, *yāsap+ʿal*[2]*+kōl* [2]
more and more, 3578, *yāsap* [2]
more, 4027, *kēn*[2] [2]
even more than, 4946, *min* [2]
more, 6330+6409, *ʿad*[2]*+ʿôlām* [2]
more, 6388+337, *ʿôd+ʾaḥēr*[1] [2]
more than, 6584, *ʿal*[2] [2]
one more, 7193, *paʿam* [2]
more and more unfaithful, 8049+5085+5086, *rābâ*[1]*+māʿal+maʿal*[1] [2]
more and more, 8049, *rābâ*[1] [2]
more, 8049, *rābâ*[1] [2]

once more, 8740, *šûb*[1] [2]
craves for more, 203+9294, *'āwâ*[1]*+ta'^{a}wâ*[1] [1]
no more, 361, *'ê* [1]
am no more, 401, *'ayin*[1] [1]
more[s], 408, *'îš*[1] [1]
once more, 421+2021+7193, *'ak+ha+pa'am* [1]
do so more, 665, *'āsap* [1]
no more, 1172, *b^{e}lî* [1]
no more, 1194, *biltî* [1]
no more, 1698, *gāmar* [1]
once more, 2256, *w^{e}-* [1]
how much more, 2256+677+3954, *w^{e}+'ap*[1]*+kî*[2] [1]
no more than, 2256, *w^{e}-* [1]
no more, 2532, *ḥādal*[1] [1]
said no more, 3087, *ḥārēš*[2] [1]
mean more, 3202, *ṭôb*[2] [1]
in little more than, 3427+6584, *yôm*[1]*+'al*[2] [1]
make more prosperous, 3512, *yāṭab* [1]
given even more, 3578+3869+2179+2256+3869+2179, *yāsap+k^{e}+hēnnâ*[2]*+w^{e}+k^{e}+hēnnâ*[2] [1]
making more, 3578, *yāsap* [1]
more besides, 3578, *yāsap* [1]
more, 3578+8041, *yāsap+rab*[1] [1]
still more, 3578, *yāsap* [1]
stirring up more, 3578, *yāsap* [1]
more, 3855, *yātar* [1]
how many more, 3869+4537, *k^{e}+mâ* [1]
more, 3869+889, *k^{e}+'^{a}šer* [1]
more, 3869, *k^{e}-* [1]
nothing more than, 3869, *k^{e}-* [1]
what more, 3954+4537, *kî*[2]*+mâ* [1]
more, 3972, *kōl* [1]
more for, 4200, *l^{e-1}* [1]
more quickly than, 4200+7156, *l^{e-1}+pāneh* [1]
more readily than, 4200+7156, *l^{e-1}+pāneh* [1]
more than, 4200+401, *l^{e-1}+'ayin*[1] [1]
more, 4200+401, *l^{e-1}+'ayin*[1] [1]
more, 4200+5087+2025, *l^{e-1}+ma'al*[2]*+-â*[2] [1]
more, 4200+8044, *l^{e-1}+rōb* [1]
even more, 4394, *m^{e}'ōd* [1]
more than, 4394, *m^{e}'ōd* [1]
more, 4394, *m^{e}'ōd* [1]
more than, 4946+4200+963, *min+l^{e-1}+bad*[1] [1]
more, 4946, *min* [1]
much more than, 4946, *min* [1]
no more, 4946, *min* [1]
till no more, 4946, *min* [1]
little more, 5071, *m^{e}'aṭ* [1]
give more space, 5602, *nāgaš* [1]
more favored, 5838, *nā'ēm* [1]
even more, 6388, *'ôd* [1]
once more, 6388, *'ôd* [1]
more, 6793, *'āṣam*[1] [1]
built more, 8049, *rābâ*[1] [1]
done more, 8049, *rābâ*[1] [1]
get more, 8049, *rābâ*[1] [1]
give more, 8049, *rābâ*[1] [1]
yet more, 8049, *rābâ*[1] [1]
have more than enough, 8425, *śāba'* [1]
more, 9101, *šānâ*[1] [1]
more than thirteen feet, 9596+564, *tēša'+'ammâ*[1] [1]
any more than, 10195+10341+10168, *hē'+k^{e}+dî* [1]
more than, 10427, *min* [1]
even more, 10678, *śaggî'* [1]
once more, 10766, *tinyānût* [1]

MOREH [3]
Moreh, 4622, *môreh*[4] [3]

MOREOVER [29]
moreover, 2256, *w^{e}-* [8]
moreover, 2256+1685, *w^{e}+gam* [8]
moreover, 1685, *gam* [5]
moreover, 10221, *w^{e}-* [3]
moreover, 677, *'ap*[1] [1]
moreover, 3954+1685, *kî*[2]*+gam* [1]
moreover, 3954, *kî*[2] [1]
moreover, 6388, *'ôd* [1]
moreover, 8370, *raq*[2] [1]

MORESHETH [2]
of Moresheth, 4629, *môraštî* [2]

MORESHETH GATH [1]
Moresheth Gath, 4628, *môrešet gat* [1]

MORIAH [2]
Moriah, 5317, *mōriyyâ* [2]

MORNING [198]
morning, 1332, *bōqer*[2] [179]
every morning, 928+2021+1332+928+2021+1332, *b^{e}+ha+bōqer*[2]*+b^{e}+ha+bōqer*[2] [4]
early in the morning, 8899, *šākam* [3]
early the next morning, 8899, *šākam* [2]
morning, 245, *'ôrâ*[1] [1]
each morning, 928+2021+1332+928+2021+1332, *b^{e}+ha+bōqer*[2]*+b^{e}+ha+bōqer*[2] [1]
morning light, 1332, *bōqer*[2] [1]
morning star, 2122, *hêlēl* [1]
each morning, 4200+2021+1332+4200+2021+1332, *l^{e-1}+ha+bōqer*[2]*+l^{e-1}+ha+bōqer*[2] [1]
morning, 5974, *nešep* [1]
morning mist, 6727, *'ānān*[1] [1]
morning, 8840, *šaḥar* [1]
early morning get up, 8899, *šākam* [1]
morning, 8899, *šākam* [1]

MORNING'S [2]
morning's, 1332, *bōqer*[2] [2]

MORNINGS [2]
mornings, 1332, *bōqer*[2] [2]

MORSELS [2]
choice morsels, 4269, *lāham* [2]

MORTAL [12]
mortal, 632, *'^{e}nôš*[1] [4]
mortal men, 1201+132, *bēn*[1]*+'ādām*[1] [2]
mortal man, 1414, *bāśār* [2]
mortal, 928+5883, *b^{e}+nepeš* [1]
mortal, 1414, *bāśār* [1]
mortal, 4637, *mût* [1]
mortal agony, 8358, *reṣaḥ* [1]

MORTALLY [1]
mortally wounded man, 2728, *ḥālāl*[1] [1]

MORTALS [1]
mortals, 132, *'ādām*[1] [1]

MORTAR [6]
mortar, 2817, *ḥōmer*[2] [4]
mortar, 4521, *m^{e}dōkâ* [1]
mortar, 4847, *maktēš* [1]

MORTGAGING [1]
mortgaging, 6842, *'ārab*[1] [1]

MOSAIC [1]
mosaic pavement, 8367, *riṣ^{e}pâ* [1]

MOSERAH [1]
Moserah, 4594, *môsērâ*[2] [1]

MOSEROTH [2]
Moseroth, 5035, *mōsērôt* [2]

MOSES [762]
Moses, 5407, *mōšeh* [722]
Moses, *NIH/RPE* [25]
Moses[s], 2257, *-ô* [7]
Moses and Aaron[s], 2157, *-hem* [3]
Moses[s], 2084, *-hû* [2]
Moses, 4200+5407, *l^{e-1}+mōšeh* [1]
Moses and Aaron[s], 4392, *-ām* [1]
Moses, 10441, *mōšeh* [1]

MOST [146]
Most High, 6610, *'elyôn*[2] [31]
most holy, 7731+7731, *qōdeš+qōdeš* [23]
Most Holy Place, 7731+7731, *qōdeš+qōdeš* [11]
most, *AIT* [10]
Most High, 10546, *'illāy* [10]
Most Holy Place, 7731, *qōdeš* [8]
most, 4394, *m^{e}'ōd* [6]
most holy offerings, 7731+7731, *qōdeš+qōdeš* [5]
most, 4946, *min* [4]
Most High, 6583, *'al*[1] [4]
most holy things, 7731+7731, *qōdeš+qōdeš* [3]
Most High, 10548, *'elyôn* [3]
most, *NIH/RPE* [2]
most, 5270, *marbît* [2]
most beautiful, 7382, *ṣ^{e}bî*[1] [2]
most important, 1524, *gādôl* [1]
most, 1540, *gādal* [1]
Most Holy Place, 1808+7731, *d^{e}bîr*[1]*+qōdeš* [1]
most excellent, 3636, *yāpâ* [1]
most, 3855, *yātar* [1]
most of, 4946, *min* [1]
most unfaithful, 5085+5086, *mā'al+ma'al*[1] [1]
Most Holy Place, 5219+7731, *miqdāš+qōdeš* [1]
most rebellious, 5286+5286, *mārâ*[1]*+mārâ*[1] [1]
most beautiful of jewels, 6344+6344, *'^{a}dî+'^{a}dî* [1]
Most High, 6584, *'al*[2] [1]
most exalted, 6609, *'elyôn*[1] [1]
most profound, 6678+6678, *'āmōq+'āmōq* [1]
most noble, 7312, *part^{e}mîm* [1]
most beautiful, 7382+7382, *ṣ^{e}bî*[1]*+ṣ^{e}bî*[1] [1]
most sacred food, 7731+7731, *qōdeš+qōdeš* [1]
most sacred, 7731+7731, *qōdeš+qōdeš* [1]
most distant land, 7895, *qāṣeh* [1]
most certainly tear away, 7973+7973, *qāra'+qāra'* [1]
most, 8041, *rab*[1] [1]
most exalted, 9366+5092, *tôr*[1]*+ma'^{a}lâ*[2] [1]
most, 10339, *yattîr* [1]

MOTH [4]
moth, 6931, *'āš*[1] [4]

MOTH'S [1]
moth's cocoon, 6931, *'āš*[1] [1]

MOTHER [152]
mother, 562, *'ēm* [134]
mother, 851, *'iššâ* [6]
mother, 3528, *yālad* [4]
mother, *NIH/RPE* [3]
queen mother, 1485, *g^{e}bîrâ* [3]
position as queen mother, 1485, *g^{e}bîrâ* [2]

MOTHER'S [61]
mother's, 562, *'ēm* [60]
mother's[s], 4849, *mālē'*[2] [1]

MOTHER-IN-LAW [12]
mother-in-law, 2792, *ḥāmôt* [11]
mother-in-law, 3165, *ḥōtenet* [1]

MOTHER-OF-PEARL [1]
mother-of-pearl, 1993, *dar* [1]

MOTHERS [12]
mothers, 562, *'ēm* [9]
expectant mothers, 2226, *hāreh* [1]
nursing mothers, 4787, *mêneqet* [1]
mothers, 8167, *reḥem* [1]

MOTHS [2]
moths, 6931, *'āš*[1] [2]

MOTIONS [1]
motions, 3723, *yārâ*[3] [1]

MOTIVE [1]
motive, 3671, *yēṣer*[1] [1]

MOTIVES [1]
motives, 8120, *rûaḥ* [1]

MOUND [5]
mound, 1195, *bāmâ*[1] [2]
mound, 1461, *gab*[1] [1]
mound, 6894, *'^{a}rēmâ* [1]
mound, 9424, *tēl* [1]

MOUNDS [3]
mounds, 1461, *gab*[1] [2]
mounds, 9424, *tēl* [1]

MOUNT [128]
mount, 2215, *har* [119]
mount, *NIH/RPE* [1]
mount, 989, *bᵉhēmâ* [1]
mount, 2118+4853, *hāyâ+milluʾâ* [1]
mount, 4848+4853, *mālēʾ*[1]*+milluʾâ* [1]
mount, 5090, *maʿᵃleh* [1]
mount up, 5951, *nāśāʾ* [1]
mount, 6590, *ʿālâ* [1]
mount, 6913, *ʿāśâ*[1] [1]
mount, 8206, *rākab* [1]

MOUNTAIN [132]
mountain, 2215, *har* [114]
mountain shrines, 2215, *har* [4]
mountain slopes, 844, *ʾăšēd* [2]
mountain, 6152, *selaʿ*[1] [2]
mountain, 10296, *ṭûr* [2]
mountain, *NIH/RPE* [1]
mountain slopes, 850, *ʾešdāt* [1]
the mountain[s], 2084, *-hû* [1]
mountain clefts, 2215, *har* [1]
mountain haunts, 2215, *har* [1]
mountain regions, 2215, *har* [1]
mountain sheep, 2378, *zemer* [1]
sacred mountain, 7600, *ṣāpôn*[1] [1]

MOUNTAINS [145]
mountains, 2215, *har* [143]
mountains, *NIH/RPE* [1]
mountains, 2065, *hᵃdûrîm* [1]

MOUNTAINSIDE [1]
mountainside, 4533, *madrēgâ* [1]

MOUNTAINTOP [1]
mountaintop, 8031+2215, *rōʾš*[1]*+har* [1]

MOUNTAINTOPS [4]
mountaintops, 8031+2215, *rōʾš*[1]*+har* [4]

MOUNTED [17]
mounted, 8206, *rākab* [6]
mounted, 4854, *milluʾîm* [3]
mounted, 8206+6061, *rākab+sûs*[1] [2]
mounted, 928+2021+6061, *bᵉ-+ha-+sûs*[1] [1]
mounted like jewels, 3782+6584+4859, *yāšab+ʿal*[2]*+millēʾt* [1]
mounted, 4848, *mālēʾ*[1] [1]
were mounted, 6015, *sābab* [1]
mounted up, 6590, *ʿālâ* [1]
mounted, 6913, *ʿāśâ*[1] [1]

MOUNTINGS [1]
mountings, 5920, *neqeb*[1] [1]

MOUNTS [1]
mounts, 989, *bᵉhēmâ* [1]

MOURN [40]
mourn, 6199, *sāpad* [12]
mourn, 61, *ʾābal*[1] [11]
mourn, 5653, *nûd* [3]
mourn, 63, *ʾābēl*[1] [2]
mourn, 65, *ʾēbel* [2]
mourn, 1134, *bākâ* [2]
mourn, 7722, *qādar* [2]
mourn, *NIH/RPE* [1]
mourn, 65+6913, *ʾēbel+ʿāśâ*[1] [1]
mourn, 458, *ʾālâ*[2] [1]
mourn loss, 5653, *nûd* [1]
mourn, 5951+7806, *nāśāʾ+qînâ*[1] [1]
mourn, 9302, *taʾᵃniyyâ* [1]

MOURNED [23]
mourned, 61, *ʾābal*[1] [9]
mourned, 6199, *sāpad* [8]
mourned, 1134, *bākâ* [3]
be mourned, 6199, *sāpad* [2]
mourned, 5629, *nāhâ*[1] [1]

MOURNERS [8]
mourners, 63, *ʾābēl*[1] [2]
mourners[s], 408, *ʾîš*[1] [2]
mourners, 230, *ʾônî* [1]
mourners, 3359+5631, *yādaʿ+nᵉhî* [1]
mourners, 6199, *sāpad* [1]
mourners, 7726, *qᵉdōrannît* [1]

MOURNFUL [1]
mournful song, 5631, *nᵉhî* [1]

MOURNFULLY [1]
moan mournfully, 2047+2047, *hāgâ*[1]*+hāgâ*[1] [1]

MOURNING [41]
mourning, 65, *ʾēbel* [15]
mourning, 5027, *mispēd* [4]
mourning, *NIH/RPE* [3]
mourning, 7722, *qādar* [3]
mourning, 61, *ʾābal*[1] [2]
pretend in mourning, 61, *ʾābal*[1] [1]
in mourning, 61, *ʾābal*[1] [1]
mourning, 63, *ʾābēl*[1] [1]
ceremony of mourning, 65, *ʾēbel* [1]
period of mourning, 65, *ʾēbel* [1]
time of mourning, 65, *ʾēbel* [1]
mourning, 627, *ʾānâ*[1] [1]
shave head in mourning, 995+7947, *bôʾ+qorḥâ* [1]
mourning, 1134, *bākâ* [1]
mourning, 1143, *bᵉkît* [1]
mourning, 2049, *hegeh* [1]
mourning, 5631, *nᵉhî* [1]
walk in mourning, 6199, *sāpad* [1]
mourning, 9302, *taʾᵃniyyâ* [1]

MOURNS [5]
mourns, 61, *ʾābal*[1] [4]
mourns, 5027, *mispēd* [1]

MOUTH [222]
mouth, 7023, *peh* [199]
mouth, 2674, *ḥēk* [6]
mouth, 10588, *pum* [4]
roof of mouth, 2674, *ḥēk* [3]
mouth, 7895, *qāṣeh* [3]
mouth, 8557, *śāpâ* [2]
mouth, *NIH/RPE* [1]
mouth, 4498, *midbār*[2] [1]
roof of mouth, 4918, *malqôḥayim* [1]
mouth, 7156, *pāneh* [1]
mouth, 7339, *petaḥ* [1]

MOUTHS [43]
mouths, 7023, *peh* [40]
mouths, 1744, *gārôn* [1]
roof of mouths, 2674, *ḥēk* [1]
mouths, 10588, *pum* [1]

MOVABLE [7]
movable stands, 4807, *mᵉkônâ* [7]

MOVE [40]
creatures that move, 8254, *remeś* [5]
move, 6047, *sûg*[1] [4]
move, 8253, *rāmaś* [4]
move, 5825, *nāsaʿ* [3]
move, 2143, *hālak* [2]
move out, 3655, *yāṣāʾ* [2]
move on, 5825, *nāsaʿ* [2]
move quickly, 3077, *ḥāraṣ*[2] [1]
made no move, 3087, *ḥārēš*[2] [1]
move quickly, 4554, *māhar*[1] [1]
move, 4631, *mûš*[2] [1]
move along, 5633, *nāhal* [1]
move about, 5825, *nāsaʿ* [1]
move out, 5825, *nāsaʿ* [1]
move, 5952, *nāśag* [1]
move back, 6073, *sûr*[1] [1]
move, 6073, *sûr*[1] [1]
move away, 6590, *ʿālâ* [1]
move, 6673, *ʿāmas* [1]
move, 6913, *ʿāśâ*[1] [1]
creatures that move, 8253, *rāmaś* [1]
creatures that move along the ground, 8254, *remeś* [1]
move about, 9237, *šāraṣ* [1]
creatures that move along the ground, 9238, *šereṣ* [1]
move along, 9238, *šereṣ* [1]

MOVED [69]
moved, 2143, *hālak* [15]
moved on, 5825, *nāsaʿ* [6]
moved on, 6296, *ʿābar*[1] [5]
be moved, 4572, *môṭ*[1] [4]
moved, 6015, *sābab* [3]
moved, 6424, *ʿûr*[3] [3]
moved, *NIH/RPE* [2]
moved about, 2143, *hālak* [2]
moved, 5825, *nāsaʿ* [2]
moved, 6980, *ʿātaq* [2]
was moved by entreaty, 6983, *ʿātar*[1] [2]
moved tents, 182, *ʾāhal*[1] [1]
moved into, 995, *bôʾ* [1]
moved out, 995, *bôʾ* [1]
moved, 995, *bôʾ* [1]
moved, 2118, *hāyâ* [1]
moved back and forth, 2143, *hālak* [1]
moved down, 3718, *yārad* [1]
deeply moved, 4023+8171, *kāmar+raḥᵃmîm* [1]
moved, 4631, *mûš*[2] [1]
moved forward, 5602, *nāgaš* [1]
moved, 5951, *nāśāʾ* [1]
moved away, 6073, *sûr*[1] [1]
moved on ahead, 6296, *ʿābar*[1] [1]
moved on beyond, 6296, *ʿābar*[1] [1]
moved away, 6590, *ʿālâ* [1]
moved up, 6590, *ʿālâ* [1]
moved on, 6980, *ʿātaq* [1]
moved, 7585, *ṣāʿan* [1]
moved out, 7756, *qûm* [1]
moved, 7756, *qûm* [1]
moved, 8206, *rākab* [1]
moved, 8253, *rāmaś* [1]
moved, 9101, *šānâ*[1] [1]

MOVEMENTS [1]
movements, 4604+2256+4569, *môṣāʾ*[1]*+wᵉ-+môbāʾ* [1]

MOVES [22]
moves, 8253, *rāmaś* [5]
moves about, 9237, *šāraṣ* [3]
moves along, 8253, *rāmaś* [2]
moves, 995, *bôʾ* [1]
moves about, 2143, *hālak* [1]
moves along, 2143, *hālak* [1]
moves, 2143, *hālak* [1]
moves to pity, 2858, *ḥānan*[1] [1]
moves, 6047, *sûg*[1] [1]
moves on, 6296, *ʿābar*[1] [1]
moves, 6980, *ʿātaq* [1]
creature that moves, 8253, *rāmaś* [1]
moves about, 8253, *rāmaś* [1]
creature that moves, 8254, *remeś* [1]
moves, 8254, *remeś* [1]

MOVING [9]
moving, *NIH/RPE* [1]
moving, 995, *bôʾ* [1]
moving about, 2143, *hālak* [1]
moving from place to place, 2143+928+889+2143, *hālak+bᵉ-+ʾᵃšer+hālak* [1]
moving from place to place, 2143, *hālak* [1]
moving, 2143, *hālak* [1]
moving, 4631, *mûš*[2] [1]
moving, 5675, *nûaʿ* [1]
moving, 8253, *rāmaś* [1]

MOWN [1]
mown field, 1600, *gēz* [1]

MOZA [5]
Moza, 4605, *môṣāʾ*[2] [5]

MOZAH [1]
Mozah, 5173, *mōṣâ* [1]

MUCH [111]
much, 2221, *harbēh* [10]
much, 8041, *rab*[1] [10]

how much less, 677+3954, *'ap[1]+kî[2]* [6]
much, *NIH/RPE* [4]
how much more, 677+3954, *'ap[1]+kî[2]* [4]
how much more, 677, *'ap[1]* [4]
much, 1524, *gādôl* [4]
much, 3972, *kōl* [4]
very much, 4394, *me'ōd* [4]
twice as much, 5467, *mišneh* [4]
much, 8044, *rōb* [4]
how much worse, 677+3954, *'ap[1]+kî[2]* [3]
much, 8049, *rābâ[1]* [3]
how much more so, 677+3954, *'ap[1]+kî[2]* [2]
how much, 889, *'ašer* [2]
as much as wanted, 1896, *day* [2]
as much as, 3869+889, *ke-+'ašer* [2]
as much as, 4200+7023, *le-[1]+peh* [2]
much, 4200+8044, *le-[1]+rōb* [2]
much, 4394, *me'ōd* [2]
as much as pleases, 5522+3338, *mattat+yād* [2]
too much, 8425, *śāba'* [2]
much, *AIT* [1]
how much better, 677+3954, *'ap[1]+kî[2]* [1]
how much less, 677+3954+4202, *'ap[1]+kî[2]+lō'* [1]
wept much, 1134+1134, *bākâ+bākâ* [1]
so much, 1524, *gādôl* [1]
boast so much, 1540+7023+3870, *gādal+peh+-kā* [1]
make so much of, 1540, *gādal* [1]
so much, 2221, *harbēh* [1]
how much more, 2256+677+3954, *we-+'ap[1]+kî[2]* [1]
as much as, 3869+7023, *ke-+peh* [1]
as much as, 3869, *ke-* [1]
so much, 4027, *kēn[2]* [1]
so much, 4394, *me'ōd* [1]
how much, 4537, *mâ* [1]
half as much, 4734, *maḥaṣît* [1]
much more than, 4946, *min* [1]
so much, 5268, *mirbâ* [1]
drink too much, 6010, *sābā'[1]* [1]
much, 6330+4394, *'ad[2]+me'ōd* [1]
so much that, 6330, *'ad[2]* [1]
so much, 6330, *'ad[2]* [1]
have too much, 6369, *'ādap* [1]
talks too much, 7331+8557, *pātâ[1]+śāpâ* [1]
much too numerous, 8041+2256+6786, *rab[1]+we-+'āṣûm* [1]
so much, 8041, *rab[1]* [1]
as much as, 8049+4946, *rābâ[1]+min* [1]
gathered much, 8049, *rābâ[1]* [1]
too much, 8049, *rābâ[1]* [1]
have too much, 8425, *śāba'* [1]

MUD [10]
mud, 3226, *ṭîṭ* [7]
mud, 2817, *hōmer[2]* [2]
mud, 1288, *bōṣ* [1]

MUDDIED [3]
muddied, 1931, *dālaḥ* [1]
what muddied, 5343, *mirpāś* [1]
muddied, 8346, *rāpaś* [1]

MUDDY [2]
muddy, 3226, *ṭîṭ* [1]
muddy, 8346, *rāpaś* [1]

MUDDYING [1]
muddying, 8346, *rāpaś* [1]

MULE [7]
mule, 7234, *pered* [4]
mule, 7235, *pirdâ* [3]

MULES [11]
mules, 7234, *pered* [11]

MULTICOLORED [1]
multicolored, 1394, *berōmîm* [1]

MULTIPLIED [7]
multiplied, 8049, *rābâ[1]* [5]
multiplied, 8143, *rāhab* [1]
multiplied, 9237, *šāraṣ* [1]

MULTIPLIES [6]
multiplies, 8049, *rābâ[1]* [3]
multiplies, 3578, *yāsap* [1]
multiplies, 3892, *kābar* [1]
multiplies, 6984, *'ātar[2]* [1]

MULTIPLY [12]
multiply, 8049, *rābâ[1]* [4]
multiply, 3578, *yāsap* [3]
multiply, 3877, *kābēd[1]* [2]
multiply, 9237, *šāraṣ* [2]
multiply the number, 8049, *rābâ[1]* [1]

MULTITUDE [5]
multitude, 2162, *hāmôn* [1]
multitude, 6107, *sāk* [1]
multitude, 6639, *'am[2]* [1]
multitude, 8041, *rab[1]* [1]
multitude, 8044, *rōb* [1]

MULTITUDES [4]
multitudes, 2162, *hāmôn* [2]
multitudes, 7372, *ṣābā'[2]* [1]
multitudes, 8041, *rab[1]* [1]

MUMBLE [1]
mumble, 8820, *šāḥaḥ* [1]

MUPPIM [1]
Muppim, 5137, *muppîm* [1]

MURDER [18]
accused of murder, 8357, *rāṣaḥ* [7]
murder, 8357, *rāṣaḥ* [6]
guilt of murder, 1947+5883, *dām+nepeš* [1]
guilty of murder, 1947, *dām* [1]
murder, 1947, *dām* [1]
murder, 2222, *hārag* [1]
murder, 4637, *mût* [1]

MURDERED [13]
murdered, 2222, *hārag* [4]
murdered, 5782, *nākâ* [4]
be murdered, 4637, *mût* [2]
murdered, 8357, *rāṣaḥ* [2]
be murdered, 8357, *rāṣaḥ* [1]

MURDERER [14]
murderer, 8357, *rāṣaḥ* [12]
murderer, 1201+8357, *bēn[1]+rāṣaḥ* [1]
murderer, 2222, *hārag* [1]

MURDERERS [2]
murderers, 2222, *hārag* [1]
murderers, 8357, *rāṣaḥ* [1]

MURDERING [2]
murdering, 1947, *dām* [1]
murdering, 2222, *hārag* [1]

MURDERS [2]
murders, 2222, *hārag* [1]
murders, 8357+5883, *rāṣaḥ+nepeš* [1]

MUSCLES [1]
muscles, 9235, *šārîr* [1]

MUSED [2]
mused, 8488, *śîaḥ[1]* [2]

MUSHI [8]
Mushi, 4633, *mûšî[1]* [8]

MUSHITE [1]
Mushite, 4634, *mûšî[2]* [1]

MUSHITES [1]
Mushites, 4634, *mûšî[2]* [1]

MUSIC [87]
director of music, 5904, *nāṣaḥ* [56]
make music, 2376, *zāmar[1]* [10]
music, 8877, *šîr[2]* [5]
music, 10233, *zemār* [4]
music, 2379, *zimrâ[1]* [2]
music of tambourines, 9512, *tōp[1]* [2]
music, *NIH/RPE* [1]
music and song, 2369, *zāmîr[1]* [1]
music, 2376, *zāmar[1]* [1]
make music, 2727, *ḥālal[3]* [1]
music of strings, 4944, *mēn[1]* [1]
music, 5593, *negînâ* [1]
music, 7754, *qôl* [1]
music of tambourine, 9512, *tōp[1]* [1]

MUSICAL [7]
musical, 8877, *šîr[2]* [6]
musical, *AIT* [1]

MUSICIAN [1]
musician, 8876, *šîr[1]* [1]

MUSICIANS [7]
musicians, 8876, *šîr[1]* [6]
musicians, 5594, *nāgan* [1]

MUST [627]
must, *AIT* [545]
must, *NIH/RPE* [19]
must be put to death, 4637+4637, *mût+mût* [18]
must, 3523, *yākōl* [4]
must die, 4637+4637, *mût+mût* [4]
must drink, 9272+9272, *šātâ[2]+šātâ[2]* [3]
must make restitution, 8966+8966, *šālēm[1]+šālēm[1]* [2]
must eat, 430+430, *'ākal+'ākal* [1]
must die, 1201+4638, *bēn[1]+māwet* [1]
must certainly put to death, 2222+2222, *hārag+hārag* [1]
must demolish, 2238+2238, *hāras+hāras* [1]
must have fought, 2991+2991, *ḥārēb[2]+ḥārēb[2]* [1]
must destroy totally, 3049+3049, *ḥāram[1]+ḥāram[1]* [1]
must understand, 3359+3359, *yāda'+yāda'* [1]
how long must wait, 3869+4537+3427, *ke-+mâ+yôm[1]* [1]
it must be, 4027, *kēn[2]* [1]
must surely be cut off, 4162+4162, *kārat+kārat* [1]
must pay bride-price, 4555+4555, *māhar[2]+māhar[2]* [1]
must be circumcised, 4576+4576, *mûl[1]+mûl[1]* [1]
must be put to death, 4637, *mût* [1]
must put to death, 4637+4637, *mût+mût* [1]
must be sold, 4835+4929, *mākar+mimkeret* [1]
must sell, 4835+4835+928+2021+4084, *mākar+mākar+be-+ha-+kesep* [1]
must report, 5583+5583, *nāgad+nāgad* [1]
must certainly put, 5782+5782, *nākâ+nākâ* [1]
must be punished, 5933+5933, *nāqam+nāqam* [1]
must be carried, 5951+5951, *nāśā'+nāśā'* [1]
must certainly give, 5989+5989, *nātan+nātan* [1]
must be stoned to death, 6232+6232, *sāqal+sāqal* [1]
must be fined, 6740+6740, *'ānaš+'ānaš* [1]
must redeem, 7009+7009, *pādâ+pādâ* [1]
must shave, 7942+7947, *qāraḥ+qorḥâ* [1]
must stone, 8083+8083, *rāgam+rāgam* [1]
must very far, 8178+8178, *rāḥaq+rāḥaq* [1]
must observe a sabbath, 8697+8701, *šābat[1]+šabbāt* [1]
must certainly make restitution, 8966+8966, *šālēm[1]+šālēm[1]* [1]
must pay, 8966+8966, *šālēm[1]+šālēm[1]* [1]
must, 9068, *šāmar* [1]
must, 10201, *hawâ* [1]

MUSTACHE [1]
mustache, 8559, *śāpām* [1]

MUSTER [4]
muster, 599, *'āmēṣ* [1]
muster, 665, *'āsap* [1]
muster, 6641, *'āmad* [1]
muster forces, 7212, *pāqad* [1]

MUSTERED [16]
mustered, 7212, *pāqad* [8]
mustered, 665, *'āsap* [3]
mustered, 7735, *qāhal* [2]

were mustered, 665, *'āsap* [1]
mustered, 7213, *pᵉquddâ* [1]
mustered, 7695, *qābaṣ* [1]

MUSTERING [1]
mustering, 7212, *pāqad* [1]

MUTE [4]
mute, 522, *'illēm* [4]

MUTTER [2]
mutter, 2047, *hāgâ¹* [1]
mutter, 2053, *higgāyôn* [1]

MUTTERS [1]
mutters, 2047, *hāgâ¹* [1]

MUZZLE [2]
muzzle, 2888, *ḥāsam* [1]
muzzle, 4727, *maḥsôm* [1]

MY [3923]
my, 3276, *-î* [3488]
my, *NIH/RPE* [130]
my, 4200+3276, *lᵉ-¹+-î* [77]
my own, 3276, *-î* [43]
my, *AIT* [40]
my, 10307, *-î* [33]
myˢ, 2021, *ha-* [31]
my, 5761, *-nî* [28]
my wrathˢ, 5647, *-nû²* [8]
my, 3870, *-kā* [4]
my own, 4200+3276, *lᵉ-¹+-î* [4]
my, 5883+3276, *nepeš+-î* [4]
my peopleˢ, 2157, *-hem* [3]
my, 638, *'ᵃnî* [2]
my, 928+8079+3276, *bᵉ-+regel+-î* [2]
my, 2257, *-ô* [2]
my peopleˢ, 4392, *-ām* [2]
mark my words, 9048, *šāma'* [2]
myˢ, 10002, *-ā'* [2]
my life, 638, *'ᵃnî* [1]
my peopleˢ, 889, *'ᵃšer* [1]
my, 907+3276, *'ēt²+-î* [1]
my, 928+3276, *bᵉ-+-î* [1]
myˢ, 1201+2257, *bēn¹+-ô* [1]
my lawˢ, 2023, *-āh* [1]
my, 2084, *-hû* [1]
my vowˢ, 2085, *hû'* [1]
my accusersˢ, 2157, *-hem* [1]
my companionˢ, 2257, *-ô* [1]
my life's, 3276, *-î* [1]
my life, 3276, *-î* [1]
my, 4200+7156+3276, *lᵉ-¹+pāneh+-î* [1]
my enemiesˢ, 4564, *-mô* [1]
my, 6640+3276, *'im+-î* [1]
my, 7156+3276, *pāneh+-î* [1]
my own, 8611+4200+3276, *ša-+lᵉ-¹+-î* [1]
my, 10621+10307, *qᵒdām+-î* [1]

MYRIADS [1]
myriads, 8047, *rᵉbābâ* [1]

MYRRH [14]
myrrh, 5255, *mōr* [12]
myrrh, 4320, *lōṭ* [2]

MYRTLE [5]
myrtle trees, 2072, *hᵃdas* [3]
myrtle, 2072, *hᵃdas* [2]

MYRTLES [1]
myrtles, 2072, *hᵃdas* [1]

MYSELF [111]
myself, 3276, *-î* [27]
myself, 638, *'ᵃnî* [21]
myself, 5883+3276, *nepeš+-î* [9]
myself, *AIT* [7]
show myself holy, 7727, *qādaš* [7]
myself, 644, *'ānōkî* [5]
make myself known, 3359, *yāda'* [3]
myself, 4213+3276, *lēb+-î* [3]
myself, 5761, *-nî* [3]
myself, *NIH/RPE* [2]
revealed myself, 3359, *yāda'* [2]
kept myself, 9068, *šāmar* [2]
held myself back, 706, *'āpaq* [1]
myself, 963+3276, *bad¹+-î* [1]
myself, 1414+3276, *bāśār+-î* [1]
clearly reveal myself, 1655+1655, *gālâ+gālâ* [1]
make myself like, 1948, *dāmâ¹* [1]
revealed myself, 2011, *dāraš* [1]
myself, 3338+3276, *yād+-î* [1]
reveal myself, 3359, *yāda'* [1]
station myself, 3656, *yāṣab* [1]
gain glory for myself, 3877, *kābēd¹* [1]
all by myself, 4200+963+3276, *lᵉ-¹+bad¹+-î* [1]
by myself, 4200+963+3276, *lᵉ-¹+bad¹+-î* [1]
by myself, 4946+907+3276, *min+'ēt²+-î* [1]
shake myself free, 5850, *nā'ar²* [1]
avenge myself, 5933, *nāqam* [1]
avenged myself, 5933, *nāqam* [1]
present myself, 8011, *rā'â¹* [1]
seen for myself, 8011+7156, *rā'â¹+pāneh* [1]
washed myself, 8175, *rāḥaṣ* [1]
myself, 10380+10307, *lēb+-î* [1]

MYSTERIES [4]
mysteries, 10661, *rāz* [3]
mysteries, 2984, *ḥēqer* [1]

MYSTERY [6]
mystery, 10661, *rāz* [6]

NAAM [1]
Naam, 5839, *na'am* [1]

NAAMAH [5]
Naamah, 5841, *na'ᵃmâ¹* [4]
Naamah, 5842, *na'ᵃmâ²* [1]

NAAMAN [19]
Naaman, 5845, *na'ᵃmān* [14]
Naaman, *NIH/RPE* [4]
Naamanˢ, 2085, *hû'* [1]

NAAMAN'S [3]
Naaman's, 5845, *na'ᵃmān* [2]
Naaman'sˢ, 2257, *-ô* [1]

NAAMATHITE [4]
Naamathite, 5847, *na'ᵃmātî* [4]

NAAMITE [1]
Naamite, 5844, *na'ᵃmî* [1]

NAARAH [4]
Naarah, 5856, *na'ᵃrâ²* [3]
Naarah, 5857, *na'ᵃrâ³* [1]

NAARAI [1]
Naarai, 5858, *na'ᵃray* [1]

NAARAN [1]
Naaran, 5860, *na'ᵃrān* [1]

NABAL [18]
Nabal, 5573, *nābāl²* [18]

NABAL'S [2]
Nabal's, 5573, *nābāl²* [2]

NABOTH [17]
Naboth, 5559, *nābôt* [17]

NABOTH'S [5]
Naboth's, 5559, *nābôt* [4]
Naboth'sˢ, 2257, *-ô* [1]

NACON [1]
Nacon, 5789, *nākôn³* [1]

NADAB [20]
Nadab, 5606, *nādāb* [19]
Nadabˢ, 2084, *-hû* [1]

NADAB'S [1]
Nadab's, 5606, *nādāb* [1]

NAGGING [1]
nagging, 7439, *ṣûq¹* [1]

NAHALAL [2]
Nahalal, 5634, *nahᵃlāl* [2]

NAHALIEL [2]
Nahaliel, 5712, *naḥᵃlî'ēl* [2]

NAHALOL [1]
Nahalol, 5636, *nahᵃlōl²* [1]

NAHAM [1]
Naham, 5715, *naḥam* [1]

NAHAMANI [1]
Nahamani, 5720, *naḥᵃmānî* [1]

NAHARAI [2]
Naharai, 5726, *naḥray* [2]

NAHASH [8]
Nahash, 5731, *nāḥāš³* [8]

NAHATH [5]
Nahath, 5740, *naḥat³* [5]

NAHBI [1]
Nahbi, 5696, *naḥbî* [1]

NAHOR [16]
Nahor, 5701, *nāḥôr* [16]

NAHOR'S [2]
Nahor's, 5701, *nāḥôr* [2]

NAHSHON [10]
Nahshon, 5732, *naḥšôn* [10]

NAHUM [1]
Nahum, 5699, *naḥûm* [1]

NAILS [7]
nails, 5021, *masmēr* [3]
nails down, 2616+928+5021, *ḥāzaq+bᵉ-+masmēr* [1]
nails, 5383, *maśmērâ* [1]
nails, 7632, *ṣippōren* [1]
nails, 10303, *ṭᵉpar* [1]

NAIOTH [6]
Naioth, 5766, *nāyôt* [6]

NAKED [25]
naked, 6873, *'ārôm* [12]
naked, 6567, *'ērōm* [9]
naked bodies, 5067, *mā'ôr* [1]
naked, 5122, *ma'ᵃrōm* [1]
stripped naked, 6867, *'ārâ¹* [1]
naked, 6872, *'erwâ* [1]

NAKEDNESS [15]
nakedness, 6872, *'erwâ* [11]
nakedness, 3338, *yād* [1]
nakedness, 5113, *ma'ar* [1]
nakedness, 6567, *'ērōm* [1]
nakedness, 6880, *'eryâ* [1]

NAME [596]
name, 9005, *šēm¹* [563]
name, *NIH/RPE* [9]
name, 7924+9005, *qārā'¹+šēm¹* [4]
name, 10721, *šum* [4]
name, 606, *'āmar¹* [2]
the nameˢ, 889, *'ᵃšer* [2]
name, 2352, *zēker* [2]
gave name, 7924, *qārā'¹* [2]
in the name of, 928, *bᵉ-* [1]
use name as a curse, 928+8678, *bᵉ-+šāba'* [1]
God's nameˢ, 2257, *-ô* [1]
name by which remembered, 2352, *zēker* [1]
name of renown, 2352, *zēker* [1]
name, 5918, *nāqab¹* [1]
name, 7924, *qārā'¹* [1]
name, 8507, *šekel* [1]

NAME'S [7]
name's, 9005, *šēm¹* [7]

NAMED [117]
named, 7924+9005, *qārā'¹+šēm¹* [54]
named, 9005, *šēm¹* [44]
named, *NIH/RPE* [6]
named, 7924, *qārā'¹* [3]
named, 8492+9005, *śîm+šēm¹* [3]

be named, 606, *'āmar*[1] [1]
named, 1819, *dābar*[2] [1]
be named, 7924+9005, *qārā'*[1]*+šēm*[1] [1]
been named, 7924+9005, *qārā'*[1]*+šēm*[1] [1]
named, 7924+928+9005, *qārā'*[1]*+b^{e}-+šēm*[1] [1]
named, 9005+7924, *šēm*[1]*+qārā'*[1] [1]
named, 10721, *šum* [1]

NAMELESS [1]
nameless, 1172+9005, *b^{e}lî+šēm*[1] [1]

NAMES [68]
names, 9005, *šēm*[1] [62]
names, 10721, *šum* [3]
names, *NIH/RPE* [2]
names in the genealogical records, 3509, *yāḥaś* [1]

NAOMI [26]
Naomi, 5843, *no'^{o}mî* [19]
Naomi, *NIH/RPE* [5]
Naomi^{s}, 2021+851, *ha-+'iššâ* [1]
Naomi^{s}, 2085, *hû'* [1]

NAOMI'S [1]
Naomi's, 5843, *no'^{o}mî* [1]

NAPHISH [3]
Naphish, 5874, *nāpîš* [3]

NAPHOTH [1]
Naphoth, 5868, *nāpôt* [1]

NAPHOTH DOR [3]
Naphoth Dor, 5869, *nāpôt dō'r* [3]

NAPHTALI [50]
Naphtali, 5889, *naptālî* [44]
Naphtali, 1201+5889, *bēn*[1]*+naptālî* [5]
Naphtali, 824+5889, *'ereṣ+naptālî* [1]

NAPHTALITES [1]
Naphtalites, *NIH/RPE* [1]

NAPHTUHITES [2]
Naphtuhites, 5888, *naptuḥîm* [2]

NARD [2]
nard, 5948, *nērd* [2]

NARROW [9]
narrow, 357, *'āṭam* [4]
narrow, 7639, *ṣar*[1] [3]
narrow, *NIH/RPE* [1]
narrow path, 5469, *miš'ôl* [1]

NARROWER [1]
narrower, 7900, *qāṣûr* [1]

NATHAN [42]
Nathan, 5990, *nātān* [42]

NATHAN-MELECH [1]
Nathan-Melech, 5994, *n^{e}tan-melek* [1]

NATION [129]
nation, 1580, *gôy* [114]
nation, 6639, *'am*[2] [9]
nation, *NIH/RPE* [2]
that nation^{s}, 2257, *-ô* [1]
nation, 4211, *l^{e}'ōm* [1]
nation, 5476, *mišpāḥâ* [1]
nation, 10040, *'ummâ* [1]

NATIONAL [1]
each national group, 1580+1580, *gôy+gôy* [1]

NATIONALITIES [2]
nationalities, 6639, *'am*[2] [1]
other nationalities, 6639+2021+824, *'am*[2]*+ha-+'ereṣ* [1]

NATIONALITY [5]
nationality, 6639, *'am*[2] [4]
nationality, *NIH/RPE* [1]

NATIONS [521]
nations, 1580, *gôy* [410]
nations, 6639, *'am*[2] [90]
nations, 4211, *l^{e}'ōm* [9]
nations, 10040, *'ummâ* [6]
nations, *NIH/RPE* [1]
nations, 824, *'ereṣ* [1]
nations, 1580+824, *gôy+'ereṣ* [1]
pagan nations, 1580, *gôy* [1]
the nations^{s}, 4392, *-ām* [1]
those nations^{s}, 4392, *-ām* [1]

NATIVE [9]
native, 4580, *môledet* [4]
native land, 141, *'^{a}dāmâ*[1] [2]
native soil, 275, *'ezrāḥ* [1]
native land, 824, *'ereṣ* [1]
native, 1201+6639, *bēn*[1]*+'am*[2] [1]

NATIVE-BORN [15]
native-born, 275, *'ezrāḥ* [12]
native-born, 275+2021+824, *'ezrāḥ+ha-+'ereṣ* [1]
native-born, 275+824, *'ezrāḥ+'ereṣ* [1]
native-born, 3528+928+2021+824, *yālad+b^{e}-+ha-+'ereṣ* [1]

NATIVES [1]
natives, 4580, *môledet* [1]

NATURAL [3]
died a natural death, 4637, *mût* [2]
natural, 3869+3972+2021+132, *k^{e}-+kōl+ha-+'ādām*[1] [1]

NAUGHT [1]
naught, 401, *'ayin*[1] [1]

NAVEL [1]
navel, 9219, *šōr* [1]

NAZIRITE [11]
Nazirite, 5687, *nāzîr* [8]
Nazirite, 5694, *nēzer* [2]
Nazirite, 5693, *nāzar*[2] [1]

NAZIRITES [2]
Nazirites, 5687, *nāzîr* [2]

NEAH [1]
Neah, 5828, *nē'â* [1]

NEAR [239]
near, 7940, *qārôb* [38]
near, 6584, *'al*[2] [26]
near, 928, *b^{e}-* [18]
near, 6640, *'im* [12]
come near, 5602, *nāgaš* [11]
come near, 7928, *qārab* [11]
near, 6584+7156, *'al*[2]*+pāneh* [8]
near, 448, *'el* [7]
near, 907, *'ēt*[2] [7]
go near, 7928, *qārab* [7]
near, 725, *'ēṣel*[1] [6]
near, 4200+7156, *l^{e}-*[1]*+pāneh* [6]
near, 4200, *l^{e}-*[1] [6]
near, 7928, *qārab* [6]
near, *AIT* [5]
near, *NIH/RPE* [5]
near, 928+7931, *b^{e}-+qereb* [4]
near head, 5265, *m^{e}ra'^{a}šôt* [4]
near, 5584, *neged* [3]
brought near, 7928, *qārab* [3]
came near, 7928, *qārab* [3]
drew near, 7928, *qārab* [3]
near, 928+6298, *b^{e}-+'ēber*[1] [2]
near, 4578, *mûl*[3] [2]
bring near, 7928, *qārab* [2]
draw near, 7929, *qārēb* [2]
near of kin, 1457, *gā'al*[1] [1]
near, 2143+907, *hālak+'ēt*[2] [1]
near the time of delivery, 3528, *yālad* [1]
near, 4946+7396, *min+ṣad*[1] [1]
near, 4946, *min* [1]
draws near, 5595, *nāga'* [1]
drew near, 5595, *nāga'* [1]
near, 5595, *nāga'* [1]
bring near, 5602, *nāgaš* [1]
came near, 5602, *nāgaš* [1]
draw near, 5602, *nāgaš* [1]
drew near, 5602, *nāgaš* [1]
go near, 5602, *nāgaš* [1]
near, 6330, *'ad*[2] [1]
near, 6584+3338, *'al*[2]*+yād* [1]
bringing near, 7928, *qārab* [1]
cause to come near, 7928, *qārab* [1]
comes near, 7928, *qārab* [1]
draw near, 7928, *qārab* [1]
draws near, 7928, *qārab* [1]
gone near, 7928, *qārab* [1]
have come near, 7928, *qārab* [1]
went near, 7928, *qārab* [1]
comes near, 7929, *qārēb* [1]
even comes near, 7929+7929, *qārēb+qārēb* [1]
goes near, 7929, *qārēb* [1]
come near, 7932, *qirbâ* [1]
near, 7932, *qirbâ* [1]
come near, 7940, *qārôb* [1]
no near, 8178, *rāḥaq* [1]
near, 10378+10619, *l^{e}-+q^{o}bēl* [1]
came near, 10638, *q^{e}rēb* [1]

NEARBY [8]
nearby, 4946+5584, *min+neged* [2]
nearby, 2178, *hēnnâ*[1] [1]
nearby, 4946+7940, *min+qārôb* [1]
nearby, 6584+3338, *'al*[2]*+yād* [1]
nearby, 6584, *'al*[2] [1]
nearby, 7940, *qārôb* [1]
nearby, 9004, *šām* [1]

NEARED [1]
neared, 2143+725, *hālak+'ēṣel*[1] [1]

NEARER [1]
nearer, 7940, *qārôb* [1]

NEAREST [7]
nearest, 7940, *qārôb* [5]
as nearest relative duty, 1460, *g^{e}'ullâ* [1]
nearest, 6584+7156, *'al*[2]*+pāneh* [1]

NEARIAH [3]
Neariah, 5859, *n^{e}'aryâ* [3]

NEARLY [2]
nearly over, 2837, *ḥānâ*[1] [1]
nearly, 3869+401, *k^{e}-+'ayin*[1] [1]

NEBAI [1]
Nebai, 5763, *nêbāy* [1]

NEBAIOTH [5]
Nebaioth, 5568, *n^{e}bāyôt* [5]

NEBALLAT [1]
Neballat, 5579, *n^{e}ballāṭ* [1]

NEBAT [25]
Nebat, 5565, *n^{e}bāṭ* [25]

NEBO [13]
Nebo, 5549, *n^{e}bô*[1] [11]
Nebo, 5550, *n^{e}bô*[2] [1]
Nebo, 5551, *n^{e}bô*[3] [1]

NEBO-SARSEKIM [1]
Nebo-Sarsekim, 5552, *n^{e}bû śar-s^{e}kîm* [1]

NEBUCHADNEZZAR [89]
Nebuchadnezzar, 5557, *n^{e}bûkadre'ṣṣar* [31]
Nebuchadnezzar, 10453, *n^{e}bûkadneṣṣar* [28]
Nebuchadnezzar, 5556, *n^{e}bûkadne'ṣṣar* [26]
Nebuchadnezzar, *NIH/RPE* [2]
Nebuchadnezzar^{s}, 2257, *-ô* [2]

NEBUCHADNEZZAR'S [1]
Nebuchadnezzar's, 4200+5557, *l^{e}-*[1]*+n^{e}bûkadre'ṣṣar* [1]

NEBUSHAZBAN [1]
Nebushazban, 5558, *n^{e}bûšazbān* [1]

NEBUZARADAN [16]
Nebuzaradan, 5555, *n^{e}bûzar'^{a}dān* [15]
Nebuzaradan, *NIH/RPE* [1]

NECK [48]
neck, 7418, *ṣawwā'r* [25]

neck, 1738, *gargerôt* [4]
neck, 6902, *ʿōrep* [4]
break neck, 6904, *ʿārap*[2] [3]
neck, 10611, *ṣawwaʾr* [3]
neck, 5883, *nepeš* [2]
neck, *NIH/RPE* [1]
neck, 1744, *gārôn* [1]
neck, 4305, *leḥî*[1] [1]
neck, 5154, *mapreqet* [1]
breaks neck, 6904, *ʿārap*[2] [1]
neck was broken, 6904, *ʿārap*[2] [1]
neck, 7023, *peh* [1]

NECK-IRONS [1]
neck-irons, 7485, *ṣînōq* [1]

NECKLACE [3]
necklace, 6735, *ʿānaq* [1]
necklace, 7454, *ṣawwerōnîm* [1]
necklace, 8054, *rābîd* [1]

NECKLACES [2]
necklaces, 3921, *kûmāz* [1]
crescent necklaces, 8448, *śaharōnîm* [1]

NECKS [8]
necks, 7418, *ṣawwāʾr* [7]
necks, 1744, *gārôn* [1]

NECO [10]
Neco, 5786, *nekô* [4]
Neco, 5785, *nekōh* [3]
Neco, *NIH/RPE* [2]
Neco[s], 2257, *-ô* [1]

NECTAR [1]
nectar, 6747, *ʿāsîs* [1]

NEDABIAH [1]
Nedabiah, 5608, *nedabyâ* [1]

NEED [22]
need, *AIT* [11]
in need, 1937, *dālal*[1] [2]
need, 4728, *maḥsôr* [2]
need, *NIH/RPE* [1]
need, 1821, *dābār* [1]
in great need, 1937, *dālal*[1] [1]
need, 4374, *lāqaḥ* [1]
need, 7664, *ṣōrek* [1]
need not, 8697, *šābat*[1] [1]
need, 10287, *ḥ ašaḥ* [1]

NEEDED [7]
needed, 430, *ʾākal* [2]
needed, *NIH/RPE* [1]
needed, 1504, *gābar* [1]
determine amount needed, 4082, *kāsas* [1]
needed, 10288, *ḥašḥâ* [1]
needed, 10289, *ḥašḥû* [1]

NEEDLESS [2]
needless, 2855, *ḥinnām* [2]

NEEDS [7]
needs, 5883, *nepeš* [3]
needs, *AIT* [1]
needs, 430, *ʾākal* [1]
needs, 4728+2893, *maḥsôr+ḥāsēr*[1] [1]
supplied all needs, 8425, *śābaʿ* [1]

NEEDY [52]
needy, 36, *ʾebyôn* [46]
needy, 6714, *ʿānî* [3]
needy, 36+132, *ʾebyôn+ʾādām*[1] [1]
needy, 1924, *dal*[2] [1]
needy, 6705, *ʿānāw* [1]

NEGEV [38]
Negev, 5582, *negeb* [36]
Negev, 824+5582, *ʾereṣ+negeb* [2]

NEGLECT [6]
neglect, 6440, *ʿāzab*[1] [3]
neglect, 5877, *nāpal* [1]
neglect, 8894, *šākaḥ* [1]
neglect, 10712+10522, *šālû+ʿabad* [1]

NEGLECTED [2]
neglected, 4202+5757, *lōʾ+nāṭar*[1] [1]
is neglected, 6440, *ʿāzab*[1] [1]

NEGLIGENT [2]
negligent, 8922, *šālâ*[1] [1]
negligent, 10712, *šālû* [1]

NEHELAMITE [3]
Nehelamite, 5713, *neḥelāmî* [3]

NEHEMIAH [9]
Nehemiah, 5718, *neḥemyâ* [8]
Nehemiah, *NIH/RPE* [1]

NEHUM [1]
Nehum, 5700, *neḥûm* [1]

NEHUSHTA [1]
Nehushta, 5735, *neḥuštāʾ* [1]

NEHUSHTAN [1]
Nehushtan, 5736, *neḥuštān* [1]

NEIEL [1]
Neiel, 5832, *neʿîʾēl* [1]

NEIGH [1]
neigh, 7412, *ṣāhal*[1] [1]

NEIGHBOR [65]
neighbor, 8276, *rēaʿ*[2] [52]
neighbor, 6660, *ʿāmît* [4]
neighbor, 8907, *šākēn* [3]
neighbor[s], 408, *ʾîš*[1] [2]
the neighbor[s], 2257, *-ô* [2]
his neighbor[s], 2257, *-ô* [1]
neighbor, 7940, *qārôb* [1]

NEIGHBOR'S [20]
neighbor's, 8276, *rēaʿ*[2] [18]
neighbor's, 408, *ʾîš*[1] [1]
neighbor's, 6660, *ʿāmît* [1]

NEIGHBORING [10]
neighboring, 824, *ʾereṣ* [4]
neighboring, 6017, *sābîb* [2]
neighboring, 8907, *šākēn* [2]
neighboring territory, 1473, *gebûl* [1]
neighboring peoples, 8907, *šākēn* [1]

NEIGHBORS [28]
neighbors, 8907, *šākēn* [11]
neighbors, 8276, *rēaʿ*[2] [8]
neighbors, 6017, *sābîb* [5]
neighbors, 7940, *qārôb* [3]
neighbors, 824, *ʾereṣ* [1]

NEIGHING [2]
neighing, 7412, *ṣāhal*[1] [1]
neighing, 7754+5177, *qôl+miṣhālôt* [1]

NEIGHINGS [1]
lustful neighings, 5177, *miṣhālôt* [1]

NEITHER [77]
neither, 4202, *lōʾ* [42]
neither, *NIH/RPE* [5]
neither, 401, *ʾayin*[1] [5]
neither, 1194, *biltî* [4]
neither, 1685+4202, *gam+lōʾ* [4]
neither, 561, *ʾim* [3]
neither, 2256+4202, *we-+lōʾ* [3]
neither, 440, *ʾal*[1] [2]
neither, 1685, *gam* [2]
neither, 2256, *we-* [2]
there is neither, 401, *ʾayin*[1] [1]
neither, 2256+440, *we-+ʾal*[1] [1]
neither, 4202+2296, *lōʾ+zeh* [1]
neither, 4946+401, *min+ʾayin*[1] [1]
neither, 10379, *lāʾ* [1]

NEKODA [4]
Nekoda, 5928, *neqôdāʾ* [4]

NEMUEL [3]
Nemuel, 5803, *nemûʾēl* [3]

NEMUELITE [1]
Nemuelite, 5804, *nemûʾēlî* [1]

NEPHEG [4]
Nepheg, 5863, *nepeg* [4]

NEPHEW [2]
nephew, 1201+278, *bēn*[1]*+ʾāḥ*[2] [2]

NEPHEWS [1]
nephews, 1201+2157, *bēn*[1]*+-hem* [1]

NEPHILIM [3]
Nephilim, 5872, *nepîlîm* [3]

NEPHTOAH [2]
Nephtoah, 5886, *neptôaḥ* [2]

NEPHUSSIM [2]
Nephussim, 5866, *nepûsîm* [1]
Nephussim, 5867, *nepûšsîm* [1]

NER [18]
Ner, 5945, *nēr*[2] [17]
Ner, *NIH/RPE* [1]

NERGAL [1]
Nergal, 5946, *nēregal* [1]

NERGAL-SHAREZER [3]
Nergal-Sharezer, 5947, *nērgal śar-ʾeṣer* [3]

NERIAH [10]
Neriah, 5949, *nēriyyâ* [7]
Neriah, 5950, *nēriyyāhû* [3]

NEST [17]
nest, 7860, *qēn* [11]
nest, 8905, *šākan* [3]
nest, 4402, *meʿûrâ* [1]
makes nest, 7873, *qānan* [1]
nest, 7873, *qānan* [1]

NESTED [1]
nested, 7873, *qānan* [1]

NESTING [1]
nesting places, 10709, *šekan* [1]

NESTLED [1]
nestled, 7873, *qānan* [1]

NESTS [2]
nests, 748, *ʾarubbâ* [1]
make nests, 7873, *qānan* [1]

NET [25]
net, 8407, *rešet* [16]
net, 3052, *ḥērem*[2] [5]
his net[s], 2156, *hēm* [1]
net, 4821, *mikmār* [1]
net, 5178, *māṣôd*[1] [1]
net, 5182, *meṣôdâ*[1] [1]

NETAIM [1]
Netaim, 5751, *neṭāʿîm* [1]

NETHANEL [14]
Nethanel, 5991, *netanʾēl* [14]

NETHANIAH [20]
Nethaniah, 5992, *netanyâ* [15]
Nethaniah, 5993, *netanyāhû* [5]

NETOPHAH [2]
Netophah, 5756, *neṭōpâ* [2]

NETOPHATHITE [8]
Netophathite, 5743, *neṭôpātî* [8]

NETOPHATHITES [3]
Netophathites, 5743, *neṭôpātî* [3]

NETS [3]
nets, 3052, *ḥērem*[2] [1]
nets, 4821, *mikmār* [1]
nets, 4823, *mikmeret* [1]

NETTLES [1]
nettles, 7853, *qimmôś* [1]

NETWORK [16]
network, 8422, *šebākâ* [12]
network, 5126+8407, *ma'aśeh+rešet* [2]
network, 8407, *rešet* [1]
network, 8422+5126+8422, *šebākâ+ma'aśeh+šebākâ* [1]

NEVER [239]
never, 4202, *lō'* [155]
never, 440, *'al*[1] [11]
never, 401, *'ayin*[1] [7]
never, 4202+4200+6409, *lō'+le-[1]+'ôlām* [5]
never, 4202+6388, *lō'+'ôd* [5]
never, 561, *'im* [4]
never, 1153, *bal*[1] [3]
never, 2721, *ḥālîl*[2] [3]
never, 4200+6409+4202, *le-[1]+'ôlām+lō'* [3]
never, 4202+4200+5905, *lō'+le-[1]+nēṣaḥ*[1] [3]
never, *NIH/RPE* [2]
never, 440+4200+6409, *'al*[1]*+le-[1]+'ôlām* [2]
never, 1153+4200+5905, *bal*[1]*+le-[1]+nēṣaḥ*[1] [2]
never, 1194, *biltî* [2]
never marry, 1436, *betûlîm* [2]
never again, 4202+4200+6409, *lō'+le-[1]+'ôlām* [2]
never, 4202+3578, *lō'+yāsap* [2]
never, 4202+3972+2021+3427, *lō'+kōl+ha-+yôm*[1] [2]
never, 4202+6330+6409, *lō'+'ad*[2]*+'ôlām* [2]
never, 4946, *min* [2]
never, 10379, *lā'* [2]
is never, 401, *'ayin*[1] [1]
never, 401+4200+6409, *'ayin*[1]*+le-[1]+'ôlām* [1]
never, 561+4200+5905, *'im+le-[1]+nēṣaḥ*[1] [1]
never, 561+6330+6409, *'im+'ad*[2]*+'ôlām* [1]
never fail, 586, *'āman*[1] [1]
never, 1153+4200+6409, *bal*[1]*+le-[1]+'ôlām* [1]
never, 1153+6409+2256+6329, *bal*[1]*+'ôlām+we+'ad*[1] [1]
never, 2721+561, *ḥālîl*[2]*+'im* [1]
never, 4200+6409+1153, *le-[1]+'ôlām+bal*[1] [1]
never, 4202+4200+7156, *lō'+le-[1]+pāneh* [1]
never, 4202+4946+3427, *lō'+min+yôm*[1] [1]
never, 4202+8041, *lō'+rab*[1] [1]
never, 6330+5905+4202, *'ad*[2]*+nēṣaḥ*[1]*+lō'* [1]
never, 6409+4202, *'ôlām+lō'* [1]
never, 6524+440, *'ayin*[1]*+'al*[1] [1]
never, 9458+4202, *tāmîd+lō'* [1]
never, 10378+10550+10379, *le-+'ālam+lā'* [1]
never end, 10527+10509+10002, *'ad+sôp+-ā'* [1]

NEVER-FAILING [1]
never-failing, 419, *'ētān*[1] [1]

NEVERTHELESS [26]
nevertheless, 2256, *we-* [9]
nevertheless, 421, *'ak* [5]
nevertheless, 8370, *raq*[2] [4]
nevertheless, 219, *'ûlām*[1] [2]
nevertheless, 3954, *kî*[2] [2]
nevertheless, *NIH/RPE* [1]
nevertheless, 2180, *hinnēh* [1]
nevertheless, 4200+4027, *le-[1]+kēn*[2] [1]
nevertheless, 10124, *beram* [1]

NEW [134]
new, 2543, *ḥādāš* [50]
new wine, 9408, *tîrôš* [34]
new moon, 2544, *ḥōdeš*[1] [8]
New Moons, 2544, *ḥōdeš*[1] [7]
new, *NIH/RPE* [4]
New Moon festivals, 2544, *ḥōdeš*[1] [4]
New Moon festival, 2544, *ḥōdeš*[1] [3]
new, 2736, *ḥālap*[1] [3]
new wine, 6747, *'āsîs* [3]
new grain, 4152, *karmel*[4] [2]
new growth, 4, *'ēb* [1]
new day, 240, *'ôr*[2] [1]
new, 337, *'aḥēr*[1] [1]
something totally new, 1375, *berî'â* [1]
new grass, 2013, *deše'* [1]
new growth, 2013, *deše'* [1]
bring new, 2542, *ḥādaš* [1]
new, 2722, *ḥalîpâ* [1]
new, 3273, *ṭārāp* [1]
new shoots, 3438, *yôneqet* [1]
new owners, 3769, *yāraš*[1] [1]
heads of new grain, 4152, *karmel*[4] [1]
new life, 4695, *miḥyâ* [1]
New Quarter, 5467, *mišneh* [1]
New Moon festivals, 8031+2544, *rō'š*[1]*+ḥōdeš*[1] [1]
new, 9408, *tîrôš* [1]

NEWBORN [1]
newborn, 3528, *yālad* [1]

NEWLY [1]
newly built, 1215, *bānâ* [1]

NEWS [36]
news, 9019, *šemû'â* [8]
news, 1415, *besōrâ* [3]
bringing good news, 1413, *bāśar* [2]
brought the news, 1413, *bāśar* [2]
proclaim the news, 1413, *bāśar* [2]
take the news, 1413, *bāśar* [2]
good news, 1415, *besōrâ* [2]
news, 9051, *šēma'* [2]
news, 606, *'āmar*[1] [1]
bring good news, 1413, *bāśar* [1]
bringing news, 1413, *bāśar* [1]
brings good news, 1413, *bāśar* [1]
hear good news, 1413, *bāśar* [1]
preach good news, 1413, *bāśar* [1]
reward for news, 1415, *besōrâ* [1]
news, 1821, *dābār* [1]
news, 2245+265, *hašmā'ût+'ōzen* [1]
tell the news, 5583, *nāgad* [1]
news, 7754, *qôl* [1]
shouted the news, 7924, *qārā'*[1] [1]
bad news, 7997, *qāšeh* [1]

NEXT [149]
next, *NIH/RPE* [32]
next day, 4740, *moḥorāt* [22]
next to, 339, *'aḥar* [17]
next, 2256, *we-* [11]
next to, 6584+3338, *'al*[2]*+yād* [7]
next to, 6584, *'al*[2] [6]
next in rank, 5467, *mišneh* [5]
next section, 6584+3338, *'al*[2]*+yād* [5]
next, 337, *'aḥēr*[1] [4]
next, 340, *'aḥarôn* [4]
next, 285, *'eḥād* [3]
next, 4740, *moḥorāt* [3]
next, 6584+3338, *'al*[2]*+yād* [3]
next to, 448+3338, *'el+yād* [2]
next to, 448+6298, *'el+'ēber*[1] [2]
next to, 725, *'ēṣel*[1] [2]
next year, 2645, *ḥay*[2] [2]
next year, 6961+2645, *'ēt+ḥay*[2] [2]
early the next morning, 8899, *šākam* [2]
next after, 339, *'aḥar* [1]
next in line, 339, *'aḥar* [1]
next, 339, *'aḥar* [1]
next[s], 465, *'ēlleh* [1]
next to, 907, *'ēt*[2] [1]
next, 1685, *gam* [1]
next to, 4200+5584, *le-[1]+neged* [1]
next to, 4200+6298, *le-[1]+'ēber*[1] [1]
next to, 4200, *le-[1]* [1]
next to, 4946+4578, *min+mûl*[3] [1]
next to, 4946+725, *min+'ēṣel*[1] [1]
next to, 4946+7396, *min+ṣad*[1] [1]
next, 6388, *'ôd* [1]
next, 9108, *šēnî* [1]
next, 10221, *we-* [1]

NEZIAH [2]
Neziah, 5909, *neṣîaḥ* [2]

NEZIB [1]
Nezib, 5908, *neṣîb*[2] [1]

NIBHAZ [1]
Nibhaz, 5563, *nibḥaz* [1]

NIBSHAN [1]
Nibshan, 5581, *nibšān* [1]

NIGHT [255]
night, 4326, *laylâ* [189]
spend the night, 4328, *lîn* [17]
night, 4325, *layil* [6]
spent the night, 4328, *lîn* [6]
night, 10391, *lêlê* [5]
last night, 621, *'emeš* [3]
watches of the night, 874, *'ašmûrâ* [3]
stay at night, 4328, *lîn* [2]
night, 6847, *'ereb*[2] [2]
night, *NIH/RPE* [1]
at night, 621, *'emeš* [1]
night, 696, *'apēlâ* [1]
last watch of the night, 874+1332, *'ašmûrâ+bōqer*[2] [1]
last watch of the night, 874+2021+1332, *'ašmûrâ+ha-+bōqer*[2] [1]
all night long, 928+2021+4326, *be-+ha-+laylâ* [1]
went in to spend the night with, 995+448, *bō'+'el* [1]
last night, 2021+4326, *ha-+laylâ* [1]
night, 3427, *yôm*[1] [1]
stayed night, 3782+2256+4328, *yāšab+we-+lîn* [1]
night creatures, 4327, *lîlît* [1]
for the night, 4328, *lîn* [1]
lie all night, 4328, *lîn* [1]
stay night, 4328, *lîn* [1]
stays at night, 4328, *lîn* [1]
stopped for the night, 4328, *lîn* [1]
place where they stopped for the night, 4869, *mālôn* [1]
place where we stopped for the night, 4869, *mālôn* [1]
stays only a night, 5742+4328, *nāṭâ+lîn* [1]
night, 5974, *nešep* [1]
deepest night, 6547+4017+694, *'êpâ*[1]*+kemô+'ōpel* [1]
spent the night, 10102, *bît* [1]

NIGHTFALL [2]
nightfall, 2021+4326, *ha-+laylâ* [1]
nightfall, 4326, *laylâ* [1]

NIGHTS [16]
nights, 4326, *laylâ* [14]
spend nights, 4328, *lîn* [1]
spent the nights, 4328, *lîn* [1]

NIGHTTIME [1]
nighttime, 4326, *laylâ* [1]

NILE [32]
Nile, 3284, *ye'ōr* [31]
streams of the Nile, 3284, *ye'ōr* [1]

NIMRAH [1]
Nimrah, 5809, *nimrâ* [1]

NIMRIM [2]
Nimrim, 5810, *nimrîm* [2]

NIMROD [4]
Nimrod, 5808, *nimrōd* [4]

NIMSHI [5]
Nimshi, 5811, *nimšî* [5]

NINE [14]
nine, 9596, *tēša'* [12]
over nine feet, 9252+564+2256+2455, *šēš*[1]*+'ammâ*[1]*+we+zeret* [1]
nine feet, 10039+10747, *'ammâ+šēt* [1]

NINE-AND-A-HALF [1]
nine-and-a-half, 9596+2256+2942, *tēša'+we-+ḥaṣî* [1]

NINETEEN [2]
nineteen, 9596+6925, *tēša'+'āśār* [1]
nineteen, 9596+6926, *tēša'+'eśrēh* [1]

NINETEENTH [4]
nineteenth, 9596+6925, *tēša'+'āśār* [2]
nineteenth, 9596+6926, *tēša'+'eśrēh* [2]

NINETY [5]
ninety feet, 10039+10749, *ʾammâ+šittîn* [3]
ninety, 9596, *tēšaʿ* [2]

NINETY-EIGHT [1]
ninety-eight, 9596+2256+9046, *tēšaʿ+we-+šemōneh* [1]

NINETY-NINE [2]
ninety-nine, 9596+2256+9596, *tēšaʿ+we-+tēšaʿ* [2]

NINETY-SIX [2]
ninety-six, 9596+2256+9252, *tēšaʿ+we-+šēš*[1] [2]

NINEVEH [20]
Nineveh, 5770, *nînewēh* [16]
Nineveh, *NIH/RPE* [3]
Nineveh[s], 5226+2023, *māqôm+-āh* [1]

NINEVITES [1]
Ninevites, 408+5770, *ʾîš*[1]*+nînewēh* [1]

NINTH [23]
ninth, 9595, *tešîʿî* [18]
ninth, 9596, *tēšaʿ* [5]

NISAN [2]
Nisan, 5772, *nîsān* [2]

NISROCH [2]
Nisroch, 5827, *nisrōk* [2]

NO [1255]
no, 4202, *lōʾ* [613]
no, 401, *ʾayin*[1] [209]
there is no, 401, *ʾayin*[1] [98]
no, 440, *ʾal*[1] [52]
there was no, 401, *ʾayin*[1] [29]
no, 3972+4202, *kōl+lōʾ* [25]
no, *NIH/RPE* [20]
no, 1194, *biltî* [14]
no, 4946, *min* [12]
no, 10379, *lāʾ* [10]
no, 1172, *belî* [9]
there will be no, 401, *ʾayin*[1] [8]
be no more, 401, *ʾayin*[1] [7]
no, 561, *ʾim* [7]
no, 4202+3972, *lōʾ+kōl* [6]
are no more, 401, *ʾayin*[1] [5]
is no more, 401, *ʾayin*[1] [5]
no, 700, *ʾepes* [5]
no, 1153, *bal*[1] [5]
is there no, 401, *ʾayin*[1] [4]
be no, 401, *ʾayin*[1] [4]
is no, 401, *ʾayin*[1] [4]
there were no, 401, *ʾayin*[1] [4]
for no reason, 2855, *ḥinnām* [4]
no, 4946+401, *min+ʾayin*[1] [4]
no, 10353+10379, *kōl+lāʾ* [4]
no sooner, 677+1153, *ʾap*[1]*+bal*[1] [3]
there is no, 1172+401, *belî+ʾayin*[1] [3]
no, 7153, *pen* [3]
there are no, 401, *ʾayin*[1] [2]
was no more, 401, *ʾayin*[1] [2]
was there no, 401, *ʾayin*[1] [2]
no longer shine, 665+5586, *ʾāsap+nōgah*[1] [2]
no, 1685, *gam* [2]
no, 3954, *kî*[2] [2]
no, 4202+4027, *lōʾ+kēn*[2] [2]
no, 4202+4946+3972, *lōʾ+min+kōl* [2]
no, 4946+1172, *min+belî* [2]
no wonder, 6584+4027, *ʿal*[2]*+kēn*[2] [2]
that no, 7153, *pen* [2]
no good, 8273, *raʿ*[1] [2]
have no, 6+4946, *ʾābad+min* [1]
no more, 361, *ʾê* [1]
am no more, 401, *ʾayin*[1] [1]
no account, 401, *ʾayin*[1] [1]
here are no, 401, *ʾayin*[1] [1]
was no, 401, *ʾayin*[1] [1]
no cure, 631, *ʾānûš* [1]
no, 677, *ʾap*[1] [1]
in order that no, 1153, *bal*[1] [1]
no longer, 1172, *belî* [1]
no more, 1172, *belî* [1]
there were no, 1172+401, *belî+ʾayin*[1] [1]
no more, 1194, *biltî* [1]
there are no, 1615, *gāzar*[1] [1]
no sooner than, 1685, *gam* [1]
no more, 1698, *gāmar* [1]
no meaning, 2039, *hebel*[1] [1]
no more than, 2256, *we-* [1]
no enough, 2532, *ḥādal*[1] [1]
no more, 2532, *ḥādal*[1] [1]
at no cost, 2855, *ḥinnām* [1]
have no, 2894, *ḥāsēr*[2] [1]
made no move, 3087, *ḥārēš*[2] [1]
said no more, 3087, *ḥārēš*[2] [1]
no yet, 3270, *ṭerem* [1]
no use, 3286, *yāʾaš* [1]
by no means, 3480+4202, *yaḥad+lōʾ* [1]
no sooner than, 3869+889, *ke-+ʾăšer* [1]
no sooner than, 3869, *ke-* [1]
no end, 3869+1896, *ke-+day* [1]
no yet, 3972+3270, *kōl+ṭerem* [1]
there is no, 3972+401, *kōl+ʾayin*[1] [1]
leave no, 4162, *kārat* [1]
of no account, 4202, *lōʾ* [1]
can no longer, 4206, *lāʾâ* [1]
lost no time, 4554, *māhar*[1] [1]
no more, 4946, *min* [1]
so that no, 4946, *min* [1]
there is no, 4946+401, *min+ʾayin*[1] [1]
till no more, 4946, *min* [1]
no less than, 5070, *māʿaṭ* [1]
no understanding, 5572, *nābāl*[1] [1]
no longer be, 6073+4946, *sûr*[1]*+min* [1]
shows no, 6073, *sûr*[1] [1]
have no, 6259+4946+6524, *sātar+min+ʾayin*[1] [1]
have no limit, 6296, *ʿābar*[1] [1]
know no limits, 6296, *ʿābar*[1] [1]
so that no, 7153, *pen* [1]
no longer stirred, 7296, *pārar*[1] [1]
bear no longer, 7918, *qāṣar*[2] [1]
no near, 8178, *rāḥaq* [1]
no purpose, 8198, *rîq*[2] [1]
have no compassion, 8317+6524, *rāʿaʿ*[1]*+ʾayin*[1] [1]
no, 8697, *šābat*[1] [1]
no longer, 8740, *šûb*[1] [1]

NOADIAH [2]
Noadiah, 5676, *nôʿadyâ* [2]

NOAH [46]
Noah, 5695, *nōaḥ* [40]
Noah, 5829, *nōʿâ* [4]
Noah[s], 2257, *-ô* [2]

NOAH'S [4]
Noah's, 5695, *nōaḥ* [3]
Noah's, *NIH/RPE* [1]

NOB [6]
Nob, 5546, *nōb* [6]

NOBAH [3]
Nobah, 5562, *nōbaḥ*[2] [2]
Nobah, 5561, *nōbaḥ*[1] [1]

NOBILITY [2]
nobility, 7312, *partemîm* [1]
women of nobility, 8576, *śārâ*[2] [1]

NOBLE [11]
noble character, 2657, *ḥayil* [3]
noble, 5618, *nādîb* [2]
noble, 5619, *nedîbâ* [2]
noble, 2657, *ḥayil* [1]
noble, 2985, *ḥōr*[1] [1]
noble, 3202, *ṭôb*[2] [1]
most noble, 7312, *partemîm* [1]

NOBLEMAN [1]
nobleman, 5618, *nādîb* [1]

NOBLES [60]
nobles, 8569, *śar* [18]
nobles, 2985, *ḥōr*[1] [12]
nobles, 5618, *nādîb* [8]
nobles, 10652, *rabrebānîn* [8]
nobles, 129, *ʾaddîr* [7]
nobles, 3877, *kābēd*[1] [2]
nobles, *NIH/RPE* [1]
nobles, 1524, *gādôl* [1]
nobles, 2077, *hādār* [1]
the nobles and officials[s], 4392, *-ām* [1]
nobles, 5592, *nāgîd* [1]

NOBLEST [1]
noblest, 4946+1475, *min+gibbôr* [1]

NOBODY [2]
nobody, 132+4202, *ʾādām*[1]*+lōʾ* [1]
be a nobody, 7829, *qālâ*[2] [1]

NOCTURNAL [1]
nocturnal, 4326, *laylâ* [1]

NOD [1]
Nod, 5655, *nôd*[2] [1]

NODAB [1]
Nodab, 5656, *nôdāb* [1]

NOGAH [2]
Nogah, 5587, *nōgah*[2] [2]

NOHAH [1]
Nohah, 5666, *nôḥâ* [1]

NOISE [20]
noise, 7754, *qôl* [11]
noise, 2162, *hāmôn* [2]
noise, *NIH/RPE* [1]
noise, 2166, *hemyâ* [1]
noise, 7754+2159, *qôl+hāmâ* [1]
made noise, 8131+9558, *rûaʿ+terûʿâ* [1]
noise, 8323, *raʿaš* [1]
loud noise, 8623, *šāʾôn*[2] [1]
noise, 8623, *šāʾôn*[2] [1]

NOISY [6]
noisy, 2162, *hāmôn* [2]
noisy boasters, 1201+8623, *bēn*[1]*+šāʾôn*[2] [1]
noisy, 2159, *hāmâ* [1]
noisy din, 7754+1524, *qôl+gādôl* [1]
noisy crowd, 8095, *rigšâ* [1]

NOMAD [1]
nomad, 6862, *ʿărābî* [1]

NOMADS [2]
nomads, 1591, *gûr*[1] [1]
nomads, 8905+928+185, *šākan+be-+ʾōhel*[1] [1]

NONE [87]
none, 4202, *lōʾ* [29]
none, 401, *ʾayin*[1] [10]
none, 3972+4202, *kōl+lōʾ* [10]
there is none, 401, *ʾayin*[1] [6]
none, 700, *ʾepes* [5]
there was none, 401, *ʾayin*[1] [4]
none, 4202+3972, *lōʾ+kōl* [4]
none, 4202+408, *lōʾ+ʾîš*[1] [3]
none, *NIH/RPE* [2]
none, 401+408, *ʾayin*[1]*+ʾîš*[1] [2]
there will be none, 401, *ʾayin*[1] [2]
none, 408+4202, *ʾîš*[1]*+lōʾ* [2]
none, 285+4202, *ʾeḥād+lōʾ* [2]
none[s], 408, *ʾîš*[1] [1]
none, 3972+5883+4202, *kōl+nepeš+lōʾ* [1]
none, 4202+4399, *lōʾ+meʾûmâ* [1]
none, 4202+4946+3972, *lōʾ+min+kōl* [1]
none will be, 4946+401, *min+ʾayin*[1] [1]
none, 4946+401, *min+ʾayin*[1] [1]
none, 10353+10379, *kōl+lāʾ* [1]

NONSENSE [2]
nonsense, 2039, *hebel*[1] [1]
turns into nonsense, 6118, *sākal* [1]

NOON [13]
noon, 7416, *ṣohorayim* [11]
noon, 4734+2021+3427, *maḥăṣît+ha-+yôm*[1] [1]
high noon, 7416, *ṣohorayim* [1]

NOONDAY [4]
noonday, 7416, *ṣohorayim* [3]

costs nothing, 2855, *ḥinnām* [1]
had nothing, 2893+3972, *ḥāsēr1+kōl* [1]
say nothing, 3087, *ḥārēš2* [1]
saying nothing, 3087, *ḥārēš2* [1]
says nothing, 3087+3087, *ḥārēš2+ḥārēš2* [1]
doing nothing, 3120, *ḥāšâ* [1]
nothing but, 3869, *ke-* [1]
nothing more than, 3869, *ke-* [1]
nothing but, 3972, *kōl* [1]
nothing, 3972+1821+4202, *kōl+dābār+lō'* [1]
nothing, 4202+3972+1821, *lō'+kōl+dābār* [1]
nothing, 4202+1821+7785+2256+1524, *lō'+dābār+qāṭōn2+we+gādôl* [1]
nothing, 4202+2021+3972, *lō'+ha+kōl* [1]
nothing, 4202+3972+889, *lō'+kōl+'ašer* [1]
nothing, 4202+4027, *lō'+kēn2* [1]
nothing, 4202+4312, *lō'+leḥem* [1]
nothing, 4202+5126, *lō'+ma'aśeh* [1]
nothing, 4399+4202, *me'ûmâ+lō'* [1]
to nothing, 4946+8024, *min+ro'î* [1]
reduce to nothing, 5070, *mā'aṭ* [1]
nothing, 5610, *nādad* [1]
nothing but skin, 6425+2256+1414, *'ôr+we+bāśār* [1]
have nothing to do, 8178, *rāḥaq* [1]
nothing but, 8370, *raq2* [1]
nothing, 8736, *šāw'* [1]
nothing but, 9417, *taklît* [1]
nothing, 10269+10379, *ḥalāq+lā'* [1]
nothing, 10379, *lā'* [1]

NOTICE [10]
take notice, 3359, *yāda'* [2]
notice, 8011, *rā'â1* [2]
notice, 3359, *yāda'* [1]
notice, 5795, *nākar1* [1]
took notice, 5795, *nākar1* [1]
took notice, 5951+6524, *nāśā'+'ayin1* [1]
take notice, 6951, *'āšat2* [1]
notice, 7155, *pānâ* [1]

NOTICED [6]
noticed, 8011, *rā'â1* [4]
noticed, 1067, *bîn* [1]
noticed, 3359, *yāda'* [1]

NOTIONS [1]
notions, 1981, *da'at1* [1]

NOURISH [2]
nourish, 2644, *ḥay1* [1]
nourish, 8286, *rā'â1* [1]

NOURISHED [4]
nourished, 1374+1414, *bārî'+bāśār* [1]
nourished, 1540, *gādal* [1]
nourished, 3567, *yānaq* [1]
well nourished, 4848+2692, *mālē'1+ḥālāb* [1]

NOURISHMENT [1]
nourishment, 9198, *šiqqûy* [1]

NOW [843]
now, 6964, *'attâ* [317]
now, 2256, *we-* [246]
now, *NIH/RPE* [56]
now, 2180, *hinnēh* [33]
now, 5528, *nā'1* [22]
now, *AIT* [18]
now, 2021+3427+2021+2296, *ha-+yôm1+ha-+zeh* [17]
now, 2021+3427, *ha-+yôm1* [14]
and now, 2256, *we-* [11]
now, 3954, *kî2* [8]
but now, 2256, *we-* [6]
now, 10363, *ke'an* [6]
now, 1685, *gam* [5]
now, 10221, *we-* [5]
now, 339, *'aḥar* [4]
now, 2176, *hēn1* [4]
now that, 2256, *we-* [4]
now, 686, *'ēpô'* [3]
now, 2256+1685, *we-+gam* [3]
now, 2296, *zeh* [3]
now that, 3954, *kî2* [3]
come now, 6964+5528, *'attâ+nā'1* [3]
now, 7193, *pa'am* [3]
now, 7756, *qûm* [3]
now, 255, *'āz* [2]
now, 677, *'ap1* [2]
now, 928+2021+3427+2021+465, *be-+ha-+yôm1+ha-+'ēlleh* [2]
go now, 2143+995, *hālak+bô'* [2]
now, 2178, *hēnnâ1* [2]
now when, 2256, *we-* [2]
now, 3869+2021+6961, *ke-+ha-+'ēt* [2]
now, 6961, *'ēt* [2]
now, 66, *'abāl* [1]
but now, 677, *'ap1* [1]
now, 928, *be-* [1]
from now, 928+6388, *be-+'ôd* [1]
and now, 1685, *gam* [1]
now, 2021+7193, *ha-+pa'am* [1]
just now, 2021+3427, *ha-+yôm1* [1]
now, 2151, *halōm* [1]
here now, 2180, *hinnēh* [1]
now then, 2180, *hinnēh* [1]
right now, 2180, *hinnēh* [1]
now, 2256+6964, *we-+'attâ* [1]
now that, 3869+889, *ke-+'ašer* [1]
now, 3893, *kebār1* [1]
now, 3907, *kōh* [1]
now, 3954+2296, *kî2+zeh* [1]
from now on, 3972+2021+3427, *kōl+ha-+yôm1* [1]
do now, 4554, *māhar1* [1]
now, 4946+255, *min+'āz* [1]
right now, 5528, *nā'1* [1]
from now on, 6388, *'ôd* [1]
left now, 6388, *'ôd* [1]
now, 6388, *'ôd* [1]
now then, 6964, *'attâ* [1]
now, 6964+2296, *'attâ+zeh* [1]
right now, 6964, *'attâ* [1]
now, 10008, *'edayin* [1]
and now, 10221, *we-* [1]
now then, 10363, *ke'an* [1]
now, 10364, *ke'enet* [1]

NOWHERE [4]
nowhere, 4202, *lō'* [2]
have nowhere, 6+4946, *'ābad+min* [1]
nowhere to be found, 6372, *'ādar3* [1]

NUBIANS [1]
Nubians, 3934, *kûšî1* [1]

NUGGETS [2]
nuggets, 1309, *beṣer1* [1]
nuggets of gold, 2298, *zāhāb* [1]

NULLIFIED [1]
nullified, 7296, *pārar1* [1]

NULLIFIES [3]
nullifies, 7296+7296, *pārar1+pārar1* [2]
nullifies, 7296, *pārar1* [1]

NULLIFY [1]
nullify, 7296, *pārar1* [1]

NUMBER [120]
number, 5031, *mispār1* [47]
number, 7212, *pāqad* [19]
number, *NIH/RPE* [9]
increase in number, 8049, *rābâ1* [9]
number, *AIT* [4]
number, 7023, *peh* [3]
number, 8041, *rab1* [3]
number, 4948, *mānâ1* [2]
number, 5031+5152, *mispār1+mipqād* [2]
increase the number, 8049, *rābâ1* [2]
reduce the number, 1757, *gāra'1* [1]
large number, 2221, *harbēh* [1]
number is less than, 2893, *ḥāsēr1* [1]
great number, 4200+8044, *le-1+rōb* [1]
number, 4500, *middâ1* [1]
number, 4831, *miksâ* [1]
presented the full number, 4848, *mālē'1* [1]
make few in number, 5070, *mā'aṭ* [1]
few in number, 5493+5071, *mōt1+me'aṭ* [1]
number, 5504, *matkōnet* [1]
exceed number, 6369, *'ādap* [1]
exceeded number, 6369, *'ādap* [1]
number, 7897, *qēṣeh* [1]
beyond number, 8041+4394, *rab1+me'ōd* [1]
larger number, 8041, *rab1* [1]
great number, 8044, *rōb* [1]
increase in number, 8045, *rābab1* [1]
increased in number, 8049, *rābâ1* [1]
increased number, 8049, *rābâ1* [1]
multiply the number, 8049, *rābâ1* [1]

NUMBERED [31]
numbered, 7212, *pāqad* [13]
numbered, *NIH/RPE* [6]
numbered, 2118, *hāyâ* [4]
numbered, 3869+285, *ke-+'eḥād* [2]
numbered, 5031, *mispār1* [2]
numbered, 3972, *kōl* [1]
numbered, 4848, *mālē'1* [1]
was numbered, 4948, *mānâ1* [1]
numbered, 10431, *menâ* [1]

NUMBERING [2]
numbering, *NIH/RPE* [1]
numbering, 7212, *pāqad* [1]

NUMBERLESS [1]
numberless, *AIT* [1]

NUMBERS [38]
numbers, 7212, *pāqad* [12]
increase numbers, 8049, *rābâ1* [8]
large numbers, 4200+8044, *le-1+rōb* [3]
numbers, 5031, *mispār1* [2]
great numbers, 8044, *rōb* [2]
great numbers, 2221+4394, *harbēh+me'ōd* [1]
great numbers, 3878+4394, *kābēd2+me'ōd* [1]
great numbers, 4200+8044, *le-1+rōb* [1]
in large numbers, 4200+8044, *le-1+rōb* [1]
numbers decreased, 5070, *mā'aṭ* [1]
numbers, 8041, *rab1* [1]
acquire great numbers, 8049, *rābâ1* [1]
add to numbers, 8049, *rābâ1* [1]
increased numbers, 8049, *rābâ1* [1]
numbers increased greatly, 8049+2256+7238, *rābâ1+we-+pārâ1* [1]
numbers increased, 8049, *rābâ1* [1]

NUMEROUS [44]
numerous, 8041, *rab1* [13]
numerous, 8049, *rābâ1* [8]
numerous, 8044, *rōb* [6]
numerous, 8045, *rābab1* [4]
make numerous, 8049, *rābâ1* [4]
numerous, 6793, *'āṣam1* [3]
numerous, *NIH/RPE* [1]
numerous, 4200+8044, *le-1+rōb* [1]
made numerous, 6793, *'āṣam1* [1]
much too numerous, 8041+2256+6786, *rab1+we-+'āṣûm* [1]
made numerous, 8049, *rābâ1* [1]
make numerous, 8049+8049, *rābâ1+rābâ1* [1]

NUN [30]
Nun, 5673, *nûn2* [30]

NURSE [14]
nurse, 3567, *yānaq* [7]
nurse, 4787, *mêneqet* [4]
nurse, 587, *'āman2* [2]
his nurses, 2023, *-āh* [1]

NURSED [5]
nursed, 3567, *yānaq* [4]
nursed, 3437, *yônēq* [1]

NURSING [3]
nursing, 3437, *yônēq* [1]
nursing mothers, 4787, *mêneqet* [1]
nursing young, 6402, *'ûl2* [1]

NURTURED [1]
nurtured, 587, *'āman2* [1]

NUT [1]
nut trees, 100, *'egôz* [1]

NUTS [1]
pistachio nuts, 1063, *boṭnâ* [1]

O [950]
O, *NIH/RPE* [870]
O, 2021, *ha-* [35]
O, 10002, *-ā’* [26]
O, 629, *’onnâ* [6]
O, 626, *’onnā’* [5]
O, 1065, *bî* [4]
O, 4537, *mâ* [3]
O, 5528, *nā’*^{1} [1]

OAK [14]
oak, 461, *’ēlâ*^{1} [6]
oak, 473, *’allôn*^{1} [4]
oak tree, 461, *’ēlâ*^{1} [3]
oak, 464, *’allâ* [1]

OAKS [9]
oaks, 381, *’ayil*^{2} [4]
oaks, 473, *’allôn*^{1} [4]
sacred oaks, 381, *’ayil*^{2} [1]

OARS [3]
oars, 5414, *māšôṭ* [1]
oars, 5415, *miššôṭ* [1]
oars, 8868, *šayiṭ* [1]

OARSMEN [2]
oarsmen, 8763, *šûṭ*^{1} [2]

OATH [107]
promised on oath, 8678, *šāba‘* [21]
oath, 8652, *š^{e}bû‘â* [17]
oath, 460, *’ālâ*^{4} [10]
took an oath, 8678, *šāba‘* [7]
swore an oath, 8678, *šāba‘* [6]
made swear an oath, 8678, *šāba‘* [3]
made take an oath, 8678, *šāba‘* [3]
oath, 8678, *šāba‘* [3]
put under oath, 8678, *šāba‘* [3]
taken an oath, 8678, *šāba‘* [3]
swears the oath, 457, *’ālâ*^{1} [2]
take an oath, 457, *’ālâ*^{1} [2]
swore oath, 8678, *šāba‘* [2]
takes an oath, 8678, *šāba‘* [2]
oath, *NIH/RPE* [1]
bound under an oath, 457, *’ālâ*^{1} [1]
put under oath, 460+9048, *’ālâ*^{4}*+šāma‘* [1]
under oath, 1251+8652, *ba‘al*^{1}*+š^{e}bû‘â* [1]
raised and taken an oath, 8123, *rûm*^{1} [1]
oath swore, 8652, *š^{e}bû‘â* [1]
bound under a strict oath, 8678+8678, *šāba‘+šāba‘* [1]
bound with the oath, 8678, *šāba‘* [1]
confirmed by oath, 8678, *šāba‘* [1]
declared on oath, 8678, *šāba‘* [1]
gave oath, 8678, *šāba‘* [1]
gave solemn oath, 8678, *šāba‘* [1]
given oath, 8678, *šāba‘* [1]
made swear an oath, 8678+8678, *šāba‘+šāba‘* [1]
pledged on oath, 8678, *šāba‘* [1]
pronounced solemn oath, 8678, *šāba‘* [1]
put oath, 8678+8652, *šāba‘+š^{e}bû‘â* [1]
ratified by oath, 8678, *šāba‘* [1]
sworn an oath, 8678, *šāba‘* [1]
taken oath, 8678, *šāba‘* [1]
takes an oath, 8678+8652, *šāba‘+š^{e}bû‘â* [1]
took oath, 8678, *šāba‘* [1]
took the oath, 8678, *šāba‘* [1]

OATHS [5]
take oaths, 8678, *šāba‘* [4]
take oaths, 457, *’ālâ*^{1} [1]

OBADIAH [22]
Obadiah, 6281, *‘ōbadyâ* [11]
Obadiah, 6282, *‘ōbadyāhû* [9]
Obadiah, *NIH/RPE* [2]

OBAL [2]
Obal, 6382, *‘ôbāl* [2]

OBED [10]
Obed, 6381, *‘ôbēd* [10]

OBED-EDOM [19]
Obed-Edom, 6273, *‘ōbēd-’^{e}dôm* [18]
Obed-Edom^{s}, 2257, *-ô* [1]

OBEDIENCE [5]
in obedience to, 928, *b^{e}-* [2]
obedience, 3682, *y^{e}qāhâ* [2]
obedience, 9048, *šāma‘* [1]

OBEDIENT [2]
obedient, 9048, *šāma‘* [2]

OBEY [116]
obey, 9048+928+7754, *šāma‘+b^{e}-+qôl* [33]
obey, 6913, *‘āśâ*^{1} [22]
obey, 9068, *šāmar* [21]
obey, 9048, *šāma‘* [19]
obey, 5915, *nāṣar* [4]
obey, 928+7754+9048, *b^{e}-+qôl+šāma‘* [3]
obey, *NIH/RPE* [2]
fully obey, 9048+9048+928+7754, *šāma‘+šāma‘+b^{e}-+qôl* [2]
obey, 2143+928, *hālak+b^{e}-* [1]
obey, 4200+7754+9048, *l^{e}-^{1}+qôl+šāma‘* [1]
obey, 4200, *l^{e}-^{1}* [1]
careful to obey, 9048+9048, *šāma‘+šāma‘* [1]
diligently obey, 9048+9048+928+7754, *šāma‘+šāma‘+b^{e}-+qôl* [1]
faithfully obey, 9048+9048, *šāma‘+šāma‘* [1]
obey fully, 9048+9048+928+7754, *šāma‘+šāma‘+b^{e}-+qôl* [1]
obey, 9068+2256+6913, *šāmar+w^{e}-+‘āśâ*^{1} [1]
obey, 10522, *‘^{a}bad* [1]
obey, 10725, *š^{e}ma‘* [1]

OBEYED [40]
obeyed, 9048+928+7754, *šāma‘+b^{e}-+qôl* [17]
obeyed, 9048, *šāma‘* [13]
obeyed, 9068, *šāmar* [5]
obeyed, 6913, *‘āśâ*^{1} [2]
obeyed, 928+7754+9048, *b^{e}-+qôl+šāma‘* [1]
obeyed, 7756+3869, *qûm+k^{e}-* [1]
fully obeyed, 9048+2256+6913, *šāma‘+w^{e}-+‘āśâ*^{1} [1]

OBEYING [4]
obeying, 9048, *šāma‘* [2]
obeying, 9048+928+7754, *šāma‘+b^{e}-+qôl* [1]
obeying, 9068, *šāmar* [1]

OBEYS [9]
obeys, 6913, *‘āśâ*^{1} [5]
obeys, 9068, *šāmar* [2]
obeys, 9048+928+7754, *šāma‘+b^{e}-+qôl* [1]
obeys, 9048, *šāma‘* [1]

OBIL [1]
Obil, 201, *’ôbîl* [1]

OBJECT [35]
object of scorn, 3075, *ḥerpâ* [5]
object of horror, 9014, *šammâ*^{1} [5]
object of cursing, 7839, *q^{e}lālâ* [4]
object of cursing, 460, *’ālâ*^{4} [3]
object, 3998, *k^{e}lî* [3]
object of ridicule, 8468, *ś^{e}ḥôq* [3]
object of ridicule, 9110, *š^{e}nînâ* [3]
object of dread, 2317, *z^{e}wā‘â* [1]
object of horror, 2997, *ḥōreb*^{2} [1]
object, 4720, *maḥmāl* [1]
object of horror, 4745, *m^{e}ḥittâ* [1]
object of scorn, 5442, *māšāl*^{1} [1]
object of horror, 5457, *m^{e}šammâ* [1]
object of malicious talk, 6590+6584+8557+4383, *‘ālâ+‘al*^{2}*+śāpâ+lāšôn* [1]
object of scorn, 9240, *š^{e}rēqâ* [1]
object of scorn, 9241, *š^{e}riqâ* [1]

OBJECTED [1]
objected, 606, *’āmar*^{1} [1]

OBJECTS [10]
objects, 3998, *k^{e}lî* [4]
objects, 5126, *ma‘^{a}śeh* [2]
sacred objects, 7731, *qōdeš* [2]
objects, *NIH/RPE* [1]
objects of reproach, 3075, *ḥerpâ* [1]

OBLIGATE [1]
obligate, 673, *’āsar* [1]

OBLIGATED [4]
obligated, 673, *’āsar* [4]

OBLIGATES [5]
obligates, 673, *’āsar* [4]
obligates, 6584, *‘al*^{2} [1]

OBLIGATION [3]
obligation taken, 673, *’āsar* [1]
free from obligation, 5929, *nāqî* [1]
under obligation, 10420+10419, *m^{e}laḥ*^{2}*+m^{e}laḥ*^{1} [1]

OBLIGATIONS [2]
obligations, 5466, *mišmeret* [1]
fulfilled obligations, 8966, *šālēm*^{1} [1]

OBLIVION [1]
oblivion, 5964, *n^{e}šiyyâ* [1]

OBOTH [4]
Oboth, 95, *’ōbōt* [4]

OBSCURE [4]
obscure, 6680, *‘āmēq* [2]
obscure, 3126, *ḥāšōk* [1]
obscure, 6680+4946+9048, *‘āmēq+min+šāma‘* [1]

OBSCURES [1]
obscures, 6623, *‘ālam* [1]

OBSERVANCE [2]
observance, *NIH/RPE* [1]
observance, 6913, *‘āśâ*^{1} [1]

OBSERVE [43]
observe, 9068, *šāmar* [20]
observe, 6913, *‘āśâ*^{1} [9]
observe, 3359, *yāda‘* [3]
observe, 8011, *rā’â*^{1} [3]
observe, 1067, *bîn* [1]
observe, 2118, *hāyâ* [1]
observe, 5564, *nābaṭ* [1]
observe, 5915, *nāṣar* [1]
observe, 6268, *‘ābad* [1]
must observe a sabbath, 8697+8701, *šābat*^{1}*+šabbāt* [1]
observe sabbath, 8697+8701, *šābat*^{1}*+šabbāt* [1]
carefully observe, 9068+9068, *šāmar+šāmar* [1]

OBSERVED [14]
observed, 6913, *‘āśâ*^{1} [4]
observed, 9068, *šāmar* [3]
observed, *NIH/RPE* [2]
been observed, 6913, *‘āśâ*^{1} [2]
observed, 8011, *rā’â*^{1} [2]
observed, 2600, *ḥāzâ* [1]

OBSERVES [1]
observes, 2600, *ḥāzâ* [1]

OBSERVING [2]
observing, *NIH/RPE* [1]
observing, 9068, *šāmar* [1]

OBSTACLES [2]
obstacles, 4842, *mikšôl* [2]

OBSTINATE [5]
obstinate, 6253, *sārar*^{1} [2]
obstinate, 599, *’āmēṣ* [1]
obstinate, 7997+4213, *qāšeh+lēb* [1]
obstinate, 7997+7156, *qāšeh+pāneh* [1]

OBTAIN [3]
obtain, *NIH/RPE* [1]
obtain decisions, 8626, *šā’al* [1]
obtain, 10708, *š^{e}kaḥ* [1]

OBTAINED [1]
obtained, *AIT* [1]

OBTAINS [1]
obtains, 7049, *pûq^{2}* [1]

OCCASION [6]
occasion, 1821, *dābār* [2]
occasion, 4595, *môʿēd* [1]
occasion, 6961, *ʿēt* [1]
occasion, 9301, *tōʾ^{a}nâ* [1]
have occasion, 10484, *n^{e}pal* [1]

OCCASIONS [1]
glad occasions, 8525, *śimḥâ* [1]

OCCUPANTS [1]
occupants, 3782, *yāšab* [1]

OCCUPATION [2]
occupation, 5126, *maʿ^{a}śeh* [2]

OCCUPIED [12]
occupied, 3782, *yāšab* [8]
occupied, 299, *ʾăḥuzzâ* [1]
occupied, 3769, *yāraš^{1}* [1]
occupied, 6641+448, *ʿāmad+ʾel* [1]
keeps occupied, 6701, *ʿānâ^{3}* [1]

OCCUPY [8]
occupy, 3769, *yāraš^{1}* [4]
occupy, 3782, *yāšab* [2]
occupy, 995+448, *bôʾ+ʾel* [1]
occupy, 9530, *tāpaś* [1]

OCCUR [2]
occur, 2118, *hāyâ* [2]

OCCURRED [1]
occurred, 2118, *hāyâ* [1]

OCCURS [1]
occurs, 6913, *ʿāśâ^{1}* [1]

OCEAN [2]
ocean depths, 9333, *t^{e}hôm* [2]

OCEANS [1]
oceans, 9333, *t^{e}hôm* [1]

OCRAN [5]
Ocran, 6581, *ʿokrān* [5]

ODED [3]
Oded, 6389, *ʿôdēd* [3]

ODIOUS [1]
so odious, 944+944, *bāʾaš+bāʾaš* [1]

OF [20524]*
of, *AIT* [15716]
of, *NIH/RPE* [1152]
of, 4200, *l^{e}-^{1}* [756]
of, 4946, *min* [592]
of, 928, *b^{e}-* [303]
of, 6584, *ʿal^{2}* [61]
of, 10168, *dî* [46]
of, 448, *ʾel* [18]
of, 4946+7156, *min+pāneh* [17]
of, 10378, *l^{e}-* [11]
of, 10427, *min* [8]
of, 4946+907, *min+ʾēt^{2}* [7]
of, 10089, *b^{e}-* [6]
of, 339, *ʾaḥar* [4]
of, 889, *ʾ^{a}šer* [4]
of, 4946+6640, *min+ʿim* [4]
of, 4946+9348, *min+tāwek* [4]
of, 10542, *ʿal* [3]
of, 907, *ʾēt^{2}* [2]
of, 4200+7156, *l^{e}-^{1}+pāneh* [2]
of, 4946+4200+7156, *min+l^{e}-^{1}+pāneh* [2]
of, 6330, *ʿad^{2}* [2]
of, 10427+10135, *min+gaw* [1]
of, 10554, *ʿim* [1]

OF BETH SHEMESH [4]
of Beth Shemesh, 1128, *bêt-šimšî* [4]

OFF [364]
cut off, 4162, *kārat* [56]
be cut off, 4162, *kārat* [37]
off, 4946+6584, *min+ʿal^{2}* [8]
better off, 3202, *ṭôb^{2}* [6]
carried off, 4374, *lāqaḥ* [6]
carried off, 5951, *nāśāʾ* [6]
cut off, 6073, *sûr^{1}* [6]
count off, 6218, *sāpar* [6]
shave off, 1662, *gālaḥ* [5]
went off, 2143, *hālak* [5]
measured off, 4499, *mādad* [5]
off, 4946, *min* [5]
carried off, 995, *bôʾ* [4]
carried off, 1024, *bāzaz* [4]
carry off, 1024, *bāzaz* [4]
go off, 2143, *hālak* [4]
carry off, 5951, *nāśāʾ* [4]
took off, 6073, *sûr^{1}* [4]
take off, 7320, *pāšaṭ* [4]
cut off, 7915, *qāṣaṣ^{1}* [4]
carried off, 8647, *šābâ* [4]
cut off, 8689, *šābar^{1}* [4]
sent off, 8938, *šālaḥ* [4]
cut off, 1298, *bāṣaʿ* [3]
cut off, 1548, *gādaʿ* [3]
shaved off, 1662, *gālaḥ* [3]
measure off, 4499, *mādad* [3]
cut off, 4577, *mûl^{2}* [3]
carried off, 5627, *nāhag^{1}* [3]
be carried off, 5951, *nāśāʾ* [3]
are cut off, 1615, *gāzar^{1}* [2]
cut off, 1757, *gāraʿ^{1}* [2]
going off duty, 3655, *yāṣāʾ* [2]
was cut off, 4162, *kārat* [2]
take off, 5970, *nāšal* [2]
take off, 6073, *sûr^{1}* [2]
take off, 7293, *pāraq* [2]
stripped off, 7320, *pāšaṭ* [2]
took off, 7320, *pāšaṭ* [2]
takes off, 7337, *pātaḥ^{1}* [2]
got off, 7563+4946+6584, *ṣānaḥ+min+ʿal^{2}* [2]
rode off, 8206, *rākab* [2]
was broken off, 8689, *šābar^{1}* [2]
off goes, 261, *ʾāzal* [1]
carry off, 928+2021+8660+995,
  b^{e}-+ha-+š^{e}bî+bôʾ [1]
far off, 928+8158, *b^{e}-+rāḥôq* [1]
off, 928, *b^{e}-* [1]
carry off, 995, *bôʾ* [1]
partitioned off, 1215, *bānâ* [1]
seals off, 1237+3159, *baʿad^{1}+ḥātam* [1]
cut off, 1299, *beṣaʿ* [1]
ran off, 1368, *bāraḥ^{1}* [1]
run off, 1368, *bāraḥ^{1}* [1]
be cut off, 1548, *gādaʿ* [1]
be sheared off, 1548, *gādaʿ* [1]
is cut off, 1548, *gādaʿ* [1]
cut off, 1605, *gāzaz* [1]
be cut off, 1605, *gāzaz* [1]
be cut off, 1615, *gāzar^{1}* [1]
was cut off, 1615, *gāzar^{1}* [1]
been torn off, 1655, *gālâ* [1]
carry off, 1655, *gālâ* [1]
strip off, 1655, *gālâ* [1]
take off, 1655, *gālâ* [1]
was forcibly carried off, 1704+1704,
  gānab+gānab [1]
am cut off, 1746, *gāraz* [1]
going off, 2143, *hālak* [1]
gone off, 2143+2143, *hālak+hālak* [1]
off, 2143, *hālak* [1]
rode off, 2143, *hālak* [1]
set off, 2143, *hālak* [1]
cut off, 2386, *zānab* [1]
cast off, 2396, *zānaḥ^{2}* [1]
take off, 2740, *ḥālaṣ^{1}* [1]
stripped off bark, 3106+3106, *ḥāśap^{1}+ḥāśap^{1}* [1]
well off, 3201, *ṭôb^{1}* [1]
well off, 3202, *ṭôb^{2}* [1]
go off duty, 3655, *yāṣāʾ* [1]
go off to war, 3655, *yāṣāʾ* [1]
go off, 3655, *yāṣāʾ* [1]
got off, 3718+4946+6584,
  yārad+min+ʿal^{2} [1]
take off, 3718+4946+6584,
  yārad+min+ʿal^{2} [1]
ward off with a ransom, 4105, *kāpar^{1}* [1]
are cut off, 4162, *kārat* [1]
been broken off, 4162, *kārat* [1]
been cut off, 4162, *kārat* [1]
cutting off, 4162, *kārat* [1]
killing off, 4162, *kārat* [1]
must surely be cut off, 4162+4162,
  kārat+kārat [1]
were cut off, 4162, *kārat* [1]
killing off, 4637, *mût* [1]
wash off, 4681, *māḥâ^{1}* [1]
are cut off, 4909, *mālal^{2}* [1]
wring off, 4916, *mālaq* [1]
off, 4946+4578, *min+mûl^{3}* [1]
dragged off, 5432, *māšak* [1]
drags off, 5432, *māšak* [1]
put off, 5612, *nādâ* [1]
get off, 5742, *nāṭâ* [1]
killed off, 5782, *nākâ* [1]
shake off, 5850, *nāʿar^{2}* [1]
am shaken off, 5850, *nāʿar^{2}* [1]
stripped off, 5911, *nāṣal* [1]
carries off, 5951, *nāśāʾ* [1]
is carried off, 5951, *nāśāʾ* [1]
drop off, 5970, *nāšal* [1]
fly off, 5970, *nāšal* [1]
drag off, 5998, *nātaq* [1]
pull off, 5998, *nātaq* [1]
tear off, 5998, *nātaq* [1]
tore off, 5998, *nātaq* [1]
torn off, 5998, *nātaq* [1]
strip off, 6073, *sûr^{1}* [1]
made come off, 6073, *sûr^{1}* [1]
ward off, 6073, *sûr^{1}* [1]
lop off, 6188, *sāʿap* [1]
take off, 6200, *sāpâ* [1]
blocking off, 6258, *sātam* [1]
cast off, 6296, *ʿābar^{1}* [1]
counted off, 6296+928+5031,
  ʿābar^{1}+b^{e}-+mispār^{1} [1]
took off, 6296, *ʿābar^{1}* [1]
fly off, 6414, *ʿûp^{1}* [1]
went off, 6590, *ʿālâ* [1]
marks off, 6913, *ʿāśâ^{1}* [1]
carry off, 7117, *pālaṭ* [1]
cast off restraint, 7277, *pāraʿ^{2}* [1]
tearing off, 7293, *pāraq* [1]
throw off, 7293, *pāraq* [1]
took off, 7293, *pāraq* [1]
strip off clothes, 7320+2256+6910,
  pāšaṭ+w^{e}-+ʿārar [1]
strip off, 7320, *pāšaṭ* [1]
taken off, 7320, *pāšaṭ* [1]
take off, 7337, *pātaḥ^{1}* [1]
marched off, 7575, *ṣāʿad* [1]
break off, 7786, *qāṭap* [1]
broke off, 7786, *qāṭap* [1]
were carried off, 7855, *qāmaṭ* [1]
cutting off, 7894, *qāṣâ^{1}* [1]
scraped off, 7894, *qāṣâ^{1}* [1]
stripped off, 7915, *qāṣaṣ^{1}* [1]
cut off, 7973, *qāraʿ* [1]
tear off, 7973, *qāraʿ* [1]
branches off, 8031, *rōʾš^{1}* [1]
ran off, 8132, *rûṣ* [1]
far off, 8158, *rāḥôq* [1]
far off, 8178, *rāḥaq* [1]
ride off, 8206, *rākab* [1]
marked off, 8492, *śîm* [1]
are broken off, 8689, *šābar^{1}* [1]
be broken off, 8689, *šābar^{1}* [1]
broke off, 8689, *šābar^{1}* [1]
broken off, 8689, *šābar^{1}* [1]
cut off, 8697, *šābat^{1}* [1]
broke off, 8740+4946, *šûb^{1}+min* [1]
ward off, 8740, *šûb^{1}* [1]
clip off, 8845, *šāḥat* [1]
throw off, 8938, *šālaḥ* [1]
throw off, 8959, *šālak* [1]
took off, 8990, *šālap* [1]
cut off, 9012, *šāmad* [1]
marked off, 9419, *tākan* [1]
wandering off, 9494, *tāʿâ* [1]
were torn off, 10440, *m^{e}raṭ* [1]
strip off, 10499, *n^{e}tar* [1]
trim off, 10635, *q^{e}ṣaṣ* [1]

OFFAL [6]
offal, 7302, *pereš*[1] [6]

OFFEND [1]
offend, 2472, *ḥābal*[2] [1]

OFFENDED [2]
offended, 2627, *ḥāṭā'* [1]
offended, 7321, *pāšaʿ* [1]

OFFENDER [1]
the offender[s], 2257, *-ô* [1]

OFFENSE [12]
offense, 7322, *pešaʿ* [5]
offense, 6411, *ʿāwōn* [2]
offense, 2633, *ḥaṭṭā't* [1]
cover the offense, 4064+6524, *kesût+ʿayin*[1] [1]
capital offense, 5477+4638, *mišpāṭ+māwet* [1]
offense, 8288, *rāʿâ*[3] [1]
detestable offense, 9359, *tôʿēbâ* [1]

OFFENSES [18]
offenses, 7322, *pešaʿ* [14]
responsibility for offenses, 6411, *ʿāwōn* [3]
offenses, 6411, *ʿāwōn* [1]

OFFENSIVE [3]
offensive, 2320, *zûr*[3] [1]
offensive, 3075, *ḥerpâ* [1]
offensive, 6778, *ʿōšeb*[2] [1]

OFFER [101]
offer, 7928, *qārab* [22]
offer sacrifices, 2284, *zābaḥ* [17]
offer, 6590, *ʿālâ* [12]
offer, 2284, *zābaḥ* [9]
offer, 6913, *ʿāśâ*[1] [8]
offer, *NIH/RPE* [4]
offer, 5989, *nātan* [4]
offer, 5951, *nāśā'* [3]
offer, 8123, *rûm*[1] [2]
offer, 928, *be-* [1]
offer, 995, *bô'* [1]
offer sacrifice, 2284, *zābaḥ* [1]
sacrifices offer, 2284, *zābaḥ* [1]
offer, 2740, *ḥālaṣ*[1] [1]
offer yourselves for sale, 4835, *mākar* [1]
willingly offer themselves, 5605, *nādab* [1]
offer up, 6590, *ʿālâ* [1]
offer prayer, 7137+9525, *pālal*[2]*+tepillâ* [1]
offer food, 7271, *pāras*[1] [1]
offer sacrifices, 7787, *qāṭar*[1] [1]
offer, 7787, *qāṭar*[1] [1]
make an offer, 7924, *qārā'*[1] [1]
offer, 7924, *qārā'*[1] [1]
offer sacrifices, 7928, *qārab* [1]
offer up, 7928, *qārab* [1]
offer many, 8049, *rābâ*[1] [1]
offer, 8821, *šāḥaṭ*[1] [1]
offer, 8966, *šālēm*[1] [1]
offer sacrifices, 10638, *qerēb* [1]

OFFERED [64]
offered, 6590, *ʿālâ* [14]
offered, 2284, *zābaḥ* [10]
offered sacrifices, 2284, *zābaḥ* [8]
offered, 5989, *nātan* [6]
offered, 7928, *qārab* [5]
offered, *AIT* [3]
offered sacrifices, 6590, *ʿālâ* [3]
offered, 6913, *ʿāśâ*[1] [3]
offered up, 6590, *ʿālâ* [2]
offered, 606, *'āmar*[1] [1]
offered a sacrifice, 2284, *zābaḥ* [1]
offered for a sin offering, 2627, *ḥāṭā'* [1]
advice offered, 3619, *yāʿaṣ* [1]
offered, 5602, *nāgaš* [1]
offered a kiss of homage, 5975+4200+7023, *nāšaq*[1]*+le-*[1]*+peh* [1]
offered, 7381, *ṣābaṭ* [1]
offered up, 7787, *qāṭar*[1] [1]
offered, 7933, *qorbān* [1]
offered, 10638, *qerēb* [1]

OFFERING [675]
burnt offering, 6592, *ʿōlâ*[1] [159]
sin offering, 2633, *ḥaṭṭā't* [105]
grain offering, 4966, *minḥâ* [92]
offering, 7933, *qorbān* [58]
offering made by fire, 852, *'iššeh* [38]
guilt offering, 871, *'āšām* [28]
drink offering, 5821, *nesek*[1] [27]
offering, 2285, *zebaḥ*[1] [24]
wave offering, 9485, *tenûpâ* [21]
fellowship offering, 8968, *šelem* [20]
offering, 9556, *terûmâ* [19]
offering, 4966, *minḥâ* [18]
offering, *NIH/RPE* [12]
freewill offering, 5607, *nedābâ* [7]
offering, 6592, *ʿōlâ*[1] [7]
sacred offering, 7731, *qōdeš* [3]
offering by fire, 852, *'iššeh* [2]
ordination offering, 4854, *millu'îm* [2]
offering of grain, 4966, *minḥâ* [2]
offering, 6590, *ʿālâ* [2]
made an offering, 7928, *qārab* [2]
offering, 7928, *qārab* [2]
offering, *AIT* [1]
memorial offering, 260, *'azkārâ* [1]
guilt offering, 872, *'āšēm* [1]
guilt offering, 873, *'ašmâ* [1]
offering, 1821, *dābār* [1]
offering of praise, 2136, *hillûlîm* [1]
offering sacrifices, 2284, *zābaḥ* [1]
offering, 2284, *zābaḥ* [1]
offering bread, 2503, *ḥabittîm* [1]
offered for a sin offering, 2627, *ḥāṭā'* [1]
presented for a sin offering, 2627, *ḥāṭā'* [1]
purification offering, 2633, *ḥaṭṭā't* [1]
whole burnt offering, 4003, *kālîl* [1]
offering as a pledge, 6287, *ʿabôṭ* [1]
makes offering, 6590, *ʿālâ* [1]
offering body, 7316+906+8079, *pāśaq+'ēt*[1]*+regel* [1]
offering, 7731, *qōdeš* [1]
make offering, 7787, *qāṭar*[1] [1]
offering, 7792, *qeṭōret* [1]
brought offering, 7928, *qārab* [1]
offering made by fire, 7933+852, *qorbān+'iššeh* [1]
thank offering, 9343, *tôdâ* [1]
present an offering, 9556, *terûmâ* [1]
sin offering, 10260, *ḥaṭṭāyâ'* [1]
offering, 10432, *minḥâ* [1]

OFFERINGS [366]
burnt offerings, 6592, *ʿōlâ*[1] [107]
grain offerings, 4966, *minḥâ* [42]
drink offerings, 5821, *nesek*[1] [32]
fellowship offerings, 8968, *šelem* [32]
offerings made by fire, 852, *'iššeh* [19]
offerings, 2285, *zebaḥ*[1] [15]
freewill offerings, 5607, *nedābâ* [10]
offerings, 4966, *minḥâ* [9]
sin offerings, 2633, *ḥaṭṭā't* [8]
sacred offerings, 7731, *qōdeš* [8]
thank offerings, 9343, *tôdâ* [8]
offerings, 7933, *qorbān* [7]
offerings, 9556, *terûmâ* [7]
offerings, *NIH/RPE* [5]
guilt offerings, 871, *'āšām* [5]
holy offerings, 7731, *qōdeš* [5]
most holy offerings, 7731+7731, *qōdeš+qōdeš* [5]
offerings, 6590, *ʿālâ* [3]
Passover offerings, 7175, *pesaḥ* [3]
offerings for dedication, 2853, *ḥanukkâ* [2]
make offerings, 7787, *qāṭar*[1] [2]
offerings made with fire, 852, *'iššeh* [1]
such offerings[s], 2296, *zeh* [1]
festival offerings, 2504, *ḥag* [1]
sin offerings, 2627, *ḥāṭā'* [1]
sin offerings, 2631, *ḥaṭā'â* [1]
wine offerings, 3516, *yayin* [1]
whole burnt offerings, 4003, *kālîl* [1]
his offerings[s], 4392, *-ām* [1]
these offerings[s], 4392, *-ām* [1]
festival offerings, 4595, *môʿēd* [1]
ordination offerings, 4854, *millu'îm* [1]
bowls used for drink offerings, 4984, *menaqqît* [1]
brought as freewill offerings, 5605+5607, *nādab+nedābâ* [1]
freewill offerings, 5605, *nādab* [1]
gave freewill offerings, 5605, *nādab* [1]
drink offerings, 5816, *nāsîk*[1] [1]
pouring out of drink offerings, 5818, *nāsak*[1] [1]
pouring out of offerings, 5818, *nāsak*[1] [1]
burnt offerings, 6590, *ʿālâ* [1]
make offerings, 6590, *ʿālâ* [1]
presented offerings, 6590, *ʿālâ* [1]
offerings, 6592, *ʿōlâ*[1] [1]
burnt offerings, 6608, *ʿaliyyâ* [1]
offerings, 7731, *qōdeš* [1]
burn offerings, 7787, *qāṭar*[1] [1]
presented offerings, 7787, *qāṭar*[1] [1]
made offerings, 7928, *qārab* [1]
wave offerings, 9485, *tenûpâ* [1]
grain offerings, 10432, *minḥâ* [1]
freewill offerings, 10461, *nedab* [1]
drink offerings, 10483, *nesak*[2] [1]
burnt offerings, 10545, *ʿalāwâ* [1]

OFFERS [13]
offers, 7928, *qārab* [7]
offers, 7933, *qorbān* [2]
offers, 2284, *zābaḥ* [1]
offers, 2627, *ḥāṭā'* [1]
offers, 6590, *ʿālâ* [1]
offers, 8492, *śîm* [1]

OFFICE [6]
priestly office, 3914, *kehunnâ* [2]
in office, 2118, *hāyâ* [1]
office, 5163, *maṣṣāb* [1]
judge in office, 9149, *šāpaṭ* [1]
judges in office, 9149, *šāpaṭ* [1]

OFFICER [30]
officer, 6247, *sārîs* [5]
chief officer, 7224, *pāqîd* [3]
officer, 8957, *šālîš*[3] [3]
commanding officer, 10116+10302, *beʿēl+teʿēm*[2] [3]
officer, 6269, *ʿebed*[1] [2]
officer, 7068, *peḥâ* [2]
officer, 7224, *pāqîd* [2]
chief officer, 8569+2021+7372, *śar+ha-+ṣābā'*[2] [2]
officer in charge, 5592, *nāgîd* [1]
officer, 5592, *nāgîd* [1]
chief officer, 6221, *sōpēr* [1]
officer in charge, 6221, *sōpēr* [1]
officer, 8569, *śar* [1]
officer, 8853, *šāṭar* [1]
chariot officer, 8957, *šālîš*[3] [1]
officer, 10718, *šallîṭ* [1]

OFFICERS [79]
officers, 8569, *śar* [31]
officers, 6269, *ʿebed*[1] [16]
officers, 8853, *šāṭar* [6]
officers, 8957, *šālîš*[3] [5]
young officers, 5853, *naʿar*[2] [4]
officers, 5592, *nāgîd* [2]
district officers, 5893, *nāṣab*[1] [2]
officers, 6247, *sārîs* [2]
officers, 7212, *pāqad* [2]
officers, 8042, *rab*[2] [2]
chariot officers, 8957, *šālîš*[3] [2]
officers, 1475, *gibbôr* [1]
officers, 6036, *segen* [1]
fellow officers, 6269+123, *ʿebed*[1]*+'ādôn* [1]
officers, 7068, *peḥâ* [1]
chief officers, 8957, *šālîš*[3] [1]

OFFICIAL [19]
official, 6247, *sārîs* [9]
official, 6269, *ʿebed*[1] [4]
official, 4454, *māg* [2]
official in charge, 5592, *nāgîd* [2]
official, 1469, *gābōah* [1]
official, 4855, *malʾāk* [1]

OFFICIALS [215]
officials, 8569, *śar* [78]
officials, 6269, *ʿebed*[1] [77]

officials, 6036, *segen* [12]
officials, 8853, *šāṭar* [10]
officials, 6247, *sārîs* [9]
court officials, 6247, *sārîs* [4]
officials in charge, 8569, *śar* [3]
officials, 5893, *nāṣab*[1] [2]
officials, 8097, *rādâ*[1] [2]
officials, 10061, *'ᵃparsᵉkāy* [2]
officials, 10716, *šilṭōn* [2]
officials, 408, *'îš*[1] [1]
officials[s], 2157, *-hem* [1]
officials, 3261, *ṭipsār* [1]
the nobles and officials[s], 4392, *-ām* [1]
officials, 5618, *nādîb* [1]
palace officials, 6247, *sārîs* [1]
government officials, 6269, *'ebed*[1] [1]
officials, 7213, *pᵉquddâ* [1]
officials, 7951, *qārî'* [1]
chief officials, 8037, *ri'šôn* [1]
chief officials, 8569, *śar* [1]
serve as officials, 8853, *šāṭar* [1]
officials, 9250, *šārat* [1]
officials, 10062, *'ᵃparsatkāy* [1]

OFFICIATE [1]
officiate, 6913, *'āśâ*[1] [1]

OFFSET [1]
offset ledges, 4492, *migrā'ôt* [1]

OFFSHOOTS [1]
offshoots, 7617, *ṣᵉpî'â* [1]

OFFSPRING [50]
offspring, 2446, *zera'* [35]
first offspring, 7081, *peṭer* [5]
offspring, 7368, *ṣe'ᵉṣā'îm* [4]
offspring, 5769, *nîn*[2] [2]
offspring, 1061, *beṭen*[1] [1]
first male offspring, 1147+7081+8167, *bᵉkōr+peṭer+reḥem* [1]
first male offspring, 1147, *bᵉkōr* [1]
offspring, 7262, *pᵉrî* [1]

OFTEN [8]
often, *NIH/RPE* [2]
how often, 3869+4537, *kᵉ-+mâ* [2]
as often as, 4946+1896, *min+day* [2]
often, 4946+1896, *min+day* [1]
often, 9458, *tāmîd* [1]

OG [20]
Og, 6384, *'ôg* [20]

OG'S [2]
Og's, 6384, *'ôg* [2]

OH [36]
oh, *NIH/RPE* [15]
oh, 4769+5989, *mî+nātan* [8]
oh, 177, *'ᵃhāh* [3]
oh, 2098, *hôy* [2]
oh that, 20, *'ābî*[1] [1]
oh, 277, *'āḥ*[1] [1]
oh that, 332, *'aḥᵃlay* [1]
oh, 626, *'onnā'* [1]
oh, 2176, *hēn*[1] [1]
oh, 4273, *lû* [1]
oh how I wish, 4769+5989, *mî+nātan* [1]
oh, 4769+5989+686, *mî+nātan+'ēpô'* [1]

OHAD [2]
Ohad, 176, *'ōhad* [2]

OHEL [1]
Ohel, 186, *'ōhel*[2] [1]

OHOLAH [5]
Oholah, 188, *'ohᵒlâ* [5]

OHOLIAB [5]
Oholiab, 190, *'ohᵒlî'āb* [5]

OHOLIBAH [6]
Oholibah, 191, *'ohᵒlîbâ* [6]

OHOLIBAMAH [8]
Oholibamah, 192, *'ohᵒlîbāmâ* [8]

OIL [197]
oil, 9043, *šemen* [155]
oil, 3658, *yiṣhār*[1] [20]
olive oil, 9043, *šemen* [13]
oil, *NIH/RPE* [2]
oil, *AIT* [1]
oil, 2016, *dešen* [1]
olive oil, 3658, *yiṣhār*[1] [1]
oil, 5417, *māšaḥ* [1]
the oils[s], 5647, *-nû*[2] [1]
oil, 10442, *mᵉšaḥ*[1] [1]
olive oil, 10442, *mᵉšaḥ*[1] [1]

OILS [1]
oils, 9043, *šemen* [1]

OINTMENT [1]
pot of ointment, 5350, *merqāḥâ* [1]

OINTMENTS [1]
ointments, 9043, *šemen* [1]

OLD [286]
old, 1201, *bēn*[1] [153]
old, 2418, *zāqēn*[2] [32]
old, 2416, *zāqēn*[1] [22]
of old, 7710, *qedem* [8]
old, 1524, *gādôl* [7]
of old, 6409, *'ôlām* [7]
old age, 8484, *śêbâ* [6]
old age, 2421, *zᵉqunîm* [4]
old, *NIH/RPE* [3]
old age, 2420, *ziqnâ* [3]
old, 3824, *yāšān* [3]
old, 6409, *'ôlām* [3]
old, 1165, *bāleh* [2]
old, 1170, *bᵉlôy* [2]
old, 2420, *ziqnâ* [2]
old, 8037, *ri'šôn* [2]
old, *AIT* [1]
of old, 255, *'āz* [1]
old, 255, *'āz* [1]
made grow old, 1162, *bālâ*[1] [1]
old, 1426, *bat*[1] [1]
grew old, 2416, *zāqēn*[1] [1]
grow old, 2416, *zāqēn*[1] [1]
very old, 2416+995+928+2021+3427, *zāqēn*[1]*+bô'+bᵉ-+ha-+yôm*[1] [1]
of ripe old age, 2418, *zāqēn*[2] [1]
old age, 2419, *zōqen* [1]
grew old, 2420, *ziqnâ* [1]
old, 3427+9102+2644, *yôm*[1]*+šānâ*[2]*+ḥay*[1] [1]
old wine, 3516, *yayin* [1]
old men, 3813, *yāšîš* [1]
old, 3813, *yāšîš* [1]
old, 4946+3427+7710, *min+yôm*[1]*+qedem* [1]
old, 5087+2025, *ma'al*[2]*+-â*[2] [1]
of old, 6329, *'ad*[1] [1]
old, 6961, *'ēt* [1]
growing old, 6980, *'ātaq* [1]
days of old, 7710, *qedem* [1]
old, 7712, *qadmâ* [1]
old, 7719, *qadmōnî*[1] [1]
days of old, 8037, *ri'šôn* [1]
of old, 8037, *ri'šôn* [1]
old, 8041, *rab*[1] [1]
three years old, 8992, *šālaš* [1]

OLDER [23]
older, 1524, *gādôl* [9]
older, 1142, *bᵉkîrâ* [6]
older, 1524+4946, *gādôl+min* [1]
grew older, 1540, *gādal* [1]
older, 2418+4200+3427, *zāqēn*[2]*+lᵉ-*[1]*+yôm*[1] [1]
older, 2418, *zāqēn*[2] [1]
older, 3888+3427, *kabbîr+yôm*[1] [1]
older, 5087+2025, *ma'al*[2]*+-â*[2] [1]
older, 8037, *ri'šôn* [1]
older, 8041, *rab*[1] [1]

OLDEST [8]
oldest, 1524, *gādôl* [4]
oldest, 1147, *bᵉkōr* [3]
oldest, 8031, *rō'š*[1] [1]

OLIVE [52]
olive oil, 9043, *šemen* [13]
olive, 2339, *zayit* [9]
olive tree, 2339, *zayit* [8]
olive groves, 2339, *zayit* [7]
olive trees, 2339, *zayit* [4]
olive, 9043, *šemen* [4]
olive grove, 2339, *zayit* [1]
olive trees, 2339+3658, *zayit+yiṣhār*[1] [1]
olive oil, 3658, *yiṣhār*[1] [1]
pressed olive, 4184, *kātît* [1]
olive, 6770+9043, *'ēṣ+šemen* [1]
wild olive, 9043, *šemen* [1]
olive oil, 10442, *mᵉšaḥ*[1] [1]

OLIVES [12]
olives, 2339, *zayit* [7]
pressed olives, 4184, *kātît* [2]
olives, 1737, *gargar* [1]
olives from trees, 2339, *zayit* [1]
crush olives, 7414, *ṣāhar* [1]

OMAR [3]
Omar, 223, *'ômār* [3]

OMEN [2]
omen, 7876, *qāsam* [1]
seek an omen, 7876+7877, *qāsam+qesem* [1]

OMENS [1]
interprets omens, 5727, *nāḥaš* [1]

OMER [5]
omer, 6685, *'ōmer*[2] [5]

OMERS [1]
omers, 6685, *'ōmer*[2] [1]

OMIT [1]
omit, 1757, *gāra'*[1] [1]

OMRI [15]
Omri, 6687, *'omrî* [15]

OMRI'S [2]
Omri's, 6687, *'omrî* [2]

ON [3608]*
on, 6584, *'al*[2] [1150]
on, 928, *bᵉ-* [956]
on, *AIT* [300]
on, 4200, *lᵉ-*[1] [137]
on, 448, *'el* [114]
on, *NIH/RPE* [107]
on, 4946, *min* [98]
on, 2025, *-â*[2] [95]
on, 6584+7156, *'al*[2]*+pāneh* [13]
on, 10542, *'al* [13]
on, 4946+6584, *min+'al*[2] [9]
on, 10089, *bᵉ-* [9]
on, 6640, *'im* [5]
on, 2134, *hālᵉ'â* [4]
on, 2256, *wᵉ-* [4]
On, 228, *'ôn*[3] [3]
on, 2006, *derek* [3]
on, 5087+2025, *ma'al*[2]*+-â*[2] [3]
on, 448+4578, *'el+mûl*[3] [2]
on, 928+7931, *bᵉ-+qereb* [2]
on, 4946+4578, *min+mûl*[3] [2]
on, 9393, *taḥat*[1] [2]
on, 10378, *lᵉ-* [2]
On, 227, *'ôn*[2] [1]
on, 906, *'ēt*[1] [1]
on, 928+9348, *bᵉ-+tāwek* [1]
on, 1068, *bayin* [1]
on, 1237, *ba'ad*[1] [1]
on, 6017, *sābîb* [1]
on, 6330+6964, *'ad*[2]*+'attâ* [1]
on, 6388, *'ôd* [1]
on, 6584+7023, *'al*[2]*+peh* [1]
on, 10089+10135, *bᵉ-+gaw* [1]
on, 10427, *min* [1]
on, 10527, *'ad* [1]

ONAM [4]
Onam, 231, *'ônām* [4]

ONAN [7]
Onan, 232, *'ônān* [7]

ONCE [101]
once, *NIH/RPE* [13]
once, *AIT* [10]
at once, 7756, *qûm* [8]
once, 285, *'eḥād* [6]
once more, 3578, *yāsap* [5]
at once, 4554, *māhar^{1}* [4]
once again, 6388, *'ôd* [4]
bring at once, 4554, *māhar^{1}* [3]
once more, 7193, *pa'am* [3]
once, 7193+285, *pa'am+'eḥād* [3]
once again, 3578+6388, *yāsap+'ôd* [2]
once more, 3578+6388, *yāsap+'ôd* [2]
once again, 3578, *yāsap* [2]
at once, 3869+8092, *k^{e}-+rega'* [2]
at once, 4559, *m^{e}hērâ* [2]
once more, 8740, *šûb^{1}* [2]
once, 255, *'āz* [1]
once for all, 285, *'eḥād* [1]
once more, 421+2021+7193, *'ak+ha-+pa'am* [1]
at once, 928+2021+3427+2021+2085, *b^{e}-+ha-+yôm^{1}+ha-+hû'* [1]
at once, 928+2021+6961+2021+2085, *b^{e}-+ha-+'ēt+ha-+hû'* [1]
once, 928, *b^{e}-* [1]
at once, 928+2021+3427, *b^{e}-+ha-+yôm^{1}* [1]
leave at once, 1368, *bāraḥ^{1}* [1]
at once, 2021+3427, *ha-+yôm^{1}* [1]
once, 2118, *hāyâ* [1]
go at once, 2143+2143, *hālak+hālak* [1]
go at once, 2143+2256+995, *hālak+w^{e}-+bô'* [1]
all at once, 2180+2296, *hinnēh+zeh* [1]
once more, 2256, *w^{e}-* [1]
once, 2296, *zeh* [1]
once again, 3869+2021+8037, *k^{e}-+ha-+ri'šôn* [1]
once, 3954, *kî^{2}* [1]
once for all, 4200+5905, *l^{e}-^{1}+nēṣaḥ^{1}* [1]
go at once, 4554, *māhar^{1}* [1]
act at once, 4554, *māhar^{1}* [1]
all at once, 4554, *māhar^{1}* [1]
once, 4946, *min* [1]
go at once, 5432, *māšak* [1]
once again, 6015, *sābab* [1]
once more, 6388, *'ôd* [1]
once, 7193, *pa'am* [1]
all at once, 7328, *pit'ōm* [1]
at once, 7328, *pit'ōm* [1]
at once, 10097, *b^{e}hal* [1]
once more, 10766, *tinyānût* [1]

ONE [1615]
one, *AIT* [560]
one, 285, *'eḥād* [467]
one, *NIH/RPE* [126]
one, 408, *'îš^{1}* [106]
Holy One, 7705, *qādôš* [43]
one, 4946, *min* [32]
one, 2021, *ha-* [26]
one, 2296, *zeh* [17]
one, 132, *'ādām^{1}* [13]
one, 2257, *-ô* [13]
one, 3972, *kōl* [13]
one, 2085, *hû'* [11]
the one^{s}, 889, *'^{a}šer* [10]
of one piece with, 4946, *min* [9]
one by one, 4200+1653+4392, *l^{e}-^{1}+gulgōlet+-ām* [8]
only one, 4200+963, *l^{e}-^{1}+bad^{1}* [8]
Mighty One, 51, *'ābîr* [6]
one, 851, *'iššâ* [6]
one, 10248, *ḥad* [5]
one day, 2256+2118, *w^{e}-+hāyâ* [4]
one day, 2256, *w^{e}-* [4]
one, 5883, *nepeš* [4]
the one^{s}, 8611, *ša-* [4]
one and the same, 285, *'eḥād* [3]
Mighty One, 446, *'ēl^{5}* [3]
one^{s}, 1201, *bēn^{1}* [3]
one, 1505, *geber^{1}* [3]
one, 2023, *-āh* [3]
Mighty One, 129, *'addîr* [2]
one group^{s}, 465, *'ēlleh* [2]
one^{s}, 889, *'^{a}šer* [2]
one by one, 928+5031, *b^{e}-+mispār^{1}* [2]
one^{s}, 2021+6639, *ha-+'am^{2}* [2]
one^{s}, 3998, *k^{e}lî* [2]
one, 4769, *mî* [2]
of one piece, 4946, *min* [2]
one^{s}, 5709, *naḥ^{a}lâ^{1}* [2]
one more, 7193, *pa'am* [2]
Righteous One, 7404, *ṣaddîq* [2]
one, 10427, *min* [2]
each one, 285, *'eḥād* [1]
one time, 285, *'eḥād* [1]
same one, 285, *'eḥād* [1]
one and all, 408, *'îš^{1}* [1]
one party^{s}, 408, *'îš^{1}* [1]
one^{s}, 408+2424, *'îš^{1}+zār* [1]
not one, 561, *'im* [1]
one, 632, *'^{e}nôš^{1}* [1]
one, 838, *'iš* [1]
one, 889, *'^{a}šer* [1]
as one, 928+9348, *b^{e}-+tāwek* [1]
one way, 928+285, *b^{e}-+'eḥād* [1]
one of^{s}, 928, *b^{e}-* [1]
one, 928, *b^{e}-* [1]
one^{s}, 989, *b^{e}hēmâ* [1]
one^{s}, 1014, *bôr* [1]
one who will inherit, 1201+5479, *bēn^{1}+mešeq* [1]
one, 1201, *bēn^{1}* [1]
one who destroys, 1251+5422, *ba'al^{1}+mašḥît* [1]
one who gives, 1251, *ba'al^{1}* [1]
one^{s}, 1266+200, *ba'^{a}lâ^{1}+'ôb^{2}* [1]
one^{s}, 1469, *gābōah* [1]
one^{s}, 1483, *gābîa'* [1]
each one, 1653, *gulgōlet* [1]
one^{s}, 1821, *dābār* [1]
one another, 2021+6639, *ha-+'am^{2}* [1]
one^{s}, 2021+4131, *ha-+k^{e}rûb^{1}* [1]
one^{s}, 2021+5566, *ha-+nābî'* [1]
one^{s}, 2257, *-ô* [1]
the one, 2257, *-ô* [1]
one condition^{s}, 2296, *zeh* [1]
the first one^{s}, 2296, *zeh* [1]
the younger one^{s}, 2296, *zeh* [1]
one, 2297, *zōh* [1]
one^{s}, 2424, *zār* [1]
one^{s}, 2657, *ḥayil* [1]
one fifth, 2797, *ḥ^{a}mîšî* [1]
loved one, 3351, *yādîd* [1]
one to give counsel, 3446, *yô'ēṣ* [1]
with one accord, 3481, *yaḥdāw* [1]
one piece with, 3669, *y^{e}ṣuqâ* [1]
one month, 3732+3427, *yeraḥ^{1}+yôm^{1}* [1]
one for each, 3869+5031, *k^{e}-+mispār^{1}* [1]
one^{s}, 3870, *-kā* [1]
one^{s}, 3972+1414, *kōl+bāśār* [1]
one^{s}, 4190, *kātēp* [1]
into one set, 4200+963, *l^{e}-^{1}+bad^{1}* [1]
one kind after another, 4200+5476+2157, *l^{e}-^{1}+mišpāḥâ+-hem* [1]
one^{s}, 4200+2157, *l^{e}-^{1}+-hem* [1]
only one, 4200+963+2257, *l^{e}-^{1}+bad^{1}+-ô* [1]
this one, 4200+963, *l^{e}-^{1}+bad^{1}* [1]
one taught, 4341, *limmud* [1]
one piece with, 4609, *mûṣāqâ* [1]
one^{s}, 4751, *maṭṭeh* [1]
one born of a forbidden marriage, 4927, *mamzēr* [1]
one, 5626, *-nâ* [1]
one, 5646, *-nû^{1}* [1]
one, 5647, *-nû^{2}* [1]
put to one side, 5825, *nāsa'* [1]
one of the other peoples, 6639+2256+6639, *'am^{2}+w^{e}-+'am^{2}* [1]
one^{s}, 6647, *'ammûd* [1]
one^{s}, 7228, *par* [1]
one^{s}, 7339, *petaḥ* [1]
one^{s}, 7521, *ṣēlā'^{1}* [1]
Holy One, 7731, *qōdeš* [1]
one^{s}, 7953, *qiryâ* [1]
became one with, 8003, *qāšar* [1]
one in the lead, 8037, *ri'šôn* [1]
one^{s}, 8148, *r^{e}ḥōb^{1}* [1]
upper one, 8207, *rekeb* [1]
one way^{s}, 8273, *ra'^{1}* [1]
one who is close, 8291, *rē'eh* [1]
one in the wrong, 8401, *rāšā'* [1]
one^{s}, 8445, *śeh* [1]
one^{s}, 8802, *šôr* [1]
one living in, 8907, *šākēn* [1]
one, 9108, *šēnî* [1]
one, 10023, *'oḥ^{o}rî* [1]
one, 10025, *'oḥ^{o}rān* [1]
one, 10168, *dî* [1]
one, 10204, *-hî* [1]

ONE'S [8]
one's, *AIT* [2]
one's, 2021, *ha-* [2]
one's, *NIH/RPE* [1]
one's, 2084, *-hû* [1]
one's, 2257, *-ô* [1]
one's own, 4392, *-ām* [1]

ONE-TENTH [5]
one-tenth, 6928, *'iśśārôn* [4]
one-tenth, 6928+285, *'iśśārôn+'eḥād* [1]

ONE-THIRD [1]
one-third, 8958, *š^{e}lîšî* [1]

ONES [62]
ones, *AIT* [46]
little ones, 3251, *ṭap^{1}* [4]
ones, *NIH/RPE* [2]
the ones^{s}, 889, *'^{a}šer* [2]
young ones, 711, *'eprōaḥ* [1]
ones^{s}, 1821, *dābār* [1]
ones^{s}, 2651, *ḥayyâ^{1}* [1]
little ones, 3529, *yeled* [1]
little ones, 6407, *'ôlēl* [1]
little ones, 7592, *ṣā'ar* [1]
holy ones, 7731, *qōdeš* [1]
ones^{s}, 9300, *t^{e}'ēnâ* [1]

ONIONS [1]
onions, 1294, *bāṣāl* [1]

ONLY [325]
only, *NIH/RPE* [119]
only, 8370, *raq^{2}* [30]
only, 421, *'ak* [16]
only, 4200+963, *l^{e}-^{1}+bad^{1}* [16]
only, 3954, *kî^{2}* [12]
only, 3954+561, *kî^{2}+'im* [11]
only, 2256, *w^{e}-* [10]
if only, 4769+5989, *mî+nātan* [10]
only, *AIT* [8]
only one, 4200+963, *l^{e}-^{1}+bad^{1}* [8]
only, 561, *'im* [7]
if only, 4273, *lû* [7]
but only, 421, *'ak* [5]
only son, 3495, *yāḥîd* [5]
only a few, 5071, *m^{e}'aṭ* [5]
only, 285, *'eḥād* [4]
only if, 561, *'im* [3]
only child, 3495, *yāḥîd* [3]
if only, 4769, *mî* [3]
only, 700, *'epes* [2]
only, 2085, *hû'* [2]
but only, 3954+561, *kî^{2}+'im* [2]
but only, 3954, *kî^{2}* [2]
only, 4946, *min* [2]
only a few, 285, *'eḥād* [1]
if only, 332, *'aḥ^{a}lay* [1]
if only, 561, *'im* [1]
only if, 928, *b^{e}-* [1]
only, 928+1727+2257, *b^{e}-+gap^{2}+-ô* [1]
not only, 2022, *h^{a}-* [1]
only, 2022+4202, *h^{a}-+lō'* [1]
only, 2176, *hēn^{1}* [1]
only, 2314+4200+963, *zûlâ+l^{e}-^{1}+bad^{1}* [1]
only, 2314, *zûlâ* [1]
not only, 3463, *yôtēr* [1]
if only, 3869+889, *k^{e}-+'^{a}šer* [1]
only, 3869, *k^{e}-* [1]
not only, 3954, *kî^{2}* [1]
only, 3972, *kōl* [1]

only exception, 4200+963, *l[e-1]+bad[1]* [1]
only one, 4200+963+2257, *l[e-1]+bad[1]+-ô* [1]
if only, 4202, *lō'* [1]
only, 4202+2314, *lō'+zûlâ* [1]
only, 4202+8370, *lō'+raq[2]* [1]
only[s], 4202, *lō'* [1]
only, 4202+1194, *lō'+biltî* [1]
only a few, 5031, *mispār[1]* [1]
only a little, 5071, *m[e]'aṭ* [1]
only a few, 5203, *miṣ'ār[1]* [1]
only a few, 5493+5031, *mōt[1]+mispār[1]* [1]
only wear out, 5570+5570, *nābēl[1]+nābēl[1]* [1]
stays only a night, 5742+4328, *nāṭâ+lîn* [1]
only, 6330, *'ad[2]* [1]
only, 6388, *'ôd* [1]
only look, 8011+8011, *rā'â[1]+rā'â[1]* [1]
but only, 8370, *raq[2]* [1]
only, 8370+421, *raq[2]+'ak* [1]

ONO [5]
Ono, 229, *'ônô* [5]

ONTO [8]
onto, 448, *'el* [2]
onto, 6584, *'al[2]* [2]
onto, *AIT* [1]
onto, *NIH/RPE* [1]
onto, 448+9348, *'el+tāwek* [1]
onto, 2025, *-â[2]* [1]

ONYCHA [1]
onycha, 8829, *š[e]ḥēlet* [1]

ONYX [11]
onyx, 8732, *šōham[1]* [9]
onyx, 74+8732, *'eben+šōham[1]* [2]

OOZING [1]
oozing out, 2144, *hēlek* [1]

OPEN [124]
open, 7337, *pātaḥ[1]* [44]
open, 7156, *pāneh* [8]
open country, 8441, *śādeh* [8]
open, 7219, *pāqaḥ* [7]
open, 7080, *pāṭar* [4]
open, 8441, *śādeh* [4]
ripped open, 1324, *bāqa'* [3]
open, 1655, *gālâ* [3]
open, 4497, *midbār[1]* [3]
open area, 4965, *munnāḥ* [3]
open, *NIH/RPE* [2]
open, 6913, *'āśâ[1]* [2]
open, 7196, *pā'ar* [2]
open wide, 7198, *pāṣâ* [2]
open field, 8441, *śādeh* [2]
rip open, 1324, *bāqa'* [1]
tore open, 1324, *bāqa'* [1]
open, 3269, *ṭārî* [1]
open, 3972, *kōl* [1]
open, 4200+7156, *l[e-1]+pāneh* [1]
open to, 4374, *lāqaḥ* [1]
open land, 4494, *migrāš* [1]
open country, 4497, *midbār[1]* [1]
open, 5157, *miptāḥ* [1]
open before, 5790+7156, *nōkaḥ+pāneh* [1]
open, 5989+7341, *nātan+pittāḥôn* [1]
swung open, 6015, *sābab* [1]
open, 7198, *pāṣâ* [1]
torn open, 7204, *pāṣam* [1]
breaks open, 7287, *pāraṣ* [1]
split open, 7297, *pārar[2]* [1]
break open, 7337, *pātaḥ[1]* [1]
open wide, 7337, *pātaḥ[1]* [1]
throw open, 7337, *pātaḥ[1]* [1]
thrown open, 7337, *pātaḥ[1]* [1]
wide open, 7337+7337, *pātaḥ[1]+pātaḥ[1]* [1]
open, 7341, *pittāḥôn* [1]
stay open, 7709, *qādam* [1]
rip open, 7973+6033+4213, *qāra'+s[e]gôr+lēb* [1]
open wide, 8143, *rāḥab* [1]
open square, 8148, *r[e]ḥōb[1]* [1]
tear open, 9117, *šāsa'* [1]

OPENED [61]
opened, 7337, *pātaḥ[1]* [33]
opened, 7219, *pāqaḥ* [4]
be opened, 7337, *pātaḥ[1]* [4]
opened, 1655, *gālâ* [3]
opened, 7198, *pāṣâ* [3]
opened up, 1324, *bāqa'* [2]
be opened, 7219, *pāqaḥ* [2]
were opened, 7337, *pātaḥ[1]* [2]
opened wide, 7198, *pāṣâ* [1]
were opened, 7219, *pāqaḥ* [1]
are opened, 7337, *pātaḥ[1]* [1]
opened up, 7337, *pātaḥ[1]* [1]
was opened, 7337, *pātaḥ[1]* [1]
opened wide, 8143, *rāḥab* [1]
opened, 10602, *p[e]taḥ* [1]
were opened, 10602, *p[e]taḥ* [1]

OPENHANDED [2]
openhanded, 7337+7337+906+3338, *pātaḥ[1]+pātaḥ[1]+'ēt[1]+yād* [2]

OPENING [13]
opening, 7023, *peh* [8]
key for opening, 5158, *maptēaḥ* [1]
opening of the womb, 5402+1201, *mašbēr+bēn[1]* [1]
opening, 7156, *pāneh* [1]
parapet opening, 7339, *petaḥ* [1]
opening, 10776, *t[e]ra'* [1]

OPENINGS [8]
openings, 2707, *ḥallôn* [7]
parapet openings, 2707, *ḥallôn* [1]

OPENLY [1]
carried on openly, 1655, *gālâ* [1]

OPENS [7]
opens, 7198, *pāṣâ* [2]
opens, 7196, *pā'ar* [1]
opens, 7219, *pāqaḥ* [1]
opens, 7298, *pāraś* [1]
opens, 7337, *pātaḥ[1]* [1]
opens the way, 8143, *rāḥab* [1]

OPHEL [5]
hill of Ophel, 6755, *'ōpel[2]* [4]
Ophel, 6755, *'ōpel[2]* [1]

OPHIR [12]
Ophir, 234, *'ôpîr[1]* [9]
Ophir, 235, *'ôpîr[2]* [2]
gold of Ophir, 234, *'ôpîr[1]* [1]

OPHNI [1]
Ophni, 6756, *'opnî* [1]

OPHRAH [8]
Ophrah, 6764, *'oprâ[2]* [7]
Ophrah, 6763, *'oprâ[1]* [1]

OPINION [1]
give opinion, 1819, *dābar[2]* [1]

OPINIONS [2]
opinions, 4213, *lēb* [1]
opinions, 6191, *s[e]'ippîm* [1]

OPPONENT [3]
opponent, 408, *'îš[1]* [1]
opponent, 7640, *ṣar[2]* [1]
opponent, 8276, *rēa'[2]* [1]

OPPONENT'S [1]
opponent's, 8276, *rēa'[2]* [1]

OPPONENTS [1]
opponents, *AIT* [1]

OPPORTUNITY [2]
opportunity, *AIT* [1]
opportunity, 4595, *mô'ēd* [1]

OPPOSE [17]
oppose, 6584, *'al[2]* [3]
oppose, 7925, *qārā'[2]* [2]
oppose, 8477, *śāṭān* [2]
oppose, 8740, *šûb[1]* [2]
oppose, 907, *'ēt[2]* [1]
oppose, 995+928, *bô'+b[e]-* [1]
oppose, 6643, *'immād* [1]
oppose, 7444, *ṣûr[2]* [1]
oppose, 7675, *ṣārar[2]* [1]
oppose, 8189+6643, *rîb[1]+'immād* [1]
oppose, 8189, *rîb[1]* [1]
oppose, 8190, *rîb[2]* [1]

OPPOSED [4]
opposed, 599+6584, *'āmēṣ+'al[2]* [1]
opposed, 1741, *gārâ* [1]
opposed, 6641+6584, *'āmad+'al[2]* [1]
opposed, 7756, *qûm* [1]

OPPOSING [1]
opposing, 4946, *min* [1]

OPPOSITE [44]
opposite, 5584, *neged* [15]
opposite, 5790, *nōkaḥ* [5]
opposite, 4200+7156, *l[e-1]+pāneh* [3]
opposite, 4200+5584, *l[e-1]+neged* [2]
opposite, 4578, *mûl[3]* [2]
opposite sides, 7521+7396, *ṣēlā'[1]+ṣad[1]* [2]
opposite, 7691, *qābal* [2]
opposite, 448+7156, *'el+pāneh* [1]
opposite, 448, *'el* [1]
opposite, 2178, *hēnnâ[1]* [1]
opposite, 2201, *hēpek* [1]
very opposite, 2201, *hēpek* [1]
opposite[s], 2257, *-ô* [1]
directly opposite, 4200+7156+5790, *l[e-1]+pāneh+nōkaḥ* [1]
opposite, 4200+6645, *l[e-1]+'ummâ[1]* [1]
opposite direction, 4578, *mûl[3]* [1]
opposite, 4946+5584, *min+neged* [1]
opposite, 7709, *qādam* [1]
opposite, 7925, *qārā'[2]* [1]
opposite[s], 9133, *ša'ar[1]* [1]

OPPOSITION [4]
in opposition to, 6584, *'al[2]* [3]
in opposition to, 4200, *l[e-1]* [1]

OPPRESS [28]
oppress, 6943, *'āšaq* [7]
oppress, 3561, *yānâ* [5]
oppress, 6700, *'ānâ[2]* [5]
oppress, 4315, *lāḥaṣ* [4]
oppress, *NIH/RPE* [1]
oppress, 1162, *bālâ[1]* [1]
oppress, 4198, *kātat* [1]
oppress each other, 5601, *nāgaś* [1]
oppress, 5601, *nāgaś* [1]
oppress, 7674, *ṣārar[1]* [1]
oppress, 10106, *b[e]lâ* [1]

OPPRESSED [45]
oppressed, 6943, *'āšaq* [7]
oppressed, 4315, *lāḥaṣ* [6]
oppressed, 6714, *'ānî* [5]
oppressed, 6700, *'ānâ[2]* [4]
oppressed, 8368, *rāṣaṣ* [4]
oppressed, 1916, *dak* [3]
oppressed, 4316, *laḥaṣ* [2]
oppressed, 6705, *'ānāw* [2]
oppressed, 7675, *ṣārar[2]* [2]
oppressed, *NIH/RPE* [1]
oppressed, 1201+6715, *bēn[1]+'[o]nî* [1]
oppressed, 2787, *ḥāmôṣ* [1]
was oppressed, 5601, *nāgaś* [1]
oppressed, 6913+928+2021+6945, *'āśâ[1]+b[e]-+ha-+'ōšeq* [1]
oppressed, 6945, *'ōšeq* [1]
oppressed, 7650, *ṣārâ[1]* [1]
oppressed, 7674, *ṣārar[1]* [1]
brutally oppressed, 8368, *rāṣaṣ* [1]
oppressed, 10559, *'[a]nēh* [1]

OPPRESSES [4]
oppresses, 6943, *'āšaq* [3]
oppresses, 3561, *yānâ* [1]

OPPRESSING [3]
oppressing, 4315, *lāḥaṣ* [1]

severely oppressing, 4316+4315, laḥaṣ+lāḥaṣ [1]
oppressing, 7675, ṣārar[2] [1]

OPPRESSION [19]
oppression, 6945, ʿōšeq [6]
oppression, 6935, ʿᵃšûqîm [3]
oppression, 4316, laḥaṣ [2]
oppression, 6808, ʿōṣer [2]
oppression, 8719, šōd[2] [2]
oppression, *NIH/RPE* [1]
oppression, 5362, maśśāʾ[1] [1]
oppression, 6943, ʿāšaq [1]
oppression, 9412, tōk [1]

OPPRESSIVE [3]
oppressive, 6662, ʿāmāl[1] [2]
oppressive, 6451, ʿāzaz [1]

OPPRESSOR [14]
oppressor, 3561, yānâ [3]
oppressor, 5601, nāgaś [3]
oppressor, 6943, ʿāšaq [2]
oppressor, 7439, ṣûq[1] [2]
oppressor, 408+9412, ʾîš[1]+tōk [1]
oppressor, 5160, mēṣ [1]
oppressor, 6934, ʿāšôq [1]
oppressor, 7640, ṣar[2] [1]

OPPRESSORS [9]
oppressors, 3561, yānâ [2]
oppressors, 4315, lāḥaṣ [2]
oppressors, 6943, ʿāšaq [2]
oppressors, 5601, nāgaś [1]
oppressors, 6700, ʿānâ[2] [1]
oppressors, 8806, šōrēr [1]

OPTIONS [2]
options, *AIT* [2]

OR [1504]
or, 2256, wᵉ- [931]
or, 196, ʾô [247]
or, *NIH/RPE* [101]
or, 7153, pen [49]
or, 561, ʾim [39]
or, 10221, wᵉ- [20]
or, 2256+4202, wᵉ-+lōʾ [14]
or, 4202, lōʾ [14]
whether or, 196, ʾô [13]
whether or, 2256, wᵉ- [10]
or, 6330, ʿad[2] [8]
either or, 2256, wᵉ- [7]
or, 1685, gam [6]
or, 440, ʾal[1] [5]
or, 2256+561, wᵉ-+ʾim [5]
either or, 196, ʾô [4]
or, 2256+1685, wᵉ-+gam [4]
or, 3954, kî[2] [3]
or, 1068, bayin [2]
or, 2022, hᵃ- [2]
or, 2256+3954, wᵉ-+kî[2] [2]
sheep goats or, 7366, ṣōʾn [2]
or else, 196, ʾô [1]
or so, 196, ʾô [1]
or, 401, ʾayin[1] [1]
or, 677, ʾap[1] [1]
or, 889+4202, ʾᵃšer+lōʾ [1]
or, 889, ʾᵃšer [1]
or even, 2256, wᵉ- [1]
or, 2256+440, wᵉ-+ʾal[1] [1]
or, 2256+561+401, wᵉ-+ʾim+ʾayin[1] [1]
or, 2256+700, wᵉ-+ʾepes [1]
or, 3869, kᵉ- [1]
or, 3954+1685, kî[2]+gam [1]
or, 4017, kᵉmô [1]
or, 4946, min [1]
grapes or raisins, 6694+4300+2256+3313, ʿēnāb+laḥ+wᵉ-+yābēš[2] [1]
or else, 7153, pen [1]

ORACLE [44]
oracle, 5363, maśśāʾ[2] [27]
oracle, 5536, nᵉʾum [9]
oracle, 5442, māšāl[1] [7]
oracle, 7877, qesem [1]

ORACLES [1]
oracles, 5363, maśśāʾ[2] [1]

ORCHARD [1]
orchard, 7236, pardēs [1]

ORCHARDS [2]
orchards, 4149, karmel[1] [2]

ORDAIN [3]
ordain, 4848+3338, mālēʾ[1]+yād [2]
ordain, 4848+906+3338, mālēʾ[1]+ʾēt[1]+yād [1]

ORDAINED [13]
ordained, 4848+906+3338, mālēʾ[1]+ʾēt[1]+yād [3]
ordained, 3569, yāsad[1] [2]
ordained, 6913, ʿāśâ[1] [2]
ordained, 7422, ṣāwâ [2]
ordained, 3670, yāṣar [1]
ordained, 3922, kûn[1] [1]
ordained, 4848+3338, mālēʾ[1]+yād [1]
ordained, 5989, nātan [1]

ORDER [89]
in order to, 4200, lᵉ-[1] [21]
gave order, 7422, ṣāwâ [7]
in order to, 4200+5100, lᵉ-[1]+maʿan [5]
order, 7422, ṣāwâ [5]
put in order, 7422, ṣāwâ [3]
order, 10302, ṭᵉʿēm[2] [3]
order, 606, ʾāmar[1] [2]
in order to, 928+6288, bᵉ-+ʿᵃbûr[1] [2]
order, 1821, dābār [2]
in the order of, 3869, kᵉ- [2]
in order that, 4200, lᵉ-[1] [2]
order, 5466, mišmeret [2]
appointed order, 7213, pᵉquddâ [2]
given order, 7422, ṣāwâ [2]
order, *NIH/RPE* [1]
gave an order, 606, ʾāmar[1] [1]
gave the order, 606, ʾāmar[1] [1]
in order that no, 1153, bal[1] [1]
order, 1826, dibrâ [1]
order, 2017, dāt [1]
in order for, 2256, wᵉ- [1]
set in order, 3922, kûn[1] [1]
in order to, 3954, kî[2] [1]
order, 4026, kēn[1] [1]
in the same order, 4027, kēn[2] [1]
order be written, 4180, kātab [1]
in order, 4200, lᵉ-[1] [1]
order of march, 5023, massaʿ [1]
order, 5184, miṣwâ [1]
in order that not, 7153, pen [1]
gave an order, 7422, ṣāwâ [1]
gave the order, 7422, ṣāwâ [1]
give the order, 7422, ṣāwâ [1]
given an order, 7422, ṣāwâ [1]
issue an order, 7422, ṣāwâ [1]
order, 8934, šālôm [1]
give an order, 8938, šālaḥ [1]
issued an order, 9048, šāmaʿ [1]
order of birth, 9352, tôlēdôt [1]
set in order, 9545, tāqan [1]
gave the order, 10042, ʾᵃmar [1]
order, 10302+10002+10682, ṭᵉʿēm[2]+-āʾ+śîm [1]
order, 10682+10302, śîm+ṭᵉʿēm[2] [1]

ORDERED [63]
ordered, 606, ʾāmar[1] [28]
ordered, 7422, ṣāwâ [22]
ordered, 5184, miṣwâ [4]
ordered, 10042, ʾᵃmar [2]
ordered, 1819, dābar[2] [1]
ordered, 1821, dābār [1]
ordered, 3338, yād [1]
ordered, 3585, yāʿad [1]
what ordered, 5184, miṣwâ [1]
ordered, 8938, šālaḥ [1]
ordered, 10558, ʿᵃnâ [1]

ORDERS [35]
gave orders, 7422, ṣāwâ [10]
gave orders, 606, ʾāmar[1] [5]
orders, 7422, ṣāwâ [4]
give orders, 7422, ṣāwâ [3]
given orders, 7422, ṣāwâ [2]
giving orders, 7422, ṣāwâ [2]
gave orders, 8938, šālaḥ [2]
gave orders, 10042, ʾᵃmar [2]
orders, *NIH/RPE* [1]
issued orders, 606, ʾāmar[1] [1]
orders, 2017, dāt [1]
orders, 5184, miṣwâ [1]
orders, 7023, peh [1]

ORDINANCE [29]
ordinance, 2978, ḥuqqâ [23]
ordinance, 5477, mišpāṭ [3]
ordinance, 2976, ḥōq [2]
ordinance, *NIH/RPE* [1]

ORDINANCES [7]
ordinances, 5477, mišpāṭ [7]

ORDINARY [2]
ordinary, 632, ʾᵉnôš[1] [1]
ordinary, 2687, ḥōl [1]

ORDINATION [13]
ordination, 4854, milluʾîm [7]
ordination, 4848+906+3338, mālēʾ[1]+ʾēt[1]+yād [2]
ordination offering, 4854, milluʾîm [2]
ordination offerings, 4854, milluʾîm [1]
ordination ram, 4854, milluʾîm [1]

ORE [3]
ore, 74, ʾeben [2]
ore, 4450, mibṣār[3] [1]

OREB [7]
Oreb, 6855, ʿōrēb[2] [7]

OREN [1]
Oren, 816, ʾōren[2] [1]

ORIGIN [1]
origin, 2446, zeraʿ [1]

ORIGINAL [1]
original design, 5504, matkōnet [1]

ORIGINS [1]
origins, 4606, môṣāʾâ [1]

ORION [3]
Orion, 4068, kᵉsîl[2] [3]

ORNAMENT [2]
ornament, 2717, ḥᵃlî[1] [1]
ornament to grace, 2834, ḥēn[1] [1]

ORNAMENTED [5]
richly ornamented, 7168, pas [3]
ornamented, 7168, pas [2]

ORNAMENTS [10]
ornaments, 6344, ʿᵃdî [5]
ornaments, 8448, śahᵃrōnîm [2]
ornaments, 3921, kûmāz [1]
ornaments jingling, 6576, ʿākas [1]
wedding ornaments, 8005, qiššurîm [1]

ORPAH [2]
Orpah, 6905, ʿorpâ [2]

ORPHAN [1]
orphan, 3846, yātôm [1]

ORPHAN'S [1]
orphan's, 3846, yātôm [1]

ORPHANS [2]
orphans, 3846, yātôm [2]

OSPREY [2]
osprey, 8164, rāḥām [1]
osprey, 8168, rāḥāmâ [1]

OSTRICH [1]
ostrich, 8266, rᵉnānîm [1]

OSTRICHES [1]
ostriches, 3612, yāʿēn [1]

OTHER [553]

other, *NIH/RPE* [153]
other, 337, *'aḥēr^{1}* [83]
other, 3856, *yeter^{1}* [45]
other, 9108, *šēnî* [33]
other^{s}, 8276, *rēa'^{2}* [29]
other^{s}, 285, *'eḥād* [27]
other, *AIT* [24]
other^{s}, 2021, *ha-* [17]
other^{s}, 278, *'āḥ^{2}* [15]
other, 6388, *'ôd* [11]
other^{s}, 3972, *kōl* [9]
other side, 6298, *'ēber^{1}* [6]
other^{s}, 2296, *zeh* [5]
other^{s}, 295, *'āḥôt* [4]
the other^{s}, 2296, *zeh* [4]
other^{s}, 3749, *y^{e}rî'â* [4]
other^{s}, 7895, *qāṣeh* [4]
the other^{s}, 285, *'eḥād* [2]
anyone other than a priest, 2424, *zār* [2]
each other, 3480, *yaḥad* [2]
other than, 3954+561, *kî^{2}+'im* [2]
facing each other, 4691+448+4691, *meḥ^{e}zâ+'el+meḥ^{e}zâ* [2]
other than, 4946+1187, *min+bal'^{a}dê* [2]
other^{s}, 7023, *peh* [2]
other^{s}, 7024, *pōh* [2]
the other^{s}, 7895+2021+824, *qāṣeh+ha-+'ereṣ* [2]
faced each other, 8011+7156, *rā'â^{1}+pāneh* [2]
other^{s}, 9109, *š^{e}nayim* [2]
other, 10692, *š^{e}'ār* [2]
other^{s}, 132, *'ādām^{1}* [1]
crave other food, 203+9294, *'āwâ^{1}+ta'^{a}wâ^{1}* [1]
craved other food, 203, *'āwâ^{1}* [1]
some other^{s}, 285, *'eḥād* [1]
other gods, 337, *'aḥēr^{1}* [1]
turned the other way, 345, *'^{a}ḥōrannît* [1]
each other, 465, *'ēlleh* [1]
other than, 561, *'im* [1]
other^{s}, 889+907, *'^{a}šer+'ēt^{2}* [1]
some other place^{s}, 889, *'^{a}šer* [1]
other than, 1194+4200+963, *biltî+l^{e-1}+bad^{1}* [1]
other^{s}, 1478, *gabbaḥat* [1]
arguing with each other, 1906, *dîn^{1}* [1]
other^{s}, 1947, *dām* [1]
other^{s}, 2085, *hû'* [1]
the other half of Manasseh^{s}, 2257, *-ô* [1]
the other man^{s}, 2257, *-ô* [1]
other, 2424, *zār* [1]
the other^{s}, 3202, *ṭôb^{2}* [1]
other days, 3427+3427, *yôm^{1}+yôm^{1}* [1]
each other, 3481, *yaḥdāw* [1]
each other^{s}, 3870, *-kā* [1]
other than, 3954, *kî^{2}* [1]
other^{s}, 3998, *k^{e}lî* [1]
other^{s}, 4053, *kānāp* [1]
other than, 4202, *lō'* [1]
other^{s}, 4211, *l^{e}'ōm* [1]
each other^{s}, 4564, *-mô* [1]
on the other side of, 4946+6298+2256+2134, *min+'ēber^{1}+w^{e}-+hāl^{e}'â* [1]
other than, 4946+4200+963, *min+l^{e-1}+bad^{1}* [1]
other^{s}, 5464, *mišmār^{1}* [1]
other, 5467, *mišneh* [1]
oppress each other, 5601, *nāgaś* [1]
came to the other side, 6296, *'ābar^{1}* [1]
pass into other hands, 6296, *'ābar^{1}* [1]
one of the other peoples, 6639+2256+6639, *'am^{2}+w^{e}-+'am^{2}* [1]
other nationalities, 6639+2021+824, *'am^{2}+ha-+'ereṣ* [1]
other^{s}, 6660, *'āmît* [1]
other people, 6850, *'ēreb^{2}* [1]
at other times, 7193+928+7193, *pa'am+b^{e}-+pa'am* [1]
other^{s}, 7193, *pa'am* [1]
other^{s}, 7396, *ṣad^{1}* [1]
other^{s}, 7895+9028, *qāṣeh+šāmayim* [1]
other^{s}, 7896, *qāṣâ^{2}* [1]
facing each other, 7925+5120, *qārā'^{2}+ma'^{a}rākâ* [1]
looking at each other, 8011, *rā'â^{1}* [1]
each other^{s}, 8276, *rēa'^{2}* [1]
jostled each other, 8368, *rāṣaṣ* [1]
other, 8637, *š^{e}'ār* [1]
other, 8642, *š^{e}'ērît* [1]
each other^{s}, 9109+2157, *š^{e}nayim+-hem* [1]
each other, 9109+5646, *š^{e}nayim+-nû^{1}* [1]
other^{s}, 9133, *ša'ar^{1}* [1]
other, 10023, *'oḥ^{o}rî* [1]
other, 10025, *'oḥ^{o}rān* [1]
other^{s}, 10353, *kōl* [1]

OTHERS [68]

others, 337, *'aḥēr^{1}* [12]
others, *AIT* [11]
others, *NIH/RPE* [10]
others^{s}, 465, *'ēlleh* [7]
others^{s}, 6639, *'am^{2}* [4]
others^{s}, 278, *'āḥ^{2}* [2]
others^{s}, 889, *'^{a}šer* [2]
others^{s}, 1856, *dôd* [2]
others^{s}, 132, *'ādām^{1}* [1]
the others^{s}, 465, *'ēlleh* [1]
others^{s}, 1469, *gābōah* [1]
others^{s}, 2021+851, *ha-+'iššâ* [1]
others^{s}, 2021, *ha-* [1]
the others^{s}, 2156, *hēm* [1]
others^{s}, 2257, *-ô* [1]
others^{s}, 2645, *ḥay^{2}* [1]
others, 3856, *yeter^{1}* [1]
others^{s}, 4211, *l^{e}'ōm* [1]
the others^{s}, 4392, *-ām* [1]
others^{s}, 4769, *mî* [1]
others^{s}, 4946+2157, *min+-hem* [1]
others, 6388, *'ôd* [1]
the others^{s}, 10036, *'illên* [1]
others^{s}, 10154, *dā'* [1]
the others^{s}, 10214, *-hēn* [1]
others, 10246, *ḥabrâ* [1]

OTHERWISE [17]

otherwise, 7153, *pen* [9]
otherwise, 2256, *w^{e}-* [3]
otherwise, 219, *'ûlām^{1}* [1]
otherwise, 561+401, *'im+'ayin^{1}* [1]
otherwise, 2256+4202, *w^{e}-+lō'* [1]
for otherwise, 3954, *kî^{2}* [1]
otherwise, 4200+5100+889+4202, *l^{e-1}+ma'an+'^{a}šer+lō'* [1]

OTHNI [1]

Othni, 6978, *'otnî* [1]

OTHNIEL [10]

Othniel, 6979, *'otnî'ēl* [7]
Othniel, *NIH/RPE* [2]
Othniel^{s}, 2257, *-ô* [1]

OUGHT [2]

ought, *AIT* [2]

OUR [795]

our, 5646, *-nû^{1}* [670]
our, *NIH/RPE* [26]
our, 3276, *-î* [25]
our, 4200+5646, *l^{e-1}+-nû^{1}* [22]
our, *AIT* [17]
our^{s}, 2021, *ha-* [14]
our own, 5646, *-nû^{1}* [12]
our, 4392, *-ām* [3]
our fathers^{s}, 4392, *-ām* [2]
our, 636, *'^{a}naḥnû* [1]
our own^{s}, 2156, *hēm* [1]
our own, 3276, *-î* [1]
our, 10450, *-nā'* [1]

OURS [11]

ours, 5646, *-nû^{1}* [7]
ours, 4200+5646, *l^{e-1}+-nû^{1}* [2]
ours, 4200+3276, *l^{e-1}+-î* [1]
ours, 4200+7156+5646, *l^{e-1}+pāneh+-nû^{1}* [1]

OURSELVES [20]

ourselves, 5646, *-nû^{1}* [10]
ourselves, 5883+5646, *nepeš+-nû^{1}* [3]
ourselves, *NIH/RPE* [2]
ourselves, *AIT* [1]
arm ourselves, 2741, *ḥālaṣ^{2}* [1]
keeping it to ourselves, 3120, *ḥāšâ* [1]
enjoy ourselves, 6632, *'ālas* [1]
humble ourselves, 6700, *'ānâ^{2}* [1]

OUSTED [1]

ousted, 2238, *hāras* [1]

OUT [1869]*

out of, 4946, *min* [179]
brought out, 3655, *yāṣā'* [100]
came out, 3655, *yāṣā'* [84]
went out, 3655, *yāṣā'* [82]
go out, 3655, *yāṣā'* [57]
set out, 5825, *nāsa'* [49]
come out, 3655, *yāṣā'* [39]
bring out, 3655, *yāṣā'* [35]
pour out, 9161, *šāpak* [33]
out, *NIH/RPE* [30]
drive out, 3769, *yāraš^{1}* [24]
stretch out, 5742, *nāṭâ* [22]
stretched out, 5742, *nāṭâ* [20]
carry out, 6913, *'āśâ^{1}* [20]
spread out, 7298, *pāraś* [19]
cry out, 2410, *zā'aq* [18]
sent out, 8938, *šālaḥ* [17]
cried out, 2410, *zā'aq* [16]
cried out, 7590, *ṣā'aq* [16]
out, *AIT* [15]
set out, 2143, *hālak* [15]
out of, 4946+9348, *min+tāwek* [13]
marched out, 3655, *yāṣā'* [12]
gone out, 3655, *yāṣā'* [11]
out, 3655, *yāṣā'* [11]
driven out, 3769, *yāraš^{1}* [11]
blot out, 4681, *māḥâ^{1}* [11]
set out, 7756, *qûm* [11]
called out, 7924, *qārā'^{1}* [11]
poured out, 9161, *šāpak* [11]
set out, 3655, *yāṣā'* [10]
reached out, 8938, *šālaḥ* [10]
went out, 2143, *hālak* [9]
drove out, 3769, *yāraš^{1}* [9]
cry out, 7590, *ṣā'aq* [9]
cried out, 7924, *qārā'^{1}* [9]
drive out, 1763, *gāraš^{1}* [8]
find out, 3359, *yāda'* [8]
coming out, 3655, *yāṣā'* [8]
find out, 8011, *rā'â^{1}* [8]
get out, 3655, *yāṣā'* [7]
going out, 3655, *yāṣā'* [7]
poured out, 5818, *nāsak^{1}* [7]
poured out, 5988, *nātak* [7]
call out, 7924, *qārā'^{1}* [7]
cry out, 7924, *qārā'^{1}* [7]
stretched out, 8938, *šālaḥ* [7]
weighed out, 9202, *šāqal* [7]
wear out, 1162, *bālâ^{1}* [6]
goes out, 3655, *yāṣā'* [6]
pour out, 5818, *nāsak^{1}* [6]
drove out, 1763, *gāraš^{1}* [5]
snuffed out, 1980, *dā'ak* [5]
go out, 2143, *hālak* [5]
out, 2575+2025, *ḥûṣ+-â^{2}* [5]
comes out, 3655, *yāṣā'* [5]
stretches out, 5742, *nāṭâ* [5]
out, 9362, *tôṣā'ôt* [5]
out of, 928, *b^{e}-* [4]
speak out, 1819, *dābar^{2}* [4]
cries out, 2410, *zā'aq* [4]
bringing out, 3655, *yāṣā'* [4]
brings out, 3655, *yāṣā'* [4]
march out, 3655, *yāṣā'* [4]
took out, 3655, *yāṣā'* [4]
poured out, 3668, *yāṣaq* [4]
out of, 4946+6584, *min+'al^{2}* [4]
out, 4946+2575, *min+ḥûṣ* [4]
carried out, 6913, *'āśâ^{1}* [4]
pours out, 7032, *pûaḥ^{2}* [4]
broken out, 7287, *pāraṣ* [4]
spied out, 8078, *rāgal* [4]
spy out, 8078, *rāgal* [4]
stretch out, 8938, *šālaḥ* [4]
called out, 606, *'āmar^{1}* [3]
cried out, 606, *'āmar^{1}* [3]
search out, 1335, *bāqaš* [3]

gushed out, 2307, *zûb* [3]
spy out, 2916, *ḥapar[1]* [3]
worn out, 3333, *yāga'* [3]
lead out, 3655, *yāṣā'* [3]
led out, 3655, *yāṣā'* [3]
marching out, 3655, *yāṣā'* [3]
send out, 3655, *yāṣā'* [3]
go out, 3882, *kābâ* [3]
worn out, 4206, *lā'â* [3]
be blotted out, 4681, *māḥâ[1]* [3]
out, 4946+9004, *min+šām* [3]
set out on the table, 5121, *ma'[a]reket* [3]
spread out, 5742, *nāṭâ* [3]
spread out, 5759, *nāṭaš* [3]
pouring out, 5818, *nāsak[1]* [3]
out to, 6330, *'ad[2]* [3]
put out, 6422, *'āwar[1]* [3]
spread out, 7233, *pārad* [3]
broken out, 7255, *pāraḥ[1]* [3]
cries out, 7590, *ṣā'aq* [3]
carried out, 7756, *qûm* [3]
called out, 7924+928+7754+1524, *qārā'[1]+b[e]-+qôl+gādôl* [3]
spread out, 8392, *rāqa'* [3]
cry out, 8775, *šāwa'* [3]
reach out, 8938, *šālaḥ* [3]
pours out, 9161, *šāpak* [3]

OUTBREAK [1]
outbreak, 8609, *śātar* [1]

OUTCAST [1]
outcast, 5615, *nādaḥ[1]* [1]

OUTCOME [3]
final outcome, 344, *'aḥ[a]rît* [1]
outcome, 344, *'aḥ[a]rît* [1]
outcome different, 4202+3869, *lō'+k[e]-* [1]

OUTCRY [8]
outcry, 2411, *z[e]'āqâ* [3]
outcry, 7591, *ṣ[e]'āqâ* [3]
outcry, 7754+7591, *qôl+ṣ[e]'āqâ* [1]
outcry, 8784, *šaw'â* [1]

OUTDOOR [1]
outdoor, 928+2021+2575, *b[e]-+ha-+ḥûṣ* [1]

OUTER [44]
outer, 2667, *ḥîṣôn* [20]
outer sanctuary, 2121, *hêkāl* [7]
outer, *NIH/RPE* [4]
outer, 2575, *ḥûṣ* [3]
outer wall, 1230, *binyān* [2]
outer fortifications, 2658, *ḥêl* [1]
both outer, 2667, *ḥîṣôn* [1]
outer, 4200+2021+2575, *l[e]-[1]+ha-+ḥûṣ* [1]
outer, 4946+4200+5087+2025, *min+l[e]-[1]+ma'al[2]+-â[2]* [1]
outer court, 6478, *'[a]zārâ* [1]
outer, 7156, *pāneh* [1]
outer fringe, 7896, *qāṣâ[2]* [1]
inner and outer[s], 9109, *š[e]nayim* [1]

OUTLAW [1]
outlaw, 8401, *rāšā'* [1]

OUTLET [1]
outlet, 4604, *môṣā'[1]* [1]

OUTLINE [1]
makes an outline, 9306, *tā'ar[2]* [1]

OUTLIVED [2]
outlived, 799+3427+339, *'ārak+yôm[1]+'aḥar* [2]

OUTLYING [2]
outlying villages, 1426, *bat[1]* [1]
outlying districts, 8441, *śādeh* [1]

OUTNUMBER [2]
outnumber, 4946+8049, *min+rābâ[1]* [1]
outnumber, 8045+4946, *rābab[1]+min* [1]

OUTPOST [8]
outpost, 5163, *maṣṣāb* [4]
outpost, 5907, *n[e]ṣîb[1]* [3]
outpost, 5165, *maṣṣābâ* [1]

OUTPOSTS [2]
outposts, 5163, *maṣṣāb* [1]
outposts, 7895+2821, *qāṣeh+ḥāmaš* [1]

OUTPOURED [3]
outpoured, 9161, *šāpak* [3]

OUTPOURING [1]
outpouring, 9161, *šāpak* [1]

OUTRAGEOUS [1]
outrageous things, 5576, *n[e]bālâ* [1]

OUTRAN [1]
outran, 6296, *'ābar[1]* [1]

OUTSIDE [87]
outside, 4946+2575, *min+ḥûṣ* [49]
outside, 2575+2025, *ḥûṣ+-â[2]* [8]
outside, 2575, *ḥûṣ* [8]
outside, 928+2021+2575, *b[e]-+ha-+ḥûṣ* [7]
outside, 4946+2575+2025, *min+ḥûṣ+-â[2]* [2]
outside, 6584, *'al[2]* [2]
outside the family, 2021+2575+2025+2424, *ha-+ḥûṣ+-â[2]+zār* [1]
outside a priest's family, 2424, *zār* [1]
outside, 2667+2025, *ḥîṣôn+-â[2]* [1]
outside, 2667, *ḥîṣôn* [1]
ever goes outside, 3655+3655, *yāṣā'+yāṣā'* [1]
went outside, 3655, *yāṣā'* [1]
outside, 4946+1946, *min+delet* [1]
outside, 4946+2134, *min+hāl[e]'â* [1]
outside walls, 6017, *sābîb* [1]
outside, 7339+2025, *petaḥ+-â[2]* [1]
outside, 7339, *petaḥ* [1]

OUTSKIRTS [4]
outskirts, 7895, *qāṣeh* [3]
outskirts, 4427, *mābô'* [1]

OUTSPREAD [1]
outspread, 5742, *nāṭâ* [1]

OUTSTANDING [3]
outstanding, 1838, *dāgal[1]* [1]
outstanding, 8031, *rō'š[1]* [1]
outstanding, 10339, *yattîr* [1]

OUTSTRETCHED [19]
outstretched, 5742, *nāṭâ* [18]
outstretched, 6981, *'ātāq* [1]

OUTWARD [1]
outward appearance, 6524, *'ayin[1]* [1]

OUTWEIGH [1]
outweigh, 4946+3877, *min+kābēd[1]* [1]

OUTWEIGHS [1]
outweighs, 3701+4946, *yāqār+min* [1]

OVEN [8]
oven, 9486, *tannûr* [8]

OVENS [3]
ovens, 9486, *tannûr* [3]

OVER [979]*
over, 6584, *'al[2]* [376]
over, 928, *b[e]-* [89]
over, 4200, *l[e]-[1]* [40]
hand over, 5989+928+3338, *nātan+b[e]-+yād* [35]
over, *AIT* [33]
over, 448, *'el* [23]
cross over, 6296, *'ābar[1]* [23]
handed over, 5989+928+3338, *nātan+b[e]-+yād* [20]
crossed over, 6296, *'ābar[1]* [17]
over, 6584+7156, *'al[2]+pāneh* [10]
over, *NIH/RPE* [9]
over, 4848, *mālē'[1]* [8]
hand over, 5989, *nātan* [8]
over, 10542, *'al* [8]
be handed over, 5989+928+3338, *nātan+b[e]-+yād* [7]
give over, 5989, *nātan* [7]
go over, 6296, *'ābar[1]* [7]
over, 10089, *b[e]-* [7]
take over, 3769, *yāraš[1]* [6]
took over, 3769, *yāraš[1]* [6]
left over, 3855, *yātar* [6]
over, 4946, *min* [6]
watches over, 9068, *šāmar* [6]
taken over, 3769, *yāraš[1]* [5]
watch over, 9068, *šāmar* [5]
gone over, 5877, *nāpal* [4]
gave over, 5989, *nātan* [4]
handed over, 928+3338+5989, *b[e]-+yād+nātan* [3]
over, 4946+4200+5087+2025, *min+l[e]-[1]+ma'al[2]+-â[2]* [3]
gave over, 6037, *sāgar* [3]
come over, 6296, *'ābar[1]* [3]
over, 6296, *'ābar[1]* [3]
pass over, 7173, *pāsaḥ[1]* [3]
watched over, 9068, *šāmar* [3]
over, 928+8031, *b[e]-+rō'š[1]* [2]
went over, 2143, *hālak* [2]
had left over, 3855, *yātar* [2]
put over, 4059, *kāsâ* [2]
over, 4946+5087, *min+ma'al[2]* [2]
over, 4946+6584, *min+'al[2]* [2]
watch over, 5915, *nāṣar* [2]
certainly be handed over, 5989+5989+928+3338, *nātan+nātan+b[e]-+yād* [2]
deliver over, 5989, *nātan* [2]
delivered over, 5989, *nātan* [2]
given over, 5989, *nātan* [2]
handed over, 5989, *nātan* [2]
turn over, 5989, *nātan* [2]
hand over, 6037+928+3338, *sāgar+b[e]-+yād* [2]
hand over, 6037, *sāgar* [2]
handed over, 6037+928+3338, *sāgar+b[e]-+yād* [2]
turn over, 6296, *'ābar[1]* [2]
rule over, 6584, *'al[2]* [2]
look over, 8011, *rā'â[1]* [2]
gave over, 8938, *šālaḥ* [2]
watching over, 9068, *šāmar* [2]
over, 9462, *tāmam* [2]

OVERAWED [1]
overawed, 3707, *yārē'[1]* [1]

OVERBOARD [1]
overboard, 448+2021+3542, *'el+ha-+yām* [1]

OVERCAME [3]
overcame, 3523, *yākōl* [2]
overcame, 2765, *ḥālaš[2]* [1]

OVERCOME [11]
overcome, 3523, *yākōl* [5]
overcome, 2200, *hāpak* [1]
was overcome, 2200, *hāpak* [1]
overcome, 3899, *kābaš* [1]
overcome, 3983, *kālâ[1]* [1]
overcome, 5162, *māṣā'* [1]
overcome, 6296, *'ābar[1]* [1]

OVERFED [1]
overfed, 8430+4312, *śib'â+leḥem* [1]

OVERFLOW [14]
overflow, 3718, *yārad* [3]
overflow, 7046, *pûṣ[1]* [2]
overflow, 8319, *rā'ap* [2]
overflow, 8796, *šûq[1]* [2]
overflow, 8851, *šāṭap* [2]
overflow, 5580, *nāba'* [1]
overflow, 6296, *'ābar[1]* [1]
overflow, 6590+6584, *'ālâ+'al[2]* [1]

OVERFLOWING [5]
overflowing, 2329, *zîz[2]* [1]
overflowing, 3718, *yārad* [1]
overflowing, 4848, *mālē'[1]* [1]
overflowing, 8426, *śābā'* [1]
overflowing, 8851, *šāṭap* [1]

OVERFLOWS [1]
overflows, 8122, *r[e]wāyâ* [1]

OVERGROWN [3]
overgrown, *AIT* [1]
overgrown, *NIH/RPE* [1]
overgrown, 6590, *ʿālâ* [1]

OVERHANG [1]
overhang, 6264, *ʿāb*[1] [1]

OVERHANGING [3]
overhanging, 6186, *sāʿîp*[1] [2]
overhanging roof, 6264, *ʿāb*[1] [1]

OVERHANGS [1]
overhangs, 6264, *ʿāb*[1] [1]

OVERHEAD [1]
hovering overhead, 6414, *ʿûp*[1] [1]

OVERHEARD [2]
overheard, 9048, *šāmaʿ* [1]
was overheard, 9048, *šāmaʿ* [1]

OVERJOYED [1]
overjoyed, 10678+10293, *śaggîʾ+ṭᵉʾēb* [1]

OVERLAID [33]
overlaid, 7596, *ṣāpâ*[2] [27]
overlaid, 2902, *ḥāpâ* [3]
overlaid, 7599, *ṣippûy* [3]

OVERLAY [13]
overlay, 7596, *ṣāpâ*[2] [11]
overlay, 7599, *ṣippûy* [2]

OVERLAYING [1]
overlaying, 3212, *ṭûaḥ* [1]

OVERLAYS [1]
overlays, 8392, *rāqaʿ* [1]

OVERLOOK [3]
overlook, 440+7155, *ʾal*[1]*+pānâ* [1]
overlook, 6296, *ʿābar*[1] [1]
overlook, 8894, *šākaḥ* [1]

OVERLOOKING [3]
overlooking, 9207, *šāqap* [2]
overlooking, 4200+7156, *lᵉ-*[1]*+pāneh* [1]

OVERLOOKS [3]
overlooks, 4059, *kāsâ* [1]
place that overlooks, 5205, *miṣpeh*[1] [1]
overlooks, 9207, *šāqap* [1]

OVERNIGHT [5]
overnight, 1201+4326, *bēn*[1]*+laylâ* [2]
hold back overnight, 4328+6330+1332, *lîn+ʿad*[2]*+bōqer*[2] [1]
leave overnight, 4328, *lîn* [1]
camp overnight, 4869, *mālôn* [1]

OVERPOWER [8]
overpower, 3523, *yākōl* [3]
overpower, 4309+6584, *lāḥam*[1]*+ʿal*[2] [1]
overpower, 4309, *lāḥam*[1] [1]
overpower, 5877, *nāpal* [1]
overpower, 8948, *šālaṭ* [1]
overpower, 9548, *tāqap* [1]

OVERPOWERED [7]
overpowered, 5782, *nākâ* [2]
overpowered, 1504, *gābar* [1]
overpowered, 2616, *ḥāzaq* [1]
overpowered, 6451+3338+6584, *ʿāzaz+yād+ʿal*[2] [1]
overpowered, 9548, *tāqap* [1]
overpowered, 10715, *šᵉlēṭ* [1]

OVERPOWERING [1]
overpowering, 3214, *ṭûl* [1]

OVERRAN [1]
overran, 2005, *dārak* [1]

OVERRIGHTEOUS [1]
overrighteous, 7404+2221, *ṣaddîq+harbēh* [1]

OVERRULED [2]
overruled, 2616+448, *ḥāzaq+ʾel* [1]
overruled, 2616+6584, *ḥāzaq+ʿal*[2] [1]

OVERRULING [1]
overruling, 8740, *šûb*[1] [1]

OVERRUN [4]
overrun, 928, *bᵉ-* [1]
overrun, 6017, *sābîb* [1]
overrun, 6296, *ʿābar*[1] [1]
overrun, 6590, *ʿālâ* [1]

OVERSEER [1]
overseer, 8853, *šāṭar* [1]

OVERSHADOWED [1]
overshadowed, 6114, *sākak*[1] [1]

OVERSHADOWING [3]
overshadowing, 6114, *sākak*[1] [2]
overshadowing, 7511, *ṣālal*[3] [1]

OVERSIGHT [1]
oversight, 7213, *pᵉquddâ* [1]

OVERSTEP [1]
overstep, 6296, *ʿābar*[1] [1]

OVERTAKE [25]
overtake, 5952, *nāśag* [14]
overtake, 995, *bôʾ* [4]
overtake, 1815, *dābaq* [1]
overtake, 4200, *lᵉ-*[1] [1]
overtake, 5162, *māṣāʾ* [1]
overtake, 5602, *nāgaš* [1]
certainly overtake, 5952+5952, *nāśag+nāśag* [1]
overtake, 6047, *sûg*[1] [1]
overtake, 7936, *qārâ*[1] [1]

OVERTAKEN [4]
overtaken, 5952, *nāśag* [2]
be overtaken, 5602, *nāgaš* [1]
overtaken, 9462, *tāmam* [1]

OVERTAKES [5]
overtakes, 995, *bôʾ* [3]
overtakes, 4200, *lᵉ-*[1] [1]
overtakes, 7936, *qārâ*[1] [1]

OVERTAKING [1]
overtaking, 5952, *nāśag* [1]

OVERTHREW [8]
overthrew, 2200, *hāpak* [5]
overthrew, 4550, *mahpēkâ* [2]
overthrew, 2238, *hāras* [1]

OVERTHROW [14]
overthrow, 2200, *hāpak* [4]
overthrow, 2238, *hāras* [3]
overthrow, 4173, *kāšal* [2]
overthrow, 3312, *yābēš* [1]
overthrow, 4742, *maḥᵃšābâ* [1]
overthrow, 5782, *nākâ* [1]
overthrow, 8845, *šāḥat* [1]
overthrow, 10400, *mᵉgar* [1]

OVERTHROWN [9]
overthrown, 4550, *mahpēkâ* [3]
overthrown, 2200, *hāpak* [1]
was overthrown, 2200, *hāpak* [1]
overthrown, 2238, *hāras* [1]
overthrown, 3721, *yārâ*[1] [1]
overthrown, 4173, *kāšal* [1]
be overthrown, 9012, *šāmad* [1]

OVERTHROWS [4]
overthrows, 6156, *sālap* [2]
overthrows, 2200, *hāpak* [1]
overthrows, 8740+294, *šûb*[1]*+ʾāḥôr* [1]

OVERTOOK [10]
overtook, 5952, *nāśag* [6]
overtook, 5162, *māṣāʾ* [1]
overtook, 995+448, *bôʾ+ʾel* [1]
overtook, 1815, *dābaq* [1]

OVERTURN [1]
overturn, 2200, *hāpak* [1]

OVERTURNED [3]
be overturned, 2200, *hāpak* [1]
overturned, 2200+4200+5087+2025, *hāpak+lᵉ-*[1]*+maʿal*[2]*+-â*[2] [1]
be overturned, 2238, *hāras* [1]

OVERTURNS [1]
overturns, 2200, *hāpak* [1]

OVERWEENING [3]
overweening, 4394, *mᵉʾōd* [2]
overweening pride, 6301+2295, *ʿebrâ+zādôn* [1]

OVERWHELM [7]
overwhelm, 995+6584, *bôʾ+ʿal*[2] [1]
overwhelm, 1286, *bāʿat* [1]
overwhelm, 2200, *hāpak* [1]
overwhelm, 4059, *kāsâ* [1]
overwhelm, 8104, *rāhab* [1]
overwhelm, 8425, *śābaʿ* [1]
overwhelm, 9548, *tāqap* [1]

OVERWHELMED [13]
overwhelmed, 1286, *bāʿat* [2]
overwhelmed with dread, 7064+7065, *pāḥad+paḥad*[1] [2]
overwhelmed, 1504, *gābar* [1]
overwhelmed, 4059, *kāsâ* [1]
overwhelmed, 4202+2118+6388+928+8120, *lōʾ+hāyâ+ʿôd+bᵉ+rûaḥ* [1]
overwhelmed, 4202+2118+928+6388+8120, *lōʾ+hāyâ+bᵉ-+ʿôd+rûaḥ* [1]
overwhelmed, 5877+6584, *nāpal+ʿal*[2] [1]
overwhelmed, 6296+8031, *ʿābar*[1]*+rōʾš*[1] [1]
overwhelmed, 6700, *ʿānâ*[2] [1]
overwhelmed, 7429, *ṣûp*[1] [1]
overwhelmed, 9037, *šāmēm*[1] [1]

OVERWHELMING [6]
overwhelming, 8851, *šāṭap* [3]
overwhelming, 8852, *šeṭep* [2]
overwhelming, 6296, *ʿābar* [1]

OVERWHELMS [2]
overwhelms, 4059, *kāsâ* [2]

OVERWICKED [1]
overwicked, 8399+2221, *rāšaʿ+harbēh* [1]

OVERWISE [1]
overwise, 2681+3463, *ḥākam+yôtēr* [1]

OWES [1]
owes, 2118, *hāyâ* [1]

OWL [22]
desert owl, 7684, *qāʾat* [4]
great owl, 3568, *yanšûp* [3]
horned owl, 1426+3613, *bat*[1]*+yaʿᵃnâ* [2]
owl, 1426+3613, *bat*[1]*+yaʿᵃnâ* [2]
little owl, 3927, *kôs*[2] [2]
screech owl, 7887, *qippōd* [2]
screech owl, 9379, *taḥmās* [2]
white owl, 9492, *tinšemet*[2] [2]
owl, 3927, *kôs*[2] [1]
owl, 7684, *qāʾat* [1]
owl, 7889, *qippôz* [1]

OWLS [5]
owls, 1426+3613, *bat*[1]*+yaʿᵃnâ* [4]
owls, 7887, *qippōd* [1]

OWN [478]
his own, 2257, *-ô* [140]
your own, 3870, *-kā* [65]
my own, 3276, *-î* [43]
their own, 4392, *-ām* [43]
their own, 2157, *-hem* [20]
your own, 4013, *-kem* [18]
our own, 5646, *-nû*[1] [12]
own, *AIT* [11]
its own, 2257, *-ô* [10]
their own, 2257, *-ô* [10]
own, *NIH/RPE* [9]
his own, 4200+2257, *lᵉ-*[1]*+-ô* [8]
his own, 2084, *-hû* [6]
her own, 2023, *-āh* [5]

their own, 4200+2157, *le-[1]+-hem* [5]
his own[s], 2021, *ha-* [4]
my own, 4200+3276, *le-[1]+-î* [4]
your own, 4200+3870, *le-[1]+-kā* [4]
his own[s], 2021+4889, *ha-+melek[1]* [3]
your own, 4200+4013, *le-[1]+-kem* [3]
your own, 911, *ʾattâ* [2]
his own[s], 2021+3913, *ha-+kōhēn* [2]
their own[s], 2021, *ha-* [2]
its own, 2157, *-hem* [2]
their own, 2177, *-hēn[2]* [2]
own, 2257, *-ô* [2]
your own, 2257, *-ô* [2]
your own flesh and blood, 3655+4946+3870,
yāṣāʾ+min+-kā [2]
own, 3772, *yeruššâ* [2]
your own, 3871, *-k* [2]
own, 4200, *le-[1]* [2]
their own, 4200+2257, *le-[1]+-ô* [2]
your very own, 4200+3870, *le-[1]+-kā* [2]
very own brother, 278+1201+562+3870,
ʾāḥ[2]+bēn[1]+ʾēm+-kā [1]
own, 907, *ʾēt[2]* [1]
his own[s], 2021+367, *ha-+ʾōyēb* [1]
his own[s], 2021+5566+2021+2418,
ha-+nābîʾ+ha-+zāqēn[2] [1]
its own, 2023, *-āh* [1]
your own, 2023, *-āh* [1]
their own, 2084, *-hû* [1]
own, 2118+4200, *hāyâ+le-[1]* [1]
our own[s], 2156, *hēm* [1]
strengthening his own position, 2616, *ḥāzaq* [1]
her own, 3276, *-î* [1]
our own, 3276, *-î* [1]
of his own, 3655+3751+2257,
yāṣāʾ+yārēk+-ô [1]
own, 3769, *yāraš[1]* [1]
your own self, 3870, *-kā* [1]
your own, 4032, *-ken* [1]
his own, 4392, *-ām* [1]
one's own, 4392, *-ām* [1]
his own, 4946+4213+2257, *min+lēb+-ô* [1]
his own, 5647, *-nû[2]* [1]
their own, 5647, *-nû[2]* [1]
his own, 5883+2257, *nepeš+-ô* [1]
its own, 5883+2257, *nepeš+-ô* [1]
their own, 7156+2157, *pāneh+-hem* [1]
my own, 8611+4200+3276, *ša-+le-[1]+-î* [1]
persist in own way, 9244+4213, *šerirût+lēb* [1]
drink in own way, 9276, *šetiyyâ* [1]
his own, 10192, *-ēh* [1]
their own, 10203, *-hôn* [1]

OWNED [10]
owned, 4200, *le-[1]* [4]
owned, 3780+4200, *yēš+le-[1]* [2]
owned, 1251, *baʿal[1]* [1]
owned, 1266, *baʿalâ[1]* [1]
owned, 2118+5238, *hāyâ+miqneh* [1]
owned, 5238+2118, *miqneh+hāyâ* [1]

OWNER [21]
owner, 1251, *baʿal[1]* [14]
owner, *NIH/RPE* [4]
owner, 4200+2257, *le-[1]+-ô* [2]
owner, 123, *ʾādôn* [1]

OWNER'S [1]
owner's, 1251, *baʿal[1]* [1]

OWNERS [1]
new owners, 3769, *yāraš[1]* [1]

OWNING [1]
owning, 4200, *le-[1]* [1]

OWNS [6]
owns, 4200, *le-[1]* [4]
owns, 2750, *ḥēleq[2]* [1]
owns, 3780+4200, *yēš+le-[1]* [1]

OX [48]
ox, 8802, *šôr* [38]
wild ox, 8028, *reʾēm* [6]
ox, 1330, *bāqār* [4]

OXEN [41]
oxen, 1330, *bāqār* [31]
oxen, 546, *ʾelep[1]* [2]
wild oxen, 8028, *reʾēm* [2]
oxen, 8802, *šôr* [2]
oxen, 476, *ʾallûp[1]* [1]
oxen, 7228, *par* [1]
oxen, 7538, *ṣemed* [1]
yoke of oxen, 7538, *ṣemed* [1]

OXGOAD [1]
oxgoad, 4913+1330, *malmad+bāqār* [1]

OZEM [2]
Ozem, 730, *ʾōṣem* [2]

OZNI [1]
Ozni, 269, *ʾoznî[1]* [1]

OZNITE [1]
Oznite, 270, *ʾoznî[2]* [1]

PAARAI [1]
Paarai, 7197, *paʿaray* [1]

PACE [1]
pace, 8079, *regel* [1]

PACIFIES [1]
pacifies, *NIH/RPE* [1]

PACIFY [1]
pacify, 4105+7156, *kāpar[1]+pāneh* [1]

PACK [2]
pack, 6913, *ʿāśâ[1]* [2]

PACKED [3]
packed, 3998, *kelî* [2]
packed, 7472, *ṣîd* [1]

PACT [1]
made a pact, 4162, *kārat* [1]

PAD [1]
pad, 4946+9393, *min+taḥat[1]* [1]

PADDAN [1]
Paddan, 7019, *paddān* [1]

PADDAN ARAM [10]
Paddan Aram, 7020, *paddan ʾarām* [10]

PADON [2]
Padon, 7013, *pādôn* [2]

PAGAN [5]
pagan nations, 1580, *gôy* [1]
pagan symbols, 2355, *zikkārôn* [1]
pagan, 3238, *ṭāmēʾ[2]* [1]
pagan priests, 4024, *kōmer* [1]
pagan, 4024, *kōmer* [1]

PAGANS [1]
pagans, 3529+5799, *yeled+nokrî* [1]

PAGIEL [5]
Pagiel, 7005, *pagʿîʾēl* [5]

PAHATH-MOAB [6]
Pahath-Moab, 7075, *paḥat môʾāb* [6]

PAID [44]
paid, 5989, *nātan* [5]
paid attention, 9048, *šāmaʿ* [4]
paid out, 5988, *nātak* [2]
paid attention, 7992, *qāšab* [2]
paid, *AIT* [1]
paid attention, 263, *ʾāzan[1]* [1]
paid, 928, *be-* [1]
paid homage, 2556, *ḥāwâ[2]* [1]
paid honor, 2556, *ḥāwâ[2]* [1]
paid, 3655, *yāṣāʾ* [1]
based on the rate paid, 3869+3427,
ke-+yôm[1] [1]
what paid, 4084, *kesep* [1]
be paid in full, 4848, *mālēʾ[1]* [1]
paid, 5239, *miqnâ* [1]
paid any attention, 5742+265+4200+9048,
nāṭâ+ʾōzen+le-[1]+šāmaʿ [1]
paid attention, 5742+265, *nāṭâ+ʾōzen* [1]
paid regard, 5795, *nākar[1]* [1]
paid, 5989+5486, *nātan+mišqāl* [1]
paid, 6590, *ʿālâ* [1]
be paid back, 6913, *ʿāśâ[1]* [1]
paid attention, 7993, *qešeb* [1]
paid attention, 8011, *rāʾâ[1]* [1]
been paid for, 8355, *rāṣâ[2]* [1]
money paid for hire, 8510, *śākār[1]* [1]
paid back, 8740, *šûb[1]* [1]
paid, 8740+868, *šûb[1]+ʾeškār* [1]
paid, 8740, *šûb[1]* [1]
paid back, 8966, *šālēm[1]* [1]
paid attention, 9068, *šāmar* [1]
paid, 9202+8510, *šāqal+śākār[1]* [1]
be paid, 10314, *yehab* [1]
paid, 10314, *yehab* [1]
were paid, 10314, *yehab* [1]
paid, 10498, *netan* [1]
paid honor, 10504, *segid* [1]

PAIN [35]
pain, 4799, *makʾōb* [7]
pain, 2659, *ḥîl[3]* [5]
pain, 2477, *ḥēbel* [3]
pain, 3873, *keʾēb* [3]
writhe in pain, 2655, *ḥîl[1]* [2]
in pain, 3872, *kāʾab* [2]
pain, *NIH/RPE* [1]
felt pain, 2655, *ḥîl[1]* [1]
writhed in pain, 2655, *ḥîl[1]* [1]
pain, 2660, *ḥîlâ* [1]
pain, 2714, *ḥalḥālâ* [1]
feels pain, 3872, *kāʾab* [1]
pain, 6772, *ʿāṣab[2]* [1]
was filled with pain, 6772, *ʿāṣab[2]* [1]
pain, 6776, *ʿeṣeb[2]* [1]
pain, 6778, *ʿōṣeb[2]* [1]
pain, 7496, *ṣîr[4]* [1]
searing pain, 7828, *qālâ[1]* [1]
pain, 9377, *taḥaluʾîm* [1]

PAINFUL [6]
painful toil, 6779, *ʿiṣṣābôn* [2]
painful, 8273, *raʿ[1]* [2]
painful, 4421, *māʾar* [1]
painful, 5344, *māraṣ* [1]

PAINS [8]
pains, 2477, *ḥēbel* [2]
taken great pains, 928+6715, *be-+ʿonî* [1]
labor pains, 2477, *ḥēbel* [1]
pains, 4799, *makʾōb* [1]
pains, 6779, *ʿiṣṣābôn* [1]
gnawing pains, 6908, *ʿāraq* [1]
labor pains, 7496, *ṣîr[4]* [1]

PAINT [1]
paint, 7037, *pûk* [1]

PAINTED [2]
painted, 3949, *kāḥal* [1]
painted, 8531+928+2021+7037,
śāmam+be-+ha-+pûk [1]

PAIR [15]
pair, 9109, *šenayim* [9]
pair, *AIT* [2]
pair, 7538, *ṣemed* [2]
pair, *NIH/RPE* [1]
pair of millstones, 8160, *rēḥayim* [1]

PAIRS [3]
pairs, 9109+9109, *šenayim+šenayim* [2]
pairs, *NIH/RPE* [1]

PALACE [157]
palace, 1074, *bayit[1]* [120]
palace, 1074+4889, *bayit[1]+melek[1]* [15]
palace, 2121, *hêkāl* [7]
palace, 10206, *hêkal* [5]
palace, 1131, *bîtān* [3]
palace grounds, 1074+4889, *bayit[1]+melek[1]* [2]
palace, 810, *ʾarmôn* [1]

palace, 1074+4895, *bayit[1]+malkût* [1]
lofty palace, 5092, *ma'alâ[2]* [1]
summer palace, 5249, *meqērâ* [1]
palace officials, 6247, *sārîs* [1]

PALACES [8]
palaces, 2121, *hêkāl* [4]
palaces, 810, *'armôn* [3]
palaces, 1074, *bayit[1]* [1]

PALAL [1]
Palal, 7138, *pālāl* [1]

PALATIAL [2]
palatial structure, 1072, *bîrâ* [2]

PALE [9]
face pale, 10228, *zîw* [3]
grow pale, 2578, *ḥāwar[1]* [1]
deathly pale, 3766, *yērāqôn* [1]
deathly pale, 5422, *mašḥît* [1]
grows pale, 7695+6999, *qābaṣ+pā'rûr* [1]
turns pale, 7695+6999, *qābaṣ+pā'rûr* [1]
look so pale, 10228+10731, *zîw+šenâ[1]* [1]

PALLU [5]
Pallu, 7112, *pallû'* [5]

PALLUITE [1]
Palluite, 7101, *pallu'î* [1]

PALM [37]
palm trees, 9474, *timōrâ* [14]
palm, 4090, *kap* [6]
palm, 9469, *tāmār[1]* [3]
palm of hand, 4090, *kap* [2]
palm branch, 4093, *kippâ* [2]
palm trees, 9469, *tāmār[1]* [2]
palm tree, 9469, *tāmār[1]* [2]
palm tree decorations, 9474, *timōrâ* [2]
palm tree, 9474, *timōrâ* [2]
palm, 9472, *tōmer[1]* [1]
palm tree designs, 9474, *timōrâ* [1]

PALMS [6]
palms, 9469, *tāmār[1]* [5]
palms of hands, 4090, *kap* [1]

PALTI [1]
Palti, 7120, *palṭî[1]* [1]

PALTIEL [3]
Paltiel, 7123, *palṭî'ēl* [2]
Paltiel, 7120, *palṭî[1]* [1]

PALTITE [1]
Paltite, 7121, *palṭî[2]* [1]

PAMPERS [1]
pampers, 7167, *pānaq* [1]

PAN [6]
pan, 5306, *marḥešet* [2]
pan, 3963, *kiyyôr* [1]
pan, 4679, *maḥabat* [1]
pan, 5389, *maśrēt* [1]
pan, 6105, *sîr* [1]

PANELED [2]
paneled, 2902, *ḥāpâ* [1]
paneled, 6211, *sāpan* [1]

PANELING [2]
carved paneling, 7334, *pittûaḥ* [1]
paneling, 7596+6770, *śāpâ[2]+'ēṣ* [1]

PANELS [9]
panels, 4995, *misgeret* [5]
side panels, 4995, *misgeret* [2]
panels, 4283, *lûaḥ* [1]
panels, 6211, *sāpan* [1]

PANGS [2]
pangs, 2477, *ḥēbel* [1]
pangs, 7496, *ṣîr[4]* [1]

PANIC [11]
panic, 4539, *mehûmâ* [4]
panic, 3010, *ḥarādâ[1]* [2]
threw into a panic, 2169, *hāmam[1]* [1]
panic, 3169, *ḥātat* [1]
give way to panic, 6907, *'āraṣ* [1]
panic, 8185, *reṭeṭ* [1]
panic, 9451, *timmāhôn* [1]

PANS [2]
pans, 4709, *maḥalāp* [1]
pans, 7505, *ṣallaḥat* [1]

PANT [5]
pant, 8634, *šā'ap[1]* [3]
pant, 6864, *'ārag* [1]
pant, 8634+8120, *šā'ap[1]+rûaḥ* [1]

PANTS [2]
pants, 6864, *'ārag* [2]

PAPYRUS [5]
papyrus, 1687, *gōme'* [4]
papyrus, 15, *'ēbeh* [1]

PARABLE [2]
parable, 5442, *māšāl[1]* [2]

PARABLES [4]
parables, 5442, *māšāl[1]* [2]
told parables, 1948, *dāmâ[1]* [1]
parables, 4886, *melîṣâ* [1]

PARADE [1]
parade, 5583, *nāgad* [1]

PARAH [1]
Parah, 7240, *pārâ[3]* [1]

PARALLEL [5]
parallel to, 4200+6645, *le-1+'ummâ[1]* [2]
set parallel, 8917, *šālab* [2]
parallel, 928+7156, *be-+pāneh* [1]

PARALYZED [1]
paralyzed, 7028, *pûg* [1]

PARAN [10]
Paran, 7000, *pā'rān* [10]

PARAPET [3]
parapet openings, 2707, *ḥallôn* [1]
parapet, 5111, *ma'aqeh* [1]
parapet opening, 7339, *petaḥ* [1]

PARCEL [2]
parcel out, 2745, *ḥālaq[2]* [2]

PARCELED [1]
parceled out, 2936, *ḥāṣâ* [1]

PARCHED [18]
parched, 7480, *ṣiyyâ* [4]
parched, 62, *'ābal[2]* [3]
parched, 2990, *ḥārēb[1]* [2]
parched land, 7480, *ṣiyyâ* [2]
parched, 3081, *ḥārar[1]* [1]
parched places, 3083, *ḥarērîm* [1]
parched, 3312, *yābēš[1]* [1]
parched, 5980, *nāšat* [1]
parched, 6546, *'āyēp* [1]
parched, 7457, *ṣiḥeh* [1]
parched ground, 7533, *ṣāmā'* [1]

PARDON [4]
pardon, 4105, *kāpar[1]* [1]
pardon, 5927, *nāqâ* [1]
pardon, 5951, *nāśā'* [1]
pardon, 6142, *sālaḥ* [1]

PARDONED [2]
pardoned, 5927, *nāqâ* [1]
pardoned, 5951, *nāśā'* [1]

PARDONS [1]
pardons, 5951, *nāśā'* [1]

PARENTS [6]
parents, 3+2256+562, *'āb+we-+'ēm* [3]
parents, 3, *'āb* [2]
parents, *NIH/RPE* [1]

PARKS [1]
parks, 7236, *pardēs* [1]

PARMASHTA [1]
Parmashta, 7269, *parmaštā'* [1]

PARNACH [1]
Parnach, 7270, *parnāk* [1]

PAROSH [6]
Parosh, 7283, *par'ōš[2]* [6]

PARSHANDATHA [1]
Parshandatha, 7309, *paršandātā'* [1]

PARSIN [1]
parsin, 10593, *perēs* [1]

PART [64]
part, 4946, *min* [11]
part, *AIT* [9]
part, *NIH/RPE* [3]
part, 5709, *naḥalâ[1]* [3]
lower part of face, 8559, *śāpām* [3]
part, 7895, *qāṣeh* [2]
part, 9556, *terûmâ* [2]
latter part of life, 344, *'aḥarît* [1]
latter part, 344, *'aḥarît* [1]
part of, 928, *be-* [1]
take part, 995, *bô'* [1]
bowl-shaped part, 1061, *beṭen[1]* [1]
part, 1473, *gebûl* [1]
that part[s], 2085, *hû'* [1]
had part in, 2118+4946, *hāyâ+min* [1]
take part, 2143+6640, *hālak+'im* [1]
the contaminated part[s], 2257, *-ô* [1]
part, 2750, *ḥēleq[2]* [1]
took part in, 3655+4200, *yāṣā'+le-1* [1]
part, 3772, *yeruššâ* [1]
have part, 4200, *le-1* [1]
in the front part, 4578, *mûl[3]* [1]
part, 4856, *melā'kâ* [1]
designated part, 5152, *mipqād* [1]
part, 5742, *nāṭâ* [1]
as part of, 6584, *'al[2]* [1]
part of, 6584, *'al[2]* [1]
part, 6584, *'al[2]* [1]
take part in, 6618, *'ālal[1]* [1]
part, 7115, *pelaḥ* [1]
part company, 7233, *pārad* [1]
take part, 7371+7372, *ṣābā'[1]+ṣābā'[2]* [1]
every part, 7895, *qāṣeh* [1]
take part, 7928+6913, *qārab+'āśâ[1]* [1]
fourth part, 8065, *rōba'[1]* [1]
another part, 9108, *šēnî* [1]
inner part, 9348, *tāwek* [1]
part, 10717, *šolṭān* [1]

PARTED [6]
parted, 5742, *nāṭâ* [2]
be parted, 7233, *pārad* [1]
parted company, 7233, *pārad* [1]
parted, 7233, *pārad* [1]
were parted, 7233, *pārad* [1]

PARTIAL [1]
partial, 5951+7156, *nāśā'+pāneh* [1]

PARTIALITY [13]
show partiality, 5795+7156, *nākar[1]+pāneh* [4]
show partiality, 5951+7156, *nāśā'+pāneh* [2]
shows partiality, 5951+7156, *nāśā'+pāneh* [2]
show partiality, 7156+5951, *pāneh+nāśā'* [2]
partiality, 5365+7156, *maśśō'+pāneh* [1]
shown partiality, 5951+7156, *nāśā'+pāneh* [1]
showed partiality, 7156+5951, *pāneh+nāśā'* [1]

PARTICIPATE [1]
participate in, 2118+448, *hāyâ+'el* [1]

PARTICULARLY [1]
particularly, 4200+4027, *le-1+kēn[2]* [1]

PARTIES [5]
raiding parties, 8845, *šāḥat* [2]
parties, *AIT* [1]

the parties, 408+2256+8276+2084, ʾîš[1]+we-+rēaʿ[2]+-hû [1]
raiding parties, 8031, rōʾš[1] [1]

PARTING [1]
parting gifts, 8933, šillûḥîm [1]

PARTITIONED [1]
partitioned off, 1215, bānâ [1]

PARTLY [8]
partly, 10427, min [7]
partly, 10427+10636, min+qeṣāt [1]

PARTNER [3]
partner, 476, ʾallûp[1] [1]
partner, 2492, ḥābēr [1]
partner, 2500, ḥaberet [1]

PARTRIDGE [2]
partridge, 7926, qōrēʾ[1] [2]

PARTS [34]
inner parts, 7931, qereb [16]
parts, 2750, ḥēleq[2] [3]
inmost parts, 2540+1061, ḥeder+beṭen[1] [2]
upper parts, 6608, ʿaliyyâ [2]
parts, NIH/RPE [1]
parts, 963, bad[1] [1]
parts, 1473, gebûl [1]
inner parts, 3219, ṭuḥôt [1]
private parts, 4434, mebûšîm [1]
parts, 4519, medînâ [1]
parts, 4869, mālôn [1]
parts, 5984, nētaḥ [1]
inner parts, 7687, qēbâ [1]
choice parts, 8040, rēʾšît [1]
distant parts, 10509, sôp [1]

PARTY [4]
raiding party, 1522, gedûd[2] [2]
one party[s], 408, ʾîš[1] [1]
be a willing party, 5951+5883, nāśāʾ+nepeš [1]

PARUAH [1]
Paruah, 7245, pārûaḥ [1]

PARVAIM [1]
Parvaim, 7246, parwayim [1]

PAS DAMMIM [1]
Pas Dammim, 7169, pas dammîm [1]
at Pas Dammim[s], 9004, šām [1]

PASACH [1]
Pasach, 7179, pāsak [1]

PASEAH [4]
Paseah, 7176, pāsēaḥ [4]

PASHHUR [13]
Pashhur, 7319, pašḥûr [13]

PASS [95]
pass, 6296, ʿābar[1] [30]
pass by, 6296, ʿābar[1] [8]
pass through, 6296, ʿābar[1] [8]
pass, 5090, maʿaleh [7]
pass by, 6296+2006, ʿābar[1]+derek [4]
pass by, 10268, ḥalap [4]
pass away, 6296, ʿābar[1] [3]
pass over, 7173, pāsaḥ[1] [3]
brought to pass, 995, bôʾ [2]
came to pass, 995, bôʾ [2]
pass, 5045, maʿbārâ [2]
pass, 6015, sābab [2]
had pass, 6296, ʿābar[1] [2]
pass on, 6296, ʿābar[1] [2]
pass, NIH/RPE [1]
pass, 910, ʾātâ [1]
pass, 995, bôʾ [1]
pass, 1577, gûz [1]
pass, 5044, maʿabār [1]
pass on as an inheritance, 5706, nāḥal [1]
pass away, 6073, sûr[1] [1]
cause to pass, 6296, ʿābar[1] [1]
had pass by, 6296, ʿābar[1] [1]
let pass, 6296, ʿābar[1] [1]
pass into other hands, 6296, ʿābar[1] [1]
take note as pass, 6296, ʿābar[1] [1]
pass away, 7155, pānâ [1]
pass again, 8740, šûb[1] [1]
pass judgment, 9149, šāpaṭ [1]
pass away, 10528, ʿadâ [1]

PASSAGEWAY [3]
passageway, 2006, derek [2]
passageway, 4544, mahalāk [1]

PASSED [52]
passed, 6296, ʿābar[1] [21]
passed by, 6296, ʿābar[1] [9]
passed, AIT [4]
passed, NIH/RPE [3]
passed through, 6296, ʿābar[1] [3]
passed, 4848, mālēʾ[1] [2]
passed along, 6296, ʿābar[1] [2]
passed, 995, bôʾ [1]
passed, 2118, hāyâ [1]
passed away, 2143, hālak [1]
passed away, 6296, ʿābar[1] [1]
passed, 6590, ʿālâ [1]
passed over, 7173, pāsaḥ[1] [1]
passed, 7891, qēṣ [1]
passed, 8740, šûb[1] [1]

PASSER-BY [2]
passer-by, 6296, ʿābar[1] [2]

PASSES [5]
passes, 6296, ʿābar[1] [2]
what passes, 4604, môṣāʾ[1] [1]
passes by, 6296, ʿābar[1] [1]
passes through, 6913, ʿāśâ[1] [1]

PASSING [8]
passing by, 6296, ʿābar[1] [2]
passing through, 6296, ʿābar[1] [2]
passing, NIH/RPE [1]
passing, 2143, hālak [1]
passing, 3655, yāṣāʾ [1]
passing, 6296, ʿābar[1] [1]

PASSION [1]
passion, 678, ʾap[2] [1]

PASSOVER [47]
Passover, 7175, pesaḥ [36]
Passover lamb, 7175, pesaḥ [4]
Passover lambs, 7175, pesaḥ [3]
Passover offerings, 7175, pesaḥ [3]
Passover animals, 7175, pesaḥ [1]

PAST [35]
past, 6584, ʿal[2] [3]
past, NIH/RPE [2]
go past, 6296, ʿābar[1] [2]
past, 6296, ʿābar[1] [2]
distant past, 255, ʾāz [1]
past, 255, ʾāz [1]
in the past, 1685+919+1685+8997, gam+ʾetmôl+gam+šilšôm [1]
review the past, 2349, zākar[1] [1]
past, 2532, ḥādal[1] [1]
glided past, 2736, ḥālap[1] [1]
skim past, 2736, ḥālap[1] [1]
sweep past, 2736, ḥālap[1] [1]
past, 3427+8037, yôm[1]+riʾšôn [1]
as in times past, 3869+3972, ke-+kōl [1]
past, 4202, lōʾ [1]
past, 4946+6584, min+ʿal[2] [1]
past, 4946+907, min+ʾēt[2] [1]
past, 6073, sûr[1] [1]
marched past, 6296+6584+3338, ʿābar[1]+ʿal[2]+yād [1]
ran past, 6296, ʿābar[1] [1]
past, 6961+8037, ʿēt+riʾšôn [1]
past, 7710, qedem [1]
past, 7712, qadmâ [1]
past, 7719, qadmōnî[1] [1]
past, 8037, riʾšôn [1]
past, 8103, rādap [1]
past, 8158, rāḥôq [1]
generations long past, 9102+1887+2256+1887, šānâ[2]+dôr[2]+we-+dôr[2] [1]
in the past, 9453+8997, temôl+šilšôm [1]
past, 9453+8997, temôl+šilšôm [1]

PASTURE [40]
pasture, 5337, mirʿeh [12]
pasture, 5659, nāweh[1] [9]
pasture, 5338, marʿît [8]
pasture, 8286, rāʿâ[1] [5]
pasture, 1824, dōber [2]
find pasture, 8286, rāʿâ[1] [2]
pasture, 6912, ʿēśeb [1]
enjoy pasture, 8286, rāʿâ[1] [1]

PASTURE-FED [1]
pasture-fed, 8297, reʿî [1]

PASTURED [2]
pastured, 8286, rāʿâ[1] [2]

PASTURELAND [8]
pastureland, 4494, migrāš [5]
pastureland, 5659, nāweh[1] [2]
pastureland, 8441+4494, śādeh+migrāš [1]

PASTURELANDS [43]
pasturelands, 4494, migrāš [41]
fertile pasturelands, 4149, karmel[1] [1]
pasturelands, 5661, nāwâ[3] [1]

PASTURES [10]
pastures, 5661, nāwâ[3] [7]
pastures, NIH/RPE [1]
rich pastures, 168, ʾadderet [1]
pastures, 5659, nāweh[1] [1]

PATCH [1]
melon patch, 5252, miqšâ[2] [1]

PATCHED [1]
patched, 3229, ṭālāʾ [1]

PATH [53]
path, 2006, derek [21]
path, 784, ʾōraḥ [17]
path, 5985, nātîb [3]
path, 5986, netîbâ [3]
path, 5047, maʿgāl[2] [2]
path, 7576, ṣaʿad [2]
path, 2006+784, derek+ʾōraḥ [1]
path, 2141, hālîk [1]
in path, 4200+7156, le-1+pāneh [1]
narrow path, 5469, mišʿôl [1]
hidden path, 5985, nātîb [1]

PATHRUSITES [2]
Pathrusites, 7357, patrusîm [2]

PATHS [35]
paths, 784, ʾōraḥ [11]
paths, 5986, netîbâ [11]
paths, 5047, maʿgāl[2] [8]
paths, 2006, derek [4]
paths, 8666, šebîl [1]

PATIENCE [5]
try patience, 4206, lāʾâ [2]
gives patience, 799+678, ʾārak+ʾap[2] [1]
patience, 800+8120, ʾārēk+rûaḥ [1]
patience, 802+678, ʾōrek+ʾap[2] [1]

PATIENT [5]
patient, 800+678, ʾārēk+ʾap[2] [3]
patient, 799, ʾārak [1]
patient, 5432, māšak [1]

PATIENTLY [4]
wait patiently, 2565, ḥûl[1] [1]
wait patiently, 5663, nûaḥ[1] [1]
waited patiently for, 7747+7747, qāwâ[1]+qāwâ[1] [1]
waited patiently, 8750, šāwâ[1] [1]

PATTERN [3]
pattern, 9322, tabnît [2]
pattern, 5260, marʾeh [1]

PAU [2]
Pau, 7185, *pā'û* [2]

PAVEMENT [8]
pavement, 8367, *riṣ^{e}pâ* [5]
pavement, 4246, *l^{e}bēnâ* [1]
brick pavement, 4861, *malbēn* [1]
mosaic pavement, 8367, *riṣ^{e}pâ* [1]

PAVILION [2]
pavilion, 2903, *ḥuppâ^{1}* [1]
pavilion, 6109, *sukkâ* [1]

PAW [2]
paw, 3338, *yād* [2]

PAWS [2]
paws, 2916, *ḥāpar^{1}* [1]
paws, 4090, *kap* [1]

PAY [105]
pay, 5989, *nātan* [14]
pay attention, 7992, *qāšab* [12]
pay, 8966, *šālēm^{1}* [9]
pay honor, 2556, *ḥāwâ^{2}* [7]
pay attention, 5742+265, *nāṭâ+'ōzen* [7]
pay back, 8966, *šālēm^{1}* [6]
pay back, 8740, *šûb^{1}* [4]
pay, *NIH/RPE* [3]
pay attention, 263, *'āzan^{1}* [3]
pay attention, 9048, *šāma'* [3]
pay, 5951, *nāšā'* [2]
pay for, 8355, *rāṣâ^{2}* [2]
pay, 8492, *śîm* [2]
pay, 8510, *śākār^{1}* [2]
pay, 8740, *šûb^{1}* [2]
pay, 9202, *šāqal* [2]
pay for it, 870, *'āšam* [1]
pay, 921, *'etnâ* [1]
pay, 924+5989, *'etnan+nātan* [1]
pay with, 928, *b^{e}-* [1]
pay for it, 2472, *ḥābal^{2}* [1]
pay, 4084+8740, *kesep+šûb^{1}* [1]
pay, 4084+9202, *kesep+šāqal* [1]
pay, 4200, *l^{e}-^{1}* [1]
must pay bride-price, 4555+4555, *māhar^{2}+māhar^{2}* [1]
poor to pay, 4575, *mûk* [1]
pay, 5989+4084, *nātan+kesep* [1]
pay, 5989+4836, *nātan+meker* [1]
pay, 5989+8510, *nātan+śākār^{1}* [1]
pay close attention, 7992+2256+9048, *qāšab+w^{e}-+šāma'* [1]
pay for, 8690, *šābar^{2}* [1]
made pay for, 8740+928+8031, *šûb^{1}+b^{e}-+rō'š^{1}* [1]
pay a ransom, 8815, *šāḥad* [1]
pay, 8883, *šît^{1}* [1]
make pay, 8966, *šālēm^{1}* [1]
must pay, 8966+8966, *šālēm^{1}+šālēm^{1}* [1]
pay back in full, 8966, *šālēm^{1}* [1]
pay for the loss, 8966, *šālēm^{1}* [1]
pay attention, 9068, *šāmar* [1]
pay attention, 9120, *šā'â* [1]
pay, 10682, *śîm* [1]

PAYING [7]
paying, 5989, *nātan* [3]
paying back, 1694, *gāmal* [1]
without paying anything, 2855, *ḥinnām* [1]
insist on paying for, 7864+7864+928+4697, *qānâ^{1}+qānâ^{1}+b^{e}-+m^{e}ḥîr^{1}* [1]
insist on paying, 7864+7864, *qānâ^{1}+qānâ^{1}* [1]

PAYMENT [13]
payment, 924, *'etnan* [2]
require payment, 5601, *nāgaś* [2]
payment, *NIH/RPE* [1]
requiring payment, 873, *'ašmâ* [1]
in payment for, 928, *b^{e}-* [1]
demanded payment, 1335, *bāqaš* [1]
without any payment, 2855+401, *ḥinnām+'ayin^{1}* [1]
payment, 4084, *kesep* [1]
payment, 4111, *kōper^{4}* [1]
measure the full payment, 4499, *mādad* [1]
payment, 7190, *p^{e}'ullâ* [1]

PAYS [8]
pays attention, 263, *'āzan^{1}* [1]
pays heed, 1067, *bîn* [1]
pays attention, 7155, *pānâ* [1]
pays back, 8740+8740, *šûb^{1}+šûb^{1}* [1]
pays back, 8740, *šûb^{1}* [1]
pays attention, 8800, *šûr^{1}* [1]
pays back, 8966, *šālēm^{1}* [1]
pays, 10682, *śîm* [1]

PEACE [155]
peace, 8934, *šālôm* [113]
come in peace, 8934, *šālôm* [5]
at peace, 9200, *šāqaṭ* [5]
at peace, 8966, *šālēm^{1}* [4]
made peace, 8966, *šālēm^{1}* [3]
had peace, 9200, *šāqaṭ* [3]
peace, 1388, *b^{e}rākâ^{1}* [2]
in peace, 8934, *šālôm* [2]
made a treaty of peace, 8966, *šālēm^{1}* [2]
have peace, 9200, *šāqaṭ* [2]
in peace, 9200, *šāqaṭ* [2]
peace and rest, 4957, *m^{e}nûḥâ* [1]
at peace, 5341, *marpē'^{2}* [1]
give peace, 5663, *nûaḥ^{1}* [1]
peace, 5739, *naḥat^{2}* [1]
peace, 8092, *rega'* [1]
have peace, 8922, *šālâ^{1}* [1]
peace and quiet, 8932, *šalwâ* [1]
peace and prosperity, 8934, *šālôm* [1]
perfect peace, 8934+8934, *šālôm+šālôm* [1]
make peace, 8966, *šālēm^{1}* [1]
makes live at peace, 8966, *šālēm^{1}* [1]
enjoyed peace, 9200, *šāqaṭ* [1]

PEACEABLY [2]
peaceably, 928+8934, *b^{e}-+šālôm* [1]
peaceably, 8934, *šālôm* [1]

PEACEFUL [8]
peaceful, 9200, *šāqaṭ* [3]
peaceful, 8934, *šālôm* [2]
peaceful, 8633, *ša'ᵃnān* [1]
peaceful relations, 8934, *šālôm* [1]
peaceful, 8966, *šālēm^{1}* [1]

PEACEFULLY [3]
peacefully, 8934, *šālôm* [2]
peacefully, 928+8934, *b^{e}-+šālôm* [1]

PEACETIME [1]
peacetime, 8934, *šālôm* [1]

PEAKS [2]
peaks, 8031, *rō'š^{1}* [1]
peaks, 9361, *tô'āpôt* [1]

PEBBLE [1]
pebble, 7656, *ṣ^{e}rôr^{2}* [1]

PEBBLES [1]
pebbles, 7326, *pat* [1]

PECKED [1]
pecked out, 5941, *nāqar* [1]

PEDAHEL [1]
Pedahel, 7010, *p^{e}dah'ēl* [1]

PEDAHZUR [5]
Pedahzur, 7011, *p^{e}dāhṣûr* [5]

PEDAIAH [8]
Pedaiah, 7015, *p^{e}dāyâ* [7]
Pedaiah, 7016, *p^{e}dāyāhû* [1]

PEDESTAL [1]
pedestal, 3962, *kiyyûn* [1]

PEELED [1]
peeled, 7202, *pāṣal* [1]

PEELING [1]
peeling, 7202, *pāṣal* [1]

PEELS [1]
peels, 4946+6584, *min+'al^{2}* [1]

PEERED [1]
peered, 9207, *šāqap* [1]

PEERING [1]
peering, 7438, *ṣûṣ^{2}* [1]

PEG [7]
peg, 3845, *yātēd* [4]
tent peg, 3845, *yātēd* [3]

PEGS [8]
tent pegs, 3845, *yātēd* [7]
pegs, 3845, *yātēd* [1]

PEKAH [11]
Pekah, 7220, *peqaḥ* [10]
Pekah, *NIH/RPE* [1]

PEKAH'S [1]
Pekah's, 7220, *peqaḥ* [1]

PEKAHIAH [5]
Pekahiah^{s}, 2084, *-hû* [2]
Pekahiah, 7222, *p^{e}qaḥyâ* [2]
Pekahiah, *NIH/RPE* [1]

PEKAHIAH'S [1]
Pekahiah's, 7222, *p^{e}qaḥyâ* [1]

PEKOD [2]
Pekod, 7216, *p^{e}qôd* [2]

PELAIAH [3]
Pelaiah, 7102, *p^{e}lā'yâ* [2]
Pelaiah, 7126, *p^{e}lāyâ* [1]

PELALIAH [1]
Pelaliah, 7139, *p^{e}lalyâ* [1]

PELATIAH [5]
Pelatiah, 7124, *p^{e}laṭyâ* [3]
Pelatiah, 7125, *p^{e}laṭyāhû* [2]

PELEG [7]
Peleg, 7105, *peleg^{2}* [7]

PELET [2]
Pelet, 7118, *peleṭ* [2]

PELETH [2]
Peleth, 7150, *pelet* [2]

PELETHITES [7]
Pelethites, 7152, *p^{e}lētî* [7]

PELONITE [3]
Pelonite, 7113, *p^{e}lônî* [3]

PELT [1]
pelt, 8959, *šālak* [1]

PELTED [1]
pelted, 6232, *sāqal* [1]

PELUSIUM [2]
Pelusium, 6096, *sîn^{1}* [2]

PEN [6]
pen, 6485, *'ēṭ* [2]
pen up, 1074+2025, *bayit^{1}+-â^{2}* [1]
pen, 1312, *boṣrâ^{1}* [1]
pen, 3032, *ḥereṭ* [1]
pen, 4813, *miklā'* [1]

PENALTIES [1]
penalties, 9150, *šepeṭ* [1]

PENALTY [8]
penalty, 871, *'āšām* [4]
penalty for lewdness, 2365, *zimmâ^{1}* [1]
penalty, 6741, *'ōneš* [1]
penalty of sin, 7322, *peša'* [1]
penalty, 10186, *dāt* [1]

PENDANTS [1]
pendants, 5755, *n^{e}ṭipâ* [1]

PENIEL [6]
Peniel, 7159, *p^{e}nû'ēl^{2}* [5]
Peniel, 7161, *p^{e}nî'ēl^{2}* [1]

PENINNAH [3]
Peninnah, 7166, peninnâ [3]

PENITENT [1]
penitent, 8740, šûb[1] [1]

PENNED [3]
penned up, 3973+928+2021+1074, kālā‘[1]+be+ha+bayit[1] [1]
keep penned up, 9068, šāmar [1]
kept penned up, 9068, šāmar [1]

PENS [8]
pens, 1556, gedērâ[1] [4]
pens, 4813, miklā’ [2]
pens, 774, ’urwâ [1]
pens, 1556+7366, gedērâ[1]+ṣō’n [1]

PENT-UP [1]
pent-up, 7639, ṣar[1] [1]

PENUEL [2]
Penuel, 7158, penû’ēl[1] [2]

PEOPLE [1816]
people, 6639, ‘am[2] [1293]
people, *AIT* [93]
people, 1201, bēn[1] [85]
people, 3782, yāšab [73]
people, *NIH/RPE* [54]
people, 1074, bayit[1] [21]
people, 132, ’ādām[1] [20]
people, 408, ’îš[1] [16]
people, 1426+6639, bat[1]+‘am[2] [14]
the people[s], 2157, -hem [11]
people, 5883, nepeš [11]
the people[s], 4392, -ām [9]
people, 1201+6639, bēn[1]+‘am[2] [8]
people, 1580, gôy [8]
people, 10553, ‘am [7]
people, 1414, bāśār [5]
people, 2446, zera‘ [4]
people, 4211, le’ōm [4]
people, 6337, ‘ēdâ[1] [4]
people, 278, ’āḥ[2] [3]
people of Geshur, 1771, gešûrî [3]
my people[s], 2157, -hem [3]
each people, 6639+2256+6639, ‘am[2]+we-+‘am[2] [3]
people, 10050, ’enāš [3]
people of Ashdod, 847, ’ašdôdî [2]
common people, 1201+6639, bēn[1]+‘am[2] [2]
lay people, 1201+6639, bēn[1]+‘am[2] [2]
people[s], 2157, -hem [2]
my people[s], 4392, -ām [2]
people, 4580, môledet [2]
people, 5476, mišpāḥâ [2]
foreign people, 6850, ‘ēreb[2] [2]
people from Benjamin, 278+2157, ’āḥ[2]+-hem [1]
people from Judah, 278+2157, ’āḥ[2]+-hem [1]
people, 438, ’ikkār [1]
my people[s], 889, ’ašer [1]
people of Asher, 896, ’āšērî [1]
people[s], 917, ’attem [1]
people of Beeroth, 943, be’ērōtî [1]
his people[s], 1201+3147, bēn[1]+ḥēt [1]
people, 1201+132, bēn[1]+’ādām[1] [1]
people, 1251, ba‘al[1] [1]
people, 1426, bat[1] [1]
people of time, 1887, dôr[2] [1]
people, 1887, dôr[2] [1]
people[s], 2021, ha- [1]
its people[s], 2023, -āh [1]
people[s], 2156, hēm [1]
the people[s], 2156, hēm [1]
people, 2162, hāmôn [1]
people[s], 2179, hēnnâ[2] [1]
the people[s], 2257, -ô [1]
wicked people, 2629, ḥaṭṭā’ [1]
people, 2653, ḥayyâ[3] [1]
people, 2728, ḥālāl[1] [1]
people[s], 3481, yaḥdāw [1]
people[s], 3972+889+928, kōl+’ašer+be- [1]
the people[s], 4013, -kem [1]
its people[s], 4392, -ām [1]
the people, 4392, -ām [1]
his people[s], 4564, -mô [1]
people, 5493, mōt[1] [1]
people, 5883+132, nepeš+’ādām[1] [1]
people of Gaza, 6484, ‘azzātî [1]
common people, 6639, ‘am[2] [1]
people of Ekron, 6834, ‘eqrônî [1]
other people, 6850, ‘ēreb[2] [1]
people of Sidon, 7479, ṣîdōnî [1]
people, 7736, qāhāl [1]
people who live in, 8907, šākēn [1]
people of Samaria, 9085, šōmerōnî [1]
people[s], 9109+8993, šenayim+šālōš [1]
people living, 9369, tôšāb [1]
people, 10040, ’ummâ [1]
people, 10120+10050, bar[2]+’enāš [1]
people, 10120, bar[2] [1]
people, 10240+10050, zera‘+’enāš [1]

PEOPLE’S [8]
people’s, 6639, ‘am[2] [7]
people’s, 4200+6639, le-[1]+‘am[2] [1]

PEOPLED [1]
peopled, 3782, yāšab [1]

PEOPLES [150]
peoples, 6639, ‘am[2] [100]
peoples, 4211, le’ōm [18]
peoples, 5476, mišpāḥâ [8]
peoples, 10553, ‘am [6]
peoples, 1201, bēn[1] [5]
peoples[s], 889, ’ašer [2]
peoples, 1580, gôy [2]
peoples, 10163, dûr [2]
peoples, *AIT* [1]
peoples, 569, ’ummâ [1]
peoples, 824, ’ereṣ [1]
one of the other peoples, 6639+2256+6639, ‘am[2]+we-+‘am[2] [1]
various peoples, 6639+2256+6639, ‘am[2]+we-+‘am[2] [1]
peoples, 8657, šēbeṭ [1]
neighboring peoples, 8907, šākēn [1]

PEOR [9]
Peor, 7186, pe‘ôr [9]

PER [1]
per, 4200, le-[1] [1]

PERATH [4]
Perath, 7310, perāt [4]

PERAZIM [1]
Perazim, 7292, perāṣîm [1]

PERCEIVE [5]
perceive, 1067, bîn [3]
perceive, 3359, yāda‘ [1]
perceive, 8800, šûr[1] [1]

PERCEIVED [1]
ear perceived, 263, ’āzan[1] [1]

PERCEIVING [1]
perceiving, 3359, yāda‘ [1]

PERES [1]
Peres, 10593, perēs [1]

PERESH [1]
Peresh, 7303, pereš[2] [1]

PEREZ [15]
Perez, 7289, pereṣ[2] [15]

PEREZ UZZAH [2]
Perez Uzzah, 7290, pereṣ ‘uzzā’ [2]

PEREZITE [1]
Perezite, 7291, parṣî [1]

PERFECT [16]
perfect, 9459, tāmîm [8]
perfect, 4003, kālîl [3]
perfect, 590, ’ōmen [1]
perfect, 4817, miklāl [1]
perfect peace, 8934+8934, šālôm+šālôm [1]
perfect, 9447, tām [1]
perfect, 9462, tāmam [1]

PERFECTION [5]
brought to perfection, 4005, kālal [2]
perfection, 4003, kālîl [1]
perfection, 9416, tiklâ [1]
perfection, 9422, toknît [1]

PERFORM [19]
perform, 6913, ‘āśâ[1] [6]
perform, *NIH/RPE* [5]
perform, 6641, ‘āmad [2]
perform, 9068, šāmar [2]
perform, 5989, nātan [1]
perform, 6268, ‘ābad [1]
perform, 8471, śāḥaq [1]
perform, 8883, šît[1] [1]

PERFORMANCE [1]
performance, 5126, ma‘aśeh [1]

PERFORMED [20]
performed, 6913, ‘āśâ[1] [9]
performed, 8492, śîm [3]
performed, *NIH/RPE* [2]
performed, 4856, melā’kâ [1]
performed, 6641, ‘āmad [1]
performed exploits, 7189, pō‘al [1]
performed, 7464, ṣāḥaq [1]
performed, 9068, šāmar [1]
performed, 10522, ‘abad [1]

PERFORMING [1]
performing, 9068, šāmar [1]

PERFORMS [4]
performs, 6913, ‘āśâ[1] [3]
performs, 10522, ‘abad [1]

PERFUME [10]
perfume, 9043, šemen [3]
perfume, 5349, merqāḥ [1]
perfume, 5883, nepeš [1]
perfume, 5948, nērd [1]
perfume, 6057, sûk[2] [1]
makes perfume, 8379, rāqaḥ [1]
fine perfume, 9043, šemen [1]
perfume, 9043+8379, šemen+rāqaḥ [1]

PERFUME-MAKERS [1]
perfume-makers, 8382, raqqāḥ [1]

PERFUMED [2]
perfumed, 5678, nûp[2] [1]
perfumed, 7787, qāṭar[1] [1]

PERFUMER [3]
perfumer, 8379, rāqaḥ [3]

PERFUMERS [1]
perfumers, 8384, raqqāḥâ [1]

PERFUMES [4]
perfumes, 1411, bōśem [1]
perfumes, 5351+5126, mirqaḥat+ma‘aśeh [1]
perfumes, 8383, riqquaḥ [1]
perfumes, 9043, šemen [1]

PERHAPS [30]
perhaps, 218, ’ûlay[2] [25]
perhaps, 3954, kî[2] [2]
perhaps, *NIH/RPE* [1]
but perhaps, 218, ’ûlay[2] [1]
perhaps, 7153, pen [1]

PERIDA [1]
Perida, 7263, perîdā’ [1]

PERIL [2]
peril, 7065, paḥad[1] [1]
peril, 8288, rā‘â[3] [1]

PERIOD [26]
period, 3427, yôm[1] [9]
period, 5614, niddâ [7]
monthly period, 5614, niddâ [3]

period of mourning, 65, *ʾēbel* [1]
monthly period, 1865+5614, *dāweh+niddâ* [1]
monthly period, 1865, *dāweh* [1]
period, 2006+851, *derek+ʾiššâ* [1]
impurity of monthly period, 5614, *niddâ* [1]
monthly period, 5614+1864, *niddâ+dāwâ* [1]
period of time, 10232+10221+10530, *z^{e}man^{2}+w^{e}-+ʿiddān* [1]

PERIODS [1]
seven-day periods, 8679+2021+3427, *šebaʿ^{1}+ha-+yôm^{1}* [1]

PERISH [69]
perish, 6, *ʾābad* [43]
perish, 3983, *kālâ^{1}* [6]
perish, 1588, *gāwaʿ* [3]
perish, 9462, *tāmam* [3]
perish, 1950, *dāmâ^{3}* [2]
perish, 4637, *mût* [2]
perish, *NIH/RPE* [1]
perish, 6+6, *ʾābad+ʾābad* [1]
doomed to perish, 1959, *dāmam^{3}* [1]
perish, 1959, *dāmam^{3}* [1]
perish, 3948, *kāḥad* [1]
perish, 5877, *nāpal* [1]
perish, 6200, *sāpâ* [1]
perish, 6296, *ʿābar^{1}* [1]
perish, 8720, *šādad* [1]
perish, 10005, *ʾ^{a}bad* [1]

PERISHED [14]
perished, 6, *ʾābad* [9]
perished, 1588, *gāwaʿ* [2]
perished, 6200, *sāpâ* [1]
perished, 9012, *šāmad* [1]
perished, 9462, *tāmam* [1]

PERISHES [4]
perishes, 6, *ʾābad* [4]

PERISHING [7]
perishing, 6, *ʾābad* [4]
perishing, 3948, *kāḥad* [1]
perishing, 6296, *ʿābar^{1}* [1]
perishing, 9462, *tāmam* [1]

PERIZZITES [23]
Perizzites, 7254, *p^{e}rizzî* [23]

PERJURERS [1]
perjurers, 8678+4200+2021+9214, *šābaʿ+l^{e-1}+ha-+šeqer* [1]

PERJURY [1]
perjury, 8678+4200+2021+9214, *šābaʿ+l^{e-1}+ha-+šeqer* [1]

PERMANENT [2]
permanent, 6409, *ʿôlām* [2]

PERMANENTLY [2]
permanently, 4200+2021+7552, *l^{e-1}+ha-+ṣ^{e}mitut* [1]
permanently, 4200+7552, *l^{e-1}+ṣ^{e}mitut* [1]

PERMISSION [7]
permission, *AIT* [1]
asked for permission, 1335, *bāqaš* [1]
gave permission, 4200, *l^{e-1}* [1]
permission, 4946, *min* [1]
give permission, 5989, *nātan* [1]
earnestly asked for permission, 8626+8626, *šāʾal+šāʾal* [1]
earnestly asked permission, 8626+8626, *šāʾal+šāʾal* [1]

PERMIT [2]
permit, 5989, *nātan* [2]

PERMITS [1]
permits, 5663, *nûaḥ^{1}* [1]

PERMITTED [2]
permitted, *AIT* [1]
permitted to do, 5989, *nātan* [1]

PERPETUATE [1]
perpetuate memory, 2349+9005, *zākar^{1}+šēm^{1}* [1]

PERPLEXED [1]
greatly perplexed, 10724, *š^{e}mam* [1]

PERSECUTE [6]
persecute, 8103, *rādap* [5]
persecute, 6715, *ʿ^{o}nî* [1]

PERSECUTORS [4]
persecutors, 8103, *rādap* [4]

PERSIA [29]
Persia, 7273, *pāras^{2}* [26]
Persia, 10594, *pāras* [2]
Persia, 10060, *ʾ^{a}pār^{e}sāy* [1]

PERSIAN [4]
Persian, 7273, *pāras^{2}* [2]
Persian, 7275, *pār^{e}sî* [1]
Persian, 10595, *parsāy* [1]

PERSIANS [4]
Persians, 10594, *pāras* [4]

PERSIST [4]
persist, 3578, *yāsap* [1]
persist, 6913, *ʿāśâ^{1}* [1]
persist in doing evil, 8317+8317, *rāʿaʿ^{1}+rāʿaʿ^{1}* [1]
persist in own way, 9244+4213, *š^{e}rirût+lēb* [1]

PERSISTED [3]
persisted, 2143, *hālak* [1]
persisted in, 3869+6913, *k^{e}-+ʿāśâ^{1}* [1]
persisted, 7210, *pāṣar* [1]

PERSISTS [1]
persists, 6641, *ʿāmad* [1]

PERSON [81]
person, 5883, *nepeš* [22]
person, *AIT* [15]
person, *NIH/RPE* [9]
person, 408, *ʾîš^{1}* [8]
person, 132, *ʾādām^{1}* [5]
infected person, 5596, *negaʿ* [3]
the person^{s}, 2257, *-ô* [2]
the person^{s}, 889, *ʾ^{a}šer* [1]
in person, 928+265, *b^{e}-+ʾōzen* [1]
person, 1653, *gulgōlet* [1]
person^{s}, 1947, *dām* [1]
that person^{s}, 2085, *hûʾ* [1]
the person^{s}, 2085, *hûʾ* [1]
person^{s}, 2257, *-ô* [1]
that person^{s}, 2257, *-ô* [1]
the person, 2257, *-ô* [1]
unauthorized person, 2424, *zār* [1]
that person^{s}, 4392, *-ām* [1]
infected person, 5596+5999, *negaʿ+neteq* [1]
person^{s}, 5596, *negaʿ* [1]
person^{s}, 5782, *nākâ* [1]
person, 6639, *ʿam^{2}* [1]
person^{s}, 7665, *ṣāraʿ* [1]
killed a person, 8357, *rāṣaḥ* [1]

PERSON'S [1]
person's, *AIT* [1]

PERSONAL [6]
personal adviser, 5335, *mērēaʿ^{1}* [1]
personal attendants, 5853+9250, *naʿar^{2}+šārat* [1]
personal servant, 5853+9250, *naʿar^{2}+šārat* [1]
personal vows, 5883+6886, *nepeš+ʿērek* [1]
personal treasures, 6035, *s^{e}gullâ* [1]
personal adviser, 8291, *rēʿeh* [1]

PERSONALLY [1]
personally, *AIT* [1]

PERSONS [6]
persons, 132, *ʾādām^{1}* [3]
persons, 5883, *nepeš* [3]

PERSPIRE [1]
perspire, 3472, *yezaʿ* [1]

PERSUADE [3]
let persuade to trust, 1053, *bāṭaḥ^{1}* [2]
persuade, 1819+6584+4213, *dābar^{2}+ʿal^{2}+lēb* [1]

PERSUADED [3]
persuaded to trust, 1053, *bāṭaḥ^{1}* [1]
persuaded, 7210, *pāṣar* [1]
be persuaded, 7331, *pātâ^{1}* [1]

PERSUASIVE [1]
persuasive words, 4375, *leqaḥ* [1]

PERTAINING [1]
pertaining, *AIT* [1]

PERUDA [1]
Peruda, 7243, *p^{e}rûdāʾ* [1]

PERVERSE [15]
perverse, 6836, *ʿiqqēš^{1}* [6]
perverse, 9337, *tahpukôt* [6]
perverse, 4279, *lûz^{1}* [1]
perverse, 6390, *ʿāwâ^{1}* [1]
perverse, 6835, *ʿāqaš* [1]

PERVERSENESS [1]
perverseness, 9337, *tahpukôt* [1]

PERVERSION [2]
perversion, 9316, *tebel* [2]

PERVERSITY [2]
perversity, 6838, *ʿiqq^{e}šût* [1]
perversity, 9337, *tahpukôt* [1]

PERVERT [7]
pervert, 5742, *nāṭâ* [3]
pervert, 6430, *ʿāwat* [3]
pervert, 6913+6404, *ʿāśâ^{1}+ʿāwel* [1]

PERVERTED [4]
perverted, 6390, *ʿāwâ^{1}* [2]
perverted, 5742, *nāṭâ* [1]
perverted, 6823, *ʿāqal* [1]

PESTILENCE [4]
pestilence, 1822, *deber^{1}* [2]
pestilence, 8404, *rešep^{1}* [2]

PESTLE [1]
pestle, 6605, *ʿelî* [1]

PESTS [1]
pests, 430, *ʾākal* [1]

PET [1]
make a pet, 8471, *śāḥaq* [1]

PETHAHIAH [4]
Pethahiah, 7342, *p^{e}taḥyâ* [4]

PETHOR [2]
Pethor, 7335, *p^{e}tôr* [2]

PETHUEL [1]
Pethuel, 7333, *p^{e}tûʾēl* [1]

PETITION [16]
petition, 8629, *š^{e}ʾēlâ* [6]
petition, 9382, *t^{e}ḥinnâ^{1}* [4]
petition, 2349, *zākar^{1}* [2]
petition, 9525, *t^{e}pillâ* [2]
make petition, 2349, *zākar^{1}* [1]
petition, 9384, *taḥ^{a}nûn* [1]

PETITIONED [1]
petitioned, 1335, *bāqaš* [1]

PETITIONS [1]
petitions, 9384, *taḥ^{a}nûn* [1]

PEULLETHAI [1]
Peullethai, 7191, *p^{e}ʿull^{e}tay* [1]

PHANTOM [1]
phantom, 7513, *ṣelem^{2}* [1]

PHARAOH [211]
Pharaoh, 7281, *par'ōh* [206]
Pharaoh, *NIH/RPE* [5]

PHARAOH'S [54]
Pharaoh's, 7281, *par'ōh* [51]
Pharaoh's, 4200+7281, *le-[1]+par'ōh* [2]
Pharaoh's[s], 2257, *-ô* [1]

PHARPAR [1]
Pharpar, 7286, *parpar* [1]

PHICOL [3]
Phicol, 7087, *pîkōl* [3]

PHILISTIA [8]
Philistia, 7148, *pelešet* [7]
Philistia, 7149, *pelištî* [1]

PHILISTINE [62]
Philistine, 7149, *pelištî* [62]

PHILISTINE'S [5]
Philistine's, 7149, *pelištî* [4]
the Philistine's[s], 2257, *-ô* [1]

PHILISTINES [210]
Philistines, 7149, *pelištî* [200]
Philistines, *NIH/RPE* [6]
Philistines, 7148, *pelešet* [2]
Philistines, 824+7149, *'ereṣ+pelištî* [1]
the Philistines[s], 2157, *-hem* [1]

PHINEHAS [25]
Phinehas, 7090, *pînehās* [25]

PHOENICIA [1]
Phoenicia, 4046, *kena'an[1]* [1]

PHYSICAL [1]
physical defect, 4583, *mûm* [1]

PHYSICIAN [1]
physician, 8324, *rāpā'[1]* [1]

PHYSICIANS [4]
physicians, 8324, *rāpā'[1]* [4]

PI HAHIROTH [4]
Pi Hahiroth, 7084, *pî haḥîrôt* [4]

PICK [13]
pick up, 5951, *nāśā'* [4]
pick up, 4377, *lāqaṭ* [3]
trying to pick a quarrel, 628, *'ānâ[2]* [1]
pick, 768, *'ārâ* [1]
pick out, 1329, *bāqar* [1]
pick up, 2715, *ḥālaṭ* [1]
pick, 4436, *mibḥār[1]* [1]
pick, 7786, *qāṭap* [1]

PICKED [10]
picked up, 5951, *nāśā'* [3]
picked up, 4374, *lāqaḥ* [2]
picked troops, 129, *'addîr* [1]
picked up scraps, 4377, *lāqaṭ* [1]
picked up, 4377, *lāqaṭ* [1]
picked up, 7695, *qābaṣ* [1]
picked up, 8123, *rûm[1]* [1]

PICKERS [2]
grape pickers, 1305, *bāṣar[1]* [2]

PICKS [6]
picks up, 5951, *nāśā'* [4]
picks, 3044, *ḥārîṣ[2]* [2]

PIECE [32]
of one piece with, 4946, *min* [9]
piece by piece, 4200+5984, *le-[1]+nētaḥ* [2]
of one piece, 4946, *min* [2]
piece, 5984, *nētaḥ* [2]
piece, 7326, *pat* [2]
piece, *AIT* [1]
piece, 102, *'agôrâ* [1]
piece, 977, *bādāl* [1]
piece[s], 2023, *-āh* [1]
piece, 2754, *ḥelqâ[2]* [1]
piece of broken pottery, 3084, *ḥereś* [1]
one piece with, 3669, *yeṣuqâ* [1]
piece, 4053, *kānāp* [1]
one piece with, 4609, *mûṣāqâ* [1]
piece of meat, 4950, *mānâ[2]* [1]
piece of wood, 6770, *'ēṣ* [1]
piece of string, 7348+5861, *pātîl+ne'ōret* [1]
piece, 7656, *ṣerôr[2]* [1]
piece of silver, 7988, *qeśîṭâ* [1]
piece of straw, 7990, *qaš* [1]

PIECES [79]
shoulder pieces, 4190, *kātēp* [8]
pieces, 5984, *nētaḥ* [8]
tear to pieces, 3271, *ṭārap* [4]
cut into pieces, 5983, *nātaḥ* [4]
pieces, *AIT* [3]
pieces, 1440, *beter[1]* [2]
cut to pieces, 1548, *gāda'* [2]
pieces, 7974, *qerā'îm* [2]
pieces of silver, 7988, *qeśîṭâ* [2]
breaking to pieces, 8689, *šābar[1]* [2]
pieces, 10197, *haddām* [2]
pieces, *NIH/RPE* [1]
were dashed to pieces, 1324, *bāqa'* [1]
hack to pieces, 1438, *bātaq* [1]
pieces, 1617, *gezer[1]* [1]
break in pieces, 1751, *gāram[2]* [1]
break to pieces, 1990, *dāqaq* [1]
broke to pieces, 1990, *dāqaq* [1]
cut in pieces, 2933, *ḥāṣēb[1]* [1]
cut to pieces, 2933, *ḥāṣēb[1]* [1]
pieces, 3084, *ḥereś* [1]
been torn to pieces, 3271+3271, *ṭārap+ṭārap* [1]
surely been torn to pieces, 3271+3271, *ṭārap+ṭārap* [1]
torn to pieces, 3271, *ṭārap* [1]
was torn to pieces by a wild animal, 3271+3271, *ṭārap+ṭārap* [1]
to pieces, 3512, *yāṭab* [1]
are broken to pieces, 4198, *kātat* [1]
be broken to pieces, 4198, *kātat* [1]
broke into pieces, 4198, *kātat* [1]
cut to pieces, 4730, *māḥaṣ* [1]
pieces, 4845, *mekittâ* [1]
crushed to pieces, 5879, *nāpaṣ[1]* [1]
dash to pieces, 5879, *nāpaṣ[1]* [1]
pieces of meat, 5984, *nētaḥ* [1]
break in pieces, 7200, *pāṣaḥ[2]* [1]
breaks in pieces, 7207, *pāṣaṣ* [1]
rip to pieces, 7293, *pāraq* [1]
pieces, 7326, *pat* [1]
be dashed to pieces, 8187, *rāṭaš* [1]
were dashed to pieces, 8187, *rāṭaš* [1]
pieces, 8269, *rāsîs[2]* [1]
smashed to pieces, 8368, *rāṣaṣ* [1]
battered to pieces, 8625+4198, *še'iyyâ+kātat* [1]
broken in pieces, 8646, *šebābîm* [1]
break to pieces, 8689+8689, *šābar[1]+šābar[1]* [1]
break to pieces, 8689, *šābar[1]* [1]
breaks in pieces, 8689, *šābar[1]* [1]
break in pieces, 8691, *šeber[1]* [1]
broke to pieces, 10182, *deqaq* [1]
broken to pieces, 10182, *deqaq* [1]
breaks to pieces, 10671, *re'a'* [1]

PIERCE [8]
pierce, 5918, *nāqab[1]* [2]
pierce, 928, *be-* [1]
pierce, 995+928, *bô'+be-* [1]
pierce, 2726, *ḥālal[2]* [1]
pierce, 4532, *madqērâ* [1]
pierce, 4730, *māḥaṣ* [1]
pierce, 8361, *rāṣa'* [1]

PIERCED [12]
pierced, 4125, *kārâ[1]* [2]
pierced, 995+928, *bô'+be-* [1]
pierced, 1991, *dāqar* [1]
pierced through, 2726, *ḥālal[2]* [1]
pierced, 2726, *ḥālal[2]* [1]
was pierced, 2726, *ḥālal[2]* [1]
pierced, 2737, *ḥālap[2]* [1]
pierced, 3249, *ṭā'an[1]* [1]
pierced, 3655, *yāṣā'* [1]
pierced, 5737+928, *nāḥat+be-* [1]
pierced, 5918, *nāqab[1]* [1]

PIERCES [7]
pierces, 5918, *nāqab[1]* [2]
pierces, 7114, *pālaḥ* [2]
pierces, 2737, *ḥālap[2]* [1]
pierces, 5595, *nāga'* [1]
pierces, 5941, *nāqar* [1]

PIERCING [1]
fastens piercing, 4323, *lāṭaš* [1]

PIETY [3]
piety, 3711, *yir'â* [3]

PIG [2]
pig, 2614, *ḥazîr* [2]

PIG'S [2]
pig's, 2614, *ḥazîr* [2]

PIGEON [3]
pigeon, 3433, *yônâ[1]* [2]
young pigeon, 1578, *gôzāl* [1]

PIGEONS [8]
pigeons, 3433, *yônâ[1]* [8]

PIGS [2]
pigs, 2614, *ḥazîr* [2]

PILDASH [1]
Pildash, 7109, *pildāš* [1]

PILE [9]
pile, 1643, *gal[1]* [2]
pile high, 1540, *gādal* [1]
pile of rocks, 1643, *gal[1]* [1]
pile wood, 1883, *dûr[1]* [1]
pile, 5989, *nātan* [1]
pile up, 6148, *sālal[2]* [1]
grain pile, 6894, *'arēmâ* [1]
pile of rubble, 10470, *newālû* [1]

PILED [7]
piled up, 5893, *nāṣab[1]* [1]
piled, 5989, *nātan* [1]
piled up, 6890, *'āram[1]* [1]
piled, 6913, *'āśâ[1]* [1]
piled, 7392, *ṣābar* [1]
piled up, 7756, *qûm* [1]
piled, 8492, *śîm* [1]

PILES [9]
piles of stone, 1643+5898, *gal[1]+nāṣāṣ[2]* [2]
piles of rubble, 10470, *newālû* [2]
piles of stones, 1643, *gal[1]* [1]
piles, 3880, *kōbed* [1]
piles, 3922, *kûn[1]* [1]
piles, 7393, *ṣibbur* [1]
piles up, 8049, *rābâ[1]* [1]

PILGRIMAGE [3]
pilgrimage, 4472, *māgôr[2]* [2]
pilgrimage, 5019, *mesillâ* [1]

PILHA [1]
Pilha, 7116, *pilḥā'* [1]

PILLAGE [2]
pillage, 1023, *bizzâ* [1]
pillage, 9115, *šāsâ* [1]

PILLAGED [2]
pillaged, 1011, *bûqâ* [1]
pillaged, 1239, *bā'â[1]* [1]

PILLAR [42]
pillar, 6647, *'ammûd* [25]
pillar, 5167, *maṣṣēbâ* [10]
pillar, 5170, *maṣṣebet[2]* [2]
pillar[s], 2257, *-ô* [1]
the pillar[s], 2257, *-ô* [1]
pillar, 5164, *muṣṣāb* [1]
pillar, 5907, *neṣîb[1]* [1]
pillar, 6642, *'ōmed* [1]

PILLARS [43]
pillars, 6647, *'ammûd* [38]

pillars, 2312, *zāwît* [1]
tops of the pillars, 4117, *kaptōr*^{2} [1]
pillars, 5167, *maṣṣēbâ* [1]
sacred pillars, 5167, *maṣṣēbâ* [1]
stone pillars, 5167, *maṣṣēbâ* [1]

PILTAI [1]
Piltai, 7122, *pilṭāy* [1]

PIN [6]
pin, 3845, *yātēd* [3]
pin, 5782, *nākâ* [3]

PINE [18]
pine, 1360, *b*^{e}*rôš* [7]
pine trees, 1360, *b*^{e}*rôš* [4]
pine tree, 1360, *b*^{e}*rôš* [3]
pine away, 581, *'āmal*^{1} [1]
pine, 815, *'ōren*^{1} [1]
spears of pine, 1360, *b*^{e}*rôš* [1]
pine, 6770+1360, *'ēṣ+b*^{e}*rôš* [1]

PINES [4]
pines, 1360, *b*^{e}*rôš* [3]
pines away, 581, *'āmal*^{1} [1]

PINIONS [2]
pinions, 89, *'ebrâ* [2]

PINON [2]
Pinon, 7091, *pînōn* [2]

PIPES [4]
pipes, 10507, *sûmpōn*^{e}*yâ* [3]
pipes, 7574, *ṣantārôt* [1]

PIRAM [1]
Piram, 7231, *pir'ām* [1]

PIRATHON [2]
Pirathon, 7284, *pir'ātôn* [1]
from Pirathon, 7285, *pir'ātônî* [1]

PIRATHONITE [3]
Pirathonite, 7285, *pir'ātônî* [3]

PISGAH [8]
Pisgah, 7171, *pisgâ* [8]

PISHON [1]
Pishon, 7093, *pîšôn* [1]

PISPAH [1]
Pispah, 7183, *pispâ* [1]

PISTACHIO [1]
pistachio nuts, 1063, *boṭnâ* [1]

PIT [62]
pit, 1014, *bôr* [26]
pit, 8846, *šaḥat* [17]
pit, 7074, *paḥat* [7]
pit, 8757, *šûḥâ*^{1} [4]
pit, 931, *b*^{e}*'ēr*^{1} [2]
slimy pit, 1014+8622, *bôr+šā'ôn*^{1} [1]
pit, 1585, *gûmmāṣ* [1]
the pit^{s}, 2023, *-āh* [1]
fire pit, 4509, *m*^{e}*dûrâ* [1]
slime pit, 8846, *šaḥat* [1]
pit, 8864, *šîḥâ* [1]

PITCH [11]
pitch, 2413, *zepet* [3]
pitch, 5742, *nāṭâ* [2]
pitch tent, 182, *'āhal*^{1} [1]
pitch darkness, 854+3125, *'*^{e}*šûn+ḥōšek* [1]
pitch, 4109, *kōper*^{2} [1]
pitch, 5749, *nāṭa'* [1]
pitch, 5989, *nātan* [1]
pitch, 9546, *tāqa'* [1]

PITCH-DARK [1]
pitch-dark, 695, *'āpēl* [1]

PITCHED [15]
pitched, 5742, *nāṭâ* [10]
pitched camp, 2837, *ḥānâ*^{1} [2]
pitched tents, 182, *'āhal*^{1} [1]
pitched, 8492, *śîm* [1]
pitched, 9546, *tāqa'* [1]

PITCHER [1]
pitcher, 3902, *kad* [1]

PITCHERS [3]
pitchers, 7987, *qaśwâ* [3]

PITFALLS [2]
pitfalls, 7074, *paḥat* [1]
pitfalls, 8864, *šîḥâ* [1]

PITHOM [1]
Pithom, 7351, *pitōm* [1]

PITHON [2]
Pithon, 7094, *pîtôn* [2]

PITIED [1]
pitied, 8171, *raḥ*^{a}*mîm* [1]

PITS [5]
full of pits, 931+931, *b*^{e}*'ēr*^{1}*+b*^{e}*'ēr*^{1} [1]
pits, 2987, *ḥur* [1]
miry pits, 4549, *mah*^{a}*mōrôt* [1]
pits, 4838, *mikreh* [1]
pits, 7663, *ṣ*^{e}*rîaḥ* [1]

PITTANCE [1]
pittance, 4202+2104, *lō'+hôn* [1]

PITY [38]
look with pity, 2571+6524, *ḥûs+'ayin*^{1} [6]
pity, 2798, *ḥāmal* [6]
show pity, 2571+6524, *ḥûs+'ayin*^{1} [4]
looked with pity, 2571+6524, *ḥûs+'ayin*^{1} [2]
had pity, 2798, *ḥāmal* [2]
have pity, 2798, *ḥāmal* [2]
have pity, 2858, *ḥānan*^{1} [2]
pity, 365, *'î*^{4} [1]
have pity, 2571, *ḥûs* [1]
showing pity, 2571+6524, *ḥûs+'ayin*^{1} [1]
take pity, 2571, *ḥûs* [1]
allow pity, 2798, *ḥāmal* [1]
take pity, 2798, *ḥāmal* [1]
moves to pity, 2858, *ḥānan*^{1} [1]
pity, 2858, *ḥānan*^{1} [1]
take pity, 2858, *ḥānan*^{1} [1]
have pity, 5714, *nāḥam* [1]
pity, 5714, *nāḥam* [1]
showed pity, 5714, *nāḥam* [1]
pity, 8163, *rāḥam* [1]
pity, 8171, *raḥ*^{a}*mîm* [1]

PLACE [641]
place, 5226, *māqôm* [268]
in place of, 9393, *taḥat*^{1} [24]
in place, 9393, *taḥat*^{1} [23]
high place, 1195, *bāmâ*^{1} [20]
place, *NIH/RPE* [28]
place, 5989, *nātan* [14]
holy place, 7731, *qōdeš* [14]
place, *AIT* [11]
place, 4806, *mākôn* [11]
Most Holy Place, 7731+7731, *qōdeš+qōdeš* [11]
dwelling place, 5438, *miškān* [8]
Most Holy Place, 7731, *qōdeš* [8]
place, 8492, *śîm* [7]
place, 1074, *bayit*^{1} [6]
resting place, 4957, *m*^{e}*nûḥâ* [6]
took place, 2118, *hāyâ* [4]
dwelling place, 5061, *mā'ôn*^{2} [4]
place, 5663, *nûaḥ*^{1} [4]
put in place, 6641, *'āmad* [4]
put in place, 8492, *śîm* [4]
set in place, 3922, *kûn*^{1} [3]
dwelling place, 5226, *māqôm* [3]
spacious place, 5303, *merḥāb* [3]
set in place, 6641, *'āmad* [3]
place, 9393, *taḥat*^{1} [3]
place, 299, *'*^{a}*ḥuzzâ* [2]
take place, 2118, *hāyâ* [2]
moving from place to place, 2143+928+889+2143, *hālak+b*^{e}*-+'*^{a}*šer+hālak* [2]
moving from place to place, 2143, *hālak* [2]
place, 3338, *yād* [2]
from place to place, 4200+5023, *l*^{e}*-*^{1}*+massa'* [2]
place where sets, 4427, *mābô'* [2]
lodging place, 4869, *mālôn* [2]
resting place, 4955, *mānôaḥ*^{1} [2]
place of rest, 4957, *m*^{e}*nûḥâ* [2]
traveled from place to place, 5023, *massa'* [2]
traveling from place to place, 5023, *massa'* [2]
holy place, 5219, *miqdāš* [2]
place to spread, 5427, *mišṭōaḥ* [2]
hiding place, 6260, *sēter* [2]
place, 7756, *qûm* [2]
prominent place, 8031, *rō'š*^{1} [2]
resting place, 8070, *rēbeṣ* [2]
distant place, 8158, *rāḥôq* [2]
place, 8883, *šît*^{1} [2]
that place^{s}, 9004, *šām* [2]
desolate place, 9039, *š*^{e}*māmâ* [2]
place, 419, *'ētān*^{1} [1]
place, 824, *'ereṣ* [1]
place^{s}, 889, *'*^{a}*šer* [1]
some other place^{s}, 889, *'*^{a}*šer* [1]
the place^{s}, 889, *'*^{a}*šer* [1]
place to stand, 892, *'*^{a}*šur* [1]
place, 995, *bô'* [1]
taken place, 995, *bô'* [1]
takes place, 995, *bô'* [1]
Most Holy Place, 1808+7731, *d*^{e}*bîr*^{1}*+qōdeš* [1]
place, 2006, *derek* [1]
the place^{s}, 2021, *ha-* [1]
that place^{s}, 2023, *-āh* [1]
the place^{s}, 2023, *-āh* [1]
surely take place, 2118, *hāyâ* [1]
slaughter takes place, 2222+2223, *hārag+hereg* [1]
dark place, 3125, *ḥōšek* [1]
were settled in place, 3190, *ṭāba'* [1]
place, 3227, *ṭîrâ* [1]
made a place, 3569, *yāsad*^{1} [1]
place, 3656, *yāṣab* [1]
take place, 3656, *yāṣab* [1]
place, 3657, *yāṣag* [1]
took place, 3782, *yāšab* [1]
firm place, 3845, *yātēd* [1]
put in place, 3922, *kûn*^{1} [1]
place, 4030, *kēn*^{5} [1]
hiding place, 4422, *ma'*^{a}*rāb* [1]
place of ambush, 4422, *ma'*^{a}*rāb* [1]
place, 4544, *mah*^{a}*lāk* [1]
certain place, 4595, *mô'ēd* [1]
place of meeting, 4595, *mô'ēd* [1]
place where met, 4595, *mô'ēd* [1]
place where worshiped, 4595, *mô'ēd* [1]
place, 4625, *môrāš*^{1} [1]
left place, 4631, *mûš*^{2} [1]
dwelling place, 4632, *môšāb* [1]
place, 4632, *môšāb* [1]
place to slaughter, 4749, *maṭbēaḥ* [1]
dwelling place, 4806, *mākôn* [1]
place, 4807, *m*^{e}*kônâ* [1]
hollow place, 4847, *maktēš* [1]
place where they stopped for the night, 4869, *mālôn* [1]
place where we stopped for the night, 4869, *mālôn* [1]
place, 4869, *mālôn* [1]
place, 4940, *mimšāq* [1]
place to set, 4955, *mānôaḥ*^{1} [1]
place to rest, 4957, *m*^{e}*nûḥâ* [1]
hiding place, 5039, *mistôr* [1]
dwelling place, 5104, *m*^{e}*'ōnâ* [1]
place of setting, 5115, *ma'*^{a}*rāb*^{2} [1]
place of shelter, 5144, *miplāṭ* [1]
place that overlooks, 5205, *miṣpeh*^{1} [1]
Most Holy Place, 5219+7731, *miqdāš+qōdeš* [1]
proper place, 5226+889+2118+9004, *māqôm+'*^{a}*šer+hāyâ+šām* [1]
place of refuge, 5236, *miqlāṭ* [1]
resting place, 5271, *marbēṣ* [1]
place of repose, 5276, *margē'â* [1]
place where fed, 5337, *mir'eh* [1]
place where dwell, 5438, *miškān* [1]
resting place, 5438, *miškān* [1]
place of judgment, 5477, *mišpāṭ* [1]

proper place, 5477, *mišpāṭ* [1]
place, 5602, *nāgaš* [1]
dwelling place, 5659, *nāweh*[1] [1]
pleasant place, 5659, *nāweh*[1] [1]
place, 5661, *nāwâ*[3] [1]
resting place, 5665, *nôaḥ* [1]
place, 5709, *naḥᵃlâ*[1] [1]
set in place, 5749, *nāṭaʿ* [1]
takes place, 5893, *nāṣab*[1] [1]
put in place, 5989, *nātan* [1]
inmost place, 6258, *sātam* [1]
hiding place, 6259, *sātar* [1]
secret place, 6260, *sēter* [1]
bring to a place of shelter, 6395, *ʿûz* [1]
putting in place, 6641, *ʿāmad* [1]
place where standing, 6642, *ʿōmed* [1]
take place, 6913, *ʿāśâ*[1] [1]
taking place, 6913, *ʿāśâ*[1] [1]
place to escape, 7129, *pᵉlēṭâ* [1]
place of leadership, 7213, *pᵉquddâ* [1]
treasured place, 7621, *ṣāpan* [1]
burial place, 7700, *qeber* [1]
take place, 7756, *qûm* [1]
dwelling place, 8070, *rēbeṣ* [1]
place of abundance, 8122, *rᵉwāyâ* [1]
spacious place, 8144, *raḥab* [1]
lofty place, 8420, *śᵉʾēt*[1] [1]
place, 8441, *śādeh* [1]
place, 8463, *śôrâ* [1]
set in place, 8492, *śîm* [1]
gave a place, 8883, *šît*[1] [1]
in that place[s], 9004, *šām* [1]
place, 9004, *šām* [1]
in the place of, 9393, *taḥat*[1] [1]
take the place of, 9393+2118, *taḥat*[1]*+hāyâ* [1]
take the place of, 9393, *taḥat*[1] [1]
place, 10087, *ʾᵃtar* [1]
place[s], 10089+10135+10193, *bᵉ-+gaw+-ah* [1]
place[s], 10089+10193, *bᵉ-+-ah* [1]
take place, 10201, *hᵃwâ* [1]
were set in place, 10667, *rᵉmâ* [1]

PLACED [67]
placed, 5989, *nātan* [23]
placed, 8492, *śîm* [16]
placed, *NIH/RPE* [5]
placed, 5663, *nûaḥ*[1] [4]
placed, 995, *bôʾ* [2]
placed, 3657, *yāṣag* [2]
placed, *AIT* [1]
placed seal, 3159+928+2597, *ḥātam+bᵉ-+ḥôtām*[1] [1]
placed at birth, 3528, *yālad* [1]
placed, 3585, *yāʿad* [1]
placed a heavy burden, 3877, *kābēd*[1] [1]
placed, 5951, *nāśāʾ* [1]
placed on, 6584, *ʿal*[2] [1]
placed, 7212, *pāqad* [1]
was placed, 8492, *śîm* [1]
placed, 8883, *šît*[1] [1]
placed, 8905, *šākan* [1]
windows placed high, 9209, *šequpîm* [1]
placed, 10314, *yᵉhab* [1]
placed in a high position, 10648, *rᵉbâ* [1]
placed, 10682, *śîm* [1]

PLACES [124]
high places, 1195, *bāmâ*[1] [62]
places, 5226, *māqôm* [12]
places, *AIT* [4]
places, 6991, *pēʾâ*[1] [3]
places, *NIH/RPE* [2]
places trust, 586, *ʾāman*[1] [2]
secret places, 5041, *mistār* [2]
dwelling places, 5438, *miškān* [2]
took places, 6641, *ʿāmad* [2]
the places[s], 889, *ʾᵃšer* [1]
places, 1473, *gᵉbûl* [1]
places[s], 2021, *ha-* [1]
the places[s], 2156, *hēm* [1]
places lying in ruins, 2999, *ḥorbâ* [1]
parched places, 3083, *ḥᵃrērîm* [1]
took places, 3656, *yāṣab* [1]
took places, 3782, *yāšab* [1]
fortified places, 4448, *mibṣār*[1] [1]
places for fire, 4453, *mᵉbaššᵉlôt* [1]
places where lived, 4632, *môšāb* [1]
hiding places, 4676, *maḥᵃbōʾ* [1]
dark places, 4743, *maḥšāk* [1]
places of rest, 4955, *mānôaḥ*[1] [1]
places of rest, 4957, *mᵉnûḥâ* [1]
hiding places, 5041, *mistār* [1]
places, 5096, *maʿᵃmād* [1]
rough places, 5112, *maʿᵃqaššîm* [1]
holy places, 5219, *miqdāš* [1]
watering places, 5393, *mašʾāb* [1]
places for spreading, 5427, *mišṭôaḥ* [1]
places where turned loose, 5448, *mišlāḥ* [1]
dwelling places, 5659, *nāweh*[1] [1]
hiding places, 6260, *sēter* [1]
places, 6551, *ʿîr*[1] [1]
stood in places, 6641, *ʿāmad* [1]
places, 6642, *ʿōmed* [1]
broken places, 7288, *pereṣ*[1] [1]
exposed places, 7460, *ṣāḥîaḥ* [1]
rugged places, 8221, *rekes* [1]
in such places[s], 9004, *šām* [1]
places, 10087, *ʾᵃtar* [1]
nesting places, 10709, *šᵉkan* [1]

PLACING [3]
placing, 995, *bôʾ* [1]
placing, 8883, *šît*[1] [1]
placing, 10682, *śîm* [1]

PLAGUE [80]
plague, 1822, *deber*[1] [43]
plague, 4487, *maggēpâ* [19]
plague, 5598, *negep* [6]
plague, 7776, *qeṭeb* [2]
plague, *NIH/RPE* [1]
plague, 1815, *dābaq* [1]
deadly plague, 4638, *māwet* [1]
plague, 4638, *māwet* [1]
plague, 4804, *makkâ* [1]
plague, 5596, *negaʿ* [1]
plague, 5597, *nāgap* [1]
strike with a plague, 5597, *nāgap* [1]
struck with a plague, 5597, *nāgap* [1]
plague, 8103, *rādap* [1]

PLAGUED [2]
are plagued, 5595, *nāgaʿ* [1]
plagued, 5595, *nāgaʿ* [1]

PLAGUES [6]
plagues, 1822, *deber*[1] [3]
plagues, 4804, *makkâ* [2]
plagues, 4487, *maggēpâ* [1]

PLAIN [25]
plain, 3971, *kikkār* [10]
plain, 1326, *biqʿâ* [9]
plain, 6677, *ʿēmeq* [2]
plain, 824+6677, *ʾereṣ+ʿēmeq* [1]
make plain, 930, *bāʾar* [1]
plain, 4793, *mîšôr* [1]
plain, 10117, *biqʿâ* [1]

PLAINS [20]
plains, 6858, *ʿᵃrābâ*[2] [17]
plains, 4793, *mîšôr* [2]
plains, 6677, *ʿēmeq* [1]

PLAN [26]
plan, 1821, *dābār* [4]
plan, 3108, *ḥāšab* [4]
plan, 6783, *ʿēṣâ*[1] [4]
plan, 4742, *maḥᵃšābâ* [3]
plan, 9322, *tabnît* [2]
plan, 606, *ʾāmar*[1] [1]
plan, 1948, *dāmâ*[1] [1]
plan, 2372, *zāmam* [1]
plan, 2925, *ḥēpeś* [1]
plan, 3086, *ḥāraš*[1] [1]
plan, 4659, *mᵉzimmâ* [1]
plan, 5477, *mišpāṭ* [1]
plan, 6051, *sôd* [1]
plan, 9422, *toknît* [1]

PLANE [2]
plane trees, 6895, *ʿermôn* [2]

PLANKS [2]
planks, 7521, *ṣēlāʿ*[1] [1]
planks, 8444, *śᵉdērâ* [1]

PLANNED [16]
planned, 3670, *yāṣar* [4]
planned, 3619, *yāʿaṣ* [3]
planned, 6783+3619, *ʿēṣâ*[1]*+yāʿaṣ* [2]
planned, 1948, *dāmâ*[1] [1]
planned evil, 2372, *zāmam* [1]
planned, 2372, *zāmam* [1]
planned, 3108, *ḥāšab* [1]
things planned, 4742, *maḥᵃšābâ* [1]
planned, 6783, *ʿēṣâ*[1] [1]
planned, 10575, *ʿᵃšat* [1]

PLANNING [4]
planning, 3108, *ḥāšab* [2]
planning, 3113, *ḥešbôn*[1] [1]
planning, 6783+3619, *ʿēṣâ*[1]*+yāʿaṣ* [1]

PLANS [38]
plans, 4742, *maḥᵃšābâ* [9]
plans, 6783, *ʿēṣâ*[1] [9]
plans, 9322, *tabnît* [3]
plans, *NIH/RPE* [2]
the plans[s], 889, *ʾᵃšer* [1]
plans, 1335, *bāqaš* [1]
plans, 1821, *dābār* [1]
plans[s], 2179, *hēnnâ*[2] [1]
plans, 2365, *zimmâ*[1] [1]
plans, 2373, *zāmām* [1]
devise plans, 3108, *ḥāšab* [1]
make plans, 3108+4742, *ḥāšab+maḥᵃšābâ* [1]
plans, 3108, *ḥāšab* [1]
makes plans, 3619, *yāʿaṣ* [1]
made plans, 3922, *kûn*[1] [1]
plans, 4600, *môʿēṣâ* [1]
plans have, 4742+3108, *maḥᵃšābâ+ḥāšab* [1]
plans, 5119, *maʿᵃrāk* [1]
plans, 6955, *ʿeštōnet* [1]

PLANT [53]
plant, 5749, *nāṭaʿ* [28]
plant, 2445, *zāraʿ* [9]
plant, 6912, *ʿēśeb* [4]
plant, 9278, *šātal* [2]
plant seed, 2445, *zāraʿ* [1]
plant with seed, 2445, *zāraʿ* [1]
plant, 2446+2445, *zeraʿ+zāraʿ* [1]
plant, 2446, *zeraʿ* [1]
plant, 5750, *neṭaʿ* [1]
plant, 5989, *nātan* [1]
plant life, 6770, *ʿēṣ* [1]
plant, 7542, *ṣemaḥ* [1]
well-watered plant, 8183, *rāṭōb* [1]
plant, 8492, *śîm* [1]

PLANTED [39]
planted, 5749, *nāṭaʿ* [19]
planted, 9278, *šātal* [5]
planted, 2445, *zāraʿ* [4]
planted crops, 2445, *zāraʿ* [2]
planted, 4760, *maṭṭāʿ* [2]
planted, 8492, *śîm* [2]
be planted, 2445, *zāraʿ* [1]
planted, 3086, *ḥāraš*[1] [1]
are planted, 5749, *nāṭaʿ* [1]
been planted, 9278, *šātal* [1]
is planted, 9278, *šātal* [1]

PLANTER [1]
planter, 5432+2446, *māšak+zeraʿ* [1]

PLANTING [4]
planting, 4760, *maṭṭāʿ* [2]
planting, 2445, *zāraʿ* [1]
planting, 2446, *zeraʿ* [1]

PLANTS [19]
plants, 6912, *ʿēśeb* [8]
plants, *NIH/RPE* [1]
mandrake plants, 1859, *dûdāʾîm* [1]
plants, 3764, *yereq* [1]

plants, 5745, *nāṭîaʿ* [1]
plants, 5749, *nāṭaʿ* [1]
plants, 5750, *neṭaʿ* [1]
plants, 6868, *ʿārâ^2* [1]
tender plants, 6912, *ʿēśeb* [1]
lotus plants, 7365, *ṣeʾ^{e}lîm* [1]
plants, 8945, *š^{e}lāḥîm* [1]
plants, 10572, *ʿ^{a}śab* [1]

PLASTER [5]

plaster, 8487, *śîd^2* [2]
plaster, 3212, *ṭûaḥ* [1]
plaster, 6760, *ʿāpār* [1]
plaster, 10142, *gîr* [1]

PLASTERED [3]

been plastered, 3212, *ṭûaḥ* [1]
plastered, 3212, *ṭûaḥ* [1]
plastered over, 3220, *ṭāḥaḥ* [1]

PLATE [16]

plate, 7883, *q^{e}ʿārâ* [13]
plate, 7488, *ṣîṣ^1* [3]

PLATEAU [10]

plateau, 4793, *mîšôr* [9]
plateau, 824+4793, *ʾereṣ+mîšôr* [1]

PLATES [4]

plates, 7883, *q^{e}ʿārâ* [4]

PLATFORM [3]

the platforms, 2257, *-ô* [1]
platform, 3963, *kiyyôr* [1]
high platform, 4463, *migdāl^1* [1]

PLAY [14]

play, *NIH/RPE* [4]
play the harp, 5594, *nāgan* [2]
play, 5594+928+3338, *nāgan+b^e-+yād* [2]
play, 5594, *nāgan* [2]
play, 8471, *śāḥaq* [1]
play, 9130, *šāʿaʿ^2* [1]
play the judge, 9149+9149, *šāpaṭ+šāpaṭ* [1]
play, 9530, *tāpaś* [1]

PLAYED [3]

played, *NIH/RPE* [1]
played, 2955, *ḥaṣṣar* [1]
played the fool, 5571, *nābal^2* [1]

PLAYING [10]

playing, *NIH/RPE* [3]
playing the harp, 5594+928+3338, *nāgan+b^e-+yād* [2]
playing, 2727, *ḥālal^3* [1]
playing, 5594, *nāgan* [1]
playing, 8471, *śāḥaq* [1]
playing, 9048, *šāmaʿ* [1]
playing tambourines, 9528, *tāpap* [1]

PLAYS [2]

plays an instrument, 5594, *nāgan* [1]
plays, 5594, *nāgan* [1]

PLEA [24]

plea, 9382, *t^{e}ḥinnâ^1* [10]
plea, 7754, *qôl* [3]
plea, 8262, *rinnâ^1* [2]
plea for mercy, 9382, *t^{e}ḥinnâ^1* [2]
plea, *NIH/RPE* [1]
plea, 1819, *dābar^2* [1]
yield to the plea, 2011, *dāraš* [1]
press plea, 8104, *rāhab* [1]
plea, 8191, *rîbâ* [1]
empty plea, 8736, *šāwʾ* [1]
plea, 9525, *t^{e}pillâ* [1]

PLEAD [18]

plead, 2858, *ḥānan^1* [3]
plead, 1906, *dîn^1* [2]
plead, 7003, *pāgaʿ* [2]
plead, 606, *ʾāmar^1* [1]
plead with, 1335, *bāqaš* [1]
plead for mercy, 2858, *ḥānan^1* [1]
make plead, 7003, *pāgaʿ* [1]
plead, 7137, *pālal^2* [1]
plead case, 8189, *rîb^1* [1]
plead cause, 8189, *rîb^1* [1]
plead the case, 8189, *rîb^1* [1]
plead, 8189, *rîb^1* [1]
plead for relief, 8775, *šāwaʿ* [1]
plead, 10114, *b^{e}ʿâ* [1]

PLEADED [5]

pleaded, 2858, *ḥānan^1* [2]
pleaded with, 1335, *bāqaš* [1]
pleaded, 1335, *bāqaš* [1]
pleaded, 1819, *dābar^2* [1]

PLEADING [3]

pleading, 609, *ʾēmer^1* [1]
pleading, 5877+9382, *nāpal+t^{e}ḥinnâ^1* [1]
pleading, 9384, *taḥ^{a}nûn* [1]

PLEADS [5]

pleads, *NIH/RPE* [1]
pleads, 1819, *dābar^2* [1]
pleads, 3519, *yākaḥ* [1]
pleads, 8189, *rîb^1* [1]
pleads case, 9149, *šāpaṭ* [1]

PLEAS [2]

respond to pleas, 6983, *ʿātar^1* [1]
pleas, 9382, *t^{e}ḥinnâ^1* [1]

PLEASANT [18]

pleasant, 5833, *nāʿîm^1* [4]
pleasant, 2775, *ḥemdâ* [3]
pleasant, 5838, *nāʿēm* [2]
pleasant, 5840, *nōʿam* [2]
pleasant, 2747, *ḥālāq^1* [1]
pleasant, 2774, *ḥemed* [1]
pleasant, 3202, *ṭôb^2* [1]
pleasant, 5518, *mātēq* [1]
pleasant place, 5659, *nāweh^1* [1]
pleasant, 6844, *ʿārab^3* [1]
pleasant, 9503, *taʿ^{a}nûg* [1]

PLEASANTNESS [1]

pleasantness, 5518, *mātēq* [1]

PLEASE [88]

please, 5528, *nāʾ^1* [59]
please, 2914, *ḥēpeṣ* [5]
please, 1065, *bî* [3]
please, 3202+928+6524, *ṭôb^2+b^e-+ʿayin^1* [2]
please, 3202, *ṭôb^2* [2]
please, 3837+928+6524, *yāšar+b^e-+ʿayin^1* [2]
please, 6844, *ʿārab^3* [2]
please, 8354, *rāṣâ^1* [2]
please, 205, *ʾawwâ* [1]
please, 561, *ʾim* [1]
please, 1065+5528, *bî+nāʾ^1* [1]
please, 3202+2256+3838+928+6524, *ṭôb^2+w^e+yāšār^1+b^e-+ʿayin^1* [1]
please, 3283+5528, *yāʾal^2+nāʾ^1* [1]
please, 3512, *yāṭab* [1]
please, 3838+928+6524, *yāšār^1+b^e-+ʿayin^1* [1]
please, 8011, *rāʾâ^1* [1]
not please, 8317+928+6524, *rāʿaʿ^1+b^e-+ʿayin^1* [1]
please, 8356, *rāṣôn* [1]
please, 8464, *śûś* [1]

PLEASED [55]

pleased, 2911, *ḥāpēṣ^1* [9]
pleased, 3512+928+6524, *yāṭab+b^e-+ʿayin^1* [7]
pleased with, 5162+2834+928+6524, *māṣāʾ+ḥēn^1+b^e-+ʿayin^1* [5]
pleased with, 8354, *rāṣâ^1* [4]
pleased, 8356, *rāṣôn* [4]
pleased, 3283, *yāʾal^2* [3]
pleased, 8354, *rāṣâ^1* [3]
pleased, 3837+928+6524, *yāšar+b^e-+ʿayin^1* [2]
pleased, 8523, *śāmaḥ* [2]
pleased, 10739, *š^{e}par* [2]
pleased, *NIH/RPE* [1]
pleased, 928+6524+3202, *b^e-+ʿayin^1+ṭôb^2* [1]
pleased, 2914, *ḥēpeṣ* [1]
pleased, 3201+928+6524, *ṭôb^1+b^e-+ʿayin^1* [1]
pleased with, 3202+928+6524, *ṭôb^2+b^e-+ʿayin^1* [1]
pleased, 3202+928+6524, *ṭôb^2+b^e-+ʿayin^1* [1]
pleased with, 3512+928+6524, *yāṭab+b^e-+ʿayin^1* [1]
pleased, 3512, *yāṭab* [1]
pleased with, 3837+928+6524, *yāšar+b^e-+ʿayin^1* [1]
pleased, 3838+928+6524, *yāšār^1+b^e-+ʿayin^1* [1]
pleased, 5883, *nepeš* [1]
pleased with, 5951+2834+928+6524, *nāśāʾ+ḥēn^1+b^e-+ʿayin^1* [1]
pleased, 8464, *śûś* [1]
pleased, 8525, *śimḥâ* [1]

PLEASES [34]

pleases, 3201, *ṭôb^1* [7]
pleases, 3202, *ṭôb^2* [6]
pleases, 2911, *ḥāpēṣ^1* [5]
pleases, 3202+928+6524, *ṭôb^2+b^e-+ʿayin^1* [5]
pleases, 8356, *rāṣôn* [4]
as much as pleases, 5522+3338, *mattat+yād* [2]
pleases, 203, *ʾāwâ^1* [1]
pleases, 205, *ʾawwâ* [1]
pleases, 3512+928+6524, *yāṭab+b^e-+ʿayin^1* [1]
pleases, 10294, *ṭāb* [1]
pleases, 10605, *ṣ^{e}bâ* [1]

PLEASING [52]

pleasing, 5767, *nîḥōaḥ* [39]
pleasing, 3202, *ṭôb^2* [2]
pleasing, 2773, *ḥāmad* [1]
pleasing, 3201, *ṭôb^1* [1]
pleasing, 4718, *maḥmād* [1]
pleasing, 5833, *nāʿîm^1* [1]
pleasing, 5838, *nāʿēm* [1]
pleasing, 5840, *nōʿam* [1]
pleasing, 6844, *ʿārab^3* [1]
pleasing, 8354, *rāṣâ^1* [1]
pleasing, 8356, *rāṣôn* [1]
pleasing, 9294, *taʾ^{a}wâ^1* [1]
pleasing, 10478, *nîḥôaḥ* [1]

PLEASURE [27]

pleasure, 8525, *śimḥâ* [5]
pleasure, 2914, *ḥēpeṣ* [3]
take pleasure, 2911, *ḥāpēṣ^1* [2]
pleasure, 8356, *rāṣôn* [2]
find pleasure, 2911, *ḥāpēṣ^1* [1]
finds pleasure, 2911, *ḥāpēṣ^1* [1]
found pleasure, 2911, *ḥāpēṣ^1* [1]
have pleasure, 2911, *ḥāpēṣ^1* [1]
pleasure, 2911, *ḥāpēṣ^1* [1]
take any pleasure in, 2911+2911, *ḥāpēṣ^1+ḥāpēṣ^1* [1]
takes pleasure in, 2913, *ḥāpēṣ^3* [1]
pleasure, 6366, *ʿednâ* [1]
found pleasure, 6844, *ʿārab^3* [1]
take pleasure in, 8354, *rāṣâ^1* [1]
take pleasure, 8354, *rāṣâ^1* [1]
good pleasure, 8356, *rāṣôn* [1]
pleasure, 8468, *ś^{e}ḥôq* [1]
take pleasure, 8523, *śāmaḥ* [1]
pleasure, 10739, *š^{e}par* [1]

PLEASURES [1]

pleasures, 5833, *nāʿîm^1* [1]

PLEDGE [30]

pledge, 674, *ʾissār* [6]
pledge, 6860, *ʿērābôn* [3]
hold in pledge, 2471, *ḥābal^1* [2]
pledge, 6287, *ʿ^{a}bôṭ* [2]
strikes in pledge, 9546, *tāqaʿ* [2]
take as a pledge, 2471+2471, *ḥābal^1+ḥābal^1* [1]
take as a pledge, 2471, *ḥābal^1* [1]
take in pledge, 2471, *ḥābal^1* [1]
taken in pledge, 2471, *ḥābal^1* [1]
require a pledge for a loan, 2478+2471, *ḥ^{a}bōl+ḥābal^1* [1]
what took in pledge for a loan, 2478, *ḥ^{a}bōl* [1]
what took in pledge, 2478, *ḥ^{a}bōl* [1]
what took in pledge, 2481, *ḥ^{a}bōlâ* [1]
gave in pledge, 5989, *nātan* [1]
given in pledge, 5989, *nātan* [1]
offering as a pledge, 6287, *ʿ^{a}bôṭ* [1]
had pledge, 6641, *ʿāmad* [1]
pledge, 6842, *ʿārab^1* [1]

strike hands in pledge, 9364, *tôqᵉʿîm* [1]
struck in pledge, 9546, *tāqaʿ* [1]

PLEDGED [10]
pledged to be married, 829, *ʾāraś* [4]
is pledged to be married, 829, *ʾāraś* [1]
pledged, 829, *ʾāraś* [1]
pledged to marry, 4374, *lāqaḥ* [1]
pledged, 5989+3338, *nātan+yād* [1]
pledged, 6641, *ʿāmad* [1]
pledged on oath, 8678, *šābaʿ* [1]

PLEDGES [5]
pledges, 674, *ʾissār* [5]

PLEIADES [3]
Pleiades, 3966, *kîmâ* [3]

PLENTIFUL [6]
plentiful, 4200+8044, *lᵉ-*[1]*+rōb* [4]
make plentiful, 8049, *rābâ*[1] [1]
plentiful, 9045, *šāmēn*[2] [1]

PLENTIFULLY [1]
plentifully, 4200+7859, *lᵉ-*[1]*+qōmeṣ* [1]

PLENTY [13]
plenty, 8041, *rab*[1] [3]
plenty, 4200+8044, *lᵉ-*[1]*+rōb* [2]
plenty, *NIH/RPE* [1]
have plenty to eat, 430+430, *ʾākal+ʾākal* [1]
plenty, 1896, *day* [1]
plenty of room, 8146+3338, *rāḥāb*[1]*+yād* [1]
enjoy plenty, 8425, *śābaʿ* [1]
had plenty, 8425, *śābaʿ* [1]
have plenty, 8425, *śābaʿ* [1]
plenty, 8565, *śēpeq* [1]

PLIGHT [2]
plight, *NIH/RPE* [2]

PLOT [33]
plot, 3108, *ḥāšab* [5]
plot, 2047, *hāgâ*[1] [3]
plot, 3086, *ḥāraš*[1] [3]
plot, 2372, *zāmam* [2]
plot of ground, 2750, *ḥēleq*[2] [2]
plot of ground, 2754, *ḥelqâ*[2] [2]
plot, 2754, *ḥelqâ*[2] [2]
plot, 3619, *yāʿaṣ* [2]
plot, 6870, *ʿᵃrûgâ* [2]
plot, *NIH/RPE* [1]
plot, 1821, *dābār* [1]
the plot[s], 2023, *-āh* [1]
plot, 2750, *ḥēleq*[2] [1]
plot, 2924, *ḥāpaś* [1]
plot against, 3108+928+4222, *ḥāšab+bᵉ-+lēbāb* [1]
plot, 5742, *nāṭâ* [1]
plot, 6168, *sāman* [1]
plot, 6783, *ʿēṣâ*[1] [1]
plot, 7188, *pāʿal* [1]

PLOTS [11]
plots, 3108, *ḥāšab* [4]
plots, 4742, *maḥᵃšābâ* [3]
plots, 3086, *ḥāraš*[1] [1]
plots, 4125, *kārâ*[1] [1]
plots, 6783, *ʿēṣâ*[1] [1]
plots, 9048, *šāmaʿ* [1]

PLOTTED [14]
plotted, 8003, *qāšar* [7]
plotted, 3619, *yāʿaṣ* [2]
plotted, 1948, *dāmâ*[1] [1]
plotted, 3108+4742, *ḥāšab+maḥᵃšābâ* [1]
plotted, 3108, *ḥāšab* [1]
plotted, 3619+6783, *yāʿaṣ+ʿēṣâ*[1] [1]
plotted, 5792, *nākal* [1]

PLOTTING [5]
plotting, 3108, *ḥāšab* [3]
plotting, 3086+2021+8288, *ḥāraš*[1]*+ha-+rāʿâ*[3] [1]
plotting, 4742, *maḥᵃšābâ* [1]

PLOW [7]
plow, 3086, *ḥāraš*[1] [6]
plow, *NIH/RPE* [1]

PLOWED [8]
be plowed, 3086, *ḥāraš*[1] [2]
plowed, 3086, *ḥāraš*[1] [2]
plowed, 9439, *telem* [2]
be plowed, 6268, *ʿābad* [1]
been plowed, 6268, *ʿābad* [1]

PLOWING [5]
plowing, 3086, *ḥāraš*[1] [2]
plowing, 1330, *bāqār* [1]
plowing season, 3045, *ḥārîš* [1]
plowing, 3045, *ḥārîš* [1]

PLOWMAN [1]
plowman, 3086, *ḥāraš*[1] [1]

PLOWMEN [1]
plowmen, 3086, *ḥāraš*[1] [1]

PLOWS [2]
plows, 3086, *ḥāraš*[1] [1]
plows, 7114, *pālaḥ* [1]

PLOWSHARES [5]
plowshares, 908, *ʾēt*[3] [3]
plowshares, 4739, *maḥᵃrēšâ* [2]

PLUCKED [1]
freshly plucked, 3273, *ṭārāp* [1]

PLUMAGE [2]
plumage, 5681, *nôṣâ* [2]

PLUMB [8]
plumb line, 643, *ʾᵃnāk* [3]
plumb line, 5487, *mišqelet* [2]
plumb line, 74+974, *ʾeben+bᵉdîl* [1]
plumb line, 74, *ʾeben* [1]
true to plumb, 643, *ʾᵃnāk* [1]

PLUNDER [104]
plunder, 8965, *šālāl* [49]
plunder, 1020, *baz* [15]
plunder, 1024, *bāzaz* [11]
plunder, 1023, *bizzâ* [7]
plunder, 8964, *šālal*[2] [4]
plunder, 4917, *malqôaḥ* [2]
plunder, 8964+8965, *šālal*[2]*+šālāl* [2]
plunder, 1024+1020, *bāzaz+baz* [1]
taken plunder, 1024, *bāzaz* [1]
taking as plunder, 1024, *bāzaz* [1]
took as plunder, 1024, *bāzaz* [1]
plunder, 1299, *beṣaʿ* [1]
plunder, 1611, *gᵉzēlâ* [1]
plunder, 2805, *ḥāmās* [1]
plunder, 5178, *māṣôd*[1] [1]
plunder, 5911, *nāṣal* [1]
plunder, 7294, *pereq* [1]
plunder, 7693+5883, *qābaʿ+nepeš* [1]
plunder, 7693, *qābaʿ* [1]
share of plunder, 8965, *šālāl* [1]
plunder, 9116, *šāsas* [1]

PLUNDERED [27]
plundered, 1020, *baz* [4]
plundered, 8964, *šālal*[2] [4]
plundered, 9115, *šāsâ* [4]
plundered, 1024, *bāzaz* [3]
plundered, 5468, *mᵉšissâ* [3]
plundered, 9116, *šāsas* [3]
plundered, 1023, *bizzâ* [1]
be plundered, 1024, *bāzaz* [1]
totally plundered, 1024+1024, *bāzaz+bāzaz* [1]
plundered, 4433, *mᵉbûqâ* [1]
plundered, 5911, *nāṣal* [1]
plundered, 8965, *šālāl* [1]

PLUNDERERS [2]
plunderers, 1024, *bāzaz* [1]
plunderers, 9115, *šāsâ* [1]

PLUNGE [4]
plunge, 3188, *ṭābal* [1]
plunge, 5782, *nākâ* [1]
plunge, 5877, *nāpal* [1]
plunge, 8175, *rāḥaṣ* [1]

PLUNGED [3]
plunged, 9546, *tāqaʿ* [2]
plunged, 5782, *nākâ* [1]

PLUS [2]
plus, *NIH/RPE* [2]

PLY [1]
ply her trade, 2388, *zānâ*[1] [1]

POCKET [1]
pocket, 4090, *kap* [1]

PODS [1]
seed pods, 1807, *dibyônîm* [1]

POETS [1]
poets, 5439, *māšal*[1] [1]

POINT [17]
point, *NIH/RPE* [5]
at the point of, 4200, *lᵉ-*[1] [2]
point of birth, 5402, *mašbēr* [2]
gleaming point, 1398, *bārāq*[1] [1]
highest point, 1726+5294, *gap*[1]*+mārôm* [1]
to the point of, 4200, *lᵉ-*[1] [1]
point, 4259, *lehābâ* [1]
highest point, 5294, *mārôm* [1]
at the point of, 6330, *ʿad*[2] [1]
to the point of, 6330, *ʿad*[2] [1]
point, 7632, *ṣippōren* [1]

POINTING [1]
pointing, 8938, *šālaḥ* [1]

POINTS [1]
points, 5226, *māqôm* [1]

POISED [2]
hang poised, 5146, *miplāś* [1]
poised, 6969, *ʿātîd* [1]

POISON [7]
poison, 8032, *rōʾš*[2] [5]
poison, 2779, *ḥēmâ* [2]

POISONED [3]
poisoned, 8032, *rōʾš*[2] [3]

POISONOUS [1]
poisonous weeds, 8032, *rōʾš*[2] [1]

POISONS [1]
poisons, 7301, *pāraš*[2] [1]

POKERETH-HAZZEBAIM [2]
Pokereth-Hazzebaim, 7097, *pōkeret haṣṣᵉbāyîm* [2]

POLE [20]
Asherah pole, 895, *ʾᵃšērâ* [14]
pole[s], 5145, *mipleṣet* [2]
pole, 5812, *nēs* [2]
pole, 4573, *môṭ*[2] [1]
pole, 7771, *qôrâ* [1]

POLES [56]
poles, 964, *bad*[2] [31]
Asherah poles, 895, *ʾᵃšērâ* [22]
carrying poles, 964, *bad*[2] [2]
poles, 4574, *môṭâ* [1]

POLISH [1]
polish, 5347, *māraq* [1]

POLISHED [9]
polished, 5307, *māraṭ* [5]
polished, 1406, *bārar*[2] [1]
polished, 5347, *māraq* [1]
polished, 6952, *ʿešet* [1]
polished, 7410, *ṣāhab* [1]

POLLUTE [1]
pollute, 2866, *ḥānēp*[1] [1]

POLLUTED [2]
polluted, 5614, *niddâ* [1]
polluted, 8845, *šāḥat* [1]

POLLUTES [1]
pollutes, 2866, *ḥānēp*[1] [1]

POMEGRANATE [5]
pomegranate, 8232, *rimmôn*[1] [4]
pomegranate tree, 8232, *rimmôn*[1] [1]

POMEGRANATES [24]
pomegranates, 8232, *rimmôn*[1] [24]

POMP [4]
pomp, 3883, *kābôd*[1] [3]
pomp, 1454, *gā'ôn* [1]

PONDER [4]
ponder, 1067, *bîn* [2]
ponder, 2047, *hāgâ*[1] [1]
ponder, 8505, *śākal*[1] [1]

PONDERED [4]
pondered, 264, *'āzan*[2] [1]
are pondered, 2011, *dāraš* [1]
pondered, 4888, *mālak*[2] [1]
pondered, 8492, *śîm* [1]

PONDERS [1]
ponders, 8492, *śîm* [1]

PONDS [2]
ponds, 106, *'ᵃgam*[1] [2]

POOL [17]
pool, 1391, *bᵉrēkâ* [13]
pool, 106+4784, *'ᵃgam*[1]*+mayim* [1]
pool, 106, *'ᵃgam*[1] [1]
pool, 1391+4784, *bᵉrēkâ+mayim* [1]
pool, 4784, *mayim* [1]

POOLS [6]
pools, 106, *'ᵃgam*[1] [3]
pools, 1391, *bᵉrēkâ* [2]
pools, 6524, *'ayin*[1] [1]

POOR [135]
poor, 6714, *'ānî* [39]
poor, 1924, *dal*[2] [36]
poor, 8133, *rûš* [20]
poor, 36, *'ebyôn* [14]
poor, 4575, *mûk* [4]
poor, 5014, *miskēn* [4]
poor, 6705, *'ānāw* [4]
poor, 8273, *ra'*[1] [3]
poor, *NIH/RPE* [1]
poorest of the poor, 1147+1924, *bᵉkōr+dal*[2] [1]
become poor, 3769, *yāraš*[1] [1]
grow poor, 3769, *yāraš*[1] [1]
poor, 3769, *yāraš*[1] [1]
poor to pay, 4575, *mûk* [1]
poor, 4728, *maḥsôr* [1]
too poor, 6123, *sākan*[2] [1]
pretends to be poor, 8133, *rûš* [1]
poor, 8136, *rāzeh* [1]
poor, 9135, *šō'ār* [1]

POOREST [6]
poorest, 1930, *dallâ*[2] [5]
poorest of the poor, 1147+1924, *bᵉkōr+dal*[2] [1]

POPLAR [3]
poplar, 4242, *libneh* [2]
poplar trees, 6857, *'ᵃrābâ*[1] [1]

POPLARS [4]
poplars, 6857, *'ᵃrābâ*[1] [3]
poplars, 6857+5707, *'ᵃrābâ*[1]*+naḥal*[1] [1]

POPULACE [1]
populace, 2162, *hāmôn* [1]

POPULATION [1]
population, 6639, *'am*[2] [1]

PORATHA [1]
Poratha, 7054, *pôrātā'* [1]

PORCH [2]
temple porch, 395, *'êlām* [1]
porch, 4997, *misdᵉrôn* [1]

PORPHYRY [1]
porphyry, 985, *bahaṭ* [1]

PORT [1]
that port[s], 9576, *taršîš*[1] [1]

PORTENT [2]
portent, 4603, *môpēt* [2]

PORTICO [44]
portico, 395, *'êlām* [44]

PORTICOES [1]
porticoes, 395, *'êlām* [1]

PORTION [72]
portion, 2750, *ḥēleq*[2] [14]
portion, *AIT* [13]
portion, 9556, *tᵉrûmâ* [12]
memorial portion, 260, *'azkārâ* [6]
portion, *NIH/RPE* [4]
portion, 2475, *hebel*[2] [3]
portion, 2754, *ḥelqâ*[2] [2]
portion, 4987, *mᵉnāt* [2]
double portion, 5467, *mišneh* [2]
give a portion, 2745, *ḥālaq*[2] [1]
prescribed portion, 2976, *ḥōq* [1]
portion, 3338, *yād* [1]
assigned portion, 4595, *mô'ēd* [1]
portion, 4950, *mānâ*[2] [1]
portion, 5368, *maś'ēt* [1]
portion, 5419, *mišḥâ*[2] [1]
portion, 5421, *mošḥâ*[2] [1]
the sacred portion[s], 5647, *-nû*[2] [1]
portion, 7023, *peh* [1]
sacred portion, 7731, *qōdeš* [1]
present a portion, 8123, *rûm*[1] [1]
portion as a special gift, 9556, *tᵉrûmâ* [1]
special portion, 9556, *tᵉrûmâ* [1]

PORTIONS [23]
fat portions, 2693, *ḥēleb*[1] [7]
portions, 2750, *ḥēleq*[2] [4]
portions, 4987, *mᵉnāt* [3]
allotted portions, 1474, *gᵉbûlâ* [1]
portions, 1598, *gôrāl* [1]
portions, 2475, *hebel*[2] [1]
portions, 2976, *ḥōq* [1]
portions, 4713, *mahᵃlōqet* [1]
portions of food, 4950, *mānâ*[2] [1]
portions of meat, 4950, *mānâ*[2] [1]
portions, 4950, *mānâ*[2] [1]
portions, 5368, *maś'ēt* [1]

PORTRAYED [3]
portrayed, 2977, *ḥāqâ* [2]
portrayed, 2980, *ḥāqaq* [1]

POSES [1]
poses as a prophet, 5547, *nābā'* [1]

POSITION [17]
position as queen mother, 1485, *gᵉbîrâ* [2]
position, 4030, *kēn*[5] [2]
royal position, 4895, *malkût* [2]
strengthen position, 2616, *ḥāzaq* [1]
strengthening his own position, 2616, *ḥāzaq* [1]
position as king, 4895, *malkût* [1]
position, 5096, *ma'ᵃmād* [1]
position, 5226, *māqôm* [1]
position, 5482, *mašqeh*[1] [1]
position, 6641, *'āmad* [1]
in position, 9393, *taḥat*[1] [1]
position, 9393, *taḥat*[1] [1]
placed in a high position, 10648, *rᵉbâ* [1]
high position, 10650, *rᵉbû* [1]

POSITIONS [22]
took up positions, 6885, *'ārak* [5]
took up positions, 2837, *ḥānâ*[1] [3]
take positions, 3656, *yāṣab* [2]
take up positions, 6885, *'ārak* [2]
took up concealed positions, 741, *'ārab* [1]
assigned to positions, 3569, *yāsad*[1] [1]
take up positions, 3656, *yāṣab* [1]
battle positions, 5120, *ma'ᵃrākâ* [1]
positions, 5226, *māqôm* [1]
high positions, 5294, *mārôm* [1]
positions, 5466, *mišmeret* [1]
positions, 6642, *'ōmed* [1]
had take up positions, 8492, *śîm* [1]
take up positions, 8492, *śîm* [1]

POSSESS [62]
possess, 3769, *yāraš*[1] [48]
possess, *NIH/RPE* [4]
possess, 299, *'ᵃḥuzzâ* [4]
possess, 3772, *yᵉruššâ* [1]
possess, 5162, *māṣā'* [1]
possess, 5706, *nāḥal* [1]
allow to possess, 5989, *nātan* [1]
possess, 10089+10311, *bᵉ-+yad* [1]
possess, 10277, *ḥᵃsan* [1]

POSSESSED [5]
possessed, 3769, *yāraš*[1] [2]
possessed, 5706, *nāḥal* [1]
possessed, 7871, *qinyān* [1]
possessed, 10277, *ḥᵃsan* [1]

POSSESSION [96]
take possession, 3769, *yāraš*[1] [31]
take possession, 299, *'ᵃḥuzzâ* [14]
took possession, 3769, *yāraš*[1] [9]
possession, 4627, *môrāšâ* [9]
possession, 3772, *yᵉruššâ* [7]
treasured possession, 6035, *sᵉgullâ* [6]
possession, 3338, *yād* [4]
taken possession, 3769, *yāraš*[1] [4]
accept possession, 296, *'āḥaz*[1] [1]
hold as a possession, 299, *'ᵃḥuzzâ* [1]
in possession, 907, *'ēt*[2] [1]
in possession, 928, *bᵉ-* [1]
take possession, 2143, *hālak* [1]
possession, 2750, *ḥēleq*[2] [1]
had difficulty taking possession of, 3655+4946, *yāṣā'+min* [1]
gain possession, 3769, *yāraš*[1] [1]
in possession, 4200, *lᵉ-*[1] [1]
taking possession, 4334, *lākad* [1]
take possession, 5706, *nāḥal* [1]
illegal possession, 7322, *peša'* [1]

POSSESSIONS [23]
possessions, 8214, *rᵉkûš* [11]
possessions, 5794, *nᵉkāsîm* [2]
family possessions, 3, *'āb* [1]
possessions[s], 889, *'ᵃšer* [1]
possessions, 1074, *bayit*[1] [1]
possessions, 2104, *hôn* [1]
possessions, 3330, *yᵉgîa'* [1]
take away possessions, 3769, *yāraš*[1] [1]
possessions, 3885, *kᵉbûddâ* [1]
possessions, 3998, *kᵉlî* [1]
choice possessions, 4436, *mibḥār*[1] [1]
possessions, 4978, *minleh* [1]

POSSESSOR [1]
possessor, 1251, *ba'al*[1] [1]

POSSIBLE [1]
as far as possible, 3869+1896, *kᵉ-+day* [1]

POSSIBLY [1]
possibly, *AIT* [1]

POST [4]
post, 5226, *māqôm* [1]
post, 5466, *mišmeret* [1]
post, 6641, *'āmad* [1]
post, 7212, *pāqad* [1]

POSTED [6]
posted, 8492, *śîm* [2]
posted, *NIH/RPE* [1]
posted, 6641, *'āmad* [1]
posted, 7212, *pāqad* [1]
posted, 8883+8883, *šît*[1]*+šît*[1] [1]

POSTERITY [2]
posterity, 2446, *zeraʿ* [2]

POSTING [1]
posting, 6641, *ʿāmad* [1]

POSTS [42]
posts, 6647, *ʿammûd* [36]
the posts[s], 2157, *-hem* [2]
posts, 4647, *mᵉzûzâ* [1]
posts, 5464, *mišmār*[1] [1]
posts, 6275, *ʿᵃbōdâ* [1]
posts, 6642, *ʿōmed* [1]

POT [34]
pot, 6105, *sîr* [11]
pot, 3998, *kᵉlî* [9]
pot, 7248, *pārûr* [3]
pot, *NIH/RPE* [2]
cooking pot, 6105, *sîr* [2]
pot, 1857, *dûd* [1]
the pot[s], 2257, *-ô* [1]
pot, 3671, *yēṣer*[1] [1]
cooking pot, 3968, *kîr* [1]
pot of ointment, 5350, *merqāḥâ* [1]
pot, 6775, *ʿeṣeb*[1] [1]
pot, 7831, *qallaḥat* [1]

POTENT [1]
potent, 6800, *ʿoṣmâ* [1]

POTIPHAR [4]
Potiphar, 7035, *pôṭîpar* [2]
Potiphar, *NIH/RPE* [1]
Potiphar[s], 2257, *-ô* [1]

POTIPHERA [3]
Potiphera, 7036, *pôṭî peraʿ* [3]

POTS [15]
pots, 6105, *sîr* [11]
the pots[s], 2157, *-hem* [1]
pots, 3998, *kᵉlî* [1]
pots, 5574, *nēbel*[1] [1]
cooking pots, 6105, *sîr* [1]

POTSHERD [3]
potsherd, 3084, *ḥereś* [2]
potsherd, 3068, *ḥarsît* [1]

POTSHERDS [2]
potsherds, 3084, *ḥereś* [2]

POTTER [11]
potter, 3450, *yôṣēr* [11]

POTTER'S [4]
potter's, 3450, *yôṣēr* [4]

POTTERS [1]
potters, 3450, *yôṣēr* [1]

POTTERY [6]
pottery, 3998, *kᵉlî* [2]
piece of broken pottery, 3084, *ḥereś* [1]
pottery, 3450, *yôṣēr* [1]
pottery, 3998+3450, *kᵉlî+yôṣēr* [1]
pottery, 5574+3450, *nēbel*[1]*+yôṣēr* [1]

POUCH [2]
pouch, 3541, *yalqûṭ* [1]
pouch, 7655, *ṣᵉrôr*[1] [1]

POUCHES [1]
pouches, 7655, *ṣᵉrôr*[1] [1]

POULTICE [2]
poultice, 1811, *dᵉbēlâ* [2]

POULTRY [1]
poultry, 7606, *ṣippôr*[1] [1]

POUNCE [2]
pounce, 6513, *ʿîṭ*[2] [1]
pounce, 9212, *šāqaq* [1]

POUNCED [1]
pounced, 6513, *ʿîṭ*[2] [1]

POUND [1]
pound, 2159, *hāmâ* [1]

POUNDED [2]
pounded, 1990, *dāqaq* [1]
pounded, 8074, *rāgaz* [1]

POUNDING [2]
pounding waves, 1922, *dᵒkî* [1]
pounding, 1985, *dāpaq* [1]

POUNDS [3]
pounds, 2159, *hāmâ* [1]
pounds, 3006, *ḥarad* [1]
pounds, 6086, *sāḥar* [1]

POUR [73]
pour out, 9161, *šāpak* [33]
pour, 3668, *yāṣaq* [11]
pour out, 5818, *nāsak*[1] [6]
pour out, 5988, *nātak* [2]
pour out, 8197, *rîq*[1] [2]
pour, 9161, *šāpak* [2]
pour out tears, 1940, *dālap*[1] [1]
pour out, 2313, *zûl* [1]
pour out, 3655, *yāṣāʾ* [1]
pour out, 3668, *yāṣaq* [1]
pour down, 4763, *māṭar* [1]
pour forth, 5580, *nābaʿ* [1]
pour out, 5580, *nābaʿ* [1]
pour, 5599, *nāgar* [1]
pour down moisture, 5688, *nāzal* [1]
pour, 5818, *nāsak*[1] [1]
pour out, 5989, *nātan* [1]
pour, 5989, *nātan* [1]
pour, 6057, *sûk*[2] [1]
pour out, 7579, *ṣāʿâ* [1]
pour, 7579, *ṣāʿâ* [1]
pour, 8197, *rîq*[1] [1]
makes pour, 8938, *šālaḥ* [1]

POURED [65]
poured out, 9161, *šāpak* [11]
poured out, 5818, *nāsak*[1] [7]
poured out, 5988, *nātak* [7]
poured, 3668, *yāṣaq* [6]
poured out, 3668, *yāṣaq* [4]
poured, *NIH/RPE* [2]
poured down, 5988, *nātak* [2]
poured out, 8197, *rîq*[1] [2]
be poured out, 9161, *šāpak* [2]
poured, 995, *bôʾ* [1]
poured, 1176, *bālal*[1] [1]
poured down, 2442, *zāram*[2] [1]
poured, 3718, *yārad* [1]
poured into measures, 4499, *mādad* [1]
poured, 5007, *māsak* [1]
poured out, 5580, *nābaʿ* [1]
poured down rain, 5752, *nāṭap* [1]
poured down, 5752, *nāṭap* [1]
poured, 5752, *nāṭap* [1]
be poured out, 5988, *nātak* [1]
been poured out, 5988, *nātak* [1]
is poured out, 5988, *nātak* [1]
poured effort, 6661, *ʿāmal* [1]
is poured, 6867, *ʿārâ* [1]
poured out, 6867, *ʿārâ* [1]
be poured out, 7337, *pātaḥ*[1] [1]
poured, 8197, *rîq*[1] [1]
poured, 8492, *śîm* [1]
am poured out, 9161, *šāpak* [1]
be poured, 9161, *šāpak* [1]
poured out, 9161+4946, *šāpak+min* [1]

POURING [9]
pouring out, 5818, *nāsak*[1] [3]
pouring, 3668, *yāṣaq* [2]
pouring out of drink offerings, 5818, *nāsak*[1] [1]
pouring out of offerings, 5818, *nāsak*[1] [1]
pouring, 6203, *sāpaḥ*[2] [1]
pouring out, 9161, *šāpak* [1]

POURS [13]
pours out, 7032, *pûaḥ*[2] [4]
pours out, 9161, *šāpak* [3]
pours out, 7981, *qārar*[1] [2]
pours, 9161, *šāpak* [2]
pours, 3655, *yāṣāʾ* [1]
pours out, 5599, *nāgar* [1]

POVERTY [15]
poverty, 8203, *rêš* [7]
poverty, 4728, *maḥsôr* [4]
poverty, 2895, *ḥeser* [1]
poverty, 2896, *ḥōser* [1]
sends poverty, 3769, *yāraš*[1] [1]
poverty, 8133, *rûš* [1]

POWDER [7]
powder, 1990, *dāqaq* [3]
powder, 6760, *ʿāpār* [2]
powder, 85, *ʾābāq* [1]
ground to powder, 3221+3512, *ṭāḥan+yāṭab* [1]

POWER [155]
power, 3338, *yād* [34]
power, 3946, *kōaḥ*[1] [31]
power, 1476, *gᵉbûrâ* [16]
power, 6437, *ʿōz* [11]
came in power, 7502, *ṣālaḥ*[1] [6]
power, 2432, *zᵉrôaʿ* [4]
power, 226, *ʾôn*[1] [3]
power, 445+3338, *ʾēl*[4]*+yād* [3]
power, 2617, *ḥāzāq* [2]
power, 2657, *ḥayil* [2]
power, 4938, *mimšāl* [2]
power, 6449, *ʿezûz* [2]
rise to power, 7756, *qûm* [2]
power, 10130, *gᵉbûrâ* [2]
power, 10717, *šolṭān* [2]
power, *NIH/RPE* [1]
acts of power, 1476, *gᵉbûrâ* [1]
mighty power, 1476, *gᵉbûrâ* [1]
power, 1524, *gādôl* [1]
great power, 1542, *gōdel* [1]
arm of power, 2432, *zᵉrôaʿ* [1]
gave power, 2616, *ḥāzaq* [1]
power, 2620, *ḥōzeq* [1]
gained power, 2621, *ḥezqâ* [1]
power, 3856, *yeter*[1] [1]
power, 3946+2432, *kōaḥ*[1]*+zᵉrôaʿ* [1]
power to destroy, 3986, *kālâ*[3] [1]
came to power, 4887, *mālak*[1] [1]
royal power, 4930, *mamlākâ* [1]
great power, 5124, *maʿᵃrāṣâ* [1]
power, 5445, *mōšel*[2] [1]
power, 6435, *ʿāz* [1]
great power, 6437, *ʿōz* [1]
power, 6786, *ʿāṣûm* [1]
height of power, 6793, *ʿāṣam*[1] [1]
power, 6793, *ʿāṣam*[1] [1]
power, 6800, *ʿoṣmâ* [1]
display awesome power, 7098, *pālāʾ* [1]
come in power, 7502, *ṣālaḥ*[1] [1]
came to power, 7756, *qûm* [1]
greater power, 8041, *rab*[1] [1]
power, 8950, *šiltôn* [1]
power, 8954, *šallîṭ* [1]
power, 9549, *tōqep* [1]
power, 10278, *ḥᵉsēn* [1]
power, 10311, *yad* [1]
sovereign power, 10424, *malkû* [1]
power, 10774, *tᵉqāp* [1]

POWERFUL [43]
powerful, 6786, *ʿāṣûm* [7]
powerful, 2617, *ḥāzāq* [6]
powerful, 1524, *gādôl* [4]
powerful, 3946, *kōaḥ*[1] [4]
powerful, 2616, *ḥāzaq* [3]
powerful, 6434, *ʿaz* [3]
powerful, 600, *ʾāmōṣ* [2]
powerful, 1475, *gibbôr* [2]
became more and more powerful, 2143+2143+2256+1524, *hālak+hālak+wᵉ-+gādôl* [2]
powerful, 10768, *taqqîp* [2]
powerful, 1540, *gādal* [1]
became more and more powerful, 2143+2256+1524, *hālak+wᵉ-+gādôl* [1]

more and more powerful, 2143+2256+1541+6330+4200+5087+2025, *hālak+wᵉ-+gādēl+ʿad[2]+lᵉ-[1]+maʿal[2]+-â[2]* [1]
powerful, 2432, *zᵉrôaʿ* [1]
became powerful, 2621, *ḥezqâ* [1]
makes powerful, 6451, *ʿāzaz* [1]
powerful, 6793, *ʿāṣam[1]* [1]
powerful, 8041, *rab[1]* [1]

POWERLESS [7]
powerless, 4202+3946, *lōʾ+kōaḥ[1]* [2]
powerless, 401+3946, *ʾayin[1]+kōaḥ[1]* [1]
powerless, 401+4200+445+3338, *ʾayin[1]+lᵉ-[1]+ʾēl[4]+yād* [1]
powerless, 401+4200+445, *ʾayin[1]+lᵉ-[1]+ʾēl[4]* [1]
powerless, 4202+3523, *lōʾ+yākōl* [1]
powerless, 4202, *lōʾ* [1]

POWERS [2]
powers, 7372, *ṣābāʾ[2]* [1]
powers, 10264, *ḥayil* [1]

PRACTICE [15]
practice, 6913, *ʿāśâ[1]* [3]
practice, 5477, *mišpāṭ* [2]
put into practice, 6913, *ʿāśâ[1]* [2]
practice, *AIT* [1]
practice, 1251, *baʿal[1]* [1]
practice divination, 5727, *nāḥaš* [1]
practice divination, 6726, *ʿānan[2]* [1]
practice sorcery, 6726, *ʿānan[2]* [1]
practice extortion, 6943+6945, *ʿāšaq+ʿōšeq* [1]
practice, 7188, *pāʿal* [1]
practice divination, 7877+7876, *qesem+qāsam* [1]

PRACTICED [6]
practiced sorcery, 6726, *ʿānan[2]* [2]
were practiced, 6913, *ʿāśâ[1]* [1]
practiced extortion, 6943+6945, *ʿāšaq+ʿōšeq* [1]
practiced divination, 7876+7877, *qāsam+qesem* [1]
practiced divination, 7876, *qāsam* [1]

PRACTICES [49]
detestable practices, 9359, *tôʿēbâ* [30]
practices, 2978, *ḥuqqâ* [3]
practices, 5095, *maʿᵃlāl* [3]
practices, 5126, *maʿᵃśeh* [3]
practices, 5477, *mišpāṭ* [2]
practices, 6913, *ʿāśâ[1]* [2]
practices, *NIH/RPE* [1]
unclean practices, 3240, *ṭumʾâ* [1]
evil practices, 5095, *maʿᵃlāl* [1]
practices, 6613, *ʿᵃlîlâ* [1]
practices divination, 7876+7877, *qāsam+qesem* [1]
corrupt practices, 8845, *šāḥat* [1]

PRAISE [299]
praise, 2146, *hālal[2]* [89]
praise, 1385, *bārak[2]* [63]
praise, 9335, *tᵉhillâ* [46]
praise, 3344, *yādâ[2]* [44]
sing praise, 2376, *zāmar[1]* [18]
worthy of praise, 2146, *hālal[2]* [6]
praise, *NIH/RPE* [4]
give praise, 2146, *hālal[2]* [3]
praise, 6437, *ʿōz* [2]
praise, 8128, *rômām* [2]
praise, 9343, *tôdâ* [2]
praise, 10122, *bᵉrak[2]* [2]
praise, 10693, *šᵉbaḥ* [2]
praise, 2035, *hab[1]* [1]
offering of praise, 2136, *hillûlîm* [1]
bring praise, 2146, *hālal[2]* [1]
giving praise, 2146, *hālal[2]* [1]
sing praise, 2146, *hālal[2]* [1]
praise, 2349, *zākar[1]* [1]
praise, 2376, *zāmar[1]* [1]
brings praise, 3344, *yādâ[2]* [1]
praise, 4545, *mahᵃlāl* [1]
psalm of praise, 5380, *maśkîl* [1]
praise, 5658, *nāwâ[2]* [1]
praise, 5762, *nîb* [1]
receive praise, 8655, *šābaḥ[1]* [1]
hymn of praise, 9335, *tᵉhillâ* [1]
psalm of praise, 9335, *tᵉhillâ* [1]
theme of praise, 9335, *tᵉhillâ* [1]

PRAISED [28]
praised, 1385, *bārak[2]* [8]
praised, 2146, *hālal[2]* [7]
be praised, 2146, *hālal[2]* [2]
praised, 9335, *tᵉhillâ* [2]
praised, 10122, *bᵉrak[2]* [2]
praised, 10693, *šᵉbaḥ* [2]
praised, *NIH/RPE* [1]
be praised, 1385, *bārak[2]* [1]
is praised, 2146, *hālal[2]* [1]
praised, 3344, *yādâ[2]* [1]
praised in song, 8876, *šîr[1]* [1]

PRAISES [16]
sing praises, 2376, *zāmar[1]* [8]
praises, 2146, *hālal[2]* [3]
praises, 9335, *tᵉhillâ* [2]
sang praises, 2146, *hālal[2]* [1]
sing praises, 2146, *hālal[2]* [1]
praises, 3344, *yādâ[2]* [1]

PRAISEWORTHY [1]
praiseworthy deeds, 9335, *tᵉhillâ* [1]

PRAISING [3]
praising, 2146, *hālal[2]* [2]
praising, 3344, *yādâ[2]* [1]

PRAY [48]
pray, 7137, *pālal[2]* [30]
pray, 6983, *ʿātar[1]* [7]
pray, 5951+9525, *nāśāʾ+tᵉpillâ* [2]
pray, 9384, *taḥᵃnûn* [2]
pray, *NIH/RPE* [1]
I pray, 5528, *nāʾ[1]* [1]
we pray, 5528, *nāʾ[1]* [1]
pray, 7924, *qārāʾ[1]* [1]
pray, 8626, *šāʾal* [1]
pray, 9525, *tᵉpillâ* [1]
pray, 10612, *ṣᵉlâ* [1]

PRAYED [44]
prayed, 7137, *pālal[2]* [28]
prayed, 606, *ʾāmar[1]* [6]
prayed, 6983, *ʿātar[1]* [4]
prayed, *NIH/RPE* [1]
prayed, 2858, *ḥānan[1]* [1]
prayed, 7924, *qārāʾ[1]* [1]
prayed, 8626, *šāʾal* [1]
prayed for, 8629, *šᵉʾēlâ* [1]
prayed, 10612, *ṣᵉlâ* [1]

PRAYER [73]
prayer, 9525, *tᵉpillâ* [60]
prayer, *NIH/RPE* [4]
answered prayer, 6983, *ʿātar[1]* [4]
prayer, 7137, *pālal[2]* [2]
prayer, 614, *ʾimrâ* [1]
offer prayer, 7137+9525, *pālal[2]+tᵉpillâ* [1]
barely whisper a prayer, 7440+4318, *ṣûq[2]+laḥaš* [1]

PRAYERS [11]
prayers, 9525, *tᵉpillâ* [10]
answered prayers, 6983, *ʿātar[1]* [1]

PRAYING [16]
praying, 7137, *pālal[2]* [10]
praying, 1819, *dābar[2]* [4]
praying, 7003, *pāgaʿ* [1]
praying, 10114, *bᵉʿâ* [1]

PRAYS [9]
prays, 7137, *pālal[2]* [5]
prays, 10114+10115, *bᵉʿâ+bāʿû* [2]
prays, 6983, *ʿātar[1]* [1]
prays, 10114, *bᵉʿâ* [1]

PREACH [4]
preach, 5752, *nāṭap* [2]
preach good news, 1413, *bāśar* [1]
preach, 7924, *qārāʾ[1]* [1]

PREACHED [3]
preached, 1819, *dābar[2]* [3]

PREACHING [2]
preaching, 5752, *nāṭap* [1]
preaching, 10452, *nᵉbûʾâ* [1]

PRECEDED [4]
preceded, 2118+4200+7156, *hāyâ+lᵉ-[1]+pāneh* [2]
preceded, 4200+7156, *lᵉ-[1]+pāneh* [2]

PRECEDING [1]
preceding, 4200+7156, *lᵉ-[1]+pāneh* [1]

PRECEPTS [27]
precepts, 7218, *piqqûdîm* [24]
his precepts[s], 2157, *-hem* [1]
precepts, 2976, *ḥōq* [1]
precepts, 5477, *mišpāṭ* [1]

PRECINCTS [1]
holy precincts, 7731, *qōdeš* [1]

PRECIOUS [37]
precious, 3701, *yāqār* [18]
precious, 3202, *ṭôb[2]* [4]
precious, 3700, *yāqar* [4]
precious stones, 74, *ʾeben* [3]
precious life, 3495, *yāḥîd* [2]
precious, 2773, *ḥāmad* [1]
precious, 2776, *ḥᵃmudôt* [1]
precious, 2914, *ḥēpeṣ* [1]
precious things, 3702, *yᵉqār* [1]
precious, 4202+5877, *lōʾ+nāpal* [1]
precious, 4458, *meged* [1]

PREDECESSOR [1]
predecessor, 889+2118+4200+7156, *ʾᵃšer+hāyâ+lᵉ-[1]+pāneh* [1]

PREDECESSORS [2]
predecessors, 8037, *riʾšōn* [1]
predecessors, 10003, *ʾab* [1]

PREDICTED [1]
predicted, 1819, *dābar[2]* [1]

PREDICTING [2]
predicting, 1821, *dābār* [2]

PREDICTION [1]
prediction, 1821, *dābār* [1]

PREDICTIONS [2]
make predictions, 3359, *yādaʿ* [1]
predictions, 6783, *ʿēṣâ[1]* [1]

PREEMINENT [1]
preeminent, 1524, *gādôl* [1]

PREFECTS [4]
prefects, 10505, *sᵉgan* [4]

PREFER [6]
prefer, 1047, *bāḥar[1]* [3]
prefer, 2913, *ḥāpēṣ[3]* [1]
prefer, 3202+928+6524, *ṭôb[2]+bᵉ-+ʿayin[1]* [1]
prefer, 4374, *lāqaḥ* [1]

PREFERENCE [1]
in preference to, 6584+7156, *ʿal[2]+pāneh* [1]

PREGNANCY [1]
pregnancy, 1061, *beṭen[1]* [1]

PREGNANT [27]
pregnant, 2225, *hārâ* [16]
pregnant, 2226, *hāreh* [7]
pregnant women, 2226, *hāreh* [1]
pregnant women, 2230, *hāriyyâ* [1]
pregnant, 2445, *zāraʿ* [1]
pregnant, 2473, *ḥābal[3]* [1]

PREMATURELY [1]
gives birth prematurely, 3655+3529, *yāṣāʾ+yeled* [1]

PREPARATION [3]
preparation, *NIH/RPE* [1]
make preparation, 3922, *kûn*[1] [1]
in preparation for, 4200, *l^{e}-*[1] [1]

PREPARATIONS [5]
made preparations, 3922, *kûn*[1] [4]
make preparations, 3922, *kûn*[1] [1]

PREPARE [78]
prepare, 6913, *ʿāśâ*[1] [30]
prepare, *NIH/RPE* [16]
prepare, 3922, *kûn*[1] [10]
prepare, 7727, *qādaš* [5]
prepare, 7155, *pānâ* [4]
prepare, 6885, *ʿārak* [3]
prepare for battle, 273, *ʾāzar* [2]
prepare, 8492, *śîm* [2]
prepare food to eat, 430, *ʾākal* [1]
prepare for war, 1741, *gārâ* [1]
prepare, 2118+3922, *hāyâ+kûn*[1] [1]
prepare, 2933, *ḥāṣēb*[1] [1]
prepare, 4374, *lāqaḥ* [1]
prepare, 5951, *nāśāʾ* [1]

PREPARED [49]
prepared, 3922, *kûn*[1] [14]
prepared, 6913, *ʿāśâ*[1] [13]
prepared, 6885, *ʿārak* [4]
prepared, 7756, *qûm* [4]
prepared, *NIH/RPE* [2]
be prepared, 6913, *ʿāśâ*[1] [2]
prepared, 3180, *ṭābaḥ* [1]
are prepared, 3922, *kûn*[1] [1]
were prepared, 3922, *kûn*[1] [1]
prepared a feast, 4127+4130, *kārâ*[3]*+kērâ* [1]
prepared without yeast, 5174, *maṣṣâ*[1] [1]
been prepared, 6885, *ʿārak* [1]
were prepared, 6913, *ʿāśâ*[1] [1]
prepared, 7142, *pālas*[1] [1]
prepared, 7155, *pānâ* [1]
prepared, 8492, *śîm* [1]

PREPARES [3]
prepares, 8492, *śîm* [2]
prepares, 430, *ʾākal* [1]

PREPARING [5]
preparing, 2284, *zābaḥ* [2]
preparing, 3670, *yāṣar* [2]
preparing, 3922, *kûn*[1] [1]

PRESCRIBED [22]
prescribed, 5477, *mišpāṭ* [4]
prescribed, 5184, *miṣwâ* [3]
prescribed way, 5477, *mišpāṭ* [3]
prescribed, *AIT* [1]
prescribed, 2017, *dāt* [1]
prescribed portion, 2976, *ḥōq* [1]
prescribed, 3869+5477, *k^{e}-+mišpāṭ* [1]
prescribed, 4181, *k^{e}tāb* [1]
way prescribed, 5184, *miṣwâ* [1]
regulations prescribed, 5477, *mišpāṭ* [1]
way prescribed, 5477, *mišpāṭ* [1]
as prescribed by, 6584+3338, *ʿal*[2]*+yād* [1]
prescribed, 7212, *pāqad* [1]
prescribed, 7422, *ṣāwâ* [1]
prescribed, 10427+10302, *min+t^{e}ʿēm*[2] [1]

PRESENCE [172]
presence, 7156, *pāneh* [108]
presence, 4200+7156, *l^{e}-*[1]*+pāneh* [19]
presence, 6524, *ʿayin*[1] [14]
in the presence of, 5584, *neged* [7]
presence, 5584, *neged* [3]
into presence, 448, *ʾel* [2]
in presence, 4200+5584+6524, *l^{e}-*[1]*+neged+ʿayin*[1] [2]
in the presence of, 5584+2025, *neged+-â*[2] [2]
presence, 9348, *tāwek* [2]
into presence, 10621, *q^{o}dām* [2]
presence, *NIH/RPE* [1]
in presence, 4946, *min* [1]
presence, 4946+6584, *min+ʿal*[2] [1]
in the presence of, 5790+7156, *nōkaḥ+pāneh* [1]
in presence of, 6584, *ʿal*[2] [1]
in presence, 6584, *ʿal*[2] [1]
in the presence of, 6584, *ʿal*[2] [1]
in the presence of, 6640, *ʿim* [1]
presence, 7931, *qereb* [1]
come into presence, 8011+906+7156, *rāʾâ*[1]*+ʾēt*[1]*+pāneh* [1]
in presence, 10621, *q^{o}dām* [1]

PRESENT [106]
present, 7928, *qārab* [36]
present, 8123, *rûm*[1] [10]
present, 6913, *ʿāśâ*[1] [7]
present, 6641, *ʿāmad* [6]
present, 5162, *māṣāʾ* [5]
present, *NIH/RPE* [3]
present, 6590, *ʿālâ* [3]
present, 995, *bôʾ* [2]
present, 1388, *b^{e}rākâ* [2]
present themselves, 3656, *yāṣab* [2]
present yourselves, 3656, *yāṣab* [2]
present, 5677, *nûp*[1] [2]
present himself, 8011, *rāʾâ*[1] [2]
present, 340, *ʾaḥ^{a}rôn* [1]
present in, 928, *b^{e}-* [1]
the present time, 2178, *hēnnâ*[1] [1]
present case, 3519, *yākaḥ* [1]
present himself, 3656, *yāṣab* [1]
present, 4200+7156, *l^{e}-*[1]*+pāneh* [1]
present, 4481, *māgan* [1]
present, 5368, *maśʾēt* [1]
present, 5602, *nāgaš* [1]
present, 5877+4200+7156, *nāpal+l^{e}-*[1]*+pāneh* [1]
present yourself, 5893, *nāṣab*[1] [1]
present, 6640, *ʿim* [1]
present, 7156, *pāneh* [1]
present, 7787, *qāṭar*[1] [1]
present yourselves, 7928, *qārab* [1]
present myself, 8011, *rāʾâ*[1] [1]
present yourself, 8011, *rāʾâ*[1] [1]
present, 8011, *rāʾâ*[1] [1]
present, 8123+9556, *rûm*[1]*+t^{e}rûmâ* [1]
present a portion, 8123, *rûm*[1] [1]
present, 8966, *šālēm*[1] [1]
present an offering, 9556, *t^{e}rûmâ* [1]
present, 10156, *d^{e}baḥ*[1] [1]
the present, 10363, *k^{e}ʿan* [1]

PRESENTED [49]
presented, 7928, *qārab* [9]
presented, 6590, *ʿālâ* [5]
presented, *NIH/RPE* [4]
presented, 9556, *t^{e}rûmâ* [4]
presented, 5677, *nûp*[1] [3]
presented, 6641, *ʿāmad* [3]
presented, 995, *bôʾ* [2]
presented themselves, 3656, *yāṣab* [2]
presented, 5602, *nāgaš* [2]
presented, 5989, *nātan* [2]
presented, *AIT* [1]
presented, 2272, *zābad* [1]
presented for a sin offering, 2627, *ḥāṭāʾ* [1]
presented, 3657, *yāṣag* [1]
presented the full number, 4848, *mālēʾ*[1] [1]
presented offerings, 6590, *ʿālâ* [1]
be presented, 6641, *ʿāmad* [1]
be presented, 6913, *ʿāśâ*[1] [1]
presented offerings, 7787, *qāṭar*[1] [1]
presented, 8123, *rûm*[1] [1]
presented, 8492, *śîm* [1]
was presented, 9556+8123, *t^{e}rûmâ+rûm*[1] [1]
presented, 10482, *n^{e}sak*[1] [1]

PRESENTING [5]
presenting, 8123, *rûm*[1] [2]
presenting, *NIH/RPE* [1]
presenting, 7787, *qāṭar*[1] [1]
presenting, 7928, *qārab* [1]

PRESENTS [6]
presents, *NIH/RPE* [2]
presents of food, 4950, *mānâ*[2] [1]
presents, 4950, *mānâ*[2] [1]
presents, 6913, *ʿāśâ*[1] [1]
presents, 7928, *qārab* [1]

PRESERVE [23]
preserve life, 2649, *ḥāyâ* [12]
preserve, 2649, *ḥāyâ* [3]
preserve, 5915, *nāṣar* [2]
preserve, 2616, *ḥāzaq* [1]
preserve, 3104, *ḥāśak* [1]
preserve, 3828, *yāšaʿ* [1]
preserve, 3855, *yātar* [1]
preserve, 8492, *śîm* [1]
preserve, 9068, *šāmar* [1]

PRESERVED [3]
preserved life, 2649, *ḥāyâ* [1]
preserved, 8492+928+2021+2645, *śîm+b^{e}-+ha-+ḥay*[2] [1]
preserved, 9068, *šāmar* [1]

PRESERVES [3]
preserves life, 2649, *ḥāyâ* [2]
preserves, 5915, *nāṣar* [1]

PRESIDES [1]
presides, 5893, *nāṣab*[1] [1]

PRESS [7]
press, 2005, *dārak* [1]
press, 2616, *ḥāzaq* [1]
press, 4315, *lāḥaṣ* [1]
press, 7439, *ṣûq*[1] [1]
press on, 8103, *rādap* [1]
press plea, 8104, *rāhab* [1]
press charges, 8492, *śîm* [1]

PRESSED [14]
pressed olives, 4184, *kātît* [2]
pressed, 4184, *kātît* [2]
pressed, *NIH/RPE* [1]
cake of pressed figs, 1811, *d^{e}bēlâ* [1]
cakes of pressed figs, 1811, *d^{e}bēlâ* [1]
pressed hard after, 1815, *dābaq* [1]
pressed hard, 1815, *dābaq* [1]
pressed olive, 4184, *kātît* [1]
pressed attack, 4309, *lāḥam*[1] [1]
pressed close, 4315, *lāḥaṣ* [1]
hard pressed, 5601, *nāgaś* [1]
pressed, 8492, *śîm* [1]

PRESSES [2]
presses, 3676, *yeqeb* [2]

PRESSING [2]
pressing, 237, *ʾûṣ* [1]
pressing, 1815, *dābaq* [1]

PRESSURE [1]
kept bringing pressure, 7210+4394, *pāṣar+m^{e}ʾōd* [1]

PRESUMES [1]
presumes, 2326, *zîd* [1]

PRESUMPTION [1]
presumption, 6753, *ʿāpal*[2] [1]

PRESUMPTUOUSLY [1]
presumptuously, 928+2295, *b^{e}-+zādôn* [1]

PRETEND [4]
pretend in mourning, 61, *ʾābal*[1] [1]
pretend to be ill, 2703, *ḥālâ*[1] [1]
pretend to be somebody, 3877, *kābēd*[1] [1]
pretend to be someone else, 5796, *nākar*[2] [1]

PRETENDED [4]
pretended to be insane, 9101+3248, *šānâ*[1]*+ṭaʿam* [2]
pretended to be ill, 2703, *ḥālâ*[1] [1]
pretended to be a stranger, 5796, *nākar*[2] [1]

PRETENDS [2]
pretends to be rich, 6947, *ʿāšar* [1]
pretends to be poor, 8133, *rûš* [1]

PRETENSE [2]
pretense, 5796, *nākar*[2] [1]
pretense, 9214, *šeqer* [1]

PREVAIL [5]
prevail, 3523, *yākōl* [3]
prevail, 6806, *ʿāṣar* [1]
prevail, 7503, *ṣālaḥ*^{2} [1]

PREVAILED [3]
prevailed, 1504, *gābar* [1]
prevailed upon, 2616+928, *ḥāzaq+b*^{e}*-* [1]
prevailed, 3523, *yākōl* [1]

PREVAILS [3]
prevails, 1504, *gābar* [1]
prevails, 3655, *yāṣāʾ* [1]
prevails, 7756, *qûm* [1]

PREVENT [4]
prevent, 1194+5989, *biltî+nātan* [2]
prevent, 1721, *gāʿar* [1]
prevent from, 4946, *min* [1]

PREVIOUS [2]
previous, 4200+7156, *l*$^{e-1}$*+pāneh* [1]
previous, 8037, *riʾšôn* [1]

PREVIOUSLY [2]
previously, *AIT* [1]
previously, 3869+919+8997,
k^{e}*-+ʾetmôl+šilšôm* [1]

PREY [29]
prey, 3272, *ṭerep* [13]
bird of prey, 6514, *ʿayiṭ* [3]
birds of prey, 6514, *ʿayiṭ* [3]
prey, *NIH/RPE* [1]
prey, 431, *ʾōkel* [1]
prey, 3271, *ṭārap* [1]
tearing prey, 3271, *ṭārap* [1]
prey, 3274, *ṭ*^{e}*rēpâ* [1]
prey, 5180, *m*^{e}*ṣûdâ*^{1} [1]
prey, 6331, *ʿad*^{3} [1]
prey on, 8286, *rāʿâ*^{1} [1]
becomes prey, 8964, *šālal*^{2} [1]
prey, 8965, *šālāl* [1]

PREYS [1]
preys upon, 7421, *ṣûd* [1]

PRICE [24]
price, 4084, *kesep* [7]
price, 4697, *m*^{e}*ḥîr*^{1} [6]
price, *NIH/RPE* [3]
price, 5239, *miqnâ* [2]
price, 3702, *y*^{e}*qār* [1]
price for bride, 4558, *mōhar* [1]
price for the bride, 4558, *mōhar* [1]
price, 5433, *mešek*^{1} [1]
price set, 6886, *ʿērek* [1]
price, 9203, *šeqel* [1]

PRICED [1]
priced, 3700, *yāqar* [1]

PRICELESS [1]
priceless, 3701, *yāqār* [1]

PRIDE [61]
pride, 1454, *gāʾôn* [23]
pride, 1452, *gaʾ ăwâ* [7]
pride, 2295, *zādôn* [4]
pride, 5294, *mārôm* [3]
pride, 1455, *gēʾût* [2]
pride, 1575, *gēwâ*^{1} [2]
pride, 8124, *rûm*^{2} [2]
pride, *NIH/RPE* [1]
pride, 1447, *gēʾ* [1]
pride, 1449, *gēʾâ* [1]
pride, 1450, *gēʾeh* [1]
pride, 1467+4213, *gābah+lēb* [1]
pride, 1467, *gābah* [1]
pride, 1468+8120, *gābēah+rûaḥ* [1]
pride, 1470+678, *gōbah+ʾap*^{2} [1]
pride, 1470, *gōbah* [1]
take pride, 2038, *hābal* [1]
overweening pride, 6301+2295,
ʿebrâ+zādôn [1]
willful pride, 7262+1542, *p*^{e}*rî+gōdel* [1]
filled with pride, 8123+4222, *rûm*^{1}*+lēbāb* [1]
pride, 8262, *rinnâ*^{1} [1]
pride, 8480, *śîʾ* [1]
pride, 9514, *tipʾeret* [1]
pride, 10136, *gēwâ* [1]
pride, 10225, *zûd* [1]

PRIEST [406]
priest, 3913, *kōhēn* [390]
priest, *NIH/RPE* [5]
anyone other than a priest, 2424, *zār* [2]
priest, 3912, *kāhan* [2]
serve as priest, 3912, *kāhan* [2]
priest, 10347, *kāhēn* [2]
the priest^{s}, 2257, *-ô* [1]
high priest, 3912, *kāhan* [1]
served as priest, 3912, *kāhan* [1]

PRIEST'S [6]
priest's, 3913, *kōhēn* [5]
outside a priest's family, 2424, *zār* [1]

PRIESTHOOD [10]
priesthood, 3914, *k*^{e}*hunnâ* [9]
priesthood, 3913, *kōhēn* [1]

PRIESTLY [6]
priestly, 3913, *kōhēn* [2]
priestly office, 3914, *k*^{e}*hunnâ* [2]
priestly, *NIH/RPE* [1]
priestly service, 3914, *k*^{e}*hunnâ* [1]

PRIESTS [341]
priests, 3913, *kōhēn* [301]
serve as priests, 3912, *kāhan* [12]
priests, *NIH/RPE* [6]
priests, 10347, *kāhēn* [6]
priests, 3912, *kāhan* [2]
served as priests, 3912, *kāhan* [2]
priests, 3914, *k*^{e}*hunnâ* [2]
priests^{s}, 278+2157, *ʾāḥ*^{2}*+-hem* [1]
priests^{s}, 2085, *hûʾ* [1]
the priests^{s}, 2156, *hēm* [1]
serving as priests, 3912, *kāhan* [1]
idolatrous priests, 3913, *kōhēn* [1]
idolatrous priests, 4024, *kōmer* [1]
pagan priests, 4024, *kōmer* [1]
priests rooms, 4384+7731, *liškâ+qōdeš* [1]
priests^{s}, 4392, *-ām* [1]
the priests^{s}, 4392, *-ām* [1]

PRIME [3]
in the prime of life, 408, *ʾîš*^{1} [1]
prime, 1953, *d*^{e}*mî* [1]
prime, 3074, *ḥōrep* [1]

PRINCE [46]
prince, 5954, *nāśîʾ* [29]
prince, 8569, *śar* [10]
prince, 5592, *nāgîd* [3]
prince, 5687, *nāzîr* [2]
prince, 1201+4889, *bēn*^{1}*+melek*^{1} [1]
prince, 8138, *rāzôn*^{2} [1]

PRINCE'S [1]
prince's, 5618, *nādîb* [1]

PRINCELY [1]
princely mansions, 2292, *z*^{e}*bul*^{2} [1]

PRINCES [71]
princes, 8569, *śar* [41]
princes, 5954, *nāśîʾ*^{1} [10]
princes, 5618, *nādîb* [5]
princes, 1201+4889, *bēn*^{1}*+melek*^{1} [3]
princes, 1201, *bēn*^{1} [3]
princes, 5817, *nāsîk*^{2} [3]
princes, 2980, *ḥāqaq* [1]
princes, 5687, *nāzîr* [1]
princes, 7278, *peraʿ*^{1} [1]
princes, 7312, *part*^{e}*mîm* [1]
princes, 8142, *rāzan* [1]
choose princes, 8606, *śārar* [1]

PRINCESS [1]
princess, 1426+4889, *bat*^{1}*+melek*^{1} [1]

PRINCIPAL [1]
principal, 1475, *gibbôr* [1]

PRIOR [1]
prior, 6330, *ʿad*^{2} [1]

PRISON [30]
prison, 1074+2021+6045, *bayit*^{1}*+ha-+sōhar* [6]
prison, 1074+2021+3975, *bayit*^{1}*+ha-+keleʾ* [4]
prison, 4993, *masgēr*^{1} [3]
prison, 1074+2021+3989, *bayit*^{1}*+ha-+k*^{e}*lûʾ* [2]
prison, 1074+3975, *bayit*^{1}*+keleʾ* [2]
prison, 1074+673, *bayit*^{1}*+ʾāsar* [2]
prison, 3975, *keleʾ* [2]
be kept in prison, 673, *ʾāsar* [1]
prison, 1074+2021+4551,
bayit^{1}*+ha-+mahpeket* [1]
prison, 1074+2021+673, *bayit*^{1}*+ha-+ʾāsar* [1]
prison, 1074+2021+7213,
bayit^{1}*+ha-+p*^{e}*quddâ* [1]
prison, 1074+5464, *bayit*^{1}*+mišmār*^{1} [1]
prison, 1074, *bayit*^{1} [1]
prison, 5180, *m*^{e}*ṣûdâ*^{1} [1]
prison, 5182, *m*^{e}*ṣôdâ*^{1} [1]
confines in prison, 6037, *sāgar* [1]

PRISONER [5]
take prisoner, 673, *ʾāsar* [1]
were taken prisoner, 673, *ʾāsar* [1]
took prisoner, 4334, *lākad* [1]
took prisoner, 4374, *lāqaḥ* [1]
prisoner, 8660, *š*^{e}*bî* [1]

PRISONERS [21]
prisoners, 659, *ʾāsîr* [8]
prisoners, 8664, *šibyâ* [3]
prisoners, 673, *ʾāsar* [2]
took as prisoners, 4374, *lāqaḥ* [2]
prisoners, 8660, *š*^{e}*bî* [2]
prisoners, 660, *ʾassîr*^{1} [1]
cowering prisoners, 7579, *ṣāʿâ* [1]
took as prisoners, 8647+8664, *šābâ+šibyâ* [1]
taken as prisoners, 8664+8647, *šibyâ+šābâ* [1]

PRISONS [1]
prisons, 1074+3975, *bayit*^{1}*+keleʾ* [1]

PRIVATE [2]
private room, 2540, *ḥeder* [1]
private parts, 4434, *m*^{e}*bûšîm* [1]

PRIVATELY [4]
privately, 928+2021+6260, *b*^{e}*-+ha-+sēter* [2]
privately, 928+2021+4319, *b*^{e}*-+ha-+lāṭ* [1]
privately, 928+2021+8952, *b*^{e}*-+ha-+šelî* [1]

PRIZES [1]
prizes, 3701, *yāqār* [1]

PROBE [5]
probe, 1043, *bāḥan* [1]
probe, 2011, *dāraš* [1]
probe, 2983, *ḥāqar* [1]
probe, 5162, *māšāʾ* [1]
probe, 8011, *rāʾâ*^{1} [1]

PROBLEMS [3]
difficult problems, 10626, *q*^{e}*ṭar* [2]
problems, 3268, *ṭōraḥ* [1]

PROCEDURE [2]
proper procedure, 5477, *mišpāṭ* [2]

PROCEED [1]
proceed, 2143, *hālak* [1]

PROCEEDED [7]
proceeded, 7756, *qûm* [3]
proceeded, *AIT* [2]
proceeded, 2143, *hālak* [1]
proceeded, 2725, *ḥālal*^{1} [1]

PROCESSION [9]
procession, 2142, *h*^{a}*lîkâ* [2]
procession, 2474, *hebel*^{1} [2]
in procession, 1839, *dāgal*^{2} [1]
the procession^{s}, 2157, *-hem* [1]
festal procession, 2504, *ḥag* [1]

the procession^{s}, 4392, -*ām* [1]
led in triumphal procession, 5627, *nāhag*^{1} [1]

PROCLAIM [69]
proclaim, 7924, *qārā'*^{1} [23]
proclaim, 9048, *šāma'* [15]
proclaim, 5583, *nāgad* [11]
proclaim, 1413, *bāśar* [4]
proclaim, 6218, *sāpar* [4]
proclaim the news, 1413, *bāśar* [2]
proclaim, 1819, *dābar*^{2} [2]
proclaim, 2349, *zākar*^{1} [2]
proclaim, 5989, *nātan* [2]
proclaim, *NIH/RPE* [1]
proclaim, 3359, *yāda'* [1]
proclaim, 4910, *mālal*^{3} [1]
proclaim, 7924+928, *qārā'*^{1}*+b*^{e}*-* [1]

PROCLAIMED [31]
proclaimed, 7924, *qārā'*^{1} [12]
proclaimed, 1819, *dābar*^{2} [5]
proclaimed king, 4887, *mālak*^{1} [3]
proclaimed, 9048, *šāma'* [3]
proclaimed, 1413, *bāśar* [1]
proclaimed, 6218, *sāpar* [1]
proclaimed, 6913, *'āśâ*^{1} [1]
proclaimed, 7924+928, *qārā'*^{1}*+b*^{e}*-* [1]
been proclaimed, 9048, *šāma'* [1]
is proclaimed, 9048, *šāma'* [1]
proclaimed, 10371, *k*^{e}*raz* [1]
proclaimed, 10637, *q*^{e}*rā'* [1]

PROCLAIMING [10]
proclaiming, 7924, *qārā'*^{1} [4]
proclaiming, 9048, *šāma'* [2]
proclaiming, 606, *'āmar*^{1} [1]
proclaiming, 1413, *bāśar* [1]
proclaiming, 1819, *dābar*^{2} [1]
proclaiming, 5583, *nāgad* [1]

PROCLAIMS [2]
proclaims, 1819, *dābar*^{2} [1]
proclaims, 9048, *šāma'* [1]

PROCLAMATION [8]
proclamation, 7754, *qôl* [5]
issued a proclamation, 2410, *zā'aq* [1]
make proclamation, 7924, *qārā'*^{1} [1]
made proclamation, 9048, *šāma'* [1]

PRODDED [1]
prodded, 552, *'ālaṣ* [1]

PRODUCE [33]
produce, 6913, *'āśâ*^{1} [5]
produce, 7262, *p*^{e}*rî* [4]
produce, 9311, *t*^{e}*bû'â* [4]
produce, *NIH/RPE* [3]
produce, 5989, *nātan* [3]
produce, 3655, *yāṣā'* [2]
produce, 995, *bô'* [1]
produce, 1006, *bûl*^{3} [1]
produce, 2012, *dāšā'* [1]
rich produce, 3206, *ṭûb* [1]
produce, 3292, *y*^{e}*bûl* [1]
produce, 3330, *y*^{e}*gîa'* [1]
produce, 5951, *nāśā'* [1]
produce, 6289, *'*^{a}*bûr*^{2} [1]
produce, 7541, *ṣāmaḥ* [1]
produce, 7756, *qûm* [1]
the produce^{s}, 8611, *ša-* [1]
produce, 9311+2446+3655, *t*^{e}*bû'â+zera'+yāṣā'* [1]

PRODUCED [7]
produced, 6913, *'āśâ*^{1} [3]
produced, 1694, *gāmal* [1]
produced, 2118, *hāyâ* [1]
produced, 3655, *yāṣā'* [1]
produced, 9311, *t*^{e}*bû'â* [1]

PRODUCES [8]
produces, 3655, *yāṣā'* [4]
produces, *AIT* [1]
produces, 5989, *nātan* [1]
produces, 7238, *pārā*^{1} [1]
produces, 9311, *t*^{e}*bû'â* [1]

PRODUCING [1]
producing, 5989, *nātan* [1]

PRODUCT [1]
product, 9311, *t*^{e}*bû'â* [1]

PRODUCTS [5]
products, 3330, *y*^{e}*gîa'* [2]
products, 5126, *ma'*^{a}*śeh* [2]
best products, 2380, *zimrâ*^{2} [1]

PROFANE [12]
profane, 2725, *ḥālal*^{1} [11]
profane, 2729, *ḥālāl*^{2} [1]

PROFANED [13]
profaned, 2725, *ḥālal*^{1} [7]
being profaned, 2725, *ḥālal*^{1} [3]
am profaned, 2725, *ḥālal*^{1} [1]
been profaned, 2725, *ḥālal*^{1} [1]
let be profaned, 2725, *ḥālal*^{1} [1]

PROFIT [9]
profit, 4639, *môtār* [2]
profit, 2657, *ḥayil* [1]
profit, 3463, *yôtēr* [1]
profit, 3603, *yā'al* [1]
profit, 3862, *yitrôn* [1]
profit, 5270, *marbît* [1]
profit, 6087, *saḥar* [1]
profit, 6122, *sākan*^{1} [1]

PROFITABLE [2]
profitable, 3202+6087, *ṭôb*^{2}*+saḥar* [1]
profitable, 3202, *ṭôb*^{2} [1]

PROFITS [3]
profits, 6087, *saḥar* [1]
profits, 6122, *sākan*^{1} [1]
profits, 6268, *'ābad* [1]

PROFLIGATE [1]
profligate, 2361, *zālal*^{1} [1]

PROFOUND [3]
profound, 4222, *lēbāb* [1]
profound, 6676, *'āmaq* [1]
most profound, 6678+6678, *'āmōq+'āmōq* [1]

PROGRESS [1]
making rapid progress, 10613, *ṣ*^{e}*laḥ* [1]

PROGRESSED [1]
progressed, 6590, *'ālâ* [1]

PROJECT [3]
project, 4856, *m*^{e}*lā'kâ* [2]
project upward, 4200+5087+2025, *l*^{e}*-*^{1}*+ma'al*^{2}*+-â*^{2} [1]

PROJECTED [1]
projected, 8145, *rōḥab* [1]

PROJECTING [17]
projecting walls, 382, *'ayil*^{3} [9]
projecting, 3655, *yāṣā'* [3]
projecting, *NIH/RPE* [2]
projecting walls, 4190, *kātēp* [2]
projecting from, 4946, *min* [1]

PROJECTION [2]
projection, 3338, *yād* [2]

PROJECTIONS [2]
projections, 3338, *yād* [2]

PROJECTS [2]
projects, 4856, *m*^{e}*lā'kâ* [1]
projects, 5126, *ma'*^{a}*śeh* [1]

PROLONG [5]
prolong, 799, *'ārak* [2]
prolong, 802, *'ōrek* [1]
prolong, 3578, *yāsap* [1]
prolong, 5432, *māšak* [1]

PROLONGED [2]
prolonged, 586, *'āman*^{1} [1]
be prolonged, 5432, *māšak* [1]

PROMINENT [6]
prominent, 2607, *ḥāzût* [2]
prominent place, 8031, *rō'š*^{1} [2]
prominent, 1524, *gādôl* [1]
prominent, 5951+7156, *nāśā'+pāneh* [1]

PROMISCUITY [5]
promiscuity, 9373, *taznût* [5]

PROMISCUOUS [2]
promiscuous, 2388, *zānâ*^{1} [1]
promiscuous, 9373, *taznût* [1]

PROMISE [37]
promise, 1821, *dābār* [15]
promise, 614, *'imrâ* [11]
promise, 1819, *dābar*^{2} [4]
promise, *NIH/RPE* [2]
rash promise, 4439, *mibṭā'* [2]
promise, 608, *'ōmer* [1]
make promise, 1821+1819, *dābār+dābar*^{2} [1]
promise, 1821+1819, *dābār+dābar*^{2} [1]

PROMISED [96]
promised, 1819, *dābar*^{2} [51]
promised on oath, 8678, *šāba'* [21]
promised, 606, *'āmar*^{1} [10]
promised, 1821, *dābār* [4]
promised, *AIT* [2]
promised, 3655+4946+7023, *yāṣā'+min+peh* [2]
promised, 606+606, *'āmar*^{1}*+'āmar*^{1} [1]
promised, 1819+928+7023, *dābar*^{2}*+b*^{e}*-+peh* [1]
promised, 3072, *ḥārap*^{4} [1]
what promised, 5624, *nēder* [1]
promised, 7198, *pāṣâ* [1]
solemnly promised, 8678, *šāba'* [1]

PROMISES [13]
promises, 1821, *dābār* [5]
promises, 614, *'imrâ* [2]
promises made, 1819, *dābar*^{2} [2]
promises, *AIT* [1]
make many promises, 1819+1821, *dābar*^{2}*+dābār* [1]
promises, 1819, *dābar*^{2} [1]
promises, 1821+1819, *dābār+dābar*^{2} [1]

PROMOTE [6]
promote, 3578, *yāsap* [2]
promote, *NIH/RPE* [1]
promote, 1335, *bāqaš* [1]
promote, 3619, *yā'aṣ* [1]
promote, 3655, *yāṣā'* [1]

PROMOTED [3]
promoted wickedness, 7277, *pāra'*^{2} [1]
promoted, 10613, *ṣ*^{e}*laḥ* [1]
promoted, 10659, *rûm*^{1} [1]

PROMOTES [1]
promotes, 1335, *bāqaš* [1]

PROMPT [1]
prompt to answer, 8740, *šûb*^{1} [1]

PROMPTS [2]
prompts, 544, *'ālap*^{1} [1]
prompts to give, 5605, *nādab* [1]

PRONE [1]
prone to, 928, *b*^{e}*-* [1]

PRONOUNCE [30]
pronounce clean, 3197, *ṭāhēr* [9]
pronounce unclean, 3237, *ṭāmē'*^{1} [8]
pronounce blessings, 1385, *bārak*^{2} [3]
pronounce, 1819, *dābar*^{2} [3]
pronounce, *NIH/RPE* [1]
pronounce blessing, 1385, *bārak*^{2} [1]
pronounce ceremonially unclean, 3237, *ṭāmē'*^{1} [1]
pronounce unclean, 3237+3237, *ṭāmē'*^{1}*+ṭāmē'*^{1} [1]
pronounce guilty, 6835, *'āqaš* [1]
pronounce a curse on, 7837, *qālal* [1]
pronounce curses, 7839, *q*^{e}*lālâ* [1]

PRONOUNCED [20]
pronounced, 1819, *dābar*[2] [6]
pronounced on, 1819+907, *dābar*[2]*+'ēt*[2] [3]
pronounced clean, 3200, *ṭohorâ* [2]
pronounced, 7023, *peh* [2]
pronounced, 1385, *bārak*[2] [1]
pronounced, 3076, *ḥāraṣ*[1] [1]
pronounced unclean, 3237, *ṭāmē'*[1] [1]
pronounced, 7924, *qārā'*[1] [1]
pronounced solemn oath, 8678, *šāba'* [1]
pronounced, 9048, *šāma'* [1]
pronounced, 10314, *yehab* [1]

PRONOUNCES [1]
pronounces clean, 3197, *ṭāhēr* [1]

PRONOUNCING [1]
pronouncing clean, 3197, *ṭāhēr* [1]

PROOF [4]
proof of virginity, 1436, *betûlîm* [3]
proof that a virgin, 1436, *betûlîm* [1]

PROPER [16]
proper value, 6886, *'ērek* [3]
proper, *AIT* [2]
proper procedure, 5477, *mišpāṭ* [2]
proper time, 6961, *'ēt* [2]
proper, 3637, *yāpeh* [1]
proper kind, 5120, *ma'arākâ* [1]
proper place, 5226+889+2118+9004, *māqôm+'ašer+hāyâ+šām* [1]
proper place, 5477, *mišpāṭ* [1]
proper, 5791, *nākōaḥ* [1]
proper burial, 7690, *qebûrâ* [1]
proper, 10071, *'arîk* [1]

PROPERTY [58]
property, 299, *'aḥuzzâ* [28]
lost property, 8, *'abēdâ* [3]
property, 5709, *naḥalâ*[1] [3]
property, 8214, *rekûš* [3]
the property[s], 889, *'ašer* [2]
property, 4856, *melā'kâ* [2]
acquire property, 296, *'āḥaz*[1] [1]
acquired property, 296, *'āḥaz*[1] [1]
family property, 299, *'aḥuzzâ* [1]
property, 824+299, *'ereṣ+'aḥuzzâ* [1]
property[s], 889+2118+4200, *'ašer+hāyâ+le-*[1] [1]
property[s], 889, *'ašer* [1]
get share of property, 2745, *ḥālaq*[2] [1]
seized property, 3769, *yāraš*[1] [1]
property, 4084, *kesep* [1]
property, 5126, *ma'aśeh* [1]
property, 5239, *miqnâ* [1]
property, 5659, *nāweh*[1] [1]
ancestral property, 5709, *naḥalâ*[1] [1]
property, 7871, *qinyān* [1]
property, 8965, *šālāl* [1]
transfer of property, 9455+3972+1821, *temûrâ+kōl+dābār* [1]
property, 10479, *nekas* [1]

PROPHECIES [1]
prophecies, 5363, *maśśā'*[2] [1]

PROPHECY [5]
prophecy, 5553, *nebû'â* [2]
prophecy, 1821, *dābār* [1]
prophecy, 5363, *maśśā'*[2] [1]
prophecy, 5566, *nābî'* [1]

PROPHESIED [28]
prophesied, 5547, *nābā'* [26]
prophesied, 5553+1819, *nebû'â+dābar*[2] [1]
prophesied, 10451, *nebā'* [1]

PROPHESIES [8]
prophesies, 5547, *nābā'* [8]

PROPHESY [53]
prophesy, 5547, *nābā'* [47]
prophesy, 5752, *nāṭap* [3]
prophesy, 2600, *ḥāzâ* [1]
prophesy, 5566, *nābî'* [1]
those who prophesy, 5566, *nābî'* [1]

PROPHESYING [29]
prophesying, 5547, *nābā'* [28]
frantic prophesying, 5547, *nābā'* [1]

PROPHET [173]
prophet, 5566, *nābî'* [152]
prophet, *NIH/RPE* [14]
prophet, 10455, *nebî'* [3]
the prophet[s], 2085, *hû'* [1]
acts like a prophet, 5547, *nābā'* [1]
poses as a prophet, 5547, *nābā'* [1]
prophet, 5752, *nāṭap* [1]

PROPHET'S [2]
prophet's garment, 168, *'adderet* [1]
prophet's, 5566, *nābî'* [1]

PROPHETESS [6]
prophetess, 5567, *nebî'â* [6]

PROPHETIC [1]
prophetic, 5547, *nābā'* [1]

PROPHETS [156]
prophets, 5566, *nābî'* [150]
false prophets, 967, *bad*[5] [2]
prophets, 2602, *ḥōzeh*[1] [1]
prophets[s], 4392, *-ām* [1]
prophets say, 5752, *nāṭap* [1]
prophets, 10455, *nebî'* [1]

PROPORTION [3]
in proportion to, 3869+7023, *ke-+peh* [1]
in proportion to, 3869, *ke-* [1]
in proportion to, 5002+3869+889, *missâ+ke-+'ašer* [1]

PROPOSAL [1]
proposal, 1821, *dābār* [1]

PROPOSE [2]
propose, 1819, *dābar*[2] [2]

PROPOSED [3]
proposed, *NIH/RPE* [1]
proposed, 606, *'āmar*[1] [1]
proposed, 1821, *dābār* [1]

PROPPED [2]
propped up, 6641, *'āmad* [2]

PROSPECT [1]
prospect, 9347, *tôḥelet* [1]

PROSPECTS [1]
prospects, 7891, *qēṣ* [1]

PROSPER [29]
prosper, 7503, *ṣālaḥ*[2] [7]
make prosper, 3512, *yāṭab* [3]
prosper, 8505, *śākal*[1] [3]
prosper, 2014, *dāšēn*[1] [2]
prosper, 8934, *šālôm* [2]
prosper, 10720, *šelām* [2]
prosper, 1215, *bānâ* [1]
make prosper, 3201, *ṭôb*[1] [1]
prosper, 3201, *ṭôb*[1] [1]
prosper, 3202, *ṭôb*[2] [1]
prosper, 3206, *ṭûb* [1]
prosper, 3512, *yāṭab* [1]
surely make prosper, 3512+3512, *yāṭab+yāṭab* [1]
prosper, 4848, *mālē'*[1] [1]
prosper, 5162+3202, *māṣā'+ṭôb*[2] [1]
prosper, 10613, *ṣelaḥ* [1]

PROSPERED [7]
prospered, 7503, *ṣālaḥ*[2] [5]
prospered, 3202, *ṭôb*[2] [1]
prospered, 10613, *ṣelaḥ* [1]

PROSPERITY [31]
prosperity, 3202, *ṭôb*[2] [9]
prosperity, 3208, *ṭôbâ* [9]
prosperity, 8934, *šālôm* [5]
prosperity, 3206, *ṭûb* [3]
prosperity, 7407, *ṣedāqâ* [2]
prosperity, 8044+3972, *rōb+kōl* [1]
peace and prosperity, 8934, *šālôm* [1]
prosperity, 10713, *šelēwâ* [1]

PROSPEROUS [11]
prosperous, 2656, *ḥîl*[2] [1]
prosperous, 3202, *ṭôb*[2] [1]
prosperous, 3208, *ṭôbâ* [1]
make more prosperous, 3512, *yāṭab* [1]
prosperous, 3769+6807, *yāraš*[1]*+'ēṣer* [1]
prosperous, 7287, *pāraṣ* [1]
prosperous, 7503, *ṣālaḥ*[2] [1]
prosperous, 8436, *śāgâ* [1]
made prosperous again, 8740+8654, *šûb*[1]*+šebût* [1]
prosperous, 8929, *šālēw* [1]
prosperous, 10670, *ra'anan* [1]

PROSPERS [6]
prospers, 5162+3202, *māṣā'+ṭôb*[2] [2]
prospers, 5952+3338, *nāśag+yād* [2]
prospers, 7503, *ṣālaḥ*[2] [1]
prospers, 8934, *šālôm* [1]

PROSTITUTE [44]
prostitute, 2390, *zōnâ* [20]
prostitute, 2388, *zānâ*[1] [12]
shrine prostitute, 7728, *qādēš*[1] [4]
hire as a prostitute, 924, *'etnan* [1]
wages of a prostitute, 924, *'etnan* [1]
caused to prostitute themselves, 2388, *zānâ*[1] [1]
led to prostitute themselves, 2388, *zānâ*[1] [1]
making a prostitute, 2388, *zānâ*[1] [1]
use as a prostitute, 2388+9373, *zānâ*[1]*+taznût* [1]
male prostitute, 3978, *keleb* [1]
prostitute, 9373, *taznût* [1]

PROSTITUTE'S [1]
prostitute's, 2390, *zōnâ* [1]

PROSTITUTED [5]
prostituted, 2388, *zānâ*[1] [5]

PROSTITUTES [15]
prostitutes, 2390, *zōnâ* [7]
shrine prostitutes, 7728, *qādēš*[1] [5]
prostitutes, 2388, *zānâ*[1] [2]
prostitutes of the shrines, 7728, *qādēš*[1] [1]

PROSTITUTING [1]
prostituting, 2388, *zānâ*[1] [1]

PROSTITUTION [35]
prostitution, 9373, *taznût* [8]
prostitution, 2394, *zenût* [7]
engaged in prostitution, 2388, *zānâ*[1] [4]
prostitution, 2393, *zenûnîm* [4]
turn to prostitution, 2388, *zānâ*[1] [3]
prostitution, 2390, *zōnâ* [2]
carried on prostitution, 2388, *zānâ*[1] [1]
continue prostitution, 2388+2388, *zānâ*[1]*+zānâ*[1] [1]
engage in prostitution, 2388, *zānâ*[1] [1]
engaging in prostitution, 2388, *zānâ*[1] [1]
guilty of prostitution, 2388, *zānâ*[1] [1]
prostitution, 2388, *zānâ*[1] [1]
turned to prostitution, 2388, *zānâ*[1] [1]

PROSTRATE [11]
falls prostrate, 5877, *nāpal* [2]
fell prostrate, 5877, *nāpal* [2]
prostrate, 6584+7156, *'al*[2]*+pāneh* [2]
fell prostrate, 2556, *ḥāwâ*[2] [1]
prostrate, 3718, *yārad* [1]
lay prostrate, 5877, *nāpal* [1]
fall prostrate, 8817, *šāḥâ* [1]
prostrate, 10542+10049, *'al+'anap* [1]

PROSTRATED [2]
prostrated himself, 2556, *ḥāwâ*[2] [2]

PROTECT [25]
protect, 5915, *nāṣar* [8]
protect, 9068, *šāmar* [5]
protect, 8435, *śāgab* [4]
protect, 5911, *nāṣal* [2]
protect, 6641+6584, *'āmad+'al*[2] [2]
protect lives, 2649, *ḥāyâ* [1]

protect, 5057, *mā'ôz* [1]
protect, 6468, *'āzar* [1]
protect, 8883+928+3829, *šît*[1]*+be-+yēša'* [1]

PROTECTED [5]
protected, 9068, *šāmar* [2]
be protected, 2461, *ḥābā'* [1]
protected, 5911, *nāṣal* [1]
be protected, 9068, *šāmar* [1]

PROTECTION [9]
protection, 5057, *mā'ôz* [2]
protection, 7498, *ṣēl* [2]
wall of protection, 1555, *gādēr* [1]
protection from, 4946+7156, *min+pāneh* [1]
protection, 5236, *miqlāṭ* [1]
spread protection, 6114, *sākak*[1] [1]
protection, 6644, *'emdâ* [1]

PROTECTIVE [1]
protective shield, 6116, *sōkēk* [1]

PROTECTS [4]
protects, 9068, *šāmar* [3]
protects, 6641+6584, *'āmad+'al*[2] [1]

PROTEST [1]
protest, 606, *'āmar* [1]

PROUD [36]
proud, 1450, *gē'eh* [7]
proud, 1454, *gā'ôn* [5]
proud, 1467, *gābah* [5]
proud, 2086, *hôd*[1] [2]
proud, 8123, *rûm*[1] [2]
proud, 8146, *rāḥāb*[1] [2]
proud beasts, 1201+8832, *bēn*[1]*+šaḥaṣ* [1]
proud, 1201+8832, *bēn*[1]*+šaḥaṣ* [1]
proud, 1452, *ga'awâ* [1]
proud, 1468, *gābēah* [1]
proud, 1469, *gābōah* [1]
proud, 2294, *zēd* [1]
proud, 3877, *kābēd*[1] [1]
proud mockers, 4370, *lēṣ* [1]
proud, 6913+1452, *'āśâ*[1]*+ga'awâ* [1]
proud, 8107, *rāhāb* [1]
proud, 8123+4213, *rûm*[1]*+lēb* [1]
proud, 8123+4222, *rûm*[1]*+lēbāb* [1]
proud, 8633, *ša'anān* [1]

PROUDLY [3]
tower proudly, 1467, *gābah* [1]
so proudly, 1469+1469, *gābōah+gābōah* [1]
proudly, 8127, *rômâ* [1]

PROVE [9]
prove false, 3941, *kāzab* [2]
prove, *NIH/RPE* [1]
prove to be, 2118, *hāyâ* [1]
prove, 3519, *yākaḥ* [1]
prove a liar, 3941, *kāzab* [1]
prove to be, 5989, *nātan* [1]
prove innocence, 7405, *ṣādaq* [1]
prove right, 7405, *ṣādaq* [1]

PROVED [8]
been proved, 3922, *kûn*[1] [2]
proved, *NIH/RPE* [1]
proved to be, 2118, *hāyâ* [1]
proved stronger, 2616, *ḥāzaq* [1]
proved wrong, 3519, *yākaḥ* [1]
proved right, 7405, *ṣādaq* [1]
proved true, 7671, *ṣārap* [1]

PROVERB [8]
proverb, 5442, *māšāl*[1] [7]
quote proverb, 5439, *māšal*[1] [1]

PROVERBS [8]
proverbs, 5442, *māšāl*[1] [7]
quotes proverbs, 5439, *māšal*[1] [1]

PROVES [1]
proves, *NIH/RPE* [1]

PROVIDE [44]
provide, 6913, *'āśâ*[1] [14]
provide, 5989, *nātan* [4]
provide, 3920, *kûl* [3]
provide, 3922, *kûn*[1] [3]
provide, 8492, *śîm* [3]
provide, *NIH/RPE* [2]
provide, 8011, *rā'â*[1] [2]
provide, 273, *'āzar* [1]
provide, 995, *bô'* [1]
provide justice, 1906, *dîn*[1] [1]
provide a foundation, 3569, *yāsad*[1] [1]
provide supplies, 3920, *kûl* [1]
provide with, 4200, *le-*[1] [1]
provide, 4252, *lābaš* [1]
provide, 4848, *mālē'*[1] [1]
provide, 5951, *nāśā'* [1]
provide safe-conduct, 6296, *'ābar*[1] [1]
provide, 7756, *qûm* [1]
provide, 10498, *netan* [1]
provide, 10522, *'abad* [1]

PROVIDED [37]
provided, 3922, *kûn*[1] [9]
provided, 4948, *mānâ*[1] [4]
provided, 5989, *nātan* [4]
provided, 6913, *'āśâ*[1] [4]
provided, 8123, *rûm*[1] [4]
provided, 3920, *kûl* [3]
provided, *NIH/RPE* [2]
provided, 561+421, *'im+'ak* [1]
provided, 606, *'āmar*[1] [1]
provided for, 2118+4200+4312+2256+430,
hāyâ+le-[1]*+leḥem+we-+'ākal* [1]
well provided for, 3512, *yāṭab* [1]
provided with clothes, 4252, *lābaš* [1]
be provided, 8011, *rā'â*[1] [1]
provided, 8492, *śîm* [1]
provided, 8938, *šālaḥ* [1]

PROVIDENCE [1]
providence, 7213, *pequddâ* [1]

PROVIDES [9]
provides, 5989, *nātan* [4]
provides, 4059, *kāsâ* [2]
provides, 3922, *kûn*[1] [1]
provides for, 4200, *le-*[1] [1]
provides, 6913, *'āśâ*[1] [1]

PROVIDING [5]
providing, *NIH/RPE* [2]
providing, 5989, *nātan* [2]
providing, 6913, *'āśâ*[1] [1]

PROVINCE [22]
province, 4519, *medînâ* [10]
province, 10406, *medînâ* [7]
each province, 4519+2256+4519,
medînâ+we-+medînâ [3]
every province, 4519+2256+4519,
medînâ+we-+medînâ [1]
that province[s], 10526+10468+10191,
'abar+nehar+-â [1]

PROVINCES [22]
provinces, 4519, *medînâ* [20]
various provinces, 4519+2256+4519,
medînâ+we-+medînâ [1]
provinces, 10406, *medînâ* [1]

PROVINCIAL [7]
provincial, 4519, *medînâ* [5]
provincial, 10406, *medînâ* [2]

PROVISION [3]
provision, *NIH/RPE* [1]
make provision, 6913, *'āśâ*[1] [1]
provision, 7049, *pûq*[2] [1]

PROVISIONS [19]
provisions, 7476, *ṣêdâ* [6]
supplied provisions, 3920, *kûl* [2]
provisions, 4312, *leḥem* [2]
provisions, 4648, *māzôn* [2]
provisions, 7474, *ṣayid*[2] [2]
eaten provisions, 430+430, *'ākal+'ākal* [1]
provisions, 786, *'aruḥâ* [1]
given provisions, 3920, *kûl* [1]
supplied provisions, 3922, *kûn*[1] [1]
provisions, 7329, *pat-bag* [1]

PROVOCATION [1]
provocation, 4088, *ka'as* [1]

PROVOKE [14]
provoke to anger, 4087, *kā'as* [7]
provoke to war, 1741, *gārâ* [2]
provoke, 4087, *kā'as* [2]
provoke, 1741, *gārâ* [1]
provoke to anger, 4088+4087, *ka'as+kā'as* [1]
provoke, 8074, *rāgaz* [1]

PROVOKED [27]
provoked to anger, 4087, *kā'as* [19]
provoked, 4087, *kā'as* [4]
provoked to anger, 4088+4087, *ka'as+kā'as* [2]
provoked to anger, 4088, *ka'as* [1]
provoked to anger, 7911, *qāṣap* [1]

PROVOKES [1]
provokes to jealousy, 7861, *qānā'* [1]

PROVOKING [8]
provoking to anger, 4087, *kā'as* [6]
kept provoking, 4087+1685+4088,
kā'as+gam+ka'as [1]
provoking, 4087, *kā'as* [1]

PROWL [4]
prowl about, 6015, *sābab* [3]
prowl, 8253, *rāmaś* [1]

PROWLED [1]
prowled, 2143, *hālak* [1]

PROWLING [1]
prowling, 2143, *hālak* [1]

PROWLS [1]
prowls, 6334, *'ādâ*[1] [1]

PRUDENCE [5]
prudence, 6893, *'ormâ* [3]
learn prudence, 6891, *'āram*[2] [1]
shows prudence, 6891, *'āram*[2] [1]

PRUDENT [12]
prudent, 6874, *'ārûm* [8]
prudent, 8505, *śākal*[1] [3]
prudent, 1067, *bîn*[1] [1]

PRUNE [2]
prune, 2377, *zāmar*[2] [2]

PRUNED [1]
pruned, 2377, *zāmar*[2] [1]

PRUNING [4]
pruning hooks, 4661, *mazmērâ* [3]
pruning knives, 4661, *mazmērâ* [1]

PSALM [60]
psalm, 4660, *mizmôr* [57]
psalm of thanks, 3344, *yādâ*[2] [1]
psalm of praise, 5380, *maśkîl* [1]
psalm of praise, 9335, *tehillâ* [1]

PUAH [5]
Puah, 7025, *pû'â* [4]
Puah, 7045, *pû'â* [1]

PUBLIC [12]
public square, 8148, *reḥōb*[1] [6]
public squares, 8148, *reḥōb*[1] [5]
public charge, 460, *'ālâ*[4] [1]

PUBLISH [1]
publish, 10673, *rešam* [1]

PUBLISHED [2]
been published, 5989, *nātan* [1]
been published, 10673, *rešam* [1]

PUFFED [1]
puffed up, 6752, *'āpal*[1] [1]

PUITE [1]
Puite, 7027, *pû'î* [1]

PUL [2]
Pul, 7040, *pûl*^{2} [2]

PULL [11]
pull down, 3718, *yārad* [2]
pull down, 2238, *hāras* [1]
pull up, 3106, *ḥāśap*^{1} [1]
pull in, 5432, *māšak* [1]
pull up, 5951, *nāśā'* [1]
pull off, 5998, *nātaq* [1]
pull out, 6590, *'ālâ* [1]
pull back, 8740, *šûb*^{1} [1]
pull out, 8963+8963, *šālal*^{1}*+šālal*^{1} [1]
pull out, 8990, *šālap* [1]

PULLED [15]
pulled up, 5825, *nāsa'* [2]
pulled down, 5997, *nātaṣ* [2]
pulled back, 995, *bô'* [1]
pulled over, 4286, *lûṭ* [1]
pulled out beard, 5307, *māraṭ* [1]
pulled out hair, 5307, *māraṭ* [1]
pulled, 5307, *māraṭ* [1]
pulled up, 5432, *māšak* [1]
pulled, 5432, *māšak* [1]
are pulled up, 5825, *nāsa'* [1]
been pulled down, 5825, *nāsa'* [1]
pulled, 5989, *nātan* [1]
be pulled, 10481, *n*^{e}*saḥ* [1]

PULLS [3]
pulls down, 3718, *yārad* [1]
pulls up, 6590, *'ālâ* [1]
pulls, 8990, *šālap* [1]

PUNISH [64]
punish, 7212, *pāqad* [45]
punish, 3579, *yāsar*^{1} [5]
punish, 3519, *yākaḥ* [3]
punish, 5782, *nākâ* [2]
punish, *AIT* [1]
punish, *NIH/RPE* [1]
punish, 1906, *dîn*^{1} [1]
punish, 6700, *'ānâ*^{2} [1]
punish, 6740, *'ānaš* [1]
punish, 6913+5477, *'āśâ*^{1}*+mišpāṭ* [1]
punish, 8657, *šēbeṭ* [1]
punish, 9149, *šāpaṭ* [1]
punish, 9350, *tôkaḥat* [1]

PUNISHED [26]
punished, 7212, *pāqad* [5]
punished, 7213, *p*^{e}*quddâ* [4]
punished, 5782, *nākâ* [3]
be punished, 7212, *pāqad* [2]
punished, 872, *'āšēm* [1]
punished for sins, 2628, *ḥēṭ'* [1]
punished less, 3104+4200+4752, *ḥāśak+l*^{e}*-*^{1}*+maṭṭâ* [1]
punished, 4592, *mûsār* [1]
be punished, 5933, *nāqam* [1]
must be punished, 5933+5933, *nāqam+nāqam* [1]
punished, 5933, *nāqam* [1]
punished, 6411, *'āwōn* [1]
punished, 6740, *'ānaš* [1]
punished, 7936+6411, *qārâ*^{1}*+'āwōn* [1]
punished, 9350, *tôkaḥat* [1]
punished, 10170+10191+10522, *dîn*^{2}*+-â+'*^{a}*bad* [1]

PUNISHES [4]
punishes, 7212, *pāqad* [3]
punishes, 6215, *sāpaq*^{1} [1]

PUNISHING [4]
punishing, 7212, *pāqad* [2]
punishing, *NIH/RPE* [1]
punishing, 4592, *mûsār* [1]

PUNISHMENT [45]
punishment, 6411, *'āwōn* [9]
punishment, 9150, *šepeṭ* [9]
punishment, 5477, *mišpāṭ* [6]
punishment, 2633, *ḥaṭṭā't* [3]
punishment, 7213, *p*^{e}*quddâ* [3]
punishment, 4592, *mûsār* [2]
punishment, *NIH/RPE* [1]
punishment, 224, *'āwen*^{1} [1]
due punishment, 1334, *biqqōret* [1]
punishment for sins, 6411, *'āwōn* [1]
punishment, 6961, *'ēt* [1]
bestow punishment, 7212, *pāqad* [1]
bring punishment, 7212, *pāqad* [1]
punishment, 8288, *rā'â*^{3} [1]
inflicted punishment, 8399, *rāša'* [1]
bring punishment, 8966, *šālēm*^{1} [1]
punishment, 8974, *šillumâ* [1]
punishment, 9144, *š*^{e}*pôṭ* [1]
punishment, 9349, *tôkēḥâ* [1]

PUNISHMENTS [1]
punishments come, 7212, *pāqad* [1]

PUNON [2]
Punon, 7044, *pûnōn* [2]

PUR [3]
pur, 7052, *pûr*^{2} [3]

PURAH [2]
Purah, 7242, *purâ* [2]

PURCHASE [6]
purchase, 5239, *miqnâ* [3]
purchase, 7864, *qānâ*^{1} [2]
purchase, *NIH/RPE* [1]

PURCHASED [4]
purchased, 4374+928+4697, *lāqaḥ+b*^{e}*-+m*^{e}*ḥîr*^{1} [2]
purchased, 7864, *qānâ*^{1} [2]

PURE [81]
pure, 3196, *ṭāhôr* [42]
pure, 6034, *sāgûr* [8]
pure, 2341, *zak* [6]
pure gold, 7058, *paz* [5]
pure, 1338, *bar*^{2} [3]
pure, 1405, *bārar*^{1} [3]
show yourself pure, 1405, *bārar*^{1} [2]
pure gold, 2298+2298, *zāhāb+zāhāb* [2]
kept pure, 2342, *zākâ* [2]
pure, 2342, *zākâ* [2]
pure, 2348, *zākak* [2]
keep pure, 2342, *zākâ* [1]
pure, 3197, *ṭāhēr* [1]
pure gold, 4188, *ketem* [1]
pure, 10294, *ṭāb* [1]

PUREST [1]
purest gold, 4188+7058, *ketem+paz* [1]

PURGE [16]
purge, 1278, *bā'ar*^{2} [12]
purge, *NIH/RPE* [1]
purge, 1405, *bārar*^{1} [1]
purge, 3197, *ṭāhēr* [1]
thoroughly purge away, 7671+3869+2021+1342, *ṣārap+k*^{e}*+ha-+bōr*^{2} [1]

PURGED [2]
purged, 3197, *ṭāhēr* [1]
are purged out, 5998, *nātaq* [1]

PURIFICATION [6]
purification, 3198, *ṭōhar* [2]
purification, 3200, *ṭoh*^{o}*râ* [2]
purification from sin, 2633, *ḥaṭṭā't* [1]
purification offering, 2633, *ḥaṭṭā't* [1]

PURIFIED [18]
purified, 3197, *ṭāhēr* [4]
purified, 2627, *ḥāṭā'* [2]
purified themselves, 3197, *ṭāhēr* [2]
purified, 3200, *ṭoh*^{o}*râ* [2]
be purified, 1405, *bārar*^{1} [1]
purified, 1405, *bārar*^{1} [1]
purified, 2423, *zāqaq* [1]
be purified, 2627, *ḥāṭā'* [1]
purified themselves, 2627, *ḥāṭā'* [1]
purified themselves ceremonially, 3197, *ṭāhēr* [1]
have purified, 7727, *qādaš* [1]
purified herself, 7727, *qādaš* [1]

PURIFIER [1]
purifier, 3197, *ṭāhēr* [1]

PURIFY [25]
purify, 2627, *ḥāṭā'* [9]
purify, 3197, *ṭāhēr* [7]
purify himself, 2627, *ḥāṭā'* [3]
purify themselves, 3197, *ṭāhēr* [3]
purify, 2200+1359, *hāpak+bārûr* [1]
purify yourselves, 2627, *ḥāṭā'* [1]
purify yourselves, 3197, *ṭāhēr* [1]

PURIFYING [1]
purifying, 2627, *ḥāṭā'* [1]

PURIM [5]
Purim, 7052, *pûr*^{2} [5]

PURITY [1]
purity, 5931, *niqqāyôn* [1]

PURPLE [42]
purple, 763, *'argāmān* [36]
purple, 10066, *'arg*^{e}*wān* [3]
purple, 760, *'arg*^{e}*wān* [1]
purple material, 763, *'argāmān* [1]
purple, 9355, *tôlā'*^{1} [1]

PURPOSE [16]
purpose, 6783, *'ēṣâ*^{1} [3]
purpose, *NIH/RPE* [2]
purpose, *AIT* [1]
for this purpose, 928+6288, *b*^{e}*-+'*^{a}*bûr*^{1} [1]
that purpose^{s}, 2146, *hālal*^{2} [1]
carry out purpose, 2372, *zāmam* [1]
purpose, 2914, *ḥēpeṣ* [1]
purpose, 4213, *lēb* [1]
purpose, 4222, *lēbāb* [1]
purpose, 4659, *m*^{e}*zimmâ* [1]
purpose, 4856, *m*^{e}*lā'kâ* [1]
achieve purpose, 7503, *ṣālaḥ*^{2} [1]
no purpose, 8198, *rîq*^{2} [1]

PURPOSED [4]
purposed, 3619, *yā'aṣ* [2]
purposed, 4742+3108, *maḥ*^{a}*šābâ+ḥāšab* [2]

PURPOSES [7]
purposes, 4742, *maḥ*^{a}*šābâ* [3]
purposes, 4659, *m*^{e}*zimmâ* [2]
purposes, 6783, *'ēṣâ*^{1} [2]

PURSE [3]
purse, 7655, *ṣ*^{e}*rôr*^{1} [2]
purse, 3967, *kîs* [1]

PURSES [2]
purses, 3038, *ḥārîṭ* [1]
purses, 7975, *qāraṣ* [1]

PURSUE [46]
pursue, 8103, *rādap* [33]
pursue, 339, *'aḥar* [5]
hotly pursue, 8634, *šā'ap*^{1} [2]
pursue, 8938+339, *šālaḥ+'aḥar* [2]
pursue, 339+2143, *'aḥar+hālak* [1]
pursue, 1335, *bāqaš* [1]
pursue, 3655+339, *yāṣā'+'aḥar* [1]
pursue, 8634, *šā'ap*^{1} [1]

PURSUED [28]
pursued, 8103, *rādap* [27]
pursued, 2143+339, *hālak+'aḥar* [1]

PURSUER [1]
pursuer, 8103, *rādap* [1]

PURSUERS [7]
pursuers, 8103, *rādap* [7]

PURSUES [11]
pursues, 8103, *rādap* [9]
pursues, 1335, *bāqaš* [1]
pursues, 8740+928, *šûb*^{1}*+b*^{e}*-* [1]

PURSUING [20]
pursuing, 8103, *rādap* [11]
pursuing, 339, *'aḥar* [5]
pursuing, 4946+339, *min+'aḥar* [2]
pursuing, 1335, *bāqaš* [1]
pursuing, 2143+339, *hālak+'aḥar* [1]

PURSUIT [13]
pursuit, 8103, *rādap* [3]
went in pursuit, 8103, *rādap* [3]
in pursuit, 8103, *rādap* [2]
in hot pursuit, 339, *'aḥar* [1]
pursuit, 339, *'aḥar* [1]
give up pursuit, 6073, *sûr*[1] [1]
came by in pursuit, 8103, *rādap* [1]
set out in pursuit, 8103, *rādap* [1]

PUSH [5]
push away, 2074, *hādap* [1]
push down, 2074, *hādap* [1]
push out, 3769, *yāraš*[1] [1]
push back, 5590, *nāgaḥ* [1]
push, 5989, *nātan* [1]

PUSHED [5]
was pushed back, 1890+1890, *dāḥâ+dāḥâ* [1]
pushed, 5742, *nāṭâ* [1]
pushed, 8938, *šālaḥ* [1]
pushed back, 8959, *šālak* [1]
pushed down, 8959, *šālak* [1]

PUSHING [1]
pushing, 5615, *nādaḥ*[1] [1]

PUT [811]
put, 5989, *nātan* [169]
put, 8492, *śîm* [106]
put to death, 4637, *mût* [43]
put to shame, 1017, *bôš*[1] [41]
be put to death, 4637, *mût* [26]
put, 5782, *nākâ* [24]
put on, 4252, *lābaš* [23]
must be put to death, 4637+4637, *mût+mût* [18]
put, *NIH/RPE* [17]
put hope, 3498, *yāḥal* [14]
put an end, 8697, *šābat*[1] [14]
put on, 2520, *ḥāgar* [13]
put back, 8740, *šûb*[1] [10]
put, 8883, *šît*[1] [9]
put, 5663, *nûaḥ*[1] [8]
put, 995, *bô'* [7]
put to death, 2222, *hārag* [7]
Put, 7033, *pûṭ* [7]
put to, 5448, *mišlāḥ* [6]
put to the test, 5814, *nāsâ* [6]
put in charge, 7212, *pāqad* [6]
put in isolation, 6037, *sāgar* [5]
put, 8959, *šālak* [5]
put, *AIT* [4]
put trust, 1053, *bāṭaḥ*[1] [4]
put an end, 3983, *kālâ*[1] [4]
put, 4374, *lāqaḥ* [4]
shall be put to death, 4637+4637, *mût+mût* [4]
surely be put to death, 4637+4637, *mût+mût* [4]
put in place, 6641, *'āmad* [4]
put, 6913, *'āśâ*[1] [4]
put, 8206, *rākab* [4]
put in place, 8492, *śîm* [4]
put up, 8492, *śîm* [4]
put to death, 10625, *q^{e}ṭal* [4]
put, 2118, *hāyâ* [3]
put, 2222, *hārag* [3]
put on, 4059, *kāsâ* [3]
put to death, 5782, *nākâ* [3]
put, 5877, *nāpal* [3]
put, 5951, *nāśā'* [3]
put out, 6422, *'āwar*[1] [3]
put in order, 7422, *ṣāwâ* [3]
put under oath, 8678, *šāba'* [3]
put on, 9189, *šāpat* [3]
put trust, 586, *'āman*[1] [2]
put, 665, *'āsap* [2]
put a curse on, 826, *'ārar* [2]
put in, 995, *bô'* [2]
put confidence, 1053, *bāṭaḥ*[1] [2]
put, 2502, *ḥābaš* [2]
put heavy, 3877, *kābēd*[1] [2]
put out, 3882, *kābâ* [2]
put over, 4059, *kāsâ* [2]
put an end, 4162, *kārat* [2]
put[s], 4637, *mût* [2]
put down, 5663, *nûaḥ*[1] [2]
been put, 5989, *nātan* [2]
put away, 6073, *sûr*[1] [2]
put, 6296, *'ābar*[1] [2]
put into practice, 6913, *'āśâ*[1] [2]
put to silence, 7551, *ṣāmat* [2]
put a curse on, 7686, *qābab* [2]
put heavy, 7996, *qāšâ* [2]
put away, 8178, *rāḥaq* [2]
put a stop, 8697, *šābat*[1] [2]
put, 8886, *šākab* [2]
put aside, 9101, *šānâ*[1] [2]
put an end, 9462, *tāmam* [2]
put in writing, 10673+10375, *r^{e}šam+k^{e}tāb* [2]
put an end, 430, *'ākal* [1]
put under oath, 460+9048, *'ālâ[4]+šāma'* [1]
put in bonds, 673, *'āsar* [1]
put in chains, 673, *'āsar* [1]
put, 673, *'āsar* [1]
put in charge of the storerooms, 732+6584+238, *'āṣar+'al[2]+'ôṣār* [1]
put, 995+4200+7156, *bô'+l^{e-1}+pāneh* [1]
let be put to shame, 1017, *bôš*[1] [1]
put to flight, 1368, *bāraḥ*[1] [1]
put limits around, 1487, *gābal* [1]
put limits, 1487, *gābal* [1]
put, 2035, *hab*[1] [1]
put, 2063, *hādâ* [1]
must certainly put to death, 2222+2222, *hārag+hārag* [1]
put to death, 2222+2222, *hārag+hārag* [1]
put to death, 2222+4638, *hārag+māwet* [1]
put sackcloth around, 2520, *ḥāgar* [1]
put away, 3655, *yāṣā'* [1]
put out, 3655+2021+2575, *yāṣā'+ha+ḥûṣ* [1]
put to sleep, 3822, *yāšēn*[1] [1]
put in place, 3922, *kûn*[1] [1]
be put to shame, 4007, *kālam* [1]
put to shame, 4007, *kālam* [1]
put in writing, 4180, *kātab* [1]
put up security, 4200+3338+9546, *l^{e-1}+yād+tāqa'* [1]
put on, 4230, *l^{e}bûš* [1]
put clothes on, 4252, *lābaš* [1]
put on as clothing, 4252, *lābaš* [1]
put on clothes, 4252, *lābaš* [1]
put on robes, 4252, *lābaš* [1]
put on, 4252+9432, *lābaš+tilbōšet* [1]
put on, 4534, *midrāk* [1]
certainly be put to death, 4637+4637, *mût+mût* [1]
is put to death, 4637, *mût* [1]
must be put to death, 4637, *mût* [1]
must put to death, 4637+4637, *mût+mût* [1]
put death, 4637, *mût* [1]
put to death, 4637+4637, *mût+mût* [1]
was put to death, 4637, *mût* [1]
were put to death, 4637, *mût* [1]
put on throne, 4887, *mālak*[1] [1]
put, 5595, *nāga'* [1]
put off, 5612, *nādâ* [1]
put, 5633, *nāhal* [1]
put to flight, 5674, *nûs* [1]
put, 5677, *nûp*[1] [1]
must certainly put, 5782+5782, *nākâ+nākâ* [1]
was put to death, 5782, *nākâ* [1]
put to one side, 5825, *nāsa'* [1]
put sandals on, 5836, *nā'al[2]* [1]
put himself forward, 5951, *nāśā'* [1]
put in jeopardy, 5951+1414+928+9094, *nāśā'+bāśār+b^{e}+šēn*[1] [1]
put, 5952, *nāśag* [1]
are put, 5989, *nātan* [1]
put in place, 5989, *nātan* [1]
put on, 5989+4230, *nātan+l^{e}bûš* [1]
put out, 5989, *nātan* [1]
put up, 5989, *nātan* [1]
put around, 6015, *sābab* [1]
put on lotions, 6057, *sûk*[2] [1]
put on, 6057, *sûk*[2] [1]
put aside, 6073, *sûr*[1] [1]
put out, 6073, *sûr*[1] [1]
put to work, 6268, *'ābad* [1]
put a yoke, 6296, *'ābar*[1] [1]
put an end, 6296, *'ābar*[1] [1]
put on jewelry, 6335+6344, *'ādâ[2]+'^{a}dî* [1]
put on, 6335, *'ādâ*[2] [1]
put on, 6590, *'ālâ* [1]
put in charge, 6641+6584+3338, *'āmad+'al[2]+yād* [1]
put on, 6698, *'ānad* [1]
put up security, 6842, *'ārab*[1] [1]
put forth, 6913, *'āśâ*[1] [1]
put in jeopardy, 6913+9214, *'āśâ[1]+šeqer* [1]
put away, 7212, *pāqad* [1]
put, 7212, *pāqad* [1]
put away, 7296, *pārar*[1] [1]
put in charge, 7422, *ṣāwâ* [1]
put into bags, 7443, *ṣûr*[1] [1]
put on, 7571, *ṣānap* [1]
put trust, 7747, *qāwâ*[1] [1]
put a curse on, 7837, *qālal* [1]
put on a leash, 8003, *qāšar* [1]
put on, 8003, *qāšar* [1]
put to flight, 8103, *rādap* [1]
put in, 8354, *rāṣâ*[1] [1]
put to death, 8357, *rāṣaḥ* [1]
were put in chains, 8415+928+2414, *rātaq+b^{e}+zēq*[1] [1]
put a hedge, 8455, *śûk* [1]
put in charge, 8492, *śîm* [1]
put on, 8492+928+5516, *śîm+b^{e}+motnayim* [1]
put oath, 8678+8652, *šāba'+š^{e}bû'â* [1]
put out, 8938, *šālaḥ* [1]
put, 8938, *šālaḥ* [1]
put, 9068, *šāmar* [1]
put to death, 9119, *šāsap* [1]
put, 9202+4200+995, *šāqal+l^{e-1}+bô'* [1]
put a mark, 9344+9338, *tāwâ[1]+tāw* [1]
put in writing, 10673, *r^{e}šam* [1]

PUTHITES [1]
Puthites, 7057, *pûtî* [1]

PUTIEL [1]
Putiel, 7034, *pûṭî'ēl* [1]

PUTS [18]
puts, 8492, *śîm* [5]
puts up security, 6842, *'ārab*[1] [4]
puts, 5989, *nātan* [2]
puts on armor, 2520, *ḥāgar* [1]
puts, 3718, *yārad* [1]
puts to shame, 4007, *kālam* [1]
puts on, 4252, *lābaš* [1]
puts up a bold front, 6451+928+7156, *'āzaz+b^{e}+pāneh* [1]
puts up security, 6842+6859, *'ārab[1]+'^{a}rubbâ* [1]
puts in command, 7422, *ṣāwâ* [1]

PUTTING [18]
putting, 8492, *śîm* [4]
putting to death, 4637, *mût* [3]
putting, 5989, *nātan* [2]
putting, 995, *bô'* [1]
putting marks, 2977, *ḥāqâ* [1]
putting in writing, 4180, *kātab* [1]
putting on, 4252, *lābaš* [1]
putting, 5616, *nādaḥ*[2] [1]
putting to death, 5782, *nākâ* [1]
putting to rout, 5782, *nākâ* [1]
putting in place, 6641, *'āmad* [1]
putting, 8938, *šālaḥ* [1]

QUAIL [4]
quail, 8513, *ś^{e}lāw* [4]

QUAKE [6]
quake, 8321, *rā'aš*[1] [3]
quake, 4570, *mûg* [1]
quake, 8074, *rāgaz* [1]
quake, 8344, *rāpap* [1]

QUAKED [4]
quaked, 8321, *rā'aš*[1] [3]
quaked, 2362, *zālal*[2] [1]

QUAKING [3]
quaking with fear, 3006, *ḥārad* [1]
quaking, 4572, *môṭ*^{1} [1]
quaking, 8321, *raʿaš*^{1} [1]

QUALIFIED [1]
qualified, 3946, *kōaḥ*^{1} [1]

QUALITIES [1]
qualities, 10658, *rûaḥ* [1]

QUALITY [4]
judge quality, 6885, *ʿārak* [2]
good quality, 3701, *yāqār* [1]
quality, 3701, *yāqār* [1]

QUANTITIES [9]
quantities, 2221, *harbēh* [2]
large quantities, 4200+8044, *l*$^{e-1}$*+rōb* [2]
quantities, *NIH/RPE* [1]
great quantities, 4200+8044+4394, *l*$^{e-1}$*+rōb+meʾōd* [1]
quantities, 4200+8044, *l*$^{e-1}$*+rōb* [1]
great quantities, 8041, *rab*^{1} [1]
quantities, 8041, *rab*^{1} [1]

QUANTITY [7]
great quantity, 2221+4394, *harbēh+meʾōd* [4]
measurements of quantity, 5374, *m*^{e}*śûrâ* [1]
quantity, 5374, *m*^{e}*śûrâ* [1]
quantity, 8041, *rab*^{1} [1]

QUARREL [12]
quarrel, 4506, *mādôn*^{1} [2]
quarrel, 8189, *rîb*^{1} [2]
quarrel, 8190, *rîb*^{2} [2]
trying to pick a quarrel, 628, *ʾānâ*^{2} [1]
quick to quarrel, 1679, *gālaʿ* [1]
quarrel between, 4200, *l*$^{e-1}$ [1]
quarrel, 5175, *maṣṣâ*^{2} [1]
quarrel, 8074, *rāgaz* [1]
quarrel, 8189+8189, *rîb*^{1}*+rîb*^{1} [1]

QUARRELED [7]
quarreled, 8189, *rîb*^{1} [7]

QUARRELING [3]
quarreling, 8190, *rîb*^{2} [2]
quarreling, 5312, *m*^{e}*rîbâ*^{1} [1]

QUARRELS [3]
quarrels, 1907, *dîn*^{2} [1]
quarrels, 5175, *maṣṣâ*^{2} [1]
quarrels, 8189, *rîb*^{1} [1]

QUARRELSOME [6]
quarrelsome, 4506, *mādôn*^{1} [6]

QUARRIES [2]
quarries, 5825, *nāsaʿ* [1]
stone quarries, 8696, *š*^{e}*bārîm* [1]

QUARRY [3]
quarry, 5024, *massāʿ*^{1} [1]
quarry, 5217+1014, *maqqebet*^{2}*+bôr* [1]
removed from quarry, 5825, *nāsaʿ* [1]

QUARTER [13]
quarter, 8055, *r*^{e}*bîʿî* [9]
quarter, 8063, *rebaʿ*^{1} [2]
New Quarter, 5467, *mišneh* [1]
quarter, 8065, *rōbaʿ*^{1} [1]

QUARTERS [5]
quarters, 1074, *bayit*^{1} [2]
quarters, 4053, *kānāp* [1]
living quarters, 5969, *niškâ* [1]
quarters, 7896, *qāṣâ*^{2} [1]

QUEEN [49]
queen, 4893, *malkâ* [30]
queen, 4906, *m*^{e}*leket* [5]
queen mother, 1485, *g*^{e}*bîrâ* [3]
position as queen mother, 1485, *g*^{e}*bîrâ* [2]
queen, 1509, *g*^{e}*beret* [2]
queen, 1485, *g*^{e}*bîrâ* [1]
queen, 4867, *m*^{e}*lûkâ* [1]
made queen, 4887, *mālak*^{1} [1]
queen, 4887, *mālak*^{1} [1]
queen, 8576, *śārâ*^{2} [1]
queen, 8712, *šēgal* [1]
queen, 10423, *malkâ* [1]

QUEEN'S [2]
queen's, 4893, *malkâ* [2]

QUEENS [4]
queens, 4893, *malkâ* [2]
queens^{s}, 851, *ʾiššâ* [1]
queens, 8576, *śārâ*^{2} [1]

QUENCH [6]
quench, 3882, *kābâ* [4]
quench fire, 3882, *kābâ* [1]
quench, 8689, *šābar*^{1} [1]

QUENCHED [8]
quenched, 3882, *kābâ* [7]
quenched its thirst, 8115, *rāwâ* [1]

QUESTION [8]
question, 8626, *šāʾal* [6]
question, 606, *ʾāmar*^{1} [1]
question, 1821, *dābār* [1]

QUESTIONED [6]
questioned, 8626, *šāʾal* [3]
questioned, 1335, *bāqaš* [1]
questioned closely, 8626+8626, *šāʾal+šāʾal* [1]
questioned, 10689, *š*^{e}*ʾēl* [1]

QUESTIONS [7]
questions, 1821, *dābār* [3]
hard questions, 2648, *ḥîdâ* [2]
such questions^{s}, 2296, *zeh* [1]
questions, 2983, *ḥāqar* [1]

QUICK [11]
quick, 4554, *māhar*^{1} [6]
quick, 987, *bāhal* [1]
quick to understand, 1067+4529, *bîn+maddāʿ* [1]
quick to quarrel, 1679, *gālaʿ* [1]
quick, 5528, *nāʿ*^{1} [1]
quick, 7709, *qādam* [1]

QUICK-TEMPERED [2]
quick-tempered, 7920+678, *qāṣēr+ʾap*^{2} [1]
quick-tempered, 7920+8120, *qāṣēr+rûaḥ* [1]

QUICKLY [59]
quickly, 4554, *māhar*^{1} [26]
come quickly, 2590, *ḥûš*^{1} [7]
quickly, 4559, *m*^{e}*hērâ* [7]
quickly, *NIH/RPE* [1]
quickly, 928+4559, *b*^{e}*-+m*^{e}*hērâ* [1]
so quickly, 928+7328, *b*^{e}*-+pitʾōm* [1]
quickly gained, 987, *bāhal* [1]
quickly, 987, *bāhal* [1]
go quickly, 2590, *ḥûš*^{1} [1]
quickly, 2673, *ḥîš* [1]
move quickly, 3077, *ḥāraš*^{2} [1]
how quickly, 3869+5071, *k*^{e}*-+m*^{e}*ʿaṭ* [1]
more quickly than, 4200+7156, *l*$^{e-1}$*+pāneh* [1]
quickly, 4394, *m*^{e}*ʾōd* [1]
come quickly, 4554+4394, *māhar*^{1}*+m*^{e}*ʾōd* [1]
come quickly, 4554, *māhar*^{1} [1]
coming quickly, 4554+4394, *māhar*^{1}*+m*^{e}*ʾōd* [1]
move quickly, 4554, *māhar*^{1} [1]
quickly, 6429, *ʿûš* [1]
go quickly, 8132, *rûṣ* [1]
quickly brought, 8132, *rûṣ* [1]
served quickly, 8132, *rûṣ* [1]

QUIET [22]
quiet, 3087, *ḥārēš*^{2} [8]
quiet, 9200, *šāqaṭ* [5]
keeps quiet, 1957, *dāmam*^{1} [1]
quiet, 2187, *has* [1]
kept quiet, 3087, *ḥārēš*^{2} [1]
quiet, 4957, *m*^{e}*nûḥâ* [1]
quiet, 5739, *naḥat*^{2} [1]
quiet, 8929, *šālēw* [1]
peace and quiet, 8932, *šalwâ* [1]
quiet, 9201, *šeqeṭ* [1]
quiet, 9447, *tām* [1]

QUIETED [1]
quieted, 1957, *dāmam*^{1} [1]

QUIETLY [5]
quietly, 928+2021+4319, *b*^{e}*-+ha-+lāṭ* [2]
quietly, 1876, *dûmām* [1]
quietly, 1957, *dāmam*^{1} [1]
live quietly, 8091, *rāgēaʿ* [1]

QUIETNESS [3]
quietness, 9200, *šāqaṭ* [3]

QUITE [1]
quite innocently, 4200+9448, *l*$^{e-1}$*+tōm* [1]

QUIVER [6]
quiver, 880, *ʾašpâ* [5]
quiver, 9437, *t*^{e}*lî* [1]

QUIVERED [1]
quivered, 7509, *ṣālal*^{1} [1]

QUIVERS [1]
quivers, 880, *ʾašpâ* [1]

QUOTA [3]
quota, *NIH/RPE* [1]
quota, 2976, *ḥōq* [1]
full quota, 9420, *tōken*^{1} [1]

QUOTAS [1]
quotas, 3869+5477, *k*^{e}*-+mišpāṭ* [1]

QUOTE [3]
quote, 5439, *māšal*^{1} [2]
quote proverb, 5439, *māšal*^{1} [1]

QUOTES [1]
quotes proverbs, 5439, *māšal*^{1} [1]

QUOTING [1]
quoting, 5439, *māšal*^{1} [1]

RAAMAH [5]
Raamah, 8311, *raʿmâ*^{2} [3]
Raamah, 8309, *raʿmāʾ* [2]

RAAMIAH [1]
Raamiah, 8313, *raʿamyâ* [1]

RABBAH [15]
Rabbah, 8051, *rabbâ* [15]

RABBIT [2]
rabbit, 817, *ʾarnebet* [2]

RABBITH [1]
Rabbith, 8056, *rabbît* [1]

RABBLE [2]
rabble, 671, *ʾ*^{a}*sapsup* [1]
rabble, 8044+132, *rōb+ʾādām*^{1} [1]

RACAL [1]
Racal, 8218, *rākāl* [1]

RACE [2]
race, 2446, *zeraʿ* [1]
race, 5296, *mērôṣ* [1]

RACED [2]
raced, 987, *bāhal* [1]
raced, 8132, *rûṣ* [1]

RACHEL [41]
Rachel, 8162, *rāḥēl*^{2} [40]
Rachel, *NIH/RPE* [1]

RACHEL'S [5]
Rachel's, 8162, *rāḥēl*^{2} [5]

RACKED [2]
racked with hunger, 1991, *dāqar* [1]
racked with, 4848, *māleʾ*^{1} [1]

RADDAI [1]
Raddai, 8099, *radday* [1]

RADIANCE [3]
radiance, 5586, *nōgah*[1] [2]
radiance, 2145, *hālal*[1] [1]

RADIANT [8]
radiant, 7966, *qāran* [3]
radiant, 5642, *nāhar*[2] [2]
radiant, 239, *'ôr*[1] [1]
radiant, 1338, *bar*[2] [1]
radiant, 7456, *ṣaḥ* [1]

RAFTERS [2]
rafters, 5248, *meqāreh* [1]
rafters, 8112, *rāhîṭ* [1]

RAFTS [2]
rafts, 1827, *dōberôt* [1]
rafts, 8343, *rapsōdôt* [1]

RAGE [21]
rage, 2779, *ḥēmâ* [5]
rage, 8074, *rāgaz* [4]
rage, 2159, *hāmâ* [2]
rage, 2408, *za'ap* [2]
rage, 6301, *'ebrâ* [2]
in a rage, 2801+4222, *ḥāmam+lēbāb* [1]
rage, 3013, *ḥārâ*[1] [1]
great rage, 3034+678, *ḥorî+'ap*[2] [1]
rage, 5352, *mārar* [1]
rage, 8120, *rûaḥ* [1]
rage, 10654, *regaz*[2] [1]

RAGED [5]
raged, 6590, *'ālâ* [2]
raged, 1277, *bā'ar*[1] [1]
raged, 3013, *ḥārâ*[1] [1]
raged, 3271, *ṭārap* [1]

RAGES [4]
rages, 2406, *zā'ap*[1] [1]
rages, 6943, *'āšaq* [1]
rages, 8074, *rāgaz* [1]
tempest rages, 8548+4394, *śā'ar*[2]*+me'ōd* [1]

RAGING [6]
raging, 2408, *za'ap* [2]
raging, 2159, *hāmâ* [1]
raging, 2162, *hāmôn* [1]
raging, 2327, *zêdôn* [1]
raging, 2406, *zā'ap*[1] [1]

RAGS [4]
rags, 6080, *seḥābâ* [2]
rags, 955, *beged*[2] [1]
rags, 7974, *qerā'îm* [1]

RAHAB [11]
Rahab, 8105, *rahab* [6]
Rahab, 8147, *rāḥāb*[2] [5]

RAHAM [2]
Raham, *NIH/RPE* [1]
Raham, 8165, *raḥam*[1] [1]

RAID [2]
raid, 1522, *gedûd*[2] [1]
raid, 8720, *šādad* [1]

RAIDED [7]
raided, 7320, *pāšaṭ* [7]

RAIDERS [7]
raiders, 1522, *gedûd*[2] [3]
band of raiders, 1522, *gedûd*[2] [2]
raiders, 9115, *šāsâ* [2]

RAIDING [11]
raiding bands, 1522, *gedûd*[2] [3]
raiding party, 1522, *gedûd*[2] [2]
raiding parties, 8845, *šāḥat* [2]
raiding, 995+928, *bô'+be-* [1]
go raiding, 7320, *pāšaṭ* [1]
raiding, 7320, *pāšaṭ* [1]
raiding parties, 8031, *rō'š*[1] [1]

RAIL [1]
rail, 2147, *hālal*[3] [1]

RAIN [79]
rain, 4764, *māṭār* [34]
rain, 1773, *gešem*[1] [24]
rain, 4784, *mayim* [3]
had rain, 4763, *māṭar* [2]
rain down, 4763, *māṭar* [2]
sent rain, 4763, *māṭar* [2]
rain, *NIH/RPE* [1]
bring rain, 1772, *gāšam* [1]
driving rain, 2443+4784, *zerem+mayim* [1]
rain, 4763+4764, *māṭar+māṭār* [1]
rain, 4763, *māṭar* [1]
send rain, 4763, *māṭar* [1]
rain in spring, 4919, *malqôš* [1]
spring rain, 4919, *malqôš* [1]
poured down rain, 5752, *nāṭap* [1]
abundant rain, 8053, *rebîbîm* [1]
rain down, 8319, *rā'ap* [1]
torrents of rain, 8852, *šeṭep* [1]

RAINBOW [4]
rainbow, 8008, *qešet* [4]

RAINED [4]
rained down, 4763, *māṭar* [3]
rained, 4763, *māṭar* [1]

RAINS [10]
spring rains, 4919, *malqôš* [5]
autumn [rains], 4620, *môreh*[2] [3]
rains, 1773, *gešem*[1] [2]
autumn [rains], 3453, *yôreh*[2] [2]
winter rains, 1773, *gešem*[1] [1]
rains, 2443, *zerem* [1]

RAINY [3]
rainy, 1773, *gešem*[1] [2]
rainy, 6039, *sagrîr* [1]

RAISE [45]
raise up, 7756, *qûm* [11]
raise, 5951, *nāśā'* [10]
raise, 8123, *rûm*[1] [5]
raise, *NIH/RPE* [2]
raise, 7756, *qûm* [2]
raise, 8938, *šālaḥ* [2]
raise, 9048, *šāma'* [2]
raise, 2118, *hāyâ* [1]
raise, 4948, *mānâ*[1] [1]
raise, 5677, *nûp*[1] [1]
raise, 5989, *nātan* [1]
raise up, 6424, *'ûr*[3] [1]
raise, 6641, *'āmad* [1]
raise itself, 6995, *pā'ar*[2] [1]
raise the battle cry, 7658, *ṣāraḥ* [1]
raise the battle cry, 8131, *rûa'* [1]
raise the war cry, 8131, *rûa'* [1]
raise hopes, 8922, *šālâ*[1] [1]

RAISED [52]
raised up, 7756, *qûm* [9]
raised, 8123, *rûm*[1] [6]
raised, 6424, *'ûr*[3] [4]
raised, 6641, *'āmad* [3]
raised up, 8123, *rûm*[1] [3]
raised up, 599, *'āmēṣ* [2]
be raised, 5951, *nāśā'* [2]
raised, 5989, *nātan* [2]
raised, 1470, *gōbah* [1]
raised, 1540, *gādal* [1]
raised, 2118, *hāyâ* [1]
raised, 2649, *ḥāyâ* [1]
raised, 5677, *nûp*[1] [1]
raised, 5742, *nāṭâ* [1]
raised sheep, 5924, *nōqēd* [1]
be raised up, 5951, *nāśā'* [1]
raised, 5951+2256+5989, *nāśā'+we-+nātan* [1]
raised, 5951, *nāśā'* [1]
was raised, 5951, *nāśā'* [1]
raised up, 6641, *'āmad* [1]
raised, 7756, *qûm* [1]
raised a cry, 7924, *qārā'*[1] [1]
raised up, 8027, *rā'am* [1]
raised and taken an oath, 8123, *rûm*[1] [1]
raised a shout, 8131+9558, *rûa'+terû'â* [1]
raised the battle cry, 8131, *rûa'* [1]
raised, 8740, *šûb*[1] [1]
raised, 10475, *neṭal* [1]
was raised up, 10624, *qûm* [1]

RAISES [5]
raises, 7756, *qûm* [2]
raises, 5677, *nûp*[1] [1]
raises, 5989, *nātan* [1]
raises up, 6590, *'ālâ* [1]

RAISIN [2]
raisin, 6694, *'ēnāb* [1]
raisin cakes, 7540, *ṣimmûqîm* [1]

RAISING [6]
raising up, 7756, *qûm* [2]
raising, 1540, *gādal* [1]
raising, 5951, *nāśā'* [1]
raising, 5989, *nātan* [1]
raising a conspiracy, 8003, *qāšar* [1]

RAISINS [7]
cakes of raisins, 7540, *ṣimmûqîm* [3]
cake of raisins, 862, *'ašîšâ* [2]
raisins, 862, *'ašîšâ* [1]
grapes or raisins, 6694+4300+2256+3313, *'ēnāb+laḥ+we-+yābēš*[2] [1]

RAKEM [1]
Rakem, 8388, *rāqem* [1]

RAKKATH [1]
Rakkath, 8395, *raqqat* [1]

RAKKON [1]
Rakkon, 8378, *raqqôn* [1]

RALLIED [3]
rallied, 665, *'āsap* [1]
rallied strength, 2616, *ḥāzaq* [1]
rallied, 7695, *qābaṣ* [1]

RALLY [1]
rally, 2011, *dāraš* [1]

RAM [98]
ram, 380, *'ayil*[1] [88]
Ram, 8226, *rām*[2] [7]
ram, *NIH/RPE* [2]
ordination ram, 4854, *millu'îm* [1]

RAM'S [3]
ram's horn, 8795, *šôpār* [2]
ram's horn, 3413, *yôbēl* [1]

RAMAH [33]
Ramah, 8230, *rāmâ*[4] [33]

RAMATH LEHI [1]
Ramath Lehi, 8257, *rāmat leḥî* [1]

RAMATH MIZPAH [1]
Ramath Mizpah, 8256, *rāmat hammiṣpeh* [1]

RAMATHAIM [1]
Ramathaim, 8259, *rāmātayim* [1]

RAMATHITE [1]
Ramathite, 8258, *rāmātî* [1]

RAMESES [5]
Rameses, 8314, *ra'mesēs* [5]

RAMIAH [1]
Ramiah, 8243, *ramyâ* [1]

RAMOTH [7]
Ramoth, 8030, *rā'môt*[2] [5]
Ramoth, 8230, *rāmâ*[4] [2]

RAMOTH GILEAD [20]
Ramoth Gilead, 8240, *rāmôt gil'ād* [20]

RAMOTH NEGEV [1]
Ramoth Negev, 8241, *rāmôt-negeb* [1]

RAMP [7]
ramp, 6149, *sōlelâ* [3]
siege ramp, 6149, *sōlelâ* [3]
siege ramp, 2006, *derek* [1]

RAMPART [1]
rampart, 6089, *sōḥērâ* [1]

RAMPARTS [4]
ramparts, 2658, *ḥêl* [3]
ramparts, 5189, *māṣôr¹* [1]

RAMPS [7]
siege ramps, 6149, *sōlᵉlâ* [4]
siege ramps, 784+369, *'ōraḥ+'êd* [1]
ramps, 6149, *sōlᵉlâ* [1]
earthen ramps, 6760, *'āpār* [1]

RAMS [70]
rams, 380, *'ayil¹* [61]
battering rams, 4119, *kar¹* [3]
rams, 10175, *dᵉkar* [3]
rams horns, 3413, *yôbēl* [1]
battering rams, 7692, *qᵉbōl* [1]
rams horns, 8795, *šôpār* [1]

RAN [42]
ran, 8132, *rûṣ* [19]
ran, 5674, *nûs* [7]
ran, 2143, *hālak* [3]
ran away, 1368, *bāraḥ¹* [1]
ran off, 1368, *bāraḥ¹* [1]
ran through, 1991, *dāqar* [1]
ran down, 2143, *hālak* [1]
ran, 3668, *yāṣaq* [1]
ran down, 3718, *yārad* [1]
turned and ran, 5674, *nûs* [1]
ran past, 6296, *'ābar¹* [1]
ran, 6296, *'ābar¹* [1]
ran up, 6590, *'ālâ* [1]
ran, 6590, *'ālâ* [1]
ran off, 8132, *rûṣ* [1]
ran, 8740, *šûb¹* [1]

RANDOM [3]
at random, 4200+9448, *lᵉ-¹+tōm* [2]
at random, 3972, *kōl* [1]

RANGE [5]
range, 8763, *šût¹* [2]
range, *NIH/RPE* [1]
range, 2215, *har* [1]
letting range free, 8938+8079, *šālaḥ+regel* [1]

RANGES [1]
ranges, 9365, *tûr* [1]

RANK [10]
next in rank, 5467, *mišneh* [5]
men of rank, 3883, *kābôd¹* [1]
second in rank, 5467, *mišneh* [1]
man of rank, 5951+7156, *nāśā'+pāneh* [1]
men of high rank, 7924, *qārā'¹* [1]
gave a high rank in, 8492+6584, *śîm+'al²* [1]

RANKS [12]
ranks, 5120, *ma'ᵃrākâ* [3]
ranks, 8444, *śᵉdērâ* [3]
ranks, *NIH/RPE* [1]
breaking ranks, 1298, *bāṣa'* [1]
in ranks, 2951, *ḥāṣaṣ¹* [1]
ranks, 4596, *mô'ād* [1]
ranks, 7931, *qereb* [1]
ranks, 9348, *tāwek* [1]

RANSACKED [2]
be ransacked, 2924, *ḥāpaś* [1]
ransacked, 9116, *šāsas* [1]

RANSOM [16]
ransom, 4111, *kōper⁴* [8]
ransom, 7009, *pādâ* [4]
ward off with a ransom, 4105, *kāpar¹* [1]
ransom, 7014, *pᵉdût* [1]
ransom, 7018, *pidyôn* [1]
pay a ransom, 8815, *šāḥad* [1]

RANSOMED [4]
ransomed, 7009, *pādâ* [2]
be ransomed, 7009, *pādâ* [1]
been ransomed, 7009+7009, *pādâ+pādâ* [1]

RANSOMS [1]
ransoms, 7009, *pādâ* [1]

RAPED [5]
raped, 6700, *'ānâ²* [2]
raped, 3359, *yāda'* [1]
raped, 6700+2256+8886, *'ānâ²+wᵉ-+šākab* [1]
raped, 8711, *šāgal* [1]

RAPES [2]
rapes, 2616+2256+8886+6640, *ḥāzaq+wᵉ-+šākab+'im* [1]
rapes, 9530+2256+8886+6640, *tāpaś+wᵉ-+šākab+'im* [1]

RAPHA [7]
Rapha, 8335, *rāpâ³* [4]
Rapha, 8325, *rāpā'²* [3]

RAPHAH [1]
Raphah, 8334, *rāpâ²* [1]

RAPHU [1]
Raphu, 8336, *rāpû'* [1]

RAPID [1]
making rapid progress, 10613, *ṣᵉlaḥ* [1]

RARE [4]
rare, 3701, *yāqār* [2]
rare, *NIH/RPE* [1]
rare, 3702, *yᵉqār* [1]

RASH [10]
rash, 5030, *mispaḥat* [3]
rash promise, 4439, *mibṭā'* [2]
rash, 6204, *sappaḥat* [2]
harmless rash, 993, *bōhaq* [1]
rash words came, 1051, *bāṭā'* [1]
rash, 4554, *māhar¹* [1]

RASHLY [2]
rashly, 4362, *lā'a'¹* [1]
speaks rashly, 7316+8557, *pāśaq+śāpâ* [1]

RAT [1]
rat, 6572, *'akbār* [1]

RATE [1]
based on the rate paid, 3869+3427, *kᵉ-+yôm¹* [1]

RATHER [27]
rather than, 4946, *min* [10]
rather, 2022, *hᵃ-* [2]
rather than, 2256+4202, *wᵉ-+lō'* [2]
rather than, 4202, *lō'* [2]
rather, *NIH/RPE* [1]
rather than, 196, *'ô* [1]
rather, 561, *'im* [1]
would rather be, 1047, *bāḥar¹* [1]
rather, 2256+1685, *wᵉ-+gam* [1]
rather, 2256, *wᵉ-* [1]
rather, 2911, *ḥāpēṣ¹* [1]
rather, 3954+561, *kî²+'im* [1]
rather, 3954, *kî²* [1]
rather, 4202+3954, *lō'+kî²* [1]
rather than, 10379, *lā'* [1]

RATIFIED [1]
ratified by oath, 8678, *šāba'* [1]

RATIONED [2]
rationed, 928+5374, *bᵉ-+mᵉśûrâ* [1]
rationed, 928+5486, *bᵉ-+mišqāl* [1]

RATS [5]
rats, 6572, *'akbār* [5]

RATTLES [1]
rattles, 8261, *rānâ* [1]

RATTLING [2]
rattling sound, 8323, *ra'aš* [1]
rattling, 8323, *ra'aš* [1]

RAVAGE [6]
ravage, 8845, *šāḥat* [2]
ravage, 2222, *hārag* [1]
ravage, 3983, *kālâ¹* [1]
ravage, 4155, *kirsēm* [1]
ravage, 8720, *šādad* [1]

RAVAGED [3]
be ravaged, 2222, *hārag* [1]
ravaged, 9037, *šāmēm¹* [1]
ravaged, 9039, *šᵉmāmâ* [1]

RAVAGES [2]
ravages, 8738, *šô'* [1]
ravages, 9377, *taḥᵃlu'îm* [1]

RAVAGING [1]
ravaging, 8845, *šāḥat* [1]

RAVEN [6]
raven, 6854, *'ōrēb¹* [6]

RAVENING [1]
ravening, 8845, *šāḥat* [1]

RAVENOUS [2]
ravenous, 3271, *ṭārap* [1]
ravenous beasts, 4266, *lāhaṭ²* [1]

RAVENS [4]
ravens, 6854, *'ōrēb¹* [4]

RAVINE [13]
ravine, 5707, *naḥal¹* [11]
ravine, 5185, *mᵉṣōlâ* [1]
ravine, 6260, *sēter* [1]

RAVINES [17]
ravines, 5707, *naḥal¹* [9]
ravines, 692, *'āpîq¹* [8]

RAVISH [1]
ravish, 8711, *šāgal* [1]

RAVISHED [3]
ravished, 6700, *'ānâ²* [1]
been ravished, 8711, *šāgal* [1]
ravished, 8711, *šāgal* [1]

RAW [9]
raw, 2645, *ḥay²* [5]
raw flesh, 4695, *miḥyâ* [1]
raw, 4695+2645, *miḥyâ+ḥay²* [1]
made raw, 5307, *māraṭ* [1]
raw, 5529, *nā'²* [1]

RAWBONED [1]
rawboned, 1752, *gerem* [1]

RAY [1]
ray of brightness, 5586, *nōgah¹* [1]

RAYS [3]
first rays, 6757, *'ap'appayim* [1]
rays, 6757, *'ap'appayim* [1]
rays, 7967, *qeren* [1]

RAZOR [7]
razor, 9509, *ta'ar* [4]
razor, 4623, *môrâ¹* [3]

REACH [22]
reach out, 8938, *šālaḥ* [3]
reach, 995+6330, *bô'+'ad²* [2]
reach, 5162, *māṣā'* [2]
reach, 5595, *nāga'* [2]
reach, 995+448, *bô'+'el* [1]
reach, 995, *bô'* [1]
fails to reach, 2627, *ḥāṭā'* [1]
reach outˢ, 3578, *yāsap* [1]
reach, 5877, *nāpal* [1]
reach, 5952, *nāśag* [1]
reach to, 6330, *'ad²* [1]
to reach, 6584, *'al²* [1]
reach, 6641, *'āmad* [1]
reach, 7337, *pātaḥ¹* [1]
reach, 7928, *qārab* [1]
beyond reach, 8158, *rāḥôq* [1]
reach down, 8938, *šālaḥ* [1]

REACHED [78]
reached, 995+448, *bô'+'el* [13]

reached, 995+6330, *bô'+ʿad*^{2} [11]
reached out, 8938, *šālaḥ* [10]
reached, *NIH/RPE* [7]
reached, 995, *bô'* [6]
reached, 995+2025, *bô'+-â*^{2} [4]
reached, 5595, *nāgaʿ* [4]
reached, 995+928, *bô'+b*^{e}*-* [2]
reached, 2118, *hāyâ* [2]
reached, 6590, *ʿālâ* [2]
reached down, 8938, *šālaḥ* [2]
reached, 8938, *šālaḥ* [2]
reached, 928+9048, *b*^{e}*-+šāmaʿ* [1]
reached, 995+4200, *bô'+l*^{e}*-*^{1} [1]
reached, 1540+6330, *gādal+ʿad*^{2} [1]
reached, 2118+928, *hāyâ+b*^{e}*-* [1]
reached, 3655, *yāṣā'* [1]
reached toward, 4369, *lāpat* [1]
reached, 6590+448, *ʿālâ+'el* [1]
reached, 7003, *pāgaʿ* [1]
reached, 7928, *qārab* [1]
reached height, 8003+6330, *qāšar+ʿad*^{2} [1]
reached out, 8938+3338, *šālaḥ+yād* [1]
reached, 9048, *šāmaʿ* [1]
reached, 10413, *m*^{e}*ṭā'* [1]

REACHES [17]
reaches, 5595, *nāgaʿ* [3]
reaches to, 6330, *ʿad*^{2} [3]
reaches, 6590, *ʿālâ* [2]
reaches, *NIH/RPE* [1]
reaches to, 928, *b*^{e}*-* [1]
reaches, 995+448, *bô'+'el* [1]
reaches, 5162, *māṣā'* [1]
reaches, 5952, *nāśag* [1]
reaches to, 6584, *ʿal*^{2} [1]
reaches, 8031, *rō'š*^{1} [1]
reaches out, 8938+3338, *šālaḥ+yād* [1]
reaches, 10413, *m*^{e}*ṭā'* [1]

REACHING [5]
reaching, 5595, *nāgaʿ* [2]
reaching, 2118, *hāyâ* [1]
reaching to, 6330, *ʿad*^{2} [1]
reaching, 8938+3338, *šālaḥ+yād* [1]

READ [49]
read, 7924, *qārā'*^{1} [33]
read, 10637, *q*^{e}*rā'* [4]
read, 606, *'āmar*^{1} [2]
read aloud, 7924, *qārā'*^{1} [2]
can read, 3359+6219, *yādaʿ+sēper*^{1} [1]
know how to read, 3359+6219, *yādaʿ+sēper*^{1} [1]
cannot read, 4202+3359+6219, *lō'+yādaʿ+sēper*^{1} [1]
read, 5246, *miqrā'* [1]
was read aloud, 7924, *qārā'*^{1} [1]
read, 10374, *k*^{e}*tab* [1]
been read, 10637, *q*^{e}*rā'* [1]
was read, 10637, *q*^{e}*rā'* [1]

READILY [1]
more readily than, 4200+7156, *l*^{e}*-*^{1}*+pāneh* [1]

READING [1]
reading, 7924, *qārā'*^{1} [1]

READS [1]
reads, 10637, *q*^{e}*rā'* [1]

READY [57]
ready, *AIT* [5]
ready, 3922, *kûn*^{1} [5]
get ready, 3922, *kûn*^{1} [4]
ready, *NIH/RPE* [3]
ready, 6969, *ʿātîd* [3]
ready for military service, 3655+7372, *yāṣā'+ṣābā'*^{2} [2]
ready to go out, 3655+7372, *yāṣā'+ṣābā'*^{2} [2]
get ready, 7756, *qûm* [2]
got ready, 7756, *qûm* [2]
get ready, 273+5516, *'āzar+motnayim* [1]
ready for battle, 408+7372+4200+2021+4878, *'îš*^{1}*+ṣābā'*^{2}*+l*^{e}*-*^{1}*+ha-+milḥāmâ* [1]
had made ready, 673, *'āsar* [1]
made ready, 673, *'āsar* [1]
ready to burst, 1324, *bāqaʿ* [1]
men ready for battle, 1522+7372+4878, *g*^{e}*dûd*^{2}*+ṣābā'*^{2}*+milḥāmâ* [1]
make ready to shoot, 2005, *dārak* [1]
ready, 2118, *hāyâ* [1]
ready to do, 2180, *hinnēh* [1]
ready, 2180, *hinnēh* [1]
ready, 2590, *ḥûš*^{1} [1]
been made ready, 3922, *kûn*^{1} [1]
have ready, 3922, *kûn*^{1} [1]
is made ready, 3922, *kûn*^{1} [1]
made ready, 3922, *kûn*^{1} [1]
ready for, 4200, *l*^{e}*-*^{1} [1]
ready, 4595, *mô'ēd* [1]
ready to die, 4637, *mût* [1]
ready, 5893, *nāṣab*^{1} [1]
made ready, 5989, *nātan* [1]
ready, 6885, *ʿārak* [1]
get ready, 6913, *ʿāśâ*^{1} [1]
got ready, 6913, *ʿāśâ*^{1} [1]
ready, 6913, *ʿāśâ*^{1} [1]
get ready, 6963, *ʿātad* [1]
makes ready, 7188, *pāʿal* [1]
ready for battle, 7372+928+2021+4878, *ṣābā'*^{2}*+b*^{e}*-+ha-+milḥāmâ* [1]
have get ready, 9462, *tāmam* [1]
ready, 10577, *ʿ*^{a}*tîd* [1]

REAFFIRM [2]
reaffirm, 2542, *ḥādaš* [1]
had reaffirm, 3578, *yāsap* [1]

REAIAH [4]
Reaiah, 8025, *r*^{e}*'āyâ* [4]

REALIZE [17]
realize, 3359, *yādaʿ* [12]
realize, 606+4200+4222, *'āmar*^{1}*+l*^{e}*-*^{1}*+lēbāb* [1]
realize, 1067, *bîn* [1]
realize, 3359+2256+8011, *yādaʿ+w*^{e}*-+rā'â*^{1} [1]
realize, 8011, *rā'â*^{1} [1]
realize, 10255, *ḥ*^{a}*zâ* [1]

REALIZED [19]
realized, 8011, *rā'â*^{1} [9]
realized, 3359, *yādaʿ* [5]
realized, 1067, *bîn* [2]
realized, 2180, *hinnēh* [1]
realized, 5795, *nākar*^{1} [1]
realized, 8011+2256+3359, *rā'â*^{1}*+w*^{e}*-+yādaʿ* [1]

REALIZING [2]
realizing, 3359, *yādaʿ* [1]
realizing, 8011, *rā'â*^{1} [1]

REALLY [23]
really, *NIH/RPE* [5]
really, 598, *'umnām* [3]
really, 2296, *zeh* [3]
really, *AIT* [2]
really, 421, *'ak* [1]
really, 593, *'omnâ*^{1} [1]
really, 677+3954, *'ap*^{1}*+kî*^{2} [1]
really, 677+598, *'ap*^{1}*+'umnām* [1]
really, 677, *'ap*^{1} [1]
really, 928+622, *b*^{e}*-+'*^{e}*met* [1]
really change, 3512+3512, *yāṭab+yāṭab* [1]
really, 3954, *kî*^{2} [1]
that really, 3954, *kî*^{2} [1]
really, 8370, *raq*^{2} [1]

REALM [11]
realm, 4895, *malkût* [5]
realm, 4931, *mamlākût* [3]
realm, 1074, *bayit*^{1} [1]
realm of death, 8619, *š*^{e}*'ôl* [1]
realm, 10424, *malkû* [1]

REAP [16]
reap, 7917, *qāṣar*^{1} [15]
reap, 7907+7917, *qāṣîr*^{1}*+qāṣar*^{1} [1]

REAPED [2]
reaped, 5162, *māṣā'* [1]
reaped, 7917, *qāṣar*^{1} [1]

REAPER [5]
reaper, 7917, *qāṣar*^{1} [3]
reaper, 7907, *qāṣîr*^{1} [1]
reaper, 9530, *tāpaś* [1]

REAPERS [1]
reapers, 7917, *qāṣar*^{1} [1]

REAPING [1]
reaping, 7907, *qāṣîr*^{1} [1]

REAPPEARS [2]
reappears, 8011+6388, *rā'â*^{1}*+ʿôd* [1]
reappears, 8740+2256+7255, *šûb*^{1}*+w*^{e}*-+pāraḥ*^{1} [1]

REAPS [2]
reaps, *NIH/RPE* [1]
reaps, 7917, *qāṣar*^{1} [1]

REAR [17]
rear guard, 665, *'āsap* [5]
rear, 294, *'āḥôr* [2]
rear, 339, *'aḥar* [2]
rear, 340, *'aḥ*^{a}*rôn* [2]
rear, *AIT* [1]
rear, 1540, *gādal* [1]
attack from the rear, 2386, *zānab* [1]
rear, 3752, *y*^{e}*rēkâ* [1]
rear, 5951, *nāśā'* [1]
rear, 6067, *sôp* [1]

REARED [6]
reared, 1540, *gādal* [4]
reared, 8049, *rābâ*^{1} [2]

REARING [1]
rearing, 1540, *gādal* [1]

REASON [13]
for no reason, 2855, *ḥinnām* [4]
without reason, 2855, *ḥinnām* [2]
without any reason, 2855, *ḥinnām* [1]
reason together, 3519, *yākaḥ* [1]
this reason, 4027, *kēn*^{2} [1]
reason, 4213, *lēb* [1]
reason, 6584, *ʿal*^{2} [1]
reason, 8011, *rā'â*^{1} [1]
without reason, 9214, *šeqer* [1]

REASONING [1]
reasoning, 9312, *t*^{e}*bûnâ* [1]

REASSIGN [1]
reassign, 5706, *nāhal* [1]

REASSURE [2]
reassure, *NIH/RPE* [2]

REASSURED [1]
reassured, 5714, *nāḥam* [1]

REBA [2]
Reba, 8064, *rebaʿ*^{2} [2]

REBEKAH [30]
Rebekah, 8071, *ribqâ* [29]
Rebekah, *NIH/RPE* [1]

REBEKAH'S [1]
Rebekah's, 8071, *ribqâ* [1]

REBEL [16]
rebel, 5277, *mārad* [7]
rebel, 5286, *mārâ*^{1} [3]
rebel, 7321, *pāšaʿ* [2]
rebel, *NIH/RPE* [1]
rebel, 2118+5308, *hāyâ+m*^{e}*rî* [1]
rebel, 5352, *mārar* [1]
rebel, 5951, *nāśā'* [1]

REBELLED [51]
rebelled, 5286, *mārâ*^{1} [20]
rebelled, 7321, *pāšaʿ* [13]
rebelled, 5277, *mārad* [12]
rebelled, 5897, *nāṣâ*^{1} [2]
rebelled, 8123+3338, *rûm*^{1}*+yād* [2]
rebelled, 5312, *m*^{e}*rîbâ*^{1} [1]

rebelled, 7756, *qûm* [1]

REBELLING [2]
rebelling, 5277, *mārad* [1]
rebelling, 5286, *mārâ*^{1} [1]

REBELLION [33]
rebellion, 7322, *peša'* [13]
rebellion, 6240, *sārâ*^{2} [4]
in rebellion, 7321, *pāša'* [4]
rebellion, 5308, *m*^{e}*rî* [3]
rebellion, 7321, *pāša'* [2]
rebellion, 5277, *mārad* [1]
rebellion, 5278, *mered*^{1} [1]
rebellion, 5286, *mārâ*^{1} [1]
guilt of rebellion, 7322, *peša'* [1]
rebellion, 8004, *qešer* [1]
rebellion, 10083, *'eštaddûr* [1]
rebellion, 10438, *m*^{e}*rad* [1]

REBELLIOUS [41]
rebellious, 5308, *m*^{e}*rî* [17]
rebellious, 5286, *mārâ*^{1} [9]
rebellious, 6253, *sārar*^{1} [4]
rebellious, 7322, *peša'* [3]
rebellious, 10439, *mārād* [2]
rebellious, 1201+5308, *bēn*^{1}+*m*^{e}*rî* [1]
rebellious, 5277, *mārad* [1]
rebellious, 5280, *mardût* [1]
most rebellious, 5286+5286, *mārâ*^{1}+*mārâ*^{1} [1]
rebellious, 7321, *pāša'* [1]
rebellious, 9101, *šānâ*^{1} [1]

REBELS [11]
rebels, 7321, *pāša'* [3]
rebels, 5286, *mārâ*^{1} [2]
rebels, *NIH/RPE* [1]
band of rebels, 1522, *g*^{e}*dûd*^{2} [1]
hardened rebels, 6073+6253, *sûr*^{1}+*sārar*^{1} [1]
rebels, 6253, *sārar*^{1} [1]
rebels, 7322, *peša'* [1]
rebels, 8473, *śēṭ* [1]

REBUILD [23]
rebuild, 1215, *bānâ* [14]
rebuild, 10111, *b*^{e}*nâ* [7]
rebuild, 8123, *rûm*^{1} [1]
rebuild, 8740+2256+1215, *šûb*^{1}+*w*^{e}-+*bānâ* [1]

REBUILDING [6]
rebuilding, 1215, *bānâ* [3]
rebuilding, 10111, *b*^{e}*nâ* [2]
rebuilding, 6641, *'āmad* [1]

REBUILT [42]
rebuilt, 1215, *bānâ* [23]
be rebuilt, 1215, *bānâ* [12]
been rebuilt, 1215, *bānâ* [2]
rebuilt, 8740+2256+1215, *šûb*^{1}+*w*^{e}-+*bānâ* [2]
be rebuilt, 10111, *b*^{e}*nâ* [2]
rebuilt, 6641, *'āmad* [1]

REBUKE [51]
rebuke, 3519, *yākaḥ* [14]
rebuke, 1722, *g*^{e}*'ārâ* [12]
rebuke, 9350, *tôkaḥat* [8]
rebuke, 1721, *gā'ar* [7]
rebuke, 8189, *rîb*^{1} [2]
rebuke, 9349, *tôkēḥâ* [2]
rebuke frankly, 3519+3519, *yākaḥ*+*yākaḥ* [1]
surely rebuke, 3519+3519, *yākaḥ*+*yākaḥ* [1]
rebuke, 4007, *kālam* [1]
rebuke, 4486, *mig'eret* [1]
rebuke, 4592, *mûsār* [1]
rebuke, 7754, *qôl* [1]

REBUKED [10]
rebuked, 1721, *gā'ar* [3]
rebuked, 3519, *yākaḥ* [3]
rebuked, 8189, *rîb*^{1} [3]
rebuked, 9117, *šāsa'* [1]

REBUKES [7]
rebukes, 3519, *yākaḥ* [3]
rebukes, 1721, *gā'ar* [2]
rebukes, 1819, *dābar*^{2} [1]
rebukes, 9350, *tôkaḥat* [1]

REBUKING [1]
rebuking, 3070, *ḥārap*^{2} [1]

RECAB [13]
Recab, 8209, *rēkāb* [13]

RECABITE [2]
Recabite, 8211, *rēkābî* [2]

RECABITES [2]
Recabites, 8211, *rēkābî* [2]

RECAH [1]
Recah, 8212, *rēkâ* [1]

RECALLED [2]
recalled, 2349, *zākar*^{1} [2]

RECALLING [1]
recalling, 2349, *zākar*^{1} [1]

RECAPTURE [1]
recapture, 9530, *tāpaś* [1]

RECAPTURED [1]
recaptured, 8740+2256+4374, *šûb*^{1}+*w*^{e}-+*lāqaḥ* [1]

RECEDE [1]
recede, 2893, *ḥāsēr*^{1} [1]

RECEDED [4]
receded, 7837, *qālal* [2]
receded steadily, 8740+2143+2256+8740, *šûb*^{1}+*hālak*+*w*^{e}-+*šûb*^{1} [1]
receded, 8896, *šākak* [1]

RECEIVE [32]
receive, 4374, *lāqaḥ* [11]
receive, *NIH/RPE* [2]
receive, 2118+4200, *hāyâ*+*l*$^{e-1}$ [2]
receive inheritance, 5706, *nāḥal* [2]
receive, 5951, *nāśā'* [2]
receive, 10618, *q*^{e}*bal* [2]
receive, 665, *'āsap* [1]
receive, 4200, *l*$^{e-1}$ [1]
receive inheritance, 5706+5709, *nāḥal*+*naḥ*^{a}*lâ* [1]
receive, 5706, *nāḥal* [1]
receive, 5951+7156, *nāśā'*+*pāneh* [1]
receive, 5989, *nātan* [1]
receive help, 6468+6469, *'āzar*+*'ēzer*^{1} [1]
receive tithes, 6923, *'āśar* [1]
receive, 7709, *qādam* [1]
receive praise, 8894, *šākaḥ* [1]
receive due, 8966, *šālēm*^{1} [1]

RECEIVED [53]
received, 4374, *lāqaḥ* [11]
received, *NIH/RPE* [10]
received, 4200, *l*$^{e-1}$ [4]
received, *AIT* [2]
received, 995+448, *bô'*+*'el* [2]
received inheritance, 5706, *nāḥal* [2]
received, 5706, *nāḥal* [2]
received, 5989, *nātan* [2]
received, 7691, *qābal* [2]
received a report, 9048, *šāma'* [2]
received, 995+4200, *bô'*+*l*$^{e-1}$ [1]
received, 995, *bô'* [1]
received, 2118+4200, *hāyâ*+*l*$^{e-1}$ [1]
received, 2118, *hāyâ* [1]
received, 2600, *ḥāzâ* [1]
received, 2745, *ḥālaq*^{2} [1]
received from, 4946, *min* [1]
received as an inheritance, 5706, *nāḥal* [1]
received, 6913, *'āśâ*^{1} [1]
received favorably, 8354, *rāṣâ*^{1} [1]
received gladly, 8523+6584, *śāmaḥ*+*'al*^{2} [1]
received message, 9048, *šāma'* [1]
received, 9048, *šāma'* [1]
received, 10754, *ṭûb* [1]

RECEIVES [6]
receives, 7049, *pûq*^{2} [2]
receives, *AIT* [1]
receives, *NIH/RPE* [1]
receives, 4200+5989, *l*$^{e-1}$+*nātan* [1]
receives, 4374, *lāqaḥ* [1]

RECEIVING [1]
receiving, *NIH/RPE* [1]

RECENTLY [3]
recently, 2021+3427, *ha-*+*yôm*^{1} [1]
recently, 2543+4946+7940, *ḥādāš*+*min*+*qārôb* [1]
recently, 2543, *ḥādāš* [1]

RECESSES [2]
recesses, 2984, *ḥēqer* [1]
farthest recesses, 3972+9417, *kōl*+*taklît* [1]

RECITE [4]
recite, 606, *'āmar*^{1} [1]
recite, 6218, *sāpar* [1]
recite, 6699+2256+606, *'ānâ*^{1}+*w*^{e}-+*'āmar*^{1} [1]
recite, 9480, *tānâ*^{2} [1]

RECITED [1]
recited, 1819, *dābar*^{2} [1]

RECITING [1]
reciting, 1819, *dābar*^{2} [1]

RECKLESS [5]
reckless words, 1051, *bāṭā'* [1]
reckless, 1053, *bāṭaḥ*^{1} [1]
reckless, 3740, *yāraṭ* [1]
reckless, 7071, *paḥ*^{a}*zût* [1]
reckless, 8199, *rêq* [1]

RECKONED [5]
be reckoned, 3108, *ḥāšab* [2]
be reckoned, 7924, *qārā'*^{1} [2]
reckoned, *NIH/RPE* [1]

RECKONING [3]
reckoning, 7213, *p*^{e}*quddâ* [1]
reckoning, 8936, *šillûm* [1]
reckoning, 9349, *tôkēḥâ* [1]

RECLAIM [1]
reclaim, 7864, *qānâ*^{1} [1]

RECLAIMED [1]
reclaimed, 6296, *'ābar*^{1} [1]

RECLINING [1]
reclining, 6584, *'al*^{2} [1]

RECOGNITION [1]
recognition, 1525, *g*^{e}*dûllâ* [1]

RECOGNIZE [6]
recognize, 5795, *nākar*^{1} [5]
recognize, 8011, *rā'â*^{1} [1]

RECOGNIZED [13]
recognized, 5795, *nākar*^{1} [9]
recognized, 3359, *yāda'* [2]
be recognized, 3359, *yāda'* [1]
are recognized, 5795, *nākar*^{1} [1]

RECOGNIZES [1]
recognizes, 3359, *yāda'* [1]

RECOIL [1]
recoil, 8740, *šûb*^{1} [1]

RECOILS [1]
recoils, 8740, *šûb*^{1} [1]

RECOMMENDED [1]
recommended, 1819, *dābar*^{2} [1]

RECOMPENSE [2]
recompense, 7190, *p*^{e}*'ullâ* [2]

RECONSECRATED [1]
be reconsecrated, 7405, *ṣādaq* [1]

RECONSIDER [2]
reconsider, 5714, *nāḥam* [1]
reconsider, 8740+6388, *šûb*^{1}+*'ôd* [1]

RECORD [14]
record, *NIH/RPE* [1]
record, 1821, *dābār* [1]
record, 2349, *zākar*^{1} [1]
be listed in the genealogical record, 3509, *yāḥaś* [1]
genealogical record listed, 3509, *yāḥaś* [1]
kept a genealogical record, 3509, *yāḥaś* [1]
record, 4180, *kātab* [1]
record, 4180+9005, *kātab+šēm*^{1} [1]
record, 6218, *sāpar* [1]
record, 6219, *sēper*^{1} [1]
record, 6225, *siprâ* [1]
kept on record, 7621, *ṣāpan* [1]
kept a record, 9068, *šāmar* [1]
genealogical record, 9352, *tôlēdôt* [1]

RECORDED [20]
recorded, 4180, *kātab* [9]
were recorded, 4180, *kātab* [3]
was recorded, 4180, *kātab* [2]
be recorded, 6218, *sāpar* [2]
were recorded in the genealogies, 3509, *yāḥaś* [1]
been recorded, 4180, *kātab* [1]
are recorded, 6590, *'ālâ* [1]
were recorded, 7212, *pāqad* [1]

RECORDER [9]
recorder, 4654, *mazkîr* [9]

RECORDS [35]
records, 9352, *tôlēdôt* [14]
records, 1821, *dābār* [7]
records, 4181, *k^{e}tāb* [3]
genealogical records, 9352, *tôlēdôt* [2]
records, *NIH/RPE* [1]
enrolled in the genealogical records, 3509, *yāḥaś* [1]
listed in genealogical records, 3509, *yāḥaś* [1]
names in the genealogical records, 3509, *yāḥaś* [1]
were entered in the genealogical records, 3509, *yāḥaś* [1]
keeping records, 6218, *sāpar* [1]
records, 6219, *sēper*^{1} [1]
town records, 9133+5226, *ša'ar*^{1}*+māqôm* [1]
records, 10515+10177, *s^{e}par+dokrān* [1]

RECOUNT [3]
recount, 6218, *sāpar* [2]
recount, 6885, *'ārak* [1]

RECOUNTED [1]
recounted, 6218, *sāpar* [1]

RECOVER [13]
recover, 2649, *ḥāyâ* [6]
recover, 8324, *rāpā'*^{1} [3]
certainly recover, 2649+2649, *ḥāyâ+ḥāyâ* [2]
recover, 4695, *miḥyâ* [1]
recover, 8740, *šûb*^{1} [1]

RECOVERED [11]
recovered, 8740, *šûb*^{1} [6]
recovered, 5911, *nāṣal* [2]
be recovered, 665, *'āsap* [1]
recovered, 2649, *ḥāyâ* [1]
recovered from grief, 5714, *nāḥam* [1]

RECOVERY [2]
recovery, 2616, *ḥāzaq* [1]
recovery, 2649+4946+2716, *ḥāyâ+min+ḥ^{o}lî* [1]

RECTANGULAR [2]
rectangular, 8062, *rāba'*^{2} [2]

RED [46]
Red, 6068, *sûp*^{2} [24]
red, 137, *'ādōm* [7]
dyed red, 131, *'ādēm* [6]
red, 131, *'ādēm* [3]
red, 9266, *šāšar* [2]
red, 145, *'admônî* [1]
red kite, 1798, *dā'â*^{2} [1]
red, 2813, *ḥāmar*^{2} [1]
red kite, 8012, *rā'â*^{2} [1]

REDDISH [2]
reddish, 140, *'^{a}damdām* [2]

REDDISH-WHITE [4]
reddish-white, 4237+140, *lābān*^{1}*+'^{a}damdām* [4]

REDEEM [50]
redeem, 7009, *pādâ* [22]
redeem, 1457, *gā'al*^{1} [17]
redeem, 1460, *g^{e}'ullâ* [3]
redeem, 1457+1457, *gā'al*^{1}*+gā'al*^{1} [2]
redeem himself, 1457, *gā'al*^{1} [1]
right to redeem, 1460, *g^{e}'ullâ* [1]
must redeem, 7009+7009, *pādâ+pādâ* [1]
redeem, 7009+7009, *pādâ+pādâ* [1]
redeem, 7012, *p^{e}dûyim* [1]
redeem, 7018, *pidyôn* [1]

REDEEMABLE [1]
redeemable, 1457, *gā'al*^{1} [1]

REDEEMED [40]
redeemed, 1457, *gā'al*^{1} [18]
redeemed, 7009, *pādâ* [15]
be redeemed, 1457, *gā'al*^{1} [3]
is redeemed, 1457, *gā'al*^{1} [1]
redeemed, 1460, *g^{e}'ullâ* [1]
be redeemed, 7009, *pādâ* [1]
let be redeemed, 7009, *pādâ* [1]

REDEEMER [17]
Redeemer, 1457, *gā'al*^{1} [17]

REDEEMS [4]
redeems, 1457, *gā'al*^{1} [2]
redeems, 1457+1457, *gā'al*^{1}*+gā'al*^{1} [1]
redeems, 7009, *pādâ* [1]

REDEMPTION [13]
redemption, 1460, *g^{e}'ullâ* [4]
right of redemption, 1460, *g^{e}'ullâ* [2]
redemption, 7012, *p^{e}dûyim* [2]
redemption, 7014, *p^{e}dût* [2]
redemption, 1453, *g^{e}'ûlîm* [1]
redemption, 7009, *pādâ* [1]
redemption, 7017, *pidyôm* [1]

REDUCE [7]
reduce, 8492, *śîm* [2]
reduce the number, 1757, *gāra'*^{1} [1]
reduce, 1757, *gāra'*^{1} [1]
reduce to silence, 3087, *ḥārēš*^{2} [1]
reduce to nothing, 5070, *mā'aṭ* [1]
reduce size, 7894, *qāṣā*^{1} [1]

REDUCED [11]
reduced, *NIH/RPE* [2]
be reduced, 1757, *gāra'*^{1} [2]
reduced, 8492, *śîm* [2]
reduced, 1757, *gāra'*^{1} [1]
reduced to, 1815, *dābaq* [1]
reduced to, 5439, *māšal*^{1} [1]
reduced, 5989, *nātan* [1]
reduced to servitude, 6268+4200+6269, *'ābad+l^{e-1}+'ebed*^{1} [1]

REDUCES [2]
reduces to, 6330, *'ad*^{2} [1]
reduces, 6913, *'āśâ*^{1} [1]

REED [8]
reed, 7866, *qāneh* [5]
reed, 109, *'agmôn* [3]

REEDS [10]
reeds, 7866, *qāneh* [4]
reeds, 286, *'āḥû* [3]
reeds, 6068, *sûp*^{2} [2]
reeds, 109, *'agmôn* [1]

REEKED [1]
reeked, 944, *bā'aš* [1]

REEL [2]
reel, 9494, *tā'â* [2]

REELAIAH [1]
Reelaiah, 8305, *r^{e}'ēlāyâ* [1]

REELED [1]
reeled, 2510, *ḥāgag* [1]

REELING [1]
reeling, 8303, *ra'al* [1]

REELS [1]
reels, 5675+5675, *nûa'+nûa'* [1]

REENTERED [1]
reentered, 995+2256+8740, *bô'+w^{e}-+šûb*^{1} [1]

REESTABLISHED [1]
was reestablished, 3922, *kûn*^{1} [1]

REFERRING [1]
referring to, 4200, *l^{e-1}* [1]

REFINE [3]
refine, 7671, *ṣārap* [2]
refine, 2423, *zāqaq* [1]

REFINED [8]
refined, 7671, *ṣārap* [5]
refined, 2423, *zāqaq* [3]

REFINER [1]
refiner, 7671, *ṣārap* [1]

REFINER'S [1]
refiner's, 7671, *ṣārap* [1]

REFINING [1]
refining goes on, 7671+7671, *ṣārap+ṣārap* [1]

REFLECT [1]
reflect on, 2349, *zākar*^{1} [1]

REFLECTED [1]
reflected on, 5989+448+4213, *nātan+'el+lēb* [1]

REFLECTS [3]
reflects a face, 2021+7156+4200+2021+7156, *ha-+pāneh+l^{e-1}+ha-+pāneh* [1]
reflects on, 2349, *zākar*^{1} [1]
reflects the man, 4200+2021+132, *l^{e-1}+ha-+'ādām*^{1} [1]

REFORM [4]
reform, 3512, *yāṭab* [4]

REFRAIN [9]
refrain, 2532, *ḥādal*^{1} [5]
refrain, 1821, *dābār* [1]
refrain from, 2532, *ḥādal*^{1} [1]
refrain, 8178, *rāḥaq* [1]
refrain, 8332, *rāpâ*^{1} [1]

REFRAINED [2]
refrained, 2798, *ḥāmal* [1]
refrained, 6806, *'āṣar* [1]

REFRESH [5]
refresh, 6184, *sā'ad* [2]
refresh, 8115, *rāwâ* [1]
refresh, 8331, *rāpad* [1]
refresh, 9272, *šātâ*^{2} [1]

REFRESHED [5]
be refreshed, 3722, *yārā*^{2} [1]
refreshed, 3922, *kûn*^{1} [1]
be refreshed, 5882, *nāpaš* [1]
refreshed himself, 5882, *nāpaš* [1]
refreshed, 6184+4213, *sā'ad+lēb* [1]

REFRESHES [2]
refreshes, 8115, *rāwâ* [1]
refreshes, 8740, *šûb*^{1} [1]

REFUGE [93]
take refuge, 2879, *ḥāsâ* [23]
refuge, 4726, *maḥseh* [18]
refuge, 5236, *miqlāṭ* [17]
refuge, 5057, *mā'ôz* [8]
refuge, 4960, *mānôs* [4]
find refuge, 2879, *ḥāsâ* [3]

takes refuge, 2879, *ḥāsâ* [3]
taken refuge, 2879, *ḥāsâ* [2]
refuge, 5104, *m^{e}ʿōnâ* [2]
refuge, 5369, *miśgāb^{1}* [2]
refuge, 6260, *sēter* [2]
have a refuge, 2879, *ḥāsâ* [1]
makes refuge, 2879, *ḥāsâ* [1]
refuge, 2879, *ḥāsâ* [1]
took refuge, 2879, *ḥāsâ* [1]
refuge, 5061, *māʿôn^{2}* [1]
place of refuge, 5236, *miqlāṭ* [1]
taken refuge, 5911, *nāṣal* [1]
take refuge, 6259, *sātar* [1]
takes refuge, 6259, *sātar* [1]

REFUGEES [2]
refugees, 5610, *nādad* [1]
refugees, 7128, *pālêṭ* [1]

REFUND [1]
refund, 8740, *šûb^{1}* [1]

REFUSE [42]
refuse, 4412, *māʾan* [15]
refuse, 1961, *dōmen* [6]
refuse, 4202, *lōʾ* [5]
refuse, 8740, *šûb^{1}* [4]
refuse, 4202+14, *lōʾ+ʾābâ* [2]
refuse, 4979, *mānaʿ* [2]
refuse, *NIH/RPE* [1]
refuse, 2532, *ḥādal^{1}* [1]
refuse, 2534, *ḥādēl* [1]
refuse, 3973, *kālāʾ^{1}* [1]
refuse, 4400, *māʾôs* [1]
refuse, 4415, *māʾas^{1}* [1]
refuse, 5648, *nûʾ* [1]
refuse, 6054, *sûḥâ* [1]

REFUSED [43]
refused, 4412, *māʾan* [22]
refused, 4202+14, *lōʾ+ʾābâ* [11]
refused, 4202, *lōʾ* [7]
refused, 4202+9048, *lōʾ+šāmaʿ* [1]
refused, 4979, *mānaʿ* [1]
stubbornly refused, 7996, *qāšâ* [1]

REFUSES [4]
refuses, 4412, *māʾan* [2]
absolutely refuses, 4412+4412, *māʾan+māʾan* [1]
refuses, 8533, *śānēʾ* [1]

REFUSING [3]
refusing, 4412, *māʾan* [2]
refusing, 1194, *biltî* [1]

REFUTE [3]
way to refute, 5101, *maʿ^{a}neh^{1}* [1]
refute, 5622, *nādap* [1]
refute, 8399, *rāšaʿ* [1]

REGAIN [5]
regain, 8740, *šûb^{1}* [3]
regain, 6806+6388, *ʿāṣar+ʿôd* [1]
regain favor, 8354, *rāṣâ^{1}* [1]

REGARD [32]
have regard for, 8011, *rāʾâ^{1}* [4]
show regard, 1067, *bîn* [2]
regard as, 2118+4200, *hāyâ+l^{e}-^{1}* [2]
in regard to, 4946, *min* [2]
have regard for, 5564, *nābaṭ* [2]
regard as holy, 7727, *qādaš* [2]
regard, 8492+4200+5584, *śîm+l^{e}-^{1}+neged* [2]
regard, *AIT* [1]
regard, *NIH/RPE* [1]
in regard to, 928, *b^{e}-* [1]
regard, 1067, *bîn* [1]
regard, 2118+4200+7156, *hāyâ+l^{e}-^{1}+pāneh* [1]
regard, 3108, *ḥāšab* [1]
had regard for, 3359, *yādaʿ* [1]
have regard for, 5564+4200, *nābaṭ+l^{e}-^{1}* [1]
paid regard, 5795, *nākar^{1}* [1]
regard, 5795, *nākar^{1}* [1]
regard as forbidden, 6887+6889, *ʿāral+ʿorlâ* [1]
regard, 8011, *rāʾâ^{1}* [1]
had regard for, 8505, *śākal^{1}* [1]
has regard for, 8505, *śākal^{1}* [1]
have regard, 9120, *šāʿâ* [1]
with regard to, 10089, *b^{e}-* [1]

REGARDED [11]
are regarded, 3108, *ḥāšab* [3]
highly regarded, 1524+4394, *gādôl+m^{e}ʾōd* [1]
regarded, 3108, *ḥāšab* [1]
regarded in the sight of, 4200+7156, *l^{e}-^{1}+pāneh* [1]
regarded, 4200, *l^{e}-^{1}* [1]
highly regarded, 5951+7156, *nāśāʾ+pāneh* [1]
was highly regarded, 5951, *nāśāʾ* [1]
regarded, 8011, *rāʾâ^{1}* [1]
are regarded, 10285, *ḥ^{a}šab* [1]

REGARDING [4]
regarding, *AIT* [1]
regarding, *NIH/RPE* [1]
regarding, 928, *b^{e}-* [1]
regarding, 6584, *ʿal^{2}* [1]

REGARDLESS [1]
regardless, 401+4200+9068, *ʾayin^{1}+l^{e}-^{1}+šāmar* [1]

REGARDS [2]
regards, 5162+4200+7156, *māṣāʾ+l^{e}-^{1}+pāneh* [1]
regards, 5162+928+6524, *māṣāʾ+b^{e}-+ʿayin^{1}* [1]

REGEM [1]
Regem, 8084, *regem* [1]

REGEM-MELECH [1]
Regem-Melech, 8085, *regem melek* [1]

REGION [36]
region, 824, *ʾereṣ* [18]
region, 2475, *ḥebel^{2}* [4]
region, 1473, *g^{e}bûl* [3]
region, 8441, *śādeh* [3]
region, *AIT* [1]
region, *NIH/RPE* [1]
region, 1666, *g^{e}lîlâ* [1]
region, 3971, *kikkār* [1]
surrounding region, 3971, *kikkār* [1]
whole region, 3971, *kikkār* [1]
region where lived, 4632, *môšāb* [1]
region, 7156, *pāneh* [1]

REGIONS [5]
regions, 1666, *g^{e}lîlâ* [2]
mountain regions, 2215, *har* [1]
regions, 4519, *m^{e}dînâ* [1]
regions, 5226, *māqôm* [1]

REGISTER [1]
register, 4180, *kātab* [1]

REGISTERED [5]
registered, 3509, *yāḥaś* [1]
were registered by genealogy, 3509, *yāḥaś* [1]
were registered, 3509, *yāḥaś* [1]
were registered, 5918, *nāqab^{1}* [1]
were registered, 7212, *pāqad* [1]

REGISTRATION [1]
registration by families, 3509, *yāḥaś* [1]

REGRET [1]
regret, 2775, *ḥemdâ* [1]

REGROUPED [1]
regrouped, 665+3480, *ʾāsap+yaḥad* [1]

REGULAR [55]
regular, 9458, *tāmîd* [23]
regular work, 4856+6275, *m^{e}lāʾkâ+ʿ^{a}bōdâ* [12]
regular, 6409, *ʿôlām* [9]
regular, *NIH/RPE* [2]
regular, *AIT* [1]
regular^{s}, 2085, *hûʾ* [1]
regular flow, 2307+928+1414, *zûb+b^{e}-+bāśār* [1]
regular allotment, 2976, *ḥōq* [1]
regular share, 2976, *ḥōq* [1]
regular, 2978, *ḥuqqâ* [1]
regular, 3972+2021+3427, *kōl+ha-+yôm^{1}* [1]
at regular intervals, 4500, *middâ^{1}* [1]
regular service, 7372+6275, *ṣābāʾ^{2}+ʿ^{a}bōdâ* [1]

REGULARLY [13]
regularly, 9458, *tāmîd* [12]
regularly, 4200+3427+928+3427, *l^{e}-^{1}+yôm^{1}+b^{e}-+yôm^{1}* [1]

REGULATED [1]
regulated, 591, *ʾ^{a}mānâ^{1}* [1]

REGULATION [1]
regulation, 5477, *mišpāṭ* [1]

REGULATIONS [39]
regulations, 9368, *tôrâ* [15]
regulations, 5477, *mišpāṭ* [11]
regulations, 2978, *ḥuqqâ* [7]
regulations, 1821, *dābār* [2]
regulations, 6343, *ʿēdût* [2]
regulations, 2976, *ḥōq* [1]
regulations prescribed, 5477, *mišpāṭ* [1]

REHABIAH [4]
Rehabiah, 8152, *r^{e}ḥabyâ* [2]
Rehabiah, 8153, *r^{e}ḥabyāhû* [2]

REHOB [10]
Rehob, 8149, *r^{e}ḥōb^{2}* [7]
Rehob, 8150, *r^{e}ḥōb^{3}* [3]

REHOBOAM [48]
Rehoboam, 8154, *r^{e}ḥabʿām* [43]
Rehoboam, *NIH/RPE* [4]
Rehoboam^{s}, 2257, *-ô* [1]

REHOBOAM'S [3]
Rehoboam's, 8154, *r^{e}ḥabʿām* [3]

REHOBOTH [3]
Rehoboth, 8151, *r^{e}ḥōbôt* [3]

REHOBOTH IR [1]
Rehoboth Ir, 8155, *r^{e}ḥōbōt ʿîr* [1]

REHUM [8]
Rehum, 8156, *r^{e}ḥûm* [4]
Rehum, 10662, *r^{e}ḥûm* [4]

REI [1]
Rei, 8298, *rēʿî* [1]

REIGN [141]
reign, *NIH/RPE* [52]
reign, 4887, *mālak^{1}* [37]
reign, 4895, *malkût* [19]
reign, 3427, *yôm^{1}* [17]
reign, 10424, *malkû* [5]
reign, 4889, *melek^{1}* [3]
reign, 3782, *yāšab* [2]
reign, 4930, *mamlākâ* [2]
intend to reign, 4887+4887, *mālak^{1}+mālak^{1}* [1]
reign, 4931, *mamlākût* [1]
reign over, 6584, *ʿal^{2}* [1]
reign, 8699, *šebet^{1}* [1]

REIGNED [90]
reigned, 4887, *mālak^{1}* [70]
reigned, *NIH/RPE* [11]
reigned, 3782, *yāšab* [8]
reigned, 4887+4889, *mālak^{1}+melek^{1}* [1]

REIGNS [16]
reigns, 4887, *mālak^{1}* [9]
reigns, 3427, *yôm^{1}* [6]
reigns, 3782, *yāšab* [1]

REIN [1]
give free rein, 6440, *ʿāzab^{1}* [1]

REINFORCE [1]
reinforce, 2616, *ḥāzaq* [1]

REINFORCED [2]
reinforced, 599, *ʾāmēṣ* [1]
reinforced, 2616, *ḥāzaq* [1]

REINFORCEMENTS [1]
reinforcements, 6450, *'izzûz* [1]

REJECT [24]
reject, 4415, *mā'as^1* [12]
reject, 2396, *zānaḥ^2* [4]
reject, 5759, *nāṭaš* [3]
reject, 8740+7156, *šûb^1+pāneh* [2]
reject, 6136, *sālâ^1* [1]
reject, 8938+4946+6584+7156, *šālaḥ+min+'al^2+pāneh* [1]
reject, 8959+4946+6584+7156, *šālak+min+'al^2+pāneh* [1]

REJECTED [61]
rejected, 4415, *mā'as^1* [34]
rejected, 2396, *zānaḥ^2* [11]
rejected, 6440, *'āzab^1* [4]
rejected, 6073, *sûr^1* [2]
rejected, 2534, *ḥādēl* [1]
rejected, 4412, *mā'an* [1]
be rejected, 4415, *mā'as^1* [1]
rejected completely, 4415+4415, *mā'as^1+mā'as^1* [1]
utterly rejected, 4415+4415, *mā'as^1+mā'as^1* [1]
rejected, 5540, *nā'aṣ* [1]
rejected, 5571, *nābal^2* [1]
rejected, 5759, *nāṭaš* [1]
rejected, 6136, *sālâ^1* [1]
rejected, 9493, *tā'ab* [1]

REJECTING [3]
rejecting, 6440, *'āzab^1* [2]
rejecting, 5540, *nā'aṣ* [1]

REJECTS [1]
rejects, 4415, *mā'as^1* [1]

REJOICE [103]
rejoice, 8523, *śāmaḥ* [42]
rejoice, 1635, *gîl^1* [25]
rejoice, 8464, *śûś* [11]
rejoice, 6600, *'ālaz* [7]
rejoice, 6636, *'ālaṣ* [3]
rejoice, 8525, *śimḥâ* [3]
rejoice, 6611, *'allîz* [2]
rejoice, 8264, *rānan* [2]
rejoice, *NIH/RPE* [1]
rejoice, 1158, *bālag* [1]
rejoice greatly, 1635+677+1638, *gîl^1+'ap^1+gîlâ* [1]
rejoice, 5642, *nāhar^2* [1]
rejoice greatly, 8464+5375, *śûś+māśôś^1* [1]
given cause to rejoice, 8523, *śāmaḥ* [1]
made rejoice, 8523, *śāmaḥ* [1]
rejoice, 8524, *śāmēaḥ* [1]

REJOICED [15]
rejoiced, 8523, *śāmaḥ* [11]
rejoiced, 8525, *śimḥâ* [2]
rejoiced, 1635, *gîl^1* [1]
rejoiced, 8523+8525, *śāmaḥ+śimḥâ* [1]

REJOICES [13]
rejoices, 8523, *śāmaḥ* [5]
rejoices, 1635, *gîl^1* [3]
rejoices, 5375, *māśôś^1* [2]
rejoices, 6636, *'ālaṣ* [2]
rejoices, *NIH/RPE* [1]

REJOICING [19]
rejoicing, 8525, *śimḥâ* [6]
rejoicing, 8471, *śāḥaq* [3]
rejoicing, 8523, *śāmaḥ* [3]
rejoicing, 8464, *śûś* [2]
rejoicing, 8524, *śāmēaḥ* [2]
rejoicing, 8262, *rinnâ^1* [1]
rejoicing, 8524+8525, *śāmēaḥ+śimḥâ* [1]
rejoicing, 8607, *śāśôn* [1]

REJOINED [1]
rejoined, 2143+448, *hālak+'el* [1]

REKEM [5]
Rekem, 8390, *reqem^2* [4]
Rekem, 8389, *reqem^1* [1]

RELATED [9]
related to, 4200, *l^e-^{1}* [3]
related, *AIT* [2]
related by marriage, 1251, *ba'al^1* [1]
related^s, 2157, *-hem* [1]
related by marriage, 3163, *ḥātān* [1]
closely related, 7940, *qārôb* [1]

RELATING [1]
relating to, 4200, *l^e-^{1}* [1]

RELATION [1]
relation to, 4200, *l^e-^{1}* [1]

RELATIONS [31]
have sexual relations with, 6872+1655, *'erwâ+gālâ* [10]
have sexual relations, 1655+6872, *gālâ+'erwâ* [3]
have relations with, 1655+6872, *gālâ+'erwâ* [2]
have sexual relations with, 8061, *rāba'^{1}* [2]
has sexual relations with, 8886+6640, *šākab+'im* [2]
abstain from sexual relations, 440+5602+448+851, *'al^1+nāgaš+'el+'iššâ* [1]
has sexual relations with, 1655+906+6872, *gālâ+'ēt^1+'erwâ* [1]
have sexual relations with, 1655+6872, *gālâ+'erwâ* [1]
had intimate relations with, 3359, *yāda'* [1]
has sexual relations, 5989+8888, *nātan+š^{e}kōbet* [1]
have sexual relations, 5989+8888+4200+2446, *nātan+š^{e}kōbet+l^e-^{1}+zera'* [1]
have sexual relations, 5989+8888, *nātan+š^{e}kōbet* [1]
dishonor by having sexual relations with, 6872+1655, *'erwâ+gālâ* [1]
dishonor by to have sexual relations, 6872+1655, *'erwâ+gālâ* [1]
have sexual relations, 8011+906+6872, *rā'â^1+'ēt^1+'erwâ* [1]
friendly relations, 8934, *šālôm* [1]
peaceful relations, 8934, *šālôm* [1]

RELATIONSHIP [2]
relationship, 1821, *dābār* [2]

RELATIONSHIPS [1]
relationships between, 1068, *bayin* [1]

RELATIVE [19]
relative, 278, *'āḥ^2* [5]
close relative, 8638, *š^e'ēr* [3]
relative, 1457, *gā'al^1* [2]
close relative, 1457, *gā'al^1* [1]
as nearest relative duty, 1460, *g^e'ullâ* [1]
relative, 1856, *dôd* [1]
relative, 4530, *mōdā'* [1]
close relative, 7940, *qārôb* [1]
blood relative, 8638+1414, *š^e'ēr+bāśār* [1]
close relative, 8638+1414, *š^e'ēr+bāśār* [1]
close relative, 8638+7940, *š^e'ēr+qārôb* [1]
relative, 8638, *š^e'ēr* [1]

RELATIVES [72]
relatives, 278, *'āḥ^2* [67]
relatives, 4580, *môledet* [3]
blood relatives, 408+1460, *'îš^1+g^e'ullâ* [1]
close relatives, 8638, *š^e'ēr* [1]

RELEASE [13]
release, 8938, *šālaḥ* [4]
release, 6142, *sālaḥ* [3]
release, *NIH/RPE* [1]
release, 3655, *yāṣā'* [1]
release, 4880, *mālaṭ^1* [1]
release, 4928, *mimkār* [1]
release, 7337, *pātaḥ^1* [1]
release from darkness, 7223, *p^{e}qaḥ-qôaḥ* [1]

RELEASED [15]
released, 3655, *yāṣā'* [4]
be released, 5927, *nāqâ* [2]
released, 5929, *nāqî* [2]
released, 5951+8031, *nāśā'+rō'š^1* [2]
released, *NIH/RPE* [1]
released, 6002, *nātar^3* [1]
released, 7080, *pāṭar* [1]
be released, 7337, *pātaḥ^1* [1]
released, 8938, *šālaḥ* [1]

RELEASES [1]
releases, 8938, *šālaḥ* [1]

RELENT [12]
relent, 5714, *nāḥam* [5]
relent, 8740, *šûb^1* [4]
relent and do not bring, 5714, *nāḥam* [1]
relent and not bring, 5714, *nāḥam* [1]
relent so that not bring, 5714, *nāḥam* [1]

RELENTED [4]
relented, 5714, *nāḥam* [3]
relented and did not, 5714, *nāḥam* [1]

RELENTLESS [1]
relentless, 1172+3104, *b^{e}lî+ḥāśak* [1]

RELENTS [2]
relents, 5714, *nāḥam* [2]

RELIABLE [4]
reliable, 622, *'^{e}met* [2]
reliable, 586, *'āman^1* [1]
reliable, 3838, *yāšār^1* [1]

RELIANCE [1]
reliance, 4440, *mibṭāḥ* [1]

RELIED [7]
relied, 9128, *šā'an* [3]
relied, 1053, *bāṭaḥ^1* [2]
relied on, 4438, *mabbāṭ* [1]
relied, 6164, *sāmak* [1]

RELIEF [19]
relief, 8121, *r^{e}wāḥâ* [2]
relief, 2198, *h^{a}pugâ* [1]
bring relief, 3104, *ḥāśak* [1]
relief, 3202, *ṭôb^2* [1]
relief, 4695, *miḥyâ* [1]
for relief from, 4946+4200+7156, *min+l^e-^{1}+pāneh* [1]
get relief, 5663, *nûaḥ^1* [1]
gives relief, 5663, *nûaḥ^1* [1]
got relief, 5663, *nûaḥ^1* [1]
get relief, 5714, *nāḥam* [1]
come to relief, 6699, *'ānâ^1* [1]
relief, 7029, *pûgâ* [1]
find relief, 8118, *rāwaḥ* [1]
relief come, 8118, *rāwaḥ* [1]
relief, 8119, *rewaḥ* [1]
give relief, 8143, *rāḥab* [1]
plead for relief, 8775, *šāwa'* [1]
grant relief, 9200, *šāqaṭ* [1]

RELIES [1]
what relies on, 4440, *mibṭāḥ* [1]

RELIEVE [3]
relieve, *NIH/RPE* [1]
relieve yourself, 3782+2575, *yāšab+ḥûṣ* [1]
relieve himself, 6114+906+8079+2257, *sākak^1+'ēt^1+regel+-ô* [1]

RELIEVED [1]
is relieved, 3104, *ḥāśak* [1]

RELIEVING [1]
relieving himself, 6114+906+8079+2257, *sākak^1+'ēt^1+regel+-ô* [1]

RELIGIOUS [2]
religious feasts, 2504, *ḥag* [2]

RELISH [1]
relish, 5951+5883, *nāśā'+nepeš* [1]

RELY [10]
rely, 9128, *šā'an* [5]
rely, 1053, *bāṭaḥ^1* [3]
rely, 6164, *sāmak* [1]
rely, 6641, *'āmad* [1]

REMAIN [77]
remain, 2118, *hāyâ* [14]
remain, *NIH/RPE* [9]
remain, 3782, *yāšab* [9]
remain, 8636, *šā'ar* [9]
remain, *AIT* [6]
remain, 3855, *yātar* [5]
remain, 4328, *lîn* [4]
remain, 6641, *ʿāmad* [3]
remain, 2143, *hālak* [2]
remain, 6388, *ʿôd* [2]
remain, 8642, *š^{e}'ērît* [2]
remain, 8905, *šākan* [2]
remain in camp, 2837, *ḥānâ^{1}* [1]
remain silent, 3087+3087, *ḥārēš^{2}+ḥārēš^{2}* [1]
allow to remain, 3855, *yātar* [1]
allowed to remain, 5663, *nûaḥ^{1}* [1]
let remain, 5663, *nûaḥ^{1}* [1]
remain, 5663, *nûaḥ^{1}* [1]
remain unmarried, 6328+4200+1194+2118+4200+408, *ʿāgan+l^{e}-^{1}+biltî+hāyâ+l^{e}-^{1}+'îš^{1}* [1]
remain, 7756, *qûm* [1]
remain, 10201, *h^{a}wâ* [1]
remain, 10697, *š^{e}baq* [1]

REMAINDER [1]
remainder, 8637, *š^{e}'ār* [1]

REMAINED [53]
remained, 3782, *yāšab* [18]
remained, 8636, *šā'ar* [10]
remained, 2118, *hāyâ* [8]
remained, *AIT* [7]
remained, 6388, *ʿôd* [2]
remained, 6641, *ʿāmad* [2]
remained, *NIH/RPE* [1]
remained, 336, *'āḥar* [1]
remained, 799, *'ārak* [1]
remained in camp, 2837, *ḥānâ^{1}* [1]
remained, 3855, *yātar* [1]
remained childless, 4202+3528, *lō'+yālad* [1]

REMAINING [14]
remaining, 3855, *yātar* [7]
remaining, 3856, *yeter^{1}* [2]
remaining, 8642, *š^{e}'ērît* [2]
remaining, *NIH/RPE* [1]
remaining, 3338, *yād* [1]
remaining, 8637, *š^{e}'ār* [1]

REMAINS [30]
remains, *NIH/RPE* [9]
remains, *AIT* [3]
remains, 6641, *ʿāmad* [3]
remains, 3855, *yātar* [2]
remains, 6388, *ʿôd* [2]
remains, 2118, *hāyâ* [1]
remains unclean, 3237+3238, *ṭāmē'^{1}+ṭāmē'^{2}* [1]
remains, 3274, *ṭ^{e}rēpâ* [1]
remains, 3782, *yāšab* [1]
remains, 3869, *k^{e}-* [1]
remains, 4328, *lîn* [1]
remains, 7756, *qûm* [1]
remains, 8239, *rāmût* [1]
smoldering remains, 8599, *ś^{e}rēpâ* [1]
remains, 8636, *šā'ar* [1]
remains, 9068, *šāmar* [1]

REMALIAH [11]
Remaliah, 8248, *r^{e}malyāhû* [11]

REMALIAH'S [2]
Remaliah's, 8248, *r^{e}malyāhû* [2]

REMEDIES [1]
remedies, 8337, *r^{e}pû'â* [1]

REMEDY [6]
remedy, 5340, *marpē'^{1}* [3]
remedy, 2502, *ḥābaš* [1]
beyond all remedy, 5344, *māraṣ* [1]
remedy, 8337, *r^{e}pû'â* [1]

REMEMBER [130]
remember, 2349, *zākar^{1}* [116]
remember, *NIH/RPE* [4]
remember, 8011, *rā'â^{1}* [3]
remember, 2180, *hinnēh* [2]
remember well, 2349+2349, *zākar^{1}+zākar^{1}* [1]
remember, 2349+2349, *zākar^{1}+zākar^{1}* [1]
well remember, 2349+2349, *zākar^{1}+zākar^{1}* [1]
remember, 3359, *yādaʿ* [1]
remember, 10313, *y^{e}daʿ* [1]

REMEMBERED [46]
remembered, 2349, *zākar^{1}* [23]
be remembered, 2349, *zākar^{1}* [15]
remembered, 2352, *zēker* [2]
remembered, 2355, *zikkārôn* [2]
are remembered, 2349, *zākar^{1}* [1]
name by which remembered, 2352, *zēker* [1]
something remembered, 2355, *zikkārôn* [1]
be remembered, 3359, *yādaʿ* [1]

REMEMBERS [10]
remembers, 2349, *zākar^{1}* [8]
remembers, 2352, *zēker* [1]
remembers, 5795, *nākar^{1}* [1]

REMEMBRANCE [2]
remembrance, 2355, *zikkārôn* [2]

REMETH [1]
remeth, 8255, *remet* [1]

REMIND [3]
remind, 2349, *zākar^{1}* [2]
remind, 2355, *zikkārôn* [1]

REMINDED [1]
reminded, 2349, *zākar^{1}* [1]

REMINDER [4]
reminder, 2355, *zikkārôn* [3]
reminder, 2349, *zākar^{1}* [1]

REMNANT [62]
remnant, 8642, *š^{e}'ērît* [44]
remnant, 8637, *š^{e}'ār* [9]
remnant, 7129, *p^{e}lêṭâ* [6]
remnant, 3856, *yeter^{1}* [1]
remnant spare, 8636, *šā'ar* [1]
remnant, 8636, *šā'ar* [1]

REMOTE [2]
remote area, 3752, *y^{e}rēkâ* [2]

REMOTEST [3]
remotest, 7891, *qēṣ* [2]
remotest frontiers, 6992, *pē'â^{2}* [1]

REMOVAL [1]
removal, 6073, *sûr^{1}* [1]

REMOVE [51]
remove, 6073, *sûr^{1}* [28]
remove, 8123, *rûm^{1}* [5]
remove, 8697, *šābat^{1}* [3]
remove ashes, 2014, *dāšēn^{1}* [2]
remove, 2048, *hāgâ^{2}* [2]
remove, 3655, *yāṣā'* [2]
remove far, 8178, *rāḥaq* [2]
remove, 665, *'āsap* [1]
remove, 1655, *gālâ* [1]
remove, 4631, *mûš^{2}* [1]
remove, 6232, *sāqal* [1]
remove, 6296, *ʿābar^{1}* [1]
remove, 7320, *pāšaṭ* [1]
remove, 8938, *šālaḥ* [1]

REMOVED [62]
removed, 6073, *sûr^{1}* [31]
removed, *NIH/RPE* [4]
removed, 3655, *yāṣā'* [4]
removed, 1278, *bā'ar^{2}* [2]
removed, 4572, *môṭ^{1}* [2]
is removed, 6073, *sûr^{1}* [2]
removed, 1655, *gālâ* [1]
removed, 1763, *gāraš^{1}* [1]
removed, 2396, *zānaḥ^{2}* [1]
been removed, 3325, *yāgâ^{2}* [1]
removed, 3718, *yārad* [1]
removed, 4374, *lāqaḥ* [1]
removed from quarry, 5825, *nāsaʿ* [1]
been removed, 6073, *sûr^{1}* [1]
removed, 6296, *ʿābar^{1}* [1]
removed, 7320, *pāšaṭ* [1]
removed, 7337, *pātaḥ^{1}* [1]
is removed, 8123, *rûm^{1}* [1]
far removed, 8178, *rāḥaq* [1]
removed, 8697, *šābat^{1}* [1]
had removed, 8938+2256+4374, *šālaḥ+w^{e}+lāqaḥ* [1]
removed, 8990, *šālap* [1]
removed, 10485, *n^{e}paq* [1]

REMOVES [1]
removes, 6073, *sûr^{1}* [1]

REND [2]
rend, 7973, *qāraʿ* [2]

RENDER [2]
render judgment, 5477+9149, *mišpāṭ+šāpaṭ* [1]
render, 6913, *ʿāśâ^{1}* [1]

RENDERING [1]
rendering decisions, 7133, *p^{e}lîliyyâ* [1]

RENEGADES [1]
renegades, 7127, *pālîṭ* [1]

RENEW [8]
renew, 2542, *ḥādaš* [4]
renew, 2649, *ḥāyâ* [1]
let renew, 2736, *ḥālap^{1}* [1]
renew, 2736, *ḥālap^{1}* [1]
renew, 8740, *šûb^{1}* [1]

RENEWAL [2]
renewal, 2652, *ḥayyâ^{2}* [1]
renewal, 2722, *ḥ^{a}lîpâ* [1]

RENEWED [4]
renewed, 4162, *kārat* [2]
is renewed, 2542, *ḥādaš* [1]
is renewed, 8186, *ruṭ^{a}paš* [1]

RENOUNCE [2]
renounce, 8740+7156, *šûb^{1}+pāneh* [1]
renounce, 10596, *p^{e}raq* [1]

RENOUNCED [1]
renounced, 5545, *nā'ar* [1]

RENOUNCES [1]
renounces, 6440, *ʿāzab^{1}* [1]

RENOWN [12]
renown, 9005, *šēm^{1}* [6]
renown, 2352, *zēker* [3]
renown, 2146, *hālal^{2}* [1]
name of renown, 2352, *zēker* [1]
renown, 9335, *t^{e}hillâ* [1]

RENOWNED [3]
renowned, 3877, *kābēd^{1}* [2]
renowned, 4200+9005, *l^{e}-^{1}+šēm^{1}* [1]

REOPENED [1]
reopened, 8740+2256+2916, *šûb^{1}+w^{e}+ḥāpar^{1}* [1]

REPAID [5]
repaid, 8740, *šûb^{1}* [2]
fully repaid, 8425, *śābaʿ* [1]
be repaid, 8966, *šālēm^{1}* [1]
repaid, 8966, *šālēm^{1}* [1]

REPAIR [14]
repair, 2616, *ḥāzaq* [10]
repair, 1553, *gādar* [2]
repair, 2616+981, *ḥāzaq+bedeq* [1]
repair, 6641, *ʿāmad* [1]

REPAIRED [24]
repaired, 2616, *ḥāzaq* [18]
repaired, *NIH/RPE* [2]
repaired, 980, *bādaq* [1]
repaired, 2542, *ḥādaš* [1]
be repaired, 8324, *rāpā'^{1}* [1]
repaired, 8324, *rāpā'^{1}* [1]

REPAIRER [1]
Repairer of Walls, 1553, *gādar* [1]

REPAIRING [4]
repairing, 981, *bedeq* [1]
repairing, 1215, *bānâ* [1]
repairing, 2616, *ḥāzaq* [1]
repairing, 10253, *ḥûṭ* [1]

REPAIRS [22]
made repairs, 2616, *ḥāzaq* [14]
repairs made, 2616, *ḥāzaq* [4]
repairs, 776, *ʾᵃrûkâ* [2]
repairs, *NIH/RPE* [1]
carried out repairs, 2616, *ḥāzaq* [1]

REPAY [38]
repay, 8966, *šālēm*[1] [18]
repay, 8740, *šûb*[1] [8]
repay, 5989, *nātan* [6]
repay, 1694, *gāmal* [2]
repay, 8492, *śîm* [1]
repay, 8740+6584+8031, *šûb*[1]*+ʿal*[2]*+rōʾš*[1] [1]
repay, 8740+928+8031, *šûb*[1]*+bᵉ+rōʾš*[1] [1]
repay in full, 8966+8966, *šālēm*[1]*+šālēm*[1] [1]

REPAYING [4]
repaying, 8966, *šālēm*[1] [2]
repaying, 1694, *gāmal* [1]
repaying, 8740, *šûb*[1] [1]

REPAYS [3]
repays, 8966, *šālēm*[1] [3]

REPEALED [3]
repealed, 10528, *ʿᵃdâ* [2]
repealed, 6296, *ʿābar*[1] [1]

REPEATED [7]
repeated, 1819, *dābar*[2] [5]
repeated, 606, *ʾāmar*[1] [1]
repeated, 6218, *sāpar* [1]

REPEATEDLY [1]
repeatedly, 8049, *rābâ*[1] [1]

REPEATS [2]
repeats, 9101, *šānâ*[1] [2]

REPENT [12]
repent, 8740, *šûb*[1] [10]
repent, *NIH/RPE* [1]
repent, 5714, *nāḥam* [1]

REPENTANCE [1]
repentance, 8746, *šûbâ* [1]

REPENTED [4]
repented, 8740, *šûb*[1] [2]
repented, 4044, *kānaʿ* [1]
repented, 5714, *nāḥam* [1]

REPENTS [2]
repents, 5714, *nāḥam* [1]
repents, 8740, *šûb*[1] [1]

REPHAEL [1]
Rephael, 8330, *rᵉpāʾēl* [1]

REPHAH [1]
Rephah, 8338, *repaḥ* [1]

REPHAIAH [5]
Rephaiah, 8341, *rᵉpāyâ* [5]

REPHAIM [8]
Rephaim, 8329, *rᵉpāʾîm*[3] [8]

REPHAITES [10]
Rephaites, 8328, *rᵉpāʾîm*[2] [10]

REPHIDIM [5]
Rephidim, 8340, *rᵉpîdîm* [5]

REPLACE [6]
replace, 9393, *taḥat*[1] [3]
replace, 995+448+9393, *bôʾ+ʾel+taḥat*[1] [1]
replace, 2736, *ḥālap*[1] [1]
replace, 8492+9393, *śîm+taḥat*[1] [1]

REPLACED [3]
replaced, 5989+9393, *nātan+taḥat*[1] [1]
replaced, 6641+9393, *ʿāmad+taḥat*[1] [1]
replaced, 8492, *śîm* [1]

REPLANTED [1]
replanted, 5749, *nāṭaʿ* [1]

REPLICA [1]
replica, 9322, *tabnît* [1]

REPLIED [238]
replied, 606, *ʾāmar*[1] [185]
replied, 6699, *ʿānâ*[1] [41]
replied, 1819, *dābar*[2] [5]
replied, 10558, *ʿᵃnâ* [5]
replied, 8938+606, *šālaḥ+ʾāmar*[1] [2]

REPLIES [2]
replies, 606, *ʾāmar*[1] [1]
replies[s], 889, *ʾᵃšer* [1]

REPLY [18]
reply, 606, *ʾāmar*[1] [4]
reply, 6699, *ʿānâ*[1] [4]
said in reply, 6699, *ʿānâ*[1] [2]
reply, 8740, *šûb*[1] [2]
giving an apt reply, 5101+7023,
maʿᵃneh[1]*+peh* [1]
reply, 5101, *maʿᵃneh*[1] [1]
written reply, 5981, *ništᵉwān* [1]
reply, 8740+4863, *šûb*[1]*+millâ* [1]
reply, 9350, *tôkaḥat* [1]
reply, 10601, *pitgām* [1]

REPOINTING [1]
repointing, 5893, *nāṣab*[1] [1]

REPORT [37]
report, 1821, *dābār* [8]
report, 9019, *šᵉmûʿâ* [7]
report, 5583, *nāgad* [5]
report, 9051, *šēmaʿ* [3]
bad report, 1804, *dibbâ* [2]
report, 1804, *dibbâ* [2]
brought report, 5583, *nāgad* [2]
received a report, 9048, *šāmaʿ* [2]
report, 606, *ʾāmar*[1] [1]
report back, 995, *bôʾ* [1]
must report, 5583+5583, *nāgad+nāgad* [1]
report came back, 5583, *nāgad* [1]
report, 10302, *ṭᵉʿēm*[2] [1]
report, 10601, *pitgām* [1]

REPORTED [37]
reported, 5583, *nāgad* [15]
reported, 1819, *dābar*[2] [6]
reported, 8740+1821, *šûb*[1]*+dābār* [6]
reported, 606, *ʾāmar*[1] [4]
reported, 5989, *nātan* [2]
reported, 995, *bôʾ* [1]
was reported, 5583, *nāgad* [1]
reported, 6699, *ʿānâ*[1] [1]
is reported, 9048, *šāmaʿ* [1]

REPORTING [1]
reporting, 606, *ʾāmar*[1] [1]

REPORTS [7]
reports, 9051, *šēmaʿ* [3]
reports, 9053, *šōmaʿ* [2]
reports, 1821, *dābār* [1]
reports, 9019, *šᵉmûʿâ* [1]

REPOSE [3]
place of repose, 5276, *margēʿâ* [1]
find repose, 8089, *rāgaʿ*[2] [1]
repose, 8089, *rāgaʿ*[2] [1]

REPOSES [1]
reposes, 5663, *nûaḥ*[1] [1]

REPRESENT [3]
represent, *NIH/RPE* [1]
represent, 4200, *lᵉ-*[1] [1]
represent, 6641, *ʿāmad* [1]

REPRESENTATIVE [2]
representative, *NIH/RPE* [1]
representative, 4946+907, *min+ʾēt*[2] [1]

REPRESENTED [2]
represented, 4200, *lᵉ-*[1] [1]
represented, 4946, *min* [1]

REPRESENTING [2]
representing, 4200, *lᵉ-*[1] [2]

REPRESENTS [1]
represents, *NIH/RPE* [1]

REPRIMANDED [1]
reprimanded, 1721, *gāʿar* [1]

REPROACH [20]
reproach, 3075, *ḥerpâ* [16]
reproach, 3070, *ḥārap*[2] [2]
objects of reproach, 3075, *ḥerpâ* [1]
reproach, 7841, *qeles* [1]

REPROACHED [1]
reproached, 4007, *kālam* [1]

REPROVES [1]
reproves, 3519, *yākaḥ* [1]

REPTILES [1]
reptiles, 8254, *remeś* [1]

REPULSE [2]
repulse, 8740+7156, *šûb*[1]*+pāneh* [2]

REPULSIVE [6]
repulsive, 5145, *mipleṣet* [2]
finds repulsive, 2299, *zāham* [1]
repulsive, 9359, *tôʿēbâ* [1]
repulsive, 9493, *tāʿab* [1]
repulsive thing, 9524, *tiplâ* [1]

REPUTATION [2]
bad reputation, 1804, *dibbâ* [1]
reputation, 9053, *šōmaʿ* [1]

REQUEST [25]
request, 1336, *baqqāšâ* [7]
request, 8626, *šāʾal* [4]
request, 1821, *dābār* [3]
have request to make, 8629+8626,
šᵉʾēlâ+šāʾal [2]
request, 830, *ʾᵃrešet* [1]
made request, 1819, *dābar*[2] [1]
make request, 1819, *dābar*[2] [1]
request, 1819+1821, *dābar*[2]*+dābār* [1]
granted request, 5951+7156, *nāśāʾ+pāneh* [1]
have request, 8626+8629, *šāʾal+šᵉʾēlâ* [1]
request, 8629, *šᵉʾēlâ* [1]
request, 9382, *tᵉḥinnâ*[1] [1]
request, 10114, *bᵉʿâ* [1]

REQUESTED [3]
requested, 1819, *dābar*[2] [1]
requested, 1821, *dābār* [1]
requested, 10397, *mēʾmar* [1]

REQUESTS [4]
requests, *NIH/RPE* [1]
requests, 5399, *mišʾālâ* [1]
granted requests, 5989, *nātan* [1]
requests, 9384, *taḥᵃnûn* [1]

REQUIRE [8]
require, 2011, *dāraš* [2]
require payment, 5601, *nāgaś* [2]
require a pledge for a loan, 2478+2471,
ḥᵃbōl+ḥābal[1] [1]
require an accounting, 3108, *ḥāšab* [1]
require, 8492, *śîm* [1]
require, 8626, *šāʾal* [1]

REQUIRED [18]
required, *AIT* [7]
required, 1821, *dābār* [2]
required, 5957+928+460, *nāšāʾ*[1]*+bᵉ+ʾālâ*[4] [2]
required, 7023, *peh* [2]
required, *NIH/RPE* [1]

required, 2011+6584, *dāraš+ʿal*[2] [1]
required, 2118, *hāyâ* [1]
required, 6275, *ʿabōdâ* [1]
required of, 6584, *ʿal*[2] [1]

REQUIREMENT [5]
requirement, 2978, *ḥuqqâ* [3]
requirement, 1821, *dābār* [2]

REQUIREMENTS [15]
requirements, 5466, *mišmeret* [7]
requirements, 5477, *mišpāṭ* [3]
requirements, 1821, *dābār* [2]
requirements, 6343, *ʿēdût* [2]
requirements, 2978, *ḥuqqâ* [1]

REQUIRES [6]
what requires, 5477, *mišpāṭ* [3]
what requires, 5466, *mišmeret* [2]
requires, 7023, *peh* [1]

REQUIRING [1]
requiring payment, 873, *ʾašmâ* [1]

RESCUE [76]
rescue, 5911, *nāṣal* [42]
rescue, 3828, *yāšaʿ* [8]
rescue, 7117, *pālaṭ* [5]
rescue, 10706, *šêzib* [5]
rescue, 4635, *môšîaʿ* [3]
rescue, 4880, *mālaṭ*[1] [3]
rescue, 1457, *gāʾal*[1] [2]
rescue, 2740, *ḥālaṣ*[1] [1]
rescue, 3802, *yešûʿâ* [1]
came to rescue, 3828, *yāšaʿ* [1]
come to rescue, 5911, *nāṣal* [1]
succeed in the rescue, 5911+5911, *nāṣal+nāṣal* [1]
came to rescue, 6468, *ʿāzar* [1]
rescue, 8740, *šûb*[1] [1]
rescue, 9591, *tešûʿâ* [1]

RESCUED [29]
rescued, 5911, *nāṣal* [12]
rescued, 4880, *mālaṭ*[1] [4]
rescued, 2740, *ḥālaṣ*[1] [3]
rescued, 3828, *yāšaʿ* [3]
rescued, 10706, *šêzib* [2]
is rescued, 2740, *ḥālaṣ*[1] [1]
be rescued, 5911, *nāṣal* [1]
rescued at all, 5911+5911, *nāṣal+nāṣal* [1]
rescued, 6913+9591, *ʿāśâ*[1]*+tešûʿâ* [1]
rescued, 7009, *pādâ* [1]

RESCUES [4]
rescues, 5911, *nāṣal* [2]
rescues, 4635, *môšîaʿ* [1]
rescues, 10706, *šêzib* [1]

RESCUING [1]
rescuing, 5911, *nāṣal* [1]

RESEN [1]
Resen, 8271, *resen*[2] [1]

RESENT [1]
resent, 7762, *qûṣ*[1] [1]

RESENTMENT [3]
resentment, 678, *ʾap*[2] [1]
resentment, 4089, *kaʿaś* [1]
resentment, 8120, *rûaḥ* [1]

RESENTS [1]
resents, 4202+170, *lōʾ+ʾāhab* [1]

RESERVE [4]
reserve, 3104, *ḥāśak* [1]
kept in reserve, 4022, *kāmas* [1]
held in reserve, 7214, *piqqādôn* [1]
reserve, 8636, *šāʾar* [1]

RESERVED [2]
reserved, *AIT* [1]
reserved, 724, *ʾāṣal* [1]

RESERVOIR [1]
reservoir, 5225, *miqwâ* [1]

RESERVOIRS [2]
reservoirs, 1391+4784, *berēkâ+mayim* [1]
reservoirs, 5224+4784, *miqweh*[2]*+mayim* [1]

RESETTLE [2]
resettle, 3782, *yāšab* [2]

RESETTLED [2]
resettled, 3782, *yāšab* [2]

RESHEPH [1]
Resheph, 8405, *rešep*[2] [1]

RESIDE [1]
reside, 5226, *māqôm* [1]

RESIDENCE [5]
residence, 1074, *bayit*[1] [2]
took up residence, 3782, *yāšab* [2]
residence, 10103, *bayit* [1]

RESIDENT [5]
temporary resident, 9369, *tôšāb* [5]

RESIDENTS [3]
residents, 3782, *yāšab* [2]
temporary residents, 9369, *tôšāb* [1]

RESIDES [3]
resides, 4328, *lîn* [1]
resides, 5663, *nûaḥ*[1] [1]
resides, 8905, *šākan* [1]

RESIN [3]
aromatic resin, 978, *bedōlaḥ* [1]
resin, 978, *bedōlaḥ* [1]
gum resin, 5753, *nāṭāp* [1]

RESIST [8]
resist, 6641+4200+7156, *ʿāmad+le-*[1]*+pāneh* [2]
resist, 1741, *gārâ* [1]
resist, 2616, *ḥāzaq* [1]
resist, 4412, *māʾan* [1]
resist, 6641, *ʿāmad* [1]
resist, 6913, *ʿāśâ*[1] [1]
resist, 7156, *pāneh* [1]

RESISTED [2]
resisted, 6641+4200+5584, *ʿāmad+le-*[1]*+neged* [1]
resisted, 7996, *qāšâ* [1]

RESOLVED [3]
resolved, 2372, *zāmam* [1]
resolved, 5989+7156, *nātan+pāneh* [1]
resolved, 8492+6584+4213, *śîm+ʿal*[2]*+lēb* [1]

RESORT [1]
resort to, 2143+4200+7925, *hālak+le-*[1]*+qārāʾ*[2] [1]

RESORTED [1]
resorted, 6913, *ʿāśâ*[1] [1]

RESOUND [9]
resound, 8306, *rāʿam*[1] [3]
resound, 9048, *šāmaʿ* [3]
resound, 995, *bôʾ* [1]
resound, 5989, *nātan* [1]
resound, 7754, *qôl* [1]

RESOUNDED [3]
resounded, 5989, *nātan* [3]

RESOUNDING [1]
resounding, 9558, *terûʿâ* [1]

RESOUNDS [2]
resounds, 2169, *hāmam*[1] [1]
resounds, 9048, *šāmaʿ* [1]

RESOURCES [1]
resources, 3946, *kōaḥ*[1] [1]

RESPECT [13]
have respect for, 3700+928+6524, *yāqar+be-+ʿayin*[1] [2]
respect, *NIH/RPE* [1]
show respect, 2075, *hādar* [1]
respect, 3707, *yārēʾ*[1] [1]
respect, 3883, *kābôd*[1] [1]
respect, 4616, *môrāʾ* [1]
treat with respect, 5692, *nāzar*[1] [1]
have respect for, 5951, *nāśāʾ* [1]
respect, 5951+7156, *nāśāʾ+pāneh* [1]
respect, 5989+3702, *nātan+yeqār* [1]
are shown respect, 7156+2075, *pāneh+hādar* [1]
respect, 8011, *rāʾâ*[1] [1]

RESPECTED [7]
respected, 3359, *yādaʿ* [2]
highly respected, 3877, *kābēd*[1] [2]
respected, 3108, *ḥāšab* [1]
is respected, 3359, *yādaʿ* [1]
highly respected, 8777, *šōaʿ*[1] [1]

RESPECTS [1]
respects, 3707, *yārēʾ*[1] [1]

RESPITE [1]
respite, 8929, *šālēw* [1]

RESPLENDENT [2]
resplendent with light, 239, *ʾôr*[1] [1]
resplendent, 7437, *ṣûṣ*[1] [1]

RESPOND [15]
respond, 6699, *ʿānâ*[1] [7]
respond to, 4374, *lāqaḥ* [3]
respond, 606, *ʾāmar*[1] [1]
respond, 5101, *maʿaneh*[1] [1]
respond to pleas, 6983, *ʿātar*[1] [1]
respond, 7155, *pānâ* [1]
respond, 8740, *šûb*[1] [1]

RESPONDED [11]
responded, 6699, *ʿānâ*[1] [6]
responded, 606, *ʾāmar*[1] [2]
responded, 1821, *dābār* [1]
responded to, 4374, *lāqaḥ* [1]
responded, 8740, *šûb*[1] [1]

RESPONDING [1]
responding to, 4200+6645, *le-*[1]*+ʿummâ*[1] [1]

RESPONSE [6]
response, 7754, *qôl* [2]
in response to, 928, *be-* [1]
willing response, 5605, *nādab* [1]
get response, 6699, *ʿānâ*[1] [1]
response, 7993, *qešeb* [1]

RESPONSIBILITIES [4]
responsibilities, 5466, *mišmeret* [4]

RESPONSIBILITY [9]
responsibility for offenses, 6411, *ʿāwōn* [3]
responsibility, *NIH/RPE* [2]
responsibility for, 6584, *ʿal*[2] [1]
responsibility, 5466, *mišmeret* [1]
assume the responsibility for carrying out, 6641+6584, *ʿāmad+ʿal*[2] [1]

RESPONSIBLE [42]
held responsible, 6411+5951, *ʿāwōn+nāśāʾ* [4]
responsible, 9068, *šāmar* [4]
responsible, 5466, *mišmeret* [3]
held responsible, 5951+6411, *nāśāʾ+ʿāwōn* [3]
responsible for, 6584, *ʿal*[2] [3]
responsible for care, 5466, *mišmeret* [2]
responsible, 6913, *ʿāśâ*[1] [2]
responsible, *AIT* [1]
responsible, *NIH/RPE* [1]
responsible for, 928+8611+4200, *be-+ša+le-*[1] [1]
responsible for, 928+889+4200, *be-+ʾašer+le-*[1] [1]
held responsible, 2628+5951, *ḥēṭʾ+nāśāʾ* [1]
responsible for, 4200+5584, *le-*[1]*+neged* [1]
responsible for, 4200, *le-*[1] [1]
responsible, 4856+6275, *melāʾkâ+ʿabōdâ* [1]
responsible, 4856, *melāʾkâ* [1]
hold responsible, 4946+3338+1335, *min+yād+bāqaš* [1]
not be held responsible, 5927, *nāqâ* [1]
not held responsible, 5929, *nāqî* [1]

not responsible, 5929, *nāqî* [1]
held responsible, 5951+2628, *nāśā'+ḥēṭ'* [1]
responsible for, 5951, *nāśā'* [1]
responsible for, 6015+928, *sābab+b^e-* [1]
responsible, 6275, *ʿ^{a}bōdâ* [1]
responsible, 6584, *ʿal*[2] [1]
responsible, 7213, *p^{e}quddâ* [1]
responsible for, 9068, *šāmar* [1]
responsible, 9068+5466, *šāmar+mišmeret* [1]

RESPONSIVE [2]
responsive, 8216, *rākak* [2]

REST [225]
rest, 3856, *yeter*[1] [21]
rest, 3855, *yātar* [20]
rest, 3972, *kōl* [13]
rest, 8637, *š^e'ār* [10]
rest, *NIH/RPE* [8]
given rest, 5663, *nûaḥ*[1] [8]
rest, 8886, *šākab* [8]
rest, 5663, *nûaḥ*[1] [7]
rest, 8642, *š^e'ērît* [7]
rest, 8702, *šabbātôn* [7]
rest, *AIT* [6]
rest, 4957, *m^{e}nûḥâ* [6]
rest, 8636, *šā'ar* [5]
rest, 10692, *š^e'ār* [5]
rest, 2118, *hāyâ* [4]
at rest, 5663, *nûaḥ*[1] [4]
give rest, 5663, *nûaḥ*[1] [4]
day of rest, 8702, *šabbātôn* [4]
rest, 9200, *šāqaṭ* [4]
the rest[s], 4392, *-ām* [3]
find rest, 5663, *nûaḥ*[1] [3]
gave rest, 5663, *nûaḥ*[1] [3]
gives rest, 5663, *nûaḥ*[1] [3]
rest, 8697, *šābat*[1] [3]
rest, 1954, *d^{o}mî* [2]
at rest, 3782, *yāšab* [2]
rest, 3972+3427, *kōl+yôm*[1] [2]
place of rest, 4957, *m^{e}nûḥâ* [2]
came to rest, 5663, *nûaḥ*[1] [2]
granted rest, 5663, *nûaḥ*[1] [2]
rest, 5739, *naḥat*[2] [2]
rest, 8069, *rābaṣ* [2]
rest, 8905, *šākan* [2]
rest, 9128, *šā'an* [2]
had rest, 9200, *šāqaṭ* [2]
come to rest, 995, *bô'* [1]
rest, 995, *bô'* [1]
rest, 1875, *dûmiyyâ* [1]
find rest, 1957, *dāmam*[1] [1]
rest, 1957, *dāmam*[1] [1]
rest, 3463, *yôtēr* [1]
rest, 3782, *yāšab* [1]
rest[s], 3972, *kōl* [1]
rest, 4328, *lîn* [1]
rest of, 4946, *min* [1]
came to rest, 4955, *mānôaḥ*[1] [1]
places of rest, 4955, *mānôaḥ*[1] [1]
rest, 4955, *mānôaḥ*[1] [1]
peace and rest, 4957, *m^{e}nûḥâ* [1]
place to rest, 4957, *m^{e}nûḥâ* [1]
places of rest, 4957, *m^{e}nûḥâ* [1]
rest, 5226, *māqôm* [1]
rest, 5273, *margôaʿ* [1]
at rest, 5657, *nāwâ*[1] [1]
comes to rest, 5663, *nûaḥ*[1] [1]
giving rest, 5663, *nûaḥ*[1] [1]
have rest, 5663, *nûaḥ*[1] [1]
lay to rest, 5663, *nûaḥ*[1] [1]
rest on, 6584, *ʿal*[2] [1]
rest[s], 7366, *ṣō'n* [1]
rest flocks, 8069, *rābaṣ* [1]
bring rest, 8089, *rāgaʿ*[2] [1]
give rest, 8089, *rāgaʿ*[2] [1]
at rest, 8631, *ša'an* [1]
have rest, 8697, *šābat*[1] [1]
rest, 8740, *šûb*[1] [1]
laid to rest, 8886, *šākab* [1]
take rest, 8886, *šākab* [1]
taking rest, 8886+5435, *šākab+miškāb* [1]
at rest, 8905, *šākan* [1]
came to rest, 8905, *šākan* [1]
lie down to rest, 8905, *šākan* [1]

RESTED [52]
rested, 8886, *šākab* [36]
rested, 5663, *nûaḥ*[1] [5]
rested, 8697, *šābat*[1] [4]
rested on, 6584, *ʿal*[2] [3]
rested, 2118, *hāyâ* [1]
rested, 3782, *yāšab* [1]
rested, 5882, *nāpaš* [1]
rested, 6164, *sāmak* [1]

RESTING [19]
resting place, 4957, *m^{e}nûḥâ* [6]
resting place, 4955, *mānôaḥ*[1] [2]
resting place, 8070, *rēbeṣ* [2]
resting, 4328, *lîn* [1]
resting on, 4946+9393, *min+taḥat*[1] [1]
resting, 4957, *m^{e}nûḥâ* [1]
resting place, 5271, *marbēṣ* [1]
resting place, 5438, *miškān* [1]
resting, 5663, *nûaḥ*[1] [1]
resting place, 5665, *nôaḥ* [1]
resting, 5893, *nāṣab*[1] [1]
resting, 8886, *šākab* [1]

RESTITUTION [14]
make restitution, 8966, *šālēm*[1] [6]
must make restitution, 8966+8966, *šālēm*[1]*+šālēm*[1] [2]
restitution, 871+8740, *'āšām+šûb*[1] [1]
make restitution, 5989, *nātan* [1]
make full restitution, 8740+928+8031, *šûb*[1]*+b^e-+rō'š*[1] [1]
restitution made, 8740, *šûb*[1] [1]
must certainly make restitution, 8966+8966, *šālēm*[1]*+šālēm*[1] [1]
restitution, 8966, *šālēm*[1] [1]

RESTLESS [4]
restless, 5675, *nûaʿ* [2]
restless, 1796, *d^e'āgâ* [1]
restless, 8113, *rûd* [1]

RESTORATION [1]
restoration, 3572, *y^{e}sôd* [1]

RESTORE [54]
restore, 8740, *šûb*[1] [34]
restore, 7756, *qûm* [7]
restore, 2542, *ḥādaš* [2]
restore, 8966, *šālēm*[1] [2]
restore, 10354, *k^{e}lal* [2]
restore, 2200, *hāpak* [1]
restore life, 2649, *ḥāyâ* [1]
restore, 3782, *yāšab* [1]
restore wall, 6441, *ʿāzab*[2] [1]
restore, 6590, *ʿālâ* [1]
restore again, 8740, *šûb*[1] [1]
forced to restore, 8740, *šûb*[1] [1]

RESTORED [32]
restored, 8740, *šûb*[1] [14]
restored to life, 2649, *ḥāyâ* [3]
are restored, 10354, *k^{e}lal* [2]
restored, 10754, *tûb* [2]
be restored, 910, *'ātâ* [1]
be restored, 1215, *bānâ* [1]
restored, 1215, *bānâ* [1]
restored, 2118, *hāyâ* [1]
restored, 2616, *ḥāzaq* [1]
restored, 2649, *ḥāyâ* [1]
restored to health, 2730, *ḥālam*[1] [1]
be restored, 3922, *kûn*[1] [1]
restored, 6441, *ʿāzab*[2] [1]
restored, 10629, *qayyām* [1]
was restored, 10771, *t^{e}qan* [1]

RESTORER [1]
Restorer, 8740, *šûb*[1] [1]

RESTORES [3]
restores, 8740, *šûb*[1] [3]

RESTORING [2]
restoring, 2616, *ḥāzaq* [1]
restoring, 10354, *k^{e}lal* [1]

RESTRAIN [5]
restrain, 8740, *šûb*[1] [2]
restrain, 3104, *ḥāśak* [1]
restrain, 3909, *kāhâ*[2] [1]
restrain, 4979, *mānaʿ* [1]

RESTRAINED [5]
were restrained, 3973, *kālā'*[1] [2]
restrained himself, 706, *'āpaq* [1]
restrained, 2520, *ḥāgar* [1]
restrained, 8740, *šûb*[1] [1]

RESTRAINING [2]
restraining, 7621, *ṣāpan* [2]

RESTRAINT [6]
show restraint, 2532, *ḥādal*[1] [1]
uses with restraint, 3104, *ḥāśak* [1]
without restraint, 6330+4394, *ʿad*[2]*+m^e'ōd* [1]
without restraint, 6984, *ʿātar*[2] [1]
cast off restraint, 7277, *pāraʿ*[2] [1]
restraint, 8270, *resen*[1] [1]

RESTRICTED [1]
restricted, 6806, *ʿāṣar* [1]

RESTRICTION [1]
restriction, 4608, *mûṣāq*[2] [1]

RESTS [6]
rests on, 6584, *ʿal*[2] [2]
rests with, 4200, *l^e-*[1] [1]
rests, 4328, *lîn* [1]
sabbath rests, 8701, *šabbāt* [1]
rests, 8905, *šākan* [1]

RESULT [6]
result, *NIH/RPE* [1]
result of, 928, *b^e-* [1]
as a result, 4200, *l^e-*[1] [1]
as a result of, 6584+1821, *ʿal*[2]*+dābār* [1]
result, 7262, *p^{e}rî* [1]
as a direct result, 9393+3338, *taḥat*[1]*+yād* [1]

RETAIN [2]
retain, 6806, *ʿāṣar* [2]

RETAINS [2]
retains, 2118+4200, *hāyâ+l^e-*[1] [1]
retains, 2118, *hāyâ* [1]

RETAKE [2]
retake, 4374, *lāqaḥ* [1]
retake, 5911, *nāṣal* [1]

RETINUE [2]
retinue, 6269, *ʿebed*[1] [2]

RETIRE [1]
retire, 8740, *šûb*[1] [1]

RETREAT [5]
retreat, 8740, *šûb*[1] [2]
retreat, 2627, *ḥāṭā'* [1]
retreat, 5674, *nûs* [1]
made retreat, 8740+294, *šûb*[1]*+'āḥôr* [1]

RETREATED [1]
retreated, 6590, *ʿālâ* [1]

RETREATING [1]
retreating, 6047+294, *sûg*[1]*+'āḥôr* [1]

RETREATS [1]
retreats, 8740, *šûb*[1] [1]

RETRIBUTION [5]
retribution, 1691, *g^{e}mûl* [2]
retribution, 8936, *šillûm* [2]
retribution, 1692, *g^{e}mûlâ* [1]

RETRIEVED [1]
retrieved, 4880, *mālaṭ*[1] [1]

RETURN [196]
return, 8740, *šûb*[1] [157]
return, 995, *bô'* [4]
return, 6590, *ʿālâ* [4]
return, 7155, *pānâ* [3]

make return, 8740, *šûb*^{1} [3]
in return for, 9393, *taḥat*^{1} [3]
return, *NIH/RPE* [2]
in return for, 928, *b*^{e}- [2]
return, 2143, *hālak* [2]
ever return, 8740+8740, *šûb*^{1}*+šûb*^{1} [2]
return, *AIT* [1]
return, 665, *'āsap* [1]
return, 995+6388, *bô'+'ôd* [1]
return, 995+995, *bô'+bô'* [1]
return, 2143+8740, *hālak+šûb*^{1} [1]
return, 2143+995, *hālak+bô'* [1]
in return for, 2739, *ḥēlep*^{2} [1]
return, 6073, *sûr*^{1} [1]
return, 7155+2256+2143, *pānâ+w*^{e}*-+hālak* [1]
return, 8510, *śākār*^{1} [1]
return, 8740+8740, *šûb*^{1}*+šûb*^{1} [1]
surely return, 8740+8740, *šûb*^{1}*+šûb*^{1} [1]
return, 8938, *šālaḥ* [1]
return, 9455, *t*^{e}*mûrâ* [1]

RETURNED [149]
returned, 8740, *šûb*^{1} [99]
returned, 995, *bô'* [29]
returned, 2143, *hālak* [5]
returned, 3655, *yāṣā'* [4]
returned, 6590, *'ālâ* [3]
returned, 10016, *'^{a}zal* [2]
returned, 10754, *tûb* [2]
returned, *NIH/RPE* [1]
returned, 665, *'āsap* [1]
returned unanswered, 2668+8740, *ḥêq+šûb*^{1} [1]
returned home, 6015, *sābab* [1]
been returned, 8740, *šûb*^{1} [1]

RETURNING [7]
returning, 995, *bô'* [3]
returning, 8740, *šûb*^{1} [3]
returning, *NIH/RPE* [1]

RETURNS [8]
returns, 8740, *šûb*^{1} [6]
returns, 8966, *šālēm*^{1} [1]
yields returns, 9311, *t*^{e}*bû'â* [1]

REU [5]
Reu, 8293, *r*^{e}*'û* [5]

REUBEN [55]
Reuben, 8017, *r*^{e}*'ûbēn* [45]
Reuben, 1201+8017, *bēn*^{1}*+r*^{e}*'ûbēn* [6]
Reuben, 8018, *r*^{e}*'ûbēnî* [2]
Reuben, 1201+8018, *bēn*^{1}*+r*^{e}*'ûbēnî* [1]
men of Reuben, 8018, *r*^{e}*'ûbēnî* [1]

REUBENITE [2]
Reubenite, 1201+8017, *bēn*^{1}*+r*^{e}*'ûbēn* [1]
Reubenite, 8018, *r*^{e}*'ûbēnî* [1]

REUBENITES [30]
Reubenites, 1201+8017, *bēn*^{1}*+r*^{e}*'ûbēn* [17]
Reubenites, 8018, *r*^{e}*'ûbēnî* [13]

REUEL [10]
Reuel, 8294, *r*^{e}*'û'ēl* [10]

REUMAH [1]
Reumah, 8020, *r*^{e}*'ûmâ* [1]

REUNITED [1]
be reunited, 7695+3481, *qābaṣ+yaḥdāw* [1]

REVEAL [4]
clearly reveal myself, 1655+1655, *gālâ+gālâ* [1]
reveal myself, 3359, *yāda'* [1]
reveal, 10144, *g*^{e}*lâ* [1]
reveal, 10252, *ḥ*^{a}*wâ* [1]

REVEALED [25]
revealed, 5583, *nāgad* [4]
revealed, 1655, *gālâ* [3]
be revealed, 1655, *gālâ* [2]
been revealed, 1655, *gālâ* [2]
revealed himself, 1655, *gālâ* [2]
revealed, 1655+265, *gālâ+'ōzen* [2]
revealed myself, 3359, *yāda'* [2]
revealed, 8011, *rā'â*^{1} [2]
revealed, *NIH/RPE* [1]
revealed, 1655+906+265, *gālâ+'ēt*^{1}*+'ōzen* [1]
revealed myself, 2011, *dāraš* [1]
revealed, 3359, *yāda'* [1]
been revealed, 10144, *g*^{e}*lâ* [1]
was revealed, 10144, *g*^{e}*lâ* [1]

REVEALER [2]
revealer, 10144, *g*^{e}*lâ* [2]

REVEALING [2]
revealing, 1655, *gālâ* [1]
revealing, 8011, *rā'â*^{1} [1]

REVEALS [5]
reveals, 10144, *g*^{e}*lâ* [2]
reveals, 1655, *gālâ* [1]
reveals, 5583, *nāgad* [1]
reveals, 8011, *rā'â*^{1} [1]

REVELATION [6]
revelation, 2606, *ḥāzôn* [4]
revelation, 1821, *dābār* [1]
revelation, 2612, *ḥizzāyôn* [1]

REVELED [1]
reveled, 6357, *'ādan* [1]

REVELERS [3]
revelers, 6601, *'ālēz* [1]
revelers, 6611, *'allîz* [1]
revelers, 8471, *śāḥaq* [1]

REVELING [2]
reveling, 2510, *ḥāgag* [1]
reveling, 6600, *'ālaz* [1]

REVELRY [5]
revelry, 6611, *'allîz* [3]
indulge in revelry, 7464, *ṣāḥaq* [1]
revelry, 8525, *śimḥâ* [1]

REVENGE [10]
took revenge, 5933+5934, *nāqam+nāqām* [2]
bent on revenge, 5933, *nāqam* [1]
get revenge, 5933+5934, *nāqam+nāqām* [1]
get revenge, 5933, *nāqam* [1]
seek revenge, 5933, *nāqam* [1]
take revenge, 5933+5934, *nāqam+nāqām* [1]
take revenge, 5933, *nāqam* [1]
revenge, 5934, *nāqām* [1]
revenge, 5935, *n*^{e}*qāmâ* [1]

REVENUE [2]
took revenue, 9202, *šāqal* [1]
revenue, 9311, *t*^{e}*bû'â* [1]

REVENUES [4]
revenues, *NIH/RPE* [1]
revenues, 5006, *misḥār* [1]
revenues, 10063, *'app*^{e}*tōm* [1]
revenues, 10402, *middâ* [1]

REVERE [17]
revere, 3707, *yārē'*^{1} [11]
revere, *NIH/RPE* [2]
revere, 1593, *gûr*^{3} [2]
revere, 3710, *yārē'*^{4} [1]
revere, 3711, *yir'â* [1]

REVERED [4]
revered, 3707, *yārē'*^{1} [4]

REVERENCE [8]
have reverence, 3707, *yārē'*^{1} [2]
reverence, 3711, *yir'â* [2]
reverence, 2556, *ḥāwâ*^{2} [1]
shown reverence, 3707, *yārē'*^{1} [1]
reverence, 4616, *môrā'* [1]
reverence, 10167, *d*^{e}*ḥal* [1]

REVERENT [1]
reverent, 3707, *yārē'*^{1} [1]

REVERING [2]
revering, 3707, *yārē'*^{1} [2]

REVERSE [1]
reverse, 8740, *šûb*^{1} [1]

REVERSED [1]
reversed, 8740, *šûb*^{1} [1]

REVERT [3]
revert, 8740, *šûb*^{1} [2]
revert, 8697, *šābat*^{1} [1]

REVIEW [1]
review the past, 2349, *zākar*^{1} [1]

REVILE [5]
revile, 5540, *nā'aṣ* [2]
revile, 1552, *gādap* [1]
revile, 7837, *qālal* [1]
revile, 8475, *śāṭam* [1]

REVILED [1]
reviled, 5540, *nā'aṣ* [1]

REVILES [1]
reviles, 5540, *nā'aṣ* [1]

REVIVE [5]
revive, 2649, *ḥāyâ* [5]

REVIVED [3]
revived, 2649, *ḥāyâ* [2]
revived, 8740+8120, *šûb*^{1}*+rûaḥ* [1]

REVIVING [1]
reviving, 8740, *šûb*^{1} [1]

REVOKE [1]
revoke, 8740, *šûb*^{1} [1]

REVOKED [3]
revoked, 8740, *šûb*^{1} [2]
was revoked, 7296, *pārar*^{1} [1]

REVOKING [1]
revoking, 7296, *pārar*^{1} [1]

REVOLT [5]
revolt, 5277, *mārad* [2]
revolt, 6240, *sārâ*^{2} [1]
in revolt, 7321, *pāša'* [1]
revolt, 10492, *n*^{e}*śā'* [1]

REVOLTED [4]
revolted, 7321, *pāša'* [2]
revolted against, 6240, *sārâ*^{2} [1]
revolted, 7756, *qûm* [1]

REWARD [31]
reward, 8510, *śākār*^{1} [6]
reward, 8966, *šālēm*^{1} [6]
reward, 2750, *ḥēleq*^{2} [3]
reward, 5989, *nātan* [2]
reward, 7190, *p*^{e}*'ullâ* [2]
reward for news, 1415, *b*^{e}*śōrâ* [1]
reward, 1694, *gāmal* [1]
reward handsomely, 3877+3877+4394, *kābēd*^{1}*+kābēd*^{1}*+m*^{e}*'ōd* [1]
reward handsomely, 3877+3877, *kābēd*^{1}*+kābēd*^{1} [1]
reward, 3877, *kābēd*^{1} [1]
reward, 4200, *l*^{e}*-*^{1} [1]
bring a reward, 5162, *māṣā'* [1]
reward, 5989+7190, *nātan+p*^{e}*'ullâ* [1]
reward, 6813, *'ēqeb* [1]
reward earned, 7262+3338, *p*^{e}*rî+yād* [1]
reward, 8512, *śeker* [1]
reward, 8816, *šōḥad* [1]

REWARDED [12]
rewarded, 8740, *šûb*^{1} [4]
rewarded, 8510, *śākār*^{1} [2]
rewarded, *NIH/RPE* [1]
rewarded, 3883, *kābôd*^{1} [1]
rewarded, 5382, *maśkōret* [1]
rewarded, 5989+8510, *nātan+śākār*^{1} [1]
rewarded, 7262, *p*^{e}*rî* [1]
is rewarded, 8966, *šālēm*^{1} [1]

REWARDS [4]
rewards, 8740, *šûb*^{1} [2]
rewards, 10454, *n*^{e}*bizbâ* [2]

REZEPH [2]
Rezeph, 8364, *reṣep*[2] [2]

REZIN [10]
Rezin, 8360, *r^{e}ṣîn* [10]

REZIN'S [1]
Rezin's, 8360, *r^{e}ṣîn* [1]

REZON [3]
Rezon, *NIH/RPE* [2]
Rezon, 8139, *r^{e}zôn* [1]

RHODES [1]
Rhodes, 8102, *rōdān* [1]

RIB [1]
rib, 7521, *ṣēlāʿ*[1] [1]

RIBAI [2]
Ribai, 8192, *rîbay* [2]

RIBBON [1]
ribbon, 2562, *ḥûṭ* [1]

RIBLAH [11]
Riblah, 8058, *riblâ* [11]

RIBS [2]
ribs, 7521, *ṣēlāʿ*[1] [1]
ribs, 10552, *ʿ^{a}laʿ* [1]

RICH [57]
rich, 6938, *ʿāšîr* [21]
rich, 6947, *ʿāšar* [7]
rich, 9045, *šāmēn*[2] [3]
rich, 419, *ʾētān*[1] [2]
rich, 3202, *ṭôb*[2] [2]
rich, *AIT* [1]
rich, *NIH/RPE* [1]
rich, 159, *ʾeder* [1]
rich pastures, 168, *ʾadderet* [1]
rich, 1524, *gādôl* [1]
rich, 1540, *gādal* [1]
rich, 2015, *dāšēn*[2] [1]
rich, 2016, *dešen* [1]
rich, 2104, *hôn* [1]
rich store, 2890, *ḥōsen* [1]
rich produce, 3206, *ṭûb* [1]
rich, 4671, *mēaḥ* [1]
rich garments, 4711, *mah^{a}lāṣôt* [1]
rich, 5952+3338, *nāśag+yād* [1]
rich, 6913, *ʿāśā*[1] [1]
get rich, 6947, *ʿāšar* [1]
made rich, 6947, *ʿāšar* [1]
pretends to be rich, 6947, *ʿāšar* [1]
rich, 8041, *rab*[1] [1]
rich, 8777, *šôaʿ*[1] [1]
rich food, 9043, *šemen* [1]
rich, 9197, *šāqâ* [1]

RICHER [1]
richer, 6947+6948, *ʿāšar+ʿōšer* [1]

RICHES [34]
riches, 6948, *ʿōšer* [14]
riches, 2657, *ḥayil* [5]
riches, 238, *ʾôṣār* [2]
riches, 3702, *y^{e}qār* [2]
riches, 3883, *kābôd*[1] [2]
riches, 5794, *n^{e}kāsîm* [2]
riches, 2104, *hôn* [1]
riches[s], 2257, *-ô* [1]
riches, 2776, *h^{a}mudôt* [1]
riches, 2890, *ḥōsen* [1]
riches, 4759, *maṭmôn* [1]
riches, 6217, *sepeq* [1]
riches, 8214, *r^{e}kûš* [1]

RICHEST [3]
richest of fare, 2016, *dešen* [1]
richest of foods, 2693+2256+2016, *ḥēleb*[1]*+w^{e}+dešen* [1]
richest, 5458, *mišmān* [1]

RICHLY [6]
richly ornamented, 7168, *pas* [3]
richly bless, 1385+1385, *bārak*[2]*+bārak*[2] [1]
richly, 8041, *rab*[1] [1]
richly, 8969, *šālēm*[2] [1]

RICHNESS [2]
richness, 9044, *šāmān* [2]

RID [23]
got rid of, 6073, *sûr*[1] [4]
rid, 1278, *bāʿar*[2] [3]
get rid of, 6073, *sûr*[1] [3]
rid, 6073, *sûr*[1] [2]
get rid of, 8959, *šālak* [2]
got rid of, 1278, *bāʿar*[2] [1]
get rid of, 1763, *gāraš*[1] [1]
get rid of, 2143, *hālak* [1]
got rid of, 3948, *kāḥad* [1]
be rid of, 4162, *kārat* [1]
rid, 8697, *šābat*[1] [1]
rid, 8896, *šākak* [1]
rid, 8959+4946+6584, *šālak+min+ʿal*[2] [1]
get rid of, 9012, *šāmad* [1]

RIDDEN [2]
ridden, 8206, *rākab* [2]

RIDDLE [8]
riddle, 2648, *ḥîdâ* [8]

RIDDLES [3]
riddles, 2648, *ḥîdâ* [2]
riddles, 10019, *ʾ^{a}ḥîdâ* [1]

RIDE [13]
ride, 8206, *rākab* [3]
ride on, 8206, *rākab* [2]
ride, 2143+928, *hālak+b^{e}-* [1]
cause to ride, 8206, *rākab* [1]
had ride along, 8206, *rākab* [1]
had ride, 8206, *rākab* [1]
let ride, 8206, *rākab* [1]
made ride, 8206, *rākab* [1]
ride forth, 8206, *rākab* [1]
ride off, 8206, *rākab* [1]

RIDER [6]
rider, 8206, *rākab* [6]

RIDERS [7]
riders, 8206, *rākab* [3]
riders, 8207, *rekeb* [3]
riders, 1251+7304, *baʿal*[1]*+pārāš*[1] [1]

RIDES [5]
rides, 8206, *rākab* [3]
rides, 2143, *hālak* [1]
rides on, 8206, *rākab* [1]

RIDGE [1]
ridge of land, 8900, *š^{e}kem*[1] [1]

RIDGES [1]
ridges, 1521, *g^{e}dûd*[1] [1]

RIDICULE [13]
object of ridicule, 8468, *ś^{e}ḥôq* [3]
object of ridicule, 9110, *š^{e}nînâ* [3]
ridicule, 3070, *ḥārap*[2] [2]
ridicule, 1819, *dābar*[2] [1]
ridicule, 4353, *laʿag* [1]
ridicule, 4886, *m^{e}līṣâ* [1]
ridicule, 5951+5442, *nāśāʾ+māšāl*[1] [1]
ridicule, 9110, *š^{e}nînâ* [1]

RIDICULED [7]
ridiculed, 4352, *lāʿag* [2]
ridiculed, 4353, *laʿag* [2]
ridiculed, 1022, *bāzâ* [1]
ridiculed, 4415, *māʿas*[1] [1]
ridiculed, 8468, *ś^{e}ḥôq* [1]

RIDING [13]
riding, 8206, *rākab* [10]
came riding, 8206, *rākab* [1]
riding in chariots, 8206, *rākab* [1]
riding, 9393, *taḥat*[1] [1]

RIFTS [1]
rifts, 8757, *šûḥâ*[1] [1]

RIGGING [2]
rigging, 2475, *hebel*[2] [1]
rigging, 2479, *ḥibbēl* [1]

RIGHT [321]
right, 3545, *yāmîn*[1] [118]
right, 3838, *yāšār*[1] [44]
right, 3556, *y^{e}mānî* [24]
right, 7407, *ṣ^{e}dāqâ* [20]
right, 5477, *mišpāṭ* [13]
all right, 8934, *šālôm* [9]
right, 3202, *ṭôb*[2] [7]
right, 4026, *kēn*[1] [7]
right, 7406, *ṣedeq* [7]
right, 4797, *mêšārîm* [6]
right, *NIH/RPE* [3]
right, 3837, *yāšar* [3]
right, 3922, *kûn*[1] [3]
right, 5791, *nākōaḥ* [3]
right, 622, *ʾemet* [2]
right of redemption, 1460, *g^{e}ʾullâ* [2]
right[s], 2178, *hēnnâ*[1] [2]
do what is right, 3512, *yāṭab* [2]
turn to the right, 3554, *yāman* [2]
right, 7404, *ṣaddîq* [2]
right behind, 339, *ʾaḥar* [1]
right in, 448, *ʾel* [1]
keep right, 886, *ʾāšar*[1] [1]
be right there, 995, *bôʾ* [1]
has the right to do it[s], 1457, *gāʾal*[1] [1]
right to redeem, 1460, *g^{e}ʾullâ* [1]
right now, 2180, *hinnēh* [1]
right where, 2296, *zeh* [1]
historic right, 2355, *zikkārôn* [1]
just right, 2914, *ḥēpeṣ* [1]
have any right, 3512, *yāṭab* [1]
do right, 3512, *yāṭab* [1]
have a right, 3512, *yāṭab* [1]
go to the right, 3554, *yāman* [1]
to the right, 3554, *yāman* [1]
consider right, 3837, *yāšar* [1]
right and true, 3838, *yāšār*[1] [1]
right, 3841, *yōšer* [1]
thinks right, 4178, *kāšēr* [1]
have right, 4200, *l^{e}-*[1] [1]
have the right, 4200, *l^{e}-*[1] [1]
right before, 4200+5584, *l^{e}-*[1]*+neged* [1]
right before, 4200, *l^{e}-*[1] [1]
right for, 4200, *l^{e}-*[1] [1]
what right have you, 4537+4200+3870, *mâ+l^{e}-*[1]*+-kā* [1]
has right, 5440, *māšal*[2] [1]
right way, 5477, *mišpāṭ* [1]
all right, 5528, *nāʾ*[1] [1]
right now, 5528, *nāʾ*[1] [1]
have a right to get even, 5927, *nāqâ* [1]
right now, 6964, *ʿattâ* [1]
in the right, 7404, *ṣaddîq* [1]
admit in the right, 7405, *ṣādaq* [1]
prove right, 7405, *ṣādaq* [1]
proved right, 7405, *ṣādaq* [1]
right, 7405, *ṣādaq* [1]
all right do it[s], 7756, *qûm* [1]
make right, 8740, *šûb*[1] [1]
right there, 9004, *šām* [1]
right answer, 9459, *tāmîm* [1]
right, 10610, *ṣidqâ* [1]
right, 10643, *q^{e}šōṭ* [1]

RIGHT-HANDED [1]
right-handed, 3554, *yāman* [1]

RIGHTEOUS [238]
righteous, 7404, *ṣaddîq* [178]
righteous, 7406, *ṣedeq* [16]
righteous, 7405, *ṣādaq* [11]
righteous, 7407, *ṣ^{e}dāqâ* [9]
righteous acts, 7407, *ṣ^{e}dāqâ* [7]
righteous things, 7407, *ṣ^{e}dāqâ* [4]
Righteous One, 7404, *ṣaddîq* [2]
righteous, *NIH/RPE* [1]
righteous, 2446+7404, *zeraʿ+ṣaddîq* [1]
righteous, 3838, *yāšār*[1] [1]
appear righteous, 7405, *ṣādaq* [1]
made appear righteous, 7405, *ṣādaq* [1]

made seem righteous, 7405, *ṣādaq* [1]
righteous act, 7407, *ṣ^{e}dāqâ* [1]
righteous deeds, 7407, *ṣ^{e}dāqâ* [1]
righteous state, 7407, *ṣ^{e}dāqâ* [1]
righteous will, 7407, *ṣ^{e}dāqâ* [1]
righteous, 9448, *tōm* [1]

RIGHTEOUSLY [3]
righteously, 7406, *ṣedeq* [2]
righteously, 7407, *ṣ^{e}dāqâ* [1]

RIGHTEOUSNESS [159]
righteousness, 7407, *ṣ^{e}dāqâ* [98]
righteousness, 7406, *ṣedeq* [58]
his former righteousness[s], 2023, *-āh* [1]
righteousness, 7404, *ṣaddîq* [1]
lead to righteousness, 7405, *ṣādaq* [1]

RIGHTFUL [1]
rightful, 7406, *ṣedeq* [1]

RIGHTFULLY [1]
rightfully, 5477, *mišpāṭ* [1]

RIGHTLY [1]
rightly, 3954, *kî^2* [1]

RIGHTS [14]
rights, 5477, *mišpāṭ* [4]
rights, 1907, *dîn^2* [3]
give the rights of the firstborn, 1144, *bākar* [1]
rights as firstborn, 1148, *b^{e}kōrâ* [1]
rights of the firstborn, 1148, *b^{e}kōrâ* [1]
defend rights, 1906, *dîn^1* [1]
marital rights, 6703, *ʿōnâ* [1]
maintain rights, 7405, *ṣādaq* [1]
rights, 7406, *ṣedeq* [1]

RIM [24]
rim, 8557, *śāpâ* [14]
rim, 4995, *misgeret* [6]
rim, 1473, *g^{e}bûl* [3]
the rim[s], 2257, *-ô* [1]

RIMMON [13]
Rimmon, 8234, *rimmôn^3* [8]
Rimmon, 8233, *rimmôn^2* [3]
Rimmon, 8235, *rimmôn^4* [2]

RIMMON PEREZ [2]
Rimmon Perez, 8236, *rimmôn pereṣ* [2]

RIMMONO [1]
Rimmono, 8237, *rimmônô* [1]

RIMS [3]
rims, 1461, *gab^1* [3]

RING [21]
ring, 3192, *ṭabbaʿat* [5]
signet ring, 3192, *ṭabbaʿat* [5]
ring, 5690, *nezem* [5]
signet ring, 2597, *ḥôtām^1* [2]
nose ring, 5690, *nezem* [2]
ring, 6584, *ʿal^2* [1]
signet ring, 10536, *ʿizqâ* [1]

RINGED [1]
ringed about, 6017, *sābîb* [1]

RINGS [42]
rings, 3192, *ṭabbaʿat* [34]
rings, 5690, *nezem* [4]
signet rings, 3192, *ṭabbaʿat* [2]
rings, 1664, *gālîl^1* [1]
rings, 10536, *ʿizqâ* [1]

RINNAH [1]
Rinnah, 8263, *rinnâ^2* [1]

RINSED [3]
rinsed, 1866, *dûaḥ* [1]
be rinsed, 8851, *šāṭap* [1]
rinsed, 8851, *šāṭap* [1]

RINSING [1]
rinsing, 8851, *šāṭap* [1]

RIP [3]
rip open, 1324, *bāqaʿ* [1]
rip to pieces, 7293, *pāraq* [1]
rip open, 7973+6033+4213, *qāraʿ+s^{e}gôr+lēb* [1]

RIPE [9]
ripe fruit, 7811, *qayiṣ* [2]
time is ripe, 995+7891, *bôʾ+qēṣ* [1]
fig ripe, 1136, *bikkûrâ* [1]
first ripe fruit, 1137, *bikkûrîm* [1]
first ripe grain, 1137, *bikkûrîm* [1]
first ripe, 1137, *bikkûrîm* [1]
ripe, 1418, *bāšal* [1]
of ripe old age, 2418, *zāqēn^2* [1]

RIPEN [2]
ripen later, 689, *ʾāpîl* [1]
ripen early, 1136, *bikkûrâ* [1]

RIPENED [3]
ripened fruit, 7811, *qayiṣ* [2]
ripened, 1418, *bāšal* [1]

RIPENING [1]
ripening, 1694, *gāmal* [1]

RIPENS [1]
ripens, 6961, *ʿēt* [1]

RIPHATH [2]
Riphath, 8196, *rîpat* [2]

RIPPED [3]
ripped open, 1324, *bāqaʿ* [3]

RISE [92]
rise, 7756, *qûm* [28]
rise up, 7756, *qûm* [28]
rise, 6590, *ʿālâ* [8]
makes rise, 6590, *ʿālâ* [3]
rise, 2436, *zāraḥ* [2]
rise up, 5951, *nāśāʾ* [2]
rise, 5951, *nāśāʾ* [2]
rise, 6641, *ʿāmad* [2]
rise to power, 7756, *qûm* [2]
rise, 10624, *qûm* [2]
rise, *AIT* [1]
rise, *NIH/RPE* [1]
rise again, 5951, *nāśāʾ* [1]
rise up, 6641, *ʿāmad* [1]
rise, 7709, *qādam* [1]
makes rise, 7756, *qûm* [1]
rise, 7810, *qîṣ* [1]
rise up, 8104, *rāhab* [1]
rise up, 8123, *rûm^1* [1]
rise, 8123, *rûm^1* [1]
rise up, 8129, *rômēmut* [1]
rise, 8852, *šeṭep* [1]
rise early, 8899, *šākam* [1]

RISEN [5]
risen up, 7756, *qûm* [2]
risen, 1448, *gāʾâ* [1]
risen, 3655, *yāṣāʾ* [1]
risen, 7756, *qûm* [1]

RISES [28]
rises, 6590, *ʿālâ* [8]
rises, 2436, *zāraḥ* [5]
rises up, 7756, *qûm* [3]
rises, 7756, *qûm* [3]
rises, 2806, *ḥāmēṣ^1* [1]
rises, 3655, *yāṣāʾ* [1]
rises, 4604, *môṣāʾ^1* [1]
rises high, 5951, *nāśāʾ* [1]
rises, 5989, *nātan* [1]
rises, 6641, *ʿāmad* [1]
rises, 8123, *rûm^1* [1]
rises up, 8420, *ś^{e}ʾēt^1* [1]
sun rises, 8840, *šaḥar* [1]

RISING [14]
rising, 4667, *mizrāḥ* [6]
rising, 6590, *ʿālâ* [5]
rising up, 2936, *ḥāṣâ* [1]
rising, 3655, *yāṣāʾ* [1]
rising, 6424, *ʿûr^3* [1]

RISK [4]
at the risk of, 928, *b^e-* [3]
could risk, 3523, *yākōl* [1]

RISKED [3]
risked, 928, *b^e-* [1]
risked, 3070+4200+4637, *ḥārap^2+l^e-^{1}+mût* [1]
risked, 8959+4946+5584, *šālak+min+neged* [1]

RISSAH [2]
Rissah, 8267, *rissâ* [2]

RITHMAH [2]
Rithmah, 8414, *ritmâ* [2]

RIVAL [4]
rival, *NIH/RPE* [1]
rival, 6669, *ʿāmam^1* [1]
rival, 7651, *ṣārâ^2* [1]
rival wife, 7675, *ṣārar^2* [1]

RIVER [100]
river, 5643, *nāhār* [58]
river, 5707, *naḥal^1* [17]
river, 3284, *y^{e}ʾōr* [13]
river, *NIH/RPE* [4]
river, 3542, *yām* [2]
river, 3720, *yardēn* [2]
river, 4784, *mayim* [2]
river crossings, 5045, *maʿbārâ* [1]
river, 10468, *n^{e}har* [1]

RIVERBANK [1]
riverbank, 8557+3284, *śāpâ+y^{e}ʾōr* [1]

RIVERBED [2]
riverbed, 5643, *nāhār* [2]

RIVERS [26]
rivers, 5643, *nāhār* [23]
rivers, 3284, *y^{e}ʾōr* [1]
rivers, 5643+5707, *nāhār+naḥal^1* [1]
rivers, 5707, *naḥal^1* [1]

RIZIA [1]
Rizia, 8359, *riṣyāʾ* [1]

RIZPAH [4]
Rizpah, 8366, *riṣpâ^2* [4]

ROAD [78]
road, 2006, *derek* [61]
road, 5019, *m^{e}sillâ* [10]
road down, 4618, *môrād* [2]
main road, 2006+2006, *derek+derek* [1]
road down, 3718, *yārad* [1]
main road, 5019, *m^{e}sillâ* [1]
road, 5986, *n^{e}tîbâ* [1]
road signs, 7483, *ṣiyyûn* [1]

ROADS [15]
roads, 2006, *derek* [9]
roads, 5019, *m^{e}sillâ* [3]
roads, 784, *ʾōraḥ* [2]
roads, 5986, *n^{e}tîbâ* [1]

ROADSIDE [3]
roadside, 2006, *derek* [3]

ROAM [4]
roam, 2143+2256+3718, *hālak+w^e+yārad* [1]
roam, 6296, *ʿābar^1* [1]
roam, 8113, *rûd* [1]
caused to roam, 8740, *šûb^1* [1]

ROAMED [2]
roamed, 2143, *hālak* [1]
roamed, 6908, *ʿāraq* [1]

ROAMING [3]
roaming, 8763, *šûṭ^1* [2]
roaming, *NIH/RPE* [1]

ROAR [33]
roar, 8613, *šāʾag* [7]
roar, 2159, *hāmâ* [5]
roar, 7754, *qôl* [5]
roar, 8614, *š^{e}ʾāgâ* [3]

roar, 2162, *hāmôn* [2]
roar, 5638, *naham* [2]
roar, 8616, *šā'ā*[2] [2]
roar, 8623, *šā'ôn*[2] [2]
roar, 5637, *nāham* [1]
roar, 8075, *rōgez* [1]
comes roar, 8613, *šā'ag* [1]
roar mightily, 8613+8613, *šā'ag+šā'ag* [1]
roar of battle, 8623, *šā'ôn*[2] [1]

ROARED [4]
roared, 8613, *šā'ag* [3]
roared, 5989+7754, *nātan+qôl* [1]

ROARING [13]
roaring, 8613, *šā'ag* [4]
roaring, 8623, *šā'ôn*[2] [3]
roaring, 2159, *hāmâ* [2]
roaring, 2162, *hāmôn* [1]
roaring, 5637, *nāham* [1]
roaring, 5639, *nᵉhāmâ* [1]
roaring, 7754+8614, *qôl+šᵉ'āgâ* [1]

ROARS [3]
roars, 8613, *šā'ag* [2]
roars, 5989+928+7754, *nātan+bᵉ-+qôl* [1]

ROAST [4]
roast, 1418, *bāšal* [1]
roast, 3047, *ḥārak* [1]
roast, 7499, *ṣālâ* [1]
roast, 7507, *ṣālî* [1]

ROASTED [10]
roasted grain, 7833, *qālî* [4]
roasted, 1418, *bāšal* [1]
roasted, 7499, *ṣālâ* [1]
roasted, 7507, *ṣālî* [1]
roasted grain, 7828, *qālâ*[1] [1]
roasted, 7828, *qālâ*[1] [1]
roasted, 7833, *qālî* [1]

ROASTS [1]
roasts, 7499, *ṣālâ* [1]

ROB [9]
rob, 1608, *gāzal* [3]
rob, 7693, *qāba'* [3]
rob, 3769, *yāraš*[1] [1]
rob, 7320, *pāšaṭ* [1]
rob of children, 8897, *šākal* [1]

ROBBED [10]
been robbed, 1608, *gāzal* [2]
robbed of cubs, 8891, *šakkûl* [2]
are robbed, 1608, *gāzal* [1]
robbed, 1608+1609, *gāzal+gēzel* [1]
robbed, 1608, *gāzal* [1]
robbed, 2740, *ḥālaṣ*[1] [1]
be robbed, 7212, *pāqad* [1]
robbed, 8891, *šakkûl* [1]

ROBBERS [3]
robbers, 7265, *pārîṣ*[2] [2]
robbers, 8720, *šādad* [1]

ROBBERY [5]
commit robbery, 1611+1608, *gᵉzēlâ+gāzal* [2]
commit robbery, 1608+1610, *gāzal+gāzēl* [1]
robbery, 1610, *gāzēl* [1]
commits robbery, 1611+1608, *gᵉzēlâ+gāzal* [1]

ROBBING [2]
robbing, 1024, *bāzaz* [1]
robbing, 7693, *qāba'* [1]

ROBE [47]
robe, 5077, *mᵉ'îl* [20]
robe, 4189, *kuttōnet* [13]
robe, 4230, *lᵉbûš* [4]
robe, 168, *'adderet* [2]
robe[s], 889, *'ᵃšer* [1]
the robe[s], 2257, *-ô* [1]
folds of robe, 2950, *ḥōṣen* [1]
hem of robe, 4053, *kānāp* [1]
robe, 4252, *lābaš* [1]
robe, 8515, *śalmâ*[1] [1]
train of robe, 8767, *šûl* [1]
robe, 9423, *takrîk* [1]

ROBED [4]
robed, 4252, *lābaš* [3]
robed, 4230, *lᵉbûš* [1]

ROBES [33]
robes, 955, *beged*[2] [17]
robes, 4860, *malbûš* [4]
robes, 5077, *mᵉ'îl* [2]
robes, 8515, *śalmâ*[1] [2]
robes, 10517, *sarbāl* [2]
royal robes, 168, *'adderet* [1]
robes, 4230, *lᵉbûš* [1]
put on robes, 4252, *lābaš* [1]
robes, 4496, *mad* [1]
fine robes, 4711, *maḥᵃlāṣôt* [1]
robes, 6078, *sût*[2] [1]

ROBS [2]
robs, 1608, *gāzal* [1]
robs, 8720, *šādad* [1]

ROCK [104]
rock, 7446, *ṣûr*[4] [60]
rock, 6152, *sela'*[1] [30]
rock, 74, *'eben* [8]
rock, 10006, *'eben* [3]
rock, *NIH/RPE* [1]
flinty rock, 2734, *ḥallāmîš* [1]
hard rock, 2734, *ḥallāmîš* [1]

ROCKS [27]
rocks, 6152, *sela'*[1] [9]
rocks, 7446, *ṣûr*[4] [8]
rocks, 74, *'eben* [7]
rocks, 4091, *kēp* [2]
pile of rocks, 1643, *gal*[1] [1]

ROCKY [6]
rocky, 7446, *ṣûr*[4] [3]
rocky crags, 6152, *sela'*[1] [1]
rocky crag, 6152, *sela'*[1] [1]
rocky, 6152, *sela'*[1] [1]

ROD [48]
rod, 8657, *šēbeṭ* [23]
rod, 7866, *qāneh* [12]
rod, 4751, *maṭṭeh* [6]
rod, 4962, *mānôr* [4]
rod, 2643, *ḥōṭer* [1]
measuring rod, 7866, *qāneh* [1]
shepherd's rod, 8657, *šēbeṭ* [1]

RODANIM [2]
Rodanim, 8102, *rōdān* [2]

RODE [10]
rode, 8206, *rākab* [4]
rode, 2143, *hālak* [2]
rode off, 8206, *rākab* [2]
rode off, 2143, *hālak* [1]
rode out, 3655, *yāṣā'* [1]

RODENTS [1]
rodents, 2923, *ḥᵃparpārâ* [1]

RODS [2]
rods, 1664, *gālîl*[1] [1]
rods, 4758, *māṭîl* [1]

ROE [1]
roe deer, 3502, *yaḥmûr* [1]

ROEBUCKS [1]
roebucks, 3502, *yaḥmûr* [1]

ROGELIM [2]
Rogelim, 8082, *rōgᵉlîm* [2]

ROHGAH [1]
Rohgah, 8108, *rohgâ* [1]

ROLL [12]
roll, 1670, *gālal*[1] [4]
roll, 7147, *pālaš* [4]
roll on, 1670, *gālal*[1] [1]
roll, 1723, *gā'aš* [1]
roll up tightly, 7571+7571+7572, *ṣānap+ṣānap+ṣᵉnēpâ* [1]
roll back, 8740, *šûb*[1] [1]

ROLLED [8]
rolled, 1670, *gālal*[1] [3]
rolled away, 1670, *gālal*[1] [1]
rolled up, 1670, *gālal*[1] [1]
rolled up, 1676, *gālam* [1]
is rolled, 6015, *sābab* [1]
rolled up, 7886, *qāpad* [1]

ROLLING [1]
come rolling in, 1670, *gālal*[1] [1]

ROLLS [2]
rolls upward, 60, *'ābak* [1]
rolls, 1670, *gālal*[1] [1]

ROMAMTI-EZER [2]
Romamti-Ezer, 8251, *rōmamtî 'ezer* [2]

ROOF [30]
roof, 1511, *gāg* [18]
roof of mouth, 2674, *ḥēk* [3]
roof, *NIH/RPE* [1]
roof of house, 1511, *gāg* [1]
roof of mouths, 2674, *ḥēk* [1]
roof of mouth, 4918, *malqôḥayim* [1]
the roof[s], 5647, *-nû*[2] [1]
overhanging roof, 6264, *'āb*[1] [1]
roof, 7415, *ṣōhar* [1]
roof, 7771, *qôrâ* [1]
roof, 7815, *qîr*[1] [1]

ROOFED [1]
was roofed, 6211, *sāpan* [1]

ROOFING [2]
roofing over, 3233, *ṭālal* [1]
roofing, 6211, *sāpan* [1]

ROOFS [7]
roofs, 1511, *gāg* [7]

ROOM [59]
room, 4384, *liškâ* [13]
room, 2540, *ḥeder* [6]
upper room, 6608, *'ᵃliyyâ* [6]
room, 5226, *māqôm* [5]
room, 1074, *bayit*[1] [4]
inner room, 2540+928+2540, *ḥeder+bᵉ-+ḥeder* [4]
room, 6608, *'ᵃliyyâ* [4]
room, *NIH/RPE* [2]
room above, 6608, *'ᵃliyyâ* [2]
room, *AIT* [1]
room enough, 1896, *day* [1]
room, 2006, *derek* [1]
inner room, 2540, *ḥeder* [1]
private room, 2540, *ḥeder* [1]
make room for, 4946+7156, *min+pāneh* [1]
be room enough, 5162, *māṣā'* [1]
room, 5969, *niškâ* [1]
room over, 6608, *'ᵃliyyâ* [1]
side room, 7521, *ṣēlā'*[1] [1]
given room, 8143, *rāḥab* [1]
plenty of room, 8146+3338, *rāḥāb*[1]*+yād* [1]
upstairs room, 10547, *'illî* [1]

ROOMS [46]
rooms, 4384, *liškâ* [21]
side rooms, 7521, *ṣēlā'*[1] [9]
rooms, 2540, *ḥeder* [3]
rooms, *AIT* [2]
rooms, *NIH/RPE* [2]
side rooms, 4384, *liškâ* [2]
upper rooms, 6608, *'ᵃliyyâ* [2]
the rooms[s], 2177, *-hēn*[2] [1]
side rooms, 3666, *yāṣîa'* [1]
priests rooms, 4384+7731, *liškâ+qōdeš* [1]
the rooms[s], 5527, *-ān* [1]
rooms, 7860, *qēn* [1]

ROOST [1]
roost, 4328, *lîn* [1]

ROOSTER [1]
strutting rooster, 2435+5516, *zarzîr+motnayim* [1]

ROOT [18]
root, 9247, *šōreš* [12]
root, 4035, *kannâ* [1]
take root, 9245+1614, *šāraš+gezaʿ* [1]
take root, 9245, *šāraš* [1]
taken root, 9245, *šāraš* [1]
taking root, 9245, *šāraš* [1]
took root, 9245+9247, *šāraš+šōreš* [1]

ROOTS [19]
roots, 9247, *šōreš* [15]
roots, 10743, *šᵉrōš* [3]
roots, 7893, *qeṣeb* [1]

ROPE [6]
rope, 6310, *ʿᵃbōt* [3]
rope, 2475, *ḥebel^{2}* [2]
rope, 5940, *niqpâ* [1]

ROPES [25]
ropes, 2475, *ḥebel^{2}* [9]
ropes, 4798, *mêtār* [7]
ropes, 6310, *ʿᵃbōt* [7]
the ropes^{s}, 4392, *-ām* [1]
ropes, 4593, *môsērâ^{1}* [1]

ROSE [53]
rose, 7756, *qûm* [16]
rose up, 7756, *qûm* [7]
rose, 5951, *nāśāʾ* [4]
rose, 6590, *ʿālâ* [4]
rose, 1504, *gābar* [3]
rose early, 8899, *šākam* [3]
rose, 8899, *šākam* [3]
rose, 2436, *zāraḥ* [2]
rose up, 6641, *ʿāmad* [2]
rose, 8123, *rûm^{1}* [2]
rose, 8250, *rāmam^{2}* [2]
rose, *NIH/RPE* [1]
rose, 995, *bôʾ* [1]
rose, 2483, *ḥᵃbaṣṣelet* [1]
rose, 7503, *ṣālaḥ^{2}* [1]
rose upward, 8250, *rāmam^{2}* [1]

ROSH [1]
Rosh, 8033, *rōʾš^{3}* [1]

ROT [7]
rot, 5245, *māqaq* [3]
rot, 8372, *rāqab* [2]
rot, 944, *bāʾaš* [1]
rot, 8373, *rāqāb* [1]

ROTS [1]
rots, 8373, *rāqāb* [1]

ROTTEN [2]
something rotten, 8373, *rāqāb* [1]
rotten, 8375, *riqqābôn* [1]

ROUGH [2]
rough places, 5112, *maʿᵃqaššîm* [1]
rough, 6815, *ʿāqōb^{2}* [1]

ROUGHER [2]
rougher and rougher, 2143+2256+6192, *hālak+wᵉ-+sāʿar* [2]

ROUGHS [1]
roughs out, 6913, *ʿāśâ^{1}* [1]

ROUND [6]
round, 6015, *sābab* [2]
round, 6318, *ʿāgōl* [2]
round about, 6017, *sābîb* [1]
round loaf, 7501, *ṣᵉlûl* [1]

ROUNDABOUT [1]
roundabout, 6015, *sābab* [1]

ROUNDED [2]
rounded, 6044, *sahar* [1]
rounded, 6318, *ʿāgōl* [1]

ROUNDS [2]
made rounds, 6015, *sābab* [2]

ROUSE [12]
rouse, 6424, *ʿûr^{3}* [6]
rouse, 7756, *qûm* [2]
rouse, 7810, *qîṣ* [2]
rouse themselves, 5951, *nāśāʾ* [1]
rouse, 8074, *rāgaz* [1]

ROUSED [5]
be roused, 6424, *ʿûr^{3}* [2]
roused himself, 6424, *ʿûr^{3}* [1]
roused, 6424, *ʿûr^{3}* [1]
roused, 7810, *qîṣ* [1]

ROUSES [1]
rouses, 6424, *ʿûr^{3}* [1]

ROUT [3]
rout, *NIH/RPE* [1]
rout, 2169, *hāmam^{1}* [1]
putting to rout, 5782, *nākâ* [1]

ROUTE [7]
route, 2006, *derek* [7]

ROUTED [12]
routed, 2169, *hāmam^{1}* [3]
been routed, 5597, *nāgap* [2]
was routed, 5597, *nāgap* [2]
routed, 2200+6902, *hāpak+ʿōrep* [1]
routed, 5597, *nāgap* [1]
were routed, 5597, *nāgap* [1]
routed, 5674, *nûs* [1]
routed, 5782, *nākâ* [1]

ROUTES [1]
routes, 2006, *derek* [1]

ROUTING [1]
routing, 3006, *ḥārad* [1]

ROUTS [1]
routs, 8103, *rādap* [1]

ROVING [1]
roving, 2143, *hālak* [1]

ROW [15]
row, 3215, *ṭûr* [9]
row, *NIH/RPE* [2]
row, 5121, *maʿᵃreket* [2]
row, 3168, *ḥātar* [1]
row, 5120, *maʿᵃrākâ* [1]

ROWS [11]
rows, 3215, *ṭûr* [9]
rows, 692, *ʾāpîq^{1}* [1]
rows, 5121, *maʿᵃreket* [1]

ROYAL [131]
royal, 4889, *melek^{1}* [65]
royal, 4895, *malkût* [16]
royal, 10421, *melek* [9]
royal, *NIH/RPE* [7]
royal, 4867, *mᵉlûkâ* [7]
royal, 4930, *mamlākâ* [7]
royal, 10424, *malkû* [4]
royal position, 4895, *malkût* [2]
royal robes, 168, *ʾadderet* [1]
royal, 350, *ʾᵃḥaštᵉrān* [1]
royal, 683, *ʾappeden* [1]
royal^{s}, 2257, *-ô* [1]
royal advisers, 3913, *kōhēn* [1]
royal power, 4930, *mamlākâ* [1]
royal, 4931, *mamlākût* [1]
royal, 5618, *nādîb* [1]
royal, 7281, *parʿōh* [1]
of royal birth, 8576, *śārâ^{2}* [1]
royal bride, 8712, *šēgal* [1]
royal canopy, 9188, *šaprîr* [1]
royal interests, 10421, *melek* [1]
royal authority, 10424, *malkû* [1]

ROYALTY [1]
royalty, 4895, *malkût* [1]

RUBBED [3]
were rubbed with salt, 4873+4873, *mālaḥ^{2}+mālaḥ^{2}* [1]
rubbed, 5417, *māšaḥ* [1]
was rubbed bare, 7942, *qāraḥ* [1]

RUBBLE [16]
rubble, 6760, *ʿāpār* [5]
heap of rubble, 6505, *ʿî* [3]
piles of rubble, 10470, *nᵉwālû* [2]
heap of rubble, 1643, *gal^{1}* [1]
rubble, 1643, *gal^{1}* [1]
rubble, 2997, *ḥōreb^{2}* [1]
heaps of rubble, 4843, *makšēlâ* [1]
rubble, 6505, *ʿî* [1]
pile of rubble, 10470, *nᵉwālû* [1]

RUBIES [8]
rubies, 7165, *pᵉnînîm* [6]
rubies, 3905, *kadkōd* [2]

RUBY [3]
ruby, 138, *ʾōdem* [3]

RUDDY [4]
ruddy, 145, *ʾadmônî* [2]
ruddy, 131, *ʾādēm* [1]
ruddy, 137, *ʾādōm* [1]

RUGGED [4]
rugged, 1493, *gabnōn* [2]
rugged, 1441, *beter^{2}* [1]
rugged places, 8221, *rekes* [1]

RUGS [2]
rugs, 1710, *genez^{2}* [1]
rugs, 7620, *ṣāpît* [1]

RUIN [77]
ruin, 8288, *rāʿaʿ^{3}* [8]
ruin, 2999, *ḥorbâ* [7]
ruin, 4745, *mᵉhittâ* [4]
ruin, 8719, *šōd^{2}* [4]
ruin, 9014, *šammâ^{1}* [4]
ruin, 6392, *ʿawwâ^{1}* [3]
ruin, 8739, *šōʾâ* [3]
ruin, 8845, *šāḥat* [3]
ruin, 7, *ʾōbēd* [2]
ruin, 2095, *hawwâ^{2}* [2]
ruin, 2992, *ḥārēb^{3}* [2]
comes to ruin, 4231, *lābaṭ* [2]
ruin, 5143, *mappēlâ* [2]
ruin, 8273, *raʿ^{1}* [2]
ruin, 9037, *šāmēm^{1}* [2]
ruin, *NIH/RPE* [1]
brought ruin, 6, *ʾābad* [1]
come to ruin, 6, *ʾābad* [1]
ruin, 6, *ʾābad* [1]
ruin, 369, *ʾêd* [1]
ruin, 1180, *bālaʿ^{1}* [1]
ruin, 1327, *bāqaq^{1}* [1]
ruin, 2169, *hāmam^{1}* [1]
ruin, 2472, *ḥābal^{2}* [1]
ruin, 3872, *kāʾab* [1]
bring to ruin, 4173, *kāšal* [1]
come to ruin, 4231, *lābaṭ* [1]
ruin, 4510, *midḥeh* [1]
ruin, 4681, *māḥâ^{1}* [1]
ruin, 5397, *maššuʾôt* [1]
ruin, 5409, *mᵉšōʾâ* [1]
surely come to ruin, 5877+5877, *nāpal+nāpal* [1]
bring down to ruin, 5997, *nātaṣ* [1]
brings to ruin, 6156+4200+2021+8273, *sālap+lᵉ-^{1}+ha-+raʿ^{1}* [1]
ruin, 6390, *ʿāwâ^{1}* [1]
ruin, 7896, *qāṣâ^{2}* [1]
come to ruin, 8318, *rāʿaʿ^{2}* [1]
ruin, 8643, *šēʾt* [1]
ruin, 8691, *šeber^{1}* [1]
allowed to fall into ruin, 8845, *šāḥat* [1]
brought to ruin, 9012, *šāmad* [1]
ruin, 9424, *tēl* [1]

RUINED [39]
ruined, 6, *ʾābad* [4]

ruined, 8720, *šādad* [4]
ruined, 1950, *dāmâ*[3] [3]
ruined, 2990, *ḥārēb*[1] [3]
ruined, 8845, *šāḥat* [3]
be ruined, 4162, *kārat* [2]
ruined, 1278, *bā'ar*[2] [1]
ruined, 2472+2256+2476, *ḥābal*[2]+*w^{e}-*+*hebel*[3] [1]
utterly ruined, 2990+2990, *ḥārēb*[1]+*ḥārēb*[1] [1]
ruined, 2992, *ḥārēb*[3] [1]
ruined, 2997, *ḥōreb*[2] [1]
ruined homes, 2999, *ḥorbâ* [1]
ruined, 2999, *ḥorbâ* [1]
ruined, 3948, *kāhad* [1]
ruined, 4200+7914, *l^{e}-*[1]+*q^{e}ṣāpâ* [1]
ruined, 4745, *m^{e}ḥittâ* [1]
lie ruined, 8615, *šā'â*[1] [1]
ruined, 8615, *šā'â*[1] [1]
ruined, 8697, *šābat*[1] [1]
are ruined, 8720, *šādad* [1]
be ruined, 8720, *šādad* [1]
utterly ruined, 8720+8720, *šādad*+*šādad* [1]
was ruined, 8845, *šāḥat* [1]
ruined, 9037, *šāmēm*[1] [1]
ruined, 9039, *š^{e}māmâ* [1]
ruined, 9332, *tōhû* [1]

RUINS [55]
ruins, 2999, *ḥorbâ* [21]
in ruins, 2992, *ḥārēb*[3] [3]
in ruins, 2999, *ḥorbâ* [3]
ruins, 9039, *š^{e}māmâ* [3]
heap of ruins, 1643, *gal*[1] [2]
in ruins, 2238, *hāras* [2]
lie in ruins, 5898, *nāṣâ*[2] [2]
ruins, 430, *'ākal* [1]
ruins, 2232, *h^{a}rîsâ* [1]
left in ruins, 2238, *hāras* [1]
lies in ruins, 2990, *ḥārēb*[1] [1]
places lying in ruins, 2999, *ḥorbâ* [1]
ruins, 4745, *m^{e}ḥittâ* [1]
heap of ruins, 4843, *makšēlâ* [1]
ruins, 5142, *mappālâ* [1]
ruins, 5397, *maššu'ôt* [1]
lay in ruins, 5997, *nātaṣ* [1]
ruins, 6156, *sālap* [1]
in ruins, 8720, *šādad* [1]
lies in ruins, 8720, *šādad* [1]
ruins, 8739, *šô'â* [1]
in ruins, 8959, *šālak* [1]
in ruins, 9014, *šammâ*[1] [1]
in ruins, 9037, *šāmēm*[1] [1]
heap of ruins, 9424, *tēl* [1]
ruins, 9424, *tēl* [1]

RULE [76]
rule, 5440, *māšal*[2] [28]
rule, 8097, *rādâ*[1] [11]
rule, 7742, *qāw*[1] [8]
rule, 4887, *mālak*[1] [5]
rule, 2118+6584, *hāyâ*+*'al*[2] [2]
rule over, 6584, *'al*[2] [2]
rule, 8286, *rā'â*[1] [2]
rule, 9149, *šāpaṭ* [2]
rule, *NIH/RPE* [1]
rule, 1821, *dābār* [1]
rule, 3782, *yāšab* [1]
rule, 4867, *m^{e}lûkâ* [1]
rule over, 4889, *melek*[1] [1]
rule, 4895, *malkût* [1]
rule, 4939, *memšālâ* [1]
actually rule, 5440+5440, *māšal*[2]+*māšal*[2] [1]
rule, 5445, *mōšel*[2] [1]
rule, 5477, *mišpāṭ* [1]
rule over, 8097, *rādâ*[1] [1]
rule, 8606, *śārar* [1]
let rule, 8948, *šālaṭ* [1]
rule, 10542, *'al* [1]
rule, 10715, *š^{e}lēṭ* [1]
authority to rule, 10717, *šolṭān* [1]

RULED [30]
ruled, 4887, *mālak*[1] [9]
ruled, 5440, *māšal*[2] [6]
ruled, 8097, *rādâ*[1] [3]
ruled, 4889, *melek*[1] [2]
ruled, 4939, *memšālâ* [2]
ruled, *NIH/RPE* [1]
ruled over, 1249, *bā'al*[1] [1]
ruled, 1249, *bā'al*[1] [1]
ruled, 2118+4889, *hāyâ*+*melek*[1] [1]
ruled over, 4887, *mālak*[1] [1]
ruled, 4939+3338, *memšālâ*+*yād* [1]
ruled over, 6584, *'al*[2] [1]
ruled, 9149, *šāpaṭ* [1]

RULER [64]
ruler, 5440, *māšal*[2] [16]
ruler, 8569, *śar* [14]
ruler, 5592, *nāgîd* [12]
ruler, 5954, *nāśî'*[1] [3]
ruler, 5601, *nāgaś* [2]
ruler, 5618, *nādîb* [2]
ruler, 9149, *šāpaṭ* [2]
made ruler, 10715, *š^{e}lēṭ* [2]
ruler, 10715, *š^{e}lēṭ* [2]
ruler, 380, *'ayil*[1] [1]
was made ruler, 4887, *mālak*[1] [1]
made ruler, 5440, *māšal*[2] [1]
ruler, 7903, *qāṣîn* [1]
ruler, 8031, *rō'š*[1] [1]
ruler, 8097, *rādâ*[1] [1]
ruler, 8606, *śārar* [1]
ruler, 8954, *šallîṭ* [1]
ruler, 10718, *šallîṭ* [1]

RULER'S [4]
ruler's, 5440, *māšal*[2] [3]
ruler's staff, 2980, *ḥāqaq* [1]

RULERS [61]
rulers, 6249, *seren*[2] [21]
rulers, 9149, *šāpaṭ* [8]
rulers, 8569, *śar* [7]
rulers, 8142, *rāzan* [5]
rulers, 5440, *māšal*[2] [4]
rulers, 7903, *qāṣîn* [3]
rulers, 5954, *nāśî'*[1] [2]
rulers, 446, *'ēl*[5] [1]
rulers, 1251, *ba'al*[1] [1]
rulers, 4482, *māgēn*[1] [1]
rulers, 4889, *melek*[1] [1]
make rulers, 5440, *māšal*[2] [1]
rulers, 5592, *nāgîd* [1]
rulers, 6036, *segen* [1]
rulers, 8031, *rō'š*[1] [1]
rulers, 8657, *šēbeṭ* [1]
rulers, 8954, *šallîṭ* [1]
rulers, 10717, *šolṭān* [1]

RULES [14]
rules, 5440, *māšal*[2] [7]
rules, 2978, *ḥuqqâ* [3]
rules, *NIH/RPE* [1]
according to the rules, 3869, *k^{e}-* [1]
rules, 5184, *miṣwâ* [1]
rules, 10718, *šallîṭ* [1]

RULING [7]
ruling, 3782, *yāšab* [2]
ruling, 5440, *māšal*[2] [2]
ruling, 4887, *mālak*[1] [1]
gave ruling, 6699, *'ānâ*[1] [1]
ruling, 10718, *šallîṭ* [1]

RUMAH [1]
Rumah, 8126, *rûmâ* [1]

RUMBLE [1]
rumble, 2162, *hāmôn* [1]

RUMBLING [3]
rumbling, 8323, *ra'aš* [2]
rumbling, 2049, *hegeh* [1]

RUMOR [4]
rumor, 9019, *š^{e}mû'â* [3]
rumor, 9051, *šēma'* [1]

RUMORS [2]
rumors, *NIH/RPE* [1]
rumors, 9019, *š^{e}mû'â* [1]

RUN [60]
run, 8132, *rûṣ* [20]
run, *NIH/RPE* [6]
run, 2143, *hālak* [5]
run, 5674, *nûs* [5]
run, 4880, *mālaṭ*[1] [4]
run through, 1991, *dāqar* [3]
run dry, 2893, *ḥāsēr*[1] [2]
run a line, 204, *'āwâ*[2] [1]
run, 237, *'ûṣ* [1]
spreads feathers to run, 928+2021+5294+5257, *b^{e}-*+*ha-*+*mārôm*+*mārā'*[2] [1]
run away, 1368, *bāraḥ*[1] [1]
run off, 1368, *bāraḥ*[1] [1]
run, 2118, *hāyâ* [1]
makes run dry, 2990, *ḥārēb*[1] [1]
letting run down, 3718, *yārad* [1]
run, 4554, *māhar*[1] [1]
do not run, 4979, *māna'* [1]
where run, 5330, *mirmās* [1]
on the run, 5674, *nûs* [1]
run course, 5938, *nāqap*[2] [1]
run after, 8103, *rādap* [1]
run a line, 9292, *tā'â* [1]

RUNNER [1]
runner, 8132, *rûṣ* [1]

RUNNING [20]
running, 8132, *rûṣ* [5]
running, *NIH/RPE* [4]
running away, 1368, *bāraḥ*[1] [3]
running sores, 3539, *yallepet* [2]
running sore, 2307, *zûb* [1]
running down, 3718, *yārad* [1]
running away, 5674, *nûs* [1]
running water, 5689, *nōzēl* [1]
running wild, 7277, *pāra'*[2] [1]
running here and there, 8592+2006, *śārak*+*derek* [1]

RUNS [4]
runs after for favors, 339+2388, *'aḥar*+*zānâ*[1] [1]
runs along, 2143, *hālak* [1]
runs, 5297, *m^{e}rûṣâ*[1] [1]
runs, 8132, *rûṣ* [1]

RURAL [1]
rural, 7253, *p^{e}rāzî* [1]

RUSE [1]
ruse, 6893, *'ormâ* [1]

RUSH [6]
rush, 8132, *rûṣ* [3]
rush, 3655, *yāṣā'* [1]
rush here and there, 8763, *šûṭ*[1] [1]
rush, 9212, *šāqaq* [1]

RUSHED [6]
rushed, 1894, *dāhap* [1]
rushed out, 3655, *yāṣā'* [1]
rushed forward, 7320, *pāšaṭ* [1]
rushed, 7320, *pāšaṭ* [1]
rushed, 7502, *ṣālaḥ*[1] [1]
rushed forward, 8132, *rûṣ* [1]

RUSHES [3]
rushes, 2590, *ḥûš*[1] [1]
rushes, 6068, *sûp*[2] [1]
rushes, 8132, *rûṣ* [1]

RUSHING [7]
rushing, 5599, *nāgar* [2]
rushing, 8041, *rab*[1] [2]
rushing, 8851, *šāṭap* [1]
rushing, 8938, *šālaḥ* [1]
rushing back and forth, 9212, *šāqaq* [1]

RUTH [20]
Ruth, 8134, *rût* [12]
Ruth, *NIH/RPE* [7]
Ruth[s], 2085, *hû'* [1]

RUTHLESS [19]
ruthless, 6883, *'ārîṣ* [17]
ruthless, 2805, *ḥāmās* [1]

ruthless, 5253, *mar^{1}* [1]

RUTHLESSLY [6]

ruthlessly, 928+7266, *b^{e}-+perek* [5]
ruthlessly, 4200+425, *l^{e-1}+'akzār* [1]

SABBATH [74]

sabbath, 8701, *šabbāt* [66]
Sabbath after Sabbath, 928+3427+2021+8701 +928+3427+2021+8701, *b^{e}-+yôm^{1}+ha-+šabbāt+b^{e}-+yôm^{1}+ha-+šabbāt* [2]
must observe a sabbath, 8697+8701, *šābat^{1}+šabbāt* [1]
observe sabbath, 8697+8701, *šābat^{1}+šabbāt* [1]
every Sabbath, 8701+8701, *šabbāt+šabbāt* [1]
every Sabbath, 8701+928+8701, *šabbāt+b^{e}-+šabbāt* [1]
Sabbath days, 8701, *šabbāt* [1]
sabbath rests, 8701, *šabbāt* [1]

SABBATHS [30]

sabbaths, 8701, *šabbāt* [30]

SABEANS [4]

Sabeans, 6014, *s^{e}bā'î* [2]
Sabeans, 8644, *š^{e}bā'* [1]
Sabeans, 8645, *š^{e}bā'îm* [1]

SABTA [1]

Sabta, 6029, *sabtā'* [1]

SABTAH [1]

Sabtah, 6030, *sabtâ* [1]

SABTECA [2]

Sabteca, 6031, *sabt^{e}kā'* [2]

SACAR [2]

Sacar, 8511, *śākār^{2}* [2]

SACHET [1]

sachet, 7655, *ṣ^{e}rōr^{1}* [1]

SACK [10]

sack, 623, *'amtaḥat* [7]
sack, 8566, *śaq* [3]

SACKCLOTH [45]

sackcloth, 8566, *śaq* [42]
sackcloth, *NIH/RPE* [1]
put sackcloth around, 2520, *ḥāgar* [1]
sackcloth, 4680+8566, *maḥ^{a}gōret+śaq* [1]

SACKED [1]

sacked, 5782, *nākâ* [1]

SACKS [10]

sacks, 623, *'amtaḥat* [7]
sacks, 8566, *śaq* [2]
sacks, 3998, *k^{e}lî* [1]

SACRED [124]

sacred, 7731, *qōdeš* [65]
sacred stones, 5167, *maṣṣēbâ* [14]
sacred offerings, 7731, *qōdeš* [8]
sacred, *NIH/RPE* [6]
sacred stone, 5167, *maṣṣēbâ* [5]
sacred, 7705, *qādôš* [4]
sacred offering, 7731, *qōdeš* [3]
sacred assembly, 6809, *'aṣārâ* [2]
sacred, 7727, *qādaš* [2]
sacred gifts, 7731, *qōdeš* [2]
sacred objects, 7731, *qōdeš* [2]
sacred oaks, 381, *'ayil^{2}* [1]
sacred, 466, *'^{e}lōhîm* [1]
sacred cakes, 862, *'^{a}šîšâ* [1]
sacred bowls, 4670, *mizrāq* [1]
sacred pillars, 5167, *maṣṣēbâ* [1]
the sacred portion^{s}, 5647, *-nû^{2}* [1]
sacred mountain, 7600, *ṣāpôn^{1}* [1]
most sacred food, 7731+7731, *qōdeš+qōdeš* [1]
most sacred, 7731+7731, *qōdeš+qōdeš* [1]
sacred portion, 7731, *qōdeš* [1]
sacred things, 7731, *qōdeš* [1]

SACRIFICE [143]

sacrifice, 2285, *zebaḥ^{1}* [47]
sacrifice, 2284, *zābaḥ* [39]
sacrifice, 6913, *'āśâ^{1}* [16]
sacrifice, 6590, *'ālâ* [11]
sacrifice, 4966, *minḥâ* [5]
daily sacrifice, 9458, *tāmîd* [5]
sacrifice, 6296, *'ābar^{1}* [4]
sacrifice made by fire, 852, *'iššeh* [2]
sacrifice, 2284+2285, *zābaḥ+zebaḥ^{1}* [2]
sacrifice, 6592, *'ōlâ^{1}* [2]
sacrifice, *NIH/RPE* [1]
offer sacrifice, 2284, *zābaḥ* [1]
offered a sacrifice, 2284, *zābaḥ* [1]
sacrifice, 5602, *nāgaš* [1]
evening sacrifice, 6590+4966, *'ālâ+minḥâ* [1]
sacrifice, 6590+4966, *'ālâ+minḥâ* [1]
sacrifice, 6592+6590, *'ōlâ^{1}+'ālâ* [1]
sacrifice, 7933, *qorbān* [1]
sacrifice, 8821, *šāḥaṭ^{1}* [1]
sacrifice, 10638, *q^{e}rēb* [1]

SACRIFICED [56]

sacrificed, 2284, *zābaḥ* [18]
sacrificed, 2285, *zebaḥ^{1}* [13]
sacrificed, 6590, *'ālâ* [13]
sacrificed, 6296, *'ābar^{1}* [6]
sacrificed, 7928, *qārab* [2]
sacrificed, 1277, *bā'ar^{1}* [1]
sacrificed, 5989+928+6296, *nātan+b^{e}-+'ābar^{1}* [1]
sacrificed, 6913, *'āśâ^{1}* [1]
sacrificed, 8821, *šāḥaṭ^{1}* [1]

SACRIFICES [119]

sacrifices, 2285, *zebaḥ^{1}* [57]
offer sacrifices, 2284, *zābaḥ* [17]
offered sacrifices, 2284, *zābaḥ* [8]
sacrifices, *NIH/RPE* [5]
sacrifices, 2284, *zābaḥ* [4]
burned sacrifices, 7787, *qāṭar^{1}* [4]
offered sacrifices, 6590, *'ālâ* [3]
burn sacrifices, 7787, *qāṭar^{1}* [3]
made sacrifices, 2284+2285, *zābaḥ+zebaḥ^{1}* [2]
sacrifices, 4966, *minḥâ* [2]
sacrifices, 8821, *šāḥaṭ^{1}* [2]
offering sacrifices, 2284, *zābaḥ* [1]
sacrifices offer, 2284, *zābaḥ* [1]
festival sacrifices, 2504, *ḥag* [1]
sacrifices, 6296, *'ābar^{1}* [1]
sacrifices, 6592, *'ōlâ^{1}* [1]
offer sacrifices, 7787, *qāṭar^{1}* [1]
offer sacrifices, 7928, *qārab* [1]
burn as sacrifices, 8596, *śārap* [1]
burned as sacrifices, 8596, *śārap* [1]
sacrifices slaughtered, 8821, *šāḥaṭ^{1}* [1]
sacrifices, 10157, *d^{e}baḥ^{2}* [1]
offer sacrifices, 10638, *q^{e}rēb* [1]

SACRIFICING [11]

sacrificing, 2284, *zābaḥ* [6]
sacrificing, 6590, *'ālâ* [5]

SAD [5]

sad, 8273, *ra'^{1}* [2]
look sad, 8273, *ra'^{1}* [1]
sad, 8278, *rōa'* [1]
look sad, 8317, *rā'a'^{1}* [1]

SADDLE [5]

saddle, 2502, *ḥābaš* [2]
saddle, 4121, *kar^{3}* [1]
saddle blankets, 4496, *mad* [1]
saddle, 8210, *rikbâ* [1]

SADDLEBAGS [1]

two saddlebags, 5478, *mišp^{e}tayim* [1]

SADDLED [10]

saddled, 2502, *ḥābaš* [9]
have saddled, 2502, *ḥābaš* [1]

SADNESS [1]

sadness, 8278, *rōa'* [1]

SAFE [24]

safe, 8934, *šālôm* [9]
keep safe, 7621, *ṣāpan* [2]
keep safe, 9068, *šāmar* [2]
safe, *NIH/RPE* [1]
safe, 575, *'^{e}mûnâ* [1]
safe, 1053, *bāṭaḥ^{1}* [1]
kept safe, 3828, *yāša'* [1]
safe, 3838, *yāšār^{1}* [1]
is kept safe, 4880, *mālaṭ^{1}* [1]
safe, 5466, *mišmeret* [1]
safe, 5911, *nāṣal* [1]
keep safe, 5915, *nāṣar* [1]
is kept safe, 8435, *śāgab* [1]
safe, 8435, *śāgab* [1]

SAFE-CONDUCT [1]

provide safe-conduct, 6296, *'ābar^{1}* [1]

SAFEKEEPING [2]

safekeeping, 9068, *šāmar* [2]

SAFELY [15]

safely, 928+8934, *b^{e}-+šālôm* [9]
safely, 4200+1055, *l^{e-1}+beṭaḥ^{1}* [2]
safely, 4200+2021+8934, *l^{e-1}+ha-+šālôm* [1]
safely, 4200+8934, *l^{e-1}+šālôm* [1]
safely, 5663, *nûaḥ^{1}* [1]
safely, 8969, *šālēm^{2}* [1]

SAFETY [32]

safety, 1055, *beṭaḥ^{1}* [24]
safety, 3829, *yēša'* [2]
flee for safety, 6395, *'ûz* [2]
safety, *NIH/RPE* [1]
safety, 3802, *y^{e}šû'â* [1]
guarantee safety, 6842, *'ārab^{1}* [1]
guaranteed safety, 6842, *'ārab^{1}* [1]

SAFFRON [1]

saffron, 4137, *karkōm* [1]

SAG [1]

sag, 4812, *mākak* [1]

SAID [2295]

said, 606, *'āmar^{1}* [1958]
said, 1819, *dābar^{2}* [197]
said, *NIH/RPE* [29]
said, 6699, *'ānâ^{1}* [29]
what said, 1821, *dābār* [21]
said, 10558, *'^{a}nâ* [13]
said, 1821, *dābār* [10]
said, 10042, *'^{a}mar* [6]
said, 5583, *nāgad* [4]
be said, 606, *'āmar^{1}* [3]
is said, 606, *'āmar^{1}* [2]
said, 3655+4946+7023, *yāṣā'+min+peh* [2]
said in reply, 6699, *'ānâ^{1}* [2]
said, 7023, *peh* [2]
was said, 606, *'āmar^{1}* [1]
what said, 609+7023, *'ēmer^{1}+peh* [1]
are said, 1819, *dābar^{2}* [1]
said a word, 1819, *dābar^{2}* [1]
said, 1821+1819, *dābār+dābar^{2}* [1]
that said, 1821, *dābār* [1]
said, 2021+1821+1819, *ha-+dābār+dābar^{2}* [1]
said no more, 3087, *ḥārēš^{2}* [1]
said, 4863, *millâ* [1]
said, 4910, *mālal^{3}* [1]
said a word, 6699, *'ānâ^{1}* [1]
said in interpretation, 7354, *pātar* [1]
what said, 7754+1821, *qôl+dābār* [1]
what said, 7754, *qôl* [1]
what said, 8557, *śāpâ* [1]
said, 8626, *šā'al* [1]
what said, 10418, *millâ* [1]

SAIL [6]

set sail, 2143, *hālak* [2]
sail, 2143+928+2021+641, *hālak+b^{e}-+ha-+'^{o}niyyâ* [1]
sail, 5155, *miprāś* [1]
sail, 5812, *nēs* [1]
sail, 6296, *'ābar^{1}* [1]

SAILED [3]

sailed, 995, *bô'* [3]

SAILORS [4]

sailors, 4876, *mallāḥ* [2]
sailors, *NIH/RPE* [1]

sailors, 408+641, *'îš[1]+'ᵒniyyâ* [1]

SAINTS [24]
saints, 2883, *ḥāsîd* [15]
saints, 10620, *qaddîš* [5]
saints, *NIH/RPE* [2]
saints, 7705, *qādôš* [2]

SAKE [74]
for the sake of, 4200+5100, *lᵉ-[1]+ma'an* [22]
for sake, 4200+5100, *lᵉ-[1]+ma'an* [21]
for the sake of, 928+6288, *bᵉ-+'ᵃbûr[1]* [11]
for sake, 6584, *'al[2]* [5]
for sake, 928+6288, *bᵉ-+'ᵃbûr[1]* [4]
for sake, 4200, *lᵉ-[1]* [4]
sake, *NIH/RPE* [1]
for the sake of, 448, *'el* [1]
for the sake of, 4200, *lᵉ-[1]* [1]
sake, 4200, *lᵉ-[1]* [1]
for sake, 4769, *mî* [1]
for sake, 4946+7156, *min+pāneh* [1]
for sake, 6584+128, *'al[2]+'ōdôt* [1]

SAKIA [1]
Sakia, 8499, *śākᵉyâ* [1]

SALE [4]
sale, 4697, *mᵉḥîr[1]* [1]
offer yourselves for sale, 4835, *mākar* [1]
money from sale, 4928, *mimkār* [1]
sale, 4928, *mimkār* [1]

SALECAH [4]
Salecah, 6146, *salkâ* [4]

SALEM [2]
Salem, 8970, *šālēm[3]* [2]

SALIVA [1]
saliva, 8202, *rîr[2]* [1]

SALLAI [1]
Sallai, 6144, *sallay* [1]

SALLU [3]
Sallu, 6132, *sallu'* [2]
Sallu, 6139, *sallû* [1]

SALLU'S [1]
Sallu's, 6139, *sallû* [1]

SALMA [2]
Salma, 8514, *śalmā'* [2]

SALMON [4]
Salmon, 8517, *śalmôn* [4]

SALT [38]
salt, 4875, *melaḥ[2]* [29]
salt, 10420, *mᵉlaḥ[2]* [2]
salt, *NIH/RPE* [1]
salt herbs, 4865, *mallûaḥ* [1]
were rubbed with salt, 4873+4873, *mālaḥ[2]+mālaḥ[2]* [1]
salt flats, 4877, *mᵉlēḥâ* [1]
salt waste, 4877, *mᵉlēḥâ* [1]
salt, 4877, *mᵉlēḥâ* [1]
salt, 7490, *ṣîṣ[3]* [1]

SALTED [1]
be salted, 4873, *mālaḥ[2]* [1]

SALU [1]
Salu, 6140, *sālû'* [1]

SALVATION [80]
salvation, 3802, *yᵉšû'â* [47]
salvation, 3829, *yēša'* [15]
salvation, 9591, *tᵉšû'â* [12]
worked salvation, 3828, *yāša'* [3]
having salvation, 3828, *yāša'* [1]
salvation, 3828, *yāša'* [1]
salvation, 7407, *ṣᵉdāqâ* [1]

SAMARIA [109]
Samaria, 9076, *šōmᵉrôn* [105]
Samaria, 10726, *šāmᵉrayin* [2]
Samaria[s], 9004, *šām* [1]
people of Samaria, 9085, *šōmᵉrōnî* [1]

SAME [156]
same, 285, *'eḥād* [32]
same, 4027, *kēn[2]* [23]
that same, 2085, *hû'* [19]
same, 3869, *kᵉ-* [16]
same as, 3869, *kᵉ-* [11]
same, 2085, *hû'* [10]
same, *NIH/RPE* [5]
same, *AIT* [3]
one and the same, 285, *'eḥād* [3]
same[s], 2257, *-ô* [3]
same, 2296, *zeh* [3]
that same, 2296, *zeh* [3]
same, 6795, *'eṣem[1]* [3]
in the same way, 3970, *kākâ* [2]
all the same, 285, *'eḥād* [1]
same one, 285, *'eḥād* [1]
same as, 889, *'ᵃšer* [1]
this same, 2085, *hû'* [1]
those same, 2156, *hēm* [1]
same amount[s], 2296, *zeh* [1]
lead to do the same[s], 2388+339+466+2177, *zānā[1]+'aḥar+'ᵉlōhîm+-hēn[2]* [1]
did the same[s], 2489+285+448+285, *ḥābar[2]+'eḥād+'el+'eḥād* [1]
do the same[s], 2489, *ḥābar[2]* [1]
same, 3869+889, *kᵉ-+'ᵃšer* [1]
the same as, 3869, *kᵉ-* [1]
same, 3907, *kōh* [1]
same, 4017, *kᵉmô* [1]
in the same way, 4027, *kēn[2]* [1]
in the same order, 4027, *kēn[2]* [1]
same as, 4200, *lᵉ-[1]* [1]
treated the same as, 4200+6645, *lᵉ-[1]+'ummâ[1]* [1]
born in the same home, 4580+1074, *môledet+bayit[1]* [1]
same[s], 10192, *-ēh* [1]
same, 10248, *ḥad* [1]

SAMGAR [1]
Samgar, 6161, *samgar* [1]

SAMLAH [4]
Samlah, 8528, *śamlâ* [4]

SAMPLE [1]
sample, 2983, *ḥāqar* [1]

SAMPLED [1]
sampled, 4374, *lāqaḥ* [1]

SAMSON [36]
Samson, 9088, *šimšôn* [33]
Samson, *NIH/RPE* [3]

SAMSON'S [3]
Samson's, 9088, *šimšôn* [3]

SAMUEL [137]
Samuel, 9017, *šᵉmû'ēl* [127]
Samuel, *NIH/RPE* [10]

SAMUEL'S [4]
Samuel's, 9017, *šᵉmû'ēl* [4]

SANBALLAT [10]
Sanballat, 6172, *sanballaṭ* [10]

SANCTUARIES [4]
sanctuaries, 5219, *miqdāš* [4]

SANCTUARY [171]
sanctuary, 7731, *qōdeš* [72]
sanctuary, 5219, *miqdāš* [61]
inner sanctuary, 1808, *dᵉbîr[1]* [14]
outer sanctuary, 2121, *hêkāl* [7]
sanctuary, *NIH/RPE* [5]
sanctuary, 1074, *bayit[1]* [2]
inner sanctuary, 7164, *pᵉnîmî* [2]
sanctuary, 185, *'ōhel[1]* [1]
sanctuary, 1074+5219, *bayit[1]+miqdāš* [1]
sanctuary, 2121, *hêkāl* [1]
inner sanctuary[s], 2257, *-ô* [1]
at sanctuary[s], 4200+7156, *lᵉ-[1]+pāneh* [1]
sanctuary, 5226+7731, *māqôm+qōdeš* [1]
inner sanctuary, 7163, *pᵉnîmâ* [1]
sanctuary area, 7731, *qōdeš* [1]

SAND [25]
sand, 2567, *ḥôl[1]* [21]
grains of sand, 2567, *ḥôl[1]* [2]
sand, 6760, *'āpār* [1]
burning sand, 9220, *šārāb* [1]

SANDAL [6]
sandal, 5837, *na'al* [6]

SANDALED [1]
sandaled, 928+2021+5837, *bᵉ-+ha-+na'al* [1]

SANDALS [16]
sandals, 5837, *na'al* [14]
put sandals on, 5836, *nā'al[2]* [1]
sandals, 5836, *nā'al[2]* [1]

SANG [18]
sang, 8876, *šîr[1]* [5]
sang, 6702, *'ānâ[4]* [4]
sang, 1819, *dābar[2]* [2]
sang, 9048, *šāma'* [2]
sang praises, 2146, *hālal[2]* [1]
sang, 2146, *hālal[2]* [1]
sang lament, 7801, *qîn* [1]
sang, 8264, *rānan* [1]
sang song, 8876, *šîr[1]* [1]

SANITY [2]
sanity, 10430, *manda'* [2]

SANK [12]
sank, 4156, *kāra'* [3]
sank, 3655, *yāṣā'* [2]
sank in, 995, *bô'* [1]
sank down, 3190, *ṭāba'* [1]
sank, 3190, *ṭāba'* [1]
sank down, 3718, *yārad* [1]
sank, 3718, *yārad* [1]
sank, 4125, *kārā[1]* [1]
sank, 7510, *ṣālal[2]* [1]

SANSANNAH [1]
Sansannah, 6179, *sansannâ* [1]

SAP [1]
sap, 430, *'ākal* [1]

SAPH [1]
Saph, 6198, *sap[4]* [1]

SAPPED [2]
was sapped, 2200, *hāpak* [1]
sapped, 4173, *kāšal* [1]

SAPPHIRE [6]
sapphire, 6209, *sappîr* [4]
sapphire, 74+6209, *'eben+sappîr* [2]

SAPPHIRES [5]
sapphires, 6209, *sappîr* [5]

SARAH [35]
Sarah, 8577, *śārâ[3]* [35]

SARAH'S [1]
Sarah's, 8577, *śārâ[3]* [1]

SARAI [15]
Sarai, 8584, *śāray* [15]

SARAPH [1]
Saraph, 8598, *śārāp[2]* [1]

SARGON [1]
Sargon, 6236, *sargôn* [1]

SARID [2]
Sarid, 8587, *śārîd[2]* [2]

SASH [8]
sash, 77, *'abnēṭ* [6]
sash, 258, *'ēzôr* [1]
sash, 2514, *ḥᵃgôrâ* [1]

SASHES [5]
sashes, 77, *'abnēṭ* [3]

sashes, 2512, ḥ^a^gôr [1]
sashes, 8005, qiššurîm [1]

SAT [57]
sat, 3782, *yāšab* [31]
sat down, 3782, *yāšab* [22]
sat, *NIH/RPE* [1]
sat, 430, *'ākal* [1]
sat up, 3782, *yāšab* [1]
sat waiting, 3782, *yāšab* [1]

SATAN [18]
Satan, 8477, *śāṭān* [18]

SATED [1]
sated, 8115, *rāwâ* [1]

SATISFACTION [4]
satisfaction, 3202, *ṭôb²* [2]
satisfaction, 3208, *ṭôbâ* [1]
gives satisfaction, 8750, *šāwâ¹* [1]

SATISFIED [35]
satisfied, 8425, *śāba'* [30]
satisfied, *NIH/RPE* [1]
satisfied, 928+8934, *bᵉ-+šālôm* [1]
are fully satisfied, 2014, *dāšēn¹* [1]
satisfied, 3512+928+6524, *yāṭab+bᵉ-+'ayin¹* [1]
is satisfied, 4848, *mālē'¹* [1]

SATISFIES [3]
satisfies, 8425, *śāba'* [3]

SATISFY [16]
satisfy, 8425, *śāba'* [9]
satisfy, 4848, *mālē'¹* [3]
satisfy, 8115, *rāwâ* [2]
satisfy fully, 8425, *śāba'* [1]
satisfy, 8429, *śōb'a* [1]

SATRAPS [13]
satraps, 10026, *'ᵃḥašdarpan* [9]
satraps, 346, *'ᵃḥašdarpān* [4]

SAUL [341]
Saul, 8620, *šā'ûl* [327]
Saul, *NIH/RPE* [12]
Saulˢ, 2257, *-ô* [2]

SAUL'S [42]
Saul's, 8620, *šā'ûl* [34]
Saul's, 4200+8620, *lᵉ-¹+šā'ûl* [4]
Saul'sˢ, 2257, *-ô* [3]
Saul'sˢ, 2021, *ha-* [1]

SAVAGE [1]
savage, 8273, *ra'¹* [1]

SAVE [150]
save, 3828, *yāša'* [86]
save, 5911, *nāṣal* [32]
save, 4880, *mālaṭ¹* [7]
save life, 2649, *ḥāyâ* [5]
save lives, 2649, *ḥāyâ* [2]
save, 2649, *ḥāyâ* [2]
save, 3802, *yᵉšû'â* [2]
save, 7117, *pālaṭ* [2]
save, 10489, *nᵉṣal* [2]
save, *NIH/RPE* [1]
save, 3829, *yēša'* [1]
save, 4631, *mûš²* [1]
save, 4635, *môšîa'* [1]
save lives, 4695, *miḥyâ* [1]
save, 4880+4880, *mālaṭ¹+mālaṭ¹* [1]
save, 5663, *nûaḥ¹* [1]
save, 6699, *'ānâ¹* [1]
save, 9591, *tᵉšû'â* [1]
save, 10706, *šêzib* [1]

SAVED [53]
saved, 3828, *yāša'* [22]
be saved, 3828, *yāša'* [11]
saved, 5911, *nāṣal* [6]
saved, 4880, *mālaṭ¹* [3]
be saved, 5911, *nāṣal* [3]
am saved, 3828, *yāša'* [2]
saved lives, 2649, *ḥāyâ* [1]
are saved, 3828, *yāša'* [1]
is saved, 3828, *yāša'* [1]
be saved, 4880, *mālaṭ¹* [1]
were saved, 4880, *mālaṭ¹* [1]
saved, 5663, *nûaḥ¹* [1]

SAVES [18]
saves, 3828, *yāša'* [10]
saves, 5911, *nāṣal* [2]
saves, *NIH/RPE* [1]
saves, 3802, *yᵉšû'â* [1]
saves, 4636, *môšā'â* [1]
saves, 7117, *pālaṭ* [1]
saves, 9591, *tᵉšû'â* [1]
saves, 10489, *nᵉṣal* [1]

SAVING [4]
saving, 2649, *ḥāyâ* [1]
saving, 3802, *yᵉšû'â* [1]
saving, 3828, *yāša'* [1]
saving, 3829, *yēša'* [1]

SAVIOR [31]
Savior, 3829, *yēša'* [13]
savior, 4635, *môšîa'* [11]
Savior, 3802, *yᵉšû'â* [6]
Savior, 9591, *tᵉšû'â* [1]

SAW [378]
saw, 8011, *rā'â¹* [306]
saw, 2180, *hinnēh* [43]
saw, 10255, *ḥᵃzâ* [7]
saw, 2600, *ḥāzâ* [5]
saw, *NIH/RPE* [3]
saw, 928+6524, *bᵉ-+'ayin¹* [3]
saw, 10646, *rē'š* [2]
saw visions, 2600+2606, *ḥāzâ+ḥāzôn* [1]
vision saw, 2600, *ḥāzâ* [1]
saw, 4490, *mᵉgērâ* [1]
saw, 5260+6524, *mar'eh+'ayin¹* [1]
saw, 5373, *maśśôr* [1]
saw, 5951+906+6524, *nāśā'+'ēt¹+'ayin¹* [1]
saw to it that was lacking, 6372, *'ādar³* [1]
saw clearly, 8011+8011, *rā'â¹+rā'â¹* [1]
saw, 8812, *šāzap* [1]

SAWS [2]
saws, 4490, *mᵉgērâ* [2]

SAY [671]
say, 606, *'āmar¹* [506]
say, 1819, *dābar²* [67]
say, *NIH/RPE* [35]
say, 1821, *dābār* [13]
what say, 1821, *dābār* [8]
say, 1819+1821, *dābar²+dābār* [3]
say, 606+606, *'āmar¹+'āmar¹* [2]
what say, 609+7023, *'ēmer¹+peh* [2]
say, 1821+1819, *dābār+dābar²* [2]
what say, 7754, *qôl* [2]
say, 7924, *qārā'¹* [2]
say, 10042, *'ᵃmar* [2]
what say, 289, *'aḥᵃwâ²* [1]
what say, 609, *'ēmer¹* [1]
what have to say, 614, *'imrâ* [1]
what say, 614, *'imrâ* [1]
used to say, 1819+1819, *dābar²+dābar²* [1]
ever say, 1821+1819, *dābār+dābar²* [1]
something to say, 1821, *dābār* [1]
what have to say, 1821, *dābār* [1]
say nothing, 3087, *ḥārēš²* [1]
say, 3655+4946+7023, *yāṣā'+min+peh* [1]
anything to say, 4863, *millâ* [1]
say, 4863, *millâ* [1]
what say, 4863, *millâ* [1]
say, 4910, *mālal³* [1]
say, 5101, *ma'ᵃneh¹* [1]
prophets say, 5752, *nāṭap* [1]
say, 6386, *'ûd¹* [1]
have say, 6699+2750, *'ānâ¹+ḥēleq²* [1]
say, 6699+2256+606, *'ānâ¹+wᵉ-+'āmar¹* [1]
say, 6699, *'ānâ¹* [1]
say, 7023, *peh* [1]
say, 7337+7023, *pātaḥ¹+peh* [1]
say, 7422, *ṣāwâ* [1]
say, 7754, *qôl* [1]
what have to say, 7754, *qôl* [1]
don't say a word, 8492+3338+6584+7023, *śîm+yād+'al²+peh* [1]
say, 8740, *šûb¹* [1]

SAYING [178]
saying, 606, *'āmar¹* [138]
saying, *NIH/RPE* [18]
saying, 1819, *dābar²* [10]
saying, 1821, *dābār* [2]
saying, 5442, *māšāl¹* [2]
keep saying, 606+606, *'āmar¹+'āmar¹* [1]
without saying a word, 3087, *ḥārēš²* [1]
saying nothing, 3087, *ḥārēš²* [1]
not saying, 3120, *ḥāšâ* [1]
saying, 4200+606, *lᵉ-¹+'āmar¹* [1]
what saying, 7754, *qôl* [1]
keeps saying, 8740+609, *šûb¹+'ēmer¹* [1]
saying, 10042, *'ᵃmar* [1]

SAYINGS [9]
sayings, 1821, *dābār* [4]
sayings, *NIH/RPE* [3]
collected sayings, 1251+670, *ba'al¹+'ᵃsuppâ* [1]
sayings, 7023, *peh* [1]

SAYS [644]
says, 606, *'āmar¹* [610]
says, 1819, *dābar²* [14]
says, *NIH/RPE* [7]
says nothing, 3087, *ḥārēš²* [3]
says, 5536, *nᵉ'um* [3]
what says, 7754, *qôl* [2]
says, 1821, *dābār* [1]
what says, 1821, *dābār* [1]
says nothing, 3087+3087, *ḥārēš²+ḥārēš²* [1]
says, 6699, *'ānâ¹* [1]
sort of things he says, 8490, *śîaḥ³* [1]

SCABBARD [5]
scabbard, 9509, *ta'ar* [5]

SCABS [1]
scabs, 1599+6760, *gûš+'āpār* [1]

SCALE [4]
scale, 1925, *dālag* [2]
scale, 6590, *'ālâ* [1]
coat of scale armor, 9234+7989, *širyôn+qaśqeśet* [1]

SCALES [23]
scales, 4404, *mō'znayim* [12]
scales, 7989, *qaśqeśet* [7]
set of scales, 4404+5486, *mō'znayim+mišqāl* [1]
scales, 7144, *peles* [1]
scales, 7866, *qāneh* [1]
scales, 10396, *mō'znē'* [1]

SCALP [1]
scalp, 7156, *pāneh* [1]

SCALPS [1]
scalps, 7327, *pōt* [1]

SCAPEGOAT [4]
scapegoat, 6439, *'ᵃzā'zēl* [4]

SCAR [2]
scar, 7648, *ṣārebet* [2]

SCARCE [2]
scarce, 928+5017+430, *bᵉ-+miskēnut+'ākal* [1]
scarce, 2893, *ḥāsēr¹* [1]

SCARCELY [3]
scarcely, 421, *'ak* [1]
scarcely, 3869+5071, *kᵉ-+mᵉ'aṭ* [1]
scarcely, 4202, *lō'* [1]

SCARCER [1]
make scarcer, 3700, *yāqar* [1]

SCARCITY [2]
scarcity, 4728, *maḥsôr* [2]

SCARECROW [1]
scarecrow, 9473, *tōmer²* [1]

SCARLET [43]
scarlet yarn, 9357+9106, *tôlē'â+šānî^{1}* [26]
scarlet, 9106, *šānî^{1}* [7]
scarlet yarn, 9106+9357, *šānî^{1}+tôlē'â* [5]
scarlet thread, 9106, *šānî^{1}* [2]
scarlet wool, 9106+9357, *šānî^{1}+tôlē'â* [1]
scarlet, 9357+9106, *tôlē'â+šānî^{1}* [1]
clad in scarlet, 9443, *tāla'* [1]

SCATTER [39]
scatter, 2430, *zārâ^{1}* [18]
scatter, 7046, *pûṣ^{1}* [11]
scatter, 2450, *zāraq^{1}* [2]
scatter, 1029, *bāzar* [1]
scatter, 2445, *zāra'* [1]
scatter, 2745, *ḥālaq^{2}* [1]
scatter, 5615, *nādaḥ^{1}* [1]
scatter, 5880, *nāpaṣ^{2}* [1]
scatter, 6990, *pā'â* [1]
scatter, 8959, *šālak* [1]
scatter, 10095, *b^{e}dar* [1]

SCATTERED [68]
scattered, 7046, *pûṣ^{1}* [21]
scattered, 2430, *zārâ^{1}* [5]
were scattered, 7046, *pûṣ^{1}* [5]
scattered, 7061, *pāzar* [5]
been scattered, 7046, *pûṣ^{1}* [4]
been scattered, 5615, *nādaḥ^{1}* [3]
scattered, 7298, *pāraś* [3]
are scattered, 2430, *zārâ^{1}* [1]
is scattered, 2430, *zārâ^{1}* [1]
were scattered, 2430, *zārâ^{1}* [1]
scattered, 2445, *zāra'* [1]
scattered, 2450, *zāraq^{1}* [1]
scattered, 2745, *ḥālaq^{2}* [1]
scattered, 5615, *nādaḥ^{1}* [1]
scattered, 5759, *nāṭaš* [1]
scattered, 5880, *nāpaṣ^{2}* [1]
scattered with a whirlwind, 6192, *sā'ar* [1]
be scattered, 7046, *pûṣ^{1}* [1]
is scattered, 7046, *pûṣ^{1}* [1]
scattered, 7056, *pûṣ^{2}* [1]
been scattered, 7061, *pāzar* [1]
scattered abroad, 7061, *pāzar* [1]
are scattered, 7233, *pārad* [1]
be scattered, 7233, *pārad* [1]
scattered, 7233, *pārad* [1]
be scattered, 7298, *pāraś* [1]
scattered, 8848, *šāṭaḥ* [1]
scattered, 8959, *šālak* [1]
scattered, 9161, *šāpak* [1]

SCATTERING [2]
scattering, 5880, *nāpaṣ^{2}* [1]
scattering, 7046, *pûṣ^{1}* [1]

SCATTERS [3]
scatters, 7046, *pûṣ^{1}* [1]
scatters, 7061, *pāzar* [1]
scatters, 7298, *pāraś* [1]

SCENT [2]
catches the scent, 8193, *rîaḥ* [1]
scent, 8194, *rêaḥ* [1]

SCEPTER [23]
scepter, 8657, *šēbeṭ* [15]
scepter, 9222, *šarbîṭ* [4]
scepter, 2980, *ḥāqaq* [2]
scepter, 4751, *maṭṭeh* [2]

SCEPTERS [1]
scepters, 2980, *ḥāqaq* [1]

SCHEME [4]
scheme of things, 3113, *ḥešbôn^{1}* [2]
scheme, 4742, *maḥ^{a}šābâ* [2]

SCHEMER [1]
schemer, 1251+4659, *ba'al^{1}+m^{e}zimmâ* [1]

SCHEMES [18]
schemes, 6783, *'ēṣâ^{1}* [3]
wicked schemes, 2365, *zimmâ^{1}* [2]
schemes, 4659, *m^{e}zimmâ* [2]
wicked schemes, 4659, *m^{e}zimmâ* [2]
schemes, 4742, *maḥ^{a}šābâ* [2]
schemes, *NIH/RPE* [1]
schemes, 2326, *zîd* [1]
evil schemes, 2365, *zimmâ^{1}* [1]
schemes, 2365, *zimmâ^{1}* [1]
schemes, 3115, *ḥiššābôn* [1]
schemes, 4600, *mô'ēṣâ* [1]
evil schemes, 4659, *m^{e}zimmâ* [1]

SCHEMING [1]
scheming, 3108, *ḥāšab* [1]

SCOFF [10]
scoff, 9239, *šāraq* [7]
scoff, 4352, *lā'ag* [1]
scoff, 4610, *mûq* [1]
scoff, 5377, *miśḥāq* [1]

SCOFFED [1]
scoffed, 9506, *tā'a'* [1]

SCOFFERS [1]
scoffers, 408+4371, *'îš^{1}+lāṣôn* [1]

SCOFFS [2]
scoffs, 4352, *lā'ag* [1]
scoffs, 8471, *śāḥaq* [1]

SCOOP [1]
scoop, 3149, *ḥātâ* [1]

SCOOPED [1]
scooped out, 8098, *rādâ^{2}* [1]

SCOOPING [1]
scooping, 3106, *ḥāśap^{1}* [1]

SCOOPS [1]
scoops out, 2916, *ḥāpar^{1}* [1]

SCORCHED [9]
scorched, 8728, *šādap* [3]
scorched, 8729, *š^{e}dēpâ* [2]
being scorched, 3917, *kāwâ* [1]
be scorched, 6977, *'āṭam* [1]
be scorched, 7646, *ṣārab* [1]
scorched, 10731, *š^{e}nâ^{1}* [1]

SCORCHING [6]
scorching, 2363, *zal'āpâ* [1]
scorching heat, 3031, *ḥarḥur* [1]
scorching, 3046, *ḥ^{a}rîšî* [1]
scorching, 6522, *'^{a}yām* [1]
scorching, 7456, *ṣaḥ* [1]
scorching, 7647, *ṣārāb* [1]

SCORN [37]
scorn, 3075, *ḥerpâ* [10]
object of scorn, 3075, *ḥerpâ* [5]
scorn, 9240, *š^{e}rēqâ* [5]
scorn, 4009, *k^{e}limmâ* [3]
scorn, 4353, *la'ag* [3]
scorn, 996, *bûz^{1}* [1]
scorn, 1246, *bā'aṭ* [1]
scorn, 1526, *giddûp* [1]
scorn, 2648, *ḥîdâ* [1]
scorn, 4415, *mā'as^{1}* [1]
object of scorn, 5442, *māšāl^{1}* [1]
shake head in scorn, 5653, *nûd* [1]
shake heads in scorn, 5653, *nûd* [1]
scorn, 7465, *ṣ^{e}ḥōq* [1]
object of scorn, 9240, *š^{e}rēqâ* [1]
object of scorn, 9241, *š^{e}riqâ* [1]

SCORNED [7]
scorned, 3075, *ḥerpâ* [3]
utterly scorned, 996+996, *bûz^{1}+bûz^{1}* [1]
scorned the idea, 1022+928+6524,
bāzâ+b^{e}-+'ayin^{1} [1]
scorned, 7840, *qālas* [1]
scorned, 8471, *śāḥaq* [1]

SCORNFULLY [1]
scornfully claps hands, 6215, *sāpaq^{1}* [1]

SCORNS [2]
scorns, 996, *bûz^{1}* [2]

SCORPION [3]
scorpion, 6832, *'aqrāb* [3]

SCORPIONS [6]
scorpions, 6832, *'aqrāb* [6]

SCOUNDREL [4]
scoundrel, 132+1175, *'ādām^{1}+b^{e}liyya'al* [1]
scoundrel, 408+1175, *'îš^{1}+b^{e}liyya'al* [1]
scoundrel, 408+2021+1175, *'îš^{1}+ha-+b^{e}liyya'al* [1]
scoundrel, 3964, *kîlay* [1]

SCOUNDREL'S [1]
scoundrel's, 3964, *kîlay* [1]

SCOUNDRELS [3]
scoundrels, 1201+1175, *bēn^{1}+b^{e}liyya'al* [3]

SCOURED [1]
be scoured, 5347, *māraq* [1]

SCOURGE [8]
scourge, 8765, *šôṭ^{1}* [3]
scourge, *NIH/RPE* [2]
scourge, 3579, *yāsar^{1}* [2]
scourge, 5596, *nega'* [1]

SCOURGED [4]
scourged, 3579, *yāsar^{1}* [4]

SCOUTS [2]
scouts, *NIH/RPE* [1]
scouts, 8078, *rāgal* [1]

SCRAPE [1]
scrape away, 6081, *sāḥâ* [1]

SCRAPED [4]
scraped himself, 1740, *gārad* [1]
scraped off, 7894, *qāṣâ^{1}* [1]
scraped, 7894, *qāṣâ^{1}* [1]
have scraped, 7909, *qāṣa'^{1}* [1]

SCRAPS [2]
picked up scraps, 4377, *lāqaṭ* [1]
scraps, 7336, *p^{e}tôt* [1]

SCRAWNY [1]
scrawny, 1924, *dal^{2}* [1]

SCREAM [2]
scream for help, 7590, *ṣā'aq* [1]
scream for help, 8123+7754+2256+7924,
rûm^{1}+qôl+w^{e}-+qārā'^{1} [1]

SCREAMED [3]
screamed, 7590, *ṣā'aq* [1]
screamed, 7924+928+7754+1524,
qārā'^{1}+b^{e}-+qôl+gādôl [1]
screamed for help, 8123+7754+2256+7924,
rûm^{1}+qôl+w^{e}-+qārā'^{1} [1]

SCREECH [4]
screech owl, 7887, *qippōd* [2]
screech owl, 9379, *taḥmās* [2]

SCRIBE [11]
scribe, 6221, *sōpēr* [11]

SCRIBE'S [1]
scribe's, 6221, *sōpēr* [1]

SCRIBES [3]
scribes, 6221, *sōpēr* [2]
scribes, 8853, *šāṭar* [1]

SCRIPT [5]
script, 4181, *k^{e}tāb* [5]

SCRIPTURES [1]
Scriptures, 6219, *sēper^{1}* [1]

SCROLL [49]
scroll, 6219, *sēper^{1}* [23]
scroll, 4479, *m^{e}gillâ* [17]
scroll, 4479+6219, *m^{e}gillâ+sēper^{1}* [4]
scroll, *NIH/RPE* [1]
scroll, 1663, *gillāyôn* [1]

the scroll^s^, 2257, *-ô* [1]
scroll, 5532, *nō'd* [1]
scroll, 10399, *m^e^gillâ* [1]

SCULPTURED [1]
sculptured, 5126+7589, *ma'^a^śeh+ṣa'^a^ṣu'îm* [1]

SCUM [1]
scum, 6082, *s^e^ḥî* [1]

SEA [285]
sea, 3542, *yām* [262]
sea cows, 9391, *taḥaš^1^* [12]
sea, *NIH/RPE* [2]
sea, 4784, *mayim* [2]
sea, 10322, *yam* [2]
the seas^s^, 2157, *-hem* [1]
sea creatures, 8254, *remeś* [1]
hides of sea cows, 9391, *taḥaš^1^* [1]
creatures of the sea, 9490, *tannîn* [1]
great sea creatures, 9490, *tannîn* [1]

SEAFARERS [1]
seafarers, 6296+3542, *'ābar^1^+yām* [1]

SEAH [3]
seah, 6006, *s^e^'â* [3]

SEAHS [6]
seahs, 6006, *s^e^'â* [6]

SEAL [18]
seal, 2597, *ḥôtām^1^* [10]
seal up, 3159, *ḥātam* [2]
seal, 3159, *ḥātam* [2]
placed seal, 3159+928+2597, *ḥātam+b^e^-+ḥôtām^1^* [1]
seal, 3160, *ḥōtemet* [1]
seal, 3973, *kālā'^1^* [1]
seal up, 6258, *sātam* [1]

SEALED [17]
sealed, 3159, *ḥātam* [12]
be sealed up, 3159, *ḥātam* [1]
sealed, 5835, *nā'al^1^* [1]
sealed together, 6037+2597, *sāgar+ḥôtām^1^* [1]
sealed, 6794, *'āṣam^2^* [1]
sealed, 10291, *ḥ^a^tam* [1]

SEALING [1]
sealing, *NIH/RPE* [1]

SEALS [2]
seals off, 1237+3159, *ba'ad^1^+ḥātam* [1]
affixing seals, 3159, *ḥātam* [1]

SEAM [2]
seam, 4678, *maḥberet* [2]

SEAMEN [4]
seamen, 2480, *ḥōbēl* [3]
seamen, 2480+3542, *ḥōbēl+yām* [1]

SEAMS [1]
seams, 981, *bedeq* [1]

SEARCH [41]
search for, 1335, *bāqaš* [10]
search out, 1335, *bāqaš* [3]
search, 1335, *bāqaš* [3]
search, 2924, *ḥāpaś* [3]
search, 2983, *ḥāqar* [3]
in search of, 1335, *bāqaš* [2]
search for, 2011, *dāraš* [2]
a search made, 10118, *b^e^qar* [2]
search, 606+928, *'āmar^1^+b^e^-* [1]
gone in search of, 1335, *bāqaš* [1]
search be made for, 1335, *bāqaš* [1]
search made for, 1335, *bāqaš* [1]
went in search of, 1335, *bāqaš* [1]
search was made, 2011, *dāraš* [1]
search for, 2916, *ḥāpar^1^* [1]
search for, 2924, *ḥāpaś* [1]
search out, 2983, *ḥāqar* [1]
search, 5162, *māṣā'* [1]
search for, 8838, *šāḥar^2^* [1]
search out, 9365, *tûr* [1]
a search be made, 10118, *b^e^qar* [1]

SEARCHED [20]
searched for, 1335, *bāqaš* [7]
searched, 1335, *bāqaš* [4]
searched through, 5491, *māšaš* [2]
searched, 2011, *dāraš* [1]
searched, 2924, *ḥāpaś* [1]
be searched out, 2983, *ḥāqar* [1]
searched out, 2983, *ḥāqar* [1]
searched, 2983, *ḥāqar* [1]
searched out, 9365, *tûr* [1]
searched, 10118, *b^e^qar* [1]

SEARCHES [8]
searches, 2011, *dāraš* [2]
searches, 2924, *ḥāpaś* [2]
searches, *NIH/RPE* [1]
searches, 1043, *bāḥan* [1]
searches for, 2011, *dāraš* [1]
searches for, 2983, *ḥāqar* [1]

SEARCHING [6]
searching for, 1335, *bāqaš* [2]
searching, 2984, *ḥēqer* [2]
searching, 1335, *bāqaš* [1]
searching for, 2983, *ḥāqar* [1]

SEARING [1]
searing pain, 7828, *qālâ^1^* [1]

SEAS [29]
seas, 3542, *yām* [21]
high seas, 4213+3542, *lēb+yām* [3]
seas, 5643, *nāhār* [3]
seas, 4784, *mayim* [1]
seas, 9333, *t^e^hôm* [1]

SEASHORE [11]
seashore, 3542, *yām* [5]
seashore, 8557+3542, *śāpâ+yām* [5]
seashore, 2572+3542, *ḥôp+yām* [1]

SEASON [16]
season, 6961, *'ēt* [12]
plowing season, 3045, *ḥārîš* [1]
season, 3074, *ḥōrep* [1]
season, 3427, *yôm^1^* [1]
season, 4873, *mālaḥ^2^* [1]

SEASONS [5]
seasons, 4595, *mô'ēd* [2]
appointed seasons, 4595, *mô'ēd* [1]
seasons, 6961, *'ēt* [1]
seasons, 10232, *z^e^man^2^* [1]

SEAT [19]
seat of honor, 4058, *kissē'* [3]
seat, 4058, *kissē'* [3]
seat, 4632, *môšāb* [3]
seat, 3782, *yāšab* [2]
took seat, 3782, *yāšab* [2]
seat, 5226+8699, *māqôm+šebet^1^* [2]
taken seat, 3782, *yāšab* [1]
takes seat, 3782, *yāšab* [1]
seat, 5323, *merkāb* [1]
took seat, 10338, *y^e^tib* [1]

SEATED [11]
seated, 3782, *yāšab* [9]
seated, 5989+5226, *nātan+māqôm* [1]
seated, 10338, *y^e^tib* [1]

SEATING [2]
seating, 4632, *môšāb* [2]

SEATS [3]
seats, 3782, *yāšab* [2]
took seats, 3782, *yāšab* [1]

SEAWEED [1]
seaweed, 6068, *sûp^2^* [1]

SEBA [4]
Seba, 6013, *s^e^bā'* [4]

SEBAM [1]
Sebam, 8423, *śebām* [1]

SECACAH [1]
Secacah, 6117, *s^e^kākâ* [1]

SECOND [125]
second, 9108, *šēnî* [75]
second, 9109, *š^e^nayim* [12]
second time, 9108, *šēnî* [10]
second, 5467, *mišneh* [8]
second, *NIH/RPE* [4]
Second District, 5467, *mišneh* [3]
second, 285, *'eḥād* [2]
second, 340, *'aḥ^a^rôn* [2]
second, *AIT* [1]
second, 337, *'aḥēr^1^* [1]
second crop, 4381, *leqeš* [1]
second in rank, 5467, *mišneh* [1]
go over a second time, 6618, *'ālal^1^* [1]
go over the branches a second time, 6994+339, *pā'ar^1^+'aḥar* [1]
second in command, 9108, *šēnî* [1]
second, 10765, *tinyān* [1]
second, 10775, *t^e^rēn* [1]

SECOND-IN-COMMAND [1]
second-in-command, 5467, *mišneh* [1]

SECRET [29]
secret, 6260, *sēter* [8]
secret, 928+4537, *b^e^-+mâ* [3]
secret arts, 4319, *lāṭ* [3]
secret places, 5041, *mistār* [2]
secret, 6259, *sātar* [2]
secret, *NIH/RPE* [1]
kept secret, 401+5583, *'ayin^1^+nāgad* [1]
secret, 1821, *dābār* [1]
secret, 2668, *ḥēq* [1]
secret arts, 4268, *l^e^hāṭîm* [1]
secret, 5041, *mistār* [1]
keeping secret vigil, 5915, *nāṣar* [1]
secret place, 6260, *sēter* [1]
secret, 6623, *'ālam* [1]
secret, 7621, *ṣāpan* [1]
secret messengers, 8078, *rāgal* [1]

SECRETARIES [4]
secretaries, 6221, *sōpēr* [4]

SECRETARY [32]
secretary, 6221, *sōpēr* [28]
secretary, 10516, *sāpar* [4]

SECRETARY'S [1]
secretary's, 6221, *sōpēr* [1]

SECRETLY [11]
secretly, 928+2021+6260, *b^e^-+ha-+sēter* [6]
taken secretly, 1704, *gānab* [1]
was secretly brought, 1704, *gānab* [1]
secretly, 2461, *ḥābā'* [1]
secretly did, 2901, *ḥāpā'* [1]
secretly, 3089, *ḥereš^2^* [1]

SECRETS [2]
secrets, 9502, *ta'^a^lumâ* [2]

SECTION [20]
section, 4500, *middâ^1^* [7]
section, *NIH/RPE* [6]
next section, 6584+3338, *'al^2^+yād* [5]
section, 5464, *mišmār^1^* [1]
adjoining section, 6584+3338, *'al^2^+yād* [1]

SECTIONS [3]
sections, 1817, *debeq* [2]
sections, *AIT* [1]

SECU [1]
Secu, 8497, *śekû* [1]

SECURE [34]
feel secure, 1053, *bāṭaḥ^1^* [4]
secure, 1055, *beṭaḥ^1^* [4]
secure, 1053, *bāṭaḥ^1^* [3]
feel secure, 8932, *šalwâ* [3]
secure, *NIH/RPE* [2]
secure, 4440, *mibṭāḥ* [2]
secure, 419, *'ētān^1^* [1]

secure, 1058, *baṭṭuḥâ* [1]
held secure, 2616, *ḥāzaq* [1]
be secure, 3922, *kûn^{1}* [1]
make secure, 3922, *kûn^{1}* [1]
makes secure, 3922, *kûn^{1}* [1]
secure, 3922, *kûn^{1}* [1]
secure, 6164, *sāmak* [1]
made secure, 6184, *sāʿad* [1]
feel secure, 8633, *šaʾ^{a}nān* [1]
secure, 8916, *šalʾ^{a}nan* [1]
secure, 8922, *šālâ^{1}* [1]
felt secure, 8930, *šālû* [1]
felt secure, 8932, *šalwâ* [1]
secure, 8934, *šālôm* [1]
made secure, 9461, *tāmak* [1]

SECURED [1]
secured, 9068, *šāmar* [1]

SECURELY [7]
securely, 1055, *beṭaḥ^{1}* [2]
ties securely, 673+673, *ʾāsar+ʾāsar* [1]
live securely, 3782, *yāšab* [1]
securely, 3782, *yāšab* [1]
fixed securely, 6451, *ʿāzaz* [1]
bound securely, 7674, *ṣārar^{1}* [1]

SECURES [1]
secures, 6913, *ʿāśâ^{1}* [1]

SECURITY [20]
puts up security, 6842, *ʿārab^{1}* [4]
security, 622, *ʾ^{e}met* [3]
security, 4440, *mibṭāḥ* [2]
security, 8631, *šāʾan* [2]
feeling of security, 1055, *beṭaḥ^{1}* [1]
security, 1055, *beṭaḥ^{1}* [1]
demanded security, 2471, *ḥābal^{1}* [1]
take as security for a debt, 2471, *ḥābal^{1}* [1]
taking as security, 2471, *ḥābal^{1}* [1]
put up security, 4200+3338+9546,
l^{e}-^{1}+yād+tāqaʿ [1]
put up security, 6842, *ʿārab^{1}* [1]
puts up security, 6842+6859, *ʿārab^{1}+ʿ^{a}rubbâ* [1]
security, 8932, *šalwâ* [1]

SEDITION [1]
sedition, 10083, *ʾeštaddûr* [1]

SEDUCED [1]
seduced, 5615, *nādaḥ^{1}* [1]

SEDUCES [1]
seduces, 7331, *pātâ^{1}* [1]

SEDUCTIVE [2]
seductive, 2744, *ḥālaq^{1}* [2]

SEE [517]
see, 8011, *rāʾâ^{1}* [342]
see, 2180, *hinnēh* [81]
see, *NIH/RPE* [15]
see, 2600, *ḥāzâ* [14]
see, 2176, *hēn^{1}* [6]
see, *AIT* [5]
see, 8800, *šûr^{1}* [5]
see, 3359, *yādaʿ* [4]
see visions, 2600, *ḥāzâ* [3]
see, 3359+2256+8011, *yādaʿ+w^{e}-+rāʾâ^{1}* [3]
see, 5564, *nābaṭ* [3]
see, 10255, *ḥ^{a}zâ* [3]
see, 4200+7156, *l^{e}-^{1}+pāneh* [2]
let see, 8011, *rāʾâ^{1}* [2]
see, 9068, *šāmar* [2]
see how, 377, *ʾêkâ* [1]
see, 448+6524, *ʾel+ʿayin^{1}* [1]
see, 1067, *bîn* [1]
let see, 1655, *gālâ* [1]
see to it, 4200+6524, *l^{e}-^{1}+ʿayin^{1}* [1]
see, 4200+6524, *l^{e}-^{1}+ʿayin^{1}* [1]
see, 5260+6524, *marʾeh+ʿayin^{1}* [1]
see, 5260, *marʾeh* [1]
examine to see, 5795, *nākar^{1}* [1]
see, 5795, *nākar^{1}* [1]
what see, 6524, *ʿayin^{1}* [1]
see for yourselves, 6524+4013+8011,
ʿayin^{1}+-kem+rāʾâ^{1} [1]
see, 6524+8011, *ʿayin^{1}+rāʾâ^{1}* [1]
see, 7212, *pāqad* [1]
see, 7221, *piqqēaḥ* [1]
see that gets justice, 7405, *ṣādaq* [1]
see visions, 8011, *rāʾâ^{1}* [1]
allowed to see, 8011, *rāʾâ^{1}* [1]
made see, 8011, *rāʾâ^{1}* [1]
make see, 8011, *rāʾâ^{1}* [1]
see, 8011+4200+2021+6524,
rāʾâ^{1}+l^{e}-^{1}+ha-+ʿayin^{1} [1]
see, 8011+7156, *rāʾâ^{1}+pāneh* [1]
see that is completely healed, 8324+8324,
rāpāʾ^{1}+rāpāʾ^{1} [1]
see, 8492+6524, *śîm+ʿayin^{1}* [1]
see on way, 8938, *šālaḥ* [1]
see, 9004, *šām* [1]
see to it, 9068, *šāmar* [1]

SEED [31]
seed, 2446, *zeraʿ* [25]
seed pods, 1807, *dibyōnîm* [1]
plant seed, 2445, *zāraʿ* [1]
plant with seed, 2445, *zāraʿ* [1]
seed, 2445+2446, *zāraʿ+zeraʿ* [1]
sowing seed, 2445, *zāraʿ* [1]
seed to sow, 5433+2446, *mešek^{1}+zeraʿ* [1]

SEED-BEARING [2]
seed-bearing, 2445+2446, *zāraʿ+zeraʿ* [2]

SEEDS [4]
seeds, 2433, *zērûaʿ* [1]
seeds, 2446+2433, *zeraʿ+zērûaʿ* [1]
seeds, 3079, *ḥarṣān* [1]
seeds, 7237, *p^{e}rudōt* [1]

SEEDTIME [1]
seedtime, 2446, *zeraʿ* [1]

SEEING [12]
seeing, 8011, *rāʾâ^{1}* [8]
seeing, *NIH/RPE* [2]
ever seeing, 8011+8011, *rāʾâ^{1}+rāʾâ^{1}* [1]
seeing visions, 8015, *rōʾeh^{2}* [1]

SEEK [112]
seek, 1335, *bāqaš* [58]
seek, 2011, *dāraš* [34]
seek out, 1335, *bāqaš* [2]
seek help, 2011, *dāraš* [2]
seek out, 2011, *dāraš* [2]
earnestly seek, 8838, *šāḥar^{2}* [2]
seek, 1329, *bāqar* [1]
seek an audience with, 1335+7156,
bāqaš+pāneh [1]
seek help, 1335, *bāqaš* [1]
seek to, 1335, *bāqaš* [1]
seek will, 2011, *dāraš* [1]
seek favor, 2704+906+7156,
ḥālâ^{2}+ʾēt^{1}+pāneh [1]
seek, 2984, *ḥēqer* [1]
seek revenge, 5933, *nāqam* [1]
seek favor, 7156+2704, *pāneh+ḥālâ^{2}* [1]
seek to destroy, 7551, *ṣāmat* [1]
seek an omen, 7876+7877, *qāsam+qesem* [1]
seek, 8838, *šāḥar^{2}* [1]

SEEKING [20]
seeking, 1335, *bāqaš* [12]
seeking, 2011, *dāraš* [5]
seeking, *NIH/RPE* [1]
seeking guidance, 1329, *bāqar* [1]
seeking advice, 3619, *yāʿaṣ* [1]

SEEKS [9]
seeks, 1335, *bāqaš* [4]
seeks, 2011, *dāraš* [2]
seeks out, 2916, *ḥāpar^{1}* [1]
seeks, 4200, *l^{e}-^{1}* [1]
seeks, 8838, *šāḥar^{2}* [1]

SEEM [15]
seem, *AIT* [4]
seem, 928+6524, *b^{e}-+ʿayin^{1}* [4]
seem, 3108, *ḥāšab* [2]
seem, 2118+928+6524, *hāyâ+b^{e}-+ʿayin^{1}* [1]
seem, 2118, *hāyâ* [1]
seem, 4017+928+6524, *k^{e}mô+b^{e}-+ʿayin^{1}* [1]
seem, 5260, *marʾeh* [1]
made seem righteous, 7405, *ṣādaq* [1]

SEEMED [10]
seemed, 928+6524, *b^{e}-+ʿayin^{1}* [8]
seemed, 2118+928+6524, *hāyâ+b^{e}-+ʿayin^{1}* [1]
seemed, 2118, *hāyâ* [1]

SEEMS [19]
seems, 928+6524, *b^{e}-+ʿayin^{1}* [10]
seems, *NIH/RPE* [3]
seems, 3108, *ḥāšab* [2]
seems to, 4200+7156, *l^{e}-^{1}+pāneh* [2]
seems, 8011, *rāʾâ^{1}* [1]
seems best, 10320, *y^{e}ṭab* [1]

SEEN [129]
seen, 8011, *rāʾâ^{1}* [102]
be seen, 8011, *rāʾâ^{1}* [9]
seen, 2600, *ḥāzâ* [5]
been seen, 8011, *rāʾâ^{1}* [3]
seen, 5564, *nābaṭ* [2]
were seen, 3359, *yādaʿ* [1]
be seen, 5162, *māṣāʾ* [1]
watched over and seen, 7212+7212,
pāqad+pāqad [1]
being seen, 8011, *rāʾâ^{1}* [1]
indeed seen, 8011+8011, *rāʾâ^{1}+rāʾâ^{1}* [1]
seen for myself, 8011+7156, *rāʾâ^{1}+pāneh* [1]
was seen, 8011, *rāʾâ^{1}* [1]
seen, 8812, *šāzap* [1]

SEER [21]
seer, 2602, *ḥōzeh^{1}* [11]
seer, 8014, *rōʾeh^{1}* [10]

SEER'S [1]
seer's, 8014, *rōʾeh^{1}* [1]

SEERS [6]
seers, 2602, *ḥōzeh^{1}* [5]
seers, 8014, *rōʾeh^{1}* [1]

SEES [40]
sees, 8011, *rāʾâ^{1}* [27]
sees, 2600, *ḥāzâ* [3]
sees, 928+6524, *b^{e}-+ʿayin^{1}* [2]
what sees, 5260, *marʾeh* [2]
sees clearly, 9280, *šātam* [2]
sees through, 2983, *ḥāqar* [1]
sees, 3247, *ṭāʿam* [1]
sees, 5564, *nābaṭ* [1]
sees, 8024, *r^{o}ʾî* [1]

SEGUB [3]
Segub, 8437, *ś^{e}gûb* [3]

SEIR [39]
Seir, 8541, *śēʿîr^{1}* [35]
Seir, 8543, *śēʿîr^{3}* [3]
Seir, 8542, *śēʿîr^{2}* [1]

SEIRAH [1]
Seirah, 8545, *ś^{e}ʿîrâ^{2}* [1]

SEIZE [25]
seize, 4374, *lāqaḥ* [4]
seize, 9530, *tāpaś* [4]
seize, 296, *ʾāḥaz^{1}* [2]
seize, 2616, *ḥāzaq* [2]
seize, 8964, *šālal^{2}* [2]
seize, *NIH/RPE* [1]
terror seize, 987, *bāhal* [1]
seize, 1608, *gāzal* [1]
seize, 2642, *ḥāṭap* [1]
seize, 3769, *yāraš^{1}* [1]
seize, 4334, *lākad* [1]
seize, 5162, *māṣāʾ* [1]
seize, 5595, *nāgaʿ* [1]
seize, 5943, *nāqaš* [1]
seize, 8492+928+3338, *śîm+b^{e}-+yād* [1]
seize, 8938, *šālaḥ* [1]

SEIZED [30]
seized, 296, *ʾāḥaz^{1}* [9]
seized, 4374, *lāqaḥ* [4]

seized, 9530, *tāpaś* [4]
seized, 1608, *gāzal* [2]
seized, 5877+6584, *nāpal+ʿal*[2] [2]
seized, 8492+3338, *śîm+yād* [2]
seized for a debt, 2471, *ḥābal*[1] [1]
seized, 2616, *ḥāzaq* [1]
seized property, 3769, *yāraš*[1] [1]
seized, 5162, *māṣāʾ* [1]
seized, 6806, *ʿāṣar* [1]
seized, 7925, *qārāʾ*[2] [1]
seized, 8647, *šābâ* [1]

SEIZES [6]
seizes, 296, *ʾāḥaz*[1] [3]
seizes, 2616, *ḥāzaq* [3]

SELA [4]
Sela, 6153, *selaʿ*[2] [4]

SELA HAMMAHLEKOTH [1]
Sela Hammahlekoth, 6154, *selaʿ hammaḥl^{e}qôt* [1]

SELAH [74]
Selah, 6138, *selâ* [74]

SELDOM [2]
seldom, 3700, *yāqar* [1]
seldom, 4202+2221, *lōʾ+harbēh* [1]

SELECT [6]
select, 4374, *lāqaḥ* [3]
select, 2600, *ḥāzâ* [1]
select a day, 4946+3427+4200+3427, *min+yôm*[1]*+l^{e}-*[1]*+yôm*[1] [1]
select, 7936, *qārā*[1] [1]

SELECTED [11]
selected, 4374, *lāqaḥ* [6]
selected, 1047, *bāḥar*[1] [2]
selected, 976, *bādal* [1]
selected, 3585, *yāʿad* [1]
selected, 8011, *rāʾâ*[1] [1]

SELECTS [3]
selects, 1047, *bāḥar*[1] [1]
selects, 2011, *dāraš* [1]
selects, 3585, *yāʿad* [1]

SELED [2]
Seled, 6135, *seled* [2]

SELF [1]
your own self, 3870, *-kā* [1]

SELF-ABASEMENT [1]
self-abasement, 9504, *taʿ^{a}nît* [1]

SELF-CONFIDENCE [1]
lost self-confidence, 5877+4394+928+6524, *nāpal+m^{e}ʿōd+b^{e}-+ʿayin*[1] [1]

SELF-CONTROL [1]
self-control, 5110+4200+8120, *maʿṣār+l^{e}-*[1]*+rûaḥ* [1]

SELFISH [2]
selfish gain, 1299, *beṣaʿ* [1]
selfish ends, 9294, *taʾ^{a}wâ*[1] [1]

SELL [32]
sell, 4835, *mākar* [17]
sell, 5989, *nātan* [6]
sell, 8690, *šābar*[2] [3]
sell, 5989+928+4084, *nātan+b^{e}-+kesep* [2]
sell, *NIH/RPE* [1]
sell for, 928+2118, *b^{e}-+hāyâ* [1]
must sell, 4835+4835+928+2021+4084, *mākar+mākar+b^{e}-+ha-+kesep* [1]
sell land, 4835+4928, *mākar+mimkār* [1]

SELLER [3]
seller, 4835, *mākar* [3]

SELLERS [1]
sellers, 4835, *mākar* [1]

SELLING [8]
selling, 4835, *mākar* [7]
selling, 8690, *šābar*[2] [1]

SELLS [10]
sells, 4835, *mākar* [7]
sells himself, 4835, *mākar* [3]

SEMAKIAH [1]
Semakiah, 6165, *s^{e}makyāhû* [1]

SEMEN [6]
semen, 2446, *zeraʿ* [5]
semen, *NIH/RPE* [1]

SENAAH [2]
Senaah, 6171, *s^{e}nāʾâ* [2]

SEND [194]
send, 8938, *šālaḥ* [113]
send, 5989, *nātan* [9]
send back, 8740, *šûb*[1] [9]
send away, 8938, *šālaḥ* [9]
send on way, 8938, *šālaḥ* [5]
send up, 6590, *ʿālâ* [4]
send word, 8938, *šālaḥ* [4]
send out, 3655, *yāṣāʾ* [3]
send, *NIH/RPE* [2]
send, 6296, *ʿābar*[1] [2]
send, 7422, *ṣāwâ* [2]
send back, 8938, *šālaḥ* [2]
send forth, 8938, *šālaḥ* [2]
send for, 8938+2256+4374, *šālaḥ+w^{e}-+lāqaḥ* [2]
send out, 8938, *šālaḥ* [2]
send, 995, *bôʾ* [1]
send forth lightning, 1397+1398, *bāraq+bārāq*[1] [1]
send into exile, 1655, *gālâ* [1]
send away, 3655, *yāṣāʾ* [1]
send down, 3718, *yārad* [1]
send rain, 4763, *māṭar* [1]
send, 4763, *māṭar* [1]
send, 4946+907+995, *min+ʾēt*[2]*+bôʾ* [1]
send down, 5782, *nākâ* [1]
send down, 5989, *nātan* [1]
send out, 5989, *nātan* [1]
send out, 6296, *ʿābar*[1] [1]
send, 6590, *ʿālâ* [1]
send fearful, 7098, *pālāʾ* [1]
send, 7212, *pāqad* [1]
send, 7727, *qādaš* [1]
send, 7756, *qûm* [1]
send far, 8178, *rāḥaq* [1]
by all means send, 8740+8740, *šûb*[1]*+šûb*[1] [1]
send, 8740, *šûb*[1] [1]
send a message, 8938, *šālaḥ* [1]
send for, 8938, *šālaḥ* [1]
send urgent, 8938+8938, *šālaḥ+šālaḥ* [1]
send, 10714, *š^{e}laḥ* [1]

SENDING [27]
sending, 8938, *šālaḥ* [20]
sending, *NIH/RPE* [2]
sending on, 2143, *hālak* [1]
sending, 2143, *hālak* [1]
sending back, 8740, *šûb*[1] [1]
sending away, 8938, *šālaḥ* [1]
sending message, 10714, *š^{e}laḥ* [1]

SENDS [20]
sends, 8938, *šālaḥ* [10]
sends, 6913, *ʿāśâ*[1] [3]
sends, *AIT* [1]
sends, *NIH/RPE* [1]
sends, 3297, *yābal* [1]
sends, 3718, *yārad* [1]
sends poverty, 3769, *yāraš*[1] [1]
sends out, 8938, *šālaḥ* [1]
sends wandering, 9494, *tāʿâ* [1]

SENEH [1]
Seneh, 6175, *senneh* [1]

SENIR [4]
Senir, 8536, *ś^{e}nîr* [4]

SENNACHERIB [15]
Sennacherib, 6178, *sanḥērîb* [13]
Sennacherib, *NIH/RPE* [2]

SENNACHERIB'S [1]
Sennacherib's^{s}, 2257, *-ô* [1]

SENSE [3]
good sense, 1069, *bînâ* [1]
sense, 4213, *lēb* [1]
sense, 6783, *ʿēṣâ*[1] [1]

SENSELESS [12]
senseless, 1279, *bāʿar*[3] [5]
senseless, 1280, *baʿar* [3]
senseless, 401+4213, *ʾayin*[1]*+lēb* [2]
give senseless, 1279, *bāʿar*[3] [1]
senseless, 6119, *sākāl* [1]

SENSIBLE [1]
sensible, 1067, *bîn* [1]

SENSITIVE [3]
sensitive, 6697, *ʿānōg* [2]
sensitive, 6695, *ʿānag* [1]

SENT [459]
sent, 8938, *šālaḥ* [310]
sent away, 8938, *šālaḥ* [22]
sent out, 8938, *šālaḥ* [17]
sent word, 8938, *šālaḥ* [11]
sent, 10714, *š^{e}laḥ* [9]
sent, 5989, *nātan* [7]
sent for, 8938+2256+7924+4200, *šālaḥ+w^{e}-+qārāʾ*[1]*+l^{e}-*[1] [5]
sent on way, 8938, *šālaḥ* [5]
sent off, 8938, *šālaḥ* [4]
sent, *NIH/RPE* [3]
sent, 3655, *yāṣāʾ* [3]
sent back, 8938, *šālaḥ* [3]
sent for, 8938+2256+7924, *šālaḥ+w^{e}-+qārāʾ*[1] [3]
sent for, 8938, *šālaḥ* [3]
sent, *AIT* [2]
sent into exile, 1655, *gālâ* [2]
sent, 2143, *hālak* [2]
sent rain, 4763, *māṭar* [2]
sent far away, 8178, *rāḥaq* [2]
sent back, 8740, *šûb*[1] [2]
sent, 8740, *šûb*[1] [2]
been sent, 8938, *šālaḥ* [2]
sent message, 8938, *šālaḥ* [2]
was sent, 8938, *šālaḥ* [2]
sent word, 606, *ʾāmar*[1] [1]
sent, 995, *bôʾ* [1]
sent up a cry, 2410, *zāʿaq* [1]
sent, 3214, *ṭûl* [1]
sent out, 3655, *yāṣāʾ* [1]
sent down, 3718, *yārad* [1]
sent out, 4102, *kāpan* [1]
sent for, 4374, *lāqaḥ* [1]
sent by, 4946+907, *min+ʾēt*[2] [1]
sent around, 6015, *sābab* [1]
sent away, 6073, *sûr*[1] [1]
sent across, 6296, *ʿābar*[1] [1]
sent over, 6296, *ʿābar*[1] [1]
sent throughout, 6296, *ʿābar*[1] [1]
sent, 6296, *ʿābar*[1] [1]
sent word, 7422, *ṣāwâ* [1]
sent, 7422, *ṣāwâ* [1]
sent away, 8933, *šillûḥîm* [1]
be sent, 8938, *šālaḥ* [1]
being sent, 8938, *šālaḥ* [1]
sent a message, 8938, *šālaḥ* [1]
sent for help, 8938, *šālaḥ* [1]
sent forth, 8938, *šālaḥ* [1]
sent for, 8938+2256+4374, *šālaḥ+w^{e}-+lāqaḥ* [1]
sent for, 8938+4200+7924, *šālaḥ+l^{e}-*[1]*+qārāʾ*[1] [1]
sent messengers, 8938, *šālaḥ* [1]
sent on way, 8938+906, *šālaḥ+ʾēt*[1] [1]
sent word, 8938+2256+5583, *šālaḥ+w^{e}-+nāgad* [1]
sent word, 8938+2256+7924, *šālaḥ+w^{e}-+qārāʾ*[1] [1]
was sent away, 8938, *šālaḥ* [1]
were sent on way, 8938, *šālaḥ* [1]
were sent, 8938, *šālaḥ* [1]

sent to spy out, 9365, *tûr* [1]
are sent, 10714, *šᵉlaḥ* [1]

SENTENCE [8]
sentence, 5477, *mišpāṭ* [5]
sentence, 9149, *šāpaṭ* [2]
sentence, 7330, *pitgām* [1]

SENTENCED [2]
sentenced, 5477, *mišpāṭ* [2]

SEORIM [1]
Seorim, 8556, *śᵉʿōrîm* [1]

SEPARATE [15]
separate, 976, *bādal* [5]
separate yourselves, 976, *bādal* [2]
separate, 2931, *ḥopšît* [2]
kept themselves separate, 976, *bādal* [1]
separate, 3657+4200+963, *yāṣag+lᵉ-1+bad1* [1]
separate, 4200+963, *lᵉ-1+bad1* [1]
keep separate, 5692, *nāzar1* [1]
separate, 5879, *nāpaṣ1* [1]
separate, 5911+1068, *nāṣal+bayin* [1]

SEPARATED [16]
separated, 976, *bādal* [4]
separated themselves, 976, *bādal* [3]
separated from, 4946+6584, *min+ʿal2* [2]
separated into divisions, 2745, *ḥālaq2* [1]
separated, 7046, *pûṣ1* [1]
be separated, 7233, *pārad* [1]
separated, 7233+1068, *pārad+bayin* [1]
separated, 7233, *pārad* [1]
was separated, 7233, *pārad* [1]
separated, 8492, *śîm* [1]

SEPARATES [4]
separates, 7233, *pārad* [3]
separates himself, 5692, *nāzar1* [1]

SEPARATION [10]
separation, 5694, *nēzer* [6]
separation, 5693, *nāzar2* [2]
separation, 5687, *nāzîr* [1]
symbol of separation, 5694, *nēzer* [1]

SEPHAR [1]
Sephar, 6223, *sᵉpār2* [1]

SEPHARAD [1]
Sepharad, 6224, *sᵉpārad* [1]

SEPHARVAIM [6]
Sepharvaim, 6226, *sᵉparwayim* [6]

SEPHARVITES [1]
Sepharvites, 6227, *sᵉparwîm* [1]

SERAH [3]
Serah, 8580, *śeraḥ* [3]

SERAIAH [18]
Seraiah, 8588, *śᵉrāyâ* [17]
Seraiah, 8589, *śᵉrāyāhû* [1]

SERAIAH'S [1]
Seraiah's, 8588, *śᵉrāyâ* [1]

SERAPHS [2]
seraphs, 8597, *śārāp1* [2]

SERED [2]
Sered, 6237, *sered* [2]

SEREDITE [1]
Seredite, 6238, *sardî* [1]

SERIOUS [6]
serious injury, 656, *ʾāsôn* [2]
not serious, 7837, *qālal* [2]
serious, 1524, *gādôl* [1]
serious, 8273, *raʿ1* [1]

SERPENT [14]
serpent, 5729, *nāḥāš1* [11]
serpent, 9490, *tannîn* [2]
venomous serpent, 8597, *śārāp1* [1]

SERPENT'S [2]
serpent's, 5729, *nāḥāš1* [2]

SERPENTS [3]
serpents, 7352, *peten* [2]
serpents, 9490, *tannîn* [1]

SERUG [5]
Serug, 8578, *śᵉrûg* [5]

SERVANT [416]
servant, 6269, *ʿebed1* [325]
servant, 5853, *naʿar2* [29]
servant, 9148, *šipḥâ* [19]
servant, 563, *ʾāmâ* [14]
servant, *NIH/RPE* [7]
servant girls, 5855, *naʿărâ1* [5]
servant girl, 9148, *šipḥâ* [3]
servant, 9250, *šārat* [3]
the servants, 5647, *-nû2* [2]
servant bound by contract, 8502, *śākîr* [2]
servant, 1201, *bēn1* [1]
servants, 2257, *-ô* [1]
the servants, 2257, *-ô* [1]
personal servant, 5853+9250, *naʿar2+šārat* [1]
servant, 6268, *ʿābad* [1]
servant girls, 9148, *šipḥâ* [1]
servant, 10523, *ʿăbēd* [1]

SERVANT'S [10]
servant's, 6269, *ʿebed1* [7]
servant's, 563, *ʾāmâ* [2]
servant's, 5853, *naʿar2* [1]

SERVANTS [206]
servants, 6269, *ʿebed1* [157]
temple servants, 5987, *nātîn* [15]
servants, 5853, *naʿar2* [14]
servants, 10523, *ʿăbēd* [6]
servants, 9250, *šārat* [4]
servants, 408, *ʾîš1* [2]
servants, 6276, *ʿăbuddâ* [2]
servants, 4200+6269, *lᵉ-1+ʿebed1* [1]
the servants, 4392, *-ām* [1]
servants men, 6269, *ʿebed1* [1]
servants the, 6269, *ʿebed1* [1]
servants, 7582, *ṣāʿîr1* [1]
temple servants, 10497, *nᵉtîn* [1]

SERVE [183]
serve, 6268, *ʿābad* [88]
serve, 3655, *yāṣāʾ* [14]
serve as priests, 3912, *kāhan* [12]
serve, 9250, *šārat* [8]
serve, 10586, *pᵉlaḥ* [7]
serve, 2118, *hāyâ* [6]
serve, 6641+4200+7156, *ʿāmad+lᵉ-1+pāneh* [5]
serve, 7372, *ṣābāʾ2* [4]
serve, 6641, *ʿāmad* [3]
serve, *NIH/RPE* [2]
serve, *AIT* [2]
serve as, 2118, *hāyâ* [2]
serve, 3656, *yāšab* [2]
serve as priest, 3912, *kāhan* [2]
serve, 6269, *ʿebed1* [2]
serve, 6913, *ʿāśâ1* [2]
serve, 9068, *šāmar* [2]
serve, 2118+4200+7156, *hāyâ+lᵉ-1+pāneh* [1]
serve, 2118+4200, *hāyâ+lᵉ-1* [1]
serve in, 3655, *yāṣāʾ* [1]
serve, 3655+2256+995, *yāṣāʾ+wᵉ+bôʾ* [1]
serve, 3668, *yāṣaq* [1]
serve, 4200+7156+6641, *lᵉ-1+pāneh+ʿāmad* [1]
serve, 4200+7156, *lᵉ-1+pāneh* [1]
serve as slaves, 6268, *ʿābad* [1]
volunteered to serve, 6370, *ʿādar1* [1]
serve, 6590, *ʿālâ* [1]
had serve, 6641, *ʿāmad* [1]
serve, 6641+6584, *ʿāmad+ʿal2* [1]
serve, 7371+7372, *ṣābāʾ1+ṣābāʾ2* [1]
serve, 7372+6913, *ṣābāʾ2+ʿāśâ1* [1]
serve, 8492, *śîm* [1]
make serve, 8492+4200, *śîm+lᵉ-1* [1]
serve as officials, 8853, *šāṭar* [1]
serve, 9148, *šipḥâ* [1]
serve as judges, 9149, *šāpaṭ* [1]
serve as judge, 9149, *šāpaṭ* [1]

SERVED [57]
served, 6268, *ʿābad* [28]
served, 9250, *šārat* [4]
served, 2118, *hāyâ* [2]
served as priests, 3912, *kāhan* [2]
served, 6641+4200+7156, *ʿāmad+lᵉ-1+pāneh* [2]
served, 6641, *ʿāmad* [2]
served, 8492, *śîm* [2]
served, *NIH/RPE* [1]
served as, 2118, *hāyâ* [1]
served, 2118+4200+7156, *hāyâ+lᵉ-1+pāneh* [1]
served, 3668, *yāṣaq* [1]
served as priest, 3912, *kāhan* [1]
served, 5951, *nāśāʾ* [1]
served, 6269, *ʿebed1* [1]
served, 6275, *ʿăbōdâ* [1]
served, 6641+907+7156, *ʿāmad+ʾēt2+pāneh* [1]
served, 7371+7371, *ṣābāʾ1+ṣābāʾ1* [1]
served, 7371, *ṣābāʾ1* [1]
served quickly, 8132, *rûṣ* [1]
served as judges, 9149, *šāpaṭ* [1]
served, 9149, *šāpaṭ* [1]
wine served, 9197, *šāqâ* [1]

SERVES [2]
serves, 6268, *ʿābad* [2]

SERVICE [56]
service, 6275, *ʿăbōdâ* [24]
service, 9250, *šārat* [5]
service, 5466, *mišmeret* [3]
hard service, 7372, *ṣābāʾ2* [3]
ready for military service, 3655+7372, *yāṣāʾ+ṣābāʾ2* [2]
service, 4856, *mᵉlāʾkâ* [2]
various kinds of service, 6275+2256+6275, *ʿăbōdâ+wᵉ+ʿăbōdâ* [2]
entered service, 6641+4200+7156, *ʿāmad+lᵉ-1+pāneh* [2]
took into service, 665, *ʾāsap* [1]
priestly service, 3914, *kᵉhunnâ* [1]
in service, 4200+7156, *lᵉ-1+pāneh* [1]
service of, 4200, *lᵉ-1* [1]
volunteered himself for service, 5605, *nādab* [1]
in service, 6269, *ʿebed1* [1]
service, 6269, *ʿebed1* [1]
enter service, 6641+4200+7156, *ʿāmad+lᵉ-1+pāneh* [1]
entered the service, 6641+4200+7156, *ʿāmad+lᵉ-1+pāneh* [1]
regular service, 7372+6275, *ṣābāʾ2+ʿăbōdâ* [1]
service, 8079, *regel* [1]
service, 9251, *šārēt* [1]
service, 10525, *ʿăbîdâ* [1]

SERVICES [3]
services, 5464, *mišmār1* [1]
services, 5466, *mišmeret* [1]
services, 6268, *ʿābad* [1]

SERVING [19]
serving, 6268, *ʿābad* [8]
serving, 6275, *ʿăbōdâ* [5]
serving, 6641+4200+7156, *ʿāmad+lᵉ-1+pāneh* [2]
serving, 2118, *hāyâ* [1]
serving as priests, 3912, *kāhan* [1]
serving, 5466, *mišmeret* [1]
serving, 9250, *šārat* [1]

SERVITUDE [1]
reduced to servitude, 6268+4200+6269, *ʿābad+lᵉ-1+ʿebed1* [1]

SET [537]
set, 8492, *śîm* [50]
set out, 5825, *nāsaʿ* [49]
set, 5989, *nātan* [36]
set up, 7756, *qûm* [17]
set, *NIH/RPE* [15]
set out, 2143, *hālak* [15]
set up, 8492, *śîm* [13]
set out, 7756, *qûm* [11]

set out, 3655, *yāṣā'* [10]
set up, 5893, *nāṣab^{1}* [9]
set up, 10624, *qûm* [9]
set, 2118, *hāyâ* [8]
set apart, 976, *bādal* [7]
set, 995, *bô'* [7]
set on fire, 3675+928+2021+836, *yāṣat+b^{e}+ha-+'ēš^{1}* [7]
set, 8883, *šît^{1}* [7]
set, *AIT* [6]
set, 4678, *maḥberet* [6]
set up, 6590, *'ālâ* [6]
set apart, 7727, *qādaš* [6]
set, 5663, *nûaḥ^{1}* [5]
set, 5893, *nāṣab^{1}* [5]
set up, 5989, *nātan* [5]
set free, 8938, *šālaḥ* [5]
set, 2501, *ḥōberet* [4]
set up camp, 2837, *ḥānâ^{1}* [4]
set, 3657, *yāṣag* [4]
set fire, 3675+836, *yāṣat+'ēš^{1}* [4]
set, 6641, *'āmad* [4]
set on fire, 8596+928+2021+836, *śārap+b^{e}+ha-+'ēš^{1}* [4]
set, 8938, *šālaḥ* [4]
set an ambush, 741, *'ārab* [3]
set aside, 976, *bādal* [3]
set in place, 3922, *kûn^{1}* [3]
set, 3922, *kûn^{1}* [3]
set, 4848, *mālē'^{1}* [3]
set out on the table, 5121, *ma'^{a}reket* [3]
set in place, 6641, *'āmad* [3]
set value, 6886, *'ērek* [3]
set on edge, 7733, *qāhâ* [3]
set, 7756, *qûm* [3]
set fire to, 8596, *śārap* [3]
set, 606, *'āmar^{1}* [2]
set on fire, 928+2021+836+3675, *b^{e}+ha-+'ēš^{1}+yāṣat* [2]
set, 963, *bad^{1}* [2]
set out, 995, *bô'* [2]
set up, 1215, *bānâ* [2]
set ablaze, 1277, *bā'ar^{1}* [2]
set, 2005, *dārak* [2]
set sail, 2143, *hālak* [2]
set, 2374, *zāman* [2]
set up tents, 2837, *ḥānâ^{1}* [2]
set apart for destruction, 3051, *ḥērem^{1}* [2]
set affection, 3137, *ḥāšaq^{1}* [2]
set, 3569, *yāsad^{1}* [2]
set up king, 4887+4889, *mālak^{1}+melek^{1}* [2]
at set times, 4946+6961+6330+6961, *min+'ēt+'ad^{2}+'ēt* [2]
set up, 5663, *nûaḥ^{1}* [2]
set on, 6584, *'al^{2}* [2]
set up, 6641, *'āmad* [2]
set out, 6885, *'ārak* [2]
set, 6885, *'ārak* [2]
set up, 6913, *'āśâ^{1}* [2]
set aside, 7727, *qādaš* [2]
set, 8206, *rākab* [2]
set up, 8905, *šākan* [2]
set parallel, 8917, *šālab* [2]
set aside, 9556, *t^{e}rûmâ* [2]
set desire on, 203, *'āwâ^{1}* [1]
set aside, 665, *'āsap* [1]
ambush set, 741, *'ārab* [1]
set ablaze, 928+2021+836+3675, *b^{e}-+ha-+'ēš^{1}+yāṣat* [1]
set on, 928, *b^{e}-* [1]
set with, 928, *b^{e}-* [1]
was set apart, 976, *bādal* [1]
set foot, 995, *bô'* [1]
set out, 1335, *bāqaš* [1]
set up, 1487, *gābal* [1]
set up to be great, 1540, *gādal* [1]
set out, 1655, *gālâ* [1]
set on fire, 1944, *dālaq* [1]
set feet, 2005, *dārak* [1]
set foot on, 2005, *dārak* [1]
set off, 2143, *hālak* [1]
set forth, 2554, *ḥûd* [1]
set up, 2837, *ḥānâ^{1}* [1]
set apart, 2930, *ḥopšî* [1]
set apart, 2936, *ḥāṣâ* [1]
set farther back, 2958+2021+337, *ḥāṣēr^{1}+ha-+'aḥēr^{1}* [1]
set, 3137, *ḥāšaq^{1}* [1]
were set, 3190, *ṭāba'* [1]
set, 3243, *ṭāman* [1]
set, 3585, *yā'ad* [1]
set free, 3655, *yāṣā'* [1]
set down, 3668, *yāṣaq* [1]
set on fire, 3675+836, *yāṣat+'ēš^{1}* [1]
set on fire, 3675, *yāṣat* [1]
set a trap, 3704, *yāqaš* [1]
set up, 3721, *yārâ^{1}* [1]
set up, 3782, *yāšab* [1]
be set, 3922, *kûn^{1}* [1]
set in order, 3922, *kûn^{1}* [1]
set on, 3922, *kûn^{1}* [1]
set up, 3922, *kûn^{1}* [1]
into another set, 4200+963, *l^{e}-^{1}+bad^{1}* [1]
into one set, 4200+963, *l^{e}-^{1}+bad^{1}* [1]
set afire, 4265, *lāhaṭ^{1}* [1]
set on fire, 4265, *lāhaṭ^{1}* [1]
set of scales, 4404+5486, *mō'znayim+mišqāl* [1]
set aside, 4426, *mibdālôt* [1]
set time, 4595+3427, *mô'ēd+yôm^{1}* [1]
time set, 4595, *mô'ēd* [1]
set apart, 4848+3338, *mālē'^{1}+yād* [1]
set a king, 4887+4889, *mālak^{1}+melek^{1}* [1]
set up kings, 4887, *mālak^{1}* [1]
place to set, 4955, *mānôaḥ^{1}* [1]
not set, 4979, *māna'* [1]
having set out, 5023, *massa'* [1]
set out, 5121, *ma'^{a}reket* [1]
set forth, 5602, *nāgaš* [1]
set, 5602, *nāgaš* [1]
be set, 5663, *nûaḥ^{1}* [1]
set down, 5663, *nûaḥ^{1}* [1]
set trembling, 5675, *nûa'* [1]
set, 5742, *nāṭâ* [1]
set in place, 5749, *nāṭa'* [1]
set out, 5749, *nāṭa'* [1]
set up, 5749, *nāṭa'* [1]
set out, 5750, *n^{e}ṭa'* [1]
set a trap, 5943, *nāqaš* [1]
set traps, 5943, *nāqaš* [1]
set yourselves, 5951, *nāśā'* [1]
set, 5998, *nātaq* [1]
set aside, 6073, *sûr^{1}* [1]
set yourself, 6147, *sālal^{1}* [1]
set free, 6296, *'ābar^{1}* [1]
set against, 6584, *'al^{2}* [1]
set out, 6885+6886, *'ārak+'ērek* [1]
set up, 6885, *'ārak* [1]
set value, 6885, *'ārak* [1]
price set, 6886, *'ērek* [1]
set, 6913, *'āśâ^{1}* [1]
be sure to set aside a tenth, 6923+6923, *'āśar+'āśar* [1]
set apart, 7111, *pālâ* [1]
set apart by themselves, 7233, *pārad* [1]
be set free, 7337, *pātaḥ^{1}* [1]
set free, 7337, *pātaḥ^{1}* [1]
set on fire, 7455, *ṣût* [1]
set, 7621, *ṣāpan* [1]
set apart as holy, 7727, *qādaš* [1]
set apart, 7731, *qōdeš* [1]
set to work, 7756, *qûm* [1]
was set up, 7756, *qûm* [1]
set out in pursuit, 8103, *rādap* [1]
as a special gift set aside, 8123, *rûm^{1}* [1]
set apart, 8123, *rûm^{1}* [1]
set high, 8123, *rûm^{1}* [1]
set up, 8123, *rûm^{1}* [1]
set free, 8143, *rāḥab* [1]
set in place, 8492, *śîm* [1]
was set, 8492, *śîm* [1]
set fire to, 8596+928+2021+836, *śārap+b^{e}+ha-+'ēš^{1}* [1]
set heart, 8751, *šāwâ^{2}* [1]
set, 8751, *šāwâ^{2}* [1]
set out, 8883, *šît^{1}* [1]
set fire to, 8938+928+2021+836, *šālaḥ+b^{e}+ha-+'ēš^{1}* [1]
set free, 8938+2930, *šālaḥ+ḥopšî* [1]
set free, 8938+4946+3338, *šālaḥ+min+yād* [1]
set down, 8959, *šālak* [1]
was set aside, 9068, *šāmar* [1]
set up camp, 9381, *taḥ^{a}nâ* [1]
set in order, 9545, *tāqan* [1]
set times, 10232, *z^{e}man^{2}* [1]
set, 10431, *m^{e}nâ* [1]
set to work, 10624+10221+10742, *qûm+w^{e}-+š^{e}râ* [1]
set, 10624, *qûm* [1]
set up, 10659, *rûm^{1}* [1]
were set in place, 10667, *r^{e}mâ* [1]

SETH [8]
Seth, 9269, *šēt^{2}* [8]

SETHUR [1]
Sethur, 6256, *s^{e}tûr* [1]

SETS [40]
sets, 2722, *ḥ^{a}lîpâ* [6]
sets, *AIT* [5]
sets, 995, *bô'* [2]
sets ablaze, 4265, *lāhaṭ^{1}* [2]
place where sets, 4427, *mābô'* [2]
sets up, 6590, *'ālâ* [2]
sets, 8492, *śîm* [2]
sets, 10624, *qûm* [2]
sets, *NIH/RPE* [1]
sets ablaze, 1277, *bā'ar^{1}* [1]
sets about work, 2520+5516, *ḥāgar+motnayim* [1]
sets, 3215, *ṭûr* [1]
sets, 3569, *yāsad^{1}* [1]
sets free, 3655, *yāṣā'* [1]
sets ablaze, 3675, *yāṣat* [1]
sets, 3782, *yāšab* [1]
sets, 3922, *kûn^{1}* [1]
sets free, 6002, *nātar^{3}* [1]
sets up, 6641, *'āmad* [1]
value sets, 6885, *'ārak* [1]
sets, 7193, *pa'am* [1]
sets, 7212, *pāqad* [1]
sets ablaze, 7706, *qādaḥ* [1]
sets up, 8492, *śîm* [1]
sets up, 10624, *qûm* [1]

SETTING [19]
setting, 5989, *nātan* [4]
setting, 995, *bô'* [3]
setting, 4427, *mābô'* [2]
setting, *NIH/RPE* [1]
setting the time, 4200+5503, *l^{e}-^{1}+mātay* [1]
setting out, 5023, *massa'* [1]
place of setting, 5115, *ma'^{a}rāb^{2}* [1]
setting out the consecrated bread, 5121, *ma'^{a}reket* [1]
setting free, 5303, *merḥāb* [1]
setting out, 5825, *nāsa'* [1]
setting aside a tenth, 6923+5130, *'āśar+ma'^{a}śēr* [1]
setting up, 7756, *qûm* [1]
setting, 8492, *śîm* [1]

SETTINGS [12]
settings, 5401, *mišb^{e}ṣôt* [3]
filigree settings, 5401, *mišb^{e}ṣôt* [2]
settings, 6015, *sābab* [2]
settings, 4853, *millu'â* [1]
settings, 4854, *millu'îm* [1]
settings, 4856+9513, *m^{e}lā'kâ+tōp^{2}* [1]
settings, 5381, *maśkît* [1]
filigree settings, 8687, *šābaṣ* [1]

SETTLE [39]
settle, 3782, *yāšab* [12]
settle, 1591, *gûr^{1}* [6]
settle down, 3782, *yāšab* [5]
where settle, 4632, *môšāb* [3]
settle, 5663, *nûaḥ^{1}* [3]
settle disputes, 3519, *yākaḥ* [2]
settle, 8905, *šākan* [2]
settle, *NIH/RPE* [1]
settle, 2837, *ḥānâ^{1}* [1]
settle in, 3782, *yāšab* [1]
settle on, 3782, *yāšab* [1]
let settle, 8905, *šākan* [1]

let settle, 9205, *šāqa'* [1]

SETTLED [67]
settled, 3782, *yāšab* [43]
settled, 8905, *šākan* [5]
settled, *NIH/RPE* [4]
settled, 1591, *gûr*[1] [2]
settled, 2118, *hāyâ* [2]
settled, 2837, *ḥānâ*[1] [1]
were settled in place, 3190, *ṭāba'* [1]
settled, 3718, *yārad* [1]
settled, 3983, *kālâ*[1] [1]
settled, 4632, *môšāb* [1]
settled down, 5663, *nûaḥ*[1] [1]
settled, 5697, *nāḥâ*[1] [1]
settled, 5877, *nāpal* [1]
settled in, 8905, *šākan* [1]
settled, 9462, *tāmam* [1]
settled, 10338, *yetib* [1]

SETTLEMENT [1]
settlement, 5659, *nāweh*[1] [1]

SETTLEMENTS [29]
surrounding settlements, 1426, *bat*[1] [10]
settlements, 1426, *bat*[1] [9]
settlements, 4632, *môšāb* [5]
settlements, 2557, *ḥawwâ*[1] [3]
settlements, 2958, *ḥāṣēr*[1] [2]

SETTLES [4]
settles, 1591, *gûr*[1] [1]
settles, 3782, *yāšab* [1]
settles, 5877, *nāpal* [1]
settles, 8697, *šābat*[1] [1]

SEVEN [299]
seven, 8679, *šeba'*[1] [286]
seven, 10696, *šeba'* [6]
seven, 8651, *šābûa'* [3]
seven, 8679+8679, *šeba'*[1]*+šeba'*[1] [2]
seven and a half feet, 2822+928+2021+564, *ḥāmēš+be+ha-+'ammâ*[1] [1]
seven, 8685, *šib'ānâ* [1]

SEVEN-DAY [2]
seven-day periods, 8679+2021+3427, *šeba'*[1]*+ha-+yôm*[1] [1]
seven-day, 8679+3427, *šeba'*[1]*+yôm*[1] [1]

SEVENFOLD [1]
sevenfold, 8679, *šeba'*[1] [1]

SEVENS [4]
sevens, 8651, *šābûa'* [4]

SEVENTEEN [8]
seventeen, 8679+6926, *šeba'*[1]*+'eśrēh* [5]
seventeen hundred, 547+2256+8679+4395, *'elep*[2]*+we-+šeba'*[1]*+mē'â*[1] [2]
seventeen, 8679+2256+6927, *šeba'*[1]*+we-+'aśārâ* [1]

SEVENTEENTH [6]
seventeenth, 8679+6925, *šeba'*[1]*+'āśār* [4]
seventeenth, 8679+6926, *šeba'*[1]*+'eśrēh* [2]

SEVENTH [106]
seventh, 8668, *šebî'î* [97]
seventh, 8679, *šeba'*[1] [9]

SEVENTY [57]
seventy, 8679, *šeba'*[1] [57]

SEVENTY-FIVE [5]
seventy-five feet, 2822+564, *ḥāmēš+'ammâ*[1] [2]
seventy-five, 2822+2256+8679, *ḥāmēš+we-+šeba'*[1] [2]
seventy-five, 8679+2256+2822, *šeba'*[1]*+we-+ḥāmēš* [1]

SEVENTY-SEVEN [3]
seventy-seven, 8679+2256+8679, *šeba'*[1]*+we-+šeba'*[1] [3]

SEVERAL [3]
several, *AIT* [3]

SEVERE [14]
severe, 2616, *ḥāzaq* [5]
severe, 3878, *kābēd*[2] [4]
severe, 2617, *ḥāzāq* [1]
severe, 3878+4394, *kābēd*[2]*+me'ōd* [1]
severe, 4200+5087+2025, *le-*[1]*+ma'al*[2]*+-â*[2] [1]
severe, 8041+4394, *rab*[1]*+me'ōd* [1]
severe, 8273, *ra'*[1] [1]

SEVERED [1]
is severed, 8178, *rāḥaq* [1]

SEVERELY [15]
severely, 3578, *yāsap* [12]
chastened severely, 3579+3579, *yāsar*[1]*+yāsar*[1] [1]
severely oppressing, 4316+4315, *laḥaṣ+lāḥaṣ* [1]
severely, 8041, *rab*[1] [1]

SEVERING [2]
severing completely, 976, *bādal* [2]

SEW [1]
sew, 9529, *tāpar* [1]

SEWED [2]
sewed together, 9529, *tāpar* [1]
sewed, 9529, *tāpar* [1]

SEX [2]
have sex with, 3359, *yāda'* [2]

SEXUAL [27]
have sexual relations with, 6872+1655, *'erwâ+gālâ* [10]
have sexual relations, 1655+6872, *gālâ+'erwâ* [3]
have sexual relations with, 8061, *rāba'*[1] [2]
has sexual relations with, 8886+6640, *šākab+'im* [2]
abstain from sexual relations, 440+5602+448+851, *'al*[1]*+nāgaš+'el+'iššâ* [1]
has sexual relations with, 1655+906+6872, *gālâ+'ēt*[1]*+'erwâ* [1]
have sexual relations with, 1655+6872, *gālâ+'erwâ* [1]
indulge in sexual immorality, 2388, *zānâ*[1] [1]
has sexual relations, 5989+8888, *nātan+šekōbet* [1]
have sexual relations, 5989+8888+4200+2446, *nātan+šekōbet+le-*[1]*+zera'* [1]
have sexual relations, 5989+8888, *nātan+šekōbet* [1]
dishonor by having sexual relations with, 6872+1655, *'erwâ+gālâ* [1]
dishonor by to have sexual relations, 6872+1655, *'erwâ+gālâ* [1]
have sexual relations, 8011+906+6872, *rā'â*[1]*+'ēt*[1]*+'erwâ* [1]

SHAALABBIN [1]
Shaalabbin, 9125, *ša'alabbîn* [1]

SHAALBIM [2]
Shaalbim, 9124, *ša'albîm* [2]

SHAALBONITE [2]
Shaalbonite, 9126, *ša'albōnî* [2]

SHAALIM [1]
Shaalim, 9127, *ša'alîm* [1]

SHAAPH [2]
Shaaph, 9131, *ša'ap* [2]

SHAARAIM [3]
Shaaraim, 9139, *ša'arayim* [3]

SHAASHGAZ [1]
Shaashgaz, 9140, *ša'ašgaz* [1]

SHABBETHAI [3]
Shabbethai, 8703, *šabbetay* [3]

SHACKLES [12]
bronze shackles, 5733, *neḥōšet*[1] [5]
shackles, 3890, *kebel* [2]
shackles, 6040, *sad* [2]
shackles, *AIT* [1]
shackles, 4591, *môsēr* [1]
shackles, 4593, *môsērâ*[1] [1]

SHADE [18]
shade, 7498, *ṣēl* [16]
shade, 6290, *'ābôt*[1] [1]
shade, 7973, *qāra'* [1]

SHADOW [34]
shadow, 7498, *ṣēl* [27]
deep shadow, 7516, *ṣalmāwet* [4]
shadow of death, 7516, *ṣalmāwet* [3]

SHADOWS [10]
shadows, 7498, *ṣēl* [4]
deep shadows, 7516, *ṣalmāwet* [2]
shadows, 694, *'ōpel* [1]
deep shadows, 696, *'apēlâ* [1]
evening shadows, 7498, *ṣēl* [1]
evening shadows fell, 7511, *ṣālal*[3] [1]

SHADRACH [14]
Shadrach, 10701, *šadrak* [13]
Shadrach, 8731, *šadrak* [1]

SHAFT [8]
shaft, 6770, *'ēṣ* [4]
shaft, 7866, *qāneh* [2]
shaft, 5707, *naḥal*[1] [1]
water shaft, 7562, *ṣinnôr* [1]

SHAGEE [1]
Shagee, 8707, *šāgēh* [1]

SHAGGY [1]
shaggy, 8537, *śā'îr*[1] [1]

SHAHARAIM [1]
Shaharaim, 8844, *šaḥarayim* [1]

SHAHAZUMAH [1]
Shahazumah, 8833, *šaḥaṣûmâ* [1]

SHAKE [26]
shake, 8321, *rā'aš*[1] [6]
shake, 5675, *nûa'* [5]
shake, 6907, *'āraṣ* [2]
shake, 4572, *môṭ*[1] [1]
shake, 4954, *mānôd* [1]
shake head in scorn, 5653, *nûd* [1]
shake heads in scorn, 5653, *nûd* [1]
shake, 5653, *nûd* [1]
shake, 5667, *nûṭ* [1]
shake, 5677, *nûp*[1] [1]
shake off, 5850, *nā'ar*[2] [1]
shake myself free, 5850, *nā'ar*[2] [1]
shake out, 5850, *nā'ar*[2] [1]
shake, 5850, *nā'ar*[2] [1]
made shake, 7064, *pāḥad* [1]
shake, 8074, *rāgaz* [1]

SHAKEN [22]
be shaken, 4572, *môṭ*[1] [8]
shaken, 5675, *nûa'* [3]
shaken, 4631, *mûš*[2] [2]
was shaken, 987, *bāhal* [1]
are shaken, 1723, *gā'aš* [1]
are shaken, 4572, *môṭ*[1] [1]
is thoroughly shaken, 4572+4572, *môṭ*[1]*+môṭ*[1] [1]
is shaken, 5675, *nûa'* [1]
am shaken off, 5850, *nā'ar*[2] [1]
shaken out, 5850, *nā'ar*[2] [1]
shaken, 8074, *rāgaz* [1]
shaken, 8321, *rā'aš*[1] [1]

SHAKES [6]
shakes, 2655, *ḥîl*[1] [2]
shakes, 8074, *rāgaz* [2]
shakes, 5677, *nûp*[1] [1]
shakes, 5742, *nāṭâ* [1]

SHAKING [1]
shaking, 5675, *nûa'* [1]

SHALISHA [1]
Shalisha, 8995, *šālišâ* [1]

SHALL [392]
shall, *AIT* [379]
shall, *NIH/RPE* [9]
shall be put to death, 4637+4637, *mût+mût* [4]

SHALLEKETH [1]
Shalleketh, 8962, *šalleket^{2}* [1]

SHALLUM [25]
Shallum, 8935, *šallûm* [25]

SHALLUM'S [1]
Shallum's, 8935, *šallûm* [1]

SHALLUN [1]
Shallun, 8937, *šallûn* [1]

SHALMAI [2]
Shalmai, 8978, *šalmay* [2]

SHALMAN [1]
Shalman, 8986, *šalman* [1]

SHALMANESER [3]
Shalmaneser, 8987, *šalman'eser* [2]
Shalmaneser^{s}, 4889+855, *melek^{1}+'aššûr* [1]

SHALMANESER'S [1]
Shalmaneser's^{s}, 4200+2257, *l^{e}-^{1}+-ô* [1]

SHAMA [1]
Shama, 9052, *šāmā'* [1]

SHAME [116]
put to shame, 1017, *bôš^{1}* [41]
shame, 1425, *bōšet* [20]
shame, 4009, *k^{e}limmâ* [9]
shame, 7830, *qālôn* [9]
shame, 1017, *bôš^{1}* [6]
shame, 1019, *bûšâ* [4]
shame, 3075, *ḥerpâ* [4]
have shame at all, 1017+1017, *bôš^{1}+bôš^{1}* [2]
shame, 4583, *mûm* [2]
shame, 6872, *'erwâ* [2]
shame, 873, *'ašmâ* [1]
bring shame, 944, *bā'aš* [1]
bear shame, 1017, *bôš^{1}* [1]
bring shame, 1017, *bôš^{1}* [1]
brings shame, 1017, *bôš^{1}* [1]
felt shame, 1017, *bôš^{1}* [1]
let be put to shame, 1017, *bôš^{1}* [1]
suffer shame, 1017, *bôš^{1}* [1]
utter shame, 1017+1425, *bôš^{1}+bōšet* [1]
shame, 1425+6872, *bōšet+'erwâ* [1]
shame, 2873, *ḥāsad^{1}* [1]
covered with shame, 2917, *ḥāpar^{2}* [1]
be put to shame, 4007, *kālam* [1]
blush with shame, 4007, *kālam* [1]
put to shame, 4007, *kālam* [1]
puts to shame, 4007, *kālam* [1]
shame, 4010, *k^{e}limmût* [1]

SHAMED [5]
shamed, 1017, *bôš^{1}* [4]
shamed, 4009, *k^{e}limmâ* [1]

SHAMEFUL [9]
shameful, 1017, *bôš^{1}* [1]
shameful gods, 1425, *bōšet* [1]
shameful god, 1425, *bōšet* [1]
shameful idol, 1425, *bōšet* [1]
shameful crimes, 2365, *zimmâ^{1}* [1]
shameful, 2365, *zimmâ^{1}* [1]
shameful treatment, 4007, *kālam* [1]
shameful, 4202+4083, *lō'+kāsap* [1]
shameful ways, 7830, *qālôn* [1]

SHAMEFULLY [1]
shamefully, 928+2365, *b^{e}-+zimmâ^{1}* [1]

SHAMELESS [1]
shameless, 2365, *zimmâ^{1}* [1]

SHAMELESSLY [1]
shamelessly, 4202+1017, *lō'+bôš^{1}* [1]

SHAMGAR [2]
Shamgar, 9011, *šamgar* [2]

SHAMHUTH [1]
Shamhuth, 9016, *šamhût* [1]

SHAMING [1]
shaming, 1425, *bōšet* [1]

SHAMIR [4]
Shamir, 9034, *šāmîr^{4}* [3]
Shamir, 9033, *šāmîr^{3}* [1]

SHAMMA [1]
Shamma, 9007, *šammā'* [1]

SHAMMAH [9]
Shammah, 9015, *šammâ^{2}* [7]
Shammah, *NIH/RPE* [1]
Shammah, 9007, *šammā'* [1]

SHAMMAI [5]
Shammai, 9025, *šammay* [5]

SHAMMAI'S [1]
Shammai's, 9025, *šammay* [1]

SHAMMOTH [1]
Shammoth, 9021, *šammôt* [1]

SHAMMUA [6]
Shammua, 9018, *šammûa'* [5]
Shammua, 9055, *šim'ā'* [1]

SHAMSHERAI [1]
Shamsherai, 9091, *šams^{e}ray* [1]

SHAPE [12]
shape of a calf, 6319, *'ēgel* [3]
shape, 5126, *ma'^{a}śeh* [2]
circular in shape, 6318+6017, *'āgōl+sābîb* [2]
shape, 7893, *qeṣeb* [2]
takes shape, 2200, *hāpak* [1]
shape, 6166, *semel* [1]
shape of calves, 6319, *'ēgel* [1]

SHAPED [5]
shaped like almond flowers, 5481, *m^{e}šuqqād* [4]
shaped, 6771, *'āṣab^{1}* [1]

SHAPES [4]
shapes, 3670, *yāṣar* [2]
shapes, 5126+3338, *ma'^{a}śeh+yād* [1]
shapes, 6913, *'āśâ^{1}* [1]

SHAPHAM [1]
Shapham, 9171, *šāpām* [1]

SHAPHAN [30]
Shaphan, 9177, *šāpān^{2}* [30]

SHAPHAT [8]
Shaphat, 9151, *šāpāṭ* [8]

SHAPHIR [1]
Shaphir, 9160, *šāpîr* [1]

SHAPING [2]
shaping, 6913, *'āśâ^{1}* [2]

SHARAI [1]
Sharai, 9232, *šāray* [1]

SHARAR [1]
Sharar, 9243, *šārār* [1]

SHARE [67]
share, 2750, *ḥēleq^{2}* [16]
share, 2976, *ḥōq* [11]
share, 2745, *ḥālaq^{2}* [3]
share, 4950, *mānâ^{2}* [3]
share, 5951+928, *nāśā'+b^{e}-* [3]
share, 2475, *ḥebel^{2}* [2]
share, *AIT* [1]
share, 296, *'āḥaz^{1}* [1]
share in, 430, *'ākal* [1]
share, 995, *bô'* [1]
share, 2118+4200, *hāyâ+l^{e}-^{1}* [1]
share with, 2490, *ḥeber^{1}* [1]
share, 2490, *ḥeber^{1}* [1]
get share of property, 2745, *ḥālaq^{2}* [1]
give a share, 2745, *ḥālaq^{2}* [1]
regular share, 2976, *ḥōq* [1]
share, 2978, *ḥuqqâ* [1]
share, 3512, *yāṭab* [1]
share in the inheritance, 3769, *yāraš^{1}* [1]
share, 3869+889+4200, *k^{e}-+'^{a}šer+l^{e}-^{1}* [1]
share, 4374, *lāqaḥ* [1]
half share, 4734, *maḥ^{a}ṣît* [1]
share, 4945, *mēn^{2}* [1]
larger share of, 4946, *min* [1]
share, 5477, *mišpāṭ* [1]
share in, 5951+6584, *nāśā'+'al^{2}* [1]
share, 5951, *nāśā'* [1]
share, 5989, *nātan* [1]
share, 6202, *sāpaḥ^{1}* [1]
share their duties, 6640+465, *'im+'ēlleh* [1]
share, 6843, *'ārab^{2}* [1]
share, 7023, *peh* [1]
share, 7271, *pāras^{1}* [1]
share joy, 8523+8525, *śāmaḥ+śimḥâ* [1]
share of plunder, 8965, *šālāl* [1]

SHARED [4]
shared, 430, *'ākal* [2]
shared with, 907, *'ēt^{2}* [1]
shared hardships, 6700+928+889+6700, *'ānâ^{2}+b^{e}-+'^{a}šer+'ānâ^{2}* [1]

SHARES [2]
shares, 3338, *yād* [1]
shares, 5989, *nātan* [1]

SHAREZER [3]
Sharezer, 8570, *śar'eṣer* [3]

SHARING [1]
sharing, 430+4946, *'ākal+min* [1]

SHARON [6]
Sharon, 9227, *šārôn* [6]

SHARONITE [1]
Sharonite, 9228, *šārônî* [1]

SHARP [10]
sharp, 9111, *šānan^{1}* [4]
sharp, 2521, *ḥad^{1}* [3]
sharp, 3023, *ḥārûṣ^{3}* [1]
sharp, 3872, *kā'ab* [1]
make sharp, 9111, *šānan^{1}* [1]

SHARPEN [4]
sharpen, 9111, *šānan^{1}* [2]
sharpen, 1406, *bārar^{2}* [1]
sharpen, 4323, *lāṭaš* [1]

SHARPENED [6]
sharpened, 2523, *ḥādad* [2]
sharpened, 4323, *lāṭaš* [2]
sharpened, 2521, *ḥad^{1}* [1]
is sharpened, 2523, *ḥādad* [1]

SHARPENING [2]
sharpening, *NIH/RPE* [1]
sharpening, 7201, *p^{e}ṣîrâ* [1]

SHARPENS [2]
sharpens, 2523, *ḥādad* [2]

SHARPLY [1]
sharply, 928+2622, *b^{e}-+ḥozqâ* [1]

SHARUHEN [1]
Sharuhen, 9226, *šārûḥen* [1]

SHASHAI [1]
Shashai, 9258, *šāšay* [1]

SHASHAK [2]
Shashak, 9265, *šāšāq* [2]

SHATTER [13]
shatter, 5879, *nāpaṣ^{1}* [9]
shatter, 3169, *ḥātat* [2]
shatter, 8720, *šādad* [1]
shatter, 9012, *šāmad* [1]

SHATTERED [24]
shattered, 3169, *ḥātat* [7]
shattered, 8689, *šābar*[1] [4]
be shattered, 3169, *ḥātat* [2]
shattered, 8320, *rāʿaṣ* [2]
shattered, *NIH/RPE* [1]
shattered, 4198, *kātat* [1]
shattered, 4730, *māḥaṣ* [1]
shattered, 5997, *nātaṣ* [1]
are shattered, 5998, *nātaq* [1]
shattered, 7297, *pārar*[2] [1]
are shattered, 8689, *šābar*[1] [1]
is shattered, 8689, *šābar*[1] [1]
shattered, 9518, *tᵉpûṣâ* [1]

SHATTERING [1]
shattering, 8689, *šābar*[1] [1]

SHATTERS [2]
shatters, 7915, *qāṣaṣ*[1] [1]
shatters, 8318, *rāʿaʿ*[2] [1]

SHAUL [9]
Shaul, 8620, *šāʾûl* [9]

SHAUL'S [1]
Shaul's[s], 2257, *-ô* [1]

SHAULITE [1]
Shaulite, 8621, *šāʾûlî* [1]

SHAVE [19]
shave off, 1662, *gālaḥ* [5]
shave, 1662, *gālaḥ* [5]
shave head in mourning, 995+7947, *bôʾ+qorḥâ* [1]
have shave, 6296+9509, *ʿābar*[1]*+taʿar* [1]
shave, 6296, *ʿābar*[1] [1]
shave, 6584+7947, *ʿal*[2]*+qorḥâ* [1]
shave heads, 7942+1605, *qāraḥ+gāzaz* [1]
must shave, 7942+7947, *qāraḥ+qorḥâ* [1]
shave heads, 7942+7947, *qāraḥ+qorḥâ* [1]
shave head, 7942, *qāraḥ* [1]
shave, 8492+7947, *śîm+qorḥâ* [1]

SHAVED [13]
shaved off, 1662, *gālaḥ* [3]
shaved, 7947, *qorḥâ* [3]
shaved, 1662, *gālaḥ* [2]
shaved, 1605, *gāzaz* [1]
be shaved, 1662, *gālaḥ* [1]
been shaved, 1662, *gālaḥ* [1]
were shaved, 1662, *gālaḥ* [1]
shaved, 8286, *rāʿâ*[1] [1]

SHAVEH [1]
Shaveh, 8753, *šāwēh* [1]

SHAVEH KIRIATHAIM [1]
Shaveh Kiriathaim, 8754, *šāwēh qiryātayim* [1]

SHAVSHA [1]
Shavsha, 8807, *šawšāʾ* [1]

SHAWL [1]
shawl, 4762, *miṭpaḥat* [1]

SHAWLS [1]
shawls, 8100, *rᵉdîd* [1]

SHE [815]
she, *AIT* [580]
she, 2085, *hûʾ* [82]
she, 2023, *-āh* [66]
she, *NIH/RPE* [38]
she[s], 2021+851, *ha-+ʾiššâ* [6]
she[s], 676, *ʾestēr* [4]
she, 2257, *-ô* [4]
she[s], 2021+5855, *ha-+naʿᵃrâ*[1] [3]
she, 4392, *-ām* [3]
she, 5626, *-nâ* [3]
she[s], 562+2257, *ʾēm+-ô* [2]
she, 2296, *zeh* [2]
she, 5883+2023, *nepeš+-āh* [2]
she[s], 374, *ʾîzebel* [1]
she, 465, *ʾēlleh* [1]
she[s], 851+2257, *ʾiššâ+-ô* [1]
she[s], 889, *ʾᵃšer* [1]
she[s], 1167, *bilhâ*[1] [1]
she[s], 1426+7281, *bat*[1]*+parʿōh* [1]
she[s], 2021, *ha-* [1]
she[s], 2021+4893, *ha-+malkâ* [1]
she[s], 2021+912, *ha-+ʾātôn* [1]
she[s], 2057, *hāgār* [1]
she, 2084, *-hû* [1]
she[s], 3304+2257, *yᵉbāmâ+-ô* [1]
she[s], 5319, *miryām* [1]
she[s], 5843, *noʿᵒmî* [1]
she[s], 5855, *naʿᵃrâ*[1] [1]
she[s], 7108+2257, *pilegeš+-ô* [1]
she[s], 8162, *rāḥēl*[2] [1]
she[s], 8577, *śārâ*[3] [1]
she[s], 8584, *śāray* [1]
she[s], 10423+10002, *malkâ+-āʾ* [1]

SHE'S [1]
she's, 2085, *hûʾ* [1]

SHE-CAMEL [1]
she-camel, 1149, *bikrâ* [1]

SHEAF [6]
sheaf, 6684, *ʿōmer*[1] [4]
sheaf, 524, *ʾᵃlummâ* [1]
sheaf of grain, 6684, *ʿōmer*[1] [1]

SHEAL [1]
Sheal, 8627, *šᵉʾāl* [1]

SHEALTIEL [10]
Shealtiel, 8630, *šᵉʾaltîʾēl* [6]
Shealtiel, 9003, *šaltîʾēl* [3]
Shealtiel, 10691, *šᵉʾaltîʾēl* [1]

SHEAR [3]
shear, 1605, *gāzaz* [3]

SHEAR-JASHUB [1]
Shear-Jashub, 8639, *šᵉʾār yāšûb* [1]

SHEARED [1]
be sheared off, 1548, *gādaʿ* [1]

SHEARERS [3]
shearers, 1605, *gāzaz* [3]

SHEARIAH [2]
Sheariah, 9138, *šᵉʿaryâ* [2]

SHEARING [4]
shearing, 1605, *gāzaz* [3]
wool from shearing, 1600, *gēz* [1]

SHEATH [3]
sheath, *NIH/RPE* [1]
sheath, 5620, *nādān*[1] [1]
sheath, 9509, *taʿar* [1]

SHEATHED [1]
are sheathed, 2902, *ḥāpâ* [1]

SHEAVES [9]
sheaves, 6684, *ʿōmer*[1] [3]
sheaves, 524, *ʾᵃlummâ* [2]
sheaves, 6658, *ʿāmîr* [2]
sheaves of grain, 524, *ʾᵃlummâ* [1]
sheaves, 1538, *gādîš*[1] [1]

SHEBA [34]
Sheba, 8644, *šᵉbāʾ* [22]
Sheba, 8680, *šebaʿ*[2] [9]
Sheba, *NIH/RPE* [1]
Sheba[s], 2257, *-ô* [1]
Sheba, 8681, *šebaʿ*[3] [1]

SHEBANIAH [6]
Shebaniah, 8676, *šᵉbanyâ* [5]
Shebaniah, 8677, *šᵉbanyāhû* [1]

SHEBAT [1]
Shebat, 8658, *šᵉbāṭ* [1]

SHEBER [1]
Sheber, 8693, *šeber*[3] [1]

SHEBNA [9]
Shebna, 8674, *šebnāʾ* [7]
Shebna, 8675, *šebnâ* [2]

SHECANIAH [10]
Shecaniah, 8908, *šᵉkanyâ* [8]
Shecaniah, 8909, *šᵉkanyāhû* [2]

SHECANIAH'S [1]
Shecaniah's, 8908, *šᵉkanyâ* [1]

SHECHEM [60]
Shechem, 8901, *šᵉkem*[2] [43]
Shechem, 8902, *šᵉkem*[3] [12]
Shechem, 8903, *šekem* [3]
Shechem, *NIH/RPE* [2]

SHECHEM'S [3]
Shechem's, 8902, *šᵉkem*[3] [3]

SHECHEMITE [1]
Shechemite, 8904, *šikmî* [1]

SHED [40]
shed, 9161, *šāpak* [25]
shed, *NIH/RPE* [6]
be shed, 9161, *šāpak* [2]
shed, *AIT* [1]
shed, 995, *bôʾ* [1]
blood shed, 1947, *dām* [1]
shed, 2118, *hāyâ* [1]
is shed, 2445, *zāraʿ* [1]
shed by, 4946+3338, *min+yād* [1]
been shed, 9161, *šāpak* [1]

SHEDDING [9]
shedding, 9161, *šāpak* [4]
guilt of shedding blood, 1947, *dām* [2]
shedding of blood, 1947, *dām* [1]
shedding, 8492, *śîm* [1]
shedding, 8959, *šālak* [1]

SHEDEUR [5]
Shedeur, 8725, *šᵉdêʾûr* [5]

SHEDS [2]
sheds, 9161, *šāpak* [2]

SHEEP [159]
sheep, 7366, *ṣōʾn* [97]
sheep, 8445, *śeh* [26]
sheep and goats, 7366, *ṣōʾn* [11]
sheep, 4166, *keśeb* [4]
sheep, *NIH/RPE* [3]
sheep, 3897, *kebeś* [3]
sheep, 8161, *rāḥēl*[1] [3]
choice sheep, 1374, *bārîʾ* [1]
mountain sheep, 2378, *zemer* [1]
sheep and goats, 5238+7366, *miqneh+ṣōʾn* [1]
raised sheep, 5924, *nōqēd* [1]
sheep, 6373, *ʿēder*[1] [1]
sheep, 6402, *ʿûl*[2] [1]
sheep goats or, 7366, *ṣōʾn* [1]
sheep or goats, 7366, *ṣōʾn* [1]
sheep, 7366+3897, *ṣōʾn+kebeś* [1]
sheep just shorn, 7892, *qāṣab* [1]
sheep, 8445+4166, *śeh+keśeb* [1]
tended sheep, 9068, *šāmar* [1]

SHEEP-SHEARING [1]
sheep-shearing time, 1605, *gāzaz* [1]

SHEEPSHEARERS [1]
sheepshearers, 1605, *gāzaz* [1]

SHEER [1]
sheer, 8370, *raq*[2] [1]

SHEERAH [1]
Sheerah, 8641, *šeʾĕrâ* [1]

SHEET [1]
sheet, 5012, *massēkâ*[2] [1]

SHEETS [2]
sheets, 7063, *paḥ*[2] [1]
thin sheets, 7063, *paḥ*[2] [1]

SHEHARIAH [1]
Shehariah, 8843, *š[e]ḥaryâ* [1]

SHEKEL [41]
shekel, 9203, *šeqel* [39]
shekel, *NIH/RPE* [1]
two thirds of a shekel, 7088, *pîm* [1]

SHEKELS [105]
shekels, *NIH/RPE* [58]
shekels, 9203, *šeqel* [45]
shekels, 4084, *kesep* [2]

SHELAH [18]
Shelah, 8941, *šelaḥ[3]* [9]
Shelah, 8925, *šēlâ[2]* [8]
of Shelah, 8989, *šēlānî* [1]

SHELANITE [1]
Shelanite, 8989, *šēlānî* [1]

SHELEMIAH [10]
Shelemiah, 8982, *šelemyâ* [5]
Shelemiah, 8983, *šelemyāhû* [5]

SHELEPH [2]
Sheleph, 8991, *šelep* [2]

SHELESH [1]
Shelesh, 8994, *šēleš* [1]

SHELOMI [1]
Shelomi, 8979, *š[e]lōmî* [1]

SHELOMITH [8]
Shelomith, 8984, *š[e]lōmît[1]* [6]
Shelomith, 8985, *š[e]lōmît[2]* [2]

SHELOMOTH [3]
Shelomoth, 8977, *š[e]lōmôt* [3]

SHELTER [24]
shelter, 6260, *sēter* [5]
shelter, 6109, *sukkâ* [3]
shelter, 1074, *bayit[1]* [2]
shelter, 3749, *y[e]rî'â* [2]
shelter, 4726, *maḥseh* [2]
shelter, 7498, *ṣēl* [2]
give shelter, 2118+6261, *hāyâ+sitrâ* [1]
shelter, 4675, *maḥ[a]bē'* [1]
place of shelter, 5144, *miplāṭ* [1]
shelter, 6114, *sākak[1]* [1]
bring to a place of shelter, 6395, *'ûz* [1]
find shelter, 8905, *šākan* [1]
shelter, 10163, *dûr* [1]
found shelter, 10300, *ṭ[e]lal* [1]

SHELTERED [1]
be sheltered, 6259, *sātar* [1]

SHELTERS [3]
shelters, 3749, *y[e]rî'â* [1]
shelters, 4953, *minhārâ* [1]
shelters, 6109, *sukkâ* [1]

SHELUMIEL [5]
Shelumiel, 8981, *š[e]lumî'ēl* [5]

SHEM [19]
Shem, 9006, *šēm[2]* [17]
Shem[s], 2085, *hû'* [1]
Shem[s], 4564, *-mô* [1]

SHEMA [6]
Shema, 9050, *šema'[2]* [5]
Shema, 9054, *š[e]ma'* [1]

SHEMAAH [1]
Shemaah, 9057, *š[e]mā'â* [1]

SHEMAIAH [39]
Shemaiah, 9061, *š[e]ma'yâ* [32]
Shemaiah, 9062, *š[e]ma'yāhû* [7]

SHEMAIAH'S [1]
Shemaiah's, 9061, *š[e]ma'yâ* [1]

SHEMARIAH [4]
Shemariah, 9079, *š[e]maryâ* [3]
Shemariah, 9080, *š[e]maryāhû* [1]

SHEMEBER [1]
Shemeber, 9008, *šem'ēber* [1]

SHEMED [1]
Shemed, 9013, *šemed* [1]

SHEMER [3]
Shemer, 9070, *šemer[2]* [3]

SHEMIDA [3]
Shemida, 9026, *š[e]mîdā'* [3]

SHEMIDAITE [1]
Shemidaite, 9027, *š[e]mîdā'î* [1]

SHEMINITH [3]
sheminith, 9030, *š[e]mînît* [3]

SHEMIRAMOTH [4]
Shemiramoth, 9035, *š[e]mîrāmôt* [4]

SHEMUEL [1]
Shemuel, 9017, *š[e]mû'ēl* [1]

SHEN [1]
Shen, 9095, *šēn[2]* [1]

SHENAZZAR [1]
Shenazzar, 9100, *šen'aṣṣar* [1]

SHEPHAM [2]
Shepham, 9172, *š[e]pām* [2]

SHEPHATIAH [13]
Shephatiah, 9152, *š[e]paṭyâ* [10]
Shephatiah, 9153, *š[e]paṭyāhû* [3]

SHEPHER [2]
Shepher, 9184, *šeper[2]* [2]

SHEPHERD [46]
shepherd, 8286, *rā'â[1]* [42]
shepherd, 1012, *bôqēr* [1]
shepherd, 7695, *qābaṣ* [1]
shepherd flock, 8286, *rā'â[1]* [1]
shepherd, 9068, *šāmar* [1]

SHEPHERD'S [3]
shepherd's, 8286, *rā'â[1]* [2]
shepherd's rod, 8657, *šēbeṭ* [1]

SHEPHERDED [1]
shepherded, 8286, *rā'â[1]* [1]

SHEPHERDESS [1]
shepherdess, 8286, *rā'â[1]* [1]

SHEPHERDS [43]
shepherds, 8286, *rā'â[1]* [37]
shepherds, 8286+7366, *rā'â[1]+ṣō'n* [3]
shepherds, *NIH/RPE* [1]
the shepherds[s], 2157, *-hem* [1]
shepherds, 5924, *nōqēd* [1]

SHEPHO [2]
Shepho, 9143, *š[e]pô* [2]

SHEPHUPHAN [1]
Shephuphan, 9146, *š[e]pûpān* [1]

SHEREBIAH [8]
Sherebiah, 9221, *šērēbyâ* [8]

SHEREBIAH'S [1]
Sherebiah's[s], 2257, *-ô* [1]

SHERESH [1]
Sheresh, 9246, *šereš* [1]

SHESHACH [2]
Sheshach, 9263, *šēšak* [2]

SHESHAI [3]
Sheshai, 9259, *šēšay* [3]

SHESHAN [4]
Sheshan, 9264, *šēšān* [4]

SHESHBAZZAR [4]
Sheshbazzar, 9256, *šēšbaṣṣar* [2]
Sheshbazzar, 10746, *šēšbaṣṣar* [2]

SHETH [1]
Sheth, 9269, *šēt[2]* [1]

SHETHAR [1]
Shethar, 9285, *šētār* [1]

SHETHAR-BOZENAI [4]
Shethar-Bozenai, 10750, *š[e]tar bôz[e]nay* [4]

SHEVA [2]
Sheva, 8737, *š[e]wā'* [2]

SHIBAH [1]
Shibah, 8683, *šib'â* [1]

SHIBBOLETH [1]
Shibboleth, 8672, *šibbōlet[1]* [1]

SHIELD [50]
shield, 4482, *māgēn[1]* [34]
shield, 7558, *ṣinnâ[2]* [9]
shield, 1713, *gānan* [4]
shield, 4059, *kāsâ* [1]
shield, 6114, *sākak[1]* [1]
protective shield, 6116, *sōkēk* [1]

SHIELDED [2]
shielded, 6015, *sābab* [1]
shielded, 6114, *sākak[1]* [1]

SHIELDING [3]
shielding, 5009, *māsāk* [3]

SHIELDS [43]
shields, 4482, *māgēn[1]* [17]
large [shields], 7558, *ṣinnâ[2]* [7]
small shields, 4482, *māgēn[1]* [6]
shields, 8949, *šeleṭ* [6]
shields, 7558, *ṣinnâ[2]* [3]
the shields[s], 4392, *-ām* [2]
shields, 2910, *ḥāpap* [1]
shields small, 4482, *māgēn[1]* [1]
shields, 5009, *māsāk* [1]
shields, 6114, *sākak[1]* [1]
shields, 6317, *'[a]gilâ* [1]
small shields, 8949, *šeleṭ* [1]

SHIFTLESS [1]
shiftless, 8244, *r[e]miyyâ[1]* [1]

SHIFTS [1]
shifts, 2722, *ḥ[a]lîpâ* [1]

SHIGGAION [1]
shiggaion, 8710, *šiggāyôn* [1]

SHIGIONOTH [1]
shigionoth, 8710, *šiggāyôn* [1]

SHIHOR [4]
Shihor, 8865, *šîḥôr* [4]

SHIHOR LIBNATH [1]
Shihor Libnath, 8866, *šîḥôr libnāt* [1]

SHIKKERON [1]
Shikkeron, 8914, *šikkārôn[2]* [1]

SHILHI [2]
Shilhi, 8944, *šilḥî* [2]

SHILHIM [1]
Shilhim, 8946, *šilḥîm* [1]

SHILLEM [3]
Shillem, 8973, *šillēm[2]* [3]

SHILLEMITE [1]
Shillemite, 8980, *šillēmî* [1]

SHILOAH [1]
Shiloah, 8942, *šilōaḥ* [1]

SHILOH [32]
Shiloh, 8926, *šilōh* [22]
Shiloh, 8931, *šilô* [6]

Shiloh, 8870, *šîlô* [3]
of Shiloh, 8872, *šîlōnî* [1]

SHILONITE [4]
Shilonite, 8872, *šîlōnî* [4]

SHILONITES [1]
Shilonites, 8872, *šîlōnî* [1]

SHILSHAH [1]
Shilshah, 8996, *šilšâ* [1]

SHIMEA [4]
Shimea, 9055, *šimʿāʾ* [4]

SHIMEAH [4]
Shimeah, 9056, *šimʿâ* [3]
Shimeah, 9009, *šimʾâ* [1]

SHIMEAM [1]
Shimeam, 9010, *šimʾām* [1]

SHIMEATH [2]
Shimeath, 9064, *šimʿāt* [2]

SHIMEATHITES [1]
Shimeathites, 9065, *šimʿātî* [1]

SHIMEI [44]
Shimei, 9059, *šimʿî*^{1} [42]
Shimei^{s}, 2257, *-ô* [1]
Shimei, 9060, *šimʿî*^{2} [1]

SHIMEI'S [1]
Shimei's, 4200+9059, *l*$^{e-1}$+*šimʿî*^{1} [1]

SHIMEITES [1]
Shimeites, 9060, *šimʿî*^{2} [1]

SHIMEON [1]
Shimeon, 9058, *šimʿôn* [1]

SHIMMERING [1]
shimmering, 7456, *ṣaḥ* [1]

SHIMON [1]
Shimon, 8873, *šîmôn* [1]

SHIMRATH [1]
Shimrath, 9086, *šimrāt* [1]

SHIMRI [4]
Shimri, 9078, *šimrî* [4]

SHIMRITH [1]
Shimrith, 9083, *šimrît* [1]

SHIMRON [5]
Shimron, 9075, *šimrôn*^{2} [3]
Shimron, 9074, *šimrôn*^{1} [2]

SHIMRON MERON [1]
Shimron Meron, 9077, *šimrôn m*^{e}*rʾôn* [1]

SHIMRONITE [1]
Shimronite, 9084, *šimrōnî* [1]

SHIMSHAI [4]
Shimshai, 9089, *šimšay* [4]

SHINAB [1]
Shinab, 9098, *šinʾāb* [1]

SHINAR [4]
Shinar, 824+9114, *ʾereṣ+šinʿār* [2]
Shinar, 9114, *šinʿār* [2]

SHINE [27]
make shine, 239, *ʾôr*^{1} [6]
shine, 239, *ʾôr*^{1} [6]
shine, 240, *ʾôr*^{2} [2]
no longer shine, 665+5586, *ʾāsap+nōgah*^{1} [2]
shine forth, 3649, *yāpaʿ* [2]
made light shine, 239, *ʾôr*^{1} [1]
shine, 2118+240, *hāyâ+ʾôr*^{2} [1]
shine, 2301, *zāhar*^{1} [1]
shine, 2436, *zāraḥ* [1]
shine, 3649, *yāpaʿ* [1]
make shine, 3655, *yāṣāʾ* [1]
shine, 5585, *nāgah* [1]
let shine, 5951, *nāśāʾ* [1]
make shine, 7413, *ṣāhal*^{2} [1]

SHINES [3]
shines forth, 3649, *yāpaʿ* [1]
shines out, 3655, *yāṣāʾ* [1]
shines brightly, 8523, *śāmaḥ* [1]

SHINING [6]
shining, 240, *ʾôr*^{2} [2]
shining ever brighter, 2143+2256+239, *hālak+w*^{e}*-+ʾôr*^{1} [1]
shining, 2436, *zāraḥ* [1]
shining splendor, 3650, *yipʿâ* [1]
shining, 3768, *y*^{e}*raqraq* [1]

SHION [1]
Shion, 8858, *šîʾōn* [1]

SHIP [6]
ship, 641, *ʾ*^{o}*niyyâ* [3]
ship, *NIH/RPE* [1]
trading ship, 641+9576, *ʾ*^{o}*niyyâ+taršîš*^{1} [1]
ship, 7469, *ṣî*^{1} [1]

SHIPHI [1]
Shiphi, 9181, *šipʿî* [1]

SHIPHMITE [1]
Shiphmite, 9175, *šipmî* [1]

SHIPHRAH [1]
Shiphrah, 9186, *šiprâ*^{2} [1]

SHIPHTAN [1]
Shiphtan, 9154, *šipṭān* [1]

SHIPS [27]
ships, 641, *ʾ*^{o}*niyyâ* [16]
ships, 639, *ʾ*^{o}*nî* [3]
ships, 7469, *ṣî*^{1} [3]
fleet of trading ships, 639+9576, *ʾ*^{o}*nî+taršîš*^{1} [1]
fleet of ships, 641, *ʾ*^{o}*niyyâ* [1]
fleet of trading ships, 641+2143+9576, *ʾ*^{o}*niyyâ+hālak+taršîš*^{1} [1]
fleet of trading ships, 641+4200+2143+9576, *ʾ*^{o}*niyyâ+l*$^{e-1}$*+hālak+taršîš*^{1} [1]
fleet of trading ships, 641+9576, *ʾ*^{o}*niyyâ+taršîš*^{1} [1]

SHIPWRECK [1]
shipwreck, 5147, *mappelet* [1]

SHIPWRIGHTS [2]
shipwrights, *NIH/RPE* [1]
shipwrights, 2616+981, *ḥāzaq+bedeq* [1]

SHISHA [1]
Shisha, 8881, *šîšāʾ* [1]

SHISHAK [7]
Shishak, 8882, *šîšaq* [7]

SHITRAI [1]
Shitrai, 8855, *šiṭray* [1]

SHITTIM [4]
Shittim, 8850, *šiṭṭîm* [4]

SHIZA [1]
Shiza, 8862, *šîzāʾ* [1]

SHOA [1]
Shoa, 8778, *šôaʿ*^{2} [1]

SHOBAB [4]
Shobab, 8744, *šôbāb*^{2} [4]

SHOBACH [2]
Shobach, 8747, *šôbak* [2]

SHOBAI [2]
Shobai, 8662, *šōbay* [2]

SHOBAL [9]
Shobal, 8748, *šôbāl* [9]

SHOBEK [1]
Shobek, 8749, *šôbēq* [1]

SHOBI [1]
Shobi, 8661, *šōbî* [1]

SHOCKED [1]
were shocked, 4007, *kālam* [1]

SHOCKING [1]
shocking thing, 9136, *šaʿ*^{a}*rûr* [1]

SHOCKS [2]
shocks of grain, 1538, *gādîš*^{1} [1]
shocks, 1538, *gādîš*^{1} [1]

SHOHAM [1]
Shoham, 8733, *šōham*^{2} [1]

SHOMER [3]
Shomer, 9071, *šōmēr* [3]

SHONE [2]
shone, 2145, *hālal*^{1} [1]
shone forth, 3649, *yāpaʿ* [1]

SHOOK [11]
shook, 8074, *rāgaz* [4]
shook, 8321, *rāʿaš*^{1} [2]
shook, 1324, *bāqaʿ* [1]
shook, 2101, *hûm* [1]
shook, 4571, *môd* [1]
shook, 5675, *nûaʿ* [1]
shook out, 5850, *nāʿar*^{2} [1]

SHOOT [23]
shoot, 3721, *yārâ*^{1} [10]
shoot, 8938, *šālaḥ* [3]
shoot, 928+2021+8008, *b*^{e}*-+ha-+qešet* [1]
make ready to shoot, 2005, *dārak* [1]
shoot, 2643, *ḥōṭer* [1]
shoot, 3343, *yādâ*^{1} [1]
tender shoot, 3437, *yônēq* [1]
shoot, 3566, *y*^{e}*nîqâ* [1]
shoot arrows, 3721, *yārâ*^{1} [1]
shoot out, 4880, *mālaṭ*^{1} [1]
shoot, 5916, *nēṣer* [1]
shoot, 7550, *ṣammeret* [1]

SHOOTING [2]
shooting, 3721, *yārâ*^{1} [1]
shooting, 8938, *šālaḥ* [1]

SHOOTS [12]
shoots, 3438, *yôneqet* [4]
tender shoots, 3764, *yereq* [2]
shoots, 2360, *zalzal* [1]
new shoots, 3438, *yôneqet* [1]
young shoots, 3438, *yôneqet* [1]
shoots, 7908, *qāṣîr*^{2} [1]
shoots, 8943, *š*^{e}*luḥôt* [1]
shoots, 9277, *šātîl* [1]

SHOPHACH [2]
Shophach, 8791, *šôpak* [2]

SHORE [5]
shore, 362, *ʾî*^{1} [1]
shore, 824, *ʾereṣ* [1]
the shore^{s}, 2257, *-ô* [1]
shore, 8557+3542, *śāpâ+yām* [1]
shore, 8557, *śāpâ* [1]

SHORELANDS [1]
shorelands, 4494, *migrāš* [1]

SHORES [4]
distant shores, 362+3542, *ʾî*^{1}*+yām* [1]
distant shores, 362, *ʾî*^{1} [1]
shores, 362, *ʾî*^{1} [1]
shores, 3338, *yād* [1]

SHORN [1]
sheep just shorn, 7892, *qāṣab* [1]

SHORT [15]
cut short, 7918, *qāṣar*^{2} [3]
short distance, 5071, *meʿaṭ* [2]
short, 7918, *qāṣar*^{2} [2]
cut short, 1548, *gādaʿ* [1]
are cut short, 2403, *zāʿak* [1]

short, 2894, *ḥāsēr*[2] [1]
short, 5071, *mᵉʿaṭ* [1]
in a very short time, 6388+5071+4663, *ʿôd+mᵉʿaṭ+mizʿār* [1]
short, 7918+7918, *qāṣar*[2]*+qāṣar*[2] [1]
too short, 7918, *qāṣar*[2] [1]
short, 8137, *rāzôn*[1] [1]

SHORTCOMINGS [1]
shortcomings, 2628, *ḥēṭʾ* [1]

SHORTER [1]
shorter, 7940, *qārôb* [1]

SHORTLY [1]
shortly after, 339, *ʾaḥar* [1]

SHOT [9]
shot, 3721, *yārâ*[1] [3]
shot, 8938, *šālaḥ* [2]
shot arrows, 3721, *yārâ*[1] [1]
shot with arrows, 3721+3721, *yārâ*[1]*+yārâ*[1] [1]
shot, 5782, *nākâ* [1]
shot, 8046, *rābab*[2] [1]

SHOULD [216]
should, *AIT* [206]
should, *NIH/RPE* [7]
determined should die, 3051, *ḥērem*[1] [1]
in the way should go, 6584+7023+2006, *ʿal*[2]*+peh+derek* [1]
should go up, 6590+6590, *ʿālâ+ʿālâ* [1]

SHOULDER [25]
shoulder pieces, 4190, *kātēp* [8]
shoulder, 8900, *šᵉkem*[1] [7]
shoulder, 4190, *kātēp* [5]
shoulder, 2432, *zᵉrôaʿ* [2]
shoulder to shoulder, 8900+285, *šᵉkem*[1]*+ʾeḥād* [2]
shoulder, *NIH/RPE* [1]

SHOULDERS [22]
shoulders, 4190, *kātēp* [10]
shoulders, 8900, *šᵉkem*[1] [9]
shoulders, *NIH/RPE* [1]
shoulders, 2432, *zᵉrôaʿ* [1]
shoulders, 7418, *ṣawwāʾr* [1]

SHOULDN'T [2]
shouldn't, 4202, *lōʾ* [2]

SHOUT [59]
shout for joy, 8264, *rānan* [11]
shout, 8131, *rûaʿ* [8]
shout aloud, 8131, *rûaʿ* [4]
shout for joy, 8131, *rûaʿ* [4]
shout, 606, *ʾāmar*[1] [2]
shout, 7754, *qôl* [2]
gave a shout, 8131+9558, *rûaʿ+tᵉrûʿâ* [2]
shout in triumph, 8131, *rûaʿ* [2]
shout, 2116, *hêdād* [1]
shout, 3946, *kōaḥ*[1] [1]
shout with laughter, 6600, *ʿālaz* [1]
shout, 6699, *ʿānâ*[1] [1]
shout in triumph, 6702+2116, *ʿānâ*[4]*+hêdād* [1]
shout aloud, 7412, *ṣāhal*[1] [1]
shout for joy, 7412, *ṣāhal*[1] [1]
shout, 7412, *ṣāhal*[1] [1]
shout, 7423, *ṣāwaḥ* [1]
shout, 7590, *ṣāʿaq* [1]
shout aloud, 7924+928+1744, *qārāʾ*[1]*+bᵉ+gārôn* [1]
shout, 7924+928+7754, *qārāʾ*[1]*+bᵉ+qôl* [1]
shout, 7924+7754+1524, *qārāʾ*[1]*+qôl+gādôl* [1]
shout, 7924, *qārāʾ*[1] [1]
shout, 8123+7754, *rûm*[1]*+qôl* [1]
shout with joy, 8131, *rûaʿ* [1]
give a shout, 8131+9558, *rûaʿ+tᵉrûʿâ* [1]
raised a shout, 8131+9558, *rûaʿ+tᵉrûʿâ* [1]
shout, 8264, *rānan* [1]
shout of joy, 8265, *rᵉnānâ* [1]
shout, 8308, *raʿam* [1]
shout for joy, 9558, *tᵉrûʿâ* [1]
shout, 9558, *tᵉrûʿâ* [1]
shout, 9583, *tᵉšuʾâ* [1]

SHOUTED [27]
shouted, 606, *ʾāmar*[1] [9]
shouted, 7924, *qārāʾ*[1] [6]
shouted, 8131, *rûaʿ* [3]
shouted, 928+9558+8123+7754, *bᵉ+tᵉrûʿâ+rûm*[1]*+qôl* [1]
shouted, 1819, *dābar*[2] [1]
shouted, 5951+7754+2256+7924, *nāśāʾ+qôl+wᵉ+qārāʾ*[1] [1]
shouted, 6699, *ʿānâ*[1] [1]
shouted the news, 7924, *qārāʾ*[1] [1]
shouted, 7924+928+7754, *qārāʾ*[1]*+bᵉ+qôl* [1]
shouted for joy, 8131, *rûaʿ* [1]
shouted for joy, 8264, *rānan* [1]
shouted, 10558, *ʿᵃnâ* [1]

SHOUTING [9]
shouting, 606, *ʾāmar*[1] [2]
shouting, 8131, *rûaʿ* [2]
shouting, 2116, *hêdād* [1]
shouting, 7658, *ṣāraḥ* [1]
shouting, 7754+9558, *qôl+tᵉrûʿâ* [1]
shouting, 8275, *rēaʿ*[1] [1]
shouting, 9558, *tᵉrûʿâ* [1]

SHOUTS [20]
shouts of joy, 2116, *hêdād* [3]
shouts of joy, 8262, *rinnâ*[1] [3]
shouts of joy, 9558, *tᵉrûʿâ* [3]
shouts, 9558, *tᵉrûʿâ* [3]
shouts of joy, 7754+8262, *qôl+rinnâ*[1] [2]
shouts, 2116, *hêdād* [1]
shouts, 2411, *zᵉʿāqâ* [1]
shouts, 7754, *qôl* [1]
shouts, 8131, *rûaʿ* [1]
shouts for joy, 9558, *tᵉrûʿâ* [1]
shouts, 9583, *tᵉšuʾâ* [1]

SHOVE [1]
shove, 2074, *hādap* [1]

SHOVEL [1]
shovel, 4665, *mizreh* [1]

SHOVELS [9]
shovels, 3582, *yāʿ* [9]

SHOVES [2]
shoves, 2074, *hādap* [2]

SHOW [133]
show, 8011, *rāʾâ*[1] [23]
show, 6913, *ʿāśâ*[1] [21]
show, 3359, *yādaʿ* [7]
show myself holy, 7727, *qādaš* [7]
show, 5989, *nātan* [5]
show pity, 2571+6524, *ḥûs+ʿayin*[1] [4]
show partiality, 5795+7156, *nākar*[1]*+pāneh* [4]
show love, 8163, *rāḥam* [4]
show, *NIH/RPE* [3]
show, 5583, *nāgad* [3]
show compassion, 8163, *rāḥam* [3]
show regard, 1067, *bîn* [2]
show yourself pure, 1405, *bārar*[1] [2]
show mercy, 2571, *ḥûs* [2]
show mercy, 2858, *ḥānan*[1] [2]
show yourself faithful, 2874, *ḥāsad*[2] [2]
show partiality, 5951+7156, *nāśāʾ+pāneh* [2]
show partiality, 7156+5951, *pāneh+nāśāʾ* [2]
show mercy, 8163, *rāḥam* [2]
show yourself blameless, 9462, *tāmam* [2]
show love, 170, *ʾāhab* [1]
show, 907, *ʾēt*[2] [1]
show contempt, 1022, *bāzâ* [1]
show favor, 1067, *bîn* [1]
show, 1067, *bîn* [1]
show greatness, 1540, *gādal* [1]
show favoritism, 2075, *hādar* [1]
show respect, 2075, *hādar* [1]
show, 2118+4200, *hāyâ+lᵉ*-[1] [1]
show, 2145, *hālal*[1] [1]
show restraint, 2532, *ḥādal*[1] [1]
show, 2555, *ḥāwâ*[1] [1]
show mercy, 2798, *ḥāmal* [1]
show favor, 2858, *ḥānan*[1] [1]
show how to distinguish, 3359, *yādaʿ* [1]
show kindness, 3512, *yāṭab* [1]
show, 4200+7156, *lᵉ*-[1]*+pāneh* [1]
made show utter contempt, 5540+5540, *nāʾaṣ+nāʾaṣ* [1]
show sympathy, 5653, *nûd* [1]
show compassion, 5714, *nāḥam* [1]
show strength, 6451, *ʿāzaz* [1]
show, 6524, *ʿayin*[1] [1]
surely show, 6913+6913, *ʿāśâ*[1]*+ʿāśâ*[1] [1]
show wonder, 7098, *pālāʾ* [1]
show yourself shrewd, 7349, *pātal* [1]
show himself holy, 7727, *qādaš* [1]
show holiness, 7727, *qādaš* [1]
show himself, 8011, *rāʾâ*[1] [1]
show ill will, 8317+6524, *rāʿaʿ*[1]*+ʿayin*[1] [1]
show favor, 8354, *rāṣâ*[1] [1]
show yourself shrewd, 9520, *tāpal* [1]

SHOWED [43]
showed, 8011, *rāʾâ*[1] [17]
showed, 6913, *ʿāśâ*[1] [5]
showed, *NIH/RPE* [1]
showed love, 170, *ʾāhab* [1]
showed themselves, 1655, *gālâ* [1]
showed, 2180, *hinnēh* [1]
showed fear, 2316, *zûaʿ* [1]
showed strength, 2616, *ḥāzaq* [1]
showed, 3359, *yādaʿ* [1]
showed, 3723, *yārâ*[3] [1]
unfaithfulness showed, 5086+5085, *maʿal*[1]*+māʿal* [1]
showed, 5583, *nāgad* [1]
showed pity, 5714, *nāḥam* [1]
showed, 5742, *nāṭâ* [1]
showed fear, 7064, *pāḥad* [1]
showed wonderful, 7098, *pālāʾ* [1]
showed concern for, 7155+448, *pānâ+ʾel* [1]
showed partiality, 7156+5951, *pāneh+nāśāʾ* [1]
showed himself holy, 7727, *qādaš* [1]
showed favor, 8354, *rāṣâ*[1] [1]
showed, 8492, *śîm* [1]
showed understanding, 8505+8507, *śākal*[1]*+śekel* [1]
showed, 10313, *yᵉdaʿ* [1]

SHOWER [2]
shower, 1773, *gešem*[1] [1]
shower down, 5688, *nāzal* [1]

SHOWERING [1]
showering, 6759, *ʿāpar* [1]

SHOWERS [15]
showers, 8053, *rᵉbîbîm* [5]
showers, 1773, *gešem*[1] [3]
showers, 4764, *māṭār* [2]
showers, 1772, *gāšam* [1]
abundant showers, 1773, *gešem*[1] [1]
showers, 3722, *yārâ*[2] [1]
showers fall, 8319, *rāʿap* [1]
showers, 8540, *śāʿîr*[4] [1]

SHOWING [7]
showing, 6913, *ʿāśâ*[1] [3]
showing pity, 2571+6524, *ḥûs+ʿayin*[1] [1]
stopped showing, 6440, *ʿāzab*[1] [1]
showing, 8011, *rāʾâ*[1] [1]
showing aptitude, 8505, *śākal*[1] [1]

SHOWN [43]
shown, 8011, *rāʾâ*[1] [12]
shown, 6913, *ʿāśâ*[1] [9]
shown, *NIH/RPE* [2]
be shown, 8011, *rāʾâ*[1] [2]
shown, 10313, *yᵉdaʿ* [2]
shown, *AIT* [1]
shown contempt, 1022, *bāzâ* [1]
been shown, 1655, *gālâ* [1]
fury shown, 2404, *zaʿam* [1]
grace is shown, 2858, *ḥānan*[1] [1]
shown himself, 3359, *yādaʿ* [1]
shown, 3359, *yādaʿ* [1]
shown reverence, 3707, *yārēʾ*[1] [1]
shown, 4848, *mālēʾ*[1] [1]
been shown, 5583, *nāgad* [1]
shown, 5583, *nāgad* [1]

shown, 5742, *nāṭâ* [1]
shown partiality, 5951+7156, *nāśāʾ+pāneh* [1]
are shown respect, 7156+2075, *pāneh+hādar* [1]
shown honor, 7156+5951, *pāneh+nāśāʾ* [1]
were shown, 8011, *rāʾâ*^{1} [1]

SHOWS [15]
shows, 6913, *ʿāśâ*^{1} [3]
shows contempt, 3070, *ḥārap*^{2} [2]
shows partiality, 5951+7156, *nāśāʾ+pāneh* [2]
shows, *NIH/RPE* [1]
shows, 606, *ʾāmar*^{1} [1]
shows to be, 2118+4200, *hāyâ+lᵉ-*^{1} [1]
shows favor, 2858, *ḥānan*^{1} [1]
shows mercy, 2858, *ḥānan*^{1} [1]
shows, 3359, *yādaʿ* [1]
shows no, 6073, *sûr*^{1} [1]
shows prudence, 6891, *ʿāram*^{2} [1]

SHREWD [3]
show yourself shrewd, 7349, *pātal* [2]
shrewd, 2682, *ḥākām* [1]

SHREWDLY [1]
deal shrewdly, 2681, *ḥākam* [1]

SHRINE [16]
shrine prostitutes, 7728, *qādēš*^{1} [5]
shrine prostitute, 7728, *qādēš*^{1} [4]
shrine, 1074+466, *bayit*^{1}*+ʾᵉlōhîm* [1]
shrine, 1074, *bayit*^{1} [1]
shrine, 2540, *ḥeder* [1]
shrine, 5219, *miqdāš* [1]
shrine, 6109, *sukkâ* [1]
inner shrine, 6551, *ʿîr*^{1} [1]
lofty shrine, 8229, *rāmâ*^{3} [1]

SHRINES [14]
shrines, 1074, *bayit*^{1} [5]
mountain shrines, 2215, *har* [4]
lofty shrines, 8229, *rāmâ*^{3} [3]
shrines, 1195, *bāmâ*^{1} [1]
prostitutes of the shrines, 7728, *qādēš*^{1} [1]

SHRIVEL [2]
made shrivel, 3312, *yābēš*^{1} [1]
shrivel up, 5570, *nābēl*^{1} [1]

SHRIVELED [4]
shriveled up, 3312, *yābēš*^{1} [1]
shriveled, 5570, *nābēl*^{1} [1]
shriveled, 6308, *ʿābaš* [1]
shriveled, 7594, *ṣāpad* [1]

SHROUD [2]
shroud, 2502, *ḥābaš* [1]
shroud, 4287, *lôṭ*^{1} [1]

SHROUDED [2]
is shrouded, 4059, *kāsâ* [1]
shrouded, 8492, *śîm* [1]

SHRUB [1]
shrub, 3972+8489, *kōl+śîaḥ*^{2} [1]

SHUA [4]
Shua, 8781, *šûaʿ*^{2} [3]
Shua, 8783, *šûʿāʾ* [1]

SHUAH [2]
Shuah, 8756, *šûaḥ*^{2} [2]

SHUAL [2]
Shual, 8786, *šûʿāl*^{2} [1]
Shual, 8787, *šûʿāl*^{3} [1]

SHUBAEL [6]
Shubael, 8742, *šûbāʾēl* [6]

SHUDDER [6]
shudder, 8547, *śāʿar*^{1} [3]
shudder, 3006, *ḥārad* [1]
shudder, 8074, *rāgaz* [1]
shudder, 8077, *rogzâ* [1]

SHUHAH'S [1]
Shuhah's, 8758, *šûḥâ*^{2} [1]

SHUHAM [1]
Shuham, 8761, *šûḥām* [1]

SHUHAMITE [2]
Shuhamite, 8762, *šûḥāmî* [2]

SHUHITE [5]
Shuhite, 8760, *šûḥî* [5]

SHULAMMITE [2]
Shulammite, 8769, *šûlammît* [2]

SHUMATHITES [1]
Shumathites, 9092, *šumātî* [1]

SHUN [2]
shun, 6073, *sûr*^{1} [2]

SHUNAMMITE [8]
Shunammite, 8774, *šûnammî* [8]

SHUNEM [3]
Shunem, 8773, *šûnēm* [3]

SHUNI [2]
Shuni, 8771, *šûnî*^{1} [2]

SHUNITE [1]
Shunite, 8772, *šûnî*^{2} [1]

SHUNNED [3]
shunned, 6073, *sûr*^{1} [1]
are shunned, 8533, *śānēʾ* [1]
shunned, 8533, *śānēʾ* [1]

SHUNS [4]
shuns, 6073, *sûr*^{1} [4]

SHUPHAM [1]
Shupham, 8792, *šûpām* [1]

SHUPHAMITE [1]
Shuphamite, 8793, *šûpāmî* [1]

SHUPPIM [1]
Shuppim, 9157, *šuppîm*^{1} [1]

SHUPPITES [2]
Shuppites, 9158, *šuppîm*^{2} [2]

SHUR [6]
Shur, 8804, *šûr*^{4} [6]

SHUT [44]
shut, 6037, *sāgar* [21]
be shut, 6037, *sāgar* [4]
shut up, 6806, *ʿāṣar* [4]
be shut up, 6037, *sāgar* [2]
shut, 7890, *qāpaṣ* [2]
shut, 1589, *gûp* [1]
shut in, 3159, *ḥātam* [1]
hold shut, 4315, *lāḥaṣ* [1]
shut yourself, 6037, *sāgar* [1]
tightly shut up, 6037+2256+6037, *sāgar+wᵉ-+sāgar* [1]
shut up, 6114, *sākak*^{1} [1]
make shut, 6623, *ʿālam* [1]
shut, 6623, *ʿālam* [1]
shut, 6806, *ʿāṣar* [1]
was shut in, 6806, *ʿāṣar* [1]
shut, 10506, *sᵉgar* [1]

SHUTHELAH [4]
Shuthelah, 8811, *šûtelaḥ* [4]

SHUTHELAHITE [1]
Shuthelahite, 9279, *šutalḥî* [1]

SHUTS [5]
shuts, 357, *ʾāṭam* [1]
shuts, 6037, *sāgar* [1]
shuts, 6794, *ʿāṣam*^{2} [1]
shuts, 7890, *qāpaṣ* [1]
shuts out, 8608, *šātam* [1]

SHUTTLE [1]
weaver's shuttle, 756, *ʾereg* [1]

SHY [1]
shy away, 8740, *šûb*^{1} [1]

SIA [1]
Sia, 6103, *sîʿāʾ* [1]

SIAHA [1]
Siaha, 6104, *sîʿᵃhāʾ* [1]

SIBBECAI [4]
Sibbecai, 6021, *sibbᵉkay* [4]

SIBBOLETH [1]
Sibboleth, 6027, *sibbōlet* [1]

SIBMAH [5]
Sibmah, 8424, *śibmâ* [5]

SIBRAIM [1]
Sibraim, 6028, *sibrayim* [1]

SICK [4]
sick, 108, *ʾāgēm* [1]
makes sick, 2703, *ḥālâ*^{1} [1]
sick, 2703, *ḥālâ*^{1} [1]
sick, 5823, *nāsas*^{1} [1]

SICKBED [1]
sickbed, 6911+1867, *ʿereś+dᵉway* [1]

SICKLE [4]
sickle, 3058, *ḥermēš* [2]
sickle, 4478, *maggāl* [2]

SICKLES [1]
sickles, 3058, *ḥermēš* [1]

SICKNESS [6]
sickness, 2716, *ḥᵒlî* [4]
sickness, 4700, *maḥᵃleh* [1]
sickness, 4701, *maḥᵃlâ* [1]

SIDDIM [3]
Siddim, 8443, *śiddîm* [3]

SIDE [259]
side, 6991, *pēʾâ*^{1} [33]
side, *AIT* [27]
side, 4190, *kātēp* [18]
on every side, 4946+6017, *min+sābîb* [16]
side, 7396, *ṣad*^{1} [14]
side, *NIH/RPE* [10]
on each side, 4946+7024+2256+4946+7024, *min+pōh+wᵉ-+min+pōh* [10]
side, 7521, *ṣēlāʿ*^{1} [10]
side, 3751, *yārēk* [9]
on every side, 6017, *sābîb* [9]
side, 6298, *ʿēber*^{1} [9]
side rooms, 7521, *ṣēlāʿ*^{1} [9]
other side, 6298, *ʿēber*^{1} [6]
side, 3338, *yād* [5]
on side, 4200, *lᵉ-*^{1} [5]
side, 725, *ʾēṣel*^{1} [4]
side, 2006, *derek* [4]
side^{s}, 2296, *zeh* [4]
on either side, 4946+7024+2256+4946+7024, *min+pōh+wᵉ-+min+pōh* [4]
side, 5516, *motnayim* [4]
every side, 6017, *sābîb* [4]
side, 8120, *rûaḥ* [4]
at side, 725, *ʾēṣel*^{1} [2]
side by side, 3480, *yaḥad* [2]
side rooms, 4384, *liškâ* [2]
from every side, 4946+6017, *min+sābîb* [2]
side panels, 4995, *misgeret* [2]
side, 7024, *pōh* [2]
side, 7815, *qîr*^{1} [2]
far side, 339, *ʾaḥar* [1]
far side, 344, *ʾaḥᵃrît* [1]
on the side of, 448, *ʾel* [1]
on side, 907, *ʾēt*^{2} [1]
on each side, 928, *bᵉ-* [1]
on side, 928, *bᵉ-* [1]
cousins on their father's side, 1201+1856, *bēn*^{1}*+dôd* [1]
on this side, 2178, *hēnnâ*^{1} [1]
your side^{s}, 2257, *-ô* [1]

closing in from every side, 2539, *ḥādar* [1]
side rooms, 3666, *yāṣîaʿ* [1]
on each side,
4946+2021+6298+4946+2296+4946+2021+6298+4946+2296,
min+ha-+ʿēber[1]*+min+zeh+min+ha-+ʿēber*[1]*+min+zeh* [1]
bordering each side[s],
4946+2296+2256+4946+2296,
min+zeh+w^{e}-+min+zeh [1]
on each side[s], 4946+2296+2256+4946+2296, *min+zeh+w^{e}-+min+zeh* [1]
on the other side of, 4946+6298+2256+2134, *min+ʿēber*[1]*+w^{e}-+hāl^{e}ʾâ* [1]
on this side of, 4946+6298, *min+ʿēber*[1] [1]
side, 4946+6298, *min+ʿēber*[1] [1]
put to one side, 5825, *nāsaʿ* [1]
on every side, 6015, *sābab* [1]
came to the other side, 6296, *ʿābar*[1] [1]
east side, 6298, *ʿēber*[1] [1]
this side, 6298, *ʿēber*[1] [1]
against side, 6584, *ʿal*[2] [1]
at side, 6584, *ʿal*[2] [1]
on side, 6584, *ʿal*[2] [1]
side room, 7521, *ṣēlāʿ*[1] [1]
side[s], 7949, *qāraḥat* [1]

SIDED [3]
sided with, 1047+4200, *bāḥar*[1]*+l^{e}-*[1] [1]
sided with, 3338+6640, *yād+ʿim* [1]
sided, 3656, *yāṣab* [1]

SIDES [49]
on all sides, 6017, *sābîb* [13]
on both sides[s], 4946+2296+2256+4946+2296, *min+zeh+w^{e}-+min+zeh* [6]
sides, 7396, *ṣad*[1] [5]
sides, 7521, *ṣēlāʿ*[1] [4]
sides, 7815, *qîr*[1] [3]
sides, 8120, *rûaḥ* [3]
opposite sides, 7521+7396, *ṣēlāʿ*[1]*+ṣad*[1] [2]
sides, 9109, *š^{e}nayim* [2]
two sides, 4101, *kepel* [1]
sides, 4190, *kātēp* [1]
on both sides[s], 4946+2296+2256+2296, *min+zeh+w^{e}-+zeh* [1]
waged against from all sides, 6015, *sābab* [1]
sides, 6298+4946+6017, *ʿēber*[1]*+min+sābîb* [1]
sides, 6298, *ʿēber*[1] [1]
sides, 6991, *pēʾâ*[1] [1]
on both sides, 7156+2256+294, *pāneh+w^{e}-+ʾāḥôr* [1]
sides, 8063, *rebaʿ*[1] [1]
both sides, 9109, *š^{e}nayim* [1]
sides, 10680, *ś^{e}ṭar* [1]

SIDEWALLS [1]
sidewalls, 4190, *kātēp* [1]

SIDING [1]
siding, 5742, *nāṭâ* [1]

SIDON [21]
Sidon, 7477, *ṣîdôn* [20]
people of Sidon, 7479, *ṣîdōnî* [1]

SIDONIANS [15]
Sidonians, 7479, *ṣîdōnî* [15]

SIEGE [49]
siege, 5189, *māṣôr*[1] [15]
siege works, 1911, *dāyēq* [6]
laid siege, 7443, *ṣûr*[1] [5]
siege ramps, 6149, *sōl^{e}lâ* [4]
siege ramp, 6149, *sōl^{e}lâ* [3]
lay siege, 7443, *ṣûr*[1] [3]
siege, *NIH/RPE* [1]
siege ramps, 784+369, *ʾōraḥ+ʿēd* [1]
laid siege, 995+928+2021+5189, *bôʾ+b^{e}-+ha-+māṣôr*[1] [1]
siege towers, 1032, *baḥûn* [1]
siege ramp, 2006, *derek* [1]
laid siege to, 2837+6584, *ḥānâ*[1]*+ʿal*[2] [1]
siege works, 5189, *māṣôr*[1] [1]
siege works, 5193, *m^{e}ṣûrâ* [1]
laid siege, 6164, *sāmak* [1]
siege, 7443, *ṣûr*[1] [1]
under siege, 7443, *ṣûr*[1] [1]
lay siege, 7674, *ṣārar*[1] [1]
under siege, 9068, *šāmar* [1]

SIEGEWORKS [1]
siegeworks, 5189, *māṣôr*[1] [1]

SIEVE [2]
sieve, 3895, *k^{e}bārâ*[1] [1]
sieve, 5864, *nāpâ*[1] [1]

SIFT [1]
sift, 7671, *ṣārap* [1]

SIGHING [5]
sighing, 635, *ʾ^{a}nāḥâ* [4]
sighing, 2052, *hāgîg* [1]

SIGHT [102]
sight, 6524, *ʿayin*[1] [63]
sight, 7156, *pāneh* [17]
sight, 4200+7156, *l^{e}-*[1]*+pāneh* [3]
sight, *NIH/RPE* [2]
sight, 5260, *marʾeh* [2]
in the sight of, 5584, *neged* [2]
sight, *AIT* [1]
gives sight, 239, *ʾôr*[1] [1]
at the sight of, 448, *ʾel* [1]
in sight, 907+7156, *ʾēt*[2]*+pāneh* [1]
within sight of, 907+7156, *ʾēt*[2]*+pāneh* [1]
in the sight of, 4200, *l^{e}-*[1] [1]
regarded in the sight of, 4200+7156, *l^{e}-*[1]*+pāneh* [1]
in sight, 5584, *neged* [1]
gives sight, 7219, *pāqaḥ* [1]
sight, 7221, *piqqēaḥ* [1]
caught sight of, 8011, *rāʾâ*[1] [1]
sight, 8011, *rāʾâ*[1] [1]
in sight, 10621, *q^{o}dām* [1]

SIGHTLESS [1]
sightless, 9129, *šāʿaʿ*[1] [1]

SIGHTS [3]
sights, *AIT* [1]
sights, 5260+6524, *marʾeh+ʿayin*[1] [1]
sights, 5260, *marʾeh* [1]

SIGN [53]
sign, 253, *ʾôt*[1] [36]
sign, 4603, *môpēt* [7]
miraculous sign, 253, *ʾôt*[1] [3]
miraculous sign, 4603, *môpēt* [2]
sign, *AIT* [1]
sign of strength, 226, *ʾôn*[1] [1]
took as a good sign, 5727, *nāḥaš* [1]
warning sign, 5812, *nēs* [1]
sign, 9338, *tāw* [1]

SIGNAL [5]
signal, 5368, *maśʾēt* [1]
signal, 5812, *nēs* [1]
signal, 8131, *rûaʿ* [1]
signal, 9239, *šāraq* [1]
signal, 9546, *tāqaʿ* [1]

SIGNALING [1]
signaling, 9558, *t^{e}rûʿâ* [1]

SIGNALS [1]
signals, 4911, *mālal*[4] [1]

SIGNED [3]
signed, 4180, *kātab* [3]

SIGNET [10]
signet ring, 3192, *ṭabbaʿat* [5]
signet ring, 2597, *ḥôtām*[1] [2]
signet rings, 3192, *ṭabbaʿat* [2]
signet ring, 10536, *ʿizqâ* [1]

SIGNPOST [1]
signpost, 3338, *yād* [1]

SIGNS [35]
miraculous signs, 253, *ʾôt*[1] [17]
signs, 253, *ʾôt*[1] [14]
signs, 10084, *ʾāt* [2]
road signs, 7483, *ṣiyyûn* [1]
miraculous signs, 10084, *ʾāt* [1]

SIHON [34]
Sihon, 6095, *sîḥôn* [34]

SIHON'S [1]
Sihon's, 6095, *sîḥôn* [1]

SILENCE [14]
put to silence, 7551, *ṣāmat* [2]
silence, 6, *ʾābad* [1]
silence of death, 1872, *dûmâ*[1] [1]
silence, 1872, *dûmâ*[1] [1]
in silence, 1876, *dûmām* [1]
silence, 1949, *dāmâ*[2] [1]
silence, 1957, *dāmam*[1] [1]
waiting in silence, 1957, *dāmam*[1] [1]
silence, 2187, *has* [1]
reduce to silence, 3087, *ḥārēš*[2] [1]
silence, 4044, *kānaʿ* [1]
silence, 7551, *ṣāmat* [1]
silence, 8697, *šābat*[1] [1]

SILENCED [10]
be silenced, 1957, *dāmam*[1] [3]
be silenced, 519, *ʾālam*[1] [1]
be silenced, 1949, *dāmâ*[2] [1]
silenced, 1951, *dumâ* [1]
silenced, 1957, *dāmam*[1] [1]
silenced, 2188, *hāsâ* [1]
be silenced, 6126, *sākar*[1] [1]
silenced, 7551, *ṣāmat* [1]

SILENCES [1]
silences, 6073, *sûr*[1] [1]

SILENT [47]
silent, 3087, *ḥārēš*[2] [15]
silent, 3120, *ḥāšâ* [8]
silent, 519, *ʾālam*[1] [6]
silent, 1957, *dāmam*[1] [6]
be silent, 2187, *has* [2]
silent, 1875, *dûmiyyâ* [1]
silent, 1954, *d^{o}mî* [1]
silent, 2532, *ḥādal*[1] [1]
altogether silent, 3087+3087, *ḥārēš*[2]*+ḥārēš*[2] [1]
keeps silent, 3087, *ḥārēš*[2] [1]
remain silent, 3087+3087, *ḥārēš*[2]*+ḥārēš*[2] [1]
keep silent, 3104+7023, *ḥāśak+peh* [1]
silent, 4202+1819, *lōʾ+dābar*[2] [1]
silent, 6129, *sākat* [1]
silent, 9200, *šāqaṭ* [1]

SILLA [1]
Silla, 6133, *sillāʾ* [1]

SILOAM [1]
Siloam, 8940, *šelaḥ*[2] [1]

SILVER [327]
silver, 4084, *kesep* [303]
silver, 10362, *k^{e}sap* [12]
silver, *NIH/RPE* [7]
silver, 4084+4084, *kesep+kesep* [2]
pieces of silver, 7988, *q^{e}śîṭâ* [2]
piece of silver, 7988, *q^{e}śîṭâ* [1]

SILVERSMITH [2]
silversmith, 7671, *ṣārap* [2]

SIMEON [37]
Simeon, 9058, *šimʿôn* [30]
Simeon, 1201+9058, *bēn*[1]*+šimʿôn* [5]
Simeon, 9063, *šimʿōnî* [2]

SIMEONITE [1]
Simeonite, 9063, *šimʿōnî* [1]

SIMEONITES [8]
Simeonites, 1201+9058, *bēn*[1]*+šimʿôn* [4]
Simeonites, 9058, *šimʿôn* [3]
Simeonites, 9063, *šimʿōnî* [1]

SIMILAR [8]
similar, 3869, *k^{e}-* [6]
similar, 3869+2021+5260, *k^{e}+ha+marʾeh* [1]

similar, 4027, *kēn*[2] [1]

SIMILARLY [1]
similarly, 2256, *wᵉ-* [1]

SIMPLE [21]
simple, 7343, *petî*[1] [15]
simple ways, 7344, *petî*[2] [2]
simple, 7785, *qāṭōn*[2] [2]
simple, 7331, *pātâ*[1] [1]
simple, 7837, *qālal* [1]

SIMPLEHEARTED [1]
simplehearted, 7343, *petî*[1] [1]

SIMPLY [1]
simply, 6584+7023, *'al*[2]*+peh* [1]

SIN [346]
sin offering, 2633, *ḥaṭṭā't* [105]
sin, 2633, *ḥaṭṭā't* [85]
sin, 6411, *'āwōn* [59]
sin, 2627, *ḥāṭā'* [23]
sin offerings, 2633, *ḥaṭṭā't* [8]
sin, 7322, *peša'* [7]
sin, 2628, *ḥēṭ'* [5]
caused to sin, 2627, *ḥāṭā'* [4]
Sin, 6097, *sîn*[2] [4]
sin, 6404, *'āwel* [4]
sin, 224, *'āwen*[1] [3]
guilty of sin, 2628, *ḥēṭ'* [3]
consequences of sin, 6411, *'āwōn* [3]
sin, *NIH/RPE* [2]
sin, 870, *'āšam* [2]
led into sin, 2627, *ḥāṭā'* [2]
consequences of sin, 2628, *ḥēṭ'* [2]
sin, 2631, *ḥªṭā'â* [2]
sin, 7321, *pāša'* [2]
sin, 8273, *ra'*[1] [2]
making amends for sin, 871, *'āšām* [1]
a sin committed, 2627+2631, *ḥāṭā'+ḥªṭā'â* [1]
bring sin, 2627, *ḥāṭā'* [1]
cause to sin, 2627, *ḥāṭā'* [1]
commit a sin, 2627, *ḥāṭā'* [1]
commits sin, 2627, *ḥāṭā'* [1]
committed a sin, 2627+2631, *ḥāṭā'+ḥªṭā'â* [1]
lead into sin, 2627, *ḥāṭā'* [1]
make sin, 2627, *ḥāṭā'* [1]
offered for a sin offering, 2627, *ḥāṭā'* [1]
presented for a sin offering, 2627, *ḥāṭā'* [1]
sin offerings, 2627, *ḥāṭā'* [1]
sin offerings, 2631, *ḥªṭā'â* [1]
sin, 2632, *ḥaṭṭā'â* [1]
purification from sin, 2633, *ḥaṭṭā't* [1]
sin, 6296, *'ābar*[1] [1]
penalty of sin, 7322, *peša'* [1]
sin, 8288, *rā'â*[3] [1]
sin offering, 10260, *ḥaṭṭāyā'* [1]

SINAI [35]
Sinai, 6099, *sînay* [35]

SINCE [158]
since, 3954, *kî*[2] [46]
since, 4946, *min* [21]
since, 2256, *wᵉ-* [19]
since, *NIH/RPE* [11]
since, 561, *'im* [6]
since, 339, *'aḥar* [5]
since, 889, *'ªšer* [5]
and since, 2256, *wᵉ-* [3]
since, 3610+889, *ya'an*[1]*+'ªšer* [3]
ever since, 4946, *min* [3]
ever since, 6330+2021+3427+2021+2296, *'ad*[2]*+ha-+yôm*[1]*+ha-+zeh* [3]
since, 2176, *hēn*[1] [2]
ever since, 4946+255, *min+'āz* [2]
since, 4946+255, *min+'āz* [2]
since, 4974, *minnî*[2] [2]
since, *AIT* [1]
since, 339+889, *'aḥar+'ªšer* [1]
since, 928+889, *bᵉ-+'ªšer* [1]
since, 1685, *gam* [1]
since, 2180, *hinnēh* [1]
but since, 3610, *ya'an*[1] [1]
since, 3610, *ya'an*[1] [1]
long since, 3893, *kᵉbār*[1] [1]
since, 3954+3610, *kî*[2]*+ya'an*[1] [1]
since, 3954+6584+4027, *kî*[2]*+'al*[2]*+kēn*[2] [1]
ever since, 4200+4946, *lᵉ-*[1]*+min* [1]
since, 4200+4946+3427, *lᵉ-*[1]*+min+yôm*[1] [1]
since, 4202, *lō'* [1]
since, 4946+889, *min+'ªšer* [1]
ever since, 4946+3427, *min+yôm*[1] [1]
ever since, 4974, *minnî*[2] [1]
since, 6330+2178, *'ad*[2]*+hēnnâ*[1] [1]
since, 6330, *'ad*[2] [1]
since then, 6388, *'ôd* [1]
since, 6584, *'al*[2] [1]
since, 6584+4027, *'al*[2]*+kēn*[2] [1]
since, 8611, *ša-* [1]
since, 9393+3954, *taḥat*[1]*+kî*[2] [1]
since, 9393+889, *taḥat*[1]*+'ªšer* [1]
since, 10353+10619+10168, *kōl+qᵒbēl+dî* [1]

SINCERE [1]
not sincere, 2761, *ḥªlaqlaq* [1]

SINCERELY [1]
sincerely, 1359, *bārûr* [1]

SINEWS [3]
sinews, 1630, *gîd* [3]

SINFUL [12]
sinful, 2627, *ḥāṭā'* [2]
sinful, 2628, *ḥēṭ'* [2]
sinful, 6411, *'āwōn* [2]
sinful folly, 222, *'iwwelet* [1]
sinful, 2629, *ḥaṭṭā'* [1]
sinful thing, 2633, *ḥaṭṭā't* [1]
sinful, 4202+3202, *lō'+ṭôb*[2] [1]
sinful, 7322, *peša'* [1]
sinful, 8278, *rōa'* [1]

SINFULNESS [1]
sinfulness, 7322, *peša'* [1]

SING [114]
sing, 8876, *šîr*[1] [33]
sing praise, 2376, *zāmar*[1] [18]
sing for joy, 8264, *rānan* [15]
sing, 8264, *rānan* [9]
sing praises, 2376, *zāmar*[1] [8]
sing, 2376, *zāmar*[1] [7]
sing, 6702, *'ānâ*[4] [6]
sing, *NIH/RPE* [5]
sing praises, 2146, *hālal*[2] [1]
sing praise, 2146, *hālal*[2] [1]
sing, 5594, *nāgan* [1]
sing, 5951, *nāśā'* [1]
sing, 5989+7754, *nātan+qôl* [1]
sing, 8262, *rinnâ*[1] [1]
sing joyfully, 8264, *rānan* [1]
ever sing for joy, 8264+8264, *rānan+rānan* [1]
joyfully sing, 8264, *rānan* [1]
made sing, 8264, *rānan* [1]
sing, 8492+928+7023, *śîm+bᵉ+peh* [1]
sing, 8877, *šîr*[2] [1]
sing songs, 9048+4200+8123+928+7754, *šāma'+lᵉ-*[1]*+rûm*[1]*+bᵉ-+qôl* [1]

SINGED [1]
was singed, 10283, *ḥªrak* [1]

SINGER [1]
singer, 5834, *nā'îm*[2] [1]

SINGERS [31]
singers, 8876, *šîr*[1] [27]
singers, 1201+8876, *bēn*[1]*+šîr*[1] [1]
singers, 2952, *ḥāṣaṣ*[2] [1]
singers, 8877, *šîr*[2] [1]
singers, 10234, *zammār* [1]

SINGING [18]
singing, 8262, *rinnâ*[1] [4]
singing, 8877, *šîr*[2] [4]
singing, 2369, *zāmîr*[1] [2]
singing, 2379, *zimrâ*[1] [2]
singing, 5362, *maśśā'*[1] [2]
singing, 3938, *kôšārâ* [1]
singing, 6702, *'ānâ*[4] [1]
singing, 8265, *rᵉnānâ* [1]
singing, 8876, *šîr*[1] [1]

SINGLE [15]
single, 285, *'eḥād* [13]
single, *AIT* [1]
single out, 976, *bādal* [1]

SINGLED [1]
singled out, 976, *bādal* [1]

SINGLENESS [1]
singleness, 285, *'eḥād* [1]

SINGS [3]
sings, *NIH/RPE* [1]
sings, 8264, *rānan* [1]
sings, 8876, *šîr*[1] [1]

SINITES [2]
Sinites, 6098, *sînî* [2]

SINK [6]
sink, 3190, *ṭāba'* [2]
sink, 9205, *šāqa'* [2]
sink, 3718, *yārad* [1]
sink, 5877, *nāpal* [1]

SINKS [2]
sinks down, 8332, *rāpâ*[1] [1]
sinks, 9205, *šāqa'* [1]

SINNED [74]
sinned, 2627, *ḥāṭā'* [68]
sinned, 7321, *pāša'* [2]
sinned greatly, 2628+2627, *ḥēṭ'+ḥāṭā'* [1]
sinned, 2629, *ḥaṭṭā'* [1]
sinned, 7322, *peša'* [1]
sinned, 8317, *rā'a'*[1] [1]

SINNER [7]
sinner, 2627, *ḥāṭā'* [5]
sinner, 2629, *ḥaṭṭā'* [1]
sinner, 2633, *ḥaṭṭā't* [1]

SINNER'S [1]
sinner's, 2627, *ḥāṭā'* [1]

SINNERS [14]
sinners, 2629, *ḥaṭṭā'* [13]
sinners, 7321, *pāša'* [1]

SINNING [10]
sinning, 2627, *ḥāṭā'* [6]
sinning, 2629, *ḥaṭṭā'* [1]
sinning, 2630, *ḥeṭ'â* [1]
sinning, 2633, *ḥaṭṭā't* [1]
sinning, 6390, *'āwâ*[1] [1]

SINS [189]
sins, 2633, *ḥaṭṭā't* [74]
sins, 6411, *'āwōn* [49]
sins, 7322, *peša'* [20]
sins, 2627, *ḥāṭā'* [19]
sins, 2628, *ḥēṭ'* [8]
sins, *NIH/RPE* [2]
sins unintentionally, 8706, *šāgā* [2]
sins, 224, *'āwen*[1] [1]
sins, 871, *'āšām* [1]
guilty of sins, 873, *'ašmâ* [1]
sins, 1821+6411, *dābār+'āwōn* [1]
willful sins, 2294, *zēd* [1]
consequences of sins, 2628, *ḥēṭ'* [1]
punished for sins, 2628, *ḥēṭ'* [1]
sins, 2631, *ḥªṭā'â* [1]
sins, 5095, *ma'ªlāl* [1]
punishment for sins, 6411, *'āwōn* [1]
sins defiantly, 6913+928+3338+8123, *'āśâ*[1]*+bᵉ-+yād+rûm*[1] [1]
sins unintentionally, 6913+928+8705, *'āśâ*[1]*+bᵉ-+šᵉgāgâ* [1]
sins, 8288, *rā'â*[3] [1]
detestable sins, 9359, *tô'ēbâ* [1]
sins, 10259, *ḥªṭāy* [1]

SIPHMOTH [1]
Siphmoth, 8560, *śipmôt* [1]

SIPPAI [1]
Sippai, 6205, *sippay* [1]

SIR [3]
sir, 123, *'ādôn* [3]

SIRAH [1]
Sirah, 6241, *sirâ* [1]

SIRION [2]
Sirion, 8590, *śiryôn* [2]

SISERA [20]
Sisera, 6102, *sîs[e]rā'* [20]

SISERA'S [1]
Sisera's, 6102, *sîs[e]rā'* [1]

SISMAI [2]
Sismai, 6183, *sismay* [2]

SISTER [91]
sister, 295, *'āḥôt* [88]
sister, 1426, *bat[1]* [1]
father's sister, 1860, *dôdâ* [1]
the woman and her sister[s], 2177, *-hēn[2]* [1]

SISTER'S [4]
sister's, 295, *'āḥôt* [4]

SISTER-IN-LAW [1]
sister-in-law, 3304, *y[e]bāmâ* [1]

SISTERS [11]
sisters, 295, *'āḥôt* [11]

SISTRUMS [1]
sistrums, 4983, *m[e]na'an'îm* [1]

SIT [73]
sit, 3782, *yāšab* [59]
sit enthroned, 3782, *yāšab* [5]
sit down, 3782, *yāšab* [3]
sit, *NIH/RPE* [2]
sit as judge, 3782, *yāšab* [1]
sit down, 6015, *sābab* [1]
sit up, 7756, *qûm* [1]
sit, 10338, *y[e]tib* [1]

SITE [13]
site, 5226, *māqôm* [4]
site, 299, *'[a]ḥuzzâ* [2]
site, 10087, *'[a]tar* [2]
site, *NIH/RPE* [1]
tent site, 185, *'ōhel[1]* [1]
site, 4806, *mākôn* [1]
burial site, 7700, *qeber* [1]
site, 8699, *šebet[1]* [1]

SITES [2]
sites, 5226, *māqôm* [2]

SITHRI [1]
Sithri, 6262, *sitrî* [1]

SITNAH [1]
Sitnah, 8479, *śiṭnâ[2]* [1]

SITS [16]
sits, 3782, *yāšab* [11]
sits enthroned, 3782, *yāšab* [4]
sits, 5323, *merkāb* [1]

SITTING [40]
sitting, 3782, *yāšab* [39]
sitting, 8069, *rābaṣ* [1]

SITUATED [3]
situated, 3782, *yāšab* [2]
situated, 4632, *môšāb* [1]

SITUATION [5]
situation, *AIT* [1]
situation, *NIH/RPE* [1]
situation, 1821, *dābār* [1]
situation, 10530, *'iddān* [1]
situation, 10606, *ṣ[e]bû* [1]

SIVAN [1]
Sivan, 6094, *sîwān* [1]

SIX [119]
six, 9252, *šēš[1]* [116]
about six hundred feet, 752+4395+564,
'arba'[1]+mē'â[1]+'ammâ[1] [2]
six feet, 752+564, *'arba'[1]+'ammâ[1]* [1]

SIXTEEN [18]
sixteen, 9252+6926, *šēš[1]+'eśrēh* [14]
sixteen, 9252+6925, *šēš[1]+'āśār* [4]

SIXTEENTH [3]
sixteenth, 9252+6925, *šēš[1]+'āśār* [3]

SIXTH [31]
sixth, 9261, *šiššî* [28]
sixth, 9252, *šēš[1]* [1]
sixth, 9257, *šāšā* [1]
sixth, 10747, *šēt* [1]

SIXTY [23]
sixty, 9252, *šēš[1]* [23]

SIXTY-EIGHT [1]
sixty-eight, 9252+2256+9046,
šēš[1]+w[e]-+š[e]mōneh [1]

SIXTY-FIVE [1]
sixty-five, 9252+2256+2822,
šēš[1]+w[e]-+ḥāmēš [1]

SIXTY-SIX [2]
sixty-six, 9252+2256+9252, *šēš[1]+w[e]-+šēš[1]* [2]

SIXTY-TWO [3]
sixty-two, 9252+2256+9109,
šēš[1]+w[e]-+š[e]nayim [2]
sixty-two, 10749+10221+10775,
šittîn+w[e]-+t[e]rên [1]

SIYON [1]
Siyon, 8481, *śî'ôn* [1]

SIZE [14]
size, 4500, *middâ[1]* [10]
great size, 4500, *middâ[1]* [1]
reduce size, 7894, *qāṣā[1]* [1]
size, 8044, *rōb* [1]
size, 9420, *tōken[1]* [1]

SKETCH [1]
sketch, 1952, *d[e]mût* [1]

SKIES [19]
skies, 8836, *šaḥaq* [8]
skies, 9028, *šāmayim* [6]
skies, *NIH/RPE* [1]
skies, 5294, *mārôm* [1]
skies, 8385, *rāqîa'* [1]
skies above, 8836, *šaḥaq* [1]
skies above, 9028+9028,
šāmayim+šāmayim [1]

SKILL [12]
skill, 2683, *ḥokmâ* [7]
skill, *NIH/RPE* [1]
skill, 2681, *ḥākam* [1]
great skill, 2682+3359+1069,
ḥākām+yāda'+bînâ [1]
skill, 2683+4213, *ḥokmâ+lēb* [1]
skill, 4179, *kišrôn* [1]

SKILLED [35]
skilled craftsman, 3110, *ḥōšēb* [8]
skilled, 2682, *ḥākām* [7]
skilled, 2682+4213, *ḥākām+lēb* [6]
skilled, 3359, *yāda'* [3]
skilled, 1067, *bîn* [2]
skilled craftsmen, 2682, *ḥākām* [2]
skilled, 2683, *ḥokmâ* [2]
skilled, 3093, *ḥārāš* [1]
skilled, 3512+2006, *yāṭab+derek* [1]
skilled, 3512, *yāṭab* [1]
skilled, 4542, *māhîr* [1]
skilled, 8505, *śākal[1]* [1]

SKILLFUL [8]
skillful, 2681, *ḥākam* [2]
skillful, 1067, *bîn* [1]
skillful, 2682, *ḥākām* [1]
skillful men, 3110, *ḥōšēb* [1]
skillful, 3359, *yāda'* [1]
skillful, 4542, *māhîr* [1]
skillful, 9312, *t[e]bûnâ* [1]

SKILLFULLY [5]
skillfully woven, 682, *'[a]puddâ* [2]
skillfully, *NIH/RPE* [1]
skillfully woven waistband, 3109, *ḥēšeb* [1]
skillfully, 3512, *yāṭab* [1]

SKILLS [1]
skills, 2657, *ḥayil* [1]

SKIM [1]
skim past, 2736, *ḥālap[1]* [1]

SKIMPING [1]
skimping, 7781, *qāṭōn[1]* [1]

SKIN [75]
skin, 6425, *'ôr* [39]
skin disease, 7669, *ṣāra'at* [10]
skin, 6425+1414, *'ôr+bāśār* [6]
skin, 2827, *ḥēmet* [3]
skin, 5574, *nēbel[1]* [3]
skin, 1414+6425, *bāśār+'ôr* [2]
skin, 1414, *bāśār* [2]
skin, 5532, *nō'd* [2]
skin, 7320, *pāšaṭ* [2]
skin, *AIT* [1]
skin, 1654, *gēled* [1]
nothing but skin, 6425+2256+1414,
'ôr+w[e]-+bāśār [1]
has an infectious skin disease, 7665, *ṣāra'* [1]
infectious skin disease, 7665, *ṣāra'* [1]
infectious skin diseases and mildew, 7669,
ṣāra'at [1]

SKINK [1]
skink, 2793, *ḥōmeṭ* [1]

SKINNED [1]
skinned, 7320, *pāšaṭ* [1]

SKINS [8]
skins, 6425, *'ôr* [6]
skins, 2293, *zāg* [1]
skins, 5574, *nēbel[1]* [1]

SKIP [1]
makes skip, 8376, *rāqad* [1]

SKIPPED [2]
skipped, 8376, *rāqad* [2]

SKIRTED [1]
skirted, 6015, *sābab* [1]

SKIRTS [5]
skirts, 8767, *šûl* [4]
skirts, 8670, *šōbel* [1]

SKULL [2]
skull, 1653, *gulgōlet* [2]

SKULLS [2]
skulls, 7721, *qodqōd* [2]

SKY [52]
sky, 9028, *šāmayim* [46]
sky, 10723, *š[e]mayin* [3]
clouds of the sky, 6265+8836, *'āb[2]+šaḥaq* [2]
sky, 8836, *šaḥaq* [1]

SLACK [1]
slack, 8332, *rāpâ[1]* [1]

SLAIN [56]
slain, 2728, *ḥālāl[1]* [38]
slain, 2222, *hārag* [9]
slain, 5782, *nākâ* [4]
slain, 4637, *mût* [2]
was slain, 10625, *q[e]ṭal* [2]

slain in battle, 2728, ḥālāl[1] [1]

SLANDER [13]
slander, 1804, *dibbâ* [3]
slander, 8806, *šōrēr* [2]
slander, 224, *'āwen*[1] [1]
slander, 1819, *dābar*[2] [1]
slander, 4387, *lāšan* [1]
slander, 5989+1984, *nātan+d[e]pî* [1]
slander, 8078, *rāgal* [1]
slander, 8215, *rākîl* [1]
spreading slander, 8215, *rākîl* [1]
slander, 8476, *śāṭan* [1]

SLANDERED [3]
slandered, 7973, *qāra'* [1]
slandered, 8078, *rāgal* [1]
slandered, 8492+6613+1821, *śîm+'[a]lîlâ+dābār* [1]

SLANDERER [1]
slanderer, 8215+2143, *rākîl+hālak* [1]

SLANDERERS [2]
slanderers, 408+4383, *'îš*[1]*+lāšôn* [1]
slanderers, 8806, *šōrēr* [1]

SLANDEROUS [1]
slanderous, 8215, *rākîl* [1]

SLANDERS [2]
slanders, 4387, *lāšan* [1]
slanders, 8492+6613+1821, *śîm+'[a]lîlâ+dābār* [1]

SLAPPED [2]
slapped, 5782, *nākâ* [2]

SLASH [1]
slash, 284, *'āḥad* [1]

SLASHED [2]
slashed themselves, 1517, *gādad*[1] [1]
slashed, 1523, *g[e]dûdâ* [1]

SLAUGHTER [61]
slaughter, 8821, *šāḥaṭ*[1] [23]
slaughter, 3181, *ṭebaḥ*[1] [9]
slaughter, 2224, *h[a]rēgâ* [5]
slaughter, 2284, *zābaḥ* [3]
slaughter, 3180, *ṭābaḥ* [3]
slaughter, 2222, *hārag* [2]
slaughter, 2223, *hereg* [2]
slaughter, 2728, *ḥālāl*[1] [2]
slaughter, 4804, *makkâ* [2]
slaughter, 18, *'ibḥâ* [1]
slaughter, 2222+4200+5422, *hārag+l[e]-[1]+mašḥît* [1]
slaughter takes place, 2222+2223, *hārag+hereg* [1]
slaughter, 3180+3181, *ṭābaḥ+ṭebaḥ*[1] [1]
slaughter, 4487, *maggēpâ* [1]
place to slaughter, 4749, *maṭbēaḥ* [1]
slaughter, 5877, *nāpal* [1]
slaughter, 7780, *qeṭel* [1]
slaughter, 8358, *reṣaḥ* [1]
slaughter, 8823, *šaḥ[a]ṭâ* [1]

SLAUGHTERED [51]
slaughtered, 8821, *šāḥaṭ*[1] [35]
slaughtered, 2284, *zābaḥ* [3]
slaughtered, 3180, *ṭābaḥ* [3]
slaughtered, 5782, *nākâ* [3]
slaughtered, 2222, *hārag* [1]
be slaughtered, 3180, *ṭābaḥ* [1]
slaughtered, 3186, *ṭibḥâ* [1]
slaughtered, 4804, *makkâ* [1]
be slaughtered, 8821, *šāḥaṭ*[1] [1]
sacrifices slaughtered, 8821, *šāḥaṭ*[1] [1]
were slaughtered, 8821, *šāḥaṭ*[1] [1]

SLAUGHTERING [5]
slaughtering, 5782, *nākâ* [2]
slaughtering, *NIH/RPE* [1]
slaughtering, 2222, *hārag* [1]
slaughtering, 8821, *šāḥaṭ*[1] [1]

SLAUGHTERS [1]
slaughters, 3180, *ṭābaḥ* [1]

SLAVE [55]
slave, 6269, *'ebed*[1] [15]
slave drivers, 5601, *nāgaś* [5]
slave, 6806, *'āṣar* [5]
slave girls, 563, *'āmâ* [4]
slave, *NIH/RPE* [3]
slave girl, 563, *'āmâ* [2]
slave, 4989, *mas* [2]
male slave, 6269, *'ebed*[1] [2]
female [slave], 563, *'āmâ* [2]
slave girl, 9148, *šipḥâ* [2]
slave woman's, 563, *'āmâ* [1]
slave woman, 563, *'āmâ* [1]
slave born in household, 1201+563, *bēn*[1]*+'āmâ* [1]
that slave[s], 2085, *hû'* [1]
the slave[s], 2085, *hû'* [1]
the slave[s], 2257, *-ô* [1]
slave by birth, 3535+1074, *yālîd+bayit*[1] [1]
slave labor force, 4989, *mas* [1]
slave labor, 4989, *mas* [1]
slave driver's, 5601, *nāgaś* [1]
slave, 5883, *nepeš* [1]
slave, 6268, *'ābad* [1]
as a slave, 6275+6269, *'[a]bōdâ+'ebed*[1] [1]
treat as a slave, 6683, *'āmar*[2] [1]
treats as a slave, 6683, *'āmar*[2] [1]

SLAVERY [17]
slavery, 6269, *'ebed*[1] [14]
slavery, 6275, *'[a]bōdâ* [2]
slavery, 6285, *'abdut* [1]

SLAVES [49]
slaves, 6269, *'ebed*[1] [30]
male slaves, 6269, *'ebed*[1] [7]
female [slaves], 9148, *šipḥâ* [7]
slaves, 6269+2256+9148, *'ebed*[1]*+w[e]-+šipḥâ* [2]
slaves, *NIH/RPE* [1]
freedom for slaves, 2002, *d[e]rôr*[3] [1]
make men slaves, 3899+6269, *kābaš+'ebed*[1] [1]
slaves, 5883+132, *nepeš+'ādām*[1] [1]
make slaves, 6268, *'ābad* [1]
serve as slaves, 6268, *'ābad* [1]
lowest of slaves, 6269+6269, *'ebed*[1]*+'ebed*[1] [1]
slaves male, 6269, *'ebed*[1] [1]
slaves, 6269+2256+563, *'ebed*[1]*+w[e]-+'āmâ* [1]
slaves, 6275, *'[a]bōdâ* [1]

SLAY [15]
slay, 2222, *hārag* [4]
slay, 4637, *mût* [4]
slay, 7779, *qāṭal* [2]
slay, 2726, *ḥālal*[2] [1]
slay, 3180, *ṭābaḥ* [1]
slay, 5782, *nākâ* [1]
slay, 5877, *nāpal* [1]
slay, 8821, *šāḥaṭ*[1] [1]

SLAYER [2]
slayer, 2222, *hārag* [2]

SLAYS [1]
slays, 4637, *mût* [1]

SLEDGE [3]
sledge, 3023, *ḥārûṣ*[3] [1]
threshing sledge, 3023, *ḥārûṣ*[3] [1]
threshing sledge, 4617, *môrag* [1]

SLEDGES [3]
threshing sledges, 4617, *môrag* [2]
sledges, 3023, *ḥārûṣ*[3] [1]

SLEEK [6]
sleek, 3637+5260, *yāpeh+mar'eh* [2]
sleek, 3637+9307, *yāpeh+tō'ar* [1]
sleek, 4170, *kāśâ* [1]
sleek, 6950, *'āšat*[1] [1]
sleek, 9045, *šāmēn*[2] [1]

SLEEP [67]
sleep, 9104, *šēnâ* [18]
sleep, 3822, *yāšēn*[1] [8]
deep sleep, 9554, *tardēmâ* [6]
sleep with, 995+448, *bô'+'el* [5]
sleep, 8886, *šākab* [5]
sleep, 3822+9104, *yāšēn*[1]*+šēnâ* [2]
sleep, 3825, *yāšēn*[3] [2]
sleep, 5670, *nûm* [2]
fell into a deep sleep, 8101, *rādam* [2]
sleep with, 8886+6640, *šākab+'im* [2]
sleep with, 448+995, *'el+bô'* [1]
go sleep with, 995+448, *bô'+'el* [1]
sleep with, 3359, *yāda'* [1]
put to sleep, 3822, *yāšēn*[1] [1]
sleep with, 6584+4156, *'al*[2]*+kāra'* [1]
in a deep sleep, 8101, *rādam* [1]
sleep, 8101, *rādam* [1]
deep sleep, 8120+9554, *rûaḥ+tardēmâ* [1]
go to sleep, 8886, *šākab* [1]
lay down to sleep, 8886, *šākab* [1]
make sleep, 8905, *šākan* [1]
sleep, 9097, *šēnā'* [1]
last sleep, 9104, *šēnâ* [1]
sleep of death, 9104, *šēnâ* [1]
sleep, 10733, *š[e]nâ*[3] [1]

SLEEPING [9]
sleeping, 3822, *yāšēn*[1] [2]
sleeping, 3825, *yāšēn*[3] [2]
sleeping, 4328, *lîn* [1]
sleeping with, 5989+928+8888, *nātan+b[e]-+š[e]kōbet* [1]
sleeping with, 8886+6640, *šākab+'im* [1]
sleeping with, 8886+907+8887+2446, *šākab+'ēt*[2]*+šikbâ+zera'* [1]
sleeping, 8886, *šākab* [1]

SLEEPS [13]
sleeps with, 8886+6640, *šākab+'im* [5]
sleeps with, 8886+907, *šākab+'ēt*[2] [3]
sleeps with, 995+448, *bô'+'el* [1]
sleeps, 3822, *yāšēn*[1] [1]
sleeps, 8101, *rādam* [1]
sleeps with, 8886+907+8887+2446, *šākab+'ēt*[2]*+šikbâ+zera'* [1]
sleeps, 8886, *šākab* [1]

SLEET [1]
sleet, 2857, *ḥ[a]nāmal* [1]

SLEPT [21]
slept with, 995+448, *bô'+'el* [5]
slept with, 8886+907, *šākab+'ēt*[2] [4]
slept with, 8886+6640, *šākab+'im* [3]
slept, 8886, *šākab* [2]
slept with, 907+8886, *'ēt*[2]*+šākab* [1]
slept with, 3359+408+4200+5435, *yāda'+'îš*[1]*+l[e]-[1]+miškāb* [1]
slept with, 3359+4200+5435+2351, *yāda'+l[e]-[1]+miškāb+zākār* [1]
slept with, 3359+5435+2351, *yāda'+miškāb+zākār* [1]
slept with, 3359+5435, *yāda'+miškāb* [1]
slept with, 3359, *yāda'* [1]
slept, 3825, *yāšēn*[3] [1]

SLEW [1]
slew, 2222, *hārag* [1]

SLIME [1]
slime pit, 8846, *šaḥat* [1]

SLIMY [1]
slimy pit, 1014+8622, *bôr+šā'ôn*[1] [1]

SLING [6]
sling, 7845, *qela'*[1] [3]
sling stones, 928+2021+74, *b[e]-+ha-+'eben* [1]
sling, 5275, *margēmâ* [1]
sling, 7843, *qāla'*[1] [1]

SLINGS [1]
men armed with slings, 7847, *qallā'* [1]

SLINGSTONES [3]
slingstones, 74+7845, *'eben+qela'*[1] [3]

SLIP [7]
slip, 4572, *môṭ*[1] [2]

slip out, 3655, yāṣāʾ [1]
slip out, 4880, mālaṭ[1] [1]
slip, 5048, māʿad [1]
slip, 6073, sûr[1] [1]
slip, 7520, ṣelaʿ [1]

SLIPPED [3]
slipped, 4572, môṭ[1] [1]
slipped away, 4880, mālaṭ[1] [1]
slipped, 5742, nāṭâ [1]

SLIPPERY [3]
slippery, 2761, h[a]laqlaq [2]
slippery, 2747, ḥālāq[1] [1]

SLIPPING [3]
slipping, 4572, môṭ[1] [2]
slipping, 5048, māʿad [1]

SLIPS [1]
slips, 4572, môṭ[1] [1]

SLOPE [9]
slope, 4190, kātēp [8]
slope, 4618, môrād [1]

SLOPES [12]
slopes, 844, ʾăšēd [5]
mountain slopes, 844, ʾăšēd [2]
slopes, 4190, kātēp [2]
mountain slopes, 850, ʾēšdāt [1]
slopes, 4618, môrād [1]
slopes, 8442, śāday [1]

SLOW [13]
slow, 800, ʾārēk [9]
slow, 336, ʾāḥar [2]
slow, 3878, kābēd[2] [1]
slow down, 6806+4200+8206, ʿāṣar+l[e-1]+rākab [1]

SLOWLY [1]
slowly, 4200+351, l[e-1]+ʾaṭ[1] [1]

SLUG [1]
slug, 8671, šabb[e]lûl [1]

SLUGGARD [13]
sluggard, 6789, ʿāṣēl [13]

SLUGGARD'S [1]
sluggard's, 6789, ʿāṣēl [1]

SLUMBER [9]
slumber, 9484, t[e]nûmâ [5]
slumber, 5670, nûm [3]
slumber, 9104, šēnâ [1]

SLUMBERS [1]
slumbers, 5670, nûm [1]

SLUMPED [1]
slumped down, 4156, kāraʿ [1]

SLUNG [2]
slung on back, 1068+4190, bayin+kātēp [1]
slung, 7843, qālaʿ[1] [1]

SLUR [1]
slur, 3075, ḥerpâ [1]

SLY [1]
sly, 6260, sēter [1]

SMALL [48]
small, 7785, qāṭōn[2] [14]
small, 7783, qāṭān[1] [12]
small shields, 4482, māgēn[1] [6]
small, 7639, ṣar[1] [3]
small, 5203, miṣʿār[1] [2]
small, 7582, ṣāʿîr[1] [2]
small, 237, ʾûṣ [1]
small flocks, 3105, ḥāśip [1]
shields small, 4482, māgēn[1] [1]
small, 5070, māʿaṭ [1]
small, 7674, ṣārar[1] [1]
small, 7829, qālâ[2] [1]
small, 7837, qālal [1]
small creatures, 8254, remeś [1]
small shields, 8949, šeleṭ [1]

SMALLER [7]
smaller, 5071, m[e]ʿaṭ [3]
smaller, 5070, māʿaṭ [2]
smaller, 724, ʾāṣal [1]
smaller, 7783, qāṭān[1] [1]

SMALLEST [2]
smallest, 7582, ṣāʿîr[1] [1]
smallest, 7783, qāṭān[1] [1]

SMASH [7]
smash, 8689, šābar[1] [4]
smash, 5879, nāpaṣ[1] [2]
smash, 5782, nākâ [1]

SMASHED [14]
smashed, 8689, šābar[1] [10]
smashed, 2150, hālam [1]
smashed to pieces, 8368, rāṣaṣ [1]
be smashed, 8689, šābar[1] [1]
smashed, 10182, d[e]qaq [1]

SMASHES [1]
smashes, 10290, ḥ[a]šal [1]

SMEAR [1]
smear, 3260, ṭāpal [1]

SMEARED [1]
smeared, 3260, ṭāpal [1]

SMELL [9]
smell, 8193, rîaḥ [2]
smell, 8194, rêaḥ [2]
give a bad smell, 944+5580, bāʾaš+nābaʿ [1]
smell, 944, bāʾaš [1]
smell, 7462, ṣaḥ[a]nâ [1]
caught the smell, 8193+8194, rîaḥ+rêaḥ [1]
smell, 10666, rêaḥ [1]

SMELLED [2]
smelled bad, 944, bāʾaš [1]
smelled, 8193, rîaḥ [1]

SMELTED [1]
is smelted, 3668, yāṣaq [1]

SMILE [2]
smile, 1158, bālag [1]
smile, 3649, yāpaʿ [1]

SMILED [1]
smiled, 8471, śāḥaq [1]

SMITE [1]
smite, 4730, māḥaṣ [1]

SMITTEN [1]
smitten, 5782, nākâ [1]

SMOKE [34]
smoke, 6940, ʿāšān[1] [23]
smoke, 6939, ʿāšan [2]
smoke, 7798, qîṭôr [2]
clouds of smoke, 5366, maśśāʾâ [1]
smoke, 5368, maśʾēt [1]
smoke, 6727, ʿānān[1] [1]
covered with smoke, 6939, ʿāšan [1]
cloud of smoke, 6940, ʿāšān[1] [1]
in smoke, 6942, ʿāšēn [1]
dense smoke, 7798, qîṭôr [1]

SMOKING [1]
smoking, 6940, ʿāšān[1] [1]

SMOLDER [2]
anger smolder, 6939, ʿāšan [1]
smolder, 6939, ʿāšan [1]

SMOLDERING [3]
smoldering, 3910, kēheh [1]
smoldering, 6942, ʿāšēn [1]
smoldering remains, 8599, śerēpâ [1]

SMOLDERS [1]
smolders, 3822, yāšēn[1] [1]

SMOOTH [9]
smooth, 2747, ḥālāq[1] [2]
smooth, 2753, ḥelqâ[1] [2]
smooth, 2744, ḥālaq[1] [1]
smooth, 2749, ḥēleq[1] [1]
smooth, 2752, ḥalluq [1]
smooth, 4793, mîšôr [1]
make smooth, 7142, pālas[1] [1]

SMOOTH-SKINNED [2]
smooth-skinned, 5307, māraṭ [2]

SMOOTHER [1]
smoother, 2747, ḥālāq[1] [1]

SMOOTHLY [1]
smoothly, 928+4797, b[e]-+mêšārîm [1]

SMOOTHS [1]
smooths, 2744, ḥālaq[1] [1]

SNAKE [19]
snake, 5729, nāḥāš[1] [14]
snake, 9490, tannîn [3]
the snake[s], 2257, -ô [1]
snake, 8597, śārāp[1] [1]

SNAKES [5]
snakes, 5729, nāḥāš[1] [3]
venomous snakes, 5729, nāḥāš[1] [1]
snakes, 8597, śārāp[1] [1]

SNAPPED [3]
snapped, 5998, nātaq [2]
are snapped, 5998, nātaq [1]

SNAPS [1]
snaps, 5998, nātaq [1]

SNARE [34]
snare, 7062, paḥ[1] [14]
snare, 4613, môqēš [12]
snare, 5180, m[e]ṣûdâ[1] [2]
snare, 1335, bāqaš [1]
snare, 3338, yād [1]
men who snare birds, 3687, yāqûš [1]
snare, 5178, māṣôd[1] [1]
snare, 7545, ṣammîm [1]
snare, 8407, rešet [1]

SNARED [4]
be snared, 3704, yāqaš [1]
snared, 3704, yāqaš [1]
snared, 4335, leked [1]
snared, 4613, môqēš [1]

SNARES [13]
snares, 4613, môqēš [6]
snares, 7062, paḥ[1] [5]
snares, 7062+3687, paḥ[1]+yāqûš [1]
lay snares, 8938, šālaḥ [1]

SNARLING [2]
snarling, 2159, hāmâ [2]

SNATCH [6]
snatch, 1024, bāzaz [1]
snatch away, 1608, gāzal [1]
snatch up, 3149, ḥātâ [1]
snatch, 5911, nāṣal [1]
snatch up, 5951, nāśāʾ [1]
snatch away, 6073, sûr[1] [1]

SNATCHED [9]
snatched, 1608, gāzal [3]
snatched, 5911, nāṣal [3]
been snatched, 4162, kārat [1]
snatched, 4374, lāqaḥ [1]
snatched, 8959, šālak [1]

SNATCHES [3]
snatches, NIH/RPE [1]
snatches away, 1704, gānab [1]
snatches away, 3166, ḥātap [1]

SNEER [1]
sneer, 8143+7023, rāḥab+peh [1]

SNEERS [1]
sneers, 7032, *pûaḥ*[2] [1]

SNEEZED [1]
sneezed, 2453, *zārar*[2] [1]

SNIFF [1]
sniff contemptuously, 5870, *nāpaḥ* [1]

SNIFFING [1]
sniffing, 8634, *šā’ap*[1] [1]

SNORTING [3]
snorting, 5724, *naḥar* [1]
snorting, 5725, *naḥ[a]râ* [1]
snorting, 6490, *‘[a]ṭîšâ* [1]

SNORTS [1]
snorts, 606, *’āmar*[1] [1]

SNOUT [1]
snout, 678, *’ap*[2] [1]

SNOW [18]
snow, 8920, *šeleg*[1] [16]
snow fallen, 8919, *šālag* [1]
snow, 10758, *t[e]lag* [1]

SNOWS [1]
snows, 8920, *šeleg*[1] [1]

SNOWY [2]
snowy, 8920, *šeleg*[1] [2]

SNUFF [2]
snuff out, 3882, *kābâ* [2]

SNUFFED [6]
snuffed out, 1980, *dā‘ak* [5]
snuffed out, 3882, *kābâ* [1]

SO [2205]
so, 2256, *w[e]-* [1179]
so that, 2256, *w[e]-* [236]
so, *NIH/RPE* [122]
so, 4027, *kēn*[2] [88]
so that, 4200+5100, *l[e]-[1]+ma‘an* [77]
so, *AIT* [64]
so that, 4200, *l[e]-[1]* [60]
and so, 2256, *w[e]-* [44]
so, 4200, *l[e]-[1]* [26]
so, 6584+4027, *‘al[2]+kēn[2]* [25]
so, 4200+5100, *l[e]-[1]+ma‘an* [18]
so, 3954, *kî*[2] [14]
ever so, 3907, *kōh* [12]
so that, 889, *’ašer* [11]
so, 4200+4027, *l[e]-[1]+kēn[2]* [10]
so, 4946, *min* [9]
so, 10089+10008, *b[e]-+’[e]dayin* [8]
so, 4394, *m[e]’ōd* [7]
so, 889, *’[a]šer* [6]
so that not, 7153, *pen* [6]
so that, 10168, *dî* [6]
so that, 928+6288, *b[e]-+‘[a]bûr[1]* [5]
so, 3970, *kākâ* [5]
so, 10221, *w[e]-* [5]
so that, 10221, *w[e]-* [5]
so when, 2256, *w[e]-* [4]
so then, 2256, *w[e]-* [3]
so, 3869, *k[e]-* [3]
so, 3907, *kōh* [3]
so that, 4946, *min* [3]
so, 6584+2296, *‘al[2]+zeh* [3]
so, 10008, *’[e]dayin* [3]
so, 255, *’āz* [2]
so, 421, *’ak* [2]
how much more so, 677+3954, *’ap[1]+kî[2]* [2]
so, 686, *’ēpô’* [2]
so long, 799, *’ārak* [2]
so, 928+6288, *b[e]-+‘[a]bûr[1]* [2]
so long, 1018, *bôš*[2] [2]
so, 2180, *hinnēh* [2]
so, 2256+1685, *w[e]-+gam* [2]
and so that, 2256, *w[e]-* [2]
so, 3869+2296, *k[e]-+zeh* [2]
so that, 3954, *kî*[2] [2]
so many, 4946+8044, *min+rōb* [2]
so not, 4946, *min* [2]
so that not, 4946, *min* [2]
get so close, 5602, *nāgaš* [2]
do so[s], 5989, *nātan* [2]
so that, 6584+4027, *‘al[2]+kēn[2]* [2]
so not, 7153, *pen* [2]
so great, 8041, *rab*[1] [2]
so many, 8041, *rab*[1] [2]
not so, 177, *’[a]hāh* [1]
or so, 196, *’ô* [1]
did so[s], 296, *’āḥaz*[1] [1]
so[s], 401, *’ayin*[1] [1]
so, 561+4202+3610, *’im+lō’+ya‘an[1]* [1]
amen so be it, 589+589, *’āmēn+’āmēn* [1]
so sure, 606+606, *’āmar[1]+’āmar[1]* [1]
do so more, 665, *’āsap* [1]
so long, 802+3427, *’ōrek+yôm[1]* [1]
so quickly, 928+7328, *b[e]-+pit’ōm* [1]
so odious, 944+944, *bā’aš+bā’aš* [1]
done so[s], 995+448+7931, *bô’+’el+qereb* [1]
do so[s], 1385, *bārak*[2] [1]
do so[s], 1413, *bāśar* [1]
do so[s], 1457, *gā’al*[1] [1]
so proudly, 1469+1469, *gābōah+gābōah* [1]
so much, 1524, *gādôl* [1]
boast so much, 1540+7023+3870,
gādal+peh+-kā [1]
make so much of, 1540, *gādal* [1]
so, 1685, *gam* [1]
so, 2022, *h[a]-* [1]
doing so[s], 2157, *-hem* [1]
so much, 2221, *harbēh* [1]
so, 2296, *zeh* [1]
did so[s], 2502, *ḥābaš* [1]
be so kind as, 3283, *yā’al*[2] [1]
so that, 3610+889, *ya‘an[1]+’ašer* [1]
do so[s], 3718, *yārad* [1]
so[s], 3718, *yārad* [1]
so[s], 3780, *yēš* [1]
did so[s], 3782, *yāšab* [1]
so, 3869+889, *k[e]-+’ašer* [1]
so many, 3869+4537, *k[e]-+mâ* [1]
so that, 3869+7023, *k[e]-+peh* [1]
so with, 3869+889, *k[e]-+’ašer* [1]
so with, 3869, *k[e]-* [1]
so, 3869+6584, *k[e]-+‘al[2]* [1]
if so, 3954+6964, *kî[2]+‘attâ* [1]
so, 3954+4394, *kî[2]+m[e]’ōd* [1]
even so, 4017, *k[e]mô* [1]
so much, 4027, *kēn*[2] [1]
so then, 4200+4027, *l[e]-[1]+kēn[2]* [1]
so as to, 4200, *l[e]-[1]* [1]
so as, 4200, *l[e]-[1]* [1]
so far as, 4200+3972, *l[e]-[1]+kōl* [1]
so many, 4200+8044, *l[e]-[1]+rōb* [1]
did so[s], 4374+8008+2256+2932,
lāqaḥ+qešet+w[e]-+ḥēṣ [1]
did so[s], 4374, *lāqaḥ* [1]
so highly, 4394, *m[e]’ōd* [1]
so much, 4394, *m[e]’ōd* [1]
so, 4394+4394, *m[e]’ōd+m[e]’ōd* [1]
ever so, 4537, *mâ* [1]
did so[s], 4576, *mûl*[1] [1]
so cannot, 4946, *min* [1]
so that no, 4946, *min* [1]
so many, 5031+8041, *mispār[1]+rab[1]* [1]
so much, 5268, *mirbâ* [1]
so, 5528, *nā’*[1] [1]
do so[s], 5583, *nāgad* [1]
done so[s], 5602, *nāgaš* [1]
so[s], 5626, *-nâ* [1]
relent so that not bring, 5714, *nāḥam* [1]
doing so, 5933, *nāqam* [1]
wept so loudly, 5989+906+7754+928+1140,
nātan+’ēt[1]+qôl+b[e]-+b[e]kî [1]
So, 6046, *sô’* [1]
did so[s], 6296, *‘ābar*[1] [1]
lasted so long, 6330, *‘ad*[2] [1]
so much that, 6330, *‘ad*[2] [1]
so much, 6330, *‘ad*[2] [1]
and so, 6584+4027, *‘al[2]+kēn[2]* [1]
did so[s], 6913+906+2021+7175,
‘āśâ[1]+’ēt[1]+ha-+pesaḥ [1]
so, 6964, *‘attâ* [1]
so cannot, 7153, *pen* [1]
so that no, 7153, *pen* [1]
so much, 8041, *rab*[1] [1]
so, 8041, *rab*[1] [1]
so many, 8044, *rōb* [1]
so does[s], 8049, *rābâ*[1] [1]
so increase, 8049+8049, *rābâ[1]+rābâ[1]* [1]
so that, 8611, *ša-* [1]
do so[s], 8740+4946+2006, *šûb[1]+min+derek* [1]
doing so[s], 8845, *šāḥat* [1]
was left so desolate, 9037, *šāmēm*[1] [1]
look so pale, 10228+10731, *zîw+š[e]nâ[1]* [1]
so, 10339, *yattîr* [1]
so, 10353+10619+10180, *kōl+q[o]bēl+d[e]nâ* [1]
do so[s], 10353+10544+10708, *kōl+‘illâ+š[e]kaḥ*
[1]
so that, 10378, *l[e]-* [1]
so then, 10385, *lāhēn*[1] [1]
so, 10385, *lāhēn*[1] [1]
so that, 10527+10159+10168, *‘ad+dibrâ+dî* [1]
so that, 10542+10159+10168, *‘al+dibrâ+dî* [1]
so, 10678, *śaggî’* [1]

SOAKED [3]
be soaked, 2014, *dāšēn*[1] [1]
soaked, 3188, *ṭābal* [1]
be soaked, 5022, *māsas* [1]

SOAP [3]
soap, 1383, *bōrît* [2]
soap, 8921, *šeleg*[2] [1]

SOAR [4]
soar, 1467, *gābah* [2]
soar, 6590, *‘ālâ* [2]

SOARED [2]
soared, 1797, *dā’â*[1] [2]

SOB [1]
sob, 1134, *bākâ* [1]

SOBBING [1]
sobbing, 1134, *bākâ* [1]

SOBER [1]
sober, 3655+2021+3516+4946,
yāṣā’+ha-+yayin+min [1]

SOCKET [3]
socket, 4090, *kap* [3]

SOCKETS [3]
turned in sockets, 1664, *gālîl*[1] [1]
sockets, 2986, *ḥōr*[2] [1]
sockets, 7327, *pōt* [1]

SOCO [3]
Soco, 8459, *śôkô* [3]

SOCOH [5]
Socoh, 8458, *śôkōh* [5]

SODA [3]
soda, 6003, *neter* [2]
washing soda, 1342, *bōr*[2] [1]

SODI [1]
Sodi, 6052, *sôdî* [1]

SODOM [38]
Sodom, 6042, *s[e]dōm* [38]

SOFTEN [1]
soften, 4570, *mûg* [1]

SOIL [25]
soil, 141, *’[a]dāmâ*[1] [11]
soil, 824, *’ereṣ* [4]
soil, 6760, *‘āpār* [4]
soil, 8441, *śādeh* [2]
native soil, 275, *’ezrāḥ* [1]
soil, 3245, *ṭānap* [1]
soil, 6760+824, *‘āpār+’ereṣ* [1]
soil, 8073, *regeb* [1]

SOLD [50]
sold, 4835, *mākar* [19]
be sold, 4835, *mākar* [5]
sold himself, 4835, *mākar* [4]

sold for, 2118+928, *hāyâ+bᵉ-* [2]
been sold, 4835, *mākar* [2]
were sold, 4835, *mākar* [2]
sold, 4928, *mimkār* [2]
what sold, 4928, *mimkār* [2]
sold, 6037, *sāgar* [2]
sold grain, 8690, *šābar*[2] [2]
sold, 9479, *tānâ*[1] [2]
sold, *NIH/RPE* [1]
be sold back, 4835, *mākar* [1]
must be sold, 4835+4929, *mākar+mimkeret* [1]
sold themselves, 4835, *mākar* [1]
sold yourself, 4835, *mākar* [1]
land sold, 4928, *mimkār* [1]

SOLDIER [6]
valiant soldier, 1475+2657, *gibbôr+ḥayil* [2]
soldier, 408+7372, *ʾîš[1]+ṣābāʾ[2]* [1]
bravest soldier, 1201+2657, *bēn[1]+ḥayil* [1]
soldier[s], 2257, *-ô* [1]
soldier, 6639, *ʿam[2]* [1]

SOLDIERS [48]
soldiers, 408+4878, *ʾîš[1]+milḥāmâ* [12]
soldiers, 6639, *ʿam[2]* [10]
foot soldiers, 8081, *raglî* [5]
foot soldiers, 408+8081, *ʾîš[1]+raglî* [3]
soldiers, 2657, *ḥayil* [3]
experienced soldiers, 3655+7372, *yāṣāʾ+ṣābāʾ[2]* [2]
great soldiers, 408+4878, *ʾîš[1]+milḥāmâ* [1]
soldiers, 408+7372, *ʾîš[1]+ṣābāʾ[2]* [1]
soldiers, 408+8081, *ʾîš[1]+raglî* [1]
soldiers, 1201+2657, *bēn[1]+ḥayil* [1]
soldiers, 1475, *gibbôr* [1]
soldiers, 1505+408+4878, *geber[1]+ʾîš[1]+milḥāmâ* [1]
soldiers, 2741, *ḥālaṣ[2]* [1]
soldiers, 6639+7372, *ʿam[2]+ṣābāʾ[2]* [1]
foot soldiers, 7305, *pārāš[2]* [1]
soldiers, 7372, *ṣābāʾ[2]* [1]
soldiers, 9530+4878, *tāpaś+milḥāmâ* [1]
soldiers, 10131, *gᵉbar* [1]
strongest soldiers, 10132+10264, *gibbar+ḥayil* [1]

SOLE [4]
sole, 4090, *kap* [4]

SOLEMN [4]
solemn, 1524, *gādôl* [1]
solemn, 3878, *kābēd[2]* [1]
gave solemn oath, 8678, *šābaʿ* [1]
pronounced solemn oath, 8678, *šābaʿ* [1]

SOLEMNLY [7]
solemnly swore, 8678, *šābaʿ* [2]
solemnly declared, 6386, *ʿûd[1]* [1]
warn solemnly, 6386+6386, *ʿûd[1]+ʿûd[1]* [1]
warned solemnly, 6386+6386, *ʿûd[1]+ʿûd[1]* [1]
solemnly consecrate, 7727+7727, *qādaš+qādaš* [1]
solemnly promised, 8678, *šābaʿ* [1]

SOLES [7]
soles, 4090, *kap* [6]
soles, 9247, *šōreš* [1]

SOLID [3]
solid, 3972, *kōl* [1]
solid, 4003, *kālîl* [1]
solid, 4816, *miklôt* [1]

SOLITARY [1]
solitary, 1620, *gᵉzērâ* [1]

SOLOMON [241]
Solomon, 8976, *šᵉlōmōh* [235]
Solomon, *NIH/RPE* [3]
Solomon[s], 2257, *-ô* [3]

SOLOMON'S [36]
Solomon's, 8976, *šᵉlōmōh* [26]
Solomon's, 4200+8976, *lᵉ-[1]+šᵉlōmōh* [7]
Solomon's[s], 2257, *-ô* [2]
Solomon's, 8611+4200+8976, *ša-+lᵉ-[1]+šᵉlōmōh* [1]

SOLVE [2]
solve, 10742, *šᵉrâ* [2]

SOLVED [1]
solved, 5162, *māṣāʾ* [1]

SOME [331]
some, 4946, *min* [123]
some, *AIT* [99]
some, *NIH/RPE* [16]
some[s], 408, *ʾîš[1]* [10]
some[s], 2021, *ha-* [9]
some time later, 339+2021+1821+2021+465, *ʾaḥar+ha-+dābār+ha-+ʾēlleh* [6]
some, 465, *ʾēlleh* [5]
some, 4946+3972, *min+kōl* [4]
some, 285, *ʾeḥād* [3]
some time later, 339+4027, *ʾaḥar+kēn[2]* [3]
some, 928, *bᵉ-* [3]
some time, 3427, *yôm[1]* [3]
some[s], 10131, *gᵉbar* [3]
some[s], 74, *ʾeben* [2]
some, 1821, *dābār* [2]
some, 3855, *yātar* [2]
some, 4200, *lᵉ-[1]* [2]
some time later, 4946+3427, *min+yôm[1]* [2]
some of, 4946, *min* [2]
some, 4946+7921, *min+qᵉṣāt* [2]
some other[s], 285, *ʾeḥād* [1]
some time later, 339, *ʾaḥar* [1]
some time after, 339, *ʾaḥar* [1]
some of them[s], 408, *ʾîš[1]* [1]
some[s], 889, *ʾᵃšer* [1]
some other place[s], 889, *ʾᵃšer* [1]
some of, 928, *bᵉ-* [1]
some[s], 1201, *bēn[1]* [1]
for some time, 1685+9453+1685+8997, *gam+tᵉmôl+gam+šilšôm* [1]
some distance away, 2134, *hālᵉʾâ* [1]
took some of the things, 2745, *ḥālaq[2]* [1]
had some left over, 3855, *yātar* [1]
some, 3869+5071, *kᵉ-+mᵉʿaṭ* [1]
some, 3869, *kᵉ-* [1]
some distance, 3896+2021+824, *kᵉbārâ[2]+ha-+ʾereṣ* [1]
some distance, 3896+824, *kᵉbārâ[2]+ʾereṣ* [1]
some years later, 4200+7891+9102, *lᵉ-[1]+qēṣ+šānâ[2]* [1]
some day, 4737, *māḥār* [1]
some distance away, 4946+8158, *min+rāḥôq* [1]
some distance from, 4946+7156, *min+pāneh* [1]
some, 4946+907, *min+ʾēt[2]* [1]
some[s], 4950, *mānâ[2]* [1]
some, 5071, *mᵉʿaṭ* [1]
some distance away, 5305, *merḥāq* [1]
some distance, 5584, *neged* [1]
some, 7326, *pat* [1]
gone some distance, 8178, *rāḥaq* [1]
some distance away, 8178+4946, *rāḥaq+min* [1]
some[s], 9109, *šᵉnayim* [1]
some, 10427, *min* [1]

SOMEBODY [2]
somebody, *AIT* [1]
pretend to be somebody, 3877, *kābēd[1]* [1]

SOMEONE [64]
someone, *AIT* [16]
someone, 408, *ʾîš[1]* [12]
someone, *NIH/RPE* [7]
someone, 132, *ʾādām[1]* [3]
someone, 2084, *-hû* [3]
someone, 5883, *nepeš* [3]
someone[s], 2021, *ha-* [2]
someone, 2021, *ha-* [2]
someone, 4769, *mî* [2]
someone, 285+2021+6639, *ʾeḥād+ha-+ʿam[2]* [1]
someone, 285, *ʾeḥād* [1]
someone else's, 337, *ʾaḥēr[1]* [1]
someone else, 337, *ʾaḥēr[1]* [1]
someone, 889, *ʾᵃšer* [1]
someone else[s], 928+3338, *bᵉ-+yād* [1]
someone[s], 2021+5877, *ha-+nāpal* [1]
someone[s], 2021+8011, *ha-+rāʿâ[1]* [1]
someone, 2257, *-ô* [1]
someone[s], 4637, *mût* [1]
pretend to be someone else, 5796, *nākar[2]* [1]
someone else, 5799, *nokrî* [1]
someone else, 8295, *rēʿût[1]* [1]
someone else, 10025, *ʾoḥᵒrān* [1]

SOMEONE'S [3]
someone's, *NIH/RPE* [2]
someone's, 2257, *-ô* [1]

SOMETHING [62]
something, *AIT* [9]
something, *NIH/RPE* [9]
something, 889, *ʾᵃšer* [4]
something, 1821, *dābār* [4]
something[s], 4312, *leḥem* [3]
something[s], 2021, *ha-* [2]
something, 3972, *kōl* [2]
something to eat, 7326+4312, *pat+leḥem* [2]
something holy, 7731, *qōdeš* [2]
something totally new, 1375, *bᵉrîʾâ* [1]
something done, 1691, *gᵉmûl* [1]
something to say, 1821, *dābār* [1]
something[s], 2085, *hûʾ* [1]
something[s], 2257, *-ô* [1]
something remembered, 2355, *zikkārôn* [1]
aren't do something, 3120, *ḥāšâ* [1]
something dreadful, 3170, *ḥᵃṭat[1]* [1]
something to dig with, 3845, *yātēd* [1]
something, 3972+3998, *kōl+kᵉlî* [1]
something made, 4382, *lāšād* [1]
something, 4399, *mᵉʾûmâ* [1]
something to eat, 4407, *maʾᵃkāl* [1]
something useful, 4856, *mᵉlāʾkâ* [1]
something happened, 5247, *miqreh* [1]
have something to eat, 6184, *sāʿad* [1]
something else, 6388, *ʿôd* [1]
do something, 6913, *ʿāśâ[1]* [1]
something, 7189, *pōʿal* [1]
something entrusted, 7214, *piqqādôn* [1]
something desperate, 8288, *rāʿâ[3]* [1]
something rotten, 8373, *rāqāb* [1]
something else, 8740, *šûb[1]* [1]
something horrible, 9136, *šaʿᵃrûr* [1]
something to do with, 10089, *bᵉ-* [1]

SOMETIMES [2]
sometimes, 3780+889, *yēš+ʾᵃšer* [2]

SOMEWHERE [1]
somewhere, 5226, *māqôm* [1]

SON [1909]
son, 1201, *bēn[1]* [1846]
son, *NIH/RPE* [20]
son, *AIT* [14]
only son, 3495, *yāḥîd* [5]
son, 10120, *bar[2]* [5]
son, 1337, *bar[1]* [4]
son, 2351, *zākār* [3]
had a son, 3528, *yālad* [2]
son, 132, *ʾādām[1]* [1]
son, 408, *ʾîš[1]* [1]
son[s], 889, *ʾᵃšer* [1]
that son[s], 2085, *hûʾ* [1]
her son[s], 2257, *-ô* [1]
son, 2446+408, *zeraʿ+ʾîš[1]* [1]
has son, 3528, *yālad* [1]
have a son, 3528, *yālad* [1]
son be born, 3528, *yālad* [1]
son, 3529, *yeled* [1]

SON'S [12]
son's, 1201, *bēn[1]* [12]

SON-IN-LAW [11]
son-in-law, 3163, *ḥātān* [6]
son-in-law, 3161, *ḥātan* [5]

SONG [76]
song, 8877, *šîr[2]* [47]
song, 8878, *šîrâ* [11]
song, 8262, *rinnâ[1]* [4]
song, 2379, *zimrâ[1]* [3]
mock in song, 5593, *nᵉgînâ* [2]
music and song, 2369, *zāmîr[1]* [1]

song, 2369, *zāmîr*[1] [1]
theme of song, 2369, *zāmîr*[1] [1]
song, 5593, *nᵉgînâ* [1]
mournful song, 5631, *nᵉhî* [1]
song, 7754, *qôl* [1]
jubilant song, 8264, *rānan* [1]
praised in song, 8876, *šîr*[1] [1]
sang song, 8876, *šîr*[1] [1]

SONGS [33]
songs, 8877, *šîr*[2] [11]
songs of joy, 8262, *rinnâ*[1] [4]
songs, 2369, *zāmîr*[1] [2]
songs of thanksgiving, 9343, *tôdâ* [2]
songs, *NIH/RPE* [1]
songs, 1426+8877, *bat*[1]*+šîr*[2] [1]
songs, 1821+8877, *dābār+šîr*[2] [1]
songs of thanksgiving, 2117, *huyyᵉdôt* [1]
had wedding songs, 2146, *hālal*[2] [1]
mock in songs, 4947, *mangînâ* [1]
songs, 5593, *nᵉgînâ* [1]
songs, 8260, *rōn* [1]
call forth songs of joy, 8264, *rānan* [1]
songs of joy, 8264, *rānan* [1]
joyful songs, 8265, *rᵉnānâ* [1]
joyful songs, 8525, *śimḥâ* [1]
songs, 8878, *šîrâ* [1]
sing songs, 9048+4200+8123+928+7754,
šāmaʿ+lᵉ-[1]*+rûm*[1]*+bᵉ-+qôl* [1]

SONS [841]
sons, 1201, *bēn*[1] [820]
sons, *NIH/RPE* [5]
sons, *AIT* [4]
sons, 3529, *yeled* [2]
sons, 10120, *bar*[2] [2]
sons, 1033, *bāḥûr*[1] [1]
sons, 2446, *zeraʿ* [1]
had sons, 3528, *yālad* [1]
sons, 3665+5055, *yāṣîʾ+mēʿeh* [1]
his sons[s], 4392, *-ām* [1]
their sons[s], 4392, *-ām* [1]
your sons[s], 4392, *-ām* [1]
sons, 5853, *naʿar*[2] [1]

SONS-IN-LAW [3]
sons-in-law, 3163, *ḥātān* [3]

SOON [65]
as soon as, 3869, *kᵉ-* [24]
soon, *NIH/RPE* [4]
as soon as, 2256, *wᵉ-* [3]
soon, 3869+5071, *kᵉ-+mᵉʿaṭ* [3]
as soon as, 4200, *lᵉ-*[1] [3]
soon, 4554, *māhar*[1] [3]
as soon as, 928, *bᵉ-* [2]
as soon as, 2180, *hinnēh* [2]
as soon as, 3869+889, *kᵉ-+ʾašer* [2]
soon, 4559, *mᵉhērâ* [2]
soon, 6388+5071, *ʿôd+mᵉʿaṭ* [2]
soon, 6964, *ʿattâ* [2]
soon, *AIT* [1]
as soon as, 889, *ʾašer* [1]
soon, 928+7940, *bᵉ-+qārôb* [1]
soon, 2180, *hinnēh* [1]
as soon as, 3869+4027, *kᵉ-+kēn*[2] [1]
soon, 3869+5071+7775, *kᵉ-+mᵉʿaṭ+qāṭ* [1]
very soon, 4559, *mᵉhērâ* [1]
very soon, 6388+5071+4663,
ʿôd+mᵉʿaṭ+mizʿār [1]
soon, 7756, *qûm* [1]
soon, 7928, *qārab* [1]
as soon as, 10008+10427+10168,
ʾᵉdayin+min+dî [1]
as soon as, 10089+10530+10002+10168,
bᵉ-+ʿiddān+-āʾ+dî [1]
as soon as, 10232+10002+10341+10168,
zᵉman[2]*+-āʾ+kᵉ-+dî* [1]

SOONER [6]
no sooner, 677+1153, *ʾap*[1]*+bal*[1] [3]
no sooner than, 1685, *gam* [1]
no sooner than, 3869+889, *kᵉ-+ʾašer* [1]
no sooner than, 3869, *kᵉ-* [1]

SOOT [3]
soot, 7086, *pîaḥ* [2]
soot, 8818, *šᵉḥôr* [1]

SOOTHED [1]
soothed, 8216, *rākak* [1]

SOOTHES [1]
soothes, 4092, *kāpâ* [1]

SOOTHING [1]
soothing, 8216, *rākak* [1]

SOOTHSAYER [1]
soothsayer, 7876, *qāsam* [1]

SOOTHSAYERS [1]
soothsayers, 6726, *ʿānan*[2] [1]

SOPHERETH [1]
Sophereth, 6072, *sôperet* [1]

SORCERERS [4]
sorcerers, 4175, *kāšap* [3]
sorcerers, 4177, *kaššāp* [1]

SORCERESS [2]
sorceress, 4175, *kāšap* [1]
sorceress, 6726, *ʿānan*[2] [1]

SORCERIES [3]
sorceries, 4176, *kešep* [3]

SORCERY [8]
sorcery, 5728, *naḥaš* [2]
practiced sorcery, 6726, *ʿānan*[2] [2]
sorcery, 6726, *ʿānan*[2] [2]
sorcery, 5727, *nāḥaš* [1]
practice sorcery, 6726, *ʿānan*[2] [1]

SORE [14]
sore, 5596, *negaʿ* [11]
running sore, 2307, *zûb* [1]
sore, 4649, *māzôr*[1] [1]
this kind of sore, 5596+2021+5999,
negaʿ+ha-+neteq [1]

SOREK [1]
Sorek, 8604, *śōrēq*[2] [1]

SORES [9]
running sores, 3539, *yallepet* [2]
sores, 4649, *māzôr*[1] [2]
festering sores, 1734, *gārāb* [1]
sores, 4804, *makkâ* [1]
sores, 5596, *negaʿ* [1]
bring sores on, 8558, *śāpaḥ* [1]
sores, 8825, *šᵉḥîn* [1]

SORROW [23]
sorrow, 3326, *yāgôn* [13]
sorrow, 4088, *kaʿas* [4]
sorrow, *NIH/RPE* [1]
sorrow, 16, *ʾᵃbôy* [1]
sorrow, 65, *ʾēbel* [1]
sorrow, 224, *ʾāwen*[1] [1]
sorrow, 1790, *dāʾab* [1]
sorrow, 9342, *tûgâ* [1]

SORROWS [4]
sorrows, 4799, *makʾōb* [2]
sorrows, 5652, *nûg* [1]
sorrows, 6780, *ʿaṣṣebet* [1]

SORRY [1]
felt sorry, 2798, *ḥāmal* [1]

SORT [2]
sort, 3869, *kᵉ-* [1]
sort of things he says, 8490, *śîaḥ*[3] [1]

SORTS [4]
all sorts, 7896, *qāṣâ*[2] [2]
sorts, *AIT* [1]
all sorts, 4946+7896, *min+qāṣâ*[2] [1]

SOTAI [2]
Sotai, 6055, *sôṭay* [2]

SOUGHT [32]
sought, 2011, *dāraš* [11]
sought, 1335, *bāqaš* [5]
sought the favor of, 2704+906+7156,
ḥālâ[2]*+ʾēt*[1]*+pāneh* [3]
sought, *NIH/RPE* [2]
sought out, 1335, *bāqaš* [2]
sought out, 2011, *dāraš* [2]
be sought, 1335, *bāqaš* [1]
sought to, 1335, *bāqaš* [1]
Sought After, 2011, *dāraš* [1]
sought favor, 2704+906+7156,
ḥālâ[2]*+ʾēt*[1]*+pāneh* [1]
sought, 2704, *ḥālâ*[2] [1]
sought favor, 7156+2704, *pāneh+ḥālâ*[2] [1]
sought out, 10114, *bᵉʿâ* [1]

SOUL [110]
soul, 5883, *nepeš* [105]
soul, 3883, *kābôd*[1] [2]
heart and soul, 3869+4222, *kᵉ-+lēbāb* [1]
living soul, 5883, *nepeš* [1]
harmless soul, 5929+2855, *nāqî+ḥinnām* [1]

SOULS [4]
souls, 5883, *nepeš* [4]

SOUND [99]
sound, 7754, *qôl* [62]
sound, 9546, *tāqaʿ* [7]
sound, 10631, *qāl* [4]
sound, 9048, *šāmaʿ* [3]
sound judgment, 9370, *tûšiyyâ* [3]
sound, *NIH/RPE* [2]
sound, 7754+6702, *qôl+ʿānâ*[4] [2]
sound, 622, *ʾemet* [1]
utter a sound, 2047, *hāgâ*[1] [1]
sound out, 2983, *ḥāqar* [1]
sound, 3202, *ṭôb*[2] [1]
sound, 3972, *kōl* [1]
sound long, 5432, *māšak* [1]
sound, 6296, *ʿābar*[1] [1]
sound, 8123+7754, *rûm*[1]*+qôl* [1]
sound a blast, 8131, *rûaʿ* [1]
sound alarm, 8131, *rûaʿ* [1]
sound of battle cry, 8131, *rûaʿ* [1]
sound, 8131, *rûaʿ* [1]
rattling sound, 8323, *raʿaš* [1]
sound, 8934, *šālôm* [1]
sound be heard, 9048, *šāmaʿ* [1]
sound the trumpets, 9558, *tᵉrûʿâ* [1]

SOUNDED [12]
sounded, 9546, *tāqaʿ* [10]
have sounded, 6296, *ʿābar*[1] [1]
sounded blast, 9546, *tāqaʿ* [1]

SOUNDING [8]
sounding, 9546, *tāqaʿ* [3]
sounding, 7754, *qôl* [2]
sounding, 2955, *ḥaṣṣar* [1]
sounding, 9048, *šāmaʿ* [1]
sounding, 9547, *tēqaʿ* [1]

SOUNDNESS [2]
soundness, 5507, *mᵉtōm* [1]
soundness, 8934, *šālôm* [1]

SOUNDS [9]
sounds, 7754, *qôl* [6]
sounds, 9546, *tāqaʿ* [2]
sounds a long blast, 5432, *māšak* [1]

SOUR [4]
sour grapes, 1235, *bōser* [3]
sour, *NIH/RPE* [1]

SOURCE [5]
source of strength, 1476, *gᵉbûrâ* [1]
source of confidence, 4440, *mibṭāḥ* [1]
source of contention, 4506, *mādôn*[1] [1]
source of, 5227, *māqôr* [1]
source of grief, 5289+8120, *mōrâ+rûaḥ* [1]

SOURCES [2]
distant sources, 2424, *zār* [1]
sources, 4441, *mabbāk* [1]

SOUTH [117]
south, 5582, *negeb* [38]
south, 1999, *dārôm* [17]
south, 3545, *yāmîn*[1] [13]
south, 3556, *y*[e]*mānî* [9]
south, 5582+2025, *negeb+-â*[2] [9]
south, 9402, *têmān*[1] [8]
south, 9402+2025, *têmān*[1]*+-â*[2] [5]
south, 4946+5582, *min+negeb* [4]
south, 5582+9402+2025, *negeb+têmān*[1]*+-â*[2] [3]
the king of the South[s], 2257, *-ô* [2]
south, 4946+3545, *min+yāmîn*[1] [2]
south, 5582+9402, *negeb+têmān*[1] [2]
south wind, 9402, *têmān*[1] [2]
south wind, 1999, *dārôm* [1]
south, 5582+2025+9402+2025, *negeb+-â*[2]*+têmān*[1]*+-â*[2] [1]
south, 9402+2025+5582+2025, *têmān*[1]*+-â*[2]*+negeb+-â*[2] [1]

SOUTHEAST [2]
southeast, 7711+2025+5582+2025, *qēdem+-â*[2]*+negeb+-â*[2] [1]
southeast, 7711+2025+5582, *qēdem+-â*[2]*+negeb* [1]

SOUTHERN [11]
southern, 5582, *negeb* [6]
southern, 5582+2025, *negeb+-â*[2] [3]
southern, 448+6991+5582, *'el+pē'â*[1]*+negeb* [1]
southern, 4946+5582, *min+negeb* [1]

SOUTHERNMOST [1]
southernmost, 4946+7895, *min+qāṣeh* [1]

SOUTHLAND [2]
southland, 5582, *negeb* [1]
southland, 8441+5582, *śādeh+negeb* [1]

SOUTHWARD [3]
southward, 448+2021+3545, *'el+ha-+yāmîn*[1] [1]
southward, 1999, *dārôm* [1]
southward, 4946+9402, *min+têmān*[1] [1]

SOVEREIGN [298]
Sovereign, 151, *'adōnāy* [291]
sovereign, 10718, *šallîṭ* [4]
Sovereign, 123, *'ādôn* [2]
sovereign power, 10424, *malkû* [1]

SOVEREIGNTY [2]
sovereignty, 10424, *malkû* [2]

SOW [19]
sow, 2445, *zāra'* [16]
sow, 3655, *yāṣā'* [1]
seed to sow, 5433+2446, *mešek*[1]*+zera'* [1]
sow, 7046, *pûṣ*[1] [1]

SOWED [1]
sowed, 2445, *zāra'* [1]

SOWER [2]
sower, 2445, *zāra'* [2]

SOWING [1]
sowing seed, 2445, *zāra'* [1]

SOWN [5]
sown, 2445, *zāra'* [4]
sown field, 4669, *mizrā'* [1]

SOWS [2]
sows, 2445, *zāra'* [2]

SPACE [10]
space, 5226, *māqôm* [2]
space, *NIH/RPE* [1]
took space, 430, *'ākal* [1]
floor space, 824, *'ereṣ* [1]
available space, 5113, *ma'ar* [1]
give more space, 5602, *nāgaš* [1]
space, 6298, *'ēber*[1] [1]
space, 8119, *rewaḥ* [1]
empty space, 9332, *tōhû* [1]

SPACIOUS [11]
spacious, 8146+3338, *rāḥāb*[1]*+yād* [4]
spacious place, 5303, *merḥāb* [3]
spacious, 8146, *rāḥāb*[1] [2]
spacious, 8118, *rāwaḥ* [1]
spacious place, 8144, *raḥab* [1]

SPAN [9]
span, 2455, *zeret* [5]
span of years, 2698, *ḥeled* [1]
span of life, 3427, *yôm*[1] [1]
life span, 5031+3427, *mispār*[1]*+yôm*[1] [1]
span, 8145, *rōḥab* [1]

SPARE [36]
spare, 2798, *ḥāmal* [12]
spare, *NIH/RPE* [3]
spare, 3855, *yātar* [3]
spare, 2649, *ḥāyâ* [2]
spare, 5951, *nāśā'* [2]
spare, 6296, *'ābar*[1] [2]
spare, 8636, *šā'ar* [2]
spare, 2571, *ḥûs* [1]
spare life, 2649, *ḥāyâ* [1]
spare lives, 2649, *ḥāyâ* [1]
spare, 3104, *ḥāśak* [1]
spare, 3828, *yāša'* [1]
spare, 7003, *pāga'* [1]
spare, 7021, *pāda'* [1]
have to spare, 8425, *śāba'* [1]
remnant spare, 8636, *šā'ar* [1]
spare, 9068, *šāmar* [1]

SPARED [25]
spared, 2649, *ḥāyâ* [10]
spared, 2798, *ḥāmal* [4]
spared, *NIH/RPE* [1]
spared, 2571, *ḥûs* [1]
spared lives, 2649, *ḥāyâ* [1]
is spared, 3104, *ḥāśak* [1]
spared, 4880, *mālaṭ*[1] [1]
spared from, 4946+7156, *min+pāneh* [1]
spared, 5911, *nāṣal* [1]
was spared, 5911, *nāṣal* [1]
is spared, 5915, *nāṣar* [1]
spared, 8938, *šālaḥ* [1]
spared, 10262, *ḥ*[a]*yâ* [1]

SPARES [2]
in compassion spares, 2798, *ḥāmal* [1]
spares, 3104, *ḥāśak* [1]

SPARING [4]
sparing, 2649, *ḥāyâ* [1]
sparing, 3104, *ḥāśak* [1]
sparing, 3855, *yātar* [1]
sparing, 8636, *šā'ar* [1]

SPARK [1]
spark, 5773, *nîṣôṣ* [1]

SPARKLE [1]
sparkle, 5824, *nāsas*[2] [1]

SPARKLED [2]
sparkled, 6524, *'ayin*[1] [2]

SPARKLES [1]
sparkles, 5989+6524, *nātan+'ayin*[1] [1]

SPARKLING [2]
sparkling jewels, 74+734, *'eben+'eqdāḥ* [1]
sparkling, 6524, *'ayin*[1] [1]

SPARKS [2]
sparks, 1201+8404, *bēn*[1]*+rešep*[1] [1]
sparks, 3958, *kîdôd* [1]

SPARROW [2]
sparrow, 7606, *ṣippôr*[1] [2]

SPATTERED [3]
spattered, 5684, *nāzâ*[1] [2]
is spattered, 5684, *nāzâ*[1] [1]

SPEAK [226]
speak, 1819, *dābar*[2] [170]
speak, 606, *'āmar*[1] [12]
speak, *NIH/RPE* [5]
speak out, 1819, *dābar*[2] [4]
speak, 1821, *dābār* [3]
speak, 8488, *śîaḥ*[1] [3]
speak up, 1819, *dābar*[2] [2]
not speak, 3120, *ḥāšâ* [2]
speak, 4946+7023, *min+peh* [2]
speak, 5583, *nāgad* [2]
speak, 7023, *peh* [2]
speak up, 7337+7023, *pātaḥ*[1]*+peh* [2]
speak, *AIT* [1]
that cannot speak, 522, *'illēm* [1]
those who cannot speak, 522, *'illēm* [1]
speak, 928+7023, *b*[e]*-+peh* [1]
speak, 1655, *gālâ* [1]
speak well, 1819+1819, *dābar*[2]*+dābar*[2] [1]
speak with words, 1819, *dābar*[2] [1]
speak up, 1821, *dābār* [1]
speak, 2047, *hāgâ*[1] [1]
speak deceit, 2744, *ḥālaq*[1] [1]
fail to speak, 3087, *ḥārēš*[2] [1]
speak, 3655, *yāṣā'* [1]
speak, 4910, *mālal*[3] [1]
speak up, 5583, *nāgad* [1]
speak, 6218, *sāpar* [1]
those who speak up for, 6332, *'ēd* [1]
speak, 10418+10425, *millâ+m*[e]*lal* [1]

SPEAKING [44]
speaking, 1819, *dābar*[2] [38]
speaking, 4863, *millâ* [2]
speaking, *NIH/RPE* [1]
speaking, 1821, *dābār* [1]
speaking, 7754+1821, *qôl+dābār* [1]
speaking, 10425, *m*[e]*lal* [1]

SPEAKS [26]
speaks, 1819, *dābar*[2] [18]
speaks, 1821, *dābār* [2]
speaks, 606, *'āmar*[1] [1]
speaks, 1655+265, *gālâ+'ōzen* [1]
speaks, 2047, *hāgâ*[1] [1]
speaks, 7023+7337, *peh+pātaḥ*[1] [1]
speaks, 7032, *pûaḥ*[2] [1]
speaks rashly, 7316+8557, *pāśaq+śāpâ* [1]

SPEAR [46]
spear, 2851, *ḥ*[a]*nît* [38]
spear, 8242, *rōmaḥ* [5]
spear, *NIH/RPE* [1]
spear, 3959, *kîdôn* [1]
spear, 4751, *maṭṭeh* [1]

SPEARHEAD [1]
spearhead, 7802, *qayin*[1] [1]

SPEARS [21]
spears, 8242, *rōmaḥ* [10]
spears, 2851, *ḥ*[a]*nît* [8]
spears of pine, 1360, *b*[e]*rôš* [1]
spears, 3959, *kîdôn* [1]
spears, 7528, *ṣilṣāl*[2] [1]

SPECIAL [25]
special guard, 1475, *gibbôr* [3]
special gifts, 9556+3338, *t*[e]*rûmâ+yād* [3]
special favor, 1388, *b*[e]*rākâ*[1] [2]
special gift, 9556, *t*[e]*rûmâ* [2]
special ability, 2657, *ḥayil* [1]
make special bread, 4221+4223, *lābab*[2]*+l*[e]*bibâ* [1]
special food, 4950, *mānâ*[2] [1]
fulfill a special vow, 7098+5624, *pālā'+nēder* [1]
make a special vow, 7098+5623, *pālā'+nādar* [1]
makes a special vow, 7098+5624, *pālā'+nēder* [1]
special vows, 7098+5624, *pālā'+nēder* [1]
special vow, 7098+5624, *pālā'+nēder* [1]
had special access to, 8011+7156, *rā'â*[1]*+pāneh* [1]
special, 8031, *rō'š*[1] [1]
as a special gift set aside, 8123, *rûm* [1]
portion as a special gift, 9556, *t*[e]*rûmâ* [1]
special gifts, 9556, *t*[e]*rûmâ* [1]

special portion, 9556, t^{e}*rûmâ* [1]
special gift, 9557, t^{e}*rûmiyyâ* [1]

SPECIFIC [1]
specific things, 3998+5466, *k^{e}lî+mišmeret* [1]

SPECIFICATIONS [2]
specifications, 5477, *mišpāṭ* [2]

SPECIFIED [9]
specified, 5477, *mišpāṭ* [8]
specified amount, 6886, *ʿērek* [1]

SPECIFY [1]
specify, 8938, *šālaḥ* [1]

SPECKLED [10]
speckled, 5923, *nāqōd* [9]
speckled, 7380, *ṣābûaʿ* [1]

SPECTACLE [2]
spectacle, 8019, *raʾ^{a}wâ* [1]
spectacle, 8024, *r^{o}ʾî* [1]

SPED [1]
sped forth, 8351, *rāṣāʾ^{1}* [1]

SPEECH [22]
speech, 8557, *śāpâ* [5]
speech, 7023, *peh* [4]
speech, 608, *ʾōmer* [2]
speech, 614, *ʾimrâ* [2]
strange speech, 7743+7743, *qāw^{2}+qāw^{2}* [2]
speech, 7754, *qôl* [2]
makes speech, 609+606, *ʾēmer^{1}+ʾāmar^{1}* [1]
speech, 1821, *dābār* [1]
speech, 2674, *ḥēk* [1]
speech, 4383, *lāšôn* [1]
speech, 4537+1819, *mâ+dābar^{2}* [1]

SPEECHES [4]
speeches, 4863, *millâ* [2]
speeches, 1821, *dābār* [1]
make fine speeches, 2488+928+4863, *ḥābar^{1}+b^{e}-+millâ* [1]

SPEECHLESS [1]
speechless, 519, *ʾālam^{1}* [1]

SPEEDILY [3]
speedily, 4559, *m^{e}hērâ* [1]
speedily, 7824, *qal* [1]
speedily, 8088, *rāgaʿ^{1}* [1]

SPEEDS [1]
speeds, 4542, *māhîr* [1]

SPELLS [4]
casts spells, 2489+2490, *ḥābar^{2}+ḥeber^{1}* [1]
magic spells, 2490, *ḥeber^{1}* [1]
spells, 2490, *ḥeber^{1}* [1]
cast spells, 6726, *ʿānan^{2}* [1]

SPELT [3]
spelt, 4081, *kussemet* [3]

SPEND [33]
spend the night, 4328, *lîn* [17]
spend, 3983, *kālâ^{1}* [8]
spend, 4328, *lîn* [2]
went in to spend the night with, 995+448, *bôʾ+ʾel* [1]
spend days, 4328, *lîn* [1]
spend nights, 4328, *lîn* [1]
spend, 5989, *nātan* [1]
spend, 7049, *pûq^{2}* [1]
spend, 9202, *šāqal* [1]

SPENT [22]
spent the night, 4328, *lîn* [6]
spent, *AIT* [3]
spent, 3983, *kālâ^{1}* [3]
spent, 4328, *lîn* [3]
spent, 2118, *hāyâ* [2]
spent, 3782, *yāšab* [1]
spent the nights, 4328, *lîn* [1]
was spent for making, 6913+4946, *ʿāśâ^{1}+min* [1]
spent, 9462, *tāmam* [1]
spent the night, 10102, *bît* [1]

SPEW [3]
spew, *NIH/RPE* [1]
make spew out, 3655+4946+7023, *yāṣāʾ+min+peh* [1]
spew, 5580, *nābaʿ* [1]

SPEWED [1]
spewed out, 5615, *nādaḥ^{1}* [1]

SPICE [3]
spice, 1411, *bōśem* [3]

SPICE-LADEN [1]
spice-laden, 1411, *bōśem* [1]

SPICED [1]
spiced, 8380, *reqaḥ* [1]

SPICES [27]
spices, 1411, *bōśem* [21]
spices, 5780, *n^{e}kōʾt* [2]
spices, 86, *ʾ^{a}bāqâ* [1]
mixed with spices, 5008, *mesek* [1]
spices, 5350, *merqāḥâ* [1]
fragrant spices, 6160, *sam* [1]

SPIDER'S [2]
spider's, 6571, *ʿakkābîš* [2]

SPIED [4]
spied out, 8078, *rāgal* [4]

SPIES [13]
spies, 8078, *rāgal* [8]
spies, 408+8078, *ʾîš^{1}+rāgal* [1]
the spies^{s}, 2156, *hēm* [1]
the spies^{s}, 2157, *-hem* [1]
spies, 4855, *malʾāk* [1]
spies, 9068, *šāmar* [1]

SPILLED [3]
spilled, 5599, *nāgar* [1]
spilled, 8845, *šāḥat* [1]
spilled out, 9161, *šāpak* [1]

SPILLS [1]
spills, 9161, *šāpak* [1]

SPIN [1]
spin, 755, *ʾārag* [1]

SPINDLE [1]
spindle, 7134, *pelek^{1}* [1]

SPIRIT [195]
spirit, 8120, *rûaḥ* [176]
spirit, 10658, *rûaḥ* [6]
spirit, 5883, *nepeš* [5]
spirit, *NIH/RPE* [2]
spirit, 5972, *n^{e}šāmâ* [2]
spirit, 200, *ʾôb^{2}* [1]
spirit, 466, *ʾ^{e}lōhîm* [1]
spirit, 4000, *kilyâ* [1]
spirit, 4213, *lēb* [1]

SPIRITIST [2]
spiritist, 3362, *yidd^{e}ʿōnî* [2]

SPIRITISTS [9]
spiritists, 3362, *yidd^{e}ʿōnî* [9]

SPIRITS [14]
in high spirits, 3201+4213, *ṭôb^{1}+lēb* [4]
spirits, 8120, *rûaḥ* [4]
spirits of the dead, 356, *ʾiṭṭîm* [1]
in good spirits, 3512+4213, *yāṭab+lēb* [1]
in high spirits, 4213+3201, *lēb+ṭôb^{1}* [1]
departed spirits, 8327, *r^{e}pāʾîm^{1}* [1]
spirits of the dead, 8327, *r^{e}pāʾîm^{1}* [1]
spirits of the departed, 8327, *r^{e}pāʾîm^{1}* [1]

SPIT [5]
spit, 3762+3762, *yāraq+yāraq* [1]
spit, 3762, *yāraq* [1]
spit out, 7794, *qîʾ^{1}* [1]
spit, 8371, *rōq* [1]
spit, 9531, *tōpet^{1}* [1]

SPITE [13]
in spite of, 928, *b^{e}-* [8]
in spite of, 6584, *ʿal^{2}* [3]
in spite of, 1685, *gam* [1]
in spite of, 6640, *ʿim* [1]

SPITS [1]
spits, 8394, *rāqaq* [1]

SPITTING [1]
spitting, 8371, *rōq* [1]

SPLENDID [3]
splendid, 129, *ʾaddîr* [1]
splendid, 168, *ʾadderet* [1]
splendid, 3883, *kābôd^{1}* [1]

SPLENDOR [63]
splendor, 2077, *hādār* [12]
splendor, 2086, *hôd^{1}* [10]
splendor, 9514, *tipʾeret* [9]
splendor, 3883, *kābôd^{1}* [6]
splendor, 2079, *h^{a}dārâ* [4]
display splendor, 6995, *pāʾar^{2}* [3]
splendor, 1454, *gāʾôn* [2]
endowed with splendor, 6995, *pāʾar^{2}* [2]
splendor, 8420, *śeʾēt^{1}* [2]
splendor, *NIH/RPE* [1]
splendor, 1470, *gōbah* [1]
splendor, 2075, *hādar* [1]
splendor, 2078, *heder* [1]
splendor, 3199, *ṭ^{e}hār* [1]
shining splendor, 3650, *yipʿâ* [1]
splendor, 3650, *yipʿâ* [1]
splendor, 3701, *yāqār* [1]
splendor, 3702, *y^{e}qār* [1]
splendor, 5586, *nōgah^{1}* [1]
splendor, 5905, *nēṣaḥ^{1}* [1]
splendor, 10199, *h^{a}dar^{2}* [1]
splendor, 10228, *zîw* [1]

SPLINT [1]
splint, 3151, *ḥittûl* [1]

SPLINTERED [3]
splintered, 8368, *rāṣaṣ* [3]

SPLIT [22]
split, 7271, *pāras^{1}* [11]
split, 1324, *bāqaʿ* [3]
split apart, 1324, *bāqaʿ* [2]
be split, 1324, *bāqaʿ* [1]
were split, 2745, *ḥālaq^{2}* [1]
is split asunder, 7297+7297, *pārar^{2}+pārar^{2}* [1]
split open, 7297, *pārar^{2}* [1]
be split apart, 7973, *qāraʿ* [1]
was split apart, 7973, *qāraʿ* [1]

SPLITS [1]
splits, 1324, *bāqaʿ* [1]

SPOIL [2]
make spoil, 1024, *bāzaz* [1]
spoil, 8965, *šālāl* [1]

SPOILS [8]
spoils, 4917, *malqôaḥ* [4]
spoils, 8965, *šālāl* [4]

SPOKE [121]
spoke, 1819, *dābar^{2}* [85]
spoke, 606, *ʾāmar^{1}* [14]
spoke up, 1819, *dābar^{2}* [3]
spoke, 6699, *ʿānâ^{1}* [3]
spoke, *NIH/RPE* [2]
spoke, 1821, *dābār* [2]
spoke up, 6699, *ʿānâ^{1}* [2]
spoke, 10425, *m^{e}lal* [2]
spoke up, 606, *ʾāmar^{1}* [1]
spoke well of, 887, *ʾāšar^{2}* [1]
what spoke, 1821, *dābār* [1]
spoke, 3655, *yāṣāʾ* [1]
spoke the word, 4946+7023, *min+peh* [1]
spoke, 5583, *nāgad* [1]
spoke, 10042, *ʾ^{a}mar* [1]

spoke, 10754, *tûb* [1]

SPOKEN [114]
spoken, 1819, *dābar*[2] [99]
spoken, 606, *ʾămar*[1] [4]
spoken, 7023, *peh* [4]
spoken, *AIT* [1]
spoken, *NIH/RPE* [1]
is spoken, 1819, *dābar*[2] [1]
spoken kindly, 1819+6584+4213, *dābar*[2]*+ʿal*[2]*+lēb* [1]
spoken, 1819+1821, *dābar*[2]*+dābār* [1]
spoken, 1821, *dābār* [1]
spoken, 7023+1819, *peh+dābar*[2] [1]

SPOKES [1]
spokes, 3140, *ḥiššuq* [1]

SPOKESMAN [1]
spokesman, 3869+7023, *k*^{e}*+peh* [1]

SPOKESMEN [1]
spokesmen, 4885, *mēlîṣ* [1]

SPORT [3]
make sport, 7464, *ṣāḥaq* [2]
make sport of, 2118+4200+5442, *hāyâ+l*$^{e-1}$*+māšāl*[1] [1]

SPOT [15]
spot, 994, *baheret* [7]
spot, 5226, *māqôm* [4]
bright spot, 994, *baheret* [2]
at the spot, 9393, *taḥat*[1] [1]
on the spot, 9393, *taḥat*[1] [1]

SPOTLESS [2]
made spotless, 4235, *lāban*[1] [2]

SPOTS [3]
spots, 994, *baheret* [2]
spots, 2494, *ḥ*^{a}*barburôt* [1]

SPOTTED [8]
spotted, 3229, *ṭālāʾ* [6]
spotted, 1353, *bārōd* [2]

SPRANG [1]
sprang up, 2118, *hāyâ* [1]

SPREAD [132]
spread, 7298, *pāraś* [21]
spread out, 7298, *pāraś* [19]
spread, 7313, *pāśâ* [14]
spread, 5989, *nātan* [9]
spread, 3655, *yāṣāʾ* [7]
spread, 2118, *hāyâ* [4]
spread, 5417, *māšaḥ* [4]
spread, 5951, *nāśāʾ* [4]
spread, 2430, *zārâ*[1] [3]
spread out, 5742, *nāṭâ* [3]
spread out, 5759, *nāṭaš* [3]
spread, 6296, *ʿābar*[1] [3]
spread, 6885, *ʿārak* [3]
spread out, 7233, *pārad* [3]
spread out, 8392, *rāqaʿ* [3]
spread, 2143, *hālak* [2]
place to spread, 5427, *mišṭôaḥ* [2]
spread, 5742, *nāṭâ* [2]
spread out, 7287, *pāraṣ* [2]
spread, 7287, *pāraṣ* [2]
spread, 7313+7313, *pāśâ+pāśâ* [2]
spread out, 2430, *zārâ*[1] [1]
spread out, 3253, *ṭāpaḥ*[1] [1]
are spread out, 3667, *yāṣaʿ* [1]
spread out, 3668, *yāṣaq* [1]
spread, 3922, *kûn*[1] [1]
spread out, 5432, *māšak* [1]
spread abroad, 5688, *nāzal* [1]
spread, 5759, *nāṭaš* [1]
spread protection, 6114, *sākak*[1] [1]
spread out, 7046, *pûṣ*[1] [1]
spread, 7596, *ṣāpâ*[2] [1]
spread out, 8146, *rāḥāb*[1] [1]
spread out, 8331, *rāpad* [1]
spread, 8492, *śîm* [1]
spread out, 8848+8848, *šāṭaḥ+šāṭaḥ* [1]
spread out, 8848, *šāṭaḥ* [1]
spread, 9494, *tāʿâ* [1]

SPREADING [38]
spreading, 8316, *ra*^{a}*nān* [11]
spreading, 7298, *pāraś* [5]
spreading, 3655, *yāṣāʾ* [4]
spreading out, 7298, *pāraś* [2]
spreading, 7313+7313, *pāśâ+pāśâ* [2]
spreading, *AIT* [1]
spreading, 802, *ʾōrek* [1]
spreading, 1328, *bāqaq*[2] [1]
places for spreading, 5427, *mišṭôaḥ* [1]
spreading mildew, 5596+7669, *negaʿ+ṣāraʿat* [1]
spreading branches, 5746, *n*^{e}*ṭîšôt* [1]
spreading out, 5759, *nāṭaš* [1]
spreading, 6243, *sāraḥ*[1] [1]
spreading among, 6296, *ʿābar*[1] [1]
spreading, 7255, *pāraḥ*[1] [1]
spreading mildew, 7669, *ṣāraʿat* [1]
spreading slander, 8215, *rākîl* [1]
spreading out, 8392, *rāqaʿ* [1]
spreading, 8938, *šālaḥ* [1]

SPREADS [11]
spreads, 1819, *dābar*[2] [2]
spreads feathers to run, 928+2021+5294+5257, *b*^{e}*+ha+mārôm+mārāʾ*[2] [1]
spreads, 3655, *yāṣāʾ* [1]
spreads out, 5155, *miprāś* [1]
spreads, 5162, *māṣāʾ* [1]
spreads out, 5501, *mātaḥ* [1]
spreads out, 5742, *nāṭâ* [1]
spreads, 5989, *nātan* [1]
spreads out, 7298, *pāraś* [1]
spreads, 7298, *pāraś* [1]

SPRIG [1]
sprig, *AIT* [1]

SPRING [53]
spring, 6524, *ʿayin*[1] [10]
spring, 5078, *maʿyān* [5]
spring rains, 4919, *malqôš* [4]
spring, 5227, *māqôr* [3]
spring, 9588+9102, *t*^{e}*šûbâ+šānâ*[2] [3]
spring, *NIH/RPE* [2]
spring, 4604+4784, *môṣāʾ*[1]*+mayim* [2]
spring, 4784, *mayim* [2]
spring, 6524+4784, *ʿayin*[1]*+mayim* [2]
spring up, 6590, *ʿālâ* [2]
spring up, 7255, *pāraḥ*[1] [2]
every spring, 995+9102, *bôʾ+šānâ*[2] [1]
the spring[s], 2023, *-āh* [1]
spring up, 3655, *yāṣāʾ* [1]
spring, 3655, *yāṣāʾ* [1]
spring, 4432, *mabbûaʿ* [1]
spring of water, 4784, *mayim* [1]
rain in spring, 4919, *malqôš* [1]
spring rain, 4919, *malqôš* [1]
spring, 4919, *malqôš* [1]
spring, 6524+2021+4784, *ʿayin*[1]*+ha+mayim* [1]
spring, 6961+9588+9102, *ʿēt+t*^{e}*šûbâ+šānâ*[2] [1]
spring up, 7238, *pārâ*[1] [1]
make spring up, 7541, *ṣāmaḥ* [1]
spring into being, 7541, *ṣāmaḥ* [1]
spring up, 7541, *ṣāmaḥ* [1]
spring, 9588+2021+9102, *t*^{e}*šûbâ+ha+šānâ*[2] [1]

SPRINGING [1]
springing out, 2397, *zānaq* [1]

SPRINGS [38]
springs, 5078, *maʿyān* [10]
springs, 1657, *gullâ* [4]
springs, 5078+4784, *maʿyān+mayim* [3]
flowing springs, 4604+4784, *môṣāʾ*[1]*+mayim* [2]
springs, 6524+4784, *ʿayin*[1]*+mayim* [2]
deep springs, 9333, *t*^{e}*hôm* [2]
springs, *NIH/RPE* [1]
hot springs, 3553, *yēmim* [1]
springs up, 3655, *yāṣāʾ* [1]
bubbling springs, 4432+4784, *mabbûaʿ+mayim* [1]
springs, 4432, *mabbûaʿ* [1]
springs, 4604+4784, *môṣāʾ*[1]*+mayim* [1]
springs, 5227, *māqôr* [1]
springs, 5569, *nēbek* [1]
what springs from, 6084, *sāḥîš* [1]
springs, 6524, *ʿayin*[1] [1]
springs up, 7437, *ṣûṣ*[1] [1]
springs forth, 7541, *ṣāmaḥ* [1]
springs up, 7541, *ṣāmaḥ* [1]
what springs from, 8826, *šāḥîs* [1]
springs, 9333, *t*^{e}*hôm* [1]

SPRINGTIME [1]
springtime, 6961+4919, *ʿēt+malqôš* [1]

SPRINKLE [31]
sprinkle, 5684, *nāzâ*[1] [17]
sprinkle, 2450, *zāraq*[1] [11]
sprinkle, *NIH/RPE* [1]
sprinkle, 6590, *ʿālâ* [1]
sprinkle, 8959, *šālak* [1]

SPRINKLED [21]
sprinkled, 2450, *zāraq*[1] [15]
been sprinkled, 2450, *zāraq*[1] [2]
sprinkled, 5684, *nāzâ*[1] [2]
sprinkled, 6590, *ʿālâ* [2]

SPRINKLES [2]
sprinkles, 2450, *zāraq*[1] [1]
sprinkles, 5684, *nāzâ*[1] [1]

SPRINKLING [30]
sprinkling bowls, 4670, *mizrāq* [15]
sprinkling bowl, 4670, *mizrāq* [13]
sprinkling, 2450, *zāraq*[1] [1]
bowl used for sprinkling, 4670, *mizrāq* [1]

SPROUT [7]
make sprout, 7541, *ṣāmaḥ* [2]
sprout, 2736, *ḥālap*[1] [1]
surely sprout, 6913+6913, *ʿāśâ*[1]*+ʿāśâ*[1] [1]
sprout, 7255, *pāraḥ*[1] [1]
sprout, 7541, *ṣāmaḥ* [1]
sprout, 7542, *ṣemaḥ* [1]

SPROUTED [4]
sprouted, 7541, *ṣāmaḥ* [3]
sprouted, 7255, *pāraḥ*[1] [1]

SPROUTING [3]
sprouting, *AIT* [2]
sprouting, 7541, *ṣāmaḥ* [1]

SPRUNG [1]
sprung up, 7541, *ṣāmaḥ* [1]

SPUN [3]
spun, 3211, *ṭāwâ* [2]
what spun, 4757, *maṭweh* [1]

SPURN [1]
spurn, 4415, *māʾas*[1] [1]

SPURNED [6]
spurned, 5540, *nāʾaṣ* [5]
spurned, 4415, *māʾas*[1] [1]

SPURNS [1]
spurns, 5540, *nāʾaṣ* [1]

SPURRED [3]
spurred on, 1894, *dāḥap* [2]
spurred on, 6056, *sûk*[1] [1]

SPURS [1]
spurs, *NIH/RPE* [1]

SPY [8]
spy out, 8078, *rāgal* [4]
spy out, 2916, *ḥāpar*[1] [3]
sent to spy out, 9365, *tûr* [1]

SPYING [2]
spying, 8078, *rāgal* [2]

SQUANDERS [1]
squanders, 6, *ʾābad* [1]

STARED [1]
stared with a fixed gaze, 6641+906+7156+2256+8492, *ʿāmad+ʾēt[1]+pāneh+w^e+śîm* [1]

STARES [1]
stares, 6821, *ʿāqâ* [1]

STARGAZERS [1]
stargazers, 2600+928+3919, *ḥāzâ+b^e+kôkāb* [1]

STARRY [15]
starry, 9028, *šāmayim* [9]
starry host, 7372, *ṣābāʾ[2]* [4]
starry, 3919, *kôkāb* [1]
starry hosts, 7372, *ṣābāʾ[2]* [1]

STARS [38]
stars, 3919, *kôkāb* [33]
stars, 7372, *ṣābāʾ[2]* [4]
stars, *NIH/RPE* [1]

START [5]
start, 7756, *qûm* [2]
start, *AIT* [1]
start, 673, *ʾāsar* [1]
start, 2118, *hāyâ* [1]

STARTED [14]
started, 2725, *ḥālal[1]* [4]
started back, 8740, *šûb[1]* [3]
started, *AIT* [2]
started, 1277, *bāʿar[1]* [1]
started, 2118, *hāyâ* [1]
started, 4200+6991, *l^e-[1]+pēʾâ[1]* [1]
started, 4946, *min* [1]
started, 7756, *qûm* [1]

STARTING [3]
starting, 3655, *yāṣāʾ* [1]
starting out from, 4946, *min* [1]
starting, 8040, *rēʾšît* [1]

STARTLE [1]
startle, 1286, *bāʿat* [1]

STARTLED [1]
startled, 3006, *ḥārad* [1]

STARVATION [2]
starvation, 8280, *rāʿāb* [2]

STARVE [2]
starve, 8280, *rāʿāb* [2]

STARVING [4]
starving, 8282, *r^{e}ʿābôn* [2]
starving, 8279, *rāʿēb[1]* [1]
starving, 8281, *rāʿēb[2]* [1]

STATE [5]
state, 1819, *dābar[2]* [1]
state, 6218, *sāpar* [1]
state, 6885, *ʿārak* [1]
righteous state, 7407, *ṣ^{e}dāqâ* [1]
lie in state, 8886+928+3883, *šākab+b^e+kābôd[1]* [1]

STATELY [4]
stately, 129, *ʾaddîr* [1]
stately, 2775, *ḥemdâ* [1]
stately bearing, 3512, *yāṭab* [1]
stately, 3512, *yāṭab* [1]

STATION [4]
station myself, 3656, *yāṣab* [1]
station yourselves, 5938, *nāqap[2]* [1]
station themselves, 5938, *nāqap[2]* [1]
station, 7756, *qûm* [1]

STATIONED [16]
stationed, 6641, *ʿāmad* [8]
stationed, 5989, *nātan* [3]
stationed at, 928, *b^e-* [1]
stationed at, 4200, *l^e-[1]* [1]
stationed around, 6017, *sābîb* [1]
stationed, 6885, *ʿārak* [1]
stationed, 8492, *śîm* [1]

STATUE [5]
statue, 10614, *ṣ^{e}lēm* [5]

STATURE [2]
stature, 1541, *gādēl* [1]
stature, 7757, *qômâ* [1]

STATUTE [3]
statute, 6343, *ʿēdût* [2]
statute, 2976, *ḥōq* [1]

STATUTES [39]
statutes, 6343, *ʿēdût* [29]
statutes, 2978, *ḥuqqâ* [5]
statutes, 2976, *ḥōq* [4]
statutes, 5477, *mišpāṭ* [1]

STAY [101]
stay, 3782, *yāšab* [40]
stay, *NIH/RPE* [7]
stay, 6641, *ʿāmad* [7]
stay, 4328, *lîn* [6]
stay, 2118, *hāyâ* [5]
stay, 1591, *gûr[1]* [4]
stay for a while, 1591, *gûr[1]* [2]
stay, 1815, *dābaq* [2]
stay, 2143, *hālak* [2]
stay, 3656, *yāṣab* [2]
stay at night, 4328, *lîn* [2]
stay up late, 336, *ʾāḥar* [1]
stay for a meal, 430+4312, *ʾākal+leḥem* [1]
stay, 673, *ʾāsar* [1]
stay there, 2461, *ḥābāʾ* [1]
stay, 2616, *ḥāzaq* [1]
stay alive, 2649, *ḥāyâ* [1]
stay, 2837, *ḥānâ[1]* [1]
stay in, 3782, *yāšab* [1]
stay up, 3782, *yāšab* [1]
stay, 4202+995, *lōʾ+bôʾ* [1]
stay night, 4328, *lîn* [1]
stay tonight, 4328, *lîn* [1]
stay, 5742, *nāṭâ* [1]
stay, 5893, *nāṣab[1]* [1]
stay, 6073, *sûr[1]* [1]
stay, 6806, *ʿāṣar* [1]
stay awake, 7219+6524, *pāqaḥ+ʿayin[1]* [1]
stay open, 7709, *qādam* [1]
stay, 8740+3782, *šûb[1]+yāšab* [1]
stay, 8859, *šîbâ[1]* [1]
stay, 8905, *šākan* [1]
stay, 10201, *h^{a}wâ* [1]

STAYED [61]
stayed, 3782, *yāšab* [32]
stayed, 2118, *hāyâ* [5]
stayed, 6641, *ʿāmad* [4]
stayed, 1591, *gûr[1]* [3]
stayed, 8905, *šākan* [3]
stayed, *NIH/RPE* [2]
stayed behind, 6641, *ʿāmad* [2]
stayed, *AIT* [1]
stayed, 799+8905, *ʾārak+šākan* [1]
for a while stayed, 1591, *gûr[1]* [1]
stayed close, 1815, *dābaq* [1]
stayed, 1815, *dābaq* [1]
stayed at home, 3782, *yāšab* [1]
stayed night, 3782+2256+4328, *yāšab+w^e+lîn* [1]
stayed away, 4202+995, *lōʾ+bôʾ* [1]
stayed, 4472, *māgôr[2]* [1]
stayed, 8886, *šākab* [1]

STAYING [14]
staying, 3782, *yāšab* [8]
staying, 1591, *gûr[1]* [2]
staying, *NIH/RPE* [1]
staying, 2118, *hāyâ* [1]
staying, 4472, *māgôr[2]* [1]
staying, 6641, *ʿāmad* [1]

STAYS [6]
stays, 3782, *yāšab* [2]
stays at night, 4328, *lîn* [1]
stays only a night, 5742+4328, *nāṭâ+lîn* [1]
stays, 6641, *ʿāmad* [1]
stays far, 8178, *rāḥaq* [1]

STEAD [1]
in stead, 9393, *taḥat[1]* [1]

STEADFAST [8]
steadfast, 3922, *kûn[1]* [6]
steadfast, 6164, *sāmak* [2]

STEADFASTLY [1]
steadfastly, 3922, *kûn[1]* [1]

STEADILY [2]
steadily, *AIT* [1]
receded steadily, 8740+2143+2256+8740, *šûb[1]+hālak+w^e+šûb[1]* [1]

STEADY [4]
steady, 296, *ʾāḥaz[1]* [1]
steady, 419, *ʾêtān[1]* [1]
steady, 575, *ʾ^{e}mûnâ* [1]
steady, 599, *ʾāmēṣ* [1]

STEAL [14]
steal, 1704, *gānab* [9]
steal away, 665, *ʾāsap* [1]
steal, 1608, *gāzal* [1]
steal away, 1704, *gānab* [1]
steal in, 1704, *gānab* [1]
steal, 8845, *šāḥat* [1]

STEALING [1]
stealing, 1704, *gānab* [1]

STEALS [3]
steals, 1704, *gānab* [2]
steals forth, 2118, *hāyâ* [1]

STEEDS [3]
steeds, *NIH/RPE* [1]
steeds, 52, *ʾabbîr* [1]
steeds, 7304, *pārāš[1]* [1]

STEEP [1]
steep, 1431, *battâ* [1]

STENCH [10]
stench, 944, *bāʾaš* [3]
stench, 945, *b^{e}ʾōš* [3]
made stench, 944+8194, *bāʾaš+rêaḥ* [1]
made yourself a stench, 944, *bāʾaš* [1]
making a stench, 944, *bāʾaš* [1]
stench, 5215, *maq* [1]

STEP [13]
step, 7576, *ṣaʿad* [5]
step, *NIH/RPE* [2]
step, 2005, *dārak* [1]
step down, 3718, *yārad* [1]
step forward, 5602, *nāgaš* [1]
step, 6811, *ʿāqēb[1]* [1]
step, 7315, *pešaʿ* [1]
step, 8079, *regel* [1]

STEPPED [11]
stepped forward, 3655, *yāṣāʾ* [2]
stepped forward, 7756, *qûm* [2]
stepped, 995, *bôʾ* [1]
stepped aside, 2461, *ḥābāʾ* [1]
stepped out, 3655, *yāṣāʾ* [1]
stepped down, 3718, *yārad* [1]
stepped forward, 5602, *nāgaš* [1]
stepped aside, 6015, *sābab* [1]
stepped out, 6590, *ʿālâ* [1]

STEPPING [2]
avoid stepping, 1925, *dālag* [1]
stepping, 6576, *ʿākas* [1]

STEPS [44]
steps, 5092, *maʿ^{a}lâ[2]* [22]
steps, 7576, *ṣaʿad* [5]
steps, 892, *ʾăšur* [4]
steps, 8079, *regel* [3]
steps, 5202, *miṣʿād* [2]
steps, 7193, *paʿam* [2]
steps, *NIH/RPE* [1]

tripping along with mincing steps, 2143+2256+3262, *hālak+we-+ṭāpap* [1]
steps, 5019, *mesillâ* [1]
steps, 6590, *'ālâ* [1]
steps, 6811, *'āqēb[1]* [1]
taken steps, 7575+7576, *ṣā'ad+ṣa'ad* [1]

STERILE [2]
sterile, 6829, *'āqār* [2]

STERN [1]
stern, 8273, *ra'[1]* [1]

STERN-FACED [1]
stern-faced, 6434+7156, *'az+pāneh* [1]

STEW [7]
stew, 5686, *nāzîd* [6]
stew, *AIT* [1]

STEWARD [9]
the stewards[s], 889+6584, *'ašer+'al[2]* [2]
steward, 5853, *na'ar[2]* [2]
steward, *NIH/RPE* [1]
stewards[s], 408, *'îš[1]* [1]
stewards[s], 889+6584+1074, *'ašer+'al[2]+bayit[1]* [1]
stewards[s], 2021+408+889+6584+1074, *ha-+'îš[1]+'ašer+'al[2]+bayit[1]* [1]
steward, 6125, *sōkēn* [1]

STEWARDS [1]
wine stewards, 8042+1074, *rab[2]+bayit[1]* [1]

STICK [19]
stick, 6770, *'ēṣ* [7]
stick of wood, 6770, *'ēṣ* [3]
burning stick, 202, *'ûd* [2]
make stick, 1815, *dābaq* [2]
stick out, 799, *'ārak* [1]
stick together, 1815, *dābaq* [1]
stick of wood, 5234, *maqqēl* [1]
stick, 8657, *šēbeṭ* [1]
stick out, 9142, *šāpâ* [1]

STICKING [1]
sticking, 1815, *dābaq* [1]

STICKS [7]
sticks, 6770, *'ēṣ* [3]
sticks, 1815, *dābaq* [2]
sticks closer, 1816, *dābēq* [1]
sticks, 5234, *maqqēl* [1]

STIFF-NECKED [18]
stiff-necked, 7996+6902, *qāšâ+'ōrep* [9]
stiff-necked, 7997+6902, *qāšeh+'ōrep* [6]
stiff-necked, 6902+7996, *'ōrep+qāšâ* [2]
stiff-necked, 6902+7997, *'ōrep+qāšeh* [1]

STIFLING [1]
stifling, 8845, *šāḥat* [1]

STILL [182]
still, 6388, *'ôd* [54]
still, *AIT* [29]
still, *NIH/RPE* [26]
while still, 6388, *'ôd* [16]
stood still, 6641, *'āmad* [6]
still, 6330, *'ad[2]* [4]
be still, 1957, *dāmam[1]* [2]
be still, 2187, *has* [2]
still, 2256, *we-* [2]
still, 3954, *kî[2]* [2]
still, 5162, *māṣā'* [2]
still, 6330+2021+3427+2021+2296, *'ad[2]+ha-+yôm[1]+ha-+zeh* [2]
still another, 6388, *'ôd* [2]
stand still, 586, *'āman[1]* [1]
still, 1875, *dûmiyyâ* [1]
stand still, 1957, *dāmam[1]* [1]
still, 1957, *dāmam[1]* [1]
stood still, 1957, *dāmam[1]* [1]
it is still there, 2180, *hinnēh* [1]
and still, 2256, *we-* [1]
still, 2256+1685, *we-+gam* [1]
still, 3087, *ḥārēš[2]* [1]
still not, 3270, *ṭerem* [1]
carried still further, 3578, *yāsap* [1]
still another, 3578+6388, *yāsap+'ôd* [1]
still more, 3578, *yāsap* [1]
stand still, 3656, *yāṣab* [1]
still, 3855, *yātar* [1]
still, 3869+2021+3427+2021+2296, *ke-+ha-+yôm[1]+ha-+zeh* [1]
still, 3972+6388, *kōl+'ôd* [1]
still, 4200+4027, *le-1+kēn[2]* [1]
still to come, 4202+6913, *lō'+'āśâ[1]* [1]
still, 4295, *lûlē'* [1]
still hunger, 4848+1061, *mālē'[1]+beṭen[1]* [1]
still out, 5162, *māṣā'* [1]
while still, 6330, *'ad[2]* [1]
still in force, 6330, *'ad[2]* [1]
still, 6364, *'adenā* [1]
still, 6388+8636, *'ôd+šā'ar* [1]
while still alive, 6584+7156, *'al[2]+pāneh* [1]
lie still, 8101, *rādam* [1]
still, 8332, *rāpâ[1]* [1]
still, 8636, *šā'ar* [1]
still, 8656, *šābaḥ[2]* [1]
still, 9200, *šāqaṭ* [1]
still, 10531, *'ôd* [1]

STILLBORN [4]
stillborn child, 5878, *nēpel* [2]
stillborn infant, 4637, *mût* [1]
stillborn child, 5878+851, *nēpel+'iššâ* [1]

STILLED [6]
stilled, 5877, *nāpal* [1]
stilled, 6700, *'ānâ[2]* [1]
stilled, 7756, *qûm* [1]
stilled, 8656, *šābaḥ[2]* [1]
stilled, 8697, *šābat[1]* [1]
stilled, 8750, *šāwâ[1]* [1]

STINGING [1]
stinging, 2779, *ḥēmâ* [1]

STINGY [2]
stingy man, 8273+6524, *ra'[1]+'ayin[1]* [1]
stingy, 8273+6524, *ra'[1]+'ayin[1]* [1]

STINK [3]
stink, 944, *bā'aš* [2]
stink, 2395, *zānaḥ[1]* [1]

STIPULATIONS [4]
stipulations, 6343, *'ēdût* [4]

STIR [16]
stir up, 6424, *'ûr[3]* [8]
stir up, 1592, *gûr[2]* [1]
stir up, 6056, *sûk[1]* [1]
stir, 6424, *'ûr[3]* [1]
stir up, 6590, *'ālâ* [1]
stir up, 6913, *'āśâ[1]* [1]
stir up, 7032, *pûaḥ[2]* [1]
stir, 7192, *pā'am* [1]
stir up, 7756, *qûm* [1]

STIRRED [14]
stirred up, 6424, *'ûr[3]* [6]
be stirred up, 1764, *gāraš[2]* [1]
stirred, 1931, *dālaḥ* [1]
stirred, 2101, *hûm* [1]
being stirred up, 6424, *'ûr[3]* [1]
stirred up, 6641, *'āmad* [1]
no longer stirred, 7296, *pārar[1]* [1]
stirred up jealous anger, 7861, *qānā'* [1]
stirred, 8180, *rāḥaš* [1]

STIRRING [3]
stirring up more, 3578, *yāsap* [1]
stirring up, 4790, *mîş* [1]
stirring up, 7443, *ṣûr[1]* [1]

STIRS [12]
stirs up, 1741, *gārâ* [3]
stirs up, 8938, *šālaḥ* [3]
stirs up, 6424, *'ûr[3]* [2]
stirs up, 5959, *nāšab* [1]
stirs up, 6590, *'ālâ* [1]
stirs up, 8088, *rāga'[1]* [1]
stirs up, 8492, *śîm* [1]

STOCK [2]
stock, 2446, *zera'* [1]
take stock of, 7212, *pāqad* [1]

STOCKS [3]
stocks, 4551, *mahpeket* [3]

STOLE [5]
stole away, 1704, *gānab* [2]
stole, 1704, *gānab* [2]
stole into, 1704+4200+995, *gānab+le-1+bô'* [1]

STOLEN [16]
stolen, 1704, *gānab* [3]
stolen heart, 4220, *lābab[1]* [2]
stolen, 1608, *gāzal* [1]
stolen goods, 1610, *gāzēl* [1]
stolen, 1610, *gāzēl* [1]
stolen, 1611+1608, *gezēlâ+gāzal* [1]
what stolen, 1611, *gezēlâ* [1]
are stolen, 1704, *gānab* [1]
be considered stolen, 1704, *gānab* [1]
was stolen, 1704+1704, *gānab+gānab* [1]
was stolen, 1704, *gānab* [1]
stolen, 1706, *genēbâ* [1]
stolen goods, 4202+4200+2257, *lō'+le-1+-ô* [1]

STOMACH [11]
stomach, 1061, *beṭen[1]* [3]
stomach, 2824, *ḥōmeš[2]* [3]
stomach, 5055, *mē'eh* [2]
stomach, 2743, *ḥalāṣayim* [1]
stomach, 4160, *kārēś* [1]
stomach, 7931, *qereb* [1]

STOMACHS [2]
stomachs, 5055, *mē'eh* [1]
empty stomachs, 5931+9094, *niqqāyôn+šēn[1]* [1]

STONE [133]
stone, 74, *'eben* [93]
sacred stone, 5167, *maṣṣēbâ* [5]
stone, 6232, *sāqal* [5]
boundary stone, 1473, *gebûl* [4]
stone, 8083+928+2021+74, *rāgam+be-+ha-+'eben* [4]
dressed stone, 1607, *gāzît* [3]
stone, 10006, *'eben* [3]
piles of stone, 1643+5898, *gal[1]+nāṣâ[2]* [2]
stone, 6232+928+2021+74, *sāqal+be-+ha-+'eben* [2]
stone, *NIH/RPE* [1]
stone, 928+2021+74+8083, *be-+ha-+'eben+rāgam* [1]
blocks of stone, 1607, *gāzît* [1]
stone, 1607, *gāzît* [1]
ledge of stone, 3215, *ṭûr* [1]
stone pillars, 5167, *maṣṣēbâ* [1]
stone, 6152, *sela'[1]* [1]
must stone, 8083+8083, *rāgam+rāgam* [1]
stone, 8083+74, *rāgam+'eben* [1]
stone, 8083, *rāgam* [1]
stone quarries, 8696, *šebārîm* [1]
hardest stone, 9032, *šāmîr[2]* [1]

STONECUTTERS [6]
stonecutters, 2935, *ḥōṣēb* [5]
stonecutters, 2935+74, *ḥōṣēb+'eben* [1]

STONED [14]
stoned, 8083+74, *rāgam+'eben* [4]
be stoned, 6232, *sāqal* [2]
been stoned, 6232, *sāqal* [2]
stoned, 6232+928+2021+74, *sāqal+be-+ha-+'eben* [2]
must be stoned to death, 6232+6232, *sāqal+sāqal* [1]
surely be stoned, 6232+6232, *sāqal+sāqal* [1]
stoned to death, 8083+74, *rāgam+'eben* [1]
stoned, 8083+928+2021+74, *rāgam+be-+ha-+'eben* [1]

STONEMASONS [2]
stonemasons, 3093+74+7815, *ḥārāš+'eben+qîr[1]* [1]
stonemasons, 3093+7815, *ḥārāš+qîr[1]* [1]

STONES [114]
stones, 74, *'eben* [86]
sacred stones, 5167, *maṣṣēbâ* [14]
precious stones, 74, *'eben* [3]
large stones, 10006+10146, *'eben+g^{e}lāl* [2]
stones, *NIH/RPE* [1]
sling stones, 928+2021+74, *b^{e}-+ha-+'eben* [1]
boundary stones, 1473, *g^{e}bûl* [1]
boundary stones, 1474, *g^{e}bûlâ* [1]
dressed stones, 1607, *gāzît* [1]
piles of stones, 1643, *gal[1]* [1]
the stones^{s}, 4392, *-ām* [1]
costly stones, 6090, *sōḥeret* [1]
cleared of stones, 6232, *sāqal* [1]

STONING [2]
stoning, 6232, *sāqal* [1]
stoning, 8083+928+2021+74, *rāgam+b^{e}-+ha-+'eben* [1]

STOOD [147]
stood, 6641, *'āmad* [82]
stood, *NIH/RPE* [8]
stood up, 7756, *qûm* [8]
stood, 3656, *yāṣab* [6]
stood still, 6641, *'āmad* [6]
stood, 5893, *nāṣab[1]* [5]
stood up, 6641, *'āmad* [5]
stood, 7756, *qûm* [5]
stood, 10624, *qûm* [4]
stood still, 1957, *dāmam[1]* [1]
stood in awe, 3169, *ḥātat* [1]
stood in awe, 3707+4394, *yārē'[1]+m^{e}'ōd* [1]
stood, 3922, *kûn[1]* [1]
stood, 4632, *môšāb* [1]
stood, 5163+8079+3922, *maṣṣāb+regel+kûn[1]* [1]
stood, 5163+8079, *maṣṣāb+regel* [1]
stood, 5187, *māṣûq* [1]
stood by, 5893, *nāṣab[1]* [1]
stood firm, 5893, *nāṣab[1]* [1]
stood upright, 5893, *nāṣab[1]* [1]
stood on end, 6169, *sāmar* [1]
stood by, 6641, *'āmad* [1]
stood firm, 6641, *'āmad* [1]
stood in places, 6641, *'āmad* [1]
stood waiting, 6641, *'āmad* [1]
stood ground, 7756, *qûm* [1]
stood, 7928, *qārab* [1]

STOOL [1]
delivery stool, 78, *'obnayim* [1]

STOOP [4]
stoop, 6430, *'āwat* [1]
stoop down, 6700, *'ānâ[2]* [1]
stoop down, 6708, *'^{a}nāwâ* [1]
stoop, 7970, *qāras* [1]

STOOPS [2]
stoops low, 7970, *qāras* [1]
stoops down, 9164, *šāpēl[1]* [1]

STOP [45]
stop, 2532, *ḥādal[1]* [8]
stop, 6641, *'āmad* [7]
stop, 6073, *sûr[1]* [4]
stop, 8697, *šābat[1]* [3]
stop, 8740, *šûb[1]* [3]
stop, 440, *'al[1]* [2]
put a stop, 8697, *šābat[1]* [2]
stop, 10098, *b^{e}ṭal* [2]
stop, 1194, *biltî* [1]
stop trusting in, 2532+4946, *ḥādal[1]+min* [1]
stop, 3087, *hārēš[2]* [1]
stop, 3973, *kālā'[1]* [1]
stop, 4202+3578, *lō'+yāsap* [1]
stop, 4202, *lō'* [1]
stop, 5801, *nālâ* [1]
stop up, 6258, *sātam* [1]
stop, 6440, *'āzab[1]* [1]
stop, 8123, *rûm[1]* [1]
stop, 8332, *rāpâ[1]* [1]
cause to stop, 8697, *šābat[1]* [1]
stop, 9462, *tāmam* [1]
stop work, 10098, *b^{e}ṭal* [1]

STOPPED [61]
stopped, 6641, *'āmad* [19]
stopped, 2532, *ḥādal[1]* [10]
stopped, 8697, *šābat[1]* [4]
stopped up, 6258, *sātam* [3]
stopped, 8740, *šûb[1]* [3]
stopped, 6073, *sûr[1]* [2]
be stopped, 6806, *'āṣar* [2]
stopped, 6806, *'āṣar* [2]
was stopped, 6806, *'āṣar* [2]
stopped, 357, *'āṭam* [1]
stopped up, 3877+4946+9048, *kābēd[1]+min+šāma'* [1]
stopped falling, 3973, *kālā'[1]* [1]
stopped, 3983, *kālâ[1]* [1]
stopped, 4202+3578+6388, *lō'+yāsap+'ôd* [1]
stopped, 4202+3855, *lō'+yātar* [1]
stopped for the night, 4328, *lîn* [1]
place where they stopped for the night, 4869, *mālôn* [1]
place where we stopped for the night, 4869, *mālôn* [1]
stopped, 4946, *min* [1]
stopped thinking, 5759, *nāṭaš* [1]
stopped showing, 6440, *'āzab[1]* [1]
stopped, 6590+4946, *'ālâ+min* [1]
stopped, 10098, *b^{e}ṭal* [1]

STOPPING [2]
stopping, 3782, *yāšab* [1]
stopping, 8697, *šābat[1]* [1]

STOPS [6]
stops, 357, *'āṭam* [1]
stops, 1957, *dāmam[1]* [1]
stops, 3159, *ḥātam* [1]
stops, 4202, *lō'* [1]
stops, 6806, *'āṣar* [1]
stops to think, 8740+448+4213, *šûb[1]+'el+lēb* [1]

STORAGE [2]
storage jars, 3998, *k^{e}lî* [1]
storage jar, 3998, *k^{e}lî* [1]

STORE [22]
store, 5016, *misk^{e}nôt* [6]
store up, 7621, *ṣāpan* [3]
store away, 665, *'āsap* [1]
rich store, 2890, *ḥōsen* [1]
store up, 3922, *kûn[1]* [1]
buildings to store, 5016, *misk^{e}nôt* [1]
store up, 5663, *nûaḥ[1]* [1]
store, 5663, *nûaḥ[1]* [1]
store, 5989, *nātan* [1]
store up, 6047, *sûg[1]* [1]
in store for, 6584, *'al[2]* [1]
in store, 6640, *'im* [1]
store, 7212, *pāqad* [1]
store up, 7392, *ṣābar* [1]
holds in store, 7621, *ṣāpan* [1]

STORED [14]
stored up, 7621, *ṣāpan* [3]
stored up, 732, *'āṣar* [2]
stored, *AIT* [1]
be stored up, 732, *'āṣar* [1]
stored, 5989, *nātan* [1]
stored up, 7213, *p^{e}quddâ* [1]
stored up, 7392, *ṣābar* [1]
is stored up, 7621, *ṣāpan* [1]
stored up, 7674, *ṣārar[1]* [1]
stored up, 7695, *qābaṣ* [1]
stored, 10474, *n^{e}ḥat* [1]

STOREHOUSE [5]
storehouse, 238, *'ôṣār* [2]
storehouse, 667, *'āsōp* [1]
storehouse, 1074+238, *bayit[1]+'ôṣār* [1]
storehouse, 1074+667, *bayit[1]+'āsōp* [1]

STOREHOUSES [12]
storehouses, 238, *'ôṣār* [9]
storehouses, 1074+5800, *bayit[1]+n^{e}kōt* [2]
the storehouses^{s}, 3972+889+928+2157, *kōl+'^{a}šer+b^{e}-+-hem* [1]

STOREROOMS [11]
storerooms, 4384, *liškâ* [5]
storerooms, 238, *'ôṣār* [1]
storerooms, 667, *'āsōp* [1]
put in charge of the storerooms, 732+6584+238, *'āṣar+'al[2]+'ôṣār* [1]
storerooms, 1711, *ganzak* [1]
the storerooms^{s}, 2157, *-hem* [1]
storerooms, 5969+4200+238, *niškâ+l^{e}-[1]+'ôṣār* [1]

STORES [3]
stores, 238, *'ôṣār* [1]
stores, 3922, *kûn[1]* [1]
stores up, 7621, *ṣāpan* [1]

STORING [1]
storing up wealth, 4043, *kānas* [1]

STORK [6]
stork, 2884, *ḥ^{a}sîdâ* [6]

STORM [27]
storm, 6194, *s^{e}'ārâ* [5]
storm, 2443, *zerem* [4]
storm, 6193, *sa'ar* [4]
storm, 6070, *sûpâ[1]* [2]
storm, 8554, *ś^{e}'ārâ* [2]
storm, 8739, *šō'â* [2]
taken by storm, 1324, *bāqa'* [1]
storm, 1352, *bārād* [1]
storm, 2147, *hālal[3]* [1]
storm, 2167, *h^{a}mullâ* [1]
the coming storm^{s}, 2257, *-ô* [1]
storm clouds, 2613, *ḥ^{a}zîz* [1]
storm out, 8548, *śā'ar[2]* [1]
storm, 9583, *t^{e}šu'â* [1]

STORMED [2]
stormed, 4309, *lāḥam[1]* [1]
stormed out, 6192, *sā'ar* [1]

STORMS [2]
lashed by storms, 6192, *sā'ar* [1]
storms, 6194, *s^{e}'ārâ* [1]

STORMY [2]
stormy, 6070, *sûpâ[1]* [1]
stormy, 6194, *s^{e}'ārâ* [1]

STORY [2]
story, 1821, *dābār* [2]

STOUTHEARTED [1]
stouthearted, 5883+6437, *nepeš+'ōz* [1]

STRAGGLER [1]
straggler, 969, *bādad* [1]

STRAIGHT [27]
make straight, 3837, *yāšar* [4]
straight ahead, 448+6298+7156, *'el+'ēber[1]+pāneh* [3]
straight, 3838, *yāšār[1]* [2]
straight, 3841, *yōšer* [2]
straight in, 5584, *neged* [2]
go straight up, 6590, *'ālâ* [2]
go straight, 3837, *yāšar* [1]
keeps straight, 3837, *yāšar* [1]
makes straight, 3837, *yāšar* [1]
went straight, 3837, *yāšar* [1]
straight ahead, 4200+5790, *l^{e}-[1]+nōkaḥ* [1]
straight to, 4200, *l^{e}-[1]* [1]
straight, 4793, *mîšôr* [1]
straight, 4797, *mêšārîm* [1]
straight ahead, 5019, *m^{e}sillâ* [1]
straight through, 5584, *neged* [1]
straight, 5584, *neged* [1]
lead straight, 9461, *tāmak* [1]

STRAIGHTEN [1]
straighten, 9545, *tāqan* [1]

STRAIGHTENED [1]
straightened, 9545, *tāqan* [1]

STRAIN [1]
stand the strain, 6641, *'āmad* [1]

STRAINING [1]
straining, 1335, *bāqaš* [1]

STRANDS [3]
strands, *AIT* [1]
strands, *NIH/RPE* [1]
strands, 7348, *pātîl* [1]

STRANGE [7]
strange, 2424, *zār* [2]
strange speech, 7743+7743, *qāw*[2]+*qāw*[2] [2]
strange, 337, *ʾaḥēr*[1] [1]
strange, 1524, *gādôl* [1]
strange, 4352, *lāʿag* [1]

STRANGER [12]
stranger, 1731, *gēr* [3]
stranger, 2424, *zār* [3]
stranger, 9369, *tôšāb* [2]
stranger, 2319, *zûr*[2] [1]
stranger, 4202+3359, *lōʾ+yādaʿ* [1]
pretended to be a stranger, 5796, *nākar*[2] [1]
stranger, 5799, *nokrî* [1]

STRANGERS [12]
strangers, 2424, *zār* [7]
strangers, 1591, *gûr*[1] [2]
strangers, 1731, *gēr* [1]
strangers, 4202+3359, *lōʾ+yādaʿ* [1]
strangers, 9369, *tôšāb* [1]

STRANGLED [1]
strangled, 2871, *ḥānaq* [1]

STRANGLING [1]
strangling, 4725, *maḥanāq* [1]

STRAP [1]
strap, 8492, *śîm* [1]

STRAPPED [2]
strapped, 2520, *ḥāgar* [1]
strapped, 7537, *ṣāmad* [1]

STRAPS [1]
yoke of straps, 4593, *môsērâ*[1] [1]

STRATEGY [3]
strategy, 6783, *ʿēṣâ*[1] [3]

STRAW [21]
straw, 9320, *teben* [17]
straw, 7990, *qaš* [2]
straw, 5495, *matbēn* [1]
piece of straw, 7990, *qaš* [1]

STRAY [9]
stray, 8706, *šāgâ* [3]
stray, 6073, *sûr*[1] [2]
stray, 9494, *tāʿâ* [2]
let stray, 8706, *šāgâ* [1]
lets stray, 8938, *šālaḥ* [1]

STRAYED [6]
strayed, 9494, *tāʿâ* [2]
strayed, 5610, *nādad* [1]
strayed, 5742, *nāṭâ* [1]
strayed far, 8178, *rāḥaq* [1]
strayed, 8740, *šûb*[1] [1]

STRAYING [1]
straying, 5615, *nādaḥ*[1] [1]

STRAYS [5]
strays, 5610, *nādad* [2]
strays, 5615, *nādaḥ*[1] [2]
strays, 9494, *tāʿâ* [1]

STREAKED [7]
streaked, 6819, *ʿāqōd* [7]

STREAM [16]
stream, 5707, *naḥal*[1] [8]
stream, 5641, *nāhar*[1] [3]
flowing stream, 419, *ʾêtān*[1] [1]
stream, 2143, *hālak* [1]
stream, 3414, *yûbal*[1] [1]
stream, 4784, *mayim* [1]
stream beds, 5707, *naḥal*[1] [1]

STREAMING [1]
streaming down, 5688, *nāzal* [1]

STREAMS [58]
streams, 5643, *nāhār* [12]
streams, 5707, *naḥal*[1] [12]
streams, 3284, *yeʾōr* [10]
streams, 7104, *peleg*[1] [9]
streams, 692, *ʾāpîq*[1] [4]
streams, 5689, *nōzēl* [3]
streams, 116, *ʾēd* [2]
streams, 692+5707, *ʾāpîq*[1]+*naḥal*[1] [1]
streams of the Nile, 3284, *yeʾōr* [1]
flowing streams, 3298+4784, *yābāl*[1]+*mayim* [1]
streams, 5688, *nāzal* [1]
intermittent streams, 5707, *naḥal*[1] [1]
streams, 7106, *pelaggâ* [1]

STREET [18]
street, 2575, *ḥûṣ* [13]
street, 2006, *derek* [2]
street, 8798, *šûq*[2] [2]
street corner, 7157, *pinnâ* [1]

STREETS [58]
streets, 2575, *ḥûṣ* [38]
streets, 8148, *reḥōb*[1] [15]
streets, 8798, *šûq*[2] [2]
streets, *NIH/RPE* [1]
streets, 2006, *derek* [1]
streets, 5986, *netîbâ* [1]

STRENGTH [168]
strength, 3946, *kōaḥ*[1] [56]
strength, 6437, *ʿōz* [38]
strength, 1476, *gebûrâ* [14]
strength, 2657, *ḥayil* [11]
strength, 2432, *zerôaʿ* [6]
strength, 3338, *yād* [3]
strength, 4394, *meʾōd* [2]
strength, 6797, *ʿōṣem*[1] [2]
strength, 9361, *tôʿāpôt* [2]
sign of strength, 226, *ʾôn*[1] [1]
strength, 226, *ʾôn*[1] [1]
strength, 384, *ʾeyāl* [1]
strength, 394, *ʾeyālût* [1]
strength, 579, *ʾammîṣ* [1]
source of strength, 1476, *gebûrâ* [1]
strength, 1542, *gōdel* [1]
strength, 1801, *dōbeʾ* [1]
strength, 2006, *derek* [1]
best strength, 2086, *hôd*[1] [1]
found strength, 2616, *ḥāzaq* [1]
gave strength, 2616, *ḥāzaq* [1]
give strength, 2616, *ḥāzaq* [1]
given strength, 2616, *ḥāzaq* [1]
grew in strength, 2616, *ḥāzaq* [1]
have strength, 2616, *ḥāzaq* [1]
helped find strength, 2616+906+3338, *ḥāzaq+ʾēt*[1]*+yād* [1]
marshaled strength, 2616, *ḥāzaq* [1]
rallied strength, 2616, *ḥāzaq* [1]
showed strength, 2616, *ḥāzaq* [1]
strength, 2619, *ḥēzeq* [1]
strength, 2620, *ḥōzeq* [1]
strength, 4301, *lēaḥ* [1]
strength, 4382, *lāšād* [1]
strength, 5057, *māʿôz* [1]
strength, 6434, *ʿaz* [1]
show strength, 6451, *ʿāzaz* [1]
strength, 6469, *ʿēzer*[1] [1]
strength, 6786, *ʿāṣûm* [1]
strength, 6793, *ʿāṣam*[1] [1]
strength, 7446, *ṣûr*[4] [1]
strength, 8120, *rûaḥ* [1]
strength, 9508, *taʿaṣumôt* [1]
strength, 10487, *niṣbâ* [1]

STRENGTHEN [23]
strengthen, 2616, *ḥāzaq* [12]
strengthen, 599, *ʾāmēṣ* [3]
strengthen, 1504, *gābar* [2]
strengthen, 273, *ʾāzar* [1]
strengthen, 1307, *bāšar*[3] [1]
strengthen position, 2616, *ḥāzaq* [1]
strengthen, 2741, *ḥālaṣ*[2] [1]
strengthen, 6164, *sāmak* [1]
strengthen, 7756, *qûm* [1]

STRENGTHENED [11]
strengthened, 2616, *ḥāzaq* [5]
strengthened, 599, *ʾāmēṣ* [1]
strengthened himself, 2616, *ḥāzaq* [1]
strengthened, 2616+2432, *ḥāzaq+zerôaʿ* [1]
was strengthened, 2616, *ḥāzaq* [1]
strengthened, 3946, *kōaḥ*[1] [1]
strengthened, 8435, *śāgab* [1]

STRENGTHENING [1]
strengthening his own position, 2616, *ḥāzaq* [1]

STRENGTHENS [1]
strengthens, 2616, *ḥāzaq* [1]

STRESS [1]
stress, 5186, *māṣôq* [1]

STRETCH [30]
stretch out, 5742, *nāṭâ* [22]
stretch out, 8938, *šālaḥ* [4]
stretch, 3655, *yāṣaʿ* [1]
stretch wide, 5742, *nāṭâ* [1]
stretch out, 7298, *pāraś* [1]
stretch out, 8594, *śāraʿ* [1]

STRETCHED [35]
stretched out, 5742, *nāṭâ* [20]
stretched out, 8938, *šālaḥ* [7]
stretched out, 1566, *gāhar* [2]
stretched, 2118, *hāyâ* [1]
stretched out, 3838, *yāšār*[1] [1]
stretched himself out, 4499, *mādad* [1]
stretched out, 5599, *nāgar* [1]
be stretched out, 5742, *nāṭâ* [1]
stretched, 5742, *nāṭâ* [1]

STRETCHES [7]
stretches out, 5742, *nāṭâ* [5]
stretches afar, 5305, *merḥāq* [1]
stretches out, 7298, *pāraś* [1]

STRETCHING [3]
stretching, *AIT* [2]
stretching out, 7298, *pāraś* [1]

STREWN [2]
strewn with, 4849, *mālēʾ*[2] [1]
strewn, 5877, *nāpal* [1]

STRICKEN [3]
stricken, *AIT* [1]
stricken, 5595, *nāgaʿ* [1]
stricken, 5596, *negaʿ* [1]

STRICT [1]
bound under a strict oath, 8678+8678, *šābaʿ+šābaʿ* [1]

STRIDE [1]
stride, 7576, *ṣaʿad* [1]

STRIDING [1]
striding forward, 7579, *ṣāʿâ* [1]

STRIFE [10]
strife, 8190, *rîb*[2] [7]
strife, 4506, *mādôn*[1] [2]
strife, 5175, *maṣṣâ*[2] [1]

STRIKE [70]
strike, 5782, *nākâ* [28]
strike down, 5782, *nākâ* [9]
strike, 5597, *nāgap* [5]
strike down, 7003, *pāgaʿ* [4]
strike down, 5597, *nāgap* [3]
strike, 5595, *nāgaʿ* [2]
strike together, 5782, *nākâ* [2]
strike, 7003, *pāgaʿ* [2]
strike, *NIH/RPE* [1]
strike, 2118+928, *hāyâ+be-* [1]
strike, 2118, *hāyâ* [1]
strike, 2150, *hālam* [1]

strike with terror, 3006, *ḥarad* [1]
strike twice, 4100, *kāpal* [1]
strike with a plague, 5597, *nāgap* [1]
strike, 5989, *nātan* [1]
strike, 6584, *ʿal^{2}* [1]
strike mark, 7003, *pāgaʿ* [1]
strike down, 8187, *rāṭaš* [1]
strike, 8790, *šûp^{2}* [1]
strike, 8883, *šît^{1}* [1]
strike twice, 9101, *šānâ^{1}* [1]
strike hands in pledge, 9364, *tôqᵉʿîm* [1]

STRIKES [13]
strikes, 5782, *nākâ* [3]
strikes, *NIH/RPE* [2]
strikes, 5595, *nāgaʿ* [2]
strikes in pledge, 9546, *tāqaʿ* [2]
strikes, 2150, *hālam* [1]
strikes, 2934, *ḥāṣab^{2}* [1]
strikes down, 5782, *nākâ* [1]
strikes the blow, 5782, *nākâ* [1]

STRIKING [6]
striking down, 5782, *nākâ* [2]
striking, 5782, *nākâ* [2]
striking, *NIH/RPE* [1]
striking, 2118+928, *hāyâ+bᵉ-* [1]

STRING [4]
string, 2005, *dārak* [1]
string, 3922, *kûn^{1}* [1]
piece of string, 7348+5861, *pātîl+nᵉʿōret* [1]
string, 7538, *ṣemed* [1]

STRINGED [9]
stringed instruments, 5593, *nᵉgînâ* [9]

STRINGS [4]
strings of jewels, 3016, *ḥᵃrûzîm* [1]
strings, 3857, *yeter^{2}* [1]
music of strings, 4944, *mēn^{1}* [1]
strings, 4944, *mēn^{1}* [1]

STRIP [19]
strip, 7320, *pāšaṭ* [7]
strip off, 1655, *gālâ* [1]
strip, 1655+6872, *gālâ+ʿerwâ* [1]
strip bare, 3106, *ḥāśap^{1}* [1]
strip bare, 3983, *kālâ^{1}* [1]
strip of, 4374, *lāqaḥ* [1]
strip off, 6073, *sûr^{1}* [1]
strip off clothes, 7320+2256+6910, *pāšaṭ+wᵉ-+ʿārar* [1]
strip off, 7320, *pāšaṭ* [1]
strip the dead, 7320, *pāšaṭ* [1]
strip, 7337, *pātaḥ^{1}* [1]
strip, 9037, *šāmēm^{1}* [1]
strip off, 10499, *nᵉtar* [1]

STRIPES [1]
stripes, 7203, *pᵉṣālôt* [1]

STRIPPED [30]
stripped, 7320, *pāšaṭ* [4]
stripped, 6873, *ʿārôm* [3]
stripped off, 7320, *pāšaṭ* [2]
stripped, 8768, *šôlāl* [2]
stripped, 10528, *ʿᵃdâ* [2]
stripped clean, 430, *ʾākal* [1]
stripped, 430, *ʾākal* [1]
stripped, 1191, *bālaq* [1]
stripped away, 1655, *gālâ* [1]
stripped, 1655, *gālâ* [1]
stripped, 2803, *ḥāmas^{1}* [1]
stripped off bark, 3106+3106, *ḥāśap^{1}+ḥāśap^{1}* [1]
stripped, 4374, *lāqaḥ* [1]
stripped off, 5911, *nāṣal* [1]
stripped naked, 6867, *ʿārâ^{1}* [1]
stripped, 6867, *ʿārâ^{1}* [1]
stripped bare, 6910, *ʿārar* [1]
was stripped, 7293, *pāraq* [1]
stripped, 7878, *qāsas* [1]
stripped off, 7915, *qāṣaṣ^{1}* [1]
stripped, 8689, *šābar^{1}* [1]
stripped, 9037, *šāmēm^{1}* [1]

STRIPS [1]
strips bare, 3106, *ḥāśap^{1}* [1]

STRIVES [2]
strives, 6424, *ʿûr^{3}* [1]
strives, 8190, *rîb^{2}* [1]

STRIVING [1]
anxious striving, 8301+4213, *raʿyôn+lēb* [1]

STRODE [1]
strode through, 7575, *ṣāʿad* [1]

STROKE [2]
stroke, 3338, *yād* [1]
stroke, 5044, *maʿᵃbār* [1]

STRONG [128]
strong, 2616, *ḥāzaq* [41]
strong, 2617, *ḥāzāq* [12]
strong, 6437, *ʿōz* [12]
strong, 6434, *ʿaz* [5]
strong, 599, *ʾāmēṣ* [4]
strong, 1475, *gibbôr* [4]
strong, 1524, *gādôl* [4]
strong, 6786, *ʿāṣûm* [4]
strong, 2657, *ḥayil* [3]
strong lion, 4097, *kᵉpîr* [3]
strong, 10772, *tᵉqip* [3]
strong, *NIH/RPE* [2]
strong, 6451, *ʿāzaz* [2]
strong, 10768, *taqqîp* [2]
strong, 52, *ʾabbîr* [1]
strong, 579, *ʾammîṣ* [1]
strong, 602, *ʾamṣâ* [1]
strong, 875, *ʾašmān* [1]
strong young men, 1033, *bāḥûr^{1}* [1]
strong fortress, 1074+5181, *bayit^{1}+mᵉṣûdâ^{2}* [1]
strong, 1374, *bārîʾ* [1]
strong, 1461, *gab^{1}* [1]
strong man, 1475, *gibbôr* [1]
strong man, 1505, *geber^{1}* [1]
strong arms, 2432+3338, *zᵉrôaʿ+yād* [1]
gave strong support, 2616+6640, *ḥāzaq+ʿim* [1]
made strong, 2616, *ḥāzaq* [1]
strong, 2616+3338, *ḥāzaq+yād* [1]
become strong, 2621, *ḥezqâ* [1]
strong, 2621, *ḥezqâ* [1]
grow strong, 2730, *ḥālam^{1}* [1]
strong, 2891, *ḥāsōn* [1]
strong, 3878, *kābēd^{2}* [1]
strong, 4849, *mālēʾ^{2}* [1]
strong, 5057, *māʿôz* [1]
strong, 6450, *ʿizzûz* [1]
making strong, 6641, *ʿāmad* [1]
very strong, 6793+3946, *ʿāṣam^{1}+kōaḥ^{1}* [1]
strong, 7997, *qāšeh* [1]
strong, 8003, *qāšar* [1]
strong, 8435, *śāgab* [1]

STRONGER [26]
stronger, 6786, *ʿāṣûm* [6]
stronger, 2616, *ḥāzaq* [5]
grew stronger and stronger, 2143+2256+2618, *hālak+wᵉ-+ḥāzēq* [2]
grew stronger and stronger, 2143+2256+7997, *hālak+wᵉ-+qāšeh* [2]
stronger, 2617, *ḥāzāq* [2]
stronger, 599, *ʾāmēṣ* [1]
stronger, 1504, *gābar* [1]
stronger, 1524, *gādôl* [1]
proved stronger, 2616, *ḥāzaq* [1]
grow stronger, 3578+601, *yāsap+ʾōmeṣ* [1]
stronger, 6434, *ʿaz* [1]
stronger, 8003, *qāšar* [1]
stronger, 8041, *rab^{1}* [1]
stronger, 9544, *taqqîp* [1]

STRONGEST [3]
strongest defenders, 408+2657, *ʾîš^{1}+ḥayil* [1]
strongest, 1504, *gābar* [1]
strongest soldiers, 10132+10264, *gibbar+ḥayil* [1]

STRONGHOLD [31]
stronghold, 5057, *māʿôz* [7]
stronghold, 5181, *mᵉṣûdâ^{2}* [7]
stronghold, 5369, *miśgāb^{1}* [5]
stronghold, 6437, *ʿōz* [3]
stronghold, 5171, *mᵉṣād* [2]
stronghold, 7663, *ṣᵉrîaḥ* [2]
stronghold, 810, *ʾarmôn* [1]
stronghold, 5190, *māṣôr^{2}* [1]
stronghold, 6152, *selaʿ^{1}* [1]
stronghold, 6434, *ʿaz* [1]
stronghold, 6755, *ʿōpel^{2}* [1]

STRONGHOLDS [18]
strongholds, 5171, *mᵉṣād* [7]
strongholds, 4448, *mibṣār^{1}* [5]
strongholds, 528, *ʾalmān^{2}* [2]
strongholds, 4995, *misgeret* [2]
strongholds, 6437, *ʿōz* [1]
strongholds, 7157, *pinnâ* [1]

STRONGLY [1]
strongly, 4394, *mᵉʾōd* [1]

STRUCK [125]
struck down, 5782, *nākâ* [57]
struck, 5782, *nākâ* [34]
struck down, 7003, *pāgaʿ* [4]
struck down, 4804, *makkâ* [3]
struck, 5595, *nāgaʿ* [3]
struck down, 5597, *nāgap* [3]
struck, 2118+928, *hāyâ+bᵉ-* [2]
struck, 5597, *nāgap* [2]
struck, 10411, *mᵉḥāʾ* [2]
struck, *NIH/RPE* [1]
struck, 2150, *hālam* [1]
be struck down, 4162, *kārat* [1]
struck, 4200, *lᵉ-^{1}* [1]
struck down and died, 4637, *mût* [1]
struck with a plague, 5597, *nāgap* [1]
be struck down, 5782, *nākâ* [1]
had struck down, 5782, *nākâ* [1]
is struck, 5782, *nākâ* [1]
struck down, 5782+4804, *nākâ+makkâ* [1]
struck the blow, 5782, *nākâ* [1]
struck, 5782+5782, *nākâ+nākâ* [1]
struck together, 6215, *sāpaq^{1}* [1]
struck down, 8845, *šāḥat* [1]
struck in pledge, 9546, *tāqaʿ* [1]

STRUCTURE [7]
palatial structure, 1072, *bîrâ* [2]
structure, 10082, *ʾuššarnāʾ* [2]
structure, *AIT* [1]
structure, 3666, *yāṣîaʿ* [1]
structure, 5126, *maʿᵃśeh* [1]

STRUCTURES [1]
structures, *AIT* [1]

STRUGGLE [4]
struggle, 3333, *yāgaʿ* [1]
struggle, 4878, *milḥāmâ* [1]
had a struggle, 5887+7349, *naptûlîm+pātal* [1]
struggle, 8190, *rîb^{2}* [1]

STRUGGLED [3]
struggled, 8575, *śārâ^{1}* [3]

STRUGGLES [1]
struggles, 3078, *ḥarṣōb* [1]

STRUM [1]
strum away, 7260, *pāraṭ* [1]

STRUNG [2]
strung, 2005, *dārak* [2]

STRUT [1]
freely strut, 2143, *hālak* [1]

STRUTTING [1]
strutting rooster, 2435+5516, *zarzîr+motnayim* [1]

STUBBLE [7]
stubble, 7990, *qaš* [7]

STUBBORN [13]
stubborn, 6253, *sārar^{1}* [6]

stubborn, 7997, *qāšeh* [2]
stubborn, 9244, *š^{e}rirût* [2]
stubborn, 2617+4213, *ḥāzāq+lēb* [1]
stubborn, 6437, *ʿōz* [1]
made stubborn, 7996, *qāšâ* [1]

STUBBORN-HEARTED [1]
stubborn-hearted, 52+4213, *ʾabbîr+lēb* [1]

STUBBORNLY [3]
stubbornly, 6253, *sārar*[1] [2]
stubbornly refused, 7996, *qāšâ* [1]

STUBBORNNESS [8]
stubbornness, 9244, *š^{e}rirût* [7]
stubbornness, 8001, *q^{e}šî* [1]

STUBS [1]
stubs, 2387, *zānāb* [1]

STUCK [2]
stuck, 1815, *dābaq* [1]
stuck, 5080, *māʿak* [1]

STUDDED [1]
studded, 5925, *n^{e}quddâ* [1]

STUDENT [1]
student, 9441, *talmîd* [1]

STUDY [3]
study, 2011, *dāraš* [2]
study, 4261, *lahag* [1]

STUMBLE [34]
stumble, 4173, *kāšal* [23]
stumble, 5597, *nāgap* [2]
stumble, 1054, *bāṭaḥ*[2] [1]
caused to stumble, 4173, *kāšal* [1]
made stumble, 4173, *kāšal* [1]
stumble and fall, 4173+4173, *kāšal+kāšal* [1]
make stumble, 4842, *mikšôl* [1]
stumble, 4842, *mikšôl* [1]
causes to stumble, 5598, *negep* [1]
stumble, 5877, *nāpal* [1]
stumble, 7048, *pûq*[1] [1]

STUMBLED [7]
stumbled, 4173, *kāšal* [4]
stumbled, 9023, *šāmaṭ* [2]
stumbled, 7520, *ṣelaʿ* [1]

STUMBLES [3]
stumbles, 4173, *kāšal* [3]

STUMBLING [8]
stumbling block, 4842, *mikšôl* [4]
stumbling, 1892, *d^{e}ḥî* [2]
stumbling, 4173, *kāšal* [1]
stumbling blocks, 4842, *mikšôl* [1]

STUMP [6]
stump, 10567, *ʿiqqar* [3]
stump, 1614, *gezaʿ* [2]
stump, 5169, *maṣṣebet*[1] [1]

STUMPS [1]
stumps, 5169, *maṣṣebet*[1] [1]

STUNNED [2]
stunned, 7028+4213, *pûg+lēb* [1]
stunned, 9449, *tāmah* [1]

STUNTED [1]
stunted, 7832, *qālaṭ* [1]

STUPID [3]
stupid, 1280, *baʿar* [1]
considered stupid, 3241, *ṭāmâ* [1]
stupid, 6119, *sākāl* [1]

STUPIDITY [1]
stupidity, 4073, *kesel*[2] [1]

STUPOR [1]
wakes from stupor, 8130, *rûn* [1]

STURDIEST [1]
sturdiest, 5458, *mišmān* [1]

STURDY [1]
sturdy, 5458, *mišmān* [1]

SUAH [1]
Suah, 6053, *sûaḥ* [1]

SUBDIVISION [1]
subdivision, 7107, *p^{e}luggâ* [1]

SUBDIVISIONS [1]
subdivisions, 5141, *miplaggâ* [1]

SUBDUE [9]
subdue, 4044, *kānaʿ* [3]
subdue, 6700, *ʿānâ*[2] [3]
subdue, 3899, *kābaš* [1]
subdue, 8096, *rādad* [1]
subdue, 10737, *š^{e}pal*[1] [1]

SUBDUED [19]
subdued, 4044, *kānaʿ* [5]
subdued, 5782, *nākâ* [4]
is subdued, 3899, *kābaš* [2]
were subdued, 4044, *kānaʿ* [2]
subdued, 1818, *dābar*[1] [1]
subdued, 3718, *yārad* [1]
subdued, 3899, *kābaš* [1]
was subdued, 4044, *kānaʿ* [1]
subdued, 6700, *ʿānâ*[2] [1]
subdued, 8097, *rādâ*[1] [1]

SUBDUES [3]
subdues, 1818, *dābar*[1] [1]
subdues, 8096, *rādad* [1]
subdues, 8097, *rādâ*[1] [1]

SUBDUING [1]
subduing, *NIH/RPE* [1]

SUBJECT [26]
subject to, 6268, *ʿābad* [8]
subject, 6269, *ʿebed*[1] [7]
subject, 6268, *ʿābad* [3]
subject, *NIH/RPE* [1]
is subject, 3899, *kābaš* [1]
subject, 3899, *kābaš* [1]
made subject to, 4044+9393+3338,
kānaʿ+taḥat[1]*+yād* [1]
subject to, 4200, *l^{e-1}* [1]
subject to, 5463, *mišmaʿat* [1]
subject to tribute, 5957, *nāšāʾ*[1] [1]
to subject, 6268, *ʿābad* [1]

SUBJECTED [4]
subjected, 4044, *kānaʿ* [2]
been subjected, 5989, *nātan* [1]
subjected, 5989, *nātan* [1]

SUBJECTS [5]
subjects, 6269, *ʿebed*[1] [3]
subjects, 4211, *l^{e}ʾōm* [1]
subjects, 6268, *ʿābad* [1]

SUBJUGATE [1]
subjugate, 6268, *ʿābad* [1]

SUBJUGATED [1]
were subjugated, 4044, *kānaʿ* [1]

SUBMISSION [2]
submission, 5202, *miṣʿād* [1]
submission, 9393, *taḥat*[1] [1]

SUBMIT [7]
submit, 14, *ʾābâ* [1]
submit, 5976, *nāšaq*[2] [1]
submit, 5989+3338, *nātan+yād* [1]
submit, 6122, *sākan*[1] [1]
submit, 6268, *ʿābad* [1]
submit, 6700, *ʿānâ*[2] [1]
submit, 8132+3338, *rûṣ+yād* [1]

SUBMITTED [1]
submitted, 5989+3338, *nātan+yād* [1]

SUBORDINATES [1]
subordinates, 6269, *ʿebed*[1] [1]

SUBSIDE [3]
subside, 5663, *nûaḥ*[1] [3]

SUBSIDED [4]
subsided, 8896, *šākak* [2]
subsided, 5663, *nûaḥ*[1] [1]
subsided, 8332, *rāpâ*[1] [1]

SUBSIDES [1]
subsides, 8740, *šûb*[1] [1]

SUBSTANCE [1]
substance, 10646+10418, *rēʾš+millâ* [1]

SUBSTITUTE [4]
substitute, 9455, *t^{e}mûrâ* [2]
substitute, 4614+4614, *mûr*[1]*+mûr*[1] [1]
substitute, 4614, *mûr*[1] [1]

SUBSTITUTION [2]
make a substitution, 4614+4614, *mûr*[1]*+mûr*[1] [1]
make substitution, 4614, *mûr*[1] [1]

SUBTRACT [1]
subtract, 1757, *gāraʿ*[1] [1]

SUCATHITES [1]
Sucathites, 8460, *śûkātî* [1]

SUCCEED [28]
succeed, 7503, *ṣālaḥ*[2] [7]
succeed, 9393, *taḥat*[1] [5]
succeed, 339, *ʾaḥar* [3]
succeed, 3523, *yākōl* [3]
succeed, 3603, *yāʿal* [2]
succeed, 3922, *kûn*[1] [1]
succeed, 4178, *kāšēr* [1]
succeed against, 4200+5584, *l^{e-1}+neged* [1]
make succeed, 4848, *mālēʾ*[1] [1]
succeed in the rescue, 5911+5911,
nāṣal+nāṣal [1]
succeed, 6641, *ʿāmad* [1]
let succeed, 7049, *pûq*[2] [1]
succeed, 7756, *qûm* [1]

SUCCEEDED [72]
succeeded, 9393, *taḥat*[1] [65]
succeeded, 7756+9393, *qûm+taḥat*[1] [2]
succeeded, 339, *ʾaḥar* [1]
succeeded, 3782, *yāšab* [1]
succeeded, 6641+6584+4030,
ʿāmad+ʿal[2]*+kēn*[5] [1]
succeeded in carrying out, 7503, *ṣālaḥ*[2] [1]
succeeded, 7503, *ṣālaḥ*[2] [1]

SUCCEEDS [2]
succeeds, 8505, *śākal*[1] [1]
succeeds, 9393, *taḥat*[1] [1]

SUCCESS [25]
gave success, 7503, *ṣālaḥ*[2] [3]
success, 8934, *šālôm* [3]
success, 3202, *ṭôb*[2] [2]
give success, 7503, *ṣālaḥ*[2] [2]
grant success, 7503, *ṣālaḥ*[2] [2]
have success, 7503, *ṣālaḥ*[2] [2]
success, 9370, *tûšiyyâ* [2]
brought success, 3512, *yāṭab* [1]
success, 3862, *yitrôn* [1]
without success, 4173, *kāšal* [1]
granted success, 7503, *ṣālaḥ*[2] [1]
make success, 7503, *ṣālaḥ*[2] [1]
gave success, 7936, *qārâ*[1] [1]
give success, 7936, *qārâ*[1] [1]
had great success, 8505, *śākal*[1] [1]
met with success, 8505, *śākal*[1] [1]

SUCCESSFUL [8]
successful, 8505, *śākal*[1] [4]
successful, 7503, *ṣālaḥ*[2] [3]
made successful, 7503, *ṣālaḥ*[2] [1]

SUCCESSFULLY [1]
successfully, 8505, *śākal*[1] [1]

SUCCESSIVE [2]
- at each successive level, 4200+5087+2025+4200+5087+2025, *l^{e-1}+maʿal^{2}+-â^{2}+l^{e-1}+maʿal^{2}+-â^{2}* [1]
- successive years, 9102+339+9102, *šānâ^{2}+ʾaḥar+šānâ^{2}* [1]

SUCCESSOR [6]
- successor, 132+8611+995+339, *ʾādām^{1}+ša-+bôʾ+ʾaḥar* [1]
- successor, 339, *ʾaḥar* [1]
- the successor^{s}, 2257, *-ô* [1]
- successor, 3782, *yāšab* [1]
- successor, 6641+6584+4030, *ʿāmad+ʿal^{2}+kēn^{5}* [1]
- successor, 6641+9393, *ʿāmad+taḥat^{1}* [1]

SUCCESSORS [1]
- successors, 1201, *bēn^{1}* [1]

SUCCOTH [18]
- Succoth, 6111, *sukkôt* [18]

SUCCOTH BENOTH [1]
- Succoth Benoth, 6112, *sukkôt b^{e}nôt* [1]

SUCH [133]
- such, *NIH/RPE* [19]
- such, 2296, *zeh* [16]
- such, *AIT* [15]
- such, 3869, *k^{e}-* [15]
- such, 465, *ʾēlleh* [10]
- such as, 3869, *k^{e}-* [8]
- such, 4027, *kēn^{2}* [7]
- such, 3869+2296, *k^{e}-+zeh* [3]
- such, 889, *ʾ^{a}šer* [2]
- such, 1524, *gādôl* [2]
- such^{s}, 2156, *hēm* [2]
- such a thing, 3970, *kākâ* [2]
- such and such, 3970, *kākâ* [2]
- in such a way that, 4200, *l^{e-1}* [2]
- such and such, 7141+532, *p^{e}lōnî+ʾalmōnî* [2]
- such as, 889, *ʾ^{a}šer* [1]
- such, 1524+2296, *gādôl+zeh* [1]
- such^{s}, 1821, *dābār* [1]
- such^{s}, 2021+6913, *ha-+ʿāśâ^{1}* [1]
- such, 2021, *ha-* [1]
- such, 2085, *hûʾ* [1]
- such things^{s}, 2157, *-hem* [1]
- such, 2179, *hēnnâ^{2}* [1]
- any such thing^{s}, 2257, *-ô* [1]
- such^{s}, 2257, *-ô* [1]
- such offerings^{s}, 2296, *zeh* [1]
- such questions^{s}, 2296, *zeh* [1]
- such, 2306, *zû* [1]
- such things^{s}, 2914, *ḥēpeṣ* [1]
- such, 3869+2297, *k^{e}-+zōh* [1]
- such, 3907, *kōh* [1]
- such, 3970, *kākâ* [1]
- such, 3972, *kōl* [1]
- such as, 4017, *k^{e}mô* [1]
- such, 4027+4017, *kēn^{2}+k^{e}mô* [1]
- such as, 4200, *l^{e-1}* [1]
- such, 4946+3972, *min+kōl* [1]
- such force^{s}, 5877, *nāpal* [1]
- such^{s}, 6402, *ʿûl^{2}* [1]
- in such places^{s}, 9004, *šām* [1]
- such, 10341+10180, *k^{e}-+d^{e}nâ* [1]

SUCK [1]
- suck, 3567, *yānaq* [1]

SUCKLING [1]
- suckling, 2692, *ḥālāb* [1]

SUDDEN [10]
- sudden, 7328, *pitʾōm* [4]
- sudden, 987, *bāhal* [1]
- sudden terror, 988, *behālâ* [1]
- sudden terror, 1166, *ballāhâ* [1]
- sudden, 2590, *ḥûš^{1}* [1]
- sudden, 4554, *māhar^{1}* [1]
- sudden, 8092, *regaʿ* [1]

SUDDENLY [28]
- suddenly, 7328, *pitʾōm* [13]
- suddenly, 2180, *hinnēh* [6]
- suddenly, 7353, *petaʿ* [3]
- suddenly, 928+285, *b^{e}-+ʾeḥād* [1]
- suddenly, 928+7353+7328, *b^{e}-+petaʿ+pitʾōm* [1]
- suddenly, 928+7353, *b^{e}-+petaʿ* [1]
- suddenly appeared, 2180, *hinnēh* [1]
- suddenly, 3869+8092, *k^{e}-+regaʿ* [1]
- suddenly, 10734+10191, *šāʿâ+-â* [1]

SUFFER [21]
- suffer, 5951, *nāśāʾ* [4]
- suffer, 6740, *ʿānaš* [2]
- suffer, 928, *b^{e}-* [1]
- suffer shame, 1017, *bôš^{1}* [1]
- suffer, 2118, *hāyâ* [1]
- cause to suffer, 2703, *ḥālâ^{1}* [1]
- suffer, 3359, *yādaʿ* [1]
- suffer, 4374, *lāqaḥ* [1]
- suffer vengeance, 5933, *nāqam* [1]
- suffer for, 5951, *nāśāʾ* [1]
- suffer, 5989+6584, *nātan+ʿal^{2}* [1]
- made suffer, 6700, *ʿānâ^{2}* [1]
- suffer, 6714, *ʿānî* [1]
- suffer thirst, 7532, *ṣāmēʾ^{1}* [1]
- surely suffer, 8273+8317, *raʿ^{1}+rāʿaʿ^{1}* [1]
- suffer loss, 10472, *n^{e}zaq* [1]
- suffer, 10472, *n^{e}zaq* [1]

SUFFERED [9]
- suffered, 5951, *nāśāʾ* [2]
- suffered, 2118+4200, *hāyâ+l^{e-1}* [1]
- suffered, 2118+928, *hāyâ+b^{e}-* [1]
- suffered, 5352, *mārar* [1]
- suffered affliction, 6700, *ʿānâ^{2}* [1]
- suffered, 6700, *ʿānâ^{2}* [1]
- suffered, 8011, *rāʾâ^{1}* [1]
- suffered, 8689, *šābar^{1}* [1]

SUFFERING [27]
- suffering, 6715, *ʿ^{o}nî* [9]
- suffering, 4799, *makʾōb* [4]
- suffering, 5186, *māṣôq* [2]
- bitter suffering, 5253, *mar^{1}* [2]
- suffering, *AIT* [1]
- suffering, 224, *ʾāwen^{1}* [1]
- suffering, 870, *ʾāšam* [1]
- suffering, 2703, *ḥālâ^{1}* [1]
- suffering, 2716, *ḥ^{o}lî* [1]
- suffering, 3873, *k^{e}ʾēb* [1]
- suffering for, 5951, *nāśāʾ* [1]
- suffering, 6662, *ʿāmāl^{1}* [1]
- suffering, 6713, *ʿenût* [1]
- suffering, 6778, *ʿōṣeb^{2}* [1]

SUFFERINGS [1]
- sufferings, 6780, *ʿaṣṣebet* [1]

SUFFERS [2]
- suffers torment, 2655, *ḥîl^{1}* [1]
- suffers harm, 8317, *rāʿaʿ^{1}* [1]

SUFFICIENT [2]
- sufficient, 1896, *day* [1]
- sufficient means, 3869+1896, *k^{e}-+day* [1]

SUGGEST [1]
- suggest, 606, *ʾāmar^{1}* [1]

SUGGESTED [5]
- suggested, 606, *ʾāmar^{1}* [3]
- suggested, 1819, *dābar^{2}* [1]
- suggested, 2021+1821+2021+2296, *ha-+dābār+ha-+zeh* [1]

SUGGESTION [1]
- suggestion, 1821, *dābār* [1]

SUITABLE [4]
- suitable, 824, *ʾereṣ* [1]
- suitable for, 3869+5584, *k^{e}-+neged* [1]
- suitable, 3869+5584, *k^{e}-+neged* [1]
- suitable, 5226, *māqôm* [1]

SUKKITES [1]
- Sukkites, 6113, *sukkiyyîm* [1]

SULFUR [7]
- burning sulfur, 1730, *goprît* [4]
- sulfur, 1730, *goprît* [3]

SULKING [1]
- sulking, 6015+906+7156, *sābab+ʾēt^{1}+pāneh* [1]

SULLEN [3]
- sullen, 6234, *sar* [3]

SUM [1]
- sum, 8031, *rōʾš^{1}* [1]

SUMMER [16]
- summer, 7811, *qayiṣ* [10]
- summer fruit, 7811, *qayiṣ* [3]
- summer palace, 5249, *m^{e}qērâ* [1]
- summer, 7797, *qayiṭ* [1]
- all summer, 7810, *qîṣ* [1]

SUMMIT [4]
- summit, 8031, *rōʾš^{1}* [3]
- summit, *NIH/RPE* [1]

SUMMON [27]
- summon, 7924, *qārāʾ^{1}* [18]
- summon, 2410, *zāʿaq* [2]
- summon, 9048, *šāmaʿ* [2]
- summon, 665, *ʾāsap* [1]
- summon, 3585, *yāʿad* [1]
- summon, 7422, *ṣāwâ* [1]
- summon, 8938+2256+4374, *šālaḥ+w^{e}-+lāqaḥ* [1]
- summon, 8938, *šālaḥ* [1]

SUMMONED [63]
- summoned, 7924, *qārāʾ^{1}* [45]
- summoned, 7735, *qāhal* [2]
- were summoned, 7924, *qārāʾ^{1}* [2]
- summoned, 8938+2256+7924, *šālaḥ+w^{e}-+qārāʾ^{1}* [2]
- summoned, *NIH/RPE* [1]
- summoned, 2410, *zāʿaq* [1]
- summoned, 7212, *pāqad* [1]
- summoned, 7590, *ṣāʿaq* [1]
- were summoned, 7590, *ṣāʿaq* [1]
- summoned to assemble, 7735, *qāhal* [1]
- being summoned, 7924, *qārāʾ^{1}* [1]
- summoned, 8938+4200+7924, *šālaḥ+l^{e-1}+qārāʾ^{1}* [1]
- summoned, 8938, *šālaḥ* [1]
- summoned, 9048, *šāmaʿ* [1]
- summoned, 10042+10378+10085, *ʾ^{a}mar+l^{e}-+ʾ^{a}tâ* [1]
- summoned, 10714+10378+10359, *š^{e}laḥ+l^{e}-+k^{e}naš* [1]

SUMMONING [1]
- summoning, 2410, *zāʿaq* [1]

SUMMONS [5]
- summons, 7924, *qārāʾ^{1}* [4]
- summons, 2349, *zākar^{1}* [1]

SUN [112]
- sun, 9087, *šemeš* [102]
- sun, 2780, *ḥammâ* [4]
- sun, 240, *ʾôr^{2}* [2]
- sun, 3064, *ḥeres^{2}* [1]
- sun, 3427, *yôm^{1}* [1]
- noonday sun, 7416, *ṣoh^{o}rayim* [1]
- sun rises, 8840, *šaḥar* [1]

SUN-SCORCHED [2]
- sun-scorched land, 7461, *ṣ^{e}ḥîḥâ* [1]
- sun-scorched land, 7463, *ṣaḥṣāḥôt* [1]

SUNDOWN [1]
- sundown, 10436+10728+10002, *meʿāl+š^{e}maš^{2}+-āʾ* [1]

SUNG [1]
- be sung, 8876, *šîr^{1}* [1]

SUNK [3]
- sunk, 3190, *ṭābaʿ* [2]
- sunk deep, 6676, *ʿāmaq* [1]

SUNLIGHT [2]
sunlight, 240+2780, *’ôr[2]+ḥammâ* [1]
sunlight, 9087, *šemeš* [1]

SUNRISE [12]
sunrise, 4667, *mizrāḥ* [5]
sunrise, 4667+9087, *mizrāḥ+šemeš* [3]
sunrise, 2436+2021+9087, *zāraḥ+ha-+šemeš* [2]
sunrise, 240, *’ôr[2]* [1]
sunrise, 2436+9087, *zāraḥ+šemeš* [1]

SUNSET [9]
sunset, 995+2021+9087, *bô’+ha-+šemeš* [6]
sunset, 6961+995+2021+9087, *ʿēt+bô’+ha-+šemeš* [2]
sunset, 995+2021+3064, *bô’+ha-+ḥeres[2]* [1]

SUNSHINE [2]
sunshine, 240, *’ôr[2]* [1]
sunshine, 9087, *šemeš* [1]

SUPERIOR [1]
superior, 1540, *gādal* [1]

SUPERSTITIONS [1]
superstitions, *NIH/RPE* [1]

SUPERVISE [5]
supervise, 6913, *ʿāśâ[1]* [3]
supervise, 5904, *nāṣaḥ* [2]

SUPERVISED [2]
supervised, 5904, *nāṣaḥ* [1]
supervised, 6584, *ʿal[2]* [1]

SUPERVISING [3]
supervising, 928, *b[e]-* [2]
supervising, 5904, *nāṣaḥ* [1]

SUPERVISION [6]
supervision, 3338, *yād* [5]
under supervision, 4200+7156, *l[e]-[1]+pāneh* [1]

SUPERVISOR [1]
supervisor, 5592, *nāgîd* [1]

SUPERVISORS [4]
supervisors, 7212, *pāqad* [2]
supervisors, 123, *’ādôn* [1]
supervisors, 7224, *pāqîd* [1]

SUPH [1]
Suph, 6069, *sûp[3]* [1]

SUPHAH [1]
Suphah, 6071, *sûpâ[2]* [1]

SUPPLICATION [5]
making supplication, 2858, *ḥānan[1]* [2]
supplication, 9382, *t[e]ḥinnâ[1]* [2]
supplication, 9384, *taḥ[a]nûn* [1]

SUPPLICATIONS [2]
supplications, 9382, *t[e]ḥinnâ[1]* [1]
supplications, 9384, *taḥ[a]nûn* [1]

SUPPLIED [10]
supplied provisions, 3920, *kûl* [2]
supplied, 3920, *kûl* [2]
supplied provisions, 3922, *kûn[1]* [1]
supplied, 5034, *māsar* [1]
supplied, 5951, *nāśā’* [1]
be supplied, 5989, *nātan* [1]
supplied, 5989, *nātan* [1]
supplied all needs, 8425, *śābaʿ* [1]

SUPPLIES [16]
supplies, 3998, *k[e]lî* [4]
supplies, 238, *’ôṣār* [2]
supplies, 5472, *mišʿān* [2]
distributing supplies, 2745, *ḥālaq[2]* [1]
provide supplies, 3920, *kûl* [1]
supplies, 3922, *kûn[1]* [1]
supplies, 4407, *ma’[a]kāl* [1]
supplies, 4751, *maṭṭeh* [1]
supplies, 4856, *m[e]lā’kâ* [1]
supplies, 5989, *nātan* [1]
supplies, 7476, *ṣêdâ* [1]

SUPPLY [18]
supply, 4751, *maṭṭeh* [4]
supply, *NIH/RPE* [1]
supply, 2118+4200, *hāyâ+l[e]-[1]* [1]
abundant supply, 2221, *harbēh* [1]
supply with food, 3920, *kûl* [1]
supply, 3922, *kûn[1]* [1]
water supply, 4784, *mayim* [1]
supply, 5473, *mašʿēn* [1]
supply, 5989, *nātan* [1]
supply liberally, 6735+6735, *ʿānaq+ʿānaq* [1]
food supply, 7474, *ṣayid[2]* [1]
supply, 8740, *šûb[1]* [1]
supply, 9250, *šārat* [1]
supply, 9414, *t[e]kûnâ* [1]
supply, 10498, *n[e]tan* [1]

SUPPORT [18]
support, 5472, *mišʿān* [2]
support, 5951, *nāśā’* [2]
gain support, 2118+3338+907, *hāyâ+yād+’ēt[2]* [1]
gave strong support, 2616+6640, *ḥāzaq+ʿim* [1]
support, 2616, *ḥāzaq* [1]
support, 3922, *kûn[1]* [1]
unable to support, 4572+3338, *môṭ[1]+yād* [1]
support, 5474, *mašʿēnâ* [1]
gave support, 6164, *sāmak* [1]
grant support, 6184, *sāʿad* [1]
gave support, 6468+339, *ʿāzar+’aḥar* [1]
give support, 6468, *ʿāzar* [1]
support, 6468, *ʿāzar* [1]
support, 6476, *ʿezrâ[1]* [1]
support, 6640, *ʿim* [1]
support, 9461, *tāmak* [1]

SUPPORTED [10]
supported, 7756, *qûm* [2]
supported, 339, *’aḥar* [1]
supported, 599, *’āmēṣ* [1]
supported, 2118+339, *hāyâ+’aḥar* [1]
supported, 2616, *ḥāzaq* [1]
supported, 3338+2118+907, *yād+hāyâ+’ēt[2]* [1]
supported, 6184, *sāʿad* [1]
supported, 6468, *ʿāzar* [1]
supported, 9393, *taḥat[1]* [1]

SUPPORTING [7]
supporting terraces, 4864, *millô’* [6]
supporting, 6584, *ʿal[2]* [1]

SUPPORTS [7]
supports, 296, *’āḥaz[1]* [2]
supports, 3338, *yād* [2]
supports, 2616+6640, *ḥāzaq+ʿim* [1]
supports, 5026, *misʿād* [1]
supports, 7193+4190, *paʿam+kātēp* [1]

SUPPOSE [7]
suppose, 2180, *hinnēh* [2]
suppose, 3954, *kî[2]* [2]
suppose, *NIH/RPE* [1]
suppose, 561, *’im* [1]
suppose, 2256, *w[e]-* [1]

SUPPOSED [1]
supposed to dine, 3782+3782+430, *yāšab+yāšab+’ākal* [1]

SUPPOSEDLY [1]
supposedly, *NIH/RPE* [1]

SUPREME [4]
supreme commander, 9580, *tartān* [2]
supreme, 8040, *rē’šît* [1]
supreme, 8950, *šilṭôn* [1]

SUR [1]
Sur, 6075, *sûr[3]* [1]

SURE [48]
sure, 622, *’[e]met* [5]
be sure, 3359+3359, *yādaʿ+yādaʿ* [5]
sure, *NIH/RPE* [4]
be sure, 3359, *yādaʿ* [3]
be sure, 9068, *šāmar* [3]
sure, *AIT* [2]
be sure of this, 3338+4200+3338, *yād+l[e]-[1]+yād* [2]
be sure to take back, 8740+8740, *šûb[1]+šûb[1]* [2]
make sure, 9068, *šāmar* [2]
be sure, 421, *’ak* [1]
sure foundation, 575, *’[e]mûnâ* [1]
sure, 586, *’āman[1]* [1]
so sure, 606+606, *’āmar[1]+’āmar[1]* [1]
be sure, 2180, *hinnēh* [1]
sure, 2180, *hinnēh* [1]
be sure, 2616, *ḥāzaq* [1]
be sure know, 3359+3359, *yādaʿ+yādaʿ* [1]
sure, 3569, *yāsad[1]* [1]
be sure to tell, 5583+5583, *nāgad+nāgad* [1]
be sure help, 6441+6441, *ʿāzab[2]+ʿāzab[2]* [1]
be sure to set aside a tenth, 6923+6923, *ʿāśar+ʿāśar* [1]
be sure to bury, 7699+7699, *qābar+qābar* [1]
be sure, 8370, *raq[2]* [1]
be sure to appoint, 8492+8492, *śîm+śîm* [1]
make sure hears, 8492+928+265, *śîm+b[e]-+’ōzen* [1]
sure to become utterly corrupt, 8845+8845, *šāḥat+šāḥat* [1]
be sure to let go, 8938+8938, *šālaḥ+šālaḥ* [1]
be sure to keep, 9068+9068, *šāmar+šāmar* [1]
be sure, 10056, *’osparnā’* [1]

SURELY [276]
as surely as lives, 2644, *ḥay[1]* [46]
surely, 3954, *kî[2]* [43]
surely, 2180, *hinnēh* [24]
as surely as live, 2644, *ḥay[1]* [23]
surely, 421, *’ak* [21]
surely, 561+4202, *’im+lō’* [14]
surely live, 2649+2649, *ḥāyâ+ḥāyâ* [9]
surely, 434, *’ākēn[1]* [7]
surely, 2176, *hēn[1]* [7]
surely die, 4637+4637, *mût+mût* [7]
surely be put to death, 4637+4637, *mût+mût* [4]
surely, *NIH/RPE* [3]
surely, 677, *’ap[1]* [3]
surely come to aid, 7212+7212, *pāqad+pāqad* [3]
surely, 8370, *raq[2]* [3]
surely go into exile, 1655+1655, *gālâ+gālâ* [2]
surely, 1685, *gam* [2]
as surely as, 2256, *w[e]-* [2]
as surely as live, 2644+5883, *ḥay[1]+nepeš* [2]
surely, 3954+561, *kî[2]+’im* [2]
surely, 4200+4027, *l[e]-[1]+kēn[2]* [2]
surely deliver, 5911+5911, *nāṣal+nāṣal* [2]
surely be destroyed, 6+6, *’ābad+’ābad* [1]
surely, 66, *’[a]bāl* [1]
surely, 421+6964, *’ak+ʿattâ* [1]
as surely as, 421, *’ak* [1]
because surely, 434, *’ākēn[1]* [1]
surely, 561+401, *’im+’ayin[1]* [1]
surely gather, 665+665, *’āsap+’āsap* [1]
surely exclude, 976+976, *bādal+bādal* [1]
surely bless, 1385+1385, *bārak[2]+bārak[2]* [1]
surely, 2022, *h[a]-* [1]
surely, 2026, *hē’* [1]
surely become, 2118+2118, *hāyâ+hāyâ* [1]
surely take place, 2118, *hāyâ* [1]
surely leave, 2143+2143+4946+6584, *hālak+hālak+min+ʿal[2]* [1]
surely, 2256, *w[e]-* [1]
as surely as live, 2644+2256+2644+5883, *ḥay[1]+w[e]-+ḥay[1]+nepeš* [1]
as surely as live, 2645, *ḥay[2]* [1]
surely been torn to pieces, 3271+3271, *ṭārap+ṭārap* [1]
surely make prosper, 3512+3512, *yāṭab+yāṭab* [1]
surely rebuke, 3519+3519, *yākaḥ+yākaḥ* [1]
surely triumph, 3523+3523, *yākōl+yākōl* [1]
surely come out, 3655+3655, *yāṣā’+yāṣā’* [1]
surely march out, 3655+3655, *yāṣā’+yāṣā’* [1]
as surely as, 3869, *k[e]-* [1]
for surely, 3954, *kî[2]* [1]
surely, 3954+2180, *kî[2]+hinnēh* [1]
surely, 3954+6964, *kî[2]+ʿattâ* [1]

must surely be cut off, 4162+4162, *kārat+kārat* [1]
surely, 4202, *lō'* [1]
surely be king, 4887+4887, *mālak[1]+mālak[1]* [1]
surely come to ruin, 5877+5877, *nāpal+nāpal* [1]
surely forget, 5960+5960, *nāšā[1]+nāšā[1]* [1]
surely hand over, 5989+5989+928+3338, *nātan+nātan+b[e]+yād* [1]
surely be stoned, 6232+6232, *sāqal+sāqal* [1]
surely bring back, 6590+6590, *'ālâ+'ālâ* [1]
surely show, 6913+6913, *'āśâ[1]+'āśâ[1]* [1]
surely sprout, 6913+6913, *'āśâ[1]+'āśâ[1]* [1]
surely bring together, 7695+7695, *qābaṣ+qābaṣ* [1]
surely stand, 7756+7756, *qûm+qûm* [1]
surely suffer, 8273+8317, *ra'[1]+rā'a'[1]* [1]
surely return, 8740+8740, *šûb[1]+šûb[1]* [1]
surely heard, 9048+9048, *šāma'+šāma'* [1]
surely be captured, 9530+9530, *tāpaś+tāpaś* [1]
surely, 10056, *'osparnā'* [1]
surely, 10427+10643+10168, *min+q[e]šōṭ+dî* [1]

SURFACE [11]
surface, 7156, *pāneh* [10]
surface, *NIH/RPE* [1]

SURFACES [1]
surfaces, 4283, *lûaḥ* [1]

SURGE [2]
surge, 1631, *gîaḥ[1]* [1]
surge, 9192, *šeṣep* [1]

SURGED [1]
surged forward, 7756, *qûm* [1]

SURGING [7]
surging, 1723, *gā'aš* [2]
surging, 1452, *ga'[a]wâ* [1]
surging, 1455, *gē'ût* [1]
surging, 1644, *gal[2]* [1]
surging, 5689, *nōzēl* [1]
surging, 8041, *rab[1]* [1]

SURLY [1]
surly, 7997, *qāšeh* [1]

SURMOUNTED [1]
surmounted by, 448, *'el* [1]

SURPASS [1]
surpass, 6590, *'ālâ* [1]

SURPASSES [1]
surpasses, 4946, *min* [1]

SURPASSING [1]
surpassing, 8044, *rōb* [1]

SURPRISE [4]
taken by surprise, 1850, *dāham* [1]
by surprise, 4202+3359, *lō'+yāda'* [1]
take by surprise, 5958, *nāšā'[2]* [1]
by surprise, 7328, *pit'ōm* [1]

SURPRISED [1]
surprised, 9449, *tāmah* [1]

SURRENDER [13]
surrender, 3655, *yāṣā'* [4]
surrender, 5989, *nātan* [3]
surrender, 5877, *nāpal* [2]
surrender, 6037, *sāgar* [2]
surrender, 3655+3655, *yāṣā'+yāṣā'* [1]
surrender, 6037+928+3338, *sāgar+b[e]+yād* [1]

SURRENDERED [1]
surrendered, 3655, *yāṣā'* [1]

SURRENDERS [2]
surrenders, 5877, *nāpal* [1]
surrenders, 5989+3338, *nātan+yād* [1]

SURROUND [21]
surround, 6015, *sābab* [10]
surround, 6017, *sābîb* [5]
surround, 705, *'āpap* [1]
surround, 2118+4946+6017, *hāyâ+min+sābîb* [1]
surround, 4990, *mēsab* [1]
surround, 5938, *nāqap[2]* [1]
surround, 6496, *'āṭar[1]* [1]
surround, 6643, *'immād* [1]

SURROUNDED [24]
surrounded, 6015, *sābab* [15]
surrounded, 6017, *sābîb* [4]
surrounded, 5938, *nāqap[2]* [2]
surrounded by, 928+9348, *b[e]+tāwek* [1]
surrounded, 4193, *kātar[2]* [1]
surrounded, 6296, *'ābar[1]* [1]

SURROUNDING [49]
surrounding, 6017, *sābîb* [27]
surrounding settlements, 1426, *bat[1]* [10]
surrounding villages, 1426, *bat[1]* [6]
surrounding, *NIH/RPE* [1]
surrounding villages, 2958, *ḥāṣēr[1]* [1]
surrounding region, 3971, *kikkār* [1]
surrounding, 6015, *sābab* [1]
completely surrounding, 6017+6017, *sābîb+sābîb* [1]
surrounding, 6017+6017, *sābîb+sābîb* [1]

SURROUNDS [3]
surrounds, 6017, *sābîb* [2]
surrounds, 6015, *sābab* [1]

SURVEY [2]
make a survey of, 2143+928, *hālak+b[e]-* [2]

SURVEYED [1]
surveyed, 7155, *pānâ* [1]

SURVIVE [13]
survive, 8586, *śārîd[1]* [4]
survive, 8636, *šā'ar* [3]
survive, 2649, *ḥāyâ* [2]
survive, 7756, *qûm* [2]
survive, 7117, *pālaṭ* [1]
survive, 7128, *pālêṭ* [1]

SURVIVED [9]
survived, 8636, *šā'ar* [5]
survived, 2649, *ḥāyâ* [2]
survived, 3855, *yātar* [1]
survived, 8586, *śārîd[1]* [1]

SURVIVES [3]
survives, 5162, *māṣā'* [2]
survives, 8636, *šā'ar* [1]

SURVIVING [3]
surviving, 3856+889+3855, *yeter[1]+'[a]šer+yātar* [1]
surviving, 3856, *yeter[1]* [1]
surviving, 6641, *'āmad* [1]

SURVIVOR [5]
survivor, 8586, *śārîd[1]* [2]
survivor, 7127, *pālîṭ* [1]
survivor, 7129, *p[e]lêṭâ* [1]
left survivor, 8636, *šā'ar* [1]

SURVIVORS [40]
survivors, 8586, *śārîd[1]* [17]
survivors, 8642, *š[e]'ērît* [7]
survivors, 7129, *p[e]lêṭâ* [4]
survivors, 3856, *yeter[1]* [3]
survivors, 8636, *šā'ar* [3]
survivors, 8637, *š[e]'ār* [3]
band of survivors, 7129, *p[e]lêṭâ* [2]
survivors, 3855, *yātar* [1]

SUSA [22]
Susa, 8809, *šûšan[2]* [21]
of Susa, 10704, *šûšankāy* [1]

SUSI [1]
Susi, 6064, *sûsî* [1]

SUSPECTS [3]
suspects, 7861, *qānā'* [3]

SUSPENDS [1]
suspends, 9434, *tālâ* [1]

SUSPENSE [1]
suspense, 9428, *tālā'* [1]

SUSTAIN [10]
sustain, 3920, *kûl* [2]
sustain, 6022, *sābal* [2]
sustain, 6164, *sāmak* [2]
sustain, 3922, *kûn[1]* [1]
sustain, 6184, *sā'ad* [1]
sustain, 6468, *'āzar* [1]
sustain, 6885, *'ārak* [1]

SUSTAINED [4]
sustained, 6164, *sāmak* [3]
sustained, 3920, *kûl* [1]

SUSTAINS [8]
sustains, 6164, *sāmak* [2]
sustains, 6184, *sā'ad* [2]
sustains, 6386, *'ûd[1]* [2]
sustains, 3920, *kûl* [1]
sustains, 6431, *'ût* [1]

SWALLOW [13]
swallow up, 1180, *bāla'[1]* [7]
swallow, 1180, *bāla'[1]* [3]
swallow, 2000, *d[e]rôr[1]* [2]
swallow up, 4312, *leḥem* [1]

SWALLOWED [20]
swallowed up, 1180, *bāla'[1]* [9]
swallowed, 1180, *bāla'[1]* [7]
be swallowed up, 1180, *bāla'[1]* [2]
is swallowed up, 1180, *bāla'[1]* [1]
what swallowed, 1183, *bela'[1]* [1]

SWALLOWS [2]
swallows, 1180, *bāla'[1]* [2]

SWAMPLAND [1]
swampland, 106+4784, *'[a]gam[1]+mayim* [1]

SWAMPS [1]
swamps, 1289, *biṣṣâ* [1]

SWARM [11]
locust swarm, 1612, *gāzām* [2]
swarm, 995, *bô'* [1]
swarm of bees, 1805, *d[e]bôrâ[1]* [1]
swarm of locusts, 3540, *yeleq* [1]
swarm, 5480, *maššāq* [1]
swarm, 6170, *sāmār* [1]
swarm, 6337, *'ēdâ* [1]
swarm, 6590, *'ālâ* [1]
swarm, 9237, *šāraṣ* [1]
insects that swarm, 9238, *šereṣ* [1]

SWARMED [1]
swarmed around, 6015, *sābab* [1]

SWARMING [1]
swarming things, 9238, *šereṣ* [1]

SWARMS [10]
swarms of flies, 6856, *'ārōb* [5]
swarms of locusts, 1479, *gōbay* [1]
swarms, 1571, *gôb[2]* [1]
swarms, 1896, *day* [1]
swarms of locusts, 7526, *ṣ[e]lāṣal* [1]
swarms, 9237, *šāraṣ* [1]

SWAY [4]
hold sway, 5675, *nûa'* [3]
sway, 8321, *rā'aš[1]* [1]

SWAYING [2]
swaying, 5653, *nûd* [1]
swaying, 7837, *qālal* [1]

SWAYS [3]
sways, 2912, *ḥāpaṣ[2]* [1]
sways, 5653, *nûd* [1]
sways, 5675, *nûa'* [1]

SWEAR [46]
swear, 8678, *šābaʿ* [29]
made swear, 8678, *šābaʿ* [4]
made swear an oath, 8678, *šābaʿ* [3]
make swear, 8678, *šābaʿ* [3]
swear, 8652, *šebûʿâ* [2]
swear, 606, *ʾāmar[1]* [1]
swear with uplifted, 5951, *nāśāʾ* [1]
made swear an oath, 8678+8678, *šābaʿ+šābaʿ* [1]
swear allegiance, 8678, *šābaʿ* [1]
want to swear, 8678, *šābaʿ* [1]

SWEARING [1]
swearing, 8678, *šābaʿ* [1]

SWEARS [5]
swears the oath, 457, *ʾālâ[1]* [2]
swears, 8678, *šābaʿ* [2]
swears falsely, 8678, *šābaʿ* [1]

SWEAT [1]
sweat, 2399, *zēʿâ* [1]

SWEEP [20]
sweep away, 6066, *sûp[1]* [2]
sweep away, 6200, *sāpâ* [2]
sweep through, 6296, *ʿābar[1]* [2]
sweep away, 665+6066, *ʾāsap+sûp[1]* [1]
sweep on, 995+995, *bôʾ+bôʾ* [1]
sweep, 2143, *hālak* [1]
sweep away, 2442, *zāram[2]* [1]
sweep on, 2736, *ḥālap[1]* [1]
sweep past, 2736, *ḥālap[1]* [1]
sweep, 3173, *ṭēʾṭēʾ* [1]
sweep away, 3589, *yāʿâ* [1]
sweep, 5677, *nûp[1]* [1]
sweep away, 5951, *nāśāʾ* [1]
sweep, 6296, *ʿābar[1]* [1]
sweep through, 7502, *ṣālaḥ[1]* [1]
sweep away, 7674+928+4053, *ṣārar[1]+be-+kānāp* [1]
sweep over, 8851, *šāṭap* [1]

SWEEPING [1]
sweeping, 2736, *ḥālap[1]* [1]

SWEEPINGS [1]
sweepings, 5139, *mappāl* [1]

SWEEPS [7]
sweeps by, 6296, *ʿābar[1]* [2]
sweeps over, 910, *ʾātâ* [1]
sweeps away, 5951, *nāśāʾ* [1]
sweeps away, 6200, *sāpâ* [1]
sweeps on, 6296, *ʿābar[1]* [1]
sweeps out, 8548, *śāʿar[2]* [1]

SWEET [24]
sweet, 5498, *mātôq* [10]
sweet, 5517, *mātaq* [4]
sweet, 6844, *ʿārab[3]* [2]
sweet, 3203, *ṭôb[3]* [1]
also sweet[s], 4027, *kēn[2]* [1]
sweet, 4914, *mālaṣ* [1]
sweet, 4941, *mamtaqqîm* [1]
enjoyed sweet, 5517, *mātaq* [1]
sweet, 5519, *mōteq* [1]
sweet, 6853, *ʿārēb* [1]
tastes sweet, 6853, *ʿārēb* [1]

SWEETER [3]
sweeter, 5498, *mātôq* [2]
sweeter, *NIH/RPE* [1]

SWEETNESS [2]
sweetness, 4941, *mamtaqqîm* [1]
sweetness as the honeycomb, 5885, *nōpet* [1]

SWELL [4]
swell, 1301, *bāṣēq[1]* [1]
swell, 7377, *ṣābâ* [1]
swell, 7379, *ṣābeh* [1]
swell with joy, 8143, *rāḥab* [1]

SWELLING [6]
swelling, 8421, *śeʾēt[2]* [6]

SWELLS [1]
swells, 7377, *ṣābâ* [1]

SWELTER [1]
swelter, 2768, *ḥām[2]* [1]

SWEPT [27]
swept, 6296, *ʿābar[1]* [5]
be swept away, 6200, *sāpâ* [4]
swept, 5850, *nāʿar[2]* [2]
swept by, 6296, *ʿābar[1]* [2]
swept, 6, *ʾābad* [1]
swept in, 995, *bôʾ* [1]
swept away, 1704, *gānab* [1]
swept away, 1759, *gārap* [1]
are swept away, 4554, *māhar[1]* [1]
swept away, 4681, *māḥâ[1]* [1]
being swept away, 6200, *sāpâ* [1]
swept away, 6200, *sāpâ* [1]
swept away, 6296, *ʿābar[1]* [1]
swept down, 7320, *pāšaṭ* [1]
swept away, 8548, *śāʿar[2]* [1]
be swept away, 8851, *šāṭap* [1]
swept away, 8851, *šāṭap* [1]
swept away, 10492, *neśāʾ* [1]

SWERVE [2]
swerve, 5742, *nāṭâ* [2]

SWERVING [1]
swerving, 6293, *ʿābaṭ[2]* [1]

SWIFT [14]
swift, 7824, *qal* [7]
swift, 4554, *māhar[1]* [3]
swift, 6101, *sîs* [2]
swift flight, 3616+3618, *yāʿēp[2]+yeʿāp* [1]
swift, 7837, *qālal* [1]

SWIFTER [6]
swifter, 7837, *qālal* [5]
swifter, 7824, *qal* [1]

SWIFTLY [4]
do swiftly, 2590, *ḥûš[1]* [1]
swiftly, 4559, *mehērâ* [1]
swiftly, 6330+4559, *ʿad[2]+mehērâ* [1]
swiftly, 7824, *qal* [1]

SWIM [3]
swim, 6296, *ʿābar[1]* [1]
swim, 8466, *śāḥâ* [1]
deep enough to swim in, 8467, *śāḥû* [1]

SWIMMER [1]
swimmer, 8466, *śāḥâ* [1]

SWING [3]
swing out, 2322, *zāḥaḥ* [2]
swing, 8938, *šālaḥ* [1]

SWINGS [2]
swings, 2933, *ḥāṣēb[1]* [1]
swings, 5616, *nādaḥ[2]* [1]

SWIRL [1]
swirl, 2200, *hāpak* [1]

SWIRLED [2]
swirled about, 705, *ʾāpap* [1]
swirled about, 6015, *sābab* [1]

SWIRLING [4]
swirling down, 2565, *ḥûl[1]* [2]
swirling, 6192, *sāʿar* [1]
swirling over, 8851, *šāṭap* [1]

SWOLLEN [3]
swollen, 1301, *bāṣēq[1]* [1]
swollen, 6623, *ʿālam* [1]
swollen, 8421, *śeʾēt[2]* [1]

SWOOP [2]
swoop down, 1797, *dāʾâ[1]* [1]
swoop down, 6414, *ʿûp[1]* [1]

SWOOPING [4]
swooping down, 1797, *dāʾâ[1]* [2]
swooping, 2590, *ḥûš[1]* [1]
swooping down, 3216, *ṭûś* [1]

SWORD [373]
sword, 2995, *ḥereb* [362]
sword, *NIH/RPE* [6]
sword, 8939, *šelaḥ[1]* [2]
sword[s], 337, *ʾaḥēr[1]* [1]
the sword[s], 2023, *-āh* [1]
drawn sword, 7339, *petaḥ* [1]

SWORDS [33]
swords, 2995, *ḥereb* [31]
swords, 4839, *mekērâ* [1]
drawn swords, 7347, *petîḥâ* [1]

SWORDSMEN [5]
swordsmen, 408+8990+2995, *ʾîš[1]+šālap+ḥereb* [5]

SWORE [55]
swore, 8678, *šābaʿ* [35]
swore an oath, 8678, *šābaʿ* [6]
swore with uplifted, 5951, *nāśāʾ* [5]
with uplifted swore, 5951, *nāśāʾ* [2]
solemnly swore, 8678, *šābaʿ* [2]
swore oath, 8678, *šābaʿ* [2]
swore, *NIH/RPE* [1]
swore, 5951+3338, *nāśāʾ+yād* [1]
oath swore, 8652, *šebûʿâ* [1]

SWORN [30]
sworn, 8678, *šābaʿ* [21]
sworn with uplifted, 5951, *nāśāʾ* [3]
sworn agreement, 460, *ʾālâ[4]* [1]
sworn, 5951+906+3338, *nāśāʾ+ʾēt[1]+yād* [1]
sworn judgments, 8652, *šebûʿâ* [1]
sworn, 8652, *šebûʿâ* [1]
sworn allegiance, 8678+8652, *šābaʿ+šebûʿâ* [1]
sworn an oath, 8678, *šābaʿ* [1]

SWUNG [1]
swung open, 6015, *sābab* [1]

SYCAMORE-FIG [5]
sycamore-fig trees, 9204, *šiqmâ* [5]

SYCAMORE-FIGS [1]
sycamore-figs, 9204, *šiqmâ* [1]

SYMBOL [2]
symbol, 3213, *ṭôṭāpōt* [1]
symbol of separation, 5694, *nēzer* [1]

SYMBOLIC [1]
symbolic of things to come, 4603, *môpēt* [1]

SYMBOLS [4]
symbols, 253, *ʾôt[1]* [2]
pagan symbols, 2355, *zikkārôn* [1]
symbols, 4603, *môpēt* [1]

SYMPATHIZE [1]
sympathize, 5653, *nûd* [1]

SYMPATHY [8]
express sympathy, 5714, *nāḥam* [5]
show sympathy, 5653, *nûd* [1]
sympathy, 5653, *nûd* [1]
sympathy, 8171, *raḥamîm* [1]

TAANACH [7]
Taanach, 9505, *taʿanak* [7]

TAANATH SHILOH [1]
Taanath Shiloh, 9304, *taʾanat šilōh* [1]

TABALIAH [1]
Tabaliah, 3189, *ṭebalyāhû* [1]

TABBAOTH [2]
Tabbaoth, 3191, *ṭabbāʿôt* [2]

TABBATH [1]
Tabbath, 3195, *ṭabbāt* [1]

TABEEL [2]
Tabeel, 3174, *ṭābeʾal* [1]
Tabeel, 3175, *ṭābeʾēl* [1]

TABERAH [2]
Taberah, 9323, *tab'ērâ* [2]

TABERNACLE [104]
tabernacle, 5438, *miškān* [102]
tabernacle, 185, *'ōhel*[1] [2]

TABERNACLES [9]
Tabernacles, 6109, *sukkâ* [9]

TABLE [63]
table, 8947, *šulḥān* [52]
set out on the table, 5121, *ma'areket* [3]
the tables, 2257, *-ô* [2]
at tables, 4200+7156, *le-*[1]*+pāneh* [2]
table, 4990, *mēsab* [1]
table, 5492, *mišteh* [1]
tables, 7156, *pāneh* [1]
each table, 8947+2256+8947, *šulḥān+we-+šulḥān* [1]

TABLES [13]
tables, 8947, *šulḥān* [12]
the tables were turned, 2200, *hāpak* [1]

TABLET [4]
tablet, 4283, *lûaḥ* [3]
clay tablet, 4246, *lebēnâ* [1]

TABLETS [33]
tablets, 4283, *lûaḥ* [33]

TABOR [10]
Tabor, 9314, *tābôr* [10]

TABRIMMON [1]
Tabrimmon, 3193, *ṭabrimmōn* [1]

TACT [1]
tact, 10302, *ṭe'ēm*[2] [1]

TADMOR [2]
Tadmor, 9330, *tadmōr* [2]

TAHAN [2]
Tahan, 9380, *taḥan* [2]

TAHANITE [1]
Tahanite, 9385, *taḥanî* [1]

TAHASH [1]
Tahash, 9392, *taḥaš*[2] [1]

TAHATH [6]
Tahath, 9394, *taḥat*[2] [4]
Tahath, 9395, *taḥat*[3] [2]

TAHKEMONITE [1]
Tahkemonite, 9376, *taḥkemōnî* [1]

TAHPANHES [7]
Tahpanhes, 9387, *taḥpanḥēs* [7]

TAHPENES [3]
Tahpenes, 9388, *taḥpenês* [3]

TAHREA [1]
Tahrea, 9390, *taḥrēa'* [1]

TAHTIM HODSHI [1]
Tahtim Hodshi, 9398, *taḥtîm ḥodšî* [1]

TAIL [14]
tail, 2387, *zānāb* [9]
fat tail, 487, *'alyâ* [5]

TAILS [1]
tails, 2387, *zānāb* [1]

TAKE [693]
take, 4374, *lāqaḥ* [238]
take possession, 3769, *yāraš*[1] [31]
take, *NIH/RPE* [25]
take refuge, 2879, *ḥāsâ* [23]
take, 995, *bô'* [14]
take up, 5951, *nāśā'* [14]
take away, 4374, *lāqaḥ* [12]
take, 2143, *hālak* [10]
take down, 3718, *yārad* [7]
take, 5951, *nāśā'* [7]
take away, 6073, *sûr*[1] [7]
take back, 8740, *šûb*[1] [7]
take, 3655, *yāṣā'* [6]
take over, 3769, *yāraš*[1] [6]
take away, 5951, *nāśā'* [5]
take, 5989, *nātan* [5]
take, 6073, *sûr*[1] [5]
take up, 6590, *'ālâ* [5]
take care of, 9068, *šāmar* [5]
take away, 665, *'āsap* [4]
take hold, 2616, *ḥāzaq* [4]
take, 4334, *lākad* [4]
take, 5602, *nāgaš* [4]
take, 5782, *nākâ* [4]
take away, 6296, *'ābar*[1] [4]
take off, 7320, *pāšaṭ* [4]
take oaths, 8678, *šāba'* [4]
take, 8740, *šûb*[1] [4]
take, 9530, *tāpaś* [4]
take warning, 2302, *zāhar*[2] [3]
take a census, 5951+906+8031, *nāśā'+'ēt*[1]*+rō'š*[1] [3]
take care of, 8286, *rā'â*[1] [3]
take, 8492, *śîm* [3]
made take an oath, 8678, *šāba'* [3]
take, 296, *'āḥaz*[1] [2]
take an oath, 457, *'ālâ*[1] [2]
take, 1335, *bāqaš* [2]
trying to take, 1335, *bāqaš* [2]
take the news, 1413, *bāśar* [2]
take place, 2118, *hāyâ* [2]
take, 2616, *ḥāzaq* [2]
take pleasure, 2911, *ḥāpēṣ*[1] [2]
take notice, 3359, *yāda'* [2]
take advantage of, 3561, *yānâ* [2]
take warning, 3579, *yāsar*[1] [2]
take out, 3655, *yāṣā'* [2]
take positions, 3656, *yāṣab* [2]
take, 3769, *yāraš*[1] [2]
take a census, 4948, *mānâ*[1] [2]
take a census, 5951+8031, *nāśā'+rō'š*[1] [2]
take off, 5970, *nāšal* [2]
take off, 6073, *sûr*[1] [2]
take, 6590, *'ālâ* [2]
take stand, 6641, *'āmad* [2]
take up positions, 6885, *'ārak* [2]
take a tenth, 6923, *'āśar* [2]
take off, 7293, *pāraq* [2]
take a handful, 7858+4850+7859, *qāmaṣ+melō'+qōmeṣ* [2]
take many, 8049, *rābâ*[1] [2]
take, 8123, *rûm*[1] [2]
take up, 8189, *rîb*[1] [2]
take captive, 8647, *šābâ* [2]
be sure to take back, 8740+8740, *šûb*[1]*+šûb*[1] [2]
take, 8883, *šît*[1] [2]
take flight, 87, *'ābar* [1]
take hold, 296, *'āḥaz*[1] [1]
take on, 296, *'āḥaz*[1] [1]
take oaths, 457, *'ālâ*[1] [1]
take heart, 599+4213, *'āmēṣ+lēb* [1]
take heart, 599+4222, *'āmēṣ+lēbāb* [1]
take, 665, *'āsap* [1]
take prisoner, 673, *'āsar* [1]
take, 724, *'āṣal* [1]
take in, 928, *be-* [1]
take along, 995, *bô'* [1]
take back, 995, *bô'* [1]
take home, 995, *bô'* [1]
take into, 995, *bô'* [1]
take out, 995, *bô'* [1]
take part, 995, *bô'* [1]
take, 995+1198, *bô'+bemô* [1]
take, 995+6584, *bô'+'al*[2] [1]
take, 1024, *bāzaz* [1]
take heed, 1067, *bîn* [1]
take note, 1067, *bîn* [1]
tried to take, 1335, *bāqaš* [1]
take by force, 1608, *gāzal* [1]
take off, 1655, *gālâ* [1]
take away, 1757, *gāra'*[1] [1]
take, 1757, *gāra'*[1] [1]
take pride, 2038, *hābal* [1]
take care of, 2118+4200+5466, *hāyâ+le-*[1]*+mišmeret* [1]
take, 2118+4200, *hāyâ+le-*[1] [1]
surely take place, 2118, *hāyâ* [1]
take care of, 2118+6125, *hāyâ+sōkēn* [1]
take command, 2118+4200+5464, *hāyâ+le-*[1]*+mišmār*[1] [1]
take hold of, 2118+928, *hāyâ+be-* [1]
take, 2118, *hāyâ* [1]
take back, 2143, *hālak* [1]
take part, 2143+6640, *hālak+'im* [1]
take possession, 2143, *hālak* [1]
take turns, 2143+3427, *hālak+yôm*[1] [1]
take as a pledge, 2471+2471, *ḥābal*[1]*+ḥābal*[1] [1]
take as a pledge, 2471, *ḥābal*[1] [1]
take as security for a debt, 2471, *ḥābal*[1] [1]
take in pledge, 2471, *ḥābal*[1] [1]
take pity, 2571, *ḥûs* [1]
take up, 2616, *ḥāzaq* [1]
take courage, 2616, *ḥāzaq* [1]
take firm hold, 2616, *ḥāzaq* [1]
take off, 2740, *ḥālaṣ*[1] [1]
take pity, 2798, *ḥāmal* [1]
take a fifth, 2821, *ḥāmaš* [1]
take pity, 2858, *ḥānan*[1] [1]
take any pleasure in, 2911+2911, *ḥāpēṣ*[1]*+ḥāpēṣ*[1] [1]
take delight, 2911, *ḥāpēṣ*[1] [1]
take advice, 3619, *yā'aṣ* [1]
take counsel, 3619, *yā'aṣ* [1]
take back, 3655, *yāṣā'* [1]
take up positions, 3656, *yāṣab* [1]
take a stand, 3656, *yāṣab* [1]
take stand, 3656, *yāṣab* [1]
take off, 3718+4946+6584, *yārad+min+'al*[2] [1]
take, 3718, *yārad* [1]
take away possessions, 3769, *yāraš*[1] [1]
take, 4033, *kānâ* [1]
take away, 4162, *kārat* [1]
take up, 4374, *lāqaḥ* [1]
take up, 4848, *mālē'*[1] [1]
take, 4850, *melō'* [1]
take turns, 5005, *massāḥ* [1]
take away, 5432, *māšak* [1]
take care of, 5466, *mišmeret* [1]
take, 5627, *nāhag*[1] [1]
take as inheritance, 5706, *nāḥal* [1]
take possession, 5706, *nāḥal* [1]
take care of, 5757, *nāṭar*[1] [1]
take away, 5911+5362, *nāṣal+maśśā'*[1] [1]
take back, 5911, *nāṣal* [1]
take, 5911, *nāṣal* [1]
take vengeance, 5933+5935, *nāqam+neqāmâ* [1]
take revenge, 5933+5934, *nāqam+nāqām* [1]
take revenge, 5933, *nāqam* [1]
take vengeance, 5933, *nāqam* [1]
take vengeance, 5934+8740, *nāqām+šûb*[1] [1]
take in marriage, 5951, *nāśā'* [1]
take by surprise, 5958, *nāšā'*[2] [1]
take for, 5989+4200+7156, *nātan+le-*[1]*+pāneh* [1]
take place, 5989, *nātan* [1]
take back, 6073, *sûr*[1] [1]
take off, 6200, *sāpâ* [1]
take, 6200, *sāpâ* [1]
take refuge, 6259, *sātar* [1]
take note as pass, 6296, *'ābar*[1] [1]
take over, 6296, *'ābar*[1] [1]
take up, 6335, *'ādâ*[2] [1]
take cover, 6395, *'ûz* [1]
take firm hold, 6487+6487, *'āṭâ*[2]*+'āṭâ*[2] [1]
take care of, 6584, *'al*[2] [1]
take away, 6590, *'ālâ* [1]
take part in, 6618, *'ālal*[1] [1]
take advantage of, 6700, *'ānâ*[2] [1]
take action, 6913, *'āśâ*[1] [1]
take place, 6913, *'āśâ*[1] [1]
take, 6913, *'āśâ*[1] [1]
take advantage, 6943, *'āšaq* [1]
take notice, 6951, *'āšat*[2] [1]
take care of, 7212, *pāqad* [1]
take stock of, 7212, *pāqad* [1]
take the lead, 7276, *pāra'*[1] [1]
take, 7296, *pārar*[1] [1]

take off, 7337, *pātaḥ*[1] [1]
take part, 7371+7372, *ṣābā'*[1]*+ṣābā'*[2] [1]
take, 7443, *ṣûr*[1] [1]
take choice, 7691, *qābal* [1]
take place, 7756, *qûm* [1]
take up a lament, 7801, *qîn* [1]
take a handful, 7858, *qāmaṣ* [1]
take part, 7928+6913, *qārab+'āśâ*[1] [1]
take out, 8123, *rûm*[1] [1]
take up, 8123, *rûm*[1] [1]
take delight, 8193, *rîaḥ* [1]
take, 8206, *rākab* [1]
take delight in, 8354, *rāṣâ*[1] [1]
take pleasure in, 8354, *rāṣâ*[1] [1]
take pleasure, 8354, *rāṣâ*[1] [1]
take delight, 8464, *śûś* [1]
take great delight, 8464+928+8525, *śûś+be-+śimḥâ* [1]
had take up positions, 8492, *śîm* [1]
take up positions, 8492, *śîm* [1]
take pleasure, 8523, *śāmaḥ* [1]
take captives, 8647+8660, *šābâ+šebî* [1]
take away, 8740, *šûb*[1] [1]
take back, 8740+8740, *šûb*[1]*+šûb*[1] [1]
take vengeance, 8740+5934, *šûb*[1]*+nāqām* [1]
take note, 8883+4213, *šît*[1]*+lēb* [1]
take rest, 8886, *šākab* [1]
take care, 9068, *šāmar* [1]
take root, 9245+1614, *šāraš+geza'* [1]
take root, 9245, *šāraš* [1]
take care of, 9250, *šārat* [1]
take charge of, 9393+3338, *taḥat*[1]*+yād* [1]
take the place of, 9393+2118, *taḥat*[1]*+hāyâ* [1]
take the place of, 9393, *taḥat*[1] [1]
take captive, 9530, *tāpaś* [1]
take hold, 9530, *tāpaś* [1]
take place, 10201, *hawâ* [1]
take, 10308, *yebal* [1]
take, 10492, *neśā'* [1]
take, 10549, *'alal* [1]

TAKEN [200]

taken, 4374, *lāqaḥ* [32]
taken, *NIH/RPE* [6]
was taken, 4334, *lākad* [6]
taken over, 3769, *yāraš*[1] [5]
taken possession, 3769, *yāraš*[1] [4]
taken away, 4374, *lāqaḥ* [4]
was taken, 4374, *lāqaḥ* [4]
taken captive, 8647, *šābâ* [4]
are taken away, 665, *'āsap* [3]
taken, 995, *bô'* [3]
taken captive, 1655, *gālâ* [3]
taken into exile, 1655, *gālâ* [3]
taken, 2118, *hāyâ* [3]
taken, 4334, *lākad* [3]
be taken, 4374, *lāqaḥ* [3]
taken away, 6073, *sûr*[1] [3]
taken an oath, 8678, *šāba'* [3]
taken, 10485, *nepaq* [3]
be taken, 1757, *gāra'*[1] [2]
taken refuge, 2879, *ḥāsâ* [2]
taken out, 3655, *yāṣā'* [2]
taken, 3655, *yāṣā'* [2]
am taken, 4374, *lāqaḥ* [2]
is taken, 4374, *lāqaḥ* [2]
was taken away, 4374, *lāqaḥ* [2]
were taken, 4374, *lāqaḥ* [2]
taken, 5951, *nāśā'* [2]
taken away, 6296, *'ābar*[1] [2]
taken, 6590, *'ālâ* [2]
taken, 8178, *rāḥaq* [2]
taken, 9530, *tāpaś* [2]
taken, *AIT* [1]
are taken, 296, *'āḥaz*[1] [1]
being taken, 296, *'āḥaz*[1] [1]
taken away, 665, *'āsap* [1]
taken, 665, *'āsap* [1]
obligation taken, 673, *'āsar* [1]
were taken prisoner, 673, *'āsar* [1]
be taken captive, 928+2021+4090+9530, *be-+ha+kap+tāpaś* [1]
taken great pains, 928+6715, *be+'onî* [1]
taken into account, 928, *be-* [1]
taken, 928+3338, *be-+yād* [1]
be taken, 995, *bô'* [1]
been taken into, 995, *bô'* [1]
taken place, 995, *bô'* [1]
was taken, 995, *bô'* [1]
were taken, 995, *bô'* [1]
taken captive, 1020, *baz* [1]
taken plunder, 1024, *bāzaz* [1]
taken by storm, 1324, *bāqa'* [1]
be forcibly taken, 1608, *gāzal* [1]
taken, 1655, *gālâ* [1]
were taken captive, 1655, *gālâ* [1]
taken secretly, 1704, *gānab* [1]
be taken away, 1757, *gāra'*[1] [1]
taken, 1757, *gāra'*[1] [1]
taken by surprise, 1850, *dāham* [1]
taken, 2143, *hālak* [1]
taken warning, 2302, *zāhar*[2] [1]
taken in pledge, 2471, *ḥābal*[1] [1]
be taken, 3108, *ḥāšab* [1]
taken, 3297, *yābal* [1]
been taken down, 3718, *yārad* [1]
taken, 3718, *yārad* [1]
was taken down, 3718, *yārad* [1]
taken seat, 3782, *yāšab* [1]
be taken, 4162, *kārat* [1]
taken, 4200, *le-*[1] [1]
be taken captive, 4334, *lākad* [1]
were taken, 4334, *lākad* [1]
are taken, 4374, *lāqaḥ* [1]
be taken away, 4374, *lāqaḥ* [1]
been taken away, 4374, *lāqaḥ* [1]
been taken, 4374, *lāqaḥ* [1]
taken from, 4946+4200+7156, *min+le-*[1]*+pāneh* [1]
taken, 4946, *min* [1]
taken away, 5911, *nāṣal* [1]
taken refuge, 5911, *nāṣal* [1]
taken anything, 5951+5951, *nāśā'+nāśā'* [1]
taken as wives, 5951, *nāśā'* [1]
taken away, 5951, *nāśā'* [1]
taken up, 5951, *nāśā'* [1]
taken, 6073, *sûr*[1] [1]
census taken, 6222+6218, *sepār*[1]*+sapar* [1]
taken from, 6296, *'ābar*[1] [1]
taken over, 6296, *'ābar*[1] [1]
taken up, 6590, *'ālâ* [1]
taken care of, 6913, *'āśâ*[1] [1]
taken by extortion, 6945+6943, *'ōšeq+'āšaq* [1]
taken, 6972, *'attîq* [1]
taken off, 7320, *pāšaṭ* [1]
taken steps, 7575+7576, *ṣā'ad+ṣa'ad* [1]
taken, 7864, *qānâ*[1] [1]
been taken, 7975, *qāraṣ* [1]
taken, 8098, *rādâ*[2] [1]
raised and taken an oath, 8123, *rûm*[1] [1]
taken, 8206, *rākab* [1]
be taken captive, 8647, *šābâ* [1]
been taken captive, 8647, *šābâ* [1]
is taken away, 8647, *šābâ* [1]
taken, 8647, *šābâ* [1]
taken as prisoners, 8664+8647, *šibyâ+šābâ* [1]
taken oath, 8678, *šāba'* [1]
taken back, 8740, *šûb*[1] [1]
taken root, 9245, *šāraš* [1]
what is taken, 9311, *tebû'â* [1]
taken hold, 9461, *tāmak* [1]
taken over, 9530, *tāpaś* [1]
taken away, 10528, *'adâ* [1]
taken, 10528, *'adâ* [1]

TAKES [57]

takes, 4374, *lāqaḥ* [6]
takes, *NIH/RPE* [5]
takes, 4334, *lākad* [4]
takes refuge, 2879, *ḥāsâ* [3]
takes away, 4374, *lāqaḥ* [2]
takes life, 5782+5883, *nākâ+nepeš* [2]
takes vengeance, 5933, *nāqam* [2]
takes off, 7337, *pātaḥ*[1] [2]
takes captive, 8647+8647, *šābâ+šābâ* [2]
takes an oath, 8678, *šāba'* [2]
takes place, 995, *bô'* [1]
takes to flight, 1368, *bāraḥ*[1] [1]
takes shape, 2200, *hāpak* [1]
slaughter takes place, 2222+2223, *hārag+hereg* [1]
takes hold, 2616, *ḥāzaq* [1]
takes pleasure in, 2913, *ḥāpēṣ*[3] [1]
takes seat, 3782, *yāšab* [1]
takes, 3782+6584, *yāšab+'al*[2] [1]
takes life, 4374, *lāqaḥ* [1]
takes, 4631, *mûš*[2] [1]
takes note of, 5795, *nākar*[1] [1]
takes place, 5893, *nāṣab*[1] [1]
takes stand, 5893, *nāṣab*[1] [1]
takes up, 5951, *nāśā'* [1]
takes, 5951, *nāśā'* [1]
takes refuge, 6259, *sātar* [1]
takes away, 6334, *'ādâ*[1] [1]
takes crooked, 6835, *'āqaš* [1]
takes captive, 7695, *qābaṣ* [1]
takes the stand, 7756+928, *qûm+be-* [1]
takes delight, 8354, *rāṣâ*[1] [1]
takes note, 8505, *śākal*[1] [1]
takes captive, 8647, *šābâ* [1]
takes an oath, 8678+8652, *šāba'+šebû'â* [1]
takes loot, 8720, *šādad* [1]
takes back, 8740+8740, *šûb*[1]*+šûb*[1] [1]
takes away, 8923, *šālâ*[2] [1]

TAKING [38]

taking, 4374, *lāqaḥ* [14]
taking, *NIH/RPE* [7]
taking, 2143, *hālak* [3]
taking with, 928+3338, *be-+yād* [2]
taking, 995, *bô'* [1]
taking as plunder, 1024, *bāzaz* [1]
taking as security, 2471, *ḥābal*[1] [1]
taking, 3149, *ḥāṭā* [1]
had difficulty taking possession of, 3655+4946, *yāṣā'+min* [1]
taking possession, 4334, *lākad* [1]
taking hold, 4374, *lāqaḥ* [1]
taking full, 4848, *mālē'*[1] [1]
taking place, 6913, *'āśâ*[1] [1]
taking away, 7277, *pāra'*[2] [1]
taking rest, 8886+5435, *šākab+miškāb* [1]
taking root, 9245, *šāraš* [1]

TALENT [9]

talent, 3971, *kikkār* [9]

TALENTS [39]

talents, 3971, *kikkār* [38]
talents, 10352, *kakkar* [1]

TALK [23]

talk, 1819, *dābar*[2] [11]
talk, 6218, *sāpar* [2]
talk, 8557, *śāpâ* [2]
idle talk, 966, *bad*[4] [1]
mere talk, 1821+8557, *dābār+śāpâ* [1]
empty talk, 2039, *hebel*[1] [1]
meaningless talk, 2039+2038, *hebel*[1]*+hābal* [1]
corrupt talk, 4299, *lāzût* [1]
object of malicious talk, 6590+6584+8557+4383, *'ālâ+'al*[2]*+śāpâ+lāšôn* [1]
big talk, 7023, *peh* [1]
talk, 7023, *peh* [1]

TALKED [19]

talked, 1819, *dābar*[2] [17]
talked, 606, *'āmar*[1] [2]

TALKER [1]

talker, 408+8557, *'îš*[1]*+śāpâ* [1]

TALKING [16]

talking, 1819, *dābar*[2] [14]
talking, 606, *'āmar*[1] [1]
talking together, 1819, *dābar*[2] [1]

TALKS [1]

talks too much, 7331+8557, *pātâ*[1]*+śāpâ* [1]

TALL [15]

tall, 8123, *rûm*[1] [4]
tall, 1469, *gābōah* [2]
tall, 1470, *gōbah* [2]
tall, 5432, *māšak* [2]

tall, 408+4500, *ʾîš[1]+middâ[1]* [1]
grow tall, 1448, *gāʾâ* [1]
make grow tall, 1467, *gābah* [1]
tall, 4500, *middâ[1]* [1]
made grow tall, 8123, *rûm[1]* [1]

TALLER [3]
taller, 1467, *gābah* [1]
taller, 1469, *gābōah* [1]
taller, 8123, *rûm[1]* [1]

TALLEST [2]
tallest, 7757, *qômâ* [2]

TALMAI [6]
Talmai, 9440, *talmay* [6]

TALMON [5]
Talmon, 3236, *ṭalmôn* [5]

TAMAR [25]
Tamar, 9470, *tāmār[2]* [22]
Tamar, 9471, *tāmār[3]* [3]

TAMARISK [3]
tamarisk tree, 869, *ʾēšel* [3]

TAMBOURINE [5]
tambourine, 9512, *tōp[1]* [4]
music of tambourine, 9512, *tōp[1]* [1]

TAMBOURINES [12]
tambourines, 9512, *tōp[1]* [9]
music of tambourines, 9512, *tōp[1]* [2]
playing tambourines, 9528, *tāpap* [1]

TAMMUZ [1]
Tammuz, 9452, *tammûz* [1]

TANHUMETH [2]
Tanhumeth, 9489, *tanḥumet* [2]

TAPESTRY [1]
tapestry, 763, *ʾargāmān* [1]

TAPHATH [1]
Taphath, 3264, *ṭāpat* [1]

TAPPUAH [6]
Tappuah, 9517, *tappûaḥ[3]* [5]
Tappuah, 9516, *tappûaḥ[2]* [1]

TAR [3]
tar, 2819, *ḥēmār* [3]

TARALAH [1]
Taralah, 9550, *tarʾălâ* [1]

TAREA [1]
Tarea, 9308, *taʾrēaʿ* [1]

TARGET [4]
target, 4766, *maṭṭārâ* [3]
target, 5133, *mipgāʿ* [1]

TARSHISH [19]
Tarshish, 9576, *taršîš[1]* [15]
Tarshish, 9578, *taršîš[3]* [4]

TARTAK [1]
Tartak, 9581, *tartāq* [1]

TASK [8]
task, 4856, *m^elāʾkâ* [3]
task, 6275, *ʿăbōdâ* [2]
task, 6721, *ʿinyān* [1]
appointed for the task, 6967, *ʿittî* [1]
took to task, 8189, *rîb[1]* [1]

TASKS [2]
tasks, *NIH/RPE* [1]
tasks, 6275, *ʿăbōdâ* [1]

TASSEL [1]
tassel, 7492, *ṣîṣit* [1]

TASSELS [3]
tassels, 7492, *ṣîṣit* [2]
tassels, 1544, *gādil* [1]

TASTE [10]
taste, 3247, *ṭāʿam* [4]
taste, 2674, *ḥēk* [3]
taste, 430, *ʾākal* [1]
made taste bitterness, 5352, *mārar* [1]
taste, 7023, *peh* [1]

TASTED [6]
tasted, 3247, *ṭāʿam* [2]
tasted, 3248, *ṭaʿam* [2]
tasted, 2118, *hāyâ* [1]
merely tasted, 3247+3247, *ṭāʿam+ṭāʿam* [1]

TASTELESS [1]
tasteless, 9522, *tāpēl[2]* [1]

TASTES [5]
tastes, 3247, *ṭāʿam* [2]
tastes, *NIH/RPE* [1]
tastes, 3248, *ṭaʿam* [1]
tastes sweet, 6853, *ʿārēb* [1]

TASTY [6]
tasty food, 4761, *maṭʿām* [6]

TATTENAI [4]
Tattenai, 10779, *tatt^enay* [4]

TATTOO [1]
tattoo, 7882, *qaʿăqaʿ* [1]

TAUGHT [24]
taught, 4340, *lāmad* [14]
taught, 3723, *yārâ[3]* [2]
taught, 1819, *dābar[2]* [1]
taught, 2118+3723, *hāyâ+yārâ[3]* [1]
taught a lesson, 3359, *yādaʿ* [1]
taught, 3579, *yāsar[1]* [1]
one taught, 4341, *limmud* [1]
taught, 4341, *limmud* [1]
taught, 4592, *mûsār* [1]
taught to walk, 8078, *rāgal* [1]

TAUNT [8]
taunt, 3070, *ḥārap[2]* [2]
taunt, 1527, *g^edûpâ* [1]
taunt, 2252, *hātal* [1]
taunt, 4088, *kaʿas* [1]
taunt, 5442+5951, *māšāl[1]+nāśāʾ* [1]
taunt, 5442, *māšāl[1]* [1]
taunt, 5629, *nāhâ[1]* [1]

TAUNTED [4]
taunted, 3070, *ḥārap[2]* [4]

TAUNTS [6]
taunts, *NIH/RPE* [1]
taunts, 1526, *giddûp* [1]
taunts, 3070, *ḥārap[2]* [1]
taunts, 4009, *k^elimmâ* [1]
taunts, 7754, *qôl* [1]
taunts, 8190, *rîb[2]* [1]

TAX [4]
tax, 5368, *maśʾēt* [2]
tax, 4501, *middâ[2]* [1]
tax collector, 5601, *nāgaś* [1]

TAXED [1]
taxed, 6885, *ʿārak* [1]

TAXES [4]
taxes, 10402, *middâ* [3]
exempt from taxes, 6913+2930, *ʿāśâ[1]+ḥopšî* [1]

TEACH [75]
teach, 4340, *lāmad* [30]
teach, 3723, *yārâ[3]* [25]
teach, 3359, *yādaʿ* [13]
teach, *NIH/RPE* [1]
teach, 544, *ʾālap[1]* [1]
what teach, 1981, *daʿat[1]* [1]
teach, 2302, *zāhar[2]* [1]
teach wisdom, 2681, *ḥākam* [1]
teach, 3723+1978, *yārâ[3]+dēʿâ* [1]
teach, 10313, *y^edaʿ* [1]

TEACHER [13]
Teacher, 7738, *qōhelet* [7]
teacher, 6221, *sōpēr* [2]
teacher, 10516, *sāpar* [2]
teacher, 1067, *bîn* [1]
teacher, 4621, *môreh[3]* [1]

TEACHERS [3]
teachers, 4621, *môreh[3]* [2]
teachers, 4340, *lāmad* [1]

TEACHES [8]
teaches, 3723, *yārâ[3]* [3]
teaches, 4340, *lāmad* [3]
teaches, 544, *ʾālap[1]* [1]
teaches, 4592, *mûsār* [1]

TEACHING [15]
teaching, 9368, *tôrâ* [8]
teaching, 4340, *lāmad* [2]
teaching, 2006, *derek* [1]
teaching, 3359, *yādaʿ* [1]
teaching, 4375, *leqaḥ* [1]
teaching of law, 9368, *tôrâ* [1]
teaching of the law, 9368, *tôrâ* [1]

TEACHINGS [1]
teachings, 9368, *tôrâ* [1]

TEAM [2]
team, 7538, *ṣemed* [1]
team, 8224, *rekeš* [1]

TEAMS [1]
teams, 7538, *ṣemed* [1]

TEAR [47]
tear, 7973, *qāraʿ* [10]
tear down, 2238, *hāras* [7]
tear to pieces, 3271, *ṭārap* [4]
tear, 3271, *ṭārap* [3]
tear down, 5997, *nātaṣ* [3]
tear down, 6867, *ʿārâ[1]* [2]
tear, 7268, *pāram* [2]
tear apart, 1324, *bāqaʿ* [1]
tear, 1608, *gāzal* [1]
tear, 1889, *dûš* [1]
tear down, 5782, *nākâ* [1]
tear, 5815, *nāsaḥ* [1]
tear out, 5997, *nātaṣ* [1]
tear away, 5998, *nātaq* [1]
tear off, 5998, *nātaq* [1]
tear, 5998, *nātaq* [1]
tear down, 7287, *pāraṣ* [1]
tear apart, 7763, *qûṣ[2]* [1]
tear out hair, 7947, *qorḥâ* [1]
most certainly tear away, 7973+7973, *qāraʿ+qāraʿ* [1]
tear off, 7973, *qāraʿ* [1]
tear down, 8845, *šāḥat* [1]
tear open, 9117, *šāsaʿ* [1]

TEARING [5]
tearing, 3271, *ṭārap* [3]
tearing prey, 3271, *ṭārap* [1]
tearing off, 7293, *pāraq* [1]

TEARS [35]
tears, 1965, *dimʿâ* [21]
tears down, 2238, *hāras* [3]
tears, 4784, *mayim* [3]
tears, *NIH/RPE* [1]
tears, 1134, *bākâ* [1]
wet with tears, 1134, *bākâ* [1]
tears, 1140, *b^ekî* [1]
pour out tears, 1940, *dālap[1]* [1]
tears, 3271, *ṭārap* [1]
tears down, 5815, *nāsaḥ* [1]
tears down, 5997, *nātaṣ* [1]

TEBAH [3]
Tebah, 3182, *ṭebaḥ[2]* [1]
Tebah, 3183, *ṭebaḥ[3]* [1]
Tebah, 3187, *ṭibḥat* [1]

TEBETH [1]
Tebeth, 3194, *ṭēbēt* [1]

TEEM [2]
teem, 9237+9238, *šāraṣ+šereṣ* [1]
teem, 9237, *šāraṣ* [1]

TEEMED [1]
teemed, 9237, *šāraṣ* [1]

TEEMING [1]
teeming creatures, 8254, *remeś* [1]

TEEMS [1]
teems, 9237, *šāraṣ* [1]

TEETH [31]
teeth, 9094, *šēn*[1] [26]
teeth, 10730, *šēn* [3]
teeth, *NIH/RPE* [1]
many teeth, 7092, *pîpiyyôt* [1]

TEHINNAH [1]
Tehinnah, 9383, *tᵉḥinnâ*[2] [1]

TEKEL [2]
tekel, 10770, *tᵉqēl* [2]

TEKOA [13]
Tekoa, 9541, *tᵉqôaʿ* [7]
from Tekoa, 9542, *tᵉqôʿî* [4]
men of Tekoa, 9542, *tᵉqôʿî* [2]

TEKOITE [1]
Tekoite, 9542, *tᵉqôʿî* [1]

TEL ABIB [1]
Tel Abib, 9425, *tēl ʾābîb* [1]

TEL ASSAR [2]
Tel Assar, 9431, *tᵉlaʾśśār* [2]

TEL HARSHA [2]
Tel Harsha, 9426, *tēl ḥaršāʾ* [2]

TEL MELAH [2]
Tel Melah, 9427, *tēl melaḥ* [2]

TELAH [1]
Telah, 9436, *telaḥ* [1]

TELAIM [1]
Telaim, 3230, *ṭᵉlāʾîm* [1]

TELEM [2]
Telem, 3234, *ṭelem*[1] [1]
Telem, 3235, *ṭelem*[2] [1]

TELL [321]
tell, 606, *ʾāmar*[1] [93]
tell, 5583, *nāgad* [93]
tell, 1819, *dābar*[2] [49]
tell, 6218, *sāpar* [18]
tell, 3359, *yādaʿ* [11]
tell, *NIH/RPE* [9]
tell, 10313, *yᵉdaʿ* [8]
tell, 10042, *ʾᵃmar* [6]
tell, 7422, *ṣāwâ* [5]
tell, 10252, *ḥᵃwâ* [4]
tell, 2555, *ḥāwâ*[1] [3]
tell, 2349, *zākar*[1] [2]
tell, 2554, *ḥûd* [2]
tell, 5439, *māšal*[1] [2]
tell, 8488, *śîaḥ*[1] [2]
tell the meaning, 1067, *bîn* [1]
tell, 1655+906+265, *gālâ+ʾēt*[1]*+ʾōzen* [1]
tell, 1819+928+265, *dābar*[2]*+bᵉ+ʾōzen* [1]
tell, 1821+606, *dābār+ʾāmar*[1] [1]
tell, 2047, *hāgâ*[1] [1]
tell the difference, 3359, *yādaʿ* [1]
be sure to tell, 5583+5583, *nāgad+nāgad* [1]
tell answer, 5583, *nāgad* [1]
tell the news, 5583, *nāgad* [1]
tell, 5795, *nākar*[1] [1]
tell, 6699, *ʿānâ*[1] [1]
tell fortunes, 7876, *qāsam* [1]
tell, 8626, *šāʾal* [1]
tell, 9048, *šāmaʿ* [1]

TELLING [13]
telling, 1819, *dābar*[2] [3]
telling, 6218, *sāpar* [3]
telling, 606, *ʾāmar*[1] [2]
telling, 5583, *nāgad* [2]
telling, *NIH/RPE* [1]
telling, 3655, *yāṣāʾ* [1]
telling, 5439, *māšal*[1] [1]

TELLS [12]
tells, 606, *ʾāmar*[1] [4]
tells, 1655+906+265, *gālâ+ʾēt*[1]*+ʾōzen* [2]
tells, 1819, *dābar*[2] [2]
tells, 5583, *nāgad* [2]
tells, *NIH/RPE* [1]
tells, 10252, *ḥᵃwâ* [1]

TEMA [5]
Tema, 9401, *têmāʾ* [4]
Tema, 824+9401, *ʾereṣ+têmāʾ* [1]

TEMAH [2]
Temah, 9457, *temaḥ* [2]

TEMAN [11]
Teman, 9403, *têmān*[2] [11]

TEMANITE [6]
Temanite, 9404, *têmānî* [6]

TEMANITES [2]
Temanites, 9404, *têmānî* [2]

TEMENI [1]
Temeni, 9405, *têmᵉnî* [1]

TEMPER [2]
loses temper, 3013+3013, *ḥārâ*[1]*+ḥārâ*[1] [1]
temper, 8120, *rûaḥ* [1]

TEMPEST [7]
tempest, 6070, *sûpâ*[1] [2]
tempest, 6193, *saʿar* [1]
tempest, 6194, *sᵉʿārâ* [1]
tempest, 8120+6185, *rûaḥ+sāʿâ* [1]
tempest, 8120+6194, *rûaḥ+sᵉʿārâ* [1]
tempest rages, 8548+4394, *śāʿar*[2]*+mᵉʾōd* [1]

TEMPLE [562]
temple, 1074, *bayit*[1] [436]
temple, 2121, *hêkāl* [54]
temple, *NIH/RPE* [21]
temple, 10103, *bayit* [16]
temple servants, 5987, *nātîn* [15]
temple, 10206, *hêkal* [8]
temple, 8377, *raqqâ* [3]
temple area, 1074, *bayit*[1] [2]
temple porch, 395, *ʾêlām* [1]
the temple[s], 889, *ʾᵃšer* [1]
temple gifts, 924, *ʾetnan* [1]
the temple[s], 2023, *-āh* [1]
temple, 5219, *miqdāš* [1]
temple, 7731, *qōdeš* [1]
temple servants, 10497, *nᵉtîn* [1]

TEMPLES [6]
temples, 1074, *bayit*[1] [2]
temples, 8377, *raqqâ* [2]
temples, 2121, *hêkāl* [1]
their temples[s], 4392, *-ām* [1]

TEMPORARY [6]
temporary resident, 9369, *tôšāb* [5]
temporary residents, 9369, *tôšāb* [1]

TEN [170]
ten, 6927, *ʿᵃśārâ* [59]
ten, 6924, *ʿeśer* [57]
ten, 6930, *ʿᵃśeret* [39]
ten thousand, 8047, *rᵉbābâ* [6]
ten, 10573, *ʿᵃśar* [4]
ten thousand, 10649, *ribbô* [2]
ten, 6917, *ʿāśôr* [1]
ten thousands, 8047, *rᵉbābâ* [1]
ten thousand, 8052, *ribbôʾ* [1]

TEN-ACRE [1]
ten-acre, 6930+7538, *ʿᵃśeret+ṣemed* [1]

TEN-STRINGED [3]
ten-stringed, 6917, *ʿāśôr* [3]

TENANTS [3]
tenants, 1251, *baʿal*[1] [1]
tenants, 5757, *nāṭar*[1] [1]
tenants, 9369, *tôšāb* [1]

TEND [12]
tend, 8286, *rāʿâ*[1] [8]
tend livestock, 408+5238+2118, *ʾîš*[1]*+miqneh+hāyâ* [1]
tend, 5757, *nāṭar*[1] [1]
tend, 6661, *ʿāmal* [1]
tend, 6885, *ʿārak* [1]

TENDED [3]
tended livestock, 408+5238+2118, *ʾîš*[1]*+miqneh+hāyâ* [1]
tended, 6885, *ʿārak* [1]
tended sheep, 9068, *šāmar* [1]

TENDER [9]
tender, 8205, *rak* [5]
tender shoots, 3764, *yereq* [2]
tender shoot, 3437, *yônēq* [1]
tender plants, 6912, *ʿēśeb* [1]

TENDERLY [3]
tenderly, 6584+4213, *ʿal*[2]*+lēb* [3]

TENDERNESS [1]
tenderness, 2162+5055, *hāmôn+mēʿeh* [1]

TENDING [8]
tending, 8286, *rāʿâ*[1] [6]
tending, 339, *ʾaḥar* [2]

TENDON [2]
tendon, 1630+5962, *gîd+nāšeh* [2]

TENDONS [2]
tendons, 1630, *gîd* [2]

TENDS [3]
tends, 3512, *yāṭab* [1]
tends, 5915, *nāṣar* [1]
tends, 8286, *rāʿâ*[1] [1]

TENS [10]
tens of thousands, 8047, *rᵉbābâ* [5]
tens, 6930, *ʿᵃśeret* [3]
tens of thousands, 8045, *rābab*[1] [1]
tens of thousands, 8052, *ribbôʾ* [1]

TENT [281]
tent, 185, *ʾōhel*[1] [260]
tent pegs, 3845, *yātēd* [7]
tent, 3749, *yᵉrîʿâ* [3]
tent peg, 3845, *yātēd* [3]
pitch tent, 182, *ʾāhal*[1] [1]
tent site, 185, *ʾōhel*[1] [1]
tent curtains, 3749, *yᵉrîʿâ* [1]
cords of tent, 3857, *yeter*[2] [1]
tent, 5438, *miškān* [1]
tent, 6108, *sōk* [1]
tent, 6109, *sukkâ* [1]
tent, 7688, *qubbâ* [1]

TENT-DWELLING [1]
tent-dwelling, 928+2021+185, *bᵉ+ha+ʾōhel*[1] [1]

TENTH [55]
tenth, 6920, *ʿᵃśîrî* [29]
tenth, 6917, *ʿāśôr* [12]
tenth, 5130, *maʿᵃśēr* [5]
tenth, 6928, *ʿiśśārôn* [4]
take a tenth, 6923, *ʿāśar* [2]
be sure to set aside a tenth, 6923+6923, *ʿāśar+ʿāśar* [1]
give a tenth, 6923+6923, *ʿāśar+ʿāśar* [1]
setting aside a tenth, 6923+5130, *ʿāśar+maʿᵃśēr* [1]

TENTS [57]
tents, 185, *ʾōhel*[1] [45]
tents, 5438, *miškān* [5]

tents, 6109, *sukkâ* [3]
set up tents, 2837, *ḥānā*[1] [2]
moved tents, 182, *ʾāhal*[1] [1]
pitched tents, 182, *ʾāhal*[1] [1]

TERAH [12]
Terah, 9561, *teraḥ* [10]
Terah, 9562, *tāraḥ* [2]

TEREBINTH [2]
terebinth, 461, *ʾēlâ*[1] [2]

TERESH [2]
Teresh, 9575, *tereš* [2]

TERMS [12]
terms, 1821, *dābār* [7]
terms, *AIT* [1]
on friendly terms, 170, *ʾāhab* [1]
the terms[s], 889, *ʾašer* [1]
on terms, 4946+6640, *min+ʿim* [1]
terms, 5184, *miṣwâ* [1]

TERRACES [8]
supporting terraces, 4864, *millôʾ* [6]
terraces, 8727, *šedēmâ* [1]
terraces, 8805, *šûrâ* [1]

TERRIBLE [8]
terrible, 1524, *gādôl* [5]
terrible, 8273, *raʿ*[1] [2]
terrible, 3878+4394, *kābēd*[2]*+meʾōd* [1]

TERRIFIED [41]
terrified, 987, *bāhal* [10]
terrified, 3169, *ḥātat* [9]
terrified, 3707+4394, *yārēʾ*[1]*+meʾōd* [4]
terrified, 6907, *ʿāraṣ* [4]
terrified, 10097, *behal* [3]
terrified, 1286, *bāʿat* [2]
terrified, 1593, *gûr*[3] [2]
terrified, 7064, *pāḥad* [2]
terrified, 2905, *ḥāpaz* [1]
terrified, 3146, *ḥat*[2] [1]
terrified, 3707+3711+1524, *yārēʾ*[1]*+yirʾâ+gādôl* [1]
terrified, 3707+4394+4394, *yārēʾ*[1]*+meʾōd+meʾōd* [1]
were terrified, 9037, *šāmēm*[1] [1]

TERRIFIES [2]
terrifies, 987, *bāhal* [2]

TERRIFY [9]
terrify, 3169, *ḥātat* [3]
terrify, 1286, *bāʿat* [2]
terrify, 987, *bāhal* [1]
terrify, 3006, *ḥārad* [1]
terrify, 3707, *yārēʾ*[1] [1]
terrify, 6907, *ʿāraṣ* [1]

TERRIFYING [3]
terrifying, 10167, *deḥal* [2]
terrifying, 7065, *paḥad*[1] [1]

TERRITORIES [5]
territories, 824, *ʾereṣ* [4]
territories, 5709, *naḥalâ*[1] [1]

TERRITORY [96]
territory, 1473, *gebûl* [57]
territory, 824, *ʾereṣ* [17]
territory, *NIH/RPE* [4]
territory, 8441, *śādeh* [4]
territory[s], 889, *ʾašer* [3]
territory, 5709, *naḥalâ*[1] [2]
territory, 299, *ʾaḥuzzâ* [1]
the territory[s], 889, *ʾašer* [1]
allotted territory, 1473, *gebûl* [1]
neighboring territory, 1473, *gebûl* [1]
territory, 1474, *gebûlâ* [1]
territory allotted, 1598, *gôrāl* [1]
territory, 2976, *ḥōq* [1]
territory inherit, 5709, *naḥalâ*[1] [1]
extend the territory, 7332, *pātâ*[2] [1]

TERROR [71]
terror, 7065, *paḥad*[1] [13]
terror, 3154, *ḥittît* [8]
terror, 399, *ʾêmâ* [7]
terror, 4471, *māgôr*[1] [7]
filled with terror, 3169, *ḥātat* [3]
terror, 4616, *môrāʾ* [3]
terror, 4745, *meḥittâ* [3]
terror, 988, *behālâ* [2]
terror, 1287, *beʿātâ* [2]
terror, 3010, *ḥarādâ*[1] [2]
terror seize, 987, *bāhal* [1]
terror, 987, *bāhal* [1]
sudden terror, 988, *behālâ* [1]
sudden terror, 1166, *ballāhâ* [1]
fill with terror, 1286, *bāʿat* [1]
terror, 2317, *zewāʿâ* [1]
terror, 2400, *zaʿawâ* [1]
terror, 2505, *ḥoggāʾ* [1]
terror, 2805, *ḥāmās* [1]
strike with terror, 3006, *ḥārad* [1]
terror filled, 3006+4394, *ḥārad+meʾōd* [1]
terror, 3150, *ḥittâ* [1]
terror, 3169, *ḥātat* [1]
terror, 3707, *yārēʾ*[1] [1]
terror, 4428, *mebûkâ* [1]
cause terror, 6907, *ʿāraṣ* [1]
brought down to terror, 7064, *pāḥad* [1]
live in terror, 7064, *pāḥad* [1]
terror, 7146, *pallāṣût* [1]
terror, 7888, *qepādâ* [1]
terror, 9526, *tipleṣet* [1]

TERRORS [14]
terrors, 1166, *ballāhâ* [6]
terrors, 399, *ʾêmâ* [4]
terrors, 1243, *biʿût* [2]
terrors, 4471, *māgôr*[1] [1]
terrors, 7065, *paḥad*[1] [1]

TEST [33]
test, 5814, *nāsâ* [14]
test, 1043, *bāḥan* [11]
put to the test, 5814, *nāsâ* [6]
test, 2983, *ḥāqar* [1]
test, 7671, *ṣārap* [1]

TESTED [19]
tested, 5814, *nāsâ* [8]
be tested, 1043, *bāḥan* [3]
tested, 1043, *bāḥan* [3]
tested, *NIH/RPE* [1]
tested, 1046, *bōḥan*[2] [1]
tested, 1047, *bāḥar*[1] [1]
tested, 2983, *ḥāqar* [1]
been tested, 7671, *ṣārap* [1]

TESTER [1]
tester of metals, 1031, *bāḥôn* [1]

TESTICLES [2]
testicles, *NIH/RPE* [1]
testicles, 863, *ʾešek* [1]

TESTIFIED [2]
testified, 6386, *ʿûd*[1] [1]
testified, 6699, *ʿānâ*[1] [1]

TESTIFIES [4]
testifies, 6699, *ʿānâ*[1] [4]

TESTIFY [16]
testify, 6699, *ʿānâ*[1] [5]
testify, 6386, *ʿûd*[1] [3]
testify, 6332, *ʿēd* [3]
testify, 2118+6332, *hāyâ+ʿēd* [1]
testify, 5583, *nāgad* [1]
call to testify, 6386, *ʿûd*[1] [1]
have testify, 6386, *ʿûd*[1] [1]
testify, 6699+4200+6332, *ʿānâ*[1]*+le-*[1]*+ʿēd* [1]

TESTIMONY [51]
testimony, 6343, *ʿēdût* [37]
testimony, 7023, *peh* [4]
testimony, 6332, *ʿēd* [3]
testimony, 9496, *teʿûdâ* [2]
testimony, *NIH/RPE* [1]
testimony, 5583, *nāgad* [1]
give testimony, 6699, *ʿānâ*[1] [1]
giving testimony, 6699, *ʿānâ*[1] [1]
testimony, 6699, *ʿānâ*[1] [1]

TESTING [2]
testing, 1043, *bāḥan* [1]
testing, 5814, *nāsâ* [1]

TESTINGS [1]
testings, 4999, *massâ*[1] [1]

TESTS [3]
tests, 1043, *bāḥan* [2]
tests, 1405, *bārar*[1] [1]

TETHER [1]
tether, 673, *ʾāsar* [1]

TETHERED [1]
tethered, 673, *ʾāsar* [1]

TEXT [4]
text, 4181, *ketāb* [3]
text, 1821, *dābār* [1]

THAN [384]
than, 4946, *min* [182]
more than, 4946, *min* [93]
rather than, 4946, *min* [10]
than, *NIH/RPE* [9]
better than, 4946, *min* [7]
than, *AIT* [6]
greater than, 4946, *min* [5]
than, 6584, *ʿal*[2] [4]
more than, 4202, *lōʾ* [3]
higher than, 4946+6584, *min+ʿal*[2] [3]
than, 4974, *minnî*[2] [3]
rather than, 2256+4202, *we-+lōʾ* [2]
anyone other than a priest, 2424, *zār* [2]
other than, 3954+561, *kî*[2]*+ʾim* [2]
than, 3954+561, *kî*[2]*+ʾim* [2]
rather than, 4202, *lōʾ* [2]
even more than, 4946, *min* [2]
less than, 4946, *min* [2]
other than, 4946+1187, *min+balʿadê* [2]
more than, 6584, *ʿal*[2] [2]
rather than, 196, *ʾô* [1]
than, 401, *ʾayin*[1] [1]
better than, 440, *ʾal*[1] [1]
other than, 561, *ʾim* [1]
other than, 1194+4200+963, *biltî+le-*[1]*+bad*[1] [1]
no sooner than, 1685, *gam* [1]
no more than, 2256, *we-* [1]
than, 2256+1685, *we-+gam* [1]
than, 2256+4202, *we-+lōʾ* [1]
number is less than, 2893, *ḥāsēr*[1] [1]
in little more than, 3427+6584, *yôm*[1]*+ʿal*[2] [1]
than, 3463+4946, *yôtēr+min* [1]
no sooner than, 3869+889, *ke-+ʾašer* [1]
no sooner than, 3869, *ke-* [1]
nothing more than, 3869, *ke-* [1]
than, 3869, *ke-* [1]
other than, 3954, *kî*[2] [1]
more quickly than, 4200+7156, *le-*[1]*+pāneh* [1]
more readily than, 4200+7156, *le-*[1]*+pāneh* [1]
more than, 4200+401, *le-*[1]*+ʾayin*[1] [1]
than, 4200, *le-*[1] [1]
better than, 4202, *lōʾ* [1]
other than, 4202, *lōʾ* [1]
more than, 4394, *meʾōd* [1]
more than, 4946+4200+963, *min+le-*[1]*+bad*[1] [1]
much more than, 4946, *min* [1]
other than, 4946+4200+963, *min+le-*[1]*+bad*[1] [1]
than deserved, 4946, *min* [1]
than, 4946+889, *min+ʾašer* [1]
worse than, 4946, *min* [1]
no less than, 5070, *māʿaṭ* [1]
better than, 6584, *ʿal*[2] [1]
higher than, 8049+4200+5087+2025, *rābâ*[1]*+le-*[1]*+maʿal*[2]*+-â*[2] [1]
have more than enough, 8425, *śābaʿ* [1]
than, 8611, *ša-* [1]
more than thirteen feet, 9596+564, *tēšaʿ+ʾammâ*[1] [1]
any more than, 10195+10341+10168, *hēʾ+ke-+dî* [1]
rather than, 10379, *lāʾ* [1]

greater than, 10427, *min* [1]
more than, 10427, *min* [1]
than, 10542, *ʿal* [1]

THANK [16]
thank offerings, 9343, *tôdâ* [8]
thank, 9343, *tôdâ* [4]
thank, 1385, *bārak*^{2} [1]
thank, 3344, *yādâ*^{2} [1]
thank offering, 9343, *tôdâ* [1]
thank, 10312, *y^{e}dâ* [1]

THANKFULNESS [1]
expression of thankfulness, 9343, *tôdâ* [1]

THANKING [1]
thanking, 3344, *yādâ*^{2} [1]

THANKS [43]
give thanks, 3344, *yādâ*^{2} [35]
gave thanks, 2146, *hālal*^{2} [1]
gave thanks, 3344, *yādâ*^{2} [1]
psalm of thanks, 3344, *yādâ*^{2} [1]
thanks, 3344, *yādâ*^{2} [1]
choirs that gave thanks, 9343, *tôdâ* [1]
choirs to give thanks, 9343, *tôdâ* [1]
giving thanks, 9343, *tôdâ* [1]
giving thanks, 10312, *y^{e}dâ* [1]

THANKSGIVING [16]
thanksgiving, 9343, *tôdâ* [9]
thanksgiving, 3344, *yādâ*^{2} [3]
songs of thanksgiving, 9343, *tôdâ* [2]
songs of thanksgiving, 2117, *huyy^{e}dôt* [1]
led in thanksgiving, 9378+3344, *t^{e}hillâ+yādâ*^{2} [1]

THAT [3693]*
that, 3954, *kî*^{2} [564]
that, 889, *ʾ^{a}šer* [538]
that, *NIH/RPE* [510]
that, 2085, *hûʾ* [379]
that, *AIT* [285]
so that, 2256, *w^{e}-* [236]
that, 2021, *ha-* [205]
that, 2256, *w^{e}-* [175]
so that, 4200+5100, *l^{e}-^{1}+maʿan* [77]
that, 4200, *l^{e}-^{1}* [75]
so that, 4200, *l^{e}-^{1}* [60]
that, 2296, *zeh* [49]
that, 10168, *dî* [46]
that is, 2085, *hûʾ* [34]
that is why, 6584+4027, *ʿal^{2}+kēn^{2}* [34]
that, 4200+5100, *l^{e}-^{1}+maʿan* [24]
that, 4027, *kēn*^{2} [20]
that same, 2085, *hûʾ* [19]
that, 8611, *ša-* [16]
at that time, 255, *ʾāz* [11]
so that, 889, *ʾ^{a}šer* [11]
after that, 339, *ʾaḥar* [10]
that, 2156, *hēm* [10]
that, 561, *ʾim* [8]
and that, 2256, *w^{e}-* [8]
that, 928, *b^{e}-* [7]
that, 2257, *-ô* [6]
so that not, 7153, *pen* [6]
so that, 10168, *dî* [6]
so that, 928+6288, *b^{e}-+ʿ^{a}bûr*^{1} [5]
that^{s}, 2257, *-ô* [5]
so that, 10221, *w^{e}-* [5]
that^{s}, 1074, *bayit*^{1} [4]
that is why, 2256, *w^{e}-* [4]
now that, 2256, *w^{e}-* [4]
that is, 2256, *w^{e}-* [4]
that, 4946, *min* [4]
that, 2180, *hinnēh* [3]
after that, 2256, *w^{e}-* [3]
that same, 2296, *zeh* [3]
now that, 3954, *kî*^{2} [3]
that is what, 4027, *kēn*^{2} [3]
that^{s}, 4392, *-ām* [3]
so that, 4946, *min* [3]
that^{s}, 5260, *marʾeh* [3]
that, 5626, *-nâ* [3]
that, 10002, *-āʾ* [3]
that, 10221, *w^{e}-* [3]
is that not, 401, *ʾayin*^{1} [2]
that, 465, *ʾēlleh* [2]
that, 561+4202, *ʾim+lōʾ* [2]
that, 928+6288, *b^{e}-+ʿ^{a}bûr*^{1} [2]
that^{s}, 2023, *-āh* [2]
that man^{s}, 2085, *hûʾ* [2]
that very, 2085, *hûʾ* [2]
that, 2137, *hallāz* [2]
that, 2138, *hallāzeh* [2]
at that time, 2256, *w^{e}-* [2]
and so that, 2256, *w^{e}-* [2]
so that, 3954, *kî*^{2} [2]
like that, 4027, *kēn*^{2} [2]
that is how, 4027, *kēn*^{2} [2]
that is the way, 4027, *kēn*^{2} [2]
in order that, 4200, *l^{e}-^{1}* [2]
in such a way that, 4200, *l^{e}-^{1}* [2]
that, 4392, *-ām* [2]
so that not, 4946, *min* [2]
so that, 6584+4027, *ʿal^{2}+kēn^{2}* [2]
that not, 7153, *pen* [2]
that no, 7153, *pen* [2]
except that, 8370, *raq*^{2} [2]
that, 10180, *d^{e}nâ* [2]
oh that, 20, *ʾābî*^{1} [1]
that, 10174, *dikkēn* [1]
that, 10191, *-â* [1]
that, 10200, *hûʾ* [1]
and that, 10221, *w^{e}-* [1]
so that, 10378, *l^{e}-* [1]
so that, 10527+10159+10168, *ʿad+dibrâ+dî* [1]
that is why, 10542+10180, *ʿal+d^{e}nâ* [1]
so that, 10542+10159+10168, *ʿal+dibrâ+dî* [1]

THAT'S [8]
that's, *NIH/RPE* [4]
that's, 2023, *-āh* [1]
that's, 2085, *hûʾ* [1]
that's, 2296, *zeh* [1]
that's why, 6584+4027, *ʿal^{2}+kēn^{2}* [1]

THAWING [1]
thawing, *NIH/RPE* [1]

THE [44840]*
the, *NIH/RPE* [19619]
the, 2021, *ha-* [16202]
the LORD, 3378, *yhwh* [6030]
the, 10002, *-āʾ* [412]
the, *AIT* [376]
the^{s}, 2257, *-ô* [336]
the LORD's, 3378, *yhwh* [242]
the^{s}, 4392, *-ām* [124]
the^{s}, 2023, *-āh* [95]
the Lord, 151, *ʾ^{a}dōnāy* [91]
the^{s}, 3870, *-kā* [85]
the^{s}, 2157, *-hem* [54]
the^{s}, 3276, *-î* [52]
the^{s}, 4013, *-kem* [52]
the LORD, 3363, *yāh* [44]
the LORD's, 4200+3378, *l^{e}-^{1}+yhwh* [27]
for the sake of, 4200+5100, *l^{e}-^{1}+maʿan* [22]
the, 10191, *-â* [15]
the^{s}, 3871, *-k* [13]
the^{s}, 2084, *-hû* [10]
the, 285, *ʾeḥād* [6]
the LORD^{s}, 2257, *-ô* [6]
the^{s}, 5646, *-nû*^{1} [6]
the^{s}, 10192, *-ēh* [5]
the, 465, *ʾēlleh* [4]
the, 2296, *zeh* [4]
the, 2306, *zû* [4]
the one^{s}, 8611, *ša-* [4]
the^{s}, 2177, *-hēn*^{2} [3]
the^{s}, 10203, *-hôn* [3]
the, 2157, *-hem* [2]
the, 2257, *-ô* [2]
the^{s}, 4564, *-mô* [2]
the^{s}, 5626, *-nâ* [2]

THEBES [5]
Thebes, 5530, *nōʾ* [4]
Thebes, 5531, *nōʾ ʾāmôn* [1]

THEBEZ [2]
Thebez, 9324, *tēbēṣ* [2]

THEFT [1]
theft, 1706, *g^{e}nēbâ* [1]

THEIR [3132]*
their, 4392, *-ām* [1012]
their, 2157, *-hem* [915]
their, *NIH/RPE* [303]
their, 2257, *-ô* [285]
their^{s}, 2021, *ha-* [95]
their, *AIT* [93]
their, 2177, *-hēn*^{2} [77]
their, 2023, *-āh* [67]
their own, 4392, *-ām* [43]
their, 4200+2157, *l^{e}-^{1}+-hem* [35]
their, 4564, *-mô* [23]
their own, 2157, *-hem* [20]
their, 2084, *-hû* [19]
their, 10203, *-hôn* [17]
their own, 2257, *-ô* [10]
their, 5527, *-ān* [9]
their, 4200+4564, *l^{e}-^{1}+-mô* [6]
their^{s}, 1201+2257, *bēn^{1}+-ô* [5]
their own, 4200+2157, *l^{e}-^{1}+-hem* [5]
their, 10209, *-hōm* [5]
their, 4013, *-kem* [4]
their, 4200+2257, *l^{e}-^{1}+-ô* [4]
their, 10192, *-ēh* [3]
their^{s}, 408, *ʾîš*^{1} [2]
their own^{s}, 2021, *ha-* [2]
their own, 2177, *-hēn*^{2} [2]
their, 3870, *-kā* [2]
their, 3871, *-k* [2]
their own, 4200+2257, *l^{e}-^{1}+-ô* [2]
their, 4200+2177, *l^{e}-^{1}+-hēn^{2}* [2]
their, 448+2157, *ʾel+-hem* [1]
their^{s}, 928+4090+2157, *b^{e}-+kap+-hem* [1]
their^{s}, 2021+465, *ha-+ʾēlleh* [1]
their, 2021, *ha-* [1]
their land^{s}, 2023, *-āh* [1]
their lands^{s}, 2023, *-āh* [1]
their, 2024, *-ōh* [1]
their own, 2084, *-hû* [1]
their idols^{s}, 2156, *hēm* [1]
their^{s}, 2257, *-ô* [1]
their, 4200+2179, *l^{e}-^{1}+hēnnâ^{2}* [1]
their, 4200+4013, *l^{e}-^{1}+-kem* [1]
their, 4946+2157, *min+-hem* [1]
their, 5626, *-nâ* [1]
their own, 5647, *-nû*^{2} [1]
their, 5647, *-nû*^{2} [1]
their, 6584+2157, *ʿal^{2}+-hem* [1]
share their duties, 6640+465, *ʿim+ʾēlleh* [1]
their own, 10203, *-hôn* [1]

THEIRS [13]
theirs, 2157, *-hem* [4]
theirs, 4200+2157, *l^{e}-^{1}+-hem* [3]
theirs, *NIH/RPE* [1]
theirs, 2084, *-hû* [1]
theirs, 2177, *-hēn*^{2} [1]
theirs, 4200+2257, *l^{e}-^{1}+-ô* [1]
theirs, 4392, *-ām* [1]
theirs, 4946+2157, *min+-hem* [1]

THEM [3986]*
them, 4392, *-ām* [1550]
them, 2157, *-hem* [1103]
them, *NIH/RPE* [559]
them, 2257, *-ô* [182]
them, *AIT* [121]
them, 5647, *-nû*^{2} [48]
them, 4564, *-mô* [47]
them, 2177, *-hēn*^{2} [46]
them, 2084, *-hû* [36]
them, 2023, *-āh* [28]
them, 10203, *-hôn* [17]
them, 2156, *hēm* [14]
them, 465, *ʾēlleh* [12]
them, 5626, *-nâ* [9]
them^{s}, 889, *ʾ^{a}šer* [6]
them, 10210, *himmô* [6]
them^{s}, 408, *ʾîš*^{1} [5]
them, 5883+4392, *nepeš+-ām* [5]
them, 10193, *-ah* [5]
them, 2179, *hēnnâ*^{2} [4]

them, 5527, *-ān* [4]
them, 10209, *-hōm* [4]
them, 2024, *-ōh* [3]
them[s], 2021+408, *ha-+ʾîš[1]* [2]
them[s], 2021, *ha-* [2]
them, 2085, *hûʾ* [2]
them, 2296, *zeh* [2]
them, 2181, *-h[e]nâ* [1]
them, 4013, *-kem* [1]
them, 10214, *-hēn* [1]

THEME [3]

theme, 1821, *dābār* [1]
theme of song, 2369, *zāmîr[1]* [1]
theme of praise, 9335, *t[e]hillâ* [1]

THEMSELVES [168]*

themselves, *AIT* [36]
themselves, 2157, *-hem* [27]
themselves, 5883+4392, *nepeš+-ām* [9]
themselves, 4392, *-ām* [6]
themselves, *NIH/RPE* [5]
themselves, 4564, *-mô* [5]
themselves, 2156, *hēm* [4]
by themselves, 4200+963+4392, *l[e-1]+bad[1]+-ām* [4]
themselves, 5647, *-nû[2]* [2]
themselves, 2023, *-āh* [1]
themselves, 2179, *hēnnâ[2]* [1]
themselves, 4213+4392, *lēb+-ām* [1]
themselves, 4222+4392, *lēbāb+-ām* [1]
themselves, 5626, *-nâ* [1]

THEN [2224]

then, 2256, *w[e]-* [1821]
then, *NIH/RPE* [99]
and then, 2256, *w[e]-* [91]
then, 255, *ʾāz* [65]
then, 10089+10008, *b[e]-+ʾ[e]dayin* [13]
then, 10008, *ʾ[e]dayin* [11]
then, 339, *ʾaḥar* [10]
then, 4200+5100, *l[e-1]+maʿan* [10]
then, 6964, *ʿattâ* [10]
then, 1685, *gam* [9]
then, 10221, *w[e]-* [9]
then, 686, *ʾēpôʾ* [7]
but then, 2256, *w[e]-* [6]
then, 3954, *kî[2]* [4]
then, 5528, *nāʾ[1]* [4]
then, *AIT* [3]
so then, 2256, *w[e]-* [3]
then when, 2256, *w[e]-* [3]
then, 2256+1685, *w[e]-+gam* [3]
then, 4200+4027, *l[e-1]+kēn[2]* [3]
then, 339+4027, *ʾaḥar+kēn[2]* [2]
then, 677, *ʾap[1]* [2]
then, 928+2021+340, *b[e]-+ha-+ʾaḥ[a]rôn* [2]
very well then, 2180, *hinnēh* [2]
just then, 2256+2180, *w[e]-+hinnēh* [2]
then, 340, *ʾaḥ[a]rôn* [1]
then, 889, *ʾ[a]šer* [1]
then, 928+6288, *b[e]-+ʿ[a]bûr[1]* [1]
then[s], 928+2021+3427+2021+2085, *b[e]-+ha-+yôm[1]+ha-+hûʾ* [1]
then, 928+2296, *b[e]-+zeh* [1]
then[s], 2021+6961+2021+2085, *ha-+ʿēt+ha-+hûʾ* [1]
then, 2178, *hēnnâ[1]* [1]
come then, 2180, *hinnēh* [1]
now then, 2180, *hinnēh* [1]
then, 2180, *hinnēh* [1]
by then, 2256, *w[e]-* [1]
even then, 2256, *w[e]-* [1]
if then, 2256, *w[e]-* [1]
then, 2256+339, *w[e]-+ʾaḥar* [1]
then, 2256+6964, *w[e]-+ʿattâ* [1]
then, 2296, *zeh* [1]
then, 3869+889, *k[e]-+ʾ[a]šer* [1]
very well then, 3954, *kî[2]* [1]
then, 4027, *kēn[2]* [1]
so then, 4200+4027, *l[e-1]+kēn[2]* [1]
for then, 4200+5100, *l[e-1]+maʿan* [1]
from then on, 4946+339+4027, *min+ʾaḥar+kēn[2]* [1]
by then, 6330, *ʿad[2]* [1]
since then, 6388, *ʿôd* [1]
then, 6584+4027, *ʿal[2]+kēn[2]* [1]
now then, 6964, *ʿattâ* [1]
then, 10213, *hēn* [1]
then, 10353+10619+10180, *kōl+q[o]bēl+d[e]nâ* [1]
now then, 10363, *k[e]ʿan* [1]
so then, 10385, *lāhēn[1]* [1]

THERE [1408]*

there, 9004, *šām* [400]
there, *NIH/RPE* [316]
there, *AIT* [198]
there is no, 401, *ʾayin[1]* [98]
there, 9004+2025, *šām+-â[2]* [58]
there, 2180, *hinnēh* [57]
there was no, 401, *ʾayin[1]* [29]
there[s], 928+2023, *b[e]-+-āh* [28]
there is, 3780, *yēš* [27]
there will be no, 401, *ʾayin[1]* [8]
is there, 3780, *yēš* [8]
there is none, 401, *ʾayin[1]* [6]
there[s], 928+3731, *b[e]-+y[e]rûšālaim* [6]
there[s], 6584+2023, *ʿal[2]+-āh* [6]
there, 10067, *ʾ[a]rû* [5]
is there no, 401, *ʾayin[1]* [4]
there is not, 401, *ʾayin[1]* [4]
there was none, 401, *ʾayin[1]* [4]
there were no, 401, *ʾayin[1]* [4]
there, 10035, *ʾ[a]lû* [4]
there is no, 1172+401, *b[e]lî+ʾayin[1]* [3]
there are, 3780, *yēš* [3]
there was, 3780, *yēš* [3]
there is, 10029, *ʾîtay* [3]
is there not, 401, *ʾayin[1]* [2]
there was nothing, 401, *ʾayin[1]* [2]
there are no, 401, *ʾayin[1]* [2]
there is nothing, 401+4399, *ʾayin[1]+m[e]ʾûmâ* [2]
there is nothing, 401, *ʾayin[1]* [2]
there was not, 401, *ʾayin[1]* [2]
there will be none, 401, *ʾayin[1]* [2]
was there no, 401, *ʾayin[1]* [2]
there, 889, *ʾ[a]šer* [2]

THERE'S [1]

there's, 2137, *hallāz* [1]

THEREFORE [287]

therefore, 4200+4027, *l[e-1]+kēn[2]* [146]
therefore, 2256, *w[e]-* [58]
therefore, 6584+4027, *ʿal[2]+kēn[2]* [52]
therefore, *NIH/RPE* [8]
therefore, 4200+5100, *l[e-1]+maʿan* [4]
therefore, 3954, *kî[2]* [3]
therefore, 6964, *ʿattâ* [3]
therefore, 2256+1685, *w[e]-+gam* [2]
therefore, 6584+2296, *ʿal[2]+zeh* [2]
therefore, 1685, *gam* [1]
therefore, 2180, *hinnēh* [1]
therefore, 4200+4027+3610, *l[e-1]+kēn[2]+yaʿan[1]* [1]
therefore, 5528, *nāʾ[1]* [1]
therefore, 6584+1826+8611, *ʿal[2]+dibrâ+ša-* [1]
therefore, 10089+10008, *b[e]-+ʾ[e]dayin* [1]
therefore, 10221, *w[e]-* [1]
therefore, 10353+10619+10180, *kōl+q[o]bēl+d[e]nâ* [1]
therefore, 10385, *lāhēn[1]* [1]

THESE [828]

these, 465, *ʾēlleh* [481]
these, 2296, *zeh* [109]
these, *NIH/RPE* [70]
these, 2021, *ha-* [54]
these, *AIT* [25]
these, 2156, *hēm* [13]
these, 4392, *-ām* [12]
these, 2157, *-hem* [9]
these, 10037, *ʾillēk* [8]
these, 447, *ʾēl[6]* [7]
these, 2179, *hēnnâ[2]* [5]
these, 2085, *hûʾ* [4]
these, 10002, *-āʾ* [4]
these, 889, *ʾ[a]šer* [3]
these, 2257, *-ô* [3]
these articles[s], 4392, *-ām* [2]
these[s], 641, *ʾ[o]niyyâ* [1]
these men[s], 1201+2021+5566, *bēn[1]+ha-+nābîʾ* [1]
these[s], 2021+2693, *ha-+ḥēleb[1]* [1]
these[s], 2021+74, *ha-+ʾeben* [1]
these, 2023, *-āh* [1]
these days[s], 2157, *-hem* [1]
these men[s], 2157, *-hem* [1]
these things[s], 2157, *-hem* [1]
these, 2177, *-hēn[2]* [1]
these, 3871, *-k* [1]
these things[s], 3972, *kōl* [1]
these[s], 3972, *kōl* [1]
these offerings[s], 4392, *-ām* [1]
these tithes[s], 5647, *-nû[2]* [1]
these[s], 5883, *nepeš* [1]
these men[s], 6913+2021+4856, *ʿāśâ[1]+ha-+m[e]lāʾkâ* [1]
these, 10032, *ʾēl* [1]
these, 10180, *d[e]nâ* [1]

THEY [4796]*

they, *AIT* [3531]
they, 2156, *hēm* [321]
they, *NIH/RPE* [294]
they, 4392, *-ām* [252]
they, 2157, *-hem* [116]
they, 2085, *hûʾ* [40]
they, 2257, *-ô* [31]
they[s], 2021, *ha-* [18]
they, 465, *ʾēlleh* [12]
they[s], 2021+408, *ha-+ʾîš[1]* [9]
they, 2177, *-hēn[2]* [8]
they, 2179, *hēnnâ[2]* [8]
they, 5647, *-nû[2]* [8]
they[s], 408, *ʾîš[1]* [7]
they, 5527, *-ān* [5]
they, 2024, *-ōh* [4]
they, 2084, *-hû* [4]
they, 5626, *-nâ* [4]
they, 5883+4392, *nepeš+-ām* [4]
they, 408, *ʾîš[1]* [3]
they, 4564, *-mô* [3]
they[s], 889, *ʾ[a]šer* [2]
they, 2181, *-h[e]nâ* [1]
they[s], 2257, *-ô* [1]
they, 10203, *-hôn* [1]
they, 10210, *himmô* [1]

THICK [27]

thick foliage, 6291, *ʿābôt[2]* [4]
thick darkness, 6906, *ʿ[a]rāpel* [4]
thick, *NIH/RPE* [3]
thick, 8145, *rōḥab* [3]
thick darkness, 694, *ʾōpel* [2]
thick, 6295, *ʿ[a]bî* [2]
thick, 1524, *gādôl* [1]
thick, 3878, *kābēd[2]* [1]
thick cloth, 4802, *makbēr* [1]
thick clouds, 6265, *ʿāb[2]* [1]
thick darkness, 7516, *ṣalmāwet* [1]
thick, 7931, *qereb* [1]
thick, 8044, *rōb* [1]
thick, 8146, *rāḥāb[1]* [1]
thick branches, 8449, *śôbek* [1]

THICKER [2]

thicker, 6286, *ʿābâ* [2]

THICKET [6]

thicket, 3623, *yaʿar[1]* [2]
lush thicket, 1454, *gāʾôn* [1]
thicket, 6019, *s[e]bak* [1]
thicket, 6020, *s[e]bōk* [1]
thicket, 6109, *sukkâ* [1]

THICKETS [11]

thickets, 1454, *gāʾôn* [3]
thickets, 3623, *yaʿar[1]* [3]
thickets, 6019, *s[e]bak* [2]
thickets, 2560, *ḥôaḥ[1]* [1]
thickets, 3091, *ḥōreš[1]* [1]
thickets, 6266, *ʿāb[3]* [1]

THICKNESS [2]

thickness, 6295, *ʿ[a]bî* [2]

THIEF [11]
thief, 1705, *gannāb* [9]
thief, *NIH/RPE* [1]
thief, 1704, *gānab* [1]

THIEVES [7]
thieves, 1705, *gannāb* [7]

THIGH [21]
thigh, 8797, *šôq* [12]
thigh, 3751, *yārēk* [9]

THIGHS [2]
thighs, 7066, *paḥad*^{2} [1]
thighs, 10334, *yarkâ* [1]

THIN [8]
thin, 1987, *daq* [6]
thin, 3950, *kāḥaš* [1]
thin sheets, 7063, *paḥ*^{2} [1]

THING [112]
thing, 1821, *dābār* [27]
thing, *AIT* [26]
detestable thing, 9359, *tô'ēbâ* [7]
disgraceful thing, 5576, *n*^{e}*bālâ* [4]
thing, *NIH/RPE* [3]
thing^{s}, 2296, *zeh* [3]
unclean thing, 5614, *niddâ* [3]
done a foolish thing, 6118, *sākal* [3]
living thing, 1414, *bāśār* [2]
great thing, 1525, *g*^{e}*dûllâ* [2]
good thing, 3208, *ṭôbâ* [2]
living thing, 3685, *y*^{e}*qûm* [2]
such a thing, 3970, *kākâ* [2]
thing, 5883, *nepeš* [2]
evil thing, 8288, *rā'â*^{3} [2]
horrible thing, 9137, *ša'*^{a}*rûrî* [2]
thing loved, 171, *'ōhab* [1]
living thing^{s}, 889, *'ašer* [1]
any such thing^{s}, 2257, *-ô* [1]
thing of horror, 2400, *za'*^{a}*wâ* [1]
sinful thing, 2633, *ḥaṭṭā't* [1]
living thing, 2645, *ḥay*^{2} [1]
green thing, 3728, *yārôq* [1]
thing, 3998, *k*^{e}*lî* [1]
living thing, 4695, *miḥyâ* [1]
wicked thing, 5576, *n*^{e}*bālâ* [1]
green thing, 6912, *'ēśeb* [1]
awful thing, 8288, *rā'â*^{3} [1]
wicked thing, 8288, *rā'â*^{3} [1]
do wicked thing, 8317, *rā'a'*^{1} [1]
thing of horror, 9014, *šammâ*^{1} [1]
shocking thing, 9136, *ša'*^{a}*rûr* [1]
crawling thing, 9238, *šereṣ* [1]
thing detestable, 9359, *tô'ēbâ* [1]
repulsive thing, 9524, *tiplâ* [1]
thing, 10418, *millâ* [1]

THINGS [322]
things, *AIT* [122]
things, 1821, *dābār* [33]
things, *NIH/RPE* [19]
detestable things, 9359, *tô'ēbâ* [18]
holy things, 7731, *qōdeš* [10]
good things, 3206, *ṭûb* [7]
good things, 3208, *ṭôbâ* [7]
things, 5126, *ma'*^{a}*śeh* [7]
devoted things, 3051, *ḥērem*^{1} [6]
things, 3998, *k*^{e}*lî* [6]
things, 889, *'*^{a}*šer* [4]
righteous things, 7407, *ṣ*^{e}*dāqâ* [4]
things^{s}, 2156, *hēm* [3]
most holy things, 7731+7731, *qōdeš+qōdeš* [3]
things detestable, 9359, *tô'ēbâ* [3]
things^{s}, 1476, *g*^{e}*bûrâ* [2]
things^{s}, 2179, *hēnnâ*^{2} [2]
mighty things, 2657, *ḥayil* [2]
scheme of things, 3113, *ḥešbôn*^{1} [2]
things^{s}, 4392, *-ām* [2]
dedicated things, 7731, *qōdeš* [2]
things dedicated, 7731, *qōdeš* [2]
things^{s}, 9359, *tô'ēbâ* [2]
things, 10418, *millâ* [2]
things^{s}, 465, *'ēlleh* [1]
things to come, 910, *'ātâ* [1]
glorious things, 1455, *gē'ût* [1]
great things done, 1540, *gādal* [1]
things did, 2006, *derek* [1]
things^{s}, 2085, *hû'* [1]
valuable things, 2104+3701, *hôn+yāqār* [1]
such things^{s}, 2157, *-hem* [1]
these things^{s}, 2157, *-hem* [1]
things, 2177, *-hēn*^{2} [1]
things, 2306, *zû* [1]
hidden things, 2648, *ḥîdâ* [1]
living things, 2651, *ḥayyâ*^{1} [1]
took some of the things, 2745, *ḥālaq*^{2} [1]
such things^{s}, 2914, *ḥēpeṣ* [1]
condemned things, 3051, *ḥērem*^{1} [1]
best things, 3206, *ṭûb* [1]
things that make unclean, 3240, *ṭum'â* [1]
precious things, 3702, *y*^{e}*qār* [1]
very things, 3869+889+4027, *k*^{e}*-+'*^{a}*šer+kēn*^{2} [1]
these things^{s}, 3972, *kōl* [1]
things, 3972+3998, *kōl+k*^{e}*lî* [1]
specific things, 3998+5466, *k*^{e}*lî+mišmeret* [1]
the things^{s}, 4392, *-ām* [1]
how find things, 4537, *mâ* [1]
symbolic of things to come, 4603, *môpēt* [1]
things planned, 4742, *maḥ*^{a}*šābâ* [1]
things did, 5126+3338, *ma'*^{a}*śeh+yād* [1]
things did, 5126, *ma'*^{a}*śeh* [1]
holy things, 5219, *miqdāš* [1]
bitter things, 5353, *mārōr* [1]
contemptible things, 5542, *ne'āṣâ* [1]
outrageous things, 5576, *n*^{e}*bālâ* [1]
worthy things, 5592, *nāgîd* [1]
find things out by divination, 5727+5727, *nāḥaš+nāḥaš* [1]
things^{s}, 6662, *'āmāl*^{1} [1]
do great things, 6913+6913, *'āśâ*^{1}*+'āśâ*^{1} [1]
astonishing things, 7099, *pele'* [1]
marvelous things, 7099, *pele'* [1]
consecrated things, 7731, *qōdeš* [1]
sacred things, 7731, *qōdeš* [1]
things^{s}, 7731, *qōdeš* [1]
looked things over, 8011, *rā'â*^{1} [1]
crawling things, 8254, *remeś* [1]
sort of things he says, 8490, *śîaḥ*^{3} [1]
worthless things, 8736, *šāw'* [1]
detestable things, 9199, *šiqqûṣ* [1]
abominable things, 9211, *šeqeṣ* [1]
swarming things, 9238, *šereṣ* [1]
confusing things, 9337, *tahpukôt* [1]
hidden things, 9502, *ta'*^{a}*lumâ* [1]
things, 10408, *mâ* [1]

THINK [37]
think, 928+6524, *b*^{e}*-+'ayin*^{1} [8]
think, 606, *'āmar*^{1} [6]
think, 3108, *ḥāšab* [6]
think, *NIH/RPE* [1]
think, 606+928+4213, *'āmar*^{1}*+b*^{e}*-+lēb* [1]
think, 606+928+4222, *'āmar*^{1}*+b*^{e}*-+lēbāb* [1]
think, 1067, *bîn* [1]
think, 1948, *dāmâ*^{1} [1]
think, 2047, *hāgâ*^{1} [1]
think, 2180, *hinnēh* [1]
think about, 2349, *zākar*^{1} [1]
think it over, 3359, *yāda'* [1]
think over, 3359, *yāda'* [1]
think, 3359, *yāda'* [1]
think, 5989+4213, *nātan+lēb* [1]
think, 5989+4222, *nātan+lēbāb* [1]
think about, 6590+6584+4213, *'ālâ+'al*^{2}*+lēb* [1]
think, 6590+6584+4222, *'ālâ+'al*^{2}*+lēbāb* [1]
think, 8492+4200+4013, *śîm+l*$^{e-1}$*+-kem* [1]
stops to think, 8740+448+4213, *šûb*^{1}*+'el+lēb* [1]

THINKING [14]
thinking, 606, *'āmar*^{1} [7]
thinking, *NIH/RPE* [1]
thinking, 1067, *bîn* [1]
thinking it easy, 2103, *hûn* [1]
what thinking, 4742, *maḥ*^{a}*šābâ* [1]
stopped thinking, 5759, *nāṭaš* [1]
thinking, 9132, *šā'ar* [1]
thinking, 10683, *ś*^{e}*kal* [1]

THINKS [4]
thinks, 606, *'āmar*^{1} [2]
thinks, 928+4222+606, *b*^{e}*-+lēbāb+'āmar*^{1} [1]
thinks right, 4178, *kāšēr* [1]

THIRD [124]
third, 8958, *š*^{e}*lîšî* [93]
third, 8993, *šālōš* [12]
third generation, 9000, *šillēšîm* [5]
third, *NIH/RPE* [4]
third highest, 10761, *taltā'* [3]
third^{s}, 285, *'eḥād* [1]
third^{s}, 4850, *m*^{e}*lō'* [1]
do a third time, 8992, *šālaš* [1]
did the third time, 8992, *šālaš* [1]
third, 8992, *šālaš* [1]
third, 10759, *t*^{e}*lîtāy* [1]
third, 10760, *t*^{e}*lāt* [1]

THIRDS [1]
two thirds of a shekel, 7088, *pîm* [1]

THIRST [20]
thirst, 7533, *ṣāmā'* [15]
thirst, 7532, *ṣāmē'*^{1} [2]
thirst, 5883, *nepeš* [1]
suffer thirst, 7532, *ṣāmē'*^{1} [1]
quenched its thirst, 8115, *rāwâ* [1]

THIRSTS [3]
thirsts, 7532, *ṣāmē'*^{1} [2]
thirsts, *NIH/RPE* [1]

THIRSTY [20]
thirsty, 7534, *ṣāmē'*^{2} [9]
thirsty, 7532, *ṣāmē'*^{1} [5]
thirsty ground, 7536, *ṣimmā'ôn* [2]
thirsty, 5883+8799, *nepeš+šôqēq* [1]
thirsty, 6546, *'āyēp* [1]
thirsty, 7533, *ṣāmā'* [1]
thirsty, 7536, *ṣimmā'ôn* [1]

THIRTEEN [13]
thirteen, 8993+6926, *šālōš+'eśrēh* [10]
thirteen, 8993+6925, *šālōš+'āśār* [2]
more than thirteen feet, 9596+564, *tēša'+'ammâ*^{1} [1]

THIRTEENTH [11]
thirteenth, 8993+6925, *šālōš+'āśār* [8]
thirteenth, 8993+6926, *šālōš+'eśrēh* [3]

THIRTIETH [1]
thirtieth, 8993, *šālōš* [1]

THIRTY [86]
thirty, 8993, *šālōš* [83]
thirty, 10762, *t*^{e}*lātîn* [2]
thirty feet, 6929+928+2021+564, *'eśrîm+b*^{e}*-+ha-+'ammâ*^{1} [1]

THIRTY-EIGHT [2]
thirty-eight, 8993+2256+9046, *šālōš+w*^{e}*-+š*^{e}*mōneh* [2]

THIRTY-EIGHTH [2]
thirty-eighth, 8993+2256+9046, *šālōš+w*^{e}*-+š*^{e}*mōneh* [2]

THIRTY-FIFTH [1]
thirty-fifth, 8993+2256+2822, *šālōš+w*^{e}*-+ḥāmēš* [1]

THIRTY-FIRST [1]
thirty-first, 8993+2256+285, *šālōš+w*^{e}*-+'eḥād* [1]

THIRTY-FIVE [3]
thirty-five, 8993+2256+2822, *šālōš+w*^{e}*-+ḥāmēš* [3]

THIRTY-NINTH [3]
thirty-ninth, 8993+2256+9596, *šālōš+w*^{e}*-+tēša'* [3]

THIRTY-ONE [3]
thirty-one, 8993+2256+285, *šālōš+w*^{e}*-+'eḥād* [3]

THIRTY-SECOND [2]
thirty-second, 8993+2256+9109, *šālōš+we-+šenayim* [2]

THIRTY-SEVEN [2]
thirty-seven, 8993+2256+8679, *šālōš+we-+šeba'[1]* [2]

THIRTY-SEVENTH [3]
thirty-seventh, 8993+2256+8679, *šālōš+we-+šeba'[1]* [3]

THIRTY-SIX [2]
thirty-six hundred, 8993+547+2256+9252+4395, *šālōš+'elep[2]+we-+šēš[1]+mē'â[1]* [1]
thirty-six, 8993+2256+9252, *šālōš+we-+šēš[1]* [1]

THIRTY-SIXTH [1]
thirty-sixth, 8993+2256+9252, *šālōš+we-+šēš[1]* [1]

THIRTY-THREE [7]
thirty-three, 8993+2256+8993, *šālōš+we-+šālōš* [6]
thirty-three hundred, 8993+547+2256+8993+4395, *šālōš+'elep[2]+we-+šālōš+mē'â[1]* [1]

THIRTY-TWO [6]
thirty-two, 8993+2256+9109, *šālōš+we-+šenayim* [5]
thirty-two, 9109+2256+8993, *šenayim+we-+šālōš* [1]

THIS [2579]*
this, 2296, *zeh* [1082]
this is what, 3907, *kōh* [471]
this, *NIH/RPE* [289]
this, 2021, *ha-* [150]
this, *AIT* [96]
this, 465, *'ēlleh* [55]
this, 2085, *hû'* [54]
this[s], 2021+1821+2021+2296, *ha+dābār+ha+zeh* [44]
this, 4027, *kēn[2]* [32]
this, 10180, *denâ* [30]
in this way, 2256, *we-* [17]
this, 3907, *kōh* [16]
at this, 2256, *we-* [14]
this[s], 2021+1821+2021+465, *ha+dābār+ha+'ēlleh* [12]
this, 10173, *dēk* [12]
this, 2023, *-āh* [10]
this, 10002, *-ā'* [7]
this is how, 928+2296, *be-+zeh* [6]
this, 2257, *-ô* [6]
this very, 2296, *zeh* [6]
this, 2297, *zōh* [6]
this[s], 2021+1821, *ha+dābār* [5]
this is why, 6584+4027, *'al[2]+kēn[2]* [5]
this, 2180, *hinnēh* [4]
this is what, 3970, *kākâ* [4]
this is how, 3970, *kākâ* [4]
this, 3970, *kākâ* [4]
this, 4392, *-ām* [4]
this, 889, *'ašer* [3]
this, 2137, *hallāz* [3]
in this way, 3970, *kākâ* [3]
in this way, 4027, *kēn[2]* [3]
this is what, 4027, *kēn[2]* [3]
after this, 339, *'aḥar* [2]
this very, 2021, *ha-* [2]
this, 2156, *hēm* [2]
this is how, 2296, *zeh* [2]
this, 3276, *-î* [2]
be sure of this, 3338+4200+3338, *yād+le-[1]+yād* [2]
this, 3870, *-kā* [2]
this is how, 3907, *kōh* [2]
this[s], 3972, *kōl* [2]
this is how, 4027, *kēn[2]* [2]
like this, 4027, *kēn[2]* [2]
this, 5626, *-nā* [2]
this far, 6330+2151, *'ad[2]+halōm* [2]
this, 10154, *dā'* [2]
this, 10357, *kēn* [2]
this, 10174, *dikkēn* [1]
this, 10191, *-â* [1]
this, 10205, *hî'* [1]
at this, 10221, *we-* [1]
this, 10358, *kenēmā'* [1]

THISTLE [4]
thistle, 2560, *ḥôaḥ[1]* [4]

THISTLES [2]
thistles, 1998, *dardar* [2]

THONG [2]
thong, 8579, *śerôk* [2]

THONGS [3]
thongs, 3857, *yeter[2]* [3]

THORN [1]
thorn hedge, 5004, *mesûkâ* [1]

THORNBUSH [5]
thornbush, 353, *'āṭād[1]* [3]
thornbush, 2560, *ḥôaḥ[1]* [1]
thornbush, 5848, *na'aṣûṣ* [1]

THORNBUSHES [4]
thornbushes, 7764, *qôṣ[1]* [2]
thornbushes, 5848, *na'aṣûṣ* [1]
thornbushes, 6106, *sîrâ* [1]

THORNS [32]
thorns, 7764, *qôṣ[1]* [10]
thorns, 8885, *šayit* [7]
thorns, 6106, *sîrâ* [3]
thorns, 2560, *ḥôaḥ[1]* [2]
thorns, 7553, *ṣēn* [2]
thorns, 7564, *ṣenînîm* [2]
thorns, *NIH/RPE* [1]
thorns, 353, *'āṭād[1]* [1]
thorns[s], 2157, *-hem* [1]
thorns, 2537, *ḥēdeq* [1]
thorns, 6141, *sillôn* [1]
thorns, 7853, *qimmôś* [1]

THOROUGH [1]
thorough, 3512, *yāṭab* [1]

THOROUGHLY [9]
thoroughly, 3512, *yāṭab* [2]
thoroughly, 4394, *me'ōd* [2]
is thoroughly shaken, 4572+4572, *môṭ[1]+môṭ[1]* [1]
glean thoroughly, 6618+6618, *'ālal[1]+'ālal[1]* [1]
thoroughly purge away, 7671+3869+2021+1342, *ṣārap+ke-+ha+bōr[2]* [1]
thoroughly hated, 8533+8533, *śānē'+śānē'* [1]
bake thoroughly, 8596+4200+8599, *śārap+le-[1]+śerēpâ* [1]

THOSE [888]
those, *AIT* [465]
those, 2021, *ha-* [145]
those, 889, *'ašer* [41]
those, *NIH/RPE* [40]
those, 2156, *hēm* [39]
those, 2157, *-hem* [18]
those, 465, *'ēlleh* [15]
those, 4392, *-ām* [12]
those[s], 3972, *kōl* [9]
those[s], 408, *'îš[1]* [6]
those, 2085, *hû'* [6]
those[s], 2021+6639, *ha+'am[2]* [5]
those, 10168, *dî* [5]
those[s], 1887, *dôr[2]* [4]
those[s], 2021+408, *ha+'îš[1]* [4]
those[s], 2257, *-ô* [4]
those, 2257, *-ô* [4]
those, 2296, *zeh* [3]
those[s], 3427, *yôm[1]* [3]
those born, 3535, *yālîd* [3]
those[s], 5883, *nepeš* [3]
those, 447, *'ēl[6]* [2]
those[s], 1074, *bayit[1]* [2]
those[s], 2021+5877, *ha+nāpal* [2]
those, 2179, *hēnnâ[2]* [2]
those[s], 3845, *yātēd* [2]
those[s], 4058, *kissē'* [2]
those[s], 6639, *'am[2]* [2]
those[s], 7983, *qereš* [2]
those[s], 132, *'ādām[1]* [1]
those[s], 149, *'eden* [1]
those who cannot speak, 522, *'illēm* [1]
those[s], 609, *'ēmer[1]* [1]
those[s], 955, *beged[2]* [1]
those who deserve, 1251, *ba'al[1]* [1]
those who get, 1251, *ba'al[1]* [1]
those who have, 1251, *ba'al[1]* [1]
those[s], 1414, *bāśār* [1]
those[s], 2021+8636, *ha+šā'ar* [1]
those[s], 2021+1583, *ha+gôlâ* [1]
those[s], 2021+2651, *ha+ḥayyâ[1]* [1]
those[s], 2021+6639+889+339, *ha+'am[2]+'ašer+'aḥar* [1]
those[s], 2021+7156, *ha+pāneh* [1]
those[s], 2021+7239, *ha+pārā[2]* [1]
those[s], 2021+8599, *ha+śerēpâ* [1]
those, 2023, *-āh* [1]
those, 2024, *-ōh* [1]
those same, 2156, *hēm* [1]
those Israelites[s], 2157, *-hem* [1]
those[s], 2682, *ḥăkām* [1]
those[s], 3338, *yād* [1]
those[s], 4053, *kānāp* [1]
those[s], 4090+8079, *kap+regel* [1]
those nations[s], 4392, *-ām* [1]
those, 4564, *-mô* [1]
those[s], 4946, *min* [1]
those who prophesy, 5566, *nābî'* [1]
those[s], 5647, *-nû[2]* [1]
those[s], 5877, *nāpal* [1]
those who speak up for, 6332, *'ēd* [1]
those[s], 6524, *'ayin[1]* [1]
those[s], 6795, *'eṣem[1]* [1]
those[s], 7496, *ṣîr[4]* [1]
those who love bribes, 8816, *šōḥad* [1]
those[s], 9300, *te'ēnâ* [1]
those, 10036, *'illēn* [1]
those, 10045, *'innûn* [1]

THOUGH [239]
though, 3954, *kî[2]* [54]
though, 2256, *we-* [39]
though, *NIH/RPE* [38]
though, 561, *'im* [22]
even though, 2256, *we-* [22]
though, 889, *'ašer* [8]
as though, 3869, *ke-* [8]
and though, 2256, *we-* [7]
even though, 3954, *kî[2]* [6]
though, 1685, *gam* [5]
though, *AIT* [4]
though, 928, *be-* [3]
though, 219, *'ûlām[1]* [2]
even though, 889, *'ašer* [2]
though, 2176, *hēn[1]* [2]
though, 3954+561, *kî[2]+'im* [2]
as though, 6584, *'al[2]* [2]
though, 6584, *'al[2]* [2]
though, 421, *'ak* [1]
even though, 561, *'im* [1]
though, 677, *'ap[1]* [1]
though, 2180, *hinnēh* [1]
and even though, 2256, *we-* [1]
as though, 3869+889, *ke-+'ašer* [1]
though, 3869, *ke-* [1]
as though, 4017, *kemô* [1]
even though, 4200+963, *le-[1]+bad[1]* [1]
though, 6330, *'ad[2]* [1]
though, 10353+10619+10168, *kōl+qobēl+dî* [1]

THOUGHT [73]
thought, 606, *'āmar[1]* [47]
give careful thought, 8492+4222, *śîm+lēbāb* [5]
thought, *NIH/RPE* [3]
thought, 3108, *ḥāšab* [3]
thought, 928+6524, *be-+'ayin[1]* [2]
gives thought, 1067, *bîn* [2]
thought, 606+448+3276, *'āmar[1]+'el+-î* [1]
give thought, 1067, *bîn* [1]

thought, 1819, *dābar*[2] [1]
thought, 1821, *dābār* [1]
thought, 1948, *dāmâ*[1] [1]
thought, 2349, *zākar*[1] [1]
is thought, 3108, *ḥāšab* [1]
were thought, 3108, *ḥāšab* [1]
gives thought, 7143, *pālas*[2] [1]
deep in thought, 8490, *śîaḥ*[3] [1]
gave thought, 8505, *śākal*[1] [1]

THOUGHTLESSLY [1]
thoughtlessly, 4200+1051+928+8557, *lᵉ-*[1]*+bāṭā'+bᵉ-+śāpâ* [1]

THOUGHTS [30]
thoughts, 4742, *maḥᵃšābâ* [14]
thoughts, 1821, *dābār* [2]
thoughts, 4213, *lēb* [2]
thoughts, 8277, *rēa'*[3] [2]
thoughts, 10669, *ra'yôn* [2]
thoughts, *NIH/RPE* [1]
thoughts, 4529, *maddā'* [1]
thoughts, 4659, *mᵉzimmâ* [1]
thoughts, 6783+928+5883, *'ēṣā*[1]*+bᵉ-+nepeš* [1]
thoughts, 8465, *śēaḥ* [1]
thoughts, 8490, *śîaḥ*[3] [1]
troubled thoughts, 8546, *śe'ippîm* [1]
anxious thoughts, 8595, *śar'appîm* [1]

THOUSAND [238]
thousand, 547, *'elep*[2] [223]
ten thousand, 8047, *rᵉbābâ* [6]
units of a thousand, 547, *'elep*[2] [2]
ten thousand, 10649, *ribbô* [2]
three thousand feet, 547+564, *'elep*[2]*+'ammâ*[1] [1]
eighteen thousand, 8052+2256+9046+547, *ribbô'+wᵉ-+šᵉmōneh+'elep*[2] [1]
ten thousand, 8052, *ribbô'* [1]
hundred and twenty thousand, 9109+6926+8052, *šᵉnayim+'eśrēh+ribbô'* [1]
thousand, 10038, *'ᵃlap* [1]

THOUSANDS [45]
thousands, 547, *'elep*[2] [31]
tens of thousands, 8047, *rᵉbābâ* [5]
thousands, 10038, *'ᵃlap* [2]
increase by thousands, 545, *'ālap*[2] [1]
tens of thousands, 8045, *rābab*[1] [1]
ten thousands, 8047, *rᵉbābâ* [1]
thousands, 8047, *rᵉbābâ* [1]
many thousands, 8052, *ribbô'* [1]
tens of thousands, 8052, *ribbô'* [1]
thousands, 9099, *šin'ān* [1]

THRASHING [2]
thrashing about, 1631, *gîaḥ*[1] [1]
thrashing, 8691, *šeber*[1] [1]

THREAD [3]
scarlet thread, 9106, *šānî*[1] [2]
thread, 2562, *ḥûṭ* [1]

THREADS [1]
threads, 2562, *ḥûṭ* [1]

THREAT [6]
threat, 1722, *gᵉ'ārâ* [3]
this threat[s], 2157, *-hem* [1]
threat, 7065, *paḥad*[1] [1]
threat, 10244, *ḥᵃbāl* [1]

THREATEN [2]
threaten, 1819, *dābar*[2] [2]

THREATENED [6]
threatened, 1819, *dābar*[2] [3]
threatened, 1821, *dābār* [1]
threatened, 3108, *ḥāšab* [1]
threatened, 6330+5883, *'ad*[2]*+nepeš* [1]

THREATS [4]
threats, 9412, *tōk* [2]
made threats, 1540, *gādal* [1]
threats, 1821, *dābār* [1]

THREE [310]
three, 8993, *šālōš* [282]
three, 10760, *tᵉlāt* [10]
three, 8958, *šᵉlîšî* [7]
three, *AIT* [3]
three, 8998, *šālîšî* [2]
three, *NIH/RPE* [1]
three thousand feet, 547+564, *'elep*[2]*+'ammâ*[1] [1]
three feet, 564, *'ammâ*[1] [1]
divide into three, 8992, *šālaš* [1]
three years old, 8992, *šālaš* [1]
three, 8992, *šālaš* [1]

THREE-DAY [4]
three-day, 8993+3427, *šālōš+yôm*[1] [4]

THREE-PRONGED [1]
three-pronged, 8993+9094, *šālōš+šēn*[1] [1]

THREE-TENTHS [8]
three-tenths, 8993+6928, *šālōš+'iśśārôn* [8]

THREE-YEAR-OLD [1]
three-year-old, 8992, *šālaš* [1]

THRESH [4]
thresh, 1889, *dûš* [3]
thresh, 2468, *ḥābaṭ* [1]

THRESHED [4]
threshed, 1889, *dûš* [2]
is threshed, 1889, *dûš* [1]
threshed, 2468, *ḥābaṭ* [1]

THRESHING [49]
threshing floor, 1755, *gōren* [32]
threshing floors, 1755, *gōren* [3]
threshing sledges, 4617, *môrag* [2]
threshing, *AIT* [1]
threshing floor, 1755+1841, *gōren+dāgān* [1]
go on threshing, 1889+1889, *dûš+dûš* [1]
threshing grain, 1889, *dûš* [1]
threshing time, 1889, *dûš* [1]
threshing, 1889, *dûš* [1]
threshing, 1912, *dayiš* [1]
threshing, 2468, *ḥābaṭ* [1]
threshing sledge, 3023, *ḥārûṣ*[3] [1]
threshing sledge, 4617, *môrag* [1]
threshing cart, 6322, *'ᵃgālâ* [1]
threshing floor, 10010, *'iddar* [1]

THRESHOLD [15]
threshold, 5159, *miptān* [8]
threshold, 6197, *sap*[3] [7]

THRESHOLDS [5]
thresholds, 6197, *sap*[3] [5]

THREW [49]
threw, 8959, *šālak* [26]
threw, *NIH/RPE* [2]
threw into confusion, 2169, *hāmam*[1] [2]
threw, 3214, *ṭûl* [2]
threw arms around, 5877+6584+7418, *nāpal+'al*[2]*+ṣawwā'r* [2]
threw down, 5877, *nāpal* [2]
threw, 5877, *nāpal* [2]
threw down, 8959, *šālak* [2]
threw, 10667, *rᵉmâ* [2]
threw into a panic, 2169, *hāmam*[1] [1]
threw down, 2238, *hāras* [1]
threw, 3343, *yādâ*[1] [1]
threw arms around, 5877+6584, *nāpal+'al*[2] [1]
threw away, 8959, *šālak* [1]
threw out, 8959, *šālak* [1]
threw down, 9023, *šāmaṭ* [1]

THRIVE [11]
thrive, 8049, *rābâ*[1] [4]
thrive, 7503, *ṣālaḥ*[2] [2]
thrive, 2014, *dāšēn*[1] [1]
make thrive, 5649, *nûb* [1]
thrive, 6424, *'ûr*[3] [1]
thrive, 7255, *pāraḥ*[1] [1]
thrive, 8436, *śāgâ* [1]

THRIVES [1]
thrives, 7229, *pārā'* [1]

THRIVING [1]
thriving, 8316, *ra'ᵃnān* [1]

THROAT [4]
throat, 1744, *gārôn* [3]
throat, 4350, *lōa'* [1]

THROATS [2]
throats, 1744, *gārôn* [1]
throats, 5883, *nepeš* [1]

THROB [1]
throb, 7064, *pāḥad* [1]

THROES [1]
throes of death, 8688, *šābāṣ* [1]

THRONE [117]
throne, 4058, *kissē'* [110]
throne, 10372, *korsē'* [2]
lofty throne, 2292, *zᵉbul*[2] [1]
throne, 3782, *yāšab* [1]
throne, 4632, *môšāb* [1]
put on throne, 4887, *mālak*[1] [1]
throne, 10424, *malkû* [1]

THRONES [10]
thrones, 4058, *kissē'* [8]
thrones, 3782, *yāšab* [1]
thrones, 10372, *korsē'* [1]

THRONG [10]
throng, 7736, *qāhāl* [3]
throng, *AIT* [1]
throng, *NIH/RPE* [1]
throng, 2101, *hûm* [1]
throng, 2162, *hāmôn* [1]
throng, 3972, *kōl* [1]
great throng, 8086, *rigmâ* [1]
throng, 8094, *regeš* [1]

THRONGED [1]
thronged, 1518, *gādad*[2] [1]

THRONGS [1]
throngs, 6786, *'āṣûm* [1]

THROUGH [465]
through, 928, *bᵉ-* [183]
through, 4200, *lᵉ-*[1] [79]
through, 928+3338, *bᵉ-+yād* [62]
through, *NIH/RPE* [18]
through, *AIT* [14]
through, 4946, *min* [13]
through, 928+9348, *bᵉ-+tāwek* [8]
through, 1237, *ba'ad*[1] [8]
through, 2006, *derek* [8]
pass through, 6296, *'ābar*[1] [8]
through, 4946+907, *min+'ēt*[2] [4]
through, 928+7931, *bᵉ-+qereb* [3]
was broken through, 1324, *bāqa'* [3]
run through, 1991, *dāqar* [3]
passed through, 6296, *'ābar*[1] [3]
through, 6330, *'ad*[2] [3]
force way through, 2238, *hāras* [2]
searched through, 5491, *māšaš* [2]
broke through, 5782, *nākâ* [2]
winds through, 6015, *sābab* [2]
get through, 6296, *'ābar*[1] [2]
led through, 6296, *'ābar*[1] [2]
passing through, 6296, *'ābar*[1] [2]
sweep through, 6296, *'ābar*[1] [2]
through, 907, *'ēt*[2] [1]
through fault, 928, *bᵉ-* [1]
through, 1198, *bᵉmô* [1]
been broken through, 1324, *bāqa'* [1]
break through, 1324, *bāqa'* [1]
cut through, 1548, *gāda'* [1]
cuts through, 1548, *gāda'* [1]
through all generations, 1887+1887, *dôr*[2]*+dôr*[2] [1]
be thrust through, 1991, *dāqar* [1]
drove through, 1991, *dāqar* [1]
ran through, 1991, *dāqar* [1]

till, 4202, *lō'* [1]
till no more, 4946, *min* [1]
till, 6330+3954, *'ad^{2}+kî^{2}* [1]
till, 6330+561, *'ad^{2}+'im* [1]
till, 6330+6961, *'ad^{2}+'ēt* [1]
till, 6330+889, *'ad^{2}+'ăšer* [1]
till, 8440, *šādad* [1]
till, 10221, *w^{e}-* [1]

TILON [1]
Tilon, 9400, *tîlôn* [1]

TILTING [1]
tilting away from, 4946+7156, *min+pāneh* [1]

TIMBER [12]
timber, 6770, *'ēṣ* [12]

TIMBERS [5]
timbers, 6770, *'ēṣ* [2]
timbers, 10058, *'ā'* [2]
timbers, 4283, *lûaḥ* [1]

TIME [514]
time, 6961, *'ēt* [179]
time, 3427, *yôm^{1}* [122]
time, *NIH/RPE* [21]
appointed time, 4595, *mô'ēd* [15]
time, 7193, *pa'am* [14]
at that time, 255, *'āz* [11]
second time, 9108, *šēnî* [10]
in the course of time, 339+4027, *'aḥar+kēn^{2}* [8]
time, *AIT* [7]
time, 4595, *mô'ēd* [7]
some time later, 339+2021+1821+2021+465, *'aḥar+ha-+dābār+ha-+'ēlleh* [6]
time, 10232, *z^{e}man^{2}* [5]
some time later, 339+4027, *'aḥar+kēn^{2}* [3]
at the time of, 928, *b^{e}-* [3]
some time, 3427, *yôm^{1}* [3]
time, 10317, *yôm* [3]
time, 10530, *'iddān* [3]
time, 255, *'āz* [2]
long time, 801, *'ārōk* [2]
at that time, 2256, *w^{e}-* [2]
time, 2375, *z^{e}mān* [2]
first time, 2725, *ḥālal^{1}* [2]
some time later, 4946+3427, *min+yôm^{1}* [2]
proper time, 6961, *'ēt* [2]
harvest time, 7907, *qāṣîr^{1}* [2]
time after time, 8041+6961, *rab^{1}+'ēt* [2]
time after time, 8049, *rābā^{1}* [2]
first time, 9378, *t^{e}ḥillâ* [2]
time of mourning, 65, *'ēbel* [1]
time of happiness, 245, *'ôrâ^{1}* [1]
about this time, 255, *'āz* [1]
one time, 285, *'eḥād* [1]
time to come, 294, *'āḥôr* [1]
lost time, 336, *'āḥar* [1]
after the time of, 339, *'aḥar* [1]
some time later, 339, *'aḥar* [1]
some time after, 339, *'aḥar* [1]
time, 340, *'aḥ^{a}rôn* [1]
time, 564, *'ammâ^{1}* [1]
lives a long time, 799, *'ārak* [1]
at the time, 928, *b^{e}-* [1]
from the time, 928, *b^{e}-* [1]
later in time, 928+344, *b^{e}+'aḥ^{a}rît* [1]
time is ripe, 995+7891, *bô'+qēṣ* [1]
sheep-shearing time, 1605, *gāzaz* [1]
for some time, 1685+9453+1685+8997, *gam+t^{e}môl+gam+šilšôm* [1]
all time, 1887+2256+1887, *dôr^{2}+w^{e}-+dôr^{2}* [1]
people of time, 1887, *dôr^{2}* [1]
threshing time, 1889, *dûš* [1]
at this time, 2021+3427, *ha-+yôm^{1}* [1]
that time^{s}, 2023, *-āh* [1]
all this time, 2143, *hālak* [1]
the present time, 2178, *hēnnâ^{1}* [1]
by the time, 2256, *w^{e}-* [1]
time appointed, 2375, *z^{e}mān* [1]
mating time, 2544, *ḥōdeš^{1}* [1]
appointed time, 2976, *ḥōq* [1]
time, 2976, *ḥōq* [1]
during that time, 3427, *yôm^{1}* [1]
allotted time, 3427, *yôm^{1}* [1]
have time, 3523+4538, *yākōl+māhah* [1]
near the time of delivery, 3528, *yālad* [1]
lived a long time, 3823, *yāšēn^{2}* [1]
by the time, 3869, *k^{e}-* [1]
in the course of time, 4200+3427+4946+3427, *l^{e}-^{1}+yôm^{1}+min+yôm^{1}* [1]
setting the time, 4200+5503, *l^{e}-^{1}+mātay* [1]
time and again, 4202+285+2256+4202+9109, *lō'+'eḥād+w^{e}-+lō'+š^{e}nayim* [1]
lost no time, 4554, *māhar^{1}* [1]
set time, 4595+3427, *mô'ēd+yôm^{1}* [1]
time set, 4595, *mô'ēd* [1]
length of time, 4632, *môšāb* [1]
time of war, 4878, *milḥāmâ* [1]
in the course of time, 4946+339+4027, *min+'aḥar+kēn^{2}* [1]
before time, 4946+4200+7156, *min+l^{e}-^{1}+pāneh* [1]
until the time for, 6330, *'ad^{2}* [1]
in a very short time, 6388+5071+4663, *'ôd+m^{e}'aṭ+miz'ār* [1]
long time, 6388, *'ôd* [1]
time, 6388, *'ôd* [1]
all time, 6409, *'ôlām* [1]
any time, 6409, *'ôlām* [1]
long time, 6409, *'ôlām* [1]
go over a second time, 6618, *'ālal^{1}* [1]
appointed time, 6961, *'ēt* [1]
due time, 6961, *'ēt* [1]
that time on, 6964, *'attâ* [1]
this time on, 6964, *'attâ* [1]
go over the branches a second time, 6994+339, *pā'ar^{1}+'aḥar* [1]
time of fasting, 7427, *ṣôm* [1]
at another time, 8092, *rega'* [1]
at any time, 8092, *rega'* [1]
loss of time, 8700, *šebet^{2}* [1]
do a third time, 8992, *šālaš* [1]
did the third time, 8992, *šālaš* [1]
time for canceling debts, 9024, *š^{e}miṭṭā* [1]
this time^{s}, 9102+8993, *šānâ^{2}+šālōš* [1]
time, 9102, *šānâ^{2}* [1]
this time, 9108, *šēnî* [1]
two at a time, 9109+9109, *š^{e}nayim+š^{e}nayim* [1]
period of time, 10232+10221+10530, *z^{e}man^{2}+w^{e}-+'iddān* [1]
time, 10734, *šā'â* [1]

TIMELY [1]
timely, 928+6961, *b^{e}-+'ēt* [1]

TIMES [133]
times, 7193, *pa'am* [44]
times, 6961, *'ēt* [26]
times, *AIT* [16]
times, 3427, *yôm^{1}* [10]
times, 10530, *'iddān* [6]
times, 8079, *regel* [4]
times, 3338, *yād* [2]
at set times, 4946+6961+6330+6961, *min+'ēt+'ad^{2}+'ēt* [2]
times, 4951, *mōneh* [2]
ancient times, 6409, *'ôlām* [2]
times, 10232, *z^{e}man^{2}* [2]
times, 1821, *dābār* [1]
designated times, 2375, *z^{e}mān* [1]
as in times past, 3869+3972, *k^{e}+kōl* [1]
in earlier times, 4200+7156, *l^{e}-^{1}+pāneh* [1]
appointed times, 4595, *mô'ēd* [1]
early times, 6409, *'ôlām* [1]
from ancient times, 6972, *'attîq* [1]
earlier times, 7156, *pāneh* [1]
at other times, 7193+928+7193, *pa'am+b^{e}-+pa'am* [1]
ancient times, 7710, *qedem* [1]
desperate times, 7997, *qāšeh* [1]
many times, 8049, *rābā^{1}* [1]
at all times, 9458, *tāmîd* [1]
set times, 10232, *z^{e}man^{2}* [1]
times, 10248, *ḥad* [1]
times, 10317, *yôm* [1]

TIMNA [6]
Timna, 9465, *timna'* [6]

TIMNAH [11]
Timnah, 9463, *timnâ* [11]

TIMNATH HERES [1]
Timnath Heres, 9466, *timnat-ḥeres* [1]

TIMNATH SERAH [2]
Timnath Serah, 9467, *timnat-seraḥ* [2]

TIMNITE'S [1]
Timnite's, 9464, *timnî* [1]

TIN [4]
tin, 974, *b^{e}dîl* [4]

TINDER [1]
tinder, 5861, *n^{e}'ōret* [1]

TINGLE [3]
tingle, 7509, *ṣālal^{1}* [2]
make tingle, 7509, *ṣālal^{1}* [1]

TIP [6]
tip, 7896, *qāṣâ^{2}* [2]
on the tip of tongue, 4383+928+2674, *lāšôn+b^{e}-+ḥēk* [1]
tip, 7895, *qāṣeh* [1]
tip, 8031, *rō'š^{1}* [1]
tip over, 8886, *šākab* [1]

TIPHSAH [3]
Tiphsah, 9527, *tipsaḥ* [2]
Tiphsah, *NIH/RPE* [1]

TIRAS [2]
Tiras, 9410, *tîrās* [2]

TIRATHITES [1]
Tirathites, 9571, *tir'ātîm* [1]

TIRE [1]
tire, 3615, *yā'ēp^{1}* [1]

TIRED [7]
tired, 3615, *yā'ēp^{1}* [2]
tired, 6546, *'āyēp* [2]
tired, 3333, *yāga'* [1]
tired, 3878, *kābēd^{2}* [1]
tired, 7918, *qāṣar^{2}* [1]

TIRHAKAH [2]
Tirhakah, 9555, *tirhāqâ* [2]

TIRHANAH [1]
Tirhanah, 9563, *tirḥ^{a}nâ* [1]

TIRIA [1]
Tiria, 9409, *tîr^{e}yā'* [1]

TIRZAH [18]
Tirzah, 9574, *tirṣâ^{2}* [14]
Tirzah, 9573, *tirṣâ^{1}* [4]

TISHBE [1]
Tishbe, 9586, *tišbê* [1]

TISHBITE [6]
Tishbite, 9585, *tišbî* [6]

TITHE [15]
tithe, 5130, *ma'^{a}śēr* [13]
tithe, *NIH/RPE* [1]
your tithe^{s}, 2257, *-ô* [1]

TITHES [16]
tithes, 5130, *ma'^{a}śēr* [13]
these tithes^{s}, 5647, *-nû^{2}* [1]
collect tithes, 6923, *'āśar* [1]
receive tithes, 6923, *'āśar* [1]

TITLE [1]
bestow a title of honor, 4033, *kānâ* [1]

TIZITE [1]
Tizite, 9407, *tîṣî* [1]

TO [15370]*
to, 4200, *l^{e}-^{1}* [4730]
to, *AIT* [3395]
to, 448, *'el* [3052]

to, *NIH/RPE* [902]
to, 6330, *ʿad^{2}* [322]
to, 6584, *ʿal^{2}* [319]
to, 2025, *-â^{2}* [292]
to, 928, *b^{e}-* [281]
to, 10378, *l^{e}-* [102]
according to, 3869, *k^{e}-* [86]
to, 6640, *ʿim* [63]
according to, 4200, *l^{e}-^{1}* [61]
according to, 928, *b^{e}-* [50]
to, 4200+7156, *l^{e}-^{1}+pāneh* [50]
to, 4200+5100, *l^{e}-^{1}+maʿan* [37]
to, 4946, *min* [37]
to, 907, *ʾēt^{2}* [28]
belongs to, 4200, *l^{e}-^{1}* [28]
belong to, 4200, *l^{e}-^{1}* [25]
belonging to, 4200, *l^{e}-^{1}* [25]
to, 4200+7023, *l^{e}-^{1}+peh* [25]
in order to, 4200, *l^{e}-^{1}* [21]
to, 928+265, *b^{e}-+ʾōzen* [19]
belonged to, 4200, *l^{e}-^{1}* [16]
to, 10542, *ʿal* [16]
to, 928+3338, *b^{e}-+yād* [15]
to, 928+7754, *b^{e}-+qôl* [15]
to, 339, *ʾaḥar* [13]
to, 3869, *k^{e}-* [12]
to, 6584+3338, *ʿal^{2}+yād* [12]
to, 10621, *q^{o}dām* [11]
to, 4200+7754, *l^{e}-^{1}+qôl* [9]
to, 6643, *ʿimmād* [6]
to, 2256, *w^{e}-* [5]
to, 10427, *min* [5]
to, 928+6288, *b^{e}-+ʿ^{a}bûr^{1}* [4]
to, 928+6524, *b^{e}-+ʿayin^{1}* [4]
to, 2006, *derek* [4]
to belong, 4200, *l^{e}-^{1}* [4]
to, 906, *ʾēt^{1}* [3]
to belonged, 4200, *l^{e}-^{1}* [3]
to, 9393, *taḥat^{1}* [2]
to, 10089, *b^{e}-* [2]
to, 10554, *ʿim* [2]
according to, 10341, *k^{e}-* [1]
to, 10527, *ʿad* [1]
up to, 10527, *ʿad* [1]

TOAH [1]
Toah, 9346, *tôaḥ* [1]

TOB [4]
Tob, 3204, *ṭôb^{4}* [4]

TOB-ADONIJAH [1]
Tob-Adonijah, 3207, *ṭôb ʾ^{a}dôniyyâ* [1]

TOBIAH [14]
Tobiah, 3209, *ṭôbiyyâ* [14]

TOBIAH'S [1]
Tobiah's, 3209, *ṭôbiyyâ* [1]

TOBIJAH [3]
Tobijah, 3209, *ṭôbiyyâ* [2]
Tobijah, 3210, *ṭôbiyyāhû* [1]

TODAY [178]
today, 2021+3427, *ha-+yôm^{1}* [137]
today, 2021+3427+2021+2296, *ha-+yôm^{1}+ha-+zeh* [39]
today, 2296+3427, *zeh+yôm^{1}* [1]
today, 3427, *yôm^{1}* [1]

TOE [5]
big toe, 991, *bōhen* [5]

TOES [8]
big toes, 991, *bōhen* [2]
big toes, 8079, *regel* [2]
toes, *NIH/RPE* [1]
toes, 720, *ʾeṣbaʿ* [1]
toes, 10064+10655, *ʾeṣbaʿ+r^{e}gal* [1]
toes, 10064, *ʾeṣbaʿ* [1]

TOGARMAH [2]
Togarmah, 9328, *tōgarmâ* [2]

TOGETHER [293]
together with, 2256, *w^{e}-* [73]
together, 3481, *yaḥdāw* [57]
together, 3480, *yaḥad* [14]
together with, 6584, *ʿal^{2}* [8]
together with, 6640, *ʿim* [8]
together, *NIH/RPE* [7]
together, *AIT* [7]
brought together, 665, *ʾāsap* [4]
gathered together, 665, *ʾāsap* [4]
called together, 7695, *qābaṣ* [4]
called together, 7924, *qārāʾ^{1}* [4]
called together, 8938+2256+665, *šālaḥ+w^{e}-+ʾāsap* [4]
together, 285+448+285, *ʾeḥād+ʾel+ʾeḥād* [3]
gather together, 665, *ʾāsap* [3]
banded together, 3585, *yāʿad* [3]
brought together, 7695, *qābaṣ* [3]
gather together, 7695, *qābaṣ* [3]
came together, 7735, *qāhal* [3]
together, 9109, *š^{e}nayim* [3]
together with, 10221, *w^{e}-* [3]
together, 851+448+295, *ʾiššâ+ʾel+ʾāḥôt* [2]
together with, 2256+1685, *w^{e}-+gam* [2]
fasten together, 2489, *ḥābar^{2}* [2]
together with, 3481, *yaḥdāw* [2]
together, 3972, *kōl* [2]
hands together, 4090+448+4090, *kap+ʾel+kap* [2]
strike together, 5782, *nākâ* [2]
knit together, 6115, *sākak^{2}* [2]
came together, 7695, *qābaṣ* [2]
come together, 7695, *qābaṣ* [2]
gathered together, 7735, *qāhal* [2]
gather together, 8006, *qāšaš^{1}* [2]
together, 408+907+8276+2084, *ʾîš^{1}+ʾēt^{2}+rēaʿ^{2}+-hû* [1]
banded together, 665+4200+2021+2653, *ʾāsap+l^{e}-^{1}+ha-+ḥayyâ^{3}* [1]
be herded together, 665+669, *ʾāsap+ʾ^{a}sēpâ* [1]
called together, 665, *ʾāsap* [1]
came together, 665, *ʾāsap* [1]
got together, 665, *ʾāsap* [1]
massing together, 665, *ʾāsap* [1]
together, 665, *ʾāsap* [1]
were brought together, 665, *ʾāsap* [1]
and together, 907, *ʾēt^{2}* [1]
together with, 907, *ʾēt^{2}* [1]
together, 907, *ʾēt^{2}* [1]
together with, 928, *b^{e}-* [1]
together, 1068, *bayin* [1]
band together, 1518, *gādad^{2}* [1]
gather together, 1591, *gûr^{1}* [1]
stick together, 1815, *dābaq* [1]
talking together, 1819, *dābar^{2}* [1]
together with, 2256+6330, *w^{e}-+ʿad^{2}* [1]
together with, 2256+677, *w^{e}-+ʾap^{1}* [1]
gathered together, 2410, *zāʿaq* [1]
were called together, 2410, *zāʿaq* [1]
join together, 2489, *ḥābar^{2}* [1]
together in unity, 3480, *yaḥad* [1]
reason together, 3519, *yākaḥ* [1]
all together, 3869+408+285, *k^{e}-+ʾîš^{1}+ʾeḥād* [1]
together, 3869+285, *k^{e}-+ʾeḥād* [1]
gather together, 4043, *kānas* [1]
together with, 4200, *l^{e}-^{1}* [1]
cling together, 4334, *lākad* [1]
calling together, 5246, *miqrāʾ* [1]
called together, 5989, *nātan* [1]
sealed together, 6037+2597, *sāgar+ḥôtām^{1}* [1]
struck together, 6215, *sāpaq^{1}* [1]
flocking together, 6337, *ʿēdâ^{1}* [1]
joined together, 6641+3869+285, *ʿāmad+k^{e}-+ʾeḥād* [1]
meet together, 7008, *pāgaš* [1]
together, 7538, *ṣemed* [1]
bring together, 7695, *qābaṣ* [1]
came together, 7695+3481, *qābaṣ+yaḥdāw* [1]
gathered together, 7695, *qābaṣ* [1]
surely bring together, 7695+7695, *qābaṣ+qābaṣ* [1]
called together, 7735, *qāhal* [1]
gather together, 7735, *qāhal* [1]
is called together, 7924, *qārāʾ^{1}* [1]
came together, 7928, *qārab* [1]
was woven together, 8387, *rāqam* [1]
woven together, 8571, *śārag* [1]
calling together, 8938+2256+995, *šālaḥ+w^{e}-+bôʾ* [1]
sewed together, 9529, *tāpar* [1]
together, 10154+10378+10154, *dāʾ+l^{e}-+dāʾ* [1]

TOHU [1]
Tohu, 9375, *tōḥû* [1]

TOIL [13]
toil, 6662, *ʿāmāl^{1}* [5]
toil, 3333, *yāgaʿ* [2]
painful toil, 6779, *ʿiṣṣābôn* [2]
toil, 3330, *y^{e}gîaʿ* [1]
toil, 5951, *nāśāʾ* [1]
toil, 6665, *ʿāmēl^{2}* [1]
toil, 6776, *ʿeṣeb^{2}* [1]

TOILED [5]
toiled, 3333, *yāgaʿ* [1]
what toiled for, 3334, *yāgāʿ* [1]
toiled, 6661, *ʿāmal* [1]
what toiled for, 6662, *ʿāmāl^{1}* [1]
toiled for, 6665, *ʿāmēl^{2}* [1]

TOILING [2]
toiling, 6665, *ʿāmēl^{2}* [1]
toiling, 6776, *ʿeṣeb^{2}* [1]

TOILS [2]
toils, 6661, *ʿāmal* [2]

TOILSOME [3]
toilsome, 6662, *ʿāmāl^{1}* [2]
toilsome, 6665, *ʿāmēl^{2}* [1]

TOKEN [1]
Token, 9421, *tōken^{2}* [1]

TOKHATH [1]
Tokhath, 9534, *toqhat* [1]

TOLA [6]
Tola, 9356, *tôlāʿ^{2}* [6]

TOLAD [1]
Tolad, 9351, *tôlād* [1]

TOLAITE [1]
Tolaite, 9358, *tôlāʿî* [1]

TOLD [286]
told, 5583, *nāgad* [87]
told, 606, *ʾāmar^{1}* [84]
told, 1819, *dābar^{2}* [37]
was told, 5583, *nāgad* [23]
told, 6218, *sāpar* [17]
told, 7422, *ṣāwâ* [8]
told, 10042, *ʾ^{a}mar* [5]
told, 1821, *dābār* [4]
told, *NIH/RPE* [3]
be told, 6218, *sāpar* [2]
were told, 6218, *sāpar* [2]
be told, 606, *ʾāmar^{1}* [1]
was told, 606, *ʾāmar^{1}* [1]
told, 1819+928+265, *dābar^{2}+b^{e}-+ʾōzen* [1]
told parables, 1948, *dāmâ^{1}* [1]
told, 3359, *yādaʿ* [1]
been told about, 5583+5583, *nāgad+nāgad* [1]
been told, 5583, *nāgad* [1]
told answer, 5583, *nāgad* [1]
were clearly told, 5583+5583, *nāgad+nāgad* [1]
told, 6699, *ʿānâ^{1}* [1]
told, 8492+928+7023, *śîm+b^{e}-+peh* [1]
told, 8938+4200+606, *šālaḥ+l^{e}-^{1}+ʾāmar^{1}* [1]
told, 9048+4946+907, *šāmaʿ+min+ʾēt^{2}* [1]
told, 9048, *šāmaʿ* [1]

TOLERATE [4]
tolerate, 5564, *nābaṭ* [3]
tolerate, 5663, *nûaḥ^{1}* [1]

TOLERATED [1]
tolerated, 6641, *ʿāmad* [1]

TOMB [23]
tomb, 7700, *qeber* [16]
tomb, 7690, *q^{e}bûrâ* [5]
tomb, 1074, *bayit^{1}* [1]

tomb, 1539, *gādîš*^{2} [1]

TOMBS [9]

tombs, 7700, *qeber* [9]

TOMBSTONE [1]

tombstone, 7483, *ṣiyyûn* [1]

TOMORROW [47]

tomorrow, 4737, *māḥār* [43]
tomorrow^{s}, 2021, *ha-* [1]
tomorrow, 3427+4737, *yôm*^{1}+*māḥār* [1]
day after tomorrow, 8958, *š*^{e}*lîšî* [1]
the day after tomorrow, 8992, *šālaš* [1]

TONGS [3]

tongs, 4920, *melqāḥayim* [3]

TONGUE [71]

tongue, 4383, *lāšôn* [62]
tongue, 2674, *ḥēk* [2]
tongue, 8557, *śāpâ* [2]
tongue^{s}, 2023, *-āh* [1]
holds tongue, 3087, *ḥārēš*^{2} [1]
tongue, 3883, *kābôd*^{1} [1]
foreign tongue, 4357, *lā'az* [1]
on the tip of tongue, 4383+928+2674,
lāšôn+b^{e}*-+ḥēk* [1]

TONGUES [23]

tongues, 4383, *lāšôn* [23]

TONIGHT [11]

tonight, 2021+4326, *ha-+laylâ* [10]
stay tonight, 4328, *lîn* [1]

TOO [204]

too, 1685, *gam* [62]
too, 4946, *min* [54]
too, *NIH/RPE* [15]
too, *AIT* [11]
too, 2256, *w*^{e}*-* [9]
too, 677, *'ap*^{1} [7]
and too, 2256, *w*^{e}*-* [7]
too, 2256+1685, *w*^{e}*-+gam* [4]
too, 2256+677, *w*^{e}*-+'ap*^{1} [2]
too, 3954, *kî*^{2} [2]
too, 6584, *'al*^{2} [2]
gone too far, 8041, *rab*^{1} [2]
too much, 8425, *śāba'* [2]
too, 375, *'êk* [1]
too, 401, *'ayin*^{1} [1]
but too, 421, *'ak* [1]
too, 2180, *hinnēh* [1]
but too, 2256, *w*^{e}*-* [1]
have too little, 2893, *ḥāsēr*^{1} [1]
too easy on, 3104, *ḥāśak* [1]
too, 3869, *k*^{e}*-* [1]
too, 4027, *kēn*^{2} [1]
too heavy a burden to carry, 4202+3523+5951,
lō'+yākōl+nāśā' [1]
too, 4202, *lō'* [1]
too, 4394, *m*^{e}*'ōd* [1]
too few, 5071, *m*^{e}*'aṭ* [1]
too little, 5071, *m*^{e}*'aṭ* [1]
drink too much, 6010, *sābā'*^{1} [1]
too poor, 6123, *sākan*^{2} [1]
have too much, 6369, *'ādap* [1]
too, 7153, *pen* [1]
talks too much, 7331+8557, *pātā*^{1}*+śāpâ* [1]
too short, 7918, *qāṣar*^{2} [1]
too long, 8041, *rab*^{1} [1]
much too numerous, 8041+2256+6786,
rab^{1}*+w*^{e}*-+'āṣûm* [1]
too much, 8049, *rābâ*^{1} [1]
have too much, 8425, *śāba'* [1]
too difficult, 10330, *yaqqîr* [1]

TOOK [533]

took, 4374, *lāqaḥ* [238]
took, 995, *bô'* [22]
took, 4334, *lākad* [17]
took, *NIH/RPE* [16]
took, 5951, *nāśā'* [12]
took away, 4374, *lāqaḥ* [10]
took possession, 3769, *yāraš*^{1} [9]
took hold, 2616, *ḥāzaq* [7]
took an oath, 8678, *šāba'* [7]
took over, 3769, *yāraš*^{1} [6]
took up, 5951, *nāśā'* [6]
took, 3655, *yāṣā'* [5]
took up positions, 6885, *'ārak* [5]
took back, 8740, *šûb*^{1} [5]
took place, 2118, *hāyâ* [4]
took, 2616, *ḥāzaq* [4]
took out, 3655, *yāṣā'* [4]
took down, 3718, *yārad* [4]
took off, 6073, *sûr*^{1} [4]
took, 6590, *'ālâ* [4]
took, 8492, *śîm* [4]
took, 9530, *tāpaś* [4]
took up positions, 2837, *ḥānâ*^{1} [3]
took stand, 3656, *yāṣab* [3]
took hold, 4374, *lāqaḥ* [3]
took aside, 5742, *nāṭâ* [3]
took, 7691, *qābal* [3]
took away, 7915, *qāṣaṣ*^{1} [3]
took captive, 8647, *šābâ* [3]
took, *AIT* [2]
took hold, 296, *'āḥaz*^{1} [2]
took, 296, *'āḥaz*^{1} [2]
took, 1024, *bāzaz* [2]
took captive, 1655, *gālâ* [2]
took into exile, 1655, *gālâ* [2]
took, 2143, *hālak* [2]
took courage, 2616, *ḥāzaq* [2]
took from, 3655, *yāṣā'* [2]
took seat, 3782, *yāšab* [2]
took up residence, 3782, *yāšab* [2]
took as prisoners, 4374, *lāqaḥ* [2]
took revenge, 5933+5934, *nāqam+nāqām* [2]
took away, 6073, *sûr*^{1} [2]
took, 6073, *sûr*^{1} [2]
took places, 6641, *'āmad* [2]
took stand, 6641, *'āmad* [2]
took off, 7320, *pāšaṭ* [2]
took longer, 336, *'āḥar* [1]
took space, 430, *'ākal* [1]
took into service, 665, *'āsap* [1]
took, 665, *'āsap* [1]
took, 724, *'āṣal* [1]
took up concealed positions, 741, *'ārab* [1]
took with, 928+3338, *b*^{e}*-+yād* [1]
took, 928, *b*^{e}*-* [1]
took back, 995, *bô'* [1]
took into, 995, *bô'* [1]
took, 995+448, *bô'+'el* [1]
took as plunder, 1024, *bāzaz* [1]
took care of, 1179, *bālas* [1]
took care of, 2118+6125, *hāyâ+sōkēn* [1]
took to, 2143, *hālak* [1]
took, 2143+1583, *hālak+gôlâ* [1]
took warning, 2302, *zāhar*^{2} [1]
what took in pledge for a loan, 2478, *ḥ*^{a}*bōl* [1]
what took in pledge, 2478, *ḥ*^{a}*bōl* [1]
what took in pledge, 2481, *ḥ*^{a}*bōlâ* [1]
took some of the things, 2745, *ḥālaq*^{2} [1]
took refuge, 2879, *ḥāsâ* [1]
took to flight, 2905, *ḥāpaz* [1]
took up, 2983, *ḥāqar* [1]
took part in, 3655+4200, *yāṣā'+l*^{e}*-*^{1} [1]
took places, 3656, *yāṣab* [1]
took places, 3782, *yāšab* [1]
took place, 3782, *yāšab* [1]
took seats, 3782, *yāšab* [1]
took, 3922, *kûn*^{1} [1]
took prisoner, 4334, *lākad* [1]
took down, 4374, *lāqaḥ* [1]
took in marriage, 4374+4200+851,
lāqaḥ+l^{e}*-*^{1}*+'iššâ* [1]
took out, 4374, *lāqaḥ* [1]
took over, 4374, *lāqaḥ* [1]
took prisoner, 4374, *lāqaḥ* [1]
took a handful, 4848+4090, *mālē'*^{1}*+kap* [1]
took control, 4887, *mālak*^{1} [1]
took, 5162, *māšā'* [1]
took, 5602, *nāgaš* [1]
took care of, 5633, *nāhal* [1]
took as a good sign, 5727, *nāḥaš* [1]
took note, 5795, *nākar*^{1} [1]
took notice, 5795, *nākar*^{1} [1]
took away, 5911, *nāṣal* [1]
took away, 5951, *nāśā'* [1]
took notice, 5951+6524, *nāśā'+'ayin*^{1} [1]
took away, 6015, *sābab* [1]
took a census, 6218, *sāpar* [1]
took off, 6296, *'ābar*^{1} [1]
took, 6296, *'ābar*^{1} [1]
took up, 6590, *'ālâ* [1]
took care of, 6640, *'im* [1]
took up, 6641+6584, *'āmad+'al*^{2} [1]
took, 6641, *'āmad* [1]
took off, 7293, *pāraq* [1]
took up lament, 7801+7806, *qîn+qînâ*^{1} [1]
took note, 8011, *rā'â*^{1} [1]
took away, 8123, *rûm*^{1} [1]
took up, 8123, *rûm*^{1} [1]
took to task, 8189, *rîb*^{1} [1]
took up, 8189, *rîb*^{1} [1]
took by chariot, 8206, *rākab* [1]
took care of mixing, 8379+5351,
rāqaḥ+mirqaḥat [1]
took, 8626, *šā'al* [1]
took as prisoners, 8647+8664, *šābâ+šibyâ* [1]
took oath, 8678, *šāba'* [1]
took the oath, 8678, *šāba'* [1]
took back, 8938+2256+995, *šālaḥ+w*^{e}*-+bô'* [1]
took off, 8990, *šālap* [1]
took revenue, 9202, *šāqal* [1]
took root, 9245+9247, *šāraš+šōreš* [1]
took hold, 9461, *tāmak* [1]
took hold, 9530, *tāpaś* [1]
took seat, 10338, *y*^{e}*tib* [1]
took, 10485, *n*^{e}*paq* [1]
took up, 10513, *s*^{e}*laq* [1]
took, 10549, *'*^{a}*lal* [1]
took over, 10618, *q*^{e}*bal* [1]

TOOL [9]

iron tool, 1366, *barzel* [2]
tool, 6485, *'ēṭ* [2]
tool of iron, 1366, *barzel* [1]
tool, 2995, *ḥereb* [1]
tool, 3032, *ḥereṭ* [1]
tool, 3998, *k*^{e}*lî* [1]
tool, 5108, *ma'*^{a}*ṣād* [1]

TOOLS [1]

tools, 3086, *ḥāraš*^{1} [1]

TOOTH [9]

tooth, 9094, *šēn*^{1} [9]

TOP [83]

top, 8031, *rō'š*^{1} [45]
on top of, 6584, *'al*^{2} [8]
top, 1511, *gāg* [3]
top, 6584, *'al*^{2} [3]
top, 7550, *ṣammeret* [3]
top of head, 7721, *qodqōd* [3]
top, 4946+4200+5087+2025,
min+l^{e}*-*^{1}*+ma'al*^{2}*+-â*^{2} [2]
top, 5485, *mašqôp* [2]
top, 6609, *'elyôn*^{1} [2]
top, 7156, *pāneh* [2]
top, 10660, *rûm*^{2} [2]
top, *AIT* [1]
top of the wall, 1511, *gāg* [1]
top, 1524, *gādôl* [1]
top, 4200+5087+2025, *l*^{e}*-*^{1}*+ma'al*^{2}*+-â*^{2} [1]
top of, 4946+4200+5087+2025,
min+l^{e}*-*^{1}*+ma'al*^{2}*+-â*^{2} [1]
top, 5087+2025, *ma'al*^{2}*+-â*^{2} [1]
top, 5087, *ma'al*^{2} [1]
very top, 8123, *rûm*^{1} [1]

TOPAZ [4]

topaz, 7077, *piṭdâ* [4]

TOPHEL [1]

Tophel, 9523, *tōpel* [1]

TOPHETH [10]

Topheth, 9532, *tōpet*^{2} [9]
Topheth, 9533, *topteh* [1]

TOPMOST [3]

topmost, 8031, *rō'š*^{1} [3]

TOPPLE [3]
topple, 4572, *môṭ^{1}* [2]
topple, 5615, *nādaḥ^{1}* [1]

TOPS [14]
tops, 8031, *rō'š^{1}* [10]
tops, 1195, *bāmâ^{1}* [1]
tops of the pillars, 4117, *kaptôr^{2}* [1]
tops, 5485, *mašqôp* [1]
tops, 7550, *ṣammeret* [1]

TORCH [4]
torch, 4365, *lappîd* [4]

TORCHES [8]
torches, 4365, *lappîd* [5]
flaming torches, 2338, *zîqôt* [1]
torches, 2338, *zîqôt* [1]
flaming torches, 4365, *lappîd* [1]

TORE [40]
tore, 7973, *qāra'* [26]
tore down, 5997, *nātaṣ* [6]
tore away, 7973, *qāra'* [2]
tore open, 1324, *bāqa'* [1]
tore loose, 5825, *nāsa'* [1]
tore off, 5998, *nātaq* [1]
tore apart, 7293, *pāraq* [1]
tore apart, 7973+4200+9109+7974, *qāra'+l^{e}-^{1}+š^{e}nayim+q^{e}rā'îm* [1]
tore apart, 9117, *šāsa'* [1]

TORMENT [6]
in torment, 2813, *ḥāmar^{2}* [2]
suffers torment, 2655, *ḥîl^{1}* [1]
torment, 3324, *yāgâ^{1}* [1]
torment, 5107, *ma'^{a}ṣēbâ* [1]
torment, 6907, *'āraṣ* [1]

TORMENTED [2]
tormented, 1286, *bā'at* [1]
tormented, 6943, *'āšaq* [1]

TORMENTING [1]
tormenting, 1286, *bā'at* [1]

TORMENTORS [2]
tormentors, 3324, *yāgâ^{1}* [1]
tormentors, 9354, *tôlāl* [1]

TORN [44]
torn, 7973, *qāra'* [12]
torn by wild animals, 3274, *ṭ^{e}rēpâ* [5]
torn down, 5997, *nātaṣ* [3]
torn down, 2238, *hāras* [2]
torn out, 2740, *ḥālaṣ^{1}* [2]
torn, *NIH/RPE* [1]
torn, 1180, *bāla'^{1}* [1]
been torn off, 1655, *gālâ* [1]
are torn down, 2238, *hāras* [1]
been torn to pieces, 3271+3271, *ṭārap+ṭārap* [1]
surely been torn to pieces, 3271+3271, *ṭārap+ṭārap* [1]
torn to pieces, 3271, *ṭārap* [1]
was torn to pieces by a wild animal, 3271+3271, *ṭārap+ṭārap* [1]
torn, 3272, *ṭerep* [1]
animal torn by beasts, 3274, *ṭ^{e}rēpâ* [1]
animals torn by wild beasts, 3274, *ṭ^{e}rēpâ* [1]
torn, 5815, *nāsaḥ* [1]
been torn down, 5997, *nātaṣ* [1]
is torn, 5998, *nātaq* [1]
torn off, 5998, *nātaq* [1]
torn, 5998, *nātaq* [1]
torn open, 7204, *pāšam* [1]
torn, 7268, *pāram* [1]
torn, 9117, *šāsa'* [1]
were torn off, 10440, *m^{e}raṭ* [1]

TORRENT [3]
torrent, 5707, *naḥal^{1}* [3]

TORRENTS [8]
torrents, 8851, *šāṭap* [3]
torrents, 5707, *naḥal^{1}* [2]
torrents, 2443, *zerem* [1]
torrents, 6207, *sāpîaḥ^{2}* [1]
torrents of rain, 8852, *šeṭep* [1]

TOSS [5]
toss, 8959, *šālak* [2]
toss, 2450, *zāraq^{1}* [1]
toss about, 4570, *mûg* [1]
toss, 8425+5611, *śāba'+n^{e}dudîm* [1]

TOSSED [1]
tossed, 2450, *zāraq^{1}* [1]

TOSSES [2]
tosses, 5675, *nûa'* [2]

TOSSING [1]
tossing, 1764, *gāraš^{2}* [1]

TOTAL [23]
total, 3972, *kōl* [11]
total, 7212, *pāqad* [2]
total, *NIH/RPE* [1]
the total^{s}, 465, *'ēlleh* [1]
the total^{s}, 889, *'^{a}šer* [1]
total, 1524+4394, *gādôl+m^{e}'ōd* [1]
total, 1653, *gulgōlet* [1]
total darkness, 3125+696, *ḥōšek+'^{a}pēlâ* [1]
total, 3972+4200+5031, *kōl+l^{e}-^{1}+mispār^{1}* [1]
total wingspan, 4053+802, *kānāp+'ōrek* [1]
total, 4200, *l^{e}-^{1}* [1]
total, 7212+3972, *pāqad+kōl* [1]

TOTALED [2]
totaled, 3972, *kōl* [2]

TOTALLY [25]
totally destroyed, 3049, *ḥāram^{1}* [13]
totally destroy, 3049, *ḥāram^{1}* [3]
totally plundered, 1024+1024, *bāzaz+bāzaz* [1]
something totally new, 1375, *b^{e}rî'â* [1]
destroy totally, 3049, *ḥāram^{1}* [1]
must destroy totally, 3049+3049, *ḥāram^{1}+ḥāram^{1}* [1]
totally destroyed, 3051, *ḥērem^{1}* [1]
totally blinded, 3908+3908, *kāhâ^{1}+kāhâ^{1}* [1]
totally, 3986, *kālā^{3}* [1]
totally, 4003, *kālîl* [1]
totally destroy, 9012+9012, *šāmad+šāmad* [1]

TOTTER [1]
totter, 7048, *pûq^{1}* [1]

TOTTERING [1]
tottering, 1890, *dāḥâ* [1]

TOU [4]
Tou, 9495, *tō'û* [2]
Tou, 9497, *tō'î* [2]

TOUCH [27]
touch, 5595, *nāga'* [17]
touch, 2118+928, *hāyâ+b^{e}-* [4]
let touch, 928+995, *b^{e}-+bō'* [1]
touch, 995, *bō'* [1]
touch, 3657, *yāšag* [1]
touch, 4630, *mûš^{1}* [1]
touch, 5602, *nāgaš* [1]
touch, 5663, *nûaḥ^{1}* [1]

TOUCHED [36]
touched, 5595, *nāga'* [24]
touched, 7003, *pāga'* [6]
touched, 995+448, *bō'+'el* [1]
touched, 1816, *dābēq* [1]
touched, 2489, *ḥābar^{2}* [1]
touched, 3188, *ṭābal* [1]
touched, 5491, *māšaš* [1]
touched, 10413, *m^{e}ṭā'* [1]

TOUCHES [46]
touches, 5595, *nāga'* [43]
touches, *NIH/RPE* [1]
touches, 2118+6584, *hāyâ+'al^{2}* [1]
touches, 5491, *māšaš* [1]

TOUCHING [3]
touching, 2489, *ḥābar^{2}* [1]
touching, 5595, *nāga'* [1]
touching, 10413, *m^{e}ṭā'* [1]

TOWARD [209]
toward, 448, *'el* [57]
toward, 2025, *-â^{2}* [25]
toward, *AIT* [20]
toward, 4200, *l^{e}-^{1}* [17]
toward, 2006, *derek* [15]
toward, 6640, *'im* [10]
toward, 6584, *'al^{2}* [9]
toward, 928, *b^{e}-* [7]
toward, *NIH/RPE* [6]
toward, 4946, *min* [5]
toward, 995+3870+2025, *bō'+-kā+-â^{2}* [3]
favorably disposed toward, 2834+928+6524, *ḥēn^{1}+b^{e}+'ayin^{1}* [3]
toward, 6584+7156, *'al^{2}+pāneh* [3]
toward, 7925, *qārā'^{2}* [3]
toward, 4578, *mûl^{3}* [2]
came toward, 7925, *qārā'^{2}* [2]
toward, 339, *'aḥar* [1]
toward, 448+2006, *'el+derek* [1]
toward, 448+5790, *'el+nōkaḥ* [1]
toward, 448+7156, *'el+pāneh* [1]
toward, 907, *'ēt^{2}* [1]
toward, 995+3870, *bō'+-kā* [1]
toward it, 2178, *hēnnâ^{1}* [1]
toward evening, 3718+4394, *yārad+m^{e}'ōd* [1]
reached toward, 4369, *lāpat* [1]
favorable toward, 5162+2834+928+6524, *māṣā'+ḥēn^{1}+b^{e}+'ayin^{1}* [1]
toward, 6330+5790, *'ad^{2}+nōkaḥ* [1]
toward, 6330, *'ad^{2}* [1]
extend toward, 6584, *'al^{2}* [1]
in hostility toward, 6584+7156, *'al^{2}+pāneh* [1]
lived in hostility toward, 6584+7156+5877, *'al^{2}+pāneh+nāpal* [1]
toward, 6584+2006, *'al^{2}+derek* [1]
toward, 6584+7156+2006, *'al^{2}+pāneh+derek* [1]
toward, 6643, *'immād* [1]
toward, 7156, *pāneh* [1]
toward, 10378, *l^{e}-* [1]
toward, 10458, *neged* [1]
toward, 10542, *'al* [1]

TOWER [29]
tower, 4463, *migdāl^{1}* [28]
tower proudly, 1467, *gābah* [1]

TOWERED [4]
towered, 1467, *gābah* [3]
towered, 1468, *gābēah* [1]

TOWERING [1]
towering, 8123, *rûm^{1}* [1]

TOWERS [19]
towers, 4463, *migdāl^{1}* [13]
towers, 859, *'ošyâ* [1]
siege towers, 1032, *baḥûn* [1]
towers, 1469, *gābōah* [1]
towers, 3227, *ṭîrâ* [1]
towers, 5164, *muṣṣāb* [1]
towers, 7610, *ṣippiyyâ* [1]

TOWN [120]
town, 6551, *'îr^{1}* [100]
town, 7953, *qiryâ* [5]
town, *NIH/RPE* [3]
town, 9133, *ša'ar^{1}* [3]
the town^{s}, 2023, *-āh* [2]
town gate, 9133, *ša'ar^{1}* [2]
town^{s}, 889, *'^{a}šer* [1]
town, 1074, *bayit^{1}* [1]
town, 5226, *māqôm* [1]
each town, 6551+2256+6551, *'îr^{1}+w^{e}+'îr^{1}* [1]
town records, 9133+5226, *ša'ar^{1}+māqôm* [1]

TOWNS [287]
towns, 6551, *'îr^{1}* [262]
towns, 9133, *ša'ar^{1}* [18]
towns, *NIH/RPE* [6]
each towns, 6551+6551, *'îr^{1}+'îr^{1}* [1]

TOWNSMEN [2]
fellow townsmen, 408+6551, *'îš^{1}+'îr^{1}* [1]
fellow townsmen, 9133+6639, *ša'ar^{1}+'am^{2}* [1]

TOWNSPEOPLE [1]
townspeople, 408+6551, *'îš*[1]+*'îr*[1] [1]

TRACE [1]
trace, 10087, *'atar* [1]

TRACK [2]
track down, 2924, *ḥāpaś* [1]
keep track of, 9068, *šāmar* [1]

TRACKED [1]
tracked down, 892, *'āšur* [1]

TRACKLESS [2]
trackless, 4202+2006, *lō'+derek* [2]

TRACKS [1]
tracks, 6811, *'āqēb*[1] [1]

TRACT [1]
tract, 2754, *ḥelqâ*[2] [1]

TRACTS [1]
tracts of land, 824, *'ereṣ* [1]

TRADE [9]
trade, 6086, *sāḥar* [3]
trade, 8219, *rekullâ* [2]
ply her trade, 2388, *zānâ*[1] [1]
who trade with, 5744, *nāṭîl* [1]
trade, 6842, *'ārab*[1] [1]
trade, 9576, *taršîš*[1] [1]

TRADED [8]
traded, 8217, *rākal* [6]
traded, 5989, *nātan* [1]
traded with, 8217, *rākal* [1]

TRADERS [5]
traders, 8217, *rākal* [2]
traders, 2493, *ḥabbār* [1]
traders, 4048, *kin'ān* [1]
traders, 6086, *sāḥar* [1]

TRADING [8]
fleet of trading ships, 639+9576, *'onî+taršîš*[1] [1]
fleet of trading ships, 641+2143+9576, *'oniyyâ+hālak+taršîš*[1] [1]
fleet of trading ships, 641+4200+2143+9576, *'oniyyâ+le-[1]+hālak+taršîš*[1] [1]
fleet of trading ships, 641+9576, *'oniyyâ+taršîš*[1] [1]
trading ship, 641+9576, *'oniyyâ+taršîš*[1] [1]
trading, 6087, *saḥar* [1]
trading, 8219, *rekullâ* [1]
trading, 9455, *temûrâ* [1]

TRADITION [1]
tradition, 2976, *ḥōq* [1]

TRADITIONS [1]
traditions, 4600, *mô'ēṣâ* [1]

TRAFFICKED [1]
trafficked, 6086, *sāḥar* [1]

TRAGEDY [1]
brought tragedy, 8317, *rā'a'*[1] [1]

TRAIL [1]
leaving a trail, 8331, *rāpad* [1]

TRAIN [5]
train, 4340, *lāmad* [2]
train, 2852, *ḥānak* [1]
led in train, 8647, *šābâ* [1]
train of robe, 8767, *šûl* [1]

TRAINED [8]
trained, 4340, *lāmad* [2]
trained, 1540, *gādal* [1]
trained men, 2849, *ḥānîk* [1]
trained, 3359, *yāda'* [1]
trained, 3579, *yāsar*[1] [1]
were trained, 4340, *lāmad* [1]
trained, 6913, *'āśâ*[1] [1]

TRAINS [3]
trains, 4340, *lāmad* [3]

TRAITOR [3]
traitor, 953, *bāgad* [2]
traitor, 8004, *qešer* [1]

TRAITORS [2]
traitors, 953, *bāgad* [1]
traitors, 8745, *šôbēb* [1]

TRAMPLE [18]
trample down, 1008, *bûs* [4]
trample, 8252, *rāmas* [4]
trample, 8635, *šā'ap*[2] [2]
trample, 1008, *bûs* [1]
trample, 1424, *bāšas* [1]
trample, 1889, *dûš* [1]
trample down, 2005, *dārak* [1]
trample down, 6748, *'āsas* [1]
trample the grapes, 8097, *rādâ*[1] [1]
trample down, 8252, *rāmas* [1]
trample down, 8492+5330, *śîm+mirmās* [1]

TRAMPLED [27]
trampled, 2005, *dārak* [4]
trampled, 8252, *rāmas* [4]
trampled underfoot, 8252, *rāmas* [3]
trampled underfoot, 5330, *mirmās* [2]
trampled, 10672, *repas* [2]
trampled down, 1008, *bûs* [1]
trampled underfoot, 1008, *bûs* [1]
trampled, 1008, *bûs* [1]
be trampled, 1889, *dûš* [1]
is trampled down, 1889, *dûš* [1]
trampled down, 2150, *hālam* [1]
trampled, 4115, *kāpaš* [1]
trampled, 5330, *mirmās* [1]
what trampled, 5330+8079, *mirmās+regel* [1]
be trampled, 8252, *rāmas* [1]
trampled, 8368, *rāṣaṣ* [1]
trampled, 8392, *rāqa'* [1]

TRAMPLING [4]
trampling, 1008, *bûs* [1]
trampling, 4431, *mebûsâ* [1]
trampling, 8252, *rāmas* [1]
trampling down, 10165, *dûš* [1]

TRANQUILLITY [1]
tranquillity, 5739, *naḥat*[2] [1]

TRANS-EUPHRATES [17]
Trans-Euphrates, 10526+10468+10191, *'abar+nehar+-â* [12]
Trans-Euphrates, 6298+2021+5643, *'ēber*[1]*+ha-+nāhār* [4]
Trans-Euphrates, 10526+10468+10002, *'abar+nehar+-ā'* [1]

TRANSACTION [1]
have the transaction witnessed, 6386+6332, *'ûd*[1]*+'ēd* [1]

TRANSACTIONS [1]
method of legalizing transactions, 9496, *te'ûdâ* [1]

TRANSFER [2]
transfer, 6296, *'ābar*[1] [1]
transfer of property, 9455+3972+1821, *temûrâ+kōl+dābār* [1]

TRANSFORMED [1]
is transformed, 2200, *hāpak* [1]

TRANSGRESSED [1]
transgressed, 6296, *'ābar*[1] [1]

TRANSGRESSION [8]
transgression, 7322, *peša'* [8]

TRANSGRESSIONS [11]
transgressions, 7322, *peša'* [11]

TRANSGRESSORS [3]
transgressors, 7321, *pāša'* [3]

TRANSLATED [1]
translated, 10597, *peraš* [1]

TRANSPLANTED [1]
is transplanted, 9278, *šātal* [1]

TRANSPORT [1]
transport, 5951, *nāśā'* [1]

TRAP [15]
trap, 7062, *paḥ*[1] [4]
trap, 4613, *môqēš* [3]
trap, 744, *'ōreb* [1]
trap, 3052, *ḥērem*[2] [1]
set a trap, 3704, *yāqaš* [1]
trap, 4650, *māzôr*[2] [1]
trap, 4892, *malkōdet* [1]
set a trap, 5943, *nāqaš* [1]
trap, 8407, *rešet* [1]
trap, 8819, *šeḥût* [1]

TRAPPED [8]
was trapped, 9530, *tāpaś* [2]
are trapped, 3704, *yāqaš* [1]
been trapped, 3704, *yāqaš* [1]
are trapped, 4334, *lākad* [1]
trapped, 4334, *lākad* [1]
trapped, 4613, *môqēš* [1]
trapped, 7072, *pāḥaḥ* [1]

TRAPS [6]
traps, 4613, *môqēš* [3]
traps, 5422, *mašḥît* [1]
set traps, 5943, *nāqaš* [1]
traps, 8827, *šeḥît* [1]

TRAVEL [7]
travel, 2143, *hālak* [2]
travel, 6296, *'ābar*[1] [2]
travel along, 2143, *hālak* [1]
travel about, 3655+2256+995, *yāṣā'+we-+bô'* [1]
travel, 6296+2006, *'ābar*[1]*+derek* [1]

TRAVELED [18]
traveled, 2143, *hālak* [5]
traveled, 5825, *nāsa'* [5]
traveled, 6296, *'ābar*[1] [3]
traveled, 995, *bô'* [1]
traveled, 2006, *derek* [1]
traveled, 2143+2006, *hālak+derek* [1]
traveled from place to place, 5023, *massa'* [1]
traveled along, 6296, *'ābar*[1] [1]

TRAVELER [5]
traveler, 782, *'āraḥ*[1] [4]
traveler, 2144, *hēlek* [1]

TRAVELERS [4]
travelers, 6296, *'ābar*[1] [2]
travelers, 782, *'āraḥ*[1] [1]
travelers, 2143+5986, *hālak+netîbâ* [1]

TRAVELING [5]
traveling, 2006, *derek* [1]
traveling merchants, 2142, *halîkâ* [1]
traveling, 2143, *hālak* [1]
traveling from place to place, 5023, *massa'* [1]
traveling through, 6296, *'ābar*[1] [1]

TRAVELS [4]
travels, 5023, *massa'* [2]
travels, 6296, *'ābar*[1] [2]

TRAYS [3]
trays, 4746, *maḥtâ* [3]

TREACHEROUS [6]
treacherous, 953, *bāgad* [4]
how treacherous, 953+953, *bāgad+bāgad* [1]
treacherous, 956, *bōgedôt* [1]

TREACHEROUSLY [1]
acted treacherously, 953, *bāgad* [1]

TREACHERY [4]
treachery, 954, *beged*[1] [1]
treachery, 3950, *kāḥaš* [1]
treachery, 5086+5085, *ma'al*[1]*+mā'al* [1]
treachery, 5327, *mirmâ*[1] [1]

TREAD [5]
- tread, 2005, *dārak* [3]
- tread underfoot, 3899, *kābaš* [1]
- tread, 8252, *rāmas* [1]

TREADING [5]
- treading, 2005, *dārak* [3]
- treading out grain, 1889, *dûš* [1]
- treading, 8252, *rāmas* [1]

TREADS [6]
- treads, 2005, *dārak* [4]
- treads, 995, *bôʾ* [1]
- treads out, 2005, *dārak* [1]

TREASON [4]
- treason, 8004, *qešer* [4]

TREASURE [9]
- treasure, 238, *ʾôṣār* [2]
- treasure, 2773, *ḥāmad* [2]
- hidden treasure, 4759, *maṭmôn* [2]
- treasure, 2890, *ḥōsen* [1]
- treasure, 4759, *maṭmôn* [1]
- treasure, 6035, *s^{e}gullâ* [1]

TREASURED [9]
- treasured possession, 6035, *s^{e}gullâ* [6]
- treasured, 4718, *maḥmād* [1]
- treasured place, 7621, *ṣāpan* [1]
- treasured, 7621, *ṣāpan* [1]

TREASURER [1]
- treasurer, 1601, *gizbār* [1]

TREASURERS [5]
- treasurers, 4837, *makkār* [2]
- treasurers, 10133, *g^{e}dābar* [2]
- treasurers, 10139, *gizbar* [1]

TREASURES [38]
- treasures, 238, *ʾôṣār* [22]
- treasures, 4718, *maḥmād* [4]
- treasures, 3998+2775, *k^{e}lî+ḥemdâ* [2]
- treasures, 2104, *hôn* [1]
- treasures, 2890, *ḥōsen* [1]
- treasures, 3702, *y^{e}qār* [1]
- treasures, 4719, *maḥmōd* [1]
- treasures, 4819, *mikmān* [1]
- hidden treasures, 5208, *maṣpôn* [1]
- personal treasures, 6035, *s^{e}gullâ* [1]
- treasures, 6965, *ʿātûd* [1]
- treasures, 7621, *ṣāpan* [1]
- treasures hidden, 8561+3243, *śāpan+ṭāman* [1]

TREASURIES [20]
- treasuries, 238, *ʾôṣār* [20]

TREASURY [14]
- treasury, 238, *ʾôṣār* [7]
- treasury, 1709, *genez*[1] [2]
- treasury, 1074+238, *bayit*[1]*+ʾôṣār* [1]
- treasury, 10103+10148, *bayit+g^{e}naz* [1]
- treasury, 10103, *bayit* [1]
- treasury, 10148, *g^{e}naz* [1]
- treasury, 10479, *n^{e}kas* [1]

TREAT [22]
- treat, 6913, *ʿāśâ*[1] [7]
- treat, 5989, *nātan* [3]
- treat, *NIH/RPE* [1]
- treat with honor, 2290, *zābal* [1]
- treat well, 3512, *yāṭab* [1]
- treat with contempt, 5540, *nāʾaṣ* [1]
- treat with contempt, 5571, *nābal*[2] [1]
- treat with respect, 5692, *nāzar*[1] [1]
- treat as a slave, 6683, *ʿāmar*[2] [1]
- treat as enemies, 7675, *ṣārar*[2] [1]
- treat with contempt, 7837, *qālal* [1]
- treat worse, 8317, *rāʿaʿ*[1] [1]
- treat, 8492, *śîm* [1]
- treat, 8883, *šît*[1] [1]

TREATED [27]
- treated, 6913, *ʿāśâ*[1] [8]
- treated, 1694, *gāmal* [2]
- treated well, 3512, *yāṭab* [2]
- treated with contempt, 5540, *nāʾaṣ* [2]
- be treated as, 2118, *hāyâ* [1]
- treated, 2118+6640, *hāyâ+ʿim* [1]
- treated, 2118, *hāyâ* [1]
- arrogantly treated, 2326, *zîd* [1]
- treated arrogantly, 2326, *zîd* [1]
- treated as, 3869, *k^{e}-* [1]
- treated the same as, 4200+6645, *l^{e}-*[1]*+ʿummâ*[1] [1]
- treated, 5989, *nātan* [1]
- treated harshly, 6618, *ʿālal*[1] [1]
- treated, 6618, *ʿālal*[1] [1]
- treated, 6913+6640, *ʿāśâ*[1]*+ʿim* [1]
- treated as enemies, 7675, *ṣārar*[2] [1]
- treated with contempt, 7837, *qālal* [1]

TREATING [5]
- treating, *AIT* [1]
- treating, *NIH/RPE* [1]
- treating, 2118, *hāyâ* [1]
- treating with contempt, 2725, *ḥālal*[1] [1]
- treating with contempt, 5540, *nāʾaṣ* [1]

TREATMENT [2]
- shameful treatment, 4007, *kālam* [1]
- harsh treatment, 9500, *taʿ^{a}lûlîm* [1]

TREATMENTS [3]
- beauty treatments, 9475, *tamrûq* [2]
- beauty treatments, 5299, *m^{e}rûqîm* [1]

TREATS [4]
- treats with contempt, 3070, *ḥārap*[2] [1]
- treats, 3108, *ḥāšab* [1]
- treats as a slave, 6683, *ʿāmar*[2] [1]
- treats harshly, 7998, *qāšaḥ* [1]

TREATY [31]
- treaty, 1382, *b^{e}rît* [26]
- treaty of friendship, 8934+2256+3208, *šālôm+w^{e}-+ṭôbâ* [2]
- made a treaty of peace, 8966, *šālēm*[1] [2]
- make a treaty, 4162, *kārat* [1]

TREE [130]
- tree, 6770, *ʿēṣ* [61]
- fig tree, 9300, *t^{e}ʾēnâ* [15]
- olive tree, 2339, *zayit* [8]
- tree, 10027, *ʾîlān* [6]
- great tree, 471, *ʾēlôn*[1] [4]
- oak tree, 461, *ʾēlâ*[1] [3]
- tamarisk tree, 869, *ʾēšel* [3]
- pine tree, 1360, *b^{e}rôš* [3]
- broom tree, 8413, *rōtem* [3]
- apple tree, 9515, *tappûaḥ*[1] [3]
- tree, *NIH/RPE* [2]
- almond tree, 9196, *šāqēd* [2]
- palm tree, 9469, *tāmār*[1] [2]
- palm tree decorations, 9474, *timōrâ* [2]
- palm tree, 9474, *timōrâ* [2]
- great tree, 461, *ʾēlâ*[1] [1]
- tree, 461, *ʾēlâ*[1] [1]
- large tree, 471, *ʾēlôn*[1] [1]
- tree, 471, *ʾēlôn*[1] [1]
- tree, 7771, *qôrâ* [1]
- pomegranate tree, 8232, *rimmôn*[1] [1]
- green tree, 8316, *raʿ^{a}nān* [1]
- tree, 8413, *rōtem* [1]
- tree, 9300, *t^{e}ʾēnâ* [1]
- palm tree designs, 9474, *timōrâ* [1]
- that tree^{s}, 10200, *hûʾ* [1]

TREES [128]
- trees, 6770, *ʿēṣ* [69]
- palm trees, 9474, *timōrâ* [14]
- fig trees, 9300, *t^{e}ʾēnâ* [6]
- sycamore-fig trees, 9204, *šiqmâ* [5]
- trees, *NIH/RPE* [4]
- great trees, 471, *ʾēlôn*[1] [4]
- balsam trees, 1132, *bākāʾ*[1] [4]
- pine trees, 1360, *b^{e}rôš* [4]
- olive trees, 2339, *zayit* [4]
- myrtle trees, 2072, *h^{a}das* [3]
- plane trees, 6895, *ʿermôn* [2]
- palm trees, 9469, *tāmār*[1] [2]
- nut trees, 100, *ʾ^{e}gôz* [1]
- olive trees, 2339+3658, *zayit+yiṣhār*[1] [1]
- olives from trees, 2339, *zayit* [1]
- trees, 6785, *ʿēṣâ*[3] [1]
- poplar trees, 6857, *ʿ^{a}rābâ*[1] [1]
- lofty trees, 8123+7757, *rûm*[1]*+qômâ* [1]
- fig trees, 9204, *šiqmâ* [1]

TREMBLE [39]
- tremble, 8074, *rāgaz* [7]
- tremble, 8321, *rāʿaš*[1] [6]
- tremble, 3006, *ḥārad* [5]
- tremble, 2655, *ḥîl*[1] [4]
- made tremble, 8321, *rāʿaš*[1] [2]
- tremble, 987, *bāhal* [1]
- makes tremble, 1286, *bāʿat* [1]
- make tremble, 2316, *zûaʿ* [1]
- tremble, 2316, *zûaʿ* [1]
- tremble, 2362, *zālal*[2] [1]
- tremble, 2714, *ḥalḥālâ* [1]
- tremble, 3007, *ḥārēd* [1]
- tremble, 5675, *nûaʿ* [1]
- made tremble, 6001, *nātar*[2] [1]
- tremble, 7064, *pāḥad* [1]
- makes tremble, 7145, *pālaṣ* [1]
- made tremble, 8074, *rāgaz* [1]
- make tremble, 8074, *rāgaz* [1]
- tremble, 8173, *rāḥap*[1] [1]
- tremble, 8323, *raʿaš* [1]

TREMBLED [15]
- trembled, 1723, *gāʿaš* [4]
- trembled, 3006, *ḥārad* [4]
- trembled, 8074, *rāgaz* [2]
- trembled, 2362, *zālal*[2] [1]
- trembled violently, 3006+3010+1524+6330+4394, *ḥārad+h^{a}rādâ*[1]*+gādôl+ʿad*[2]*+m^{e}ʾōd* [1]
- trembled, 3007, *ḥārēd* [1]
- trembled, 5675, *nûaʿ* [1]
- trembled, 8417, *r^{e}ṭēṭ* [1]

TREMBLES [13]
- trembles, 8321, *rāʿaš*[1] [4]
- trembles, 3007, *ḥārēd* [2]
- trembles, 2655, *ḥîl*[1] [1]
- trembles, 3006, *ḥārad* [1]
- trembles, 5951, *nāśāʾ* [1]
- trembles, 6169, *sāmar* [1]
- trembles, 7064, *pāḥad* [1]
- trembles, 8074, *rāgaz* [1]
- trembles, 8283, *rāʿad* [1]

TREMBLING [17]
- trembling, 8285, *r^{e}ʿādâ* [4]
- come trembling, 3004, *ḥārag* [2]
- come trembling, 3006, *ḥārad* [2]
- trembling, 3006, *ḥārad* [2]
- trembling, 8284, *raʿad* [2]
- set trembling, 5675, *nûaʿ* [1]
- come trembling, 7064, *pāḥad* [1]
- trembling, 7146, *pallāṣût* [1]
- come trembling, 8074, *rāgaz* [1]
- trembling, 8283, *rāʿad* [1]

TRENCH [4]
- trench, 9498, *t^{e}ʿālâ*[1] [3]
- trench, 3022, *ḥārûṣ*[2] [1]

TRESSES [1]
- tresses, 8111, *rahaṭ*[2] [1]

TRIAL [4]
- trial, 5477, *mišpāṭ* [2]
- standing trial, 6641, *ʿāmad* [1]
- brought to trial, 9149, *šāpaṭ* [1]

TRIALS [2]
- trials, 4999, *massâ*[1] [2]

TRIBAL [18]
- tribal, 4751, *maṭṭeh* [8]
- tribal, *NIH/RPE* [3]
- tribal, 8657, *šēbeṭ* [3]
- tribal, 569, *ʾummâ* [2]
- tribal divisions, 4713, *maḥ^{a}lōqet* [2]

TRIBE [181]
tribe, 4751, *maṭṭeh* [124]
tribe, 8657, *šēbeṭ* [44]
tribe, *NIH/RPE* [2]
tribe, 1074, *bayit*^{1} [2]
tribe of Benjamin, 1228, *binyāmîn* [2]
tribe^s, 2257, *-ô* [2]
tribe of Benjamin, 408+3549, *'îš*^{1}*+y*^{e}*mînî* [1]
tribe, 1201, *bēn*^{1} [1]
the tribe^s, 2257, *-ô* [1]
tribe of Manasseh, 4985, *m*^{e}*naššeh* [1]
tribe, 7259, *pirḥaḥ* [1]

TRIBES [103]
tribes, 8657, *šēbeṭ* [74]
tribes, 4751, *maṭṭeh* [21]
tribes, *NIH/RPE* [2]
tribes, 1074, *bayit*^{1} [2]
tribes, 1201, *bēn*^{1} [1]
tribes, 4722, *maḥ*^{a}*neh* [1]
desert tribes, 7470, *ṣî*^{2} [1]
tribes, 10694, *š*^{e}*baṭ* [1]

TRIBUTE [27]
tribute, 4966, *minḥâ* [13]
tribute, 4830, *mekes* [6]
tribute, 10107, *b*^{e}*lô* [3]
tribute, *NIH/RPE* [2]
tribute, 4989, *mas* [1]
tribute, 5362, *maśśā'*^{1} [1]
subject to tribute, 5957, *nāšā'*^{1} [1]

TRICKING [1]
tricking, 9506, *tā'a'* [1]

TRIED [18]
tried, 1335, *bāqaš* [5]
tried, *AIT* [4]
tried, 1043, *bāḥan* [1]
tried to take, 1335, *bāqaš* [1]
tried, 3108, *ḥāšab* [1]
tried, 3283, *yā'al*^{2} [1]
tried, 5814, *nāsâ* [1]
tried, 6913+4027, *'āśâ*^{1}*+kēn*^{2} [1]
is tried, 9149, *šāpaṭ* [1]
tried, 9365+928+4213, *tûr+b*^{e}*-+lēb* [1]
tried, 10114, *b*^{e}*'â* [1]

TRIES [1]
tries, *AIT* [1]

TRIFLING [1]
trifling, 5070, *mā'aṭ* [1]

TRIM [2]
trim, 6913, *'āśâ*^{1} [1]
trim off, 10635, *q*^{e}*ṣaṣ* [1]

TRIMMED [6]
trimmed beams, 4164, *k*^{e}*rutôt* [3]
trimmed, 1760, *gārar* [1]
keep hair trimmed, 4080+4080, *kāsam+kāsam* [1]
trimmed, 6913, *'āśâ*^{1} [1]

TRIMMERS [8]
wick trimmers, 4662, *m*^{e}*zammeret* [5]
wick trimmers, 4920, *melqāḥayim* [3]

TRIP [1]
trip, 1890, *dāḥâ* [1]

TRIPOLIS [1]
men from Tripolis, 10305, *ṭarp*^{e}*lāy* [1]

TRIPPING [1]
tripping along with mincing steps, 2143+2256+3262, *hālak+w*^{e}*-+ṭāpap* [1]

TRIUMPH [22]
triumph, *NIH/RPE* [4]
triumph, 1504, *gābar* [3]
triumph, 6600, *'ālaz* [2]
triumph, 6636, *'ālaṣ* [2]
shout in triumph, 8131, *rûa'* [2]
triumph, 8934, *šālôm* [2]
triumph, 1452, *ga'*^{a}*wâ* [1]
surely triumph, 3523+3523, *yākōl+yākōl* [1]
triumph, 6451, *'āzaz* [1]
shout in triumph, 6702+2116, *'ānâ*^{4}*+hêdād* [1]
let triumph, 8123, *rûm*^{1} [1]
triumph, 8123, *rûm*^{1} [1]
triumph, 8131, *rûa'* [1]

TRIUMPHAL [1]
led in triumphal procession, 5627, *nāhag*^{1} [1]

TRIUMPHANT [1]
triumphant, 6451, *'āzaz* [1]

TRIUMPHED [3]
triumphed, 1540, *gādal* [1]
triumphed, 2616, *ḥāzaq* [1]
triumphed, 8123, *rûm*^{1} [1]

TRIVIAL [2]
considered trivial, 7837, *qālal* [1]
trivial, 7837, *qālal* [1]

TROD [2]
trod, 2005, *dārak* [1]
trod down, 8252, *rāmas* [1]

TRODDEN [2]
trodden, 2005, *dārak* [2]

TROOP [2]
troop, 1522, *g*^{e}*dûd*^{2} [2]

TROOPS [64]
troops, 6639, *'am*^{2} [31]
troops, 111, *'*^{a}*gap* [7]
troops, 1522, *g*^{e}*dûd*^{2} [5]
troops, 2657, *ḥayil* [4]
troops, 4722, *maḥ*^{a}*neh* [3]
troops, *AIT* [2]
troops, 7372, *ṣābā'*^{2} [2]
troops, 9180, *šip'â* [2]
picked troops, 129, *'addîr* [1]
troops, 1201+1522, *bēn*^{1}*+g*^{e}*dûd*^{2} [1]
troops, 1475+2657, *gibbôr+ḥayil* [1]
marshal troops, 1518, *gādad*^{2} [1]
troops with banners, 1839, *dāgal*^{2} [1]
your troops^s, 2157, *-hem* [1]
troops, 2162, *hāmôn* [1]
troops, 4422, *ma'*^{a}*rāb* [1]

TROUBLE [112]
trouble, 7650, *ṣārâ*^{1} [24]
trouble, 8288, *rā'â*^{3} [17]
trouble, 6662, *'āmāl*^{1} [15]
trouble, 7639, *ṣar*^{1} [11]
trouble, 8273, *ra'*^{1} [8]
brings trouble, 6579, *'ākar* [4]
brought trouble, 6579, *'ākar* [3]
brought trouble, 8317, *rā'a'*^{1} [3]
trouble, 1314, *baṣṣārâ* [2]
bring trouble, 6579, *'ākar* [2]
made trouble, 6579, *'ākar* [2]
trouble, *NIH/RPE* [1]
in trouble, 208, *'ôy* [1]
trouble, 224, *'āwen*^{1} [1]
trouble, 1821, *dābār* [1]
gone to trouble, 3006+3010, *ḥārad+ḥ*^{a}*rādâ*^{1} [1]
trouble, 4087, *kā'as* [1]
trouble, 5126, *ma'*^{a}*śeh* [1]
making trouble, 6662, *'āmāl*^{1} [1]
trouble, 6776, *'eṣeb*^{2} [1]
trouble, 7441, *ṣôq* [1]
trouble, 7442, *ṣûqâ* [1]
gave trouble, 7674, *ṣārar*^{1} [1]
trouble, 7674, *ṣārar*^{1} [1]
give trouble, 7675, *ṣārar*^{2} [1]
in trouble, 7997+3427, *qāšeh+yôm*^{1} [1]
trouble, 8075, *rōgez* [1]
trouble, 8113, *rûd* [1]
bring trouble, 8317, *rā'a'*^{1} [1]
trouble came, 8317, *rā'a'*^{1} [1]
trouble, 8739, *šô'â* [1]
trouble, 9360, *tō'â* [1]

TROUBLED [12]
troubled, 7192, *pā'am* [3]
troubled, 928+6524+8273, *b*^{e}*-+'ayin*^{1}*+ra'*^{1} [1]
troubled, 1793, *dā'ag* [1]
troubled, 3013, *ḥārâ*^{1} [1]
troubled, 6946, *'ošqâ* [1]
deeply troubled, 7997+8120, *qāšeh+rûaḥ* [1]
troubled thoughts, 8546, *śe'ippîm* [1]
troubled, 9200+4202+3523, *šāqaṭ+lō'+yākōl* [1]
troubled, 10097, *b*^{e}*hal* [1]
troubled, 10369, *k*^{e}*râ* [1]

TROUBLEMAKER [1]
troublemaker, 408+1175, *'îš*^{1}*+b*^{e}*liyya'al* [1]

TROUBLEMAKERS [2]
troublemakers, 1175, *b*^{e}*liyya'al* [1]
troublemakers, 1201+1175, *bēn*^{1}*+b*^{e}*liyya'al* [1]

TROUBLER [1]
troubler, 6579, *'ākar* [1]

TROUBLES [14]
troubles, 7650, *ṣārâ*^{1} [8]
troubles, 8288, *rā'â*^{3} [4]
troubles, 4200, *l*^{e}*-*^{1} [1]
troubles, 7192, *pā'am* [1]

TROUBLESOME [1]
troublesome, 10472, *n*^{e}*zaq* [1]

TROUBLING [3]
troubling, *NIH/RPE* [1]
troubling, 2169, *hāmam*^{1} [1]
what is troubling, 4537, *mâ* [1]

TROUGH [3]
kneading trough, 5400, *miš'eret* [2]
trough, 9216, *šōqet* [1]

TROUGHS [5]
kneading troughs, 5400, *miš'eret* [2]
troughs, 8110, *rahaṭ*^{1} [2]
troughs, 8110+9216, *rahaṭ*^{1}*+šōqet* [1]

TROUSERS [1]
trousers, 10582, *paṭṭîš* [1]

TRUDGE [1]
trudge, 2143, *hālak* [1]

TRUE [58]
true, 622, *'emet* [20]
true, 597, *'omnām* [4]
true, 4027, *kēn*^{2} [4]
true, *NIH/RPE* [3]
comes true, 995, *bô'* [3]
not true, 9214, *šeqer* [3]
come true, 586, *'āman*^{1} [2]
come true, 995, *bô'* [2]
true, 593, *'omnâ*^{1} [1]
true to plumb, 643, *'*^{a}*nāk* [1]
true, 677, *'ap*^{1} [1]
comes true, 995+995, *bô'+bô'* [1]
certainly come true, 2118+2118, *hāyâ+hāyâ* [1]
right and true, 3838, *yāšār*^{1} [1]
true, 3970, *kākâ* [1]
found to be true, 5162, *māṣā'* [1]
true, 7406, *ṣedeq* [1]
proved true, 7671, *ṣārap* [1]
come true, 7936, *qārâ*^{1} [1]
true, 7999, *qōšṭ* [1]
true wisdom, 9370, *tûšiyyâ* [1]
is it true, 10190+10609, *h*^{a}*-+ṣ*^{e}*dā'* [1]
know the true meaning, 10326, *y*^{e}*ṣab* [1]
true meaning, 10327, *yaṣṣîb* [1]
true, 10327, *yaṣṣîb* [1]

TRULY [5]
truly, 928+622, *b*^{e}*-+'emet* [2]
truly, 434, *'ākēn*^{1} [1]
truly, 3954, *kî*^{2} [1]
truly, 4026, *kēn*^{1} [1]

TRUMPET [48]
trumpet, 8795, *šôpār* [44]
trumpet, 8795+9558, *šôpār+t*^{e}*rû'â* [1]
trumpet, 9540, *tāqôa'* [1]
trumpet blasts, 9558, *t*^{e}*rû'â* [1]
trumpet blast, 9558, *t*^{e}*rû'â* [1]

TRUMPETERS [4]
trumpeters, 2956, ḥᵃṣōṣᵉrâ [3]
trumpeters, 2955, ḥaṣṣar [1]

TRUMPETS [50]
trumpets, 2956, ḥᵃṣōṣᵉrâ [25]
trumpets, 8795, šôpār [18]
trumpets, 8795+3413, šôpār+yôbēl [3]
blew trumpets, 2955, ḥaṣṣar [1]
trumpets, 7967+3413, qeren+yôbēl [1]
blow trumpets, 9546, tāqaʿ [1]
sound the trumpets, 9558, tᵉrûʿâ [1]

TRUST [79]
trust, 1053, bāṭaḥ[1] [45]
trust, 586, ʾāman[1] [8]
put trust, 1053, bāṭaḥ[1] [4]
trust, 4440, mibṭāḥ [4]
trust, 4073, kesel[2] [3]
places trust, 586, ʾāman[1] [2]
put trust, 586, ʾāman[1] [2]
let persuade to trust, 1053, bāṭaḥ[1] [2]
trust, 2879, ḥāsâ [2]
trust, NIH/RPE [1]
trust, 575, ʾᵉmûnâ [1]
made trust, 1053, bāṭaḥ[1] [1]
persuaded to trust, 1053, bāṭaḥ[1] [1]
trust, 1057, biṭḥâ [1]
trust, 2349, zākar[1] [1]
put trust, 7747, qāwâ[1] [1]

TRUSTED [21]
trusted, 1053, bāṭaḥ[1] [10]
trusted, 7747, qāwâ[1] [2]
trusted friends, 408+8934, ʾîš[1]+šālôm [1]
be trusted, 586, ʾāman[1] [1]
trusted advisers, 586, ʾāman[1] [1]
trusted, 586, ʾāman[1] [1]
be trusted, 3922, kûn[1] [1]
trusted in, 4438, mabbāṭ [1]
trusted, 4440, mibṭāḥ [1]
trusted, 10041, ʾᵃman [1]
trusted, 10665, rᵉḥaṣ [1]

TRUSTFULLY [1]
trustfully, 4200+1055, lᵉ-[1]+beṭaḥ[1] [1]

TRUSTING [4]
trusting, 1053, bāṭaḥ[1] [2]
trusting, 586, ʾāman[1] [1]
stop trusting in, 2532+4946, ḥādal[1]+min [1]

TRUSTS [18]
trusts, 1053, bāṭaḥ[1] [15]
trusts, 586, ʾāman[1] [1]
trusts, 1670, gālal[1] [1]
trusts in, 4073, kesel[2] [1]

TRUSTWORTHY [12]
trustworthy, 586, ʾāman[1] [4]
trustworthy, 575, ʾᵉmûnâ [2]
trustworthy, 622, ʾᵉmet [2]
trustworthy, 10041, ʾᵃman [2]
trustworthy, 574, ʾēmûn[2] [1]
trustworthy, 586+8120, ʾāman[1]+rûaḥ [1]

TRUTH [41]
truth, 622, ʾᵉmet [29]
truth, 575, ʾᵉmûnâ [6]
truth, 589, ʾāmēn [2]
truth, 7406, ṣedeq [2]
truth, 3838, yāšār[1] [1]
truth, 9459, tāmîm [1]

TRUTHFUL [6]
truthful, 622, ʾᵉmet [3]
truthful, 575, ʾᵉmûnâ [2]
truthful, 574, ʾēmûn[2] [1]

TRY [14]
try, *AIT* [5]
try patience, 4206, lāʾâ [2]
try, *NIH/RPE* [1]
try, 237, ʾûṣ [1]
try to find, 1335, bāqaš [1]
try to get, 1335, bāqaš [1]
try, 5814, nāsâ [1]
try again, 8740, šûb[1] [1]
try, 10503, sᵉbar [1]

TRYING [14]
trying, *AIT* [6]
trying, 1335, bāqaš [3]
trying to take, 1335, bāqaš [2]
trying to pick a quarrel, 628, ʾānâ[2] [1]
trying to get, 1335, bāqaš [1]
trying to, 1335, bāqaš [1]

TUBAL [8]
Tubal, 9317, tubal [8]

TUBAL-CAIN [1]
Tubal-Cain, 9340, tûbal qayin [1]

TUBAL-CAIN'S [1]
Tubal-Cain's, 9340, tûbal qayin [1]

TUBES [1]
tubes, 692, ʾāpîq[1] [1]

TUCK [3]
tuck cloak into belt, 2520+5516, ḥāgar+motnayim [2]
tuck away, 7443, ṣûr[1] [1]

TUCKED [1]
cloak tucked into belt, 5516+2520, motnayim+ḥāgar [1]

TUCKING [1]
tucking cloak into belt, 9113+5516, šānas+motnayim [1]

TUMBLES [1]
tumbles, 5877, nāpal [1]

TUMBLEWEED [2]
tumbleweed, 1650, galgal[2] [2]

TUMBLING [1]
came tumbling, 2200, hāpak [1]

TUMORS [8]
tumors, 6754, ʿōpel[1] [6]
tumors, 3224, ṭᵉḥōrîm [2]

TUMULT [6]
tumult, 2159, hāmâ [1]
tumult, 2162, hāmôn [1]
tumult, 4539, mᵉhûmâ [1]
tumult, 7754+2167, qôl+hᵃmullâ [1]
great tumult, 8623, šāʾôn[2] [1]
tumult, 8623, šāʾôn[2] [1]

TUNE [12]
tune, *NIH/RPE* [11]
tune, 7754, qôl [1]

TUNED [1]
tuned to, 4200, lᵉ-[1] [1]

TUNIC [11]
tunic, 4189, kuttōnet [5]
tunic, 4496, mad [3]
tunic, 955, beged[2] [2]
military tunic, 4496+4230, mad+lᵉbûš [1]

TUNICS [6]
tunics, 4189, kuttōnet [6]

TUNNEL [1]
tunnel, 9498, tᵉʿālâ[1] [1]

TUNNELS [1]
tunnels, 3284+1324, yᵉʾōr+bāqaʿ [1]

TURBAN [15]
turban, 5200, miṣnepet [11]
turban, 7565, ṣānîp [3]
turban, 6996, pᵉʾēr [1]

TURBANS [4]
turbans, 6996, pᵉʾēr [2]
turbans, 3178, ṭᵉbûlîm [1]
turbans, 10368, karbᵉlâ [1]

TURBULENT [1]
turbulent, 7070, paḥaz [1]

TURMOIL [7]
turmoil, 4539, mᵉhûmâ [3]
turmoil, 8075, rōgez [3]
turmoil, 2162, hāmôn [1]

TURN [284]
turn, 8740, šûb[1] [50]
turn back, 8740, šûb[1] [34]
turn away, 6073, sûr[1] [22]
turn, 7155, pānâ [18]
turn away, 8740, šûb[1] [15]
turn, 5742, nāṭâ [12]
turn, 6073, sûr[1] [10]
turn, 6015, sābab [9]
turn, 2200, hāpak [8]
turn, *NIH/RPE* [7]
turn, 8492, śîm [7]
turn aside, 6073, sûr[1] [6]
turn to prostitution, 2388, zānâ[1] [3]
turn aside, 5742, nāṭâ [3]
turn, 5989, nātan [3]
in turn, 1685, gam [2]
turn to, 2118, hāyâ [2]
in turn, 2256, wᵉ- [2]
turn to the right, 3554, yāman [2]
turn, 3922, kûn[1] [2]
turn, 5048, māʿad [2]
made turn, 5989, nātan [2]
turn into, 5989, nātan [2]
turn over, 5989, nātan [2]
turn about, 6015, sābab [2]
turn over, 6296, ʿābar[1] [2]
turn, 8474, śāṭâ [2]
turn into, 8492, śîm [2]
turn around, 8740, šûb[1] [2]
turn away, 8740+8740, šûb[1]+šûb[1] [2]
turn, 8883, šît[1] [2]
turn, 9366, tôr[1] [2]
turn, 9543, tᵉqûpâ [2]
turn, 995, bôʾ [1]
turn, 1182, bālaʿ[3] [1]
turn against, 2118+4200+8477, hāyâ+lᵉ-[1]+śāṭān [1]
turn into, 2200, hāpak [1]
turn upside down, 2201, hēpek [1]
turn a deaf ear, 3087, ḥārēš[2] [1]
turn to wailing, 3536, yālal [1]
turn away, 3697, yāqaʿ [1]
turn into, 4200, lᵉ-[1] [1]
turn aside, 4369, lāpat [1]
turn away, 5412, mᵉšûbâ [1]
turn from, 5412, mᵉšûbâ [1]
turn away, 5615, nādaḥ[1] [1]
turn, 5615, nādaḥ[1] [1]
turn away, 5742, nāṭâ [1]
turn of events, 5813, nᵉsibbâ [1]
turn, 5951, nāśāʾ [1]
make turn, 5989+448, nātan+ʾel [1]
turn against, 6015, sābab [1]
turn away, 6015+7156, sābab+pāneh [1]
turn over, 6015, sābab [1]
turn of events, 6016, sibbâ [1]
turn away, 6047, sûg[1] [1]
turn back, 6047, sûg[1] [1]
turn, 6047, sûg[1] [1]
turn into foolishness, 6118, sākal [1]
turn away, 6296, ʿābar[1] [1]
turn from, 6440, ʿāzab[1] [1]
turn away, 6623, ʿālam [1]
turn in fear, 7064, pāḥad [1]
turn around, 7155, pānâ [1]
turn back, 7155, pānâ [1]
turn to help, 7155, pānâ [1]
in turn, 7756, qûm [1]
turn, 8011, rāʿâ[1] [1]
turn, 8123, rûm[1] [1]
turn aside, 8454, śûṭ [1]
caused to turn, 8492, śîm [1]
turn again, 8740, šûb[1] [1]
make turn, 8883, šît[1] [1]
turn away, 9120, šāʿâ [1]

TURNED [221]
turned, 7155, *pānâ* [27]
turned, 2200, *hāpak* [21]
turned, 8740, *šûb*[1] [16]
turned away, 8740, *šûb*[1] [13]
turned, 6015, *sābab* [12]
turned away, 6073, *sûr*[1] [10]
turned back, 8740, *šûb*[1] [10]
turned, 5742, *nāṭâ* [7]
be turned, 6047, *sûg*[1] [5]
turned, 6073, *sûr*[1] [5]
turned aside, 6073, *sûr*[1] [4]
turned, 8492, *śîm* [4]
turned away, 5742, *nāṭâ* [3]
turned, 5989, *nātan* [3]
turned around, 8740, *šûb*[1] [3]
turned, 9305, *tāʿar*[1] [3]
turned into, 2118+4200, *hāyâ+l^e-*[1] [2]
be turned, 2200, *hāpak* [2]
turned back, 2200, *hāpak* [2]
turned, 2319, *zûr*[2] [2]
turned away in disgust, 3697, *yāqaʿ* [2]
turned away in disgust, 5936, *nāqaʿ* [2]
turned around, 6015, *sābab* [2]
turned away, 6015, *sābab* [2]
turned in, 6073, *sûr*[1] [2]
turned back, 7155, *pānâ* [2]
turned into, 8615, *šāʾâ*[1] [2]
turned, 10731, *š^{e}nâ*[1] [2]
turned, *AIT* [1]
turned, *NIH/RPE* [1]
turned the other way, 345, *ʾ^{a}ḥōrannît* [1]
turned in sockets, 1664, *gālîl*[1] [1]
turned out, 2118, *hāyâ* [1]
turned, 2118, *hāyâ* [1]
turned, 2143, *hālak* [1]
been turned over, 2200, *hāpak* [1]
the tables were turned, 2200, *hāpak* [1]
turned about, 2200+3338, *hāpak+yād* [1]
turned and became, 2200, *hāpak* [1]
turned around, 2200, *hāpak* [1]
turned into, 2200, *hāpak* [1]
turned over, 2200, *hāpak* [1]
was turned, 2200, *hāpak* [1]
turned to prostitution, 2388, *zānâ*[1] [1]
turned, 2565, *ḥûl*[1] [1]
turned, 3585, *yāʿad* [1]
turned out, 3655, *yāṣāʾ* [1]
to turned, 4200, *l^e-*[1] [1]
turned a deaf ear, 4202+263, *lōʾ+ʾāzan*[1] [1]
turned, 4369, *lāpat* [1]
places where turned loose, 5448, *mišlāḥ* [1]
turned and ran, 5674, *nûs* [1]
turned aside, 5742, *nāṭâ* [1]
turned away, 5936, *nāqaʿ* [1]
turned into, 5989, *nātan* [1]
turned over, 5989, *nātan* [1]
turned, 5989+7156, *nātan+pāneh* [1]
be turned over, 6015, *sābab* [1]
turned over, 6015, *sābab* [1]
turned, 6015+7156, *sābab+pāneh* [1]
turned over, 6037, *sāgar* [1]
turned away, 6047, *sûg*[1] [1]
turned, 6047, *sûg*[1] [1]
turned aside, 6296, *ʿābar*[1] [1]
turned crooked, 6835, *ʿāqaš* [1]
turned around, 7155, *pānâ* [1]
turned away, 7155, *pānâ* [1]
turned, 7155+8900, *pānâ+š^{e}kem*[1] [1]
turned, 7756, *qûm* [1]
as it turned out, 7936+5247, *qārāʾ*[1]*+miqreh* [1]
turned into, 8492, *śîm* [1]
turned, 8492+7156, *śîm+pāneh* [1]
turned again, 8740, *šûb*[1] [1]
turned to go, 8740, *šûb*[1] [1]
turned, 8883, *šît*[1] [1]
turned, 8938, *šālaḥ* [1]
turned, 10513, *s^{e}laq* [1]
turned into, 10682, *śîm* [1]
be turned into, 10702, *š^{e}wâ* [1]

TURNING [25]
turning, 6015, *sābab* [3]
turning aside, 6073, *sûr*[1] [3]
turning, 6073, *sûr*[1] [3]
turning, 7155, *pānâ* [3]
turning from, 4946, *min* [2]
turning, 8740, *šûb*[1] [2]
turning, *NIH/RPE* [1]
turning, 2143, *hālak* [1]
turning, 2200, *hāpak* [1]
turning away, 5086, *maʿal*[1] [1]
turning aside, 5742, *nāṭâ* [1]
turning, 5742, *nāṭâ* [1]
turning, 6047, *sûg*[1] [1]
turning, 7992, *qāšab* [1]
turning away, 8740, *šûb*[1] [1]

TURNS [37]
turns away, 8740, *šûb*[1] [7]
turns, 8740, *šûb*[1] [7]
turns, 7155, *pānâ* [3]
turns into light, 5585, *nāgah* [2]
turns, 6015, *sābab* [2]
turns away, 7155, *pānâ* [2]
turns, *NIH/RPE* [1]
take turns, 2143+3427, *hālak+yôm*[1] [1]
turns into a fool, 2147, *hālal*[3] [1]
turns, 2200, *hāpak* [1]
take turns, 5005, *massāḥ* [1]
turns, 5989, *nātan* [1]
turns away, 6073, *sûr*[1] [1]
turns, 6073, *sûr*[1] [1]
turns into nonsense, 6118, *sākal* [1]
turns, 6493, *ʿāṭap*[1] [1]
turns to gloom, 6845, *ʿārab*[4] [1]
turns to, 6913, *ʿāśâ*[1] [1]
turns back, 7155, *pānâ* [1]
turns pale, 7695+6999, *qābaṣ+pāʾrûr* [1]

TURQUOISE [6]
turquoise, 5876, *nōpek* [4]
turquoise, 7037, *pûk* [2]

TUSKS [1]
tusks, 7967, *qeren* [1]

TWELFTH [22]
twelfth, 9109+6925, *š^{e}nayim+ʿāśār* [15]
twelfth, 9109+6926, *š^{e}nayim+ʿeśrēh* [7]

TWELVE [84]
twelve, 9109+6925, *š^{e}nayim+ʿāśār* [51]
twelve, 9109+6926, *š^{e}nayim+ʿeśrēh* [29]
twelve, 10775+10573, *t^{e}rên+ʿ^{a}śar* [2]
twelve hundred, 547+2256+4395, *ʾelep*[2]*+w^e-+mēʾâ*[1] [1]
twelve, 9109, *š^{e}nayim* [1]

TWENTIETH [9]
twentieth, 6929, *ʿeśrîm* [9]

TWENTY [121]
twenty, 6929, *ʿeśrîm* [119]
twenty feet, 2822+6926+564, *ḥāmēš+ʿeśrēh+ʾammâ*[1] [1]
hundred and twenty thousand, 9109+6926+8052, *š^{e}nayim+ʿeśrēh+ribbôʾ* [1]

TWENTY-EIGHT [4]
twenty-eight, 6929+2256+9046, *ʿeśrîm+w^e-+š^{e}mōneh* [2]
twenty-eight, 9046+2256+6929, *š^{e}mōneh+w^e-+ʿeśrîm* [2]

TWENTY-FIFTH [3]
twenty-fifth, 6929+2256+2822, *ʿeśrîm+w^e-+ḥāmēš* [3]

TWENTY-FIRST [4]
twenty-first, 285+2256+6929, *ʾeḥād+w^e-+ʿeśrîm* [3]
twenty-first, 6929+2256+285, *ʿeśrîm+w^e-+ʾeḥād* [1]

TWENTY-FIVE [23]
twenty-five, 6929+2256+2822, *ʿeśrîm+w^e-+ḥāmēš* [16]
twenty-five, 2822+2256+6929, *ḥāmēš+w^e-+ʿeśrîm* [7]

TWENTY-FOUR [5]
twenty-four, 6929+2256+752, *ʿeśrîm+w^e-+ʾarbaʿ*[1] [5]

TWENTY-FOURTH [9]
twenty-fourth, 6929+2256+752, *ʿeśrîm+w^e-+ʾarbaʿ*[1] [7]
twenty-fourth, 752+2256+6929, *ʾarbaʿ*[1]*+w^e-+ʿeśrîm* [2]

TWENTY-NINE [5]
twenty-nine, 6929+2256+9596, *ʿeśrîm+w^e-+tēšaʿ* [5]

TWENTY-ONE [4]
twenty-one, 6929+2256+285, *ʿeśrîm+w^e-+ʾeḥād* [4]

TWENTY-SECOND [2]
twenty-second, 9109+2256+6929, *š^{e}nayim+w^e-+ʿeśrîm* [2]

TWENTY-SEVEN [4]
twenty-seven, 6929+2256+8679, *ʿeśrîm+w^e-+šebaʿ*[1] [2]
twenty-seven hundred, 547+2256+8679+4395, *ʾelep*[2]*+w^e-+šebaʿ*[1]*+mēʾâ*[1] [1]
twenty-seven feet, 9046+6926+564, *š^{e}mōneh+ʿeśrēh+ʾammâ*[1] [1]

TWENTY-SEVENTH [6]
twenty-seventh, 6929+2256+8679, *ʿeśrîm+w^e-+šebaʿ*[1] [5]
twenty-seventh, 8679+2256+6929, *šebaʿ*[1]*+w^e-+ʿeśrîm* [1]

TWENTY-SIX [2]
twenty-six hundred, 547+2256+9252+4395, *ʾelep*[2]*+w^e-+šēš*[1]*+mēʾâ*[1] [1]
twenty-six, 6929+2256+9252, *ʿeśrîm+w^e-+šēš*[1] [1]

TWENTY-SIXTH [1]
twenty-sixth, 6929+2256+9252, *ʿeśrîm+w^e-+šēš*[1] [1]

TWENTY-THIRD [7]
twenty-third, 8993+2256+6929, *šālōš+w^e-+ʿeśrîm* [4]
twenty-third, 6929+2256+8993, *ʿeśrîm+w^e-+šālōš* [3]

TWENTY-THREE [6]
twenty-three, 6929+2256+8993, *ʿeśrîm+w^e-+šālōš* [3]
twenty-three, 8993+2256+6929, *šālōš+w^e-+ʿeśrîm* [3]

TWENTY-TWO [15]
twenty-two, 6929+2256+9109, *ʿeśrîm+w^e-+š^{e}nayim* [15]

TWICE [15]
twice, 7193, *paʿam* [5]
twice as much, 5467, *mišneh* [4]
twice, 9109, *š^{e}nayim* [2]
strike twice, 4100, *kāpal* [1]
twice, 5467, *mišneh* [1]
twice over, 7193, *paʿam* [1]
strike twice, 9101, *šānâ*[1] [1]

TWIG [1]
twig, 7913, *qeṣep*[2] [1]

TWIGS [2]
twigs, 2173, *h^{a}māsîm* [1]
twigs, 7908, *qāṣîr*[2] [1]

TWILIGHT [14]
at twilight, 1068+2021+6847, *bayin+ha-+ʿereb*[2] [11]
twilight, 5974, *nešep* [3]

TWIN [5]
twin, 9339, *tôʾ^{a}mîm* [3]
has twin, 9298, *tāʾam* [2]

TWINS [1]
twins, 9339, *tô'amîm* [1]

TWIST [1]
twist, 6772, *'āṣab*[2] [1]

TWISTED [23]
finely twisted, 8813, *šāzar* [21]
twisted, 2502, *ḥābaš* [1]
is twisted, 6430, *'āwat* [1]

TWISTING [1]
twisting, 4790, *mîṣ* [1]

TWISTS [3]
twists, 6156, *sālap* [2]
twists, 2655, *ḥîl*[1] [1]

TWO [478]
two, 9109, *šenayim* [374]
two, *AIT* [75]
two, *NIH/RPE* [6]
two kinds, 3977, *kil'ayim* [3]
two, 2942, *ḥaṣî* [2]
two, 7538, *ṣemed* [2]
two differing weights, 74+2256+74, *'eben+we-+'eben* [1]
two differing measures, 406+2256+406, *'êpâ+we-+'êpâ* [1]
two[s], 465, *'ēlleh* [1]
the two of them[s], 1192+2256+1189, *bālāq+we-+bil'ām*[1] [1]
cut in two, 1615, *gāzar*[1] [1]
two[s], 2021, *ha-* [1]
two[s], 3427, *yôm*[1] [1]
two men, 3481+408+2256+278, *yaḥdāw+'îš*[1]*+we-+'āḥ*[2] [1]
two sides, 4101, *kepel* [1]
two hundred, 4395, *mē'â*[1] [1]
two handfuls, 4850+2908, *melō'+ḥōpen* [1]
two saddlebags, 5478, *mišpetayim* [1]
two thirds of a shekel, 7088, *pîm* [1]
two[s], 8169, *raḥamâ* [1]
two at a time, 9109+9109, *šenayim+šenayim* [1]
two, 9348, *tāwek* [1]

TWO-AND-A-HALF [1]
two-and-a-half, 9109+2256+2942, *šenayim+we-+ḥaṣî* [1]

TWO-HORNED [2]
two-horned, 1251+2021+7967, *ba'al*[1]*+ha-+qeren* [2]

TWO-TENTHS [11]
two-tenths, 9109+6928, *šenayim+'iśśārôn* [11]

TWO-THIRDS [1]
two-thirds, 7023+9109, *peh+šenayim* [1]

TYING [1]
tying, 7674, *ṣārar*[1] [1]

TYPE [2]
type, *AIT* [2]

TYRANNICAL [1]
tyrannical, 8041+5131, *rab*[1]*+ma'ašaqqôt* [1]

TYRANNY [1]
tyranny, 6945, *'ōšeq* [1]

TYRE [48]
Tyre, 7450, *ṣōr* [42]
Tyre, *NIH/RPE* [1]
Tyre[s], 2023, *-āh* [1]
men from Tyre, 7660, *ṣōrî* [1]
Tyre, 7660, *ṣōrî* [1]
from Tyre, 7660, *ṣōrî* [1]
of Tyre, 7660, *ṣōrî* [1]

TYRIANS [1]
Tyrians, 7660, *ṣōrî* [1]

UCAL [1]
Ucal, 432, *'ukāl* [1]

UEL [1]
Uel, 198, *'û'ēl* [1]

UGLY [7]
ugly, 8273, *ra'*[1] [3]
ugly, 8273+5260, *ra'*[1]*+mar'eh* [2]
ugly, 8273+9307, *ra'*[1]*+tō'ar* [1]
ugly, 8278, *rōa'* [1]

ULAI [2]
Ulai, 217, *'ûlay*[1] [2]

ULAM [4]
Ulam, 220, *'ûlām*[2] [4]

ULLA [1]
Ulla, 6587, *'ullā'* [1]

UMMAH [1]
Ummah, 6646, *'ummâ*[2] [1]

UNABLE [6]
unable, 4202, *lō'* [2]
unable, 1194, *biltî* [1]
unable, 4202+3523, *lō'+yākōl* [1]
unable to support, 4572+3338, *môṭ*[1]*+yād* [1]
unable, 10379+10321, *lā'+yekil* [1]

UNAFRAID [1]
unafraid, 4202+7064, *lō'+pāḥad* [1]

UNANSWERED [2]
returned unanswered, 2668+8740, *ḥêq+šûb*[1] [1]
go unanswered, 4202+6699, *lō'+'ānâ*[1] [1]

UNAUTHORIZED [4]
unauthorized, 2424, *zār* [3]
unauthorized person, 2424, *zār* [1]

UNAWARE [6]
unaware of, 6623+4946, *'ālam+min* [3]
unaware, 4202+3359, *lō'+yāda'* [2]
unaware, 6623+4946+6524, *'ālam+min+'ayin*[1] [1]

UNBORN [1]
yet unborn, 3528, *yālad* [1]

UNBOUND [1]
unbound, 10742, *šerâ* [1]

UNCEASING [1]
unceasing, 1194+6239, *biltî+sārâ*[1] [1]

UNCEASINGLY [1]
unceasingly, 4202+1949, *lō'+dāmâ*[2] [1]

UNCHANGED [5]
unchanged, 6641, *'āmad* [2]
unchanged, 9393+6641, *taḥat*[1]*+'āmad* [2]
unchanged, 4202+4614, *lō'+mûr*[1] [1]

UNCHECKED [1]
flamed unchecked, 9068+5905, *šāmar+nēṣaḥ*[1] [1]

UNCIRCUMCISED [29]
uncircumcised, 6888, *'ārēl* [29]

UNCLE [12]
uncle, 1856, *dôd* [11]
uncle, 278, *'āḥ*[2] [1]

UNCLE'S [1]
uncle's, 278+562, *'āḥ*[2]*+'ēm* [1]

UNCLEAN [186]
unclean, 3238, *ṭāmē'*[2] [64]
unclean, 3237, *ṭāmē'*[1] [62]
ceremonially unclean, 3238, *ṭāmē'*[2] [12]
pronounce unclean, 3237, *ṭāmē'*[1] [8]
unclean, 3240, *ṭum'â* [6]
ceremonially unclean, 3237, *ṭāmē'*[1] [3]
make himself unclean, 3237, *ṭāmē'*[1] [3]
unclean, 4202+3196, *lō'+ṭāhôr* [3]
unclean thing, 5614, *niddâ* [3]
unclean, 1458, *gā'al*[2] [2]
make himself ceremonially unclean, 3237, *ṭāmē'*[1] [2]
make yourselves unclean, 3237, *ṭāmē'*[1] [2]
unclean, *NIH/RPE* [1]
unclean, 401+3196, *'ayin*[1]*+ṭāhôr* [1]
ceremonially unclean, 1194+3196, *biltî+ṭāhôr* [1]
be made unclean, 3237, *ṭāmē'*[1] [1]
make unclean, 3237, *ṭāmē'*[1] [1]
pronounce ceremonially unclean, 3237, *ṭāmē'*[1] [1]
pronounce unclean, 3237+3237, *ṭāmē'*[1]*+ṭāmē'*[1] [1]
pronounced unclean, 3237, *ṭāmē'*[1] [1]
remains unclean, 3237+3238, *ṭāmē'*[1]*+ṭāmē'*[2] [1]
ceremonially unclean, 3240, *ṭum'â* [1]
things that make unclean, 3240, *ṭum'â* [1]
unclean practices, 3240, *ṭum'â* [1]
unclean, 4202+3197, *lō'+ṭāhēr* [1]
unclean, 5765, *nîdâ* [1]
unclean meat, 7002, *piggûl* [1]
unclean, 7002, *piggûl* [1]

UNCLEANNESS [17]
uncleanness, 3240, *ṭum'â* [16]
woman's monthly uncleanness, 3240+2021+5614, *ṭum'â+ha-+niddâ* [1]

UNCONCERNED [1]
unconcerned, 8932+9200, *šalwâ+šāqaṭ* [1]

UNCOVER [2]
uncover, 1655, *gālâ* [2]

UNCOVERED [9]
uncovered, 1655, *gālâ* [4]
uncovered, 401+4064, *'ayin*[1]*+kesût* [1]
was uncovered, 1655, *gālâ* [1]
uncovered, 5162, *māṣā'* [1]
uncovered, 6880+6423, *'eryâ+'ûr*[2] [1]
uncovered, 8011, *rā'â*[1] [1]

UNCOVERS [2]
uncovers, 6867, *'ārâ*[1] [1]
uncovers, 7337, *pātaḥ*[1] [1]

UNCUT [2]
uncut, 4202+7786, *lō'+qāṭap* [1]
uncut, 8969, *šālēm*[2] [1]

UNDEPENDABLE [1]
undependable, 953, *bāgad* [1]

UNDER [280]
under, 9393, *taḥat*[1] [150]
under, 928, *be-* [33]
under, 6584, *'al*[2] [15]
under, 4200, *le-*[1] [10]
under, *NIH/RPE* [8]
under, 4946+9393, *min+taḥat*[1] [7]
under, *AIT* [6]
under, 10757, *teḥôt* [4]
under, 928+3338, *be-+yād* [3]
under, 4946, *min* [3]
put under oath, 8678, *šāba'* [3]
under, 448, *'el* [2]
under a curse, 826, *'ārar* [2]
under, 4200+7156, *le-*[1]*+pāneh* [2]
under head, 5265, *mera'ašôt* [2]
under, 10089, *be-* [2]
under the command of, 339, *'aḥar* [1]
bound under an oath, 457, *'ālâ*[1] [1]
put under oath, 460+9048, *'ālâ*[4]*+šāma'* [1]
under, 889, *'ašer* [1]
under care, 907, *'ēt*[2] [1]
under, 907+7156, *'ēt*[2]*+pāneh* [1]
under, 907, *'ēt*[2] [1]
under cover, 928+9564, *be-+tormâ* [1]
under control, 928+294, *be-+'āḥôr* [1]
under oath, 1251+8652, *ba'al*[1]*+šebû'â* [1]
under the wrath, 2404, *zā'am* [1]
under wrath, 2404, *zā'am* [1]
under care, 3338, *yād* [1]
was brought under control, 3899, *kābaš* [1]
under direction, 4200+7156, *le-*[1]*+pāneh* [1]
under blessing, 4200+7156, *le-*[1]*+pāneh* [1]
under supervision, 4200+7156, *le-*[1]*+pāneh* [1]
under, 4200+1074, *le-*[1]*+bayit*[1] [1]

under, 4946+3338, *min+yād* [1]
under, 4946+7156, *min+pāneh* [1]
under guard, 5466, *mišmeret* [1]
under guard, 6584+5464, *ʿal^{2}+mišmār^{1}* [1]
been under, 6590+6584, *ʿālâ+ʿal^{2}* [1]
under siege, 7443, *ṣûr^{1}* [1]
bound under a strict oath, 8678+8678, *šābaʿ+šābaʿ* [1]
under siege, 9068, *šāmar* [1]
under construction, 10111, *b^{e}nâ* [1]
under obligation, 10420+10419, *m^{e}laḥ^{2}+m^{e}laḥ^{1}* [1]

UNDERFOOT [11]
trampled underfoot, 8252, *rāmas* [3]
trampled underfoot, 5330, *mirmās* [2]
underfoot, 10089+10655, *b^{e}-+r^{e}gal* [2]
underfoot, 928+8079, *b^{e}-+regel* [1]
trampled underfoot, 1008, *bûs* [1]
tread underfoot, 3899, *kābaš* [1]
underfoot, 9393+8079, *taḥat^{1}+regel* [1]

UNDERGARMENTS [5]
undergarments, 4829, *miknās* [4]
undergarments, 4829+965, *miknās+bad^{3}* [1]

UNDERGO [1]
undergo circumcision, 4576+906+1414+6889, *mûl^{1}+ʾēt^{1}+bāśār+ʿorlâ* [1]

UNDERGROWTH [2]
undergrowth, 580, *ʾāmîr* [1]
undergrowth, 3017, *ḥārûl* [1]

UNDERLINGS [2]
underlings, 5853, *naʿar^{2}* [2]

UNDERMINE [1]
undermine, 7296, *pārar^{1}* [1]

UNDERNEATH [4]
underneath, 9393, *taḥat^{1}* [2]
underneath, 4946+1074, *min+bayit^{1}* [1]
underneath, 4946+9393, *min+taḥat^{1}* [1]

UNDERSIDES [1]
undersides, 9393, *taḥat^{1}* [1]

UNDERSTAND [67]
understand, 1067, *bîn* [29]
understand, 3359, *yādaʿ* [15]
understand, 9048, *šāmaʿ* [8]
understand, 8505, *śākal^{1}* [6]
understand, 10313, *y^{e}daʿ* [2]
let understand, 1067, *bîn* [1]
quick to understand, 1067+4529, *bîn+maddāʿ* [1]
understand clearly, 1067+1069, *bîn+bînâ* [1]
understand, 1069, *bînâ* [1]
must understand, 3359+3359, *yādaʿ+yādaʿ* [1]
understand, 3359+1069, *yādaʿ+bînâ* [1]
understand, 8011, *rāʾâ^{1}* [1]

UNDERSTANDING [99]
understanding, 9312, *t^{e}bûnâ* [28]
understanding, 1069, *bînâ* [24]
understanding, 1067, *bîn* [11]
understanding, 4213, *lēb* [5]
give understanding, 1067, *bîn* [4]
have understanding, 1067, *bîn* [4]
understanding, 3359, *yādaʿ* [4]
understanding, 8507, *śekel* [4]
understanding, 8505, *śākal^{1}* [3]
gain understanding, 1067, *bîn* [2]
gives understanding, 1067, *bîn* [2]
understanding, 4222, *lēbāb* [2]
understanding, 1981, *daʿat^{1}* [1]
no understanding, 5572, *nābāl^{1}* [1]
beyond understanding, 7100, *pilʾî* [1]
gave understanding, 8505, *śākal^{1}* [1]
showed understanding, 8505+8507, *śākal^{1}+śekel* [1]
understanding, 10684, *śokl^{e}tānû* [1]

UNDERSTANDS [6]
understands, 1067, *bîn* [4]
understands, 3359, *yādaʿ* [1]
understands, 8505, *śākal^{1}* [1]

UNDERSTOOD [9]
understood, 1067, *bîn* [5]
understood, 3359, *yādaʿ* [2]
understood, 3359+1069, *yādaʿ+bînâ* [1]
understood, 9419, *tākan* [1]

UNDERTAKEN [2]
undertaken, 6913, *ʿāśâ^{1}* [2]

UNDERTAKES [1]
undertakes, 7756, *qûm* [1]

UNDERTOOK [4]
undertook great, 1540, *gādal* [1]
undertook, 2725, *ḥālal^{1}* [1]
undertook, 3655, *yāṣāʾ* [1]
undertook, 5126, *maʿ^{a}śeh* [1]

UNDESERVED [1]
undeserved, 2855, *ḥinnām* [1]

UNDESIRABLE [1]
undesirable, 8273, *raʿ^{1}* [1]

UNDETECTED [1]
undetected, 6259, *sātar* [1]

UNDIGNIFIED [1]
become undignified, 7837, *qālal* [1]

UNDISCIPLINED [1]
undisciplined, 7346, *p^{e}tayyût* [1]

UNDISTURBED [2]
undisturbed, 8633, *šaʾ^{a}nān* [1]
undisturbed, 8922, *šālâ^{1}* [1]

UNDIVIDED [3]
undivided, 285, *ʾeḥād* [1]
give undivided, 3479, *yāḥad* [1]
undivided loyalty, 4202+4213+2256+4213, *lōʾ+lēb+w^{e}-+lēb* [1]

UNDOING [2]
undoing, 4745, *m^{e}ḥittâ* [1]
undoing, 5422, *mašḥît* [1]

UNDONE [1]
left undone, 6073, *sûr^{1}* [1]

UNDULY [1]
unduly, 4946+3841, *min+yōšer* [1]

UNEATEN [1]
uneaten, 4202+1180, *lōʾ+bālaʿ^{1}* [1]

UNENDING [1]
unending, 5905, *nēṣaḥ^{1}* [1]

UNEXPECTEDLY [1]
unexpectedly, 7328, *pitʾōm* [1]

UNFAILING [35]
unfailing love, 2876, *ḥesed^{2}* [32]
unfailing kindness, 2876, *ḥesed^{2}* [3]

UNFAITHFUL [50]
unfaithful, 953, *bāgad* [16]
unfaithful, 5085, *māʿal* [13]
unfaithful, 5085+5086, *māʿal+maʿal^{1}* [6]
unfaithful, 2388, *zānâ^{1}* [5]
unfaithful, 957, *bāgôd* [2]
unfaithful, 8745, *šôbēb* [2]
utterly unfaithful, 953+953, *bāgad+bāgad* [1]
unfaithful, 3950, *kāḥaš* [1]
unfaithful, 4202+574, *lōʾ+ʾēmûn^{2}* [1]
most unfaithful, 5085+5086, *māʿal+maʿal^{1}* [1]
unfaithful, 5086+5085, *maʿal^{1}+māʿal* [1]
more and more unfaithful, 8049+5085+5086, *rābâ^{1}+māʿal+maʿal^{1}* [1]

UNFAITHFULLY [3]
acted unfaithfully, 5085+5086, *māʿal+maʿal^{1}* [2]
acted unfaithfully, 5085, *māʿal* [1]

UNFAITHFULNESS [12]
unfaithfulness, 5086, *maʿal^{1}* [6]
unfaithfulness, 2393, *z^{e}nûnîm* [1]
unfaithfulness, 2394, *z^{e}nût* [1]
unfaithfulness guilty of, 5086+5085, *maʿal^{1}+māʿal* [1]
unfaithfulness showed, 5086+5085, *maʿal^{1}+māʿal* [1]
unfaithfulness, 5086+5085, *maʿal^{1}+māʿal* [1]
unfaithfulness, 5538, *naʿ^{a}pûpîm* [1]

UNFAMILIAR [1]
unfamiliar, 4202+3359, *lōʾ+yādaʿ* [1]

UNFANNED [1]
unfanned, 4202+5870, *lōʾ+nāpaḥ* [1]

UNFAVORABLE [1]
unfavorable, 8273, *raʿ^{1}* [1]

UNFEELING [1]
unfeeling, 3263, *ṭāpaš* [1]

UNFILLED [1]
unfilled, 8200, *rêqām* [1]

UNFOLDING [1]
unfolding, 7340, *pētaḥ* [1]

UNFORMED [1]
unformed body, 1677, *gōlem* [1]

UNFRIENDLY [1]
unfriendly, 7233, *pārad* [1]

UNFULFILLED [1]
hope unfulfilled, 3498, *yāḥal* [1]

UNFURLED [1]
be unfurled, 5824, *nāsas^{2}* [1]

UNGODLINESS [2]
ungodliness, 2869, *ḥōnep* [1]
ungodliness, 2870, *ḥ^{a}nuppâ* [1]

UNGODLY [5]
ungodly, 2868, *ḥānēp^{3}* [3]
ungodly, 4202+2883, *lōʾ+ḥāsîd* [1]
ungodly, 8401, *rāšāʿ* [1]

UNHARMED [4]
unharmed, 928+8934, *b^{e}-+šālôm* [1]
unharmed, 3208, *ṭôbâ* [1]
unharmed, 8934, *šālôm* [1]
unharmed, 10244+10379+10029, *ḥ^{a}bāl+lāʾ+ʾîtay* [1]

UNHEARD-OF [2]
unheard-of, 285, *ʾeḥād* [1]
unheard-of, 7098, *pālāʾ* [1]

UNINTENTIONAL [1]
unintentional wrong, 8705, *š^{e}gāgâ* [1]

UNINTENTIONALLY [17]
unintentionally, 928+8705, *b^{e}-+š^{e}gāgâ* [6]
unintentionally, 928+1172+1981, *b^{e}-+b^{e}lî+daʿat^{1}* [4]
sins unintentionally, 8706, *šāgâ* [2]
unintentionally, 928+4202+7402, *b^{e}-+lōʾ+ṣ^{e}diyyâ* [1]
unintentionally, 4200+8705, *l^{e-1}+š^{e}gāgâ* [1]
sins unintentionally, 6913+928+8705, *ʿāśâ^{1}+b^{e}-+š^{e}gāgâ* [1]
wrong committed unintentionally, 8705+8704, *š^{e}gāgâ+šāgag* [1]
unintentionally, 8706, *šāgâ* [1]

UNION [2]
Union, 2482, *ḥōb^{e}lîm* [2]

UNIQUE [2]
unique, 285, *ʾeḥād* [2]

UNISON [1]
in unison, 3869+285, *k^{e}-+ʾeḥād* [1]

UNIT [5]
unit, 285, *ʾeḥād* [4]

unit, 548, *'elep3* [1]

UNITE [3]
unite, 2118+4222+4200+3480, *hāyâ+lēbāb+le-1+yaḥad* [1]
unite, 4848, *mālē'1* [1]
unite, 6202, *sāpaḥ1* [1]

UNITED [3]
united, 1815, *dābaq* [1]
united, 2492, *ḥābēr* [1]
united, 10158+10180+10554+10180, *debaq+denâ+'im+denâ* [1]

UNITS [13]
units of a hundred, 4395, *mē'â1* [6]
units of a thousand, 547, *'elep2* [2]
units of hundreds, 4395, *mē'â1* [2]
units of 1,000, 547, *'elep2* [1]
units, 548, *'elep3* [1]
units, 4722, *maḥaneh* [1]

UNITY [2]
unity, 285, *'eḥād* [1]
together in unity, 3480, *yaḥad* [1]

UNJUST [14]
unjust, 4202+9419, *lō'+tākan* [4]
unjust gain, 1299, *beṣa'* [2]
unjust, 224, *'āwen1* [1]
make unjust gain, 1298+1299, *bāṣa'+beṣa'* [1]
make unjust gain, 1298, *bāṣa'* [1]
unjust, 4202+5477, *lō'+mišpāṭ* [1]
unjust, 6404, *'āwel* [1]
unjust, 6405, *'awwāl* [1]
unjust, 6406, *'awlâ* [1]
unjust, 8273, *ra'1* [1]

UNJUSTLY [1]
unjustly, 4202+4026, *lō'+kēn1* [1]

UNKEMPT [3]
unkempt, 7277, *pāra'2* [3]

UNKNOWN [3]
unknown, 4202+3359, *lō'+yāda'* [3]

UNLEASH [3]
unleash, 1324, *bāqa'* [1]
unleash, 7046, *pûṣ1* [1]
unleash, 8938, *šālaḥ* [1]

UNLEASHED [2]
unleashed, 8938, *šālaḥ* [2]

UNLEASHES [1]
unleashes, 9223, *šārâ1* [1]

UNLEAVENED [22]
unleavened bread, 5174, *maṣṣâ1* [20]
Feast of Unleavened Bread, 5174, *maṣṣâ1* [1]
unleavened, 5174, *maṣṣâ1* [1]

UNLESS [24]
unless, 3954+561, *kî2+'im* [6]
unless, 561+4202, *'im+lō'* [4]
unless, *NIH/RPE* [2]
unless, 1194, *biltî* [2]
unless, 4295, *lûlē'* [2]
unless, 401, *'ayin1* [1]
unless, 561+4202+3954, *'im+lō'+kî2* [1]
unless, 1194+561, *biltî+'im* [1]
unless, 2022+4202, *ha-+lō'* [1]
unless, 2180, *hinnēh* [1]
unless, 3954+561+4200+7156, *kî2+'im+le-1+pāneh* [1]
unless, 4202, *lō'* [1]
unless, 10386, *lāhēn2* [1]

UNLIKE [7]
unlike, 4202+3869, *lō'+ke-* [4]
unlike, *NIH/RPE* [1]
unlike, 4202+6913+4027, *lō'+'āśâ1+kēn2* [1]
unlike, 4202, *lō'* [1]

UNLOADED [1]
unloaded, 7337, *pātaḥ1* [1]

UNLOCKED [1]
unlocked, 7337, *pātaḥ1* [1]

UNLOVED [2]
unloved, 8533, *śānē'* [2]

UNMARRIED [3]
unmarried, 1435, *betûlâ* [1]
unmarried, 4202+2118+4200+408, *lō'+hāyâ+le-1+'îš1* [1]
remain unmarried, 6328+4200+1194+2118+4200+408, *'āgan+le-1+biltî+hāyâ+le-1+'îš1* [1]

UNMINDFUL [1]
unmindful, 8894, *šākaḥ* [1]

UNNI [3]
Unni, 6716, *'unnî* [3]

UNNOTICED [2]
unnoticed, 928+2021+4319, *be-+ha-+lāṭ* [1]
unnoticed, 4946+1172+8492, *min+belî+śîm* [1]

UNPLOWED [3]
unplowed ground, 5776, *nîr3* [2]
lie unplowed, 9023, *šāmaṭ* [1]

UNPRODUCTIVE [2]
make unproductive, 8897, *šākal* [1]
unproductive, 8897, *šākal* [1]

UNPROFITABLE [1]
unprofitable, 4202+3603, *lō'+yā'al* [1]

UNPROTECTED [2]
unprotected, 6872, *'erwâ* [2]

UNPUNISHED [18]
go unpunished, 5927, *nāqâ* [9]
leave the guilty unpunished, 5927+5927, *nāqâ+nāqâ* [3]
let go entirely unpunished, 5927+5927, *nāqâ+nāqâ* [2]
unpunished, 4202+870, *lō'+'āšam* [1]
go unpunished, 5927+5927, *nāqâ+nāqâ* [1]
indeed go unpunished, 5927+5927, *nāqâ+nāqâ* [1]
let go unpunished, 5927, *nāqâ* [1]

UNQUENCHABLE [1]
unquenchable, 4202+3882, *lō'+kābâ* [1]

UNQUENCHED [1]
unquenched, 8799, *šôqēq* [1]

UNRELENTING [1]
unrelenting, 4202+2798, *lō'+ḥāmal* [1]

UNRELIABLE [1]
unreliable, 2200, *hāpak* [1]

UNREST [2]
unrest, 4539, *mehûmâ* [1]
unrest, 8074, *rāgaz* [1]

UNRIGHTEOUS [1]
unrighteous, 6405, *'awwāl* [1]

UNRIGHTEOUSNESS [1]
unrighteousness, 4202+7406, *lō'+ṣedeq* [1]

UNRIPE [1]
unripe grapes, 1235, *bōser* [1]

UNROLLED [1]
unrolled, 7298, *pāraś* [1]

UNRULY [3]
unruly, 2171, *hāman* [1]
unruly, 4202+4340, *lō'+lāmad* [1]
unruly, 8113, *rûd* [1]

UNSANDALED [1]
Unsandaled, 2740+5837, *ḥālaṣ1+na'al* [1]

UNSATISFIED [1]
unsatisfied, 8200, *rêqām* [1]

UNSCALABLE [1]
unscalable, 8435, *śāgab* [1]

UNSCATHED [3]
unscathed, 928+8934, *be-+šālôm* [1]
unscathed, 8934, *šālôm* [1]
unscathed, 8966, *šālēm1* [1]

UNSEALED [3]
unsealed, 1655, *gālâ* [2]
unsealed, 7337, *pātaḥ1* [1]

UNSEARCHABLE [2]
unsearchable, 401+2984, *'ayin1+ḥēqer* [1]
unsearchable, 1290, *bāṣûr* [1]

UNSHARPENED [1]
unsharpened, 4202+7837, *lō'+qālal* [1]

UNSHEATHED [1]
unsheathed, 3655+4946+9509, *yāṣā'+min+ta'ar* [1]

UNSTOPPED [1]
unstopped, 7337, *pātaḥ1* [1]

UNSTRUNG [1]
unstrung, 7337, *pātaḥ1* [1]

UNSUCCESSFUL [1]
unsuccessful, 4202+7503, *lō'+ṣālaḥ2* [1]

UNSUITED [1]
unsuited, 4202+5534, *lō'+nā'weh* [1]

UNSUSPECTING [6]
unsuspecting, 1053, *bāṭaḥ1* [2]
unsuspecting, 1055, *beṭaḥ1* [2]
unsuspecting, 4200+1055, *le-1+beṭaḥ1* [1]
unsuspecting, 9200, *šāqaṭ* [1]

UNSWERVING [1]
unswerving, 2616, *ḥāzaq* [1]

UNTENDED [2]
untended vines, 5687, *nāzîr* [2]

UNTHINKABLE [1]
unthinkable, 597+4202, *'omnām+lō'* [1]

UNTIE [1]
untie, 6002, *nātar3* [1]

UNTIED [1]
untied, 7337, *pātaḥ1* [1]

UNTIL [312]
until, 6330, *'ad2* [224]
until, 6330+889, *'ad2+'ašer* [30]
until, 2256, *we-* [17]
until, 10527+10168, *'ad+dî* [8]
until, 6330+8611, *'ad2+ša-* [6]
until, 4946, *min* [4]
until, 10527, *'ad* [4]
until, 4200, *le-1* [3]
until, 6330+3954, *'ad2+kî2* [3]
until, 6330+561, *'ad2+'im* [3]
continue until, 5952, *nāśag* [2]
until, 6330+889+561, *'ad2+'ašer+'im* [2]
until, *NIH/RPE* [1]
until, 3954+561, *kî2+'im* [1]
won't until, 3954+561, *kî2+'im* [1]
until the end of, 6330, *'ad2* [1]
until the time for, 6330, *'ad2* [1]
until, 10221, *we-* [1]

UNTIRING [1]
untiring, 4202+7028, *lō'+pûg* [1]

UNTO [1]
unto, 4200, *le-1* [1]

UNTOUCHED [1]
untouched, 1153+7212, *bal1+pāqad* [1]

UNTRAVELED [1]
untraveled, 4946+1172+408+6296, *min+belî+'îš1+'ābar1* [1]

UNTRUE [1]
untrue, 3950, *kāḥaš* [1]

UNUSED [1]
unused, 5759, *nāṭaš* [1]

UNWALLED [3]
unwalled, 4722, *maḥᵃneh* [1]
unwalled villages, 7252, *pᵉrāzôt* [1]
unwalled, 7253, *pᵉrāzî* [1]

UNWEIGHED [1]
left unweighed, 5663, *nûaḥ*[1] [1]

UNWILLING [7]
unwilling, 4202+14, *lō'+'ābâ* [7]

UNWISE [1]
unwise, 4202+2682, *lō'+ḥākām* [1]

UNWORTHY [2]
unworthy, 7781, *qāṭōn*[1] [1]
unworthy, 7837, *qālal* [1]

UNYIELDING [5]
unyielding, *NIH/RPE* [1]
unyielding, 3877, *kābēd*[1] [1]
unyielding, 3878, *kābēd*[2] [1]
unyielding, 7156+2617, *pāneh+ḥāzāq* [1]
unyielding, 7997, *qāšeh* [1]

UP [1466]*
went up, 6590, *'ālâ* [111]
go up, 6590, *'ālâ* [76]
got up, 7756, *qûm* [50]
brought up, 6590, *'ālâ* [46]
lift up, 5951, *nāśā'* [32]
came up, 6590, *'ālâ* [31]
rise up, 7756, *qûm* [27]
up, 5951, *nāśā'* [26]
get up, 7756, *qûm* [24]
bring up, 6590, *'ālâ* [23]
come up, 6590, *'ālâ* [23]
up to, 6330, *'ad*[2] [21]
set up, 7756, *qûm* [17]
lifted up, 5951, *nāśā'* [16]
dried up, 3312, *yābēš*[1] [15]
up, *NIH/RPE* [14]
take up, 5951, *nāśā'* [14]
set up, 8492, *śîm* [13]
built up, 1215, *bānâ* [12]
up, 6590, *'ālâ* [12]
raise up, 7756, *qûm* [11]
gone up, 6590, *'ālâ* [10]
swallowed up, 1180, *bāla'*[1] [9]
set up, 5893, *nāṣab*[1] [9]
coming up, 6590, *'ālâ* [9]
raised up, 7756, *qûm* [9]
set up, 10624, *qûm* [9]
stir up, 6424, *'ûr*[3] [8]
stood up, 7756, *qûm* [8]
lift up, 8123, *rûm*[1] [8]
swallow up, 1180, *bāla'*[1] [7]
build up, 1215, *bānâ* [7]
grown up, 1540, *gādal* [7]
dry up, 3312, *yābēš*[1] [7]
rose up, 7756, *qûm* [7]
stand up, 7756, *qûm* [7]
grew up, 1540, *gādal* [6]
took up, 5951, *nāśā'* [6]
stirred up, 6424, *'ûr*[3] [6]
led up, 6590, *'ālâ* [6]
marched up, 6590, *'ālâ* [6]
set up, 6590, *'ālâ* [6]
dried up, 2990, *ḥārēb*[1] [5]
went up, 5602, *nāgaš* [5]
give up, 5989, *nātan* [5]
set up, 5989, *nātan* [5]
wake up, 6424, *'ûr*[3] [5]
take up, 6590, *'ālâ* [5]
stand up, 6641, *'āmad* [5]
stood up, 6641, *'āmad* [5]
took up positions, 6885, *'ārak* [5]
got up early, 8899, *šākam* [5]
up, *AIT* [4]
ate up, 430, *'ākal* [4]
be burned up, 928+2021+836+8596, *bᵉ-+ha-+'ēš*[1]*+śārap* [4]
set up camp, 2837, *ḥānâ*[1] [4]
dry up, 2990, *ḥārēb*[1] [4]
pick up, 5951, *nāśā'* [4]
picks up, 5951, *nāśā'* [4]
build up, 6148, *sālal*[2] [4]
climb up, 6590, *'ālâ* [4]
goes up, 6590, *'ālâ* [4]
going up, 6590, *'ālâ* [4]
send up, 6590, *'ālâ* [4]
shut up, 6806, *'āṣar* [4]
puts up security, 6842, *'ārab*[1] [4]
wake up, 7810, *qîṣ* [4]
put up, 8492, *śîm* [4]
burned up, 8596+928+2021+836, *śārap+bᵉ-+ha-+'ēš*[1] [4]
get up early, 8899, *šākam* [4]
got up, 8899, *šākam* [4]
came up, 10513, *sᵉlaq* [4]
up to, 448, *'el* [3]
gathered up, 665, *'āsap* [3]
burn up, 1277, *bā'ar*[1] [3]
stirs up, 1741, *gārâ* [3]
spoke up, 1819, *dābar*[2] [3]
bind up, 2502, *ḥābaš* [3]
binds up, 2502, *ḥābaš* [3]
give up, 2532, *ḥādal*[1] [3]
took up positions, 2837, *ḥānâ*[1] [3]
stand up, 3656, *yāṣab* [3]
woke up, 3699, *yāqaṣ* [3]
cover up, 4059, *kāsâ* [3]
pick up, 4377, *lāqaṭ* [3]
picked up, 5951, *nāśā'* [3]
stopped up, 6258, *sātam* [3]
up to, 6584, *'al*[2] [3]
climbed up, 6590, *'ālâ* [3]
grew up, 6590, *'ālâ* [3]
store up, 7621, *ṣāpan* [3]
stored up, 7621, *ṣāpan* [3]
help up, 7756, *qûm* [3]
rises up, 7756, *qûm* [3]
up, 7756, *qûm* [3]
raised up, 8123, *rûm*[1] [3]
early got up, 8899, *šākam* [3]
stirs up, 8938, *šālaḥ* [3]
dries up, 62, *'ābal*[2] [2]
eat up, 430, *'ākal* [2]
raised up, 599, *'āmēṣ* [2]
gather up, 665, *'āsap* [2]
gathers up, 665, *'āsap* [2]
hitch up, 673, *'āsar* [2]
tie up, 673, *'āsar* [2]
stored up, 732, *'āṣar* [2]
up to, 928, *bᵉ-* [2]
be swallowed up, 1180, *bāla'*[1] [2]
set up, 1215, *bānâ* [2]
burned up, 1277, *bā'ar*[1] [2]
opened up, 1324, *bāqa'* [2]
speak up, 1819, *dābar*[2] [2]
went up, 2143, *hālak* [2]
lifts up, 2422, *zāqap* [2]
set up tents, 2837, *ḥānâ*[1] [2]
seal up, 3159, *ḥātam* [2]
dries up, 3312, *yābēš*[1] [2]
come up, 3655, *yāṣā'* [2]
took up residence, 3782, *yāšab* [2]
used up, 3983, *kālâ*[1] [2]
up, 4200+5087+2025, *lᵉ-*[1]*+ma'al*[2]*+-â*[2] [2]
picked up, 4374, *lāqaḥ* [2]
licked up, 4379, *lāqaq* [2]
set up king, 4887+4889, *mālak*[1]*+melek*[1] [2]
dried up, 5457, *mᵉšammâ* [2]
look up, 5564, *nābaṭ* [2]
came up, 5602, *nāgaš* [2]
go up, 5602, *nāgaš* [2]
set up, 5663, *nûaḥ*[1] [2]
break up, 5774, *nîr*[1] [2]
pulled up, 5825, *nāsa'* [2]
be lifted up, 5951, *nāśā'* [2]
rise up, 5951, *nāśā'* [2]
catch up, 5952, *nāśag* [2]
be shut up, 6037, *sāgar* [2]
close up, 6037, *sāgar* [2]
closed up, 6037, *sāgar* [2]
up, 6330, *'ad*[2] [2]
stirs up, 6424, *'ûr*[3] [2]
go on up, 6590, *'ālâ* [2]
carried up, 6590, *'ālâ* [2]
carry up, 6590, *'ālâ* [2]
go straight up, 6590, *'ālâ* [2]
offered up, 6590, *'ālâ* [2]
sets up, 6590, *'ālâ* [2]
spring up, 6590, *'ālâ* [2]
propped up, 6641, *'āmad* [2]
rose up, 6641, *'āmad* [2]
set up, 6641, *'āmad* [2]
spoke up, 6699, *'ānâ*[1] [2]
drew up line, 6885, *'ārak* [2]
drew up, 6885, *'ārak* [2]
take up positions, 6885, *'ārak* [2]
set up, 6913, *'āśâ*[1] [2]
spring up, 7255, *pāraḥ*[1] [2]
speak up, 7337+7023, *pātaḥ*[1]*+peh* [2]
gets up, 7756, *qûm* [2]
raising up, 7756, *qûm* [2]
risen up, 7756, *qûm* [2]
grows up, 7850, *qāmâ* [2]
brought up, 8123, *rûm*[1] [2]
lifted up, 8123, *rûm*[1] [2]
take up, 8189, *rîb*[1] [2]
been burned up, 8596, *śārap* [2]
burn up, 8596+928+2021+836, *śārap+bᵉ-+ha-+'ēš*[1] [2]
burn up, 8596, *śārap* [2]
broke up, 8689, *šābar*[1] [2]
set up, 8905, *šākan* [2]

UPHAZ [1]
Uphaz, 233, *'ûpāz* [1]

UPHELD [4]
be upheld, 586, *'āman*[1] [1]
upheld, 6673, *'āmas* [1]
upheld, 6913, *'āśâ*[1] [1]
upheld, 8189, *rîb*[1] [1]

UPHOLD [15]
uphold, 6913, *'āśâ*[1] [5]
uphold, 9461, *tāmak* [3]
uphold, 6184, *sā'ad* [1]
uphold, 6641, *'āmad* [1]
uphold holiness, 7727, *qādaš* [1]
uphold, 7756, *qûm* [1]
uphold cause, 8189, *rîb*[1] [1]
uphold, 8189, *rîb*[1] [1]
uphold, 9149, *šāpaṭ* [1]

UPHOLDING [1]
upholding, 6184, *sā'ad* [1]

UPHOLDS [6]
upholds, 6164, *sāmak* [3]
upholds, *NIH/RPE* [1]
upholds, 6913, *'āśâ*[1] [1]
upholds, 9461, *tāmak* [1]

UPHOLSTERED [1]
upholstered, *NIH/RPE* [1]

UPLIFTED [13]
swore with uplifted, 5951, *nāśā'* [5]
sworn with uplifted, 5951, *nāśā'* [3]
with uplifted swore, 5951, *nāśā'* [2]
swear with uplifted, 5951, *nāśā'* [1]
uplifted, 5951, *nāśā'* [1]
uplifted, 9485, *tᵉnûpâ* [1]

UPON [324]
upon, 6584, *'al*[2] [166]
upon, 928, *bᵉ-* [34]
upon, *AIT* [28]
upon, 4200, *lᵉ-*[1] [25]
upon, 448, *'el* [20]
upon, *NIH/RPE* [8]
come upon, 5162, *māṣā'* [7]
upon, 907, *'ēt*[2] [4]
upon, 6584+7156, *'al*[2]*+pāneh* [4]
call upon, 7924, *qārā'*[1] [4]
upon, 928+7931, *bᵉ-+qereb* [3]
came upon, 4252, *lābaš* [3]

came upon, 5162, *māṣāʾ* [3]
upon, 4946, *min* [2]
come upon, 7925, *qārāʾ*[2] [2]
almost upon, 1815, *dābaq* [1]
upon, 2256, *wᵉ-* [1]
prevailed upon, 2616+928, *ḥāzaq+bᵉ-* [1]
wave upon wave, 2722, *ḥᵃlîpâ* [1]
brings upon, 5162, *māṣāʾ* [1]
bring defeat upon, 5597, *nāgap* [1]
fell upon, 5782, *nākâ* [1]
bring upon, 5951, *nāśāʾ* [1]
preys upon, 7421, *ṣûd* [1]
brought upon, 7925, *qārāʾ*[2] [1]
fall upon, 7925, *qārāʾ*[2] [1]

UPPER [43]
upper, 6609, *ʿelyôn*[1] [15]
upper room, 6608, *ʿᵃliyyâ* [6]
upper, *NIH/RPE* [3]
Upper Egypt, 7356, *patrôs* [3]
Upper Egypt, 824+7356, *ʾereṣ+patrôs* [2]
upper, 6606, *ʿillî* [2]
upper chambers, 6608, *ʿᵃliyyâ* [2]
upper parts, 6608, *ʿᵃliyyâ* [2]
upper rooms, 6608, *ʿᵃliyyâ* [2]
upper, 8207, *rekeb* [2]
upper, 6590, *ʿālâ* [1]
upper one, 8207, *rekeb* [1]
got the upper hand, 8948, *šālaṭ* [1]
upper, 8958, *šᵉlîšî* [1]

UPRAISED [6]
upraised, 5742, *nāṭâ* [5]
upraised, 8123, *rûm*[1] [1]

UPRIGHT [63]
upright, 3838, *yāšār*[1] [48]
upright, 3841, *yōšer* [4]
upright, *NIH/RPE* [2]
upright, 6641, *ʿāmad* [2]
upright, 7404, *ṣaddîq* [2]
upright, 2341, *zak* [1]
upright, 3837, *yāšar* [1]
upright, 3838+2006, *yāšār*[1]*+derek* [1]
upright, 3842, *yišrâ* [1]
stood upright, 5893, *nāṣab*[1] [1]

UPRIGHTLY [3]
uprightly, 4797, *mêšārîm* [2]
uprightly, 5791, *nākōaḥ* [1]

UPRIGHTNESS [5]
uprightness, 3841, *yōšer* [2]
uprightness, 3838, *yāšār*[1] [1]
uprightness, 4793, *mîšôr* [1]
uprightness, 5791, *nākōaḥ* [1]

UPRIGHTS [3]
uprights, 8918, *šālāb* [3]

UPROAR [8]
uproar, 8623, *šāʾôn*[2] [5]
in uproar, 2159, *hāmâ* [1]
uproar, 7754+2162, *qôl+hāmôn* [1]
uproar, 7754+9558, *qôl+tᵉrûʿâ* [1]

UPROOT [14]
uproot, 6004, *nātaš* [11]
completely uproot, 6004+6004, *nātaš+nātaš* [1]
uproot, 6827, *ʿāqar*[1] [1]
uproot, 9245, *šāraš* [1]

UPROOTED [15]
be uprooted, 6004, *nātaš* [3]
uprooted, 6004, *nātaš* [3]
be uprooted, 4572, *môṭ*[1] [1]
be uprooted, 5815, *nāsaḥ* [1]
was uprooted, 6004, *nātaš* [1]
uprooted, 6827, *ʿāqar*[1] [1]
be uprooted, 9245, *šāraš* [1]
uprooted, 9245, *šāraš* [1]
be uprooted, 9247+4572, *šōreš+môṭ*[1] [1]
uprooted, 9247+5998, *šōreš+nātaq* [1]
were uprooted, 10566, *ʿᵃqar* [1]

UPROOTS [1]
uproots, 5825, *nāsaʿ* [1]

UPSET [1]
upset, 8317+928+6524, *rāʿaʿ*[1]*+bᵉ+ʿayin*[1] [1]

UPSIDE [2]
turn upside down, 2201, *hēpek* [1]
upside down, 6584+7156, *ʿal*[2]*+pāneh* [1]

UPSTAIRS [1]
upstairs room, 10547, *ʿillî* [1]

UPSTREAM [1]
upstream, 4200+5087+2025, *lᵉ-*[1]*+maʿal*[2]*+-â*[2] [1]

UPWARD [11]
upward, 4200+5087+2025, *lᵉ-*[1]*+maʿal*[2]*+-â*[2] [6]
rolls upward, 60, *ʾābak* [1]
upward, 1467, *gābah* [1]
project upward, 4200+5087+2025, *lᵉ-*[1]*+maʿal*[2]*+-â*[2] [1]
upward, 4946+4200+5087+2025, *min+lᵉ-*[1]*+maʿal*[2]*+-â*[2] [1]
rose upward, 8250, *rāmam*[2] [1]

UR [5]
Ur, 243, *ʾûr*[3] [4]
Ur, 244, *ʾûr*[4] [1]

URGE [2]
urge, 7003, *pāgaʿ* [1]
urge, 7422, *ṣāwâ* [1]

URGED [15]
urged, 6077, *sût*[1] [3]
urged, 7287, *pāraṣ* [3]
urged, 2616, *ḥāzaq* [2]
urged, *NIH/RPE* [1]
urged, 237, *ʾûṣ* [1]
urged, 606, *ʾāmar*[1] [1]
urged to eat, 1356, *bārâ*[1] [1]
urged on, 6077, *sût*[1] [1]
urged, 7003, *pāgaʿ* [1]
urged, 7210, *pāṣar* [1]

URGENT [3]
urgent, 5722, *nāḥaṣ* [1]
send urgent, 8938+8938, *šālaḥ+šālaḥ* [1]
urgent, 10280, *ḥᵃsap* [1]

URGENTLY [1]
urgently, 928+2622, *bᵉ-+ḥozqâ* [1]

URGING [2]
urging, 1819, *dābar*[2] [1]
urging, 7287, *pāraṣ* [1]

URI [8]
Uri, 247, *ʾûrî* [7]
Uri, 788, *ʾurî* [1]

URIAH [33]
Uriah, 249, *ʾûriyyâ* [29]
Uriah, 250, *ʾûriyyāhû* [3]
Uriah, *NIH/RPE* [1]

URIAH'S [2]
Uriah's, 249, *ʾûriyyâ* [2]

URIEL [4]
Uriel, 248, *ʾûrîʾēl* [4]

URIM [7]
Urim, 242, *ʾûr*[2] [7]

URINE [2]
urine, 8875, *šayin* [2]

US [950]
us, 5646, *-nû*[1] [701]
us, *AIT* [120]
us, *NIH/RPE* [67]
us, 3276, *-î* [18]
us, 5761, *-nî* [12]
us, 10450, *-nāʾ* [7]
us, 636, *ʾᵃnaḥnû* [6]
us, 4392, *-ām* [4]
us, 4564, *-mô* [3]
us, 5883+5646, *nepeš+-nû*[1] [3]
us[s], 465, *ʾēlleh* [2]
us, 3276+2256+3870, *-î+wᵉ+-kā* [2]
each of us, 638+2256+2085, *ʾᵃnî+wᵉ+hûʾ* [1]
us, 3276+2256+2157, *-î+wᵉ+-hem* [1]
us, 3276+2256+4013, *-î+wᵉ+-kem* [1]
us deserve, 5646, *-nû*[1] [1]
us, 6524+5646, *ʿayin*[1]*+-nû*[1] [1]

USE [62]
use, 928, *bᵉ-* [6]
use, 6275, *ʿᵃbōdâ* [5]
use, *AIT* [4]
use, 6913, *ʿāśâ*[1] [4]
use, 2118, *hāyâ* [3]
use, 4374, *lāqaḥ* [3]
use, 6057, *sûk*[2] [3]
use, *NIH/RPE* [2]
use for fuel, 1277+836, *bāʿar*[1]*+ʾēš*[1] [2]
use, 2118+4200, *hāyâ+lᵉ-*[1] [2]
use, 5677, *nûp*[1] [2]
use, 6913+4856, *ʿāśâ*[1]*+mᵉlāʾkâ* [2]
use, 430, *ʾākal* [1]
use, 606, *ʾāmar*[1] [1]
use name as a curse, 928+8678, *bᵉ-+šābaʿ* [1]
use for fuel, 1277, *bāʿar*[1] [1]
use, 2005, *dārak* [1]
use, 2143+448, *hālak+ʾel* [1]
use as a prostitute, 2388+9373, *zānâ*[1]*+taznût* [1]
common use, 2687, *ḥōl* [1]
no use, 3286, *yāʾaš* [1]
use, 3286, *yāʾaš* [1]
use[s], 3519, *yākaḥ* [1]
of what use, 4200+4537+2296, *lᵉ-*[1]*+mâ+zeh* [1]
of what use, 4200+4537, *lᵉ-*[1]*+mâ* [1]
for the use of, 4200, *lᵉ-*[1] [1]
use as, 4374, *lāqaḥ* [1]
use, 5417, *māšaḥ* [1]
use, 5466, *mišmeret* [1]
use, 5989, *nātan* [1]
use, 6700, *ʿānâ*[2] [1]
use to make, 6913, *ʿāśâ*[1] [1]
use an abundance, 8049, *rābâ*[1] [1]
use, 8492, *śîm* [1]
use to do, 8938, *šālaḥ* [1]
use, 8938, *šālaḥ* [1]

USED [95]
used, *AIT* [21]
used, 928, *bᵉ-* [14]
used, *NIH/RPE* [7]
used to, 4200+7156, *lᵉ-*[1]*+pāneh* [5]
used, 6913, *ʿāśâ*[1] [4]
used, 2118, *hāyâ* [3]
used, 6590, *ʿālâ* [3]
used to make, 6913, *ʿāśâ*[1] [3]
used up, 3983, *kālâ*[1] [2]
used to, 4200+2021+8037, *lᵉ-*[1]*+ha-+riʾšôn* [2]
used to, 5814, *nāsâ* [2]
used, 6268, *ʿābad* [2]
used up, 430+430, *ʾākal+ʾākal* [1]
used, 606, *ʾāmar*[1] [1]
used up, 699, *ʾāpēs* [1]
used for, 928, *bᵉ-* [1]
used, 928+3338, *bᵉ-+yād* [1]
were used, 1215, *bānâ* [1]
used to say, 1819+1819, *dābar*[2]*+dābar*[2] [1]
used to, 2118, *hāyâ* [1]
used to be, 3427+6409, *yôm*[1]*+ʿôlām* [1]
used as, 4200, *lᵉ-*[1] [1]
used by, 4200, *lᵉ-*[1] [1]
used for, 4200, *lᵉ-*[1] [1]
used in, 4200, *lᵉ-*[1] [1]
bowl used for sprinkling, 4670, *mizrāq* [1]
used, 4946, *min* [1]
bowls used for drink offerings, 4984, *mᵉnaqqît* [1]
used, 5677, *nûp*[1] [1]
used lotions at all, 6057+6057, *sûk*[2]*+sûk*[2] [1]
used, 6296, *ʿābar*[1] [1]
used for, 6584, *ʿal*[2] [1]
used, 6584, *ʿal*[2] [1]
be used, 6913, *ʿāśâ*[1] [1]
been used, 6913+4856, *ʿāśâ*[1]*+mᵉlāʾkâ* [1]
used to, 8037, *riʾšôn* [1]
used, 8492, *śîm* [1]

used for fuel, 8596+1198+836, śārap+b^{e}mô+'ēš^{1} [1]
again be used, 8740, šûb^{1} [1]

USEFUL [4]
anything useful, 4856, m^{e}lā'kâ [1]
something useful, 4856, m^{e}lā'kâ [1]
useful, 6913, 'āśâ^{1} [1]
useful, 7503, ṣālaḥ^{2} [1]

USELESS [11]
useless, 2855, ḥinnām [2]
useless, 4202+7503, lō'+ṣālaḥ^{2} [2]
utterly useless, 2039+2256+8198, hebel^{1}+w^{e}-+rîq^{2} [1]
useless, 4200+2021+9214, l^{e-1}+ha-+šeqer [1]
useless, 4202+3603, lō'+yā'al [1]
useless, 4202+6122, lō'+sākan^{1} [1]
useless, 4202, lō' [1]
useless idols, 9332, tōhû [1]
useless, 9332, tōhû [1]

USES [7]
uses, 928+3338, b^{e}-+yād [1]
uses^{s}, 2461, ḥābā' [1]
uses with restraint, 3104, ḥāśak [1]
uses, 4200, l^{e-1} [1]
uses, 4848, mālē'^{1} [1]
uses, 5677, nûp^{1} [1]
uses for divination, 5727+5727, nāḥaš+nāḥaš [1]

USHERS [1]
ushers, 5697, nāḥâ^{1} [1]

USING [11]
using, 928, b^{e}- [5]
using^{s}, 1215, bānâ [2]
using, AIT [1]
using, 1068, bayin [1]
using, 2118, hāyâ [1]
using, 6584, 'al^{2} [1]

USUAL [5]
usual, NIH/RPE [1]
as usual, 3869+9453+8997, k^{e}-+t^{e}môl+šilšôm [1]
usual, 3869, k^{e}- [1]
usual way of dealing, 9368, tôrâ [1]
usual, 10255, ḥ^{a}zâ [1]

USUALLY [4]
usually, AIT [1]
as usually did, 3869+3427+928+3427, k^{e}-+yôm^{1}+b^{e}-+yôm^{1} [1]
as usually, 3869, k^{e}- [1]
what usually happens, 7213, p^{e}quddâ [1]

USURY [8]
usury, 5968, nešek [5]
exacting of usury, 5391, maššā' [1]
usury, 5391, maššā' [1]
usury charging, 5957, nāšā'^{1} [1]

UTENSILS [13]
utensils, 3998, k^{e}lî [13]

UTHAI [2]
Uthai, 6433, 'ûtay [2]

UTMOST [5]
utmost heights, 3752, y^{e}rēkâ [4]
utmost, 5905, nēṣaḥ^{1} [1]

UTTER [17]
utter, 3655, yāṣā' [2]
utter, NIH/RPE [1]
utter a curse, 457, 'ālâ^{1} [1]
utter darkness, 696, '^{a}pēlâ [1]
utter shame, 1017+1425, bôš^{1}+bōšet [1]
utter, 1819, dābar^{2} [1]
utter a sound, 2047, hāgâ^{1} [1]
utter, 2047, hāgâ^{1} [1]
utter, 3972, kōl [1]
utter, 4394, m^{e}'ōd [1]
utter, 4604, môṣā'^{1} [1]
made show utter contempt, 5540+5540, nā'aṣ+nā'aṣ [1]
utter, 5580, nāba' [1]
utter, 5583, nāgad [1]
utter, 6218, sāpar [1]
utter divinations, 7876, qāsam [1]

UTTERANCE [1]
utterance, 2050, hāgût [1]

UTTERED [11]
uttered, 5951+2256+606, nāśā'+w^{e}-+'āmar^{1} [7]
uttered, 606, 'āmar^{1} [1]
uttered a word, 3076+906+4383, ḥāraṣ^{1}+'ēt^{1}+lāšôn [1]
uttered, 3655+4946, yāṣā'+min [1]
what uttered, 4604, môṣā'^{1} [1]

UTTERING [1]
uttering, 2047, hāgâ^{1} [1]

UTTERLY [18]
utterly, 4394, m^{e}'ōd [2]
utterly, 6330+4394, 'ad^{2}+m^{e}'ōd [2]
utterly unfaithful, 953+953, bāgad+bāgad [1]
utterly scorned, 996+996, bûz^{1}+bûz^{1} [1]
utterly, 1524, gādôl [1]
utterly meaningless, 2039+2039, hebel^{1}+hebel^{1} [1]
utterly useless, 2039+2256+8198, hebel^{1}+w^{e}-+rîq^{2} [1]
utterly ruined, 2990+2990, ḥārēb^{1}+ḥārēb^{1} [1]
utterly rejected, 4415+4415, mā'as^{1}+mā'as^{1} [1]
utterly, 4946, min [1]
utterly, 8045, rābab^{1} [1]
utterly ruined, 8720+8720, šādad+šādad [1]
sure to become utterly corrupt, 8845+8845, šāḥat+šāḥat [1]
utterly desolate, 9039, š^{e}māmâ [1]
utterly abhor, 9210+9210, šāqaṣ+šāqaṣ [1]
utterly amazed, 9449+9449, tāmah+tāmah [1]

UTTERS [1]
utters, 2047, hāgâ^{1} [1]

UZ [8]
Uz, 6419, 'ûṣ^{2} [5]
Uz, 6420, 'ûṣ^{3} [2]
Uz, 824+6420, 'ereṣ+'ûṣ^{3} [1]

UZAI [1]
Uzai, 206, 'ûzay [1]

UZAL [3]
Uzal, 207, 'ûzāl [3]

UZZA [5]
Uzza, 6438, 'uzzā' [5]

UZZAH [9]
Uzzah, 6438, 'uzzā' [6]
Uzzah, 6446, 'uzzâ [3]

UZZEN SHEERAH [1]
Uzzen Sheerah, 267, 'uzzēn še'^{e}râ [1]

UZZI [12]
Uzzi, 6454, 'uzzî [11]
Uzzi, NIH/RPE [1]

UZZIA [1]
Uzzia, 6455, 'uzziyyā' [1]

UZZIAH [26]
Uzziah, 6460, 'uzziyyāhû [17]
Uzziah, 6459, 'uzziyyâ [8]
Uzziah^{s}, 2257, -ô [1]

UZZIAH'S [1]
Uzziah's, 6460, 'uzziyyāhû [1]

UZZIEL [16]
Uzziel, 6457, 'uzzî'ēl [16]

UZZIELITES [2]
Uzzielites, 6458, 'ozzî'ēlî [2]

VAIN [25]
in vain, 2039, hebel^{1} [5]
in vain, 4200+2021+8736, l^{e-1}+ha-+šāw' [4]
in vain, 4200+8198, l^{e-1}+rîq^{2} [4]
in vain, 8736, šāw' [3]
in vain, 8198, rîq^{2} [2]
vain, NIH/RPE [1]
in vain, 401, 'ayin^{1} [1]
in vain, 448+2855, 'el+ḥinnām [1]
in vain, 4202, lō' [1]
in vain, 9214, šeqer [1]
vain hope, 9214, šeqer [1]
in vain, 9332, tōhû [1]

VAIZATHA [1]
Vaizatha, 2262, way^{e}zātā' [1]

VALIANT [11]
valiant, 2657, ḥayil [4]
valiant fighters, 408+2657, 'îš^{1}+ḥayil [2]
valiant fighter, 1201+408+2657, bēn^{1}+'îš^{1}+ḥayil [2]
valiant soldier, 1475+2657, gibbôr+ḥayil [2]
valiant men, 52+4213, 'abbîr+lēb [1]

VALIANTLY [1]
valiantly, 2657, ḥayil [1]

VALID [1]
valid, 3202, ṭôb^{2} [1]

VALLEY [144]
valley, 6677, 'ēmeq [52]
valley, 1628, gay' [50]
valley, 5707, naḥal^{1} [34]
valley, 1326, biq'â [7]
valley, NIH/RPE [1]

VALLEYS [26]
valleys, 6677, 'ēmeq [11]
valleys, 1628, gay' [7]
valleys, 1326, biq'â [4]
valleys, 692, 'āpîq^{1} [2]
valleys, 5707, naḥal^{1} [2]

VALUABLE [4]
valuable gifts, 4458, meged [2]
valuable things, 2104+3701, hôn+y^{e}qār [1]
valuable, 2775, ḥemdâ [1]

VALUABLES [2]
valuables, 2775, ḥemdâ [1]
valuables, 3702, y^{e}qār [1]

VALUE [44]
value, 6886, 'ērek [11]
the value^{s}, 2257, -ô [5]
proper value, 6886, 'ērek [3]
set value, 6886, 'ērek [3]
of value, 3603, yā'al [2]
value, 4084+6886, kesep+'ērek [2]
value, 170, 'āhab [1]
value, 1540+928+6524, gādal+b^{e}-+'ayin^{1} [1]
value, 2775, ḥemdâ [1]
value, 2776, ḥ^{a}mudôt [1]
determine the value, 3108, ḥāšab [1]
have value, 3603, yā'al [1]
of little value, 3869+5071, k^{e}-+m^{e}'aṭ [1]
value, 4084, kesep [1]
little value, 4202+4399, lō'+m^{e}'ûmâ [1]
little value, 4399, m^{e}'ûmâ [1]
articles of value, 4458, meged [1]
value, 4718+6524, maḥmād+'ayin^{1} [1]
value, 4718, maḥmād [1]
value, 4831+6886, miksâ+'ērek [1]
value, 5625, nōah [1]
set value, 6885, 'ārak [1]
value sets, 6885, 'ārak [1]
value, 8965, šālāl [1]

VALUED [2]
valued, 1540+928+6524, gādal+b^{e}-+'ayin^{1} [1]
valued at, 4200, l^{e-1} [1]

VALUES [1]
equivalent values, 6886, 'ērek [1]

VANIAH [1]
Vaniah, 2264, wanyâ [1]

VANISH [14]
vanish, 3983, kālâ[1] [3]
vanish, 9462, tāmam [2]
vanish, 699, ʾāpēs [1]
vanish away, 700, ʾepes [1]
vanish, 1980, dāʿak [1]
vanish, 4416, māʾas[2] [1]
vanish, 4631, mûš[2] [1]
vanish, 4872, mālaḥ[1] [1]
vanish, 6073, sûr[1] [1]
vanish, 6259, sātar [1]
vanish, 6440, ʿāzab[1] [1]

VANISHED [4]
vanished, 6, ʾābad [1]
vanished, 699, ʾāpēs [1]
vanished, 4162, kārat [1]
vanished, 7182, pāsas [1]

VANISHES [2]
vanishes, 3983, kālâ[1] [1]
vanishes, 6296, ʿābar[1] [1]

VAPOR [1]
vapor, 2039, hebel[1] [1]

VARIED [1]
varied colors, 8391, riqmâ [1]

VARIOUS [15]
various, *AIT* [2]
various, 3972, kōl [2]
various kinds of service, 6275+2256+6275, ʿᵃbōdâ+wᵉ-+ʿᵃbōdâ [2]
various, *NIH/RPE* [1]
various, 337, ʾaḥēr[1] [1]
various, 2385, zan [1]
various kinds, 2446, zeraʿ [1]
various provinces, 4519+2256+4519, mᵉdînâ+wᵉ-+mᵉdînâ [1]
various kinds, 4786, mîn [1]
various peoples, 6639+2256+6639, ʿam[2]+wᵉ-+ʿam[2] [1]
various colors, 8391, riqmâ [1]
various gates, 9133+2256+9133, šaʿar[1]+wᵉ-+šaʿar[1] [1]

VASHTI [10]
Vashti, 2267, waštî [10]

VASSAL [3]
vassal, 6269, ʿebed[1] [2]
vassal, 1201, bēn[1] [1]

VASSALS [2]
vassals, 6269, ʿebed[1] [2]

VAST [25]
vast, 1524, gādôl [7]
vast, 8041, rab[1] [6]
vast army, 2162, hāmôn [2]
vast, 3883, kābôd[1] [1]
vast, 547+547, ʾelep[2]+ʾelep[2] [1]
vast, 579, ʾammîṣ [1]
vast, 1524+4394+4394, gādôl+mᵉʾōd+mᵉʾōd [1]
vast, 1524+4394, gādôl+mᵉʾōd [1]
vast, 3972, kōl [1]
vast, 6793, ʿāṣam[1] [1]
vast array, 7372, ṣābāʾ[2] [1]
vast expanses, 8144, raḥab [1]

VAT [1]
wine vat, 3676, yeqeb [1]

VATS [5]
vats, 3676, yeqeb [3]
vats, 238, ʾôṣār [1]
vats, 1964, demaʿ [1]

VAULTED [2]
vaulted, 2553, ḥûg[2] [1]
vaulted cell, 2844, ḥānût [1]

VAULTS [1]
vaults, 238, ʾôṣār [1]

VAUNTS [1]
vaunts himself, 1504, gābar [1]

VEGETABLE [2]
vegetable, 3763, yārāq [2]

VEGETABLES [3]
vegetables, 2447, zērōʿîm [1]
vegetables, 2448, zērʿōnîm [1]
vegetables, 3763, yārāq [1]

VEGETATION [6]
vegetation, 2013, dešeʾ [3]
vegetation, 6912, ʿēśeb [2]
vegetation, 7542, ṣemaḥ [1]

VEIL [12]
veil, 7539, ṣammâ [4]
veil, 5003, masweh [3]
veil, 7581, ṣāʿîp [3]
veil, 4485, mᵉginnâ [1]
veil, 6260, sēter [1]

VEILED [1]
veiled, 6486, ʿāṭā[1] [1]

VEILS [3]
veils, 5029, mispāḥâ [2]
veils, 8304, rᵉʿālâ [1]

VENGEANCE [33]
vengeance, 5935, nᵉqāmâ [17]
vengeance, 5934, nāqām [7]
takes vengeance, 5933, nāqam [2]
blood vengeance, 1947, dām [1]
take vengeance, 5933+5935, nāqam+nᵉqāmâ [1]
suffer vengeance, 5933, nāqam [1]
take vengeance, 5933, nāqam [1]
vengeance, 5933, nāqam [1]
take vengeance, 5934+8740, nāqām+šûb[1] [1]
take vengeance, 8740+5934, šûb[1]+nāqām [1]

VENOM [5]
venom, 2779, ḥēmâ [4]
venom, 5355, mᵉrōrâ [1]

VENOMOUS [4]
venomous, 8597, śārāp[1] [2]
venomous snakes, 5729, nāḥāš[1] [1]
venomous serpent, 8597, śārāp[1] [1]

VENT [5]
vent fury, 2404, zāʿam [1]
gives vent to, 3655, yāṣāʾ [1]
given full vent, 3983, kālâ[1] [1]
vent, 8740, šûb[1] [1]
vent, 8938, šālaḥ [1]

VENTURE [2]
venture out, 3655, yāṣāʾ [1]
venture, 5814, nāsâ [1]

VENTURES [1]
ventures, 5814, nāsâ [1]

VERDANT [1]
verdant, 8316, raʿᵃnān [1]

VERDICT [5]
verdict, 1821+5477, dābār+mišpāṭ [2]
verdict, 5477, mišpāṭ [1]
verdict, 6783, ʿēṣâ[1] [1]
verdict, 10690, šᵉʾēlâ [1]

VERIFIED [1]
be verified, 586, ʾāman[1] [1]

VERSED [1]
well versed, 4542, māhîr [1]

VERSES [1]
verses, 5126, maʿᵃśeh [1]

VERY [204]
very, 4394, mᵉʾōd [71]
very, *NIH/RPE* [23]
very, 6795, ʿeṣem[1] [11]
very, 1524, gādôl [6]
this very, 2296, zeh [6]
very, 6330+4394, ʿad[2]+mᵉʾōd [6]
very angry, 3013+678, ḥārâ[1]+ʾap[2] [4]
very much, 4394, mᵉʾōd [4]
very angry, 6297, ʿābar[2] [4]
very, 2296, zeh [3]
very, 928+4394+4394, bᵉ-+mᵉʾōd+mᵉʾōd [2]
this very, 2021, ha- [2]
that very, 2085, hûʾ [2]
very well then, 2180, hinnēh [2]
very well, 2180, hinnēh [2]
very well, 3202, ṭôb[2] [2]
very, 3983, kālâ[1] [2]
very well, 4200+4027, lᵉ-[1]+kēn[2] [2]
very, 4200+5087+2025, lᵉ-[1]+maʿal[2]+-â[2] [2]
your very own, 4200+3870, lᵉ-[1]+-kā [2]
very zealous, 7861+7861, qānāʾ+qānāʾ [2]
very, *AIT* [1]
very own brother, 278+1201+562+3870, ʾāḥ[2]+bēn[1]+ʾēm+-kā [1]
very, 421, ʾak [1]
very, 465, ʾēlleh [1]
very few, 632+4663, ʾᵉnôš[1]+mizʿār [1]
very, 677, ʾap[1] [1]
very guilty, 870+870, ʾāšam+ʾāšam [1]
very capable men, 1475+2657, gibbôr+ḥayil [1]
very well, 1685, gam [1]
very, 2085, hûʾ [1]
very well go, 2143+2143, hālak+hālak [1]
very well, 2180+5528, hinnēh+nāʾ[1] [1]
very opposite, 2201, hēpek [1]
very, 2221+4394, harbēh+mᵉʾōd [1]
very old, 2416+995+928+2021+3427, zāqēn[1]+bôʾ+bᵉ-+ha-+yôm[1] [1]
acted very wickedly, 2472+2472, ḥābal[2]+ḥābal[2] [1]
very being, 2652, ḥayyâ[2] [1]
knows very well, 3359+3359, yādaʿ+yādaʿ [1]
very, 3512, yāṭab [1]
very, 3701, yāqār [1]
very things, 3869+889+4027, kᵉ-+ʾᵃšer+kēn[2] [1]
very well then, 3954, kî[2] [1]
very well, 4027, kēn[2] [1]
to the very end, 4200+6409+6813, lᵉ-[1]+ʿôlām+ʿēqeb [1]
very, 4200+466, lᵉ-[1]+ʾᵉlōhîm [1]
very, 4213, lēb [1]
very soon, 4559, mᵉhērâ [1]
very few, 5071+4663, mᵉʿaṭ+mizʿār [1]
very few, 5493+5031, mōt[1]+mispār[1] [1]
very, 6330+4200+5087+2025, ʿad[2]+lᵉ-[1]+maʿal[2]+-â[2] [1]
in a very short time, 6388+5071+4663, ʿôd+mᵉʿaṭ+mizʿār [1]
very soon, 6388+5071+4663, ʿôd+mᵉʿaṭ+mizʿār [1]
very, 6786+4394, ʿāṣûm+mᵉʾōd [1]
very strong, 6793+3946, ʿāṣam[1]+kōaḥ[1] [1]
very crafty, 6891+6891, ʿāram[2]+ʿāram[2] [1]
very, 7754, qôl [1]
very angry, 7911+7912, qāṣap+qeṣep[1] [1]
very well, 8011, rāʾâ[1] [1]
very, 8041, rab[1] [1]
very top, 8123, rûm[1] [1]
must very far, 8178+8178, rāḥaq+rāḥaq [1]
very disturbed, 8317+8288, rāʿaʿ[1]+rāʿâ[3] [1]
made very glad, 8523+8523, śāmaḥ+śāmaḥ [1]
very, 10339, yattîr [1]

VESSEL [1]
vessel, 8500, śᵉkiyyâ [1]

VESSELS [3]
vessels, 3998, kᵉlî [3]

VESTMENTS [1]
vestments, 4252, lābaš [1]

VETERAN [1]
veteran, 2418, zāqēn[2] [1]

VEXED [2]
vexed, 4087, kāʿas [1]
vexed, 9345, tāwâ[2] [1]

VICINITY [8]
- vicinity, 1473, gebûl [2]
- vicinity, 824, 'ereṣ [1]
- vicinity, 3338, yād [1]
- in the vicinity of, 4578, mûl[3] [1]
- vicinity, 5790, nōkaḥ [1]
- to the vicinity of, 6330+995+3870, 'ad[2]+bô'+-kā [1]
- vicinity, 7396, ṣad[1] [1]

VICIOUSLY [1]
- attacked viciously, 5782+8797+6584+3751, nākâ+šôq+'al[2]+yārēk [1]

VICTIM [2]
- victim, 2724, ḥēlkâ [1]
- victim, 5468, mešissâ [1]

VICTIMS [10]
- victims, 2728, ḥālāl[1] [3]
- victims, *NIH/RPE* [2]
- victims, 2724, ḥēlkâ [2]
- victims, 3272, ṭerep [2]
- victims, 665, 'āsap [1]

VICTORIES [5]
- victories, 3802, yešû'â [5]

VICTORIOUS [8]
- victorious, 7503, ṣālaḥ[2] [4]
- victorious, 3802, yešû'â [2]
- victorious, 599, 'āmēṣ [1]
- victorious, 2616, ḥāzaq [1]

VICTORIOUSLY [1]
- victoriously, 7503, ṣālaḥ[2] [1]

VICTORY [35]
- victory, 9591, tešû'â [12]
- gave victory, 3828, yāša' [4]
- victory, 2657, ḥayil [2]
- bring victory, 3828, yāša' [2]
- give victory, 3828, yāša' [2]
- victory, 3829, yēša' [2]
- victory, 5782, nākâ [2]
- victory, 9370, tûšiyyâ [2]
- victory, *NIH/RPE* [1]
- victory, 1476, gebûrâ [1]
- gained the victory, 3523, yākōl [1]
- victory, 3802, yešû'â [1]
- brought about victory, 3828+9591, yāša'+tešû'â [1]
- victory, 4804, makkâ [1]
- gave victory, 5989+928+3338, nātan+be-+yād [1]

VIEW [10]
- full view, 6524, 'ayin[1] [2]
- view, 8011, rā'â[1] [2]
- in view, 907+7156, 'ēt[2]+pāneh [1]
- in view of, 928, be- [1]
- in full view, 5790+6524, nōkaḥ+'ayin[1] [1]
- view, 7170, pāsag [1]
- come into view, 8011, rā'â[1] [1]
- view, 8800, šûr[1] [1]

VIEWED [2]
- viewed, 5564, nābaṭ [1]
- viewed, 8011, rā'â[1] [1]

VIEWS [1]
- views, 5564, nābaṭ [1]

VIGIL [3]
- vigil, 9081, šimmurîm [2]
- keeping secret vigil, 5915, nāṣar [1]

VIGOR [7]
- vigor, 226, 'ôn[1] [1]
- vigor, 2006, derek [1]
- full vigor, 3995, kelaḥ[1] [1]
- vigor, 3995, kelaḥ[1] [1]
- youthful vigor, 6596, 'alûmîm [1]
- vigor, 6795, 'eṣem[1] [1]
- vigor, 8841, šaḥarût [1]

VIGOROUS [4]
- vigorous, 2645, ḥay[2] [1]
- vigorous, 2650, ḥāyeh [1]
- vigorous, 3946, kōaḥ[1] [1]
- vigorous, 9045, šāmēn[2] [1]

VIGOROUSLY [2]
- vigorously, 928+6437, be-+'ōz [1]
- vigorously defend, 8189+8189, rîb[1]+rîb[1] [1]

VILE [23]
- vile images, 9199, šiqqûṣ [9]
- vile, 9493, tā'ab [4]
- vile, 1175, beliyya'al [2]
- what is vile, 2359, zullût [1]
- vile, 4415, mā'as[1] [1]
- vile, 7837, qālal [1]
- vile, 8273, ra'[1] [1]
- vile, 8317, rā'a'[1] [1]
- vile goddess, 9199, šiqqûṣ [1]
- vile god, 9199, šiqqûṣ [1]
- vile, 9199, šiqqûṣ [1]

VILENESS [2]
- vileness, 5576, nebālâ [2]

VILEST [2]
- guilty of the vilest adultery, 2388+2388, zānâ[1]+zānâ[1] [1]
- behaved in the vilest manner, 9493+4394, tā'ab+me'ōd [1]

VILLAGE [1]
- village life, 7251, perāzôn [1]

VILLAGES [78]
- villages, 2958, ḥāṣēr[1] [45]
- villages, 6551, 'îr[1] [8]
- villages, 1426, bat[1] [7]
- surrounding villages, 1426, bat[1] [6]
- villages, *NIH/RPE* [3]
- villages, 4099, kepîrîm [2]
- villages, 4107, kāpār [2]
- outlying villages, 1426, bat[1] [1]
- surrounding villages, 2958, ḥāṣēr[1] [1]
- villages, 4108, kōper[1] [1]
- villages, 6551+7252, 'îr[1]+perāzôt [1]
- unwalled villages, 7252, perāzôt [1]

VILLAIN [1]
- villain, 408+224, 'îš[1]+'āwen[1] [1]

VINDICATE [6]
- vindicate, 9149, šāpaṭ [4]
- vindicate, 1906, dîn[1] [2]

VINDICATED [5]
- vindicated, 7405, ṣādaq [2]
- vindicated, 1906, dîn[1] [1]
- are vindicated, 3519, yākaḥ [1]
- vindicated, 3655+7407, yāṣā'+ṣedāqâ [1]

VINDICATES [1]
- vindicates, 7405, ṣādaq [1]

VINDICATION [4]
- vindication, 7407, ṣedāqâ [2]
- vindication, 5477, mišpāṭ [1]
- vindication, 7406, ṣedeq [1]

VINE [46]
- vine, 1728, gepen [36]
- vine, 7813, qîqāyôn [5]
- fruitful vine, 1201+7238, bēn[1]+pārâ[1] [2]
- vine, *NIH/RPE* [1]
- vine growers, 4144, kōrēm [1]
- choice vine, 8603, śōrēq[1] [1]

VINEGAR [5]
- vinegar, 2810, ḥōmeṣ [4]
- wine vinegar, 2810, ḥōmeṣ [1]

VINES [23]
- vines, 1728, gepen [16]
- vines, 2367, zemôrâ [2]
- untended vines, 5687, nāzîr [2]
- go over the vines again, 6618+339, 'ālal[1]+'aḥar [1]
- choicest vines, 8602, śārōq[2] [1]
- choicest vines, 8603, śōrēq[1] [1]

VINEYARD [43]
- vineyard, 4142, kerem[1] [41]
- the vineyard[s], 889, 'ašer [1]
- vineyard, 1292, bāṣîr[1] [1]

VINEYARDS [54]
- vineyards, 4142, kerem[1] [49]
- work vineyards, 4144, kōrēm [2]
- vineyards, 4144, kōrēm [1]
- working fields and vineyards, 4144, kōrēm [1]
- vineyards, 9224, šārâ[2] [1]

VINTAGE [1]
- vintage, 4142, kerem[1] [1]

VIOLATE [5]
- violate, 2725, ḥālal[1] [2]
- violate, 6296, 'ābar[1] [1]
- violate women, 6700, 'ānâ[2] [1]
- violate, 7296, pārar[1] [1]

VIOLATED [12]
- violated, 6296, 'ābar[1] [6]
- violated, 6700, 'ānâ[2] [2]
- violated, 2736, ḥālap[1] [1]
- violated, 8399, rāša' [1]
- violated, 8845, šāḥat [1]
- violated, 8886+2256+6700, šākab+we-+'ānâ[2] [1]

VIOLATES [2]
- violates, 2725, ḥālal[1] [1]
- violates, 6700, 'ānâ[2] [1]

VIOLATING [1]
- violating the ban, 5085, mā'al [1]

VIOLATION [2]
- commits a violation, 5085+5086, mā'al+ma'al[1] [1]
- violation, 6296, 'ābar[1] [1]

VIOLENCE [51]
- violence, 2805, ḥāmās [43]
- violence, 8719, šōd[2] [3]
- do violence, 2803, ḥāmas[1] [2]
- violence, 2803, ḥāmas[1] [1]
- violence, 6449, 'ezûz [1]
- violence, 8273, ra'[1] [1]

VIOLENT [14]
- violent, 2805, ḥāmās [5]
- violent, 7265, pārîṣ[2] [3]
- violent, 1524, gādôl [1]
- violent, 2728, ḥālāl[1] [1]
- violent, 4848+2805, mālē'[1]+ḥāmās [1]
- violent winds, 6193, sa'ar [1]
- violent winds, 8120+6194, rûaḥ+se'ārâ [1]
- violent wind, 8120+6194, rûaḥ+se'ārâ [1]

VIOLENTLY [2]
- trembled violently, 3006+3010+1524+6330+4394, ḥārad+ḥarādâ[1]+gādôl+'ad[2]+me'ōd [1]
- violently, 4394, me'ōd [1]

VIPER [3]
- viper, 7625, ṣepa' [1]
- viper, 7626, ṣip'ōnî [1]
- viper, 9159, šepîpōn [1]

VIPER'S [1]
- viper's, 7626, ṣip'ōnî [1]

VIPERS [4]
- vipers, 7626, ṣip'ōnî [2]
- vipers, *NIH/RPE* [1]
- vipers, 6582, 'akšûb [1]

VIRGIN [32]
- virgin, 1435, betûlâ [25]
- be a virgin, 928+1436, be-+betûlîm [1]
- proof that a virgin, 1436, betûlîm [1]
- to be a virgin, 1436, betûlîm [1]
- virgin, 1436, betûlîm [1]

WANTON [2]
wanton lust, 2393, *zᵉnûnîm* [1]
wanton, 6349, *ʿādîn*[1] [1]

WANTS [10]
wants, *AIT* [5]
wants, 2914, *ḥēpeṣ* [3]
wants, *NIH/RPE* [1]
wants to give, 5952+3338, *nāśag+yād* [1]

WAR [123]
war, 4878, *milḥāmâ* [73]
war, 7372, *ṣābāʾ*[2] [6]
make war, 4309, *lāḥam*[1] [5]
war, 7930, *qᵉrāb* [5]
war, 4309, *lāḥam*[1] [3]
at war with, 408+4878, *ʾîš*[1]*+milḥāmâ* [2]
provoke to war, 1741, *gārâ* [2]
war, 2995, *ḥereb* [2]
made war, 4309, *lāḥam*[1] [2]
war horses, 7304, *pārāš*[1] [2]
war cries, 9558, *tᵉrûʿâ* [2]
war, *NIH/RPE* [1]
prepare for war, 1741, *gārâ* [1]
wage war, 1741+4200+2021+4878,
gārâ+lᵉ-1+ha-+milḥāmâ [1]
go off to war, 3655, *yāṣāʾ* [1]
at war, 4309, *lāḥam*[1] [1]
waging war, 4309, *lāḥam*[1] [1]
war, 4311, *lāḥem* [1]
at war, 4878, *milḥāmâ* [1]
time of war, 4878, *milḥāmâ* [1]
war cry, 4878, *milḥāmâ* [1]
weapons of war, 4878, *milḥāmâ* [1]
war club, 5151, *mappēṣ* [1]
war clubs, 5234+3338, *maqqēl+yād* [1]
at war, 6913+4878, *ʿāśâ*[1]*+milḥāmâ* [1]
went to war, 6913+4878, *ʿāśâ*[1]*+milḥāmâ* [1]
war cry, 7754, *qôl* [1]
raise the war cry, 8131, *rûaʿ* [1]
give a war cry, 8131, *rûaʿ* [1]
war, 10639, *qᵉrāb* [1]

WAR-HORSES [2]
war-horses, 6061, *sûs*[1] [2]

WARD [3]
ward off with a ransom, 4105, *kāpar*[1] [1]
ward off, 6073, *sûr*[1] [1]
ward off, 8740, *šûb*[1] [1]

WARDEN [3]
warden, 8569, *śar* [3]

WARDROBE [3]
wardrobe, 955, *beged*[2] [2]
wardrobe, 4921, *meltāḥâ* [1]

WARES [9]
wares, 5114, *maʿᵃrāb*[1] [8]
finest wares, 3206, *ṭûb* [1]

WARFARE [4]
warfare, 4878, *milḥāmâ* [3]
warfare, 6009, *saʾsᵉʾâ* [1]

WARM [10]
warm, 2801, *ḥāmam* [8]
warm, 2768, *ḥām*[2] [1]
lets warm, 2801, *ḥāmam* [1]

WARMING [1]
warming, 2801, *ḥāmam* [1]

WARMS [2]
warms, 2801, *ḥāmam* [2]

WARN [14]
warn, 2302, *zāhar*[2] [8]
warn, 6386, *ʿûd*[1] [4]
warn, 3619, *yāʿaṣ* [1]
warn solemnly, 6386+6386, *ʿûd*[1]*+ʿûd*[1] [1]

WARNED [20]
warned, 1819, *dābar*[2] [5]
warned, 6386, *ʿûd*[1] [5]
warned, 5583, *nāgad* [2]
warned, 606, *ʾāmar*[1] [1]
be warned, 2302, *zāhar*[2] [1]
is warned, 2302, *zāhar*[2] [1]
warned, 2302, *zāhar*[2] [1]
be warned, 3579, *yāsar*[1] [1]
been warned, 6386, *ʿûd*[1] [1]
warned solemnly, 6386+6386, *ʿûd*[1]*+ʿûd*[1] [1]
warned, 6386+6386, *ʿûd*[1]*+ʿûd*[1] [1]

WARNING [14]
take warning, 2302, *zāhar*[2] [3]
give warning, 2302, *zāhar*[2] [2]
take warning, 3579, *yāsar*[1] [2]
warning, 606, *ʾāmar*[1] [1]
taken warning, 2302, *zāhar*[2] [1]
took warning, 2302, *zāhar*[2] [1]
warning, 3579, *yāsar*[1] [1]
warning, 4592, *mûsār* [1]
warning sign, 5812, *nēs* [1]
give warning, 6386, *ʿûd*[1] [1]

WARNINGS [3]
warnings, 4592, *mûsār* [1]
warnings gave, 6343+6386, *ʿēdût+ʿûd*[1] [1]
warnings given, 6343+6386, *ʿēdût+ʿûd*[1] [1]

WARPED [2]
warped, 6390, *ʿāwâ*[1] [1]
warped, 6836, *ʿiqqēš*[1] [1]

WARRIOR [21]
warrior, 1475, *gibbôr* [12]
warrior, 408+4878, *ʾîš*[1]*+milḥāmâ* [5]
mighty warrior, 1475, *gibbôr* [2]
brave warrior, 1475+2657, *gibbôr+ḥayil* [1]
mighty warrior, 1475+2657, *gibbôr+ḥayil* [1]

WARRIOR'S [4]
warrior's, 1475, *gibbôr* [2]
warrior's belt, 2514, *ḥᵃgôrâ* [1]
warrior's, 6008, *sāʾan* [1]

WARRIORS [47]
warriors, 1475, *gibbôr* [27]
brave warriors, 1475+2657, *gibbôr+ḥayil* [6]
warriors, 52, *ʾabbîr* [2]
warriors, 408+2657, *ʾîš*[1]*+ḥayil* [2]
mighty warriors, 1475, *gibbôr* [2]
warriors, 7940, *qārôb* [2]
warriors, *AIT* [1]
warriors, 1201+2657, *bēn*[1]*+ḥayil* [1]
warriors, 1475+2657, *gibbôr+ḥayil* [1]
warriors, 1476, *gᵉbûrâ* [1]
warriors, 7250, *pārāz* [1]
warriors, 7251, *pᵉrāzôn* [1]

WARS [7]
wars, 4878, *milḥāmâ* [6]
wars, 4309, *lāḥam*[1] [1]

WARTS [1]
anything with warts, 3301, *yabbelet* [1]

WAS [2795]*
was, *NIH/RPE* [1192]
was, *AIT* [888]
was, 2118, *hāyâ* [305]
there was no, 401, *ʾayin*[1] [29]
was, 10201, *hᵃwâ* [7]
there was none, 401, *ʾayin*[1] [4]
was not, 401, *ʾayin*[1] [3]
there was, 3780, *yēš* [3]
there was nothing, 401, *ʾayin*[1] [2]
there was not, 401, *ʾayin*[1] [2]
was no more, 401, *ʾayin*[1] [2]
was there no, 401, *ʾayin*[1] [2]

WASH [64]
wash, 3891, *kābas* [36]
wash, 8175, *rāḥaṣ* [23]
wash away, 8851, *šāṭap* [2]
wash away, 3891, *kābas* [1]
wash off, 4681, *māḥâ*[1] [1]
wash away, 8175, *rāḥaṣ* [1]

WASHBASIN [2]
washbasin, 6105+8176, *sîr+raḥaṣ* [2]

WASHED [25]
washed, 8175, *rāḥaṣ* [10]
washed, 3891, *kābas* [5]
be washed, 3891, *kābas* [2]
been washed, 3891, *kābas* [2]
washed, 8851, *šāṭap* [2]
washed, 1866, *dûaḥ* [1]
washed away, 3668, *yāṣaq* [1]
washed myself, 8175, *rāḥaṣ* [1]
were washed, 8175, *rāḥaṣ* [1]

WASHERMAN'S [3]
Washerman's, 3891, *kābas* [3]

WASHING [7]
washing, 8175, *rāḥaṣ* [4]
washing, 8177, *raḥṣâ* [2]
washing soda, 1342, *bōr*[2] [1]

WASN'T [2]
wasn't, 4202+2118, *lōʾ+hāyâ* [1]
wasn't enough, 5071, *mᵉʿaṭ* [1]

WASTE [71]
waste, 9014, *šammâ*[1] [7]
laid waste, 2990, *ḥārēb*[1] [6]
waste, 9039, *šᵉmāmâ* [5]
waste away, 5245, *māqaq* [4]
waste, 5457, *mᵉšammâ* [4]
lay waste, 9037, *šāmēm*[1] [4]
laid waste, 9014, *šammâ*[1] [3]
waste away, 5877, *nāpal* [2]
waste away, 8140, *rāzî* [2]
was laid waste, 9037, *šāmēm*[1] [2]
laid waste, 9039, *šᵉmāmâ* [2]
waste, 9332, *tōhû* [2]
waste away, 581, *ʾāmal*[1] [1]
laid waste, 1278, *bāʿar*[2] [1]
be completely laid waste, 1327+1327,
bāqaq[1]*+bāqaq*[1] [1]
laid waste, 1327, *bāqaq*[1] [1]
lay waste, 1327, *bāqaq*[1] [1]
will be laid waste, 1959, *dāmam*[3] [1]
waste, 2233, *hᵃrîsût* [1]
laid waste, 2238+2256+2990,
hāras+wᵉ+ḥārēb[1] [1]
waste away, 2307, *zûb* [1]
laid waste, 2803, *ḥāmas*[1] [1]
lay waste, 2990, *ḥārēb*[1] [1]
desolate waste, 2992, *ḥārēb*[3] [1]
waste, 2997, *ḥōreb*[2] [1]
waste, 2999, *ḥorbâ* [1]
waste, 3810, *yᵉšîmôn* [1]
made waste away, 4570, *mûg* [1]
salt waste, 4877, *mᵉlēḥâ* [1]
waste away, 5022, *māsas* [1]
waste away, 5071, *mᵉʿaṭ* [1]
laid waste, 5898, *nāṣâ*[2] [1]
laid waste, 5898+5898, *nāṣâ*[2]*+nāṣâ*[2] [1]
be laid waste, 6440, *ʿāzab*[1] [1]
waste away, 8135, *rāzâ* [1]
burning waste, 8599, *śᵉrēpâ* [1]
laid waste, 8845, *šāḥat* [1]
be laid waste, 9037, *šāmēm*[1] [1]
laid waste, 9037, *šāmēm*[1] [1]
desolate waste, 9039, *šᵉmāmâ* [1]

WASTED [5]
wasted away, 581, *ʾāmal*[1] [1]
wasted away, 1162, *bālâ*[1] [1]
wasted away, 3532, *yālah* [1]
wasted away, 4812, *mākak* [1]
wasted, 8845, *šāḥat* [1]

WASTELAND [21]
wasteland, 3810, *yᵉšîmôn* [7]
wasteland, 6858, *ʿᵃrābâ*[2] [3]
wasteland, 9039, *šᵉmāmâ* [3]
wasteland, 4497, *midbār*[1] [2]
wasteland, 1429, *bātâ* [1]
wasteland, 2999, *ḥorbâ* [1]
wasteland, 5118, *mᵉʿārâ*[2] [1]
wasteland, 5409, *mᵉšōʾâ* [1]
wasteland, 9014, *šammâ*[1] [1]
wasteland, 9332, *tōhû* [1]

WASTELANDS [4]
wastelands, 6858, ʿarābâ^{2} [2]
wastelands, 3810, yešîmôn [1]
wastelands, 5409, mešōʾâ [1]

WASTES [5]
wastes away, 581, ʾāmal^{1} [1]
wastes away, 1162, bālâ^{1} [1]
wastes away, 3983, kālâ^{1} [1]
wastes away, 5022, māsas [1]
wastes away, 5877, nāpal [1]

WASTING [6]
wasting disease, 8137, rāzôn^{1} [2]
wasting, 4642, māzeh [1]
wasting away, 5245, māqaq [1]
wasting diseases, 8831, šaḥepet [1]
wasting disease, 8831, šaḥepet [1]

WATCH [52]
watch, 9068, šāmar [9]
watch, 8011, rāʾâ^{1} [5]
watch over, 9068, šāmar [5]
watch, 4200+6524, le-^{1}+ʿayin^{1} [3]
watch, 7595, ṣāpâ^{1} [3]
watch, 874, ʾašmûrâ [2]
watch over, 5915, nāṣar [2]
last watch of the night, 874+1332, ʾašmûrâ+bōqer^{2} [1]
last watch of the night, 874+2021+1332, ʾašmûrâ+ha-+bōqer^{2} [1]
watch, 5466, mišmeret [1]
watch, 5564, nābaṭ [1]
keep watch over, 5915, nāṣar [1]
watch, 5917, niṣṣerâ [1]
watch, 6524+928, ʿayin^{1}+be- [1]
watch, 6524, ʿayin^{1} [1]
watch over, 7212, pāqad [1]
keep watch, 7595, ṣāpâ^{1} [1]
keeping watch, 7595, ṣāpâ^{1} [1]
standing watch, 7595, ṣāpâ^{1} [1]
watch in hope, 7595, ṣāpâ^{1} [1]
keeping watch, 8011+928+6524, rāʾâ^{1}+be-+ʿayin^{1} [1]
watch over, 8492+6584, śîm+ʿal^{2} [1]
keep watch, 8788, šôʿēr [1]
keep close watch on, 9068, šāmar [1]
keeps close watch, 9068, šāmar [1]
kept watch, 9068, šāmar [1]
watch carefully, 9068, šāmar [1]
watch kept, 9193, šāqad^{1} [1]
watch, 9193, šāqad^{1} [1]
watch, 10255, ḥazâ [1]

WATCHED [21]
watched, 8011, rāʾâ^{1} [4]
watched, 4200+6524, le-^{1}+ʿayin^{1} [3]
watched over, 9068, šāmar [3]
watched, 10255, ḥazâ [3]
watched, 9207, šāqap [2]
watched over, 3359, yādaʿ [1]
watched, 4200+7156, le-^{1}+pāneh [1]
watched over and seen, 7212+7212, pāqad+pāqad [1]
watched, 7595, ṣāpâ^{1} [1]
watched closely, 8617, šāʾâ^{3} [1]
watched, 9193, šāqad^{1} [1]

WATCHER [1]
watcher, 5915, nāṣar [1]

WATCHES [16]
watches over, 9068, šāmar [6]
watches of the night, 874, ʾašmûrâ [3]
watches, 9068, šāmar [2]
watches over, 3359, yādaʿ [1]
watches over, 5564, nābaṭ [1]
watches, 6524, ʿayin^{1} [1]
watches over, 7595, ṣāpâ^{1} [1]
watches, 8708, śāgaḥ [1]

WATCHFUL [1]
keep watchful, 7219, pāqaḥ [1]

WATCHING [23]
watching, 8011, rāʾâ^{1} [7]
watching, 6524, ʿayin^{1} [3]
watching, 9193, šāqad^{1} [3]
watching, 4200+6524, le-^{1}+ʿayin^{1} [2]
watching over, 9068, šāmar [2]
watching, 9068, šāmar [2]
watching, NIH/RPE [1]
watching, 5564, nābaṭ [1]
watching, 7595, ṣāpâ^{1} [1]
watching, 10255, ḥazâ [1]

WATCHMAN [15]
watchman, 7595, ṣāpâ^{1} [11]
watchman, 9068, šāmar [3]
watchman, 5915, nāṣar [1]

WATCHMEN [13]
watchmen, 9068, šāmar [8]
watchmen, 7595, ṣāpâ^{1} [4]
watchmen, 5915, nāṣar [1]

WATCHTOWER [6]
watchtower, 4463+5915, migdāl^{1}+nāṣar [2]
watchtower, 4463, migdāl^{1} [2]
watchtower, 1044, baḥan [1]
watchtower, 5205, miṣpeh^{1} [1]

WATCHTOWERS [1]
watchtowers, 4463, migdāl^{1} [1]

WATER [403]
water, 4784, mayim [359]
water, NIH/RPE [11]
water, 9197, šāqâ [10]
draw water, 8612, šāʾab [5]
draw water, 1926, dālâ^{1} [1]
drew water, 1926+1926, dālâ^{1}+dālâ^{1} [1]
the water^{s}, 2084, -hû [1]
water, 3722, yārâ^{2} [1]
the water^{s}, 4392, -ām [1]
water^{s}, 4564, -mô [1]
water, 4763, māṭar [1]
spring of water, 4784, mayim [1]
water supply, 4784, mayim [1]
water, 5482, mašqeh^{1} [1]
water jars, 5574, nēbel^{1} [1]
water holes, 5635, nahalōl^{1} [1]
running water, 5689, nōzēl [1]
water shaft, 7562, ṣinnôr [1]
drew water, 8612, šāʾab [1]
water, 8796, šûq^{1} [1]
gave water, 9197, šāqâ [1]
give water, 9197, šāqâ [1]

WATER'S [1]
water's, 4784, mayim [1]

WATERCOURSE [1]
watercourse, 7104+4784, peleg^{1}+mayim [1]

WATERED [9]
watered, 9197, šāqâ [6]
well watered, 5482, mašqeh^{1} [1]
watered land, 8116, rāweh [1]
well watered, 8425, śābaʿ [1]

WATERFALLS [1]
waterfalls, 7562, ṣinnôr [1]

WATERING [5]
watering, 2449, zārap [1]
watering, 4784, mayim [1]
watering places, 5393, mašʾāb [1]
watering, 8115, rāwâ [1]
watering, 9197, šāqâ [1]

WATERLESS [2]
waterless, 401+4784, ʾayin^{1}+mayim [2]

WATERS [151]
waters, 4784, mayim [140]
waters, NIH/RPE [3]
deep waters, 9333, tehôm [3]
waters, 5643, nāhār [2]
the waters, 2157, -hem [1]
waters, 3542, yām [1]
waters, 9197, šāqâ [1]

WATERY [1]
watery deep, 7425, ṣûlâ [1]

WAVE [36]
wave offering, 9485, tenûpâ [21]
wave, 5677, nûp^{1} [12]
wave upon wave, 2722, ḥalîpâ [2]
wave offerings, 9485, tenûpâ [1]

WAVED [10]
waved, 9485, tenûpâ [5]
waved, 5677, nûp^{1} [4]
was waved, 9485+5677, tenûpâ+nûp^{1} [1]

WAVER [1]
waver, 7174, pāsaḥ^{2} [1]

WAVERING [1]
wavering, 5048, māʿad [1]

WAVES [20]
waves, 1644, gal^{2} [13]
waves, 5403, mišbār [3]
waves, 1195, bāmâ^{1} [1]
pounding waves, 1922, dokî [1]
waves, 3338, yād [1]
waves, 4784, mayim [1]

WAVY [1]
wavy, 9446, taltāl [1]

WAX [4]
wax, 1880, dônag [4]

WAY [377]
way, 2006, derek [177]
in this way, 2256, we- [17]
all the way to, 6330, ʿad^{2} [12]
way, NIH/RPE [10]
way, 784, ʾōraḥ [9]
way, AIT [6]
send on way, 8938, šālaḥ [5]
sent on way, 8938, šālaḥ [5]
way, 1821, dābār [3]
on way, 2143, hālak [3]
in this way, 3970, kākâ [3]
in this way, 4027, kēn^{2} [3]
prescribed way, 5477, mišpāṭ [3]
all the way to, 448, ʾel [2]
which way, 625+2025, ʾān+-â^{2} [2]
the way^{s}, 889, ʾašer [2]
be on way, 2143, hālak [2]
go way, 2143, hālak [2]
way, 2143, hālak [2]
went on way, 2143, hālak [2]
were on way, 2143, hālak [2]
force way through, 2238, hāras [2]
in way, 3869, ke- [2]
just the way, 3869+889, ke-+ʾašer [2]
way, 3869, ke- [2]
in the same way, 3970, kākâ [2]
in way, 4027, kēn^{2} [2]
that is the way, 4027, kēn^{2} [2]
give way, 4173, kāšal [2]
in such a way that, 4200, le-^{1} [2]
in way, 4200+7156, le-^{1}+pāneh [2]
way, 5090, maʿaleh [2]
way, 5986, netîbâ [2]
made way around, 6015, sābab [2]
go on way, 6296, ʿābar^{1} [2]
long way, 8158, rāḥôq [2]
make way, 91, ʾabrēk [1]
turned the other way, 345, ʾaḥōrannît [1]
which way, 361+2296+2021+2006, ʾê+zeh+ha-+derek [1]
which way, 361+2296, ʾê+zeh [1]
this is the way, 928+4392, be-+-ām [1]
one way, 928+285, be-+ʾeḥād [1]
all the way to, 995, bôʾ [1]
way^{s}, 1692, gemûlâ [1]
feeling way, 1779, gāšaš [1]
by way of, 2006, derek [1]
way, 2134, hălēʾâ [1]
way, 2142, halîkâ [1]
all the way, 2143, hālak [1]
go on way, 2143, hālak [1]

keeping all the way, 2143+2143, *hālak+hālak* [1]
made way, 2143, *hālak* [1]
miss the way, 2627, *ḥāṭā'* [1]
block the way, 2888, *ḥāsam* [1]
led the way, 3338+2118+8037, *yād+hāyâ+ri'šôn* [1]
on the way, 3655, *yāṣā'* [1]
on way, 3655, *yāṣā'* [1]
in the way, 3869, *k^{e}-* [1]
this way, 3907, *kōh* [1]
every way, 3972, *kōl* [1]
in the same way, 4027, *kēn^{2}* [1]
this way, 4027, *kēn^{2}* [1]
in this way, 4200+5100, *l^{e-1}+ma'an* [1]
in this way, 4200, *l^{e-1}* [1]
gives way, 4202+6641, *lō'+'āmad* [1]
way^{s}, 4316, *laḥaṣ* [1]
gives way, 4572, *môṭ^{1}* [1]
give way, 4614, *mûr^{1}* [1]
give way, 4631, *mûš^{2}* [1]
across the way, 4946+5584, *min+neged* [1]
all the way from, 4946, *min* [1]
out of way, 4946+4200+7156, *min+l^{e-1}+pāneh* [1]
way, 5023, *massa'* [1]
way, 5047, *ma'gāl^{2}* [1]
way up, 5090, *ma'^{a}leh* [1]
way to refute, 5101, *ma'^{a}neh^{1}* [1]
way, 5126, *ma'^{a}śeh* [1]
way prescribed, 5184, *miṣwâ* [1]
way, 5226, *māqôm* [1]
lead the way, 5432, *māšak* [1]
right way, 5477, *mišpāṭ* [1]
way prescribed, 5477, *mišpāṭ* [1]
be on way, 5825+2256+2143, *nāsa'+w^{e}+hālak* [1]
on the way, 6296, *'ābar^{1}* [1]
on way, 6296, *'ābar^{1}* [1]
all the way to, 6330+995+3870, *'ad^{2}+bô'+-kā* [1]
all the way to, 6330+995, *'ad^{2}+bô'* [1]
all the way up, 6330, *'ad^{2}* [1]
all the way to, 6584, *'al^{2}* [1]
in the way should go, 6584+7023+2006, *'al^{2}+peh+derek* [1]
which way, 6584+3545+196+6584+8520, *'al^{2}+yāmîn^{1}+'ô+'al^{2}+ś^{e}mō'l* [1]
on way, 6590, *'ālâ* [1]
is on way, 6590, *'ālâ* [1]
on way up, 6590, *'ālâ* [1]
that way^{s}, 6873, *'ārôm* [1]
give way to panic, 6907, *'āraṣ* [1]
on way, 6913+2006, *'āśâ^{1}+derek* [1]
way, 7156, *pāneh* [1]
give way, 7211, *piq* [1]
opens the way, 8143, *rāḥab* [1]
long way, 8158+4394, *rāḥôq+m^{e}'ōd* [1]
one way^{s}, 8273, *ra'^{1}* [1]
way, 8666, *š^{e}bîl* [1]
see on way, 8938, *šālaḥ* [1]
sent on way, 8938+906, *šālaḥ+'ēt^{1}* [1]
were sent on way, 8938, *šālaḥ* [1]
persist in own way, 9244+4213, *š^{e}rirût+lēb* [1]
drink in own way, 9276, *š^{e}tiyyâ* [1]
usual way of dealing, 9368, *tôrâ* [1]
in way, 10341, *k^{e}-* [1]
gave way, 10742, *š^{e}râ* [1]

WAYLAID [1]
waylaid, 8492+928+2021+2006, *śîm+b^{e}+ha-+derek* [1]

WAYLAY [2]
waylay, 7621, *ṣāpan* [2]

WAYS [210]
ways, 2006, *derek* [180]
ways, *AIT* [5]
ways, 784, *'ōraḥ* [5]
detestable ways, 9359, *tô'ēbâ* [3]
ways, *NIH/RPE* [2]
the ways^{s}, 889, *'^{a}šer* [2]
simple ways, 7344, *petî^{2}* [2]
ways, 10068, *'^{a}raḥ* [2]
ways, 2142, *h^{a}lîkâ* [1]
ways, 2143, *hālak* [1]
ways, 4742, *maḥ^{a}šābâ* [1]
ways, 5019, *m^{e}sillâ* [1]
ways, 5047, *ma'gāl^{2}* [1]
ways, 5095, *ma'^{a}lāl* [1]
ways, 6404, *'āwel* [1]
crooked ways, 6824, *'^{a}qalqāl* [1]
shameful ways, 7830, *qālôn* [1]

WAYWARD [8]
wayward, 5799, *nokrî* [6]
wayward, 9494, *tā'â* [2]

WAYWARDNESS [2]
waywardness, 5412, *m^{e}šûbâ* [2]

WE [941]
we, *AIT* [658]
we, 636, *'^{a}naḥnû* [103]
we, 5646, *-nû^{1}* [94]
we, *NIH/RPE* [56]
we, 638, *'^{a}nî* [6]
we, 5721, *naḥnû* [5]
we, 5883+5646, *nepeš+-nû^{1}* [5]
we, 10047, *'^{a}naḥnā'* [4]
we, 3276, *-î* [3]
we, 5761, *-nî* [2]
we, 644, *'ānōkî* [1]
we, 3972+5646, *kōl+-nû^{1}* [1]
place where we stopped for the night, 4869, *mālôn* [1]
we pray, 5528, *nā'^{1}* [1]
we, 10450, *-nā'* [1]

WE'LL [12]
we'll, *AIT* [11]
we'll, *NIH/RPE* [1]

WE'RE [4]
we're, 636, *'^{a}naḥnû* [2]
we're, *AIT* [1]
we're, 5646, *-nû^{1}* [1]

WE'VE [2]
we've, *AIT* [2]

WEAK [35]
weak, 2703, *ḥālâ^{1}* [8]
weak, 1924, *dal^{2}* [4]
weak, 6949, *'āšaš* [3]
weak, 2143, *hālak* [2]
weak, 3908, *kāhâ^{1}* [2]
weak, 6714, *'ānî* [2]
weak, 8205, *rak* [2]
weak, 401+226, *'ayin^{1}+'ôn^{1}* [1]
weak, 1937, *dālal^{1}* [1]
weak, 3910, *kēheh* [1]
weak, 4173, *kāšal* [1]
weak, 5022, *māsas* [1]
make weak, 5070, *mā'aṭ* [1]
weak, 6488, *'āṭûp* [1]
weak, 6494, *'āṭap^{2}* [1]
weak, 8133, *rûš* [1]
weak, 8332, *rāpâ^{1}* [1]
weak, 8333+3338, *rāpeh+yād* [1]
weak, 8333, *rāpeh* [1]

WEAK-WILLED [1]
weak-willed, 581+4226, *'āmal^{1}+libbâ* [1]

WEAKENED [1]
weakened, 7674, *ṣārar^{1}* [1]

WEAKER [2]
grew weaker and weaker, 2143+2256+1924, *hālak+w^{e}+dal^{2}* [2]

WEAKEST [1]
weakest, 1924, *dal^{2}* [1]

WEAKLING [1]
weakling, 2766, *ḥallāš* [1]

WEAKNESS [1]
weakness, 4202+3946, *lō'+kōaḥ^{1}* [1]

WEALTH [99]
wealth, 2657, *ḥayil* [25]
wealth, 6948, *'ōšer* [21]
wealth, 2104, *hôn* [15]
wealth, 2162, *hāmôn* [5]
wealth, 3883, *kābôd^{1}* [3]
wealth of goods, 2104, *hôn* [2]
wealth, 3856, *yeter^{1}* [2]
wealth, 3860, *yitrâ* [2]
wealth, 3946, *kōaḥ^{1}* [2]
wealth, 8214, *r^{e}kûš* [2]
wealth, *NIH/RPE* [1]
wealth, 226, *'ôn^{1}* [1]
wealth, 238, *'ôṣār* [1]
wealth, 1541, *gādēl* [1]
wealth, 2155, *hām^{2}* [1]
wealth, 2773, *ḥāmad* [1]
wealth, 2890, *ḥōsen* [1]
wealth, 3202, *ṭôb^{2}* [1]
wealth, 3330, *y^{e}gîa'* [1]
wealth, 3780, *yēš* [1]
storing up wealth, 4043, *kānas* [1]
wealth, 5733, *n^{e}ḥōšet^{1}* [1]
wealth, 5794, *n^{e}kāsîm* [1]
wealth, 6938, *'āšîr* [1]
bring wealth, 6947, *'āšar* [1]
brings wealth, 6947, *'āšar* [1]
give wealth, 6947+6948, *'āšar+'ōšer* [1]
wealth, 6947, *'āšar* [1]
heaps up wealth, 7392, *ṣābar* [1]
wealth, 8782, *šûa'^{3}* [1]

WEALTHY [9]
wealthy, 1524, *gādôl* [2]
wealthy, 1540, *gādal* [2]
wealthy, 226, *'ôn^{1}* [1]
wealthy, 2657, *ḥayil* [1]
makes wealthy, 3877, *kābēd^{1}* [1]
wealthy, 3877, *kābēd^{1}* [1]
wealthy, 6938, *'āšîr* [1]

WEANED [10]
weaned, 1694, *gāmal* [7]
was weaned, 1694, *gāmal* [2]
is weaned, 1694, *gāmal* [1]

WEAPON [15]
weapon, 3998, *k^{e}lî* [7]
weapon, 8939, *šelaḥ^{1}* [3]
weapon, *NIH/RPE* [1]
weapon, 3998+4878, *k^{e}lî+milḥāmâ* [1]
weapon, 3998+5424, *k^{e}lî+mašḥēt* [1]
weapon, 3998+7372+4878, *k^{e}lî+ṣābā'^{2}+milḥāmâ* [1]
weapon, 5977, *nešeq^{1}* [1]

WEAPONS [26]
weapons, 3998, *k^{e}lî* [14]
weapons, 5977, *nešeq^{1}* [6]
weapons, 2210, *hōṣen* [1]
weapons, 2723, *ḥ^{a}lîṣâ* [1]
weapons, 2995, *ḥereb* [1]
weapons, 3998+4878, *k^{e}lî+milḥāmâ* [1]
weapons of war, 4878, *milḥāmâ* [1]
weapons, 8939, *šelaḥ^{1}* [1]

WEAR [34]
wear, 4252, *lābaš* [9]
wear out, 1162, *bālâ^{1}* [6]
wear, 2118+6584, *hāyâ+'al^{2}* [3]
wear, 2118, *hāyâ* [2]
wear, 2520, *ḥāgar* [2]
wear, 5951, *nāśā'* [2]
wear themselves out, 2703, *ḥālâ^{1}* [1]
wear out, 3333, *yāga'* [1]
wear out, 3985, *kāleh* [1]
wear, 4059, *kāsâ* [1]
wear, 4200, *l^{e-1}* [1]
wear clothes, 4252, *lābaš* [1]
only wear out, 5570+5570, *nābēl^{1}+nābēl^{1}* [1]
make wear, 6590+6584+5516, *'ālâ+'al^{2}+motnayim* [1]
wear, 6590+6584, *'ālâ+'al^{2}* [1]
wear, 6590, *'ālâ* [1]

WEARIED [6]
- wearied, 3333, *yāga'* [6]

WEARIES [2]
- wearies, 3331, *y^{e}gî'â* [1]
- wearies, 3333, *yāga'* [1]

WEARING [24]
- wearing, 6584, *'al^{2}* [7]
- wearing, 928, *b^{e}-* [4]
- wearing, 2520, *ḥāgar* [4]
- wearing, 4059, *kāsâ* [3]
- wearing, 296, *'āḥaz^{1}* [1]
- wearing, 928+265, *b^{e}-+'ōzen* [1]
- wearing, 5951, *nāśā'* [1]
- wearing, 6486, *'āṭâ^{1}* [1]
- wearing around, 6584, *'al^{2}* [1]
- wearing, 10089, *b^{e}-* [1]

WEARISOME [1]
- wearisome, 3335, *yāgēa'* [1]

WEARS [3]
- wears herself out, 4206, *lā'â* [1]
- wears out, 7551, *ṣāmat* [1]
- wears away, 8835, *šāḥaq* [1]

WEARY [24]
- weary, 6546, *'āyēp* [6]
- weary, 3333, *yāga'* [5]
- weary, 4206, *lā'â* [3]
- weary, 3617, *yā'ēp^{3}* [2]
- weary, 1941, *dālap^{2}* [1]
- weary, 3329+3946, *yāgîa'+kōaḥ^{1}* [1]
- weary, 3335, *yāgēa'* [1]
- grow weary, 3983, *kālâ^{1}* [1]
- weary with longing, 4001, *killāyôn* [1]
- weary themselves, 4206, *lā'â* [1]
- weary, 5883+6546, *nepeš+'āyēp* [1]
- grew weary, 7918, *qāṣar^{2}* [1]

WEASEL [1]
- weasel, 2700, *ḥōled* [1]

WEAVE [2]
- weave, 755, *'ārag* [1]
- weave, 8687, *šābaṣ* [1]

WEAVER [3]
- weaver, 755, *'ārag* [3]

WEAVER'S [5]
- weaver's, 755, *'ārag* [4]
- weaver's shuttle, 756, *'ereg* [1]

WEAVERS [2]
- weavers, 755, *'ārag* [2]

WEAVING [1]
- did weaving, 755+1428, *'ārag+bat^{3}* [1]

WEB [3]
- web, 1074, *bayit^{1}* [2]
- web, 7770, *qûr^{2}* [1]

WEDDING [6]
- had wedding songs, 2146, *hālal^{2}* [1]
- wedding, 3164, *ḥ^{a}tunnâ* [1]
- wedding, 3353, *y^{e}dîdôt* [1]
- wedding ornaments, 8005, *qiššurîm* [1]
- attended at wedding, 8287, *rā'â^{2}* [1]
- wedding gift, 8933, *šillûḥîm* [1]

WEDGE [2]
- wedge, 4383, *lāšôn* [2]

WEEDS [4]
- weeds, 3017, *ḥārûl* [2]
- weeds, 947, *bo'šâ* [1]
- poisonous weeds, 8032, *rō'š^{2}* [1]

WEEK [2]
- bridal week, 8651, *šābûa'* [1]
- week, 8651, *šābûa'* [1]

WEEKS [11]
- weeks, 8651, *šābûa'* [7]
- weeks, 8651+3427, *šābûa'+yôm^{1}* [2]
- Feast of Weeks, 8651, *šābûa'* [1]
- weeks, 8701, *šabbāt* [1]

WEEP [38]
- weep, 1134, *bākâ* [26]
- weep, 1140, *b^{e}kî* [4]
- weep, 65, *'ēbel* [1]
- weep at all, 1134+1134, *bākâ+bākâ* [1]
- weep bitterly, 1134+1134, *bākâ+bākâ* [1]
- weep, 1134+1134, *bākâ+bākâ* [1]
- weep bitterly, 1963+1963, *dāma'+dāma'* [1]
- weep, 3536, *yālal* [1]
- weep, 5951+1140, *nāśā'+b^{e}kî* [1]
- weep, 6199, *sāpad* [1]

WEEPING [41]
- weeping, 1134, *bākâ* [16]
- weeping, 1140, *b^{e}kî* [14]
- weeping, 1965, *dim'â* [2]
- weeping, 5027, *mispēd* [2]
- weeping, *NIH/RPE* [1]
- weeping, 63, *'ābēl^{1}* [1]
- weeping, 1134+1140, *bākâ+b^{e}kî* [1]
- weeping bitterly, 1140+1140, *b^{e}kî+b^{e}kî* [1]
- weeping aloud, 2410, *zā'aq* [1]
- weeping, 7754, *qôl* [1]
- weeping, 7806, *qînâ^{1}* [1]

WEEPS [3]
- weeps, 1140, *b^{e}kî* [2]
- bitterly weeps, 1134+1134, *bākâ+bākâ* [1]

WEIGH [6]
- weigh out, 9202, *šāqal* [2]
- weigh, 9202, *šāqal* [2]
- weigh out, 5484, *mišqôl* [1]
- weigh down, 6584, *'al^{2}* [1]

WEIGHED [29]
- weighed out, 9202, *šāqal* [7]
- weighed, 5486, *mišqāl* [6]
- weighed, *NIH/RPE* [5]
- weighed, 2118, *hāyâ* [1]
- weighed down, 3877, *kābēd^{1}* [1]
- weighed down, 4849, *mālē'^{2}* [1]
- weighed out, 5486, *mišqāl* [1]
- weighed, 6590, *'ālâ* [1]
- be weighed, 9202+9202, *šāqal+šāqal* [1]
- be weighed, 9202, *šāqal* [1]
- weighed, 9202, *šāqal* [1]
- are weighed, 9419, *tākan* [1]
- weighed, 9419, *tākan* [1]
- been weighed, 10769, *t^{e}qal* [1]

WEIGHING [42]
- weighing, *NIH/RPE* [26]
- weighing, 5486, *mišqāl* [16]

WEIGHS [10]
- weighs, *NIH/RPE* [2]
- weighs heavily, 8041, *rab^{1}* [2]
- weighs, 9419, *tākan* [2]
- weighs, 2047, *hāgâ^{1}* [1]
- weighs, 5747, *nāṭal* [1]
- weighs down, 8817, *šāḥâ* [1]
- weighs, 9203, *šeqel* [1]

WEIGHT [27]
- weight, 5486, *mišqāl* [20]
- weight, *NIH/RPE* [4]
- exact weight, 5486, *mišqāl* [1]
- worth their weight, 6131, *sālā'* [1]
- according to the weight current, 6296, *'ābar^{1}* [1]

WEIGHTS [8]
- weights, 74, *'eben* [5]
- differing weights, 74+2256+74, *'eben+w^{e}-+'eben* [2]
- two differing weights, 74+2256+74, *'eben+w^{e}-+'eben* [1]

WELCOME [1]
- welcome, 8934, *šālôm* [1]

WELCOMED [2]
- welcomed, 7709, *qādam* [1]
- welcomed, 7925, *qārā'^{2}* [1]

WELDING [1]
- welding, 1817, *debeq* [1]

WELFARE [2]
- welfare, 3208, *ṭôbâ* [1]
- welfare, 8934, *šālôm* [1]

WELL [219]
- as well as, 2256, *w^{e}-* [41]
- well, 931, *b^{e}'ēr^{1}* [30]
- go well, 3512, *yāṭab* [14]
- well, 3202, *ṭôb^{2}* [10]
- well advanced, 995, *bô'* [7]
- well, 1014, *bôr* [7]
- and as well, 2256, *w^{e}-* [7]
- well, *NIH/RPE* [6]
- as well, 1685, *gam* [4]
- well, 8934, *šālôm* [4]
- as well as, 2256+1685, *w^{e}-+gam* [3]
- well, 3208, *ṭôbâ* [3]
- well, 3512, *yāṭab* [3]
- very well then, 2180, *hinnēh* [2]
- very well, 2180, *hinnēh* [2]
- did well, 3201, *ṭôb^{1}* [2]
- very well, 3202, *ṭôb^{2}* [2]
- as well as, 3481, *yaḥdāw* [2]
- treated well, 3512, *yāṭab* [2]
- very well, 4200+4027, *l^{e}-^{1}+kēn^{2}* [2]
- as well as, 4200+963+4946, *l^{e}-^{1}+bad^{1}+min* [2]
- as well as, 6584, *'al^{2}* [2]
- as well as, 6640, *'im* [2]
- well, *AIT* [1]
- well, 66, *'^{a}bāl* [1]
- spoke well of, 887, *'āšar^{2}* [1]
- as well as, 907, *'ēt^{2}* [1]
- well, 931+4784, *b^{e}'ēr^{1}+mayim* [1]
- note well, 1067+1067, *bîn+bîn* [1]
- well, 1067, *bîn* [1]
- very well, 1685, *gam* [1]
- as well as, 1685, *gam* [1]
- speak well, 1819+1819, *dābar^{2}+dābar^{2}* [1]
- very well go, 2143+2143, *hālak+hālak* [1]
- full well, 2176, *hēn^{1}* [1]
- very well, 2180+5528, *hinnēh+nā'^{1}* [1]
- well, 2180, *hinnēh* [1]
- as well as, 2256+3869, *w^{e}-+k^{e}-* [1]
- as well, 2256, *w^{e}-* [1]
- remember well, 2349+2349, *zākar^{1}+zākar^{1}* [1]
- well remember, 2349+2349, *zākar^{1}+zākar^{1}* [1]
- well, 2876, *ḥesed^{2}* [1]
- done well, 3201, *ṭôb^{1}* [1]
- go well, 3201, *ṭôb^{1}* [1]
- well off, 3201, *ṭôb^{1}* [1]
- well off, 3202, *ṭôb^{2}* [1]
- knows very well, 3359+3359, *yāda'+yāda'* [1]
- well informed, 3359+1981, *yāda'+da'at^{1}* [1]
- goes well, 3512, *yāṭab* [1]
- treat well, 3512, *yāṭab* [1]
- well provided for, 3512, *yāṭab* [1]
- well known, 3700+4394, *yāqar+m^{e}'ōd* [1]
- as well as, 3869, *k^{e}-* [1]
- might well have, 3869+5071, *k^{e}-+m^{e}'aṭ* [1]
- very well then, 3954, *kî^{2}* [1]
- well, 3954, *kî^{2}* [1]
- as well, 3954, *kî^{2}* [1]
- how well, 3954, *kî^{2}* [1]
- as well as, 4017, *k^{e}mô* [1]
- very well, 4027, *kēn^{2}* [1]
- as well, 4027, *kēn^{2}* [1]
- as well as, 4200+6645, *l^{e}-^{1}+'ummâ^{1}* [1]
- wish well, 4200+8934, *l^{e}-^{1}+šālôm* [1]
- learn well, 4340+4340, *lāmad+lāmad* [1]
- full well, 4394, *m^{e}'ōd* [1]
- well versed, 4542, *māhîr* [1]
- well nourished, 4848+2692, *mālē'^{1}+ḥālāb* [1]
- well, 5078, *ma'yān* [1]
- well, 5227, *māqôr* [1]
- well watered, 5482, *mašqeh^{1}* [1]
- listen well, 5742+265, *nāṭâ+'ōzen* [1]
- go well, 5838, *nā'ēm* [1]
- well, 5838, *nā'ēm* [1]
- guard well, 5915, *nāṣar* [1]
- well, 6524, *'ayin^{1}* [1]
- very well, 8011, *rā'â^{1}* [1]
- well watered, 8425, *śāba'* [1]

consider well, 8883+4213, *šît^{1}+lēb* [1]
well, 8929, *šālēw* [1]
all is well, 8934, *šālôm* [1]
grow well, 8934, *šālôm* [1]
cook well, 9462, *tāmam* [1]
as well as, 10554, *ʿim* [1]

WELL'S [1]
well's, 931, *b^{e}'ēr^{1}* [1]

WELL-BEING [4]
well-being, 3202, *ṭôb^{2}* [1]
well-being, 3208, *ṭôbâ* [1]
well-being, 8934, *šālôm* [1]
well-being, 10261, *ḥay* [1]

WELL-BUILT [1]
well-built, 3637+9307, *yāpeh+tō'ar* [1]

WELL-DRESSED [1]
well-dressed hair, 5126+5250, *maʿ^{a}śeh+miqšeh* [1]

WELL-FED [1]
well-fed, 8889, *śākā* [1]

WELL-KNEADED [1]
well-kneaded, 8057, *rābak* [1]

WELL-KNOWN [1]
well-known, 408+9005, *'îš^{1}+šēm^{1}* [1]

WELL-MIXED [1]
well-mixed, 8057, *rābak* [1]

WELL-NOURISHED [1]
well-nourished, 9042, *šāmēn^{1}* [1]

WELL-NURTURED [1]
well-nurtured, 1540, *gādal* [1]

WELL-TO-DO [1]
well-to-do, 1524, *gādôl* [1]

WELL-TRAINED [1]
well-trained, 6913+4878, *ʿāśâ^{1}+milḥāmâ* [1]

WELL-WATERED [6]
well-watered, 8116, *rāweh* [2]
well-watered, 9272+4784, *šātâ^{2}+mayim* [2]
well-watered, 5482, *mašqeh^{1}* [1]
well-watered plant, 8183, *rāṭōb* [1]

WELLS [8]
wells, 931, *b^{e}'ēr^{1}* [2]
wells, 1014, *bôr* [2]
dug wells, 7769, *qûr^{1}* [2]
wells, 931+4784, *b^{e}'ēr^{1}+mayim* [1]
wells, 5078, *maʿyān* [1]

WELLSPRING [1]
wellspring, 9362, *tôṣā'ôt* [1]

WELTS [1]
welts, 2467, *ḥabbûrâ* [1]

WENT [876]
went, 995, *bô'* [174]
went, 2143, *hālak* [171]
went up, 6590, *ʿālâ* [111]
went out, 3655, *yāṣā'* [82]
went down, 3718, *yārad* [63]
went, *NIH/RPE* [24]
went back, 8740, *šûb^{1}* [21]
went, 3655, *yāṣā'* [20]
went in, 995, *bô'* [18]
went away, 2143, *hālak* [11]
went into, 995, *bô'* [10]
went, 6296, *ʿābar^{1}* [10]
went out, 2143, *hālak* [9]
went on, 6296, *ʿābar^{1}* [8]
went, 6590, *ʿālâ* [8]
went back, 995, *bô'* [6]
went, 2118, *hāyâ* [6]
went off, 2143, *hālak* [5]
went on, 2143, *hālak* [5]
went up, 5602, *nāgaš* [5]
went, 5825, *nāsaʿ* [5]
went, 7928, *qārab* [5]
went, *AIT* [3]
went on, 3655, *yāṣā'* [3]
went, 5602, *nāgaš* [3]
went in pursuit, 8103, *rādap* [3]
went astray, 9494, *tāʿâ* [3]
went as a group, 10656, *r^{e}gaš* [3]
went into captivity, 1655, *gālâ* [2]
went into exile, 1655, *gālâ* [2]
went on way, 2143, *hālak* [2]
went over, 2143, *hālak* [2]
went up, 2143, *hālak* [2]
went, 3718, *yārad* [2]
went around, 6015, *sābab* [2]
went, 7756, *qûm* [2]
went, 10016, *'^{a}zal* [2]
went, 10549, *'^{a}lal* [2]
went into, 673, *'āsar* [1]
entered and went, 995, *bô'* [1]
went in to spend the night with, 995+448, *bô'+'el* [1]
went inside, 995, *bô'* [1]
went on, 995, *bô'* [1]
went out, 995, *bô'* [1]
went over, 995, *bô'* [1]
went in search of, 1335, *bāqaš* [1]
went about, 2143, *hālak* [1]
went along, 2143+2143, *hālak+hālak* [1]
went around, 2143, *hālak* [1]
went back, 2143, *hālak* [1]
went down, 2143, *hālak* [1]
went forth, 2143, *hālak* [1]
went forward, 2143, *hālak* [1]
went home, 2143, *hālak* [1]
went in, 2143, *hālak* [1]
went out, 2143+2143, *hālak+hālak* [1]
went, 2143+2143, *hālak+hālak* [1]
went away, 3655, *yāṣā'* [1]
went outside, 3655, *yāṣā'* [1]
went aboard, 3718+928, *yārad+b^{e}-* [1]
went out, 3718, *yārad* [1]
went straight, 3837, *yāšar* [1]
went into labor, 4156, *kāraʿ* [1]
went, 5595, *nāgaʿ* [1]
went close, 5602, *nāgaš* [1]
went over, 5602, *nāgaš* [1]
went over, 5742, *nāṭâ* [1]
went out, 5825, *nāsaʿ* [1]
went throughout, 6015, *sābab* [1]
went, 6015, *sābab* [1]
went over, 6017+2118, *sābîb+hāyâ* [1]
went over, 6073, *sûr^{1}* [1]
went up, 6073, *sûr^{1}* [1]
went as far as, 6296, *ʿābar^{1}* [1]
went away, 6296, *ʿābar^{1}* [1]
went forward, 6296, *ʿābar^{1}* [1]
went over, 6296, *ʿābar^{1}* [1]
went up, 6296, *ʿābar^{1}* [1]
went back, 6590, *ʿālâ* [1]
went off, 6590, *ʿālâ* [1]
went over, 6590, *ʿālâ* [1]
went about, 6913, *ʿāśâ^{1}* [1]
went on, 6913, *ʿāśâ^{1}* [1]
went to war, 6913+4878, *ʿāśâ^{1}+milḥāmâ* [1]
went on, 6980, *ʿātaq* [1]
went out, 7287, *pāraṣ* [1]
went out, 7756, *qûm* [1]
went to work, 7756, *qûm* [1]
went to meet, 7925, *qārā'^{2}* [1]
went near, 7928, *qārab* [1]
went far, 8178, *rāḥaq* [1]
went astray, 8704, *šāgag* [1]
went around, 8763, *šûṭ^{1}* [1]
went, 8801, *šûr^{2}* [1]
went down, 9305, *tāʿar^{1}* [1]
went back, 9588, *t^{e}šûbâ* [1]
went, 10085, *'^{a}tâ* [1]
went in, 10549, *'^{a}lal* [1]
went, 10638, *q^{e}rēb* [1]

WEPT [44]
wept, 1134, *bākâ* [36]
wept, 1134+1140, *bākâ+b^{e}kî* [3]
wept, *NIH/RPE* [1]
wept aloud, 1134, *bākâ* [1]
wept bitterly, 1134+2221+1135, *bākâ+harbēh+bekeh* [1]
wept much, 1134+1134, *bākâ+bākâ* [1]
wept so loudly, 5989+906+7754+928+1140, *nātan+'ēt^{1}+qôl+b^{e}-+b^{e}kî* [1]

WERE [1797]*
were, *NIH/RPE* [809]
were, *AIT* [577]
were, 2118, *hāyâ* [159]
there were no, 401, *'ayin^{1}* [4]
were not, 401, *'ayin^{1}* [4]
were, 10201, *h^{a}wâ* [2]

WEREN'T [1]
weren't, 10379, *lā'* [1]

WEST [91]
west, 3542, *yām* [37]
west, 3542+2025, *yām+-â^{2}* [28]
west, 5115, *maʿ^{a}rāb^{2}* [12]
west, 339, *'aḥar* [4]
west, 294, *'āḥōr* [2]
west, 4427+9087, *mābô'+šemeš* [2]
west, 340, *'aḥ^{a}rôn* [1]
west, 928+6298, *b^{e}-+ʿēber^{1}* [1]
on the west, 4427+2021+9087, *mābô'+ha-+šemeš* [1]
west, 4946+6298, *min+ʿēber^{1}* [1]
west, 5115+2025, *maʿ^{a}rāb^{2}+-â^{2}* [1]
west, 6298, *ʿēber^{1}* [1]

WESTERN [26]
western foothills, 9169, *š^{e}pēlâ* [13]
western, 3542, *yām* [5]
western, 340, *'aḥ^{a}rôn* [4]
western, 3542+2025, *yām+-â^{2}* [2]
western coastlands, 4183, *kittiyyîm* [1]
western^{s}, 4667+2025, *mizrāḥ+-â^{2}* [1]

WESTWARD [4]
westward, 3542+2025, *yām+-â^{2}* [3]
extend westward, 3542+2025, *yām+-â^{2}* [1]

WET [1]
wet with tears, 1134, *bākâ* [1]

WHAT [1708]*
this is what, 3907, *kōh* [471]
what, 4537, *mâ* [343]
what, 889, *'^{a}šer* [178]
what, *AIT* [121]
what, *NIH/RPE* [95]
what, 2021, *ha-* [67]
what^{s}, 2021+1821, *ha-+dābār* [31]
what said, 1821, *dābār* [21]
what, 3869, *k^{e}-* [21]
what, 3869+889, *k^{e}-+'^{a}šer* [18]
what, 4769, *mî* [17]
what^{s}, 1821, *dābār* [11]
what done, 5126, *maʿ^{a}śeh* [11]
what made, 5126, *maʿ^{a}śeh* [10]
what if, 218, *'ûlay^{2}* [9]
what say, 1821, *dābār* [8]
what done, 2006, *derek* [5]
what, 2296, *zeh* [5]
what, 4200+4537, *l^{e-1}+mâ* [5]
what done, 6613, *ʿ^{a}lîlâ* [5]
what, 10408, *mâ* [5]
what, 375, *'ēk* [4]
what done, 1691, *g^{e}mûl* [4]
this is what, 3970, *kākâ* [4]
what, 4027, *kēn^{2}* [4]
what mean, 4537, *mâ* [4]
what done, 7189, *pōʿal* [4]
what, 361+2296, *'ê+zeh* [3]
what^{s}, 2021, *ha-* [3]
that is what, 4027, *kēn^{2}* [3]
this is what, 4027, *kēn^{2}* [3]
what, 928+4537, *b^{e}-+mâ* [2]
what, 928, *b^{e}-* [2]
what, 2085, *hû'* [2]
what, 2180, *hinnēh* [2]
what, 3954, *kî^{2}* [2]
what, 10168, *dî* [2]
what, 10426, *man* [2]

WHAT'S [5]
what's the matter, 4537, *mâ* [3]
what's the meaning of, 4508, *maddûaʿ* [1]
what's, 4537, *mâ* [1]

WHATEVER [124]
whatever, 3972+889, *kōl+ʾ[a]šer* [30]
whatever, 889, *ʾ[a]šer* [18]
whatever, 3972, *kōl* [17]
whatever, 2021, *ha-* [11]
whatever, *AIT* [7]
whatever, 3869+889, *k[e]-+ʾ[a]šer* [7]
whatever, 4537, *mâ* [7]
whatever, 3869+3972+889, *k[e]-+kōl+ʾ[a]šer* [5]
whatever, *NIH/RPE* [3]
whatever, 3869, *k[e]-* [3]
whatever, 3869+3972, *k[e]-+kōl* [2]
whatever, 3869+889+4027, *k[e]-+ʾ[a]šer+kēn[2]* [2]
whatever, 10353+10168, *kōl+dî* [2]
whatever[s], 285, *ʾeḥād* [1]
nothing whatever, 401+3972+1821, *ʾayin[1]+kōl+dābār* [1]
whatever, 928+3972+889, *b[e]-+kōl+ʾ[a]šer* [1]
whatever, 1821+4537, *dābār+mâ* [1]
whatever, 1896, *day* [1]
whatever[s], 2021+3655, *ha-+yāṣāʾ* [1]
whatever, 3869+3972+889+4027, *k[e]-+kōl+ʾ[a]šer+kēn[2]* [1]
whatever do, 5126, *maʿ[a]śeh* [1]
whatever, 10408, *mâ* [1]
whatever, 10408+10168, *mâ+dî* [1]

WHEAT [34]
wheat, 2636, *ḥiṭṭâ* [30]
wheat, 1339, *bar[3]* [2]
wheat, 10272, *ḥinṭā* [2]

WHEEL [12]
wheel, 236, *ʾôpan* [8]
wheel around, 2200+3338, *hāpak+yād* [2]
wheel, 78, *ʾobnayim* [1]
wheel, 1649, *galgal[1]* [1]

WHEELS [32]
wheels, 236, *ʾôpan* [23]
wheels, 1649, *galgal[1]* [3]
wheels, *NIH/RPE* [2]
chariot wheels, 1649, *galgal[1]* [1]
whirling wheels, 1649, *galgal[1]* [1]
wheels, 1651, *gilgāl[1]* [1]
wheels, 10143, *galgal* [1]

WHEN [1991]
when, 2256, *w[e]-* [596]
when, 928, *b[e]-* [497]
when, 3954, *kî[2]* [221]
when, *AIT* [118]
when, 3869, *k[e]-* [112]
when, *NIH/RPE* [82]
and when, 2256, *w[e]-* [64]
when, 928+3427, *b[e]-+yôm[1]* [45]
when, 889, *ʾ[a]šer* [41]
when, 3869+889, *k[e]-+ʾ[a]šer* [38]
when, 561, *ʾim* [27]
but when, 2256, *w[e]-* [25]
when, 4200, *l[e-1]* [25]
when, 928+6961, *b[e]-+ʿēt* [11]
when, 5503, *mātay* [11]
when, 4946, *min* [9]
when, 2022, *h[a]-* [4]
when, 2176, *hēn[1]* [4]
so when, 2256, *w[e]-* [4]
when, 196, *ʾô* [3]
then when, 2256, *w[e]-* [3]
when, 6330, *ʿad[2]* [3]
when, 6584, *ʿal[2]* [3]
when, 6961, *ʿēt* [3]
when, 10341+10168, *k[e]-+dî* [3]
when, 928+2021+3427, *b[e]-+ha-+yôm[1]* [2]
when, 2180, *hinnēh* [2]
now when, 2256, *w[e]-* [2]
even when, 2256, *w[e]-* [2]
when, 4200+6961, *l[e-1]+ʿēt* [2]
when, 4200+7023, *l[e-1]+peh* [2]
when, 6964, *ʿattâ* [2]
when, 10089+10008, *b[e]-+ʾ[e]dayin* [2]
when, 339, *ʾaḥar* [1]
when, 928+8040, *b[e]-+rēʾšît* [1]
when began, 928+3427, *b[e]-+yôm[1]* [1]
when, 1685, *gam* [1]
when also, 2256, *w[e]-* [1]
when, 3427, *yôm[1]* [1]
when, 3954+4200+7023, *kî[2]+l[e-1]+peh* [1]
even when, 3954, *kî[2]* [1]
when, 4946+2118, *min+hāyâ* [1]
when, 4946+255, *min+ʾāz* [1]
when, 4946+3427, *min+yôm[1]* [1]
when, 6330+625+2025, *ʿad[2]+ʾān+-â[2]* [1]
when, 6330+4537, *ʿad[2]+mâ* [1]
when, 6330+8611, *ʿad[2]+ša-* [1]
when, 6584+889, *ʿal[2]+ʾ[a]šer* [1]
when, 6640, *ʿim* [1]
when, 9004, *šām* [1]
when, 9393, *taḥat[1]* [1]
when, 10089+10530+10002, *b[e]-+ʿiddān+-āʾ* [1]
and when, 10221, *w[e]-* [1]
when, 10221, *w[e]-* [1]
when, 10341, *k[e]-* [1]
when, 10427+10168, *min+dî* [1]

WHENEVER [60]
whenever, 928, *b[e]-* [20]
whenever, 2256, *w[e]-* [6]
whenever, 3954, *kî[2]* [5]
whenever, 4946+1896, *min+day* [5]
whenever, 561, *ʾim* [4]
whenever, 3869, *k[e]-* [4]
whenever, 928+3972, *b[e]-+kōl* [3]
whenever, *NIH/RPE* [2]
whenever, *AIT* [1]
whenever, 928+3972+889, *b[e]-+kōl+ʾ[a]šer* [1]
whenever, 928+6961, *b[e]-+ʿēt* [1]
whenever, 928+3427, *b[e]-+yôm[1]* [1]
whenever, 928+3972+6961, *b[e]-+kōl+ʿēt* [1]
and whenever, 2256, *w[e]-* [1]
whenever, 3869+889, *k[e]-+ʾ[a]šer* [1]
whenever, 3954+4946+1896, *kî[2]+min+day* [1]
whenever, 3972, *kōl* [1]
whenever, 4200+7023, *l[e-1]+peh* [1]
whenever, 4200+3972, *l[e-1]+kōl* [1]

WHERE [482]
where, 9004, *šām* [101]
where, 889, *ʾ[a]šer* [79]
where, *NIH/RPE* [70]
where, 372, *ʾayyēh* [43]
where, *AIT* [19]
where, 625+2025, *ʾān+-â[2]* [17]
where, 361, *ʾê* [16]
where, 9004+2025, *šām+-â[2]* [16]
where, 402, *ʾayin[2]* [12]
where, 928, *b[e]-* [10]
where, 361+2296, *ʾê+zeh* [9]
where, 407, *ʾêpōh* [8]
where, 4946+402, *min+ʾayin[2]* [5]
where[s], 5226, *māqôm* [4]
where, 9393, *taḥat[1]* [4]
where settle, 4632, *môšāb* [3]
where, 180, *ʾ[e]hî* [2]
where, 377, *ʾêkâ* [2]
where, 625, *ʾān* [2]
where[s], 928+2023, *b[e]-+-āh* [2]
where, 928+889, *b[e]-+ʾ[a]šer* [2]
where[s], 2021+5226, *ha-+māqôm* [2]
where, 2256, *w[e]-* [2]
place where sets, 4427, *mābôʾ* [2]
where, 4946+9004, *min+šām* [2]
where dwells, 5438, *miškān* [2]
where, 180+686, *ʾ[e]hî+ʾēpôʾ* [1]
where, 378, *ʾêkōh* [1]
where from, 407, *ʾêpōh* [1]
where[s], 824, *ʾereṣ* [1]
where[s], 928+2021+5226, *b[e]-+ha-+māqôm* [1]
where[s], 928+2177, *b[e]-+-hēn[2]* [1]
where[s], 928+2257, *b[e]-+-ô* [1]
where[s], 928+396, *b[e]-+ʾêlim* [1]
where[s], 928+5226, *b[e]-+māqôm* [1]
where[s], 928+6152+8234, *b[e]-+selaʿ[1]+rimmôn[3]* [1]
where[s], 1074, *bayit[1]* [1]
where[s], 2021+2006, *ha-+derek* [1]
where[s], 2021+2958+2021+2667, *ha-+ḥāṣēr[1]+ha-+ḥîṣôn* [1]
do not know where am going, 2143+6584+889+2143, *hālak+ʿal[2]+ʾ[a]šer+hālak* [1]
right where, 2296, *zeh* [1]
where, 2306, *zû* [1]
where, 3954, *kî[2]* [1]
where[s], 4200+4564, *l[e-1]+-mô* [1]
where[s], 4200+7156, *l[e-1]+pāneh* [1]
where lived, 4472, *māgôr[2]* [1]
where, 4537, *mâ* [1]
place where met, 4595, *môʿēd* [1]
place where worshiped, 4595, *môʿēd* [1]
where dawns, 4604, *môṣāʾ[1]* [1]
places where lived, 4632, *môšāb* [1]
region where lived, 4632, *môšāb* [1]
place where they stopped for the night, 4869, *mālôn* [1]
place where we stopped for the night, 4869, *mālôn* [1]
where live, 5061, *māʿôn[2]* [1]
where dwells, 5226, *māqôm* [1]
where lived, 5226, *māqôm* [1]
where, 5226+361, *māqôm+ʾê* [1]
where run, 5330, *mirmās* [1]
place where fed, 5337, *mirʿeh* [1]
place where dwell, 5438, *miškān* [1]
places where turned loose, 5448, *mišlāḥ* [1]
where[s], 6584+2157, *ʿal[2]+-hem* [1]
where[s], 6584+6642, *ʿal[2]+ʿōmed* [1]
where, 6640, *ʿim* [1]
place where standing, 6642, *ʿōmed* [1]
where[s], 6801, *ʿaṣmôn* [1]
where[s], 7730+2025, *qedeš+-â[2]* [1]
where lay, 8070, *rēbeṣ* [1]
where, 8611, *ša-* [1]
where thrown, 9162, *šepek* [1]
where stand, 9393, *taḥat[1]* [1]

WHEREVER [56]
wherever, 928+3972+889, *b[e]-+kōl+ʾ[a]šer* [10]
wherever, 928+3972, *b[e]-+kōl* [10]
wherever, 448+3972+889, *ʾel+kōl+ʾ[a]šer* [3]
wherever, 928+2021+2006+889, *b[e]-+ha-+derek+ʾ[a]šer* [3]
wherever, 928+5226+889, *b[e]-+māqôm+ʾ[a]šer* [3]
wherever, 889, *ʾ[a]šer* [2]
wherever, 928+3972+2021+5226+889, *b[e]-+kōl+ha-+māqôm+ʾ[a]šer* [2]
wherever, 928, *b[e]-* [2]
wherever, 9004+2025, *šām+-â[2]* [2]
wherever, *AIT* [1]
wherever, 625+2025, *ʾān+-â[2]* [1]
wherever, 889+9004+2025, *ʾ[a]šer+šām+-â[2]* [1]
wherever, 928+3972+2021+5226, *b[e]-+kōl+ha-+māqôm* [1]
wherever goes, 928+3655+2256+928+995, *b[e]-+yāṣāʾ+w[e]-+b[e]-+bôʾ* [1]
wherever goes, 928+995+2256+928+3655, *b[e]-+bôʾ+w[e]-+b[e]-+yāṣāʾ* [1]
wherever, 928+2021+5226+889, *b[e]-+ha-+māqôm+ʾ[a]šer* [1]
wherever, 928+285+2021+5226+889, *b[e]-+ʾeḥād+ha-+māqôm+ʾ[a]šer* [1]
wherever, 928+889, *b[e]-+ʾ[a]šer* [1]
wherever, 3972+889+9004, *kōl+ʾ[a]šer+šām* [1]
wherever, 4200+8079, *l[e-1]+regel* [1]
wherever, 4200, *l[e-1]* [1]
wherever, 4946+3972+2021+5226, *min+kōl+ha-+māqôm* [1]
wherever, 4946+889, *min+ʾ[a]šer* [1]
wherever[s], 5226+889, *māqôm+ʾ[a]šer* [1]
wherever, 6584+3972+2021+5226+889, *ʿal[2]+kōl+ha-+māqôm+ʾ[a]šer* [1]
wherever, 6584+3972+889, *ʿal[2]+kōl+ʾ[a]šer* [1]
wherever, 9004, *šām* [1]
wherever, 10089+10353+10168, *b[e]-+kōl+dî* [1]

WHETHER [83]
whether, 561, *ʾim* [16]
whether or, 196, *ʾô* [13]
whether, 2022, *h[a]-* [12]
whether or, 2256, *w[e]-* [10]
whether, 4946, *min* [7]

whether, 928, *b^{e}-* [4]
whether, 196, *'ô* [3]
whether, *NIH/RPE* [2]
whether, 561+4202, *'im+lō'* [2]
whether, 1068, *bayin* [2]
whether, 3954, *kî^{2}* [2]
whether, *AIT* [1]
whether, 677, *'ap^{1}* [1]
whether, 1685, *gam* [1]
whether, 2022+561+4202, *h^{a}-+'im+lō'* [1]
whether, 2256+700, *w^{e}-+'epes* [1]
whether, 2256, *w^{e}-* [1]
whether, 3869, *k^{e}-* [1]
whether, 4017, *k^{e}mô* [1]
whether, 4200, *l^{e}-^{1}* [1]
whether, 4537, *mâ* [1]

WHICH [462]
which, 889, *'^{a}šer* [222]
which, *NIH/RPE* [56]
which, *AIT* [47]
which, 2021, *ha-* [18]
which^{s}, 9004, *šām* [18]
which, 4769, *mî* [11]
which, 2085, *hû'* [9]
which, 10168, *dî* [9]
which^{s}, 2023, *-āh* [7]
which^{s}, 4392, *-ām* [7]
which, 8611, *ša-* [7]
which^{s}, 5626, *-nâ* [5]
in which^{s}, 9004, *šām* [5]
which, 2084, *-hû* [4]
which, 2157, *-hem* [4]
which, 2257, *-ô* [4]
which, 4392, *-ām* [3]
which, 361+2296, *'ê+zeh* [2]
which way, 625+2025, *'ān+-â^{2}* [2]
which, 2023, *-āh* [2]
which, 2296, *zeh* [2]
which way, 361+2296+2021+2006, *'ê+zeh+ha-+derek* [1]
which way, 361+2296, *'ê+zeh* [1]
which^{s}, 678+2257, *'ap^{2}+-ô* [1]
which^{s}, 2021+7366, *ha-+ṣō'n* [1]
which^{s}, 2021+8965, *ha-+šālāl* [1]
which^{s}, 2085, *hû'* [1]
which^{s}, 2177, *-hēn^{2}* [1]
which, 2177, *-hēn^{2}* [1]
name by which remembered, 2352, *zēker* [1]
that which is devoted, 3051, *ḥērem^{1}* [1]
which, 4537, *mâ* [1]
which, 5626, *-nâ* [1]
which^{s}, 6551, *'îr^{1}* [1]
which way, 6584+3545+196+6584+8520, *'al^{2}+yāmîn^{1}+'ô+'al^{2}+ś^{e}mō'l* [1]
which^{s}, 7366+2257, *ṣō'n+-ô* [1]
among which^{s}, 9004, *šām* [1]
which^{s}, 9203, *šeqel* [1]
which, 10193, *-ah* [1]

WHILE [271]
while, 2256, *w^{e}-* [113]
while, 928, *b^{e}-* [48]
while, *NIH/RPE* [23]
while still, 6388, *'ôd* [16]
while, *AIT* [12]
while, 3869, *k^{e}-* [9]
while, 4200, *l^{e}-^{1}* [5]
while, 6330, *'ad^{2}* [5]
while, 3954, *kî^{2}* [3]
little while, 5071, *m^{e}'aṭ* [3]
while married to, 9393, *taḥat^{1}* [3]
while, 928+3427, *b^{e}-+yôm^{1}* [2]
live for a while, 1591, *gûr^{1}* [2]
stay for a while, 1591, *gûr^{1}* [2]
while, 6388, *'ôd* [2]
after a while, 339+2021+1821+2021+465, *'aḥar+ha-+dābār+ha-+'ēlleh* [1]
while, 561, *'im* [1]
while, 889, *'^{a}šer* [1]
while, 928+6288, *b^{e}-+'^{a}bûr^{1}* [1]
for a while stayed, 1591, *gûr^{1}* [1]
but while, 2256, *w^{e}-* [1]
even while, 2256, *w^{e}-* [1]
for a while, 3427+285, *yôm^{1}+'eḥād* [1]
while, 3610, *ya'an^{1}* [1]
while, 3869+889, *k^{e}-+'^{a}šer* [1]
while continues, 3972+3427, *kōl+yôm^{1}* [1]
while, 3972+3427, *kōl+yôm^{1}* [1]
while, 4200+6961, *l^{e}-^{1}+'ēt* [1]
while, 4946, *min* [1]
little while, 5071+8092, *m^{e}'aṭ+rega'* [1]
little while, 5203, *miṣ'ār^{1}* [1]
while still, 6330, *'ad^{2}* [1]
while, 6330+8611, *'ad^{2}+ša-* [1]
little while, 6388+5071, *'ôd+m^{e}'aṭ* [1]
while still alive, 6584+7156, *'al^{2}+pāneh* [1]
while, 10089, *b^{e}-* [1]
while, 10221, *w^{e}-* [1]
while, 10527+10168, *'ad+dî* [1]

WHIP [2]
whip, 8765, *šôṭ^{1}* [2]

WHIPS [6]
whips, 8765, *šôṭ^{1}* [5]
whips, 8849, *šōṭēṭ* [1]

WHIRLING [1]
whirling wheels, 1649, *galgal^{1}* [1]

WHIRLWIND [13]
whirlwind, 6070, *sûpâ^{1}* [6]
whirlwind, 6194, *s^{e}'ārâ* [3]
whirlwind, 1649, *galgal^{1}* [1]
scattered with a whirlwind, 6192, *sā'ar* [1]
whirlwind, 6193, *sa'ar* [1]
whirlwind, 8120, *rûaḥ* [1]

WHIRLWINDS [1]
whirlwinds, 6070, *sûpâ^{1}* [1]

WHIRRING [1]
whirring, 7527, *ṣilṣāl^{1}* [1]

WHISPER [9]
whisper, 7627, *ṣāpap* [2]
whisper, 1821, *dābār* [1]
whisper, 1960, *d^{e}māmâ* [1]
whisper, 4317, *lāḥaš* [1]
barely whisper a prayer, 7440+4318, *ṣûq^{2}+laḥaš* [1]
whisper, 7754+1960, *qôl+d^{e}māmâ* [1]
whisper, 8557, *šāpâ* [1]
whisper, 9066, *šēmeṣ* [1]

WHISPERING [2]
whispering, 1804, *dibbâ* [1]
whispering among themselves, 4317, *lāḥaš* [1]

WHISTLE [1]
whistle, 9239, *šāraq* [1]

WHISTLES [1]
whistles, 9239, *šāraq* [1]

WHISTLING [1]
whistling, 9241, *š^{e}riqâ* [1]

WHITE [37]
white, 4237, *lābān^{1}* [24]
white, 2580, *ḥûr^{1}* [2]
white owl, 9492, *tinšemet^{2}* [2]
white, *NIH/RPE* [1]
white linen, 1009, *bûṣ* [1]
leaving white, 4235, *lāban^{1}* [1]
white, 4235, *lāban^{1}* [1]
white, 7467, *ṣāḥōr* [1]
white, 8202, *rîr^{2}* [1]
white hair, 8484, *śêbâ* [1]
white, 10254, *ḥiwwār* [1]
white, 10490, *n^{e}qē'* [1]

WHITER [3]
whiter, 4235, *lāban^{1}* [1]
whiter, 4237, *lābān^{1}* [1]
whiter, 7458, *ṣāḥaḥ* [1]

WHITEWASH [6]
whitewash, 9521, *tāpēl^{1}* [4]
whitewash, 3212+9521, *ṭûaḥ+tāpēl^{1}* [1]
whitewash, 3225, *ṭîaḥ* [1]

WHITEWASHED [1]
whitewashed, 3212, *ṭûaḥ* [1]

WHO [3366]*
who, *AIT* [1737]
who, 889, *'^{a}šer* [527]
who, 2021, *ha-* [468]
who, 4769, *mî* [285]
who, *NIH/RPE* [189]
who, 2085, *hû'* [32]
who, 10168, *dî* [18]
who, 8611, *ša-* [15]
who, 2257, *-ô* [13]
who, 2156, *hēm* [6]
who, 2157, *-hem* [6]
who, 4392, *-ām* [6]
who^{s}, 2021+3913, *ha-+kōhēn* [4]
who, 4537, *mâ* [4]
who, 408, *'îš^{1}* [3]
who, 465, *'ēlleh* [3]
who^{s}, 2061, *h^{a}dad'ezer* [2]
who, 2296, *zeh* [2]
who, 10426, *man* [2]

WHOEVER [111]
whoever, *AIT* [41]
whoever, 3972, *kōl* [22]
whoever, 2021, *ha-* [18]
whoever, 4769, *mî* [6]
whoever, 889, *'^{a}šer* [4]
whoever, 408+889, *'îš^{1}+'^{a}šer* [2]
whoever, 408, *'îš^{1}* [2]
whoever, 4769+2021+408, *mî+ha-+'îš^{1}* [2]
whoever, 4769+889, *mî+'^{a}šer* [2]
whoever, 10426+10168, *man+dî* [2]
whoever, *NIH/RPE* [1]
whoever^{s}, 265, *'ōzen* [1]
whoever^{s}, 1505, *geber^{1}* [1]
whoever^{s}, 2021, *ha-* [1]
whoever, 2085, *hû'* [1]
whoever, 3972+408+889, *kōl+'îš^{1}+'^{a}šer* [1]
whoever, 3972+2021+132, *kōl+ha-+'ādām^{1}* [1]
whoever he may be, 6424+2256+6699, *'ûr^{3}+w^{e}-+'ānâ^{1}* [1]
whoever, 10353+10050+10168, *kōl+'^{e}nāš+dî* [1]
whoever, 10353+10168, *kōl+dî* [1]

WHOLE [298]
whole, 3972, *kōl* [265]
whole, 10353, *kōl* [7]
whole, *NIH/RPE* [3]
whole, 4003, *kālîl* [3]
whole, *AIT* [2]
whole, 3427, *yôm^{1}* [2]
whole, 8969, *šālēm^{2}* [2]
whole, 9459, *tāmîm* [2]
whole month, 2544+3427, *ḥōdeš^{1}+yôm^{1}* [1]
the whole land^{s}, 3776, *yiśrā'ēl* [1]
whole region, 3971, *kikkār* [1]
whole burnt offerings, 4003, *kālîl* [1]
whole burnt offering, 4003, *kālîl* [1]
whole band, 4850, *m^{e}lō'* [1]
whole, 5303, *merḥāb* [1]
whole assembly, 7736+2256+6337, *qāhāl+w^{e}-+'ēdâ^{1}* [1]
whole, 8041, *rab^{1}* [1]
whole, 8049, *rābâ^{1}* [1]
whole earth, 9315+824, *tēbēl+'ereṣ* [1]
whole world, 9315+824, *tēbēl+'ereṣ* [1]

WHOLEHEARTED [4]
wholehearted devotion, 4213+8969, *lēb+šālēm^{2}* [2]
wholehearted devotion, 4222+8969, *lēbāb+šālēm^{2}* [2]

WHOLEHEARTEDLY [14]
wholeheartedly, 4848, *mālē'^{1}* [7]
wholeheartedly, 928+3972+4213, *b^{e}-+kōl+lēb* [2]
wholeheartedly, 928+3972+4222, *b^{e}-+kōl+lēbāb* [2]
wholeheartedly, 928+4222+8969, *b^{e}-+lēbāb+šālēm^{2}* [2]

wholeheartedly, 928+4213+8969,
b^{e}-+lēb+šālēm^{2} [1]

WHOLESOME [1]

wholesome, 8324, *rāpāʾ^{1}* [1]

WHOLLY [2]

be given wholly, 5989+5989, *nātan+nātan* [2]

WHOM [228]

whom, 889, *ʾ^{a}šer* [120]
whom, 4769, *mî* [34]
whom, 2257, *-ô* [26]
whom, *NIH/RPE* [13]
whom, 10168, *dî* [8]
whom, *AIT* [7]
whom, 2157, *-hem* [4]
whom, 8611, *ša-* [3]
whom, 4392, *-ām* [2]
whom, 5647, *-nû^{2}* [2]
whom^{s}, 9004, *šām* [2]
whom^{s}, 367, *ʾōyēb* [1]
whom, 2021, *ha-* [1]
whom, 2023, *-āh* [1]
whom, 2084, *-hû* [1]
whom, 2296, *zeh* [1]
whom, 3871, *-k* [1]
whom^{s}, 3937, *kûšan rišʿātayim* [1]

WHOSE [218]

whose, 2257, *-ô* [56]
whose, 889, *ʾ^{a}šer* [42]
whose, *NIH/RPE* [23]
whose, *AIT* [21]
whose, 4392, *-ām* [15]
whose, 2023, *-āh* [12]
whose, 4769, *mî* [11]
whose, 2157, *-hem* [7]
whose, 8611, *ša-* [4]
whose^{s}, 1201, *bēn^{1}* [3]
whose, 2021, *ha-* [3]
whose, 4200+2257, *l^{e}-^{1}+-ô* [3]
whose, 4200+4769, *l^{e}-^{1}+mî* [3]
whose^{s}, 2021, *ha-* [2]
whose, 2084, *-hû* [2]
whose, 3871, *-k* [2]
whose^{s}, 465+1426+2257, *ʾēlleh+bat^{1}+-ô* [1]
whose^{s}, 1426+7524, *bat^{1}+s^{e}lopḥād* [1]
whose^{s}, 2021+285+2021+9108,
ha-+ʾeḥād+ha-+šēnî [1]
whose, 2085, *hûʾ* [1]
whose, 2306, *zû* [1]
whose, 3870, *-kā* [1]
whose, 4200+889, *l^{e}-^{1}+ʾ^{a}šer* [1]
whose^{s}, 6690, *ʿ^{a}māśāʾ* [1]
whose, 10168, *dî* [1]

WHY [394]

why, 4200+4537, *l^{e}-^{1}+mâ* [165]
why, 4508, *maddûaʿ* [70]
why, *NIH/RPE* [35]
that is why, 6584+4027, *ʿal^{2}+kēn^{2}* [34]
why, 4537, *mâ* [33]
why, 6584+4537, *ʿal^{2}+mâ* [13]
why, 3954, *kî^{2}* [8]
why, 375, *ʾêk* [6]
this is why, 6584+4027, *ʿal^{2}+kēn^{2}* [5]
that is why, 2256, *w^{e}-* [4]
why, *AIT* [2]
why, 10378+10408, *l^{e}-+mâ* [2]
why, 361+4200+2296, *ʾê+l^{e}-^{1}+zeh* [1]
why, 561+4027+4200+4537,
ʾim+kēn^{2}+l^{e}-^{1}+mâ [1]
why, 928+4537, *b^{e}-+mâ* [1]
why, 1821, *dābār* [1]
this is why, 2180, *hinnēh* [1]
and that is why, 2256, *w^{e}-* [1]
why, 3610+4537, *yaʿan^{1}+mâ* [1]
is that why, 3954, *kî^{2}* [1]
but why, 4200+4537, *l^{e}-^{1}+mâ* [1]
that is why, 4200+5100, *l^{e}-^{1}+maʿan* [1]
this is why, 6584+465, *ʿal^{2}+ʾēlleh* [1]
that's why, 6584+4027, *ʿal^{2}+kēn^{2}* [1]
why, 6584+2296, *ʿal^{2}+zeh* [1]
why, 8611+4200+4537, *ša-+l^{e}-^{1}+mâ* [1]
why, 9393+4537, *taḥat^{1}+mâ* [1]
that is why, 10542+10180, *ʿal+d^{e}nâ* [1]
why, 10542+10408, *ʿal+mâ* [1]

WICK [10]

wick trimmers, 4662, *m^{e}zammeret* [5]
wick trimmers, 4920, *melqāḥayim* [3]
wick, 7325, *pištâ* [2]

WICKED [342]

wicked, 8401, *rāšāʿ* [237]
wicked, 8273, *raʿ^{1}* [24]
wicked, 8317, *rāʿaʿ^{1}* [10]
wicked, 6406, *ʿawlâ* [7]
wicked, 224, *ʾāwen^{1}* [6]
wicked, 1175, *b^{e}liyyaʿal* [6]
wicked, 8288, *rāʿâ^{3}* [6]
wicked, 8400, *rešaʿ* [5]
wicked, *NIH/RPE* [4]
wicked, 6411, *ʿāwōn* [4]
wicked, 1201+1175, *bēn^{1}+b^{e}liyyaʿal* [3]
wicked schemes, 2365, *zimmâ^{1}* [2]
the wicked^{s}, 4392, *-ām* [2]
wicked schemes, 4659, *m^{e}zimmâ* [2]
wicked, 6405, *ʿawwāl* [2]
wicked, 8278, *rōaʿ* [2]
wicked, 8399, *rāšaʿ* [2]
wicked fools, 211, *ʾ^{e}wîl^{1}* [1]
the wicked^{s}, 2257, *-ô* [1]
wicked, 2365, *zimmâ^{1}* [1]
wicked, 2627, *ḥaṭṭāʾ* [1]
wicked people, 2629, *ḥaṭṭāʾ* [1]
wicked, 4202+3202, *lōʾ+ṭôb^{2}* [1]
wicked deeds, 5095, *maʿ^{a}lāl* [1]
wicked, 5360, *miršaʿat* [1]
wicked fools, 5572, *nābāl^{1}* [1]
wicked thing, 5576, *n^{e}bālâ* [1]
the wicked^{s}, 5647, *-nû^{2}* [1]
wicked, 6836, *ʿiqqēš^{1}* [1]
wicked men, 7188+224, *pāʿal+ʾāwen^{1}* [1]
wicked thing, 8288, *rāʿâ^{3}* [1]
do wicked thing, 8317, *rāʿaʿ^{1}* [1]
wicked, 8402, *rišʿâ* [1]
wicked, 10090, *bʾyš* [1]
wicked, 10705, *š^{e}ḥat* [1]

WICKEDLY [7]

acted wickedly, 8399, *rāšaʿ* [3]
acted very wickedly, 2472+2472,
ḥābal^{2}+ḥābal^{2} [1]
wickedly, 6406, *ʿawlâ* [1]
acted wickedly, 8317, *rāʿaʿ^{1}* [1]
wickedly, 8317, *rāʿaʿ^{1}* [1]

WICKEDNESS [94]

wickedness, 8288, *rāʿâ^{3}* [32]
wickedness, 8400, *rešaʿ* [16]
wickedness, 6411, *ʿāwōn* [13]
wickedness, 8402, *rišʿâ* [11]
wickedness, 6406, *ʿawlâ* [7]
wickedness, 2365, *zimmâ^{1}* [3]
wickedness, 8401, *rāšāʿ* [3]
wickedness, 224, *ʾāwen^{1}* [1]
wickedness, 1175, *b^{e}liyyaʿal* [1]
wickedness, 2632, *ḥaṭṭāʾâ* [1]
wickedness, 2633, *ḥaṭṭāʾt* [1]
promoted wickedness, 7277, *pāraʿ^{2}* [1]
wickedness, 7317, *paš* [1]
wickedness is great, 8288+8288, *rāʿâ^{3}+rāʿâ^{3}* [1]
guilty of wickedness, 8399, *rāšaʿ* [1]
wickedness, 10532, *ʿ^{a}wāyâ* [1]

WIDE [98]

wide, 8145, *rōḥab* [69]
wide, *NIH/RPE* [9]
wide, 802, *ʾōrek* [2]
far and wide, 4946+2085+2256+2134,
min+hûʾ+w^{e}-+hālēʾâ [2]
open wide, 7198, *pāṣâ* [2]
wide, 10603, *p^{e}tāy* [2]
wide, *AIT* [1]
stretch wide, 5742, *nāṭâ* [1]
far and wide, 6330+4200+4946+8158,
ʿad^{2}+l^{e}-^{1}+min+rāḥôq [1]
far and wide, 6330+8158, *ʿad^{2}+rāḥôq* [1]
opened wide, 7198, *pāṣâ* [1]
far and wide, 7287, *pāraṣ* [1]
open wide, 7337, *pātaḥ^{1}* [1]
wide open, 7337+7337, *pātaḥ^{1}+pātaḥ^{1}* [1]
wide, 8041, *rab^{1}* [1]
open wide, 8143, *rāḥab* [1]
opened wide, 8143, *rāḥab* [1]
wide, 8143, *rāḥab* [1]

WIDELY [1]

widely, 8158, *rāḥôq* [1]

WIDENED [1]

widened, 8145, *rōḥab* [1]

WIDER [2]

wider, 8143, *rāḥab* [1]
wider, 8146, *rāḥāb^{1}* [1]

WIDESPREAD [1]

widespread, 8044, *rōb* [1]

WIDOW [40]

widow, 530, *ʾalmānâ* [31]
widow, 851, *ʾiššâ* [6]
widow, 851+4637, *ʾiššâ+mût* [1]
brother's widow, 3304, *y^{e}bāmâ* [1]
widow^{s}, 5626, *-nâ* [1]

WIDOW'S [6]

widow's, 530, *ʾalmānâ* [4]
widow's, 531, *ʾalmānût* [2]

WIDOWHOOD [2]

widowhood, 529, *ʾalmōn* [1]
widowhood, 531, *ʾalmānût* [1]

WIDOWS [19]

widows, 530, *ʾalmānâ* [18]
widows, 531, *ʾalmānût* [1]

WIDTH [11]

width, 8145, *rōḥab* [11]

WIELD [1]

wield, 5677, *nûp^{1}* [1]

WIELDING [1]

wielding, 995+4200+5087+2025,
bôʾ+l^{e}-^{1}+maʿal^{2}+-â^{2} [1]

WIFE [270]

wife, 851, *ʾiššâ* [253]
wife, *AIT* [6]
wife, *NIH/RPE* [6]
wife, 851+1249, *ʾiššâ+baʿal^{1}* [1]
your wife^{s}, 2023, *-āh* [1]
brother's wife, 3304, *y^{e}bāmâ* [1]
become wife, 4374+4200+851,
lāqaḥ+l^{e}-^{1}+ʾiššâ [1]
rival wife, 7675, *ṣārar^{2}* [1]

WIFE'S [9]

wife's, 851, *ʾiššâ* [9]

WILD [86]

wild, 8441, *śādeh* [24]
wild, 824, *ʾereṣ* [6]
wild animals, 2651, *ḥayyâ^{1}* [6]
wild ox, 8028, *r^{e}ʾēm* [6]
torn by wild animals, 3274, *ṭ^{e}rēpâ* [5]
wild donkey, 7230, *pereʾ* [4]
wild, 8273, *raʿ^{1}* [4]
wild, 928+2021+8441, *b^{e}-+ha-+śādeh* [3]
wild donkeys, 7230, *pereʾ* [3]
wild, 10119, *bar^{1}* [3]
wild beasts, 2651, *ḥayyâ^{1}* [2]
wild goats, 3604, *yāʿēl^{1}* [2]
wild game, 7473, *ṣayid^{1}* [2]
wild oxen, 8028, *r^{e}ʾēm* [2]
wild goats, 8538, *śāʿîr^{2}* [2]
wild goat, 735, *ʾaqqô* [1]
wild beasts, 989, *b^{e}hēmâ* [1]
wild animal, 2651, *ḥayyâ^{1}* [1]
was torn to pieces by a wild animal, 3271+3271,
ṭārap+ṭārap [1]
animals torn by wild beasts, 3274, *t^{e}rēpâ* [1]
wild, 5799, *nokrî* [1]
wild donkey's, 7230, *pereʾ* [1]
wild donkey, 7241, *pereh* [1]

running wild, 7277, *pāra'*[2] [1]
wild, 8442, *śāday* [1]
wild olive, 9043, *šemen* [1]
wild donkeys, 10570, *'ᵃrād* [1]

WILDER [1]
grew even wilder, 2143+2256+6192, *hālak+wᵉ-+sā'ar* [1]

WILDERNESS [5]
wilderness, 4497, *midbār*[1] [2]
wilderness, 6858, *'ᵃrābâ*[2] [2]
barren wilderness, 4497, *midbār*[1] [1]

WILDS [1]
wilds, 1340, *bar*[4] [1]

WILL [8418]
will, *AIT* [7846]
will, *NIH/RPE* [502]
will, 2118, *hāyâ* [19]
there will be no, 401, *'ayin*[1] [8]
will, 3780, *yēš* [4]
will, 8356, *rāṣôn* [4]
will, 14, *'ābâ* [2]
there will be none, 401, *'ayin*[1] [2]
will, 2911, *ḥāpēṣ*[1] [2]
will, 4213, *lēb* [2]
that will mean, 255, *'āz* [1]
there will not be, 401, *'ayin*[1] [1]
will not, 401, *'ayin*[1] [1]
will[s], 995, *bô'* [1]
one who will inherit, 1201+5479, *bēn*[1]*+mešeq* [1]
will[s], 1819+1821, *dābar*[2]*+dābār* [1]
will be laid waste, 1959, *dāmam*[3] [1]
seek will, 2011, *dāraš* [1]
will[s], 2143, *hālak* [1]
will[s], 2649, *ḥāyâ* [1]
will, 2914, *ḥēpeṣ* [1]
will, 3523, *yākōl* [1]
will[s], 3718, *yārad* [1]
there will be, 3780, *yēš* [1]
because that will mean, 3954, *kî*[2] [1]
life will not be worth living, 4200+4537+2644, *lᵉ-*[1]*+mâ+ḥay*[1] [1]
will, 4273, *lû* [1]
none will be, 4946+401, *min+'ayin*[1] [1]
will, 4946, *min* [1]
if you will, 5528, *nā'*[1] [1]
will, 5706, *nāḥal* [1]
will[s], 6037, *sāgar* [1]
will, 6584+7023, *'al*[2]*+peh* [1]
righteous will, 7407, *ṣᵉdāqâ* [1]
show ill will, 8317+6524, *rā'a'*[1]*+'ayin*[1] [1]
will be left with, 10029+10378, *'îtay+lᵉ-* [1]
will, 10668, *rᵉ'û* [1]

WILLFUL [3]
willful sins, 2294, *zēd* [1]
willful, 4213, *lēb* [1]
willful pride, 7262+1542, *pᵉrî+gōdel* [1]

WILLFULLY [1]
willfully, 928+4222, *bᵉ-+lēbāb* [1]

WILLING [32]
willing, 14, *'ābâ* [11]
willing, 5618, *nādîb* [3]
willing, *AIT* [2]
willing, 5607, *nᵉdābâ* [2]
willing, 5618+4213, *nādîb+lēb* [2]
willing, 5951+4213, *nāśā'+lēb* [2]
willing, 2911, *ḥāpēṣ*[1] [1]
willing, 2913, *ḥāpēṣ*[3] [1]
willing, 3283, *yā'al*[2] [1]
willing response, 5605, *nādab* [1]
willing volunteers, 5605, *nādab* [1]
willing, 5605+4213, *nādab+lēb* [1]
willing, 5605+8120, *nādab+rûaḥ* [1]
willing, 5605, *nādab* [1]
willing, 5883, *nepeš* [1]
be a willing party, 5951+5883, *nāśā'+nepeš* [1]

WILLINGLY [5]
willingly, 4946+4213, *min+lēb* [1]
gave willingly, 5605, *nādab* [1]
given willingly, 5605, *nādab* [1]
willingly given, 5605, *nādab* [1]
willingly offer themselves, 5605, *nādab* [1]

WILLOW [1]
willow, 7628, *ṣapṣāpâ* [1]

WILLS [1]
wills, 5706, *nāḥal* [1]

WILY [1]
wily, 7349, *pātal* [1]

WIN [2]
win, 5162, *māṣā'* [1]
win, 7503, *ṣālaḥ*[2] [1]

WIND [99]
wind, 8120, *rûaḥ* [79]
east wind, 7708, *qādîm* [7]
wind, *NIH/RPE* [3]
south wind, 9402, *têmān*[1] [2]
south wind, 1999, *dārôm* [1]
wind, 6193, *sa'ar* [1]
north wind, 7600, *ṣāpôn*[1] [1]
desert wind, 7708, *qādîm* [1]
hot east wind, 7708, *qādîm* [1]
violent wind, 8120+6194, *rûaḥ+sᵉ'ārâ* [1]
wind, 8551, *śa'ar*[2] [1]
wind, 10658, *rûaḥ* [1]

WINDBLOWN [3]
windblown, 5622, *nādap* [3]

WINDING [1]
winding, 6824, *'ᵃqalqāl* [1]

WINDOW [14]
window, 2707, *ḥallôn* [13]
window, 748, *'ᵃrubbâ* [1]

WINDOWS [13]
windows, 2707, *ḥallôn* [10]
windows, 748, *'ᵃrubbâ* [1]
windows placed high, 9209, *šᵉqupîm* [1]
windows, 10348, *kawwâ* [1]

WINDS [20]
winds, 8120, *rûaḥ* [13]
winds through, 6015, *sābab* [2]
driving winds, 4668, *mᵉzārîm* [1]
violent winds, 6193, *sa'ar* [1]
east winds, 7708, *qādîm* [1]
violent winds, 8120+6194, *rûaḥ+sᵉ'ārâ* [1]
winds, 10658, *rûaḥ* [1]

WINDSTORM [2]
windstorm, 6070, *sûpâ*[1] [1]
windstorm, 8120+6194, *rûaḥ+sᵉ'ārâ* [1]

WINE [194]
wine, 3516, *yayin* [132]
new wine, 9408, *tîrôš* [34]
wine, 10271, *ḥᵃmar* [6]
wine, *NIH/RPE* [5]
new wine, 6747, *'āsîs* [3]
bowls of mixed wine, 4932, *mimsāk* [2]
wine vinegar, 2810, *ḥōmeṣ* [1]
old wine, 3516, *yayin* [1]
wine offerings, 3516, *yayin* [1]
wine vat, 3676, *yeqeb* [1]
blended wine, 4641, *mezeg* [1]
choice wine, 6011, *sōbe'* [1]
wine, 6011, *sōbe'* [1]
wine, 6747, *'āsîs* [1]
wine stewards, 8042+1074, *rab*[2]*+bayit*[1] [1]
aged wine, 9069, *šemer*[1] [1]
wine served, 9197, *šāqâ* [1]
wine, 9408, *tîrôš* [1]

WINEPRESS [12]
winepress, 3676, *yeqeb* [7]
winepress, 1780, *gat*[1] [4]
winepress, 7053, *pûrâ* [1]

WINEPRESSES [4]
winepresses, 3676, *yeqeb* [3]
winepresses, 1780, *gat*[1] [1]

WINES [1]
wines, 9069, *šemer*[1] [1]

WINESKIN [4]
wineskin, 5574, *nēbel*[1] [2]
wineskin, 2827, *ḥēmet* [1]
wineskin, 5532, *nō'd* [1]

WINESKINS [3]
wineskins, 5532+3516, *nō'd+yayin* [2]
wineskins, 199, *'ôb*[1] [1]

WING [16]
wing, 4053, *kānāp* [14]
wing, *NIH/RPE* [1]
bird on the wing, 1251+4053, *ba'al*[1]*+kānāp* [1]

WINGED [4]
winged, 6416, *'ôp* [2]
winged, 4053, *kānāp* [1]
winged creature, 6416, *'ôp* [1]

WINGS [67]
wings, 4053, *kānāp* [56]
wings, *NIH/RPE* [6]
wings, 10149, *gap* [3]
wings, 88, *'ēber* [2]

WINGSPAN [1]
total wingspan, 4053+802, *kānāp+'ōrek* [1]

WINK [1]
maliciously wink, 7975, *qāraṣ* [1]

WINKS [3]
winks, 6781, *'āṣâ* [1]
winks maliciously, 7975+6524, *qāraṣ+'ayin*[1] [1]
winks, 7975, *qāraṣ* [1]

WINNING [2]
winning, 1504, *gābar* [2]

WINNOW [4]
winnow, 2430, *zārâ*[1] [4]

WINNOWING [2]
winnowing, 2430, *zārâ*[1] [1]
winnowing fork, 4665, *mizreh* [1]

WINNOWS [2]
winnows out, 2430, *zārâ*[1] [2]

WINS [2]
wins, 4374, *lāqaḥ* [1]
wins, 5989, *nātan* [1]

WINTER [8]
winter, 3074, *ḥōrep* [5]
winter rains, 1773, *gešem*[1] [1]
all winter, 3069, *ḥārap*[1] [1]
winter, 6255, *sᵉtāw* [1]

WIPE [11]
wipe out, 6, *'ābad* [2]
wipe, 4681, *māḥâ*[1] [2]
wipe out, 9012, *šāmad* [2]
wipe out, 3948, *kāḥad* [1]
wipe, 3983, *kālâ*[1] [1]
wipe out, 4162, *kārat* [1]
wipe away, 4681, *māḥâ*[1] [1]
wipe out, 4681, *māḥâ*[1] [1]

WIPED [10]
wiped out, 4681, *māḥâ*[1] [2]
wiped out, 6, *'ābad* [1]
be wiped out, 1950, *dāmâ*[3] [1]
wiped, 3948, *kāḥad* [1]
wiped out, 3983, *kālâ*[1] [1]
wiped, 3983, *kālâ*[1] [1]
be wiped away, 4681, *māḥâ*[1] [1]
be wiped out, 4681, *māḥâ*[1] [1]
were wiped, 4681, *māḥâ*[1] [1]

WIPES [2]
wipes, 4681, *māḥâ*[1] [2]

WIPING [1]
wiping, 4681, *māḥâ*[1] [1]

WISDOM [166]
wisdom, 2683, *ḥokmâ* [131]
wisdom, 10266, *ḥokmâ* [7]
wisdom, 2682, *ḥākām* [4]
wisdom, 2684, *ḥokmôt* [4]
wisdom, 8507, *śekel* [3]
wisdom, 1069, *bînâ* [2]
wisdom[s], 2023, *-āh* [2]
wisdom, 2681, *ḥākam* [2]
wisdom, 9370, *tûšiyyâ* [2]
wisdom, *NIH/RPE* [1]
teach wisdom, 2681, *ḥākam* [1]
wisdom, 4213, *lēb* [1]
wisdom, 8120+2683, *rûaḥ+ḥokmâ* [1]
gaining wisdom, 8505, *śākal*[1] [1]
wisdom[s], 8611, *ša-* [1]
wisdom, 9312, *tᵉbûnâ* [1]
true wisdom, 9370, *tûšiyyâ* [1]
wisdom, 10539, *ʿēṭâ* [1]

WISE [155]
wise, 2682, *ḥākām* [105]
wise, 10265, *ḥakkîm* [14]
wise, 2681, *ḥākam* [13]
wise, 8505, *śākal*[1] [13]
wise, 4213, *lēb* [2]
wise, *NIH/RPE* [1]
making wise, 2681, *ḥākam* [1]
extremely wise, 2682+2681, *ḥākām+ḥākam* [1]
wise, 2682+4213, *ḥākām+lēb* [1]
wise advice, 2683, *ḥokmâ* [1]
wise, 2683, *ḥokmâ* [1]
become wise, 4220, *lābab*[1] [1]
wise, 8507, *śekel* [1]

WISELY [3]
acted wisely, 1067, *bîn* [1]
act wisely, 8505, *śākal*[1] [1]
wisely, 8505, *śākal*[1] [1]

WISER [7]
wiser, 2681, *ḥākam* [2]
wiser, 2682, *ḥākām* [2]
wiser, *NIH/RPE* [1]
make wiser, 2681, *ḥākam* [1]
makes wiser, 2681, *ḥākam* [1]

WISEST [1]
wisest, 2682, *ḥākām* [1]

WISH [9]
wish, *AIT* [1]
wish, 2914, *ḥēpeṣ* [1]
wish, 3202+928+6524, *ṭôb*[2]*+bᵉ-+ʿayin*[1] [1]
wish, 3512+928+6524, *yāṭab+bᵉ-+ʿayin*[1] [1]
wish well, 4200+8934, *lᵉ-*[1]*+šālôm* [1]
I wish, 4769+5989, *mî+nātan* [1]
oh how I wish, 4769+5989, *mî+nātan* [1]
wish, 8626, *šāʾal* [1]
wish, 10461, *nᵉdab* [1]

WISHED [4]
wished, 2911, *ḥāpēṣ*[1] [1]
wished, 3202+928+6524, *ṭôb*[2]*+bᵉ-+ʿayin*[1] [1]
wished, 5883, *nepeš* [1]
wished, 8356, *rāṣôn* [1]

WISHES [7]
wishes, 10605, *ṣᵉbâ* [4]
wishes, *AIT* [2]
wishes, 5883, *nepeš* [1]

WITCHCRAFT [5]
witchcraft, 4176, *kešep* [3]
engages in witchcraft, 4175, *kāšap* [1]
witchcraft, 4175, *kāšap* [1]

WITH [4557]*
with, 928, *bᵉ-* [1047]
with, *AIT* [703]
with, 6640, *ʿim* [527]
with, 907, *ʾēt*[2] [406]
with, *NIH/RPE* [336]
with, 2256, *wᵉ-* [333]
with, 4200, *lᵉ-*[1] [219]
with, 6584, *ʿal*[2] [79]
together with, 2256, *wᵉ-* [73]
with, 448, *ʾel* [51]
along with, 2256, *wᵉ-* [48]
with, 4946, *min* [44]
in accordance with, 3869, *kᵉ-* [30]
with, 928+3338, *bᵉ-+yād* [20]
with, 928+9348, *bᵉ-+tāwek* [17]
with, 339, *ʾaḥar* [16]
with, 6643, *ʿimmād* [16]
along with, 907, *ʾēt*[2] [13]
with, 928+7931, *bᵉ-+qereb* [11]
along with, 6640, *ʿim* [11]
with, 10089, *bᵉ-* [11]
with, 10554, *ʿim* [10]
with, 3869, *kᵉ-* [8]
along with, 6584, *ʿal*[2] [8]
together with, 6584, *ʿal*[2] [8]
together with, 6640, *ʿim* [8]
with, 4200+7156, *lᵉ-*[1]*+pāneh* [7]
along with, 928+9348, *bᵉ-+tāwek* [6]
have to do with, 4200, *lᵉ-*[1] [5]
with, 4200+7023, *lᵉ-*[1]*+peh* [5]
with, 928+6524, *bᵉ-+ʿayin*[1] [4]
lay with, 3359, *yādaʿ* [4]
with, 9393, *taḥat*[1] [4]
with, 4974, *minnî*[2] [3]
with, 10168, *dî* [3]
together with, 10221, *wᵉ-* [3]
with, 10221, *wᵉ-* [3]
with, 10427, *min* [3]
along with, 448, *ʾel* [2]
with, 725, *ʾēṣel*[1] [2]
with, 889, *ʾᵃšer* [2]
with, 1068, *bayin* [2]
with, 1198, *bᵉmô* [2]
with, 1251, *baʿal*[1] [2]
with, 4017, *kᵉmô* [2]
with, 10378+10619, *lᵉ-+qᵒbēl* [1]
with, 10378, *lᵉ-* [1]

WITHDRAW [12]
withdraw, 6590, *ʿālâ* [3]
withdraw, 665, *ʾāsap* [2]
withdraw, 8332, *rāpâ*[1] [2]
withdraw, 8740, *šûb*[1] [2]
withdraw favor, 1757, *gāraʿ*[1] [1]
withdraw, 2143, *hālak* [1]
withdraw far, 8178, *rāḥaq* [1]

WITHDRAWN [5]
withdrawn, 6590, *ʿālâ* [2]
withdrawn, 665, *ʾāsap* [1]
withdrawn, 2740, *ḥālaṣ*[1] [1]
withdrawn, 8740+294, *šûb*[1]*+ʾāḥôr* [1]

WITHDRAWS [1]
withdraws, 665, *ʾāsap* [1]

WITHDREW [19]
withdrew, 8740, *šûb*[1] [4]
withdrew, 2143, *hālak* [3]
withdrew, 3655, *yāṣāʾ* [3]
withdrew, 6590, *ʿālâ* [3]
withdrew, 5825, *nāsaʿ* [2]
withdrew, 665, *ʾāsap* [1]
withdrew, 2143+4946, *hālak+min* [1]
withdrew, 3782, *yāšab* [1]
withdrew, 7756, *qûm* [1]

WITHER [17]
wither, 3312, *yābēš*[1] [6]
wither, 5570, *nābēl*[1] [3]
wither, 581, *ʾāmal*[1] [2]
wither away, 3312, *yābēš*[1] [2]
wither, 4908, *mālal*[1] [2]
wither completely, 3312+3312, *yābēš*[1]*+yābēš*[1] [1]
wither, 7857, *qāmal* [1]

WITHERED [14]
withered, 3312, *yābēš*[1] [8]
withered, 581, *ʾāmal*[1] [1]
completely withered, 3312+3312, *yābēš*[1]*+yābēš*[1] [1]
withered away, 3312, *yābēš*[1] [1]
withered, 5570, *nābēl*[1] [1]
withered away, 6634, *ʿālap* [1]
withered, 7568, *ṣānum* [1]

WITHERS [11]
withers, 3312, *yābēš*[1] [5]
withers, 5570, *nābēl*[1] [2]
withers, 581, *ʾāmal*[1] [1]
withers away, 4908, *mālal*[1] [1]
withers away, 5376, *māśôś*[2] [1]
withers, 7857, *qāmal* [1]

WITHHELD [14]
withheld, 4979, *mānaʿ* [4]
withheld, 3104, *ḥāśak* [3]
withheld, *NIH/RPE* [1]
are withheld, 706, *ʾāpaq* [1]
withheld, 3973, *kālāʾ*[1] [1]
withheld[s], 4202+4763, *lōʾ+māṭar* [1]
been withheld, 4979, *mānaʿ* [1]
withheld, 7890, *qāpaṣ* [1]
withheld, 8740, *šûb*[1] [1]

WITHHOLD [8]
withhold, 4979, *mānaʿ* [4]
withhold, 1608, *gāzal* [1]
withhold, 3973, *kālāʾ*[1] [1]
withhold, 4202, *lōʾ* [1]
withhold, 8740, *šûb*[1] [1]

WITHHOLDS [5]
withholds, 8740, *šûb*[1] [2]
withholds, 2893, *ḥāsēr*[1] [1]
withholds, 3104, *ḥāśak* [1]
withholds, 5742, *nāṭâ* [1]

WITHIN [99]
within, 928+7931, *bᵉ-+qereb* [20]
within, 928, *bᵉ-* [20]
within, 928+9348, *bᵉ-+tāwek* [15]
within, 6584, *ʿal*[2] [10]
within, 928+6388, *bᵉ-+ʿôd* [6]
within, 9348, *tāwek* [5]
within, 4200, *lᵉ-*[1] [4]
within, 4946, *min* [4]
within, *AIT* [3]
within, 907, *ʾēt*[2] [2]
within, 5055, *mēʿeh* [2]
within, 7163, *pᵉnîmâ* [2]
to within, 448, *ʾel* [1]
within sight of, 907+7156, *ʾēt*[2]*+pāneh* [1]
within, 928+2668, *bᵉ-+ḥēq* [1]
within, 928+3752, *bᵉ-+yᵉrēkâ* [1]
within, 928+9348+5055, *bᵉ-+tāwek+mēʿeh* [1]
within, 1061, *beṭen*[1] [1]

WITHOUT [274]
without, 4202, *lōʾ* [67]
without defect, 9459, *tāmîm* [47]
without, 401, *ʾayin*[1] [29]
bread made without yeast, 5174, *maṣṣâ*[1] [14]
without, 4946, *min* [13]
without, 4946+401, *min+ʾayin*[1] [9]
without cause, 2855, *ḥinnām* [7]
without, 1172, *bᵉlî* [6]
without, 928+4202, *bᵉ-+lōʾ* [5]
without yeast, 5174, *maṣṣâ*[1] [5]
without, 4202+928, *lōʾ+bᵉ-* [4]
without cause, 9214, *šeqer* [4]
without, 10379, *lāʾ* [4]
without, 440, *ʾal*[1] [3]
without, 928+700, *bᵉ-+ʾepes* [3]
without, 1194, *biltî* [3]
without, 4200+4202, *lᵉ-*[1]*+lōʾ* [3]
bread without yeast, 5174, *maṣṣâ*[1] [3]
without, 928+401, *bᵉ-+ʾayin*[1] [2]
without reason, 2855, *ḥinnām* [2]
without, 3954+561, *kî*[2]*+ʾim* [2]
without, 4200+1172, *lᵉ-*[1]*+bᵉlî* [2]
without, 4946+1187, *min+balʿᵃdê* [2]
made without yeast, 5174, *maṣṣâ*[1] [2]
without, 6, *ʾābad* [1]
without equal, 401+3202+4946, *ʾayin*[1]*+ṭôb*[2]*+min* [1]
without, 401+4200, *ʾayin*[1]*+lᵉ-*[1] [1]

without meaning, 928+2021+2039, *b*^{e}*-+ha-+hebel*^{1} [1]
without, 928+1172, *b*^{e}*-+b*^{e}*lî* [1]
without a care, 1055, *beṭaḥ*^{1} [1]
without, 1153, *bal*^{1} [1]
without, 1187, *bal'*^{a}*dê* [1]
without, 2575+4946, *ḥûṣ+min* [1]
without any payment, 2855+401, *ḥinnām+'ayin*^{1} [1]
without any reason, 2855, *ḥinnām* [1]
without paying anything, 2855, *ḥinnām* [1]
without saying a word, 3087, *ḥārēš*^{2} [1]
without, 3869+1172, *k*^{e}*-+b*^{e}*lî* [1]
be without, 4162+4946, *kārat+min* [1]
without success, 4173, *kāšal* [1]
without, 4631, *mûš*^{2} [1]
without being aware, 4946+6524, *min+'ayin*^{1} [1]
without, 4946+1172, *min+b*^{e}*lî* [1]
prepared without yeast, 5174, *maṣṣâ*^{1} [1]
without guilt, 5929, *nāqî* [1]
cross over without fail, 6296+6296, *'ābar*^{1}*+'ābar*^{1} [1]
without restraint, 6330+4394, *'ad*^{2}*+m*^{e}*'ōd* [1]
without, 6330+401, *'ad*^{2}*+'ayin*^{1} [1]
without young, 6829, *'āqār* [1]
without restraint, 6984, *'ātar*^{2} [1]
city without walls, 7252, *p*^{e}*rāzôt* [1]
without cause, 8200, *rêqām* [1]
without excuse, 8200, *rêqām* [1]
left without, 8697, *šābat*^{1} [1]
without help, 9037, *šāmēm*^{1} [1]
without reason, 9214, *šeqer* [1]
without eating, 10297, *ṭ*^{e}*wāt* [1]

WITHSTAND [8]
withstand, 995+928, *bô'+b*^{e}*-* [2]
withstand, 4200+7156+6641, *l*$^{e-1}$*+pāneh+'āmad* [2]
withstand, 6641+928+7156, *'āmad+b*^{e}*-+pāneh* [2]
withstand, 6640+3656, *'im+yāṣab* [1]
withstand, 7756, *qûm* [1]

WITHSTOOD [1]
withstood, 6641+928+7156, *'āmad+b*^{e}*-+pāneh* [1]

WITLESS [1]
witless, 5554, *nābûb* [1]

WITNESS [48]
witness, 6332, *'ēd* [38]
witness, 6338, *'ēdâ*^{2} [4]
witness, *NIH/RPE* [3]
acting as witness, 6386, *'ûd*^{1} [1]
witness, 7032, *pûaḥ*^{2} [1]
witness, 9048+1068, *šāma'+bayin* [1]

WITNESSED [3]
had witnessed, 6386+6332, *'ûd*^{1}*+'ēd* [1]
have the transaction witnessed, 6386+6332, *'ûd*^{1}*+'ēd* [1]
witnessed, 6386+6332, *'ûd*^{1}*+'ēd* [1]

WITNESSES [22]
witnesses, 6332, *'ēd* [18]
call as witnesses, 6386, *'ûd*^{1} [2]
witnesses, 6338, *'ēdâ*^{2} [1]
call in as witnesses, 6386+6332, *'ûd*^{1}*+'ēd* [1]

WITS [1]
at wits end, 3972+2683+1182, *kōl+ḥokmâ+bāla'*^{3} [1]

WIVES [100]
wives, 851, *'iššâ* [91]
wives, 10699, *šēgal* [3]
wives, *NIH/RPE* [2]
brought in as wives, 995, *bô'* [1]
choose as wives, 4374, *lāqaḥ* [1]
taken as wives, 5951, *nāśā'* [1]
wives, 10493, *n*^{e}*šîn* [1]

WOE [60]
woe, 2098, *hôy* [36]
woe, 208, *'ôy* [19]
woe, *NIH/RPE* [1]
woe, 210, *'ôyâ* [1]
woe, 365, *'î*^{4} [1]
woe, 518, *'allay* [1]
woe, 2113, *hî* [1]

WOES [1]
woes, 4799, *mak'ōb* [1]

WOKE [3]
woke up, 3699, *yāqaṣ* [3]

WOLF [4]
wolf, 2269, *z*^{e}*'ēb*^{1} [4]

WOLVES [3]
wolves, 2269, *z*^{e}*'ēb*^{1} [3]

WOMAN [236]
woman, 851, *'iššâ* [167]
woman, *AIT* [46]
woman, 1426, *bat*^{1} [5]
woman, *NIH/RPE* [4]
woman, 5922, *n*^{e}*qēbâ* [3]
young woman, 5855, *na'*^{a}*râ*^{1} [2]
slave woman, 563, *'āmâ* [1]
young woman, 1435, *b*^{e}*tûlâ* [1]
the first woman^{s}, 2023, *-āh* [1]
the woman^{s}, 2085, *hû'* [1]
the man and the woman^{s}, 2157, *-hem* [1]
the woman and her sister^{s}, 2177, *-hēn*^{2} [1]
woman, 2296, *zeh* [1]
woman^{s}, 6303, *'ibrî*^{1} [1]
woman, 8167, *reḥem* [1]

WOMAN'S [6]
woman's, 851, *'iššâ* [4]
slave woman's, 563, *'āmâ* [1]
woman's monthly uncleanness, 3240+2021+5614, *ṭum'â+ha-+niddâ* [1]

WOMB [52]
womb, 1061, *beṭen*^{1} [28]
womb, 8167, *reḥem* [20]
womb, *NIH/RPE* [1]
womb, 1068+8079, *bayin+regel* [1]
womb, 5055, *mē'eh* [1]
opening of the womb, 5402+1201, *mašbēr+bēn*^{1} [1]

WOMBS [1]
wombs, 8167, *reḥem* [1]

WOMEN [169]
women, 851, *'iššâ* [103]
women, *AIT* [22]
women, 1426, *bat*^{1} [15]
women and children, 3251, *ṭap*^{1} [6]
women^{s}, 8876, *šîr*^{1} [5]
young women, 1435, *b*^{e}*tûlâ* [4]
young women, 1426, *bat*^{1} [2]
women, 9148, *šipḥâ* [2]
women, *NIH/RPE* [1]
women, 1435, *b*^{e}*tûlâ* [1]
women^{s}, 2157, *-hem* [1]
pregnant women, 2226, *hāreh* [1]
pregnant women, 2230, *hāriyyâ* [1]
women^{s}, 2418, *zāqēn*^{2} [1]
women^{s}, 3528, *yālad* [1]
women, 5922, *n*^{e}*qēbâ* [1]
violate women, 6700, *'ānâ*^{2} [1]
women of nobility, 8576, *śārâ*^{2} [1]

WOMEN'S [1]
women's, 851, *'iššâ* [1]

WON [7]
won, 5951+4200+7156, *nāśā'+l*$^{e-1}$*+pāneh* [2]
won, 3523, *yākōl* [1]
won, 3769, *yāraš*^{1} [1]
won over, 5742, *nāṭâ* [1]
won, 5951+928+6524, *nāśā'+b*^{e}*-+'ayin*^{1} [1]
won, 6913, *'āśâ*^{1} [1]

WON'T [18]
won't, 4202, *lō'* [13]
won't, 401, *'ayin*^{1} [2]
won't, *AIT* [1]
won't until, 3954+561, *kî*^{2}*+'im* [1]
won't, 7153, *pen* [1]

WONDER [8]
wonder, 4603, *môpēt* [3]
no wonder, 6584+4027, *'al*^{2}*+kēn*^{2} [2]
show wonder, 7098, *pālā'* [1]
wonder, 7098, *pālā'* [1]
wonder, 7099, *pele'* [1]

WONDERFUL [21]
wonderful, 7098, *pālā'* [15]
wonderful, 7099, *pele'* [2]
wonderful, *NIH/RPE* [1]
are wonderful, 7098, *pālā'* [1]
showed wonderful, 7098, *pālā'* [1]
wonderful, 7100, *pil'î* [1]

WONDERFULLY [1]
am wonderfully made, 7098, *pālā'* [1]

WONDERS [48]
wonders, 4603, *môpēt* [17]
wonders, 7098, *pālā'* [17]
wonders, 7099, *pele'* [4]
awesome wonders, 3707, *yārē'*^{1} [3]
wonders, 10763, *t*^{e}*mah* [3]
wonders, 1524, *gādôl* [2]
wonders, 253, *'ôt*^{1} [1]
wonders, 5140, *miplā'ôt* [1]

WOOD [116]
wood, 6770, *'ēṣ* [100]
stick of wood, 6770, *'ēṣ* [3]
acacia wood, 8847, *šiṭṭâ* [3]
wood, 10058, *'ā* [2]
wood, *AIT* [1]
cypress wood, 855, *'aššûr* [1]
pile wood, 1883, *dûr*^{1} [1]
the wood^{s}, 2257, *-ô* [1]
wood, 4509, *m*^{e}*dûrâ* [1]
stick of wood, 5234, *maqqēl* [1]
loads of wood, 6770, *'ēṣ* [1]
piece of wood, 6770, *'ēṣ* [1]

WOODCUTTERS [3]
woodcutters, 2634+6770, *ḥāṭab+'ēṣ* [3]

WOODED [1]
wooded areas, 3091, *ḥōreš*^{1} [1]

WOODEN [13]
wooden, 6770, *'ēṣ* [10]
wooden, *NIH/RPE* [1]
wooden idol, 6770, *'ēṣ* [1]
wooden idols, 6785, *'ēṣâ*^{3} [1]

WOODPILE [1]
woodpile, 6770, *'ēṣ* [1]

WOODS [3]
woods, 3623, *ya'ar*^{1} [3]

WOODSMAN [1]
woodsman, *AIT* [1]

WOODSMEN [1]
woodsmen, 2634, *ḥāṭab* [1]

WOODWORK [1]
woodwork, 6770, *'ēṣ* [1]

WOOING [1]
wooing, 6077, *sût*^{1} [1]

WOOL [16]
wool, 7547, *ṣemer* [13]
wool from shearing, 1600, *gēz* [1]
scarlet wool, 9106+9357, *šānî*^{1}*+tôlē'â* [1]
wool, 10556, *'*^{a}*mar* [1]

WOOLEN [3]
woolen, 7547, *ṣemer* [2]
woolen garment, 7547, *ṣemer* [1]

WORD [414]
word, 1821, *dābār* [339]
word, 614, *'imrâ* [13]

sent word, 8938, *šālaḥ* [11]
word, 606, *ʾāmar*[1] [8]
word, 7023, *peh* [5]
word, *NIH/RPE* [4]
send word, 8938, *šālaḥ* [4]
word, 7754, *qôl* [3]
word, *AIT* [2]
word, 4863, *millâ* [2]
sent word, 606, *ʾāmar*[1] [1]
word, 608, *ʾōmer* [1]
word come, 1655, *gālâ* [1]
said a word, 1819, *dābar*[2] [1]
the word, 1821, *dābār* [1]
word, 1825, *dibbēr* [1]
word^s^, 2023, *-āh* [1]
uttered a word, 3076+906+4383, *ḥāraṣ*[1]*+ʾēt*[1]*+lāšôn* [1]
without saying a word, 3087, *ḥārēš*[2] [1]
word that comes from, 4604, *môṣāʾ*[1] [1]
spoke the word, 4946+7023, *min+peh* [1]
word came, 5583, *nāgad* [1]
said a word, 6699, *ʿānâ*[1] [1]
given word, 7198+906+7023, *pāṣâ+ʾēt*[1]*+peh* [1]
sent word, 7422, *ṣāwâ* [1]
word, 7924, *qārāʾ*[1] [1]
don't say a word, 8492+3338+6584+7023, *śîm+yād+ʿal*[2]*+peh* [1]
sent word, 8938+2256+5583, *šālaḥ+wᵉ-+nāgad* [1]
sent word, 8938+2256+7924, *šālaḥ+wᵉ-+qārāʾ*[1] [1]
word, 9005, *šēm*[1] [1]
bring word, 9048, *šāmaʿ* [1]
word came, 9048, *šāmaʿ* [1]
word, 9051, *šēmaʿ* [1]

WORDS [318]
words, 1821, *dābār* [226]
words, 609, *ʾēmer*[1] [33]
words, 4863, *millâ* [24]
words, 614, *ʾimrâ* [4]
words, 1819, *dābar*[2] [4]
words, *NIH/RPE* [3]
words, 10418, *millâ* [3]
words, 609+7023, *ʾēmer*[1]*+peh* [2]
empty words, 1821+8557, *dābār+śāpâ* [2]
words, 4383, *lāšôn* [2]
words, 7754, *qôl* [2]
mark my words, 9048, *šāmaʿ* [2]
words, *AIT* [1]
words, 606, *ʾāmar*[1] [1]
reckless words, 1051, *bāṭāʾ* [1]
rash words came, 1051, *bāṭāʾ* [1]
speak with words, 1819, *dābar*[2] [1]
words, 1821+7023, *dābār+peh* [1]
words, 4180, *kātab* [1]
persuasive words, 4375, *leqaḥ* [1]
words, 7339+7023, *petaḥ+peh* [1]
words, 8557, *śāpâ* [1]
words of insight, 9312, *tᵉbûnâ* [1]

WORE [8]
wore, 4252, *lābaš* [2]
wore, 6584, *ʿal*[2] [2]
wore, *NIH/RPE* [1]
wore, 673, *ʾāsar* [1]
wore, 4229, *lābûš* [1]
wore, 5951, *nāśāʾ* [1]

WORK [294]
work, 4856, *mᵉlāʾkâ* [87]
work, 5126, *maʿăśeh* [60]
work, 6275, *ʿᵃbōdâ* [39]
regular work, 4856+6275, *mᵉlāʾkâ+ʿᵃbōdâ* [12]
work, 6268, *ʿābad* [10]
work, *NIH/RPE* [8]
work, 6662, *ʿāmāl*[1] [8]
work, 6913, *ʿāśâ*[1] [8]
work, 7189, *pōʿal* [7]
work, *AIT* [3]
work for, 6268, *ʿābad* [3]
do work, 6913, *ʿāśâ*[1] [3]
work, 10525, *ʿᵃbîdâ* [3]
work, 3098, *ḥᵃrōšet*[1] [2]
work vineyards, 4144, *kōrēm* [2]
work, 6268+6275, *ʿābad+ʿᵃbōdâ* [2]
work, 7190, *pᵉʿullâ* [2]
floral work, 7258, *peraḥ* [2]
embroidered work, 8391, *riqmâ* [2]
work fields, 438, *ʾikkār* [1]
work, 995, *bôʾ* [1]
did work, 1215, *bānâ* [1]
work, 1691, *gᵉmûl* [1]
work, 1821, *dābār* [1]
work, 2118, *hāyâ* [1]
work havoc, 2472, *ḥābal*[2] [1]
sets about work, 2520+5516, *ḥāgar+motnayim* [1]
good work, 3208, *ṭôbâ* [1]
heavy work, 3330, *yᵉgîaʿ* [1]
work, 3330, *yᵉgîaʿ* [1]
work, 5095, *maʿᵃlāl* [1]
work, 5126+6913, *maʿᵃśeh+ʿāśâ*[1] [1]
work, 6026, *siblôt* [1]
work horses, 6061, *sûs*[1] [1]
do work, 6268, *ʿābad* [1]
make work, 6268, *ʿābad* [1]
making work, 6268, *ʿābad* [1]
put to work, 6268, *ʿābad* [1]
doing work, 6275, *ʿᵃbōdâ* [1]
made work, 6268, *ʿābad* [1]
work, 6721, *ʿinyān* [1]
hard work, 6776, *ʿeṣeb*[2] [1]
at work, 6913, *ʿāśâ*[1] [1]
work, 6913+4856, *ʿāśâ*[1]*+mᵉlāʾkâ* [1]
set to work, 7756, *qûm* [1]
went to work, 7756, *qûm* [1]
abstained from work, 8697, *šābat*[1] [1]
do not work, 8697, *šābat*[1] [1]
stop work, 10098, *bᵉṭal* [1]
set to work, 10624+10221+10742, *qûm+wᵉ-+šᵉrâ* [1]

WORKED [30]
worked, 6913, *ʿāśâ*[1] [6]
worked, 5126, *maʿᵃśeh* [4]
worked salvation, 3828, *yāšaʿ* [3]
worked for, 6268, *ʿābad* [3]
worked, 6268, *ʿābad* [3]
worked, *NIH/RPE* [1]
worked, 1215, *bānâ* [1]
worked for, 2011, *dāraš* [1]
worked hard, 2616, *ḥāzaq* [1]
worked, 3330, *yᵉgîaʿ* [1]
worked, 4856, *mᵉlāʾkâ* [1]
worked, 4946, *min* [1]
been worked, 6268, *ʿābad* [1]
worked, 6590, *ʿālâ* [1]
worked, 6641, *ʿāmad* [1]
worked, 6661, *ʿāmal* [1]

WORKER [5]
hired worker, 8502, *śākîr* [4]
worker, 6913, *ʿāśâ*[1] [1]

WORKERS [17]
workers, 6913+4856, *ʿāśâ*[1]*+mᵉlāʾkâ* [7]
workers, 6268, *ʿābad* [2]
workers, *AIT* [1]
workers, 1074+6275, *bayit*[1]*+ʿᵃbōdâ* [1]
workers, 3093, *ḥārāš* [1]
workers, 5853, *naʿar*[2] [1]
workers, 6774, *ʿaṣṣāb* [1]
workers, 6913, *ʿāśâ*[1] [1]
workers in cloth, 9271, *šātâ*[1] [1]
workers, 10586, *pᵉlaḥ* [1]

WORKING [12]
working, 6913, *ʿāśâ*[1] [4]
working, *NIH/RPE* [2]
working, 5126, *maʿᵃśeh* [2]
working fields and vineyards, 4144, *kōrēm* [1]
working, 6026, *siblôt* [1]
keep working, 6268, *ʿābad* [1]
working, 6913+4856, *ʿāśâ*[1]*+mᵉlāʾkâ* [1]

WORKMAN'S [1]
workman's, 6664, *ʿāmēl*[1] [1]

WORKMEN [5]
workmen, 6913+4856, *ʿāśâ*[1]*+mᵉlāʾkâ* [3]
workmen, 4856, *mᵉlāʾkâ* [1]
workmen, 6913+928+2021+4856, *ʿāśâ*[1]*+bᵉ-+ha-+mᵉlāʾkâ* [1]

WORKS [48]
works, 5126, *maʿᵃśeh* [17]
siege works, 1911, *dāyēq* [6]
works, 7189, *pōʿal* [5]
works, 2006, *derek* [3]
works, 6913, *ʿāśâ*[1] [3]
works, 6268, *ʿābad* [2]
works, *AIT* [1]
mighty works, 1476, *gᵉbûrâ* [1]
awesome works, 3707, *yārēʾ*[1] [1]
works, 5149, *mipʿālâ* [1]
siege works, 5189, *māṣôr*[1] [1]
siege works, 5193, *mᵉṣûrâ* [1]
works, 6613, *ʿᵃlîlâ* [1]
works, 6661, *ʿāmal* [1]
works out, 6913, *ʿāśâ*[1] [1]
works out, 7188, *pāʿal* [1]
works, 7188, *pāʿal* [1]
works, 7190, *pᵉʿullâ* [1]

WORLD [55]
world, 9315, *tēbēl* [30]
world, 824, *ʾereṣ* [20]
world, 2698, *ḥeled* [3]
whole world, 9315+824, *tēbēl+ʾereṣ* [1]
world, 10075, *ʾᵃraʿ* [1]

WORLD'S [1]
world's, 9315, *tēbēl* [1]

WORM [8]
worm, 9357, *tôlēʿâ* [5]
worm, 8231, *rimmâ* [2]
worm, 6182, *sās* [1]

WORMS [4]
worms, 8231, *rimmâ* [2]
worms, 9357, *tôlēʿâ* [2]

WORN [18]
worn, *NIH/RPE* [3]
worn out, 3333, *yāgaʿ* [3]
worn out, 4206, *lāʾâ* [3]
worn out, 1162, *bālâ*[1] [2]
worn out, 1165, *bāleh* [1]
worn, 1165, *bāleh* [1]
worn out, 3335, *yāgēaʿ* [1]
worn, 4252, *lābaš* [1]
worn, 5432+928, *māšak+bᵉ-* [1]
worn out, 6546, *ʿāyēp* [1]
worn, 6584, *ʿal*[2] [1]

WORN-OUT [3]
worn-out, *NIH/RPE* [1]
worn-out, 1165, *bāleh* [1]
worn-out, 1170, *bᵉlôy* [1]

WORRIED [1]
worried, 1793, *dāʾag* [1]

WORRIES [1]
has worries, 1793, *dāʾag* [1]

WORRY [1]
worry, 8492+906+4213, *śîm+ʾēt*[1]*+lēb* [1]

WORRYING [1]
worrying, 1793, *dāʾag* [1]

WORSE [10]
how much worse, 677+3954, *ʾap*[1]*+kî*[2] [3]
grew worse and worse, 2118+2716+2617+4394, *hāyâ+ḥōlî+ḥāzāq+mᵉʾōd* [2]
looking worse, 2407, *zāʿap*[2] [1]
worse, 4017+4202, *kᵉmô+lōʾ* [1]
worse than, 4946, *min* [1]
worse, 8273, *raʿ*[1] [1]
treat worse, 8317, *rāʿaʿ*[1] [1]

WORSHIP [111]
worship, 2556, *ḥāwâ*[2] [39]

worship, 6268, *ʿābad* [37]
worship, 3707, *yārēʾ*^{1} [10]
worship, 10504, *sᵉgid* [10]
Baal worship, 1251, *baʿal*^{1} [3]
bowed in worship, 2556, *ḥāwâ*^{2} [2]
worship, 6913, *ʿāśâ*^{1} [2]
worship, *NIH/RPE* [1]
bow down to worship, 2556, *ḥāwâ*^{2} [1]
worship, 3710, *yārēʾ*^{4} [1]
worship, 4200+7156, *lᵉ-*^{1}*+pāneh* [1]
worship, 6268+6275, *ʿābad+ʿᵃbōdâ* [1]
worship, 6269, *ʿebed*^{1} [1]
worship, 10586, *pᵉlaḥ* [1]
worship, 10587, *polḥān* [1]

WORSHIPED [44]
worshiped, 2556, *ḥāwâ*^{2} [23]
worshiped, 6268, *ʿābad* [13]
worshiped, 3707, *yārēʾ*^{1} [2]
worshiped, 3710, *yārēʾ*^{4} [2]
worshiped leaned, 2556, *ḥāwâ*^{2} [1]
place where worshiped, 4595, *môʿēd* [1]
worshiped, 10504, *sᵉgid* [1]
worshiped, 10586, *pᵉlaḥ* [1]

WORSHIPERS [1]
worshipers, 6985, *ʿātār*^{1} [1]

WORSHIPING [17]
worshiping, 2556, *ḥāwâ*^{2} [7]
worshiping, *NIH/RPE* [3]
worshiping, 6268, *ʿābad* [3]
joined in worshiping, 7537, *ṣāmad* [2]
worshiping, 339, *ʾaḥar* [1]
worshiping, 3710, *yārēʾ*^{4} [1]

WORSHIPS [3]
worships, 2556, *ḥāwâ*^{2} [2]
worships, 1385, *bārak*^{2} [1]

WORST [4]
worst, 3878+4394, *kābēd*^{2}*+mᵉʾōd* [2]
worst, 8273, *raʿ*^{1} [1]
worst, 8288, *rāʿâ*^{3} [1]

WORTH [9]
worth, *NIH/RPE* [1]
worth, 928, *bᵉ-* [1]
worth, 4017, *kᵉmô* [1]
life will not be worth living, 4200+4537+2644, *lᵉ-*^{1}*+mâ+ḥay*^{1} [1]
worth, 4697, *mᵉḥîr*^{1} [1]
worth, 4836, *meker* [1]
worth their weight, 6131, *sālāʾ* [1]
worth, 6886, *ʿērek* [1]
worth, 8510, *śākār*^{1} [1]

WORTHLESS [37]
worthless idols, 2039, *hebel*^{1} [9]
worthless, 2039, *hebel*^{1} [4]
worthless, 8736, *šāwʾ* [4]
worthless, 496, *ʾelîl* [2]
worthless, 2038, *hābal* [2]
worthless idols, 4202+3603, *lōʾ+yāʿal* [2]
worthless, 8199, *rêq* [2]
worthless, 401+2914, *ʾayin*^{1}*+ḥēpeṣ* [1]
worthless, 703, *ʾepaʿ* [1]
worthless, 1153+3603, *bal*^{1}*+yāʿal* [1]
worthless, 1175, *bᵉliyyaʿal* [1]
worthless, 1194+3603, *biltî+yāʿal* [1]
worthless idols, 2039+8736, *hebel*^{1}*+šāwʾ* [1]
worthless, 2361, *zālal*^{1} [1]
worthless, 4202+3603, *lōʾ+yāʿal* [1]
worthless idols, 8736, *šāwʾ* [1]
worthless things, 8736, *šāwʾ* [1]
worthless, 9332, *tōhû* [1]
worthless, 9522, *tāpēl*^{2} [1]

WORTHWHILE [1]
worthwhile, 3202, *ṭôb*^{2} [1]

WORTHY [12]
worthy of praise, 2146, *hālal*^{2} [6]
worthy, 2657, *ḥayil* [2]
worthy of mention, 2349, *zākar*^{1} [1]
worthy, 3701, *yāqār* [1]
worthy, 3838, *yāšār*^{1} [1]
worthy things, 5592, *nāgîd* [1]

WOULD [484]
would, *AIT* [418]
would, *NIH/RPE* [45]
would, 14, *ʾābâ* [13]
I would like, 5528, *nāʾ*^{1} [2]
would have, 14, *ʾābâ* [1]
would^{s}, 430, *ʾākal* [1]
would rather be, 1047, *bāḥar*^{1} [1]
would^{s}, 1655+1655, *gālâ+gālâ* [1]
would, 2011, *dāraš* [1]
would, 7153, *pen* [1]

WOULDN'T [5]
wouldn't, 4202, *lōʾ* [4]
wouldn't, 401, *ʾayin*^{1} [1]

WOUND [17]
wound, 8691, *šeber*^{1} [7]
wound, 4804, *makkâ* [4]
wound, 7206, *peṣaʿ* [2]
incurable wound, 631, *ʾānûš* [1]
healing for wound, 776, *ʾᵃrûkâ* [1]
wound, 5782, *nākâ* [1]
wound, 10244, *ḥᵃbāl* [1]

WOUNDED [22]
wounded, 2728, *ḥālāl*^{1} [5]
wounded, 2703, *ḥālâ*^{1} [3]
wounded, 2655, *ḥîl*^{1} [2]
been wounded, 2703, *ḥālâ*^{1} [2]
wounded, 5782, *nākâ* [2]
wounded, *NIH/RPE* [1]
fatally wounded, 1991, *dāqar* [1]
wounded, 1991, *dāqar* [1]
wounded, 2726, *ḥālal*^{2} [1]
mortally wounded man, 2728, *ḥālāl*^{1} [1]
wounded, 4708, *mahᵃluyîm* [1]
wounded, 4730, *māḥaṣ* [1]
wounded, 7205, *pāṣaʿ* [1]

WOUNDING [1]
wounding, 7206, *peṣaʿ* [1]

WOUNDS [24]
wounds, 4804, *makkâ* [9]
wounds, 7206, *peṣaʿ* [4]
wounds, 995+928, *bôʾ+bᵉ-* [2]
wounds, 2467, *ḥabbûrâ* [2]
wounds, *NIH/RPE* [1]
wounds, 2726, *ḥālal*^{2} [1]
wounds, 3872, *kāʾab* [1]
wounds, 4731, *maḥaṣ* [1]
wounds, 5596, *negaʿ* [1]
wounds was given, 5782, *nākâ* [1]
wounds, 6780, *ʿaṣṣebet* [1]

WOVE [1]
wove, 755, *ʾārag* [1]

WOVEN [23]
woven, 9274, *šᵉtî*^{1} [9]
woven, 8573, *śᵉrād* [4]
skillfully woven, 682, *ʾᵃpuddâ* [2]
woven, *NIH/RPE* [1]
skillfully woven waistband, 3109, *ḥēšeb* [1]
woven, 5126+755, *maʿᵃśeh+ʾārag* [1]
was woven together, 8387, *rāqam* [1]
woven together, 8571, *śārag* [1]
woven material, 9122, *šaʿaṭnēz* [1]
woven, 9122, *šaʿaṭnēz* [1]
woven, 9587, *tašbēṣ* [1]

WRAP [4]
wrap, 5989, *nātan* [2]
wrap around, 4043, *kānas* [1]
wrap around himself, 6486, *ʿāṭâ*^{1} [1]

WRAPPED [9]
wrapped, 6486, *ʿāṭâ*^{1} [2]
wrapped around, 2502, *ḥābaš* [1]
wrapped in cloths, 3156+3156, *ḥātal+ḥātal* [1]
wrapped, 3157, *ḥᵃtullâ* [1]
wrapped, 4286, *lûṭ* [1]
wrapped himself, 6486, *ʿāṭâ*^{1} [1]
wrapped up, 7674, *ṣārar*^{1} [1]
wrapped, 7674, *ṣārar*^{1} [1]

WRAPS [3]
wraps around him, 6486, *ʿāṭâ*^{1} [1]
wraps himself, 6486, *ʿāṭâ*^{1} [1]
wraps up, 7674, *ṣārar*^{1} [1]

WRATH [166]
wrath, 2779, *ḥēmâ* [75]
wrath, 6301, *ʿebrâ* [21]
wrath, 678, *ʾap*^{2} [15]
wrath, 2405, *zaʿam* [15]
wrath, 7912, *qeṣep*^{1} [13]
my wrath^{s}, 5647, *-nû*^{2} [8]
wrath, 3019, *ḥārôn* [5]
wrath, 7288, *pereṣ*^{1} [2]
wrath, *NIH/RPE* [1]
wrath, 399, *ʾêmâ* [1]
expresses wrath, 2404, *zāʿam* [1]
under the wrath, 2404, *zāʿam* [1]
under wrath, 2404, *zāʿam* [1]
great wrath, 2405+2256+7912, *zaʿam+wᵉ-+qeṣep*^{1} [1]
wrath, 2408, *zaʿap* [1]
maintains wrath, 5757, *nāṭar*^{1} [1]
wrath, 6552, *ʿîr*^{2} [1]
aroused wrath, 7911, *qāṣap* [1]
wrath, 8075, *rōgez* [1]
wrath, 10634, *qᵉṣap*^{2} [1]

WREATH [3]
wreath, 6498, *ʿᵃṭārâ*^{1} [3]

WREATHS [3]
wreaths, 4324, *lōyâ* [3]

WRECKED [2]
were wrecked, 8689, *šābar*^{1} [2]

WRENCHED [2]
wrenched, 3697, *yāqaʿ* [1]
wrenched, 5048, *māʿad* [1]

WRESTLE [1]
wrestle, 8883, *šît*^{1} [1]

WRESTLED [2]
wrestled, 84, *ʾābaq* [2]

WRETCHED [3]
wretched, 6579, *ʿākar* [1]
wretched, 6714, *ʿānî* [1]
wretched, 8273, *raʿ*^{1} [1]

WRING [2]
wring off, 4916, *mālaq* [1]
wring, 4916, *mālaq* [1]

WRIST [2]
wrist, 3338, *yād* [2]

WRISTS [2]
wrists, 723+3338, *ʾaṣṣîl+yād* [1]
wrists, 3338, *yād* [1]

WRITE [35]
write, 4180, *kātab* [25]
write down, 4180, *kātab* [6]
write a description, 4180, *kātab* [2]
write, 6218, *sāpar* [1]
write down, 10374, *kᵉtab* [1]

WRITER [1]
writer, 6221, *sōpēr* [1]

WRITES [2]
writes, 4180, *kātab* [2]

WRITHE [6]
writhe in pain, 2655, *ḥîl*^{1} [2]
writhe, 2655, *ḥîl*^{1} [2]
writhe in agony, 2655+2655, *ḥîl*^{1}*+ḥîl*^{1} [1]
writhe in agony, 2655+4394, *ḥîl*^{1}*+mᵉʾōd* [1]

WRITHED [3]
writhed, 2655, *ḥîl*^{1} [2]
writhed in pain, 2655, *ḥîl*^{1} [1]

WRITHES [2]
writhes, 2655, *ḥîl*[1] [2]

WRITING [21]
writing, 4844, *miktāb* [5]
writing, 10375, *k^{e}tāb* [5]
writing, 6221, *sōpēr* [2]
put in writing, 10673+10375, *r^{e}šam+k^{e}tāb* [2]
writing, *NIH/RPE* [1]
put in writing, 4180, *kātab* [1]
putting in writing, 4180, *kātab* [1]
writing, 4180, *kātab* [1]
writing, 4181, *k^{e}tāb* [1]
writing kit, 7879, *qeset* [1]
put in writing, 10673, *r^{e}šam* [1]

WRITTEN [132]
written, 4180, *kātab* [107]
be written, 4180, *kātab* [3]
written, *NIH/RPE* [2]
what written, 1821, *dābār* [2]
written, 1821, *dābār* [2]
were written, 4180, *kātab* [2]
written, 6219, *sēper*[1] [2]
were written, 2980, *ḥāqaq* [1]
order be written, 4180, *kātab* [1]
was written down, 4180, *kātab* [1]
was written, 4180, *kātab* [1]
written descriptions, 4180, *kātab* [1]
directions written, 4181, *k^{e}tāb* [1]
written, 4844, *miktāb* [1]
written reply, 5981, *ništ^{e}wān* [1]
written, 8398, *rāšam* [1]
was written, 10374, *k^{e}tab* [1]
what written, 10375, *k^{e}tāb* [1]
was written, 10673, *r^{e}šam* [1]

WRONG [72]
wrong, 8273, *ra'*[1] [10]
wrong, 8288, *rā'â*[3] [8]
done wrong, 6390, *'āwâ*[1] [6]
wrong, 6406, *'awlâ* [5]
wrong, 224, *'āwen*[1] [3]
wrong, 6404, *'āwel* [3]
wrong, 871, *'āšām* [2]
do wrong, 2627, *ḥāṭā'* [2]
done wrong, 2627, *ḥāṭā'* [2]
wrong, 6411, *'āwōn* [2]
wrong, 6662, *'āmāl*[1] [2]
wrong, 9214, *šeqer* [2]
wrong, 2803, *ḥāmas*[1] [1]
wrong, 2805, *ḥāmās* [1]
proved wrong, 3519, *yākaḥ* [1]
do wrong, 3561, *yānâ* [1]
wrong, 4202+3202, *lō'+ṭôb*[2] [1]
what is wrong, 4537, *mâ* [1]
did wrong, 6390, *'āwâ*[1] [1]
does wrong, 6390, *'āwâ*[1] [1]
doing wrong, 6404, *'āwel* [1]
wrong done, 6432, *'awwātâ* [1]
do wrong, 7321, *pāša'* [1]
wrong, 7322, *peša'* [1]
doing wrong, 8317, *rā'a'*[1] [1]
done wrong, 8317+8317, *rā'a'*[1]*+rā'a'*[1] [1]
did wrong, 8399, *rāša'* [1]
do wrong, 8399, *rāša'* [1]
doing wrong, 8399, *rāša'* [1]
done wrong, 8399, *rāša'* [1]
in the wrong, 8401, *rāšā'* [1]
one in the wrong, 8401, *rāšā'* [1]
unintentional wrong, 8705, *š^{e}gāgâ* [1]
wrong committed unintentionally, 8705+8704, *š^{e}gāgâ+šāgag* [1]
wrong, 8705, *š^{e}gāgâ* [1]
wrong, 8706, *šāgâ* [1]
wrong, 10242, *ḥ^{a}bûlâ* [1]

WRONGDOING [10]
wrongdoing, 8288, *rā'â*[3] [4]
wrongdoing, 9524, *tiplâ* [2]
guilty of wrongdoing, 870+870, *'āšam+'āšam* [1]
wrongdoing, 5126, *ma'^{a}śeh* [1]
wrongdoing, 6411, *'āwōn* [1]
wrongdoing, 6913+8400, *'āśâ*[1]*+reša'* [1]

WRONGDOINGS [1]
wrongdoings, 6411, *'āwōn* [1]

WRONGED [9]
wronged, 2627, *ḥāṭā'* [4]
wronged, 870, *'āšam* [1]
wronged, 2633, *ḥaṭṭā't* [1]
wronged, 2805, *ḥāmās* [1]
wronged, 6430, *'āwat* [1]
wronged, 8317, *rā'a'*[1] [1]

WRONGING [1]
wronging, 6430, *'āwat* [1]

WRONGS [9]
wrongs, 2627, *ḥāṭā'* [2]
wrongs, 2633, *ḥaṭṭā't* [1]
avenge wrongs, 5933, *nāqam* [1]
wrongs, 6411, *'āwōn* [1]
wrongs, 6913+2633, *'āśâ*[1]*+ḥaṭṭā't* [1]
wrongs, 7321, *pāša'* [1]
wrongs, 7322, *peša'* [1]
wrongs, 8288, *rā'â*[3] [1]

WROTE [38]
wrote, 4180, *kātab* [23]
wrote down, 4180, *kātab* [5]
wrote, 10374, *k^{e}tab* [4]
wrote out, 4180, *kātab* [2]
wrote, *NIH/RPE* [1]
wrote description, 4180, *kātab* [1]
wrote down, 10374, *k^{e}tab* [1]
wrote, 10673, *r^{e}šam* [1]

WROUGHT [1]
wrought, 6936, *'āšôt* [1]

WRUNG [1]
wrung out, 5172, *māṣâ* [1]

XERXES [31]
Xerxes, 347, *'^{a}ḥašwērôš* [31]

YARDS [2]
five hundred yards, 547+564, *'elep*[2]*+'ammâ*[1] [1]
yards, 564, *'ammâ*[1] [1]

YARN [34]
scarlet yarn, 9357+9106, *tôlē'â+šānî*[1] [26]
scarlet yarn, 9106+9357, *šānî*[1]*+tôlē'â* [5]
blue yarn, 9418, *t^{e}kēlet* [3]

YAUDI [1]
Yaudi, 3375, *y^{e}hûdî*[2] [1]

YEAR [332]
year, 9102, *šānâ*[2] [303]
year, 3427, *yôm*[1] [7]
year, 10732, *š^{e}nâ*[2] [5]
year, *NIH/RPE* [3]
each year, 9102+928+9102, *šānâ*[2]*+b^{e}-+šānâ*[2] [3]
next year, 2645, *ḥay*[2] [2]
each year, 4946+3427+3427+2025, *min+yôm*[1]*+yôm*[1]*+-â*[2] [2]
next year, 6961+2645, *'ēt+ḥay*[2] [2]
year, 1821+9102, *dābār+šānâ*[2] [1]
over a year, 2296+3427+196+2296+9102, *zeh+yôm*[1]*+'ô+zeh+šānâ*[2] [1]
Year of Jubilee, 3413, *yôbēl* [1]
year, 4200+2021+3427, *l^{e}-*[1]*+ha-+yôm*[1] [1]
each year, 9102+9102, *šānâ*[2]*+šānâ*[2] [1]

YEAR'S [2]
last year's harvest, 3824+3823, *yāšān+yāšēn*[2] [1]
year's, 9102, *šānâ*[2] [1]

YEAR-OLD [7]
year-old, 1201+9102, *bēn*[1]*+šānâ*[2] [5]
year-old, 1426+9102, *bat*[1]*+šānâ*[2] [2]

YEARLING [1]
yearling, 5309, *m^{e}rî* [1]

YEARLY [3]
yearly, 928+9102+285, *b^{e}-+šānâ*[2]*+'eḥād* [2]
yearly festivals, 2504, *ḥag* [1]

YEARNS [4]
yearns for, 203, *'āwâ*[1] [1]
yearns, 2159, *hāmâ* [1]
yearns, 3983, *kālâ*[1] [1]
yearns, 4083, *kāsap* [1]

YEARS [452]
years, 9102, *šānâ*[2] [409]
years, 3427, *yôm*[1] [21]
years, *NIH/RPE* [5]
years, 3427+9102, *yôm*[1]*+šānâ*[2] [4]
years, 9102+3427, *šānâ*[2]*+yôm*[1] [4]
many years, 802+3427, *'ōrek+yôm*[1] [1]
years, 2021+6961+9102, *ha-+'ēt+šānâ*[2] [1]
span of years, 2698, *heled* [1]
many years, 3427+2256+9102, *yôm*[1]*+w^{e}-+šānâ*[2] [1]
some years later, 4200+7891+9102, *l^{e}-*[1]*+qēṣ+šānâ*[2] [1]
three years old, 8992, *šālaš* [1]
full years, 9102+3427, *šānâ*[2]*+yôm*[1] [1]
successive years, 9102+339+9102, *šānâ*[2]*+'aḥar+šānâ*[2] [1]
years, 10732, *š^{e}nâ*[2] [1]

YEAST [44]
bread made without yeast, 5174, *maṣṣâ*[1] [14]
without yeast, 5174, *maṣṣâ*[1] [5]
yeast, 8419, *śe'ōr* [5]
yeast, 2809, *ḥāmēṣ*[4] [3]
bread without yeast, 5174, *maṣṣâ*[1] [3]
anything containing yeast, 2809, *ḥāmēṣ*[4] [2]
made without yeast, 5174, *maṣṣâ*[1] [2]
yeast added, 2806, *ḥāmēṣ*[1] [1]
yeast, 2806, *ḥāmēṣ*[1] [1]
anything with yeast in it, 2809, *ḥāmēṣ*[4] [1]
bread made with yeast, 2809, *ḥāmēṣ*[4] [1]
containing yeast, 2809, *ḥāmēṣ*[4] [1]
made with yeast, 2809, *ḥāmēṣ*[4] [1]
with yeast in it, 2809, *ḥāmēṣ*[4] [1]
anything with yeast in it, 4721, *maḥmeṣet* [1]
made with yeast, 4721, *maḥmeṣet* [1]
prepared without yeast, 5174, *maṣṣâ*[1] [1]

YELLOW [3]
yellow, 7411, *ṣāhōb* [3]

YES [51]
yes, *NIH/RPE* [15]
yes, 2180, *hinnēh* [9]
yes, 1685, *gam* [6]
yes, 3954, *kî*[2] [5]
yes, 2256, *w^{e}-* [4]
yes, 677, *'ap*[1] [2]
yes, 2256+1685, *w^{e}-+gam* [2]
yes but, 66, *'^{a}bāl* [1]
yes[s], 638, *'^{a}nî* [1]
yes, 3780, *yēš* [1]
yes, 4026, *kēn*[1] [1]
yes, 4027, *kēn*[2] [1]
yes, 4202+3954, *lō'+kî*[2] [1]
yes[s], 8934, *šālôm* [1]
yes, 10221, *w^{e}-* [1]

YESTERDAY [5]
yesterday, 9453, *t^{e}môl* [4]
yesterday, 621, *'emeš* [1]

YET [268]
yet, 2256, *w^{e}-* [143]
yet, *NIH/RPE* [27]
yet, 3954, *kî*[2] [19]
yet, *AIT* [10]
and yet, 2256, *w^{e}-* [10]
yet, 6388, *'ôd* [7]
yet, 421, *'ak* [5]
yet if, 561, *'im* [4]
not yet, 3270, *ṭerem* [4]
yet, 8370, *raq*[2] [3]
yet, 434, *'ākēn*[1] [2]
yet, 1685, *gam* [2]
yet, 2176, *hēn*[1] [2]
yet, 2256+1685, *w^{e}-+gam* [2]
may yet, 218, *'ûlay*[2] [1]

yet, 219, *ʾûlām*^{1} [1]
yet to come, 340, *ʾaḥ*^{a}*rôn* [1]
yet, 700+3954, *ʾepes+kî*^{2} [1]
yet, 889, *ʾ*^{a}*šer* [1]
not yet created, 1343, *bārāʾ*^{1} [1]
yet, 2021+3427, *ha-+yôm*^{1} [1]
yet also, 2256, *w*^{e}*-* [1]
yet, 2256+677, *w*^{e}*-+ʾap*^{1} [1]
yet, 2256+6964, *w*^{e}*-+ʿattâ* [1]
no yet, 3270, *ṭerem* [1]
yet unborn, 3528, *yālad* [1]
yet, 3869, *k*^{e}*-* [1]
yet, 3954+561, *kî*^{2}*+ʾim* [1]
no yet, 3972+3270, *kōl+ṭerem* [1]
yet, 4027, *kēn*^{2} [1]
yet, 4200+4027, *l*^{e}*-*^{1}*+kēn*^{2} [1]
yet, 4946+1172+889, *min+b*^{e}*lî+ʾ*^{a}*šer* [1]
yet, 6330+2021+3427+2021+2085, *ʿad*^{2}*+ha-+yôm*^{1}*+ha-+hûʾ* [1]
yet, 6330+2021+3427+2021+2156, *ʿad*^{2}*+ha-+yôm*^{1}*+ha-+hēm* [1]
yet, 6330+2178, *ʿad*^{2}*+hēnnâ*^{1} [1]
yet, 6330+6964, *ʿad*^{2}*+ʿattâ* [1]
yet, 6330, *ʿad*^{2} [1]
yet, 6362, *ʿ*^{a}*den* [1]
yet to come, 6388, *ʿôd* [1]
yet, 6584, *ʿal*^{2} [1]
yet more, 8049, *rābâ*^{1} [1]
yet, 10221, *w*^{e}*-* [1]

YIELD [24]
yield, 5989, *nātan* [13]
yield, 6913, *ʿāśâ*^{1} [4]
yield, *AIT* [1]
yield, 14, *ʾābâ* [1]
yield, 1765, *gereš* [1]
yield to the plea, 2011, *dāraš* [1]
yield, 3946, *kōaḥ*^{1} [1]
yield, 5742, *nāṭâ* [1]
yield, 9311, *t*^{e}*bûʾâ* [1]

YIELDED [2]
yielded, 6913, *ʿāśâ*^{1} [2]

YIELDING [1]
yielding, 1540, *gādal* [1]

YIELDS [5]
yields, *NIH/RPE* [2]
yields, 5989, *nātan* [2]
yields returns, 9311, *t*^{e}*bûʾâ* [1]

YOKE [55]
yoke, 6585, *ʿōl* [36]
yoke, 4574, *môṭâ* [8]
yoke, 7538, *ṣemed* [3]
yoke, *NIH/RPE* [2]
yoke, 6026, *siblôt* [2]
yoke, 4573, *môṭ*^{2} [1]
yoke of straps, 4593, *môsērâ*^{1} [1]
put a yoke, 6296, *ʿābar*^{1} [1]
yoke of oxen, 7538, *ṣemed* [1]

YOKED [3]
yoked, *NIH/RPE* [1]
yoked, 6590+6585, *ʿālâ+ʿōl* [1]
yoked themselves, 7537, *ṣāmad* [1]

YOKES [1]
yokes, 3998, *k*^{e}*lî* [1]

YOU [9725]*
you, *AIT* [3679]
you, 3870, *-kā* [2610]
you, 4013, *-kem* [1268]
you, 911, *ʾattâ* [621]
you, *NIH/RPE* [581]
you, 3871, *-k* [487]
you, 917, *ʾattem* [244]
you, 905, *ʾatt* [50]
you, 10342, *-k* [40]
you, 5883+3870, *nepeš+-kā* [21]
you^s, 2021, *ha-* [13]
you, 10052, *ʾantâ* [13]
you, 4392, *-ām* [11]
you, 2257, *-ô* [9]
you, 10349, *-kôn* [8]
you, 4032, *-ken* [5]
I beg you, 5528, *nāʾ*^{1} [5]
you, 920, *ʾattēn* [4]
you, 5883+3871, *nepeš+-k* [4]
you^s, 123+3276, *ʾādôn+-î* [3]
you, 10355, *-kōm* [3]
you^s, 408, *ʾîš*^{1} [2]
you, 2023, *-āh* [2]
you, 2085, *hûʾ* [2]
you, 2157, *-hem* [2]
you, 3276, *-î* [2]
you, 3338+3870, *yād+-kā* [2]
you, 5883+4013, *nepeš+-kem* [2]
you, 7156+3871, *pāneh+-k* [2]
you, 1414+3870, *bāśār+-kā* [1]
you, 2084, *-hû* [1]
you, 2118, *hāyâ* [1]
you, 2156, *hēm* [1]
you^s, 3870, *-kā* [1]
you, 3870+561, *-kā+ʾim* [1]
you, 4213+3870, *lēb+-kā* [1]
you, 5527, *-ān* [1]
you, 5646, *-nû*^{1} [1]
you, 6795+4013, *ʿeṣem*^{1}*+-kem* [1]
you yourself, 7156+3870, *pāneh+-kā* [1]
you, 7156+4013, *pāneh+-kem* [1]
you, 8120+3870, *rûaḥ+-kā* [1]
you, 10053, *ʾantûn* [1]

YOU'LL [1]
you'll, 911, *ʾattâ* [1]

YOU'RE [3]
you're, 911, *ʾattâ* [2]
you're, 4013, *-kem* [1]

YOU'VE [4]
you've, *AIT* [4]

YOUNG [268]
young, 1201, *bēn*^{1} [54]
young men, 1033, *bāḥûr*^{1} [34]
young, 5853, *naʿar*^{2} [25]
young man, 5853, *naʿar*^{2} [23]
young men, 3529, *yeled* [11]
young men, 5853, *naʿar*^{2} [11]
young goat, 1531+6436, *g*^{e}*dî+ʿēz* [7]
young, 7785, *qāṭōn*^{2} [7]
young man, 1033, *bāḥûr*^{1} [6]
young goat, 1531, *g*^{e}*dî* [5]
young, 5830, *n*^{e}*ʿûrîm* [5]
young, 7783, *qāṭān*^{1} [5]
young women, 1435, *b*^{e}*tûlâ* [4]
young lions, 4097, *k*^{e}*pîr* [4]
young officers, 5853, *naʿar*^{2} [4]
young, 7262, *p*^{e}*rî* [4]
young, *AIT* [3]
young, 3529, *yeled* [3]
young, 5855, *naʿ*^{a}*râ*^{1} [3]
young stag, 6762+385, *ʿōper+ʾayyāl* [3]
young bulls, 7228, *par* [3]
young, 7582, *ṣāʿîr*^{1} [3]
young, 711, *ʾeprōaḥ* [2]
young men, 1201, *bēn*^{1} [2]
young women, 1426, *bat*^{1} [2]
young locusts, 3540, *yeleq* [2]
young woman, 5855, *naʿ*^{a}*râ*^{1} [2]
young, *NIH/RPE* [1]
young ones, 711, *ʾeprōaḥ* [1]
strong young men, 1033, *bāḥûr*^{1} [1]
young camels, 1145, *bēker* [1]
young, 1426, *bat*^{1} [1]
young woman, 1435, *b*^{e}*tûlâ* [1]
young goats, 1531+6436, *g*^{e}*dî+ʿēz* [1]
young goats, 1531, *g*^{e}*dî* [1]
young goats, 1537, *g*^{e}*diyyâ* [1]
young pigeon, 1578, *gôzāl* [1]
young, 1578, *gôzāl* [1]
young, 1594, *gûr*^{4} [1]
young child, 1694, *gāmal* [1]
care for young, 1842, *dāgar* [1]
young locusts, 2885, *ḥāsîl* [1]
young shoots, 3438, *yôneqet* [1]
bore young, 3528, *yālad* [1]
young man, 3529, *yeled* [1]
young, 3531, *yaldût* [1]
young locust, 3540, *yeleq* [1]
young lion, 4097+787, *k*^{e}*pîr+ʾ*^{a}*rî* [1]
young lion, 4097, *k*^{e}*pîr* [1]
young, 4097, *k*^{e}*pîr* [1]
young of the flock, 4166, *keśeb* [1]
young cow, 6320+1330, *ʿeglâ*^{1}*+bāqār* [1]
have young, 6402, *ʿûl*^{2} [1]
nursing young, 6402, *ʿûl*^{2} [1]
young goat, 6436, *ʿēz* [1]
young man, 6624, *ʿelem* [1]
without young, 6829, *ʿāqār* [1]
young, 10120, *bar*^{2} [1]

YOUNGER [21]
younger, 7783, *qāṭān*^{1} [8]
younger, 7582, *ṣāʿîr*^{1} [7]
younger, 7785, *qāṭōn*^{2} [3]
younger men, 1033, *bāḥûr*^{1} [1]
the younger one^s, 2296, *zeh* [1]
younger, 7582+4200+3427, *ṣāʿîr*^{1}*+l*^{e}*-*^{1}*+yôm*^{1} [1]

YOUNGEST [21]
youngest, 7785, *qāṭōn*^{2} [14]
youngest, 7783, *qāṭān*^{1} [4]
youngest, 7582, *ṣāʿîr*^{1} [3]

YOUR [5687]*
your, 3870, *-kā* [3459]
your, 4013, *-kem* [940]
your, 3871, *-k* [615]
your, *NIH/RPE* [204]
your, *AIT* [81]
your own, 3870, *-kā* [65]
your^s, 2021, *ha-* [59]
your, 4200+4013, *l*^{e}*-*^{1}*+-kem* [48]
your, 10342, *-k* [46]
your, 4200+3870, *l*^{e}*-*^{1}*+-kā* [36]
your, 2257, *-ô* [26]
your own, 4013, *-kem* [18]
your, 4032, *-ken* [13]
your, 4200+3871, *l*^{e}*-*^{1}*+-k* [10]
your, 2023, *-āh* [6]
your, 911, *ʾattâ* [4]
your own, 4200+3870, *l*^{e}*-*^{1}*+-kā* [4]
your, 917, *ʾattem* [3]
your own, 4200+4013, *l*^{e}*-*^{1}*+-kem* [3]
your, 4392, *-ām* [3]
your own, 911, *ʾattâ* [2]
your, 2084, *-hû* [2]
your, 2157, *-hem* [2]
your own, 2257, *-ô* [2]
your own, 3871, *-k* [2]
your^s, 3972, *kōl* [2]
your very own, 4200+3870, *l*^{e}*-*^{1}*+-kā* [2]
your, 10349, *-kôn* [2]
your, 10355, *-kōm* [2]
your, 907+3870, *ʾēt*^{2}*+-kā* [1]
your, 928+2257, *b*^{e}*-+-ô* [1]
your, 928+3870, *b*^{e}*-+-kā* [1]
your own, 2023, *-āh* [1]
your, 3276, *-î* [1]
your own self, 3870, *-kā* [1]
your own, 4032, *-ken* [1]
your, 4946+3871, *min+-k* [1]
your, 4946+4013, *min+-kem* [1]
your, 6584+3871, *ʿal*^{2}*+-k* [1]
your, 6584+4013, *ʿal*^{2}*+-kem* [1]

YOURS [61]
yours, 4200+3870, *l*^{e}*-*^{1}*+-kā* [24]
yours, 3870, *-kā* [19]
yours, *NIH/RPE* [4]
yours, 4200+4013, *l*^{e}*-*^{1}*+-kem* [4]
yours, 4013, *-kem* [3]
yours, 917, *ʾattem* [2]
yours, 3871, *-k* [2]
yours, 911, *ʾattâ* [1]
yours, 4200+3871, *l*^{e}*-*^{1}*+-k* [1]
yours, 10342, *-k* [1]

YOURSELF [141]
yourself, 3870, *-kā* [43]
yourself, *AIT* [19]
yourself, 911, *ʾattâ* [17]
yourself, 4222+3870, *lēbāb+-kā* [4]

yourself, 5883+3870, *nepeš+-kā* [4]
humbled yourself, 4044, *kānaʿ* [3]
yourself, *NIH/RPE* [2]
show yourself pure, 1405, *bārar*[1] [2]
show yourself faithful, 2874, *ḥasad*[2] [2]
defiled yourself, 3237, *ṭāmēʾ*[1] [2]
yourself, 3871, *-k* [2]
yourself, 4213+3870, *lēb+-kā* [2]
free yourself, 5911, *nāṣal* [2]
humble yourself, 6700, *ʿānâ*[2] [2]
guard yourself, 9068, *šāmar* [2]
show yourself blameless, 9462, *tāmam* [2]
armed yourself, 273, *ʾāzar* [1]
hold yourself back, 706, *ʾāpaq* [1]
you yourself, 911, *ʾattâ* [1]
made yourself a stench, 944, *bāʾaš* [1]
exalt yourself, 2075, *hādar* [1]
yourself, 2257, *-ô* [1]
adorn yourself, 3636, *yāpâ* [1]
relieve yourself, 3782+2575, *yāšab+hûṣ* [1]
gained glory for yourself, 3877, *kābēd*[1] [1]
yourself, 4213+2257, *lēb+-ô* [1]
yourself, 4213+3871, *lēb+-k* [1]
yourself, 4222+2023, *lēbāb+-āh* [1]
yourself, 4222+3871, *lēbāb+-k* [1]
sold yourself, 4835, *mākar* [1]
yourself, 5883+2257, *nepeš+-ô* [1]
present yourself, 5893, *nāṣab*[1] [1]
exalted yourself, 5951, *nāśāʾ* [1]
shut yourself, 6037, *sāgar* [1]
set yourself, 6147, *sālal*[1] [1]
hide yourself, 6259, *sātar* [1]
delight yourself, 6695, *ʿānag* [1]
you yourself, 7156+3870, *pāneh+-kā* [1]
free yourself, 7337, *pātaḥ*[1] [1]
show yourself shrewd, 7349, *pātal* [1]
present yourself, 8011, *rāʾâ*[1] [1]
humble yourself, 8346, *rāpaś* [1]
destroy yourself, 9037, *šāmēm*[1] [1]
disguise yourself, 9101, *šānâ*[1] [1]
show yourself shrewd, 9520, *tāpal* [1]
yourself, 10342, *-k* [1]
yourself, 10381+10342, *lebab+-k* [1]

YOURSELVES [128]
yourselves, 4013, *-kem* [36]
yourselves, *AIT* [13]
yourselves, 5883+4013, *nepeš+-kem* [12]
yourselves, 917, *ʾattem* [10]
consecrate yourselves, 7727, *qādaš* [9]
yourselves, 3870, *-kā* [7]
defile yourselves, 3237, *ṭāmēʾ*[1] [6]
separate yourselves, 976, *bādal* [2]
cut yourselves, 1517, *gādad*[1] [2]
make yourselves unclean, 3237, *ṭāmēʾ*[1] [2]
present yourselves, 3656, *yāṣab* [2]
yourselves, 3871, *-k* [2]
yourselves, 4222+3870, *lēbāb+-kā* [2]
yourselves, 5883+3870, *nepeš+-kā* [2]
yourselves, 7156+4013, *pāneh+-kem* [2]
among yourselves, 408+448+278, *ʾîš*[1]*+ʾel+ʾāḥ*[2] [1]
make yourselves clean, 2342, *zākâ* [1]
hide yourselves, 2461, *ḥābāʾ* [1]
brace yourselves, 2616+5516, *ḥāzaq+motnayim* [1]
purify yourselves, 2627, *ḥāṭāʾ* [1]
arm yourselves, 2741, *ḥālaṣ*[2] [1]
purify yourselves, 3197, *ṭāhēr* [1]
defiled yourselves, 3237, *ṭāmēʾ*[1] [1]
yourselves, 4222+4013, *lēbāb+-kem* [1]
circumcise yourselves, 4576, *mûl*[1] [1]
offer yourselves for sale, 4835, *mākar* [1]
station yourselves, 5938, *nāqap*[2] [1]
set yourselves, 5951, *nāśāʾ* [1]
see for yourselves, 6524+4013+8011, *ʿayin*[1]*+-kem+rāʾâ*[1] [1]
yourselves, 7418+4013, *ṣawwāʾr+-kem* [1]
assemble yourselves, 7695, *qābaṣ* [1]
call yourselves, 7924, *qārāʾ*[1] [1]
present yourselves, 7928, *qārab* [1]
blind yourselves, 9129, *šāʿaʿ*[1] [1]

YOUTH [55]
youth, 5830, *neʿûrîm* [37]
youth, 5853, *naʿar*[2] [3]
youth, 5854, *nōʿar* [3]
youth, 6596, *ʿalûmîm* [3]
youth, 1035, *behûrôt* [2]
youth, 3529, *yeled* [2]
youth, 3531, *yaldût* [2]
youth, *NIH/RPE* [1]
youth, 1036, *behûrîm* [1]
youth, 5831, *neʿûrôt* [1]

YOUTHFUL [1]
youthful vigor, 6596, *ʿalûmîm* [1]

YOUTHS [4]
youths, 3529, *yeled* [1]
youths, 5853+7783, *naʿar*[2]*+qāṭān*[1] [1]
youths, 5853, *naʿar*[2] [1]
youths, 6620, *ʿālal*[3] [1]

ZAANAN [1]
Zaanan, 7367, *ṣaʾanān* [1]

ZAANANNIM [2]
Zaanannim, 7588, *ṣaʿanannîm* [2]

ZAAVAN [2]
Zaavan, 2401, *zaʿawān* [2]

ZABAD [8]
Zabad, 2274, *zābād* [8]

ZABBAI [2]
Zabbai, 2287, *zabbay* [2]

ZABDI [3]
Zabdi, 2275, *zabdî* [3]

ZABDIEL [2]
Zabdiel, 2276, *zabdîʾēl* [2]

ZABUD [1]
Zabud, 2280, *zābûd* [1]

ZACCAI [2]
Zaccai, 2347, *zakkay* [2]

ZACCUR [10]
Zaccur, 2346, *zakkûr* [10]

ZADOK [51]
Zadok, 7401, *ṣādôq* [51]

ZADOKITES [1]
Zadokites, 1201+7401, *bēn*[1]*+ṣādôq* [1]

ZAHAM [1]
Zaham, 2300, *zaham* [1]

ZAHAR [1]
Zahar, 7466, *ṣāḥar* [1]

ZAIR [1]
Zair, 7583, *ṣāʿîr*[2] [1]

ZALAPH [1]
Zalaph, 7523, *ṣālāp* [1]

ZALMON [3]
Zalmon, 7515, *ṣalmôn*[2] [2]
Zalmon, 7514, *ṣalmôn*[1] [1]

ZALMONAH [2]
Zalmonah, 7517, *ṣalmōnâ* [2]

ZALMUNNA [10]
Zalmunna, 7518, *ṣalmunnāʿ* [10]

ZAMZUMMITES [1]
Zamzummites, 2368, *zamzummîm* [1]

ZANOAH [5]
Zanoah, 2391, *zānôaḥ*[1] [4]
Zanoah, 2392, *zānôaḥ*[2] [1]

ZAPHENATH-PANEAH [1]
Zaphenath-Paneah, 7624, *ṣāpenat paʿnēaḥ* [1]

ZAPHON [3]
Zaphon, 7601, *ṣāpôn*[2] [3]

ZAREPHATH [3]
Zarephath, 7673, *ṣārepat* [3]

ZARETHAN [4]
Zarethan, 7681, *ṣāretān* [4]

ZATTU [5]
Zattu, 2456, *zattûʾ* [5]

ZAZA [1]
Zaza, 2321, *zāzāʾ* [1]

ZEAL [17]
zeal, 7863, *qinʾâ* [15]
zeal, 5883, *nepeš* [1]
zeal, 7861, *qānāʾ* [1]

ZEALOUS [6]
very zealous, 7861+7861, *qānāʾ+qānāʾ* [2]
zealous, 7861, *qānāʾ* [2]
zealous, *NIH/RPE* [1]
zealous, 7861+7863, *qānāʾ+qinʾâ* [1]

ZEALOUSLY [1]
zealously, 3013, *ḥārâ*[1] [1]

ZEBADIAH [9]
Zebadiah, 2277, *zebadyâ* [6]
Zebadiah, 2278, *zebadyāhû* [3]

ZEBAH [10]
Zebah, 2286, *zebaḥ*[2] [10]

ZEBIDAH [1]
Zebidah, 2288, *zebîdâ* [1]

ZEBINA [1]
Zebina, 2289, *zebînāʾ* [1]

ZEBOIIM [5]
Zeboiim, 7375, *ṣebōʾîm* [5]

ZEBOIM [2]
Zeboim, 7391, *ṣebōʿîm* [2]

ZEBUL [6]
Zebul, 2291, *zebul*[1] [6]

ZEBULUN [46]
Zebulun, 2282, *zebûlûn* [40]
Zebulun, 1201+2282, *bēn*[1]*+zebûlûn* [5]
Zebulun, 2283, *zebûlōnî* [1]

ZEBULUNITE [1]
Zebulunite, 2283, *zebûlōnî* [1]

ZECHARIAH [43]
Zechariah, 2357, *zekaryâ* [24]
Zechariah, 2358, *zekaryāhû* [16]
Zechariah, 10230, *zekaryâ* [2]
Zechariah[s], 2257, *-ô* [1]

ZECHARIAH'S [2]
Zechariah's[s], 2257, *-ô* [1]
Zechariah's, 2357, *zekaryâ* [1]

ZEDAD [2]
Zedad, 7398, *ṣedād* [2]

ZEDEKIAH [60]
Zedekiah, 7409, *ṣidqiyyāhû* [53]
Zedekiah, 7408, *ṣidqiyyâ* [7]

ZEDEKIAH'S [5]
Zedekiah's[s], 2257, *-ô* [2]
Zedekiah's, 7409, *ṣidqiyyāhû* [2]
Zedekiah's, 4200+7409, *le-*[1]*+ṣidqiyyāhû* [1]

ZEEB [6]
Zeeb, 2270, *zeʾēb*[2] [6]

ZEKER [1]
Zeker, 2353, *zeker*[1] [1]

ZELA [1]
Zela, 7522, *ṣēlāʿ*[2] [1]

ZELAH [1]
Zelah, 7522, *ṣēlāʿ*[2] [1]

ZELEK [2]
Zelek, 7530, *ṣeleq* [2]

ZELOPHEHAD [5]
Zelophehad, 7524, *ṣelopḥād* [5]

ZELOPHEHAD'S [4]
Zelophehad's, 7524, *ṣelopḥād* [4]

ZELZAH [1]
Zelzah, 7525, *ṣelṣaḥ* [1]

ZEMARAIM [2]
Zemaraim, 7549, *ṣemārayim* [2]

ZEMARITES [2]
Zemarites, 7548, *ṣemārî* [2]

ZEMIRAH [1]
Zemirah, 2371, *zemîrâ* [1]

ZENAN [1]
Zenan, 7569, *ṣenān* [1]

ZEPHANIAH [11]
Zephaniah, 7622, *ṣepanyâ* [8]
Zephaniah, 7623, *ṣepanyāhû* [2]
Zephaniah, *NIH/RPE* [1]

ZEPHATH [1]
Zephath, 7634, *ṣepat* [1]

ZEPHATHAH [1]
Zephathah, 7635, *ṣepatâ* [1]

ZEPHO [3]
Zepho, 7598, *ṣepô* [3]

ZEPHON [2]
Zephon, 7602, *ṣepôn* [2]

ZEPHONITE [1]
Zephonite, 7604, *ṣepônî*[2] [1]

ZER [1]
Zer, 7643, *ṣēr* [1]

ZERAH [20]
Zerah, 2438, *zeraḥ*[2] [20]

ZERAHIAH [5]
Zerahiah, 2440, *zeraḥyâ* [5]

ZERAHITE [4]
Zerahite, 2439, *zarḥî* [4]

ZERAHITES [3]
Zerahites, 2439, *zarḥî* [2]
Zerahites, 1201+2438, *bēn*[1]*+zeraḥ*[2] [1]

ZERED [3]
Zered, 2429, *zered* [3]

ZEREDAH [1]
Zeredah, 7649, *ṣerēdâ* [1]

ZERERAH [1]
Zererah, 7678, *ṣerērâ* [1]

ZERESH [4]
Zeresh, 2454, *zereš* [4]

ZERETH [1]
Zereth, 7679, *ṣeret* [1]

ZERETH SHAHAR [1]
Zereth Shahar, 7680, *ṣeret haššaḥar* [1]

ZERI [1]
Zeri, 7662, *ṣerî* [1]

ZEROR [1]
Zeror, 7657, *ṣerôr*[3] [1]

ZERUAH [1]
Zeruah, 7654, *ṣerû'â* [1]

ZERUBBABEL [22]
Zerubbabel, 2428, *zerubbābel* [21]
Zerubbabel, 10239, *zerubbābel* [1]

ZERUIAH [25]
Zeruiah, 7653, *ṣerûyâ* [25]

ZERUIAH'S [1]
Zeruiah's, 7653, *ṣerûyâ* [1]

ZETHAM [2]
Zetham, 2457, *zētām* [2]

ZETHAN [1]
Zethan, 2340, *zêtān* [1]

ZETHAR [1]
Zethar, 2458, *zētar* [1]

ZIA [1]
Zia, 2333, *zîa'* [1]

ZIBA [16]
Ziba, 7471, *ṣîbā'* [15]
Ziba, *NIH/RPE* [1]

ZIBA'S [1]
Ziba's, 7471, *ṣîbā'* [1]

ZIBEON [8]
Zibeon, 7390, *ṣib'ôn* [8]

ZIBIA [1]
Zibia, 7384, *ṣibyā'* [1]

ZIBIAH [2]
Zibiah, 7385, *ṣibyâ* [2]

ZICRI [12]
Zicri, 2356, *zikrî* [12]

ZIDDIM [1]
Ziddim, 7403, *ṣiddîm* [1]

ZIHA [3]
Ziha, 7484, *ṣîḥā'* [3]

ZIKLAG [15]
Ziklag, 7637, *ṣiqlag* [14]
Ziklag[s], 2021+6551, *ha-+'îr*[1] [1]

ZILLAH [3]
Zillah, 7500, *ṣillâ* [3]

ZILLETHAI [2]
Zillethai, 7531, *ṣilletay* [2]

ZILPAH [7]
Zilpah, 2364, *zilpâ* [7]

ZIMMAH [3]
Zimmah, 2366, *zimmâ*[2] [3]

ZIMRAN [2]
Zimran, 2383, *zimrān* [2]

ZIMRI [17]
Zimri, 2381, *zimrî*[1] [16]
Zimri, 2382, *zimrî*[2] [1]

ZIMRI'S [1]
Zimri's, 2381, *zimrî*[1] [1]

ZIN [10]
Zin, 7554, *ṣin* [10]

ZION [156]
Zion, 7482, *ṣiyyôn* [152]
in Zion[s], 9004, *šām* [2]
Zion, *NIH/RPE* [1]
Zion[s], 2023, *-āh* [1]

ZION'S [2]
Zion's, 7482, *ṣiyyôn* [2]

ZIOR [1]
Zior, 7486, *ṣî'ōr* [1]

ZIPH [9]
Ziph, 2334, *zîp*[1] [7]
Ziph, 2335, *zîp*[2] [2]

ZIPHAH [1]
Ziphah, 2336, *zîpâ* [1]

ZIPHITES [3]
Ziphites, 2337, *zîpî* [3]

ZIPHRON [1]
Ziphron, 2412, *ziprôn* [1]

ZIPPOR [7]
Zippor, 7607, *ṣippôr*[2] [7]

ZIPPORAH [4]
Zipporah, 7631, *ṣippōrâ* [3]
Zipporah, *NIH/RPE* [1]

ZITHER [4]
zither, 10630, *qîterōs* [4]

ZIV [2]
Ziv, 2304, *ziw* [2]

ZIZ [1]
Ziz, 7489, *ṣîṣ*[2] [1]

ZIZA [4]
Ziza, 2330, *zîzā'* [3]
Ziza, 2331, *zîzâ* [1]

ZOAN [7]
Zoan, 7586, *ṣō'an* [7]

ZOAR [10]
Zoar, 7593, *ṣō'ar* [10]

ZOBAH [13]
Zobah, 7420, *ṣôbâ* [10]
Zobah, 7419, *ṣôbā'* [2]
Zobah, *NIH/RPE* [1]

ZOHAR [5]
Zohar, 7468, *ṣōḥar* [5]

ZOHELETH [1]
Zoheleth, 2325, *zōḥelet* [1]

ZOHETH [1]
Zoheth, 2311, *zôḥēt* [1]

ZOPHAH [2]
Zophah, 7432, *ṣôpaḥ* [2]

ZOPHAI [1]
Zophai, 7433, *ṣôpay* [1]

ZOPHAR [4]
Zophar, 7436, *ṣôpar* [4]

ZOPHIM [1]
Zophim, 7614, *ṣōpîm* [1]

ZORAH [10]
Zorah, 7666, *ṣor'â* [10]

ZORATHITES [2]
Zorathites, 7670, *ṣāre'ātî* [2]

ZORITES [1]
Zorites, 7668, *ṣor'î* [1]

ZUAR [5]
Zuar, 7428, *ṣû'ār* [5]

ZUPH [3]
Zuph, 7431, *ṣûp*[3] [3]

ZUPHITE [1]
Zuphite, 7434, *ṣûpî* [1]

ZUR [5]
Zur, 7448, *ṣûr*[6] [5]

ZURIEL [1]
Zuriel, 7452, *ṣûrî'ēl* [1]

ZURISHADDAI [5]
Zurishaddai, 7453, *ṣûrîšadday* [5]

ZUZITES [1]
Zuzites, 2309, *zûzîm* [1]

KEY FEATURES OF THE HEBREW-ENGLISH AND ARAMAIC-ENGLISH DICTIONARIES

HEBREW OR ARAMAIC WORD
Each entry begins with three designations for the Hebrew or Aramaic word: the G/K number, the word in Hebrew, and in transliteration. See the introduction, page xiii.

DEFINITION
The concise definition is based on NIV translations and the standard lexicons. See the introduction, page xiii.

3 אָב, *'āb*, father, grandfather, forefather, ancestor, S: 1, B: 3A, K: 1C, H: 1A

170 אָהַב, *'āhab*, [A] to love, like, be a friend; [C] to be loved; [D] be a lover, an ally, S: 157, B: 12C, K: 15C, H: 5B & 76A

RESOURCE REFERENCES
Each word is referenced to Strong's numbering system and the lexicons of Brown, Driver, and Briggs; Koehler and Baumgartner; and Holladay. An asterisk (*) means there is no reference. See the introduction, page xiii.

VERB STEM CODES
Definitions of verbs are organized by verb stems. See the introduction, page xiii, and the abbreviations at the foot of each page spread.

A Concise Hebrew-English Dictionary to the Old Testament

1 א ', letter of the Hebrew alphabet, S: 3, B: 1A, K: 1A, H*

2 אָ- *-ā'*, she, her, S*, B*, K*, H*

3 אָב *'āb*, father, grandfather; forefather, ancestor, S: 1, B: 3A, K: 1C, H: 1A

4 אֵב *'ēb*, new (plant) growth, shoot, S: 3, B: 1A, K: 2B, H: 1A

5 אֲבַגְתָא *'^{a}bagtā'*, Abagtha, S: 5, B: 1B, K: 2B, H: 1A

6 אָבַד *'ābad*, [A] perish, [D, G] destroy, demolish, annihilate, S: 6, B: 1B, K: 2B, H: 1B

7 אֹבֵד *'ōbēd*, ruin, S: 8, B: 2B, K: 3B, H: 1C

8 אֲבֵדָה *'^{a}bēdâ*, lost item, S: 9, B: 2B, K: 3B, H: 1C

9 אֲבַדֹּה *'^{a}baddōh*, destruction, S: 10, B: 2B, K: 3C, H: 1C

10 אֲבַדּוֹ *'^{a}baddô*, variant: destruction, S: 11†, B: 2B, K: 3C, H: 1C

11 אֲבַדּוֹן *'^{a}baddôn*, destruction, S: 11, B: 2B, K: 3C, H: 1C

12 אַבְדָן *'abdān*, destruction, S: 12, B: 2B, K: 3C, H: 1C

13 אָבְדָן *'obdān*, destruction, S: 13, B: 2B, K: 3C, H: 1C

14 אָבָה *'ābâ*, [A] to be willing, consent, yield, S: 14, B: 2C, K: 3C, H: 1C

15 אֵבֶה *'ēbeh*, papyrus or reed (boat), S: 16, B: 3C, K: 4A, H: 1D

16 אֲבוֹי *'^{a}bôy*, sorrow, S: 17, B: 5A, K: 4A, H: 1D

17 אֵבוּס *'ēbûs*, manger, S: 18, B: 7B, K: 4A, H: 1D

18 אִבְחָה *'ibḥâ*, slaughter, S: 19, B: 5A, K: 4A, H: 1D

19 אֲבַטִּיחַ *'^{a}baṭṭîaḥ*, melon, S: 20, B: 105C, K: 4A, H: 1D

20 אָבִי[1] *'ābî[1]*, Oh, that!, S: 15†, B: 2C, K: 4A, H: 1D

21 אָבִי[2] *'ābî[2]*, variant: Abi, S*, B: 27C, K: 4B, H: 1D

22 אָבִי[3] *'ābî[3]*, variant: see 995, S*, B: 97C, K: 4A, H: 1D

23 אֲבִי *'^{a}bî*, Abijah, Abiezrite, S: 21, B: 4A, K: 4B, H: 2A

24 אֲבִיאֵל *'^{a}bî'ēl*, Abiel, S: 22, B: 3D, K: 4B, H: 2A

25 אֲבִיאָסָף *'^{a}bî'āsāp*, Abiasaph, S: 23, B: 4A, K: 4B, H: 2A

26 אָבִיב *'ābîb*, (month of) Abib; head (of grain), S: 24, B: 1B, K: 4B, H: 2A

27 אֲבִיבַעַל *'^{a}bîba'al*, variant: Abi-Baal, S*, B: 3D, K: 4C, H: 2B

28 אֲבִיגַיִל *'^{a}bîgayil*, Abigail, S: 26, B: 4A, K: 4C, H: 2A

29 אֲבִידָן *'^{a}bîdān*, Abidan, S: 27, B: 4A, K: 4C, H: 2A

30 אֲבִידָע *'^{a}bîdā'*, Abida, S: 28, B: 4A, K: 4C, H: 2A

31 אֲבִיָּה *'^{a}biyyâ*, Abijah, S: 29, B: 4A, K: 4C, H: 2A

32 אֲבִיָּהוּ *'^{a}biyyāhû*, Abijah, S: 29, B: 4A, K: 4D, H: 2A

33 אֲבִיהוּא *'^{a}bîhû'*, Abihu, S: 30, B: 4B, K: 4D, H: 2A

34 אֲבִיהוּד *'^{a}bîhûd*, Abihud, S: 31, B: 4B, K: 4D, H: 2A

35 אֲבִיהַיִל *'^{a}bîhayil*, Abihail, S: 32, B: 4B, K: 4D, H: 2A

36 אֶבְיוֹן *'ebyôn*, poor, needy, S: 34, B: 2D, K: 4D, H: 2A

37 אֲבִיּוֹנָה *'^{a}biyyônâ*, caper berry (that stimulates desire), S: 35, B: 2D, K: 5A, H: 2A

38 אֲבִיחַיִל *'^{a}bîḥayil*, Abihail, S: 32, B: 4B, K: 5A, H: 2A

39 אֲבִיטוּב *'^{a}bîṭûb*, Abitub, S: 36, B: 4B, K: 5A, H: 2A

40 אֲבִיטָל *'^{a}bîṭāl*, Abital, S: 37, B: 4B, K: 5A, H*

41 אֲבִיָּם *'^{a}biyyām*, variant: Abiyam, S: 38, B: 4A, K: 5A, H: 2B

42 אֲבִימָאֵל *'^{a}bîmā'ēl*, Abimael, S: 39, B: 4B, K: 5B, H: 2B

43 אֲבִימֶלֶךְ *'^{a}bîmelek*, Abimelech, S: 40, B: 4B, K: 5B, H: 2B

44 אֲבִינָדָב *'^{a}bînādāb*, Abinadab, S: 41, B: 4C, K: 5B, H: 2B

45 אֲבִינֹעַם *'^{a}bînō'am*, Abinoam, S: 42, B: 4C, K: 5B, H: 2B

46 אֲבִינֵר *'^{a}bînēr*, Abner, S: 74, B: 4C, K: 5B, H: 2B

47 אֶבְיָסָף *'ebyāsāp*, Ebiasaph, S: 43, B: 4A, K: 5C, H: 2B

48 אֲבִיעֶזֶר *'^{a}bî'ezer*, Abiezer, S: 44, B: 4C, K: 5C, H: 2B

49 אֲבִי עֶזְרִי *'^{a}bî 'ezrî*, Abiezrite, S: 33†, B: 4C, K: 5C, H*

50 אֲבִי־עַלְבוֹן *'^{a}bî-'albôn*, Abi-Albon, S: 45, B: 3D, K: 5C, H: 2B

51 אָבִיר *'ābîr*, mighty, powerful; (as a divine title) the Mighty One, S: 46, B: 7C, K: 5C, H: 2B

52 אַבִּיר *'abbîr*, mighty, powerful, S: 47, B: 7D, K: 5C, H: 2B

53 אֲבִירָם *'^{a}bîrām*, Abiram, S: 48, B: 4D, K: 5D, H: 2B

54 אֲבִישַׁג *'^{a}bîšag*, Abishag, S: 49, B: 4D, K: 5D, H: 2B

55 אֲבִישׁוּעַ *'^{a}bîšûa'*, Abishua, S: 50, B: 4D, K: 5D, H: 2B

56 אֲבִישׁוּר *'^{a}bîšûr*, Abishur, S: 51, B: 4D, K: 5D, H: 2C

57 אֲבִישַׁי *'^{a}bîšay*, Abishai, S: 52, B: 5A, K: 6A, H: 2C

58 אֲבִישָׁלוֹם *'^{a}bîšālôm*, Abishalom, S: 53, B: 5A, K: 6A, H: 2C

59 אֶבְיָתָר *'ebyātār*, Abiathar, S: 54, B: 5A, K: 6A, H: 2C

60 אָבַךְ *'ābak*, [F] to roll upward, to be borne along, S: 55, B: 5B, K: 6A, H: 2C

61 אָבַל[1] *'ābal[1]*, [A, F] to mourn, lament, grieve, [G] cause to mourn, S: 56, B: 5B, K: 6A, H: 2C

62 אָבַל[2] *'ābal[2]*, [A] to dry up, lie parched, S: 56, B: 5B, K: 6C, H: 2C

63 אָבֵל[1] *'ābēl[1]*, mourning, grieving, weeping, S: 57 & 59†, B: 5D, K: 6C, H: 2C

64 אָבֵל[2] *'ābēl[2]*, Abel, S: 58 & 59†, B: 5D, K: 6C, H: 2C

65 אֵבֶל *'ēbel*, ceremony of mourning, period of mourning, S: 60, B: 5C, K: 6D, H: 2C

66 אֲבָל *'^{a}bāl*, but; however, surely, indeed, S: 61, B: 6A, K: 7A, H: 2D

67 אֻבָל *'ubāl*, canal, S: 180†, B: 385C, K: 7A, H: 2D

68 אָבֵל בֵּית מַעֲכָה *'ābēl bêt ma'^{a}kâ*, Abel Beth Maacah, S: 62, B: 6A, K: 6C 5., H: 2C

[F] Hitpael (hitpoel, hitpoal, hitpolel, hitpolal, hitpalel, hitpalal, hitpalpel, hitpalpal, hotpael, hotpaal) [G] Hiphil (hiphtil) [H] Hophal [I] Hishtaphel

69 אָבֵל הַשִּׁטִּים *'ābēl haššiṭṭîm*, Abel Shittim, S: 63, B: 6A, K: 6C 2., H: 2C

70 אָבֵל כְּרָמִים *'ābēl kerāmîm*, Abel Keramim, S: 64, B: 6A, K: 6C 3., H: 2C

71 אָבֵל מְחוֹלָה *'ābēl meḥôlâ*, Abel Meholah, S: 65, B: 6A, K: 6C 4., H: 2C

72 אָבֵל מַיִם *'ābēl mayim*, Abel Maim, S: 66, B: 6A, K: 6C 6., H: 2C

73 אָבֵל מִצְרַיִם *'ābēl miṣrayim*, Abel Mizraim, S: 67, B: 6A, K: 6C 1., H: 2C

74 אֶבֶן *'eben*, stone, rock; gem, jewel; hailstone, S: 68, B: 6B, K: 7A, H: 2D

75 אֶבֶן הָעֵזֶר *'eben hā'ēzer*, Ebenezer, S: 72, B: 7A, K: 696C, H*

76 אֲבָנָה *'abānâ*, Abana, S: 71, B: 7B, K: 7D, H: 3A

77 אַבְנֵט *'abnēṭ*, sash, S: 73, B: 126A, K: 7D, H: 3A

78 אָבְנַיִם *'obnayim*, potter's wheel; delivery stool, S: 70†, B: 7A, K: 7D, H: 3A

79 אַבְנֵר *'abnēr*, Abner, S: 74, B: 4C, K: 8A, H: 3A

80 אָבַס *'ābas*, [B] to be fattened, S: 75, B: 7B, K: 8A, H: 3C

81 אֲבַעְבֻּעֹת *'aba'bu'ōt*, festers, blisters, S: 76†, B: 101B, K: 8A, H: 3A

82 אֶבֶץ *'ebeṣ*, Ebez, S: 77, B: 7B, K: 8A, H: 3A

83 אִבְצָן *'ibṣān*, Ibzan, S: 78, B: 7B, K: 8B, H: 3A

84 אָבַק *'ābaq*, [C] to wrestle (with), S: 79, B: 7C, K: 8B, H: 3A

85 אָבָק *'ābāq*, fine dust, powder, S: 80, B: 7B, K: 8B, H: 3B

86 אֲבָקָה *'abāqâ*, spice, S: 81, B: 7C, K: 8B, H: 3B

87 אָבַר *'ābar*, [G] to take flight, soar upward, S: 82, B: 7C, K: 8C, H: 3B

88 אֵבֶר *'ēber*, feather, wing, S: 83, B: 7C, K: 8C, H: 3B

89 אֶבְרָה *'ebrâ*, feather, pinion, wing, S: 84, B: 7C, K: 8C, H: 3B

90 אַבְרָהָם *'abrāhām*, Abraham, S: 85, B: 4D, K: 8C, H: 3B

91 אַבְרֵךְ *'abrēk*, Make way!, S: 86, B: 7D, K: 8D, H: 3B

92 אַבְרָם *'abrām*, Abram, S: 87, B: 4D, K: 8D, H: 3B

93 אַבְשַׁי *'abšay*, Abishai, S: 52, B: 5A, K: 8D, H: 3B

94 אַבְשָׁלוֹם *'abšālôm*, Absalom, S: 53†, B: 5A, K: 8D, H: 3B

95 אֹבֹת *'ōbōt*, Oboth, S: 88, B: 15C, K: 8D, H: 3B

96 אָגֵא *'āgē'*, Agee, S: 89, B: 8A, K: 9A, H: 3B

97 אֲגַג *'agag*, Agag, S: 90, B: 8A, K: 9A, H: 3B

98 אֲגָגִי *'agāgî*, Agagite, S: 91, B: 8A, K: 9A, H: 3B

99 אֲגֻדָּה *'aguddâ*, bunch, bundle; group, band; cord, bands; foundation, structure, S: 92, B: 8A, K: 9B, H: 3C

100 אֱגוֹז *'egôz*, nut tree, S: 93, B: 8B, K: 9B, H: 3C

101 אָגוּר *'āgûr*, Agur, S: 94, B: 8D, K: 9B, H: 3C

102 אֲגוֹרָה *'agôrâ*, fee, payment, S: 95, B: 8D, K: 9B, H: 3C

103 אֵגֶל *'ēgel*, drop (of dew), S: 96†, B: 8B, K: 9B, H: 3C

104 אֶגְלַיִם *'eglayim*, Eglaim, S: 97, B: 8B, K: 9C, H: 3C

105 אָגַם *'āgam*, variant: [A] to be hot, S*, B*, K: 9C, H: 3C

106 אֲגַם[1] *'agam[1]*, swamp, pond, marsh, S: 98, B: 8B, K: 9C, H: 3C

107 אֲגַם[2] *'agam[2]*, variant: outwork (of a fort), S: 98, B: 8B, K: 9C, H: 3C

108 אָגֵם *'āgēm*, sick, grieved, S: 99, B: 8C, K: 9C, H: 3C

109 אַגְמוֹן *'agmôn*, reed; cord (made of reeds), S: 100, B: 8C, K: 9C, H: 3C

110 אַגָּן *'aggān*, bowl, goblet, S: 101, B: 8C, K: 9D, H: 3C

111 אֲגַף *'agap*, troop, band, S: 102†, B: 8C, K: 9D, H: 3C

112 אָגַר *'āgar*, [A] to gather (in), S: 103, B: 8D, K: 9D, H: 3D

113 אֲגַרְטָל *'agarṭāl*, dish, S: 105, B: 173D, K: 9D, H: 3D

114 אֶגְרֹף *'egrōp*, fist, S: 106, B: 175D, K: 10A, H: 3D

115 אִגֶּרֶת *'iggeret*, letter, document, S: 107, B: 8D, K: 10A, H: 3D

116 אֵד *'ēd*, stream, S: 108, B: 15D, K: 10A, H: 3D

117 אָדַב *'ādab*, [G] to grieve, S: 109, B: 9A, K: 10B, H: 3D

118 אַדְבְּאֵל *'adbe'ēl*, Adbeel, S: 110, B: 9A, K: 10B, H: 3D

119 אֲדַד *'adad*, Hadad, S: 111, B: 212D, K: 10B, H: 3D

120 אִדּוֹ *'iddô*, Iddo, S: 112, B: 9A, K: 10B, H: 3D

121 אֱדוֹם *'edôm*, Edom, S: 123, B: 10B, K: 10B, H: 3D

122 אֲדוֹמִי *'adômî*, Edomite, S: 130†, B: 10C, K: 10D & 14B, H: 4A

123 אָדוֹן *'ādôn*, lord, master, supervisor; the Lord, (with Yahweh [3378]) Sovereign, S: 113, B: 10D, K: 10D, H: 4A

124 אַדּוֹן *'addôn*, Addon, S: 114, B: 11D, K: 11D, H: 4B

125 אֲדוֹנִיָּה *'adôniyyâ*, variant: Adonijah, S: 138, B: 11D, K: 350B, H*

126 אֲדוֹרַיִם *'adôrayim*, Adoraim, S: 115, B: 12A, K: 11D, H: 4B

127 אֲדוֹרָם *'adôrām*, variant: Adoram, S: 151†, B: 12A, K: 11D, H: 4B

128 אֹדוֹת *'ōdôt*, on account of, because of, for the reason that, S: 182, B: 15C, K: 18C, H: 4B

129 אַדִּיר *'addîr*, mighty, noble, majestic, splendid; (as a divine title) the Mighty One, S: 117, B: 12B, K: 11D, H: 4B

130 אֲדַלְיָא *'adalyā'*, Adalia, S: 118, B: 9A, K: 12A, H: 4B

131 אָדֵם *'ādēm*, [A] be ruddy; [E] be dyed red, S: 119†, B: 10A, K: 12A, H: 4B

132 אָדָם[1] *'ādām[1]*, man, person, human, mankind, S: 120, B: 9A, K: 12B, H: 4C

133 אָדָם[2] *'ādām[2]*, variant: leather, S: 120, B: 9A, K: 12B, H: 4C

134 אָדָם[3] *'ādām[3]*, Adam, S: 121, B: 9A, K: 13A, H: 4C

135 אָדָם[4] *'ādām[4]*, variant: ground, S: 120, B: 9A, K: 12B, H: 4C

136 אָדָם[5] *'ādām[5]*, Adam, S: 121, B: 9A, K: 13A, H: 4C

137 אָדֹם *'ādōm*, red; ruddy (skin), S: 122, B: 10B, K: 13B, H: 4D

138 אֹדֶם *'ōdem*, ruby, S: 124, B: 10B, K: 13B, H: 4D

139 אֱדֹם *'edōm*, variant: Edom, S: 123, B: 10B, K: 673A, H: 262B

140 אֲדַמְדָּם *'adamdām*, reddish, reddish-white, S: 125, B: 10C, K: 13B, H: 4D

141 אֲדָמָה[1] *'adāmâ[1]*, ground, soil, dust; land, earth, S: 127, B: 9C, K: 13B, H: 4D

142 אֲדָמָה[2] *'adāmâ[2]*, Adamah, S: 128, B: 9C 7., K: 14A, H: 4D

143 אֲדָמָה[3] *'adāmâ[3]*, variant: [red] blood, S: 127, B: 9C, K: 13B, H: 4D

144 אַדְמָה *'admâ*, Admah, S: 126, B: 10A, K: 14A, H: 4D

145 אַדְמוֹנִי *'admônî*, red; ruddy (skin), S: 132 & 726†, B: 10C, K: 14B, H: 4D

146 אֲדָמִי הַנֶּקֶב *'adāmî hanneqeb*, Adami Nekeb, S: 129† + 5346†, B: 10A, K: 14B, H: 5A

147 אֲדֻמִּים *'adummîm*, Adummim, S: 131, B: 10C, K: 14B, H: 5A

148 אַדְמָתָא *'admātā'*, Admatha, S: 133, B: 10C, K: 14C, H: 5A

149 אֶדֶן *'eden*, base, footing, pedestal, S: 134, B: 10D, K: 14C, H: 5A

150 אַדָּן *'addān*, Addon, S: 135, B: 11D, K: 14C, H: 5A

151 אֲדֹנָי *'adōnāy*, the Lord, (with Yahweh [3378]) Sovereign, S: 136, B: 10D, K: 10D, H: 4A 2.

152 אֲדֹנִי בֶזֶק *'adōnî bezeq*, Adoni-Bezek, S: 137, B: 11D, K: 14C, H: 5A

153 אֲדֹנִיָּה *'adōniyyâ*, Adonijah, S: 138, B: 11D, K: 14C, H: 5A

154 אֲדֹנִיָּהוּ *'adōniyyāhû*, Adonijah, S: 138, B: 11D, K: 14D, H: 5A

155 אֲדֹנִי־צֶדֶק *'adōnî-ṣedeq*, Adoni-Zedek, S: 139, B: 11D, K: 14D, H: 5A

156 אֲדֹנִיקָם *'adōnîqām*, Adonikam, S: 140, B: 12A, K: 14D, H: 5A

157 אֲדֹנִירָם *'adōnîrām*, Adoniram, S: 141, B: 12A, K: 14D, H: 5A

158 אָדַר *'ādar*, [C] to prove oneself majestic, powerful; [G] to make glorious, make powerful, S: 142, B: 12A, K: 14D, H: 5A

159 אֶדֶר *'eder*, splendor, handsomeness, S: 145, B: 12A, K: 15A, H: 5A

160 אֲדָר *'adār*, Adar, S: 143, B: 12C, K: 15A, H: 5A

161 אַדָּר[1] *'addār[1]*, Addar, S: 146, B: 12A, K: 15A, H: 5B

162 אַדָּר[2] *'addār[2]*, Addar, S: 146, B: 12A, K: 15A, H: 5B

163 אֲדַרְכֹנִים *'adarkōnîm*, darics, S: 150†, B: 204A, K: 15A, H: 5B

164 אֲדֹרָם *'adōrām*, variant: Adoram, S: 151, B: 12A, K: 15A, H: 5B

165 אַדְרַמֶּלֶךְ[1] *'adrammelek[1]*, Adrammelech (pagan god), S: 152, B: 12C, K: 15B, H: 5B

166 אַדְרַמֶּלֶךְ[2] *'adrammelek[2]*, Adrammelech, S: 152, B: 12C, K: 15B, H: 5B

167 אֶדְרֶעִי *'edre'î*, Edrei, S: 154, B: 204C, K: 15B, H: 5B

168 אַדֶּרֶת *'adderet*, cloak, royal robe, (hairy) garment, S: 155, B: 12B, K: 15B, H: 5B

169 אָדַשׁ *'ādaš*, variant: see 1889, S: 156, B: 190B, K: 15C, H: 5B

170 אָהַב *'āhab*, [A] to love, like, be a friend; [C] to be loved; [D] be a lover, an ally, S: 157, B: 12C, K: 15C, H: 5B & 76A

171 אָהַב *'ōhab*, love; something loved, S: 159, B: 13B, K: 16C, H: 5C

172 אַהַב *'ahab*, lover (negative); loving, charming (positive), S: 158, B: 13B, K: 16C, H: 5C

173 [1]אַהֲבָה *'ahabâ[1]*, love, S: 160, B: 13B, K: 16B, H: 5C

174 [2]אַהֲבָה *'ahabâ[2]*, variant: leather, S: 160†, B: 13B, K: 16B, H: 5D

175 אֲהַבְהָבַי *'ahabhābay*, variant: ardor of love, S*, B: 396D, K: 223B, H: 5D

176 אֹהַד *'ōhad*, Ohad, S: 161, B: 13C, K: 16D, H: 5D

177 אֲהָהּ *'ahāh*, Ah!, Oh!, Alas!, S: 162, B: 13C, K: 16D, H: 5D

178 אַהֲוָא *'ahawā*, Ahava, S: 163, B: 13C, K: 16D, H: 5D

179 אֵהוּד *'ēhûd*, Ehud, S: 164, B: 13C, K: 16D, H: 5D

180 אֱהִי *'ehî*, Where?, S: 165, B: 13C, K: 16D, H: 5D

181 אֶהְיֶה *'ehyeh*, variant: I am, I will be (self-designation of God), S: 1961†, B: 218B I., K: 16D, H: 5D

182 [1]אָהַל *'āhal[1]*, [A, D] to pitch a tent, S: 167, B: 14B, K: 17A, H: 5D

183 [2]אָהַל *'āhal[2]*, [G] to be bright, S: 166, B: 14C, K: 17A, H: 5D

184 אָהָל *'āhāl*, variant: Ahal, S: 174†, B*, K*, H*

185 [1]אֹהֶל *'ōhel[1]*, tent, tent-dwelling; home, dwelling place, S: 168, B: 13D, K: 17A, H: 5D

186 [2]אֹהֶל *'ōhel[2]*, Ohel, S: 169, B: 14B, K: 17B, H: 6A

187 אֵהֶל *'ēhel*, variant: these, those, S: 428†, B: 41C, K: 50B, H: 6A

188 אָהֳלָה *'oholâ*, Oholah, S: 170, B: 14B, K: 17B, H: 6A

189 אֲהָלוֹת *'ahālôt*, aloes, S: 174, B: 14C 2, K: 17B, H: 6A

190 אָהֳלִיאָב *'oholî'āb*, Oholiab, S: 171, B: 14B, K: 17C, H: 6A

191 אָהֳלִיבָה *'oholîbâ*, Oholibah, S: 172, B: 14C, K: 17C, H: 6A

192 אָהֳלִיבָמָה *'oholîbāmâ*, Oholibamah, S: 173, B: 14C, K: 17C, H: 6A

193 [1]אֲהָלִים *'ahālîm[1]*, aloes, S: 174, B: 14C, K: 17C, H: 6A

194 [2]אֲהָלִים *'ahālîm[2]*, variant: ice plant, S*, B: 14C, K: 17C, H: 6A

195 אַהֲרֹן *'aharôn*, Aaron, S: 175, B: 14D, K: 17D, H: 6A

196 אוֹ *'ô*, or, or if, whether, S: 176, B: 14D, K: 17D, H: 6A

197 אַו *'aw*, crave, S: 176, B: 16B, K: 18A, H: 6B

198 אוּאֵל *'û'ēl*, Uel, S: 177, B: 15A, K: 18A, H: 6B

199 [1]אוֹב *'ôb[1]*, wineskin, bag, S: 178, B: 15A, K: 18A, H: 6B

200 [2]אוֹב *'ôb[2]*, medium, spiritist, S: 178, B: 15A, K: 18B, H: 6B

201 אוֹבִיל *'ôbîl*, Obil, S: 179, B: 6A, K: 18C, H: 6B

202 אוּד *'ûd*, burning stick, S: 181, B: 15C, K: 18C, H: 6B

203 [1]אָוָה *'āwâ[1]*, [D, F] to crave, desire, yearn for, long for, S: 183, B: 16A, K: 18C, H: 6B

204 [2]אָוָה *'āwâ[2]*, [F] to run a line, measure, S: 184, B: 16C, K: 18D, H: 6B

205 אַוָּה *'awwâ*, wanting, craving; earnestness, S: 185, B: 16B, K: 19A, H: 6C

206 אוּזַי *'ûzay*, Uzai, S: 186, B: 17A, K: 19A, H: 6C

207 אוּזָל *'ûzāl*, Uzal, S: 187, B: 23D, K: 19A, H: 6C

208 אוֹי *'ôy*, Woe! Alas!, S: 188, B: 17A, K: 19A, H: 6C

209 אֱוִי *'ewî*, Evi, S: 189, B: 16C, K: 19A, H: 6C

210 אוֹיָה *'ôyâ*, Woe!, Alas!, S: 190, B: 17A, K: 19B, H: 6C

211 [1]אֱוִיל *'ewîl[1]*, foolish; (as noun) a fool, S: 191, B: 17B, K: 19B, H: 6C

212 [2]אֱוִיל *'ewîl[2]*, variant: citizenry (of the land), S: 193†, B: 17C, K: 19D, H: 6C

213 אֱוִיל מְרֹדַךְ *'ewîl merōdak*, Evil-Merodach, S: 192, B: 17B, K: 19C, H: 6C

214 [1]אוּל *'ûl[1]*, body, belly, S: 193, B: 17C, K: 19D, H: 6D

215 [2]אוּל *'ûl[2]*, variant: leading man, noble, S: 193, B: 17C, K: 19D, H: 6D

216 אֱוִלִי *'ewilî*, foolish, S: 196, B: 17C, K: 19D, H: 6C

217 [1]אוּלַי *'ûlay[1]*, Ulai, S: 195, B: 19C, K: 19D, H: 6D

218 [2]אוּלַי *'ûlay[2]*, what if, perhaps, maybe, S: 194, B: 19C, K: 19D, H: 6D

219 [1]אוּלָם *'ûlām[1]*, but, however, on the other hand, nevertheless, S: 199, B: 19D, K: 20A, H: 6D

220 [2]אוּלָם *'ûlām[2]*, Ulam, S: 198, B: 17D, K: 20A, H: 6D

221 [3]אוּלָם *'ûlām[3]*, variant: portico; hall; colonnade, S: 197, B: 17C, K: 20A, H: 6D

222 אִוֶּלֶת *'iwwelet*, foolishness, folly, S: 200, B: 17C, K: 20A, H: 6D

223 אוֹמָר *'ômār*, Omar, S: 201, B: 57B, K: 20B, H: 6D

224 [1]אָוֶן *'āwen[1]*, evil, wickedness, iniquity; evildoer; calamity, trouble, injustice, S: 205, B: 19D, K: 20B, H: 6D

225 [2]אָוֶן *'āwen[2]*, Heliopolis; (Valley of) Aven, S: 206, B: 19D, K: 144B, H: 6D & 7A

226 [1]אוֹן *'ôn[1]*, power, strength, vigor, manhood; wealth, S: 202, B: 20B, K: 20D, H: 7A

227 [2]אוֹן *'ôn[2]*, On, S: 203, B: 20B, K: 20D, H: 7A

228 [3]אוֹן *'ôn[3]*, On, S: 204, B: 58A, K: 21A, H: 7A

229 אוֹנוֹ *'ônô*, Ono, S: 207, B: 20C, K: 21A, H: 7A

230 אוֹנִי *'ônî*, mourning, S: 205†, B: 122B, K: 67D, H: 7A

231 אוֹנָם *'ônām*, Onam, S: 208, B: 20C, K: 21A, H: 7A

232 אוֹנָן *'ônān*, Onan, S: 209, B: 20C, K: 21A, H: 7A

233 אוּפָז *'ûpāz*, Uphaz, S: 210, B: 20C, K: 21A, H: 7A

234 [1]אוֹפִיר *'ôpîr[1]*, Ophir, S: 211, B: 20C 2., K: 21B, H: 7A

235 [2]אוֹפִיר *'ôpîr[2]*, variant: Ophir, S: 211, B: 20C 1., K: 21B, H: 7A

236 אוֹפָן *'ôpan*, wheel, S: 212, B: 66D, K: 21C, H: 7A

237 אוּץ *'ûṣ*, [A] to be in haste, be eager; to press (for an answer); to be small, narrow; [G] to urge, insist upon, S: 213, B: 21A, K: 21C, H: 7A

238 אוֹצָר *'ôṣār*, treasury, storehouse, storeroom, storage vault, S: 214, B: 69D, K: 21C, H: 7B

239 [1]אוֹר *'ôr[1]*, [A] to shine, be bright; [G] to give light, make shine, brighten; [C] to be resplendent with light, shine on, S: 215, B: 21A, K: 21D, H: 7B

240 [2]אוֹר *'ôr[2]*, light, brightness; lightning; daylight, sunshine, S: 216, B: 21C, K: 22B, H: 7C

241 [1]אוּר *'ûr[1]*, light; east [the region of light], S: 217, B: 22A, K: 22D, H: 7C

242 [2]אוּר *'ûr[2]*, Urim, S: 224†, B: 22A, K: 22D, H: 7C

243 [3]אוּר *'ûr[3]*, Ur, S: 218, B: 22D, K: 23A, H: 7C

244 [4]אוּר *'ûr[4]*, Ur, S: 218, B: 22B, K: 23B, H: 7D

245 [1]אוֹרָה *'ôrâ[1]*, light, morning light; happiness, serenity, cheerfulness, S: 219, B: 21D, K: 23B & 90C, H: 7C

246 [2]אוֹרָה *'ôrâ[2]*, herb, mallow, S: 219, B: 21D, K: 90C, H: 7D

247 אוּרִי *'ûrî*, Uri, S: 221, B: 22B, K: 23B, H: 7D

248 אוּרִיאֵל *'ûrî'ēl*, Uriel, S: 222, B: 22B, K: 23B, H: 7D

249 אוּרִיָּה *'ûriyyâ*, Uriah, S: 223, B: 22C, K: 23B, H: 7D

250 אוּרִיָּהוּ *'ûriyyāhû*, Uriah, S: 223, B: 22C, K: 23C, H: 7D

251 אוּרִים *'ûrîm*, variant: Urim, see 242, S: 224, B: 22A, K: 22D, H: 7C

252 אוּת *'ût*, [C] to consent, agree, S: 225, B: 22D, K*, H: 7D

253 [1]אוֹת *'ôt[1]*, sign, mark, symbol, S: 226, B: 16C, K: 23C, H: 7D

254 [2]אוֹת *'ôt[2]*, variant: see 906, S: 853†, B: 84C, K: 24A, H: 8A

255 אָז *'āz*, then, at that time, meanwhile, S: 227, B: 23A & 23B, K: 24A, H: 8A

256 אֶזְבָּי *'ezbāy*, Ezbai, S: 229, B: 23C, K: 24C, H: 8A

257 אֵזוֹב *'ēzôb*, hyssop, S: 231, B: 23C, K: 24C, H: 8A

258 אֵזוֹר *'ēzôr*, belt, sash; loincloth, S: 232, B: 25B, K: 24C, H: 8A

259 אֲזַי *'azay*, (if not ...) then, S: 233, B: 23B, K: 24C, H: 8A

260 אַזְכָּרָה *'azkārâ*, memorial offering, memorial portion, S: 234, B: 272B, K: 24D, H: 8B

261 אָזַל *'āzal*, [A] to go about, go away; disappear, S: 235, B: 23C, K: 24D, H: 8B

262 אֶזֶל *'ezel*, Ezel, S: 237, B: 23D, K: 25A, H: 8B

263 [1]אָזַן *'āzan[1]*, [G] to listen, pay attention, give ear, S: 238, B: 24B, K: 25A, H: 8B

264 [2]אָזַן *'āzan[2]*, [D] to ponder, S: 239, B: 24D, K: 25B, H: 8B

265 אֹזֶן *'ōzen*, ear: the organ for hearing, listening, and hence, responding, S: 241, B: 23D, K: 25B, H: 8B

266 אָזֵן *'āzēn*, equipment, tools, S: 240, B: 24C, K: 25C, H: 8C

267 אֻזֵּן שֶׁאֱרָה *'uzzēn še'erâ*, Uzzen Sheerah, S: 242, B: 25A, K: 25D, H: 8C

268 אַזְנוֹת תָּבוֹר *'aznôt tābôr*, Aznoth Tabor, S: 243, B: 24D, K: 25C, H: 8C

269 אָזְנִי 'oznî[1], Ozni, S: 244, B: 24C, K: 25C, H: 8C

270 [2]אָזְנִי 'oznî[2], Oznite, S: 244, B: 24C, K: 25C, H: 8C

271 אֲזַנְיָה 'azanyâ, Azaniah, S: 245, B: 24D, K: 25D, H: 8C

272 אֲזִקִּים 'aziqqîm, chains, S: 246, B: 279B, K: 25D, H: 8C

273 אָזַר 'āzar, [A] to gird up, belt on; [D] to gird someone; [C, F] to gird oneself, S: 247, B: 25A, K: 25D, H: 8C

274 אֶזְרוֹעַ 'ezrôa', arm, S: 248, B: 284B, K: 26A, H: 8D

275 אֶזְרָח 'ezrāḥ, native-born, S: 249, B: 280C, K: 26A, H: 8D

276 אֶזְרָחִי 'ezrāḥî, Ezrahite, S: 250, B: 280D, K: 26B, H: 8D

277 אָח 'āḥ[1], Alas!, Oh!, S: 253, B: 25B, K: 26B, H: 8D

278 [2]אָח 'āḥ[2], brother; family, relative, kinsman; countryman; associates, S: 251, B: 26A, K: 26B, H: 8D

279 אַח 'aḥ, firepot, S: 254†, B: 28D, K: 26D, H: 9A

280 אֹחַ 'ōaḥ, jackal, S: 255, B: 28D, K: 26D, H: 9A

281 אַחְאָב 'aḥ'āb, Ahab, S: 256, B: 26C, K: 27A, H: 9A

282 אֶחָב 'eḥāb, Ahab, S: 256, B: 26C, K: 27A, H: 9A

283 אַחְבָּן 'aḥbān, Ahban, S: 257, B: 26C, K: 27A, H: 9A

284 אָחַד 'āḥad, variant: see 2523, S: 258, B: 25C, K: 27A, H: 9A

285 אֶחָד 'eḥād, one; a certain one; first, S: 259, B: 25C, K: 27A, H: 9A

286 אָחוּ 'āḥû, reeds, S: 260, B: 28A, K: 28B, H: 9C

287 אֵהוּד 'ēhûd, Ehud, S: 261, B: 26A, K: 28B, H: 9C

288 [1]אַחֲוָה 'aḥawâ[1], brotherhood, S: 264, B: 27D, K: 28B, H: 9C

289 [2]אַחֲוָה 'aḥawâ[2], what is said, declaration, S: 262, B: 296A, K: 28B, H: 9C

290 אָחוּז 'āḥûz, variant: see 296, S: 270†, B: 28A, K: 29A, H: 9C

291 אֲחוֹחַ 'aḥôaḥ, Ahoah, S: 265, B: 29A, K: 28B, H: 9C

292 אֲחוֹחִי 'aḥôḥî, Ahohite, S: 266, B: 29A, K: 28B, H: 9C

293 אֲחוּמַי 'aḥûmay, Ahumai, S: 267, B: 26C, K: 28B, H: 9C

294 אָחוֹר 'āḥôr, back, backward, rear, hindquarters, from behind; west, S: 268, B: 30C, K: 28C, H: 9C

295 אָחוֹת 'āḥôt, sister, S: 269, B: 27D, K: 28D, H: 9D

296 [1]אָחַז 'āḥaz[1], [A] grasp, seize, hold; [B] to be fastened; [C] to be caught, acquire, S: 270, B: 28A, K: 29A & 29D, H: 9D

297 [2]אָחַז 'āḥaz[2], [A] to attach, cover, panel; [H] be attached; [D] to cover, S: 270, B: 28A, K: 29C, H: 10A

298 אָחָז 'āḥāz, Ahaz, S: 271, B: 28C, K: 29D, H: 10A

299 אֲחֻזָּה 'aḥuzzâ, property, possession, S: 272, B: 28C, K: 29D, H: 10A

300 אַחְזַי 'aḥzay, Ahzai, S: 273, B: 28D, K: 30A, H: 10A

301 אֲחַזְיָה 'aḥazyâ, Ahaziah, S: 274, B: 28D, K: 30A, H: 10A

302 אֲחַזְיָהוּ 'aḥazyāhû, Ahaziah, S: 274, B: 28D, K: 30A, H: 10B

303 אֲחֻזָּם 'aḥuzzām, Ahuzzam, S: 275, B: 28D, K: 30B, H: 10B

304 אֲחֻזַּת 'aḥuzzat, Ahuzzath, S: 276, B: 28D, K: 30B, H: 10B

305 אֵחִי 'ēḥî, Ehi, S: 278, B: 29A, K: 30B, H: 10B

306 אֲחִי 'aḥî, Ahi, S: 277, B: 26D 10, K: 30B, H: 10B

307 אֲחִיאָם 'aḥî'ām, Ahiam, S: 279, B: 26C, K: 30B, H: 10B

308 אֲחִיָּה 'aḥiyyâ, Ahijah, S: 281, B: 26C, K: 30B, H: 10B

309 אֲחִיָּהוּ 'aḥiyyāhû, Ahijah, S: 281, B: 26C, K: 30C, H: 10B

310 אֲחִיהוּד 'aḥîhûd, Ahihud, S: 282, B: 26D, K: 30C, H: 10B

311 אַחְיוֹ 'aḥyô, Ahio, S: 283, B: 26D, K: 30C, H: 10B

312 אֲחִיחֻד 'aḥîḥud, Ahihud, S: 284, B: 26D, K: 30C, H: 10B

313 אֲחִיטוּב 'aḥîṭûb, Ahitub, S: 285, B: 26D, K: 30C, H: 10B

314 אֲחִילוּד 'aḥîlûd, Ahilud, S: 286, B: 27A, K: 30D, H: 10B

315 אֲחִימוֹת 'aḥîmôt, Ahimoth, S: 287, B: 27A, K: 30D, H: 10B

316 אֲחִימֶלֶךְ 'aḥîmelek, Ahimelech, S: 288, B: 27A, K: 30D, H: 10B

317 אֲחִימַן 'aḥîman, Ahiman, S: 289, B: 27A, K: 30D, H: 10B

318 אֲחִימַעַץ 'aḥîma'aṣ, Ahimaaz, S: 290, B: 27A, K: 31A, H: 10B

319 אַחְיָן 'aḥyān, Ahian, S: 291, B: 27B, K: 31A, H: 10B

320 אֲחִינָדָב 'aḥînādāb, Ahinadab, S: 292, B: 27B, K: 31A, H: 10B

321 אֲחִינֹעַם 'aḥînō'am, Ahinoam, S: 293, B: 27B, K: 31A, H: 10B

322 אֲחִיסָמָךְ 'aḥîsāmāk, Ahisamach, S: 294, B: 27B, K: 31A, H: 10C

323 אֲחִיעֶזֶר 'aḥî'ezer, Ahiezer, S: 295, B: 27B, K: 31B, H: 10C

324 אֲחִיקָם 'aḥîqām, Ahikam, S: 296, B: 27B, K: 31B, H: 10C

325 אֲחִירָם 'aḥîrām, Ahiram, S: 297, B: 27B, K: 31B, H: 10C

326 אֲחִירָמִי 'aḥîrāmî, Ahiramite, S: 298, B: 27C, K: 31B, H: 10C

327 אֲחִירַע 'aḥîra', Ahira, S: 299, B: 27C, K: 31B, H: 10C

328 אֲחִישָׁחַר 'aḥîšāḥar, Ahishahar, S: 300, B: 27C, K: 31B, H: 10C

329 אֲחִישָׁר 'aḥîšār, Ahishar, S: 301, B: 27C, K: 31C, H: 10C

330 אֲחִיתֹפֶל 'aḥîtōpel, Ahithophel, S: 302, B: 27C, K: 31C, H: 10C

331 אַחְלָב 'aḥlāb, Ahlab, S: 303, B: 317B, K: 31C, H: 10C

332 אַחֲלַי 'aḥalay, Oh that!; If only!, S: 305, B: 25B, K: 31C, H: 10C

333 אַחְלָי 'aḥlāy, Ahlai, S: 304, B: 29A, K: 31C, H: 10C

334 אַחְלָמָה 'aḥlāmâ, amethyst, S: 306, B: 29A, K: 31C, H: 10C

335 אֲחַסְבַּי 'aḥasbay, Ahasbai, S: 308, B: 29B, K: 31D, H: 10C

336 אָחַר 'āḥar, [A] to remain, stay on; [D] to detain, delay, slow down; [G] to take longer (than a set time), come late, S: 309, B: 29B, K: 31D, H: 10C

337 [1]אַחֵר 'aḥēr[1], other, another, different; next, additional, more, extra, S: 312, B: 29C, K: 32A, H: 10D

338 [2]אַחֵר 'aḥēr[2], Aher, S: 313, B: 31B, K: 32B, H: 10D

339 אַחַר 'aḥar, (temporal) after, afterward, later, some time later; (spatial) back, behind, following, S: 310, B: 29D, K: 32B, H: 10D

340 אַחֲרוֹן 'aḥarôn, (temporal) next, later, last, end; (spatial) at the back, behind, west, S: 314, B: 30D, K: 33B, H: 11B

341 אַחְרַח 'aḥraḥ, Aharah, S: 315, B: 31B, K: 33C, H: 11B

342 אֲחַרְחֵל 'aḥarḥēl, Aharhel, S: 316, B: 31C, K: 33C, H: 11B

343 אַחֲרַי 'aḥaray, in the end, afterward, S: 310†, B: 30C, K: 32B, H: 11B

344 אַחֲרִית 'aḥarît, (spatial) the far side, the other side; (temporal) at the last, at the end, (in days) to come, S: 319, B: 31A, K: 33C, H: 11B

345 אֲחֹרַנִּית 'aḥōrannît, backwardly, by turning around, in turning back, S: 322, B: 30D, K: 34A, H: 11C

346 אֲחַשְׁדַּרְפָּן 'aḥašdarpān, satraps, S: 323, B: 31C, K: 34A, H: 11C

347 אֲחַשְׁוֵרוֹשׁ 'aḥašwērôš, Ahaseurus, Xerxes, S: 325, B: 31C, K: 34A, H: 11C

348 אֲחַשְׁרֹשׁ 'aḥašērōš, variant: see 347, S: 325, B: 31C, K: 34A, H: 11C

349 אֲחַשְׁתָּרִי 'aḥaštārî, variant: Ahashtari, S: 326, B: 31C, K: 34A, H: 11C

350 אֲחַשְׁתְּרָן 'aḥašterān, royal, belonging to the king, S: 327, B: 31C, K: 34B, H: 11C

351 [1]אַט 'aṭ[1], (as adv.) gently, meekly, slowly, S: 328, B: 31D, K: 34B, H: 11C

352 [2]אַט 'aṭ[2], variant: see 5742, S*, B: 640C, K: 611B, H: 11C

353 [1]אָטָד 'āṭād[1], thornbush, S: 329, B: 31D, K: 34B, H: 11C

354 [2]אָטָד 'āṭād[2], Atad, S: 329, B: 31D, K: 34B, H*

355 אֵטוּן 'ēṭûn, linen, S: 330, B: 32A, K: 34C, H: 11D

356 אִטִּים 'iṭṭîm, spirits of the dead, S: 328†, B: 31D, K: 34C, H: 11D

357 אָטַם 'āṭam, [A] to stop up (one's ears); to hold (one's tongue); [B] to be narrow, S: 331, B: 31D, K: 34C, H: 11D

358 אָטַר 'āṭar, [A] to close, S: 332, B: 32A, K: 34D, H: 11D

359 אָטֵר 'āṭēr, Ater, S: 333, B: 32A, K: 34D, H: 11D

360 אִטֵּר 'iṭṭēr, hindered on the right hand, (thus) left-handed, S: 334, B: 32A, K: 34D, H: 11D

361 אֵי 'ê, where?, which way?, S: 335†, B: 32B, K: 34D, H: 11D

362 [1]אִי 'î[1], island; coastland; distant shores, S: 339, B: 15D, K: 35B, H: 12A

363 [2]אִי 'î[2], hyena, S: 338, B: 17B, K: 35C, H: 12A

364 [3]אִי 'î[3], not, S: 336, B: 33A, K: 35C, H: 12A

365 [4]אִי 'î[4], Woe!, S: 337, B: 33A, K: 35C, H: 12A

366 אָיַב 'āyab, [A] to be an enemy, be hostile towards, S: 340, B: 33B, K: 35D, H: 12A

367 אֹיֵב 'ōyēb, enemy, foe, S: 341, B: 33B, K: 35D, H: 12A

368 אֵיבָה 'êbâ, hostility, enmity, S: 342, B: 33C, K: 36A, H: 12B

369 אֵיד 'êd, disaster, calamity, destruction, S: 343, B: 15D, K: 36A, H: 12B

370 אַיָּה[1] 'ayyâ[1], black kite; falcon; vulture, S: 344, B: 17B, K: 36B, H: 12B
371 [2]אַיָּה 'ayyâ[2], Aiah, S: 345, B: 17B, K: 36B, H: 12B
372 אַיֵּה 'ayyēh, Where?, S: 346, B: 32C, K: 36B, H: 12B
373 אִיּוֹב 'iyyôb, Job, S: 347, B: 33C, K: 36C, H: 12B
374 אִיזֶבֶל 'îzebel, Jezebel, S: 348, B: 33B, K: 36C, H: 12B
375 אֵיךְ 'êk, How? Why?; How! Also!, S: 349, B: 32C, K: 36D, H: 12B
376 אִיכָבוֹד, אִי־כָבוֹד 'îkābôd, 'î-kābôd, Ichabod, S: 350, B: 33B, K: 36D, H: 12C
377 אֵיכָה 'êkâ, how?, where?; how! (in lament), S: 349, B: 32D, K: 37A, H: 12C
378 אֵיכֹה 'êkōh, Where?, S: 351, B: 32D, K: 37A, H: 12C
379 אֵיכָכָה 'êkākâ, How?, S: 349, B: 32D, K: 37A, H: 12C
380 אַיִל[1] 'ayil[1], ram; leading man, ruler, S: 352, B: 17D, K: 37A, H: 12C
381 [2]אַיִל 'ayil[2], oaks, S: 352, B: 18B, K: 37C, H: 12C
382 [3]אַיִל 'ayil[3], projecting wall; jamb, S: 352, B: 18A, K: 37C, H: 12D
383 [4]אַיִל 'ayil[4], variant: leader, chief, S: 352†, B: 18B, K: 37A, H: 12C 2.
384 אֱיָל 'ᵉyāl, strength, S: 353, B: 33D, K: 37C, H: 12D
385 אַיָּל 'ayyāl, deer, young stag, S: 354, B: 19B, K: 37C, H: 12D
386 אֵיל פָּארָן 'êl pā'rān, El Paran, S: 364, B: 18C, K: 750D, H: 13A
387 אַיָּלָה 'ayyālâ, deer, doe, S: 355 & 365†, B: 19B, K: 37D, H: 12D
388 אִילוֹ 'îlô, variant: woe!, alas!, S: 337†, B: 33A, K: 35C, H: 12D
389 אַיָּלוֹן 'ayyālôn, Aijalon, S: 357, B: 19C, K: 37D, H: 12D
390 אֵילוֹן[1] 'êlôn[1], Elon, S: 356, B: 19A, K: 38A, H: 12D
391 [2]אֵילוֹן 'êlôn[2], Elon, S: 356, B: 19A, K: 38A, H: 12D
392 אֵילוֹן בֵּית חָנָן 'êlôn bêt ḥānān, Elon Bethhanan, S: 358, B: 19A 4., K: 38A, H: 12D
393 אֵילוֹת 'êlôt, Elath, S: 359, B: 19A, K: 38B, H: 12D
394 אֱיָלוּת 'ᵉyālût, Strength, Power [divine title], S: 360, B: 33D, K: 38A, H: 12D
395 אֵילָם 'êlām, portico, porch, hall, S: 361, B: 19A, K: 38A, H: 12D
396 אֵילִם 'êlim, Elim, S: 362, B: 18C, K: 38B, H: 13A
397 אֵילַת 'êlat, Elath, S: 359, B: 19A, K: 38B, H: 13A
398 אָיֹם 'āyōm, fearful; majestic, S: 366, B: 33D, K: 38C, H: 13A
399 אֵימָה 'êmâ, terror, dread, fear, S: 367, B: 33D, K: 38C, H: 13A
400 אֵימִים 'êmîm, Emites, S: 368, B: 34A, K: 38D, H: 13A
401 אַיִן[1] 'ayin[1], there is no, not, none, without, S: 369, B: 34A, K: 38D, H: 13A
402 [2]אַיִן 'ayin[2], where (from)?, S: 370, B: 32D, K: 40A, H: 13C
403 אִין 'în, there is not, S: 371, B: 35B, K: 40B, H: 13C
404 אִיעֶזֶר 'î ezer, Iezer, S: 372, B: 4C, K: 40B, H: 13C
405 אִיעֶזְרִי 'î ezrî, Iezerite, S: 373, B: 4C, K: 40B, H: 13C
406 אֵיפָה 'êpâ, ephah (measure), S: 374, B: 35B, K: 40B, H: 13C
407 אֵיפֹה 'êpōh, where?, S: 375, B: 33A, K: 40C, H: 13C
408 אִישׁ[1] 'îš[1], man, husband; person (without reference to gender); (as pronoun) each, every, someone, a certain one, anyone, whoever, S: 376, B: 35D, K: 40C, H: 13C
409 [2]אִישׁ 'îš[2], variant: there is, S: 386†, B: 35D & 441B, K: 40C, H: 14A
410 אִישׁ־בֹּשֶׁת 'îš-bōšet, Ish-Bosheth, S: 378, B: 36B, K: 41D, H: 14A
411 אִישׁ־טוֹב 'îš-ṭôb, variant: Ish-Tob, S: 382, B: 36A, K: 349A, H: 14A
412 אִישְׁהוֹד 'îšhôd, Ishhod, S: 379, B: 36B, K: 41D, H: 14A
413 אִישׁוֹן 'îšôn, pupil (of the eye), S: 380, B: 36B, K: 41D, H: 14A
414 אִישַׁי 'îšay, Jesse, S: 3448†, B: 445A, K: 41D, H: 14B
415 אִיתוֹן 'îtôn, entrance, S: 2978†, B: 87C, K: 42A, H: 14B
416 אִיתַי 'îtay, Ithai, S: 863, B: 87A, K: 101B, H: 14B
417 אִיתִיאֵל 'îtî'ēl, Ithiel, S: 384, B: 87B, K: 42A, H: 14B
418 אִיתָמָר 'îtāmār, Ithamar, S: 385, B: 16A, K: 42A, H: 14B
419 אֵיתָן[1] 'êtān[1], ever-flowing, never-failing, steady, established, eternal, S: 386, B: 450D, K: 42A, H: 14B
420 [2]אֵיתָן 'êtān[2], Ethan, S: 387, B: 451A, K: 42B, H: 14B
421 אַךְ 'ak, but, surely, only, however, S: 389, B: 36C, K: 42B, H: 14B
422 אַכַּד 'akkad, Akkad, S: 390, B: 37A, K: 42D, H: 14C
423 אַכְזָב 'akzāb, deceptive, deceitful, S: 391, B: 469D, K: 42D, H: 14C
424 אַכְזִיב 'akzîb, Aczib, S: 392, B: 469D, K: 43A, H: 14C
425 אַכְזָר 'akzār, deadly, ruthless, fierce, heartless, S: 393, B: 470A, K: 43A, H: 14C
426 אַכְזָרִי 'akzārî, cruel, merciless, S: 394, B: 470A, K: 43A, H: 14C
427 אַכְזְרִיּוּת 'akzᵉriyyût, cruelty, S: 395, B: 470A, K: 43A, H: 14C
428 אֲכִילָה 'ᵃkîlâ, food, S: 396, B: 38B, K: 43A, H: 14C
429 אָכִישׁ 'ākîš, Achish, S: 397, B: 37A, K: 43B, H: 14C
430 אָכַל 'ākal, [A] to eat; [C] to be eaten; [E] be consumed, be destroyed; [G] to give to eat, feed, S: 398, B: 37A, K: 43B, H: 14C
431 אֹכֶל 'ōkel, food, S: 400, B: 38A, K: 44C, H: 15A
432 אֻכָל 'ukāl, Ucal, S: 401, B: 38B, K: 44D, H: 15A
433 אָכְלָה 'oklâ, what is consumed, food, fuel, S: 402, B: 38A, K: 44D, H: 15A
434 אָכֵן[1] 'ākēn[1], Surely! Truly!, S: 403, B: 38C, K: 44D, H: 15A
435 [2]אָכֵן 'ākēn[2], variant: so that, S: 403, B: 38C a, K: 44D, H: 15B
436 אָכַף 'ākap, [A] to drive, press hard, S: 404, B: 38C, K: 45A, H: 15B
437 אֶכֶף 'ekep, pressure, S: 405, B: 38C, K: 45A, H: 15B
438 אִכָּר 'ikkār, farmer, people who work in fields and vineyards, S: 406, B: 38D, K: 45A, H: 15B
439 אַכְשָׁף 'akšāp, Acshaph, S: 407, B: 506D, K: 45A, H: 15B
440 אַל[1] 'al[1], no, not, S: 408, B: 39A, K: 45A, H: 15B
441 [2]אַל 'al[2], variant: the (Arabic art.), S*, B*, K: 45C, H: 15C
442 אֵל[1] 'ēl[1], variant: ram, man of power, S: 352†, B: 17D, K: 45C, H: 15C
443 [2]אֵל 'ēl[2], variant: mighty tree, S: 352†, B: 18B, K: 45D, H: 15C
444 [3]אֵל 'ēl[3], variant: doorpost, S: 352†, B: 18B, K: 45D, H: 15C
445 [4]אֵל 'ēl[4], power, S: 410, B: 43A, K: 45D, H: 15C
446 [5]אֵל 'ēl[5], God, the Mighty One; god, gods, mighty ones, S: 410, B: 42B, K: 45D, H: 15C
447 [6]אֵל 'ēl[6], these, S: 411, B: 41B, K: 47D, H: 16A
448 אֶל 'el, to, toward; in, into; with regard to, S: 413, B: 39B, K: 48A, H: 16A
449 אֵל אֱלֹהֵי יִשְׂרָאֵל 'ēl 'ᵉlōhê yiśrā'ēl, El Elohe Israel, S: 415, B: 42D 6.f, K: 47A e), H*
450 אֵל בֵּית־אֵל 'ēl bêt-'ēl, El Bethel, S: 416, B: 42C 6.c, K: 123D, H: 39B 2
451 אֵל בְּרִית 'ēl bᵉrît, El-Berith, S: 1286†, B: 42C 4 & 136C I 3, K: 152A 14., H: 15C & 46A b13
452 אֵלָא 'ēlā', Ela, S: 414, B: 41D, K: 49A, H: 16B
453 אֶלְגָּבִישׁ 'elgābîš, hail, S: 417, B: 38D, K: 49A, H: 16B
454 אַלְגּוּמִּים 'algûmmîm, algum (wood), S: 418, B: 38D, K: 55B, H: 16B
455 אֶלְדָּד 'eldād, Eldad, S: 419, B: 44D, K: 49A, H: 16B
456 אֶלְדָּעָה 'eldā'â, Eldaah, S: 420, B: 44D, K: 49B, H: 16B
457 אָלָה[1] 'ālâ[1], [A] to utter a curse, swear an oath; [G] to bind under oath, take an oath, S: 422, B: 46D, K: 49B, H: 16C
458 [2]אָלָה 'ālâ[2], [A] to mourn, wail, S: 421, B: 46D, K: 49B, H: 16C
459 [3]אָלָה 'ālâ[3], variant: [A] to be unfit to, S: 428†, B: 384A 2, K: 49B, H: 16C
460 [4]אָלָה 'ālâ[4], curse, oath; sworn agreement; public charge, S: 423, B: 46D, K: 49C, H: 16C
461 אֵלָה[1] 'ēlâ[1], oak, terebinth, S: 424, B: 18C, K: 50A, H: 16C
462 [2]אֵלָה 'ēlâ[2], Elah, S: 425, B: 18D, K: 50A, H: 16C
463 [3]אֵלָה 'ēlâ[3], Elah, S: 425, B: 18C, K: 716D, H: 16C
464 אַלָּה 'allâ, oak, S: 427, B: 47C, K: 50B, H: 16C
465 אֵלֶּה 'ēlleh, these, S: 428, B: 41C, K: 50B, H: 16C
466 אֱלֹהִים 'ᵉlōhîm, God [plural of majesty]; gods; mighty one, great one, judge, S: 430, B: 43B, K: 50C, H: 16D 2.
467 אִלּוּ 'illû, if, S: 432, B: 47A, K: 50C, H: 16D
468 אֱלוֹהַּ 'ᵉlôah, God; god, S: 433, B: 43A, K: 50C, H: 16D
469 אֱלוּל[1] 'ᵉlûl[1], Elul, S: 435, B: 47A, K: 52A, H: 17B

470 [2]אֱלוּל 'ᵉlûl[2], variant: see 496, S: 434, B: 47B, K: 53D, H: 17D
471 אֵלוֹן[1] 'ēlôn[1], great tree, large tree, S: 436, B: 18D, K: 52B, H: 17B
472 אֵלוֹן[2] 'ēlôn[2], Elon, S: 356, B: 19A, K: 52B, H: 17B
473 אַלּוֹן[1] 'allôn[1], oak tree, S: 437, B: 47C, K: 52B, H: 17B
474 אַלּוֹן[2] 'allôn[2], Allon, S: 438, B: 47D, K: 52C, H: 17B
475 אַלּוֹן בָּכוּת 'allôn bākût, Allon Bacuth, S: 439, B: 47C & 113D, K: 52C & 127A, H: 17B
476 אַלּוּף[1] 'allûp[1], close friend, partner, ally, companion, S: 441, B: 48C, K: 52C, H: 17B
477 [2]אַלּוּף 'allûp[2], chief, leader, S: 441, B: 49B, K: 52C, H: 17B
478 אָלוּשׁ 'ālûš, Alush, S: 442, B: 47A, K: 52D, H: 17C
479 אֶלְזָבָד 'elzābād, Elzabad, S: 443, B: 44D, K: 52D, H: 17C
480 אלח 'ālaḥ, [C] to be, become corrupt, S: 444, B: 47A, K: 52D, H: 17C
481 אֶלְחָנָן 'elḥānān, Elhanan, S: 445, B: 44D, K: 52D, H: 17C
482 אֱלִיאָב 'ᵉlîʾāb, Eliab, S: 446, B: 45A, K: 53A, H: 17C
483 אֱלִיאֵל 'ᵉlîʾēl, Eliel, S: 447, B: 45A, K: 53A, H: 17C
484 אֱלִיאָתָה 'ᵉlîʾātâ, Eliathah, S: 448, B: 45A, K: 53A, H: 17C
485 אֱלִידָד 'ᵉlîdād, Elidad, S: 419† & 449, B: 44D, K: 53A, H: 17C
486 אֶלְיָדָע 'elyādāʿ, Eliada, S: 450, B: 45A, K: 53A, H: 17C
487 אַלְיָה 'alyâ, fat tail, S: 451, B: 46D, K: 53B, H: 17C
488 אֵלִיָּה 'ēliyyâ, Elijah, S: 452, B: 45B, K: 53B, H: 17C
489 אֵלִיָּהוּ 'ēliyyāhû, Elijah, S: 452, B: 45B, K: 53B, H: 17C
490 אֱלִיהוּ 'ᵉlîhû, Elihu, S: 453, B: 45B, K: 53B, H: 17C
491 אֱלִיהוּא 'ᵉlîhûʾ, Elihu, S: 453, B: 45B, K: 53C, H: 17C
492 אֶלְיְהוֹעֵינַי 'elyᵉhôʿênay, Eliehoenai, S: 454, B: 41B, K: 53C, H: 17C
493 אֶלְיוֹעֵינַי 'elyôʿênay, Elioenai, S: 454, B: 41B, K: 53C, H: 17C
494 אֶלְיַחְבָּא 'elyaḥbāʾ, Eliahba, S: 455, B: 45B, K: 53C, H: 17C
495 אֱלִיחֹרֶף 'ᵉlîḥōrep, Elihoreph, S: 456, B: 45B, K: 53D, H: 17C
496 אֱלִיל 'ᵉlîl, idols, images, gods, S: 457, B: 47B, K: 53D, H: 17D
497 אֱלִימֶלֶךְ 'ᵉlîmelek, Elimelech, S: 458, B: 45B, K: 54A, H: 17D
498 אֶלְיָסָף 'elyāsāp, Eliasaph, S: 460, B: 45B, K: 54A, H: 17D
499 אֱלִיעֶזֶר 'ᵉlîʿezer, Eliezer, S: 461, B: 45C, K: 54A, H: 17D
500 אֱלִיעָם 'ᵉlîʿām, Eliam, S: 463, B: 45C, K: 54A, H: 17D
501 אֱלִיעֵנַי 'ᵉlîʿēnay, Elienai, S: 462, B*, K: 54A, H: 17D
502 אֱלִיפַז 'ᵉlîpaz, Eliphaz, S: 464, B: 45C, K: 54B, H: 17D
503 אֱלִיפַל 'ᵉlîpal, Eliphal, S: 465, B: 45C, K: 54B, H: 17D
504 אֱלִיפְלֵהוּ 'ᵉlîpᵉlēhû, Eliphelehu, S: 466, B: 45C, K: 54B, H: 17D
505 אֱלִיפֶלֶט 'ᵉlîpeleṭ, Eliphelet, S: 467, B: 45C, K: 54B, H: 17D
506 אֱלִיצוּר 'ᵉlîṣûr, Elizur, S: 468, B: 45D, K: 54B, H: 17D
507 אֱלִיצָפָן 'ᵉlîṣāpān, Elizaphan, S: 469, B: 45D, K: 54B, H: 17D
508 אֱלִיקָא 'ᵉlîqāʾ, Elika, S: 470, B: 45D, K: 54C, H: 17D
509 אֶלְיָקִים 'elyāqîm, Eliakim, S: 471, B: 45D, K: 54C, H: 17D
510 אֱלִישֶׁבַע 'ᵉlîšebaʿ, Elisheba, S: 472, B: 45D, K: 54C, H: 17D
511 אֱלִישָׁה 'ᵉlîšâ, Elishah, S: 473, B: 47A, K: 54C, H: 17D
512 אֱלִישׁוּעַ 'ᵉlîšûaʿ, Elishua, S: 474, B: 46A, K: 54D, H: 18A
513 אֶלְיָשִׁיב 'elyāšîb, Eliashib, S: 475, B: 46A, K: 54D, H: 18A
514 אֱלִישָׁמָע 'ᵉlîšāmāʿ, Elishama, S: 476, B: 46A, K: 55A, H: 18A
515 אֱלִישָׁע 'ᵉlîšāʿ, Elisha, S: 477, B: 46A, K: 55A, H: 18A
516 אֱלִישָׁפָט 'ᵉlîšāpāṭ, Elishaphat, S: 478, B: 46A, K: 55A, H: 18A
517 אֱלִיָּתָה 'ᵉliyyātâ, Eliathah, S: 448, B: 45A, K: 53A, H: 18A
518 אַלְלַי 'allay, Woe!, What misery!, Alas!, S: 480, B: 47D, K: 55A, H: 18A
519 [1]אָלַם 'ālam[1], [C] to be silenced, be speechless, S: 481, B: 47D, K: 55A, H: 18A
520 [2]אָלַם 'ālam[2], [D] to bind, S: 481, B: 47D, K: 55A, H: 18A
521 אֵלֶם 'ēlem, variant: silence [?], S: 482, B: 48A, K: 55B, H: 18A
522 אִלֵּם 'illēm, mute, unable to speak, S: 483, B: 48A, K: 55B, H: 18A
523 אַלְמֻגִּים 'almuggîm, almugwood, S: 484, B: 38D, K: 55B, H: 18B
524 אֲלֻמָּה 'ᵃlummâ, sheaf, S: 485, B: 48A, K: 55C, H: 18B
525 אַלְמוֹדָד 'almôdād, Almodad, S: 486, B: 38D, K: 55C, H: 18B
526 אַלַּמֶּלֶךְ 'allammelek, Allammelech, S: 487, B: 47D, K: 55D, H: 18B
527 [1]אַלְמָן 'almān[1], widowed, S: 488, B: 48A, K: 55D, H: 18B
528 [2]אַלְמָן 'almān[2], stronghold, S: 488, B: 48A (bottom), K: 56A, H: 18B
529 אַלְמֹן 'almōn, widowhood, S: 489, B: 48A, K: 55D, H: 18B
530 אַלְמָנָה 'almānâ, widow, S: 490, B: 48A, K: 55D, H: 18B
531 אַלְמָנוּת 'almānût, widowhood, S: 491, B: 48B, K: 56A, H: 18B
532 אַלְמֹנִי 'almōnî, a certain so-and-so, whoever, wherever, S: 492, B: 48C, K: 56B, H: 18B
533 אֵלֹנִי 'ēlōnî, Elonite, S: 440†, B: 19A, K: 56B, H: 18C
534 אֶלְנָעַם 'elnaʿam, Elnaam, S: 493†, B: 46B, K: 56B, H: 18C
535 אֶלְנָתָן 'elnātān, Elnathan, S: 494, B: 46B, K: 56B, H: 18C
536 אֶלָּסָר 'ellāsār, Ellasar, S: 495, B: 48C, K: 56B, H: 18C
537 אֶלְעָד 'elʿād, Elead, S: 496, B: 46B, K: 56B, H: 18C
538 אֶלְעָדָה 'elʿādâ, Eleadah, S: 497, B: 46C, K: 56C, H: 18C
539 אֶלְעוּזַי 'elʿûzay, Eluzai, S: 498, B: 46B, K: 56C, H: 18C
540 אֶלְעָזָר 'elʿāzār, Eleazar, S: 499, B: 46B, K: 56C, H: 18C
541 אֶלְעָלֵא 'elʿālēʾ, Elealeh, S: 500, B: 46C, K: 56C, H: 18C
542 אֶלְעָלֵה 'elʿālēh, Elealeh, S: 500, B: 46C, K: 56C, H: 18C
543 אֶלְעָשָׂה 'elʿāśâ, Eleasah, S: 501, B: 46C, K: 56C, H: 18C
544 [1]אָלַף 'ālap[1], [A] to learn, become familiar with; [D] to teach, instruct, S: 502, B: 48C, K: 56C, H: 18C
545 [2]אָלַף 'ālap[2], [G] to increase by thousands, produce in abundance, S: 503, B: 1120B, K: 56D, H: 18C
546 [1]אֶלֶף 'elep[1], cattle herd; oxen, S: 504, B: 48C, K: 56D, H: 18C
547 [2]אֶלֶף 'elep[2], thousand, S: 505, B: 48D, K: 57A, H: 18C
548 [3]אֶלֶף 'elep[3], (family) clan, (military) unit, S: 505, B: 49A 2., K: 57B, H: 18D
549 [4]אֶלֶף 'elep[4], variant: Eleph, see 2030, S: 507, B: 49B, K: 57B, H*
550 אֶלְפֶּלֶט 'elpeleṭ, Elpelet, S: 467, B: 45C, K: 57B, H: 18D
551 אֶלְפַּעַל 'elpaʿal, Elpaal, S: 508, B: 46C, K: 57C, H: 18D
552 אָלַץ 'ālaṣ, [D] to prod, urge, S: 509, B: 49B, K: 57C, H: 18D
553 אֶלְצָפָן 'elṣāpān, Elzaphan, S: 469, B: 45D, K: 57C, H: 18D
554 אַלְקוּם 'alqûm, army, S: 510, B: 39A, K: 57C, H: 18D
555 אֶלְקָנָה 'elqānâ, Elkanah, S: 511, B: 46C, K: 57C, H: 18D
556 אֶלְקֹשִׁי 'elqōšî, Elkoshite, S: 512, B: 49B, K: 57C, H: 18D
557 אֶלְתּוֹלַד 'eltôlad, Eltolad, S: 513, B: 39A, K: 1021C, H: 18D
558 אֶלְתְּקֵא 'eltᵉqēʾ, Eltekeh, S: 514, B: 49C, K: 57D, H: 19A
559 אֶלְתְּקֵה 'eltᵉqēh, Eltekeh, S: 514, B: 49C, K: 57D, H: 19A
560 אֶלְתְּקוֹן 'eltᵉqôn, Eltekon, S: 515, B: 49C, K: 57D, H: 19A
561 אִם 'im, if, whether, or; whenever, as often as, S: 518, B: 49C, K: 57D, H: 19A
562 אֵם 'ēm, mother, grandmother; fork (in a road), S: 517, B: 51C, K: 58D, H: 19B
563 אָמָה 'āmâ, slave woman; female servant, maidservant, S: 519, B: 51A, K: 59A, H: 19B
564 [1]אַמָּה 'ammâ[1], cubit (measurement of length), S: 520, B: 52A, K: 59B, H: 19C
565 [2]אַמָּה 'ammâ[2], Ammah, S: 522, B: 52C, K: 59C, H: 19C
566 [3]אַמָּה 'ammâ[3], variant: mother-city, metropolis, S: 4965†, B: 52A, K: 59C, H: 222C
567 [4]אַמָּה 'ammâ[4], variant: pivot (of a door), S: 520†, B: 52C, K: 59C, H: 19C 2.
568 אֵמָה 'ēmâ, variant: see 4395, S: 367, B: 52B, K: 59C, H: 19C
569 אֻמָּה 'ummâ, tribe, clan, S: 523, B: 52C, K: 59C, H: 19C
570 [1]אָמוֹן 'āmôn[1], craftsman, S: 539 & 527 & 525, B: 54C, K: 59D, H: 19C
571 [2]אָמוֹן 'āmôn[2], Amon, S: 526, B: 54C, K: 59D, H: 19C
572 [3]אָמוֹן 'āmôn[3], Amon (pagan god), S: 527 & 528, B: 51B, K: 59D, H: 19C

573 אֵמוּן 'ēmûn[1], faithful, S: 529, B: 53C, K: 60A, H: 19C

574 אֵמוּן[2] 'ēmûn[2], faithful, trustworthy, S: 529, B: 53C, K: 62A, H: 19C

575 אֱמוּנָה 'emûnâ, faithfulness, steadiness, trustworthiness, S: 530, B: 53C, K: 60A, H: 19D

576 אָמוֹץ 'āmôṣ, Amoz, S: 531, B: 55B, K: 60B, H: 20D

577 אָמִי 'āmî, Ami, S: 532, B: 51B, K: 60B, H: 19D

578 אֲמִינוֹן 'amînôn, Amnon, S: 550, B: 54C, K: 60B, H: 19D

579 אַמִּיץ 'ammîṣ, strong, mighty, brave, S: 533, B: 55C, K: 60C, H: 19D

580 אָמִיר 'āmîr, branch, S: 534, B: 57B, K: 60C, H: 20A

581 אָמַל 'āmal[1], [B] to be weak-willed; [E] to wither, languish, fade away, S: 535, B: 51B, K: 60C, H: 20A

582 אָמַל[2] 'āmal[2], variant: [B] to be hot, feverish, S: 535, B: 51B, K: 60D, H: 20A

583 אֻמְלַל 'umlal, faint, fading away, S: 536, B: 51C, K: 60D, H: 20A

584 אֲמֵלָל 'amēlāl, feeble, fading, S: 537, B: 51C, K: 60D, H: 20A

585 אֲמָם 'amām, Amam, S: 538, B: 52C, K: 60D, H: 20A

586 אָמַן 'āman[1], [C] to be faithful, be trustworthy, be established; [G] to believe, trust, have confidence, S: 539, B: 52D, K: 60D, H: 20A

587 אָמַן[2] 'āman[2], [A] to nurse, nurture, care for; be a trustee, be a guardian; [B, C] to be nurtured, cared for, S: 539 & 541, B: 52D, K: 61D, H: 20B

588 אָמָּן 'ommān, craftsman, S: 542, B: 53B, K: 61C, H: 20C

589 אָמֵן 'āmēn, amen, surely; truth, S: 543, B: 53B, K: 61C, H: 20C

590 אֹמֶן 'ōmen, faithfulness, S: 544, B: 53B, K: 61D, H: 20C

591 אֲמָנָה 'amānâ[1], binding agreement, trustworthy agreement, S: 548, B: 53D, K: 62A, H: 20C

592 אֲמָנָה[2] 'amānâ[2], Amana, S: 549, B: 53D, K: 62A, H: 20C

593 אָמְנָה 'omnâ[1], really, truly, indeed, S: 546, B: 53D, K: 62A, H: 20C

594 אָמְנָה[2] 'omnâ[2], bringing up, caring, tending, fostering, S: 545, B: 53D, K: 62A, H: 20C

595 אֹמְנָה 'ōmenâ, doorpost, S: 547, B: 52D 4., K: 62B, H: 20C

596 אַמְנוֹן 'amnôn, Amnon, S: 550, B: 54C, K: 62B, H: 20C

597 אָמְנָם 'omnām, indeed, truly, assuredly, S: 551, B: 53D, K: 62B, H: 20D

598 אֻמְנָם 'umnām, really, indeed, S: 552, B: 53D, K: 62B, H: 20D

599 אָמֵץ 'āmēṣ, [A] to be strong, courageous; [D] to strengthen, support, establish; harden; [F] to persist, determine, S: 553†, B: 54D, K: 62B, H: 20D

600 אָמֹץ 'āmōṣ, powerful, strong, S: 554, B: 55B, K: 62D, H: 21A

601 אֹמֶץ 'ōmeṣ, strength, S: 555, B: 55B, K: 62D, H: 21A

602 אַמְצָה 'amṣâ, strength, S: 556, B: 55B, K: 62D, H: 21A

603 אַמְצִי 'amṣî, Amzi, S: 557, B: 55C, K: 63A, H: 21A

604 אֲמַצְיָה 'amaṣyâ, Amaziah, S: 558, B: 55C, K: 63A, H: 21A

605 אֲמַצְיָהוּ 'amaṣyāhû, Amaziah, S: 558, B: 55C, K: 63A, H: 21A

606 אָמַר 'āmar[1], [A, G] to say, speak, think (say to oneself); [B, C] to be said, S: 559, B: 55C, K: 63A, H: 21A

607 אָמַר[2] 'āmar[2], [F] to boast, S: 559, B: 56D, K: 64C, H: 21C

608 אֹמֶר 'ōmer, saying, word, S: 562, B: 56D, K: 64C, H: 21C

609 אֵמֶר 'ēmer[1], word, saying, S: 561, B: 57A 1., K: 64C, H: 21C

610 אֵמֶר[2] 'ēmer[2], variant: branched antlers *or* lamb, S: 561, B: 57A 2., K: 64D, H: 21D

611 אִמֵּר 'immēr[1], fawn, lamb, S: 561, B: 57A, K: 65A, H: 21D

612 אִמֵּר[2] 'immēr[2], Immer, S: 564, B: 57B, K: 65A, H: 21D

613 אִמֵּר[3] 'immēr[3], Immer, S: 564, B: 57B, K: 65A, H: 21D

614 אִמְרָה 'imrâ, word, saying, S: 565, B: 57A, K: 65A, H: 21D

615 אֶמְרָה 'emrâ, variant: see 614, S: 565, B: 57B, K: 65A, H: 21D

616 אֱמֹרִי 'emōrî, Amorite, S: 567, B: 57B, K: 65A, H: 21D

617 אִמְרִי 'imrî, Imri, S: 566, B: 57C, K: 65D, H: 21D

618 אֲמַרְיָה 'amaryâ, Amariah, S: 568, B: 57C, K: 65D, H: 21D

619 אֲמַרְיָהוּ 'amaryāhû, Amariah, S: 568, B: 57C, K: 66A, H: 21D

620 אַמְרָפֶל 'amrāpel, Amraphel, S: 569, B: 57D, K: 66A, H: 21D

621 אֶמֶשׁ 'emeš, last night; yesterday (evening), S: 570, B: 57D, K: 66A, H: 22A

622 אֱמֶת 'emet, faithfulness, reliability, trustworthiness; truth, S: 571, B: 54A, K: 66B, H: 22A

623 אַמְתַּחַת 'amtaḥat, sack, S: 572, B: 607C, K: 67A, H: 22A

624 אֲמִתַּי 'amittay, Amittai, S: 573, B: 54C, K: 67A, H: 22A

625 אָן 'ān, how long?; where?, S: 575, B: 33A, K: 67B, H: 22A

626 אָנָּא 'onnā', I ask you!, O! (preceding a request), S: 577, B: 58A, K: 67B, H: 22B

627 אָנָה 'ānâ[1], [A] to mourn, lament, groan, S: 578, B: 58B, K: 67C, H: 22B

628 אָנָה[2] 'ānâ[2], [D] to make happen; [E] to befall, have happen to; [F] to pick a quarrel against, S: 579, B: 58C, K: 67D, H: 22B

629 אָנָּה 'onnâ, I ask you!, O! (preceding a request), S: 577, B: 58A, K: 67B, H: 22B

630 אֲנוּ 'anû, variant: we, S: 580, B: 59A, K: 67D, H: 22C

631 אָנוּשׁ 'ānûš, incurable, beyond cure; despairing, S: 605†, B: 60C, K: 67D, H: 22C

632 אֱנוֹשׁ 'enôš[1], man, mankind, mortal man, S: 582, B: 60D, K: 68A, H: 22C

633 אֱנוֹשׁ[2] 'enôš[2], Enosh, S: 583, B: 60D, K: 68B, H: 22C

634 אָנַח 'ānaḥ, [C] to groan, moan, S: 584, B: 58D, K: 68B, H: 22C & 234D

635 אֲנָחָה 'anāḥâ, groaning, sighing, S: 585, B: 58D, K: 68C, H: 22C

636 אֲנַחְנוּ 'anaḥnû, we, S: 587, B: 59C, K: 68C, H: 22C

637 אֲנָחֲרַת 'anāḥarat, Anaharath, S: 588, B: 58D, K: 68C, H: 22C

638 אֲנִי 'anî, I, S: 589, B: 58D, K: 68D, H: 22C

639 אֳנִי 'onî, ships, fleet of ships, S: 590, B: 58B, K: 69A, H: 22D

640 אֲנִיָּה 'aniyyâ, lamentation, mourning, S: 592, B: 58B, K: 69A, H: 22D

641 אֳנִיָּה 'oniyyâ, ship, trading ship; (pl.) fleet of ships, S: 591, B: 58B, K: 69A, H: 22D

642 אֲנִיעָם 'anî'ām, Aniam, S: 593, B: 58B, K: 69B, H: 22D

643 אֲנָךְ 'anāk, plummet, weight for a plumb line, S: 594, B: 59D, K: 69B, H: 22D

644 אָנֹכִי 'ānōkî, I, S: 595, B: 59A, K: 69B, H: 22D

645 אָנַן 'ānan, [F] to complain, S: 596, B: 59D, K: 70A, H: 23A

646 אָנַס 'ānas, [A] to compel, S: 597, B: 60A, K: 70A, H: 23A

647 אָנַף 'ānap, [A] to be, become angry; [F] to feel angry, S: 599, B: 60A, K: 70A, H: 23A

648 אָנַף 'ānāp, variant: face, S*, B*, K*, H: 23A

649 אֲנָפָה 'anāpâ, heron, S: 601, B: 60B, K: 70B, H: 23A

650 אָנַק 'ānaq, [A, C] to groan, lament, sigh, S: 602, B: 60B, K: 70B, H: 23A

651 אֲנָקָה 'anāqâ[1], groaning, sighing, S: 603, B: 60C, K: 70C, H: 23A

652 אֲנָקָה[2] 'anāqâ[2], gecko, S: 604, B: 60C, K: 70C, H: 23A

653 אָנַשׁ 'ānaš, [C] be ill, sickly, S: 605, B: 60C, K: 70C, H: 23A

654 אָסָא 'āsā', Asa, S: 609, B: 61D, K: 70D, H: 23A

655 אָסוּךְ 'āsûk, small (oil) jar, flask, S: 610, B: 692A, K: 71A, H: 23A

656 אָסוֹן 'āsôn, serious injury, harm, S: 611, B: 62A, K: 71A, H: 23A

657 אֵסוּר 'ēsûr, bindings, chains, fetters, shackles, S: 612, B: 64A, K: 71A, H: 23B

658 אָסִיף 'āsîp, (Feast of) Ingathering; harvest, S: 614, B: 63B, K: 71A, H: 23B

659 אָסִיר 'āsîr, prisoner, captive, S: 615, B: 64A, K: 71B, H: 23B

660 אַסִּיר 'assîr[1], captive, prisoner, S: 616, B: 64B, K: 71B, H: 23B

661 אַסִּיר[2] 'assîr[2], Assir, S: 617, B: 64B, K: 71C, H: 23B

662 אָסָם 'āsām, barn, S: 618, B: 62A, K: 71C, H: 23B

663 אַסְנָה 'asnâ, Asnah, S: 619, B: 62A, K: 71C, H: 23B

664 אָסְנַת 'āsenat, Asenath, S: 621, B: 62A, K: 71C, H: 23B

665 אָסַף 'āsap, [A] to store, gather, harvest; [B] to be a victim; [C] to be gathered, assembled; [D] to be a rear guard, to bring in, gather; [E] to be gathered, collected; [F] to assemble; [G] to bring together, S: 622, B: 62A, K: 71D, H: 23B

666 אָסָף 'āsāp, Asaph, S: 623, B: 63A, K: 73A, H: 23D

667 אָסֹף 'āsōp, storehouse, storeroom, S: 624†, B: 63B, K: 73B, H: 23D

668 אֹסֶף *'ōsep*, harvest (of fruit), gathering, S: 625, B: 63A, K: 73B, H: 23D

669 אֲסֵפָה *'^{a}sēpâ*, gathering (prisoners); imprisonment, S: 626, B: 63B, K: 73B, H: 23D

670 אֲסֻפָּה *'^{a}suppâ*, collection (of sayings), S: 627, B: 63B, K: 73B, H: 23D

671 אֲסַפְסֻף *'^{a}sapsup*, rabble, collection (of grumblers), S: 628, B: 63C, K: 73B, H: 23D

672 אַסְפָּתָא *'aspātā'*, Aspatha, S: 630, B: 63C, K: 73B, H: 23D

673 אָסַר *'āsar*, [A] to bind, tie up; to obligate; [B] to be confined, be bound; [C] to be tied, be kept in prison; [E] to be captured, be taken prisoner, S: 631, B: 63C, K: 73C, H: 23D & 82D

674 אִסָּר *'issār*, pledge, S: 632, B: 64B, K: 74A, H: 24A

675 אֵסַר־חַדֹּן *'ēsar-ḥaddōn*, Esarhaddon, S: 634, B: 64D, K: 74A, H: 24A

676 אֶסְתֵּר *'estēr*, Esther, S: 635, B: 64D, K: 74B, H: 24A

677 [1]אַף *'ap*[1], how much (better, worse; more, less); really, truly; too, also, even more, S: 637, B: 64D, K: 74B, H: 24A

678 [2]אַף *'ap*[2], nose (representing the face or some part of the face); "hot of nose" = anger, S: 639, B: 60A, K: 75A, H: 24B

679 אָפַד *'āpad*, [A] to fasten, S: 640, B: 65D, K: 75D, H: 24C

680 [1]אֵפֹד *'ēpōd*[1], ephod, S: 646†, B: 65B, K: 76A, H: 24C

681 [2]אֵפֹד *'ēpōd*[2], Ephod, S: 641, B: 65D, K: 76D, H: 24C

682 אֲפֻדָּה *'^{a}puddâ*, skillfully woven covering, S: 642, B: 65D, K: 76D, H: 24C

683 אַפֶּדֶן *'appeden*, palace tent, royal tent, S: 643, B: 66A, K: 76D, H: 24D

684 אָפָה *'āpâ*, [A] to bake; [C] to be baked, S: 644, B: 66A, K: 76D, H: 24D

685 אֹפֶה *'ōpeh*, baker, S: 644†, B: 66A, K: 77A, H: 24D

686 אֵפוֹא *'ēpô'*, then, so then, S: 645, B: 66B, K: 77A, H: 24D

687 אָפוּנָה *'āpûnâ*, variant: despair [?], S: 6323†, B: 67A, K: 755A, H: 25A

688 אֲפִיחַ *'^{a}pîaḥ*, Aphiah, S: 647, B: 66C, K: 77C, H: 25A

689 אָפִיל *'āpîl*, late-ripening, S: 648, B: 66C, K: 77C, H: 25A

690 [1]אַפַּיִם *'appayim*[1], variant: face, anger, S: 639†, B: 60A, K: 77C, H: 25A

691 [2]אַפַּיִם *'appayim*[2], Appaim, S: 649, B: 60B, K: 77C, H: 25A

692 [1]אָפִיק *'āpîq*[1], stream, water channel; valley, ravine, S: 650, B: 67D, K: 77C, H: 25A

693 [2]אָפִיק *'āpîq*[2], mighty, strong, S: 650, B: 67D, K: 77D, H: 25A

694 אֹפֶל *'ōpel*, darkness, gloom, shadows, S: 652, B: 66C, K: 77D, H: 25A

695 אָפֵל *'āpēl*, dark, S: 651, B: 66C, K: 78A, H: 25A

696 אֲפֵלָה *'^{a}pēlâ*, the dark, darkness, S: 653, B: 66C, K: 78A, H: 25A

697 אֶפְלָל *'eplāl*, Ephlal, S: 654, B: 813D, K: 78A, H: 25A

698 אֹפֶן *'ōpen*, (right) time; aptly, S: 655, B: 67A, K: 78A, H: 25A

699 אָפֵס *'āpēs*, [A] to come to an end, cease, S: 656, B: 67A, K: 78B, H: 25B

700 אֶפֶס *'epes*, ends (of the earth); no, nothing; however, but, only, yet, S: 657, B: 67A, K: 78B, H: 25B

701 אֹפֶס *'ōpes*, (dual) ankles, S: 657†, B: 67B, K: 78D, H: 25B

702 אֶפֶס דַּמִּים *'epes dammîm*, Ephes Dammim, S: 658, B: 67C, K: 78D, H: 25B

703 אֶפַע *'epa'*, worthless, S: 659, B: 67C, K: 78D, H: 25B

704 אֶפְעֶה *'ep'eh*, adder, S: 660, B: 821A, K: 78D, H: 25B

705 אָפַף *'āpap*, [A] to surround, entangle, engulf, S: 661, B: 67C, K: 78D, H: 25B

706 אָפַק *'āpaq*, [F] to control oneself, restrain oneself; to feel compelled, S: 662, B: 67C, K: 79A, H: 25C

707 אֲפֵק *'^{a}pēq*, Aphek, S: 663, B: 67D, K: 79A, H: 25C

708 אֲפֵקָה *'^{a}pēqâ*, Aphekah, S: 664, B: 68A, K: 79B, H: 25C

709 אֵפֶר *'ēper*, ashes, dust, S: 665, B: 68C, K: 79B, H: 25C

710 אֲפֵר *'^{a}pēr*, headband, S: 666, B: 68A, K: 79C, H: 25C

711 אֶפְרֹחַ *'eprōaḥ*, young (of a bird), chick, S: 667, B: 827B, K: 79C, H: 25C

712 אַפִּרְיוֹן *'appiryôn*, carriage, S: 668, B: 68B, K: 79D, H: 25C

713 אֶפְרַיִם *'eprayim*, Ephraim, S: 669, B: 68B, K: 79D, H: 25C

714 [1]אֶפְרָת *'eprāt*[1], Ephrath, S: 672, B: 68C 1., K: 80B, H: 25D

715 [2]אֶפְרָת *'eprāt*[2], Ephrath, S: 672, B: 68C 4., K: 80A, H: 25D

716 [1]אֶפְרָתָה *'eprātâ*[1], Ephrathah, S: 672, B: 68C, K: 80B, H: 25D

717 [2]אֶפְרָתָה *'eprātâ*[2], Ephrathah, S: 672, B: 68C 4., K: 80A, H: 25D

718 אֶפְרָתִי *'eprātî*, Ephraimite, S: 673, B: 68D, K: 80B, H: 25D

719 אֶצְבֹּן *'eṣbōn*, Ezbon, S: 675, B: 69A, K: 80B, H: 25D

720 אֶצְבַּע *'eṣba'*, finger, toe, S: 676, B: 840C, K: 80C, H: 25D

721 [1]אָצִיל *'āṣîl*[1], far corner (of the earth), S: 678, B: 69C, K: 80C, H: 25D

722 [2]אָצִיל *'āṣîl*[2], leader, S: 678, B: 69C, K: 80D, H: 25D

723 אַצִּיל *'aṣṣîl*, joint (of shoulder or wrist); long (cubit), S: 679, B: 69C, K: 80D, H: 25D

724 אָצַל *'āṣal*, [A] to turn aside; to take away; [C] to be smaller, S: 680, B: 69B, K: 80D, H: 26A

725 [1]אֵצֶל *'ēṣel*[1], beside, near, at the side, S: 681, B: 69A, K: 81A, H: 26A

726 [2]אֵצֶל *'ēṣel*[2], variant: Ezel, see 1089, S: 1018†, B: 69B, K: 124A, H: 39B 3.

727 [1]אָצֵל *'āṣēl*[1], Azel, S: 682, B: 69B, K: 81B, H: 26A

728 [2]אָצֵל *'āṣēl*[2], Azel, S: 682, B: 69C, K: 81B, H*

729 אֲצַלְיָהוּ *'^{a}ṣalyāhû*, Azaliah, S: 683, B: 69D, K: 81B, H: 26A

730 אֹצֶם *'ōṣem*, Ozem, S: 684, B: 69D, K: 81B, H: 26A

731 אֶצְעָדָה *'eṣ'ādâ*, armlet, armband, S: 685, B: 858A, K: 81B, H: 26A

732 אָצַר *'āṣar*, [A] to store up; [C] be stored; [G] to be in charge of a storeroom, S: 686, B: 69D, K: 81C, H: 26A

733 אֵצֶר *'ēṣer*, Ezer, S: 687†, B: 69D, K: 81C, H: 26A

734 אֶקְדָּח *'eqdāḥ*, sparkling jewel, S: 688, B: 869B, K: 81C, H: 26A

735 אַקּוֹ *'aqqô*, wild goat, S: 689, B: 70A, K: 81D, H: 26B

736 אֲרָא *'^{a}rā'*, Ara, S: 690, B: 70B, K: 81D, H: 26B

737 אֶרְאֵל *'er'ēl*, brave man, hero, S: 691, B: 72A, K: 81D & 86D, H: 26B

738 אֲרִיאֵל *'^{a}ri'ēl*, best man, warrior, S: 739†, B: 72A, K: 86D, H: 26B

739 [1]אַרְאֵלִי *'ar'ēlî*[1], Areli, S: 692, B: 72A, K: 81D, H: 26B 1.

740 [2]אַרְאֵלִי *'ar'ēlî*[2], Arelite, S: 692, B: 72A, K: 81D, H: 26B 2.

741 אָרַב *'ārab*, [A] to lay in wait against, hide in ambush; [D] to ambush, waylay; [G] to set an ambush, S: 693, B: 70B, K: 81D, H: 26B

742 אֲרָב *'^{a}rāb*, Arab, S: 694, B: 70C, K: 82B, H: 26C

743 אֶרֶב *'ereb*, cover, hiding place, lair; hiding place (for an ambush), S: 695, B: 70C, K: 82B, H: 26C

744 אֹרֶב *'ōreb*, trap, intrigue, S: 696, B: 70C, K: 82B, H: 26C

745 אַרְבֵּאל *'arbē'l*, variant: Arbel, S: 1009†, B: 111A, K: 82B, H: 26C

746 אַרְבֶּה *'arbeh*, locust, mature locust, S: 697, B: 916A, K: 82C, H: 26C

747 אָרְבָּה *'orbâ*, cleverness, S: 698†, B: 70C, K: 82C, H: 26C

748 אֲרֻבָּה *'^{a}rubbâ*, floodgate; window; nest (nesting hole), S: 699, B: 70C, K: 82C, H: 26C

749 אֲרֻבּוֹת *'^{a}rubbôt*, Arubboth, S: 700, B: 70D, K: 82D, H: 26C

750 אַרְבִּי *'arbî*, Arbite, S: 701, B: 70C, K: 82D, H: 26C

751 ארנבן *'rnbn*, variant: Aranabanim, S: 1835† & 3120†, B: 75A, K*, H*

752 [1]אַרְבַּע *'arba'*[1], four, (pl.) forty; fourth, fortieth, S: 702 & 706†, B: 916D, K: 82D, H: 26C

753 [2]אַרְבַּע *'arba'*[2], variant: Arba, S: 704, B: 917B, K: 83B, H: 26D

754 אַרְבָּעִים *'arbā'îm*, variant: forty, S: 705, B: 917B, K: 82D, H: 26D

755 אָרַג *'ārag*, [A] to weave, spin (a web), S: 707, B: 70D, K: 83B, H: 26D

756 אֶרֶג *'ereg*, weaver's loom, weaver's shuttle, S: 708, B: 71A, K: 83C, H: 26D

757 אַרְגָּב *'argāb*, variant: heap, mound, S*, B: 918D, K*, H*

758 [1]אַרְגֹּב *'argōb*[1], Argob, S: 709, B: 918D 1., K: 83C, H: 26D

759 [2]אַרְגֹּב *'argōb*[2], Argob, S: 709, B: 918D 2., K: 83C, H*

760 אַרְגְּוָן *'arg^{e}wān*, purple (yarn), S: 710, B: 71A, K: 83C, H: 26D

761 אַרְגַּז *'argaz*, chest (containing objects), S: 712, B: 919C, K: 83C, H: 26D

762 אֹרְגִים *'ōr^{e}gîm*, variant: Oregim, S: 3296†, B: 421A, K: 391C, H: 139A

763 אַרְגָּמָן *'argāmān*, purple (yarn), S: 713, B: 71A, K: 83C, H: 26D

764 אַרְדְּ *'ard*, Ard, S: 714, B: 71B, K: 83D, H: 26D

765 אַרְדּוֹן *'ardôn*, Ardon, S: 715, B: 71B, K: 83D, H: 26D

766 אַרְדִּי *'ardî*, Ardite, S: 716, B: 71B, K: 83D, H: 27A

767 אֲרִדַי 'ᵃriday, Aridai, S: 742†, B: 71C, K: 84A, H: 27A

768 אָרָה 'ārâ, [A] to gather, pick (fruit), S: 717, B: 71C, K: 84A, H: 27A

769 אֲרוֹד 'ᵃrôd, variant: Arod, see 771, S: 720, B: 71B, K: 84A, H: 27A

770 אַרְוָד 'arwād, Arvad, S: 719, B: 71C, K: 84A, H: 27A

771 אֲרוֹדִי 'ᵃrôdî[1], Arodi, S: 722, B: 71B, K: 84A, H: 27A 1.

772 ²אֲרוֹדִי 'ᵃrôdî[2], Arodite, S: 722, B: 71B, K: 84A, H: 27A 2.

773 אַרְוָדִי 'arwādî, Arvadite, S: 721, B: 71C, K: 84B, H: 27A

774 אֻרְוָה 'urwâ, (animal) stall, pen, S: 220† & 723, B: 71D, K: 84B, H: 27A

775 אָרוּז 'ārûz, tight, solid, S: 729†, B: 72D, K: 84B, H: 27A

776 אֲרוּכָה 'ᵃrûkâ, healing, health; repair, S: 724, B: 74A, K: 84B, H: 27A

777 אֲרוּמָה 'ᵃrûmâ, Arumah, S: 725, B: 72B, K: 84C, H: 27A

778 אֲרוֹן 'ᵃrôn, ark, chest, box; coffin, S: 727†, B: 75B, K: 84C, H: 27A

779 אֲרַוְנָה 'ᵃrawnâ, Araunah, S: 728, B: 72B, K: 85B, H: 27B & 7D

780 אֶרֶז 'erez, cedar, S: 730, B: 72C, K: 85C, H: 27B

781 אַרְזָה 'arzâ, beam of cedar, S: 731, B: 72D, K: 85D, H: 27B

782 אָרַח 'āraḥ[1], [A] to go, travel, S: 732, B: 72D, K: 85D, H: 27C

783 ²אָרַח 'āraḥ[2], Arah, S: 733, B: 73B, K: 85D, H: 27C

784 אֹרַח 'ōraḥ, road, way, path; way, manner, conduct, S: 734, B: 73A, K: 86A, H: 27C

785 אֹרְחָה 'ōrḥâ, caravan, S: 736, B: 73C, K: 86B, H: 27C

786 אֲרֻחָה 'ᵃruḥâ, allowance, provision; portion, S: 737, B: 73C, K: 86B, H: 27C

787 אֲרִי 'ᵃrî, lion, S: 738, B: 71C, K: 86C, H: 27C

788 אֻרִי 'urî, Uri, S: 221†, B: 22B 3., K: 86C, H: 27C

789 אֲרִיאֵל 'ᵃrî'ēl[1], altar hearth, S: 741, B: 72A 4., K: 86C, H: 27D

790 ²אֲרִיאֵל 'ᵃrî'ēl[2], Ariel, S: 740, B: 72A 1., K: 86D, H: 27D

791 ³אֲרִיאֵל 'ᵃrî'ēl[3], Ariel, S: 740, B: 72A 2., K: 86D, H: 27D

792 אֲרִידָתָא 'ᵃrîdātā', Aridatha, S: 743, B: 71C, K: 86D, H: 27D

793 אַרְיֵה 'aryēh[1], lion, S: 744, B: 71D, K: 86D, H: 27D

794 ²אַרְיֵה 'aryēh[2], Arieh, S: 745, B: 72A, K: 87A, H: 27D

795 אֻרְיָה 'uryâ, variant: manger, crib, S: 723†, B: 71D, K: 87A, H: 27D

796 אַרְיוֹךְ 'aryôk, Arioch, S: 746, B: 73C, K: 87A, H: 27D

797 אֻרִים 'urîm, variant: (pl.) region of light, East, S: 224†, B: 22A, K: 87A, H: 27D

798 אֲרִיסַי 'ᵃrîsay, Arisai, S: 747, B: 1120D, K: 87A, H: 27D

799 אָרַךְ 'ārak, [A] to be, become long; [G] to lengthen, to have a long (life), S: 748, B: 73C, K: 87A, H: 27D

800 אָרֵךְ 'ārēk, slow (to anger), patient, long-suffering, S: 750, B: 74A, K: 87C, H: 28A

801 אָרֹךְ 'ārōk, length (spatial and temporal), S: 752, B: 74A, K: 87D, H: 28A

802 אֹרֶךְ 'ōrek, length (spatial and temporal), S: 753, B: 73D, K: 87C, H: 28A

803 אֶרֶךְ 'erek[1], variant: see 800, S: 750†, B: 74A, K: 87C, H: 28A

804 ²אֶרֶךְ 'erek[2], Erech, S: 751, B: 74B, K: 87D, H: 28A

805 אַרְכִּי 'arkî, Arkite, S: 757, B: 74B, K: 87D, H: 28A

806 אֲרָם 'ᵃrām, Aram, S: 758, B: 74B, K: 87D, H: 28A

807 אֲרַם מַעֲכָה 'ᵃram ma'ᵃkâ, Aram Maacah, S: 758 + 4601, B: 591A 3., K: 87D, H: 206C

808 אֲרַם נַהֲרַיִם 'ᵃram nahᵃrayim, Aram Naharaim, S: 763, B: 74C, K: 87D, H: 28A & 230B

809 אֲרַם צוֹבָה 'ᵃram ṣôbâ, Aram Zobah, S: 760, B: 74B, K: 87D, H: 28A

810 אַרְמוֹן 'armôn, fortress, citadel, palace, stronghold, S: 759, B: 74D, K: 88C, H: 28B

811 אֲרָמִי 'ᵃrāmî, in Aramaic, S: 762† & 7421†, B: 74C, K: 88C, H: 28B

812 אֲרַמִּי 'ᵃrammî, Aramean, S: 761, B: 74C, K: 88D, H: 28B

813 אַרְמֹנִי 'armōnî, Armoni, S: 764, B: 74D, K: 88D, H: 28B

814 אֲרָן 'ᵃrān, Aran, S: 765, B: 75A, K: 88D, H: 28B

815 אֹרֶן 'ōren[1], pine tree, S: 766, B: 75A, K: 88D, H: 28B

816 ²אֹרֶן 'ōren[2], Oren, S: 767, B: 75A, K: 88D, H: 28B

817 אַרְנֶבֶת 'arnebet, rabbit, S: 768, B: 58A, K: 89A, H: 28B

818 אַרְנוֹן 'arnôn, Arnon, S: 769, B: 75A, K: 89A, H: 28B

819 אֲרַנְיָה 'ᵃranyâ, variant: Aranyah, S: 728†, B: 72B, K: 89A, H: 28B

820 אַרְנָן 'arnān, Arnan, S: 770, B: 75A, K: 89A, H: 28

821 אָרְנָן 'ornān, Araunah, S: 771, B: 75A, K: 89A, H: 28B

822 אַרְפָּד 'arpād, Arpad, S: 774, B: 75D, K: 89B, H: 28B

823 אַרְפַּכְשַׁד 'arpakšad, Arphaxad, S: 775, B: 75D, K: 89B, H: 28C

824 אֶרֶץ 'ereṣ, world, earth, land, ground, soil; country, region, territory, S: 776, B: 75D, K: 89B, H: 28C

825 אַרְצָא 'arṣā', Arza, S: 777, B: 76C, K: 89D, H: 28C

826 אָרַר 'ārar, [A] to curse, place a curse; [B] to be cursed, be under a curse; [C] to be cursed; [D] to bring a curse; [H] to bring a curse upon one, S: 779, B: 76C, K: 89D, H: 28C

827 אֲרָרַט 'ᵃrāraṭ, Ararat, S: 780, B: 76D, K: 90A, H: 28D

828 אֲרָרִי 'ᵃrārî, variant: Ararite, see 2240, S: 2043†, B: 251B 1., K: 90B, H: 28D

829 אָרַשׂ 'āraś, [D] to betroth, pledge to marriage; [E] to be betrothed, be pledged to be married, S: 781, B: 76D, K: 90B, H: 28D

830 אֲרֶשֶׁת 'ᵃrešet, request, desire, S: 782, B: 77A, K: 90C, H: 28D

831 אַרְתַּחְשַׁסְתְּא 'artaḥšast', אַרְתַּחְשַׁשְׂתְּ 'artaḥšaśt, אַרְתַּחְשַׁשְׂתְּא 'artaḥšaśtā', Artaxerxes, S: 783, B: 77A, K: 90C, H: 28D

832 אֲשַׂרְאֵל 'ᵃśar'ēl, Asarel, S: 840, B: 77B, K: 90D, H: 28D

833 אֲשַׂרְאֵלָה 'ᵃśar'ēlâ, Asarelah, S: 841, B: 77B, K: 90D, H: 29A

834 אַשְׂרִאֵלִי 'aśri'ēlî, Asrielite, S: 845, B: 77B, K: 90D, H: 29A

835 אַשְׂרִיאֵל 'aśrî'ēl, Asriel, S: 844, B: 77B, K: 90D, H: 29A

836 אֵשׁ 'ēš[1], fire, flame; lightning, S: 784 & 800†, B: 77B, K: 90D, H: 29A

837 ²אֵשׁ 'ēš[2], variant: trifle, S: 748†, B: 77B, K: 90D, H: 29A

838 אִשׁ 'iš, there is, S: 786, B: 78A, K: 91B, H: 29A

839 אַשְׁבֵּל 'ašbēl, Ashbel, S: 788, B: 78A, K: 91B, H: 29A

840 אַשְׁבֵּלִי 'ašbēlî, Ashbelite, S: 789, B: 78A, K: 91C, H: 29A

841 אֶשְׁבָּן 'ešbān, Eshban, S: 790, B: 78B, K: 91C, H: 29A

842 אַשְׁבֵּעַ 'ašbēa', variant: Ashbea, see 1080, S: 791, B*, K: 91C, H: 29A

843 אֶשְׁבַּעַל 'ešba'al, Esh-Baal, S: 792, B: 36B, K: 91C, H: 29A

844 אָשֵׁד 'āšēd, slopes, mountain slopes, S: 794†, B: 78B, K: 91C, H: 29A

845 אֶשֶׁד 'ešed, variant: foundation, bottom, lower part (slope), S: 793, B: 78B, K: 91C, H: 29A

846 אַשְׁדּוֹד 'ašdôd, Ashdod, S: 795, B: 78B, K: 91D, H: 29A

847 אַשְׁדּוֹדִי 'ašdôdî, from Ashdod, S: 796, B: 78C, K: 91D, H: 29A

848 אַשְׁדּוֹדִית 'ašdôdît, language of Ashdod, S: 797, B: 78C, K: 91D, H*

849 אַשְׁדּוֹת הַפִּסְגָּה 'ašdôt happisgâ, variant: Ashdoth Pisgah, S: 798, B: 820A, K: 91C & 768D, H: 29A & 294C

850 אֵשְׁדָּת 'ēšdāt, mountain slope, S: 799, B: 77D 6. & 206D, K: 91D, H: 29A

851 אִשָּׁה 'iššâ, woman; wife, S: 802, B: 61A, K: 92A, H: 29B

852 אִשֶּׁה 'iššeh, offering made by fire, S: 801, B: 77D, K: 92C, H: 29B

853 אֲשׁוּיָה 'ᵃšûyâ, variant: see 859, S: 803, B: 78C, K: 92D, H: 29B

854 אֱשׁוּן 'ᵉšûn, approach (of darkness), S: 380†, B: 36B, K: 93A, H: 29B

855 אַשּׁוּר 'aššûr, Asshur, Assyria, S: 804, B: 78C, K: 93A, H: 29B

856 אֲשׁוּרִי 'ᵃšûrî, Ashuri, S: 805, B: 79A, K: 93B, H: 29C

857 אַשּׁוּרִם 'aššûrim, Asshurite, S: 805†, B: 78D, K: 93B, H: 29C

858 אַשְׁחוּר 'ašḥûr, Ashhur, S: 806, B: 1007B, K: 93C, H: 29C

859 אָשְׁיָה 'ošyâ, tower, S: 803†, B: 78C, K: 93C, H: 29C

860 אֲשִׁימָא 'ašîmā', Ashima, S: 807, B: 79C, K: 93C, H: 29C

861 אָשִׁישׁ 'āšîš, man, S: 808, B: 84B, K: 93C, H: 29C

862 אֲשִׁישָׁה 'ᵃšîšâ, cake of raisins, S: 809, B: 84B, K: 93C, H: 29C

863 אֶשֶׁךְ 'ešek, testicle, S: 810, B: 79A, K: 93D, H: 29C

864 אֶשְׁכּוֹל 'eškôl[1], cluster of grapes, S: 811, B: 79A, K: 93D, H: 29C

865 ²אֶשְׁכּוֹל 'eškôl[2], Eshcol, S: 812, B: 79B, K: 94A, H: 29C

866 ³אֶשְׁכֹּל 'eškōl[3], Eshcol, S: 812, B: 79B, K: 93D, H: 29C

867 אַשְׁכְּנַז *'aškᵉnaz*, Ashkenaz, S: 813, B: 79B, K: 94A, H: 29D

868 אֶשְׁכָּר *'eškār*, gifts; payment, S: 814, B: 1016C, K: 94A, H: 29D

869 אֵשֶׁל *'ēšel*, tamarisk tree, S: 815, B: 79B, K: 94A, H: 29D

870 אשׁם *'āšam*, [A] to be guilty; [C] to be suffering; [G] to declare guilty, S: 816, B: 79C, K: 94A, H: 29D

871 אָשָׁם *'āšām*, guilt offering; guilt, penalty, S: 817, B: 79D, K: 94B, H: 29D

872 אָשֵׁם *'āšēm*, guilty, bearing guilt, S: 818, B: 79D, K: 94C, H: 30A

873 אַשְׁמָה *'ašmâ*, guilt, guiltiness, S: 819, B: 80A, K: 94C, H: 30A

874 אַשְׁמוּרָה *'ašmûrâ*, watch of the night (middle or last), S: 821, B: 1038A, K: 94D, H: 30A

875 אַשְׁמָן *'ašmān*, strong one, S: 820, B: 1032C, K: 94D, H: 30A

876 אֶשְׁנָב *'ešnāb*, lattice, S: 822, B: 1039D, K: 94D, H: 30A

877 אַשְׁנָה *'ašnâ*, Ashnah, S: 823, B: 80B, K: 95A, H: 30A

878 אֶשְׁעָן *'eš'ān*, Eshan, S: 824, B: 1043D, K: 95A, H: 30A

879 אַשָּׁף *'aššāp*, enchanter, S: 825, B: 80B, K: 95A, H: 30A

880 אַשְׁפָּה *'ašpâ*, quiver (for arrows), S: 827, B: 80C, K: 95A, H: 30A

881 אַשְׁפְּנַז *'ašpᵉnaz*, Ashpenaz, S: 828, B: 80C, K: 95A, H: 30B

882 אֶשְׁפָּר *'ešpār*, cake of dates, S: 829, B: 80C, K: 95B, H: 30B

883 אַשְׁפֹּת *'ašpōt*, ash heap; Dung (Gate), S: 830, B: 1046B, K: 95B, H: 30B & 84C

884 אַשְׁקְלוֹן *'ašqᵉlôn*, Ashkelon, S: 831, B: 80C, K: 95B, H: 30B

885 אֶשְׁקְלוֹנִי *'ešqᵉlônî*, Ashkelonite, S: 832, B: 80D, K: 95B, H: 30B

886 ¹אשׁר *'āšar*[1], [A] to walk (straight); [D] to lead, guide; reprove; [E] to be guided, S: 833, B: 80D, K: 95C, H: 30B

887 ²אשׁר *'āšar*[2], [D] to call blessed, pronounce happy, speak well of; [E] to be blessed, S: 833, B: 80D, K: 95D, H: 30B

888 אָשֵׁר *'āšēr*, Asher, S: 836, B: 81A, K: 95D, H: 30C

889 אֲשֶׁר *'ᵃšer*, (as rel.) who, which, what; (as c.) that, in order that, so that, S: 834, B: 81C, K: 96A, H: 30C

890 אֶשֶׁר *'ešer*, fortune, blessedness, happiness, S: 835, B: 80D, K: 98C, H: 30D

891 אֹשֶׁר *'ōšer*, fortune, blessedness, happiness, S: 837, B: 81A, K: 98A, H: 30D

892 אֲשֻׁר *'āšur*, steps, tracks, S: 838, B: 81A, K: 98B, H: 30D

893 ¹אַשֻּׁר *'aššur*[1], variant: step, track, see 892, S: 838†, B: 81A, K: 98B, H: 30D

894 ²אַשֻּׁר *'aššur*[2], variant: Asshur, see 855, S: 838†, B: 78D 4., K: 98B, H: 30D

895 אֲשֵׁרָה *'ᵃšērâ*, Asherah (pagan god), Asherah pole, S: 842, B: 81B, K: 98B, H: 30D

896 אָשֵׁרִי *'āšērî*, people of Asher, S: 843, B: 81B, K: 98C, H: 31A

897 אַשְׁרֵי *'ašrê*, blessed!, happy!, S: 835†, B: 80D, K: 98C, H: 31A

898 אֲשֻׁרִים *'ᵃšurîm*, variant: Ashurites [?], S: 843†, B: 81B, K: 158D & 1017A, H: 386A

899 אשׁשׁ *'āšaš*, [F] to fix in one's mind, S: 377†, B: 84B, K: 98D, H: 31A

900 אֶשְׁתָּאוֹל *'eštā'ôl*, Eshtaol, S: 847, B: 84B, K: 99A, H: 31A

901 אֶשְׁתָּאֻלִי *'eštā'ulî*, Eshtaolite, S: 848, B: 84B, K: 99A, H: 31A

902 אֶשְׁתּוֹן *'eštôn*, Eshton, S: 850, B: 84C, K: 99A, H: 31A

903 אֶשְׁתְּמֹה *'eštᵉmōh*, Eshtemoh, S: 851, B: 84C, K: 99B, H: 31A

904 אֶשְׁתְּמֹעַ *'eštᵉmōa'*, Eshtemoa, S: 851, B: 84C, K: 99B, H: 31A

905 אַתְּ *'att*, you, S: 859, B: 61D, K: 99B, H: 31A

906 ¹אֵת *'ēt*[1], usually not translated: marks the direct object, S: 853, B: 84C, K: 99B, H: 31A

907 ²אֵת *'ēt*[2], with, to, upon, beside, among, against, S: 854, B: 85C, K: 100A, H: 31C

908 ³אֵת *'ēt*[3], plowshare, mattock, S: 855, B: 88A, K: 100D, H: 31C

909 אֶתְבַּעַל *'etba'al*, Ethbaal, S: 856, B: 87A, K: 100D, H: 31C

910 אתה *'ātâ*, [A] to come; [G] to bring, S: 857, B: 87B, K: 100D, H: 31C

911 אַתָּה *'attâ*, you, your, yourself, S: 859, B: 61C, K: 101A, H: 31D

912 אָתוֹן *'ātôn*, female donkey, S: 860, B: 87C, K: 101B, H: 31D

913 אַתּוּק *'attûq*, variant: see 916, S: 862, B: 87D, K: 101B, H: 31D

914 אַתִּי *'attî*, variant: see 905, S: 859, B: 61C, K: 101B, H: 31D

915 אִתַּי *'ittay*, Ittai, S: 863, B: 87A, K: 101B, H: 31D

916 אַתִּיק *'attîq*, gallery, S: 862, B: 87D, K: 101C, H: 31D

917 אַתֶּם *'attem*, you (all), yours, yourselves, S: 859, B: 61D, K: 101C, H: 31D

918 אֵתָם *'ētām*, Etham, S: 864, B: 87C, K: 101C, H: 31D

919 אֶתְמוֹל *'etmôl*, yesterday; (as adv.) before, formerly, lately, in the past, S: 865, B: 1069D, K: 101C, H: 31B

920 אַתֵּן *'attēn*, you (all), S: 859, B: 61D, K: 101C, H: 32A

921 אֶתְנָה *'etnâ*, payment (of a prostitute), S: 866, B: 1071D, K: 101D, H: 32A

922 אֶתְנִי *'etnî*, Ethni, S: 867, B: 87D, K: 101D, H: 32A

923 אֵתָנִים *'ētānîm*, Ethanim, S: 388, B: 450D, K: 42A, H: 14B

924 אֶתְנַן *'etnan*, wages, payment (of a prostitute), S: 869, B: 1072C, K: 101D, H: 32C

925 אֶתְנָן *'etnān*, Ethnan, S: 868†, B: 1072C, K: 101D, H: 32C

926 אֲתָרִים *'ᵃtārîm*, Atharim, S: 871, B: 87D, K: 101D, H: 32C

927 ב *b*, letter of the Hebrew alphabet, S*, B: 88A, K: 102A, H*

928 בְּ- *bᵉ-*, in, on, among, over, through, against; when, whenever, S*, B: 88A, K: 102A, H: 32A

929 בִּאָה *bi'â*, entrance, S: 872†, B: 99D, K: 105A, H: 32D

930 בָּאַר *bā'ar*, [D] to make plain, make clear, expound, S: 874, B: 91B, K: 105A, H: 32D

931 ¹בְּאֵר *bᵉ'ēr*[1], well, pit, S: 875, B: 91C, K: 105B, H: 32D

932 ²בְּאֵר *bᵉ'ēr*[2], Beer, S: 876, B: 91D, K: 105C, H: 32D

933 ³בְּאֵר *bᵉ'ēr*[3], variant: Beer (used in compound names), S: 884†, B: 91A ff., K: 105B ff., H: 32D

934 בֹּאר *bō'r*, variant: see 1014, S: 877, B: 92B, K: 114C, H: 36A

935 בְּאֵר אֵילִים *bᵉ'ēr 'êlîm*, Beer Elim, S: 879, B: 91C 3., K: 105C, H: 32D

936 בְּאֵר לַחַי רֹאִי *bᵉ'ēr laḥay rō'î*, Beer Lahai Roi, S: 883, B: 91D, K: 105D, H: 32D

937 בְּאֵר שֶׁבַע *bᵉ'ēr šeba'*, Beersheba, S: 884, B: 92A, K: 105D, H: 32D

938 בְּאֵרָא *bᵉ'ērā'*, Beera, S: 878, B: 92A, K: 106A, H: 32D

939 בְּאֵרָה *bᵉ'ērâ*, Beerah, S: 880, B: 92A, K: 105C, H: 32D

940 בְּאֵרוֹת *bᵉ'ērôt*, Beeroth, S: 881, B: 92A, K: 106A, H: 32D

941 בְּאֵרִי *bᵉ'ērî*, Beeri, S: 882, B: 92B, K: 106A, H: 32D

942 בְּאֵרֹת בְּנֵי־יַעֲקָן *bᵉ'ērōt bᵉnê-ya'ᵃqān*, variant: Beeroth Bene-Jaakan, S: 885, B: 92B, K: 106A, H: 33A

943 בְּאֵרֹתִי *bᵉ'ērōtî*, Beerothite, S: 886, B: 92A, K: 106A, H: 33A

944 בָּאַשׁ *bā'aš*, [A] to stink, smell; [C] to become a stench; [G] to make a stench, to cause a bad smell; [F] to make oneself a stench, S: 887, B: 92D, K: 106A, H: 33A

945 בְּאֹשׁ *bᵉ'ōš*, stench, S: 889, B: 93B, K: 106C, H: 33A

946 בְּאֻשׁ *bᵉ'uš*, bad fruit, rotten grapes, S: 891†, B: 93B, K: 106C, H: 33A

947 בָּאְשָׁה *bo'šâ*, weeds, S: 890, B: 93B, K: 106C, H: 33A

948 בַּאֲשֶׁר *ba'ᵃšer*, because, for, since; where, wherever, S: 834†, B: 84A, K: 105A, H: 33A

949 בָּבָה *bābâ*, apple (of the eye), eyeball, S: 892, B: 93B, K: 106D, H: 33A

950 בֵּבַי *bēbay*, Bebai, S: 893, B: 93C, K: 106D, H: 33A

951 בָּבֶל *bābel*, Babel, Babylon, S: 894, B: 93C, K: 106D, H: 33A

952 בַּג *bag*, variant: see 1020, S: 897, B: 93C, K: 107A, H: 33B

953 בָּגַד *bāgad*, [A] to be unfaithful, be faithless; to betray, act treacherously, S: 898, B: 93C, K: 107A, H: 33B

954 ¹בֶּגֶד *beged*[1], treachery, S: 899, B: 93D, K: 107C, H: 33B

955 ²בֶּגֶד *beged*[2], clothing, garment, cloak, robe, S: 899, B: 93D, K: 107C, H: 33B

956 בֹּגְדוֹת *bōgᵉdôt*, treachery, S: 900, B: 93D, K: 107D, H: 33C

957 בָּגוֹד *bāgôd*, unfaithful, S: 901, B: 93D, K: 107D, H: 33C

958 בִּגְוַי *bigway*, Bigvai, S: 902, B: 94A, K: 107D, H: 33C

959 בִּגְלַל *biglal*, variant: because of, S: 1559†, B: 164B, K: 185A, H: 33C

960 בִּגְתָא *bigtā'*, Bigtha, S: 903, B: 94A, K: 107D, H: 33C

961 בִּגְתָן *bigtān*, Bigthana, S: 904, B: 94B, K: 108A, H: 33C

[A] Qal [B] Qal passive [C] Niphal [D] Piel (poel, polel, pilel, pilal, pealal, pilpel) [E] Pual (poal, polal, poalal, pulal, pualal)

962 בִּגְתָנָא *bigtānā'*, Bigthana, S: 904, B: 94B, K: 108A, H: 33C

963 בַּד[1] *bad[1]*, part, member, limb; alone, apart, only; in addition to, S: 905, B: 94C, K: 108A, H: 33C

964 בַּד[2] *bad[2]*, pole, bar, S: 905, B: 94C, K: 108C, H: 33C

965 בַּד[3] *bad[3]*, linen, S: 906, B: 94B, K: 108A, H: 33C

966 בַּד[4] *bad[4]*, boasting, idle talk, S: 907, B: 95A, K: 108C, H: 33C

967 בַּד[5] *bad[5]*, false prophet, S: 907, B: 95A, K: 108C, H: 33D

968 בָּדָא *bādā'*, [A] to choose; to make up, devise, S: 908, B: 94B, K: 108D, H: 33D

969 בָּדַד *bādad*, [A] to be alone, isolated, S: 909, B: 94B, K: 108D, H: 33D

970 בָּדָד *bādād*, alone, by oneself, apart, S: 910, B: 94D, K: 108D, H: 33D

971 בְּדַד *b^{e}dad*, Bedad, S: 911, B: 95A, K: 109A, H: 33D

972 בֵּדְיָ *b^{e}dê*, variant: see 928 & 1896, S: 1767†, B: 191C 2., K: 207D, H: 33D & 70A 2.a

973 בֵּדְיָה *bēd^{e}yâ*, Bedeiah, S: 912, B: 95A, K: 109A, H: 33D

974 בְּדִיל *b^{e}dîl*, tin, S: 913, B: 95D, K: 109A, H: 33D

975 בָּדִיל *bādîl*, impurities, S: 913†, B: 95D, K: 109A, H: 33D

976 בָּדַל *bādal*, [C] separate oneself, be expelled; [G] to separate, sever completely, distinguish between, S: 914, B: 95A, K: 109A, H: 33D

977 בָּדָל *bādāl*, piece (of an ear), S: 915, B: 95C, K: 109C, H: 34A

978 בְּדֹלַח *b^{e}dōlaḥ*, aromatic resin, S: 916, B: 95D, K: 109C, H: 34A

979 בְּדָן *b^{e}dān*, Bedan, S: 917, B: 96A, K: 109D, H: 34A

980 בָּדַק *bādaq*, [A] to repair, mend, S: 918, B: 96A, K: 109D, H: 34A

981 בֶּדֶק *bedeq*, breach (of a temple or a ship), S: 919, B: 96A, K: 109D, H: 34A

982 בִּדְקַר *bidqar*, Bidkar, S: 920, B: 96A, K: 110A, H: 34A

983 בֹּהוּ *bōhû*, emptiness, desolation, S: 922, B: 96A, K: 110A, H: 34A

984 בְּהוֹן *b^{e}hôn*, thumb, big toe, S: 931†, B: 97B, K: 110A, H: 34A

985 בַּהַט *bahaṭ*, porphyry (precious stone), S: 923, B: 96B, K: 110A, H: 34A

986 בָּהִיר *bāhîr*, bright, brilliant, S: 925, B: 97C, K: 110A, H: 34B

987 בָּהַל *bāhal*, [C] to be terrified, alarmed, dismayed, bewildered; [D] to make afraid, terrify; to make haste; [E] to be hastened, made to hurry; to cause terror; to cause to hurry, S: 926, B: 96B, K: 110A, H: 34B

988 בֶּהָלָה *behālâ*, sudden terror; misfortune, S: 928, B: 96D, K: 110C, H: 34B

989 בְּהֵמָה *b^{e}hēmâ*, beast, animal, livestock, herds, cattle, S: 929, B: 96D, K: 110C, H: 34B

990 בְּהֵמוֹת *b^{e}hēmôt*, behemoth, S: 930, B: 97A, K: 111A, H: 34C

991 בֹּהֶן *bōhen*, thumb, big toe, S: 931, B: 97B, K: 111A, H: 34C

992 בֹּהַן *bōhan*, Bohan, S: 932, B: 97B, K: 111A, H: 34C

993 בֹּהַק *bōhaq*, harmless rash, S: 933, B: 97B, K: 111B, H: 34C

994 בַּהֶרֶת *baheret*, spot, bright spot (on the skin), S: 934†, B: 97B, K: 111B, H: 34C

995 בּוֹא *bô'*, [A] to come, go; [G] to bring, take; [H] to be brought, S: 935, B: 97C, K: 111C, H: 34C

996 בּוּז[1] *bûz[1]*, [A] to despise, scorn, deride, S: 936, B: 100B, K: 113C, H: 35A

997 בּוּז[2] *bûz[2]*, contempt, S: 937, B: 100B, K: 113C, H: 35C

998 בּוּז[3] *bûz[3]*, Buz, S: 938, B: 100C, K: 113C, H: 35C

999 בּוּזָה *bûzâ*, contempt, S: 939, B: 100C, K: 113C, H: 35C

1000 בּוּזִי[1] *bûzî[1]*, Buzite, S: 940, B: 100C, K: 113D, H: 35C

1001 בּוּזִי[2] *bûzî[2]*, Buzi, S: 941, B: 100C, K: 113D, H: 35C

1002 בַּוַּי *bawway*, variant: Bavvai, see 1218, S: 942, B: 100C, K: 113D, H: 35C

1003 בּוּךְ *bûk*, [C] to wander around, mill about; to be bewildered, S: 943, B: 100C, K: 113D, H: 35C

1004 בּוּל[1] *bûl[1]*, Bul (month), S: 945, B: 100D, K: 113D, H: 35C

1005 בּוּל[2] *bûl[2]*, block (of wood), S: 944, B: 385B, K: 113D, H: 35D

1006 בּוּל[3] *bûl[3]*, produce, S: 944, B: 385B, K: 113D, H: 35D

1007 בּוּנָה *bûnâ*, Bunah, S: 946, B: 107B, K: 114A, H: 35D

1008 בּוּס *bûs*, [A, D] to trample down; loathe; [F] to kick about; [H] to be trodden down, S: 947, B: 100D, K: 114A, H: 35D

1009 בּוּץ *bûṣ*, fine linen; white linen, S: 948, B: 101B, K: 114B, H: 35D

1010 בּוֹצֵץ *bôṣēṣ*, Bozez, S: 949, B: 130D, K: 114B, H: 35D

1011 בּוּקָה *bûqâ*, pillage, emptiness, S: 950, B: 101C, K: 114B, H: 35D

1012 בּוֹקֵר *bôqēr*, shepherd, S: 951, B: 133C, K: 114C, H: 35D

1013 בּוּר *bûr*, [A] to conclude, S: 952, B: 101C, K: 156B, H: 35D

1014 בּוֹר *bôr*, pit, well, cistern; dungeon, S: 953, B: 92B, K: 114C, H: 36A

1015 בּוֹר הַסִּרָה *bôr hassirâ*, variant: Bor Hasirah, see 1014 & 6241, S: 953 + 5626, B: 92C, K: 667D, H: 36A 1

1016 בּוֹר־עָשָׁן *bôr-'āšān*, Bor Ashan, S: 953 + 6228, B: 92D, K: 115A, H: 36A 1.

1017 בּוֹשׁ[1] *bôš[1]*, [A] to be put to shame, be ashamed, be disgraced; [F] to feel ashamed; [G] to bring shame, to cause disgrace, act shamefully, S: 954†, B: 101D, K: 115A, H: 36A

1018 בּוֹשׁ[2] *bôš[2]*, [E] to be delayed, be long, S: 954†, B: 101D, K: 115A, H: 36B

1019 בּוּשָׁה *bûšâ*, shame, S: 955, B: 102A, K: 115C, H: 36C

1020 בַּז *baz*, plunder, loot, despoiling, S: 957, B: 103A, K: 115C, H: 36C

1021 בָּזָא *bāzā'*, [A] to divide, S: 958, B: 102B, K: 115D, H: 36C

1022 בָּזָה *bāzâ*, [A] to despise, scorn, ridicule, show contempt for; [B] to be despised; [C] to be despised, be contemptible; [G] to cause to despise, S: 959 & 960† & 5240†, B: 102B, K: 115D, H: 36A

1023 בִּזָּה *bizzâ*, plunder, booty, S: 961, B: 103A, K: 116A, H: 36C

1024 בָּזַז *bāzaz*, [A] to plunder, loot, carry off spoils; [B, C, E] to be plundered, S: 962, B: 102D, K: 116B, H: 36C

1025 בִּזָּיוֹן *bizzāyôn*, disrespect, contempt, S: 963, B: 102C, K: 116C, H: 36D

1026 בִּזְיוֹתְיָה *bizyôt^{e}yâ*, Biziothiah, S: 964, B: 103A, K: 116C, H: 36D

1027 בָּזָק *bāzāq*, flashes of lightning, lightning, S: 65, B: 103B, K: 116C, H: 36D

1028 בֶּזֶק *bezeq*, Bezek, S: 966, B: 103, K: 116C, H: 36D

1029 בָּזַר *bāzar*, [A] to distribute; [D] to scatter, S: 967, B: 103B, K: 116C, H: 36D

1030 בִּזְּתָא *bizz^{e}tā'*, Biztha, S: 968, B: 103B, K: 116D, H: 36D

1031 בָּחוֹן *bāḥôn*, tester of metals, assayer, S: 969, B: 103D, K: 116D, H: 36D

1032 בַּחוּן *baḥûn*, siege tower, S: 971†, B: 103D, K: 116D, H: 36D

1033 בָּחוּר[1] *bāḥûr[1]*, young man, able (fighting) man; bridegroom, S: 970, B: 104C, K: 116D, H: 36D

1034 בָּחוּר[2] *bāḥûr[2]*, variant: see 1047, S: 977†, B: 103D, K: 117A, H: 37A

1035 בְּחוּרוֹת *b^{e}ḥûrôt*, youth, S: 979, B: 104C, K: 117A, H: 37A

1036 בְּחוּרִים *b^{e}ḥûrîm*, youth, S: 980, B: 104C, K: 118B, H: 37A

1037 בַּחוּרִים[1] *baḥûrîm[1]*, variant: young men, S: 970†, B: 104C, K: 116D, H: 37A

1038 בַּחוּרִים[2] *baḥûrîm[2]*, Bahurim, S: 980, B: 104C, K: 118B, H: 37A

1039 בַּחִין *baḥîn*, variant: see 1032, S: 971, B: 103D, K: 117A, H: 37A

1040 בָּחִיר *bāḥîr*, chosen one, S: 972, B: 104C, K: 117A, H: 37A

1041 בָּחַל[1] *bāḥal[1]*, [A] to detest, disdain, S: 973, B: 103B, K: 117B, H: 37A

1042 בָּחַל[2] *bāḥal[2]*, variant: [E] to be gotten by greed, S: 973, B: 103C, K: 117B, H: 37A

1043 בָּחַן *bāḥan*, [A] to test, try, probe, examine; [B, C, E] to be tested, S: 974, B: 103D, K: 117B, H: 37A

1044 בַּחַן *baḥan*, watchtower, S: 975, B: 103D, K: 117C, H: 37B

1045 בֹּחַן[1] *bōḥan[1]*, variant: testing, see 1043, S*, B: 103C, K: 117C, H: 37B

1046 בֹּחַן[2] *bōḥan[2]*, tested (stone), S: 976, B: 103D, K: 117C, H: 37B

1047 בָּחַר[1] *bāḥar[1]*, [A] to choose, select, desire, prefer; [B, C] to be chosen, choice, the best, preferred, S: 977, B: 103D, K: 117D, H: 37B

1048 בָּחַר[2] *bāḥar[2]*, variant: [A] to enter into a covenant; [E] be joined, S: 977, B: 103D, K: 117D, H: 37C

1049 בַּחֲרוּמִי *baḥ^{a}rûmî*, Baharumite, S: 978, B: 104D, K: 118B, H: 37C

1050 בַּחֻרִמִי *baḥurimî*, variant: Bahurimite, see 1372, S*, B: 104D, K: 118B, H: 37C

1051 בָּטָא *bāṭā'*, [A, D] to speak thoughtlessly, to speak rashly, recklessly, S: 981, B: 104D, K: 118B, H: 37C

1052 בָּטוּחַ *bāṭûaḥ*, variant: confident, see 1053, S*, B: 105A, K: 118C, H: 37C

[F] Hitpael (hitpoel, hitpoal, hitpolel, hitpolal, hitpalel, hitpalal, hitpalpel, hitpalpal, hotpael, hotpaal) [G] Hiphil (hiphtil) [H] Hophal [I] Hishtaphel

1053 ¹בָּטַח bāṭaḥ[1], [A] to trust, rely on, put confidence in; [B] to be confident; [G] to lead to believe, make trust, S: 982, B: 105A, K: 118C, H: 37C

1054 ²בָּטַח bāṭaḥ[2], [A] to stumble, fall to the ground, S: 982, B: 105A, K: 118C, H: 37D

1055 ¹בֶּטַח beṭaḥ[1], safety, security, S: 983, B: 105B, K: 119A, H: 37D

1056 ²בֶּטַח beṭaḥ[2], variant: Betah, see 3182, S: 984, B: 105C, K: 119A, H: 37D

1057 בִּטְחָה biṭḥâ, trust, confidence, S: 985, B: 105C, K: 119B, H: 37D

1058 בַּטֻּחָה baṭṭuḥâ, security, safety, S: 987†, B: 105C, K: 119B, H: 37D

1059 בִּטָּחוֹן biṭṭāḥôn, confidence, hope, S: 986, B: 105C, K: 119B, H: 37D

1060 בָּטַל bāṭal, [A] to cease, S: 988†, B: 105D, K: 119B, H: 37D

1061 ¹בֶּטֶן beṭen[1], inmost part, abdomen, belly, stomach, womb; heart, S: 990, B: 105D, K: 119B, H: 37D

1062 ²בֶּטֶן beṭen[2], Beten, S: 991, B: 106B, K: 119D, H: 38A

1063 בָּטְנָה boṭnâ, pistachio nut, S: 992†, B: 106B, K: 119D, H: 38A

1064 בְּטֹנִים beṭōnîm, Betonim, S: 993, B: 106B, K: 119D, H: 38A

1065 בִּי bî, O!, please!, S: 994, B: 106C, K: 120A, H: 38A

1066 בָּיַי bāyay, variant: to entreat, S: 15†, B: 106B, K: 4A, H: 1D

1067 בִּין bîn, [A] to understand, discern, realize; be prudent; [C] to be discerning, be understanding; [D] to care for; to have skill, insight; to instruct, explain; [F] to look closely, consider with full attention, ponder, S: 995, B: 106C, K: 120A, H: 38A

1068 בַּיִן bayin, between; separate from; whether ... or, S: 996†, B: 107B, K: 121B, H: 38C

1069 בִּינָה bînâ, understanding, insight, discernment, good sense, wisdom, S: 998, B: 108A, K: 121D, H: 38D

1070 בֵּיצָה bêṣâ, egg, S: 1000, B: 101B, K: 122A, H: 38D

1071 בַּיִר bayir, variant: well, S: 875†, B: 92D, K: 122A, H: 38D

1072 בִּירָה bîrâ, citadel, fort, palatial structure, S: 1002, B: 108B, K: 122A, H: 38D

1073 בִּירָנִיָּה bîrāniyyâ, variant: fortified place, S: 1003†, B: 108C, K: 122B, H: 38D

1074 ¹בַּיִת bayit[1], house, home, temple; household, family, clan, tribe, S: 1004, B: 108C, K: 122B, H: 38D

1075 ²בַּיִת bayit[2], between; among; at a crossroads, S: 996†, B: 108A, K*, H: 39C

1076 ³בַּיִת bayit[3], variant: Bayit, S*, B: 110C, K: 122B, H: 38D

1077 בֵּית אָוֶן bêt 'āwen, Beth Aven, S: 1007, B: 110C, K: 123D 1., H: 39B 1.

1078 בֵּית־אֵל bêt-'ēl, Bethel, S: 1008, B: 110D, K: 123D 2., H: 39B 2.

1079 בֵּית אַרְבֵאל bêt 'arbē'l, Beth Arbel, S: 1009, B: 111A, K: 124A 4., H: 39B 4.

1080 בֵּית אַשְׁבֵּעַ bêt 'ašbēa', Beth Ashbea, S: 1004 + 791, B*, K: 91C, H: 39B 5.

1081 בֵּית בַּעַל מְעוֹן bêt ba'al me'ôn, Beth Baal Meon, S: 1010, B: 111A, K: 124A 5., H: 39B 6.

1082 בֵּית בִּרְאִי bêt bir'î, Beth Biri, S: 1011, B: 111A, K: 124A 6., H: 39B 7.

1083 בֵּית בָּרָה bêt bārâ, Beth Barah, S: 1012, B: 111B, K: 124A 7., H: 39B 8.

1084 בֵּית־גָּדֵר bêt-gādēr, Beth Gader, S: 1013, B: 111B, K: 124A 8., H: 39B 9.

1085 בֵּית גָּמוּל bêt gāmûl, Beth Gamul, S: 1014, B: 111B, K: 124B 10., H: 39B 11.

1086 בֵּית דִּבְלָתַיִם bêt diblātayim, Beth Diblathaim, S: 1015, B: 111B, K: 124B 12., H: 39B 13.

1087 בֵּית־דָּגוֹן bêt-dāgôn, Beth Dagon, S: 1016, B: 111B, K: 124B 13., H: 39B 14.

1088 בֵּית הָאֱלִי bêt hā'elî, the Bethelite, S: 1017, B: 111A, K: 126A, H: 39B 2.

1089 בֵּית הָאֵצֶל bêt hā'ēṣel, Beth Ezel, S: 1018, B: 111A, K: 124A 3., H: 39B 3.

1090 בֵּית הַגִּלְגָּל bêt haggilgāl, Beth Gilgal, S: 1019, B: 111B & 166A, K: 124A 9., H: 39B 10.

1091 בֵּית הַגָּן bêt haggān, Beth Haggan, S: 1004 + 1588, B: 111B, K: 124B 11., H: 39B 12.

1092 בֵּית הַמֶּרְחָק bêt hammerḥāq, variant: Beth Hamerhaq; see 1074 & 5305, S: 1023, B: 112A, K: 566B, H: 39C 30.

1093 בֵּית הַיְשִׁימוֹת bêt hayešîmôt, Beth Jeshimoth, S: 1020, B: 111D, K: 124C 19., H: 39B 21.

1094 בֵּית־הַכֶּרֶם bêt-hakkerem, Beth Hakkerem, S: 1021, B: 111D, K: 124D 21., H: 39B 23.

1095 בֵּית־הַלַּחְמִי bêt-hallaḥmî, the Bethlehemite, S: 1022, B: 112A, K: 126A & 479C, H: 39C 25.

1096 בֵּית־הַמַּרְכָּבוֹת bêt-hammarkābôt, Beth Marcaboth, S: 1024, B: 112B, K: 125A 27., H: 39C 31.

1097 בֵּית הָעֵמֶק bêt hā'ēmeq, Beth Emek, S: 1025, B: 112B, K: 125A 31., H: 39C 35.

1098 בֵּית הָעֲרָבָה bêt hā'arābâ, Beth Arabah, S: 1026, B: 112C, K: 125B 35., H: 39C 39.

1099 בֵּית הָרָם bêt hārām, Beth Haram, S: 1027, B: 111B, K: 124B 14., H: 39C 15. & 45.

1100 בֵּית הָרָן bêt hārān, Beth Haran, S: 1028, B: 111C, K: 124B 15., H: 39C 45.

1101 בֵּית הַשִּׁטָּה bêt haššiṭṭâ, Beth Shittah, S: 1029, B: 112D, K: 125D 42., H: 39C 49.

1102 בֵּית־חָגְלָה bêt-ḥoglâ, Beth Hoglah, S: 1031, B: 111C, K: 124C 16., H: 39B 17.

1103 בֵּית־חוֹרוֹן bêt-ḥôrôn, Beth Horon, S: 1032, B: 111C, K: 124C 18., H: 39B 19.

1104 בֵּית חָנָן bêt ḥānān, variant: Bethhanan, S: 358†, B: 111C, K: 124C 17., H: 39B 18.

1105 בֵּית כָּר bêt kār, Beth Car, S: 1033, B: 111D, K: 124C 20., H: 39B 22.

1106 בֵּית לְבָאוֹת bêt lebā'ôt, Beth Lebaoth, S: 1034, B: 111D, K: 124D 22., H: 39B 24.

1107 בֵּית לֶחֶם bêt leḥem, Bethlehem, S: 1035, B: 111D, K: 124D 23., H: 39B 25.

1108 בֵּית לְעַפְרָה bêt le'aprâ, Beth Ophrah, S: 1036, B: 112A, K: 125A 24., H: 39C 26.

1109 בֵּית מִלּוֹא bêt millô', Beth Millo, S: 1037, B: 571C, K: 527D, H: 39C 27.

1110 בֵּית מְעוֹן bêt me'ôn, Beth Meon, S: 1010†, B: 111A, K: 125A 25., H: 39C 28.

1111 בֵּית מַעֲכָה bêt ma'akâ, variant: Beth Maacah, S: 1038, B: 112A, K: 125A 26., H: 39C 29.

1112 בֵּית מַרְכָּבוֹת bêt markābôt, Beth Marcaboth, S: 1024†, B: 112B, K: 125A 27., H: 39C 31.

1113 בֵּית נִמְרָה bêt nimrâ, Beth Nimrah, S: 1039, B: 112B, K: 125A 28., H: 39C 32.

1114 בֵּית עֶדֶן bêt 'eden, Beth Eden, S: 1040†, B: 112B, K: 125A 29., H: 39C 33.

1115 בֵּית־עַזְמָוֶת bêt-'azmāwet, Beth Azmaveth, S: 1041, B: 112B, K: 125A 30., H: 39C 34.

1116 בֵּית־עֲנוֹת bêt-'anôt, Beth Anoth, S: 1042, B: 112B, K: 125B 32., H: 39C 36.

1117 בֵּית־עֲנָת bêt-'anāt, Beth Anath, S: 1043, B: 112C, K: 125B 33., H: 39C 37.

1118 בֵּית־עֵקֶד bêt-'ēqed, Beth Eked, S: 1044, B: 112C & 785B, K: 125B 34., H: 39C 38

1119 בֵּית עַשְׁתָּרוֹת bêt 'aštārôt, variant: Beth Ashtaroth, S: 1045, B: 800A, K: 745D, H: 286C

1120 בֵּית פֶּלֶט bêt peleṭ, Beth Pelet, S: 1046, B: 112C, K: 125B 36., H: 39C 40.

1121 בֵּית פְּעוֹר bêt pe'ôr, Beth Peor, S: 1047, B: 112C, K: 125C 37., H: 39C 41.

1122 בֵּית פַּצֵּץ bêt paṣṣēṣ, Beth Pazzez, S: 1048, B: 112D, K: 125C 38., H: 39C 42.

1123 בֵּית־צוּר bêt-ṣûr, Beth Zur, S: 1049, B: 112D, K: 125C 39., H: 39C 43.

1124 בֵּית־רְחוֹב bêt-reḥôb, Beth Rehob, S: 1050, B: 112D, K: 125C 40., H: 39C 44.

1125 בֵּית רָפָא bêt rāpā', Beth Rapha, S: 1051, B: 112D, K: 903D, H: 39C 47.

1126 בֵּית־שְׁאָן bêt-šě'ān, Beth Shan, S: 1052, B: 112D, K: 125C 41., H: 39C 48.

1127 בֵּית שֶׁמֶשׁ bêt šemeš, Beth Shemesh, S: 1053, B: 112D, K: 125D 43., H: 39C 50.

1128 בֵּית־שִׁמְשִׁי bêt-šimšî, of Beth Shemesh, S: 1030†, B: 113A, K: 126A, H: 39C

1129 בֵּית תּוֹגַרְמָה *bêt tôgarmâ*, Beth Togarmah, S: 1004 + 8425, B: 1062B, K: 1018D, H: 39C 51.

1130 בֵּית־תַּפּוּחַ *bêt-tappûaḥ*, Beth Tappuah, S: 1054, B: 113A, K: 125D 44., H: 39C 52.

1131 בִּיתָן *bîtān*, palace, S: 1055, B: 113A, K: 126A, H: 39C

1132 ¹בָּכָא *bākā'*[1], balsam tree, S: 1057, B: 113A, K: 126A, H: 39C

1133 ²בָּכָא *bākā'*[2], Baca, S: 1056, B: 113A, K: 126A, H: 39C

1134 בָּכָה *bākâ*, [A] to weep, wail, cry, sob, mourn; [D] to weep for, mourn for, S: 1058, B: 113B, K: 126B, H: 39D

1135 בֶּכֶה *bekeh*, weeping, S: 1059, B: 113D, K: 126C, H: 39D

1136 בִּכּוּרָה *bikkûrâ*, early ripened fruit, S: 1063 & 1073†, B: 114C, K: 126C, H: 39D

1137 בִּכּוּרִים *bikkûrîm*, firstfruits, first ripened produce, S: 1061†, B: 114C, K: 126D, H: 39D

1138 בְּכוֹרַת *bᵉkôrat*, Becorath, S: 1064, B: 114C, K: 127A, H: 39D

1139 בָּכוּת *bākût*, variant: Bacuth, S: 439†, B: 113D, K: 127A, H: 39D

1140 בְּכִי *bᵉkî*, weeping, S: 1065, B: 113D, K: 127A, H: 40A

1141 בֹּכִים *bōkîm*, Bokim, S: 1066, B: 114A, K: 127A, H: 40A

1142 בְּכִירָה *bᵉkîrâ*, first born (daughter), S: 1067, B: 114C, K: 127B, H: 40A

1143 בְּכִית *bᵉkît*, mourning, weeping, S: 1068, B: 114A, K: 127B, H: 40A

1144 בָּכַר *bākar*, [D] bear early fruit; give the rights of the firstborn; [E] be made a firstborn (dedication); [G] to bear one's first child, S: 1069, B: 114A, K: 127B, H: 40A

1145 בֵּכֶר *bēker*, young bull camel, S: 1070†, B: 114C, K: 127C, H: 40A

1146 בֶּכֶר *beker*, Beker, S: 1071, B: 114B, K: 127C, H: 40A

1147 בְּכֹר *bᵉkōr*, firstborn, first male offspring, the oldest son, S: 1060†, B: 114A, K: 127C, H: 40A

1148 בְּכֹרָה *bᵉkōrâ*, birthright, rights of the firstborn, S: 1062, B: 114C, K: 127D, H: 40B

1149 בִּכְרָה *bikrâ*, young cow-camel, S: 1072, B: 114C, K: 127D, H: 40B

1150 בֹּכְרוּ *bōkᵉrû*, Bokeru, S: 1074, B: 114B, K: 127D, H: 40B

1151 בַּכְרִי *bakrî*, Bekerite, S: 1076, B: 114B, K: 127D, H: 40B

1152 בִּכְרִי *bikrî*, Bicri, S: 1075, B: 114B, K: 128A, H: 40B

1153 ¹בַּל *bal*[1], no, not, cannot, never, S: 1077, B: 115B, K: 128A, H: 40B

1154 ²בַּל *bal*[2], variant: surely, S: 1077, B: 115B, K: 128A, H: 40B

1155 בֵּל *bēl*, Bel, S: 1078, B: 128C, K: 128B, H: 40C

1156 בַּלְאֲדָן *bal'ᵃdān*, Baladan, S: 1081, B: 114D, K: 128B, H: 40C

1157 בֵּלְאשַׁצַּר *bēl'šaṣṣar*, Belshazzar, S: 1112, B: 128D, K: 131D, H: 41D

1158 בָּלַג *bālag*, [G] to flash, gleam; smile, rejoice, S: 1082, B: 114D, K: 128B, H: 40C

1159 בִּלְגָּה *bilgâ*, Bilgah, S: 1083, B: 114D, K: 128C, H: 40C

1160 בִּלְגַּי *bilgay*, Bilgai, S: 1084, B: 114D, K: 128C, H: 40C

1161 בִּלְדַּד *bildad*, Bildad, S: 1085, B: 115A, K: 128C, H: 40C

1162 ¹בָּלָה *bālâ*[1], [A] to wear out, waste away; [D] to enjoy, use to the full; to decay; to grow old; to oppress, S: 1086, B: 115A, K: 128C, H: 40C

1163 ²בָּלָה *bālâ*[2], Balah, S: 1088, B: 115A, K: 128D, H: 40C

1164 ³בָּלַהּ *bālah*[3], variant: [D] to be troubled, S: 1089, B: 117A, K: 128D, H: 40C

1165 בָּלֶה *bāleh*, old, worn-out, S: 1087, B: 115B, K: 128D, H: 40C

1166 בַּלָּהָה *ballāhâ*, sudden terror, horrible end, S: 1091, B: 117A, K: 129A, H: 40D

1167 ¹בִּלְהָה *bilhâ*[1], Bilhah, S: 1090, B: 117B, K: 129A, H: 40D

1168 ²בִּלְהָה *bilhâ*[2], Bilhah, S: 1090, B: 117B, K: 129A, H: 40D

1169 בִּלְהָן *bilhān*, Bilhan, S: 1092, B: 117B, K: 129A, H: 40D

1170 בְּלוֹי *bᵉlôy*, old, worn-out (things), S: 1094, B: 115B, K: 129B, H: 40D

1171 בֵּלְטְשַׁאצַּר *bēlṭᵉšā'ṣṣar*, Belteshazzar, S: 1095, B: 117B, K: 129B, H: 40D

1172 בְּלִי *bᵉlî*, lacking, without; nothing, S: 1097, B: 115C, K: 129B, H: 40D

1173 בְּלִיל *bᵉlîl*, fodder, S: 1098, B: 117D, K: 129D, H: 41A

1174 בְּלִימָה *bᵉlîmâ*, variant: nothing, S: 1099, B: 116A, K: 129D, H: 41A

1175 בְּלִיַּעַל *bᵉliyya'al*, wicked one, vile one, evil one, troublemaker, scoundrel, worthless one, S: 1100, B: 116A, K: 130A, H: 41A

1176 ¹בָּלַל *bālal*[1], [A] to confuse; feed; pour upon; [B] to mix (with); [F] to be thrown about, shaken back and forth, S: 1101, B: 117B, K: 130A, H: 41A

1177 ²בָּלַל *bālal*[2], variant: [A] to give fodder, feed, S: 1101, B: 117D, K: 130A, H: 41A

1178 בָּלַם *bālam*, [A] to be controlled, S: 1102, B: 117D, K: 130A, H: 41B

1179 בָּלַס *bālas*, [A] to nip (scratch open) unripe sycamore-fig fruit, S: 1103, B: 118A, K: 130A, H: 41B

1180 ¹בָּלַע *bāla'*[1], [A] to swallow up; [C] to be swallowed; [D] to swallow up, gulp down, devour, consume; [E] be swallowed up, be devoured, S: 1104, B: 118A, K: 130C, H: 41B

1181 ²בָּלַע *bāla'*[2], variant: [D] to communicate, spread abroad; [E] be communicated (to a person), S: 1104, B: 118C 2.c, K: 131A, H: 41B

1182 ³בָּלַע *bāla'*[3], [C] be befuddled, confused; [D] to confuse, turn away; [E] to be led astray; [F] to be confused thoroughly, S: 1104, B: 118B, K: 131A, H: 41C

1183 ¹בֶּלַע *bela'*[1], what is swallowed, S: 1105, B: 118C, K: 131B, H: 41C

1184 ²בֶּלַע *bela'*[2], harmful, S: 1105, B: 118C, K: 131B, H: 41C

1185 ³בֶּלַע *bela'*[3], Bela, S: 1106, B: 118C, K: 131B, H: 41C

1186 ⁴בֶּלַע *bela'*[4], Bela, S: 1106, B: 118D, K: 131B, H: 41C

1187 בַּלְעֲדֵי *bal'ᵃdê*, apart from, except for, besides, S: 1107, B: 116B, K: 131B, H: 41C

1188 בַּלְעִי *bal'î*, Belaite, S: 1108, B: 118D, K: 131C, H: 41C

1189 ¹בִּלְעָם *bil'ām*[1], Balaam, S: 1109, B: 118D, K: 131C, H: 41C

1190 ²בִּלְעָם *bil'ām*[2], Bileam, S: 1109, B: 118D, K: 131D, H: 41D

1191 בָּלַק *bālaq*, [A] to devastate; [E] to be stripped, devastated, S: 1110, B: 118D, K: 131D, H: 41D

1192 בָּלָק *bālāq*, Balak, S: 1111, B: 118D, K: 131D, H: 41D

1193 בִּלְשָׁן *bilšān*, Bilshan, S: 1114, B: 119A, K: 131D, H: 41D

1194 בִּלְתִּי *biltî*, no, not, without; except for; besides, S: 1115, B: 116C, K: 131D, H: 41D

1195 ¹בָּמָה *bāmâ*[1], high place, worship shrine; heights, S: 1116, B: 119A, K: 132B, H: 42A

1196 ²בָּמָה *bāmâ*[2], Bamah, S: 1117, B: 119D, K: 132B, H: 42A 4.

1197 בִּמְהָל *bimhāl*, Bimhal, S: 1118, B: 119D, K: 132D, H: 42A

1198 בְּמוֹ *bᵉmô*, by, with, in, S: 1119, B: 91B, K*, H: 42A

1199 בָּמוֹת *bāmôt*, Bamoth, S: 1120, B: 119D, K: 132D, H: 42A

1200 בָּמוֹת בַּעַל *bāmôt ba'al*, Bamoth Baal, S: 1120, B: 119D, K: 132D, H: 42C

1201 ¹בֵּן *bēn*[1], son, child, grandchild, descendant; people; one of a class or kind or nation or family, S: 1121, B: 119D, K: 133A, H: 42A

1202 ²בֵּן *bēn*[2], variant: Ben, S: 1122, B: 122A, K: 134A, H: 42C

1203 בֶּן־אֲבִינָדָב *ben-'ᵃbînādāb*, Ben-Abinadab, S: 1125, B: 122A, K: 5B, H: 2D

1204 בֶּן־אוֹנִי *ben-'ônî*, Ben-Oni, S: 1126, B: 122B, K: 134A, H: 42C

1205 בֶּן־גֶּבֶר *ben-geber*, Ben-Geber, S: 1127, B: 122B, K: 168C, H: 55A

1206 בֶּן־דֶּקֶר *ben-deqer*, Ben-Deker, S: 1128, B: 122B, K: 216D, H: 73D

1207 בֶּן־הֲדַד *ben-hᵃdad*, Ben-Hadad, S: 1130, B: 122B, K: 134A, H: 42C

1208 בֶּן־הִנֹּם *ben-hinnōm*, Ben Hinnom, S: 2011†, B: 244D, K: 179D, H: 82C

1209 בֶּן־זוֹחֵת *ben-zôḥēt*, Ben-Zoheth, S: 1132, B: 122B, K: 134B, H: 42C

1210 בֶּן־חוּר *ben-ḥûr*, Ben-Hur, S: 1133, B: 122B, K: 283D, H: 42C

1211 בֶּן־חַיִל *ben-ḥayil*, Ben-Hail, S: 1134, B: 122C, K: 134B, H: 42C

1212 בֶּן־חָנָן *ben-ḥānān*, Ben-Hanan, S: 1135, B: 122C, K: 134B, H: 42C

1213 בֶּן־חֶסֶד *ben-ḥesed*, Ben-Hesed, S: 1136, B: 122C, K: 318D, H: 111C

1214 בֶּן־עַמִּי *ben-'ammî*, Ben-Ammi, S: 1151, B: 122C, K: 710B, H*

1215 בָּנָה *bānâ*, [A] to make, build, rebuild, establish; [B, C] to be built, established, S: 1129, B: 124A, K: 134B, H: 42D

1216 בְּנֹב *bᵉnōb*, variant: Benob, S*, B: 444A, K*, H*

1217 בְּנוֹ *bᵉnô*, Beno, S: 1121, B: 122B, K*, H*

1218 בִּנּוּי *binnûy*, Binnui, S: 1131, B: 125A, K: 135A, H: 43A

1219 בְּנוֹת *b^{e}nôt*, variant: Benoth, see 6112, S: 5524†, B: 696D, K: 657B, H: 256A

1220 בָּנִי *bānî*, Bani, S: 1137, B: 125B, K: 135A, H: 43A

1221 בֻּנִּי *bunnî*, Bunni, S: 1138, B: 125B, K: 135A, H: 35D & 43A

1222 בְּנֵי־בְרַק *b^{e}nê-b^{e}raq*, Bene Berak, S: 1139, B: 122C, K: 135A, H: 43A

1223 בְּנֵי יַעֲקָן *b^{e}nê ya'^{a}qān*, Bene Jaakan, S: 1142, B: 122C, K: 135A, H: 43A

1224 בִּנְיָה *binyâ*, building, S: 1140, B: 125B, K: 135A, H: 43A

1225 בְּנָיָה *b^{e}nāyâ*, Benaiah, S: 1141, B: 125C, K: 135A, H: 43A

1226 בְּנָיָהוּ *b^{e}nāyāhû*, Benaiah, S: 1141, B: 125C, K: 135B, H: 43A

1227 בֵּנַיִם *bēnayim*, champion, single fighter, S: 1143, B: 108A, K: 135B, H: 43A

1228 בִּנְיָמִין *binyāmîn*, בֶּן־יָמִין *ben-yāmîn*, Benjamin, S: 1144, B: 122C, K: 135B, H: 43A

1229 בֶּן־יְמִינִי *ben-y^{e}mînî*, בִּנְיְמִינִי *beny^{e}mînî*, Benjamite, of Benjamin, S: 1145, B: 122D & 412B, K: 135D, H: 43A

1230 בִּנְיָן *binyān*, building, outer wall, S: 1146, B: 125C, K: 135D, H: 43A

1231 בְּנִינוּ *b^{e}nînû*, Beninu, S: 1148, B: 123A, K: 135D, H: 43A

1232 בִּנְעָא *bin'ā'*, Binea, S: 1150, B: 126A, K: 135D, H: 43A

1233 בְּסוֹדְיָה *b^{e}sôd^{e}yâ*, Besodeiah, S: 1152, B: 126A, K: 135D, H: 43A

1234 בֵּסַי *bēsay*, Besai, S: 1153, B: 126A, K: 135D, H: 43B

1235 בֹּסֶר *bōser*, unripe grapes, sour grapes, S: 1154† & 1155, B: 126A, K: 135D, H: 43B

1236 בַּעֲבוּר *ba'^{a}bûr*, variant: for the sake of; on account of; for; in order that, S*, B: 721A, K: 674B, H: 262C

1237 בַּעַד[1] *ba'ad*[1], behind; through, over; around; from; on behalf of, for (benefit of), S: 1157†, B: 126B, K: 136A, H: 43B

1238 בַּעַד[2] *ba'ad*[2], variant: price, payment, S: 1157†, B: 126B, K: 136A, H: 43C

1239 בָּעָה[1] *bā'â*[1], [A] to ask, inquire; [C] to be pillaged, searched out, S: 1158, B: 126D, K: 136C, H: 43C

1240 בָּעָה[2] *bā'â*[2], [A] to boil; [C] to bulge, be swollen, S: 1158, B: 126D, K: 136C, H: 43C

1241 בְּעוּלָה *b^{e}'ûlâ*, Beulah, S: 1166†, B: 127A, K: 137A, H: 43D

1242 בְּעוֹר *b^{e}'ôr*, Beor, S: 1160, B: 129D, K: 136D, H: 43C

1243 בִּעוּת *bi'ût*, terror, S: 1161†, B: 130A, K: 136D, H: 43C

1244 בֹּעַז[1] *bō'az*[1], Boaz, S: 1162, B: 126D, K: 136D, H: 43C

1245 בֹּעַז[2] *bō'az*[2], Boaz, S: 1162, B: 127A, K: 136D, H: 43C

1246 בָּעַט *bā'aṭ*, [A] to kick (in scorn), S: 1163, B: 127A, K: 136D, H: 43C

1247 בְּעִי *b^{e}'î*, variant: ?, S: 1164, B: 730C, K: 699A, H: 43C

1248 בְּעִיר *b^{e}'îr*, animals, livestock, cattle, S: 1165, B: 129C, K: 137A, H: 43C

1249 בָּעַל[1] *bā'al*[1], [A] to rule over; to marry, be a husband; [B, C] to be married, have a husband, S: 1166, B: 127A, K: 137A, H: 43D

1250 בָּעַל[2] *bā'al*[2], variant: [A] to make, S: 1167†, B: 127A, K: 137A, H: 43D

1251 בַּעַל[1] *ba'al*[1], 1) Baal (pagan god); 2) husband, master, owner, citizen, S: 1167, B: 127B, K: 137B, H: 43D

1252 בַּעַל[2] *ba'al*[2], Baal, S: 1168, B: 127D 2., K: 138D, H: 44B

1253 בַּעַל בְּרִית *ba'al b^{e}rît*, Baal-Berith, S: 1170, B: 127D, K: 138B & 152A, H: 43D II.2.b.

1254 בַּעַל גָּד *ba'al gād*, Baal Gad, S: 1171, B: 128A, K: 139A, H: 44B 2.

1255 בַּעַל הָמוֹן *ba'al hāmôn*, Baal Hamon, S: 1174, B: 128A, K: 139A, H: 44B 3.

1256 בַּעַל זְבוּב *ba'al z^{e}bûb*, Baal-Zebub, S: 1176, B: 127B II.4., K: 248A, H: 44B II.2.c

1257 בַּעַל חָנָן *ba'al ḥānān*, Baal-Hanan, S: 1177, B: 128A, K: 139B, H: 44B

1258 בַּעַל חָצוֹר *ba'al ḥāṣôr*, Baal Hazor, S: 1178, B: 128A, K: 139B, H: 44B 4.

1259 בַּעַל חֶרְמוֹן *ba'al ḥermôn*, Baal Hermon, S: 1179, B: 128A, K: 139B, H: 44B 5.

1260 בַּעַל מְעוֹן *ba'al m^{e}'ôn*, Baal Meon, S: 1186, B: 128B, K: 139C, H: 44B 7.

1261 בַּעַל פְּעוֹר *ba'al p^{e}'ôr*, Baal Peor, S: 1187, B: 128B, K: 770B, H: 44B 8.

1262 בַּעַל־פְּרָצִים *ba'al-p^{e}rāṣîm*, Baal Perazim, S: 1188, B: 128B, K: 139C, H: 44B 9.

1263 בַּעַל צְפֹן *ba'al ṣ^{e}pōn*, Baal Zephon, S: 1189, B: 128B & 861B, K: 139C, H: 44B 10.

1264 בַּעַל שָׁלִשָׁה *ba'al šālišâ*, Baal Shalishah, S: 1190, B: 128B, K: 139C, H: 44B 11.

1265 בַּעַל תָּמָר *ba'al tāmār*, Baal Tamar, S: 1193, B: 128B, K: 139C, H: 44B 12.

1266 בַּעֲלָה[1] *ba'^{a}lâ*[1], mistress (of sorceries); (female) owner, S: 1172 & 1180†, B: 128B, K: 139A, H: 44B

1267 בַּעֲלָה[2] *ba'^{a}lâ*[2], Baalah, S: 1173, B: 128B, K: 139A, H: 44B

1268 בְּעָלוֹת *b^{e}'ālôt*, Bealoth, S: 1175, B: 128C, K: 139B, H: 44B

1269 בְּעֶלְיָדָע *b^{e}'elyādā'*, Beeliada, S: 1182, B: 128C, K: 139B, H: 44B

1270 בְּעַלְיָה *b^{e}'alyâ*, Bealiah, S: 1183 & 1184†, B: 128C, K: 139B, H: 44C

1271 בַּעֲלִיס *ba'^{a}lîs*, Baalis, S: 1185, B: 128D, K: 139C, H: 44C

1272 בַּעֲלָת *ba'^{a}lāt*, Baalath, S: 1191, B: 128C & 127D 1., K: 139A, H: 44C

1273 בַּעֲלַת בְּאֵר *ba'^{a}lat b^{e}'ēr*, Baalath Beer, S: 1192, B: 128C, K: 139C, H: 44C

1274 בְּעֹן *b^{e}'ōn*, Beon, S: 1194, B: 111A, K: 139C, H: 44C

1275 בַּעֲנָא *ba'^{a}nā'*, Baana, S: 1195, B: 128D, K: 139D, H: 44C

1276 בַּעֲנָה *ba'^{a}nâ*, Baanah, S: 1196, B: 128D, K: 139D, H: 44C

1277 בָּעַר[1] *bā'ar*[1], [A] to burn; [D] to light a fire, set a blaze; [E] to be burning; [F] to start a fire, consume with fire, S: 1197, B: 128D, K: 139D, H: 44C

1278 בָּעַר[2] *bā'ar*[2], [C] to be purged; [D] to purge, remove, get rid of; [G] to graze, S: 1197, B: 128D, K: 140B, H: 44D

1279 בָּעַר[3] *bā'ar*[3], [A] to be senseless, to be brutal; [C] to behave senseless, S: 1197, B: 129C, K: 140C, H: 44D

1280 בַּעַר *ba'ar*, senselessness, stupidity, ignorance, S: 1198, B: 129D, K: 140D, H: 44D

1281 בַּעֲרָא *ba'^{a}rā'*, Baara, S: 1199, B: 129D, K: 140D, H: 45A

1282 בְּעֵרָה *b^{e}'ērâ*, fire, S: 1200, B: 129C, K: 140D, H: 45A

1283 בַּעֲשֵׂיָה *ba'^{a}śēyâ*, Baaseiah, S: 1202, B: 129D, K: 140D, H: 45A

1284 בַּעְשָׁא *ba'šā'*, Baasha, S: 1201, B: 129D, K: 140D, H: 45A

1285 בְּעֶשְׁתְּרָה *b^{e}'ešt^{e}râ*, Be Eshtarah, S: 1203, B: 129D, K: 140D, H: 45A

1286 בָּעַת *bā'at*, [C] to be afraid, be terrified; [D] to torment, terrify, overwhelm, S: 1204, B: 129D, K: 141A, H: 45A

1287 בְּעָתָה *b^{e}'ātâ*, terror, S: 1205, B: 130A, K: 141A, H: 45A

1288 בֹּץ *bōṣ*, mud, S: 1206, B: 130C, K: 141B, H: 45A

1289 בִּצָּה *biṣṣâ*, marsh, swamp, S: 1207, B: 130C, K: 141B, H: 45A

1290 בָּצוּר *bāṣûr*, fortified, S: 1208†, B: 130D, K: 141B, H: 45A

1291 בֵּצַי *bēṣay*, Bezai, S: 1209, B: 130A, K: 141C, H: 45A

1292 בָּצִיר[1] *bāṣîr*[1], grape harvest; grapes; vineyard, S: 1210, B: 131B, K: 141C, H: 45A

1293 בָּצִיר[2] *bāṣîr*[2], dense, inaccessible (forest), S: 1210, B: 131B, K: 141C, H: 45A

1294 בָּצָל *bāṣāl*, onion, S: 1211†, B: 130B, K: 141C, H: 45B

1295 בְּצַלְאֵל *b^{e}ṣal'ēl*, Bezalel, S: 1212, B: 130B, K: 141C, H: 45B

1296 בַּצְלוּת *baṣlût*, Bazluth, S: 1213, B: 130B, K: 141D, H: 45B

1297 בַּצְלִית *baṣlît*, variant: Bazlith, S: 1213, B: 130B, K: 141D, H: 45B

1298 בָּצַע *bāṣa'*, [A] to cut off; to be greedy, make unjust gain; [D] to cut off; to finish; to make unjust gain, S: 1214, B: 130B, K: 141D, H: 45B

1299 בֶּצַע *beṣa'*, ill-gotten gain, dishonest gain; cutting off, S: 1215, B: 130C, K: 142A, H: 45B

1300 בְּצַעֲנַנִּים *b^{e}ṣa'^{a}nannîm*, variant: Bezaanannim, S: 6815†, B: 130C, K: 142B, H: 45C

1301 בָּצֵק[1] *bāṣēq*[1], [A] to swell, become swollen, S: 1216, B: 130D, K: 142B, H: 45A

1302 בָּצֵק[2] *bāṣēq*[2], dough, S: 1217, B: 130D, K: 142B, H: 45C

1303 בִּצְקָלוֹן *biṣqālôn*, variant: head of grain, S: 6861†, B: 862D, K: 814D, H: 45C

1304 בָּצְקַת *boṣqat*, Bozkath, S: 1218, B: 130D, K: 142B, H: 45C

1305 בָּצַר[1] *bāṣar*[1], [A] to harvest, gather grapes, S: 1219, B: 130D, K: 142C, H: 45C

1306 [2]בָּצַר *bāṣar*[2], [A] to humble, break (the spirit), S: 1219, B: 130D, K: 142C, H: 45C

1307 [3]בָּצַר *bāṣar*[3], [C] to be impossible, be thwarted; [D] to strengthen, fortify, S: 1219, B: 131A, K: 142C, H: 45C

1308 [4]בָּצַר *bāṣar*[4], variant: [D] to test gold, assay, S*, B: 131C, K: 142C, H: 45C

1309 [1]בֶּצֶר *beṣer*[1], gold ore, S: 1220 & 1222†, B: 131A, K: 142D, H: 45C

1310 [2]בֶּצֶר *beṣer*[2], Bezer, S: 1221, B: 131A 2., K: 142D, H: 45D

1311 [3]בֶּצֶר *beṣer*[3], Bezer, S: 1221, B: 131A 1., K: 142D, H: 45D

1312 [1]בָּצְרָה *boṣrâ*[1], pen, sheep-fold, S: 1223, B: 131B, K: 142D, H*

1313 [2]בָּצְרָה *boṣrâ*[2], Bozrah, S: 1224, B: 131B, K: 142D, H: 45D

1314 בַּצָּרָה *baṣṣārâ*, drought; trouble, S: 1226, B: 131B, K: 143A, H: 45D

1315 בִּצָּרוֹן *biṣṣārôn*, fortress, stronghold, S: 1225, B: 131B, K: 143A, H: 45D

1316 בַּצֹּרֶת *baṣṣōret*, drought, S: 1226, B: 131B, K: 143A, H: 45D

1317 בַּקְבּוּק *baqbûq*, Bakbuk, S: 1227, B: 132D, K: 143A, H: 45D

1318 בַּקְבֻּק *baqbuq*, jar, S: 1228, B: 132D, K: 143A, H: 45D

1319 בַּקְבֻּקְיָה *baqbuqyâ*, Bakbukiah, S: 1229, B: 132D, K: 143B, H: 45D

1320 בַּקְבַּקַּר *baqbaqqar*, Bakbakkar, S: 1230, B: 131C, K: 143B, H: 45D

1321 בֻּקִּי *buqqî*, Bukki, S: 1231, B: 131C, K: 143B, H: 45D

1322 בֻּקִּיָּהוּ *buqqiyyāhû*, Bukkiah, S: 1232†, B: 131C, K: 143B, H: 45D

1323 בָּקִיעַ *bāqîa'*, breach (in a defense); bits, debris, S: 1233†, B: 132C, K: 143B, H: 45D

1324 בָּקַע *bāqa'*, [A] to divide, split, tear open; [C] to be split, burst open; [D] to split open, burst forth; [E] to be cracked open, broken through, ripped open; [G] to break through, divide; [H] to be broken through; [F] to split apart, S: 1234, B: 131D, K: 143B, H: 46A

1325 בֶּקַע *beqa'*, beka (half-shekel), S: 1235, B: 132B, K: 144A, H: 46B

1326 בִּקְעָה *biq'â*, valley, plain, S: 1237, B: 132C, K: 144B, H: 46B

1327 [1]בָּקַק *bāqaq*[1], [A] to lay waste, ruin, destroy; [C] to be laid waste; [D] to devastate, S: 1238, B: 132C, K: 144C, H: 46C

1328 [2]בָּקַק *bāqaq*[2], [A] to grow abundantly, spread out, S: 1238, B: 132C, K: 144C, H: 46C

1329 בָּקַר *bāqar*, [D] to inspect, seek; look after; consider, S: 1239, B: 133A, K: 144C, H: 46C

1330 בָּקָר *bāqār*, animal, cow, bull; cattle, oxen, herd, S: 1241, B: 133A, K: 144D, H: 46C

1331 [1]בֹּקֶר *bōqer*[1], variant: sacrifice for omens, S: 1242, B: 134A 1.d., K: 145B, H: 46D

1332 [2]בֹּקֶר *bōqer*[2], morning, S: 1242, B: 133C, K: 145B, H: 46D

1333 בַּקָּרָה *baqqārâ*, looking after, S: 1243, B: 134C, K: 145D, H: 46D

1334 בִּקֹּרֶת *biqqōret*, due punishment, S: 1244, B: 134C, K: 145D, H: 46D

1335 בָּקַשׁ *bāqaš*, [D] to seek, search, look for, inquire about; [E] be sought, be investigated, S: 1245, B: 134C, K: 145D, H: 46D

1336 בַּקָּשָׁה *baqqāšâ*, request, S: 1246, B: 135A, K: 146C, H: 47A

1337 [1]בַּר *bar*[1], son, S: 1248, B: 135A, K: 146C, H: 47B

1338 [2]בַּר *bar*[2], pure; empty; favorite; radiant, bright, S: 1249, B: 141A, K: 146C, H: 47B

1339 [3]בַּר *bar*[3], grain, wheat, S: 1250, B: 141B, K: 146C, H: 47B

1340 [4]בַּר *bar*[4], wilds, in the open field, S: 1250, B: 141B, K: 146D, H: 47B

1341 [1]בֹּר *bōr*[1], cleanness, S: 1252, B: 141B, K: 146D, H: 47B

1342 [2]בֹּר *bōr*[2], soda, potash, lye, S: 1253, B: 141B, K: 146D, H: 47B

1343 [1]בָּרָא *bārā'*[1], [A] to create, Creator; [C] to be created, S: 1254, B: 135B, K: 146D, H: 47B

1344 [2]בָּרָא *bārā'*[2], [G] to fatten, S: 1254, B: 135D, K: 147C, H: 47C

1345 [3]בָּרָא *bārā'*[3], [D] to cut, cut down, clear (a forest), S: 1254, B: 135C 3., K: 147C, H: 47C

1346 [4]בָּרָא *bārā'*[4], variant: see 1356, S: 1262, B: 136A, K: 147D, H: 47C

1347 בְּרֹאדַךְ־בַּלְאֲדָן *bᵉrō'dak-bal'ᵃdān*, variant: Berodach-Baladan, see 5282, S: 1255, B: 597D, K: 147D, H: 47C

1348 בִּרְאִי *bir'î*, variant: Biri, S: 1011†, B: 111A, K: 124A 6., H: 39B 7.

1349 בְּרָאיָה *bᵉrā'yâ*, Beraiah, S: 1256, B: 135C, K: 147D, H: 47C

1350 בַּרְבֻּר *barbur*, fowl, bird, S: 1257, B: 141B, K: 147D, H: 47C

1351 בָּרַד *bārad*, [A] to shower hail, S: 1258, B: 136A, K: 147D, H: 47C

1352 בָּרָד *bārād*, hail, hailstones, S: 1259, B: 135D, K: 148A, H: 47C

1353 בָּרֹד *bārōd*, spotted, dappled, S: 1261, B: 136A, K: 148A, H: 47C

1354 [1]בֶּרֶד *bered*[1], Bered, S: 1260, B: 136A 1., K: 148A, H: 47C

1355 [2]בֶּרֶד *bered*[2], Bered, S: 1260, B: 136A 2., K: 148A, H: 47C

1356 [1]בָּרָה *bārâ*[1], [A] to eat; [G] to give to eat, urge to eat, S: 1262 & 1274†, B: 136A, K: 148A, H: 47C

1357 [2]בָּרָה *bārâ*[2], variant: [A] to enter into a covenant, S: 1262 & 1274†, B: 136B, K: 148B, H: 47D

1358 בָּרוּךְ *bārûk*, Baruch, S: 1263, B: 140A, K: 148B, H: 47D

1359 בָּרוּר *bārûr*, pure, sincere, S: 1305†, B: 140D, K: 148C, H: 47D

1360 בְּרוֹשׁ *bᵉrôš*, pine tree, S: 1265, B: 141B, K: 148C, H: 47D

1361 בְּרוֹת *bᵉrôt*, fir tree, S: 1266†, B: 141C, K: 148D, H: 48A

1362 בָּרוּת *bārût*, food, S: 1267, B: 136A, K: 148D, H: 48A

1363 בֵּרוֹתָה *bērôtâ*, Berothah, S: 1268, B: 92D, K: 148D, H: 48A

1364 בִּרְזָוִת *birzāwit*, variant: Birzavith, see 1365, S: 1269†, B: 137B, K: 148D, H: 48A

1365 בִּרְזָיִת *birzāyit*, Birzaith, S: 1269†, B: 137B, K: 148D, H: 48A

1366 בַּרְזֶל *barzel*, iron, iron (implements), S: 1270, B: 137B, K: 148D, H: 48A

1367 בַּרְזִלַּי *barzillay*, Barzillai, S: 1271, B: 137D, K: 149B, H: 48A

1368 [1]בָּרַח *bāraḥ*[1], [A] to flee, run away, escape; [G] to drive out, make flee, S: 1272, B: 137D, K: 149B, H: 48A

1369 [2]בָּרַח *bāraḥ*[2], variant: [G] to injure, S: 1272, B: 138A, K: 149B, H: 48B

1370 [3]בָּרַח *bāraḥ*[3], variant: [G] to make impassable, S: 1272, B: 138A, K: 149B, H: 48B

1371 בָּרִחַ *bāriaḥ*, gliding; fugitive, S: 1281, B: 138A, K: 149D, H: 48B

1372 בַּרְחֻמִי *barḥumî*, Barhumite, S: 1273, B: 138C, K: 149D, H: 48B

1373 בֵּרִי *bērî*, Beri, S: 1275, B: 92D, K: 149D, H: 48B

1374 בָּרִיא *bārî'*, fat, choice, healthy, S: 1277, B: 135D, K: 149D, H: 48B

1375 בְּרִיאָה *bᵉrî'â*, created thing, S: 1278, B: 135C, K: 150A, H: 48B

1376 בִּרְיָה *biryâ*, food, S: 1279, B: 136A, K: 150A, H: 48B

1377 בָּרִיחַ *bārîaḥ*, Bariah, S: 1282, B: 138A, K: 150A, H: 48B

1378 בְּרִיחַ *bᵉrîaḥ*, bar, gate bar, crossbar, S: 1280, B: 138B, K: 150A, H: 48B

1379 בֵּרִים *bērîm*, Berite, S: 1276†, B: 138C, K: 150B, H: 48C

1380 בְּרִיעָה *bᵉrî'â*, Beriah, S: 1283, B: 140B, K: 150B, H: 48C & 50B

1381 בְּרִיעִי *bᵉrî'î*, Beriite, S: 1284, B: 140B, K: 150B, H: 48C

1382 בְּרִית *bᵉrît*, covenant, treaty, compact, agreement, S: 1285, B: 136B, K: 150C, H: 48C

1383 בֹּרִית *bōrît*, soap, S: 1287, B: 141B, K: 152D, H: 49B

1384 [1]בָּרַךְ *bārak*[1], [A] to kneel down; [G] to make kneel, S: 1288, B: 138C, K: 153A, H: 49C

1385 [2]בָּרַךְ *bārak*[2], [D] to bless, pronounce blessings, give praise, give thanks, extol; [B, C, E] to be blessed, be praised; [F] to bless oneself, be blessed, S: 1288, B: 138C, K: 153A, H: 49C

1386 בֶּרֶךְ *berek*, knee, S: 1290, B: 139C, K: 154C, H: 50A

1387 בַּרַכְאֵל *barak'ēl*, Barakel, S: 1292, B: 140A, K: 154D, H: 50A

1388 [1]בְּרָכָה *bᵉrākâ*[1], blessing; gift, S: 1293, B: 139C, K: 154D, H: 50B

1389 [2]בְּרָכָה *bᵉrākâ*[2], Beracah, S: 1294, B: 139D 2., K: 155A, H: 50B

1390 [3]בְּרָכָה *bᵉrākâ*[3], Beracah, S: 1294, B: 139D 1., K*, H*

1391 בְּרֵכָה *bᵉrēkâ*, pool, reservoir, S: 1295, B: 140A, K: 155A, H: 50B

1392 בֶּרֶכְיָה *berekyâ*, Berekiah, S: 1296, B: 140A, K: 155B, H: 50B

1393 בֶּרֶכְיָהוּ *berekyāhû*, Berekiah, S: 1296, B: 140A, K: 155B, H: 50B

1394 בְּרֹמִים *bᵉrōmîm*, multicolored, S: 1264, B: 140B, K: 155B, H: 50B

1395 בַּרְנֵעַ *barnēa'*, variant: Barnea, S: 6947†, B: 873D, K: 826D, H: 50B

1396 בֶּרַע *bera'*, Bera, S: 1298, B: 140B, K: 155C, H: 50B

1397 בָּרַק *bāraq*, [A] to flash lightning, S: 1299, B: 140B, K: 155C, H: 50B

1398 [1]בָּרָק *bārāq*[1], lightning bolt, flash of lightning, S: 1300, B: 140C, K: 155D, H: 50C

1399 [2]בָּרָק *bārāq*[2], Barak, S: 1301, B: 140C, K: 155D, H: 50C

[F] Hitpael (hitpoel, hitpoal, hitpolel, hitpolal, hitpalel, hitpalal, hitpalpel, hitpalpal, hotpael, hotpaal) [G] Hiphil (hiphtil) [H] Hophal [I] Hishtaphel

1400 בְּרַק *bᵉraq*, variant: Berak, S: 1139†, B: 122C, K: 135A, H: 50C

1401 בַּרְקוֹס *barqôs*, Barkos, S: 1302, B: 140D, K: 156A, H: 50C

1402 בַּרְקֹן *barqōn*, brier, S: 1303†, B: 140D, K: 156A, H: 50C

1403 בָּרֶקֶת *bāreqet*, beryl, S: 1304†, B: 140C, K: 156A, H: 50C

1404 בָּרְקַת *bārᵉqat*, beryl, S: 1304, B: 140D, K: 156A, H: 50C

1405 [1]בָּרַר *bārar*[1], [A] to purge; [B] to be chosen, be choice; [C] to keep clean, be pure; [D] purify; [G] to cleanse; [F] to show oneself pure, S: 1305, B: 140D, K: 156B, H: 50C

1406 [2]בָּרַר *bārar*[2], [B] to be sharpened, polished, [G] to sharpen, S: 1305, B: 140D, K: 156B, H: 50C

1407 בִּרְשַׁע *birša'*, Birsha, S: 1306, B: 141D, K: 156C, H: 50D

1408 בֵּרֹתַי *bērōtay*, Berothai, S: 1268, B: 92D, K: 156C, H: 50D

1409 בֵּרֹתִי *bērōtî*, Berothite, S: 1307, B: 92D, K: 156C, H: 50D

1410 בְּשׂוֹר *bᵉśôr*, Besor, S: 1308, B: 143A, K: 156C, H: 50D

1411 בֹּשֶׂם *bōśem*, spices, perfume, fragrance, S: 1313† & 1314, B: 141D, K: 156C, H: 50D

1412 בָּשְׂמַת *bāśᵉmat*, Basemath, S: 1315, B: 142A, K: 156D, H: 50D

1413 בָּשַׂר *bāśar*, [D] to bring (good) news, proclaim (good) news; [F] to hear news, S: 1319, B: 142A, K: 156D, H: 50D

1414 בָּשָׂר *bāśār*, flesh: living things, mankind, body, meat, S: 1320, B: 142B, K: 157A, H: 51A

1415 בְּשׂרָה *bᵉśōrâ*, news, good news, S: 1309, B: 142D, K: 157D, H: 51B

1416 בַּשֶּׁבֶת *baššebet*, variant: Basshebeth, S*, B: 444A, K: 410C, H: 146C

1417 בְּשַׁגַּם *bᵉšaggam*, variant: see 928, 8611, 1685, S: 7683†, B: 88A & 979B & 168D, K: 102A & 933D & 186B, H: 51B

1418 בָּשַׁל *bāšal*, [A] to ripen; boil; [D] to cook, boil, roast, bake; [E] to be cooked, be boiled; [G] ripen, S: 1310, B: 143A, K: 157D, H: 51B

1419 בָּשֵׁל *bāšēl*, cooked, boiled, S: 1311, B: 143B, K: 158A, H: 51B

1420 בִּשְׁלָם *bišlām*, Bishlam, S: 1312, B: 143B, K: 158A, H: 51B

1421 [1]בָּשָׁן *bāšān*[1], Bashan, S: 1316, B: 143B, K: 158B, H: 51C

1422 [2]בָּשָׁן *bāšān*[2], variant: serpent, S: 1316, B: 143B, K: 158A, H: 51C

1423 בָּשְׁנָה *bošnâ*, disgrace, shame, S: 1317, B: 102A, K: 158C, H: 51C

1424 בָּשַׁס *bāšas*, [D] to trample, S: 1318, B: 143C, K: 158C, H: 51C

1425 בֹּשֶׁת *bōšet*, shame, disgrace, humiliation, S: 1322, B: 102A, K: 158C, H: 51C

1426 [1]בַּת *bat*[1], daughter, granddaughter; girl, woman; outlying village or settlement, S: 1323, B: 123A, K: 158D, H: 51C

1427 [2]בַּת *bat*[2], bath (liquid measure), S: 1324, B: 144C, K: 159D, H: 51D

1428 [3]בַּת *bat*[3], woven garment, S: 1004, B: 123A, K: 158D, H: 51D

1429 בָּתָה *bātâ*, wasteland, S: 1326, B: 144D, K: 159D, H: 51D

1430 בֹּתָה *bōtâ*, variant: see 2999, S*, B*, K: 159D, H: 51D

1431 בַּתָּה *battâ*, steep ravine, face of a cliff, S: 1327, B: 144C, K: 159D, H: 51D

1432 [1]בְּתוּאֵל *bᵉtû'ēl*[1], Bethuel, S: 1328, B: 143D, K: 159D, H: 51D

1433 [2]בְּתוּאֵל *bᵉtû'ēl*[2], Bethuel, S: 1328, B: 143D, K: 159D, H: 51D

1434 בְּתוּל *bᵉtûl*, Bethul, S: 1329, B: 143D, K: 160A, H: 51D

1435 בְּתוּלָה *bᵉtûlâ*, virgin, maiden, (unmarried) young women, S: 1330, B: 143D, K: 160A, H: 52A

1436 בְּתוּלִים *bᵉtûlîm*, virginity, proof of virginity, S: 1331, B: 144A, K: 160B, H: 52A

1437 בִּתְיָה *bityâ*, Bithiah, S: 1332, B: 124A, K: 160C, H: 52A

1438 בָּתַק *bātaq*, [D] to hack to pieces, slaughter, S: 1333, B: 144A, K: 160C, H: 52C

1439 בָּתַר *bātar*, [A, D] to cut in pieces, S: 1334, B: 144A, K: 160C, H: 52C

1440 [1]בֶּתֶר *beter*[1], piece, S: 1335, B: 144A 1., K: 160C, H: 52C

1441 [2]בֶּתֶר *beter*[2], ruggedness, S: 1336, B: 144A 2., K: 160D, H: 52C

1442 בַּת־רַבִּים *bat-rabbîm*, Bath Rabbim, S: 1337, B: 123D, K: 159D 5., H: 51C

1443 בִּתְרוֹן *bitrôn*, Bithron, S: 1338, B: 144C, K: 160D, H: 52C

1444 בַּת־שֶׁבַע *bat-šeba'*, Bathsheba, S: 1339, B: 124A, K: 160D, H: 52C

1445 בַּת־שׁוּעַ *bat-šûa'*, variant: Bath-Shua, S: 1340, B: 124A, K: 160D, H: 52C

1446 ג *g*, letter of the Hebrew alphabet, S*, B: 144B, K: 161A, H*

1447 גֵּא *gē'*, proud, S: 1341, B: 144B, K: 161C, H: 52A

1448 גָּאָה *gā'â*, [A] to grow tall, be high, to rise up; to be exalted, S: 1342, B: 144B, K: 161C, H: 52A

1449 גֵּאָה *gē'â*, pride, S: 1344, B: 144D, K: 161C, H: 52A

1450 גֵּאֶה *gē'eh*, proud, S: 1343, B: 144B, K: 161D, H: 52A

1451 גְּאוּאֵל *gᵉ'û'ēl*, Geuel, S: 1345, B: 145B, K: 161D, H: 52B

1452 גַּאֲוָה *ga'ᵃwâ*, surging; majesty, glory, triumph; pride, arrogance, conceit, S: 1346, B: 144D, K: 161D, H: 52B

1453 גְּאוּלִים *gᵉ'ûlîm*, redemption, S: 1350†, B: 145D, K: 162A, H: 52B

1454 גָּאוֹן *gā'ôn*, surging (waves), lush (high) thickets; majesty, splendor, glory; pride, arrogance, S: 1347, B: 144D, K: 162A, H: 52B

1455 גֵּאוּת *gē'ût*, surging (sea), rising (smoke); majesty, glory; pride, arrogance, S: 1348, B: 145A, K: 162B, H: 52B

1456 גַּאֲיוֹן *ga'ᵃyôn*, arrogant, S: 1349, B: 145B, K: 162B, H: 52C

1457 [1]גָּאַל *gā'al*[1], [A] to redeem, deliver (as noun) avenger; kinsman-redeemer; [B] to be redeemed; [C] to be redeemed, redeem oneself, S: 1350, B: 145B, K: 162C, H: 52C

1458 [2]גָּאַל *gā'al*[2], [C] to be stained, defiled; [D] to defile; [E] to be unclean, defiled; [G] to stain; [F] to defile oneself, S: 1351, B: 146A, K: 163B, H: 53A

1459 גֹּאַל *gō'al*, defilement, S: 1352, B: 146A, K: 163B, H: 53A

1460 גְּאֻלָּה *gᵉ'ullâ*, redemption, right of redemption; blood relatives, S: 1353, B: 145D, K: 163C, H: 53A & 52B

1461 [1]גַּב *gab*[1], eyebrow; rim (of a wheel); mound, back, S: 1354, B: 146B, K: 163C, H: 53B

1462 [2]גַּב *gab*[2], defense, S: 1354, B: 146B, K: 163C, H: 53B

1463 [1]גֵּב *gēb*[1], ditch; cistern, S: 1356, B: 155D, K: 163D, H: 53B

1464 [2]גֵּב *gēb*[2], beam, S: 1356, B: 155D, K: 163D, H: 53B

1465 גֶּבֶא *gebe'*, cistern; marsh, S: 1360, B: 146B, K: 163D, H: 53B

1466 גֵּבָה *gēbâ*, swarm (of locust), S: 1357†, B: 146D, K: 164A, H: 53B & 53B

1467 גָּבַהּ *gābah*, [A] to be tall, tower high; to exalt; to be proud, haughty, arrogant; [G] to make high, grow tall; exalt, S: 1361, B: 146D, K: 164A, H: 53B

1468 גָּבֵהַּ *gābēah*, proud, haughty; high, towered, S: 1362 & 1364, B: 147A, K: 164B, H: 53C

1469 גָּבֹהַּ *gābōah*, proud, haughty; high, tall, S: 1364, B: 147A, K: 164B, H: 53C

1470 גֹּבַהּ *gōbah*, tallness, height; splendor, majesty; pride, haughtiness, conceit, S: 1363, B: 147B, K: 164C, H: 53C

1471 גַּבְהוּת *gabhût*, arrogance, S: 1365, B: 147B, K: 164D, H: 53C

1472 גָּבוֹל *gābôl*, variant: boundary [?], S: 1366†, B: 147C, K: 164D, H: 53C

1473 גְּבוּל *gᵉbûl*, territory, boundary, border, S: 1366, B: 147C & D, K: 164D, H: 53C

1474 גְּבוּלָה *gᵉbûlâ*, boundary stone, border marker, S: 1367, B: 148B, K: 165A, H: 53D

1475 גִּבּוֹר *gibbôr*, mighty one, mighty warrior, special guard, S: 1368, B: 150A, K: 165B, H: 53D

1476 גְּבוּרָה *gᵉbûrâ*, power, strength, might, achievement, S: 1369, B: 150B, K: 165C, H: 54A

1477 גִּבֵּחַ *gibbēaḥ*, bald forehead, S: 1371, B: 147C, K: 166A, H: 54A

1478 גַּבַּחַת *gabbaḥat*, forehead, S: 1372, B: 147C, K: 166A, H: 54A

1479 גֹּבַי *gōbay*, swarm of locust, S: 1462†, B: 146D, K: 166A, H: 54B

1480 גַּבַּי *gabbay*, Gabbai, S: 1373, B: 146C, K: 166A, H: 54B

1481 גֵּבִים *gēbîm*, Gebim, S: 1374, B: 155D, K: 166A, H: 54B

1482 גְּבִינָה *gᵉbînâ*, cheese, S: 1385, B: 148C, K: 166A, H: 54B

1483 גָּבִיעַ *gābîa'*, cup, (drinking) bowl, S: 1375, B: 149B, K: 166B, H: 54B

1484 גְּבִיר *gᵉbîr*, lord, master, S: 1376, B: 150C, K: 166B, H: 54B

1485 גְּבִירָה *gᵉbîrâ*, mistress (female lord); queen, S: 1377, B: 150C, K: 166B, H: 54B

1486 גָּבִישׁ *gābîš*, jasper, S: 1378, B: 150D, K: 166C, H: 54B

1487 גָּבַל *gābal*, [A] to set up a boundary; [G] to put limits around (a geographical area), S: 1379, B: 148B, K: 166C, H: 54B

1488 גְּבַל *g^{e}bal*, Gebal, S: 1380, B: 148B, K: 166D, H: 54C

1489 גְּבָל *g^{e}bāl*, Gebal, S: 1381, B: 148C, K: 166D, H: 54C

1490 גִּבְלִי *giblî*, Gebalite, S: 1382, B: 148C, K: 166D, H: 54C

1491 גַּבְלֻת *gablut*, braided (gold chain), S: 1383, B: 148B, K: 166D, H: 54C

1492 גִּבֵּן *gibbēn*, hunchbacked, S: 1384, B: 148C, K: 167A, H: 54C

1493 גַּבְנֹן *gabnôn*, ruggedness, S: 1386, B: 148D, K: 167A, H: 54C

1494 גֶּבַע *geba'*, Geba, S: 1387, B: 148D, K: 167A, H: 54C

1495 גִּבְעָא *gib'ā'*, Gibea, S: 1388, B: 148D, K: 167B, H: 54C

1496 [1]גִּבְעָה *gib'â*[1], hill, hill top, height, S: 1389, B: 148D, K: 167B, H: 54C

1497 [2]גִּבְעָה *gib'â*[2], Gibeah, S: 1390, B: 149B, K: 167B, H: 54D

1498 גִּבְעוֹנִי *gib'ônî*, Gibeonite, of Gibeon, S: 1393, B: 149C, K: 167C, H: 54D

1499 גִּבְעֹל *gib'ōl*, bloom, S: 1392, B: 149C, K: 167D, H: 54D

1500 גִּבְעוֹן *gib'ōn*, Gibeon, S: 1391, B: 149C, K: 167C, H: 54D

1501 גִּבְעַת *gib'at*, variant: Gibeath, S: 1394, B: 149B, K: 167D, H: 54C

1502 גִּבְעַת הָעֲרָלוֹת *gib'at hā'^{a}rālôt*, Gibeath Haaraloth, S: 1394†, B: 149A 4., K: 167B, H: 54C 7.

1503 גִּבְעָתִי *gib'ātî*, Gibeathite, S: 1395, B: 149B, K: 167D, H*

1504 גָּבַר *gābar*, [A] to rise, flood; to be greater, stronger; to prevail, overwhelm; [D] to strengthen; [G] to cause to triumph, confirm (a covenant); [F] to show oneself as a victor, S: 1396 & 1399†, B: 149C, K: 167D, H: 54D

1505 [1]גֶּבֶר *geber*[1], (strong, young) man, S: 1397, B: 149D, K: 168A, H: 55A

1506 [2]גֶּבֶר *geber*[2], Geber, S: 1398, B: 150A, K: 168C, H: 55A

1507 גִּבָּר *gibbār*, Gibbar, S: 1402, B: 150A, K: 168C, H: 55A

1508 גַּבְרִיאֵל *gabrî'ēl*, Gabriel, S: 1403, B: 150C, K: 168C, H: 55A

1509 גְּבֶרֶת *g^{e}beret*, queen, S: 1404, B: 150C, K: 168C, H: 55A

1510 גִּבְּתוֹן *gibb^{e}tôn*, Gibbethon, S: 1405, B: 146D, K: 168C, H: 55B

1511 גָּג *gāg*, roof, top, S: 1406, B: 150D, K: 168C, H: 55B

1512 [1]גַּד *gad*[1], coriander, S: 1407, B: 151B, K: 168D, H: 55B

1513 [2]גַּד *gad*[2], good fortune; (as a pagan god) Fortune, S: 1408 & 1409†, B: 151C, K: 169A, H: 55B

1514 גָּד *gād*, Gad, S: 1410, B: 151C, K: 169A, H: 55B

1515 גִּדְגָּד *gidgād*, variant: Gidgad, see 2988, S: 2735†, B: 151D, K: 169B, H: 55B

1516 גֻּדְגֹּדָה *gudgōdâ*, Gudgodah, S: 1412, B: 151D, K: 169B, H: 55B

1517 [1]גָּדַד *gādad*[1], [F] to cut oneself, slash oneself, S: 1413, B: 151A, K: 169B, H: 55B

1518 [2]גָּדַד *gādad*[2], [A] to band together; [F] to marshall, band together against, S: 1413, B: 151A, K: 169B, H: 55C

1519 גָּדָה *gādâ*, variant: bank (of a river), S: 1415, B: 152A, K: 170D, H: 56A

1520 גַּדָּה *gaddâ*, variant: Gaddah, S: 2693†, B: 347C, K: 169C, H: 55C

1521 [1]גְּדוּד *g^{e}dûd*[1], ridge (of a furrow), S: 1417, B: 151B, K: 169B, H: 55C

1522 [2]גְּדוּד *g^{e}dûd*[2], band of raiders; band of rebels; bandits; troops, divisions, S: 1416, B: 151B, K: 169C, H: 55C

1523 גְּדוּדָה *g^{e}dûdâ*, slash, cut (of the skin), S: 1418, B: 151B, K: 169C, H: 55C

1524 גָּדוֹל *gādôl*, great, large; much, more, S: 1419, B: 152D, K: 169D, H: 55C

1525 גְּדוּלָּה *g^{e}dûllâ*, greatness, majesty, recognition, honor, S: 1420, B: 153C, K: 170B, H: 56A

1526 גִּדּוּף *giddûp*, taunt, scorn, S: 1421, B: 154D, K: 170C, H: 56A

1527 גְּדוּפָה *g^{e}dûpâ*, taunt, scorn, S: 1422, B: 154D, K: 170C, H: 56A

1528 גִּדּוּפָה *giddûpâ*, insult, S: 1421, B: 154D, K: 170C, H: 56A

1529 [1]גְּדוֹר *g^{e}dôr*[1], Gedor, S: 1446, B: 155B 3., K: 170C, H: 56A

1530 [2]גְּדוֹר *g^{e}dôr*[2], Gedor, S: 1446, B: 155B 1. & 2., K: 173A, H: 57A

1531 גְּדִי *g^{e}dî*, (male) young goat, S: 1423, B: 152A, K: 170C, H: 56A

1532 [1]גָּדִי *gādî*[1], Gadite, of Gad, S: 1425, B: 151D, K: 170D, H: 56A 1.

1533 [2]גָּדִי *gādî*[2], Gadi, S: 1424, B: 151D, K: 170D, H: 56A 2.

1534 גַּדִּי *gaddî*, Gaddi, S: 1426, B: 151D, K: 170D, H: 56A

1535 גַּדִּיאֵל *gaddî'ēl*, Gaddiel, S: 1427, B: 151D, K: 170D, H: 56A

1536 גִּדְיָה *gidyâ*, bank (of a river), S: 1428, B: 152A, K: 170D, H: 56A

1537 גְּדִיָּה *g^{e}diyyâ*, (female) young goat, S: 1429, B: 152A, K: 170C, H: 56A

1538 [1]גָּדִישׁ *gādîš*[1], shock of grain, sheaf of grain, S: 1430, B: 155C, K: 171A, H: 56A

1539 [2]גָּדִישׁ *gādîš*[2], tomb, S: 1430, B: 155C, K: 171A, H: 56B

1540 גָּדַל *gādal*, [A] to grow up; be great, exalted; [D] to grow long, make great; to exalt, honor, glorify; [E] to be well-nurtured; [G] to make great, cause greatness; [F] to magnify oneself, show greatness, S: 1431, B: 152B, K: 171A, H: 56B

1541 גָּדֵל *gādēl*, great, powerful, S: 1432, B: 152C, K: 172A, H: 56C

1542 גֹּדֶל *gōdel*, greatness, majesty, strength; pride, arrogance, S: 1433, B: 152D, K: 171D, H: 56C

1543 גִּדֵּל *giddēl*, Giddel, S: 1435, B: 153C, K: 172A, H: 56D

1544 גָּדִל *gādil*, tassel, festoon, S: 1434, B: 152D, K: 172A, H: 56D

1545 גְּדַלְיָה *g^{e}dalyâ*, Gedaliah, S: 1436, B: 153D, K: 172A, H: 56D

1546 גְּדַלְיָהוּ *g^{e}dalyāhû*, Gedaliah, S: 1436, B: 153D, K: 172A, H: 56D

1547 גִּדַּלְתִּי *giddaltî*, Giddalti, S: 1437, B: 153D, K: 172B, H: 56D

1548 גָּדַע *gāda'*, [A] to cut short, cut off, break; [D] to cut down, cut to pieces; [B, C, E] to be cut off, be cut down, S: 1438, B: 154B, K: 172B, H: 56D

1549 גִּדְעוֹן *gid'ôn*, Gideon, S: 1439, B: 154C, K: 172C, H: 57A

1550 גִּדְעֹם *gid'ōm*, Gidom, S: 1440, B: 154C, K: 172C, H: 57A

1551 גִּדְעֹנִי *gid'ōnî*, Gideoni, S: 1441, B: 154C, K: 172C, H: 57A

1552 גָּדַף *gādap*, [D] to blaspheme, revile, S: 1442, B: 154C, K: 172C, H: 57A

1553 גָּדַר *gādar*, [A] to built a stone wall, heap up stones for a wall, S: 1443, B: 154D, K: 172D, H: 57A

1554 גֶּדֶר *geder*, Geder, S: 1445, B: 155A, K: 172D, H: 57A

1555 גָּדֵר *gādēr*, wall, fence, S: 1444† & 1447, B: 154D, K: 173A, H: 57A

1556 [1]גְּדֵרָה *g^{e}dērâ*[1], wall, pen (for sheep), S: 1448, B: 155A, K: 173A, H: 57A

1557 [2]גְּדֵרָה *g^{e}dērâ*[2], Gederah, S: 1449, B: 155B, K: 173B, H: 57A

1558 גְּדֵרוֹת *g^{e}dērôt*, Gederoth, S: 1450, B: 155B, K: 173B, H: 57B

1559 גְּדֵרִי *g^{e}dērî*, Gederite, S: 1451, B: 155B, K: 173B, H: 57B

1560 גְּדֶרֶת *g^{e}deret*, variant: wall of stones, S: 1448†, B: 155A, K: 173B, H: 57B

1561 גְּדֵרָתִי *g^{e}dērātî*, Gederathite, S: 1452, B: 155B, K: 173B, H: 57B

1562 גְּדֵרֹתַיִם *g^{e}dērōtayim*, Gederothaim, S: 1453, B: 155B, K: 173B, H: 57B

1563 גֵּה *gēh*, variant: see 2296, S: 1454, B: 155C, K: 173C, H: 57B

1564 גָּהָה *gāhâ*, [A] to heal, S: 1455, B: 155C, K: 173C, H: 57B

1565 גֵּהָה *gēhâ*, medicine, S: 1456, B: 155C, K: 173C, H: 57B

1566 גָּהַר *gāhar*, [A] to bow down; stretch out in prostration, S: 1457, B: 155C, K: 173C, H: 57B

1567 גַּו *gaw*, back (of the body), S: 1458, B: 156A, K: 173C, H: 57B

1568 [1]גֵּו *gēw*[1], back (of the body), S: 1460, B: 156B, K: 173D, H: 57B

1569 [2]גֵּו *gēw*[2], fellow people, community, S: 1460, B: 156B, K: 173D, H: 57B

1570 [1]גּוֹב *gôb*[1], Gob, S: 1359, B: 146C, K: 173D, H: 57B

1571 [2]גּוֹב *gôb*[2], locust, S: 1462, B: 146D, K: 173D, H: 57B

1572 גּוּב *gûb*, variant: [A] to dig, S: 1461, B: 155C, K: 361A, H: 127A

1573 גּוֹג *gôg*, Gog, S: 1463, B: 155D, K: 174A, H: 57B

1574 גּוּד *gûd*, [A] to attack, invade, S: 1464, B: 156A, K: 174A, H: 57B

1575 [1]גֵּוָה *gēwâ*[1], pride, lifting up, S: 1467, B: 145B, K: 174A, H: 57C

1576 [2]גֵּוָה *gēwâ*[2], back (of the body), S: 1465 & 1466, B: 156B, K: 174A, H: 57C

1577 גּוּז *gûz*, [A] to pass along, pass away, S: 1468, B: 156D, K: 174B, H: 57C

1578 גּוֹזָל *gôzāl*, young bird, S: 1469, B: 160A, K: 174B, H: 57C

1579 גּוֹזָן *gôzān*, Gozan, S: 1470, B: 157A, K: 174B, H: 57C

1580 גּוֹי *gôy*, people, nation, the Gentiles, S: 1471, B: 156C, K: 174C, H: 57C

1581 גְּוִיָּה *g^{e}wiyyâ*, dead body, corpse; carcass, S: 1472, B: 156B, K: 174D, H: 57D

[F] Hitpael (hitpoel, hitpoal, hitpolel, hitpolal, hitpalel, hitpalal, hitpalpel, hitpalpal, hotpael, hotpaal) [G] Hiphil (hiphtil) [H] Hophal [I] Hishtaphel

1582 גּוֹיִם *gôyim*, Goiim, Goyim, S: 1471†, B: 157A, K: 175A, H: 57D

1583 גּוֹלָה *gôlâ*, exile, captive, S: 1473, B: 163C, K: 175A, H: 57D

1584 גּוֹלָן *gôlān*, Golan, S: 1474, B: 157B, K: 175B, H: 57D

1585 גּוּמָּץ *gûmmāṣ*, pit, S: 1475, B: 170A, K: 175C, H: 57D

1586 גּוּנִי[1] *gûnî[1]*, Guni, S: 1476, B: 157B, K: 175C, H: 57D

1587 [2]גּוּנִי *gûnî[2]*, Gunite, S: 1477, B: 157B, K: 175C, H: 57D

1588 גָּוַע *gāwaʿ*, [A] to perish, die, breath one's last, S: 1478, B: 157B, K: 175C, H: 58A

1589 גּוּף *gûp*, [G] to shut (a door), S: 1479, B: 157C, K: 175C, H: 58A

1590 גּוּפָה *gûpâ*, dead body, corpse, S: 1480, B: 157C, K: 175D, H: 58A

1591 גּוּר[1] *gûr[1]*, [A] to live as an alien, dwell as a stranger; [F] to stay, gather together, S: 1481, B: 157C, K: 175D, H: 58A

1592 [2]גּוּר *gûr[2]*, [A] to attack, stir up, S: 1481, B: 158D, K: 176B, H: 58A

1593 [3]גּוּר *gûr[3]*, [A] to be terrified, be afraid, fear; to revere, S: 1481, B: 158D, K: 176B, H: 58B

1594 [4]גּוּר *gûr[4]*, cub (young of lions, jackals), S: 1482, B: 158D, K: 176C, H: 58B

1595 [5]גּוּר *gûr[5]*, Gur, S: 1483, B: 158A, K: 176C, H: 58B

1596 גּוֹר *gôr*, cub (of lion), S: 1484, B: 158D, K: 176C, H: 58B

1597 גּוּר־בַּעַל *gûr-baʿal*, Gur Baal, S: 1485, B: 158A, K: 176C, H: 58B

1598 גּוֹרָל *gôrāl*, lot (device by which a decision was made); allotment, S: 1486, B: 174A, K: 176D, H: 58B

1599 גּוּשׁ *gûš*, scab, S: 1487, B: 159A, K: 177B, H: 58C

1600 גֵּז *gēz*, fleece, sheared wool; grass mowed, S: 1488, B: 159C, K: 177B, H: 58C

1601 גִּזְבָּר *gizbār*, treasurer, S: 1489, B: 159B, K: 177B, H: 58C

1602 גָּזָה *gāzâ*, [A] to bring forth, cut off (the umbilical cord), S: 1491, B: 159B, K: 177C, H: 58C

1603 גִּזָּה *gizzâ*, wool fleece, S: 1492†, B: 159C, K: 177C, H: 58C

1604 גִּזוֹנִי *gizônî*, Gizonite, S: 1493, B: 159B, K: 177C, H: 58C

1605 גָּזַז *gāzaz*, [A] to shear sheep; to shave one's head (in mourning), S: 1494, B: 159C, K: 177C, H: 58C

1606 גָּזֵז *gāzēz*, Gazez, S: 1495, B: 159C, K: 177D, H: 58C

1607 גָּזִית *gāzît*, dressed stone, stone hewn or cut for masonry, S: 1496, B: 159B, K: 177D, H: 58C

1608 גָּזַל *gāzal*, [A] to rob, seize, snatch, take way; [B, C] to be robbed, be forcibly taken from, S: 1497, B: 159D, K: 177D, H: 58C

1609 גֵּזֶל *gēzel*, denial of rights, S: 1499, B: 160A, K: 178A, H: 58D

1610 גָּזֵל *gāzēl*, stealing, robbery, S: 1498, B: 160A, K: 178B, H: 58D

1611 גְּזֵלָה *gᵉzēlâ*, plunder, spoil, stolen things, S: 1500, B: 160A, K: 178B, H: 58D

1612 גָּזָם *gāzām*, locust swarm, S: 1501, B: 160B, K: 178B, H: 58D

1613 גַּזָּם *gazzām*, Gazzam, S: 1502, B: 160B, K: 178B, H: 58D

1614 גֶּזַע *gezaʿ*, stump, root stock, S: 1503, B: 160B, K: 178C, H: 58D

1615 גָּזַר[1] *gāzar[1]*, [A] to cut in two, divide, cut down; decide on; to disappear; [C] to be cut off, be excluded, S: 1504, B: 160B, K: 178C, H: 59A

1616 [2]גָּזַר *gāzar[2]*, [A] to devour, eat, S: 1504, B: 160B, K: 178D, H: 59A

1617 גֶּזֶר[1] *gezer[1]*, pieces, S: 1506, B: 160C, K: 178D, H: 59A

1618 [2]גֶּזֶר *gezer[2]*, Gezer, S: 1507, B: 160C, K: 178D, H: 59A

1619 גִּזְרָה *gizrâ*, courtyard; appearance, S: 1508, B: 160D, K: 179A, H: 59A

1620 גְּזֵרָה *gᵉzērâ*, variant: solitary place, unfertile land, S: 1509, B: 160C, K: 179A, H: 59A

1621 גִּזְרִי *gizrî*, variant: Gizrite, see 1747, S: 1511, B: 160C, K: 179A, H: 59A

1622 גָּחָה *gāḥâ*, variant: [A] to draw out (from womb), S: 1518†, B: 161C, K: 179A, H: 59A

1623 גָּחוֹן *gāḥôn*, belly (of reptile), S: 1512, B: 161A, K: 179A, H: 59A

1624 גַּחַל *gaḥal*, burning coals, hot embers, S: 1513†, B: 160D, K: 179B, H: 59B

1625 גַּחֶלֶת *gaḥelet*, burning coals, S: 1513†, B: 160D, K: 179C, H: 59B

1626 גַּחַם *gaḥam*, Gaham, S: 1514, B: 161A, K: 179C, H: 59B

1627 גַּחַר *gaḥar*, Gahar, S: 1515, B: 161A, K: 179C, H: 59B

1628 גַּיְא *gayʾ*, valley, S: 1516, B: 161A, K: 179C, H: 59B

1629 גֵּיא חֲרָשִׁים *gêʾ ḥᵃrāšîm*, Ge Harashim, S: 2798†, B: 161A, K: 180A (f), H: 59C 2.f

1630 גִּיד *gîd*, sinew, tendon, S: 1517, B: 161C, K: 180B, H: 59C

1631 גִּיחַ[1] *gîaḥ[1]*, [A] to burst forth, surge, bring forth (a baby); [G] to charge; to thrash about, S: 1518, B: 161C, K: 180B, H: 59C

1632 [2]גִּיחַ *gîaḥ[2]*, Giah, S: 1520, B: 161D, K: 180C, H: 59C

1633 גִּיחוֹן *gîḥôn*, Gihon, S: 1521, B: 161D, K: 180C, H: 59C

1634 גֵּיחֲזִי *gêḥᵃzî*, Gehazi, S: 1522, B: 161C, K: 180C, H: 59C

1635 גִּיל[1] *gîl[1]*, [A] to rejoice, be glad, be joyful, S: 1523, B: 162A, K: 180C, H: 59C

1636 [2]גִּיל *gîl[2]*, age, stage in life, S: 1524, B: 162B, K: 180D, H: 59D

1637 [3]גִּיל *gîl[3]*, gladness, delight, jubilance, S: 1524, B: 162B, K: 180D, H: 59D

1638 גִּילָה *gîlâ*, rejoicing, delight, S: 1525, B: 162B, K: 181A, H: 59D

1639 גִּילֹנִי *gîlōnî*, Gilonite, S: 1526, B: 162B, K: 181A, H: 59D

1640 גִּינַת *gînat*, Ginath, S: 1527, B: 171B, K: 181A, H: 59D

1641 גִּישׁ *gîš*, variant: see 1599, S: 1487, B: 162C, K: 181A, H: 58C

1642 גֵּישָׁן *gêšān*, Geshan, S: 1529, B: 162C, K: 181A, H: 59D

1643 גַּל[1] *gal[1]*, heap, pile (of rocks, rubble), S: 1530, B: 164C, K: 181B, H: 59D

1644 [2]גַּל *gal[2]*, waves, breaker waves, surging waves; fountain, S: 1530, B: 164C, K: 181B, H: 59D

1645 גֵּל *gēl*, dung, excrement, S: 1561†, B: 165A, K: 181B, H: 60A

1646 גֹּל *gōl*, variant: see 1657, S: 1531, B: 165A, K: 181C, H: 60A

1647 גַּלָּב *gallāb*, barber, S: 1532, B: 162C, K: 181C, H: 60A

1648 גִּלְבֹּעַ *gilbōaʿ*, Gilboa, S: 1533, B: 162C, K: 181C, H: 60A

1649 גַּלְגַּל[1] *galgal[1]*, wheel; whirlwind, S: 1534, B: 165D, K: 181C, H: 60A

1650 [2]גַּלְגַּל *galgal[2]*, tumbleweed, S: 1534, B: 165D, K: 181D, H: 60A

1651 גִּלְגָּל[1] *gilgāl[1]*, wheel, S: 1536, B: 166A, K: 181D, H: 60A

1652 [2]גִּלְגָּל *gilgāl[2]*, Gilgal, S: 1537, B: 166A, K: 181D, H: 60A

1653 גֻּלְגֹּלֶת *gulgōlet*, skull; individual, person, S: 1538, B: 166B, K: 182A, H: 60A

1654 גֶּלֶד *gēled*, skin, S: 1539†, B: 162D, K: 182A, H: 60A

1655 גָּלָה *gālâ*, [A] to tell, uncover, reveal; depart, leave, be exiled, banished; [B] to be opened, unseal; be made known; [C] to be revealed, be exposed; [D] to reveal, expose (nakedness) = sexual relations; [E] to be opened, exiled; [G] to deport, exile, S: 1540, B: 162D, K: 182A, H: 60A

1656 גִּלֹה *gilōh*, Giloh, S: 1542, B: 162B, K: 183B, H: 60D

1657 גֻּלָּה *gullâ*, spring (of water); bowl-shaped capital (of a pillar), S: 1543, B: 165A, K: 183C, H: 60D

1658 גִּלּוּלִים *gillûlîm*, (pl.) idols, S: 1544†, B: 165C, K: 183C, H: 60D

1659 גְּלוֹם *gᵉlôm*, fabric, S: 1545, B: 166B, K: 183D, H: 60D

1660 גָּלוֹן *gālôn*, variant: Galon, see 1584, S*, B: 157B, K: 183D, H: 60D

1661 גָּלוּת *gālût*, exile, captive, S: 1546, B: 163C, K: 183D, H: 60D

1662 גָּלַח *gālaḥ*, [D] to shave off, cut off; [E] be shaved off; [F] to have oneself shaven, shave oneself, S: 1548, B: 164A, K: 183D, H: 61A

1663 גִּלָּיוֹן *gillāyôn*, scroll; mirror, S: 1549, B: 163D, K: 184A, H: 61B

1664 גָּלִיל[1] *gālîl[1]*, turnable (door); rings; rods, S: 1550, B: 165B, K: 184B, H: 61A

1665 [2]גָּלִיל *gālîl[2]*, Galilee, S: 1551, B: 165B, K: 184B, H: 61A

1666 גְּלִילָה *gᵉlîlâ*, region, district, S: 1552, B: 165B, K: 184B, H: 61B

1667 גְּלִילוֹת *gᵉlîlôt*, Geliloth, S: 1553, B: 165C, K: 184C, H: 61B

1668 גַּלִּים *gallîm*, Gallim, S: 1554, B: 164D, K: 184C, H: 61B

1669 גָּלְיָת *golyāt*, Goliath, S: 1555, B: 163D, K: 184C, H: 61B

1670 גָּלַל[1] *gālal[1]*, [A] to roll down, roll away; to commit, turn over; [C] to be rolled; [D] to roll; [E] to be rolled; [F] to roll about, wallow, S: 1556, B: 164B, K: 184C, H: 61B

1671 [2]גָּלַל *gālal[2]*, variant: [E, F] to be befouled, S: 1556, B: 164B, K: 184C, H: 61C

1672 גָּלָל[1] *gālāl[1]*, dung, filth, S: 1557, B: 165B, K: 185A, H: 61C

1673 [2]גָּלָל *gālāl[2]*, because of, on account of, for the sake of, S: 1558, B: 164B, K: 185A, H: 61C

1674 ³גָּלָל *gālāl[3]*, Galal, S: 1559, B: 165B, K: 185A, H: 61C
1675 גִּלְלַי *gil[a]lay*, Gilalai, S: 1562, B: 165B, K: 185B, H: 61C
1676 גָּלַם *gālam*, [A] to roll up, S: 1563, B: 166B, K: 185B, H: 61C
1677 גֹּלֶם *gōlem*, unformed body, embryo, S: 1564, B: 166B, K: 185B, H: 61C
1678 גַּלְמוּד *galmûd*, barren, haggard, S: 1565, B: 166C, K: 185B, H: 61D
1679 גָּלַע *gāla'*, [F] to burst out (in quarrel); to defy, S: 1566, B: 166C, K: 185C, H: 61D
1680 גִּלְעָד *gil'ād*, Gilead, S: 1568, B: 166D, K: 185C, H: 61D
1681 גַּלְעֵד *gal'ēd*, Galeed, S: 1567, B: 165A, K: 186A, H: 61D
1682 גִּלְעָדִי *gil'ādî*, Gileadite, of Gilead, S: 1569, B: 167C, K: 186A, H: 61D
1683 גָּלַשׁ *gālaš*, [A] to descend, S: 1570, B: 167C, K: 186A, H: 61D
1684 גֻּלֹּת *gullōt*, variant: Gullot, S: 1543†, B: 165A, K: 186B, H: 61D
1685 גַּם *gam*, also, surely, too; and, but, yet, even, moreover, S: 1571, B: 168D, K: 186B, H: 61D
1686 גָּמָא *gāmā'*, [D] to eat up, swallow up; [G] to give water (to sip), S: 1572, B: 167C, K: 187D, H: 62B
1687 גֹּמֶא *gōme'*, papyrus, S: 1573, B: 167D, K: 187D, H: 62B
1688 גֹּמֶד *gōmed*, unit of measure, about 18 inches, S: 1574, B: 167D, K: 188A, H: 62C
1689 גַּמָּדִים *gammādîm*, men of Gammad, S: 1575†, B: 167D, K: 188A, H: 62C
1690 גָּמוּל *gāmûl*, Gamul, S: 1577, B: 168C, K: 188A, H: 62C
1691 גְּמוּל *g[e]mûl*, what is done; benefit; what is deserved, recompense, S: 1576, B: 168B, K: 188A, H: 62C
1692 גְּמוּלָה *g[e]mûlâ*, what is done; retribution, recompense, S: 1578, B: 168C, K: 188B, H: 62C
1693 גִּמְזוֹ *gimzô*, Gimzo, S: 1579, B: 168A, K: 188B, H: 62C
1694 גָּמַל *gāmal*, [A] to do, produce, deal fully; to wean; to repay (what is deserved); [B, C] to be weaned, S: 1580, B: 168A, K: 188B, H: 62C
1695 גָּמָל *gāmāl*, camel, S: 1581, B: 168C, K: 188D, H: 62D
1696 גְּמַלִּי *g[e]mallî*, Gemalli, S: 1582, B: 168D, K: 189A, H: 62D
1697 גַּמְלִיאֵל *gamlî'ēl*, Gamaliel, S: 1583, B: 168C, K: 189A, H: 62D
1698 גָּמַר *gāmar*, [A] to bring to an end, fail; fulfill, S: 1584, B: 170A, K: 189A, H: 62D
1699 ¹גֹּמֶר *gōmer[1]*, Gomer, S: 1586, B: 170A, K: 189B, H: 62D
1700 ²גֹּמֶר *gōmer[2]*, Gomer, S: 1586, B: 170A, K: 189B, H: 62D
1701 גְּמַרְיָה *g[e]maryâ*, Gemariah, S: 1587, B: 170B, K: 189B, H: 63A
1702 גְּמַרְיָהוּ *g[e]maryāhû*, Gemariah, S: 1587, B: 170B, K: 189B, H: 63A
1703 גַּן *gan*, garden, S: 1588, B: 171A, K: 189C, H: 63A
1704 גָּנַב *gānab*, [A] to steal, be a thief, kidnap; to deceive; [B, C, E] to be stolen, forcibly carried off; [F] to steal oneself away, sneak in, S: 1589, B: 170B, K: 189D, H: 63A
1705 גַּנָּב *gannāb*, thief; kidnapper, S: 1590, B: 170C, K: 190A, H: 63B
1706 גְּנֵבָה *g[e]nēbâ*, stolen possession, S: 1591, B: 170C, K: 190A, H: 63B
1707 גְּנֻבַת *g[e]nubat*, Genubath, S: 1592, B: 170C, K: 190A, H: 63B
1708 גַּנָּה *gannâ*, garden, grove, S: 1593 & 1594†, B: 171B, K: 190B, H: 63B
1709 ¹גֶּנֶז *genez[1]*, (royal) treasury, S: 1595, B: 170D, K: 190B, H: 63B
1710 ²גֶּנֶז *genez[2]*, rug, S: 1595, B: 170D, K: 190B, H: 63B
1711 גַּנְזַךְ *ganzak*, (temple) storeroom, S: 1597†, B: 170D, K: 190B, H: 63B
1712 גַּנִּים *gannîm*, variant: Gannim, S: 5873†, B: 745C, K: 700C, H: 271D 4.d
1713 גָּנַן *gānan*, [A] to defend, shield, protect, S: 1598, B: 170D, K: 190C, H: 63B
1714 גִּנְּתוֹי *ginn[e]tôy*, variant: Ginnethoi, see 1715, S: 1599†, B: 171B, K: 190C, H: 63B
1715 גִּנְּתוֹן *ginn[e]tôn*, Ginnethon, S: 1599, B: 171B, K: 190C, H: 63B
1716 גָּעָה *gā'â*, [A] to bellow, low (of cattle), S: 1600, B: 171D, K: 190C, H: 63C
1717 גֹּעָה *gō'â*, Goah, S: 1601, B: 171D, K: 190C, H: 63C
1718 גָּעַל *gā'al*, [A] to abhor, despise, loathe; [C] to be defiled; [G] to cause defiling = fail to impregnate, S: 1602, B: 171D, K: 190D, H: 63C
1719 גֹּעַל *gō'al*, despising, loathing, S: 1604, B: 172A, K: 190D, H: 63C
1720 גַּעַל *ga'al*, Gaal, S: 1603, B: 172A, K: 190D, H: 63C
1721 גָּעַר *gā'ar*, [A] to rebuke, reprimand; prevent (insects), S: 1605, B: 172A, K: 191A, H: 63C
1722 גְּעָרָה *g[e]'ārâ*, rebuke; threat, S: 1606, B: 172A, K: 191A, H: 63C
1723 גָּעַשׁ *gā'aš*, [A] to shake, tremble; [E] to be shaken; [F] to shake back and forth, stagger, surge, tremble back and forth, S: 1607, B: 172B, K: 191B, H: 63C
1724 גַּעַשׁ *ga'aš*, Gaash, S: 1608, B: 172B, K: 191B, H: 63D
1725 גַּעְתָּם *ga'tām*, Gatam, S: 1609, B: 172B, K: 191C, H: 63D
1726 ¹גַּף *gap[1]*, height, elevation, S: 1610, B: 172D, K: 191C, H: 63D
1727 ²גַּף *gap[2]*, body; by oneself [with 928], S: 1610, B: 172D, K: 191C, H: 63D
1728 גֶּפֶן *gepen*, vine, grapevine, S: 1612, B: 172B, K: 191C, H: 63D
1729 גֹּפֶר *gōper*, cypress (wood), S: 1613, B: 172D, K: 191D, H: 63D
1730 גָּפְרִית *goprît*, sulfur, S: 1614, B: 172D, K: 192A, H: 63D
1731 גֵּר *gēr*, alien, stranger (in a foreign land), S: 1616, B: 158A, K: 192A, H: 63D
1732 גִּר *gir*, chalk, S: 1615, B: 162C, K: 192C, H: 64A
1733 גֵּרָא *gērā'*, Gera, S: 1617, B: 173A, K: 192C, H: 64A
1734 גָּרָב *gārāb*, festering sore, S: 1618, B: 173A, K: 192C, H: 64A
1735 ¹גָּרֵב *gārēb[1]*, Gareb, S: 1619, B: 173A 1., K: 192D, H: 64A
1736 ²גָּרֵב *gārēb[2]*, Gareb, S: 1619, B: 173A 2., K: 192D, H: 64A
1737 גַּרְגַּר *gargar*, ripe olives, S: 1620, B: 176B, K: 192D, H: 64A
1738 גַּרְגְּרוֹת *garg[e]rôt*, neck, S: 1621, B: 176B, K: 192D, H: 64A
1739 גִּרְגָּשִׁי *girgāšî*, Girgashite, S: 1622, B: 173A, K: 193A, H: 64A
1740 גָּרַד *gārad*, [F] to scrape oneself (with a broken piece of pottery), S: 1623, B: 173B, K: 193A, H: 64A
1741 גָּרָה *gārâ*, [D] to stir up (a dispute); [F] to provoke (to war), engage (to battle), S: 1624, B: 173B, K: 193A, H: 64A
1742 ¹גֵּרָה *gērâ[1]*, cud, S: 625, B: 176A, K: 193B, H: 64B
1743 ²גֵּרָה *gērâ[2]*, gerah (measure), S: 1626, B: 176A, K: 193B, H: 64B
1744 גָּרוֹן *gārôn*, throat, neck, mouth, S: 1627, B: 173C, K: 193B, H: 64B
1745 גֵּרוּת כִּמְהָם *gērût kimhām*, Geruth Kimham, S: 1628† + 3643†, B: 158A, K: 193C, H: 64B
1746 גָּרַז *gāraz*, [C] to be cut off, S: 1629, B: 173D, K: 193C, H: 64B
1747 גִּרְזִי *girzî*, Girzite, S: 1511, B: 173D, K: 193C, H: 64B
1748 גְּרִזִים *g[e]rizîm*, Gerizim, S: 1630, B: 173D, K: 193C, H: 64B
1749 גַּרְזֶן *garzen*, ax, chisel, S: 1631, B: 173D, K: 193D, H: 64B
1750 ¹גָּרַם *gāram[1]*, [A] to leave, reserve, S: 1633, B: 175A, K: 193D, H: 64C
1751 ²גָּרַם *gāram[2]*, [D] to break, to break bones, S: 1633, B: 175A, K: 193D, H: 64C
1752 גֶּרֶם *gerem*, bone, rawboned, bony; bareness, S: 1634, B: 175A, K: 194A, H: 64C
1753 גַּרְמִי *garmî*, Garmite, S: 1636, B: 175A, K: 194A, H: 64C
1754 גָּרֹל *gārōl*, variant: see 1524, S: 1632, B: 175A, K: 176D, H: 64B
1755 גֹּרֶן *gōren*, threshing floor, S: 1637, B: 175B, K: 194A, H: 64C
1756 גָּרַס *gāras*, [A] to be crushed; [G] to break, crush, S: 1638, B: 176B, K: 194C, H: 64C
1757 ¹גָּרַע *gāra'[1]*, [A] to take away, reduce, hinder; [B] to be cut off (of a beard); [C] to be reduced, be taken away, to disappear, S: 1639, B: 175C, K: 194C, H: 64C
1758 ²גָּרַע *gāra'[2]*, [D] to draw up (drops of water), S: 1639, B: 175C, K: 194C, H: 64D
1759 גָּרַף *gārap*, [A] to sweep away (of a river), S: 1640, B: 175D, K: 194D, H: 64D
1760 גָּרַר *gārar*, [A] to chew; to drag away; [E] to be sawn; [F] to drive, swirl, S: 1641, B: 176A, K: 194D, H: 64D
1761 גְּרָר *g[e]rār*, Gerar, S: 1642, B: 176B, K: 195A, H: 64D
1762 גֶּרֶשׂ *gereś*, crushed grain, S: 1643, B: 176C, K: 195A, H: 64D
1763 ¹גָּרַשׁ *gāraš[1]*, [A] to drive out; [B] to be divorced; [C] to be banished; [D] to drive out, expel [E] to be banished, S: 1644, B: 176C, K: 195B, H: 65A

[F] Hitpael (hitpoel, hitpoal, hitpolel, hitpolal, hitpalel, hitpalal, hitpalpel, hitpalpal, hotpael, hotpaal) [G] Hiphil (hiphtil) [H] Hophal [I] Hishtaphel

1764 ²גָּרַשׁ *gāraš²*, [A] to cast up, toss up; [C] to be tossed, be stirred up, S: 1644, B: 176C, K: 195B, H: 65A

1765 גֶּרֶשׁ *gereš*, yield, produce, S: 1645, B: 177A, K: 195C, H: 65A

1766 גְּרֻשָׁה *gᵉrušâ*, dispossession, S: 1646, B: 177A, K: 195C, H: 65A

1767 גֵּרְשׁוֹן *gēršôn*, Gershon, S: 1648, B: 177A, K: 195C, H: 65A

1768 גֵּרְשֹׁם *gēršōm*, Gershom, Gershon, S: 1647, B: 177A, K: 195D, H: 65A

1769 גֵּרְשֻׁנִּי *gēršunnî*, Gershonite, S: 1649, B: 177B, K: 195D, H: 65A

1770 גְּשׁוּר *gᵉšûr*, Geshur, S: 1650, B: 178A, K: 195D, H: 65A

1771 גְּשׁוּרִי *gᵉšûrî*, Geshurite, people of Geshur, S: 1651, B: 178C, K: 196A, H: 65B

1772 גָּשַׁם *gāšam*, [G] to bring rain, S: 1652, B: 177D, K: 196A, H: 65B

1773 ¹גֶּשֶׁם *gešem¹*, rain, shower, downpour, S: 1653, B: 177C, K: 196A, H: 65B

1774 ²גֶּשֶׁם *gešem²*, Geshem, S: 1654, B: 177C, K: 196B, H: 65C

1775 גֹּשֶׁם *gōšem*, shower, rain, S: 1656, B: 177D, K: 196C, H: 65C

1776 גַּשְׁמוּ *gašmû*, Geshem, S: 1654, B: 177C, K: 196C, H: 65C

1777 גֹּשֶׁן *gōšen*, Goshen, S: 1657, B: 177D, K: 196C, H: 65C

1778 גִּשְׁפָּא *gišpā'*, Gishpa, S: 1658, B: 177D, K: 196C, H: 65C

1779 גָּשַׁשׁ *gāšaš*, [D] to grope along, feel one's way (as if blind), S: 1659, B: 178C, K: 196D, H: 65C

1780 ¹גַּת *gat¹*, winepress, S: 1660, B: 387C, K: 196D, H: 65C

1781 ²גַּת *gat²*, Gath, S: 1661, B: 387D, K: 196D, H: 65C

1782 ³גַּת *gat³*, variant: Gath, see 1783, 1784, S: 1662 & 1667, B: 387C, K: 196D, H: 65C

1783 גַּת הַחֵפֶר גַּת חֵפֶר רְפָאָה *gat* גַּת חֵפֶר *gat ḥēper*, Gath Hepher, S: 1662, B: 387D, K: 197A, H: 65C 1.

1784 גַּת־רִמּוֹן *gat-rimmôn*, Gath Rimmon, S: 1667, B: 387D, K: 197C, H: 65C 2.

1785 גִּתִּי *gittî*, Gittite, S: 1663, B: 388A, K: 197A, H: 65D

1786 גִּתַּיִם *gittayim*, Gittaim, S: 1664, B: 388A, K: 197C, H: 65D

1787 גִּתִּית *gittît*, gittith: unknown musical term, possibly the name of the tune, or the name of the instrument that played it, S: 1665, B: 388A, K: 197C, H: 65D

1788 גֶּתֶר *geter*, Gether, S: 1666, B: 178C, K: 197C, H: 65D

1789 ד *d*, letter of the Hebrew alphabet, S*, B: 178A, K: 197A, H*

1790 דָּאַב *dā'ab*, [A] to be dim (of eyes); to sorrow, S: 1669, B: 178A, K: 197B, H: 65B

1791 דְּאָבָה *dᵉ'ābâ*, dismay, despair, S: 1670, B: 178B, K: 197B, H: 65B

1792 דְּאָבוֹן *dᵉ'ābôn*, despair, S: 1671, B: 178B, K: 197B, H: 65B

1793 דָּאַג *dā'ag*, [A] to worry, dread, be troubled, be afraid, S: 1672, B: 178B, K: 197C, H: 65B

1794 דָּאג *dā'g*, fish, S: 1709, B: 185C, K: 197B, H: 65D

1795 דֹּאֵג *dō'ēg*, Doeg, S: 1673, B: 178C, K: 204B, H: 65D & 68D

1796 דְּאָגָה *dᵉ'āgâ*, fear, anxiety, restlessness, S: 1674, B: 178C, K: 197D, H: 66A

1797 ¹דָּאָה *dā'â¹*, [A] to swoop down, pounce; to soar, S: 1675, B: 178D, K: 197D, H: 66A

1798 ²דָּאָה *dā'â²*, red kite (bird), S: 1676, B: 178D, K: 198A, H: 66A

1799 דֹּאר *dō'r*, Dor, S: 1756, B: 190B, K: 198A, H: 66A

1800 דֹּב *dōb*, bear (animal), S: 1677, B: 179A, K: 198A, H: 66A

1801 דֹּבֶא *dōbe'*, strength, S: 1679, B: 179A, K: 198B, H: 66A

1802 דְּבָאָה *dᵉbā'â*, variant: strength, S: 1670†, B: 178B, K: 197B, H: 66A

1803 דָּבַב *dābab*, [A] to flow over gently, S: 1680, B: 179A, K: 198B, H: 66A

1804 דִּבָּה *dibbâ*, bad report, slander, bad reputation, whisper, S: 1681, B: 179A, K: 198B, H: 66A

1805 ¹דְּבוֹרָה *dᵉbôrâ¹*, wild honey bee; (pl.) swarm of bees, S: 1682, B: 184B, K: 198B, H: 66A

1806 ²דְּבוֹרָה *dᵉbôrâ²*, Deborah, S: 1683, B: 184B, K: 198C, H: 66A

1807 דִּבְיֹנִים *dibyōnîm*, seed pods *or* doves' dung, S: 1686†, B: 179B, K: 198C, H: 66A

1808 ¹דְּבִיר *dᵉbîr¹*, inner sanctuary, S: 1687, B: 184B, K: 198C, H: 66A & 68A

1809 ²דְּבִיר *dᵉbîr²*, Debir, S: 1688, B: 184C 1., K: 198D, H: 66B

1810 ³דְּבִיר *dᵉbîr³*, Debir, S: 1688, B: 184C 2., K: 202C, H: 66B & 68A

1811 דְּבֵלָה *dᵉbēlâ*, pressed fig cakes; poultice of figs, S: 1690, B: 179B, K: 198D, H: 66B

1812 דִּבְלָה *diblâ*, Diblah, S: 1689, B: 179C, K: 199A, H: 66B

1813 דִּבְלַיִם *diblayim*, Diblaim, S: 1691, B: 179C, K: 198D, H: 66B

1814 דִּבְלָתַיִם *diblātayim*, variant: Diblathaim, S: 1015†, B: 179C, K: 709C, H: 66B & 39B 13.

1815 דָּבַק *dābaq*, [A] to be united, hold fast, keep, cling to; [G] to overtake, cause to cleave, press hard upon; [E] to be joined fast, be stuck together; [H] be made to cleave, stick to, S: 1692, B: 179C, K: 199A, H: 66B

1816 דָּבֵק *dābēq*, holding fast, sticking to, S: 1695, B: 180A, K: 199C, H: 66C

1817 דֶּבֶק *debeq*, welding; sections (of armor), S: 1694, B: 180A, K: 199C, H: 66C

1818 ¹דָּבַר *dābar¹*, [D] to depart; to destroy; [G] to subdue, S: 1696, B: 180B, K: 199C, H: 66D

1819 ²דָּבַר *dābar²*, [A, D, F] to say, speak, tell, command, promise; [B, E] to be spoken (of); [C] to speak together, S: 1696, B: 180B, K: 199D, H: 66D

1820 ³דָּבַר *dābar³*, variant: [D] to have descendants, S: 1696, B: 180B, K: 199D, H: 67B

1821 דָּבָר *dābār*, what is said, word; matter; thing, S: 1697, B: 182A, K: 201A, H: 67B

1822 ¹דֶּבֶר *deber¹*, plague, pestilence, disease, S: 1698, B: 184A, K: 202B, H: 68A

1823 ²דֶּבֶר *deber²*, variant: thorn, S: 1698, B: 184A, K: 202C, H: 68A

1824 דֹּבֶר *dōber*, pasture, S: 1699, B: 184A, K: 202C, H: 68A

1825 דִּבֵּר *dibbēr*, word (of God), S: 1699´, B: 184C, K: 202C, H: 68A

1826 דִּבְרָה *dibrâ*, cause; order; therefore, because, S: 1700, B: 184A, K: 202C, H: 68A

1827 דֹּבְרוֹת *dōbᵉrôt*, raft, S: 1702†, B: 184A, K: 202D, H: 68A

1828 דִּבְרִי *dibrî*, Dibri, S: 1704, B: 184C, K: 202D, H: 68A

1829 דָּבְרַת *dābᵉrat*, Daberath, S: 1705, B: 184B, K: 202D, H: 68A

1830 דַּבֶּרֶת *dabberet*, instruction, word, S: 1703†, B: 184C, K: 202D, H: 68B

1831 דְּבַשׁ *dᵉbaš*, honey, S: 1706, B: 185A, K: 203A, H: 68B

1832 ¹דַּבֶּשֶׁת *dabbešet¹*, hump (of a camel), S: 1707, B: 185C 1., K: 203A, H: 68B

1833 ²דַּבֶּשֶׁת *dabbešet²*, Dabbesheth, S: 1708, B: 185C 2., K: 203B, H: 68B

1834 דָּג *dāg*, fish, S: 1709, B: 185C, K: 203B, H: 68B

1835 ¹דָּגָה *dāgā¹*, [A] to increase, multiply, S: 1711, B: 185C, K: 203B, H: 68B

1836 ²דָּגָה *dāgā²*, fish, S: 1710, B: 185D, K: 203B, H: 68B

1837 דָּגוֹן *dāgôn*, Dagon (pagan god), S: 1712, B: 1868A, K: 203C, H: 68B

1838 ¹דָּגַל *dāgal¹*, [B] to be outstanding, be conspicuous, S: 1713, B: 186A, K: 203C, H: 68B

1839 ²דָּגַל *dāgal²*, [A] to lift a banner; [C] be gathered around the banner(s), organized as troops, S: 1713, B: 186B, K: 203C, H: 68B

1840 דֶּגֶל *degel*, standard, banner, S: 1714, B: 186B, K: 203C, H: 68C

1841 דָּגָן *dāgān*, grain, S: 1715, B: 186B, K: 203D, H: 68C

1842 דָּגַר *dāgar*, [A] to care for; hatch eggs, S: 1716, B: 186C, K: 203D, H: 68C

1843 דַּד *dad*, bosom, breast, S: 1717, B: 186D, K: 203D, H: 68C

1844 דָּדָה *dādâ*, [F] to walk, lead, S: 1718, B: 186D, K: 204A, H: 68C

1845 דֹּדָוָהוּ *dōdāwāhû*, Dodavahu, S: 1735, B: 187D, K: 205B, H: 68C

1846 דֹּדַי *dōdî*, variant: Dodai, S: 1734†, B: 187D, K: 205B, H: 68C

1847 דְּדָן *dᵉdān*, Dedan, S: 1719, B: 186D, K: 204A, H: 68C

1848 דְּדָנִי *dᵉdānî*, Dedanite, S: 1719† & 1720, B: 187A, K: 204B, H: 68C

1849 דֹּדָנִים *dōdānîm*, variant: Dodanim, S: 1721, B: 187A, K: 204B, H: 68C

1850 דָּהַם *dāham*, [C] to be taken by surprise, be astounded, S: 1724, B: 187A, K: 204B, H: 68C

1851 דָּהַר *dāhar*, [A] to gallop, S: 1725, B: 187B, K: 204B, H: 68C

1852 דַּהֲרָה *dahᵃrâ*, galloping, S: 1726, B: 187B, K: 204B, H: 68C

1853 דּוּב *dûb*, [G] to drain away, wear away, S: 1727, B: 187B, K: 204C, H: 68D

1854 דַּוָּג *dawwāg*, fisherman, S: 1728, B: 186A, K: 204C, H: 68D

1855 דּוּגָה *dûgâ*, fishing (hooks), S: 1729, B: 186A, K: 204C, H: 68D

1856 דּוֹד *dôd*, uncle, cousin, relative; beloved one, lover, S: 1730, B: 187C, K: 204C, H: 68D

1857 דּוּד *dûd*, basket; kettle, caldron, pot, S: 1731, B: 188B, K: 204D, H: 68D

1858 דָּוִד *dāwid*, David, S: 1732, B: 187D, K: 205A, H: 68D

1859 דּוּדָאִים *dûdā'îm*, mandrake plant, S: 1736†, B: 188B, K: 205B, H: 68D

1860 דּוֹדָה *dôdâ*, aunt (father's sister), S: 1733, B: 187D, K: 205B, H: 69A

1861 דּוֹדוֹ *dôdô*, Dodo, S: 1734, B: 187D, K: 205B, H: 69A

1862 דּוֹדַי *dôday*, Dodai, S: 1737, B: 187D, K: 205B, H: 69A

1863 דּוּדַי *dûday*, variant: mandrakes, S: 1736, B: 188B, K: 205B, H: 68D

1864 דָּוָה *dāwâ*, [A] to have a monthly period, menstruate, S: 1738, B: 188C, K: 205B, H: 69A

1865 דָּוֶה *dāweh*, pertaining to the menstrual cycle; fainting, S: 1739, B: 188C, K: 205C, H: 69A

1866 דּוּחַ *dûaḥ*, [G] to rinse, wash, cleanse, S: 1740, B: 188D, K: 205C, H: 69A

1867 דְּוַי *dᵉway*, illness, S: 1741, B: 188C, K: 205C, H: 69A

1868 דַּוָּי *dawwāy*, faint; afflicted, S: 1742, B: 188D, K: 205C, H: 69A

1869 דּוֹיֵג *dôyēg*, variant: Doyeg, see 1795, S: 1673†, B: 178C, K: 204B, H: 69A

1870 דּוּךְ *dûk*, [A] to crush (in a mortar), S: 1743, B: 188D, K: 205D, H: 69A

1871 דּוּכִיפַת *dûkîpat*, hoopoe, S: 1744, B: 189A, K: 205D, H: 69A

1872 דּוּמָה[1] *dûmâ*[1], silence, S: 1745, B: 189A, K: 205D, H: 69B

1873 דּוּמָה[2] *dûmâ*[2], Dumah, S: 1746, B: 189A, K: 205D, H: 69B

1874 דּוּמָה[3] *dûmâ*[3], Dumah, S: 1746, B: 189A, K: 206A, H: 69B

1875 דּוּמִיָּה *dûmiyyâ*, silence, stillness; rest, S: 1747, B: 189B, K: 206A, H: 69B

1876 דּוּמָם *dûmām*, in silence, quietly; lifeless, S: 1748, B: 189B, K: 206A, H: 69B

1877 דּוּמֶּשֶׂק *dûmmeśeq*, Damascus, S: 1834, B: 199D, K: 206A, H: 69B

1878 דּוֹן *dôn*, variant: [A] to remain [?], S: 1777†, B: 192A, K: 206A, H: 69B

1879 דּוּן *dûn*, variant: judgment, S: 1777, B: 189B, K: 206A, H: 69B

1880 דּוֹנַג *dônag*, wax, S: 1749, B: 200A, K: 206A, H: 69B

1881 דּוּץ *dûṣ*, [A] to leap, S: 1750, B: 189B, K: 206B, H: 69B

1882 דּוּק *dûq*, variant: [A] to review, S: 1751, B: 200D, K: 206B, H: 69B

1883 דּוּר[1] *dûr*[1], [A] to pile logs (around), S: 1752, B: 189C, K: 206B, H: 69B

1884 דּוּר[2] *dûr*[2], [A] to dwell, S: 1752, B: 189C, K: 206B, H: 69B

1885 דּוּר[3] *dûr*[3], all around, encircling; ball, S: 1754, B: 189C, K: 206C, H: 69C

1886 דּוֹר[1] *dôr*[1], house, dwelling, S: 1755, B: 189C, K: 206C, H: 69C

1887 דּוֹר[2] *dôr*[2], generation, generation to come; descendant, S: 1755, B: 189C, K: 206C, H: 69C

1888 דּוֹר[3] *dôr*[3], Dor, S: 1756, B: 190B, K: 207A, H: 69C

1889 דּוּשׁ *dûš*, [A] to tread, trample, thresh; [B, C, H] be trampled, be threshed, S: 1758, B: 190B, K: 207A, H: 69C

1890 דָּחָה *dāḥâ*, [A] to push, push away; trip up; [B] to totter; [C] to be brought down; [E] to be thrown down, S: 1760, B: 190D, K: 207A, H: 69D

1891 דָּחַח *dāḥaḥ*, variant: [C] to be push, pushed out, S: 1760, B: 191A, K: 207B, H: 69D

1892 דְּחִי *dᵉḥî*, stumbling, S: 1762, B: 191A, K: 207B, H: 69D

1893 דֹּחַן *dōḥan*, millet, S: 1764, B: 191A, K: 207C, H: 69D

1894 דָּחַף *dāḥap*, [B] to be spurred on, be in haste; [C] to be eager, be rushed, hurry, S: 1765, B: 191B, K: 207C, H: 70A

1895 דָּחַק *dāḥaq*, [A] to afflict, oppress, S: 1766, B: 191B, K: 207C, H: 70A

1896 דַּי *day*, enough, sufficient, S: 1767, B: 191B, K: 207D, H: 70A

1897 דִּיבוֹן *dîbôn*, Dibon, S: 1769, B: 192A, K: 208B, H: 70B

1898 דִּיבֹן גָּד *dîbôn gād*, Dibon Gad, S: 1769 + 1410, B: 192A 1., K: 208B, H: 70B

1899 דִּיג *dîg*, [A] to catch fish, S: 1770, B: 185D, K: 208B, H: 70B

1900 דַּיָּג *dayyāg*, fisherman, S: 1771, B: 186A, K: 208B, H: 70B

1901 דַּיָּה *dayyâ*, falcon, S: 1772, B: 178D, K: 208C, H: 70B

1902 דְּיוֹ *dᵉyô*, ink, S: 1773, B: 188D, K: 208C, H: 70B

1903 דִּי זָהָב *dî zāhāb*, Dizahab, S: 1774, B: 191D, K: 208C, H: 70B

1904 דִּימוֹן *dîmôn*, Dimon, S: 1775, B: 192A 1., K: 208C, H: 70B

1905 דִּימוֹנָה *dîmônâ*, Dimonah, S: 1776, B: 192A 2., K: 208C, H: 70B

1906 דִּין[1] *dîn*[1], [A] to judge, punish; to plead, defend, vindicate, contend for; [C] to argue, S: 1777, B: 192A, K: 208C, H: 70B

1907 דִּין[2] *dîn*[2], cause, legal case; judgment, justice, S: 1779, B: 192C, K: 208D, H: 70C

1908 דַּיָּן *dayyān*, defender, judge, S: 1781, B: 193A, K: 209A, H: 70C

1909 דִּינָה *dînâ*, Dinah, S: 1783, B: 192D, K: 209A, H: 70C

1910 דִּיפַת *dîpat*, variant: Diphath, see 8196, S: 7384, B: 193D, K: 209A, H: 70C

1911 דָּיֵק *dāyēq*, siege works, S: 1785, B: 189B, K: 209A, H: 70C

1912 דַּיִשׁ *dayiš*, threshing (season), S: 1786, B: 190C, K: 209A, H: 70C

1913 דִּישׁוֹן[1] *dîšôn*[1], ibex, S: 1788, B: 190D, K: 209A, H: 70C

1914 דִּישׁוֹן[2] *dîšôn*[2], Dishon, Dishan, S: 1787, B: 190D, K: 209B, H: 70C

1915 דִּישָׁן *dîšān*, Dishan, S: 1789, B: 190D, K: 209B, H: 70C

1916 דַּךְ *dak*, oppressed, S: 1790, B: 194C, K: 209B, H: 70C

1917 דָּכָא *dākā'*, [C] to be contrite; [D] to crush; [E] to be crushed, be dejected, be humbled; [F] to lie crushed, S: 1792, B: 193D, K: 209B, H: 70C

1918 דַּכָּא[1] *dakkā'*[1], crushed, contrite, S: 1793, B: 194B, K: 209C, H: 70D 1.

1919 דַּכָּא[2] *dakkā'*[2], dust, S: 1793, B: 194B, K: 209C, H: 70D 2.

1920 דָּכָה *dākâ*, [A, D] to crush; [C] to be crushed, contrite, S: 1794, B: 194B, K: 209C, H: 70D

1921 דַּכָּה *dakkâ*, variant: crushing (of testicle), S: 1795, B: 194C, K: 209D, H: 70D

1922 דֳּכִי *dᵒkî*, pounding (waves), S: 1796, B: 194B, K: 209D, H: 70D

1923 דַּל[1] *dal*[1], door, S: 1817†, B: 194D, K: 209D, H: 70D

1924 דַּל[2] *dal*[2], poor, needy, humble; weak, haggard, scrawny, S: 1800, B: 195D, K: 209D, H: 70D

1925 דָּלַג *dālag*, [A, D] to scale, ascend, leap up over, S: 1801, B: 194C, K: 210A, H: 71A

1926 דָּלָה[1] *dālâ*[1], [A, D] to draw up, draw water (from a well), S: 1802, B: 194C, K: 210A, H: 71A

1927 דָּלָה[2] *dālâ*[2], [A] to hang limp, dangle, S: 1802, B: 194C, K: 210A, H: 71A

1928 דָּלָה[3] *dālâ*[3], variant: door, S: 1817†, B: 194D, K: 211B, H: 71C

1929 דַּלָּה[1] *dallâ*[1], threads remaining on the loom; flowing hair, S: 1803, B: 195D, K: 210B, H: 71A

1930 דַּלָּה[2] *dallâ*[2], poor, S: 1803, B: 195D, K: 210B, H: 71A

1931 דָּלַח *dālaḥ*, [A] to churn, stir up, S: 1804, B: 195C, K: 210B, H: 71A

1932 דְּלִי *dᵉlî*, bucket, S: 1805, B: 194D, K: 210C, H: 71B

1933 דְּלָיָה *dᵉlāyâ*, Delaiah, S: 1806, B: 195B, K: 210C, H: 71B

1934 דְּלָיָהוּ *dᵉlāyāhû*, Delaiah, S: 1806, B: 195B, K: 210C, H: 71B

1935 דְּלִילָה *dᵉlîlâ*, Delilah, S: 1807, B: 196A, K: 210C, H: 71B

1936 דָּלִית *dālît*, branch, bough, S: 1808†, B: 194D, K: 210C, H: 71B

1937 דָּלַל[1] *dālal*[1], [A] to be in need, be weak, fade, S: 1809, B: 195C, K: 210D, H: 71A

1938 דָּלַל[2] *dālal*[2], [A] to dangle, S: 1809, B: 195C, K: 210D, H: 71B

1939 דִּלְעָן *dilʿān*, Dilean, S: 1810, B: 196A, K: 211A, H: 71B

1940 דָּלַף[1] *dālap*[1], [A] to leak; to pour out, S: 1811, B: 196A, K: 211A, H: 71B

1941 דָּלַף[2] *dālap*[2], [A] to be weary, be sleepless, S: 1811, B: 196A, K: 211A, H: 71B

1942 דֶּלֶף *delep*, leaky roof, S: 1812, B: 196A, K: 211A, H: 71C

1943 דַּלְפוֹן *dalpôn*, Dalphon, S: 1813, B: 196A, K: 211A, H: 71C

1944 דָּלַק *dālaq*, [A] to set on fire; to hunt, chase, pursue; [G] to inflame, kindle, S: 1814, B: 196A, K: 211B, H: 71C

1945 דַּלֶּקֶת *dalleqet*, inflammation, S: 1816, B: 196B, K: 211B, H: 71C

1946 דֶּלֶת *delet*, door, gate; column, lid, leaf (of a door), S: 1817, B: 195A, K: 211B, H: 71C

1947 דָּם *dām*, blood, lifeblood; bloodshed, S: 1818, B: 196B, K: 212A, H: 71D

1948 [1]דָּמָה *dāmâ[1]*, [A] to be like, liken, resemble; [C] to be like; [D] to think, plan, intend; to liken; [F] to consider oneself equal to, S: 1819, B: 197D, K: 212D, H: 72A

1949 [2]דָּמָה *dāmâ[2]*, [A] to cease; to be silent; [C] to be silenced, S: 1820, B: 198C, K: 213B, H: 72B

1950 [3]דָּמָה *dāmâ[3]*, [A] to destroy; [C] to perish, be ruined, be destroyed, be wiped out, S: 1820, B: 198C, K: 213B, H: 72C

1951 דּוּמָה *dumâ*, one silenced, S: 1822, B: 199A, K: 213B, H: 72C & 152A

1952 דְּמוּת *dᵉmût*, likeness, figure, image, form, S: 1823, B: 198B, K: 213C, H: 72C

1953 דְּמִי *dᵉmî*, prime (of life), S: 1824, B: 198C, K: 213C, H: 72C

1954 דֳּמִי *dᵒmî*, silence, rest, S: 1824, B: 198C, K: 213D, H: 72C

1955 דִּמְיוֹן *dimyôn*, likeness, S: 1825, B: 198B, K: 213D, H: 72C

1956 דַּמִּים *dammîm*, variant: Dammim, see 702, S: 658† & 6450†, B: 67C, K: 78D, H: 72C

1957 [1]דָּמַם *dāmam[1]*, [A] to be still, be silent, be quiet, rest; [C] to be silenced; [D] to quiet, S: 1826, B: 198D, K: 213D, H: 72C

1958 [2]דָּמַם *dāmam[2]*, variant: [A] to wail, S: 1826, B: 199A, K: 213D, H: 72D

1959 [3]דָּמַם *dāmam[3]*, [A] to perish; [C] to be laid waste, be silenced, be destroyed; [G] to doom to perish, S: 1826, B: 198D, K: 213D, H: 72C

1960 דְּמָמָה *dᵉmāmâ*, hush, whisper, S: 1827, B: 199A, K: 214A, H: 72D

1961 דֹּמֶן *dōmen*, refuse, dung, S: 1828, B: 199B, K: 214B, H: 72D

1962 דִּמְנָה *dimnâ*, Dimnah, S: 1829, B: 199B, K: 214B, H: 72D

1963 דָּמַע *dāma'*, [A] to weep, S: 1830, B: 199C, K: 214B, H: 72D

1964 דֶּמַע *dema'*, juice, S: 1831, B: 199C, K: 214B, H: 73A

1965 דִּמְעָה *dim'â*, tears, weeping, S: 1832, B: 199C, K: 214C, H: 73A

1966 דַּמֶּשֶׂק *dammeśeq*, Damascus, S: 1834, B: 199D, K: 214C, H: 73A

1967 דְּמֶשֶׁק *dᵉmešeq*, variant: Damascus, damask [?], S: 1833, B: 200A, K: 214C, H: 73A

1968 [1]דָּן *dān[1]*, Dan, S: 1835, B: 192D, K: 214D, H: 73A 1. & 2.

1969 [2]דָּן *dān[2]*, Dan, S: 1835, B: 192D, K: 214D, H: 73A 3.

1970 דָּן יַעַן *dān ya'an*, Dan Jaan, S: 1842, B: 193A (note), K: 214D & 389C, H: 73A 3.

1971 דָּנִאֵל *dāni'ēl*, variant: Danel, Daniel, see 1975, S: 1840, B: 193A, K: 215B, H: 73A

1972 דַּנָּה *dannâ*, Dannah, S: 1837, B: 200A, K: 215A, H: 73A

1973 דִּנְהָבָה *dinhābâ*, Dinhabah, S: 1838, B: 200B, K: 215A, H: 73A

1974 דָּנִי *dānî*, Danite, men of Dan, S: 1839, B: 193A, K: 215A, H: 73A

1975 דָּנִיֵּאל *dāniyyē'l*, Daniel, S: 1840, B: 193A, K: 215B, H: 73A

1976 דֵּעַ *dēa'*, what is known, knowledge, S: 1843, B: 395B, K: 215B, H: 73A

1977 דָּעָה *dā'â*, variant: [A] to seek, ask about, S: 3045†, B: 393B, K: 215B, H: 73A

1978 דֵּעָה *dē'â*, knowledge, S: 1844, B: 395C, K: 215B, H: 73A

1979 דְּעוּאֵל *dᵉ'û'ēl*, Deuel, S: 1845, B: 396A, K: 215C, H: 73A

1980 דָּעַךְ *dā'ak*, [A] to snuff out, extinguish; [C] to vanish; [E] to die out, S: 1846, B: 200B, K: 215C, H: 73B

1981 [1]דַּעַת *da'at[1]*, knowledge; understanding, learning, S: 1847, B: 395C, K: 215C, H: 73B

1982 [2]דַּעַת *da'at[2]*, variant: claim, S: 1847, B: 395C, K: 215C, H: 73B

1983 [3]דַּעַת *da'at[3]*, variant: sweat, S: 1847, B: 395D, K: 215C, H: 73B

1984 דֳּפִי *dᵒpî*, blemish, stain; slander, S: 1848†, B: 200C, K: 216A, H: 73B

1985 דָּפַק *dāpaq*, [A] to drive hard; to knock hard (= worry); [F] to pound (on a door), S: 1849, B: 200C, K: 216A, H: 73B

1986 דָּפְקָה *dopqâ*, Dophkah, S: 1850, B: 200C, K: 216B, H: 73C

1987 דַּק *daq*, gaunt, thin, dwarfed; finely ground (incense), fine (dust), S: 1851, B: 201A, K: 216B, H: 73C

1988 דֹּק *dōq*, canopy, thin veil, S: 1852, B: 201A, K: 216B, H: 73C

1989 דִּקְלָה *diqlâ*, Diklah, S: 1853, B: 200C, K: 216C, H: 73C

1990 דָּקַק *dāqaq*, [A] to finely crush or grind; [G] to grind to powder, break to pieces; [H] to be ground (to make bread), S: 1854, B: 200D, K: 216C, H: 73C

1991 דָּקַר *dāqar*, [A] to drive through, pierce, stab; [B, C, E] to be pierced, S: 1856, B: 201A, K: 216D, H: 73C

1992 דֶּקֶר *deqer*, variant: Deker, see 1206, S: 1857, B: 201B, K: 216D, H: 73D

1993 דַּר *dar*, mother-of-pearl, S: 858, B: 204D, K: 217A, H: 73D

1994 דֵּרָאוֹן *dērā'ôn*, loathing, contempt, S: 1860, B: 201B, K: 217A, H: 73D

1995 דָּרְבָן *dorbān*, (iron) goading stick, S: 1861, B: 201C, K: 217A, H: 73D

1996 דָּרְבֹנָה *dorbōnâ*, (iron) goading stick, S: 1861†, B: 201C, K: 217A, H: 73D

1997 דַּרְדַּע *darda'*, Darda, S: 1862, B: 201C, K: 217B, H: 73D

1998 דַּרְדַּר *dardar*, thistle, S: 1863, B: 205A, K: 217B, H: 73D

1999 דָּרוֹם *dārôm*, south; south wind, S: 1864, B: 204D, K: 217B, H: 73D

2000 [1]דְּרוֹר *dᵉrôr[1]*, bird, swallow, S: 1866, B: 204D, K: 217B, H: 73D

2001 [2]דְּרוֹר *dᵉrôr[2]*, oil of myrrh, S: 1865, B: 204D 1., K: 217B, H: 73D

2002 [3]דְּרוֹר *dᵉrôr[3]*, freedom, liberty, S: 1865, B: 204D 2., K: 217C, H: 74A

2003 דָּרְיָוֶשׁ *dārᵉyāweš*, Darius, S: 1867, B: 201D, K: 217C, H: 74A

2004 דַּרְיוֹשׁ *daryôš*, variant: see 2011, S: 1875†, B: 205C, K: 217C, H*

2005 דָּרַךְ *dārak*, [A] to go out, set out, march on, walk upon, trample; to bend (a bow); [B] to string (a bow), be bent (of a bow); [G] to shoot (a bow); to cause to tread, to enable to go; to lead, guide, S: 1869, B: 201D, K: 217C, H: 74A

2006 דֶּרֶךְ *derek*, way, path, route, road, journey; conduct, way of life, S: 1870, B: 202C, K: 218A, H: 74A

2007 דַּרְכְּמוֹנִים *darkᵉmônîm*, (pl.) drachmas, S: 1871†, B: 204A, K: 219A, H: 74C

2008 דַּרְמֶשֶׂק *darmeśeq*, Damascus, S: 1834, B: 199D, K: 219A, H: 74D

2009 דָּרַע *dāra'*, variant: Daraa, see 1997, S: 1873†, B: 201C, K: 219A, H: 74D

2010 דַּרְקוֹן *darqôn*, Darkon, S: 1874, B: 204C, K: 219B, H: 74D

2011 דָּרַשׁ *dāraš*, [A] to seek, inquire, consult; [B] to ponder, be sought after; [C] to let oneself be inquired of, to allow a search to be made, S: 1875, B: 205A, K: 219B, H: 74D

2012 דָּשָׁא *dāšā'*, [A] to become green (of pastures); [G] to produce, cause to shoot forth, S: 1876, B: 205D, K: 220A, H: 75A

2013 דֶּשֶׁא *deše'*, (new) green vegetation, (new) green grass, S: 1877, B: 206A, K: 220B, H: 75A

2014 [1]דָּשֵׁן *dāšēn[1]*, [A] to thrive, grow fat; [D] to anoint, give health; to remove the (fat) ashes; [E] to prosper, be satisfied, be soaked (with fat); [F] to be covered with fat, S: 1878, B: 206A, K: 220B, H: 75C

2015 [2]דָּשֵׁן *dāšēn[2]*, rich, fresh, S: 1879, B: 206C, K: 220D, H: 75C

2016 דֶּשֶׁן *dešen*, abundance, riches, choice food; (fatty) ashes (the burned wood of the altar fire soaked with fat), S: 1880, B: 206B, K: 220C, H: 75C

2017 דָּת *dāt*, command, prescription, custom, edict, law, S: 1881, B: 206C, K: 220D, H: 75C

2018 דָּתָן *dātān*, Dathan, S: 1885, B: 206D, K: 220D, H: 75C

2019 דֹּתָן *dōtān*, Dothan, S: 1886, B: 206D, K: 220D, H: 75C

2020 ה *h*, letter of the Hebrew alphabet, S*, B: 206B, K: 221A, H*

2021 -הַ *ha-*, the, a, who, this, that; often not translated, S*, B: 206B, K: 221C, H: 75B

2022 -הֲ *hᵃ-*, introduces a question; usually translated as a question mark, S*, B: 209C, K: 222C, H: 75D

2023 -ָה *-āh*, -הָ *-hā*, -ָהִי *-â[1]*, -הָא *-hā'*, she, her; it, its, S*, B*, K*, H*

2024 -הֹ *-ōh*, he, his, him, S*, B*, K*, H*

2025 [2]-ָה *-â[2]*, to, toward, S*, B*, K*, H*

2026 הֵא *hē'*, surely! see!, S: 1887, B: 210C, K: 223A, H: 76A

2027 הֶאָח *he'āḥ*, Ah!, Aha!, S: 1889, B: 210C, K: 223A, H: 76A

2028 הָאֲחַשְׁתָּרִי *hā'ᵃḥaštārî*, Haahashtari, S: 326†, B: 31C, K: 34A, H: 11C

2029 הָאֵלִי *hā'ēlî*, variant: see 1088, S: 1017†, B: 111A, K: 126A, H: 39B 2.

2030 הָאֶלֶף *hā'elep*, Haeleph, S: 507†, B: 49B, K: 57B, H*

[A] Qal [B] Qal passive [C] Niphal [D] Piel (poel, polel, pilel, pilal, pealal, pilpel) [E] Pual (poal, polal, poalal, pulal, pualal)

2031 הָאַמָּה *hā'ammâ*, variant: Ha-Ammah, see 5497, S: 4965†, B: 52A, K: 59C, H: 222C

2032 הָאֵצֶל *hā'ēṣel*, variant: Ha-Ezel, see 1089, S: 1018†, B: 69B, K: 124A 3., H*

2033 הָאַרְבַּע *hā'arba'*, variant: Arba, S: 7151† + 704†, B: 900B, K: 856A, H: 325D 1.

2034 הָאֲרָרִי *hā'rārî*, variant: see 2240, S: 2043, B: 210C & 251B, K: 90B, H: 84C

2035 [1]הַב *hab*[1], come!, give!, put!, ascribe!, S: 3051†, B: 396C, K: 223B, H: 76A

2036 [2]הַב *hab*[2], variant: elephant [?], S: 8143†, B: 1042B, K: 997D, H: 76A

2037 הַבְהָב *habhab*, gift, S: 1890, B: 396D, K: 223B, H: 76A

2038 הָבַל *hābal*, [A] to be worthless, meaningless; be proud, vain; [G] to fill with false hopes, cause to become vain, S: 1891, B: 211A, K: 223C, H: 76A

2039 [1]הֶבֶל *hebel*[1], meaninglessness, worthlessness, vanity, emptiness, futility, S: 1892, B: 210C, K: 223C, H: 76B

2040 [2]הֶבֶל *hebel*[2], Abel, S: 1893, B: 211A, K: 224A, H: 76B

2041 הָבְנִים *hobnîm*, ebony, S: 1894†, B: 211B, K: 224A, H: 76B

2042 הָבַר *hābar*, [A] (ptcp.) astrologer, S: 1895, B: 211B, K: 224A, H: 76B

2043 הֵגֵא *hēgē'*, Hegai, S: 1896, B: 211B, K: 224C, H: 76B

2044 הַגִּדְגָּד *haggidgād*, variant: Haggidgad, see 2988, S: 2735†, B: 301B & 151D, K: 329B, H: 115B

2045 הַגְּדוֹלִים *hagg^{e}dôlîm*, Haggedolim, S: 1419†, B: 153A, K*, H*

2046 הַגּוֹיִם *haggôyim*, variant: Haggoyim, S: 2800† + 1471†, B: 361D, K: 338C, H: 118C

2047 [1]הָגָה *hāgā*[1], [A] to utter a sound, moan, meditate; [G] to mutter, S: 1897, B: 211C, K: 224A, H: 76C

2048 [2]הָגָה *hāgā*[2], [A] to expel, remove, S: 1898, B: 212A, K: 224C, H: 76C

2049 הֶגֶה *hegeh*, moaning, mourning, rumbling, S: 1899, B: 211D, K: 224C, H: 76C

2050 הָגוּת *hāgût*, utterance, meditation, S: 1900, B: 212A, K: 224C, H: 76C

2051 הֵגַי *hēgay*, Hegai, S: 1896, B: 211B, K: 224C, H: 76C

2052 הָגִיג *hāgîg*, sighing, meditation, S: 1901, B: 211C, K: 224C, H: 76C

2053 הִגָּיוֹן *higgāyôn*, muttering, meditation; Higgaion, melody, S: 1902, B: 212A, K: 224D, H: 76C

2054 הָגִין *hāgîn*, corresponding, S: 1903, B: 212B, K: 224D, H: 76D

2055 הַגִּלְגָּל *haggilgāl*, variant: Gilgal, S: 1537†, B: 111B, K: 181D, H: 39B 10.

2056 הַגָּן *haggān*, variant: Haggan, see 1091, S: 1588†, B: 111B, K: 124B, H: 39B 12.

2057 הָגָר *hāgār*, Hagar, S: 1904, B: 212B, K: 224D, H: 76D

2058 הַגְרִי *hagrî*, Hagrites, of Hagri, S: 1905, B: 212B, K: 225A, H: 76D

2059 הֵד *hēd*, joyous shout, S: 1906, B: 212D, K: 225A, H: 76D

2060 הֲדַד *h^{a}dad*, Hadad, S: 1908, B: 212D, K: 225A, H: 76D

2061 הֲדַדְעֶזֶר *h^{a}dad'ezer*, Hadadezer, S: 1909, B: 212D, K: 225B, H: 76D

2062 הֲדַד־רִמּוֹן *h^{a}dad-rimmôn*, Hadad Rimmon, S: 1910, B: 213A, K: 225B, H: 76D

2063 הָדָה *hādâ*, [A] to put, stretch out, S: 1911, B: 213A, K: 225B, H: 76D

2064 הֹדּוּ *hōddû*, India, S: 1912, B: 213A, K: 225B, H: 76D

2065 הֲדוּרִים *h^{a}dûrîm*, mountains, S: 1921†, B: 213D, K: 225C, H: 76D

2066 [1]הֲדוֹרָם *h^{a}dôrām*[1], Hadoram, S: 1913, B: 213B 1., K: 225C, H: 76D

2067 [2]הֲדוֹרָם *h^{a}dôrām*[2], Hadoram; Adoniram, S: 1913, B: 213B 2. & 214C, K: 225C, H: 76D

2068 הִדַּי *hidday*, Hiddai, S: 1914, B: 213B, K: 225C, H: 76D

2069 הוֹדַיְוָהוּ *hōdaywāhû*, variant: Hodayvahu, see 2089, S: 1939, B: 1124A, K: 227D, H: 76D

2070 הָדַךְ *hādak*, [A] to crush by treading upon, S: 1915, B: 213B, K: 225C, H: 76D

2071 הֲדֹם *h^{a}dōm*, footstool, S: 1916, B: 213B, K: 225C, H: 76D

2072 הֲדַס *h^{a}das*, myrtle tree, S: 1918, B: 213C, K: 225D, H: 77A

2073 הֲדַסָּה *h^{a}dassâ*, Hadassah, S: 1919, B: 213C, K: 225D, H: 77A

2074 הָדַף *hādap*, [A] to shove, push, thrust, drive out, S: 1920, B: 213C, K: 225D, H: 77A

2075 הָדַר *hādar*, [A] to show favoritism; show respect; [B] to be in splendor; [C] to be shown respect; [F] to exalt oneself, S: 1921, B: 213D, K: 226A, H: 77A

2076 הֲדַר *h^{a}dar*, variant: Hadar, see 2060, S: 1924, B: 214C, K: 225A, H: 77A

2077 הָדָר *hādār*, majesty, splendor, glory, nobility, S: 1926, B: 214A, K: 226A, H: 77A

2078 הֶדֶר *heder*, splendor, S: 1925, B: 214A, K: 226C, H: 77A

2079 הֲדָרָה *h^{a}dārâ*, splendor, glory, S: 1927, B: 214C, K: 226C, H: 77B

2080 הֲדַרְעֶזֶר *h^{a}dar'ezer*, variant: Hadarezer, see 2061, S: 1928, B: 214C, K: 225B, H: 76D

2081 הָהּ *hāh*, Alas!, S: 1929, B: 214C, K: 226C, H: 77B

2082 הוֹ *hô*, ah! (doubled for emphasis), S: 1930, B: 214C, K: 226C, H: 77B

2083 הוּ *hû*, he, she, it; that, which, S*, B: 214D, K: 226C, H: 77B

2084 ־הוּ *-hû*, he, his, him; it, its, S*, B*, K: 226C, H*

2085 הוּא *hû'*, he, it; this, that, S: 1931, B: 214D, K: 226C, H: 77B

2086 [1]הוֹד *hôd*[1], splendor, majesty, glory, strength, S: 1935, B: 217A, K: 227C, H: 77C

2087 [2]הוֹד *hôd*[2], Hod, S: 1936, B: 217B, K: 227D, H: 77C

2088 הוֹדְוָה *hôd^{e}wâ*, Hodaviah, S: 1937, B: 217B, K: 227D, H: 77D

2089 הוֹדַוְיָה *hôdawyâ*, Hodaviah, S: 1938, B: 217A, K: 227D, H: 77D

2090 הוֹדַוְיָהוּ *hôdawyāhû*, Hodaviah, S: 1939, B: 217C, K: 227D, H: 77D

2091 הוֹדִיָּה *hôdiyyâ*, Hodiah, S: 1940 & 1941, B: 217C, K: 227D, H: 77D

2092 [1]הָוָה *hāwâ*[1], [A] to fall (on), S: 1933, B: 216D, K: 227D, H: 77C & D

2093 [2]הָוָה *hāwâ*[2], [A] to be, become; to get, have, S: 1933, B: 217C, K: 228A, H: 77D

2094 [1]הַוָּה *hawwâ*[1], (evil) desire, craving, S: 1942, B: 217C, K: 228A, H: 77D

2095 [2]הַוָּה *hawwâ*[2], destruction, ruin, corruption, S: 1942, B: 217C, K: 228A, H: 77D

2096 הֹוָה *hōwâ*, calamity, disaster, S: 1943, B: 217D, K: 228A, H: 77D

2097 הוֹהָם *hôhām*, Hoham, S: 1944, B: 222D, K: 228B, H: 77D

2098 הוֹי *hôy*, woe!, ah!, oh!, alas!; (to invite) come!, S: 1945, B: 222D, K: 228B, H: 77D

2099 הוֹלֵלוֹת *hôlēlôt*, madness, delusion, folly, S: 1947†, B: 239C, K: 228B, H: 78A

2100 הוֹלֵלוּת *hôlēlût*, madness, delusion, folly, S: 1948, B: 239C, K: 228B, H: 78A

2101 הוּם *hûm*, [A] to throw into confusion; [C] to be stirred up, be shook; [G] to be distraught; to throng, S: 1949, B: 223A, K: 228C, H: 78A

2102 הוֹמָם *hômām*, Homam, S: 1950, B: 243A, K: 228C, H: 78A

2103 הוּן *hûn*, [G] to think it easy, S: 1951, B: 223B, K: 228C, H: 78A

2104 הוֹן *hôn*, wealth, riches, possessions, S: 1952, B: 223C, K: 228C, H: 78A

2105 הוֹר *hôr*, variant: mountain, S: 2029†, B: 223C, K: 241B, H: 83B

2106 הוֹשָׁמָע *hôšāmā'*, Hoshama, S: 1953, B: 221D, K: 228D, H: 78A

2107 הוֹשֵׁעַ *hôšēa'*, Hoshea; Joshua, S: 1954, B: 448A, K: 228D, H: 78A

2108 הוֹשַׁעְיָה *hôša'yâ*, Hoshaiah, S: 1955†, B: 448A, K: 229A, H: 78A

2109 הוּת *hût*, [D] to assault, S: 2050†, B: 223D, K: 243D, H: 78B

2110 הוֹתִיר *hôtîr*, Hothir, S: 1956, B: 452D, K: 229A, H: 78B

2111 הָזָה *hāzâ*, [A] to dream, S: 1957, B: 223D, K: 229A, H: 78B

2112 הַחִירֹת *haḥîrôt*, variant: Hahiroth, S: 6367†, B: 809D, K: 759A, H: 291B

2113 הִי *hî*, woe!, S: 1958, B: 223D & 624D, K: 229A, H: 78B

2114 ־הִי *-hî*, his, him, S*, B*, K*, H*

2115 הִיא *hî'*, variant: she, see 2085, S: 1931, B: 214D, K: 226C, H: 78B

2116 הֵידָד *hêdād*, shout (of joy), S: 1959, B: 212C, K: 229A, H: 78B

2117 הֻיְּדוֹת *huyy^{e}dôt*, (pl.) songs of thanksgiving, S: 1960†, B: 392D, K: 229B, H: 78B

2118 הָיָה *hāyâ*, [A] to be, become, happen; [C] to be done, happen, S: 1961, B: 224A, K: 229B, H: 78B

2119 הַיָּה *hayyâ*, variant: destruction, S: 1962, B: 228A & 217D, K: 230D, H: 79A

2120 הֵיךְ *hêk*, how?, S: 1963, B: 228A, K: 230D, H: 79A

2121 הֵיכָל *hêkāl*, temple, sanctuary, palace; main hall, S: 1964, B: 228A, K: 230D, H: 79A

2122 הֵילֵל *hêlēl*, morning star, S: 1966, B: 237D, K: 231B, H: 79B

2123 הֵימָם *hêmām*, Homam, S: 1967, B: 243A, K: 231B, H: 79B

2124 הֵימָן *hêmān*, Homam, S: 1968, B: 54C, K: 231B, H: 79B

2125 הִין *hîn*, hin (liquid measure), S: 1969, B: 228D, K: 231C, H: 79B

2126 הַיַּרְקוֹן *hayyarqôn*, variant: Jarkon, S: 4313†, B: 566A, K: 518D, H: 193A

2127 הַיְשִׁימוֹת *hayᵉšîmôt*, variant: Jeshimoth, S: 1020†, B: 111D, K: 124C, H: 39B b. 21.

2128 הָכַר *hākar*, variant: see 2686, S: 1970, B: 229A, K: 231C, H: 79B

2129 הַכָּרָה *hakkārâ*, look (on a face), S: 1971, B: 648B, K: 231C, H: 79B

2130 הַכֶּרֶם *hakkerem*, variant: Hakkerem, S: 1021†, B: 111D, K: 124D 21., H: 39B b 23.

2131 הַל *hal*, variant: interrogative particle, S: 1973, B: 210B, K: 222C & 462B, H: 75D & 167B

2132 הֲלֹא *hᵃlō'*, variant: see 2022 & 4202, S: 3808†, B: 518B, K: 466B, H: 79B

2133 הָלָא *hālā'*, [C] to be driven away, be removed, S: 1972, B: 229C, K: 231C, H: 79B

2134 הָלְאָה *hālᵉ'â*, beyond; far (and wide), some distance away; out of the way!, S: 1973, B: 229B, K: 231C, H: 79C

2135 הַלּוֹחֵשׁ *hallōḥēš*, Hallohesh, S: 3873†, B: 538A, K: 476C, H: 174C

2136 הִלּוּלִים *hillûlîm*, offering of praise; festival (related to a god), S: 1974†, B: 239B, K: 231D, H: 79C

2137 הַלָּז *hallāz*, this, S: 1975, B: 229C, K: 231D, H: 79C

2138 הַלָּזֶה *hallāzeh*, this, S: 1976, B: 229C, K: 232A, H: 79C

2139 הַלֵּזוּ *hallēzû*, variant: this, S: 1977, B: 229D, K: 232A, H: 79C

2140 הַלַּחְמִי *hallaḥmî*, variant: see 1095, S: 1022†, B: 112A, K: 479C, H: 175D

2141 הָלִיךְ *hālîk*, path, steps, S: 1978, B: 237B, K: 232A, H: 79C

2142 הֲלִיכָה *hᵃlîkâ*, procession, way, walk; traveling merchants; affairs, S: 1979, B: 237B, K: 232A, H: 79C

2143 הָלַךְ *hālak*, [A] to walk, go, travel; [C] to fade away; [D] to walk about, go about, [G] to drive back, get rid of; enable to walk; to lead; bring; [F] to move to and fro, wander, walk about, S: 1980 & 3212†, B: 229D, K: 232B, H: 79D

2144 הֵלֶךְ *hēlek*, oozing, flowing; visitor, S: 1982, B: 237A, K: 235A, H: 80D

2145 ¹הָלַל *hālal¹*, [G] to flash, radiate, shine, S: 1984, B: 237C, K: 235A, H: 80D

2146 ²הָלַל *hālal²*, [D] to praise; give thanks; cheer, extol; [E] to be praised, be worthy of praise, be of renown; [F] to make one's boast in (the name of God), S: 1984, B: 237D, K: 235A, H: 80B

2147 ³הָלַל *hālal³*, [A] to be arrogant; [D] to make a fool of, to mock, rail against; [E] to be foolish; [F] to act like a madman; act furiously, S: 1984, B: 237D, K: 235D, H: 81A

2148 הִלֵּל *hillēl*, Hillel, S: 1985, B: 239B, K: 236A, H: 81B

2149 הַלְלוּיָהּ *halᵉlûyāh*, variant: hallelujah (praise Yahweh), S: 1984 + 3050, B: 238B 2.d & 219C, K: 236A, H: 81B

2150 הָלַם *hālam*, [A] to strike, smash, beat, trample, S: 1986, B: 240C, K: 236A, H: 81B

2151 הֲלֹם *hᵃlōm*, to here, S: 1988, B: 240D, K: 236B, H: 81B

2152 הֵלֶם *hēlem*, Helem, S: 1987†, B: 240C, K: 236B, H: 81B

2153 הַלְמוּת *halmût*, hammer, S: 1989, B: 240D, K: 236B, H: 81B

2154 ¹חָם *hām¹*, Ham, S: 1990, B: 241A, K: 236C, H: 81B

2155 ²הָם *hām²*, wealth, S: 1991†, B: 241A, K: 237A, H*

2156 הֵם *hēm*, they, them, S: 1992, B: 241A, K: 236C, H: 81B & 82A

2157 -הֶם *-hem*, -הֵם *-hēm*, they, them, their, S*, B*, K*, H*

2158 הַמְּדָתָא *hammᵉdātā'*, Hammedatha, S: 4099†, B: 241A, K: 236C, H: 81C

2159 הָמָה *hāmâ*, [A] to make a noise, be tumultuous, S: 1993, B: 242A, K: 236C, H: 81C

2160 הֵמָּה *hēmmâ*, variant: they, S: 1992, B: 241A, K: 237A, H: 81C

2161 -הֵמָה *-hēmâ*, they, them, S: 1992†, B*, K*, H*

2162 הָמוֹן *hāmôn*, commotion, tumult, confusion; many, populace, hoards, army, S: 1995, B: 242B, K: 237A, H: 81C

2163 הֲמוֹן גּוֹג *hᵃmôn gôg*, Hamon Gog, S: 1996, B: 155D & 242B, K: 174A & 237A, H: 81C

2164 הֲמוֹנָה *hᵃmônâ*, Hamonah, S: 1997, B: 242D, K: 237C, H: 81D

2165 הַמַּחְלְקוֹת *hammaḥlᵉqôt*, variant: Hammahlekoth, S: 5555†, B: 325D, K: 513B, H: 257B II. 2.

2166 הֶמְיָה *hemyâ*, noise, sound, tone, S: 1998, B: 242D, K: 237C, H: 81D

2167 הֲמֻלָּה *hᵃmullâ*, tumult, sound, noise, S: 1999, B: 242D, K: 237C, H: 81D & C

2168 הַמֹּלֶכֶת *hammōleket*, Hammoleketh, S: 4447†, B: 574C, K: 532C, H: 199A

2169 ¹הָמַם *hāmam¹*, [A] to throw into confusion; to rout, S: 2000, B: 243A, K: 237C, H: 81D

2170 ²הָמַם *hāmam²*, variant: [A] to drain, S: 2000, B: 243A, K: 237C, H: 81D

2171 הָמַן *hāman*, [A] to rage, be turbulent, S: 1995†, B: 243A, K: 237D, H: 82A

2172 הָמָן *hāmān*, Haman, S: 2001, B: 243B, K: 237D, H: 81D

2173 הֲמָסִים *hᵃmāsîm*, twigs, brushwood, S: 2003†, B: 243B, K: 238A, H: 82A

2174 הַמִּצְפֶּה *hammiṣpeh*, variant: Ha-Mizpah, see 8256, S: 7434†, B: 859D, K: 557D, H: 211B

2175 הַמַּרְכָּבוֹת *hammarkābôt*, variant: Ha-Marcaboth, S: 1024†, B: 112B, K: 125A 27., H: 39C b 31.

2176 ¹הֵן *hēn¹*, see!, surely!; if, yet, but, then, S: 2005 & 3860†, B: 243B, K: 238A, H: 82A

2177 -²הֵן *-hēn²*, -הֶן *-hen*, they, them, their, S: 2004†, B*, K*, H*

2178 ¹הֵנָּה *hēnnâ¹*, here, to here; on this side, on the opposite side, S: 2008, B: 244C, K: 238C, H: 82A

2179 ²הֵנָּה *hēnnâ²*, they, these, those, S: 2007, B: 244D, K: 238D, H: 82B

2180 הִנֵּה *hinnēh*, look!, now!, here, there, S: 2009, B: 243D, K: 238D, H: 82B

2181 -הֶנָה *-hᵉnâ*, -הֵנָה *-henâ*, they, them, S*, B*, K: 226C, H*

2182 הֲנָחָה *hᵃnāḥâ*, holiday, S: 2010, B: 629C, K: 239C, H: 82C

2183 הִנֹּם *hinnōm*, Hinnom, S: 2011, B: 244D, K: 179D, H: 82C

2184 הֵנַע *hēna'*, Hena, S: 2012, B: 245A, K: 239D, H: 82C

2185 הֲנָפָה *hᵃnāpâ*, variant: shaking, see 5677, S: 5130†, B: 632A, K: 239D, H: 82C

2186 הַנְּקֶב *hanneqeb*, variant: Nekeb, S: 5346†, B: 10A, K: 631D, H: 5A

2187 הַס *has*, Silence!, Quiet!, Hush!, S: 2013†, B: 245A, K: 239D, H: 82C

2188 הָסָה *hāsâ*, [G] to silence, cause to be still, S: 2013, B: 245A, K: 239D, H: 82C

2189 הַסְּנָאָה *hassᵉnā'â*, Hassenaah, S: 5570†, B: 702D, K: 661D, H: 257D

2190 הַסְּנֻאָה *hassᵉnu'â*, Hassenuah, S: 5570†, B: 703A, K: 662A, H: 258A

2191 הַסֹּפֶרֶת *hassōperet*, Hassophereth, S: 5618†, B: 709B, K: 667A, H: 260A

2192 הָעֲבָרִים *hā'ᵃbārîm*, variant: Abarim, S: 5863†, B: 743D, K: 699C, H: 271C

2193 הָעֵזֶר *hā'ēzer*, variant: Ha-Ezer, see 75, S: 72†, B: 7A, K: 696C, H: 270C

2194 הָעַמֹּנִי *hā'ammōnî*, variant: Ha-Ammoni, see 4112, S: 3726†, B: 770A, K: 714C, H: 276B

2195 הָעֵמֶק *hā'ēmeq*, variant: Ha-Emek, see 1097, S: 1025†, B: 112B, K: 716C, H: 39C b 35.

2196 הָעֲרָבָה *hā'ᵃrābâ*, variant: Ha-Arabah, see 1098, S: 1026†, B: 112C, K: 125B 35., H: 39C b 39.

2197 הָעֲרָלוֹת *hā'ᵃrālôt*, variant: Haaraloth, see 1502, S: 6190†, B: 790B, K: 737B, H: 283D

2198 הֲפֻגָה *hᵃpugâ*, relief, stopping, S: 2014, B: 806B, K: 239D, H: 82D

2199 הַפּוּךְ *happûk*, variant: Happuch, S: 7163†, B: 902A, K: 857A, H: 326A

2200 הָפַךְ *hāpak*, [A] to overthrow, overturn, turn around, change; [B] to be turned over; [C] to be changed, transformed, turned into; [H] to be overwhelmed; [F] to tumble around, flash back and forth, swirl, S: 2015, B: 245B, K: 240A, H: 82D

2201 הֵפֶךְ *hēpek*, opposite, turning of things upside down, perversion, S: 2016 & 2017†, B: 246A, K: 241A, H: 83A

2202 הֲפֵכָה *h^a pēkâ*, catastrophe, demolition, S: 2018, B: 246B, K: 241A, H: 83A

2203 הֲפַכְפַּךְ *h^a pakpak*, devious, crooked, S: 2019, B: 246B, K: 241A, H: 83A

2204 הַפִּצֵּץ *happiṣṣēṣ*, Happizzez, S: 6483†, B: 823A, K: 772D, H: 295D

2205 הֻצַּב *huṣṣab*, variant: see 5893, S: 5324†, B: 662C, K: 628D, H: 243C

2206 הַצֹּבֵבָה *haṣṣōbēbâ*, Hazzobebah, S: 6637†, B: 839D, K: 791C, H: 302C

2207 הַצְּבָיִים *haṣṣ^e bāyîm*, variant: Hazzebaim, S: 6380†, B: 810B, K: 759D, H: 291C

2208 הַצָּלָה *haṣṣālâ*, deliverance, S: 2020, B: 665A, K: 241A, H: 83B

2209 הַצְּלֶלְפּוֹנִי *haṣṣ^e lelpônî*, Hazzelelponi, S: 6753†, B: 853C, K: 241A, H: 83B

2210 הֹצֶן *hōṣen*, weapon, S: 2021, B: 246C, K: 241A, H: 83B

2211 הַצֻּרִים *haṣṣurîm*, variant: Hazzurim, S: 2521†, B: 324D, K: 307D, H: 305B

2212 הַקּוֹץ *haqqôṣ*, Hakkoz, S: 6976†, B: 881A 2., K: 834A, H: 83B

2213 הַקֹּורֵא *haqqōrē'*, variant: Hakkore, see 6530, S: 5875†, B: 745B, K: 700C, H: 271D 4.k

2214 הַקָּטָן *haqqāṭān*, Hakkatan, S: 6997†, B: 882A, K: 835C, H: 317C

2215 הַר *har*, hill, mountain, range (of hills, mountains), S: 2022 & 2042†, B: 249A, K: 241B, H: 83B

2216 הֹר *hōr*, Hor, S: 2023, B: 246D, K: 241D, H: 83B

2217 הָרָא *hārā'*, Hara, S: 2024, B: 246D, K: 241D, H: 83B

2218 הָרֹאֶה *hārō'eh*, Haroeh, S: 7204†, B: 909B, K: 864A, H: 329A

2219 הַרְאֵל *har'ēl*, altar hearth, S: 2025, B: 72B, K: 241D, H: 83B

2220 הַרְבָּה *harbâ*, variant: see 8049, S: 7235†, B: 915C, K: 242A, H: 83B

2221 הַרְבֵּה *harbēh*, great (number), many, much, abundance, S: 7235†, B: 915A, K: 869D, H: 83C

2222 הָרַג *hārag*, [A] to kill, put to death, murder, slaughter; [B, C, E] to be slain, be put to death, be slaughtered, S: 2026, B: 246D, K: 242A, H: 83C

2223 הֶרֶג *hereg*, slaughter, killing, S: 2027, B: 247C, K: 242C, H: 83D

2224 הֲרֵגָה *h^a rēgâ*, slaughter, S: 2028, B: 247C, K: 242C, H: 83D

2225 הָרָה *hārâ*, [A] to conceive, become pregnant, be with child; [B, E] to be conceived, born, S: 2029, B: 247C, K: 242C, H: 83D

2226 הָרֶה *hāreh*, pregnant, expecting (child), S: 2030, B: 248A, K: 242D, H: 83D

2227 הָרוּם *hārûm*, Harum, S: 2037, B: 248B, K: 243A, H: 84A

2228 הֵרוֹן *hērôn*, childbearing, pregnancy, S: 2032, B: 248A, K: 243A, H: 84A

2229 הֲרוֹרִי *h^a rôrî*, Harorite, S: 2033, B: 248B, K: 243A, H: 84A

2230 הָרִיָּה *hāriyyâ*, pregnant, expecting, S: 2030†, B: 248A, K: 243A, H: 83D

2231 הֵרָיוֹן *hērāyôn*, conception, pregnancy, S: 2032, B: 248A, K: 243A, H: 84A

2232 הֲרִיסָה *h^a rîsâ*, ruin, S: 2034, B: 249A, K: 243A, H: 84A

2233 הֲרִיסוּת *h^a rîsût*, waste, ruin, destruction, S: 2035, B: 249A, K: 243A, H: 84A

2234 הָרָם *hārām*, variant: Haram, S: 1027†, B: 111B, K: 124B 14., H: 84A & 39B 45.

2235 הֹרָם *hōrām*, Horam, S: 2036, B: 248B, K: 243B, H: 84A

2236 הַרְמוֹן *harmôn*, Harmon, S: 2038, B: 248B, K: 243B, H: 84A

2237 הָרָן *hārān*, Haran, S: 2039, B: 248C, K: 243B, H: 84A

2238 הָרַס *hāras*, [A] to tear down, break down, destroy; [B] to be in ruins; [C] to be destroyed, in ruins; [D] to destroy, S: 2040, B: 248C, K: 243B, H: 84A

2239 הֶרֶס *heres*, destruction (= Heliopolis), S: 2041, B: 249A, K: 243C, H: 84C

2240 הֲרָרִי *h^a rārî*, Hararite, S: 2043, B: 251C, K: 243C, H: 84C

2241 הַשַּׁחַר *haššaḥar*, variant: Ha-Shahar, see 7680, S: 6890†, B: 866C, K: 818D, H: 311C

2242 הַשִּׁטָּה *haššiṭṭâ*, variant: Ha-Shittah, see 1101, S: 1029†, B: 112D, K: 125D 42., H: 39C 49.

2243 הַשִּׁטִּים *haššiṭṭîm*, variant: Ha-Shittim, see 69, S: 63†, B: 1008D, K: 964A, H: 367A

2244 הָשֵׁם *hāšēm*, Hashem, S: 2044, B: 251C, K: 243D, H: 84C

2245 הַשְׁמָעוּת *hašmā'ût*, news, communication, information, S: 2045, B: 1036A, K: 243D, H: 84C

2246 הַתַּאֲוָה *hatta'^a wâ*, variant: Hattaavah, S: 6914†, B: 869A, K: 821C, H: 312C

2247 הִתּוּךְ *hittûk*, melting, S: 2046, B: 678A, K: 243D, H: 84C

2248 הִתְחַבְּרוּת *hitḥabb^e rût*, variant: alliance, see 2489, S: 2266†, B: 288C, K: 273A, H: 84C

2249 הִתְיַחֵשׂ *hityaḥēś*, variant: registration, S: 3188†, B: 405B, K: 378C, H: 84C

2250 הַתִּיכוֹן *hattîkôn*, variant: Hatticon, S: 2694†, B: 347C, K: 1027B, H: 389D

2251 הֲתָךְ *h^a tāk*, Hathach, S: 2047, B: 251C, K: 243D, H: 84C

2252 הָתַל *hātal*, [D] to taunt, mock, S: 2048, B: 251C, K: 243D, H: 84C

2253 הֲתֻלִים *h^a tulîm*, mockery, S: 2049†, B: 251D, K: 243D, H: 84D

2254 הָתַת *hātat*, variant: [D] to overwhelm with reproaches, S: 2050, B: 223D, K: 243D, H: 84D

2255 ו *w*, letter of the Hebrew alphabet, S*, B: 251B, K: 244A, H*

2256 -וְ *w^e-*, and, but, yet, also, S*, B: 251B, K: 244C, H: 84B

2257 -וֹ *-ô*, -ו *-w*, -וּ *-û*, he, him, his; it, its, S*, B*, K*, H*

2258 וְדָן *w^e dān*, variant: see 1968, S: 2051, B: 255A, K: 246D, H: 85D

2259 וָהֵב *wāhēb*, Waheb, S: 2052, B: 255A, K: 246D, H: 85D

2260 וָו *wāw*, hook, peg, S: 2053, B: 255B, K: 246D, H: 85D

2261 וָזָר *wāzār*, guilty, S: 2054, B: 255C, K: 246D, H: 85D

2262 וַיְזָתָא *way^e zātā'*, Vaizatha, S: 2055, B: 255C, K: 246D, H: 85D

2263 וָלָד *wālād*, child, S: 2056, B: 409B, K: 246D, H: 85D

2264 וַנְיָה *wanyâ*, Vaniah, S: 2057, B: 255C, K: 247C, H: 85D

2265 וָפְסִי *wopsî*, Vophsi, S: 2058, B: 255C, K: 247C, H: 85D

2266 וַשְׁנִי *wašnî*, variant: see 9108, S: 2059, B: 255C, K: 247C, H: 85D

2267 וַשְׁתִּי *waštî*, Vashti, S: 2060, B: 255D, K: 247C, H: 85D

2268 ז *z*, letter of the Hebrew alphabet, S*, B: 255B, K: 247A, H*

2269 זְאֵב¹ *z^e 'ēb^1*, wolf, S: 2061, B: 255B, K: 247B, H: 85B

2270 זְאֵב² *z^e 'ēb^2*, Zeeb, S: 2062, B: 255D, K: 247B, H: 85B

2271 זֹאת *zō't*, variant: this, these, S: 2063, B: 260A, K: 247B, H: 85D

2272 זָבַד *zābad*, [A] to give (a gift), bestow, S: 2064, B: 256A, K: 247C, H: 85D

2273 זֵבֶד *zēbed*, gift, S: 2065†, B: 256B, K: 247D, H: 86A

2274 זָבָד *zābād*, Zabad, S: 2066, B: 256B, K: 247D, H: 86A

2275 זַבְדִּי *zabdî*, Zabdi, S: 2067, B: 256C, K: 247D, H: 86A

2276 זַבְדִּיאֵל *zabdî'ēl*, Zabdiel, S: 2068, B: 256C, K: 247D, H: 86A

2277 זְבַדְיָה *z^e badyâ*, Zebadiah, S: 2069, B: 256C, K: 247D, H: 86A

2278 זְבַדְיָהוּ *z^e badyāhû*, Zebadiah, S: 2069, B: 256C, K: 248A, H: 86A

2279 זְבוּב *z^e bûb*, fly (insect), S: 2070, B: 256A, K: 248A, H: 86A

2280 זָבוּד *zābûd*, Zabud, S: 2071, B: 256B, K: 248A, H: 86A

2281 זְבוּדָּה *z^e bûddâ*, variant: Zebuddah, see 2288, S: 2072†, B: 256B, K: 248A, H: 86A

2282 זְבוּלוּן *z^e bûlûn*, Zebulun, S: 2074, B: 259D, K: 248A, H: 86A

2283 זְבוּלֹנִי *z^e bûlōnî*, Zebulunite, S: 2075, B: 259D, K: 248B, H: 86A

2284 זָבַח *zābaḥ*, [A, D] to offer a sacrifice; to slaughter, butcher, S: 2076, B: 256D, K: 248C, H: 86A

2285 זֶבַח¹ *zebaḥ^1*, sacrifice, offering, S: 2077, B: 257B, K: 249A, H: 86A

2286 זֶבַח² *zebaḥ^2*, Zebah, S: 2078, B: 258A, K: 250A, H: 86C

2287 זַבַּי *zabbay*, Zabbai, S: 2079, B: 256A, K: 250A, H: 86C

2288 זְבִידָה *z^e bîdâ*, Zebidah, S: 2080, B: 256B, K: 250A, H: 86C

2289 זְבִינָא *z^e bînā'*, Zebina, S: 2081, B: 259B, K: 250A, H: 86C

2290 זָבַל *zābal*, [A] to honor, exalt, S: 2082, B: 259C, K: 250A, H: 86C

2291 זְבֻלִ¹ *z^e bul^1*, Zebul, S: 2073 & 2083, B: 259D, K: 250B, H: 86C

2292 [2]זְבֻל *zebul[2]*, magnificent dwelling, princely mansion, lofty dwelling, S: 2073, B: 259C, K: 250B, H: 86C

2293 זָג *zāg*, skin, peel (of grape), S: 2085, B: 260A, K: 250B, H: 86C

2294 זֵד *zēd*, arrogant, proud, haughty, S: 2086, B: 267D, K: 250B, H: 86D

2295 זָדוֹן *zādôn*, pride, arrogance, contempt, presumption, S: 2087, B: 268A, K: 250C, H: 86D

2296 זֶה *zeh*, this, these, such, S: 2088, B: 260A, K: 250C, H: 86D

2297 זֹה *zōh*, this, S: 2090, B: 262B, K: 251D, H: 87A

2298 זָהָב *zāhāb*, gold, nugget of gold, S: 2091, B: 262C, K: 251D, H: 87A

2299 זָהַם *zāham*, [D] to make repulsive, loathsome (to someone), S: 2092, B: 263D, K: 252A, H: 87B

2300 זַהַם *zaham*, Zaham, S: 2093, B: 263D, K: 252B, H: 87B

2301 [1]זָהַר *zāhar[1]*, [G] to shine, S: 2094, B: 263D, K: 252B, H: 87B

2302 [2]זָהַר *zāhar[2]*, [C] to be warned, take warning; [G] to give warning, dissuade, S: 2094, B: 264A, K: 252B, H: 87B

2303 זֹהַר *zōhar*, brightness, shining, S: 2096, B: 264A, K: 252C, H: 87B

2304 זִו *ziw*, Ziv, S: 2099, B: 264C, K: 252C, H: 87B

2305 זוֹ *zô*, this, S: 2097, B: 262B, K: 252C, H: 87B

2306 זוּ *zû*, who, which, that, S: 2098, B: 262B, K: 252C, H: 87B

2307 זוּב *zûb*, [A] to flow, gush out; discharge (of body fluids), S: 2100, B: 264C, K: 252D, H: 87C

2308 זוֹב *zôb*, discharge (of body fluids), S: 2101, B: 264D, K: 253A, H: 87C

2309 זוּזִים *zûzîm*, Zuzite, S: 2104, B: 265C, K: 253A, H: 87C

2310 זוּחַ *zûaḥ*, variant: [C] to come loose, get out of place, S: 2118†, B: 267B, K: 254A, H: 87C

2311 זוֹחֵת *zôḥēt*, Zoheth, S: 2105, B: 265D, K: 253A, H: 87C

2312 זָוִית *zāwît*, corner (of a palace, altar), pillar, S: 2106, B: 265A, K: 253A, H: 87C

2313 זוּל *zûl*, [A] to pour out, weigh out, S: 2107, B: 266A, K: 253B, H: 87C

2314 זוּלָה *zûlâ*, but, only, except; apart from, besides, S: 2108, B: 265D, K: 253B, H: 87C

2315 זוּן *zûn*, variant: [A] to feed, S: 2109, B: 266A, K: 253B, H: 87D

2316 זוּעַ *zûaʿ*, [A] to show fear, tremble; [D] to make tremble, S: 2111, B: 266A, K: 253C, H: 87D

2317 זְוָעָה *zewāʿâ*, abhorrence, terror, object of dread, S: 2113, B: 266B, K: 253C, H: 87D

2318 [1]זוּר *zûr[1]*, [A] to squeeze, press upon, crush, S: 2115 & 2116†, B: 266D, K: 253D, H: 87D

2319 [2]זוּר *zûr[2]*, [A, C, H] to go astray, turn aside, be estranged, S: 2114, B: 266B, K: 253D, H: 87D

2320 [3]זוּר *zûr[3]*, [A] be offensive, stink, S: 2114, B: 266D, K: 253D, H: 88A

2321 זָזָא *zāzāʾ*, Zaza, S: 2117, B: 265B, K: 254A, H: 88A

2322 זָחַח *zāḥaḥ*, [C] to swing out, S: 2118, B: 267B, K: 254A, H: 87C

2323 [1]זָחַל *zāḥal[1]*, [A] to crawl, glide (of a snake), S: 2119, B: 267B, K: 254A, H: 88A

2324 [2]זָחַל *zāḥal[2]*, [A] to be afraid, S: 2119, B: 267C, K: 254A, H: 88A

2325 זֹחֶלֶת *zōḥelet*, Zoheleth, S: 2120, B: 267B, K: 254B, H: 88A

2326 זִיד *zîd*, [A] to treat arrogantly, defy; [G] to cook; to act arrogantly, be contemptuous, S: 2102, B: 267C, K: 254B, H: 88A

2327 זֵידוֹן *zêdôn*, raging (water), S: 2121, B: 268A, K: 254C, H: 88A

2328 [1]זִיז *zîz[1]*, creatures, S: 2123, B: 265A, K: 254C, H: 88A

2329 [2]זִיז *zîz[2]*, nipple (of a lactating breast), S: 2123, B: 265C, K: 254C, H: 88A

2330 זִיזָא *zîzāʾ*, Ziza, S: 2124, B: 265B, K: 254C, H: 88B

2331 זִיזָה *zîzâ*, Ziza, S: 2125, B: 265B, K: 254C, H: 88B

2332 זִינָא *zînāʾ*, variant: Zina, see 2330, S: 2126, B: 265B, K: 254C, H: 88B

2333 זִיעַ *zîaʿ*, Zia, S: 2127, B: 266B, K: 254C, H: 88B

2334 [1]זִיף *zîp[1]*, Ziph, S: 2128, B: 268B 1., K: 254D, H: 88B

2335 [2]זִיף *zîp[2]*, Ziph, S: 2128, B: 268B 2., K: 254D, H: 88B

2336 זִיפָה *zîpâ*, Ziphah, S: 2129, B: 268B, K: 254D, H: 88B

2337 זִיפִי *zîpî*, Ziphite, S: 2130, B: 268B, K: 254D, H: 88B

2338 זִיקוֹת *zîqôt*, flaming torch, S: 2131†, B: 278A, K: 254D, H: 88B

2339 זַיִת *zayit*, olive (tree, grove, oil, leaf), S: 2132, B: 268B, K: 255A, H: 88B

2340 זֵיתָן *zêtān*, Zethan, S: 2133, B: 268D, K: 255B, H: 88B

2341 זַךְ *zak*, pure, clear; flawless, innocent, upright, S: 2134, B: 269A, K: 255B, H: 88B

2342 זָכָה *zākâ*, [A] to be pure; be justified, be acquitted; [D] to keep pure; [F] to make oneself clean, pure, S: 2135, B: 269A, K: 255B, H: 88C

2343 זְכוֹכִית *zekôkît*, crystal, S: 2137, B: 269B, K: 255C, H: 88C

2344 זְכוּר *zekûr*, male, S: 2138, B: 271D, K: 255C, H: 88C

2345 זָכוּר *zākûr*, variant: male, S: 2138, B: 271D, K: 255C, H: 88C

2346 זַכּוּר *zakkûr*, Zaccur, S: 2139, B: 271D, K: 255C, H: 88C

2347 זַכַּי *zakkay*, Zaccai, S: 2140, B: 269B, K: 255D, H: 88C

2348 זָכַךְ *zākak*, [A] to be pure, bright, clean, S: 2141, B: 269A, K: 255D, H: 88C

2349 [1]זָכַר *zākar[1]*, [A] to remember, commemorate, consider; [B] to remember; [C] to be remembered, be mentioned; [G] to bring to remembrance, remind, mention, S: 2142, B: 269C, K: 255D, H: 88C

2350 [2]זָכַר *zākar[2]*, [C] to be born male, S: 2142, B: 271C, K: 256C, H: 88C

2351 זָכָר *zākār*, male, man, S: 2145, B: 271B, K: 257A, H: 89A

2352 זֵכֶר *zēker*, memory, remembrance; fame, renown, S: 2143, B: 271B, K: 257C, H: 89A

2353 [1]זֶכֶר *zeker[1]*, Zeker, S: 2144, B: 271A, K: 257C, H: 89A

2354 [2]זֶכֶר *zeker[2]*, variant: memorial, S: 2143, B: 271A, K: 257C, H: 89A

2355 זִכָּרוֹן *zikkārôn*, memorial, remembrance, commemoration, reminder, S: 2146, B: 272A, K: 257D, H: 89A

2356 זִכְרִי *zikrî*, Zicri, S: 2147, B: 271D, K: 258A, H: 89B

2357 זְכַרְיָה *zekaryâ*, Zechariah, S: 2148, B: 272A, K: 258A, H: 89B

2358 זְכַרְיָהוּ *zekaryāhû*, Zechariah, S: 2148, B: 272A, K: 258B, H: 89B

2359 זֻלּוּת *zullût*, vileness, S: 2149, B: 273A, K: 258D, H: 89B

2360 זַלְזַל *zalzal*, shoots, sprigs, S: 2150, B: 272D, K: 258C, H: 89B

2361 [1]זָלַל *zālal[1]*, [A] to profligate, be a glutton, to gorge oneself; [G] to despise, treat contemptibly, S: 2151, B: 272D, K: 258C, H: 89B

2362 [2]זָלַל *zālal[2]*, [C] to tremble (of mountains), S: 2151, B: 272D, K: 258C, H: 89C

2363 זַלְעָפָה *zalʿāpâ*, raging (wind); indignation; fits of hunger, S: 2152, B: 273A, K: 258D, H: 89C

2364 זִלְפָּה *zilpâ*, Zilpah, S: 2153, B: 273A, K: 258D, H: 89C

2365 [1]זִמָּה *zimmâ[1]*, lewdness, shamelessness, evil, S: 2154, B: 273B, K: 258D, H: 89C

2366 [2]זִמָּה *zimmâ[2]*, Zimmah, S: 2155, B: 273C, K: 259A, H: 89C

2367 זְמוֹרָה *zemôrâ*, vine branch, S: 2156, B: 274D, K: 259A, H: 89C

2368 זַמְזֻמִּים *zamzummîm*, Zamzummite, S: 2157†, B: 273D, K: 259B, H: 89C

2369 [1]זָמִיר *zāmîr[1]*, song, music and song, S: 2158, B: 274B, K: 259B, H: 89D

2370 [2]זָמִיר *zāmîr[2]*, variant: pruning (of vines); vintage, S: 2159, B: 274D, K: 259B, H: 89D

2371 זְמִירָה *zemîrâ*, Zemirah, S: 2160, B: 275B, K: 259C, H: 89D

2372 זָמַם *zāmam*, [A] to determine, plan, plot, intend, resolve, S: 2161, B: 273A, K: 259C, H: 89D

2373 זָמָם *zāmām*, plan, plot, S: 162, B: 273B, K: 259C, H*

2374 זָמַן *zāman*, [E] to be set, be designated, appointed, S: 2163, B: 273D, K: 259D, H: 89D

2375 זְמָן *zemān*, time, appointed time, S: 2165, B: 273D, K: 259D, H: 89D

2376 [1]זָמַר *zāmar[1]*, [D] to sing, sing praises, to make music, S: 2167, B: 274A, K: 259D, H: 89D

2377 [2]זָמַר *zāmar[2]*, [A] to prune (vines); [C] to be pruned, S: 2168, B: 274D, K: 260A, H: 90A

2378 זֶמֶר *zemer*, mountain sheep, S: 2169, B: 275A, K: 260B, H: 90A

2379 [1]זִמְרָה *zimrâ[1]*, singing, song, (instrumental) music, S: 2172, B: 274B, K: 260B, H: 90A

2380 [2]זִמְרָה *zimrâ[2]*, best products, S: 2173, B: 275A, K: 260B, H: 90A

2381 [1]זִמְרִי *zimrî[1]*, Zimri, S: 2174, B: 275B, K: 260C, H: 90A

2382 [2]זִמְרִי *zimrî*[2], Zimri, S: 2174, B: 275B, K: 260C, H: 90A

2383 זִמְרָן *zimrān*, Zimran, S: 2175, B: 275B, K: 260C, H: 90A

2384 זִמְרָת *zimrāt*, variant: song *or* strength, S: 2176, B: 274B, K: 260D, H: 90A

2385 זַן *zan*, kind, sort, S: 2177, B: 275B, K: 260D, H: 90A

2386 זָנַב *zānab*, [D] to cut off from the rear position, attack from the rear, S: 2179, B: 275C, K: 260D, H: 90A

2387 זָנָב *zānāb*, tail; stump, S: 2180, B: 275B, K: 260D, H: 90A

2388 [1]זָנָה *zānâ*[1], [A] to be, become a prostitute; to be sexually immoral, be promiscuous, commit adultery; [E] to be solicited for prostitution; [G] to make a prostitute, to turn to prostitution, S: 2181, B: 275C, K: 261A, H: 90A

2389 [2]זָנָה *zānâ*[2], variant: [A] to feel a dislike for, S: 2181, B: 275C, K: 261D, H: 90C

2390 זֹנָה *zōnâ*, prostitute, harlot, S: 2181† & 2185†, B: 275C, K: 261A, H: 90C

2391 [1]זָנוֹחַ *zānôaḥ*[1], Zanoah, S: 2182, B: 276C, K: 261D, H: 90C

2392 [2]זָנוֹחַ *zānôaḥ*[2], Zanoah, S: 2182, B: 276C, K: 261D, H: 90C

2393 זְנוּנִים *z^{e}nûnîm*, wanton lust, prostitution, adultery, S: 2183†, B: 276A, K: 261D, H: 90C

2394 זְנוּת *z^{e}nût*, prostitution, sexual immorality, unfaithfulness, S: 2184, B: 276A, K: 262A, H: 90C

2395 [1]זָנַח *zānaḥ*[1], [G] to stink, S: 2186, B: 276C, K: 262A, H: 90C

2396 [2]זָנַח *zānaḥ*[2], [A] to reject, cast out; [G] to declare rejected; to remove, S: 2186, B: 276B, K: 262A, H: 90C

2397 זָנַק *zānaq*, [D] to spring out, S: 2187, B: 276C, K: 262B, H: 90D

2398 זָעָה *zā'â*, variant: [D] to terrify, S: 2111†, B: 266A, K: 253C, H: 90D

2399 זֵעָה *zē'â*, sweat, S: 2188, B: 402C, K: 262B, H: 90D

2400 זַעֲוָה *za'^{a}wâ*, thing of horror, terror, S: 2189, B: 266B, K: 262B, H: 90D

2401 זַעֲוָן *za'^{a}wān*, Zaavan, S: 2190, B: 266B & 276C, K: 262B, H: 90D

2402 זְעֵיר *z^{e}'êr*, variant: little; a little longer, S: 2191, B: 277D, K: 262C, H: 90D

2403 זָעַךְ *zā'ak*, [C] to be extinguished, S: 2193, B: 276C, K: 262C, H: 90D

2404 זָעַם *zā'am*, [A] to express wrath, show fury, denounce; [B] to be under wrath, be accursed; [C] to be scolded, be cursed, S: 2194, B: 276D, K: 262C, H: 90D

2405 זַעַם *za'am*, wrath, anger, indignation, insolence, S: 2195, B: 276D, K: 262D, H: 91A

2406 [1]זָעַף *zā'ap*[1], [A] to rage against, become angry, S: 2196, B: 277A, K: 262D, H: 91A

2407 [2]זָעַף *zā'ap*[2], [A] to look dejected, look pitiful, S: 2196, B: 277A, K: 262D, H: 91A

2408 זַעַף *za'ap*, rage, wrath, S: 2197, B: 277A, K: 263A, H: 91A

2409 זָעֵף *zā'ēp*, angry, raging, S: 2198, B: 277C, K: 263A, H: 91A

2410 זָעַק *zā'aq*, [A] to cry out, call to, weep aloud, howl; [C] to be called, be summoned; be assembled; [G] to summon, cause to gather together, issue a proclamation, S: 2199, B: 277A, K: 263A, H: 91A

2411 זְעָקָה *z^{e}'āqâ*, outcry, shout, lament, wail, S: 2201, B: 277C, K: 263C, H: 91B

2412 זִפְרֹן *ziprôn*, Ziphron, S: 2202, B: 277D, K: 263C, H: 91B

2413 זֶפֶת *zepet*, pitch (resin), S: 2203, B: 278A, K: 263C, H: 91B

2414 [1]זֵק *zēq*[1], chains, fetters, S: 2131, B: 278A, K: 263D, H: 91B

2415 [2]זֵק *zēq*[2], firebrands, S: 2131, B: 278A, K: 263D, H: 91B

2416 [1]זָקֵן *zāqēn*[1], [A] to be old; [G] to grow old, S: 2204, B: 278B, K: 263D, H: 91B

2417 זָקָן *zāqān*, beard, whiskers; chin, S: 2206, B: 278B, K: 264A, H: 91B

2418 [2]זָקֵן *zāqēn*[2], elder, old, aged, veteran; (as noun) elder, leader, dignitary, S: 2205, B: 278C, K: 264A, H: 91C

2419 זֹקֶן *zōqen*, old age, S: 2207, B: 279A, K: 264C, H: 91C

2420 זִקְנָה *ziqnâ*, old age, growing old, S: 2209, B: 279A, K: 264C, H: 91C

2421 זְקֻנִים *z^{e}qunîm*, old age, S: 2208†, B: 279A, K: 264C, H: 91C

2422 זָקַף *zāqap*, [A] to lift up, S: 2210, B: 279A, K: 264D, H: 91C

2423 זָקַק *zāqaq*, [A] to refine, distill; [D] to refine; [E] to be refined, be purified, S: 2212, B: 279B, K: 264D, H: 91C

2424 זָר *zār*, strange, foreign, alien, one of a different kind; unauthorized, illegitimate, S: 2214†, B: 266C 2c., K: 265A, H: 91D

2425 זֵר *zēr*, molding, S: 2213, B: 267A, K: 265C, H: 92A

2426 זָרָא *zārā'*, loathsome thing, S: 2214, B: 266D, K: 265C, H: 92A

2427 זָרַב *zārab*, [E] to become dry, S: 2215, B: 279C, K: 265C, H: 92A

2428 זְרֻבָּבֶל *z^{e}rubbābel*, Zerubbabel, S: 2216, B: 279C, K: 265D, H: 92A

2429 זֶרֶד *zered*, Zered, S: 2218, B: 279C, K: 265D, H: 92A

2430 [1]זָרָה *zārâ*[1], [A, D] to scatter, spread out; winnow; [C, E] to be scattered, spread out, S: 2219, B: 279D, K: 265D, H: 92A

2431 [2]זָרָה *zārâ*[2], [D] to measure off, discern, S: 2219, B: 279D, K: 266B, H: 92B

2432 זְרוֹעַ *z^{e}rôa'*, arm, forearm, shoulder; power, strength, force, S: 2220, B: 283D, K: 266B, H: 92B

2433 זֵרוּעַ *zērûa'*, (plants from) seeds, S: 2221, B: 283B, K: 266D, H: 92B

2434 זַרְזִיף *zarzîp*, variant: dripping, S: 2222, B: 284B, K: 266D, H: 92B

2435 זַרְזִיר *zarzîr*, rooster, horse, greyhound [?], S: 2223, B: 267A, K: 266D, H: 92B

2436 זָרַח *zāraḥ*, [A] to rise, dawn (of the sun); to appear bright red (as with a skin disorder), S: 2224, B: 280B, K: 266D, H: 92B

2437 [1]זֶרַח *zeraḥ*[1], dawning (of light), S: 2225, B: 280B, K: 267A, H: 92C

2438 [2]זֶרַח *zeraḥ*[2], Zerah, S: 2226, B: 280B, K: 267A, H: 92C

2439 זַרְחִי *zarḥî*, Zerahite, S: 2227, B: 280C, K: 267B, H: 92C

2440 זְרַחְיָה *z^{e}raḥyâ*, Zerahiah, S: 2228, B: 280C, K: 267B, H: 92C

2441 [1]זָרַם *zāram*[1], [A] to sweep away, put an end to, S: 2229, B: 281A, K: 267B, H: 92C

2442 [2]זָרַם *zāram*[2], [A] to sweep away (=2441?); [D] to pour down, S: 2229, B: 281A, K: 267B, H: 92C

2443 זֶרֶם *zerem*, rain, rainstorm, thunderstorm, torrent rains, S: 2230, B: 281B, K: 267C, H: 92C

2444 זִרְמָה *zirmâ*, male genitals *or* emission, S: 2231, B: 281B, K: 267C, H: 92C

2445 זָרַע *zāra'*, [A] to sow seed, plant seed; [B] to be sown upon; [E] to be sown; [C] to be sown, be planted, to have children, have descendants; [G] to yield seed, to become pregnant, S: 2232, B: 281B, K: 267C, H: 92C

2446 זֶרַע *zera'*, seed, semen; child, offspring, descendant, line, race, S: 2233, B: 282A, K: 268A, H: 92D

2447 זֵרֹעִים *zērō'îm*, vegetables, S: 2235†, B: 283B, K: 268D, H: 93A

2448 זֵרְעֹנִים *zēr'ōnîm*, vegetables, S: 2235†, B: 283B, K: 268D, H: 93A

2449 זָרַף *zārap*, [D] to water, shower, S: 2222†, B: 284B, K: 268D, H: 93A

2450 [1]זָרַק *zāraq*[1], [A] to sprinkle, to scatter, to toss (in the air); [E] to be sprinkled, S: 2236, B: 284C, K: 268D, H: 93C

2451 [2]זָרַק *zāraq*[2], variant: [A] to creep in, S: 2236, B: 284C, K: 269A, H: 93C

2452 [1]זָרַר *zārar*[1], variant: [B] to be pressed out, S: 2237, B: 284D, K: 269B, H: 93C

2453 [2]זָרַר *zārar*[2], [D] to sneeze, S: 2237, B: 284D, K: 269B, H: 93C

2454 זֶרֶשׁ *zereš*, Zeresh, S: 2238, B: 284D, K: 269C, H: 93C

2455 זֶרֶת *zeret*, span, handbreadth, S: 2239, B: 284D, K: 269C, H: 93C

2456 זַתּוּא *zattû'*, Zattu, S: 2240, B: 285C, K: 269C, H: 93C

2457 זֵתָם *zētām*, Zetham, S: 2241, B: 268D & 285C, K: 269C, H: 93C

2458 זֵתַר *zētar*, Zethar, S: 2242, B: 285C, K: 269D, H: 93C

2459 ח *ḥ*, letter of the Hebrew alphabet, S*, B: 285A, K: 269C, H*

2460 חֹב *ḥōb*, heart, S: 2243, B: 285C, K: 270A, H: 93B

2461 חָבָא *ḥābā'*, [C] to be hidden, to hide oneself; [E] to keep oneself in hiding; [G] to hide (another); [H] to be hidden away; [F] to keep oneself hidden, S: 2244, B: 285A, K: 270B, H: 93B

2462 חָבַב *ḥābab*, [A] to love, S: 2245, B: 285C, K: 270C, H: 93B

2463 חֹבָב *ḥōbāb*, Hobab, S: 2246, B: 285D, K: 270C, H: 93B

2464 חָבָה *ḥābâ*, [A] to hide; [C] to conceal oneself, S: 2247, B: 285D, K: 270C, H: 93B

2465 חֻבָּה *ḥubbâ*, Hubbah, S: 3160†, B: 285D, K: 270D, H: 93D

2466 חָבוֹר *ḥābôr*, Habor, S: 2249, B: 289C, K: 270D, H: 93D

2467 חַבּוּרָה *ḥabbûrâ*, bruise, welt, wound, injury, S: 2250, B: 289A, K: 270D, H: 93D

2468 חָבַט *ḥābaṭ*, [A] to thresh, beat out; [C] to be beaten, S: 2251, B: 286A, K: 271A, H: 93D

2469 חֳבַיָּה *ḥ[o]bayyâ*, Hobaiah, S: 2252, B: 285D, K: 271A, H: 93D

2470 חֶבְיוֹן *ḥebyôn*, hiding, covering, S: 2253, B: 285D, K: 271A, H: 93D

2471 [1]חָבַל *ḥābal*[1], [A] to require a pledge, demand a security, S: 2254, B: 286B, K: 271A, H: 93D

2472 [2]חָבַל *ḥābal*[2], [A] to act wickedly, to offend; [D] to destroy, ruin, work havoc; [E] to be broken, S: 2254, B: 287B, K: 271B, H: 94A

2473 [3]חָבַל *ḥābal*[3], [D] to conceive, be pregnant, to be in labor, S: 2254, B: 286B, K: 271C, H: 94A

2474 [1]חֶבֶל *ḥebel*[1], procession, group, S: 2256, B: 286C, K: 271D, H: 94A

2475 [2]חֶבֶל *ḥebel*[2], rope, cord, line, rigging; share, portion, region, district, S: 2256, B: 286C, K: 271D, H: 94B

2476 [3]חֶבֶל *ḥebel*[3], destruction, ruin, S: 2256, B: 287C, K: 272B, H: 94B

2477 חֵבֶל *ḥēbel*, labor pains, anguish of birth pangs, S: 2256, B: 286D, K: 272B, H: 94B

2478 חֲבֹל *ḥ[a]bōl*, pledge for a loan, S: 2258, B: 287A, K: 272B, H: 94B

2479 חִבֵּל *ḥibbēl*, (ship's) rigging, S: 2260, B: 287A, K: 272B, H: 94B

2480 חֹבֵל *ḥōbēl*, seaman, sailor, S: 2259, B: 287A, K: 272C, H: 94B

2481 חֲבֹלָה *ḥ[a]bōlâ*, pledge for a loan, S: 2258, B: 287A, K: 272C, H: 94C

2482 חֹבְלִים *ḥōb[e]lîm*, union, S: 2256, B: 287A, K: 272C, H: 94C

2483 חֲבַצֶּלֶת *ḥ[a]baṣṣelet*, rose; crocus, S: 2261, B: 287C, K: 272C, H: 94C

2484 חֲבַצִּנְיָה *ḥ[a]baṣṣinyâ*, Habazziniah, S: 2262, B: 287C, K: 272C, H: 94C

2485 חָבַק *ḥābaq*, [A] to hold in one's arms, embrace; to fold one's hands; [D] to embrace, hug, S: 2263, B: 287D, K: 272D, H: 94C

2486 חִבֻּק *ḥibbuq*, folding (of idle hands), S: 2264, B: 287D, K: 272D, H: 94C

2487 חֲבַקּוּק *ḥ[a]baqqûq*, Habakkuk, S: 2265, B: 287D, K: 273A, H: 94C

2488 [1]חָבַר *ḥābar*[1], [G] to make fine speeches, S: 2266, B: 287D, K: 273A, H: 94C

2489 [2]חָבַר *ḥābar*[2], [A] to join, unite, be attached, to be touching; to cast spells, to enchant; [B] to be joined; [D] to fasten, join; [E] to be fastened, be closely compacted; [F] to make an alliance, become allies, S: 2266, B: 287D, K: 273A, H: 94C

2490 [1]חֶבֶר *ḥeber*[1], sharing; band, group; magic spell, S: 2267, B: 288C, K: 273D, H: 94D

2491 [2]חֶבֶר *ḥeber*[2], Heber, S: 2268, B: 288C, K: 273D, H: 94D

2492 חָבֵר *ḥābēr*, companion, associate, partner, friend, S: 2270, B: 288D, K: 273D, H: 94D

2493 חַבָּר *ḥabbār*, (fellow) trader, S: 2271, B: 289A, K: 274A, H: 94D

2494 חֲבַרְבֻּרוֹת *ḥ[a]barburôt*, spots (of a leopard), S: 2272†, B: 289A, K: 274A, H: 95A

2495 חֶבְרָה *ḥebrâ*, company, association, S: 2274, B: 288D, K: 274A, H: 95A

2496 [1]חֶבְרוֹן *ḥebrôn*[1], Hebron, S: 2275 & 5683†, B: 289B, K: 274A, H: 95A

2497 [2]חֶבְרוֹן *ḥebrôn*[2], Hebron, S: 2275, B: 289B, K: 274C, H: 95A

2498 חֶבְרוֹנִי *ḥebrônî*, Hebronite, S: 2276, B: 289C, K: 274C, H: 95A

2499 חֶבְרִי *ḥebrî*, Heberite, S: 2277, B: 288D, K: 274C, H: 95A

2500 חֲבֶרֶת *ḥ[a]beret*, partner, (marriage) companion, S: 2278, B: 289A, K: 274C, H: 95A

2501 חֹבֶרֶת *ḥōberet*, set (of curtains), S: 2279, B: 289A, K: 274C, H: 95A

2502 חָבַשׁ *ḥābaš*, [A] to tie, bind, saddle; [B] to be saddled; to be twisted, wrapped around; [D] to bind up; [E] to be bound, bandaged, S: 2280, B: 289C, K: 274D, H: 95A

2503 חֲבִתִּים *ḥ[a]bittîm*, offering bread (flat cakes), S: 2281†, B: 290A, K: 275A, H: 95B

2504 חַג *ḥag*, religious feast, festival; festal procession, S: 2282, B: 290D, K: 275B, H: 95B

2505 חָגָּא *ḥoggā'*, terror, S: 2283, B: 291B, K: 275C, H: 95B

2506 [1]חָגָב *ḥāgāb*[1], grasshopper, locust, S: 2284, B: 290B, K: 275C, H: 95B

2507 [2]חָגָב *ḥāgāb*[2], Hagab, S: 2285, B: 290C, K: 275D, H: 95C

2508 חֲגָבָא *ḥ[a]gābā'*, variant: Hagaba, S: 2286, B: 290C, K: 275D, H: 95C

2509 חֲגָבָה *ḥ[a]gābâ*, Hagabah, S: 2286, B: 290C, K: 275D, H: 95C

2510 חָגַג *ḥāgag*, [A] to hold a festival, celebrate a festival, S: 2287, B: 290C, K: 275D, H: 95C

2511 חָגוּ *ḥāgû*, clefts (of a rock), S: 2288†, B: 291C, K: 276A, H: 95C

2512 חֲגוֹר *ḥ[a]gôr*, belt, sash, S: 2290, B: 292A, K: 276B, H: 95C

2513 חָגוֹר *ḥāgôr*, belted (around the waist), S: 2289, B: 292A, K: 276B, H: 95C

2514 חֲגוֹרָה *ḥ[a]gôrâ*, covering; belt, sash, S: 2290, B: 292A, K: 276B, H: 95C

2515 חַגִּי *ḥaggî*, Haggi, S: 2291, B: 291B, K: 276B, H: 95C

2516 חַגַּי *ḥaggay*, Haggai, S: 2292, B: 291B, K: 276B, H: 95C

2517 חַגִּיָּה *ḥaggiyyâ*, Haggiah, S: 2293, B: 291B, K: 276C, H: 95C

2518 חַגִּית *ḥaggît*, Haggith, S: 2294, B: 291B, K: 276C, H: 95C

2519 חָגְלָה *ḥoglâ*, Hoglah, S: 2295, B: 291C, K: 276C, H: 95D

2520 חָגַר *ḥāgar*, [A] to tie, strap, fasten; to tuck (lower robe) into one's belt, gird; [B] to be tucked in, girded, S: 2296, B: 291C, K: 276C, H: 95D

2521 [1]חַד *ḥad*[1], sharp (sword), S: 2299, B: 292B, K: 277A, H: 95D

2522 [2]חַד *ḥad*[2], one, each, S: 2297, B: 26A, K: 277A, H: 96A

2523 חָדַד *ḥādad*, [A] to be fierce, sharp; [H] to be sharpened; [F] to slash, S: 2300, B: 292B, K: 277B, H: 96A

2524 חֲדַד *ḥ[a]dad*, Hadad, S: 2301, B: 292C, K: 277B, H: 96A

2525 [1]חָדָה *ḥādâ*[1], [A] to be delighted; [D] to make glad, S: 2302, B: 292D, K: 277C, H: 96A

2526 [2]חָדָה *ḥādâ*[2], [C] to be seen, S: 2302, B: 292D, K: 277C, H: 96A

2527 [3]חָדָה *ḥādâ*[3], [A] to sharpen; [G] to sharpen, S: 2300, B: 292C, K: 277B, H: 96A

2528 חַדָּה *ḥaddâ*, variant: Haddah, S: 5876†, B: 745C, K: 700C(e), H: 271D 4.f

2529 חַדּוּד *ḥaddûd*, jagged, pointed, S: 2303, B: 292C, K: 277C, H: 96A

2530 חֶדְוָה *ḥedwâ*, joy, S: 2304, B: 292D, K: 277C, H: 96A

2531 חָדִיד *ḥādîd*, Hadid, S: 2307, B: 292C, K: 277C, H: 96A

2532 [1]חָדַל *ḥādal*[1], [A] to stop, cease, refrain, fail, S: 2308, B: 292D, K: 277D, H: 96A

2533 [2]חָדַל *ḥādal*[2], variant: [A] to become fat, have success, S: 2308, B: 292D, K: 277D, H: 96B

2534 חָדֵל *ḥādēl*, refused, rejected, fleeting, S: 2310, B: 293B, K: 278A, H: 96B

2535 חֶדֶל *ḥedel*, world (of the living), S: 2309, B: 293B, K: 278B, H: 96C

2536 חַדְלָי *ḥadlāy*, Hadlai, S: 2311, B: 293B, K: 278B, H: 96C

2537 חֵדֶק *ḥēdeq*, brier, thorn, S: 2312, B: 293B, K: 278B, H: 96C

2538 חִדֶּקֶל *ḥiddeqel*, Hidekel = Tigris, S: 2313, B: 293C, K: 278B, H: 96C

2539 חָדַר *ḥādar*, [A] to close in on every side, surround, S: 2314, B: 293C, K: 278B, H: 96C

2540 חֶדֶר *ḥeder*, room, chamber, bedroom; shrine, S: 2315 & 2316†, B: 293C, K: 278C, H: 96C

2541 חַדְרָךְ *ḥadrāk*, Hadrach, S: 2317, B: 293D, K: 278D, H: 96D

2542 חָדַשׁ *ḥādaš*, [A] to renew, restore, repair, reaffirm; [F] to renew oneself, S: 2318, B: 293D, K: 279A, H: 96D

2543 חָדָשׁ *ḥādāš*, new, recent, fresh, S: 2319, B: 294A, K: 279A, H: 96D

2544 [1]חֹדֶשׁ *ḥōdeš*[1], month; new moon, new moon festival, S: 2320, B: 294B, K: 279C, H: 96D

2545 [2]חֹדֶשׁ *ḥōdeš*[2], Hodesh, S: 2321, B: 295A, K: 280A, H: 97A

2546 חֲדָשָׁה *ḥ[a]dāšâ*, Hadashah, S: 2322, B: 295A, K: 280A, H: 97A

2547 חָדְשִׁי *ḥodšî*, variant: Hodshi, S: 8483†, B: 295A, K: 280A, H: 97A

2548 חֲדַתָּה *ḥ[a]dattâ*, variant: Hadattah, S: 2675†, B: 347D, K: 280A, H: 97A

2549 חוּב *ḥûb*, [D] to forfeit (one's head), S: 2325, B: 295A, K: 280A, H: 97A

2550 חוֹב *ḥôb*, loan, debt, S: 2326, B: 295A, K: 280B, H: 97A

2551 חוֹבָה *ḥôbâ*, Hobah, S: 2327, B: 295B, K: 280B, H: 97B

2552 [1]חוּג *ḥûg*[1], [A] to encircle, S: 2328, B: 295B, K: 280B, H: 97B

2553 [2]חוּג *ḥûg*[2], circle, horizon, S: 2329, B: 295B, K: 280B, H: 97B

2554 חוּד *ḥûd*, [A] to tell a riddle, set forth an allegory, S: 2330, B: 295C, K: 280C, H: 97B

2555 [1]חָוָה *ḥāwâ*[1], [D] to tell, explain, show, display, S: 2331, B: 296A, K: 280C, H: 97B

2556 [2]חָוָה *ḥāwā*[2], [I] to bow down low in worship; prostrate oneself; pay one honor, homage, S: 2331, B: 1005B, K: 959B, H: 97B

2557 [1]חַוָּה *ḥawwâ*[1], settlement, camp, S: 2333, B: 295D, K: 280C, H: 97C

2558 [2]חַוָּה *ḥawwâ*[2], Eve, S: 2332, B: 295C, K: 280D, H: 97C

2559 חוֹזָי *ḥôzāy*, variant: Hozai, S: 2335, B: 302C, K: 281A, H: 97C

2560 [1]חוֹחַ *ḥôaḥ*[1], thicket, thistle, thornbush, bramble, briers; hook, S: 2336, B: 296A, K: 281A, H: 97C

2561 [2]חוֹחַ *ḥôaḥ*[2], variant: hollows, cleft in rock, S: 2337†, B: 296B 1a, K: 281A, H: 97C

2562 חוּט *ḥûṭ*, line, cord, ribbon, thread, S: 2339, B: 296C, K: 281B, H: 97C

2563 חִוִּי *ḥiwwî*, Hivite, S: 2340, B: 295D, K: 281B, H: 97D

2564 חֲוִילָה *ḥ[a]wîlâ*, Havilah, S: 2341, B: 296C, K: 281C, H: 97D

2565 [1]חוּל *ḥûl*[1], [A] to swirl, turn, fall, dance; [D] to wait; to dance (the round dance); [F] to wait patiently; to swirl down, S: 2342, B: 296D, K: 281C, H: 97D

2566 [2]חוּל *ḥûl*[2], Hul, S: 2343, B: 299A, K: 281D, H: 97D

2567 [1]חוֹל *ḥôl*[1], sand, grains of sand, S: 2344, B: 297C, K: 282A, H: 97D

2568 [2]חוֹל *ḥôl*[2], variant: palm tree *or* phoenix bird, S: 2344, B: 297C, K: 282A, H: 97D

2569 חוּם *ḥûm*, dark-colored, S: 2345, B: 299B, K: 282A, H: 97D

2570 חוֹמָה *ḥômâ*, wall, S: 2346, B: 327B, K: 282A, H: 97D

2571 חוּס *ḥûs*, [A] to show pity, mercy, have compassion, spare, S: 347, B: 299B, K: 282D, H: 98A

2572 חוֹף *ḥôp*, coast, seashore, haven (for ships), S: 2348, B: 342B, K: 282D, H: 98A

2573 חוּפָם *ḥûpām*, Hupham, S: 2349, B: 299C, K: 283A, H: 98A

2574 חוּפָמִי *ḥûpāmî*, Huphamite, S: 2350, B: 299C, K: 283A, H: 98A

2575 חוּץ *ḥûṣ*, out, outside; street, market area; countryside, fields, outdoors, S: 2351, B: 299C, K: 283A, H: 98A

2576 חוֹק *ḥôq*, variant: see 2668, S: 2436, B: 300C, K: 283D, H: 98C

2577 חוּקֹק *ḥûqōq*, Hukok, S: 2712†, B: 301A & 350C, K: 283D, H: 98C

2578 [1]חָוַר *ḥāwar*[1], [A] to grow pale, S: 2357, B: 301A, K: 283D, H: 98C

2579 [2]חָוַר *ḥāwar*[2], variant: [A] to become less, S: 2787†, B: 359B, K: 332A, H: 98C

2580 [1]חוּר *ḥûr*[1], white garments, white linen, S: 2353, B: 301A, K: 283D, H: 98C

2581 [2]חוּר *ḥûr*[2], Hur, S: 2354, B: 301B, K: 283D, H: 98C

2582 חוֹרוֹן *ḥôrôn*, variant: Horon, S: 1032†, B: 111C, K: 124C 18., H: 116B

2583 חוֹרָי *ḥôrāy*, fine linen, S: 2355†, B: 301A, K: 284A, H: 98C

2584 חוּרַי *ḥûray*, Hurai, S: 2360, B: 301B, K: 284A, H: 98C

2585 חוּרִי *ḥûrî*, Huri, S: 2359, B: 301B, K: 284A, H: 98C

2586 חוּרָם *ḥûrām*, Huram, Hiram, S: 2361, B: 27C, K: 284A, H: 98C

2587 חוּרָם אָבִי *ḥûrām 'ābî*, Huram-Abi, S: 2361†, B: 27C, K: 296C, H: 98C

2588 חַוְרָן *ḥawrān*, Hauran, S: 2362, B: 301C, K: 284A, H: 98C

2589 חוֹרֹנַיִם *ḥôrōnayim*, Horonaim, S: 2773, B: 357B, K: 332C, H: 98C

2590 [1]חוּשׁ *ḥûš*[1], [A] to go quickly, hasten, rush upon; [B] to be ready; [G] to make hurry, hasten, S: 2363 & 2439†, B: 301C, K: 284B, H: 98C

2591 [2]חוּשׁ *ḥûš*[2], [A] to be greatly disturbed; to find enjoyment; [G] to be dismayed, S: 2363, B: 301D, K: 284B, H: 98D

2592 חוּשָׁה *ḥûšâ*, Hushah, S: 2364, B: 302A, K: 284C, H: 98D

2593 חוּשַׁי *ḥûšay*, Hushai, S: 2365, B: 302A, K: 284C, H: 98D

2594 חוּשִׁים *ḥûšîm*, Hushim, S: 2366, B: 302A, K: 284C, H: 98D

2595 חוּשָׁם *ḥûšām*, Husham, S: 2367, B: 302A, K: 284C & 342B, H: 98D & 119D

2596 חַוֹּת יָאִיר *ḥawwōt yā'îr*, Havvoth Jair, S: 2334†, B: 22C & 295D, K: 358A, H: 97C 2.

2597 [1]חוֹתָם *ḥôtām*[1], seal, signet ring, S: 2368, B: 368A, K: 284C, H: 98D

2598 [2]חוֹתָם *ḥôtām*[2], Hotham, S: 2369, B: 368B, K: 284D, H: 98D

2599 חֲזָאֵל *ḥ[a]zā'ēl*, Hazael, S: 2371, B: 303C, K: 284D, H: 98D

2600 חָזָה *ḥāzâ*, [A] to see, to look, observe, gaze; to have visions, prophecy, S: 2372, B: 302A, K: 284D, H: 98D

2601 חָזֶה *ḥāzeh*, breast (portion of sacrifice), S: 2373, B: 303D, K: 285B, H: 99A

2602 [1]חֹזֶה *ḥōzeh*[1], seer, S: 2374, B: 302C, K: 285B, H: 99A

2603 [2]חֹזֶה *ḥōzeh*[2], agreement, S: 2374, B: 302C, K: 285B, H: 99A

2604 חֲזָהאֵל *ḥ[a]zāh'ēl*, variant: Haziel, see 2609, S: 2371, B: 303C, K: 284D, H: 99A

2605 חֲזוֹ *ḥ[a]zô*, Hazo, S: 2375, B: 303D, K: 285C, H: 99A

2606 חָזוֹן *ḥāzôn*, vision, revelation, S: 2377, B: 302D, K: 285C, H: 99A

2607 חָזוּת *ḥāzût*, vision; prominent appearance, S: 2380, B: 303A, K: 285D, H: 99B

2608 חֲזֹות *ḥ[a]zôt*, visions, S: 2378†, B: 303A, K: 285D, H: 99B

2609 חֲזִיאֵל *ḥ[a]zî'ēl*, Haziel, S: 2381, B: 303C, K: 285D, H: 99B

2610 חֲזָיָה *ḥ[a]zāyâ*, Hazaiah, S: 2382, B: 303C, K: 285D, H: 99B

2611 חֶזְיוֹן *ḥezyôn*, Hezion, S: 2383, B: 303C, K: 285D, H: 99B

2612 חִזָּיוֹן *ḥizzāyôn*, vision, dream, revelation, S: 2384, B: 303B, K: 285D, H: 99B

2613 חֲזִיז *ḥ[a]zîz*, storm cloud, S: 2385, B: 304A, K: 286A, H: 99B

2614 חֲזִיר *ḥ[a]zîr*, pig, boar, S: 2386, B: 306B, K: 286A, H: 99B

2615 חֵזִיר *ḥēzîr*, Hezir, S: 2387, B: 306C, K: 286A, H: 99B

2616 חָזַק *ḥāzaq*, [A] to be strong, hard, harsh, severe; [D] to harden (one's heart); to give strength, repair, encourage; [G] to grasp, seize, hold; to make repairs; [F] to establish oneself firmly; to encourage, to rally strength, S: 2388, B: 304A, K: 286B, H: 99C

2617 חָזָק *ḥāzāq*, mighty, powerful, strong, hard, severe, S: 2389, B: 305C, K: 288A, H: 100A

2618 חָזֵק *ḥāzēq*, strong, loud, S: 2390, B: 305D, K: 288B, H: 100B

2619 חֵזֶק *ḥēzeq*, strength, S: 2391, B: 305D, K: 288B, H: 100B

2620 חֹזֶק *ḥōzeq*, might, strength, power, S: 2392, B: 305D, K: 288B, H: 100B

2621 חֶזְקָה *ḥezqâ*, strength, power, S: 2393, B: 305D, K: 288B, H: 100B

2622 חָזְקָה *ḥozqâ*, force, harshness, urgency, S: 2394, B: 306A, K: 288C, H: 100B

2623 חִזְקִי *ḥizqî*, Hizki, S: 2395, B: 306A, K: 288C, H: 100B

2624 חִזְקִיָּה *ḥizqiyyâ*, Hezekiah, S: 2396, B: 306A, K: 288C, H: 100B

2625 חִזְקִיָּהוּ *ḥizqiyyāhû*, Hezekiah, S: 2396, B: 306A, K: 288C, H: 100C

2626 חָח *ḥāḥ*, hook; brooch, S: 2397, B: 296B, K: 288D, H: 100C

2627 חָטָא *ḥāṭā'*, [A] to sin, do wrong, miss the way; [D] to purify, cleanse, to offer a sin offering; [G] to bring a sin upon, cause to commit a sin; [F] to purify oneself, S: 2398, B: 306C, K: 288D, H: 100C

2628 חֵטְא *ḥēṭ'*, sin, guilt, error, S: 2399, B: 307D, K: 289D, H: 100D

2629 חַטָּא *ḥaṭṭā'*, sinful, guilty; (as noun) sinner, wicked, S: 2400, B: 308B, K: 290A, H: 101A

2630 חֶטְאָה *ḥeṭ'â*, sin, S: 2398, B: 307A 2b, K: 290A, H: 101A

2631 חֲטָאָה *ḥ[a]ṭā'â*, sin, guilt, condemnation; sin offering, S: 2401, B: 308B, K: 290A, H: 101A

2632 חַטָּאָה *ḥaṭṭā'â*, variant: sin, wickedness, fault, S: 2402, B: 308B, K: 290B, H: 101A

2633 חַטָּאת *ḥaṭṭā't*, sin, wrong, iniquity; sin offering, purification offering, S: 2403, B: 308B, K: 290B, H: 101A

2634 חָטַב *ḥāṭab*, [A] to cut, chop (wood); (as noun) woodcutter, woodsman; [E] to carve, S: 2404, B: 310A, K: 290C, H: 101B

2635 חֲטֻבוֹת *ḥ[a]ṭubôt*, colored, embroidered (fabric), S: 2405†, B: 310B, K: 290D, H: 101B

2636 חִטָּה *ḥiṭṭâ*, wheat, S: 2406, B: 334D, K: 290D, H: 101B

2637 חַטּוּשׁ *ḥaṭṭûš*, Hattush, S: 2407, B: 310D, K: 291A, H: 101C

2638 חֲטִיטָא *ḥ[a]ṭîṭā'*, Hatita, S: 2410, B: 310B, K: 291B, H: 101C

2639 חַטִּיל *ḥaṭṭîl*, Hattil, S: 2411, B: 310B, K: 291B, H: 101C

2640 חֲטִיפָא *ḥ[a]ṭîpā'*, Hatipha, S: 2412, B: 310C, K: 291B, H: 101C

2641 חָטַם *ḥāṭam*, [A] to hold back, restrain, S: 2413, B: 310C, K: 291B, H: 101C

2642 חָטַף *ḥāṭap*, [A] to seize, carry off (by force), S: 2414, B: 310C, K: 291B, H: 101C

2643 חֹטֶר *ḥōṭer*, rod, switch; shoot, twig, S: 2415, B: 310D, K: 291C, H: 101C

2644 ¹חַי ḥay¹, life, state of living, lifetime, S: 2416, B: 311D & 313A, K: 291C & 294A, H: 101C

2645 ²חַי ḥay², living, alive, S: 2416, B: 311D & 313A, K: 291C, H: 101D

2646 ³חַי ḥay³, family, kin, S: 2416, B: 312C, K: 292C, H: 101D

2647 חִיאֵל ḥî'ēl, Hiel, S: 2419, B: 27D & 313C, K: 292C, H: 102A

2648 חִידָה ḥîdâ, riddle, hard question, allegory; hidden things, intrigue; scorn, S: 2420, B: 295A, K: 292C, H: 102A

2649 חָיָה ḥāyâ, [A] to live; recover, revive; [D] to keep alive, preserve life; [G] to keep alive, save a life, spare a life, restore a life, S: 2421 & 2425†, B: 310D, K: 292D, H: 102

2650 חָיֶה ḥāyeh, vigorous, S: 2422, B: 313A, K: 293B, H: 102B

2651 ¹חַיָּה ḥayyâ¹, animal, beast, livestock, living creature, S: 2416†, B: 312C, K: 293B, H: 102B

2652 ²חַיָּה ḥayyâ², life, one's very being; hunger (of lions), S: 2416†, B: 312C, K: 293D, H: 102C

2653 ³חַיָּה ḥayyâ³, band, army; people, home, S: 2416†, B: 312D, K: 293B, H: 102C

2654 חַיּוּת ḥayyût, lifetime, S: 2424, B: 313C, K: 293D, H: 102C

2655 ¹חִיל ḥîl¹, [A] to writhe, tremble, be in labor, give birth; [D] to give birth, bring forth; be in deep anguish, to twist; [E] to be brought forth, be given birth; [G] to shake; [H] to be born; [F] to be in distress, in torment, S: 2342, B: 296D, K: 294B, H: 102C

2656 ²חִיל ḥîl², [A] to endure, prosper, S: 2342, B: 298C, K: 295A, H: 102D

2657 חַיִל ḥayil, strength, capability, skill, valor, wealth; army, troop, warrior, S: 2428, B: 298C, K: 295A, H: 102D

2658 חֵיל ḥêl, ramparts, outer fortification, defense walls, S: 2426 & 2430†, B: 298A, K: 295D, H: 103A

2659 ³חִיל ḥîl³, pain, anguish, S: 2427, B: 297D, K: 295D, H: 103A

2660 חִילָה ḥîlâ, pain, S: 2427, B: 297D, K: 296A, H: 103A

2661 חִילֵז ḥîlēz, variant: Hilez, see 2664, S: 2432†, B: 298A, K: 296A, H: 103A

2662 חֵילֵךְ ḥêlēk, Helech, S: 2428†, B: 299A 4, K: 296A, H: 103A

2663 חֵילָם ḥêlām, Helam, S: 2431, B: 298A, K: 296A, H: 103A

2664 חִילֵן ḥîlēn, Hilen, S: 2432, B: 298B, K: 296A, H: 103B

2665 חִין ḥîn, gracefulness, S: 2433, B: 336D, K: 296A, H: 103B

2666 חַיִץ ḥayiṣ, flimsy wall, inner wall, S: 2434, B: 300C, K: 296A, H: 103B

2667 חִיצוֹן ḥîṣôn, outer, outside, exterior, S: 2435, B: 300B, K: 296A, H: 103B

2668 חֵיק ḥêq, lap, heart, bosom, seat of affection; fold of a cloak, gutter, S: 2436, B: 300C, K: 296B, H: 103B

2669 חִירָה ḥîrâ, Hirah, S: 2437, B: 301B, K: 296C, H: 103B

2670 חִירוֹם ḥîrôm, Hiram, S: 2438, B: 27C, K: 296C, H: 103B

2671 חִירָם ḥîrām, Hiram, S: 2438, B: 27C, K: 296C, H: 103B

2672 חִירֹת ḥîrōt, variant: Hiroth, S: 6367†, B: 809D, K: 759A, H: 103C

2673 חִישׁ ḥîš, quickly, in haste, S: 2440, B: 301D, K: 296D, H: 103C

2674 חֵךְ ḥēk, (area of the) mouth: lips, tongue (taste), roof of the mouth, S: 2441, B: 335A, K: 296D, H: 103C

2675 חָכָה ḥākâ, [A] to wait; [D] to lie in wait (ambush); hope for, long for, S: 2442, B: 314A, K: 297A, H: 103C

2676 חַכָּה ḥakkâ, fishhook, S: 2443, B: 335D, K: 297A, H: 103C

2677 חֲכִילָה ḥᵃkîlâ, Hakilah, S: 2444, B: 314B, K: 297A, H: 103C

2678 חֲכַלְיָה ḥᵃkalyâ, Hacaliah, S: 2446, B: 314B, K: 297B, H: 103C

2679 חַכְלִילִי ḥaklîlî, darker, S: 2447†, B: 314B, K: 297B, H: 103C

2680 חַכְלִלוּת ḥaklilût, bloodshot (eyes), S: 2448, B: 314B, K: 297B, H: 103C

2681 חָכַם ḥākam, [A] to be wise, be skillful, gain wisdom; [D] to make wiser, to teach wisdom; [E] to be skillful; [G] to make wise; [F] to deal shrewdly; to show oneself wise, S: 2449, B: 314B, K: 297B, H: 103C

2682 חָכָם ḥākām, wise, skilled, shrewd, craftsman, S: 2450, B: 314C, K: 297D, H: 103D

2683 חָכְמָה ḥokmâ, wisdom, skill, learning, S: 2451, B: 315B, K: 298A, H: 104A

2684 חָכְמוֹת ḥokmôt, wisdom, S: 2454, B: 315B, K: 298B, H: 104A

2685 חַכְמֹנִי ḥakmōnî, Hacmoni; Hacmonite, S: 2453, B: 315D, K: 298C, H: 104A

2686 חָכַר ḥākar, [A] to attack (vigorously), S: 1970†, B: 229A, K: 298C, H: 104A

2687 חֹל ḥōl, common use, not holy, ordinary, S: 2455, B: 320D, K: 298C, H: 104A

2688 חָלָא ḥālā', [A] to be ill, S: 2456, B: 316A, K: 298C, H: 104B

2689 ¹חֶלְאָה ḥel'â¹, deposit, encrustation, rust, S: 2457, B: 316A, K: 298D, H: 104B

2690 ²חֶלְאָה ḥel'â², Helah, S: 2458, B: 316A, K: 298D, H: 104B

2691 חֵלָאם ḥēlā'm, variant: Helam, see 2663, S: 2431, B: 298A, K: 296A, H: 104B

2692 חָלָב ḥālāb, milk, S: 2461, B: 316B, K: 298D, H: 104B

2693 ¹חֵלֶב ḥēleb¹, fat, fat portions; finest, best part; callous heart, S: 2459, B: 316D, K: 299A, H: 104B

2694 ²חֵלֶב ḥēleb², variant: Heleb, see 2699, S: 2460, B: 317A, K: 299C, H: 104B

2695 חֶלְבָּה ḥelbâ, Helbah, S: 2462, B: 317A, K: 299C, H: 104B

2696 חֶלְבּוֹן ḥelbôn, Helbon, S: 2463, B: 317A, K: 299C, H: 104C

2697 חֶלְבְּנָה ḥelbᵉnâ, galbanum, S: 2464, B: 317B, K: 299C, H: 104C

2698 חֶלֶד ḥeled, life, duration of life; this world, S: 2465, B: 317B, K: 299D, H: 104C

2699 חֵלֶד ḥēled, Heled, S: 2466, B: 317C, K: 299D, H: 104C

2700 חֹלֶד ḥōled, weasel, S: 2467, B: 317C, K: 299D, H: 104C

2701 חֻלְדָּה ḥuldâ, Huldah, S: 2468, B: 317C, K: 300A, H: 104C

2702 חֶלְדַּי ḥelday, Heldai, S: 2469, B: 317C, K: 300A, H: 104C

2703 ¹חָלָה ḥālâ¹, [A] to be ill, be weak, be faint, become diseased, be wounded; [C] to be made sick, be incurable; [D] to afflict; [E] to become weak; [G] to make ill, to cause to suffer; [H] to be wounded; [F] to pretend to be ill, to feel sick, S: 2470, B: 317C, K: 300A, H: 104C

2704 ²חָלָה ḥālâ², [D] to entreat, implore, seek favor, intercede, S: 2470, B: 318C, K*, H: 105A

2705 חַלָּה ḥallâ, (ring-shaped) bread cakes, S: 2471, B: 319C, K: 300D, H: 104D

2706 חֲלוֹם ḥᵃlôm, dream, dreamer, S: 2472, B: 321C, K: 300D, H: 105A

2707 חַלּוֹן ḥallôn, window, narrow openings, parapet openings, S: 2474, B: 319D, K: 301A, H: 105A

2708 חֹלוֹן ḥōlôn, Holon, S: 2473, B: 298B, K: 301B, H: 105A

2709 חַלּוֹנָי ḥallônāy, variant: window, S: 2474†, B: 319D, K: 301B, H: 105A

2710 חֲלוֹף ḥᵃlôp, destitute, vanishing, S: 2475, B: 322B, K: 301B, H: 106B

2711 חֲלוּשָׁה ḥᵃlûšâ, defeat, S: 2476, B: 325D, K: 301B, H: 105A

2712 חֲלַח ḥᵃlaḥ, Halah, S: 2477, B: 318D, K: 301B, H: 105A

2713 חַלְחוּל ḥalḥûl, Halhul, S: 2478, B: 319A, K: 301B, H: 105A

2714 חַלְחָלָה ḥalḥālâ, anguish, pain, trembling, S: 2479, B: 298B, K: 301C, H: 105A

2715 חָלַט ḥālaṭ, [A] to accept a statement, S: 2480, B: 319A, K: 301C, H: 105A

2716 חֳלִי ḥᵒlî, illness, sickness, affliction; wound, injury, S: 2483, B: 318B, K: 301C, H: 105A

2717 ¹חֲלִי ḥᵃlî¹, ornament, jewel, S: 2481, B: 318D, K: 301D, H: 105B

2718 ²חֲלִי ḥᵃlî², Hali, S: 2482, B: 318D, K: 301D, H: 105B

2719 חֶלְיָה ḥelyâ, jewelry, ornament, S: 2484, B: 318D, K: 301D, H: 105B

2720 ¹חָלִיל ḥālîl¹, flute, S: 2485, B: 319D, K: 301D, H: 105B

2721 ²חָלִילָה ḥālîl², far be it!, never!, S: 2486†, B: 321A, K: 301D, H: 105B

2722 חֲלִיפָה ḥᵃlîpâ, set, sequence, shift; renewal, relief, S: 2487, B: 322B, K: 302A, H: 105B

2723 חֲלִיצָה ḥᵃlîṣâ, belongings, equipment, S: 2488, B: 322D, K: 302B, H: 105C

2724 חֵלְכָה ḥēlkâ, victim, S: 2489, B: 319A, K: 302B, H: 105C

2725 ¹חָלַל ḥālal¹, [C] to defile oneself, be profaned, be desecrated; [D] to defile, profane, desecrate; to enjoy; [E] to be defiled; [G] to begin, to proceed, launch; [H] to be begun, S: 2490, B: 320A, K: 302C, H: 105C

2726 ²חָלַל ḥālal², [A] to be wounded; [D] to pierce, wound; [E] to be wounded; to be killed, S: 2490, B: 319B, K: 303B, H: 105D

2727 ³חָלַל ḥālal³, [A, D] to play the flute, S: 2490, B: 320A, K: 303C, H: 106A

2728 [1]חָלָל *ḥālāl*[1], dead, slain, casualty, S: 2491, B: 319C, K: 303C, H: 106A

2729 [2]חָלָל *ḥālāl*[2], defiled, profane, S: 2491, B: 321A, K: 303C, H: 106A

2730 [1]חָלַם *ḥālam*[1], [A] to grow strong; [G] to restore to health, S: 2492, B: 321B, K: 303D, H: 106A

2731 [2]חָלַם *ḥālam*[2], [A] to dream; [G] to encourage one to have dreams, S: 2492, B: 321B, K: 303D, H: 106A

2732 חֵלֶם *ḥēlem*, variant: Helem, see 2702, S: 2494, B: 321B, K: 304A, H: 106B

2733 חַלָּמוּת *ḥallāmût*, egg *or* mallow, S: 2495, B: 321D, K: 304A, H: 106B

2734 חַלָּמִישׁ *ḥallāmîš*, flinty rock, hard rock, S: 2496, B: 321D, K: 304B, H: 106B

2735 חֵלֹן *ḥēlōn*, Helon, S: 2497, B: 298B, K: 304B, H: 106B

2736 [1]חָלַף *ḥālap*[1], [A] to go by, pass on, sweep by; to be new; [D] to change; [G] to change, exchange, replace, renew, S: 2498, B: 322A, K: 304B, H: 106B

2737 [2]חָלַף *ḥālap*[2], [A] to pierce, cut through, S: 2498, B: 322A, K: 304D, H: 106C

2738 [1]חֵלֶף *ḥēlep*[1], Heleph, S: 2501†, B: 322B, K: 304D, H: 106C

2739 [2]חֵלֶף *ḥēlep*[2], in return for, S: 2500, B: 322B, K: 304D, H: 106C

2740 [1]חָלַץ *ḥālaṣ*[1], [A] to take off; [B] to be taken off; [C] to be delivered, be rescued; [D] to rescue, deliver; to tear out, rob, S: 2502, B: 322C, K: 305A, H: 106C

2741 [2]חָלַץ *ḥālaṣ*[2], [B] to be armed (for battle); [C] to arm oneself; [G] to strengthen, S: 2502, B: 323A, K: 305A, H: 106C

2742 חֶלֶץ *ḥeleṣ*, Helez, S: 2503, B: 323B, K: 305B, H: 106D

2743 חֲלָצַיִם *ḥᵃlāṣayim*, waist, stomach, heart; body, flesh, S: 2504†, B: 323B, K: 305C, H: 106D

2744 [1]חָלַק *ḥālaq*[1], [A] to be smooth, slippery; deceitful; [G] to speak deceit, flatter, be seductive, S: 2505, B: 323C, K: 305C, H: 106D

2745 [2]חָלַק *ḥālaq*[2], [A] to divide, apportion, assign; [C] to be divided, be dispersed, be distributed; [D] to divide, allot, apportion; [E] to be divided; [G] to get one's share; [F] to divide among themselves, S: 2505, B: 325A, K: 305D, H: 106D

2746 [3]חָלַק *ḥālaq*[3], variant: [D] to destroy, S: 2505, B: 323D 3, K: 305D, H: 107A

2747 [1]חָלָק *ḥālāq*[1], smooth, slippery, pleasant, flattering, S: 2509 & 2511†, B: 325B, K: 306B 5., H: 107A

2748 [2]חָלָק *ḥālāq*[2], Halak, S: 2510, B: 325B, K: 306B, H: 107A 4.

2749 [1]חֵלֶק *ḥēleq*[1], smoothness, S: 2506, B: 325B, K: 306C, H: 107B

2750 [2]חֵלֶק *ḥēleq*[2], share, portion, allotment, plot of ground, S: 2506, B: 324A, K: 306C, H: 107B

2751 [3]חֵלֶק *ḥēleq*[3], Helek, S: 2507, B: 324C, K: 307A, H: 107C

2752 חַלֻּק *ḥalluq*, smooth (stones), S: 2512, B: 325C, K: 307B, H: 107C

2753 [1]חֶלְקָה *ḥelqâ*[1], smoothness, S: 2513, B: 325C, K: 307B, H: 107C

2754 [2]חֶלְקָה *ḥelqâ*[2], plot, field, tract, S: 2513, B: 324C, K: 307B, H: 107C

2755 חֲלֻקָּה *ḥᵃluqqâ*, part, portion, division, S: 2515, B: 324C, K: 307C, H: 107C

2756 חֲלַקְלַקָּה *ḥᵃlaqqâ*, variant: smoothness, flattery, S: 2514, B: 325C, K: 306B, H: 107C

2757 חֶלְקִי *ḥelqî*, Helekite, S: 2516, B: 324C, K: 307C, H: 107C

2758 חֶלְקַי *ḥelqāy*, Helkai, S: 2517, B: 324D, K: 307C, H: 107C

2759 חִלְקִיָּה *ḥilqiyyâ*, Hilkiah, S: 2518, B: 324D, K: 307C, H: 107C

2760 חִלְקִיָּהוּ *ḥilqiyyāhû*, Hilkiah, S: 2518, B: 324D, K: 307C, H: 107C

2761 חֲלַקְלַק *ḥᵃlaqlaq*, slippery; intrigue; not sincere, S: 2519, B: 325C, K: 307D, H: 107C

2762 חֶלְקַת *ḥelqat*, Helkath, S: 2520, B: 324D, K: 307D, H: 107D

2763 חֶלְקַת הַצֻּרִים *ḥelqat haṣṣurîm*, Helkath Hazzurim, S: 2521, B: 324D, K: 307D, H: 107D

2764 [1]חָלַשׁ *ḥālaš*[1], [A] to be laid low, S: 2522, B: 325D, K: 307D, H: 107D

2765 [2]חָלַשׁ *ḥālaš*[2], [A] to overcome, defeat, S: 2522, B: 325D, K: 307D, H: 107D

2766 חַלָּשׁ *ḥallāš*, weak, S: 2523, B: 325D, K: 308A, H: 107D

2767 [1]חָם *ḥām*[1], father-in-law, S: 2524, B: 327A, K: 308A, H: 107D

2768 [2]חָם *ḥām*[2], hot, sweltering, S: 2525, B: 328D, K: 308A, H: 107D

2769 [3]חָם *ḥām*[3], Ham, S: 2526, B: 325D, K: 308A, H: 107D

2770 חֹם *ḥōm*, heat, S: 2527, B: 328D, K: 308B, H: 107D

2771 חֵמָא *ḥēmā'*, variant: see 2779, S: 2534, B: 404B, K: 309B, H: 107D

2772 חֶמְאָה *ḥem'â*, curds, curdled milk; butter, cream, S: 2529, B: 326A, K: 308B, H: 107D

2773 חָמַד *ḥāmad*, [A] to covet, lust, desire; delight in; [B] (as noun) what is coveted: treasure, wealth; [C] to be pleasing, be desirable; [D] to delight, S: 2530, B: 326B, K: 308C, H: 107D

2774 חֶמֶד *ḥemed*, fruitfulness, lushness; pleasantness; handsomeness, S: 2531, B: 326C, K: 308D, H: 108A

2775 חֶמְדָּה *ḥemdâ*, desirable, pleasant, fine, valuable (things), S: 2532, B: 326C, K: 308D, H: 108A

2776 חֲמֻדוֹת *ḥᵃmudôt*, esteemed, precious, costly (things), S: 2530†, B: 326D, K: 309A, H: 108A

2777 חֶמְדָּן *ḥemdān*, Hemdan, S: 2533, B: 326D, K: 309A, H: 108A

2778 חָמָה *ḥāmâ*, [A] to watch, be careful, S: 2534†, B: 404B, K: 309A, H: 108A

2779 חֵמָה *ḥēmâ*, anger, wrath, fury, rage, venom, S: 2534, B: 404B, K: 309B, H: 108B

2780 חַמָּה *ḥammâ*, heat (of the sun), S: 2535, B: 328D, K: 309C, H: 108B

2781 חַמּוּאֵל *ḥammû'ēl*, Hammuel, S: 2536, B: 329B, K: 309D, H: 108B

2782 חֲמוּטַל *ḥᵃmûṭal*, Hamutal, S: 2537, B: 327D, K: 309D, H: 108B

2783 חָמוּל *ḥāmûl*, Hamul, S: 2538, B: 328B, K: 309D, H: 108B

2784 חָמוּלִי *ḥāmûlî*, Hamulite, S: 2539, B: 328B, K: 309D, H*

2785 חַמּוֹן *ḥammôn*, Hammon, S: 2540, B: 329A, K: 309D, H: 108B

2786 חָמוּץ *ḥāmûṣ*, variant: crimson, see 2808, S: 2556†, B: 330A, K: 310A, H: 108B

2787 חָמוֹץ *ḥāmôṣ*, oppressor; oppressed, S: 2541, B: 330B, K: 310A, H: 108B

2788 חַמּוּק *ḥammûq*, gracefulness, curve, S: 2542, B: 330B, K: 310A, H: 108C

2789 [1]חֲמוֹר *ḥᵃmôr*[1], donkey, S: 2543, B: 331A, K: 310A, H: 108C

2790 [2]חֲמוֹר *ḥᵃmôr*[2], variant: heap, S: 2543, B: 331A, K: 310A, H: 108C

2791 [3]חֲמוֹר *ḥᵃmôr*[3], Hamor, S: 2544, B: 331C, K: 310B, H: 108C

2792 חָמוֹת *ḥāmôt*, mother-in-law, S: 2545, B: 327B, K: 310B, H: 108C

2793 חֹמֶט *ḥōmeṭ*, skink, S: 2546, B: 328A, K: 310B, H: 108C

2794 חֻמְטָה *ḥumṭâ*, Humtah, S: 2547, B: 328A, K: 310C, H: 108C

2795 חֲמִיטַל *ḥᵃmîṭal*, variant: Hamital, see 2782, S: 2537, B: 327D, K: 310C, H: 108C

2796 חָמִיץ *ḥāmîṣ*, mash, fodder, S: 2548, B: 330A, K: 310C, H: 108C

2797 חֲמִישִׁי *ḥᵃmîšî*, fifth, S: 2549, B: 332C, K: 310C, H: 108C

2798 חָמַל *ḥāmal*, [A] to spare, take pity on, have mercy on, S: 2550 & 2565†, B: 328A, K: 310D, H: 108D

2799 חֶמְלָה *ḥemlâ*, mercy, S: 2551, B: 328B, K: 311A, H: 108D

2800 חֻמְלָה *ḥumlâ*, variant: compassion, S: 2550†, B: 328B, K: 311A, H: 108D

2801 חָמַם *ḥāmam*, [A] to be hot, be warm; be aroused; be in a rage; [C] to burn with lust; [D] to let warm; [F] to warm oneself, S: 2552, B: 328C, K: 311A, H: 108D

2802 חַמָּן *ḥammān*, incense altar, S: 2553, B: 329A, K: 311C, H: 109A

2803 [1]חָמַס *ḥāmas*[1], [A] to do violence, harm, to lay waste; to be stripped off; [C] to be mistreated, S: 2554, B: 329B, K: 311C, H: 109A

2804 [2]חָמַס *ḥāmas*[2], variant: [A] to think up, devise, S: 2554, B: 329B 2, K: 311C, H: 109A

2805 חָמָס *ḥāmās*, violence, destruction, malice, ruthlessness, fierceness, S: 2555, B: 329C, K: 311D, H: 109A

2806 [1]חָמֵץ *ḥāmēṣ*[1], [A] to have yeast added, be leavened; [F] to be grieved, embittered, S: 2556, B: 329D, K: 312A, H: 109B

2807 [2]חָמֵץ *ḥāmēṣ*[2], [A] to be cruel, oppress, S: 2556, B: 330A, K: 312A, H: 109B

2808 [3]חָמֵץ *ḥāmēṣ*[3], [B] to be stained crimson, S: 2556, B: 330A, K: 310A, H: 108B

2809 [4]חָמֵץ *ḥāmēṣ*[4], something leavened, made with yeast, S: 2557, B: 329D, K: 312B, H: 109B

2810 חֹמֶץ *ḥōmeṣ*, vinegar, wine vinegar, S: 2558, B: 330A, K: 312B, H: 109B

2811 חָמַק *ḥāmaq*, [A] to leave, turn away; [F] to wander, turn here and there, S: 2559, B: 330B, K: 312B, H: 109B

2812 [1] חָמַר *ḥāmar*[1], [A] to foam, S: 2560, B: 330B, K: 312C, H: 109B

2813 [2] חָמַר *ḥāmar*[2], [E] to be reddened, glow, S: 2560, B: 331A, K: 312D, H: 109C

2814 [3] חָמַר *ḥāmar*[3], [A] to coat, cover, S: 2560, B: 330D, K: 312C, H: 109C

2815 חֶמֶר *ḥemer*, (foaming, fermenting) wine, S: 2561, B: 330C, K: 312D, H: 109C

2816 [1] חֹמֶר *ḥōmer*[1], churning, storming (sea waters), S: 2563, B: 330D, K: 312D, H: 109C

2817 [2] חֹמֶר *ḥōmer*[2], clay, mortar, mud, S: 2563, B: 330C, K: 312D, H: 109C

2818 [3] חֹמֶר *ḥōmer*[3], homer (measure), S: 2563, B: 330D, K: 312D, H: 109C

2819 חֵמָר *ḥēmār*, tar, S: 2564, B: 330C, K: 313A, H: 109C

2820 חַמְרָן *ḥamrān*, variant: Hamran, see 2777, S: 2566, B: 331C, K: 313A, H: 109D

2821 חָמַשׁ *ḥāmaš*, [B] to be organized for war; [D] to take a fifth, S: 2567 & 2571†, B: 332B & 332D, K: 313A, H: 109D

2822 חָמֵשׁ *ḥāmēš*, five, (pl.) fifty, S: 2568, B: 331C, K: 313B, H: 109D

2823 [1] חֹמֶשׁ *ḥōmeš*[1], fifth, S: 2569, B: 332B, K: 313C, H: 109D

2824 [2] חֹמֶשׁ *ḥōmeš*[2], stomach, belly, S: 2570, B: 332D, K: 313C, H: 109D

2825 חֲמִשִּׁים *ḥ^{a}miššîm*, variant: fifty, S: 2572, B: 332B, K: 313B, H: 109D

2826 חֲמֻשִׁים *ḥ^{a}mušîm*, variant: in battle array, S: 2572†, B: 332D, K: 313A, H: 109D

2827 חֵמֶת *ḥēmet*, skin (for water or wine), S: 2573, B: 332D, K: 313C, H: 109D

2828 חֲמָת *ḥ^{a}māt*, Hamath, S: 2574, B: 333A, K: 313D, H: 109D

2829 [1] חַמַּת *ḥammat*[1], Hammath, S: 2575, B: 329A, K: 313D, H: 109D

2830 [2] חַמַּת *ḥammat*[2], Hammath, S: 2575, B: 329B, K: 313D, H: 110A

2831 חַמֹּת דֹּאר *ḥammōt dō'r*, Hammoth Dor, S: 2576, B: 329B, K: 207A, H: 66A

2832 חֲמָת צוֹבָה *ḥ^{a}māt ṣôbâ*, Hamath Zobah, S: 2578, B: 333A & 844C, K: 796D, H: 304A

2833 חֲמָתִי *ḥ^{a}mātî*, Hamathite, S: 2577, B: 333B, K: 314A, H: 110A

2834 [1] חֵן *ḥēn*[1], favor, grace; charm, S: 2580, B: 336B, K: 314A, H: 110A

2835 [2] חֵן *ḥēn*[2], Hen, S: 2581, B: 336D, K: 314A, H*

2836 חֵנָדָד *ḥēnādād*, Henadad, S: 2582, B: 337B, K: 314C, H: 110A

2837 [1] חָנָה *ḥānâ*[1], [A] to set up camp, pitch camp, encamp, S: 2583, B: 333B, K: 314C, H: 110A

2838 [2] חָנָה *ḥānâ*[2], variant: see 2858, S: 2589†, B: 335D, K: 314D, H: 110B

2839 חַנָּה *ḥannâ*, Hannah, S: 2584, B: 336D, K: 314D, H: 110B

2840 [1] חֲנוֹךְ *ḥ^{a}nôk*[1], Enoch; Hanoch, S: 585, B: 335C, K: 314D, H: 110B

2841 [2] חֲנוֹךְ *ḥ^{a}nôk*[2], variant: Enoch, S: 2585, B: 335C 1, K: 314D, H: 110B

2842 חָנוּן *ḥānûn*, Hanun, S: 2586, B: 337A, K: 315A, H: 110B

2843 חַנּוּן *ḥannûn*, gracious, compassionate, S: 2587, B: 337A, K: 315A, H: 110B

2844 חָנוּת *ḥānût*, vaulted cell, S: 2588, B: 333D, K: 315A, H: 110B

2845 [1] חָנַט *ḥānaṭ*[1], [A] to ripen, S: 2590, B: 334C, K: 315A, H: 110B

2846 [2] חָנַט *ḥānaṭ*[2], [A] to embalm, S: 2590, B: 334C, K: 315A, H: 110B

2847 חֲנֻטִים *ḥ^{a}nuṭîm*, embalming, S: 2590†, B: 334D, K: 315B, H: 110B

2848 חַנִּיאֵל *ḥannî'ēl*, Hanniel, S: 2592, B: 337A, K: 315B, H: 110B

2849 חָנִיךְ *ḥānîk*, trained (men), S: 2593, B: 335C, K: 315B, H: 110B

2850 חֲנִינָה *ḥ^{a}nînâ*, favor, kindness, S: 2594, B: 337A, K: 315B, H: 110B

2851 חֲנִית *ḥ^{a}nît*, spear, S: 2595, B: 333D, K: 315B, H: 110B

2852 חָנַךְ *ḥānak*, [A] to dedicate, train, S: 2596, B: 335B, K: 315D, H: 110C

2853 חֲנֻכָּה *ḥ^{a}nukkâ*, dedication, offering for dedication, S: 2598, B: 335C, K: 315D, H: 110C

2854 חֲנֹכִי *ḥ^{a}nōkî*, Hanochite, S: 2599, B: 335C, K: 314D, H: 110C

2855 חִנָּם *ḥinnām*, without cause, for no reason; for nothing, S: 2600, B: 336C, K: 316A, H: 110C

2856 חֲנַמְאֵל *ḥ^{a}nam'ēl*, Hanamel, S: 2601, B: 335D, K: 316A, H: 110C

2857 חֲנָמַל *ḥ^{a}nāmal*, sleet, S: 2602†, B: 335D, K: 316A, H: 110C

2858 [1] חָנַן *ḥānan*[1], [A] to be gracious, to have mercy, to take pity, be kind; [D] to move to pity, be kind, be charming; [H] to be shown compassion, mercy; [F] to plead for grace, beg for mercy, S: 2603, B: 335D, K: 316B, H: 110C

2859 [2] חָנַן *ḥānan*[2], [A] to be loathsome, S: 2603, B: 337D, K: 316D, H: 110D

2860 חָנָן *ḥānān*, Hanan, S: 2605, B: 336D, K: 316D, H: 110D

2861 חֲנַנְאֵל *ḥ^{a}nan'ēl*, Hananel, S: 2606, B: 337A, K: 316D, H: 111A

2862 חֲנָנִי *ḥ^{a}nānî*, Hanani, S: 2607, B: 337B, K: 317A, H: 111A

2863 חֲנַנְיָה *ḥ^{a}nanyâ*, Hananiah, S: 2608, B: 337B, K: 317A, H: 111A

2864 חֲנַנְיָהוּ *ḥ^{a}nanyāhû*, Hananiah, S: 2608, B: 337B, K: 317A, H: 111A

2865 חָנֵס *ḥānēs*, Hanes, S: 2609, B: 337D, K: 317A, H: 111A

2866 [1] חָנֵף *ḥānēp*[1], [A] to be desecrated, be defiled; [G] to corrupt, defile, pollute, S: 2610, B: 337D, K: 317B, H: 111A

2867 [2] חָנֵף *ḥānēp*[2], variant: [A] to limp, see 2868, S: 2611†, B: 338B, K: 317C, H: 111A

2868 [3] חָנֵף *ḥānēp*[3], godless, ungodly, S: 2611, B: 338A, K: 317C, H: 111A

2869 חֹנֶף *ḥōnep*, ungodliness, godlessness, S: 2612, B: 338A, K: 317C, H: 111A

2870 חֲנֻפָּה *ḥ^{a}nuppâ*, ungodliness, godlessness, S: 2613, B: 338B, K: 317C, H: 111A

2871 חָנַק *ḥānaq*, [C] to hang oneself; [D] to strangle, S: 2614, B: 338B, K: 317C, H: 111A

2872 חַנָּתֹן *ḥannātôn*, Hannathon, S: 2615, B: 337B, K: 317D, H: 111A

2873 [1] חָסַד *ḥāsad*[1], [D] to put to shame, reproach, S: 2616, B: 340A, K: 317D, H: 111A

2874 [2] חָסַד *ḥāsad*[2], [F] to conduct oneself as faithful, S: 2616, B: 340A, K: 317D, H: 111B

2875 [1] חֶסֶד *ḥesed*[1], disgrace, S: 2617, B: 340A, K: 317D, H: 111B

2876 [2] חֶסֶד *ḥesed*[2], unfailing love, loyal love, devotion, kindness, S: 2617, B: 338C, K: 318A, H: 111B

2877 [3] חֶסֶד *ḥesed*[3], variant: Hesed, S: 2618, B: 122C, K: 318D, H: 111C

2878 חֲסַדְיָה *ḥ^{a}sadyâ*, Hasadiah, S: 2619, B: 339D, K: 318D, H: 111C

2879 חָסָה *ḥāsâ*, [A] to take refuge in, to trust in, S: 2620, B: 340A, K: 318D, H: 111C

2880 [1] חֹסָה *ḥōsâ*[1], Hosah, S: 2621, B: 340B 1., K: 319A, H: 111D

2881 [2] חֹסָה *ḥōsâ*[2], Hosah, S: 2621, B: 340B 2., K: 319A, H: 111D

2882 חָסוּת *ḥāsût*, variant: refuge, S: 2622, B: 340B, K: 319A, H: 111D

2883 חָסִיד *ḥāsîd*, saints; faithful ones; godly, S: 2623, B: 339C, K: 319A, H: 111D

2884 חֲסִידָה *ḥ^{a}sîdâ*, stork, S: 2624, B: 339D, K: 319B, H: 111D

2885 חָסִיל *ḥāsîl*, grasshoppers, locusts, S: 2625, B: 340C, K: 319B, H: 111D

2886 חָסִין *ḥ^{a}sîn*, mighty, strong, S: 2626, B: 340D, K: 319B & 319D, H: 111D

2887 חָסַל *ḥāsal*, [A, G] to devour, consume, S: 2628, B: 340C, K: 319C, H: 111D

2888 חָסַם *ḥāsam*, [A] to muzzle (an animal); to block (the way), S: 2629, B: 340C, K: 319C, H: 111D

2889 חָסַן *ḥāsan*, [C] to be stored up, S: 2630, B: 340D, K: 319D, H: 112A

2890 חֹסֶן *ḥōsen*, stored treasure, riches, wealth, S: 2633, B: 340D, K: 319D, H: 112A

2891 חָסֹן *ḥāsōn*, mighty, strong, S: 2634, B: 340D, K: 319D, H: 112A

2892 חַסְפַּס *ḥaspas*, [E] to flake, S: 2636, B: 341A, K: 319D, H: 112A

2893 [1] חָסֵר *ḥāsēr*[1], [A] to lack; to have nothing; to go down, recede; [D] to make lower; to deprive; [G] to cause to lack, withhold, S: 2637, B: 341A, K: 320A, H: 112A

2894 [2] חָסֵר *ḥāsēr*[2], lacking; wanting, S: 2638, B: 341C, K: 320B, H: 112A

2895 חֶסֶר *ḥeser*, poverty, lack, S: 2639, B: 341C, K: 320B, H: 112A

2896 חֹסֶר *ḥōser*, poverty, lack, S: 2640, B: 341C, K: 320B, H: 112A

2897 חַסְרָה *ḥasrâ*, Hasrah, S: 2641, B: 341C, K: 320B, H: 112A

2898 חֶסְרוֹן *ḥesrôn*, what is lacking, S: 2642, B: 341C, K: 320B, H: 112B

2899 [1] חַף *ḥap*[1], clean, pure, S: 2643, B: 342C, K: 320C, H: 112B

2900 [2] חַף *ḥap*[2], variant: Apis, S: 5502†, B: 695A, K: 320C, H: 112B

2901 חָפָא *ḥāpā'*, [D] to do secretly, S: 2644, B: 341D, K: 320C, H: 112B

2902 חָפָה *ḥāpâ*, [A] to cover; [B] to be covered; [C] to be sheathed, be covered; [D] to panel, overlay, cover, S: 2645, B: 341D, K: 320C, H: 112B

2903 [1]חֻפָּה *ḥuppâ*[1], canopy, shelter; chamber, pavilion (of marriage ceremony), S: 2646, B: 342C, K: 320D, H: 112B

2904 [2]חֻפָּה *ḥuppâ*[2], Huppah, S: 2647, B: 342C, K: 320D, H: 112B

2905 חָפַז *ḥāpaz*, [A] to hurry away (in alarm or terror), S: 2648, B: 342A, K: 320D, H: 112B

2906 חִפָּזוֹן *ḥippāzôn*, haste, S: 2649, B: 342A, K: 320D, H: 112C

2907 חֻפִּים *ḥuppîm*, Huppim; Huppite, S: 2650, B: 342C, K: 321A, H: 112C

2908 חֹפֶן *ḥōpen*, hollow of the hand, handful, S: 2651, B: 342B, K: 321A, H: 112C

2909 חָפְנִי *ḥopnî*, Hophni, S: 2652, B: 342B, K: 321A, H: 112C

2910 חָפַף *ḥāpap*, [A] to shield, shelter, S: 2653, B: 342B, K: 321A, H: 112C

2911 [1]חָפֵץ *ḥāpēṣ*[1], [A] to desire, delight in, be pleased with, have pleasure, S: 2654, B: 342C, K: 321B, H: 112C

2912 [2]חָפֵץ *ḥāpaṣ*[2], [A] to sway, S: 2654, B: 343C, K: 321C, H: 112C

2913 [3]חָפֵץ *ḥāpēṣ*[3], desire, delight, pleasure, S: 2655, B: 343A, K: 321C, H: 112C

2914 חֵפֶץ *ḥēpeṣ*, desire, delight, pleasure, S: 2656, B: 343A, K: 321D, H: 112D

2915 חֶפְצִי־בָהּ *ḥepṣî-bāh*, Hephzibah, S: 2657†, B: 343B, K: 322A, H: 112D

2916 [1]חָפַר *ḥāpar*[1], [A] to dig; to spy out, search for, look about, seek out; to paw, scoop, S: 2658, B: 343C, K: 322A, H: 112D

2917 [2]חָפֵר *ḥāpar*[2], [A] to feel dismay, be disgraced, be humiliated, be in confusion; [G] to bring disgrace, be ashamed, be humiliated, S: 2659†, B: 344A, K: 322B, H: 112D

2918 [1]חֵפֶר *ḥēper*[1], Hepher, S: 2660, B: 343D, K: 322B, H: 113A

2919 [2]חֵפֶר *ḥēper*[2], Hepher, S: 2660, B: 343D, K: 322B, H: 113A

2920 חֶפְרִי *ḥeprî*, Hepherite, S: 2662, B: 343D, K: 322C, H: 113A

2921 חֲפָרַיִם *ḥ[a]pārayim*, Hapharaim, S: 2663, B: 343D, K: 322C, H: 113A

2922 חָפְרַע *ḥopra'*, Hophra, S: 6548†, B: 344B, K: 322C, H: 113A

2923 חֲפַרְפָּרָה *ḥ[a]parpārâ*, rodent, S: 2661† + 6512†, B: 344A, K: 322C, H: 113A

2924 חָפַשׂ *ḥāpaś*, [A] to search for, examine, plot; [C] to be ransacked; [D] to search, look around, track down, hunt down; [E] to go into hiding, to devise; [F] to disguise oneself, become like, S: 2664, B: 344B, K: 322C, H: 113A

2925 חֵפֶשׂ *ḥēpeś*, plan, plot, S: 2665, B: 344C, K: 323A, H: 113B

2926 חָפַשׁ *ḥāpaš*, [E] to be freed, S: 2666, B: 344D, K: 323A, H: 113B

2927 חֹפֶשׁ *ḥōpeš*, material (for saddle blanket), S: 2667, B: 344D, K: 323A, H: 113B

2928 חֻפְשָׁה *ḥupšâ*, freedom, S: 2668, B: 344D, K: 323A, H: 113B

2929 חָפְשׁוּת *ḥopšût*, variant: see 2931, S: 2669, B: 345A, K: 323A, H: 113B

2930 חָפְשִׁי *ḥopšî*, free; set apart, exempt, S: 2670, B: 344D, K: 323A, H: 113B

2931 חָפְשִׁית *ḥopšît*, separation, exemption (from duties), S: 2669, B: 345A, K: 323B, H: 113B

2932 חֵץ *ḥēṣ*, arrow; archer, S: 2671, B: 346B, K: 323B, H: 113B

2933 [1]חָצֵב *ḥāṣēb*[1], [A] to dig; hew out, cut out; [B, C, E] to be dug, be engraved, be cut out; [G] to cut in pieces, S: 2672, B: 345A, K: 323C, H: 113B

2934 [2]חָצֵב *ḥāṣab*[2], [A] to strike (with lightning), S: 2672, B: 345A 3, K: 323C, H: 113C

2935 חֹצֵב *ḥōṣēb*, stonecutter, mason, S: 2672†, B: 345A, K: 323C, H: 113C

2936 חָצָה *ḥāṣâ*, [A] to divide; set apart; to rise up to; [C] to be divided, be parceled out, S: 2673, B: 345B, K: 324A, H: 113C

2937 [1]חָצוֹר *ḥāṣôr*[1], Hazor, S: 2674, B: 347D, K: 324B, H: 113D

2938 [2]חָצוֹר *ḥāṣôr*[2], variant: sedentary Arabs, S: 2674, B: 347D, K: 324B, H: 113D

2939 חָצוֹר חֲדַתָּה *ḥāṣôr ḥ[a]dattâ*, Hazor Hadattah, S: 2675, B: 347D, K: 324B, H: 113D & 97A

2940 חֲצוֹת *ḥ[a]ṣôt*, middle (of the night), mid(night), S: 2676, B: 345C, K: 324B, H: 113D

2941 חֻצוֹת *ḥuṣôt*, variant: Huzoth, S: 7155†, B: 900C, K: 856A 3., H: 325D

2942 חֲצִי *ḥ[a]ṣî*, half, halfway, middle, midst, S: 2677†, B: 345C, K: 324B, H: 113D

2943 [1]חֵצִי *ḥēṣî*[1], arrow, S: 2678, B: 345D, K: 324C, H: 113D

2944 [2]חֵצִי *ḥēṣî*[2], variant: see 2942, S: 2677, B: 345C, K: 324B, H: 113D

2945 [1]חָצִיר *ḥāṣîr*[1], grass; hay, S: 2682, B: 348B, K: 324C, H: 113D

2946 [2]חָצִיר *ḥāṣîr*[2], leeks, S: 2682, B: 348B, K: 324D, H: 113D

2947 [3]חָצִיר *ḥāṣîr*[3], variant: reed, S: 2682, B: 347D & 348B 1 & 2, K: 324D, H: 113D

2948 [4]חָצִיר *ḥāṣîr*[4], home, abode, haunt, S: 2681, B: 347D, K: 324C, H: 113D

2949 חֵצֶן *ḥēṣen*, variant: bosom (of a garment), S: 2683, B: 346A, K: 324D, H: 113D

2950 חֹצֶן *ḥōṣen*, arms, folds of a robe, S: 2684, B: 346A, K: 324D, H: 113D

2951 [1]חָצַץ *ḥāṣaṣ*[1], [A] to be in order, in ranks; [D] to divide, share; [E] to come to an end, S: 2686, B: 346B, K: 325A, H: 113D

2952 [2]חָצַץ *ḥāṣaṣ*[2], [D] to sing, S: 2686, B: 346D, K: 325A, H: 113D

2953 חָצָץ *ḥāṣāṣ*, gravel, S: 2687, B: 346B, K: 325A, H: 114A

2954 חַצְצוֹן תָּמָר *ḥaṣ[e]ṣôn tāmār*, Hazazon Tamar, S: 2688, B: 346C, K: 325A, H: 114A

2955 חצצר *ḥaṣṣar*, [D] to sound a trumpet, play a trumpet, S: 2690†, B: 348D, K: 325A, H: 114A

2956 חֲצֹצְרָה *ḥ[a]ṣōṣ[e]râ*, trumpet, S: 2689, B: 348C, K: 325B, H: 114A

2957 חָצַר *ḥāṣar*, variant: see 2955, S: 2690, B: 348D, K: 325A, H: 114A

2958 [1]חָצֵר *ḥāṣēr*[1], courtyard, court of a house, enclosed areas; village, S: 2691 & 2699†, B: 346D & 347B, K: 325C, H: 114A a.

2959 [2]חָצֵר *ḥāṣēr*[2], variant: Hazar, S: 2694†, B: 347B, K: 326A Nomina loci, H: 114A b

2960 חֲצַר־אַדָּר *ḥ[a]ṣar-'addār*, Hazar Addar, S: 2692, B: 347B, K: 326A 1., H: 114B b.1.

2961 חֲצַר גַּדָּה *ḥ[a]ṣar gaddâ*, Hazar Gaddah, S: 2693, B: 347C, K: 326A 2., H: 114B b.2.

2962 חָצֵר הַתִּיכוֹן *ḥāṣēr hattîkôn*, Hazer Hatticon, S: 2694, B: 347C, K: 326A, H: 114B b.

2963 חֲצַר סוּסָה *ḥ[a]ṣar sûsâ*, Hazar Susah, S: 2701, B: 347C, K: 326A 3., H: 114B b. 3.

2964 חֲצַר סוּסִים *ḥ[a]ṣar sûsîm*, Hazar Susim, S: 2702, B: 347C, K: 326A 3., H: 114B b.

2965 חֲצַר עֵינוֹן *ḥ[a]ṣar 'ênôn*, Hazar Enan, S: 2703, B: 347C, K: 326A 4., H: 114B b.4.

2966 חֲצַר עֵינָן *ḥ[a]ṣar 'ênān*, Hazar Enan, S: 2704, B: 347C, K: 326A 4., H: 114B b

2967 חֲצַר שׁוּעָל *ḥ[a]ṣar šû'āl*, Hazar Shual, S: 2705, B: 347C, K: 326A 5., H: 114B b.5.

2968 חֶצְרוֹ *ḥeṣrô*, Hezro, S: 2695, B: 347D, K: 326A, H: 114B

2969 [1]חֶצְרוֹן *ḥeṣrôn*[1], Hezron, S: 2696, B: 348A 2., K: 326A, H: 114B

2970 [2]חֶצְרוֹן *ḥeṣrôn*[2], Hezron, S: 2696, B: 348A 1., K: 326B, H: 114B

2971 חֶצְרוֹנִי *ḥeṣrônî*, Hezronite, S: 2697, B: 348A, K: 326B, H: 114B

2972 חֲצֵרוֹת *ḥ[a]ṣērôt*, Hazeroth, S: 2698, B: 348A, K: 326B, H: 114B

2973 חֲצֵרִים *ḥ[a]ṣērîm*, variant: Hazerim, S: 2691†, B: 347B, K: 325C, H: 114A

2974 חֶצְרַי *ḥeṣray*, variant: Hezrai, see 2968, S: 2695†, B: 347D, K: 326B, H: 114B

2975 חֲצַרְמָוֶת *ḥ[a]ṣarmāwet*, Hazarmaveth, S: 2700, B: 348A, K: 326B, H: 114B

2976 חֹק *ḥōq*, decree, statute, prescription; allotment, share, portion, S: 2706, B: 349A, K: 326C, H: 114B

2977 חָקָה *ḥāqâ*, [E] to be carved, be portrayed; [F] mark for oneself, S: 2707, B: 348D, K: 327B, H: 114C

2978 חֻקָּה *ḥuqqâ*, decree, ordinance, regulation, statute, S: 2708, B: 349D, K: 327C, H: 114C

2979 חֲקוּפָא *ḥ[a]qûpā'*, Hakupha, S: 2709, B: 349A, K: 328A, H: 114C

2980 חָקַק *ḥāqaq*, [A] to mark out, inscribe, chisel, engrave; [B] to be portrayed; [D] to command, be a leader, ruler; staff (of a commander); [E] to be decreed; [H] to be written, S: 2710, B: 349A, K: 328A, H: 114C

2981 חֵקֶק *ḥēqeq*, variant: see 2976, S: 2711, B*, K*, H: 114D

2982 חֻקֹּק *ḥuqqōq*, Hukkok, S: 2712, B: 301A & 350C, K: 328C, H: 98C

2983 חָקַר *ḥāqar*, [A] to explore, search out, probe; [C] to be determined, be searched; [D] to search out, S: 2713, B: 350C, K: 328C, H: 114D

2984 חֵקֶר *ḥēqer*, searching, finding out, S: 2714, B: 350D, K: 328D, H: 115A

2985 [1]חֹרִי *ḥōr*[1], noble, free person, S: 2715, B: 359D, K: 329A, H: 115A

2986 [2]חֹר *ḥōr*[2], hole (in various forms), S: 2356, B: 359D, K: 329A, H: 115A

2987 חֻר *ḥur*, hole, pit, S: 2352, B: 359D, K: 329B, H: 115A

2988 חֹר הַגִּדְגָּד *ḥōr haggidgād*, Hor Haggidgad, S: 2735, B: 301B, K: 329B, H: 115B

2989 חֲרָאִים *ḥarā'îm*, filth, excrement, S: 2716†, B: 351A, K: 329B, H: 115B

2990 [1]חָרֵב *ḥārēb*[1], [A] to be dried up, be parched; be desolate, lay in ruins; [C] to be ruined, be desolate; [E] to be dried up; [G] to lay waste, devastate, cause to dry up; [H] to lie in ruins, S: 2717, B: 351A & 351C, K: 328C, H: 115B

2991 [2]חָרֵב *ḥārēb*[2], [A] to kill; [C] to be slaughtered, S: 2717, B: 352B, K: 329D, H: 115C

2992 [3]חָרֵב *ḥārēb*[3], dry, desolate, wasted, in ruins, S: 2720, B: 351A & 351D, K: 330A, H: 115C

2993 [4]חָרֵב *ḥārēb*[4], variant: to be desolate, S: 2717, B: 351B & 351D, K: 330A, H: 115C

2994 [5]חָרֵב *ḥārēb*[5], variant: waste, desolate, S*, B*, K*, H*

2995 חֶרֶב *ḥereb*, sword; dagger; knife; cutting tool, S: 2719, B: 352B, K: 330A & 330D, H: 115C

2996 [1]חֹרֶב *ḥōreb*[1], heat, dryness, drought, fever, S: 2721, B: 351B, K: 330B, H: 115C 1.

2997 [2]חֹרֶב *ḥōreb*[2], waste, rubble, object of horror, desolation, S: 2721, B: 351D, K: 330B, H: 115C 2.

2998 חֹרֵב *ḥōrēb*, Horeb, S: 2722, B: 352A, K: 330C, H: 115C

2999 חָרְבָּה *ḥorbâ*, ruins, desolate place, S: 2723, B: 352A, K: 330C, H: 115C

3000 חָרָבָה *ḥārābâ*, dry land, dry ground, S: 2724, B: 351C, K: 330D, H: 115D

3001 חֲרָבוֹן *ḥarābôn*, dry heat, S: 2725, B: 351C, K: 330D, H: 115D

3002 חַרְבוֹנָא *ḥarbônā'*, Harbona, S: 2726, B: 353A, K: 330D, H: 115D

3003 חַרְבוֹנָה *ḥarbônâ*, Harbona, S: 2726, B: 353A, K: 330D, H: 115D

3004 חָרַג *ḥārag*, [A] to come out trembling, S: 2727, B: 353A, K: 330D, H: 115D

3005 חַרְגֹּל *ḥargōl*, cricket, S: 2728, B: 353B, K: 331A, H: 115D

3006 חָרַד *ḥārad*, [A] to tremble, quake, shudder, be startled; [G] to make afraid, frighten, make tremble, S: 2729, B: 353B, K: 331A, H: 115D

3007 חָרֵד *ḥārēd*, trembling, fearful, S: 2730, B: 353D, K: 331B, H: 116A

3008 [1]חֲרֹד *ḥarōd*[1], Harod, S: 5878†, B: 353D, K: 331B, H: 116A

3009 [2]חֲרֹד *ḥarōd*[2], variant: see 3012, S: 2733†, B: 248B, K: 331C, H: 116A

3010 [1]חֲרָדָה *ḥarādâ*[1], panic, fear, terror, horror, S: 2731, B: 353D, K: 331C, H: 116A

3011 [2]חֲרָדָה *ḥarādâ*[2], Haradah, S: 2732, B: 354A, K: 331C, H: 116A

3012 חֲרֹדִי *ḥarōdî*, Harodite, S: 2733, B: 353D, K: 331C, H: 116A

3013 [1]חָרָה *ḥārâ*[1], [A] to be angry, be aroused; to burn with anger; [C] to rage; [G] to be jealous; [Tiphel] to compete, contend with; [F] to fret, S: 2734 & 8474†, B: 354A, K: 331C, H: 116A

3014 [2]חָרָה *ḥārâ*[2], variant: [A] to become few in number, S: 2787†, B: 359B 2, K: 332A, H: 116B

3015 חַרְהֲיָה *ḥarhayâ*, Harhaiah, S: 2736, B: 354D, K: 332A, H: 116B

3016 חֲרוּזִים *ḥarûzîm*, string of jewels, S: 2737†, B: 354D, K: 332A, H: 116B

3017 חָרוּל *ḥārûl*, weeds, undergrowth, S: 2738, B: 355B, K: 332A, H: 116B

3018 חֲרוּמַף *ḥarûmap*, Harumaph, S: 2739, B: 354C, K: 332B, H: 116B

3019 חָרוֹן *ḥārôn*, fierce (anger), burning (anger), wrath, S: 2740, B: 354C, K: 332B, H: 116B

3020 חֲרוּפִי *ḥarûpî*, Haruphite, S: 2741, B: 358B, K: 332C, H: 116C

3021 [1]חָרוּץ *ḥārûṣ*[1], gold, S: 2742, B: 359A, K: 332C, H: 116C

3022 [2]חָרוּץ *ḥārûṣ*[2], trench, ditch, S: 2742, B: 358D, K: 332C, H: 116C

3023 [3]חָרוּץ *ḥārûṣ*[3], threshing sledge, sharp instrument for harvest, S: 2742, B: 358D, K: 332D, H: 116C

3024 [4]חָרוּץ *ḥārûṣ*[4], maimed, mutilated, S: 2782†, B: 358C, K: 332D, H: 116C

3025 [5]חָרוּץ *ḥārûṣ*[5], decision, S: 2742, B: 358D, K: 336B, H: 116C

3026 [6]חָרוּץ *ḥārûṣ*[6], diligent, industrious, S: 2742, B: 358D, K: 332D, H: 116C

3027 [7]חָרוּץ *ḥārûṣ*[7], Haruz, S: 2743, B: 358D, K: 332D, H: 116C

3028 חַרְחוּר *ḥarḥûr*, Harhur, S: 2744, B: 359C, K: 333A, H: 116C

3029 חַרְהֲיָה *ḥarhayâ*, variant: see 3015, S: 2736†, B: 354D, K: 332D, H: 116C

3030 חַרְחַס *ḥarḥas*, Harhas, S: 2745, B: 354D, K: 333A, H: 116C

3031 חַרְחֻר *ḥarḥur*, scorching heat, S: 2746, B: 359C, K: 333A, H: 116C

3032 חֶרֶט *ḥereṭ*, pen; fashioning tool, stylus, S: 2747, B: 354D, K: 333A, H: 116C

3033 חַרְטֹם *ḥarṭōm*, magician, S: 2748, B: 355A, K: 333A, H: 116C

3034 חֳרִי *ḥorî*, hot, burning, fierce (anger), S: 2750, B: 354C, K: 333B, H: 116D

3035 [1]חֹרִי *ḥōrî*[1], (white) bread or cake, S: 2751, B: 301A, K: 333B, H: 116D

3036 [2]חֹרִי *ḥōrî*[2], Hori, S: 2752, B: 360A 3., K: 333B, H: 116D

3037 [3]חֹרִי *ḥōrî*[3], Horite, S: 2753, B: 360A 1. & 2., K: 333C, H: 116D

3038 חָרִיט *ḥārîṭ*, bag, purse, S: 2754, B: 355A, K: 333C, H: 116D

3039 חִרְייוֹנִים *ḥiryyônîm*, variant: dove's dung [?], see 2989, S: 2755†, B: 351A, K: 333C, H: 116D

3040 חָרִיף *ḥārîp*, Hariph, S: 2756, B: 358B, K: 333C, H: 116D

3041 חֲרִיפוֹת *ḥarîpôt*, variant: grains of sand, S*, B: 937D, K: 333C, H: 116D

3042 חֲרִיפִי *ḥarîpî*, variant: Hariphite, see 3020, S: 2741†, B: 358B, K: 333C, H: 116D

3043 [1]חָרִיץ *ḥārîṣ*[1], portion, slice, S: 2757, B: 358D, K: 333D, H: 116D

3044 [2]חָרִיץ *ḥārîṣ*[2], pick (iron tool), S: 2757, B: 358D, K: 333D, H: 116D

3045 חָרִישׁ *ḥārîš*, plowing, time of plowing, S: 2758, B: 361A, K: 333D, H: 116D

3046 חֲרִישִׁי *ḥarîšî*, scorching, S: 2759, B: 362A, K: 333D, H: 117A

3047 חָרַךְ *ḥārak*, [A] to roast, S: 2760, B: 355A, K: 333D, H: 117A

3048 חֲרַכִּים *ḥarakkîm*, lattice, S: 2762†, B: 355B, K: 334A, H: 117A

3049 [1]חָרַם *ḥāram*[1], [G] to completely destroy, devote to destruction, exterminate, annihilate [H] to be destroyed, be devoted to destruction, S: 2763, B: 355C, K: 334A, H: 117A

3050 [2]חָרַם *ḥāram*[2], [B] to be disfigured, mutilated, S: 2763, B: 356D, K: 334B, H: 117A

3051 [1]חֵרֶם *ḥērem*[1], devoted (to the LORD), set apart for destruction, S: 2764, B: 356A, K: 334C, H: 117B

3052 [2]חֵרֶם *ḥērem*[2], net, fishnet, trap, S: 2764, B: 357A, K: 334D, H: 117B

3053 חָרִם *ḥārim*, Harim, S: 2766, B: 356C, K: 334D, H: 117B

3054 חֳרֵם *ḥorēm*, Horem, S: 2765, B: 356C, K: 334D, H: 117B

3055 חָרְמָה *ḥormâ*, Hormah, S: 2767, B: 356C, K: 334D, H: 117B

3056 חֶרְמוֹן *ḥermôn*, Hermon, S: 2768, B: 356D, K: 335A, H: 117B

3057 חֶרְמוֹנִים *ḥermônîm*, variant: heights of Hermon, see 3056, S: 2769, B: 356D, K: 335A, H: 117B

3058 חֶרְמֵשׁ *ḥermēš*, sickle (for harvest of grain), S: 2770, B: 357A, K: 335A, H: 117B

3059 [1]חָרָן *ḥārān*[1], Haran, S: 2771, B: 357A, K: 335B, H: 117B

3060 [2]חָרָן *ḥārān*[2], Haran, S: 2771, B: 357B, K: 335B, H: 117B

3061 חֹרֹנִי *ḥōrōnî*, Horonite, S: 2772, B: 111C & 357B, K: 335B, H: 117B

3062 חַרְנֶפֶר *ḥarneper*, Harnepher, S: 2774, B: 357B, K: 335B, H: 117C

3063 [1]חֶרֶס *ḥeres*[1], itch, S: 2775, B: 360B, K: 335B, H: 117C

3064 [2]חֶרֶס *ḥeres*[2], sun, S: 2775, B: 357B, K: 335C, H: 117C

3065 [3]חֶרֶס *ḥeres*[3], Heres, S: 2776, B: 357C, K: 335C, H: 117C

3066 חַרְסָה *harесâ*, variant: sun, see 3064, S: 2775†, B: 357B, K: 335C, H: 117C

3067 חַרְסוּת *ḥarsût*, variant: potsherd, see 3068, S: 2777, B: 360B, K: 335C, H: 117C

3068 חַרְסִית *ḥarsît*, potsherd, S: 2777†, B: 360B, K: 335C, H: 117C

3069 [1]חָרַף *ḥārap*[1], [A] (to spend the time of) winter, S: 2778, B: 358B, K: 335C, H: 117C

3070 [2]חָרַף *ḥārap*[2], [A] to treat with contempt, insult, reproach, taunt; [D] to defy, ridicule, taunt, mock, insult, S: 2778, B: 357C, K: 335D, H: 117C

3071 [3]חָרַף *ḥārap*[3], variant: [D] to disillusion, confuse, S: 2778, B: 357C, K: 335D, H: 117C

3072 [4]חָרַף *ḥārap*[4], [C] to be promised to a man, engaged, S: 2778, B: 358B, K: 335C, H: 117C

3073 חָרֵף *ḥārēp*, Hareph, S: 2780, B: 358B, K: 336A, H: 117D

3074 חֹרֶף *ḥōrep*, winter; prime (of one's youth), S: 2779, B: 358A, K: 336A, H: 117D

3075 חֶרְפָּה *ḥerpâ*, disgrace, contempt, scorn, insult, S: 2781, B: 357D, K: 336A, H: 117D

3076 [1]חָרַץ *ḥāras*[1], [A] to pronounce, determine; [B, C] to be determined, be decreed, S: 2782, B: 358C, K: 336B, H: 117D

3077 [2]חָרַץ *ḥāras*[2], [A] to pay attention, act quickly, S: 2782, B: 358C, K: 336C, H: 117D

3078 חַרְצֹב *harṣōb*, struggle; chains, S: 2784†, B: 359A, K: 336C, H: 117D

3079 חַרְצָן *harṣān*, seeds (of grapes), S: 2785†, B: 359A, K: 336C, H: 118A

3080 חָרַק *ḥāraq*, [A] to gnash, grind (teeth), S: 2786, B: 359B, K: 336D, H: 118A

3081 [1]חָרַר *ḥārar*[1], [A] to burn; (heated metal) glow; [C] to be parched, burned, charred; [D] to kindle, cause to burn, glow, S: 2787, B: 359B, K: 336D, H: 118A

3082 [2]חָרַר *ḥārar*[2], variant: [C] to be hoarse, S: 2787†, B: 359B, K: 337A, H: 118A

3083 חֲרֵרִים *ḥarērîm*, parched place, S: 2788†, B: 359C, K: 337A, H: 118A

3084 חֶרֶשׂ *ḥereś*, clay pot, earthenware; potsherd, fragment of pottery, S: 2789, B: 360A, K: 337A, H: 118A

3085 חֲרֶשֶׂת *ḥareśet*, variant: Hareseth, see 7819, S: 7025†, B: 885B, K: 337B, H: 318B

3086 [1]חָרַשׁ *ḥāraš*[1], [A] to plow; engrave; plan, plot; [B] to be inscribed; [C] to be plowed; [G] to plot against, S: 2790 & 2794†, B: 360B, K: 337B, H: 118A

3087 [2]חָרֵשׁ *ḥārēš*[2], [A] to be silent, be quiet; to become deaf; [G] to be quiet, say nothing, be silent; [F] to make no moves, keep silent, S: 2790, B: 361A, K: 337C, H: 118B

3088 [1]חֶרֶשׁ *ḥereš*[1], variant: magic, sorcery, S: 2796†, B: 361D, K: 338A, H: 118B

3089 [2]חֶרֶשׁ *ḥereš*[2], secretly, silently, S: 2791, B: 361C, K: 338A, H: 118B

3090 [3]חֶרֶשׁ *ḥereš*[3], Heresh, S: 2792, B: 361D, K: 338A, H*

3091 [1]חֹרֶשׁ *ḥōreš*[1], wooded place, forest, thicket, S: 2793, B: 361C, K: 338A, H: 118B

3092 [2]חֹרֶשׁ *ḥōreš*[2], Horesh, S: 2793, B: 361C, K: 338C, H: 118C

3093 חָרָשׁ *ḥārāš*, skilled craftsman: blacksmith, carpenter, stonemason, etc., S: 2796, B: 360D, K: 338A, H: 118C

3094 חֵרֵשׁ *ḥērēš*, deaf (one), S: 2795, B: 361B, K: 338B, H: 118C

3095 חַרְשָׁא *ḥaršā'*, Harsha, S: 2797, B: 361D, K: 338C, H: 118C

3096 חֲרָשִׁים *ḥarāšîm*, variant: Harashim, see 1629, S: 2798, B: 161B d., K: 338A, H: 59C II f.

3097 חֲרֶשֶׁת *ḥarešet*, variant: Haresheth, see 7819, S: 7025†, B: 885B, K: 838D, H: 318B

3098 [1]חֲרֹשֶׁת *ḥarōšet*[1], cutting (stone), working (wood), S: 2799, B: 360D, K: 338C, H: 118C

3099 חֲרֹשֶׁת הַגּוֹיִם *ḥarōšet haggôyim*, Harosheth Haggoyim, S: 2800† + 1471†, B: 361D, K: 338C, H: 118C

3100 חָרַת *ḥārat*, [B] to be engraved, S: 2801, B: 362A, K: 338C, H: 118C

3101 חֶרֶת *ḥeret*, Hereth, S: 2802, B: 362A, K: 338C, H: 118C

3102 חֲשׂוּפָא *ḥaśûpā'*, Hasupha, S: 2817, B: 362D, K: 338D, H: 118C

3103 חֲשׂוּפַי *ḥaśûpay*, variant: see 3106, S: 2834†, B: 362C, K: 338D, H: 118C

3104 חָשַׂךְ *ḥāśak*, [A] to keep back, to withhold, halt, spare; [C] to be spared, be relieved, S: 2820, B: 362A, K: 338D, H: 118C

3105 חֲשִׂף *ḥāśip*, small flock, S: 2835, B: 362C, K: 339C, H: 118D

3106 [1]חָשַׂף *ḥāśap*[1], [A] to strip bare, lay bare; to scoop out, draw out; [B] to be bared, S: 2834, B: 362C, K: 339A, H: 118D

3107 [2]חָשַׂף *ḥāśap*[2], variant: [D] to bring to premature birth, S: 2834†, B: 362C, K: 339B, H: 118D

3108 חָשַׁב *ḥāšab*, [A] to plan, plot, purpose, consider; to credit, account, impute; [C] to be thought, considered, regarded; be reckoned, accounted; [D] to determine, plan, plot; to compute, account; [F] to consider oneself, S: 2803, B: 362B, K: 339C, H: 118D

3109 חֵשֶׁב *ḥēšeb*, waistband, S: 2805, B: 363D, K: 340C, H: 119B

3110 חֹשֵׁב *ḥōšēb*, skilled craftsman, designer, S: 2803†, B: 362D I 5., K: 340A 11. & 12., H: 119B

3111 חַשְׁבַּדָּנָה *ḥašbaddānâ*, Hashbaddanah, S: 2806, B: 364C, K: 340C, H: 119B

3112 חֲשֻׁבָה *ḥašubâ*, Hashubah, S: 2807, B: 363D, K: 340C, H: 119B

3113 [1]חֶשְׁבּוֹן *ḥešbôn*[1], scheme, plan, S: 2808, B: 363D, K: 340C, H: 119B

3114 [2]חֶשְׁבּוֹן *ḥešbôn*[2], Heshbon, S: 2809, B: 363D, K: 340C, H: 119B

3115 חִשָּׁבוֹן *ḥiššābôn*, machine (for hurling against ramparts); scheme, S: 2810, B: 364A, K: 340D, H: 119B

3116 חֲשַׁבְיָה *ḥašabyâ*, Hashabiah, S: 2811, B: 364A, K: 340D, H: 119B

3117 חֲשַׁבְיָהוּ *ḥašabyāhû*, Hashabiah, S: 2811, B: 364A, K: 341A, H: 119B

3118 חֲשַׁבְנָה *ḥašabnâ*, Hashabnah, S: 2812, B: 364B, K: 341A, H: 119B

3119 חֲשַׁבְנְיָה *ḥašabneyâ*, Hashabneiah, S: 2813, B: 364B, K: 341A, H: 119B

3120 חָשָׁה *ḥāšâ*, [A] to be silent, be hushed; [G] to keep silent; to do nothing, hesitate, S: 2814, B: 364C, K: 341A, H: 119C

3121 חַשּׁוּב *ḥaššûb*, Hasshub, S: 2815, B: 363D, K: 341B, H: 119C

3122 חָשׁוּק *ḥāšûq*, band, binding, S: 2838, B: 366A, K: 341B, H: 119C

3123 חֻשִׁים *ḥušîm*, Hushim, S: 2366, B: 302A, K: 284C, H: 119C

3124 חָשַׁךְ *ḥāšak*, [A] to grow dark, be dim, be black; [G] to darken, make dark, S: 2821, B: 364D, K: 341B, H: 119C

3125 חֹשֶׁךְ *ḥōšek*, darkness, dark; blackness, gloom, S: 2822, B: 365A, K: 341C, H: 119D

3126 חָשֹׁךְ *ḥāšōk*, obscure, dark, unknown, S: 2823, B: 365B, K: 342A, H: 119D

3127 חָשְׁכָה *ḥoškâ*, darkness, S: 2821†, B: 365B, K: 341B & 342A, H: 119D

3128 חֲשֵׁכָה *ḥašēkâ*, darkness, S: 2824† & 2825, B: 365B, K: 342A, H: 119D

3129 חָשַׁל *ḥāšal*, [C] to lag (behind), be worn out, S: 2826, B: 365B, K: 342A, H: 119D

3130 חָשֻׁם *ḥāšum*, Hashum, S: 2828, B: 365C, K: 342A, H: 119D

3131 חֻשִׁם *ḥušim*, Hushite, S: 2366, B: 302A, K: 342B, H: 119D

3132 חֶשְׁמוֹן *ḥešmôn*, Heshmon, S: 2829, B: 365C, K: 342B, H: 119D

3133 חַשְׁמַל *ḥašmal*, glowing metal, S: 2830, B: 365C, K: 342B, H: 119D

3134 חַשְׁמַן *ḥašman*, envoy, S: 2831, B: 365C, K: 342B, H: 120A

3135 חַשְׁמֹנָה *ḥašmōnâ*, Hashmonah, S: 2832, B: 365C, K: 342B, H: 120A

3136 חֹשֶׁן *ḥōšen*, breastpiece, S: 2833, B: 365D, K: 342C, H: 120A

3137 [1]חָשַׁק *ḥāšaq*[1], [A] to set one's affection, desire, love, be attached to, S: 2836, B: 365D, K: 342C, H: 120A

3138 [2]חָשַׁק *ḥāšaq*[2], [D] to make bands, make joints for binding; [E] to have bands, S: 2836, B: 366A, K: 342C, H: 120A

3139 חֵשֶׁק *ḥēšeq*, thing desired, thing longed for, S: 2837, B: 366A, K: 342D, H: 120A

3140 חִשֻּׁק *ḥiššuq*, spokes (of a wheel), S: 2839, B: 366B, K: 342D, H: 120A

3141 חִשֻּׁר *ḥiššur*, hub (of a wheel), S: 2840, B: 366B, K: 342D, H: 120A

3142 חַשְׁרָה *ḥašrâ*, variant: collection, mass, S: 2841, B: 366B, K: 342D, H: 120A

3143 חֲשַׁשׁ *ḥašaš*, chaff, dry grass, S: 2842, B: 366B, K: 343A, H: 120A

3144 חֻשָׁתִי *ḥušātî*, Hushathite, S: 2843, B: 302A, K: 343A, H: 120A

3145 [1]חַת *ḥat*[1], fear, dread, terror, S: 2844, B: 369C, K: 343A, H: 120A

3146 [2]חַת *ḥat*[2], terrified, broken, S: 2844, B: 369C, K: 343A, H: 120B

3147 חֵת *ḥēt*, Hittite, S: 2845, B: 366C, K: 343A, H: 120B

3148 חָתָא *ḥātā'*, variant: [C] to be destroyed, see 9393, S: 2398, B*, K: 343A, H: 120B

3149 חָתָה *ḥātâ*, [A] to get, snatch, take away, S: 2846, B: 367A, K: 343B, H: 120B

3150 חִתָּה *ḥittâ*, terror, S: 2847, B: 369D, K: 343B, H: 120B

3151 חִתּוּל *ḥittûl*, splint, bandage, S: 2848, B: 367C, K: 343B, H: 120B

3152 חַתְחַת *ḥatḥat*, horror, terror, danger, S: 2849, B: 369D, K: 343B, H: 120B

3153 חִתִּי *ḥittî*, Hittite, S: 2850, B: 366C, K: 343C, H: 120B

3154 חִתִּית *ḥittît*, terror, S: 2851, B: 369D, K: 343D, H: 120B

3155 חָתַךְ *ḥātak*, [C] to be decreed, S: 2852, B: 367B, K: 343D, H: 120B

3156 חָתַל *ḥātal*, [E, G] to be wrapped in strips of cloth, S: 2853, B: 367C, K: 343D, H: 120B

3157 חֲתֻלָּה *ḥ[a]tullâ*, band (of cloth) for wrapping, S: 2854, B: 367C, K: 344A, H: 120C

3158 חֶתְלוֹן *ḥetlôn*, Hethlon, S: 2855, B: 367C, K: 344A, H: 120C

3159 חָתַם *ḥātam*, [A] to seal (with a signet ring); to seal up; [B] to be sealed, be enclosed; [C] to be sealed; [D] to seal in; [G] to block, obstruct, S: 2856, B: 367C, K: 344A, H: 120C

3160 חֹתֶמֶת *ḥōtemet*, signet ring seal, S: 2858, B: 368B, K: 344B, H: 120C

3161 חָתַן *ḥātan*, [A, F] to intermarry; to become a son-in-law, S: 2859, B: 368D, K: 344B, H: 120C

3162 חֹתֵן *ḥōtēn*, father-in-law, S: 2859†, B: 368C, K: 344B, H: 120D

3163 חָתָן *ḥātān*, son-in-law; bridegroom, S: 2860, B: 368C, K: 344C, H: 120D

3164 חֲתֻנָּה *ḥ[a]tunnâ*, wedding, marriage, S: 2861, B: 368D, K: 345A, H: 120D

3165 חֹתֶנֶת *ḥōtenet*, mother-in-law, S: 2859†, B: 368C 2, K: 344B, H: 120D

3166 חָתַף *ḥātap*, [A] to snatch away, S: 2862, B: 368D, K: 345A, H: 120D

3167 חֶתֶף *ḥetep*, bandit, robber, S: 2863, B: 369A, K: 345A, H: 120D

3168 חָתַר *ḥātar*, [A] to dig, break into; row (in rough seas), S: 2864, B: 369A, K: 345A, H: 120D

3169 חָתַת *ḥātat*, [A] to be shattered, dismayed, terrified; [C] to be discouraged, terrified; [D] to frighten; break; [G] to shatter, terrify, S: 2865, B: 369A, K: 345B, H: 121A

3170 [1]חֲתַת *ḥ[a]tat[1]*, something dreadful, horrible, S: 2866, B: 369C, K: 345D, H: 121C

3171 [2]חֲתַת *ḥ[a]tat[2]*, Hathath, S: 2867, B: 369D, K: 345D, H: 121C

3172 ט *ṭ*, letter of the Hebrew alphabet, S*, B: 370A, K: 345B, H*

3173 טֵאטֵא *ṭē'ṭē'*, [D] to sweep away, S: 2894†, B: 370A, K: 346A, H: 121A

3174 טָבְאַל *ṭāb[e]'al*, Tabeel, S: 2870†, B: 370B, K: 346A, H: 121A

3175 טָבְאֵל *ṭāb[e]'ēl*, Tabeel, S: 2870, B: 370B, K: 346A, H: 121A

3176 טָבַב *ṭābab*, variant: [A] to speak, S: 2896†, B: 375A 1., K: 349A, H: 121A

3177 טִבָּה *ṭibbâ*, variant: rumor, S: 2896†, B: 375C 3., K: 346A, H: 121A

3178 טְבוּלִים *ṭ[e]bûlîm*, turban, S: 2871†, B: 371B, K: 346B, H: 121A

3179 טַבּוּר *ṭabbûr*, center of (the land), S: 2872, B: 371D, K: 346B, H: 121A

3180 טָבַח *ṭābaḥ*, [A] to slaughter, butcher; [B] to be slaughtered, S: 2873, B: 370B, K: 346B, H: 121B

3181 [1]טֶבַח *ṭebaḥ[1]*, slaughtering, S: 2874, B: 370D, K: 346C, H: 121B

3182 [2]טֶבַח *ṭebaḥ[2]*, Tebah, S: 2875, B: 370D, K: 346C, H: 121B

3183 [3]טֶבַח *ṭebaḥ[3]*, Tebah, S: 2874, B: 105C, K: 346C, H: 121B

3184 טַבָּח *ṭabbāḥ*, cook, butcher; guard, imperial guard; executioner, S: 2876, B: 371A, K: 346C, H: 121B

3185 טַבָּחָה *ṭabbāḥâ*, (female) cook (of meat), S: 2879, B: 371A, K: 346D, H: 121B

3186 טִבְחָה *ṭibḥâ*, slaughtered meat, butchered meat, S: 2878, B: 370D, K: 346D, H: 121B

3187 טִבְחַת *ṭibḥat*, Tebah, S: 2880, B: 371A, K: 346D, H: 121C

3188 טָבַל *ṭābal*, [A] to dip, plunge; bathe, soak; [C] to be dipped, S: 2881, B: 371A, K: 346D, H: 121C

3189 טְבַלְיָהוּ *ṭ[e]balyāhû*, Tabaliah, S: 2882, B: 371B, K: 347A, H: 121D

3190 טָבַע *ṭāba'*, [A] to sink down, to fall into; [E] to be drowned; [H] to be sunk, be settled into, S: 2883, B: 371C, K: 347A, H: 121D

3191 טַבָּעוֹת *ṭabbā'ôt*, Tabbaoth, S: 2884, B: 371D, K: 347B, H: 121D

3192 טַבַּעַת *ṭabba'at*, ring; signet ring, S: 2885, B: 371C, K: 347B, H: 121D

3193 טַבְרִמּוֹן *ṭabrimmōn*, Tabrimmon, S: 2886, B: 372A, K: 347C, H: 121D

3194 טֵבֵת *ṭēbēt*, Tebeth, S: 2887†, B: 372A, K: 347C, H: 121D

3195 טַבָּת *ṭabbāt*, Tabbath, S: 2888, B: 372A, K: 347C, H: 121D

3196 טָהוֹר *ṭāhôr*, clean, pure, flawless, free from impurity, S: 2889 & 2890†, B: 373A, K: 348B, H: 121D

3197 טָהֵר *ṭāhēr*, [A] to be (ceremonially) clean, purified; [D] to pronounce clean, cleanse, make ceremonially clean, to purify; [F] to cleanse oneself, purify oneself, S: 2891, B: 372A, K: 347C, H: 122A

3198 טֹהַר *ṭōhar*, purity; cleanness; clearness, brightness, S: 2892, B: 372D, K: 348A, H: 122B

3199 טְהָר *ṭ[e]hār*, splendor, purity, S: 2892†, B: 372D, K: 348B, H: 122B

3200 טָהֳרָה *ṭoh[o]râ*, cleansing, purification; pronouncement of (ceremonial) cleansing, S: 2893, B: 372D, K: 348C, H: 122B

3201 [1]טוֹב *ṭôb[1]*, [A] to be good, well, pleasing; [G] to do well, do good, prosper, S: 2896, B: 373A, K: 348C, H: 122B

3202 [2]טוֹב *ṭôb[2]*, good, pleasing, desirable; goodness, S: 2896†, B: 373C & 375A, K: 349A, H: 122C

3203 [3]טוֹב *ṭôb[3]*, sweet(-smelling), perfume, S: 2897, B: 373C, K: 349D, H: 123A

3204 [4]טוֹב *ṭôb[4]*, Tob, S: 2897, B: 376A, K: 350A, H: 123A

3205 [5]טוֹב *ṭôb[5]*, variant: see 3202, S: 2896†, B: 375A, K: 349D, H: 123A

3206 טוּב *ṭûb*, good, best; goodness, prosperity, S: 2898, B: 375C, K: 350A, H: 123A

3207 טוֹב אֲדוֹנִיָּה *ṭôb '[a]dôniyyâ*, Tob-Adonijah, S: 2899, B: 375B, K: 350B, H*

3208 טוֹבָה *ṭôbâ*, good, well-being, S: 2896†, B: 375C, K: 350B, H: 123A

3209 טוֹבִיָּה *ṭôbiyyâ*, Tobiah; Tobijah, S: 2900, B: 375D, K: 350C, H: 123B

3210 טוֹבִיָּהוּ *ṭôbiyyāhû*, Tobijah, S: 2900, B: 375D, K: 350D, H: 123B

3211 טָוָה *ṭāwâ*, [A] to spin (yarn), S: 2901, B: 376A, K: 350D, H: 123B

3212 טוּחַ *ṭûaḥ*, [A] to cover with whitewash; overlay with plaster; [C] to be plastered, be coated, S: 2902, B: 376A, K: 350D, H: 123B

3213 טוֹטָפֹת *ṭôṭāpōt*, symbol, sign (later, phylactery), S: 2903†, B: 377D, K: 351A, H: 123B

3214 טוּל *ṭûl*, [D] to hurl; [G] to thrown, hurl; [H] to be overpowered, be fallen, be hurled, S: 2904, B: 376C, K: 351A, H: 123B

3215 טוּר *ṭûr*, row, course, S: 2905, B: 377A, K: 351B, H: 123C

3216 טוּשׂ *ṭûś*, [A] to swoop down, S: 2907, B: 377B, K: 351B, H: 123C

3217 טָחָה *ṭāḥâ*, [D] to shoot (an arrow the distance of a bowshot), S: 2909, B: 377B, K: 351C, H: 123C

3218 טְחוֹן *ṭ[e]ḥôn*, hand-mill, grinding-mill, S: 2911, B: 377C, K: 351C, H: 123C

3219 טֻחוֹת *ṭuḥôt*, inner parts; heart, S: 2910†, B: 376B, K: 351C, H: 123C

3220 טָחַח *ṭāḥaḥ*, [A] to be smeared over, S: 2902†, B: 377C, K: 351C, H: 123C

3221 טָחַן *ṭāḥan*, [A] to grind to flour, crush to powder, S: 2912, B: 377C, K: 351C, H: 123C

3222 טַחֲנָה *ṭaḥ[a]nâ*, grinding-mill, S: 2913, B: 377D, K: 351D, H: 123D

3223 טֹחֲנָה *ṭōḥ[a]nâ*, grinder (= molar tooth), S: 2912†, B: 377C, K: 351D, H: 123D

3224 טְחֹרִים *ṭ[e]ḥōrîm*, tumor, hemorrhoids, S: 2914†, B: 377D, K: 351D, H: 123D

3225 טִיחַ *ṭîaḥ*, coating (of whitewash), S: 2915, B: 376B, K: 352A, H: 123D

3226 טִיט *ṭîṭ*, mud, dirt, mire, clay, S: 2916, B: 376C, K: 352A, H: 123D

3227 טִירָה *ṭîrâ*, camp (protected by stone walls); tower, battlement, S: 2918, B: 377A, K: 352B, H: 123D

3228 טַל *ṭal*, dew, night mist, S: 2919, B: 378B, K: 352B, H: 123D

3229 טָלָא *ṭālā'*, [B] to be spotted; be variegated; [E] to be patched, S: 2921, B: 378A, K: 352C, H: 123D

3230 טְלָאִים *ṭ[e]lā'îm*, Telaim, S: 2923, B: 378A, K: 352C, H: 124A

3231 טָלֶה *ṭāleh*, lamb, S: 2922† & 2924, B: 378B, K: 352D & 352D, H: 124A

3232 טַלְטֵלָה *ṭalṭēlâ*, hurling, throwing, S: 2925, B: 376D, K: 352D, H: 124A

3233 טָלַל *ṭālal*, [D] to cover with a roof, S: 2926, B: 378D, K: 353A, H: 124A

3234 [1]טֶלֶם *ṭelem[1]*, Telem, S: 2928, B: 378D 1., K: 353A, H: 124A

3235 [2]טֶלֶם *ṭelem[2]*, Telem, S: 2928, B: 378D, K: 353A, H: 124A

3236 טַלְמוֹן *ṭalmôn*, Talmon, S: 2929, B: 379A, K: 353A, H: 124A

3237 [1]טָמֵא *ṭāmē'[1]*, [A] to be unclean, defiled; [C] to be made unclean, become defiled, impure; [D] to make unclean, defile, desecrate; [E] to become defiled; [F] to make oneself unclean, defiled; to be defiled, S: 2930, B: 379A, K: 353A, H: 124A

[A] Qal [B] Qal passive [C] Niphal [D] Piel (poel, polel, pilel, pilal, pealal, pilpel) [E] Pual (poal, polal, poalal, pulal, pualal)

3238 [2]טָמֵא *ṭāmē'*[2], unclean, defiled, impure, S: 2931, B: 379D, K: 353D, H: 124B

3239 טָמְאָה *ṭom'â*, variant: uncleanness, see 3237, S: 2930†, B: 380A, K: 353B, H: 124C

3240 טֻמְאָה *ṭum'â*, uncleanness, impurity, filthiness, S: 2932, B: 380A, K: 354A, H: 124C

3241 טָמָה *ṭāmâ*, [C] to be considered stupid, S: 2933, B: 380B, K: 354B, H: 124C

3242 טָמַם *ṭāmam*, variant: [C] to be stopped up, S: 2933†, B: 380B, K: 354B, H: 124C

3243 טָמַן *ṭāman*, [A] to hide; bury; [B] to be hidden; [C] to hide oneself; [G] to keep hidden, S: 2934, B: 380B, K: 354B, H: 124C

3244 טֶנֶא *ṭene'*, basket, S: 2935, B: 380D, K: 354C, H: 124D

3245 טָנַף *ṭānap*, [D] to soil, make dirty, S: 2936, B: 380D, K: 354C, H: 124D

3246 טָעָה *ṭā'â*, [G] to lead astray, S: 2937, B: 380D, K: 354D, H: 124D

3247 טָעַם *ṭā'am*, [A] to taste; to see, discover by experience, S: 2938, B: 380D, K: 354D, H: 124D

3248 טַעַם *ṭa'am*, taste; discretion; discernment; decree, judgment, S: 2940, B: 381A, K: 355A, H: 124D

3249 טָעַן[1] *ṭā'an*[1], [E] to be pierced, S: 2944, B: 381B, K: 355B, H: 124D

3250 [2]טָעַן *ṭā'an*[2], [A] to load, S: 2943, B: 381B, K: 355B, H: 124D

3251 טַף[1] *ṭap*[1], (little) children, women and children, S: 2945, B: 381D, K: 355B, H: 125A

3252 [2]טַף *ṭap*[2], variant: drops, S: 2945, B: 381D, K: 355B, H: 125A

3253 טָפַח[1] *ṭāpaḥ*[1], [D] to spread out, S: 2946, B: 381B, K: 355C, H: 125A

3254 [2]טָפַח *ṭāpaḥ*[2], [D] to care for, S: 2946, B: 381B, K: 355D, H: 125A

3255 טֶפַח *ṭepaḥ*, handbreadth, span of the hand, S: 2947†, B: 381C, K: 355D, H: 125A

3256 טֹפַח *ṭōpaḥ*, handbreadth, span of the hand, S: 2948, B: 381C, K: 355D, H: 125A

3257 טִפְחָה[1] *ṭapḥâ*[1], handbreadth, S: 2947†, B: 381C 1, K: 356A, H: 125A

3258 [2]טִפְחָה *ṭapḥâ*[2], eaves, S: 2947†, B: 381C, K: 356A, H: 125A

3259 טִפֻּחִים *ṭippuḥîm*, caring for, S: 2949†, B: 381C, K: 356A, H: 125A

3260 טָפַל *ṭāpal*, [A] to smear, cover, S: 2950, B: 381C, K: 356A, H: 125B

3261 טִפְסָר *ṭipsār*, official, clerk, S: 2951, B: 381D, K: 356A, H: 125B

3262 טָפַף *ṭāpap*, [A] to take little steps, trip along, S: 2952, B: 381D, K: 356A, H: 125B

3263 טָפַשׁ *ṭāpaš*, [A] to be unfeeling, insensible, S: 2954, B: 382A, K: 356B, H: 125B

3264 טָפַת *ṭāpat*, Taphath, S: 2955, B: 382A, K: 356B, H: 125B

3265 טָרַד *ṭārad*, [A] to constantly drip, S: 2956, B: 382A, K: 356B, H: 125B

3266 טְרוֹם *ṭ^{e}rôm*, variant: before, S: 2958, B: 382C, K: 356C, H: 125C

3267 טָרַח *ṭāraḥ*, [G] to load down, burden with, S: 2959, B: 382B, K: 356C, H: 125C

3268 טֹרַח *ṭōraḥ*, burden, problem, load, S: 2960, B: 382B, K: 356C, H: 125C

3269 טָרִי *ṭārî*, fresh (bone); open, moist (sore), S: 2961, B: 382B, K: 356C, H: 125C

3270 טֶרֶם *ṭerem*, before; not, not yet, S: 2962, B: 382C, K: 356D, H: 125C

3271 טָרַף *ṭārap*, [A] to tear, mangle; [B, C, E] to be torn (to pieces); [G] to provide (to enjoy), S: 2963, B: 382D, K: 356D, H: 125C

3272 טֶרֶף *ṭerep*, prey (food for wild animals), S: 2964, B: 383A, K: 357C, H: 125D

3273 טָרָף *ṭārāp*, fresh-picked (leaf or vegetation), S: 2965, B: 383A, K: 357C, H: 125D

3274 טְרֵפָה *ṭ^{e}rēpâ*, animal torn by wild beasts, S: 2966, B: 383C, K: 356D, H: 125D

3275 י *y*, letter of the Hebrew alphabet, S*, B: 383B, K: 357B, H*

3276 ִי־ *-î*, I, me, my, S*, B*, K*, H*

3277 יָאַב *yā'ab*, [A] to long for, S: 2968, B: 383B, K: 357B, H: 125B

3278 יָאָה *yā'â*, [A] to be fitting, be proper, S: 2969, B: 383B, K: 357D, H: 125B

3279 יַאֲזַנְיָה *ya'^{a}zanyâ*, Jaazaniah, S: 2970, B: 24D, K: 357D, H: 125D

3280 יַאֲזַנְיָהוּ *ya'^{a}zanyāhû*, Jaazaniah, S: 2970, B: 24D, K: 357D, H: 125D

3281 יָאִיר *yā'îr*, Jair, S: 2971, B: 22C, K: 358A, H: 126A

3282 יָאַל[1] *yā'al*[1], [C] to become foolish, act foolish, S: 2973, B: 383B, K: 358A, H: 126A

3283 [2]יָאַל *yā'al*[2], [G] to begin; to determine; be intent upon; to agree to; to be content, be pleased; to be bold, S: 2974, B: 383D, K: 358A & 49B, H: 126A

3284 יְאֹר *y^{e}'ōr*, river, stream, the Nile river, S: 2975, B: 384B, K: 358B, H: 126A

3285 יָאִרִי *yā'irî*, Jairite, S: 2972, B: 22C, K: 358A, H: 126A

3286 יָאַשׁ *yā'aš*, [C] to be despairing of, be without hope, give up; [D] to let despair, S: 2976, B: 384C, K: 358C, H: 126B

3287 יֹאשִׁיָּה *yō'šiyyâ*, Josiah, S: 2977, B: 78C, K: 358D, H: 126B

3288 יֹאשִׁיָּהוּ *yō'šiyyāhû*, Josiah, S: 2977, B: 78C, K: 358D, H: 126B

3289 יְאתוֹן *yi'tôn*, variant: see 415, S: 2978†, B: 87C, K: 358D, H: 126B

3290 יְאָתְרַי *y^{e}'āt^{e}ray*, Jeatherai, S: 2979, B: 384C, K: 358D, H: 126B

3291 יָבַב *yābab*, [D] to cry out, lament, S: 2980, B: 384D, K: 358D, H: 126B

3292 יְבוּל *y^{e}bûl*, crops, produce, harvest, S: 2981, B: 385B, K: 359A, H: 126B

3293 יְבוּס *y^{e}bûs*, Jebus, S: 2982, B: 101A, K: 359A, H: 126B

3294 יְבוּסִי *y^{e}bûsî*, Jebusite, S: 2983, B: 101A, K: 359A, H: 126B

3295 יִבְחָר *yibḥār*, Ibhar, S: 2984†, B: 104D, K: 359B, H: 126B

3296 יָבִין *yābîn*, Jabin, S: 2985, B: 108A, K: 359B, H: 126B

3297 יָבַל *yābal*, [G] to bring, take (a gift); [H] to be brought, be led, be carried off, S: 2986, B: 384D, K: 359B, H: 126C

3298 יָבָל[1] *yābāl*[1], stream, watercourse, S: 2988, B: 385A, K: 359C, H: 126C

3299 [2]יָבָל *yābāl*[2], Jabal, S: 2989, B: 385A, K: 359C, H: 126C

3300 יִבְלְעָם *yibl^{e}'ām*, Ibleam, S: 2991, B: 385D, K: 359C, H: 126C

3301 יַבֶּלֶת *yabbelet*, wart, S: 2990†, B: 385C, K: 359D, H: 126C

3302 יָבַם *yābam*, [D] to fulfill the procreational duty of the brother-in-law, S: 2992, B: 386A, K: 359D, H: 126C

3303 יָבָם *yābām*, husband's brother, S: 2993, B: 386A, K: 359D, H: 126C

3304 יְבָמָה *y^{e}bāmâ*, brother's widow; sister-in-law, husband's brother's widow, S: 2994†, B: 386A, K: 360A, H: 126C

3305 יַבְנְאֵל *yabn^{e}'ēl*, Jabneel, S: 2995, B: 125C, K: 360A, H: 126D

3306 יַבְנֵה *yabnēh*, Jabneh, S: 2996†, B: 125C, K: 360A, H: 126D

3307 יִבְנְיָה *yibn^{e}yâ*, Ibneiah, S: 2997, B: 125C, K: 360A, H: 126D

3308 יִבְנִיָּה *yibniyyâ*, Ibnijah, S: 2998, B: 125C, K: 360A, H: 126D

3309 יַבֹּק *yabbōq*, Jabbok, S: 2999, B: 132D, K: 360A, H: 126D

3310 יְבֶרֶכְיָהוּ *y^{e}berekyāhû*, Jeberekiah, S: 3000, B: 140A, K: 360B, H: 126D

3311 יִבְשָׂם *yibśām*, Ibsam, S: 3005, B: 142A, K: 360B, H: 126D

3312 יָבֵשׁ[1] *yābēš*[1], [A] to dry up, be dry, be withered, be shriveled up; [D] to make wither, dry up; [G] to make wither, dry up, S: 3001, B: 386B, K: 360B, H: 126D

3313 [2]יָבֵשׁ *yābēš*[2], dry, withered, S: 3002, B: 386D, K: 360C, H: 127A

3314 [3]יָבֵשׁ *yābēš*[3], Jabesh, S: 3003, B: 386D 2., K: 360D, H: 126C 2. & 127A

3315 [4]יָבֵשׁ *yābēš*[4], Jabesh, S: 3003, B: 386D 1., K: 360D, H: 126C 1. & 127A

3316 יָבֵשׁ גִּלְעָד *yābēš gil'ād*, Jabesh Gilead, S: 3003†, B: 386D 1., K: 360D, H: 127A

3317 יַבָּשָׁה *yabbāšâ*, dry ground, dry land, S: 3004, B: 387A, K: 360D, H: 127A

3318 יַבֶּשֶׁת *yabbešet*, dry ground, dry land, S: 3006, B: 387A, K: 360D, H: 127A

3319 יִגְאָל *yig'āl*, Igal, S: 3008, B: 145D, K: 360D, H: 127A

3320 יָגַב *yāgab*, [A] to work a field, S: 3009, B: 387A, K: 361A, H: 127A

3321 יָגֵב *yāgēb*, field, S: 3010, B: 387A, K: 361A, H: 127A

3322 יָגְבְּהָה *yogb^{e}hâ*, Jogbehah, S: 3011, B: 147B, K: 361A, H: 127A

3323 יִגְדַּלְיָהוּ *yigdalyāhû*, Igdaliah, S: 3012, B: 153D, K: 361A, H: 127A

3324 יָגָה[1] *yāgâ*[1], [C] to be grieved; [D] to bring grief; [G] to torment, bring grief, S: 3013, B: 387A, K: 361A, H: 127B

3325 יָגָה[2] *yāgâ*[2], [G] to remove, S: 3014, B: 387C, K: 224C, H: 127B

3326 יָגוֹן *yāgôn*, sorrow, anguish, grief, S: 3015, B: 387B, K: 361B, H: 127B

3327 יָגוּר *yāgûr*, Jagur, S: 3017, B: 158C, K: 361B, H: 127B

[F] Hitpael (hitpoel, hitpoal, hitpolel, hitpolal, hitpalel, hitpalal, hitpalpel, hitpalpal, hotpael, hotpaal) [G] Hiphil (hiphtil) [H] Hophal [I] Hishtaphel

3328 יָגוֹר *yāgôr*, fearing, filled with fear, S: 3016, B: 388D, K: 361B, H: 127B

3329 יָגִיעַ *yāgîa'*, weary, exhausted, S: 3019, B: 388C, K: 361C, H: 127B

3330 יְגִיעַ *yegîa'*, labor, heavy work; produce, gain, S: 3018, B: 388C, K: 361C, H: 127B

3331 יְגִעָה *yegî'â*, weariness, S: 3024†, B: 388B, K: 362A, H: 127B

3332 יָגְלִי *yoglî*, Jogli, S: 3020, B: 163D, K: 361C, H: 127B

3333 יָגַע *yāga'*, [A] to labor, toil, be weary; [D] to make weary; [G] to make weary, S: 3021, B: 388A, K: 361C, H: 127B

3334 יָגָע *yāgā'*, what is toiled for, the produce of labor, S: 3022, B: 388B, K: 361D, H: 127C

3335 יָגֵעַ *yāgēa'*, worn out, weary, wearisome, S: 3023, B: 388B, K: 362A, H: 127C

3336 יָגֹר *yāgōr*, [A] to fear, dread, S: 3025, B: 388C, K: 362A, H: 127C

3337 יְגַר שָׂהֲדוּתָא *yegar śāhadûtā'*, Jegar Sahadutha, S: 3026, B: 1094D & 962A, K: 1080C, H: 127C

3338 יָד *yād*, hand, arm; direction; (figurative of) power, control, S: 3027, B: 388D, K: 362A, H: 127C

3339 יִדְאֲלָה *yid'alâ*, Idalah, S: 3030, B: 391D, K: 363C, H: 128B

3340 יִדְבָּשׁ *yidbāš*, Idbash, S: 3031, B: 185C, K: 363C, H: 128B

3341 יָדַד *yādad*, [A] to cast (lots for decision making), S: 3032, B: 391D, K: 363C, H: 128B

3342 יְדִדוּת *yedidût*, loved one, beloved, S: 3033, B: 392A, K: 363D, H: 128B

3343 1יָדָה *yādâ[1]*, [A] to shoot (a bow); [D] to throw (down), S: 3034, B: 392A, K: 363D, H: 128B

3344 2יָדָה *yādâ[2]*, [G] to express praise, give thanks, extol, make a public confession, make an admission, S: 3034, B: 392A, K: 363D, H: 128C

3345 יַדּוֹ *yaddaw*, variant: Jaddaw, see 3350, S: 3035†, B: 392A 2, K: 364C, H: 128C

3346 יִדּוֹ *yiddô*, Iddo, S: 3035, B: 392A, K: 364C, H: 128C

3347 יָדוֹן *yādôn*, Jadon, S: 3036, B: 193D, K: 364C, H: 128C

3348 יַדּוּעַ *yaddûa'*, Jaddua, S: 3037, B: 396A, K: 364C, H: 128C

3349 יְדוּתוּן *yedûtûn*, Jeduthun, S: 3038, B: 393A, K: 364C, H: 128C

3350 יַדַּי *yadday*, Jaddai, S: 3035†, B: 392A, K: 364C, H: 128C

3351 יָדִיד *yādîd*, lovely, beloved, S: 3039, B: 391D, K: 364C, H: 128C

3352 יְדִידָה *yedîdâ*, Jedidah, S: 3040, B: 392A, K: 364D, H: 128D

3353 יְדִידֹת *yedîdôt*, love (song), S: 038†, B: 391D 3, K: 364D, H: 128D

3354 יְדִידְיָהּ *yedîdeyāh*, Jedidiah, S: 3041†, B: 392A, K: 364D, H: 128D

3355 יְדָיָה *yedāyâ*, Jedaiah, S: 3042, B: 393A, K: 364D, H: 128D

3356 יְדִיעֲאֵל *yedî'a'ēl*, Jediael, S: 3043, B: 396A, K: 364D, H: 128D

3357 יְדִיתוּן *yedîtûn*, Jeduthun, S: 3038, B: 393A, K: 364D, H: 128D

3358 יִדְלָף *yidlāp*, Jidlaph, S: 3044, B: 393B, K: 364D, H: 128D

3359 יָדַע *yāda'*, [A] to know, recognize, understand; to have sexual relations; [B] to be respected; [C] to be known, make oneself known; [D] to cause to know; [E] to be well known; [G] to show, teach, make known; [H] to be made aware; [F] to make oneself known, S: 3045, B: 393B, K: 364D, H: 128D

3360 יָדָע *yādā'*, Jada, S: 3047, B: 395B, K: 367A, H: 129D

3361 יְדַעְיָה *yeda'yâ*, Jedaiah, S: 3048, B: 396A, K: 367A, H: 129D

3362 יִדְּעֹנִי *yidde'ōnî*, spiritist, soothsayer, S: 3049, B: 396B, K: 367A, H: 129D

3363 יָהּ *yāh*, LORD (Yahweh), S: 3050, B: 219C, K: 367A, H: 129D

3364 יָהַב *yāhab*, variant: [A] to give; see 2035, S: 3051, B: 396C, K: 367B & 223B, H: 407B

3365 יְהָב *yehāb*, care, burden, S: 3053, B: 396D, K: 367B, H: 129D

3366 יָהַד *yāhad*, [F] to become a Jew, S: 3054, B: 397C, K: 367B, H: 129D

3367 יָהְדַּי *yāhday*, Jahdai, S: 3056, B: 213A, K: 367B, H: 130A

3368 יְהֻדִיָּה *yehudiyyâ*, variant: Jewish, Judean, S: 3057, B: 397C, K: 368A, H: 130A

3369 יֵהוּא *yēhû'*, Jehu, S: 3058, B: 219C, K: 367B, H: 130A

3370 יְהוֹאָחָז *yehô'āḥāz*, Jehoahaz, S: 3059, B: 219D, K: 367C, H: 130A

3371 יְהוֹאָשׁ *yehô'āš*, Joash; Jehoash, S: 3060, B: 219D, K: 367C, H: 130A

3372 יְהוּד *yehûd*, Jehud, S: 3055†, B: 397A, K: 367C, H: 130A

3373 יְהוּדָה *yehûdâ*, Judah, Jew; Yaudi, S: 3063, B: 397A, K: 367C, H: 130A

3374 1יְהוּדִי *yehûdî[1]*, (men) of Judah, Judean, Jew, Jewish, S: 3064, B: 397C, K: 368A, H: 130A

3375 2יְהוּדִי *yehûdî[2]*, Jehudi, S: 3065, B: 397C, K: 368A, H: 130A

3376 1יְהוּדִית *yehûdît[1]*, in Hebrew (language), in the language of Judah, S: 3066, B: 397C, K: 368A, H*

3377 2יְהוּדִית *yehûdît[2]*, Judith, S: 3067, B: 397C, K: 368A, H: 130A

3378 יהוה *yhwh*, יֱהוִה *yehwih*, LORD (Yahweh), S: 3068 & 3069, B: 217D, K: 368B & 369A, H: 130A

3379 יְהוֹזָבָד *yehôzābād*, Jehozabad, S: 3075, B: 220A, K: 369D, H: 130A

3380 יְהוֹחָנָן *yehôḥānān*, Jehohanan, S: 3076, B: 220B, K: 369D, H: 130A

3381 יְהוֹיָדָע *yehôyādā'*, Jehoiada, S: 3077, B: 220B, K: 369D, H: 130A

3382 יְהוֹיָכִין *yehôyākîn*, Jehoiachin, S: 3078, B: 220C, K: 369D, H: 130A

3383 יְהוֹיָקִים *yehôyāqîm*, Jehoiakim, S: 3079, B: 220C, K: 370A, H: 130B

3384 יְהוֹיָרִיב *yehôyārîb*, Jehoiarib, S: 3080, B: 220D, K: 370A, H: 130B

3385 יְהוּכַל *yehûkal*, Jehucal, S: 3081, B: 220D, K: 370A, H: 130B

3386 יְהוֹנָדָב *yehônādāb*, Jonadab; Jehonadab, S: 3082, B: 220D, K: 370A, H: 130B

3387 יְהוֹנָתָן *yehônātān*, Jonathan; Jehonathan, S: 3083, B: 220D, K: 370B, H: 130B

3388 יְהוֹסֵף *yehôsēp*, Joseph, S: 3084, B: 415C, K: 370B, H: 130B

3389 יְהוֹעַדָּה *yehô'addâ*, Jehoaddah, S: 3085, B: 221A, K: 370B, H: 130B

3390 יְהוֹעַדִּין *yehô'addîn*, Jehoaddin, S: 3086, B: 221A, K: 370B, H: 130B

3391 יְהוֹעַדָּן *yehô'addān*, Jehoaddin, S: 3086, B: 221A, K: 370B, H: 130B

3392 יְהוֹצָדָק *yehôṣādāq*, Jehozadak, S: 3087, B: 221B, K: 370C, H: 130B

3393 יְהוֹרָם *yehôrām*, Joram; Jehoram, S: 3088, B: 221B, K: 370C, H: 130B

3394 יְהוֹשֶׁבַע *yehôšeba'*, Jehosheba, S: 3089, B: 221B, K: 370C, H: 130B

3395 יְהוֹשַׁבְעַת *yehôšab'at*, Jehosheba, S: 3090, B: 221B, K: 370C, H: 130B

3396 יְהוֹשָׁמָע *yehôšāmā'*, variant: Jehoshama, S*, B: 221D, K: 228D, H: 78A

3397 יְהוֹשֻׁעַ *yehôšua'*, Joshua, S: 3091, B: 221C, K: 370C, H: 130B

3398 1יְהוֹשָׁפָט *yehôšāpāṭ[1]*, Jehoshaphat, S: 3092, B: 221D 1-6., K: 370D, H: 130B

3399 2יְהוֹשָׁפָט *yehôšāpāṭ[2]*, Jehoshaphat, S: 3092, B: 221D 7., K: 370D, H: 130B

3400 יָהִיר *yāhîr*, arrogant, haughty, S: 3093, B: 397D, K: 370D, H: 130B

3401 יְהַלֶּלְאֵל *yehallel'ēl*, Jehallelel, S: 3094, B: 239C, K: 371A, H: 130B

3402 יַהֲלֹם *yāhalōm*, emerald (precious stone), S: 3095, B: 240D, K: 371A, H: 130C

3403 יַהַץ *yahaṣ*, Jahaz, S: 3096, B: 397D, K: 371A, H: 130C

3404 יַהְצָה *yahṣâ*, Jahzah, S: 3096, B: 397D, K: 371A, H: 130C

3405 יוֹאָב *yô'āb*, Joab, S: 3097, B: 222A, K: 371A, H: 130C

3406 יוֹאָח *yô'āḥ*, Joah, S: 3098, B: 222A, K: 371A, H: 130C

3407 יוֹאָחָז *yô'āḥāz*, Jehoahaz; Joahaz, S: 3099, B: 219D, K: 371B, H: 130C

3408 יוֹאֵל *yô'ēl*, Joel, S: 3100, B: 222A, K: 371B, H: 130C

3409 יוֹאָשׁ *yô'āš*, Joash; Jehoash, S: 3101, B: 219D, K: 371B, H: 130C

3410 יוֹב *yôb*, variant: Job, S: 3102, B: 398A, K: 371B, H: 130C

3411 1יוֹבָב *yôbāb[1]*, Jobab, S: 3103, B: 384D, K: 371B, H: 130C

3412 2יוֹבָב *yôbāb[2]*, Jobab, S: 3103, B: 384D, K: 371C, H: 130C

3413 יוֹבֵל *yôbēl*, ram's horn; (blowing of ram's horn) jubilee, (Year of) Jubilee, S: 3104, B: 385C, K: 371C, H: 130C

3414 1יוּבַל *yûbal[1]*, stream, watercourse, S: 3105, B: 385B, K: 371D, H: 130C

3415 2יוּבָל *yûbāl[2]*, Jubal, S: 3106, B: 385B, K: 371D, H: 130C

3416 יוֹזָבָד *yôzābād*, Jozabad, S: 3107, B: 220A, K: 371D, H: 130C

3417 יוֹזָכָר *yôzākār*, variant: Jozakar, S: 3108, B: 222B, K: 371D, H: 130C

3418 יוֹחָא *yôḥā'*, Joha, S: 3109, B: 398A, K: 371D, H: 130D

3419 יוֹחָנָן *yôḥānān*, Johanan, S: 3110, B: 220B, K: 371D, H: 130D

3420 יוּטָּה *yûṭṭâ*, Juttah, S: 3194, B: 641A, K: 372A, H: 130D

3421 יוֹיָדָע *yôyādā'*, Joiada, S: 3111, B: 220B, K: 372A, H: 130D

3422 יוֹיָכִין *yôyākîn*, Jehoiachin, S: 3112, B: 220C, K: 372A, H: 130D

3423 יוֹיָקִים *yôyāqîm*, Joiakim, S: 3113, B: 220C, K: 372A, H: 130D

3424 יוֹיָרִיב *yôyārîb*, Joiarib, S: 3114, B: 220D, K: 372A, H: 130D

3425 יוֹכֶבֶד *yôkebed*, Jochebed, S: 3115, B: 222C, K: 372A, H: 130D

3426 יוּכַל *yûkal*, Jehucal, S: 3116, B: 220D, K: 372A, H: 130D

3427 יוֹם[1] *yôm*[1], day, today, indefinite period of time, S: 3117, B: 398A, K: 372A, H: 130D

3428 יוֹם[2] *yôm*[2], variant: storm, wind; breath, S: 3117, B: 398A, K: 372A, H: 131C

3429 יוֹמָם *yômām*, day; in the daytime, by day, S: 3119, B: 401B, K: 374A, H: 131C

3430 יָוָן *yāwān*, Javan; Greeks; Greece, S: 3120, B: 402A, K: 374A, H: 131C

3431 יָוֵן *yāwēn*, mire, mud, sediment, S: 3121, B: 401C, K: 374B, H: 131D

3432 יוֹנָדָב *yônādāb*, Jonadab, S: 3122, B: 220D, K: 374B, H: 131D

3433 יוֹנָה[1] *yônâ*[1], dove; pigeon, S: 3123, B: 401D, K: 374B, H: 131D

3434 יוֹנָה[2] *yônâ*[2], Jonah, S: 3124, B: 402A, K: 374C, H: 131D

3435 יוֹנָה[3] *yônâ*[3], variant: see 3561, S: 3238†, B: 402A & 413A, K: 385C, H: 131D

3436 יְוָנִי *yᵉwānî*, Javanite = Greek, S: 3125, B: 402B, K: 374C, H: 131D

3437 יוֹנֵק *yônēq*, infant, one nursing; tender shoot, S: 3126, B: 413C, K: 374C, H: 131D

3438 יוֹנֶקֶת *yôneqet*, new shoot, young shoot (of a plant), S: 3127, B: 413C, K: 374C, H: 131D

3439 יוֹנַת אֵלֶם רְחֹקִים *yônat 'ēlem rᵉḥōqîm*, variant: Dove of the Distant Oaks, S: 3128, B: 401D, K: 374B & 55B & 885A, H: 131D

3440 יוֹנָתָן *yônātān*, Jonathan, S: 3129, B: 220D, K: 374D, H: 131D

3441 יוֹסֵף *yôsēp*, Joseph, S: 3130, B: 415C, K: 374D, H: 131D

3442 יוֹסִפְיָה *yôsipyâ*, Josiphiah, S: 3131, B: 415D, K: 375A, H: 132A

3443 יוֹעֵאלָה *yô'ē'lâ*, Joelah, S: 3132, B: 418D, K: 375A, H: 132A

3444 יוֹעֵד *yô'ēd*, Joed, S: 3133, B: 222C, K: 375A, H: 132A

3445 יוֹעֶזֶר *yô'ezer*, Joezer, S: 3134, B: 222C, K: 375A, H: 132A

3446 יוֹעֵץ *yô'ēṣ*, counselor, adviser, S: 3289†, B: 419C, K: 390A, H: 132A

3447 יוֹעָשׁ *yô'āš*, Joash, S: 3135, B: 222C, K: 375A, H: 132A

3448 יוֹצֵאת *yôṣē't*, going into captivity, departure, S: 3318†, B: 422B, K: 375B, H: 132A

3449 יוֹצָדָק *yôṣādāq*, Jozadak, S: 3136, B: 221B, K: 375B, H: 132A

3450 יוֹצֵר *yôṣēr*, potter, S: 3335†, B: 427C, K: 375B, H: 132A

3451 יוֹקִים *yôqîm*, Jokim, S: 3079† & 3137, B: 220C, K: 375B, H: 132A

3452 יוֹרֶה[1] *yôreh*[1], archer, S: 3384†, B: 434D, K: 402C, H: 132A

3453 יוֹרֶה[2] *yôreh*[2], autumn (i.e., the time of the early rains), S: 3138, B: 435C, K: 375B, H: 132B

3454 יוֹרָה *yôrâ*, Jorah, S: 3088† & 3139, B: 435C, K: 375C, H: 132B

3455 יוֹרַי *yôray*, Jorai, S: 3140, B: 436C, K: 375C, H: 132B

3456 יוֹרָם *yôrām*, Joram; Jehoram, S: 3141, B: 221B, K: 375C, H: 132B

3457 יוּשַׁב חֶסֶד *yûšab ḥesed*, Jushab-Hesed, S: 3142, B: 1000B, K: 375C, H: 132B

3458 יוֹשִׁבְיָה *yôšibyâ*, Joshibiah, S: 3143, B: 444A, K: 375C, H: 132B

3459 יוֹשָׁה *yôšâ*, Joshah, S: 3144, B: 444D, K: 375C, H: 132B

3460 יוֹשַׁוְיָה *yôšawyâ*, Joshaviah, S: 3145, B: 444D, K: 375C, H: 132B

3461 יוֹשָׁפָט *yôšāpāṭ*, Joshaphat, S: 3146, B: 221D, K: 375D, H: 132B

3462 יוֹתָם *yôtām*, Jotham, S: 3147, B: 222D, K: 375D, H: 132B

3463 יוֹתֵר *yôtēr*, the rest; gain, advantage, profit; more than, S: 3148, B: 452C, K: 375D, H: 132B

3464 יְזוּאֵל *yᵉzû'ēl*, variant: Jezuel, see 3465, S: 3149†, B: 402B, K: 376A, H: 132C

3465 יְזִיאֵל *yᵉzî'ēl*, Jeziel, S: 3149†, B: 402B, K: 376A, H: 132C

3466 יִזִּיָּה *yizziyyâ*, Izziah, S: 3150, B: 633C, K: 376A, H: 132C

3467 יָזִיז *yāzîz*, Jaziz, S: 3151, B: 265C, K: 376A, H: 132C

3468 יִזְלִיאָה *yizlî'â*, Izliah, S: 3152, B: 272C, K: 376A, H: 132C

3469 יָזַן *yāzan*, [E] to be lusty, be in the rut, S: 2109†, B: 402C, K: 376A, H: 132C

3470 יְזַנְיָה *yᵉzanyâ*, Jezaniah, S: 3153, B: 24D, K: 376A, H: 132C

3471 יְזַנְיָהוּ *yᵉzanyāhû*, Jaazaniah, S: 3153, B: 24D, K: 376A, H: 132C

3472 יֶזַע *yeza'*, perspiration, sweat, S: 3154, B: 402C, K: 376B, H: 132C

3473 יִזְרָח *yizrāḥ*, Izrahite, S: 3155, B: 280D, K: 376B, H: 132C

3474 יִזְרַחְיָה *yizraḥyâ*, Izrahiah; Jezrahiah, S: 3156, B: 280D, K*, H: 132C

3475 יִזְרְעֶאל[1] *yizrᵉ'e'l*[1], Jezreel, S: 3157, B: 283B 2., K: 376B, H: 132C

3476 יִזְרְעֶאל[2] *yizrᵉ'e'l*[2], Jezreel, S: 3157, B: 283B, K: 376B, H: 132C

3477 יִזְרְעֵאלִי *yizrᵉ'ē'lî*, Jezreelite, of Jezreel, S: 3158 & 3159†, B: 283C, K: 376C, H: 132C

3478 יְחֻבָּה *yᵉḥubbâ*, variant: Jehubbah, see 2465, S: 3160, B: 285D, K: 376C, H: 132C

3479 יָחַד *yāḥad*, [A] to join, be united; [D] to unite, S: 3161, B: 402C, K: 376C, H: 132C

3480 יַחַד *yaḥad*, together, in unity, along with, S: 3162, B: 403A, K: 376C, H: 132D

3481 יַחְדָּו *yaḥdāw*, together; altogether; at the same time, S: 3162†, B: 403B, K: 377A, H: 132D

3482 יַחְדּוֹ *yaḥdô*, Jahdo, S: 3163, B: 403C, K: 377A, H: 132D

3483 יַחְדַּי *yaḥdōy*, variant: see 3482, S*, B: 403C, K: 377A, H: 132D

3484 יַחְדִּיאֵל *yaḥdî'ēl*, Jahdiel, S: 3164, B: 292D, K: 377A, H: 132D

3485 יֶחְדְּיָהוּ *yeḥdᵉyāhû*, Jehdeiah, S: 3165, B: 292D, K: 377A, H: 132D

3486 יְחוּאֵל *yᵉḥû'ēl*, variant: Jehuel, see, S: 3171, B: 313C, K: 377B, H: 133A

3487 יַחֲזִיאֵל *yaḥᵃzî'ēl*, Jahaziel, S: 3166, B: 303C, K: 377B, H: 133A

3488 יַחְזְיָה *yaḥzᵉyâ*, Jahzeiah, S: 3167, B: 303C, K: 377B, H: 133A

3489 יְחֶזְקֵאל *yᵉḥezqē'l*, Ezekiel; Jehezkel, S: 3168, B: 306B, K: 377B, H: 133A

3490 יְחִזְקִיָּה *yᵉḥizqiyyâ*, Hezekiah, S: 3169, B: 306A, K: 377B, H: 133A

3491 יְחִזְקִיָּהוּ *yᵉḥizqiyyāhû*, Hezekiah; Jehizkiah, S: 3169, B: 306A, K: 377B, H: 133A

3492 יַחְזֵרָה *yaḥzērâ*, Jahzerah, S: 3170, B: 306C & 403D, K: 377C, H: 133A

3493 יְחִיאֵל *yᵉḥî'ēl*, Jehiel, S: 3171, B: 313C, K: 377C, H: 133A

3494 יְחִיאֵלִי *yᵉḥî'ēlî*, Jehieli, S: 3172, B: 313D, K: 377C, H*

3495 יָחִיד *yāḥîd*, only son, only child; precious life; alone, solitary, S: 3173, B: 402D, K: 377C, H: 133A

3496 יְחִיָּה *yᵉḥiyyâ*, Jehiah, S: 3174, B: 313D, K: 377D, H: 133A

3497 יָחִיל *yāḥîl*, waiting, S: 3175, B: 404A, K: 377D, H: 133A

3498 יָחַל *yāḥal*, [C] to wait; [D] to wait for, put hope in, expect; [G] to wait, put hope in, S: 3176, B: 403D, K: 377D, H: 133A

3499 יַחְלְאֵל *yaḥlᵉ'ēl*, Jahleel, S: 3177, B: 404B, K: 378A, H: 133B

3500 יַחְלְאֵלִי *yaḥlᵉ'ēlî*, Jahleelite, S: 3178, B: 404B, K: 378A, H*

3501 יָחַם *yāḥam*, [A] to be in (breeding) heat, be in the rut; [D] to be in (breeding) heat, to mate, to conceive, S: 3179, B: 404B, K: 378A, H: 133B

3502 יַחְמוּר *yaḥmûr*, roebuck, the roe deer, S: 3180, B: 331C, K: 378B, H: 133B

3503 יַחְמַי *yaḥmay*, Jahmai, S: 3181, B: 327D, K: 378B, H: 133B

3504 יָחֵף *yāḥēp*, barefoot, S: 3182, B: 405A, K: 378B, H: 133B

3505 יַחְצְאֵל *yaḥṣᵉ'ēl*, Jahziel, Jahzeel, S: 3183, B: 345D, K: 378B, H: 133B

3506 יַחְצְאֵלִי *yaḥṣᵉ'ēlî*, Jahzeelite, S: 3184, B: 345D, K: 378B, H*

3507 יַחֲצִיאֵל *yaḥᵃṣî'ēl*, Jahziel, S: 3185, B: 345D, K: 378C, H: 133B

3508 יָחַר *yāḥar*, variant: see 336, S: 3186, B: 405A, K: 378C, H: 133C

3509 יָחַשׂ *yāḥaś*, [F] to enroll oneself in a genealogical record, be in a family register, S: 3187, B: 405B, K: 378C, H: 133C

3510 יַחַשׂ *yaḥaś*, (book of) genealogy, S: 3188, B: 405B, K: 378D, H: 133C

3511 יַחַת *yaḥat*, Jahath, S: 3189, B: 367A, K: 378D, H: 133C

3512 יָטַב *yāṭab*, [A] to be good, go well; to be glad, pleased; [G] to do good, right; to make successful, cause to prosper, S: 2895† & 3190, B: 405C, K: 378D, H: 133C

3513 יָטְבָה *yoṭbâ*, Jotbah, S: 3192, B: 406A, K: 379C, H: 133D

3514 יָטְבָתָה *yoṭbātâ*, Jotbathah, S: 3193, B: 406A, K: 379C, H: 133D

3515 יְטוּר *yᵉṭûr*, Jetur, S: 3195, B: 377B, K: 379C, H: 134A

3516 יַיִן *yayin*, wine, S: 3196, B: 406B, K: 379D, H: 134A

[F] Hitpael (hitpoel, hitpoal, hitpolel, hitpolal, hitpalel, hitpalal, hitpalpel, hitpalpal, hotpael, hotpaal) [G] Hiphil (hiphtil) [H] Hophal [I] Hishtaphel

3517 יַךְ *yak*, variant: see 3338, S: 3197, B: 406D, K: 380B, H: 134A

3518 יְכָנְיָה *yekôneyâ*, variant: Jeconiah, S: 3204, B: 467C, K: 380B, H: 134A

3519 יָכַח *yākaḥ*, [C] to reason together (in a legal case); to be vindicated; [G] to rebuke, discipline, punish; decide, argue, defend, judge; [H] to be chastened; [F] to lodge a charge against, S: 3198, B: 406D, K: 380B, H: 134A

3520 יָכִין[1] *yākîn*[1], Jakin, S: 3199, B: 467C, K: 380D, H: 134B

3521 [2]יָכִין *yākîn*[2], Jakin, S: 3199, B: 467C 2., K: 380D, H*

3522 יָכִינִי *yākînî*, Jakinite, S: 3200, B: 467C, K: 380D, H: 134B

3523 יָכֹל *yākōl*, [A] to be able, capable; overcome, prevail, have victory, S: 3201, B: 407B, K: 381D, H: 134B

3524 יְכָלְיָה *yekolyâ*, Jecoliah, S: 3203, B: 408A, K: 381B, H: 134B

3525 יְכָלְיָהוּ *yekolyāhû*, Jecoliah, S: 3203, B: 408A, K: 381B, H: 134C

3526 יְכָנְיָה *yekonyâ*, Jehoiachin, S: 3204, B: 467C, K: 381B, H: 134C

3527 יְכָנְיָהוּ *yekonyāhû*, Jehoiachin, S: 3204, B: 467C, K: 381B, H: 134C

3528 יָלַד *yālad*, [A] to give birth to, have a child, become the father of; [B, C, E, G] to be born, be a descendant; [D] to assist in childbirth, be a midwife; [G] to become the father of, cause to come to birth, S: 3205, B: 408A, K: 381B, H: 134C

3529 יֶלֶד *yeled*, male child, young boy, S: 3206, B: 409B, K: 382B, H: 135A

3530 יַלְדָּה *yaldâ*, female child, young girl, S: 3207, B: 409C, K: 382C, H: 135B

3531 יַלְדוּת *yaldûṯ*, youth, childhood, S: 3208, B: 409C, K: 382C, H: 135B

3532 יָלַהּ *yālah*, [A] to waste away, languish, S: 3856†, B: 529C, K: 382C, H: 135B

3533 יִלּוֹד *yillôd*, born (children), S: 3209, B: 409C, K: 382C, H: 135B

3534 יָלוֹן *yālôn*, Jalon, S: 3210, B: 1124A, K: 382D, H: 135B

3535 יָלִיד *yālîd*, born (child, slave child); (pl.) descendants, children, S: 3211, B: 409C, K: 382D, H: 135B

3536 יָלַל *yālal*, [G] to wail, howl, S: 3213, B: 410A, K: 382D, H: 135B

3537 יְלֵל *yelēl*, howling, wailing-cry, S: 3214, B: 410B, K: 383A, H: 135C

3538 יְלָלָה *yelālâ*, wailing, lamentation, howling, S: 3215, B: 410B, K: 383A, H: 135C

3539 יַלֶּפֶת *yallepet*, running sore, S: 3217, B: 410C, K: 383A, H: 135C

3540 יֶלֶק *yeleq*, locust, grasshopper; young locust, S: 3218, B: 410C, K: 383B, H: 135C

3541 יַלְקוּט *yalqûṭ*, pouch, S: 3219, B: 545A, K: 383B, H: 135C

3542 יָם *yām*, sea; seashore; (direction) the west, S: 3220, B: 410D, K: 383B, H: 135C

3543 יְמוּאֵל *yemû'ēl*, Jemuel, S: 3223, B: 410C, K: 384B, H: 135D

3544 יְמִימָה *yemîmâ*, Jemimah, S: 3224, B: 410D, K: 384A, H: 136A

3545 יָמִין[1] *yāmîn*[1], (direction) right; south, southward, S: 3225, B: 411C, K: 384A, H: 136A

3546 [2]יָמִין *yāmîn*[2], Jamin, S: 3226, B: 412C, K: 384C, H: 136A

3547 יָמִינִי *yāmînî*, Jaminite, S: 3228†, B: 412C, K: 384D, H*

3548 יְמָינִי *yemāynî*, variant: see 3556, S: 3233†, B: 412A, K: 384D, H: 136A

3549 יְמִינִי *yemînî*, Benjamite, S: 3227, B: 412B, K: 384D, H: 136B

3550 יִמְלָא *yimlā'*, Imlah, S: 3229, B: 571C, K: 384D, H: 136B

3551 יִמְלָה *yimlâ*, Imlah, S: 3229, B: 571C, K: 384D, H: 136B

3552 יַמְלֵךְ *yamlēk*, Jamlech, S: 3230, B: 576A, K: 384D, H: 136B

3553 יֵמִם *yēmim*, hot springs, S: 3222†, B: 411B, K: 385A, H: 136B

3554 יָמַן *yāman*, [G] to go the right; (ptcp.) right-handed, S: 3231, B: 412B, K: 385A, H: 136B

3555 יִמְנָה *yimnâ*, Imnah; Imnite, S: 3232, B: 412C, K: 385A, H: 136B

3556 יְמָנִי *yemānî*, (direction) right, S: 3233, B: 412B, K: 385A, H: 136B

3557 יִמְנָע *yimnā'*, Imna, S: 3234, B: 586B, K: 385B, H: 136B

3558 יָמַר *yāmar*, [G] to change, exchange, S: 3235, B: 413A, K: 385C, H: 136B

3559 יִמְרָה *yimrâ*, Imrah, S: 3236, B: 598C, K: 385C, H: 136C

3560 יָמַשׁ *yāmaš*, variant: [G] to touch, S: 3237, B: 413A, K: 385C, H: 136C

3561 יָנָה *yānâ*, [A] to oppress, to crush; [G] to mistreat, take advantage of, oppress, S: 3238, B: 413A, K: 385C, H: 136C

3562 יָנוֹחַ *yānôaḥ*, Janoah, S: 3239, B: 629C, K: 385C, H: 136C

3563 יָנוֹחָה *yānôḥâ*, variant: Janohah, S: 3239, B: 629C, K: 385C, H: 136C

3564 יָנוּם *yānûm*, variant: Janum, S: 3241†, B: 630B, K: 385D, H: 136C

3565 יָנִים *yānîm*, Janim, S: 3241, B: 630B, K: 385D, H: 136C

3566 יְנִיקָה *yenîqâ*, shoot (of a plant), S: 3242, B: 413C, K: 385D, H: 136C

3567 יָנַק *yānaq*, [A] to suck, be nursing; [G] to give nourishment, nurse, S: 3243 & 5134†, B: 413B, K: 385D, H: 136C

3568 יַנְשׁוּף *yanšûp*, great owl, S: 3244, B: 676A, K: 386A, H: 136D

3569 יָסַד[1] *yāsad*[1], [A] to lay a foundation, establish, ordain; [C] to be founded; [D] to lay a foundation, establish; [E, G] to be founded, have a foundation laid, S: 3245, B: 413D, K: 386A, H: 136D

3570 [2]יָסַד *yāsad*[2], [C] to associate, conspire (together), S: 3245, B: 413D, K: 386C, H: 137A

3571 יְסֻד *yesud*, variant: foundation, beginning, S: 3246, B: 414B, K: 386C, H: 137A

3572 יְסוֹד *yesôd*, foundation; base (of an altar); foot (base of the body); what is firm, S: 3247, B: 414B, K: 386D, H: 137A

3573 יְסוּדָה *yesûdâ*, foundation, S: 3248, B: 414B, K: 386D, H: 137A

3574 יִסּוֹר *yissôr*, corrector, fault-finder, reprover, S: 3250, B: 416B, K: 386D, H: 137A

3575 יָסַךְ *yāsak*, variant: see 6057, S: 3251, B: 414C, K: 651C, H: 254A

3576 יִסְכָּה *yiskâ*, Iscah, S: 3252, B: 414C, K: 386D, H: 137A

3577 יִסְמַכְיָהוּ *yismakyāhû*, Ismakiah, S: 3253, B: 702B, K: 386D, H: 137A

3578 יָסַף *yāsap*, [A] to add to, to do once more, to do again; [C] to be added to, to gain more, to be joined; [G] to increase, to cause to add to, to continue on, to add to, to happen again, S: 3254, B: 414D, K: 386D, H: 137A

3579 יָסַר[1] *yāsar*[1], [A] to correct, discipline; [C] to accept correction, be warned, be disciplined; [D] to punish, correct, discipline; to instruct, train, discipline; [G] to catch; [Nitpael] to let oneself take warning, S: 3256, B: 415D, K: 387C, H: 137C

3580 [2]יָסַר *yāsar*[2], variant: [D] to strengthen, S: 3256, B: 415D, K: 387C, H: 137D

3581 יָסֹר *yāsōr*, variant: inspector, instructor, S: 3256†, B: 416A, K: 387C, H: 137D

3582 יָעֶ *yā'*, shovel (for altar fires), S: 3257, B: 418B, K: 388D, H: 137D

3583 יַעְבֵּץ[1] *ya'bēṣ*[1], Jabez, S: 3258, B: 716D 2., K: 388A, H: 137D 1.

3584 [2]יַעְבֵּץ *ya'bēṣ*[2], Jabez, S: 3258, B: 716D 1., K: 388A, H: 137D 2.

3585 יָעַד *yā'ad*, [A] to select, appoint, set out; [C] to meet with, assemble, band together, join forces; [G] to summon, challenge; [H] to be set, be ordered, S: 3259, B: 416D, K: 388A, H: 137D

3586 יַעְדָּה *ya'dâ*, Jadah, S: 3294†, B: 421A, K: 388B, H: 138A

3587 יֶעְדּוֹ *ye'dô*, Iddo, S: 3260†, B: 418A, K: 388B, H: 138A

3588 יֶעְדִּי *ye'dî*, variant: Iddi, S: 3260, B: 418A, K: 388B, H: 138A

3589 יָעָה *yā'â*, [A] to sweep away, S: 3261, B: 418A, K: 388B, H: 138A

3590 יְעוּאֵל *ye'û'ēl*, Jeuel, S: 3262, B: 418B, K: 388C, H: 138A

3591 יְעוּץ *ye'ûṣ*, Jeuz, S: 3263, B: 734B, K: 388C, H: 138A

3592 יָעוּר *yā'ûr*, variant: Jaur, S: 3265, B: 735D, K: 388C, H: 138A

3593 יְעוּשׁ *ye'ûš*, Jeush, S: 3266, B: 736B, K: 388C, H: 138A

3594 יָעַז *yā'az*, [C] to be arrogant, be insolent, S: 3267, B: 418B, K: 388C, H: 138A

3595 יַעֲזִיאֵל *ya'azî'ēl*, Jaaziel, S: 3268, B: 739D, K: 388D, H: 138A

3596 יַעֲזִיָּהוּ *ya'aziyyāhû*, Jaaziah, S: 3269, B: 739D, K: 388D, H: 138A

3597 יַעְזֵיר *ya'zēr*, Jazer, S: 3270, B: 741B, K: 388D, H: 138A

3598 יָעַט *yā'aṭ*, [A] to array, cover, S: 3271, B: 418C, K: 388D, H: 138A

3599 יְעִיאֵל *ye'î'ēl*, Jeiel, S: 3273, B: 418B, K: 388D, H: 138A

3600 יָעִיר *yā'îr*, Jair, S: 3265†, B: 735D, K: 389A, H: 138B

3601 יְעִישׁ *ye'îš*, variant: Jeish, S: 3274, B: 736B, K: 389A, H: 138B

3602 יַעְכָּן *ya'kān*, Jacan, S: 3275, B: 747C, K: 389A, H: 138B

3603 יָעַל *yā'al*, [G] to have value, have use, have value, have benefit, S: 3276†, B: 418C, K: 389A, H: 138B

3604 יָעֵל[1] *yā'ēl*[1], mountain goat, wild goat, S: 3277, B: 418D, K: 389B, H: 138B

[A] Qal [B] Qal passive [C] Niphal [D] Piel (poel, polel, pilel, pilal, pealal, pilpel) [E] Pual (poal, polal, poalal, pulal, pualal)

3605 [2]יָעֵל *yā'ēl*[2], Jael, S: 3278, B: 418D, K: 389B, H: 138B

3606 יַעֲלָא *ya'^{a}lā'*, Jaala, S: 3279, B: 419A, K: 389B, H: 138B

3607 יַעֲלָה *ya'^{a}lâ*[1], (female) mountain goat, ibex; deer, S: 3280, B: 418D, K: 389B, H: 138B

3608 [2]יַעֲלָה *ya'^{a}lâ*[2], Jaala, S: 3279, B: 419A, K: 389B, H: 138B

3609 יַעְלָם *ya'lām*, Jalam, S: 3281, B: 761C, K: 389B, H: 138B

3610 יַעַן *ya'an*[1], for, because, since, S: 3282, B: 774C, K: 389C, H: 138B

3611 [2]יַעַן *ya'an*[2], variant: Jaan, see 1970, S*, B: 193A (note), K: 214D, H: 73A 3.

3612 יָעֵן *yā'ēn*, ostrich, S: 3283, B: 419A, K: 389C, H: 138C

3613 יַעֲנָה *ya'^{a}nâ*, owl; horned owl, S: 3284, B: 419A, K: 389C, H: 138C

3614 יַעְנַי *ya'nay*, Janai, S: 3285, B: 775A, K: 389D, H: 138C

3615 יָעֵף *yā'ēp*[1], [A] to grow tired, be faint, exhaust oneself, S: 3286†, B: 419B, K: 389D, H: 138C

3616 [2]יָעֵף *yā'ēp*[2], [H] to be in swift flight, S: 3288†, B: 419B, K: 390A, H: 138C

3617 [3]יָעֵף *yā'ēp*[3], weary, exhausted, fatigued, S: 3287, B: 419B, K: 390A, H: 138C

3618 יְעָף *y^e'āp*, flight, S: 3288, B: 419B, K: 390A, H: 138C

3619 יָעַץ *yā'aṣ*, [A] to give advise, give counsel; to purpose, plan, plot, determine; [B] to be determined; [C] to seek advise, consult; to confer, to plot (together); [F] to consult together, conspire against, S: 3289, B: 419C, K: 390A, H: 138C

3620 יַעֲקֹב *ya'^{a}qōb*, Jacob, S: 3290, B: 784D, K: 390C, H: 138D

3621 יַעֲקֹבָה *ya'^{a}qōbâ*, Jaakobah, S: 3291, B: 785A, K: 391A, H: 138D

3622 יַעֲקָן *ya'^{a}qān*, Jaakan, S: 3292, B: 122C, K: 391A, H: 138D

3623 יַעַר *ya'ar*[1], forest, woods, thicket; tree groves, S: 3264† & 3293, B: 420C, K: 391A, H: 138D

3624 [2]יַעַר *ya'ar*[2], honeycomb, S: 3293, B: 421A, K: 391C, H: 139A

3625 [3]יַעַר *ya'ar*[3], Jaar, S: 3293, B: 421A, K: 391C, H: 138D

3626 יַעְרָה *ya'^{a}râ*[1], honeycomb, S: 3295, B: 421A, K: 391C, H: 139A

3627 [2]יַעְרָה *ya'^{a}râ*[2], variant: forest, S: 3295†, B: 420D c, K: 391C, H: 139A

3628 יַעְרָה *ya'râ*, variant: Jarah, see 3586, S: 3294, B: 421A, K: 391C, H: 139A

3629 יַעְרֵי אֹרְגִים *ya'^{a}rê 'ōr^{e}gîm*, Jaare-Oregim, S: 3296, B: 421A, K: 391C, H: 139A

3630 יְעָרִים *y^e'ārîm*, Jearim, S: 3297, B: 421B, K: 855D 2. & 241B, H*

3631 יַעֲרֶשְׁיָה *ya'^{a}rešyâ*, Jaareshiah, S: 3298, B: 793B, K: 391D, H: 139A

3632 יַעֲשׂוּ *ya'^{a}śû*, Jaasu, S: 3299, B: 795C, K: 391D, H: 139A

3633 יַעֲשַׂי *ya'^{a}śāy*, variant: Jaasai, S: 3299†, B: 795C, K: 391D, H: 139A

3634 יַעֲשִׂיאֵל *ya'^{a}śî'ēl*, Jaasiel, S: 3300, B: 795C, K: 391D, H: 139A

3635 יִפְדְיָה *yipd^{e}yâ*, Iphdeiah, S: 3301, B: 804C, K*, H: 139A

3636 יָפָה *yāpâ*, [A] to be beautiful, delightful; [D] to adorn, make beautiful; [F] to adorn oneself, S: 3302, B: 421B, K: 391D, H: 139A

3637 יָפֶה *yāpeh*, beautiful, fair, lovely, handsome, S: 3303, B: 421C, K: 392A, H: 139A

3638 יְפֵה־פִיָּה *y^{e}pēh-piyyâ*, variant: beautiful, pretty, S: 3304, B: 421D, K: 392A, H: 139B

3639 יָפוֹ *yāpô*, Joppa, S: 3305, B: 421D, K: 392B, H: 139B

3640 יָפַח *yāpaḥ*, [F] to gasp for breath, S: 3306, B: 422A, K: 392B, H: 139B

3641 יָפֵחַ *yāpēaḥ*, breathing out, S: 3307, B: 422A, K: 392B, H: 139B

3642 יְפִי *y^{e}pî*, beauty, S: 3308, B: 421D, K: 392B, H: 139B

3643 יָפִיעַ *yāpîa'*[1], Japhia, S: 3309, B: 422B 2., K: 392C, H: 139B

3644 [2]יָפִיעַ *yāpîa'*[2], Japhia, S: 3309, B: 422B 1., K: 392C, H: 139B

3645 יְפֵהפִיָּה *y^{e}pêpiyyâ*, beautiful, S: 3304†, B: 421D, K: 392A, H: 139B

3646 יַפְלֵט *yaplēṭ*, Japhlet, S: 3310, B: 812D, K: 392C, H: 139B

3647 יַפְלֵטִי *yaplēṭî*, Japhletite, S: 3311, B: 812D, K: 392C, H: 139B

3648 יְפֻנֶּה *y^{e}punneh*, Jephunneh, S: 3312, B: 819C, K: 392C, H: 139B

3649 יָפַע *yāpa'*, [G] to shine forth, flash; smile, S: 3313, B: 422A, K: 392C, H: 139B

3650 יִפְעָה *yip'â*, shining splendor, S: 3314, B: 422B, K: 392D, H: 139C

3651 יֶפֶת *yepet*, Japheth, S: 3315, B: 834D, K: 392D, H: 139C

3652 יִפְתָּח *yiptāḥ*[1], Iphtah, S: 3316, B: 836B 2., K: 392D, H: 139C

3653 [2]יִפְתָּח *yiptāḥ*[2], Jephthah, S: 3316, B: 836B 1., K: 392D, H: 139C

3654 יִפְתַּח־אֵל *yiptaḥ-'ēl*, Iphtah El, S: 3317, B: 836B, K: 392D, H: 139C

3655 יָצָא *yāṣā'*, [A] to go out, come out; [G] to bring out, lead forth; produce; [H] to be brought out; emptied, S: 3318, B: 422B, K: 393A, H: 139C

3656 יָצַב *yāṣab*, [F] to stand one's ground, confront; to stand before, present oneself, commit oneself, S: 3320, B: 426A, K: 394C, H: 140C

3657 יָצַג *yāṣag*, [G] to set, place, present; touch; [H] to be left behind, S: 3322, B: 426C, K: 395A, H: 140C

3658 יִצְהָר *yiṣhār*[1], olive oil, S: 3323, B: 844A, K: 395B, H: 140D

3659 [2]יִצְהָר *yiṣhār*[2], Izhar, S: 3324, B: 844B, K: 395B, H: 140D

3660 יִצְהָרִי *yiṣhārî*, Izharite, S: 3325, B: 844B, K: 395B, H: 140D

3661 יָצוּעַ *yāṣûa'*[1], bed, couch, S: 3326, B: 426D, K: 395C, H: 140D

3662 [2]יָצוּעַ *yāṣûa'*[2], variant: see 3666, S: 3326, B: 426D, K*, H: 140D

3663 יִצְחָק *yiṣḥāq*, Isaac, S: 3327, B: 850C, K: 395C, H: 140D

3664 יִצְחָר *yiṣḥār*, variant: Jizhar, S: 3328†, B: 850D, K: 395C, H: 140D

3665 יָצִיא *yāṣî'*, coming forth, S: 3329, B: 425C, K: 395C, H: 140D

3666 יָצִיעַ *yāṣîa'*, structure, room, S: 3326†, B: 427A, K: 395C, H: 140D

3667 יָצַע *yāṣa'*, [G] to spread out bedding; [H] to be spread out, S: 3331†, B: 426D, K: 395D, H: 141A

3668 יָצַק *yāṣaq*, [A] to pour out, cast out; [B] be cast out, be poured out, be smelted; [G] to pour out, spread out; [H] to be poured out, be washed away; be anointed, S: 3332, B: 427A, K: 395D, H: 141A

3669 יְצֻקָה *y^{e}ṣuqâ*, casting (of metal), S: 3333, B: 427C, K: 396B, H: 141B

3670 יָצַר *yāṣar*, [A] to form, fashion, shape, create; (of God) the Maker, the Creator; [C] to be formed; [E] to be formed; [H] to be forged, be formed, S: 3335, B: 427C, K: 396B, H: 141B

3671 יֵצֶר *yēṣer*[1], something formed, creation; inclination, disposition, motivation, S: 3336, B: 428A, K: 396D, H: 141B

3672 [2]יֵצֶר *yēṣer*[2], Jezer, S: 3337 & 3340†, B: 428A, K: 396D, H: 141C

3673 יִצְרִי *yiṣrî*, Izri; Jezerite, S: 3339, B: 428B, K: 397A, H*

3674 יְצֻרִים *y^{e}ṣurîm*, frame, body, limbs, S: 3338†, B: 428B, K: 397A, H: 141C

3675 יָצַת *yāṣat*, [A] to set ablaze; [C] to burn, be burned; [G] to kindle, set on fire, S: 3341, B: 428B, K: 397A, H: 141C

3676 יֶקֶב *yeqeb*, winepress; (wine or oil) vat, S: 3342, B: 428C, K: 397B, H: 141C

3677 יְקַבְצְאֵל *y^{e}qabs^e'ēl*, Jekabzeel, S: 3343, B: 868B, K: 397C, H: 141D

3678 יָקַד *yāqad*, [A] to burn; to kindle a fire; [H] to be burning, be kindled, S: 3344, B: 428D, K: 397C, H: 141D

3679 יְקֹד *y^{e}qōd*, blazing, burning, S: 3350†, B: 428D, K: 397D, H: 141D

3680 יָקְדְעָם *yoqd^e'ām*, Jokdeam, S: 3347, B: 429A, K: 397D, H: 141D

3681 יָקֶה *yāqeh*, Jakeh, S: 3348, B: 429A, K: 397D, H: 141D

3682 יְקָהָה *y^{e}qāhâ*, obedience, S: 3349, B: 429B, K: 397D, H: 141D

3683 יָקוּד *yāqûd*, hearth (of a fireplace), S: 3344, B: 428D, K: 397D, H: 141D

3684 יָקוֹט *yāqôṭ*, fragile, S: 2901† & 6990†, B: 876C, K: 398A, H: 141D

3685 יְקוּם *y^{e}qûm*, living thing, living creature, S: 3351, B: 879C, K: 398A, H: 141D

3686 יָקוֹשׁ *yāqôš*, variant: fowler, bait-layer, S: 3352, B: 430C, K: 398A, H: 142A

3687 יָקוּשׁ *yāqûš*, fowler, one who snares birds, S: 3353, B: 430C, K: 398A, H: 142A

3688 יְקוּתִיאֵל *y^{e}qûtî'ēl*, Jekuthiel, S: 3354, B: 429A, K: 398A, H: 142A

3689 יָקַח *yāqaḥ*, [G] to become insolent, S: 3947†, B: 542C, K: 485C, H: 142A

3690 יָקְטָן *yoqṭān*, Joktan, S: 3355, B: 429B, K: 398A, H: 142A

3691 יָקִים *yāqîm*, Jakim, S: 3356, B: 879C, K: 398A, H: 142A

3692 יַקִּיר *yaqqîr*, dear, precious, S: 3357, B: 430B, K: 398A, H: 142A

3693 יְקַמְיָה *y^{e}qamyâ*, Jekamiah, S: 3359, B: 880C, K: 398B, H: 142A

3694 יְקַמְעָם *y^{e}qam'ām*, Jekameam, S: 3360, B: 880C, K: 398B, H: 142A

3695 יָקְמְעָם *yoqm^e'ām*, Jokmeam, S: 3361, B: 880C, K: 398B, H: 142A

3696 יָקְנְעָם *yoqneʿām*, Jokneam, S: 3362, B: 429B, K: 398B, H: 142A

3697 יָקַע *yāqaʿ*, [A] to turn (away), wrench; [G] to kill and expose; [H] to be killed and exposed, S: 3363, B: 429B, K: 398B, H: 142A

3698 יְקִפָּאוֹן *yeqippāʾôn*, variant: see 7885, S: 3368†, B: 891A, K: 845C, H: 142B

3699 יָקַץ *yāqaṣ*, [A] to wake up, awake, S: 3364, B: 429C, K: 398C, H: 142B

3700 יָקַר *yāqar*, [A] to be precious, be costly; become well known; [G] to make scarce, S: 3365, B: 429C, K: 398C, H: 142B

3701 יָקָר *yāqār*, precious, valuable, quality, S: 3368, B: 429D, K: 398D, H: 142B

3702 יְקָר *yeqār*, honor, splendor, riches, valuable things, S: 3366, B: 430B, K: 399A, H: 142C

3703 יִקְרָה *yiqrâ*, variant: meeting, S: 3368†, B: 429A, K: 399A, H: 142B

3704 יָקֹשׁ *yāqaš*, [A] to lay a bird snare, set a trap; [C, E] to be ensnared, be trapped, S: 3369†, B: 430B, K: 399B, H: 142C

3705 יָקְשָׁן *yoqšān*, Jokshan, S: 3370, B: 430D, K: 399B, H: 142C

3706 יָקְתְאֵל *yoqteʾēl*, Joktheel, S: 3371, B: 430D, K: 399B, H: 142C

3707 יָרֵא *yārēʾ*[1], [A] to be afraid, be frightened; to revere, respect; [C] to be awesome, be dreadful, be feared; [D] to frighten, terrify, intimidate, S: 3372, B: 431A, K: 399C, H: 142C

3708 יָרֵא *yārēʾ*[2], variant: see 3721, S: 3372, B: 432B, K: 400B, H: 143A

3709 יָרֵא *yārēʾ*[3], variant: see 3722, S: 3384†, B: 432B & 434D, K: 400B, H: 143A

3710 יָרֵא *yārēʾ*[4], fear; worship, S: 3373, B: 431D, K: 400B, H: 143A

3711 יִרְאָה *yirʾâ*, fear, reverence, piety, S: 3374, B: 432A, K: 400C, H: 143A

3712 יִרְאוֹן *yirʾôn*, Iron, S: 3375, B: 432A, K: 400D, H: 143A

3713 יִרְאִיָּיה *yirʾiyyāyh*, Irijah, S: 3376, B: 909D, K: 400D, H: 143A

3714 יָרֵב *yārēb*, great (king), S: 3377, B: 937A, K: 400D, H: 143A

3715 יְרֻבַּעַל *yerubbaʿal*, Jerub-Baal, S: 3378, B: 937C, K: 401A, H: 143B

3716 יָרָבְעָם *yārobʿām*, Jeroboam, S: 3379, B: 914C, K: 401A, H: 143B

3717 יְרֻבֶּשֶׁת *yerubbešet*, Jerub-Besheth, S: 3380, B: 937C, K: 401A, H: 143B

3718 יָרַד *yārad*, [A] to come down, go down, descend; [G] to bring down, lower; [H] to be brought down, be taken down, S: 3381, B: 432C, K: 401A, H: 143B

3719 יֶרֶד *yered*, Jared; Jered, S: 3382, B: 434B, K: 402B, H: 143D

3720 יַרְדֵּן *yardēn*, Jordan, S: 3383, B: 434C, K: 402B, H: 143D

3721 יָרָה *yārâ*[1], [A] to throw, cast; shoot; [C] to be shot through; [G] to shoot (an arrow), to hurl, S: 3384, B: 432B & 434D, K: 402C, H: 143D

3722 יָרָה *yārâ*[2], [G] to water upon, rain, shower; [H] to be refreshed, S: 3384, B: 432B & 434D, K: 403A, H: 132A & 144A

3723 יָרָה *yārâ*[3], [G] to teach, instruct, give guidance, S: 3384, B: 434D, K: 403A, H: 144A

3724 יָרַהּ *yārah*, [A] to be frozen in fear, S: 7297†, B: 436C, K: 403C, H: 144B

3725 יְרוּאֵל *yerûʾēl*, Jeruel, S: 3385, B: 436C, K: 403C, H: 144B

3726 יָרוֹחַ *yārôaḥ*, Jaroah, S: 3386, B: 437B, K: 403C, H: 144B

3727 יָרוּם *yārûm*, variant: high, exalted, S: 7311†, B: 926C, K: 879D, H: 144B

3728 יָרוֹק *yārôq*, green plant, S: 3387, B: 438D, K: 403D, H: 144B

3729 יְרוּשָׁא *yerûšāʾ*, Jerusha, S: 3388, B: 440B, K: 403D, H: 144B

3730 יְרוּשָׁה *yerûšâ*, Jerusha, S: 3388, B: 440B, K: 403D, H: 144B

3731 יְרוּשָׁלַםִ *yerûšālaim*, Jerusalem, S: 3389, B: 436C, K: 403D, H: 144B

3732 יֶרַח *yeraḥ*[1], moon; (lunar) month, S: 3391, B: 437B, K: 404A, H: 144C

3733 יֶרַח *yeraḥ*[2], Jerah, S: 3392, B: 437B, K: 404B, H: 144C

3734 יָרֵחַ *yārēaḥ*, moon, S: 3394, B: 437A, K: 404B, H: 144C

3735 יְרִחוֹ *yeriḥô*, Jericho, S: 3405, B: 437D, K: 404C, H: 144C

3736 יְרֹחָם *yerōḥām*, Jeroham, S: 3395, B: 934A, K: 404C, H: 144C

3737 יְרַחְמְאֵל *yeraḥmeʾēl*, Jerahmeel, S: 3396, B: 934A, K: 404D, H: 144C

3738 יְרַחְמְאֵלִי *yeraḥmeʾēlî*, Jerahmeelite, S: 3397, B: 934A, K: 404D, H: 144C

3739 יַרְחָע *yarḥāʿ*, Jarha, S: 3398, B: 437C, K: 404D, H: 144C

3740 יָרַט *yāraṭ*, [A] to throw (into someone's custody); to be reckless, S: 3399, B: 437C, K: 404D, H: 144C

3741 יְרִיאֵל *yerîʾēl*, Jeriel, S: 3400, B: 436C, K: 404D, H: 144C

3742 יָרִיב *yārîb*[1], contender, accuser, adversary, opponent, S: 3401, B: 937A, K: 404D, H: 144C

3743 יָרִיב *yārîb*[2], Jarib, S: 3402, B: 937B, K: 405A, H: 144C

3744 יְרִיבַי *yerîbay*, Jeribai, S: 3403, B: 937B, K: 405A, H: 144C

3745 יְרִיָּה *yeriyyâ*, Jeriah, S: 3404, B: 436C, K: 405A, H: 144C

3746 יְרִיָּהוּ *yeriyyāhû*, Jeriah, S: 3404, B: 436C, K: 405A, H: 144C

3747 יְרִיחֹה *yerîḥōh*, variant: Jericho, S: 3405, B: 437C, K: 405A, H: 144C

3748 יְרִימוֹת *yerîmôt*, Jerimoth, S: 3406, B: 438B 1a, K: 405A, H: 144C

3749 יְרִיעָה *yerîʿâ*, tent curtain; tent, shelter, dwelling, S: 3407, B: 438C, K: 405A, H: 144D

3750 יְרִיעוֹת *yerîʿôt*, Jerioth, S: 3408, B: 438C, K: 405B, H: 144D

3751 יָרֵךְ *yārēk*, thigh, hip, breast, leg; side, base, S: 3409, B: 437D, K: 405B, H: 144D

3752 יְרֵכָה *yerēkâ*, far end, ends (of the earth); remote area: heights, depths, S: 3411, B: 438A, K: 405C, H: 144D

3753 יָרַם *yāram*, variant: [B] to be high, exalted, S: 7311†, B: 926C, K: 879D, H: 145A

3754 יַרְמוּת *yarmût*, Jarmuth, S: 3412, B: 438B, K: 405D, H: 145A

3755 יְרָמוֹת *yerāmôt*, variant: Jeramoth, S: 3406†, B: 438B, K: 405D, H: 145A

3756 יְרֵמוֹת *yerēmôt*, Jeremoth; Jerimoth, S: 3406, B: 438B, K: 405A, H: 145A

3757 יְרֵמַי *yerēmay*, Jeremai, S: 3413, B: 438B, K: 405D, H: 145A

3758 יִרְמְיָה *yirmeyâ*, Jeremiah, S: 3414, B: 941C, K: 405D, H: 145A

3759 יִרְמְיָהוּ *yirmeyāhû*, Jeremiah, S: 3414, B: 941C, K: 406A, H: 145A

3760 יָרַע *yāraʿ*, [A] to tremble, be faint-hearted, S: 3415, B: 438C, K: 406A, H: 145A

3761 יִרְפְּאֵל *yirpeʾēl*, Irpeel, S: 3416, B: 951B, K: 406A, H: 145A

3762 יָרַק *yāraq*, [A] to spit (in the face as an act of contempt), S: 3417†, B: 439A, K: 406A, H: 145A

3763 יָרָק *yārāq*, vegetables, vegetable greens, S: 3419, B: 438D, K: 406B, H: 145A

3764 יֶרֶק *yereq*, green (of plants, foliage, shoots, grass), S: 3418, B: 438D, K: 406B, H: 145A

3765 יַרְקוֹן *yarqôn*, variant: Jarkon, S: 4313†, B: 566A, K: 406B, H: 145A

3766 יֵרָקוֹן *yērāqôn*, paleness (of face); mildew (of grain), S: 3420, B: 439A, K: 406C, H: 145A

3767 יָרְקְעָם *yorqoʿām*, Jorkeam, S: 3421, B: 439A, K: 406C, H: 145B

3768 יְרַקְרַק *yeraqraq*, yellowish-green, pale-green (mildew); shining-yellowish (gold), S: 3422, B: 439A, K: 406C, H: 145B

3769 יָרַשׁ *yāraš*[1], [A] to be an heir, gain an inheritance, have as a possession; [C] to become destitute, to be poor; [D] to take possession of; [G] to drive away, push out, destroy; to cause to inherit, S: 3423, B: 439A, K: 406C, H: 145B

3770 יָרַשׁ *yāraš*[2], variant: [A] to press (grapes), S: 8492†, B: 440D, K: 1027D, H: 145C

3771 יְרֵשָׁה *yerēšâ*, possession conquered, S: 3424, B: 440B, K: 407B, H: 145C

3772 יְרֻשָּׁה *yeruššâ*, possession, inheritance, S: 3425, B: 440B, K: 407B, H: 145C

3773 יִשְׂחָק *yiśḥāq*, Isaac, S: 3446, B: 850C, K: 407C, H: 145C

3774 יְשִׂימִאֵל *yeśîmiʾēl*, Jesimiel, S: 3450†, B: 964D, K: 407C, H: 145C

3775 יָשַׂם *yāśam*, variant: see 8492, S: 3455, B: 441A, K: 920A, H: 351A

3776 יִשְׂרָאֵל *yiśrāʾēl*, Israel, S: 3478, B: 441A & 975B, K: 407C, H: 145D

3777 יְשַׂרְאֵלָה *yeśarʾēlâ*, Jesarelah, S: 3480, B: 441A, K: 408B, H: 29A

3778 יִשְׂרְאֵלִי *yiśreʾēlî*, Israelite, S: 3481 & 3482†, B: 976A, K: 408B, H: 145D

3779 יִשָּׂשכָר *yiśśāśkār*, Issachar, S: 3485, B: 441A, K: 408B, H: 145D

3780 יֵשׁ *yēš*, there is, it exists, S: 3426, B: 441B, K: 408C, H: 145D

3781 יִשְׁאָל *yišʾāl*, variant: Ishal, S*, B: 982B, K: 409B, H: 357A

3782 יָשַׁב *yāšab*, [A] to live, inhabit, dwell, stay; [C] to be settled, be inhabited; [D] to set up; to cause to settle, make dwell, to cause to sit; to marry, S: 3427, B: 442A, K: 409B, H: 146A

3783 יֹשֵׁב בַּשֶּׁבֶת *yōšēb baššebet*, Josheb-Basshebeth, S: 3429, B: 444A, K: 410C, H: 146C

3784 יֶשֶׁבְאָב *yešeb'āb*, Jeshebeab, S: 3428, B: 444A, K: 410C, H: 146C

3785 יִשְׁבּוֹ בְנֹב *yišbô benōb*, variant: Ishbo-Benob, S: 3430, B: 444A, K*, H*

3786 יִשְׁבָּח *yišbāḥ*, Ishbah, S: 3431†, B: 986D, K: 410C, H: 146C

3787 יִשְׁבִּי בְנֹב *yišbî benōb*, Ishbi-Benob, S: 3430†, B: 444A, K*, H*

3788 יָשֻׁבִי לֶחֶם *yāšubî leḥem*, Jashubi Lehem, S: 3433, B: 1000B, K: 410C, H*

3789 יִשְׁבַּעַל *yišba'al*, variant: Ish-Baal, S*, B: 36B, K: 410C, H: 146C

3790 יָשָׁבְעָם *yāšob'ām*, Jashobeam, S: 3434, B: 1000B, K: 410C, H: 146C

3791 יִשְׁבָּק *yišbāq*, Ishbak, S: 3435, B: 990B, K: 410C, H: 146C

3792 יָשְׁבְּקָשָׁה *yošbeqāšâ*, Joshbekashah, S: 3436, B: 444A, K: 410C, H: 146C

3793 יָשׁוּב[1] *yāšûb*[1], Jashub, S: 3437, B: 1000B, K: 410D, H: 146C

3794 2יָשׁוּב *yāšûb*[2], variant: Jashub, S: 3427†, B: 442A, K: 410D, H: 146C

3795 יָשׁוּבִי *yāšûbî*, Jashubite, S: 3432†, B: 1000B, K: 410D, H: 146C

3796 יִשְׁוָה *yišwâ*, Ishvah, S: 3438, B: 1001A, K: 410D, H: 146C

3797 יְשׁוֹחָיָה *yešôḥāyâ*, Jeshohaiah, S: 3439, B: 1006A, K: 410D, H: 146C

3798 יִשְׁוִי[1] *yišwî*[1], Ishvi, S: 3440, B: 1001A, K: 410D, H: 146C

3799 2יִשְׁוִי *yišwî*[2], Ishvite, S: 3441, B: 1001A, K: 410D, H: 146C

3800 יֵשׁוּעַ[1] *yēšûa'*[1], Jeshua, S: 3442, B: 221C, K: 410D, H: 146D

3801 2יֵשׁוּעַ *yēšûa'*[2], Jeshua, S: 3442, B: 221C, K: 410D, H: 146D

3802 יְשׁוּעָה *yešû'â*, salvation, deliverance, help, S: 3444, B: 447B, K: 411A, H: 146D

3803 יֶשַׁח *yešaḥ*, emptiness, S: 3445, B: 445A, K: 411B, H: 146D

3804 יָשַׁט *yāšaṭ*, [G] to extend; hold out, S: 3447, B: 445A, K: 411A, H: 146D

3805 יִשַׁי *yišay*, Jesse, S: 3448, B: 445A, K: 411B, H: 146D

3806 יָשִׁיב *yāšîb*, variant: Jashib, S: 3437, B: 1000B 1, K: 411C, H: 146D

3807 יִשִּׁיָּה *yiššiyyâ*, Isshiah; Ishijah, S: 3449, B: 674D, K: 411C, H: 146D

3808 יִשִּׁיָּהוּ *yiššiyyāhû*, Isshiah, S: 3449, B: 674D, K: 411C, H: 146D

3809 יְשִׁימָה *yešîmâ*, variant: desolation, S: 3451, B: 445B, K*, H*

3810 יְשִׁימוֹן *yešîmôn*, Jeshimon; wasteland, S: 3452, B: 445B, K: 411C, H: 146D

3811 יְשִׁימוֹת *yešîmôt*, variant: Jeshimoth, S: 1020†, B: 111D, K: 124C 19., H: 147A & 39B 21.

3812 יַשִּׁימָוֶת *yaššîmāwet*, variant: devastation, S: 3451†, B: 445B, K: 411C, H: 147A

3813 יָשִׁישׁ *yāšîš*, old, aged, S: 3453, B: 450A, K: 411D, H: 147A

3814 יְשִׁישַׁי *yešîšay*, Jeshishai, S: 3454†, B: 450B, K: 411D, H: 147A

3815 יָשַׁם *yāšam*, variant: [A] to be desolate, S: 3456, B: 445B, K: 411D, H: 375D

3816 יִשְׁמָא *yišmā'*, Ishma, S: 3457, B: 445C, K: 411D, H: 147A

3817 יִשְׁמָעֵאל *yišmā'ē'l*, Ishmael, S: 3458, B: 1035D, K: 411D, H: 147A

3818 יִשְׁמְעֵאלִי *yišme'ē'lî*, Ishmaelite, S: 3459, B: 1035D, K: 412A, H: 147A

3819 יִשְׁמַעְיָה *yišma'yâ*, Ishmaiah, S: 3460, B: 1036A, K: 412A, H: 147A

3820 יִשְׁמַעְיָהוּ *yišma'yāhû*, Ishmaiah, S: 3460, B: 1036A, K: 412A, H: 147A

3821 יִשְׁמְרַי *yišmeray*, Ishmerai, S: 3461, B: 1038B, K: 412A, H: 147A

3822 יָשֵׁן[1] *yāšēn*[1], [A] to sleep, fall asleep; [D] to put to sleep, S: 3462 & 8153†, B: 445C, K: 412A, H: 147A

3823 2יָשֵׁן *yāšēn*[2], [C] to live a long time, be old, chronic, S: 3462, B: 445D, K: 412B, H: 147A

3824 יָשָׁן *yāšān*, old; pertaining to last year, S: 3465, B: 445D, K: 412C, H: 147B

3825 3יָשֵׁן *yāšēn*[3], sleeping, pertaining to sleep, S: 3463, B: 445D, K: 412C, H: 147B

3826 4יָשֵׁן *yāšēn*[4], Jashen, S: 3464, B: 445D, K: 412C, H: 147B

3827 יְשָׁנָה *yešānâ*, Jeshanah, S: 3466, B: 446A, K: 412C, H: 147B

3828 יָשַׁע *yāša'*, [C] to be rescued, be delivered, be saved; [G] to save, rescue, deliver, S: 3467, B: 446B, K: 412D, H: 147B

3829 יֵשַׁע *yēša'*, salvation, deliverance, protection; (of God) Savior, S: 3468, B: 447A, K: 413B, H: 147C

3830 יֹשַׁע *yōša'*, variant: help, S: 3467†, B: 446B, K: 412D, H: 147C

3831 יִשְׁעִי *yiš'î*, Ishi, S: 3469, B: 447D, K: 413C, H: 147C

3832 יְשַׁעְיָה *yeša'yâ*, Jeshaiah, S: 3470, B: 447D, K: 413C, H: 147D

3833 יְשַׁעְיָהוּ *yeša'yāhû*, Isaiah; Jeshaiah, S: 3470, B: 447D, K: 413C, H: 147D

3834 יִשְׁפָּה *yišpâ*, Ishpah, S: 3472, B: 1046A, K: 413D, H: 147D

3835 יָשְׁפֵה *yāšepēh*, jasper, S: 3471, B: 448C, K: 413D, H: 147D

3836 יִשְׁפָּן *yišpān*, Ishpan, S: 3473, B: 1051A, K: 413D, H: 147D

3837 יָשַׁר *yāšar*, [A] to do good, do right, be straight; [D] to make straight, make smooth; [E] to be evenly hammered; [G] to make straight, gaze straight, S: 3474, B: 448C, K: 413D, H: 147D

3838 יָשָׁר[1] *yāšār*[1], straight; right, upright, innocent, S: 3477, B: 449A, K: 414B, H: 148A

3839 2יָשָׁר *yāšār*[2], Jashar, S: 3477, B: 449B 3c2, K: 414B, H: 148A

3840 יֵשֶׁר *yēšer*, Jesher, S: 3475, B: 449C, K: 414D, H: 148A

3841 יֹשֶׁר *yōšer*, uprightness, straightness, honesty, integrity, S: 3476, B: 449C, K: 414D, H: 148A

3842 יִשְׁרָה *yišrâ*, uprightness, S: 3483, B: 449C, K: 414D, H: 148B

3843 יְשֻׁרוּן *yešurûn*, Jeshurun, S: 3484, B: 449C, K: 414D, H: 148B

3844 יָשֵׁשׁ *yāšēš*, aged, decrepit, S: 3486, B: 450A, K: 415A, H: 148B

3845 יָתֵד *yātēd*, tent peg, stake, pin (of a loom); tool for digging, S: 3489, B: 450B, K: 415A, H: 148B

3846 יָתוֹם *yātôm*, fatherless, orphan, S: 3490, B: 450C, K: 415B, H: 148B

3847 יְתוּר *yetûr*, variant: see 9365, S: 3491, B: 1064D, K: 1023A, H: 148C

3848 יַתִּיר *yattîr*, Jattir, S: 3492, B: 452D, K: 415C, H: 148C

3849 יִתְלָה *yitlâ*, Ithlah, S: 3494, B: 1068B, K: 415C, H: 148C

3850 יִתְמָה *yitmâ*, Ithmah, S: 3495, B: 450D, K: 415C, H: 148C

3851 יָתַן[1] *yātan*[1], variant: [A] to be constant, be durable, S: 5414†, B: 679C 1t & 681C 1c, K: 415C, H: 148C

3852 2יָתַן *yātan*[2], variant: [A] to give, S: 5414†, B: 681A 3a, K: 642A, H: 148C

3853 יַתְנִיאֵל *yatnî'ēl*, Jathniel, S: 3496, B: 1072A, K: 415C, H: 148C

3854 יִתְנָן *yitnān*, Ithnan, S: 3497, B: 451A, K: 415C, H: 148C

3855 יָתַר *yātar*, [C] to remain, be left over, the rest; [G] to have left over, spare, preserve, S: 3498, B: 451A, K: 415D, H: 148C

3856 יֶתֶר[1] *yeter*[1], remainder, remnant, the rest, what is left over, S: 3499, B: 451D, K: 416B, H: 148D

3857 2יֶתֶר *yeter*[2], thong, cord, bowstring, S: 3499, B: 452A, K: 416A, H: 148D

3858 3יֶתֶר *yeter*[3], Jether; Jethro, S: 3500, B: 452B, K: 416B, H: 148D

3859 יִתְרָא *yitrā'*, Jether, S: 3501, B: 452B, K: 416C, H: 148D

3860 יִתְרָה *yitrâ*, wealth, abundance, S: 3502, B: 452B, K: 416C, H: 148D

3861 יִתְרוֹ *yitrô*, Jethro, S: 3503, B: 452B, K: 416C, H: 148D

3862 יִתְרוֹן *yitrôn*, profit, gain, increase, S: 3504, B: 452C, K: 416C, H: 149A

3863 יִתְרִי *yitrî*, Ithrite, S: 3505, B: 452B, K: 416D, H: 149A

3864 יִתְרָן *yitrān*, Ithran, S: 3506, B: 452D, K: 416D, H: 149A

3865 יִתְרְעָם *yitre'ām*, Ithream, S: 3507, B: 453C, K: 416D, H: 149A

3866 יֹתֶרֶת *yōteret*, covering, lobe (of certain animal livers), S: 3508, B: 452C, K: 416D, H: 149C

3867 יְתֵת *yetēt*, Jetheth, S: 3509, B: 453C, K: 416D, H: 149C

3868 כ *k*, letter of the Hebrew alphabet, S*, B: 453A, K: 417A, H*

3869 -כְּ *ke-*, as, like, according to, S*, B: 453A, K: 417A, H: 149A

3870 ךָ- *-kā*, ךְ- *-āk*, כָה- *-kēh*, you, your, S*, B*, K*, H*

3871 ךְ- *-k*, כִי- *-kî*, you, your, S*, B*, K*, H*

3872 כָּאַב *kā'ab*, [A] to feel pain, ache; [G] to bring pain, S: 3510, B: 456A, K: 418B, H: 149C

3873 כְּאֵב *ke'ēb*, pain, anguish, suffering, S: 3511, B: 456B, K: 418C, H: 149D

3874 כָּאָה *kā'â*, [C] to be brokenhearted, lose heart; [G] to dishearten, cause to lose heart, S: 3512, B: 456C, K: 418C, H: 149D

3875 כָּאֶה *kā'eh*, variant: disheartened, S: 2489†, B: 456C, K: 302B, H: 105C

3876 כַּאֲשֶׁר *ka'ašer*, variant: as, just as, because, S: 834†, B: 455B, K: 418D, H: 149D

3877 כָּבֵד¹ *kābēd¹*, [A] to be heavy; to be wealthy, honored, glorified; to be failing, dull; [C] to be glorified, honored, renowned; [D] to honor, glorify, reward; [E] to be honored; [G] to make heavy, make hard; [F] to make numerous; honor oneself, S: 3513, B: 457A, K: 418D, H: 150A

3878 כָּבֵד² *kābēd²*, heavy, severe, difficult, S: 3515, B: 458A, K: 419D, H: 150C

3879 כָּבֵד³ *kābēd³*, liver; heart, S: 3516, B: 458B, K: 420A, H: 150C

3880 כֹּבֶד *kōbed*, heaviness; heavy mass (density, piles), S: 3514, B: 458C, K: 420B, H: 150D

3881 כְּבֵדֻת *kᵉbēdut*, difficulty, awkwardness, S: 3517, B: 459C, K: 420B, H: 150D

3882 כָּבָה *kābâ*, [A] to be quenched, snuffed out; [D] to quench, put out, snuff out, S: 3518, B: 459C, K: 420B, H: 150D

3883 כָּבוֹד¹ *kābôd¹*, glory, honor, splendor, wealth, S: 3519, B: 458C, K: 420C, H: 150D

3884 כָּבוֹד² *kābôd²*, glorious, elegant, S: 3520†, B: 458C, K: 422A, H: 150D

3885 כְּבוּדָּה *kᵉbûddâ*, possession, valuable property, S: 3520, B: 459C, K: 422A, H: 151B

3886 כָּבוּל *kābûl*, Cabul, S: 3521, B: 459D, K: 422A, H: 151B

3887 כַּבּוֹן *kabbôn*, Cabbon, S: 3522, B: 460A, K: 422A, H: 151B

3888 כַּבִּיר *kabbîr*, great, mighty, S: 3524, B: 460B, K: 422A, H: 151B

3889 כָּבִיר *kābîr*, something braided, S: 3523, B: 460D, K: 422B, H: 151B

3890 כֶּבֶל *kebel*, shackles, fetters, S: 3525, B: 459D, K: 422B, H: 151B

3891 כָּבַס *kābas*, [A] (ptcp.) washer, fuller; [D] to wash, launder; [E] to be washed; [F] to be washed off, S: 3526, B: 460A, K: 422B, H: 151B

3892 כָּבַר *kābar*, [G] to multiply; provide in abundance, S: 3527 & 4342†, B: 460B, K: 422D, H: 151C

3893 כְּבָר¹ *kᵉbār¹*, already, before, S: 3528, B: 460C, K: 422D, H: 151C

3894 כְּבָר² *kᵉbār²*, Kebar, S: 3529, B: 460C, K: 422D, H: 151C

3895 כְּבָרָה¹ *kᵉbārâ¹*, sieve, S: 3531, B: 460D, K: 423A, H: 151C

3896 כִּבְרָה² *kᵉbārâ²*, (a certain) distance, S: 3530†, B: 460C, K: 423A, H: 151C

3897 כֶּבֶשׂ *kebeś*, ram-lamb, young ram sheep, S: 3532, B: 461A, K: 423A, H: 151C

3898 כִּבְשָׂה *kibśâ*, ewe-lamb, young female sheep, S: 3535, B: 461A, K: 423B, H: 151C

3899 כָּבַשׁ *kābaš*, [A] to subdue, overcome, enslave; [C] be subdued, be subject, be brought under control; [D] to subdue; [G] subdue, subjugate, S: 3533, B: 461B, K: 423B, H: 151C

3900 כֶּבֶשׁ *kebeš*, footstool, S: 3534, B: 461C, K: 423C, H: 151D

3901 כִּבְשָׁן *kibšān*, furnace, S: 3536, B: 461C, K: 423C, H: 151D

3902 כַּד *kad*, jar, pitcher, S: 3537, B: 461C, K: 423C, H: 151D

3903 כַּדּוּר *kaddûr*, variant: ball, S: 1754†, B: 462A, K: 423D, H: 151D

3904 כְּדֵי *kᵉdê*, variant: see 1896 & 3869, S: 1767†, B: 191C 2b, K: 423D, H: 151D

3905 כַּדְכֹּד *kadkōd*, ruby, S: 3539, B: 461D, K: 423D, H: 151D

3906 כְּדָרְלָעֹמֶר *kᵉdorlāʿōmer*, כְּדָר־לָעֹמֶר *kᵉdor-lāʿōmer*, Kedorlaomer, S: 3540, B: 462A, K: 423D, H: 152A

3907 כֹּה *kōh*, this is what, thus, S: 3541, B: 462A, K: 423D, H: 152A

3908 כָּהָה¹ *kāhâ¹*, [A] to grow dim, be weak; [D] to fade, become faint, S: 3543, B: 462C, K: 424B, H: 152A

3909 כָּהָה² *kāhâ²*, [D] to rebuke, set (someone) right, S: 3543, B: 462D, K: 424B, H: 152B

3910 כֵּהֶה *kēheh*, dull; weak; smoldering; despairing, S: 3544, B: 462D, K: 424C, H: 152B

3911 כֵּהָה *kēhâ*, healing, relief, S: 3545, B: 462D, K: 424C, H: 152B

3912 כָּהַן *kāhan*, [D] to serve as a priest, S: 3547, B: 464C, K: 424C, H: 152B

3913 כֹּהֵן *kōhēn*, priest, S: 3548, B: 463A, K: 424D, H: 152B

3914 כְּהֻנָּה *kᵉhunnâ*, priesthood, priestly office, S: 3550, B: 464D, K: 425C, H: 152C

3915 כּוּב *kûb*, variant: Kub, S: 3552, B: 464D, K: 425C, H: 152C

3916 כּוֹבַע *kôbaʿ*, helmet, S: 3553, B: 464D, K: 425D, H: 152C

3917 כָּוָה *kāwâ*, [C] to be burned, be scorched, S: 3554, B: 464D, K: 425D, H: 152D

3918 כְּוִיָּה *kᵉwiyyâ*, burn spot, scar (of a burn), S: 3555, B: 465A, K: 425D, H: 152D

3919 כּוֹכָב *kôkāb*, star, S: 3556, B: 456D, K: 426A, H: 152D

3920 כּוּל *kûl*, [A] to hold, seize; [D] to hold; to provide, supply, sustain; [G] to hold; to bear, endure, S: 3557, B: 465A, K: 426A, H: 152D

3921 כּוּמָז *kûmāz*, ornament, necklace, S: 3558, B: 484D, K: 426C, H: 153A

3922 כּוּן¹ *kûn¹*, [C] to be established, be steadfast, be firm, be prepared; [D] to establish, set in place, make secure; [E] to be made firm, be prepared; [G] to establish, make preparations, provide; [H] to be made ready, be established, be attached, S: 3559, B: 465C, K: 426C, H: 153A

3923 כּוּן² *kûn²*, Cun, S: 3560, B: 467B, K: 428B, H: 153D

3924 כַּוָּן *kawwān*, cake of bread (presented as an offering), S: 3561, B: 467D, K: 428B, H: 153D

3925 כּוֹנַנְיָהוּ *kônanyāhû*, variant: Conaniah, S: 3562, B: 467B, K: 428B, H: 153D

3926 כּוֹס¹ *kôs¹*, cup, S: 3563, B: 468A, K: 428B, H: 154A

3927 כּוֹס² *kôs²*, little owl, S: 3563, B: 468A, K: 428C, H: 154A

3928 כּוּר¹ *kûr¹*, variant: [A] to bore, dig, hew, S: 3738†, B: 468C, K: 454B, H: 164B

3929 כּוּר² *kûr²*, furnace (for smelting metals), S: 3564, B: 468B, K: 428D, H: 154A

3930 כּוֹר עָשָׁן *kôr ʿāšān*, variant: Kor Ashan, S: 3565, B: 468B, K: 428D, H: 154A

3931 כּוֹרֶשׁ *kôreš*, Cyrus, S: 3566, B: 468D, K: 428D, H: 154A

3932 כּוּשׁ¹ *kûš¹*, Cush, S: 3568, B: 468D, K: 429A, H: 154A

3933 כּוּשׁ² *kûš²*, Cush, S: 3568, B: 469A, K: 429B, H: 154A

3934 כּוּשִׁי¹ *kûšî¹*, Cushite, S: 3569 & 3571†, B: 469A, K: 458D, H: 154A

3935 כּוּשִׁי² *kûšî²*, Cushi, S: 3570, B: 469B, K: 429B, H: 154A

3936 כּוּשָׁן *kûšān*, Cushan, S: 3572, B: 469B, K: 429B, H: 154A

3937 כּוּשַׁן רִשְׁעָתַיִם *kûšan rišʿātayim*, Cushan-Rishathaim, S: 3573, B: 469B, K: 429B, H: 154A

3938 כּוֹשָׁרָה *kôšārâ*, singing *or* prosperity, fortune, S: 3574, B: 507A, K: 429C, H: 154A

3939 כּוּת *kût*, Cuthah, S: 3575, B: 469B, K: 429C, H: 154B

3940 כּוּתָה *kûtâ*, Cuthah, S: 3575, B: 469B, K: 429C, H: 154B

3941 כָּזַב *kāzab*, [A] to lie; [C] to be proven a liar, be false; [D] to lie, deceive, prove false; to fail; [G] to prove someone a liar, S: 3576, B: 469B, K: 429C, H: 154B

3942 כָּזָב *kāzāb*, lie, falsehood; delusion (false god), S: 3577, B: 469C, K: 429D, H: 154B

3943 כֹּזֵבָא *kōzēbāʾ*, Cozeba, S: 3578, B: 469D, K: 429D, H: 154C

3944 כָּזְבִּי *kozbî*, Cozbi, S: 3579, B: 469D, K: 430A, H: 154C

3945 כְּזִיב *kᵉzîb*, Kezib, S: 3580, B: 469D, K: 430A, H: 154C

3946 כֹּחַ¹ *kōaḥ¹*, strength, power, might, ability, S: 3581, B: 470C, K: 430A, H: 154C

3947 כֹּחַ² *kōaḥ²*, monitor lizard, S: 3581, B: 470A, K: 430C, H: 154C

3948 כָּחַד *kāḥad*, [C] to be hidden; be destroyed, perish; [D] to hide, conceal, keep from; [G] to hide; to destroy, annihilate, get rid of, S: 3582, B: 470B, K: 430C, H: 154C

3949 כָּחַל *kāḥal*, [A] to paint (eyes), S: 3583, B: 471A, K: 430D, H: 154D

3950 כָּחַשׁ *kāḥaš*, [A] to be thin; [C] to cringe, feign obedience; [D] to lie, deceive; fail; to cringe, feign obedience; [F] to cringe, feign obedience, S: 3584, B: 471A, K: 431A, H: 154D

3951 כַּחַשׁ *kaḥaš*, lie, deception; gauntness, thinness, leanness, S: 3585, B: 471C, K: 431B, H: 155A

3952 כֶּחָשׁ *keḥāš*, deceitful, untruthful, S: 3586, B: 471C, K: 431B, H: 155A

3953 כִּי¹ *kî¹*, branding, S: 3587, B: 465A, K: 431B, H: 155A

3954 כִּי² *kî²*, for, that, because, S: 3588, B: 471C, K: 431C, H: 155A

3955 כִּי־אִם *kî-ʾim*, variant: but, except, S: 3588 + 518†, B: 474C, K: 433A, H: 156A

3956 כִּי עַל כֵּן *kî ʿal kēn*, variant: forasmuch as, S: 3588 + 408 + 3651†, B: 475C, K: 432B, H: 155A

3957 כִּיד *kîd*, destruction, S: 3589, B: 475D, K: 433B, H: 156A

3958 כִּידוֹד *kîdôd*, spark, S: 3590, B: 461C, K: 433B, H: 156B

3959 כִּידוֹן *kîdôn*, javelin, lance, spear, S: 3591, B: 475D, K: 433C, H: 156B

3960 כִּידוֹר *kîdôr*, attack, battle, S: 3593, B: 461D, K: 433C, H: 156B

3961 כִּידֹן *kîdōn*, Kidon, S: 3592†, B: 475D, K: 433C, H: 156B

3962 כִּיּוּן *kiyyûn*, pedestal, S: 3594, B: 475D, K: 433C, H: 156B

3963 כִּיּוֹר *kiyyôr*, basin, pan, firepot, S: 3595, B: 468C, K: 433D, H: 156B

3964 כִּילַי *kîlay*, scoundrel, S: 3596, B: 647D, K: 433D, H: 156B

3965 כֵּילַפּוֹת *kêlappôt*, ax, S: 3597†, B: 476A, K: 433D, H: 156C

3966 כִּימָה *kîmâ*, Pleiades, S: 3598, B: 465B, K: 434A, H: 156C

3967 כִּיס *kîs*, bag, purse, S: 3599, B: 476A, K: 434A, H: 156C

3968 כִּיר *kîr*, cooking pot, stove, S: 3600, B: 468C, K: 434A, H: 156C

3969 כִּישׁוֹר *kîšôr*, distaff, spindle, S: 3601, B: 507A, K: 434B, H: 156C

3970 כָּכָה *kākâ*, this is what, this is how, thus, S: 3602, B: 462B, K: 434B, H: 156C

3971 כִּכָּר *kikkār*, plain (geographical area); loaf of bread; cover (of lead); talent (unit of weight or value), S: 3603, B: 503A, K: 434C, H: 156C

3972 כֹּל *kōl*, all, every; everyone, everything, S: 3605, B: 481A, K: 435A, H: 156D

3973 כָּלָא[1] *kālā'*[1], [A] to stop, withhold, contain; [B] to be confined; [C] to be restrained, S: 3607, B: 476B, K: 436B, H: 157C

3974 כָּלָא[2] *kālā'*[2], [D] to finish, S: 3607, B: 477B, K: 437B, H: 157C

3975 כֶּלֶא *kele'*, prison, (house of) imprisonment, S: 3608, B: 476C, K: 436C, H: 157D

3976 כִּלְאָב *kil'āb*, Kileab, S: 3609, B: 476D, K: 436C, H: 157D

3977 כִּלְאַיִם *kil'ayim*, (things of) two kinds, S: 3610, B: 476C, K: 436D, H: 157D

3978 כֶּלֶב *keleb*, dog; male prostitute, S: 3611, B: 476D, K: 436D, H: 157D

3979 כָּלֵב *kālēb*, Caleb, S: 3612, B: 477A, K: 437A, H: 158A

3980 כָּלֵב אֶפְרָתָה *kālēb 'eprātâ*, Caleb Ephrathah, S: 3613, B: 68D 2 & 477A, K: 80A, H: 25D & 158A

3981 כָּלִבּוֹ *kālibbiw*, variant: see 3982, S: 3612†, B: 477A, K: 437B, H: 158A

3982 כָּלִבִּי *kālibbî*, Calebite, S: 3614†, B: 477A, K: 437B, H: 158A

3983 כָּלָה[1] *kālâ*[1], [A] to finish, fulfill, complete; to fail, cease, perish; [D] to finish, complete, fulfill; to destroy, end, wipe out; [E] to be completed, be concluded, S: 3615, B: 477B, K: 437B, H: 158A

3984 כָּלָה[2] *kālâ*[2], variant: see 3973, S: 3607†, B: 476B, K: 438B, H: 158C

3985 כָּלֶה *kāleh*, variant: failing with desire, longing, S: 3616, B: 479A, K: 438B, H: 158C

3986 כָּלָה[3] *kālâ*[3], destruction, complete destruction, S: 3617, B: 478D, K: 438B, H: 158C

3987 כַּלָּה *kallâ*, (before marriage) bride; daughter-in-law, S: 3618, B: 483C, K: 438C, H: 158C

3988 כְּלֻהַי *k^{e}luhî*, Keluhi, S: 3622†, B: 479A, K: 438C, H: 158C

3989 כְּלוּא *k^{e}lû'*, imprisonment, S: 3628, B: 476C & 109A ae(2), K: 436C, H: 158C

3990 כְּלוּב[1] *k^{e}lûb*[1], (fruit) basket; (bird) cage, S: 3619, B: 477B, K: 438D, H: 158C

3991 כְּלוּב[2] *k^{e}lûb*[2], Kelub, S: 3620, B: 477B, K: 438D, H: 158C

3992 כְּלוּבָי *k^{e}lûbāy*, Caleb, S: 3621, B: 477B, K: 438D, H: 158C

3993 כְּלוּהוּ *k^{e}lûhû*, variant: Keluhu, S: 3622†, B: 479A, K: 438C, H: 158C

3994 כְּלוּלֹת *k^{e}lûlōt*, time of betrothal, state of betrothal, S: 3623†, B: 483C, K: 438D, H: 158C

3995 כֶּלַח[1] *kelah*[1], full vigor, S: 3624, B: 480C, K: 438D, H: 158C

3996 כֶּלַח[2] *kelaḥ*[2], Calah, S: 3625, B: 480D, K: 439A, H: 158C

3997 כָּל־חֹזֶה *kol-ḥōzeh*, Col-Hozeh, S: 3626, B: 480D, K: 439A, H: 158D

3998 כְּלִי *k^{e}lî*, article, utensil, thing, S: 3627, B: 479B, K: 439A, H: 158D

3999 כְּלִיא *k^{e}lî'*, variant: imprisonment, S: 3628, B: 476C, K: 439C, H: 159A

4000 כִּלְיָה *kilyâ*, kidney; inmost being: heart, mind, spirit; kernel (of wheat), S: 3629, B: 480B, K: 439D, H: 159A

4001 כִּלָּיוֹן *killāyôn*, destruction, annihilation; weariness, failure (of the eyes), S: 3631, B: 479A, K: 439D, H: 159A

4002 כִּלְיוֹן *kilyôn*, Kilion, S: 3630, B: 479A, K: 439D, H: 159A

4003 כָּלִיל *kālîl*, entire, whole, perfect; whole burnt offering, S: 3632, B: 483A, K: 440A, H: 159A

4004 כַּלְכֹּל *kalkōl*, Calcol, S: 3633, B: 465B, K: 440A, H: 159A

4005 כָּלַל *kālal*, [A] to bring to perfection, make complete, S: 3634, B: 480D, K: 440B, H: 159A

4006 כְּלָל *k^{e}lāl*, Kelal, S: 3636, B: 483C, K: 440B, H: 159A

4007 כָּלַם *kālam*, [C] to be disgraced, be humiliated, be put to shame; [G] to disgrace, humble, bring to shame; [H] to be mistreated, be despairing, S: 3637, B: 483C, K: 440B, H: 159B

4008 כִּלְמַד *kilmad*, Kilmad, S: 3638, B: 484B, K: 440C, H: 159B

4009 כְּלִמָּה *k^{e}limmâ*, disgrace, shame, scorn, S: 3639, B: 484A, K: 440D, H: 159B

4010 כְּלִמּוּת *k^{e}limmût*, shame, disgrace, insult, S: 3640, B: 484B, K: 440D, H: 159B

4011 כַּלְנֵה *kalnēh*, Calneh, S: 3641, B: 484C, K: 440D, H: 159B

4012 כַּלְנוֹ *kalnô*, Calno, S: 3641, B: 484C, K: 441A, H*

4013 ־כֶם *-kem*, you, your, S*, B*, K*, H*

4014 כָּמַהּ *kāmah*, [A] to long for, yearn for, S: 3642, B: 484C, K: 441A, H: 159B

4015 כַּמָּה *kammâ*, variant: why?, see 3869 & 4537, S: 3588 + 4100†, B: 553C 4c, K: 498A, H: 159C

4016 כִּמְהָם *kimhām*, Kimham, S: 3643, B: 484C, K: 441A, H: 159C

4017 כְּמוֹ *k^{e}mô*, like, as; for, with, when, S: 3644, B: 455D, K: 441B, H: 159C

4018 כִּמְוֹהָם *kimwhām*, variant: Kimuham, S: 3643†, B: 484C, K: 441C, H: 159C

4019 כְּמוֹשׁ *k^{e}môš*, Chemosh (pagan god), S: 3645, B: 484D, K: 441C, H: 159C

4020 כְּמִישׁ *k^{e}mîš*, variant: see 4019, S: 3645, B: 484D, K: 441D, H: 159C

4021 כַּמֹּן *kammōn*, cummin, S: 3646, B: 485A, K: 441D, H: 159C

4022 כָּמַס *kāmas*, [B] to be kept in reserve, S: 3647, B: 485A, K: 441D, H: 159C

4023 כָּמַר *kāmar*, [C] to become hot; become aroused, be excited (with compassion), S: 3648, B: 485A, K: 441D, H: 159C

4024 כֹּמֶר *kōmer*, pagan priest, priest of foreign gods, S: 3649†, B: 485C, K: 442A, H: 159C

4025 כִּמְרִיר *kamrîr*, blackness, deep gloom, S: 3650†, B: 485B, K: 442B, H: 159D

4026 כֵּן[1] *kēn*[1], honest; right, correct, orderly, S: 3651, B: 467A, K: 442B, H: 159D

4027 כֵּן[2] *kēn*[2], so, thus, S: 3651, B: 485D, K: 442C, H: 159D

4028 כֵּן[3] *kēn*[3], variant: which, S: 3651, B*, K*, H: 160A

4029 כֵּן[4] *kēn*[4], stand (of a basin), S: 3653, B: 487C, K: 443B, H: 160A

4030 כֵּן[5] *kēn*[5], position; place, S: 3653, B: 487C, K: 443B, H: 160A

4031 כֵּן[6] *kēn*[6], gnats, flies, S: 3654, B: 487D, K: 443B, H: 160A

4032 ־כֶן, ־כֶנָה *-ken, -kenâ*, you, your, S*, B*, K*, H*

4033 כָּנָה *kānâ*, [D] to bestow a title or name of honor; to flatter by giving a name of honor, S: 3655, B: 487B, K: 443B, H: 160A

4034 כַּנֵּה *kannēh*, Canneh, S: 3656†, B: 487C, K: 443C, H: 160A

4035 כַּנָּה *kannâ*, root, S: 3657, B: 488A, K: 443C, H: 160A

4036 כִּנּוֹר *kinnôr*, harp, lyre, lute, S: 3658, B: 490A, K: 443C, H: 160B

4037 כָּנְיָהוּ *konyāhû*, Jehoiachin, S: 3659, B: 220C, K: 443D, H: 160B

4038 כִּנָּם *kinnām*, gnats, S: 3654†, B: 487D, K: 443D, H: 160B

4039 כְּנָנִי *k^{e}nānî*, Kenani, S: 3662, B: 487D, K: 443D, H: 160B

4040 כְּנַנְיָה *k^{e}nanyâ*, Kenaniah, S: 3663, B: 487D, K: 443D, H: 160B

4041 כְּנַנְיָהוּ *k^{e}nanyāhû*, Kenaniah, S: 3663, B: 487D, K: 443D, H: 160B

4042 כָּנַנְיָהוּ *kānanyāhû*, Conaniah, S: 3663†, B: 467B, K: 428B, H: 153D

4043 כָּנַס *kānas*, [A, D] to assemble, gather, store up; [F] to wrap around, S: 3664, B: 488A, K: 443D, H: 160B

4044 כָּנַע *kāna'*, [C] to be humbled, be subdued, be subjected; [G] to subdue, humble, subject, S: 3665, B: 488B, K: 444A, H: 160B

4045 כִּנְעָה *kin'â*, bundle of belongings, S: 666, B: 488C, K: 444B, H: 160C

4046 כְּנַעַן[1] *k^{e}na'an*[1], Canaan; Canaanite, S: 3667, B: 488C, K: 444B, H: 160C

[F] Hitpael (hitpoel, hitpoal, hitpolel, hitpolal, hitpalel, hitpalal, hitpalpel, hitpalpal, hotpael, hotpaal) [G] Hiphil (hiphtil) [H] Hophal [I] Hishtaphel

4047 [2]כְּנַעַן *kᵉna'an*[2], merchant, trader, S: 3667, B: 488D, K: 444B, H: 160C

4048 כִּנְעָן *kin'ān*, trader, merchant, S: 3669†, B: 1124C, K: 445A, H: 160C

4049 כְּנַעֲנָה *kᵉna'ᵃnâ*, Kenaanah, S: 3668, B: 489B, K: 444D, H: 160C

4050 [1]כְּנַעֲנִי *kᵉna'ᵃnî*[1], Canaanite, of Canaan, in Canaan, S: 3669, B: 489A, K: 444D, H: 160C 1.

4051 [2]כְּנַעֲנִי *kᵉna'ᵃnî*[2], merchant, trader, S: 3669, B: 489B, K: 444D, H: 160C 2.

4052 כָּנַף *kānap*, [C] to hide oneself, be hidden, S: 3670, B: 489D, K: 445A, H: 160C

4053 כָּנָף *kānāp*, wing (of creatures that fly); corner, hem (of garment); ends (of the earth), S: 3671, B: 489B, K: 445B, H: 160C

4054 כִּנְרוֹת *kinrôt*, כִּנֲּרוֹת *kinᵃrôt*, Kinnereth, S: 3672, B: 490B, K: 445D, H: 160D

4055 כִּנֶּרֶת *kinneret*, Kinnereth, S: 3672, B: 490B, K: 445D, H: 160D

4056 כְּנָת *kᵉnāt*, associate, companion, S: 3674, B: 490C, K: 446A, H: 160D

4057 כֶּסֶא *kese'*, full moon, S: 3677, B: 490C, K: 446A, H: 160D

4058 כִּסֵּא *kissē'*, throne, seat, chair, place of authority, S: 3676† & 3678, B: 490A, K: 446A, H: 160D

4059 כָּסָה *kāsâ*, [B] to be covered; [C] to be covered; [D] to cover, conceal; to decorate; to overwhelm; [E] to be covered, be shrouded; [F] to cover oneself, put on clothing, S: 3680, B: 491B, K: 446C, H: 161A

4060 כֵּסֶה *kēseh*, variant: full moon, S: 3677†, B: 490C, K: 446A, H: 161B

4061 כִּסֵּה *kissēh*, variant: see 4057, S: 3678, B: 490C, K: 446A, H: 161B

4062 כָּסוּי *kāsûy*, covering, S: 3681, B: 492B, K: 447B, H: 161C

4063 כְּסוּלּוֹת *kᵉsûlôt*, Kesulloth, S: 3694, B: 493B, K: 448A, H: 161C

4064 כְּסוּת *kᵉsût*, covering, cloak, clothing, S: 3682, B: 492B, K: 447B, H: 161C

4065 כָּסַח *kāsaḥ*, [B] to be cut down (of brush), S: 3683, B: 492D, K: 447B, H: 161C

4066 כֵּסְיָה *kēsyāh*, variant: see 3363 & 4058, S: 3678† + 3050†, B: 490D 1b, K: 447B, H: 161C

4067 [1]כְּסִיל *kᵉsîl*[1], foolish, stupid, insolent; (as noun) fool, insolent person, S: 3684, B: 493A, K: 447C, H: 161C

4068 [2]כְּסִיל *kᵉsîl*[2], Orion (and its adjoining constellations), S: 3685, B: 493A, K: 447C, H: 161C

4069 [3]כְּסִיל *kᵉsîl*[3], Kesil, S: 3686, B: 493B, K: 447C, H: 161C

4070 כְּסִילוּת *kᵉsîlût*, folly, stupidity, insolence, S: 3687, B: 493A, K: 447C, H: 161C

4071 כָּסַל *kāsal*, [A] to be foolish, be stupid, S: 3688, B: 492D, K: 447C, H: 161D

4072 [1]כֶּסֶל *kesel*[1], waist, back; (pl.) loins, S: 3689, B: 492D, K: 447D, H: 161D

4073 [2]כֶּסֶל *kesel*[2], trust, confidence; stupidity, S: 3689, B: 492D, K: 447D, H: 161D

4074 כִּסְלָה *kislâ*, confidence; folly, S: 3690†, B: 493A, K: 447D, H: 161D

4075 כִּסְלֵו *kislēw*, Kislev, S: 3691, B: 493B, K: 447D, H: 161D

4076 כְּסָלוֹן *kᵉsālôn*, Kesalon, S: 3693, B: 493B, K: 448A, H: 161D

4077 כִּסְלוֹן *kislôn*, Kislon, S: 3692, B: 493B, K: 448A, H: 161D

4078 כַּסְלֻחִים *kasluḥîm*, Casluhite, S: 3695, B: 493B, K: 448A, H: 161D

4079 כִּסְלֹת תָּבֹר *kislōt tābôr*, Kisloth Tabor, S: 3696, B: 493B & 1061D 3, K: 448A, H: 161D

4080 כָּסַם *kāsam*, [A] to trip, clip (hair), S: 3697, B: 493C, K: 448A, H: 161D

4081 כֻּסֶּמֶת *kussemet*, spelt, emmer wheat, S: 3698, B: 493C, K: 448B, H: 161D

4082 כָּסַס *kāsas*, [A] to determine, reckon, compute, S: 3699, B: 493C, K: 448B, H: 162A

4083 כָּסַף *kāsap*, [A] to long for; be hungry; [C] to long for, yearn for; to be ashamed, S: 3700, B: 493D, K: 448B, H: 162A

4084 כֶּסֶף *kesep*, silver, money, S: 3701, B: 494A, K: 448C, H: 162A

4085 כָּסִפְיָא *kāsipyā'*, Casiphia, S: 3703, B: 494D, K: 449A, H: 162A

4086 כֶּסֶת *keset*, magic charm band, S: 3704, B: 492C, K: 449A, H: 162A

4087 כָּעַס *kā'as*, [A] to be angry, be vexed, be incensed; [D] to anger, provoke; [G] to provoke to anger, S: 3707, B: 494D, K: 449A, H: 162B

4088 כַּעַס *ka'as*, sorrow, grief, anxiety; anger, displeasure, annoyance, S: 3708, B: 495B, K: 449B, H: 162B

4089 כַּעַשׂ *ka'aś*, anguish, grief; anger, resentment, S: 3708, B: 495B, K: 449B, H: 162C

4090 כַּף *kap*, hand (or paw), palm of the hand, sole of the foot; (something hollowed) socket; dish, S: 3709, B: 496A, K: 449C, H: 162C

4091 כֵּף *kēp*, rock, S: 3710, B: 495B, K: 450B, H: 162D

4092 כָּפָה *kāpâ*, [A] to soothe, avert (anger), S: 3711, B: 495C, K: 450B, H: 162D

4093 כִּפָּה *kippâ*, palm branch, palm frond, S: 3712, B: 497A, K: 450C, H: 162D

4094 [1]כְּפוֹר *kᵉpôr*[1], bowl, dish (made of gold or silver), S: 3713, B: 499B, K: 450C, H: 162D

4095 [2]כְּפוֹר *kᵉpôr*[2], frost, S: 3713, B: 499B, K: 450C, H: 163A

4096 כָּפִיס *kāpîs*, beam (of woodwork), S: 3714, B: 496A, K: 450C, H: 163A

4097 כְּפִיר *kᵉpîr*, young lion, S: 3715, B: 498D, K: 450C, H: 163A

4098 כְּפִירָה *kᵉpîrâ*, Kephirah, S: 3716, B: 499A, K: 450D, H: 163A

4099 כְּפִירִים *kᵉpîrîm*, villages, S: 3715†, B: 499A, K: 452D, H: 163A

4100 כָּפַל *kāpal*, [A] to fold double; [B] to be folded double; [C] to be doubled, S: 3717, B: 495C, K: 450D, H: 163A

4101 כֶּפֶל *kepel*, double; two sides, S: 3718, B: 495C, K: 451A, H: 163A

4102 כָּפַן *kāpan*, [A] to hunger, send out roots in hunger, S: 3719, B: 495D, K: 451A, H: 163A

4103 כָּפָן *kāpān*, hunger, famine, S: 3720, B: 495D, K: 451A, H: 163A

4104 כָּפַף *kāpap*, [A] to bow down in distress; [B] be bowed down; [C] bow down (before), S: 3721, B: 496A, K: 451B, H: 163A

4105 [1]כָּפַר *kāpar*[1], [Nitpael] to be atoned (for); [D] to make atonement; make amends, pardon, release, appease, forgive; [E] to be atoned for, be annulled; [F] to allow for atonement, S: 3722, B: 497B, K: 451B, H: 163A

4106 [2]כָּפַר *kāpar*[2], [A] to coat, cover (with pitch), S: 3722, B: 498D, K: 451B, H: 163A

4107 כָּפָר *kāpār*, (unwalled) village, S: 3723, B: 499A, K: 452D, H: 163D

4108 [1]כֹּפֶר *kōper*[1], (unwalled) village, S: 3724, B: 499A, K: 452D, H: 163D

4109 [2]כֹּפֶר *kōper*[2], pitch (to seal the ark of Noah), S: 3724, B: 498D, K: 453A, H: 163D

4110 [3]כֹּפֶר *kōper*[3], henna, henna blossom, S: 3724, B: 499A, K: 453A, H: 163D

4111 [4]כֹּפֶר *kōper*[4], ransom, compensation, payment; bribe, S: 3724, B: 497A, K: 453A, H: 163D

4112 כְּפַר הָעַמֹּנִי *kᵉpar hā'ammōnî*, Kephar Ammoni, S: 3726, B: 499A, K: 714C, H: 163D

4113 כִּפֻּרִים *kippurîm*, atonement, S: 3725†, B: 498C, K: 453B, H: 163D

4114 כַּפֹּרֶת *kappōret*, atonement cover, S: 3727, B: 498C, K: 453B, H: 163D

4115 כָּפַשׁ *kāpaš*, [G] to trample down, S: 3728, B: 499B, K: 453B, H: 164A

4116 [1]כַּפְתּוֹר *kaptôr*[1], Caphtor, S: 3731, B: 499C, K: 453C, H: 164A

4117 [2]כַּפְתּוֹר *kaptôr*[2], bud; top of a pillar or column, S: 3730, B: 499B, K: 453C, H: 164A

4118 כַּפְתֹּרִי *kaptôrî*, Caphtorite, S: 3732, B: 499C, K: 453C, H: 164A

4119 [1]כַּר *kar*[1], ram-lamb, (young) ram; battering ram, S: 3733, B: 503A, K: 453D, H: 164A

4120 [2]כַּר *kar*[2], meadow, pastureland, S: 3733, B: 499C, K: 453D, H: 164A

4121 [3]כַּר *kar*[3], saddle, saddle-bag, S: 3733, B: 468B, K: 453D, H: 164A

4122 כָּר *kār*, variant: Car, S: 1033†, B: 111D, K: 124D 20., H: 39B 22.

4123 כֹּר *kōr*, cor (measure), S: 3734, B: 499D, K: 453D, H: 164A

4124 כִּרְבֵּל *kirbēl*, [E] to be clothed, be wrapped, S: 3736, B: 499D, K: 454A, H: 164A

4125 [1]כָּרָה *kārā*[1], [A] to dig; to hew (stone); to hollow out, S: 3738, B: 500A, K: 454A, H: 164A

4126 [2]כָּרָה *kārâ*[2], [A] to barter; purchase, S: 3739, B: 500B, K: 454B, H: 164B

4127 [3]כָּרָה *kārâ*[3], [A] to prepare a feast, S: 3738, B: 500B, K: 454B, H: 164B

4128 [4]כָּרָה *kārâ*[4], variant: [A] to tie together, S: 3738†, B: 500B & 468C, K: 454B, H: 164B

4129 [5]כָּרָה *kārâ*[5], variant: cistern, well, S: 3741, B: 500B, K*, H*

4130 כֵּרָה *kērâ*, feast, banquet, S: 3740, B: 500C, K: 454B, H: 164B

4131 [1]כְּרוּב *k^{e}rûb*[1], cherub, (pl.) cherubim, S: 3742, B: 500C, K: 454C, H: 164B

4132 [2]כְּרוּב *k^{e}rûb*[2], Kerub, S: 3743, B: 500C, K: 454D, H: 164B

4133 כָּרִי *kārî*, Carite, S: 3746, B: 501B, K: 454D, H: 164B

4134 כְּרִית *k^{e}rît*, Kerith, S: 3747, B: 504D, K: 454D, H: 164C

4135 כְּרִיתוּת *k^{e}rîtût*, divorce, S: 3748, B: 504D, K: 454D, H: 164C

4136 כַּרְכֹּב *karkōb*, ledge, rim, edge, S: 3749, B: 501B, K: 455A, H: 164C

4137 כַּרְכֹּם *karkōm*, saffron (plant), S: 3750, B: 501B, K: 455A, H: 164C

4138 כַּרְכְּמִישׁ *kark^{e}mîš*, Carchemish, S: 3751, B: 501C, K: 455A, H: 164C

4139 כַּרְכַּס *karkas*, Carcas, S: 3752, B: 501C, K: 455A, H: 164C

4140 כִּרְכָּרָה *kirkārâ*, (fast running) female camel, S: 3753, B: 503A, K: 455A, H: 164C

4141 כָּרַם *kāram*, variant: [A] to tend a vineyard, S: 3755†, B*, K*, H*

4142 [1]כֶּרֶם *kerem*[1], vineyard, S: 3754, B: 501C, K: 455B, H: 164C

4143 [2]כֶּרֶם *kerem*[2], variant: Kerem, S*, B*, K*, H: 164C

4144 כֹּרֵם *kōrēm*, worker in the vineyard, vine growers, vinedressers, S: 3755, B: 501D, K: 455C, H: 164C

4145 [1]כַּרְמִי *karmî*[1], Carmi, S: 3756, B: 501D, K: 455C, H: 164C 1.

4146 [2]כַּרְמִי *karmî*[2], Carmite, S: 3757, B: 502A, K: 455C, H: 164C 2.

4147 כַּרְמִיל *karmîl*, crimson (yarn), S: 3758, B: 502B, K: 455C, H: 164D

4148 כְּרָמִים *k^{e}rāmîm*, variant: Keramim, S: 3754†, B: 6A 4., K: 6C 3., H: 2C & 164C

4149 [1]כַּרְמֶל *karmel*[1], fertile land, fruitful land, S: 3759, B: 502A, K: 455C, H: 164D

4150 [2]כַּרְמֶל *karmel*[2], Carmel (city), S: 3760, B: 502A, K: 455D, H: 164D

4151 [3]כַּרְמֶל *karmel*[3], Carmel (hill), S: 3760, B: 502A 1, K: 455D, H: 164D

4152 [4]כַּרְמֶל *karmel*[4], new grain, newly ripe grain, S: 3759, B: 502A 2., K: 455D, H: 164D

4153 כַּרְמְלִי *karm^{e}lî*, Carmelite, of Carmel, S: 3761 & 3762†, B: 502B, K: 456A, H: 164D

4154 כְּרָן *k^{e}rān*, Keran, S: 3763, B: 502B, K: 456A, H: 164D

4155 כִּרְסֵם *kirsēm*, [D] to ravage, eat away, S: 3765, B: 493C, K: 456A, H: 164D

4156 כָּרַע *kāra'*, [A] to kneel down, crouch; [G] to make bow down, make kneel, make miserable, S: 3766, B: 502C, K: 456A, H: 165A

4157 כְּרַע *kera'*, leg bone (the shank bone, between the knee and ankle), S: 3767†, B: 502D, K: 456C, H: 165A

4158 כַּרְפַּס *karpas*, (fine) linen, S: 3768, B: 502D, K: 456C, H: 165A

4159 כָּרַר *kārar*, [D] to dance, S: 3769, B: 502D, K: 456C, H: 165A

4160 כָּרֵשׂ *kārēś*, stomach, belly, S: 3770†, B: 503C, K: 456D, H: 165A

4161 כַּרְשְׁנָא *karš^{e}nā'*, Carshena, S: 3771, B: 503C, K: 456D, H: 165A

4162 כָּרַת *kārat*, [A] to cut off, cut down; to make (a covenant, agreement); [B] to be cut off, broken off; [C] to be cut off, be destroyed; [E] to be cut down; [G] to cut off, get rid of, destroy, kill; [H] to be cut off, S: 3772, B: 503C, K: 456D, H: 165A

4163 כְּרֹת *k^{e}rōt*, variant: see 4165, S*, B: 504D, K: 458A, H: 165D

4164 כְּרֻתוֹת *k^{e}rutôt*, beams (trimmed and cut), S: 3773†, B: 503D 3, K: 458A, H: 165D

4165 כְּרֵתִי *k^{e}rētî*, Kerethite, S: 3774, B: 504D, K: 458A, H: 165D

4166 כֶּשֶׂב *keśeb*, ram-lamb, young sheep, S: 3775, B: 461A, K: 458B, H: 165D

4167 כִּשְׂבָּה *kiśbâ*, ewe-lamb, young sheep, S: 3776, B: 461B, K: 458B, H: 165D

4168 כֶּשֶׂד *keśed*, Kesed, S: 3777, B: 505A, K: 458B, H: 165D

4169 כַּשְׂדִּים *kaśdîm*, Chaldean, Babylonian, astrologers, S: 3778†, B: 505A, K: 458B, H: 165D

4170 כָּשָׂה *kāśâ*, [A] to become sleek, heavy; stubborn, S: 3780, B: 505B, K: 458C, H: 166A

4171 כָּשַׁח *kāšaḥ*, variant: [A] to become lame, crippled, S: 7911†, B: 1013A 1b, K: 458D, H: 166A

4172 כַּשִּׁיל *kaššîl*, axe, S: 3781, B: 506A, K: 459A, H: 166A

4173 כָּשַׁל *kāšal*, [A] to stumble, falter, fail; [C] to be caused to stumble, be brought down; [G] to cause to stumble, overthrow, bring to ruin; [H] to be overthrown, S: 3782, B: 505B, K: 459A, H: 166A

4174 כִּשָּׁלוֹן *kiššālôn*, falling down, stumbling, S: 3783, B: 506A, K: 459C, H: 166A

4175 כָּשַׁף *kāšap*, [D] to engage in witchcraft, be a sorcerer, S: 3784, B: 506C, K: 459C, H: 166B

4176 כֶּשֶׁף *kešep*, witchcraft, sorcery, S: 3785, B: 506C, K: 459C, H: 166B

4177 כַּשָּׁף *kaššāp*, sorcerer, S: 3786, B: 506C, K: 459C, H: 166B

4178 כָּשֵׁר *kāšēr*, [A] to be right, successful; [G] to bring success, S: 3787, B: 506D, K: 459C, H: 166B

4179 כִּשְׁרוֹן *kišrôn*, skill, achievement; benefit, S: 3788, B: 507A, K: 459D, H: 166B

4180 כָּתַב *kātab*, [A] to write, engrave (on stone tablets); [B] to be written, be inscribed; [C] to be written down, be listed, be recorded; [D] to issue a written statement, S: 3789, B: 507A, K: 459D, H: 166C

4181 כְּתָב *k^{e}tāb*, writing: script, text, records, book, S: 3791†, B: 508B, K: 460D, H: 166D

4182 כְּתֹבֶת *k^{e}tōbet*, tattoo mark, S: 3793, B: 508B, K: 460D, H: 166D

4183 כִּתִּיִּים *kittiyyîm*, Kittim, Cyprus; western coastlands, S: 3794†, B: 508C, K: 460D, H: 166D

4184 כָּתִית *kātît*, beaten or pressed olives, S: 3795, B: 510C, K: 461A, H: 167A

4185 כֹּתֶל *kōtel*, wall (of a house), S: 3796, B: 508C, K: 461A, H: 167A

4186 כִּתְלִישׁ *kitlîš*, Kitlish, S: 3798, B: 508C, K: 461A, H: 167A

4187 כָּתַם *kātam*, [C] to be stained, be defiled, S: 3799, B: 508D, K: 461A, H: 167A

4188 כֶּתֶם *ketem*, gold, pure gold, S: 3800, B: 508D, K: 461B, H: 167A

4189 כֻּתֹּנֶת *kuttōnet*, garment, robe, tunic, S: 3801, B: 509A, K: 461B, H: 167A

4190 כָּתֵף *kātēp*, shoulder, shoulder piece; slope, side, wall, S: 3802, B: 509B, K: 461C, H: 167B

4191 כְּתֹף *k^{e}tōp*, variant: see 3869 & 9512, S: 8596†, B: 1074B, K: 1036C, H: 167C

4192 [1]כָּתַר *kātar*[1], [D] to bear with, have patience with, S: 3803, B: 509C, K: 462A, H: 167C

4193 [2]כָּתַר *kātar*[2], [D] to surround, encircle; [G] to gather about; hem in, S: 3803, B: 509C, K: 462A, H: 167C

4194 [3]כָּתַר *kātar*[3], [G] to crown, wear as a headdress, S: 3803, B: 509C, K: 462A, H: 167C

4195 כֶּתֶר *keter*, crown, royal headdress, crest, S: 3804, B: 509D, K: 462B, H: 167C

4196 כֹּתֶרֶת *kōteret*, capital (of a pillar or column), S: 3805, B: 509D, K: 462B, H: 167C

4197 כָּתַשׁ *kātaš*, [A] to grind, pound (in a mortar), S: 3806, B: 509D, K: 462C, H: 167C

4198 כָּתַת *kātat*, [A] to crush, beat; [B] to be crushed, be shattered; [D] to beat, crush, break to pieces; [E] to be crushed; [G] to beat down; [H] to be battered to pieces, S: 3807, B: 510A, K: 462C, H: 167D

4199 ל *l*, letter of the Hebrew alphabet, S*, B: 510B, K: 462B, H*

4200 [1]לְ- *l^{e}-1*, to, toward; in, through; before, at, with; by means of, S*, B: 510A, K: 462B, H: 167B

4201 [2]לְ- *l^{e}-2*, variant: emphatic, vocative prefix, S*, B: 510A, K: 462B, H: 169D

4202 לֹא *lō'*, no, not, S: 3808, B: 518B, K: 466B, H: 170A

4203 לֹא דְבָר ,לוֹ דְבָר ,לִדְבִר *lō' d^{e}bār*, Lo Debar, S: 3810, B: 520D, K: 467D, H: 170D

4204 לֹא עַמִּי *lō' 'ammî*, Lo-Ammi, S: 3818, B: 520D, K: 468D, H: 171B

4205 לֹא רֻחָמָה *lō' ruḥāmâ*, Lo-Ruhamah, S: 3819, B: 520D, K: 468D, H: 171B

4206 לָאָה *lā'â*, [A] to be weary; [C] to wear oneself out, be weary; [G] to wear someone out, try one's patience, frustrate, S: 3811, B: 521A, K: 468A, H: 170D

4207 לֵאָה *lē'â*, Leah, S: 3812, B: 521B, K: 468B, H: 171A

4208 לָאז *lā'z*, variant: see 262, S: 1975†, B: 229C, K: 468B, H: 171A

4209 לָאט *lā'aṭ*, variant: [A] to cover, S: 3813, B: 521B, K: 476D, H: 171A

4210 לָאֵל *lā'ēl*, Lael, S: 3815, B: 522B, K: 468C, H: 171B

4211 לְאֹם *le'ōm*, people, nation, S: 3816, B: 522C, K: 468C, H: 171B

4212 לְאֻמִּים *le'ummîm*, Leummite, S: 3817, B: 522C, K: 468C, H: 171B

4213 לֵב *lēb*, heart; thus conscience, courage, mind, understanding, S: 3820, B: 524B, K: 468D, H: 171B

4214 לֵב קָמָי *lēb qāmāy*, Leb Kamai, S: 3820 + 6965, B: 525D, K: 470D, H: 173A & 172A 13.

4215 לָבֹא *lābō'*, variant: entrance, see 4217, S: 935†, B: 333A, K: 470D, H: 172A

4216 לְבֶא *lebe'*, lion, S: 3833†, B: 522B, K: 470D, H: 172A

4217 לְבֹא חֲמָת *lebō' ḥamāt*, Lebo Hamath, S: 2574†, B: 333A, K: 470D, H: 109D

4218 לִבְאָה *lib'â*, lioness, S: 3833†, B: 522D, K: 470D, H: 172B

4219 לְבָאוֹת *lebā'ôt*, Lebaoth, S: 3822, B: 522D, K: 471A, H: 172B

4220 לָבַב¹ *lābab¹*, [C] to be made wise, be made intelligent; [D] to steal one's heart (from a lover's glance), S: 3823, B: 525D, K: 471A, H: 172B

4221 לָבַב² *lābab²*, [D] to make special bread (heart-shaped?), S: 3823, B: 525D, K: 471A, H: 172B

4222 לֵבָב *lēbāb*, heart; thus conscience, courage, mind, understanding, S: 3824, B: 523A, K: 471A, H: 172B

4223 לְבִבָה *lebibâ*, special bread (heart-shaped?), S: 3834, B: 525D, K: 471B, H: 172B

4224 לְבַד *lebad*, variant: alone, see 963 & 4200, S: 905†, B: 94C, K: 471B, H: 172B

4225 לַבָּה *labbâ*, flame, S: 3827, B: 529B, K: 471C, H: 172C

4226 לִבָּה *libbâ*, rage, S: 3826, B: 525D, K: 471C, H: 172C

4227 לְבוֹנָה¹ *lebônâ¹*, variant: frankincense, S: 3828†, B: 526C, K: 473A, H: 172C

4228 לְבוֹנָה² *lebônâ²*, Lebonah, S: 3829, B: 526D, K: 471C, H: 172C

4229 לָבוּשׁ *lābûš*, clothing, garments, S: 3830†, B: 528C, K: 471C, H: 172C

4230 לְבוּשׁ *lebûš*, clothing, garment, robe, S: 3830, B: 528C, K: 471C, H: 172C

4231 לָבַט *lābaṭ*, [C] to come to ruin, be trampled, S: 3832, B: 526A, K: 471D, H: 172C

4232 לְבִי *lebî*, variant: lion, S: 3833†, B: 522D, K: 470D, H: 172A & 172B

4233 לָבִיא *lābî'*, lion, lioness, S: 3833, B: 522D, K: 472A, H: 172C

4234 לְבִיָּא *lebiyyā'*, lioness, S: 3833, B: 522D, K: 472A, H: 172C

4235 לָבַן¹ *lāban¹*, [G] to make white, be whitened; [F] to show oneself spotless, purified, S: 3835, B: 526A, K: 472A, H: 172C

4236 לָבַן² *lāban²*, [A] to make bricks, S: 3835, B: 527C, K: 472B, H: 172D

4237 לָבָן¹ *lābān¹*, white, S: 3836, B: 526B, K: 472B, H: 172D

4238 לָבָן² *lābān²*, Laban, S: 3837, B: 526C, K: 472C, H: 172D

4239 לָבָן³ *lābān³*, Laban, S: 3837, B: 526C, K: 472C, H: 172D

4240 לַבֵּן *labbēn*, variant: of the son [?], S: 4192†, B: 527C, K: 462B & 221A & 133A, H: 167B & 75B & 42A

4241 לְבָנָהא *lebānāh'*, variant: Lebana, see 4245, S: 3838, B: 526C, K*, H*

4242 לִבְנֶה *libneh*, poplar tree, S: 3839, B: 527B, K: 472C, H: 172D

4243 לִבְנָה *libnâ*, Libnah, S: 3841, B: 526C, K: 472C, H: 172D

4244 לְבָנָה¹ *lebānâ¹*, bright (full) moon, S: 3842, B: 526B, K: 472D, H: 172D

4245 לְבָנָה² *lebānâ²*, Lebanah; Lebana, S: 3838, B: 526C, K: 472D, H: 172D

4246 לְבֵנָה *lebēnâ*, brick; tablet, S: 3840† & 3843, B: 527B, K: 472D, H: 172D

4247 לְבֹנָה *lebōnâ*, frankincense, S: 3828, B: 526C, K: 473A, H: 173A

4248 לְבָנוֹן *lebānôn*, Lebanon, S: 3844, B: 526D, K: 473A, H: 173A

4249 לִבְנִי¹ *libnî¹*, Libni, S: 3845, B: 526D, K: 473C, H: 173A

4250 לִבְנִי² *libnî²*, Libnite, S: 3846, B: 526D, K: 473C, H: 173A

4251 לִבְנָת *libnāt*, variant: Libnath, see 8866, S: 7884†, B: 1009D, K: 473C, H: 173A

4252 לָבַשׁ *lābaš*, [A] to put on clothing, dress, clothe; [B] to be dressed; [E] to be dressed; [G] to dress another, clothe someone, S: 3847, B: 527D, K: 473C, H: 173A

4253 לֹג *lōg*, log (liquid measure), S: 3849, B: 528D, K: 474A, H: 173B

4254 לֹד *lōd*, Lod, S: 3850, B: 528D, K: 474B, H: 173B

4255 לִדְבִר *lidbir*, variant: Lidbir, see 1810 & 4200, S: 1688†, B: 529A, K: 474B, H: 173B

4256 לֵדָה *lēdâ*, delivery (of birth), S: 3205†, B: 408B, K: 474B, H: 173B

4257 לֹה *lōh*, variant: not, S: 3808, B: 520B 4b(beta), K: 474B, H: 173C

4258 לַהַב *lahab*, flame of fire; flash (of a blade), S: 3851, B: 529A, K: 474C, H: 173C

4259 לֶהָבָה *lehābâ*, flame, blaze, flash; (iron) point (of a blade), S: 3852, B: 529B, K: 474C, H: 173C

4260 לְהָבִים *lehābîm*, Lehabite, S: 3853, B: 529C, K: 474C, H: 173C

4261 לַהַג *lahag*, study, devotion to books, S: 3854, B: 529C, K: 474D, H: 173C

4262 לַהַד *lāhad*, Lahad, S: 3855, B: 529C, K: 474D, H: 173C

4263 לָהַהּ *lāhah*, [F] to behave like a madman, S: 3856, B: 529C, K: 474D, H: 173C

4264 לָהָה *lāhâ*, variant: [A] to languish, faint, S: 3856†, B: 529C, K: 382C, H: 173C

4265 לָהַט¹ *lāhaṭ¹*, [A] to burn, flame; [D] to set afire, set ablaze, consume, S: 3857, B: 529D, K: 474D, H: 173C

4266 לָהַט² *lāhaṭ²*, [A] to devour; (as noun) ravenous beast, S: 3857, B: 529C, K: 474D, H: 173D

4267 לַהַט *lahaṭ*, flame, S: 3858, B: 529D, K: 475A, H: 173D

4268 לְהָטִים *lehāṭîm*, secret arts, sorceries, S: 3858†, B: 532B 2, K: 475A, H: 173D

4269 לָהַם *lāham*, [F] to let oneself swallow greedily; (ptcp.) choice morsels, S: 3859, B: 529D, K: 475A, H: 173D

4270 לָהֵן *lāhēn*, variant: therefore, S: 3860, B: 530A, K: 475A, H: 173D

4271 לְהִלֵהַּ *lihlēah*, variant: [F] to amaze, startle; (as noun) madman, S: 3856†, B: 529C, K: 474D, H: 173C

4272 לַהֲקָה *lahaqâ*, group, community, S: 3862, B: 530A, K: 475B, H: 173D

4273 לוּ *lû*, if! if only!; O that!, S: 3863, B: 530A, K: 475B, H: 174A

4274 לוֹ דְבָר *lô debār*, Lo Debar, S: 3810, B: 520D, K: 475D, H: 174A

4275 לוּב *lûb*, Libya, Libyan, S: 3864†, B: 530C, K: 475C, H: 174A

4276 לוּד *lûd*, Lud, Ludite; Lydia, Lydians, S: 3865 & 3866†, B: 530D, K: 475C, H: 174D

4277 לָוָה¹ *lāwâ¹*, [A] to accompany; [C] to be joined, be attached, be bound to, S: 3867, B: 530D, K: 475D, H: 174A

4278 לָוָה² *lāwâ²*, [A] to borrow; [G] to lend, S: 3867, B: 531A, K: 476A, H: 174B

4279 לוּז¹ *lûz¹*, [A] to depart (from one's sight); [C] to be devious, be perverse, be deceitful; [G] to depart (from one's sight), S: 3868, B: 531B, K: 476A, H: 174B

4280 לוּז² *lûz²*, almond tree (branch), S: 3869, B: 531C, K: 476B, H: 174B

4281 לוּז³ *lûz³*, Luz, S: 3870, B: 531C, K: 476B, H: 174B

4282 לוּזָה *lûzâ*, variant: Luzah, see 4281, S*, B: 531C, K: 476B, H: 174B

4283 לוּחַ *lûaḥ*, tablets (of stone); board, panel (of wood), S: 3871, B: 531D, K: 476B, H: 174C

4284 לוּחִית *lûḥît*, Luhith, S: 3872, B: 532A, K: 476C, H: 174C & 175B

4285 לוֹחֵשׁ *lôḥēš*, variant: Lohesh, see 2135, S: 3873, B: 538A, K: 476C, H: 174C

4286 לוּט *lûṭ*, [A] to cover, enfold; [B] to be wrapped up; [G] to cover, wrap up, S: 3874, B: 532A, K: 476C, H: 174C

4287 לוֹט¹ *lôṭ¹*, shroud, covering, S: 3875, B: 532B, K: 476D, H: 174C

4288 לוֹט² *lôṭ²*, Lot, S: 3876, B: 532B, K: 476D, H: 174C

4289 לוֹטָן *lôṭān*, Lotan, S: 3877, B: 532B, K: 476D, H: 174C

4290 לֵוִי¹ *lēwî¹*, Levi; Levite, S: 3878, B: 532B, K: 476D, H: 174C 1.

4291 לֵוִי² *lēwî²*, Levite, of Levi, S: 3878 & 3881†, B: 532D, K: 476D, H: 174C 2-4

4292 לִוְיָה *liwyâ*, garland, wreath, S: 3880, B: 531A, K: 477C, H: 174C

4293 לִוְיָתָן *liwyātān*, Leviathan, sea-monster, S: 3882, B: 531B, K: 477C, H: 174D

4294 לוּל *lûl*, stairway, S: 3883, B: 533B, K: 477C, H: 174D

4295 לוּלֵא *lûlē'*, if not, unless, S: 3884, B: 530B, K: 477C, H: 174D

4296 לוּן *lûn*, [C] to grumble against, blame; [G] to grumble against, blame, S: 3885, B: 534A, K: 477D, H: 174D

4297 לוּשׁ *lûš*, [A] to knead (bread dough), S: 3888, B: 534C, K: 477D, H: 175A

4298 לָוִשׁ *lāwiš*, variant: Lawish, see 4331, S: 3919† & 3889†, B: 539D, K: 481C, H: 175A

4299 לָזוּת *lāzût*, crookedness, perversity, S: 3891†, B: 531C, K: 478A, H: 175A

4300 לַח *laḥ*, fresh, fresh-cut, still moist, S: 3892, B: 535A, K: 478A, H: 175A

4301 לֵחַ *lēaḥ*, strength, S: 3893, B: 535A, K: 478A, H: 175A

4302 1לְחוּם *lᵉḥûm*[1], entrails, S: 3894†, B: 535D, K: 478B, H: 175A

4303 2לְחוּם *lᵉḥûm*[2], blow, wound, S: 3894†, B: 535D, K: 478B, H: 175A

4304 לֻחוֹת *luḥôt*, variant: Luhoth, see 4284, S: 3872, B: 532A, K: 476C, H: 174C

4305 1לְחִי *lᵉḥî*[1], jaw, jawbone; cheek, jowl, S: 3895, B: 534C, K: 478B, H: 175B

4306 2לְחִי *lᵉḥî*[2], Lehi, S: 3896†, B: 534D, K: 478C, H: 175B

4307 לַחַי רֹאִי *laḥay rō'î*, variant: Lahai Roi, S: 883†, B: 91D, K: 864C, H: 175B

4308 לָחַךְ *lāḥak*, [A] to lick up; [D] to lick up, subdue, S: 3897, B: 535A, K: 478C, H: 175B

4309 1לָחַם *lāḥam*[1], [A] to fight against, attack; [C] to fight against, attack, S: 3898, B: 535A, K: 478C, H: 175C

4310 2לָחַם *lāḥam*[2], [A] to eat, dine; [B] to be consumed, S: 3898, B: 536D, K: 479A, H: 175C

4311 לָחֶם *lāḥem*, war, S: 3901, B: 535D, K: 479B, H*

4312 לֶחֶם *leḥem*, bread, bread loaf, food, meal, S: 3899, B: 536D, K: 479B, H: 175D

4313 לַחְמִי *laḥmî*, Lahmi, S: 3902, B: 537C, K: 479C, H: 175D

4314 לַחְמָס *laḥmās*, Lahmas, S: 3903, B: 537C, K: 479D, H: 175D

4315 לָחַץ *lāḥaṣ*, [A] to oppress, crush, confine; [C] to be pressed close, S: 3905, B: 537D, K: 479D, H: 176A

4316 לַחַץ *laḥaṣ*, oppression, affliction; short ration (of bread or water), S: 3906, B: 537D, K: 479D, H: 176A

4317 לָחַשׁ *lāḥaš*, [D] to charm, enchant (i.e., whisper); [F] to whisper together, S: 3907, B: 538A, K: 480A, H: 176A

4318 לַחַשׁ *laḥaš*, charming, whispering; charm, enchanter, S: 3908, B: 538A, K: 480A, H: 176A

4319 לָט *lāṭ*, quietly, privately, secretly; (pl.) secret arts, S: 3814† & 3909, B: 532A, K: 480B, H: 176A

4320 לֹט *lōṭ*, myrrh, S: 3910, B: 538B, K: 480B, H: 176B

4321 לְטָאָה *lᵉṭā'â*, wall lizard, S: 3911, B: 538B, K: 480B, H: 176B

4322 לְטוּשִׁים *lᵉṭûšîm*, Letushite, S: 3912, B: 538C, K: 480B, H: 176B

4323 לָטַשׁ *lāṭaš*, [A] to sharpen; to forge, hammer; to pierce (with the eyes); [E] to be sharpened, S: 3913, B: 538B, K: 480B, H: 176B

4324 לֹיָה *lōyâ*, wreath, garland, S: 3914, B: 531A, K: 480C, H: 176B

4325 לַיִל *layil*, night, S: 3915, B: 538C, K: 480C, H: 176B

4326 לַיְלָה *laylâ*, night, tonight, S: 3915, B: 538C, K: 480C, H: 176B

4327 לִילִית *lîlît*, night creature; Lilith, S: 3917, B: 539B, K: 480D, H: 176C

4328 לִין *lîn*, [A] to spend the night, stay the night; [G] to hold back overnight, leave overnight; [F] to stay for the night, S: 3885, B: 533C, K: 481A, H: 176C & 175A

4329 לִיץ *lîṣ*, [A] to mock, scorn, talk big; [G] to mock; [F] to show oneself a mocker, S: 3887†, B: 539B, K: 481B, H: 176D

4330 1לַיִשׁ *layiš*[1], lion, S: 3918, B: 539D, K: 481C, H: 176D

4331 2לַיִשׁ *layiš*[2], Laish, S: 3919, B: 539D, K: 481C, H: 176D

4332 3לַיִשׁ *layiš*[3], Laish, S: 3919, B: 539D, K: 481C, H: 176D

4333 לַיְשָׁה *layᵉšâ*, Laishah, S: 3919†, B: 539D, K: 481D, H: 177A

4334 לָכַד *lākad*, [A] to capture, seize, take as a possession; [C] to be taken captive, be seized, be taken, S: 3920, B: 539D, K: 481D, H: 177A

4335 לֶכֶד *leked*, snaring, capturing, S: 3921, B: 540B, K: 482B, H: 177B

4336 לֵכָה *lēkâ*, Lecah, S: 3922, B: 540B, K: 482B, H: 177B

4337 לָכִישׁ *lākîš*, Lachish, S: 3923, B: 540B, K: 482B, H: 177B

4338 לָכֵן *lākēn*, variant: therefore, see 4200 & 4027, S: 3651†, B: 485D, K: 482B, H: 177B

4339 לֻלָאֹת *lulā'ōt*, (pl.) loops, S: 3924†, B: 533B, K: 482C, H: 177B

4340 לָמַד *lāmad*, [A] to learn, train for; [B] to be trained; [D] to teach, instruct, cause to learn; [E] to be trained, S: 3925, B: 540C, K: 482C, H: 177B

4341 לִמֻּד *limmud*, accustomed to; (as noun) a disciple, one who is taught, S: 3928, B: 541A, K: 483B, H: 177D

4342 לָמָּה *lāmmâ*, variant: why?, see 4200 & 4537, S: 4100†, B: 552B, K: 498A, H: 177D

4343 לָמוֹ *lāmô*, variant: to him, his, see 4200 & 4564, S*, B: 510A, K: 483B, H: 177D

4344 לְמוֹ *lᵉmô*, for, in, over, S: 3926, B: 530C, K: 462B, H: 177D

4345 לְמוּאֵל *lᵉmû'ēl*, Lemuel, S: 3927, B: 541A, K: 483C, H: 177D

4346 לְמוֹאֵל *lᵉmô'l*, variant: see 4200 & 4578, S: 4136†, B: 541A, K: 483C, H: 177D

4347 לֶמֶךְ *lemek*, Lamech, S: 3929, B: 541A, K: 483C, H: 177D

4348 לְמַעַן *lᵉma'an*, variant: so that, that; to; for the sake of, S: 4616†, B: 775A, K: 549B, H: 177D

4349 לֵן *lēn*, variant: spending the night, see 4328, S: 3885†, B: 533C, K: 483C, H: 178A

4350 לֹעַ *lōa'*, throat, S: 3930, B: 534B, K: 483C, H: 178A

4351 לָעַב *lā'ab*, [G] to mock, make sport of (someone), make a game of (someone), S: 3931, B: 541B, K: 483D, H: 178A

4352 לָעַג *lā'ag*, [A] to mock, scoff, ridicule; [C] to stammer, speak as a foreigner; [G] to mock, ridicule, S: 3932, B: 541B, K: 483D, H: 178A

4353 לַעַג *la'ag*, scorn, ridicule, derision, S: 3933, B: 541C, K: 484A, H: 178A

4354 לָעֵג *lā'ēg*, variant: people of stammering lips or foreign language, S: 3934, B: 541D, K: 484A, H: 178A

4355 לַעְדָּה *la'dâ*, Laadah, S: 3935, B: 541D, K: 484A, H: 178A

4356 לַעְדָּן *la'dān*, Ladan, S: 3936, B: 541D, K: 484A, H: 178A

4357 לָעַז *lā'az*, [A] to speak a foreign tongue, speak an unintelligible language, S: 3937, B: 541D, K: 484B, H: 178A

4358 לָעַט *lā'aṭ*, [G] to let (someone) gulp down, S: 3938, B: 542A, K: 484B, H: 178B

4359 לָעִיר *lā'îr*, variant: Laair, see 4200 & 6551, S*, B: 746B, K: 701B, H: 178B

4360 לַעֲנָה *la'ᵃnâ*, bitterness, gall, S: 3939, B: 542A, K: 484B, H: 178B

4361 לְעַנּוֹת *lᵉ'annôt*, leannoth [t.t. in Psalms], S: 6030†, B: 777B, K: 720A, H: 278B

4362 1לָעַע *lā'a'*[1], [A] to talk impetuously, to dedicate (something) rashly, S: 3886†, B: 534B, K: 484C, H: 178B

4363 2לָעַע *lā'a'*[2], [A] to sip, lap, slurp, S: 3216†, B: 534B, K: 484C, H: 178B

4364 לְעָפְרָה *lᵉ'aprâ*, variant: Ophrah, S: 1036†, B: 112A, K: 125A 24., H: 39C 26.

4365 לַפִּיד *lappîd*, torch, firebrand; lightning, S: 3940, B: 542A, K: 484C, H: 178B

4366 לַפִּידוֹת *lappîdôt*, Lappidoth, S: 3941, B: 542B, K: 484D, H: 178B

4367 לִפְנֵי *lipnê*, variant: to, for, before, see 4200 & 7155, S: 6440†, B: 815D, K: 766A, H: 293D

4368 לִפְנָי *lipnāy*, variant: see 4200 & 7156, S: 6440†, B: 819B, K: 462B & 766A, H: 167B & 293D

4369 לָפַת *lāpat*, [A] to reach toward; [C] be turned aside, S: 3943, B: 542B, K: 484D, H: 178C

4370 לֵץ *lēṣ*, mocker, babbler, scoffer, S: 3887†, B: 539B, K: 484D, H: 178C

4371 לָצוֹן *lāṣôn*, mockery, scoffing, S: 3944, B: 539C, K: 484D, H: 178C

4372 לָצַץ *lāṣaṣ*, mocker, scoffer, S: 3945, B: 539C, K: 481C, H: 178C

4373 לַקּוּם *laqqûm*, Lakkum, S: 3946, B: 542C, K: 485A, H: 178C

4374 לָקַח *lāqaḥ*, [A] to take, receive; [B] to be led away; [C] to be captured, taken away; [E] to be taken away, brought; [F] to flash back and forth, S: 3947, B: 542C, K: 485A, H: 178C

4375 לֶקַח *leqaḥ*, teaching, instruction, learning, S: 3948, B: 544B, K: 486A, H: 179A

4376 לִקְחִי *liqḥî*, Likhi, S: 3949, B: 544B, K: 486A, H: 179A

4377 לָקַט *lāqaṭ*, [A] to gather; [D] to gather, pick up, glean; [E] to be gathered up; [F] to gather oneself about, S: 3950, B: 544C, K: 486A, H: 179A

4378 לֶקֶט *leqeṭ*, gleanings (of a harvest), S: 3951, B: 545A, K: 486B, H: 179B

4379 לָקַק *lāqaq*, [A, D] to lap up, lick up, S: 3952, B: 545A, K: 486C, H: 179B

4380 לָקַשׁ *lāqaš*, [D] to glean, S: 3953, B: 545C, K: 486C, H: 179C

4381 לֶקֶשׁ *leqeš*, second crop, late grass at spring time, S: 3954, B: 545B, K: 486C, H: 179C

4382 לָשָׁד *lāšād*, moist (food), strength, S: 3955†, B: 545C, K: 486D, H: 179C

4383 לָשׁוֹן *lāšôn*, tongue; something tongue-shaped: wedge, bay, gulf; language, speech, S: 3956, B: 546A, K: 486D, H: 179C

4384 לִשְׁכָּה *liškâ*, room, chamber; hall; storeroom, S: 3957, B: 545C, K: 487B, H: 179D

4385 ¹לֶשֶׁם *lešem[1]*, jacinth, S: 3958, B: 545D, K: 487C, H: 179D

4386 ²לֶשֶׁם *lešem[2]*, Leshem, S: 3959, B: 546A, K: 487C, H: 179D

4387 לָשַׁן *lāšan*, [D] to slander; [G] to slander, S: 3960, B: 546D, K: 487C, H: 179D

4388 לֶשַׁע *leša'*, Lasha, S: 3962, B: 546D, K: 487C, H: 179D

4389 לַשָּׁרוֹן *laššārôn*, Lasharon, S: 8289†, B: 450A, K: 487D, H: 179D

4390 לֶתֶךְ *lētek*, lethek (a dry measure), S: 3963†, B: 547C, K: 487D, H: 179D

4391 מ *m*, letter of the Hebrew alphabet, S*, B: 547A, K: 488A, H: 180A

4392 ־ָם *-ām*, ־ם *-m*, they, them, their, S*, B*, K*, H*

4393 מַאֲבוּס *ma'ᵃbûs*, granary, S: 3965, B: 7B, K: 488A, H: 180A

4394 מְאֹד *mᵉ'ōd*, strength, greatness, much; very, greatly, exceedingly, S: 3966, B: 547A, K: 488B, H: 180A

4395 ¹מֵאָה *mē'â[1]*, hundred, S: 3967, B: 547C, K: 488C, H: 180A

4396 ²מֵאָה *mē'â[2]*, (the Tower of) the Hundred, S: 3968, B: 548C, K: 489A, H: 180B

4397 מַאֲוַיִּים *ma'ᵃwiyyîm*, desires, S: 3970†, B: 16C, K: 489A, H: 180B

4398 מְאוּם *mᵉ'ûm*, variant: defect, blemish, see 4583, S: 3971, B: 548C, K: 489A, H: 180B

4399 מְאוּמָה *mᵉ'ûmâ*, something, anything; (with negation) nothing, S: 3972, B: 548D, K: 489B, H: 180B

4400 מָאוֹס *mā'ôs*, refuse, trash, S: 3973, B: 549D, K: 490D 4., H: 180B

4401 מָאוֹר *mā'ôr*, light source, luminary, light-bearer, S: 3974, B: 22C, K: 489C, H: 180B

4402 מְאוּרָה *mᵉ'ûrâ*, nest hole (of a viper), S: 3975, B: 22D, K: 489C, H: 180B

4403 מֵאָז *mē'āz*, variant: from that time, ever since; of long ago, see 4946 & 255, S*, B: 23B, K: 24A, H: 8A 4.

4404 מֹאזְנַיִם *mō'znayim*, set of scales; (two) balance pans for weight measurement, S: 3976†, B: 24D, K: 489C, H: 180C

4405 מְאָיוֹת *mᵉ'āyôt*, variant: see 4395, S: 3967†, B: 547C, K: 488C, H: 180C

4406 מֵאַיִן *mē'ayin*, variant: from where?, see 402 & 4946, S: 369†, B: 32D, K: 40A, H: 180C

4407 מַאֲכָל *ma'ᵃkāl*, food, supplies, something to eat, S: 3978, B: 38B, K: 489D, H: 180C

4408 מַאֲכֶלֶת *ma'ᵃkelet*, (butcher) knife, S: 3979, B: 38B, K: 490A, H: 180C

4409 מַאֲכֹלֶת *ma'ᵃkōlet*, fuel (for a fire), S: 3980, B: 38C, K: 490A, H: 180C

4410 מַאֲמָץ *ma'ᵃmāṣ*, effort, exertion, S: 3981, B: 55C, K: 490A, H: 180C

4411 מַאֲמָר *ma'ᵃmār*, command, decree, instruction, S: 3982†, B: 57C, K: 490A, H: 180C

4412 מָאַן *mā'an*, [D] to refuse, reject, S: 3985†, B: 549A, K: 490A, H: 180C

4413 מָאֵן *mā'ēn*, variant: refusing, S: 3986, B: 549B, K: 490B, H: 180C

4414 מֵאֵן *mē'ēn*, variant: refusing, S: 3987†, B: 549B, K: 490B, H: 180C

4415 ¹מָאַס *mā'as[1]*, [A] to reject, despise, spurn, disdain; [C] to be rejected, become vile, S: 3988, B: 549B, K: 490B, H: 180D

4416 ²מָאַס *mā'as[2]*, [C] to be festering, be dissolving; be vanishing, S: 3988, B: 549D, K: 490D, H: 180D

4417 מְאַסֵּף *mᵉ'assēp*, variant: rear guard, see 665, S: 622†, B: 62A, K: 72D, H: 181A

4418 מַאֲפֶה *ma'ᵃpeh*, something baked, S: 3989, B: 66B, K: 490D, H: 181A

4419 מַאֲפֵל *ma'ᵃpēl*, darkness, S: 3990, B: 66D, K: 490D, H: 181A

4420 מַאְפֵּלְיָה *ma'pēlyâ*, great darkness, S: 3991, B: 66D, K: 490D, H: 181A

4421 מָאַר *mā'ar*, [G] to be destructive; to be painful, S: 3992, B: 549D, K: 491A, H: 181A

4422 מַאֲרָב *ma'ᵃrāb*, ambush; troops in an ambush, S: 3993, B: 70D, K: 491A, H: 181A

4423 מְאֵרָה *mᵉ'ērâ*, curse, S: 3994, B: 76D, K: 491A, H: 181A

4424 מֵאֲשֶׁר *mē'ᵃšer*, variant: from which, from whom, see 889 & 4946, S: 834†, B: 84A, K: 96A, H: 200B & 30C

4425 מֵאֵת *mē'ēt*, variant: from (with), see 4946 & 907, S: 854†, B: 86C 4, K: 535A, H: 181A

4426 מִבְדָּלוֹת *mibdālôt*, set aside, selected, singled out, S: 3995†, B: 95D, K: 491A, H: 181A

4427 מָבוֹא *mābô'*, entrance, entryway, gateway; west, the place of the setting of the sun, S: 3996 & 3997†, B: 99D, K: 491B, H: 181A

4428 מְבוּכָה *mᵉbûkâ*, confusion, confused terror, S: 3998, B: 100D, K: 491B, H: 181B

4429 מַבּוּל *mabbûl*, flood (waters), S: 3999, B: 550A, K: 491B, H: 181B

4430 מְבוֹנִים *mᵉbônîm*, variant: see 1067, S: 4000†, B: 108A, K: 491C, H: 181B

4431 מְבוּסָה *mᵉbûsâ*, trampling down, S: 4001, B: 101B, K: 491C, H: 181B

4432 מַבּוּעַ *mabbûa'*, (a bubbling) spring (of water), S: 4002, B: 616A, K: 491C, H: 181B

4433 מְבוּקָה *mᵉbûqâ*, plundering, devastation, desertion, S: 4003, B: 101C, K: 491C, H: 181B

4434 מְבוּשִׁים *mᵉbûšîm*, private parts, genitals (of a male person), S: 4016†, B: 102B, K: 491C, H: 181B

4435 מִבְחוֹר *mibḥôr*, choicest (trees); major (towns), S: 4004, B: 104D, K: 491C, H: 181B

4436 ¹מִבְחָר *mibḥār[1]*, choicest, best, elite, finest (persons or things), S: 4005, B: 104D, K: 491C, H: 181B

4437 ²מִבְחָר *mibḥār[2]*, Mibhar, S: 4006, B: 104D, K: 491D, H: 181B

4438 מַבָּט *mabbāṭ*, hope, trust in, relying on, S: 4007, B: 613D, K: 491D, H: 181B

4439 מִבְטָא *mibṭā'*, rash promise, rashness, S: 4008, B: 105A, K: 491D, H: 181C

4440 מִבְטָח *mibṭāḥ*, security, trust, confidence, S: 4009, B: 105C, K: 491D, H: 181C

4441 מַבָּךְ *mabbāk*, source, S*, B: 614A, K: 491D, H: 181C

4442 מַבֵּל *mabbēl*, fire, S: 1097†, B: 116A c γ, K: 129B, H*

4443 מַבְלִיגִית *mablîgît*, comfort, smile, cheerfulness, S: 4010, B: 114D, K: 492A, H: 181C

4444 מְבֻלָקָה *mᵉbulāqâ*, variant: destruction, see 1191, S: 1110†, B: 118D, K: 131D, H: 181C

4445 מִבְנֶה *mibneh*, building, structure, S: 4011, B: 125D, K: 492A, H: 181C

4446 מְבֻנַּי *mᵉbunnay*, Mebunnai, S: 4012, B: 125D, K: 492A, H: 181C

4447 מַבְנִית *mabnît*, variant: structure, frame, body, S*, B: 108A, K: 121D, H: 181C

4448 ¹מִבְצָר *mibṣār[1]*, fortress, fortification, stronghold, S: 4013, B: 131B, K: 492A, H: 181C

4449 ²מִבְצָר *mibṣār[2]*, Mibzar, S: 4014, B: 550B, K: 492B, H: 181D

4450 ³מִבְצָר *mibṣār[3]*, ore, S: 4013, B: 131B, K: 492A, H*

4451 מִבְרָח *mibrāḥ*, fleeing, refugee, S: 4015, B: 138B, K: 492B, H: 181D

4452 מִבְשָׂם *mibśām*, Mibsam, S: 4017, B: 142A, K: 492B, H: 181D

4453 מְבַשְּׁלוֹת *mᵉbaššᵉlôt*, places for fire, cooking-places, S: 4018†, B: 143B, K: 492B, H: 181D

4454 מָג *māg*, official (used with 8042), S: 7248†, B: 550B, K: 492B, H: 181D

4455 מַגְבִּישׁ *magbîš*, Magbish, S: 4019, B: 150D, K: 492B, H: 181D

4456 מִגְבָּלוֹת *migbālôt*, (braided) chains, (twisted) cords, S: 4020†, B: 148B, K: 492C, H: 181D

4457 מִגְבָּעָה *migbā'â*, headband, S: 4021, B: 149B, K: 492C, H: 181D

4458 מֶגֶד *meged*, choice things, best gifts, S: 4022 & 4030†, B: 550C, K: 492C, H: 181D

4459 מְגִדּוֹ *mᵉgiddô*, Megiddo, S: 4023, B: 151D, K: 492C, H: 182A

4460 מִגְדּוֹל *migdôl*, variant: great, see 1540, S: 4024, B: 154A, K: 492D, H: 182A

4461 מְגִדּוֹן *mᵉgiddôn*, Megiddo, S: 4023, B: 151D, K: 492D, H: 182A

4462 מַגְדִּיאֵל *magdî'ēl*, Magdiel, S: 4025, B: 550C, K: 492D, H: 182A

4463 מִגְדָּלִי *migdāl*[1], tower, watchtower, high platform, S: 4026, B: 153D, K: 492D, H: 182A

4464 [2]מִגְדָּל *migdāl*[2], variant: Migdal, S: 4027† & 4028†, B: 154A, K: 493A, H: 182A

4465 מִגְדֹּל *migdōl*, Migdol, S: 4024, B: 154A, K: 493B, H: 182A

4466 מִגְדַּל־אֵל *migdal-'ēl*, Migdal El, S: 4027, B: 154A, K: 493A, H: 182A 1.

4467 מִגְדַּל־גָּד *migdal-gad*, Migdal Gad, S: 4028, B: 154A, K: 493A, H: 182A 2.

4468 מִגְדַּל־עֵדֶר *migdal-'ēder*, Migdal Eder, S: 4029, B: 154A, K: 493A, H: 182A 3.

4469 מִגְדָּנוֹת *migdānôt*, variant: costly gifts, articles of value, S: 4030†, B: 550C, K: 493B, H: 182A

4470 מָגוֹג *māgôg*, Magog, S: 4031, B: 156A, K: 493B, H: 182A

4471 מָגוֹרִי *māgôr*[1], terror, horror, S: 4032, B: 159A, K: 493B, H: 182A

4472 [2]מָגוֹר *māgôr*[2], to live as an alien, stay as a stranger; place to live, place to lodge, S: 4033†, B: 158C, K: 493C, H: 182A

4473 [3]מָגוֹר *māgôr*[3], variant: grain pit, storage chamber = heart, mind, S: 4033†, B: 158C, K: 493C, H: 182B

4474 מָגוֹר מִסָּבִיב *māgôr missābîb*, Magor-Missabib, S: 4036, B: 159A & 686D 1.d., K: 493B, H: 182A & 252C 3.

4475 מְגוֹרָה *m^{e}gôrâ*, dread, fear, S: 4034, B: 159A, K: 493C, H: 182B

4476 מְגוּרָה *m^{e}gûrâ*, barn, grain-pit, storage chamber, S: 4035, B: 158C, K: 493C, H: 182B

4477 מַגְזֵרָה *magzērâ*, ax, S: 4037, B: 160D, K: 493C, H: 182B

4478 מַגָּל *maggāl*, sickle, S: 4038, B: 618C, K: 493D, H: 182B

4479 מְגִלָּה *m^{e}gillâ*, scroll, S: 4039, B: 166B, K: 493D, H: 182B

4480 מְגַמָּה *m^{e}gammâ*, horde, S: 4041, B: 169D, K: 493D, H: 182B

4481 מָגַן *māgan*, [D] to hand over, deliver to, present with, S: 4042, B: 171C, K: 493D, H: 182B

4482 מָגֵןי *māgēn*[1], (small) shield, S: 4043, B: 171B, K: 494A, H: 182B

4483 [2]מָגֵן *māgēn*[2], variant: insolent, S: 4043†, B: 171B, K: 494B, H: 182C

4484 מֶגֶן *megen*, variant: gift, present (gifts made in return), S: 4043†, B: 171B, K: 494B, H: 182C

4485 מְגִנָּה *m^{e}ginnâ*, veil, covering, S: 4044, B: 171C, K: 494B, H: 182C

4486 מִגְעֶרֶת *mig'eret*, rebuke, reproach, S: 4045, B: 172A, K: 494C, H: 182C

4487 מַגֵּפָה *maggēpâ*, plague; blow, strike, slaughter, S: 4046, B: 620A, K: 494C, H: 182C

4488 מַגְפִּיעָשׁ *magpî'āš*, Magpiash, S: 4047, B: 550D, K: 494C, H: 182C

4489 מָגַר *māgar*, [B] to be thrown; [D] to cast, throw down, S: 4048, B: 550D, K: 494C, H: 182C

4490 מְגֵרָה *m^{e}gērâ*, saw (stone-cutting tool), S: 4050, B: 176B, K: 494C, H: 182C

4491 מִגְרוֹן *migrôn*, Migron, S: 4051, B: 550D, K: 494D, H: 182C

4492 מִגְרָעוֹת *migrā'ôt*, offset ledge, recess, rebatement (of a wall), S: 4052†, B: 175D, K: 494D, H: 182C

4493 מֶגְרָפָה *megrāpâ*, clods (of earth) *or* hoe, spade, S: 4053, B: 175D, K: 494D, H: 182D

4494 מִגְרָשׁ *migrāš*, pastureland, untilled open land (belonging to a town), S: 4054, B: 177B, K: 494D, H: 182D

4495 מִגְרְשׁוֹת *migr^{e}šôt*, variant: see 4494, S: 4054†, B: 177B, K: 495A, H: 182D

4496 מַד *mad*, clothing, garment; measure, decree, S: 4055, B: 551B, K: 495A, H: 182D

4497 מִדְבָּרי *midbār*[1], desert, wasteland, barren wilderness, open country, S: 4057, B: 184C, K: 495A, H: 182D

4498 [2]מִדְבָּר *midbār*[2], mouth, instrument of speech, S: 4057, B: 184D, K: 495B, H: 182D

4499 מָדַד *mādad*, [A] to measure a distance; consider a plan; [C] to be measured; [D] to measure off; [F] to stretch oneself out, S: 4058 & 4059†, B: 551A, K: 495B, H: 182D

4500 מִדָּהי *middâ*[1], measurement, size, length; section (of a wall), S: 4060, B: 551C, K: 495D, H: 183A

4501 [2]מִדָּה *middâ*[2], tax, S: 4060, B: 551D, K: 496A, H: 183A

4502 מַדְהֵבָה *madhēbâ*, fury, S: 4062, B: 923C, K: 496A, H: 183B

4503 מַדוּ *madû*, מַדְוֶהי *madweh*[1], garment, S: 4063†, B: 551D, K: 496A, H: 183B

4504 [2]מַדְוֶה *madweh*[2], disease, sickness, S: 4064, B: 188C, K: 496A, H: 183B

4505 מַדּוּחִים *maddûḥîm*, misleading, S: 4065†, B: 623B, K: 496B, H: 183B

4506 מָדוֹןי *mādôn*[1], dissension, quarrel, strife, contention, S: 4066 & 4079† & 4090†, B: 193B, K: 496B, H: 183B

4507 [2]מָדוֹן *mādôn*[2], Madon, S: 4068, B: 193C, K: 496B, H: 183B

4508 מַדּוּעַ *maddûa'*, Why?, What is the meaning?, S: 4069, B: 396C, K: 496C, H: 183B

4509 מְדוּרָה *m^{e}dûrâ*, (circular) pile of wood, fire pit, S: 4071, B: 190B, K: 496C, H: 183B

4510 מִדְחֶה *midḥeh*, ruin, downfall, S: 4072, B: 191A, K: 496C, H: 183B

4511 מַדְחֵפָה *madḥēpâ*, blow, thrust; (pl.) blow after blow, S: 4073†, B: 191B, K: 496C, H: 183B

4512 מָדַי *māday*, Madai; Media, Medes, S: 4074, B: 552A, K: 496C, H: 183B

4513 מָדִי *mādî*, Mede, S: 4075†, B: 552A, K: 496C, H: 183C

4514 מַדַּי *madday*, variant: see 4537 *or* 4946 & 1896, S: 1767†, B: 191C 2., K: 207D, H: 183C

4515 מָדִין *mādîn*, variant: see 4506 *or* 4500, S: 4060†, B: 193B, K: 496B, H: 183B

4516 מִדִּין *middîn*, Middin, S: 4081, B: 551D, K: 496D, H: 183C

4517 מִדְיָןי *midyān*[1], variant: quarrel, strife, contention, S: 4067†, B: 193B, K: 496D, H: 183C

4518 [2]מִדְיָן *midyān*[2], Midian, Midianite, S: 4080, B: 193C, K: 496D, H: 183C

4519 מְדִינָה *m^{e}dînâ*, province, district, region, S: 4082, B: 193D, K: 497A, H: 183C

4520 מִדְיָנִי *midyānî*, Midianite, S: 4084 & 4092†, B: 193C, K: 497B, H: 183C

4521 מְדֹכָה *m^{e}dōkâ*, mortar, S: 4085, B: 189A, K: 497B, H: 183C

4522 מַדְמֵן *madmēn*, Madmen, S: 4086, B: 199B, K: 497B, H: 183C

4523 מַדְמֵנָהי *madmēnâ*[1], manure-pile, dung-heap, S: 4087, B: 199B, K: 497B, H: 183C

4524 [2]מַדְמֵנָה *madmēnâ*[2], Madmenah, S: 4088, B: 199B, K: 497C, H: 183C

4525 מַדְמַנָּהי *madmannâ*[1], Madmannah, S: 4089, B: 199B 2., K: 497C, H: 183C

4526 [2]מַדְמַנָּה *madmannâ*[2], Madmannah, S: 4089, B: 199B 1., K: 497C, H: 183C

4527 מְדָןי *m^{e}dān*[1], Medan, S: 4091, B: 193C, K: 497C, H: 183C

4528 [2]מְדָן *m^{e}dān*[2], variant: dissension, see 4506, S: 4067†, B: 193B, K: 496B, H: 183C

4529 מַדָּע *maddā'*, knowledge, S: 4093, B: 396B, K: 497C, H: 183C

4530 מֹדָע *mōdā'*, (distant) relative, kinsman, S: 4129, B: 396B, K: 497C, H: 183C

4531 מֹדַעַת *mōda'at*, (distant) kinsman, S: 4130, B: 396B, K: 497D, H: 183D

4532 מַדְקֵרָה *madqērâ*, piercing (of a sword), S: 4094†, B: 201B, K: 497D, H: 183D

4533 מַדְרֵגָה *madrēgâ*, cliff, (steep) mountainside, S: 4095, B: 201C, K: 497D, H: 183D

4534 מִדְרָךְ *midrāk*, foot-width, footprint, S: 4096, B: 204A, K: 497D, H: 183D

4535 מִדְרָשׁ *midrāš*, annotation, study, writing, exposition, S: 4097, B: 205D, K: 497D, H: 183D

4536 מְדֻשָׁה *m^{e}dušâ*, that which is crushed (by trampling on a threshing floor), S: 4098, B: 190D, K: 498A, H: 183D

4537 מָה *mâ*, why?, what?, how?; O!, who, whoever, whatever, S: 4100, B: 552B, K: 498A, H: 183D

4538 מָהַהּ *māhah*, [F] to wait, delay, linger, hesitate, S: 4102, B: 554C, K: 499B, H: 184C

4539 מְהוּמָה *m^{e}hûmâ*, turmoil, confusion, panic, discomfiture, S: 4103, B: 223B, K: 499C, H: 184C

4540 מְהוּמָן *m^{e}hûmān*, Mehuman, S: 4104, B: 54D, K: 499C, H: 184C

4541 מְהֵיטַבְאֵל *m^{e}hêṭab'ēl*, Mehetabel, S: 4105, B: 406B, K: 499C, H: 184C

4542 מָהִיר *māhîr*, skilled, well versed, experienced; speedy, prompt, S: 4106, B: 555B, K: 499C, H: 184C

4543 מָהַל *māhal*, [B] to be diluted, changed to an adulterated state, S: 4107, B: 554C, K: 499D, H: 184C

[F] Hitpael (hitpoel, hitpoal, hitpolel, hitpolal, hitpalel, hitpalal, hitpalpel, hitpalpal, hotpael, hotpaal) [G] Hiphil (hiphtil) [H] Hophal [I] Hishtaphel

4544 מַהֲלָךְ *mah^{a}lāk*, passageway; journey, S: 4108† & 4109, B: 237B, K: 499D, H: 184C

4545 מַהֲלָל *mah^{a}lāl*, praise, good reputation, S: 4110, B: 239C, K: 499D, H: 184D

4546 מַהֲלַלְאֵל *mah^{a}lal'ēl*, Mahalalel, S: 4111, B: 239D, K: 500A, H: 184D

4547 מַהֲלֻמוֹת *mah^{a}lumôt*, (pl.) beating, thrashing, S: 4112†, B: 240D, K: 500A, H: 184D

4548 מָהֵם *māhēm*, variant: see 4537 & 2156, S*, B: 552B & 241D 7, K: 498A & 236C, H: 184D

4549 מַהֲמֹרוֹת *mah^{a}mōrôt*, miry pits, pits filled with rain water, S: 4113†, B: 243B, K: 500A, H: 184D

4550 מַהְפֵּכָה *mahpēkâ*, overthrow, destruction, demolishing, S: 4114, B: 246B, K: 500A, H: 184D

4551 מַהְפֶּכֶת *mahpeket*, stocks (confining a prisoner, suggesting in a crooked posture or distortion), S: 4115, B: 246B, K: 500A, H: 184D

4552 מְהוֹלָה *m^{e}hôlâ*, variant: Meholah, S: 65†, B: 6A 5., K: 6C 4, H: 2C

4553 מְהֻקְצָעוֹת *m^{e}huqṣā'ôt*, variant: made with corners, S*, B: 893B, K: 848B, H: 184D

4554 [1]מָהַר *māhar*[1], [C] to be swept away; to be impetuous, rash, disturbed; [D] to be quick, hasten, hurry, do at once, S: 4116, B: 554D, K: 500B, H: 184D

4555 [2]מָהַר *māhar*[2], [A] to pay the purchase price for a bride, S: 4117, B: 555C, K: 500C, H: 185B

4556 [1]מָהֵר *mahēr*[1], variant: swift, S: 4117†, B: 555A, K: 500B, H: 184D

4557 [2]מָהֵר *mahēr*[2], variant: swiftly, S: 4118, B: 555A, K: 500B, H: 184D

4558 מֹהַר *mōhar*, bride-price, compensation to the father of the bride, S: 4119, B: 555C, K: 500D, H: 185B

4559 מְהֵרָה *m^{e}hērâ*, haste, quickness, speed; (as adv.) quickly, swiftly, soon, at once, S: 4120, B: 555B, K: 500D, H: 185B

4560 מַהֲרַי *mah^{a}ray*, Maharai, S: 4121, B: 555B, K: 501A, H: 185B

4561 מַהֵר שָׁלָל חָשׁ בַּז *mahēr šālāl ḥāš baz*, Maher-Shalal-Hash-Baz, S: 4122, B: 555B, K: 979B & 115C, H: 185B

4562 מַהֲתַלָּה *mah^{a}tallâ*, illusion, deception, S: 4123, B: 1122C, K: 501A, H: 185B

4563 מוֹ *mô*, variant: see 4784, S*, B: 555C, K: 441B, H: 42A & 159C & 177D

4564 ־מוֹ, ־מוּ *-mô, -mû*, he, him; they, them, S*, B*, K*, H*

4565 [1]מוֹאָב *mô'āb*[1], Moab, S: 4124, B: 555D, K: 501A, H: 185B 1.

4566 [2]מוֹאָב *mô'āb*[2], Moab, Moabite, S: 4124, B: 555D, K: 501A, H: 185B 2.

4567 מוֹאָבִי *mô'ābî*, Moabite, from Moab, S: 4125, B: 555D, K: 501C, H: 185B

4568 מוֹאל *mô'l*, variant: see 4578, S: 4136, B: 557B, K: 502D, H: 185B

4569 מוֹבָא *môbā'*, coming in; entrance (way), S: 4126, B: 100A, K: 501C, H: 185B

4570 מוּג *mûg*, [A] to melt, waste away; [C] to melt away (in fear), be disheartened; to collapse; [D] to soften; to toss about; [F] to melt away, flow from, S: 4127, B: 556A, K: 501C, H: 185C

4571 מוּד *môd*, [D] to shake, convulse, set into motion, S: 4128†, B: 556D, K: 501D, H: 185C

4572 [1]מוֹט *môṭ*[1], [A] to slip, fall, totter, stagger; [C] to be shaken, be caused to move, be toppled; [G] to bring down, to cause to fall; [F] to be thoroughly shaken, be continually shaken, S: 4131, B: 556D, K: 502A, H: 185C

4573 [2]מוֹט *môṭ*[2], carrying frame; pole; yoke bar, S: 4132, B: 557A, K: 502B, H: 185D

4574 מוֹטָה *môṭâ*, yoke bar, pole, bar, S: 4133, B: 557B, K: 502B, H: 185D

4575 מוּךְ *mûk*, [A] to become poor, S: 4134, B: 557B, K: 502B, H: 185D

4576 [1]מוּל *mûl*[1], [A] to circumcise; [B] to be circumcised; [C] to be circumcised, undergo circumcision, circumcise oneself, S: 4135, B: 557D, K: 502C, H: 185D

4577 [2]מוּל *mûl*[2], [G] to cut off, ward off, S: 4135, B: 557D, K: 502C, H: 186A

4578 [3]מוּל *mûl*[3], before, opposite, in front of, S: 4136, B: 557B, K: 502D, H: 186A

4579 מוֹלָדָה *môlādâ*, Moladah, S: 4137, B: 409D, K: 502D, H: 186A

4580 מוֹלֶדֶת *môledet*, family, relatives, children; (land of) birth, native (land), S: 4138, B: 409D, K: 503A, H: 186A

4581 מוּלָה *mûlâ*, circumcision, S: 4139, B: 558A, K: 503A, H: 186B

4582 מוֹלִיד *môlîd*, Molid, S: 4140, B: 410A, K: 503A, H: 186B

4583 מוּם *mûm*, defect, blemish, flaw, injury; shame, defilement, S: 3971, B: 548C, K: 489A, H: 186B

4584 מְמוּכָן *m^{e}wmukān*, variant: Mumecan, see 4925, S: 4462†, B: 577A, K: 533C, H: 186B

4585 מוּסָב *mûsāb*, variant: encompassing, surrounding, S: 5439†, B: 687C, K: 503B, H: 186B

4586 מוּסָד *mûsād*, foundation, laying the foundation stone, S: 4143, B: 414B, K: 503B, H: 186B

4587 מוֹסָד *môsād*, foundation, S: 4144, B: 414C, K: 503B, H: 186B

4588 מוּסָדָה *mûsādâ*, foundation, S: 4145 & 4328†, B: 414C, K: 503B, H: 186B

4589 מוֹסָדָה *môsādâ*, foundation, S: 4146, B: 414C, K: 503B, H: 186B

4590 מוּסָךְ *mûsāk*, canopy, S: 4329†, B: 697B, K: 519D, H: 186B

4591 מוֹסֵר *môsēr*, chains, shackles, fetters, S: 4147, B: 64C, K: 503C, H: 186C

4592 מוּסָר *mûsār*, discipline, instruction, correction, S: 4148, B: 416B, K: 503C, H: 186C

4593 [1]מוֹסֵרָה *môsērâ*[1], bonds, shackles, straps, chains, fetters, S: 4147, B: 64C, K: 503A, H: 186C

4594 [2]מוֹסֵרָה *môsērâ*[2], Moserah, S: 4149, B: 64C, K*, H: 186C

4595 מוֹעֵד *mô'ēd*, (Tent of) Meeting; appointed time, designated time, season, S: 4150, B: 417B, K: 503D, H: 186C

4596 מוֹעָד *mô'ād*, ranks, appointed place of a soldier, S: 4151, B: 418A, K: 504C, H: 186D

4597 מוּעָדָה *mû'ādâ*, designation, appointment, S: 4152, B: 418A, K: 504C, H: 186D

4598 מוֹעַדְיָה *mô'adyâ*, Moadiah, S: 4153, B: 588C, K: 544D, H: 186D

4599 מוּעָף *mû'āp*, gloom, darkness, S: 4155, B: 734A, K: 504D, H: 186D

4600 מוֹעֵצָה *mô'ēṣâ*, plan, scheme, device, intrigue, S: 4156, B: 420B, K: 504D, H: 186D

4601 מוּעָקָה *mû'āqâ*, burden, misery, hardship, S: 4157, B: 734C, K: 504D, H: 187A

4602 מוֹפַעַת *môpa'at*, variant: Mophaath, see 4789, S: 4158, B: 422B, K: 519D, H: 187A

4603 מוֹפֵת *môpēt*, wonder, sign, miracle, portent; symbol, S: 4159, B: 68D, K: 504D, H: 187A

4604 [1]מוֹצָא *môṣā'*[1], act of going out, springing out, exiting, moving on, S: 4161, B: 425C, K: 505A, H: 187A

4605 [2]מוֹצָא *môṣā'*[2], Moza, S: 4162, B: 426A, K: 505B, H: 187A

4606 מוֹצָאָה *môṣā'â*, origin, coming out; latrine, S: 4163, B: 426A, K: 505B, H: 187A

4607 [1]מוּצָק *mûṣāq*[1], casting (of metal), S: 4164, B: 427C, K: 505C, H: 187A

4608 [2]מוּצָק *mûṣāq*[2], restriction, constraint; distress, hardship, S: 4165, B: 848A, K: 505C, H: 187A

4609 מוּצָקָה *mûṣāqâ*, casting (into one piece); channel, spout or lip (of a lamp), S: 4166, B: 427C, K: 505C, H: 187B

4610 מוּק *mûq*, [G] to scoff, S: 4167, B: 558B, K: 505C, H: 187B

4611 מוֹקֵד *môqēd*, glowing embers, burning embers, S: 4168, B: 428D, K: 505C, H: 187B

4612 מוֹקְדָה *môq^{e}dâ*, hearth, place of burning, S: 4169, B: 429A, K: 505C, H: 187B

4613 מוֹקֵשׁ *môqēš*, snare, trap; ensnarement, entrapment, S: 4170, B: 430C, K: 505C, H: 187B

4614 [1]מוּר *mûr*[1], [C] to be changed; [G] to exchange, substitute, change, S: 4171, B: 558C, K: 505D, H: 187B

4615 [2]מוּר *mûr*[2], [C] to shake, quake, S: 4171, B: 558C 1, K: 505D, H: 187B

4616 מוֹרָא *môrā'*, fear, terror, respect, reverence; awesome deed, S: 4172, B: 432A, K: 506A, H: 187C

4617 מוֹרַג *môrag*, threshing sledge, S: 4173, B: 558D, K: 506A, H: 187C

4618 מוֹרָד *môrād*, slope, road going down; something hammered down, S: 4174, B: 434B, K: 506B, H: 187C

4619 [1]מוֹרֶה *môreh*[1], archer, S: 4175, B: 435B 2, K: 402D, H: 187C

4620 [2]מוֹרֶה *môreh*[2], autumn rains, S: 4175, B: 435C, K: 506B, H: 187C

4621 [3]מוֹרֶה *môreh*[3], teacher, S: 4175, B: 435D, K: 506B, H: 187C

[A] Qal [B] Qal passive [C] Niphal [D] Piel (poel, polel, pilel, pilal, pealal, pilpel) [E] Pual (poal, polal, poalal, pulal, pualal)

4622 מוֹרֶה *môreh*[4], Moreh, S: 4176, B: 435C, K: 506B, H: 187C

4623 מוֹרָה *môrâ*[1], razor, S: 4177, B: 559A, K: 506B, H: 187D

4624 מוֹרָה *môrâ*[2], variant: terror, see 4616, S: 4172, B: 432B, K: 506C, H: 187D

4625 מוֹרָשׁ *môrāš*[1], possession, inheritance, S: 4180, B: 440C, K: 506C, H: 187D

4626 מוֹרָשׁ *môrāš*[2], desire, S: 4180, B: 440C, K: 506C, H: 187D

4627 מוֹרָשָׁה *môrāšâ*, possession, S: 4181, B: 440C, K: 506C, H: 187D

4628 מוֹרֶשֶׁת גַּת *môrešet gat*, Moresheth Gath, S: 4182, B: 440C, K: 506C, H: 187D

4629 מוֹרַשְׁתִּי *môraštî*, of Moresheth, S: 4183, B: 440D, K: 506C, H: 187D

4630 מוּשׁ *mûš*[1], [A] to touch, feel; [G] to be able to feel, touch, S: 4184, B: 559B, K: 506C, H: 187D

4631 מוּשׁ *mûš*[2], [A] to depart, leave, move away, vanish; [G] to remove, S: 4185, B: 559A, K: 506D, H: 187D

4632 מוֹשָׁב *môšāb*, dwelling, settlement, place to live, place, S: 4186, B: 444A, K: 507A, H: 188A

4633 מוּשִׁי *mûšî*[1], Mushi, S: 4187, B: 559B, K: 507B, H: 188A 1.

4634 מוּשִׁי *mûšî*[2], Mushite, S: 4188, B: 559B, K: 507B, H: 188A 2.

4635 מוֹשִׁיעַ *môšîa'*, savior, deliverer, rescuer, S: 3467†, B: 446B, K: 412D, H: 188A

4636 מוֹשָׁעָה *môšā'â*, act of salvation, act of helping, S: 4190, B: 448A, K: 507B, H: 188B

4637 מוּת *mût*, [A] to die, be killed, be dead; [D] to kill, slay, put to death; [G] to kill, make die, put to death, assassinate; [H] to be put to death, be murdered, S: 4191 & 4192, B: 559B, K: 507B, H: 188B

4638 מָוֶת *māwet*, death, dying, S: 4194, B: 560C, K: 508A, H: 188D

4639 מוֹתָר *môtār*, profit, advantage, S: 4195, B: 452D, K: 508C, H: 188D

4640 מִזְבֵּחַ *mizbēaḥ*, altar, S: 4196, B: 258A, K: 508C, H: 188D

4641 מֶזֶג *mezeg*, blended wine, mixed wine, S: 4197, B: 561A, K: 509A, H: 189A

4642 מָזֶה *māzeh*, empty (from hunger), S: 4198, B: 561A, K: 509A, H: 189A

4643 מַזֶּה *mazzeh*, variant: see 4537 & 2296, S: 4100† + 2088†, B: 552B & 260A, K: 509B, H: 189A

4644 מִזֶּה *mizzeh*, variant: from this, from here, see 4946 & 2296, S: 4100† + 2088†, B: 577C & 260A, K: 535A & 250C, H: 189A

4645 מִזָּה *mizzâ*, Mizzah, S: 4199, B: 561A, K: 509B, H: 189A

4646 מָזוּ *māzû*, barn, granary, S: 4200†, B: 265A, K: 509B, H: 189A

4647 מְזוּזָה *m^{e}zûzâ*, doorframe, doorpost, doorjamb, S: 4201, B: 265B, K: 509B, H: 189A

4648 מָזוֹן *māzôn*, provisions, food, S: 4202, B: 266A, K: 509B, H: 189A

4649 מָזוֹר *māzôr*[1], sore, boil, ulcer, S: 4205, B: 267A, K: 509A, H: 189A

4650 מָזוֹר *māzôr*[2], trap, ambush, S: 4204, B: 561C, K: 509C, H: 189A

4651 מֵזַח *mēzaḥ*[1], harbor, S: 4206, B: 561A, K: 509C, H: 189A

4652 מֵזַח *mēzaḥ*[2], belt, leather girdle worn next to the skin, S: 4206, B: 561A, K: 509C, H: 189A

4653 מָזִיחַ *māzîaḥ*, belt, girdle, S: 4206, B: 561B, K: 509D, H: 189A

4654 מַזְכִּיר *mazkîr*, recorder, clerk, secretary, S: 2142†, B: 272C & 271A, K: 255D, H: 189B

4655 מַזָּל *mazzāl*, constellation (possibly of the zodiac signs), S: 4208†, B: 561B, K: 509D, H: 189B

4656 מִזְלָג *mizlāg*, variant: (three-tined) meat fork, S: 4207†, B: 272C, K: 509D, H: 189B

4657 מַזְלֵג *mazlēg*, (three-tined) meat fork, S: 4207, B: 272C, K: 509D, H: 189B

4658 מִזְלָגָה *mizlāgâ*, variant: (three-tined) meat fork, see 4656, S: 4207, B: 272C, K: 509D, H: 189B

4659 מְזִמָּה *m^{e}zimmâ*, discretion; scheme, plan, purpose, intent, S: 4209, B: 273C, K: 510A, H: 189B

4660 מִזְמוֹר *mizmôr*, psalm, melody, S: 4210, B: 274C, K: 510A, H: 189B

4661 מַזְמֵרָה *mazmērâ*, pruning hook, pruning knife, vine-knife, S: 4211, B: 275A, K: 510B, H: 189B

4662 מְזַמֶּרֶת *m^{e}zammeret*, wick trimmer, S: 4212†, B: 275A, K: 510B, H: 189B

4663 מִזְעָר *miz'ār*, small matter, few, S: 4213, B: 277D, K: 510B, H: 189B

4664 מָזַר *māzar*, variant: [B] to be spread out (a net), S: 2219†, B: 279D, K: 510B, H: 189B

4665 מִזְרֶה *mizreh*, winnowing fork, shovel, S: 4214, B: 280A, K: 510C, H: 189C

4666 מַזָּרוֹת *mazzārôt*, constellations, S: 4216†, B: 561D, K: 510C, H: 189C

4667 מִזְרָח *mizrāḥ*, direction of the sunrise, east, eastern, S: 4217, B: 280D, K: 510C, H: 189C

4668 מְזָרִים *m^{e}zārîm*, driving (north) winds, S: 2219† & 4215†, B: 279D, K: 511A, H: 189C

4669 מִזְרָע *mizrā'*, seeded field, land sown, S: 4218, B: 283C, K: 511A, H: 189C

4670 מִזְרָק *mizrāq*, sacred bowl used for sprinkling (the altar), S: 4219, B: 284D, K: 511A, H: 189C

4671 מֵחַ *mēaḥ*, fat sheep; (representing) the rich, S: 4220, B: 562D, K: 511A, H: 189C

4672 מֹחַ *mōaḥ*, marrow, S: 4221, B: 562D, K: 511B, H: 189C

4673 מָחָא *māḥā'*[1], [A] to clap (hands in joy), S: 4222, B: 561D, K: 511B, H: 189C

4674 מָחָא *māḥā'*[2], variant: see 4683, S: 4229†, B: 562D, K: 511B, H: 189D

4675 מַחֲבֵא *maḥ^{a}bē'*, shelter, hiding place (from wind), S: 4224, B: 285C, K: 511B, H: 189D

4676 מַחֲבֹא *maḥ^{a}bō'*, hiding place, S: 4224, B: 285C, K: 511B, H: 189D

4677 מְחַבְּרוֹת *m^{e}ḥabb^{e}rôt*, fittings, joists, S: 4226†, B: 289C, K: 511B, H: 189D

4678 מַחְבֶּרֶת *maḥberet*, place of joining, seam, set (of curtains), S: 4225, B: 289C, K: 511C, H: 189D

4679 מַחֲבַת *maḥ^{a}bat*, (metal) griddle *or* baking pan, S: 4227, B: 290A, K: 511C, H: 189D

4680 מַחֲגֹרֶת *maḥ^{a}gōret*, girding (of sackcloth), S: 4228, B: 292B, K: 511C, H: 189D

4681 מָחָה *māḥâ*[1], [A] to wash off, wipe out, blot out, destroy; [C] to be blotted out, be wiped out, be exterminated; [G] to cause to blot out, S: 4229, B: 562A, K: 511C, H: 189D

4682 מָחָה *māḥâ*[2], [A] to continue along, stretch along, S: 4229, B: 562B, K: 512A, H: 190A

4683 מָחָה *māḥâ*[3], [E] (choice food-dishes) to be filled with marrow, S: 4229, B: 562D, K: 512A, H: 190A

4684 מְחוּגָה *m^{e}ḥûgâ*, compass (for making circles), S: 4230, B: 295B, K: 512A, H: 190A

4685 מָחוֹז *māḥôz*, haven, harbor, S: 4231, B: 562C, K: 512A, H: 190A

4686 מְחוּיָאֵל *m^{e}ḥûyā'ēl*, Mehujael, S: 4232, B: 562C, K: 512A, H: 190A

4687 מַחֲוִים *maḥ^{a}wîm*, Mahavite, S: 4233, B: 296A, K: 512A, H: 190A

4688 מָחוֹל *māḥôl*[1], circle-dancing, round-dancing, S: 4234, B: 298B, K: 512B, H: 190A

4689 מָחוֹל *māḥôl*[2], Mahol, S: 4235, B: 562D, K: 512B, H: 190A

4690 מַחֲזֶה *maḥ^{a}zeh*, vision, S: 4236, B: 303C, K: 512B, H: 190A

4691 מֶחֱזָה *meḥ^{e}zâ*, light, place of seeing, window, S: 4237, B: 303D, K: 512B, H: 190B

4692 מַחֲזִיאוֹת *maḥ^{a}zî'ôt*, Mahazioth, S: 4238, B: 303D, K: 512B, H: 190B

4693 מְחִי *m^{e}ḥî*, blow (of a battering ram), S: 4239, B: 562C, K: 512C, H: 190B

4694 מְחִידָא *m^{e}ḥîdā'*, Mehida, S: 4240, B: 563A, K: 512C, H: 190B

4695 מִחְיָה *miḥyâ*, saving of a life; raw flesh; food, sustenance; relief, recovering, S: 4241, B: 313C, K: 512C, H: 190B

4696 מְחִיָּיאֵל *m^{e}ḥiyyā'ēl*, variant: Mehijael, S: 4232, B: 562C, K: 512C, H: 190B

4697 מְחִיר *m^{e}ḥîr*[1], price, cost, money, S: 4242, B: 564B, K: 512C, H: 190B

4698 מְחִיר *m^{e}ḥîr*[2], Mehir, S: 4243, B: 564B, K: 512D, H: 190B

4699 מַחֲלֵב *maḥ^{a}lēb*, variant: Mahaleb, see 2475, S: 2256† + 392†, B*, K: 512D, H*

4700 מַחֲלֶה *maḥ^{a}leh*, sickness, disease, S: 4245, B: 318B, K: 512D, H: 190B

4701 מַחֲלָה *maḥ^{a}lâ*, disease, sickness, S: 4245, B: 318B, K: 512D, H: 190B

4702 מַחְלָה *maḥlâ*, Mahlah, S: 4244, B: 563A, K: 512D, H: 190B

4703 מְחֹלָה *m^{e}ḥōlâ*, circle-dance, round-dance, S: 4246, B: 298B, K: 512D, H: 190C

4704 מְחִלָּה *mᵉḥillâ*, hole, S: 4247, B: 320A, K: 513A, H: 190C

4705 מַחְלוֹן *maḥlôn*, Mahlon, S: 4248, B: 563A, K: 513A, H: 190C

4706 מַחְלִי *maḥlî*[1], Mahli, S: 4249, B: 563A, K: 513A, H: 190C 1.

4707 מַחְלִי *maḥlî*[2], Mahlite, S: 4250, B: 563A, K: 513A, H: 190C 2.

4708 מַחֲלֻיִים *maḥᵃluyîm*, sickness (caused by wounding), S: 4251†, B: 318C, K: 513A, H: 190C

4709 מַחֲלָף *maḥᵃlāp*, utensil: pan *or* knife, S: 4252, B: 322C, K: 513A, H: 190C

4710 מַחְלָפָה *maḥᵃlāpâ*, braids (of hair), S: 4253, B: 322C, K: 513A, H: 190C

4711 מַחֲלָצוֹת *maḥᵃlāṣôt*, fine robes, fine, white, festival garments, S: 4254†, B: 323A, K: 513A, H: 190C

4712 מַחְלְקוֹת *maḥlᵉqôt*, variant: smoothness, slipperiness, see 6154, S: 5555†, B: 325D, K: 660D d), H: 190C 3.

4713 מַחֲלֹקֶת *maḥᵃlōqet*, portion, share (of land); division, group (of people), S: 4256, B: 324D, K: 513B, H: 190C

4714 מָחֲלַת *māḥᵃlat*[1], mahalath (t.t. in the Psalms), S: 4257, B: 318D, K: 513B, H: 190D

4715 מָחֲלַת *māḥᵃlat*[2], Mahalath, S: 4258, B: 563B, K: 513B, H: 190D

4716 מְחֹלָתִי *mᵉḥōlātî*, Meholathite, of Meholah, S: 4259, B: 563B, K: 513B, H: 190D

4717 מַחְמָאֹת *maḥmā'ōt*, butter, S: 4260†, B: 563B, K: 513C, H: 190D

4718 מַחְמָד *maḥmād*, thing of value, something of delight, treasure, S: 4261, B: 326D, K: 513C, H: 190D

4719 מַחְמֹד *maḥmōd*, treasure, something precious, S: 4262†, B: 327A, K: 513C, H: 190D

4720 מַחְמָל *maḥmāl*, yearning, S: 4263, B: 328C, K: 513C, H: 190D

4721 מַחְמֶצֶת *maḥmeṣet*, something made with yeast, S: , B: 330A, K: 513C, H: 190D

4722 מַחֲנֶה *maḥᵃneh*, camp, group (military or civilian), S: 4264, B: 334A, K: 513D, H: 190D

4723 מַחֲנֵה־דָן *maḥᵃnēh-dān*, Mahaneh Dan, S: 4265, B: 334B, K: 513D, H: 191A

4724 מַחֲנַיִם *maḥᵃnayim*, Mahanaim, S: 4266, B: 334B, K: 514A, H: 191A

4725 מַחֲנָק *maḥᵃnāq*, strangling, suffocation, S: 4267, B: 338B, K: 514A, H: 191A

4726 מַחְסֶה *maḥseh*, refuge, shelter, S: 4268, B: 340B, K: 514A, H: 191A

4727 מַחְסוֹם *maḥsôm*, muzzle, S: 4269, B: 340D, K: 514B, H: 191A

4728 מַחְסוֹר *maḥsôr*, need, lack of, scarcity, *hence* poverty, S: 4270, B: 341D, K: 514B, H: 191A

4729 מַחְסֵיָה *maḥsēyâ*, Mahseiah, S: 4271, B: 340C, K: 514B, H: 191A

4730 מָחַץ *māḥaṣ*, [A] to beat to pieces, crush, shatter, S: 4272, B: 563C, K: 514B, H: 191A

4731 מַחַץ *maḥaṣ*, wound, S: 4273, B: 563D, K: 514C, H: 191B

4732 מַחְצֵב *maḥṣēb*, dressed (stone), hewn (stone), S: 4274, B: 345B, K: 514C, H: 191B

4733 מֶחֱצָה *meḥᵉṣâ*, half, S: 4275, B: 345D, K: 514C, H: 191B

4734 מַחֲצִית *maḥᵃṣît*, half; noon, middle of the day, S: 4276, B: 345D, K: 514C, H: 191B

4735 מָחַק *māḥaq*, [A] to crush, smash, S: 4277, B: 563D, K: 514D, H: 191B

4736 מֶחְקָר *meḥqār*, (unexplored) depths (of the earth), S: 4278, B: 350D, K: 514D, H: 191B

4737 מָחָר *māḥār*, tomorrow, the next day, in the future, S: 4279, B: 563D, K: 514D, H: 191B

4738 מַחֲרָאָה *maḥᵃrā'â*, latrine, S: 4280, B: 351A, K: 515A, H: 191C

4739 מַחֲרֵשָׁה *maḥᵃrēšâ*, plowshare, S: 4281 & 4282†, B: 361A, K: 515A, H: 191C

4740 מָחֳרָת *moḥᵒrāt*, the next day, the day after, S: 4283, B: 564A, K: 515A, H: 191C

4741 מַחְשֹׂף *maḥśōp*, exposing, laying bare (of wood), S: 4286, B: 362D, K: 515A, H: 191C

4742 מַחֲשָׁבָה *maḥᵃšābâ*, thought, plan, scheme, plot, design, S: 4284, B: 364B, K: 515B, H: 191C

4743 מַחְשָׁךְ *maḥšāk*, place of darkness, hiding place, S: 4285, B: 365B, K: 515C, H: 191D

4744 מַחַת *maḥat*, Mahath, S: 4287, B: 367B, K: 515C, H: 191D

4745 מְחִתָּה *mᵉḥittâ*, ruin, undoing; terror, horror, S: 4288, B: 369D, K: 515C, H: 191D

4746 מַחְתָּה *maḥtâ*, censer, firepan, tray, S: 4289, B: 367B, K: 515C, H: 191D

4747 מַחְתֶּרֶת *maḥteret*, (the act of) breaking into (a house), S: 4290, B: 369A, K: 515D, H: 191D

4748 מַטְאֲטֵא *maṭ'ᵃṭē'*, broom, S: 4292, B: 370A, K: 515D, H: 191D

4749 מַטְבֵּחַ *maṭbēaḥ*, place of slaughter, slaughter yard, S: 4293, B: 371A, K: 515D, H: 191D

4750 מָטֶה *māṭeh*, variant: one approaching death, S*, B: 556D, K: 515D, H: 185C

4751 מַטֶּה *maṭṭeh*, tribe; staff, scepter, rod; club, S: 4294, B: 641C, K: 515D, H: 191D

4752 מַטָּה *maṭṭâ*, below, beneath, lower, bottom, S: 4295, B: 641B, K: 516B, H: 192A

4753 מִטָּה *miṭṭâ*, bed, couch, bier, carriage, S: 4296, B: 641D, K: 516C, H: 192A

4754 מֻטֶּה *muṭṭeh*, injustice, warping (of justice), crookedness (of law), S: 4297, B: 642A, K: 516D, H: 192A

4755 מֻטָּה *muṭṭâ*, variant: outspreading (of wings), S: 4298, B: 642A, K: 516D, H: 192A

4756 מִטְהָר *miṭhār*, variant: purity, splendor, S: 2892†, B: 372D, K: 348B, H: 192B

4757 מַטְוֶה *maṭweh*, that which is spun, yarn, S: 4299, B: 376A, K: 516D, H: 192B

4758 מָטִיל *māṭîl*, (iron) rod, S: 4300†, B: 564C, K: 516D, H: 192B

4759 מַטְמוֹן *maṭmôn*, (hidden) treasure, (hidden) riches, S: 4301, B: 380C, K: 517A, H: 192B

4760 מַטָּע *maṭṭā'*, (the act or place of) planting, S: 4302, B: 642D, K: 517A, H: 192B

4761 מַטְעָם *maṭ'ām*, tasty food, delicacy, S: 4303†, B: 381B, K: 517A, H: 192B

4762 מִטְפַּחַת *miṭpaḥat*, cloak, shawl, S: 4304, B: 381C, K: 517A, H: 192B

4763 מָטַר *māṭar*, [C] to be rained upon; [G] to send rain down on; [H] to be rained upon, S: 4305, B: 565A, K: 517A, H: 192B

4764 מָטָר *māṭār*, rain, rain shower, S: 4306, B: 564D, K: 517B, H: 192C

4765 מַטְרֵד *maṭrēd*, Matred, S: 4308, B: 382B, K: 517D, H: 192C

4766 מַטָּרָה *maṭṭārâ*, (the court of the) guard, i.e., place of confinement; (the Gate of the) Guard (a place); target, S: 4307, B: 643C, K: 517C, H: 192C

4767 מַטְרִי *maṭrî*, Matri, S: 4309, B: 565A, K: 517D, H: 192C

4768 מַי *may*, variant: see 4537, S: 4100†, B*, K: 518A, H: 192C

4769 מִי *mî*, who?, what?, which?; anyone, whoever, S: 4310, B: 566A, K: 518B, H: 192C

4770 מֵי הַיַּרְקוֹן *mê hayyarqôn*, Me Jarkon, S: 4313, B: 566A, K: 518D, H: 193A

4771 מֵי זָהָב *mê zāhāb*, Me-Zahab, S: 4314, B: 566A, K: 518D, H: 193A

4772 מֵידְבָא *mêdᵉbā'*, Medeba, S: 4311, B: 567D, K: 518D, H: 193A

4773 מֵידָד *mêdād*, Medad, S: 4312, B: 392A, K: 518D, H: 193A

4774 מֵיטָב *mêṭāb*, best (part of something), S: 4315, B: 406B, K: 519A, H: 193A

4775 מִיכָא *mîkā'*, Mica, S: 4316, B: 567D, K: 519A, H: 193A

4776 מִיכָאֵל *mîkā'ēl*, Michael, S: 4317, B: 567C, K: 519A, H: 193A

4777 מִיכָה *mîkâ*, Micah; Mica; Micaiah, S: 4318, B: 567D, K: 519A, H: 193A

4778 מִיכָהוּ *mîkāhû*, variant: Micahu, see 4780, S: 4319, B: 567C, K: 519B, H: 193A

4779 מִיכָיָה *mîkāyâ*, Micaiah, S: 4320, B: 567C, K: 519B, H: 193A

4780 מִיכָיָהוּ *mîkāyāhû*, Micaiah, S: 4322, B: 567C, K: 519B, H: 193A

4781 מִיכָיְהוּ *mîkāyᵉhû*, Micaiah; Micah, S: 4321, B: 567C, K: 519B, H: 193A

4782 מִיכָל *mîkāl*, brook, stream, S: 4323, B: 568A, K: 519B, H: 193A

4783 מִיכַל *mîkal*, Michal, S: 4324†, B: 568A, K: 519B, H: 193A

4784 מַיִם *mayim*, water, S: 4325, B: 565A, K: 517D, H: 193A

4785 מִיָּמִן *miyyāmîn*, Mijamin, S: 4326†, B: 568A, K: 519C, H: 193B

4786 מִין *mîn*, kind: genus *or* species, S: 4327, B: 568B, K: 519C, H: 193B

4787 מֵינֶקֶת *mêneqet*, nursing woman, wet-nurse, S: 3243†, B: 413B, K: 519C, H: 193B

4788 מֵיסָךְ *mêsāk*, variant: see 4590, S: 4329, B: 697B, K: 519D, H: 193C

4789 מֵיפַעַת *mêpa'at*, Mephaath, S: 4158, B: 422B, K: 519D, H: 193C

4790 מִיץ *mîṣ*, pressing, squeezing, S: 4330, B: 568C, K: 519D, H: 193C

4791 מֵישָׁא *mêšā'*, Mesha, S: 4331, B: 568C, K: 519D, H: 193C

4792 מִישָׁאֵל *mîšā'ēl*, Mishael, S: 4332, B: 567D, K: 519D, H: 193C

4793 מִישׁוֹר *mîšôr*, (geographical) plateau, plain, level ground; (of ruling and right living) uprightness, justice, straightness, S: 4334, B: 449D, K: 520A, H: 193C

4794 מֵישַׁךְ *mêšak*, Meshach, S: 4335, B: 568D, K: 520B, H: 193C

4795 מֵישַׁע *mêša'*, Mesha, S: 4338, B: 448A, K: 520B, H: 193C

4796 מֵישָׁע *mêšā'*, Mesha, S: 4337, B: 448A, K: 520B, H: 193C

4797 מֵישָׁרִים *mêšārîm*, uprightness, fairness, equity, justice, S: 4339†, B: 449C, K: 520B, H: 193C

4798 מֵיתָר *mêtār*, rope, cord; bow-string, S: 4340, B: 452D, K: 520C, H: 193D

4799 מַכְאֹב *mak'ōb*, pain, grief, sorrow, suffering, S: 4341, B: 456B, K: 520C, H: 193D

4800 מַכְבֵּנָה *makbēnâ*, Macbenah, S: 4343†, B: 460A, K: 520D, H: 193D

4801 מַכְבַּנַּי *makbannay*, Macbannai, S: 4344, B: 460C, K: 520D, H: 193D

4802 מַכְבֵּר *makbēr*, thick cloth, S: 4346†, B: 460D, K: 520D, H: 193D

4803 מִכְבָּר *mikbār*, grating, lattice-work, S: 4345†, B: 460D, K: 520D, H: 193D

4804 מַכָּה *makkâ*, wound, injury; plague, affliction, calamity, disaster, S: 4347, B: 646D, K: 520D, H: 193D

4805 מִכְוָה *mikwâ*, burn (on the skin), S: 4348, B: 465A, K: 521A, H: 194A

4806 מָכוֹן *mākôn*, (established) place, site; foundation (of earth or throne), S: 4349, B: 467C, K: 521A, H: 194A

4807 מְכוֹנָה *m^{e}kônâ*, movable stand; (established) place, foundation, S: 4350 & 4369†, B: 467D, K: 521A, H: 194A

4808 מְכוּרָה *m^{e}kûrâ*, ancestry, origin, parentage, S: 4351, B: 468D, K: 521B, H: 194A

4809 מָכִי *mākî*, Maki, S: 4352, B: 568D, K: 521B, H: 194A

4810 מָכִיר *mākîr*, Makir, Makirite, S: 4353, B: 569C, K: 521B, H: 194B

4811 מָכִירִי *mākîrî*, Makirite, S: 4354, B: 569C, K: 521B, H: 194B

4812 מָכַךְ *mākak*, [A] to sink, go down, waste away; [C] to sag, be sunk down; [H] to be brought low, S: 4355, B: 568D, K: 521C, H: 194B

4813 מִכְלָא *miklā'*, pen, fold (for sheep or goats), S: 4356†, B: 476C, K: 521C, H: 194B

4814 מִכְלוֹל *miklôl*, fullness, completeness, perfection, S: 4358, B: 483B, K: 521C, H: 194B

4815 מַכְלוּל *maklûl*, beautiful garment, finery, S: 4360†, B: 483B, K: 521D, H: 194B

4816 מִכְלוֹת *miklôt*, solid (gold), purest (gold), S: 4357†, B: 479A, K: 521C, H: 194B

4817 מִכְלָל *miklāl*, perfection, S: 4359, B: 483B, K: 521D, H: 194B

4818 מַכֹּלֶת *makkōlet*, food, S: 4361, B: 38C, K: 521D, H: 194B

4819 מִכְמָן *mikmān*, (hidden) treasure, S: 4362, B: 485A, K: 521D, H: 194C

4820 מִכְמָס *mikmās*, Micmash, S: 4363, B: 485A, K: 521D, H: 194C

4821 מִכְמָר *mikmār*, net, snare (for capture of game), S: 4364, B: 485B, K: 522A, H: 194C

4822 מַכְמֹר *makmōr*, variant: net, snare, S: 4365†, B: 485C, K: 522A, H: 194C

4823 מִכְמֶרֶת *mikmeret*, fishing net, dragnet (for fish), S: 4365, B: 485C, K: 522A, H: 194C

4824 מִכְמֹרֶת *mikmōret*, variant: fishing net, dragnet (for fish), S: 4365, B: 485C, K: 522A, H: 194C

4825 מִכְמָשׂ *mikmāś*, Micmash, S: 4363, B: 485A, K: 521D, H: 194C

4826 מִכְמְתָת *mikm^{e}tāt*, Micmethath, S: 4366, B: 485C, K: 522A, H: 194C

4827 מַכְנַדְבַי *maknadbay*, Macnadebai, S: 4367, B: 569A, K: 522A, H: 194C

4828 מְכֹנָה *m^{e}kōnâ*, Meconah, S: 4368, B: 569A, K: 522A, H: 194C

4829 מִכְנָס *miknās*, undergarment, S: 4370, B: 488B, K: 522A, H: 194C

4830 מֶכֶס *mekes*, tribute, cultic dues *or* taxes, S: 4371, B: 493D, K: 522B, H: 194C

4831 מִכְסָה *miksâ*, number (of persons); amount, valuation (of a thing), S: 4373, B: 493D, K: 522B, H: 194C

4832 מִכְסֶה *mikseh*, covering, S: 4372, B: 492C, K: 522B, H: 194C

4833 מְכַסֶּה *m^{e}kasseh*, covering; layer of fat (on the kidneys), S: 4374, B: 492C, K: 522B, H: 194C

4834 מַכְפֵּלָה *makpēlâ*, Machpelah, S: 4375, B: 495D, K: 522C, H: 194D

4835 מָכַר *mākar*, [A] to sell; [C] to be sold; [F] to sell oneself, S: 4376, B: 569A, K: 522C, H: 194D

4836 מֶכֶר *meker*, worth, value; merchandise, S: 4377, B: 569C, K: 523A, H: 195A

4837 מַכָּר *makkār*, treasurer, S: 4378, B: 648C, K: 523B, H: 195A

4838 מִכְרֶה *mikreh*, (salt) pit, S: 4379, B: 500B, K: 523B, H: 195A

4839 מְכֵרָה *m^{e}kērâ*, sword, weapon, S: 4380, B: 468D, K: 523B, H: 195A

4840 מִכְרִי *mikrî*, Micri, S: 4381, B: 569D, K: 523B, H: 195A

4841 מְכֵרָתִי *m^{e}kērātî*, Mekerathite, S: 4382, B: 569D, K: 523B, H: 195A

4842 מִכְשׁוֹל *mikšôl*, stumbling block, obstacle; (occasion of) stumbling, downfall, S: 4383, B: 506A, K: 523B, H: 195A

4843 מַכְשֵׁלָה *makšēlâ*, heap of ruins, heap of rubble, S: 4384, B: 506B, K: 523C, H: 195A

4844 מִכְתָּב *miktāb*, writing, inscription, letter, S: 4385, B: 508B, K: 523C, H: 195A

4845 מְכִתָּה *m^{e}kittâ*, pieces, crushed fragments, S: 4386, B: 510C, K: 523C, H: 195B

4846 מִכְתָּם *miktām*, miktam (t.t. in the Psalms), S: 4387, B: 508D, K: 523C, H: 195B

4847 מַכְתֵּשׁ *maktēš*, hollow place; mortar; market district, S: 4388 & 4389, B: 509D, K: 523D, H: 195B

4848 מָלֵא[1] *mālē'*[1], [A] to fill up, be full; [B] to be ordained, fulfilled; [C] to be filled, become filled up; [D] to fill up, satisfy; ordain, consecrate; [E] to be set; [F] to unite together, S: 4390, B: 569D, K: 523D, H: 195B

4849 מָלֵא[2] *mālē'*[2], filled, full, S: 4392, B: 570D, K: 525A, H: 196A

4850 מְלֹא *m^{e}lō'*, what fills, what makes something full; fullness, everything, S: 4393, B: 571A, K: 525B, H: 196A

4851 מִלֹּא *millō'*, variant: Millo, S: 4407, B: 571C, K: 525B, H: 196B

4852 מְלֵאָה *m^{e}lē'â*, full yield (of crops), S: 4395, B: 571B, K: 525C, H: 196B

4853 מִלֻּאָה *millu'â*, mounting (of jewels), setting (of jewels), S: 4396, B: 571B, K: 525C, H: 196B

4854 מִלֻּאִים *millu'îm*, ordination, consecration (of a priest); mounting, setting (of gem stones), S: 4394†, B: 571B, K: 525C, H: 196B

4855 מַלְאָךְ *mal'āk*, angel, messenger, envoy, S: 4397, B: 521C, K: 525D, H: 196B

4856 מְלָאכָה *m^{e}lā'kâ*, work, deed, duty, craft, service; thing, something, S: 4399, B: 521D, K: 526B, H: 196C

4857 מַלְאָכוּת *mal'ākût*, message (from a commissioned messenger), S: 4400†, B: 522B, K: 527B, H: 196D

4858 מַלְאָכִי *mal'ākî*, Malachi, S: 4401, B: 522B, K: 527B, H: 196D

4859 מִלֵּאת *millē't*, setting, mounting, S: 4402, B: 571C, K: 527B, H: 196D

4860 מַלְבּוּשׁ *malbûš*, clothing, robe, attire, garment, S: 4403, B: 528C, K: 527B, H: 196D

4861 מַלְבֵּן *malbēn*, brickwork, brick pavement; (the act of) brickmaking, S: 4404, B: 527C, K: 527C, H: 197A

4862 מָלָה *mālâ*, variant: [D] to fill; [C] be filled, S: 4390†, B: 570B 2, K: 523D, H: 197A

4863 מִלָּה *millâ*, word, speech, what is said, S: 4405, B: 576B, K: 527C, H: 197A

4864 מִלּוֹא *millô'*, supporting terrace (cf. Beth Millo), S: 4407, B: 571C, K: 527D, H: 197A

4865 מַלּוּחַ *mallûaḥ*, salt herb (collected by the destitute and banished), S: 4408, B: 572A, K: 527D, H: 197A

4866 מַלּוּךְ *mallûk*, Malluch, S: 4409, B: 576A, K: 527D, H: 197B

4867 מְלוּכָה *m^{e}lûkâ*, kingship, rulership, royalty, S: 4410, B: 574C, K: 528A, H: 197B

4868 מַלּוּכִי *mallûkî*, Malluch, S: 4409, B: 576A, K: 528A, H: 197B

4869 מָלוֹן *mālôn*, place of overnight lodging, place where one spends the night, S: 4411, B: 533D, K: 528A, H: 197B

4870 מְלוּנָה *m^elûnâ*, hut, structure (of a watchman in the field), S: 4412, B: 534A, K: 528B, H: 197B

4871 מַלּוֹתִי *mallôtî*, Mallothi, S: 4413, B: 576C, K: 528B, H: 197B

4872 מָלַח[1] *mālaḥ*[1], [C] to vanish, be dispersed, S: 4414, B: 571D, K: 528B, H: 197B

4873 מָלַח[2] *mālaḥ*[2], [A] to season with salt; [E] to be salted; [H] to be rubbed with salt, S: 4414, B: 572A, K: 528B, H: 197C

4874 מֶלַח[1] *melaḥ*[1], worn-out clothes, rags, S: 4418†, B: 571D, K: 528C, H: 197C

4875 מֶלַח[2] *melaḥ*[2], salt, S: 4417, B: 571D, K: 528C, H: 197C

4876 מַלָּח *mallāḥ*, sailor, mariner, S: 4419, B: 572A, K: 528C, H: 197C

4877 מְלֵחָה *m^elēḥâ*, salt flat, salt waste-lands, barren country, S: 4420, B: 572A, K: 528D, H: 197C

4878 מִלְחָמָה *milḥāmâ*, battle, war, fighting, S: 4421, B: 536A, K: 528D, H: 197C

4879 מֶלֶט *meleṭ*, clay flooring, S: 4423, B: 572D, K: 529D, H: 198A

4880 מָלַט[1] *mālaṭ*[1], [C] to deliver oneself, escape, flee; [D] to save, deliver, rescue; [G] to rescue; to deliver (a child); [F] to shoot out (of sparks); to escape, S: 4422, B: 572B, K: 529B, H: 197D

4881 מָלַט[2] *mālaṭ*[2], variant: [F] to be bald, S: 4422, B: 572B, K: 529C, H: 198A

4882 מְלַטְיָה *m^elaṭyâ*, Melatiah, S: 4424, B: 572D, K: 529D, H: 198A

4883 מְלִיכוּ *m^elîkû*, variant: Melichu, see 4868, S: 4409†, B: 576A, K: 529D, H: 198A

4884 מְלִילָה *m^elîlâ*, (rubbed) kernels (of grain), S: 4425, B: 576C, K: 529D, H: 198A

4885 מֵלִיץ *mēlîṣ*, intercessor, mediator (in various capacities), S: 3887† & 3945†, B: 539B, K: 481B, H: 198A

4886 מְלִיצָה *m^elîṣâ*, allusive saying, parable; ridicule, S: 4426, B: 539C, K: 529D, H: 198A

4887 מָלַךְ[1] *mālak*[1], [A] to reign as king; [G] to make one a king, have a coronation; [H] be made a king, S: 4427, B: 573D, K: 529D, H: 198A

4888 מָלַךְ[2] *mālak*[2], [C] to ponder, consider carefully within oneself, S: 4427, B: 576A, K: 530C, H: 198C

4889 מֶלֶךְ[1] *melek*[1], king, royal ruler, S: 4428 & 4429, B: 572D, K: 530C, H: 198C

4890 מֶלֶךְ[2] *melek*[2], Melech, S: 4429, B: 574B, K: 531A, H: 198D

4891 מֹלֶךְ *mōlek*, Molech (pagan god), S: 4432, B: 574A, K: 531B, H: 198D

4892 מַלְכֹּדֶת *malkōdet*, trap, snare, S: 4434, B: 540B, K: 531B, H: 198D

4893 מַלְכָּה *malkâ*, queen (outside Israel), wife of a king, S: 4436, B: 573C, K: 531B, H: 198D

4894 מִלְכָּה *milkâ*, Milcah, S: 4435, B: 574C, K: 531C, H: 198D

4895 מַלְכוּת *malkût*, kingdom, empire, realm; reign, royal power, position as a king, S: 4438, B: 574D, K: 531C, H: 198D

4896 מַלְכִּיאֵל *malkî'ēl*, Malkiel, S: 4439, B: 575C, K: 531D, H: 199A

4897 מַלְכִּיאֵלִי *malkî'ēlî*, Malkielite, S: 4440, B: 575C, K: 532A, H*

4898 מַלְכִּיָּה *malkiyyâ*, Malkijah, S: 4441, B: 575D, K: 532A, H: 199A

4899 מַלְכִּיָּהוּ *malkiyyāhû*, Malkijah, S: 4441, B: 575C, K: 532A, H: 199A

4900 מַלְכִּי־צֶדֶק *malkî-ṣedeq*, Melchizedek, S: 4442, B: 575D, K: 532A, H: 199A

4901 מַלְכִּירָם *malkîrām*, Malkiram, S: 4443, B: 575D, K: 532A, H: 199A

4902 מַלְכִּי־שׁוּעַ *malkî-šûa'*, Malki-Shua, S: 4444†, B: 575D, K: 532B, H: 199A

4903 מַלְכָּם *malkām*, Malcam, Molech, S: 4445, B: 575D, K: 532B, H: 199A

4904 מִלְכֹּם *milkōm*, Milcom, Molech, S: 4445, B: 575D, K: 532B, H: 199A

4905 מַלְכֵּן *malkēn*, variant: see 4861, S: 4404†, B: 527C 1, K: 532B, H: 199A

4906 מְלֶכֶת *m^eleket*, Queen (of Heaven), S: 4446, B: 573D, K: 532B, H: 199A

4907 מֹלֶכֶת *mōleket*, variant: Moleketh, see 2168, S: 4447, B: 574C, K: 532C, H: 199A

4908 מָלַל[1] *mālal*[1], [A] to wither away; [D] to wither; [F] be blunted (of arrows), S: 5243†, B: 576C, K: 532C, H: 199B

4909 מָלַל[2] *mālal*[2], [A] to circumcise; [C] to be cut off, S: 5243†, B: 576D, K: 532C, H: 199B

4910 מָלַל[3] *mālal*[3], [D] to say, speak, proclaim, S: 4448, B: 576B, K: 532C, H: 199B

4911 מָלַל[4] *mālal*[4], [A] to signal by rubbing or scraping, S: 4448, B: 576C, K: 532C, H: 199B

4912 מִלְלַי *mil^elay*, Milalai, S: 4450, B: 576C, K: 532D, H: 199B

4913 מַלְמָד *malmād*, oxgoad, S: 4451, B: 541A, K: 532D, H: 199B

4914 מָלַץ *mālaṣ*, [C] to be smooth, pleasant, palatable, sweet, S: 4452, B: 576D, K: 532D, H: 199B

4915 מֶלְצַר *melṣar*, guard, guardian, official, S: 4453, B: 576D, K: 533A, H: 199C

4916 מָלַק *mālaq*, [A] to wring off, pinch off (the head of a bird), S: 4454, B: 577A, K: 533A, H: 199C

4917 מַלְקוֹחַ *malqôaḥ*, spoils of war, plunder, war-booty, S: 4455, B: 544B, K: 533A, H: 199C

4918 מַלְקוֹחַיִם *malqôḥayim*, roof of the mouth, palate, S: 4455†, B: 544C, K: 533B, H: 199C

4919 מַלְקוֹשׁ *malqôš*, spring rains, latter rains of March-April, S: 4456, B: 545B, K: 533B, H: 199C

4920 מֶלְקָחַיִם *melqāḥayim*, (pair of) wick trimmers; (pair of) tongs, S: 4457†, B: 544C, K: 533B, H: 199C

4921 מֶלְתָּחָה *meltāḥâ*, wardrobe, S: 4458, B: 547A, K: 533B, H: 199C

4922 מַלְתָּעוֹת *maltā'ôt*, fangs, teeth, S: 4459†, B: 1069A, K: 582C, H: 199C

4923 מַמְּגֻרָה *mamm^egûrâ*, granary, grain-pit, S: 4460, B: 158C, K: 533C, H: 199C

4924 מֵמַד *mēmād*, dimensions, measurement, S: 4461†, B: 551D, K: 533C, H: 199C

4925 מְמוּכָן *m^emûkān*, Memucan, S: 4462, B: 577A, K: 533C, H: 199C

4926 מָמוֹת *māmôt*, death, S: 4463, B: 560D, K: 533C, H: 199C

4927 מַמְזֵר *mamzēr*, one born of a forbidden marriage; foreigner, S: 4464, B: 561C, K: 533C, H: 199C

4928 מִמְכָּר *mimkār*, what is sold, goods, merchandise, S: 4465, B: 569D, K: 533D, H: 199D

4929 מִמְכֶּרֶת *mimkeret*, selling, sale, S: 4466, B: 569D, K: 533D, H: 199D

4930 מַמְלָכָה *mamlākâ*, kingdom, royal dominion, reign, S: 4467, B: 575A, K: 533D, H: 199D

4931 מַמְלָכוּת *mamlākût*, kingdom, realm, royal dominion, S: 4468, B: 575C, K: 534A, H: 199D

4932 מִמְסָךְ *mimsāk*, bowl of mixed wine, S: 4469, B: 587C, K: 534A, H: 199D

4933 מֶמֶר *memer*, bitterness, annoyance, S: 4470, B: 601B, K: 534B, H: 200A

4934 מַמְרֵא[1] *mamrē'*[1], Mamre, S: 4471, B: 577B 1. & 3., K: 534B, H: 200A

4935 מַמְרֵא[2] *mamrē'*[2], Mamre, S: 4471, B: 577B 2., K: 534B, H: 200A

4936 מַמְּרֹרִים *mamm^erōrîm*, misery, bitterness, S: 4472†, B: 601B, K: 534B, H: 200A

4937 מִמְשַׁח *mimšaḥ*, anointing, S: 4473, B: 603D, K: 534B, H: 200A

4938 מִמְשָׁל *mimšāl*, leader, ruler; power, dominion, sovereign authority, S: 4474, B: 606A, K: 534B, H: 200A

4939 מֶמְשָׁלָה *memšālâ*, dominion, power to govern, authority to rule, S: 4475, B: 606A, K: 534C, H: 200A

4940 מִמְשָׁק *mimšāq*, place (overgrown with weeds), S: 4476, B: 606C, K: 534C, H: 200A

4941 מַמְתַקִּים *mamtaqqîm*, sweetness, sweet things, S: 4477†, B: 609A, K: 534C, H: 200A

4942 מָן[1] *mān*[1], manna, S: 4478, B: 577B, K: 534C, H: 200A

4943 מָן[2] *mān*[2], what?, S: 4478, B: 577C, K: 534D, H: 200B

4944 מֵן[1] *mēn*[1], (music of) stringed instruments, S: 4482, B: 577C, K: 535A, H: 200A

4945 מֵן[2] *mēn*[2], share, portion, S: 4482, B: 585D, K: 534D, H*

4946 מִן *min*, from, out of, of; since, after; more than; because of, S: 4480, B: 577C, K: 535A, H: 200B

4947 מַנְגִּינָה *mangînâ*, mocking song, S: 4485, B: 618D, K: 536D, H: 201B

4948 מָנָה[1] *mānā*[1], [A] to count, number, take a census; [C] to be counted, be numbered; [D] to assign, appoint, provide; [E] to be assigned, be appointed, S: 4487, B: 584A, K: 536D, H: 201B

4949 מָנֶה *māneh*, mina (unit of weight of precious metal), S: 4488, B: 584B, K: 537B, H: 201C

4950 [2]מָנָה *mānā*[2], share, portion, piece, S: 4490, B: 584B, K: 537B, H: 201C

4951 מֹנֶה *mōneh*, time, occurrence, S: 4489, B: 584C, K: 537B, H: 201C

4952 מִנְהָג *minhāg*, driving (of a chariot), S: 4491, B: 624C, K: 537C, H: 201C

4953 מִנְהָרָה *minhārâ*, shelter, hole (in mountain clefts), S: 4492, B: 626A, K: 537C, H: 201C

4954 מָנוֹד *mānôd*, shaking of the head (in scorn or derision), S: 4493, B: 627B, K: 537C, H: 201C

4955 [1]מָנוֹחַ *mānôaḥ*[1], resting place, S: 4494, B: 629C, K: 537C, H: 201C

4956 [2]מָנוֹחַ *mānôaḥ*[2], Manoah, S: 4495, B: 629D, K: 537D, H: 201D

4957 מְנוּחָה *menûḥâ*, resting place, S: 4496, B: 629D, K: 537D, H: 201D

4958 מָנוֹל *mānôl*, variant: property, possessions, S: 5186† + 4512†, B: 649B, K: 539C, H: 201D

4959 מָנוֹן *mānôn*, grief, S: 4497, B: 584D, K: 537D, H*

4960 מָנוֹס *mānôs*, place to flee, place of escape, refuge, S: 4498, B: 631A, K: 537D, H: 201D

4961 מְנוּסָה *menûsâ*, flight, fleeing, S: 4499, B: 631A, K: 538A, H: 202A

4962 מָנוֹר *mānôr*, (weaver's) rod, beam (of weavers), S: 4500, B: 644D, K: 538A, H: 202A

4963 מְנוֹרָה *menôrâ*, lampstand, S: 4501, B: 633A, K: 538A, H: 202A

4964 מִנְּזָר *minnezār*, guard, watchman, S: 4502, B: 634D, K: 538A, H: 202A

4965 מֻנָּח *munnāḥ*, open area, S: 3240† & 5117†, B: 629A, K: 602C, H: 202A

4966 מִנְחָה *minḥâ*, grain offering; animal offering or sacrifice; gift, tribute, present, S: 4503, B: 585A, K: 538B, H: 202A

4967 מְנֻחוֹת *menuḥôt*, variant: Manuhoth, see 4971, S: 4496†, B: 629D, K: 537D, H: 202B

4968 מְנַחֵם *menaḥēm*, Menahem, S: 4505, B: 637C, K: 539A, H: 202B

4969 [1]מָנַחַת *mānaḥat*[1], Manahath, S: 4506, B: 630A, K: 539A, H: 202B

4970 [2]מָנַחַת *mānaḥat*[2], Manahath, S: 4506, B: 630A, K: 539A, H: 202B

4971 מָנַחְתִּי *mānaḥtî*, Manahathite, S: 2679† & 2680†, B: 630A, K: 539B, H: 202B

4972 מְנִי *menî*, Destiny (pagan god), S: 4507, B: 584C, K: 539B, H: 202B

4973 [1]מִנִּי *minnî*[1], Minni, S: 4508, B: 585D, K: 539B, H: 202B

4974 [2]מִנִּי *minnî*[2], from, out of; more than, S: 4480, B: 577C, K: 535A, H: 202B

4975 מִנְיָמִין *minyāmîn*, Miniamin, S: 4509, B: 568B, K: 539B, H: 202B

4976 [1]מִנִּית *minnît*[1], Minnith, S: 4511, B: 585D, K: 539C, H: 202B

4977 [2]מִנִּית *minnît*[2], variant: rice [?], S: 4511†, B: 585D, K: 539C, H: 202B

4978 מִנְלֶה *minleh*, possession, acquisition, S: 4512, B: 649B, K: 539C, H: 202C

4979 מָנַע *māna'*, [A] to keep from, withhold, deny, refuse; [C] to be kept from, be withheld, be denied, S: 4513, B: 586A, K: 539C, H: 202C

4980 מַנְעוּל *man'ûl*, bolt, lock (of a door), S: 4514, B: 653B, K: 539D, H: 202C

4981 מִנְעָל *min'āl*, bolt (on a gate), S: 4515, B: 653B, K: 539D, H: 202C

4982 מַנְעַמִּים *man'ammîm*, (edible) delicacies, S: 4516†, B: 654B, K: 539D, H: 202C

4983 מְנַעַנְעִים *mena'an'îm*, sistrum, S: 4517†, B: 631C, K: 539D, H: 202C

4984 מְנַקִּית *menaqqît*, bowl used for drink offering, S: 4518, B: 667D, K: 540A, H: 202C

4985 מְנַשֶּׁה *menaššeh*, Manasseh, S: 4519, B: 586B, K: 540A, H: 202C

4986 מְנַשִּׁי *menaššî*, Manassite, of Manasseh, S: 4520, B: 586D, K: 540B, H: 202D

4987 מְנָת *menāt*, portion, lot, assigned share, S: 4521, B: 584C, K: 540B, H: 202D

4988 מָס *mās*, despairing (man), S: 4523, B: 588A, K: 540C, H: 202D

4989 מַס *mas*, forced labor, slave labor, S: 4522, B: 586D, K: 540C, H: 202D

4990 מֵסַב *mēsab*, surrounding; round table, circle of feasters; (as adv.) around, round about, S: 4524, B: 687B, K: 540D, H: 203A

4991 מְסִבָּה *mesibbâ*, (as adv.) around, round about, S: 4524†, B: 687B, K: 540D, H: 203A

4992 מִסָּבִיב *missābîb*, variant: Missabib, see 4474, S: 4036†, B: 687A 1d, K: 493B, H: 182A

4993 [1]מַסְגֵּר *masgēr*[1], prison, dungeon, S: 4525, B: 689D, K: 540D, H: 203A

4994 [2]מַסְגֵּר *masgēr*[2], artisan, S: 4525, B: 689D, K: 541A, H: 203A

4995 מִסְגֶּרֶת *misgeret*, side panels (of a building); rim (of a table and base); stronghold; den, S: 4526, B: 689D, K: 541A, H: 203A

4996 מַסַּד *massad*, foundation, S: 4527, B: 414C, K: 541A, H: 203A

4997 מִסְדְּרוֹן *misderôn*, porch, vestibule, S: 4528, B: 690C, K: 541A, H: 203A

4998 מָסָה *māsâ*, [G] to melt, dissolve; to consume; to drench (with tears), S: 4529, B: 587B, K: 541A, H: 203A

4999 [1]מַסָּה *massâ*[1], trial, test, temptation, S: 531, B: 650B, K: 541B, H: 203B

5000 [2]מַסָּה *massâ*[2], despair, S: 4531, B: 588A, K: 541B, H: 203B

5001 [3]מַסָּה *massâ*[3], Massah, S: 4532, B: 650C, K: 541B, H: 203B

5002 מִסָּה *missâ*, proportion, measure, S: 4530, B: 588B, K: 541B, H: 203B

5003 מַסְוֶה *masweh*, veil, covering, S: 4533, B: 691D, K: 541C, H: 203B

5004 מְסוּכָה *mesûkâ*, thorn hedge, S: 4534, B: 692B, K: 541C, H: 203B

5005 מַסָּח *massāḥ*, in turn, taking turns, S: 4535, B: 587B, K: 541C, H: 203B

5006 מִסְחָר *misḥār*, revenue, S: 4536†, B: 695C, K: 541C, H: 203B

5007 מָסַךְ *māsak*, [A] to mingle, mix (substances into drinks), S: 4537, B: 587C, K: 541C, H: 203B

5008 מֶסֶךְ *mesek*, mixture (of spices), S: 4538, B: 587C, K: 541D, H: 203B

5009 מָסָךְ *māsāk*, curtain, covering; shield, defense, S: 4539, B: 697A, K: 541D, H: 203B

5010 מְסֻכָּה *mesukâ*, covering, S: 4540, B: 697B, K: 541D, H: 203C

5011 [1]מַסֵּכָה *massēkâ*[1], image, idol (of cast metal), S: 4541, B: 651A, K: 541D, H: 203C

5012 [2]מַסֵּכָה *massēkâ*[2], (woven) blanket, (interwoven) covering, S: 4541, B: 651B, K: 542A, H: 203C

5013 [3]מַסֵּכָה *massēkâ*[3], variant: alliance, S: 4541, B: 651B, K: 542A, H: 203C

5014 מִסְכֵּן *miskēn*, poor, needy (one), S: 4542, B: 587C, K: 542A, H: 203C

5015 מְסֻכָּן *mesukkān*, variant: a kind of tree [?], see 6123, S: 5533†, B: 698C, K: 658B, H: 203C

5016 מִסְכְּנוֹת *miskenôt*, storage places, warehouses, S: 4543†, B: 698B, K: 542B, H: 203D

5017 מִסְכֵּנֻת *miskēnut*, scarcity, poverty, S: 4544, B: 587D, K: 542B, H: 203D

5018 מַסֶּכֶת *masseket*, warp-threads (the lengthwise threads of a loom), S: 4545, B: 651C, K: 542B, H: 203D

5019 מְסִלָּה *mesillâ*, main road, (raised) highway, S: 4546, B: 700C, K: 542B, H: 203D

5020 מַסְלוּל *maslûl*, highway, S: 4547, B: 700C, K: 542C, H: 203D

5021 מַסְמֵר *masmēr*, nail, S: 4548, B: 702C & 971B, K: 542C, H: 203D

5022 מָסַס *māsas*, [A] to waste away, dissolve; [C] to be melted, dissolved; [G] to cause to melt, S: 4549, B: 587D, K: 542D, H: 203D

5023 מַסַּע *massa'*, journey, travels from place to place, S: 4550, B: 652C, K: 543A, H: 204A

5024 [1]מַסָּע *massā'*[1], quarry, S: 4551, B: 652D, K: 543A, H: 204A

5025 [2]מַסָּע *massā'*[2], dart, weapon, S: 4551, B: 652D, K: 543A, H: 204A

5026 מִסְעָד *mis'ād*, supports (for a building), S: 4552, B: 703C, K: 543A, H: 204A

5027 מִסְפֵּד *mispēd*, wailing, howling, weeping, mourning, S: 4553, B: 704D, K: 543B, H: 204B

5028 מִסְפּוֹא *mispô'*, fodder, animal feed, S: 4554, B: 704C, K: 543B, H: 204B

5029 מִסְפָּחָה *mispāḥâ*, veil, (head) covering, S: 4555, B: 705D, K: 543B, H: 204B

5030 מִסְפַּחַת *mispaḥat*, (uninfectious) breaking out of skin, rash or scab, S: 4556, B: 705C, K: 543B, H: 204B

5031 [1]מִסְפָּר *mispār*[1], number, quantity; listing, inventory, census, S: 4557, B: 708D, K: 543B, H: 204B

5032 [2]מִסְפָּר *mispār*[2], Mispar, S: 4558, B: 709A, K: 544A, H: 204D

5033 מִסְפֶּרֶת *misperet*, Mispereth, S: 4559, B: 709A, K: 544A, H: 204D

5034 מָסַר *māsar*, [A] to supply, deliver; [C] to be supplied, S: 4560, B: 588A, K: 544A, H: 204D

5035 מֹסֵרוֹת *mōsērôt*, Moseroth, S: 4149, B: 64C, K: 544A, H: 204D

5036 מֹסָרָם *mōsārām*, variant: see 4592, S: 4561†, B: 416C, K: 544A, H: 204D

5037 מָסֹרֶת *māsōret*, bond, obligation, duty, S: 4562, B: 64B, K: 544A, H: 204D

5038 מִסַּת *missat*, variant: see 5002, S*, B*, K*, H*

5039 מִסְתּוֹר *mistôr*, hiding place, shelter (from the elements), S: 4563, B: 712C, K: 544B, H: 204D

5040 מַסְתֵּר *mastēr*, (the act of) hiding, S: 4564, B: 712C, K: 544B, H: 204D

5041 מִסְתָּר *mistār*, hiding place, covered place (from which to ambush), S: 4565, B: 712C, K: 544B, H: 205A

5042 מַעֲבָד *ma'^{a}bād*, deed, action, S: 4566†, B: 716A, K: 544B, H: 205A

5043 מַעֲבֶה *ma'^{a}beh*, mold, foundry, S: 4568, B: 716B, K: 544B, H: 205A

5044 מַעֲבָר *ma'^{a}bār*, stroke (of a rod); (geographical) pass; ford (of a river), S: 4569, B: 721B, K: 544B, H: 205A

5045 מַעְבָּרָה *ma'bārâ*, ford, river crossing; (geographical) pass, S: 4569†, B: 721B, K: 544C, H: 205A

5046 [1]מַעְגָּל *ma'gāl*[1], (circled) camp, encampment, S: 4570, B: 722D, K: 544C, H: 205A

5047 [2]מַעְגָּל *ma'gāl*[2], (rutted) path (of a cart or wagon), S: 4570, B: 722D, K: 544C, H: 205A

5048 מָעַד *mā'ad*, [A] to slip, waver, wobble; [E] to become lame; [G] cause to wobble, to bend, wrench (one's back), S: 4154† & 4571 & 5976†, B: 588C, K: 544C, H: 205A

5049 מַעֲדַי *ma'^{a}day*, Maadai, S: 4572, B: 588C, K: 544D, H: 205B

5050 מַעַדְיָה *ma'adyâ*, Moadiah, S: 4573, B: 588C, K: 544D, H: 205B

5051 מַעֲדַנּוֹת *ma'^{a}dannôt*, beautiful; (as adv.) confidently, S: 4575†, B: 588D & 772C, K: 544D, H: 205B

5052 מַעֲדַנִּים *ma'^{a}dannîm*, delicacy; delight, S: 4574†, B: 726D, K: 544D, H: 205B

5053 מַעְדֵּר *ma'dēr*, hoe (to cultivate ground), S: 4576, B: 727C, K: 545A, H: 205B

5054 מָעָה *mā'â*, grain (of sand), S: 4579†, B: 589A, K: 545A, H: 205B

5055 מֵעֶה *mē'eh*, body, viscera: stomach, heart, bowels, womb; emotion: anguish, tenderness, S: 4578, B: 588D, K: 547A, H: 205B

5056 מָעוֹג *mā'ôg*, provision, supply, S: 4580, B: 728B, K: 545A, H: 205B

5057 מָעוֹז *mā'ôz*, refuge, stronghold, fortress, place of protection; (used with head) helmet, S: 4581, B: 731D, K: 545A, H: 205C

5058 מָעוֹזֶן *mā'ôzen*, fortress, refuge, S: 4581†, B: 732A 1, K: 545D, H: 205C

5059 מָעוֹךְ *mā'ôk*, Maoch, S: 4582, B: 590D, K: 545B, H: 205C

5060 [1]מָעוֹן *mā'ôn*[1], variant: help, S: 4583, B: 732D, K*, H: 205C

5061 [2]מָעוֹן *mā'ôn*[2], dwelling place, S: 4583, B: 732D, K: 545B, H: 205C

5062 [3]מָעוֹן *mā'ôn*[3], Maon; Maonite, S: 4584, B: 733A 2. & 3., K: 545C, H: 205C

5063 [4]מָעוֹן *mā'ôn*[4], Maon, S: 4584, B: 733A 1., K: 545C, H: 205C

5064 מְעוּנִים *m^{e}'ûnîm*, Meunim, Meunite, S: 4586†, B: 589B, K: 545C, H: 205D

5065 מְעוֹנֹתַי *m^{e}'ônōtay*, Meonothai, S: 4587, B: 733B, K: 545D, H: 205D

5066 מָעוּף *mā'ûp*, gloom, darkness, S: 4588, B: 734A, K: 545D, H: 205D

5067 מָעוֹר *mā'ôr*, exposed genitals, nakedness, S: 4589, B: 735D, K: 545D, H: 205D

5068 מַעַזְיָה *ma'azyâ*, Maaziah, S: 4590, B: 589B, K: 545D, H: 205D

5069 מַעַזְיָהוּ *ma'azyāhû*, Maaziah, S: 4590, B: 589B, K: 545D, H: 205D

5070 מָעַט *mā'aṭ*, [A] to dwindle, decrease, become few; [D] to become few; [G] to let reduce, make diminish, make collect little, S: 4591, B: 589B, K: 545D, H: 205D

5071 מְעַט *m^{e}'aṭ*, little, few (of time and things), S: 4592, B: 589D, K: 546B, H: 206A

5072 מְעֻטָּה *m^{e}'uṭṭâ*, variant: see 6487, S*, B: 598D 2, K: 546C, H: 206B

5073 מַעֲטֶה *ma'^{a}ṭeh*, garment, mantle, wrap, S: 4594, B: 742A, K: 546D, H: 206B

5074 מַעֲטֶפֶת *ma'^{a}ṭepet*, cape, outer garment, S: 4595†, B: 742C, K: 546D, H: 206B

5075 מְעִי *m^{e}'î*, heap (of ruins), S: 4596, B: 590C & 730D, K: 546D, H: 206B

5076 מָעַי *mā'ay*, Maai, S: 4597, B: 590C, K: 546D, H: 206B

5077 מְעִיל *m^{e}'îl*, robe, cloak, S: 4598, B: 591C, K: 546D, H: 206B

5078 מַעְיָן *ma'yān*, spring, fountain, well, S: 4599, B: 745D, K: 547B, H: 206C

5079 מְעִינִים *m^{e}'înîm*, variant: Meinites, see 5064, S: 4583†, B: 589B, K: 545C, H: 205D

5080 מָעַךְ *mā'ak*, [B] to be pressed (into the ground), be crushed, be bruised; [E] be fondled, S: 4600, B: 590C, K: 547B, H: 206C

5081 [1]מַעֲכָה *ma'^{a}kâ*[1], Maacah, S: 4601, B: 590D 3., K: 547C, H: 206C

5082 [2]מַעֲכָה *ma'^{a}kâ*[2], Maacah, S: 4601, B: 590D, K: 547C, H: 206C

5083 מַעֲכָת *ma'^{a}kāt*, Maacah, S: 4601, B: 591A, K: 547C, H: 206C

5084 מַעֲכָתִי *ma'^{a}kātî*, Maacathite, of Maacah, S: 4602, B: 591A, K: 547C, H: 206C

5085 מָעַל *mā'al*, [A] to act unfaithfully, break faith, commit a violation, S: 4603, B: 591A, K: 547D, H: 206C

5086 [1]מַעַל *ma'al*[1], unfaithfulness, S: 4604, B: 591B, K: 548A, H: 206D

5087 [2]מַעַל *ma'al*[2], above, beyond, S: 4605, B: 751C, K: 548A, H: 206D

5088 מֵעַל *mē'al*, variant: see 4946 & 6584, S: 4480† + 5921†, B: 577C & 752B, K: 200B & 703C, H: 207A

5089 מֹעַל *mō'al*, lifting (of hands), S: 4607, B: 751B, K: 548B, H: 207A

5090 מַעֲלֶה *ma'^{a}leh*, and ascent: hill, mount, (geographical) pass; stairs, S: 4608, B: 751B, K: 548C, H: 207A

5091 [1]מַעֲלָה *ma'^{a}lâ*[1], what goes through (or rises into) one's mind, S: 4609, B: 752A, K: 548C, H: 207A

5092 [2]מַעֲלָה *ma'^{a}lâ*[2], ascent: steps, stairway, S: 4609, B: 752A, K: 548C, H: 207A

5093 מַעְלָה *ma'^{e}lâ*, variant: above, S: 4605†, B: 751C 2., K: 548A, H: 207A

5094 מַעֲלִיל *ma'^{a}lîl*, variant: see 5095, S: 4611†, B: 760B, K: 548D, H: 207B

5095 מַעֲלָל *ma'^{a}lāl*, deeds, actions, practices, what is done, S: 4611, B: 760B, K: 548D, H: 207B

5096 מַעֲמָד *ma'^{a}mād*, attendance, serving; position of attendant, S: 4612, B: 765B, K: 549A, H: 207B

5097 מָעֳמָד *mo'^{o}mād*, foothold, firm ground, S: 4613, B: 765C, K: 549A, H: 207B

5098 מַעֲמָסָה *ma'^{a}māsâ*, heavy stone, hard-to-lift rock, S: 4614, B: 770C, K: 549B, H: 207B

5099 מַעֲמַקִּים *ma'^{a}maqqîm*, depths (of waters or seas), S: 4615†, B: 771B, K: 549B, H: 207B

5100 מַעַן *ma'an*, for the sake of, on account of, because; therefore, so that, S: 4616, B: 775A, K: 549B, H: 207B

5101 [1]מַעֲנֶה *ma'^{a}neh*[1], reply, answer, response, S: 4617, B: 775A, K: 549D, H: 207C

5102 [2]מַעֲנֶה *ma'^{a}neh*[2], purpose, S: 4617, B: 775A, K: 549D, H: 207C

5103 מַעֲנָה *ma'^{a}nâ*, furrow, plow path, S: 4618, B: 776A, K: 549D, H: 207C

5104 מְעֹנָה *m^{e}'ōnâ*, hiding place, refuge; dwelling place, (animal) den, S: 4585, B: 733A, K: 549D, H: 207C

5105 מַעֲנִית *ma'^{a}nît*, variant: see 5103, S: 4618†, B: 776A, K: 550A, H: 207C

5106 מַעַץ *ma'aṣ*, Maaz, S: 4619, B: 591D, K: 550A, H: 207C

5107 מַעֲצֵבָה *ma'^{a}ṣēbâ*, place of torment, place of pain, S: 4620, B: 781A, K: 550A, H: 207C

5108 מַעֲצָד *ma'^{a}ṣād*, chiseling tool (for wood carving), S: 4621, B: 781B, K: 550A, H: 207D

5109 מַעְצוֹר *ma'ṣôr*, hindrance, S: 4622†, B: 784A, K: 550A, H: 207D

5110 מַעְצָר *ma'ṣār*, self-control, S: 4623, B: 784A, K: 550A, H: 207D

5111 מַעֲקֶה *ma'^{a}qeh*, parapet, S: 4624, B: 785B, K: 550B, H: 207D

5112 מַעֲקַשִּׁים *ma'^{a}qaššîm*, rough places, uneven terrain, S: 4625†, B: 786A, K: 550B, H: 207D

5113 מַעַר *ma'ar*, nakedness; available space, S: 4626, B: 789A, K: 550B, H: 207D

5114 [1]מַעֲרָב *ma'^{a}rāb*[1], wares, goods (for trade, exchange, or barter), S: 4627, B: 786D, K: 550B, H: 207D

5115 [2]מַעֲרָב *ma'^{a}rāb*[2], west (the place of the sunset), S: 4628, B: 788A, K: 550B, H: 207D

5116 מַעֲרֶה *ma'^{a}reh*, variant: approaches, vicinity, S: 4629†, B: 788A, K: 550C, H: 207D

5117 [1]מְעָרָה *m^{e}'ārâ*[1], cave, S: 4631, B: 792C, K: 550C, H: 208A

5118 ²מְעָרָה *me'ārâ²*, wasteland, bare field, S: 4632, B: 792C, K: 550D, H: 208A

5119 מַעֲרָךְ *ma'ᵃrāk*, plan, consideration, arrangement, S: 4633, B: 790A, K: 550D, H: 208A

5120 מַעֲרָכָה *ma'ᵃrākâ*, battle line, rows of army ranks; row, layer (of things), S: 4630† & 4634, B: 790A, K: 550D, H: 208A

5121 מַעֲרֶכֶת *ma'ᵃreket*, (consecrated) bread set in rows, S: 4635, B: 790B, K: 550D, H: 208A

5122 מַעֲרֹם *ma'ᵃrōm*, nakedness, naked person, S: 4636, B: 736A, K: 551A, H: 208A

5123 מַעֲרָץ *ma'ᵃrāṣ*, variant: terror, see 6907, S: 6206†, B*, K*, H: 208A

5124 מַעֲרָצָה *ma'ᵃrāṣâ*, terrifying power, S: 4637, B: 792B, K: 551A, H: 208A

5125 מַעֲרָת *ma'ᵃrāt*, Maarath, S: 4638, B: 789B, K: 551A, H: 208A

5126 מַעֲשֶׂה *ma'ᵃśeh*, work, labor, deed; something made, something done, S: 4639, B: 795C, K: 551A, H: 208B

5127 מַעְשַׂי *ma'śay*, Maasai, S: 4640, B: 796B, K: 551D, H: 208C

5128 מַעֲשֵׂיָה *ma'ᵃśēyâ*, Maaseiah, S: 4641, B: 796B, K: 551D, H: 208C

5129 מַעֲשֵׂיָהוּ *ma'ᵃśēyāhû*, Maaseiah, S: 4641, B: 796B, K: 552A, H: 208C

5130 מַעֲשֵׂר *ma'ᵃśēr*, tithe, setting aside a tenth, S: 4643, B: 798B, K: 552A, H: 208C

5131 מַעֲשַׁקּוֹת *ma'ᵃšaqqôt*, (col.pl) extortion, S: 4642†, B: 799A, K: 552B, H: 208D

5132 מֹף *mōp*, Moph = Memphis, S: 4644, B: 592A, K: 552B, H: 208D

5133 מִפְגָּע *mipgā'*, target, S: 4645, B: 803C, K: 552B, H: 208D

5134 מַפָּח *mappāḥ*, (a dying) gasp, exhaling (of soul), S: 4646, B: 656A, K: 552B, H: 208D

5135 מַפֻּחַ *mappuaḥ*, bellows, S: 4647, B: 656A, K: 552B, H: 208D

5136 מְפִיבֹשֶׁת *mᵉpîbōšet*, מְפִי־בֹשֶׁת *mᵉpî-bōšet*, Mephibosheth, S: 4648, B: 937C, K: 552B, H: 208D

5137 מֻפִּים *muppîm*, Muppim, S: 4649, B: 592B, K: 552C, H: 208D

5138 מֵפִיץ *mēpîṣ*, war club, S: 4650, B: 807B, K: 552C, H: 208D

5139 מַפָּל *mappāl*, sweepings, waste, refuse (of wheat); (fleshy) folds (of the leviathan), S: 4651, B: 658C, K: 552C, H: 208D

5140 מִפְלָאוֹת *miplā'ôt*, wonders, marvelous works, S: 4652†, B: 811A, K: 552C, H: 208D

5141 מִפְלַגָּה *miplaggâ*, division (of family groups), S: 4653, B: 811B, K: 552C, H: 208D

5142 מַפָּלָה *mappālâ*, ruin, heap of rubble, S: 4654, B: 658C, K: 552C, H: 209A

5143 מַפֵּלָה *mappēlâ*, ruin, heap of rubble, S: 4654, B: 658C, K: 552C, H: 209A

5144 מִפְלָט *miplāṭ*, place of shelter, refuge, escape, S: 4655, B: 812D, K: 552C, H: 209A

5145 מִפְלֶצֶת *mipleṣet*, repulsive image, disgraceful (idol), S: 4656, B: 814A, K: 552D, H: 209A

5146 מִפְלָשׂ *miplāś*, floating, hovering (clouds), S: 4657, B: 814A, K: 552D, H: 209A

5147 מַפֶּלֶת *mappelet*, downfall, collapse; (something downfallen) a shipwreck; carcass, S: 4658, B: 658C, K: 552D, H: 209A

5148 מִפְעָל *mip'āl*, deed, work, S: 4659, B: 821D, K: 552D, H: 209A

5149 מִפְעָלָה *mip'ālâ*, deed, work, S: 4659, B: 821D, K: 552D, H: 209A

5150 מַפָּץ *mappāṣ*, shattering, wrecking (weapon), S: 4660, B: 658D, K: 553A, H: 209A

5151 מַפֵּץ *mappēṣ*, war club, S: 4661, B: 659A, K: 553A, H: 209A

5152 מִפְקָד *mipqād*, appointment (by a king); number, counting (of the people); Inspection (Gate), S: 4662 & 4663, B: 824C, K: 553A, H: 209A

5153 מִפְרָץ *miprāṣ*, cove, inlet, landing-place, S: 4664, B: 830A, K: 553A, H: 209B

5154 מַפְרֶקֶת *mapreqet*, neck, S: 4665†, B: 830B, K: 553A, H: 209B

5155 מִפְרָשׂ *miprāś*, spreading (used of clouds and canvas sail), S: 4666, B: 831C, K: 553A, H: 209B

5156 מִפְשָׂעָה *mipśā'â*, buttocks, posterior area, S: 4667, B: 832C, K: 553B, H: 209B

5157 מִפְתָּח *miptāḥ*, opening (of lips), S: 4669, B: 836B, K: 553B, H: 209B

5158 מַפְתֵּחַ *maptēaḥ*, key, S: 4668, B: 836B, K: 553B, H: 209B

5159 מִפְתָּן *miptān*, threshold, S: 4670, B: 837A, K: 553B, H: 209B

5160 מֵץ *mēṣ*, oppressor, S: 4160†, B: 568C, K: 553B, H: 209B

5161 מֹץ *mōṣ*, chaff, S: 4671, B: 558B, K: 553B, H: 209B

5162 מָצָא *māṣā'*, [A] to find, find out, discover, uncover; [C] to be found out; be caught; [G] to hand over, present; to bring upon, cause to encounter, S: 4672, B: 592C, K: 553C, H: 209B

5163 מַצָּב *maṣṣāb*, standing place; office; outpost, garrison, S: 4673, B: 662D, K: 554B, H: 210A

5164 מֻצָּב *muṣṣāb*, pillar, tower, S: 4674, B: 663A, K: 554C, H: 210A

5165 מַצָּבָה *maṣṣābâ*, outpost, S: 4675, B: 663A, K: 554C, H: 210A

5166 מִצָּבָה *miṣṣābâ*, variant: guard, watch, S: 4675, B: 663A, K*, H*

5167 מַצֵּבָה *maṣṣēbâ*, sacred (upright) stone, stone pillar, S: 4676, B: 663A, K: 554C, H: 210A

5168 מְצֹבָיָה *mᵉṣōbāyâ*, Mezobaite, S: 4677, B: 594B, K: 554D, H: 210A

5169 ¹מַצֶּבֶת *maṣṣebet¹*, (tree) stump, S: 4678, B: 663A, K: 555A, H: 210B

5170 ²מַצֶּבֶת *maṣṣebet²*, sacred (upright) stone, stone pillar, S: 4678, B: 663A, K: 555A, H: 210B

5171 מְצָד *mᵉṣād*, stronghold, fortress (with difficult access), S: 4679, B: 844D, K: 555A, H: 210B

5172 מָצָה *māṣâ*, [A] to squeeze out; to drain dry; [C] to be drained out, S: 4680, B: 594C, K: 555A, H: 210B

5173 מֹצָה *mōṣâ*, Mozah, S: 4681, B: 594C, K: 555B, H: 210B

5174 ¹מַצָּה *maṣṣâ¹*, unleavened bread, bread made without yeast, S: 4682, B: 595A, K: 555B, H: 210B

5175 ²מַצָּה *maṣṣâ²*, quarrel, strife, S: 4683, B: 663C, K: 555C, H: 210C

5176 מֻצְהָב *muṣhāb*, variant: brass, see 7410, S: 6668†, B: 843C, K: 795D, H: 210C

5177 מִצְהָלוֹת *miṣhālôt*, neighing, S: 4684†, B: 843D, K: 555D, H: 210C

5178 ¹מָצוֹד *māṣôd¹*, (hunting) snare, net, S: 4685, B: 844D, K: 555D, H: 210C

5179 ²מָצוֹד *māṣôd²*, plunder; stronghold, S: 4685, B: 844D, K: 555D, H: 210C

5180 ¹מְצוּדָה *mᵉṣûdâ¹*, (hunting) snare, net; prey, S: 4686, B: 845A, K: 555D, H: 210C

5181 ²מְצוּדָה *mᵉṣûdâ²*, stronghold, fortress, prison (a place difficult to access), S: 4686, B: 845A, K: 555D, H: 210C

5182 ¹מְצוֹדָה *mᵉṣôdâ¹*, net, S: 4685, B: 845A, K: 556A, H: 210D

5183 ²מְצוֹדָה *mᵉṣôdâ²*, fortress, prison (a place difficult to access), S: 4685, B: 845A, K: 556A, H*

5184 מִצְוָה *miṣwâ*, command, order, prescription, instruction, S: 4687, B: 846B, K: 556A, H: 210D

5185 מְצוֹלָה *mᵉṣôlâ*, depths, the deep, S: 4688 & 4699†, B: 846D & 847A, K: 556C, H: 210D

5186 מָצוֹק *māṣôq*, distress, suffering, stress, hardship, S: 4689, B: 848A, K: 556C, H: 210D

5187 מָצוּק *māṣûq*, foundation, pillar, support, S: 4690, B: 848B, K: 556D, H: 211A

5188 מְצוּקָה *mᵉṣûqâ*, distress, anguish, stress, affliction, S: 4691, B: 848A, K: 556D, H: 211A

5189 ¹מָצוֹר *māṣôr¹*, siege; siege works, ramparts, S: 4692, B: 848D, K: 556D, H: 211A

5190 ²מָצוֹר *māṣôr²*, stronghold, fortification, defense, S: 4692, B: 849A, K: 557D, H: 211A

5191 ³מָצוֹר *māṣôr³*, Egypt, S: 4693, B: 596A, K: 557A, H: 211A

5192 ⁴מָצוֹר *māṣôr⁴*, variant: lock up, custody, S: 4686†, B: 848D, K: 557A, H: 211A

5193 מְצוּרָה *mᵉṣûrâ*, fortification, defense, fortress, S: 4694, B: 849A, K: 557B, H: 211A

5194 מַצּוּת *maṣṣût*, enemy, person of strife, S: 4695, B: 663C, K: 558D, H: 211A

5195 מֵצַח *mēṣaḥ*, forehead, S: 4696, B: 594D, K: 557B, H: 211B

5196 מִצְחָה *miṣḥâ*, greaves (armor for the front or back of leg from ankle to knee), S: 4697, B: 595A, K: 557B, H: 211B

5197 מְצִלָּה *mᵉṣillâ*, (small) bell (on a horse), S: 4698, B: 853A, K: 557C, H: 211B

5198 מְצֻלָה *meṣulâ*, variant: depth, the deep, S: 4688, B: 846D, K: 556C, H: 210D

5199 מְצִלְתַּיִם *meṣiltayim*, (pair of) cymbals, S: 4700†, B: 853A, K: 557C, H: 211B

5200 מִצְנֶפֶת *miṣnepet*, turban, S: 4701, B: 857B, K: 557C, H: 211B

5201 מַצָּע *maṣṣā'*, bed, couch, S: 4702, B: 427A, K: 557C, H: 211B

5202 מִצְעָד *miṣ'ād*, step; (position of submission in a) train, S: 703, B: 857D, K: 557D, H: 211B

5203 מִצְעָרי *miṣ'ār*[1], small quantity, few, S: 4705, B: 859B, K: 557D, H: 211B 1.

5204 מִצְעָר[2] *miṣ'ār*[2], Mizar, S: 4706, B: 859B, K: 557D, H: 211B 3.

5205 מִצְפֶּהי *miṣpeh*[1], watchtower, place that overlooks, S: 4707, B: 859D, K: 557D, H: 211B

5206 מִצְפֶּה[2] *miṣpeh*[2], Mizpah, S: 4708, B: 859D, K: 557D, H: 211B

5207 מִצְפָּה *miṣpâ*, Mizpah, S: 4709, B: 859D, K: 558A, H: 211C

5208 מַצְפּוֹן *maṣpôn*, hidden treasure, hiding place, S: 4710†, B: 861B, K: 558A, H: 211C

5209 מָצַץ *māṣaṣ*, [A] to drink deeply, quaff, S: 4711, B: 595A, K: 558A, H: 211C

5210 מֵצַר *mēṣar*, anguish, distress, hardship, S: 4712, B: 865C, K: 558A, H: 211C

5211 מַצָּרָה *maṣṣārâ*, variant: guard, watch, S: 4694†, B: 849C, K: 558B, H: 211A

5212 מִצְרִי *miṣrî*, Egyptian, S: 4713, B: 596A, K: 558B, H: 211C

5213 מִצְרַיִם *miṣrayim*, Mizraim; Egypt, Egyptian, S: 4714, B: 595C, K: 558B, H: 211C

5214 מַצְרֵף *maṣrēp*, crucible, melting pot for metal, S: 4715†, B: 864C, K: 558D, H: 211C

5215 מַק *maq*, stench, smell of decay, S: 4716, B: 597A, K: 558D, H: 211C

5216 מַקֶּבֶתי *maqqebet*[1], hammer, S: 4717† & 4718, B: 666C, K: 558D, H: 211D 2.

5217 מַקֶּבֶת[2] *maqqebet*[2], quarry, S: 4718, B: 666C, K: 559A, H: 211D 1.

5218 מַקֵּדָה *maqqēdâ*, Makkedah, S: 4719, B: 596B, K: 559A, H: 211D

5219 מִקְדָּשׁ *miqdāš*, sanctuary, shrine, holy place, S: 4720, B: 874A, K: 559A, H: 211D

5220 מַקְהֵל *maqhēl*, assembly, congregation, S: 4721, B: 875B, K: 559B, H: 211D

5221 מַקְהֵלוֹת *maqhēlôt*, Makheloth, S: 4722, B: 875B, K: 559C, H: 212A

5222 מִקְוֵא *miqwē'*, variant: see 2256 & 7745, S*, B: 577C & 875C, K: 559C, H: 212A

5223 מִקְוֶהי *miqweh*[1], hope, S: 4723, B: 876A, K: 559C, H: 212A

5224 מִקְוֶה[2] *miqweh*[2], collection (of water), reservoir, S: 4723, B: 876C, K: 559C, H: 212A

5225 מִקְוָה *miqwâ*, reservoir, S: 4724, B: 876C, K: 559C, H: 212A

5226 מָקוֹם *māqôm*, place, site, S: 4725, B: 879D, K: 559C, H: 212A

5227 מָקוֹר *māqôr*, fountain, spring, source (of a flow), S: 4726, B: 881B, K: 560B, H: 212B

5228 מִקָּח *miqqāḥ*, taking, accepting (a bribe), S: 4727, B: 544C, K: 560C, H: 212C

5229 מַקָּחוֹת *maqqāḥôt*, (pl.) merchandise, wares, S: 4728†, B: 544C, K: 560C, H: 212C

5230 מִקְטָר *miqṭār*, burning, S: 4729, B: 883B, K: 560C, H: 212C

5231 מֻקְטָר *muqṭār*, incense, S: 6999†, B: 883B, K: 836C, H: 212C

5232 מְקַטֶּרֶת *meqaṭṭeret*, incense altar, S: 6999†, B: 883B, K: 560C, H: 212C

5233 מִקְטֶרֶת *miqṭeret*, censer, incense burner, S: 4730, B: 883B, K: 560C, H: 212C

5234 מַקֵּל *maqqēl*, branch, stick; staff, S: 4731, B: 596B, K: 560D, H: 212C

5235 מִקְלוֹת *miqlôt*, Mikloth, S: 4732, B: 596C, K: 560D, H: 212C

5236 מִקְלָט *miqlāṭ*, refuge, place of protection, S: 4733, B: 886A, K: 560D, H: 212C

5237 מִקְלַעַת *miqla'at*, carving, engraving (on wood), S: 4734, B: 887C, K: 561A, H: 212D

5238 מִקְנֶה *miqneh*, livestock, (animals from) herds and flocks, S: 4735, B: 889B, K: 561A, H: 212D

5239 מִקְנָה *miqnâ*, something bought, purchased, acquisition, S: 4736, B: 889B, K: 561C, H: 212D

5240 מִקְנֵיָהוּ *miqnēyāhû*, Mikneiah, S: 4737, B: 889C, K: 561C, H: 213A

5241 מִקְסָם *miqsām*, divination, S: 4738, B: 890D, K: 561C, H: 213A

5242 מָקַץ *māqaṣ*, Makaz, S: 4739, B: 596D, K: 561C, H: 213A

5243 מִקְצוֹעַ *miqṣôa'*, corner (of a base); angle of a wall, S: 4740, B: 893A, K: 561D, H: 213A

5244 מַקְצֻעָה *maqṣu'â*, (wood) chisel, S: 4741, B: 893A, K: 561D, H: 213A

5245 מָקַק *māqaq*, [C] to rot, waste away, fester; dissolve; [G] to cause to rot, S: 4743, B: 596D, K: 561D, H: 213A

5246 מִקְרָא *miqrā'*, assembly, calling the community together, S: 4744, B: 896D, K: 562A, H: 213B

5247 מִקְרֶה *miqreh*, happening by chance; fate, destiny, S: 4745, B: 899D, K: 562A, H: 213B

5248 מְקָרֶה *meqāreh*, rafters, roof beams, S: 4746, B: 900A, K: 562B, H: 213B

5249 מְקֵרָה *meqērâ*, coolness; cool room, summer home, S: 4747, B: 903B, K: 562B, H: 213B

5250 מִקְשֶׁה *miqšeh*, well-dressed hair, S: 4748, B: 904D, K: 562B, H: 213B

5251 מִקְשָׁהי *miqšâ*[1], hammered work, S: 4749, B: 904D, K: 562B, H: 213B

5252 מִקְשָׁה[2] *miqšâ*[2], melon field, cucumber field, S: 4750, B: 903D, K: 562B, H: 213B

5253 מַרי *mar*[1], bitter; bitterness, S: 4751, B: 600C, K: 562C, H: 213C

5254 מַר[2] *mar*[2], drop (in a bucket), S: 4752, B: 601C, K: 562C, H: 213C

5255 מֹר *mōr*, myrrh, S: 4753, B: 600D, K: 562D, H: 213C

5256 מָרָאי *mārā'*[1], variant: [H] to be obstinate, S: 4754, B: 598A, K: 563A, H: 213C

5257 מָרָא[2] *mārā'*[2], [A] to flap, spread the feathers as it runs, S: 4754, B: 597A, K: 563A, H: 213D

5258 מָרָא[3] *mārā'*[3], variant: [A] to fatten, graze, S: 4806†, B: 597B, K: 563B, H: 213D

5259 מָרָא[4] *mārā'*[4], Mara, S: 4755, B: 600C, K: 562C, H: 213D

5260 מַרְאֶה *mar'eh*, what is seen with the eye, appearance; vision, S: 4758, B: 909C, K: 563B, H: 213D

5261 מַרְאָהי *mar'â*[1], vision, S: 4759, B: 909B, K: 563C, H: 214A 1.

5262 מַרְאָה[2] *mar'â*[2], mirror, S: 4759, B: 909C, K: 563C, H: 214A 2.

5263 מֻרְאָה *mur'â*, crop (of a bird), S: 4760, B: 597B, K: 563D, H: 214A

5264 מֵרְאוֹן *mer'ôn*, variant: Meron, S: 8112†, B: 1038A, K: 563D, H: 214A

5265 מְרַאֲשׁוֹת *mera'ašôt*, head rest, place near the head, S: 4761† & 4763†, B: 912B, K: 563D, H: 214A

5266 מֵרַב *mērab*, Merab, S: 4764†, B: 597B, K: 564A, H: 214A

5267 מַרְבַד *marbad*, covering, S: 4765, B: 915A, K: 564A, H: 214A

5268 מִרְבָּה *mirbâ*, so much, S: 4767, B: 916B, K: 564A, H: 214A

5269 מַרְבֶּה *marbeh*, abundance, increase, S: 4766, B: 916A, K: 564A, H: 214A

5270 מַרְבִּית *marbît*, great number; most, majority; profit, S: 4768, B: 916B, K: 564A, H: 214A

5271 מַרְבֵּץ *marbēṣ*, lair, resting place, place to lie down, S: 4769, B: 918C, K: 564A&B, H: 214B

5272 מַרְבֵּק *marbēq*, fattening (of a calf), S: 4770, B: 918D, K: 564B, H: 214B

5273 מַרְגּוֹעַ *margôa'*, resting place, S: 4771, B: 921B, K: 564B, H: 214B

5274 מַרְגְּלוֹת *margelôt*, (place of) the feet, S: 4772†, B: 920B, K: 564B, H: 214B

5275 מַרְגֵּמָה *margēmâ*, sling, S: 4773, B: 920C, K: 564B, H: 214B

5276 מַרְגֵּעָה *margē'â*, place of repose, resting-place, S: 4774, B: 921C, K: 564B, H: 214B

5277 מָרַד *mārad*, [A] to rebel, revolt, S: 4775, B: 597C, K: 564C, H: 214B

5278 מֶרֶדי *mered*[1], rebellion, S: 4777, B: 597D, K: 564C, H: 214C

5279 מֶרֶד[2] *mered*[2], Mered, S: 4778, B: 597D, K: 564C, H: 214C

5280 מַרְדּוּת *mardût*, rebellion, revolt, S: 4780, B: 597D, K: 564D, H: 214C

5281 מְרֹדָךְ *merōdāk*, Marduk, Merodak (pagan god), S: 4781, B: 597D, K: 564D, H: 214C

5282 מְרֹדַךְ־בַּלְאֲדָן *m^{e}rōdak-bal'^{a}dān*, Merodach-Baladan, S: 4757†, B: 597D, K: 564D, H: 214C

5283 מָרְדֳּכַי *mord^{o}kay*, Mordecai, S: 4782†, B: 598A, K: 564D, H: 214C

5284 מֻרְדָּף *murdāp*, aggression, S: 4783, B: 922A & 923A, K: 564D, H: 214C

5285 מָרָּה *morrâ*, variant: bitterness, S: 4787, B: 601A, K: 565B, H: 214D

5286 [1]מָרָה *mārâ[1]*, [A] to rebel, defy, become disobedient; [G] to act as a rebel, defy by one's action, S: 4784, B: 598A, K: 565A, H: 214C

5287 [2]מָרָה *mārâ[2]*, variant: bitter[ness], S: 4751, B: 600C, K: 565B, H: 214D

5288 [3]מָרָה *mārâ[3]*, Marah, S: 4785, B: 600D, K: 565B, H: 214D

5289 מֹרָה *mōrâ*, bitterness, grief, S: 4786, B: 601A, K: 565B, H: 214D

5290 מַרְהֵבָה *marhēbâ*, variant: attack, assault, S: 4062†, B: 923C, K: 565C, H: 214D

5291 מָרוּד *mārûd*, wandering; wanderer, S: 4788, B: 924A, K: 565C, H: 214D

5292 מֵרוֹז *mērôz*, Meroz, S: 4789, B: 72D, K: 565C, H: 214D

5293 מָרוֹחַ *mārôaḥ*, damaged (by pounding or grinding), S: 4790†, B: 598C, K: 565C, H: 214D

5294 מָרוֹם *mārôm*, heights, place on high; pride, haughtiness, arrogance, S: 4791, B: 928D, K: 565C, H: 214D

5295 מֵרוֹם *mērôm*, Merom, S: 4792, B: 598C, K: 566A, H: 215A

5296 מֵרוֹץ *mērôṣ*, foot race, running, S: 4793, B: 930C, K: 566A, H: 215A

5297 [1]מְרוּצָה *m^{e}rûṣâ[1]*, manner or mode of running; course of a race, S: 4794, B: 930C, K: 566A, H: 215A

5298 [2]מְרוּצָה *m^{e}rûṣâ[2]*, extortion, S: 4835, B: 954D, K: 566A, H: 215A

5299 מְרוּקִים *m^{e}rûqîm*, beauty treatments (including massage and ointments), S: 4795†, B: 599D, K: 566A, H: 215A

5300 מָרוֹת *mārôt*, Maroth, S: 4796, B: 598C, K: 566A, H: 215A

5301 מַרְזֵחַ *marzēaḥ*, funeral meal; cultic feast, S: 4797† & 4798, B: 931A, K: 566A, H: 215A

5302 מָרַח *māraḥ*, [A] to apply by spreading on or rubbing in, S: 4799, B: 598D, K: 566B, H: 215A

5303 מֶרְחָב *merḥāb*, spaciousness, wideness, S: 4800, B: 932C, K: 566B, H: 215A

5304 מֶרְחָבְיָה *merḥobyâ*, variant: see 3378 & 5303, S: 4800† + 3050†, B: 932C, K: 566B, H: 215A

5305 מֶרְחָק *merḥāq*, distance, far away, S: 4801, B: 935D, K: 566B, H: 215B

5306 מַרְחֶשֶׁת *marḥešet*, cooking pan, S: 4802, B: 935D, K: 566C, H: 214B

5307 מָרַט *māraṭ*, [A] to pull out (hair); [B] to be polished, rubbed; [C] to lose one's hair, become bald; [E] to be polished, burnished, smooth (skinned), S: 4178† & 4803, B: 598D, K: 566C, H: 215B

5308 מְרִי *m^{e}rî*, rebellion, S: 4805, B: 598B, K: 566D, H: 215C

5309 מְרִיא *m^{e}rî'*, fattened animal (choice for consumption), S: 4806, B: 597A, K: 566D, H: 215C

5310 מֵרִיב *mērîb*, variant: antagonist (of Baal), S: 4807† & 4810†, B: 937C, K: 567A, H: 215C

5311 מְרִיב בַּעַל *m^{e}rîb ba'al*, Merib-Baal, S: 4807 & 4810†, B: 937C, K: 567A, H: 215C

5312 [1]מְרִיבָה *m^{e}rîbâ[1]*, quarreling, strife, S: 4808, B: 937B, K: 567A, H: 215C

5313 [2]מְרִיבָה *m^{e}rîbâ[2]*, Meribah, S: 4809, B: 937B, K: 567A, H: 215C

5314 מְרִי־בַעַל *m^{e}rî-ba'al*, Merib-Baal, S: 4807†, B: 937C, K: 567A, H: 215C

5315 מְרִיבַת קָדֵשׁ *m^{e}rîbat qādēš*, Meribah Kadesh, S: 4809 + 6946, B: 937B & 873D, K: 567A, H: 215C & 314B

5316 מְרָיָה *m^{e}rāyâ*, Meraiah, S: 4811, B: 599A, K: 567A, H: 215C

5317 מֹרִיָּה *mōriyyâ*, Moriah, S: 4179, B: 599A, K: 567B, H: 215C

5318 מְרָיוֹת *m^{e}rāyôt*, Meraioth, S: 4812, B: 599A, K: 567B, H: 215C

5319 מִרְיָם *miryām*, Miriam, S: 4813, B: 599B, K: 567B, H: 215C

5320 מְרִירוּת *m^{e}rîrût*, bitterness, S: 4814, B: 601B, K: 567B, H: 215C

5321 מְרִירִי *m^{e}rîrî*, bitter, S: 4815, B: 601B, K: 567B, H: 215D

5322 מֹרֶךְ *mōrek*, fearfulness, despondency, S: 4816, B: 940B, K: 567C, H: 215D

5323 מֶרְכָּב *merkāb*, seat, saddle, chariot, S: 4817, B: 939C, K: 567C, H: 215D

5324 מֶרְכָּבָה *merkābâ*, chariot, S: 4818, B: 939C, K: 567C, H: 215D

5325 מַרְכָּבוֹת *markābôt*, variant: Marcaboth, S*, B: 112A, K: 125A 27., H: 39C 31.

5326 מַרְכֹּלֶת *markōlet*, marketplace, place of merchandizing, S: 4819, B: 940C, K: 567D, H: 215D

5327 [1]מִרְמָה *mirmâ[1]*, deceit, deception, dishonesty, treachery, S: 4820, B: 941B, K: 567D, H: 215D

5328 [2]מִרְמָה *mirmâ[2]*, Mirmah, S: 4821, B: 599B, K: 568A, H: 216A

5329 מְרֵמוֹת *m^{e}rēmôt*, Meremoth, S: 4822, B: 599B, K: 568A, H: 216A

5330 מִרְמָס *mirmās*, trampling down, running over, S: 4823, B: 942D, K: 568A, H: 216A

5331 מֵרֹנֹתִי *mērōnōtî*, Meronothite, of Meronoth, S: 4824, B: 599C, K: 568A, H: 216A

5332 מֶרֶס *meres*, Meres, S: 4825, B: 599C, K: 568A, H: 216A

5333 מַרְסְנָא *mars^{e}nā'*, Marsena, S: 4826, B: 599C, K: 568A, H: 216A

5334 מֵרַע *mēra'*, evil, atrocity, S: 4827, B: 949D, K: 568A, H: 216A

5335 [1]מֵרֵעַ *mērēa'[1]*, close friend, companion, personal adviser, S: 4828, B: 946C & B, K: 568A, H: 216A

5336 [2]מֵרֵעַ *mērēa'[2]*, variant: see 8317, S: 7489†, B*, K*, H: 216A

5337 מִרְעֶה *mir'eh*, pasture, grazing place, S: 4829, B: 945C, K: 568B, H: 216A

5338 מַרְעִית *mar'ît*, pasture, place of grazing, S: 4830†, B: 945C, K: 568B, H: 216A

5339 מַרְעֲלָה *mar'^{a}lâ*, Maralah, S: 4831, B: 599C, K: 568C, H: 216A

5340 [1]מַרְפֵּא *marpē'[1]*, healing, remedy, S: 4832, B: 951B, K: 568C, H: 216A

5341 [2]מַרְפֵּא *marpē'[2]*, calmness, composure, S: 4832, B: 951B, K: 568C, H: 216B

5342 מַרְפֵּה *marpēh*, variant: healing, see 5340, S: 4832†, B: 951B, K: 568C, H: 216B

5343 מִרְפָּשׂ *mirpāś*, what is muddy, fouled (by trampling), S: 4833, B: 952C, K: 568C, H: 216B

5344 מָרַץ *māraṣ*, [C] to be painful, hurtful; [G] to provoke, irritate, S: 4834, B: 599C, K: 568C, H: 216B

5345 מַרְצֵעַ *marṣēa'*, awl (piercing tool), S: 4836, B: 954A, K: 568D, H: 216B

5346 מַרְצֶפֶת *marṣepet*, (stone) base, stone-layer, S: 4837, B: 954B, K: 568D, H: 216B

5347 מָרַק *māraq*, [A] to polish; [B] to be polished; [E] to be thoroughly scoured; [G] to cleanse, S: 4838, B: 599D, K: 568D, H: 216B

5348 מָרָק *mārāq*, broth (juice stewed out of meat), S: 4839, B: 600A, K: 569A, H: 216C

5349 מֶרְקָח *merqāḥ*, aromatic herb, scented spice, S: 4840, B: 955C, K: 569A, H: 216C

5350 מֶרְקָחָה *merqāḥâ*, ointment jar, spice-pot, S: 4841, B: 955C, K: 569A, H: 216C

5351 מִרְקַחַת *mirqaḥat*, mixture of fragrant spices, blend of perfumes, S: 4842, B: 955C, K: 569A, H: 216C

5352 מָרַר *mārar*, [A] to be bitter; suffer anguish; [D] to make bitter, weep bitterly; [G] to make bitter; to grieve bitterly; [F] to enrage oneself, be furious, S: 4843, B: 600A, K: 569A, H: 216C

5353 מָרֹר *mārōr*, bitter things, S: 4844, B: 601A, K: 569C, H: 216D

5354 מְרֵרָה *m^{e}rērâ*, gall, S: 4845, B: 601A, K: 569C, H: 216D

5355 מְרֹרָה *m^{e}rōrâ*, gall-bladder; venom, poison (of snakes), S: 4846, B: 601A, K: 569C, H: 216D

5356 [1]מְרָרִי *m^{e}rārî[1]*, Merari; Merarite, S: 4847, B: 601B, K: 569C, H: 216D

5357 [2]מְרָרִי *m^{e}rārî[2]*, Merarite, S: 4848, B: 601B, K: 569D, H: 216D

5358 [1]מָרֵשָׁה *mārēšâ[1]*, Mareshah, S: 4762, B: 601C, K: 569D, H: 214A & 216D

5359 [2]מָרֵשָׁה *mārēšâ[2]*, Mareshah, S: 4762, B: 601C, K: 569D, H: 216D

5360 מִרְשַׁעַת *mirša'at*, wickedness, of a person (that) wicked woman, S: 4849, B: 958A, K: 569D, H: 216D

5361 מְרָתַיִם *m^{e}rātayim*, Merathaim, S: 4850, B: 601C, K: 569D, H: 216D

5362 [1]מַשָּׂא *maśśā'[1]*, burden, load, what is carried, oppression; singing, S: 4853, B: 672C, K: 569D, H: 217A

5363 [2]מַשָּׂא *maśśā'[2]*, oracle, prophetic utterance, pronouncement, S: 4853, B: 672D, K: 570A, H: 217A

5364 [3]מַשָּׂא *maśśā'[3]*, Massa, S: 4854, B: 601D, K: 570B, H: 217A

5365 מַשֹּׂא *maśśō'*, partiality, S: 4856, B: 673A, K: 570C, H: 217A

5366 מַשָּׂאָה *maśśā'â*, uplifted (clouds), S: 4858, B: 673A, K: 570C, H: 217A

5367 מַשְׂאוֹת *maś'ôt*, variant: see 5363 & 5368, S: 4864†, B: 673A & 672D & 669D, K: 570C, H: 217A

5368 מַשְׂאֵת *maś'ēt*, what is lifted up: portion (of food), tax, tribute, gift, burden, S: 4864, B: 673A, K: 570C, H: 217B

5369 מִשְׂגָּב¹ *miśgāb*[1], fortress, refuge, stronghold, S: 4869, B: 960D, K: 570D, H: 217D 1.

5370 ²מִשְׂגָּב *miśgāb*[2], variant: Misgab, see 5369, S: 4869, B: 960D, K: 570D, H: 217B

5371 מַשֶּׂגֶת *maśśeget*, variant: overtaking, see 5952, S: 5381†, B: 673B, K: 570D, H: 217B

5372 מְשֻׂכָּה *meśûkkâ*, thorn-hedge, S: 4881, B: 968A, K: 570D, H: 217B

5373 מַשּׂוֹר *maśśôr*, saw (cutting tool), S: 4883, B: 673D, K: 570D, H: 217B

5374 מְשׂוּרָה *meśûrâ*, (liquid) measure of quantity, measure of capacity, S: 4884, B: 601D, K: 570D, H: 217B

5375 ¹מָשׂוֹשׂ *māśôś*[1], joy, delight, celebration, S: 4885, B: 965C, K: 570D, H: 217C

5376 ²מָשׂוֹשׂ *māśôś*[2], wasting away, rotting away, S: 4885, B: 965C, K: 570D, H: 217C

5377 מִשְׂחָק *miśḥāq*, (scoffing) laughter, S: 4890, B: 966A, K: 571A, H: 217C

5378 מַשְׂטֵמָה *maśṭēmâ*, hostility, animosity, enmity, S: 4895, B: 966B, K: 571A, H: 217C

5379 מְשֻׂכָה *meśukâ*, (thorn) hedge (which impedes movement), S: 4881, B: 962B, K: 571A, H: 217C

5380 מַשְׂכִּיל *maśkîl*, maskil (t.t. in the Psalms, perhaps "wisdom song"), S: 4905, B: 968D, K: 571A, H: 217C

5381 מַשְׂכִּית *maśkît*, carved image, sculpture, figurine; what is imagined, imagination, S: 4906, B: 967C, K: 571B, H: 217C

5382 מַשְׂכֹּרֶת *maśkōret*, wage, S: 4909, B: 969B, K: 571B, H: 217C

5383 מַשְׂמֵרָה *maśmērâ*, nail (on the end of a goad), S: 4930†, B: 702C, K: 571B, H: 217C

5384 מִשְׂפָּח *miśpāḥ*, bloodshed, S: 4939, B: 705C, K: 571B, H: 217C

5385 מִשְׂרָה *miśrâ*, dominion, rule, S: 4951, B: 976A, K: 571B, H: 217C

5386 מִשְׂרָפוֹת *miśrāpôt*, (complete) burning, funeral fire, S: 4955†, B: 977C, K: 571C, H: 217C 1.

5387 מִשְׂרְפוֹת מַיִם *miśrepôt mayim*, Misrephoth Maim, S: 4956, B: 977C, K: 571C, H: 217C 2.

5388 מַשְׂרֵקָה *maśrēqâ*, Masrekah, S: 4957, B: 977D, K: 571C, H: 217D

5389 מַשְׂרֵת *maśrēt*, cooking pan, S: 4958, B: 602A, K: 571C, H: 217D

5390 מַשׁ *maš*, variant: see 5434, S: 4851, B: 602A, K: 571C, H: 217D

5391 מַשָּׁא *maššā'*, debt; exacting of usury, S: 4855, B: 673D, K: 571D, H: 217D

5392 מֵשָׁע *mēšā'*, Mesha, S: 4852, B: 602A, K: 571D, H: 217D

5393 מַשְׁאָב *maš'āb*, watering channel, place to draw water, S: 4857, B: 980C, K: 571D, H: 217D

5394 מַשָּׁאָה *maššā'â*, (secured) loan, S: 4859, B: 673D, K: 571D, H: 217D

5395 מַשֻּׁאָה *maššu'â*, variant: deceiving, see 8420, S*, B: 577C & 673B, K: 571D, H: 348A

5396 מַשָּׁאוֹן *maššā'ôn*, deception, S: 4860, B: 674A, K: 571D, H: 218A

5397 מַשֻּׁאוֹת *maššu'ôt*, ruin, rubble, desolation, S: 4876†, B: 674B, K: 572A, H: 218A

5398 מִשְׁאָל *miš'āl*, Mishal, S: 4861, B: 602B, K: 572A, H: 218A

5399 מִשְׁאָלָה *miš'ālâ*, desire, S: 4862, B: 982C, K: 572A, H: 218A

5400 מִשְׁאֶרֶת *miš'eret*, kneading trough, S: 4863, B: 602B, K: 572A, H: 218A

5401 מִשְׁבְּצוֹת *mišbeṣôt*, filigree settings (ornamental work with fine gold wire usually for setting jewels), S: 4865†, B: 990B, K: 572A, H: 218A

5402 מַשְׁבֵּר *mašbēr*, opening of the womb, the point where birth first occurs, S: 4866†, B: 991B, K: 572A, H: 218A

5403 מִשְׁבָּר *mišbār*, breakers, waves, S: 4867, B: 991C, K: 572A, H: 218A

5404 מִשְׁבָּת *mišbāt*, destruction, cessation, finish, S: 4868, B: 992D, K: 572B, H: 218A

5405 מִשְׁגֶּה *mišgeh*, inadvertent mistake, oversight, S: 4870', B: 993B, K: 572B, H: 218A

5406 מָשָׁה *māšâ*, [A] to draw out; [G] to cause to draw out, S: 4871, B: 602B, K: 572B, H: 218B

5407 מֹשֶׁה *mōšeh*, Moses, S: 4872, B: 602C, K: 572B, H: 218B

5408 מַשֶּׁה *maššeh*, credit, loan, S: 4874, B: 674C, K: 572D, H: 218B

5409 מְשׁוֹאָה *mešô'â*, wasteland, desolate land, S: 4875, B: 996C, K: 572D, H: 218B

5410 מַשּׁוּאָה *maššû'â*, variant: deception, S: 4876, B: 674B, K: 572D, H: 218B

5411 מְשׁוֹבָב *mešôbāb*, Meshobab, S: 4877, B: 1000C, K: 572D, H: 218B

5412 מְשׁוּבָה *mešûbâ*, waywardness, backsliding, faithlessness, apostasy, S: 4878, B: 1000B, K: 572D, H: 218B

5413 מְשׁוּגָה *mešûgâ*, error, S: 4879, B: 1000C, K: 573A, H: 218B

5414 מָשׁוֹט *māšôṭ*, oar, S: 4880, B: 1002B, K: 573A, H: 218B

5415 מִשּׁוֹט *miššôṭ*, oar, S: 4880, B: 1002B, K: 573A, H: 218B

5416 מְשִׁוסָּה *mešiwssâ*, variant: see 5468, S: 4882, B: 1042C, K: 573A, H: 218B

5417 מָשַׁח *māšaḥ*, [A] to anoint; [B] to be spread, be anointed; [C] to be anointed, S: 4886, B: 602D, K: 573A, H: 218B

5418 ¹מִשְׁחָה *mišḥâ*[1], anointing (oil), anointment, S: 4888, B: 603B, K: 573C, H: 218C

5419 ²מִשְׁחָה *mišḥâ*[2], portion, S: 4888, B: 603B, K: 573C, H: 218C

5420 ¹מָשְׁחָה *mošḥâ*[1], anointing, S: 4888, B: 602D, K: 573D, H: 218C

5421 ²מָשְׁחָה *mošḥâ*[2], portion, S: 4888, B: 603C, K: 573D, H: 218C

5422 מַשְׁחִית *mašḥît*, destroyer, one who destroys; destruction, corruption; bird trap, S: 4889, B: 1008C, K: 573D, H: 218C

5423 מִשְׁחָר *mišḥār*, dawn, early morning light, S: 4891, B: 1007D, K: 573D, H: 218D

5424 מַשְׁחֵת *mašḥēt*, destruction, annihilation, S: 4892, B: 1008C, K: 574A, H: 218D

5425 מִשְׁחַת *mišḥat*, disfigurement, S: 4893†, B: 1008C, K: 574A, H: 218D

5426 מָשְׁחָת *mošḥāt*, deformity, defect, corruption, S: 4893, B: 1008C, K: 574A, H: 218D

5427 מִשְׁטוֹחַ *mišṭôaḥ*, place for spreading out nets, drying yard for nets, S: 4894, B: 1009A, K: 574A, H: 218D

5428 מִשְׁטָר *mišṭār*, dominion, rule, S: 4896, B: 1009C, K: 574A, H: 218D

5429 מֶשִׁי *mešî*, costly fabric for garments, S: 4897, B: 603D, K: 574B, H: 218D

5430 מְשֵׁיזַבְאֵל *mešêzab'ēl*, Meshezabel, S: 4898, B: 604A, K: 574B, H: 218D

5431 מָשִׁיחַ *māšîaḥ*, anointed (one); the Anointed One, S: 4899, B: 603C, K: 574B, H: 218D

5432 מָשַׁךְ *māšak*, [A] to draw up, drag; to extend, spread out; [C] to be prolonged, delayed; [E] to be deferred; to be tall, S: 4900, B: 604A, K: 574C, H: 219A

5433 ¹מֶשֶׁךְ *mešek*[1], (leather) bag, pouch (= price), S: 4901, B: 604D, K: 575A, H: 219B

5434 ²מֶשֶׁךְ *mešek*[2], Meshech, S: 4902, B: 604D, K: 575A, H: 219B

5435 מִשְׁכָּב *miškāb*, bed, couch, S: 4904, B: 1012D, K: 575B, H: 219B

5436 מֹשְׁכוֹת *mōšekôt*, cords, chains, fetters, S: 4189†, B: 604D, K: 575C, H: 219B

5437 מְשַׁכֶּלֶת *mešakkelet*, variant: miscarriage, S: 7921†, B: 1014A, K: 969C, H: 369B

5438 מִשְׁכָּן *miškān*, tabernacle; dwelling place, habitat, tent, S: 4908, B: 1015C, K: 575C, H: 219C

5439 ¹מָשַׁל *māšal*[1], [A] to quote (a proverb or saying), to make up a proverb; [C] to liken, be like; [D] to tell a proverb; [G] to liken, compare to; [F] to show oneself like, S: 4911, B: 605A, K: 575D, H: 219C

5440 ²מָשַׁל *māšal*[2], [A] to rule, govern, control; [G] make one a ruler, (as noun) dominion, S: 4910, B: 605C, K: 576B, H: 219C

5441 ³מָשַׁל *māšal*[3], variant: [A, D] to speak a proverb, S: 4911, B: 605B, K: 575D, H: 219C

5442 ¹מָשָׁל *māšāl*[1], proverb, parable; oracle; taunt, ridicule, S: 4912, B: 605A, K: 576D, H: 219D

5443 ²מָשָׁל *māšāl*[2], Mashal, S: 4913, B: 602B, K: 577A, H: 220A

5444 ¹מֹשֶׁל *mōšel*[1], likeness, similarity, S: 4915, B: 605C, K: 577A, H: 220A

5445 ²מֹשֶׁל *mōšel*[2], power, dominion, S: 4915, B: 606A, K: 577A, H: 220A

[A] Qal [B] Qal passive [C] Niphal [D] Piel (poel, polel, pilel, pilal, pealal, pilpel) [E] Pual (poal, polal, poalal, pulal, pualal)

5446 מְשֹׁל *mᵉšōl*, variant: byword, see 5439, S: 4914, B: 605C, K: 576A, H: 219C

5447 מִשְׁלוֹחַ *mišlôaḥ*, giving, sending (presents); laying (hands), S: 4916, B: 1020A, K: 577A, H: 220A

5448 מִשְׁלָח *mišlāḥ*, stretching out (of the hand), S: 4916, B: 1020A, K: 577B, H: 220A

5449 מִשְׁלַחַת *mišlaḥat*, discharge (from military); band, company (of angels), S: 4917, B: 1020A, K: 577B, H: 220A

5450 מְשֻׁלָּם *mᵉšullām*, Meshullam, S: 4918, B: 1024C, K: 577B, H: 220B

5451 מְשִׁלֵּמוֹת *mᵉšillēmôt*, Meshillemoth, S: 4919, B: 1024C, K: 577B, H: 220B

5452 מְשֶׁלֶמְיָה *mᵉšelemyâ*, Meshelemiah, S: 4920, B: 1024C, K: 577C, H: 220B

5453 מְשֶׁלֶמְיָהוּ *mᵉšelemyāhû*, Meshelemiah, S: 4920, B: 1024C, K: 577C, H: 220B

5454 מְשִׁלֵּמִית *mᵉšillēmît*, Meshillemith, S: 4921, B: 1024C 2., K: 577C, H: 220B

5455 מְשֻׁלֶּמֶת *mᵉšullemet*, Meshullemeth, S: 4922, B: 1024C, K: 577C, H: 220B

5456 מִשְׁלֹשׁ *mišlōš*, variant: period of three (months), see 8993, S: 7969†, B: 577C & 1025C, K: 535A & 982B, H: 220B

5457 מְשַׁמָּה *mᵉšammâ*, object of horror, desolate waste, dried up place, S: 4923, B: 1031D, K: 577C, H: 220B

5458 מִשְׁמָן *mišmān*, fatness; sturdiness, stoutness; richness, fertileness, S: 4924†, B: 1032C, K: 577D, H: 220B

5459 מִשְׁמַנָּה *mišmannâ*, Mishmannah, S: 4925, B: 1032D, K: 577D, H: 220B

5460 מַשְׁמַנִּים *mašmannîm*, choice food, festive food, S: 4924†, B: 1032D, K: 577D, H: 220C

5461 מִשְׁמָעִ *mišmā'¹*, what one hears, rumor, hearsay, S: 4926, B: 1036A, K: 577D, H: 220C

5462 ²מִשְׁמָע *mišmā'²*, Mishma, S: 4927, B: 1036A, K: 577D, H: 220C

5463 מִשְׁמַעַת *mišma'at*, bodyguard; subject, one obligated to allegiance, S: 4928, B: 1036A, K: 578A, H: 220C

5464 ¹מִשְׁמָר *mišmār¹*, guard *or* guarding, custody, imprisonment, S: 4929, B: 1038B, K: 578A, H: 220C

5465 ²מִשְׁמָר *mišmār²*, variant: muzzle, S: 4929, B: 1038B, K: 578A, H: 220C

5466 מִשְׁמֶרֶת *mišmeret*, responsibility, duty, service; requirement, obligation; guard, watch, what is cared for, S: 4931, B: 1038B, K: 578B, H: 220C

5467 מִשְׁנֶה *mišneh*, second, next (in a series); twice, double, S: 4932, B: 1041C, K: 578C, H: 220D

5468 מְשִׁסָּה *mᵉšissâ*, plunder, loot, booty, S: 4933, B: 1042D, K: 579A, H: 221A

5469 מִשְׁעוֹל *miš'ôl*, narrow path, S: 4934, B: 1043C, K: 579A, H: 221A

5470 מִשְׁעִי *miš'î*, cleansing, S: 4935, B: 606B, K: 579A, H: 221A

5471 מִשְׁעָם *miš'ām*, Misham, S: 4936, B: 606C, K: 579A, H: 221B

5472 מִשְׁעָן *miš'ān*, support, supplies, S: 4937, B: 1044A, K: 579A, H: 221B

5473 מַשְׁעֵן *maš'ēn*, support, supply, S: 4937, B: 1044A, K: 579B, H: 221B

5474 מַשְׁעֵנָה *maš'ēnâ*, support, supply, S: 4938, B: 1044A, K: 579B, H: 221B

5475 מִשְׁעֶנֶת *miš'enet*, staff, stick, S: 4938, B: 1044A, K: 579B, H: 221B

5476 מִשְׁפָּחָה *mišpāḥâ*, clan, family, people, S: 4940, B: 1046C, K: 579B, H: 221B

5477 מִשְׁפָּט *mišpāṭ*, justice, judgment; law, regulation, prescription, specification, S: 4941, B: 1048B, K: 579C, H: 221C

5478 מִשְׁפְּתַיִם *mišpᵉtayim*, (dual) campfires *or* two saddlebags, S: 4942†, B: 1046B, K: 580C, H: 221D

5479 מֶשֶׁק *mešeq*, inheritance, possession, S: 4943, B: 606C, K: 580C, H: 221D

5480 מַשָּׁק *maššāq*, onslaught, assault, S: 4944, B: 1055B, K: 580C, H: 221D

5481 מְשֻׁקָּד *mᵉšuqqād*, shape of almond flowers, S: 8246, B: 1052B, K: 580C, H: 222A

5482 ¹מַשְׁקֶה *mašqeh¹*, cupbearer; drink (liquid); drinking vessel, S: 4945, B: 1052D, K: 580C, H: 222A 1.

5483 ²מַשְׁקֶה *mašqeh²*, variant: irrigation, drink, S: 4945, B: 1052D, K: 580C 2., H: 222A 2.

5484 מִשְׁקוֹל *mišqôl*, weight, S: 4946, B: 1054A, K: 580D, H: 222A

5485 מַשְׁקוֹף *mašqôp*, top (upper crosspiece of a door), lintel, S: 4947, B: 1054D, K: 580D, H: 222A

5486 מִשְׁקָל *mišqāl*, weight, S: 4948, B: 1054A, K: 580D, H: 222A

5487 מִשְׁקֶלֶת *mišqelet*, plumb line, leveling instrument, S: 4949, B: 1054A, K: 581A, H: 222A

5488 מִשְׁקָע *mišqā'*, clear (settled) water, S: 4950, B: 1054B, K: 581A, H: 222A

5489 מִשְׁרָה *mišrâ*, (grape) juice, S: 4952, B: 1056A, K: 581A, H: 222B

5490 מִשְׁרָעִי *mišrā'î*, Mishraite, S: 4954, B: 606D, K: 581A, H: 222B

5491 מָשַׁשׁ *māšaš*, [A] to touch, feel; [D] to grope, search thoroughly; [G] to let one feel, S: 4959, B: 606D, K: 581B, H: 222B

5492 מִשְׁתֶּה *mišteh*, feast, banquet, dinner; drink, S: 4960, B: 1059C, K: 581B, H: 222B

5493 ¹מֹתִי *mōt¹*, men; few (people), S: 4962†, B: 607A, K: 581C, H: 222C

5494 ²מֹת *mōt²*, variant: louse (insect), S: 4962†, B: 607B, K: 581C, H: 222C

5495 מַתְבֵּן *matbēn*, heap of straw, S: 4963, B: 1062A, K: 581D, H: 222C

5496 מֶתֶג *meteg*, bridle, S: 4964, B: 607C, K: 582A, H: 222C

5497 מֶתֶג הָאַמָּה *meteg hā'ammâ*, Metheg Ammah, S: 4965, B: 607C & 52C, K: 582A, H: 222C

5498 מָתוֹק *mātôq*, sweet, sweetness, S: 4966, B: 608D, K: 582A, H: 222C

5499 מְתוּשָׁאֵל *mᵉtûšā'ēl*, Methushael, S: 4967, B: 607B, K: 582A, H: 222C

5500 מְתוּשֶׁלַח *mᵉtûšelaḥ*, Methuselah, S: 4968, B: 607B, K: 582A, H: 222C

5501 מָתַח *mātaḥ*, [A] to spread out, S: 4969, B: 607C, K: 582B, H: 222C

5502 מִתְחָה *mitḥâ*, variant: spreading out, S: 8478†, B: 577C & 1065A, K: 582B, H: 200B & 389B

5503 מָתַי *mātay*, How long?; When?, S: 4970, B: 607D, K: 582B, H: 222C

5504 מַתְכֹּנֶת *matkōnet*, measure, formula, S: 4971, B: 1067C, K: 582C, H: 222D

5505 מַתְּלָאָה *mattᵉlā'â*, variant: see 4537 & 9430, S: 4972, B: 552B & 521B, K: 582C, H: 222D

5506 מְתַלְּעוֹת *mᵉtalle'ôt*, jaw; teeth, S: 4973†, B: 1069A, K: 582C, H: 222D

5507 מְתֹם *mᵉtōm*, health, soundness, S: 4974, B: 1071B, K: 582C, H: 222D

5508 ¹מַתָּן *mattān¹*, gift, present, S: 4976, B: 682B, K: 582D, H: 222D

5509 ²מַתָּן *mattān²*, Mattan, S: 4977, B: 682B, K: 582D, H: 222D

5510 ¹מַתָּנָה *mattānâ¹*, gift, something give, bribe, S: 4979, B: 682B, K: 582D, H: 222D

5511 ²מַתָּנָה *mattānâ²*, Mattanah, S: 4980, B: 682C, K: 583A, H: 223A

5512 מִתְנִי *mitnî*, Mithnite, S: 4981, B: 608C, K: 583A, H: 223A

5513 מַתְּנַי *mattᵉnay*, Mattenai, S: 4982, B: 682D, K: 583A, H: 223A

5514 מַתַּנְיָה *mattanyâ*, Mattaniah, S: 4983, B: 682C, K: 583A, H: 223A

5515 מַתַּנְיָהוּ *mattanyāhû*, Mattaniah, S: 4983, B: 682C, K: 583A, H: 223A

5516 מָתְנַיִם *motnayim*, (dual) waist, lower back (lumbar region), loins, S: 4975†, B: 608A, K: 583B, H: 223A

5517 מָתַק *mātaq*, [A] to be, become sweet; [G] to taste sweet, enjoy sweetness, S: 4985 & 4988†, B: 608C, K: 583C, H: 223A

5518 מָתֵק *mātēq*, sweetness, S: 4986†, B: 608D, K: 583C, H: 223C

5519 מֹתֶק *mōteq*, sweetness, S: 4987, B: 608D, K: 583C, H: 223C

5520 מִתְקָה *mitqâ*, Mithcah, S: 4989, B: 609A, K: 583C, H: 223C

5521 מִתְרְדָת *mitrᵉdāt*, Mithredath, S: 4990, B: 609C, K: 583D, H: 223C

5522 מַתַּת *mattat*, gift, S: 4991†, B: 682C, K: 583D, H: 223C

5523 מַתַּתָּה *mattattâ*, Mattattah, S: 4992, B: 683A, K: 583D, H: 223C

5524 מַתִּתְיָה *mattityâ*, Mattithiah, S: 4993, B: 682D, K: 583D, H: 223C

5525 מַתִּתְיָהוּ *mattityāhû*, Mattithiah, S: 4993, B: 682D, K: 583D, H: 223C

5526 נ *n*, letter of the Hebrew alphabet, S*, B: 609A, K: 584A, H*

5527 ָן- *-ān*, ן- *-n*, they, them, their, S*, B*, K*, H*

5528 ¹נָא *nā'¹*, often not translated, marks entreaty or exhortation: please!, I beg you!, now!, S: 4994, B: 609A, K: 584A, H: 223A

5529 ²נָא *nā'²*, raw (meat), S: 4995, B: 644B, K: 584D, H: 223B

5530 נֹא *nō'*, No = Thebes, S: 4996, B: 609D, K: 584D, H: 223B

5531 נֹא אָמוֹן *nō' 'āmôn*, No Amon = Thebes, S: 527 + 4996, B: 51B, K: 584D, H: 19C

5532 נֹאד *nō'd*, skin vessel (skinned in one piece, the appendages tied or sewn, the neck the funnel, used to hold liquid), S: 4997, B: 609D, K: 584D, H: 223C

5533 נָאָה *nā'â*, [D] to be beautiful, adorn, S: 4998, B: 610A, K: 585A, H: 223D

5534 נָאוֶה *nā'weh*, lovely, fitting, suited, S: 5000, B: 610A, K: 585A, H: 223D

5535 נָאַם *nā'am*, [A] to declare as a prophet, S: 5001, B: 610C, K: 585A, H*

5536 נְאֻם *n[e]'um*, declaration, oracle, utterance, S: 5002, B: 610B, K: 585B, H: 223D

5537 נָאַף *nā'ap*, [A, D] to commit adultery; (ptcp.) adulterer, adulteress, S: 5003, B: 610C, K: 585B, H: 224A

5538 נַאֲפוּפִים *na'[a]pûpîm*, (marks of) unfaithfulness, adultery, S: 5005†, B: 610D, K: 585D, H: 224A

5539 נִאֻפִים *ni'upîm*, adultery, S: 5004†, B: 610D, K: 585D, H: 224A

5540 נָאַץ *nā'aṣ*, [A] to spurn, despise, reject; [D] to treat with contempt, revile, despise; [F] be blasphemed, be reviled, S: 5006, B: 610D, K: 585D, H: 224B

5541 נְאָצָה *n[e]'āṣâ*, disgrace, shame, S: 5007, B: 611A, K: 586A, H: 224B

5542 נֶאָצָה *ne'āṣâ*, contemptible things, blasphemies, S: 5007, B: 611A, K: 586A, H: 224B

5543 נָאַק *nā'aq*, [A] to groan, S: 5008, B: 611A, K: 586A, H: 224B

5544 נְאָקָה *n[e]'āqâ*, groaning, S: 5009, B: 611A, K: 586A, H: 224B

5545 נֵאַר *nā'ar*, [D] to renounce, abandon, S: 5010, B: 611B, K: 586B, H: 224B

5546 נֹב *nōb*, Nob, S: 5011, B: 611B, K: 586B, H: 224C

5547 נָבָא *nābā'*, [C, F] to prophesy, speak as a prophet, S: 5012, B: 612A, K: 586B, H: 224C

5548 נָבַב *nābab*, variant: [A] to hollow out, S: 5014, B: 612C, K: 587A, H: 224D

5549 [1]נְבוֹ *n[e]bô[1]*, Nebo, S: 5015, B: 612D, K: 587B, H: 224D

5550 [2]נְבוֹ *n[e]bô[2]*, Nebo (pagan god), S: 5015, B: 612D, K: 587B, H: 224D

5551 [3]נְבוֹ *n[e]bô[3]*, Nebo, S: 5015, B: 612D, K: 587B, H*

5552 נְבוּ שַׂר־סְכִים *n[e]bû śar-s[e]kîm*, Nebo-Sarsekim, S: 5562†, B: 701C, K: 660D, H: 224D & 354C

5553 נְבוּאָה *n[e]bû'â*, prophesy, the word of the prophet, S: 5016, B: 612C, K: 587C, H: 224D

5554 נָבוּב *nābûb*, hollow thing; witless person, S: 5014†, B: 612C, K: 587A, H: 224D

5555 נְבוּזַרְאֲדָן *n[e]bûzar'[a]dān*, נְבוּזַר־אֲדָן *n[e]bûzar-'[a]dān*, Nebuzaradan, S: 5018, B: 613A, K: 587C, H: 224D

5556 נְבוּכַדְנֶאצַּר *n[e]bûkadne'ṣṣar*, נְבוּכַדְנֶצַּר *n[e]bûkadneṣṣar*, נְבוּכַדְנֶצּוֹר *n[e]bûkadneṣṣôr*, Nebuchadnezzar, S: 5019, B: 613A, K: 587C, H: 224D

5557 נְבוּכַדְרֶאצַּר *n[e]bûkadre'ṣṣar*, נְבוּכַדְרֶאצּוֹר *n[e]bûkadre'ṣṣôr*, Nebuchadnezzar, S: 5019, B: 613A, K: 587C, H: 224D

5558 נְבוּשַׁזְבָּן *n[e]bûšazbān*, נְבוּשַׁז־בָּן *n[e]bûšaz-bān*, Nebushazban, S: 5021, B: 613D, K: 587D, H: 224D

5559 נָבוֹת *nābôt*, Naboth, S: 5022, B: 613B, K: 587D, H: 224D

5560 נָבַח *nābaḥ*, [A] to bark, S: 5024, B: 613B, K: 587D, H: 224D

5561 [1]נֹבַח *nōbaḥ[1]*, Nobah, S: 5025, B: 613B, K: 587D, H: 225A

5562 [2]נֹבַח *nōbaḥ[2]*, Nobah, S: 5025, B: 613B, K: 587D, H: 225A

5563 נִבְחַז *nibḥaz*, Nibhaz (pagan god), S: 5026, B: 613B, K: 588A, H: 225A

5564 נָבַט *nābaṭ*, [D] to look at; [G] to look at, gaze at, consider, S: 5027, B: 613C, K: 588A, H: 225A

5565 נְבָט *n[e]bāṭ*, Nebat, S: 5028, B: 614A, K: 588C, H: 225B

5566 נָבִיא *nābî'*, prophet, S: 5030, B: 611C, K: 588C, H: 225B

5567 נְבִיאָה *n[e]bî'â*, prophetess, S: 5031, B: 612C, K: 589A, H: 225B

5568 נְבָיוֹת *n[e]bāyôt*, Nebaioth, S: 5032, B: 614A, K: 589A, H: 225B

5569 נֵבֶךְ *nēbek*, source springs (of the sea), S: 5033, B: 614A, K: 589B, H: 225B

5570 [1]נָבֵל *nābēl[1]*, [A] to wither, shrivel, fade, decay, S: 5034, B: 615B, K: 589B, H: 225B & 225D

5571 [2]נָבֵל *nābal[2]*, [A] to play the fool, act disdainfully; [D] to treat with contempt, dishonor, reject, S: 5034, B: 614C, K: 589B, H: 225C

5572 [1]נָבָל *nābāl[1]*, foolish, lacking understanding, S: 5036, B: 614D, K: 589C, H: 225C

5573 [2]נָבָל *nābāl[2]*, Nabal, S: 5037, B: 615A, K: 589D, H: 225C

5574 [1]נֵבֶל *nēbel[1]*, (wine) skin; water jar, jug, pot (of clay), S: [5035], B: 614B, K: 589D, H: 225C

5575 [2]נֵבֶל *nēbel[2]*, lyre, harp (stringed instrument), S: [5035], B: 614B, K: 589D, H: 225C

5576 נְבָלָה *n[e]bālâ*, (very) wicked thing, disgraceful thing; vileness, S: 5039, B: 615A, K: 590A, H: 225C

5577 נְבֵלָה *n[e]bēlâ*, dead body, carcass, S: 5038, B: 615C, K: 590A, H: 225C

5578 נַבְלוּת *nablût*, (female) genitals, S: 5040, B: 615B, K: 590B, H: 225D

5579 נְבַלָּט *n[e]ballāṭ*, Neballat, S: 5041, B: 615D, K: 590B, H: 225D

5580 נָבַע *nāba'*, [G] to gush forth, bubble out, spew forth, S: 5042, B: 615D, K: 590B, H: 225D

5581 נִבְשָׁן *nibšān*, Nibshan, S: 5044, B: 143C, K: 590C, H: 225D

5582 נֶגֶב *negeb*, south, the Negev, S: 5045, B: 616A, K: 590C, H: 225D

5583 נָגַד *nāgad*, [G] to tell, report, inform; [H] to be told, have reported to, S: 5046, B: 616C, K: 591A, H: 226A

5584 נֶגֶד *neged*, before, in front of, opposite of, beyond, S: 5048, B: 617A, K: 591C, H: 226B

5585 נָגַהּ *nāgah*, [A] to shine; [G] to cause to shine, give light, S: 5050, B: 618B, K: 592B, H: 226C

5586 [1]נֹגַהּ *nōgah[1]*, brightness, radiance, splendor, brilliance, S: 5051, B: 618B, K: 592B, H: 226C

5587 [2]נֹגַהּ *nōgah[2]*, Nogah, S: 5052, B: 618B, K: 592B, H: 226C

5588 נְגֹהָה *n[e]gōhâ*, brightness, luster, S: 5054, B: 618C, K: 592B, H: 226C

5589 נְגוֹ *n[e]gô*, variant: Nego, see 6284, S: 5664†, B: 715A, K: 673A, H: 262B

5590 נָגַח *nāgaḥ*, [A] to gore (a bull into a person); [D] to gore, push back, butt; to engage in pushing back, butting, thrusting, S: 5055, B: 618C, K: 592B, H: 226C

5591 נַגָּח *naggāḥ*, (the act of) goring (a bull into a person), S: 5056, B: 618C, K: 592C, H: 226D

5592 נָגִיד *nāgîd*, leader, ruler, official, officer, S: 5057, B: 617D, K: 592C, H: 226D

5593 נְגִינָה *n[e]gînâ*, stringed instrument; song that mocks, taunts, S: 5058, B: 618D, K: 592D, H: 227A

5594 נָגַן *nāgan*, [A] to play a stringed instrument, (as noun) musician; [D] to play a stringed instrument, S: 5059, B: 618D, K: 593A, H: 227A

5595 נָגַע *nāga'*, [A] to touch; to strike; [B] to be plagued, be stricken; [C] to let oneself be driven back (in a battle); [D] to inflict, afflict; [E] to be plagued; [G] to extend, reach out, cause to touch, S: 5060, B: 619A, K: 593B, H: 227A

5596 נֶגַע *nega'*, plague, blow (of various kinds): mildew, infection, sores, scourge, disaster, S: 5061, B: 619C, K: 593D, H: 227B

5597 נָגַף *nāgap*, [A] to strike, afflict (with a plague); [C] to be defeated, S: 5062, B: 619D, K: 594A, H: 227C

5598 נֶגֶף *negep*, plague; stumbling (caused by a stone), S: 5063, B: 620A, K: 594B, H: 227C

5599 נָגַר *nāgar*, [C] to be spilled, flow; [G] to pour out, hand over, deliver over; [H] to be poured down (a slope), S: 5064, B: 620B, K: 594C, H: 227C

5600 נִגֶּרֶת *niggeret*, variant: torrent, see 5599, S: 5064†, B: 620B, K: 594C, H: 227D

5601 נָגַשׂ *nāgaś*, [A] to oppress, exploit, (as noun) a slave driver; [C] to be oppressed, be hard pressed, S: 5065, B: 620B, K: 594C, H: 227D

5602 נָגַשׁ *nāgaš*, [A] to come near, approach; [C] to come near, approach; [G] to bring forth, present; [H] to be brought, be presented; [F] to draw near, assemble, S: 5066, B: 620C, K: 594D, H: 227D

5603 נֵד *nēd*, heap, wall, barrier, S: 5067, B: 622D, K: 595C, H: 228B

5604 נָדָא *nādā'*, variant: [G] detach, remove from, S: 5077, B: 621B, K: 595D, H: 228B

5605 נָדַב *nādab*, [A] to be willing; to prompt, incite; [F] to willingly offer oneself, volunteer, give a freewill offering, S: 5068, B: 621C, K: 595D, H: 228B

5606 נָדָב *nādāb*, Nadab, S: 5070, B: 621C, K: 596A, H: 228C

5607 נְדָבָה *n[e]dābâ*, free, voluntary; freewill offering, S: 5071, B: 621D, K: 596A, H: 228C

5608 נְדַבְיָה *n^{e}dabyâ*, Nedabiah, S: 5072, B: 622A, K: 596B, H: 228C

5609 נִדְגָּלוֹת *nidgālôt*, variant: see 1839, S: 1713†, B: 186B, K: 203C [NIPHAL PARTICIPLE], H: 228C

5610 נָדַד *nādad*, [A] to flee, be a fugitive; to wander, stray; [D] to flee away; [G] to banish, put to flight; [H] to be banished, be cast aside, S: 5074, B: 622B, K: 596B, H: 228C

5611 נְדֻדִים *n^{e}dudîm*, tossing and turning, restlessness (in bed in the night), S: 5076†, B: 622C, K: 596C, H: 228D

5612 נָדָה *nādâ*, [D] to exclude; to put off thoughts, suppose to be far off, S: 5077, B: 622D, K: 596C, H: 228D

5613 נֵדֶה *nēdeh*, gift, reward, S: 5078, B: 622D, K: 596D, H: 228D

5614 נִדָּה *niddâ*, period of menstruation; (water used in) cleansing, unclean water; (act of) impurity, corruption, defilement, S: 5079, B: 622C, K: 596D, H: 228D

5615 [1]נָדַח *nādaḥ*[1], [C] to be scattered, be exiled, be outcast; [E] be thrust into; [G] to cause to scatter, banish, drive out; [H] to be driven, be hunted, S: 5080, B: 623A, K: 597A, H: 229A

5616 [2]נָדַח *nādaḥ*[2], [A] to wield (an ax); (to have hand) be put (to the ax); [G] to bring, S: 5080, B: 623A, K: 597A, H: 229B

5617 נֹדִי *nōdî*, variant: see 5654, S: 5112†, B: 627A, K: 597C, H: 229B

5618 נָדִיב *nādîb*, willing, generous; prince, noble, ruler, official, S: 5081, B: 622A, K: 597C, H: 229B

5619 נְדִיבָה *n^{e}dîbâ*, something noble; dignity, nobility, S: 5082, B: 622A, K: 597C, H: 229B

5620 [1]נָדָן *nādān*[1], sheath (of a sword), S: 5084, B: 623C, K: 597D, H: 229B

5621 [2]נָדָן *nādān*[2], gift, wages of illicit sexual favors, S: 5083, B: 623C, K: 597D, H: 229B

5622 נָדַף *nādap*, [A] to blow away, scatter; [C] to be windblown, be fleeting, S: 5086, B: 623C, K: 597D, H: 229C

5623 נָדַר *nādar*, [A] to make a vow, S: 5087, B: 623D, K: 598A, H: 229C

5624 נֶדֶר *neder*, vow, S: 5088, B: 634D, K: 598A, H: 229C

5625 נֹהַּ *nōah*, value, distinction, S: 5089, B: 627B, K: 598C, H: 229C

5626 -נָה *-nâ*, her; it, its, S*, B*, K*, H*

5627 [1]נָהַג *nāhag*[1], [A] to drive, lead, guide; [B] to be led; [D] to drive, lead forth, guide, S: 5090, B: 624A, K: 598C, H: 229C

5628 [2]נָהַג *nāhag*[2], [D] to moan, sob, lament, S: 5090, B: 624C, K: 598D, H: 229D

5629 [1]נָהָה *nāhâ*[1], [A] to mourn, wail; [C] to be taunted (with a mournful song), S: 5091, B: 624C, K: 598D, H: 229D

5630 [2]נָהָה *nāhâ*[2], variant: [C] to keep close, stay loyal, S: 5091, B: 624C, K: 599A, H: 229D

5631 נְהִי *n^{e}hî*, wailing, mourning, lamentation, S: 5092, B: 624C, K: 599A, H: 229D

5632 נִהְיָה *nihyâ*, variant: wailing, lamentation, mourning, S: 5093, B: 624D, K: 230D, H: 79A

5633 נָהַל *nāhal*, [D] guide, bring along, lead; [F] to move along, S: 5095, B: 624D, K: 599A, H: 230A

5634 נַהֲלָל *nah^{a}lāl*, Nahalal, S: 5096, B: 625B, K: 599B, H: 230A

5635 [1]נַהֲלֹל *nah^{a}lōl*[1], watering hole, S: 5097, B: 625B, K: 599B, H: 230A

5636 [2]נַהֲלֹל *nah^{a}lōl*[2], Nahalol, S: 5096, B: 625B, K: 599B, H: 230A

5637 נָהַם *nāham*, [A] to growl, roar; to groan, S: 5098, B: 625B, K: 599B, H: 230A

5638 נַהַם *naham*, roaring, growling, S: 5099, B: 625B, K: 599C, H: 230A

5639 נְהָמָה *n^{e}hāmâ*, roaring, growling; anguish, groaning, S: 5100, B: 625B, K: 599C, H: 230A

5640 נָהַק *nāhaq*, [A] to bray (of a donkey), S: 5101, B: 625C, K: 599C, H: 230A

5641 [1]נָהַר *nāhar*[1], [A] to stream to (like a river flow), S: 5102, B: 625C, K: 599C, H: 230B

5642 [2]נָהַר *nāhar*[2], [A] to be radiant (with joy), beam (with joy), S: 5102, B: 626A, K: 599C, H: 230B

5643 נָהָר *nāhār*, river, stream, canal; the River (Euphrates, Tigris or Nile), S: 5104, B: 625C, K: 599D, H: 230B

5644 נְהָרָה *n^{e}hārâ*, (beaming) light, S: 5105, B: 626A, K: 600A, H: 230B

5645 נַהֲרַיִם *nah^{a}rayim*, variant: Naharaim, see 808, S: 763†, B: 74B, K: 600A, H: 230B

5646 [1]-נוּ *-nû*[1], us, our, S*, B*, K*, H*

5647 [2]-נוּ -נוֹ *-nû*[2], *-nô*, him, his; it, its, S*, B*, K*, H*

5648 נוּא *nû'*, [A] to hinder; [G] to forbid, thwart, discourage, S: 5106, B: 626B, K: 600B, H: 230C

5649 נוּב *nûb*, [A] to bring forth, bear fruit, increase; [D] to make thrive, S: 5107, B: 626B, K: 600B, H: 230C

5650 נֹב *nôb*, variant: see 5762, S: 5108, B: 626C, K: 614C, H: 230C

5651 נוֹבָי *nôbāy*, variant: Nobai, see 5763, S: 5109, B: 626C, K: 600C, H: 230C

5652 נוּג *nûg*, sorrow, S: 3013†, B: 387B, K: 600C, H: 230C

5653 נוּד *nûd*, [A] to sway, wander, be aimless, become homeless; to mourn, express sympathy (by shaking the head), S: 5110, B: 626C, K: 600C, H: 230C

5654 [1]נוֹדִי *nôd*[1], lament, S: 5112, B: 627A, K: 597C, H: 229B

5655 [2]נוֹד *nôd*[2], Nod, S: 5113, B: 627A, K: 600D, H: 230D

5656 נוֹדָב *nôdāb*, Nodab, S: 5114, B: 622A, K: 601A, H: 230D

5657 [1]נָוָה *nāwâ*[1], [A] to be at rest, reach one's aim, S: 5115, B: 627D, K: 601A, H: 230D

5658 [2]נָוָה *nāwâ*[2], [G] to praise, S: 5115, B: 627B, K: 601A, H: 230D

5659 [1]נָוֶה *nāweh*[1], pasture, pastureland; (generally) abode, dwelling, house, S: 5116, B: 627C, K: 601A, H: 230D

5660 [2]נָוֶה *nāweh*[2], variant: dwelling, abiding, S: 5116, B: 627D, K: 601B, H*

5661 [3]נָוָה *nāwâ*[3], pasture, pastureland; (generally) abode, dwelling, camp, place, S: 4999, B: 627D, K: 601C, H: 231A

5662 נָוֹת *nāwôt*, variant: Navoth, see 5766, S: 5121†, B: 627D, K: 614C, H: 231A

5663 [1]נוּחַ *nûaḥ*[1], [A] to settle, rest, wait; [G] to put, keep, settle, rest; to leave, allow; [H] to be placed, find rest, S: 5117, B: 628A, K: 601C, H: 231A

5664 [2]נוּחַ *nûaḥ*[2], variant: [A] to lament, wail, S: 5117, B: 628A, K: 602C, H: 231C

5665 נֹחַ *nôaḥ*, resting place, S: 5118, B: 629D, K: 602C, H: 231C

5666 נוֹחָה *nôḥâ*, Nohah, S: 5119, B: 629A, K: 602C, H: 231C

5667 נוּט *nûṭ*, [A] to shake, quake, S: 5120, B: 630A, K: 602C, H: 231C

5668 נָוִית *nāwît*, variant: Navith, see 5766, S: 5121, B: 627D, K: 614C, H: 231C

5669 נָוֶל *nāwel*, variant: thread, S*, B*, K: 602D, H: 231C

5670 נוּם *nûm*, [A] to sleep, slumber, S: 5123, B: 630B, K: 602D, H: 231D

5671 נוּמָה *nûmâ*, drowsiness, S: 5124, B: 630B, K: 602D, H: 231D

5672 [1]נוּן *nûn*[1], [C] to propagate, increase, S: 5125, B: 630C, K: 614D, H*

5673 [2]נוּן *nûn*[2], Nun, S: 5126, B: 630C, K: 602D, H: 231D

5674 נוּס *nûs*, [A] to flee away, escape; [D] to drive along; [G] to put to flight, get to safety, S: 5127, B: 630C, K: 603A, H: 231D

5675 נוּעַ *nûa'*, [A] to shake, sway, swagger, wander; [C] to be shaken; [G] to make wander, to set trembling, shake, toss, S: 5128, B: 631A, K: 603B, H: 231D

5676 נוֹעַדְיָה *nô'adyâ*, Noadiah, S: 5129, B: 418A, K: 603D, H: 232A

5677 [1]נוּף *nûp*[1], [D] to wave (the fist) threateningly; [G] to wave, present (an offering) by waving; to shake, wield, sweep; [H] to be waved, S: 5130, B: 631D, K: 603D, H: 232A

5678 [2]נוּף *nûp*[2], [A] to sprinkle with myrrh (a bed); [G] to cause (rain) to fall, S: 5130, B: 631D, K: 604B, H: 232B

5679 נוֹף *nôp*, loftiness, elevation, height, S: 5131, B: 632C, K: 604B, H: 232B

5680 נוּץ *nûṣ*, [A] to leave, go away, S: 5132, B: 663B, K: 604B, H: 232B

5681 נוֹצָה *nôṣâ*, plumage, feathers, S: 5133, B: 663B, K: 604C, H: 232B

5682 נוּק *nûq*, variant: [G] to suckle, nurse, S: 3243†, B: 632D, K*, H: 232C

5683 נוּשׁ *nûš*, [A] to be sick, S: 5136, B: 633B, K: 604C, H: 232C

5684 [1]נָזָה *nāzâ*[1], [A] to spatter; [G] to sprinkle, S: 5137, B: 633B, K: 604C, H: 232C

5685 [2]נָזָה *nāzâ*[2], variant: [G] to leap, spring, S: 5137, B: 633C, K: 604C, H: 232C

5686 נָזִיד *nāzîd*, stew, thick boiled food, S: 5138, B: 268A, K: 604D, H: 232C

5687 נָזִיר *nāzîr*, Nazirite, separation; untended vine, S: 5139, B: 634C, K: 604D, H: 232C

5688 נָזַל *nāzal*, [A] to flow down, pour down, stream down; [G] to make flow, S: 5140, B: 633C, K: 605A, H: 232D

5689 נֹזֵל *nōzēl*, streams; surging waters, S: 5140†, B: 633C, K: 605A, H: 232D

5690 נֶזֶם *nezem*, ring (in the nose or ear of male or female), S: 5141, B: 633D, K: 605A, H: 232D

5691 נֵזֶק *nēzeq*, burden, trouble, S: 5143, B: 634A, K: 605B, H: 232D

5692 [1]נָזַר *nāzar*[1], [C] to separate oneself, consecrate oneself; [G] to keep separate, S: 5144, B: 634A, K: 605B, H: 232D

5693 [2]נָזַר *nāzar*[2], [G] to abstain, separate as a Nazirite, S: 5144, B: 634C, K: 605B, H: 233A

5694 נֵזֶר *nēzer*, separation, dedication; diadem, crown (as a sign of consecration); Nazirite, S: 5145, B: 634B, K: 605C, H: 233A

5695 נֹחַ *nōaḥ*, Noah, S: 5146, B: 629B, K: 605D, H: 233A

5696 נַחְבִּי *naḥbî*, Nahbi, S: 5147, B: 286A, K: 605D, H: 233A

5697 [1]נָחָה *nāḥâ*[1], [A, G] to lead, guide, S: 5148, B: 634D, K: 606A, H: 233A

5698 [2]נָחָה *nāḥâ*[2], variant: [A] lean upon, S: 5117†, B: 628A, K: 606A, H: 231A

5699 נַחוּם *naḥûm*, Nahum, S: 5151, B: 637B, K: 606B, H: 233B

5700 נְחוּם *nᵉḥûm*, Nehum, S: 5149, B: 637B, K: 606B, H: 233B

5701 נָחוֹר *nāḥôr*, Nahor, S: 5152, B: 637D, K: 606B, H: 233B

5702 נָחוּשׁ *nāḥûš*, (made) of bronze, S: 5153, B: 639A, K: 606B, H: 233B

5703 נְחוּשָׁה *nᵉḥûšâ*, copper, bronze, S: 5154, B: 639A, K: 606C, H: 233B

5704 נְחִילוֹת *nᵉḥîlôt*, flutes, S: 5155†, B: 636A, K: 606C, H: 233B

5705 נָחִיר *nāḥîr*, (dual) nostrils, S: 5156, B: 638A, K: 606C, H: 233B

5706 נָחַל *nāḥal*, [A] to take as an appearance, take possession; [D] to assign an inheritance, allot; [G] to cause to inherit, give an inheritance; [H] to be allotted; [F] to obtain an inheritance for oneself; to distribute an inheritance, S: 5157, B: 635C, K: 606C, H: 233B

5707 [1]נַחַל *naḥal*[1], river, stream, brook, wadi torrent; ravine, gorge, valley, S: 5158, B: 636A, K: 607C, H: 233D

5708 [2]נַחַל *naḥal*[2], variant: date palm, S: 5158, B: 636D, K: 607D, H: 234A

5709 [1]נַחֲלָה *naḥᵃlâ*[1], inheritance, property, S: 5159, B: 635A, K: 607D, H: 234A

5710 [2]נַחֲלָה *naḥᵃlâ*[2], disease, S*, B: 317C, K: 607D, H: 234A

5711 [3]נַחֲלָה *naḥᵃlâ*[3], wadi (of Egypt), S: 5158, B: 636C, K: 607C, H: 234B

5712 נַחֲלִיאֵל *naḥᵃlî'ēl*, Nahaliel, S: 5160, B: 636D, K: 608C, H: 234B

5713 נֶחֱלָמִי *neḥᵉlāmî*, Nehelamite, S: 5161, B: 636D, K: 608C, H: 234B

5714 נָחַם *nāḥam*, [C] to relent, repent, change one's mind; be grieved; [D] to comfort, console, express sympathy; [E] to be comforted, be consoled; [F] to console oneself; to change one's mind; avenge oneself, S: 5162, B: 636D, K: 608C, H: 234B

5715 נַחַם *naḥam*, Naham, S: 5163, B: 637B, K: 609B, H: 234C

5716 נֹחַם *nōḥam*, compassion, pity, S: 5164, B: 637B, K: 609B, H: 234D

5717 נֶחָמָה *neḥāmâ*, comfort, consolation, S: 5165, B: 637C, K: 609B, H: 234D

5718 נְחֶמְיָה *nᵉḥemyâ*, Nehemiah, S: 5166, B: 637C, K: 609C, H: 234D

5719 נִחֻמִים *niḥumîm*, comfort, compassion, S: 5150†, B: 637B, K: 609C, H: 234D

5720 נַחֲמָנִי *naḥᵃmānî*, Nahamani, S: 5167, B: 637C, K: 609C, H: 234D

5721 נַחְנוּ *naḥnû*, we, S: 5168, B: 59D, K: 609C, H: 234D

5722 נָחַץ *nāḥaṣ*, [B] to be urgent, S: 5169, B: 637D, K: 609C, H: 234D

5723 נָחַר *nāḥar*, [A] to blow; [D] to snort, S: 2734† & 2787†, B: 637D, K: 609C, H: 234D

5724 נַחַר *naḥar*, snorting (of a horse), S: 5170, B: 637D, K: 609D, H: 234D

5725 נַחֲרָה *naḥᵃrâ*, snorting (of a horse), S: 5170, B: 637D, K: 609D, H: 234D

5726 נַחְרַי *naḥray*, Naharai, S: 5171, B: 638A, K: 609D, H: 234D

5727 נָחַשׁ *nāḥaš*, [D] to practice divination, interpret omens and signs, S: 5172, B: 638C, K: 609D, H: 235A

5728 נַחַשׁ *naḥaš*, sorcery, magic curse, spell, S: 5173, B: 638D, K: 610A, H: 235A

5729 [1]נָחָשׁ *nāḥāš*[1], snake, serpent, S: 5175, B: 638A, K: 610A, H: 235A

5730 [2]נָחָשׁ *nāḥāš*[2], variant: Nahash, see 6560, S: 5904†, B: 638B, K: 610B, H: 235A

5731 [3]נָחָשׁ *nāḥāš*[3], Nahash, S: 5176, B: 638B, K: 610B, H: 235A

5732 נַחְשׁוֹן *naḥšôn*, Nahshon, S: 5177, B: 638B, K: 610B, H: 235A

5733 [1]נְחֹשֶׁת *nᵉḥōšet*[1], copper, bronze, S: 5178, B: 638D, K: 610C, H: 235A

5734 [2]נְחֹשֶׁת *nᵉḥōšet*[2], variant: menstruation, S: 5178, B: 639B, K: 610D, H: 235A

5735 נְחֻשְׁתָּא *nᵉḥuštā'*, Nehushta, S: 5179, B: 639A, K: 610D, H: 235B

5736 נְחֻשְׁתָּן *nᵉḥuštān*, Nehushtan, S: 5180, B: 639B, K: 610D, H: 235B

5737 נָחַת *nāḥat*, [A] to descend, go down; [C] to be pierced, penetrate; [D] to bend (a bow); to level off; [G] to bring down, S: 5181, B: 639B, K: 611A, H: 235B

5738 [1]נַחַת *naḥat*[1], coming down, descending, S: 5183, B: 639C, K: 611A, H: 235B

5739 [2]נַחַת *naḥat*[2], rest, peace, tranquility, S: 5183, B: 629B, K: 611B, H: 235B

5740 [3]נַחַת *naḥat*[3], Nahath, S: 5184, B: 639C, K: 611B, H: 235B

5741 נָחֵת *nāḥēt*, going down, descending, S: 5185, B: 639C, K: 611B, H: 235B

5742 נָטָה *nāṭâ*, [A] to spread out, stretch out; [B] to be outstretched, be spread out, be extended; [C] to be spread out, be stretched out; [G] to turn aside, pervert, lead astray; [H] to be outspread, S: 5186, B: 639D, K: 611B, H: 235C

5743 נְטֹפָתִי *nᵉṭôpātî*, Netophathite, S: 5200, B: 643B, K: 612C, H: 236A

5744 נָטִיל *nāṭîl*, weighing (of silver), S: 5187, B: 642B, K: 612C, H: 236A

5745 נָטִיעַ *nāṭîa'*, shoot (of a young plant), S: 5195, B: 642D, K: 612C, H: 236A

5746 נְטִישׁוֹת *nᵉṭîšôt*, spreading branches, tendrils, S: 5189†, B: 644A, K: 612D, H: 236A

5747 נָטַל *nāṭal*, [A] to lay upon; to weigh; [D] to lift, S: 5190, B: 642A, K: 612D, H: 236A

5748 נֵטֶל *nēṭel*, burden, load, S: 5192, B: 642B, K: 612D, H: 236B

5749 נָטַע *nāṭa'*, [A] to plant, S: 5193, B: 642B, K: 612D, H: 236B

5750 נֶטַע *neṭa'*, garden, plants; young plant, S: 5194, B: 642C, K: 613B, H: 236B

5751 נְטָעִים *nᵉṭā'îm*, Netaim, S: 5196, B: 642D, K: 613B, H: 236B

5752 נָטַף *nāṭap*, [A] to pour down; gently fall, drip; [G] to (drip words) preach, prophesy, S: 5197, B: 642D, K: 613B, H: 236B

5753 נָטָף *nāṭāp*, gum resin, drops of stacte, S: 5198, B: 643A, K: 613C, H: 236C

5754 נֶטֶף *neṭep*, drop (of water), S: 5198†, B: 643A, K: 613C, H: 236C

5755 נְטִפָה *nᵉṭipâ*, pendant, S: 5188, B: 643B, K: 613C, H: 236C

5756 נְטֹפָה *nᵉṭōpâ*, Netophah, S: 5199, B: 643B, K: 613C, H: 236C

5757 [1]נָטַר *nāṭar*[1], [A] to care for, tend; to be angry, harbor a grudge, S: 5201, B: 643B, K: 613D, H: 236A

5758 [2]נָטַר *nāṭar*[2], [A] to be angry, harbor a grudge, S: 5201, B: 643B, K: 613D, H: 236C

5759 נָטַשׁ *nāṭaš*, [A] to abandon, forsake, reject; [B] to be scattered; [C] to spread out; to be deserted; [E] to be abandoned, S: 5203, B: 643C, K: 613D, H: 236C

5760 נִי *nî*, wailing, S: 5204, B: 624D, K: 614C, H: 237A

5761 -נִי *-nî*, I, me, my, S*, B*, K*, H*

5762 נִיב *nîb*, fruit, S: 5108†, B: 626C, K: 614C, H: 237A

5763 נֵיבָי *nêbāy*, Nebai, S: 5109†, B: 626C, K: 614C, H: 237A

5764 נִיד *nîd*, comfort, S: 5205, B: 627A, K: 614C, H: 237A

5765 נִידָה *nîdâ*, uncleanness, impurity, S: 5206, B: 622C, K: 614C, H: 237A

5766 נָיוֹת *nāyôt*, Naioth, S: 5121, B: 627D, K: 614C, H: 231A

5767 נִיחֹחַ *nîḥōaḥ*, pleasing, soothing, appeasing, S: 5207, B: 629B, K: 614D, H: 237A

5768 [1]נִין *nîn*[1], variant: [A] to sprout forth, S: 5125†, B: 630C, K: 614D, H*

5769 [2]נִין *nîn*[2], offspring, children, posterity, S: 5209, B: 630C, K: 615A, H: 237A

5770 נִינְוֵה *nînᵉwēh*, Nineveh, S: 5210, B: 644B, K: 615A, H: 237A

5771 נִיס *nîs*, variant: flight, fleeing, S: 5211, B: 630C, K: 615A, H: 237A

5772 נִיסָן *nîsān*, Nisan, S: 5212, B: 644C, K: 615A, H: 237A

5773 נִיצוֹץ *nîṣôṣ*, spark, S: 5213, B: 665B, K: 615A, H: 237A

5774 [1]נִיר *nîr*[1], [A] to break up, bring into cultivation, S: 5214, B: 644C, K: 615B, H: 237B

5775 [2]נִיר *nîr*[2], lamp, S: 5216, B: 633A, K: 615B, H: 237B

5776 [3]נִיר *nîr*[3], unplowed ground, S: 5215, B: 644C, K: 615B, H: 237B

5777 [1]נָכָא *nākāʾ*[1], [C] to be driven out (by whipping or scourging), S: 5217, B: 644D, K: 615B, H: 237B

5778 [2]נָכָא *nākāʾ*[2], grieving (as one unmercifully beaten), S: 5218, B: 644D, K: 615C, H: 237B

5779 נָכֵא *nākēʾ*, crushed, beaten, broken, S: 5218, B: 644D, K: 615C, H: 237B

5780 נְכֹאת *nᵉkōʾt*, spices, resin, S: 5219, B: 644D, K: 615C, H: 237B

5781 נֶכֶד *neked*, descendant, progeny, S: 5220, B: 645A, K: 615C, H: 237C

5782 נָכָה *nākâ*, [C] to be struck; [E] to be destroyed; [G] to kill, slaughter, destroy, defeat; [H] to be beat, be struck, be wounded, be killed, S: 5221, B: 645A, K: 615C, H: 237C

5783 נָכֶה *nākeh*, lame, crippled; contrite, S: 5223, B: 646D, K: 616C, H: 238A

5784 נֵכֶה *nēkeh*, attacker, S: 5222, B: 646D, K: 616C, H: 238A

5785 נְכֹה *nᵉkōh*, Neco, S: 5224 & 6549†, B: 647A, K: 616D, H: 238A

5786 נְכוֹ *nᵉkô*, Neco, S: 5224, B: 647A, K: 616D, H: 238A

5787 [1]נָכוֹן *nākôn*[1], variant: strike, blow, S: 3559†, B: 646D, K: 616D, H: 238A

5788 [2]נָכוֹן *nākôn*[2], something prepared, fate, S: 3559†, B: 465C, K: 426C, H: 238A

5789 [3]נָכוֹן *nākôn*[3], Nacon, S: 5225, B: 467D, K: 616D, H: 238A

5790 נֹכַח *nōkaḥ*, opposite, before, in front of, S: 5226† & 5227, B: 647A, K: 616D, H: 238A

5791 נָכֹחַ *nākōaḥ*, proper, right, honest, what is straight, S: 5228 & 5229†, B: 647C, K: 617A, H: 238B

5792 נָכַל *nākal*, [A, D] to cheat, treat cunningly; [F] to conspire, plot, S: 5230, B: 647C, K: 617B, H: 238B

5793 נֵכֶל *nēkel*, deception, cunning, S: 5231, B: 647D, K: 617C, H: 238C

5794 נְכָסִים *nᵉkāsîm*, riches, wealth, possessions, S: 5233†, B: 647D, K: 617C, H: 238C

5795 [1]נָכַר *nākar*[1], [C] to disguise oneself, be not recognized; [D] to regard, consider; to favor; to misunderstand; [G] to recognize, acknowledge; [F] to make known, S: 5234, B: 647D, K: 617C, H: 238C

5796 [2]נָכַר *nākar*[2], [D] to treat as foreign; [F] to pretend to be a stranger, S: 5234, B: 649A, K: 617C, H: 238C

5797 נֵכָר *nēkār*, (one from a foreign land) foreigner, alien, stranger, S: 5236, B: 648C, K: 618B, H: 238D

5798 נֵכֶר *nēker*, misfortune, disaster, S: 5235†, B: 648C, K: 618A, H: 238D

5799 נָכְרִי *nokrî*, foreign, alien; (as noun) foreigner, S: 5237, B: 648D, K: 618B, H: 239A

5800 נְכֹת *nᵉkōt*, treasure, storage, S: 5238, B: 649B, K: 618C, H: 239A

5801 נָלָה *nālâ*, [G] to stop, S: 5239, B: 649B, K: 618D, H: 239A

5802 נְמִבְזָה *nᵉmibzâ*, variant: see 1022, S: 959†, B: 102B, K: 618D, H: 239A

5803 נְמוּאֵל *nᵉmûʾēl*, Nemuel, S: 5241, B: 649C, K: 618D, H: 239A

5804 נְמוּאֵלִי *nᵉmûʾēlî*, Nemuelite, S: 5242, B: 649C, K: 618D, H: 239A

5805 נְמָלָה *nᵉmālâ*, ant, S: 5244, B: 649C, K: 618D, H: 239A

5806 נָמֵס *nāmēs*, variant: see 5022, S: 3988†, B: 587D, K: 542D, H: 239A

5807 נָמֵר *nāmēr*, leopard, S: 5246, B: 649C, K: 618D, H: 239A

5808 נִמְרֹד *nimrōd*, Nimrod, S: 5248, B: 650A, K: 619A, H: 239A

5809 נִמְרָה *nimrâ*, Nimrah, S: 5247, B: 649D, K: 619A, H: 239B

5810 נִמְרִים *nimrîm*, Nimrim, S: 5249, B: 649D, K: 619A, H: 239B

5811 נִמְשִׁי *nimšî*, Nimshi, S: 5250, B: 650A, K: 619A, H: 239B

5812 נֵס *nēs*, banner, standard, signal pole, S: 5251, B: 651D, K: 619B, H: 239B

5813 נְסִבָּה *nᵉsibbâ*, turn of events, S: 5252, B: 687C, K: 619B, H: 239B

5814 נָסָה *nāsâ*, [D] to test, try, S: 5254, B: 650A, K: 619B, H: 239B

5815 נָסַח *nāsaḥ*, [A] to tear down; [C] to be uprooted, be torn down, S: 5255, B: 650C, K: 619D, H: 239C

5816 [1]נָסִיךְ *nāsîk*[1], drink offering; metal image, idol, S: 5257, B: 651A, K: 619D, H: 239C

5817 [2]נָסִיךְ *nāsîk*[2], prince, leader, S: 5257, B: 651C, K: 619D, H: 239C

5818 [1]נָסַךְ *nāsak*[1], [A] to pour out; [C] to be poured out; [D] to pour out; [G] to pour out; [H] to be poured out, S: 5258, B: 650D, K: 620A, H: 239C

5819 [2]נָסַךְ *nāsak*[2], [B] to be woven, S: 5259, B: 651B, K: 620B, H: 239D

5820 [3]נָסַךְ *nāsak*[3], [A] to install, set; [C] to be appointed, S: 5258, B: 651C, K: 620A, H: 239D & 239C

5821 [1]נֶסֶךְ *nesek*[1], drink offering, S: 5262, B: 651A, K: 620B, H: 239D

5822 [2]נֶסֶךְ *nesek*[2], metal image, idol, S: 5262, B: 651A, K: 620C, H: 240A

5823 [1]נָסַס *nāsas*[1], [A] to falter, S: 5263, B: 651C, K: 620C, H: 240A

5824 [2]נָסַס *nāsas*[2], [F] to unfurl; to sparkle, S: 5264, B: 651C, K: 620C, H: 240A

5825 נָסַע *nāsaʿ*, [A] to set out, move on, leave, travel on; [C] to be pulled up; [G] to lead, bring out; to pull out, S: 5265, B: 652A, K: 620D, H: 240A

5826 נָסַק *nāsaq*, variant: see 6158, S: 5266, B: 652D, K: 660C, H: 257C

5827 נִסְרֹךְ *nisrōk*, Nisroch (pagan god), S: 5268†, B: 652D, K: 621A, H: 240B

5828 נֵעָה *nēʿâ*, Neah, S: 5269, B: 631C, K: 621A, H: 240B

5829 נֹעָה *nōʿâ*, Noah, S: 5270, B: 631C, K: 621A, H: 240B

5830 נְעוּרִים *nᵉʿûrîm*, youth, childhood, boyhood, S: 5271†, B: 655B, K: 621A, H: 240B

5831 נְעוּרוֹת *nᵉʿûrôt*, youth, S: 5271†, B: 655C, K: 623D, H: 241B

5832 נְעִיאֵל *nᵉʿîʾēl*, Neiel, S: 5272, B: 653A, K: 621C, H: 240B

5833 [1]נָעִים *nāʿîm*[1], pleasant, charming, S: 5273, B: 653D, K: 621C, H: 240B

5834 [2]נָעִים *nāʿîm*[2], singing, sweetly sounding, musical, S: 5273, B: 654B, K: 621C, H*

5835 [1]נָעַל *nāʿal*[1], [A] to lock up, bolt; [B] to be locked up, be sealed, S: 5274, B: 653A, K: 621C, H: 240C

5836 [2]נָעַל *nāʿal*[2], [A] to put on a sandal; [G] to provide with sandals, S: 5274, B: 653B, K: 621C, H: 240C

5837 נַעַל *naʿal*, sandal, S: 5275, B: 653A, K: 621D, H: 240C

5838 נָעֵם *nāʿēm*, [A] to be pleasant, be dear, be favored, S: 5276, B: 653C, K: 622A, H: 240C

5839 נַעַם *naʿam*, Naam, S: 5277, B: 653D, K: 622B, H: 240D

5840 נֹעַם *nōʿam*, pleasantness, favor, S: 5278, B: 653C, K: 622B, H: 240D

5841 [1]נַעֲמָה *naʿᵃmâ*[1], Naamah, S: 5279, B: 653D, K: 622C, H: 240D

5842 [2]נַעֲמָה *naʿᵃmâ*[2], Naamah, S: 5279, B: 654A, K: 622C, H: 240D

5843 נָעֳמִי *noʿᵒmî*, Naomi, S: 5281, B: 654A, K: 622C, H: 240D

5844 נַעֲמִי *naʿᵃmî*, Naamite, S: 5280, B: 654B, K: 622C, H: 240D

5845 נַעֲמָן *naʿᵃmān*, Naaman, S: 5283, B: 654A, K: 622C, H: 240D

5846 נַעֲמָנִים *naʿᵃmānîm*, finest (of Adonis [?]), S: 5282†, B: 654A, K: 622C, H: 240D

5847 נַעֲמָתִי *naʿᵃmātî*, Naamathite, S: 5284, B: 654B, K: 622D, H: 240D

5848 נַעֲצוּץ *naʿᵃṣûṣ*, thornbush, S: 5285, B: 654C, K: 622D, H: 240D

5849 [1]נָעַר *nāʿar*[1], [A] to growl, S: 5286, B: 654C, K: 622D, H: 240D

5850 [2]נָעַר *nāʿar*[2], [A] to shake off; to refuse; [B] to be shaken out; [C] to shake oneself free, be shaken off; [D] to shake off, sweep away; [F] to shake oneself free, S: 5287, B: 654C, K: 622D, H: 240D

5851 [3]נָעַר *nāʿar*[3], variant: [A] to dry out, S: 5287, B: 654C, K: 622D, H: 241A

5852 [1]נַעַר *naʿar*[1], variant: scattering, shaking; (as noun) scattered ones, S: 5289, B: 654D, K: 623C, H: 241A

5853 [2]נַעַר *naʿar*[2], young man, boy, child; servant, attendant, steward, S: 5288, B: 654D, K: 623A, H: 241A

5854 נֹעַר *nōʿar*, youth, S: 5290, B: 655A, K: 623C, H*

5855 [1]נַעֲרָה *naʿᵃrâ*[1], young woman, girl; servant, maid, S: 5291, B: 655A, K: 623C, H: 241A

5856 [2]נַעֲרָה *naʿᵃrâ*[2], Naarah, S: 5292, B: 655C, K: 623D, H: 241B

5857 [3]נַעֲרָה *naʿᵃrâ*[3], Naarah, S: 5292, B: 655C, K: 623D, H: 241B

5858 נַעֲרַי *naʿᵃray*, Naarai, S: 5293, B: 655C, K: 623D, H: 241B

5859 נְעַרְיָה *nᵉʿaryâ*, Neariah, S: 5294, B: 655D, K: 624A, H: 241B

5860 נַעֲרָן *naʿᵃrān*, Naaran, S: 5295, B: 655D, K: 624A, H: 241B

[F] Hitpael (hitpoel, hitpoal, hitpolel, hitpolal, hitpalel, hitpalal, hitpalpel, hitpalpal, hotpael, hotpaal) [G] Hiphil (hiphtil) [H] Hophal [I] Hishtaphel

5861 נְעֹרֶת *nᵉʿōret*, tinder (broken fibers shaken off flax), S: 5296, B: 654D, K: 624A, H: 241B

5862 נֹף *nōp*, Noph = Memphis, S: 5297, B: 592A, K: 624A, H: 241B

5863 נֶפֶג *nepeg*, Nepheg, S: 5298, B: 655D, K: 624A, H: 241B

5864 [1]נָפָה *nāpâ*[1], sieve (winnowing device), S: 5299, B: 632B, K: 624A, H: 241B

5865 [2]נָפָה *nāpâ*[2], variant: height, yoke, S: 5299, B: 632C, K: 624A, H: 241C

5866 נְפוּסִים *nᵉpûsîm*, Nephussim, S: 5300†, B: 656B, K: 624B, H: 241C

5867 נְפוּשְׁסִים *nᵉpûšsîm*, Nephushsim, S: 5300, B: 656B, K: 624B, H: 241C

5868 נָפוֹת *nāpôt*, Naphoth, S: 5316†, B: 190B, K: 624A, H: 66A

5869 נָפוֹת דֹּאר רְ(ד) נָפוֹת דּוֹר *nāpôt dôr*, Naphoth Dor, S: 5299† + 1756†, B: 190B, K: 624A, H: 66A

5870 נָפַח *nāpaḥ*, [A] to blow upon, breathe upon; [B, E] to be blown upon; [G] to sniff out; to cause to breathe out, S: 5301, B: 655D, K: 624B, H: 241C

5871 נֹפַח *nōpaḥ*, Nophah, S: 5302, B: 656A, K: 624C, H: 241C

5872 נְפִילִים *nᵉpîlîm*, Nephilim, S: 5303†, B: 658C, K: 624C, H: 241C

5873 נְפִיסִים *nᵉpîsîm*, variant: Nephissim, S: 5304, B: 656B, K: 624B, H: 241D

5874 נָפִישׁ *nāpîš*, Naphish, S: 5305, B: 661C, K: 624C, H: 241D

5875 נְפִישְׁסִים *nᵉpîšᵉsîm*, variant: Nephishsim [?], S: 5300†, B: 656B, K: 624B, H: 241D

5876 נֹפֶךְ *nōpek*, turquoise (green semi-precious stone), S: 5306, B: 656C, K: 624C, H: 241D

5877 נָפַל *nāpal*, [A] to fall, fail; [E?] to fall; [G] to cause to fall, to cast down, drop; (used of casting lots) to allocate; [F] to fall prostrate (to worship); to fall upon (to attack), S: 5307, B: 656C, K: 624D, H: 241D

5878 נֵפֶל *nēpel*, stillborn child, miscarriage, S: 5309, B: 658B, K: 626A, H: 242C

5879 [1]נָפַץ *nāpaṣ*[1], [A] to shatter; [D] to shatter; (of log raft) to separate; [E] to be crushed, S: 5310, B: 658C, K: 626A, H: 242C

5880 [2]נָפַץ *nāpaṣ*[2], [A] to scatter, S: 5310, B: 659A, K: 626A, H: 242C

5881 נֶפֶץ *nepeṣ*, bursting (of rain), S: 5311, B: 658D, K: 626B, H: 242C

5882 נָפַשׁ *nāpaš*, [C] to be refreshed, refresh oneself, S: 5314, B: 661C, K: 626B, H: 242C

5883 נֶפֶשׁ *nepeš*, soul, life, self; person, someone, S: 5315, B: 659B, K: 626C, H: 242D

5884 נֶפֶת *nepet*, variant: Nephet *or* hill, see 5868, S: 5316, B: 632C, K: 628B, H: 243B

5885 נֹפֶת *nōpet*, honey of the honeycomb, S: 5317, B: 661D, K: 628B, H: 243B

5886 נֶפְתּוֹחַ *neptôaḥ*, Nephtoah, S: 5318, B: 836B, K: 628B, H: 243B

5887 נַפְתּוּלִים *naptûlîm*, struggles, wrestlings, S: 5319†, B: 836D, K: 628B, H: 243B

5888 נַפְתֻּחִים *naptuḥîm*, Naphtuhite, S: 5320, B: 661D, K: 628C, H: 243B

5889 נַפְתָּלִי *naptālî*, Naphtali, S: 5321, B: 836D, K: 628C, H: 243B

5890 [1]נֵץ *nēṣ*[1], blossom, S: 5322, B: 665B, K: 628D, H: 243C

5891 [2]נֵץ *nēṣ*[2], hawk (bird of prey), S: 5322, B: 665C, K: 628D, H: 243C

5892 נָצָא *nāṣāʾ*, variant: [A] to fly, S: 5323, B: 661D, K: 629C, H: 243D

5893 [1]נָצַב *nāṣab*[1], [C] to stand oneself before; (as noun) officer, official; [G] to station, set up, establish; [H] to be set up, be decreed, S: 5324, B: 662A, K: 628D, H: 243C

5894 [2]נָצַב *nāṣab*[2], variant: [C] to be wretched, exhausted, S: 5324, B: 662A, K: 628D, H: 243D

5895 [1]נִצָּב *niṣṣāb*[1], variant: see 5893, S: 5324†, B: 662A, K: 628D, H: 243D

5896 [2]נִצָּב *niṣṣāb*[2], handle, hilt (of sword, dagger *or* knife), S: 5325, B: 662C, K: 629C, H: 243D

5897 [1]נָצָה *nāṣâ*[1], [C] to fight (quarreling that can come to blows and struggles); [G] to rebel, engage in a struggle, S: 5327, B: 663C, K: 629C, H: 243D

5898 [2]נָצָה *nāṣâ*[2], [A] to lie in ruins; [C] to be laid waste, be desolate, S: 5327, B: 663D, K: 629C, H: 243D

5899 [3]נָצָה *nāṣâ*[3], variant: [A] to fly, S*, B: 663B, K: 629C, H: 243D

5900 נִצָּה *niṣṣâ*, blossom, S: 5328, B: 665B, K: 629D, H: 243D

5901 [1]נֹצָה *nōṣâ*[1], contents (of a bird's crop), S: 5133, B: 663C, K: 629D, H: 243D

5902 [2]נֹצָה *nōṣâ*[2], variant: falcon, S: 5133, B: 663B, K: 604C, H: 243D

5903 נְצוּרִים *nᵉṣûrîm*, variant: secret places, see 5915, S: 5341†, B: 665C, K: 629D, H: 244A

5904 נָצַח *nāṣaḥ*, [C] to be enduring, lasting; [D] to direct, supervise; (as noun) director (of music), S: 5329, B: 663D, K: 629D, H: 244A

5905 [1]נֵצַח *nēṣaḥ*[1], glory, majesty, splendor; forever, unending, everlasting, always, S: 5331, B: 664B, K: 630A, H: 244A

5906 [2]נֵצַח *nēṣaḥ*[2], juice (= blood), S: 5332, B: 664C, K: 630B, H: 244A

5907 [1]נְצִיב *nᵉṣîb*[1], garrison, outpost; pillar, S: 5333, B: 662C, K: 630B, H: 244A

5908 [2]נְצִיב *nᵉṣîb*[2], Nezib, S: 5334, B: 662D, K: 630B, H: 244A

5909 נְצִיחַ *nᵉṣîaḥ*, Neziah, S: 5335, B: 664C, K: 630C, H: 244A

5910 נָצִיר *nāṣîr*, variant: preserved, see 5915, S: 5336, B: 666A, K: 630C, H: 244B

5911 נָצַל *nāṣal*, [C] to be saved, be delivered, be spared; [D] to plunder, take away, tear away; [G] to deliver, save, rescue; [H] to be snatched; [F] to strip off oneself, S: 5337, B: 664C, K: 630C, H: 244B

5912 נִצָּנִים *niṣṣānîm*, variant: blossom, S: 5339†, B: 665B, K: 631A, H: 244C

5913 [1]נָצַץ *nāṣaṣ*[1], [A] to gleam, sparkle, S: 5340, B: 665A, K: 631A, H: 244C

5914 [2]נָצַץ *nāṣaṣ*[2], [G] to bloom, blossom, S: 5006† & 5132†, B: 665B, K: 631A, H: 244C

5915 נָצַר *nāṣar*, [A] to guard, watch, protect, keep, preserve; [B] to be kept secret, be hidden, S: 5341, B: 665C, K: 631A, H: 244C

5916 נֵצֶר *nēṣer*, branch, shoot (of a plant), S: 5342, B: 666A, K: 631C, H: 244D

5917 נִצְּרָה *niṣṣᵉrâ*, watching, guarding, S: 5341†, B: 665D, K*, H: 244D

5918 [1]נָקַב *nāqab*[1], [A] to bore (a hole), pierce; to designate, bestow; [B] to have a hole; to be notable; [C] to be designated, be registered, S: 5344, B: 666A, K: 631C, H: 244D 1. & 2.

5919 [2]נָקַב *nāqab*[2], [A] to blaspheme, S: +, B: 666C, K: 631C, H: 244D 3.

5920 [1]נֶקֶב *neqeb*[1], mounting (used in gold jewelry), S: 5345, B: 666B, K: 631D, H: 244D 2.

5921 [2]נֶקֶב *neqeb*[2], variant: Nekeb, S: 5346, B: 666C, K: 631D 1, H: 244D 1

5922 נְקֵבָה *nᵉqēbâ*, female, woman, S: 5347, B: 666C, K: 632A, H: 245A

5923 נָקֹד *nāqōd*, speckled, spotted, S: 5348, B: 666D, K: 632A, H: 245A

5924 נֹקֵד *nōqēd*, shepherd, one who raises sheep, S: 5349, B: 667A, K: 632A, H: 245A

5925 נְקֻדָּה *nᵉquddâ*, point, drops (of silver on a gold earring), S: 5351, B: 667A, K: 632B, H: 245A

5926 נִקֻּדִים *niqqudîm*, (small) cakes; crumbling (food supplies), S: 5350†, B: 666D, K: 632B, H: 245A

5927 נָקָה *nāqâ*, [A] to go unpunished; [C] to be innocent, be released, go unpunished; [D] to leave unpunished, consider innocent, pardon, S: 5352, B: 667A, K: 632B, H: 245A

5928 נְקוֹדָא *nᵉqôdāʾ*, Nekoda, S: 5353, B: 667A, K: 632D, H: 245B

5929 נָקִי *nāqî*, innocent, free of blame, not guilty, S: 5355, B: 667C, K: 632D, H: 245B

5930 נָקִיא *nāqîʾ*, variant: innocent, S: 5355, B: 667D, K: 632D, H: 245B

5931 נִקָּיוֹן *niqqāyôn*, innocence, purity, cleanness; whiteness (of teeth) = empty stomach, S: 5356, B: 667D, K: 632D, H: 245B

5932 נָקִיק *nāqîq*, crevice, cleft, crack, S: 5357, B: 669B, K: 633A, H: 245B

5933 נָקַם *nāqam*, [A] to seek vengeance, avenge; [C] to be avenged, avenge oneself; [D] to avenge; [G or B] to be avenged; [F] to take one's own vengeance, S: 5358, B: 667D, K: 633A, H: 245B

5934 נָקָם *nāqām*, vengeance, revenge, S: 5359, B: 668B, K: 633C, H: 245C

5935 נְקָמָה *nᵉqāmâ*, vengeance, revenge, S: 5360, B: 668C, K: 633C, H: 245D

5936 נָקַע *nāqaʿ*, [A] to turn away in disgust, S: 5361, B: 668C, K: 633D, H: 245D

5937 [1]נָקַף *nāqap*[1], [D] to cut down; to be destroyed, S: 5362, B: 668C, K: 633D, H: 245D

5938 [2]נָקַף *nāqap*[2], [A] to go through a yearly cycle; [G] to surround, encircle, engulf, S: 5362, B: 668D, K: 634A, H: 245D

5939 נֹקֶף *nōqep*, beating (fruit off olive tree in harvest), S: 5363, B: 668D, K: 634B, H: 246A

5940 נִקְפָּה *niqpâ*, rope (around waist), S: 5364, B: 669A, K: 634B, H: 246A

5941 נָקַר *nāqar*, [A] to gouge out, peck out (an eye); [D] to gouge out; to pierce; [E] to be hewn out (of quarry rock), S: 5365, B: 669B, K: 634B, H: 246A

5942 נְקָרָה *nᵉqārâ*, cleft; cavern, S: 5366, B: 669B, K: 634C, H: 246A

5943 נָקַשׁ *nāqaš*, [C] to be ensnared; [D] to lay out snares; [F] to lay out traps, set a trap, S: 5367, B: 669B, K: 634C, H: 246A

5944 נֵר¹ *nēr*[1], lamp, S: 5216, B: 632D, K: 634C, H: 246A

5945 ²נֵר *nēr*[2], Ner, S: 5369, B: 633A, K: 634D, H: 246B

5946 נֵרְגַל *nērᵉgal*, Nergal (pagan god), S: 5370, B: 669C, K: 635A, H: 246B

5947 נֵרְגַל שַׂר־אֶצֶר *nērgal śar-ʾeṣer*, Nergal-Sharezer, S: 5371†, B: 669C, K: 635A, H: 246B

5948 נֵרְדְּ *nērd*, nard (aromatic ointment), S: 5373, B: 669D, K: 635A, H: 246B

5949 נֵרִיָּה *nēriyyâ*, Neriah, S: 5374, B: 633A, K: 635B, H: 246B

5950 נֵרִיָּהוּ *nēriyyāhû*, Neriah, S: 5374, B: 633A, K: 635B, H: 246B

5951 נָשָׂא *nāśāʾ*, [A] to bear, carry, lift up; forgive; [B] to be forgiven, honored, carried; [C] to be carried off, lifted up; [D] to elevate, carry along; [G] to cause to carry, to bring; [F] to exalt oneself, lift up oneself, S: 4984† & 5375 & 5379† & 7721†, B: 669D, K: 635B, H: 246B & 239C

5952 נָשַׂג *nāśag*, [G] to overtake, catch up, attain; to reach, to be able to afford, S: 5381, B: 673B, K: 637C, H: 247C

5953 נְשׂוּאָה *nᵉśûʾâ*, burden, load (of images that are carried about), S: 5385, B: 672B, K: 637D, H: 247C

5954 נָשִׂיא¹ *nāśîʾ*[1], leader, ruler, chief, prince, S: 5387, B: 672B, K: 637D, H: 247C

5955 ²נָשִׂיא *nāśîʾ*[2], rising mist, damp fog, S: 5387, B: 672C, K: 638A, H: 247D

5956 נָשַׂק *nāśaq*, [C] to be kindled; [G] to kindle a fire, burn, S: 5400, B: 1005, K: 638A, H: 247D

5957 נָשָׁא¹ *nāšāʾ*[1], [A] to give a loan, be a creditor; [G] to make a loan; to subject one to tribute, S: 5378 & 5383, B: 673D, K: 638B, H: 247D

5958 ²נָשָׁא *nāšāʾ*[2], [C] to be deceived; [G] to deceive, S: 5377, B: 674A, K: 638C, H: 248A

5959 נָשַׁב *nāšab*, [A] to blow; [G] to cause to blow; to drive away, S: 5380, B: 674B, K: 638D, H: 248A

5960 נָשָׁה¹ *nāšâ*[1], [A] to forget; [C] to be forgotten; [D] to make forget; [G] to make one forget; to allow one to forget, S: 5382, B: 674C, K: 638D, H: 248A

5961 ²נָשָׁה *nāšâ*[2], variant: see 5957, S: 5378†, B: 674B, K: 639A, H: 248A

5962 נָשֶׁה *nāšeh*, tendon (attached to the hip), S: 5384, B: 674D, K: 639A, H: 248A

5963 נְשִׁי *nᵉšî*, debt, S: 5386, B: 674C, K: 639B, H: 248A

5964 נְשִׁיָּה *nᵉšiyyâ*, oblivion, place forgotten (by the LORD), S: 5388, B: 674D, K: 639B, H: 248A

5965 נְשִׁיקָה *nᵉšîqâ*, kiss, S: 5390, B: 676C, K: 639B, H: 248B

5966 נָשַׁךְ¹ *nāšak*[1], [A] to bite; [B] to be bitten; [D] to bite, S: 5391, B: 675A, K: 639B, H: 248B

5967 ²נָשַׁךְ *nāšak*[2], [A] to earn interest; to claim interest against one; [G] to charge interest, S: 5391, B: 675B, K: 639C, H: 248B

5968 נֶשֶׁךְ *nešek*, interest, usury, S: 5392, B: 675B, K: 639C, H: 248B

5969 נִשְׁכָּה *niškâ*, room (for various uses: living, storage, etc.), S: 5393, B: 675B, K: 639C, H: 248C

5970 נָשַׁל *nāšal*, [A] to take off, come off; to drive out, S: 5394, B: 675B, K: 639C, H: 248C

5971 נָשַׁם *nāšam*, [A] to gasp, pant, S: 5395, B: 675C, K: 639D, H: 248C

5972 נְשָׁמָה *nᵉšāmâ*, breath, blast of breath; spirit, life, S: 5397, B: 675C, K: 639D, H: 248C

5973 נָשַׁף *nāšap*, [A] to blow, S: 5398, B: 676A, K: 640A, H: 248C

5974 נֶשֶׁף *nešep*, dusk, dawn (of morning); twilight (of evening), S: 5399, B: 676A, K: 640A, H: 248C

5975 נָשַׁק¹ *nāšaq*[1], [A] to kiss; [D] to kiss (repeatedly or intensely), S: 5401, B: 676B, K: 640B, H: 248C

5976 ²נָשַׁק *nāšaq*[2], [A] to be equipped, arm oneself; [G] to brush against, touch up against, S: 5401, B: 676C, K: 640D, H: 248D

5977 נֶשֶׁק¹ *nešeq*[1], weapon; armory, S: 5402, B: 676D, K: 640D, H: 248D

5978 ²נֶשֶׁק *nešeq*[2], variant: kind of fragrance substance, S: 5402, B: 676D, K: 640D, H: 248D

5979 נֶשֶׁר *nešer*, eagle; vulture, S: 5404, B: 676D, K: 640D, H: 249A

5980 נָשַׁת *nāšat*, [A] to be dry, be parched; [C] to be dried up, S: 5405, B: 677A, K: 641A, H: 249A

5981 נִשְׁתְּוָן *ništᵉwān*, variant: letter, writing, see 10496, S: 5406, B: 677A, K: 641A, H: 249A

5982 נְתוּנִים *nᵉtûnîm*, variant: see 5989 & 5987, S: 5411†, B: 678A, K: 641B, H: 249A

5983 נָתַח *nātaḥ*, [D] to cut into pieces, S: 5408, B: 677C, K: 641B, H: 249A

5984 נֵתַח *nētaḥ*, piece (of butchered things or persons), S: 5409, B: 677C, K: 641B, H: 249A

5985 נָתִיב *nātîb*, path, S: 5410, B: 677A, K: 641B, H: 249A

5986 נְתִיבָה *nᵉtîbâ*, path, way, road, S: 5410, B: 677B, K: 641C, H: 249A

5987 נָתִין *nātîn*, servant, S: 5411, B: 682A, K: 641C, H: 249A

5988 נָתַךְ *nātak*, [A] to pour out; [C] to be poured out, be melted; [G] to pour out (liquid or money); to melt; [H] to be melted, S: 5413, B: 677C, K: 641D, H: 249A

5989 נָתַן *nātan*, [A] to give, put; [B] to be given, dedicated; [C] to be given; [G or B] to be given, S: 5414, B: 687A, K: 642A, H: 249B

5990 נָתָן *nātān*, Nathan, S: 5416, B: 681D, K: 644A, H: 250B

5991 נְתַנְאֵל *nᵉtanʾēl*, Nethanel, S: 5417, B: 682A, K: 644A, H: 250B

5992 נְתַנְיָה *nᵉtanyâ*, Nethaniah, S: 5418, B: 682B, K: 644A, H: 250B

5993 נְתַנְיָהוּ *nᵉtanyāhû*, Nethaniah, S: 5418, B: 682B, K: 644A, H: 250C

5994 נְתַן־מֶלֶךְ *nᵉtan-melek*, Nathan-Melech, S: 5419, B: 682A, K: 644B, H: 250C

5995 נָתַס *nātas*, [A] to break up, tear up, S: 5420, B: 683A, K: 644B, H: 250C

5996 נָתַע *nātaʿ*, [C] to be broken down, be knocked out (of teeth), S: 5421, B: 683A, K: 644B, H: 250C

5997 נָתַץ *nātaṣ*, [A] to break down, tear down, demolish; [B] to be broken down; [C] to be shattered, lay in ruins; [D] to tear down, break down, shatter, destroy; [E] to be demolished; [H] to be broken up, S: 5422, B: 683A, K: 644B, H: 250C

5998 נָתַק *nātaq*, [A] to draw away, pull off; [B] to be torn; [C] to be lured away, be shattered, be torn, be broken; [D] to break, tear; [G] to lure away, drag off; [H] to be drawn away, S: 5423, B: 683C, K: 644C, H: 250D

5999 נֶתֶק *neteq*, diseased area of skin: itch, S: 5424, B: 683D, K: 645A, H: 251A

6000 נָתַר¹ *nātar*[1], [G] to let loose, withdraw, S: 5425, B: 684A, K: 645A, H: 251A

6001 ²נָתַר *nātar*[2], [A] to leap up; [D] to hop up; [G] to make leap up, jump up, S: 5425, B: 684A, K: 645A, H: 251A

6002 ³נָתַר *nātar*[3], [G] to set free, release, untie, S: 5425, B: 684A, K: 645A, H: 251A

6003 נֶתֶר *neter*, natron (a sodium carbonate for washing), S: 5427, B: 684A, K: 645C, H: 251C

6004 נָתַשׁ *nātaš*, [A] to uproot; [C] to be uprooted; [H] to be uprooted, S: 5428, B: 684C, K: 645C, H: 251C

6005 ס *s*, letter of the Hebrew alphabet, S*, B: 684B, K: 645B, H*

6006 סְאָה *sᵉʾâ*, seah (measure of capacity), S: 5429, B: 684B, K: 645D, H: 251A

6007 סְאוֹן *sᵉʾôn*, boot, S: 5430, B: 684B, K: 646A, H: 251B

6008 סָאַן *sāʾan*, [A] to tramp along in boots, S: 5431, B: 684D, K: 646A, H: 251B

6009 סַאסְּאָה *saʾssᵉʾâ*, warfare, chasing away, S: 5432†, B: 684D, K: 646A, H: 251B

6010 סָבָא¹ *sābāʾ*[1], [A] to be a drunkard, drink too much; [B] to be drunk, S: 5433, B: 684D, K: 646B, H: 251B

6011 סֹבֶא *sōbeʾ*, wine, drink, S: 5435, B: 685A, K: 646B, H: 251B

6012 ²סָבָא *sābāʾ*[2], variant: bind-weed, shrub, S: 5433, B: 685A, K: 646B, H: 251B

6013 סְבָא *sᵉbāʾ*, Seba, S: 5434, B: 685B, K: 646C, H: 251B

6014 סְבָאִי *sᵉbāʾî*, Sabean, S: 5436, B: 685B, K: 646C, H: 251B

6015 סָבַב *sābab*, [A] to go around, surround, encircle, engulf; [C] to change direction; to be surrounded; [D] to change; to surround, shield, go about; [G] to turn about, circle around; [H] to be set, mounted, surrounded; to be changed, S: 4141† & 4142† & 5437, B: 685B, K: 646C, H: 251C & 239B

6016 סִבָּה *sibbâ*, turning, arrangement (of events), S: 5438, B: 686D, K: 647D, H: 252B

6017 סָבִיב *sābîb*, all around, on all sides, surrounding, encircling, S: 5439, B: 686D, K: 647D, H: 252B

6018 סָבַךְ *sābak*, [B, E] to be entangled, entwined, S: 5440, B: 687C, K: 648B, H: 252C

6019 סְבַךְ *s^{e}bak*, thicket, underbrush, S: 5442†, B: 687C, K: 648B, H: 252C

6020 סְבֹךְ *s^{e}bōk*, thicket, underbrush, S: 5441†, B: 687C, K: 648B, H: 252C

6021 סִבְּכַי *sibb^{e}kay*, Sibbecai, S: 5444, B: 687C, K: 648B, H: 252C

6022 סָבַל *sābal*, [A] to bear, carry, sustain; [E] to be (heavy) laden; [F] to drag oneself along, S: 5445, B: 687D, K: 648B, H: 252C

6023 סֵבֶל *sēbel*, burden; forced labor, S: 5447, B: 687D, K: 648C, H: 252D

6024 סֹבֶל *sōbel*, burden, S: 5448, B: 687D, K: 648C, H: 252D

6025 סַבָּל *sabbāl*, carrier, burden-bearer, S: 5449, B: 688A, K: 648C, H: 252D

6026 סִבְלוֹת *siblôt*, forced labor, burden-bearer, S: 5450†, B: 688A, K: 648D, H: 252D

6027 סִבֹּלֶת *sibbōlet*, Sibboleth, S: 5451, B: 688A, K: 648D, H: 252D

6028 סִבְרַיִם *sibrayim*, Sibraim, S: 5453, B: 688A, K: 648D, H: 253A

6029 סַבְתָּא *sabtā'*, Sabta, S: 5454, B: 688B, K: 648D, H: 253A

6030 סַבְתָּה *sabtâ*, Sabtah, S: 5454, B: 688B, K: 648D, H: 253A

6031 סַבְתְּכָא *sabt^{e}kā'*, Sabteca, S: 5455, B: 688B, K: 648D, H: 253A

6032 סָגַד *sāgad*, [A] to bow down (in worship), S: 5456, B: 688B, K: 648D, H: 253A

6033 סְגוֹר *s^{e}gôr*, enclosure, closing (of the heart), S: 5458, B: 689C, K: 649A, H: 253A

6034 סָגוּר *sāgûr*, purity (of gold), S: 5462†, B: 688D, K: 649A, H: 253A

6035 סְגֻלָּה *s^{e}gullâ*, treasured possession, personal property, S: 5459, B: 688C, K: 649A, H: 253A

6036 סֶגֶן *segen*, official, officer, commander, S: 5461†, B: 688C, K: 649B, H: 253A

6037 סָגַר *sāgar*, [A] to shut, close; [B] to be shut; [C] to be confined, to be shut up, be imprisoned; [D] to deliver; [E] to be shut up, be barred, be closed; [G] to surrender, give over, deliver up; to put in isolation, S: 5462, B: 688D, K: 649B, H: 253A

6038 סָגָר *sāgār*, javelin, ax, S: 5462†, B: 688D, K: 650A, H: 253C

6039 סַגְרִיר *sagrîr*, heavy rain, downpour of rain, S: 5464, B: 690A, K: 650A, H: 253C

6040 סַד *sad*, shackles, S: 5465, B: 690A, K: 650A, H: 253C

6041 סָדִין *sādîn*, linen garment, S: 5466, B: 690B, K: 650B, H: 253C

6042 סְדֹם *s^{e}dōm*, Sodom, S: 5467, B: 690A, K: 650B, H: 253C

6043 סֵדֶר *sēder*, order, arrangement, S: 5468†, B: 690B, K: 650C, H: 253C

6044 סַהַר *sahar*, roundness, S: 5469, B: 690C, K: 650C, H: 253C

6045 סֹהַר *sōhar*, prison, S: 5470, B: 690C, K: 650C, H: 253D

6046 סוֹא *sō'*, So, S: 5471, B: 690D, K: 650C, H: 253D

6047 [1]סוּג *sûg[1]*, [A] to turn away, be faithless, be disloyal; [C] to be turned back, be disloyal, be faithless; [G] to move, displace; [H] to be driven back, S: 5472 & 7734†, B: 690D, K: 650C, H: 253D

6048 [2]סוּג *sûg[2]*, [B] to be encircled, be bordered (by lilies), S: 5473, B: 691B, K: 651A, H: 253D

6049 [3]סוּג *sûg[3]*, variant: dross, see 6092, S: 5509, B: 691A, K: 651A, H: 254A

6050 סוּגַר *sûgar*, cage, S: 5474, B: 689C, K: 651A, H: 254A

6051 סוֹד *sôd*, confidential talk, conspiracy; council, confidant, S: 5475, B: 691C, K: 651A, H: 254A

6052 סוֹדִי *sôdî*, Sodi, S: 5476, B: 691D, K: 651B, H: 254A

6053 סוּחַ *sûaḥ*, Suah, S: 5477, B: 691D, K: 651B, H: 254A

6054 סוּחָה *sûḥâ*, refuse, garbage, offal, S: 5478, B: 691D, K: 651B, H: 254A

6055 סוֹטַי *sôṭay*, Sotai, S: 5479, B: 691D, K: 651C, H: 254A

6056 [1]סוּךְ *sûk[1]*, [D] to spur on, stir up, S: 5526†, B: 1127A, K: 651C, H: 254A

6057 [2]סוּךְ *sûk[2]*, [A] to anoint, to use oils or perfumes or lotions; [G] to put on lotions; [H] to be poured on, S: 5480, B: 691D, K: 651C, H: 254A

6058 [3]סוּךְ *sûk[3]*, variant: [A, G] to hedge about, fence in, S: 5526†, B: 692A, K: 657B, H: 256A

6059 סְוֵנֵה *s^{e}wēnēh*, Syene = Aswan, S: 5482, B: 692B, K: 651D, H: 254A

6060 סְוֵנִים *s^{e}wēnîm*, variant: of Syene (Aswan), S: 5515†, B: 692B, K: 656B, H: 255C

6061 [1]סוּס *sûs[1]*, (male) horse, stallion, S: 5483, B: 692B, K: 651D, H: 254A

6062 [2]סוּס *sûs[2]*, variant: swallow, swift, S: 5483, B: 692B, K: 651D, H: 254B

6063 סוּסָה *sûsâ*, (female) horse, mare, S: 5484, B: 692D, K: 652B, H: 254B

6064 סוּסִי *sûsî*, Susi, S: 5485, B: 692D, K: 652B, H: 254B

6065 סוּסִים *sûsîm*, variant: Susim, S: 2702†, B: 347C, K: 326A 3., H: 114A B3

6066 [1]סוּף *sûp[1]*, [A] to come to an end; demolish; die; [G] to sweep away, S: 5486, B: 692D, K: 652B, H: 254B

6067 סוֹף *sôp*, end, conclusion, destiny; rear guard, S: 5490, B: 693A, K: 652C, H: 254B

6068 [2]סוּף *sûp[2]*, reed; Reed Sea (*trad.* Red Sea), S: 5488, B: 693A, K: 652C, H: 254B

6069 [3]סוּף *sûp[3]*, Suph, S: 5489, B: 693B, K: 652D, H: 254B

6070 [1]סוּפָה *sûpâ[1]*, storm wind, whirlwind, tempest, gale, S: 5492, B: 693A, K: 652D, H: 254B

6071 [2]סוּפָה *sûpâ[2]*, Suphah, S: 5492, B: 693B, K: 652D, H: 254B

6072 סֹפֶרֶת *sōperet*, Sophereth, S: 5618†, B: 709B, K: 667A, H: 254B

6073 [1]סוּר *sûr[1]*, [A] to turn away, depart, leave; [B] to be rejected; [D] to drag from, turn aside; [G] to remove, get rid of, take off; [H] to be removed, be abolished, S: 3249† & 5493, B: 693B, K: 652D, H: 254C

6074 [2]סוּר *sûr[2]*, corrupt, S: 5494, B: 694C, K: 654A, H: 255A

6075 [3]סוּר *sûr[3]*, Sur, S: 5495, B: 694C, K: 654A, H*

6076 סוּרִי *sôrî*, variant: stinking, foul-smelling, S: 5494†, B: 693B, K: 654A, H: 255A

6077 [1]סוּת *sût[1]*, [G] to incite, entice, urge, mislead, S: 5496, B: 694C, K: 654B, H: 255A

6078 [2]סוּת *sût[2]*, robe, garment, S: 5497, B: 691D, K: 654B, H: 255A

6079 סָחַב *sāḥab*, [A] to drag down, S: 5498, B: 694D, K: 654B, H: 255A

6080 סְחָבָה *s^{e}ḥābâ*, rag, S: 5499, B: 695A, K: 654C, H*

6081 סָחָה *sāḥâ*, [D] to scrape away, S: 5500, B: 695A, K: 654C, H: 255A

6082 סְחִי *s^{e}ḥî*, scum, refuse, S: 5501, B: 695A, K: 654C, H: 255A

6083 סְחִיפָה *s^{e}ḥîpâ*, variant: downpour (of rain), S*, B: 705B, K: 654C, H: 255A

6084 סָחִישׁ *sāḥîš*, grain that shoots up on its own (in the second year), S: 7823, B: 695A, K: 654D, H: 255A

6085 סָחַף *sāḥap*, [A] to wash away (of rain); [C] to be washed away, be laid low, S: 5502, B: 695A, K: 654D, H: 255B

6086 סָחַר *sāḥar*, [A] to be a trader, a merchant; [D] to pound, throb (of the heart), S: 5503 & 5505, B: 695A, K: 654D, H: 255B

6087 סַחַר *saḥar*, profit (from merchandising in the marketplace), S: 5504, B: 695C, K: 655B, H: 255B

6088 סְחֹרָה *s^{e}ḥōrâ*, customer, S: 5506, B: 695C, K: 655B, H: 255B

6089 סֹחֵרָה *sōḥērâ*, rampart, wall, S: 5507, B: 695C, K: 655B, H: 255B

6090 סֹחֶרֶת *sōḥeret*, costly stone (not specifically defined), S: 5508, B: 695C, K: 655B, H: 255C

6091 סֵט *sēṭ*, faithlessness, transgression, S: 7750†, B: 962B, K: 655C, H: 255C

6092 סִיג *sîg*, dross (usually of silver), S: 5509, B: 691A, K: 655C, H: 255C

6093 סִיד *sîd*, variant: lime, S: 7875†, B: 690A, K: 655C, H: 253C

6094 סִיוָן *sîwān*, Sivan, S: 5510, B: 695D, K: 655C, H: 255C

6095 סִיחוֹן *sîḥôn*, Sihon, S: 5511, B: 695D, K: 655C, H: 255C

6096 [1]סִין *sîn[1]*, Sin = Pelusium, S: 5512, B: 695D, K: 655D, H: 255C

6097 [2]סִין *sîn[2]*, Sin, S: 5512, B: 695D, K: 655D, H: 255C

6098 סִינִי *sînî*, Sinite, S: 5513, B: 696B, K: 655D, H: 255C

6099 סִינַי *sînay*, Sinai, S: 5514, B: 696A, K: 656A, H: 255C

6100 סִינִים *sînîm*, variant: Sinim, Chinese [?], S: 5515†, B: 696B, K: 656B, H: 255C

6101 סִיס *sîs*, swift, swallow, S: 5483†, B: 692B, K: 656B, H: 255C

6102 סִיסְרָא *sîsᵉrāʾ*, Sisera, S: 5516, B: 696B, K: 656B, H: 255C

6103 סִיעָא *sîʿāʾ*, Sia, S: 5517, B: 696B, K: 656B, H: 255C

6104 סִיעֲהָא *sîʿᵃhāʾ*, Siaha, S: 5517, B: 696B, K: 656B, H: 255C

6105 סִיר *sîr*, pot, pan, caldron, washbasin, S: 5518, B: 696C, K: 656B, H: 255C

6106 סִירָה *sîrâ*, thorn, thornbush; fishhook, barb, S: 5518, B: 696C, K: 656C, H: 255D

6107 סָךְ *sāk*, multitude, throng, S: 5519, B: 697C, K: 656C, H: 255D

6108 סֹךְ *sōk*, covering, dwelling (of human or lion), S: 5520, B: 697C, K: 656D, H: 255D

6109 סֻכָּה *sukkâ*, tabernacle, shrine; booth, shelter, dwelling, tent, S: 5521, B: 697C, K: 656D, H: 255D

6110 סִכּוּת *sikkût*, variant: Sikkut (pagan god?), see 6109, S: 5522, B: 696D, K: 657A, H: 256A

6111 סֻכּוֹת *sukkôt*, Succoth, S: 5523, B: 697D, K: 657A, H: 256A

6112 סֻכּוֹת בְּנוֹת *sukkôt bᵉnôt*, Succoth Benoth (pagan god), S: 5524, B: 696D, K: 657B, H: 256A

6113 סֻכִּיִּים *sukkiyyîm*, Sukkite, S: 5525†, B: 696D, K: 657B, H: 256A

6114 ¹סָכַךְ *sākak¹*, [A] to cover, conceal, overshadow, shield; [G] to cover, shield; to relieve oneself, S: 5526, B: 696D, K: 657B, H: 256A

6115 ²סָכַךְ *sākak²*, [A] to knit together; [D] to knit together, S: 5526, B: 697B, K: 657B, H: 256B

6116 סֹכֵךְ *sōkēk*, protective shield (a portable roof), S: 5526†, B: 697D, K: 657C, H: 256B

6117 סְכָכָה *sᵉkākâ*, Secacah, S: 5527, B: 698A, K: 657D, H: 256B

6118 סָכַל *sākal*, [C] to do a foolish thing; [D] to turn into foolishness; [G] to act like a fool, S: 5528, B: 698A, K: 657D, H: 256B

6119 סָכָל *sākāl*, foolish (one), senseless, stupid, S: 5530, B: 698A, K: 657D, H: 256B

6120 סֶכֶל *sekel*, foolishness, fool, S: 5529, B: 698A, K: 657D, H: 256B

6121 סִכְלוּת *siklût*, folly, S: 5531, B: 698A, K: 657D, H: 256B

6122 ¹סָכַן *sākan¹*, [A] to be of use, benefit, profit; [G] to be in the habit; be familiar with; to get along well with, S: 5532, B: 698B, K: 658A, H: 256B

6123 ²סָכַן *sākan²*, [E] to be poor, S: 5533, B: 698C, K: 658B, H: 256C

6124 ³סָכַן *sākan³*, [C] to be endangered, S: 5533, B: 698B, K: 658A, H: 256B

6125 סֹכֵן *sōkēn*, steward, nurse, attendant, S: 5532†, B: 698B, K: 658B, H: 256C

6126 ¹סָכַר *sākar¹*, [C] to be closed; be silent, S: 5534, B: 698C, K: 658B, H: 256C

6127 ²סָכַר *sākar²*, [D] to hand over, deliver, S: 5534, B: 698C, K: 658B, H: 256C

6128 ³סָכַר *sākar³*, [A] to hire, S: 7936†, B: 698D, K: 658C, H: 256C

6129 סָכַת *sākat*, [G] to be silent, be still, S: 5535, B: 698D, K: 658C, H: 256C

6130 סַל *sal*, basket, S: 5536, B: 700D, K: 658C, H: 256C

6131 סָלָא *sālāʾ*, [E] to be weighed (in correlation to gold), S: 5537, B: 698D, K: 658C, H: 256C

6132 סַלֻּא *salluʾ*, Sallu, S: 5543, B: 699A, K: 659A, H: 256C

6133 סִלָּא *sillāʾ*, Silla, S: 5538, B: 698D, K: 658C, H: 256D

6134 סָלַד *sālad*, [D] to skip (for joy), S: 5539, B: 698D, K: 658D, H: 256D

6135 סֶלֶד *seled*, Seled, S: 5540, B: 699A, K: 658D, H: 256D

6136 ¹סָלָה *sālâ¹*, [A] to reject, toss aside; [D] to reject, S: 5541, B: 699A, K: 658D, H: 256D

6137 ²סָלָה *sālâ²*, [E] to be bought, be paid for, S: 5541, B: 699A, K: 658D, H: 256D

6138 סֶלָה *selâ*, selah (t.t. in the Psalms), S: 5542, B: 699D, K: 659A, H: 256D

6139 סַלּוּ *sallû*, Sallu, S: 5543, B: 699A, K: 659C, H: 256D

6140 סָלוּא *sālûʾ*, Salu, S: 5543, B: 699A, K: 659A, H: 256D

6141 סִלּוֹן *sillôn*, thorn, brier, S: 5544, B: 699B, K: 659B, H: 256D

6142 סָלַח *sālaḥ*, [A] to forgive, release, pardon; [C] to be forgiven, S: 5545, B: 699B, K: 659B, H: 256D

6143 סַלָּח *sallāḥ*, forgiving, S: 5546, B: 699C, K: 659C, H: 257A

6144 סַלַּי *sallay*, Sallai, S: 5543, B: 699A, K: 659C, H: 257A

6145 סְלִיחָה *sᵉlîḥâ*, forgiveness, pardon, S: 5547, B: 699C, K: 659C, H: 257A

6146 סַלְכָה *salkâ*, Salecah, S: 5548, B: 699C, K: 659C, H: 257A

6147 ¹סָלַל *sālal¹*, [D] to esteem, cherish; [F] to behave haughtily, insolently, S: 5549, B: 699C, K: 659C, H: 257A

6148 ²סָלַל *sālal²*, [A] to build up, heap up (a highway), extol; to pile up, S: 5549, B: 699C, K: 659C, H: 257A

6149 סֹלְלָה *sōlᵉlâ*, siege ramp, siege mound, S: 5550, B: 700C, K: 659D, H: 257A

6150 סֻלָּם *sullām*, stairway, S: 5551, B: 700C, K: 660A, H: 257B

6151 סַלְסִלָּה *salsillâ*, branch, shoot, S: 5552, B: 700D, K: 660A, H: 257B

6152 ¹סֶלַע *selaʿ¹*, rock, cliff, crag, S: 5553, B: 700D, K: 660A, H: 257B 1.

6153 ²סֶלַע *selaʿ²*, Sela, S: 5554, B: 701A, K: 660A, H: 257B 2.

6154 סֶלַע הַמַּחְלְקוֹת *selaʿ hammaḥlᵉqôt*, Sela Hammahlekoth, S: 5555, B: 325D, K: 660A, H: 257B 2.(2)

6155 סָלְעָם *solʿām*, edible locust *or* katydid, S: 5556, B: 701B, K: 660C, H: 257B

6156 סָלַף *sālap*, [D] to twist; to overthrow; to frustrate, S: 5557, B: 701B, K: 660C, H: 257B

6157 סֶלֶף *selep*, duplicity, perversity, deceit, S: 5558, B: 701B, K: 660C, H: 257C

6158 סָלַק *sālaq*, [A] to go up, ascend, climb up, S: 5927†, B: 701B, K: 660C, H: 257C

6159 סֹלֶת *sōlet*, fine flour, S: 5560, B: 701C, K: 660D, H: 257C

6160 סַם *sam*, fragrant perfume, S: 5561, B: 702C, K: 660D, H: 257C

6161 סַמְגַּר *samgar*, Samgar, S: 5562†, B: 701C, K: 660D, H: 257C

6162 סַמְגַּר־נְבוֹ *samgar-nᵉbô*, variant: Samgar-Nebo, see 5552 & 6161, S: 5562†, B: 701C, K: 660D, H: 257C

6163 סְמָדַר *sᵉmādar*, blossom (of a vine), S: 5563, B: 701D, K: 660D, H: 257C

6164 סָמַךְ *sāmak*, [A] to sustain, uphold; to lay (one's hand upon); [B] to be braced, be steadfast; [C] to lean upon, rely upon, gain confidence; [D] to strengthen, refresh, S: 5564, B: 701D, K: 661A, H: 257C

6165 סְמַכְיָהוּ *sᵉmakyāhû*, Semakiah, S: 5565, B: 702B, K: 661C, H: 257D

6166 סֶמֶל *semel*, image, idol, S: 5566, B: 702B, K: 661C, H: 257D

6167 סָמַם *sāmam*, variant: [G] to dye (i.e., to smear with paste or perfume), S*, B: 962C, K: 661C, H: 257D

6168 סָמַן *sāman*, [C] to be appointed, apportioned, S: 5567, B: 702C, K: 661C, H: 257D

6169 סָמַר *sāmar*, [A] to tremble, shudder (i.e., to have goose bumps, gooseflesh); [D] to bristle, stand on end (of hair), S: 5568, B: 702C, K: 661C, H: 257D

6170 סָמָר *sāmār*, bristling (locust), S: 5569, B: 702C, K: 661D, H: 257D

6171 סְנָאָה *sᵉnāʾâ*, Senaah, S: 5570, B: 702D, K: 661D, H: 257D

6172 סַנְבַלַּט *sanballaṭ*, Sanballat, S: 5571, B: 702D, K: 661D, H: 258A

6173 סַנָּה *sannâ*, variant: Sannah, S: 7158†, B: 900D, K: 856A 5., H: 258A

6174 סְנֶה *sᵉneh*, bush, thorny shrub, S: 5572†, B: 702D, K: 661D, H: 258A

6175 סֶנֶּה *senneh*, Seneh, S: 5573†, B: 702D, K: 662A, H: 258A

6176 סְנוּאָה *sᵉnûʾâ*, variant: Senuah, see 2190, S: 5574†, B: 703A, K: 662A, H: 258A

6177 סַנְוֵרִים *sanwērîm*, blindness, S: 5575†, B: 703A, K: 662A, H: 258A

6178 סַנְחֵרִיב *sanḥērîb*, Sennacherib, S: 5576, B: 703A, K: 662A, H: 258A

6179 סַנְסַנָּה *sansannâ*, Sansannah, S: 5578, B: 703A, K: 662A, H: 258A

6180 סַנְסִנָּה *sansinnâ*, fruit cluster (of date tree), S: 5577†, B: 703B, K: 662B, H: 258A

6181 סְנַפִּיר *sᵉnappîr*, fin, S: 5579, B: 703B, K: 662B, H: 258A

6182 סָס *sās*, (garment) moth, S: 5580, B: 703B, K: 662B, H: 258A

6183 סִסְמַי *sismay*, Sismai, S: 5581, B: 703B, K: 662B, H: 258A

6184 סָעַד *sāʿad*, [A] to sustain, support, refresh, S: 5582, B: 703C, K: 662B, H: 258A

6185 סָעָה *sāʿâ*, [A] to slander, defame, S: 5584, B: 703C, K: 662C, H: 258B

6186 ¹סָעִיף *sāʿîp¹*, cleft, crag, S: 5585, B: 703D 1., K: 662C, H: 258B

6187 ²סָעִיף *sāʿîp²*, bough, branch, S: 5585, B: 703D 2., K: 662D, H: 258B

6188 סָעַף *sā'ap*, [D] to lop off, trim down, S: 5586, B: 703D, K: 662D, H: 258B

6189 סֵעֵף *sē'ēp*, double-minded, divided in heart, S: 5588, B: 704A, K: 662D, H: 258B

6190 סְעַפָּה *sᵉ'appâ*, bough, S: 5589, B: 703D, K: 663A, H: 258B

6191 סְעִפִּים *sᵉ'ippîm*, division, divided opinion, S: 5587†, B: 704A, K: 663A, H: 258B

6192 סָעַר *sā'ar*, [A] to grow stormier, rougher; [C] to be enraged; [D] to scatter in a wind; swirl; [E] to be lashed by storms, S: 5590, B: 704A, K: 663A, H: 258B

6193 סַעַר *sa'ar*, windstorm, tempest, gale, S: 5591, B: 704B, K: 663B, H: 258C

6194 סְעָרָה *sᵉ'ārâ*, windstorm, tempest, gale, S: 5591, B: 704B, K: 663B, H: 258C

6195 1סַף *sap*[1], basin, bowl, S: 5592, B: 706B, K: 663B, H: 258C

6196 2סַף *sap*[2], variant: wool, hide, skin, S: 5592, B: 706B, K: 663B, H: 258C

6197 3סַף *sap*[3], threshold, door frame, entrance, doorway; doorkeeper, S: 5592, B: 706B, K: 663C, H: 258C

6198 4סַף *sap*[4], Saph, S: 5593, B: 706C, K: 663D, H: 258D

6199 סָפַד *sāpad*, [A] to beat the breast, mourn, lament, weep; [C] to be mourned, S: 5594, B: 704C, K: 663D, H: 258D

6200 סָפָה *sāpâ*, [A] to sweep away; take away; bring disaster; [C] to be swept away; be destroyed, S: 5595, B: 705A, K: 664A, H: 258D

6201 סָפוּן *sāpôn*, variant: panelling, S: 5603†, B: 706A, K: 664B, H: 259A

6202 1סָפַח *sāpaḥ*[1], [A] to associate, attach to; [C] to be attached, be united; [E] be joined together; [F] to feel oneself attached to, S: 5596, B: 705B, K: 664B, H: 258D

6203 2סָפַח *sāpaḥ*[2], [D] to pour out, S: 5596, B: 705B, K: 664B, H: 258D

6204 סַפַּחַת *sappaḥat*, rash, skin eruption, S: 5597, B: 705C, K: 664C, H: 259A

6205 סִפַּי *sippay*, Sippai, S: 5598, B: 706C, K: 663D, H: 259A

6206 1סָפִיחַ *sāpîaḥ*[1], what grows on its own, after-growth in a fallow year, S: 5599, B: 705C, K: 664C, H: 259A

6207 2סָפִיחַ *sāpîaḥ*[2], torrent, downpour, S: 5599, B: 705B, K: 664C, H: 259A

6208 סְפִינָה *sᵉpînâ*, ship (with a covering or deck), S: 5600, B: 706B, K: 664C, H: 259A

6209 סַפִּיר *sappîr*, sapphire, S: 5601, B: 705D, K: 664C, H: 259A

6210 סֵפֶל *sēpel*, bowl (for water or curdled milk), S: 5602, B: 705D, K: 664D, H: 259A

6211 סָפַן *sāpan*, [A] to cover; [B] to be roofed, be paneled, be roofed, S: 5603, B: 706A, K: 664D, H: 259A

6212 סִפֻּן *sippun*, ceiling, S: 5604, B: 706A, K: 665A, H: 259A

6213 סַפְסִיג *sapsîg*, glaze, S: 5509†, B: 691A, K: 655C, H: 259A

6214 סָפַף *sāpap*, [F] to stand at the threshold, S: 5605, B: 706C, K: 665A, H: 259B

6215 1סָפַק *sāpaq*[1], [A] to clap hands; beat one's breast; to punish, slap, S: 5606, B: 706C, K: 665A, H: 259B

6216 2סָפַק *sāpaq*[2], [A] to wallow, splash, S: 5606, B: 706C, K: 665A, H: 259B

6217 סֶפֶק *sepeq*, riches, abundance, S: 5607, B: 706D, K: 928D, H: 259B

6218 סָפַר *sāpar*, [A] to count, number, take a census; [C] to be counted, be recorded; [D] to tell, proclaim, recount; [E] to be told, S: 5608, B: 707D, K: 665B, H: 259B

6219 1סֵפֶר *sēper*[1], book, scroll, letter, certificate, deed, dispatch, S: 5612, B: 706D, K: 665D, H: 259C

6220 2סֵפֶר *sēper*[2], variant: plate, panel, S: 5612†, B: 706D, K: 665D, H: 259D

6221 סֹפֵר *sōpēr*, learned writer, scribe, secretary, S: 5608†, B: 708B, K: 666C, H: 259D

6222 1סְפָר *sᵉpār*[1], census, S: 5610, B: 708C, K: 666D, H: 259D

6223 2סְפָר *sᵉpār*[2], Sephar, S: 5611, B: 708C, K: 666D, H: 259D

6224 סְפָרַד *sᵉpārad*, Sepharad, S: 5614†, B: 709B, K: 666D, H: 259D

6225 סִפְרָה *siprâ*, record, writing, scroll, S: 5612, B: 707C, K: 666D, H: 260A

6226 סְפַרְוַיִם *sᵉparwayim*, Sepharvaim, S: 5617, B: 709B, K: 667A, H: 260A

6227 סְפַרְוִים *sᵉparwîm*, Sepharvite, S: 5616†, B: 709C, K: 667A, H: 260A

6228 סְפֹרוֹת *sᵉpōrôt*, measure, number, S: 5615†, B: 708D, K: 667A, H: 260A

6229 סֹפְרִים *sōpᵉrîm*, variant: see 6221, S*, B: 708B, K: 665D, H: 260A

6230 סֹפֶרֶת *sōperet*, variant: (office of) scribes, S: 5618, B: 709B, K: 667A, H: 260A

6231 סֶפֶת *sepet*, variant: see 3578, S: 3254†, B: 414D, K: 386D, H: 260A

6232 סָקַל *sāqal*, [A] to stone (as an execution); [C] to be stoned; [D] to throw stones (out or away), pelt with stones; [E] to be stoned, S: 5619, B: 709C, K: 667A, H: 260A

6233 סָר *sār*, captain, S: 8269†, B: 694A 4, K: 929B, H: 354C

6234 סַר *sar*, sullen, dejected, discouraged, S: 5620, B: 711A, K: 667B, H: 260A

6235 סָרָב *sārāb*, briers, S: 5621, B: 709D, K: 667C, H: 260B

6236 סַרְגוֹן *sargôn*, Sargon, S: 5623, B: 709D, K: 667C, H: 260B

6237 סֶרֶד *sered*, Sered, S: 5624, B: 710A, K: 667C, H: 260B

6238 סַרְדִּי *sardî*, Seredite, S: 5625, B: 710A, K: 667C, H: 260B

6239 1סָרָה *sārâ*[1], ceasing, stopping, S: 5627, B: 694C, K: 667C, H: 260B

6240 2סָרָה *sārâ*[2], rebellion, revolt, S: 5627, B: 694C, K: 667C, H: 260B

6241 סִרָה *sirâ*, Sirah, S: 5626, B: 694C, K: 667D, H: 260B

6242 סָרוּחַ *sārûaḥ*, flowing, lounging, S: 5628†, B: 710A, K: 667D, H: 260B

6243 1סָרַח *sāraḥ*[1], [A] to hang down, overhang, spread over; [B] to be overhanged, S: 5628, B: 710A, K: 667D, H: 260B

6244 2סָרַח *sāraḥ*[2], [C] to be decayed, be spoiled, become stinking, S: 5628, B: 710A, K: 668A, H: 260B

6245 סֶרַח *seraḥ*, overhang, what projects over, S: 5629, B: 710B, K: 668A, H: 260B

6246 סִרְיוֹן *siryôn*, (scale) armor, coat of mail, S: 5630†, B: 710B, K: 668A, H: 260B

6247 סָרִיס *sārîs*, court official, palace officer, eunuch, S: 5631, B: 710, K: 668A, H: 260C

6248 1סֶרֶן *seren*[1], axle, S: 5633, B: 710D, K: 668B, H: 260C

6249 2סֶרֶן *seren*[2], ruler, prince, S: 5633, B: 710C, K: 668B, H: 260C

6250 סַרְעַפָּה *sar'appâ*, bough, S: 5634, B: 703D, K: 668C, H: 260C

6251 סָרַף *sārap*, [D] to burn, S: 5635, B: 977A, K: 668C, H: 260C

6252 סִרְפָּד *sirpād*, briers, stinging nettles, S: 5636, B: 710D, K: 668C, H: 260C

6253 1סָרַר *sārar*[1], [A] to be stubborn, be obstinate, be rebellious, S: 5637, B: 710D, K: 668C, H: 260C

6254 2סָרַר *sārar*[2], [A] to be in charge, superintend, S: 8269†, B: 979A, K: 387C, H: 260C

6255 סְתָו *sᵉtāw*, winter, rainy season, S: 5638, B: 711A, K: 668D, H: 260C

6256 סְתוּר *sᵉtûr*, Sethur, S: 5639, B: 712C, K: 668D, H: 260D

6257 סְתָיו *sᵉtāyw*, variant: winter, see 6255, S: 5638†, B: 711A, K: 668D, H: 260C

6258 סָתַם *sātam*, [A] to stop up, block off, seal; [B] to be closed up, be in a secret place; [C] to be closed; [D] to stop up, S: 5640, B: 711A, K: 668D, H: 260D

6259 סָתַר *sātar*, [A] to be hidden, be concealed, have a refuge; [D] to hide; [E] to be hidden; [G] to hide, conceal; [F] to hide oneself, keep oneself hidden, S: 5641, B: 711B, K: 669A, H: 260D

6260 סֵתֶר *sēter*, hiding place, secret place, shelter; covering, veil; (as adv.) secretly, in secret, S: 5643, B: 712A, K: 669C, H: 261C

6261 סִתְרָה *sitrâ*, shelter, hiding-place, refuge, S: 5643, B: 712C, K: 669D, H: 261C

6262 סִתְרִי *sitrî*, Sithri, S: 5644, B: 712C, K: 669D, H: 261C

6263 ע *'*, letter of the Hebrew alphabet, S*, B: 712B, K: 670A, H*

6264 1עָב *'āb*[1], overhang, overhanging roof, S: 5646, B: 712B, K: 670B, H: 261A

6265 2עָב *'āb*[2], clouds, S: 5645, B: 728A, K: 670B, H: 261B

6266 3עָב *'āb*[3], thicket, S: 5645, B: 728A, K: 670C, H: 261B

6267 עַב *'ab*, variant: denseness, see 6295, S: 5645†, B: 716A, K: 670C, H: 261B

6268 עָבַד ʿābad, [A] to work, serve, labor, do; to worship, minister, work in ministry; [C] to be plowed, be cultivated; [E] to be worked; [G] to reduce to servitude, enslave, cause to serve; [H] to be caused to serve, worship (a god), S: 5647, B: 712B, K: 670C, H: 261B

6269 עֶבֶד¹ ʿebed[1], servant, slave, attendant, S: 5650, B: 713D, K: 671D, H: 262A

6270 עֶבֶד² ʿebed[2], Ebed, S: 5651, B: 714C, K: 672D, H: 262B

6271 עֲבָד ʿabād, what is done, deed, act, S: 5652, B: 714D, K: 672D, H: 262B

6272 עַבְדָּא ʿabdā', Abda, S: 5653, B: 715A, K: 673A, H: 262B

6273 עֹבֵד־אֱדוֹם ʿōbēd-'edôm, Obed-Edom, S: 5654†, B: 714D, K: 673A, H: 262B

6274 עַבְדְּאֵל ʿabde'ēl, Abdeel, S: 5655, B: 715A, K: 673A, H: 262B

6275 עֲבֹדָה ʿabōdâ, work, service, labor, task, duty, job; ministerial duties, S: 5656, B: 715A, K: 673B, H: 262B

6276 עֲבֻדָּה ʿabuddâ, servant, slave, S: 5657, B: 715C, K: 673C, H: 262C

6277 עַבְדּוֹן¹ ʿabdôn[1], Abdon, S: 5658, B: 715C 1., K: 673D, H: 262C

6278 עַבְדּוֹן² ʿabdôn[2], Abdon, S: 5658, B: 715C, K: 673D, H: 262C

6279 עַבְדִּי ʿabdî, Abdi, S: 5660, B: 715D, K: 673D, H: 262C

6280 עַבְדִּיאֵל ʿabdî'ēl, Abdiel, S: 5661, B: 715D, K: 673D, H: 262C

6281 עֹבַדְיָה ʿōbadyâ, Obadiah, S: 5662, B: 715D, K: 673D, H: 262C

6282 עֹבַדְיָהוּ ʿōbadyāhû, Obadiah, S: 5662, B: 715D, K: 674A, H: 262C

6283 עֶבֶד־מֶלֶךְ ʿebed-melek, Ebed-Melech, S: 5663†, B: 715A, K: 673A, H: 262B

6284 עֲבֵד נְגוֹ ʿabēd negô, Abednego, S: 5664, B: 715A, K: 673A, H: 262B

6285 עַבְדֻת ʿabdut, slavery, servitude, S: 5659, B: 715C, K: 674A, H: 262C

6286 עָבָה ʿābâ, [A] to be thick, S: 5666, B: 716A, K: 674A, H: 262C

6287 עֲבוֹט ʿabôt, pledge, (garment) security (for a loan), S: 5667, B: 716B, K: 674B, H: 262C

6288 עֲבוּר¹ ʿabûr[1], for, because, on account of; in order to, S: 5668, B: 721A, K: 674B, H: 262C

6289 עֲבוּר² ʿabûr[2], produce, yield, S: 5669, B: 721A, K: 674C, H: 262D

6290 עָבֹת¹ ʿābôt[1], leafy, dense, interwoven foliage, S: 5687, B: 721C, K: 674C, H: 262D

6291 עָבוֹת² ʿābôt[2], thick foliage, S: 5688†, B: 721C, K: 674C, H: 262D

6292 עָבַט¹ ʿābaṭ[1], [A] to borrow, i.e., take or receive a pledge; [G] to lend on a pledge, S: 5670, B: 716B, K: 674D, H: 262D

6293 עָבַט² ʿābaṭ[2], [D] to swerve, change (a course), S: 5670, B: 716B, K: 674D, H: 262D

6294 עַבְטִיט ʿabṭîṭ, heavy pledges, excessive mortgage for a debt, S: 5671, B: 716B, K: 674D, H: 262D

6295 עֲבִי ʿabî, thickness, density, mold, S: 5672, B: 716A, K: 675A, H: 263A

6296 עָבַר¹ ʿābar[1], [A] to pass over, cross over, travel through; [C] to be crossed; [D] to extend; to breed; [G] to make pass through, let pass over, send over, S: 5674, B: 716D, K: 675A, H: 263A

6297 עָבַר² ʿābar[2], [F] to be very angry, show oneself angry, S: 5674, B: 720D, K: 676C, H: 263D

6298 עֵבֶר¹ ʿēber[1], what is on the other side, what is beyond, across; i.e., east or west; Trans-Euphrates, S: 5676, B: 719B, K: 676D, H: 263D

6299 עֵבֶר² ʿēber[2], Eber, S: 5677, B: 720A, K: 677B, H: 264A

6300 עָבָר ʿābār, variant: crossing, see 6305, S: 863†, B: 743D & 720D, K: 677C, H: 264A

6301 עֶבְרָה ʿebrâ, wrath, anger, fury, rage, S: 5678, B: 720C, K: 677C, H: 264A

6302 עֲבָרָה ʿabārâ, ford, crossing, S: 5679, B: 720B, K: 677D, H: 264A

6303 עִבְרִי¹ ʿibrî[1], Hebrew, S: 5680, B: 720A, K: 677D, H: 264A

6304 עִבְרִי² ʿibrî[2], Ibri, S: 5681, B: 720B, K: 677D, H: 264A

6305 עֲבָרִים ʿabārîm, Abarim, S: 5682, B: 720D, K: 678B, H: 264A

6306 עֶבְרֹן ʿebrōn, variant: Ebron, see 6278, S: 2275†, B: 720D, K: 673D, H: 262C

6307 עַבְרֹנָה ʿabrōnâ, Abronah, S: 5684, B: 720D, K: 678B, H: 264B

6308 עָבַשׁ ʿābaš, [A] to shrivel, wither, dry up, S: 5685, B: 721B, K: 678C, H: 264B

6309 עָבַת ʿābat, [D] to conspire, twist, S: 5686, B: 721B, K: 678C, H: 264B

6310 עֲבֹת ʿabōt, rope, cord, chains, ties; fetters, harness, S: 5688, B: 721C, K: 678C, H: 264B

6311 עָגַב ʿāgab, [A] to lust, have sensual desire for, S: 5689, B: 721D, K: 678C, H: 264B

6312 עֲגָבָה ʿagābâ, lust, sensual desire, S: 5691, B: 721D, K: 678D, H: 264B

6313 עֲגָבִים ʿagābîm, devotion, love, S: 5690†, B: 721D, K: 678D, H: 264B

6314 עֻגָה ʿugâ, (round, flat) bread cakes, S: 5692, B: 728A, K: 678D, H: 264C

6315 עָגוּר ʿāgûr, (short footed) thrush (a bird), S: 5693, B: 723A, K: 679A, H: 264C

6316 עָגִיל ʿāgîl, earring, S: 5694, B: 722D, K: 679A, H: 264C

6317 עֲגִילָה ʿagîlâ, circular shield, S: 5699†, B: 722C, K: 679A, H: 264C

6318 עָגֹל ʿāgōl, circular, round, S: 5696, B: 722C, K: 679B, H: 264C

6319 עֵגֶל ʿēgel, bull-calf; calf-shaped idol, S: 5695, B: 722A, K: 679B, H: 264C

6320 עֶגְלָה¹ ʿeglâ[1], heifer-calf, young cow, S: 5697, B: 722B, K: 679B, H: 264C

6321 עֶגְלָה² ʿeglâ[2], Eglah, S: 5698, B: 722C, K: 679C, H: 264C

6322 עֲגָלָה ʿagālâ, cart, S: 5699, B: 722C, K: 679C, H: 264C

6323 עֶגְלוֹן¹ ʿeglôn[1], Eglon, S: 5700, B: 722D 1., K: 679C, H: 264D

6324 עֶגְלוֹן² ʿeglôn[2], Eglon, S: 5700, B: 722D 2., K: 679C, H: 264D

6325 עֶגְלַיִם ʿeglayim, variant: Eglaim, S: 5882†, B: 745C, K: 700C i, H: 264D

6326 עֶגְלַת שְׁלִשִׁיָּה ʿeglat šelišiyyâ, Eglath Shelishiyah, S: 5697† + 7992†, B: 722C, K: 978A, H: 264D

6327 עָגַם ʿāgam, [A] to grieve for, have pity on, S: 5701, B: 723A, K: 679D, H: 264D

6328 עָגַן ʿāgan, [C] to keep withdrawn (from marital relations), S: 5702, B: 723A, K: 679D, H: 264D

6329 עַד¹ ʿad[1], forever, eternal, for ever and ever; continual, always; old ancient, S: 5703, B: 723C, K: 679D, H: 264D

6330 עַד² ʿad[2], until, up to, as far as, S: 5704, B: 723D, K: 680B, H: 264D

6331 עַד³ ʿad[3], prey, plunder, S: 5706, B: 723D, K: 681B, H: 265B

6332 עֵד ʿēd, witness, testimony, S: 5707, B: 729C, K: 681B, H: 265B

6333 עִדֹּא ʿiddō', Iddo, S: 5714, B: 723B, K: 682A, H: 265C

6334 עָדָה¹ ʿādâ[1], [A] to prowl; [G] to take away, remove, S: 5710, B: 723C, K: 682B, H: 265D

6335 עָדָה² ʿādâ[2], [A] to adorn oneself, put on jewelry, S: 5710, B: 725C, K: 682B, H: 265D

6336 עָדָה³ ʿādâ[3], Adah, S: 5711, B: 725D, K: 682C, H: 265D

6337 עֵדָה¹ ʿēdâ[1], community, assembly, S: 5712, B: 417A, K: 682C, H: 265D

6338 עֵדָה² ʿēdâ[2], witness, S: 5713, B: 729D, K: 683A, H: 265D

6339 עֵדָה³ ʿēdâ[3], variant: testimony, S*, B: 730A, K: 683A, H: 266A

6340 עִדָּה ʿiddâ, menstruation, S: 5708, B: 723B, K: 683A, H: 265D

6341 עִדּוֹ ʿiddô, Iddo, S: 5714, B: 723B, K: 683A, H: 265D

6342 עִדּוֹא ʿiddô', Iddo, S: 5714, B: 723B, K: 682A, H: 265D

6343 עֵדוּת ʿēdût, testimony, statute, stipulation, regulation, S: 5715, B: 730B, K: 683A, H: 266A

6344 עֲדִי ʿadî, ornament, beautiful jewelry, S: 5716, B: 725D, K: 683C, H: 266A

6345 עֲדָיָא ʿadāyā', variant: Adaia, see 6342, S: 5714†, B: 723B 4, K: 683C, H: 266A

6346 עֲדִיאֵל ʿadî'ēl, Adiel, S: 5717, B: 726A, K: 683C, H: 266A

6347 עֲדָיָה ʿadāyâ, Adaiah, S: 5718, B: 726A, K: 683C, H: 266A

6348 עֲדָיָהוּ ʿadāyāhû, Adaiah, S: 5718, B: 726A, K: 683D, H: 266A

6349 עָדִין¹ ʿādîn[1], voluptuous, wantonness, S: 5719, B: 726D, K: 683D, H: 266A

6350 עָדִין² ʿādîn[2], Adin, S: 5720, B: 726D, K: 683D, H: 266C

6351 עֲדִינָא ʿadînā', Adina, S: 5721, B: 726D, K: 683D, H: 266A

6352 עֲדִינוֹ ʿadînô, variant: Adino, S: 5722†, B: 726D & 734D, K: 683D & 690C, H*

6353 עֲדִיתַיִם ʿadîtayim, Adithaim, S: 5723, B: 726A, K: 683D, H: 266A

6354 עַדְלַי ʿadlay, Adlai, S: 5724, B: 726B, K: 683D, H: 266A

6355 עֲדֻלָּם ʿadullām, Adullam, S: 5725, B: 726B, K: 684A, H: 266A

6356 עֲדֻלָּמִי *ʿadullāmî*, Adullamite, of Adullam, S: 5726, B: 726C, K: 684A, H: 266A

6357 עָדַן *ʿādan*, [F] to revel in the good life, luxuriate, S: 5727, B: 726C, K: 684A, H: 266A

6358 ¹עֵדֶן *ʿēden*[1], delight, delicacy; finery, S: 5730, B: 726C, K: 684A, H: 266A

6359 ²עֵדֶן *ʿēden*[2], Eden, S: 5731, B: 727A, K: 684A, H: 266B

6360 ³עֵדֶן *ʿēden*[3], Eden, S: 5731, B: 726C, K: 684B, H: 266B

6361 עֶדֶן *ʿeden*, Eden, S: 5729, B: 727A, K: 684B, H: 266B

6362 עֲדֶן *ʿaden*, yet, S: 5728, B: 725C, K: 684B, H: 266B

6363 עַדְנָא *ʿadnāʾ*, Adna, S: 5733, B: 726C, K: 684B, H: 266B

6364 עֲדֶנָה *ʿadenâ*, still, S: 5728, B: 725C, K: 684B, H: 266B

6365 עַדְנָה *ʿadnâ*, Adnah, S: 5734, B: 726D, K: 684C, H: 266B

6366 עֶדְנָה *ʿednâ*, (sexual) pleasure, delight, S: 5730, B: 726C, K: 684C, H: 266B

6367 עַדְנַח *ʿadnaḥ*, Adnah, S: 5734†, B: 726D 2, K: 684C, H: 266B

6368 עַדְעָדָה *ʿadʿādâ*, Adadah, S: 5735, B: 793A 3, K: 684C, H: 266B

6369 עָדַף *ʿādap*, [A] (ptcp.) what is left over, what is additional; [G] to have a surplus, S: 5736, B: 727A, K: 684C, H: 266B

6370 ¹עדר *ʿādar*[1], [A] to help, serve, S: 5737, B: 727B, K: 684C, H: 266B

6371 ²עָדַר *ʿādar*[2], [C] to be cultivated, be weeded, S: 5737, B: 727B, K: 684D, H: 266C

6372 ³עָדַר *ʿādar*[3], [C] to be missing; be lacking; [D] to let be lacking, S: 5737, B: 727C, K: 684D, H: 266C

6373 ¹עֵדֶר *ʿēder*[1], flock, herd, S: 5739, B: 727C, K: 685A, H: 266C

6374 ²עֵדֶר *ʿēder*[2], Eder, S: 5740, B: 727D, K: 685A, H: 266C

6375 ³עֵדֶר *ʿēder*[3], Eder, S: 5740, B: 727D, K: 685B, H: 266C

6376 עֶדֶר *ʿeder*, Eder, S: 5738, B: 727D, K: 685B, H: 266C

6377 עַדְרִיאֵל *ʿadrîʾēl*, Adriel, S: 5741, B: 727B, K: 685B, H: 266C

6378 עֲדָשִׁים *ʿadāšîm*, lentils, S: 5742†, B: 727D, K: 685B, H: 266C

6379 עַוָּא *ʿawwāʾ*, Avva, S: 5755, B: 731D, K: 685B, H: 266C

6380 עוב *ʿûb*, [G] to cover with a cloud, S: 5743, B: 728A, K: 685B, H: 266C

6381 עוֹבֵד *ʿôbēd*, Obed, S: 5744, B: 714D, K: 685C, H: 266C

6382 עוֹבָל *ʿôbāl*, Obal, S: 5745, B: 716C, K: 685C, H: 266D

6383 עוג *ʿûg*, [A] to bake a (round, flat) cake of bread, S: 5746, B: 728B, K: 685C, H: 266D

6384 עוֹג *ʿôg*, Og, S: 5747, B: 728B, K: 685D, H: 266D

6385 עוּגָב *ʿûgāb*, flute, S: 5748, B: 721D, K: 685D, H: 266D

6386 ¹עוד *ʿûd*[1], [D] to surround (with ropes); to sustain, relieve; [G] to admonish, warn, charge, declare; to testify, to call on a witness; [H] to be warned; [F] to hold each other up, S: 5749, B: 729D, K: 685D, H: 266D

6387 ²עוד *ʿûd*[2], variant: [A, G] to bear witness, S: 5749, B: 728C, K: 685D, H: 266D

6388 עוֹד *ʿôd*, longer, again, still, more, S: 5750, B: 728C, K: 686B, H: 267A

6389 עוֹדֵד *ʿôdēd*, Oded, S: 5752, B: 729C, K: 686D, H: 267B

6390 ¹עָוָה *ʿāwâ*[1], [A] to do wrong; [C] to be perverse, be warped; [D] to ruin, make crooked; [G] to do wrong, pervert, S: 5753, B: 730C, K: 686D, H: 267B

6391 ²עָוָה *ʿāwâ*[2], variant: [A] to do wrong; [G] to commit iniquity, S: 5753, B: 731C, K: 686D, H: 267B

6392 ¹עַוָּה *ʿawwâ*[1], ruin, wreckage, rubble, S: 5754, B: 730C, K: 687A, H: 267B

6393 ²עַוָּה *ʿawwâ*[2], variant: Avvah, see 6394, S: 5755, B: 731D, K: 687A, H: 267B

6394 עִוָּה *ʿiwwâ*, Ivvah, S: 5755, B: 731D, K: 687A, H: 267B

6395 עוז *ʿûz*, [A] to take refuge; [G] to bring to refuge, give shelter, S: 5756, B: 731D, K: 687B, H: 267B

6396 ¹עֲוִיל *ʿawîl*[1], little boys, S: 5759, B: 732B, K: 687B, H: 267C

6397 ²עֲוִיל *ʿawîl*[2], evil one, unjust one, S: 5760, B: 732D, K: 687B, H: 267C

6398 ¹עַוִּים *ʿawwîm*[1], Avvite, S: 5757† & 5761, B: 731D & 732A, K: 687B, H: 267C

6399 ²עַוִּים *ʿawwîm*[2], Avvim, S: 5761, B: 732A 2., K: 687B, H: 267C

6400 עֲוִית *ʿawît*, Avith, S: 5762, B: 732A, K: 687B, H: 267C

6401 עָוַל *ʿāwal*[1], [D] to do evil, act wrong, S: 5765, B: 732C, K: 687C, H: 267C

6402 ²עול *ʿûl*[2], [A] to nurse, suckle, S: 5763, B: 732B, K: 687C, H: 267C

6403 ³עוּל *ʿûl*[3], nursing infant, baby, S: 5764, B: 732B, K: 687C, H: 267C

6404 עָוֶל *ʿāwel*, wrong, evil, sin, injustice, S: 5766, B: 732B, K: 687D, H: 267C

6405 עַוָּל *ʿawwāl*, wicked one, evil one, unjust one, S: 5767, B: 732D, K: 687D, H: 267C

6406 עַוְלָה *ʿawlâ*, wickedness, evil, injustice, S: 5766, B: 732C, K: 687D, H: 267C

6407 עוֹלֵל *ʿôlēl*, child, little one, S: 5768, B: 760C, K: 688A, H: 267D

6408 עוֹלָל *ʿôlāl*, child, little one, S: 5768†, B: 760C, K: 688A, H: 267D

6409 עוֹלָם *ʿôlām*, everlasting, forever, eternity; from of old, ancient, lasting, for a duration, S: 5769, B: 761D, K: 688B, H: 267D

6410 עון *ʿûn*, variant: [A] to dwell, S: 6030†, B: 732D, K: 720A & 547B, H: 278B & 206C

6411 עָוֹן *ʿāwōn*, sin, guilt, wickedness, iniquity, S: 5771, B: 730D, K: 689A, H: 268A

6412 עוֹנָה *ʿônâ*, variant: sin, see 6411, S: 5869†, B: 733B, K: 689A, H: 268A

6413 עִוְעִים *ʿiwʿîm*, (col. pl.) dizziness, staggering, frenzy, S: 5773†, B: 730C, K: 689C, H: 268A

6414 ¹עוף *ʿûp*[1], [A] to fly; [D] to dart about (of a flying bird or a snake); [G] to let (eyes) glance; [F] to fly away, S: 5774, B: 733B, K: 689C, H: 268A

6415 ²עוף *ʿûp*[2], variant: [A] to be dark, S: 5774, B: 734A, K: 689D, H: 268B

6416 עוֹף *ʿôp*, bird, winged creatures, flying creatures, S: 5775, B: 733D, K: 690A, H: 268B

6417 עוֹפַי *ʿôpay*, variant: Ophai, see 6550, S: 5778, B: 734A, K: 701B, H: 268B

6418 ¹עוץ *ʿûṣ*[1], [A] to consider, devise, plan, S: 5779, B: 734A, K: 690A, H: 268B

6419 ²עוּץ *ʿûṣ*[2], Uz, S: 5780, B: 734B 1., K: 690B, H: 268B

6420 ³עוּץ *ʿûṣ*[3], Uz, S: 5780, B: 734B 2., K: 690B, H: 268B

6421 עוק *ʿûq*, [A] to crush, totter; [G] to crush, cause to totter, S: 5781, B: 734B, K: 690B, H: 268B

6422 ¹עור *ʿāwar*[1], [D] to make blind, S: 5786, B: 734C, K: 690C, H: 268C

6423 ²עור *ʿûr*[2], [C] to be uncovered, be laid bare, S: 5783, B: 735D, K: 690C, H: 268C

6424 ³עור *ʿûr*[3], [A] to awake; [C] to be aroused, stirred up, wakened; [D] to awaken, arouse, raise up; to keep up; [G] to stir up, rouse, waken; [F] to rouse oneself, S: 5782, B: 734D, K: 690C, H: 268C

6425 עוֹר *ʿôr*, skin, hide, leather, S: 5785, B: 736A, K: 691B, H: 268D

6426 עִוֵּר *ʿiwwēr*, blind, S: 5787, B: 734C, K: 691C, H: 268D

6427 עִוָּרוֹן *ʿiwwārôn*, blindness, blinding, S: 5788, B: 734D, K: 691C, H: 269A

6428 עַוֶּרֶת *ʿawweret*, blindness, S: 5788, B: 734D, K: 691D, H: 269A

6429 עוש *ʿûš*, [A] to be quick *or* to help, S: 5789, B: 736B, K: 691D, H: 269A

6430 עָוַת *ʿāwat*, [D] to make crooked, pervert; [E] to be twisted, be made crooked; [F] to stoop down, bend over, S: 5791, B: 736C, K: 691D, H: 269A

6431 עות *ʿût*, [A] to sustain, help, S: 5790, B: 736C, K: 692A, H: 269A

6432 עַוָּתָה *ʿawwātâ*, wrong, S: 5792, B: 736C, K: 692A, H: 269A

6433 עוּתַי *ʿûtay*, Uthai, S: 5793, B: 736D, K: 692A, H: 269A

6434 עַז *ʿaz*, strong, mighty, powerful, fierce, S: 5794, B: 738C, K: 692A, H: 269A

6435 עָז *ʿāz*, power, strength, S: 5794, B: 738D, K: 692B, H: 269A

6436 עֵז *ʿēz*, goat; goat hair, S: 5795, B: 777C, K: 692B, H: 269A

6437 עֹז *ʿōz*, strength, power, might, S: 5797, B: 738D, K: 692C & 693A, H: 269B

6438 עֻזָּא *ʿuzzāʾ*, Uzza, Uzzah, S: 5798, B: 739B, K: 693A, H: 269B

6439 עֲזָאזֵל *ʿazāʾzēl*, scapegoat, S: 5799, B: 736D, K: 693B, H: 269B

6440 ¹עָזַב *ʿāzab*[1], [A] to leave, abandon, reject, desert; [B] to be left, be abandoned, be freed; [C] to be abandoned, be forsaken, be neglected; [E] to be deserted, be abandoned, S: 5800, B: 736D, K: 693B, H: 269B

6441 עָזַב[2] *ʿāzab*[2], [A] to restore, help, S: 5800, B: 738A, K: 694B, H: 269D

6442 עִזְבוֹנִים *ʿizbônîm*, merchandise, goods, S: 5801†, B: 738A, K: 694B, H: 269D

6443 עַזְבּוּק *ʿazbûq*, Azbuk, S: 5802, B: 739D, K: 694B, H: 269D

6444 עַזְגָּד *ʿazgād*, Azgad, S: 5803, B: 739D, K: 694B, H: 269D

6445 עַזָּה *ʿazzâ*, Gaza, S: 5804, B: 738B, K: 694B, H: 269D

6446 עֻזָּה *ʿuzzâ*, Uzzah, S: 5798, B: 739C, K: 694C, H: 269D

6447 עֲזוּבָה[1] *ʿᵃzûbâ*[1], variant: forsaking, desolation, S: 5805, B: 737D, K: 693B, H: 269B

6448 עֲזוּבָה[2] *ʿᵃzûbâ*[2], Azubah, S: 5806, B: 738A, K: 694C, H: 269D

6449 עֱזוּז *ʿᵉzûz*, power, strength, S: 5807, B: 739B, K: 694C, H: 269D

6450 עִזּוּז *ʿizzûz*, strong, powerful, S: 5808, B: 739B, K: 694C, H: 269D

6451 עָזַז *ʿāzaz*, [A] to be strong, overpower; [G] to put on a bold face, be brazen, S: 5810, B: 738B, K: 694D, H: 270A

6452 עָזָז *ʿāzāz*, Azaz, S: 5811, B: 739B, K: 695A, H: 270A

6453 עֲזַזְיָהוּ *ʿᵃzazyāhû*, Azaziah, S: 5812, B: 739C, K: 695A, H: 270A

6454 עֻזִּי *ʿuzzî*, Uzzi, S: 5813, B: 739D, K: 695A, H: 270A

6455 עֻזִּיָּא *ʿuzziyyāʾ*, Uzzia, S: 5814, B: 739D, K: 695A, H: 270A

6456 עֲזִיאֵל *ʿᵃzîʾēl*, Aziel, S: 5815, B: 739D, K: 695A, H: 270A

6457 עֻזִּיאֵל *ʿuzzîʾēl*, Uzziel, S: 5816, B: 739C, K: 695B, H: 270A

6458 עָזִּיאֵלִי *ʿozzîʾēlî*, Uzzielite, S: 5817, B: 739C, K: 695B, H: 270A

6459 עֻזִּיָּה *ʿuzziyyâ*, Uzziah, S: 5818, B: 739C, K: 695B, H: 270A

6460 עֻזִּיָּהוּ *ʿuzziyyāhû*, Uzziah, S: 5818, B: 739C, K: 695B, H: 270A

6461 עֲזִיזָא *ʿᵃzîzāʾ*, Aziza, S: 5819, B: 739C, K: 695B, H: 270A

6462 עַזְמָוֶת[1] *ʿazmāwet*[1], Azmaveth, S: 5820, B: 740A, K: 695C, H: 270A

6463 עַזְמָוֶת[2] *ʿazmāwet*[2], Azmaveth, S: 5820, B: 740A & 112B, K: 125A 30., H: 270A

6464 עַזָּן *ʿazzān*, Azzan, S: 5821, B: 740A, K: 695C, H: 270B

6465 עָזְנִיָּה *ʿozniyyâ*, black vulture, S: 5822, B: 740A, K: 695C, H: 270B

6466 עָזַק *ʿāzaq*, [D] to dig, S: 5823, B: 740A, K: 695C, H: 270B

6467 עֲזֵקָה *ʿᵃzēqâ*, Azekah, S: 5825, B: 740A, K: 695D, H: 270B

6468 עָזַר *ʿāzar*, [A] to help, support; [B] to be helped; [C] to be helped, S: 5826, B: 740A, K: 695D, H: 270B

6469 עֵזֶר[1] *ʿēzer*[1], help, helper, S: 5828, B: 740C, K: 696B, H: 270C

6470 עֵזֶר[2] *ʿēzer*[2], Ezer, S: 5827† & 5829, B: 740D, K: 696C, H: 270C

6471 עֶזֶר[1] *ʿezer*[1], variant: Ezer, see 75, S: 7320†, B: 7A 9, K: 696C, H: 270C

6472 עֶזֶר[2] *ʿezer*[2], Ezer, S: 5829†, B: 740D 2., K: 696C, H: 270C

6473 עַזֻּר *ʿazzur*, Azzur, S: 5809, B: 741A, K: 696C, H: 270C

6474 עֶזְרָא *ʿezrāʾ*, Ezra, S: 5830, B: 740D, K: 696C, H: 270C

6475 עֲזַרְאֵל *ʿᵃzarʾēl*, Azarel, S: 5832, B: 741A, K: 696D, H: 270C

6476 עֶזְרָה[1] *ʿezrâ*[1], help, aid, support, S: 5833, B: 740D, K: 696D, H: 270C

6477 עֶזְרָה[2] *ʿezrâ*[2], Ezrah, S: 5834, B: 741A, K: 696D, H: 270C

6478 עֲזָרָה *ʿᵃzārâ*, court, enclosure; ledge, barrier, S: 5835, B: 741C, K: 696D, H: 270C

6479 עֶזְרִי *ʿezrî*, Ezri, S: 5836, B: 741B, K: 697A, H: 270C

6480 עַזְרִיאֵל *ʿazrîʾēl*, Azriel, S: 5837, B: 741A, K: 697A, H: 270C

6481 עֲזַרְיָה *ʿᵃzaryâ*, Azariah, S: 5838, B: 741A, K: 697B, H: 270C

6482 עֲזַרְיָהוּ *ʿᵃzaryāhû*, Azariah; Azariahu, S: 5838, B: 741A, K: 697B, H: 270D

6483 עַזְרִיקָם *ʿazrîqām*, Azrikam, S: 5840, B: 741B, K: 697B, H: 270D

6484 עַזָּתִי *ʿazzātî*, Gazite, S: 5841, B: 738B, K: 697B, H: 270D

6485 עֵט *ʿēṭ*, (iron) engraving tool; (reed) pen, S: 5842, B: 741C, K: 697B, H: 270D

6486 עָטָה[1] *ʿāṭâ*[1], [A] to cover, wrap oneself; [G] cover, wrap another (thing), S: 5844, B: 741D, K: 697B, H: 270D

6487 עָטָה[2] *ʿāṭâ*[2], [A] to grasp; [E] to be grasped, S: 4593† & 5844, B: 742A, K: 697C, H: 270D

6488 עָטוּף *ʿāṭûp*, weak, faint, S: 5848†, B: 742C, K: 697D, H: 270D

6489 עֲטִין *ʿᵃṭîn*, body, part of body *or* pail, bucket, S: 5845, B: 742B, K: 697D, H: 270D

6490 עֲטִישָׁה *ʿᵃṭîšâ*, snorting, sneezing, S: 5846, B: 743A, K: 697D, H: 271A

6491 עֲטַלֵּף *ʿᵃṭallēp*, bat (animal), S: 5847, B: 742A, K: 697D, H: 271A

6492 עָטָם *ʿāṭām*, variant: thigh, S*, B: 782C, K: 698A, H: 271A

6493 עָטַף[1] *ʿāṭap*[1], [A] to clothe, mantle; to turn aside, S: 5848, B: 742B, K: 698A, H: 271A

6494 עָטַף[2] *ʿāṭap*[2], [A] to grow faint; [C] to be faint; [G] to be feeble; [F] to ebb away, grow faint, S: 5848, B: 742C, K: 698A, H: 271A

6495 עָטַף[3] *ʿāṭap*[3], variant: [B, C, F, G] to be feeble, S*, B: 742B, K: 698A, H: 271A

6496 עָטַר[1] *ʿāṭar*[1], [A] to surround, close in upon, S: 5849, B: 742C, K: 698B, H: 271A

6497 עָטַר[2] *ʿāṭar*[2], [D] to crown, place a wreath (on the head); [G] to bestow a crown, S: 5849, B: 742D, K: 698B, H: 271A

6498 עֲטָרָה[1] *ʿᵃṭārâ*[1], crown, wreath, S: 5850, B: 742D, K: 698C, H: 271B

6499 עֲטָרָה[2] *ʿᵃṭārâ*[2], Atarah, S: 5851, B: 742D, K: 698D, H: 271B

6500 עֲטָרוֹת *ʿᵃṭārôt*, Ataroth, S: 5852, B: 743A, K: 698D, H: 271B

6501 עַטְרוֹת אַדָּר *ʿaṭrôt ʾaddār*, Ataroth Addar, S: 5853, B: 743A 2a, K: 698D, H: 271B

6502 עַטְרוֹת בֵּית יוֹאָב *ʿaṭrôt bêt yôʾāb*, Atroth Beth Joab, S: 5854, B: 743A 2c, K: 698D, H: 271B

6503 עַטְרוֹת שׁוֹפָן *ʿaṭrôt šôpān*, Atroth Shophan, S: 5855, B: 743A 1b, K: 698D, H: 271B

6504 עַי *ʿay*, Ai, S: 5857, B: 743A, K: 698D, H: 271B

6505 עִי *ʿî*, heap of rubble; (of a person) a broken man, S: 5856, B: 730C, K: 699A, H: 271B

6506 עֵיבָל[1] *ʿêbāl*[1], Ebal, S: 5858, B: 716C, K: 699A, H: 271B

6507 עֵיבָל[2] *ʿêbāl*[2], Ebal, S: 5858, B: 716C, K: 699B, H: 271B

6508 עֵיבָל[3] *ʿêbāl*[3], variant: Ebal, see 6382, S: 5858, B: 716C, K: 685C, H: 266D

6509 עַיָּה *ʿayyâ*, Ayyah; Aija, S: 5857†, B: 743B 1, K: 699B, H: 271B

6510 עִיּוֹן *ʿiyyôn*, Ijon, S: 5859, B: 743B, K: 699B, H: 271B

6511 עֲיוֹת *ʿᵃyôt*, variant: Aioth, see 6400, S: 5762, B: 732B, K: 687B, H: 267C

6512 עִיט[1] *ʿîṭ*[1], [A] to hurl insults, S: 5860, B: 743B, K: 699B, H: 271B

6513 עִיט[2] *ʿîṭ*[2], [A] to pounce upon (with shrieks and screams), S: 5860, B: 743C, K: 699B, H: 271B

6514 עַיִט *ʿayiṭ*, (coll) birds of prey, carrion birds, S: 5861, B: 743C, K: 699C, H: 271C

6515 עֵיטָם *ʿêṭām*, Etam, S: 5862, B: 743C, K: 699C, H: 271C

6516 עִיֵּי הָעֲבָרִים *ʿiyyê hāʿᵃbārîm*, Iye Abarim, S: 5863, B: 743D, K: 699C, H: 271C

6517 עִיִּים *ʿiyyîm*, Iyim; Iim, S: 5864, B: 743D, K: 699C, H: 271C

6518 עֵילוֹם *ʿêlôm*, variant: forever, see 6409, S: 5865†, B: 761D, K: 699C, H: 271C

6519 עִילַי *ʿîlay*, Ilai, S: 5866, B: 743D, K: 699C, H: 271C

6520 עֵילָם[1] *ʿêlām*[1], Elam, S: 5867, B: 743D, K: 699D, H: 271C

6521 עֵילָם[2] *ʿêlām*[2], Elam, S: 5867, B: 743D, K: 699D, H: 271C

6522 עֲיָם *ʿᵃyām*, scorching (of wind), S: 5868, B: 744A, K: 137A, H: 43C

6523 עָיַן *ʿāyan*, [A] to keep an eye on, look at (with suspicion or jealousy), S: 5770†, B: 745A, K: 699D, H: 271C

6524 עַיִן[1] *ʿayin*[1], eye, sight; spring, fountain, S: 5869, B: 744A, K: 699D, H: 271C 1-3.

6525 עַיִן[2] *ʿayin*[2], variant: spring, fountain, S: 5872 to 5887†, B: 745A, K: 700B 3ff., H: 271D 4

6526 עַיִן[3] *ʿayin*[3], Ain, S: 5871, B: 745B, K: 699D, H: 271C

6527 עֵין גֶּדִי *ʿên gedî*, En Gedi, S: 5872, B: 745B, K: 700B a., H: 271D 4.c.

6528 עֵין גַּנִּים *ʿên gannîm*, En Gannim, S: 5873, B: 745C, K: 700C b, H: 271D 4.b

6529 עֵין־דֹּאר *ʿên-dōʾr*, עֵין־דּוֹר *ʿên-dôr*, Endor, S: 5874, B: 745C, K: 700C d., H: 271D 4.e

6530 עֵין הַקּוֹרֵא *ʿên haqqôrēʾ*, En Hakkore, S: 5875, B: 745B b., K: 700C j., H: 271D 4.k

6531 עֵין הַתַּנִּין *ʿên hattannîn*, variant: En Hattannin, see 6524 & 9490, S*, B: 745B d, K: 700C n., H: 271D 4.o

[F] Hitpael (hitpoel, hitpoal, hitpolel, hitpolal, hitpalel, hitpalal, hitpalpel, hitpalpal, hotpael, hotpaal) [G] Hiphil (hiphtil) [H] Hophal [I] Hishtaphel

6532 עֵין חַדָּה ʿên ḥaddâ, En Haddah, S: 5876, B: 745C, K: 700C e., H: 271D 4.f.

6533 עֵין חָצוֹר ʿên ḥāṣôr, En Hazor, S: 5877, B: 745C, K: 700C f., H: 271D 4.g

6534 עֵין חֲרֹד ʿên ḥ^{a}rōd, variant: En Harod, see 6524 & 3008, S: 5878, B: 745B a, K: 700C g., H: 271D 4.h

6535 עֵין מִשְׁפָּט ʿên mišpāṭ, En Mishpat, S: 5880, B: 745C, K: 700C h., H: 271D 4.i

6536 עֵין עֶגְלַיִם ʿên ʿeglayim, En Eglaim, S: 5882, B: 745C, K: 700C i., H: 271D 4.j.

6537 עֵין רֹגֵל ʿên rōgēl, En Rogel, S: 5883, B: 745B c, K: 700C k., H: 271D 4.l.

6538 עֵין רִמּוֹן ʿên rimmôn, En Rimmon, S: 5884, B: 745C, K: 700C l., H: 271D 4.m.

6539 עֵין שֶׁמֶשׁ ʿên šemeš, En Shemesh, S: 5885, B: 745D, K: 700C m., H: 271D 4.n.

6540 עֵין תַּפּוּחַ ʿên tappûaḥ, En Tappuah, S: 5887, B: 745D, K: 700C o., H: 271D 4.p.

6541 עֵינוֹן ʿênôn, variant: Enan, S: 2703†, B: 347C, K: 326A 4., H: 271D

6542 עֵינַיִם ʿênayim, Enaim, S: 5879, B: 745D, K: 700D, H: 271D

6543 עֵינָם ʿênām, Enam, S: 5879, B: 745D, K: 700D, H: 271D

6544 עֵינָן ʿênān, Enan, S: 5881, B: 745D, K: 700D, H: 271D

6545 עִיף ʿîp, [A] to be faint, be exhausted, S: 5774† & 5888†, B: 746A, K: 700D, H: 271D

6546 עָיֵף ʿāyēp, weary, faint; famished, parched, S: 5889, B: 746A, K: 701A, H: 271D

6547 ¹עֵיפָה ʿêpâ¹, darkness, S: 5890, B: 734A, K: 701A, H: 271D

6548 ²עֵיפָה ʿêpâ², Ephah, S: 5891, B: 734A 1., K: 701A, H: 271D

6549 ³עֵיפָה ʿêpâ³, Ephah, S: 5891, B: 734A 2. & 3., K: 701A, H: 271D

6550 עֵיפַי ʿêpay, Ephai, S: 5778†, B: 734A, K: 701B, H: 272A

6551 ¹עִיר ʿîr¹, city, town, village, S: 5892, B: 746B, K: 701B, H: 272A

6552 ²עִיר ʿîr², anguish, terror, wrath, S: 5892, B: 735C, K: 702A, H: 272A

6553 ³עִיר ʿîr³, Ir, S: 5893, B: 746D, K: 702A, H: 272A

6554 ⁴עִיר ʿîr⁴, (male) donkey (young and robust), S: 5895†, B: 747A, K: 702A, H: 272A

6555 עַיִר ʿayir, (male) donkey, S: 5895†, B: 747A, K: 702A, H: 272B

6556 עִיר הַהֶרֶס ʿîr haheres, variant: Ir Haheres, see 6551 & 2021 & 2239, S: 5892† + 2041†, B: 746B & 249A, K: 701D a., H: 272A a.

6557 עִיר הַחֶרֶס ʿîr haḥeres, variant: Ir Haheres, see 6551 & 2021 & 3064, S*, B*, K: 701D b., H: 272A b.

6558 עִיר הַמֶּלַח ʿîr hammelaḥ, variant: Ir Hammelak, see 6551 & 2021 & 4875, S: 5898, B: 746D, K: 701D c., H: 272A c.

6559 עִיר הַתְּמָרִים ʿîr hatt^{e}mārîm, variant: Ir Hattemarim, see 6551 & 2021 & 9468, S: 5899, B: 437C, K: 701D f., H: 272A f.

6560 עִיר נָחָשׁ ʿîr nāḥāš, Ir Nahash, S: 5904, B: 638B 3., K: 610B, H: 272A d.

6561 עִיר שֶׁמֶשׁ ʿîr šemeš, Ir Shemesh, S: 5905, B: 746D, K: 701D e., H: 272A e.

6562 עִירָא ʿîrāʾ, Ira, S: 5896, B: 747A, K: 702B, H: 272B

6563 עִירָד ʿîrād, Irad, S: 5897, B: 747A, K: 702B, H: 272B

6564 עִירוּ ʿîrû, Iru, S: 5900, B: 747A, K: 702B, H: 272B

6565 עִירִי ʿîrî, Iri, S: 5901, B: 747A, K: 702B, H: 272B

6566 עִירָם ʿîrām, Iram, S: 5902, B: 747A, K: 702B, H: 272B

6567 עֵירֹם ʿêrōm, naked; nakedness, S: 5903, B: 735D, K: 702B, H: 272B

6568 עַיִשׁ ʿayiš, constellation: the Bear *or* the Lion, S: 5906, B: 747A, K: 702C, H: 272D

6569 עַיַּת ʿayyat, Aiath, S: 5857, B: 743A 1., K: 699B, H: 272B

6570 עַכְבּוֹר ʿakbôr, Acbor, S: 5907, B: 747B, K: 702C, H: 272B

6571 עַכָּבִישׁ ʿakkābîš, spider, S: 5908, B: 747B, K: 702C, H: 272B

6572 עַכְבָּר ʿakbār, (jumping) rat, jerboa, S: 5909, B: 747B, K: 702D, H: 272B

6573 עַכּוֹ ʿakkô, Acco, S: 5910, B: 747B, K: 702D, H: 272C

6574 עָכוֹר ʿākôr, Achor, S: 5911, B: 747D, K: 702D, H: 272C

6575 עָכָן ʿākān, Achan, S: 5912, B: 747C, K: 703A, H: 272C

6576 עכס ʿākas, [D] to jingle, rattle (of ankle ornaments), S: 5913, B: 747C, K: 703A, H: 272C

6577 עֶכֶס ʿekes, bangle, ankle ornament, S: 5914, B: 747C, K: 703A, H: 272C

6578 עַכְסָה ʿaksâ, Acsah, S: 5915, B: 747C, K: 703A, H: 272C

6579 עכר ʿākar, [A] to bring trouble, make trouble; [C] to be troubled, be anguished, S: 5916, B: 747C, K: 703B, H: 272C

6580 עָכָר ʿākār, Achar, S: 5917, B: 747D, K: 703B, H: 272C

6581 עָכְרָן ʿokrān, Ocran, S: 5918, B: 747D, K: 703B, H: 272C

6582 עַכְשׁוּב ʿakšûb, (horned) viper, S: 5919, B: 747D, K: 703C, H: 272C

6583 ¹עַל ʿal¹, (the) Most High, S: 5920, B: 752B I., K: 703C, H: 272C

6584 ²עַל ʿal², on, upon, over, against; because of, according to, S: 5921, B: 752C II & III., K: 703C, H: 272C

6585 עֹל ʿōl, yoke, S: 5923, B: 760D, K: 705A, H: 273A

6586 עַל־כֵּן ʿal-kēn, variant: see 6584 & 4027, S: 5921† + 3651†, B: 752B & 487B, K: 708C, H: 274C

6587 עֻלָּא ʿullāʾ, Ulla, S: 5925, B: 748A, K: 705B, H: 273A

6588 עַלְבוֹן ʿalbôn, variant: Albon, see 50, S: 45†, B: 3D, K: 705B, H: 273B

6589 עִלֵּג ʿillēg, speaking inarticulately; (pl., as noun) stammerers, S: 5926, B: 748A, K: 705B, H: 273B

6590 עָלָה ʿālâ, [A] to go up, ascend, rise; [C] to be lifted up, withdraw, be exalted; [G] to take up, set up, offer a sacrifice; [H] to be offered up, be carried away, be recorded; [F] to raise oneself up, S: 5927, B: 748A, K: 705B, H: 273B

6591 עָלֶה ʿāleh, leaves, foliage, S: 5929, B: 750A, K: 706D, H: 273D

6592 ¹עֹלָה ʿōlâ¹, burnt offering, S: 5930, B: 750B, K: 706D, H: 273D

6593 ²עֹלָה ʿōlâ², variant: see 6406, S: 5766†, B: 751A, K: 707A, H: 273D

6594 ¹עַלְוָה ʿalwâ¹, evil, wickedness, S: 5932, B: 759B, K: 707A, H: 274A

6595 ²עַלְוָה ʿalwâ², Alvah, S: 5933, B: 759B, K: 707A, H: 274A

6596 עֲלוּמִים ʿ^{a}lûmîm, (abst.pl.) youthfulness, (the vigor of) youth, S: 5934†, B: 761C, K: 707B, H: 274A

6597 עַלְוָן ʿalwān, Alvan, S: 5935, B: 759B, K: 707B, H: 274A

6598 עֲלוּקָה ʿ^{a}lûqâ, leech, S: 5936, B: 763C, K: 707B, H: 274A

6599 עָלוֹת ʿālôt, Aloth, S: 1175†, B: 128C, K: 139B, H: 44B

6600 עלז ʿālaz, [A] to rejoice, be jubilant, S: 5937, B: 759C, K: 707B, H: 274A

6601 עָלֵז ʿālēz, reveling, exultant; (as noun) reveler, S: 5938, B: 759C, K: 707C, H: 274A

6602 עֲלָטָה ʿ^{a}lāṭâ, darkness, dusk, S: 5939, B: 759C, K: 707C, H: 274A

6603 ¹עֵלִי ʿēlî¹, Eli, S: 5941, B: 750A, K: 707C, H: 274A

6604 ²עֵלִי ʿēlî², Most High, S: 5942†, B: 753D II 1d, K: 703C, H: 272C

6605 עֱלִי ʿ^{e}lî, pestle (of a mortar), S: 5940, B: 750A, K: 707C, H: 274A

6606 עִלִּי ʿillî, upper, S: 5942, B: 751A, K: 707C, H: 274A

6607 עַלְיָה ʿalyâ, variant: Aliah, see 6595, S: 5933, B: 759B, K: 707C, H: 274A

6608 עֲלִיָּה ʿ^{a}liyyâ, upper room, upper parts, S: 5944, B: 751A, K: 707D, H: 274A

6609 ¹עֶלְיוֹן ʿelyôn¹, upper, the Upper, S: 5945, B: 751B, K: 707D, H: 274A 1.

6610 ²עֶלְיוֹן ʿelyôn², (the) Most High, S: 5945, B: 751B, K: 707D, H: 274A 2.

6611 עַלִּיז ʿallîz, rejoicing, exulting; reveling, wild, S: 5947, B: 759C, K: 708B, H: 274B

6612 עֲלִיל ʿ^{a}lîl, furnace, S: 5948, B: 760D, K: 708B, H: 274B

6613 עֲלִילָה ʿ^{a}lîlâ, what is done, deed, action, S: 5949, B: 760A, K: 708B, H: 274B

6614 עֲלִילִיָּה ʿ^{a}lîliyyâ, deed, S: 5950, B: 760B, K: 708C, H: 274B

6615 עַלְיָן ʿalyān, variant: Alian, see 6597, S: 5935, B: 759B, K: 708C, H: 274B

6616 עָלִיץ ʿālîṣ, variant: haughty, insolent, S*, B: 792B, K: 708C, H: 274B

6617 עֲלִיצֻת ʿ^{a}lîṣut, haughtiness, presumption, S: 5951, B: 763C, K: 708C, H: 274B

6618 ¹עלל ʿālal¹, [D] to deal with; to glean, go over a second time; [E] to be dealt with (in a way that causes suffering); [F] to deal harshly, abuse, mistreat; to take part in (wickedness), S: 5953, B: 759D, K: 708D, H: 274C

6619 [2]עָלַל *ʿālal*[2], [D] to thrust (in), S: 5953, B: 760C, K: 709A, H: 274C

6620 [3]עָלַל *ʿālal*[3], [D] to act or play the child; (as noun) youths, S: 5953, B: 760C, K: 708D, H: 274C

6621 [4]עָלַל *ʿālal*[4], variant: [D] to glean, S: 5953, B: 760A, K: 708D, H: 274C

6622 עֹלֵלוֹת *ʿōlēlôt*, gleanings, S: 5955†, B: 760A, K: 709A, H: 274C

6623 עָלַם *ʿālam*, [B] to be in secret; [C] to be concealed, be hidden, be unaware; [G] to hide, shut off, conceal; [F] to hide oneself from, ignore, S: 5956, B: 761A, K: 709A, H: 274D

6624 עֶלֶם *ʿelem*, boy, young man, S: 5958, B: 761C, K: 709B, H: 274D

6625 עַלְמָה *ʿalmâ*, girl, young woman, (in certain contexts) virgin, S: 5959, B: 761C, K: 709C, H: 274D

6626 עַלְמוֹן *ʿalmôn*, Almon, S: 5960, B: 761B, K: 709C, H: 274D

6627 עַלְמֹן דִּבְלָתָיְמָה *ʿalmôn diblātayim*, Almon Diblathaim, S: 5963†, B: 761B, K: 709C, H: 274D & 66D

6628 עֲלָמוֹת *ʿalāmôt*, alamoth (t.t. in the Psalms), S: 5961, B: 761C, K: 709C, H: 274C

6629 עַל־מוּת *ʿal-mût*, variant: Al-Muth, see 6584 & 4637, S: 5921† + 4192†, B*, K: 709C, H: 274D

6630 [1]עָלֶמֶת *ʿālemet*[1], Alemeth, S: 5964, B: 761B 2., K: 709D, H: 275A

6631 [2]עָלֶמֶת *ʿālemet*[2], Alemeth, S: 5964, B: 761B 1., K: 709D, H: 275A

6632 עָלַס *ʿālas*, [A] to enjoy; [C] to appear glad; [F] to enjoy one another, S: 5965, B: 763A, K: 709D, H: 275A

6633 עָלַע *ʿālaʿ*, [D] to drink, feast on, S: 5966, B: 763A, K: 709D, H: 275A

6634 עָלַף *ʿālap*, [E] to faint; to be withered; be decorated, covered; [F] to disguise oneself; to grow faint, S: 5968, B: 763B, K: 709D, H: 275A

6635 עֻלְפֶּה *ʿulpeh*, variant: see 6634, S: 5969, B: 763B, K: 710A, H: 275A

6636 עָלַץ *ʿālaṣ*, [A] to rejoice, be jubilant, S: 5970, B: 763B, K: 710A, H: 275A

6637 עֹלָתָה *ʿōlātâ*, injustice, S: 5766†, B: 732C 2, K: 710B, H: 275A

6638 [1]עַם *ʿam*[1], father's relatives, one's people, S: 5971, B: 769B, K: 710B, H: 275A

6639 [2]עַם *ʿam*[2], people, nation, countrymen; army, troop, S: 5971, B: 766B, K: 710C, H: 275B

6640 עִם *ʿim*, with, among; to, toward, S: 5973, B: 767A, K: 711B, H: 275B

6641 עָמַד *ʿāmad*, [A] to stand, stand up, stand still; [G] to cause to stand, present; to appoint, assign; [H] to be presented, be caused to stand, S: 5975, B: 763C, K: 712A, H: 275C

6642 עֹמֶד *ʿōmed*, standing-place (a position, station, or post), S: 5977, B: 765A, K: 713C, H: 276A

6643 עִמָּד *ʿimmād*, with, S: 5978, B: 767A, K: 713D, H: 276A

6644 עֶמְדָּה *ʿemdâ*, place to stand, protection, S: 5979, B: 765A, K: 713D, H: 276A

6645 [1]עֻמָּה *ʿummâ*[1], close by; alongside; adjoining, S: 5980, B: 769C, K: 713D, H: 276A

6646 [2]עֻמָּה *ʿummâ*[2], Ummah, S: 5981, B: 769D, K: 714A, H: 276B

6647 עַמּוּד *ʿammûd*, pillar, post, column, S: 5982, B: 765A, K: 714A, H: 276B

6648 עַמּוֹן *ʿammôn*, Ammonite; Ammon, S: 5983, B: 769D, K: 714B, H: 276B

6649 עַמּוֹנִי *ʿammônî*, Ammonite, from Ammon, S: 5984 & 5985†, B: 770A, K: 714C, H: 276B

6650 עָמוֹס *ʿāmôs*, Amos, S: 5986, B: 770C, K: 714C, H: 276B

6651 עָמוֹק *ʿāmôq*, Amok, S: 5987, B: 771B, K: 714D, H: 276B

6652 עַמִּי *ʿammî*, variant: Ammi, S: 3818†, B: 520D, K: 468D, H: 276B

6653 עַמִּיאֵל *ʿammîʾēl*, Ammiel, S: 5988, B: 770A, K: 714D, H: 276B

6654 עַמִּיהוּד *ʿammîhûd*, Ammihud, S: 5989, B: 770A, K: 714D, H: 276B

6655 עַמִּיזָבָד *ʿammîzābād*, Ammizabad, S: 5990, B: 770B, K: 714D, H: 276C

6656 עַמִּיחוּר *ʿammîḥûr*, variant: Ammihur, see 6654, S: 5991, B: 770A, K: 714D, H: 276C

6657 עַמִּינָדָב *ʿammînādāb*, Amminadab, S: 5992, B: 770B, K: 714D, H: 276C

6658 עָמִיר *ʿāmîr*, (newly) cut grain, S: 5995, B: 771C, K: 715A, H: 276C

6659 עַמִּישַׁדָּי *ʿammîšaddāy*, Ammishaddai, S: 5996, B: 770B, K: 715A, H: 276C

6660 עָמִית *ʿāmît*, neighbor, countryman, associate (one in close, united relation), S: 5997, B: 765C, K: 715A, H: 276C

6661 עָמַל *ʿāmal*, [A] to labor, toil, pour forth effort, S: 5998, B: 765C, K: 715A, H: 276C

6662 [1]עָמָל *ʿāmāl*[1], trouble, work, labor, toil, S: 5999, B: 765D, K: 715B, H: 276C

6663 [2]עָמָל *ʿāmāl*[2], Amal, S: 6000, B: 765D, K: 715C, H: 276C

6664 [1]עָמֵל *ʿāmēl*[1], misery; workman, laborer, S: 6001, B: 766A, K: 715C, H: 276C 1.

6665 [2]עָמֵל *ʿāmēl*[2], toiling, laboring, S: 6001, B: 766A, K: 715C, H: 276C 2.

6666 עַמְלָץ *ʿamlāṣ*, variant: shark, S*, B: 766B & 510A & 850D, K: 715C, H: 275B & 167B & 305D

6667 עֲמָלֵק *ʿamālēq*, Amalek; Amalekite, S: 6002, B: 766A, K: 715C, H: 276C

6668 עֲמָלֵקִי *ʿamālēqî*, Amalekite, S: 6003, B: 766A, K: 715D, H: 276C

6669 [1]עָמַם *ʿāmam*[1], [A] to be rival to, be equal to, S: 6004, B: 770B, K: 715D, H: 276C

6670 [2]עָמַם *ʿāmam*[2], [A] to grow dark; [H] to lose luster, grow dark, S: 6004, B: 770B, K: 715D, H: 276D

6671 עַמֹּנָה *ʿammōnâ*, variant: see 4112, S: 3726†, B: 499A, K: 714C, H: 163D

6672 עִמָּנוּ אֵל *ʿimmānû ʾēl*, Immanuel, S: 6005, B: 769B, K: 716A, H: 276D

6673 עָמַס *ʿāmas*, [A] to load a burden, carry a burden; [B] to be burdensome, be upheld; [G] to lay a burden upon, S: 6006, B: 770C, K: 716A, H: 276D

6674 עֲמַסְיָה *ʿamasyâ*, Amasiah, S: 6007, B: 770C, K: 716B, H: 276D

6675 עַמְעָד *ʿamʿād*, Amad, S: 6008, B: 770C, K: 716B, H: 276D

6676 עָמַק *ʿāmaq*, [A] to be profound; [G] to make deep (in various senses), S: 6009, B: 770D, K: 716B, H: 276D

6677 עֵמֶק *ʿēmeq*, valley; (low-lying) plain, S: 6010, B: 770D, K: 716C, H: 277A

6678 עָמֹק *ʿāmōq*, deep; profound, S: 6013, B: 771B, K: 717A, H: 277A

6679 עֹמֶק *ʿōmeq*, depth, S: 6011, B: 771B, K: 717A, H: 277A

6680 עָמֵק *ʿāmēq*, obscure, unintelligible, S: 6012, B: 771B, K: 717A, H: 277A

6681 עֵמֶק קְצִיץ *ʿēmeq qeṣîṣ*, Emek Keziz, S: 7104†, B: 894A, K: 716C, H: 322A

6682 [1]עָמַר *ʿāmar*[1], [D] to bind sheaves (of newly cut grain), S: 6014, B: 771C, K: 717A, H: 277A

6683 [2]עָמַר *ʿāmar*[2], [F] to treat brutally, deal tyrannically with, S: 6014, B: 771C, K: 717B, H: 277B

6684 [1]עֹמֶר *ʿōmer*[1], sheaf of grain, S: 6016, B: 771B, K: 717B, H: 277B

6685 [2]עֹמֶר *ʿōmer*[2], omer (a measure), S: 6016, B: 771C, K: 717B, H: 277B

6686 עֲמֹרָה *ʿamōrâ*, Gomorrah, S: 6017, B: 771C, K: 717C, H: 277B

6687 עָמְרִי *ʿomrî*, Omri, S: 6018, B: 771D, K: 717C, H: 277B

6688 עַמְרָם *ʿamrām*, Amram, S: 6019, B: 771D, K: 717C, H: 277B

6689 עַמְרָמִי *ʿamrāmî*, Amramite, S: 6020, B: 771D, K: 717C, H: 277B

6690 עֲמָשָׂא *ʿamāśāʾ*, Amasa, S: 6021, B: 771D, K: 717C, H: 277B

6691 עֲמָשַׂי *ʿamāśay*, Amasai, S: 6022, B: 772A, K: 717D, H: 277B

6692 עֲמַשְׁסַי *ʿamašsay*, Amashai, S: 6023, B: 772A, K: 717D, H: 277B

6693 עֲנָב *ʿanāb*, Anab, S: 6024, B: 772B, K: 717D, H: 277B

6694 עֵנָב *ʿēnāb*, cluster of grapes, S: 6025, B: 772A, K: 717D, H: 277B

6695 עָנַג *ʿānag*, [E] to be delicate; [F] to delight oneself, enjoy, to mock, S: 6026, B: 772B, K: 718A, H: 277C

6696 עֹנֶג *ʿōneg*, delight, luxury, enjoyment, S: 6027, B: 772B, K: 718B, H: 277C

6697 עָנֹג *ʿānōg*, sensitive, delicate, S: 6028, B: 772B, K: 718B, H: 277C

6698 עָנַד *ʿānad*, [A] to bind around, bind upon, S: 6029, B: 772C, K: 718B, H: 277C

6699 [1]עָנָה *ʿānâ*[1], [A] to answer, reply, respond; [C] to be answered, S: 6030, B: 772C, K: 718B, H: 277C

6700 [2]עָנָה *ʿānâ*[2], [A] to be afflicted; to stoop down; [C] to be afflicted, humbled, oppressed; [D] to afflict, oppress, subdue, humble, mistreat; [E] to be afflicted, deny oneself; [G] to afflict another, oppress; [F] to humble oneself, S: 6031, B: 776A, K: 719A, H: 277D

6701 [3]עָנָה *ʿānâ*[3], [A] to be concerned about, be worried about; [G] to keep occupied, keep oneself busy, S: 6031, B: 775D, K: 719D, H: 278A

6702 עָנָה⁴ *ʿānâ⁴*, [A] to sing; [D] to sing to *or* sing about, S: 6030, B: 777A, K: 719D, H: 278B

6703 עֹנָה *ʿōnâ*, marital rights (of intercourse), S: 5772†, B: 773B, K: 720A, H: 278B

6704 עֲנָה *ʿᵃnâ*, Anah, S: 6034, B: 777B, K: 720A, H: 278B

6705 עָנָו *ʿānāw*, humble, afflicted, poor, oppressed, S: 6035, B: 776C, K: 720B, H: 278B

6706 עֻנּוֹ *ʿunnô*, variant: Unno, see 6716, S: 6042†, B: 777D, K: 720B, H: 278B

6707 עָנוּב *ʿānûb*, Anub, S: 6036, B: 772B, K: 720B, H: 278B

6708 עֲנָוָה *ʿᵃnāwâ*, humility, S: 6038, B: 776C, K: 720C, H: 278B

6709 עַנְוָה *ʿanwâ*, variant: humility, S: 6037, B: 776C, K: 720C, H: 278C

6710 עֲנוֹק *ʿᵃnôq*, Anak, S: 6061†, B: 778C, K: 720C, H: 278C

6711 עֲנוּשִׁים *ʿᵃnûšîm*, (punishing) fines, S: 6064†, B: 778D, K: 720C, H: 278C

6712 עֲנוֹת *ʿᵃnôt*, variant: Anoth, see 1116, S: 1042†, B: 779A & 112B, K: 720C, H: 278C

6713 עֱנוּת *ʿᵉnût*, suffering, affliction, S: 6039, B: 776D, K: 720C, H: 278C

6714 עָנִי *ʿānî*, needy, poor, afflicted, oppressed, S: 6041, B: 776D, K: 720C, H: 278C

6715 עֳנִי *ʿᵒnî*, affliction, suffering, misery, S: 6040, B: 777A, K: 721A, H: 278C

6716 עֻנִּי *ʿunnî*, Unni, S: 6042, B: 777D, K: 721A, H: 278C

6717 עֲנָיָה *ʿᵃnāyâ*, Anaiah, S: 6043, B: 777D, K: 721A, H: 278C

6718 עָנָיו *ʿānāyw*, variant: see 6705, S: 6035, B: 776C 4, K: 721B, H: 278C

6719 עָנִים *ʿānîm*, Anim, S: 6044, B: 745D, K: 721B, H: 278C

6720 עֵנִים *ʿēnîm*, variant: see 3612, S: 3283†, B: 419A, K: 389C, H: 138C

6721 עִנְיָן *ʿinyān*, task, work, labor; misfortune, cares, troubles, S: 6045, B: 775D, K: 721B, H: 278C

6722 עָנֵם *ʿānēm*, Anem, S: 6046, B: 745C 2, K: 721B, H: 278C

6723 עֲנָמִים *ʿᵃnāmîm*, Anamite, S: 6047, B: 777D, K: 721B, H: 278C

6724 עֲנַמֶּלֶךְ *ʿᵃnammelek*, Anammelech (pagan god), S: 6048, B: 777D, K: 721B, H: 278C

6725 עָנַן¹ *ʿānan¹*, [D] to bring clouds, S: 6049, B: 778A, K: 721C, H: 278C

6726 עָנַן² *ʿānan²*, [D] to practice sorcery, practice divination, cast spells, S: 6049, B: 778A, K: 721C, H: 278C

6727 עָנָן¹ *ʿānān¹*, cloud, S: 6051, B: 777D, K: 721C, H: 278D

6728 עָנָן² *ʿānān²*, Anan, S: 6052, B: 778B, K: 721D, H: 278D

6729 עֲנָנָה *ʿᵃnānâ*, cloud, S: 6053, B: 778A, K: 721D, H: 278D

6730 עֲנָנִי *ʿᵃnānî*, Anani, S: 6054, B: 778B, K: 722A, H: 278D

6731 עֲנָנְיָהּ¹ *ʿᵃnānᵉyâ¹*, Ananiah, S: 6055, B: 778B 1., K: 722A, H: 278D

6732 עֲנָנְיָה² *ʿᵃnānᵉyâ²*, Ananiah, S: 6055, B: 778B, K: 722A, H: 278D

6733 עָנָף *ʿānāp*, branches, S: 6057, B: 778C, K: 722A, H: 278D

6734 עָנֵף *ʿānēp*, full of branches, S: 6058, B: 778C, K: 722A, H: 278D

6735 עָנַק *ʿānaq*, [A] to put on (as a necklace); [G] to supply (as putting on one's neck), S: 6059, B: 778D, K: 722A, H: 278D

6736 עֲנָק¹ *ʿᵃnāq¹*, necklace chain, S: 6060†, B: 778C, K: 722B, H: 279A

6737 עֲנָק² *ʿᵃnāq²*, Anak, Anakites (with 1201), S: 6062†, B: 778C, K: 722B, H: 279A

6738 עָנֵר¹ *ʿānēr¹*, Aner, S: 6063, B: 778D, K: 722C, H: 279A

6739 עָנֵר² *ʿānēr²*, Aner, S: 6063, B: 778D, K: 722C, H: 279A

6740 עָנַשׁ *ʿānaš*, [A] to levy a fine (as a punishment or recompense); [C] to be fined, be punished, S: 6064, B: 778D, K: 722C, H: 279A

6741 עֹנֶשׁ *ʿōneš*, levy, penalty, fine, S: 6066, B: 778D, K: 722C, H: 279A

6742 עֲנָת *ʿᵃnāt*, Anath, S: 6067, B: 779A, K: 722C, H: 279A

6743 עֲנָתוֹת¹ *ʿᵃnātôt¹*, Anathoth, S: 6068, B: 779A 1., K: 722D, H: 279A

6744 עֲנָתוֹת² *ʿᵃnātôt²*, Anathoth, S: 6068, B: 779A, K: 722D, H: 279A

6745 עַנְּתֹתִי *ʿannᵉtōtî*, Anathothite, from Anathoth, S: 6069, B: 779A, K: 722D, H: 279A

6746 עַנְתֹתִיָּה *ʿantōtiyyâ*, Anthothijah, S: 6070, B: 779A, K: 722D, H: 279A

6747 עָסִיס *ʿāsîs*, new wine; nectar, S: 6071, B: 779B, K: 723A, H: 279A

6748 עָסַס *ʿāsas*, [A] to trample down, S: 6072, B: 779A, K: 723A, H: 279A

6749 עָעַר *ʿāʿar*, variant: see 6424, S: 5782†, B: 735A, K: 723A, H: 279B

6750 עֳפָאִים *ʿᵒpāʾyim*, variant: foliage, S*, B: 779B, K: 723A, H: 279B

6751 עֳפִי *ʿᵒpî*, branch, S: 6073†, B: 779B, K: 723A, H: 279B

6752 עָפַל¹ *ʿāpal¹*, [E] to be puffed up, be swelled, S: 6075, B: 779B, K: 723B, H: 279B

6753 עָפַל² *ʿāpal²*, [G] to have presumption, to have the audacity to, S: 6075, B: 779C, K: 723B, H: 279B

6754 עֹפֶל¹ *ʿōpel¹*, tumor, hemorrhoid, abscess, S: 6076, B: 779B, K: 723B, H: 279B

6755 עֹפֶל² *ʿōpel²*, hill; (as a proper name) the hill of Ophel, S: 6077, B: 779B, K: 723B, H: 279B

6756 עָפְנִי *ʿopnî*, Ophni, S: 6078, B: 779C, K: 723C, H: 279B

6757 עַפְעַפַּיִם *ʿapʿappayim*, flashing rays (of dawn); glances or flitting of eyes or eyelids, S: 6079†, B: 733D, K: 723C, H: 279B

6758 עָפַף *ʿāpap*, [D] to brandish, cause to fly to and fro, S: 5774†, B: 733B, K: 723C, H: 279B

6759 עָפַר *ʿāpar*, [D] to shower (with dust or dirt), S: 6080, B: 780A, K: 723C, H: 279B

6760 עָפָר *ʿāpār*, dust, earth, soil, S: 6083, B: 779C, K: 723D, H: 279B

6761 עֵפֶר *ʿēper*, Epher, S: 6081, B: 780B, K: 724B, H: 279C

6762 עֹפֶר *ʿōper*, fawn (of a deer or gazelle), S: 6082, B: 780A, K: 724B, H: 279C

6763 עָפְרָה¹ *ʿoprâ¹*, Ophrah, S: 6084, B: 780B 2., K: 724B, H: 279C

6764 עָפְרָה² *ʿoprâ²*, Ophrah, S: 6084, B: 780B, K: 724C, H: 279C

6765 עַפְרָה *ʿaprâ*, variant: Ophrah, S: 1036†, B: 112A, K: 724C, H: 279C

6766 עֶפְרוֹן¹ *ʿeprôn¹*, Ephron, S: 6085, B: 780B 1., K: 724C, H: 279C

6767 עֶפְרוֹן² *ʿeprôn²*, Ephron, S: 6085, B: 780B 2. & 3., K: 724C, H: 279C

6768 עֶפְרַיִן *ʿeprayin*, variant: Ephrayin, see 6761, S: 6085†, B: 780B, K: 724C, H: 279C

6769 עֹפֶרֶת *ʿōperet*, lead (a mineral), S: 5777, B: 780B, K: 724D, H: 279C

6770 עֵץ *ʿēṣ*, tree, wood, wooden things (timber, lumber, gallows), S: 6086, B: 781C, K: 724D, H: 279C

6771 עָצַב¹ *ʿāṣab¹*, [D] to shape; [G] to make an image (of the Queen of Heaven), S: 6087, B: 781A, K: 725C, H: 279D

6772 עָצַב² *ʿāṣab²*, [A] to interfere with; [B] to be distressed; [C] to be grieved, be distressed; [D] to grieve; [G] to grieve; [F] to be filled with grief, be filled with pain, S: 6087, B: 780C, K: 725D, H: 279D

6773 עָצָב *ʿāṣāb*, idol, image, S: 6091, B: 781B, K: 726A, H: 280A

6774 עַצָּב *ʿaṣṣāb*, (hard) worker, toiler, S: 6092†, B: 780D, K: 726A, H: 280A

6775 עֶצֶב¹ *ʿeṣeb¹*, pot, vessel, S: 6089, B: 781A, K: 726A, H: 280A

6776 עֶצֶב² *ʿeṣeb²*, pain, toil, hard work, S: 6089, B: 780D, K: 726B, H: 280A

6777 עֹצֶב¹ *ʿōṣeb¹*, idol, S: 6090, B: 781B, K: 726B, H: 280A

6778 עֹצֶב² *ʿōṣeb²*, pain, toil, S: 6090, B: 780D, K: 726B, H: 280A

6779 עִצָּבוֹן *ʿiṣṣābôn*, pain, hardship, distress, S: 6093, B: 781A, K: 726B, H: 280B

6780 עַצֶּבֶת *ʿaṣṣebet*, pain, sorrow, grief, S: 6094, B: 781A, K: 726B, H: 280B

6781 עָצָה *ʿāṣâ*, [A] to wink (the eye), S: 6095, B: 781B, K: 726C, H: 280B

6782 עָצֶה *ʿāṣeh*, backbone, tailbone, S: 6096, B: 782B, K: 726C, H: 280B

6783 עֵצָה¹ *ʿēṣâ¹*, advice, counsel, plan, purpose, scheme, S: 6098, B: 420A, K: 726C, H: 280B

6784 עֵצָה² *ʿēṣâ²*, variant: revolt, resistance, disobedience, S: 6098†, B: 420A, K: 726D, H: 280B

6785 עֵצָה³ *ʿēṣâ³*, (coll) wood, S: 6097, B: 782A, K: 727A, H: 280B

6786 עָצוּם *ʿāṣûm*, strong, mighty, powerful, S: 6099, B: 783A, K: 727A, H: 280B

6787 עֶצְיוֹן גֶּבֶר *ʿeṣyôn geber*, Ezion Geber, S: 6100, B: 782B, K: 727B, H: 280C

6788 עָצַל *ʿāṣal*, [C] to hesitate, be sluggish, be slow, S: 6101, B: 782B, K: 727B, H: 280C

6789 עָצֵל *ʿāṣēl*, sluggish, slow, lazy, S: 6102, B: 782B, K: 727B, H: 280C

6790 עַצְלָה *ʿaṣlâ*, laziness, slowness, sluggishness, S: 6103, B: 782B, K: 727C, H: 280C

6791 עַצְלוּת *ʿaṣlût*, idleness, sluggishness, laziness, S: 6104, B: 782C, K: 727C, H: 280C

6792 עֲצַלְתַּיִם *ʿaṣaltayim*, extreme laziness, indolence, S: 6103†, B: 782B, K: 727C, H: 280C

6793 [1]עָצַם *ʿāṣam*[1], [A] to be vast, powerful, numerous; [D] to crush his bone; [G] to make numerous, make powerful, make vast, S: 6105, B: 782C, K: 727C, H: 280C

6794 [2]עָצַם *ʿāṣam*[2], [A] to close (the eyes); [D] to tightly shut (the eyes), S: 6105, B: 783B, K: 727D, H: 280C

6795 [1]עֶצֶם *ʿeṣem*[1], bone, bones; body, limb, blood; (as adv.) that very (day), S: 6106, B: 782C, K: 728A, H: 280D

6796 [2]עֶצֶם *ʿeṣem*[2], Ezem, S: 6107, B: 783A, K: 728B, H: 280D

6797 [1]עֹצֶם *ʿōṣem*[1], might, strength, S: 6108, B: 782C, K: 728B, H: 280D

6798 [2]עֹצֶם *ʿōṣem*[2], framework (of bones of the human body), S: 6108, B: 782C, K: 728C, H: 280D

6799 עַצְמָה *ʿaṣmâ*, variant: evil deeds; severe suffering, S: 6106†, B: 782C, K: 728C, H: 280D

6800 עָצְמָה *ʿoṣmâ*, power, potency, might, S: 6109, B: 782C, K: 728C, H: 280D

6801 עַצְמוֹן *ʿaṣmôn*, Azmon, S: 6111, B: 783B, K: 728C, H: 281A

6802 עֲצֻמוֹת *ʿaṣumôt*, defensive arguments, strong words, S: 6110†, B: 783B, K: 728C, H: 281A

6803 עֵצֶן *ʿēṣen*, variant: Ezen, see 2851, S*, B*, K: 728D, H: 281A

6804 עֶצְנִי *ʿeṣnî*, variant: Eznite, see 2851, S: , B*, K: 728D, H: 281A

6805 עָצַץ *ʿāṣaṣ*, variant: [A] to fix one's eyes on, S: 3289†, B: 419C, K: 728D, H: 138C

6806 עָצַר *ʿāṣar*, [A] to refrain, hold back, restrain; [B] to be enslaved, be constrained; [C] to be stopped, be detained, S: 6113†, B: 783C, K: 728D, H: 281A

6807 עֶצֶר *ʿeṣer*, restraint, oppression, S: 6114, B: 783D, K: 729B, H: 281B

6808 עֹצֶר *ʿōṣer*, oppression; barrenness, S: 6115, B: 783D, K: 729B, H: 281B

6809 עֲצָרָה *ʿaṣārâ*, assembly, S: 6116, B: 783D, K: 729C, H: 281B

6810 עָקַב *ʿāqab*, [A] to deceive; to grasp at the heel; [D] to hold the heel, to hold back, S: 6117, B: 784B, K: 729C, H: 281B

6811 [1]עָקֵב *ʿāqēb*[1], heel, hoof; footstep, footprint, S: 6119, B: 784A, K: 729D, H: 281B

6812 [2]עָקֵב *ʿāqēb*[2], deceiver, S: 6120, B: 784C, K: 729D, H*

6813 עֵקֶב *ʿēqeb*, (as c.) because; (as noun) a reward; unto the end, S: 6118, B: 784C, K: 729D, H: 281C

6814 [1]עָקֹב *ʿāqōb*[1], footprint, S: 6121, B: 784C 2, K: 730A, H*

6815 [2]עָקֹב *ʿāqōb*[2], deceitful; rough, bumpy, S: 6121, B: 784C, K: 730A, H: 281C

6816 עֹקֶב *ʿōqeb*, variant: insidiousness, S*, B: 780D, K: 730A, H: 280A

6817 עָקְבָה *ʿoqbâ*, deceptiveness, cunning, craftiness, S: 6122†, B: 784C, K: 730A, H: 281C

6818 עָקַד *ʿāqad*, [A] to bind (feet), S: 6123, B: 785B, K: 730A, H: 281C

6819 עָקֹד *ʿāqōd*, streaked, striped, S: 6124, B: 785B, K: 730B, H: 281C

6820 עֵקֶד *ʿēqed*, variant: Eked, see 1118, S: 1044†, B: 112C, K: 730B, H: 39C

6821 עָקָה *ʿāqâ*, pressure, S: 6125, B: 734B, K: 730B, H: 281C

6822 עַקּוּב *ʿaqqûb*, Akkub, S: 6126, B: 784D, K: 730B, H: 281C

6823 עָקַל *ʿāqal*, [E] to be perverted, be distorted, be crooked, S: 6127, B: 785B, K: 730C, H: 281C

6824 עֲקַלְקַל *ʿaqalqāl*, crooked, winding, S: 6128, B: 785C, K: 730C, H: 281C

6825 עֲקַלָּתוֹן *ʿaqallātôn*, coiling (serpent), S: 6129, B: 785C, K: 730C, H: 281C

6826 עֲקָן *ʿaqān*, Akan, S: 6130†, B: 785C, K: 730C, H: 281C

6827 [1]עָקַר *ʿāqar*[1], [A] to root up; [C] to be uprooted, S: 6131, B: 785C, K: 730D, H: 281D

6828 [2]עָקַר *ʿāqar*[2], [D] to hamstring, S: 6131, B: 785C, K: 730D, H: 281D

6829 עָקָר *ʿāqār*, barren, sterile, without children, S: 6135, B: 785D, K: 730D, H: 281D

6830 [1]עֵקֶר *ʿēqer*[1], offspring, S: 6133, B: 785C, K: 731A, H: 281D

6831 [2]עֵקֶר *ʿēqer*[2], Eker, S: 6134, B: 785D, K: 731A, H: 281D

6832 עַקְרָב *ʿaqrāb*, scorpion, S: 6137, B: 785D, K: 731A, H: 281D

6833 עֶקְרוֹן *ʿeqrôn*, Ekron, S: 6138, B: 785D, K: 731A, H: 281D

6834 עֶקְרוֹנִי *ʿeqrônî*, Ekronite, of Ekron, S: 6139, B: 785D, K: 731B, H: 281D

6835 עָקַשׁ *ʿāqaš*, [C] to be perverse, be crooked; [D] to take crooked paths; to distort; [G] to pronounce guilty, S: 6140, B: 786A, K: 731B, H: 281D

6836 [1]עִקֵּשׁ *ʿiqqēš*[1], perverse, crooked, warped, S: 6141, B: 786A, K: 731C, H: 282A

6837 [2]עִקֵּשׁ *ʿiqqēš*[2], Ikkesh, S: 6142, B: 786A, K: 731C, H: 282A

6838 עִקְּשׁוּת *ʿiqqᵉšût*, perversion, corruption, crookedness, S: 6143, B: 786A, K: 731C, H: 282A

6839 [1]עָר *ʿār*[1], enemy, adversary, S: 6145, B: 786B, K: 731C, H: 282A

6840 [2]עָר *ʿār*[2], Ar, S: 6144, B: 786A, K: 731D, H: 282A

6841 עֵר *ʿēr*, Er, S: 6147, B: 735C, K: 731D, H: 282A

6842 [1]עָרַב *ʿārab*[1], [A] to put up a security, make a guarantee, give a pledge; [F] to make a bargain, make a wager, S: 6148, B: 786C, K: 731D, H: 282A

6843 [2]עָרַב *ʿārab*[2], [F] to mingle, join in with, share with, S: 6148, B: 786C, K: 732A, H: 282B

6844 [3]עָרַב *ʿārab*[3], [A] to be pleasing, be pleasant, be acceptable, S: 6149†, B: 787A, K: 732B, H: 282B

6845 [4]עָרַב *ʿārab*[4], [A] to become evening; (opposite of joy) turn to gloom; [G] to do something in the evening, S: 6150, B: 788A, K: 732B, H: 282B

6846 [1]עֶרֶב *ʿereb*[1], variant: see 6850, S: 6152†, B: 787B, K: 732C, H: 282B

6847 [2]עֶרֶב *ʿereb*[2], evening, twilight, dusk, the fading of the day, S: 6153, B: 787D, K: 732C, H: 282B

6848 [3]עֶרֶב *ʿereb*[3], variant: see 6851, S: 6154, B: 786B, K: 733A, H: 282B

6849 [1]עֵרֶב *ʿēreb*[1], knitted material, S: 6154, B: 786C, K: 733A, H: 282B

6850 [2]עֵרֶב *ʿēreb*[2], foreign people, S: 6154, B: 786B, K: 733A, H: 282C

6851 [1]עֲרָב *ʿarab*[1], Arabia, Arab, S: 6152, B: 787A, K: 733A, H: 282C

6852 [2]עֲרָב *ʿarab*[2], variant: see 6851 & 6858, S: 6152, B: 787B, K: 733A, H: 282C

6853 עָרֵב *ʿārēb*, pleasant, sweet (voice), S: 6156, B: 787A, K: 733B, H: 282C

6854 [1]עֹרֵב *ʿōrēb*[1], raven, S: 6158, B: 788B, K: 733B, H: 282C

6855 [2]עֹרֵב *ʿōrēb*[2], Oreb, S: 6159, B: 1126A, K: 733B, H: 282C

6856 עָרֹב *ʿārōb*, swarms of flies, S: 6157, B: 786C, K: 733B, H: 282C

6857 [1]עֲרָבָה *ʿarābâ*[1], poplar tree, S: 6155†, B: 788B, K: 733B, H: 282C

6858 [2]עֲרָבָה *ʿarābâ*[2], plains (a geographical region of desert, wilderness or wasteland); (as a proper name) Arabah, S: 6160, B: 787B, K: 733C, H: 282C

6859 עֲרֻבָּה *ʿarubbâ*, security, pledge; assurance, S: 6161, B: 786D, K: 733D, H: 282C

6860 עֵרָבוֹן *ʿērābôn*, pledge, security, S: 6162†, B: 786D, K: 734A, H: 282D

6861 עַרְבִי *ʿarbî*, Arab, of Arabia, S: 6163, B: 787B, K: 734A, H: 282D

6862 עֲרָבִי *ʿarābî*, Arab, nomad, S: 6163, B: 787B, K: 734A, H: 282D

6863 עַרְבָתִי *ʿarbātî*, Arbathite, S: 6164, B: 112C, K: 734A, H: 282D

6864 עָרַג *ʿārag*, [A] to pant for, long for (as a thirsty animal), S: 6165, B: 788B, K: 734A, H: 282D

6865 [1]עֲרָד *ʿarād*[1], Arad, S: 6166, B: 788C, K: 734B, H: 282D

6866 [2]עֲרָד *ʿarād*[2], Arad, S: 6166, B: 788C, K: 734B, H: 282D

6867 [1]עָרָה *ʿārâ*[1], [C] to be poured; [D] to lat bare, empty, expose, strip; [G] to make exposed; to cause to pour out; to dishonor; [F] to show oneself naked, S: 6168, B: 788C, K: 734B, H: 282D

6868 [2]עָרָה *ʿārâ*[2], plants, bulrushes, S: 6169, B: 788D, K: 734C, H: 283A

6869 [3]עָרָה *ʿārâ*[3], Arah, S: 4632†, B: 788D, K: 550C, H: 208A

6870 עֲרוּגָה *ʿarûgâ*, garden bed, garden plot, S: 6170, B: 788C, K: 734D, H: 283A

6871 עָרוֹד *ʿārôd*, wild donkey, S: 6171, B: 789B, K: 734D, H: 283A

6872 עֶרְוָה *ʿerwâ*, nakedness (which the showing of was indecent or shameful in certain situations), S: 6172, B: 788D, K: 734D, H: 283A

6873 עָרוֹם *ʿārôm*, naked, stripped, S: 6174, B: 736A, K: 735A, H: 283A

6874 עָרוּם *ʿārûm*, prudent, crafty, clever, S: 6175, B: 791A, K: 735A, H: 283A

6875 [1]עֲרוֹעֵר *ʿarôʿēr*[1], variant: bush, S: 6176†, B: 792D, K: 735B, H: 283A

6876 [2]עֲרוֹעֵר *ʿarôʿēr*[2], Aroer, S: 6177, B: 792D, K: 735B, H: 283A

6877 עָרוּץ *ʿārûṣ*, dry *or* dreadful, S: 6178, B: 792A, K: 735B, H: 283A

[F] Hitpael (hitpoel, hitpoal, hitpolel, hitpolal, hitpalel, hitpalal, hitpalpel, hitpalpal, hotpael, hotpaal) [G] Hiphil (hiphtil) [H] Hophal [I] Hishtaphel

6878 עֵרִי *ʿērî*[1], Eri, S: 6179, B: 735C, K: 735B, H: 283A

6879 [2]עֵרִי *ʿērî*[2], Erite, S: 6180, B: 735C, K: 735C, H: 283A

6880 עֶרְיָה *ʿeryâ*, bareness, nakedness, uncoveredness, S: 6181, B: 789A, K: 735C, H: 283A

6881 עֲרִיסָה *ʿărîsâ*, ground meal (dough in the first phase of bread making), S: 6182, B: 791B, K: 735C, H: 283B

6882 עֲרִיפִים *ʿărîpîm*, cloud, S: 6183†, B: 791D, K: 735C, H: 283B

6883 עָרִיץ *ʿārîṣ*, ruthless, cruel, fierce, S: 6184, B: 792A, K: 735C, H: 283B

6884 עֲרִירִי *ʿărîrî*, childless, S: 6185, B: 792D, K: 735D, H: 283B

6885 עָרַךְ *ʿārak*, [A] to arrange in rows; put in order, take up (battle) positions; [B] to be arranged, be put in order, be put in formation; [G] to set a value, S: 6186, B: 789B & 790A, K: 735D, H: 283B

6886 עֵרֶךְ *ʿērek*, proper estimated value, S: 6187, B: 789D, K: 736B, H: 283C

6887 עָרֵל *ʿāral*, [A] to regard as forbidden, leave unharvested, S: 6188†, B: 790C, K: 736D, H: 283C

6888 עָרֵל *ʿārēl*, uncircumcised (i.e., having a foreskin of the penis), S: 6189, B: 790C, K: 736D, H: 283D

6889 עָרְלָה *ʿorlâ*, foreskin (of the penis), S: 6190, B: 790B, K: 737B, H: 283D

6890 [1]עָרַם *ʿāram*[1], [C] to be piled up, be dammed up, S: 6192, B: 790D, K: 737B, H: 283D

6891 [2]עָרַם *ʿāram*[2], [A] to be crafty, show prudence; [G] to initiate cunning plans, S: 6191, B: 791A, K: 737C, H: 284A

6892 עֹרֶם *ʿōrem*, variant: craftiness, S: 6193, B: 791A, K: 737C, H: 284A

6893 עָרְמָה *ʿormâ*, prudence, cunning, S: 6195, B: 791A, K: 737D, H: 284A

6894 עֲרֵמָה *ʿărēmâ*, heap, mound (of grain), S: 6194, B: 790D, K: 737D, H: 284A

6895 עֶרְמוֹן *ʿermôn*, plane tree, S: 6196†, B: 790D, K: 737D, H: 284A

6896 עֵרָן *ʿērān*, Eran, S: 6197, B: 735D, K: 737D, H: 284A

6897 עֵרָנִי *ʿērānî*, Eranite, S: 6198, B: 735D, K: 738A, H: 284A

6898 עַרְעוֹר *ʿarʿôr*, variant: variant, see 6876, S: 6176†, B: 792D, K: 738A, H: 284A

6899 עַרְעָר *ʿarʿār*, destitute, naked, stripped; (juniper) bush, S: 6199, B: 792D, K: 738A, H: 284A

6900 עַרְעָרָה *ʿarʿārâ*, variant: Ararah, see 6899 & 6368, S: 5735†, B: 792D 3, K: 738A, H: 283A

6901 עֲרֹעֵרִי *ʿărōʿērî*, Aroerite, S: 6200, B: 793A, K: 738A, H: 284A

6902 עֹרֶף *ʿōrep*, neck, (stiff-)necked, S: 6203, B: 791B, K: 738B, H: 284B

6903 [1]עָרַף *ʿārap*[1], [A] to trickle, drip, S: 6201, B: 791C, K: 738A, H: 284A

6904 [2]עָרַף *ʿārap*[2], [A] to break; [B] be broken, S: 6202, B: 791C, K: 738B, H: 284B

6905 עָרְפָּה *ʿorpâ*, Orpah, S: 6204, B: 791C, K: 738C, H: 284B

6906 עֲרָפֶל *ʿărāpel*, dark *or* thick clouds; deep gloom, S: 6205, B: 791D, K: 738D, H: 284B

6907 עָרַץ *ʿāraṣ*, [A] to shake, to shake in terror; [C] to be feared; [G] to dread, stand in awe, S: 6206, B: 791D, K: 738D, H: 284B

6908 עָרַק *ʿāraq*, [A] to gnaw, S: 6207, B: 792B, K: 739A, H: 284C

6909 עַרְקִי *ʿarqî*, Arkite, S: 6208, B: 792B, K: 739A, H: 284C

6910 עָרַר *ʿārar*, [A] to strip off; [D] to strip; to level, demolish; [F] to be laid utterly bare, S: 6209, B: 792C, K: 739A, H: 284C

6911 עֶרֶשׂ *ʿereś*, bed, couch, S: 6210, B: 793A, K: 739B, H: 284C

6912 עֵשֶׂב *ʿēśeb*, green plant, vegetation, grass, S: 6212, B: 793B, K: 739C, H: 284C

6913 [1]עָשָׂה *ʿāśâ*[1], [A] to do, make; [B] to be done; [C] to be done, be made; [E] to be made, S: 6213, B: 793C, K: 739D, H: 284D

6914 [2]עָשָׂה *ʿāśâ*[2], [D] to caress, squeeze, S: 6213, B: 796B, K: 741C, H: 285C

6915 עֲשָׂהאֵל *ʿăśāhʾēl*, עֲשָׂה־אֵל *ʿăśāh-ʾēl*, Asahel, S: 6214, B: 795C, K: 741C, H: 285C

6916 עֵשָׂו *ʿēśāw*, Esau, S: 6215, B: 796C, K: 741C, H: 285C

6917 עָשׂוֹר *ʿāśôr*, (group of) ten, S: 6218, B: 797C, K: 741D, H: 285C

6918 עֲשִׂיאֵל *ʿăśîʾēl*, Asiel, S: 6221, B: 795C, K: 741D, H: 285C

6919 עֲשָׂיָה *ʿăśāyâ*, Asaiah, S: 6222, B: 795C, K: 741D, H: 285C

6920 עֲשִׂירִי *ʿăśîrî*, tenth, S: 6224, B: 798A, K: 742A, H: 285C

6921 עָשַׂק *ʿāśaq*, [F] to dispute, quarrel, S: 6229, B: 796C, K: 742A, H: 285D

6922 עֵשֶׂק *ʿēśeq*, Esek, S: 6230, B: 796C, K: 742B, H: 285D

6923 עָשַׂר *ʿāśar*, [A] to take a tenth; [D] to give a tenth, set aside a tenth; [G] to give or receive a tenth, S: 6237, B: 797C, K: 742B, H: 285D

6924 עֶשֶׂר *ʿeśer*, ten, S: 6235, B: 796C, K: 742C, H: 285D

6925 עָשָׂר *ʿāśār*, ten (always used in combined numbers), S: 6240, B: 797A, K: 742C, H: 285D

6926 עֶשְׂרֵה *ʿeśrēh*, ten (used in compound numbers), S: 6240†, B: 797A, K: 742D, H: 285D

6927 עֲשָׂרָה *ʿăśārâ*, ten, S: 6235, B: 796D, K: 743A, H: 285D

6928 עִשָּׂרוֹן *ʿiśśārôn*, tenth part, S: 6241, B: 798A, K: 743A, H: 286A

6929 עֶשְׂרִים *ʿeśrîm*, twenty, S: 6242, B: 797D, K: 743B, H: 286A

6930 עֲשֶׂרֶת *ʿăśeret*, (group of) ten, S: 6240†, B: 796A, K: 743B, H: 286A

6931 [1]עָשׁ *ʿāš*[1], moth, S: 6211, B: 799C, K: 743B, H: 286A

6932 [2]עָשׁ *ʿāš*[2], variant: pus, S: 6211, B: 799C, K: 743C, H: 286A

6933 [3]עָשׁ *ʿāš*[3], Bear *or* Lion (a constellation), S: 6211, B: 798B, K: 743C, H: 286A

6934 עָשׁוֹק *ʿāšôq*, oppressor, S: 6216, B: 799A, K: 743C, H: 286A

6935 עֲשׁוּקִים *ʿăšûqîm*, oppression, S: 6217†, B: 799A, K: 743C, H: 286A

6936 עָשׁוֹת *ʿāšôt*, wrought, fashioned (iron), S: 6219, B: 799D, K: 743C, H: 286A

6937 עַשְׁוָת *ʿašwāt*, Ashvath, S: 6220, B: 798B, K: 743C, H: 286A

6938 עָשִׁיר *ʿāšîr*, rich, wealthy; (as noun) the rich, rich person, S: 6223, B: 799B, K: 743C, H: 286A

6939 עָשַׁן *ʿāšan*, [A] to envelope in smoke, smolder, S: 6225, B: 798C, K: 743D, H: 286A

6940 [1]עָשָׁן *ʿāšān*[1], smoke (billowing, ascending, blowing), S: 6227, B: 798C, K: 744A, H: 286A

6941 [2]עָשָׁן *ʿāšān*[2], Ashan, S: 6228, B: 798C, K: 115A, H: 286B

6942 עָשֵׁן *ʿāšēn*, smoking, smoldering, S: 6226, B: 798C, K: 744B, H: 286B

6943 עָשַׁק *ʿāšaq*, [A] to oppress, mistreat; to defraud, extort; [B] to be oppressed, be tormented; [E] to be crushed, S: 6231, B: 798D, K: 744B, H: 286B

6944 עֵשֶׁק *ʿēšeq*, Eshek, S: 6232, B: 799A, K: 744C, H: 286B

6945 עֹשֶׁק *ʿōšeq*, oppression, tyranny; extortion, S: 6233, B: 799A, K: 744C, H: 286B

6946 עָשְׁקָה *ʿošqâ*, trouble, oppression, S: 6234, B: 799A, K: 744C, H: 286B

6947 עָשַׁר *ʿāšar*, [A] to be, become rich; [G] to make rich, bring wealth, S: 6238, B: 799A, K: 744C, H: 286B

6948 עֹשֶׁר *ʿōšer*, wealth, riches, S: 6239, B: 799B, K: 744D, H: 286C

6949 עָשֵׁשׁ *ʿāšaš*, [A] to grow weak, S: 6244†, B: 799C, K: 745A, H: 286C

6950 [1]עָשַׁת *ʿāšat*[1], [A] to grow sleek (i.e., smooth *or* shiny), S: 6245, B: 799C, K: 745A, H: 286C

6951 [2]עָשַׁת *ʿāšat*[2], [F] to take notice, S: 6245, B: 799D, K: 745A, H: 286C

6952 עֶשֶׁת *ʿešet*, polished piece, slab, plate, S: 6247, B: 799D, K: 745A, H: 286C

6953 עַשְׁתּוּת *ʿaštût*, thought, S: 6248, B: 799D, K: 745B, H: 286C

6954 עַשְׁתֵּי *ʿaštê*, eleven, eleventh, S: 6249, B: 799D, K: 745B, H: 286C

6955 עֶשְׁתֹּנֹת *ʿeštōnet*, plan, thought, S: 6250†, B: 799D, K: 745B, H: 286C

6956 עַשְׁתֹּרֶת *ʿaštōret*, Ashtoreth (pagan god), S: 6253, B: 800A, K: 745C, H: 286C

6957 עַשְׁתֶּרֶת *ʿašteret*, lamb *or* ewe, S: 6251†, B: 800B, K: 745C, H: 286D

6958 עַשְׁתָּרֹת *ʿaštārōt*, Ashtaroth, S: 6252†, B: 800B, K: 745D, H: 286C

6959 עַשְׁתְּרֹת קַרְנַיִם *ʿaštᵉrōt qarnayim*, Ashteroth Karnaim, S: 6255, B: 800B, K: 745D, H: 286D

6960 עַשְׁתְּרָתִי *ʿaštᵉrātî*, Ashterathite, S: 6254, B: 800C, K: 745D, H: 286D

6961 עֵת *ʿēt*, time, season (of various lengths), S: 6256, B: 773B, K: 745D, H: 286D

6962 עֵת קָצִין *ʿēt qāṣîn*, Eth Kazin, S: 6278, B: 773D, K: 747A, H: 287A

6963 עָתַד *ʿātad*, [D] to make ready; [F] to be destined, S: 6257, B: 800C, K: 747A, H: 287A

6964 עַתָּה *ʿattâ*, now, S: 6258, B: 773D, K: 747A, H: 287A

6965 עָתוּד *ʿātûd*, supply, treasure, S: 6259, B: 800C, K: 747D, H: 287B

[A] Qal [B] Qal passive [C] Niphal [D] Piel (poel, polel, pilel, pilal, pealal, pilpel) [E] Pual (poal, polal, poalal, pulal, pualal)

6966 עַתּוּד *'attûd*, male goat; (of humans) a leader, S: 6260, B: 800C, K: 747D, H: 287B

6967 עִתִּי *'ittî*, available, S: 6261, B: 774C, K: 748A, H: 287B

6968 עַתַּי *'attay*, Attai, S: 6262, B: 774C, K: 748A, H: 287C

6969 עָתִיד *'ātîd*, ready, prepared, S: 6264, B: 800C, K: 748A, H: 287C

6970 עֲתָיָה *'ᵃtāyâ*, Athaiah, S: 6265, B: 800D, K: 748A, H: 287C

6971 עָתִיק *'ātîq*, fine, choice, select, S: 6266, B: 801B, K: 748A, H: 287C

6972 עַתִּיק *'attîq*, taken, removed (from place or time), S: 6267, B: 801C, K: 748A, H: 287C

6973 עֲתָךְ *'ᵃtāk*, Athach, S: 6269, B: 800D, K: 748B, H: 287C

6974 עַתְלָי *'atlāy*, Athlai, S: 6270, B: 800D, K: 748B, H: 287C

6975 עֲתַלְיָה *'ᵃtalyâ*, Athaliah, S: 6271, B: 800D, K: 748B, H: 287C

6976 עֲתַלְיָהוּ *'ᵃtalyāhû*, Athaliah, S: 6271, B: 800D, K: 748B, H: 287C

6977 עָתַם *'ātam*, [C] to be scorched, S: 6272, B: 801A, K: 748B, H: 287C

6978 עָתְנִי *'otnî*, Othni, S: 6273, B: 801A, K: 748C, H: 287C

6979 עָתְנִיאֵל *'otnî'ēl*, Othniel, S: 6274, B: 801A, K: 748C, H: 287C

6980 עָתַק *'ātaq*, [A] to move; to grow old, grow weak; [G] to move on; to fail; to copy, S: 6275, B: 801A, K: 748C, H: 287C

6981 עָתָק *'ātāq*, arrogant, insolent, outstretched, S: 6277, B: 801B, K: 748D, H: 287D

6982 עָתֵק *'ātēq*, enduring (wealth), S: 6276, B: 801B, K: 748D, H: 287D

6983 ¹עָתַר *'ātar¹*, [A] to pray; [C] to respond to prayer, be moved by an entreaty; [G] to pray, make entreaty, S: 6279, B: 801C, K: 748D, H: 287D

6984 ²עָתַר *'ātar²*, [C] to be multiplied; [G] to multiply, S: 6280, B: 801D, K: 748D, H: 287D

6985 ¹עָתָר *'ātār¹*, worshiper, S: 6282, B: 801C, K: 749C, H: 287D

6986 ²עָתָר *'ātār²*, fragrance, perfume, S: 6282, B: 801D, K: 749C, H: 287D

6987 עֶתֶר *'eter*, Ether, S: 6281, B: 801D, K: 749C, H: 287D

6988 עֲתֶרֶת *'ᵃteret*, abundance, S: 6283, B: 801D, K: 749C, H: 287D

6989 פ *p*, letter of the Hebrew alphabet, S*, B: 802A, K: 749B, H*

6990 פָּאָה *pā'â*, [G] to split into pieces, scatter, S: 6284, B: 802A, K: 749B, H: 288A

6991 ¹פֵּאָה *pē'â¹*, side, edge, boundary, S: 6285, B: 802A, K: 749B, H: 288A

6992 ²פֵּאָה *pē'â²*, piece, part, S: 6285, B: 802A, K: 750A, H: 288A

6993 ³פֵּאָה *pē'â³*, variant: splendor, luxury, S: 6285, B: 802A, K: 750A, H: 288A

6994 ¹פָּאַר *pā'ar¹*, [D] to knock down olives a second time, S: 6286, B: 802D, K: 750A, H: 288A

6995 ²פָּאַר *pā'ar²*, [D] to honor, adorn, endow with splendor; [F] to glorify oneself, display one's splendor; (negatively) to boast, S: 6286, B: 802B, K: 750B, H: 288B

6996 פְּאֵר *pᵉ'ēr*, turban, headdress, S: 6287, B: 802C, K: 750B, H: 288B

6997 פֹּארָה *pō'râ*, branch, leafy bough, S: 6288, B: 802D, K: 750C, H: 288B

6998 פֻּארָה *pu'râ*, bough, S: 6288, B: 802D, K: 750C, H: 288B

6999 פָּארוּר *pā'rûr*, growing pale, turning pale, S: 6289, B: 802D, K: 750C, H: 288B

7000 פָּארָן *pā'rān*, Paran, S: 6290, B: 803A, K: 750D, H: 288B

7001 פַּג *pag*, early fruit, S: 6291, B: 803A, K: 750D, H: 288C

7002 פִּגּוּל *piggûl*, impurity, unclean meat, S: 6292, B: 803B, K: 750D, H: 288C

7003 פָּגַע *pāga'*, to strike, touch; intercede for, plead with; [G] to make intercession, intervene; strike; cause to encounter, S: 6293, B: 803B, K: 751A, H: 288C

7004 פֶּגַע *pega'*, chance, occurrence, S: 6294, B: 803C, K: 751B, H: 288D

7005 פַּגְעִיאֵל *pag'î'ēl*, Pagiel, S: 6295, B: 803C, K: 751C, H: 288D

7006 פָּגַר *pāgar*, [D] to be exhausted, S: 6296, B: 803C, K: 751C, H: 288D

7007 פֶּגֶר *peger*, dead body, corpse; carcass, S: 6297, B: 803D, K: 751C, H: 288D

7008 פָּגַשׁ *pāgaš*, [A] to meet; to attack; [C] to have in common, to meet together; [D] to come upon, encounter, S: 6298, B: 803D, K: 751D, H: 288D

7009 פָּדָה *pādâ*, [A] to redeem, ransom, deliver, rescue, buy; [B] to be redeemed, be ransomed; [C] to be ransomed, be redeemed; [G] to let be ransomed; [H] to be brought to ransomed, S: 6299, B: 804A, K: 751D, H: 289A

7010 פְּדַהְאֵל *pᵉdah'ēl*, Pedahel, S: 6300, B: 804B, K: 752C, H: 289A

7011 פְּדָהצוּר, פְּדָה־צוּר *pᵉdāhṣûr*, *pᵉdāh-ṣûr*, Pedahzur, S: 6301, B: 804C, K: 752C, H: 289A

7012 פְּדוּיִם *pᵉdûyim*, redemption, ransom, S: 6302†, B: 804B, K: 752C, H: 289A

7013 פָּדוֹן *pādôn*, Padon, S: 6303, B: 804B, K: 752C, H: 289A

7014 פְּדוּת *pᵉdût*, redemption, ransom, S: 6304, B: 804B, K: 752C, H: 289B

7015 פְּדָיָה *pᵉdāyâ*, Pedaiah, S: 6305, B: 804C, K: 752C, H: 289B

7016 פְּדָיָהוּ *pᵉdāyāhû*, Pedaiah, S: 6305, B: 804C, K: 752D, H: 289B

7017 פִּדְיוֹם *pidyôm*, redemption, ransom, S: 6306, B: 804B, K: 752D, H: 289B

7018 פִּדְיוֹן *pidyôn*, redemption money, ransom payment, S: 6306, B: 804B, K: 752D, H: 289B

7019 פַּדָּן *paddān*, Paddan, S: 6307, B: 804C, K: 752D, H: 289B

7020 פַּדַּן אֲרָם *paddan 'ᵃrām*, Paddan Aram, S: 6307, B: 804C, K: 752D, H: 289B

7021 פָּדַע *pāda'*, [A] to spare, deliver, S: 6308, B: 804C, K: 753A, H: 289B

7022 פֶּדֶר *peder*, suet (the hard fat about kidney's and loins of animals), S: 6309, B: 804D, K: 753A, H: 289B

7023 פֶּה *peh*, mouth, opening, edge (of a sword); speech: command, testimony, S: 6310 & 6366†, B: 804D, K: 753A, H: 289B

7024 פֹּה *pōh*, here, S: 6311, B: 805D, K: 754A, H: 289C

7025 פּוּאָה *pû'â*, Puah, S: 6312, B: 806A, K: 754A, H: 289D

7026 פּוּאָה *puû'â*, Puah, S: 6312†, B: 806A, K: 754B, H: 289D

7027 פּוּאִי *pû'î*, Puite, S: 6324†, B: 806A, K: 755A, H*

7028 פּוּג *pûg*, [A] to grow numb, be feeble; [C] to be benumbed, be feeble, S: 6313, B: 806A, K: 754A, H: 289D

7029 פּוּגָה *pûgâ*, relief, relaxation, S: 6314, B: 806B, K: 754B, H: 289D

7030 פֻּוָּה *puwwâ*, variant: Puvah, see 7026, S: 6312, B: 806A, K: 754B, H: 289D

7031 ¹פּוּחַ *pûaḥ¹*, [A] to blow, become dawn (of the day); [G] to blow (of wind), S: 6315, B: 806B, K: 754B, H: 289D

7032 ²פּוּחַ *pûaḥ²*, [A] to breathe out; [G] to breathe out, sneer, malign, S: 6315, B: 806B, K: 754B, H: 289D

7033 פּוּט *pûṭ*, Put, S: 6316, B: 806C, K: 754C, H: 289D

7034 פּוּטִיאֵל *pûṭî'ēl*, Putiel, S: 6317, B: 806C, K: 754C, H: 289D

7035 פּוֹטִיפַר *pôṭîpar*, Potiphar, S: 6318, B: 806C, K: 754D, H: 289D

7036 פּוֹטִי פֶרַע *pôṭî pera'*, Potiphera, S: 6319, B: 806C, K: 754D, H: 289D

7037 פּוּךְ *pûk*, (eye) paint; turquoise, S: 6320, B: 806C, K: 754D, H: 290A

7038 פּוֹל *pôl*, beans, S: 6321, B: 806D, K: 754D, H: 290A

7039 ¹פּוּל *pûl¹*, variant: see 4275, S: 6322, B: 806D, K: 755A, H: 290A

7040 ²פּוּל *pûl²*, Pul, S: 6322, B: 806D, K: 755A, H: 290A

7041 פּוּן *pûn*, [A] to be in despair, S: 6323, B: 806D, K: 755A, H: 290A

7042 פּוֹנֶה *pôneh*, variant: see 7157, S: 6437†, B: 806D, K: 755A, H: 290A

7043 פּוּנִי *pûnî*, variant: Punite, see 7027, S: 6324, B: 806A, K: 755A, H: 290A

7044 פּוּנֹן *pûnōn*, Punon, S: 6325, B: 806D, K: 755A, H: 290A

7045 פּוּעָה *pû'â*, Puah, S: 6326, B: 806D, K: 755A, H: 290A

7046 ¹פּוּץ *pûṣ¹*, [A] to be scattered; [B] to be scattered; [C] to be scattered; [G] to cause to scatter, S: 6327, B: 806D, K: 755B, H: 290A

7047 ²פּוּץ *pûṣ²*, variant: [A] flow, overflow, S: 6327, B: 807B, K: 755B, H: 290A

7048 ¹פּוּק *pûq¹*, [A] to stumble, totter; [G] to totter, S: 6328 & 6329, B: 807B, K: 755D, H: 290B

7049 ²פּוּק *pûq²*, [G] to bring out, furnish, promote, S: 6329, B: 807C, K: 755D, H: 290B

7050 פּוּקָה *pûqâ*, staggering, stumbling, S: 6330, B: 807C, K: 755D, H: 290B

7051 ¹פּוּר *pûr¹*, variant: [G] to destroy, S: 6331 & 6512†, B: 830B, K: 755D, H: 290B

7052 ²פּוּר *pûr²*, pur (the lot); (pl.) Purim, S: 6332, B: 807C, K: 756A, H: 290C

7053 פּוּרָה *pûrâ*, trough of the winepress; measure (equal to the filling of the winepress), S: 6333, B: 807D, K: 756A, H: 290C

7054 פּוֹרָתָא *pôrātā'*, Poratha, S: 6334, B: 807D, K: 756A, H: 290C

7055 ¹פּוּשׁ *pûš*[1], [A] to leap, frolic, gallop, S: 6335, B: 807D, K: 756A, H: 290C

7056 ²פּוּשׁ *pûš*[2], [C] to be scattered, S: 6335, B: 807D, K: 756A, H: 290C

7057 פּוּתִי *pûtî*, Puthite, S: 6336, B: 807D, K: 756B, H: 290C

7058 פַּז *paz*, pure gold, S: 6337†, B: 808A, K: 756B, H: 290C

7059 ¹פָּזַז *pāzaz*[1], [H] to be set with pure gold, S: 6338, B: 808A, K: 756B, H: 290C

7060 ²פָּזַז *pāzaz*[2], [A] to be limber; [D] to leap, S: 6339, B: 808A, K: 756C, H: 290C

7061 פָּזַר *pāzar*, [B] to be scattered; [D] to scatter; [C] to be scattered; [E] to be dispersed, S: 6340, B: 808A, K: 756C, H: 290C

7062 ¹פַּח *paḥ*[1], snare, bird-trap, S: 6341, B: 809A, K: 756D, H: 290D

7063 ²פַּח *paḥ*[2], thin sheets (of hammered metal), S: 6341, B: 809A, K: 756D, H: 290D

7064 פָּחַד *pāḥad*, [A] to tremble, be afraid; [D] to live in terror, fear; [G] to make shake, make tremble, S: 6342, B: 808B, K: 757A, H: 290D

7065 ¹פַּחַד *paḥad*[1], fear, terror, dread, S: 6343, B: 808B, K: 757B, H: 290D

7066 ²פַּחַד *paḥad*[2], thigh, S: 6344, B: 808C, K: 757D, H: 291A

7067 פַּחְדָּה *paḥdâ*, awe, dread, S: 6345, B: 808C, K: 757D, H: 291A

7068 פֶּחָה *peḥâ*, governor, officer, S: 6346, B: 808C, K: 757D, H: 291A

7069 פָּחַז *pāḥaz*, [A] to be arrogant, be insolent, S: 6348, B: 808D, K: 757D, H: 291A

7070 פַּחַז *paḥaz*, turbulence, recklessness, S: 6349, B: 808D, K: 758A, H: 291A

7071 פַּחֲזוּת *paḥ*ª*zût*, recklessness, S: 6350, B: 808D, K: 758A, H: 291A

7072 פָּחַח *pāḥaḥ*, [G] to trap; [H] to be entrapped, S: 6351, B: 809A, K: 758A, H: 291A

7073 פֶּחָם *peḥām*, coal, charcoal, S: 6352, B: 809B, K: 758A, H: 291A

7074 פַּחַת *paḥat*, pit, cave, S: 6354, B: 809B, K: 758B, H: 291A

7075 פַּחַת מוֹאָב *paḥat mô'āb*, Pahath-Moab, S: 6355, B: 809B, K: 758B, H: 291A

7076 פְּחֶתֶת *p*ᵉ*ḥetet*, mildew (that eats away at a garment), S: 6356, B: 809B, K: 758B, H: 291A

7077 פִּטְדָה *piṭdâ*, topaz, S: 6357, B: 809B, K: 758B, H: 291A

7078 פְּטִירִים *p*ᵉ*ṭîrîm*, variant: see 7080, S: 6359†, B: 809C 2., K: 758C, H: 291A

7079 פַּטִּישׁ *paṭṭîš*, (sledge-)hammer, S: 6360, B: 809C, K: 758C, H: 291A

7080 פָּטַר *pāṭar*, [A] to elude, escape, release; [B] to be opened; [G] to open wide the mouth (as an insult), S: 6358† & 6362, B: 809C, K: 758C, H: 291B

7081 פֶּטֶר *peṭer*, first offspring, firstborn, S: 6363, B: 809D, K: 758D, H: 291B

7082 פִּטְרָה *piṭrâ*, firstborn, S: 6363, B: 809D, K: 758D, H: 291B

7083 פִּי־בֶסֶת *pî-beset*, Bubastis (Piy-Beset), S: 6364, B: 809D, K: 759A, H: 291B

7084 פִּי הַחִירֹת *pî haḥîrôt*, Pi Hahiroth, S: 6367, B: 809D, K: 759A, H: 291B

7085 פִּיד *pîd*, misfortune, distress, calamity, S: 6365, B: 810A, K: 759A, H: 291B

7086 פִּיחַ *pîaḥ*, soot (from a furnace), S: 6368, B: 806B, K: 759A, H: 291B

7087 פִּיכֹל *pîkōl*, Phicol, S: 6369, B: 810A, K: 759B, H: 291B

7088 פִּים *pîm*, pim (about 2/3 of a shekel in weight), S*, B*, K: 759B, H: 291C

7089 פִּימָה *pîmâ*, fat, S: 6371, B: 810A, K: 759B, H: 291C

7090 פִּינְחָס *pînᵉḥās*, Phinehas, S: 6372, B: 810A, K: 759B, H: 291C

7091 פִּינֹן *pînōn*, Pinon, S: 6373, B: 810A, K: 759C, H: 291C

7092 פִּיפִיּוֹת *pîpiyyôt*, double-edged, with many teeth, S: 6374†, B: 804D, K: 759C, H: 291C

7093 פִּישׁוֹן *pîšôn*, Pishon, S: 6376, B: 810B, K: 759C, H: 291C

7094 פִּיתוֹן *pîtôn*, Pithon, S: 6377, B: 810B, K: 759C, H: 291C

7095 פַּךְ *pak*, flask, (small) jug, S: 6378, B: 810B, K: 759C, H: 291C

7096 פָּכָה *pākâ*, [D] to trickle, S: 6379, B: 810B, K: 759D, H: 291C

7097 פֹּכֶרֶת הַצְּבָיִים *pōkeret haṣṣᵉbāyîm*, Pokereth-Hazzebaim, S: 6380, B: 810B, K: 759D, H: 291C

7098 פָּלָא *pālā'*, [C] to be wonderful, be marvelous, be amazing; to be hard, be amazing; [D] to fulfill; [G] to show a wonder, to cause to astound; [F] to show oneself marvelous, S: 6381, B: 810C, K: 759D, H: 291C

7099 פֶּלֶא *pele'*, wonder, miracle, astounding thing, S: 6382, B: 810B, K: 760C, H: 291D

7100 פִּלְאִי *pil'î*, wonderful, beyond understanding, S: 6383, B: 811A, K: 760D, H: 291D

7101 פַּלֻּאִי *pallu'î*, Palluite, S: 6384, B: 811A, K: 760D, H: 292A

7102 פְּלָאיָה *pᵉlā'yâ*, Pelaiah, S: 6411, B: 811A, K: 760D, H: 292A

7103 פָּלַג *pālag*, [C] to be divided; [D] to cut open, divide, S: 6385, B: 811A, K: 760D, H: 292A

7104 ¹פֶּלֶג *peleg*[1], stream, artificial irrigation canal, S: 6388, B: 811B, K: 761A, H: 292A

7105 ²פֶּלֶג *peleg*[2], Peleg, S: 6389, B: 811B, K: 761A, H: 292A

7106 פְּלַגָּה *pᵉlaggâ*, district, division; stream, S: 6390, B: 811B, K: 761B, H: 292A

7107 פְּלֻגָּה *pᵉluggâ*, division, S: 6391, B: 811B, K: 761B, H: 292A

7108 פִּילֶגֶשׁ *pilegeš*, concubine, S: 6370, B: 811B, K: 761B, H: 292A

7109 פִּלְדָּשׁ *pildāš*, Pildash, S: 6394, B: 811C, K: 761C, H: 292A

7110 פְּלָדֹת *pᵉlādōt*, metal, S: 6393†, B: 811C, K: 761C, H: 292A

7111 פָּלָה *pālâ*, [C] to be distinguished; [G] to deal differently, make a distinction, S: 6395, B: 811C, K: 761C, H: 292A

7112 פַּלּוּא *pallû'*, Pallu, S: 6396, B: 811A, K: 761D, H: 292B

7113 פְּלוֹנִי *pᵉlônî*, Pelonite, S: 6397, B: 813D, K: 764A, H: 293A

7114 פָּלַח *pālaḥ*, [A] to plow; [D] to cut up, pierce; to bring forth (from the womb), S: 6398, B: 812A, K: 761D, H: 292B

7115 פֶּלַח *pelaḥ*, millstone; half (of a pomegranate); slice (of a cake), S: 6400, B: 812A, K: 762A, H: 292B

7116 פִּלְחָא *pilḥā'*, Pilha, S: 6401, B: 812B, K: 762A, H: 292B

7117 פָּלַט *pālaṭ*, [A] to escape; [D] to rescue, deliver; [G] to bring to safety, S: 6403, B: 812B, K: 762A, H: 292B

7118 פֶּלֶט *peleṭ*, Pelet, S: 6404, B: 812B, K: 762B, H: 292C

7119 פַּלֵּט *pallēṭ*, deliverance, S: 6405, B: 812C, K: 762A, H: 292B

7120 ¹פַּלְטִי *palṭî*[1], Palti; Paltiel, S: 6406, B: 812D, K: 762B, H: 292C

7121 ²פַּלְטִי *palṭî*[2], Paltite, S: 6407, B: 112C & 812C, K: 762C, H: 292C

7122 פִּלְטָי *pilṭāy*, Piltai, S: 6408, B: 812D, K: 762C, H: 292C

7123 פַּלְטִיאֵל *palṭî'ēl*, Paltiel, S: 6409, B: 812D, K: 762C, H: 292C

7124 פְּלַטְיָה *pᵉlaṭyâ*, Pelatiah, S: 6410, B: 812D, K: 762C, H: 292C

7125 פְּלַטְיָהוּ *pᵉlaṭyāhû*, Pelatiah, S: 6410, B: 812D, K: 762C, H: 292C

7126 פְּלָיָה *pᵉlāyâ*, Pelaiah, S: 6411, B: 811A, K: 762C, H: 292C

7127 פָּלִיט *pālîṭ*, fugitive, one who escapes, S: 6412, B: 812C, K: 762C, H: 292C

7128 פָּלֵיט *pālêṭ*, fugitive, one who escapes, S: 6412, B: 812C, K: 762D, H: 292C

7129 פְּלֵיטָה *pᵉlêṭâ*, fugitive, one who escapes, survivors, remnant, S: 6413, B: 812C, K: 762D, H: 292C

7130 פָּלִיל *pālîl*, judge, S: 6414, B: 813C, K: 762D, H: 292D

7131 פְּלִילָה *pᵉlîlâ*, decision, S: 6415, B: 813D, K: 763A, H: 292D

7132 פְּלִילִי *pᵉlîlî*, for a judge, calling for judgment, S: 6416, B: 813D, K: 763A, H: 292D

7133 פְּלִילִיָּה *pᵉlîliyyâ*, rendering of a decision, the calling for a judgment, S: 6417, B: 813D, K: 763A, H: 292D

7134 ¹פֶּלֶךְ *pelek*[1], spindle-whorl, S: 6418, B: 813A, K: 763A, H: 292D

7135 ²פֶּלֶךְ *pelek*[2], district, S: 6418, B: 813A, K: 763B, H: 292D

7136 ¹פָּלַל *pālal*[1], [D] to mediate, intervene; to expect; to furnish justification, S: 6419, B: 813A, K: 763B, H: 292D

7137 ²פָּלַל *pālal*[2], [F] to pray, S: 6419, B: 813A, K: 763B, H: 292D

7138 פָּלָל *pālāl*, Palal, S: 6420, B: 813A, K: 763D, H: 293A

7139 פְּלַלְיָה *pᵉlalyâ*, Pelaliah, S: 6421, B: 813D, K: 763D, H: 293A

7140 פַּלְמֹנִי *palmōnî*, certain one, S: 6422, B: 811D, K: 763D, H: 293A

7141 פלני *p^{e}lōnî*, certain one, S: 6423, B: 811D, K: 764A, H: 293A

7142 [1]פלס *pālas*[1], [D] to make level, make smooth, prepare, S: 6424, B: 814A, K: 764A, H: 293A

7143 [2]פלס *pālas*[2], [D] to examine, observe, S: 6424, B: 814A, K: 764A, H: 293A

7144 פלס *peles*, balance, scale, S: 6425, B: 813D, K: 764B, H: 293A

7145 פלץ *pālaṣ*, [F] to tremble, shake, S: 6426, B: 814A, K: 764B, H: 293A

7146 פלצות *pallāṣût*, trembling, shuddering, shaking, S: 6427, B: 814A, K: 764B, H: 293A

7147 פלש *pālaš*, [F] to roll oneself (in the dust or ash), S: 6428, B: 814B, K: 764B, H: 293A

7148 פלשת *p^{e}lešet*, Philistia; Philistine, S: 6429, B: 814B, K: 764C, H: 293A

7149 פלשתי *p^{e}lištî*, Philistine, S: 6430, B: 814B, K: 764C, H: 293A

7150 פלת *pelet*, Peleth, S: 6431, B: 814C, K: 764D, H: 293A

7151 פלת *p^{e}lut*, distinction, S: 6304†, B: 804B, K: 764D, H: 289B

7152 פלתי *p^{e}lētî*, Pelethite, S: 6432, B: 814C, K: 764D, H: 293A

7153 פן *pen*, lest, not, S: 6435†, B: 814C, K: 764D, H: 293B

7154 פנג *pannag*, food, confection, S: 6436, B: 815A, K: 765B, H: 293B

7155 פנה *pānâ*, [A] to turn (in various senses); [D] to prepare; to turn away; [G] to turn; [H] to be caused to turn, S: 6437, B: 815A, K: 765B, H: 293B

7156 פנה *pāneh*, face, appearance; (as pp.) before, in front of, in the presence of, S: 3942† & 6440, B: 815D, K: 766A, H: 293D

7157 פנה *pinnâ*, corner (of a structure), cornerstone (as a crucial element); stronghold; leader, S: 6434† & 6438, B: 819C, K: 767D, H: 294B

7158 [1]פנואל *p^{e}nûʾēl*[1], Penuel, S: 6439, B: 819C 2., K: 768A, H: 294B

7159 [2]פנואל *p^{e}nûʾēl*[2], Peniel, S: 6439, B: 819C 1., K: 768A, H: 294B

7160 [1]פניאל *p^{e}nîʾēl*[1], variant: Peniel, see 7158, S: 6439, B: 819C 2, K: 768B, H: 294B

7161 [2]פניאל *p^{e}nîʾēl*[2], Peniel, S: 6439, B: 819C 1, K: 768B, H: 294B

7162 פניים *p^{e}nîyyim*, variant: see 7165, S: 6443†, B: 819D, K: 768B, H: 294B

7163 פנימה *p^{e}nîmâ*, inner, inside, within, S: 6441, B: 819B, K: 768B, H: 294B

7164 פנימי *p^{e}nîmî*, inner, S: 6442, B: 819B, K: 768C, H: 294C

7165 פנינים *p^{e}nînîm*, rubies *or* corals, S: 6443†, B: 819D, K: 768C, H: 294C

7166 פננה *p^{e}ninnâ*, Peninnah, S: 6444, B: 819D, K: 768C, H: 294C

7167 פנק *pānaq*, [D] to pamper, S: 6445, B: 819D, K: 768C, H: 294C

7168 פס *pas*, ornamentation, many-colored *or* long-sleeved garment, S: 6446, B: 821A, K: 768D, H: 294C

7169 פס דמים *pas dammîm*, Pas Dammim, S: 6450, B: 67C, K: 78D, H: 25B

7170 פסג *pāsag*, [D] to look over *or* to walk among, S: 6448, B: 819D, K: 768D, H: 294C

7171 פסגה *pisgâ*, Pisgah, S: 6449, B: 820A, K: 768D, H: 294C

7172 פסה *pissâ*, abundance, plenty, S: 6451, B: 821A, K: 769A, H: 294C

7173 [1]פסח *pāsaḥ*[1], [A] to pass over, S: 6452, B: 820A, K: 769A, H: 294C

7174 [2]פסח *pāsaḥ*[2], [A] to be limp; [C] to become crippled; to worship in a limping dance, S: 6452, B: 820C, K: 769A, H: 294C

7175 פסח *pesaḥ*, Passover, S: 6453, B: 820A, K: 769A, H: 294C

7176 פסח *pāsēaḥ*, Paseah, S: 6454, B: 820C, K: 769C, H: 294D

7177 פסח *pissēaḥ*, lame, crippled, S: 6455, B: 820C, K: 769C, H: 294D

7178 פסיל *pāsîl*, idol, carved image, S: 6456, B: 820D, K: 769D, H: 294D

7179 פסך *pāsak*, Pasach, S: 6457, B: 820D, K: 769D, H: 294D

7180 פסל *pāsal*, [A] to chisel out, carve, S: 6458, B: 820D, K: 769D, H: 294D

7181 פסל *pesel*, idol, carved image, S: 6459, B: 820D, K: 770A, H: 294D

7182 פסס *pāsas*, [A] to vanish, S: 6461, B: 821A, K: 770A, H: 294D

7183 פספה *pispâ*, Pispah, S: 6462, B: 821A, K: 770A, H: 294D

7184 פעה *pāʿâ*, [A] to cry out, groan (in childbirth), S: 6463, B: 821A, K: 770B, H: 294D

7185 פעו *pāʿû*, Pau, S: 6464, B: 821B, K: 770B, H: 294D

7186 פעור *p^{e}ʿôr*, Peor, S: 6465, B: 822B, K: 770B, H: 294D

7187 פעי *pāʿî*, variant: Pai, see 7185, S: 6464†, B: 821B, K: 770C, H: 294D

7188 פעל *pāʿal*, [A] to do, make, S: 6466, B: 821B, K: 770C, H: 295A

7189 פעל *pōʿal*, work, deed, labor, S: 6467, B: 821C, K: 770D, H: 295A

7190 פעלה *p^{e}ʿullâ*, work, deed, recompense, S: 6468, B: 821C, K: 771A, H: 295A

7191 פעלתי *p^{e}ʿull^{e}tay*, Peullethai, S: 6469, B: 821D, K: 771B, H: 295B

7192 פעם *pāʿam*, [A] to push, impel; [C] to be troubled; [F] to be troubled, S: 6470, B: 821D, K: 771B, H: 295B

7193 פעם *paʿam*, step, foot; time, occurrence, S: 6471, B: 821D, K: 771B, H: 295B

7194 פעמון *paʿ^{a}môn*, bell (on a robe), S: 6472†, B: 822B, K: 771D, H: 295C

7195 פענח *paʿnēaḥ*, variant: Paneah, S: 6847†, B: 861B, K: 771D, H: 295C

7196 פער *pāʿar*, [A] to open wide (mouth), S: 6473, B: 822B, K: 771D, H: 295C

7197 פערי *paʿ^{a}ray*, Paarai, S: 6474, B: 822B, K: 772A, H: 295C

7198 פצה *pāṣâ*, [A] to open (mouth); to deliver, set free, S: 6475, B: 822C, K: 772A, H: 295C

7199 [1]פצח *pāṣaḥ*[1], variant: [A] to be serene, S: 476, B: 822C, K: 772B, H: 295C

7200 [2]פצח *pāṣaḥ*[2], [A] to break forth, burst forth; [D] to break (in pieces), S: 6476, B: 822C, K: 772B, H: 295C

7201 פצירה *p^{e}ṣîrâ*, sharpening (of plowshare), S: 6477, B: 823A, K: 772B, H: 295C

7202 פצל *pāṣal*, [D] to peel (bark off boughs), S: 6478, B: 822D, K: 772B, H: 295D

7203 פצלות *p^{e}ṣālôt*, stripes (made by peeling bark), S: 6479†, B: 822D, K: 772C, H: 295D

7204 פצם *pāṣam*, [A] to tear open, S: 6480, B: 822D, K: 772C, H: 295D

7205 פצע *pāṣaʿ*, [A] to bruise, wound; [B] to be emasculated (by crushing), S: 6481, B: 822D, K: 772C, H: 295D

7206 פצע *peṣaʿ*, wound, bruise, S: 6482, B: 822D, K: 772C, H: addenda XVII

7207 פצץ *pāṣaṣ*, [D] to break to pieces, shatter, crush; [F] to be crumbled, be shattered, S: 6327†, B: 822D, K: 772D, H: 295D

7208 פצץ *paṣṣēṣ*, variant: Pazzez, see 1122, S: 1048†, B: 112D, K: 125C 38. & 772D, H: 39C 42.

7209 פצץ *piṣṣēṣ*, variant: Pizzez, see 2204, S: 6483, B: 823A, K: 772D, H: 295D

7210 פצר *pāṣar*, [A] to insist on, bring pressure, persuade; [G] to be arrogant, S: 6484, B: 823A, K: 772D, H: 295D

7211 פק *piq*, giving way, shaking (of knees), S: 6375†, B: 807C, K: 773A, H: 295D

7212 פקד *pāqad*, [A] to count, number; to punish; [B] to be counted, listed; [C] to be missing, empty; [D] to muster; [E] to be robbed; to be recorded; [G] to appoint, give a charge; [H] to be appointed; [F] to be mustered, counted, S: 6485, B: 823A, K: 773A, H: 296A

7213 פקדה *p^{e}quddâ*, appointment, charge; punishment, S: 6486, B: 824A, K: 774B, H: 296C

7214 פקדון *piqqādôn*, something entrusted, something in reserve, S: 6487, B: 824C, K: 774C, H: 296C

7215 פקדת *p^{e}qidut*, (captain of the) guard, S: 6488, B: 824B, K: 774D, H: 296C

7216 פקוד *p^{e}qôd*, Pekod, S: 6489, B: 824C, K: 774D, H: 296C

7217 פקודים *p^{e}qûdîm*, accounting (of materials), S: 6485†, B: 824B, K: 773A, H: 296C

7218 פקודים *piqqûdîm*, precepts, directions, orders, S: 6490†, B: 824B, K: 774D, H: 296C

7219 פקח *pāqaḥ*, [A] to open; [B] to be opened; [C] to be opened, S: 6491, B: 824C, K: 774D, H: 296C

7220 פקח *peqaḥ*, Pekah, S: 6492, B: 824D, K: 775A, H: 296D

7221 פקח *piqqēaḥ*, (normal) sighted, S: 6493, B: 824D, K: 775A, H: 296D

7222 פקחיה *p^{e}qaḥyâ*, Pekahiah, S: 6494, B: 824D, K: 775A, H: 296D

7223 פקח־קוח *p^{e}qaḥ-qôaḥ*, opening (of eyesight), S: 6495, B: 824D, K: 775A, H: 296D

7224 פקיד *pāqîd*, chief officer, supervisor, commissioner, S: 6496, B: 824B, K: 775B, H: 296D

7225 פקעים *p^{e}qāʿîm*, gourds, S: 6497†, B: 825A, K: 775B, H: 296D

7226 פקעת *paqquʿōt*, gourds, S: 6498†, B: 825A, K: 775B, H: 296D

7227 פֶּקֶר *peqer*, variant: licentiousness, S: 6485†, B: 824A, K: 775C, H: 296A

7228 פַּר *par*, bull, S: 6499, B: 830D, K: 775C, H: 296D

7229 פָּרָא *pārā'*, [G] to thrive in fruitfulness, S: 6500, B: 826A, K: 775D, H: 296D

7230 פֶּרֶא *pere'*, wild donkey, S: 6501, B: 825B, K: 775D, H: 296D

7231 פִּרְאָם *pir'ām*, Piram, S: 6502, B: 825B, K: 776A, H: 297A

7232 פַּרְבָּר *parbār*, court (of the temple), S: 6503, B: 826C, K: 776A, H: 297A

7233 פָּרַד *pārad*, [B] to be spread out; [C] to be separated, be parted; [D] to consort with; [E] to be scattered; [G] to set apart, divide, separate; [F] to be scattered, be parted, S: 6504, B: 825B, K: 776A, H: 297A

7234 פֶּרֶד *pered*, mule, S: 6505, B: 825D, K: 776C, H: 297B

7235 פִּרְדָּה *pirdâ*, (female) mule, S: 6506, B: 825D, K: 776C, H: 297B

7236 פַּרְדֵּס *pardēs*, park, forest, orchard, S: 6508, B: 825D, K: 776D, H: 297B

7237 פְּרֻדֹת *pᵉrudōt*, grain (of seed), S: 6507†, B: 825C, K: 776D, H: 297B

7238 פָּרָה *pārâ[1]*, [A] to be fruitful, flourish; [G] to make fruitful, S: 6509, B: 826A, K: 776D, H: 297B

7239 2פָּרָה *pārâ[2]*, cow, heifer, S: 6510, B: 831A, K: 777A, H: 297B

7240 3פָּרָה *pārâ[3]*, Parah, S: 6511, B: 831A, K: 777A, H: 297B

7241 פֶּרֶה *pereh*, wild donkey, S: 6501, B: 825A, K: 777A, H: 297B

7242 פֻּרָה *purâ*, Purah, S: 6513, B: 826C, K: 777B, H: 297B

7243 פְּרוּדָא *pᵉrûdā'*, Peruda, S: 6514, B: 825C, K: 777B, H: 297B

7244 פְּרוֹזִים *pᵉrôzîm*, variant: see 7253, S: 6519†, B: 826D, K: 777B, H: 297C

7245 פָּרוּחַ *pārûaḥ*, Paruah, S: 6515, B: 827C, K: 777B, H: 297C

7246 פַּרְוַיִם *parwayim*, Parvaim, S: 6516, B: 826C, K: 777B, H: 297C

7247 פַּרְוָר *parwār*, court, S: 6503, B: 826C, K: 777C, H: 297C

7248 פָּרוּר *pārûr*, cooking pot, S: 6517, B: 807D, K: 777C, H: 297C

7249 פֵּרוֹת *pērôt*, variant: see 2923, S: 2661†, B: 344A, K: 322C, H: 113A

7250 פָּרָז *pārāz*, warrior, S: 6518, B: 826D, K: 777C, H: 297C

7251 פְּרָזוֹן *pᵉrāzôn*, dwellers in the open country; warriors, S: 6520, B: 826D, K: 777C, H: 297C

7252 פְּרָזוֹת *pᵉrāzôt*, rural, open country, S: 6519†, B: 826D, K: 777C, H: 297C

7253 פְּרָזִי *pᵉrāzî*, rural, open country, S: 6521, B: 826D, K: 777D, H: 297C

7254 פְּרִזִּי *pᵉrizzî*, Perizzite, S: 6522, B: 827A, K: 777D, H: 297C

7255 פָּרַח *pāraḥ[1]*, [A] to sprout, blossom; break out, flourish; [G] to make flourish, bring to bud, S: 6524, B: 827A, K: 777D, H: 297C

7256 2פָּרַח *pāraḥ[2]*, [A] to fly; (as noun) a bird, S: 6524, B: 827C, K: 778B, H: 297D

7257 3פָּרַח *pāraḥ[3]*, variant: [A] to break out, S: 6524, B: 827B, K: 777D, H: 297C

7258 פֶּרַח *peraḥ*, blossom, bud; floral work, S: 6525, B: 827B, K: 778B, H: 297D

7259 פִּרְחַח *pirḥaḥ*, tribe, offspring, S: 6526, B: 827B, K: 778B, H: 297D

7260 פָּרַט *pāraṭ*, [A] to strum, improvise (on a musical instrument), S: 6527, B: 827C, K: 778B, H: 297D

7261 פֶּרֶט *pereṭ*, fallen grapes, S: 6528, B: 827C, K: 778C, H: 297D

7262 פְּרִי *pᵉrî*, fruit, produce, crops, S: 6529, B: 826B, K: 778C, H: 297D

7263 פְּרִידָא *pᵉrîdā'*, Perida, S: 6514, B: 825C, K: 778D, H: 297D

7264 פָּרִיץ *pārîṣ[1]*, ferocious (animal), S: 6530, B: 829D, K: 778D, H: 298A

7265 2פָּרִיץ *pārîṣ[2]*, robber; violent one, S: 6530, B: 829D, K: 778D, H: 298A

7266 פֶּרֶךְ *perek*, ruthlessness, brutality, violence, S: 6531, B: 827D, K: 779A, H: 298A

7267 פָּרֹכֶת *pārōket*, curtain, S: 6532†, B: 827D, K: 779A, H: 298A

7268 פָּרַם *pāram*, [A] to tear; [B] to be torn, S: 6533, B: 827D, K: 779A, H: 298A

7269 פַּרְמַשְׁתָּא *parmaštā'*, Parmashta, S: 6534, B: 828A, K: 779B, H: 298A

7270 פַּרְנָךְ *parnāk*, Parnach, S: 6535, B: 828A, K: 779B, H: 298A

7271 פָּרַס *pāras[1]*, [A] to offer food, share food; [G] to have a divided hoof, S: 6536, B: 828A, K: 779B, H: 298A

7272 פֶּרֶס *peres*, vulture, S: 6538, B: 828B, K: 779C, H: 298A

7273 2פָּרַס *pāras[2]*, Persia; Persian, S: 6539, B: 828A, K: 779C, H: 298B

7274 פַּרְסָה *parsâ*, hoof, S: 6541, B: 828B, K: 779C, H: 298B

7275 פָּרְסִי *pārᵉsî*, Persian, S: 6542, B: 828A, K: 779D, H: 298B

7276 פָּרַע *pāra'[1]*, [A] to take the lead, S: 6544, B: 828C, K: 779D, H: 298B

7277 2פָּרַע *pāra'[2]*, [A] to be out of control, be unkempt; to ignore, avoid; [B] to be unkempt, be running wild; [C] be unrestrained; [G] to let neglect; to promote wickedness, S: 6544, B: 828D, K: 779D, H: 298B

7278 פֶּרַע *pera'[1]*, leader, prince, S: 6546†, B: 828C, K: 780A, H: 298B

7279 2פֶּרַע *pera'[2]*, long hair of head, S: 6545, B: 828D, K: 780A, H: 298C

7280 3פֶּרַע *pera'[3]*, variant: Pera, see 7036, S: 6319†, B: 806C, K: 754D, H: 289D

7281 פַּרְעֹה *par'ōh*, Pharaoh, S: 6547, B: 829A, K: 780A, H: 298C

7282 פַּרְעֹשׁ *par'ōš[1]*, flea, S: 6550, B: 829A, K: 780B, H: 298C

7283 2פַּרְעֹשׁ *par'ōš[2]*, Parosh, S: 6551, B: 829B, K: 780B, H: 298C

7284 פִּרְעָתוֹן *pir'ātôn*, Pirathon, S: 6552, B: 828C, K: 780B, H: 298C

7285 פִּרְעָתוֹנִי *pir'ātônî*, Pirathonite, from Pirathon, S: 6553, B: 828D, K: 780B, H: 298C

7286 פַּרְפַּר *parpar*, Pharpar, S: 6554, B: 829B, K: 780C, H: 298C

7287 פָּרַץ *pāraṣ*, [A] to break out, burst forth; [B] to be broken through; [C] to be spread abroad; [E] to be broken down; [F] to break oneself away, S: 6555, B: 829B, K: 780C, H: 298C

7288 פֶּרֶץ *pereṣ[1]*, breech, break, gap, S: 6556, B: 829C, K: 781A, H: 298D

7289 2פֶּרֶץ *pereṣ[2]*, Perez, S: 6557, B: 829D, K: 781B, H: 298D

7290 פֶּרֶץ עֻזָּא (פֶּרֶץ עֻזָּה) *pereṣ 'uzzā*, Perez Uzzah, S: 6560, B: 829D, K: 781B, H: 298D

7291 פַּרְצִי *parṣî*, Perezite, S: 6558, B: 829D 1., K: 781B, H: 298D

7292 פְּרָצִים *pᵉrāṣîm*, Perazim, S: 6559, B: 829D 2b, K: 781B, H: 298D

7293 פָּרַק *pāraq*, [A] to rip to pieces; to free (by tearing away); [D] to take off, tear off; [F] to take off from oneself, tear off from oneself, S: 6561, B: 830A, K: 781B, H: 298D

7294 פֶּרֶק *pereq*, crossroad; plunder, S: 6563, B: 830A, K: 781C, H: 299A

7295 פָּרָק *pārāq*, variant: fragment, S: 6564, B: 830A, K: 781C, H: 299A

7296 פָּרַר *pārar[1]*, [G] to break, violate, nullify; [H] to be broken, revoked, thwarted, S: 6565, B: 830B, K: 781C, H: 299A

7297 2פָּרַר *pārar[2]*, [A] to split asunder; [D] to shatter; to split open; [F] to split asunder, S: 6565, B: 830C, K: 782A, H: 299A

7298 פָּרַשׂ *pāraś*, [A] to spread out, scatter; [B] to be spread out; [C] to be scattered; [D] to scatter, spread out, S: 6566, B: 831A, K: 782B, H: 299B

7299 פַּרְשֵׁז *paršēz*, spreading, S: 6576†, B: 831C, K: 782D, H: 299C

7300 פָּרַשׁ *pāraš[1]*, [A] to make clear; [C] to be given; [E] to be made clear, S: 6567, B: 831C, K: 782D, H: 299C

7301 2פָּרַשׁ *pāraš[2]*, [G] to secrete poison, S: 6567, B: 831D, K: 782D, H: 299C

7302 פֶּרֶשׁ *pereš[1]*, offal, S: 6569, B: 831D, K: 783A, H: 299C

7303 2פֶּרֶשׁ *pereš[2]*, Peresh, S: 6570, B: 831D, K: 783B, H: 299C

7304 פָּרָשׁ *pārāš[1]*, horse, S: 6571, B: 832A, K: 783B, H: 299C 2.

7305 2פָּרָשׁ *pārāš[2]*, horseman, S: 6571, B: 832A, K: 783B, H: 299C 1.

7306 פַּרְשֶׁגֶן *paršegen*, copy, S: 6572, B: 832B, K: 783C, H: 418C

7307 פַּרְשְׁדֹן *paršᵉdōn*, back (of a person), back door [?], S: 6574, B: 832B, K: 783C, H: 299D

7308 פָּרָשָׁה *pārāšâ*, exact amount, exact statement, S: 6575, B: 831D, K: 783D, H: 299D

7309 פַּרְשַׁנְדָּתָא *paršandātā'*, Parshandatha, S: 6577, B: 832B, K: 783D, H: 299D

7310 פְּרָת *pᵉrāt*, Euphrates, Perath, S: 6578, B: 832B, K: 783D, H: 299D

7311 פֹּרָת *pōrāt*, variant: see 7238, S: 6509†, B: 826A 2, K: 784A, H: 299D

7312 פַּרְתְּמִים *partᵉmîm*, nobles, princes, S: 6579†, B: 832C, K: 784A, H: 299D

7313 פָּשָׂה *pāśâ*, [A] to spread, S: 6581, B: 832C, K: 784A, H: 299D

7314 פָּשַׂע *pāśa'*, [A] to march, step forth, S: 6585, B: 832C, K: 784A, H: 299D

7315 פֶּשַׂע *peśa'*, step, S: 6587, B: 832C, K: 784B, H: 299D

7316 פָּשַׂק *pāśaq*, [A] to open wide (the lips in talking or smirking); [D] to spread the feet or legs (in immorality), S: 6589, B: 832D, K: 784B, H: 299D

7317 פַּשׁ *paš*, wickedness *or* weakness, foolishness, S: 6580, B: 832D, K: 784B, H: 299D

7318 פָּשַׁח *pāšaḥ*, [D] to mangle, S: 6582, B: 832D, K: 784B, H: 299D

7319 פַּשְׁחוּר *pašḥûr*, Pashhur, S: 6583, B: 832D, K: 784B, H: 300A

7320 פָּשַׁט *pāšaṭ*, [A] to take off, strip; to make a sudden dash, raid; [D] to strip; [G] to take off, strip off; [F] to strip oneself, S: 6584, B: 832D, K: 784C, H: 300A

7321 פָּשַׁע *pāša'*, [A] to rebel, revolt, S: 6586, B: 833B, K: 785A, H: 300A

7322 פֶּשַׁע *peša'*, rebellion, revolt, sin, transgression, S: 6588, B: 833B, K: 785B, H: 300B

7323 פֵּשֶׁר *pēšer*, explanation, interpretation, S: 6592, B: 833D, K: 785C, H: 300A

7324 פֵּשֶׁת *pēšet*, flax, linen (made of flax), S: 6593†, B: 833D, K: 785D, H: 300B

7325 פִּשְׁתָּה *pištâ*, flax, wick (made of flax), S: 6594, B: 834A, K: 785D, H: 300B

7326 פַּת *pat*, little piece, morsel (of food), S: 6595, B: 837D, K: 785D, H: 300B

7327 פֹּת *pōt*, scalp, forehead; socket (for doors), S: 6596, B: 834A, K: 786A, H: 300C

7328 פִּתְאֹם *pit'ōm*, suddenly, unexpectedly, all at once, in an instant, S: 6597, B: 837B, K: 786A, H: 300C

7329 פַּת־בַּג *pat-bag*, (fine) food, choice provisions, S: 6598, B: 834A, K: 786B, H: 300C

7330 פִּתְגָם *pitgām*, edict, decree; sentence (for a crime), S: 6599, B: 834A, K: 786B, H: 300C

7331 [1]פָּתָה *pātâ*[1], [A] to be simple, easily deceived, enticed; [D] to seduce, entice, deceive, allure; [C] to be enticed, deceived; [E] to be deceived, enticed, persuaded, S: 6601, B: 834B & C, K: 786B, H: 300C

7332 [2]פָּתָה *pātâ*[2], [G] to provide ample space, S: 6601, B: 834B, K: 786C, H: 300D

7333 פְּתוּאֵל *p^{e}tû'ēl*, Pethuel, S: 6602, B: 834D, K: 786D, H: 300D

7334 פִּתּוּחַ *pittûaḥ*, engraving, inscription, S: 6603, B: 836C, K: 786D, H: 300D

7335 פְּתוֹר *p^{e}tôr*, Pethor, S: 6604, B: 834D, K: 786D, H: 300D

7336 פְּתוֹת *p^{e}tôt*, scrap, morsel (of food), S: 6595†, B: 837D, K: 786D, H: 300D

7337 [1]פָּתַח *pātaḥ*[1], [A] to open; [B] to be opened; [C] to be opened; [D] to loosen, release, take off; [F] to free oneself, S: 6605, B: 834D, K: 787A, H: 300D

7338 [2]פָּתַח *pātaḥ*[2], [D] to engrave, carve; [E] to be engraved, S: 6605, B: 836B, K: 787D, H: 301A

7339 פֶּתַח *petaḥ*, entrance, opening, door, S: 6607, B: 835D, K: 787D, H: 301B

7340 פֵּתַח *pētaḥ*, unfolding, opening, S: 6608, B: 836A, K: 788A, H: 301B

7341 פִּתְחוֹן *pittāḥôn*, opening (of mouth for communication), S: 6610, B: 836A, K: 788B, H: 301B

7342 פְּתַחְיָה *p^{e}taḥyâ*, Pethahiah, S: 6611, B: 836A, K: 788B, H: 301C

7343 [1]פְּתִי *petî*[1], simple, naive, S: 6612, B: 834B, K: 788B, H: 301C

7344 [2]פְּתִי *petî*[2], simple ways, simplemindedness, S: 6612, B: 834C, K: 788C, H: 301C

7345 פְּתִיגִיל *p^{e}tîgîl*, fine clothing, S: 6614, B: 836C, K: 788C, H: 301C

7346 פְּתַיּוּת *p^{e}tayyût*, undisciplined, deceptive, S: 6615, B: 834C, K: 788C, H: 301C

7347 פְּתִיחָה *p^{e}tîḥâ*, drawn sword, S: 6609†, B: 836A, K: 788C, H: 301C

7348 פָּתִיל *pātîl*, cord, strands, string, S: 6616, B: 836D, K: 788C, H: 301C

7349 פָּתַל *pātal*, [C] to have a struggle; to be wily, be crooked; [F] to show oneself shrewd, S: 6617, B: 836C, K: 788D, H: 301C

7350 פְּתַלְתֹּל *p^{e}taltōl*, crooked, perverse, S: 6618, B: 836D, K: 788D, H: 301C

7351 פִּתֹם *pitōm*, Pithom, S: 6619, B: 837A, K: 788D, H: 301C

7352 פֶּתֶן *peten*, cobra, serpent, S: 6620, B: 837A, K: 789A, H: 301C

7353 פֶּתַע *peta'*, instant; (as adv.) suddenly, in an instant, S: 6621, B: 837B, K: 789A, H: 301C

7354 פָּתַר *pātar*, [A] to interpret, give the meaning (of a dream), S: 6622, B: 837C, K: 789A, H: 301D

7355 פִּתְרוֹן *pittārôn*, interpretation, meaning, S: 6623†, B: 837C, K*, H: 301D

7356 פַּתְרוֹס *patrôs*, Upper Egypt (Patros), S: 6624, B: 837C, K: 789C, H: 301D

7357 פַּתְרֻסִים *patrusîm*, Pathrusite, S: 6625†, B: 837D, K: 789C, H: 301D

7358 פַּתְשֶׁגֶן *patšegen*, copy (of a text), S: 6572, B: 837D, K: 789C, H: 301D

7359 פָּתַת *pātat*, [A] to crumble, S: 6626, B: 837D, K: 789C, H: 301D

7360 צ *ṣ*, letter of the Hebrew alphabet, S*, B: 838A, K: 789B, H*

7361 צֵא *ṣē'*, variant: dirt, S*, B: 422B, K: 789D, H: 301B

7362 צֵאָה *ṣē'â*, excrement, dung, S: 6627, B: 844B, K: 789D, H: 301B

7363 צֹאָה *ṣō'â*, filth, excrement, dung, S: 6675, B: 844B, K: 789D, H: 301D

7364 צֹאִי *ṣō'î*, filthy, befouled (with excrement), S: 6674†, B: 844B, K: 790A, H: 302A

7365 צֶאֱלִים *ṣe'^{e}lîm*, lotus plant, S: 6628†, B: 838A, K: 790A, H: 302A

7366 צֹאן *ṣō'n*, flock, sheep, goats, S: 6629, B: 838A, K: 790A, H: 302A

7367 צַאֲנָן *ṣa'^{a}nān*, Zaanan, S: 6630, B: 838C, K: 790B, H: 302A

7368 צֶאֱצָאִים *ṣe'^{e}ṣā'îm*, offspring, descendant, S: 6631†, B: 425C, K: 790B, H: 302A

7369 [1]צָב *ṣāb*[1], (covered) wagon, S: 6632, B: 839D, K: 790B, H: 302A

7370 [2]צָב *ṣāb*[2], lizard, S: 6632, B: 839D, K: 790C, H: 302A

7371 [1]צָבָא *ṣābā'*[1], [A] to fight, do battle; to serve in (temple) corps, S: 6633, B: 838C, K: 790C, H: 302A

7372 [2]צָבָא *ṣābā'*[2], army, host, divisions (of an army); (as a title of God) the Almighty, S: 6635, B: 838D, K: 790D, H: 302B

7373 [3]צְבָא *ṣābā'*[3], gazelle, S: 6643†, B: 840A, K: 791C, H: 302B

7374 צְבָאָה *ṣ^{e}bā'â*, (female) gazelle, S: 6643†, B: 840A, K: 791C, H: 302B

7375 צְבֹאִים *ṣ^{e}bō'îm*, Zeboiim, S: 6636, B: 840B, K: 791C, H: 302C

7376 צֹבֵבָה *ṣōbēbâ*, variant: Zobebah, see 2206, S: 6637†, B: 839D, K: 791C, H: 302C

7377 צָבָה *ṣābâ*, [A] to swell; [G] to cause to swell, S: 6638, B: 839D, K: 791D, H: 302C

7378 צֹבֶה *ṣōbeh*, variant: see 7371, S: 6635†, B: 838D, K: 791D, H: 302C

7379 צָבֶה *ṣābeh*, swollen, S: 6639, B: 839D, K: 791D, H: 302C

7380 צָבוּעַ *ṣābûa'*, speckled, variegated, S: 6641, B: 840C, K: 791D, H: 302C

7381 צָבַט *ṣābaṭ*, [A] to offer (food to another person), S: 6642, B: 840B, K: 792A, H: 302C

7382 [1]צְבִי *ṣ^{e}bî*[1], ornament, beautiful (thing), glory, S: 6643, B: 840A, K: 792A, H: 302C

7383 [2]צְבִי *ṣ^{e}bî*[2], gazelle, S: 6643, B: 840A, K: 792A, H: 302C

7384 צִבְיָא *ṣibyā'*, Zibia, S: 6644, B: 840B, K: 792B, H: 302C

7385 צִבְיָה *ṣibyâ*, Zibiah, S: 6645, B: 840B, K: 792B, H: 302C

7386 צְבִיָּה *ṣ^{e}biyyâ*, (female) gazelle, S: 6646, B: 840B, K: 792B, H: 302D

7387 צְבֹיִים *ṣ^{e}bōyîm*, variant: Zeboiim, see 7375, S: 6636†, B: 840B, K: 792B, H: 302D

7388 צָבַע *ṣāba'*, variant: [F] to be dyed, S: 3320†, B: 426B b, K: 792B, H: 302D

7389 צֶבַע *ṣeba'*, colorful (dyed) garment, S: 6648, B: 840C, K: 792C, H: 302D

7390 צִבְעוֹן *ṣib'ôn*, Zibeon, S: 6649, B: 840D, K: 792C, H: 302D

7391 צְבֹעִים *ṣ^{e}bō'îm*, Zeboim, S: 6650, B: 840D, K: 792C, H: 302D

7392 צָבַר *ṣābar*, [A] to store up, heap up, pile up, S: 6651, B: 840D, K: 792C, H: 302D

7393 צִבֻּר *ṣibbur*, pile, heap, S: 6652, B: 840D, K: 792D, H: 302D

7394 צִבָּרוֹן *ṣibbārôn*, variant: heap, S: 1225†, B: 131B, K: 792D, H: 45D

7395 צֶבֶת *ṣebet*, bundle (of grain with the stalk), S: 6653, B: 841A, K: 792D, H: 302D

7396 [1]צַד *ṣad*[1], side (of something), S: 6654, B: 841A, K: 792D, H: 302D

7397 [2]צַד *ṣad*[2], variant: snare, S: 6654, B: 841A, K: 793A, H: 302D

7398 צְדָד *ṣādād*, Zedad, S: 6657†, B: 841A, K: 793A, H: 302D

7399 [1]צָדָה *ṣādâ*[1], [A] to lie in wait, hunt down a person, S: 6658, B: 841B, K: 793A, H: 302D

7400 [2]צָדָה *ṣādâ*[2], [C] to be destroyed, be laid waste, S: 6658, B: 841B, K: 793B, H: 303A

7401 צָדוֹק *ṣādôq*, Zadok, S: 6659, B: 843B, K: 793B, H: 303A

7402 צְדִיָּה *ṣᵉdiyyâ*, ambush, lying-in-wait (with malicious intent), S: 6660, B: 841B, K: 793C, H: 303A

7403 צִדִּים *ṣiddîm*, Ziddim, S: 6661, B: 841A, K: 793C, H: 303A

7404 צַדִּיק *ṣaddîq*, righteous, upright, just, innocent, S: 6662, B: 843A, K: 793C, H: 303A

7405 צָדַק *ṣādaq*, [A] to be righteous, be innocent, be vindicated, S: 6663, B: 842C, K: 794A, H: 303A

7406 צֶדֶק *ṣedeq*, righteousness, justice, rightness, S: 6664, B: 841C, K: 794C, H: 303C

7407 צְדָקָה *ṣᵉdāqâ*, righteousness, S: 6666, B: 842A, K: 795A, H: 303C

7408 צִדְקִיָּה *ṣidqiyyâ*, Zedekiah, S: 6667, B: 843B, K: 795C, H: 303D

7409 צִדְקִיָּהוּ *ṣidqiyyāhû*, Zedekiah, S: 6667, B: 843B, K: 795D, H: 303D

7410 צָהַב *ṣāhab*, [H] to be polished, gleaming copper color, S: 6668, B: 843C, K: 795D, H: 303D

7411 צָהֹב *ṣāhōb*, yellow, S: 6669, B: 843C, K: 795D, H: 303D

7412 [1]צָהַל *ṣāhal*[1], [A] to shout out, celebrate; to neigh (of a horse), S: 6670, B: 843C, K: 796A, H: 303D

7413 [2]צָהַל *ṣāhal*[2], [G] to make shine, S: 6670, B: 843D, K: 796A, H: 304A

7414 צָהַר *ṣāhar*, [G] to press olives, S: 6671, B: 844A, K: 796A, H: 304A

7415 צֹהַר *ṣōhar*, roof, covering (for ark vessel), S: 6672, B: 844A, K: 796B, H: 304A

7416 צָהֳרַיִם *ṣohᵒrayim*, noon, noonday, midday, S: 6672†, B: 843D, K: 796B, H: 304A

7417 צַו *ṣaw*, worthless thing = idol *or* command, utterance, S: 6673, B: 846C, K: 796C, H: 304A

7418 צַוָּאר *ṣawwā'r*, (back of) neck, S: 6677, B: 848B, K: 796C, H: 304A

7419 צוֹבָא *ṣôbā'*, Zobah, S: 6678, B: 844B, K: 796D, H: 304A

7420 צוֹבָה *ṣôbâ*, Zobah, S: 6678, B: 844B, K: 796D, H: 304A

7421 צוּד *ṣûd*, [A] to hunt, stalk; [D] to ensnare, S: 6679, B: 844C, K: 796D, H: 304A

7422 צָוָה *ṣāwâ*, [D] to command, order, instruct, give direction; [E] to be commanded, be directed, be ordered, S: 6680, B: 845B, K: 797A, H: 304B

7423 צָוַח *ṣāwaḥ*, [A] to shout, cry aloud, S: 6681, B: 846D, K: 797D, H: 304C

7424 צְוָחָה *ṣᵉwāḥâ*, cry of distress, wail, S: 6682, B: 846D, K: 797D, H: 304C

7425 צוּלָה *ṣûlâ*, the watery deep, the ocean abyss, S: 6683, B: 846D, K: 797D, H: 304C

7426 צוּם *ṣûm*, [A] to fast, S: 6684, B: 847A, K: 797D, H: 304C

7427 צוֹם *ṣôm*, fast, time of fasting, act of fasting, S: 6685, B: 847B, K: 798A, H: 304C

7428 צוּעָר *ṣû'ār*, Zuar, S: 6686, B: 859B, K: 798B, H: 304C

7429 [1]צוּף *ṣûp*[1], [A] to flow; [G] to make float; to overwhelm (with water), S: 6687, B: 847B, K: 798B, H: 304D

7430 [2]צוּף *ṣûp*[2], honeycomb (dripping with honey), S: 6688, B: 847B, K: 798B, H: 304D

7431 [3]צוּף *ṣûp*[3], Zuph, S: 6689, B: 847C, K: 798B, H: 304D

7432 צוֹפַח *ṣôpaḥ*, Zophah, S: 6690, B: 860C, K: 798C, H: 304D

7433 צוֹפַי *ṣôpay*, Zophai, S: 6689, B: 847C, K: 798C, H: 304D

7434 צוּפִי *ṣûpî*, Zuphite, S: 6689†, B: 847C, K: 798C, H: 304D

7435 צוֹפִים *ṣôpîm*, variant: Zophim, S: 7436†, B: 847C, K: 798C, H: 304D

7436 צוֹפַר *ṣôpar*, Zophar, S: 6691, B: 862B, K: 798C, H: 304D

7437 [1]צוּץ *ṣûṣ*[1], [A] to bud, blossom; [G] to put forth blossoms; to cause to flourish, S: 6692, B: 847C, K: 798C, H: 304D

7438 [2]צוּץ *ṣûṣ*[2], [G] to peer at, look at, S: 6692, B: 847D, K: 798D, H: 304D

7439 [1]צוּק *ṣûq*[1], [G] to oppress, compel, nag, inflict, S: 6693, B: 847D, K: 798D, H: 304D

7440 [2]צוּק *ṣûq*[2], [A] to pour out, S: 6694, B: 848B, K: 798D, H: 310B

7441 צוֹק *ṣôq*, trouble, oppression, S: 6695, B: 848A, K: 798D, H: 305A

7442 צוּקָה *ṣûqâ*, trouble, distress, oppression, S: 6695, B: 848A, K: 799A, H: 305A

7443 [1]צוּר *ṣûr*[1], [A] to siege, besiege, enclose, S: 6696, B: 848D, K: 799A, H: 305A

7444 [2]צוּר *ṣûr*[2], [A] to oppose, harass, S: 6696, B: 849A, K: 799B, H: 305A

7445 [3]צוּר *ṣûr*[3], [A] to fashion, shape, S: 6697, B: 849B, K: 799B, H: 305A

7446 [4]צוּר *ṣûr*[4], rock, rocky crag, S: 6697, B: 849C, K: 799C, H: 305A

7447 [5]צוּר *ṣûr*[5], variant: pebble, flint, S: 6697, B: 849C 1a, K: 799D, H: 305B

7448 [6]צוּר *ṣûr*[6], Zur, S: 6698, B: 849D, K: 800A, H: 305B

7449 [7]צוּר *ṣûr*[7], variant: Zur, see 1123, S: 1049†, B: 112D, K: 800A, H: 305B

7450 צוֹר *ṣôr*, Tyre, S: 6865, B: 862D, K: 815C, H: 305B

7451 צוּרָה *ṣûrâ*, design, form, S: 6699, B: 849B, K: 800A, H: 305B

7452 צוּרִיאֵל *ṣûrî'ēl*, Zuriel, S: 6700, B: 849D, K: 800A, H: 305B

7453 צוּרִישַׁדָּי *ṣûrîšadday*, צוּרִי־שַׁדָּי *ṣûrî-šadday*, Zurishaddai, S: 6701, B: 849D, K: 800A, H: 305B

7454 צַוְּרֹנִים *ṣawwᵉrōnîm*, necklace, S: 6677†, B: 848C, K: 800B, H: 305B

7455 צוּת *ṣût*, [G] to set on fire, S: 6702, B*, K: 800B, H: 305B

7456 צַח *ṣaḥ*, radiant, shimmering, scorching, clear, S: 6703, B: 850A, K: 800B, H: 305B

7457 צִחֶה *ṣiḥeh*, parched, S: 6704, B: 850A, K: 800B, H: 305C

7458 צָחַח *ṣāḥaḥ*, [A] to be white, S: 6705, B: 850A, K: 800C, H: 305C

7459 צְחִחִי *ṣᵉḥiḥî*, variant: see 7460, S: 6708, B: 850A, K: 800C, H: 305C

7460 צָחִיחַ *ṣāḥîaḥ*, bare (rock *or* place in a wall), S: 6706, B: 850A, K: 800C, H: 305C

7461 צְחִיחָה *ṣᵉḥîḥâ*, bare, (sun-)scorched land, S: 6707, B: 850B, K: 800C, H: 305C

7462 צַחֲנָה *ṣaḥᵃnâ*, putrid smell, stench, S: 6709, B: 850B, K: 800D, H: 305C

7463 צַחְצָחוֹת *ṣaḥṣāḥôt*, bare, (sun-)scorched land, S: 6710†, B: 850B, K: 800D, H: 305C

7464 צָחַק *ṣāḥaq*, [A] to laugh; [D] to mock, make sport, caress, S: 6711, B: 850B, K: 800D, H: 305C

7465 צְחֹק *ṣᵉḥōq*, laughter, scorn, S: 6712, B: 850B, K: 801A, H: 305C

7466 צָחַר *ṣāḥar*, Zahar, S: 6713†, B: 850C, K: 801A, H: 305C

7467 צָחֹר *ṣāḥōr*, white, yellowish red, tawny, S: 6715, B: 850C, K: 801A, H: 305C

7468 צֹחַר *ṣōḥar*, Zohar, S: 6714, B: 850C, K: 801B, H: 305D

7469 [1]צִי *ṣî*[1], ship, S: 6716, B: 850D, K: 801B, H: 305D

7470 [2]צִי *ṣî*[2], desert creature; tribes of the desert, S: 6728†, B: 850D, K: 801B, H: 305D

7471 צִיבָא *ṣîbā'*, Ziba, S: 6717, B: 850D, K: 801B, H: 305D

7472 צִיד *ṣîd*, [F] to pack provisions for oneself, S: 6679†, B: 845B, K: 801B, H: 305D

7473 [1]צַיִד *ṣayid*[1], (hunting) game; hunter, S: 6718, B: 844D, K: 801C, H: 305D

7474 [2]צַיִד *ṣayid*[2], food supply, provision, S: 6718, B: 845B, K: 801C, H: 305D

7475 צַיָּד *ṣayyād*, hunter, S: 6719, B: 844D, K: 801C, H: 305D

7476 צֵידָה *ṣêdâ*, food, provisions, supplies, S: 6720, B: 845B, K: 801D, H: 305D

7477 צִידוֹן *ṣîdôn*, Sidon, S: 6721, B: 850D, K: 801D, H: 305D

7478 צִידוֹן רַבָּה *ṣîdôn rabbâ*, Greater Sidon, S: 7227† + 6721†, B: 850D, K: 801D, H: 305D

7479 צִידֹנִי *ṣîdōnî*, Sidonian, people of Sidon, S: 6722, B: 851A, K: 801D, H: 305D

7480 צִיָּה *ṣiyyâ*, desert, parched land, dry land, waterless region, S: 6723, B: 851A, K: 801A, H: 305D

7481 צָיוֹן *ṣāyôn*, desert, waterless country, S: 6724, B: 851B, K: 802A, H: 306A

7482 צִיּוֹן *ṣiyyôn*, Zion, S: 6726, B: 851B, K: 802A, H: 306A

7483 צִיּוּן *ṣiyyûn*, sign, stone marker, S: 6725, B: 846B, K: 802C, H: 306A

7484 צִיחָא *ṣîḥā'*, Ziha, S: 6727, B: 851C, K: 802C, H: 306A

7485 צִינֹק *ṣînōq*, neck-iron, iron collar, S: 6729, B: 857B, K: 802C, H: 306A

7486 צִיעֹר *ṣî'ōr*, Zior, S: 6730, B: 859B, K: 802C, H: 306A

7487 צִיף *ṣîp*, variant: Ziph, see 7431, S: 6689, B: 847C, K: 802D, H: 306A

7488 צִיץ *ṣîṣ*[1], flower, blossom; (ornamental) plate, S: 6731, B: 847C, K: 802D, H: 306A

7489 [2]צִיץ *ṣîṣ*[2], Ziz, S: 6732, B: 851D, K: 802D, H: 306A

7490 [3]צִיץ *ṣîṣ*[3], salt, S: 6731, B: 851C, K: 802D, H: 306A

7491 צִיצָה *ṣîṣâ*, flower, S: 6733, B: 847D, K: 802D, H: 306A

7492 צִיצִת *ṣîṣit*, tassel; tuft of hair, S: 6734, B: 851D, K: 802D, H: 306A

7493 צִיר *ṣîr*[1], [F] to act as a delegation, S: 6735 & 6737†, B: 864B, K: 803A, H: 306A

7494 [2]צִיר *ṣîr*[2], hinge, (door-)pivot, S: 6735 & 6737†, B: 852A, K: 803A, H: 306A

7495 [3]צִיר *ṣîr*[3], envoy, messenger, S: 6735 & 6737†, B: 851D, K: 803A, H: 306B

7496 [4]צִיר *ṣîr*[4], pains, pangs, anguish, S: 6735 & 6737†, B: 852A, K: 803B, H: 306B

7497 [5]צִיר *ṣîr*[5], idol, S: 6736, B: 849C, K: 803B, H: 306B

7498 צֵל *ṣēl*, shadow, shade, protection, S: 6738 & 6752†, B: 853B, K: 803B, H: 306B

7499 צָלָה *ṣālâ*, [A] to roast (meat), S: 6740, B: 852A, K: 803C, H: 306B

7500 צִלָּה *ṣillâ*, Zillah, S: 6741, B: 853C, K: 803D, H: 306B

7501 צְלוּל *ṣᵉlûl*, round loaf, S: 6742, B: 853D, K: 803D, H: 306B

7502 צָלַח *ṣālaḥ*[1], [A] to be powerful, come forcefully; to rush, S: 6743, B: 852B, K: 803D, H: 306B

7503 [2]צָלַח *ṣālaḥ*[2], [A] to prosper, prevail, succeed, avail; [G] to make a success, grant prosperity, make victorious, S: 6743, B: 852B, K: 803D, H: 306B

7504 צְלֹחִית *ṣᵉlōḥît*, bowl, S: 6746, B: 852D, K: 804B, H: 306C

7505 צַלַּחַת *ṣallaḥat*, dish, pan, S: 6745† & 6747, B: 852C, K: 804B, H: 306C

7506 צֵלַחַת *ṣēlaḥat*, variant: pot for cooking, S: 6747†, B: 852C, K: 804B, H: 306C

7507 צָלִי *ṣālî*, roasted (meat), S: 6748, B: 852A, K: 804B, H: 306C

7508 צְלִיל *ṣᵉlîl*, variant: cake, round loaf, S: 6742†, B: 853D, K: 804B, H: 306C

7509 צָלַל *ṣālal*[1], [A] to tingle; to quiver, S: 6750, B: 852D, K: 804B, H: 306C

7510 [2]צָלַל *ṣālal*[2], [A] to sink down, S: 6749, B: 853A, K: 804C, H: 306C

7511 [3]צָלַל *ṣālal*[3], [A] to grow dark; [G] to give shade, S: 6751, B: 853A, K: 804C, H: 306C

7512 צֶלֶם *ṣelem*[1], image, idol, S: 6754, B: 853D, K: 804D, H: 306D

7513 [2]צֶלֶם *ṣelem*[2], phantom, fantasy, shadowy thing, S: 6754, B: 853D, K: 804D, H: 306D

7514 צַלְמוֹן *ṣalmôn*[1], Zalmon, S: 6756, B: 854A, K: 804D, H: 306D

7515 [2]צַלְמוֹן *ṣalmôn*[2], Zalmon, S: 6756, B: 854A, K: 804D, H: 306D

7516 צַלְמָוֶת *ṣalmāwet*, shadow, darkness, gloom, blackness, S: 6757, B: 853C, K: 805A, H: 306D

7517 צַלְמֹנָה *ṣalmōnâ*, Zalmonah, S: 6758, B: 854A, K: 805A, H: 306D

7518 צַלְמֻנָּע *ṣalmunnāʿ*, Zalmunna, S: 6759, B: 854A, K: 805A, H: 306D

7519 צָלַע *ṣālaʿ*, [A] to be lame, limp, S: 6760, B: 854B, K: 805A, H: 306D

7520 צֶלַע *ṣelaʿ*, stumbling, falling, slipping, S: 6761, B: 854C, K: 805B, H: 306D

7521 צֵלָע *ṣēlāʿ*[1], side, S: 6763, B: 854B, K: 805B, H: 306D

7522 [2]צֶלַע *ṣēlāʿ*[2], Zela, Zelah, S: 6762, B: 854B, K: 805C, H: 307A

7523 צָלָף *ṣālāp*, Zalaph, S: 6764, B: 854C, K: 805C, H: 307A

7524 צְלָפְחָד *ṣᵉlopḥād*, Zelophehad, S: 6765, B: 854C, K: 805C, H: 307A

7525 צֶלְצַח *ṣelṣaḥ*, Zelzah, S: 6766, B: 854C, K: 805C, H: 307A

7526 צְלָצַל *ṣᵉlāṣal*, (swarm of) locust, S: 6767, B: 852D, K: 805C, H: 307A

7527 צִלְצָל *ṣilṣāl*[1], whirring, buzzing, S: 6767†, B: 852D, K: 805D, H: 307A

7528 [2]צִלְצָל *ṣilṣāl*[2], (fishing) spear, S: 6767†, B: 852D, K: 805D, H: 307A

7529 צֶלְצְלִים *ṣelṣelîm*, cymbals, S: 6767†, B: 852D, K: 805D, H: 307A

7530 צֶלֶק *ṣeleq*, Zelek, S: 6768, B: 854C, K: 806A, H: 307A

7531 צִלְּתַי *ṣillᵉtay*, Zillethai, S: 6769, B: 853C, K: 806A, H: 307A

7532 צָמֵא *ṣāmēʾ*[1], [A] to thirst, be thirsty, S: 6770, B: 854C, K: 806A, H: 307B

7533 צָמָא *ṣāmāʾ*, thirst, S: 6772, B: 854D, K: 806A, H: 307B

7534 [2]צָמֵא *ṣāmēʾ*[2], thirsty, S: 6771, B: 854D, K: 806B, H: 307B

7535 צִמְאָה *ṣimʾâ*, thirst, S: 6773, B: 854D, K: 806B, H: 307B

7536 צִמָּאוֹן *ṣimmāʾôn*, thirsty ground, S: 6774, B: 855A, K: 806B, H: 307B

7537 צָמַד *ṣāmad*, [C] to be joined together; [E] to be strapped on; [G] to harness, attach to, S: 6775, B: 855A, K: 806B, H: 307B

7538 צֶמֶד *ṣemed*, yoke, team of two, pair, S: 6776, B: 855A, K: 806C, H: 307B

7539 צַמָּה *ṣammâ*, veil, S: 6777, B: 855D, K: 806D, H: 307C

7540 צִמּוּקִים *ṣimmûqîm*, raisin cakes, S: 6778†, B: 856A, K: 806D, H: 307C

7541 צָמַח *ṣāmaḥ*, [A] to sprout up, spring up; [D] to grow; [G] to cause to grow, bring to fruition, S: 6779, B: 855B, K: 806D, H: 307C

7542 צֶמַח *ṣemaḥ*, growth (which sprouts); (as a messianic title) the Branch, S: 6780, B: 855C, K: 807A, H: 307C

7543 צָמִיד *ṣāmîd*[1], bracelet, S: 6781, B: 855B, K: 807B, H: 307D

7544 [2]צָמִיד *ṣāmîd*[2], lid, cover, S: 6781, B: 855B, K: 807B, H: 307D

7545 צַמִּים *ṣammîm*, snare, S: 6782, B: 855D, K: 807B, H: 307D

7546 צָמַק *ṣāmaq*, [A] to be dry, shriveled (of breasts), S: 6784, B: 855D, K: 807C, H: 307D

7547 צֶמֶר *ṣemer*, wool, S: 6785, B: 856A, K: 807C, H: 307D

7548 צְמָרִי *ṣᵉmārî*, Zemarite, S: 6786, B: 856A, K: 807D, H: 307D

7549 צְמָרַיִם *ṣᵉmārayim*, Zemaraim, S: 6787, B: 856A, K: 807D, H: 307D

7550 צַמֶּרֶת *ṣammeret*, top (of a tree), S: 6788, B: 856A, K: 807D, H: 307D

7551 צָמַת *ṣāmat*, [A] to silence; [C] to be silenced; [D] to destroy; to wear out; [G] to put to silence, destroy, S: 6789, B: 856B, K: 807D, H: 307D

7552 צְמִתֻת *ṣᵉmitut*, permanence, finality, S: 6783, B: 856C, K: 808A, H: 307D

7553 צֵן *ṣēn*, thorn; hook, S: 6791, B: 856D, K: 808A, H: 308A

7554 צִן *ṣin*, Zin, S: 6790, B: 856C, K: 808A, H: 308A

7555 צֹנָא *ṣōnāʾ*, variant: flocks, S: 6792†, B: 856C, K: 808B, H: 308A

7556 צֹנֶה *ṣōneh*, flocks (of sheep and goats), S: 6792, B: 856C, K: 808B, H: 308A

7557 צִנָּה *ṣinnâ*[1], coolness, S: 6793, B: 856D, K: 808B, H: 308A

7558 [2]צִנָּה *ṣinnâ*[2], (large) shield, S: 6793, B: 857A, K: 808B, H: 308A

7559 [3]צִנָּה *ṣinnâ*[3], variant: hook, see 7553, S: 6793, B: 856D, K: 808A, H: 308A

7560 צָנוּעַ *ṣānûaʿ*, humble, modest, S: 6800†, B: 857A, K: 808C, H: 308A

7561 צָנוּף *ṣānûp*, variant: turban, see 7565, S: 6797†, B: 857B, K: 808C, H: 308A

7562 צִנּוֹר *ṣinnôr*, water shaft; waterfall, S: 6794†, B: 857C, K: 808C, H: 308A

7563 צָנַח *ṣānaḥ*, [A] to get down; to go down, S: 6795, B: 856C, K: 808C, H: 308A

7564 צְנִינִים *ṣᵉnînîm*, thorns, S: 6796†, B: 856D, K: 808D, H: 308A

7565 צָנִיף *ṣānîp*, turban, S: 6797, B: 857A, K: 808D, H: 308A

7566 צְנִיפָה *ṣᵉnîpâ*, turban (of woman), S: 6797, B: 857B, K: 808D, H: 308A

7567 צָנַם *ṣānam*, variant: [A] to dry up, harden, see 7568, S: 6798, B: 856D, K: 808A, H: 308A

7568 צָנֻם *ṣānum*, withered, S: 6798†, B: 856D, K: 808D, H: 308A

7569 צְנָן *ṣᵉnān*, Zenan, S: 6799, B: 838C, K: 790B, H: 302A

7570 צָנַע *ṣānaʿ*, [G] to show a humble (walk with God), S: 6800, B: 857A, K: 809A, H: 308B

7571 צָנַף *ṣānap*, [A] to wrap around, wind around, S: 6801, B: 857A, K: 809A, H: 308B

7572 צְנֵפָה *ṣᵉnēpâ*, winding, wrapping, S: 6802, B: 857B, K: 809B, H: 308B

7573 צִנְצֶנֶת *ṣinṣenet*, vessel, receptacle, S: 6803, B: 857A, K: 809B, H: 308B

7574 צַנְתָּרוֹת *ṣantārôt*, pipes, S: 6804†, B: 857C, K: 809B, H: 308B

7575 צָעַד *ṣāʿad*, [A] to step, march; [G] to make march, S: 6805, B: 857C, K: 809B, H: 308B

7576 צַעַד *ṣaʿad*, step, stride, S: 6806, B: 857D, K: 809C, H: 308B

7577 צְעָדָה *ṣᵉʿādâ*[1], marching, S: 6807, B: 857D, K: 809C, H: 308B 1.

7578 [2]צְעָדָה *ṣᵉʿādâ*[2], ankle chains, S: 6807, B: 857D, K: 809C, H: 308B 2.

[F] Hitpael (hitpoel, hitpoal, hitpolel, hitpolal, hitpalel, hitpalal, hitpalpel, hitpalpal, hotpael, hotpaal) [G] Hiphil (hiphtil) [H] Hophal [I] Hishtaphel

7579 צָעָה *ṣā'â*, [A] to lay down, stoop, incline; [D] to tip, pour out, S: 6808, B: 858A, K: 809C, H: 308C

7580 צָעוֹר *ṣā'ôr*, variant: see 7582, S: 6820†, B: 859A, K: 809D, H: 308C

7581 צָעִיף *ṣā'îp*, veil, S: 6809, B: 858B, K: 809D, H: 308C

7582 צָעִיר[1] *ṣā'îr*[1], younger, small, little, lowly, S: 4704† & 6810, B: 859A, K: 809D, H: 308C

7583 צָעִיר[2] *ṣā'îr*[2], Zair, S: 6811, B: 859A, K: 810A, H: 308C

7584 צְעִירָה *ṣe'îrâ*, youth, youngest (offspring), S: 6812, B: 859A, K: 810A, H: 308C

7585 צָעַן *ṣā'an*, [A] to pack up, move (a tent), S: 6813, B: 858A, K: 810B, H: 308C

7586 צֹעַן *ṣō'an*, Zoan, S: 6814, B: 858B, K: 810B, H: 308D

7587 צְעַנִּים *ṣe'annîm*, variant: Zeannim, see 7588, S: 6815†, B: 858B, K: 810B, H: 308D

7588 צַעֲנַנִּים *ṣa'anannîm*, Zaanannim, S: 6815, B: 858B, K: 810B, H: 308D

7589 צַעֲצֻעִים *ṣa'aṣu'îm*, sculptured work (by metal casting), S: 6816†, B: 847A, K: 810C, H: 308D

7590 צָעַק *ṣā'aq*, [A] to cry; [C] to be called out, be summoned; [D] to keep crying; [G] to call together, summon, S: 6817, B: 858B, K: 810C, H: 308D

7591 צְעָקָה *ṣe'āqâ*, cry of distress, outcry, wailing, S: 6818†, B: 858C, K: 810D, H: 308D

7592 צָעַר *ṣā'ar*, [A] to be trivial, insignificant, little, S: 6819, B: 858D, K: 811A, H: 308D

7593 צֹעַר *ṣō'ar*, Zoar, S: 6820, B: 858D, K: 811A, H: 309A

7594 צָפַד *ṣāpad*, [A] to shrivel, S: 6821, B: 859B, K: 811B, H: 309A

7595 צָפָה[1] *ṣāpâ*[1], [A] to keep watch, be a lookout; [B] to be spied out; [D] to watch, lookout, S: 6822, B: 859B, K: 811B, H: 309A

7596 צָפָה[2] *ṣāpâ*[2], [A] to arrange; [D] to overlay, cover, adorn; [E] to be overlaid, be coated, S: 6823, B: 860A, K: 811C, H: 309A

7597 צָפָה[3] *ṣāpâ*[3], out-flow, discharge, S: 6824, B: 847C, K: 811D, H: 309A

7598 צְפוֹ *ṣepô*, Zepho, S: 6825, B: 859D, K: 812A, H: 309B

7599 צִפּוּי *ṣippûy*, overlaying, (metal) plating, S: 6826, B: 860B, K: 812A, H: 309B

7600 צָפוֹן[1] *ṣāpôn*[1], north, northern, S: 6828, B: 860D, K: 812A, H: 309B

7601 צָפוֹן[2] *ṣāpôn*[2], Zaphon, S: 6829, B: 861B, K: 812C, H: 309B

7602 צְפוֹן *ṣepôn*, Zephon, S: 6827, B: 859D, K: 812C, H: 309B

7603 צְפוֹנִי[1] *ṣepônî*[1], northern; (as noun) northerner, S: 6830, B: 861A, K: 812C, H: 309B

7604 צְפוֹנִי[2] *ṣepônî*[2], Zephonite, S: 6831, B: 859D, K: 812D, H: 309C

7605 צָפוּעַ *ṣāpûa'*, variant: see 7616, S: 6832, B: 861C, K: 812D, H: 309C

7606 צִפּוֹר[1] *ṣippôr*[1], bird (individual and collective), S: 6833, B: 861D, K: 812D, H: 309C

7607 צִפּוֹר[2] *ṣippôr*[2], Zippor, S: 6834, B: 862A, K: 813A, H: 309C

7608 צַפַּחַת *ṣappaḥat*, jug, jar (for liquid), S: 6835, B: 860B, K: 813A, H: 309C

7609 צְפִי *ṣepî*, variant: Zephi, see 7598, S: 6825, B: 859D, K: 813A, H: 309C

7610 צִפִּיָּה *ṣippiyyâ*, watchtower, lookout, S: 6836, B: 859D, K: 813B, H: 309C

7611 צִפְיוֹן *ṣipyôn*, variant: Ziphion, see 7602, S: 6837, B: 859D, K: 813B, H: 309C

7612 צִפְיוֹנִי *ṣipyônî*, variant: Ziphionite, S: 6831†, B: 859D, K: 813B, H: 309C

7613 צַפִּיחִת *ṣappîḥit*, wafer, flat-cake, S: 6838, B: 860C, K: 813B, H: 309C

7614 צֹפִים *ṣōpîm*, Zophim, S: 6839, B: 859C, K: 798C, H: 309A

7615 צָפִין *ṣāpîn*, variant: see 7621, S: 6840, B: 860D, K: 813B, H: 309C

7616 צָפִיעַ *ṣāpia'*, manure, dung, S: 6832†, B: 861C, K: 813B, H: 309C

7617 צְפִיעָה *ṣepî'â*, offshoots, leaf, S: 6849†, B: 861C, K: 813B, H: 309C

7618 צָפִיר *ṣāpîr*, (male) goat, S: 6842, B: 862B, K: 813B, H: 309C

7619 צְפִירָה *ṣepîrâ*, crown, wreath; doom, S: 6843, B: 862A, K: 813C, H: 309D

7620 צָפִית *ṣāpît*, rug, carpet, S: 6844, B: 860B, K: 813C, H: 309D

7621 צָפַן *ṣāpan*, [A] to hide, conceal, store up; [B] to be treasured, be cherished; [C] to be stored up, be concealed; [G] to hide, S: 6845, B: 860C, K: 813C, H: 309D

7622 צְפַנְיָה *ṣepanyâ*, Zephaniah, S: 6846, B: 861B, K: 813D, H: 309D

7623 צְפַנְיָהוּ *ṣepanyāhû*, Zephaniah, S: 6846, B: 861B, K: 814A, H: 309D

7624 צָפְנַת פַּעְנֵחַ *ṣāpenat pa'nēaḥ*, Zaphenath-Paneah, S: 6847, B: 861B, K: 814A, H: 309D

7625 צֶפַע *ṣepa'*, viper, serpent, S: 6848, B: 861C, K: 814A, H: 310A

7626 צִפְעֹנִי *ṣip'ōnî*, viper, S: 6848, B: 861C, K: 814B, H: 310A

7627 צָפַף *ṣāpap*, [D] to chirp; to whisper, S: 6850, B: 861C, K: 814B, H: 310A

7628 צַפְצָפָה *ṣapṣāpâ*, willow, S: 6851, B: 861D, K: 814B, H: 310A

7629 צָפַר *ṣāpar*, [A] to leave, depart, S: 6852, B: 861D, K: 814B, H: 310A

7630 צְפַרְדֵּעַ *ṣepardēa'*, frogs, S: 6854, B: 862C, K: 814C, H: 310A

7631 צִפֹּרָה *ṣippōrâ*, Zipporah, S: 6855, B: 862A, K: 814C, H: 310A

7632 צִפֹּרֶן *ṣippōren*, nail (of finger or toe); (flint *or* hard stone) point (of a stylus), S: 6856, B: 862B, K: 814C, H: 310A

7633 צֶפֶת *ṣepet*, capital (of a pillar), S: 6858, B: 860B, K: 814D, H: 310A

7634 צְפַת *ṣepat*, Zephath, S: 6857, B: 862C, K: 814D, H: 310A

7635 צְפָתָה *ṣepatâ*, Zephathah, S: 6859, B: 862C, K: 814D, H: 310B

7636 צָקוּן *ṣāqûn*, variant: see 7440, S: 6845†, B: 848B, K: 814D, H: 310B

7637 צִקְלַג *ṣiqlag*, Ziklag, S: 6860, B: 862C, K: 814D, H: 310B

7638 צִקָּלוֹן *ṣiqqālôn*, garment, bag, S: 6861†, B: 862D, K: 814D, H: 310B

7639 צַר[1] *ṣar*[1], (as noun) trouble, distress, anguish; (as a.) narrow, S: 6862, B: 865A, K: 815A, H: 310B

7640 צַר[2] *ṣar*[2], enemy, foe, adversary, opponent, S: 6862, B: 865D, K: 815A, H: 310B

7641 צַר[3] *ṣar*[3], flint, S: 6862, B: 866A, K: 815B, H: 310B

7642 צַר[4] *ṣar*[4], variant: see 7639, S*, B*, K*, H*

7643 צֵר *ṣēr*, Zer, S: 6863, B: 862D, K: 815B, H: 310B

7644 צֹר[1] *ṣōr*[1], flint knife, S: 6864, B: 866A, K: 815B, H: 310B

7645 צֹר[2] *ṣōr*[2], variant: Tyre, S: 6865, B: 862D, K: 815C, H: 310B

7646 צָרַב *ṣārab*, [C] to be scorched, S: 6866, B: 863A, K: 815C, H: 310C

7647 צָרָב *ṣārāb*, scorching, S: 6867†, B: 863A, K: 815D, H: 310C

7648 צָרֶבֶת *ṣārebet*, scar, S: 6867, B: 863A, K: 815D, H: 310C

7649 צְרֵדָה *ṣerēdâ*, Zeredah, S: 6868, B: 863A, K: 815D, H: 310C

7650 צָרָה[1] *ṣārâ*[1], trouble, distress, calamity, anguish, S: 6869, B: 865B, K: 815D, H: 310C

7651 צָרָה[2] *ṣārâ*[2], rival-wife, S: 6869, B: 865D, K: 816A, H: 310C

7652 צִרָה *ṣirâ*, variant: (stone) sheep pen, fold, S: 1224†, B: 131B, K: 816A, H: 310C

7653 צְרוּיָה *ṣerûyâ*, Zeruiah, S: 6870, B: 863B, K: 816A, H: 310C

7654 צְרוּעָה *ṣerû'â*, Zeruah, S: 6871, B: 864A, K: 816B, H: 310C

7655 צְרוֹר[1] *ṣerôr*[1], pouch, purse, sachet, bag, S: 6872, B: 865C, K: 816B, H: 310C

7656 צְרוֹר[2] *ṣerôr*[2], pebble, S: 6872, B: 866C, K: 816B, H: 310C

7657 צְרוֹר[3] *ṣerôr*[3], Zeror, S: 6872, B: 866C, K: 816B, H: 310C

7658 צָרַח *ṣāraḥ*, [A] to shout, cry out; [G] to raise the battle cry, S: 6873, B: 863C, K: 816C, H: 310C

7659 צֶרַח *ṣeraḥ*, variant: war-cry, shriek, S*, B: 954A & 865B, K: 816C, H: 310C

7660 צֹרִי *ṣōrî*, Tyrian, of Tyre, S: 6876, B: 863A, K: 816C, H: 310C

7661 צֳרִי *ṣorî*, balm, mastic (resin), S: 6875, B: 863B, K: 816C, H: 310C

7662 צְרִי *ṣerî*, Zeri, S: 6874, B: 863B, K: 816D, H: 310D

7663 צְרִיחַ *ṣerîaḥ*, pit, (underground) stronghold, S: 6877, B: 863C, K: 816D, H: 310D

7664 צֹרֶךְ *ṣōrek*, need, S: 6878, B: 863D, K: 816D, H: 310D

7665 צָרַע *ṣāra'*, [B, E] to be leprous, afflicted with an infectious skin disease, S: 6879, B: 863D, K: 816D, H: 310D

7666 צָרְעָה *ṣor'â*, Zorah, S: 6881, B: 864A, K: 817A, H: 310D

7667 צִרְעָה *ṣir'â*, hornets *or* discouragement, S: 6880, B: 864A, K: 817B, H: 310D

7668 צָרְעִי *ṣor'î*, Zorite, S: 6882, B: 864A, K: 817B, H: 310D

7669 צָרַעַת *ṣāra'at*, infectious skin disease; (of clothing) mildew, S: 6883, B: 863D, K: 817B, H: 310D

7670 צָרְעָתִי *ṣāre'âtî*, Zorathite, S: 6882, B: 864A, K: 817C, H: 310D

7671 צָרַף *ṣārap*, [A] to smelt, refine (metals); (as noun) (gold- *or* silver-)smith, S: 6884, B: 864A, K: 817C, H: 311A

7672 צֹרְפִי *ṣōrepî*, (member of the) goldsmiths, S: 6885, B: 864C, K: 817D, H: 311A

7673 צָרְפַת *ṣārepat*, Zarephath, S: 6886, B: 864C, K: 817D, H: 311A

7674 [1]צָרַר *ṣārar*[1], [A] to bind up, wrap up, tie up; to hamper, oppress, be in distress; [B] be bound, be confined; [E] to be mended; [G] to bring trouble, distress, oppress, S: 3334† & 6887, B: 864C, K: 818A, H: 311A

7675 [2]צָרַר *ṣārar*[2], [A] to be a rival-wife; to be an enemy, adversary, S: 6887, B: 865C, K: 818C, H: 311C

7676 [3]צָרַר *ṣārar*[3], variant: [G] to suffer distress, S: 6869†, B: 865B, K: 818C, H: 311A

7677 [4]צָרַר *ṣārar*[4], variant: [A] to be a rival wife, S: 6887, B: 865D, K: 818C, H: 311C 2

7678 צְרֵרָה *ṣerērâ*, Zererah, S: 6888, B: 866C, K: 818D, H: 311C

7679 צֶרֶת *ṣeret*, Zereth, S: 6889, B: 866C, K: 818D, H: 311C

7680 צֶרֶת הַשַּׁחַר *ṣeret haššaḥar*, Zereth Shahar, S: 6890, B: 866C, K: 818D, H: 311C

7681 צָרְתָן *ṣāretān*, Zarethan, S: 6891, B: 866C, K: 818D, H: 311C

7682 ק *q*, letter of the Hebrew alphabet, S*, B: 866B, K: 819A, H*

7683 קֵא *qē'*, vomit, S: 6892, B: 883C, K: 819A, H: 311B

7684 קָאַת *qā'at*, desert owl, S: 6893, B: 866B, K: 819A, H: 311B

7685 קַב *qab*, cab (measure of volume), S: 6894, B: 866B, K: 819B, H: 311B

7686 קָבַב *qābab*, [A] to curse, S: 6895, B: 866D, K: 819B, H: 311B

7687 קֵבָה *qēbâ*, maw (4th stomach of cud-chewing animals); (of humans) belly, stomach area, S: 6896 & 6897†, B: 867A, K: 819B, H: 311B

7688 קֻבָּה *qubbâ*, woman's section (of a tent), S: 6898, B: 866D, K: 819C, H: 311B

7689 קִבּוּץ *qibbûṣ*, collection (of idols), S: 6899, B: 868B, K: 819C, H: 311B

7690 קְבוּרָה *qebûrâ*, tomb, grave, burial, S: 6900, B: 869A, K: 819C, H: 311D

7691 קָבַל *qābal*, [D] to receive, take; [G] to match, correspond, S: 6901, B: 867A, K: 819D, H: 311D

7692 קְבֹל *qebōl*, (something) in front of, battering ram, S: 6904† & 6905†, B: 867B, K: 820A, H: 311D

7693 קָבַע *qāba'*, [A] to rob, plunder, S: 6906, B: 867B, K: 820A, H: 311D

7694 קֻבַּעַת *qubba'at*, cup, goblet, S: 6907, B: 867C, K: 820B, H: 312A

7695 קָבַץ *qābaṣ*, [A] to collect, gather, assemble; [B] to be assembled; [C] to be gathered, be assembled, be joined; [D] to gather, assemble; [E] to be gathered; [F] to gather (themselves) together, S: 6908, B: 867C, K: 820B, H: 312A

7696 קַבְצְאֵל *qabṣe'ēl*, Kabzeel, S: 6909, B: 868B, K: 821A, H: 312B

7697 קְבֻצָה *qebuṣâ*, gathering, S: 6910, B: 868B, K: 821A, H: 312B

7698 קִבְצַיִם *qibṣayim*, Kibzaim, S: 6911, B: 868B, K: 821A, H: 312B

7699 קָבַר *qābar*, [A] to store up, pile up, heap up, S: 6912, B: 868B, K: 821A, H: 312B

7700 קֶבֶר *qeber*, burial site, tomb, grave, S: 6913, B: 868D, K: 821B, H: 312B

7701 קִבְרוֹת הַתַּאֲוָה *qibrôt hatta'awâ*, Kibroth Hattaavah, S: 6914, B: 869A, K: 821C, H: 312C

7702 קָדַד *qādad*, [A] to bow low, bow down, S: 6915, B: 869A, K: 821D, H: 312C

7703 קִדָּה *qiddâ*, cassia, S: 6916, B: 869B, K: 821D, H: 312C

7704 קְדוּמִים *qedûmîm*, age-old, ancient, S: 6917†, B: 870C, K: 822A, H: 312C

7705 קָדוֹשׁ *qādôš*, holy, sacred, consecrated, S: 6918, B: 872C, K: 822A, H: 312C

7706 קָדַח *qādaḥ*, [A] to kindle, light (a fire), S: 6919, B: 869B, K: 822D, H: 312D

7707 קַדַּחַת *qaddaḥat*, fever, inflammation, S: 6920, B: 869B, K: 822D, H: 312D

7708 קָדִים *qādîm*, east, eastern, S: 6921, B: 870B, K: 822D, H: 312D

7709 קָדַם *qādam*, [D] to be in front of, meet, confront, S: 6923, B: 869D, K: 823A, H: 312D

7710 קֶדֶם *qedem*, (as a direction) east, eastern; (used of time) ancient, eternal, long ago, S: 6924, B: 869C, K: 823C, H: 313A

7711 קֵדֶם *qēdem*, eastern, (toward the) east, S: 6924†, B: 870A, K: 824A, H: 313A

7712 קַדְמָה *qadmâ*, past, antiquity; ancient (city), S: 6927, B: 870B, K: 824A, H: 313A

7713 קִדְמָה *qidmâ*, east, S: 6926, B: 870B, K: 824B, H: 313A

7714 [1]קֵדְמָה *qēdemâ*[1], variant: eastward, see 7711 & 2025, S: 6924†, B: 870A, K: 824B, H: 313B

7715 [2]קֵדְמָה *qēdemâ*[2], Kedemah, S: 6929, B: 870B, K: 824B, H: 313B

7716 קַדְמוֹן *qadmôn*, eastern, S: 6930, B: 870C, K: 824B, H: 313B

7717 קְדֵמוֹת *qedēmôt*, Kedemoth, S: 6932, B: 870D, K: 824B, H: 313B

7718 קַדְמִיאֵל *qadmî'ēl*, Kadmiel, S: 6934, B: 870D, K: 824B, H: 313B

7719 [1]קַדְמֹנִי *qadmōnî*[1], (of a direction) eastern; (of time) old, former, past, S: 6931, B: 870C, K: 824C, H: 313B

7720 [2]קַדְמֹנִי *qadmōnî*[2], Kadmonite, S: 6935, B: 870D, K: 824C, H: 313C

7721 קָדְקֹד *qodqōd*, top or crown of the head, S: 6936, B: 869A, K: 824C, H: 313B

7722 קָדַר *qādar*, [A] to grow dark, be black; to mourn, wail, grieve; [G] to make dark, bring gloom; [F] to grow dark, S: 6937, B: 871A, K: 824D, H: 313B

7723 קֵדָר *qēdār*, Kedar, S: 6938, B: 871A, K: 824D, H: 313C

7724 קִדְרוֹן *qidrôn*, Kidron, S: 6939, B: 871B, K: 825A, H: 313C

7725 קַדְרוּת *qadrût*, darkness, blackness, S: 6940, B: 871A, K: 825A, H: 313C

7726 קְדֹרַנִּית *qedōrannît*, in mourner's attire, in an unkempt manner, S: 6941, B: 871A, K: 825A, H: 313C

7727 קָדַשׁ *qādaš*, [A] to be holy, sacred, consecrated; [C] to show oneself holy, be consecrated; [D] to consecrate, make holy; [E] to be dedicated, consecrated; [F] to consecrate oneself; [G] to set apart, consecrate, dedicate, regard as holy, S: 6942, B: 872D, K: 825A, H: 313C

7728 [1]קָדֵשׁ *qādēš*[1], (male or female) shrine prostitute, S: 6945 & 6948†, B: 873C, K: 826D, H: 314B

7729 [2]קָדֵשׁ *qādēš*[2], Kadesh, S: 6946, B: 873D, K: 826D, H: 314B

7730 קֶדֶשׁ *qedeš*, Kedesh, S: 6943, B: 873D, K: 827A, H: 314B

7731 קֹדֶשׁ *qōdeš*, holy or sacred thing, holy or sacred place, sanctuary; holiness, S: 6944, B: 871C, K: 827A, H: 314B

7732 קָדֵשׁ בַּרְנֵעַ *qādēš barnēa'*, Kadesh Barnea, S: 6947, B: 873D, K: 826D, H: 314B

7733 קָהָה *qāhâ*, [A] to be dull, blunt (of teeth); [D] to be dull, S: 6949, B: 874B, K: 828D, H: 314D

7734 קֵהָיוֹן *qēhāyôn*, variant: bluntness, S: 5356†, B: 874C, K: 632D, H: 245B

7735 קָהַל *qāhal*, [C] to be gathered, be assembled; [G] to summon, call together, cause to assemble, S: 6950, B: 874D, K: 829A, H: 314D

7736 קָהָל *qāhāl*, assembly, community, S: 6951, B: 874C, K: 829B, H: 314D

7737 קְהִלָּה *qehillâ*, assembly, meeting, S: 6952, B: 875A, K: 829D, H: 315A

7738 קֹהֶלֶת *qōhelet*, (as a title or name) the Teacher, S: 6953, B: 875A, K: 829D, H: 315A

7739 קְהֵלָתָה *qehēlātâ*, Kehelathah, S: 6954, B: 875B, K: 830A, H: 315A

7740 קְהָת *qehāt*, Kohath, Kohathite, S: 6955, B: 875B, K: 830A, H: 315A

7741 קְהָתִי *qehātî*, Kohathite, S: 6956, B: 875C, K: 830A, H: 315A

7742 [1]קַו *qāw*[1], measuring line, ruler, S: 6957, B: 875C, K: 830A, H: 315A

7743 [2]קַו *qāw*[2], strange speech, S: 6978†, B: 876A, K: 830B, H: 315B

7744 [3]קַו *qāw*[3], variant: qav (a mocking sound), S: 6957 & 6978†, B: 876A, K: 830B, H: 315B

7745 קְוֵא *qewē'*, Kue, S: 4723†, B: 875C, K: 830D, H: 315B

7746 קוֹבַע *qôba'*, helmet, S: 6959, B: 875C, K: 830B, H: 315B

7747 [1]קָוָה *qāwâ*[1], [A] to hope in; [D] to hope for, wait for, look for, S: 6960, B: 875C, K: 830B, H: 315B

7748 [2]קָוָה *qāwâ*[2], [C] to be gathered, S: 6960, B: 876B, K: 830D, H: 315B

[F] Hitpael (hitpoel, hitpoal, hitpolel, hitpolal, hitpalel, hitpalal, hitpalpel, hitpalpal, hotpael, hotpaal) [G] Hiphil (hiphtil) [H] Hophal [I] Hishtaphel

7749 קָוֶה qāweh, variant: see 7742, S: 6961, B: 876A, K: 830D, H: 315C

7750 קְוֵה qewēh, Kue, S: 4723†, B: 875C, K: 830D, H: 315C

7751 קוֹחַ qôaḥ, variant: see 7223, S: 6495†, B: 824D, K: 830D, H: 315C

7752 קוּט qûṭ, [A] to feel anger, loathing; [C] to feel loathing; [F] to loathe, abhor, S: 5354† & 6962, B: 876C, K: 831A, H: 315C

7753 קוֹט qôṭ, variant: [A] to be fragile, see 3684, S: 6962†, B: 876C, K*, H*

7754 קוֹל qôl, sound, voice, noise, S: 6963, B: 876D, K: 831A, H: 315C

7755 קוֹלָיָה qôlāyâ, Kolaiah, S: 6964, B: 877B, K: 831C, H: 315D

7756 קוּם qûm, [A] to get up, arise, stand, establish; [D] to establish, confirm, restore; to raise up; [G] to set up, establish, restore; [H] to be set up, be raised up; [F] to raise up against, S: 6965, B: 877C, K: 831D, H: 315D

7757 קוֹמָה qômâ, height, S: 6967, B: 879B, K: 833C, H: 316D

7758 קוֹמְמִיּוּת qômemiyyût, (as adv.) with head held high, S: 6968, B: 879C, K: 833C, H: 316D

7759 קוֹנֵן qônēn, variant: see 7801, S: 6969†, B: 884B, K: 833C, H: 316D

7760 קוֹעַ qôaʿ, Koa, S: 6970, B: 880C, K: 833C, H: 316D

7761 קוֹף qôp, ape, S: 6971, B: 880D, K: 833D, H: 316D

7762 קוּץ¹ qûṣ[1], [A] to detest, be disgusted, loathe, S: 6973, B: 880D, K: 833D, H: 316D

7763 קוּץ² qûṣ[2], [G] to tear apart, S: 6972 & 6974, B: 847D, K: 834A, H: 317A

7764 קוֹץ¹ qôṣ[1], thorns, thornbush, S: 6975, B: 881A, K: 834A, H: 317A

7765 קוֹץ² qôṣ[2], variant: shreds of a wick, S: 6975, B: 881A 2., K: 834A, H: 317A

7766 קוֹץ³ qôṣ[3], Koz, S: 6976, B: 881A 1., K: 834A, H: 317A

7767 קְוֻצּוֹת qewuṣṣôt, (locks) of hair, S: 6977†, B: 881B, K: 834B, H: 317A

7768 קַוְקָו qawqāw, variant: power, suppleness, strange speech, S*, B: 876A, K: 830B, H: 315B

7769 קוּר¹ qûr[1], [A] to dig (a well or water hole), S: 6979, B: 881B, K: 834B, H: 317A

7770 קוּר² qûr[2], thread (of a spider cobweb), S: 6980, B: 881C, K: 834B, H: 317A

7771 קוֹרָה qôrâ, beam, pole, roof beams, tree, S: 6982, B: 900A, K: 834B, H: 317A

7772 קוּשׁ qûš, [A] to set a snare, S: 6983†, B: 881C, K: 834C, H: 317A

7773 קוּשָׁיָהוּ qûšāyāhû, Kushaiah, S: 6984, B: 881C, K: 834C, H: 317A

7774 קָח qāḥ, variant: willow, S: 3947†, B: 542C, K: 834C, H: 317B

7775 קַט qāṭ, little; soon (with 3869 & 5071), S: 6985†, B: 881C, K: 834C, H: 317B

7776 קֶטֶב qeṭeb, plague, destruction, S: 6986 & 6987†, B: 881C, K: 834D, H: 317B

7777 קְטֹרָה qeṭôrâ, smoke (of sacrifice), S: 6988, B: 882C, K: 834D, H: 317B

7778 קְטוּרָה qeṭûrâ, Keturah, S: 6989, B: 882C, K: 834D, H: 317B

7779 קָטַל qāṭal, [A] to slay, kill, S: 6991, B: 881D, K: 834D, H: 317B

7780 קֶטֶל qeṭel, slaughter, S: 6993, B: 881D, K: 835A, H: 317B

7781 קָטֹן¹ qāṭōn[1], [A] to be unworthy, not enough, trifling; [G] to make a (measure) small, S: 6994, B: 881D, K: 835A, H: 317B

7782 קֹטֶן qōṭen, little finger, S: 6995, B: 882B, K: 835A, H: 317B

7783 קָטָן¹ qāṭān[1], small, young(est), lesser, insignificant, S: 6996, B: 881D, K: 835B, H: 317B

7784 קָטָן² qāṭān[2], variant: Katan, see 2214, S: 6997, B: 882A, K: 835C, H: 317C

7785 קָטֹן² qāṭōn[2], small, least, youngest, S: 6996, B: 882B, K: 835C, H: 317C

7786 קָטַף qāṭap, [A] to pick off (grain), break off (twigs); [C] to be picked off, S: 6998, B: 882B, K: 835D, H: 317C

7787 קָטַר¹ qāṭar[1], [D] to burn an offering (of incense smoke); [E] to be perfumed; [G] to make a burned smoking offering; [H] to be burned as an offering, S: 6999, B: 882D, K: 835D, H: 317C

7788 קָטַר² qāṭar[2], [B] to be enclosed, S: 7000, B: 883B, K: 836C, H: 317D

7789 קִטֵּר qiṭṭēr, incense, S: 7002, B: 883B, K: 836C, H: 317D

7790 קִטְרוֹן qiṭrôn, Kitron, S: 7003, B: 883C, K: 836C, H: 317D

7791 קְטֻרוֹת qeṭurôt, variant: enclosures, see 7788, S*, B: 883B, K: 836C, H: 317D

7792 קְטֹרֶת qeṭōret, incense, smoke offering, S: 7004, B: 882C, K: 836C, H: 317D

7793 קַטָּת qaṭṭāt, Kattath, S: 7005, B: 883C, K: 836D, H: 317D

7794 קִיא¹ qîʾ[1], [A] to vomit; [G] to vomit out, spit out, S: 6958 & 7006†, B: 883C & D, K: 836D, H: 317D

7795 קִיא² qîʾ[2], vomit, S: 6892, B: 883C, K: 837A, H: 318A

7796 קָיָה qāyâ, variant: [A] to vomit, S: 6958, B: 883D, K: 837A, H: 318A

7797 קַיִט qayiṭ, variant: summer, S*, B: 876C, K: 837A, H: 318A

7798 קִיטוֹר qîṭôr, smoke, S: 7008, B: 882C, K: 837A, H: 318A

7799 קִים qîm, foe, adversary, S: 7009, B: 879C, K: 837A, H: 318A

7800 קִימָה qîmâ, standing up, S: 7012, B: 879C, K: 837A, H: 318A

7801 קִין qîn, [D] to chant a lament, sing a dirge, S: 6969, B: 884B, K: 837B, H: 318A

7802 קַיִן¹ qayin[1], spearhead, spear, S: 7013, B: 883D, K: 837B, H: 318A

7803 קַיִן² qayin[2], Cain, S: 7014, B: 884A, K: 837B, H: 318A

7804 קַיִן³ qayin[3], Kenite, S: 7014, B: 883D 1., K: 837C, H: 318A

7805 קַיִן⁴ qayin[4], Kain, S: 7014, B: 883D 2., K: 837C, H: 318A

7806 קִינָה¹ qînâ[1], lament, mourning song, dirge, S: 7015, B: 884B, K: 837C, H: 318A

7807 קִינָה² qînâ[2], Kinah, S: 7016, B: 884A, K: 837C, H: 318A

7808 קֵינִי qênî, Kenite, S: 7017, B: 884A, K: 837D, H: 318A

7809 קֵינָן qênān, Kenan, S: 7018, B: 884B, K: 837D, H: 318B

7810 קִיץ qîṣ, [A] to pass the summer; [G] to rouse, awaken, S: 6974†, B: 884C, K: 837D, H: 318B

7811 קַיִץ qayiṣ, summer; summer fruit, ripe fruit, S: 7019, B: 884D, K: 838A, H: 318B

7812 קִיצוֹן qîṣôn, end, outermost, S: 7020, B: 894A, K: 838B, H: 318B

7813 קִיקָיוֹן qîqāyôn, caster-oil vine, S: 7021, B: 884D, K: 838B, H: 318B

7814 קִיקָלוֹן qîqālôn, disgrace, S: 7022, B: 887B, K: 838B, H: 318B

7815 קִיר¹ qîr[1], wall, side wall, S: 7023, B: 885A, K: 838B, H: 318B

7816 קִיר² qîr[2], Kir, S: 7024, B: 885B, K: 838D, H: 318B

7817 קִיר³ qîr[3], Kir, S: 7024, B: 885B, K: 838D, H: 318C

7818 קִיר־חֶרֶשׂ qîr-ḥereś, Kir Hareseth, S: 7025†, B: 885B, K: 838D, H: 318B

7819 קִיר חֲרֶשֶׂת qîr hareśet, Kir Hareseth, S: 7025, B: 885B, K: 838D, H: 318B

7820 קֵירֹס qêrōs, Keros, S: 7026, B: 902B, K: 839A, H: 318C

7821 קִישׁ qîš, Kish, S: 7027, B: 885C, K: 839A, H: 318C

7822 קִישׁוֹן qîšôn, Kishon, S: 7028, B: 885C, K: 839A, H: 318C

7823 קִישִׁי qîšî, Kishi, S: 7029, B: 881C, K: 839A, H: 318C

7824 קַל qal, fleet-footed, swift, speedy, S: 7031, B: 886D, K: 839A, H: 318C

7825 קֹל¹ qōl[1], lightness, (i.e., frivolity or light-heartedness), S: 6963, B: 887A, K: 839B, H: 318C

7826 קֹל² qōl[2], variant: voice, see 7754, S: 6963, B: 876D, K: 839B, H: 318C

7827 קָלָה qālah, variant: see 7735, S: 7035, B: 874D, K: 839B, H: 318C

7828 קָלָה¹ qālâ[1], [A] to burn; [B] to be roasted; [C] to have a burning sensation, S: 7033, B: 885C, K: 839B, H: 318C

7829 קָלָה² qālâ[2], [C] to lightly esteemed, to be a nobody, be degraded; [G] to dishonor, treat with contempt, S: 7034, B: 885D, K: 839B, H: 318D

7830 קָלוֹן qālôn, shame, disgrace, dishonor, S: 7036, B: 885D, K: 839C, H: 318D

7831 קַלַּחַת qallaḥat, caldron, (cooking) pot, S: 7037, B: 886A, K: 839C, H: 318D

7832 קָלַט qālaṭ, [B] to be stunted, S: 7038, B: 886A, K: 839C, H: 318D

7833 קָלִי qālî, roasted grain, parched grain, S: 7039, B: 885D, K: 839D, H: 318D

7834 קַלָּי qallāy, Kallai, S: 7040†, B: 887A, K: 839D, H: 318D

7835 קֵלָיָה qēlāyâ, Kelaiah, S: 7041, B: 886B, K: 839D, H: 318D

7836 קְלִיטָא qelîṭāʾ, Kelita, S: 7042, B: 886B, K: 839D, H: 318D

7837 קָלַל *qālal*, [A] to recede, grow smaller; to be vile, to disdain, despise; to be swift; [C] to be trivial, insignificant; to be swift; [D] to curse, blaspheme, revile; [E] to be accursed; [G] to lighten; to humble; to treat with contempt; [F] to be shaken, S: 7043, B: 886B, K: 839D, H: 318D

7838 קָלָל *qālāl*, burnished, polished, S: 7044, B: 887A, K: 840D, H: 319B

7839 קְלָלָה *qᵉlālâ*, curse, condemnation, S: 7045, B: 887A, K: 840D, H: 319B

7840 קָלַס *qālas*, [D] to scorn; [F] to make fun of, S: 7046, B: 887B, K: 841A, H: 319C

7841 קֶלֶס *qeles*, derision, reproach, S: 7047, B: 887B, K: 841B, H: 319C

7842 קַלָּסָה *qallāsâ*, laughingstock, object of derision, S: 7048, B: 887B, K: 841B, H: 319C

7843 [1]קָלַע *qāla'*[1], [A, D] to hurl a stone (from a sling), S: 7049, B: 887B, K: 841B, H: 319C

7844 [2]קָלַע *qāla'*[2], [A] to carve, S: 7049, B: 887C, K: 841B, H: 319C

7845 [1]קֶלַע *qela'*[1], sling (a weapon), S: 7050, B: 887C, K: 841C, H: 319C

7846 [2]קֶלַע *qela'*[2], curtains, S: 7050, B: 887C, K: 841C, H: 319D

7847 קַלָּע *qallā'*, slinger (one who uses a sling), S: 7051, B: 887C, K: 841D, H: 319D

7848 קְלֹקֵל *qᵉlōqēl*, miserable (food), starvation (rations), S: 7052, B: 887A, K: 841D, H: 319D

7849 קִלְּשׁוֹן *qillᵉšôn*, (sharp pointed, three-pronged) fork, S: 7053, B: 887D, K: 841D, H: 319D

7850 קָמָה *qāmâ*, standing grain, S: 7054, B: 879B, K: 842A, H: 319D

7851 קְמוּאֵל *qᵉmû'ēl*, Kemuel, S: 7055, B: 887D, K: 842A, H: 319D

7852 קָמוֹן *qāmôn*, Kamon, S: 7056, B: 879C, K: 842A, H: 319D

7853 קִמּוֹשׂ *qimmôś*, thorns, nettles, briers (weeds of all kinds), S: 7057† & 7063†, B: 888B, K: 842A, H: 319D

7854 קֶמַח *qemaḥ*, flour, S: 7058, B: 887D, K: 842B, H: 319D

7855 קָמַט *qāmaṭ*, [A] to seize; [E] to be seized, S: 7059, B: 888A, K: 842B, H: 319D

7856 קָמַי *qāmāy*, variant: Kamai, see 4214, S: 6965†, B: 525D, K: 470D, H: 173A & 172A 13.

7857 קָמַל *qāmal*, [A] to wither, S: 7060, B: 888A, K: 842B, H: 319D

7858 קָמַץ *qāmaṣ*, [A] to take a handful, S: 7061, B: 888A, K: 842C, H: 320A

7859 קֹמֶץ *qōmeṣ*, handful; (pl.) abundance, S: 7062, B: 888A, K: 842C, H: 320A

7860 קֵן *qēn*, nest, S: 7064, B: 890A, K: 842C, H: 320A

7861 קָנָא *qānā'*, [D] to be jealous, be envious, be zealous, S: 7065, B: 888C, K: 842D, H: 320A

7862 קַנָּא *qannā'*, jealous, S: 7067, B: 888D, K: 843A, H: 320A

7863 קִנְאָה *qin'â*, jealousy, envy, zeal, S: 7068, B: 888B, K: 843A, H: 320B

7864 [1]קָנָה *qānâ*[1], [A] to buy, acquire, get; [C] to be bought, S: 7069, B: 888D, K: 843B, H: 320B

7865 [2]קָנָה *qānâ*[2], [A] to create, bring forth; (as a title of God) Creator, S: 7069, B: 888D, K: 843D, H: 320C

7866 קָנֶה *qāneh*, branch, rod; (calamus) reed, stalk, shaft, cane, S: 7070, B: 889C, K: 843D, H: 320C

7867 [3]קָנָה *qānâ*[3], Kanah, S: 7071, B: 889D, K: 844B, H: 320C

7868 קַנּוֹא *qannô'*, jealous, S: 7072, B: 888D, K: 844B, H: 320C

7869 קְנַז *qᵉnaz*, Kenaz, S: 7073, B: 889D, K: 844B, H: 320C

7870 קְנִזִּי *qᵉnizzî*, Kenizzite, S: 7074, B: 889D, K: 844B, H: 320D

7871 קִנְיָן *qinyān*, goods, property, possessions, S: 7075, B: 889A, K: 844C, H: 320D

7872 קִנָּמוֹן *qinnāmôn*, cinnamon, S: 7076, B: 890A, K: 844C, H: 320D

7873 קָנַן *qānan*, [D] to make a nest; [E] to be nestled, nested, S: 7077, B: 890A, K: 844C, H: 320D

7874 קֶנֶץ *qeneṣ*, end, S: 7078, B: 890B, K: 844D, H: 320D

7875 קְנָת *qᵉnāt*, Kenath, S: 7079, B: 890B, K: 844D, H: 320D

7876 קָסַם *qāsam*, [A] to practice divination, be a soothsayer, seek an omen, S: 7080, B: 890C, K: 844D, H: 320D

7877 קֶסֶם *qesem*, divination, S: 7081, B: 890C, K: 845A, H: 320D

7878 קָסַס *qāsas*, [D] to strip off, S: 7082, B: 890D, K: 845A, H: 321A

7879 קֶסֶת *qeset*, writing kit, writing-case, S: 7083, B: 903C, K: 845A, H: 321A

7880 קָעָה *qā'â*, variant: [A] to cry out, S*, B*, K: 845B, H*

7881 קְעִילָה *qᵉ'îlâ*, Keilah, S: 7084, B: 890D, K: 845B, H: 321A

7882 קַעֲקַע *qa'ᵃqa'*, tattoo, S: 7085, B: 891A, K: 845B, H: 321A

7883 קְעָרָה *qᵉ'ārâ*, plate, dish, S: 7086, B: 891A, K: 845B, H: 321A

7884 קָפָא *qāpā'*, [A, C] to congeal, thicken; [G] to curdle, S: 7087, B: 891A, K: 845C, H: 321A

7885 קִפָּאוֹן *qippā'ôn*, frost, S: 7087†, B: 891B, K: 845C, H: 321A

7886 קָפַד *qāpad*, [D] to roll up, S: 7088, B: 891B, K: 845C, H: 321A

7887 קִפֹּד *qippōd*, screech owl, S: 7090, B: 891B, K: 845C, H: 321A

7888 קְפָדָה *qᵉpādâ*, terror, anguish, S: 7089, B: 891C, K: 845D, H: 321A

7889 קִפּוֹז *qippôz*, owl, S: 7091, B: 891C, K: 845D, H: 321B

7890 קָפַץ *qāpaṣ*, [A] to draw together, shut; [C] to be gathered up; [D] to bound, leap, S: 7092, B: 891C, K: 845D, H: 321B

7891 קֵץ *qēṣ*, end, limit, boundary, S: 7093, B: 893D, K: 846A, H: 321B

7892 קָצַב *qāṣab*, [A] to cut off; [B] to be shorn, be cut off, S: 7094, B: 891D, K: 846C, H: 321C

7893 קֶצֶב *qeṣeb*, shape, foundation, S: 7095, B: 891D, K: 846C, H: 321C

7894 [1]קָצָה *qāṣâ*[1], [D] to cut off, reduce; [G] to scrape off, S: 7096, B: 891D, K: 846C, H: 321C

7895 קָצֶה *qāṣeh*, end, limit, outskirts, edge, S: 7097, B: 892A, K: 846D, H: 321D

7896 [2]קָצָה *qāṣâ*[2], end, fringe, edge, S: 7098, B: 892B, K: 847A, H: 321D

7897 קֵצֶה *qēṣeh*, end, boundary, limit, S: 7097, B: 892C, K: 847B, H: 322A

7898 [1]קָצוּ *qāṣû*, ends, borders (of the earth), S: 7099†, B: 892C, K: 847B, H: 322A

7899 קָצוּץ *qāṣûṣ*, distant *or* cut off, S: 7112†, B: 893C, K: 848D, H: 322C

7900 קָצוּר *qāṣûr*, narrow, short, S: 7114†, B: 894A, K: 847B, H: 322A

7901 קְצוֹת *qᵉṣôt*, variant: end, S: 7098†, B: 892A, K: 847B, H: 322A

7902 קֶצַח *qeṣaḥ*, caraway, cummin, S: 7100, B: 892D, K: 847C, H: 322A

7903 קָצִין *qāṣîn*, commander, ruler, leader, S: 7101, B: 892D, K: 847C, H: 322A

7904 [1]קְצִיעָה *qᵉṣî'â*[1], cassia, S: 7102, B: 893A, K: 847C, H: 322A

7905 [2]קְצִיעָה *qᵉṣî'â*[2], Keziah, S: 7103, B: 893A, K: 847D, H: 322A

7906 קְצִיץ *qᵉṣîṣ*, variant: Keziz, S: 7104, B: 894A, K: 847D, H: 322A

7907 [1]קָצִיר *qāṣîr*[1], harvest, time of reaping, S: 7105, B: 894C, K: 847D, H: 322A

7908 [2]קָצִיר *qāṣîr*[2], branch, bough, twig, shoot, S: 7105, B: 894D, K: 848A, H: 322B

7909 [1]קָצַע *qāṣa'*[1], [G] to scrape off, S: 7106, B: 892D, K: 848A, H: 322B

7910 [2]קָצַע *qāṣa'*[2], [E, G] to be made with corners, S: 4742† & 7106, B: 893B, K: 848B, H: 322B

7911 קָצַף *qāṣap*, [A] to be angry; [G] to provoke to anger; [F] to be enraged, S: 7107, B: 893B, K: 848B, H: 322B

7912 [1]קֶצֶף *qeṣep*[1], wrath, anger, fury, S: 7110, B: 893C, K: 848C, H: 322B

7913 [2]קֶצֶף *qeṣep*[2], twig (snapped off), S: 7110, B: 893C, K: 848D, H: 322C

7914 קְצָפָה *qᵉṣāpâ*, stump, splintering, S: 7111, B: 893C, K: 848D, H: 322C

7915 [1]קָצַץ *qāṣaṣ*[1], [A] to cut off; [D] to cut off, take away; [E] to be cut off, maimed, S: 7112, B: 893C, K: 848D, H: 322C

7916 [2]קָצַץ *qāṣaṣ*[2], variant: [G] to come to an end, S*, B: 884C, K: 849A, H: 318B

7917 [1]קָצַר *qāṣar*[1], [A] to reap, harvest, gather, S: 7114, B: 894B, K: 849A, H: 322C

7918 [2]קָצַר *qāṣar*[2], [A] to be short; to be impatient, angry; [D] to cut short; [G] to shorten, cut short, S: 7114, B: 894A, K: 849B, H: 322D

7919 קֹצֶר *qōṣer*, discouragement, despondency, S: 7115, B: 894B, K: 849C, H: 322D

7920 קָצֵר *qāṣēr*, shortened: quick-tempered, impatient, S: 7116, B: 894B, K: 849C, H: 322D

7921 קְצָת *qᵉṣāt*, end, extremity, S: 7117, B: 892C, K: 849C, H: 322D

7922 קַר *qar*, cool, cold (water); cool-headed, even-tempered (of one's spirit), S: 7119, B: 903B, K: 849D, H: 323A

7923 קֹר *qōr*, cold, S: 7120, B: 903B, K: 849D, H: 323A

7924 [1]קָרָא *qārā'*[1], [A] to call, summon, announce, proclaim; [B] to be invited as a guest, be appointed; [C] to be called, be summoned; [E] to be called, S: 7121, B: 894D, K: 849A, H: 323A

7925 [2]קָרָא *qārā'*[2], [A] to meet, encounter, happen; [C] to have met, have happened, [G] to cause to happen, S: 7122 & 7125†, B: 896D, K: 851B, H: 323D

7926 [1]קֹרֵא *qōrē'*[1], partridge, S: 7124, B: 896C, K: 851C, H: 324A

7927 [2]קֹרֵא *qōrē'*[2], Kore, S: 6981, B: 896C, K: 851D, H: 324A

7928 קָרַב *qārab*, [A] to come near, approach; [C] to present oneself, be brought near; [D] to bring near, approach; [G] to bring near, offer, present, S: 7126, B: 897B, K: 851D, H: 324A

7929 קָרֵב *qārēb*, approaching, coming near, S: 7131, B: 898A, K: 853A, H: 324C

7930 קְרָב *qerāb*, war, battle, S: 7128, B: 898B, K: 853A, H: 324C

7931 קֶרֶב *qereb*, inner parts, heart, mind; interior, midst, S: 7130, B: 899A, K: 853B, H: 324C

7932 קִרְבָה *qirbâ*, nearness, approach, S: 7132†, B: 898B, K: 853C, H: 324D

7933 קָרְבָּן *qorbān*, gift, offering, sacrifice, S: 7133, B: 898D, K: 853D, H: 324D

7934 קֻרְבָּן *qurbān*, contribution, supply (of wood), S: 7133, B: 898D, K: 853D, H: 324D

7935 קַרְדֹּם *qardōm*, ax, S: 7134, B: 899C, K: 853D, H: 324D

7936 [1]קָרָה *qārâ*[1], [A] to happen, meet, encounter; [C] to meet with, have happen; [D] to make beams, build beams; [G] to give success, to select oneself, S: 7136, B: 899C, K: 853D, H: 324D

7937 קָרֶה *qāreh*, emission (at night), S: 7137, B: 899D, K: 854B, H: 325A

7938 [2]קָרָה *qārâ*[2], cold, S: 7135, B: 903B, K: 854B, H: 325A

7939 [3]קָרָה *qārâ*[3], variant: [D] to lay the beams of, S: 7136, B: 900A, K: 854B, H: 325A

7940 קָרוֹב *qārôb*, near, close, S: 7138, B: 898B, K: 854C, H: 325A

7941 קָרוּת *qārût*, variant: cold, see 7938, S: 3368†, B: 430A & 903B, K: 855A, H: 325B

7942 קָרַח *qāraḥ*, [A] to shave, make bald; [C] to shave oneself, make oneself bald; [G] to shave another, make bald; [H] to be rubbed bare, be make bald, S: 7139 & 7144†, B: 901A, K: 855A, H: 325B

7943 קֶרַח *qeraḥ*, ice, frost, hail, S: 7140, B: 901C, K: 855B, H: 325C

7944 קֵרֵחַ *qērēaḥ*, bald, baldheaded, S: 7142, B: 901B, K: 855B, H: 325C

7945 קָרֵחַ *qārēaḥ*, Kareah, S: 7143, B: 901B, K: 855B, H: 325C

7946 קֹרַח *qōraḥ*, Korah, S: 7141, B: 901B, K: 855B, H: 325C

7947 קָרְחָה *qorḥâ*, baldness, shaving the head, S: 7146†, B: 901B, K: 855C, H: 325C

7948 קָרְחִי *qorḥî*, Korahite, S: 7145, B: 901C, K: 855C, H: 325C

7949 קָרַחַת *qāraḥat*, bald spot (not the forehead area); bare spot (of articles), S: 7146, B: 901B, K: 855C, H: 325C

7950 קְרִי *qerî*, hostile encounter, hostility, S: 7147, B: 899D, K: 855C, H: 325C

7951 קָרִיא *qārî'*, summoned, called, S: 7148, B: 896C, K: 855D, H: 325C

7952 קְרִיאָה *qerî'â*, message, appeal, S: 7150, B: 896D, K: 855D, H: 325C

7953 קִרְיָה *qiryâ*, city, town, S: 7151, B: 900A, K: 855D, H: 325C

7954 קְרִיּוֹת *qeriyyôt*, Kerioth, S: 7152, B: 901A, K: 856B, H: 325D

7955 קְרִיּוֹת חֶצְרוֹן *qeriyyôt ḥeṣrôn*, Kerioth Hezron, S: 2696† + 7152†, B: 901A & 348A, K: 856B, H: 325D & 114B

7956 קִרְיַת *qiryat*, Kiriath, S: 7151†, B: 900A, K: 855D, H: 325D II

7957 קִרְיַת אַרְבַּע *qiryat 'arba'*, Kiriath Arba, S: 7153, B: 900B, K: 855D & 83B, H: 325D 2.(1)

7958 קִרְיַת־בַּעַל *qiryat-ba'al*, Kiriath Baal, S: 7154†, B: 900C, K: 855D 2., H: 325D 2.(2)

7959 קִרְיַת הָאַרְבַּע *qiryat hā'arba'*, Kiriath Arba, S: 7153†, B: 900B, K: 855D 1., H: 325D 2.(1)

7960 קִרְיַת חֻצוֹת *qiryat ḥuṣôt*, Kiriath Huzoth, S: 7155, B: 900C, K: 855D 3., H: 325D 2.(3)

7961 קִרְיַת יְעָרִים *qiryat ye'ārîm*, Kiriath Jearim, S: 7157, B: 900C, K: 855D 2., H: 325D 2.(4)

7962 קִרְיַת־סַנָּה *qiryat-sannâ*, Kiriath Sannah, S: 7158†, B: 900D, K: 855D 5., H: 325D 2.(5)

7963 קִרְיַת־סֵפֶר *qiryat-sēper*, Kiriath Sepher, S: 7158†, B: 900D, K: 855D 6., H: 325D 2.(6)

7964 קִרְיָתַיִם *qiryātayim*, Kiriathaim, S: 7156, B: 900B, K: 856B, H: 325D

7965 קָרַם *qāram*, [A] to cover with, spread; [C] to be spread over, S: 7159, B: 901C, K: 856B, H: 325D

7966 קָרַן *qāran*, [A] to be radiant; [G] to be with horns, S: 7160, B: 902A, K: 856C, H: 325D

7967 קֶרֶן *qeren*, horn, (pair) of horns, S: 7161, B: 901D, K: 856C, H: 325D

7968 קֶרֶן הַפּוּךְ *qeren happûk*, Keren-Happuch, S: 7163, B: 902A, K: 857A, H: 326A

7969 קַרְנַיִם *qarnayim*, Karnaim, S: 7161†, B: 902B, K: 857A, H: 326A

7970 קָרַס *qāras*, [A] to stoop low, bend down, S: 7164, B: 902B, K: 857A, H: 326A

7971 קֶרֶס *qeres*, clasp, hook (of curtains), S: 7165, B: 902B, K: 857A, H: 326A

7972 קַרְסֹל *qarsōl*, (dual) ankles, S: 7166, B: 902B, K: 857A, H: 326A

7973 קָרַע *qāra'*, [A] to tear, rend, rip; [B] to be torn; [C] to be torn to pieces, be split apart, S: 7167, B: 902B, K: 857B, H: 326A

7974 קְרָעִים *qerā'îm*, torn pieces (of a garment), rags, S: 7168†, B: 902D, K: 857C, H: 326B

7975 קָרַץ *qāraṣ*, [A] to maliciously wink, purse (the lips); [E] to be shaped, S: 7169, B: 902D, K: 857D, H: 326B

7976 קֶרֶץ *qereṣ*, gadfly, S: 7171, B: 903A, K: 857D, H: 326B

7977 [1]קַרְקַע *qarqa'*[1], floor, S: 7172, B: 903A, K: 857D, H: 326B

7978 [2]קַרְקַע *qarqa'*[2], Karka, S: 7173, B: 903A, K: 858A, H: 326B

7979 קַרְקַר *qarqar*, variant: see 7721, S: 6979†, B: 903A, K: 858A, H: 326B

7980 קַרְקֹר *qarqōr*, Karkor, S: 7174, B: 903A, K: 858A, H: 326B

7981 [1]קָרַר *qārar*[1], [G] to pour out *or* to keep cool, S: 6979†, B: 903B, K: 858A, H: 326C

7982 [2]קָרַר *qārar*[2], [D] to tear down, S: 6979†, B: 903B, K: 858A, H: 326C

7983 קֶרֶשׁ *qereš*, frame, S: 7175, B: 903C, K: 858B, H: 326C

7984 קֶרֶת *qeret*, city, town, S: 7176, B: 900D, K: 858B, H: 326C

7985 קַרְתָּה *qartâ*, Kartah, S: 7177, B: 900D, K: 858B, H: 326C

7986 קַרְתָּן *qartān*, Kartan, S: 7178, B: 900B, K: 858B, H: 326C

7987 קַשְׂוָה *qaśwâ*, pitcher, jar, S: 7184, B: 903C, K: 858C, H: 326C

7988 קְשִׂיטָה *qeśîṭâ*, piece of silver (unknown unit of weight or value), S: 7192, B: 903D, K: 858C, H: 326D

7989 קַשְׂקֶשֶׂת *qaśqeśet*, scales (as on skin of marine creatures); scale armor, S: 7193, B: 903D, K: 858C, H: 326C

7990 קַשׁ *qaš*, stubble, chaff, straw, S: 7179, B: 905D, K: 858D, H: 326C

7991 קִשֻּׁאָה *qiššu'â*, cucumber, S: 7180†, B: 903D, K: 858D, H: 326C

7992 קָשַׁב *qāšab*, [A] to listen; [G] to pay attention, give heed, listen, S: 7181, B: 904A, K: 858D, H: 326C

7993 קֶשֶׁב *qešeb*, paying attention, responding, S: 7182, B: 904A, K: 859A, H: 326D

7994 קַשָּׁב *qaššāb*, attentive, S: 7183, B: 904A, K: 859B, H: 326D

7995 קַשֻּׁב *qaššub*, attentive, S: 7183, B: 904B, K: 859B, H: 326D

7996 קָשָׁה *qāšâ*, [A] to be hard, harsh, cruel; [C] to be distressed; [D] to have great difficulty (in labor); [G] to make stiff, harden, be difficult, S: 7185, B: 904B, K: 859B, H: 326D

7997 קָשֶׁה *qāšeh*, hard, harsh, difficult, fierce; stubborn, stiff(-necked), obstinate, S: 7186, B: 904C, K: 859C, H: 327A

7998 קָשַׁח *qāšaḥ*, [G] to harden, S: 7188, B: 905A, K: 859D, H: 327A

7999 קֹשְׁטְ *qōšṭ*, true, S: 7189, B: 905A, K: 860A, H: 327B

8000 קֹשֶׁט *qōšeṭ*, bow (weapon), S: 7189, B: 905A, K: 860A, H: 327B

8001 קְשִׁי *qešî*, stubbornness, S: 7190, B: 904D, K: 860A, H: 327B

8002 קִשְׁיוֹן *qišyôn*, Kishion, S: 7191, B: 904D, K: 860A, H: 327B

8003 קָשַׁר *qāšar*, [A] to tie, bind; to plot, conspire; [B] to be bound up; be strong; [C] to be joined with; [D] to bind; [E] to be strong; [F] to conspire together, S: 7194, B: 905A, K: 860B, H: 327B

8004 קֶשֶׁר *qešer*, conspiracy, treason, S: 7195, B: 905C, K: 860D, H: 327C

8005 קִשֻּׁרִים *qiššurîm*, sashes, wedding ornaments, S: 7196†, B: 905C, K: 860D, H: 327C

8006 קָשַׁשׁ *qāšaš*[1], [A] to gather together; [D] to gather; [F] to gather together, S: 7197, B: 905D, K: 860D, H: 327C

8007 קָשַׁשׁ *qāšaš*[2], variant: [A, F] to gather together, assemble, S: 7197, B: 905D, K: 860D, H: 327D

8008 קֶשֶׁת *qešet*, bow (weapon), rainbow, S: 7198, B: 905D, K: 861A, H: 327D

8009 קַשָּׁת *qaššāt*, archer, S: 7199, B: 906C, K: 861D, H: 327D

8010 ר *r*, letter of the Hebrew alphabet, S*, B: 906B, K: 861B, H*

8011 רָאָה *rā'â*[1], [A] to see, look, view; to realize, know, consider; [B] to be selected; [C] to become visible, appear, show oneself; [E] to be seen; [G] to cause to see, show; [H] to be shown; [F] to look at each other, meet with, S: 7200 & 7202†, B: 906B, K: 861D, H: 327B

8012 רָאָה *rā'â*[2], red kite, S: 7201, B: 906B, K: 864A, H: 329A

8013 רָאֶה *rā'eh*, variant: seeing, S: 7200†, B: 909A, K: 876D, H: 329A

8014 רֹאֶה *rō'eh*[1], seer, S: 7203, B: 909A, K: 864A, H: 329A

8015 רֹאֶה *rō'eh*[2], vision, S: 7203, B: 909B, K: 864B, H: 329A

8016 רֹאֶה *rō'eh*[3], variant: Roeh, see 2218, S: 7211†, B: 909B, K: 864A, H*

8017 רְאוּבֵן *re'ûbēn*, Reuben, S: 7205, B: 910A, K: 864B, H: 329A

8018 רְאוּבֵנִי *re'ûbēnî*, Reubenite, of Reuben, S: 7206, B: 910A, K: 864B, H: 329A

8019 רַאֲוָה *ra'awâ*, spectacle, sight, S: 7207, B: 909B, K: 864C, H: 329A

8020 רְאוּמָה *re'ûmâ*, Reumah, S: 7208, B: 910B, K: 864C, H: 329A

8021 רְאוּת *re'ût*, look, S: 7200†, B: 909B, K: 864C, H: 329A

8022 רֳאִי *rō'î*, variant: Roi, see 936, S: 883†, B: 91D, K: 105D, H: 32D

8023 רְאִי *re'î*, mirror, S: 7209, B: 909B, K: 864C, H: 329A

8024 רֳאִי *ro'î*, appearance, spectacle, S: 7210, B: 909B, K: 864C, H: 329A

8025 רְאָיָה *re'āyâ*, Reaiah, S: 7211, B: 909D, K: 864D, H: 329B

8026 רְאִית *re'ît*, variant: look, sight, S: 7212, B: 909B, K: 864D, H: 329B

8027 רָאַם *rā'am*, [A] to rise up high, S: 7213, B: 910B, K: 864D, H: 329B

8028 רְאֵם *re'ēm*, wild oxen, S: 7214, B: 910B, K: 864D, H: 329B

8029 רָאמוֹת *rā'môt*[1], coral, S: 7215†, B: 910C, K: 865A, H: 329B

8030 רָאמוֹת *rā'môt*[2], Ramoth, S: 7216, B: 928B, K: 865A, H: 329B

8031 רֹאשׁ *rō'š*[1], head: top, leader, chief, S: 7218 & 7226†, B: 910C, K: 865B, H: 329B

8032 רֹאשׁ *rō'š*[2], poison; gall; bitterness, S: 7219, B: 912C, K: 866B, H: 329D

8033 רֹאשׁ *rō'š*[3], Rosh, S: 7220, B: 912C, K: 866B, H: 329D

8034 רֹאשׁ *rō'š*[4], variant: Rosh, S: 7218, B: 912C, K: 866B, H: 329D

8035 רִאשָׁה *ri'šâ*, beginning, before, S: 7221, B: 911C, K: 866B, H: 329D

8036 רֹאשָׁה *rō'šâ*, uppermost, cap[stone], S: 7222, B: 911C, K: 866B, H: 329D

8037 רִאשׁוֹן *ri'šôn*, (of position) first, foremost; (of time) former, beginning, earlier, S: 7223, B: 911C, K: 866C, H: 329D

8038 רִאשֹׁנִי *ri'šōnî*, first, S: 7224, B: 912A, K: 867A, H: 330A

8039 רַאֲשׁוֹת *ra'ašôt*, variant: head, place of the head, see 5265, S: 4763†, B: 912B, K: 867A, H: 330A

8040 רֵאשִׁית *rē'šît*, what is first; beginning, S: 7225, B: 912A, K: 867B, H: 330A

8041 רַב *rab*[1], many, much; great, abundant, numerous, S: 7227, B: 912D, K: 867C, H: 330A

8042 רַב *rab*[2], commander, chief officer, high official, S: 7227, B: 913C, K: 868B, H: 330C

8043 רַב *rab*[3], archer, S: 7228, B: 914D, K: 868C, H: 330C

8044 רֹב *rōb*, greatness, abundance; multitude, S: 7230, B: 913D, K: 868C, H: 330C

8045 רָבַב *rābab*[1], [A] to abound, increase, be great; [E] to increase by tens of thousands, S: 7231, B: 912C, K: 868D, H: 330D

8046 רָבַב *rābab*[2], [A] to shoot (an arrow), S: 7232, B: 914D, K: 869A, H: 330D

8047 רְבָבָה *rebābâ*, ten thousand, myriad; (virtually) countless number, S: 7233, B: 914B, K: 869A, H: 330D

8048 רָבַד *rābad*, [A] to cover, S: 7234, B: 914D, K: 869B, H: 330D

8049 רָבָה *rābâ*[1], [A] to increase in number, multiply, grow large; [D] to rear (offspring); to gain; make numerous; [G] to cause to increase, make numerous, enlarge, S: 7235, B: 915A, K: 869B, H: 330D

8050 רָבָה *rābâ*[2], [A] to shoot; (ptcp.) archer, S: 7235, B: 916C, K: 870A, H: 331B

8051 רַבָּה *rabbâ*, Rabbah, S: 7237, B: 913D, K: 870B, H: 331B

8052 רִבּוֹא *ribbô'*, ten thousand; myriad, (virtually) countless number, S: 7239, B: 914B, K: 870B, H: 331B

8053 רְבִיבִים *rebîbîm*, rain shower, abundant rain, S: 7241†, B: 914C, K: 870C, H: 331B

8054 רָבִיד *rābîd*, necklace, ornamental chain, S: 7242, B: 914D, K: 870C, H: 331B

8055 רְבִיעִי *rebî'î*, fourth, S: 7243, B: 917D, K: 870C, H: 331B

8056 רַבִּית *rabbît*, Rabbith, S: 7245, B: 914C, K: 870D, H: 331C

8057 רָבַךְ *rābak*, [H] to be kneaded, mixed (of dough), S: 7246, B: 916C, K: 870D, H: 331C

8058 רִבְלָה *riblâ*, Riblah, S: 7247, B: 916C, K: 870D, H: 331C

8059 רַב מָג *rab māg*, variant: high official, S: 7248†, B: 913C & 550B, K: 868B, H: 331C

8060 רַב־סָרִיס *rab-sārîs*, variant: chief officer, S: 7249, B: 913C & 710B, K: 868B & 668A, H: 331C

8061 רָבַע *rāba'*[1], [A] to lie down with, have sexual relations with; [G] to mate, cross-breed, S: 7250 & 7252† & 7254†, B: 918A, K: 871A, H: 331C

8062 רָבַע *rāba'*[2], [B, D] to be squared, have four corners, S: 7251, B: 917C, K: 871A, H: 331C

8063 רֶבַע *reba'*[1], fourth-part, quarter; side (of a square thing), S: 7253, B: 917D, K: 871B, H: 331C

8064 רֶבַע *reba'*[2], Reba, S: 7254, B: 918B, K: 871B, H: 331D

8065 רֹבַע *rōba'*[1], fourth-part, quarter, S: 7255, B: 917D, K: 871B, H: 331D

8066 רֹבַע *rōba'*[2], variant: dust, rubbish, S: 7255, B: 917D, K: 871B, H: 331D

8067 רִבֵּעַ *ribbēa'*, fourth; (as noun) the fourth generation, S: 7256, B: 918A, K: 871B, H: 331D

8068 רְבֻעַת *rebu'at*, variant: square, S: 7243†, B: 918A 3., K: 871C, H: 331D

8069 רָבַץ *rābaṣ*, [A] to lie down; [G] to make lie down; to cause to rest, S: 7257, B: 918B, K: 871C, H: 331D

8070 רֵבֶץ *rēbeṣ*, resting place, S: 7258, B: 918C, K: 871D, H: 332A

8071 רִבְקָה *ribqâ*, Rebekah, S: 7259, B: 918D, K: 871D, H: 332A

8072 רַב־שָׁקֵה *rab-šāqēh*, Assyrian officer: (field) commander, cupbearer, S: 7262†, B: 913C, K: 872A, H: 332A

8073 רֶגֶב *regeb*, clod of dirt, S: 7263, B: 918D, K: 872A, H: 332A

8074 רָגַז *rāgaz*, [A] to quake, shake, tremble; to be angry, be in anguish; [G] to cause to shake, make tremble, cause a disturbance; [F] to enrage oneself (against), S: 7264, B: 919A, K: 872A, H: 332A

8075 רֹגֶז *rōgez*, turmoil, excitement, tumult, S: 7267, B: 919C, K: 872C, H: 332B

8076 רַגָּז *raggāz*, anxious, trembling, S: 7268, B: 919C, K: 872C, H: 332B

8077 רָגְזָה *rogzâ*, shuddering, agitation, S: 7269, B: 919C, K: 872C, H: 332B

8078 רָגַל *rāgal*, [A] to slander; [D] to spy, explore, S: 7270 & 8637†, B: 920A, K: 872C, H: 332B

8079 רֶגֶל *regel*, foot; footstep, S: 7272, B: 919C, K: 872D, H: 332B

8080 רֹגֵל *rōgēl*, variant: Rogel, see 6537, S: 5883†, B: 745A, K: 700C k., H: 271C

8081 רַגְלִי *raglî*, (persons) on foot (i.e., not riding), S: 7273, B: 920B, K: 873B, H: 332D

8082 רֹגְלִים *rōgelîm*, Rogelim, S: 7274, B: 920C, K: 873C, H: 332D

8083 רָגַם *rāgam*, [A] to execute by hurling stones, S: 7275, B: 920C, K: 873C, H: 332D

8084 רֶגֶם *regem*, Regem, S: 7276, B: 920D, K: 873D, H: 332D

8085 רֶגֶם מֶלֶךְ *regem melek*, Regem-Melech, S: 7278, B: 920D, K: 873D, H: 332D

8086 רִגְמָה *rigmâ*, great throng, crowd, S: 7277, B: 920C, K: 873D, H: 332D

8087 רָגַן *rāgan*, [A] to complain; [C] to be grumbling, be gossiping, S: 5372† & 7279, B: 920D, K: 873D, H: 332D

8088 רָגַע *rāga'*[1], [A] to stir up, churn up; [G] to do something in an instant, S: 7280, B: 920D, K: 874A, H: 332D

8089 [2]רָגַע *rāgaʿ*[2], [C] to cease; [G] to find repose, bring rest, S: 7280, B: 921B, K: 874A, H: 332D

8090 [3]רָגַע *rāgaʿ*[3], [A] to harden, crust over, S: 7280, B: 921C, K: 874A, H: 332D

8091 רָגֵעַ *rāgēaʿ*, quiet, resting, S: 7282, B: 921B, K: 874B, H: 333A

8092 רֶגַע *regaʿ*, moment, instant; peace, tranquility, S: 7281, B: 921A, K: 874B, H: 333A

8093 רָגַשׁ *rāgaš*, [A] to be restless, be in tumult, S: 7283, B: 921C, K: 874C, H: 333A

8094 רֶגֶשׁ *regeš*, throng, S: 7285, B: 921C, K: 874C, H: 333A

8095 רִגְשָׁה *rigšâ*, crowd, throng, S: 7285, B: 921C, K: 874C, H: 333A

8096 רָדַד *rādad*, [A] to subdue, beat down; [G] to hammer out flat, S: 7286, B: 921C, K: 874C, H: 333A

8097 [1]רָדָה *rādâ*[1], [A] to rule over; [G] to cause to dominate, S: 7287, B: 921D, K: 874D, H: 333B

8098 [2]רָדָה *rādâ*[2], [A] to scoop out, scrape out, S: 7287, B: 922A, K: 875A, H: 333B

8099 רַדַּי *radday*, Raddai, S: 7288, B: 921D, K: 875A, H: 333B

8100 רְדִיד *r^{e}dîd*, cloak, shawl, S: 7289, B: 921D, K: 875B, H: 333B

8101 רָדַם *rādam*, [C] to be in a heavy sleep, S: 7290, B: 922B, K: 875B, H: 333C

8102 רֹדָן *rōdān*, Rodanim; Rhodes, S: 1721†, B: 922B, K: 875B, H: 333C

8103 רָדַף *rādap*, [A] to pursue, chase, persecute; [C] to be pursued, be hounded; [D] to pursue, chase; [E] to be chased; [G] to chase, S: 7291, B: 922C, K: 875B, H: 333C

8104 רָהַב *rāhab*, [A] to rise up against; press one's plea; [G] to overwhelm; make bold, S: 7292, B: 923B, K: 875D, H: 333D

8105 רַהַב *rahab*, Rahab, S: 7293 & 7294, B: 923C, K: 876A, H: 333D

8106 רֹהַב *rōhab*, variant: pride *or* hurry, see 8145, S: 7296†, B: 923B, K: 876A, H: 333D

8107 רָהָב *rāhāb*, proud, defiant, S: 7295, B: 923B, K: 876A, H: 333D

8108 רָהְגָּה *rohgâ*, Rohgah, S: 7303†, B: 923C, K: 876B, H: 334A

8109 רָהָה *rāhâ*, variant: [A] to fear, S: 7297, B: 923C, K: 403C, H: 144B

8110 [1]רַהַט *rahaṭ*[1], watering trough, S: 7298, B: 923D, K: 876B, H: 334A

8111 [2]רַהַט *rahaṭ*[2], tress, rafter, S: 7298, B: 923D, K: 876B, H: 334A

8112 רָהִיט *rāhîṭ*, rafters, S: 7351†, B: 923D, K: 876B, H: 334A

8113 רוּד *rûd*, [A] to roam; [G] to grow restless, cause restlessness, S: 7300, B: 923D, K: 876B, H: 334A

8114 רוֹדָנִים *rôdānîm*, variant: Rhodians, S: 1721, B: 922C, K: 876C, H: 334A

8115 רָוָה *rāwâ*, [A] to drink to satisfaction, quench the thirst; [D] to drench, refresh, satisfy; [G] to lavish upon, cause to refresh, S: 7301, B: 924A, K: 876D, H: 334A

8116 רָוֶה *rāweh*, well-watered, drenched, S: 7302, B: 924B, K: 876D, H: 334B

8117 רוֹהֲגָה *rôh^{a}gâ*, variant: Rohagah, see 8108, S: 7303, B: 923C, K: 877A, H: 334B

8118 רָוַח *rāwaḥ*, [A] to feel relief; [E] to be spacious, S: 7304, B: 926B, K: 877A, H: 334B

8119 רֶוַח *rewaḥ*, relief; space, S: 7305, B: 926C, K: 877B, H: 334C

8120 רוּחַ *rûaḥ*, spirit, the Spirit; wind; breath, life, heart, mind, S: 7307, B: 924C, K: 877B, H: 334C

8121 רְוָחָה *r^{e}wāḥâ*, relief, respite, S: 7309, B: 926C, K: 879C, H: 335A

8122 רְוָיָה *r^{e}wāyâ*, place of abundance, overflowing, S: 7310, B: 924B, K: 879C, H: 335A

8123 [1]רוּם *rûm*[1], [A] to be high, raise up; to be proud, haughty; [D] to exalt, lift high; [E] to be exalted, be lifted up; [G] to cause to lift up, present (an offering); to raise up against, rebel; [H] to be presented, be taken away; to exalt oneself, S: 7311, B: 926C, K: 879D, H: 335A

8124 [2]רוּם *rûm*[2], height; haughtiness, pride, S: 7312, B: 927D, K: 881C, H: 335D

8125 רוֹם *rôm*, on high, S: 7315, B: 927D, K: 881C, H: 335D

8126 רוּמָה *rûmâ*, Rumah, S: 7316, B: 928A, K: 881C, H: 335D

8127 רוֹמָה *rômâ*, proudly, haughtily, S: 7317, B: 928A, K: 881D, H: 335D

8128 רוֹמָם *rômām*, praise, exaltation, S: 7318, B: 928C, K: 881D, H: 335D

8129 רוֹמֵמֻת *rômēmut*, rising up, lifting up, S: 7319† & 7427†, B: 928C, K: 881D, H: 336A

8130 רוּן *rûn*, [F] to awake from a stupor, become sober, S: 7442†, B: 929C, K: 881D, H: 336A

8131 רוּעַ *rûaʿ*, [G] to raise a battle cry; sound a trumpet blast; shout in triumph or exaltation, S: 7321, B: 929C, K: 881D, H: 336A

8132 רוּץ *rûṣ*, [A] to run, hurry, be a messenger; [D] to dart about, run to and fro; [G] to chase; to bring quickly, S: 7323, B: 930A, K: 882B, H: 336A

8133 רוּשׁ *rûš*, [A] to be poor, be in poverty, be oppressed; [F] to pretend to be poor, S: 7326, B: 930D, K: 883A, H: 336B

8134 רוּת *rût*, Ruth, S: 7327, B: 946C, K: 883A, H: 336C

8135 רָזָה *rāzâ*, [A] to destroy; [C] to waste away, S: 7329, B: 930D, K: 883B, H: 336C

8136 רָזֶה *rāzeh*, lean; barren, S: 7330, B: 931A, K: 883B, H: 336C

8137 [1]רָזוֹן *rāzôn*[1], wasting disease; short, scrimped (ephah), S: 7332, B: 931A, K: 883B, H: 336C

8138 [2]רָזוֹן *rāzôn*[2], prince, dignitary, S: 7333, B: 931B, K: 883B, H: 336C

8139 רְזוֹן *r^{e}zôn*, Rezon, S: 7331, B: 931B, K: 883C, H: 336C

8140 רָזִי *rāzî*, wasting away, leanness, S: 7334, B: 931A, K: 883C, H: 336C

8141 רָזַם *rāzam*, [A] to wink, flash the eyes, S: 7335, B: 931B, K: 883C, H: 336C

8142 רָזַן *rāzan*, [A] to be a ruler; (ptcp.) a prince, ruler, S: 7336, B: 931B, K: 883C, H: 336C

8143 רָחַב *rāḥab*, [A] to be wide; to swell (with joy); to boast; [C] to be roomy, be broad; [G] to enlarge, broaden, make wide, S: 7337, B: 931B, K: 883C, H: 336C

8144 רַחַב *raḥab*, spacious place, vast expanse, S: 7338, B: 931D, K*, H*

8145 רֹחַב *rōḥab*, breadth, width, S: 7341, B: 931D, K: 884A, H: 336D

8146 [1]רָחָב *rāḥāb*[1], spacious, broad, roomy, S: 7342, B: 932A, K: 884B, H: 336D

8147 [2]רָחָב *rāḥāb*[2], Rahab, S: 7343, B: 932A, K: 884B, H: 337A

8148 [1]רְחֹב *r^{e}ḥōb*[1], public square, open street, S: 7339, B: 932A, K: 884B, H: 337A

8149 [2]רְחֹב *r^{e}ḥōb*[2], Rehob, S: 7340, B: 932B 1., K: 884C, H: 337A

8150 [3]רְחֹב *r^{e}ḥōb*[3], Rehob, S: 7340, B: 932B, K: 884C, H: 337A

8151 רְחֹבוֹת *r^{e}ḥōbôt*, Rehoboth, S: 7344, B: 932C, K: 884C, H: 337A

8152 רְחַבְיָה *r^{e}ḥabyâ*, Rehabiah, S: 7345, B: 932C, K: 884D, H: 337A

8153 רְחַבְיָהוּ *r^{e}ḥabyāhû*, Rehabiah, S: 7345, B: 932C, K: 884D, H: 337A

8154 רְחַבְעָם *r^{e}ḥabʿām*, Rehoboam, S: 7346, B: 932C, K: 884D, H: 337A

8155 רְחֹבֹת עִיר *r^{e}ḥōbōt ʿîr*, Rehoboth Ir, S: 7344† + 5892†, B: 932C 1., K: 884C 3., H: 337A

8156 רְחוּם *r^{e}ḥûm*, Rehum, S: 7348, B: 933D, K: 885A, H: 337A

8157 רַחוּם *raḥûm*, compassionate, merciful, S: 7349, B: 933D, K: 885A, H: 337A

8158 רָחוֹק *rāḥôq*, far, distant; (as noun) distance, afar, S: 7350, B: 935B, K: 885A, H: 337A

8159 רָחִיט *rāḥîṭ*, variant: see 8112, S: 7351, B: 923D, K: 885C, H: 337B

8160 רֵחַיִם *rēḥayim*, handmill; pair of mill stones, S: 7347†, B: 932D, K: 885D, H: 337B

8161 [1]רָחֵל *rāḥēl*[1], ewe-sheep, S: 7353, B: 932D, K: 885D, H: 337C

8162 [2]רָחֵל *rāḥēl*[2], Rachel, S: 7354, B: 932D, K: 885D, H: 337C

8163 רָחַם *rāḥam*, [A] to love; [D] to have compassion on, show mercy, take pity on; [E] to find compassion, be loved, S: 7355, B: 933C, K: 885D, H: 337C

8164 רָחָם *rāḥām*, carrion-vulture, S: 7360, B: 934B, K: 886B, H: 337C

8165 [1]רַחַם *raḥam*[1], Raham, S: 7357, B: 933D, K: 886B, H: 337C

8166 [2]רַחַם *raḥam*[2], variant: see 8167, S: 7356†, B: 933A, K: 886B, H: 337C

8167 רֶחֶם *reḥem*, womb, S: 7358, B: 933A, K: 886B, H: 337C

8168 רָחָמָה *rāḥāmâ*, carrion-vulture, S: 7360, B: 934B, K: 886C, H: 337D

8169 רַחֲמָה *raḥ^{a}mâ*, womb; slang for woman, S: 7361, B: 933B 2., K: 886C, H: 337D

8170 רֻחָמָה *ruḥāmâ*, variant: Ruhamah, S: 3819†, B: 520D, K: 468D, H: 171B

8171 רַחֲמִים *raḥ^{a}mîm*, compassion, mercy, pity, S: 7356†, B: 933B, K: 886C, H: 337D

8172 רַחֲמָנִי *raḥ^{a}mānî*, compassionate, S: 7362, B: 933D, K: 886D, H: 337D

8173 [1]רָחַף *rāḥap*[1], [A] to tremble, shake; [D] to hover, S: 7363, B: 934B, K: 886D, H: 337D

8174 [2]רָחַף *rāḥap*[2], variant: [A] to grow soft, relax, S: 7363, B: 934B, K: 886D, H: 337D

8175 רָחַץ *rāḥaṣ*, [A] to wash, bathe; [E] to be cleansed; [F] to wash oneself, S: 7364, B: 934B, K: 887A, H: 337D

8176 רַחַץ *raḥaṣ*, washing, S: 7366, B: 934D, K: 887C, H: 338A

8177 רַחְצָה *raḥṣâ*, washing, S: 7367, B: 934D, K: 887C, H: 338A

8178 רָחַק *rāḥaq*, [A] to be far off; to avoid, stand aloof; [D] to send far away, extend; [G] to remove far away, drive far off, go very far, S: 7368, B: 934D, K: 887C, H: 338A

8179 רָחֵק *rāḥēq*, one who is far away, S: 7369, B: 935B, K: 888A, H: 338B

8180 רָחַשׁ *rāḥaš*, [A] to be stirred up (one's heart), S: 7370, B: 935D, K: 888A, H: 338B

8181 רַחַת *raḥat*, winnowing fork, shovel, S: 7371, B: 935D, K: 888A, H: 338B

8182 רָטַב *rāṭab*, [A] to be drenched, be wet, S: 7372, B: 936A, K: 888B, H: 338B

8183 רָטֹב *rāṭōb*, well-watered (plant), S: 7373, B: 936A, K: 888B, H: 338B

8184 רָטָה *rāṭâ*, variant: [A] to wring out, S: 3399†, B: 936A, K: 888B, H: 338C

8185 רֶטֶט *reṭeṭ*, panic, S: 7374, B: 936A, K: 888B, H: 338C

8186 רֻטֲפַשׁ *ruṭ^{a}paš*, [B] to be renewed, S: 7375, B: 936A, K: 888B, H: 338C

8187 רָטַשׁ *rāṭaš*, [D] to dash to pieces; [E] to be dashed to pieces, S: 7376†, B: 936B, K: 888C, H: 338C

8188 רִי *rî*, moisture, S: 7377, B: 924B, K: 888C, H: 338C

8189 [1]רִיב *rîb*[1], [A] to quarrel, contend, plead for, S: 7378, B: 936B, K: 888D, H: 338C

8190 [2]רִיב *rîb*[2], contention, grievance, strife, legal dispute, S: 7379, B: 936D, K: 889B, H: 338D

8191 רִיבָה *rîbâ*, legal plea, S: 7379†, B: 937A, K: 889C, H: 339A

8192 רִיבַי *rîbay*, Ribai, S: 7380, B: 937A, K: 889C, H: 339A

8193 רִיחַ *rîaḥ*, [G] to smell (an aroma or odor), S: 7306†, B: 926B, K: 877A, H: 339A

8194 רֵיחַ *rêaḥ*, aroma, smell, fragrance, S: 7381, B: 926B, K: 889C, H: 339A

8195 רִיפוֹת *rîpôt*, grain, S: 7383†, B: 937D, K: 889D, H: 339A

8196 רִיפַת *rîpat*, Riphath, S: 7384, B: 937D, K: 889D, H: 339A

8197 [1]רִיק *rîq*[1], [G] to pour forth, empty out; to draw (a sword), S: 7324†, B: 937D, K: 889D, H: 339A

8198 [2]רִיק *rîq*[2], emptiness, nothingness, vanity, S: 7385, B: 938B, K: 890A, H: 339B

8199 רֵיק *rêq*, empty; idle, worthless, S: 7386, B: 938A, K: 890B, H: 339B

8200 רֵיקָם *rêqām*, empty-handed, without cause *or* satisfaction, S: 7387, B: 938B, K: 890B, H: 339B

8201 [1]רִיר *rîr*[1], [A] to flow, S: 7325†, B: 938B, K: 890C, H: 339C

8202 [2]רִיר *rîr*[2], saliva; white (of an egg), S: 7388, B: 938C, K: 890C, H: 339C

8203 רֵישׁ *rêš*, poverty, S: 7389, B: 930D, K: 890C, H: 339C

8204 רֹךְ *rōk*, gentleness, tenderness, softness, S: 7391, B: 940A, K: 890D, H: 339C

8205 רַךְ *rak*, gentle, tender, weak, soft, S: 7390, B: 940A, K: 890D, H: 339C

8206 רָכַב *rākab*, [A] to ride or mount an riding animal, S: 7392, B: 938C, K: 890D, H: 339C

8207 רֶכֶב *rekeb*, chariot; large upper mill stone, S: 7393, B: 939A, K: 891A, H: 339D

8208 רַכָּב *rakkāb*, chariot driver, horseman, S: 7395, B: 939B, K: 892A, H: 340A

8209 רֵכָב *rēkāb*, Recab, S: 7394, B: 939C, K: 892A, H: 340A

8210 רִכְבָּה *rikbâ*, act of riding, S: 7396, B: 939B, K: 892A, H: 340A

8211 רֵכָבִי *rēkābî*, Recabite, S: 7394†, B: 939C, K: 892A, H: 340A

8212 רֵכָה *rēkâ*, Recah, S: 7397, B: 939D, K: 892A, H: 340A

8213 רְכוּב *r^{e}kûb*, chariot, S: 7398, B: 939C, K: 892A, H: 340A

8214 רְכוּשׁ *r^{e}kûš*, possessions, property, goods, equipment, S: 7399, B: 940D, K: 892A, H: 340A

8215 רָכִיל *rākîl*, slanderer, gossip, S: 7400, B: 940C, K: 892B, H: 340A

8216 רָכַךְ *rākak*, [A] to be soft, faint-hearted; [E] to be soothed; [G] to make faint, S: 7401, B: 939D, K: 892B, H: 340A

8217 רָכַל *rākal*, [A] to do trade, act as a merchant; (as noun) trader, merchant, S: 7402, B: 940B, K: 892C, H: 340B

8218 רָכָל *rākāl*, Racal, S: 7403, B: 940B, K: 892D, H: 340B

8219 רְכֻלָּה *r^{e}kullâ*, trading of merchandise, S: 7404, B: 940B, K: 892D, H: 340B

8220 רָכַס *rākas*, [A] to tie, bind, S: 7405, B: 940C, K: 892D, H: 340B

8221 רֶכֶס *rekes*, rugged place, S: 7406, B: 940C, K: 892D, H: 340B

8222 רֹכֶס *rōkes*, intrigue, plot, conspiracy, S: 7407, B: 940C, K: 893A, H: 340B

8223 רָכַשׁ *rākaš*, [A] to tie, bind, S: 7408, B: 940D, K: 893A, H: 340B

8224 רֶכֶשׁ *rekeš*, team of horses; fast horses (for couriers), S: 7409, B: 940D, K: 893A, H: 340B

8225 [1]רָם *rām*[1], variant: high, exalted, S: 7311†, B: 926C, K: 893A, H: 340C

8226 [2]רָם *rām*[2], Ram, S: 7410, B: 928A, K: 893A, H: 340C

8227 [1]רָמָה *rāmâ*[1], [A] to hurl (horse and rider); to shoot (arrows), S: 7411, B: 941A, K: 893B, H: 340C

8228 [2]רָמָה *rāmâ*[2], [D] to deceive, betray, S: 7411, B: 941A, K: 893B, H: 340C

8229 [3]רָמָה *rāmâ*[3], lofty shrine; height, S: 7413, B: 928A, K: 893C, H: 340C

8230 [4]רָמָה *rāmâ*[4], Ramah; Ramoth, S: 7414, B: 928A, K: 893C, H: 340C

8231 רִמָּה *rimmâ*, worm, maggot, S: 7415, B: 942C, K: 893D, H: 340C

8232 [1]רִמּוֹן *rimmôn*[1], pomegranate, S: 7416, B: 941D, K: 893D, H: 340C

8233 [2]רִמּוֹן *rimmôn*[2], Rimmon, S: 7417, B: 942A, K: 894A, H: 340D

8234 [3]רִמּוֹן *rimmôn*[3], Rimmon, S: 7417, B: 942A, K: 894A, H: 340D

8235 [4]רִמּוֹן *rimmôn*[4], Rimmon (pagan god), S: 7417, B: 942A, K: 894A, H: 340D

8236 רִמֹּן פֶּרֶץ *rimmôn pereṣ*, Rimmon Perez, S: 7428, B: 942A, K: 894A, H: 340D

8237 רִמּוֹנוֹ *rimmônô*, Rimmono, S: 7417, B: 942B, K: 894B, H: 340D

8238 רָמוֹת *rāmôt*, Ramoth, S: 7418†, B: 928B, K: 894B, H: 340D

8239 רָמוּת *rāmût*, remains, refuse, rubbish, S: 7419, B: 928C, K: 894B, H: 340D

8240 רָמוֹת גִּלְעָד *rāmôt gil'ād*, Ramoth Gilead, S: 7433, B: 928B, K: 893D 8., H: 340C & 61D

8241 רָמוֹת־נֶגֶב *rāmôt-negeb*, Ramoth Negev, S: 7418, B: 928B 1.b., K: 893D 7., H: 340D & 225D

8242 רֹמַח *rōmaḥ*, spear, S: 7420, B: 942B, K: 894B, H: 340D

8243 רַמְיָה *ramyâ*, Ramiah, S: 7422, B: 941D, K: 894C, H: 340D

8244 [1]רְמִיָּה *r^{e}miyyâ*[1], laziness, laxness, slackness, S: 7423, B: 941C, K: 894C, H: 340D

8245 [2]רְמִיָּה *r^{e}miyyâ*[2], deceit, S: 7423, B: 941A, K: 894C, H: 340D

8246 רַמִּים *rammîm*, variant: Ramites, S: 761†, B: 942B, K: 894C, H: 340D

8247 רַמָּכָה *rammākâ*, fast mare, S: 7424†, B: 942B, K: 894D, H: 340D

8248 רְמַלְיָהוּ *r^{e}malyāhû*, Remaliah, S: 7425, B: 942B, K: 894D, H: 340D

8249 [1]רָמַם *rāmam*[1], [A] to be full of maggots, be wormy, S: 7311†, B: 942C, K: 894D, H: 341A

8250 [2]רָמַם *rāmam*[2], [A] to be exalted; [C] to rise upward; to get away, S: 7426, B: 942C, K: 894D, H: 341A

8251 רוֹמַמְתִּי עֶזֶר *rōmamtî 'ezer*, Romamti-Ezer, S: 7320, B: 928D, K: 895A, H: 341A

8252 רָמַס *rāmas*, [A] to trample, tread upon; [C] to be trampled, S: 7429, B: 942C, K: 895A, H: 341A

8253 רָמַשׂ *rāmaś*, [A] to move along (ground or in the water), S: 7430, B: 942D, K: 895B, H: 341A

8254 רֶמֶשׂ *remeś*, creatures that move along (ground or sea), S: 7431, B: 943A, K: 895C, H: 341A

8255 רֶמֶת *remet*, Remeth, S: 7432, B: 928D 1.c., K: 895C, H: 341B

8256 רָמַת הַמִּצְפֶּה *rāmat hammiṣpeh*, Ramath Mizpah, S: 7434, B: 928B, K: 557D 4, H: 211B

8257 רָמַת לְחִי *rāmat lᵉḥî*, Ramath Lehi, S: 7437, B: 928B, K: 478C, H: 175B

8258 רָמָתִי *rāmātî*, Ramathite, S: 7435, B: 928B, K: 895C, H: 341B

8259 רָמָתַיִם *rāmātayim*, Ramathaim, S: 7414†, B: 928C, K: 893C, H*

8260 רֹן *rōn*, song, S: 7438, B: 943C, K: 895C, H: 341B

8261 רָנָה *rānâ*, [A] to rattle, S: 7439, B: 943A, K: 895C, H: 341B

8262 ¹רִנָּה *rinnâ¹*, shout of joy, song of joy; cry of pleading, S: 7440, B: 943C, K: 895D, H: 341B

8263 ²רִנָּה *rinnâ²*, Rinnah, S: 7441, B: 943D, K: 895D, H: 341B

8264 רָנַן *rānan*, [A] to shout for joy, sing for joy; to cry, plead; [D] to sing for joy; [E] to sing for joy; [G] to make sing, call for songs of joy, S: 7442 & 7444†, B: 943B, K: 895D, H: 341B

8265 רְנָנָה *rᵉnānâ*, shout of joy, joyful song, S: 7445, B: 943C, K: 896B, H: 341C

8266 רְנָנִים *rᵉnānîm*, female ostrich, S: 7443†, B: 943D, K: 896B, H: 341C

8267 רִסָּה *rissâ*, Rissah, S: 7446, B: 943D, K: 896B, H: 341C

8268 ¹רָסִיס *rāsîs¹*, drop (of moisture), S: 7447, B: 944A, K: 896B, H: 341C

8269 ²רָסִיס *rāsîs²*, broken piece (of rubble), S: 7447, B: 944A, K: 896C, H: 341C

8270 ¹רֶסֶן *resen¹*, bridle, S: 7448, B: 943D, K: 896C, H: 341C

8271 ²רֶסֶן *resen²*, Resen, S: 7449, B: 944A, K: 896C, H: 341C

8272 רָסַס *rāsas*, [A] to moisten, sprinkle, S: 7450, B: 944A, K: 896C, H: 341C

8273 ¹רַע *ra'¹*, evil, bad, wicked, S: 7451, B: 948A, K: 896D, H: 341C

8274 ²רַע *ra'²*, variant: evil, distress, misery, injury, calamity, S: 7451, B: 948C, K: 896D, H: 341C

8275 ¹רֵעַ *rēa'¹*, shouting, roar, S: 7452, B: 929D, K: 897C, H: 342A

8276 ²רֵעַ *rēa'²*, neighbor; friend, companion, associate, S: 7453, B: 945D, K: 897C, H: 342A

8277 ³רֵעַ *rēa'³*, thought, intention, S: 7454, B: 946D, K: 898A, H: 342B

8278 רֹעַ *rōa'*, evil, wickedness, bad (quality), S: 7455, B: 947D, K: 898B, H: 342B

8279 ¹רָעֵב *rā'ēb¹*, [A] to be hungry, be famished, be starving, S: 7456, B: 944A, K: 898B, H: 342B

8280 רָעָב *rā'āb*, hunger, famine, starvation, S: 7457† & 7458, B: 944B, K: 898C, H: 342B

8281 ²רָעֵב *rā'ēb²*, hungry, S: 7456, B: 944C, K: 898C, H: 342B

8282 רְעָבוֹן *rᵉ'ābôn*, hunger, famine, starvation, S: 7459, B: 944C, K: 898C, H: 342B

8283 רָעַד *rā'ad*, [A, G] to tremble, S: 7460, B: 944C, K: 898D, H: 342B

8284 רַעַד *ra'ad*, trembling, S: 7461, B: 944C, K: 898D, H: 342C

8285 רְעָדָה *rᵉ'ādâ*, trembling, S: 7461, B: 944D, K: 898D, H: 342C

8286 ¹רָעָה *rā'â¹*, [A] to be a shepherd, to care for flocks as a herdsman, S: 7473†, B: 944D, K: 898D, H: 342C

8287 ²רָעָה *rā'â²*, [A] to be a companion, be a friend; [D] to be an attendant of the groom (of a wedding), S: 7462, B: 945C, K: 899C, H: 342D

8288 ³רָעָה *rā'â³*, disaster, evil, wickedness, harm, S: 7465†, B: 949A, K: 899D, H: 342D

8289 ⁴רָעָה *rā'â⁴*, variant: [D] to be an attendant of a groom, see 8287, S: 7462, B: 946B, K: 899C, H: 342B

8290 ⁵רָעָה *rā'â⁵*, variant: [A] to desire, long for, S*, B*, K*, H*

8291 רֵעֶה *rē'eh*, friend, personal advisor, S: 7463, B: 946B, K: 900A, H: 343A

8292 רֵעָה *rē'â*, companion, friend, S: 7464, B: 946B, K: 900B, H: 343A

8293 רְעוּ *rᵉ'û*, Reu, S: 7466, B: 946C, K: 900B, H: 343A

8294 רְעוּאֵל *rᵉ'û'ēl*, Reuel, S: 7467, B: 946C, K: 900B, H: 343A

8295 ¹רְעוּת *rᵉ'ût¹*, (female) neighbor; fellow (female), S: 7468, B: 946B, K: 900B, H: 343A

8296 ²רְעוּת *rᵉ'ût²*, chasing after, S: 7469, B: 946D, K: 900C, H: 343A

8297 רְעִי *rᵉ'î*, pastured (cattle), S: 7471, B: 945C, K: 900C, H: 343B

8298 רֵעִי *rē'î*, Rei, S: 7472, B: 946C, K: 900C, H: 343B

8299 רַעְיָה *ra'yâ*, darling, beloved, S: 7474, B: 946B, K: 900D, H: 343B

8300 רֵעְיָה *rē'yâ*, variant: companion, S: 7464†, B: 946B, K: 900D, H: 343B

8301 רַעְיוֹן *ra'yôn*, chasing after, striving for, S: 7475, B: 946D, K: 900D, H: 343B

8302 רָעַל *rā'al*, [H] to be made to quiver, S: 7477, B: 947A, K: 900D, H: 343B

8303 רַעַל *ra'al*, reeling, S: 7478, B: 947A, K: 900D, H: 343B

8304 רְעָלָה *rᵉ'ālâ*, veil, S: 7479†, B: 947A, K: 901A, H: 343B

8305 רְעֵלָיָה *rᵉ'ēlāyâ*, Reelaiah, S: 7480, B: 947A, K: 901A, H: 343B

8306 ¹רָעַם *rā'am¹*, [A] to storm, thunder; [G] to make thunder, make storm, S: 7481, B: 947B, K: 901A, H: 343B

8307 ²רָעַם *rā'am²*, [A] to be confused, distorted; [G] to irritate, agitate, S: 7481, B: 947B, K: 901A, H: 343C

8308 רַעַם *ra'am*, thunder; thunderous shout, S: 7482, B: 947B, K: 901B, H: 343C

8309 רַעְמָא *ra'mā'*, Raamah, S: 7483†, B: 947, K: 901B, H: 343C

8310 ¹רַעְמָה *ra'mâ¹*, mane (of a horse), S: 7483, B: 947C, K: 901B, H: 343C

8311 ²רַעְמָה *ra'mâ²*, Raamah, S: 7484, B: 947C, K: 901B, H: 343C

8312 ³רַעְמָה *ra'mâ³*, variant: thunder, S: 7484, B: 928C, K: 901B, H: 336A

8313 רַעַמְיָה *ra'amyâ*, Raamiah, S: 7485, B: 947C, K: 901C, H: 343C

8314 רַעְמְסֵס *ra'mᵉsēs*, Rameses, S: 7486, B: 947C, K: 901C, H: 343C

8315 רָעַן *rā'an*, [D] to flourish, S: 7488†, B: 947D, K: 901C, H: 343C

8316 רַעֲנָן *ra'ᵃnān*, spreading (tree), verdant, luxuriant, S: 7488, B: 947D, K: 901D, H: 343C

8317 ¹רָעַע *rā'a'¹*, [A] to be distressed, be displeased; to be bad, be evil; [C] to suffer harm; [G] to do wickedness; bring trouble, mistreat, S: 7489, B: 949B, K: 901D, H: 343C

8318 ²רָעַע *rā'a'²*, [A] to break, shatter; [F] to come to ruin, S: 7489, B: 949D, K: 902C, H: 343D

8319 רָעַף *rā'ap*, [A] to drop, fall, overflow; [G] to cause to rain, S: 7491, B: 950A, K: 902C, H: 344A

8320 רָעַץ *rā'aṣ*, [A] to shatter, S: 7492, B: 950A, K: 902D, H: 344A

8321 ¹רָעַשׁ *rā'aš¹*, [A] to shake, quake, tremble; [C] to be made to quake; [G] to cause to shake, make to tremble, S: 7493, B: 950A, K: 902D, H: 344A

8322 ²רָעַשׁ *rā'aš²*, variant: [A] to be abundant, S: 7493, B: 950A, K: 903A, H: 344A

8323 רַעַשׁ *ra'aš*, commotion, rattling, earthquake, S: 7494, B: 950B, K: 903A, H: 344A

8324 ¹רָפָא *rāpā'¹*, [A] to heal; [C] to be healed, be cured; [D] to heal, repair; [F] to recover, S: 7495, B: 950C, K: 903B, H: 344A

8325 ²רָפָא *rāpā'²*, Rapha, S: 7498, B: 951A, K: 903D, H: 344C

8326 רִפְאוּת *rip'ût*, health, healing, S: 7500, B: 951B, K: 903D, H: 344C

8327 ¹רְפָאִים *rᵉpā'îm¹*, dead, the spirits of the departed, S: 7496†, B: 952B, K: 903D, H: 344C

8328 ²רְפָאִים *rᵉpā'îm²*, Rephaite, S: 7497†, B: 952B, K: 904A, H: 344C

8329 ³רְפָאִים *rᵉpā'îm³*, Rephaim, S: 7497†, B: 952B, K: 904A, H: 344C

8330 רְפָאֵל *rᵉpā'ēl*, Rephael, S: 7501, B: 951B, K: 904A, H: 344C

8331 רָפַד *rāpad*, [A] to spread (mud, so as to leave a trail); [D] to spread out; to refresh, S: 7502, B: 951C, K: 904A, H: 344C

8332 ¹רָפָה *rāpâ¹*, [A] to hang limp, sink down, be feeble; [C] to be lazy; [D] to lower; discourage; [G] to leave alone, abandon, withdraw; [F] to show oneself slack, S: 7503, B: 951C, K: 904B, H: 344C

8333 רָפֶה *rāpeh*, weak, feeble, S: 7504, B: 952A, K: 904D, H: 345A

8334 ²רָפָה *rāpâ²*, Raphah, S: 7498, B: 951B, K: 905A, H: 345A

8335 ³רָפָה *rāpâ³*, Rapha, S: 7510†, B: 952A, K: 905A, H: 345A

8336 רָפוּא *rāpû'*, Raphu, S: 7505, B: 951B, K: 905A, H: 345A

8337 רְפוּאָה *rᵉpû'â*, healing, S: 7499, B: 951B, K: 905A, H: 345A

8338 רֶפַח *repaḥ*, Rephah, S: 7506, B: 952C, K: 905A, H: 345A

8339 רְפִידָה *rᵉpîdâ*, base (of a royal carriage), S: 7507, B: 951C, K: 905A, H: 345A

8340 רְפִידִים *rᵉpîdîm*, Rephidim, S: 7508, B: 951C, K: 905A, H: 345A

8341 רְפָיָה *rᵉpāyâ*, Rephaiah, S: 7509, B: 951B, K: 905B, H: 345A

8342 רִפָּיוֹן *rippāyôn*, hanging limp, S: 7510, B: 952A, K: 905B, H: 345A

8343 רַפְסֹדוֹת *rapsōdôt*, (log) rafts, S: 7513†, B: 952C, K: 905B, H: 345B

8344 רָפַף *rāpap*, [E] to quake, shake, S: 7322†, B: 952C, K: 905B, H: 345B

8345 רָפַק *rāpaq*, [F] to lean oneself (upon), S: 7514, B: 952D, K: 905C, H: 345B

8346 רָפַשׂ *rāpaś*, [A] to muddy (a stream by trampling through); [C] to be muddied; [F] to be humbled, humble oneself, S: 7511† & 7515, B: 952C, K: 905C, H: 345B

8347 רֶ֫פֶשׁ *repeš*, mire (of the sea), S: 7516, B: 952D, K: 905C, H: 345B

8348 רֶ֫פֶת *repet*, stall, enclosure for cattle, S: 7517, B: 952D, K: 905D, H: 345B

8349 רַץ *raṣ*, bar (of silver), S: 7518, B: 954D, K: 905D, H: 345B

8350 רָץ *rāṣ*, variant: runner, guard, see 8132, S: 7323†, B: 930A, K: 905D, H: 345B

8351 רָצָא[1] *rāṣā'*[1], [A] to run forth, S: 7519, B: 952D, K: 905D, H: 345B

8352 [2]רָצָא *rāṣā'*[2], variant: [A] to take pleasure in, accept, see 8354, S: 7521†, B: 953A, K: 905D, H: 345C

8353 רָצַד *rāṣad*, [D] to gaze in hostility, S: 7520, B: 952D, K: 905D, H: 345C

8354 רָצָה[1] *rāṣâ*[1], [A] to be pleased, delight in, accept; [B] to be favored, be esteemed; [C] to be accepted; [G] to enjoy; [F] to regain favor, S: 7521, B: 953A, K: 906A, H: 345C

8355 [2]רָצָה *rāṣâ*[2], [A] to pay for (sin); [C] to be paid for; [D] to make amends, S: 7521, B: 953A, K: 906C, H: 345D

8356 רָצוֹן *rāṣôn*, pleasure, acceptance, favor, will, S: 7522, B: 953C, K: 906D, H: 345D

8357 רָצַח *rāṣaḥ*, [A] to murder, kill; [C] to be murdered, killed; [D] to murder, kill, S: 7523, B: 953D, K: 907A, H: 346A

8358 רֶ֫צַח *reṣaḥ*, slaughter, murder, agony of death, S: 7524, B: 954A, K: 907B, H: 346A

8359 רִצְיָא *riṣyā'*, Rizia, S: 7525, B: 954A, K: 907B, H: 346A

8360 רְצִין *r^{e}ṣîn*, Rezin, S: 7526, B: 954A, K: 907B, H: 346A

8361 רָצַע *rāṣa'*, [A] to pierce (ear), S: 7527, B: 954A, K: 907C, H: 346B

8362 רָצַף *rāṣap*, [B] to be inlaid, be fitted, S: 7528, B: 954B, K: 907C, H: 346B

8363 רֶ֫צֶף[1] *reṣep*[1], hot coals, live coals, S: 7529, B: 954B, K: 907D, H: 346B

8364 [2]רֶ֫צֶף *reṣep*[2], Rezeph, S: 7530, B: 954B, K: 907D, H: 346B

8365 רִצְפָּה[1] *riṣpâ*[1], live coal, hot coal, S: 7531, B: 954B, K: 907D, H: 346B

8366 [2]רִצְפָּה *riṣpâ*[2], Rizpah, S: 7532, B: 954C, K: 907D, H: 346B

8367 רִ֫צְפָּה *riṣ^{e}pâ*, (stone) pavement, S: 7531, B: 954B, K: 907D, H: 346B

8368 רָצַץ *rāṣaṣ*, [A] break, smash, oppress; [B] to be smashed, broken, splintered, oppressed; [C] to be broken, splintered; [D] to oppress, crush; [G] to crush to pieces; [F] to jostle each other, S: 7533, B: 954C, K: 908A, H: 346B

8369 רַק[1] *raq*[1], lean, thin, lank, S: 7534, B: 956B 1., K: 908B, H: 346C

8370 [2]רַק *raq*[2], only, but, however, except, S: 7535, B: 956B 2., K: 908B, H: 346C

8371 רֹק *rōq*, spit, saliva, S: 7536, B: 956D, K: 908C, H: 346C

8372 רָקַב *rāqab*, [A] to rot, become worm-eaten, S: 7537, B: 955A, K: 908C, H: 346C

8373 רָקָב *rāqāb*, rottenness, decay, S: 7538, B: 955A, K: 908D, H: 346D

8374 רֹ֫קֶב *rōqeb*, variant: wine-skin, S: 7538†, B: 955A, K: 908D, H: 346D

8375 רִקָּבוֹן *riqqābôn*, rottenness, S: 7539, B: 955A, K: 908D, H: 346D

8376 רָקַד *rāqad*, [A] to skip, dance; [D] to leap about, dance; [G] to make skip, S: 7540, B: 955A, K: 908D, H: 346D

8377 רַקָּה *raqqâ*, temple (of the head), S: 7541, B: 956D, K: 909A, H: 346D

8378 רַקּוֹן *raqqôn*, Rakkon, S: 7542, B: 956D, K: 909A, H: 346D

8379 רָקַח *rāqaḥ*, [A] to make perfume, mix spices; [E] to be blended (of perfume); [G] to mix spices, S: 7543, B: 955B, K: 909A, H: 346D

8380 רֶ֫קַח *reqaḥ*, (powdered) spice, S: 7544, B: 955B, K: 909B, H: 347A

8381 רֹ֫קַח *rōqaḥ*, fragrant blend, spice-blend, S: 7545, B: 955B, K: 909B, H: 347A

8382 רַקָּח *raqqāḥ*, perfume-maker, ointment-mixer, S: 7546, B: 955C, K: 909B, H: 347A

8383 רִקֻּחַ *riqquaḥ*, perfume, ointment, S: 7547, B: 955C, K: 909B, H: 347A

8384 רַקָּחָה *raqqāḥâ*, perfume-maker, ointment-mixer, S: 7548, B: 955C, K: 909B, H: 347A

8385 רָקִיעַ *rāqîa'*, expanse (of the sky or heaven), S: 7549, B: 956A, K: 909B, H: 347A

8386 רָקִיק *rāqîq*, wafer, (thin, flat) cake, S: 7550, B: 956D, K: 909C, H: 347A

8387 רָקַם *rāqam*, [A] to embroider, weave colored thread; [E] to be woven together, S: 7551, B: 955C, K: 909C, H: 347A

8388 רָקֶם *rāqem*, Rakem, S: 7552†, B: 955D, K: 909D, H: 347A

8389 רֶ֫קֶם[1] *reqem*[1], Rekem, S: 7552, B: 955D 2., K: 909D, H: 347A

8390 [2]רֶ֫קֶם *reqem*[2], Rekem, S: 7552, B: 955D 1., K: 909D, H: 347A

8391 רִקְמָה *riqmâ*, embroidered work; varied colored things, S: 7553, B: 955D, K: 909D, H: 347A

8392 רָקַע *rāqa'*, [A] to spread out; stamp upon, trample; [D] to hammer out thin, overlay (with precious metal); [E] to be hammered, be beaten thin; [G] to cause to spread out, make into plated metal, S: 7554, B: 955D, K: 910A, H: 347B

8393 רִקֻּעַ *riqqua'*, sheet, something beaten thin, S: 7555, B: 956B, K: 910B, H: 347B

8394 רָקַק *rāqaq*, [A] to spit saliva, S: 7556, B: 956D, K: 910B, H: 347B

8395 רַקַּת *raqqat*, Rakkath, S: 7557, B: 957A, K: 910C, H: 347B

8396 רֹשׁ *rōš*, variant: Rosh, S: 7220†, B: 910C, K: 910C, H: 347B

8397 רִשְׁיוֹן *rišyôn*, authorization, permission, S: 7558, B: 957A, K: 910C, H: 347B

8398 רָשַׁם *rāšam*, [B] to be written, be inscribed, S: 7559, B: 957A, K: 910C, H: 347C

8399 רָשַׁע *rāša'*, [A] to do evil, act wickedly; to be guilty; [G] to declare guilty, condemn, inflict punishment; to do wrong, S: 7561, B: 957D, K: 910D, H: 347C

8400 רֶ֫שַׁע *reša'*, evil, wickedness, wrongdoing, S: 7562, B: 957C, K: 911A, H: 347C

8401 רָשָׁע *rāšā'*, wicked, evil, guilty, S: 7563, B: 957B, K: 911B, H: 347C

8402 רִשְׁעָה *riš'â*, wickedness, S: 7564, B: 958A, K: 911C, H: 347D

8403 רִשְׁעָתַ֫יִם *riš'ātayim*, variant: Rishathaim, S: 3573†, B: 469B, K: 911D, H: 347D

8404 רֶ֫שֶׁף[1] *rešep*[1], flame, S: 7565, B: 958A, K: 911D, H: 347D

8405 [2]רֶ֫שֶׁף *rešep*[2], Resheph, S: 7566, B: 958B, K: 911D, H: 347D

8406 רָשַׁשׁ *rāšaš*, [D] to destroy, shatter; [E] to be crushed, shattered, S: 7567, B: 958B, K: 912A, H: 347D

8407 רֶ֫שֶׁת *rešet*, net, snare, trap (for catching game); network (net-like metal grating), S: 7568, B: 440B, K: 912A, H: 347D

8408 רַתּוֹק *rattôq*, chain, S: 7569, B: 958D, K: 912A, H: 348A

8409 רָתַח *rātaḥ*, [D] to bring to a boil; [E] to be caused to churn; [G] to make to churn, S: 7570, B: 958B, K: 912B, H: 348A

8410 רֶ֫תַח *retaḥ*, boiling, S: 7571, B: 958C, K: 912C, H: 348A

8411 רַתִּיקָה *rattîqâ*, chain, S: 7572, B: 958D, K: 912C, H: 348C

8412 רָתַם *rātam*, [A] to tie up, harness (horse team), S: 7573, B: 958C, K: 912C, H: 348C

8413 רֹ֫תֶם *rōtem*, broom tree, S: 7574, B: 958C, K: 912C, H: 348C

8414 רִתְמָה *ritmâ*, Rithmah, S: 7575, B: 958C, K: 912C, H: 348C

8415 רָתַק *rātaq*, [E] to be bound with chains, S: 7576, B: 958C, K: 912C, H: 348C

8416 רְתֻקוֹת *r^{e}tuqôt*, chains, S: 7577†, B: 958D, K: 912D, H: 348C

8417 רְתֵת *r^{e}tēt*, trembling, fright, S: 7578, B: 958D, K: 912D, H: 348C

8418 שׂ *ś*, letter of the Hebrew alphabet, S*, B: 959A, K: 912C, H*

8419 שְׂאֹר *ś^{e}'ōr*, yeast, leaven, S: 7603, B: 959A, K: 913A, H: 348A

8420 שְׂאֵת[1] *ś^{e}'ēt*[1], splendor, honor, loftiness, acceptance, S: 7613, B: 673B, K: 913A, H: 348A

8421 [2]שְׂאֵת *ś^{e}'ēt*[2], swelling, S: 7613, B: 673B, K: 913A, H: 348B

8422 שְׂבָכָה *ś^{e}bākâ*, network, lattice, interwoven mesh, S: 7638 & 7639, B: 959A, K: 913B, H: 348B

8423 שְׂבָם *ś^{e}bām*, Sebam, S: 7643, B: 959B, K: 913B, H: 348B

8424 שִׂבְמָה *śibmâ*, Sibmah, S: 7643, B: 959B, K: 913B, H: 348B

8425 שָׂבַע *śāba'*, [A] to be satisfied, have enough, be satiated, S: 7646, B: 959B, K: 913B, H: 348B

8426 שָׂבָע *śābā'*, abundance, overflowing, S: 7647, B: 960A, K: 914A, H: 348D

[F] Hitpael (hitpoel, hitpoal, hitpolel, hitpolal, hitpalel, hitpalal, hitpalpel, hitpalpal, hotpael, hotpaal) [G] Hiphil (hiphtil) [H] Hophal [I] Hishtaphel

8427 שֹׂבַע *śōbaʿ*, one's fill to contentment, all one wants, S: 7648, B: 959D, K: 914A, H: 348D

8428 שָׂבֵעַ *śābēaʿ*, full, abounding, S: 7649, B: 960A, K: 914B, H: 348D

8429 שׇׂבְעָה *śobʿâ*, abundance, satisfaction, enough, S: 7654, B: 960A, K: 914B, H: 349A

8430 שִׂבְעָה *śibʿâ*, abundance, plenty, S: 7653, B: 960A, K: 914B, H: 349A

8431 שָׂבַר[1] *śābar*[1], [A] to examine, S: 7663, B: 960B, K: 914C, H: 349A

8432 שָׂבַר[2] *śābar*[2], [D] to wait for, hope for, S: 7663, B: 960B, K: 914C, H: 349A

8433 שֵׂבֶר *śēber*, hope, S: 7664, B: 960B, K: 914C, H: 349A

8434 שָׂגָא *śāgāʾ*, [G] to make great, extol, S: 7679, B: 960B, K: 914C, H: 349A

8435 שָׂגַב *śāgab*, [A] to be too strong for; [C] to be lofty, be exalted; [D] to lift high; to protect; [E] to be kept safe; [G] to act exalted, S: 7682, B: 960C, K: 914D, H: 349A

8436 שָׂגָה *śāgâ*, [A] to be prosperous, thrive, grow; [G] to increase (in wealth), S: 7685, B: 960D, K: 915A, H: 349B

8437 שְׂגוּב *śᵉgûb*, Segub, S: 7687, B: 960D, K: 915B, H: 349B

8438 שַׂגִּיא *śaggîʾ*, exalted, S: 7689, B: 960C, K: 915B, H: 349B

8439 שְׂגִיב *śᵉgîb*, variant: Sebig, see 8437, S: 7687†, B: 960D, K: 915B, H: 349B

8440 שָׂדַד *śādad*, [D] to till, harrow, break up the ground, S: 7702, B: 961A, K: 915B, H: 349B

8441 שָׂדֶה *śādeh*, field, open country, countryside, S: 7704, B: 961B, K: 915C, H: 349B

8442 שָׂדַי *śāday*, field, S: 7704, B: 961A, K: 916A, H: 349C

8443 שִׂדִּים *śiddîm*, Siddim, S: 7708, B: 961A, K: 916B, H: 349C

8444 שְׂדֵרָה *śᵉdērâ*, ranks, rows; planks (architectural term), S: 7713, B: 690B, K: 916B, H: 349C

8445 שֶׂה *śeh*, sheep, lamb, S: 7716 & 2089†, B: 961D, K: 916B, H: 349C

8446 שָׂהֵד *śāhēd*, witness, S: 7717, B: 962A, K: 916C, H: 349D

8447 שָׂהֲדוּתָא *śāhᵃdûtāʾ*, variant: Sahadutha, S: 3026†, B: 1113C, K: 916C, H: 349D

8448 שַׂהֲרֹנִים *śahᵃrōnîm*, ornamental crescent (or moon shaped) necklace, S: 7720, B: 962A, K: 916C, H: 349D

8449 שׂוֹבֶךְ *śôbek*, tangle of branches, S: 7730, B: 959A, K: 916D, H: 349D

8450 שׂוּג[1] *śûg*[1], variant: see 6047, S: 5253†, B: 690D, K: 916D, H: 349D

8451 שׂוּג[2] *śûg*[2], [D] to cause growth, raise, S: 7735, B: 691B, K: 916D, H: 349D

8452 שׂוּחַ *śûaḥ*, [A] to meditate, S: 7742, B: 962B & 1001D, K: 916D, H: 349D

8453 שַׂוְחָט *śawḥāṭ*, variant: see 8821, S*, B: 1006B, K: 916D, H*

8454 שׂוּט *śûṭ*, [A] to turn aside (to false gods), S: 7750, B: 962B, K: 917A, H: 349D

8455 שׂוּךְ *śûk*, [A] to block with thorn hedges, S: 7753, B: 962B, K: 917A, H: 349D

8456 שׂוֹךְ *śôk*, branch, S: 7754, B: 962C, K: 917A, H: 349D

8457 שׂוֹכָה *śôkâ*, branch, S: 7754, B: 962C, K: 917B, H: 349D

8458 שׂוֹכֹה *śôkōh*, Socoh, S: 7755, B: 962C, K: 917B, H: 350A

8459 שׂוֹכוֹ *śôkô*, Soco, S: 7755, B: 962C, K: 917B, H: 350A

8460 שׂוּכָתִי *śûkātî*, Sucathite, S: 7756, B: 962C, K: 917B, H: 350A

8461 שׂוּמָה *śûmâ*, intention, S: 7760†, B: 965A, K: 920A, H: 351A

8462 שׂוּר *śûr*, variant: [A] to saw, S: 5493, B: 965A, K: 917B, H: 350A

8463 שׂוֹרָה *śôrâ*, place, row *or* a type of grain, S: 7795, B: 965A, K: 917C, H: 350A

8464 שׂוּשׂ *śûś*, [A] to rejoice, be pleased, be delighted, S: 7797, B: 965A, K: 917C, H: 350A

8465 שֵׂחַ *śēaḥ*, thoughts, S: 7808, B: 967B, K: 917D, H: 350A

8466 שָׂחָה *śāḥâ*, [A] to swim; [G] to make swim, flood, S: 7811, B: 965C, K: 917D, H: 350A

8467 שָׂחוּ *śāḥû*, water deep enough to swim in, S: 7813, B: 965C, K: 917D, H: 350A

8468 שְׂחוֹק *śᵉḥôq*, laughter; ridicule, laughingstock, S: 7814, B: 966A, K: 918A, H: 350B

8469 שָׂחַט *śāḥaṭ*, [A] to squeeze out (juice from grapes), S: 7818, B: 965C, K: 918A, H: 350B

8470 שָׂחִיף *śāḥîp*, covered, paneled, S: 7824, B: 965D, K: 918A, H: 350B

8471 שָׂחַק *śāḥaq*, [A] to laugh, be amused; to laugh at, mock, scoff; [D] to celebrate, rejoice, frolic; [G] to scorn, S: 7832, B: 965D, K: 918A, H: 350B

8472 שֻׂחֹת *śuḥōt*, variant: filth, S*, B: 1001C, K: 918C, H: 350C

8473 שֵׂט *śēṭ*, rebel, S: 7846, B: 962B, K: 918C, H: 350C

8474 שָׂטָה *śāṭâ*, [A] to go astray, S: 7847, B: 966A, K: 918C, H: 350C

8475 שָׂטַם *śāṭam*, [A] to hold a grudge, hold hostility toward, S: 7852, B: 966B, K: 918C, H: 350C

8476 שָׂטַן *śāṭan*, [A] to accuse, slander, S: 7853, B: 966C, K: 918D, H: 350C

8477 שָׂטָן *śāṭān*, adversary, accuser, one who opposes, slanderer; (as a proper name) Satan, S: 7854, B: 966B, K: 918D, H: 350C

8478 שִׂטְנָה[1] *śiṭnâ*[1], accusation, S: 7855, B: 966C, K: 919A, H: 350C

8479 שִׂטְנָה[2] *śiṭnâ*[2], Sitnah, S: 7856, B: 966C, K: 919A, H: 350D

8480 שִׂיא *śîʾ*, height, S: 7863, B: 673B, K: 919A, H: 350D

8481 שִׂיאֹן *śîʾōn*, Siyon, S: 7865†, B: 673B, K: 919A, H: 350D

8482 שִׂיב *śîb*, [A] to be gray(-haired) (*hence*) old, S: 7867, B: 966C, K: 919A, H: 350D

8483 שֵׂיב *śêb*, gray-headedness, old age, S: 7869, B: 966C, K: 919B, H: 350D

8484 שֵׂיבָה *śêbâ*, gray-haired (person), old age, S: 7872, B: 966C, K: 919B, H: 350D

8485 שִׂיג *śîg*, busyness, *perhaps* bowel movement, S: 7873, B: 691A & 1125C, K: 919B, H: 350D

8486 שִׂיד[1] *śîd*[1], [A] to coat with (a whitewash) plaster, S: 7874, B: 966D, K: 919B, H: 350D

8487 שִׂיד[2] *śîd*[2], lime, plaster (used as a whitewash), S: 7875, B: 966D, K: 919C, H: 350D

8488 שִׂיחַ[1] *śîaḥ*[1], [A] to meditate, muse on, consider, think on, S: 7878, B: 967A, K: 919C, H: 350D

8489 שִׂיחַ[2] *śîaḥ*[2], bush, shrub, S: 7880, B: 967B, K: 919D, H: 351A

8490 שִׂיחַ[3] *śîaḥ*[3], complaint, lament, S: 7879, B: 967A, K: 919D, H: 351A

8491 שִׂיחָה *śîḥâ*, meditation, S: 7881, B: 967A, K: 919D, H: 351A

8492 שִׂים *śîm*, [A] to place, put, establish, appoint; [B] to be placed, set upon; [G] to cause to place, put; [H] to be set, S: 7760 & 7787†, B: 962C, K: 920A, H: 351A

8493 שֵׂךְ *śēk*, barb, splinter, thorn, S: 7899, B: 968A, K: 921A, H: 351D

8494 שֹׂךְ *śōk*, dwelling place, S: 7900, B: 968A, K: 921B, H: 351D

8495 שָׂכָה *śākâ*, variant: [A] to look out for, S*, B: 1013D, K: 921C, H: 351D

8496 שֻׂכָּה *śukkâ*, harpoon, S: 7905, B: 968A, K: 921C, H: 351D

8497 שֶׂכוּ *śekû*, Secu, S: 7906†, B: 967D, K: 921C, H: 351D

8498 שֶׂכְוִי *śekwî*, mind, S: 7907, B: 967C, K: 921C, H: 351D

8499 שָׂכְיָה *śākᵉyâ*, Sakia, S: 7634†, B: 967D, K: 921D, H: 351D

8500 שְׂכִיָּה *śᵉkiyyâ*, marine vessel, ship, S: 7914, B: 967C, K: 921D, H: 351D

8501 שַׂכִּין *śakkîn*, knife, S: 7915, B: 967D, K: 921D, H: 351D

8502 שָׂכִיר *śākîr*, hired worker, servant under contract, S: 7916 & 7917†, B: 969B, K: 921D, H: 351D

8503 שָׂכַךְ[1] *śākak*[1], [A] to cover (with the purpose to hide or screen), S: 5526†, B: 967D, K: 922A, H: 352A

8504 שָׂכַךְ[2] *śākak*[2], variant: [D] to knit or weave together, to be pointed, S*, B: 968A, K: 922A, H: 256B

8505 שָׂכַל[1] *śākal*[1], [A] to have success; [G] to have insight, wisdom, understanding; to prosper, successful, S: 7919, B: 968A, K: 922A, H: 352A

8506 שָׂכַל[2] *śākal*[2], [D] to cross (the hands and arms in an extended motion), S: 7919, B: 968D, K: 922C, H: 352B

8507 שֶׂכֶל *śekel*, understanding, wisdom, discretion, S: 7922, B: 968C, K: 922D, H: 352B

8508 שִׂכְלוּת *siklût*, folly, S: 5531, B: 698A, K: 922D, H: 352B

8509 שָׂכַר *śākar*, [A] to hire; [B] to be hired; [C] to hire oneself; [F] to earn wages for oneself, S: 7936, B: 968D, K: 922D, H: 352B

8510 שָׂכָר[1] *śākār*[1], wage, reward, S: 7939, B: 969A, K: 923A, H: 352B

8511 שָׂכָר[2] *śākār*[2], Sacar, S: 7940, B: 969B, K: 923B, H: 352C

8512 שֶׂכֶר *śeker*, wage, reward, S: 7938, B: 969A, K: 923B, H: 352C

8513 שְׂלָו *śelāw*, quail, S: 7958, B: 969B, K: 923B, H: 352C

8514 שַׂלְמָא *śalmā'*, Salma, S: 8007, B: 969C, K: 923C, H: 352C

8515 שַׂלְמָה¹ *śalmâ¹*, clothing, garment, cloak, robe, S: 8008, B: 971A, K: 923C, H: 352C

8516 ²שַׂלְמָה *śalmâ²*, variant: Salmah, see 8517, S: 8009, B: 969C, K: 923D, H: 352C

8517 שַׂלְמוֹן *śalmôn*, Salmon, S: 8012, B: 969C, K: 923D, H: 352D

8518 שַׂלְמַי *śalmay*, variant: Salmai, see 8978, S: 8014, B: 969C, K: 923D, H: 352C

8519 שָׂלַק *śālaq*, variant: [C] to be kindled; [G] to make a fire burn, S: 5400, B: 969C, K: 923D, H: 247D

8520 שְׂמֹאל *śemō'l*, left (opposite of right); north, S: 8040 & 8041†, B: 969D, K: 923D, H: 352C

8521 שִׂמְאֵל *śim'ēl*, [G] to go to the left; be left-handed, S: 8041†, B: 970A, K: 924B, H: 352D

8522 שְׂמָאלִי *śemā'lî*, on the left; northern, S: 8042, B: 970A, K: 924C, H: 352D

8523 שָׂמַח *śāmaḥ*, [A] to rejoice, be glad, delight in, S: 8055, B: 970A, K: 924C, H: 352D

8524 שָׂמֵחַ *śāmēaḥ*, rejoicing, gladness, delight, S: 8056, B: 970C, K: 925A, H: 353A

8525 שִׂמְחָה *śimḥâ*, joy, gladness, pleasure, delight, S: 8057, B: 970D, K: 925A, H: 353A

8526 שְׂמִיכָה *śemîkâ*, covering, S: 8063, B: 970D, K: 925B, H: 353A

8527 שָׂמַךְ *śāmak*, variant: [A] to cover, S*, B: 604A, K: 925B, H: 219A

8528 שַׂמְלָה *śamlâ*, Samlah, S: 8072, B: 971A, K: 925B, H: 353A

8529 שִׂמְלָה *śimlâ*, clothing, garment, cloak, S: 8071, B: 971A, K: 925C, H: 353A

8530 שַׂמְלַי *śamlay*, variant: Samlai, see 8978, S: 8073, B: 969C, K: 925C, H: 353B

8531 שָׂמַם *śāmam*, variant: [G] to paint or perfume, S*, B: 962C, K: 925C, H: 353B

8532 שְׂמָמִית *śemāmît*, lizard, S: 8079, B: 971B, K: 925C, H: 353B

8533 שָׂנֵא *śānē'*, [A] to hate, be an enemy; [B] to be unloved; [C] to be hated, be shunned; [D] to be an adversary, be a foe, S: 8130, B: 971B, K: 925D, H: 353B

8534 שִׂנְאָה *śin'â*, hatred, malice, S: 8135, B: 971D, K: 926B, H: 353C

8535 שָׂנִיא *śānî'*, not loved, disdained, S: 8146, B: 971D, K: 926B, H: 353C

8536 שְׂנִיר *śenîr*, Senir, S: 8149, B: 972A, K: 926B, H: 353C

8537 שָׂעִיר¹ *śā'îr¹*, hairy, shaggy, S: 8163, B: 972C, K: 926C, H: 353C

8538 ²שָׂעִיר *śā'îr²*, male goat, S: 8163, B: 972C, K: 926C, H: 353C

8539 ³שָׂעִיר *śā'îr³*, goat idol, S: 8163, B: 972D, K: 926C, H: 353C

8540 ⁴שָׂעִיר *śā'îr⁴*, rain shower, S: 8164, B: 973C, K: 926D, H: 353C

8541 שֵׂעִיר¹ *śē'îr¹*, Seir, S: 8165, B: 973A 1., K: 926D, H: 353C

8542 ²שֵׂעִיר *śē'îr²*, Seir, S: 8165, B: 973A, K: 926D, H: 353C

8543 ³שֵׂעִיר *śē'îr³*, Seir, S: 8165, B: 973A 1.d., K: 926D, H: 353C

8544 שְׂעִירָה¹ *śe'îrâ¹*, female goat, S: 8166, B: 972C, K: 927A, H: 353D

8545 ²שְׂעִירָה *śe'îrâ²*, Seirah, S: 8167, B: 972C, K: 927A, H: 353D

8546 שְׂעִפִּים *śe'ippîm*, disquieted thoughts, troubled thoughts, S: 5587†, B: 972A, K: 927A, H: 353D

8547 שָׂעַר¹ *śā'ar¹*, [A] to shudder, bristle with horror, S: 8175, B: 972B, K: 927A, H: 353D

8548 ²שָׂעַר *śā'ar²*, [A] to sweep away (by the wind); [C] to be in a storm; [D] to sweep away (by a wind); [F] to storm against, S: 8175, B: 973B, K: 927B, H: 353D

8549 ³שָׂעַר *śā'ar³*, [A] to know about, be acquainted with, S: 8175, B: 973B, K: 927B, H: 353D

8550 שַׂעַר¹ *śa'ar¹*, horror, shudder, S: 8178, B: 972C, K: 927B, H: 353D

8551 ²שַׂעַר *śa'ar²*, wind storm, gale, S: 8178, B: 973B, K: 927C, H: 353D

8552 שֵׂעָר *śē'ār*, hair, S: 8181, B: 972B, K: 927C, H: 353D

8553 שַׂעֲרָה *śa'ᵃrâ*, hair, S: 8185, B: 972B, K: 927D, H: 354A

8554 שְׂעָרָה *śe'ārâ*, storm, gale, S: 8183, B: 973B, K: 927D, H: 354A

8555 שְׂעֹרָה *śe'ōrâ*, barley, S: 8184, B: 972D, K: 927D, H: 354A

8556 שְׂעֹרִים *śe'ōrîm*, Seorim, S: 8188, B: 972D, K: 928A, H: 354A

8557 שָׂפָה *śāpâ*, lips; speech, language; edge, rim, border, S: 8193, B: 973C, K: 928A, H: 354A

8558 שָׂפַח *śāpaḥ*, [D] to bring sores, make scabby, S: 5596, B: 705C, K: 928C, H: 354B

8559 שָׂפָם *śāpām*, (the area of the) mustache; lower part of the face, S: 8222, B: 974A, K: 928C, H: 354B

8560 שִׂפְמוֹת *śipmôt*, Siphmoth, S: 8224, B: 1050D, K: 928C, H: 354B

8561 שָׂפַן *śāpan*, [B] to be hidden, S: 8226, B: 706A, K: 928C, H: 354B

8562 שָׂפַק¹ *śāpaq¹*, [A] to clap one's hands (in derision); [G] to clasp hands, S: 5606, B: 706C, K: 928D, H: 354B

8563 ²שָׂפַק *śāpaq²*, [A] to be enough, S: 5606, B: 974A, K: 928D, H: 354B

8564 שֶׂפֶק *śepeq*, variant: hand-clapping, i.e., mockery, S: 8210†, B: 706D, K: 928D, H: 354B

8565 שֵׂפֶק *śēpeq*, plenty, sufficiency, S: 5607, B: 974A, K: 928D, H*

8566 שַׂק *śaq*, sackcloth; sack, S: 8242, B: 974B, K: 929A, H: 354B

8567 שָׂקַד *śāqad*, [C] to be bound, S: 8244, B: 974B, K: 929A, H: 354C

8568 שָׂקַר *śāqar*, [D] to flirt (with the eyes), S: 8265, B: 974C, K: 929B, H: 354C

8569 שַׂר *śar*, commander, official, prince, chief, leader, S: 8269, B: 978A, K: 929B, H: 354C

8570 שַׂרְאֶצֶר *śar'eṣer*, שַׂר־אֶצֶר *śar-'eṣer*, Sharezer, S: 8272†, B: 974C, K: 930A, H: 354C

8571 שָׂרַג *śārag*, [E] to be close-knit, be intertwined; [F] to be woven together, S: 8276, B: 974D, K: 930B, H: 354D

8572 שָׂרַד *śārad*, [A] to run away, escape, S: 8277, B: 974D, K: 930B, H: 354D

8573 שְׂרָד *śerād*, woven material (with some kind of braiding woven in it), S: 8278, B: 975A, K: 930B, H: 354D

8574 שֶׂרֶד *śered*, marker (for wood chiseling), S: 8279, B: 975B, K: 930C, H: 354D

8575 שָׂרָה¹ *śārâ¹*, [A] to struggle, contend, S: 8280, B: 975B, K: 930C, H: 354D

8576 ²שָׂרָה *śārâ²*, woman of nobility, lady of royal birth, queen, S: 8282, B: 979A, K: 930D, H: 354D

8577 ³שָׂרָה *śārâ³*, Sarah, S: 8283, B: 979A, K: 930D, H: 354D

8578 שְׂרוּג *śerûg*, Serug, S: 8286, B: 974D, K: 930D, H: 354D

8579 שְׂרוֹךְ *śerôk*, thong (of a sandal), S: 8288, B: 976C, K: 930D, H: 354D

8580 שֶׂרַח *śeraḥ*, Serah, S: 8294, B: 976A, K: 931A, H: 355A

8581 שָׂרַט *śāraṭ*, [A] to make a cut, incise the skin; [C] to make oneself incised, cut oneself, S: 8295, B: 976B, K: 931A, H: 355A

8582 שֶׂרֶט *śereṭ*, cut, incision, S: 8296, B: 976B, K: 931A, H: 355A

8583 שָׂרֶטֶת *śāreṭet*, cut, incision, S: 8296, B: 976B, K: 931B, H: 355A

8584 שָׂרַי *śāray*, Sarai, S: 8297, B: 979C, K: 931B, H: 355A

8585 שָׂרִיג *śārîg*, branch (of grape vines and fig trees), S: 8299, B: 974D, K: 931B, H: 355A

8586 שָׂרִיד¹ *śārîd¹*, survivor; those left, S: 8300, B: 975A, K: 931B, H: 355A

8587 ²שָׂרִיד *śārîd²*, Sarid, S: 8301, B: 975A, K: 931C, H: 355A

8588 שְׂרָיָה *śerāyâ*, Seraiah, S: 8304, B: 976A, K: 931C, H: 355A

8589 שְׂרָיָהוּ *śerāyāhû*, Seraiah, S: 8304, B: 976A, K: 931C, H: 355A

8590 שִׂרְיוֹן *śiryôn*, Sirion, S: 8303, B: 976B, K: 931C, H: 355A

8591 שָׂרִיק *śārîq*, combed (flax), S: 8305†, B: 977C, K: 931D, H: 355A

8592 שָׂרַךְ *śārak*, [D] to run here and there (aimlessly), S: 8308, B: 976C, K: 931D, H: 355A

8593 שַׂר־סְכִים *śar-sekîm*, variant: Sarsekim, S: 8310†, B: 976C, K: 931D, H: 355A

8594 שָׂרַע *śāra'*, [B] to be deformed; [F] to stretch oneself, S: 8311, B: 976C, K: 931D, H: 355B

8595 שַׂרְעַפִּים *śar'appîm*, anxiety, anxious thoughts, S: 8312, B: 972A, K: 932A, H: 355B

8596 שָׂרַף *śārap*, [A] to burn, set a fire; [B, C, E] to be burned up, S: 8313, B: 976D, K: 932A, H: 355B

8597 שָׂרָף[1] *śārāp*[1], venomous snake; seraph (six-winged being), S: 8314, B: 977B, K: 932C, H: 355C

8598 [2]שָׂרָף *śārāp*[2], Saraph, S: 8315, B: 977B, K: 932D, H: 355C

8599 שְׂרֵפָה *ś^{e}rēpâ*, burning, S: 8316, B: 977B, K: 932D, H: 355C

8600 שָׂרַק *śāraq*, variant: to comb or card flax, S*, B: 977C, K: 932D, H: 355C

8601 שָׂרֹק[1] *śārōq*[1], brown, dark red (color of grapes), S: 8320†, B: 977D, K: 933A, H: 355C

8602 [2]שָׂרֹק *śārōq*[2], choice vines, S: 8291†, B: 977D, K: 933A, H: 355C

8603 שֹׂרֵק[1] *śōrēq*[1], choice vines, S: 8321, B: 977D, K: 933A, H: 355C

8604 [2]שֹׂרֵק *śōrēq*[2], Sorek, S: 7796† & 8291†, B: 977D, K: 917C, H: 350A

8605 שְׂרֵקָה *ś^{e}rēqâ*, choice vine, S: 8322, B: 977D, K: 933A, H: 355D

8606 שָׂרַר *śārar*, [A] to rule, govern; [G] to choose a prince; [F] to act out as a ruler, S: 7786† & 8323, B: 979A, K: 933A, H: 355D

8607 שָׂשׂוֹן *śāśôn*, joy, gladness, S: 8342, B: 965B, K: 933C, H: 355D

8608 שָׂתַם *śātam*, [A] to shut out, obstruct, S: 5640, B: 979C, K: 933C, H: 355D

8609 שָׂתַר *śātar*, [C] to be broken out (with tumors), S: 8368, B: 979C, K: 933D, H: 355D

8610 שׁ *š*, letter of the Hebrew alphabet, S*, B: 979B, K: 933B, H*

8611 -שֶׁ *ša-*, who, that, because, S: 7945†, B: 979B, K: 933D, H: 356A

8612 שָׁאַב *šā'ab*, [A] to draw and carry water, S: 7579, B: 980B, K: 934C, H: 356B

8613 שָׁאַג *šā'ag*, [A] to roar, S: 7580, B: 980C, K: 934D, H: 356B

8614 שְׁאָגָה *š^{e}'āgâ*, roar, groan, S: 7581, B: 980D, K: 934D, H: 356B

8615 שָׁאָה[1] *šā'â*[1], [A] to lie wasted; [C] to be ruined; [G] to turn into desolation, S: 7582, B: 980D, K: 935A, H: 356B

8616 [2]שָׁאָה *šā'â*[2], [C] to roar, S: 7582, B: 980D, K: 935A, H: 356C

8617 [3]שָׁאָה *šā'â*[3], [F] to watch closely, gaze at, S: 7583, B: 981B, K: 935B, H: 356C

8618 שַׁאֲוָה *ša'^{a}wâ*, variant: devastating storm, S: 7584, B: 981A, K: 935B, H: 356C

8619 שְׁאוֹל *š^{e}'ôl*, grave, realm of death, Sheol deepest depths, S: 7585, B: 982D, K: 935B, H: 356C

8620 שָׁאוּל *šā'ûl*, Saul, Shaul, S: 7586, B: 982B, K: 935D, H: 356C

8621 שָׁאוּלִי *šā'ûlî*, Shaulite, S: 7587, B: 982C, K: 935D, H: 356C

8622 שָׁאוֹן[1] *šā'ôn*[1], waste, desolation, S: 7588, B: 981A, K: 935D, H: 356C

8623 [2]שָׁאוֹן *šā'ôn*[2], roar, uproar, tumult, loud noise, S: 7588, B: 981A, K: 936A, H: 356C

8624 שְׁאָט *š^{e}'āṭ*, malice, S: 7589, B: 1002B, K: 936A, H: 356C

8625 שְׁאִיָּה *š^{e}'iyyâ*, desolation, ruin, S: 7591, B: 981A, K: 936A, H: 356D

8626 שָׁאַל *šā'al*, [A] to ask, inquire, request; [B] to be given over; [C] to ask permission; [D] to ask intently, beg; [G] to give what is asked for, S: 7592, B: 981B, K: 936B, H: 356D

8627 שְׁאָל *š^{e}'āl*, Sheal, S: 7594, B: 982B, K: 937A, H: 357A

8628 שְׁאָלָה *š^{e}'ālâ*, variant: in [the] depths, see 8619, S: 7592†, B: 983A 1, K: 937A, H: 357A

8629 שְׁאֵלָה *š^{e}'ēlâ*, petition, request, S: 7596, B: 982C, K: 937A, H: 357B

8630 שְׁאַלְתִּיאֵל *š^{e}'altî'ēl*, Shealtiel, S: 7597, B: 982C, K: 937B, H: 357B

8631 שָׁאַן *šā'an*, [D] to be at ease, be at rest, be secure, S: 7599, B: 983B, K: 937B, H: 357B

8632 שְׁאָן *š^{e}'ān*, variant: Shan, see 1126, S: 1052†, B: 112D, K: 937C, H: 357B

8633 שַׁאֲנָן *ša'^{a}nān*, at ease, complacent, secure; insolent, proud, S: 7600, B: 983B, K: 937C, H: 357B

8634 שָׁאַף[1] *šā'ap*[1], [A] to pant after, long for, pursue, S: 7602, B: 983C, K: 937C, H: 357B

8635 [2]שָׁאַף *šā'ap*[2], [A] to trample, crush, S: 7602, B: 983C, K: 937C, H*

8636 שָׁאַר *šā'ar*, [A] to remain; [C] to be left, remain; [G] to leave, spare, S: 7604, B: 983D, K: 937D, H: 357B

8637 שְׁאָר *š^{e}'ār*, remainder, remnant, the rest, S: 7605, B: 984B, K: 938B, H: 357C

8638 שְׁאֵר *š^{e}'ēr*, flesh, meat; blood relative, S: 7607, B: 984D, K: 938C, H: 357C

8639 שְׁאָר יָשׁוּב *š^{e}'ār yāšûb*, Shear-Jashub, S: 7610, B: 984C, K: 938D, H: 357D

8640 שַׁאֲרָה *ša'^{a}râ*, variant: see 8638, S: 7608, B: 985A 2., K: 938C, H: 357C

8641 שֶׁאֱרָה *še'^{e}râ*, Sheerah, S: 7609, B: 985A, K: 938D, H: 357C

8642 שְׁאֵרִית *š^{e}'ērît*, remnant, remainder, the rest, S: 7611, B: 984C, K: 938D, H: 357D

8643 שֵׁאת *šē't*, ruin, desolation, S: 7612, B: 981B, K: 939A, H: 357D

8644 שְׁבָא *š^{e}bā'*, Sheba, S: 7614, B: 985A, K: 939A, H: 357D

8645 שְׁבָאִים *š^{e}bā'îm*, Sabeans, S: 7615, B: 985B, K: 939B, H: 357D

8646 שְׁבָבִים *š^{e}bābîm*, broken pieces, splinters, S: 7616, B: 985B, K: 939C, H: 357D

8647 שָׁבָה *šābâ*, [A] to take captive; [B, C] to be taken captive, S: 7617, B: 985C, K: 939C, H: 357D

8648 שְׁבוֹ *š^{e}bô*, agate, S: 7618, B: 986B, K: 939D, H: 358A

8649 שְׁבוּאֵל *š^{e}bû'ēl*, Shubael, S: 7619, B: 986C, K: 939D, H: 358A

8650 שְׁבוּל *š^{e}bûl*, variant: path, see 8666, S*, B: 987C, K: 940A, H: 358A

8651 שָׁבוּעַ *šābûa'*, week (a time period of seven), S: 7620, B: 988D, K: 940A, H: 358A

8652 שְׁבוּעָה *š^{e}bû'â*, sworn oath, S: 7621, B: 989D, K: 940B, H: 358A

8653 שָׁבוּר *šābûr*, injury (by fracture), S: 7665†, B: 990C, K: 940C, H: 358B

8654 שְׁבוּת *š^{e}bût*, captivity, exile; fortunes, S: 7622, B: 986A, K: 940C, H: 358B

8655 שָׁבַח[1] *šābaḥ*[1], [D] to glorify, commend, extol; [F] to glory in, S: 7623, B: 986C, K: 941D, H: 358B

8656 [2]שָׁבַח *šābaḥ*[2], [D] to keep still; [G] to cause stillness, S: 7623, B: 986C, K: 941A, H: 358B

8657 שֵׁבֶט *šēbeṭ*, tribe, people; rod, staff, scepter, S: 7626, B: 986D, K: 941A, H: 358C

8658 שְׁבָט *š^{e}bāṭ*, Shebat, S: 7627, B: 987B, K: 941C, H: 358C

8659 שָׁבִי *šābî*, variant: captive, S*, B: 985D, K: 942A, H: 358C

8660 שְׁבִי *š^{e}bî*, captivity, exile; captive, prisoner, S: 7628, B: 985D, K: 941C, H: 358C

8661 שֹׁבִי *šōbî*, Shobi, S: 7629, B: 986B, K: 941D, H: 358C

8662 שֹׁבַי *šōbay*, Shobai, S: 7630, B: 986B, K: 941D, H: 358C

8663 שָׁבִיב *šābîb*, flame, S: 7632, B: 985B, K: 941D, H: 358C

8664 שִׁבְיָה *šibyâ*, captive, prisoner; captivity, S: 7633, B: 986A, K: 942A, H: 358C

8665 שְׁבִיָּה *š^{e}biyyâ*, captive, S: 7628†, B: 985D, K: 942A, H: 358C

8666 שְׁבִיל *š^{e}bîl*, way, path, S: 7635†, B: 987C, K: 942A, H: 358D

8667 שָׁבִיס *šābîs*, headband, S: 7636, B: 987D, K: 942A, H: 358D

8668 שְׁבִיעִי *š^{e}bî'î*, seventh, S: 7637, B: 988C, K: 942B, H: 358D

8669 שְׁבִית *š^{e}bît*, captivity; fortune, S: 7622, B: 986A, K: 942B, H: 358D

8670 שֹׁבֶל *šōbel*, skirt, hem of skirt, S: 7640, B: 987C, K: 942C, H: 358D

8671 שַׁבְּלוּל *šabb^{e}lûl*, slug, snail, S: 7642, B: 117D, K: 942C, H: 358D

8672 שִׁבֹּלֶת[1] *šibbōlet*[1], head of grain, S: 7641, B: 987C, K: 942C, H: 358D

8673 [2]שִׁבֹּלֶת *šibbōlet*[2], flood, torrent, flow, S: 7641, B: 987C, K: 942C, H: 358D

8674 שֶׁבְנָא *šebnā'*, Shebna, S: 7644, B: 987D, K: 942D, H: 359A

8675 שֶׁבְנָה *šebnâ*, Shebna, S: 7644, B: 987D, K: 942D, H: 359A

8676 שְׁבַנְיָה *š^{e}banyâ*, Shebaniah, S: 7645, B: 987D, K: 942D, H: 359A

8677 שְׁבַנְיָהוּ *š^{e}banyāhû*, Shebaniah, S: 7645, B: 987D, K: 942D, H: 359A

8678 שָׁבַע *šāba'*, [C] to swear an oath, make a sworn promise; [G] to make one swear an oath, give a charge, S: 7650, B: 989A, K: 942D, H: 359A

8679 שֶׁבַע[1] *šeba'*[1], seven; (pl.) seventy, S: 7651, B: 987D, K: 944A, H: 359B

8680 [2]שֶׁבַע *šeba'*[2], Sheba, S: 7652, B: 989D, K: 944C, H: 359B

8681 [3]שֶׁבַע *šeba'*[3], Sheba, S: 7652, B: 989D, K: 944C, H: 359C

8682 [4]שֶׁבַע *šeba'*[4], variant: abundance, S: 884†, B: 960A, K: 944C, H*

8683 שִׁבְעָה *šib'â*, Shibah, S: 7656, B: 988B, K: 944C, H: 359D

8684 שִׁבְעִים *šib'îm*, variant: seventy, S: 7657, B: 988C, K: 944A, H: 359B

8685 שִׁבְעָנָה *šib'ānâ*, seven, S: 7658, B: 988D, K: 944C, H: 359C

8686 שִׁבְעָתַיִם *šibʿātayim*, variant: seven-fold, seven times, S: 7659, B: 988D, K: 944A, H: 359B

8687 שָׁבַץ *šābaṣ*, [D] to weave; [E] to be woven (of fine metal), (as noun) a filigree setting, S: 7660, B: 990A, K: 944D, H: 359C

8688 שָׁבָץ *šābāṣ*, seizure, cramp, S: 7661, B: 990B, K: 944D, H: 359C

8689 [1]שָׁבַר *šābar*[1], [A] to break, destroy, crush; [B] to be broken; [C] to be destroyed, be smashed, be broken; [D] to break, smash, shatter; [G] to bring to break through (of birth); [H] to be crushed, S: 7665, B: 990C, K: 944D, H: 359C

8690 [2]שָׁבַר *šābar*[2], [A] to buy grain or food; [G] to sell, allow to buy grain, S: 7666, B: 991C, K: 945D, H: 360A

8691 [1]שֶׁבֶר *šeber*[1], destruction, brokenness, injury, S: 7667, B: 991A, K: 946A, H: 360A

8692 [2]שֶׁבֶר *šeber*[2], grain, S: 7668, B: 991C, K: 946B, H: 360B

8693 [3]שֶׁבֶר *šeber*[3], Sheber, S: 7669, B: 991B, K: 946B, H: 360B

8694 שֵׁבֶר *šēber*, interpretation (of a dream), S: 7667, B: 991B, K: 946B, H: 360B

8695 שִׁבָּרוֹן *šibbārôn*, destruction, brokenness, S: 7670†, B: 991B, K: 946B, H: 360B

8696 שְׁבָרִים *šᵉbārîm*, stone quarry, S: 7671, B: 991B, K: 946B, H: 360B

8697 [1]שָׁבַת *šābat*[1], [A] to rest, observe the Sabbath; [C] to come to an end, disappear; [G] to put to an end, stop, S: 7673, B: 991D, K: 946C, H: 360B

8698 [2]שָׁבַת *šābat*[2], variant: [A] to keep, observe (the Sabbath), S: 7673†, B: 992C, K: 946C, H: 360B

8699 [1]שֶׁבֶת *šebet*[1], place of sitting or settling, site, seat, S: 7675, B: 443D, K: 947A, H: 360C

8700 [2]שֶׁבֶת *šebet*[2], cessation, doing-nothing, S: 7674, B: 992A, K: 947A, H: 360C

8701 שַׁבָּת *šabbāt*, Sabbath, S: 7676, B: 992A, K: 947B, H: 360C

8702 שַׁבָּתוֹן *šabbātôn*, (day of) rest, S: 7677, B: 992D, K: 948A, H: 360D

8703 שַׁבְּתַי *šabbᵉtay*, Shabbethai, S: 7678, B: 992D, K: 948A, H: 360D

8704 שָׁגַג *šāgag*, [A] to err unintentionally, go astray, S: 7683, B: 992D, K: 948B, H: 360D

8705 שְׁגָגָה *šᵉgāgâ*, unintentional wrong, accidental error, S: 7684, B: 993A, K: 948B, H: 360D

8706 שָׁגָה *šāgâ*, [A] to sin unintentionally, go astray, wander, S: 7686, B: 993A, K: 948B, H: 360D

8707 שָׁגֵה *šāgēh*, Shagee, S: 7681†, B: 993B, K: 948C, H: 361A

8708 שָׁגַח *šāgaḥ*, [G] to gaze, stare, S: 7688, B: 993B, K: 948C, H: 361A

8709 שְׁגִיאָה *šᵉgîʾâ*, error, mistake, S: 7691, B: 993B, K: 948D, H: 361A

8710 שִׁגָּיוֹן *šiggāyôn*, shiggaion, shigionoth, S: 7692, B: 993C, K: 948D, H: 361A

8711 שָׁגַל *šāgal*, [A] to ravish, sexually violate; [B, C, E] to be ravished, be raped, S: 7693, B: 993C, K: 948D, H: 361A

8712 שֵׁגַל *šēgal*, queen, royal bride, S: 7694, B: 993C, K: 948D, H: 361B

8713 שָׁגַע *šāgaʿ*, [E] to be mad, act like a maniac; [F] to carry on like a madman, S: 7696, B: 993C, K: 949A, H: 361B

8714 שִׁגָּעוֹן *šiggāʿôn*, madness, S: 7697, B: 993D, K: 949A, H: 361B

8715 שֶׁגֶר *šeger*, calf, offspring (of cattle), S: 7698, B: 993D, K: 949B, H: 361B

8716 שַׁד *šad*, (female) breast, S: 7699, B: 994C, K: 949B, H: 361B

8717 שֵׁד *šēd*, demon, evil spirit, S: 7700, B: 993D, K: 949C, H: 361B

8718 [1]שֹׁד *šōd*[1], (female) breast, S: 7699, B: 994D, K: 949C, H: 361B

8719 [2]שֹׁד *šōd*[2], destruction, ruin, violence, S: 7701, B: 994C, K: 949C, H: 361C

8720 שָׁדַד *šādad*, [A] to devastate, devastate; [B] to be destroyed; [G] to be ruined; [D] to ravage, destroy; [E] to be destroyed, be ruined; [H] to be ruined, S: 7703 & 7736†, B: 994A, K: 949D, H: 361C

8721 שִׁדָּה *šiddâ*, lady, concubine, (pl.) harem, S: 7705, B: 994D, K: 950A, H: 361C

8722 שָׁדוּד *šādûd*, variant: Shadud, see 8587, S*, B: 975A, K: 950A, H: 355A

8723 שַׁדּוּן *šaddûn*, judgment, S: 1779†, B: 192C (note), K: 950C, H: 361C

8724 שַׁדַּי *šadday*, Almighty, S: 7706, B: 994D, K: 950B, H: 361C

8725 שְׁדֵיאוּר *šᵉdêʾûr*, Shedeur, S: 7707, B: 994D, K: 950B, H: 361D

8726 שַׁדִּין *šaddîn*, variant: judgment, S: 1779†, B: 192C (note), K: 950C, H: 361D

8727 שְׁדֵמָה *šᵉdēmâ*, (cultivated) field; terrace, S: 7709, B: 995A, K: 950C, H: 361D

8728 שָׁדַף *šādap*, [B] to be scorched, S: 7710, B: 995B, K: 950C, H: 361D

8729 שְׁדֵפָה *šᵉdēpâ*, scorching, S: 7711, B: 995B, K: 950C, H: 361D

8730 שִׁדָּפוֹן *šiddāpôn*, blight, S: 7711, B: 995B, K: 950D, H: 361D

8731 שַׁדְרַךְ *šadrak*, Shadrach, S: 7714, B: 995B, K: 950D, H: 361D

8732 [1]שֹׁהַם *šōham*[1], onyx, S: 7718, B: 995D, K: 950D, H: 361D

8733 [2]שֹׁהַם *šōham*[2], Shoham, S: 7719, B: 996A, K: 950D, H: 361D

8734 שַׁו *šāw*, variant: worthless, see 8736, S*, B: 996B 3, K: 951A, H: 361D

8735 שׁוּא *šûʾ*, variant: [G] to treat badly, S*, B: 673D & 674A, K: 638C, H: 361D

8736 שָׁוְא *šāwʾ*, worthlessness, vanity, falseness, S: 7723, B: 996A, K: 951A, H: 361D

8737 שְׁוָא *šᵉwāʾ*, Sheva, S: 7724, B: 996A, K: 951C, H: 362A

8738 שׁוֹא *šōʾ*, ravage, S: 7722, B: 996B, K: 951C, H: 362A

8739 שׁוֹאָה *šōʾâ*, trouble, ruin, disaster, desolation, S: 7722, B: 996B, K: 951C, H: 362A

8740 [1]שׁוּב *šûb*[1], [A] to turn back, turn to, return; [B] to return; [D] to restore, bring back; [E] to be recovered; [G] to restore, recover, bring back; [H] to be returned, be brought back, S: 7725, B: 996D, K: 951D, H: 362A

8741 [2]שׁוּב *šûb*[2], variant: see 8740, S*, B: 986A, K: 953D, H: 363D

8742 שׁוּבָאֵל *šûbāʾēl*, Shubael, S: 7619, B: 986C, K: 954A, H: 363D

8743 [1]שׁוֹבָב *šôbāb*[1], faithless, rebellious, apostate, S: 7726, B: 1000A, K: 954A, H: 363D

8744 [2]שׁוֹבָב *šôbāb*[2], Shobab, S: 7727, B: 1000A, K: 954A, H: 363D

8745 שׁוֹבֵב *šôbēb*, unfaithful, traitorous, apostate, S: 7728, B: 1000A, K: 954A, H: 364A

8746 שׁוּבָה *šûbâ*, returning, i.e., repentance, S: 7729, B: 1000A, K: 954A, H: 364A

8747 שׁוֹבַךְ *šôbak*, Shobach, S: 7731, B: 1000C, K: 954B, H: 364A

8748 שׁוֹבָל *šôbāl*, Shobal, S: 7732, B: 987C, K: 954B, H: 364A

8749 שׁוֹבֵק *šôbēq*, Shobek, S: 7733, B: 990B, K: 954B, H: 364A

8750 [1]שָׁוָה *šāwâ*[1], [A] to be like, be equal; to be appropriate, be deserved; [C] to be like; [D] to make smooth; [G] to liken; to count as equal, S: 7737, B: 1000D, K: 954B, H: 364A

8751 [2]שָׁוָה *šāwâ*[2], [D] to set, place, bestow, S: 7737, B: 1001A, K: 954C, H: 364A

8752 שָׁוֶה *šāweh*, variant: see 8753 & 8754, S*, B: 1001A, K: 954D, H: 364B

8753 שָׁוֵה *šāwēh*, Shaveh, S: 7740, B: 1001A, K: 954D, H: 364B

8754 שָׁוֵה קִרְיָתַיִם *šāwēh qiryātayim*, Shaveh Kiriathaim, S: 7741, B: 1001A, K: 954D, H: 364B

8755 [1]שׁוּחַ *šûaḥ*[1], [A] sink down, S: 7743, B: 1001B, K: 954D, H: 364B

8756 [2]שׁוּחַ *šûaḥ*[2], Shuah, S: 7744, B: 1001D, K: 954D, H: 364B

8757 [1]שׁוּחָה *šûḥâ*[1], pit, rift, S: 7745, B: 1001C, K: 955A, H: 364B

8758 [2]שׁוּחָה *šûḥâ*[2], Shuhah, S: 7746, B: 1001D, K: 955A, H: 364B

8759 שַׁוְחָט *šawḥāṭ*, variant: see 8821, S*, B: 1006A, K: 955A, H: 365D

8760 שׁוּחִי *šûḥî*, Shuhite, S: 7747, B: 1001D, K: 955A, H: 364B

8761 שׁוּחָם *šûḥām*, Shuham, S: 7748, B: 1001D, K: 955A, H: 364B

8762 שׁוּחָמִי *šûḥāmî*, Shuhamite, S: 7749, B: 1001D, K: 955A, H: 364B

8763 [1]שׁוּט *šûṭ*[1], [A] to roam, go about; to oar (a boat); [D] to wander, go here and there; [F] to rush here and there, S: 7751, B: 1001D & 1002B, K: 955A, H: 364B

8764 [2]שׁוּט *šûṭ*[2], [A] to malign, act malicious, S: 7590†, B: 1002B, K: 955B, H: 364B

8765 [1]שׁוֹט *šôṭ*[1], whip, lash, S: 7752, B: 1002A, K: 955C, H: 364C

8766 [2]שׁוֹט *šôṭ*[2], variant: (sudden) flood, S: 7752, B: 1002A, K: 955C, H: 364C

8767 שׁוּל *šûl*, hem (of a robe); skirt, S: 7757, B: 1002C, K: 955C, H: 364C

8768 שׁוֹלָל *šôlāl*, barefoot, stripped, S: 7758†, B: 1021D, K: 955D, H: 364C

8769 שׁוּלַמִּית *šûlammît*, Shulammite, S: 7759, B: 1002C, K: 955D, H: 364C

8770 שׁוּמִים *šûmîm*, garlic, S: 7762, B: 1002C, K: 955D, H: 364C

8771 [1]שׁוּנִי *šûnî*[1], Shuni, S: 7764, B: 1002C 1., K: 955D, H: 364C

8772 [2]שׁוּנִי *šûnî*[2], Shunite, S: 7765, B: 1002C 1., K: 956A, H: 364C

8773 שׁוּנֵם *šûnēm*, Shunem, S: 7766, B: 1002D, K: 956A, H: 364C

8774 שׁוּנַמִּי *šûnammî*, Shunammite, S: 7767†, B: 1002D, K: 956A, H: 364C

8775 שָׁוַע *šāwa'*, [D] to cry for help, plead, S: 7768, B: 1002D, K: 956A, H: 364C

8776 שֶׁוַע *šewa'*, cry for help, S: 7773, B: 1002D, K: 956B, H: 364C

8777 [1]שׁוֹעַ *šôa'*[1], highly respected, noble; (as noun) the rich, S: 7771, B: 447C, K: 956B, H: 364C

8778 [2]שׁוֹעַ *šôa'*[2], Shoa, S: 7772, B: 1003A, K: 956B, H: 364D

8779 [3]שׁוֹעַ *šôa'*[3], crying out, S: 7772, B: 1003A, K: 956B, H: 364C

8780 [1]שׁוּעַ *šûa'*[1], cry for help, S: 7769, B: 447D & 1002D, K: 956B, H: 364C

8781 [2]שׁוּעַ *šûa'*[2], Shua, S: 7770, B: 447C, K: 956B, H: 364D

8782 [3]שׁוּעַ *šûa'*[3], wealth, S: 7769, B: 1002D, K: 956B, H: 364C

8783 שׁוּעָא *šû'ā'*, Shua, S: 7774, B: 447D, K: 956C, H: 364D

8784 שַׁוְעָה *šaw'â*, cry for help, S: 7775, B: 1003A, K: 956C, H: 364D

8785 [1]שׁוּעָל *šû'āl*[1], fox; jackal, S: 7776, B: 1043C, K: 956C, H: 364D

8786 [2]שׁוּעָל *šû'āl*[2], Shual, S: 7777, B: 1043C, K: 956C, H: 364D

8787 [3]שׁוּעָל *šû'āl*[3], Shual, S: 7777, B: 1043C, K: 956C, H: 364D

8788 שֹׁועֵר *šô'ēr*, gatekeeper, doorkeeper, S: 7778, B: 1045B, K: 956C, H: 364D

8789 [1]שׁוּף *šûp*[1], [A] to crush, S: 7779, B: 1003A, K: 956D, H: 364D

8790 [2]שׁוּף *šûp*[2], [A] to strike, S: 7779, B: 1003A, K: 956D, H: 364D

8791 שׁוֹפָךְ *šôpak*, Shophach, S: 7780, B: 1000C, K: 957A, H: 364D

8792 שׁוּפָם *šûpām*, Shupham, S: 8197, B: 1051B, K: 957A, H: 380C

8793 שׁוּפָמִי *šûpāmî*, Shuphamite, S: 7781, B: 1051B, K: 957A, H: 364D

8794 שׁוֹפָן *šôpān*, variant: Shophan, S: 5855†, B: 743A 1b, K: 957A, H: 271B

8795 שׁוֹפָר *šôpār*, trumpet, ram's horn, S: 7782, B: 1051C, K: 957A, H: 364D

8796 [1]שׁוּק *šûq*[1], [G] to prove narrow, overflow; [D] to water abundantly, S: 7783, B: 1003B, K: 957B, H: 365A

8797 שׁוֹק *šôq*, (lower) thigh; leg, S: 7785, B: 1003B, K: 957C, H: 365A

8798 [2]שׁוּק *šûq*[2], street, S: 7784, B: 1003B, K: 957C, H: 365A

8799 שׁוֹקֵק *šôqēq*, thirsty, unquenched, S: 8264†, B: 1055B, K: 957D, H: 365A

8800 [1]שׁוּר *šûr*[1], [A] to see, look, view, S: 7789, B: 1003D, K: 957D, H: 365A

8801 [2]שׁוּר *šûr*[2], [A] to travel, descend, S: 7788, B: 1003C, K: 957D, H: 365A

8802 שׁוֹר *šôr*, bull, ox, S: 7794, B: 1004A, K: 958A, H: 365B

8803 [3]שׁוּר *šûr*[3], wall, S: 7790, B: 1004A & B, K: 958B, H: 365B

8804 [4]שׁוּר *šûr*[4], Shur, S: 7793, B: 1004B, K: 958B, H: 365B

8805 שׁוּרָה *šûrâ*, supporting wall (of a terrace), S: 7791†, B: 1004C, K: 958C, H: 365B

8806 שׁוֹרֵר *šôrēr*, enemy, adversary, S: 8324†, B: 1004A, K: 958C, H: 365B

8807 שַׁוְשָׁא *šawšā'*, Shavsha, S: 7798, B: 1004C, K: 958C, H: 365B

8808 [1]שׁוּשַׁן *šûšan*[1], lily, S: 7799, B: 1004C, K: 958C, H: 365B

8809 [2]שׁוּשַׁן *šûšan*[2], Susa, S: 7800, B: 1004D, K: 958D, H: 365B

8810 שׁוּשַׁק *šûšaq*, variant: Shushak, see 8882, S: 7895, B: 1004D, K: 958D, H: 365B

8811 שׁוּתֶלַח *šûtelaḥ*, Shuthelah, S: 7803, B: 1004D, K: 958D, H: 365B

8812 שָׁזַף *šāzap*, [A] to see; to be darkened, S: 7805, B: 1004D, K: 959A, H: 365C

8813 שָׁזַר *šāzar*, [H] to be finely twisted, S: 7806, B: 1004D, K: 959A, H: 365C

8814 שַׁח *šaḥ*, downward, bent, low, S: 7807, B: 1006A, K: 959A, H: 365C

8815 שָׁחַד *šāḥad*, [A] to give a gift; pay a bribe, S: 7809, B: 1005A, K: 959A, H: 365C

8816 שֹׁחַד *šōḥad*, bribe, gift, S: 7810†, B: 1005A, K: 959B, H: 365C

8817 שָׁחָה *šāḥâ*, [A] to bow down; [G] to weigh down, cause to bow, S: 7812, B: 1005B, K: 959B, H: 365C

8818 שְׁחוֹר *šᵉḥôr*, soot, S: 7815, B: 1007A, K: 960A, H: 365C

8819 שְׁחוּת *šᵉḥût*, trap, pit, S: 7816, B: 1005C, K: 960A, H: 365D

8820 שָׁחַח *šāḥaḥ*, [A] to bow down, bend low; [C] to be brought low; [G] to humble, bring low, S: 7817, B: 1005D, K: 960A, H: 365D

8821 [1]שָׁחַט *šāḥaṭ*[1], [A] to slaughter, kill; [B, C] to be killed, be slaughtered, S: 7819, B: 1006A, K: 960B, H: 365D

8822 [2]שָׁחַט *šāḥaṭ*[2], [B] to be hammered, beaten, S: 7819 & 7820, B: 1006A, K: 960C, H: 366A

8823 שַׁחֲטָה *šaḥᵃṭâ*, slaughter, S: 7819†, B: 1006B, K: 960D, H: 366A

8824 שְׁחִיטָה *šᵉḥîṭâ*, killing, slaughter, S: 7821, B: 1006B, K: 960D, H: 366A

8825 שְׁחִין *šᵉḥîn*, boils, skin sores, S: 7822, B: 1006C, K: 960D, H: 366A

8826 שָׁחִיס *šāḥîs*, growth, what springs up, S: 7823, B: 1006B, K: 961A, H: 366A

8827 שְׁחִית *šᵉḥît*, pit, trap, grave, S: 7825, B: 1005D, K: 961A, H: 366A

8828 שַׁחַל *šaḥal*, lion, S: 7826, B: 1006C, K: 961A, H: 366A

8829 שְׁחֵלֶת *šᵉḥēlet*, onycha (a fragrant spice), S: 7827, B: 1006C, K: 961A, H: 366A

8830 שַׁחַף *šaḥap*, gull *or possibly* bat, S: 7828, B: 1006D, K: 961B, H: 366A

8831 שַׁחֶפֶת *šaḥepet*, wasting disease, consumption, S: 7829, B: 1006D, K: 961B, H: 366A

8832 שַׁחַץ *šaḥaṣ*, pride, dignity, S: 7830, B: 1006D, K: 961B, H: 366A

8833 שַׁחֲצוּמָה *šaḥᵃṣûmâ*, Shahazumah, S: 7831†, B: 1006D, K: 961C, H: 366B

8834 שַׁחֲצִימָה *šaḥᵃṣîmâ*, variant: Shahazimah, see 8833, S: 7831†, B: 1006D, K: 961C, H: 366B

8835 שָׁחַק *šāḥaq*, [A] to grind, wear away, S: 7833, B: 1006D, K: 961C, H: 366B

8836 שַׁחַק *šaḥaq*, clouds, skies, S: 7834, B: 1007A, K: 961D, H: 366B

8837 [1]שָׁחַר *šāḥar*[1], [A] to become black, S: 7835, B: 1007A, K: 962A, H: 366B

8838 [2]שָׁחַר *šāḥar*[2], [A] to seek, look; [D] to earnestly seek, search for, S: 7836, B: 1007C, K: 962A, H: 366B

8839 שָׁחֹר *šāḥōr*, black, dark, S: 7838, B: 1007B, K: 962B, H: 366C

8840 שַׁחַר *šaḥar*, dawn, daybreak, S: 7837, B: 1007B, K: 962B, H: 366C

8841 שַׁחֲרוּת *šaḥᵃrût*, vigor, prime of youth, S: 7839, B: 1007B, K: 962C, H: 366C

8842 שְׁחַרְחֹר *šᵉḥarḥōr*, dark, swarthy (complexion), S: 7840†, B: 1007B, K: 962C, H: 366C

8843 שְׁחַרְיָה *šᵉḥaryâ*, Shehariah, S: 7841, B: 1007D, K: 962C, H: 366C

8844 שַׁחֲרַיִם *šaḥᵃrayim*, Shaharaim, S: 7842, B: 1007D, K: 962D, H: 366C

8845 שָׁחַת *šāḥat*, [C] to be corrupt, be ruined, be marred; [D] to corrupt, destroy, ruin; [G] to destroy, corrupt, bring to ruin, S: 516† & 7843, B: 1007D, K: 962D, H: 366C

8846 שַׁחַת *šaḥat*, pit, dungeon; corruption, decay, S: 7845, B: 1001C, K: 963C, H: 367A

8847 שִׁטָּה *šiṭṭâ*, acacia wood, S: 7848, B: 1008D, K: 963D, H: 367A

8848 שָׁטַח *šāṭaḥ*, [A] to spread out, enlarge, scatter; [D] to spread out, S: 7849, B: 1008D, K: 964A, H: 367A

8849 שֹׁטֵט *šōṭēṭ*, whip, scourge, S: 7850, B: 1002B, K: 964A, H: 367A

8850 שִׁטִּים *šiṭṭîm*, Shittim, S: 7851, B: 1008D, K: 964A, H: 367A

8851 שָׁטַף *šāṭap*, [A] to overflow, flood, wash away; [C] to be rinsed, be swept away; [E] to be rinsed, S: 7857, B: 1009A, K: 964B, H: 367A

8852 שֶׁטֶף *šeṭep*, flood, torrents (of rain), S: 7858, B: 1009B, K: 964C, H: 367B

8853 שָׁטַר *šāṭar*, [A] to keep a record; (as noun) official, officer, foreman, S: 7860†, B: 1009C, K: 964C, H: 367B

8854 שֹׁטֵר *šōṭēr*, variant: oversee, officer, S*, B: 1009C, K: 964C, H: 367B

8855 שִׁטְרַי *šiṭray*, Shitrai, S: 7861, B: 1009C, K: 964D, H: 367B

8856 שַׁי *šay*, gift, S: 7862, B: 1009C, K: 964D, H: 367B

8857 שְׁיָא *šᵉyā'*, variant: Sheya, see 8737, S: 7864, B: 1009D, K: 964D, H: 367B

8858 שִׁיאֹן *šî'ōn*, Shion, S: 7866†, B: 1009D, K: 964D, H: 367B

8859 [1]שִׁיבָה *šîbâ*[1], stay, S: 7871, B: 444A, K: 964D, H: 367B

8860 [2]שִׁיבָה *šîbâ*[2], captives, S: 7870, B: 1000A, K: 964D, H: 367B

8861 שָׁיָה *šāyâ*, [A] to desert, forget, S: 7876, B: 1009D, K: 964D, H: 367C

8862 שִׁיזָא *šîzā'*, Shiza, S: 7877, B: 1009D, K: 965A, H: 367C

8863 שִׂיחַ *šîaḥ*, [A] to disintegrate away (to dust), S: 7817†, B: 1005D, K: 965A, H: 367C

8864 שִׁיחָה *šîḥâ*, pit, pitfall, S: 7882, B: 1001C, K: 965A, H: 367C

8865 שִׁיחוֹר *šîḥôr*, Shihor, S: 7883, B: 1009D, K: 965A, H: 367C

8866 שִׁיחוֹר לִבְנָת *šîḥôr libnāt*, Shihor Libnath, S: 7884, B: 1009D, K: 965B, H: 367C

8867 שִׁיט *šîṭ*, variant: scourge, see 8765, S: 7752†, B: 1002B, K: 965B, H: 367C

8868 שַׁיִט *šayiṭ*, oar, S: 7885, B: 1002B, K: 965B, H: 367C

8869 שִׁילֹה *šîlōh*, variant: Shiloh, S: 7886, B: 1010A, K: 965B, H: 367C

8870 שִׁילוֹ *šîlô*, Shiloh, S: 7887, B: 1017D, K: 965B, H: 367C

8871 שֵׁילָל *šêlāl*, variant: see 8768, S: 7758, B: 1021D, K: 965C, H: 367C

8872 שִׁילֹנִי *šîlōnî*, Shilonite, of Shiloh, S: 7888†, B: 1018A, K: 965C, H: 367C

8873 שִׁימוֹן *šîmôn*, Shimon, S: 7889, B: 1010A, K: 965C, H: 367C

8874 שִׁין *šîn*, [Hiphil] to urinate (on a wall), i.e., a male, S: 8366†, B: 1010B, K: 965C, H: 367C

8875 שַׁיִן *šayin*, urine, S: 7890, B: 1010A, K: 965C, H: 367D

8876 שִׁיר[1] *šîr*[1], [A] to sing; [D] singer, musician, S: 7891, B: 1010C, K: 965D, H: 367D

8877 שִׁיר[2] *šîr*[2], song, music, S: 7892, B: 1010B, K: 966B, H: 367D

8878 שִׁירָה *šîrâ*, song, S: 7892, B: 1010C, K: 966C, H: 368A

8879 שְׁיָרָה *šᵉyārâ*, variant: caravan, see 8801, S*, B*, K: 966C, H*

8880 שַׁיִשׁ *šayiš*, alabaster, S: 7893, B: 1010D, K: 966C, H: 368A

8881 שִׁישָׁא *šîšā'*, Shisha, S: 7894, B: 1010D, K: 966D, H: 368A

8882 שִׁישַׁק *šîšaq*, Shishak, S: 7895, B: 1011A, K: 966D, H: 368A

8883 שִׁית[1] *šît*[1], [A] to place, put, set; [H] to be demanded, S: 7896, B: 1011A, K: 966D, H: 368A

8884 שִׁית[2] *šît*[2], garment, S: 7897, B: 1011C, K: 967D, H: 368C

8885 שַׁיִת *šayit*, thorns, thorn-bushes, S: 7898, B: 1011D, K: 967D, H: 368C

8886 שָׁכַב *šākab*, [A] to lie down, rest; sleep with; (as a euphemism of sexual intercourse) to lie with, sleep with; [G] to make lie down; [H] to be laid down, S: 7901, B: 1011D, K: 967D, H: 368C

8887 שִׁכְבָה *šikbâ*, emission, discharge, S: 7902†, B: 1012C, K: 968B, H: 368D

8888 שְׁכֹבֶת *šᵉkōbet*, sexual relations, sexual intercourse, S: 7903, B: 1012D, K: 968C, H: 368D

8889 שָׁכָה *šākâ*, [G] to be well-fed; lusting, S: 7904, B: 1013A, K: 968C, H: 368D

8890 שְׁכוֹל *šᵉkôl*, forlornness, loss of children, S: 7908, B: 1013D, K: 968C, H: 369A

8891 שַׁכּוּל *šakkûl*, pertaining to the loss of offspring, S: 7909, B: 1014A, K: 968D, H: 369A

8892 שְׁכוּלָה *šᵉkûlâ*, bereaved (of children), S: 7909†, B: 1014A, K: 968D, H: 369A

8893 שִׁכּוֹר *šikkôr*, drunk, drunkenness; (as noun) a drunkard, S: 7910, B: 1016C, K: 968D, H: 369A

8894 שָׁכַח *šākaḥ*, [A] to forget; [C] to be forgotten; [D] to make forget; [G] to make forget; [F] to be forgotten, S: 7911, B: 1013A, K: 968D, H: 369A

8895 שָׁכֵחַ *šākēaḥ*, forgetting, S: 7913, B: 1013C, K: 969B, H: 369B

8896 שָׁכַךְ *šākak*, [A] to recede, reside; [G] to get rid of, S: 7918, B: 1013C, K: 969C, H: 369B

8897 שָׁכֹל *šākal*, [A] to be bereaved (of children); [D] to make childless, bring bereavement, suffer miscarriage; [G] to miscarry, S: 7921†, B: 1013C, K: 969C, H: 369B

8898 שִׁכֻּלִים *šikkulîm*, (state of) bereavement (of children), S: 7923, B: 1014A, K: 969D, H: 369C

8899 שָׁכַם *šākam*, [G] to do early in the morning; to do again and again, S: 7925, B: 1014C, K: 970A, H: 369C

8900 שְׁכֶם[1] *šᵉkem*[1], shoulder (upper part of the back); ridge of land, S: 7926 & 7929†, B: 1014A, K: 970B, H: 369D

8901 שְׁכֶם[2] *šᵉkem*[2], Shechem, S: 7927, B: 1014B 1., K: 970C, H: 369D

8902 שְׁכֶם[3] *šᵉkem*[3], Shechem, S: 7927, B: 1014B 2., K: 970D, H: 369D

8903 שֶׁכֶם *šekem*, Shechem, S: 7928, B: 1014C, K: 970D, H: 369D

8904 שִׁכְמִי *šikmî*, Shechemite, S: 7930, B: 1014C, K: 970D, H: 369D

8905 שָׁכַן *šākan*, [A] to dwell, abide, live among, stay; [D] to make to dwell, make a home; [G] to cause to dwell, settle in, set up a dwelling, S: 7931 & 7933†, B: 1014D, K: 970D, H: 369D

8906 שֶׁכֶן *šeken*, variant: dwelling, S*, B: 1015C, K*, H*

8907 שָׁכֵן *šākēn*, neighbor; inhabitant, S: 7934, B: 1015C, K: 971C, H: 370A

8908 שְׁכַנְיָה *šᵉkanyâ*, Shecaniah, S: 7935, B: 1016A, K: 971C, H: 370B

8909 שְׁכַנְיָהוּ *šᵉkanyāhû*, Shecaniah, S: 7935, B: 1016A, K: 971D, H: 370B

8910 שָׁכַר *šākar*, [A] to become drunk, drink to one's fill; [D] to make drunk; [G] to make drunk; [F] to behave drunken, S: 7937, B: 1016A, K: 971D, H: 370B

8911 שֵׁכָר *šēkār*, fermented drink, beer, S: 7941, B: 1016B, K: 972A, H: 370B

8912 שָׁכֻר *šākur*, drunken, S: 7937†, B: 1016A, K: 972A, H: 370B

8913 שִׁכָּרוֹן[1] *šikkārôn*[1], drunkenness, S: 7943, B: 1016C, K: 972B, H: 370C

8914 שִׁכָּרוֹן[2] *šikkārôn*[2], Shikkeron, S: 7942†, B: 1016C, K: 972B, H: 370C

8915 שַׁל *šal*, irreverent act, S: 7944, B: 1016D, K: 972B, H: 370C

8916 שַׁלְאֲנָן *šal'ᵃnan*, secure, S: 7946†, B: 1016D, K: 972B, H: 370C

8917 שָׁלַב *šālab*, [E] to be joined, set parallel, dovetailed, S: 7947, B: 1016D, K: 972B, H: 370C

8918 שָׁלָב *šālāb*, upright, crossbar, S: 7948, B: 1016D, K: 972C, H: 370C

8919 שָׁלַג *šālag*, [G] to snow, S: 7949, B: 1017A, K: 972C, H: 370C

8920 שֶׁלֶג[1] *šeleg*[1], snow, S: 7950, B: 1017A, K: 972C, H: 370C

8921 שֶׁלֶג[2] *šeleg*[2], soap, S: 7950, B: 1017A, K: 972D, H: 370C

8922 שָׁלָה[1] *šālâ*[1], [A] to be at ease, have peace; [C] to give oneself to rest; [G] to raise hopes, S: 7951, B: 1017A, K: 972D, H: 370C

8923 שָׁלָה[2] *šālâ*[2], [A] to take away, extract, S: 7952 & 7953, B: 1017D, K: 972D, H: 370C

8924 שֵׁלָה[1] *šēlâ*[1], petition, S: 7956, B: 982C, K: 972D, H: 370C

8925 שֵׁלָה[2] *šēlâ*[2], Shelah, S: 7956, B: 1017C, K: 973A, H: 370D

8926 שִׁלֹה *šilōh*, Shiloh, S: 7887, B: 1017D, K: 973A, H: 370D

8927 שַׁלְהֶבֶת *šalhebet*, flame, S: 7957, B: 529B, K: 973A, H: 370D

8928 שַׁלְהֶבֶתְיָה *šalhebetyâ*, mighty flame (*or* 8927 + 3363), S: 7957†, B: 529B & 219C, K: 973A, H: 370D

8929 שָׁלֵו *šālēw*, quiet, at ease, carefree, S: 7961, B: 1017C, K: 973B, H: 370D

8930 שָׁלוּ *šālû*, secure feeling, ease, S: 7959†, B: 1017B, K: 973B, H: 370D

8931 שִׁלוֹ *šilô*, Shiloh, S: 7887, B: 1017D, K: 973B, H: 370D

8932 שַׁלְוָה *šalwâ*, security, ease, S: 7962, B: 1017C, K: 973B, H: 370D

8933 שִׁלּוּחִים *šillûḥîm*, parting gifts; sending away, S: 7964†, B: 1019D, K: 973B, H: 370D

8934 שָׁלוֹם *šālôm*, peace, safety, prosperity, well-being; intactness, wholeness, S: 7965, B: 1022D, K: 973C, H: 371A

8935 שַׁלּוּם *šallûm*, Shallum, S: 7967, B: 1024B, K: 974D, H: 371B

8936 שִׁלּוּם *šillûm*, retribution, reckoning; bribe, gift, S: 7966, B: 1024B, K: 974D, H: 371B

8937 שַׁלּוּן *šallûn*, Shallun, S: 7968, B: 1024C, K: 975A, H: 371C

8938 שָׁלַח *šālaḥ*, [A] to send out; [B] to be sent away; [C] to be sent; [D] to send away, let go, release; [E] to be sent away, thrust out; [G] to send out, S: 7971, B: 1018A, K: 975A, H: 371C

8939 שֶׁלַח[1] *šelaḥ*[1], weapon, sword, javelin, S: 7973, B: 1019C, K: 976C, H: 372A

8940 שֶׁלַח[2] *šelaḥ*[2], Siloam, S: 7975, B: 1019D, K: 976C, H: 372A

8941 שֶׁלַח[3] *šelaḥ*[3], Shelah, S: 7974, B: 1019D, K: 976C, H: 372B

8942 שִׁלֹחַ *šilōaḥ*, Shiloah, S: 7975, B: 1019D, K: 976D, H: 372B

8943 שְׁלֻחוֹת *šᵉluḥôt*, shoot (of a vine), S: 7976†, B: 1020A, K: 976D, H: 372B

8944 שִׁלְחִי *šilḥî*, Shilhi, S: 7977, B: 1019D, K: 976D, H: 372B

8945 שְׁלָחִים *šᵉlāḥîm*, shoots, sprouts of a plant, S: 7973†, B: 1019C 2, K: 976D, H: 372B

8946 שִׁלְחִים *šilḥîm*, Shilhim, S: 7978, B: 1019D, K: 976D, H: 372B

8947 שֻׁלְחָן *šulḥān*, table, S: 7979, B: 1020B, K: 976D, H: 372B

8948 שָׁלַט *šālaṭ*, [A] to control, lord over; [G] to let rule, enable, S: 7980, B: 1020C, K: 977B, H: 372B

8949 שֶׁלֶט *šeleṭ*, small (round) shield, S: 7982, B: 1020D, K: 977B, H: 372C

8950 שִׁלְטוֹן *šilṭôn*, supremacy, S: 7983, B: 1020D, K: 977C, H: 372C
8951 שַׁלֶּטֶת *šalleṭet*, brazen, domineering, S: 7986, B: 1020D, K: 977C, H: 372C
8952 שְׁלִי *šᵉlî*, privateness, uninterruptedness, S: 7987, B: 1017B, K: 977C, H: 372C
8953 שִׁלְיָה *šilyâ*, afterbirth, S: 7988, B: 1017D, K: 977C, H: 372C
8954 שַׁלִּיט *šallîṭ*, ruler, governor, S: 7989, B: 1020C, K: 977C, H: 372C
8955 [1]שָׁלִישׁ *šālîš*[1], bowlful, basketful (a unit of measure), S: 7991, B: 1026C, K: 977C, H: 372C
8956 [2]שָׁלִישׁ *šālîš*[2], lute, S: 7991, B: 1026C, K: 977D, H: 372C
8957 [3]שָׁלִישׁ *šālîš*[3], officer, S: 7991, B: 1026D, K: 977D, H: 372C
8958 שְׁלִישִׁי *šᵉlîšî*, third, S: 7992, B: 1026A, K: 978A, H: 372D
8959 שָׁלַךְ *šālak*, [G] to throw, hurl, scatter; [H] to be thrown, be cast, S: 7993, B: 1020D, K: 978A, H: 372D
8960 שָׁלָךְ *šālāk*, cormorant, S: 7994, B: 1021C, K: 978D, H: 373A
8961 [1]שַׁלֶּכֶת *šalleket*[1], cutting down, S: 7995, B: 1021C, K: 978D, H: 373A
8962 [2]שַׁלֶּכֶת *šalleket*[2], Shalleketh, S: 7996, B: 1021C, K: 978D, H: 373A
8963 [1]שָׁלַל *šālal*[1], [A] to pull out, S: 7997, B: 1021C, K: 979A, H: 373A
8964 [2]שָׁלַל *šālal*[2], [A] to plunder, loot; [F] to be plundered, S: 7997, B: 1021D, K: 979A, H: 373A
8965 שָׁלָל *šālāl*, plunder, spoil, loot, S: 7998, B: 1021D, K: 979A, H: 373B
8966 [1]שָׁלֵם *šālēm*[1], [A] to be finished, be completed; be at peace; [B] to be at peace; [D] to repay, make restitution, fulfill (a vow); [E] be repaid, be fulfilled; [G] to make peace; cause to fulfill; [H] to be brought into peace, S: 7999†, B: 1022B, K: 979B, H: 373B
8967 שְׁלָם *šᵉlām*, variant: agreement, S*, B: 1116A, K: 980C, H: 373D
8968 שֶׁלֶם *šelem*, fellowship (offering), S: 8002, B: 1023B, K: 980C, H: 373D
8969 [2]שָׁלֵם *šālēm*[2], safe, complete, whole, S: 8003, B: 1023D, K: 980D, H: 373D
8970 [3]שָׁלֵם *šālēm*[3], Salem, S: 8004, B: 1024A, K: 981A, H: 373D
8971 [4]שָׁלֵם *šālēm*[4], variant: [D] to make a covenant of peace, be at peace, S*, B: 1023D, K*, H*
8972 [1]שִׁלֵּם *šillēm*[1], variant: recompense, S: 8005, B: 1024A, K: 981A, H: 373D
8973 [2]שִׁלֵּם *šillēm*[2], Shillem, S: 8006, B: 1024A, K: 981A, H: 373D
8974 שִׁלֻּמָה *šillumâ*, punishment, retribution, S: 8011, B: 1024B, K: 981A, H: 374A
8975 שַׁלָּמָה *šallāmâ*, variant: see 8611 & 4200 & 4537, S: 4100†, B: 980A 3b & 510A & 552B, K: 933D & 462B & 498A, H: 374A
8976 שְׁלֹמֹה *šᵉlōmōh*, Solomon, S: 8010, B: 1024C, K: 981B, H: 374A
8977 שְׁלֹמוֹת *šᵉlōmôt*, Shelomoth, S: 8013, B: 1024D, K: 981B, H: 374A
8978 שַׁלְמַי *šalmay*, Shalmai, S: 8073, B: 969C, K: 923D, H: 352C
8979 שְׁלֹמִי *šᵉlōmî*, Shelomi, S: 8015, B: 1025A, K: 981B, H: 374A
8980 שִׁלֵּמִי *šillēmî*, Shillemite, S: 8016, B: 1024B, K: 981B, H: 374A
8981 שְׁלֻמִיאֵל *šᵉlumîʾēl*, Shelumiel, S: 8017, B: 1025A, K: 981B, H: 374A
8982 שֶׁלֶמְיָה *šelemyâ*, Shelemiah, S: 8018, B: 1025A, K: 981C, H: 374A
8983 שֶׁלֶמְיָהוּ *šelemyāhû*, Shelemiah, S: 8018, B: 1025A, K: 981C, H: 374A
8984 [1]שְׁלֹמִית *šᵉlōmît*[1], Shelomith, S: 8019, B: 1024D, K: 981C, H: 374A
8985 [2]שְׁלֹמִית *šᵉlōmît*[2], Shelomith, S: 8019, B: 1025A, K: 981C, H: 374A
8986 שַׁלְמַן *šalman*, Shalman, S: 8020, B: 1025A, K: 981C, H: 374A
8987 שַׁלְמַנְאֶסֶר *šalmanʾeser*, Shalmaneser, S: 8022, B: 1025B, K: 981C, H: 374A
8988 שַׁלְמֹנִים *šalmōnîm*, gifts, S: 8021†, B: 1024B, K: 981D, H: 374A
8989 שֵׁלָנִי *šēlānî*, Shelanite, of Shelah, S: 8023† & 8024, B: 1017C, K: 981D, H: 374A
8990 שָׁלַף *šālap*, [A] to draw out (a sword); remove (a sandal); [B] to be drawn (sword), S: 8025, B: 1025B, K: 981D, H: 374A
8991 שֶׁלֶף *šelep*, Sheleph, S: 8026, B: 1025C, K: 982A, H: 374A
8992 שָׁלַשׁ *šālaš*, [D] to do a third time, on the third day; [E] to be three years old, in three parts, S: 8027, B: 1026A, K: 982A, H: 374A
8993 שָׁלֹשׁ *šālōš*, three; (pl.) thirty, S: 7969, B: 1025C, K: 982B, H: 374B
8994 שֵׁלֶשׁ *šēleš*, Shelesh, S: 8028†, B: 1026D, K: 982D, H: 374B
8995 שָׁלִשָׁה *šālišâ*, Shalisha, S: 8031, B: 1027A, K: 982D, H: 374B
8996 שִׁלְשָׁה *šilšâ*, Shilshah, S: 8030, B: 1027A, K: 982D, H: 374C
8997 שִׁלְשׁוֹם *šilšôm*, three days ago, S: 8032, B: 1026B, K: 982D, H: 374C
8998 שָׁלִשִׁי *šālišî*, [the] Three, S: 7991†, B: 1026A, K: 978A, H: 374B
8999 שְׁלִשִׁיָּה *šᵉlišiyyâ*, variant: Shelishiyah, see 6326, S: 7992†, B: 1026A, K: 978A, H: 264D
9000 שִׁלֵּשִׁים *šillēšîm*, third (generation), S: 8029†, B: 1026D, K: 982D, H: 374C
9001 שְׁלֹשִׁים *šᵉlōšîm*, variant: thirty, S: 7970†, B: 1026C, K: 982B, H: 374B
9002 שִׁלְתָּה *šiltâ*, variant: Shiltah, S*, B: 1068B, K: 983A, H: 148C
9003 שַׁלְתִּיאֵל *šaltîʾēl*, Shealtiel, S: 7597, B: 1027A, K: 983A, H: 374C
9004 שָׁם *šām*, there, where, S: 8033, B: 1027A, K: 983A, H: 374C
9005 [1]שֵׁם *šēm*[1], name; renown, fame, S: 8034, B: 1027D, K: 983B, H: 374C
9006 [2]שֵׁם *šēm*[2], Shem, S: 8035, B: 1028D, K: 984C, H: 375A
9007 שַׁמָּא *šammāʾ*, Shamma; Shammah, S: 8037, B: 1031C, K: 984D, H: 375A
9008 שֶׁמְאֵבֶר *šemʾēber*, Shemeber, S: 8038, B: 1028D, K: 984D, H: 375A
9009 שִׁמְאָה *šimʾâ*, Shimeah, S: 8039, B: 1029A, K: 984D, H: 375A
9010 שִׁמְאָם *šimʾām*, Shimeam, S: 8043, B: 1029A, K: 984D, H: 1029A
9011 שַׁמְגַּר *šamgar*, Shamgar, S: 8044, B: 1029A, K: 984D, H: 375A
9012 שָׁמַד *šāmad*, [C] to be destroyed; [G] to destroy, demolish, annihilate, S: 8045, B: 1029A, K: 984D, H: 375A
9013 שֶׁמֶד *šemed*, Shemed, S: 8106†, B: 1029C, K: 985B, H: 375A
9014 [1]שַׁמָּה *šammâ*[1], thing of horror; desolation, devastation, what is laid waste, S: 8047, B: 1031C, K: 985B, H: 375A
9015 [2]שַׁמָּה *šammâ*[2], Shammah, S: 8048, B: 1031C, K: 985C, H: 375B
9016 שַׁמְהוּת *šamhût*, Shamhuth, S: 8049, B: 1030B, K: 985C, H: 375B
9017 שְׁמוּאֵל *šᵉmûʾēl*, Samuel; Shemuel, S: 8050, B: 1028D, K: 985C, H: 375B
9018 שַׁמּוּעַ *šammûaʿ*, Shammua, S: 8051, B: 1035B, K: 985D, H: 375B
9019 שְׁמוּעָה *šᵉmûʿâ*, message, rumor, report, S: 8052, B: 1035B, K: 985D, H: 375B
9020 שָׁמוּר *šāmûr*, variant: Shamur, see 9033, S: 8053, B: 1039A, K: 986A, H: 375B
9021 שַׁמּוֹת *šammôt*, Shammoth, S: 8054, B: 1031C 3.b., K: 986A, H: 375B
9022 שָׂמַח *šāmaḥ*, variant: [A] to be magnanimous, see 8523, S*, B*, K: 986A, H: 375B
9023 שָׁמַט *šāmaṭ*, [A] to drop down, stumble; to lie unplowed; [C] to be thrown down; [G] to cancel a debt, S: 8058, B: 1030C, K: 986B, H: 375C
9024 שְׁמִטָּה *šᵉmiṭṭâ*, canceling of debt, S: 8059, B: 1030D, K: 986B, H: 375C
9025 שַׁמַּי *šammay*, Shammai, S: 8060, B: 1031D, K: 986C, H: 375C
9026 שְׁמִידָע *šᵉmîdāʿ*, Shemida, S: 8061, B: 1029A, K: 986C, H: 375C
9027 שְׁמִידָעִי *šᵉmîdāʿî*, Shemidaite, S: 8062, B: 1029A, K: 986C, H: 375C
9028 שָׁמַיִם *šāmayim*, heaven (the realm of God); the heavens: place of the stars, sky, air, S: 8064, B: 1029C, K: 986C, H: 375C
9029 שְׁמִינִי *šᵉmînî*, eighth, S: 8066, B: 1033B, K: 988A, H: 375C
9030 שְׁמִינִית *šᵉmînît*, sheminith, S: 8067, B: 1033B, K: 988A, H: 375D
9031 [1]שָׁמִיר *šāmîr*[1], briers, S: 8068, B: 1038D, K: 988B, H: 375D
9032 [2]שָׁמִיר *šāmîr*[2], hardest stone; (other contexts) flint or emery, S: 8068, B: 1039A 2, K: 988B, H: 375D
9033 [3]שָׁמִיר *šāmîr*[3], Shamir, S: 8069, B: 1039A, K: 988B, H: 375D
9034 [4]שָׁמִיר *šāmîr*[4], Shamir, S: 8069, B: 1039A, K: 988B, H: 375D
9035 שְׁמִירָמוֹת *šᵉmîrāmôt*, Shemiramoth, S: 8070, B: 1029A, K: 988C, H: 375D
9036 שַׁמְלַי *šamlay*, variant: Shamlai, see 8978, S: 8073, B: 969C, K: 988C, H: 375D
9037 [1]שָׁמֵם *šāmēm*[1], [A] to be desolate, be appalled; [C] to become desolate, be appalled; [D] to cause desolation, be appalled; [G] to bring to devastation, cause to be appalled; [H] to lie desolate; [F] to destroy oneself, be appalled, S: 8074, B: 1030D, K: 988C, H: 375D
9038 [2]שָׁמֵם *šāmēm*[2], desolate, deserted, S: 8076, B: 1031B, K: 989B, H: 376B
9039 שְׁמָמָה *šᵉmāmâ*, desolation, ruin, wasteland, S: 8077, B: 1031B, K: 989C, H: 376B

[A] Qal [B] Qal passive [C] Niphal [D] Piel (poel, polel, pilel, pilal, pealal, pilpel) [E] Pual (poal, polal, poalal, pulal, pualal)

9040 שִׁמְמָה *šimemâ*, desolation, S: 8077, B: 1031C, K: 989C, H: 376B

9041 שִׁמָּמוֹן *šimmāmôn*, despair, S: 8078, B: 1031D, K: 989C, H: 376B

9042 [1]שָׁמֵן *šāmēn*[1], [A] to grow fat; [G] to show as well-fed; to be calloused, S: 8080†, B: 1031D, K: 989D, H: 376B

9043 שֶׁמֶן *šemen*, olive oil, oil lotions; olive (wood), S: 8081, B: 1032A, K: 989D, H: 376C

9044 שָׁמָן *šāmān*, richness, fatness, S: 4924†, B: 1032A, K: 990B, H: 376C

9045 [2]שָׁמֵן *šāmēn*[2], rich, fertile, S: 8082, B: 1032A, K: 990B, H: 376C

9046 שְׁמֹנֶה *šemōneh*, eight; (pl.) eighty, S: 8083, B: 1032D, K: 990C, H: 376C

9047 שְׁמֹנִים *šemōnîm*, variant: eighty, S: 8084, B: 1033B, K: 990C, H: 376C

9048 שָׁמַע *šāmaʿ*, [A] to hear, listen, obey; [C] to be heard; [D] to summon, call together; [G] to proclaim, summon, make hear, S: 8085, B: 1033B, K: 990D, H: 376C

9049 [1]שֶׁמַע *šemaʿ*[1], clash, sound, S: 8085†, B: 1034D, K: 992A, H: 377B

9050 [2]שֶׁמַע *šemaʿ*[2], Shema, S: 8087, B: 1034D, K: 992A, H: 377B

9051 שֵׁמַע *šēmaʿ*, what is heard, report, news, rumor, S: 8088, B: 1034D, K: 992A, H: 377B

9052 שָׁמָע *šāmāʿ*, Shama, S: 8091, B: 1035A, K: 992B, H: 377B

9053 שֹׁמַע *šōmaʿ*, report; reputation, S: 8089, B: 135A, K: 992B, H: 377B

9054 שְׁמַע *šemaʿ*, Shema, S: 8090, B: 1035A, K: 992B, H: 377B

9055 שִׁמְעָא *šimʿāʾ*, Shimea; Shammua, S: 8092, B: 1035A, K: 992B, H: 377B

9056 שִׁמְעָה *šimʿâ*, Shimeah, S: 8093, B: 1035A, K: 992B, H: 377B

9057 שְׁמָעָה *šemāʿâ*, Shemaah, S: 8094, B: 1035A, K: 992B, H: 377B

9058 שִׁמְעוֹן *šimʿôn*, Simeon, Simeonite, S: 8095, B: 1035B, K: 992B, H: 377B

9059 [1]שִׁמְעִי *šimʿî*[1], Shimei, S: 8096, B: 1035C, K: 992C, H: 377B

9060 [2]שִׁמְעִי *šimʿî*[2], Shimeites, of Shimei, S: 8097, B: 1035C, K: 992D, H: 377C

9061 שְׁמַעְיָה *šemaʿyâ*, Shemaiah, S: 8098, B: 1035C, K: 992D, H: 377C

9062 שְׁמַעְיָהוּ *šemaʿyāhû*, Shemaiah, S: 8098, B: 1035C, K: 992D, H: 377C

9063 שִׁמְעֹנִי *šimʿōnî*, Simeonite, of Simeon, S: 8099, B: 1035C, K: 993A, H: 377C

9064 שִׁמְעָת *šimʿāt*, Shimeath, S: 8100†, B: 1035A, K: 993A, H: 377C

9065 שִׁמְעָתִי *šimʿātî*, Shimeathite, S: 8101, B: 1035A, K: 993A, H: 377C

9066 שֶׁמֶץ *šēmeṣ*, whisper, S: 8102†, B: 1036B, K: 993A, H: 377C

9067 שִׁמְצָה *šimṣâ*, laughingstock, derision, S: 8103, B: 1036B, K: 993A, H: 377C

9068 שָׁמַר *šāmar*, [A] to keep, watch, observe, guard; [B] to be set aside, be secured; [C] to be careful, beware; [D] to cling to; [F] to keep oneself; to observe for oneself, S: 8104, B: 1036B, K: 993A, H: 377C

9069 [1]שֶׁמֶר *šemer*[1], dregs (of wine); aged wine, S: 8105, B: 1038D, K: 994B, H: 378A

9070 [2]שֶׁמֶר *šemer*[2], Shemer, S: 8106, B: 1037C, K: 994C, H: 378A

9071 שֹׁמֵר *šōmēr*, Shomer, S: 7763, B: 1037C, K: 994C, H: 378A

9072 שָׁמְרָה *šomrâ*, guard, watch, S: 8108, B: 1037C, K: 994C, H: 378A

9073 שְׁמֻרָה *šemurâ*, eye-lid, S: 8109, B: 1037D, K: 994C, H: 378A

9074 [1]שִׁמְרוֹן *šimrôn*[1], Shimron, S: 8110, B: 1038A, K: 994C, H: 378A

9075 [2]שִׁמְרוֹן *šimrôn*[2], Shimron, S: 8110, B: 1038A, K: 994C, H: 378A

9076 שֹׁמְרוֹן *šōmerôn*, Samaria, S: 8111, B: 1037D, K: 994C, H: 378A

9077 שִׁמְרוֹן מְראוֹן *šimrôn merʾôn*, Shimron Meron, S: 8112, B: 1038A, K: 563D, H: 378A

9078 שִׁמְרִי *šimrî*, Shimri, S: 8113, B: 1037C, K: 995A, H: 378A

9079 שְׁמַרְיָה *šemaryâ*, Shemariah, S: 8114, B: 1037D, K: 995A, H: 378B

9080 שְׁמַרְיָהוּ *šemaryāhû*, Shemariah, S: 8114, B: 1037D, K: 995A, H: 378B

9081 שִׁמֻּרִים *šimmurîm*, vigil, night-watch, S: 8107†, B: 1037D, K: 995A, H: 378B

9082 שְׁמִרִימוֹת *šemirîmôt*, variant: Shemirimoth, see 9035, S: 8070†, B: 1029A 2c, K: 988C, H: 378B

9083 שִׁמְרִית *šimrît*, Shimrith, S: 8116, B: 1037D, K: 994C, H: 378A

9084 שִׁמְרֹנִי *šimrōnî*, Shimronite, S: 8117, B: 1038A, K: 995A, H: 378B

9085 שֹׁמְרֹנִי *šōmerōnî*, of Samaria, S: 8118, B: 1038A, K*, H*

9086 שִׁמְרָת *šimrāt*, Shimrath, S: 8119, B: 1037D, K: 995A, H: 378B

9087 שֶׁמֶשׁ *šemeš*, sun, S: 8121, B: 1039A, K: 995A, H: 378B

9088 שִׁמְשׁוֹן *šimšôn*, Samson, S: 8123, B: 1039C, K: 995D, H: 378B

9089 שִׁמְשַׁי *šimšay*, variant: Shimshai, see 10729, S: 8124†, B: 1039C & 1116C, K: 995D, H: 378B

9090 שִׁמְשִׁי *šimšî*, variant: see 1128, S: 1030†, B*, K*, H*

9091 שַׁמְשְׁרַי *šamšeray*, Shamsherai, S: 8125, B: 1039C, K: 995D, H: 378B

9092 שֻׁמָתִי *šumātî*, Shumathite, S: 8126, B: 1029C, K: 995D, H: 378B

9093 שַׁן *šan*, variant: Shan, S: 1052†, B: 112D, K: 995D, H: 378B

9094 [1]שֵׁן *šēn*[1], tooth; (rocky) crag; ivory, S: 8127, B: 1042A, K: 995D, H: 378C

9095 [2]שֵׁן *šēn*[2], Shen, S: 8129, B: 1042B, K: 995D, H: 378C

9096 שָׁנֵא *šānāʾ*, [A] to become dull, S: 8132, B: 1039D, K: 996B, H: 378C

9097 שֵׁנָא *šēnāʾ*, sleep, S: 8142, B: 446A, K: 996B, H: 378C

9098 שִׁנְאָב *šinʾāb*, Shinab, S: 8134, B: 1039C, K: 996B, H: 378C

9099 שִׁנְאָן *šinʾān*, high in rank or number, S: 8136, B: 1041D, K: 996C, H: 378C

9100 שֶׁנְאַצַּר *šenʾaṣṣar*, Shenazzar, S: 8137, B: 1039C, K: 996C, H: 378C

9101 [1]שָׁנָה *šānâ*[1], [A] to repeat, do again; [C] to be repeated; [D] to change, alter; to pretend; [E] to be changed; [F] to disguise oneself, S: 8132† & 8138, B: 1039D, K: 996C, H: 378C

9102 [2]שָׁנָה *šānâ*[2], year, S: 8141, B: 1040A, K: 997A, H: 378D

9103 [3]שָׁנָה *šānâ*[3], variant: [A] to repeat, do again; [C] to be repeated, S*, B: 1040D, K: 996C, H: 378C

9104 שֵׁנָה *šēnâ*, sleep, S: 8142, B: 446A, K: 997C, H: 379A

9105 שֶׁנְהַבִּים *šenhabbîm*, ivory, S: 8143, B: 1042B, K: 997D, H: 379A

9106 [1]שָׁנִי *šānî*[1], scarlet, crimson (thread), S: 8144, B: 1040C, K: 997D, H: 379A

9107 [2]שָׁנִי *šānî*[2], variant: full grown, S*, B*, K: 998A, H: 379A

9108 שֵׁנִי *šēnî*, second, S: 8145, B: 1041B, K: 998A, H: 379A

9109 שְׁנַיִם *šenayim*, two, S: 8147, B: 1040D, K: 998B, H: 379A

9110 שְׁנִינָה *šenînâ*, object of ridicule, S: 8148, B: 1042B, K: 998D, H: 379B

9111 [1]שָׁנַן *šānan*[1], [A] to sharpen; [B] be sharpened; [F] to be embittered, S: 8150, B: 1041D, K: 998D, H: 379B

9112 [2]שָׁנַן *šānan*[2], [D] to impress, repeat, S: 8150, B: 1041D, K: 998D, H: 379B

9113 שָׁנַס *šānas*, [D] to tuck up the cloak (into the belt), S: 8151, B: 1042B, K: 999A, H: 379C

9114 שִׁנְעָר *šinʿār*, Shinar; Babylonia, S: 8152, B: 1042B, K: 999A, H: 379C

9115 שָׁסָה *šāsâ*, [A] to raid, loot, plunder; [B] to be looted, S: 8154, B: 1042C, K: 999B, H: 379C

9116 שָׁסַס *šāsas*, [A] to plunder, ransack; [C] to be looted, be ransacked, S: 8155, B: 1042C, K: 999B, H: 379C

9117 שָׁסַע *šāsaʿ*, [A] to divide; [B] be divided; [D] to tear apart, S: 8156, B: 1042D, K: 999C, H: 379C

9118 שֶׁסַע *šesaʿ*, cleft (split hoof), S: 8157, B: 1043A, K: 999D, H: 379C

9119 שָׁסַף *šāsap*, [D] to hack to pieces (for execution), S: 8158, B: 1043A, K: 999D, H: 379D

9120 שָׁעָה *šāʿâ*, [A] to look with favor, have regard for, pay attention to, S: 8159, B: 1043A, K: 999D, H: 379D

9121 שְׁעָטָה *šeʿāṭâ*, galloping, pounding (hooves), S: 8161, B: 1043B, K: 1000A, H: 379D

9122 שַׁעַטְנֵז *šaʿaṭnēz*, woven cloth, S: 8162, B: 1043B, K: 1000A, H: 379D

9123 שֹׁעַל *šōʿal*, handful, hollow of the hand, S: 8168, B: 1043B, K: 1000B, H: 379D

9124 שַׁעַלְבִים *šaʿalbîm*, Shaalbim, S: 8169, B: 1043C, K: 1000B, H: 379D

9125 שַׁעֲלַבִּין *šaʿalabbîn*, Shaalabbin, S: 8169, B: 1043C, K: 1000B, H: 380A

9126 שַׁעַלְבֹנִי *šaʿalbōnî*, Shaalbonite, S: 8170, B: 1043D, K: 1000B, H: 380A

9127 שַׁעֲלִים *šaʿalîm*, Shaalim, S: 8171, B: 1043D, K: 1000B, H: 380A

9128 שָׁעַן *šāʿan*, [C] to lean oneself upon, rely on, S: 8172, B: 1043D, K: 1000C, H: 380A

9129 [1]שָׁעַע *šāʿaʿ*[1], [A] be blinded; [G] to make close the eyes; [F] to blind oneself, S: 8173, B: 1044A, K: 1000D, H: 380A

[F] Hitpael (hitpoel, hitpoal, hitpolel, hitpolal, hitpalel, hitpalal, hitpalpel, hitpalpal, hotpael, hotpaal) [G] Hiphil (hiphtil) [H] Hophal [I] Hishtaphel

9130 ²שָׁעַע *šā'a'²*, [D] to take joy in, delight in; [E] to be dandled; [F] to delight oneself in, S: 8173, B: 1044B, K: 1000D, H: 380A

9131 שַׁעַף *ša'ap*, Shaaph, S: 8174, B: 1044C, K: 1001A, H: 380B

9132 שָׁעַר *šā'ar*, [A] to think, estimate, calculate, S: 8176, B: 1045C, K: 1001A, H: 380B

9133 ¹שַׁעַר *ša'ar¹*, gate, gateway, S: 8179, B: 1044C, K: 1001A, H: 380B

9134 ²שַׁעַר *ša'ar²*, measure (of grain), S: 8180, B: 1045C, K: 1001D, H: 380B

9135 שֹׁעָר *šō'ār*, burst open, i.e., poor quality (figs), S: 8182, B: 1045D, K: 1002A, H: 380B

9136 שַׁעֲרוּר *ša'ᵃrûr*, something horrible, shocking thing, S: 8186†, B: 1045D, K: 1002A, H: 380B

9137 שַׁעֲרוּרִי *ša'ᵃrûrî*, horrible thing, S: 8187†, B: 1045D, K: 1002A, H: 380B

9138 שְׁעַרְיָה *šᵉ'aryâ*, Sheariah, S: 8187†, B: 1045C, K: 1002A, H: 380C

9139 שַׁעֲרַיִם *ša'ᵃrayim*, Shaaraim, S: 8189, B: 1045C, K: 1002A, H: 380C

9140 שַׁעַשְׁגַז *ša'ašgaz*, Shaashgaz, S: 8190, B: 1045D, K: 1002A, H: 380C

9141 שַׁעֲשׁוּעִים *ša'ᵃšû'îm*, delight, S: 8191†, B: 1044B, K: 1002A, H: 380C

9142 שָׁפָה *šāpâ*, [C, E] to be swept bare, S: 8192, B: 1045D, K: 1002B, H: 380C

9143 שְׁפוֹ *šᵉpô*, Shepho, S: 8195, B: 1046A, K: 1002B, H: 380C

9144 שְׁפוֹט *šᵉpôṭ*, judgment, punishment, S: 8196, B: 1048A, K: 1002B, H: 380C

9145 שְׁפוּפָם *šᵉpûpām*, variant: Shephupham, S: 8197, B: 1051B, K: 1002C, H: 380C

9146 שְׁפוּפָן *šᵉpûpān*, Shephuphan, S: 8197, B: 1051B, K: 1002C, H: 380C

9147 שְׁפוֹת *šᵉpôt*, cheese, S: 8194†, B: 1045D, K: 1002C, H: 380C

9148 שִׁפְחָה *šipḥâ*, maidservant, female slave, S: 8198, B: 1046C, K: 1002C, H: 380C

9149 שָׁפַט *šāpaṭ*, [A] to judge, decide; lead, defend, vindicate; [C] to execute judgment, be brought to trial; to argue a matter; [D] (ptcp.) judge, S: 8199, B: 1047A, K: 1002D, H: 380C

9150 שֶׁפֶט *šepeṭ*, judgment, punishment, S: 8201, B: 1048A, K: 1003D, H: 381A

9151 שָׁפָט *šāpāṭ*, Shaphat, S: 8202, B: 1048B, K: 1003D, H: 381A

9152 שְׁפַטְיָה *šᵉpaṭyâ*, Shephatiah, S: 8203, B: 1049B, K: 1004A, H: 381A

9153 שְׁפַטְיָהוּ *šᵉpaṭyāhû*, Shephatiah, S: 8203, B: 1049B, K: 1004A, H: 381A

9154 שִׁפְטָן *šiptān*, Shiphtan, S: 8204, B: 1049B, K: 1004A, H: 381A

9155 ¹שְׁפִי *šᵉpî¹*, barren height, S: 8205, B: 1046D, K: 1004A, H: 381A

9156 ²שְׁפִי *šᵉpî²*, variant: Shephi, see 9143, S: 8195†, B: 1046A, K: 1004A, H: 381A

9157 ¹שֻׁפִּים *šuppîm¹*, Shuppim, S: 206, B: 1051B, K*, H*

9158 ²שֻׁפִּים *šuppîm²*, Shuppites, S: 8206, B: 1051B, K*, H*

9159 שְׁפִיפֹן *šᵉpîpōn*, viper, S: 8207, B: 1051B, K: 1004A, H: 381A

9160 שָׁפִיר *šāpîr*, Shaphir, S: 8208, B: 1051C, K: 1004B, H: 381A

9161 שָׁפַךְ *šāpak*, [A] to pour out, shed, spill; [B, C, E] to be outpoured, be shed; [F] be scattered, ebb away, S: 8210, B: 1049B, K: 1004B, H: 381A

9162 שֶׁפֶךְ *šepek*, dump (for throwing out ash refuse), S: 8211, B: 1050A, K: 1004D, H: 381B

9163 שָׁפְכָה *šopkâ*, male organ (fluid duct), S: 8212, B: 1050A, K: 1004D, H: 381B

9164 ¹שָׁפֵל *šāpēl¹*, [A] to be humbled, be brought low; [G] to humble, bring low, S: 8213, B: 1050A, K: 1004D, H: 381C

9165 שֵׁפֶל *šēpel*, low estate, humble condition, S: 8216†, B: 1050C, K: 1005A, H: 381C

9166 שָׁפָל *šāpāl*, low, deep, S: 8217, B: 1050C, K: 1005A, H: 381C

9167 ²שָׁפֵל *šāpēl²*, variant: low, S*, B: 1050A, K: 1005B, H: 381D

9168 שִׁפְלָה *šiplâ*, state of lowness, condition of humiliation, S: 8218, B: 1050C, K: 1005B, H: 381D

9169 שְׁפֵלָה *šᵉpēlâ*, foothill, S: 8219, B: 1050C, K: 1005C, H: 381D

9170 שִׁפְלוּת *šiplût*, idleness, inactivity, S: 8220, B: 1050D, K: 1005C, H: 381D

9171 שָׁפָם *šāpām*, Shapham, S: 8223, B: 1050D, K: 1005C, H: 381D

9172 שְׁפָם *šᵉpām*, Shepham, S: 8221, B: 1050D, K: 1005C, H: 381D

9173 שֻׁפָּם *šuppim*, variant: Shuppites, see 9158, S: 8309†, B: 1051B 1, K: 1005C, H: 381D

9174 שִׁפְמוֹת *šipᵃmôt*, variant: Shiphamot, see 8560, S*, B: 1050D, K: 928C, H: 354B

9175 שִׁפְמִי *šipmî*, Shiphmite, S: 8225, B: 1050D, K: 1005D, H: 381D

9176 ¹שָׁפָן *šāpān¹*, coney, S: 8227, B: 1050D, K: 1005D, H: 381D

9177 ²שָׁפָן *šāpān²*, Shaphan, S: 8227, B: 1051A, K: 1005D, H: 381D

9178 שָׁפַע *šāpa'*, variant: [A] to flow abundantly, S*, B: 798D, K: 1005D, H: 381D

9179 שֶׁפַע *šepa'*, abundance, S: 8228, B: 1051A, K: 1006A, H: 381D

9180 שִׁפְעָה *šip'â*, (of water) flood; mass (of humans or animals), S: 8229, B: 1051A, K: 1006A, H: 381D

9181 שִׁפְעִי *šip'î*, Shiphi, S: 8230, B: 1051B, K: 1006A, H: 382A

9182 שָׁפַר *šāpar*, [A] to be delightful, pleasing, S: 8231, B: 1051C, K: 1006A, H: 382A

9183 ¹שֶׁפֶר *šeper¹*, beauty, loveliness, S: 8233, B: 1051C, K: 1006B, H: 382A

9184 ²שֶׁפֶר *šeper²*, Shepher, S: 8234, B: 1051C, K: 1006B, H: 382A

9185 ¹שִׁפְרָה *šiprâ¹*, fairness, clearness (of skies), S: 8235, B: 1051C, K: 1006B, H: 382A

9186 ²שִׁפְרָה *šiprâ²*, Shiphrah, S: 8236, B: 1051C, K: 1006B, H: 382A

9187 שַׁפְרוּר *šaprûr*, variant: see 9188, S: 8237, B: 1051D, K: 1006B, H: 382A

9188 שַׁפְרִיר *šaprîr*, royal canopy, pavilion, S: 8237†, B: 1051D, K: 1006B, H: 382A

9189 שָׁפַת *šāpat*, [A] to place, put, S: 8239, B: 1046A, K: 1006C, H: 382A

9190 ¹שְׁפַתַּיִם *šᵉpattayim¹*, fireplaces, S: 8240†, B: 1046B, K: 1006C, H: 382A

9191 ²שְׁפַתַּיִם *šᵉpattayim²*, double-pronged hooks, S: 8240†, B: 1052A, K: 1006C, H: 382A

9192 שֶׁצֶף *šeṣep*, surging, flooding (of anger), S: 8241, B: 1009B, K: 1006D, H: 382A

9193 ¹שָׁקַד *šāqad¹*, [A] to be awake, watch, stand guard, S: 8245, B: 1052A, K: 1006D, H: 382A

9194 ²שָׁקַד *šāqad²*, variant: [A] to be emaciated, S: 8245, B: 1052A, K: 1006D, H: 382B

9195 ³שָׁקַד *šāqad³*, variant: [D] to be shaped like an almond blossom, S: 8245, B: 1052B, K: 580C, H*

9196 שָׁקֵד *šāqēd*, almond tree, almond nuts, S: 8247, B: 1052B, K: 1007A, H: 382B

9197 שָׁקָה *šāqâ*, [C] to be given a drink; [E] to be moistened; [G] to give a drink to, S: 8248, B: 1052B, K: 1007A, H: 382B

9198 שִׁקּוּי *šiqqûy*, drink; nourishing drink, S: 8249† & 8250, B: 1052C, K: 1007C, H: 382C

9199 שִׁקּוּץ *šiqqûṣ*, detestable thing, vileness, abomination, S: 8251, B: 1055A, K: 1007C, H: 382C

9200 שָׁקַט *šāqaṭ*, [A] to be at rest, be at peace; [G] to keep silent, remain quiet, remain calm, S: 8252, B: 1052D, K: 1007D, H: 382C

9201 שֶׁקֶט *šeqeṭ*, quietness, S: 8253, B: 1053B, K: 1008A, H: 382D

9202 שָׁקַל *šāqal*, [A] to weigh out, make payment; [C] to be weighed, S: 8254, B: 1053B, K: 1008A, H: 382D

9203 שֶׁקֶל *šeqel*, shekel (a unit of weight), S: 8255, B: 1053C, K: 1008C, H: 382D

9204 שִׁקְמָה *šiqmâ*, sycamore-fig tree, S: 8256, B: 1054A, K: 1008D, H: 383A

9205 שָׁקַע *šāqa'*, [A] to sink down; [C] to sink; [G] to make sink down, make settle, S: 8257, B: 1054B, K: 1008D, H: 383A

9206 שְׁקַעֲרוּרָה *šᵉqa'ᵃrûrâ*, depression, hollow, S: 8258, B: 891A, K: 1009A, H: 383A

9207 שָׁקַף *šāqap*, [C] to look down on, overlook; [G] to look down on, S: 8259, B: 1054C, K: 1009A, H: 383A

9208 שֶׁקֶף *šāqep*, frame work (of a door), S: 8260†, B: 1054D, K: 1009B, H: 383B

9209 שְׁקֻפִים *šᵉqupîm*, clerestory window (a high place window), S: 8261†, B: 1054D, K: 1009B, H: 383B

9210 שָׁקַץ *šāqaṣ*, [D] to detest, abhor, defile, S: 8262, B: 1055A, K: 1009C, H: 383B

9211 שֶׁקֶץ *šeqeṣ*, detestable thing, S: 8263, B: 1054D, K: 1009C, H: 383B

9212 שָׁקַק *šāqaq*, [A] to rush forth, charge forth; [F] to rush back and forth, S: 8264, B: 1055B, K: 1009C, H: 383B

9213 שָׁקַר *šāqar*, [A] to deal falsely with; [D] to deceive, lie, betray, S: 8266, B: 1055D, K: 1009D, H: 383C

9214 שֶׁקֶר *šeqer*, lie, falseness, deception; vanity, S: 8267, B: 1055B, K: 1009D, H: 383C

9215 שַׁקָּר *šaqqār*, variant: liar, slanderer, S*, B: 1055B, K: 1010C, H: 383D

9216 שֹׁקֶת *šōqet*, watering-trough, S: 8268, B: 1052D, K: 1010C, H: 383D

9217 [1]שֵׁר *šēr*[1], bracelet, S: 8285†, B: 1057B, K: 1010C, H: 383D

9218 [2]שֵׁר *šēr*[2], variant: see 9219, S: 8270†, B: 1057A, K: 1010C, H: 383D

9219 שֹׁר *šōr*, navel; umbilical cord, S: 8270, B: 1057A, K: 1010C, H: 383D

9220 שָׁרָב *šārāb*, parching heat; burning hot sand, S: 8273, B: 1055D, K: 1010D, H: 383D

9221 שֵׁרֵבְיָה *šērēbyâ*, Sherebiah, S: 8274, B: 1055D, K: 1010D, H: 383D

9222 שַׁרְבִיט *šarbîṭ*, scepter, staff, S: 8275, B: 987B, K: 1010D, H: 383D

9223 [1]שָׁרָה *šārâ*[1], [A] to unleash; to deliver, set free, S: 3474† & 8281†, B: 1056A, K: 1010D, H: 383D

9224 [2]שָׁרָה *šārâ*[2], vineyard, S: 8284 & 8281†, B: 1004B, K: 1011A, H: 383D

9225 שֵׁרָה *šērâ*, variant: bracelet, S: 8285, B: 1057B, K: 1011A, H: 383D

9226 שָׁרוּחֶן *šārûḥen*, Sharuhen, S: 8287, B: 1056B, K: 1011A, H: 383D

9227 שָׁרוֹן *šārôn*, Sharon, S: 8289, B: 450A, K: 1011A, H: 384A

9228 שָׁרוֹנִי *šārônî*, Sharonite, S: 8290, B: 1124B, K: 1011B, H: 384A

9229 שְׁרוּקָה *šᵉrûqâ*, variant: scorn, see 9241, S: 8292, B: 1057C, K: 1011B, H: 384A

9230 שֵׁרוּת *šērût*, variant: see 9223, S: 8293, B*, K*, H*

9231 שִׁרְטַי *širṭay*, variant: Shirtai, see 8855, S: 7861†, B: 1009C, K: 1011B, H: 384A

9232 שָׁרַי *šāray*, Sharai, S: 8298, B: 1056C, K: 1011B, H: 384A

9233 שִׁרְיָה *širyâ*, javelin, S: 8302, B: 1056B, K: 1011B, H: 384A

9234 שִׁרְיוֹן *širyôn*, coat of scale armor, S: 8302, B: 1056D, K: 1011B, H: 384A

9235 שָׁרִיר *šārîr*, muscle, S: 8306, B: 1057B, K: 1011B, H: 384A

9236 שְׁרֵמוֹת *šᵉrēmôt*, variant: see 8727, S: 8309†, B: 995B, K: 1011C, H: 384A

9237 שָׁרַץ *šāraṣ*, [A] to teem, swarm, move about, S: 8317, B: 1056C, K: 1011C, H: 384A

9238 שֶׁרֶץ *šereṣ*, creatures that teem, swarm, move about, S: 8318, B: 1056D, K: 1011C, H: 384A

9239 שָׁרַק *šāraq*, [A] to whistle, hiss, scoff, S: 8319, B: 1056D, K: 1011D, H: 384A

9240 שְׁרֵקָה *šᵉrēqâ*, scorn, derision, S: 8322, B: 1056D, K: 1011D, H: 384B

9241 שְׁרִקָה *šᵉriqâ*, whistling; scorn, S: 8292†, B: 1057A, K: 1011D, H: 384B

9242 שָׁרַר *šārar*, variant: [A] to be firm, hard, S: 8325, B: 1057, K: 1012A, H*

9243 שָׁרָר *šārār*, Sharar, S: 8325†, B: 1057B, K: 1012A, H: 384B

9244 שְׁרִירוּת *šᵉrirût*, stubbornness, S: 8307, B: 1057B, K: 1012A, H: 384B

9245 שָׁרַשׁ *šāraš*, [D] to uproot; to take root; [E] to be uprooted; [G] to take root, S: 8327, B: 1057D, K: 1012A, H: 384B

9246 שֶׁרֶשׁ *šereš*, Sheresh, S: 8329, B: 1058A, K: 1012B, H: 384B

9247 שֹׁרֶשׁ *šōreš*, root, S: 8326 & 8328†, B: 1057C, K: 1012B, H: 384B

9248 שַׁרְשָׁה *šaršâ*, variant: chain, see 9249, S: 8333†, B: 1057B, K: 1012C, H: 384C

9249 שַׁרְשְׁרָה *šaršᵉrâ*, chain, S: 8333, B: 1057B, K: 1012C, H: 384C

9250 שָׁרַת *šārat*, [D] to minister, serve, attend, S: 8334, B: 1058A, K: 1012D, H: 384C

9251 שָׁרֵת *šārēt*, cultic service, S: 8335, B: 1058B, K: 1013B, H: 384C

9252 [1]שֵׁשׁ *šēš*[1], six; (pl.) sixty, S: 8337, B: 995C, K: 1013B, H: 384C

9253 [2]שֵׁשׁ *šēš*[2], alabaster, S: 8336, B: 1010D, K: 1013C, H: 384D

9254 [3]שֵׁשׁ *šēš*[3], fine linen, S: 8336, B: 1058C, K: 1013C, H: 384D

9255 שָׁשָׁא *šāšā'*, [D] to lead along, S: 8338, B: 1058C, K: 1013D, H: 384D

9256 שֵׁשְׁבַּצַּר *šēšbaṣṣar*, Sheshbazzar, S: 8339, B: 1058C, K: 1013D, H: 384D

9257 שָׁשָׁה *šāšâ*, [D] to give a sixth part, S: 8341, B: 995D, K: 1013D, H: 384D

9258 שָׁשַׁי *šāšay*, Shashai, S: 8343, B: 1058D, K: 1013D, H: 384D

9259 שֵׁשַׁי *šēšay*, Sheshai, S: 8344, B: 1058D, K: 1013D, H: 384D

9260 שֵׁשִׁי *šēšî*, variant: linen, see 9254, S*, B: 1058C, K: 1013D, H: 384D

9261 שִׁשִּׁי *šiššî*, sixth, S: 8345, B: 995D, K: 1013D, H: 384C

9262 שִׁשִּׁים *šiššîm*, variant: sixty, S: 8346, B: 995D, K: 1013B, H: 384C

9263 שֵׁשַׁךְ *šēšak*, Sheshach, S: 8347, B: 1058D, K: 1014A, H: 384D

9264 שֵׁשָׁן *šēšān*, Sheshan, S: 8348, B: 1058D, K: 1014A, H: 384D

9265 שָׁשָׁק *šāšāq*, Shashak, S: 8349†, B: 1059A, K: 1014A, H: 384D

9266 שָׁשַׁר *šāšar*, red color, S: 8350, B: 1059A, K: 1014A, H: 385A

9267 שָׁת *šāt*, variant: foundation, see 9268, S*, B*, K*, H*

9268 [1]שֵׁת *šēt*[1], foundation; buttocks, S: 8351 & 8352† & 8357†, B: 1059D, K: 1014B, H: 385A

9269 [2]שֵׁת *šēt*[2], Seth, S: 8352, B: 1011C, K: 1014B, H: 385A

9270 [3]שֵׁת *šēt*[3], variant: defiance, S*, B: 1011D, K: 1014B, H: 385A

9271 [1]שָׁתָה *šātâ*[1], worker in weaving, S: 8356, B: 1011D, K: 1014B, H: 385A

9272 [2]שָׁתָה *šātâ*[2], [A] to drink, be drunk; [C] to be drunken, S: 8354, B: 1059A, K: 1014C, H: 385A

9273 שָׁתוֹת *šātôt*, variant: see 9268 & 9272, S*, B: 1011D, K: 1014D, H: 385C

9274 [1]שְׁתִי *šᵉtî*[1], woven material, S: 8359, B: 1059D, K: 1014D, H: 385A

9275 [2]שְׁתִי *šᵉtî*[2], drunkenness, drinking, S: 8358, B: 1059C, K: 1015A, H: 385C

9276 שְׁתִיָּה *šᵉtiyyâ*, (manner of) drinking, S: 8360, B: 1059C, K: 1015A, H: 385C

9277 שָׁתִיל *šātîl*, slip, cutting (of a plant), S: 8363†, B: 1060A, K: 1015A, H: 385C

9278 שָׁתַל *šātal*, [A] to plant; [B] to be planted, S: 8362, B: 1060A, K: 1015A, H: 385C

9279 שֻׁתַלְחִי *šutalḥî*, Shuthelahite, S: 8364, B: 1004D, K: 1015C, H: 385C

9280 שָׁתַם *šātam*, [B] to be opened, S: 8365, B: 1060C, K: 1015C, H: 385C

9281 שְׁתֻם *šᵉtum*, variant: see 9280, S: 8365†, B: 1060C, K: 1015C, H: 385C

9282 שָׁתַן *šātan*, variant: [G] to urinate, S: 8366, B: 1010B, K: 1015C, H: 385C

9283 שָׁתַע *šāta'*, [A] to be dismayed, S*, B: 1043A, K: 999D, H: 385C

9284 שָׁתַק *šātaq*, [A] to become calm, die down, S: 8367, B: 1060C, K: 1015C, H: 385C

9285 שֵׁתָר *šētār*, Shethar, S: 8369, B: 1060C, K: 1015C, H: 385C

9286 שָׁתַת *šātat*, [A] to be destined, appoint, lay claim, S: 8371, B: 1060C, K: 1015C, H: 385C

9287 ת *t*, letter of the Hebrew alphabet, S*, B: 1060B, K: 1015B, H*

9288 תָּא *tā'*, alcove for guards, guardroom, S: 8372, B: 1060B, K: 1015B, H: 385B

9289 [1]תָּאַב *tā'ab*[1], [A] to long for, desire, S: 8373, B: 1060B, K: 1015D, H: 385B

9290 [2]תָּאַב *tā'ab*[2], [D] to abhor, loathe, S: 8374, B: 1060D, K: 1015D, H: 385B

9291 תַּאֲבָה *ta'ᵃbâ*, longing, desiring, S: 8375, B: 1060B, K: 1015D, H: 385B

9292 תָּאָה *tā'â*, [D] to draw a line, mark out (territory), S: 8376, B: 1060D, K: 1016A, H: 385B

9293 תְּאוֹ *tᵉ'ô*, antelope, S: 8377, B: 1060D, K: 1016A, H: 385B

9294 [1]תַּאֲוָה *ta'ᵃwâ*[1], longing, desire, craving, S: 8378, B: 16C, K: 1016A, H: 385D

9295 [2]תַּאֲוָה *ta'ᵃwâ*[2], variant: boundary, S: 8379, B: 1063B, K: 1016A, H: 385D

9296 תְּאוֹמִים *tᵉ'ômîm*, variant: twins, see 9339, S: 8380†, B: 1060D, K: 1016B, H: 385D

9297 תַּאֲלָה *ta'ᵃlâ*, curse, S: 8381, B: 46D, K: 1016B, H: 385D

9298 תָּאַם *tā'am*, [G] to have twins, S: 8382, B: 1060D, K: 1016B, H: 385D

9299 תַּאֲנָה *ta'ᵃnâ*, (time of) heat, rut, S: 8385, B: 58C, K: 1016B, H: 385D

9300 תְּאֵנָה *tᵉ'ēnâ*, fig; fig tree, S: 8384, B: 1061A, K: 1016B, H: 386A

9301 תֹּאֲנָה *tō'ᵃnâ*, occasion, opportunity, S: 8385, B: 58C, K: 1016C, H: 386A

9302 תַּאֲנִיָּה *ta'ᵃniyyâ*, mourning, S: 8386, B: 58B, K: 1016C, H: 386A

9303 תְּאֻנִים *tᵉ'unîm*, efforts, toil, S: 8383, B: 20B, K: 1016C, H: 386A

9304 תַּאֲנַת שִׁלֹה *ta'ᵃnat šilōh*, Taanath Shiloh, S: 8387, B: 1061B, K: 1016C, H: 386A

9305 תָּאַר¹ *tā'ar*[1], [A] to turn toward; [E] to be turned toward, S: 8388, B: 1061B, K: 1016C, H: 386A

9306 תָּאַר² *tā'ar*[2], [D] to mark out a form, make an outline, S: 8388, B: 1061C, K: 1016C, H: 386A

9307 תֹּאַר *tō'ar*, form, shape; beauty, fine-looking person, S: 8389, B: 1061B, K: 1016D, H: 386A

9308 תַּאְרֵעַ *ta'rēa'*, Tarea, S: 8390, B: 357C, K: 1016D, H: 386A

9309 תְּאַשּׁוּר *t^{e}'aššûr*, cypress tree, cypress wood, S: 8391 & 839†, B: 81B, K: 1017A, H: 386A

9310 תֵּבָה *tēbâ*, ark, basket, S: 8392, B: 1061C, K: 1017A, H: 386A

9311 תְּבוּאָה *t^{e}bû'â*, harvest, crops, produce, S: 8393, B: 100A, K: 1017B, H: 386B

9312 תְּבוּנָה *t^{e}bûnâ*, understanding, insight; ability, skill, wisdom, S: 8394, B: 108A, K: 1017C, H: 386B

9313 תְּבוּסָה *t^{e}bûsâ*, downfall, ruin, S: 8395, B: 101B, K: 1017D, H: 386B

9314 תָּבוֹר *tābôr*, Tabor, S: 8396, B: 1061D, K: 1017D, H: 386B

9315 תֵּבֵל *tēbēl*, world, earth, S: 8398, B: 385C, K: 1017D, H: 386B

9316 תֶּבֶל *tebel*, perversion, abominable confusion, S: 8397, B: 117D, K: 1018A, H: 386C

9317 תֻּבַל *tubal*, Tubal, S: 8422, B: 1063A, K: 1018A, H: 386C

9318 תַּבְלִית *tablît*, destruction, S: 8399, B: 115B, K: 1018B, H: 386C

9319 תְּבַלֻּל *t^{e}ballul*, defect (obscuring vision), S: 8400, B: 117D, K: 1018B, H: 386C

9320 תֶּבֶן *teben*, straw, S: 8401, B: 1061D, K: 1018B, H: 386C

9321 תִּבְנִי *tibnî*, Tibni, S: 8402, B: 1062A, K: 1018C, H: 386C

9322 תַּבְנִית *tabnît*, image, form, shape, S: 8403, B: 125D, K: 1018C, H: 386C

9323 תַּבְעֵרָה *tab'ērâ*, Taberah, S: 8404, B: 129C, K: 1018C, H: 386C

9324 תֵּבֵץ *tēbēṣ*, Thebez, S: 8405, B: 1062A, K: 1018C, H: 386C

9325 תִּגְלַת פִּלְאֶסֶר *tiglat pil'eser*, Tiglath-Pileser, S: 8407, B: 1062A, K: 1018D, H: 386D

9326 תַּגְמוּל *tagmûl*, benefit, gracious act, S: 8408, B: 168C, K: 1018D, H: 386D

9327 תִּגְרָה *tigrâ*, agitation, blow, S: 8409, B: 173D, K: 1018D, H: 386D

9328 תֹּגַרְמָה *tōgarmâ*, Togarmah, S: 8425, B: 1062B, K: 1018D, H: 386D

9329 תִּדְהָר *tidhār*, fir tree, S: 8410, B: 187B, K: 1019A, H: 386D

9330 תַּדְמֹר *tadmōr*, Tadmor, S: 8412, B: 1062B, K: 1019A, H: 386D

9331 תִּדְעָל *tid'āl*, Tidal, S: 8413, B: 1062B, K: 1019A, H: 386D

9332 תֹּהוּ *tōhû*, formless, waste, empty; (of speech) useless, confused, vain, S: 8414, B: 1062C, K: 1019B, H: 386D

9333 תְּהוֹם *t^{e}hôm*, the deep, depths, S: 8415, B: 1062D, K: 1019B, H: 386D

9334 תָּהֳלָה *toh^{o}lâ*, error, S: 8417, B: 1062D, K: 1019C, H: 387A

9335 תְּהִלָּה *t^{e}hillâ*, praise, renown, glory, S: 8416, B: 239D, K: 1019D, H: 387A

9336 תַּהֲלוּכָה *tah^{a}lûkâ*, variant: procession, S: 8418, B: 237C, K: 1020A, H: 387A

9337 תַּהְפֻּכוֹת *tahpukôt*, perversity, confusing things, S: 8419†, B: 246C, K: 1020A, H*

9338 תָּו *tāw*, mark (on the forehead); signing (a document), S: 8420, B: 1063B, K: 1020B, H: 387A

9339 תּוֹאֲמִים *tô'^{a}mîm*, twins, (something) double, S: 8380†, B: 1060D, K: 1020B, H: 387A

9340 תּוּבַל קַיִן *tûbal qayin*, Tubal-Cain, S: 8423, B: 1063B, K: 1020C, H: 387B

9341 תּוּבְנָה *tûbnâ*, variant: see 9312, S: 8394†, B: 108B, K: 1020C, H: 387B

9342 תּוּגָה *tûgâ*, grief, sorrow, S: 8424, B: 387B, K: 1020C, H: 387B

9343 תּוֹדָה *tôdâ*, thank offering; thanksgiving, confession of thankfulness; song of thanksgiving, S: 8426, B: 392D, K: 1020C, H: 387B

9344 תָּוָה¹ *tāwâ*[1], [D] to put a mark, place a sign, S: 8427, B: 1063B, K: 1020D, H: 387B

9345 תָּוָה² *tāwâ*[2], [G] to vex, bring pain, S: 8428, B: 1063B, K: 1020D, H: 387B

9346 תּוֹחַ *tôaḥ*, Toah, S: 8430, B: 1063C, K: 1020D, H: 387B

9347 תּוֹחֶלֶת *tôḥelet*, hope, expectation, S: 8431, B: 404B, K: 1020D, H: 387C

9348 תָּוֶךְ *tāwek*, middle, midst, center, among, within, S: 8432, B: 1063C, K: 1021A, H: 387C

9349 תּוֹכֵחָה *tôkēḥâ*, rebuke, punishment, correction, S: 8433, B: 407B, K: 1021B, H: 387D

9350 תּוֹכַחַת *tôkaḥat*, correction, rebuke, punishment, S: 8433, B: 407B, K: 1021B, H: 387D

9351 תּוֹלָד *tôlād*, Tolad, S: 8434, B: 410A, K: 1021C, H: 387D

9352 תּוֹלֵדוֹת *tôlēdôt*, account, record, genealogy, family line, S: 8435†, B: 410A, K: 1021C, H: 387D

9353 תּוֹלוֹן *tôlôn*, variant: Tolon, see 9400, S: 8436†, B: 1066C, K: 1027B, H: 389D

9354 תּוֹלָל *tôlāl*, tormentor, oppressor, S: 8437, B: 1064A, K: 1021D, H: 387D

9355 תּוֹלָעִ¹ *tôlā'*[1], (deep) red, purple, S: 8438, B: 1068D, K: 1021D, H: 387D

9356 תּוֹלָע² *tôlā'*[2], Tola, S: 8439, B: 1069A, K: 1021D, H: 388A

9357 תּוֹלֵעָה *tôlē'â*, scarlet yarn, scarlet yarn; worm, maggot, S: 8438, B: 1069A, K: 1021D, H: 388A

9358 תּוֹלָעִי *tôlā'î*, Tolaite, S: 8440, B: 1069A, K: 1022A, H: 388A

9359 תּוֹעֵבָה *tô'ēbâ*, detestable thing, loathsome thing, abomination, S: 8441, B: 1072D, K: 1022B, H: 388A

9360 תּוֹעָה *tô'â*, trouble, error, S: 8442, B: 1073C, K: 1022D, H: 388B

9361 תּוֹעָפוֹת *tô'āpôt*, best, the choice; strength, S: 8443†, B: 419B, K: 1022D, H: 388B

9362 תּוֹצָאוֹת *tôṣā'ôt*, end, limit, starting point, S: 8444†, B: 426A, K: 1022D, H: 388B

9363 תָּוְקְהַת *towq^{e}hat*, variant: Tokehath, see 9534, S: 8445†, B: 876B 1, K: 1023A, H: 388B

9364 תּוֹקְעִים *tôq^{e}'îm*, striking of hands in pledge, S: 8628†, B: 1075C 3, K: 1023A, H: 388B

9365 תּוּר *tûr*, [A] to explore, investigate, search out; [G] to send out to spy, S: 8446, B: 1064B, K: 1023A, H: 388B

9366 תּוֹר¹ *tôr*[1], turning; earring, S: 8447 & 8448, B: 1064C, K: 1023B, H: 388C

9367 תּוֹר² *tôr*[2], dove, S: 8449, B: 1076A, K: 1023C, H: 388C

9368 תּוֹרָה *tôrâ*, law, regulation, teaching, instruction, S: 8451 & 8452†, B: 435D, K: 1023C, H: 388C

9369 תּוֹשָׁב *tôšāb*, temporary resident, stranger, alien, S: 8453, B: 444C, K: 1024D, H: 388C

9370 תּוּשִׁיָּה *tûšiyyâ*, success, victory; sound judgment, wisdom, S: 8454, B: 444D, K: 1024D, H: 388D

9371 תּוֹתָח *tôtāḥ*, (stout) club, S: 8455, B: 450C, K: 1025A, H: 388D

9372 תָּזַז *tāzaz*, [G] to cut down, S: 8456, B: 1064D, K: 1025A, H: 388D

9373 תַּזְנוּת *taznût*, promiscuity, prostitution, act of lust, S: 8457, B: 276B, K: 1025A, H: 388D

9374 תַּחְבֻּלוֹת *taḥbulôt*, guidance, advice, giving direction, S: 8458†, B: 287B, K: 1025A, H: 388D

9375 תֹּחוּ *tōḥû*, Tohu, S: 8459, B: 1063C, K: 1025B, H: 388D

9376 תַּחְכְּמֹנִי *taḥk^{e}mōnî*, Tahkemonite, S: 8461, B: 315D, K: 1025B, H: 388D

9377 תַּחֲלֻאִים *tah^{a}lu'îm*, diseases, S: 8463†, B: 316A, K: 1025B, H: 388D

9378 תְּחִלָּה *t^{e}ḥillâ*, beginning, at first, S: 8462, B: 321A, K: 1025B, H: 389A

9379 תַּחְמָס *taḥmās*, screech owl, S: 8464, B: 329D, K: 1025C, H: 389A

9380 תַּחַן *taḥan*, Tahan, S: 8465, B: 334C, K: 1025C, H: 389A

9381 תַּחֲנָה *tah^{a}nâ*, encampment, S: 8466, B: 334C, K: 1025D, H: 389A

9382 תְּחִנָּה¹ *t^{e}ḥinnâ*[1], plea, petition, request, supplication, S: 8467, B: 337C, K: 1025C, H: 389A

9383 תְּחִנָּה² *t^{e}ḥinnâ*[2], Tehinnah, S: 8468, B: 337C, K: 1025C, H: 389A

9384 תַּחֲנוּן *tah^{a}nûn*, plea for mercy, petition, supplication, S: 8469, B: 337C, K: 1025D, H: 389A

9385 תַּחֲנִי *tah^{a}nî*, Tahanite, S: 8466† & 8470, B: 334C, K: 1025D, H: 389A

9386 תַּחֲנֹתִי *tah^{a}nōtî*, variant: see 9381, S: 8466†, B: 334C, K: 1025D, H: 389A

9387 תַּחְפַּנְחֵס *taḥpanḥēs*, Tahpanhes, S: 8471, B: 1064D, K: 1025D, H: 389A

9388 תַּחְפְּנֵיס *taḥp^{e}nês*, Tahpenes, S: 8472, B: 1065A, K: 1026A, H: 389B

9389 תַּחְרָא *taḥrā'*, collar, S: 8473, B: 1065A, K: 1026A, H: 389B

9390 תַּחְרֵעַ *taḥrēaʿ*, Tahrea, S: 8475, B: 357C, K: 1026A, H: 389B

9391 [1]תַּחַשׁ *taḥaš*[1], (leather of) a sea cow, S: 8476, B: 1065A, K: 1026A, H: 389B

9392 [2]תַּחַשׁ *taḥaš*[2], Tahash, S: 8477, B: 1065A, K: 1026B, H: 389B

9393 [1]תַּחַת *taḥat*[1], under, in place of, succeeding (on a sequence), S: 8478, B: 1065A, K: 1026B, H: 389B

9394 [2]תַּחַת *taḥat*[2], Tahath, S: 8480, B: 1066C 1., K: 1026D, H: 389C

9395 [3]תַּחַת *taḥat*[3], Tahath, S: 8480, B: 1066C 2., K: 1026D, H: 389C

9396 תַּחְתּוֹן *taḥtôn*, lower, S: 8481, B: 1066B, K: 1027A, H: 389C

9397 תַּחְתִּי *taḥtî*, lower; (as noun) depths, below, S: 8482, B: 1066B, K: 1027A, H: 389C

9398 תַּחְתִּים חָדְשִׁי *taḥtîm ḥodšî*, Tahtim Hodshi, S: 8483, B: 874A, K: 1027B, H: 389D

9399 תִּיכוֹן *tîkôn*, middle, center, S: 8484, B: 1064A, K: 1027B, H: 389D

9400 תִּילוֹן *tîlôn*, Tilon, S: 8436†, B: 1066C, K: 1027B, H: 389D

9401 תֵּימָא *têmāʾ*, Tema, S: 8485, B: 1066D, K: 1027B, H: 389D

9402 [1]תֵּימָן *têmān*[1], south, southward, south wind, S: 8486, B: 412C, K: 1027B, H: 389D

9403 [2]תֵּימָן *têmān*[2], Teman, S: 8487, B: 412D, K: 1027C, H: 389D

9404 תֵּימָנִי *têmānî*, Temanite, S: 8489, B: 412D, K: 1027C, H: 389D

9405 תֵּימְנִי *têm^{e}nî*, Temeni, S: 8488, B: 412D, K: 1027D, H*

9406 תִּימָרָה *tîmārâ*, column (of smoke), S: 8490, B: 1071D, K: 1027D, H: 389D

9407 תִּיצִי *tîṣî*, Tizite, S: 8491, B: 1066D, K: 1027D, H: 389D

9408 תִּירוֹשׁ *tîrôš*, new wine, S: 8492, B: 440D, K: 1027D, H: 389D

9409 תִּירְיָא *tîr^{e}yāʾ*, Tiria, S: 8493, B: 432B & 1066D, K: 1028A, H: 389D

9410 תִּירָס *tîrās*, Tiras, S: 8494, B: 1066D, K: 1028A, H: 389D

9411 תַּיִשׁ *tayiš*, male goat, S: 8495, B: 1066D, K: 1028A, H: 390A

9412 תֹּךְ *tōk*, oppression, threat, S: 8496 & 8501†, B: 1067A, K: 1028A, H: 390A

9413 תָּכָה *tākâ*, [E] to bow down, S: 8497, B: 1067A, K: 1028B, H: 390A

9414 תְּכוּנָה *t^{e}kûnâ*, dwelling; arrangement, supply, S: 8498 & 8499, B: 467D, K: 1028B, H: 390A

9415 תֻּכִּיִּים *tukkiyyîm*, baboons, S: 8500†, B: 1067A, K: 1028B, H: 390A

9416 תִּכְלָה *tiklâ*, perfection, S: 8502, B: 479A, K: 1028C, H: 390A

9417 תַּכְלִית *taklît*, end, limit, boundary, S: 8503, B: 479B, K: 1028C, H: 390A

9418 תְּכֵלֶת *t^{e}kēlet*, blue material, S: 8504, B: 1067A, K: 1028C, H: 390A

9419 תָּכַן *tākan*, [A] to weigh, estimate; [C] to be just, be weighted; [D] to hold firm, mark off, understand; [E] to be determined, S: 8505, B: 1067B, K: 1028D, H: 390A

9420 [1]תֹּכֶן *tōken*[1], full quota, fixed measure; size, measurement, S: 8506, B: 1067C, K: 1029A, H: 390B

9421 [2]תֹּכֶן *tōken*[2], Token, S: 8507, B: 1067C, K: 1029A, H: 390B

9422 תָּכְנִית *toknît*, (perfect) example, design, S: 8508, B: 1067C, K: 1029A, H: 390B

9423 תַּכְרִיךְ *takrîk*, robe, mantle, S: 8509, B: 501B, K: 1029A, H: 390B

9424 תֵּל *tēl*, mound, heap, ruin, S: 8510, B: 1068B, K: 1029A, H: 390B

9425 תֵּל אָבִיב *tēl ʾābîb*, Tel Abib, S: 8512, B: 1068B, K: 1029B, H: 390B 2.a.

9426 תֵּל חַרְשָׁא *tēl ḥaršāʾ*, Tel Harsha, S: 8521, B: 1068B, K: 1029A, H: 390B 2.b.

9427 תֵּל מֶלַח *tēl melaḥ*, Tel Melah, S: 8528, B: 1068B, K: 1029A, H: 390B 2.c.

9428 תָּלָא *tālāʾ*, [A] to hang; [B] to be suspended, be determined, S: 8511, B: 1067D, K: 1029B, H: 390B

9429 תַּלְאֻבוֹת *talʾubôt*, burning heat, S: 8514†, B: 520D, K: 1029B, H: 390C

9430 תְּלָאָה *t^{e}lāʾâ*, hardship, burden, S: 8513, B: 521B, K: 1029C, H: 390C

9431 תְּלַאשָּׂר *t^{e}laʾśśār*, Tel Assar, S: 8515†, B: 1067D, K: 1029C, H: 390C

9432 תִּלְבֹּשֶׁת *tilbōšet*, clothing, what is worn, S: 8516, B: 528D, K: 1029C, H: 390C

9433 תִּלְּגַת פִּלְנְאֶסֶר *till^{e}gat* פִּלְנֶסֶר רֶסְנִלְגִפ תִּלְגַת פִּלְנֶסֶר *till^{e}gat pilneser*, Tiglath-Pileser (Tilgat-Pilneser), S: 8407, B: 1062A, K: 1018D, H: 390C

9434 תָּלָה *tālâ*, [A, D] to hang, suspend; [B, C] to be hung, S: 8518, B: 1067D, K: 1029C, H: 390C

9435 תָּלוּל *tālûl*, lofty, towering, S: 8524†, B: 1068C, K: 1029D, H: 390C

9436 תֶּלַח *telaḥ*, Telah, S: 8520, B: 1068B, K: 1029D, H: 390C

9437 תְּלִי *t^{e}lî*, quiver (case to hold arrows in), S: 8522, B: 1068A, K: 1029D, H: 390D

9438 תָּלַל *tālal*, [G] to make a fool of, deceive, cheat; [H] to be deluded, S: 2048†, B: 1068C, K: 1030A, H: 390D

9439 תֶּלֶם *telem*, furrow, plowed line, S: 8525, B: 1068D, K: 1030A, H: 390D

9440 תַּלְמַי *talmay*, Talmai, S: 8526, B: 1068D, K: 1030B, H: 390D

9441 תַּלְמִיד *talmîd*, student, pupil, S: 8527, B: 541A, K: 1030B, H: 390D

9442 תְּלֻנּוֹת *t^{e}lunnôt*, grumbling, complaint, S: 8519†, B: 534B, K: 1030B, H: 390D

9443 תָּלַע *tālaʿ*, [E] to be clad in scarlet material, S: 8529, B: 1069A, K: 1030B, H: 390D

9444 תַּלְפִּיּוֹת *talpiyyôt*, elegance *or* courses of stones, S: 8530†, B: 1069B, K: 1030B, H: 390D

9445 תְּלַשָּׂר *t^{e}laśśār*, variant: Telassar, see 9431, S: 8515†, B: 1067D, K: 1030C, H: 390D

9446 תַּלְתַּל *taltāl*, wavy, S: 8534†, B: 1068C, K: 1030C, H: 390D

9447 תָּם *tām*, blameless, flawless, perfect, S: 8535, B: 1070D, K: 1030C, H: 390D

9448 תֹּם *tōm*, blamelessness, integrity, innocence, S: 8537, B: 1070D, K: 1030D, H: 391A

9449 תָּמַהּ *tāmah*, [A] to be astonished, be astounded, be stunned; [F] to be stunned in oneself, S: 8539, B: 1069B, K: 1031A, H: 391A

9450 תֻּמָּה *tummâ*, integrity, blamelessness, S: 8538, B: 1070D, K: 1031A, H: 391B

9451 תִּמָּהוֹן *timmāhôn*, confusion, panic, S: 8541, B: 1069B, K: 1031A, H: 391B

9452 תַּמּוּז *tammûz*, Tammuz (pagan god), S: 8542, B: 1069C, K: 1031A, H: 391B

9453 תְּמוֹל *t^{e}môl*, yesterday; (generally) before, in the past, S: 8543, B: 1069D, K: 1031B, H: 391B

9454 תְּמוּנָה *t^{e}mûnâ*, form, image, likeness, S: 8544, B: 568B, K: 1031B, H: 391B

9455 תְּמוּרָה *t^{e}mûrâ*, substitution, transfer, exchange, S: 8545, B: 558C, K: 1031C, H: 391B

9456 תְּמוּתָה *t^{e}mûtâ*, death, S: 8546, B: 560D, K: 1031C, H: 391B

9457 תֶּמַח *temaḥ*, Temah, S: 8547, B: 1069C, K: 1031C, H: 391C

9458 תָּמִיד *tāmîd*, (as adv.) continually, constantly, regularly, daily, S: 8548, B: 556B, K: 1031C, H: 391C

9459 תָּמִים *tāmîm*, without defect, blameless, perfect, S: 8549, B: 1071A, K: 1031D, H: 391C

9460 תֻּמִּים *tummîm*, Thummim, S: 8550, B: 1070D 4, K: 1032A, H: 391C

9461 תָּמַךְ *tāmak*, [A] to take hold of, grasp, hold secure; [C] to be seized, S: 8551, B: 1069C, K: 1032B, H: 391D

9462 תָּמַם *tāmam*, [A] to complete, finish, perfect; [G] to end, stop, complete; [F] to show oneself blameless, S: 8552, B: 1070B, K: 1032B, H: 391D

9463 תִּמְנָה *timnâ*, Timnah, S: 8553, B: 584C, K: 1033A, H: 392A

9464 תִּמְנִי *timnî*, Timnite, S: 8554, B: 584D, K: 1033B, H: 392A

9465 תִּמְנָע *timnaʿ*, Timna, S: 8555, B: 586B, K: 1033B, H: 392A

9466 תִּמְנַת־חֶרֶס *timnat-ḥeres*, Timnath Heres, S: 8556†, B: 584D, K: 1033A 3, H: 392A

9467 תִּמְנַת־סֶרַח *timnat-seraḥ*, Timnath Serah, S: 8556, B: 584D, K: 1033A 3., H: 392A

9468 תֶּמֶס *temes*, melting away, S: 8557, B: 588A, K: 1033B, H: 392A

9469 [1]תָּמָר *tāmār*[1], palm tree, S: 8558, B: 1071C, K: 1033B, H: 392A

9470 [2]תָּמָר *tāmār*[2], Tamar, S: 8559, B: 1071C 1., K: 1033C, H: 392B

9471 [3]תָּמָר *tāmār*[3], Tamar, S: 8559, B: 1071C 2., K: 1033C, H: 392B

9472 [1]תֹּמֶר *tōmer*[1], the Palm (of Deborah: a location), S: 8560, B: 1071C, K: 1033C, H: 392B

9473 [2]תֹּמֶר *tōmer*[2], scarecrow, S: 8560, B: 1071C, K: 1033C, H: 392B

9474 תִּמֹרָה *timōrâ*, palm tree, S: 8561, B: 1071C, K: 1033D, H: 392B

[F] Hitpael (hitpoel, hitpoal, hitpolel, hitpolal, hitpalel, hitpalal, hitpalpel, hitpalpal, hotpael, hotpaal) [G] Hiphil (hiphtil) [H] Hophal [I] Hishtaphel

9475 תַּמְרוּק *tamrûq*, beauty treatment, cosmetics, S: 8562†, B: 600A, K: 1033D, H: 392B

9476 ¹תַּמְרוּרִים *tamrûrîm*[1], bitterness, S: 8563†, B: 601B, K: 1033D, H: 392B

9477 ²תַּמְרוּרִים *tamrûrîm*[2], guidepost, S: 8564†, B: 1071D, K: 1033D, H: 392B

9478 תַּן *tan*, jackal, S: 8565 & 8568†, B: 1072B, K: 1034A, H: 392B

9479 ¹תָּנָה *tānâ*[1], [A, G] to sell oneself as a prostitute, S: 8566, B: 1071D, K: 1034A, H: 392B

9480 ²תָּנָה *tānâ*[2], [D] to commemorate, recount, S: 8567, B: 1072A, K: 1034A, H: 392B

9481 תְּנוּאָה *t^{e}nû'â*, fault, opposition, what one has against another, S: 8569, B: 626B, K: 1034A, H: 392C

9482 תְּנוּבָה *t^{e}nûbâ*, crop, produce, S: 8570, B: 626C, K: 1034B, H: 392C

9483 תְּנוּךְ *t^{e}nûk*, lobe (of the ear), S: 8571, B: 1072A, K: 1034B, H: 392C

9484 תְּנוּמָה *t^{e}nûmâ*, slumber, sleep, S: 8572, B: 630B, K: 1034B, H: 392C

9485 תְּנוּפָה *t^{e}nûpâ*, wave offering, what it waved, S: 8573, B: 632B, K: 1034B, H: 392C

9486 תַּנּוּר *tannûr*, oven, furnace, firepot, S: 8574, B: 1072A, K: 1034C, H: 392C

9487 תַּנְחוּמוֹת *tanḥûmôt*, consolation, S: 8575†, B: 637C, K: 1034D, H: 392D

9488 תַּנְחוּמִים *tanḥûmîm*, consolation, comfort, S: 8575†, B: 637C, K: 1034D, H: 392D

9489 תַּנְחֻמֶת *tanḥumet*, Tanhumeth, S: 8576, B: 637C, K: 1034D, H: 392D

9490 תַּנִּין *tannîn*, monster of the deep; serpent, snake; (as a proper name) Jackal (Well), S: 8577, B: 1072C, K: 1034D, H: 392D

9491 ¹תִּנְשֶׁמֶת *tinšemet*[1], chameleon, S: 8580, B: 675D, K: 1035A, H: 392D

9492 ²תִּנְשֶׁמֶת *tinšemet*[2], white owl, S: 8580, B: 675D, K: 1035A, H: 392D

9493 תָּעַב *tā'ab*, [C] to be repulsive, be vile, be rejected; [D] to detest, abhor, loathe, despise; [G] to behave in a vile manner, S: 8581, B: 1073A, K: 1035A, H: 392D

9494 תָּעָה *tā'â*, [A] to wander, go astray; [C] to deceive oneself; to stagger around (as a drunk); [G] to lead astray, make wander, mislead, S: 8582, B: 1073B, K: 1035B, H: 393A

9495 תֹּעוּ *tō'û*, Tou, S: 8583, B: 1073D, K: 1035D, H: 393B

9496 תְּעוּדָה *t^{e}'ûdâ*, testimony; method of legalizing transactions (sandal transaction), S: 8584, B: 730C, K: 1035D, H: 393B

9497 תֹּעִי *tō'î*, Tou (Toi), S: 8583, B: 1073D, K: 1035D, H: 393B

9498 ¹תְּעָלָה *t^{e}'ālâ*[1], trench, channel, aqueduct, S: 8585, B: 752B, K: 1036A, H: 393B

9499 ²תְּעָלָה *t^{e}'ālâ*[2], healing, S: 8585, B: 752B, K: 1036A, H: 393B

9500 תַּעֲלוּלִים *ta'^{a}lûlîm*, wantonness; harsh treatment, S: 8586†, B: 760C, K: 1036A, H: 393B

9501 תַּעֲלֻם *ta'^{a}lum*, variant: hidden thing, S*, B: 761B, K: 1036A, H: 393B

9502 תַּעֲלֻמָה *ta'^{a}lumâ*, secret; hidden thing, S: 8587, B: 761B, K: 1036A, H: 393B

9503 תַּעֲנוּג *ta'^{a}nûg*, delight, pleasure; living in luxury, S: 8588, B: 772C, K: 1036B, H: 393C

9504 תַּעֲנִית *ta'^{a}nît*, self-abasement, mortification, S: 8589, B: 777A, K: 1036B, H: 393C

9505 תַּעְנָךְ *ta'^{a}nak*, Taanach, S: 8590, B: 1073D, K: 1036B, H: 393C

9506 תָּעַע *tā'a'*, [D] to mock; [F] to scoff at, S: 8591, B: 1073D, K: 1036B, H: 393C

9507 תְּעֻפָה *t^{e}'upâ*, darkness, S: 5774†, B: 734A, K: 1035D, H: 393C

9508 תַּעֲצֻמוֹת *ta'^{a}ṣumôt*, strength, might, S: 8592†, B: 783B, K: 1036C, H: 393C

9509 תַּעַר *ta'ar*, razor, knife, scabbard, S: 8593, B: 789B, K: 1036C, H: 393C

9510 תַּעֲרוּבוֹת *ta'^{a}rûbôt*, hostage, S: 8594†, B: 787A, K: 1036C, H: 393C

9511 תַּעְתֻּעִים *ta'tu'îm*, mockery, S: 8595†, B: 1074A, K: 1036C, H: 393C

9512 ¹תֹּף *tōp*[1], tambourine, timbrel, S: 8596, B: 1074B, K: 1036C, H: 393C

9513 ²תֹּף *tōp*[2], setting, jewelry, S: 8596, B: 1074B, K: 1036C, H: 393C

9514 תִּפְאֶרֶת *tip'eret*, glory, splendor, honor, S: 8597, B: 802C, K: 1036D, H: 393D

9515 ¹תַּפּוּחַ *tappûaḥ*[1], apple, apple tree, S: 8598, B: 656B, K: 1037A, H: 393C

9516 ²תַּפּוּחַ *tappûaḥ*[2], Tappuah, S: 8599, B: 656B, K: 1037A, H: 393D

9517 ³תַּפּוּחַ *tappûaḥ*[3], Tappuah, S: 8599, B: 656B, K: 1037A, H: 393D

9518 תְּפוּצָה *t^{e}pûṣâ*, shattering, dispersing, S: 8600†, B: 807B, K: 1037B, H: 393D

9519 תֻּפִינִים *tupînîm*, broken into pieces, S: 8601†, B: 1074A, K: 1037B, H: 393D

9520 תָּפַל *tāpal*, variant: see 7349, S: 6617†, B: 836D, K: 1037B, H: 393D

9521 ¹תָּפֵל *tāpēl*[1], whitewash, S: 8602, B: 1074B, K: 1037B, H: 394A

9522 ²תָּפֵל *tāpēl*[2], tasteless (food); worthless (prophetic visions), S: 8602, B: 1074A, K: 1037B, H: 394A

9523 תֹּפֶל *tōpel*, Tophel, S: 8603, B: 1074B, K: 1037C, H: 394A

9524 תִּפְלָה *tiplâ*, repulsiveness, wrongdoing, S: 8604, B: 1074A, K: 1037C, H: 394A

9525 תְּפִלָּה *t^{e}pillâ*, prayer, plea, petition, S: 8605, B: 813C, K: 1037C, H: 394A

9526 תִּפְלֶצֶת *tipleṣet*, terror, horror, S: 8606, B: 814A, K: 1037D, H: 394A

9527 תִּפְסַח *tipsaḥ*, Tiphsah, S: 8607, B: 820B, K: 1037D, H: 394A

9528 תָּפַף *tāpap*, [A] to tap (play) a tambourine; [D] to beat (the breast), S: 8608, B: 1074C, K: 1037D, H: 394A

9529 תָּפַר *tāpar*, [A] to sew, mend; [D] to sew (together), S: 8609, B: 1074C, K: 1038A, H: 394A

9530 תָּפַשׂ *tāpaś*, [A] to take hold of, seize, capture; [B] to be covered; [C] to be seized, be caught, be captured; [D] to catch (a lizard), S: 8610, B: 1074C, K: 1038A, H: 394B

9531 ¹תֹּפֶת *tōpet*[1], spitting, S: 8611, B: 1064B, K: 1038C, H: 394C

9532 ²תֹּפֶת *tōpet*[2], Topheth, S: 8612, B: 1075A, K: 1038C, H: 394C

9533 תָּפְתֶּה *topteh*, Topheth, S: 8613, B: 1075A, K: 1038D, H: 394C

9534 תָּקְהַת *toqhat*, Tokhath, S: 8616†, B: 876B, K: 1038D, H: 394C

9535 ¹תִּקְוָה *tiqwâ*[1], cord, S: 8615, B: 876B, K: 1038D, H: 394C

9536 ²תִּקְוָה *tiqwâ*[2], hope, expectation, S: 8615, B: 876B, K: 1038D, H: 394C

9537 ³תִּקְוָה *tiqwâ*[3], Tikvah, S: 8616, B: 876B, K: 1039A, H: 394C

9538 תְּקוּמָה *t^{e}qûmâ*, ability to stand, S: 8617, B: 879C, K: 1039A, H: 394C

9539 תְּקוֹמֵם *t^{e}qômēm*, variant: see 7756, S: 6965† & 8618, B: 878C, K: 1039A, H: 394C

9540 תָּקוֹעַ *tāqôa'*, trumpet, S: 8619, B: 1075D, K: 1039A, H*

9541 תְּקוֹעַ *t^{e}qôa'*, Tekoa, S: 8620, B: 1075D, K: 1039A, H: 394D

9542 תְּקוֹעִי *t^{e}qô'î*, Tekoite, of Tekoa, S: 8621, B: 1075D, K: 1039B, H: 394D

9543 תְּקוּפָה *t^{e}qûpâ*, turning, course, S: 8622, B: 880D, K: 1039B, H: 394D

9544 תַּקִּיף *taqqîp*, strong, mighty, S: 8623, B: 1076A, K: 1039B, H: 394D

9545 תָּקַן *tāqan*, [A] to be straight; [D] to straighten, set in order, S: 8626, B: 1075B, K: 1039C, H: 394D

9546 תָּקַע *tāqa'*, [A] to sound (a trumpet); to pitch, camp; to strike, clap; [B] to be driven; [C] to be sounded (a trumpet); to put up a security, S: 8628, B: 1075B, K: 1039C, H: 394D

9547 תֵּקַע *tēqa'*, sounding, blast (of a trumpet), S: 8629, B: 1075D, K: 1040A, H: 395A

9548 תָּקַף *tāqap*, [A] to overpower, overwhelm, S: 8630, B: 1075D, K: 1040A, H: 395A

9549 תֹּקֶף *tōqep*, power, might, authority, S: 8633, B: 1076A, K: 1040B, H: 395A

9550 תַּרְאֲלָה *tar'^{a}lâ*, Taralah, S: 8634, B: 1076A, K: 1040B, H: 395A

9551 תַּרְבּוּת *tarbût*, brood, S: 8635, B: 916B, K: 1040B, H: 395B

9552 תַּרְבִּית *tarbît*, excessive interest, exorbitant interest, S: 8636, B: 916B, K: 1040B, H: 395B

9553 תִּרְגֵּם *tirgēm*, [E] to be interpreted, be translated, S: 8638†, B: 1076A, K: 1040B, H: 395B

9554 תַּרְדֵּמָה *tardēmâ*, deep (supernatural) sleep, S: 8639, B: 922B, K: 1040C, H: 395B

9555 תִּרְהָקָה *tirhāqâ*, Tirhakah, S: 8640, B: 1076B, K: 1040C, H: 395B

9556 תְּרוּמָה *t^{e}rûmâ*, offering, special gift, contribution, S: 8641, B: 929A, K: 1040C, H: 395B

9557 תְּרוּמִיָּה *t^{e}rûmiyyâ*, special gift, tribute, S: 8642, B: 929B, K: 1041A, H: 395C

9558 תְּרוּעָה *t^{e}rû'â*, trumpet blast, battle cry, S: 8643, B: 929D, K: 1041A, H: 395C

9559 תְּרוּפָה *t^{e}rûpâ*, healing, S: 8644, B: 930A, K: 1041B, H: 395C

9560 תִּרְזָה *tirzâ*, cypress tree, S: 8645, B: 1076B, K: 1041B, H: 395C

9561 תֶּרַח *teraḥ*, Terah, S: 8646, B: 1076B 1., K: 1041B, H: 395C

9562 תָּרַח *tāraḥ*, Terah, S: 8646†, B: 1076B 2., K: 1041B, H: 395C

9563 תִּרְחֲנָה *tirḥ^{a}nâ*, Tirhanah, S: 8647, B: 934B, K: 1041C, H: 395C

9564 תָּרְמָה *tormâ*, (under) cover, S: 8649, B: 941B, K: 1041C, H: 395C

9565 תַּרְמוּק *tarmûq*, pavement, S*, B*, K*, H*

9566 תַּרְמוּת *tarmût*, variant: see 9567, S: 8649, B: 941C, K: 1041C, H: 395C

9567 תַּרְמִית *tarmît*, deceitfulness, delusion, S: 8649, B: 941C, K: 1041C, H: 395C

9568 תֹּרֶן *tōren*, (sailing) mast; flagstaff (on top of hill), S: 8650, B: 1076C, K: 1041C, H: 395C

9569 תַּרְעִית *tar'ît*, variant: speculation, S: 8649†, B: 941C, K: 1041C, H: 395C

9570 תַּרְעֵלָה *tar'ēlâ*, staggering, reeling, S: 8653, B: 947A, K: 1041D, H: 395C

9571 תִּרְעָתִים *tir'ātîm*, Tirathite, S: 8654†, B: 1076C, K: 1041D, H: 395C

9572 תְּרָפִים *t^{e}rāpîm*, household god, idol, S: 8655, B: 1076C, K: 1041D, H: 395D

9573 תִּרְצָה ^{1} *tirṣâ^{1}*, Tirzah, S: 8656, B: 953C 1., K: 1042A, H: 395D

9574 תִּרְצָה ^{2} *tirṣâ^{2}*, Tirzah, S: 8656, B: 953C 2., K: 1042A, H: 395D

9575 תֶּרֶשׁ *tereš*, Teresh, S: 8657, B: 1076D, K: 1042A, H: 395D

9576 תַּרְשִׁישׁ ^{1} *taršîš^{1}*, Tarshish, ships of Tarshish = trading ships, S: 8659, B: 1076D 1., K: 1042A, H: 395D

9577 תַּרְשִׁישׁ ^{2} *taršîš^{2}*, chrysolite, S: 8658, B: 1076D, K: 1042B, H: 395D

9578 תַּרְשִׁישׁ ^{3} *taršîš^{3}*, Tarshish, S: 8659, B: 1076D 2., K: 1042C, H: 395D

9579 תִּרְשָׁתָא *tiršātā'*, governor, S: 8660, B: 1077A, K: 1042C, H: 395D

9580 תַּרְתָּן *tartān*, supreme commander, second in command, S: 8661, B: 1077A, K: 1042C, H: 395D

9581 תַּרְתָּק *tartāq*, Tartak (pagan god), S: 8662, B: 1077B, K: 1042C, H: 395D

9582 תְּשׂוּמָה *t^{e}śûmâ*, pledge, security, S: 8667†, B: 965A, K: 1042D, H: 395D

9583 תְּשֻׁאָה *t^{e}šu'â*, shouting, commotion, thundering, S: 8663, B: 996C, K: 1042D, H: 395D

9584 תִּשְׁבֶּה *tišbeh*, variant: Tishbeh, S*, B: 986C, K: 1042D, H: 396A

9585 תִּשְׁבִּי *tišbî*, Tishbite, S: 8664, B: 986C, K: 1042D, H: 396A

9586 תִּשְׁבֵּי *tišbê*, Tishbe, S: 8664†, B: 986C, K: 1042D, H: 396A

9587 תַּשְׁבֵּץ *tašbēṣ*, woven or checkered fabric, S: 8665, B: 990B, K: 1042D, H: 396A

9588 תְּשׁוּבָה *t^{e}šûbâ*, spring [time of year]; answer, S: 8666, B: 1000C, K: 1043A, H: 396A

9589 תְּשֻׁוָּה *t^{e}šuwwâ*, variant: storm, noise, see 9583, S: 7738† & 8663†, B: 996C, K: 1043A, H: 396A

9590 תַּשְׁוִית *tašwît*, variant: cushioned couch, ottoman, S*, B: 996C, K: 1043A, H: 395D

9591 תְּשׁוּעָה *t^{e}šû'â*, deliverance, salvation, victory, S: 8668, B: 448B, K: 1043A, H: 396A

9592 תְּשׁוּקָה *t^{e}šûqâ*, desire, longing, S: 8669, B: 1003C, K: 1043C, H: 396C

9593 תְּשׁוּרָה *t^{e}šûrâ*, gift, present, S: 8670, B: 1003D, K: 1043C, H: 396C

9594 תֻּשִׁיָּה *tušiyyâ*, variant: storm, noise, see 9583, S*, B: 444D b, K: 1043C, H: 396C

9595 תְּשִׁיעִי *t^{e}ší'î*, ninth, S: 8671, B: 1077D, K: 1043C, H: 396C

9596 תֵּשַׁע *tēša'*, nine, S: 8672, B: 1077C, K: 1043C, H: 396C

9597 תִּשְׁעִים *tiš'îm*, variant: ninety, S: 8673, B: 1077D, K: 1043D, H: 396C

A Concise Aramaic-English Dictionary to the Old Testament

10001 א ', letter of the Aramaic alphabet, S*, B*, K: 1047A, H*

10002 ־ָא *-ā*, suffixed article: the, a; indicates vocative: O; indicates emphatic state, S*, B*, K*, H*

10003 אַב *'ab*, father, predecessor, S: 2, B: 1078B, K: 1047B, H: 396B

10004 אֵב *'ēb*, fruit, S: 4, B: 1078A, K: 1047C, H: 396B

10005 אֲבַד *'^{a}bad*, [J] to perish; [P] to execute; [Q] to be destroyed, S: 7, B: 1078B, K: 1047C, H: 396B

10006 אֶבֶן *'eben*, rock, stone, S: 69, B: 1078B, K: 1047D, H: 396B

10007 אִגְּרָה *'iggerâ*, letter, S: 104, B: 1078B, K: 1047D, H: 396B

10008 אֱדַיִן *'^{e}dayin*, then, thus, so then, S: 116, B: 1078C, K: 1048A, H: 396B

10009 אֲדָר *'^{a}dār*, Adar, S: 144, B: 1078D, K: 1048A, H: 396B

10010 אִדַּר *'iddar*, threshing floor, S: 147, B: 1078D, K: 1048A, H: 396B

10011 אֲדַרְגָּזַר *'^{a}dargāzar*, adviser, counselor, S: 148†, B: 1078D, K: 1048B, H: 396D

10012 אַדְרַזְדָּא *'adrazdā'*, with diligence, zealously, S: 149, B: 1079A, K: 1048B, H: 396D

10013 אֶדְרָע *'edrā'*, arm, i.e., by force, S: 153, B: 1089A, K: 1048B, H: 396D

10014 אַזְדָּא *'azdā'*, firm, assured, S: 230†, B: 1079A, K: 1048B, H: 396D

10015 אֲזָה *'^{a}zâ*, [J] to heat; [Jp] to be heated, S: 228, B: 1079A, K: 1048C, H: 396D

10016 אֲזַל *'^{a}zal*, [J] to go, return, S: 236, B: 1079B, K: 1048C, H: 396D

10017 אַח *'aḥ*, brother, S: 252, B: 1079C, K: 1048C, H: 396D

10018 אַחֲוָיָה *'ah^{a}wāyâ*, declaring, S: 263†, B: 1092B, K: 1074C, H: 396D

10019 אֲחִידָה *'^{a}ḥîdâ*, riddle, S: 280, B: 1092A, K: 1048D, H: 396D

10020 אַחְמְתָא *'aḥm^{e}tā'*, Ecbatana, S: 307†, B: 1079C, K: 1048D, H: 396D

10021 אַחַר *'aḥar*, after, in the future, S: 311, B: 1079D, K: 1049A, H: 396D

10022 אַחֲרִי *'aḥ^{a}rî*, end (of days), (days) to come, S: 320†, B: 1079D, K: 1049A, H: 397A

10023 אָחֳרִי *'oḥ^{o}rî*, other, another, S: 317, B: 1079D, K: 1049A, H: 397A

10024 אָחֳרֵין *'oḥ^{o}rên*, finally, at last, S: 318, B: 1079D, K: 1049B, H: 397A

10025 אָחֳרָן *'oḥ^{o}rān*, other, another, someone else, S: 321, B: 1079D, K: 1049B, H: 397A

10026 אֲחַשְׁדַּרְפַּן *'^{a}ḥašdarpan*, satrap, S: 324, B: 1080A, K: 1049C, H: 397A

10027 אִילָן *'îlān*, tree, S: 363, B: 1079A, K: 1049C, H: 397A

10028 אֵימְתָן *'êm^{e}tān*, frightening, terrible, S: 574†, B: 1080A, K: 1049C, H: 397A

10029 אִיתַי *'îtay*, there is, there are, S: 383, B: 1080A, K: 1049D, H: 397A

10030 אֲכַל *'^{a}kal*, [J] to eat, devour, S: 399, B: 1080B, K: 1050A, H: 397A

10031 אַל *'al*, not, S: 409, B: 1080B, K: 1050A, H: 397B

10032 אֵל *'ēl*, these, S: 412, B: 1080B, K: 1050B, H: 397B

10033 אֱלָהּ *'^{e}lāh*, God; (pl.) gods, S: 426, B: 1080C, K: 1050B, H: 397B

10034 אֵלֶּה *'ēlleh*, these, S: 429, B: 1080C, K: 1050C, H: 397B

10035 אֲלוּ *'^{a}lû*, there!, behold!, S: 431, B: 1080D, K: 1050D, H: 397C

10036 אִלֵּין *'illên*, these, S: 459, B: 1080D, K: 1050D, H: 397C

10037 אִלֵּךְ *'illēk*, these, S: 479, B: 1080D, K: 1050D, H: 397C

10038 אֲלַף *'^{a}lap*, thousand, S: 506, B: 1081A, K: 1051A, H: 397C

10039 אַמָּה *'ammâ*, cubit (measurement of distance), S: 521, B: 1081A, K: 1051A, H: 397C

10040 אֻמָּה *'ummâ*, nation, people, S: 524, B: 1081A, K: 1051A, H: 397C

10041 אֲמַן *'^{a}man*, [P] to trust in; [Pp] be trustworthy, S: 540, B: 1081A, K: 1051B, H: 397C

10042 אֲמַר *'^{a}mar*, [J] to say, tell; to command, S: 560, B: 1081A, K: 1051B, H: 397C

10043 אִמַּר *'immar*, male lamb, S: 563, B: 1081B, K*, H: 397D

10044 אֲנָה *'^{a}nâ*, I, S: 576, B: 1081B, K: 1051D, H: 397D

10045 אִנּוּן *'innûn*, they; those, S: 581, B: 1081C, K: 1051D, H: 397D

10046 אֱנוֹשׁ *'^{e}nôš*, variant: man, person, see 10050, S: 582, B: 1081D, K: 1052B, H: 397D

10047 אֲנַחְנָא *'^{a}naḥnā'*, we, S: 586, B: 1081C, K: 1052A, H: 397D

10048 אֲנַס *'^{a}nas*, [J] to oppress, make difficult, S: 598, B: 1081C, K: 1052A, H: 398A

10049 אֲנַף *'^{a}nap*, face, S: 600, B: 1081C, K: 1052A, H: 398A

10050 אֱנָשׁ *'^{e}nāš*, human, mankind, people, S: 606, B: 1081D, K: 1052B, H: 398A

10051 אַנְתְּ *'ant*, variant: you, your, see 10052, S: 607†, B: 1082A, K: 1052C, H: 398A

10052 אַנְתָּה *'antā*, you, S: 607, B: 1082A, K: 1052C, H: 398A

10053 אַנְתּוּן *'antûn*, you (all), S: 608, B: 1082A, K: 1052C, H: 398A

10054 אֱסוּר *'^{e}sûr*, bond, fetter; (pl.) imprisonment, S: 613, B: 1082B, K: 1052D, H: 398A

10055 אָסְנַפַּר *'ās^{e}nappar*, Ashurbanipal, S: 620, B: 1082A, K: 1052D, H: 398A

10056 אָסְפַּרְנָא *'osparnā'*, with diligence, surely, fully, S: 629, B: 1082A, K: 1052D, H: 398A

10057 אֱסָר *'^{e}sār*, (enforced) decree, S: 633, B: 1082B, K: 1053A, H: 398A

10058 אָע *'ā'*, wood, timber, S: 636, B: 1082B, K: 1053A, H: 398B

10059 אַף *'ap*, even, also, S: 638, B: 1082B, K: 1053A, H: 398B

10060 אֲפָרְסָי *'^{a}pār^{e}sāy*, Persian, from Persia, S: 670†, B: 1082B, K: 1053B, H: 398B

10061 אֲפָרְסְכָי *'^{a}pars^{e}kāy*, officials, S: 671†, B: 1082B, K: 1053B, H: 398B

10062 אֲפַרְסַתְכָי *'^{a}parsatkāy*, officials, S: 671†, B: 1082C, K: 1053B, H: 398B

[O] Hithpaal (Itpaal, Itpoal) [P] Haphel (Aphel, Shaphel) [Pp] Haphel passive [Q] Hophal [R] Hishtaphal

10063 אַפְּתֹם 'app^{e}tōm, revenue, treasury, S: 674, B: 1082C, K: 1053B, H: 398B

10064 אֶצְבַּע 'eṣba', toe, finger, S: 677, B: 1109C, K: 1053C, H: 398B

10065 אַרְבַּע 'arba', four, S: 703, B: 1112C, K: 1053C, H: 398B

10066 אַרְגְּוָן 'arg^{e}wān, purple (clothing), S: 711, B: 1082C, K: 1053C, H: 398B

10067 אֲרוּ '^{a}rû, there!, behold!, S: 718, B: 1082C, K: 1053D, H: 398C

10068 אֲרַח '^{a}raḥ, way, conduct of life, S: 735†, B: 1082D, K: 1053D, H: 398C

10069 אַרְיֵה 'aryēh, lion, S: 738, B: 1082C, K: 1053D, H: 398C

10070 אַרְיוֹךְ 'aryôk, Arioch, S: 746, B: 1082D, K: 1054A, H: 398C

10071 אֲרִיךְ '^{a}rîk, proper, fitting, S: 749†, B: 1082D, K: 1054A, H: 398C

10072 אַרְכֻבָּה 'arkubbâ, knee, S: 755, B: 1085C, K: 1054A, H: 398C

10073 אַרְכָה 'arkâ, continuing, prolongation, S: 754, B: 1082D, K: 1054B, H: 398C

10074 אַרְכְּוָי 'ark^{e}wāy, Erech, S: 756†, B: 1083A, K: 1054B, H: 398C

10075 אֲרַע '^{a}ra', earth, world; land, ground, S: 772, B: 1083A, K: 1054B, H: 398C

10076 אַרְעִי 'ar'î, floor, bottom, S: 773†, B: 1083A, K: 1054C, H: 398C

10077 אֲרַק '^{a}raq, earth, S: 778, B: 1083A, K: 1054C, H: 398C

10078 אַרְתַּחְשַׁשְׂתְּא 'artaḥšaśt', אַרְתַּחְשַׁסְתְּא 'artaḥšast', אַרְתַּחְשַׁשְׂתְּ 'artaḥšaśt, Artaxerxes, S: 783, B: 1083A, K: 1054C, H: 398C

10079 אֹשׁ 'ōš, foundation, S: 787, B: 1083A, K: 1054D, H: 398C

10080 אֶשָּׁא 'eššā', fire, S: 785†, B: 1083A, K: 1054D, H: 398C

10081 אָשַׁף 'āšap, enchanter, conjurer, S: 826, B: 1083B, K: 1054D, H: 398D

10082 אֻשַּׁרְנָא 'uššarnā', structure, S: 846, B: 1083B, K: 1054D, H: 398D

10083 אֶשְׁתַּדּוּר 'eštaddûr, rebellion, sedition, revolt, S: 849, B: 1083B, K: 1055A, H: 398D

10084 אָת 'āt, miraculous sign, S: 852, B: 1083B, K: 1055A, H: 398D

10085 אֲתָה '^{a}tâ, [J] to come, go; [P] to bring; [Pp] to be brought, S: 858†, B: 1114C, K: 1055B, H: 398D

10086 אַתּוּן 'attûn, furnace, S: 861, B: 1079A, K: 1055B, H: 398D

10087 אֲתַר '^{a}tar, site, place, S: 870, B: 1083C, K: 1055B, H: 398D

10088 ב b, letter of the Aramaic alphabet, S*, B: 1083C, K: 1055C, H: 399A

10089 -בְּ b^{e}-, in, with, by, S*, B: 1083C, K: 1055D, H: 399A

10090 בִּאישׁ bi'yš, wicked, evil, bad, S: 873†, B*, K: 1056A, H*

10091 בְּאֵשׁ b^{e}'ēš, [J] to be distressed, S: 888, B: 1083D, K: 1056A, H: 399A

10092 בָּאתַר bā'tar, after, S: 870†, B: 1084A, K: 1056B, H: 399B

10093 בָּבֶל bābel, Babylon, S: 895, B: 1084A, K: 1056B, H: 399B

10094 בָּבְלָי bāb^{e}lî, Babylonian, from Babylon, S: 896†, B: 1083C, K: 1056C, H: 399B

10095 בְּדַר b^{e}dar, [M] to scatter, S: 921, B: 1084A, K: 1056C, H: 399B

10096 בְּהִילוּ b^{e}hîlû, hurry, haste; (as adv.) immediately, S: 924, B: 1084A, K: 1056C, H: 399B

10097 בְּהַל b^{e}hal, [M] to frighten, terrify; [L] to hurry, be at once; [O] to be frightened, S: 927, B: 1084A, K: 1056D, H: 399B

10098 בְּטֵל b^{e}ṭal, [J] to come to a standstill; [M] to stop (another), S: 989, B: 1084B, K: 1056D, H: 399B

10099 בֵּין bên, between, among, S: 997, B: 1084A, K: 1056D, H: 399B

10100 בִּינָה bînâ, discernment, insight, S: 999, B: 1084B, K: 1057A, H: 399B

10101 בִּירָה bîrâ, citadel, fortress, S: 1001†, B: 1084B, K: 1057B, H: 399C

10102 בִּית bît, [J] to spend the night, S: 956†, B: 1084B, K: 1057B, H: 399C

10103 בַּיִת bayit, house, residence, home; temple, hall, S: 1005, B: 1084C, K: 1057B, H: 399C

10104 בָּל bāl, heart, mind, S: 1079, B: 1084C, K: 1057C, H: 399C

10105 בֵּלְשַׁאצַּר bēl'šaṣṣar, Belshazzar, S: 1113, B: 1084C, K: 1057C, H: 399D

10106 בְּלָה b^{e}lâ, [M] to oppress, wear down, S: 1080, B: 1084B, K: 1057D, H: 399D

10107 בְּלוֹ b^{e}lô, tribute, tax, S: 1093, B: 1084D, K: 1057D, H: 399D

10108 בֵּלְטְשַׁאצַּר bēlṭ^{e}ša'ṣṣar, Belteshazzar, S: 1096, B: 1084C, K: 1057D, H: 399D

10109 בֵּלְשַׁאצַּר bēlša'ṣṣar, Belshazzar, S: 1113, B: 1084C, K: 1057D, H: 399D

10110 בֵּן bēn, variant: see 10120, S: 1123, B: 1084D, K: 1058A, H: 399D

10111 בְּנָה b^{e}nâ, [J] to build, construct, rebuild; [Jp] to be built; [L] to be built, be constructed, be rebuilt, S: 1124, B: 1084D, K: 1058A, H: 399D

10112 בִּנְיָן binyān, building, S: 1147, B*, K*, H*

10113 בְּנַס b^{e}nas, [J] to become angry, S: 1149, B: 1084D, K: 1058B, H: 399D

10114 בְּעָה b^{e}'â, [J] to ask for, request, pray for, plead for, S: 1156, B: 1084D, K: 1058C, H: 400A

10115 בָּעוּ bā'û, prayer, petition, request, S: 1159, B: 1084D, K: 1058C, H: 400A

10116 בְּעֵל b^{e}'ēl, commanding officer, S: 1169, B: 1085A, K: 1058C, H: 400A

10117 בִּקְעָה biq'â, plain, (broad) valley, S: 1236†, B: 1085A, K: 1058D, H: 400A

10118 בְּקַר b^{e}qar, [M] to make a search, inquire; [O] to let a search be made, S: 1240, B: 1085A, K: 1059A, H: 400A

10119 ^{1}בַּר bar^{1}, open field, the wild, S: 1251, B: 1085A, K: 1059A, H: 400B

10120 ^{2}בַּר bar^{2}, son, child, descendant, S: 1247, B: 1085A, K: 1059A, H: 400B

10121 ^{1}בְּרַךְ b^{e}rak^{1}, [J] to kneel, S: 1289, B: 1085C, K: 1059B, H: 400C

10122 ^{2}בְּרַךְ b^{e}rak^{2}, [Jp] to be praised; [M] to praise; [Mp] to be praised, S: 1289, B: 1085B, K: 1059B, H: 400C

10123 בְּרֵךְ b^{e}rēk, knee, S: 1291†, B: 1085B, K: 1059C, H: 400C

10124 בְּרַם b^{e}ram, but, however, nevertheless, S: 1297, B: 1085B, K: 1059D, H: 400C

10125 בְּשַׂר b^{e}śar, flesh (human or creatures), S: 1321, B: 1085C, K: 1059D, H: 400C

10126 בַּת bat, bath (liquid measure), S: 1325, B: 1085C, K: 1059D, H: 400D

10127 ג g, letter of the Aramaic alphabet, S*, B: 1085C, K: 1060A, H: 400D

10128 גַּב gab, the back (body part), S: 1355, B: 1085D, K: 1060C, H: 400D

10129 גֹּב gōb, den, pit (of lions), S: 1358, B*, K: 1060A, H*

10130 גְּבוּרָה g^{e}bûrâ, power, might, strength, S: 1370, B: 1085D, K: 1060B, H: 400B

10131 גְּבַר g^{e}bar, (mighty) man, S: 1400, B: 1085D, K: 1060B, H: 400B

10132 גִּבָּר gibbar, strong man, mighty one, S: 1401†, B: 1086A, K: 1060B, H: 400D

10133 גְּדָבַר g^{e}dābar, treasurer, S: 1411†, B: 1086A, K: 1060C, H: 400D

10134 גְּדַד g^{e}dad, [J] to cut down, S: 1414, B: 1086A, K: 1060D, H: 401A

10135 גַּו gaw, middle, interior, S: 1459, B: 1086A, K: 1060D, H: 401A

10136 גֵּוָה gēwâ, pride, S: 1467, B: 1086A, K: 1061A, H: 401A

10137 גּוּחַ gûaḥ, [P] to churn up, stir up (the sea), S: 1519, B: 1086A, K: 1061A, H: 401A

10138 גּוֹן gôn, variant: see 10135 & 10464, S*, B: 1085D, K: 1061B, H: 401A

10139 גִּזְבַּר gizbar, treasurer, S: 1490†, B*, K: 1061B, H: 401A

10140 גְּזַר g^{e}zar, [J] to determine; (as noun) diviner, astrologer; [L] to cut out; S: 1505, B*, K*, H: 401A

10141 גְּזֵרָה g^{e}zērâ, decree, decision, S: 1510, B: 1086B, K: 1061C, H: 401A

10142 גִּיר gîr, plaster, S: 1528, B: 1086B, K: 1061C, H: 401A

10143 גַּלְגַּל galgal, wheel, S: 1535, B: 1086B, K: 1061D, H: 401B

10144 גְּלָה g^{e}lâ, [J] to reveal (mysteries); [K] to be revealed (i.e., mysteries); [P] to deport, S: 1541, B: 1086B, K: 1061D, H: 401C

10145 גָּלוּ gālû, exile, S: 1547†, B: 1086C, K: 1062A, H: 401C

10146 גְּלָל g^{e}lāl, (col.) stone blocks, S: 1560, B: 1086C, K: 1062A, H: 401C

10147 גְּמַר g^{e}mar, [Jp] to be finished; (as an introduction in a letter) Greetings, S: 1585, B: 1086C, K: 1062A, H: 401C

10148 גְּנַז g^{e}naz, place of treasure and archived documents, S: 1596, B: 1086C, K: 1062B, H: 401C

10149 גַּף gap, wing, S: 1611, B: 1086C, K: 1062B, H: 401C

10150 גְּרַם g^{e}ram, bone, S: 1635†, B: 1086C, K: 1062C, H: 401C

10151 גְּשֵׁם g^{e}šēm, body, S: 1655, B: 1086D, K: 1062C, H: 401C

10152 ד d, letter of the Aramaic alphabet, S*, B: 1086D, K: 1062D, H: 401C

10153 -דְּ d^{e}-, who, that, of, S*, B: 1086D, K: 1062D, H: 401C

10154 דָּא dā', this, this one, S: 1668, B*, K: 1063A, H*

10155 דֹּב dōb, bear, S: 1678, B: 1087C, K: 1064B, H: 402A

10156 דְּבַח d^{e}baḥ[1], [J] to present a sacrifice, S: 1684, B: 1086D, K: 1063A, H: 401B

10157 [2]דְּבַח d^{e}baḥ[2], sacrifice (i.e., animal), S: 1685, B: 1087A, K: 1063B, H: 401B

10158 דְּבַק d^{e}baq, [J] to be united, S: 1693, B: 1087A, K: 1063B, H: 401B

10159 דִּבְרָה dibrâ, affair, matter, S: 1701, B: 1087A, K: 1063B, H: 401B

10160 דְּהַב d^{e}hab, gold, S: 1722, B: 1087A, K: 1063C, H: 401B

10161 דְּהוּא d^{e}hû', variant: that is (10168 + 10200), S: 1723†, B: 1087A, K: 1063C, H: 401D

10162 דֶּהָיֵא dehāyē', variant: that is (10168 + 10200), S: 1723†, B: 1087A, K: 1063D, H: 401D

10163 דּוּר dûr, [J] to live, dwell, S: 1753, B: 1087A, K: 1063D, H: 401D

10164 דּוּרָא dûrā', Dura, S: 1757, B: 1087A, K: 1063D, H: 401D

10165 דּוּשׁ dûš, [J] to trample, tread down, S: 1759, B: 1087B, K: 1064A, H: 401D

10166 דַּחֲוָה dah^{a}wâ, entertainment, S: 1761, B: 1087B, K: 1064A, H: 402A

10167 דְּחַל d^{e}ḥal, [J] to fear, reverence; [Jp] to be terrified, be awesome; [M] to make afraid, S: 1763, B: 1087C, K: 1064A, H: 402A

10168 דִּי dî, who, that, of, S: 1768, B: 1087C, K: 1064A, H: 402A

10169 דִּין dîn[1], [J] to administer justice, judge, S: 1778, B: 1087C, K: 1064B, H: 402A

10170 [2]דִּין dîn[2], judgment, court (place of judgment), S: 1780, B: 1087C, K: 1064B, H: 402A

10171 דַּיָּן dayyān, judge, S: 1782, B: 1088B, K: 1065C, H: 402C

10172 דִּינָיֵא dînāyē', judge, S: 1784, B: 1088B, K: 1065C, H: 402C

10173 דֵּךְ dēk, this, S: 1791, B: 1088C, K: 1065D, H: 402C

10174 דִּכֵּן dikkēn, that, S: 1797, B: 1088C, K: 1065D, H: 402C

10175 דְּכַר d^{e}kar, ram (male animal), S: 1798, B: 1088C, K: 1065D, H: 402C

10176 דִּכְרוֹן dikrôn, memorandum, record, S: 1799, B: 1088C, K: 1066A, H: 402D

10177 דָּכְרָן dokrān, memorandum, archived record, S: 1799, B: 1088D, K: 1066A, H: 402D

10178 דְּלַק d^{e}laq, [J] to be ablaze, burn, S: 1815, B: 1088D, K: 1066B, H: 402D

10179 דְּמָה d^{e}mâ, [J] to look like, resemble, S: 1821, B: 1088D, K: 1066B, H: 402D

10180 דְּנָה d^{e}nâ, this, that, S: 1836†, B: 1088D, K: 1066B, H: 402D

10181 דָּנִיֵּאל dāniyyē'l, Daniel, S: 1841, B: 1088D, K: 1066C, H: 402D

10182 דְּקַק d^{e}qaq, [J] to break to pieces; [P] to crush, smash, pulverize, S: 1855, B: 1088D, K: 1066C, H: 402D

10183 דָּר dār, generation, S: 1859, B: 1088C, K: 1066D, H: 403A

10184 דָּרְיָוֶשׁ dār^{e}yāweš, Darius, S: 1868, B: 1089A, K: 1066D, H: 403A

10185 דְּרָע d^{e}rā', arm, S: 1872†, B: 1087B, K: 1067A, H: 403A

10186 דָּת dāt, law, decree, S: 1882, B: 1089A, K: 1067B, H: 403A

10187 דֶּתֶא dete', grass (of the open country), S: 1883, B: 1089A, K: 1067C, H: 403A

10188 דְּתָבַר d^{e}tābar, judge, S: 1884†, B: 1089B, K: 1067C, H: 403C

10189 ה h, letter of the Aramaic alphabet, S*, B: 1089B, K: 1067C, H: 403C

10190 הֲ- h^{a}-, introduces a question, not translated, S*, B: 1089B, K: 1067D, H: 403C

10191 -ָה -â, suffixed article: the, a, S*, B*, K: 1067B, H*

10192 -ֵהּ -ēh, he, him, his; it, its, S*, B: 1089B, K: 1067B, H: 403A

10193 -ַהּ -ah, she, her; it, its, S*, B*, K*, H*

10194 הָא hā', look!, there!, S: 1888, B*, K*, H*

10195 הֵא hē', just as, S: 1888, B*, K*, H*

10196 הַדָּבַר haddābar, royal adviser, official of the king, S: 1907, B: 1089C, K: 1067D, H: 403A

10197 הַדָּם haddām, pieces, members (of an execution by dismemberment), S: 1917, B: 1089C, K: 1068A, H: 403A

10198 הדר h^{a}dar[1], [M] to glorify, honor, S: 1922, B: 1089C, K: 1068A, H: 403B

10199 [2]הדר h^{a}dar[2], splendor, honor, majesty, S: 1923, B: 1089D, K: 1068A, H: 403B

10200 הוּא hû', he, it, S: 1932, B: 1089D, K: 1068B, H: 403B

10201 הֲוָה h^{a}wâ, [J] to be, become, happen, S: 1934, B: 1089D, K: 1068B, H: 403B

10202 הוּךְ hûk, variant: see 10207, S: 1946, B: 1090A, K: 1068B, H: 403B

10203 -הוֹן -hôn, they, them, their, S*, B: 1089D, K: 1068C, H: 403B

10204 -הִי -hî, he, his, him; it, its, S*, B: 1090B, K*, H*

10205 הִיא hî', she, it, S: 1932, B*, K*, H*

10206 הֵיכַל hêkal, temple, palace, S: 1965, B*, K*, H*

10207 הֲלַךְ h^{a}lak, [J] to go; [M] to walk about; [P] to walk around, S: 1981, B: 1090A, K: 1069A, H: 403D

10208 הֲלָךְ h^{a}lāk, duty, toll, tax, S: 1983, B: 1090B, K: 1069A, H: 403D

10209 -הֹם -hōm, they, them, their, S*, B: 1090B, K: 1069A, H: 403D

10210 הִמּוֹ himmô, they, them, S: 1994, B: 1090B, K: 1069B, H: 403D

10211 המונכ hmwnk, necklace, S: 2002, B*, K*, H*

10212 הַמְיָנַךְ hamyānak, chain, necklace, S: 2002†, B: 1090B, K: 1069C, H: 403D

10213 הֵן hēn, if, then, whether, S: 2006, B: 1090C, K: 1069C, H: 403D

10214 -הֵן -hēn, they, them, their, S*, B: 1090C, K: 1069C, H: 403D

10215 הַנְזָקָה hanzāqâ, injury, disadvantage, S*, B: 1090C, K: 1069D, H: 404A

10216 הַצְדָּא haṣdā', variant: truly? really?, see 10190 & 10609, S*, B*, K*, H*

10217 הַרְהֹר harhōr, mental image (in a dream-like state), S: 2031, B: 1102C, K: 1070A, H: 404A

10218 הִתְבְּהָלָה hitb^{e}hālâ, variant: hurry, see 10097, S: 927†, B: 1109C, K: 1070A, H: 404C

10219 הִתְנַדָּבוּ hitnaddābû, variant: gift, see 10461, S: 5069†, B: 1090D, K: 1070A, H: 404C

10220 ו w, letter of the Aramaic alphabet, S*, B: 1084A, K: 1070C, H: 404C

10221 -וְ w^{e}-, and, or, but, then, now, S*, B: 1102B, K: 1070C, H: 404C

10222 ז z, letter of the Aramaic alphabet, S*, B*, K: 1070B, H*

10223 זְבַן z^{e}ban, [J] to try to gain (time), buy (time), S: 2084, B: 1090D, K: 1070B, H: 404A

10224 זְהִיר z^{e}hîr, careful, cautious, S: 2095†, B*, K: 1071A, H*

10225 זוּד zûd, [P] to act proudly, act haughtily, S: 2103, B: 1091A, K: 1071A, H: 404A

10226 זוּן zûn, [L] to be fed, live on, S: 2110, B: 1091A, K: 1071B, H: 404B

10227 זוּעַ zûa', [J] to dread, fear, tremble, S: 2112, B: 1091A, K: 1071B, H: 404B

10228 זִיו zîw, dazzlingness, splendor; flushed, pale, S: 2122, B: 1091B, K: 1071B, H: 404B

10229 זָכוּ zākû, innocence, S: 2136, B: 1091B, K: 1071C, H: 404B

10230 זְכַרְיָה z^{e}karyâ, Zechariah, S: 2148, B: 1091B, K: 1071C, H: 404B

10231 זְמַן z^{e}man[1], [L] to conspire, agree to; [P] to decide, S: 2164, B: 1091B, K: 1071D, H: 404B

10232 [2]זְמָן z^{e}man[2], time, period of time, set time, season, S: 2166, B: 1091C, K: 1072A, H: 404B

10233 זְמָר z^{e}mār, music, S: 2170, B: 1091C, K: 1072A, H: 404B

10234 זַמָּר zammār, singer, S: 2171, B: 1091C, K: 1072A, H: 404B

10235 זַן zan, kind, sort, S: 2178, B: 1091C, K: 1072B, H: 404D

10236 זְעֵיר z^{e}'êr, little, small, S: 2192, B: 1091C, K: 1072B, H: 404D

10237 זְעִק z^{e}'iq, [J] to call out, shout, S: 2200, B: 1091C, K: 1072C, H: 404D

10238 זְקַף z^{e}qap, [Jp] to be lifted up, S: 2211, B: 1091D, K: 1072C, H: 404D

10239 זְרֻבָּבֶל z^{e}rubbābel, Zerubbabel, S: 2217, B: 1091C, K: 1072C, H: 404D

10240 זְרַע z^{e}ra', seed, descendant, S: 2234, B: 1091D, K: 1072C, H: 404D

10241 ח ḥ, letter of the Aramaic alphabet, S*, B: 1091D, K: 1072D, H: 404D

10242 חֲבוּלָה ḥ^{a}bûlâ, wrong, crime, S: 2248, B: 1091D, K: 1072D, H: 404D

10243 חֲבַל *ḥ^{a}bal*, [M] to destroy, hurt; [O] to be destroyed, S: 2255, B*, K: 1073A, H*

10244 חֲבָל *ḥ^{a}bāl*, harm, wound, hurt, S: 2257†, B: 1092A, K: 1073A, H: 405A

10245 חֲבַר *ḥ^{a}bar*, friend, companion, S: 2269, B: 1091D, K: 1073A, H: 405A

10246 חַבְרָה *ḥabrâ*, companion (horn), S: 2273, B: 1092A, K: 1073B, H: 405A

10247 חַגַּי *ḥaggay*, Haggai, S: 2292, B: 1092A, K: 1073B, H: 405A

10248 חַד *ḥad*, one, first, a; time, occurrence, S: 2298, B: 1092A, K: 1073B, H: 405A

10249 חֲדֵה *ḥ^{a}dēh*, chest, breast, S: 2306†, B: 1092A, K: 1073C, H: 405A

10250 חֶדְוָה *ḥedwâ*, joy, S: 2305, B: 1079C, K: 1073C, H: 405A

10251 חֲדַת *ḥ^{a}dat*, new, S: 2323†, B: 1092A, K: 1073D, H: 405A

10252 חֲוָה *ḥ^{a}wâ*, [M] to reveal, tell, show; [P] tell, explain, make known, interpret, S: 2324†, B: 1092A, K: 1074A, H: 405B

10253 חוּט *ḥûṭ*, [P] to repair, S: 2338, B: 1092A, K: 1074A, H: 405B

10254 חִוָּר *ḥiwwār*, white, S: 2358, B: 1092B, K: 1074A, H: 405B

10255 חֲזָה *ḥ^{a}zâ*, [J] to see, look, watch, realize; [Jp] to be usual, be customary, S: 2370, B: 1092B, K: 1074B, H: 405B

10256 חֱזוּ *ḥ^{e}zû*, vision, appearance, S: 2376†, B: 1092C, K: 1074C, H: 405B

10257 חֲזוֹת *ḥ^{a}zôt*, visible sight, S: 2379, B: 1092C, K: 1074C, H: 405B

10258 חַטָּאָה *ḥaṭṭā'â*, variant: sin offering, see 10260, S: 2402, B: 1092C, K: 1074D, H: 405C

10259 חֲטָי *ḥ^{a}ṭāy*, sin, S: 2408†, B: 1092D, K: 1075A, H: 405C

10260 חַטָּיָא *ḥaṭṭāyā'*, sin offering, S: 2409, B: 1092D, K: 1075A, H: 405C

10261 חַי *ḥay*, living, alive, S: 2417, B: 1092D, K: 1075A, H: 405C

10262 חֲיָה *ḥ^{a}yâ*, [J] to live; [P] to spare, let live, S: 2418, B: 1092D, K: 1075A, H: 405C

10263 חֵיוָה *ḥêwâ*, beast, animal, S: 2423, B: 1092D, K: 1075A, H: 405C

10264 חַיִל *ḥayil*, strength, power; an army, S: 2429, B: 1092D, K: 1075B, H: 405C

10265 חַכִּים *ḥakkîm*, wise man (usually pertaining to a social class), S: 2445, B: 1092D, K: 1075C, H: 405D

10266 חָכְמָה *ḥokmâ*, wisdom, S: 2452, B: 1093A, K: 1075C, H: 405D

10267 חֵלֶם *ḥēlem*, dream, S: 2493, B: 1093A, K: 1075D, H: 405D

10268 חֲלַף *ḥ^{a}lap*, [J] to pass by, pass over, S: 2499, B: 1093A, K: 1075D, H: 405D

10269 חֲלָק *ḥ^{a}lāq*, portion, lot in life, S: 2508, B: 1093A, K: 1075D, H: 405D

10270 חֲמָה *ḥ^{a}mâ*, fury, rage, S: 2528, B: 1093A, K: 1076A, H: 405D

10271 חֲמַר *ḥ^{a}mar*, wine, S: 2562, B: 1093B, K: 1076A, H: 405D

10272 חִנְטָה *ḥinṭâ*, wheat, S: 2591†, B: 1095C, K: 1076B, H: 405D

10273 חֲנֻכָּה *ḥ^{a}nukkâ*, (ceremonial religious) dedication, S: 2597†, B: 1093B, K: 1076B, H: 406A

10274 חֲנַן *ḥ^{a}nan*, [J] to be kind, show mercy; [O] to ask, implore, S: 2604, B: 1093B, K: 1076B, H: 406A

10275 חֲנַנְיָה *ḥ^{a}nanyâ*, Hananiah, S: 2608, B: 1093B, K: 1076C, H: 406A

10276 חַסִּיר *ḥassîr*, wanting, deficient, S: 2627, B: 1093B, K: 1076C, H: 406A

10277 חֲסַן *ḥ^{a}san*, [P] to take possession of, occupy, S: 2631, B: 1093B, K: 1076C, H: 406A

10278 חֱסֵן *ḥ^{e}sēn*, power, might, force, S: 2632†, B: 1093C, K: 1076D, H: 406A

10279 חֲסַף *ḥ^{a}sap*, (formed, molded) clay, baked clay, S: 2635, B: 1093C, K: 1076D, H: 406A

10280 חֲצַף *ḥ^{a}ṣap*, [P] to show harshness, S: 2685, B: 1093C, K: 1076D, H: 406A

10281 חֲרַב *ḥ^{a}rab*, [Q] to be destroyed, be devastated, S: 2718, B: 1093C, K: 1077A, H: 406A

10282 חַרְטֹם *ḥarṭōm*, magician, S: 2749, B: 1093C, K: 1077B, H: 406A

10283 חֲרַךְ *ḥ^{a}rak*, [O] to be singed (i.e., hair burnt), S: 2761, B: 1093D, K: 1077B, H: 406C

10284 חֲרַץ *ḥ^{a}raṣ*, hips, hip joints, S: 2783, B: 1093D, K: 1077B, H: 406C

10285 חֲשַׁב *ḥ^{a}šab*, [Jp] to be regarded, be respected, S: 2804, B: 1093D, K: 1077C, H: 406C

10286 חֲשׁוֹךְ *ḥ^{a}šôk*, darkness, S: 2816, B: 1093D, K: 1077C, H: 406C

10287 חֲשַׁח *ḥ^{a}šaḥ*, [J] to be in need, S: 2818, B: 1093D, K: 1077C, H: 406C

10288 חַשְׁחָה *ḥašḥâ*, need, S: 2818, B: 1094A, K: 1077D, H: 406C

10289 חַשְׁחוּ *ḥašḥû*, what is needed, S: 2819†, B: 1093D, K: 1077D, H: 406C

10290 חֲשַׁל *ḥ^{a}šal*, [J] to smash, pulverize, S: 2827, B: 1093D, K: 1077D, H: 406C

10291 חֲתַם *ḥ^{a}tam*, [J] to seal (with a signet ring), S: 2857, B: 1093D, K: 1078A, H: 406C

10292 ט *ṭ*, letter of the Aramaic alphabet, S*, B: 1094A, K: 1078A, H: 406C

10293 טְאֵב *ṭ^e'ēb*, [J] to be good = to have joy, S: 2868, B: 1094A, K: 1078C, H: 406C

10294 טָב *ṭāb*, good, pleasing, pure, S: 2869, B*, K: 1078A, H*

10295 טַבָּח *ṭabbāḥ*, (royal) body-guard, executioner, S: 2877, B: 1094A, K: 1078B, H: 406B

10296 טוּר *ṭûr*, mountain, S: 2906, B: 1094B, K: 1078B, H: 406B

10297 טְוָת *ṭ^{e}wāt*, without eating, in hunger, in fasting, S: 2908, B: 1094B, K: 1078D, H: 406B

10298 טִין *ṭîn*, (wet) clay, S: 2917, B: 1094B, K: 1078D, H: 406B

10299 טַל *ṭal*, dew, S: 2920, B: 1094B, K: 1078D, H: 406B

10300 טְלַל *ṭ^{e}lal*, [P] to find shelter, S: 2927, B: 1094B, K: 1079A, H: 406B

10301 טְעֵם¹ *ṭ^{e}ʿēm*[1], [M] to eat, S: 2939†, B: 1094B, K: 1079A, H: 406B

10302 טְעֵם² *ṭ^{e}ʿēm*[2], order, decree, command; tact, good sense; report, advice, S: 2942†, B: 1094B, K: 1079B, H: 406D

10303 טְפַר *ṭ^{e}par*, (finger & toe) nails, claws, S: 2953, B: 1094B, K: 1079B, H: 406D

10304 טְרַד *ṭ^{e}rad*, [J] to drive away (as noun) one driven away; [K] to be driven away, S: 2957, B: 1094C, K: 1079C, H: 406D

10305 טַרְפְּלָי *ṭarp^{e}lāy*, from Tripolis, S: 2967†, B: 1094C, K: 1080A, H: 407A

10306 י *y*, letter of the Aramaic alphabet, S*, B: 1094C, K: 1080A, H: 407A

10307 ־ִי *-î*, I, me, my, S*, B: 1094C, K: 1080C, H: 407C

10308 יְבַל *y^{e}bal*, [P] to bring, take, S: 2987, B*, K: 1080A, H*

10309 יַבֶּשְׁתָּא *yabb^{e}šâ*, earth, S: 3007†, B*, K*, H*

10310 יְגַר *y^{e}gar*, variant: Jegar, see 3337, S: 3026, B: 1094D, K: 1080A, H: 407A

10311 יַד *yad*, hand, power, S: 3028, B: 1094D, K: 1080B, H: 407A

10312 יְדָה *y^{e}dâ*, [P] to give thanks, confess praise, S: 3029†, B: 1094D, K: 1080C, H: 407A

10313 יְדַע *y^{e}daʿ*, [J] to know, understand, acknowledge; [Jp] to be known; [P] to make known, tell, inform, S: 3046, B: 1094D, K: 1080D, H: 407A

10314 יְהַב *y^{e}hab*, [J] to give; [Jp] to be given; [L] to be given as payment; be entrusted, S: 3052, B: 1095A, K: 1080D, H: 407B

10315 יְהוּד *y^{e}hûd*, Judah, S: 3061, B: 1095A, K: 1081A, H: 407B

10316 יְהוּדָי *y^{e}hûdāy*, Jew, S: 3062†, B: 1095B, K: 1081B, H: 407B

10317 יוֹם *yôm*, day, period of time, S: 3118, B: 1095C, K: 1081C, H: 407C

10318 יוֹצָדָק *yôṣādāq*, Jozadak, S: 3136, B: 1095C, K: 1081D, H: 407D

10319 יְחַת *y^{e}ḥat*, variant: [M] to lay a foundation, see 10253, S*, B: 1095C, K: 1081D, H: 407D

10320 יְטַב *y^{e}ṭab*, [J] to seem best, be pleasing, S: 3191, B: 1095C, K: 1082A, H: 407D

10321 יְכִל *y^{e}kil*, [J] to be able, S: 3202†, B*, K*, H*

10322 יַם *yam*, sea, S: 3221†, B: 1095D, K: 1082B, H: 407D

10323 יְסַף *y^{e}sap*, [Q] to be added, S: 3255, B: 1095D, K: 1082B, H: 407D

10324 יְעַט *y^{e}ʿaṭ*, [O] to take counsel together, S: 3272, B: 1095D, K: 1082C, H: 408A

10325 יָעֵט *yāʿēṭ*, adviser, counselor, S: 3272, B: 1095D, K: 1082C, H: 408A

10326 יְצַב *y^{e}ṣab*, [M] to make certain, S: 3321†, B: 1095D, K: 1082C, H: 408A

10327 יַצִּיב *yaṣṣîb*, certain, true, reliable, S: 3330, B: 1096A, K: 1082C, H: 408A

10328 יְקַד *y^{e}qad*, [J] to burn, S: 3345, B: 1096A, K: 1082D, H: 408A

10329 יְקֵדָה *y^{e}qēdâ*, blazing, burning, S: 3346, B: 1096A, K: 1082D, H: 408A

10330 יַקִּיר *yaqqîr*, honorable; difficult, S: 3358, B: 1096A, K: 1083A, H: 408A

10331 יְקָר *yᵉqār*, glory, honor, majesty, S: 3367, B: 1096A, K: 1083A, H: 408A

10332 יְרוּשְׁלֶם *yᵉrûšᵉlem*, Jerusalem, S: 3390†, B: 1096A, K: 1083A, H: 408A

10333 יְרַח *yᵉraḥ*, month, S: 3393, B: 1096A, K: 1083B, H: 408C

10334 יַרְכָה *yarkâ*, (upper) thigh, S: 3410†, B: 1096B, K: 1083B, H: 408C

10335 יִשְׂרָאֵל *yiśrāʾēl*, Israel, S: 3479, B: 1096B, K: 1083B, H: 408C

10336 יֵשׁוּעַ *yēšûaʿ*, Jeshua, S: 3443, B: 1096A, K: 1083C, H: 408C

10337 יָת *yāt*, not translated, indicates the direct object, S: 3487†, B: 1096B, K: 1083C, H: 408C

10338 יְתִב *yᵉtib*, [J] to live in, dwell; to sit, be seated; [P] to cause to settle, cause to dwell in, S: 3488, B: 1096B, K: 1083C, H: 408C

10339 יַתִּיר *yattîr*, exceptional, outstanding; (as adv.) so, very, exceedingly, S: 3493, B: 1096B, K: 1083D, H: 408C

10340 כ *k*, letter of the Aramaic alphabet, S*, B: 1096B, K: 1083D, H: 408C

10341 כְּ- *kᵉ-*, as, like, according to, S*, B: 1096C, K: 1084A, H: 408C

10342 ךְ- *-k*, you, your, S*, B*, K: 1084A, H*

10343 כְּדַב *kᵉdab*, misleading, false, S: 3538, B: 1096C, K: 1084B, H: 408B

10344 כִּדְבָה *kidbâ*, lie, S*, B*, K*, H*

10345 כָּה *kâ*, here, up to this point, S: 3542, B: 1096C, K: 1084B, H: 408B

10346 כְּהַל *kᵉhal*, [J] to be able, S: 3546, B: 1096C, K: 1084B, H: 408B

10347 כָּהֵן *kāhēn*, priest, S: 3549, B: 1096D, K: 1084D, H: 408B

10348 כַּוָּה *kawwâ*, window, S: 3551†, B: 1096D, K: 1084D, H: 408B

10349 כוֹן- *-kôn*, you, your, S*, B: 1096D, K: 1084D, H: 408B

10350 כּוֹרֶשׁ *kôreš*, Cyrus, S: 3567, B: 1096D, K: 1085A, H: 408B

10351 כִּיל *kîl*, variant: [L] to be fixed, S*, B*, K*, H*

10352 כַּכַּר *kakkar*, talent (unit of weight or value), S: 3604†, B: 1096D, K: 1085A, H: 408B

10353 כֹּל *kōl*, all, any, every, S: 3606, B*, K: 1085A, H: 408D

10354 כְּלַל *kᵉlal*, [P] to finish, restore; [R] to be finished, S: 3635, B: 1098A, K: 1085B, H: 408D

10355 כֹם- *-kōm*, you, your, S*, B: 1097A, K: 1085B, H: 408D

10356 כְּמָה *kᵉmâ*, variant: how?. see 10341 & 10408, S: 4101†, B: 1097A, K: 1085D, H: 409A

10357 כֵּן *kēn*, this is what, thus, S: 3652, B*, K*, H*

10358 כְּנֵמָא *kᵉnēmāʾ*, as follows, thus, S: 3660, B: 1099D 3a, K: 1086A, H: 409A

10359 כְּנַשׁ *kᵉnaš*, [J] to assemble (persons); [O] to be assembled, S: 3673†, B: 1097B, K: 1086A, H: 409A

10360 כְּנָת *kᵉnāt*, associate, colleague, S: 3675, B: 1097B, K: 1086A, H: 409A

10361 כַּסְדַּי *kasdāy*, variant: Chaldean, S: 3679, B: 1097B, K: 1086A, H: 409B

10362 כְּסַף *kᵉsap*, silver, S: 3702, B: 1097C, K: 1086B, H: 409B

10363 כְּעַן *kᵉʿan*, now, furthermore, to the present, S: 3705, B: 1098A, K: 1086B, H: 409B

10364 כְּעֶנֶת *kᵉʿenet*, (and) now, S: 3706, B: 1097C, K: 1086C, H: 409B

10365 כְּעֶת *kᵉʿet*, (and) now, S: 3706, B: 1107B, K: 1086C, H: 409B

10366 כְּפַת *kᵉpat*, [K] to be bound; [M] to tie up; [Mp] to be tied, S: 3729, B: 1107B, K: 1086D, H: 409C

10367 כֹּר *kōr*, cor (dry measure), S: 3734, B: 1107B, K: 1086D, H: 409C

10368 כַּרְבְּלָה *karbᵉlâ*, turban, cap, S: 3737†, B: 1097C, K: 1086D, H: 409C

10369 כְּרָה *kᵉrâ*, [L] to be troubled, distressed, S: 3735†, B: 1096D, K: 1087A, H: 409C

10370 כָּרוֹז *kārôz*, herald, proclaimer, S: 3744, B: 1097D, K: 1087A, H: 409C

10371 כְּרַז *kᵉraz*, [P] to proclaim, S: 3745, B: 1097C, K: 1087B, H: 409C

10372 כָּרְסֵא *korsēʾ*, throne, S: 3764, B: 1097D, K: 1087B, H: 409C

10373 כַּשְׂדַּי *kaśdāy*, Chaldean; Babylonian; (as a common noun) astrologer, S: 3779†, B: 1097D, K: 1087C, H: 409C

10374 כְּתַב *kᵉtab*, [J] to write; [Jp/K] to be written, S: 3790, B: 1097C, K: 1087C, H: 409C

10375 כְּתָב *kᵉtāb*, writing, inscription, decree, S: 3792, B: 1098A, K: 1087C, H: 409C

10376 כְּתַל *kᵉtal*, wall, S: 3797, B: 1098A, K: 1087D, H: 409D

10377 ל *l*, letter of the Aramaic alphabet, S*, B: 1098A, K: 1087D, H: 409D

10378 לְ- *lᵉ-*, to, for, toward, into; belonging to, with regard to, S*, B: 1098B, K: 1088C, H: 409D

10379 לָא *lāʾ*, no, not, never, S: 3809, B*, K: 1088A, H*

10380 לֵב *lēb*, heart, mind, S: 3821, B: 1098B, K: 1088B, H: 409B

10381 לְבַב *lᵉbab*, heart, mind, S: 3825, B: 1098C, K: 1089B, H: 410B

10382 לְבוּשׁ *lᵉbûš*, clothing, garment, S: 3831, B: 1098D, K: 1089C, H: 410C

10383 לְבַשׁ *lᵉbaš*, [J] to be clothed; [P] to clothe (another), S: 3848, B: 1098D, K: 1089D, H: 410C

10384 לָה *lâ*, variant: see 10379, S: 3809, B: 1098D, K: 1089D, H: 410C

10385 לָהֵן *lāhēn*[1], so then, therefore, S: 3861, B: 1098D, K: 1089D, H: 410C

10386 לָהֵן *lāhēn*[2], except, but, unless, S: 3861, B: 1098C, K: 1090A, H: 410C

10387 לֵוָי *lēwāy*, Levite, S: 3879†, B: 1099A, K: 1090A, H: 410C

10388 לְוָת *lᵉwāt*, near, beside, S: 3890, B: 1099A, K: 1090A, H: 410C

10389 לְחֶם *lᵉḥem*, banquet meal, S: 3900, B: 1099A, K: 1090B, H: 410C

10390 לְחֵנָה *lᵉḥēnâ*, concubine, S: 3904, B: 1099A, K: 1090B, H: 410C

10391 לֵילֵי *lêlê*, night, S: 3916†, B: 1099A, K: 1090B, H: 410D

10392 לִשָּׁן *liššān*, language, tongue, S: 3961, B: 1099B, K: 1090C, H: 410D

10393 מ *m*, letter of the Aramaic alphabet, S*, B: 1099B, K: 1090D, H: 410D

10394 מָא *māʾ*, variant: what?, see 10408, S: 3964, B: 1099B, K: 1090D, H: 410D

10395 מְאָה *mᵉʾâ*, hundred; (dual) two hundred, S: 3969, B*, K: 1091A, H*

10396 מֹאזְנֵא *mōʾznēʾ*, scale, balance, S: 3977†, B: 1099C, K: 1091A, H: 410B

10397 מֵאמַר *mēʾmar*, declaration, request, S: 3983, B: 1099B, K: 1091A, H: 410B

10398 מָאן *māʾn*, article, container, goblet, S: 3984, B: 1079B, K: 1091B, H: 410B

10399 מְגִלָּה *mᵉgillâ*, scroll, S: 4040, B: 1081B, K: 1091B, H: 410D

10400 מְגַר *mᵉgar*, [M] to overthrow, S: 4049, B: 1099C, K: 1091B, H: 410D

10401 מַדְבַּח *madbaḥ*, altar, S: 4056, B: 1086C, K: 1091B, H: 411A

10402 מִדָּה *middâ*, tax, revenue, tribute, S: 4061, B: 1099C, K: 1091C, H: 411A

10403 מְדוֹר *mᵉdôr*, living, dwelling, S: 4070, B: 1087A, K: 1091C, H: 411A

10404 מָדַי *māday*, Mede; Media, S: 4076 & 4077, B: 1101B, K: 1091D, H: 411A

10405 מָדָיָא *mādāyāʾ*, variant: the Mede, see 10404, S: 4076† & 4077@, B: 1087B, K: 1091D, H: 411A

10406 מְדִינָה *mᵉdînâ*, province, district, S: 4083, B: 1099C, K: 1091D, H: 411A

10407 מְדָר *mᵉdār*, living, dwelling (place), S: 4070, B: 1099C, K: 1091D, H: 411A

10408 מָה *mâ*, why?, what?; that which, what, S: 4101, B: 1088C, K: 1092A, H: 411A

10409 מוֹת *môt*, death, S: 4193, B: 1087B, K: 1092B, H: 411A

10410 מָזוֹן *māzôn*, food, S: 4203, B: 1099C, K: 1092B, H: 411A

10411 מְחָא *mᵉḥāʾ*, [J] to strike; [M] to hold back, prevent; [L] to be impaled, S: 4223, B: 1099D, K: 1092C, H: 411B

10412 מַחְלְקָה *maḥlᵉqâ*, group, division (of priests), S: 4255, B: 1091B, K: 1092C, H: 411B

10413 מְטָא *mᵉṭāʾ*, [J] to reach out, extend towards, S: 4291, B: 1099D, K: 1092C, H: 411B

10414 מִישָׁאֵל *mîšāʾēl*, Mishael, S: 4333, B: 1093B, K: 1092D, H: 411B

10415 מֵישַׁךְ *mêšak*, Meshach, S: 4336, B: 1100A, K: 1092D, H: 411B

10416 מְלָא *mᵉlāʾ*, [J] to fill; [L] to be filled, S: 4391, B: 1100A, K: 1093B, H: 411C

10417 מַלְאַךְ *malʾak*, angel, S: 4398, B: 1100A, K: 1093B, H: 411C

10418 מִלָּה *millâ*, word, command; matter, thing, affair, S: 4406, B: 1100A, K: 1093B, H: 411C

10419 מְלַח¹ *melaḥ*[1], [J] to eat salt (i.e., be under obligation to), S: 4415, B: 1098D, K: 1093B, H: 411C

10420 מְלַח² *melaḥ*[2], salt, S: 4416, B: 1100C, K: 1093C, H: 411C

10421 מֶלֶךְ *melek*, king, royal ruler, S: 4430, B: 1100A, K: 1093C, H: 411C

10422 מְלַךְ *melak*, advice, counsel, S: 4431, B: 1100A, K: 1093D, H: 411C

10423 מַלְכָּה *malkâ*, queen, S: 4433†, B: 1100B, K: 1094A, H: 411C

10424 מַלְכוּ *malkû*, kingdom, dominion, reign, S: 4437, B: 1100C, K: 1094B, H: 411D

10425 מְלַל *melal*, [M] to speak, S: 4449, B: 1100B, K: 1094B, H: 411D

10426 מַן *man*, who? what?; anyone, whoever, S: 4479, B: 1100B, K: 1094B, H: 411D

10427 מִן *min*, from, to, out of, more than, S: 4481, B: 1100C, K: 1094C, H: 411D

10428 מְנֵא *menē'*, mene (unit of weight), S: 4484, B: 1100D, K: 1094C, H: 412A

10429 מִנְדָּה *mindâ*, variant: tribute, see 10402, S: 4061, B: 1100D, K: 1094D, H: 412A

10430 מַנְדַּע *mandaʿ*, knowledge, understanding, S: 4486, B: 1101B, K: 1095B, H: 412B

10431 מְנָה *menâ*, [J] to number; [M] to appoint, set (over), S: 4483, B: 1101B, K: 1095C, H: 412B

10432 מִנְחָה *minḥâ*, offering, gift; grain offering, S: 4504, B: 1095B, K: 1095C, H: 412B

10433 מִנְיָן *minyān*, number, S: 4510, B: 1101B, K: 1095D, H: 412C

10434 מַעֲבָד *maʿabād*, what one does, work, S: 4567†, B: 1101C, K: 1095D, H: 412C

10435 מְעֵה *meʿēh*, belly, S: 4577, B: 1101B, K: 1095D, H: 412C

10436 מֶעָל *meʿāl*, going in, (+ 10728) sunset, S: 4606†, B: 1105A, K: 1096A, H: 412C

10437 מָרֵא *mārē'*, lord; (of God) the Lord, S: 4756, B: 1101C, K: 1096A, H: 412C

10438 מְרַד *merad*, rebellion, S: 4776, B: 1106D, K: 1096A, H: 412C

10439 מָרָד *mārād*, rebellious, S: 4779, B: 1101C, K: 1096B, H: 412C

10440 מְרַט *meraṭ*, [K] to be torn off, plucked out, S: 4804, B: 1101C, K: 1096C, H: 412C

10441 מֹשֶׁה *mōšeh*, Moses, S: 4873, B: 1101C, K: 1096C, H: 412C

10442 מְשַׁח¹ *mešaḥ*[1], olive oil, S: 4887, B: 1101D, K: 1096C, H: 412C

10443 מְשַׁח² *mešaḥ*[2], variant: measure, S: 4887, B: 1101D, K: 1096C, H: 412C

10444 מִשְׁכַּב *miškab*, bed, S: 4903, B: 1101D, K: 1096C, H: 412D

10445 מִשְׁכַּן *miškan*, dwelling, abode, S: 4907, B*, K: 1096D, H: 412D

10446 מַשְׁרוֹקִי *mašrôqî*, flute, musical pipe, S: 4953, B: 1115B, K: 1096D, H: 412D

10447 מִשְׁתֵּא *mištē'*, banquet (hall); feast (hall), S: 4961†, B: 1115C, K: 1096D, H: 412D

10448 מַתְּנָה *mattenâ*, gift, S: 4978†, B: 1117B, K: 1097A, H: 412D

10449 נ *n*, letter of the Aramaic alphabet, S*, B: 1117C, K: 1097A, H: 412D

10450 -נָא *-nā'*, we, our, S*, B: 1103D, K: 1097C, H: 412D

10451 נְבָא *nebā'*, [O] to prophesy, act as a prophet, S: 5013, B*, K: 1097A, H*

10452 נְבוּאָה *nebû'â*, prophesying, preaching, S: 5017, B*, K*, H*

10453 נְבוּכַדְנֶצַּר *nebûkadneṣṣar*, Nebuchadnezzar, S: 5020, B: 1101D, K: 1097B, H: 413A

10454 נְבִזְבָּה *nebizbâ*, present, gift, S: 5023, B: 1102A, K: 1097B, H: 413A

10455 נְבִיא *nebî'*, prophet, S: 5029, B: 1102A, K: 1097B, H: 413A

10456 נֶבְרְשָׁה *nebrešâ*, lampstand, S: 5043†, B: 1102A, K: 1097D, H: 413A

10457 נְגַד *negad*, [J] to flow, S: 5047, B: 1101D, K: 1097D, H: 413A

10458 נֶגֶד *neged*, toward, before, facing, S: 5049, B: 1102A, K: 1098A, H: 413B

10459 נְגַהּ *negah*, brightness (i.e., first light of dawn), S: 5053†, B: 1102A, K: 1098A, H: 413A

10460 נְגוֹ *negô*, variant: Nego, see 10524, S: 5665†, B: 1102A, K: 1098A, H: 413A

10461 נְדַב *nedab*, [O] to be willing, to give freely; (as noun) a freewill offering, S: 5069, B: 1102A, K: 1098B, H: 413A

10462 נִדְבָּךְ *nidbāk*, course (of timber or stone in building), S: 5073, B: 1105A, K: 1098B, H: 413A

10463 נְדַד *nedad*, [J] to flee (i.e., sleep flees = insomnia), S: 5075, B: 1102B, K: 1098B, H: 413B

10464 נִדְנֶה *nidneh*, sheath (of the spirit = the body), S: 5085, B: 1102B, K: 1098B, H: 413B

10465 נְהוֹר *nehôr*, light, S: 5094†, B: 1102B, K: 1098C, H: 413B

10466 נְהִיר *nehîr*, light, S: 5094, B: 1102B, K: 1098C, H: 413B

10467 נַהִירוּ *nahîrû*, insight, illumination (of the mind), S: 5094, B: 1102C, K: 1098C, H: 413B

10468 נְהַר *nehar*, river, stream, S: 5103, B: 1102C, K: 1098D, H: 413B

10469 נוּד *nûd*, [J] to flee, S: 5111, B: 1102C, K: 1098D, H: 413B

10470 נְוָלוּ *newālû*, pile of rubble, garbage-heap, S: 5122, B: 1102C, K: 1098D, H: 413B

10471 נוּר *nûr*, fire, S: 5135, B: 1102C, K: 1099A, H: 413C

10472 נְזַק *nezaq*, [J] to suffer loss; [P] to cause to suffer, be a detriment, be troublesome, S: 5142, B: 1102C, K: 1099A, H: 413C

10473 נְחָשׁ *neḥāš*, bronze material, S: 5174, B: 1102C, K: 1099B, H: 413C

10474 נְחַת *neḥat*, [J] to come down; [P] to deposit, store; [Q] to be deposed, S: 5182, B: 1102C, K: 1099B, H: 413C

10475 נְטַל *neṭal*, [J] to raise up, lift up; [K] to be lifted up, S: 5191, B: 1102D, K: 1099C, H: 413C

10476 נְטַר *neṭar*, [J] to keep (in one's mind or heart), S: 5202, B: 1102D, K: 1099C, H: 413C

10477 -נִי *-nî*, I, me, my, S*, B: 1102D, K: 1099B, H: 413D

10478 נִיחוֹחַ *nîḥôaḥ*, incense, pleasing scent, S: 5208, B: 1102D, K: 1099D, H: 413D

10479 נְכַס *nekas*, treasury; fine, S: 5232, B*, K*, H*

10480 נְמַר *nemar*, leopard, S: 5245, B: 1102D, K: 1100A, H: 413D

10481 נְסַח *nesaḥ*, [L] to be pulled out, S: 5256, B: 1103A, K: 1100B, H: 413D

10482 נְסַךְ¹ *nesak*[1], [M] to present (an offering), S: 5260, B: 1103A, K: 1100B, H: 413D

10483 נְסַךְ² *nesak*[2], drink offering, libation, S: 5261, B: 1103A, K: 1100B, H: 413D

10484 נְפַל *nepal*, [J] to fall, S: 5308, B: 1103A, K: 1100B, H: 413D

10485 נְפַק *nepaq*, [J] to go out, come out; [P] to take out, remove, S: 5312, B: 1103A, K: 1100C, H: 413D

10486 נִפְקָה *nipqâ*, expense, cost, S: 5313†, B: 1103A, K: 1100C, H: 414A

10487 נִצְבָּה *niṣbâ*, hardness, firmness, S: 5326, B: 1103B, K: 1100D, H: 414A

10488 נְצַח *neṣaḥ*, [O] to distinguish oneself, S: 5330, B: 1103B, K: 1101A, H: 414A

10489 נְצַל *neṣal*, [P] to save, rescue, deliver, S: 5338, B: 1103B, K: 1101A, H: 414A

10490 נְקֵא *neqē'*, pure, clean, S: 5343, B: 1103B, K: 1101A, H: 414A

10491 נְקַשׁ *neqaš*, [J] to knock (together), S: 5368, B: 1103B, K: 1101B, H: 414A

10492 נְשָׂא *neśā'*, [J] to take away, carry away; [O] to revolt, rise up, S: 5376, B: 1103C, K: 1101B, H: 414B

10493 נְשִׁין *nešîn*, wives, women, S: 5389, B: 1103C, K: 1101C, H: 414C

10494 נִשְׁמָה *nišmâ*, breath (pertaining to life), S: 5396, B: 1103C, K: 1101C, H: 414C

10495 נְשַׁר *nešar*, eagle, S: 5403, B: 1081D, K: 1101C, H: 414C

10496 נִשְׁתְּוָן *ništewān*, official letter, decree, S: 5407, B: 1103C, K: 1101D, H: 414C

10497 נְתִין *netîn*, temple servant, S: 5412, B: 1103C, K: 1101D, H: 414C

10498 נְתַן *netan*, [J] to give, provide, supply, S: 5415, B: 1103C, K: 1102A, H: 414C

10499 נְתַר *netar*, [P] to strip off, shake off, S: 5426, B: 1103C, K: 1102A, H: 414C

10500 ס *s*, letter of the Aramaic alphabet, S*, B: 1103C, K: 1102A, H: 414C

10501 סַבְּכָא *sabbekā'*, lyre, S: 5443, B: 1103D, K: 1102C, H: 414C

10502 סְבַל *sebal*, [N] to be laid, S: 5446, B*, K: 1102B, H*

10503 סְבַר *sebar*, [J] to try, strive, seek, S: 5452, B: 1113C, K: 1102B, H: 414B

10504 סְגִד *s^e^gid*, [J] to worship, pay honor, S: 5457, B: 1103D, K: 1102B, H: 414B

10505 סְגַן *s^e^gan*, prefect, governor, S: 5460, B: 1104A, K: 1102D, H: 414B

10506 סְגַר *s^e^gar*, [J] to shut, close up, S: 5463, B: 1104A, K: 1103A, H: 414B

10507 סוּמְפֹּנְיָה *sûmpōn^e^yâ*, pipe (musical instrument), S: 5481, B: 1104A, K: 1103A, H: 414B

10508 סוּף *sûp*, [J] to be fulfilled; [P] to bring to an end, S: 5487, B: 1104A, K: 1103A, H: 414D

10509 סוֹף *sôp*, end (of space, time, or circumstance), S: 5491, B: 1104B, K: 1103C, H: 414D

10510 סוּפֹּנְיָא *sûppōn^e^yā'*, variant: pipes, see 10507, S: 5481†, B: 1104B, K: 1103B, H: 414D

10511 סְטַר *s^e^ṭar*, variant: see 10680, S: 7859†, B: 1104B, K: 1103C, H: 414D

10512 סִיפֹּנְיָא *sîppōn^e^yā'*, variant: pipes, see 10507, S: 5481†, B: 1104A, K: 1103C, H: 414D

10513 סְלִק *s^e^laq*, [J] to come up, go up; [P] to lift up; [Q] to be lifted up, S: 5559† & 5267@, B: 1113D, K: 1103C, H: 414D

10514 סְעַד *s^e^'ad*, [M] to help, support, S: 5583, B: 1104A, K: 1103C, H: 414D

10515 סְפַר *s^e^par*, book, record, archive, S: 5609, B: 1104B, K: 1103C, H: 415A

10516 סָפַר *sāpar*, teacher of the Law; secretary (an official), scribe, S: 5613†, B: 1104B, K: 1103D, H: 415A

10517 סַרְבָּל *sarbāl*, robe, garment, S: 5622†, B: 1104C, K: 1104A, H: 415A

10518 סָרַךְ *sārak*, administrator, S: 5632†, B: 1104C, K: 1104A, H: 415C

10519 סְתַר¹ *s^e^tar*[1], [Mp] to be hidden; (as noun) hidden things, S: 5642, B: 1104C, K: 1104B, H: 415C

10520 ²סְתַר *s^e^tar*[2], [J] to destroy, demolish, S: 5642, B: 1104C, K: 1104C, H: 415C

10521 ע *'*, letter of the Aramaic alphabet, S*, B: 1104C, K: 1104D, H: 415C

10522 עֲבַד *'^a^bad*, [J] to do, make; [L] to be done, be made, be turned into, S: 5648, B: 1104D, K: 1104D, H: 415C

10523 עֲבֵד *'^a^bēd*, servant, S: 5649†, B*, K: 1105A, H*

10524 עֲבֵד נְגוֹ *'^a^bēd n^e^gô*, Abednego, S: 5665†, B: 1104D, K: 1105A, H: 415A

10525 עֲבִידָה *'^a^bîdâ*, work, service, administration, S: 5673, B: 1105A, K: 1105C, H: 415B

10526 עֲבַר *'^a^bar*, the opposite bank (of a river); Trans(-Euphrates), S: 5675, B: 1105A, K: 1105C, H: 415B

10527 עַד *'ad*, up to, until, S: 5705, B: 1105A, K: 1105C, H: 415B

10528 עֲדָה *'^a^dâ*, [J] to be taken, be repealed; [P] to take away, S: 5709, B: 1105A, K: 1105D, H: 415C

10529 עִדּוֹא *'iddô'*, Iddo, S: 5714, B: 1105B, K: 1106A, H: 415C

10530 עִדָּן *'iddān*, time (general or specific period), S: 5732, B: 1105B, K: 1106B, H: 415D

10531 עוֹד *'ôd*, still, yet, S: 5751, B*, K: 1106B, H: 415D

10532 עֲוָיָה *'^a^wāyâ*, wickedness, iniquity, S: 5758†, B: 1105C, K: 1106C, H: 415D

10533 עוֹף *'ôp*, bird, S: 5776, B: 1105C, K: 1106D, H: 416A

10534 עוּר *'ûr*, chaff, S: 5784, B: 1105C, K: 1106D, H: 416A

10535 עֵז *'ēz*, goat (male and female), S: 5796, B: 1105C, K: 1106D, H: 416A

10536 עִזְקָה *'izqâ*, signet-ring, S: 5824†, B: 1105C, K: 1106D, H: 416A

10537 עֶזְרָא *'ezrā'*, Ezra, S: 5831, B: 1107C, K: 1107A, H: 416A

10538 עֲזַרְיָה *'^a^zaryâ*, Azariah, S: 5839, B: 1105D, K: 1107A, H: 416A

10539 עֵטָה *'ēṭâ*, counsel, wisdom, S: 5843†, B: 1105D, K: 1107B, H: 416A

10540 עַיִן *'ayin*, eye, S: 5870, B: 1105D, K: 1107B, H: 416A

10541 עִיר *'îr*, messenger (of God), watcher, S: 5894, B: 1096A, K: 1107B, H: 416A

10542 עַל *'al*, upon, over, against, toward, concerning, S: 5922, B: 1105D, K: 1107B, H: 416A

10543 עֵלָּא *'ēllā'*, over, above, S: 5924, B: 1105D, K: 1107C, H: 416A

10544 עִלָּה *'illâ*, grounds, basis, pretext (for charges), S: 5931, B: 1106A, K: 1107C, H: 416A

10545 עֲלָוָה *'^a^lāwâ*, burnt offering, S: 5928†, B: 1106C, K: 1108A, H: 416B

10546 עִלָּי *'illāy*, highest, superior; (as a title) the Most High, S: 5943†, B: 1106C, K: 1108B, H: 416B

10547 עִלִּי *'illî*, upstairs room, S: 5952†, B: 1106A, K: 1108B, H: 416B

10548 עֶלְיוֹן *'elyôn*, highest, superior; (as a title) the Most High, S: 5946, B: 1106A, K: 1108C, H: 416C

10549 עֲלַל *'^a^lal*, [J] to go in; [P] to take in, bring before; [Q] to be brought in, introduced before, S: 5954, B: 1106A, K: 1108C, H: 416C

10550 עָלַם *'ālam*, forever, eternal, everlasting; ancient, a long time ago, S: 5957, B: 1106A, K: 1108D, H: 416C

10551 עֵלְמָי *'ēlmāy*, Elamite, S: 5962†, B: 1106C, K: 1108D, H: 416C

10552 עֲלַע *'^a^la'*, rib, S: 5967, B: 1106D, K: 1109A, H: 416C

10553 עַם *'am*, people, nation, S: 5972, B: 1106D, K: 1109B, H: 416D

10554 עִם *'im*, with, along with, to, for, S: 5974, B: 1106D, K: 1109C, H: 416D

10555 עַמִּיק *'ammîq*, deep; (as noun) the deep things, S: 5994, B: 1107A, K: 1109C, H: 416D

10556 עֲמַר *'^a^mar*, wool, S: 6015, B: 1107A, K: 1109C, H: 416D

10557 עַן *'an*, variant: see 10363, S: 3705†, B: 1107A, K: 1109D, H: 417A

10558 עֲנָה *'^a^nâ*, [J] to answer, reply, S: 6032, B: 1107A, K: 1110A, H: 417A

10559 עֲנֵה *'^a^nēh*, oppressed, needy, poor, S: 6033†, B: 1107B, K: 1110A, H: 417A

10560 עֲנָן *'^a^nān*, cloud, S: 6050†, B: 1107A, K: 1110A, H: 417A

10561 עֲנַף *'^a^nap*, branch, bough, S: 6056, B: 1107C, K: 1110B, H: 417A

10562 עֲנָשׁ *'^a^nāš*, confiscation, S: 6065†, B: 1107C, K: 1110B, H: 417A

10563 עֶנֶת *'enet*, variant: see 10364, S: 3706, B: 1107C, K: 1110C, H: 417A

10564 עֳפִי *'^o^pî*, leaves, foliage, S: 6074, B: 1107C, K: 1110C, H: 417A

10565 עֲצִיב *'^a^ṣîb*, anguished, sorrowful, S: 6088†, B: 1107B, K: 1110C, H: 417A

10566 עֲקַר *'^a^qar*, [L] to be uprooted, plucked out, S: 6132, B: 1107C, K: 1110C, H: 417A

10567 עִקַּר *'iqqar*, stump, root, S: 6136, B: 1107D, K: 1110D, H: 417B

10568 עָר *'ār*, adversary, foe, S: 6146, B: 1107D, K: 1110D, H: 417B

10569 עֲרַב *'^a^rab*, [Mp] to be mixed; [O] (ptcp.) mixture, S: 6151, B: 1107D, K: 1110D, H: 417C

10570 עֲרָד *'^a^rād*, wild donkey, S: 6167, B: 1108A, K: 1111A, H: 417C

10571 עַרְוָה *'arwâ*, dishonor, S: 6173, B: 1107D, K: 1111A, H: 417C

10572 עֲשַׂב *'^a^śab*, grass, (green) plants, S: 6211', B: 1107D, K: 1111B, H: 417C

10573 עֲשַׂר *'^a^śar*, ten, S: 6236, B: 1107D, K: 1111B, H: 417C

10574 עֶשְׂרִין *'eśrîn*, twenty, S: 6243†, B: 1108A, K: 1111B, H: 417C

10575 עֲשַׁת *'^a^šat*, [J] to plan, intend, S: 6246†, B: 1108A, K: 1111C, H: 417C

10576 עֶת *'et*, variant: see 10365, S: 3706†, B: 1108A, K: 1111C, H: 417C

10577 עֲתִיד *'^a^tîd*, ready, S: 6263, B: 1108A, K: 1111C, H: 417C

10578 עַתִּיק *'attîq*, old, ancient; (as a title) the Ancient (of Days), S: 6268, B: 1107B, K: 1086D, H: 417D

10579 פ *p*, letter of the Aramaic alphabet, S*, B: 1108A, K: 1111D, H: 417D

10580 פֶּחָה *peḥâ*, governor, S: 6347, B: 1108A, K: 1111D, H: 417D

10581 פֶּחָר *peḥār*, potter, S: 6353, B*, K: 1112A, H*

10582 פַּטִּישׁ *paṭṭîš*, trousers, leggings, S: 6361, B: 1108B, K: 1112A, H: 417B

10583 פְּלַג¹ *p^e^lag*[1], [Jp] to be divided, S: 6386, B: 1108B, K: 1112B, H: 417B

10584 ²פְּלַג *p^e^lag*[2], half, S: 6387, B: 1108B, K: 1112B, H: 417B

10585 פְּלֻגָּה *p^e^luggâ*, division (of priests), S: 6392, B: 1108B, K: 1112D, H: 417B

10586 פְּלַח *p^e^laḥ*, [J] to serve, worship, work for (deity or deities), S: 6399, B: 1108B, K: 1112D, H: 417B

10587 פָּלְחָן *polḥān*, worship, service, work (for deity), S: 6402, B: 1108C, K: 1112D, H: 417B

10588 פֻּם *pum*, mouth, S: 6433, B: 1108C, K: 1113A, H: 417D

10589 פַּס *pas*, (palm of) hand, S: 6447, B: 1108C, K: 1113A, H: 417D

10590 פְּסַנְתֵּרִין *p^e^santērîn*, harp (triangular stringed instrument), S: 6460, B: 1108C, K: 1113B, H: 417D

10591 פַּרְזֶל *parzel*, iron, S: 6523, B: 1108D, K: 1113B, H: 417D

10592 פְּרַס p^{e}ras, [K] to be divided, S: 6537, B: 1108C, K: 1113C, H: 418A

10593 פְּרֵס p^{e}rēs, parsin, peres (unit of measure & weight), S: 6537, B: 1108D, K: 1113C, H: 418A

10594 פָּרַס pāras, Persia, Persian, S: 6540, B: 1108D, K: 1113C, H: 418A

10595 פַּרְסָי parsāy, Persian, S: 6543, B: 1108D, K: 1113D, H: 418A

10596 פְּרַק p^{e}raq, [J] to renounce, S: 6562, B: 1108D, K: 1114A, H: 418A

10597 פְּרַשׁ p^{e}raš, [Mp] to be translated, be made clear, S: 6568, B: 1108D, K: 1114A, H: 417A

10598 פַּרְשֶׁגֶן paršegen, copy (of a document), S: 6573, B: 1108D, K: 1114A, H: 418A

10599 פְּשַׁר[1] p^{e}šar[1], [J] to give an interpretation; [M] to interpret; (as noun) an interpreter, S: 6590, B: 1109A, K: 1114A, H: 418A

10600 פְּשַׁר[2] p^{e}šar[2], interpretation, explanation, what something means, S: 6591, B: 1109A, K: 1114B, H: 418A

10601 פִּתְגָם pitgām, word: report, reply, edict, decision, decree, S: 6600, B: 1109A, K: 1114C, H: 418C

10602 פְּתַח p^{e}taḥ, [Jp, K] to be opened, S: 6606, B: 1109A, K: 1114C, H: 418C

10603 פְּתָי p^{e}tāy, width, breadth, S: 6613†, B: 1109B, K: 1114D, H: 418C

10604 צ ṣ, letter of the Aramaic alphabet, S*, B: 1109B, K: 1114D, H: 418C

10605 צְבָה ṣ^{e}bâ, [J] to wish, desire, want, long for, S: 6634, B: 1109B, K: 1115C, H: 418C

10606 צְבוּ ṣ^{e}bû, situation, matter, affair, thing, S: 6640, B*, K: 1115A, H*

10607 צְבַע ṣ^{e}ba', [M] to drench, make wet; [O] to be drenched, made wet, S: 6647, B: 1109B, K: 1115A, H: 418B

10608 צַד ṣad, side, S: 6655, B: 1109C, K: 1115B, H: 418B

10609 צְדָא ṣ^{e}dā', purpose, (with 10190) is it true?, S: 6656, B: 1109C, K: 1115B, H: 418B

10610 צִדְקָה ṣidqâ, what is right, S: 6665, B: 1109C, K: 1115C, H: 418B

10611 צַוַּאר ṣawwa'r, neck, S: 6676, B: 1109C, K: 1115D, H: 418B

10612 צְלָה ṣ^{e}lâ, [M] to pray, S: 6739†, B: 1109D, K: 1115D, H: 418B

10613 צְלַח ṣ^{e}laḥ, [P] to cause to prosper; to promote; to make progress, S: 6744, B: 1109D, K: 1116A, H: 418D

10614 צְלֵם ṣ^{e}lēm, sculptured image, statue, S: 6755†, B: 1109D, K: 1116B, H: 418D

10615 צְפִיר ṣ^{e}pîr, male goat, S: 6841, B: 1109D, K: 1116B, H: 418D

10616 צִפַּר ṣippar, bird, S: 6853†, B: 1109D, K: 1116C, H: 418D

10617 ק q, letter of the Aramaic alphabet, S*, B: 1110A, K: 1116D, H: 418D

10618 קְבַל q^{e}bal, [M] to receive; to take over, S: 6902, B: 1110A, K: 1116D, H: 418D

10619 קֳבֵל q^{o}bēl, before, in front of; since, because of, S: 6903, B*, K: 1117A, H*

10620 קַדִּישׁ qaddîš, holy; (as noun) holy one, saint, S: 6922, B: 1110B, K: 1117A, H: 419A

10621 קֳדָם q^{o}dām, before, in the presence of, S: 6925, B: 1110A, K: 1117B, H: 419A

10622 קַדְמָה qadmâ, before times; (as adv.) formerly, S: 6928, B: 1110D, K: 1117D, H: 419A

10623 קַדְמָי qadmāy, first; earlier, former, S: 6933†, B: 1110B, K: 1117D, H: 419A

10624 קוּם qûm, [J] to stand, rise up; [M] to issue (a decree); [P] to set up, establish; [Q] to be set up, be established, S: 6966, B: 1110C, K: 1118B, H: 419B

10625 קְטַל q^{e}ṭal, [J] to put to death, kill; [K] to be slain; [L] to be put to death; [M] to kill; [O] to be put to death, S: 6992, B: 1110C, K: 1118B, H: 419B

10626 קְטַר q^{e}ṭar, difficult problem; joint (of the hip), S: 7001, B: 1110D, K: 1118C, H: 419B

10627 קַיִט qayiṭ, summer, S: 7007, B: 1111A, K: 1119A, H: 419C

10628 קְיָם q^{e}yām, edict, statute, decree, S: 7010, B: 1111B, K: 1119B, H: 419D

10629 קַיָּם qayyām, enduring, S: 7011, B: 1111B, K: 1119C, H: 419D

10630 קִיתְרֹס qît^{e}rōs, zither, S: 7030†, B: 1111A, K: 1119C, H: 419D

10631 קָל qāl, sound, voice, S: 7032, B: 1111A, K: 1119C, H: 419D

10632 קְנָה q^{e}nâ, [J] to buy, S: 7066†, B: 1111B, K: 1119C, H: 419D

10633 קְצַף[1] q^{e}ṣap[1], [J] to become furious, S: 7108, B: 1110D, K: 1119D, H: 419D

10634 קְצַף[2] q^{e}ṣap[2], wrath, fury, S: 7109, B: 1111B, K: 1119D, H: 419D

10635 קְצַץ q^{e}ṣaṣ, [M] to trim off, cut off, S: 7113, B: 1111C, K: 1119D, H: 420A

10636 קְצָת q^{e}ṣāt, part; the end, S: 7118, B: 1111C, K: 1120A, H: 420A

10637 קְרָא q^{e}rā', [J] to call, proclaim, read out loud; [Jp/K] to be read out loud; [L] to be called, be summoned, S: 7123, B*, K: 1120A, H: 420A

10638 קְרֵב q^{e}rēb, [J] to come near, approach; [M] to offer (a sacrifice); [P] to bring near, offer (a sacrifice), S: 7127, B: 1111C, K: 1120A, H: 420A

10639 קְרָב q^{e}rāb, war, S: 7129, B: 1111C, K: 1120B, H: 420A

10640 קִרְיָה qiryâ, city, town, S: 7149†, B: 1111C, K: 1120B, H: 420A

10641 קֶרֶן qeren, horn (of an animal, also used as a musical instrument), S: 7162, B: 1111D, K: 1120C, H: 420C

10642 קְרַץ q^{e}raṣ, piece, ("to eat pieces" = slander, denouncement), S: 7170, B: 1111D, K: 1120C, H: 420C

10643 קְשֹׁט q^{e}šōṭ, truth; (as adv.) surely, truly, rightly, S: 7187†, B: 1111D, K: 1120D, H: 420C

10644 קַתְרוֹס qatrôs, variant: zither, lyre, see 10630, S: 7030, B: 1111D, K: 1121A, H: 420C

10645 ר r, letter of the Aramaic alphabet, S*, B: 1112A, K: 1121C, H: 420C

10646 רֵאשׁ rē'š, head (for functions of sight and thought); leader, S: 7217, B: 1111B, K: 1121C, H: 419D

10647 רַב rab, great, large, many, S: 7229 & 7260, B*, K: 1121B, H*

10648 רְבָה r^{e}bâ, [J] to become large, be great; [M] to place in a high position, make great, S: 7236, B: 1112A, K: 1121B, H: 420B

10649 רִבּוֹ ribbô, ten thousand, myriad, (virtually) countless number, S: 7240, B: 1112A, K: 1122A, H: 420B

10650 רְבוּ r^{e}bû, greatness, high position, S: 7238, B: 1112B, K: 1122B, H: 420B

10651 רְבִיעָי r^{e}bî'āy, fourth, S: 7244†, B: 1112B, K: 1122B, H: 420B

10652 רַבְרְבָנִין rabr^{e}bānîn, nobles, lords, S: 7261†, B: 1112C, K: 1122C, H: 420D

10653 רְגַז[1] r^{e}gaz[1], [P] to anger, enrage, S: 7265, B: 1112C, K: 1122C, H: 420D

10654 רְגַז[2] r^{e}gaz[2], rage, S: 7266, B: 1112B, K: 1122C, H: 420D

10655 רְגַל r^{e}gal, foot, S: 7271, B: 1112C, K: 1122D, H: 420D

10656 רְגַשׁ r^{e}gaš, [P] to go in as a group (causing an uproar), S: 7284, B: 1112C, K: 1122D, H: 420D

10657 רֵו rēw, appearance, S: 7299, B: 1112C, K: 1123A, H: 420D

10658 רוּחַ rûaḥ, spirit; wind, S: 7308, B: 1112C, K: 1123A, H: 420D

10659 רוּם[1] rûm[1], [J] to become arrogant; [M] to exalt, praise; [P] to promote, cause to rise (in rank); [L] to rise up (against), S: 7313, B: 1112A, K: 1123B, H: 420D

10660 רוּם[2] rûm[2], height; the top, S: 7314, B: 1112D, K: 1123B, H: 420D

10661 רָז rāz, mystery, secret, S: 7328, B: 1112D, K: 1123C, H: 421A

10662 רְחוּם r^{e}ḥûm, Rehum, S: 7348, B: 1112D, K: 1123D, H: 421A

10663 רַחִיק raḥîq, far away, S: 7352, B: 1112D, K: 1123D, H: 421A

10664 רַחֲמִין raḥ^{a}mîn, mercy, compassion, S: 7359†, B: 1113A, K: 1123D, H: 421A

10665 רְחַץ r^{e}ḥaṣ, [L] to put one's trust in, rely on, S: 7365, B: 1113A, K: 1124A, H: 421A

10666 רֵיחַ rêaḥ, (singed, scorched) smell, S: 7382, B: 1113A, K: 1124A, H: 421A

10667 רְמָה r^{e}mâ, [J] to throw; to impose; [K] to be thrown, be set in place; [L] to be thrown, S: 7412, B: 1113A, K: 1124A, H: 421A

10668 רְעוּ r^{e}'û, will, decision, S: 7470, B: 1112D, K: 1124B, H: 421A

10669 רַעְיוֹן ra'yôn, thought (in one's mind), S: 7476, B: 1113A, K: 1124C, H: 421A

10670 רַעֲנַן ra'^{a}nan, prosperous, flourishing, S: 7487, B: 1113B, K: 1124D, H: 421C

10671 רְעַע r^{e}'a', [J] to break, crush; [M] to break to pieces, shatter, S: 7490, B: 1113B, K: 1124D, H: 421C

10672 רְפַס r^{e}pas, [J] to trample down, S: 7512, B: 1113B, K: 1125A, H: 421C

10673 רְשַׁם r^{e}šam, [J] to put in writing, publish; [K] to be written, be published, S: 7560, B: 1113B, K: 1125A, H: 421C

10674 שׂ *ś*, letter of the Aramaic alphabet, S*, B: 1113B, K: 1125C, H: 421C

10675 שָׂב *śāb*, elder (of the Jewish community), S: 7868†, B: 1113B, K: 1125C, H: 421C

10676 שַׂבְּכָא *śabbᵉkā'*, lyre (triangular instrument with four strings), S: 5443, B*, K: 1125B, H*

10677 שְׂגָא *śᵉgā'*, [J] to grow great, S: 7680, B*, K: 1125B, H: 421B

10678 שַׂגִּיא *śaggî'*, great, large, abundant, S: 7690, B: 1113C, K: 1125D, H: 421B

10679 שָׂהֲדוּ *śāhᵃdû*, variant: witness, see 3337, S: 3026†, B: 1113C, K: 1125D, H: 421B

10680 שְׂטַר *śᵉṭar*, side, S: 7859, B: 1113C, K: 1126A, H: 421B

10681 שִׂיב *śîb*, variant: [J] to be gray-haired, S: 7868, B: 1113C, K: 1126B, H: 421B

10682 שִׂים *śîm*, [J] to place (an order), issue (a decree); [K] to be place, be issued; [L] to be put, be laid (to rubble), S: 7761†, B: 1113D, K: 1126B, H: 421B

10683 שְׂכַל *śᵉkal*, [O] to think about, consider, S: 7920, B: 1114A, K: 1126C, H: 421B

10684 שָׂכְלְתָנוּ *śoklᵉtānû*, intelligence, understanding, insight, S: 7924, B: 1113D, K: 1126C, H: 421B

10685 שָׂלָה *śillâ*, variant: insolence, rebellion, S: 7955†, B: 1114A, K: 1126D, H: 421D

10686 שְׂנָא *śᵉnā'*, [J] to hate; (as noun) an enemy, S: 8131, B: 1114A, K: 1127A, H: 421D

10687 שְׂעַר *śᵉ'ar*, hair (of the head or body), S: 8177, B: 1115C, K: 1127A, H: 421D

10688 שׁ *š*, letter of the Aramaic alphabet, S*, B: 1114A, K: 1127A, H: 421D

10689 שְׁאֵל *šᵉ'ēl*, [J] to ask, question, S: 7593, B: 1114A, K: 1127C, H: 421D

10690 שְׁאֵלָה *šᵉ'ēlâ*, verdict, decision, S: 7595, B*, K: 1127B, H*

10691 שְׁאַלְתִּיאֵל *šᵉ'altî'ēl*, Shealtiel, S: 7598, B: 1114A, K: 1127B, H: 422A

10692 שְׁאָר *šᵉ'ār*, the rest, remainder, S: 7606, B: 1114A, K: 1127D, H: 422A

10693 שְׁבַח *šᵉbaḥ*, [M] to praise, honor, S: 7624, B*, K: 1128A, H: 422A

10694 שְׁבַט *šᵉbaṭ*, tribe, S: 7625, B: 1114B, K: 1128A, H: 422A

10695 שְׁבִיב *šᵉbîb*, flame, S: 7631, B: 1114B, K: 1128B, H: 422A

10696 שְׁבַע *šᵉba'*, seven, S: 7655†, B: 1114B, K: 1128B, H: 422A

10697 שְׁבַק *šᵉbaq*, [J] to leave, have remain; [L] to be left, S: 7662, B: 1114B, K: 1128C, H: 422A

10698 שְׁבַשׁ *šᵉbaš*, [O] to be baffled, be perplexed, S: 7672, B: 1114B, K: 1128C, H: 422B

10699 שֵׁגַל *šēgal*, wife, concubine, S: 7695†, B: 1114C, K: 1128C, H: 422B

10700 שְׁדַר *šᵉdar*, [O] to make every effort, strive, S: 7712, B: 1114C, K: 1128D, H: 422B

10701 שַׁדְרַךְ *šadrak*, Shadrach, S: 7715, B: 1114C, K: 1129A, H: 422B

10702 שְׁוָה *šᵉwâ*, [K] to be made like; [M] to make like; [O] to be made into, S: 7739, B: 1114C, K: 1129A, H: 422B

10703 שׁוּר *šûr*, wall, S: 7792, B: 1114C, K: 1129A, H: 422B

10704 שׁוּשַׁנְכָי *šûšankāy*, of Susa, S: 7801, B: 1114D, K: 1129B, H: 422B

10705 שְׁחַת *šᵉḥat*, [Jp] to be corrupt, wicked; (as noun) corruption, S: 7844, B: 1114D, K: 1129B, H: 422C

10706 שֵׁיזִב *šêzib*, [P] to rescue, save, S: 7804†, B: 1114D, K: 1129C, H: 422C

10707 שֵׁיצִיא *šêṣî'*, [P] to complete, finish, S: 3319†, B: 1115A, K: 1129C, H: 422C

10708 שְׁכַח *šᵉkaḥ*, [P] to find; [L] to be found, S: 7912, B: 1115A, K: 1129D, H: 442C

10709 שְׁכַן *šᵉkan*, [J] to dwell; [M] to cause to dwell, S: 7932, B: 1115A, K: 1129D, H: 422C

10710 שְׁלֵה *šᵉlēh*, contented, at ease, S: 7954†, B: 1115B, K: 1130A, H: 422D

10711 שָׁלֻה *šāluh*, variant: see 10712, S: 7955†, B: 1115B, K: 1130B, H: 422D

10712 שָׁלוּ *šālû*, negligence, S: 7960, B: 1115C, K: 1130C, H: 422D

10713 שְׁלֵוָה *šᵉlēwâ*, prosperity, S: 7963, B: 1115C, K: 1130C, H: 422D

10714 שְׁלַח *šᵉlaḥ*, [J] to send out; [Jp/K] to be sent, S: 7972, B: 1115C, K: 1130C, H: 422D

10715 שְׁלֵט *šᵉlēṭ*, [J] to rule over, overpower; [P] to make rule over, S: 7981, B: 1115C, K: 1130C, H: 423A

10716 שִׁלְטֹן *šilṭōn*, high official, S: 7984†, B: 1115C, K: 1130D, H: 423A

10717 שָׁלְטָן *šolṭān*, dominion, power, authority, S: 7985, B: 1115C, K: 1131A, H: 423A

10718 שַׁלִּיט *šallîṭ*, mighty, powerful, sovereign, ruling, S: 7990, B*, K: 1131A, H: 423A

10719 שְׁלִם *šᵉlim*, [J] to be finished; [P] to (deliver) completely, bring to an end, S: 8000, B: 1115D, K: 1131B, H: 423A

10720 שְׁלָם *šᵉlām*, (as salutation) cordial greetings!; prosperity, well-being, good health, S: 8001, B: 1115D, K: 1131B, H: 423B

10721 שֻׁם *šum*, name, what someone is called, S: 8036, B: 1115D, K: 1131C, H: 423B

10722 שְׁמַד *šᵉmad*, [P] to completely destroy, exterminate, S: 8046, B: 1116A, K: 1131D, H: 423B

10723 שְׁמַיִן *šᵉmayin*, heaven (the realm of God); (of this world) the heavens, sky, air, S: 8065†, B: 1116A, K: 1131D, H: 423B

10724 שְׁמַם *šᵉmam*, [O] to be greatly perplexed, S: 8075, B: 1116A, K: 1132A, H: 423C

10725 שְׁמַע *šᵉma'*, [J] to hear; [O] to obey, S: 8086, B: 1116A, K: 1132A, H: 423C

10726 שָׁמְרַיִן *šāmᵉrayin*, Samaria, S: 8115, B: 1116B, K: 1132B, H: 423C

10727 [1]שְׁמַשׁ *šᵉmaš*[1], [M] to attend to, serve, S: 8120, B: 1116B, K: 1132C, H: 423C

10728 [2]שְׁמַשׁ *šᵉmaš*[2], sun, S: 8122†, B: 1116B, K: 1132C, H: 423C

10729 שִׁמְשַׁי *šimšay*, Shimshai, S: 8124, B: 1116B, K: 1132C, H: 423C

10730 שֵׁן *šēn*, tooth, S: 8128, B: 1116B, K: 1132D, H: 423C

10731 [1]שְׁנָה *šᵉnâ*[1], [J] to be changed, be different; [M] to change; defy; [Mp] to be different; [P] to change, alter; [O] to be changed, be turned into, S: 8133†, B: 1116C, K: 1133A, H: 423D

10732 [2]שְׁנָה *šᵉnâ*[2], year, S: 8140, B: 1116D, K: 1133A, H: 423D

10733 [3]שְׁנָה *šᵉnâ*[3], sleep, S: 8139, B: 1116C, K: 1133A, H: 423D

10734 שָׁעָה *šā'â*, moment, short time; (as adv.) immediately, suddenly, for a time, S: 8160, B: 1116D, K: 1133C, H: 424A

10735 שְׁפַט *šᵉpaṭ*, [J] to judge; (as noun) judge, S: 8200, B: 1096B, K: 1133C, H: 424A

10736 שַׁפִּיר *šappîr*, beautiful, fair, lovely, S: 8209, B: 1116D, K: 1133D, H: 424A

10737 [1]שְׁפַל *šᵉpal*[1], [P] to humble, subdue, bring low, S: 8214, B: 1117A, K: 1134A, H: 424A

10738 [2]שְׁפַל *šᵉpal*[2], low; (as superlative) lowliest, S: 8215, B: 1117A, K: 1134A, H: 424A

10739 שְׁפַר *šᵉpar*, [J] to be pleased, have pleasure, S: 8232, B: 1117A, K: 1134A, H: 424A

10740 שְׁפַרְפָּר *šᵉparpār*, dawn, S: 8238, B: 1117A, K: 1134B, H: 424A

10741 שָׁק *šāq*, lower leg, shank, S: 8243, B: 1117A, K: 1134B, H: 424A

10742 שְׁרָה *šᵉrâ*, [J] to loosen, solve (a problem); [Jp] to be loosened; to dwell; [M] to begin; [O] to be loose and shaking (of legs giving way), S: 8271†, B: 1117A, K: 1134B, H: 424A

10743 שְׁרֹשׁ *šᵉrōš*, root, S: 8330†, B: 1114D, K: 1134C, H: 424B

10744 שְׁרֹשׁוּ *šᵉrōšû*, banishment, uprooting (from community), S: 8332, B: 1117B, K: 1134C, H: 424C

10745 שְׁרֹשִׁי *šᵉrōšî*, variant: banishment, uprooting (from community), see 10744, S: 8332†, B: 1117B, K: 1134D, H: 424C

10746 שֵׁשְׁבַּצַּר *šēšbaṣṣar*, Sheshbazzar, S: 8340, B: 1117B, K: 1135A, H: 424C

10747 שֵׁת *šēt*, six, S: 8353, B: 1117B, K: 1135A, H: 424C

10748 שְׁתָה *šᵉtâ*, [J] to drink, S: 8355, B: 1058C, K: 1135A, H: 424C

10749 שִׁתִּין *šittîn*, sixty, S: 8361, B: 1114D, K: 1135A, H: 424C

10750 שְׁתַר בּוֹזְנַי *šᵉtar bôzᵉnay*, Shethar-Bozenai, S: 8370, B: 1117C, K: 1135B, H: 424C

10751 ת *t*, letter of the Aramaic alphabet, S*, B: 1114D, K: 1135C, H: 424C

10752 תְּבַר *tᵉbar*, [Jp] to be brittle, to break, S: 8406, B: 1117C, K: 1135C, H: 424D

10753 תְּדִיר *tᵉdîr*, duration, encircling; (as adv.) continually, S: 8411†, B*, K: 1135B, H*

10754 תּוּב *tûb*, [J] to return, restore; [P] to give back, return, answer, S: 8421, B: 1117C, K: 1135B, H: 424B

10755 תְּוַהּ *t*^{e}*wah*, [J] to be amazed, be alarmed, S: 8429, B: 1087B, K: 1135D, H: 424B

10756 תּוֹר *tôr*, bull, steer, ox, S: 8450, B: 1117D, K: 1136A, H: 424B

10757 תְּחוֹת *t*^{e}*ḥôt*, under, S: 8460 & 8479, B: 1117D, K: 1136B, H: 424B

10758 תְּלַג *t*^{e}*lag*, snow, S: 8517, B: 1117D, K: 1136B, H: 424D

10759 תְּלִיתָי *t*^{e}*lîtāy*, third, S: 8523†, B: 1117D, K: 1136B, H: 424D

10760 תְּלָת *t*^{e}*lāt*, three, S: 8531, B: 1117D, K: 1136C, H: 424D

10761 תַּלְתָּא *taltā'*, third highest, S: 8532, B: 1118A, K: 1136C, H: 424D

10762 תְּלָתִין *t*^{e}*lātîn*, thirty, S: 8533, B: 1118A, K: 1136D, H: 424D

10763 תְּמַהּ *t*^{e}*mah*, wonder, miracle, S: 8540, B: 1118A, K: 1136D, H: 425A

10764 תַּמָּה *tammâ*, there, S: 8536†, B: 1118A, K: 1137A, H: 425A

10765 תִּנְיָן *tinyān*, second, S: 8578, B: 1118B, K: 1137A, H: 425A

10766 תִּנְיָנוּת *tinyānût*, once more, in the second time, S: 8579, B: 1118A, K: 1137B, H: 425A

10767 תִּפְתָּי *tiptāy*, magistrate, S: 8614†, B: 1118B, K: 1137B, H: 425A

10768 תַּקִּיף *taqqîp*, strong, powerful, mighty, S: 8624, B: 1118B, K: 1137C, H: 425A

10769 תְּקַל *t*^{e}*qal*, [K] to be weighed, S: 8625, B: 1118B, K: 1137C, H: 425A

10770 תְּקֵל *t*^{e}*qēl*, tekel, (i.e., shekel of weight), S: 8625, B: 1118C, K: 1137C, H: 425A

10771 תְּקַן *t*^{e}*qan*, [Q] to be restored, be reestablished, S: 8627, B: 1118C, K: 1137C, H: 425A

10772 תְּקִף *t*^{e}*qip*, [J] to become strong, become hard; [M] to enforce, make hard, S: 8631, B: 1118C, K: 1137D, H: 425A

10773 תְּקֹף *t*^{e}*qōp*, might, strength, S: 8632, B: 1118C, K: 1137D, H: 425C

10774 תְּקָף *t*^{e}*qāp*, power, strength, S: 8632, B: 1118C, K: 1138A, H: 425C

10775 תְּרֵין *t*^{e}*rên*, two, S: 8648, B: 1118C, K: 1138A, H: 425C

10776 תְּרַע *t*^{e}*ra'*, opening (of a furnace); (royal) court, S: 8651, B: 1118C, K: 1138B, H: 425C

10777 תָּרָע *tārā'*, gatekeeper, doorkeeper, S: 8652, B: 1118B, K: 1138B, H: 425C

10778 תַּרְתֵּין *tartên*, variant: two, see 10775, S: 8648, B: 1118D, K: 1138C, H: 425C

10779 תַּתְּנַי *tatt*^{e}*nay*, Tattenai, S: 8674, B: 1118D, K: 1138D, H: 425C

[J] Peal [Jp] Peal passive [K] Peil [L] Hithpeel (Hitpolel, Itpeel) [M] Pael [Mp] Pael passive [N] Pual (Poel)